Contents

D0132060

How to Use This Book

ARTIST NAME

VITAL STATISTICS: For groups, **f.** indicates date and place of formation; **db.** indicated date disbanded. For individual performers, date and place of birth (**b.**) and death (**d.**), if known, are given.

INSTRUMENT(S) / STYLE(S): Indicates the instruments played if the artist is an individual, followed by the styles of music associated with the performer or group.

BIOGRAPHY: A quick view of the artist's life and musical career. For major performers, proportionately longer biographies are provided.

ALBUM REVIEWS: These are the albums selected by our editors and contributors.

KEY TO SYMBOLS: ● ☆ ★

☆ ESSENTIAL RECORDINGS: Albums marked with a star should be part of any good collection of the genre. Often, these are also a good first purchase (filled star). By hearing these albums, you can get a good overview of the entire genre. These are must-hear and must-have recordings. You can't go wrong with them.

●★ FIRST PURCHASE: Albums marked with either a filled circle or a filled star should be your first purchase. This is where to begin to find out if you like this particular artist. These albums are representative of the best this artist has to offer. If you don't like these picks, chances are this artist is not for you. In the case of an artist who has a number of distinct periods, you will find an essential pick marked for each period. Albums are listed chronologically when possible.

ALBUM TITLE: The name of the album is listed in bold as it appears on the original when possible. Very long titles have been abbreviated, or repeated in full as part of the comment, where needed.

DATE: The year of an album's first recording or release, if known.

RECORD LABEL: Record labels indicate the current (or most recent) release of this recording. Label numbers are not included because they change frequently.

ALBUM RATINGS: ♦ TO ♦♦♦♦♦ In addition to the stars and circles used to distinguish exceptional noteworthy albums, as explained above, all albums are rated on a scale from one to five diamonds.

REVIEWERS: The name of each review's author is given at the end of the review.

Johnny Cash

b. Feb. 26, 1932, Kingsland, AR, **d.** Sept. 12, 2003, Nashville, TN
Guitar, Songwriter, Vocals / Traditional Country, Cowboy, Country-Pop, Rockabilly, Country Gospel, Rock & Roll

Johnny Cash was one of the most imposing and influential figures in post-World War II country music. With his deep, resonant baritone and spare, percussive guitar, he had a basic, distinctive sound. Cash didn't sound like Nashville, nor did he sound like honky tonk or rock & roll. He created his own sub-genre, falling halfway between the blunt emotional honesty of folk, the rebelliousness of rock & roll, and the world weariness of country. Cash's career coincided with the birth of rock & roll, and his rebellious attitude and simple, direct musical attack shared a lot of similarities with rock. However, there was a deep sense of history—as he would later illustrate with his series of historical albums—that kept him forever tied with country. And he was one of country music's biggest stars of the '50s and '60s, scoring well over 100 hit singles.

Johnny Cash's beloved wife June Carter Cash died on May 15, 2003, of complications following heart surgery. Five months later, Johnny Cash died of complications from diabetes in Nashville, Tennessee.

☆ **At Folsom Prison** / 1968 / Columbia/Legacy ♦♦♦♦♦
At Folsom Prison was one of two legendary live albums Johnny Cash recorded in front of a prison audience in the late '60s. Part of the appeal of the records is the way Cash plays to the audience, selecting a set of songs that are all about prison, crime, murder, regret, loss, mother, God, and loneliness. Cash stimulates the audience's emotions, which in turn stimulates his performance, especially since he delivers the songs with the conviction of someone who has lived through it. There aren't many hits on the record—"Folsom Prison Blues," "I Still Miss Someone," "Jackson," "Give My Love to Rose," and "I Got Stripes" are the familiar items—but few albums come as close to capturing the darkness and rage that lays deep in Cash's music, as well as the depth of his talent. [The 1999 CD reissue of *At Folsom Prison* presents the complete concert, including three previously unreleased tracks: "Busted," "Joe Bean," and "The Legend of John Henry's Hammer."] —*Stephen*

★ **Man in Black: Greatest Hits** / Mar. 2, 1999 / Columbia/Legacy ♦♦♦♦♦
There have been no shortage of Johnny Cash compilations over the years, particularly of his classic Columbia recordings. There's something for whatever your taste—single-disc compilations with just the hits and extravagant multi-disc box sets tracing his entire career. *Man in Black: Greatest Hits* falls somewhere in between, presenting a comprehensive 30-song overview of (primarily) Cash's work for Columbia. That means the bulk of his groundbreaking Sun work is missing—"I Walk the Line," "Ballad of a Teenage Queen," and "Guess Things Happen That Way" are here, but classics such as "Get Rhythm," "Cry! Cry! Cry!," and "Folsom Prison Blues" (included in a later live version) aren't—but they're all available on Rhino's excellent *Sun Years* collection; this is notable for being an affordable and relatively exhaustive overview of the Columbia years, which is something that hasn't been attempted before this collection. There may be a few hits and cult favorites missing from this compilation, but it does a stellar job in featuring the best, most important cuts from Cash's prolific years with the label, and it makes an excellent companion to *The Sun Years* for the serious Cash fan on a budget. —*Stephen Thomas Erlewine*

Murder / May 23, 2000 / Columbia/Legacy ♦♦♦♦♦
Of the three thematic Cash CDs simultaneously released in the spring of 2000 (the others are *God* and *Love*), *Murder* is the most sensible. For one thing, there are actually far fewer Cash songs about murder than there are Cash songs about love or God, so this compilation is a more thorough retrospective of a niche in his repertoire. In addition, one has to admit that Cash's somber vocals and flair for storytelling are well-suited for tales of assassination. Also, this is a well-selected set of 16 tunes, spanning the mid-'50s to the mid-'90s. With the exception of the classics "Folsom Prison Blues" (the original Sun version), "The Long Black Veil," and "Don't Take Your Guns to Town," most of these will be unfamiliar to many Cash fans, taken as they are from LPs, B-sides, and live recordings. Most of them are moving, sometimes chilling performances, whether Cash takes on the role of the killer or an observer. One track, a 1966 cover of Harlan Howard's "The Sound of Laughter," was previously unreleased in the U.S., although it doesn't rate as one of the more notable entries on the anthology. *Murder* is also available as part of the three-CD box set *Love God Murder*, comprised of thematic discs that are available together or separately. —*Richie Unterberger*

Road Less Travelled: Sun Recordings / Mar. 13, 2001 / Varese ♦♦♦♦
Varese's *Roads Less Travelled* contains 18 hard-to-find Sun recordings from Johnny Cash and the Tennessee Two, songs that were either not released or weren't issued as A-sides or languished as album tracks. This is actually a bit of a godsend, since Cash and the Tennessee Two were at their peak at Sun and it's a little difficult to dig deep into their catalog for lost treasures, unless you're willing to delve into Bear Family's overly exhaustive *Man in Black* set. This culls many of the highlights from the set and while there are no revelations, there are finds the very best elements of that set, and while there's no revelations, there are plenty of small gems to enjoy and it's easily the best choice for serious listeners (who are not completists) after they've absorbed the very best of his Sun material. —*Stephen Thomas Erlewine*

Contributors

All Music Guide

Vladimir Bogdanov, President
Chris Woodstra, Vice President of Content
    Development, Editor-in-Chief

AMG Popular Music Department

Stephen Thomas Erlewine, Senior Editor
John Bush, Senior Editor
Joslyn Layne, Associate Editor

Assistant Editors

Al Campbell
Thom Jurek
Andy Kellman
Wade Kergan
Greg McIntosh
Heather Phares
Tim Sendra
Sean Westergaard
Mackenzie Wilson

Copy Editing

Jason Birchmeier
Amy Cloud
Ann Holter
Steve Jones
Dave Lynch
Aaron Warshaw

Data Processing

Mark Donkers, Manager
Jonathan Ball
Matt Collar
Jack "Lee" Isles
Zac Johnson
Aaron Latham
Corwin Moore
David Serra
Donn Stroud
Rob Theakston
Dan Trenz
Chris True

Contributors

Bret Adams
Greg Adams
Mark Allan
Jason Anderson
Rick Anderson
Jason Ankeny
Bill Ashford
William Ashford
Jon Azpiri
Aaron Badgley
Rodney Batdorf
Kenneth Bays
Brian Beatty
Michael Berick
Jason Birchmeier
Roxanne Blanford
Dacia A. Blodgett-Williams
Myles Boisen
Ross Boissoneau
Bret Booth
Rob Bowman
Sandra Brennan
Deanne Briggs
Brian Briscoe
Lynne Bronstein
Daniel Browne
Jeff Burger
John Bush
Nathan Bush
Bryan Buss
Becky Byrkit
Rob Caldwell
Al Campbell
Bill Carpenter
Daphne Carr
Sean Carruthers
Kenneth M. Cassidy
Evan Cater
Eugene Chadbourne
James Chrispell
Rick Cohoon
Matt Collar
Paul Collins
David Connolly
Stephen Cook
Dan Cooper

Scott Cooper
Steve Cooper
Kristi Coulter
Stephen Cramer
Jeff Crooke
Dan Cross
Michael Cusanelli
Peter J. D'Angelo
Mike DaRonco
Bill Dahl
Ben Davies
Hank Davis
Mike DeGagne
Ron DePasquale
Tom Demalon
Mark Deming
Tim DiGravina
Charlotte Dillon
Maria Konicki Dinoia
Eleanor Ditzel
Robert L. Doerschuk
Chuck Donkers
John Dougan
Brian Downing
Travis Drageset
Jimmy Draper
Ken Dryden
John Duffy
Bruce Eder
Jason Elias
Michael Erlewine
Stephen Thomas Erlewine
Todd Everett
Keith Farley
Peter Fawthrop
Kathleen C. Fennessy
Rob Ferrier
Inigo C. Figuracion
Matt Fink
Sigmund Finman
Murrday Fisher
Rebecca Flint
Brian Flota
John Floyd
Richard Foss
Michael Frey
Michael Gallucci
Richard S. Ginell

Daniel Gioffre
Rev. Keith A. Gordon
Bob Gottlieb
Mary Grady
Adam Greenberg
Matthew Greenwald
JT Griffith
Tim Griggs
Donald A. Guarisco
All Music Guide
Erik Hage
Andrew Hamilton
Chris Handyside
Shawn M. Haney
Jeff Hannusch
Craig Harris
Brett Hartenbach
Ralph Heibutzki
Alex Henderson
Matthew Hilburn
Bob Hinkle
Hal Horowitz
Steve Huey
Mark A. Humphrey
Vik Iyengar
Leon Jackson
Jesse Jarnow
Zac Johnson
Liana Jonas
Thom Jurek
Tom Kealey
Andy Kellman
Brian Kelly
Rudyard Kennedy
Kit Kiefer
Quint Kik
Cub Koda
Linda Kohanov
Todd Kristel
Peter Kurtz
Steve Kurutz
Theresa LaVeck
Matt Laferty
Ronnie D. Lankford Jr.
David Lavin
Joslyn Layne
Jack Leaver
Dan Lee
Uncle Dave Lewis
Richard Lieberson
Johnny Loftus
John Lomax

Lars Lovén
John Lupton
Megan Lynch
Dennis MacDonald
Jason MacNeil
James Manheim
Brian Mansfield
Stewart Mason
Burgin Mathews
Michael McCall
Kieran McCarthy
Kelly McCartney
Steven McDonald
Gregory McIntosh
Richard Meyer
S. Colby Miller
Martin Monkman
Stansted Montfichet
Mark Morgenstein
Jim Newsom
Jason Nickey
Chris Nickson
Ed Nimmervoll
Ben O'Connor
Brian O'Neill
Michael Ofjord
J.P. Ollio
Thom Owens
Roch Parisien
Jana Pendragon
Heather Phares
Lindsay Planer
Larry Powell
Greg Prato
Stacia Proefrock
Jose F. Promis
Jon Pruett
Jack Rabid
Ned Raggett
Matt Reasor
Chip Renner
Michael Ribas
Vince Ripol
Pemberton Roach
Joel Roberts
John Storm Roberts
Matthew Robinson
Tom Roland
Rose of Sharon Witmer
William Ruhlmann
Tom Schulte
Jeff Schwachter

K.A. Scott
Linda Seida
Tim Sendra
Tim Sheridan
Earl Simmons
Richard Skelly
Dave Sleger
Hank Small
Jim Smith
Michael Smith
Charles Spano
Leo Stanley
Don Stevens
Alex Stimmel
Doug Stone
Denise Sullivan
Kim Summers
Stanton Swihart
Sara Sytsma
Jeff Tamarkin
Robert Taylor
Bryan Thomas
Dave Thompson
Lang Thompson
Bradley Torreano
Chris M True
Ian Trumbull
John Uhl
Jeremy Ulrey
Neal Umphred
Richie Unterberger
John Vallier
Philip Van Vleck
Mark Vanderhoff
Joe Viglione
David Vinopal
Brian Wahlert
Thomas Ward
Sean Westergaard
Brian Whitener
Ann Wickstrom
Jonathan Widran
MacKenzie Wilson
Charles S. Wolfe
Kurt Wolff
Deborah Wong
Linda Woods
Chris Woodstra
Jim Worbois
Ron Wynn
Scott Yanow
Curtis Zimmermann

Introduction

Country music is not the easiest music to collect. Unlike other popular music, country never has established a clear, easily defined aesthetic for record collectors. Rock has an established canon of classic albums, even for its obscurities, so it's easy for the curious to begin listening and dig ever deeper. There are many jazz aficionados who meticulously detail every recording session, many of which are released in either officially or semi-legitimate form. Soul collectors obsessively track down rare singles, but even those listeners with less time and slimmer wallets can find many rare items on specialist reissues, along with the classic catalog that never goes out of print. The best blues is nearly always in print, with even forgotten songsters like Curly Weaver experiencing revivals when least expected.

Country music has elements of all these kinds of collecting, but they rarely gel into a cohesive aesthetic, something that is universally acknowledged as the way to collect country. There is an accepted canon, but it's of artists, not albums. Hank, Merle, Willie, Buck, Johnny, Waylon, George, Lefty, are all giants, but even their greatest albums aren't as well known as their songs, the way that the Beatles' *Sgt. Pepper* is as well-known as "I Want to Hold Your Hand." They all have albums and collections in print, but they suffer from having *too many* discs in their catalog—not only have they recorded many official albums, sometimes as many as three records a year, but they have an endless stream of budget-line compilations. On the other end of the spectrum, there are the lavish, expensive, impressive reissues from Bear Family, which treats the legacy of such country giants as Ernest Tubb, Hank Snow, Hank Thompson, Waylon Jennings, and Willie Nelson with the precision and detail of a jazz collector. Still, these sets are not only priced for the fanatical collector, they also are at mercy of the whims of what the label chooses to release, so there are iconic figures deserving of such a thorough retrospective yet not receiving it. Nevertheless, specialist labels like Bear Family, England's Ace, Proper and others specialize in unearthing fantastic historic material, such as the exemplary overview of Nashville indie labels of the '40s and '50s in *A Shot in the Dark: Tennessee Jive*, similar to the wave of rare soul collections in recent years. On a related note, such reissue labels as Varese Sarabande, Razor & Tie, Collectors Choice Music, and Koch, along with its subsidiary Audium, release great compilations and reissues of once-popular, now neglected artists, but they suffer a fate all too common to country collectors: these great discs go out of print quickly. This is a common situation not just for reissues, of course, but also for new albums, since labels cut the under-performers off very quickly in country.

This means that what's out on the market is a mess, but, historically, that's been the case with country records. Albums are rushed out to capitalize on a hit, or retitled and reissued with the album now sharing the title of the smash single. Labels license out their back catalog haphazardly, resulting in a glut of titles in both new and used record stores. Once an artist is hot, their label not only cranks out the releases, but so do labels that own earlier recordings from that musician. It takes a lot of dedication, a lot of willpower, and a lot of love to sort through what's been released, what's available in your local second-hand shop and what's currently available, not just from the big American labels, but as European imports or on specialty labels.

A lot of dedication, willpower, and love have indeed been put into the second edition of the *All Music Guide to Country*, because this is a music we love to collect, and the result is the best guide to country recordings yet assembled. Other books and encyclopedias devote their space to biographies, discographies, and the occasional album review, presenting a generalized overview. Here, we give that biographical overview and then dig deep into the discography, reviewing items both brand new and long out of print, giving as complete a picture possible of their recorded work. We concentrate on what you might actually find in stores, online or in second-hand shops, steering you toward the best collections and away from rip-offs. We also know that cheap doesn't necessarily equal lousy; there may be scores of budget-line discs that were little more than trash, but every once in a while, there's a gem.

There are numerous differences between this expanded second edition of the *All Music Guide to Country* and the first volume, published six years ago. Of course, there are the numerous new artists and new releases, but we've also found noteworthy historic artists not covered in our initial volume and made considerable effort to expand discographies of artists included the first time around. In all, we have nearly doubled the number of albums listed this time around. We have reviewed many classic albums that have yet to find their way to CD, including classic long-players by Merle Haggard, Johnny Paycheck, David Allan Coe, Tompall Glaser, and Hank Thompson, among many others. These may not currently be easily available, but they are worth a search and very well may show up on a reissue CD somewhere in this big world. Also, we have increased our coverage of those imports, so you know what to look for whenever you shop online or go to country-only stores like Ernest Tubb Record Shop in Nashville. Finally, we have not neglected noteworthy compilations that have gone out of print; if they're worth searching for, we've included them.

The reason we have included such a broad array of recordings—albums that never have made it to disc, imports, out of print titles—is because they all need to be there in order to give a full picture of both an individual artist and the music as a whole. Titles drift in and out of print, great albums aren't always circulated and essential reissues are never given release in the United States. That's what makes country music not an easy music to collect, but that can also be part of the fun, since it means that in order to hear the best albums, it requires you to be an active collector and listener, since you have to be on the hunt. And this book is what you need to guide you on the hunt, because it was made by critics, collectors and fans who have spent many, many hours digging through stacks of used records, searching high and low for the best country music on record and disc.

Keep in mind that we have had to make tough decisions regarding what artists and albums to include in the book. Unlike on our website www.allmusic.com, which contains complete biographies and discographies as well as a wealth of other historical information, we do not have an endless amount of space, so we had to keep discographies to the most noteworthy albums. At times, this means that the full discography is indeed listed, other times it means just in-print albums, and other times it's a combination of out-of-print proper albums and new compilations—it all depended on the artist, and what presented the full scope of their work. Usually, we fit as much as we could; if you believe something is missing or wish to research further, please check out our website.

There's a lot of great country music and it's just waiting to be discovered. This book will help you find the best of the lot. For us at the All Music Guide, it's been a joy assembling this book. Hopefully, it will be as much fun for you to read as it was for us to write. —*Stephen Thomas Erlewine*

Style Descriptions

ALTERNATIVE COUNTRY

Alternative Country refers to country bands that play traditional country but bend the rules slightly. They don't conform to Nashville's hitmaking traditions, nor do they follow the accepted "outlaw" route to notoriety. Instead, alternative country bands work outside of the country industry's spotlight, frequently subverting musical traditions with singer/songwriter and rock & roll lyrical (and musical) aesthetics.

ALTERNATIVE COUNTRY-ROCK

Alternative country-rock is often simply referred to as alternative country, but the two styles are actually somewhat distinct from one another—simply put, alternative country performers come from the country side of the equation, whereas alternative country-rock is rooted more in rock. It's considered a branch of alternative rock—even though it may not always sound that way on the surface—because it doesn't fit any mainstream sensibility, and also because its bands usually get their start as part of the American indie-label scene. In contrast to alternative country, which pushes the boundaries of country music from the inside, alternative country-rock is music made by outsiders who love the sound and spirit of country. They faithfully preserve traditional sounds, but reinterpret the spirit in personal, contemporary, and idiosyncratic ways that rarely appeal to straight country fans. The godfather of alternative country-rock was Gram Parsons, the single most important figure in the invention of country-rock and an enduring cult legend for his deeply emotional records. Neil Young's varying musical personalities were also an important influence, as was the progressive country movement of the '70s, particularly an Austin, TX-centered group of highly literate singer/songwriters like Townes Van Zandt, Guy Clark, and Jerry Jeff Walker, among others. The man who heralded the birth of alternative country-rock was Lyle Lovett, whose wit and eclecticism seemed to revitalize country's possibilities in the minds of many rock fans. But the first true alternative country-rock band was Uncle Tupelo, who at the start of their career fused punk and country in a far more reverent way than any band in the short-lived '80s cowpunk movement. Their cover of the A.P. Carter spiritual "No Depression" gave its name to their seminal 1990 debut album, the premier fanzine chronicling the alt-country scene, and a nickname to the movement in general. Uncle Tupelo soon became a more tradition-minded country-rock outfit, and following their 1993 landmark *Anodyne* split into two different bands, the staunchly revivalist Son Volt and the more pop-inflected Wilco; by that time, alternative country-rock itself had begun to split into several strains. One school was chiefly dedicated to reviving the Parsons/Young sound of the early '70s, sometimes adding elements of Beatlesque pop to their crunchy rockers and aching ballads. Others were sincere traditionalists, drawing from the most haunting qualities of old-time country and Appalachian folk while updating the lyrical sensibilities just enough. A related school made that old-timey sound into a soft, spare, ethereal hybrid of country and indie rock, usually featuring a female vocalist. Still other alt-country-rock bands brought a sense of humor to their traditionalist work, whether it was the good-natured wit of a twangy, rollicking bar band, or the flat-out weird irony of Lambchop. Alternative country-rock continued to produce new, critically acclaimed hybrid acts into the new millennium, with an increasing indie-rock flavor.

AMERICANA

Much like its next of kin (alternative country-rock), Americana developed during the 1990s as a roots-oriented reaction to the slick commercial sounds that dominated mainstream country during the decade. But while alternative country-rock developed out of punk, alternative rock, and country itself, Americana sprung from less raw and edgy source material. In fact, much of what fell under the Americana umbrella is in fact a revival of dormant country styles, including Western swing and rockabilly. Though considered an alternative radio format, Americana did not break with country tradition; instead, it embraced it—something, ironically enough, that the music hitting the Nashville charts throughout the era did not do.

APPALACHIAN FOLK

The folk music of rural Appalachia—primarily concentrated in western Pennsylvania, West Virginia, western North Carolina, eastern Kentucky, and Tennessee —provided much of the basis for bluegrass and country music. Centered around stringed instruments—fiddle, guitar, bass, mandolin, banjo, dulcimer, etc.—and rudimentary percussion (if any), Appalachian folk largely descended from English and Scots-Irish folk traditions, brought to the region by colonial immigrants seeking territory and farmland to call their own; there were also smaller influences from other European immigrants, African-Americans, and Native Americans. Because of the rugged landscape, transportation and communication were difficult, leaving the region's culture and music to develop in relative isolation over the course of the 1800s. Life in the mountains was often tough and lonely,

and music became the most popular means of expression and entertainment. Appalachian folk songs were simple and covered all facets of everyday life, both extraordinary and run-of-the-mill—work (especially coal mining, logging, and working on the river), love, death, religion (including many traditional hymns), and murder (the famed ballad of "Tom Dooley" originated here). Known as old-timey music or hillbilly music, Appalachian folk began to find popular acceptance during the 1920s thanks in part to its traditional values, which were also fairly well ingrained in the culture at large. The recordings of the Carter Family helped preserve crucial parts of the Appalachian folk repertoire, and helped pave the way for both country music and, especially, bluegrass (birthed in the '40s thanks to the work of Bill Monroe). Evolution of the Appalachian folk tradition was inevitable by this point, since the music's popularity was accompanied by hordes of talent scouts, opening both the region and its performers up to a great deal of outside influence. However, even if Appalachian folk is no longer a thriving tradition (due mainly to ever-increasing outside influence and a population exodus from the still-impoverished area), the music is still the subject of much preservationist fascination, and has become virtually synonymous with American folk tradition.

BAKERSFIELD SOUND

Bakersfield was the first subgenre of country music to rely heavily on electric instrumentation, as well as a defined backbeat—in other words, it was the first to be significantly influenced by rock & roll. Named after the town of Bakersfield, California, where a great majority of the artists performed, the sound was pioneered by Wynn Stewart and popularized by Buck Owens and Merle Haggard. Using telecaster guitars, the singers developed a clean, ringing sound that stood in direct opposition to the produced, string-laden Nashville sound. The Bakersfield sound became one of the most popular—and arguably the most influential—country subgenres of the '60s, setting the stage for country-rock and outlaw, as well as reviving the spirit of honky tonk.

BLUEGRASS

Bluegrass music grew out of traditional string band music that formed the roots of country music. In the '40s, country music began to splinter into different directions, as honky tonk and country-pop became subgenres of their own. A certain segment of country musicians continued playing traditional string music. Led by Bill Monroe, these musicians adhered to the songs, structures, and conventions of string bands, but they made the music faster, harder, and more technically demanding. The result was bluegrass; the genre was named after Bill Monroe's backing band, the Blue Grass Boys. After its inception in the mid-'40s, bluegrass didn't change for nearly 20 years. In the late '60s, a number of bluegrass groups began expanding the possibilities of the genre, much to the chagrin of many of the music's most popular artists and dedicated fans. Consequently, the new breed of bluegrass groups were dubbed progressive bluegrass while those that adhered to the music's heritage were tagged traditional bluegrass. Over the next three decades, progressive bluegrass changed frequently, while the sound of traditional bluegrass never varied.

BLUEGRASS-GOSPEL

Bluegrass-Gospel is naturally very similar to country gospel, sharing many of the same songs and the same basic attitude. The main difference, of course, is that it's bluegrass, so the harmonies are pitched high and lonesome, the tempos are a little faster, and the instrumental work is deft and blindingly intricate. Unlike country-gospel, which can range from old timey to country-pop, bluegrass-gospel is pretty traditional, sticking to old-time songs played in the style of traditional bluegrass. There are exceptions to the rule, but in general, that applies for much of the style. Appropriately for a music so steeped in heritage, bluegrass-gospel has been performed since the inception of bluegrass.

CLOSE HARMONY

Close Harmony is one of the most distinctive sounds in traditional country. The term refers to the keening two (occasionally three) part harmonies that acts like the Louvin Brothers and the Delmore Brothers popularized. The sound of close harmony grew out of the high, lonesome sound of bluegrass, yet most close-harmony songs were closer to traditional country than bluegrass. During the late '40s and early '50s, close-harmony acts became quite popular, thanks to a string of brother acts. The Louvin Brothers, perhaps the definitive close-harmony group, became popular at the end of the era. Their popularity was impeded by the emergence of rock & roll, which cut the country audience dramatically. Ironically, close-harmony acts in general—and the Louvins in particular—were an influence on the harmony style of the Everly Brothers, who happened to write the template for rock & roll harmonies with their late '50s singles. The Everlys' influence was as apparent in the Beatles as the Louvins were in the Everlys, and that is just one testament to the depth and influence of close harmony.

CONTEMPORARY BLUEGRASS

Contemporary Bluegrass developed during the '80s, when traditional bluegrass had incorporated the innovations of progressive bluegrass. It isn't as jazzy or experimental as progressive bluegrass—sticking to familiar traditional forms—but it is slightly less classicist than traditional bluegrass. Essentially, it is an updated and fresh version of bluegrass for modern times.

CONTEMPORARY COUNTRY

Following the rise of the pop-oriented Urban Cowboy style in the late '70s and early '80s, singers like George Strait and Randy Travis set their sights on bringing country music back to its roots, beginning a movement known as the New Traditionalists. While their sound drew primarily on classic honky tonk, it also boasted all the advantages of updated production techniques and equipment, proving that pure country music could sound authentic yet modern. At its outset, Contemporary Country built upon this revelation, taking the foundation laid by new traditionalist country and infusing it with pop/rock sensibilities—without sounding wimpy. During the late '80s and early '90s, contemporary country was still essentially country at its core, even though it was reaching a wider audience than ever, thanks in no small part to Garth Brooks and his latent rock influences. Although pop-crossover hit singles were still a rare occurrence at this point, contemporary country albums began to sell in unprecedented numbers in the wake of Brooks' success, and while contemporary country was by no means restricted to male singers, they—with a few notable exceptions—were the main early beneficiaries of the music's greater visibility. This wave of male artists dominated the early to mid-'90s, mixing country grit and simple, line-dance-ready songcraft in varying proportions, with the new traditionalist movement continuing to hold a strong influence over many; some of the less substantive in the bunch were dubbed "hat acts," after what cynics described as their most appealing attribute. All of the increased exposure eventually pulled contemporary country farther and farther into mainstream pop music, and a number of (mostly) female artists began to actively pursue crossover success; in the most pronounced cases, their music differentiated itself from full-fledged pop/rock only by a certain twang in the vocals. While shifting contemporary country away from its roots, this willingness to play to an even wider audience resulted in massive, genre-dominating popularity for acts like Shania Twain, LeAnn Rimes, the Dixie Chicks, and Faith Hill in the late '90s and early 2000s. Whether the songs were closer to neo-honky tonk or pop/rock, though, contemporary country was always marked by its shiny, radio-ready production, which occasionally incorporated synthesizers, but above all kept the music smooth and polished, helping make it more accessible to country, rock, and pop fans alike.

COUNTRY BOOGIE

Country Boogie is a cross between the bluesy inflections of honky tonk and the polished style of the Nashville sound. It has a rollicking beat and follows bluesy changes, but is played with country instruments. In essence, the genre foreshadowed rockabilly with its uptempo beat and bluesy chords.

COUNTRY COMEDY

Like any kind of humor, Country Comedy isn't suited to all tastes. For fans of more urbane music—including slickly produced country-pop—country comedy is crude, simplistic, old-fashioned, and foolish. Nevertheless, the very squareness of the genre is what makes it appealing. Country comedy grew directly out of vaudeville and burlesque, where comedians told silly jokes. Initially, country performers—including the Carter Family and Jimmie Rodgers—would perform comedy skits during their shows, and comedians like Minnie Pearl were major figures at the *Grand Ole Opry*. Often, country comedians were simply comedians, but there were several—like Grandpa Jones and Homer & Jethro—that were excellent musicians as well. From the late '40s to the mid-'60s, artists like Homer & Jethro were popular both as comedians and musicians, but by the beginning of the '70s, country comedy became the provinces of comedians. Of course, there were still novelty singles, but country comedy was largely relegated to live performances, not records. In the mid-'90s, Jeff Foxworthy renewed country comedy as a viable commercial proposition with his series of *You Might Be a Redneck If…* records. In his wake, a number of other new country comedians, most notably Cledus T. Judd, also scaled the charts.

COUNTRY GOSPEL

Along with old-timey, country gospel is the oldest, most simple and straightforward of all country subgenres. Though it somewhat changed with the times, country gospel remained the most simple and straightforward of all country subgenres. The sound of country gospel is similar to traditional country—the only difference is, the subject matter is religious, not secular. Like traditional country, the sound of country gospel became smoother and more pop-oriented as the decades progressed, and by the early '70s, it became nearly indistinguishable from the lush sounds of mainstream pop. That trend continued throughout the rest of the '70s and '80s, and by the '90s, contemporary country gospel sounded identical to the adult contemporary inclinations of CCM. Nevertheless, that music was never widely recognized as country gospel, which will always be identified with its simple arrangements, small vocal choirs, and twangy instrumentation.

COUNTRY-FOLK

Like most hybrid genres, Country-Folk draws in different proportions from each side of the equation, depending largely upon the performer's taste. Most country-folk artists write and perform the vast majority of their material themselves, and in that respect, they follow the mold of the folk artist more closely. Moreover, country-folk performers tend to find greater appreciation among folk audiences; among country fans, it's often just their songwriting skill that finds acceptance, and that only when full-fledged country singers cover their compositions. There are exceptions on both sides of the fence, of course, but the overall trend is probably due to the fact that country-folk has a mellower, gentler feel than most country, whose audience has usually been weaned on performances that are rowdier or more sentimental. Country-folk artists who compose their own material usually concentrate a great deal on crafting thoughtful, often emotionally complex lyrics, thus keeping with the singer/songwriter tradition established by folk-rock artists like Bob Dylan.

COUNTRY-POP

Prior to the rise of rock & roll, country music was rarely heard outside of its intended market, effectively isolating it from any concerns about wide accessibility. When rockabilly took off, however, country musicians were forced to consider whether their true affinities lay with traditional country or with this popular new style, which allowed artists to reach crossover audiences for the first time. This flirtation with the mainstream marked the beginnings of Country-Pop, which grew out of the realization that country-influenced music (as opposed to straight-ahead honky tonk) could be hybridized and smoothed out for mass consumption. RCA Records producer Chet Atkins was the most important figure in the initial cross-breeding of country and pop, creating a sound that was dubbed "countrypolitan" for its blend of rural sensibility and urban sophistication. Because the melodies and song structures of country music were usually very simple and catchy, they worked well when placed in a pop-oriented format; Atkins' productions often placed the songs in orchestral arrangements heavy on the strings, which sometimes blended with country instrumentation and sometimes stood alone. This approach resulted in a bevy of pop crossover hits for singers who could make the transition to Atkins' smooth, polished style, most notably Jim Reeves. Decca Records producer Owen Bradley crafted an even lusher sound for his artists, most importantly providing the sympathetic sonic environment that best showcased the angelic voice of Patsy Cline, and making her a star in the process. Countrypolitan pop eventually came to be tagged "the Nashville Sound," since nearly all of its records were produced there. But even as its practitioners racked up hit after hit, the first of many backlashes against country-pop began to form in the 1960s among artists frustrated at not fitting into the Nashville mold; the biggest came in the form of the Bakersfield sound, with its hard-driving beat, electric instrumentation, and love of old-style honky tonk. Nevertheless, the Nashville sound continued to prosper among fans of mainstream-oriented country. In fact, it became more popular than ever during the '70s thanks to producer Billy Sherrill, whose orchestrations and recordings were even more grandiose and detailed, and owed as much to "Wall of Sound" rock producer Phil Spector as they did to Atkins and Bradley; George Jones, Tammy Wynette, Charlie Rich, and Conway Twitty all benefited immensely from his touch. A simpler country-pop sound, which more closely resembled pop/rock with country trappings, also made inroads on non-country radio during the decade, thanks in part to country-rock fusion efforts by Bob Dylan, the Byrds, and the Flying Burrito Brothers; this sound was spearheaded by artists like Glen Campbell, John Denver and B.J. Thomas. The mid-'70s saw another rebellion in the edgier, more eclectic form of outlaw country, but by the end of the decade, the film *Urban Cowboy* had popularized a new variation on country-pop (named after the film), which smoothed the music out even more by blending it with soft-rock influences. During the mid- to late '80s, the new traditionalist movement sought to return country to its honky tonk roots, but its polished (yet not elaborate) production helped lay the groundwork for a new breed of country-pop that was informed by rock & roll, both in its driving beat and its big-sounding production techniques. This sound made Garth Brooks a superstar during the '90s and brought pop crossover success to Billy Ray Cyrus; toward the end of the decade, the emphasis had shifted to female vocalists like Shania Twain, LeAnn Rimes, and Faith Hill, whose brands of country-pop could encompass soft-rock covers, roots-rock, or arena-rock-style production.

COWBOY

Cowboy Music was originally handed down from the genuine Old West articles, its repertoire consisting of songs sung on the open range to pass the time on cattle drives. This tradition continued to inform country & western music long after its attendant lifestyle had all but disappeared, since romanticized cowboy mythology still held a fascination for many. That fascination resulted in the production of innumerable Western and cowboy films, and with those films came a revival of interest in cowboy music. Actually, it wasn't so much a revival as a hunger for more mythology—singer/actors like Roy Rogers and Gene Autry relied far more on new compositions which evoked similar themes of cowboy life. The performances and production of cowboy songs depend largely on the context—while movie songs were usually recorded with modern soundtrack-style orchestras, old-time groups like the Sons of the Pioneers relied on traditional, unadorned acoustic instruments. While it's the spirit of cowboy music, rather than specific standard songs, that has generally survived in country music, some artists have sought to preserve the tradition and educate their audiences about authentic cowboy songs; Michael Martin Murphey became a notable figure in these efforts during the '90s.

HONKY TONK

Birthed in the rowdy Southern bars christened with the same name, Honky Tonk is the single sound most associated with country music. It's become an enduring staple, the style to which mainstream country inevitably returns time and time again to refresh itself, a source of inspiration and renewal when popular trends begin to take country music away from its roots. The basic honky tonk sound features acoustic and/or electric guitar, fiddle, string bass, and steel guitar (which was imported from Hawaiian music), while the vocals often draw from the so-called "high lonesome" sound of traditional country, sounding either rough and nasal (Hank Williams, Ernest Tubb) or smooth and clear (Lefty Frizzell, George Jones). Like the music, honky tonk lyrics are emotionally simple and direct, often with a plain-spoken vulnerability and a sense of emotional release. Instead of depicting rural life, though, honky tonk's subject matter was rooted in its immediate surroundings—taverns. Celebrations of romance, parties, and good-times were quite common (as were novelty songs), but honky tonk became especially well-known for its fascination with the flip side: heartbreak, infidelity, pain that could only be numbed with alcohol, morning-after remorse, and religious guilt. Although it's generally thought of as a rural music, honky tonk was actually more the result of rural migration to Southern urban centers, particularly those of Texas. The music initially became popular during World War II, with Ernest Tubb becoming its first star; however, the '50s proved to be honky tonk's golden age. Singer and songwriter Hank Williams hit his absolute prime at the dawn of the decade, and Lefty Frizzell forever altered the way country music was sung with his smooth, lengthy melodic phrases and rich, pure tenor. George Jones rose to prominence in the middle of the decade, becoming a near-consensus choice for country's greatest-ever interpretive singer by adding a startling emotional intensity to Frizzell's phrasing innovations. Honky tonk slowly declined in popularity as rockabilly and country-pop captured mainstream audiences, but its signature sound informed virtually every reaction against country-pop in the decades to come: Bakersfield country in the '60s, progressive and outlaw country in the '70s, and New Traditionalist country in the '80s and '90s.

INSTRUMENTAL COUNTRY

Instrumental Country is exactly what it says it is—any form of country, from traditional honky tonk to country-rock, played strictly instrumentally and without any vocals.

JUG BAND

Although jug band music is often associated with the folk traditions of rural, predominantly white Appalachia, it was in reality performed mostly by African-Americans in urban areas. Jug bands united Appalachian folk with blues, ragtime, and very early jazz; they are best known, of course, for their novel, do-it-yourself instrumentation. The jug in question was usually a whiskey jug, and a player blew across the mouth of the jug to produce pitches in the bass register. Jug bands usually featured at least one stringed instrument from the Appalachian tradition—guitar, banjo, and/or fiddle—and used a wide variety of everyday, easily available household objects for rhythmic accompaniment. The most common were the washboard (whose slats were struck and rubbed in a way analogous to a snare drum) and the metal washtub bass, which was usually equipped with a broomstick and clothesline that produced the sounds. Other possible percussion instruments included spoons, gut buckets, bones, and saw blades; additional melodic accompaniment might have included a harmonica, kazoo, or even comb and tissue paper—whatever was available and economical, really. Jug band music originated in Louisville, Kentucky at the dawn of the 1900s, but found its greatest popularity in Memphis, Tennessee during the '10s and '20s, eventually spreading to Ohio and North Carolina as well. Given the inherent playfulness of the instrumentation, jug band music was accordingly informal, spontaneous, often humorous, and rhythmically bouncy. The most important bands included the Memphis Jug Band, Gus Cannon's Jug Stompers, and Earl McDonald's Dixieland Jug Blowers. The regional jug band fad had largely passed by the '30s, but the British skiffle movement of the '50s and America's own early-'60s folk revival brought a renewed appreciation of the style. Good-humored preservationist outfits like the Jim Kweskin Jug Band and the Even Dozen Jug Band sprang up Stateside; additionally, members of both the Grateful Dead and the Lovin' Spoonful got their start playing jug band music.

NASHVILLE SOUND/COUNTRYPOLITAN

Countrypolitan—an outgrowth of the Nashville sound of the '50s—is among the most commercially-oriented genres of country music. The Nashville sound emerged in the '50s as a way to bring country music to a broad pop audience. The movement was led by Chet Atkins, who was the head of RCA Records' country division. Atkins designed a smooth, commercial sound that relied on country song structures but abandoned all of the hillbilly and honky tonk instrumentation. He hired session musicians and coordinated pop-oriented, jazz-tinged productions. Similarly, Owen Bradley created productions—most notably with Patsy Cline—that featured sophisticated productions and smooth, textured instrumentation. Eventually, most records from Nashville featured this style of production and the Nashville sound began to incorporate strings and vocal choirs. In the late '60s, the Nashville sound metamorphosed into countrypolitan, which emphasized these kinds of pop production flourishes. Featuring layers of keyboards, guitars, strings, and vocals, countrypolitan records were designed to cross over to pop radio and they frequently did. The sound dominated the country charts in the '70s and stayed popular until the early '80s.

NEO-TRADITIONALIST COUNTRY

Neo-Traditionalist Country refers to country artists that play in the style of hardcore traditional country such as honky tonk, yet they are essentially revivalists. Since they are revivalists, they bring a variety of contemporary techniques—such as pop/rock or singer/songwriter influences—to their music, yet these are always subservient to the dominant strain of country music. Furthermore, where new traditionalists brought the sound of traditional country back to the mainstream, neo-traditionalists always operated on the fringes.

NEW TRADITIONALIST

New Traditionalist refers to the legions of young country singers that emerged in the late '80s. These artists reworked and updated the classic sounds of honky tonk and traditional country, adding contemporary production touches to make it more commercially viable—even with the flourishes, the music was essentially hardcore country. After the first wave of new traditionalists (George Strait, Randy Travis, Dwight Yoakam), the genre became a bit slicker and demonstrated more overt rock influences, but the new traditionalists continued to dominate the country charts in one form or another until the mid-'90s.

OLD-TIMEY

Old-Timey (or old-time) refers to the oldest form of country music ever recorded. Country music was first recorded in the early '20s, and its style and sound had remained consistent since the 1800s. Though it encompassed a number of different influences, the music's roots lay in British folk songs, which were played on stringed instruments, such as the fiddle. By the late 1800s, rural Americans had begun playing the folk songs on Spanish guitars and African banjos as well, adding other instruments—dobro, bass, washboards—to the mix. During the early 1900s, this country-folk music added some contemporary influences, particularly the blues and vaudeville comedy. This rurally eclectic amalgamation was the sound of country music during the '20s, and it would forever be identified as "old-time" country, because it was the music that evoked country's roots. Though the music began to evolve in the '30s, as Jimmie Rodgers brought country into the industrial age, there were groups still performing old-time into the 21st century, frequently without changing the conventions of the genre at all. One major style within old-time was bluegrass, which developed in the late '40s as a reaction to the increasing modernization of country music.

OUTLAW COUNTRY

Outlaw Country was one of the more significant trends in country music in the '70s. During that decade, many of the most popular hardcore country singers of the '60s—from George Jones to Merle Haggard—softened their sound slightly, moving away from their honky tonk roots. While the outlaws weren't strictly honky tonk—they were as much storytellers in the tradition of folk songwriters as they were honky tonk vocalists—they kept that spirit alive. Outlaws didn't play by Nashville's rules. They didn't change their music to fit the heavily produced, pop-oriented Nashville sound, nor did they go out of their way to fit into the accepted conventions of country music. Instead, they created an edgy form of hardcore country that was influenced by rock & roll, folk, and blues. Ironically, two of the leading figures of the movement—Waylon Jennings and Willie Nelson—had their roots in the music industry, but by the time they came into their own as recording artists in the mid-'70s, they had developed a unique, defiant way of performing. Several other musicians—including David Allan Coe, Billy Joe Shaver, and Tompall Glaser—followed in their footsteps, and the outlaws were quite popular for a period of three to four years. At the end of the '70s, the urban cowboy movement easily eclipsed the outlaw movement in terms of commercial appeal, but the outlaws had a lasting influence. During the '80s, certain neo-traditionalists owed a bit of their sound to the outlaws, while a whole breed of songwriters, led by Steve Earle, demonstrated a massive debt to the outlaws and their fusion of country, folk, and rock.

PROGRESSIVE BLUEGRASS

Bluegrass is one of the most rigid music genres, one that steadfastly refuses to change its direction. Therefore, Progressive Bluegrass is viewed with skepticism at best, derision at worst, by some hardcore bluegrass fans. Progressive bluegrass expands the sonic palette of bluegrass either by adding elements of jazz, folk, country, and rock, or by amplifying the instruments. The subgenre developed in the late '60s, but it flourished in the '70s, when bands like the Dillards, Boone Creek, Country Gazette, and New Grass Revival began coming to the forefront of bluegrass and folk festivals. Progressive bluegrass continued to evolve into the 21st century, moving closer toward folk and rock in some quarters and closer to jazz in others.

PROGRESSIVE COUNTRY

Progressive Country developed in the late '60s as a reaction to the increasingly polished and pop-oriented sound of mainstream, Nashville-based country. Inspired equally by the spare, twangy, hard-driving sound of Bakersfield country, the singer/songwriter introspection of Bob Dylan, classic honky tonk, and rock & roll, progressive country was the first anti-Nashville movement to emerge since the dawn of rock & roll. Progressive country was rootsier and more intellectual than many of its contemporary genres; it was more concerned with breaking boundaries than with scoring hits. The genre was also songwriter-based. Many of its key artists—Kris Kristofferson, Willie Nelson, Billy Joe Shaver, Tom T. Hall, Jimmie Dale Gilmore, Butch Hancock—were not "good" singers by conventional standards, yet they wrote distinctive, individual songs and had compelling voices. By the early '70s, such artists had developed a sizable cult following, and progressive country began to inch its way into the mainstream, usually in the form of cover versions (Sammi Smith took Kristofferson's "Help Me Make It Through the Night" to the country Top Ten). Progressive country also provided the basis for outlaw country, a harder-edged genre that shook country-pop (briefly) off the top of the charts in the mid-'70s. Even after Outlaw's five-year reign in the late '70s, progressive country continued to exist, until it eventually metamorphosed into alternative country in the '80s.

ROCKABILLY

Rockabilly was a wild, hepped-up meeting between country & western music and early rhythm & blues. It was one of the very first forms of rock & roll, and it was the first one performed predominantly by white musicians (almost all of whom came from the South). Rockabilly was played with spare instrumentation: a twangy electric guitar and an acoustic standup bass whose strings were snapped percussively in a technique dubbed "slap-back" (which sometimes made drums unnecessary). Rockabilly had a thumping, jumping beat that easily made it the most propulsive, visceral, and implicitly sexual style of "white" American music up to that point. Essentially, it made rock & roll accessible to white audiences, thus touching off a cultural revolution the effects of which are still being felt. The genesis of rockabilly dates back to the early '50s, when Bill Haley started fusing electrified country boogie with jump blues. But the style truly crystallized on Elvis Presley's 1954-56 recordings for the Sun label, which captured the manic, primal energy that would become a rockabilly staple. They also established rockabilly's signature production style: echoed vocals, loads of reverb, and a warm, crisp ambience that became the Sun label's trademark. Haley's "Rock Around the Clock" broke rockabilly into the big time in 1955, making it possible for Sun owner Sam Phillips to sell Presley's contract to RCA for a substantial sum of money. Presley became a superstar in 1956, touching off a tidal wave of copycat recordings that, while low on budget and innovation, still inspire rockabilly fanatics with their crazed DIY enthusiasm; additionally, many straight country singers began making rockabilly records, some for the style's popularity, others for its wild excitement. Meanwhile, Phillips used his Presley dollars to gather a stable of rockabilly artists that was second to none: Carl Perkins, Jerry Lee Lewis (who broke from the rockabilly norm by playing piano), Roy Orbison, and singers like Johnny Cash and Charlie Rich who were really country artists at heart. Other significant rockabilly artists were Buddy Holly, who brought melodic pop sensibilities to the music; Gene Vincent, whose crack band featured rockabilly's fastest lead guitarist in Cliff Gallup; Eddie Cochran, whose wry stories of teenage rebellion were overshadowed by his untimely death; and Johnny Burnette, who waxed some of the wildest rockabilly sides ever before finding greater acceptance as a pop idol. As rock & roll evolved into a slicker commercial enterprise, and as the music itself mutated (very quickly) into new forms, rockabilly was left in the dust, largely disappearing from the charts after 1958. However, as the "roll" was slowly siphoned out of rock & roll over the coming decades, artists looking for ways to lend their music a certain raunchiness frequently returned to rockabilly's madly swinging, hip-rolling beat. In the early '80s, there was a full-fledged rockabilly revival; some groups, like the Stray Cats, played up the retro-'50s stylization and greaser image, while others, like the Cramps, loved the raw, crude, amateurish side of the music (usually adding a campy flair) that created a modern subgenre known as psychobilly.

RODEO

Rodeo music is an uptempo, fiddle-driven version of cowboy music that is designed to be played at rodeos. Like square dancing, rodeo is essentially a functional music that is designed for a specific purpose; there are few artists that specialize in rodeo music, and it is usually only released in various-artists collections.

SQUARE DANCE

In the days before World War II, Square Dances were one of the main social gatherings for rural Americans. At these community dances, Western swing and uptempo traditional country were often played—it was all designed to get the patrons dancing. In the years after WWII, square dancing lost its popularity as honky tonks became a preferred gathering place. Square dancing survived as a nostalgic form, and the music that was played at these dances was essentially the same as before, yet like its jazz equivalent, Dixieland, it was devoid of any innovation—it was a stylistic exercise. Unlike Dixieland, where genuinely talented musicians and stylists flourished, square dancing basically served as a function, without offering musicians any place to showcase their skills. As a result, whenever square dancing reached record, it was by and large generic, and only available on albums where the musicians weren't credited.

STRING BANDS

With their intricate instrumental interplay and driving rhythms, String Bands were the most distinctive subgenre of old time country. Though all old-time artists supported themselves with stringed instruments, string bands were notable because they emphasized the instrumentation, not the singers. The popularity of string bands faded in the '30s after Jimmie Rodgers and the Carter Family became country's first stars, yet the groups provided the foundation for the harder sounds of bluegrass in the late '40s.

TRADITIONAL COUNTRY

Traditional Country is a nebulous term—it can refer to anything from Roy Acuff's simple songs to the electrified honky tonk of Johnny Paycheck—but the name does evoke a specific sound, namely the long-standing tradition of simple country songs delivered with simple instrumentation and a distinct twang. The era of traditional country didn't begin until the early '30s, when Jimmie Rodgers became the first national country music star. Rodgers brought the formerly rural music into the industrial era by streamlining the music and lyrics; in the process, he made the genre a viable commercial property. Following Rodgers' success, old-time music faded in popularity and traditional country was born. For the next 40 years, most country music fell under the traditional country umbrella, regardless if it was the big-band dance music of Western swing or driving roadhouse honky

tonk. The majority of the popular artists from the '30s and '40s—Acuff, Eddy Arnold, Ernest Tubb, Hank Williams—became the foundation of the *Grand Ole Opry*, a weekly radio broadcast that became the definitive word of country music. This generation of musicians inspired all the artists that emerged in the following two decades, who put their own spin on traditional country. Following the emergence of rock & roll, country music began to incorporate more pop production techniques, and although this Nashville sound was smoother than the music of the '40s and early '50s, it still conformed to the conventions of traditional country. During the '60s, mainstream country became progressively more pop-influenced, yet traditional country held strong until the early '70s, when country-pop became the dominant form of country music. Many fans of hard country turned toward the tougher sounds of progressive country and outlaw country, yet most of the country audience continued to listen to country-pop, especially since traditional country singers like George Jones, Conway Twitty, and Loretta Lynn had turned toward that subgenre. By the late '70s, most new country singers were either raised on country-pop or pop/rock, and consequently, the reign of traditional country came to an end. During the mid-'80s, a wave of new-traditionalist singers such as George Strait emerged, but their music tended to be influenced by contemporaries as well, making the movement as much an evolution as a revival.

TRUCK DRIVING COUNTRY

Truck Driving Country is an offshoot of honky tonk, country-rock, and Bakersfield country. It's hard-driving music, with a beat straight out of country-rock and sentiments from honky tonk. Often, the songs are about driving trucks or heartbreak. The music reached a larger audience in the late '70s, when the CB phenomenon swept pop culture and the films *Convoy* and *Smokey and the Bandit* popularized truck driving country.

URBAN COWBOY

Urban Cowboy was a 1979 film that romanticized the world of upscale, urban country fans and their lives and music. The music that comprised the soundtrack was modified outlaw and country-pop—it was slick, highly polished music that celebrated the outlaw mythology and honky tonk song structure, but it was given a glossy pop production. Consequently, the music appealed to a greater audience, even winning a number of pop music fans in the process. Following the success of *Urban Cowboy* and its soundtrack (which featured vocalists like Mickey Gilley and Johnny Lee), the country charts were dominated by acts that copied the style and sound of Urban Cowboy. Throughout the early '80s and well into the mid-'80s, Urban Cowboy was the sound of country music and it wasn't until the late '80s, when the neo-traditionalists came along, that it disappeared from the charts.

WESTERN SWING

Western Swing was the most eclectic form of country music and in its free-wheeling diversity, it set the stage for rock & roll. Based in traditional string band music, Western swing also incorporated traditional pop melodies, jazz improvisation, blues, and folk, creating a wildly entertaining and eclectic form of American music. Bob Wills and Milton Brown popularized the form in the '30s, and Wills became known as the father of the genre, since he remained popular for several decades, during which he had a remarkable string of hit singles. Although it sometimes faded away from view, Western swing remained popular into the 21st century, occasionally experiencing upswings in popularity, such as in the early '70s and the early '90s.

WESTERN SWING REVIVAL

Musically, Western Swing Revival differs little from Western swing itself—it is still the same joyous, eclectic mix of big-band jazz, country songs, and pop melodies that made the genre one of the most popular music styles in the '40s. Western swing revival simply marks the moment when the genre reasserted itself as part of country's mainstream. Following World War II, Western swing slowly lost its fanbase as honky tonk and country-pop won over the country audience. In the early '70s, the genre reappeared thanks to the dedication of Merle Haggard and Asleep at the Wheel, two acts who incorporated Western swing into their sound and brought the music back to the top of the country charts. At the beginning of the 21st century, the Western swing revival retained a popular cult following, occasionally slipping a hit single or two onto the charts.

YODELING

Yodeling is a means of vocal performance whereby the singer suddenly changes from a natural voice to a falsetto and back again, constantly alternating between chest and head voices. Originally developed centuries ago by mountain dwellers in the Swiss Alps as a means of communication, yodeling found perhaps its greatest proponent in country music legend Jimmie Rodgers, whose "Blue Yodel" records established him as one of the biggest stars of the 1920s and '30s.

Nathan Abshire

b. Jun. 23, 1913, Gueydan, LA, **d.** May 13, 1981, Basile, LA
Accordion, Vocals / Zydeco, Traditional Cajun, Louisiana Blues, Swamp Blues
Nathan Abshire helped bring the blues and honky tonk to Cajun music and repopularized the accordion with his recordings during the 1950s and '60s, but still never managed to make a living from his music. Born in Gueydan, LA, on June 23, 1913, Abshire began playing professionally in the 1920s, and he first recorded in the early '30s with Happy Fats & His Rayne-Bo Ramblers. Abshire went to work at the Basile, LA, town dump around that time, and he held the job for most of his working life.

His fortunes began looking bright by 1936, however, when the Rayne-Bo Ramblers began backing him on sides for Bluebird. After serving in World War II, Abshire cut "Pine Grove Blues"—his most famous single and later his signature song—for D.T. Records. He recorded for Khoury/Lyric, Swallow, and Kajun during the 1950s and '60s, meanwhile playing local dances and appearing on sessions by the Balfa Brothers.

A renewal of interest in Cajun and folk music during the '70s gave Abshire a chance to play several festivals and colleges and star in the 1975 PBS-TV Cajun documentary, *Good Times Are Killing Me*. The title proved prophetic, however, as Abshire fought alcoholism during his last years. Several sessions for Folkways and La Louisienne followed in the late '70s, but he died on May 13, 1981. —*John Bush*

Pine Grove Blues / 1979 / Swallow ♦♦♦
According to the liner notes on the original LP, this was Abshire's first album, although he had previously had some tracks on several various-artists collections. The Balfa Brothers back him on most of the songs on this jovial, none-too-slick-sounding Cajun recording, devoted mostly to Abshire originals. Actually the bottom end of "La Valse De Holly Beach" is a little muddily recorded by the standards of the 1970s, but if anything that adds to the appeal of music that wasn't meant to sound too finely honed in the recording studio. Joe South's "Games People Play" makes for an unexpected cover choice, though it's slotted into a standard upbeat Cajun rhythm, with infectious ensemble "la-la" backup vocals, steel guitar, accordion, and fiddle. Is there a drawback to a well-executed set by a major veteran Cajun musician in which the performers sound like they're having fun? Well, it's one that bugs many a non-Cajun obsessive: by the time you get late in the program of these 12 songs, you wish for a little more variety in this standard mix of cheery uptempo tunes and lazy, drawling slower ones. [*Pine Grove Blues* was paired with another Abshire album originally issued on Swallow, *The Good Times Are Killing Me*, on a single-disc Ace CD reissue.] —*Richie Unterberger*

The Good Times Are Killing Me / 1979 / Swallow ♦♦♦
As on Abshire's prior Swallow album *Pine Grove Blues*, the Balfa Brothers take a prominent role as accompanists. It differs from the previous record, though, in that Abshire takes just five of the lead vocals on the twelve selections. The lead singing is distributed much as it would be in a leaderless band, some vocals taken by Rodney Balfa, others by Dewey Balfa, and some by Thomas Langley. Also, the production is usually crisper this time around, and the percussion more to the forefront in the mix. In respects to repertoire and performance, though, it's pretty much the same traditionally based mix of two-steps and waltzes, uptempo and slow tempo. The alternation of different lead singers helps alleviate the similarity that causes the attention of many to drag over the course of a Cajun album. The slower, more lugubrious numbers have a welcome honky tonk country feel. The closing "La Noce a Rosalie" is the most atypical piece, sounding a little like an unplugged front-porch toss-off, with spoken sections from Abshire. [*The Good Times Are Killing Me* was paired with another Abshire album originally issued on Swallow, *Pine Grove Blues*, on a single-disc Ace CD reissue.] —*Richie Unterberger*

The Cajun Legend: Best of Nathan Abshire / 1991 / Swallow ♦♦♦♦♦
With "The Good Times Are Killing Me" emblazoned on his accordion case, Abshire embodied the Cajun musician's ethos. There are 20 two-steps and waltzes here, some with the Balfa Brothers, including a remake of the great "Pine Grove Blues" and a heartfelt "Tramp Sur La Rue" with wailing vocals from Nathan. —*Mark A. Humphrey*

★ **French Blues** / 1993 / Arhoolie ♦♦♦♦♦
Recorded between 1949 and 1956, this is prime Cajun music. The fidelity is slightly better than the best Cajun discs of the 1930s, but the approach is still satisfyingly raw and spontaneous, with waltzes, boogies, and blues. A steel guitar is present to varying degrees on most of the tracks, giving the fiddle/accordion-dominated arrangements a bit more flavor. This has a great spontaneous feel that stops short (but not that short) of raggedness, highlighted by Abshire's joyous calls and asides. Includes his big "hit," "Pine Grove Blues," although a hit by the standards of this regional style only constituted about three thousand copies sold. With 28 tracks and 78 minutes running time, it's the usual excellent value for an Arhoolie reissue. —*Richie Unterberger*

The Great Cajun Accordionist / Dec. 12, 1995 / Ace ♦♦♦♦
One time through this CD and the listener will know why Nathan Abshire was called great. The accordionist, born in 1913, was a huge force in the music of his culture from the '30s until his death in 1981, and his influence continues to this day. It was he who incorporated the blues of Creole tradition into Cajun music. His signature tune, "Pine Groves Blues," was a regional hit and made an impact on every Cajun musician thereafter. The man was ahead of his time. Cajun music would not hit the mainstream scene until shortly before his death, so he never got the acclaim that was really his due. Still, listeners have his recordings. This one contains both traditional selections and those written by Abshire himself. As always, the music is meant for dancing. Abshire's virtuosity shines on "Le Two Step de l'Acadian," as well as his own "Le Two Step de Choupique." He is in turn lyrical on waltzes such as "Le Valse du Kaplan" and his "Le Valse de Bayou Teche," hard driving on "Le Blues Francais," and poignant on "Pauvre Hobo." The songs are played with all the heart and soul of the man with "the good times are killing me" as his personal motto. The CD is worthy of this giant of Cajun accordion music. —*Rose of Sharon Witmer*

Pine Grove Blues/The Good Times Are Killing Me / Mar. 2002 / Ace ♦♦♦♦
This two-on-one CD reissue pairs two albums Nathan Abshire recorded for Swallow in the 1970s. —*Richie Unterberger*

Roy Acuff

b. Sep. 15, 1903, Maynardville, TN, **d.** Nov. 23, 1992
Vocals, Harmonica, Violin / Traditional Country, Honky Tonk
Roy Acuff was called the King of Country Music, and for more than 60 years he lived up to that title. If any performer embodied country music, it was Roy Acuff. Throughout his career, Acuff was a champion for traditional country values, enforcing his beliefs as a performer, a music publisher, and as the Grand Master of the *Grand Ole Opry*. Acuff was the first country music superstar after the death of Jimmie Rodgers, pioneering an influential vocal style that complemented the spare, simple songs he was performing. Generations of artists, from Hank Williams to George Jones, have been influenced by Acuff, and countless others have paid respect to him. At the time of his death in 1992, he was still actively involved in the *Grand Ole Opry*, and was as popular as ever.

Originally, Acuff didn't plan to be a singer. Born in the small town of Maynardville, TN, in 1903, Acuff sang in the church choir as a schoolboy, but he was more interested in sports, particularly baseball. Not only was he attracted to the sport, he had a wild streak—after his family moved to Knoxville, he was frequently arrested for fighting. Acuff continued to concentrate on playing ball, eventually becoming strong enough to earn a tryout for the major leagues. However, that tryout never took place. Before he had a chance to play, he was struck by a severe sunstroke while he was on a fishing trip; after the sunstroke, Acuff suffered a nervous breakdown. While he was recovering, he decided that a career in baseball was no longer possible, so he decided to become an entertainer. He began to learn the fiddle and became an apprentice of Doc Hauer, a local medicine showman.

While traveling with the medicine show, Acuff learned how to be a performer—he learned how to sing, how to imitate, how to entertain, how to put on a show. Soon, Acuff joined the Tennessee Crackerjacks, who had a regular slot on Knoxville radio station WROL. Although he was performing frequently, he wasn't making any significant headway, failing to become a star in Tennessee. One song changed that situation—"The Great Speckled Bird," an old gospel tune that had become popular with the Church of God sect. After another radio entertainer wrote the words out to the song, Acuff began performing it in his shows. Quickly, he became popular throughout the eastern part of Tennessee and was asked to record the song by ARC, a record label with national distribution. Acuff headed north to Chicago for a recording session, which resulted in 20 different songs. In addition to "The Great Speckled Bird," he recorded "Steamboat Whistle Blues" and "The Wabash Cannonball," another Tennessee standard that featured the singer imitating the sound of a train whistle; he also made a handful of risqué numbers during these sessions, which were released under the name the Bang Boys.

In 1938, the *Grand Ole Opry* invited Acuff to audition for the show. During the show, he sang "The Great Speckled Bird" and became an instant hit, prompting the *Opry* to hire him full-time. Before he was given his regular slot, the *Opry* insisted that he change the name of his band to the Smoky Mountain Boys. The following year, Acuff reassembled his band, with the most notable addition being Pete "Bashful Brother Oswald" Kirby, a dobro player who sang high harmonies.

Roy Acuff became a national superstar during the '40s, scoring a long string of hit records, which included the classics "The Wreck on the Highway," "The Precious Jewel," and "Beneath That Lonely Mound of Clay," among many others. During this time, he discovered that there was a potential gold mine in music publishing. Acuff had printed his own songbook, which sold a staggering 100,000 copies. Publishers in New York tried to acquire the rights to his songs, but the success of the songbook convinced

Acuff to hold on to the songs and seek out the help of Fred Rose, a professional songwriter and pianist working in Chicago. The pair founded Acuff-Rose Publications in October 1942, using Acuff's songs as its base; Rose also added his songs, including "Faded Love," "Deep Water," and "Blue Eyes Crying in the Rain." Acuff-Rose was an immediate success, and over the next two decades many of the most popular songs and songwriters were the property of the company, including the songs of Hank Williams, the Louvin Brothers, Don Gibson, Roy Orbison, the Everly Brothers, John D. Loudermilk, Boudleaux & Felice Bryant, and Redd Stewart & Pee Wee King's "Tennessee Waltz."

In the late '40s, Acuff continued to rule the country charts, as well as scoring a number of pop crossovers ("The Prodigal Son," "I'll Forgive You, But I Can't Forget"). For most of the '50s, he concentrated on touring—he didn't have a single charting record between 1947 and 1958, returning with the Top Ten hit "Once More," as well as two other Top 20 singles, "So Many Times" and "Come and Knock." In 1962, he became the first living performer to be inducted to the Country Music Hall of Fame. The '60s yielded some hits, yet he continued to concentrate on touring; by the end of the decade, he decided to leave the road, staying at the *Grand Ole Opry*.

The beginning of the '80s was a difficult period for Acuff, as he experienced the death of his wife and several longtime bandmembers, including pianist Jimmie Riddle and fiddler Howdy Forrester. In 1987, he released his final charting record, an inspirational duet with Charlie Louvin called "The Precious Jewel." As his health began to decline in the late '80s, Acuff built a house near the *Opry* so he could greet friends and fans. He passed away in 1992, leaving behind a legacy that isn't limited to his music. Through his records, his performances, and Acuff-Rose, Roy Acuff has had an enormous effect on shaping the role of country music in the 20th century; it is hard to imagine the music without him. —*Stephen Thomas Erlewine*

Fly Birdie Fly '39–41 / 1939 / Rounder ✦✦✦✦✦

The songs on *Fly Birdie Fly* were recorded in 1939-1941, as he was flying high as a new star of the *Opry*. Although these tracks are not his best-known, these blues and gospel songs are rowdier than his reputation and as good as his classics. —*Michael McCall*

Songs of the Smokey Mountains / 1955 / Capitol ✦✦✦

The Great Roy Acuff / 1964 / Capitol ✦✦✦

The original *Great Roy Acuff* LP was a reissue of material Acuff had recorded for Capitol between 1953-1955, including one song, the tragic "Please Daddy Forgive," that had not been previously released. The album begins with an excellent train song, "Sunshine Special," before running through a characteristic set of sentimental, spiritual, and moralistic songs. It's unfortunate that "Rushing Around" and "Sweep Around Your Own Back Door" were sequenced next to each other since their refrains have virtually identical melodies. [The Dualtone CD is a straight reissue of the 1964 album that reproduces the original album art and adds new notes, but it is unnecessarily brief (a two-fer would have been a better value). All of this material is duplicated and expanded on Bear Family's two-disc set, *The King of Country Music*.] —*Greg Adams*

The Voice of Country Music / 1965 / Capitol ✦✦✦

Roy Acuff's *The Voice of Country Music* LP was a reissue when it was originally released in 1965 since it compiled tracks Acuff had recorded for Capitol in the mid-'50s. Some of the most unusual music Acuff ever recorded is here, including novelties ("Sixteen Chickens and a Tambourine") and honky tonk songs (Jimmy Work's "That's What Makes the Juke Box Play"). "Streamline Heartbreaker," a song written but never recorded by the Louvin Brothers, is simply stunning and is the standout track on the album. While not representative of Acuff's typical output, *The Voice of Country Music* is easily enjoyable, and surprising when compared to Acuff's usual religious and moral music. [The 2002 CD release duplicates the original LP except for the new liner notes by Paul Kingsbury. All of the recordings here are also available on Bear Family's two-CD set *The King of Country Music*.] —*Greg Adams*

Greatest Hits / 1970 / Sony ✦✦✦✦✦

This contains the original versions of Acuff's classic, groundbreaking work—"The Great Speckled Bird," "Wabash Cannonball," "Night Train to Memphis," "Were You There When They Crucified My Lord," and "Fire Ball Mail." —*Stephen Thomas Erlewine*

Night Train to Memphis / 1970 / Harmony ✦✦✦

Arguably, Roy Acuff was the Louis Armstrong of country—a seminal figure who was a major influence on everyone from Hank Williams, Ernest Tubb, and Cowboy Copas to Lefty Frizzell, Hank Snow, and Buck Owens. And that list of heavyweights barely scratches the surface. Acuff didn't invent country any more than Armstrong invented jazz, but his impact was tremendous. Assembled by Allegro's Roots of Country label in 2001, this two-CD collection focuses on Acuff's influential recordings of the 1930s and 1940s. *Night Train to Memphis* is full of definitive hits that inspired countless country legends, including "Tennessee Waltz," "Precious Jewel," "Wreck on the Highway," and the title track. Most of the material is secular, although "Brother Take Warning," "Prodigal Son," and "I'll Reap My Harvest in Heaven" are fine examples of country gospel. While the material is superb, many of Acuff's essential recordings are missing, including "Faded Love," "Wabash Cannonball," and "The Great Speckled Bird." One thing that collectors definitely *won't* like about *Night Train to Memphis* is the total absence of recording dates and personnel—and, regrettably, several other country collections that Roots of Country provided in August 2001 had the same problem. Such laziness is inexcusable; collections of vintage material should *always* have recording dates, if available. But despite its shortcomings, this double CD has a lot of good points. All of the selections—even the ones that aren't quite essential—are captivating. *Night Train to Memphis* is hardly the last word on Acuff's legacy, but it's worth having in your collection if you can forgive the absence of recording dates and personnel. —*Alex Henderson*

☆ **Columbia Historic Edition** / 1985 / Columbia ✦✦✦✦✦

As an LP, this 16 song compilation, covering the years 1936-1951, was a supremely admirable effort at an overview of Roy Acuff's 16 years with the American Record Corporation (ARC) and Columbia Records, and was notable for the inclusion of five previously unissued sides. It was supposed to be heard, ideally, in tandem with the label's *Greatest Hits* collection, but it stands well on its own; as a CD it still holds up, presenting the earliest renditions of a brace of songs that became not only Acuff standards, but standards for country music in his hands, most notably "Wabash Cannonball" in its 1936 rendition, with Sam "Dynamite" Hatcher on vocals. Pete "Bashful Brother Oswald" Kirby shines at various points on the late-'30s sides and beyond with his rippling banjo work and distinctive, bluesy dobro sound. The most fascinating thing about this collection is how relatively little Acuff's sound changed over the decade and a half represented—his music embraced blues, folk, gospel, pop, bluegrass, and a host of other elements, but he still had an authentic, raw country sound in the early '50s, long after he had moved into very profitable and sophisticated areas behind the scenes in the business of country music. The budget price of this disc, coupled with the quality of the notes by John Rumble of the Country Music Foundation and the excellent tape research by producers Bob Pinson and Michael Brooks, make this a definite choice addition to any country collection. —*Bruce Eder*

☆ **Steamboat Whistle Blues** / 1985 / Rounder ✦✦✦✦✦

Steamboat Whistle Blues makes a nice companion to Columbia's *The Essential Roy Acuff (1936-1949)*. The Rounder Records release contains late-'30s cuts by Acuff and his Crazy Tennesseans (later the Smoky Mountain Boys) not found on the *Essential* collection and provides an excellent overview of Acuff's early and varied repertoire, including fiddle breakdown tunes ("Shout Oh Lulu"), pop covers ("Yes Sir, That's My Baby"), countrified rags ("Smokey Mountain Rag"), and some mountain blues ("Honky Tonk Mamas"). There's also a fine example of Acuff's church-hymn style here in the endearing, "modern-day" gospel tune "The Automobile of Life." Crazy Tennesseans and Smoky Mountain Boys alike (guitarist James Clell Summy and harmonica player Sam "Dynamite" Hatcher in particular) provide Acuff with rough-hewn yet tight backing on all the numbers. If you'd like a good record of Acuff's career before his star rose as both a Grand Ole Opry fixture and a country music publishing giant, then pick up a used copy (sorry, it's out of print) of *Steamboat Whistle Blues*. Listening to these great songs one can certainly understand how Acuff, along with Jimmie Rodgers and Hank Williams, have come to define what country music used to be. —*Stephen Cook*

The Best of Roy Acuff / 1991 / Curb ✦✦✦

Curb's *The Best of Roy Acuff* collects a selection of '60s hits and a number of re-recordings Acuff made in the '60s while signed to Hickory Records, a label he began with his publishing partner Fred Rose. By this point, Acuff's recording career was no longer successful; he concentrated on the *Grand Ole Opry*. Nevertheless, these re-recordings are entertaining, although they are considerably slicker and less affecting than his early, groundbreaking tracks. As a sampler of Acuff's '60s sound, *The Best of* is effective. Bear in mind, the disc only has ten tracks, so while it may be bargain-priced, it's not necessarily a bargain. —*Stephen Thomas Erlewine*

★ **The Essential Roy Acuff (1936–1949)** / 1992 / Columbia/Legacy ✦✦✦✦✦

The Essential Roy Acuff (1936–1949) contains the original versions of "The Great Speckled Bird," "Night Train to Memphis," "The Precious Jewel," and "Wabash Cannonball," and 16 other tracks that were cut for Columbia Records at the peak of his recording career. —*Stephen Thomas Erlewine*

King of Country Music / Jun. 28, 1994 / Bear Family ✦✦✦✦✦

King of Country Music (1936–1947) / Aug. 18, 1998 / ASV ✦✦✦✦✦

King of Country Music is an affordably priced import collection of some of Acuff's prime recordings, including three with the Crazy Tennesseans (before the Opry urged them to change their name to the Smoky Mountain Boys). 25 tracks from 1936-47 are presented in chronological order, including some of Acuff's signature songs: "Wabash Cannonball," "Great Speckled Bird" and "The Streamlined Cannon Ball," as well as several chart hits from the mid-'40s. Offering a greater number of tracks than Columbia's *Historic Edition*, *King of Country Music* provides a generous retrospective of Acuff's peak years. —*Greg Adams*

R.C. Cola Radio Shows, Vol. 1 / Nov. 9, 1999 / RME ✦✦✦

The first volume of a projected ten-volume series, here are Roy's 1953 radio shows sponsored by the popular soft drink. These rare acetates (only four complete sets still exist) encompassed 52 15-minute shows for the entire broadcast run and were recorded at the WSM Studios in Nashville. As such, it's classic Acuff and the Smoky Mountain Boys, expanded to include comedy from the Duke of Paducah and harmonica and fiddle features from Jimmy Riddle and Howdy Forrester. These four shows are also a reminder of what was still on the radio in the early to mid-'50s when rock & roll was taking over the airwaves. —*Cub Koda*

R.C. Cola Radio Shows, Vol. 2 / Nov. 9, 1999 / RME ✦✦✦

R.C. Cola Radio Shows, Vol. 3 / Apr. 25, 2000 / Romulan ✦✦✦

The third volume in this series of radio transcriptions catches Acuff and the Smoky Mountain Boys in top form on tunes like "Little Pal," "Mother's Not Dead, She's Sleepin'," "Take My Hand, Precious Lord," and "Mommy, Please Stay Home With Me." Comedy is provided by the Duke of Paducah, who checks in with four routines while instrumental specialties are handled by Brother Oswald and fiddler Howdy Forrester. Another valuable document of early radio from the 1950s and country music back in the good old days. —*Cub Koda*

R.C. Cola Radio Shows, Vol. 4 / Jul. 11, 2000 / RME ✦✦✦

20 Greatest Songs / Mar. 13, 2001 / Varese ✦✦✦

The Crazy Tennessean / Aug. 28, 2001 / Catfish ✦✦✦✦

Roy Acuff's transformation from a country boy in the backwoods of Tennessee to leading light of the *Grand Ole Opry* helped set the template for the classic tale of fame so often told in Nashville. Thankfully, as with many of country music's early stars, Acuff shored up his folksy aura with some of the finest raw country sides to be recorded. Standing alongside other originators like Jimmie Rodgers and Ernest Tubb, Acuff made his mark with such classics as "Great Speckled Bird," "Wabash Cannonball," and "Automobile of Life." The Catfish label's fine Acuff collection, *The Crazy Tennessean*, includes these and 20 other of the singer's best numbers, most of which were cut during the late '30s. This disc makes a fine complement to Columbia's *The Essential Roy Acuff*, which includes a good share of his '40s hits like "Wreck on the Highway" and "Blue Eyes Crying in the Rain." *—Stephen Cook*

Ryan Adams

b. Nov. 5, 1974, Jacksonville, NC

Vocals, Guitar, Piano / Alternative Country, Singer/Songwriter, Alternative Country-Rock, Americana, Alternative Pop/Rock

Mixing the heartfelt angst of a singer/songwriter with the cocky brashness of a garage rocker, Ryan Adams is at once one of the few artists to emerge from the alt-country scene to achieve mainstream commercial success; and he is the one who most strongly refused to be defined by the genre, leaping from one spot to another stylistically as he follows his increasingly prolific muse.

Ryan Adams was born in Jacksonville, NC, in 1974. While country music was a major part of his family's musical diet when he was young (he's cited Loretta Lynn, George Jones, Merle Haggard, and Johnny Cash as particular favorites), in his early teens Adams developed a taste for punk rock and he began playing electric guitar. At 15, Adams started writing songs, and a year later he formed a band called the Patty Duke Syndrome; Adams once described PDS as "an arty noise punk band," with Hüsker Dü frequently cited as a key influence and reference point. The Patty Duke Syndrome developed a following in Jacksonville, and when Adams was 19 the band relocated to the larger town of Raleigh, NC, in hopes of expanding their following. However, Adams became eager to do something more melodic that would give him a platform for his country and pop influences.

In 1994, Adams left the Patty Duke Syndrome and formed Whiskeytown with guitarist Phil Wandscher and violinist Caitlin Cary. With bassist Steve Grothman and drummer Eric "Skillet" Gilmore completing the lineup, Whiskeytown (the name came from regional slang for getting drunk) released their first album, *Faithless Street*, on the local Mood Food label. The album won reams of critical praise in the music press, and more than one writer suggested that Whiskeytown could do for the alt-country or No Depression scene what Nirvana had done for grunge. But by the time the band signed to a major label—the Geffen-distributed imprint Outpost Records—the band had undergone the first in a series of major personal shakeups; and in the summer of 1997, when Whiskeytown's Outpost debut *Stranger's Almanac* was ready for release, Adams and Wandscher were the only official members of the band left. Cary soon returned, but Wandscher left shortly afterward, and Whiskeytown had a revolving-door lineup for much of the next two years, with the band's live shows become increasingly erratic, as solid performances were often followed by noisy, audience-baiting disasters. Consequently, as strong as *Stranger's Almanac* was, Whiskeytown never fulfilled the commercial expectations created for them by others.

In 1999, the band—which was down to Adams, Cary, and a handful of session musicians—recorded their third and final album, *Pneumonia*, but when Geffen was absorbed in a merger between PolyGram and Universal, Outpost was phased out, and the album was shelved; shortly afterward, Whiskeytown quietly called it quits. Following Whiskeytown's collapse, Adams wasted no time launching a career apart from the band, and after a few solo acoustic tours, Adams went into a Nashville studio with songwriters Gillian Welch and David Rawlings and cut his first album under his own name, *Heartbreaker*, which was released by pioneering "insurgent country" label Bloodshot Records in 2000. The album received critical raves, respectable sales, and a high-profile endorsement from Elton John, and Adams was signed by Universal's new Americana imprint, Lost Highway Records. Lost Highway gave Whiskeytown's *Pneumonia* a belated release in early 2001, and later that same year, they released his second solo set, *Gold*, which displayed less of a country influence in favor of classic pop and rock styles of the 1970s. In the wake of the September 11 terrorist attacks, the album's opening track, "New York, New York," was embraced by radio as an anthem of resilience (though it actually concerned a busted romance), and Adams once again found himself touted as the "next big thing." Always a prolific songwriter, in a bit more than a year following *Gold*'s release, Adams had written and recorded enough material for four albums; Adams opted to whittle the 60 tunes down to a 13 song collection called *Demolition*, which was released in 2002 as Adams went into the studio to record his official follow-up to *Gold*. In addition, Adams has recorded in collaboration with Emmylou Harris and Beth Orton; guested on albums by Lucinda Williams and his former bandmate Caitlin Cary; and has planned albums with Nashville punk band the Pink Hearts and an all-star rock outfit called the Fucking Virgins, featuring Evan Dando, James Iha, and Melissa Auf Der Maur. *—Mark Deming*

● **Heartbreaker** / 2000 / Bloodshot ✦✦✦✦

As Whiskeytown finally ground to a halt in the wake of an astonishing number of personal changes following *Faithless Street* (coupled with record company problems that kept their final album, *Pneumonia*, from reaching stores until two years after it was recorded), Ryan Adams ducked into a Nashville studio for two weeks of sessions with Gillian Welch and David Rawlings. While arch traditionalists Welch and Rawlings would hardly seem like a likely match for alt-country's bad boy, the collaboration brought out the best in Adams; *Heartbreaker* is loose, open, and heartfelt in a way Whiskeytown's admittedly fine albums never were, and makes as strong a case for Adams' gifts as anything his band ever released. With the exception of the Stones-flavored "Shakedown on 9th Street" and the swaggering "To Be Young (Is to Be Sad, Is to Be High)," *Heartbreaker* leaves rock & roll on the shelf in favor of a sound that blends low-key folk-rock with a rootsy, bluegrass-accented undertow, and while the album's production and arrangements are subtle and spare, they make up in emotional impact whatever they lack in volume. As a songwriter, Adams concerns himself with the ups and downs of romance rather than the post-teenage angst that dominated Whiskeytown's work, and "My Winding Wheel" and "Damn, Sam (I Love a Woman That Rains)" are warmly optimistic in a way he's rarely been before, while "Come Pick Me Up" shows he's still eloquently in touch with heartbreak. Adams has always been a strong vocalist, but his duet with Emmylou Harris on "Oh My Sweet Carolina" may well be his finest hour as a singer, and the stripped-back sound of these sessions allows him to explore the nooks and crannies of his voice, and the results are pleasing. Whiskeytown fans who loved the "Replacements-go-twang" crunch of "Drank Like a River" and "Yesterday's News" might have a hard time warming up to *Heartbreaker*, but the strength of the material and the performances suggest Adams is finally gaining some much-needed maturity, and his music is all the better for it. *—Mark Deming*

Demolition / Sep. 24, 2002 / Universal ✦✦✦

On more than one occasion, Ryan Adams has played solo acoustic gigs that consisted almost entirely of songs he wrote the afternoon of the show, and after his 2001 album, *Gold*, finally gave him an audience outside the small but rabidly enthusiastic alt-country scene, the very prolific Adams seemed to waste no time laying down as many songs as he possibly could. If one believes what they read in *New Musical Express*, Adams cut about four albums' worth of material during sessions with various musicians and producers within the space of a year (not even counting the much talked about but to date unheard four-track recordings of blues versions of all the songs from the Strokes' debut disc, *Is This It?*). Sensibly enough, Adams and his record company decided that releasing such a huge flood of material wasn't in the best interest of either artist or label, and instead Adams cherry-picked these sessions into a 13-track collection, *Demolition*. Appropriately enough, *Demolition* sounds less like "the third Ryan Adams album" than a collection of stray tunes—some of which are very good, especially the lazy summer vibe of "Tennessee Sucks," the uptempo acoustic twang of "Chin Up, Cheer Up," the winsome "Cry on Demand," and the heading-off-the-rails rocker "Starting to Hurt." But more than a few of the other songs on the album sound like rough drafts rather than completed works, and *Demolition* seems to lack a strong thematic or structural center. In short, *Demolition* sounds like a bunch of demos, which of course is just what it is, and while it preserves a few strong tunes and offers an insight into Adams' creative process, it also makes clear that even the rising wunderkind of Americana can benefit from a bit of judicious editing and polishing. *—Mark Deming*

Gold / Nov. 26, 2002 / Universal ✦✦✦

One would think that being Ryan Adams would be a pretty good deal at the time of this album's release; he had a major-label deal, critics were in love with him, he got to date Winona Ryder and Alanis Morrisette, Elton John went around telling everyone he was a genius, and his record company gave him *carte blanche* to do whatever he wanted. But to listen to *Gold*, Adams' first solo album for his big-league sponsors at Lost Highway, one senses that there are about a dozen other musicians Adams would love to be, and nearly all of them were at their peak in the early to mid-'70s. Adams' final album with Whiskeytown, *Pneumonia*, made it clear that he was moving beyond the scruffy alt-country of his early work, and *Gold* documents his current fascination with '70s rock. Half the fun of the album is playing "Spot the Influence": "Answering Bell" is a dead ringer for Van Morrison (with fellow Morrison enthusiast Adam Duritz on backing vocals), "Tina Toledo's Street Walkin' Blues" is obviously modeled on the Rolling Stones, "Harder Now That It's Over" sounds like *Harvest*-period Neil Young, "New York, New York" resembles Steven Stills in his livelier moments (Steven's son, Chris Stills, plays on the album), and "Rescue Blues" and "La Cienaga Just Smiled" suggest the influence of Adams' pal Elton John. Of course, everyone has their influences, and Adams seems determined to make the most of them on *Gold*; it's a far more ambitious album than his solo debut, *Heartbreaker*. The performances are polished, Ethan Johns' production is at once elegant and admirably restrained, Adams is in strong voice throughout, and several of the songs are superb, especially the swaggering but lovelorn "New York, New York," the spare and lovely "When the Stars Go Blue," and the moody closer, "Goodnight, Hollywood Blvd." But while *Gold* sounds like a major step forward for Adams in terms of technique, it lacks the heart and soul of *Heartbreaker* or *Pneumonia*; the album seems to reflect craft rather than passion, and while it's often splendid craft, the fire that made Whiskeytown's best work so special isn't evident much of the time. *Gold* sounds like an album that could win Ryan Adams a lot of new fans (especially with listeners whose record collections go back a ways), but longtime fans may be a bit put off by the album's richly crafted surfaces and emotionally hollow core. [The first pressing of *Gold* came with a bonus five-song EP, entitled *Side Four*, that allowed Adams' twangy side to rise to the surface again for a couple of numbers, especially "The Fools We Are as Men" and "The Bar Is a Beautiful Place."] *—Mark Deming*

Eddie Adcock

b. Jun. 21, 1938, Scottsville, VA

Banjo, Guitar / Bluegrass, Progressive Bluegrass, Traditional Bluegrass

Among the major-league talent emerging from the folk music boom of the late '50s were the Country Gentlemen, a D.C.-based quartet that introduced bluegrass to a generation of city folks and college students, people who had never heard of Flatt & Scruggs or Bill Monroe or the Stanley Brothers. The Gentlemen, in playing the old bluegrass standards but playing them "different," were in a sense the first newgrass group. Eddie Adcock was the band's banjo player and he was a player of distinction—his style was as innovative as Don Reno's. Adcock's considerable talent spread to other stringed instruments when he left the Gentlemen in 1970 and began exploring new musical genres. For the next three decades, Eddie Adcock remained one of the most popular musicians in bluegrass.

Adcock was born and raised in Scottsville, VA. He bought his first banjo as child and began performing with his brother Frank shortly afterward. The duo would sing in local churches and radio stations based in the nearby Charlottesville. In his teens, he played in a band called the James River Playboys and worked at a theater in his hometown, where he had the opportunity to see major country artists of the day, including Wilma Lee and Stoney Cooper. At the age of 14, he left home after a family crisis and supported himself through semi-professional boxing. For the next seven years, he boxed and played music at nights. A few years later, he began racing cars. As a racer, Adcock racked up 34 straight wins with his car, which he named Mr. Banjo; he also had set two track records at Manassas, VA. Not only did he box and race, he also performed various blue-collar jobs to pay the rent. All the time, he played music at night.

Eddie Adcock didn't begin his professional musical career until 1953, when he joined Smokey Graves & His Blue Star Boys, who had a regular show at a radio station in Crewe, VA. His exposure with Graves led to jobs with other musicians, including Mac Wiseman, Bill Harrell, and Buzz Busby. Between 1953 and 1957, he floated between different bands. Bill Monroe offered a job to Adcock in 1957, and he played with the Blue Grass Boys for a short time—Monroe had to let him go because the band simply wasn't earning enough money to employ him. Adcock returned to working day jobs, but that was short-lived. After he started working in a sheet metal factory, Jim Cox, John Duffey, and Charlie Waller asked him to join their new band, the Country Gentlemen.

The Country Gentlemen became one of the most popular and respected bluegrass bands of the late '50s and '60s, as well as one of the most progressive. They expanded the repertoire of bluegrass bands to include contemporary country, folk, and rock songwriters, most notably Bob Dylan; usually they added this material at the urging of Adcock. The Country Gentlemen rode to popularity in the late '50s as part of the folk boom and continued to be one of the most popular bluegrass/folk bands in the country throughout the '60s.

At the end of the '60s, Adcock began to feel constrained by the Country Gentlemen. He wanted to experiment with different musical genres, which he felt the band wasn't willing to do. Consequently, he quit the Gentlemen and moved to California, where he formed a country-rock band called the Clinton Special. While he performed with the group he used the pseudonym Clinton Codack. The band recorded only one single, "Just as You Are I Love You"/"Blackberry Fence," which was released on MGM Records; the A-side of the single was featured in the 1971 film *The Horsemen*.

After the Clinton Special fell apart, Adcock headed back east, where he formed another group, II Generation with Bob White, A.L. Wood, Wendy Thatcher, and Jimmy Gaudreau, who used to play with the Country Gentlemen. II Generation's lineup changed frequently during the '70s, but it gelled around 1974 when Martha Hearon joined the group. Hearon played guitar for the band and wrote a good share of its material; she also married Adcock soon after she joined. II Generation was active throughout the '70s, releasing a handful of albums on the Rome, Rebel, and CMH labels. Adcock and Hearon disbanded the group in 1980 and moved to Tennessee, where they formed a trio called Talk of the Town with bassist Missy Raines. In the mid-'80s, Adcock launched a solo career, releasing a series of cassette-only collections on CMH. In the '90s, he began releasing albums on compact disc, as well as performing with an all-star bluegrass outfit called the Masters. After nearly 40 years in the music business, Eddie Adcock remained as popular as he ever was, touring all around the world. —*Stephen Thomas Erlewine & David Vinopal*

And Talk of the Town / 1987 / CMH ✦✦✦✦✦

Eddie Adcock and His Guitar / 1988 / CMH ✦✦✦

The Acoustic Connection / 1988 / CMH ✦✦✦

Dixie Fried / 1991 / CMH ✦✦✦✦✦

Talk to Your Heart / Jan. 15, 1995 / CMH ✦✦✦

Renaissance Man / 1996 / Pinecastle ✦✦✦
Eddie Adcock is rightly celebrated for his instrumental mastery in the world of bluegrass, but he's always been a cutting-edge player, too—as he showed in 1978 by inventing the Gitbo, a double-necked instrument that combined electric guitar and acoustic banjo. Not surprisingly, then, he rewrites the rule book yet again on this relaxed, mostly instrumental outing that features a bevy of notable contributors—starting with Ricky Skaggs, who lends deft fiddle and guitar to a high-spirited cover of Bob Wills' "San Antonio Rose." Another obvious high point is the wistful "Lost at Sea," where vocalist Alan O'Day swears to find himself first before buying anymore things he doesn't need, with Bobby Hicks' fiddle weaving a perfect counterpoint. Guest vocalists Mac Wiseman and Buck White turn up to sing a few strategic lines on "Poopsie Blue" and "Crazy Blues," which flips the instrumental-vocal conundrum on its head. Eddie's wife, Martha, also does a sparkling vocal on "Sing Banjo Sing"—one of five originals by her husband—and the traditional "Wild Swanee Home." Other surprises include a spiffy remake of Simon & Garfunkel's "Mrs. Robinson" with banjo, fiddle, mandolin, and string bass. Adcock's knack for reinterpretation also extends to "Pallet on Your Floor" (a traditional number that late jazzman Rahsaan Roland Kirk also recorded). His original instrumentals ("Mandango," "Dream Concerto") also make fine showcases for Martha's rhythm guitar, fiddling ace Glen Duncan, and upright bassist Missy Raines. All in all, there's some treats for everybody, whether they're avid bluegrass listeners or not. —*Ralph Heibutzki*

• **Spirited** / May 6, 1998 / Pinecastle ✦✦✦✦✦
Eddie Adcock boasts stints with the "classic" Country Gentlemen, Mac Wiseman and Bill Monroe, on his glittering bluegrass resumé. His wife, vocalist and guitarist Martha, joins the banjoist as well. The title track is a fiery instrumental that showcases the virtuoso

picking ability of these two players trading leads. A cunning dip in tempo brings the foray to a close. The meat of the recording is the 11 other songs that are ostensibly bluegrass hymns, still feature the stunning playing and singing (mostly from Martha) that make this collection a hallmark of contemporary bluegrass, regardless of topic. A particularly memorable track is in the Eddie-penned "What Love Can't Do." Eddie picks the melody and supports Martha with baritone harmonies as she provides guitar rhythm. The lyrics are poetic and insightful, the music skilled and melodic. —*Thomas Schulte*

Hobo Jack Adkins

Guitar / Traditional Country, Old-Timey, Traditional Folk
Hobo Jack Adkins was given his stage name by a radio station manager during an era when radio was closely involved with newly developing strains of old-time, country, and bluegrass music. It places him in the unique category of players whose names connote a rambling lifestyle—Ramblin' Jack Elliot would be the most famous example—as if all musicians weren't already partially hobos because of the wandering demands of the occupation. An orphan, Adkins grew up during the worst years of the Depression and claims to have never known any family besides a mother who died when he was 16, and a father who had apparently been poisoned when Adkins was just a baby. It was a haunting memory that he claims to have visualized while performing country & western masterpieces decades later. He went on to record some of the most beautiful examples of early bluegrass music in the company of most of the membership of the legendary Lonesome Pine Fiddlers: stellar old-time players such as mandolinist and vocalist Red Ratliff, banjoist Ray Goins, and fiddler Ray Cline. Adkins always had one foot solidly in country music despite the enormous influence of traditional Appalachian string music, and made historic early use of electric guitar on tracks such as "You Have Let Me Memories," originally cut for the Lucky label in the mid-'40s.

The memories Adkins did have were certainly ones of deprivation: his toys were rocks that he pretended were cars, the family stowed apples in the cellar in order to have something special for Christmas, and "a candy bar was really somethin' back then!" A cousin that played guitar got him into music at around the age of 12, also coinciding with the beginning of his days of hitchhiking and roaming. Around 17, he actually acquired a guitar of own, after a bit of barter involving a .22 rifle and a bushel of shelled corn. The Acme company, perhaps the same firm supplying endless ordnance and gadgetry to Wiley Coyote, made the first recordings of Hobo Jack Adkins in 1944. It was a time when the regional recording industry was operating about on the same level as moonshine, with fellows such as Jim Stanton selling his Rich-R-Tone sides out of the back of his car. "Going Back to Kentucky" was a marvelous number cut in 1945 with a sprightly bluegrass feel to it; Adkins backed simply by Ratliff on mandolin, a bassist, and a spicy banjo player identified only as "Red Onion." The Lucky company picked up on Adkins after Acme failed in the promotion department, but then the singer tossed dirt in the face of discographers by starting up his own label with the same fortunate name, Lucky. There are also theories that the Adco label was his, an abbreviation for "Adkins company." He also had a contract with the Starday label, releasing a series of singles in the late '50s including numbers such as "Kentucky School Boy" and "Country Boy Went to Town," the former number included on the label's marvelous compilation release entitled *Tragic Songs of Death and Sorrow.*

Adkins is an accomplished songwriter, and has turned out numbers that have been recorded by the Stanley Brothers, and other bluegrass and country acts. The modern Howlin' Dog Moon progressive bluegrass outfit covers his song entitled "Another Night," but may have learned it from Ricky Skaggs or Alison Krauss, both of whom have also recorded it. As he got older, Adkins focused more on this type of income, shifting almost permanently into the realm of gospel music by the '60s, when he also suffered a series of health setbacks including heart attacks. Despite these problems, he seems to have been a dynamo, eventually running three record labels and a publishing company, as well as preaching gospel as a minister. In the '70s, he fronted a gospel group called the Old Regular Baptists. —*Eugene Chadbourne*

Jack Adkins / 1962 / Starday ✦✦✦

Trace Adkins

b. Jan. 13, 1962, Sarepta, LA
Guitar, Vocals / Contemporary Country, New Traditionalist
Trace Adkins helped keep country's traditionalist flame burning during the crossover-happy late '90s, mixing classic honky tonk with elements of gospel, blues, and rock & roll. Adkins was born in the small Louisiana town of Sarepta in 1962, and took up the guitar at an early age; he went on to study music at Louisiana Tech, where he also played football, and worked on an offshore oil rig after graduating. His finger was severed in an accident while on the job, and once several years had passed, he returned to music with the gospel quartet the New Commitments. In the early '90s he began to pursue a solo career, playing honky tonk bars and clubs as often as he could, and honing a powerful, wide-ranging baritone voice in the process. He spent several years on the circuit, and finally moved to Nashville to try his luck in the industry; he was quickly signed to Capitol by Scott Hendricks, who'd produced the likes of Brooks & Dunn, Faith Hill, and Alan Jackson.

Adkins issued his debut album, *Dreamin' Out Loud*, in 1996, and it established him as a rising star. The lead single, "Every Light in the House," went to number three; "I Left Something Turned on at Home" hit number two; and "(This Ain't) No Thinkin' Thing" went all the way to number one. His 1997 follow-up album, *Big Time*, spawned another Top Five hit in "The Rest of Mine," and "Lonely Won't Leave Me Alone" just missed the Top Ten. However, it wasn't quite the commercial powerhouse of *Dreamin' Out Loud*; neither was its follow-up, 1999's *More*, which featured just one Top Ten single in the title track. Nonetheless, all three albums made the country Top Ten. *Chrome*, in 2001, brought Adkins into the Top Five of the country album charts for the first time, as the Top Ten lead single "I'm Tryin'" proved to be his biggest hit since "The Rest of Mine." In July of that year, Adkins was arrested for drunk driving and later pled guilty. The title track of *Chrome* belatedly climbed into the Top Ten in early 2003. —*Steve Huey*

• **Dreamin' Out Loud** / 1996 / Capitol ♦♦♦♦
Trace Adkins' debut *Dreamin' Out Loud* illustrates that he does indeed have a powerhouse voice, one that's big and strong and capable of handling both honky tonk and ballads. It's a voice that makes singers into stars, and his producers must have realized this. Unfortunately, they wanted to ensure that Adkins became a star, so they gave *Dreamin' Out Loud* a production that's a little too clean and songs that are a little too predictable, when it's clear that he is capable of so much more. Even so, *Dreamin' Out Loud* remains a satisfying debut. Adkins sings his heart out on even the lesser songs, and when he does have a good number ("That's a Bad Way of Saying Goodbye," "There's a Girl in Texas"), he sounds like one of the finest new traditionalists of the late '90s. *—Thom Owens*

Big Time / Oct. 21, 1997 / Capitol ♦♦♦
While Trace Adkins' second album, *Big Time*, isn't as consistently strong as his debut, *Dreamin' Out Loud*, it nevertheless establishes him a vocal talent. There are moments where the songwriting rings a little flat, but the best cuts on *Big Time*, such as the single "The Rest of Mine," are well-crafted contemporary country showcasing his booming baritone to fine effect. *—Thom Owens*

More / Nov. 2, 1999 / Capitol ♦♦♦♦
More is a very apt title for Trace Adkins' third album, since it essentially offers more of the same. For some artists, this would be a harsh criticism, but not in the case of Adkins, since he's proving himself to be one of the more reliable neo-traditionalists of the late '90s. Unlike some of his peers, Adkins doesn't pattern his singing after any of his idols; he absorbs his influences, creating his own distinctive sound that has elements of classic honky tonk as well as blues and rock. He sounds equally convincing on heartbreak songs ("Don't Lie"), rockers ("Can I Want Your Love," "More"), honky tonk ("I'm Gonna Love You Anyway," "I Can Dig It"), and Western swing ("All Hat, No Cattle"). *More* may drag a little bit in the middle, but overall, it achieves a nice balance of performance and song, proving along the way that not only does Adkins have and individual voice, but that he's more purely country than many of his peers. *—Stephen Thomas Erlewine*

Chrome / Oct. 9, 2001 / Capitol ♦♦♦
It's not uncommon for the tell-it-like-it-is, six-and-a-half-foot Adkins to say things like the following: "I'm first and foremost interested in the lyrics on anything I record. It sounds like it sounds, but the most important thing is the words." Perhaps that's why he elected to choose Nashville's "pop" producer Dann Huff, who lends himself to commercial country songs that get lots of radio airtime. That's not to say Adkins has abandoned his progressive old-time country roots. Album number four is just a little bit more of a discriminatory mix of traditional classics and uptempo contemporaries that listeners are not used to hearing from him. But the 12-track collection certainly works at that, all the while staying true to what he's known for. You've got to love the way this guy sings bass. Praiseworthy tunes include the nebulous "Chrome," the overly prideful "Once Upon a Fool Ago," and the excitable "Scream." *—Maria Konicki Dinoia*

• **Greatest Hits Collection, Vol. 1** / Jun. 3, 2003 / Capitol ♦♦♦♦

Rhett Akins

b. Valdosta, GA
Guitar, Vocals / Country-Pop, Contemporary Country, Neo-Traditionalist Country
With his Top Five single "That Ain't My Truck," Rhett Akins became a sensation, however briefly, in the summer of 1995. Like many new country singers, he wasn't able to follow the record up with an equally successful second record, but he managed to cultivate a following of dedicated fans. Aikins grew up in Valdosta, GA, learning to play guitar and forming his first band with his two younger brothers by the time he was 11. In 1992, he moved to Nashville, where he began singing on demos, as well as securing a publishing deal of his own. Eventually, Decca Records secured a demo of one of Akins' songs and the label offered him a contract.

A Thousand Memories, Akins' debut album, was released in 1994. After his first two singles—"What They're Talkin' About" and "I Brake for Brunettes"—cracked the Top 40, "That Ain't My Truck" became his breakthrough hit, rocketing to number three in the summer of 1995. "That Ain't My Truck" became his signature song and helped the album become a hit. For most of 1995, he toured as Reba McEntire's opening act, performing a few dates as a headliner as well. In the summer of 1996, Akins released his second album, *Somebody New*. Although the record sold well initially, it quickly fell out of the Top 40. He returned in January 1998 with his third album, *What Livin's All About*. *—Stephen Thomas Erlewine*

A Thousand Memories / 1995 / Decca ♦♦♦

• **Somebody New** / Jun. 1996 / Decca ♦♦♦♦♦

What Livin's All About / Jan. 13, 1998 / MCA Nashville ♦♦♦♦
As the title suggests, *What Livin's All About* finds Rhett Akins stripping back the production gloss somewhat in favor of straight-ahead, direct neo-traditional country. Of course, Akins still has his eye on the new country audience, so the album is hardly honky tonk, but it does reveal that he has a strong ear for material. Most of the songs steer away from the frothy fun of early tracks like "That Ain't My Truck" and "I Brake for Brunettes" in favor of more introspective material (most of which is written by other songwriters). The result isn't as immediate as his first two records, but it's arguably more rewarding, proving that he's more than a flash in the pan. *—Stephen Thomas Erlewine*

Friday Night in Dixie / Mar. 26, 2002 / Audium ♦♦♦
With its signings of folks like Ross Nickerson, John Anderson, and Rhett Akins, Audium Records is like the second chance home for those country neo-traditionalists squeezed out of Nashville by both the pop direction of Faith Hill or Shania Twain and the rootsier moves of the alt-country posses. Like Akins' three major-label albums of the '90s, 2002's *Friday Night in Dixie* blends George Strait and the Marshall Tucker Band for an entertaining if not particularly innovative mix of country twang and Southern rock choogle. The title track, co-written and produced by Charlie Daniels, raises the most hell, but Akins is at his best on more introspective material like the sweet "She Was" and the lonesome "Where the Blacktop Ends." Bookended by a pair of country-radio possibilities, the anonymous but catchy "Highway Sunrise" and a swell acoustic version of Akins' biggest '90s hit, "That Ain't My Truck," *Friday Night in Dixie* is a solid comeback for a journeyman singer/songwriter. *—Stewart Mason*

Alabama

f. 1977, Fort Payne, AL
Group / Contemporary Country, Urban Cowboy, Country-Pop, Country-Rock
Before Alabama, bands were usually relegated to a supporting role in country music. In the first part of the century, bands were popular with audiences across the country, but as recordings became available, nearly every popular recording artist was a vocalist, not a group. Alabama was the group that made country bands popular again. Emerging in the late '70s, the band had roots in both country and rock; in fact, many of Alabama's musical concepts, particularly the idea of a performing band, owed more to rock and pop than hardcore country. However, there is no denying that Alabama is a country band—the bandmembers' pop instincts may come from rock, but their harmonies, songwriting, and approach are indebted to country, particularly the Bakersfield sound of Merle Haggard, bluegrass, and the sound of Nashville pop. A sleek, country-rock sound made the group the most popular country group in history, selling more records than any other artist of the '80s and earning stacks of awards.

First cousins Randy Owen (b. December 14, 1949; lead vocal, rhythm guitar) and Teddy Gentry (b. January 22, 1952; vocals, bass) form the core of Alabama. Owen and Gentry grew up on separate cotton farms on Lookout Mountain in Alabama, but the pair learned how to play guitar together; the duo also had sung in church together before they were six years old. On their own, Gentry and Owen played in a number of different bands during the '60s, playing country, bluegrass, and pop on different occasions. During high-school, the duo teamed with another cousin, Jeff Cook (b. August 27, 1949; lead guitar, vocals, keyboards, fiddle), to form Young Country in 1969. Before joining his cousins, Cook had played in a number of bands and was a rock & roll DJ. Young Country's first gig was at a high-school talent contest; performing a Merle Haggard song, the band won first prize—a trip to the *Grand Ole Opry*. However, the group was fairly inactive as Owen and Cook went to college.

After Owen and Cook graduated from college, they moved with Gentry to Anniston, AL, with the intention of keeping the band together. Sharing an apartment, the band practiced at night and performed manual labor during the day. They changed their name to Wildcountry in 1972, adding drummer Bennet Vartanian to the lineup. The following year, they made the decision to become professional musicians, quitting their jobs and playing a number of bars in the Southeast. During this time, they began writing their own songs, including "My Home's in Alabama." Vartanian left soon after the band turned professional; after losing four more drummers, Rick Scott was added to the lineup in 1974.

Wildcountry changed its name to Alabama in 1977, the same year the band signed a one-record contract with GRT. The resulting single, "I Wanna Be With You Tonight," was a minor success, peaking in the Top 80. Nevertheless, the single's performance was an indication that Alabama was one of the most popular bands in the Southeast; at the end of the decade, the band was playing over 300 shows a year. After "I Wanna Be With You Tonight," the group borrowed $4,000 from a Fort Payne bank, using the money to record and release its own records, which were sold at shows. When GRT declared bankruptcy a year after the release of "I Wanna Be With You Tonight," the bandmembers discovered that they were forbidden from recording with another label because of a hidden clause in their contract. For two years, Alabama raised money to buy out its contract. In 1979, the group was finally able to begin recording again. That same year, Scott left the band. Scott was replaced by Mark Herndon, a former rock drummer who helped give Alabama its signature sound.

Later in 1979, Alabama self-recorded and released an album, hiring an independent record promoter to help get radio play for the single "I Wanna Come Over." The band also sent hundreds of hand-written letters to program directors and DJs across the country. "I Wanna Come Over" gained the attention of MDJ Records, a small label based in Dallas. MDJ released the single, and it reached number 33 on the charts. In 1980, MDJ released "My Home's in Alabama," which made it into the Top 20. Based on the single's success, Alabama performed at the *Country Music New Faces* show, where the band was spotted by an RCA Records talent scout, who signed the group after the show.

Alabama released its first RCA single, "Tennessee River," late in 1980. Produced by Harold Shedd, the song began a remarkable streak of 21 number-one hits (interrupted by the 1982 holiday single "Christmas in Dixie"), which ran until 1987; after one number-seven hit, the streak resumed for another six singles, resulting in a total of 27 number-one singles during the decade. Taken alone, the amount of chart-topping singles is proof of Alabama's popularity, but the band also won numerous awards, had seven multi-platinum albums, and crossed over to the pop charts nine times during the '80s.

In the '90s, their popularity declined somewhat, yet they were still having hit singles and gold and platinum albums with regularity. It's unlikely that any other country group will be able to surpass the success of Alabama. *—Stephen Thomas Erlewine*

My Home's in Alabama / 1980 / RCA ♦♦♦
This is the album that introduced Alabama as one of the biggest hitmaking country/pop bands of the '80s. While the disc contains what was termed "country-rock" at the time, this is nothing like Lynyrd Skynyrd or even Hank Williams Jr. at his rowdiest. The closest thing to country-rock among these ten tracks is the six-minute-and-27-second title track. The earliest representation of the band's developing sound includes the ballad "Why Lady Why" and the fiddle-heavy "Tennessee River," both hit singles. *—Al Campbell*

Feels So Right / 1981 / RCA ♦♦♦♦
On Alabama's second album, *Feels So Right*, you can hear the band becoming comfortable with their sound and finding their niche. Unlike their first release, *My Home's in*

Alabama, they don't sound like they're testing out various tempos, selections, and styles. This session has a flowing consistency which resulted in three hit singles: the mellow pop of "Feels So Right" and "Love in the First Degree," along with traditional country on "Old Flame." —*Al Campbell*

Mountain Music / 1982 / RCA ✦✦✦✦✦
This is their best effort. The group hadn't quite fallen into any formulas, and as a result, they cover the stylistic gamut pretty well. The title track practically defined what country groups have strived to accomplish, and the group slides easily from sentiment, to social relevance, to out-and-out partying. —*Tom Roland*

The Closer You Get / 1983 / RCA ✦✦✦✦
On their fourth album *The Closer You Get*, Alabama gets further away from the country roots and down-home charm responsible for their incredible chart success. One may be surprised at the unusual number of ballads, but popular country in the early '80s, in hindsight, seems more suited to adult easy listening than country with the popularity of Kenny Rogers, Crystal Gayle, and Dolly Parton. The songwriting is strong, and the vocal harmonies still blend unlike any other country band—in fact, the members of Alabama trade lead vocal roles throughout the album. However, this album suffers from glossy production and the use of synthesizers. The use of a drum machine on the opening title track is nearly unforgivable, and the arrangement distracts the listener from an otherwise good song. However, Alabama shines when they use more traditional country arrangements. Upbeat songs like "Red River" and "Dixieland Delight" are great additions to their catalog and demonstrate how they became one of country's most successful groups. This is not the place to start, but most fans should eventually own this album. —*Vik Iyengar*

Roll On / 1984 / RCA ✦✦✦
The title track and "If You're Gonna Play in Texas (You Gotta Have a Fiddle in the Band)" make this entertaining but slightly formulaic album worth pursuing. —*Stephen Thomas Erlewine*

40 Hour Week / 1985 / RCA ✦✦✦✦✦
Opening with the driving title track, *40 Hour Week* encapsulates why Alabama was the top country group of the '80s. Alternating between restrained rockers and well-crafted ballads, it captures the band at its peak. Nevertheless, it isn't quite as strong as their first albums—the performances and production are a bit too mannered—but its professionalism is appealing. And that professionalism made *40 Hour Week* the group's most popular album, as it crossed over into the pop Top Ten. —*Stephen Thomas Erlewine*

Alabama Christmas / 1985 / RCA ✦✦✦✦✦
Highlighted by the perennial "Christmas in Dixie," this collection of holiday tunes is among Alabama's strongest records, seasonal or otherwise; although at times the material is overly sappy, there's no mistaking the group's affection for the project, and cuts like "Happy Holidays," "Tennessee Christmas" and "A Candle in the Window" are all fine additions to the contemporary country Yuletide canon. —*Jason Ankeny*

The Touch / 1986 / RCA ✦
Although the album has a couple of worthwhile songs, particularly the title track, *The Touch* is the weakest record Alabama had put out to date. It follows the same formula as the band's previous records, but there isn't enough melody or hooks to make the album memorable. —*Stephen Thomas Erlewine*

★ **Greatest Hits** / 1986 / RCA ✦✦✦✦✦
Released in 1986, *Greatest Hits* runs a mere ten tracks, so it simply doesn't have enough room to chronicle all the hits they had in the early '80s; though they had years of hits still to come, they already had become a fixture at the top of the country charts, turning out too many hits to fit in this collection. That said, this does an excellent job of summarizing this early peak, containing many songs that became perennials of modern country: "Mountain Music," "Feels So Right," "Tennessee River," "40 Hour Week (For a Livin')," and "My Home's in Alabama." Later collections would offer more, but this collection provides the songs that are at the core of their sound, and, years later, it is still an excellent crystallization of what Alabama is all about. —*Stephen Thomas Erlewine*

Just Us / 1987 / RCA ✦✦
An improvement on the stilted *Touch*, *Just Us* has a number of fine moments, including the pining "(I Wish It Could Always Be) '55" and the K.T. Oslin duet "Face to Face," but it falls short of being a complete return to form, mainly because it is weighed down with too much mediocre material. —*Stephen Thomas Erlewine*

Live / 1988 / RCA ✦✦
Alabama have always been an entertaining live band, but *Live* simply doesn't capture the excitement of their concerts. —*Stephen Thomas Erlewine*

Southern Star / 1989 / RCA ✦✦✦✦✦
After eight very successful years with record producer Harold Shedd, Alabama wisely opts for change. Half the album is recorded with Josh Leo and Larry Lee, the other half with Barry Beckett, and the guys from Fort Payne attack the project with a little more energy than in some of their prior efforts. Get it on CD—three of the four "bonus" tracks are substantial. —*Tom Roland*

Pass It on Down / 1990 / RCA ✦✦✦
On the previous *Southern Star*, Alabama bounced out of their mid-'80s rut, and their winning streak continued on *Pass It on Down*. Like any of their albums, there is a fair share of filler, but that's outweighed by the best songs on the record, particularly the hit "Down Home." —*Stephen Thomas Erlewine*

Greatest Hits, Vol. 2 / 1991 / RCA ✦✦✦✦✦
Greatest Hits, Vol. 2 contains a 11-track cross-section of Alabama's hit singles from the mid- and late '80s, including the number-one singles "Dixieland Delight," "Lady Down

on Love," "The Closer You Get," "Roll On (Eighteen Wheeler)," "Fallin' Again," "Song of the South," "High Cotton," and "Take Me Down." This second volume is even stronger than the first and represents some of the best mainstream rock-influenced country of the '80s. —*Thom Owens*

American Pride / 1992 / RCA ✦✦✦
So much happened between Alabama's arrival on the scene and the country boom of the early '90s that by the time the band released *American Pride*, they were among the genre's aging veterans. As such it was a little late to expect big surprises. So everything that Alabama's known for is here: full-group harmonies, small-town Southern virtues, and common-sense patriotism. The group turned "I'm in a Hurry (And Don't Know Why)" into a big hit, but it's no surprise the best songs are about folks who settled in for the long haul, happily married parents ("Between the Two of Them"), and Richard Petty ("Richard Petty's Fans"). —*Brian Mansfield*

Cheap Seats / 1993 / RCA ✦✦✦
A charming video helped sell the way-cute title track, which offers another context for Alabama's down-home brand of nostalgia. Not to be overlooked, however, is "A Better Word for Love," a quiet, morning love song co-written by Gary Nicholson and former NRBQ guitarist Al Anderson. —*Dan Cooper*

Greatest Hits, Vol. 3 / 1994 / RCA ✦✦✦✦✦
Like most country artists, Alabama made better singles than albums, rarely releasing a bad song for a single. Their third greatest hits compilation collects their biggest and best hits of the late '80s and early '90s—including "I'm in a Hurry (And Don't Know Why)," "Tennessee River," "Angels Among Us," and "When We Make Love"—making it a worthwhile addition to a contemporary country library. —*Stephen Thomas Erlewine*

In Pictures / Aug. 15, 1995 / RCA ✦✦✦
Alabama's train hasn't run out of steam on *In Pictures*, their thirteenth album of original material. The group doesn't depart from their trademark sound at all, but as the single "She Ain't No Ordinary Girl" shows, that's a benefit. *In Pictures* may be merely another Alabama album, but the group's knack for turning out catchy, straightforward pop-inflected country has not diminished over the years. —*Stephen Thomas Erlewine*

Alabama Christmas, Vol. 2 / Sep. 17, 1996 / RCA ✦✦✦
Like its predecessor, *Alabama Christmas, Vol. 2* is a pleasant mix of traditional holiday carols ("Little Drummer Boy," "O Little Town of Bethlehem") and fine, but undistinguished, original carols like "New Year's Eve 1999" and "Christmas in Your Arms." There's not much in *Alabama Christmas, Vol. 2* for listeners who aren't already fans of the group, but for fans, it's a fine addition to their collection. —*Thom Owens*

Dancin' on the Boulevard / Apr. 8, 1997 / RCA ✦✦
Although it has a few good moments, *Dancin' on the Boulevard* finds Alabama turning a fairly predictable and routine record that only catches fire on its singles. The remainder of the album is pleasant, but unremarkable. —*Thom Owens*

The Essential / Jun. 2, 1998 / RCA ✦✦✦✦✦
Contrary to its title, *The Essential Alabama* isn't the definitive Alabama collection. The 16-track collection does contain its share of great songs—"Mountain Music," "You've Got the Touch," "I Showed Her"—but it's too short and contains too many album tracks to be truly definitive. Nevertheless, it's a nice sampler, even if it isn't a good introduction. —*Thom Owens*

★ **For the Record** / Aug. 25, 1998 / RCA ✦✦✦✦✦
Even though the title should be taken with a grain of salt—an enormous number of these 44 songs did reach number one, but a handful only peaked at two or three—there's no denying that *For the Record* is an impressive achievement. Spanning two discs and two decades, *For the Record* contains nearly every great song Alabama recorded, plus three new tunes. If any single album provides definitive proof as to why Alabama is the most popular country band of all time, this is it—they make this appealingly polished, hook-heavy, radio-ready mainstream pop sound as easy as pie. Alabama may have had a couple of album cuts every now and then that were quite good, but they were at their best turning out hits as a singles band, as such contemporary classics as "Tennessee River," "Mountain Music," "The Closer You Get," "Forty Hour Week (For a Livin')," "Jukebox on My Mind," and "Down Home" illustrate. Consequently, it's hard not to view *For the Record*, with its virtual cornucopia of hits, as the definitive Alabama collection, maybe even the definitive Alabama album. —*Stephen Thomas Erlewine*

Twentieth Century / Jun. 15, 1999 / RCA ✦✦
Two decades into their successful career, Alabama is comfortable as professionals. They know how to craft a record, even if that means relying on session musicians over the core band. They know how to select songs, knowing what songs will be ideal for radio. That means they're reliable, but it also means that they can slip into predictability, as they do on *Twentieth Century*. Immaculately constructed and utterly smooth, just like the white suits the quartet sports on the cover, *Twentieth Century* is the work of professionals: professional songwriters, professional producers (Don Cook and the band themselves), professional musicians. There's not a note out of place or a missed harmony. It's easy to marvel at the sheer technical achievement of the record, since not only is it so well made, but the songs rarely make an impression. All the tunes are so predictable and the production so carefully considered that the album flows together, with only a couple of cuts grabbing a listener's attention: the silly capsule history of "Twentieth Century"; Jeff Cook's horn-spiked, Van Morrison tribute "Mist of Desire"; the nice rocker "Life's Too Short to Love This Fast"; and the ballad "God Must Have Spent a Little More Time on You"—complete with backing vocals from fellow RCA labelmates °NSYNC. Taken individually, these particular songs sound pretty good, and would work well on the radio, but taken in the context of the record, they're nearly indistinguishable from the rest. That's the problem

with *Twentieth Century*. although it's pleasant, it never creates its own identity, even compared to latter-day Alabama records. — *Stephen Thomas Erlewine*

When It All Goes South / Jan. 9, 2001 / RCA ✦✦✦

In the Mood: The Love Songs / Feb. 4, 2003 / RCA ✦✦✦
Spanning two discs and over two decades' worth of music, Alabama's *In the Mood: The Love Songs* collects the most romantic moments from the band's body of work, including "Close Enough to Perfect," "Feels So Right," "How Do You Fall in Love," and "The Closer You Get." Indeed, love songs play a fairly significant part in the band's career— many of the tracks included here, such as "Fallin' Again," "Touch Me When We're Dancing," "Lady Down on Love," and "In Pictures," also appear on *For the Record*, Alabama's collection of chart-topping singles. All of this means *In the Mood: The Love Songs* is a consistent collection of the band's easygoing, sentimental songs, and while it doesn't replace a more straightforward greatest-hits compilation, it should please the band's fans as well as anyone partial to romantic country. — *Heather Phares*

Christine Albert
Trumpet, Vocals / Progressive Bluegrass, Singer/Songwriter
Singer/songwriter Christine Albert drew on both her family's European heritage and the musical legacy of her adopted home state of Texas to create her unique sound. Born and raised in upstate New York, Albert moved to Santa Fe, NM, at the age of 16 and began to pursue a career in music. After settling in Austin in 1982, she became a fixture on the area's club scene, but did not release her first LP, *You Are Gold*, until 1990. Her next LP, 1992's *Texafrance*, was a bilingual affair that explored her family's French roots while seeking a common ground between the music of Patsy Cline and Edith Piaf. Released in 1993, *The High Road* marked a renewed focus on straight-ahead country, a trend further developed by 1995's *Underneath the Lone Star Sky*. — *Jason Ankeny*

You Are Gold / 1990 / Gambini ✦✦✦

Texafrance / 1992 / Gambini ✦✦✦

● **Underneath the Lone Star Sky** / Oct. 1995 / Dos ✦✦✦✦

Pat Alger
Guitar, Vocals / Contemporary Country, Contemporary Folk, Contemporary Singer/ Songwriter
Pat Alger, who is among the most successful country songwriters of the late '80s and early '90s, comes from a folk background, and that colors the unusually thoughtful, articulated songs he writes. He first turned up on record himself playing guitar and singing with the loosely constructed Woodstock Mountain Revue on the album *More Music from Mud Acres* in 1977. He was a co-author of the song "Ocracoke Time," which appeared on the Revue's third album, *Pretty Lucky*, in 1978, as well as "Old Time Music" on its fourth album, *Back to Mud Acres*, in 1981, and the sole author of "Southern Crescent Line" on the same album.

But Alger really began to gain recognition as a songwriter with the release of Nanci Griffith's third album, *Once in a Very Blue Moon*, in 1985. Alger co-wrote the title song, which reached the country charts in 1986. He was also heard from on Griffith's fourth album, *The Last of the True Believers*, in 1986, for which he co-wrote the song "Goin' Gone." (He also played guitar on the album and did its graphics.) Alger was co-author of the title song on Griffith's 1987 album, *Lone Star State of Mind*, and that song became a Top 40 country hit. In 1988, Kathy Mattea's version of "Goin' Gone" hit the top of the country charts. In 1990, Mattea took Alger and Fred Koller's "She Came from Fort Worth" to number two.

It's no surprise, then, that when Alger came to record his debut album, *True Love & Other Short Stories*, in 1991, he was able to call on the help of the cream of the young Nashville writers and performers. Trisha Yearwood, Nanci Griffith, Mary Black, Ashley Cleveland, Kathy Mattea, and Lyle Lovett all turn up, though Alger himself is the focus, singing his best-known songs. "No one sings or plays Pat Alger like Pat Alger himself," Griffith writes. — *William Ruhlmann*

● **True Love & Other Short Stories** / 1991 / Sugar Hill ✦✦✦✦
This country/folk songwriter sings his own versions of such hits as "Lone Star State of Mind" and "Goin' Gone." Guests include Nanci Griffith and Kathy Mattea. — *William Ruhlmann*

Seeds / 1994 / Sugar Hill ✦✦✦
Produced by Jim Rooney, this album contains a baker's dozen of new Alger songs, including his Garth Brooks hit "The Thunder Rolls." Alger is supported by such artists as Tim O'Brien, Trisha Yearwood, Kathy Mattea and the solid Roy Husky Jr. While most of these tracks are good, straight, coverable country-folk songs, some have a deeper irony such as the final song, "Unanswered Prayers." — *Richard Meyer*

Notes & Grace Notes / Sep. 6, 1994 / Capitol ✦✦✦

Gary Allan
b. Dec. 5, 1967
Vocals / Contemporary Country, Neo-Traditionalist Country, New Traditionalist
Gary Allan hit the honky tonk circuit in his native southern California at the seasoned age of 12. Playing in and out of the smoky, sweaty bars with his dad's band led Allan to follow in his father's footsteps and start his own band. When Allan returned to those same honky tonks with his own combo, the sound was true Bakersfield country: Merle Haggard, Buck Owens, and the rest. Allan spent most of his twenties honing his skills as a new traditionalist country singer; finally, in 1996, he was picked up by the Decca label. *Used Heart for Sale* appeared that year, and even if it was a bit timid, the album established Allan as a talented performer with plenty of potential.

Two years later, he returned with *It Would Be You*. This time out, Allan suffered from slick Nashville production, which winnowed away most of his whiskey-soaked barroom charm. Nevertheless, Allan's talent shone through. In 1999, Decca closed its doors.

However, Allan's contract was picked up by MCA, who released his *Smoke Rings in the Dark* later that year. The album combined most of what Allan did best—dusty honky tonk, cracked country ballads—into a solid effort that didn't get too heavy with the Music City sheen. The album even included a rousing cover of the Del Shannon classic "Runaway" that harked back to Allan's younger days on the honky tonk circuit. With 2001's *Alright Guy*, an accomplished mix of driving, dusty swagger and slow-burn croon, Allan proved that he was only getting better with age. Its single, "Man to Man," became the singer's first number-one hit. Allan toured extensively in support of *Alright Guy* and began work on a follow-up in spring of 2003. — *Johnny Loftus*

Used Heart for Sale / Sep. 24, 1996 / Decca ✦✦✦
Gary Allan's debut *Used Heart for Sale* is a competent set of new-traditionalist country that occasionally comes to life—such as on the single "Her Man"—but often is hampered by unimaginative material and timid performances. Allan's best moments suggest that he is capable of more, yet *Used Heart for Sale* doesn't give him enough opportunity to stretch out and showcase his talents. — *Thom Owens*

It Would Be You / 1998 / Decca ✦✦✦
Gary Allan's sophomore effort shows considerable growth since the release of his 1996 debut project, *Used Heart for Sale*, which seemingly filed away Allan's sharp honky tonk edge. This time out, the project suffers from over-production and some material that reflects the soft pop fluff manufactured and sold as country music by Factory Music City. Allan is not a pop singer nor a soft rock balladeer, and these schlocky, country radio-ready tunes do not enhance his position as a traditionalist nor do they show him in the best light. There are also moments when Allan sounds too much like fellow honky tonker Mark Chesnutt for his own good. Chalk this up to the Nashville production style. Yet, this is a danger the native Californian will hopefully be able to sidestep in the future, since his musical vision has always been firmly rooted in the work of George Jones, Buck Owens, Ernest Tubb, and Merle Haggard. These influences are evident in his cover of Conway Twitty's "She Loves Me, She Don't Love You" and the Marty Stuart/Kostas co-write "Don't Leave Her Lonely Too Long." Just as listenable are "I've Got a Quarter in My Pocket," "Red Lips, Blue Eyes, Little White Lies," and the only tune on the project that Allan had a hand in writing, "Baby I Will." Sadly, Allan suffers in the face of the marketing blitz that surrounds his young career. Too often the artist is lost in the product and the artist's true potential is never realized. In this case, only time will tell. — *Jana Pendragon*

● **Smoke Rings in the Dark** / Oct. 19, 1999 / MCA ✦✦✦✦
Gary Allan grows better and more assured with each album, and his third record, *Smoke Rings in the Dark*, is his best effort yet. Similar to the Mavericks, Allan stylishly blends a number of roots styles, from his signature Bakersfield country to dusty folk and pop crooning, into a neo-traditionalist sound that is curiously out of time. Allan is considerably more mainstream than the Mavericks, which means that the production is more polished and he doesn't really take musical risks. Even if he doesn't quite hold his own against some Americana artists, he certainly is stronger than many contemporary country artists, especially since he tries many different styles and sounds throughout *Smoke Rings in the Dark*. Not every song works, but even those that don't have still something recommendable in their performance or production. It's a fine album from an artist that keeps getting better. — *Stephen Thomas Erlewine*

Alright Guy / Oct. 2, 2001 / MCA ✦✦✦
Allan's fourth album honors traditional honky tonk and American music without dripping into the sentimentality that bogs down so many of his contemporaries. The singing is better here than on anything he's ever done, and the song selection—ranging from a Todd Snider cover to a nice Bruce Robison-penned closer called "What Would Willie Do"—is sharp and smart. Country music that bucks tradition while keeping the faith. — *Michael Gallucci*

Susie Allanson
b. Mar. 17, 1952, Las Vegas, NV
Vocals / Country-Pop, Urban Cowboy
Singer and actress Susie Allanson did not have a "classic country" voice—she possessed a girlish, almost whispery quality with theatrical intonations. The latter was not surprising, as she began her professional career in the road version of *Hair* in 1970, also touring with *Jesus Christ Superstar* a year later. She stayed on for 18 months, singing on the U.S. cast album and appearing in the film. Allanson moved to southern California in 1975 to audition for a bicentennial project by Ray Ruff, who later became her husband and manager. ABC released her debut album, which contained the single "Love Is a Satisfied Woman"/"Me & Charlie Brown." Allanson released another single, "Baby Don't Keep Me Hangin' On," which led to a deal with Curb Records. They took over the single, which made it to the Top 30. Her next album, *We Belong Together*, contained two hits, the title track and her cover of Buddy Holly's "Maybe Baby," which reached number two and four, respectively, on the charts.

In 1979, she signed to the Elektra label and released the album *Heart to Heart*, which contained two major hits, "Words" and "Two Steps Forward and Three Steps Back." In 1980, Allanson moved to United Artists/Liberty for *Susie*, which contained only two minor hits. It was the last Allanson LP issued. Her 1981 singles—"Run to Her" (a cover of Bobby Vinton's "Run to Him") and "Love Is Knockin' at My Door"—both hit the Top 50, but the album upon which they appeared, *Sleepless Nights*, was never released. Allanson settled into motherhood during the 1980s, but did release the singles "Where's the Fire"/"Can't Say It on the Radio" and "She Don't Love You"/"Girls Get Lonely Too" in 1987 on the Los Angeles indie TNP. — *Sandra Brennan & Johnny Loftus*

Susie Allanson / 1976 / ABC ✦✦✦

We Belong Together / 1978 / Warner Bros. ✦✦✦✦

● **Heart to Heart** / 1979 / Elektra ✦✦✦✦

Allen Brothers

f. 1923, **db.** 1934

Group / Old-Timey, Traditional Country, Country Gospel

The Allen Brothers, Lee and Austin, were among the first of the fraternal duets that became popular in the '20s and '30s. They were known for their fast-paced, upbeat blues and old-time music-influenced songs. Offering sometimes-bawdy good-time music, droll humor, and Lee Allen's delightful kazoo leads, they created a unique blues-derived sound independent from that of country music's star bluesman of the day, Jimmie Rodgers. Between 1926-1934 the "Chattanooga Boys" recorded 89 songs and notched several hits. The brothers were born five years apart (Austin was the oldest) around the turn of the century on Monteagle Mountain, 50 miles north of Chattanooga, to a sawyer and a trained violinist.

In childhood they were influenced by a combination of contemporary and traditional music. The brothers hit the local music circuit around 1923, becoming particularly popular in isolated coal-mining camps. While traveling, the Allens began collecting all sorts of local, traditional tunes. Soon they began writing their own songs, many of which contain references to their mountain home and the Chattanooga area, and they absorbed the blues, often of the sort containing sexual double meanings, perhaps more thoroughly than any subsequent brother duet. The Allens made their recording debut on the Columbia label in 1926. Their first single was a version of "Salty Dog Blues" titled "Bow Wow Blues." It became quite popular, but when the label released their "Laughin' and Cryin' Blues" in its 14,000-numbered "Race" series instead of the 15,000 "Old-Time" series, the brothers were offended and threatened to sue the company if the records remained on the shelves.

The mistake was probably an honest one on Columbia's part; some Allen Brothers recordings sound very close to those by Southeastern African-American performers of the day, especially to those by small hokum ensembles. Nevertheless, the Allens moved to Victor and met Ralph Peer, who was reaping the fruits of his discovery of Jimmie Rodgers and was keen to mine the white blues vein further. In concerts the Allens sang a combination of uptempo and slower tunes, and became frustrated when Peer insisted that they record only the former. Still, they remained with Victor until 1933, recording such hits as "Skippin' and Flyin'" (1928) and "Jake Walk Blues" (1930), the latter a commentary on the Jamaican ginger ("jake") food-poisoning episode that made headlines that year. During the Depression, the brothers continued to record, but despite their popularity they had difficulty earning enough to support their families.

In 1933 Austin and his family moved to New York, where he became a radio announcer. Lee stayed in Tennessee and became a construction worker. They also appeared together in a play, *Bushwhacker*, and made a final stab at the music business with a session in 1934 for ARC. They cut new versions of some of their best hits, but these recordings still didn't make enough impact to justify a return to full-time music-making. Austin later became a construction worker and engineer. He died in Williamston, SC, in 1959. In the late '60s, the Allen Brothers were rediscovered by a new generation. Several LP reissues of their 78 rpm recordings appeared, and Lee Allen was coaxed into performing again. He appeared occasionally at local events near his home in Lebanon, TN, before his death in 1981. The 1990s saw the release of the brothers' complete recordings on three compact discs by Austria's Document label. —*Sandra Brennan & James Manheim*

Sweet Rumors / 1974 / Rounder ♦♦

● **Clara's Boys** / 1976 / Rounder ♦♦♦♦

Are You Feeling It Too? / 1994 / Smithsonian Folkways ♦♦♦♦

Allen Brothers, Vol. 1: 1927–1930 / Sep. 7, 2000 / Document ♦♦♦♦

The Allen Brothers (singer/banjoist Austin Allen and Lee Allen on kazoo, guitar, and occasional vocals) were one of the most popular and prolific of the early country groups. All of their music has been reissued on three Document CDs. The duo primarily played good-time music, influenced by the blues and to a small extent by hokum. Listening to their performances, one has to occasionally overlook small and unfortunate racist remarks that were part of the Southern white culture of the time. However, the sound of the duo is appealing (even if "Laughin' and Cryin' Blues" is a bit annoying), with the highlights on this first disc including "Salty Dog Blues," "Prisoner's Dream," "Jake Walk Blues," and "Frisco Blues." One session is unusual because it has the duo joined by violin and guitar, but that was the only time in their career that the Allen Brothers used other musicians. Early country collectors will want to hear this music. —*Scott Yanow*

Allen Brothers, Vol. 2: 1930–1932 / Sep. 7, 2000 / Document ♦♦♦♦♦

The second of three CDs that reissue all of the recordings by the Allen Brothers features the duo (Austin Allen on vocals and banjo, Lee Allen on kazoo, guitar, and occasional singing) performing 23 selections during seven sessions cut in Memphis, Charlotte, Atlanta, and Camden, New Jersey. The pioneering country group performs such numbers as "A New Salty Dog," "Preacher Blues," "Slide Daddy, Slide," "Shake It, Ida, Shake It," "Mother-in-Law Blues," "Crossfiring Blues," and "Fruit Jar Blues." Of their three Document discs, this is the most rewarding one. —*Scott Yanow*

Allen Brothers, Vol. 3: 1932–1934 / Jan. 9, 2001 / Document ♦♦♦♦

The last of three CDs that contain all of the recordings by the pioneering country duo the Allen Brothers has two sessions from 1932 and their four dates (from a five-day period) that ended their recording careers in October 1934. The group did not change its style at all from its first sessions in 1927, and was fortunate to record so much during the peak years of the Depression. Most of these titles were formerly quite rare, and there are three previously unreleased tracks. As usual, the interplay between Austin Allen (vocals and banjo) and Lee Allen (kazoo, guitar, and vocals) is quite appealing, and their brand of country music often shows the similarity between country, string band music, and blues. Among their 23 final recordings are "Slipping Clutch Blues," "Midnight Mama," "Long Gone From Bowling Green," "New Deal Blues," "Salty Dog, Hey Hey Hey," "Allen Brothers' Rag," and "Drunk and Nutty Blues." —*Scott Yanow*

Deborah Allen

b. Sep. 30, 1953, Memphis, TN

Vocals / Country-Pop, Urban Cowboy

A country-pop singer strongly influenced by Patsy Cline, Deborah Allen scored a few major hits in the early '80s and subsequently reinvented herself with a newly sensual image for the '90s. Born in Memphis in 1953, Allen moved to Nashville at age 17 to pursue a country-music singing career, and met Roy Orbison while working as a waitress. Orbison hired her as a backup singer, and she subsequently worked at the Opryland theme park before landing a gig as a singer and dancer in Tennessee Ernie Ford's touring revue. As a solo act in her own right, Allen went on to open for Jim Stafford, and in 1979 was handpicked by the late Jim Reeves' wife to dub duet vocals onto three unfinished Reeves tracks—"Don't Let Me Cross Over," "Oh, How I Miss You Tonight," and the Top Ten hit "Take Me in Your Arms and Hold Me."

This proved to be Allen's big break, and she signed with Capitol for her debut album, 1980's *Trouble in Paradise*. It produced a few minor hits, including "Nobody's Fool" and the Top 20 "You (Make Me Wonder Why)." However, it was the 1983 mini-album *Cheat the Night* that proved to be Allen's breakthrough; "Baby I Lied" and "I've Been Wrong Before" both made the country Top Five, and "I Hurt for You" went Top Ten; all were co-written by Allen and her husband, Rafe Van Hoy. Their collaboration continued on the 1984 full-length *Let Me Be the First*, which began to employ electronic instrumentation. In 1987, *Telepathy* went even further afield, with a title track written by Prince under the pseudonym Joey CoCo. All the stylistic experimentation served to alienate Allen's core country audience, and when she found herself without a record contract, she and Van Hoy made their living as songwriters, penning "Don't Worry 'Bout Me Baby" for Janie Fricke and "Can I See You Tonight" for Tanya Tucker, among others.

In the meantime, she worked on a new album using her own time and money, and eventually made an agreement with Warner Bros. to release it. The result, *Delta Dreamland*, appeared in 1993 and showcased a new bluesy, sexy style that was supported with a corresponding video image for the minor hit "Rock Me (In the Cradle of Love)." The follow-up, 1994's *All That I Am*, continued in a similar vein. Allen subsequently made her living behind the scenes as a songwriter and session backup singer. —*Steve Huey*

Trouble in Paradise / 1980 / Capitol ♦♦♦

Cheat the Night / 1984 / RCA ♦♦♦♦♦

An EP features her two best-known hits of the 1980s, "Baby I Lied" and "I've Been Wrong Before." It's sweeter and softer-edged than her '90s work. —*Michael McCall*

Let Me Be the First / 1984 / RCA ♦♦♦

Working again with husband/producer/co-writer Rafe Van Hoy, Allen attempts an artful, electronic style of country-pop that proved too progressive for the country mainstream. —*Michael McCall*

Delta Dreamland / 1993 / Warner Bros. ♦♦♦♦♦

Allen comes roaring back with another Van Hoy collaboration, this one produced before signing a record contract. Bluesy, sexy and intimately powerful, it rocks stronger than anything she previously offered. —*Michael McCall*

All That I Am / 1994 / Giant ♦♦♦♦♦

Allen pushes her steamy sensuality even more to the forefront here in another strong collection. —*Michael McCall*

● **Anthology** / Oct. 13, 1998 / Renaissance ♦♦♦♦♦

Anthology offers an excellent overview of Deborah Allen's career, compiling all of the singer's country-pop hits from 1979 to 1993. Beginning with her earliest Top Ten entries—three "duets" with Jim Reeves produced in the wake of his death—the set goes on to encompass not only Allen's biggest solo smashes ("I've Been Wrong Before," "Baby I Lied" and "I Hurt for You") as well as fascinating obscurities ("Telepathy," written by one Joey CoCo—a.k.a. the Artist Formerly Known as Prince). —*Hank Small*

Best of Deborah Allen / Aug. 29, 2000 / Curb ♦♦♦

Harley Allen

b. Jan. 23, 1956

Vocals / Contemporary Country, Singer/Songwriter

The son of noted bluegrass musician Red Allen, who had performed with the trio Osborne Brothers, Harley Allen has found considerable success as a performer and writer in his own right. With his brothers, he performed as the Allen Brothers, touring with them and appearing on several releases, including *My Old Kentucky Home* (1972), *Sweet Rumors* (1974), and *Clara's Boys* (1976). Relocating from Dayton, OH, to Nashville, Allen soon found work as a staff writer. Over the past two decades, he has had his songs recorded by acts such as George Jones, Alison Krauss, Linda Ronstadt, Alan Jackson, Garth Brooks, and Hal Ketchum. John Michael Montgomery's version of Allen's "This Little Girl" was nominated for three Academy of Country Music Awards in 2001. That same year, Allen also participated in the soundtrack to *O Brother, Where Art Thou?* as a member of the Soggy Bottom Boys with Union Station guitarist Dan Tyminski and Pat Enright. The album was an out-of-nowhere success, selling several million copies and walking away with a Grammy for Album of the Year. Allen has also lent his vocals to sessions for other artists throughout the years, as well as recording several solo releases, including 2001's *Live at the Bluebird*. —*Tom Demalon*

● **Another River** / Apr. 1996 / Mercury ♦♦♦

Live at the Bluebird / Jun. 12, 2001 / American Originals ♦♦♦

Jules Verne Allen

b. 1883, **d.** 1945

Main Performer, Vocals, Guitar / Cowboy, Old-Timey, Yodeling

Jules Verne Allen was one of a handful of authentic and documented cowboy singers and writers—along with Carl T. Sprague—who lived the life that his songs dealt with. He also learned those songs before radio and records carried them to the world, when they were still part of an oral tradition. A cowboy from the age of ten, and a participant in cattle drives until the end of the first decade of the new century, Allen began singing as an amateur for the pleasure of his fellow cowboys.

After a stint in law enforcement, including a possible period as a Texas Ranger, and service in the army during World War I, he began working as a professional singer in the 1920s and was appearing on radio in Dallas, San Antonio, and Los Angeles by the end of the decade, sometimes under various pseudonyms, including Longhorn Luke. Allen began cutting music for Victor starting in 1928, and cut a total of a dozen sides for the company that year and the next. He cut what were among the earliest known versions of "The Cowboy's Dream," "Home on the Range," and "Days of Forty-Nine." His recording of "The Dying Cowboy," more familiar as "Oh Bury Me Not on the Lone Prairie," is one of the more notable authentic oral tradition-derived versions of a song dating, in that form, at least since the 1830s.

Allen was also a composer and writer in his own right, and published *Cowboy Lore*, a collection of three dozen songs accompanied by details about cowboy life, in 1933—it has been reprinted several times, most recently in 1971, some 26 years after his death. —*Bruce Eder*

Red Allen

b. Feb. 12, 1930, Perry County, KY, **d.** Apr. 3, 1993
Guitar, Vocals / Bluegrass, Traditional Bluegrass
With a high lonesome sound heavily influenced by Bill and Charlie Monroe, Red Allen quietly took his place as one of the most talented and underrated bluegrass artists of the post-World War II era. Born in Perry County, KY, he later made his mark not far from there, first landing in Dayton, OH, at the age of 19 in 1949 after a two-year stint in the Marines. In Ohio, he became acquainted with several other musicians with whom he would later collaborate, including Frank Wakefield, the Osborne Brothers and Noah Crase.

In 1954, he made his recording debut on an independent Kentucky label. In March 1956, he began an incredibly fruitful partnership with the Osborne Brothers, shortly after they had signed on with the Wheeling Jamboree, a popular radio show broadcast from the *Virginia Theater* in Wheeling, WV. Four months after he joined the group, they made their first recording with MGM Records, and built their audience over the next year by a steady program of touring and recording. In the spring of 1958, their song, "Once More," hit number 13 on the country charts and helped earn the band a steady following. Allen left the Osborne Brothers at the end of 1958 and took a brief break from recording before moving to Washington, D.C., in 1959 and forming the Kentuckians with Wakefield. Their relationship was extremely fruitful creatively, but ultimately too tumultuous to sustain for long, and after producing a classic album in 1964 for Smithsonian Folkways simply titled *Bluegrass*, they parted ways.

In 1967, Allen moved to Nashville to relieve a temporarily ailing Lester Flatt in Flatt & Scruggs. The next year he and J.D. Crowe founded the Kentucky Mountain Boys. In 1969, Allen went back to Dayton and formed a band with his sons known as Red Allen & the Allen Brothers. With his boys, he found himself again on the Wheeling Jamboree, also recording for King Bluegrass and Lemco. The '70s brought international touring for Allen but little recording. In 1979, he issued another album for Smithsonian Folkways with the Kentuckians entitled *Live and Let Live*. In 1980, he issued a tribute to Lester Flatt titled *In Memory of the Man*, and followed that album with two more recordings for Folkways, 1981's *Red Allen Family & Friends* and 1983's *The Red Allen Tradition*. Throughout the rest of the '80s and early '90s, Allen typically stayed a little closer to home, playing clubs and festivals near Dayton until his death from cancer in 1993. In 2001, Folkways issued *The Folkways Years: 1964-1983*, which was essentially a reissue of the 1964 *Bluegrass* album, plus six previously unreleased songs and a number of tracks from Allen's four other Folkways albums. The collection helped highlight some of the high points in Allen's long career, and showcased his remarkable talent as a bluegrass vocalist and guitarist. —*Stacia Proefrock*

Red Allen, Frank Wakefield and the Kentuckians / 1964 / Folkways ✦✦✦✦
bluegrass / 1964 / Folkways ✦✦✦✦
Oddly, this first-rate Folkways recording—spelled "bluegrass" with a lower-case "b"—began as an attempt to interest commercial-budget labels in putting out Allen product. It came to the attention of Folkways' Moe Asch, who put it out in 1964. It was the result of two separate sessions with different personnel, always including Allen and mandolinist/vocalist Frank Wakefield; on the first session they were supported by Pete Kuykendall on banjo and Tom Morgan on bass, on the second by Bill Keith on banjo and Fred Weisz on bass. These meshed together for a dozen solid performances, highlighted not just by fine playing and harmonizing, but also by Allen's grainy, emotional lead vocals. All 12 of the songs appear on the 2001 Smithsonian Folkways compilation *The Folkways Years 1964-1983*, along with a half-dozen outtakes from the sessions, and ten performances from Allen releases on Folkways in the late '70s and early '80s. —*Richie Unterberger*

Red Allen & the Kentuckians / 1991 / County ✦✦✦✦
Red Allen & The Kentuckians is an album the bluegrass pioneer Red Allen recorded for County Records in 1966. The record is one of his best, capturing his pure and intense style through both instrumental showcases and a selection of fine material, such as "Milk Cow Blues," "I Wonder Where You Are Tonight," "Maiden's Prayer" and "If That's the Way You Feel." —*Thom Owens*

Bluegrass Reunion / May 1991 / Acoustic Disc ✦✦✦✦
Traditional bluegrass guitarist/vocalist Red Allen heads up an all-star cast for *Bluegrass Reunion*, which was a pet project for and became the fourth release on David "Dawg" Grisman's (mandolin/vocals) Acoustic Disc record label. This title aptly gathers musicians who at one time or another have crossed paths with Grisman. *Bluegrass Reunion* (1992) features 20 standards and adaptations with a revolving cast that also includes Herb Pedersen (banjo/vocals), Jim Buchanan (fiddle(s)/vocals), and

Jim Kerwin (bass). Allen was one of the first musicians to have worked with Dawg, allowing the neophyte to both play mandolin as well as produce several of his sessions in the early '60s. Jerry Garcia (guitar/vocals) turns in two affective performances. His haunting vocals and lead acoustic fretwork reinvent the Stanley Brothers' classic "The Fields Have Turned Brown." In contrast, his loose and throaty reading of "Ashes of Love" hearkens back to Johnnie & Jack's rendition. While the Acuff-Rose catalog is well-represented throughout this release, the individual leanings of each of the performers also revive some of the lesser-recorded entries. As a cohesive unit, this "reunion" interprets the legendary "high and lonesome sound" with knowing authenticity. These range from the dark and hollow-bellied reading of Helen Carter's "Is This My Destiny?" to the shuckin' and jivin' instrumental "Pigeon Roost," which, incidentally, is the album's sole original composition. "She's No Angel," "Little Maggie," and "To Love and Live Together" are likewise intense in their authenticity, yet Grisman's highly advanced recording techniques unveil a freshness and vitality that vintage sides often fail to capture. —*Lindsay Planer*

The Kitchen Tapes / 1994 / Acoustic Disc ✦✦✦✦
Red Allen and Frank Wakefield were recorded here by Wakefield's future student David Grisman in 1963. *The Kitchen Tapes* captures the two of them jamming and improvising informally—at the time, Peter K. Siegel and Grisman were college students who had simply been allowed to capture one of Allen and Wakefield's private sessions, sitting in a kitchen in Hyattsville, MD. This was purely for Siegel and Grisman to learn from, but the tapes proved so valuable through the years that 31 years later, arrangements were made to issue it commercially. Lines are blown and notes are slurred here and there, and not every harmony is as smooth as it might be with some rehearsal, but this is still a priceless document, showing off these two legends in an informal, private session playing for their own pleasure. The 25 numbers include "I'm Just Here to Get My Baby Out of Jail," "Bluegrass Breakdown," "Muskrat Song," "Crying Heart Blues," "Billy in the Low Ground" (in maybe the best version of its era), "Nine Pound Hammer," "'Tis Sweet to Be Remembered," and "Swing Low Sweet Chariot." Grisman studied copies of these tapes for years, and has now shared them with the world. —*Bruce Eder*

● **The Folkways Years: 1964–1983** / Apr. 24, 2001 / Smithsonian Folkways ✦✦✦✦✦
Other than Ralph Stanley and Jimmy Martin, the self-proclaimed "King of Bluegrass," it's difficult to conceive of a more distinctive bluegrass singer than the late Red Allen. His voice defined the high lonesome sound of the music Bill created from the ground up. This set is actually Allen's debut for Folkways in 1964, and it is rounded out with six outtakes from the same session and selections from four subsequent albums for the label—28 tracks in all. It's a hell of a value. From the opening roar of "Little Maggie," with Allen going for the top of his range, letting his voice crack just enough to wring all the drama for the song and lay it in the listener's lap. His singing is pure tradition. Unlike his pals the Country Gentlemen, Allen sticks to Monroe's original model as practiced by Stanley and him. It is noted often that to hear bluegrass in all its majesty you have to listen to the gospel tunes. Allen makes a serious case for that here with his "Are You Washed in the Blood?" His voice calls down fire and brimstone and begs the question of the listener with such intensity and purity of intent it's difficult not to be moved by the emotion. And then there's "I'm Just Here to Get My Baby out of Jail," a down in the grass blues. It's a pleading tune, one of forlorn loneliness; you can feel this man beg for his woman. At only two minutes and 11 seconds, it's one of the most powerful songs on the whole set. Allen's other gift—as if he needed another one with that voice and his rock-steady rhythm guitar playing—was his ability to take a country song, one from the tradition, and transform it into a bluegrass angel. The evidence of this is on Allen's reading of "When My Blue Moon Turns to Gold Again." I can hear Merle Haggard sing this still and cannot for the life of me fathom how Allen takes this beautiful country ballad and turns it into a midtempo bluegrass cruiser. The song remains honest, the emotion and the longing is not reduced one measure by this shape shift, but it remains a cipher, a song within a song that marries two traditions together without seams. Ultimately, this exhaustive collection is the best of Red Allen, and nothing more is needed except by fanatics. —*Thom Jurek*

Rex Allen

b. Dec. 31, 1922, Willcox, AZ, **d.** Dec. 17, 1999
Vocals, Guitar / Cowboy
Better-known as the Arizona Cowboy, Rex Allen was the last of Hollywood's singing cowboys. Between 1950 and 1954, Allen starred in 19 movies for Republic studios. The films launched a popular recording career for Allen, as he had several hit singles and albums in the early '50s, before the singing cowboys slowly disappeared from the charts. The son of a fiddle player, Rex Allen was given his first guitar when he was 11 years old; his father intended Rex to support him at dances. Shortly afterwards, Allen began singing. After he finished high-school, he was hired as a performer by a Phoenix radio station, but he only stayed there for a brief time. Instead, Allen hit the rodeo circuit. His career as a rodeo rider was short-lived, as he suffered an injury from a bull. The injury led Allen back to singing, and he was hired by WTTM in Trenton, NJ, in 1943.

After he left WTTM, Allen joined the Sleepy Hollow Ranch Gang in Pennsylvania. During the summer of 1946, Allen was spotted by Lulu Belle & Scotty; impressed, the duo recommended that he try out for the National Barn Dance and WLS in Chicago. Allen became a popular performer in the Windy City, which led him to become one of the first country & western artists signed by Mercury Records. Mercury released several of Allen's singles before he had a hit with "Afraid" in 1949. That same year, Allen went to Hollywood. Bringing along a CBS network radio program, Allen approached Republic Pictures. The studio signed the singer to a star in a film, *The Arizona Cowboy*, which was released in 1950. The movie was a success, beginning a string of 19 pictures that ran until February 1954. All of the movies were musical Westerns, starring Allen with a rotating cast of sidekicks. Frequently, he would star with Slim Pickens, but Buddy Ebsen and Fuzzy Knight also made their appearances in Allen's films.

Allen's film successes led to a hit record in 1951, "Sparrow in the Tree Top." Released on Mercury Records, the single climbed into the country Top Ten and made it into the pop Top 30. Soon after its release, Allen signed with Decca Records, which released his biggest hit, 1953's "Crying in the Chapel"; the song peaked in the Top Five and reached the Top Ten pop charts. In the latter half of the decade, he made a number of albums composed of Western songs. During this time, he acted in 39 episodes of the television program *Frontier Doctor*.

By the '60s, Rex Allen had re-signed with Mercury Records, which led to several minor hits and one major success—1962's "Don't Go Near the Indians," which returned the singer to the country Top Ten and the pop Top 20. On his '60s stint at Mercury, Allen had two other significant hits—1961's "Marines Let's Go" and "Tear After Tear" in 1964. In the late '60s, the singer went back to Decca Records, which resulted in one minor hit in 1968, "Tiny Bubbles." During this time and the early '70s, he recorded albums for Disneyland, Buena Vista, and JMI. However, he was more prominent in this era as a narrator for many Walt Disney films and television programs, as well as a voice in several Disney cartoons. In the '80s, Allen's oldest son, Rex Allen Jr., became a star in his own right. A museum in his hometown, Willcox, AZ, was dedicated to Rex Allen, and the Governor of Arizona honored him. Allen occasionally appeared in Western film fare, where he remained as popular as ever. He died December 17, 1999, after his caretaker accidentally ran him over with a car; Allen was 78. *—Stephen Thomas Erlewine*

● **Boney Kneed, Hairy Legged Cowboy Songs** / 1984 / Bear Family ♦♦♦♦♦

Hawaiian Cowboy / Apr. 1986 / Bear Family ♦♦♦

Voice of the West / Aug. 1986 / Bear Family ♦♦♦♦

Voice of the West collects songs Rex Allen recorded in the early '70s with producer Jack Clement, who cut away the cinematic strings that dominated Allen's previous recordings. Instead, he leaves the singing cowboy with simple, straight-forward production that accentuates the western roots of his music. Not only does he play traditional cowboy classics, he does a handful of contemporary country numbers. It might not have his classic hits, but *Voice of the West* gives a good sense of the scope of Allen's talents. *—Stephen Thomas Erlewine*

Rex Allen Jr.

b. Aug. 23, 1947, Chicago, IL

Vocals / Nashville Sound/Countrypolitan

Rex Allen Jr. is the son of Rex Allen, the country music singer who scored seven country hits between 1949 and 1968, the biggest of which was 1953's "Crying in the Chapel," which crossed over to number eight in the pop chart. Allen Jr. was born in Chicago and traveled with his father from the age of six. He took up the guitar and later worked as a rodeo clown. Moving to Nashville in the late '60s, he broke into the country charts himself with "The Great Mail Robbery" in 1973 and first reached the country Top Ten with "Two Less Lonely People" in 1977. *—William Ruhlmann*

● **Very Best of Rex Allen Jr.** / Nov. 8, 1994 / Warner Bros. ♦♦♦♦

Rex Allen Jr., despite his impressive string of 21 Top 40 country hits on Warner Bros. in the '70s and early '80s, has not been well represented in the digital age. *The Very Best of Rex Allen Jr.* is budget-length but mid-priced, providing less than half an hour of music. The disc collects only ten of his recordings, and some of his bigger hits are passed over in favor of lower-charting singles. One of these, "The Great Mail Robbery," failed to crack the Top 40 at all, but it was Allen's first charting single from 1973. It's a delightful track and a surprising inclusion on such a brief collection. Allen provides liner notes (including short track-by-track comments), and it's a shame that his efforts weren't enlisted for a lengthier anthology. *—Greg Adams*

Rosalie Allen (Julie Marlene Bedra)

b. Jun. 27, 1924, Old Forge, PA

Vocals / Cowboy, Yodeling

One of the first wave of female country stars, Rosalie Allen recorded several hits during the late '40s as a singing cowgirl and yodeler in the Patsy Montana tradition. Born Julie Marlene Bedra on June 27, 1924, she grew up in a large, poor Pennsylvania family. Inspired by the singing cowboys of the '30s, she taught herself to sing and play guitar, and began working on the radio in Wilkes-Barre, PA. She moved to New York in the early '40s, and sang with the Swing Billies and also with Zeke Manners, where she met her future duet partner, Elton Britt. Allen's first hit came in 1946 with RCA Victor; the update of Patsy Montana's "I Want to Be a Cowboy's Sweetheart" hit number five and was later trumped on the country charts by its B-side, "Guitar Polka (Old Monterey)," which reached number three.

During the late '40s, Allen became quite famous in New York as a major promoter of country music. She hosted a TV show in New York as well as the WOV radio program *Prairie Stars*, and her writing appeared in columns for *National Jamboree* and *Country Sound Roundup*. Her Rosalie Allen Hillbilly Music Center in New York was the first specifically country record store in the nation. Allen's final two chart hits paired her with Elton Britt, the yodeler famous in the mid-'40s for "There's a Star-Spangled Banner Waving Somewhere." Their first single, "Beyond the Sunset," hit number seven in 1950; it was followed closely by the number three "Quicksilver." The duo also recorded an album for Waldorf Records in the mid-'50s—now released as *Starring Elton Britt and Rosalie Allen* on the Grand Award label. Also, two albums of Allen's solo recordings are available as German imports. *—John Bush*

Rosalie Allen Sings Country & Western Hits / 1957 / Waldorf Music ♦♦♦

● **Songs of the Golden West** / 1957 / Grand Award ♦♦♦♦

Rodeo / 1959 / Grand Award ♦♦♦

Rosalie Allen / 1961 / RCA ♦♦♦♦

Starring Elton Britt and Rosalie Allen / 1966 / Grand Award ♦♦♦

Queen of the Yoldelers / 1983 / Cattle [Germany] ♦♦♦♦

The Coyboy's Sweetheart / 1990 / Cowgirlboy [Germany] ♦♦♦

Terry Allen

b. May 7, 1943, Wichita, KS

Keyboards, Vocals / Country-Rock, Alternative Country

There may be no greater maverick than Terry Allen in all of country music from the mid-'70s onward. Along with Jimmie Dale Gilmore, Joe Ely, and Butch Hancock—all of whom he's known and collaborated with—Allen is a standard-bearer of the Lubbock, TX, country scene. Though not widely heralded, this is perhaps the most progressive movement in all of contemporary country, digging into modern-day concerns with a gutsy, liberal perspective, while maintaining a firm musical grounding in regional country and folk traditions. Allen is perhaps the most ambitious of them all, writing complex song cycles that have been performed with the help of fellow eclectics ranging from Lowell George to David Byrne.

Allen's audience, like those of the other Lubbock pioneers, is not the country mainstream. Indeed, his principal appeal may not lie with the country audience at all (though his music definitely *is* country), but with open-minded alternative folk and rock listeners. Unlike most current country artists, his words aim to question and confront hard day-to-day realities, rather than offer conservative clichés or maudlin comforts to shield listeners from those very day-to-day realities. He does so with a humor and irreverence that will also find little sympathy in Nashville or Middle America.

Country music is just one of Allen's artistic pursuits, perhaps accounting to some degree for his wide perspective. The renaissance man is also an internationally recognized artist with three NEA grants and a Guggenheim Fellowship to his credit. He's also a true multimedia performer, having done work in the mediums of painting, sculpture, film, video, installation, theater, and poetry. Just a few of his more interesting projects, for instance, were writing the music for *Amerasia*, a film about American servicemen living in Thailand after the Vietnam War; writing a new national anthem (with Ely, Hancock, and Gilmore) in conjunction with a book about Vietnam; and collaborating with his wife, Jo Harvey Allen, as well as Ely and Hancock, on the production of the acclaimed stage play *Chippy*.

But Allen is not a country music dilettante, having written songs for Bobby Bare and Robert Earl Keen. Outside of the strict country sphere, he wrote "New Delhi Freight Train" for Little Feat, and contributed a few songs to the soundtrack of David Byrne's *True Stories* film. The cinema has always been an inspiration or influence upon Allen's work. His first album, *Juarez* (from the mid-'70s), was a conceptual work that originated as a soundtrack to an imaginary film, evolving in performance to a set of songs inspired by Mexican imagery.

Released in 1979, *Lubbock (On Everything)* is considered his most significant album. Inspired by his experiences growing up in the Texas town, it won praise for observing the details of regional life and characters with a sensitivity and wit more akin to rock and folksinger/songwriters than country ones. Allen's music (if not his lyrical content), however, remains very much in the Texan country tradition. With many artistic projects always in the works, Allen has never had the need to record frequently. His singing and songwriting prowess remained undimmed, though, on 1996's *Human Remains*. He also expanded his musical horizons significantly with support from such noted stars and cult figures as David Byrne, Lucinda Williams, Ponty Bone, Lloyd Maines, and Joe Ely. *Salivation* followed in 1999. *—Richie Unterberger*

Juarez / 1975 / Fate ♦♦♦

Terry Allen is, first and foremost, a visual artist. He just happens to make brilliant, idiosyncratic albums on the side. In fact, his first album, 1975's *Juarez*, wasn't even initially conceived as an album, but as a set of songs recorded to accompany an artwork installation. Original copies of the album were released with a set of lithographs illustrating the characters who populate the album's world, an elliptical place where motivations and desires are often shadowy to the point of inscrutability, but the characterizations are almost three-dimensional. The story of two couples on a drinking spree that turns into a murderous chase through the southern California desert, *Juarez* is a tough-as-nails narrative with the deadpan, biting humor of crime fiction writers like Jim Thompson or Chester Himes. The album was recorded quickly and on a low budget, so the musical settings are ultra-spare, with Allen's whiskey-cured vocals and thumping piano often the only musical elements. As a concept album, the individual songs don't work as well out of context, but, listened to as a whole, *Juarez* is one of the more fascinating country albums of its time, like Willie Nelson's *Red Headed Stranger* as re-imagined by Quentin Tarantino. *—Stewart Mason*

● **Lubbock (On Everything)** / 1979 / Sugar Hill ♦♦♦♦♦

Although it's all but unknown outside of a devoted cult following, Terry Allen's second album, 1979's *Lubbock (On Everything)*, is one of the finest country albums of all time, a progenitor of what would eventually be called alt-country. This is country music with a wink and a dry-as-West-Texas-dust sense of humor, but at heart, *Lubbock (On Everything)* is a thoughtful meditation on Allen's hometown. Recorded in Lubbock after Allen hadn't lived there for close to a decade with a small group headed by local legends Don Caldwell and Lloyd Maines, the songs alternate between biting character studies like "Lubbock Woman" and "The Great Joe Bob (A Regional Tragedy)," about a high-school football star who ends up robbing a liquor store, and more loving tributes like "The Thirty Years War" and "The Wolfman of Del Rio." Salted through are a handful of songs about the pretensions of the art world (something Allen knows well in his day job as a sculptor and painter) that help keep the album's more cutting lines from sounding mean-spirited. A 20-song masterpiece, *Lubbock (On Everything)* is essential listening for anyone with an interest in the outer fringes of country music. —*Stewart Mason*

Smokin' the Dummy / 1980 / Sugar Hill ♦♦

The follow-up to Terry Allen's 1979 double-album masterpiece *Lubbock (On Everything)*, 1980's *Smokin' the Dummy* largely pales in comparison to its immediate predecessor, one of the most creative and twisted country albums ever. On its own merits, however, *Smokin' the Dummy* is, for the most part, a solid piece of oddball country-rock. Opening with the Little Feat-style rocker "The Heart of California" (dedicated to the Feat's recently deceased frontman, Lowell George), the album has a much more pronounced rock edge than either of Allen's previous albums. The richer arrangements, built on Allen's keyboards and producer Lloyd Maines' overdubbed electric and acoustic guitars (with plenty of pedal steel and slide for texture and occasional dashes of fiddle and New Orleans-style horns for color), sound terrific. They're particularly appreciated, however, because lyrically this is probably Allen's weakest album. There's a few of Allen's typically unique vignettes of west Texas life; in this respect, the almost short story-like "The Night Cafe" is the best thing here, with the spookily mesmerizing "The Lubbock Tornado," an impressionistic, almost Biblical tale of an April 1970 twister that destroyed a good chunk of the west Texas college town where Allen was raised, a close second. But for every lyrically and musically inventive track like "Red Bird" and the obsessively pun-filled "Helena, Montana," there's an underwritten country-rocker like "Roll Truck Roll" or "Feelin' Easy." The nadir is "Whatever Happened to Jesus (And Maybellene)?," which starts out just fine in a dryly ironic gospel mode, but after a clever pun on a popular brand of makeup, it degenerates into a rather pointless cover of Chuck Berry's first hit, as if Allen couldn't be bothered to finish his own song. Perhaps recorded too soon after the mightily impressive *Lubbock (On Everything)* for Allen to have enough solid songs at the ready, *Smokin' the Dummy* is a frustrating mélange of ideas both terrific and terrible. —*Stewart Mason*

Bloodlines / 1983 / Fate ♦♦♦♦

A remarkable improvement over 1980's extremely spotty *Smokin' the Dummy*, 1983's *Bloodlines* often rises to the level of Terry Allen's 1979 masterpiece *Lubbock (On Everything)*. The pantheistic hymn that opens and closes the album (the first in a simple and gorgeous voice and accordion setting, the last in a swelling choral version with a full band) sets a tone for the entire song cycle, one hinted at in the cover photo of a tattered painting of a lamb (a common Christ symbol) and explicated in the second track, the joyously heretical shaggy-dog story "Gimme a Ride to Heaven, Boy," in which Allen gives a lift to a hitchhiker who turns out to be Jesus, who promptly pulls a gun and takes off with his wheels ("The Lord moves in mysterious ways, and tonight my son, he's gonna use your car"). Throughout the rest of the album, Allen returns almost obsessively to the theme of religion's place in the modern world. "Ourland" sets images of the atrocities committed on both sides of the religious conflict in Northern Ireland to a bitterly ironic Celtic death march, while "Oh Hally Lou," the gospel-style theme song for a play by Allen's wife Jo Harvey Allen, questions Jesus' love for humanity. Tragicomic vignettes like "There Oughta Be a Law Against Sunny Southern California" and "Cantina Carlotta" (both remade from Allen's 1975 debut, *Juarez*) also touch on the same themes in more idiosyncratic ways. And for all its lyrical strength, *Bloodlines* is equally impressive musically. Reeling back the rock edge of *Smokin' the Dummy* without returning to the acoustic folk setting of most of *Lubbock (On Everything)*, *Bloodlines* mixes country, rock, folk, and oddball jazz like *Music From Big Pink*-era Band without the "Americana" fetish. A satisfying and often fascinating album, *Bloodlines* is one of Allen's best. —*Stewart Mason*

Human Remains / Jan. 23, 1996 / Sugar Hill ♦♦♦♦♦

The conceptual scope of *Human Remains* is not nearly as ambitious as *Lubbock*. But the gutsier and more varied musical arrangements—crafted with help from Lloyd Maines, David Byrne, Joe Ely, Lucinda Williams, and many others—may make this a better introduction to Allen's world. There's certainly no shortage of interesting character sketches, like a one-legged dancing woman, memories of "flower children and their sh*t-eating grins," and 13-year-olds well on their way to reform school. "Gone to Texas" especially is a refreshing blast of true anti-establishment sentiment, Allen singing in even-mannered tones that he doesn't need a chickensh*t (his term) businessman telling him what to do, and dissing some country star who thinks that all it takes to be special is to wear a hat and win Grammys. —*Richie Unterberger*

Shelly Lee Alley

b. Jul. 6, 1894, Alleyton, TX, d. 1964
Fiddle, Leader, Vocals / Western Swing
During the '30s and '40s, Shelly Lee Alley and his Alley Cats were one of the most prominent Western swing bands in Texas. Born in Alleyton, Texas, singer/songwriter/fiddle player Alley began his career as the leader of a San Antonio army camp orchestra during World War I. Following military service, he went on to lead several small orchestras, which played on radio stations throughout the Lone Star State. During the early '20s, Alley was primarily interested in pop and jazz music and belonged to several small combos, including the Dixie Serenaders, which played at a Dallas radio station. In addition to performing and conducting music, Alley was also a songwriter. One of his early songs, "Travelin' Blues," became a Depression-era hit for Jimmie Rodgers; its success turned Alley more towards country & western music, and he joined a Fort Worth radio show called "The Chuck Wagon Gang."

He formed the Alley Cats in 1936 and played radio stations and local dances in the Houston and Beaumont area. The Alley Cats recorded several sessions for the American Record Corporation on the Vocalion label. Some Alley Cats members, such as Ted Daffan and Leon Selph, went on to form their own successful bands. In 1941, Alley cut a single for Bluebird, and also continued writing songs, many of which were recorded by Jimmie

Davis. During World War II, the Alley Cats broke up and Alley began playing with Patsy and the Buckaroos. He got the Cats back together and cut a single for the Globe label, but the group disbanded for good around 1946. Alley still played his fiddle occasionally and wrote songs; his stepson, Clyde Brewer, went on to become a popular Western swing musician in his own right. —*Sandra Brennan*

Dave Alvin

b. 1955, Downey, CA
Guitar, Vocals / Heartland Rock, Roots Rock, Americana, Singer/Songwriter, Alternative Country-Rock
Dave Alvin helped to kick start the American roots rock scene in the early '80s with the band the Blasters and has since gone on to a career as a solo performer, songwriter, producer, and sideman that's been as well respected as it is eclectic. Born in Downey, CA, in 1955, Alvin was raised by a family of music fans, and as teenagers Dave and his older brother Phil immersed themselves in blues, rockabilly, and vintage country sounds, collecting rare records and attending nightclub performances by the likes of T-Bone Walker, Big Joe Turner, and Lee Allen. Like many fans, the Alvin brothers wanted to play music influenced by the sounds they loved, and in 1979 the formed the Blasters with fellow Downey residents Bill Bateman and John Bazz. Combining the revved-up energy of punk rock with an enthusiastic embrace of classic American sounds, the Blasters became a sensation in Los Angeles and won an enthusiastic cult following across the United States and Europe. However, the Blasters were unable to translate their critical respect and enthusiastic fan base into mainstream success, and in 1986, Dave left the band.

While playing with the Blasters, Alvin had already displayed a broad range of enthusiasms with two side projects, Chris D.'s literate goth-punk collective the Flesh Eaters and the Knitters, an acoustic ensemble in which Alvin performed vintage country and folk numbers with John Doe and Exene Cervenka of X. Shortly after leaving the Blasters, Alvin joined X as lead guitarist after the departure of Billy Zoom; however, Alvin amicably left the group to work on a solo project shortly after the recording sessions for their album *See How We Are*. Alvin's first solo album, entitled *Romeo's Escape* in the United States and *Every Night About This Time* in England, added a purer country influence along with a larger side-portion of the blues; while the album was critically well received, it didn't fare well in the marketplace, and Alvin was dropped by his American record label, Columbia.

Alvin suffered health problems which sidelined him for a while, except for a wild tour with friends Mojo Nixon and Country Dick Montana as the Pleasure Barons, which was described as "a Las Vegas revue from acts who aren't going to be asked to play Vegas." (A live album was released of a second Pleasure Barons tour in 1993.) In 1989, Dwight Yoakam scored a hit on the country charts with Alvin's song "Long White Cadillac," and Alvin used the royalties to start work on his second solo set, *Blue Blvd.* Released by the California-based roots-music label Hightone Records, *Blue Blvd* received enthusiastic reviews and sold well enough to re-establish Alvin as a significant artist in the roots rock scene. After releasing *Museum of Heart* in 1993, Alvin began to turn his attention to acoustic music with 1994's *King of California*, and over the next several years Alvin moved back and forth between hard-edged roots rock and more introspective acoustic material that still honored his influences (and allowed him to display a greater range as a vocalist). In 2000, Alvin recorded a collection of traditional folk and blues classics, *Public Domain: Songs From the Wild Land*, which earned him a Grammy award for Best Contemporary Folk Album.

When not busy recording his own music, Alvin has also worked as a producer for several other roots-oriented acts, including Tom Russell, the Derailers, and Big Sandy & His Fly-Rite Boys, as well as collaborating with rockabilly legend Sonny Burgess. As a sideman, Alvin has recorded sessions with the likes of Ramblin' Jack Elliott, Little Milton, Katy Moffatt, and Syd Straw. —*Mark Deming*

● Romeo's Escape / Dec. 1987 / Razor & Tie ♦♦♦♦♦

After leaving the Blasters (and ending a short stint as the post-Billy Zoom guitarist in X), Dave Alvin kicked off his solo career with this album, in which he indulged in his passions for blues, country, and roots rock in stronger and grittier form than he had in his previous bands. The album's eclecticism, however, proved to be its commercial Achilles heel; in America, it was marketed as a country album under the title *Romeo's Escape*, even though the title track was the album's fiercest rocker, while in Europe it was called *Every Night About This Time* after a superb country weeper Alvin wrote for the set, but was pitched as a rock album. Needless to say, most everyone was confused and few people heard the record under either title, which is a real shame. If Alvin was still getting his sea legs as a vocalist on *Romeo's Escape*, his emotional conviction and intelligent phrasing outweigh his somewhat limited range, and he's rarely rocked harder in the studio (with Tony Gilkyson, Greg Leisz, and David Hidalgo helping to kick up some dust in his backing band). The re-recordings of several Blasters classics ("Long White Cadillac," "Border Radio," "Jubilee Train") bring out sharp new angles in the songs that are worth hearing, and the rest of the lineup proves he had lots of new material worthy of his talents (especially "Every Night About This Time" and "I Wish It Was Saturday Night"). While Dave Alvin's work would get stronger and more confident with time, *Romeo's Escape* left no doubt he had the goods to be a first-rate frontman, while his gifts as a guitarist and writer remained as strong as ever. —*Mark Deming*

Every Night About This Time / Dec. 1987 / Demon ♦♦♦♦♦

This is Dave Alvin's solo debut, which was released initially in the U.K., then picked up for U.S. release by Epic Records, which changed the album title to *Romeo's Escape*. —*William Ruhlmann*

Blue Blvd / Aug. 1991 / Hightone ♦♦♦

The only thing that mars this wonderful, rootsy singer/songwriter album is a heavy production hand and a drum sound attempting to give it a rock edge; consequently, some of the more beautiful songs like the title track suffer under the weight, but the final cut, "Dry

River," is worth the price of the disc alone. Alvin's rock & roll pals come out to play—Dwight Yoakam, David Hidalgo, saxophonist Lee Allen—making the record essential for anyone interested in the state of California roots music in the early '90s. —*Denise Sullivan*

Museum of Heart / Sep. 20, 1993 / Hightone ✦✦✦
Alvin's vision falters slightly, as none of the songs here are as instantly likable or classic as on previous outings. Perhaps stunted by more than half of the songs being co-writes ("Between the Cracks" with Tom Russell), Alvin's normally clear and simple approach is muddled, but the instrumentation is flawless and his regular all-star cast (John Doe, Syd Straw, and Katy Moffatt) is present. —*Denise Sullivan*

King of California / May 1, 1994 / Hightone ✦✦✦
From the time the Blasters began making waves on the California rock scene, the standard line always was that Dave Alvin was the group's great songwriter and Phil Alvin was the great singer. And when Dave launched his solo career in 1987, he was frequently saddled with the criticism that he wasn't much of a vocalist compared to his brother. While dozens of blues and roots rock performers have built solid careers without singing any better than Dave Alvin, it's true that on *Romeo's Escape* and *Blue Blvd* his rough, flinty voice lacked the natural grace and projection of Phil's work with the Blasters. But on 1994's *King of California*, Alvin recorded a few new songs alongside a stack of classics from his back catalog (and some well-chosen covers) with a small acoustic combo backing him up. Suddenly freed from having to shout over a high-powered rock band, Alvin proved on this release just how good of a vocalist he really was. While Alvin's natural instrument still shows certain limitations on *King of California*, when allowed to play with the nooks and crannies of his voice he reveals a subtle but dramatic sense of phrasing and a marvelous feel for the characters he created; he's still no Al Green, but as a musical storyteller he's mighty impressive. Of course, it helps that he has a bunch of superb songs to work with here, including "Barn Burning," "Fourth of July," "Border Radio," and "Little Honey," and that the great Greg Leisz is on hand to anchor the band, produce the sessions, and play marvelous slide guitar. While *King of California* was often lumped in with the then-fashionable unplugged craze, in retrospect it was the album where Dave Alvin's abilities as a performer began to catch up with his gifts as a songwriter, pointing the way for his later albums *Blackjack David* and *Public Domain*. —*Mark Deming*

Interstate City / Jul. 1996 / Hightone ✦✦✦✦
Recorded at the Continental Club in Austin, TX, with his backup band, the Guilty Men, *Interstate City* documents the nervy energy and gritty sound of Dave Alvin live in concert. Alvin tears through his back catalog with surprising gusto, touching on both the Blasters and his solo hits. Most enticing for fans, however, are the new songs he works into the set. Most of the newer numbers are on par with his finest material and they are delivered with an intoxicating rush. *Interstate City* is one of the rare live albums that actually improves on the original recordings. —*Thom Owens*

Blackjack David / Jun. 16, 1998 / Hightone ✦✦✦✦
Dave Alvin earned his crown as the King of California the hard way. A fourth-generation Californian, Alvin worked his way through various incarnations in order to arrive at this point. A longstanding monumental force in Los Angeles and California music, Alvin is essentially a blues player who writes and performs what he terms "American folk music." From Celtic and British folk tunes to early rock & roll, from classic blues and country & western to the Bakersfield sound, Alvin knows his stuff. Gleaning from all the genres, Alvin sits firmly upon his throne, creating a brand of music that is intelligent, insightful, and broad in scope. With Alvin at peace with his creative direction, *Blackjack David* picks up where *King of California* left off in 1994. More electric, *Blackjack David* almost rocks in places, as on "Abilene" and "New Highway." It ambles along nicely in other spots, too. The title cut, a traditional tune hundreds of years old, is given new life under the deft Alvin touch and a new arrangement. This effectively connects the past and the present in terms of Alvin and his place in musical history. "1968," written with fellow "405 Freeway Boy" Chris Gaffney, reveals a country twist. As interesting as anything either of them have written individually, the Tom Russell co-write "California Snow" is startling in its intensity. The final cut, "Tall Trees," is haunting and mysterious, displaying all of Alvin's power as a writer and communicator in a subtle fashion that demands attention. A Renaissance man, Dave Alvin continues to make and record music of integrity. —*Jana Pendragon*

Public Domain: Songs from the Wild Land / Aug. 15, 2000 / Hightone ✦✦✦✦✦
Drawing from the mother lode of traditional songs in the public domain, songwriter Dave Alvin brings an authentic voice and extraordinary understanding to his chosen tracks. Familiar songs from the folk canon like "Shenandoah" and "Walk Right In" are reworked by him and a full band with arrangements incorporating the roadhouse style they've honed from years of working together. He also unearthed lesser-known songs like "Mama, Ain't Long for Day" (perhaps credited to Blind Willie McTell), "Sign of Judgment," and "Railroad Bill," having learned versions from records he unearthed as a kid by obscure artists: from Will Bennett to Kid Prince Moore. This is the work of a scholar as well as a master craftsman. —*Denise Sullivan*

Out in California / May 21, 2002 / Hightone ✦✦✦✦
Recorded live in August of 2001 in Santa Barbara and in January of 2002 in Pasadena, Dave Alvin's album comes by its title honestly. As live albums tend to be, it's a curious mix of the familiar and the obscure; concerts always have to offer the hits and standbys, but they also offer the performers a chance to play old and unfamiliar songs that hold a personal significance. Thus, listeners get rawboned performances of the inevitable "Fourth of July" (an Alvin composition recorded more famously by X, of which he was a member for a while) and "American Music" (recorded more famously by the Blasters, the band with which he made his breakthrough albums in the 1980s), along

with a lascivious old Bo Carter blues, the Bo Diddley classic "Who Do You Love" (here performed in a medley with another old Blasters tune, "Little Honey") and the hoariest of old blues-rock chestnuts, "Don't Let Your Deal Go Down." The album's finest moment is a stunningly beautiful rendition of Alvin's "Abilene," which is beautiful in large part because the other bandmembers pitch in on vocals—Alvin is a fine guitarist and an even better songwriter, but he's no kind of singer. At the very end, there is a hidden track; an audience member calls for "Freebird" in an ironic tone of voice, and Alvin responds, "What, you think we can't play that?" With that, the band rips into "Freebird" with a (mercifully brief) vengeance. It's the perfect ending to a very impressive album. —*Rick Anderson*

Phil Alvin

b. Mar. 6, 1953, Downey, CA
Guitar, Vocals / Roots Rock, Americana
As the frontman of the Blasters during the early '80s, singer/guitarist Phil Alvin spearheaded the underground's return to American music traditions ranging from blues to rockabilly to country, predating the roots rock movement that bloomed in the years to follow. Born March 6, 1953, in Los Angeles, Alvin and his younger brother Dave were raised on the music of Elvis Presley, T-Bone Walker, and Big Joe Turner; together they formed the Blasters in 1979, borrowing the name from Jimmy McCracklin's Blues Blasters.

Their debut LP, 1980's *American Music*, created a major buzz among insiders for its gritty, rootsy sound, and their self-titled 1981 follow-up even cracked the Top 40. However, Dave Alvin left the Blasters in 1985, at which time the group went on hiatus as Phil returned to grad school to pursue his master's degree in mathematics and artificial intelligence. (He later earned his Ph.D. from UCLA.) Alvin resurfaced in 1986 with his solo debut, *Un "Sung" Stories*, which featured cameos by everyone from Sun Ra & His Arkestra to the Dirty Dozen Brass Band; he reconvened the Blasters a short time later, and the group continued with a revolving lineup into the following decade. A second solo effort, *County Fair 2000*, appeared in 1994, and featured members of the Alvin side project the Faultline Syncopators, a traditional jazz combo. —*Jason Ankeny*

● **Un "Sung" Stories** / 1986 / Slash ✦✦✦✦✦
Songwriter and guitarist Dave Alvin was the heart of the Blasters, one of America's greatest roots rock bands, but his brother, vocalist Phil Alvin, was the soul of the group, and anyone who wants a crash course on the importance of Phil's contribution to that fine band ought to check out his first solo album, *Un "Sung" Stories*. Here, Phil tackles ten vintage blues, jazz, and gospel tunes, sometimes accompanied a small combo (or just Phil's rudimentary guitar), while on other cuts Alvin is joined by Sun Ra & His Arkestra and the Dirty Dozen Brass Band, each of whom swing up a storm in their own truly individual ways. While the sound and approach of this set is a far cry from the Blasters potent take on America's musical history, Alvin's vocals ring out with a palpable joy, and he makes these musical museum pieces live and breathe like they were written last week; this album truly carries the spirit of the Blasters' wide-spectrum approach to American music into a very different direction. And while Phil may not have his brother's songwriting chops, you can't say that a man who would ask Sun Ra to arrange "The Old Man of the Mountain" and "Brother, Can You Spare a Dime" and then have the courage to take the lead vocal on the same is lacking in the way of a unique personal vision. Short and sweet, *Un "Sung" Stories* is a true gem that's richly felt in a way a collection of "old standards" is not expected to be. Now would someone be so kind as to reissue this on CD? —*Mark Deming*

County Fair 2000 / Oct. 25, 1994 / Hightone ✦✦✦
Phil Alvin's second solo date, *County Fair 2000* continues his thorough exploration of Americana with references to tap dancing ("Low Down Rhythm"), Ellingtonia ("the Terror"), Delta blues ("That Thing"), New Orleans brass bands ("Danny Boy's Mourning Sunset"), rockabilly/country ("County Fair 2000"), automobiles ("Wreck Your V-8 Ford"), and the Jimmy Reed-styled "Oh, Doctor." Alvin has the good taste to employ an impressive list of guests including the Dirty Dozen Brass Band, Billy Boy Arnold, Cesar Rosas from Los Lobos, James Intveld, and members of the Blasters (without brother Dave Alvin.) County Fair 2000 leaves no doubt that Phil Alvin is a premier musicologist, preserving and staying true to what he loves. —*Al Campbell*

The Amazing Rhythm Aces

f. 1974, Memphis, TN, db. 1981
Group / Country-Rock
A mainstream country-rock band similar in execution (if not commercial success) to the Eagles, the Amazing Rhythm Aces were formed in Memphis in 1974 by bassist Jeff Davis and drummer Butch McDade, who had earlier recorded and toured with the great singer/songwriter Jesse Winchester. After striking out on their own, Davis and McDade enlisted vocalist/guitarist Russell Smith, keyboardist Billy Earheart III, dobro player Barry Burton, and pianist James Hooker to develop a sound composed of equal parts pop, country and blue-eyed soul. *Stacked Deck*, the Amazing Rhythm Aces debut album, appeared in 1975; it produced two significant crossover hits, "Third Rate Romance" and "Amazing Grace (Used to Be Her Favorite Song)," the group's lone Top Ten country single. A year later, the hit "The End Is Not in Sight (The Cowboy Tune)," from the LP *Too Stuffed to Jump*, won the Aces a Grammy for Country Vocal Performance by a Group. Following the release of 1977's *Toucan Do It Too*, Burton left the group, and was replaced by Duncan Cameron.

In 1978, the Aces released *Burning the Ballroom Down*, followed a year later by a self-titled effort featuring cameos by Joan Baez, Tracy Nelson and the Muscle Shoals Horns; both were met with critical approval, but sold poorly. They released one final record, *How the Hell Do You Spell Rhythum*, before disbanding. While Smith went on to become a successful songwriter, Earheart joined Hank Williams Jr.'s Bama Band, and Cameron joined Sawyer Brown—a group which, ironically enough, would find significant chart success in the 1980s with a sound similar to what the Amazing Rhythm Aces had created a decade earlier.

After a hiatus of some 15 years, the Aces reformed in 1994. The group, now comprised of Smith, Davis, McDade, Earheart, Hooker and new guitarist/mandolinist Danny Parks, marked their return to duty by releasing *Born Again*, a collection of newly-recorded renditions of their biggest hits. In addition, they also began composing new songs for a projected comeback album; although McDade's cancer-related death on November 29, 1998, temporarily halted that plan, *Chock Full of Country Goodness* finally appeared in mid-1999. —*Jason Ankeny*

☆ **Stacked Deck** / 1975 / Valley ✦✦✦✦✦

In contrast to such '70s country-rock outfits as the Eagles and Poco, whose members had passed through the West Coast folk-rock scene dominated by the Byrds, the Amazing Rhythm Aces were a Memphis-based band. Their debut album is an edgy effort, rooted in a purer Southern sound, and embracing a soulfulness that their West Coast rivals lacked. The country gospel tune "Life's Railway to Heaven," the funky "The 'Ella B'," the stomping "Hit the Nail on the Head," and the soulful "The Beautiful Lie" would never have been done in as raw, intense, or bracing a fashion by their rivals. Russell Smith brings a vocal performance to Charlie Rich's "Who Will the Next Fool Be" that sounds like he's channeling the ghost of Sam Cooke. And between those album highlights and the hits "Third Rate Romance" and "Amazing Grace (Used to Be Her Favorite Song)," the group works in a sweetly nostalgic piece called "King of the Cowboys," all about movie and television heroes. —*Bruce Eder*

Too Stuffed to Jump / 1976 / Valley ✦✦✦✦✦

The group's second album is only slightly less inventive than its first, still very countrified compared to most country-rock, and more soulful than most of the competition. The numbers range from rocking stompers like "Typical American Boy" to the lyrical "If I Just Know What to Say," with room in between for some fine western numbers ("The End Is Not in Sight," "Out of the Snow")—the former a Grammy-winning country tune, the latter a beautiful mandolin workout—and novelty songs ("A Little Italy Rag"). —*Bruce Eder*

Toucan Do It Too / 1977 / ABC ✦✦✦✦

Although the Amazing Rhythm Aces remained firmly in touch with their country and Southern rock roots, they began shedding their twang in favor of some harder and edgier material, which they matched with equally aggressive execution. The airy and slightly calypso "Never Been to the Islands (Howard and Hugh's Blues)"—which opens their third long-player, *Toucan Do It Too*—demonstrates that the Aces had not strayed too far afield. Both "Living in a World Unknown" and "Who's Crying Now" provide a contrast with solid, propulsive rockers led by the dual electric fretwork of Russell Smith (guitar/vocals) and Barry Burton (dobro/guitar/mandolin/pedal steel/slide guitar/vocals), who left the band shortly after the Aces recorded their follow-up to this disc. They recall the sunny and carefree southern California sound of the Eagles, and blend that force with their trademark country-rock leanings. The Aces could also pull off lean blue-eyed soulful numbers, such as the midtempo "Never Been Hurt," featuring some tasty keyboard inflections from future Nanci Griffith collaborator and Blue Moon Orchestra member James Hooker (piano/electric piano/clavinet/vocals). There are a number of decidedly more traditional-sounding sides, which are among the album's zeniths. "Everybody's Talked Too Much" offers somewhat of a retreat into an increasingly laid-back country-rock vibe, while the high and lonesome "Last Letter Home" is instrumentally bolstered by Burton's lilting and acoustically lyrical mandolin runs, which are tucked behind Jeff Davis (bass) and Hooker's sonic accoutrement. "Geneva's Lullaby" is an achingly tender ballad from Smith, whose criminally underappreciated guitar work and songwriting are given a well-deserved showcase. His compositional versatility is evident on the LP's closing track, "Two Can Do It Too," which boasts a healthy syncopation that could have easily been covered by the likes of Little Feat or—thanks to the funky shuffle groove—even the Neville Brothers. [In 2000, Collectors' Choice Music issued a two-fer that paired this album with *Burning the Ballroom Down*, the Aces' final release with the original lineup.] —*Lindsay Planer*

Burning the Ballroom Down / 1978 / ABC ✦✦✦✦

On their fourth long-player, the Amazing Rhythm Aces continued the trend of presenting well-crafted pop songs leaning toward laid-back country and Southern rock. *Burning the Ballroom Down* was the final long-player from the "classic" incarnation of the band, featuring Barry Burton (dobro/guitar/mandolin/steel guitar/slide guitar/vocals), who departed shortly after this disc was recorded, Jeff Davis (bass/vocals), Billy Earheart III (organ/keyboards), James Hooker (piano/keyboards/clavinet/vocals), Butch McDade (percussion/drums/vocals), and Russell Smith (guitar/vocals). The Aces' Memphis roots are evident throughout the album and are revealed in a variety of styles, ranging from the blue-eyed soul of the opening title track to the gospel-tinged waltz balladry on "Out of Control." The even more sacred "Spirit Walk" is particularly notable for aptly displaying Burton's multi-stringed mastery. Moving away from the harder edge of their previous long-player, *Toucan Do It Too*, the Aces retreat into more regional acoustic folk and bluegrass styles on the tongue-in-cheek "I Pity the Mother and the Father (When the Kids Move Away)" as well as the tropically inspired "Ashes of Love." Along the same line is Smith's hauntingly poignant and minor-chord masterpiece "Red to Blue (When Dreams Come True)." Other highlights include the slinky rocker "A Jackass Gets His Oats," which bears some striking resemblances to a typical Lynyrd Skynyrd deep-fried rocker. The easygoing "Della's Long Brown Hair" features a sweet pedal steel solo from Burton, who had exited the combo by the time the Aces hit the road in support of *Burning the Ballroom Down*. Enthusiasts should search out the live disc *Between You & Us*, which includes a show from this tour and features Burton's replacement, Duncan Cameron, in one of his earliest gigs with the band. [In 2000, Collectors' Choice Music issued a two-fer that paired this album with its predecessor, *Toucan Do It Too*, on a single compact disc.] —*Lindsay Planer*

The Amazing Rhythm Aces / 1978 / Columbia ✦✦✦

By 1979, the Aces' recording career was winding down and their longtime label folded. As a result, this record was released on both ABC and Columbia with the only difference being the picture on the back cover. This album also saw the departure of guitarist/producer Barry Burton. Whatever the causes, this is their strongest album in some time. —*Jim Worbois*

How the Hell Do You Spell Rhythum? / 1980 / Warner Bros. ✦✦

The band goes out in tighter-than-tight style, covering "Further on Down the Road," and Delbert McClinton's "Object of My Affection," and Van Morrison's "Wild Night" and introducing the original version of "Big Ole Brew." —*Kit Kiefer*

Full House: Aces High / 1981 / MSS ✦✦

4 You 4 Ever: Best of Amazing Rhythm Aces / 1982 / M&R ✦✦✦✦✦

Ride Again / Jan. 14, 1997 / Breaker Productions ✦✦

Out of the Blue / Jul. 1, 1997 / Breaker Productions ✦✦✦

The loping bass, punctuating guitar, and drumstick slaps let you know right away that you have an Amazing Rhythm Aces release on your hands. This is the first good release of their material on disc (there was a *Ride Again*, best-of collection, that didn't quite satisfy) which contains some wonderful quality material. The Aces are purveyors of rock-inflected country music, or countrified rock, and this amalgam is flavored with a healthy dose of blues. The intelligent lyrics are backdropped by instrumentation that perfectly augments the sentiments of the lyrics. The lead voice on most songs is Russell Smith, whose voice has gotten even better and more reflective with the passing of years. The Aces have maintained the excellent lyric content of the songs, and when mixed with their simple but elegant arrangements, they produce simply great songs. Hard to find, but worth the effort. —*Bob Gottlieb*

Chock Full of Country Goodness / Aug. 24, 1999 / Valley ✦✦✦

Fans of the Amazing Rhythm Aces can start proclaiming "Yippe Yi Yo Yo!" (the first cut on the album). Back as a full-time band after a number of years out of the spotlight, the Aces serve up the same combination of classic rock, soulful blues, and stone country that made them so popular back in the '70s and '80s on *Chock Full of Country Goodness*. Perhaps best known for such colossal hits as "Third Rate Romance," "Amazing Grace (Used to Be Her Favorite Song)," and the Grammy Award-winning "The End Is Not in Sight," the Aces have recaptured the unique and emphatic sound that have kept fans loyal despite the band's 14-year hiatus (1981-1995). With 12 original songs from lead singer and songwriter Russell Smith, and with the rest of the original bandmembers intact (minus founding member and influential drummer/songwriter Butch McDade, who succumbed to cancer in 1998), the Aces rekindle their fire for cheap guitars and rednecks. With so many new country artists making the crossover to pop, *Chock Full of Country Goodness* is a refreshing reminder of our good ol' country roots. —*Maria Konicki Dinoia*

Absolutely Live / Apr. 25, 2000 / Icehouse ✦✦✦

We have here a fine aggregate of the "greatest hits" of the Amazing Rhythm Aces played live (this was recorded in Switzerland at a live show). This band has such a good feeling about it that when they hit those first notes of "The End Is Not In Sight" you will immediately begin to smile. Then the sound of Russell Smith's smooth, but with an edge of having been though it all, voice kicks in and drives the song along. This is a collection that all of the band's fans should want to get, as it gets to most of the material the band did best and has a good cross section of their more recent work. The band is in good form and solid with a core of the original band intact. There are a few personnel changes, but the exchange of players is not noticeable in their playing. The fire is still there, and, best of all, Russell Smith is still in very fine voice. This not a throwaway disc by any means, and it is worth going out and looking for. —*Bob Gottlieb*

★ **Stacked Deck/Too Stuffed to Jump** / Jul. 11, 2000 / Collectors' Choice Music ✦✦✦✦✦

The group's first two LPs assembled together on one CD from Collectors' Choice—there are no notes, but the original artwork is recreated with full music credits, and beautiful, state-of-the-art sound. The band's music has aged well, and although their master tapes evidently no longer reside with the ABC library (which is part of MCA-Universal), they haven't been lost track of either, to judge from the good results here. —*Bruce Eder*

Toucan Do It Too/Burning the Ballroom Down / Jul. 11, 2000 / Collectors' Choice Music ✦✦✦✦

The group's third and fourth albums assembled together, again with no annotation but excellent sound. In addition to being a fine showcase for the group overall, the CD gives a good account of Barry Burton's skills and development as a producer, and his ability to get some extraordinary sounds out of the group as singers as well as instrumentalists—"The Spirit Walk" by itself, which closes this disc, is one of the crowning achievements for the group and a stunning piece of white gospel music. —*Bruce Eder*

Between You & Us / Oct. 9, 2001 / Pilot ✦✦✦✦

This 1979 performance has been floating around tape-trading circles ever since it was first broadcast on KFML in Denver, CO. Likewise, a pre-FM distillation of the show surfaced in 1999 as *Concert Classics, Vol. 3*. In fact, *Between You & Us* is a U.K. reissue of that disc. Regardless of which incarnation should avail itself, the documented performance is a fiery and rollicking ride—perfectly encapsulating what made the Amazing Rhythm Aces among the finest and, ironically (if not somewhat criminally), equally overlooked American rock bands of the '70s. Even though they are on the road supporting *Burning the Ballroom Down*—their fourth album in three years—this live set includes very little from that disc, as "I Pity the Mother and the Father" is the sole representative. This show also correlates with the recent departure of founding member Barry Burton prior to commencing the tour. His replacement, Duncan Cameron, is front and center during this show and would continue with the Amazing Rhythm Aces through their various reformations in the '80s and beyond. One of the band's most endearing qualities is the uncanny ability to parley its Memphis roots far beyond traditional blue-eyed soul. As guitarists Cameron and Russell Smith trade licks throughout, at times they rival the rapport between their ABC Records labelmates Walter Becker and Jeff "Skunk" Baxter from Steely Dan. The seemingly intuitive lead guitars on "Who's Crying Now" retain the same bite as the Dan's "Kid Charlemagne." Another dynamic duo in the band consists of keyboardists Billy Earheart III (organ) and James Hooker (piano/clavinet). The two are able to enhance each other, weaving melodies and punctuations most notably on acoustic outings such as "Amazing Grace (Used to Be Her Favorite Song)" and "These Dreams of Loving You"—which additionally exemplify the Amazing Rhythm Aces' wide scope of distinctly American music. Most of the tunes featured on this set are from the *Stacked Deck* and *Too Stuffed to Jump* albums. These discs feature such fan favorites as the raucous blues shuffle "Hit the Nail on the Head" and the funky "Anything You Want"—both of which are propelled by Earheart and Hooker. The band is also looking forward to its next self-titled release—which would include a cover of Al Green's "Love and Happiness"—perfectly tethering the bandmembers back to their soul roots. *Between You & Me* is good starting point for the curious and a worthwhile addition for the converted. —*Lindsay Planer*

Eric Ambel

b. Aurora, IL

Guitar, Vocals, Producer / Roots Rock, Alternative Country-Rock

A Brooklyn-based artist known for his blistering guitar work, Eric "Roscoe" Ambel was one of the leading proponents of American roots rock, both as a musician and producer. After serving in an early incarnation of Joan Jett's Blackhearts, in 1981 Ambel formed the Del-Lords with ex-Dictator Scott Kempner. One of the more successful bands to spring up from the "roots-rock revival" of the early '80s, the Del-Lords were essentially Kempner's baby, although Ambel did occasionally take over the lead vocal reins. After debuting in 1984 with the LP *Frontier Days*, the group issued three more albums—1985's *Johnny Comes Marching Home*, 1988's *Based on a True Story*, and 1990's *Lovers Who Wander*—before Ambel's exit hastened the group's breakup.

Ambel left the Del-Lords to focus on a solo career, which he had begun in 1988 with *Roscoe's Gang*, a laid-back rock record cut with the aid of the Skeletons, Peter Holsapple, and other friends. The LP was a combination of originals as well as covers of Bob Dylan, Swamp Dogg, and Neil Young, the artist to whom Ambel has been most frequently compared throughout his career. He did not release another solo LP, however, until 1995, at which time he issued *Loud and Lonesome*. Throughout the 1990s, Ambel's greatest visibility was as a producer of likeminded musicians, including Nils Lofgren, the Bottle Rockets, Blue Mountain, the Blood Oranges, Go to Blazes, and the Dog & Pony Show. In addition, he played with ex-Georgia Satellite Dan Baird in a raucous hillbilly side project called the Yayhoos. —*Jason Ankeny*

● **Roscoe's Gang** / 1988 / Enigma ✦✦✦✦✦

On his debut solo album, Del-Lord Eric Ambel cuts songs by buddies like Scott Kempner and Peter Holsapple, not to mention fave raves like Bob Dylan's "If You Gotta Go, Go Now," and Swamp Dogg's "Total Destruction To Your Mind," and Neil Young's "Vampire Blues." "Recorded absolutely live in the studio. No overdubs, second takes or rehearsal," warns the record jacket, but that only contributes to the party atmosphere. Ambel is an authoritative singer, aided and abetted by Syd Straw, and he plays a vicious lead guitar, too. A worthy addition to the '80s roots rock library. —*William Ruhlmann*

Loud and Lonesome / 1995 / East Side Digital ✦✦✦

Be forwarned—*Loud & Lonesome* could become addictive. Ambel's mixture of roots rock and singer/songwriter influences has produced one of the finest albums in a longtime. From the rollicking "Song for the Walls" to the achingly beautiful "Autumn Rose," Ambel and the Gang come up with 11 top-notch tunes. Also, check out the hidden bonus track "Frozen Head St. Park Song" (which also appears as a bonus on the fastest Dan Baird album). —*James Chrispell*

American Flyer

f. 1976, **db.** 1978

Group / Country-Rock, Singer/Songwriter

American Flyer was a '70s folk-rock quartet made up of former members of other groups: Craig Fuller was from Pure Prairie League, Eric Kaz had been a member of Blues Magoos, Steve Katz was in Blood, Sweat & Tears, and Doug Yule had played in the Velvet Underground. Together they charted with two albums on United Artists in the mid-'70s. —*William Ruhlmann*

● **American Flyer** / 1976 / United Artists ✦✦✦✦✦

American Flyer deserved better. Eric Kaz had written great love songs for Linda Ronstadt and Bonnie Raitt, and Craig Fuller was coming off his Top 40 hit "Amie" with Pure Prairie League. As it happened, Steve Katz's "Back In '57" turned out to be one of the album's highlights, but "Let Me Down Easy," by Kaz And Fuller, was a minor hit, and there was also Kaz's classic co-composition, "Love Has No Pride." But those were just the cream of an excellent set produced by George Martin. Add it all up, and it should have meant more than a chart peak in the lower reaches of the Top 100, an early indication that, for whatever reasons, American Flyer was not destined to become the next Crosby, Stills, Nash & Young. —*William Ruhlmann*

Spirit of a Woman / 1977 / United Artists ✦✦

Maybe there was only room for one really successful country-folk-rock group with good songs and strong harmonies in the mid-'70s, and the job had already been taken by the Eagles. Who knows? American Flyer's second and final album didn't have as many great songs as the debut, and some of them were swamped by strings, but it was a pleasant work, notably featuring a version of Eric Kaz's "I'm Blowin' Away," which Bonnie Raitt had covered a couple of years earlier. —*William Ruhlmann*

Al Anderson

b. 1947, Windsor, CT

Guitar, Vocals / Bar Band, Roots Rock, Retro-Rock

Guitarist and songwriter Al Anderson is probably still best known for his 22-year stint with roots rock renegades NRBQ, though he's distinguished himself as a gifted songwriter and solo artist since striking out on his own. Born in 1947 in Windsor, CT, Anderson was raised in a musical family, and after developing a taste for country music via the radio, he picked up a guitar and was proficient enough to begin playing with a local band, the Visuals, at the age of 11. (An out of print EP, *Little Al*, featured home recordings of Anderson made the year before.) After playing with several local teen combos, Anderson ended up playing guitar with a band called the Six Packs, who in 1966 changed their name to the Wildweeds. In 1967, the first song Anderson wrote for the band, a tough R&B-influenced tune called "No Good to Cry," became a massive hit on the East Coast and was picked up for national distribution by Cadet Records. While the song briefly cracked the *Billboard* Top 100 (and was covered by a Florida band called the Hour Glass who in time would evolve into the Allman Brothers Band), the Wildweeds never managed to grow beyond their massive regional popularity, and their sole full-length album, a self-titled effort released by Vanguard in 1970, found the band moving into a country-rock direction shortly before they broke up. (A compilation of the Wildweeds' Cadet-era material was released in 2002.)

In 1971, shortly after the Wildweeds folded, Anderson signed on as guitarist with NRBQ, following the departure of original guitarist Steve Ferguson. Anderson's love of country, R&B, rockabilly, and jazz made him the perfect match for the ever-eclectic group, and along with his blazing fretboard work, Anderson contributed more than a few memorable songs to the group's catalog, including "Ridin' in My Car," "It Comes to Me Naturally," "Crazy Like a Fox," and "A Girl Like That." In 1972, still owing Vanguard an album under the Wildweeds' contract, Anderson cut his first solo set (simply called *Al Anderson*), featuring NRBQ bandmates Terry Adams and Tom Staley, and Wildweeds bassist Al Lepak Jr. In 1989, Anderson quietly released his second solo album, *Party Favors*, and collaborated on tunes with noted songwriter John Hiatt. Over the next several years, Anderson began concentrating more and more on his songwriting and became disenchanted with NRBQ's busy tour schedule. After a tune Anderson wrote for Carlene Carter, "Every Little Thing," became a massive hit on country radio, Anderson left the band, saying he had "no hard feelings. It was a great band before, and will be a great band after."

While Anderson occasionally toured as a guitarist-for-hire for a number of country acts, he devoted the bulk of his time to his songwriting, and in time landed tunes with some of the biggest Nashville hitmakers of the 1990s, including Trisha Yearwood, LeAnn Rimes, Alabama, the Mavericks, and Deana Carter. Anderson did find time to cut another solo album in 1996, the raucous roots rock set *Pay Before You Pump*. —*Mark Deming*

Al Anderson / 1972 / Vanguard ✦✦✦

The happy-go-lucky almost Mardi Gras feel of "We'll Make Love," the second track on this 1972 solo disc from the man behind the Northeast's legendary Wildweeds and their phenomenal Boston-area hit "No Good to Cry" (unfortunately, not on this disc, but an acoustic version might be a perfect addition to a future re-release), carries that distinctive almost gravel voice of Al Anderson. Though he would later join NRBQ, this earthy folk/blues/country platter was recorded between June and September of 1972 and is a wonderful snapshot of an underrated artist at that point in time. "Ain't No Woman Finer" has Jeff Potter's wailing harp that plays off of Anderson's vocal sustain and snappy guitar work. The colorful and uniquely distorted cover photo of Anderson is almost psychedelic country, but there's none of that here. His vocal on "You're Just Laughing Inside" is reminiscent of early Elton John, say the "Amoreena" or "Burn Down the Mission" period. Hank Williams' "Honky Tonkin'" is the shortest track, but one of the liveliest. "Don't Hold the Line" explodes toward the end, and it is one of the few tunes on here that gets really raucous. "I Just Want to Have You Back Again" is a simple two-and-a-half-minute tune—if Jim Croce were more laid-back, he'd probably have sounded like this, melodically it reminds one almost of early Paul McCartney solos—maybe the first McCartney meets Ringo on his *Sentimental Journey*. The closing title, "I Haven't Got the Strength to Carry On" with Tom Staley's drums and Al Lepak's bass, form a nice framework for Anderson's blues-driven guitar. Also released in "Quadrophonic" in the early '70s, it remains a sincere work by a veteran American artist. —*Joe Viglione*

Party Favors / 1988 / Twin/Tone ✦✦✦✦

● **Pay Before You Pump** / Sep. 17, 1996 / Valley ✦✦✦✦

For 22 years, Al Anderson had the dubious distinction of being the relatively normal guy in NRBQ; while the rest of the band were frequently content to wander off in a delightful but inscrutable musical direction no one seemed to full comprehend but themselves, Big Al could be counted on to keep at least one foot firmly planted on solid ground, playing blazing country-accented guitar leads and writing the band's most accessible songs, such as "Riding in My Car" and "It Comes to Me Naturally." So it should come as a shock to no one that *Pay Before You Pump*, Anderson's first solo album after leaving NRBQ, is short on quirks and long on barroom boogie and hot-rodded twangy guitar; Anderson's strengths were always based in good and greasy roots rock, and here he lets his country accents rise to the surface (and seems to be having a great time doing it). By this time, Anderson was also racking up a good number of credits as a Nashville songwriter for hire, and *Pay Before You Pump* is also something of a sampler that offers a little bit of everything Big Al likes to write—punchy rockers ("No Place in History," "That Thang"), rowdy roadhouse escapades ("Bang Bang Bang"), twangy dance numbers ("Get Done"), *faux* Cajun groovers ("After the Mardi Gras"), and even a self-reflective ballad ("A Change Is Gonna Do Me Good"). If the songs here are generally more polished and professional and less idiosyncratic than his work with NRBQ, they're still lots of fun and boast a lot more heart and soul than your average Music Row hack, while Anderson also leaves himself plenty of room for some extra-crispy chicken pickin'. *Pay Before You Pump* never quite scales the peaks of oddball wonder of NRBQ's best work, but it's never less than a rockin' good-time with great songs and stellar guitar work, and there's not a thing wrong with that. —*Mark Deming*

Bill Anderson

b. Nov. 1, 1937, Columbia, SC
Songwriter, Vocals / Country-Pop, Nashville Sound/Countrypolitan, Traditional Country
One of the most successful songwriters in country music history, Bill Anderson was also a hugely popular singer in his own right, earning the nickname "Whispering Bill" for his gentle, airy vocal style and occasional spoken narrations. Anderson was born in Columbia, SC, in 1937 and grew up mostly in Atlanta. He studied journalism at the University of Georgia, with an eye toward sports writing, and worked his way through school as a radio DJ, during which time he first tried his hand at songwriting and singing. His composition "City Lights," written when he was just 19 years old, was recorded by Ray Price in 1958 and went all the way to the top of the country charts. Anderson took full advantage of his big break, moving to Nashville and landing a record contract of his own with Decca.

His first chart hit came with 1959's "That's What It's Like to Be Lonesome," and he had his first Top Ten entry with 1960's "Tip of My Fingers." Early hits like "Po' Folks" (1961), "Mama Sang a Song" (his first number one, from 1962), and "8 X 10" (number two, 1963) still remain among his best-known. Anderson recorded his biggest hit and signature song, the partly spoken ballad "Still," in 1963, and it not only topped the country charts, but crossed over to the pop Top Ten as well. Anderson remained a regular visitor to the country Top Ten through the late '70s, and reached the Top Five a total of 19 times through 1978. Among the highlights were the number ones "I Get the Fever" (1966), "For Loving You" (a 1967 duet with regular partner Jan Howard), "My Life (Throw It Away if I Want To)" (1969), "World of Make Believe" (1974), and "Sometimes" (1976). By that point, Anderson was working often with a new duet partner, Mary Lou Turner. He had also penned numerous hits for other artists, including Connie Smith, Hank Locklin, Porter Wagoner, Jim Reeves, and Faron Young, among many others. His final Top Ten country hit came with 1978's disco-tinged "I Can't Wait Any Longer," and by 1982, Anderson's inability to score a follow-up hit led him away from both songwriting and recording.

Instead, he became a regular presence on television, hosting game shows (ABC's *The Better Sex*, TNN's *Fandango*) and spending several years in the cast of the soap opera *One Life to Live*; he also hosted the TNN talk show *Opry Backstage*. When Steve Wariner hit the Top Five in 1992 with his cover of "Tip of My Fingers," Anderson was galvanized into a return to songwriting. He partnered with various Nashville pros and saw his songs new and old recorded by Kenny Chesney, Lorrie Morgan, Collin Raye, John Michael Montgomery, Mark Wills, Brad Paisley, Vince Gill, and many others. In 1998, Anderson returned to recording as well, signing with Reprise for the all-new album *Fine Wine*; *A Lot of Things Different*, which featured Anderson's version of the title track (a hit for Kenny Chesney), followed on Varese in 2001. —*Steve Huey*

Bill Anderson Sings Country Heart Songs / 1962 / Decca ✦✦✦✦✦

Still / 1963 / Decca ✦✦✦

Bill Anderson Showcase / 1964 / Decca ✦✦

Bright Lights and Country Music / 1965 / Decca ✦✦✦✦✦

From This Pen / 1965 / Decca ✦✦✦

I Love You Drops / 1966 / Decca ✦✦

Get While the Gettin's Good / 1967 / Decca ✦✦✦

I Can Do Nothing Alone / 1967 / Decca ✦✦✦

For Loving You / 1967 / Decca ✦✦✦
Bill Anderson and Jan Howard's first duet album, *For Loving You*, was released in support of the title track, which topped the country charts for four weeks in 1967. The album seems like an afterthought since the material consists almost entirely of country standards like "Have I Told You Lately That I Love You" and "Beyond the Sunset." "I Walk the Line" is the liveliest cut on an album of love songs that were obviously chosen on the basis of their common sentiment. In that sense, the album is thematic and complements "For Loving You," but the dearth of original material from Anderson, who is a talented and prolific songwriter, is curious. —*Greg Adams*

● **Bill Anderson's Greatest Hits** / 1967 / Varese Vintage ✦✦✦✦✦
Bill Anderson's Greatest Hits contains 18 of his biggest hits and best-known songs, including "Mama Sang a Song," "Still," "I Get the Fever," "My Life (Throw It Away If You Want To)," "The Corner of My Life," and "8 X 10." Compiled by Anderson himself, the compilation hits almost all of the highlights, and represents the first thorough retrospective assembled on the country-pop crooner during the CD era. —*Stephen Thomas Erlewine*

Happy State of Mind / 1968 / Decca ✦✦✦

My Life/But You Know I Love You / 1969 / Decca ✦✦✦

The Bill Anderson Story / 1969 / Decca ✦✦✦✦✦
The 24-track collection *The Bill Anderson Story* contains the bulk of Anderson's major hits, including the number-one singles "Mama Sang a Song," "Still," and "I Get the Fever," as well as songs of his that were made famous by other performers. Several hits are missing, yet *The Bill Anderson Story* offers an effective introduction to the popular vocalist's easy-going, muted style. —*Thom Owens*

Wild Weekend / 1969 / Decca ✦✦✦
Not that there aren't plenty of other opportunities to learn the lesson that a book can't be judged by its cover, but take the idea of a *Wild Weekend* with the ever dependable country artist and songwriter Bill Anderson. There are record collectors who would acquire this side just to laugh at the cover, since the juxtaposition of the *Wild Weekend* idea with a photograph of the artist having a bad hair day creates instant belly chuckles. Put the needle on the title track, however, and the laughter will be replaced with looks of awe, especially if the listener is a country fan. The twangy guitar and pedal steel lift the song right off the ground, providing an indication of what is to come. Time and time again, the instrumental expertise of Nashville's army of unidentified pickers combined with Anderson's reliable vocal delivery bring to life tracks that on paper seem to have no potential whatsoever. A version of "Rocky Top"? Don't run for the door, it features great bluegrass banjo picking and an Anderson vocal that somehow casually gives the impression that the song is being sung for the first time and that no other versions even exist. The impact is dulled by the background singers, but one can't expect sheer perfection on a *Wild Weekend*. Another overdone song, Tom Paxton's "Last Thing on My Mind," is treated to a bouncy arrangement that discards the usual nihilistic interpretation of the lyrics for a cheerfulness that is altogether more threatening. Not everything works this well—in fact, there are cuts that are worth avoiding completely. This includes a "Gentle on My Mind" that drags in horrid strings and voices, as if the sleeping bag stuffed behind the couch wasn't bad enough, and a cover of the awful "Little Green Apples." Either of these tracks could come in handy for torturing prisoners. The final track, "Sleep," by good old Jack Clement, is a delightful surprise. It's a country classic that is once again a bit mauled in the production but includes a narrated section in which Anderson seems to have a lump in his throat the size of a cowboy hat. A hat would be a good idea: It would cover up that hairdo. —*Eugene Chadbourne*

If It's All The Same to You / 1970 / Decca ✦✦✦

Love Is a Sometimes Thing / 1970 / Decca ✦✦✦

Where Have All Our Heroes Gone / 1971 / Decca ✦✦✦

Always Remember / 1971 / Decca ✦✦✦
Considering the rate at which Bill Anderson released LPs in his heyday (roughly three a year, often one for each of his hit singles), even fans might not expect too much from his album tracks. *Always Remember* confounds expectations not only because it is a very good album, but because it achieves this out of seemingly ordinary materials. The three songs by Kris Kristofferson and one by Kenny Rogers show Anderson embracing the "new" country music, but his plain vocal style confers an aura of honesty and unaffectedness that really benefits over-exposed titles like "Help Me Make It Through the Night." Anderson's five originals are all worthwhile, and the title track became a Top Ten country hit, in addition to "bubbling under" the pop charts. —*Greg Adams*

Bill & Jan (Or Jan & Bill) / 1972 / Decca ✦✦✦

Bill Anderson Sings for "All The Lonely Women in the World" / 1972 / Decca ✦✦

Bill / 1973 / MCA ✦✦✦

● **Greatest Hits** / 1996 / Varese ✦✦✦✦✦
This is an enjoyable sampler of Bill Anderson's Decca hits. Among the 18 countrypolitan titles are his early-'60s hits "Mama Sang a Song," "The Tips of My Fingers," and "Po Folks." Whispering Bill's vocal style may not appeal to fans of hardcore honky tonk country, but this greatest-hits collection serves as a decent introduction to his laid-back style. —*Al Campbell*

Greatest Hits, Vol. 2 / Oct. 7, 1997 / Varese ✦✦✦✦✦
Bill Anderson had a few more hits in him than his standard greatest-hits package on Decca would lead you to believe, and this second volume of country chart goodies from Varese Sarabande makes a nice bookend companion to its original volume. Highlights on this 15-track collection include "Walk Out Backwards," "For Loving You" (a number-one duet with Jan Howard), "Happy State of Mind," "Quits," "World of Make Believe," "If You Can Live With It (I Can Live Without It)" and "Liars One, Believers Zero," Top Ten charters all. Whispering Bill's smooth style also works well in two duets with Mary Lou Turner, "That's What Made Me Love You" and "Sometimes." —*Cub Koda*

Fine Wine / Aug. 25, 1998 / Warner Bros. ✦✦✦

A Lot of Things Different / Aug. 7, 2001 / Varese ✦✦✦

12 Classics: Five Star Collection / Sep. 10, 2002 / Varese ✦✦✦✦

Classics / May 13, 2003 / Varese ✦✦
Bill Anderson's 2003 *Classics* collection on Varese is yet another collection of latter-day re-recordings of his big hits. Anderson has many of these in his collection and, compared to some of the cheaper sessions out there, this is pretty good—cleanly recorded, professionally played, well-sung, and very, very relaxed and mellow. As it plays, it's entirely pleasant, but it's not memorable, so when it's finished playing, there's no real reason to put it on again. Stick with a collection of the original hits. —*Stephen Thomas Erlewine*

John Anderson

b. Dec. 12, 1955, Apopka, FL
Bass, Vocals, Guitar / Honky Tonk, Outlaw Country, New Traditionalist
Neo-honky tonker John Anderson was born in Apopka, FL, in 1955, and grew up listening to rock & roll, until he discovered country music at age 15 through Merle Haggard. He moved to Nashville in the early '70s, showing up at his sister's house with no warning, and worked a variety of odd jobs (including one as a roofer for the *Grand Ole Opry*) while playing clubs at night. Eventually, all the hard work paid off with a contract for Warner Bros., and Anderson released his first single in 1978. His self-titled debut album appeared

in 1980 and helped signal the rise of the new traditionalist movement, drawing critical praise as well. Soon the hits started to pile up: "1959" and "Chicken Truck" became his first country Top Tens in 1981, and "I'm Just an Old Chunk of Coal (But I'm Gonna Be a Diamond Someday)" went Top Five later that year. "Wild and Blue" (1982) was Anderson's first chart-topper, and he duplicated that feat twice in 1983 with "Black Sheep" and the million-selling "Swingin'," the latter of which was the biggest-selling country single in Warner Bros.' history.

Anderson returned to the Top Ten several times over the next few years, most notably with 1984's "She Sure Got Away With My Heart," but by 1987, his commercial momentum had stalled, and he and Warner parted ways. Anderson continued to record steadily and mounted a major comeback in the early '90s, starting with 1992's *Seminole Wind*. Its title track went to number two, and the follow-up, "Straight Tequila Night," went all the way to number one; "When It Comes to You" also made the Top Five. Anderson scored another number one in 1993 with "Money in the Bank" and hit the Top Five three times over 1994-1995 with "I Wish I Could Have Been There," "I've Got It Made," and "Bend Until It Breaks." Though he hasn't been back to the top since, Anderson's albums and singles continue to make the lower reaches of the country charts—evidence of a still-solid fan base. *—Steve Huey*

John Anderson / 1980 / Warner Bros. ✦✦✦✦

John Anderson 2 / 1981 / Warner Bros. ✦✦✦✦✦
His second album (obviously), this traditionally minded package contrasted with the bulk of the material released in the same *Urban Cowboy*-influenced time period. His cover of Lefty Frizzell's "I Love You a Thousand Ways" shows his roots nicely, and "I'm Just an Old Chunk of Coal (But I'm Gonna Be a Diamond Someday)" is simply classic. *—Tom Roland*

Wild & Blue / 1982 / Warner Bros. ✦✦✦✦
The occasional use of strings in this album was probably master-minded by former Don Law protégé Frank Jones, who co-produced it. Twin fiddles and steel guitar dominate, though, especially in a remake of Ferlin Husky's "The Waltz You Saved for Me," featuring Emmylou Harris. It includes "Swingin'" and a new version of Lefty Frizzell's "Long Black Veil"—the very last track recorded in the legendary Columbia Studio B. *—Tom Roland*

I Just Came Home to Count the Memories / 1982 / Warner Bros. ✦✦✦

All the People Are Talkin' / 1983 / Warner Bros. ✦✦✦

★ **Greatest Hits** / 1984 / Warner Bros. ✦✦✦✦✦
Greatest Hits covers John Anderson's biggest hits from the early '80s, including the Top Ten singles "I Just Came Home to Count the Memories," "She Sure Got Away With My Heart," "Chicken Truck," "1959," "Would You Catch a Falling Star," "I'm Just an Old Chunk of Coal (But I'm Gonna Be a Diamond Someday)" and the number one hits "Wild and Blue," "Swingin'," and "Black Sheep." *—Thom Owens*

Eye of the Hurricane / 1985 / Warner Bros. ✦✦✦

Tokyo, Oklahoma / 1985 / Warner Bros. ✦✦✦

Blue Skies Again / 1987 / Universal Special Products ✦✦

Countrified / 1987 / Warner Bros. ✦✦✦

10 / 1988 / MCA ✦✦

Too Tough to Tame / 1990 / Capitol ✦✦✦

Greatest Hits, Vol. 2 / 1990 / Warner Bros. ✦✦✦✦✦

Seminole Wind / 1992 / RCA ✦✦✦✦
As his comeback, John Anderson didn't just stumble upon a couple of hit singles, he produced a solid album, full of twangy rubble raisers and moving, yearning ballads. Including the number-one hit "Straight Tequila Night," the environment-inspired title cut, and the tender, pleading "Let Go of the Stone," this album catapulted Anderson back to the forefront of country music. Of course, he wasn't just riding the crest of new country; he was harking back to its more traditional roots. But while able to bridge the gap between old and new, he also demonstrates his ability to meld the two as he mourns the poppification of country in "Look Away" and then turns around and puts a honky tonk spin on the Tina Turner cut "Steamy Windows." Being able to be faithful to both while fluidly combining them is true artistry and testament to his voice, his material, and his arrangements. This is contemporary country at top form. *—Bryan Buss*

Solid Ground / Jun. 1993 / BNA ✦✦✦✦
Solid Ground is a fitting title for this album, as John Anderson was surely in his stride when he recorded this follow-up to his comeback, *Seminole Wind*. Anderson's strongest point is that he comes across as an honest-to-God good ol' boy—which many posers of contemporary country only claim to be—and nowhere is this more evident than on the first track, "Money in the Bank." He turns the thankful tune into gold with his trademark twang, then turns right around and nails an ode to regret for what his success has cost him on "I Wish I Could Have Been There." Though there aren't any tracks as immediately accessible as "Straight Tequila Night," "Let Go of the Stone," "Look Away," or the title track, the cuts on this album are more assured, finding Anderson maturing as both a vocalist and a producer. Though he co-wrote only four of the ten tracks, he owns all of them, making this a classic country album of the early '90s. *—Bryan Buss*

Country 'til I Die / 1994 / BNA ✦✦✦

Paradise / Jan. 30, 1996 / BNA ✦✦✦
Featuring guest appearances by Levon Helm and Mark Knopfler, John Anderson's *Paradise* is a typically consistent effort from the singer, featuring a handful of great songs that cancel out the fair amount of filler on the record. *—Sara Sytsma*

Greatest Hits / Oct. 15, 1996 / BNA ✦✦✦
Greatest Hits is a 15-track compilation that features John Anderson's '90s hits for BNA Records, as well as selections from his '80s work for RCA Records. The result is a career-spanning compilation that touches on most of Anderson's best work, including hit singles like "Swingin'" and "Money in the Bank." Consequently, it's the best place to get acquainted with one of the trailblazing new traditionalists of the '80s. *—Thom Owens*

Takin' the Country Back / Jul. 29, 1997 / Mercury ✦✦✦
Although it suffers a little bit from uneven material, *Takin' the Country Back* is one of John Anderson's best latter-day efforts, thanks to his impassioned vocals and the clean, muscular production from Keith Stegall. *—Thom Owens*

The Essential / Jun. 2, 1998 / BNA ✦✦✦✦
Essential contains 16 well-chosen tracks taken from John Anderson's early- to mid-'80s recordings on Warner Bros., including the modern honky tonk hits "Straight Tequila Night," "Let Go of the Stone," "Money in the Bank," and his biggest country crossover smash, "Swingin'." This is an adequate compilation, but it's missing too many hits to be comprehensive. Pick up the double-disc John Anderson *Anthology* instead. *—Al Campbell*

Nobody's Got It All / Mar. 27, 2001 / Columbia ✦✦✦
Columbia Records, which signed John Anderson to his fifth major-label affiliation in 2000, must figure that it is once again time for the veteran country singer to make one of his comebacks. Anderson struggled early in his career until early 1981, when he began a string of hits with "1959." He cooled off in the mid-'80s, switched labels several times, and returned to the top of the charts in 1992 with "Straight Tequila Night," leading to another string of hits that lasted into 1995. Another couple of label switches landed him at Columbia for the 2000 chart single "Nobody's Got It All," followed by this identically titled album, his first new collection in nearly four years. But in or out of commercial favor, Anderson takes pretty much the same approach. His uptempo songs have a honky tonk feel, but he really shines on the ballads, which prominently feature steel guitar and fiddle in traditional country style. It's his voice, a vulnerable, slightly wheezy tenor, that works better on the slow material, whether it's a typically sentimental, quasi-religious country tearjerker like "The Call" or one of Anderson's many conservative reflections on how much better life used to be, such as "I Ain't Afraid of Dying." Producers Blake Chancey and Paul Worley (country's hottest production team of the late '90s, due to their work with the Dixie Chicks) try to vary things, having Anderson turn nearly comic on "The Big Revival" and reach for crossover with Bruce Springsteen's "Atlantic City" (which only emphasizes Anderson's vocal similarity to Levon Helm, who has recorded the same song with the Band) and giving the singer an uptempo, horn-filled arrangement on the album's second single, "You Ain't Hurt Nothin' Yet." But the real potential hits are romantic ballads like "I Love You Again" and midtempo numbers like the rueful "It Ain't Easy Being Me" (with its witty tag line, "I've had to work to be the jerk I've come to be"). And a hit is what Anderson needs to turn his career around one more time. *—William Ruhlmann*

RCA Country Legends / Sep. 10, 2002 / RCA ✦✦✦✦
John Anderson burst on the country music scene in the late '70s as one of the first of the new breed of singers known as "new traditionalists." They were dedicated to playing country the way Hank and Merle and Lefty did, and to keeping the traditions of real country alive. This collection of hits by Anderson focuses on his time at BNA Records in the 1990s. His hitmaking days had seemed over before he joined BNA, but soon he found himself back at the top of the charts. Collected here are his two number ones, "Straight Tequila Night" and "Money in the Bank"; the title track to his double platinum record, *Seminole Wind*; five more Top Ten hits; and five rare B-Sides. This disc is an ideal compilation of 1990s John Anderson and is highly recommended to lovers of traditional country music. *—Tim Sendra*

★ **Anthology** / Oct. 22, 2002 / Audium ✦✦✦✦✦
This is an excellent two-disc compilation of John Anderson's Warner Bros. recordings. These 30 tracks consist of all the radio favorites, including "I'm Just an Old Chunk of Coal," "1959," "Straight Tequila Night," "Black Sheep," and the huge country/pop crossover tune from 1982, "Swingin'." Also featured are several cuts that received radio attention but weren't officially "hits," like Mark Knopfler's "When It Comes to You" and Anderson's "Seminole Wind." *—Al Campbell*

Lynn Anderson

b. Sep. 26, 1947, Grand Forks, ND
Vocals / Country-Pop, Nashville Sound/Countrypolitan
Best-known for her Grammy-winning smash "Rose Garden," Lynn Anderson was one of the most popular female country singers of the early '70s, helped by her regular exposure on national television. Anderson was born in Grand Forks, ND, and grew up in Sacramento, CA; her mother, Liz, was a professional songwriter best-known for penning Merle Haggard's early hits "(All My Friends Are Gonna Be) Strangers" and "The Fugitive" (the latter with her husband, Carey). Naturally, Lynn picked up music too, and performed as a singer and guitarist during her teen years. In the mid-'60s, her mother got a recording contract of her own based on her demo tapes, some of which featured Lynn singing background vocals. When the two traveled to Nashville, Lynn wound up recording for the small Chart label, cutting a duet with Jerry Lane as her first single. Her first solo single was 1966's "In Person," and in 1967 she scored her first Top 40 hit with her mother's composition "Ride, Ride, Ride."

She burst into the country Top Five with 1967's "If I Kiss You (Will You Go Away)," 1968's "Promises, Promises," and 1969's "That's a No No." Her success helped her land a spot as a weekly regular on *The Lawrence Welk Show* for a time, and made her the only country singer of her time to fill such a slot on any TV program. She eventually departed amid objections to singing in stereotypical haywagon settings, but went on to appear on numerous other variety shows. In 1970, Anderson moved to Nashville with her husband, writer/producer Glenn Sutton, and signed with Columbia. She quickly scored the biggest hit of her career with the Joe South-penned "Rose Garden," which topped the country charts and went all the way to number three on the pop side. It won her a Grammy for Best Female Country Vocal, and proved a hit in 15 countries.

While Anderson never quite duplicated that crossover phenomenon, she racked up 14 more Top Ten hits on the country charts through 1974, including the number ones "How Can I Unlove You," "You're My Man," "Keep Me in Mind," and "What a Man, My Man Is." Her run of success tailed off somewhat in the latter half of the decade, but she continued to make regular appearances on the charts, and finally returned to the Top Ten with 1979's "Isn't It Always Love." She parted ways with Columbia in 1981, and scored one last Top Ten hit for Permian with 1984's "You're Welcome to Tonight." Other than a single for MCA and an album for Mercury, Anderson was silent for the remainder of the '80s; in 1992, she issued the album *Cowboy's Sweetheart* on the Laserlight label. *Live at Billy Bob's Texas* appeared from out of nowhere in 2000. —*Steve Huey*

Ride, Ride, Ride / 1967 / Chart ✦✦✦

Promises, Promises / 1968 / Chart ✦✦✦

With Love, from Lynn / 1969 / Chart ✦✦✦✦

Big Girls Don't Cry / 1969 / Chart ✦✦✦

At Home with Lynn / 1969 / Chart ✦✦✦

Songs That Made Country Girls Famous / 1969 / Chart ✦✦✦

Uptown Country Girl / 1970 / Chart ✦✦✦

Songs My Mother Wrote / 1970 / Chart ✦✦✦

Stay There 'Til I Get There / 1970 / Columbia ✦✦✦

Stay There 'Til I Get There is Lynn Anderson's first album for Columbia Records following a successful stint on the independent Chart label. Since Anderson's crossover smash "Rose Garden" was released several months later, *Stay There 'Til I Get There* sounds just like one of her Chart albums, down to the banjo picking on the hit title track. The one departure from her earlier records is the poverty of compositions by Anderson's mother, Liz Anderson. Producer Glenn Sutton takes her place to an extent, but Anderson also covers the underrated Sonny James song "True Love's a Blessing" and Bobbie Gentry's hit "Fancy." "Rose Garden" gave Anderson's sound a strong push toward pop music, so those who enjoy her early straight country recordings will also enjoy this first album for Columbia. —*Greg Adams*

No Love at All / 1970 / Columbia ✦✦✦✦

A lost gem of early-'70s countrypolitan, *No Love at All* epitomizes the genre, yet also stands tall simply as an album of first-rate tunes sung sensitively and maturely by one of the most underrated singers in country music. Lynn Anderson repeatedly performs that rarest of tricks: a vocal performance that is both full of character and passion, yet technically flawless. At times, the sheer operatic force of her voice is nothing short of astounding, but never overshadows the song's basic message. And virtually every song here is excellent. Well-known tunes include the great John D. Loudermilk's "It's My Time" and Conway Twitty's classic "Hello Darlin'," but the real surprise is that the album's best track was written by Anderson herself. Though musically framed as a jauntily humorous, throwaway foot-stomper, "Husband Hunting" is lyrically an important song that intelligently examines women's cultural disenfranchisement. Though not as direct as Loretta Lynn's "Fist City" and the like, the song is also much less cartoonish in that it manages to portray the heroine as a complex person who feels a conflicting responsibility to pre serve both her marriage and her own sanity. Though Lynn Anderson has never had quite the musical charisma and personality of contemporaries like Dolly Parton and Tammy Wynette, *No Love at All* reminds the listener that she is a formidable talent whose work deserves to be re-examined. —*Pemberton Roach*

Rose Garden / 1970 / Columbia ✦✦✦✦✦

You're My Man / 1971 / Columbia ✦✦✦✦

"Rose Garden" was Lynn Anderson's career hit, a pop song that topped the country charts for several weeks and reached number one on the *Cash Box* pop charts. Her sound up to that point had been broadly appealing but easily identifiable as country, but immediately afterward, that began to change. *You're My Man*, her first album following *Rose Garden*, made further concessions to the pop crowd with covers of "Proud Mary," "Knock Three Times," and "Joy to the World." Producer Glenn Sutton contributed "I'm Gonna Write a Song," a fine composition that became a hit for Tommy Cash that same year. Although *You're My Man* made a calculated effort to cross over, even "Proud Mary" featured steel guitar, and the title track came nowhere near the top of the pop charts, despite giving Anderson her second number-one country hit. —*Greg Adams*

The World of Lynn Anderson / 1971 / Columbia ✦✦✦

How Can I Unlove You / 1971 / Columbia ✦✦✦

Lynn Anderson With Strings / 1971 / Chart ✦✦✦

Lynn Anderson / 1971 / Chart ✦✦✦✦

Cry / 1972 / Columbia ✦✦✦

Listen to a Country Song / 1972 / Columbia ✦✦✦

Greatest Hits / 1972 / RCA ✦✦✦✦✦

With big pipes, big production, and big hits from the mid- to late '60s, this includes "Rose Garden." —*Mark A. Humphrey*

Top of the World / 1973 / Columbia ✦✦

Keep Me in Mind / 1973 / Columbia ✦✦

Flower of Love / 1973 / Pickwick ✦✦

Flower of Love is one of two albums in Pickwick's budget line of Lynn Anderson reissues (*It Makes You Happy* is the other), both of which are drawn from Anderson's early Chart recordings. The focus here is on Anderson's covers of others' hits—none of her own hits are included. There is nothing as playful and adventurous as her recordings of "I've Been Everywhere" and "The Auctioneer" (both on *Anthology, Vol. 2: The Chart Years*); Joe

South's "Games People Play" and Merle Haggard's "Okie From Muskogee" are as close as this album comes. Anderson's versions of "Stand By Your Man," Dottie West's "Paper Mansions," and Connie Smith's "Once a Day" are too close to the originals to excite, but "Lie a Little" and "A Penny for Your Thoughts" are Liz Anderson originals from Lynn Anderson's 1967 album *Promises, Promises*. Because these songs are duplicated on earlier albums, *Flower of Love* is of limited value. —*Greg Adams*

Smile for Me / 1974 / Columbia ✦✦

What a Man My Man Is / 1974 / Columbia ✦✦

It Makes You Happy / 1974 / Pickwick ✦✦

Before "Rose Garden" and her other big crossover hits on Columbia, Lynn Anderson recorded successfully for Chart Records. Chart had a licensing agreement with Pickwick, a label that repackaged previously released recordings for budget albums, so Columbia was obligated to allow Pickwick to reissue Anderson's early Chart recordings even though Columbia had purchased the masters. Three of her Chart hits are included on this nine-song album, the biggest of which is the sassy, grammatically challenged "No Another Time." A minor hit duet with Chart labelmate Jerry Lane ("Keeping Up Appearances") and the Top 30 "Too Much of You" round out the "greatest hits" content of the reissue. The remaining tracks include two other duets with Lane and the title track, which was a minor hit for another Chart artist, Kenny Vernon. Typical of Anderson's early output, half of the songs were written by her mother, Liz Anderson. The Pickwick reissues seem to have been assembled almost at random and are thoroughly redundant except for those who don't already own the Chart albums. —*Greg Adams*

I've Never Loved Anyone More / 1975 / Columbia ✦✦✦

All the King's Horses / 1976 / Columbia ✦✦✦

Cowboy's Sweetheart / Jun. 1992 / Laserlight ✦✦

One of Anderson's stronger albums, *Cowboy's Sweetheart* is a collection of songs linked by their connection to Western mythos, including "Desperado," "Even Cowgirls Get the Blues" and "Happy Trails." A surprising cover of Cole Porter's "Don't Fence Me In" is also included. —*Jason Ankeny*

Rose Garden / Apr. 22, 1997 / Kingfisher ✦✦✦✦✦

● **Golden Classics Edition** / Jul. 1, 1997 / Collectables ✦✦✦✦✦

Unlike some installments in Collectables' *Golden Classics Edition* series, Lynn Anderson's *Golden Classics Edition* is neither a proper hits collection nor an expanded version of one album. Instead, it contains the entirety of her 1970 album *Rose Garden* and its 1971 successor, *You're My Man*, augmented by four bonus tracks ("How Can I Unlove You," "Cry," "Top of the World," "What a Man, My Man Is"). This results in a disc that, in many ways, is better at capturing Anderson at her best than a hits collection, since it presents her at her peak as a recording artist. She had hits before and after these two albums, but she was at her best on these two records, and, when they're fleshed out with the mid-'70s bonus tracks, they result in a consistently enjoyable 26-track collection of mainstream, poppy country music from the early '70s, something that proves Anderson was more than a one-hit wonder. —*Stephen Thomas Erlewine*

Pure Country / Aug. 25, 1998 / Sony Special Products ✦✦✦✦

Sony Special Products' *Pure Country* is an effective sampler of Lynn Anderson's country-pop work for Columbia Records in the '70s. In fact, it works in many ways as a hits compilation, since every one of the featured songs—"Rose Garden," "How Can I Unlove You," "Sing About Love," "Cry," "Fool Me," "You're My Man," "Keep Me in Mind," "Top of the World," "What a Man, My Man Is" and "Talkin' to the Wall"—were Top Ten country hits for Anderson. Because of that, *Pure Country* is more than just a good bargain for a budget-line collection—it's a good bargain in general. —*Stephen Thomas Erlewine*

Anthology: The Columbia Years / Sep. 14, 1999 / Renaissance ✦✦✦✦

● **Anthology, Vol. 2: The Chart Years** / Sep. 28, 1999 / Renaissance ✦✦✦✦✦

Lynn Anderson made some of the best music of her career during her late-'60s period on the Chart label. Her mother, noted songwriter and recording artist Liz Anderson, supplied her with excellent material such as "Ride, Ride, Ride," her first hit, and "If I Kiss You (Will You Go Away)," her first major hit. Anderson had more of a traditional country sound during her Chart period than on her later crossover hits like "Rose Garden," but she made the country Top Ten four times and charted a total of 17 singles for the label. *Anthology, Vol. 2: The Chart Years* includes all of Anderson's Chart hits and a handful of interesting album tracks such as a delightful version of Leroy Van Dyke's "The Auctioneer" and Merle Haggard's "Strangers" (another Liz Anderson composition). In fact, Liz Anderson's fingerprints are all over this material, and the proud mother even contributed the package's liner notes. —*Greg Adams*

Live at Billy Bob's Texas / Feb. 29, 2000 / Smith Music Group ✦✦✦

Anderson sounds pretty good on this set recorded, one would guess, in the late '90s, or at any rate shortly before its 2000 release. (Like everything in the *Billy Bob's Texas* series, no date is given in the liner notes.) There's nothing extraneous to the band, either: just a pretty tight seven-piece combining electric guitar and a rhythm section with piano, fiddle, and steel. A bunch of her expected hits are on hand, including "Rose Garden," of course, as well as "You're My Man," "Even Cowgirls Get the Blues," "How Can I Unlove You," and "What a Man My Man Is." She must have done "Rose Garden" many, many times prior to this recording; at the end, she thanks the audience and acknowledges, à la that heavily accented ex-baseball playing announcer on *Saturday Night Live*'s news broadcasts, that "that song, it was very very good to me!" There are some covers that you might not expect but are not ill fits: Ian Tyson's "Someday Soon"; done country style, the Carpenters' "Top of the World"; and the Drifters' "Under the Boardwalk." This disc is not an electrifying find, but it's decent for what it is. —*Richie Unterberger*

Pete Anderson

b. Detroit, MI

Guitar, Producer / Roots Rock, Bakersfield Sound, Alternative Country

Pete Anderson was born in Detroit, and grew up to become the creative partner of one of the most significant country artists of the 1980s, Dwight Yoakam. An only child, Anderson's earliest musical memories revolve around the country & western music his father listened to and seeing Elvis on television. The sudden death of his father left the young prodigy to be raised by his mother, who also worked full-time in one of the Motor City's factories.

A natural athlete, Anderson vacillated between sports and music. His first instrument was a Hawaiian guitar, which he promptly knocked out of tune on a regular basis after imitating Elvis for the neighborhood kids who loved to watch him perform. Still, he chose to participate in sports rather than spend his time practicing the guitar. But, as a teenager, the music began to be more meaningful and Anderson joined several bands, including a jug band called the B-52 Blues when he was 17.

After high-school, Anderson traveled the U.S. by bus, went to art school, and got married. Shortly thereafter, his then-wife gave birth to a son. Working in the factories, parenting, and playing music filled his life. Gigging around Detroit provided a solid education in the blues. Muddy Waters became the young father's hero. Still, he knew there was more to life than playing in bands in his hometown. As the marriage floundered, Anderson made up his mind to pursue his music at the next level. When his mother finally retired, she moved to Arizona, where the weather was not as severe as what she had known in Detroit. Both father and son followed, and Anderson worked his way up the hierarchy of the Phoenix music scene. Again, he knew that this was not his ultimate destination. With his son in the care of his ex-wife and his mother basking in the southwestern sunshine, Pete Anderson packed up and headed for California, and more specifically, L.A., in May of 1972.

A blues and rock player of some skill, the aggressive guitarist quickly made a name for himself. Wanting to record as much as play live gigs, the future producer honed his studio skills by making tapes and arranging songs. Working with various outfits, he was an important part of Hollywood Gumbo, which broke up on the road somewhere in Canada. He eventually found that he could actually make a living playing the country music that had meant so much to his father. Developing his own rapid-fire style, Anderson was a working musician at night and painting houses when necessary during the daylight hours. His son and ex-wife came west and the small family tried to make a go of it one more time.

It was during this period that Boo Bernstein introduced Anderson to Dwight Yoakam, a struggling, skinny kid from Ohio who had a knack for writing real country songs. Needing a guitar player for a gig at the Cowboy in Orange County, Yoakam remembered Anderson and asked him to do the date with him. That was the start of a partnership that resulted in numerous platinum records, sold-out tours, and some fine music in the Bakersfield and hillbilly traditions. Anderson became known as a top-flight producer who could get the job done. Working not only in country but also in other genres, he was responsible for some outstanding projects by Rosie Flores, Michelle Shocked, the Meat Puppets, the Backsliders, the Lonesome Strangers, and Thelonious Monster. He and Dusty Wakeman were responsible for *Vol. 1* and *Vol. 2* of the *A Town South of Bakersfield* compilations, a mid-'80s landmark that resulted in a resurgence of interest in the West Coast country scene and the Bakersfield sound.

In 1993, along with Wakeman, Anderson joined Barbara Hein, a longtime Capitol Records executive with a history in the music business, and engineer Michael Dumas to form Little Dog Records. Recording his first solo CD on his own label in 1995, Anderson placed himself on the road in support of *Working Class*, a country blues-rock-roots music extravaganza produced by Wakeman. While continuing to work with Yoakam, being the president of a record label opened new worlds for Anderson. Signing artists that he and his partners believed in gave Anderson the creative freedom he craved. Having to be part businessman and part artist was a difficult part to play every day, but Anderson proved he was up to the challenge when he negotiated a distribution deal with Polygram in 1996. *—Jana Pendragon*

Working Class / 1994 / Little Dog ♦♦♦

Before moving to California and beginning his successful association with country singer Dwight Yoakam, Pete Anderson cut his musical teeth in Detroit playing rock & roll and R&B. It comes as no surprise then that on his first solo outing he would stray from the signature country string-bending style that had become his trademark. From the bluesy strut of Anderson's own "Working Class" to the gorgeous instrumental reading of the oft-covered Ruby & the Romantics classic "Our Day Will Come" along with the Texas blues shuffle take on Jimi Hendrix's "Fire," Anderson's relaxed delivery—both vocally and with his always-captivating guitar playing—emits the feeling that there was little pressure in making this record. He and his band sound like they are having a great time. There are hints of country and folk (a solo cover of Dylan's "She Belongs to Me"), but primarily this is a blues record and a fine one at that. An enjoyable and insightful look at one of country music's most innovative and influential guitarists. *—Jack Leaver*

● **Dogs in Heaven** / Apr. 8, 1997 / Little Dog ♦♦♦♦

Dogs in Heaven is Pete Anderson's second solo outing on his own Little Dog Records label. His debut effort in 1994, *Working Class*, played down his country music association and emphasized his Americana roots. *Dogs in Heaven* seemingly picks up where *Working Class* left off. This time without the steady hand of producer Dusty Wakeman, Anderson still pulls off some spectacular moments. Throughout his guitar playing is perfection; he is vocally akin to Tom Waits, which lends itself well to songs such as the Duane Jarvis co-write "110 in the Shade," which is an evocative blues number, as is "Feels Like Mississippi," written by Anderson and Kostas. For good rockin', Anderson proves himself on "Chalene" and the infectious "For You." His instrumental title track is also notable, as is his cover of the Motown hit, "Ain't That Peculiar," a nod to his Detroit roots. With his usual band, Taras Prodaniuk, Skip Edwards, and James Christie in tow, this is another fine example of Anderson's eclectic musical style. *—Jana Pendragon*

Terry Anderson

b. 1941

Drums, Vocals / Roots Rock, Alternative Country-Rock

North Carolina singer/songwriter Terry Anderson first gained local attention as the drummer and occasional vocalist of bar bands the Woods and the Fabulous Knobs. His first widespread notice, however, came when his composition "Battleship Chains" was covered by the Georgia Satellites; later, the Satellites' frontman Dan Baird made his solo debut with Anderson's "I Love You Period." In 1994, Anderson cut his first solo effort, *You Don't Like Me*; *What Else Can Go Right*, a collection of no-frills rockers and rootsy acoustic numbers, followed two years later. The new millennium saw the release of Anderson's third album, *I'll Drink to That. —Jason Ankeny*

You Don't Like Me / 1995 / East Side Digital ♦♦♦

What Else Can Go Right / Aug. 13, 1996 / East Side Digital ♦♦♦

● **I'll Drink to That** / Jan. 16, 2001 / Not Lame ♦♦♦♦

The third album from multi-instrumentalist Anderson (drums, guitar, farfisa), a Nashville expatriate frustrated with the music city's commercial songwriting, is a loose and spirited affair, inspired by a memory of a Dave Edmunds concert that knocked him out. A member of the similarly styled Yayhoos along with ex-Satellite Dan Baird, with whom he has written in the past, Anderson whips through 45 minutes of happy-go-lucky American roots rock with nods to Chuck Berry, Edmunds, the Georgia Satellites (who had a hit with his "Battleship Chains" back in the day), and NRBQ, whom he calls the best band in the world, and whose ex-guitarist Al Anderson (no relation) guests on some tracks. With a nasal voice and lyrical style somewhat similar to Joe Walsh, Anderson sings about the "Nastiest House" in the whole wide world, his "Rock and Roll Girlfriend" who'd rather listen to LPs and cassettes from 1973 instead of anything on MTV, and a humorous Bo Diddley-fueled yarn about driving "37 Miles in Reverse." This won't change the world, of course, but it's all good, relatively clean fun (with the possible exception of "Safety First," an upbeat ditty about condoms), featuring snappy word play and a feisty attitude that sounds like he and his equally energetic backing musicians were having a blast recording this no-frills album. Recommended for fans of boozy, down-to-earth guitar rocking and anyone else looking for a rollicking time. *—Hal Horowitz*

Jessica Andrews

b. Dec. 29, 1983, Tennessee

Vocals / Country-Pop, Contemporary Country

Tennessee native Jessica Andrews was born into a musical family, and found singing was her niche in a fourth-grade talent show. Her version of Dolly Parton's "I Will Always Love You" won first prize and set her on a path that took her to local fairs and carnivals—anywhere she could sing.

Word of mouth about Andrews' talents spread, and soon friends of Nashville producer Byron Gallimore insisted he listen to her. Intrigued by her range and tonal control, he and Andrews went into the studio and began choosing songs to record. Gallimore also invited DreamWorks Nashville label representatives to a showcase Andrews performed at, where she was offered a contract immediately. Her debut release for the label, *Heart Shaped World*, came out in 1999. *Who I Am* followed two years later. *Who I Am* followed two years later; the title track earned Andrews her first number-one country single. The release of *Now* (2003), introduced a slightly more down-to-earth, grown-up sound. *—Heather Phares*

Heart Shaped World / Mar. 23, 1999 / DreamWorks ♦♦♦♦

When a 15-year-old Jessica Andrews debuted with *Heart Shaped World*, the most obvious comparison was LeAnn Rimes. The parallels were certainly there—like Rimes, Andrews was a teenage country-pop singer with a wholesome, clean-cut, all-American girl image and the usual Nashville hype to go with her debut. But like Rimes, Andrews had some talent, charisma, and substance to go with the hype. Though *Heart Shaped World* isn't brilliant, the Tennessee native usually has decent material to work with. No one's going to mistake this CD for hardcore, Bakersfield honky tonk—like Rimes and Shania Twain, Andrews specializes in a sleek, commercial blend of pop, country, and rock. But as much sweetness as she projects, Andrews isn't bubblegum—when she digs into "You Go First," "I've Been Waiting for You," and "James Dean in Tennessee," you know that the singer isn't without an edge. And on Billy Burnette's ominous, bluesy "Hungry Love"—the tale of a girl who has to grow up much too fast—it's clear that Andrews is capable of depth. A few of the tunes are bland, but *Heart Shaped World*'s best moments indicate that Andrews is someone to keep an eye on. *—Alex Henderson*

Who I Am / Feb. 27, 2001 / DreamWorks ♦♦♦♦

Jessica Andrews delivers an impressive sophomore album. Upon first listen, it's easy to recognize her very maturing talent. Her vocals are strong and convincing, her songs are snappy and infectious, and there's little sign of her being just 17 years of age. Producer for the second time around, Byron Gallimore (Jo Dee Messina, Tim McGraw) says "age is never an issue with her because of the depth in her voice." Truer words were never spoken. Everything from vocal delivery to production redefines what she gave listeners on 1999's *Heart Shaped World*. Andrews' appealing new confidence comes through in just about all of the album's 12 songs, but the title track "Who I Am," "Every Time," "These Wings," and the vivacious "Never Had It So Good" make it worth setting the CD player for continuous play. *—Maria Konicki Dinoia*

● **Now** / Apr. 15, 2003 / DreamWorks ♦♦♦♦♦

Facing 20, Jessica Andrews decides to open her music on her third album, *Now*. Her hold to country was always a little tentative, particularly because it seemed like she was signed partially because she was a teenage girl who could really sing during the height of LeAnn Rimes' popularity. Like Rimes, Andrews wants to leave strict country behind as she leaves her adolescence, but unlike LeAnn, Jessica sounds in control, having a clear idea of who she is musically and where she wants to go. *Now* is grounded in country, along with other American roots music, but it's held together with an inclusive pop sensibility and a polished, professional production that nevertheless retains its identity and keeps the focus on Andrews, whose voice sounds stronger and better than ever. If initial comparisons to Rimes did not fall to her favor, she now sounds more versatile and assured than her peer, but she goes even further with *Now*, crafting an album that straddles the country-pop and adult-pop line as alluringly as the best of Faith Hill, whose *Cry* pales in comparison to this record. Why? Because this is never stifled by diva ambitions. Because this has uptempo and midtempo songs with character and color, along with catchy hooks. Because the ballads, while slick, still have substance. Ultimately, because Andrews is a hell of singer, finding her own distinctive voice and coming into her own, somewhere between Faith Hill and Sheryl Crow. If the production ever so slightly is a little too mature, a little older than her years, it's only appropriate because her voice sounds older than her years. But even if this does have an adult-pop bent, it's still done better than nearly any other adult-pop in 2003, and the times that *Now* does loosen up offer tantalizing possibilities of where Andrews could go next. And, no matter which way you cut it, as of this writing *Now* is one of the best mainstream pop albums of 2003, with only Kelly Clarkson's *Thankful* rivaling it in consistency and quality. *—Stephen Thomas Erlewine*

Anglin Brothers

f. 1933, Franklin, TN

Group / Traditional Country, Close Harmony

Red, Jim, and Jack Anglin, performing as the Anglin Twins and Red, billed themselves with some justification as "the South's favorite trio" in the 1930s. The group was something of an incubator for the next generation of country sounds, spawning the 1940s duo Johnnie & Jack and thence, indirectly, the career of Kitty Wells. The brothers were born in Franklin, TN, into a large family, but grew up in Athens, AL. Befriended and influenced by northern Alabama's Delmore Brothers while they were still young, the Anglins moved to Nashville in 1930 and were inspired to think of a performing career themselves by a Delmore Brothers performance on the *Grand Ole Opry*. By 1933, they had formed a trio consisting of Jack on guitar, Jim on string bass, and Red singing vocal harmonies with the other two.

They landed a non-paying slot on Nashville's WSIX radio in the mid-'30s, after which the Delmores paved the way for a more lucrative program featuring the brothers on Birmingham, AL's WAPI. Regional celebrity led the ARC label to the Anglins as they prepared to launch a recording operation in San Antonio in 1937, and those sessions produced the hit single "They Are All Going Home but One." The Anglins moved to Memphis station WMC in 1938, and recorded again that year, this time in Columbia, SC. Of the 34 sides the Anglin Brothers recorded, only 14 were released, all on ARC's newly acquired Vocalion imprint. After radio stints in New Orleans and Atlanta, the group broke up when Red was drafted. He was injured during the Allied invasion of France. Jim Anglin became one of the great songwriters of the 1940s and '50s, composing key items in the repertoires of Roy Acuff and later Kitty Wells. Of the three, Jack Anglin found the most success when he formed a duo with his brother-in-law, Johnnie Wright, in the early '40s. Johnnie & Jack produced numerous hits for RCA Victor until 1963, when Jack was killed in an auto wreck.

In 1979, Michigan's Old Homestead label produced a compilation containing all the Anglin Brothers' commercially released songs; the album reveals a songbag heavy with humorous and sentimental pieces in venerable molds, including several pieces that later artists may well have learned from the brothers' performances on recordings and radio. "Uncle Eph's Got the Coon" became a trademark number for Grandpa Jones, for example, and "Where the Soul of Man Never Dies" became one of Hank Williams' gospel favorites. *—James Manheim*

Dave Apollon

b. Feb. 23, 1897, Kiev, Russia, **d.** May 30, 1972

Mandolin / Traditional Bluegrass, Gypsy

Dave Apollon was born in Kiev, Russia, in 1897. Originally a student of the violin, he became acquainted with the mandolin through an old bowl-backed model his father had lying about the house. By the young age of 14, he was performing on the instrument in theaters throughout Kiev, but a stint as a soldier during the Russian Revolution stalled his burgeoning career. After the war, Apollon moved to the Philippines, where he continued playing his mandolin and dancing. After a brief stop in Japan, he headed for America. In 1919, Apollon landed in New York and began working in vaudeville. The release of his first recorded material, in 1932, was a mélange of American ragtime rhythms and Russian folk music on which Apollon was accompanied by a troupe of Philippine string musicians. It was also around this time that Apollon began his movie career, dancing and playing the mandolin in a series of "soundies" based on his vaudeville routines.

In 1937, Apollon married Danzi Goodell. He also opened a nightclub—*Club Casanova*—on Manhattan's Upper East Side. While the mandolin was still a part of his life, only a few singles were released during this period. He appeared in the 1938 Universal feature *Merry Go Round* and began a stint on Broadway with comedian Ed Wynn. He then recorded a series of performances for the Decca label, accompanied by piano and guitar. These recordings remain the best examples of his virtuosic talent on his chosen instrument. In 1946, Apollon jammed with guitarist Django Reinhardt, who was in New York with Duke Ellington's band.

Apollon moved to California in the early '50s and self-released *Lots of Love* in 1956. The album led to a performance contract with the Desert Inn in Las Vegas that would last until 1963. Billing himself as the World's Greatest Mandolin Virtuoso, Apollon's dancing and playing were a big hit with the swinging Vegas audiences. The exposure landed a deal with the Coral label, which released three Apollon albums throughout the late '50s and early '60s. His Vegas experiences were the last performances of his colorful life. Apollon passed away at home in 1972. Noted mandolin players such as David Grisman regularly list him as a significant influence. *—Johnny Loftus*

Mandolin Virtuoso / 1980 / Yazoo ✦✦✦✦✦

● **The Man with the Mandolin** / Oct. 21, 1997 / Acoustic Disc ✦✦✦✦✦

This two-CD collection, compiled and produced by the king of "Dawg Music" (a kind of swinging bluegrass jazz), David Grisman, is filled with overlooked treasures by a mandolin genius. Apollan was a bit of a novelty act in his early years, and much of the first disc is a bit bogged down with some of the promotional and film work that showcased him as a rather clownish Hungarian. But by the second disc, his fingers fly freely on masterful renditions of such wide-ranging work as "Perfidia," "Zigeunerweisen," and "The Man I Love." A must for guitar and mandolin fans. *—Tim Sheridan*

Amédé Ardoin

b. Mar. 11, 1896, L'Anse Rougeau, LA, **d.** Nov. 9, 1941, Alexandria, LA

Accordion, Vocals / Creole, Zydeco

Amédé Ardoin is to zydeco music as Robert Johnson is to the blues and Buddy Bolden is to jazz. Like Johnson and Bolden, Ardoin not only died under still mysterious conditions, but also shares the potency of their musical influence, having laid the foundation for southwest Louisiana's zydeco music.

The first Creole to be recorded, Ardoin is best remembered for his resonating, high-pitched vocals and sizzling-hot accordion playing. Although he only recorded 31 tunes, his compositions have been included in the repertoire of Cajun and zydeco bands ranging from Austin Pitre and Dewey Balfa to Beausoleil and C.J. Chenier. Iry LeJeune helped to launch a revival in Cajun music in the 1950s, when he recorded 12 of Ardoin's tunes. The great-grandson of a slave, Ardoin moved, as a child, with his family to work on the Rougeau farm in L'Anse des Rougeau near Basile. While there, he frequented the homes of his friends Adam Fontenot, who played accordion and was later the father of fiddler Canray Fontenot, and Alphonse LaFleur, who played fiddle. Together with LaFleur or Douglas Bellard, a black fiddler from Bellaire Cove, Ardoin became a frequent performer at dances, playing mostly for white audiences who paid him $2.50 per night.

In his teens, Ardoin moved frequently, working for room and board. For a while, he worked as a sharecropper on Oscar Comeaux's farm near Chataignier. While there, he met Dennis McGee, a white fiddler from Eunice. One of the first biracial Cajun duos, Ardoin and McGee began to play at house parties, often attended by Ardoin's cousin, Bois Sec Ardoin. When Comeaux sold the farm, the two musicians moved to Eunice, where they worked at Celestin Marcantel's farm. A lover of music, Marcantel often transported Ardoin and McGee to performances in his horse-drawn buggy.

Ardoin and McGee's recording debut came on December 9, 1929, when they cut seven tunes at a studio in New Orleans. They returned to the studio to record six songs on November 20 and 21, 1930. On August 8, 1934, they recorded six tunes at the Texas Hotel in San Antonio. Their fourth and final recording session, recorded at a New York studio on December 22, 1934, produced 12 new tunes. Their recordings were issued on the Brunswick, Vocalion, Decca, Melotone, and Bluebird labels.

Ardoin often performed with fiddler Sady Courville of Eunice. In the late '30s, they played every Saturday night at Abe's Palace in Eunice. Courville's mother, however, prevented them from recording together. Ardoin's death remains shrouded in mystery. One report has him being brutally beaten after wiping his brow with a handkerchief handed to him by the daughter of a white farm owner. According to McGee, Ardoin was poisoned by a jealous fiddler. More recent studies have concluded that Ardoin died of venereal disease at the Pineville Mental Institution. *—Craig Harris*

Original Recordings: 1929–1934 / 1983 / Arhoolie ✦✦✦✦✦

★ **Louisiana Cajun Music, Vol. 6: Amédé Ardoin—His Original Recordings** / Mar. 1983 / Old-Timey ✦✦✦✦✦

Amédé Ardoin's *His Original Recordings, 1928-1938* is divided between seven songs Ardoin recorded with Dennis McGee and seven solo tracks. The duets with McGee are among the most legendary Cajun recordings; McGee's fiddle perfectly meshes with Ardoin's accordion and raw, bluesy voice. These are the recordings that laid the foundation on contemporary Cajun and zydeco. Ardoin's solo recordings are nearly as influential and exciting, capturing him alone with his accordion. While these aren't quite as kinetic as the duets, they are nevertheless enjoyable. *—Thom Owens*

First Black Cajun Recording Artist / Dec. 2, 1993 / Arhoolie ✦✦✦✦

Violinist Dennis McGee is featured on this 14-track album, which contains recordings from 1929, 1930, and 1934. *—AMG*

The I'm Never Comin' Back: The Roots of Zydeco / 1995 / Arhoolie ✦✦✦

In his relatively short career, the acknowledged progenitor of Cajun and zydeco music, Amédé Ardoin, recorded only 31 songs, spread across four sessions around 1930. Of those, 26 are presented here, from all of the sessions except the first. The sound shows itself largely as what is now called "Cajun," with only hints of what would later be turned into zydeco. The accordion is jumping with energy in the dance numbers (here's where you might notice the similarities to zydeco), and toned down for the blues. Regardless of the style, Ardoin's French vocals fly out loudly and plaintively over the top of the music. The combination of accordion and vocals is what defines his music, and it does a good job of creating a texture of emotion and music together. Additional fiddling by Dennis McGee (making these the first interracial recordings of Louisiana folk music) adds to the pot in a favorable manner. While the recording quality can occasionally be less than perfect (these were recorded between 1929-1934, after all), the historical and musical value of the songs easily make up for it. For fanatics in the fields of Louisiana's folk musics, this album makes a great item to add to the collection for a look into the past. For those just starting out in the fields, more contemporary artists might make for a smoother introduction, but they'll all point back to Ardoin eventually. *—Adam Greenberg*

Area Code 615

f. 1969, Tennessee, **db.** 1971

Group / Instrumental Country, Country-Rock, Progressive Country

Area Code 615 was a Nashville studio supergroup (615 is the Nashville telephone area code) formed in 1969 in the wake of Bob Dylan's *Nashville Skyline* album, on which some of the future members played. They were a who's who of Nashville session stars: Charlie McCoy, Mac Gayden, Weldon Myrick, Kenny Buttrey, Bobby Thompson, Wayne Moss, Buddy Spicher, Norbert Putnam, and Ken Lauber. All of these appeared on their instrumental debut album, *Area Code 615*. Keyboard player Lauber was replaced by David Briggs by the time of the second and final album, *A Trip in the Country*, in 1970. Subsequently, Moss formed Barefoot Jerry, and Putnam and Briggs became producers. *—William Ruhlmann*

● **Area Code 615** / 1969 / Polydor ✦✦✦✦

This is a legendary record recorded by a legendary group of musicians. Area Code 615 was, as the name implies, the location of Cinderella Studios in Nashville (Madison, to be exact). The session players who recorded there are some of the greatest unsung heroes in popular music: Weldon Myrick (pedal steel), Bobby Thompson (banjo), Buddy Spicher (fiddle), Mac Gayden and Wayne Moss (lead guitar), Charlie McCoy (harp), Ken Buttrey (drums), David Briggs (piano), and Norman Putnam (bass). These players performed miracles on hundreds of records, including those by Johnny Cash, Bob Dylan, the Beau Brummels, Ian & Sylvia, and countless others. This, their "group" debut, is a timeless excursion into all forms of music. The record contains a lot (for then) of contemporary covers, such as an awe-inspiring version of "Hey Jude" that, in some ways, builds in intensity as much as the Beatles' version. It's soul, rock, and country at its finest, and ironically sounds as though it was a possible blueprint for Joe Cocker/Leon Russell's *Mad Dogs & Englishmen* project. Aside from the general power and groove, all of the solos are spectacular, especially Charlie McCoy and Mac Gayden's performances on "Nashville 9—NY 1." Gayden is particularly impressive, often sounding like a visiting Eric Clapton in 1969. It's that good. Buttrey and Putnam, though, are the real stars here, laying down the most solid, knee-deep funk and soul that you will ever hear. Absolutely awesome. Friends, this is one stone gas. *—Matthew Greenwald*

A Trip in the Country / 1970 / Polydor ✦✦✦

On its second album, the Nashville professional musician supergroup Area Code 615 took the opportunity to stretch out and try some really far-out things. While still nominally country, this has more in common with the freewheeling psychedelic rock and sunshine pop of 1970 than what was coming out of Nashville. Given the fuzz tones, light funk vamps, trippy interludes, and random outbursts of heavy guitars, it's little wonder that Area Code 615 was appealing to hippies, not rednecks, but even among those hippies the group was a cult item; a two-night stint at *the Fillmore West* did not spur the band's debut into greater record sales, and *A Trip in the Country* didn't even chart. Perhaps that's because they didn't cover any obvious material here. Where the first record had three Beatles tunes and numbers by Dylan and Otis Redding, this relies on new songs and a couple of bluegrass and folk songs that sound unrecognizable; Bill Monroe's "Scotland" has its boundaries blown wide open, and the result is a serious head trip. But perhaps the best-known item here is "Stone Fox Chase," whose stuttering refrain—performed by harmonica player extraordinaire Charlie McCoy—became the theme song for the BBC's fantastic music program *The Old Grey Whistle Test*. That tune also illustrates the nature of this band: it's a musician's band, the work of exceptional players whose skills are best appreciated by other players. That doesn't mean there isn't some extraordinary playing here, since there is (although the debut is a better place to just hear the band *play*, since this relies more on the structure than the solo), but only fellow musicians will find this more than a semi-interesting period piece. *—Stephen Thomas Erlewine*

Area Code 615/A Trip in the Country / 2000 / Polydor ✦✦✦✦

Armstrong Twins

b. DeWitt, AR

Group / Traditional Country, Close Harmony

The Armstrong Twins were one of the last duets to master the great harmonies of the traditional country music that came from '30s and '40s. The twins, guitarist Lloyd and mandolin player Floyd, were born in DeWitt, AR, but were raised in Little Rock. They made their radio debut at age five and by the age of nine were hosting their own radio show. Greatly influenced by the Blue Sky Boys and the Bailes Brothers, the Armstrongs were appearing on two daily radio shows and on the *Arkansas Jamboree* by 1946. Between then and 1951, they cut over a dozen songs, most of which were bluegrass covers. Occasionally, they would also record instrumentals. The twins moved to Odessa, TX, in 1952 and began appearing on local radio and television programs. They then began touring with Johnny Horton and later worked on *Louisiana Hayride*.

In the late '50s, they moved to California and began appearing on the *Town Hall Party* in Compton.They were unique in that they were most popular on the West Coast at a time when local charts were dominated by western swing and honky-tonk tunes. After that, they moved back to Little Rock. Decades later, their old recording were reissued, and the Armstrongs began a new series of festival and club engagements, even releasing a new album in 1980. Due to Floyd's ill health, the brothers had to curtail personal appearances and only played occasionally during the 1980s. *—Sandra Brennan*

Hillbilly Mandolin / 1979 / Old-Timey ✦✦✦✦

● **Just Country Boys** / 1980 / Arhoolie ✦✦✦✦

Billy Armstrong

b. Mar. 18, 1930, Streator, IL

Fiddle, Violin, Leader / Western Swing

Billy Armstrong was one of country music's premier fiddle players from 1965-1977, and was named Fiddle Player of the Year 13 years in a row by the ACM. He first played professionally in 1943 with Bob Lively's Dude Ranch Cowboys, quitting after four years to form Billy Armstrong & the Westerners, a group that included Don Hoag (drums), Bobby Wagoner (guitar), and Billy Strange (guitar). Armstrong began playing on the radio in 1948 on *Spade Cooley Presents*; the following year, he replaced "Lefty" Joe Holley in Tommy Duncan's Western All Stars. After playing on several of Duncan's recording sessions for the Intro label, he returned to L.A. and joined Hi Busse & the Frontiersmen, playing with them until 1951. Armstrong briefly played with another band until founding the Westernaires.

Following their 1957 breakup, Armstrong joined Hank Thompson's Brazos Valley Boys for six months. Road life finally exhausted him and he quit, returned to L.A., and joined Cliffie Stone's Hometown Jamboree and then Tex Williams' band. He released two singles, "Gloria" and "If You Leave While I'm Sleeping," in 1959. In 1965, Armstrong won his first ACM Fiddler of the Year award and also released the single "The Orange Blossom Special." He then played with Gene Davis on the television series *Star Route* before joining the Sons of the Pioneers in 1966, with whom he sang lead and alternating tenor. He stayed with the Pioneers until early 1972, when he joined the Chaparral Brothers. During the 1970s, Armstrong also had a solo recording career, which produced three albums. *—Sandra Brennan*

● **World's Greatest Fiddle Player** / 1976 / Hillside ✦✦✦✦

Billy Don't Sell Your Fiddle / Hillside ✦✦✦

Eddy Arnold

b. May 15, 1918, Madisonville, TN

Vocals, Guitar / Traditional Country, Cowboy, Country-Pop, Honky Tonk, Nashville Sound/Countrypolitan

Eddy Arnold moved hillbilly music to the city, creating a sleek sound that relied on his smooth voice and occasionally lush orchestrations. In the process, he became the most popular country performer of the 20th century, spending more weeks at the top of the charts than any other artist. Arnold not only had 28 number-one singles, he had more charting singles than any other artist. More than any other country performer of the postwar era, he was responsible for bringing the music to the masses, to people who wouldn't normally listen to country music. Arnold was initially influenced by cowboy singers like Gene Autry, but as his career progressed, he shaped his phrasing in the style of Pete Cassell. Nevertheless, he was more of a crooner than a hillbilly singer, which is a large reason why he was embraced by the entertainment industry at large, and frequently crossed over to the pop charts. Arnold's career ran strong into the '90s. Although his records didn't dominate the charts like they did during the '40s and '50s, he continued to fill concert halls and reissues of his older recordings sold well.

Raised on a farm in Tennessee, Arnold was given a guitar at the age of ten by his mother. His father, who had played fiddle and bass, died the following year. Arnold left school so he could help out on the farm. However, he began playing dances whenever he had a chance. Several years later, he made his first radio appearance on a station in Jackson. Arnold then moved to St. Louis, where he played in nightclubs with fiddler Speedy McNatt. In St. Louis, Arnold landed a regular spot on WMPS Memphis, spending six years at the radio station. Through the show, the singer earned a dedicated following of fans. During World War II, Eddy Arnold became part of R.J. Reynolds' Camel Caravan, which featured Redd Stewart, Pee Wee King's Golden West Cowboys, Minnie Pearl, and San Antonio Rose. The troupe performed for U.S. troops throughout America, as well some selected dates in Panama. After the Camel Caravan, Arnold became the featured singer in the Golden West Cowboys while they performed on the *Grand Ole Opry*. At first, he appeared under the name the Tennessee Plowboy, a nickname that followed him throughout his career.

Arnold recorded his first single, "Mommy Please Stay Home With Me," in 1944 for RCA Victor. At RCA, the singer received the guidance of the label's A&R head, Steve Sholes, which proved to be invaluable help for his career. Eddy Arnold pursued a solo career in 1945, the same year he got married to Sally Gayhart. "Each Minute Seems a Million Years," released on RCA's Bluebird division that same year, became his first charting record, peaking in the Top Five. Arnold's career really took off the following year, when "That's How Much I Love You" peaked in the Top Three, staying there for 16 weeks and selling over 650,000 copies; its flip side, "Chained to a Memory," also climbed into the Top Three. Arnold followed the single's success with two number-one hits in 1947, "What Is Life Without Love" and "It's a Sin." However, that didn't compare to the success of his next record, "I'll Hold You in My Heart (Till I Can Hold You in My Arms)." The single spent 46 weeks on the charts, with 21 of those weeks spent at the top; it also crossed over to the pop charts, reaching the Top 30. In the process, it became the number-one single of the decade.

"I'll Hold You in My Heart" confirmed that Arnold had become a country superstar, as did the performance of his 1948 singles. All of his nine singles went into the Top Five, and five of them went to number one, including "Anytime," "What a Fool I Was," "Texarkana Baby," "Just a Little Lovin' (Will Go a Long, Long Way)," "My Daddy Is Only a Picture," and "Bouquet of Roses," which stayed at the top for 19 weeks. In total, Arnold racked up over 40 weeks on top of the charts during 1948, becoming the number one country star in America. He headlined all the radio shows and concerts he appeared on, and he was in demand throughout the nation. By the end of the year, Colonel Tom Parker had become his manager; Parker would later become Elvis Presley's manager. Throughout 1949, he continued to dominate the charts, releasing a succession of Top Ten singles, including the number one "Don't Rob Another Man's Castle," "One Kiss Too Many," "I'm Throwing Rice (At the Girl I Love)," and "Take Me in Your Arms and Hold Me."

Eddy Arnold became a familiar face not only to country fans but also to the general public in the early '50s. He toured all of the U.S., as well as several foreign countries. All of the major television shows of the era, including *The Perry Como Show* and *Arthur Godfrey's Talent Scouts*, featured the singer. Indeed, he became so popular that he was the first country star to have his own television show, *Eddy Arnold Time*. The show originally aired on NBC, but it later moved to ABC. Through all of this, his string of Top Ten hits remained unbroken, even though he didn't have another crossover pop hit until 1954.

Nevertheless, the sheer amount of country hits was overwhelming: In 1950 he had seven, and 13 in 1951 (including the number ones "There's Been a Change in Me," "Kentucky Waltz," "I Wanna Play House With You," "Easy on the Eyes," and "A Full Time Job"). The hits, including "Eddy's Song" (composed of the titles of previous hits), "How's the World Treating You?," "I Really Don't Want to Know," "My Everything," "The Cattle Call," "That Do Make It Nice," "Just Call Me Lonesome," and "The Richest Man (In the World)," continued to come in force until 1956.

Between 1956 and 1964, Arnold continued to chart, but he wasn't reaching the Top Ten at the same frequency of the previous decade. During this time, his style was beginning to change, as he was shedding his rootsy style for a slicker, polished sound that was more appropriate for urban settings than rural territories. Arnold became a crooner, complete with subdued instrumental backings, highlighted by gentle steel guitars and the occasional orchestra. The change in musical direction was a major commercial success, sparking a new era of chart dominance that began in 1965 with "What's He Doing in My World." Not only did he return to the top of the country charts, he once again crossed over to the pop charts. Arnold's second streak of major hits ran until 1969. During this time, he earned several number-one and Top Ten singles, all of which were pop hits as well, including "Make the World Go Away," "I Want to Go With You," "The Last Word in Lonesome," "Somebody Like Me," "Lonely Again," "Turn the World Around," "Then You Can Tell Me Goodbye," "They Don't Make Love Like They Used To," and "Please Don't Go."

In the early '70s, Arnold continued to appear on the country charts, although his pop hits dried up. The singer signed with MGM in 1972, ending 27 straight years at RCA. Arnold spent only four years at MGM, landing only one major hit, 1974's "I Wish That I Had Loved You Better." Returning to RCA in 1976, he closed out the decade with two hits—"Cowboy" (1976) and "If Everyone Had Someone Like You" (1978). Arnold managed to put two songs into the Top Ten in 1980 ("Let's Get It While the Gettin's Good," "That's What I Get for Loving You"), making him one of the few artists who charted in five different decades. He continued to record in the '90s, although without charting a hit single. Nevertheless, his concert and television appearances remained popular until his retirement from the stage in 1999.

Beginning in the '60s, Eddy Arnold was bestowed with a numerous amount of awards. In 1966, he was inducted into the Country Music Hall of Fame. The following year, he was the first Entertainer of the Year named by the CMA. The ACM gave him the Pioneer Award in 1984; three years later, the Songwriters Guild gave him its President's Award. Perhaps the truest gauge of his success is his record sales. Over the course of his career, he has sold over 85 million records, making him one of the most successful artists of the 20th century. —*Stephen Thomas Erlewine*

Anytime/Eddy Arnold and His Guitar / 1952 / RCA Victor ✦✦✦✦✦
The fine, early country material ("Bouquet of Roses," "Molly Darling") features Little Roy Wiggins on steel guitar. —*Richard Lieberson*

An American Institution / 1954 / RCA Victor ✦✦✦✦

The Chapel on the Hill / 1955 / RCA Victor ✦✦✦

Wanderin' / 1955 / RCA Victor ✦✦✦✦✦
Eddy Arnold recorded a few albums devoted to folk and traditional songs in his career, and *Wanderin'* is one of them. The album, made in 1955, is one of Arnold's best LPs, featuring his exquisite baritone in an appealingly spare commercial folk setting (acoustic guitar, strings, vocal chorus) in which the pop elements are subdued enough to be inoffensive. The songs are nearly all well-worn favorites in the public domain, but Arnold elaborates on the melodies with melancholy minor-key flourishes that add new depth to songs that might otherwise be taken for granted. The 14-song program is unusually generous for the time and includes western ballads ("Home on the Range") alongside ancient traditional folk songs like "Barbara Allen." The title track gained a new life on James Taylor's 1975 album *Gorilla*, but Arnold's version is even more plaintive. Recommended. —*Greg Adams*

Anytime / 1955 / RCA Victor ✦✦✦✦✦
Anytime is an expanded reissue of a 1952 two-EP set of the same name that contains several of Eddy Arnold's biggest early hits. Seven of the 12 tracks were number-one hits, while "Molly Darling" and "That's How Much I Love You" made the Top Ten. Although Arnold did not hold his early recordings in high esteem later in his career, these are some of the hits that established his reputation as a major artist, and are among the most traditional-sounding country records he made. His easygoing vocal style is the same as ever, and the spare instrumentation—with fiddles in place of the sweet strings he would later favor—provides an appealing backdrop. It is interesting to note that there is a sameness to Arnold's early hits, just as there is a sameness to his big '60s hits. Even at this early stage, although he was working within the confines of straight country music, Arnold had a well-developed middle-of-the-road sensibility. —*Greg Adams*

A Little on the Lonely Side / 1956 / RCA Victor ✦✦✦

My Darling, My Darling / 1957 / RCA Victor ✦✦✦

When They Were Young / 1957 / RCA Victor ✦✦✦

Praise Him, Praise Him / 1958 / RCA Victor ✦✦
Eddy Arnold gives listeners that old time religion on *Praise Him, Praise Him*, a tribute to the blind songstress Fanny Crosby, composer of over 9,000 hymns in the 1800s and early 1900s. "Blessed Assurance" is one of her most famous hymns, and it is here with 11 other sacred songs like "Though Your Sins Be as Scarlet" and "He Hideth My Soul." While country gospel may hold some appeal for fans of secular country music, *Praise Him, Praise Him* is not a country gospel album at all—it contains old-fashioned church music that Arnold performs with an organ, piano, and choir. The stately arrangements and reverent performances are very good, but unless you are an avid churchgoer or collector of hymnals, *Praise Him, Praise Him* will be a challenging proposition. —*Greg Adams*

Have Guitar, Will Travel / 1959 / RCA Victor ✦✦
Based around a loose "travel" concept, *Have Guitar, Will Travel* features a collection of songs with the names of states or cities in its title. It's a cute concept, but it wears thin fast, simply because the quality of the material is so drastically uneven. Within the album, there are some gems—like a beautiful "Carry Me Back to Old Virginny"—but the record is more interesting as an artifact than as an album. —*Stephen Thomas Erlewine*

Thereby Hangs a Tale / 1959 / RCA Victor ✦✦✦✦
Thereby Hangs a Tale is devoted to songs that tell a story, from Eddy Arnold's hit version of Jimmie Driftwood's "Tennessee Stud" to older songs like "Riders in the Sky" and "The Wreck of the Old '97." Johnny Horton's "The Battle of New Orleans" was a phenomenal hit in 1959, and its influence is felt on the historical songs Arnold tackles, from "The Battle of Little Big Horn" to "Boot Hill," the latter of which was released unsuccessfully on a single. Arnold's performances are far more subdued than Horton's and lack the martial snare drum beats, giving *Thereby Hangs a Tale* a folk flavor. A version of "Tom Dooley" reinforces the folksy tone, as does "The Red Headed Stranger," a contemporary song that Willie Nelson later revived. Arnold's thematic albums are often his most interesting, and *Thereby Hangs a Tale* is no exception. —*Greg Adams*

Eddy Arnold Sings Them Again / 1960 / RCA Victor ✦✦
Many artists re-recorded their earlier mono hits in stereo as that technology became more widespread, and *Eddy Arnold Sings Them Again* is exactly that—new stereo recordings of 11 of Arnold's hits from 1947-1956. A 12th song, "I Walk Alone," wasn't a hit for Arnold but was one of his earliest recordings in 1945. This kind of re-recording project is often disposable, and *Eddy Arnold Sings Them Again* is no exception. The album package served its purpose in 1960 by providing fans with a higher-fidelity and more modern-sounding anthology of popular songs, but in most cases Arnold did not significantly update the arrangements. One exception is the remake of his 1950 hit "The Lovebug Itch," which is performed in a mild rock & roll style. —*Greg Adams*

More / 1960 / RCA Victor ✦✦✦✦
Eddy Arnold made only a handful of recordings that could be characterized as rock & roll, and one of them is "Little Bit" from his 1960 album *More Eddy Arnold*. A mild strain of pop/rock courses through the album, which stands out for its unusual production tone and strong, exclusive material. "Take Her for a Boat Ride" is another mild rocker, and "Just a Little Lovin'," a fun update of his 1948 hit, features a playful performance that exercises Arnold's entire vocal range. He sounds energized and engaged throughout the album, and a few cuts seem like they could have been successful singles. With material this good, it's astonishing that 1960 was a year without hits for Eddy Arnold. —*Greg Adams*

Let's Make Memories Tonight / 1961 / RCA Victor ✦✦

Our Man Down South / 1962 / RCA Victor ✦✦
RCA released a slew of "Our Man" albums in 1963 to promote artists from Paul Anka to Pérez Prado in association with various cities or regions. Eddy Arnold represented the South by offering, among others, interpretations of Pat Boone's tragedy hit "Moody River," Johnny Horton's "The Ballad of New Orleans," and Leroy Van Dyke's "Black Cloud." There is no theme beyond the series' concept, and there are no hits either, since these cover versions were not issued on singles. Still, it's a lively and entertaining album that bears a personal endorsement by the governor of Tennessee. —*Greg Adams*

Cattle Call / 1963 / RCA Victor ✦✦✦✦✦
Western music may live forever, but in the early '60s it had already suffered a decline. The singing cowboys had all but disappeared from the silver screen, and the days when western attire and repertoire were expected of country artists would soon be over. The album format became the new domain of commercial western music, and stalwarts like the Sons of the Pioneers and Tex Ritter continued to release moderately successful albums long after their hitmaking heydays. Eddy Arnold had a number-one hit in 1955 with one of his recordings of "Cattle Call," but this 1963 LP was his first all-western album and his first to make the *Billboard* album charts. In addition to the expected western standards on *Cattle Call*, Arnold "westernizes" popular songs like "The Wayward Wind," and his smooth baritone fits these songs just as well as that of Rex Allen or Johnny Western. The re-recording of the title track is a haunting beauty with a real yodel rather than the falsetto vocal treatment it often receives, and is the version that is frequently anthologized even though it wasn't a hit. Well made and well remembered, *Cattle Call* is perhaps the most significant western album of the '60s. —*Greg Adams*

Songs I Love to Sing / 1963 / Capitol ✦✦✦
Songs I Love to Sing illustrates in a nutshell Eddy Arnold's changing image in the '60s, from country crooner to all-around pop entertainer. The album was originally released in 1963 under the title *Country Songs I Love to Sing*, with a rustic cover photo of Arnold strumming his guitar on the porch of a log cabin. The reissue excises the word "country" from the title, replaces the original cover with a suave head shot, and offers a new set of liner notes cleansed of all references to country music. Where the original album declared Arnold "one of the great country (and pop!) singers," the reissue refers to him only as a pop singer. Likewise, the reference to his nickname (the Tennessee Plowboy) in the early notes is omitted from the reissue. The album itself is a collection of early recordings (all but two of the cuts were big hits for Arnold between 1946-1951) that are unmistakably "country" (however mild), and the attempt to sell it to the pop audience in a misleading package is simply dishonest. —*Greg Adams*

Folk Song Book / 1964 / RCA Victor ✦✦✦

Sometimes I'm Happy, Sometimes I'm Blue / 1964 / RCA Victor ✦✦✦

Eddy's Songs / 1964 / RCA Camden ✦✦
Eddy's Songs may contain several fine tracks, including "Roll Along Kentucky Moon," "When My Blue Moon Turns to Gold Again," and "Kentucky Waltz," but the LP is burdened by uneven songs and performances, making it only a fitfully entertaining listen. [The stereo editions of *Eddy's Songs* are electronically reprocessed stereo, not true stereo.] —*Thom Owens*

Pop Hits From the Country Side / 1964 / RCA Victor ♦♦

Pop Hits From the Country Side rounds up a dozen country songs that also found favor with the pop audience, as interpreted by the king of crossover music, Eddy Arnold. The twist is that the songs are presented in a "completely pop context," to quote the liner notes, and the album sounds a lot like those made by pop vocalists John Gary and Al Martino when they tackled similar material. Arnold's versions of pop-oriented country songs like "I Fall to Pieces" and "Four Walls" are even more languid than the originals, with lush orchestral arrangements that contrast with Arnold's homey baritone. The album was a departure for Arnold in that it was recorded in New York instead of Nashville and cleaves to its pure pop concept. Rosemary Clooney did this sort of thing over a decade earlier with "Half As Much," so *Pop Hits From the Country Side* can hardly be considered a groundbreaker, even though it was an experiment of sorts for Eddy Arnold. —*Greg Adams*

The Easy Way / 1965 / RCA Victor ♦♦♦♦

Despite the title, which implies that this is going to be another one of Eddy Arnold's many MOR pop albums, *The Easy Way* is actually one of the most invigorating and enjoyable of his mid-'60s LPs. "Bad News" is a funny, boastful tune that had been a minor hit for its writer, John D. Loudermilk. "Tell 'Em Where You Got Your Blues" and "Baby I've Got It" are blues-based with some ace guitar, probably played by producer Chet Atkins. "What-Cha Gonna Do" is the kind of uptempo country song that became a rarity on Arnold's later albums, and the melody of "Understand Your Man" is very close to Bob Dylan's "Don't Think Twice, It's Alright." Most of the other tracks take a laid-back approach and are more in alignment with the expectations of the mainstream listeners who made giant hits out of songs like "Make the World Go Away" and "What's He Doing in My World" around this time. Bill Walker's arrangements seem to favor the electric guitar a little more than usual, which lends a slight edge that is often lacking on Arnold's pop ballads. —*Greg Adams*

My World / 1965 / RCA Victor ♦♦♦

My World was certified gold in 1965 on the strength of Eddy Arnold's smash hits "Make the World Go Away" and "What's He Doing in My World." —*Steve Huey*

I'm Throwing Rice / 1965 / Camden ♦♦♦

I'm Throwing Rice is a budget reissue of ten Eddy Arnold sides from the mid-'50s in fake stereo. There are a few hits in the bunch, including "Casey Jones (The Brave Engineer)" and Arnold's competing version of Marvin Rainwater's "Gonna Find Me a Bluebird." Particularly interesting is "The Rockin' Mockin' Bird," an attempt at rock & roll cut in 1956. Beyond that, the album is a hodgepodge of sentimental ballads ("I Wouldn't Trade the Silver in My Mother's Hair") and a western show tune ("Wagon Wheels") from the years before Arnold became a veritable pop singer. If you can get past the reprocessed stereo effect, *I'm Throwing Rice* is a convenient anthology of assorted singles. —*Greg Adams*

The Last Word in Lonesome / 1966 / RCA Victor ♦♦♦

Eddy Arnold drifted steadily toward the pop mainstream throughout the late '50s and '60s until, with *The Last Word in Lonesome*, he arrived at his destination. "Country-pop" and "Nashville sound" do not describe the music here—it is pure MOR pop vocal material of the sort in which John Gary and Al Martino dealt. The cover photo of Arnold in an elegant black velvet jacket and white silk scarf tells the story before the needle even touches the vinyl. The songwriters, from Bob Montgomery and Dottie West to Cindy Walker and Hank Cochran, hail from the field of country music, but Arnold's smooth crooning and Bill Walker's easy listening string arrangements are bound for the supper club. "Why" is particularly lovely, and "Misty Blue" became a big hit for Arnold in 1967 (and again for Billy Jo Spears in 1976). Arnold's recording of the title track, one of Roger Miller's most affecting compositions, almost reached number one and crossed over to the pop Top 40. If country music was moving uptown in the '60s, *The Last Word in Lonesome* saw it comfortably ensconced in a Manhattan penthouse, sipping champagne and bragging about its golf scores. —*Greg Adams*

Somebody Like Me / 1966 / RCA Victor ♦♦

It is telling that *Somebody Like Me*, one of the blandest middle-of-the-road pop records Eddy Arnold made in the '60s, was also one of his most commercially successful. Its strong sales performance explains why the so-called Tennessee Plowboy came to make such an abundance of easy listening records: a lot of people were buying them. There are several good songs, but the sweet, languid arrangements lack the moodiness and atmospherics of his best easy listening records. The limp interpretation of Bill Anderson's "The Tips of My Fingers" was a number-three hit, and "Somebody Like Me" spent a month at number one. The appearance of "Lay Some Happiness on Me" a year before either Dean Martin or Bobby Wright had a hit with it is notable, but chart status notwithstanding, *Somebody Like Me* is not one of Arnold's strongest albums. —*Greg Adams*

Lonely Again / 1967 / RCA Victor ♦♦♦

"Lonely Again," a lush pop ballad that floats by in a choral mist, became a number-one hit for Eddy Arnold in 1967. The attendant album is filled with ballads in the same vein, and although Arnold made many such albums in the '60s, *Lonely Again* holds up better than some. That's because the songs are mostly original, the production is not fixed in any particular era, and there are no attempts at trendiness or conspicuous modernity. "Did It Rain" and "He's Got You" are simply lovely performances in complementary settings, and the entire album, for that matter, is an easy listening pleasure. —*Greg Adams*

Turn the World Around / 1967 / RCA Victor ♦♦♦♦

Turn the World Around begins like any other Eddy Arnold album from the late '60s, with easy listening vocal performances that connect tenuously, at best, with country music. Arnold was a popular balladeer and recorded many cherished albums in that style, but if you enjoy a little variety in your music, things pick up considerably halfway through the present album. Side two kicks off with the title track, a crossover hit that topped the country chart, and a cover of Wynn Stewart's big hit "It's Such a Pretty World Today," before

moving on to a couple of ace uptempo performances. "There's This About You" is a wonderfully catchy pop song that is grounded in the country idiom with tasteful lead guitar work, and "Love Finds a Way" is nearly as good. It is so rare to encounter spirited country music (well, country-pop...) on an Eddy Arnold LP from this period that almost anything that picks up the pace is welcomed. These two songs add enough spice to the platter to make *Turn the World Around* one of the more engaging albums from Arnold's later years. —*Greg Adams*

★ **The Best of Eddy Arnold** / 1967 / RCA ♦♦♦♦♦

Released in 1967, RCA's *The Best of Eddy Arnold* offers an excellent 12-track overview of his countrypolitan peak for the label in the '60s. Arnold had a tremendous number of hits, charting consistently from 1955-1975, but the early-'60s singles that this record chronicles are at the heart of his legacy—smooth, lush productions of sweet ballads and heartache songs, perfectly suited for his easy-rolling voice. Later collections might be more comprehensive, but this *The Best of Eddy Arnold* contains the essentials—"Bouquet of Roses," "Make the World Go Away," "Anytime," "I'll Hold You in My Heart (Till I Can Hold You in My Arms)," "Last World in Lonesome Is Me," "What's He Doing in My World," a nice re-recording of "Cattle Call"—that make this record as effective an overview now as it was back then. Other collections may be longer, but this will tell many listeners everything they need to know. —*Stephen Thomas Erlewine*

The Everlovin' World of Eddy Arnold / 1968 / RCA Victor ♦♦

The albums that flowed seemingly endlessly from Eddy Arnold in the '60s usually fell into clear categories: MOR pop albums, country-pop albums, "Eddy Arnold sings the hits" collections, and thematic sets. *The Everlovin' World of Eddy Arnold* is one of his MOR pop efforts, crafted in the manner of a John Gary or Vic Dana record with no connection whatsoever to the world of country music. Some of his easy listening albums, especially those with uncommonly good songs or particularly evocative mood music production values, hold up quite well; others, including *The Everlovin' World of Eddy Arnold*, are forgettable offerings of familiar songs with paint-by-numbers arrangements. Arnold's relaxed performances are fine, and the album made the pop charts, but there is little else to distinguish it from the uncounted MOR vocal albums from this period. —*Greg Adams*

The Romantic World of Eddy Arnold / 1968 / RCA Victor ♦♦

Walkin' in Love Land / 1968 / RCA Victor ♦♦♦

Walkin' in Love Land has an aura of nostalgia because of the number of older pop songs, like the Everly Brothers' "All I Have to Do Is Dream" and Glen Campbell's "Turn Around, Look at Me" (which was on the charts again in 1968 thanks to the Vogues). The wistful "Then You Can Tell Me Goodbye" was deservedly a number-one hit for Eddy Arnold, even if Johnny Tillotson's 1963 recording was better. The Platters' "I'll Never Smile Again" is a surprising selection that is well-suited to Arnold's style, and the title track sounds like a missed opportunity for a single. On the downside, the cloying "Apples, Raisins and Roses" and most of side two are bland pop ballads of the sort that dominate Arnold's late-'60s LPs. About half of *Walkin' in Love Land* ranges in quality from above-average to very good, which is enough to place the album among the best of Eddy Arnold's late RCA albums. —*Greg Adams*

Songs of the Young World / 1969 / RCA Victor ♦♦

Eddy Arnold's evolution from a hillbilly singer to a middle-of-the-road pop balladeer was gradual enough that he continued to be identified with country music even when his albums contained not a whit of country. His late-'60s singles often appeared simultaneously on the pop, country, and adult contemporary charts, and his repertoire came to include some surprisingly modern pop songs. His 1969 album *Songs of the Young World* contains his Top Ten hit "They Don't Make Love Like They Used To" and inevitable versions of the country-pop hits "Witchita Lineman" and "Little Green Apples." "Tender Is Her Name," with its flutes and lazy soul vibe, shows what a short distance Arnold would have had to travel at this stage to turn into a deep-voiced Bobby Goldsboro. In 1973 RCA's Camden imprint reissued *Songs of the Young World* under the title *I Love How You Love Me.* —*Greg Adams*

The Glory of Love / 1969 / RCA Victor ♦♦

Eddy Arnold's *The Glory of Love* is one of a few of his late RCA albums on which every song sounds like either Glen Campbell or Bobby Goldsboro. "Heaven Below" is melodically similar to Campbell's "Witchita Lineman," and "Then She's a Lover" (a hit for Roy Clark) is a slice-of-life song like Goldsboro's "The Straight Life," or "Honey" without the morbid ending. Veteran arranger Bill Walker's contributions are in keeping with the times and are most interesting on the hit "But for Love" with its echoey guitar leads. "Please Don't Go" was Arnold's last Top Ten hit for over a decade, and in the context of the album doesn't particularly stand out. Arnold was entering a commercial as well as creative dry spell at this point, and his best cuts are better-heard on collections. —*Greg Adams*

The Warmth of Eddy / 1969 / RCA Victor ♦♦

Love & Guitars / 1970 / RCA Victor ♦♦

Standing Alone / 1970 / RCA Victor ♦♦♦

Portrait of My Woman / 1971 / RCA Victor ♦♦♦

Welcome to My World / 1971 / RCA Victor ♦♦♦

This Is Eddy Arnold / 1971 / RCA Victor ♦♦♦

Loving Her Was Easier / 1971 / RCA Victor ♦♦

Eddy Arnold was a few years past his last major country hit when he made *Loving Her Was Easier*. The light country-folk sound was probably influenced by the contemporaneous success of artists like John Denver and James Taylor. In fact, Denver's "Take Me Home, Country Roads" is covered, as are big hits such as "Ruby, Don't Take Your Love to Town" and Freddie Hart's "Easy Loving," both of which fit well with the tone of the album, even if the performances are lackluster. A tepid run-through of Jackie DeShannon's "Put a Little Love in Your Heart" is included for Arnold's least-discerning pop fans. "I Love You Dear" was a minor hit and the only charting single from the album. A year or so after *Loving Her Was Easier*, Arnold's sagging sales resulted in his parting ways with RCA after nearly 30 years with the company. —*Greg Adams*

Lonely People / 1972 / RCA Victor ◆◆

Eddy Arnold Sings for Housewives & Other Lovers / 1972 / RCA Victor ◆◆◆

Many Tears Ago / 1985 / Capitol ◆◆◆

☆ **Cattle Call/Thereby Hangs a Tale** / 1990 / Bear Family ◆◆◆◆◆
This CD is made up of two similarly conceived albums that were among the finest LPs Arnold ever cut, when he was in the midst of the extended peak of his career. *Cattle Call* was an apparent attempt (and almost wholly successful one) to tap into the revival of interest in Western songs fostered by Marty Robbins and Johnny Cash at Columbia. In addition to Arnold's re-recording (his fourth version in less than 20 years) of the title tune, in a spare but polished rendition, he also does an excellent job with Bob Nolan's "Cool Water" and "Tumbling Tumbleweeds," the traditional "Carry Me Back to the Lone Prairie," and pieces like the singing-cowboy anthem "Leaning on the Old Top Rail." Grady Martin is the lead guitarist on these sessions, which were produced by Chet Atkins and have a clean, lean sound, not overproduced and all rather similar to the sound that Robbins got on his records. What is lacking is the tone of urgency and involvement that Robbins brought to this same material. *Thereby Hangs a Tale* grew out of the folk music boom and Arnold's successful 1959 single of Jimmie Driftwood's "Tennessee Stud." The Anita Kerr Singers turn up here and there, but are used in a fairly restrained manner. The stereo separation is extremely crisp and the instrumental textures are vivid throughout. Jimmie Driftwood's original notes on *Thereby Hangs a Tale* have been replaced by new notes, focusing more on the songs themselves. Chet Atkins produced both albums, but only played on *Tale*. —*Bruce Eder*

Hand-Holdin' Songs / 1990 / RCA ◆◆
Now in his 70s, his voice remains rich, his style reserved and low-key. —*Michael McCall*

Best of Eddy Arnold / 1990 / Curb ◆◆
Best of Eddy Arnold is somewhat of a misleading title. Although several of his greatest songs are included on this album, they are presented in re-recorded versions from the '70s. None of the new versions are particularly bad, but they aren't particularly good, either; stick with the RCA versions. —*Stephen Thomas Erlewine*

Last of the Love Song Singers: Then & Now / 1993 / RCA ◆◆◆
The double-disc box set *Last of the Love Song Singers: Then and Now* is a wasted opportunity. The first disc, called *Then*, is a quick overview of some of Arnold's biggest hits that doesn't offer enough songs. The second disc, titled *Now*, is a collection of new recordings. Though they aren't bad, the new recordings devalue the set's worth as a retrospective and as an introduction. —*Stephen Thomas Erlewine*

The Essential Eddy Arnold / Jun. 18, 1996 / RCA ◆◆◆◆◆
The Essential Eddy Arnold contains the majority of Eddy Arnold's biggest hits, including "Make the World Go Away" and "Cattle Call." It's the only single disc retrospective that offers a reasonably thorough overview of his hit singles, making it an ideal introduction and—considering that the two-disc box set *Last of the Love Song Singers* contained an entire disc of newly recorded material—the only currently available retrospective that could be considered definitive. —*Thom Owens*

Legendary Eddy Arnold / Nov. 18, 1997 / BMG Special Products ◆◆◆
The Legendary Eddy Arnold focuses on the singer's country-pop recordings, with renditions of Jimmy Webb's "By the Time I Get to Phoenix" and "Wichita Lineman," in addition to performances of "Gentle on My Mind," "Little Green Apples," and others. As a budget-line compilation, it's plainly intended to serve as an introduction to Arnold's music, but its focus is just too narrow to give a proper sense of the singer's achievements. —*Jason Ankeny*

The Hits / Mar. 31, 1998 / Mercury ◆◆
Mercury Nashville's *The Hits* contains 11 remakes of classic hits that Eddy Arnold recorded for MGM between 1973 and 1975. Arnold was in surprisingly good voice for a man approaching 60, but these versions simply pale in comparison to his original hit versions, and this collection should be avoided. —*Stephen Thomas Erlewine*

☆ **The Tennessee Plowboy & His Guitar** / Aug. 11, 1998 / Bear Family ◆◆◆◆◆
The 120 tracks on these five CDs constitute a group of Eddy Arnold songs with which few people under the age of 50 could be familiar—only about a half-dozen of them ever appeared on LP, much less CD. Recorded between 1944 and 1950, they represent his rise to country stardom (but not yet to pop stardom), and also the evolution of country music in the period immediately after the war. His performances on the early sides were heavily influenced by the work of Gene Autry, but they were much closer to hillbilly music, with thin, twangy guitars and fiddle. With the help of producer Steve Sholes, Arnold and his group (the Tennessee Plowboys) achieved a fine, lean sound that was a good compromise between hillbilly authenticity and commercial country music. Disc two, covering 1947-1948, shows Arnold consolidating his earlier success, and acquiring a greater range in the process. Disc three shows Arnold's voice mellowing into the fine instrument that it became as he later emerged into pop stardom; his low range is richer, and he reaches those high notes more easily. This was all of a piece with making Arnold accessible to the widest possible audience; what no one realized at the time was that Arnold was helping to change country music in the process. While Disc four shows Arnold moving toward an ever more mainstream sound, Disc five has a number of religious songs that come off extremely well—largely due to the quality and sincerity of Arnold's singing. By this time, Arnold's voice had evolved into a wonderfully polished baritone, turning him into

almost a countrified Bing Crosby. The sound is excellent, and the notes are extremely informative, although there is relatively little about the recording sessions themselves. The booklet is filled with wonderful photos as well. —*Bruce Eder*

Early Hits of "The Tennessee Plowboy" / Apr. 11, 2000 / ASV ◆◆◆◆◆
An excellent entry in ASV's *Living Era* series, this brings together the 25 early hits of Eddy Arnold, when he earned his nickname of "the Tennessee Plowboy" honestly. This is Arnold before he went countrypolitan in the mid- to late '50s, with stripped-down instrumentation and him singing and yodeling his heart out. Indelibly stamped with Little Roy Wiggins' signature steel guitar, these tracks—cut between 1944 and 1949—reflect Eddy's breakthrough into the country & western scene, and show the five-year development of the music itself. If you've only heard Arnold's smoother, more pop-influenced work, this set will come as a real eye-opener. —*Cub Koda*

RCA Country Legends / Nov. 7, 2000 / Buddha ◆◆◆◆
There have been many Eddy Arnold collections released over the years, but Buddha's 2000 compilation *RCA Country Legends* stands as one of the best. This is especially true because CD-era collections of his RCA countrypolitan work have been confusing, either existing as budget-line discs or as jumbled overviews that didn't hit enough of the high points. Since this collection focuses on his RCA recordings, it doesn't have any of his early, rawer sides, and since it only runs 16 tracks, it does leave off many of his hits. However, it has most of the big songs—"I'll Hold You in My Heart (Till I Can Hold You in My Arms)," "Anytime," "Bouquet of Roses," "The Cattle Call," "What's He Doing in My World," "Make the World Go Away"—and its song selection is superb, offering a good overview of his commercial peak of the late '40s through the mid-'60s. Until a more thorough overview comes along, this stands as the most thoughtful overview of Arnold's RCA work. —*Stephen Thomas Erlewine*

Looking Back / Feb. 5, 2002 / RCA ◆◆◆
Looking Back is a collection of sentimental ballads recorded in the '60s selected by Arnold himself, who offers reminiscences and reflections on each song. It's not a hits collection, but rather an assemblage of personal favorites with heavily orchestrated versions that are clearly geared toward older fans. One point of interest, though, is that most of these songs have never been available on CD, which makes *Looking Back* an interesting collector's item. —*Jim Smith*

Jimmy Arnold

b. 1952, Fries, VA, d. Dec. 24, 1992
Fiddle, Guitar, Harmonica, Vocals / Traditional Bluegrass
Although Jimmy Arnold was never well-known—during his brief life, he recorded only a handful of albums—he remained one of the most acclaimed bluegrass musicians of the '70s and '80s. As a child, Arnold became interested in music after hearing his friends practicing next door. His first instrument was a guitar, but he soon learned how to play the banjo and by age 12 had founded a bluegrass band, the Twin County Partners, with his cousin Tommy playing mandolin and his friend Wes Golden on guitar. The group became quite popular in their area, which led to appearances on local TV shows and even a single for Stark Records. They disbanded in 1965, and Arnold began performing at music festivals all over the South.

After graduating from high-school, Arnold was invited by studio musician Joe Greene to play with him in Nashville. He next teamed up with Wes Golden to play with the Virginia Cut-Ups, with whom he cut an album for Latco Records. Subsequently, Arnold joined many bands, including Keith Whitley & the New Tradition, but was frequently fired from the groups due to his excessive drinking. He recorded an album of banjo music, *Strictly Arnold*, in 1974. In 1977, he released his second album, *Jimmy Arnold Guitar*, followed six years later by *Southern Soul*. None of his albums were commercially successful, and Arnold abandoned music in 1984. He opened a tattoo parlor in North Carolina, but he soon fell into drug abuse and used the parlor as a front for selling narcotics. In 1985, he was arrested and briefly served a jail sentence. Following his release from prison, he was the resident artist at Martin Community College for a short time, but he soon returned to performing music. In 1992, he became a member of the Pentecostal Church and went completely sober. However, his body was irreparably damaged—he died of heart failure on Christmas Eve in 1992. —*Sandra Brennan*

Strictly Arnold / 1974 / Rebel ◆◆◆

Rainbow Ride / 1982 / Rebel ◆◆◆◆

● **Southern Soul** / 1983 / Rebel ◆◆◆◆

Charline Arthur (Charlene Highsmith)

b. Sep. 2, 1929, Henrietta, TX, d. 1987
Vocals / Honky Tonk, Country Boogie
Charline Arthur didn't play by the rules. During the '50s, country music wasn't particularly receptive to rowdy, racy material sung by females, much less one who refused to submit to the orders of her record company or promoters. No matter how much pressure Arthur received, she didn't change her ways. With a raging temper, she was difficult to work with, particularly angering her producer, Chet Atkins. Nevertheless, her music was frequently impressive. In some ways, Arthur was a forerunner of rockabilly, with her bluesy, raw hillbilly music and her wild stage shows. She was the first female singer in country music to perform in pants and she used the extra freedom to prowl the stage. While her career was extremely brief—she recorded for RCA for three years—her music gained a cult following over the years, as proved by the appearance of Bear Family's *Welcome to the Club* compilation in 1986.

The daughter of a Pentecostal preacher, Charline Arthur (born Charline Highsmith, September 2, 1929, in Henrietta, TX) began singing in church while she was in school. At the age of seven, she earned enough money collecting empty bottles to buy a guitar for six dollars. Influenced by the hardcore honky tonk of Ernest Tubb, she wrote her first song, "I've Got the Boogie Blues," when she was 12. By the time she was a teenager, she was performing on a local Texas radio show. Arthur won a spot on a traveling medicine show in the mid-'40s, yet her parents refused to let her leave home. She countered by marrying Jack Arthur, who would later play bass on her records.

In the late '40s, she began singing in honky tonks and nightclubs across Texas, which eventually led to a single with Bullet Records, "I've Got the Boogie Blues"/"Is Love a Game." After she recorded the single, she and Jack moved to Kermit, TX, where she was hired by a radio station as a DJ. Soon, Charline assembled a band. Performing in local clubs and the radio, Arthur gained a fan base. In 1950, she recorded a single for the small label Imperial. During this time, Eddy Arnold and his manager, Colonel Tom Parker, heard Arthur perform. Impressed with what they heard, they directed Julian and Gene Aberbach, owners of the Hill and Range music publishing company, toward the singer. The pair signed her to a publishing deal and landed her a contract with RCA Records in 1953.

Arthur made her first record for RCA early in 1953, recording with session musicians who included Floyd Cramer and Chet Atkins. Her contract with RCA led to appearances with the Louisiana Hayride, the Big D Jamboree, and the Ozark Jubilee. During this time, she frequently performed on the same stage as Elvis Presley, whose mother was a big fan of Arthur. All of her performances were gaining her acclaim—in 1955, she was the runner-up to Kitty Wells in *Country & Western Jamboree* magazine's DJ poll. However, things weren't going smoothly for Arthur. Although she appeared on the "Prince Albert" portion of the *Grand Ole Opry*, her material was frequently rejected on the grounds it was too racy. At RCA, Chet Atkins followed Steve Sholes as her record producer, and the two musicians could not get along. Furthermore, she was having no success with any of her records. After her contract expired at the end of 1956, she left RCA for Colin, but she had a similar lack of success there. Shortly after her record label switch, she parted ways with her husband, Jack.

Charline formed a trio with her sisters, Betty Sue and Dottie, but the teaming was unsuccessful. By 1960, she was broke. Arthur moved to Salt Lake City, where she met Ray Pellum, a nightclub and record label owner who landed her a regular singing job in Chubbuck, ID. During this time, she also recorded for his Eldorado label. In 1965, Arthur headed out to California. Between 1965 and 1978, she recorded for three small labels—Rustic, Wytra, and Republic—with Alice M. Michaels as her manager. Suffering from debilitating arthritis, she went back to Idaho in 1979, and stayed there until her death in 1987. Charline Arthur lived long enough to see her RCA material reissued by Germany's Bear Family Records in 1986. —*Stephen Thomas Erlewine*

Welcome to the Club / Nov. 25, 1998 / Bear Family ✦✦✦✦

Charline Arthur was a country singer who was shaking things up in a proto-feminist way long before Patsy Cline and decades before today's crop of liberated country ladies ever entertained such notions. She wore pants on-stage, jumped off amplifiers, and cavorted in a manner that later made her assert that she was "shakin' that thing on-stage long before Elvis ever thought about it." Her ahead-of-her-time stance didn't bring forth any hits, but a wealth of fine music did emerge, all of it collected on this 32-track single-disc anthology. There wasn't anything subtle or subdued in Arthur's approach; she could honky tonk howl and carry on every bit as good as Rose Maddox and then some. Her brassy and sassy demeanor contained more than a generous dollop of blues phrasing, best-heard on flag-wavers like "I've Got the Boogie Blues," "Burn That Candle," "Just Look, Don't Touch, He's Mine," "Flash Your Diamonds," "Honey Bun," and the title track. But Charline could also wrap her pipes around slow weepers full of recrimination like "Too Long, Too Many Times," "I Was Wrong," "I'm Having a Party All by Myself," and "(I'm in Love) With Somebody Else's Used to Be" with just as much enthusiasm and finesse. Bringing together tracks cut for Bullet, Imperial, RCA Victor, and Coin between 1949-1957, this is the best overview that'll probably ever hit the stands on this one-of-a-kind artist. Excellent notes by Colin Escott make this package an overall delightful surprise for folks coming to her work for the first time. —*Cub Koda*

Clarence Ashley

b. Sep. 29, 1895, Bristol, TN, d. Jun. 2, 1967
Banjo, Vocals, Vocals / Traditional Bluegrass, Old-Timey, Country-Blues, Folksongs, Appalachian Folk

A medicine show performer in the 1910s and 1920s, Clarence (Tom) Ashley influenced the urban folk revival when his early recordings were included on the Folkways album *Anthology of American Folk Music* in 1952. Although he had retired from the medicine show circuit in 1943, he made a successful comeback in the early '60s when he recorded a pair of albums that introduced influential flatpicking guitarist Arthel "Doc" Watson. Ashley, who took his last name from the maternal grandfather who raised him, was inspired by the jokes and songs that he heard played by transients who boarded in his family home. His mother's two older sister taught him songs and instructed him on the banjo. Joining his first medicine show in 1913, Ashley traveled by horse and buggy through the southern Appalachian region, playing songs while "the doc" sold his elixirs. In 1914, he married Hettie Osborne and settled in Shouns, TN.

Although he supplemented his income as a musician by farming and working at a sawmill, Ashley continued to perform. By 1927, Ashley was performing with numerous string bands, including the Blue Ridge Mountain Entertainers. He recorded as a member of Byrd Moore & His Hot Shots and the Carolina Tar Heels. His solo debut came in 1929 when he recorded "The Cuckoo Bird" and "The House Carpenter" for Columbia. Signed to a solo contract by both Columbia (as Clarence Ashley) and Victor (as Tom Ashley), he recorded for both labels until 1933. Retiring from the medicine shows in 1943, Ashley bought a truck and, with his son J.D., hauled coal, furniture, and lumber. His performances were limited to working as a comedian with Charlie Monroe's Kentucky Partners and the Stanley Brothers.

While his songs were revived by string band instrumentalists in the 1950s, Ashley disappeared almost completely from the music scene. Attending the Union Grove Old Time Fiddlers Convention in 1960, he met folklorist Ralph Rinzler, who, with folk song collector Eugene Earle, set up a recording session at Ashley's daughter's home in Saltville, VA.

Ashley invited Watson to accompany him on guitar. The session marked the acoustic guitar debut for Watson, who had previously played electric guitar in rockabilly and country bands. Beginning in 1961, Ashley and Watson, joined by fiddler Fred Price, performed at northern folk festivals, coffeehouses, and clubs. Their concert at New York's *Town Hall* was recorded and released as their second album. Ashley recorded an additional album with fiddler Tex Isley. —*Craig Harris*

● **Greenback Dollar: 1929–1933** / 2001 / County ✦✦✦✦✦

Clarence Ashley became fairly well-known during the early '60s when his career was revitalized by the Folk Revival. But Ashley had an active career during the late '20s and early '30s, both as a solo performer and with a number of groups, including the Carolina Tar Heels. Now County has collected his important early work on *Greenback Dollar*. A spunky version of "Little Sadie" gets things started, a woeful tale of cold-blooded murder and swift justice. The steady rhythm of Ashley's banjo infuses the piece with an infectious energy. This is also true of the gambling classic "Coo Coo Bird" and the murder ballad "Naomi Wise." These pieces feature Ashley performing solo, his banjo perfectly underlining and highlighting his slightly nasal vocal. It is interesting to note that some of the lyrics of these ballads are starker than in contemporary versions. John Lewis kicks and chokes Naomi before he drowns her, and "Old John Hardy" wants to "shoot out another man's brains." There are several vivacious songs by the Blue Ridge Mountain Entertainers, including "Baby All Night Long," "Short Life of Trouble," and "Corrina Corrina." String band lovers will appreciate these songs. The Carolina Tar Heels prove equally entertaining with "Rude and Rambling Man" and "You Are a Little Too Small," and Ashley performs several pieces with harmonica player Gwen Foster (who was also a member of the Blue Ridge Mountain Entertainers). Foster's expressive harp playing on the title cut and "Drunk Man Blues" is a real treat. *Greenback Dollar* is a fine collection, representative of all facets of Ashley's early career. It will be warmly welcomed by fans of old-time music. —*Ronnie Lankford Jr.*

Leon Ashley

b. May 18, 1936, Covington, GA
Songwriter, Vocals / Country-Pop, Nashville Sound/Countrypolitan

Leon Ashley has a small place in country music history as the first artist to write, record, release, distribute, and publish his own material. That record, "Laura (What's He Got That I Ain't Got)," is also part of Ashley's legacy, becoming a country standard of the '60s and '70s, as it was recorded by a variety of artists, including Marty Robbins and Kenny Rogers. In fact, Ashley had more influence as a songwriter, not a performer. Nevertheless, he had a modestly successful performing career as a country-pop singer that lasted through the '60s and '70s.

Ashley began performing at an early age. When he was nine, he performed on a Covington, GA, radio station, and by the time he was 11, he had his own show. In 1960, he recorded his first single, "He'll Never Go." Released on Goldband, the record didn't gain much attention. He signed with Imperial the following year, releasing "Teen Age Angel" and "It's Alright Baby" to a similar lack of attention. In 1962, he returned to Goldband and recorded one more single, "Not Going Home." Dot Records released his "You Gave Me Reason to Live" in 1964. Leon Ashley was paired with Margie Singleton to record "How Can We Divide These Little Hearts" in 1966. The following year, the duo married; they continued working together for the rest of their marriage.

The year 1967 was significant for Ashley for another reason—he founded his own record label, Ashley. Surprisingly, Ashley's self-owned and operated record label was more successful for his career than any of the more-established labels he had previously recorded for. "Laura (What's He Got That I Ain't Got)," the third release on Ashley, rocketed to number one on the country charts, and was followed by two other lesser hits later that year (a duet with Margie called "Hangin' On" and "Anna, I'm Taking You Home"). Ashley had two more hits in 1968—the Top 15 "Mental Journey" and the duet "You'll Never Be Lonely Again"—and 1969 brought three more hits, "While Your Lover Sleeps," "Back to Birmingham," and "Ain't Gonna Worry." However, that was the end of his brief period of chart success. Ashley had one more minor hit single, "Ease Up" in 1972. For the remainder of the decade, he toured with Margie and their manager, Linda G. Denny, and the Country Music Spectacular. Although he no longer had hits, other performers regularly recorded Leon Ashley's songs, including many co-written with Margie. —*Stephen Thomas Erlewine*

Laura (What's He Got That I Ain't Got) / 1967 / Ashley ✦✦✦✦

Ode to Billie Joe / 1968 / Hilltop ✦✦✦

Mental Journey / 1968 / Ashley ✦✦✦

A New Brand of Country / 1969 / Ashley ✦✦✦

● **The Best of Leon Ashley** / 1970 / Ashley ✦✦✦✦

Ernest Ashworth

b. Dec. 15, 1928, Huntsville, AL
Guitar, Vocals / Traditional Country, Honky Tonk

Singer/songwriter and guitarist Ernie Ashworth listened to the *Grand Ole Opry* as a youth in his native Huntsville, AL, and he began writing songs even before taking up the guitar. By 1948 he was playing in a band called the Tunetwisters and appearing on Huntsville radio station WBHP. Making the move to Nashville the following year, Ashworth earned a living as an early member of that city's fabled community of songwriters and performed on radio stations WLAC and WSIX. He became a staff writer for the Acuff-Rose publishing house, composing songs for such performers as Little Jimmy Dickens and Carl Smith and even crossing over to the pop sphere when he placed "I Wish" with rock & roll crooner Paul Anka. In 1955, Wesley Rose greased the wheels for Ashworth's signing to the MGM label as Billy Worth, but the six singles he cut for the label went nowhere on the charts. In 1957, Ashworth returned to Alabama and took a job at Huntsville's Redstone Arsenal missile plant.

Meanwhile, Rose remained determined to further Ashworth's music career and managed to get him signed to Decca in 1960. Now billed as Ernest Ashworth, he hit the Top Five with his first Decca single, "Each Moment (Spent With You)." That same year he scored a Top Ten hit with "You Can't Pick a Rose in December." In 1962, he signed with the Acuff-Rose-owned Hickory label and again hit the Top Five with "Everybody but Me." A year later, he had his only number-one hit with the John D. Loudermilk-penned "Talk Back Trembling Lips." That song was tailor-made for Ashworth's vulnerable tenor voice, influenced by Anka and by Buddy Holly but with a more distinctively country reediness; it propelled him to Most Promising Male Artist awards from *Billboard* and *Cashbox* magazines and to the stage of the *Grand Ole Opry* in 1964. With further successes, such as the self-penned "I Love to Dance With Annie," Ashworth was a consistent hitmaker up to the release of 1970's "The Look of Goodbye." After four singles on the independent O'Brien label flopped, he retired to his farm in Lewisburg, TN, continuing to appear regularly on the *Opry* and occasionally touring the country. In 1989 he became the owner of Ardmore, TN, radio station WSLV, and his occasional recording releases in the 1990s found favor among tradition-minded European country listeners. —*James Manheim*

● **The Greatest Hits** / 1991 / Curb ✦✦✦✦
The Greatest Hits is a 12-track budget-priced collection that features some of Ernest Ashworth's biggest hits from the early '60s, including "Talk Back Trembling Lips," "Everybody But Me," "I Take the Chance," "A Week in the Country," "I Love to Dance With Annie," "Pushed in a Corner," "Because I Cared" and "The DJ Cried." Although this is a budget-priced disc, it contains the bulk of Ashworth's hits, making it a solid introduction to his career. —*Stephen Thomas Erlewine*

Asleep at the Wheel

f. 1970, Paw Paw, WV
Group / Neo-Traditionalist Country, Western Swing Revival
Since the early '70s, Asleep at the Wheel has been the most important force in keeping the sound of Western swing alive. In reviving the freewheeling, eclectic sensibility of Western swing godfather Bob Wills, the Wheel earned enthusiastic critical praise throughout their lengthy career; they not only preserved classic sounds that had all but disappeared from country music, but were also able to update the music, keeping it a living, breathing art form. Typically featuring 8-11 musicians, the group has gone through myriad personnel changes (at last count, over 80 members had passed through their ranks), but 6-feet-7-inch frontman Ray Benson has held it together for over three decades, keeping Asleep at the Wheel a viable recording and touring concern and maintaining their devotion to classic-style Western swing.

Singer/guitarist Benson was born Ray Benson Seifert and grew up listening to a variety of music in Philadelphia, especially jazz. He formed Asleep at the Wheel in Paw Paw, WV, in 1970, along with longtime friend Lucky Oceans (born Reuben Gosfield; steel guitar) and Leroy Preston (rhythm guitar). They soon added a female singer in Chris O'Connell, who was fresh out of high-school. Initially, the group played straight-ahead country in local venues, but quickly switched to Western swing when they discovered the music through Merle Haggard (specifically his Bob Wills tribute album) and eclectic country-rockers Commander Cody & His Lost Planet Airmen.

In fact, Commander Cody helped the group sign with his own manager, Joe Kerr, who convinced them to move to San Francisco in late 1971. They subsequently added keyboardist Floyd Domino, and secured a residency at Berkeley's Longbranch Saloon. Praise from Van Morrison in a *Rolling Stone* article helped them land a record deal with United Artists, which released their debut album, *Comin' Right at Ya*, in 1973. In 1974, Asleep at the Wheel relocated to the roots music haven of Austin, TX, and also switched labels to Epic. Their self-titled label debut appeared that same year, and their cover of Louis Jordan's "Choo Choo Ch'Boogie" became their first single to hit the country charts. Afterwards, they added fiddler Lisa Silver and trumpeter Bobby Womack, and hopped labels again to Capitol. *Texas Gold* (1975) was their breakthrough album, climbing into the country Top Ten and producing their only Top Ten hit on the country singles charts, "The Letter That Johnny Walker Read." That year they performed on the first non-pilot episode of *Austin City Limits*, and although they continued to experience personnel shifts, they turned out a string of excellent albums over the rest of the decade: *Wheelin' and Dealin'* (1976), *The Wheel* (1977), and *Collision Course* (1978), the latter of which featured their first Grammy winner in the instrumental cover of Count Basie's "One O'Clock Jump."

Asleep at the Wheel moved to MCA for 1980's *Framed*, but all was not well: founding member Lucky Oceans left the group that year, and Chris O'Connell took a leave of absence to start a family not long after. Plus, the group was heavily in debt, forcing them to work on commercials and movie soundtracks. The financial problems conspired to keep them off record for the next few years, and when they returned on Dot/MCA with a self-titled album in 1985, they were virtually ignored. Following the small-label release *Pasture Prime* later that year, Benson did some moonlighting as a producer, and soon managed to get a second shot with Epic. By now, O'Connell had returned, and the new lineup featured fiddler Larry Franklin, steel guitarist John Ely, pianist/accordionist Tim Alexander, saxophonist Mike Francis, bassist Jon Mitchell, and drummer David Sanger. This unit recorded the major comeback effort, *10*, in 1987, which brought them back to the Top 20 of the country album and singles charts (the latter via "House of Blue Lights") for the first time in over a decade. Additionally, the album's "String of Pars" won them their second Grammy for Best Country Instrumental, and featured contributions from fiddle legend and onetime Texas Playboy Johnny Gimble. The 1988 follow-up, *Western Standard Time*, continued their momentum, winning another Best Country Instrumental Grammy for "Sugarfoot Rag."

In 1990, Asleep at the Wheel moved to Arista and recorded *Keepin' Me Up Nights*, which flopped in comparison to its two predecessors. Major personnel turnover ensued, with O'Connell leaving a second time, and Benson regrouped with Francis, Sanger, fiddler Ricky Turpin, bassist David Miller, and steel guitarist/dobroist Cyndi Cashdollar. They issued two albums on Liberty/Capitol, the acclaimed, guest-laden *A Tribute to the Music of Bob Wills & the Texas Playboys* (1993; featuring the Grammy-winning instrumental

"Red Wing") and *The Wheel Keeps on Rollin'* (1995). Their next major studio project, *Ride With Bob*, was released by DreamWorks in 1999 and featured fiddler Jason Roberts (a young relative of Johnny Gimble) and pianist/second fiddler Chris Booher. It was the group's second explicit tribute to Bob Wills, and it attracted even more positive attention than the first, winning multiple Grammys and drawing non-country collaborators like the Manhattan Transfer and Squirrel Nut Zippers. —*Steve Huey*

Comin' Right at Ya / 1973 / EMI ✦✦✦✦✦
Asleep at the Wheel did not start the Western swing revival of the '70s—Merle Haggard kicked it into gear with his tremendous 1970 album *A Tribute to the Best Damn Fiddle Player in the World*—but Asleep stuck to it so long that the band came to personify it. Though they occasionally stretched out, they never really strayed from the sound they unveiled on their 1973 debut, *Comin' Right at Ya*. The 12-song platter kicks off with a faithful but loose version of Bob Wills' "Take Me Back to Tulsa," setting the tone for not just the record, but the group's music. Asleep at the Wheel's members were disciples of Wills and the Texas Playboys, and they not only patterned their sound after them, but followed the Playboys' restless spirit in how they used Western swing as a foundation for exploring other sounds and styles. Where Wills' group often spun into jazz and blues, Asleep branched out into other kinds of country, delving into pure Texas honky tonk, country boogie, and heartache ballads, touching on Hank Williams, Hank Thompson, Hank Snow, Ernest Tubb, Ray Price, Patsy Cline, and Loretta Lynn. There's also a dash of post-hippie humor, rearing its head clearly on "Hillbilly Nut," and just the slightest touch of knowingly reverent reserve, as if the group were trying out an uncle's clothes to see if they fit. This little hint of artifice—this little echo of Commander Cody—is the only area where the record stumbles, and it's a slight one, the kind of thing that should be expected on a debut, because the group is musically powerful and nimble, re-creating the sound of pure country at a time when it often wasn't heard. Asleep at the Wheel would better this record, but that the band had such a sure grasp on its musical versatility so early in its career is impressive, and the general good spirits *Comin' Right at Ya* stirs up are infectious. Years later, after many fine records, this still stands as one of their best. —*Stephen Thomas Erlewine*

Asleep at the Wheel / 1974 / Epic ✦✦✦
Texas guitarist and singer Ray Benson started this band in the early '70s as a "longhair" tribute to Bob Wills, and they've been swinging ever since. This is their first Epic album. —*Mark A. Humphrey*

Texas Gold / 1975 / Capitol ✦✦✦✦✦
Not long after its first album, Asleep at the Wheel relocated to Austin, TX, whose freewheeling, wide-ranging music scene fit the band's sensibility perfectly. One record for Epic followed before they signed with Capitol, releasing *Texas Gold* in 1975 and setting their career into high gear in the process. *Texas Gold* wound up in the country Top Ten, sending "The Letter That Johnny Walker Read" there as well, and its success was the result of both good timing and a better band. In 1975, Texas music started to seep into the mainstream, thanks to Willie Nelson's ascendency to superstardom, thereby opening doors for bands that trafficked in Western swing and neo-traditionalist country, like Asleep at the Wheel. Still, they never would have gotten anywhere if they didn't have the goods to back it up, and this proves that their interaction had become more natural and organic, sounding closer to their idols than they did on their debut. That's not to say that they were entirely traditionalist, because the members of Asleep at the Wheel also had traces of their peers in their sound. Certainly, the Commander Cody influence is still felt—tamed down from the debut, but still apparent in the humor and freewheeling attitude—but there are also echoes of Doug Sahm and Willie Nelson in these laid-back groups. If Bob Wills & His Texas Playboys remain the towering influence here—"Fat Boy Rag" and "Trouble in Mind" are both covered—Asleep manages to capture more of their spirit than before, particularly because the group's disparate influences are synthesized, not trotted through one at a time. On top of that, the song selection is first-rate, turning *Texas Gold* into the best record Asleep at the Wheel had made to date. Arguably, it's the best, most consistent album they ever did. —*Stephen Thomas Erlewine*

Wheelin' and Dealin' / 1976 / Capitol ✦✦✦
Combining old-fashioned swing, Western swing, country ballads, Cajun and good ol' rock & roll, Asleep at the Wheel turns a wonderful performance on *Wheelin' and Dealin'*. Highlights include "Route 66," done in fine rockabilly style, "Cajun Stripper," full of fiddles and accordions, "The Trouble with Lovin' Today," a real country tearjerker, and the bawdy "They Raided the Joint." With *Wheelin' and Dealin'*, Asleep at the Wheel covers all of the bases and wins the ballgame to boot! —*James Chrispell*

The Wheel / 1977 / Capitol ✦✦✦✦
The Wheel finds Asleep at the Wheel consistently making music full of fun, along with fine musicianship and a sense of purpose. Even though anyone can simply enjoy the great batch of tunes on this recording, a more discerning listener can see that there is a higher cause, that being the preservation of Western swing and all the genres present in that form. So whether the cuts are jazz oriented ("The Wheel"), gospel ("Somebody Stole His Body"), or honky tonk ("I Can't Handle It Now"), the band is up to the task. Particularly noteworthy are the musical compositions of rhythm guitarist Leroy Preston and leader Ray Benson's distinctively raspy vocal style. What sets this record above other bands that might want to keep the spirit of Western swing alive is a sense of integrity beneath the surface. However, that sense of purpose is never so heavy-handed that a feeling of festivity is too far away. The sax, fiddle, or accordion solos may be technically sophisticated, but try not dancing to this stuff or tapping your toes and see how far you get. In other words, Asleep at the Wheel has made a fine record that will appeal to both the average fan and serious students of the Western swing tradition. —*Michael Ofjord*

Collision Course / 1978 / Capitol ✦✦✦

Served Live / 1979 / Capitol ✦✦

Framed / 1980 / MCA ✦✦

Asleep at the Wheel / 1985 / MCA ✦✦✦✦✦

Benson by now is revealing a romantic baritone as well as his usual sublime swing. Guest appearances come from Bonnie Raitt and Willie Nelson. *—Michael McCall*

Pasture Prime / 1985 / Stony Plain ✦✦✦✦

Part of Stony Plain's *Classics* series, this is actually a re-release of an album that was originally released in 1984 on vinyl in Canada and England. *Pasture Prime* was a comeback of sorts for the band; they had not recorded in five years, and—had it not been for the generosity of one Willie Nelson—this one might not have happened either. Nelson, a big fan of the band, graciously offered his Briarcliff, TX, studio for the recording of several of the songs here. *Pasture Prime* sports just two originals: founder Ray Benson's "Shorty" and "Liar's Moon." There are three Bob Wills tunes: "Across the Alley From the Alamo," the instrumental "Big Beaver," and the traditional "Deep Water." Fiddler Johnny Gimble is on board for nearly all cuts, and Junior Brown makes one of his first recording appearances, playing lap steel guitar on "Deep Water" and "That's Your Red Wagon." The entire Roomful of Blues horn section brings an extra helping of Kansas City-style swing to Big Joe Turner's "Switchin' in the Kitchen," and female vocalist Chris O'Connell is in top form throughout. Not without a laugh, Willie Nelson contributes a hilarious song he wrote as a jab at music industry executives and country "purists" called "Write Your Own Song." As a duet between Nelson and Benson, it neatly segues into the traditional "Cotton Eyed Joe," which features some very nice piano playing at the hands of Floyd Domino. This CD of classic Western swing closes with a friendly, informative, 17-minute interview with Benson, conducted by Holger Petersen just prior to the re-release. *—Ann Wickstrom*

10 / 1987 / Epic ✦✦✦

Western Standard Time / 1988 / Epic ✦✦✦✦✦

Keepin' Me Up Nights / 1990 / Arista ✦✦✦

● **Greatest Hits: Live & Kickin'** / Aug. 1991 / Arista ✦✦✦✦✦

Recorded at an Austin roadhouse, *Greatest Hits: Live & Kickin'* showcases Asleep at the Wheel running through their best-known material in a kinetic live setting. It's a great introduction to the band—they are never better than they are in concert, and the selection brings out the best in the musicians. *—Stephen Thomas Erlewine*

The Best of Asleep at the Wheel / 1992 / CEMA Special Markets ✦✦✦✦✦

The Best of Asleep at the Wheel is a concise introduction to the group's early years, including their first hit "Choo Choo Ch'Boogie," as well as favorites like "The Letter That Johnny Walker Read" and "Bump Bounce Boogie" which launched the band into the country mainstream during the mid-'70s and still sound fresh today. *—Jason Ankeny*

The Swinging Best of Asleep at the Wheel / Oct. 27, 1992 / Epic ✦✦✦✦

The Swingin' Best collects the hits from Asleep at the Wheel's two tenures on the Epic label; in addition to their first hit, 1974's "Choo Choo Ch'Boogie," the album features "House of Blue Lights," "Way Down Texas Way" and "Blowin' Like a Bandit." *—Jason Ankeny*

A Tribute to the Music of Bob Wills & the Texas Playboys / Oct. 25, 1993 / Liberty ✦✦✦✦✦

Benson and the Wheel invite a bus full of guests to pay homage to the King of Western Swing and do so with joyful, rollicking fun. Garth Brooks, Vince Gill, George Strait, Dolly Parton, Marty Stuart and Suzy Bogguss are among those enjoying themselves on this exemplary album. *—Michael McCall*

The Wheel Keeps on Rollin' / 1995 / Capitol ✦✦✦

As the title suggests, *The Wheel Keeps on Rollin'* doesn't offer anything new from Asleep at the Wheel, but that's not a bad thing at all. For over 20 years, the group has been the leading Western swing group in the United States, bringing the music to several new generations of fans. *The Wheel Keeps On Rollin'* is another first-rate collection of music. It might not have the conceptual power of their previous *Tribute to the Music of Bob Wills & the Texas Playboys*, nor is it as raw their earliest recordings, but it is an album that will satisfy their dedicated fans. *—Stephen Thomas Erlewine*

Back to the Future Now—Live at Arizona Charlie's / May 20, 1997 / Sony ✦✦✦

"Why another live record?" asks bandleader Ray Benson in his liner notes to Asleep at the Wheel's fourth concert disc, and he has two answers, both valid. First, with hundreds of gigs per year, Asleep at the Wheel is essentially a live band, and live records reflect that. Second, Benson has cooked up a reunion performance in which original bandmembers Lucky Oceans and Leroy Preston sit in with the current lineup, along with departed veterans Chris O'Connell, Floyd Domino, Tony Garnier, and Tim Alexander, as well as guest stars Tracy Byrd, Wade Hayes, the McGuire Sisters, and Johnny Lee Carpenter. Of course, the defining element in the group's sound remains Benson's big baritone, which he puts at the service of many of the band's hits, including "The Letter That Johnny Walker Read," "House of Blue Lights," "Miles and Miles of Texas," "Boogie Back to Texas," and "Hot Rod Lincoln." The recordings are taken from a December 1996 club date, which gives the show an unusual intimacy. Given that warmth and the survey the album provides of the band's career, *Back to the Future Now* makes a good primer of Asleep at the Wheel, even if the question Benson should have asked is, "Why not another live record?," to which the answer would be, "because it's redundant." *—William Ruhlmann*

Ride With Bob / Aug. 10, 1999 / DreamWorks ✦✦✦✦

Asleep at the Wheel devoted its entire career to Western swing, which is commonly known as the music Bob Wills created. They became the standard bearers for the genre, making sure that it was still an integral part of the country music mainstream. Since their entire career feels like a living monument to Wills, it almost seems unnecessary for them to record tributes to the "King of Western Swing"—that is, until you hear the records. *Ride With Bob*, their sequel to the award-winning *Tribute to the Music of Bob Wills*, has more guest appearances than its predecessor, but it's every bit as enjoyable. The fact of the matter is, Asleep at the Wheel played this music better than anybody else at the close of the century, and these are some of the greatest songs in popular music—"New San Antonio Rose," "Roly Poly," "Cherokee Maiden," "Right or Wrong," "Faded Love," "Take Me Back to Tulsa," and "Stay All Night" always sound fresh, and the band draws out excellent performances from Dwight Yoakam, the Dixie Chicks, Ray Benson, Reba McEntire, Lyle Lovett and Shawn Colvin, Clay Walker, and Mark Chesnutt, respectively, on these songs. It's a testament to both the group and the songs that nobody here—not the Squirrel Nut Zippers or Manhattan Transfer—sounds out of place. This is warm, generous, rich music that's endlessly listenable, much like Wills himself. And the Clint Black-sung cover of Waylon Jennings' tribute "Bob Wills Is Still the King" is a nice touch. *—Stephen Thomas Erlewine*

● **Comin' Right at Ya/Texas Gold** / Sep. 12, 2000 / Koch ✦✦✦✦✦

In 2000, Koch reissued Asleep at the Wheel's 1973 debut, *Comin' Right at Ya*, and 1975's *Texas Gold*, the band's third album, as a CD two-fer. While the package misses Asleep's 1974 album for Epic (different label, different rights; the two here are from EMI and Capitol, respectively), these two albums nevertheless make good companion pieces, since the first record shows a band with enormous potential and the second finds a band reaching its potential. This is the sound of a band finding its voice and riding with it, and both albums are among the very best records the group ever did, which makes this an essential—perhaps *the* essential—Asleep at the Wheel release. *—Stephen Thomas Erlewine*

23 Country Classics / Feb. 6, 2001 / EMI ✦✦✦✦

Fans of country music, especially fans of Western swing, will want to add this collection album to the spots they save for the music they play the most. Asleep at the Wheel recorded the album *23 Country Classics* in early 2001. This offering is a celebration of Texas dancehall style. You'll find several old favorites here, many flavored with jazz, honky tonk, rock, boogie, and R&B—all coated with the energetic touch that this Grammy-winning group adds to its work. Some of the outstanding tracks on *23 Country Classics* are "Bump Bounce Boogie," "Lay Down Sally," "Cherokee Boogie," "She Came to Dance," and "Still Water Runs the Deepest." It should be noted that a lot of the numbers have been spiced up into dance versions. *—Charlotte Dillon*

20th Century Masters—The Millennium Collection: The Best of Asleep at the Wheel / Jun. 19, 2001 / MCA ✦✦

Quite capable of introducing listeners to some of Asleep at the Wheel's better moments, *20th Century Masters* unfortunately overlooks many of the band's best moments. For instance, "Choo Choo Ch'Boogie" is nowhere to be found, as well as "Miles and Miles of Texas," "House of Blue Lights," "Cherokee Boogie," and a number of other songs that arguably deserve a slot on a proper best-of. This is, of course, because *20th Century Masters* culls its picks merely from Asleep at the Wheel's early- to mid-'80s recordings for MCA, most of the songs featured here coming from the group's self-titled 1985 album and 1980's *Framed*. This approach ignores far too much of the band's work, and even if the material featured here is enjoyable and of high quality, it's an insular portrait of Asleep at the Wheel. It's best to avoid this best-of in favor of the group's many other collections, such as *The Swinging Best of Asleep at the Wheel* or the excellent live album, *Greatest Hits: Live & Kickin'*. *—Jason Birchmeier*

20 Greatest Hits / Apr. 1, 2003 / Capitol ✦✦✦✦

While Ray Benson's indefatigable Western swing revival outfit Asleep at the Wheel has recorded for a handful of labels over the course of a career that's spanned four decades (so far), they've cut enough stuff for Capitol and other labels currently under their ownership (United Artists and Liberty) that this compilation, if not definitive, certainly provides a healthy and accurate overview of their career. (Capitol also licensed one track each from the band's Epic and Arista back catalogs for good measure.) Though Asleep at the Wheel has dipped its toes ever so slightly into the country mainstream over the years, Benson and his crew have always stayed true to their love for the vintage sounds of hillbilly boogie, Western swing, and twang-infused blues, and these 20 cuts prove that despite dozens of lineup changes, this group's musical vision has remained consistently strong through the decades, and that both then and now they knew how to keep the sainted spirit of Bob Wills alive and dancing. While the sheer bulk of Asleep at the Wheel's back catalog would suggest that a box set is in order for this band, *20 Greatest Hits* shows they started out with the right idea and have yet to lose it, and if it isn't the ideal AATW collection, it's a better-than-average cross section of their music and a pretty good introduction for beginners. *—Mark Deming*

Bob Atcher

b. 1914, Hardin County, KY, **d.** Oct. 31, 1993

Vocals / Old-Timey, Cowboy, Country-Folk

Bob Atcher was one of the most popular country music entertainers of the post-World War II era, enjoying a 21-year career at OKeh and Columbia Records, as well as major radio stardom on WLS' National Barn Dance out of Chicago. His range of material ran from traditional country and comic novelty songs to folk.

James Robert Owen Atcher was born and raised in Hardin County, KY, on property that was later appropriated for Fort Knox. The family, led by his father, a champion fiddle player, was musical, and he learned both the violin and the guitar. By the early '30s, he'd made his debut on radio on WHAS out of Louisville, and over the next few years appeared on several small stations across the South and Midwest. In 1939, Atcher got his first big break when he got a regular spot on WGBM in Chicago, a daily program that was picked up nationally by the CBS radio network. He quickly built a major national following with his mix of country and novelty songs. He joined the American Record Company that same year, just in time for the label to be purchased by CBS (which rechristened it Columbia Records), and passed through the label's OKeh imprint before going on to Columbia.

During the years 1939-1942, many of Atcher's singles were credited to duets with Bonnie Blue Eyes (aka Loretta Applegate)—their records together included the comical

"Answer to You Are My Sunshine" and "Pins and Needles (In My Heart)." Atcher was also joined in the studio on occasion by his younger brother, Randy Atcher—their singles together included "Papa's Going Crazy, Mama's Going Mad." Atcher served in the army during the later part of World War II and resumed his career in 1946. He charted around that time with "Why Don't You Haul Off and Love Me" and "I Must Have Been Wrong."

Atcher made his biggest career move in 1948, when he joined the *National Barn Dance* on Chicago's WLS. At that time, the *National Barn Dance* was still one of the two biggest showcases for country music, and he became one of the show's most popular stars over the next ten years. He also scored big on the charts again with "I'm Thinking Tonight of My Blue Eyes," which became a classic piece of country comedy. His recording career proceeded apace, with some notable achievements. In 1948, Atcher cut two of the earliest LPs ever released by Columbia, a pair of ten-inch discs devoted to cowboy songs and folk music (*Early American Folk Songs*, which contained one of the earliest extant commercial recordings of "Devilish Mary," a 19th century folk song that would become part of the repertoire of the members of the Grateful Dead). Atcher left Columbia in 1950 for Capitol Records, and later recorded for Kapp Records. He remained a star on the *National Barn Dance* into the 1960s, and later rejoined Columbia Records. In the interim, the label had reissued the two early LPs of folk music and cowboy songs on its budget-priced Harmony line, and during his second stint at Columbia, Atcher re-recorded his classic songs in stereo.

Like Gene Autry before him, Bob Atcher invested his earnings far outside the recording industry, and by the 1960s he owned various businesses and had a hand in the banking industry as well, as a board member of the Schaumberg State Bank in Schaumberg, IL. He also served 20 years as the mayor of Schaumberg, from 1959 until 1979. *—Bruce Eder*

Songs of the Saddle / 1953 / Harmony ♦♦♦

Early American Folk Songs / 1955 / Harmony ♦♦♦

• **The Dean of Cowboy Singers** / 1964 / Columbia ♦♦♦♦

Chet Atkins

b. Jun. 20, 1924, Luttrell, TN, **d.** Jun. 30, 2001, Nashville, TN

Guitar, Guitar (Electric), Vocals, Producer, Fiddle, Arranger / Traditional Country, Country-Pop, Nashville Sound/Countrypolitan, Instrumental Country, Country Boogie

Without Chet Atkins, country music may never have crossed over into the pop charts in the '50s and '60s. Although he recorded hundreds of solo records, Atkins' largest influence came as a session musician and a record producer. During the '50s and '60s, he helped create the Nashville sound, a style of country music that owed nearly as much to pop as it did to honky tonks. And as a guitarist, he was without parallel. Atkins' style grew out of his admiration for Merle Travis, expanding Travis' signature syncopated thumb and fingers roll into new territory. Interestingly, Atkins didn't begin his musical career by playing guitar. On the recommendation of his older brother, Lowell, he began playing the fiddle at a child. However, Chet was still attracted to the guitar, and at the age of nine he traded a pistol for a guitar. Atkins learned his instrument rapidly, becoming an accomplished player by the time he left high-school in 1941. Using a variety of contacts, he wound up performing on the Bill Carlisle Show on WNOX in Knoxville, TN, as well as becoming part of the Dixie Swingers. Atkins worked with Homer & Jethro while he was at the radio station. After three years, he moved to a radio station in Cincinnati.

Supporting Red Foley, Atkins made his first appearance at the *Grand Ole Opry* in 1946. That same year, he made his first records, recording for Bullet. Atkins also began making regular performances on the WRVA radio station in Richmond, VA, but he was repeatedly fired because his musical arrangements differed from the expectations of the station's executives. He eventually moved to Springfield, MO, working for the KWTO station. A tape of one of Atkins' performances was sent to RCA Victor's office in Chicago. Eventually, it worked its way to Steve Sholes, the head of country music at RCA. Sholes had heard Atkins previously, and had been trying to find him for several years. By the time Sholes heard the tape, Atkins had moved to Denver, and was playing with Shorty Thompson & His Rangers. Upon receiving the call from RCA, he moved to Nashville to record. Once he arrived in Nashville, Atkins recorded eight tracks for the label, five of which featured the guitarist singing. Impressed by his playing, Sholes made Atkins the studio guitarist for all of the RCA studio's Nashville sessions in 1949. The following year, Mother Maybelle and the Carter Sisters hired him as a regular on the *Grand Ole Opry*, making his place in Nashville's musical community secure. While he worked for RCA, he played on many hit records and helped fashion the Nashville sound. RCA appreciated his work and made him a consultant to the company's Nashville division in 1953. That year, the label began to issue a number of instrumental albums that showcased Atkins' considerable talents. Two years later, he scored his first hit with a version of "Mr. Sandman"; it was followed by "Silver Bell," a duet with Hank Snow. By the late '50s, Atkins was known throughout the music industry as a first-rate player. Not only did his records sell well, he designed guitars for Gibson and Gretsch; the popularity of these models continues to the present day.

Sholes left for New York in 1957 to act as head of pop A&R, leaving Atkins as the manager of RCA's Nashville division. However, the guitarist didn't abandon performing, and throughout the early '60s his star continued to rise. He played the Newport Jazz Festival in 1960; in 1961, he performed at the White House. Atkins had his first Top Five hit in 1965 with a reworking of Boots Randolph's "Yakety Sax," retitled "Yakety Axe"; in addition to being a sizable country hit, the song crossed over to the pop charts. Atkins' role behind the scenes was thriving as well. He produced hits for the majority of RCA's Nashville acts, including Elvis Presley and Eddy Arnold, and discovered a wealth of talent, including Don Gibson, Waylon Jennings, Floyd Cramer, Charley Pride, Bobby Bare, and Connie Smith. Because of his consistent track record, Atkins was promoted to vice president of RCA's country division when Sholes died in 1968.

The following year, Atkins had his last major hit single, "Country Gentleman." In the late '60s and early '70s, several minor hits followed, but only one song, "Prissy" (1968), made it into the Top 40. Instead, the guitarist's major musical contribution in the early part of the '70s was with Homer & Jethro. Under the name the Nashville String Band, the trio released five albums between 1970 and 1972. Following Homer's death, Atkins continued to work with Jethro.

Atkins continued to record for RCA throughout the '70s, although he was creatively stifled by the label by the end of the decade. The guitarist wanted to record a jazz album, but he was met with resistance by the label. In 1982, he left the label and signed with Columbia, releasing his first album for the label, *Work It Out With Chet Atkins*, in 1983. During his time at Columbia, Atkins departed from his traditional country roots, demonstrating that he was a bold and tasteful jazz guitarist as well. He did return to country on occasion, particularly on duet albums with Mark Knopfler and Jerry Reed, but by and large, Atkins' Columbia records demonstrated a more adventurous guitarist than was previously captured on his RCA albums.

Sadly, Atkins was diagnosed with cancer, and in 1997 doctors removed a tumor from his brain. In his last months, the cancer had made Atkins inactive, and he finally lost the battle on June 30, 2001, at his home in Nashville. Throughout his career, Chet Atkins earned numerous awards, including 11 Grammy awards and nine CMA Instrumentalist of the Year honors, as well as a Lifetime Achievement Award from NARAS. Although his award list is impressive, it only begins to convey his contribution to country music. *—Stephen Thomas Erlewine*

A Session with Chet Atkins / 1954 / RCA ♦♦♦♦

With a roomful of crack Nashville session men, Chet Atkins' first 12-inch album is one joyful, yet sophisticated and controlled compilation of mostly standard pop and jazz tunes all decked out country-style. Some tunes, like "South," "Indiana" and "Caravan," would turn up again and again throughout Chet's career as reference points for jamming. While occasionally doubling back to the country on "Corrine, Corrina," Chet explores the possibilities of tunes like "The Birth of the Blues," "Old Man River" and "Honeysuckle Rose" within a country framework—and with his fingerpicking technique and innate musicality, he makes everything fit. The major soloists are Dale Potter, who takes his country fiddle part of the way into jazz territory, Bud Isaacs' tasty period steel guitar, and John Gordy's straight-ahead piano. On "Caravan," Gordy also breaks a bit of ground, offering what the liner credits as the first use of a celeste on a country record. *—Richard Ginell*

Chet Atkins in Three Dimensions / 1955 / Longhorn ♦♦♦♦

In his second 12-inch album, the young master guitarist tries to transcend categories and stereotypes, dividing the album into three distinct sections. The first deals with sometimes surprising treatments of four folk tunes; "Arkansaw Traveler" is a particularly amazing *tour de force* that takes us to other strange places before reaching the tune. Part two is devoted to pop songs, again in varied treatments. His "Little Rock Getaway" at first bears a partial resemblance to the recording by Atkins' early influence Les Paul; "Blues in the Night" combines a jazz sensibility with various classic country licks; and Atkins gets away with a perfectly respectful treatment of "Tip Toe Through the Tulips." Then Atkins takes a big left turn into classical music, playing Bach quite respectably (if colorlessly) on classical guitar. He switches back to electric for Provost's "Intermezzo," Kreisler's "Schon Rosmarin," and Chopin's "Minute Waltz," using discreet tape echo effects and brandishing the country influence now and then. A all-encompassing record like this was the envy of every open-minded guitarslinger of the time. *—Richard Ginell*

Finger Style Guitar / 1956 / RCA ♦♦♦♦

As a consummate display of Atkins' refined fingerpicking style, this album sets its own lofty standards. A nearly invisible rhythm section underpins Atkins' one-man guitar ensemble with very subtle rhythm support on side one, where each number shines like a finished gem. To cite two examples, "Swedish Rhapsody" has dignity and subtle swing—the perfect expression of a country gentleman—and the note selection on "Liza" is astonishingly right every time. On side two, Atkins goes it alone, often leaning toward short, sometimes hokey classical pieces, the exception being "Unchained Melody," which has a simply stated first chorus followed by an echo-delayed overdubbed second chorus. In general, the tunes with rhythm on side one are more ingratiating than the unaccompanied pieces on side two, yet they all display a relaxed, confident musicality at all times. *—Richard Ginell*

Stringin' Along With Chet Atkins / 1956 / RCA ♦♦♦

In 1953, RCA Victor packaged some of Chet Atkins' recordings of the early '50s into the ten-inch LP *Stringin' Along With Chet Atkins*. Three years later, the label added some more tracks to fill out the album for the 12-inch format. The 1956 12-track version of *Stringin' Along* combines the master guitarist's versions of some Tin Pan Alley ("Oh! By Jingo," "Hello Ma Baby"), show music ("Indian Love Call"), and blues ("Memphis Blues," "St. Louis Blues") of the early part of the century with some Atkins originals ("Galloping on the Guitar," "Blue Gypsy") and the popular "Third Man Theme" from the 1949 movie. Atkins' playing is as distinctive as ever, and if the sources of the material are various, his style holds it together into a coherent collection. The 1967 reissue is in electronically enhanced (i.e., "phony") stereo. *—William Ruhlmann*

Chet Atkins at Home / 1957 / RCA ♦♦♦♦

The photo of Chet Atkins thoughtfully leaning on his guitar, surrounded by now-coveted vintage recording equipment in his knotty pine-paneled home recording studio, immediately conjures cozy images of the 1950s. Yet the record still sounds timeless for its musical beauty and taste, as well as a catholic repertoire that now falls completely outside the boundaries of Nashville country. There is some elegantly played Ellington ("Sophisticated Lady"), two Lecuona tunes ("Say Si Si," "Jungle Drums"), novelties like "Nagasaki," and a clever contrapuntal teaming of two tunes ("Yankee Doodle Dixie") where Atkins ends the Civil War by uniting Northern sophistication and Southern down-home feeling. As usual, he employs harmonics, the tremolo bar, electronic echo, and reverb effects with discretion and restraint. In addition, the record allegedly features an early electronic accompanying instrument that Atkins called the "Invisible Bass Man," which is almost as inaudible as it is invisible. *—Richard Ginell*

Hi Fi in Focus / 1957 / RCA ✦✦✦✦

Hi-Fi was one of the biggest buzz words of the 1950s before stereo supplanted it (the term made a comeback in the mid-'80s when the VCR reached a refined stage), and Chet Atkins was the recipient of its name value on this LP. There is nothing more inherently "hi-fi" in the sound of this album than its immediate companions in Atkins' catalog; suffice is it to say that this is another lovingly played collection of a dozen tunes from what is now considered the great guitarist's most prized period on recordings. This time, the unaccompanied pieces are mixed in with those containing a smartly recessed rhythm section, and the song selection ranges widely between pop standards, a couple of crypto-Latin arrangements ("Anna" is a particularly lovely display of strumming and staccato playing), and a Bach encore. "Portuguese Washerwoman" gets the most varied rhythmic treatment, from sophisticated jazz to two-beat country fingerpicking. Almost every line of the liner notes dwell on a now-forgotten photo contest for the abstract, high-tech art on the album cover, whereas it is the music that will be more remembered. *—Richard Ginell*

Hum & Strum Along With Chet Atkins / 1959 / RCA ✦✦

This listener participation album is more pertinent as a rival label's response to Mitch Miller's wildly popular *Sing Along With Mitch* series than as a significant addition to Chet Atkins' catalog. With a Nashville chorus singing a series of country and public domain popular songs straight and square, Atkins backs the voices with standard countrified fingerpicking, filling the spaces with tasteful obbligatos. It's an innocuous period piece through and through, notable only for some witty and elegant Atkins fills that somehow get by the concept. The original edition was an elaborate fold-out, do-it-yourself singing and playing kit; by 1961, a slimmed-down ordinary album cover would have to suffice. *—Richard Ginell*

Chet Atkins in Hollywood / 1959 / RCA ✦✦✦✦✦

If the cover of *At Home* evokes the 1950s, the music on *In Hollywood* IS the 1950s: a warm, cozy, sophisticated album of mood music in the best sense. Yet this is not an album of film music (though a handful of film themes turn up). Rather, it is exactly what the title indicates: Chet Atkins recording an album in a Hollywood studio, as opposed to the familiar haunts of Nashville. Here, he places his often affectingly lovely guitar licks in front of full, lush, sometimes inspired string arrangements by Dennis Farnon. Sometimes, Atkins appears all by himself, caressing "Estrellita" before the strings kick in, and his fingerpicking technique appears on a piquant treatment of "Armen's Theme" (originally a pre-Chipmunks hit for Ross Bagdasarian, aka David Seville). Farnon is particularly good when he hooks onto a lush string motif and repeats it seductively on the "Theme From Picnic" or follows Atkins' guitar in a broad, surpassingly lovely treatment of Fats Waller's "Jitterbug Waltz"—the two most gorgeous tracks on the record. For some, this record might fall under the category of guilty pleasures, but a pleasure it is, one of the great make-out records of its time. Mobile Fidelity re-circulated it all too briefly in the 1990s as part of a two-CD set. *—Richard Ginell*

The Other Chet Atkins / 1960 / RCA ✦✦✦

The Other Chet Atkins is something of an unusual entry in Atkins' catalog—an entire album of the guitarist playing Spanish guitar, with no electric instruments or country music to be heard. It's a gentle, lilting album, featuring understated versions of "The Streets of Laredo," "Maria Elena," "Marcheta," and "Begin the Beguine." *—Thom Owens*

Teensville / 1960 / RCA ✦✦

As the title indicates, *Teensville* is Chet Atkins' attempt to cut a record that appealed to the teenage audience weaned on rock & roll. Though he records a fair amount of rock, rockabilly, R&B, and country songs—and the Everly Brothers, who he produced, wrote the line notes—he never captures the raw spark of rock & roll. What shines through is Atkins' understated elegance. All of the numbers are arranged as pop instrumentals and his guitar playing is so tasteful that it makes the half-hearted execution almost forgivable. *—Stephen Thomas Erlewine*

A Man & His Guitar / 1961 / RCA ✦✦✦✦

Chet Atkins' Workshop / 1961 / RCA ✦✦✦✦

Chet Atkins, the country boy whose catholic tastes deserve some of the credit (or blame) for pushing country music toward the pop mainstream in the '60s, serves up exclusively pop and jazz material on his 1961 album *Chet Atkins' Workshop*. "Whispering" and "Lullaby of Birdland" are two of the jazz standards, while instrumental renditions of the Debbie Reynolds hit "Tammy" and Doris Day's "Que Sera, Sera (Whatever Will Be, Will Be)" are pure pop. Atkins' relaxed fingerpicking works the material into a smooth consistency that sometimes belies the complexity of his technique, but the album is an engaging listen and an effortless-sounding intersection of diverse styles. Atkins was an album artist, and *Chet Atkins' Workshop*, though failing to produce a charting single, made the Top Ten and became his best-selling LP. *—Greg Adams*

The Most Popular Guitar / 1961 / RCA ✦✦✦

Chet Atkins hit the jackpot with his 12th 12-inch LP release, *Chet Atkins' Workshop*, which soared into the pop Top Ten, and RCA Victor Records hopefully released his 13th one with the title *The Most Popular Guitar* and adorned it with a cover picture of a comely girl in a negligee. The notion here seems to have been to present Atkins not so much as a guitar instrumentalist (though his guitar playing was, as usual, front and center) as the leader of a lush studio orchestra and chorus playing easy-listening favorites in the manner of Percy Faith. The varied selections ranged from show tunes like the leadoff track, George and Ira Gershwin's "It Ain't Necessarily So" from *Porgy and Bess*, to recent pop hits like the Platters' "My Prayer" and Swing Era favorites such as "East of the Sun (West of the Moon)." But no matter the source, the treatment was in middle-of-the-road ballad form, with piano and harpsichord, muted horns, swirling strings, and wordless choruses augmenting Atkins' dreamy electric-guitar stylings. But perhaps Chet Atkins was not destined to become the next Ray Conniff. In any case, *The Most Popular Guitar*, despite spending ten weeks in the *Billboard* LP chart, did not match the sales of *Chet Atkins' Workshop*, and the guitarist was free to go his own way, making whatever style of record he wanted in the future. *—William Ruhlmann*

Christmas With Chet Atkins / 1961 / RCA ✦✦✦✦✦

One of the most underrated holiday platters of all-time, *Christmas With Chet Atkins* shows the father of country/rock guitar performing 16 holiday standards in his own incomparable style. Although the uptempo stuff such as "Jingle Bell Rock" and "Winter Wonderland" are excellent readings, it's in the slower-paced selections that Atkins really shines. Chet's version of "Silver Bells" is, quite simply, one of the best versions of the standard ever, and possibly one of Atkins most arresting performances of all-time. Also excellent is the medley of "The Coventry Carol" and "God Rest Ye Merry Gentleman." Overall, criminally underrated, this disc should be rated up there with such fodder as *Charlie Brown Christmas*. Gorgeous. *—Matthew Greenwald*

Caribbean Guitar / 1962 / RCA ✦✦✦

Chet Atkins' versatility and curiosity have covered a lot of ground, and you would think that his talent would be able to encompass calypso and other Caribbean styles as well. Alas, he isn't given much of a chance here, for very little of this torporously paced album actually has anything to do with the Caribbean. Sure, some of the titles suggest the region, but not their treatments. "Mayan Dance" is a lovely two-part waltz, with bad string overdubs; "Banana Boat Song" is a lazy cover of the Tarriers' version (not Belafonte's). "Come to the Mardi Gras" moves from the Gay '90s to some unidentified jazzy muted trumpet without leaving the mainland; Bobby Darin's "Come September: Theme" is Brazilian samba; "Moon Over Miami" is a soft boogie; and so on and so forth. Atkin's playing is impeccable and tasteful as always—perhaps most elegantly on "Temptation"—just not as inspired as it can be. *—Richard Ginell*

Chet Atkins Plays Back Home Hymns / 1962 / RCA ✦✦✦

A budget-priced collection clocking in at less than a half hour, *Chet Atkins Plays Back Home Hymns* is simply too brief to stand as a definitive collection of the guitarist's spiritual recordings; his instrumental work is impeccable, of course, but performances of favorites like "Amazing Grace," "Just a Closer Walk With Thee" and "The Old Rugged Cross" pass by too quickly to properly whet the listener's appetite. *—Jason Ankeny*

Down Home / Feb. 1962 / RCA ✦✦✦

After the commercial success of Chet Atkins' 12th 12-inch LP, *Chet Atkins' Workshop*, which peaked in the pop Top Ten in 1961, RCA Victor Records decided to turn the country guitarist into an easy-listening bandleader à la Ray Conniff on his next release, *The Most Popular Guitar*. But that LP didn't come close to sales of its predecessor, and after a holiday collection (*Christmas With Chet Atkins*) at the end of the year, RCA opted to let Atkins do what he wanted again. Hence, his 15th long-player, *Down Home*. The contrast from his previous secular release couldn't have been more dramatic. The scantily clad lass with the come-hither smile on the cover of *The Most Popular Guitar* was replaced by a front-porch-swing shot of Atkins himself, guitar in hand, a vintage car in the background and a faithful dog at his feet. And the strings that dominated *The Most Popular Guitar* were replaced by Atkins' free-picking studio regulars, supporting him on a varied collection that never strayed far in the arrangements from an old-time country feeling, even when a saxophone intruded here and there. "Salty Dog Rag," the leadoff track, was not the kind of material you'd have heard on *The Most Popular Guitar*, but it was no doubt closer to Atkins' taste. The rest of the album, while mixing in a current movie theme ("Never on Sunday") and a Swing Era classic ("Tuxedo Junction"), kept doubling back to country styles. And-what do you know?—*Down Home* outpolled *The Most Popular Guitar* by 88 places in the *Billboard* LP charts, returning him to the Top 40, which seemed to indicate that when you let Atkins do what he liked his fans probably would like it, too. *—William Ruhlmann*

Travelin' Guitar / 1963 / RCA ✦✦✦

Besides doing session work and helping to create the Nashville sound while at RCA, guitarist Chet Atkins cut many jazz- and pop-inflected country instrumental albums under his own name. After producing sides for country stars like Don Gibson, Connie Smith, and Eddy Arnold, Atkins would team up with pianist Floyd Cramer, tenor saxophonist Boots Randolph, and other RCA musicians to reel off smooth, but usually engaging, covers of everything from blues and schmaltzy standards to Beatles tunes. While often seen as no more than hokey, easy listening ephemera, Atkins' many sides from the '60s deserve a reassessment. The stellar jazz dates Atkins later did at Columbia may better showcase his jazz leanings, but these RCA discs still have a wealth of quality picking and a good share of top-drawer material. This time out, Atkins showcases music from around the world, mixing in warhorses like "Exodus" and "Volare" with nice surprises like Nino Rota's "La Dolce Vita." Of course, the album has a few overly glib and stiff moments but, in spite of the mire, the playing is always great. And even though it's out of print, *Travelin'* usually can be found for just a few dollars at your local vinyl emporium. *—Stephen Cook*

The Guitar Genius / 1963 / RCA Camden ✦✦✦✦✦

It features "Swanee River," "Hidden Charm," "Heartbreak Hotel," "It's Now or Never," and other hits. *—AMG*

Our Man in Nashville / 1963 / RCA ✦✦✦

If any of RCA Victor's extensive series of "Our Man in So-and-So" albums bore the ring of truth, it was this one, for Chet Atkins indeed was RCA's point man in Nashville, in charge of the operation. For all of that, Chester remains his usual unclassifiable self, dealing out the country picking, smooth easy listening guitar, jazz, and even some very mild rock & roll on this session, with some overdubbed strings discreetly decorating a few tracks. "The Old Double Shuffle" bears a slight resemblance to "If I Had a Hammer," and

"A House in New Orleans" is an Atkins paraphrase of "St. James Infirmary," which converts to his fingerpicking style, with help from trumpet and harmonica soloists. Setting an example for his A&R department, Atkins respectfully plays the tunes of Ben E. King's "Spanish Harlem" and the Burl Ives hit "A Little Bitty Tear" in perfectly straight fashion. However, the tune of "Goodnight Irene" is thoroughly dodged and embroidered in elegant style, with some nice harmonica (Charlie McCoy?). And, as on so many Atkins albums, there is at least one track that one can develop a guilty addiction to for no particular reason; here, it's the happy-go-lucky "Always on Saturday." *—Richard S. Ginell*

Teen Scene / 1963 / RCA ✦✦

Guitar Country / 1964 / RCA ✦✦✦✦

My Favorite Guitars / 1965 / RCA ✦✦✦

Whether as a reaction to the perceived chaos of rock & roll or just an extension of pop trends already at work, easy listening instrumentals (or in more current terms, lounge music) became prevalent in the '50s and '60s. They served as background for pool parties and were popularized by movie and TV soundtracks. Thankfully, besides many bland creations, there existed the provocative and even somewhat innovative work of Esquivel, Martin Denny, Henry Mancini, and others. Chet Atkins own smooth, countrypolitan hat was thrown into the ring around 1960: almost two dozen titles were released during the decade, full of a variety of standards from all types of music. And while Atkins can't be considered an exception to the elevator music pack for his arranging and compositional skills, he does deserve special mention for his top-notch pickin' and the willingness to stretch beyond his Nashville base to incorporate jazz, classical, rock, and even shades of Far Eastern, African, and South American music. *My Favorite Guitars* (1965) helps prove the point, as Atkins tours the world's guitar shop, soft shouldering Chopin, Jobim, Ellington, and various global ditties while coming up with consistently impressive solos (the favorite guitars in question, as heard throughout the disc, are his signature Gretsch "Country Gentleman" electric guitar; some vaguely indigenous, South American acoustic model he calls the "Los Indios Tabajaras"; and a Spanish classical guitar). The playing is as smooth as the musical backdrops, so don't expect any gratuitous displays of technique. Not his best effort but worth the two dollars for a used LP copy. *—Stephen Cook*

Progressive Pickin' / 1964 / RCA ✦✦✦

Chet Atkins Picks on the Beatles / 1965 / RCA ✦✦

Chet Atkins Picks on the Beatles is an entertaining, if ultimately disposable, artifact. Atkins plays a cross-section of the Beatles' early hits, dressing them up as country-pop or light rockabilly. As always, his playing is subtle and tasteful, but the album doesn't provide enough inventive or energetic performances to be of lasting interest. *—Stephen Thomas Erlewine*

From Nashville with Love / 1966 / RCA ✦✦✦

The Pops Goes Country / 1966 / RCA ✦✦✦

Chet Atkins' first collaboration with Arthur Fiedler and his mighty Boston Pops is one of those rare cases when the original idea is inferior to the sequel (the follow-up being *Chet Picks on the Pops*). In the case of *The Pops Goes Country*, the problem perhaps lies in the selection of country/folk songs, which collapse under the inflated symphonic treatment that arranger Richard Hayman drapes all over their unpretentious frameworks. Tunes like "Tennessee Waltz," "Faded Love," "Cold, Cold Heart," and "Adios Amigo" did not seem to inspire Atkins very much at this stage in his busy life either; he goes at many of them in rote fashion, without many of the nuances and harmonic twists that he would find in hit pop material in his second album with Fiedler. Not all is lost, though; "Alabama Jubilee" gets one of the better, more energetic treatments; John Loudermilk's "Windy and Warm" breathes more life into Atkins' fingerpicking; and the orchestra sounds great in Boston's resonant *Symphony Hall*. But they would do much better next time. *—Richard Ginell*

It's a Guitar World / 1967 / RCA ✦✦✦

This attractive LP from Chester Burton Atkins purports to leap international boundaries, but for the most part, he stays right home in Nashville. Categories certainly go by the boards as Atkins seamlessly translates "What'd I Say" into his fingerpicking language and Vince Guaraldi's "Cast Your Fate to the Wind" gets a lovely straight-ahead treatment. There are also then-recent hits from the Tijuana Brass ("A Taste of Honey," "What Now My Love"), a quiet solo rendering of the Beatles' "For No One," and some ventures south of the border. The most intriguing, and certainly most bizarre, international experiment is a brief session with Indian sitarist Harihar Rao, who just happened to be passing through Nashville. "January in Bombay" is really "The Battle of New Orleans" with Rao strumming wildly, incoherently, on the gopi (either Rao had gone avant-garde or, more likely, he avant garde a clue), but then Rao gets some responsive sitar licks going as the track fades. "Ranjana" has a sitar lead with Atkins playing in unison, but the tune is quite Western and the backing is straight Nashville country, with a drone and a solo on one chord by Rao, and another by Atkins in his own countrified idiom. Hey, it was 1967, and India was in, but this fusion really needed a shotgun to make it happen. *—Richard Ginell*

Solid Gold '68 / 1968 / RCA ✦✦

By 1968, Chet Atkins was so caught up in the Nashville music machine that he helped create—and perhaps so consumed with production and executive tasks—that putting much thought into his own records had to take a back seat. Either that or forces out of his control told him to do this and that. Hence *Solid Gold '68*, a mostly overproduced, perfunctory collection of period pop hits that does neither the guitarist nor the tunes much good. Atkins mostly ambles through things like "Lady Madonna," "The Sound of Silence," "Harper Valley P.T.A.," and "Grazing in the Grass" in his easygoing pop/rock mode, although he does display some Southern-tinged affinity for Laura Nyro's "Stoned Soul Picnic." The orchestrations by Nashville mainstay Bill Walker are hackwork; those by Cam Mullins are somewhat better, with more personality. Only completists who must hear everything need search for this. *—Richard Ginell*

Relaxin' With Chet / 1969 / RCA Camden ✦✦✦

Lovers Guitar / 1969 / RCA ✦✦✦

Solid Gold '69 / 1969 / RCA ✦✦

Chet Atkins & C. E. Snow / 1969 / RCA ✦✦✦

Chet Picks on the Pops / 1969 / RCA ✦✦✦✦

It was considered a badge of honor for a pop artist to play with the Boston Pops in Arthur Fiedler's day—a sure sign that he or she had made it—and Fiedler could make nearly any improbable combination of artists and styles sound zesty and original. Nevertheless, it is still surprising how well this experiment works, despite the formulaic driving idea (symphonic treatments of '60s pop hits). For that, one can thank Atkins' superb taste; Fiedler's enthusiasm; some good, idiomatically sweeping sympho-pop arrangements by Boston Pops stalwart Richard Hayman; and the fabulously resonant acoustics of Boston's Symphony Hall. With a twist or two of the harmonies and some tasty echo delay work, Chet turns Bobbie Gentry's "Ode to Billie Joe" into a haunting piece of work, just as effective in its way as the original hit single. "Wimoweh" lifts off with a fine kicking beat and some pithy fingerpicking, and as the sole nod to Atkins' Tennessee roots, the LP concludes with a medley of "The Battle of New Orleans" and "Sugarfoot Rag" that is both inflated and loads of fun. The nice thing about this album—the second Atkins/Fiedler session—is that it is a collaboration, not just a star solo turn with orchestral backing, with Atkins fitting comfortably into the Boston Pops' then-distinctive sound. *—Richard Ginell*

Yestergroovin' / 1970 / RCA ✦✦✦✦

The double-fold cover of this sleeper in Chet Atkins' huge catalog depicts an old-fashioned general store in the country—and in a sense, that's what this LP is, a throwback to some of his earlier, less-cluttered, more musical albums. It's a relaxed, friendly, assured package, where the jazz, rock, electronic and other elements in playing reveal themselves modestly within the countrified context. The leadoff track "Steeplechase Lane" is clearly the best thing on the record, a great nostalgic Jerry Reed tune, with beautiful fingerpicking, harmonics, and staccato work by Atkins. The wheezy old Jimmy Durante signature "Inka Dinka Doo" is brought up to date (as of 1970) via a wah-wah pedal and "Tennessee Pride" is actually a tense country-rocker. Of the jazz-oriented standards, "Cherokee" finds him using octaves, harmonics, sophisticated chords, and a jazz organ backing, and "How High the Moon" is easily slotted into the Chet Atkins fingerpicking groove. Lovely record; one of his best from this period. *—Richard Ginell*

Me & Jerry / 1970 / RCA ✦✦✦✦

On this casually recorded session, which justly won a Grammy for Best Country Instrumental Performance, Jerry Reed joins Chet Atkins for a series of guitar duets. (Atkins is in the right speaker, Reed in the left.) The song list is surprising, consisting of pop hits like "Bridge Over Troubled Water" and "MacArthur Park," along with standards like "Ol' Man River," though there are several Jerry Reed originals. The two play well together, with Atkins precise and tasteful, while Reed is typically brash, often interjecting a hum or a bit of the lyric. The offhand nature of the project is what makes it so impressive. *—William Ruhlmann*

Pickin' My Way / 1970 / Mobile Fidelity ✦✦✦✦✦

This Is Chet Atkins / 1971 / RCA ✦✦

Alone / 1973 / RCA ✦✦✦

Chet Atkins Picks on Jerry Reed / 1974 / RCA ✦✦✦✦

The third of the Chet Atkins/Jerry Reed collaborations finds Atkins paying tribute to his pal by going it alone on ten Reed tunes, most of which are pretty terrific country vehicles. The majority of the songs are played on acoustic guitar, many have minimal rhythm backing, and, often, the setting is stripped down to just Atkins' guitar. All of these tunes give Atkins plenty of room to display some fancy fingerpicking, classical technique, and even a bit of gentle sustained rock guitar on his instruments. While the quality of the material is fairly even, one can single out "Baby's Coming Home" and "Steeplechase Lane" (a different recording from the often-reissued one on *Yestergroovin'*) as the standouts. Since the vast majority of country albums then were considered disposable goods by the Nashville machine, this—like many a fine Atkins record—will be difficult to locate. *—Richard Ginell*

Atkins-Travis Traveling Show / 1974 / RCA ✦✦✦

The Night Atlanta Burned / 1975 / RCA ✦✦✦✦✦

A dignified John D. Loudermilk composition inspired by *General Sherman's* scorched-earth treatment of Atlanta during the Civil War, "The Night Atlanta Burned" in turn inspired this beautiful, all too brief LP credited to the Atkins String Co.—a quartet of top-notch country string players led by Chester Atkins himself. Here, Atkins was trying to achieve a fusion of classical music techniques and ideas with those of country music and its bluegrass branch, so what you have is a classy chamber country ensemble drawing tunes and influences from around the map. You can hear Vivaldi, Bach, Mozart, and Latin classical influences mixed together or side by side on the homey "San Antonio Stroll" or Bill Monroe's hoe-down "Scotland." Atkins' fluid Tennessee-smooth acoustic guitar and occasional mandolin has the most striking personality, with Lisa Silver's violin and viola, Johnny Gimble's mandolin, and Paul Yandell's rhythm guitar providing gentle companionship. With all the hype about the Yo-Yo Ma/Mark O'Connor/Edgar Meyer Appalachia Waltz projects of the 1990s, it's enlightening to discover the seeds of that classical/country/bluegrass fusion right here, some 20 years ahead of the game. *—Richard Ginell*

The Best of Chet Atkins & Friends / 1976 / RCA ✦✦✦✦✦

Here, we skim off the cream from one of the most remarkable series of duets in the history of recording. The list of partners Chet Atkins has recorded with is astonishing in its breadth, and this LP only covers the list up to 1976, with not a single weak or even middling selection. Without batting an eye, he can engage in a remarkable country-jazz flavored duet with Lenny Breau on "Sweet Georgia Brown," exchange some swinging picking and bowing with Johnny Gimble (and briefly Charlie McCoy) on "Fiddlin' Around," or sing good-naturedly in front of Ray Stevens' simulated live show on the goofy novelty tune "Frog Kissin'." Another highlight is the extended fun and games with Les Paul on "Avalon" (from *Chester and Lester*), with the hilarious studio chatter left in—and not to be missed is a sample of Atkins' successful collaboration with the massive forces of Arthur Fiedler and the Boston Pops on "The Battle of New Orleans/Sugarfoot Rag." A few of the tracks are available nowhere else, among them a cooking session with Boots Randolph ("Terry on the Turnpike"), and a cozy duet with Dolly Parton on her East Tennessee-flavored tune "Do I Ever Cross Your Mind." In addition, he trades licks with country stars like Jerry Reed, Merle Travis, Hank Snow, and Danny Davis and the Nashville Brass. All of which proves that Chet Atkins is an eclectic musician in the best sense; he fits in virtually everywhere, his curiosity about different kinds of music knows no bounds, and his musicality accompanies him at all times. *—Richard Ginell*

Chester & Lester / 1977 / RCA ✦✦✦✦

Chester & Lester is a beautiful and fun album by two masters. It was recorded in the mid-'70s when Chet Atkins was in his fifties and Les Paul was in his sixties. The latter had been in retirement for a decade before the recording of this album. Nashville studio musicians, including Randy Goodrum on piano and Larrie Londin on drums, backup the master guitarists, but this is by no means a country album. In fact, this album swings on classics such as "Birth of the Blues," "Avalon," and "Caravan." Other classic songs, including "It's Been a Long Time" and "It Had to Be You," are beautifully rendered, featuring Les Paul's instantly recognizable ringing bell tone and Chet Atkins' fluid, slightly twangy sound. The recording has an informal feel, with between song bantering (and even some joking in the middle of songs) included on the record, which adds to the enjoyment and warmth of this album. The listener knows that the musicians are having a great time. According to the liner notes, only two songs have any overdubs, so, "You hear the music just as it came down." And it all "came down" beautifully. *—Tim Griggs*

Me & My Guitar / 1977 / RCA ✦✦✦✦

With his prestige in the executive suites at RCA and in the hearts and minds of Nashville musicians never higher, Chet Atkins seems to be interested in just making music here, without any thoughts of getting a hit. He freely alternates among nylon and steel-stringed electric, classical acoustic, and resonator guitars here—perhaps the title should have been "Me & My Guitars"—sometimes using a rhythm section, sometimes hooking up with Lenny Breau, or even going it alone on Don McLean's "Vincent." He can be heard at his inventive, countrified best on "Cascade," picking on another tasty Jerry Reed tune ("Struttin'"), running his nylon string electric gently through a phase shifter on "You'd Be So Nice to Come Home To," which ultimately turns into a bossa nova. He also modestly sings a little on the title track, a James Taylor-penned vow of companionship for his instrument. There is a mild concession to the times—some sparingly applied string synths on a few tracks—and the two sentimental waltzes at the close of the album bring down the overall rating a bit. *—Richard Ginell*

Reflections / 1980 / Sugar Hill ✦✦✦

This critically acclaimed 1980 release by two musical legends has finally made it to CD, and listeners are all the more fortunate because of it. Two of the finest guitarists the world has ever produced are together on one fun-filled record. It's odd to imagine, but a fact nonetheless, that Doc Watson and Chet Atkins both sprang from the Great Smoky Mountains at almost the same time, and really didn't grow up all that far down the road from one another. It's also interesting to note that each of them idolized the guitarist Merle Travis to such an extent that both men named their children after the picker (Doc's son, Merle Watson, and Chet's daughter, Merle Atkins). Chet Atkins was by far one of the most popular guitarists of all time, and his six-string magic shines brightly here. The red-hot picking flows like water from a backyard faucet on "Dill Pickle Rag," an old '30s ragtime number. More ragtime is included in the medley "Tennessee Rag/Beaumont Rag"; "Texas Gales/Old Joe Clark," is another medley that allows both musicians to show their stuff. The flat-picking is marvelous. The same holds true for "Black and White/Ragtime Annie." "Flatt Did It" was written by Atkins and Watson to commemorate the musical accomplishments of their friend, the late Lester Flatt, and they fill the piece with enough Flatt-inspired licks to please any Flatt & Scruggs fan. There are also some really nice vocals on the record, one of the finest of which is "You're Gonna Be Sorry," an old Alton and Rabon Delmore tune from the '40s. There is also the tongue-in-cheek "Me and Chet Made a Record" and the outstanding Karl Davis composition "Don't Monkey 'Round My Widder." "Goodnight Waltz" is a beautiful old Midnight Ramblers song, and Atkins and Watson create an impressive interpretation from beginning to end. The set closes with the foot-stompin' spiritual "On My Way to Canaan's Land," with an arrangement from Atkins and Watson that incorporates a few names of fellow country music artists, adding another personal touch to an already deeply personal recording. *—Michael B. Smith*

Work It Out With Chet Atkins C.G.P. / 1983 / Columbia ✦✦✦

Frustrated with RCA for suppressing his desire to explore music beyond the realm of Nashville, Chet Atkins bolted his recording home since the 1940s for their Music Row rivals, Columbia, in 1982—only to have Columbia suggest that his first album be a background track for exercising! Well, evidently Atkins took to the idea with some enthusiasm, at least in public. Here, several medley of diverse tunes are given overall task names—"Warm Up Medley," "Strolling Medley," "Streakin' Medley," "Cross Country Medley"—and the music by and large is ultimately subservient to a rigid beat (although Atkins does subvert "Bye Bye Blues" a bit with some rhythmic changes). Individual tracks like "Walk Me Home," "Bourree," and "Run, Don't Walk" are free of athletic designations—presumably the listener/exerciser is free to decide what to do—but the idea is the same. Luckily, Atkins is in a stylistically diverse mood, ranging back and forth across the fence from country to pop, getting off many genial tasteful licks on electric or acoustic guitars. Some of the song choices are as corny as all get out—when was the last time you heard a major artist perform "My Grandfather's Clock" or "Bicycle Built for Two"?—but the performances are dignified, musical, definitely not throwaways. Bassist David Hungate would stay on through many of Atkins' Columbia projects, and producer Randy Goodrum handles both the keyboards and drums. There is a simulated applause track on the opening medley, along with strings and Chester's casual vocals; a Nashville chorus chirps now and then. A most unpretentious, even likable Columbia debut for Atkins—and yes, you can jog to it quite nicely. *—Richard Ginell*

East Tennessee Christmas / 1983 / Columbia ✦✦

Stay Tuned / 1985 / Columbia ✦✦✦✦

After decades of recording for RCA Victor, Atkins switched labels; this 1985 effort is a summit meeting of sorts with young guitar hotshots like Larry Carlton, George Benson, Mark Knopfler, Steve Lukather, and Earl Klugh, plus session A-teamers like Boots Randolph, Larry Londin, David Hungate, Mark O'Connor and others. Atkins' tone is, as usual, faultless, and his playing superb. If the "meetings" don't always come off, it's usually due to the overzealousness of the other guitar players (Lukather's over-the-top style screams '80s big hair, for instance), not Chet, whose playing always exercises the utmost in restraint in every situation. All in all, a good modern-day Chet Atkins album, but not the place to start a collection. *—Cub Koda*

Street Dreams / 1986 / Columbia ✦✦✦

This 1986 album has a production sheen to it that makes it totally of its time, and it doesn't necessarily wear too well because of it. Too many synthesizers and contemporary touches simply detract from the main reason you bought it in the first place—to hear Chet Atkins play his patented fluid guitar. Although Atkins usually sounds wonderful on gut-string guitar, here his sound is pinched and curiously restrained, being particularly roped in by the tunes written by Daryl Dybka, which account for six of the ten songs here. Only the quiet solo closer, Atkins' own "Honolulu Blue," does his soul come up for air and his individual style emerge from this commercialized dross. *—Cub Koda*

Sails / 1987 / Columbia ✦✦✦

Another of Chet Atkins' attempts to break into the jazz world during his Columbia period, this recording veers well across the line into new age wallowing of the most innocuous kind. At this point in time, when a record opened with soothing ocean waves, followed by a gentle wash of synths, you could pretty much expect the new age to be lapping at your feet throughout. As he has with so many other genres, Atkins displays an instinctive grasp of this feel-good idiom, though he has to hold back his powers of invention to conform to its clichés and repetitions. Yet even amidst the twittering sound effects and electronic drums of "Up in My Treehouse" and the listless treatment of Keith Jarrett's "My Song," Atkins' guitar always exudes dignity. Encouragingly, several of the tunes that Atkins composed himself are the most interesting ones on the disc. "Laffin' at Life" allows for some fingerpicking by the master and some OK doodling by other guitarists and keyboardists, and the succeeding, smooth-jazz "On a Roll" has other facets of the Atkins personality, with Earl Klugh apparently taking a guest solo. One of Atkins' favorite latter-day collaborators, Mark Knopfler is also on the record, to little discernable effect. Obviously, then, this is not one of the better Atkins Columbia discs. *—Richard Ginell*

The Best of Chet Atkins & Friends, Vol. 2 / 1987 / RCA ✦✦✦

The second volume includes "Give the World a Smile," "Yakety Axe," "Alley Cat," "Que Sera, Sera," and others. *—AMG*

C.G.P. / 1988 / Columbia ✦✦✦

Chet Atkins' '80s makeover into a contemporary crossover jazz guitar player continues unabated here, with a difference. With keyboardist Daryl Dybka co-producing, the level of material is somewhat higher than it had been on some earlier albums, boosted by a handful of superior rock tunes. "Chinook Wind" has an interesting, terse tune, and the track has a tension that keeps it afloat, while "Put Your Clothes On"—co-written with fiddler Johnny Gimble—brings a native country flavor into the smooth jazz recipe. There is a touching, perfectly straight rendition of John Lennon's "Imagine" for acoustic and electric guitars without rhythm section, and John Sebastian's "Daydream" is given a boogie/Latin feeling. "Knucklebusters" is a very good Atkins original, with a tense bass guitar theme, chugging electronic drums, and some of Atkins' old effects (echo delay, tremolo bar) for old times' sake. Finally, in a live concert appearance, Atkins takes to the microphone on "I Still Can't Say Goodbye," a poignant, almost tearful tune about a fellow who can't quite shake the memory of his dad. *—Richard Ginell*

Neck & Neck / Oct. 1990 / Columbia ✦✦✦✦

Working with Dire Straits guitarist Mark Knopfler had a rejuvenating influence on Chet Atkins. Knopfler has Atkins moving toward his country roots, but both guitarists still play with a tasteful, jazzy sensibility—however, Atkins has abandoned the overt jazz-fusion pretensions that sank most of his '80s records. With its direct, understated approach, *Neck & Neck* is the most focused and arguably the most rewarding record Atkins has released. *—Stephen Thomas Erlewine*

Sneakin' Around / Oct. 1991 / Columbia ✦✦✦✦

Almost two decades after their series of collaborations had apparently run its course, Chet Atkins and Jerry Reed returned for an encore—a most welcome one. This reunion starts out on Atkins' new contemporary jazz-flavored turf, with comfortable associates like bassist David Hungate, keyboardist Daryl Dybka, rhythm guitarist Paul Yandell, and familiar guests like fiddler Mark O'Connor and guitarist Mark Knopfler filling in the band. But before long, the old Atkins/Reed country ways filter in; the rapport and good humor between the two intact and bubbling on "Here We Are," trading and stealing licks from each other with acute, long-simmering telepathy. There are a few attractive Reed originals to be savored, including a remake of the picking special "The Claw" and a dignified duet on a tune entitled "Major Attempt at a Minor Thing." Knopfler again plays a key guest role on an Atkins album, giving "Cajun Stripper" much of its chugging drive and lending a hand to the most memorable tune on the CD, "Gibson Girl," a double entendre ode to a favorite guitar. A few star singers like Suzy Bogguss and Amy Grant turn up in the chorus on "Nifty Fifties"—and the sauntering title track truly sneaks up on you. *—Richard Ginell*

The RCA Years, 1947-1981 / Oct. 1992 / RCA ✦✦✦✦✦
The RCA Years—1947-1981 isn't quite a definitive compilation, but it is the closest attempt at a comprehensive retrospective to date. Chet Atkins compiled the set himself, which means it's filled with idiosyncratic selections that don't necessarily present him at his most representative. Nevertheless, *The RCA Years* does give a sense of Atkins' accomplishments and the breadth of his talents. *—Stephen Thomas Erlewine*

Galloping Guitar: The Early Years / 1993 / Bear Family ✦✦✦✦✦
A wonderful multi-disc boxed set retrospective of Atkins' earliest recordings. Casual fans will be surprised to hear that Chet was originally marketed as a vocalist/guitarist, much the same as then popular Merle Travis was on Capitol. His eventual move over to strict instrumentals doesn't come until the end of this box set, with guest vocalists flitting in and out of the picture, but Atkins' guitar is solid throughout. *—Cub Koda*

My Favorite Guitars/It's a Guitar World / May 30, 1995 / One Way ✦✦✦
Chet Atkins' albums of easy-going, easy listening guitar playing had become a standard feature of the RCA Victor release schedule by the mid-'60s, and this two-fer CD reissue combines two typical efforts, Atkins' 22nd 12-inch LP, *My Favorite Guitars* (1965), and his 26th, *It's a Guitar World* (1967). The two albums were united—nominally—by their international themes. Like such earlier efforts as *Travelin'*, both albums feature songs referring to faraway places or having vaguely exotic themes—at least, some of the time. Of course, the guitarist and his cronies never left Nashville, but that didn't keep them from referring to South Africa ("Wimoweh"), Brazil ("One Note Samba"), the South Seas ("Moon of Manakoora"), Japan ("Sukiyaki"), India ("January in Bombay"), Russia ("Lara's Theme"), and France ("Et Maintenant [What Now My Love]"), among other places. Often, of course, they were traveling no farther than the American hit parade with such choices, and the jazz ("It Don't Mean a Thing [If It Ain't Got That Swing]") and R&B ("What'd I Say") covers didn't fit the theme, but that didn't matter. The title *My Favorite Guitars* signaled that Atkins was playing his three choice instruments, an electric, an acoustic, and a classical instrument, on different songs. He also offered a fine solo version of the Beatles' "For No One" and combined with visiting sitarist Harihar Rao for "Ranjana," reflecting the mid-'60s vogue for Indian sounds. Somehow, it all came out sounding like what it was, music made by Music Row pros. But that remained hard to fault. *—William Ruhlmann*

The Most Popular Guitar/Down Home / May 30, 1995 / One Way ✦✦✦
Although 1961's *The Most Popular Guitar* and 1962's *Down Home* are nearly successive albums in Chet Atkins' catalog, separated only by the holiday collection *Christmas With Chet Atkins*, and thus would seem to make a logical pairing in One Way Records' twofer Atkins reissue campaign, they are very different collections. In 1961, Atkins hit the pop Top Ten with his 12th 12-inch LP, *Chet Atkins' Workshop*, which seems to have inspired his record label, RCA Victor, to suppose that the country guitarist could be turned into a Nashville version of Percy Faith or Ray Conniff. So, the label titled his next release *The Most Popular Guitar* and put a female model in a state of undress on the cover while filling up the grooves with lush orchestrations and a sighing chorus. Atkins got to poke his guitar neck in here and there, but the album was really an exercise in easy-listening styles. Yet the experiment didn't work; the album didn't sell very well. So, RCA seems to have let Atkins go back to his instincts on his next album, and *Down Home*, displaying on the cover a picture of the homely guitarist on a front porch with his faithful dog at his feet, was a return to the country picking for which he was known. Combining such different approaches on a single disc is odd, but the package is tied together by Atkins' playing, which is always tasteful, no matter the surroundings. *—William Ruhlmann*

Caribbean Guitar/Travelin' / May 30, 1995 / One Way ✦✦✦
One Way Records' twofer CD reissue of Chet Atkins' 16th 12-inch LP, 1962's *Caribbean Guitar*, and his 19th, 1963's *Travelin'*, combines two albums that each have international themes. *Caribbean Guitar*, subtitled "Latin favorites by the greatest pop guitar," is full of songs with tropical connections, whether they or not they actually derive directly from around the West Indies. Atkins looked to Hawaiian instrumentalist Arthur Lyman (by way of landlocked songwriters Norman Luboff, Alan Bergman, and Marilyn Keith) for "Yellow Bird," which actually was based on a West Indian folk song, while the members of the folk group the Tarriers claimed a copyright on "The Banana Boat Song," most closely identified with Jamaican native Harry Belafonte. But the relationship of Bobby Darin's "Theme from 'Come September,'" a film set in Italy, or Nacio Herb Brown and Arthur Freed's "Temptation," from the Bing Crosby picture *Going Hollywood*, is harder to discern, though the arrangements boast Latin elements. Whatever the sources of the material, Atkins and his backup band gave the tunes lively treatments, with the guitarist chording and fingerpicking his way through the melodies. *Travelin'* keyed off of Atkins' then-recent concert trek with Jim Reeves and Floyd Cramer, presenting "Smash Hit Tunes Direct from His History-Making International Tour," but it was not a live album. Rather, the theme was just an excuse to choose standards that had a foreign flavor, from "Calcutta" to Italy's "Volare" to "Baubles, Bangles and Beads," found in the musical *Kismet*, set in the Middle East. Again, "Muskrat Ramble" didn't seem to fit exactly (unless muskrats had learned to ramble across the ocean), but that reinforced the sense that the theme was just a backdrop for Atkins and company to enjoy themselves in a Nashville studio again. *—William Ruhlmann*

Almost Alone / Mar. 12, 1996 / Columbia ✦✦✦
On this album of nearly solo guitar instrumentals, Chet Atkins plays with his usual ease and dexterity, beginning with some tasty originals and gradually moving into such standards as "Mr. Bojangles" and "Cheek to Cheek." The most unusual track is the in-concert vocal performance "I Still Write Your Name in the Snow," which is a bit more risqué than you might expect, but makes a welcome change of pace. *—William Ruhlmann*

The Essential Chet Atkins / Jun. 18, 1996 / RCA ✦✦✦✦✦
Since *The Essential Chet Atkins* concentrates on his instrumental tracks—including hits like "Mr. Sandman" and "Yakety Axe"—it functions as the best single-disc retrospective of the guitarist. It is also one of the only collections that concisely demonstrates his subtly dazzling virtuosity. *—Thom Owens*

Me & My Guitar/The First Nashville Guitar Quartet / 1997 / One Way ✦✦✦✦
This CD two-fer reissue from One Way Records combines two Chet Atkins albums originally released on RCA in the mid-'70s, 1977's *Me & My Guitar* and 1979's *The First Nashville Guitar Quartet*. It's standard operating procedure on *Me & My Guitar*, another one of Atkins' dozens of albums of instrumental country tinged pop featuring his facile guitar-picking backed by a studio full of Nashville session pros. "Cascade" sets a fast pace for the playing, but the most impressive moments come on the slower, quieter moments, notably Atkins' solo acoustic guitar reading of Don McLean's "Vincent" and the title song, penned by James Taylor, with Atkins even taking a modest vocal turn. The synthesizer sounds have the odd effect of making the music seem more dated than older Atkins albums. *The First Nashville Guitar Quartet*, on the other hand, is something new, an attempt to create a new kind of chamber music using four acoustic guitars. Here, Atkins is joined by fellow string pullers John Pell, Liona Boyd, and John Knowles for a selection of arrangements of various material, from John Philip Sousa's "Washington Post March" to "Someday My Prince Will Come," the four guitars working together like a string quartet. It is a mostly successful experiment in combining a classical approach with down-home picking. It also suggests that, at this point in his career, Atkins was looking far afield for new ideas. *—William Ruhlmann*

Pickin' the Hits / 1997 / Sony Special Products ✦✦
Sony Special Products' *Pickin' the Hits* culls ten covers of pop tunes that Chet Atkins recorded for Columbia Records over the years. Although the songs date from all different eras, from Gershwin's "Summertime" and *Gone with the Wind's* "Tara's Theme" to John Lennon's "Imagine" and Don McLean's "Vincent," they were all recorded in the '80s and '90s, which gives the album some sort of sonic consistency, at least. That said, the collection remains a little weak, largely because these are tasteful but curiously flat performances. Still, fans enamored with Atkins' flirtations with smooth jazz/pop/country fusion may find this budget-priced compilation to be an enjoyable listen and perhaps even a bargain. *—Stephen Thomas Erlewine*

The Day Finger Pickers Took Over the World / Mar. 11, 1997 / Sony ✦✦✦✦✦
At 73, with hundreds of albums and countless sessions to his credit, Chet Atkins still had another great recording in him—this splendid duo session with the young Australian guitarist/composer Tommy Emmanuel. Here, Atkins leaves all of the smooth jazz experiments from the previous decade and a half behind him, choosing superior material for their acoustic guitars, with the rhythm section laying down swinging country-pie tracks underneath. Emmanuel's fingerpicking style isn't quite as tied to the rhythm as Atkins'; it's a little sharper in attack, fleeter in technique and a bit flashier in temperament, yet remarkably well-matched to that of the east Tennessee master, almost an alter ego. Indeed Atkins' tune "Tip Toe Through the Bluegrass" plays the two styles off each other quite revealingly. Emmanuel turns out to be a top-notch tunesmith in his own right, too. His "Dixie McGuire," a disarmingly affectionate midtempo tune that won't let you go, inspires a performance that is one of the high points of Atkins' Columbia period—or for that matter, equal to anything from his long RCA period, too, in sheer emotional effect. The title track, which Atkins adapted from a lyric that dealt with bass players (as opposed to fingerpickers), finds the two reciting and singing a mock-horror flick tale—and "Ode to Mel Bay" good-naturedly mocks beginning string players everywhere. As a tribute to the visitor from Down Under, there is also a slyly countrified "Waltzing Matilda." This would be Atkins' last album of new material released during the 20th century—leaving it, glory be, on a very high note. *—Richard Ginell*

Mister Guitar/Chet Atkins in Three Dimensions / Nov. 24, 1998 / One Way ✦✦✦
In 1998, One Way released *Mister Guitar/Chet Atkins in Three Dimensions*, which contained two complete albums—*Mister Guitar* (originally released on RCA Victor) and *Chet Atkins in Three Dimensions* (originally released on RCA Victor)—by Chet Atkins on one compact disc. *—Jason Birchmeier*

Picks on the Hits/Superpickers / Nov. 24, 1998 / One Way ✦✦✦
Apparently solely on the grounds that both titles have a version of the word "pick" in them, One Way Records has combined a very good Chet Atkins album with a mediocre one on this discount-priced two-fer. Good news first: On *Superpickers*, Atkins joins together with an A-list of Nashville session musicians for a set of picking extravaganzas. The players make up a well-chosen band, and Atkins gives them plenty of space to solo on folk standards like "Mr. Bojangles" and "City of New Orleans," as well as tunes that are just platforms for the many variations. Atkins himself is goaded into some wonderful playing as a result, and *Superpickers* is one of his best albums. Unfortunately, *Picks on the Hits*, originally released in the late summer of 1972, is one of those easy listening toss-offs, a collection of tunes that had been high in the pop charts recently, tarted out with strings and occasional choruses, with Atkins sticking his guitar in here and there. The album has no place on a disc with the far superior *Superpickers*, but the discount price is low enough to recommend buying the CD just to get the second album on it. *—William Ruhlmann*

Me & Chet/Me & Jerry / Nov. 24, 1998 / One Way ✦✦✦✦
This discount-priced two-fer combines the two celebrated duet albums made by Chet Atkins and Jerry Reed in the early '70s. Oddly, they are sequenced in reverse chronological order. *Me & Jerry*, which won the 1970 Grammy Award for Best Country Instrumental Performance, comes second (tracks 12-21), while 1972's *Me & Chet*, which was merely nominated for the same award, comes first (tracks 1-11). *Me & Jerry* is the more casual effort, as Atkins (in your right speaker) and Reed (in your left) pick their way through a number of pop standards, including "Bridge Over Troubled Water" and "MacArthur Park." Atkins is the more sedate of the two, as Reed can be heard humming and singing snatches of the lyrics here and there, but it's the interaction between them that makes the recordings valuable. The tracks from *Me & Chet* are perhaps a bit more considered, and thus not as impressive, though there is a reading of "Mystery Train" that has considerable fire. *—William Ruhlmann*

Finger Style Guitar/Stringin' Along With Chet Atkins / Nov. 24, 1998 / One Way ✦✦✦
If you look at Chet Atkins' album discography, it appears as if *Stringin' Along With Chet Atkins* and *Finger Style Guitar* follow each other in release in 1956, which may explain why they are paired together on this two-fer release issued 42 years later, if not why they are presented in reverse order. But the two albums do not both represent the Atkins of 1956. *Finger Style Guitar* is indeed a 1956 collection, Atkins' third 12-inch offering recorded as such, following 1954's *A Session With Chet Atkins* and *Chet Atkins in Three Dimensions* from earlier in 1956. But *Stringin' Along With Chet Atkins* was a compilation of Atkins recordings made between 1950 and 1953, originally released in a ten-inch, eight-song version in 1953 and only reissued in a 12-inch, 12-song version in 1956. *Stringin' Along* finds Atkins applying his familiar guitar style to a range of early 20th century material, including Tin Pan Alley songs, show tunes, and blues numbers, along with some of his originals, while *Finger Style Guitar* is one of his more classical outings. But the highlights of both albums, and thus of this reissue, are movie themes. "Unchained Melody" from *Finger Style Guitar* has some attractive echo effects, and "The Third Man Theme," which concludes *Stringin' Along* and thus this collection as well, is an excellent version of that attractive 1949 guitar tune. So, despite the disparate sources, the 24-track compilation can be enjoyed as a consistent selection of excellent Atkins instrumental playing. *—William Ruhlmann*

Hum & Strum Along With Chet Atkins/The Other Chet Atkins / Nov. 24, 1998 / One Way ✦✦✦
This entry in One Way Records' series of two-fer reissues of Chet Atkins' RCA catalog combines two albums that were one-offs, and thus not easy to pair with any other of his records. *Hum & Strum Along With Chet Atkins*, from 1959, was an album on which Atkins, taking a cue from Mitch Miller's popular *Sing Along With Mitch* LPs, assembled a group of folk songs and other popular tunes, and then brought in a chorus to sing them, adding his characteristic guitar work in the background, the idea being that listeners would sing (or at least hum) along. Needless to say, the result is not much of a showcase for Atkins, and after the album failed to sell, he didn't repeat the gimmick. On the other hand, 1960's *The Other Chet Atkins* is very much an Atkins showcase, albeit one on which he picks up a nylon-stringed Spanish guitar and tries his hand at a bunch of Latin (or at least Latin-esque) tunes, beginning with Cole Porter's "Begin the Beguine." The choice of a Broadway composer's take on a Latin form as the opening track should give some indication of how authentically Spanish Atkins is willing to get (he even includes a version of Marty Robbins' "Streets of Laredo," Laredo, TX, being on the Mexican border). But what matters is the playing, and Atkins proves as effective on Spanish guitar as he is on any other six-stringed instrument. *—William Ruhlmann*

Chester & Lester/Guitar Monsters / Dec. 8, 1998 / One Way ✦✦✦
In 1998, One Way released *Chester & Lester/Guitar Monsters*, which contained two complete albums—*Chester & Lester* (originally released on RCA) and *Guitar Monsters* (originally released on RCA)—by Chet Atkins on one compact disc. *—Jason Birchmeier*

• **Guitar Legend: The RCA Years** / Apr. 4, 2000 / Buddha ✦✦✦✦✦
Considering the incredible amount of influence and prestige Chet Atkins has pumped into country music in the last 50 years, it's strange that there aren't more greatest-hits packages on the market of real value. While RCA's *Essential Chet Atkins* attempts the near-impossible task of condensing the guitarist's vast 30-year output onto a single disc, Bear Family's four-disc box is characteristically too exhaustive and expensive to be practical. With 50 tracks spanning from his first recordings in 1947 to the Nashville Guitar Quartet sessions 30 years later, the two-disc retrospective *Guitar Legend* is arguably the first affordable collection to paint a comprehensive picture. Despite the inclusion of a vocal track, "Tellin' My Troubles to My Old Guitar," the set is focused on the stylistic innovations Atkins brought to Travis-picking, and thus, country music. Each phase of his development is documented, with an emphasis on his classic early group recordings. His saccharine '60s output receives minor attention, as do his ventures into straight jazz, allowing plenty of room for his trademark fingerpicking to be heard without the strings and other excesses that tended to clutter his albums. Most of his hits are here, as well as a few tracks previously unissued in the U.S. *—Jim Smith*

Guitar Country/More of That Guitar Country / Jun. 12, 2001 / Collectables ✦✦✦
Chet Atkins is a great guitar player. His fingerpicking style set the pace in the '50s, leading budding guitarists to play his LPs at slower speeds to discover the master's technique. Atkins' genius, however, has not always come across in the recording studio. As author of the Nashville sound, he has often found it expedient to add background singing, strings, and syrupy arrangements to his records. These problems crop up on *Guitar Country/More of That Guitar Country*, but they are less "problems" than distractions. Atkins, even in less than perfect situations, still plays guitar like no one else. He covers a number of classics—"Sugarfoot Rag," "Freight Train," and "Nine Pound Hammer"—but also shows himself to be a "with it" guy by tackling "Blowin' in the Wind" and Donovan's "Catch the Wind." Atkins' trademark style of combining chords with a steady bassline comes across wonderfully on Johnny Cash's "Understand Your Man" and the original "My Town." One would be remiss for not mentioning that *More of That Country Guitar* kicks off with "Yakety Axe," a lovely guitar romp like no other. It is perhaps odd, now that most music comes on CDs, to realize that many LPs lasted no more than 30 minutes. This, however, has allowed Collectables to put both of these records onto one CD, giving the listener nearly 60 minutes of prime Chet Atkins. For guitar players and fans, *Guitar Country/More of That Guitar Country* will be an enjoyable release. *—Ronnie D. Lankford Jr.*

• **RCA Country Legends** / Nov. 20, 2001 / Buddha ✦✦✦✦✦
Chet Atkins earned and held the title of "Mr. Guitar" for 50 years before passing away in the summer of 2001. Signed to RCA in 1947, he would help define the "Nashville Sound" in the late '50s while simultaneously releasing a steady string of instrumental albums. *RCA Country Legends* captures Atkins on 14 wonderful tracks recorded between 1949 and 1976. Atkins recorded the self-penned single "Barber Shop Rag" with mandolinist Jethro Burns and guitarist Homer Haynes. Burns' speedy runs work as a nice counterpoint, and bring out equally inspired work from Atkins. Curiously, Atkins and his buddies even add vocals on an infectious cut titled "Boogie Man Boogie." There's a nice duet with writer and fellow guitar picker Jerry Reed on "Twitchy," and a spunky take on "Tiger Rag" worthy of Django Reinhardt. There are also a number of solo pieces, including "Petite Waltz," "Yes Ma'am," and the closer, "Liza." These cuts capture a quintessential Atkins, just a man and his guitar, handling the rhythm and lead without blinking. A couple of rare extras also sweeten this package. "Royal Garden Blues," featuring lead guitar by jazz great George Barnes, was previously unreleased, while "One Man Boogie," recorded in 1951, was only previously available as an import. *RCA Country Legends* offers a good introduction and career overview of Chet Atkins' impeccable guitar work. *—Ronnie D. Lankford Jr.*

Chet Picks on the Grammys / Feb. 12, 2002 / Columbia ✦✦✦✦
So many gallons of ink have been spilled singing the praises of Chet Atkins that it's difficult for reviewers to find new ways to describe the quality that made his guitar style so special. There had been other good pickers before Atkins. Merle Travis used a similar style earlier, called "Travis picking," but was also known as the singer of classics like "Smoke, Smoke, Smoke That Cigarette." Joe Maphis, a contemporary of Atkins, worshiped at the alter of speedy licks, trading individual style for "fire on the strings." Atkins' style, both urban and refined, was always identifiable. This was true whether he was playing holiday songs or the Beatles. *Chet Picks on the Grammys* collects 13 instrumentals that won Grammys between 1967 and 1996. Even over such a long period with disparate changes in production, Atkins' combination of chords and thumb technique remained distinct. There are a number of choice items here and many will be familiar as hits by other artists. "Snowbird" harks back to 1971 and "Ready for the Times to Get Better" to 1981. As though to prove he wasn't just a country boy with a guitar, Atkins also tackles "The Entertainer" and offers a fascinating rendering of Duke Ellington's "Caravan." *Chet Picks on the Grammys* offers a good overview of Atkins' instrumental work and a fine excuse for reviewers to spill a few more gallons of ink singing the praises of Mister Guitar. *—Ronnie D. Lankford Jr.*

Audrey Auld

b. Australia

Guitar (Acoustic), Guitar, Main Performer, Vocals / Contemporary Country, Singer/Songwriter, Country-Rock, Country-Folk, Alternative Country

Neo-traditionalist country singer Audrey Auld first came to prominence partnering up with Bill Chambers, father to Kasey Chambers and patriarch to Australian country music's royal family. *Looking Back to See*, released under the Bill & Audrey moniker in 1999, was an album of duets released on Auld and Chambers' own Reckless Records label. In 2000, she released her solo debut *The Fallen*. The effort, produced and recorded by Auld, featured a duet with honky tonk singer Dale Watson and a cover of Fred Eaglesmith's "Alcohol and Pills."

Auld was raised in rural Tasmania and as a child endured a strict routine of classical violin and piano lessons imposed by her jazz musician father. She eventually came to country music via the unlikely route of the post-punk of such bands as the Birthday Party, Bauhaus, and the Psychedelic Furs. An art teacher friend introduced Auld to the sounds of folks such as Dwight Yoakam, Patsy Cline, Emmylou Harris, and Loretta Lynn, sparking an obsession with the genre.

As an adult, Auld moved around the Northern Territory before settling in Sydney. She initially formed an a cappella country music group with two other girls, but an interest in Western swing led her to form the Harmony Grits, which played swing with a jazz flavor. That group evolved into Audrey & the Rhythm Wranglers. Soon after, Auld met Bill Chambers and the two began writing together in 1997, forming the group Luke & the Drifters. *—Erik Hage*

• **The Fallen** / Sep. 12, 2000 / Reckless ✦✦✦✦
Imagine the saddest voice singing yet another sad tale of a man leaving a woman. The odd thing in this instance, however, is the fact that the singer doesn't really blame him. "I won't stop you when you go/'Cause I'd leave me too." "I'd Leave Me Too" is a refreshing kickoff to an album that just gets better with delicious country & western romps like "Shove It." Audrey Auld's authenticity, curiously, doesn't hail from Texas or Tennessee, but from Australia. *The Fallen*'s arrival on native shores gives notice that, first, country music has long ceased to be a strictly American phenomenon, and second, that Outback country & western may have a thing or two to teach sterile Nashville. Songs like "Too Far to Fall" and "Still Holding On" feature honest-to-God pedal steel and a jaunty country shuffle. Auld's voice cracks and breaks in the classic tradition of singers like Kitty Wells and Loretta Lynn. There's a great duet with Dale Watson on "Jackson" and a good take on

Fred Eaglesmith's "Alcohol and Pills." Drummer Doug Gallacher pushes a number of these songs into high gear with a steady backbeat, while Michel Rose lays down some lovely dobro and steel. Auld has written ten good songs, embracing every style from classic country to Western swing. Delivered with confidence and style, *The Fallen* is an excellent debut. *—Ronnie D. Lankford Jr.*

Mike Auldridge

b. Dec. 30, 1938, Washington, D.C.

Dobro, Guitar, Pedal Steel, Vocals, Slide Guitar / Bluegrass, Progressive Bluegrass, Traditional Bluegrass

With his skill and his broad definition of the meaning of bluegrass music, Mike Auldridge became known over his multi-decade career as a master of the Dobro, or resonator guitar. Raised in Kensington, MD, he began playing guitar at 12, adding banjo when he was 16 and settling on Dobro at 17. In 1954, he made his first radio appearance on a local show, playing in a band with his brother, Dave. He graduated from the University of Maryland in 1967 and became a commercial artist, while continuing to play at local clubs.

In 1969, he joined the New Shade of Green. That group soon gained a strong following and helped highlight Auldridge's unique expressive style on the Dobro. He joined the Seldom Scene in 1971, and remained with that group through multiple personnel changes up until the mid-'90s, then later re-joined them on a part-time basis in 2002. The group became pioneers of the newgrass sound which incorporated elements of jazz, folk, and rock into traditional bluegrass harmonies. Their eclectic material spanned original compositions as well as cover songs that ranged from J.J. Cale's "After Midnight" to Eric Clapton's "Lay Down Sally."

Such flexibility provided a good jumping off point for Auldridge's solo work, which was aided in the beginning by several members of the Seldom Scene. Auldridge's first two solo albums for Takoma, *Dobro* and *Blues & Bluegrass*, both feature a melding of unconventional cover songs, like Roberta Flack's "Killing Me Softly"; deep emotive playing; and the sometimes welcome, sometimes out-of-place contributions of high-profile guest stars like Ricky Skaggs and Linda Ronstadt. As he continued to record through the '70s for labels like Flying Fish, he also kept busy doing session work for Ronstadt, Emmylou Harris, Jonathan Edwards, and Jimmy Arnold. His work in the late '80s and early '90s for Sugar Hill, especially *Eight String Swing*, took his multi-genre experimentations a step further. In the mid-'90s, Auldridge transferred his energies from the Seldom Scene to Chesapeake, a more serious band with a smaller and more stable lineup. That band produced several recordings for Sugar Hill and also helped spawn a pair of trio recordings made by Auldridge, Jimmy Gaudreau, and Richard Bennett, 2000's *This Old Town* and 2001's *Blue Lonesome Wind*. *—Stacia Proefrock*

Dobro / 1972 / Takoma ♦♦♦♦

Although not as cosmic as the solo guitar odysseys of John Fahey or Robbie Basho, the early-'70s recordings of this veteran dobro picker have an equal importance to the development of acoustic-stringed music in America. The skill with which Auldridge put together vehicles for his tremendously appealing soloing style, smoothly handling transitions between members of a large and star-studded cast of supporting characters, not only resulted in a boost in interest in the dobro, but the entire civilization of soloists on various instruments benefited from such obvious evidence of potential appeal, while the Washington, D.C., bluegrass scene never quite recovered from the legendary status of these recording sessions and the magical things that went on as the tapes rolled. This was the first of a pair of projects Auldridge created for Takoma; he cut the fine *Blues & Bluegrass* several years later, using many of the same musicians. In many ways these are like adjunct Seldom Scene recordings, as a few of that group's players show up. Things couldn't get off to a livelier start than the opening track, "Hillbilly Hula," a sheer delight in its combination of both Hawaiian and bluegrass genre trademarks. "Pickaway" is one of several bluegrass numbers that is out and out hardcore in the sense of sounding like the energy of that rock style is being referenced. The banjo picking on this track is wonderful. As the album proceeds the instrumentalists keep digging deeper and deeper, splashing musical imagery in a competition that suggests a group of crack photographers trying to outdo each other at a slide show. "Rolling Fog" comes in, atmosphere galore, right before the landing on "Dobro Island," most likely a place that fans of Auldridge would love to be stranded. The latter state is how some listeners might feel if forced to sit through the entire "House of the Rising Sun," the final selection and one of a only a few misfires in the program. Another dud is the saccharine "Greensleeves," played as if trying to entertain drunks at an Appalachian ski lodge, but of course this was the track that got all the NPR airplay. *—Eugene Chadbourne*

Blues & Bluegrass / 1974 / Takoma ♦♦♦

Another winner from dobro master Mike Auldridge, this production must have seemed like a Hollywood blockbuster compared to the average Takoma release, many of them solo guitar efforts. Even on its own terms, this album suffered from the drawbacks of the masterpiece mentality and the *carte blanche* budget, at least on relative terms. Auldridge again juggles several different ensemble combinations, the challenge being to create an easily flowing and dramatically coherent set of pieces, as he had done so gracefully on the 1972 set simply entitled *Dobro*. But here, the director has earned a bigger trailer based on the huge success of this previous release. Although instrumentals are once again the main fare, there is more of a shot taken at doing vocal tracks, with several heavy-hitters from the '70s pop ballpark brought in to display their imagined ease with roots material. Eclecticism may keep the listener on the edge of their seat; early on, there is a cover of "Killing Me Softly," not at all bluegrass in delivery, that is every bit as interesting as the '90s version by the Fugees and indeed would make a fine combination for that record in a mash-up. "This Ain't Grass," sounding like an admonition to a crooked dope dealer, is an example of the slick and complex progressive bluegrass instrumentals that are the main course of these projects, allowing space for some brilliant picking as well as a sense that some kind of acoustic hillbilly cousin of electric jazz fusion is hiding in the closet. Many of these arrangements have stood up very well to the test of time, as generally does most music in which the players' minds are seriously engaged. It can be a jolt moving from such material to the Hollywood hokiness of a Linda Ronstadt vocal or the too-easy silliness of the "Walk Don't Run" cover, but this is one of the problems Auldridge worked so hard to overcome when putting together such ambitious collections of material. Here he moves from spotlighting Mike Auldridge the dobro player to Auldridge the record producer and studio genius, so of course there's a bit of a letdown. He certainly makes a good case for himself choosing material, overlooking the odd dud and coming up with nifty instrumentals from the likes of dobro forefather Tut Taylor and unique country picker Roy Nichols and a fascinating country tune from fine songwriter Dick Curless. *—Eugene Chadbourne*

● **Dobro/Blues & Bluegrass** / 1974 / Takoma ♦♦♦♦♦

This welcome reissue brings together the first two solo albums by Seldom Scene dobro player Mike Auldridge, each of which was groundbreaking in a different way. While "progressive bluegrass" was already a fully established musical convention by 1972, when *Dobro* was originally issued, instrumental bluegrass arrangements of material like "Greensleeves" and "House of the Rising Sun" were a bit unusual even in the progressive context, and, to be honest, were not quite as successful as his brilliantly flashy rendition of Lester Flatt's "Pickaway" or the weepy country standard "Silver Threads." The second album presented on this reissue, *Blues & Bluegrass*, is a bit more consistently rewarding. Most of the tracks are Seldom Scene performances in all but name, with the occasional addition of such stellar guests as Vassar Clements, Ricky Skaggs, and David Bromberg. This album veers happily between barnburning bluegrass ("New Camptown Races," "8 More Miles to Louisville") and soulful blues numbers ("Summertime," "Struttin' the Blues"), with occasional detours into sappy pop ("Killing Me Softly") and, believe it or not, surf-bluegrass fusion ("Walk Don't Run"). All of it manages to be lots and lots of fun. Highly recommended. *—Rick Anderson*

Mike Auldridge / 1976 / Flying Fish ♦♦♦♦♦

Fans of this dobro player, and they are legion, tend to champion the earlier pair of releases he created for Takoma, which among many virtues have a freshness and immediacy that would be hard to find on any Flying Fish release. For some reason much of this label's catalog, despite good intentions, has a feeling of having been protected by mothballs for several generations before being released to the general public. Despite the pervasive production stiffness, the good side in the case of this Auldridge album is that the occasional lapses that were part of his earlier, incredibly ambitious production efforts have been negated by the tighter, clearer focus. This quality is in turn enhanced by the additional maturity of the performer himself, as well as some of his associates, some of whom are the same great players that shone so brightly on earlier Auldridge projects but sound better than ever here. The cover versions of '60s and '70s pop hits are particularly worthy of attention: "Last Train to Clarkesville" comes off with a snap that is invigorating, while the mighty "California Dreamin'," having already provided a full meal for the studio pickers on the original record, has a perfect harmonic structure for bluegrass exploration, Auldridge digging into his instrument as if his slide bar was a serving spoon cracking the crust at the top of a pot of French onion soup. Some of the best fiddling on record from Vassar Clements is part of the action here, as is the steady rhythm guitar of Dick Feller. With only a few slow moments, this album is a classic of the '70s bluegrass scene. *—Eugene Chadbourne*

Mike Auldridge & Old Dog / 1978 / Flying Fish ♦♦♦

The Old Dog bluegrass band probably got a chance to release a Flying Fish record thanks to the presence in the band of dobro wizard Mike Auldridge, whose own recordings were some of the most popular in the progressive bluegrass genre of the time. When the group itself failed to make much of a splash, the recording was later reissued with the dobro picker's name added in front. While Old Dog makes a lie of its name with progressive intentions from time to time, the type of cutting-edge "newgrass" picking that Auldridge can be a master of is not really the theme here. This group mixes in a strong old-time and country feeling to much of its material, coming across less like a sterile, emotionless pack of technical bluegrass hotshots than a talented bar band whose members are benefiting from heavy eye contact with the folks in the front row. There are highlights such as the skidding "Sledd Ride," but a great deal of the material is just too ordinary. Auldridge recorded extensively during this period, so completists may even think twice about this acquisition—that is, unless they happen to hear their hero's playing, which is as grand as usual. A sludgy atmosphere develops during covers of insipid folk-rock material by Gordon Lightfoot and Jim Croce, and the band even manages to fumble a few surefire passes such as "Steel Guitar Rag." *—Eugene Chadbourne*

Slidin' Smoke / 1979 / Flying Fish ♦♦♦♦

On this mellow album, Auldridge (dobro) and Newman (steel guitar) add a touch of jazz to their bluegrass sound. *—AMG*

Eight String Swing / 1988 / Sugar Hill ♦♦♦

As the title suggests, Mike Auldridge recorded *Eight String Swing* with a specially made, eight-string dobro, which helped him ease his music out of traditional bluegrass and into country, jazz, western swing, and folk. Auldridge is joined by several of his Seldom Scene cohorts and fiddler Jimmy Arnold on the album, and the sympathetic support adds depth to both the originals and the eclectic covers (Duke Ellington's "Caravan," Willie Nelson's "Crazy," Benny Goodman's "Stompin' at the Savoy"). *—Stephen Thomas Erlewine*

Treasures Untold / 1989 / Sugar Hill ♦♦♦♦

Treasures Untold is comprised entirely of traditional country & western songs, ranging from cowboy standards ("Deep Water," "Shenandoah Waltz") to honky tonk ("Walking the Floor Over You," "Drivin' Nails in My Coffin"). Most of the record features lead vocals by Doc Watson, Tony Rice and John Starling, while Auldridge simply plays some stunning dobro, but he does step to the mike for a couple of songs, including the title track. *—Thom Owens*

High Time / 1990 / Sugar Hill ♦♦♦♦
This great dobro picker plays here with Lou Reid and Michael Coleman. *—Mark A. Humphrey*

This Old Town / Jan. 25, 2000 / Rebel ♦♦♦
Resonator guitarist Mike Auldridge and mandolin player Jimmy Gaudreau are noteworthy bluegrass musicians who are active members of the bluegrass outfit Chesapeake, and guitarist Richard Bennett is a well-respected artist who has served with a number of bands, including J.D. Crowe & the New South. This threesome, with the added services of bassist Joe Sharp, have pooled their considerable resources to create *This Old Town.* The featured numbers are mostly performed in the traditional bluegrass vein, though Charles Roehrig's "Come Sit by the River" and Kate Wolf's "Across the Great Divide" offer a contemporary lyrical style. Their most effective covers are a stirring version of Josh Dray's Civil War story "Southern Son" and a very sharp rendition of Norman Blake's "Billy Gray." Among the instrumental breakdowns on the CD, the best are Gaudreau's catchy "Old Columbus Blues," Bennett's classic guitar piece "Sally on the Treadmill," and a fine version of the hymn "Just a Closer Walk With Thee," dignified by Auldridge's evocative resonator guitar. *—Philip Van Vleck*

Blue Lonesome Wind / May 15, 2001 / Rebel ♦♦♦♦
Many progressive bluegrass musicians perform in a number of settings with a variety of players. Like jazz players, their commitment has more to do with making quality music than preserving one band. Dobroist Mike Auldridge, guitarist Richard Bennett, and mandolinist Jimmy Gaudreau are no exception. When they joined forces for *This Old Town* in 2000, no one could be sure they would record together again. In 2001, they returned with the lovely *Blue Lonesome Wind.* Bennett lends his expressive voice to the title track and to the self-penned "Satisfied to Stay," an upbeat piece featuring some superb group harmony. Bennett also continues to be one of the best guitar players in the Tony Rice mold. His picking on "New Sweet Home" and "Dog Pause" will, as the saying goes, knock your hat in the creek. Other instrumentals like "Welcome to New York" give everyone lots of room to show off their instrumental prowess. Auldridge captures the romantic flavor of the piece, laying down the quality work that always gave the Seldom Scene such a distinctive sound. Gaudreau's mandolin likewise captures all the right nuances. He's always present with the right lick, whether kicking off a piece like "Too Many Tears" or playing rhythm behind his comrades. Complaints? None really. It may confuse some that this band can vacillate between jazz-grass and bluegrass as opposed to sticking to one style, but it shouldn't. This contemporary bluegrass band succeeds where so many fail; they never allow smooth arrangements or stale material to straightjacket their music. *Blue Lonesome Wind* is a nice piece of work, guaranteed to create expectations for another album. *—Ronnie D. Lankford Jr.*

Austin Lounge Lizards

f. 1980

Group / Progressive Bluegrass

Regarding their name, Austin Lounge Lizards guitarist and founding member Conrad Deisler said: "I think it was a slang term I'd heard my grandmother use to describe gentlemen of easy virtue who hung around in bars. When we started out, that's just what we were doing—hanging out and playing for beer and tips and stuff like that." The Lounge Lizards trace their origins back to the late '70s, when Deisler, then a Princeton student, hooked up with Hank Card to indulge their shared interest in folk and country by playing in progressive folk bands. The two landed in Austin in 1980, where they met Tom Pittman, a banjo and pedal steel player who'd just moved to town from Georgia. They combined the sounds of Pittman's bluegrass heritage with the folk and country forms from Deisler and Card's college-band days up north. Unsatisfied with playing bluegrass and traditional country covers, the Lizards found they had a knack for writing bizarro social and politically themed songs, overflowing with tongue-in-cheek twang.

The band has gone through its share of mandolin players, bassists, and fiddlers, but the core of the group has remained Pittman, Deisler, and Card, with long stints from bassist Boo Resnick, drummer Paul Pearcy, and multi-instrumentalist Richard Bowden. Whatever its lineup, the Austin Lounge Lizards have long been known for their Texas-sized twisted tales and humorous songs, charming their fans for over twenty years. In their own words, "Our accents are the drawliest, our howdies are the y'alliest/Our Lone Star flag's the waviest, our fried steak's the cream graviest."

The group's first album, *Creatures From the Black Saloon*, was released in 1984, and was followed by 1988's *The Highway Cafe of the Damned*, 1991's live album *Lizard Vision*, 1993's *Paint Me on Velvet*, 1995's *Small Minds*, and 1998's *Employee of the Month*. *Never an Adult Moment* was issued in late summer 2000. *—Zac Johnson*

• **Creatures from the Black Saloon** / 1984 / Watermelon ♦♦♦♦♦
Imagine tradition-steeped Texas swing fused to Monty Python, and you have an idea what's in store with the Austin Lounge Lizards. The Lizards can serve up the tastiest country licks imaginable while at the same time trashing every old West cliché/tradition in the book. The group's debut *Creatures from the Black Lagoon* revealed such classics as "The Car Hank Died In," "Kool Whip" (Devo meets The Bonzo Dog Band), and "Saguaro" (wailing pedal steel and mock heroic baritone rendering the tale of a twerpy urban cowpoke duelling a gang of desperado cacti—and losing). *—Roch Parisien*

The Highway Cafe of the Damned / 1988 / Sugar Hill ♦♦♦♦
The Lizards second release captures both the time of its creation—the late Reagan years, underscored by a perverse ballad about the man himself—and the group's own wonderfully offbeat and definitely left-leaning vision of the universe. The opening, three-minute title track showcases the band's balanced strengths. On the one hand, they simply cook in ways that Bill Monroe would be proud of: straight-up bluegrass without gimmicks, with main singer Card possessed of a voice easily and simply described as "mighty fine." On the other hand, the tale of a purgatorial greasy-spoon, where the protagonist demands both coffee and Kafka from the demonic waitress while "the radio is playing Barry Manilow incessantly" sparkles with a rapid-fire wit that most bands could barely dream of. From there on, it's a romp through a dozen slices of Americana seen with some highly warped visions—thus the regretful musing of the gay émigré from Nebraska stuck in San Francisco in "Cornhusker Refugee" or the reverse generation-gap knee-slapper "Get a Haircut, Dad." The Lizards' grasp of musical styles is both playful and skillful. As a band, they're able to take in everything from Bob Wills-style Western swing to straight country, and other lead singers Williams and Deisler work the mike just as well as Card. From start to finish, a perfect delight. *—Ned Raggett*

Lizard Vision / 1991 / Flying Fish ♦♦♦
Combine country and bluegrass melodies with the type of irreverent, authority-questioning lyrics you'd expect from a rock & roll or folk act, and you've got the Austin Lounge Lizards, whose sense of humor is impossible to miss on *Lizard Vision.* Recorded live at the Waterloo Ice House in Austin, TX, in January 1990, this CD illustrates the Lizards' vitality and makes it clear they're far from typical of country and bluegrass acts. The band might sound a bit like the Statler Brothers at times, but lyrically, they're in a class by themselves. "Dan Stepford" has a good laugh at the expense of Dan Quayle (who was the U.S. vice president when this CD was recorded), while the doo wop-influenced "Jesus Loves Me (But He Can't Stand You)" takes aim at the hypocrisy of religious fanatics. Not all of the songs have sociopolitical references; on "He's Just a Friend" and Roger Waters' "Brain Damage," for example, the Lizards simply enjoy some healthy, good-natured goofiness for the sake of goofiness. Arguably, *Lizard Vision* is the band's most essential release. *—Alex Henderson*

Paint Me on Velvet / 1993 / Flying Fish ♦♦♦
Since their formation in 1980, the Austin Lounge Lizards have entertained themselves and a lot of other people with their brand of music, which they call "satirical bluegrass." Actually, the listener can also hear strains of rock, soul, blues, and gospel in the music. The band is composed of Conrad Deisler on acoustic lead guitar, Hank Card on acoustic guitar, Tom Pittman on banjo and pedal steel guitar, Boo Resnick on bass, and Eamon McGloughlin on mandolin and fiddle. The fact that they are master musicians is often lost in the hilarity of their lyrics. Best known for their song "Jesus Loves Me (But He Can't Stand You)," the Austin Lounge Lizards poke fun at everything and everybody in modern American culture. Their humorous take on such an easy target has spawned an enthusiastic following of fans known as Lizard Heads. *Paint Me on Velvet* follows the Lizards' formula for success: great music and funny lyrics. There are rollicking banjos and hot fiddles and beautiful harmonies. It seems so comfortably bluegrass until your ears tune into the words. The CD's title track, "Paint Me on Velvet," is a case in point, as the Lizards make fun of the tacky, while at the same time parodying the icons and styles of the genre. No idol is too big to fall before the barbs of group's sharp pens and tongues: This song finds Waylon Jennings and Willie Nelson on the hot seats. The title of "Put the Oak Ridge Boys in the Slammer" speaks for itself. "1984 Blues" shows just how good these musicians really are. Enigmatically, they then go off on a version of that long-forgotten song from the crypt, "The Purple People Eater." But then this group of former lawyers, doctors, and other ne're-do-wells is nothing if not enigmatic. Other standouts on the CD include "Going to Hell in Your Heavenly Arms," "Boudreaux Was a Nutcase," and "That Godforsaken Hellhole I Call Home." Having the musical knowledge to appreciate the group's inside jokes and puns increases the fun, but the music stands on its own, guaranteeing all listeners a good laugh along with an enjoyable musical experience. *—Rose of Sharon Witmer*

Small Minds / 1995 / Watermelon ♦♦♦
There's nothing more demented than a country band with a sense of humor, unless it's a country band with a sense of humor *and* a sense of irony. The Austin Lounge Lizards have humor, irony and satire going for them, a pretty deadly combination altogether. Targets on *Small Minds* range from Newt Gingrich (in the acidic "Gingrich the Newt," which has this Newt giving the humble newt species a bad name) to the intelligentsia of the art world. For all the bent edges, *Small Minds* is a finely played and sung album that's a pleasure to listen to and gets a definite recommendation. *—Steven McDonald*

Employee of the Month / Feb. 17, 1998 / Sugar Hill ♦♦♦♦
They're light, they're fluffy, they're as funny as all get out. Whether it's a lampoon of Very Big Texan Things in "Stupid Texas Song," a parody of Leonard Cohen in "Leonard Cohen's Day Job" (which gets funnier the more you listen to it) or acknowledging the family of the '90s ("Hey, Little Minivan"), they're sharp and smart. The satire isn't quite as biting as on *Small Minds*, their 1995 release, but they sure are funny. *—Steven McDonald*

Never an Adult Moment / Aug. 29, 2000 / Sugar Hill ♦♦♦♦
One of the more enjoyably bent elements of country music, the Lizards have a habit of being a bit too scattershot for their own good. This set is, therefore, pretty much typical for them, despite the inclusion of "Hillbillies in a Haunted House," with a way too late parody in "Grunge Song," a thematic repeat in "Forty Years Old and I'm Livin' in My Mom's Garage" (which is little more than a continuation of "Wrong End of the Gene Pool"), and so on. However, not all is lost: "Rasputin's HMO" is priceless, "Big Rio Grande River" is a gem of a parody of Tex-Mex and Marty Robbins, and "The Illusion Travels By Stock Car," which mixes Richard Petty with Luis Bunuel, qualifies for the most surreal country song ever recorded. Cumulatively, this is not the best Austin Lounge Lizards effort, but it has more than its share of good moments. *—Steven McDonald*

Chad Austin

b. Andice, TX

Main Performer, Vocals, Guitar, Piano / Neo-Traditionalist Country, Contemporary Country

Gritty hard country singer Chad Austin hails from Andice, TX, a town that, according to Austin, "had a general store in the 1880s with a sign that said 'Beer and Ice.' It was on a wooden plank and it weathered off until it just said, 'And Ice,' so that's how the community got its name." This kind of small town straightforward simplicity has transferred itself into his earthy persona and vocal style. Influenced by Marty Robbins, Charley Pride, Merle Haggard, and other classic country stylists, Austin began playing piano and guitar at age 12. By the time he was in his teens, he was joining his father and uncles in the family band that played the Texas club circuit. In 1999, he signed with Asylum Records who released his debut album All My Dreams. His self-titled follow-up arrived in late 2000. *—Zac Johnson*

All My Dreams / Oct. 26, 1999 / Asylum ♦♦♦

• **Chad Austin** / Oct. 3, 2000 / Asylum ♦♦♦♦

Country singer and proud Texan Chad Austin grew up in a musical family. His father and uncles spent plenty of nights performing at one local club or another. Austin learned to play the guitar and the piano at a young age, and then joined his father on-stage where they offered their audiences tunes that were traditional country in the style of artists like Marty Robbins and Merle Haggard. Austin never moved away from those early influences, and it shows in his music. In 1999 he recorded his first album; the title, *All My Dreams*, seemed more than appropriate for the debut. For the new millennium, Austin recorded a self-titled album that is sure to please his fans, with more of what they enjoyed from the debut. This impressive sophomore offering is all country. Some of the standout tunes from *Chad Austin* are "That's a Woman," "It's Tomorrow in Atlanta," and "Both Sides of Goodbye." *—Charlotte Dillon*

Gene Autry

b. Sep. 29, 1907, Tioga, TX, **d.** Oct. 2, 1998, Studio City, CA

Guitar, Songwriter, Vocals / Traditional Country, Cowboy

Gene Autry was more than a musician. His music, coupled with his careers in movies and on radio and television, made him a part of the mythos that has made up the American identity for the past hundred years—John Wayne with a little bit of Sam Houston and Davy Crockett all rolled into one, with a great singing voice and an ear for music added on. He defined country music for two generations of listeners, cowboy songs for much of the 20th century, and American music for much of the world. He was country music's first genuine "multimedia" star, the best-known country & western singer on records, in movies, on radio, and on television from the early '30s until the mid-'50s. His 300 songs cut between 1929 and 1964 include nine gold record awards and one platinum record; his 93 movies saved one big chunk of the movie industry, delighted millions, and made millionaires of several producers (as well as Autry himself); his radio and television shows were even more popular and successful; and a number of his songs outside of the country & western field have become American pop culture touchstones.

The biggest selling country & western singer of the middle of the 20th century was born Orvon Gene Autry on September 29, 1907, in the tiny Texas town of Tioga, the son of Delbert and Elnora Ozmont Autry. He was first taught to sing at age five by his grandfather, William T. Autry, a Baptist preacher and descendant of some of the earliest settlers in Texas, contemporaries of the Houstons and the Crocketts (an Autry had died at the Alamo). The boy's interest in music was encouraged by his mother, who taught him hymns and folk songs and read psalms to him at night. Autry got his first guitar at age 12, bought from the Sears, Roebuck & Co. catalog for eight dollars (saved from his work as a hired hand on his uncle's farm baling and stacking hay). By the time he was 15, he had played anyplace there was to perform in Tioga, including school plays and the local cafe, but made most of his living working for the railroad as an apprentice at $35 a month. Later on, as a proper telegraph operator, he was making $150 a month, which those days was a comfortable income in that part of Texas.

He was working the four-to-midnight shift at the local telegraph office in Chelsea, OK, one summer night in 1927 when, to break up the monotony, he began strumming a guitar and singing quietly to himself. A customer came into the office; rather than insisting upon immediate service, he motioned for Autry to continue singing, then sat down to watch and listen while he looked over the pages he was preparing to send. At one point, the visitor asked him to sing another. Finally, after dropping his copy on the counter, the customer told Autry that with some hard work, he might have a future on the radio, and should consider going to New York to pursue a singing career. The man, whom Autry had recognized instantly, was Will Rogers, the humorist, writer, and movie actor, and one of the most popular figures in the entertainment world of that era.

Autry didn't immediately give up his job, but just over a year later he was in New York auditioning for a representative of RCA Victor. The judgment was that he had a good voice, but should stay away from pop hits, find his own kind of songs and his own sound, and get some experience. He was back six months later, on October 9, 1929, cutting his first record, "My Dreaming of You"/"My Alabama Home," for Victor. Two weeks later, Autry was making a demo record for the Columbia label of Jimmie Rodgers' "Blue Yodel No. 5." Present that same day in the studio were two up-and-coming singers, Rudy Vallée and Kate Smith. Autry found himself being pressured to sign an exclusive contract with Victor, but chose instead to sign with the American Record Corporation. Their general manager, Arthur Satherly (who would later record Leadbelly, among many other acts), persuaded Autry that while Victor was a large company and could offer more money and a better marketing apparatus, he would be lost at Victor amid its existing stable of stars, whereas ARC would treat him as their most important star. Additionally, Satherly—through a series of arrangements involving major retail and chain stores across the country—now had the means to get Autry's records into peoples' hands as easily as Victor.

His first recordings had just been released when his mother, who'd been ill for months, died at the age of 45, apparently of cancer. Autry's father began drifting away soon afterward, and he became the head of the family and the main supporter of himself, two sisters, and a younger brother. In early December of 1929, Autry cut his first six sides for ARC. The music was a mix of hillbilly, blues, country, yodel songs, and cowboy ballads. His breakthrough record, "That Silver-Haired Daddy of Mine," co-written by Autry and his friend Jimmy Long one night at the railroad depot, was released in 1931. The song sold 30,000 copies within a month, and by the end of a year 500,000 had been sold, an occasion that American Records decided to mark with the public presentation of a gold-plated copy of the record. Autry received a second gold record when sales later broke one million. And that was where the notion of the Gold Record Award was born. The record also led him into a new career on the radio as Oklahoma's Yodeling Cowboy on the *National Barn Dance* show sponsored by WLS out of Chicago. It was there that Autry became a major national star—his record sales rose assisted by his exposure on radio.

During the early years of his career, Autry took a number of important collaborators and musicians aboard. Among them were Fred Rose, the songwriter (later responsible for "Your Cheatin' Heart") with whom he collaborated on many of his hits, and fiddle player Carl Cotner (who also played sax, clarinet, and piano), who became his arranger. Autry had a knack for knowing a good song when he heard it (though he almost passed on the biggest hit of his career), and for knowing when a song needed something extra in its arrangement, but it was Cotner who was able to translate his sensibilities into musical notes and arrangements. Mary Ford, later of Les Paul fame, was in Autry's band at one time, and in 1936 Autry signed up a 17-year-old guitar player named Merle Travis, the future country star and songwriter.

By the early '30s, Autry became one of the most beloved singers in country & western music. By 1933, he was getting fan letters by the hundreds every week, and his record sales were only going up. Autry's career might've been made right there, but fate intervened again that year, in the form of the movie business. The Western—especially the B Western, the bottom-of-the-bill, low-budget action oater—had been hit very hard by the coming of sound in the years 1927 to 1929. Audiences expected dialogue in their movies, and most Western stars up to that time were a lot better at riding, roping, and shooting than reading lines. Not only did producers and directors need something to fill up the soundtracks of their movies, especially on the limited budgets of the B Westerns, but something to substitute for violent action, which was being increasingly criticized by citizen groups.

Cowboy star Ken Maynard, who was a great trick rider and stuntman but no singer, had tried singing songs in a few of his movies, and the producers noticed that the songs had gone over well despite his vocal limitations. Maynard was making another Western, *In Old Santa Fe* (1934), for Mascot Pictures, and producer Nat Levine decided to try an experiment, putting in a musical number sung by a professional. By sheer chance, the American Record Company and Mascot Pictures were locked together financially, though indirectly, and with the help from the president of ARC, Levine was steered toward Autry. A phone call brought the young singer and another ARC performer—multi-instrumentalist/comedian Smiley Burnette—out to Hollywood, where, after a quick meeting and screen test, the two were put into *In Old Santa Fe*. Autry had only one scene, singing a song and calling a square dance, but that scene proved to be one of the most popular parts of the movie.

Levine next stuck Autry and Burnette into a Ken Maynard serial, *Mystery Mountain*, in minor supporting roles. But Autry's next appearance was much more important, as the star of the highly successful 12-chapter serial *The Phantom Empire*. Perhaps recognizing that Autry was no "actor," and that he had an audience of millions already, he, the writers, and the producer agreed that he should simply play "Gene Autry," a good-natured radio singer and sometime cowboy. The success of Autry's early films was not enough to save Mascot Pictures, which collapsed under the weight of debts held by Consolidated Film Laboratories, which did Mascot's film processing. In 1935, Consolidated forced a merger of Mascot and a handful of other small studios and formed Republic Pictures, with Consolidated's president, Herbert J. Yates, at the helm. Republic thrived in the B movie market, ultimately dominating the entire field for the next 20 years. And central to Republic's success were the Westerns of Gene Autry.

His first starring Western for the newly organized Republic Pictures, *Tumbling Tumbleweeds* (released on September 5, 1935), which also included the singing group the Sons of the Pioneers, was a huge hit, and was followed by *Melody Trail*, *The Sagebrush Troubador*, and *The Singing Vagabond*, all released during the final three months of 1935. Autry settled into a schedule of one movie every six weeks, or eight per year, at $5,000 per movie, and a formula was quickly established. The production values on these movies were modest, in keeping with their low budgets and tight shooting schedules, but within the framework of B Westerns and the context of their music, they were first-rate productions. By 1937 and for five years after—a string that was only broken when he enlisted in the army during World War II—Autry was rated in an industry survey of theater owners as one of the top ten box-office attractions in the country, alongside the likes of James Cagney and Clark Gable. Autry was the only cowboy star to make the list, and the only actor from B movies on the list.

For Republic Pictures, his movies were such a cash cow, and so popular in the southern, border, and western states, that the tiny studio was able to use them as a way to force "block booking" on theater owners and chains—that is, theaters only got access to the Autry movies scheduled each season if they bought all of Republic's titles for that season. It was Autry's discovery of this policy (which, in fairness, was practiced by every major studio at the time, and led to the anti-trust suit by the government that ultimately forced the studios to give up their theater chains) in early 1938 that led to his first break with Republic. The problems had been brewing for some time, over Autry's unhappiness at never having gotten a raise from his original Mascot-era $5,000-per-movie deal, and contractual clauses—which had never been exercised, but worried him nonetheless—giving Republic a share of his radio, personal appearance, and endorsement earnings. After trying unsuccessfully to work out the problems with Yates, Autry walked out of the studio chief's office and thereafter refused to report for the first day's shooting on a movie called *Washington Cowboy*, later retitled *Under Western Stars* when it became the debut of Roy Rogers.

After eight months of legal sparring, Autry was left enjoined from making live appearances. Republic, however, found itself with an uprising of theater owners and chains on its hands—without a guarantee that it would have any Autry movies to release, the studio's entire annual distribution plans were jeopardized. By the fall of 1938 the two sides had come to terms, with raises for Autry and freedom from the most onerous clauses in his old contract. Despite his best efforts, however, he couldn't help the theater owners over the block-booking policy, for it was now entrenched in the industry and an integral part of Republic's business plan.

Meanwhile, his recording career continued, often in tandem with the movies. Whenever Republic could, the studio licensed the rights to whatever hit song Autry had most recently recorded to use it as the title of his newest picture—when this was done, Republic always charged the theater owners somewhat more for the film, and they paid it, because the song had "pre-sold" the movie to the public. The songs kept coming, sometimes out of the movies themselves, and not always his own: Autry's friend Ray Whitley had written "Back in the Saddle Again" for a 1938 George O'Brien Western called *Border G-Man*, and when Autry was looking for a theme song for his own radio show, he went back to Whitley's song, made a few changes, and recorded it himself. Along with "That Silver-Haired Daddy of Mine," it was the song he would be most closely associated with.

Autry's career was interrupted by his service in the military during World War II, but when he returned to the recording and movie studios in 1945, he resumed both his singing and film careers without skipping a beat. He was still a name to be reckoned with at the box office, although he was never again ranked among the top ten money-making stars of movies. The cultural dislocations caused by World War II and their effect on rural and small-town America and on the movie business, as well as the impending arrival of television, had shrunk the B movie market to a shadow of its 1930s glory. His movies still made money, however, and he kept making them right into the beginning of the 1950s, after which he moved into television production—Autry had already begun buying up radio stations before the war, and by the early '50s he was owner of several television stations, a studio, and his own production company, where he made his own television program as well as others that he owned.

His singing career was bigger than ever, however. Even before the war, Autry had occasionally moved away from country music and scored big, as with his 1940 hit version of "Blueberry Hill," which predated Fats Domino's recording by 16 years. After the war, he still did cowboy and country songs such as "Silver Spurs" and "Sioux City Sue," sprinkled with occasional folk songs and pop numbers. In 1949, however, Autry scored the biggest single hit of his career—and possibly the second- or third-biggest hit song ever recorded up to that time—with "Rudolph the Red-Nosed Reindeer," a song by Johnny Marks that Autry had recorded only reluctantly, in a single take at the end of a session. That same year, he cut "(Ghost) Riders in the Sky," a number by a former forest ranger named Stan Jones, which became both a country and pop music standard, cut by everyone from Vaughan Monroe to Johnny Cash.

By the mid-'50s, Autry's career had slowed. Rock & roll and R&B were attracting younger listeners, and a new generation of country music stars, heralded by Johnny Cash and Marty Robbins, was beginning to attract serious sales. Autry, then in his forties, still had his audience, but he gradually receded from the limelight to attend to his burgeoning business interests. He died October 2, 1998. *—Bruce Eder*

Country Music Hall of Fame / 1970 / Columbia ♦♦♦♦♦

Country's first hat act was the inspiration to a generation crooning, smooth and sincere, in the Roosevelt era. *—Mark A. Humphrey*

Back in the Saddle Again / 1977 / Sony Special Products ♦♦♦♦

This 12-song budget collection covers Autry's early career at Columbia Records, much of which is not usually included on compilations—not only the expected cowboy songs ("Way Out West in Texas," "The Dying Cowgirl," etc., which feature Autry yodeling), but blues as well. Going back to 1931 and "Mississippi Valley Blues," a duet with Jimmy Long, and other, less-well-remembered songs, the sound is rougher and less sophisticated than that which he subsequently achieved in the studio. Some of the music almost has the texture of field recordings, Autry's basic, unaffected singing style and the relatively primitive recorded sound combining to give the music an authentic feel that is startling. The version of "Back in the Saddle Again" featured here is also different from that usually included in Autry collections. The age and conditions of some of the masters have made this disc a little noisier than usual, but for fans who want to hear what Autry sounded like early in his career, add an extra notch to the rating. *—Bruce Eder*

Columbia Historic Edition / 1982 / Columbia ♦♦♦♦

This ten-song, low-mid-priced collection covers yet more Autry songs that aren't on the other budget Autry releases—and, like them, includes only minimal annotation. Originally released by the Vocalion, OKeh, Banner, and Columbia labels between 1935-1944, this would be a chunk of an Autry best-of set, featuring his cover of Bob Nolan's "Tumbling Tumbleweeds," the gentle Western swing-styled "I'll Go Ridin' Down That Texas Trail," "Don't Fence Me In" (which is best-remembered as the title of a Roy Rogers B-western), the ravishingly romantic "Amapola" (which makes "South of the Border" seem tepid), and the previously unreleased romantic ballad "There's a New Moon Over My Shoulder," one of the catchiest, bounciest, most well-played songs in Autry's output. In the absence of a complete Gene Autry set from Bear Family (which would require at least eight CDs), it's worth springing for this collection, which was prepared with the assistance of the Country Music Foundation, along with the others. *—Bruce Eder*

Gene Autry's Golden Hits / 1985 / Good Music ♦♦♦♦♦

If this 20-song collection were easy to find, it would probably be a good starting point for Autry fans to start collecting him on CD. But it's not, being a product of the Good Music Company of Katonah, NY. It does have the most popular versions of many of Autry's most familiar songs, including "Back In the Saddle Again," "That Silver-Haired Daddy of Mine," "You Are My Sunshine," "South of the Border," and "Goodbye, Little Darlin' Goodbye," grouped with such standards as "Tumbling Tumbleweeds," "Home on the Range," "Sioux City Sue," "Red River Valley," and "The Last Roundup," all in good sound. *—Bruce Eder*

Christmas Favorites / 1989 / CBS Special Products ♦♦♦♦

Beyond his work as a singer of cowboy songs and pop standards, Gene Autry also had a major career as a singer of novelty songs, including Christmas songs, recording the second biggest seller of them all after "White Christmas," "Rudolph the Red-Nosed Reindeer," in 1949. He cut three other Christmas songs that day, plus a bunch more throughout his career, and 14 of them (including "Rudolph") are included here, among them such stylized pieces as "The Night Before Christmas (In Texas, That Is)" as well as familiar fare like "Here Comes Santa Claus" and "Santa Claus Is Coming to Town." The voice is so honest and unaffected that you absolutely want to believe that Santa is somewhere out there, and the arrangements are top-notch, bright, and engaging in their own right, and two of them feature Autry in duets with Rosemary Clooney (mother of George, for any youngsters reading this) when she was in her prime. *—Bruce Eder*

Greatest Hits / 1992 / Sony ♦♦♦♦

Gene Autry was the greatest Western singer who ever stepped in front of a microphone, and if anyone doubts it, they can get their minds changed by this budget-priced ten-song collection. This 27-minute CD may not offer a lot in length, and any real Autry greatest-hits collection could easily run 20 songs and still be skimpy. But the ten songs that are here are the ones for which audiences most loved Autry—"That Silver-Haired Daddy of Mine," "You Are My Sunshine," "Back in the Saddle Again," "Have I Told You Lately That I Love You," "Blueberry Hill" (he had the hit with it more than ten years before Fats Domino), "South of the Border," and Stan Jones' "(Ghost) Riders in the Sky," the latter in its most soulful and moving interpretation ever. The sound is excellent, and the particular versions (Autry recorded a couple of these numbers more than once) are definitive. There are no notes or recording dates, but the music is so beguiling that this is a must-own bargain volume. *—Bruce Eder*

★ **The Essential Gene Autry** / Aug. 18, 1992 / Columbia/Legacy ♦♦♦♦♦

This would be a perfect Autry collection but for the fact that it has only 18 songs, when there was room for about 25, and the producers evidently think that "South of the Border" and "Blueberry Hill" aren't "essential." But you do get "The Yellow Rose of Texas," "The Last Round-up," "Take Me Back To My Boots and Saddle," "The Call of the Canyon," "It Makes No Difference Now," "Deep in the Heart of Texas," "Tumbling Tumbleweeds" (featuring Jimmy Long and Smiley Burnette) and "Maria Elena," among others. And for a change, there are decent, detailed notes, though as soon as Bear Family gets around to it, their release will probably put all of these to shame. *—Bruce Eder*

South of the Border / 1994 / Castle ♦♦♦

South of the Border isn't a bad Gene Autry collection, mid-priced with 18 songs, also Mexican or Spanish theme material. There are no dates for the music listed, although all of it is in stereo and dates from long after the classic Columbia recordings. Autry's voice is less rich and attractive than those classic sides, and the cover art is tacky, but there's a lot here that isn't easy to find elsewhere on compact disc, including "You Belong to My Heart," "El Rancho Grande," "In a Little Spanish Town," "My Adobe Hacienda," and "A Gay Ranchero," as well as his recordings of "Dixie Cannon Ball," "Serenade of the Bells," and "Down in the Valley." The material tends toward the more romantic pop side of Autry's repertory, and fans of his blues and cowboy songs may want to skip this release. But anyone who likes his voice or enjoys the romantic side of singing cowboy movies will love this collection—and his performance of "Under Fiesta Stars" by itself will prove worth the price. *—Bruce Eder*

A Gene Autry Christmas / 1994 / Columbia/Legacy ♦♦♦

Released by Columbia/Legacy in 1994, *A Gene Autry Christmas* is an excellent overview of his holiday recordings for Columbia, featuring no less than 16 songs, including his classic "Here Comes Santa Claus," "Rudolph the Red-Nosed Reindeer," "If it Doesn't Snow on Christmas Day," "Santa Claus Is Coming to Town" and "Everyone's a Child at Christmas." Autry's recordings were almost always charming, and that quality was in ample display on his holiday albums. This disc does a terrific job of rounding up highlights from those many records; it very well could be the definitive Autry Christmas collection. *—Stephen Thomas Erlewine*

● **Portrait of an Artist** / 1995 / Sound Exchange ♦♦♦♦♦

Now this is more like it: The notes still aren't much, but there are 22 songs here, including most of the best material of the existing budget collections, except for the early-'30s-focused *Back in the Saddle Again* (yet another, different, even more lively version of that song is present here), and a few odd items like "Buttons and Bows" that just aren't around elsewhere. The sound is about as good as it gets, and this would be the collection to go out and buy, except that it's a mail-order item from Time Warner on its Sound Exchange imprint, and, thus, you can't find it in stores, except maybe as a used item. And who would sell anything this good? *—Bruce Eder*

Back in the Saddle Again / 1996 / ASV ♦♦♦♦♦

This is one of the more interesting and appealing of Autry's compact discs, covering his earliest hillbilly and blues numbers, including "High Steppin' Mama" and "Blue Yodel No. 5," as well as alternate versions of such standards as "You Are My Sunshine" and "South of the Border" (in versions utterly different from those on the various Sony compilations) and pop numbers like "Blueberry Hill" going right into the end of World War II. The 25 songs run from the late '20s through the mid-'40s, and the sound is generally excellent, even on the older tracks, although "That Silver-Haired Daddy of Mine" and a handful of others are pretty rough. *—Bruce Eder*

Blues Singer 1929–1931: Booger Rooger Saturday / Oct. 8, 1996 / Columbia/Legacy ♦♦♦♦♦

If your concept of a blues singer embraces the sound of country music singer Jimmie Rodgers, as well as a Muddy Waters sideman like Jimmy Rogers, then this collection will make perfect sense to you. This superlative collection of Autry's earliest recordings for various Columbia budget labels like Melotone, Banner, Velvet Tone, Diva, and Oriole casts the latter-day cowboy hero in direct competition with Rodgers, sometimes recording covers of well-known hits by the Singing Brakeman. While seven of the 23 tracks collected here are Rodgers tunes (and superlative covers they are, too), ten of them are from Autry's pen, an indication that he not only had his own ideas to impart, but had figured the game out early from a business standpoint as well. On the majority of tracks, Autry is only accompanied by his yodeling and his acoustic guitar, but the addition on certain tracks of Roy Smeck on steel guitar or banjo certainly spices things up while allowing Autry to play some nifty fills in tandem. The biggest surprise, of course, is how comfortable Autry sounds on all of this material, clearly enjoying himself while finding his own voice as the sessions progress toward his "cowboy singer" breakthrough, only a year away from the last of these recordings. Yes, Gene Autry sang the blues and was pretty good at it, too. A landmark in country music's history while clearly demonstrating the cross-genre appeal of the blues as a musical form accessible to everyone. —*Cub Koda*

Sing Cowboy Sing: The Gene Autry Collection / Mar. 18, 1997 / Rhino ♦♦♦♦♦

Sing Cowboy Sing: The Gene Autry Collection is a comprehensive overview of the most famous singing cowboy in Hollywood history. Spanning three CDs and 84 tracks, the box set contains every one of Autry's biggest hits, plus several unreleased cuts from his *Melody Ranch* radio show and a handful of rarities from his classic Columbia recordings. Though the set is far too exhaustive for the casual listener, *Sing Cowboy Sing* is a loving tribute to Autry, and it is worth the investment of any devoted fan. —*Stephen Thomas Erlewine*

Singing Cowboy, Chapter One / Sep. 23, 1997 / Varese ♦♦♦♦♦

The idea behind this 28-minute collection was OK—collect the movie versions of some of Autry's most beloved songs for CD release. Included is his abbreviated rendition of Bob Nolan's "Tumbling Tumbleweeds" and the title track from *Guns and Guitars*, and the soundtrack versions of "Ride, Ranger, Ride," "Melody Ranch," "Down Mexico Way," "Sioux City Sue," and "Ghost Riders in the Sky." These are interesting, but only for the true fanatic—several of the songs have sound effects and even dialogue over their performances, and the fidelity is rather restricted, as the masters are mostly derived from optical film sources (magnetic sound being a rarity on low-budget movies of that era). The audio is compressed and overloaded, as well as noisy, so seriously that not even Autry's voice can really survive intact, with the result that the packaging is distinctly prettier than the sound. Additionally, while it might have worked well in cinematic terms, the mixing of Autry's voice with choruses, as on "Melody Ranch," is disastrous as a pure audio production. The postwar stuff is far superior to the prewar material, and "Ghost Riders in the Sky" almost works as a full-blown production. —*Bruce Eder*

Gene Autry With the Legendary Singing Groups of the West / Sep. 23, 1997 / Varese ♦♦♦♦♦

The companion to Autry's movie song collection works far better, opening with one of the most extraordinary team-ups of its kind, Gene Autry and Roy Rogers with the Sons of the Pioneers doing "Silent Trail." The use of dialogue elsewhere is a mistake, however, especially on "Wild and Wooley West," from *The Big Show*, which is too laden with support singers. Autry's work with the Cass County Boys on "Yours" and "That's My Home" is less than exceptional, though the Cass County Boys do well on their own "The Cowboy," "Cowboy Blues," and "Great Grandad"—in fact, this is a better showcase for them than it is for Autry or the Pioneers. Autry's collaboration with the Jimmy Wakely Trio (including Johnny Bond) is bright and distinctive, but his work with the Sons of the Pioneers on "Old Pinto" is wasted, as their harmonies don't come in until very late in the song. The sound is surprisingly good, given the age of the recordings, but this is primarily a release for serious fans. —*Bruce Eder*

Always Your Pal, Gene Autry / Mar. 24, 1998 / Sony Wonder ♦♦♦

Marketed as a children's album, *Always Your Pal, Gene Autry* compiles 16 recordings, most of which were made in the '50s. Some of the selections, such as "Rusty the Rocking Horse" and "Bucky the Bucking Bronco" are children's songs, while others, including "Back in the Saddle Again" and "The Old Chisholm Trail," are simply Western songs. The package offers Gene Autry's adult fans an opportunity to collect some of his seldom-anthologized recordings (many of the children's songs are enjoyable and only marginally juvenile), while children will appreciate the many animal characters described in the lyrics. The booklet includes lyrics for all of the selections so that listeners can easily sing along. —*Greg Adams*

The Singing Cowboy, Chapter Two / May 12, 1998 / Varese ♦♦♦

Taken right from the soundtracks of various films Autry starred in between 1937 and 1952, this isn't the place for new listeners to get acquainted with his work, as the fidelity isn't as good as what his studio recordings could offer. For specialists, though, it offers a number of classic cowboy tunes in their soundtrack versions, including "South of the Border," "Mexicali Rose," "Rancho Grande," and "Mule Train." Most are Autry solo turns, but some are sung with sidekicks like Smiley Burnette, or with group backing vocals. —*Richie Unterberger*

With His Little Darlin' Mary Lee / May 12, 1998 / Varese ♦♦

Autry fans should be aware that, although the disc bears the name of Gene Autry as the artist, it's really more a collection of Mary Lee performances containing a few duets with Autry than the other way around. Autry, in fact, only appears on six of the songs; one of these, "Carry Me Back to the Lone Prairie," is about the strongest (and most western-

sounding) performance. Lee was a teenage actress who made nine films with Autry, which naturally gave her the chance to sing, both solo and with Autry, on screen. These 16 tracks from 1939-1941, taken from the films themselves (there's an additional cut with dialogue only), are typically corny soundtrack fare of the period, not always exhibiting a strong connection to cowboy music. The package is well-annotated and so forth, but really advised for Autry or Lee lovers only. —*Richie Unterberger*

Last Round-Up: 25 Cowboy Classics / Jul. 21, 1998 / ASV ♦♦♦

20 Greatest Movie Hits / Feb. 9, 1999 / Varese ♦♦♦♦♦

Whether these 20 tracks constitute Gene Autry's "greatest movie hits" is anybody's guess, but they are extremely strong performances and the range of material is truly representative of the diversity of Autry's talent. The array of songs will astonish those who are unfamiliar with Autry's true musical depth—"That Silver-Haired Daddy of Mine" is represented, as are "Back in the Saddle Again," "Melody Ranch," "I'm an Old Cowhand," "Sioux City Sue," and "Someday (You'll Want Me to Want You)," but so are "My Buddy," "Blueberry Hill," "In the Jailhouse Now," and "Oklahoma Hills." His singing is amazing, not a trained voice but an honest and expressive one, rather like that of Fred Astaire; "Carry Me Back to the Lone Prairie" is one of Autry's towering performances, gently and convincingly dramatic and honest, while "I'm an Old Cowhand" is just as impressive for its good humor and jocularity. The accompaniment varies from unobtrusive choir to straight, stripped-down Western band, and Autry is joined on some tracks by Ann Miller, Mary Lee, and Smiley Burnette. In contrast to the earlier volumes, the audio quality on this disc is remarkably good, and none of the movie-action noise intrudes on any of the songs. Indeed, in the absence of a decent, well-thought-out Columbia Records (where he spent most of his career) collection on Gene Autry, *20 Greatest Movie Hits* could be the best single disc through which to get a glimpse of the triple-threat talent that was Gene Autry, although without "Rudolph the Red-Nose Reindeer," it's not definitive either (although it does give us "Here Comes Santa Claus" as compensation). The notes by James Laredo are loving and honest in dealing with their subject. —*Bruce Eder*

Love Songs / Feb. 9, 1999 / Varese ♦♦♦

This is a decent if not ideal companion volume to Autry's *20 Greatest Movie Hits* CD, with a bit of overlap "Someday (You'll Want Me To Want You)." Generally it has the same high quality sound, but the annotation is minimal, which is understandable, since the songs rather speak for themselves. "Let Me Call You Sweetheart" is one of the more familiar numbers in this 18 songs collection—"The Girl in the Middle of My Heart," "I'm Mad About You," "You Belong to My Heart," and "You Stole My Heart" are typical of the titles, romantic ballads that are always pleasant, but not at all representative of Autry's output and, thus, not necessarily of interest to all fans. —*Bruce Eder*

Country Music Hall of Fame 1969 / Nov. 9, 1999 / King ♦♦♦

Ten selections of Gene Autry classics have been remastered as part of King's tribute to Country Music Hall of Fame inductees (Autry was inducted two years after the Music Hall's opening in 1967). This compilation includes such signature tunes as "Back in the Saddle Again," "The Yellow Rose of Texas," and "Buttons and Bows." —*Joslyn Layne*

The Gene Autry Show, Vol. 1 / 2000 / Varese ♦♦♦

The Gene Autry Show, Vol. 1 is the first of three volumes that together collect all of the music from Autry's early- to mid-'50s television program. The disc begins and ends with the program's theme music, and in between are 36 brief songs and snippets of dialogue lifted directly from first 27 episodes of the show. The Cass County Boys, a Sons of the Pioneers-style Western trio that sometimes appeared on the program, provide occasional backing and enjoy an entertaining solo turn on "Great Grand Dad." Extraneous background noises sometimes intrude, so listeners who are looking for straightforward performances of Western songs should look elsewhere, but fans of Autry (and *The Gene Autry Show* in particular) will enjoy this revival of vintage television performances. —*Greg Adams*

Gene Autry Show, Vol. 2 / 2000 / Varese ♦♦♦

Picking up where the previous volume left off, *The Gene Autry Show, Vol. 2* collects all of the music from episodes 28-64 of *The Gene Autry Show*, Autry's early- to mid-'50s television program. The compilers did a thorough job of including all of the music from the show, even incidental bits such as Pat Buttram singing "Back in the Saddle Again," which adds to the vintage television appeal of the package. Most of the songs are Autry originals, Western classics, or traditional numbers, usually given partial run-throughs because of the time limitations of the original program. More of a nostalgia item than a collection of straight Western recordings, this volume and its two companions are recommended to fans of Autry and golden age television. —*Greg Adams*

Gene Autry Show, Vol. 3 / 2000 / Varese ♦♦♦

The third and final installment of a series, *The Gene Autry Show, Vol. 3* wraps up Varese Sarabande's reissue of the music from Autry's weekly Western television program with another 35 snippets of songs and dialogue. Autry duets with the occasional female co-star, and is joined on several other songs by the Cass County Boys, who are granted a couple of solo numbers as well. This volume spans episodes 65-91, the final episode of which marked the end of the series' original run in 1955. A few songs that were performed earlier in the series are reprised here in new performances, and the remainder is in keeping with the now-familiar mix of Autry originals, Western classics, and traditional tunes. The three individual volumes of this series were also packaged together in a slipcase as a limited-edition box set. —*Greg Adams*

The Gene Autry Show: The Complete 1950s Television Recordings / Oct. 24, 2000 / Varese ♦♦♦

The Gene Autry Show was a weekly television program on which Autry, after the obligatory horse chases and shoot-outs, brought an endless parade of bad guys to justice. It was primarily a Western action series, but Autry usually managed to squeeze in one or two brief songs, mostly Western favorites and his own hits, but sometimes unusual selections. This three-disc box set collects every musical performance from the entire 1950-1955 run of the program, which amounts to over 100 songs, plus bits of dialogue and the opening and closing scores. Since these recordings were taken directly from the television series, there is often extraneous noise over the music—hammering, gunshots, and the like, and many of the tracks are mere song fragments. But the music and dialogue is wonderfully entertaining, particularly for fans of the television series, and the occasional oddball composition, such as "Crime Will Never Pay," is a hoot. This is a box set designed for fans, but it wouldn't take too much of a diehard to find enjoyment within. *—Greg Adams*

Gene Autry at the Melody Ranch / 2001 / Collectors' Choice Music ♦♦♦

Gene Autry is remembered as a movie-star cowboy, a singer of Western songs, and the person who made a huge hit out of "Rudolf the Red-Nosed Reindeer." *At the Melody Ranch* captures a number of Autry's radio performances from the 1940s, including a long skit that recalls his accidental rise to fame. "The Gene Autry Story" covers his early years, from cowhand to telegraph operator to singing star. It's kind of funny to hear Autry's wholesome, aw shucks persona explaining how no one would really enjoy listening to him sing. Really? Well, comedian Will Rogers felt differently. He encouraged the singing cowboy to go public, and a year later Autry signed with the American Recording Company, and the rest is singing-cowboy history. Of course this all may seem a little hokey today, but so what? This is how it happened. The remainder of the album is comprised of classics like "I Hate to Say Goodbye to the Prairies" and "At Sundown." The purple prose of the lyrics takes a page from Zane Grey, painting an unabashedly romantic picture of doggies, blazing trails, and endless ranges. The tasteful arrangements of guitars, fiddles, and, occasionally, horns are low key and never get in the way of Autry's resonant, upbeat vocals. There's also some fine harmony from his cowboy buddies that conjures up nights spent beneath the lonesome stars. *At the Melody Ranch* is short—32 minutes—but the material sounds great, and fans of Western music will not want to miss it. *—Ronnie Lankford Jr.*

The Western Collection / Oct. 30, 2001 / Varese ♦♦♦

Goin' Back to Texas / Oct. 30, 2001 / Varese ♦♦♦

The Cowboy Is a Patriot / Oct. 29, 2002 / Varese ♦♦♦

Hoyt Axton

b. Mar. 25, 1938, Duncan, OK, **d.** Oct. 26, 1999, Victor, MT

Guitar, Songwriter, Vocals / Country-Pop, Traditional Country

First rising to prominence as a songwriter, Hoyt Axton carved out successful careers as a singer and actor as well; rooted equally in country, folk and pop, his gravelly baritone and wry, earthy songs projected an uncommon wit, warmth, and optimism, yielding a consistently engaging body of work extending across four decades. Axton was born March 25, 1938 in Duncan, OK, the son of a naval officer and his English teacher wife. Raised primarily in Jacksonville, FL, he studied classical piano as a child before switching to guitar, writing his first songs at 15. Despite the musical impact of his mother, Mae Boren Axton—the co-author of Elvis Presley's landmark 1956 chart-topper "Heartbreak Hotel"—he initially pursued a career in athletics, attending Oklahoma State University on a football scholarship before serving a stint in the navy. From there Axton relocated to San Francisco, performing at local folk clubs and in 1962 writing his first hit, the Kingston Trio's "Greenback Dollar." Later that year he issued his first album, *The Balladeer*, a live effort recorded at the Hollywood nightspot the Troubadour; a concurrent appearance on the television western *Bonanza* also launched his acting career.

Axton resurfaced in 1963 with *Thunder & Lightnin'*, followed later that year by *Saturday's Child*; around that same time one of his best friends suffered a fatal drug overdose, inspiring his song "The Pusher," a hit for the rock band Steppenwolf subsequently included on the soundtrack to the film *Easy Rider*. Despite his success as a songwriter, Axton's performing career failed to catch fire, and after 1965's *Sings Bessie Smith* he was without a recording contract for several years before signing to Columbia in 1969 to issue *My Griffin Is Gone*. While opening for Three Dog Night in support of the album, the band heard his composition "Joy to the World"—their recording of the song topped the pop charts in the spring of 1971—and early the following year they returned to the Top Ten with Axton's "Never Been to Spain." He signed to A&M to release 1973's *Less Than the Song*; the follow-up, *Life Machine*, launched two of his biggest solo hits, the lovely "When the Morning Comes" (a duet with Linda Ronstadt) and "Boney Fingers." In 1975, Ringo Starr also notched a Top Three smash with Axton's "The No No Song."

Following the much-acclaimed 1977 album *Snowblind Friend*, Axton completed his deal with MCA with the release of *Free Sailin'*; he then formed his own label, Jeremiah Records, and with 1979's *A Rusty Old Halo* scored his biggest solo hit with the classic "Della and the Dealer." In the wake of appearances on dozens of television series including *I Dream of Jeannie* and *McCloud*, he landed his first major film work that same year in the acclaimed family drama *The Black Stallion*; Axton's subsequent movie roles included co-starring appearances in projects including 1983's *Heart Like a Wheel*, 1984's *Gremlins*, and 1989's *We're No Angels*. After 1982's *Pistol Packin' Mama*, Jeremiah folded, and Axton was noticeably absent from recording until issuing the comeback album *Spin of the Wheel* in 1990. The LP was Axton's last major new release, however, and in 1996 he suffered a stroke; his health continued to decline, and after a series of heart attacks he died October 26, 1999, at the age of 61. *—Jason Ankeny*

Thunder & Lightnin' / 1963 / Horizon ♦♦♦

Saturday's Child / 1963 / Vee-Jay ♦♦

Devoted largely to traditional folk and blues selections, this sounds more like an undernourished demo session than a proper album. Axton sings fairly well, but not exceptionally, as he plays acoustic guitar (presumably, no credits are given) and interprets familiar tunes like the title track, "Willie Jean," "St. James Infirmary," "Make Me a Pallet," and "Hoochie Coochie Man" (the last of which he is, erroneously, given the songwriting credit). What really sinks the set is the addled decision to use squiggly trad jazz-styled trombone on many of the tracks, which makes this, probably inadvertently, sound close to a novelty record. As a solo acoustic folk album, this could have been adequate; the addition of trombone (and nothing else) is a mismatch. Axton's own songwriting efforts are limited to a couple of tunes, and are in a pretty bluesy fettle; curiosity seekers should also note that he covers a couple of compositions by Rod McKuen. *—Richie Unterberger*

Explodes / 1964 / Vee-Jay ♦♦♦

Axton may have been known as something of a folksinger at the time of this release, and he may have subsequently become known as a country artist, but make no mistake: This is a rock album, albeit a pretty strange one by 1964 standards. Not so much because it's weird, but because it's an uncomfortable intersection of blues, go-go R&B-influenced rock, and hints of folk and novelty songwriting. It's *not* a folk-rock album, despite Axton's background; the arrangements are rather close to those used by Johnny Rivers on his mid-'60s material. Or, if you prefer, it's something of a much more pop-oriented John Hammond Jr. It's that hard to peg. And it's not that good, though unlike his prior Vee-Jay effort, *Saturday's Child*, it uses full electric arrangements, and Axton wrote most of the material. For much of the set he adopts a growling blues voice that's not only at odds with the peppy R&B/pop production, but also doesn't suit him too well. When he unleashes full-out-throaty growls (as he does often on this LP), he doesn't sound tough or swaggering; he just sounds like someone who really needs to clear his throat, or at least to lighten up if he doesn't want to destroy his lungs. The songs are largely routine, studly blues-pop numbers, sometimes faintly reminiscent of songs like "Hi Heel Sneakers," though there's perhaps some (very) muted anti-war protest in "Red White & Blue," and a bit of a troubadour folk gallop to the moody "Young Man." The only other cover is a ludicrously uptempo, hoarsely screamed-sung rock version of "Heartbreak Hotel," co-written by his mother, Mae Axton. The album's not that hard to listen to, but it's not that pleasant to listen to either. And it must have been even harder to market, given its indecisive stylings. *—Richie Unterberger*

Sings Betty Smith / 1965 / Exodus ♦♦♦

Mr Greenback Dollar Man / 1965 / Surrey ♦♦♦

My Griffin Is Gone / 1969 / Edsel ♦♦♦♦

Hoyt Axton was still in his first decade as a recording artist when he made this album, but it was a decade in which performing artists were certainly encouraged to think lofty thoughts. Pretension was as common on the radio in the late '60s as thongs would be in the '90s, hence we have an album, but sadly enough no song, on the theme of losing one's "griffin," typical Axton imagery that subtly invokes the wonder of childhood while pretending to be doing something else. He settles into some remarkable moods on the best parts of the album, communicating with such a sense of the natural that it makes the work of many other recording artists seem stilted. He can evoke the feeling of Colorado simply by mentioning the state as if in passing conversation; other singers would have to be recorded riding up and down a ski lift strumming in order to establish any equivalent sense of time and place. While his social commentary, such as "Beelzebub's Laughter," has the sting, if not the detail, of mid-period Phil Ochs, some of the songs—such as "Way Before the Time of Towns" and "Revelations"—ring so totally hollow, without any real sense of conviction or commitment, that the listener will be longing for one of the musicians to make a satirical raspberry. Instead it is a subdued, talented crowd doing the backup, pursuing a mood that can be quite effective when the ingredients are right—roughly about half the time on this uneven but respectable production. Lead guitar is in the capable hands of James Burton, but this cannot be said to have been one of his most rip-roaring days in the studio. *—Eugene Chadbourne*

Joy to the World / 1971 / Capitol ♦♦♦♦♦

Songwriter Hoyt Axton lets loose with a batch of original songs that have been heavily covered (resulting in hits) by artists as varied as Three Dog Night, Steppenwolf, and Waylon Jennings. Axton has a distinctive style which makes his original versions as interesting as the better-known covers. *—Jim Worbois*

Less Than the Song / 1973 / A&M ♦♦♦♦

There is a concept at work on *Less Than the Song*, at least in terms of presentation. The songs are stripped to the bone with Axton's giant voice out front, an acoustic guitar behind, and smatterings of other instruments here and there for color—but no drum kit. It's an unusual and risky blend considering that *Less Than the Song* was Axton's debut for A&M, but the result is gratifying. Many casual listeners may not even note the absence of drums, and the songs are nearly all Axton's. "Sweet Misery" was perhaps too bluesy for country radio and failed as a single, but it's one of Axton's classics. The halting piano rhythm of "Oklahoma Song" and the startling rooster sounds on "Mexico City Hangover" show that *Less Than the Song* is really a fairly quirky, experimental album disguised as a commercial country record. *—Greg Adams*

Life Machine / 1974 / A&M ♦♦♦♦♦

After the interesting but comparatively uncommercial *Less Than the Song*, Hoyt Axton justified A&M's investment with *Life Machine*, the album that generated "Boney Fingers," his biggest and most enduring hit. "When the Morning Comes," which features harmony vocals by Linda Ronstadt, also made the country Top Ten and gave Axton his only pop hit. "Geronimo's Cadillac" is a powerful album track, and modernized versions of "That's All Right" and "Maybelline" seem appropriate for the man whose mother co-wrote "Heartbreak Hotel." Elsewhere the album takes some unusual detours of the sort that Axton's fans come to either anticipate or endure, such as "Pet Parade," which is practically a children's song, and the slick, funky "Telephone Booth." Axton's four albums for A&M are usually considered his best, and of those, *Life Machine* may rate the highest for the inclusion of his two big hits. *—Greg Adams*

Southbound / 1975 / A&M ✦✦✦
By the time of this, his 13th and a relatively unlucky album, Hoyt Axton's talent was not always as strong a force as his own firm belief in the Axton legend: a genius songwriting artist with his own niche, not quite country, not quite rock, not quite pop. It is also the concept of "good old boy" charm that is wrapped around this album like yellow ribbons during a hostage crisis; it is something along the order of a Mac Davis vibe, and like the similarly well-tanned Davis, Axton comes across best when in a rowdy mode. His "Roll Your Own" is an in-your-face, unabashed pot song that would give a rasta a coughing fit, but there is equal time to drink in "Whisky," visit "Nashville," and get caught in a "Speed Trap." These titles all form an inner block inside the record when the listener may begin to feel like all is right with Axton's world—he is cooking along and the God-squad philosophies of his earlier albums have happily vamoosed. Elsewhere on the album, however, is an excruciating version of "Greensleeves" and a flabby number called "Pride of Man" which unfortunately has led jumpy discographers to credit Axton with composing a different song with the same title by the Quicksilver Messenger Service. But while that "Pride of Man" was a highlight of the latter band's debut album, the Axton song is nothing to be proud of, like several numbers in this collection that seem like half-finished throwaways. Sometimes the songs themselves actually may have had the potential to come across much better than they do due to the party-hearty studio atmosphere, in which all manner of celebrity interface and networking seems to have been going on. Cheech & Chong make an appearance and so does television hunk David Hasselhoff. There is the warbling of Linda Ronstadt as well as that of Bob Lind, the one-hit wonder behind "Elusive Butterfly." The thoughtful Axton is on to some truths and gets his musicians into worthwhile grooves on a few less of the tracks than most listeners will find satisfactory. *—Eugene Chadbourne*

Fearless / 1976 / A&M ✦✦✦

Snowblind Friend / 1977 / Edsel ✦✦✦

Road Songs / 1977 / A&M ✦✦✦✦✦
Featuring instrumental support from James Burton and backing vocals from Linda Ronstadt, *Road Songs* has a good cross-section of Axton's best-known songs, including "Boney Fingers" and "The No-No Song," making it a good introduction to the songwriter. *—Stephen Thomas Erlewine*

Free Sailin' / 1978 / MCA ✦✦✦
Although it produced no hits and has only a few originals, it's a strong album that touches on Country anthems ("Honky Tonk Music"), vintage Country (Carson Robison's "Left My Gal in the Mountains"), and another of Axton's many drug-related songs ("Them Downers"). Because of the brief running time it would have been nice if *Free Sailin'* had been issued as a two-fer with Axton's other MCA album, *Snowblind Friend* (also available on CD from Edsel), but it's worthwhile to have the album available again in any form. [England's Edsel Records, responsible for reviving so much of Hoyt Axton's catalog in latter days, likewise reissued *Free Sailin'*, his 1978 MCA album, on CD.] *—Greg Adams*

A Rusty Old Halo / 1979 / Jeremiah ✦✦✦✦
As the '70s came to a final fizzle, this songwriter had a thriving acting career and probably plenty of money. Maybe he didn't need to keep recording, and skeptics who might have been worn down by the uneven nature of his recording career would probably question whether Axton had anything more to say on record. The recording industry that had made a fortune on his work had come to such a negative conclusion, leading Axton to start his own label and put this record out himself, yet another addition to a teetering pile of sides that he began in the early '60s with Vee-Jay, progressing through stages of thought-provoking country art music that attracted musician followers, to ultra-laid-back outlaw country that attracted Hollywood airheads. Here he assembles several busloads of heavy-duty musician friends and looks back over all these developments in his music, choosing a song from 1974, another from 1978, and basically putting together a full album of the different aspects of his work with many less missteps than on his albums as a young man. His sincerity, one of his great strengths when it is present, is a strong part of the success of tracks such as the title song or the superb "So Hard to Give It All Up." Many of the tracks just don't seem to get a chance to breathe, however, such is the steamroller effect of one band in which guitarist Steve Stills, his tone dazzling and bright, fights to keep up with the rollicking New Orleans rhythms created by Dr. John, one of the masters of that city's recording studios. Such authenticity and style is a bit lost on the low-key Axton, however—a bit like laying out an enormous spread of spicy food for someone with terrible heartburn. Axton almost staggers through the likes of the corny "Wild Bull Rider" and is too old and exhausted to be wondering about what's "In a Young Girl's Mind." The presence of his old compatriot James Burton on guitar bolsters confidence, however, and is highlighted on tracks where the guitarist and his fellow session pros create a veneer that would have been smooth enough for Elvis. *—Eugene Chadbourne*

American Originals / Jan. 18, 1993 / Capitol ✦✦✦
Part of an odd, short-lived reissued series launched by Capitol in the early '90s, *American Originals* consists of two 1971 albums, *Joy to the World* and *Country Anthem*, plus one previously unreleased track. This period was a transitional one between Axton's uneven folk/rock of the '60s and his country hits of the mid-'70s, but on these recordings Axton found the voice that would serve him throughout the rest of his career. Axton's own versions of "The Pusher," "Never Been to Spain" and "Joy to the World," hits he wrote for Steppenwolf and Three Dog Night, are here. Other highlights include the wryly humorous "Have a Nice Day," and "Thomas Hall," an excellent folk ballad. *—Greg Adams*

Lonesome Road / Jul. 18, 1995 / Combo ✦✦
Originally released as an LP, *Lonesome Road* is a brief collection of ten songs drawn from two 1964 Hoyt Axton albums, *Sings Bessie Smith* and *Explodes*. In the '60s, Axton's music veered toward folk and rock & roll rather than country, with limited success. "Young Man" and "Big Red" are straight-ahead rockers, and the Bessie Smith material is performed with horns and clarinet in an approximation of the originals, although Axton's vocals are often delivered in an unappealing growl. Given the scarcity of Axton's '60s recordings on CD, serious fans may find something to enjoy here. *—Greg Adams*

● **The A&M Years** / 1998 / A&M ✦✦✦✦✦
The A&M Years is a U.K. import that collects Hoyt Axton's four albums for the label—*Less Than the Song, Life Machine, Southbound*, and *Fearless*—on two CDs. This period of Axton's career (1973-1976) is often considered his peak as a recording artist, and some of his best-known performances are here, including "Boney Fingers," "When the Morning Comes," "Flash of Fire," and "Geronimo's Cadillac." This package marks the only appearance of his classic A&M material on CD; for some, that may justify its high import price (which, in reality, is no more expensive than these four albums would cost if they'd been reissued domestically on individual CDs). *—Greg Adams*

Rusty Old Halo/Where Did the Money Go? / Oct. 13, 1998 / Edsel ✦✦✦✦
In the late '70s, Hoyt Axton founded Jeremiah Records to release his new albums, and this import two-fer reissues the label's first two offerings. The first, *A Rusty Old Halo*, takes its name from Axton's rocking remake of a song recorded decades earlier by the Maddox Brothers & Rose. That and "Della and the Dealer," the latter of which Axton performed on the television sitcom *WKRP*, were Top 20 country hits. Two other singles from this quality album, "Wild Bull Rider" and "Evangelina," also entered the country Top 40. *Where Did the Money Go?* from 1980 was much less successful, and the material is accordingly more uneven. A scarcity of Axton originals and a few outright clunkers are two of the problems with the album, which is better appreciated in tandem with *A Rusty Old Halo* than alone. *—Greg Adams*

Pistol Packin' Mama/Spin of the Wheel / Oct. 13, 1998 / Edsel ✦✦
This import CD is a reissue of Hoyt Axton's third and fourth studio albums released on his own Jeremiah label. *Pistol Packin' Mama*, from 1982, is dominated by remakes of well-known songs like the title track, "I Walk the Line," and "Don't Fence Me In." Axton's songwriting contribution is at an all-time low, and one of the few new originals is the annoying "Fearless the Wonder Dog," the melody of which is based on the "Casper the Friendly Ghost" cartoon theme song. *Spin of the Wheel* from 1990, Axton's final album, refocuses on his own songs, some of which are fine additions to his canon. "We Could've Been Sweethearts," in particular, is as good as anything he did during his mid-'70s peak. Overall these are Axton's weakest albums since the '60s, but fans will find several diamonds in the rough. *—Greg Adams*

● **Gotta Keep Rollin': The Jeremiah Years 1979–1981** / 1999 / Raven ✦✦✦✦✦
Gotta Keep Rollin': The Jeremiah Years 1979-1981 spotlights the most creatively and commercially rewarding period of Hoyt Axton's recording career—assembling 25 songs cut for his own Jeremiah label (so named in honor of his first and biggest composition, the Three Dog Night smash "Joy to the World," also covered here by its writer), the disc offers irrefutable proof that, sales and chart information to the contrary, his unique fusion of pop, country, and blues was ultimately best served not by other performers but by his own warm, grizzled baritone and devilish wit. Many of the highlights originated on the superb *Rusty Old Halo* LP, including the classic opener "Della and the Dealer"; although cameos from Linda Ronstadt ("When the Mornin' Comes")" and Cheech & Chong (the wonderful "No-No Song") sparkle, it's Axton's presence—his voice, rumbling yet intimate, and his worldview, heartfelt yet irreverent—which brings these songs to life. In a nice tip of the hat, Axton also covers "Heartbreak Hotel"—not so much a tribute to the memory of Elvis Presley but to his schoolteacher mother Mae, who co-wrote the song three decades earlier. *—Jason Ankeny*

Joy to the World/Country Anthem / Jul. 10, 2001 / Raven ✦✦✦✦
Raven Records from Australia has released exemplary discs by Ronnie Spector, the Joe Perry Project, Scott McKenzie, and a brilliant *What Goes On* boxed set of the Velvet Underground prior to Polygram's release of *Peel Slowly and See*. Here they take two Hoyt Axton 1971 Capitol albums and add a bonus track, "It's Been Fun," which really is fun as well as keyboard-heavy with uplifting backing vocals. What this single disc does not have is the usually excellent liner notes found with Raven's other releases. The music is worthy of additional notation, but credits for all the tracks except the bonus are included, as well as what appears to be the liner notes from one of the Capitol discs. The lyrics to Axton's biggest hit, "Joy to the World," are inside the booklet with Reverend W. Stevens' words to "Farther Along" printed inside the tray cover under which the CD is placed. Hoyt Axton's arrangement of "Farther Along" has his voice out front in the mix, with wonderful gospel vocals surrounding him and the simple bass guitar accompaniment. The son of the woman who wrote Elvis Presley's "Heartbreak Hotel" had more than a couple of hits in him and this document speaks volumes about the environment that nurtured a creative force. "Never Been to Spain" is amazing with Chris Darrow's fiddle; the band's swelling vocals in "Joy to the World" make it a treat. This is solid stuff beyond the familiar tunes; "Ease Your Pain" becomes as enjoyable a listening experience as Hoyt's gritty performance of "The Pusher." Sure, John Kay growled this epic and made it a '60s classic, proving the *Easy Rider* soundtrack a truly influential disc, but it is Axton's reading of this "let's storm the castle and get the dealer" composition that is truly timeless. "Indian Song" is country leaning toward pop, and that is the magic of Hoyt Axton: he had a good sense of what the public at large could absorb and he told his stories with master strokes of the brushes that were his voice and pen. David Jackson's piano playing adds much to the song and the album; he's on every track save four. "California Women" drives with heavy John Ware drums, as does "Lightnin' Bar Blues," which is almost a sequel to "Joy to the World," and had the Band followed "Up on Cripple Creek" with this tune, they might've had another big hit. The barroom brawl gets a bit silly, but the song itself works. "Farther Along" and "Old Time Religion" are a wonderful combination, displaying the multi-talents of the

eventual co-star of the film *Gremlins*. "Jambalaya (On the Bayou)" is more authentic, drawing more from Hank Williams' 1952 number, one hit than John Fogerty's 1973 party version with the Blue Ridge Rangers; Fantasy Records beat Capitol to the punch, though Hoyt Axton re-recorded the tune two years before John Fogerty. Neil Young must have been listening to this material, because his "Words" on *Harvest* is melodically flavored by "Officer Ray." Young's work with Cajun artist Rusty Kershaw was evidence that he was hip to what was going on around him. Though *Country Anthem* didn't spawn the hits that *Joy to the World* did, both albums are a perfect fit with Hoyt Axton's band as the Nashville players were on Tommy James' *My Head, My Bed, My Red Guitar* country masterpiece. Hoyt Axton may be gone, but artists like Kerry Kearney and reissues like this amazing project keep the spirit of the music he was making alive. A portion of a Hoyt Axton interview might've been nice to top off the disc with the three extra minutes available, and additional liner notes would be helpful, but those are minor quibbles. There are excellent photos of the songsmith, including one from the film *Smoky* and another with his family. *Joy to the World/Country Anthem* is a treasure chest full of gems which can inspire generations of songwriters and which is thoroughly entertaining in its own right. —*Joe Viglione*

Gold / Nov. 13, 2001 / Collectables ✦✦✦

Singer/actor/songwriter Hoyt Axton's peak period was unquestionably the early to mid-'70s; he wrote a number of hits in that era, including "Snowblind Friend," "Never Been to Spain," "No-No Song," "Joy to the World," and "The Pusher," not to mention his own laid-back baritone vocal on the chart-topping "Boney Fingers" and "Della and the Dealer." In contrast, *Gold* provides an interesting yet non-essential glimpse into the pre-country-pop of Axton's early, developing material. Performed mainly in the folk style of the early '60s, these 24 tracks were originally recorded for Vee-Jay Records. Early hits like "Greenback Dollar" and "Thunder & Lightnin'" are included, along with a version of "Heartbreak Hotel" which was co-written by Axton's mother, Mae. —*Al Campbell*

B

The Backsliders

f. 1994, North Carolina
Group / Roots Rock, Alternative Country-Rock, Alternative Country

The Backsliders were an alternative-traditional country-rock band from North Carolina made up of guitarist Steve Howell, frontman and acoustic guitarist Chip Robinson, bassman Danny Kurtz, Jeff Dennis on drums, and Brad Rice rounding things out with his guitar. In 1994, inspired by Buck Owens, Webb Pierce, and the honky tonk life, Howell and Robinson put together the Backsliders and started playing clubs in their area. Both Howell and Robinson were working with other acts at the time. Robinson was playing with a rock band and Howell was a member of the Shady Grove Band, a traditional bluegrass outfit that recorded for Flying Fish. *Mulberry Moon* was the Shady Grove release that included Howell's tune "Mansion in the Sky."

Appearances in North Carolina resulted in a popular following for the band, which was being compared to Gram Parsons, the Blasters, and Los Lobos, all pioneers in American roots music and all products of the wild West Coast. Just as wild, the Backsliders were a direct contradiction to the overly manufactured sounds coming out of Nashville, where '70s rock acts held more sway than Lefty Frizzell or George Jones. The Backsliders also provided a paradox to the whining, angry "woe is me" style of contemporary rock bands and could more often than not rock the so-called rockers off any stage.

With a positive attitude and extolling the virtues of shuffle and twang, the Backsliders started touring regularly around the Southeast. Each homecoming to the Brewery in their hometown of Raleigh was met with a full house and a satisfied crowd, who took great pleasure in seeing and hearing a band made up of their own homeboys. These live shows eventually resulted in what was to be their first release on Mammoth Records. A six-song EP, *From Raleigh, North Carolina* displayed all the power and intensity that made the Backsliders such a high-profile band. Their first full-length project on Mammoth was released in January 1997. *Throwin' Rocks at the Moon*, produced by West Coast patriarch Pete Anderson, was recorded at Mad Dog Studios during the early fall of 1996. Stating that it was the quality of the songwriting that swayed him to take on the Backsliders, Anderson proceeded to pull out all the stops and gleaned every ounce of talent and sweat that the band had to give. After completing *Throwin' Rocks at the Moon*, however, interpersonal problems began ripping the Backsliders apart at the seams, and in time Robinson was the lone remaining original member left. He proceeded to record 1999's *Southern Lines* largely as a solo project, although it still appeared under the Backsliders name. —*Jana Pendragon*

From Raleigh, North Carolina / 1996 / Mammoth ✦✦✦
Rough-hewn vocals the flavor of Billy Joe Shaver, with the reckless spirit of Gram Parsons serving his rock & roll apprenticeship with the Stones. The revved up country-honk backing is ragged, but definitely right. This six-song EP—recorded live on a hot summer night in a Southern college town—was released to give a taste of the band's fire. The result has a lot of charm, not to mention a liquid cover of the Flying Burrito Brothers' "High Fashion Queen." Cool! —*Jack Leaver*

● **Throwin' Rocks at the Moon** / 1997 / Mammoth ✦✦✦✦
The full-length debut, produced by Pete Anderson (Dwight Yoakam), from this Raleigh, NC, quintet. With a driving guitar sound that picks up where the New Riders of the Purple Sage left off in the '70s and what Jason & the Scorchers started in the '80s, the Backsliders will appeal to fans who like their country a little rough around the edges. The songwriting and musical attitude comes off as honest and sincere, and Anderson does a great job of toughening the band's already muscular live-show attack, without messing with its charm. Adding a little Hammond B-3 on the soulful rockers, the country elements are in turn accentuated by occasional pedal steel and mandolin. Standout cuts include the heartfelt "Broken Wings," the melodic honky-tonk of "Lonesome Teardrops" and the rambunctious album closer "Cowboy Boots." —*Jack Leaver*

Southern Lines / Apr. 27, 1999 / Mammoth ✦✦✦✦
Produced by Eric Ambel, and with a track by Don Dixon/Mitch Easter, Backsliders' recording comeback is strong. Singer/guitarist Chip Robinson, a trailer park denizen from Raleigh, NC, had an auspicious early '90s debut before he got sidelined after his band went up in smoke. He bears a slight vocal resemblance and songwriting style to Steve Earle; the hard-country roots are what drive the songs about small towns, lost love and the like and just like Earle, it's easy to take Robinson's bits of broken imagery and well-worn trails as gospel. But it's the classic and acoustic ballads ("It Rained on Monday," and the hidden songs that end the set) which set Robinson apart from the pack or contemporary Southern rockers. —*Denise Sullivan*

Bad Livers

f. 1990, Austin, TX
Group / Neo-Traditional Folk, Bluegrass, Alternative Country-Rock, Roots Rock, Alternative Pop/Rock, Old-Timey

The clubs of Austin, TX, proved to be fertile ground in the 1990s for bands with eclectic musical influences, but the Bad Livers may have been the least-categorizable

ensemble of all. The trio's recorded songs ran the gamut from traditional folk and bluegrass to blues, early rock & roll, punk rock, and eventually even trance music. At the height of their long touring career it was possible to hear music by the Carter Family, Iggy Pop, Monk, Mississippi John Hurt, the Misfits, and Slayer, all in the course of one concert set. They tapped into a base of music fans who could appreciate a mongrelized music, but the later stages of their career showed that "Americana" could be a musical category as confining as any other; the band's increasingly experimental outlook resonated only intermittently with the preferences of fans of traditional music. The Bad Livers' instrumentation was unique within the pop/rock realm: lead singer Danny Barnes played banjo, guitar, and tuba; Mark Rubin played bass and tuba; and in late 1996 the two were joined by Bob Grant on mandolin, guitar, and tenor banjo. Grant replaced Ralph White, who played fiddle and Cajun and Mexican accordion with the trio.

Both Rubin and Barnes grew up with bluegrass music, and that genre label was as apt for the Bad Livers as was any other. Rubin, raised in rural Oklahoma, began playing tuba as a youngster and continued his studies into high-school, when he also began playing bass. Rubin also heard klezmer music in his youth, and the soundprint of the klezmer band would become audible in the music of the Bad Livers. The group was formed in 1990, right after Rubin had attended the New Music Seminar in New York and was inspired to put together his own band; it coalesced with an ad hoc Danny Barnes Trio, which actually consisted of Barnes plus whatever other musicians he was able to raise on the phone on any given evening.

The Bad Livers gained widespread attention from Austin clubgoers in 1991 and became the sensation of the *SXSW* music conference the following year. They signed with the Chicago-based Quarterstick label, releasing *Delusions of Banjer* (1992) and *Horses in the Mines* (1994). Another recording, *Dust on the Bible*, was originally sold on cassette at the trio's live shows and was later issued on CD by Quarterstick; it was a collection of bluegrass-gospel standards that showed that the group could play it straight when they so desired. The Bad Livers moved to the North Carolina-based Sugar Hill label for *Hogs on the Highway* (1997) and 1998's *Industry and Thrift*, the latter album produced by longtime Texas music gadfly Lloyd Maines. Each subsequent release broadened the trio's musical range, and *Blood & Mood*, which appeared in early 2000, was an unclassifiable mixture of bluegrass, punk, sampling of various kinds, and other electronic techniques. The album was alternately hailed as a masterpiece and denounced as the final step in a long betrayal of traditional bluegrass; the group's website dryly noted that it was "to date the worst selling title in the catalog." By that time Barnes and Rubin had both become involved with solo projects of their own; Rubin was the music supervisor for Richard Linklater's film *The Newton Boys*, and Barnes, who had moved to Washington state, had composed music for the Seattle Symphony Orchestra. After *Blood & Mood*, though the Bad Livers never officially dissolved, the individual members' solo projects took precedence. Barnes released several left-of-center banjo albums somewhat reminiscent of the Bad Livers' early material, while Rubin remained a fixture of the Austin live-music and recording scene. —*James Manheim*

● **Delusions of Banjer** / 1992 / Quarterstick ✦✦✦✦
Upon first listen, the Bad Livers' debut recording sounds like a good, old-timey bluegrass album, but by the time the tuba enters on the third track, you begin to realize that this is not your average bluegrass combo. Danny Barnes has got the chops on both guitar and banjo, and sings in a voice no more nasal than many of the genre's stalwarts. He can even write tunes that stand rather nicely next to traditional tunes and Reno & Smiley. Then there's "Shit Creek" and "The Adventures of Pee Pee the Sailor," a Butthole Surfers cover no less; and the mere presence of tuba and accordion almost assuring turned-up noses by the hardcore bluegrass crowd. But that's the beauty of the Bad Livers—they love all sorts of music and aren't afraid to incorporate them in any way they see fit; a characteristic that would infuriate some fans later on in their career. On *Delusions of Banjer*, the sound remains mostly traditional, even when the subject matter may not be. Mark Rubin and Ralph White provide fine support, but the real focus is Danny Barnes. His songwriting ranges from "Shit Creek" to the beautiful bluegrass-gospel of "Precious Time" and "How Dark My Shadow's Grown" to the murder ballad "Pretty Daughter"; and his guitar and banjo playing are both stellar. *Delusions of Banjer* is a great record that may not appeal directly to all bluegrass fans, but whose irreverent attitude and sense of humor might be just the ticket to attract other people curious about the genre, or those simply in search of an old-timey good-time. —*Sean Westergaard*

Horses in the Mines / 1994 / Quarterstick ✦✦✦
For their second album, the Bad Livers have turned in another fine batch of tunes, but this time they've traded the crisp Paul Leary production of the first album for a slightly more murky mix, where the vocals sometimes get a bit lost. The instruments come through just fine, and once again Danny Barnes is in fine form on both guitar and banjo. The songs are top-notch. In particular, the playing and arrangement (for banjo, guitar,

dobro, and mandolin) on "He Didn't Say a Word to Me" are exquisite. They also do a wonderful job with the Kentucky Colonels' "Blue Ridge Express." "Clawhammer Fish" and "Where They Do Not Know My Name" really showcase Barnes' banjo technique, and "Horses in the Mines" is a slow country blues with slide banjo. But they also start taking some slightly experimental chances as well, hinting at what's to come on subsequent albums. About halfway through the album, "New Bad Liver Singer" is a goof-off track with someone's dog (uncredited!) howling along with a harmonica. Following that is "High, Lonesome, Dead and Gone," a song in three parts where you can clearly hear a television set droning on behind the band. The treated vocals on "Shot at a Bird, Hit Me a Stump" and "Puke Grub" pretty much guarantee that a career playing bluegrass festivals is not in the cards. *Horses in the Mines* is a small step in the evolution of the Bad Livers. While it has a largely traditional sound, its production and experimental tendencies are likely to further alienate any potential traditional bluegrass fans they may have courted, but fans of other bands on the indie label Quarterstick are just as likely to admire their DIY ethic and don't-care attitude. Ironically, this would be their last recording for Quarterstick before moving to the traditional bluegrass label Sugar Hill. *—Sean Westergaard*

Dust on the Bible / Aug. 31, 1994 / Quarterstick ♦♦♦

Originally available exclusively on cassette at Bad Livers live shows, this collection of 11 deeply traditional old-timey and bluegrass-gospel songs shows a reverential side to the band's usually slightly goofy twang-a-billy punk folk style. Relying heavily on songs made known by the Stanley Brothers, Bill Monroe, and other traditional bluegrass spirituals, songs like "I'm Using My Bible for a Roadmap" and "Jesus on the Mainline" are delivered so faithfully the music barely hints at their creativity or sense of humor. That is, unless you happen to know that bassist Mark Rubin is Jewish and that banjo player Danny Barnes grew up in the Church of Christ, which forbids instrumental music in its worship services. Although it contains what may be the only recording of "Keep Your Lamp Trimmed and Burning" with a tuba solo, the rest of *Dust on the Bible* should appeal to traditional folk aficionados, and for fans of Bad Livers' usual bizarro cowpunk, this certainly presents another facet of the band. *—Zac Johnson*

Hogs on the Highway / Feb. 18, 1997 / Sugar Hill ♦♦♦♦

Perhaps it's appropriate that the Bad Livers scaled back their punk influences and played up their traditional bluegrass roots when they moved to Sugar Hill Records for *Hogs on the Highway.* After all, the label is one of America's best independent country/bluegrass labels, so the group would have to clean up their act somewhat to fit in with the crowd. Fortunately, they haven't cleaned up too much, and *Hogs on the Highway* is a stomping, infectious collection of twisted newgrass, informed by punk energy but in the style of traditional bluegrass. *—Thom Owens*

Industry and Thrift / Sep. 15, 1998 / Sugar Hill ♦♦♦

Bluegrass with attitude. A very weird attitude, in fact. It isn't too difficult to imagine Bad Livers communing with Sugar Hill Records' other satirical cowboys, the Austin Lounge Lizards (with Terry Allen sitting in on the odd session, of course). *Industry and Thrift* manages to range all the way from the less sensible edges of bluegrass (of which there are many) to the bluegrass fringes of klezmer (which they seem to have had a hand in building themselves, with some inspiration from various worldly weirdos such as 3 Mustaphas 3). The result is an amusing and highly eclectic set that never stays in any single place long enough to get firmly categorized. A fun record. *—Steven McDonald*

Blood & Mood / Feb. 22, 2000 / Sugar Hill ♦♦♦♦

Never a band to be comfortable in a single category, on *Blood & Mood* the Bad Livers are even more perverse than usual—any illusions of bluegrass traditionalism that might have remained from their earlier work are here blown apart by found-sound sampling ("Looky Here"), East European time signatures ("New York City"), and flat-out punk aggression ("I'm Losing"). Granted, the accent is still strictly hillbilly, the chord progressions are as often Nashville as New York, and that's some genuine high-lonesome harmonizing on "One More Night in a Hotel." But this is most definitely not bluegrass. What it is exactly is unclear—but it sure is fun. *—Rick Anderson*

The Bailes Brothers

f. 1944

Group / Traditional Country, Close Harmony

From the mid-'40s through the '50s the Bailes Brothers were among the most popular close-harmony duets. There were actually four brothers—Kyle, Johnnie, Walter and Homer—but they seldom worked together as an entire group, instead pairing off for performances. The Bailes were born and raised in West Virginia, near Charleston. Their father, a minister, died when they were young and their impoverished mother had to struggle to keep them together. (Years later, Walter paid tribute to her trials with his song "Give Mother My Crown.") While working a variety of odd jobs during the Depression, the brothers were inspired to pursue music by the songs of such performers as Billy Cox and Buddy Starcher. They started out on a variety of radio programs, but didn't earn much recognition until 1942, when Johnnie and Walter began working as a duo at WSAZ Huntington. All four brothers played string instruments; after they became popular, they added other members to their group, among them Fiddlin' Arthur Smith.

It was Roy Acuff who got the Bailes their big break when he suggested to WSM Nashville executives that the brothers appear on the *Grand Ole Opry.* They made their debut on the show in 1944 and stayed in Nashville for two years. They made their recording debut in early 1945 for Columbia; among their first singles were their original songs "Dust on the Bible" and "The Drunkard's Grave." As they continued recording the brothers added more and more original songs, such as "Broken Marriage Vows." In 1947, Walter left to become a minister and Homer became the singing partner of their friend Dean Upson. They made their last recordings for Columbia at the end of the year, later becoming co-founders of the famous *Louisiana Hayride* show.

The original Bailes Brothers went their separate ways in 1949. Over the next decade, different combinations of Bailes Brothers appeared. In the early '50s Homer and Kyle teamed up to work at a Little Rock, AR, station. They also recorded a single. Later Johnnie and Walter reunited and began singing gospel in Texas. In 1953, they recorded three singles for King; Johnnie also cut a few solo records. During the 1960s, they continued the pattern, with Walter teaming up with Kyle and Homer at different times. Johnnie and Homer reunited during the early '70s, and from the mid-'70s through the '80s Walter, Kyle, and former band member Ernest Ferguson frequently played at churches and sometimes at festivals. Homer was busy working as a pastor while Johnnie ran three radio stations. Walter was also an evangelical preacher. In 1976 Walter and Kyle made an album; in 1977, all four reunited for a record, joined by their sister Minnie on a few cuts. After, Walter recorded on his Starlit and White Dove labels, while Homer also recorded solo. Much of the Bailes Brothers' early works are available on anthologies, and some of their records have been re-issued. *—Sandra Brennan*

• **Oh So Many Years** / Nov. 12, 2002 / Bear Family ♦♦♦♦♦

Oh So Many Years covers the four Bailes Brothers most commercially productive period in the 1940s. These 28 tracks originally released on Columbia records capture their unique harmonies on signature songs including "The Drunkard's Grave," "Dust on the Bible," and "Broken Marriage Vows." As an added bonus interview sections with the brothers are interspersed throughout. Fans of the Louvin Brothers should be on the lookout for this Bear Family reissue. *—Al Campbell*

The Bailey Brothers

f. 1940, Charleston, WV, **db.** 1954

Group / Bluegrass, Traditional Bluegrass, Old-Timey, Close Harmony

Charlie and Danny Bailey were extremely popular radio singers in West Virginia and Tennessee during the late '40s through the '50s who were among the few fraternal duets to successfully make the transition from old-time music to bluegrass. The Baileys were born to a large, musically inclined family in Happy Valley, TN. Charlie made his professional singing debut in 1936 when he teamed up with Charlie Cope and began touring. He and brother Danny teamed shortly after, and soon they were singing on local radio. In 1940 they went to Knoxville to play on WNOX and WROL, and soon gained a devoted following. But in 1941, just before they were to make their recording debut, Charlie was inducted into the Army. While he was gone Danny founded the Happy Valley Boys, and remained in Knoxville. By 1944, the Happy Valley Boys had moved to Nashville and were appearing on the *Grand Ole Opry.* The group changed personnel when two members were drafted. They were replaced by Charlie and Lester Cope. In 1946, Charlie returned and the Copes left to find their own fame.

Not long after, the Happy Valley Boys became a full-fledged bluegrass band; joined by fiddler L.E. White, banjo picker Wiley Birchfield and bass player Jake Tullock, Charlie played mandolin and guitar while Danny played guitar. With this line-up they waxed six songs in late 1947, among them the first recorded version of "The Sweetest Gift," by J.B. Coates. They made two more singles before moving to a radio station in Raleigh, NC. There, fiddler Clarence "Tater" Tate and banjo player Hoke Jenkins joined the Happy Valley Boys.

The Baileys founded their own Canary label before moving to play on the *Wheeling Jamboree* at WWVA Wheeling, WV, in 1952. Here the brothers were at their most popular; at one time, the Baileys and their band were even bigger than Bill Monroe & His Blue Grass Boys. About two years later, Danny began having health problems and, but for a few months in 1954, the Baileys stopped playing together. They did reunite briefly between 1957 and 1958. Danny basically remained in Knoxville after 1954 and continued working on radio and television on the *Farm and Home Hour* until the show was canceled in 1983. Meanwhile Charlie went to work in Richmond and then eventually returned to Wheeling where he founded a band featuring members of the McCumbee Family and later the Osborne Brothers. He later teamed up with Jimmy Elrod, Chubby Collier and Ray Meyers. With this line-up, he recorded a few songs at WWVA. Following his brief professional reunion with his brother in 1958, Charlie embarked upon a six-month tour of the Canadian Maritime Provinces. He retired in 1960 and went on to open an exterminating business in Delaware.

The Baileys briefly reunited in 1970 for a concert during the Smithsonian Festival of American Folklife; later in the decade they recorded two albums for Rounder. In 1975, they gathered for the the old-timer reunion at Fan Fair, and in 1982 played at the Knoxville World's Fair. The Rounder label has reissued most of the Bailey Brothers recordings done for Rich-R-Tone and Canary. *—Sandra Brennan*

Have You Forgotten / 1974 / Rounder ♦♦♦

Take Me Back to Happy Valley / 1975 / Rounder ♦♦♦♦

Originally issued on LP in the mid-'70s, this album finds Charlie and Danny Bailey continuing in the traditional yet unique style that was theirs alone. Although there was nothing new about their general approach—taking the standard mandolin-and-guitar brother-duet format and augmenting it with bluegrass banjo, fiddle, and bass—the Baileys stood out sonically from the rest of the bluegrass pack. Their unique sound was due in part to their frequent trading of harmony parts and partly to Charlie's unusual approach to the mandolin, one which eschewed chopped chordal backup in favor of quiet, single-note lines that wove gently (and, frankly, sometimes inaudibly) through the instrumental mix. On this album, which is fairly evenly divided between love songs and gospel material, particular highlights include the classic "Honeysuckle Rose" (which was later a big hit for Jim & Jesse McReynolds) and the sweetly yearning "Heaven." The only complaint one might have about this album is its lack of any previously unreleased material, given that it is being reissued at full price. Recommended. *—Rick Anderson*

• **Early Days of Bluegrass, Vol. 6—Have You Forgotten?** / 1976 / Rounder ♦♦♦♦♦

Just As the Sun Went Down / 1980 / Rounder ♦♦♦

Early Duet Stylings / 1981 / Old Homestead ♦♦♦♦♦

DeFord Bailey

b. Dec. 14, 1899, Bellwood, TN, **d.** Jul. 2, 1982, Nashville, TN

Harmonica / Prewar Country Blues

There is a gulf of Bibilical proportions between the amount of influence American black music has had on country & western and the number of black performers actually involved in country. One of the few heroes in what is sadly not a fable is this harmonica player, a victim of infantile paralysis who had to struggle with his physical handicaps as well as racism. The old-time music performer, stooped with a deformed chest, less than five feet tall and weighing under 100 pounds, was for a time a familiar act at the *Grand Ole Opry*. That is, until a tiff with *Opry* honcho George Hay led to his dismissal. After that, the only job he could get in country music in Nashville was as a shoeshine man, in itself a step below the often joked about official way of summoning a country songwriter in that town: "waiter!" And even after his death, the fight between Bailey and the Nashville establishment continues, with Roy Acuff bristling at the idea of honoring the man with a membership in the Country Music Hall of Fame, although many other old-time performers of Bailey's generation have already been inducted. After all, it was these original old-time performers who with their personality and unique music had managed to launch what would become an unstoppable institution in country music.

Bailey was a professional musician from the age of 14, by which time he was already supporting himself around Smith County, TN, by playing the harmonica. He had also picked up a few other instruments that were required items in country music from his dad and uncle. The music that was being passed around was something Bailey described as black hillbilly, old-time music that was like a bottle of half and half, with the milk country and the cream blues. And nobody listening cared if a particular number had a bit more cream than milk, or vice versa. By the end of 1925, Bailey was good enough on harmonica to place second in a WDAD French Harp Contest. Right around that time he met another harmonica player, Dr. Humphrey Bate, who was both a country physician and musician. It was Bate who would bring his fellow harp player to the attention of the *Opry* and its promotion genius George Hay. Bate and his group had been performers on the first broadcast of the *Opry*, and his relationship with the management was typical of the effect Hay and his ilk would have on the cultural perception of country music.

When Bate had arrived at the studio for this premier *Opry* broadcast, his group was known as the Augmented Orchestra, as it featured doubles of instruments such as guitar and fiddle. But when the group appeared on the air, it was announced as Dr. Humphrey Bate and His Possum Hunters. The name was a concoction of Hay, who literally made hay selling old-time music dressed up in hillbilly clothes. Hay's first reaction to a slightly hunchbacked height-challenged black harmonica player was apparently not one of high enthusiasm. Bate pressed firmly on the subject of Bailey, however, and perhaps the doc's medical credentials intimidated Hay. Bailey was given a chance and went on to become the *Opry*'s first solo star as well as its first black artist. Historians lobbying for Bailey's importance go on to point out that in 1928, the *Opry*'s first year, the harmonica player did his thing on 49 of the 52 programs. No other artist even came close to that record of appearances. A symbolically more important event was the fact that immediately after the audience heard the phrase *Grand Ole Opry* announced for the very first time, on came Bailey blowing his train imitation on the harp. He remained secure in this contract with the *Opry* for about 15 years. He recorded in the late '20s on labels such as Columbia, Brunswick, and Victor. His sessions were the first decently recorded examples of harmonica playing and were incredibly influential.

His effect on the history of the instrument itself is measurable, because his success led to opportunities for many other harmonica players to record and perform. "Pan American Blues" was one of his most popular numbers along with "John Henry." Bailey complained about never receiving royalties for these sides, which were re-released steadily through 1936, then began showing up on old-time and classic country compilations from the '70s onward. In the '30s, Bailey was involved in many tours, including a package show with old-time legend Uncle Dave Macon. Bailey helped establish several performers by appearing as a solo artist in front of their bands, including Roy Acuff. Venues at this time included tent shows and county fairs as well as theatres. Wherever the tour might lead, Bailey always had to be back in Nashville for the Saturday night *Opry* show. Since his pay was only five dollars, this situation often meant he was losing money arriving for his *Opry* shows. There are articles that also claim his rate of pay reflected racist practices, but accounts of other *Opry* artists from this era have mentioned this as a basic rate for all the artists. One thing is beyond question. Bailey was forced to eat and sleep separately from his fellow *Opry* artists due to segregation.

The number of black country artists has remained negligible, in fact they could be packed into a small car and still have room for Ernest Tubb's merchandise setup. The next one allowed on the *Opry* after Bailey would be Charlie Pride. Why the *Opry* gave Bailey the hook is often described as a matter of dispute, but the reality of the situation is pretty apparent from remarks made by Hay in his memoirs. "Like some members of his race, DeFord was lazy. He knew about a dozen numbers, which he put on the air and recorded for a major company, but he refused to learn any more." The truth is that many old-time musicians worked from a fixed repertoire, and were not interested in adding material beyond that. Of course this creates problems for record producers, publishers, or other music investors attempting to acquire copyrights. The way to ensure the survival of different types of traditional music is of course to provide performing situations for its practitioners, regardless of how many new titles might be added to their song list in a given year. The *Opry* management didn't see this, however.

He was invited back to the *Opry* for an old-timer's show in 1974, at which time he apparently blew up a storm. In between he cooled his heels while polishing other people's, working at a shoeshine stand he had opened with his uncle in 1933. He lived in the I.W. Gernert Homes, not far from the shoeshine stand, when he died four years after the final *Opry* show. So far the official Hall of Fame line is that although he will be remembered fondly for his contributions to the show, these contributions do not warrant a place in the Country Music Hall of Fame. Several music organizations and individuals who were fans of Bailey's continue to lobby on his behalf. *—Eugene Chadbourne*

The Legendary DeFord Bailey: Country Music's First Black Star / May 19, 1998 / Revenant ✦✦✦

This album's title is true. Throughout the '20s and '30s, Nashville's *Grand Ole Opry* regularly featured DeFord Bailey on its stage. His solo harmonica performances of traditional folk tunes were wildly popular, even if they were more akin to country blues music than to country music proper. Made between 1974 and 1976, when Bailey himself was in his late seventies, these recordings capture the legend with his harmonica abilities mostly in tact. His trademark tune, "Pan American," is included, as are renditions of the blues and gospel standards "John Henry" and "Swing Low, Sweet Chariot." Most of the album's tunes are harmonica solos, but Bailey also trails a pair of old-time banjo tunes and fingerpicks four blues numbers on an acoustic guitar. Bailey plays with great joy and skill throughout, offering casual and serious listeners alike something to enjoy. *—Brian Beatty*

Razzy Bailey

b. Feb. 14, 1939, Five Points, AL

Vocals / Country-Pop, Rockabilly

A singer whose vocal style fused country with blue-eyed soul, Alabama-born Rasie Michael "Razzy" Bailey cut his first recordings in 1949 at the age of ten. By 15, he led a string band, sponsored by the local chapter of the Future Farmers of America, which came in second in a talent contest held at Auburn University.

Bailey married and had children immediately after graduating high-school; as a result, his career as a performer was sporadic and unsuccessful for a number of years. In 1966, he contributed a number of songs to Atlantic Records' Bill Lowery, among them "9,999,999 Tears," which Lowery agreed to produce. While the single, on which Bailey was backed by a studio band featuring Billy Joel, Joe South, and Freddy Weller, failed to chart, it renewed the singer's interest in pursuing a recording career full time. As a result, he formed the pop-oriented trio Daily Bread in 1968, releasing a pair of albums on small labels. Another group, the Aquarians, followed in 1972; in 1974, Bailey recorded the album *I Hate Hate* simply as Razzy.

After *I Hate Hate* failed to chart, Bailey again dropped out of music, but in 1976, singer Dickey Lee hit number three with a cover of "9,999,999 Tears"; after Lee hit the Top 20 with another of his songs, "Peanut Butter," Bailey signed a new recording contract of his own. In 1978, he released the single "What Time Do You Have to Be Back in Heaven," the first of five consecutive Top Ten hits. Between August 1980 and December 1981, Bailey reached his commercial peak with a string of five number-one hits—"Loving Up a Storm," "I Keep Coming Back," "Friends," "Midnight Hauler," and "She Left Love All Over Me"—and in 1981 was named *Billboard* magazine's Country Singles Artist of the Year. The albums *Razzy* (1980), *Makin' Friends* (1981), *Feelin' Right*, and *A Little More Razzy* (both 1982) were also very successful. By the mid-'80s, however, Bailey's hit-making days were largely over; his singles landed only in the lower rungs of the charts. In 1987, he began issuing his records through his own label, SOA (Sounds of America). In 1993, the release of the album *Razzy Bailey: Fragile, Handle With Care* was marred by the suicide of Bailey's wife, Sandra. *—Jason Ankeny*

Razzy / 1980 / RCA ✦✦✦

Makin' Friends / 1981 / RCA ✦✦✦

Feelin' Right / 1982 / RCA ✦✦✦

● **Greatest Hits** / 1983 / RCA ✦✦✦✦✦

In the Midnight Hour / 1984 / RCA ✦✦✦

Baillie & the Boys

f. 1973

Group / Contemporary Country

Though originally from New Jersey, Kathy Baillie and Michael Bonagura met in Delaware through a friend who gave Bonagura a tape that featured Baillie's vocals. Fans of artists like the Four Tops, the Beatles, the Supremes, Linda Ronstadt, and James Taylor, they developed a strong harmony—both on-stage and off: They were married in 1977. Bonagura's buddy, bass player Alan LeBoeuf, joined up, and after a number of years on the Garden State's nightclub circuit, yet another friend—a driver with Allied Van Lines—persuaded them to join him on a trip to Nashville.

They stayed in Music City, and in 1982 they got their first chance to appear on a record, singing backup on Ed Bruce's "My First Taste of Texas." Bonagura co-wrote Marie Osmond's single "There's No Stopping Your Heart," and the trio sang backing vocals on a number of singles for Dan Seals and Randy Travis. Ultimately, they signed with RCA Records, making their debut in 1987. After completing their second album, LeBoeuf decided their touring schedule was too hectic and left. Baillie and Bonagura retained the original name, though Boys seems a bit misleading. *—Tom Roland*

Baillie & the Boys / 1987 / RCA ✦✦✦

Turn the Tide / 1989 / RCA ✦✦✦✦✦

Lights of Home / 1990 / RCA ✦✦✦

● **The Best of Baillie & the Boys** / 1991 / RCA ✦✦✦✦✦

This highlights the real strength of the act: tuneful melodies, pristine harmonies, and Kathy Baillie's infectious enunciations. Best cuts: "Oh Heart," "(Wish I Had A) Heart of Stone," "Long Shot," and "I Can't Turn the Tide." *—Tom Roland*

Lovin' Every Minute / Aug. 20, 1996 / Intersound ✦✦

The Road That Led Me to You / Feb. 29, 2000 / Synergy ✦✦✦

Baker & Myers

Group / Contemporary Country

Baker & Myers were professional contemporary country songwriters based in Nashville. After Alabama had a hit with the duo's "Once in a Lifetime" and John Michael Montgomery took "I Swear" to number one (the song was also a pop and R&B hit by All

4 One), Baker & Myers launched a performing career, releasing their eponymous debut on Curb Records in the fall of 1995. *—Stephen Thomas Erlewine*

Baker & Myers / Oct. 10, 1995 / Curb ♦♦♦

Though Baker & Myers are talented proffesional songwriters, they haven't quite developed into skilled performers of their own, as their eponymous debut proves. Neither has very compelling voices, while the studio musicians make the music too polished to truly stick. Still, the duo's strong point is slickness, such as John Michael Montgomery's hit "I Swear," yet slickness has to be delivered with a little more flair than the pleasant, but dull, professionalism that comprises *Baker & Myers*. *—Stephen Thomas Erlewine*

Kenny Baker

b. Jun. 26, 1926, Jenkins, KY

Fiddle / Traditional Bluegrass

Bluegrass fiddler Kenny Baker was born on June 26, 1926, in Jenkins, KY. Both his father and grandfather were fiddlers, and by eight years old, Kenny himself had picked up the instrument. After a stint in the navy, Baker returned to Kentucky, where he worked in the coal mines and played fiddle and some guitar at local dances. In 1953, country vocalist Don Gibson hired Baker for his band at WNOX in Knoxville, TN. During his tenure with Gibson, Baker expanded his stylistic range, incorporating the smoother jazz violin style of Stephane Grappelli. He also began to develop his "long-bow" style of playing, which blended and elongated notes much more than the traditional chop of bluegrass fiddle. Of his style, Baker would later comment "bluegrass is nothing but a hillbilly version of jazz."

In 1955, he released *Baker's Dozen*, a no-frills bluegrass picking album that featured a young Sam Bush. By 1957, Baker was playing bluegrass full-time as a member of Bill Monroe's band, the Blue Grass Boys. It proved to be a lasting partnership—he became the longest running Blue Grass Boy. He worked with Monroe off and on over the next 30 years, leaving during the lean times to focus on his farm or for work in the mines. But it was as a Blue Grass Boy that Baker influenced countless latter-day fiddle players with his easy, traditional style.

Baker issued another solo album, *Portrait of a Bluegrass Fiddler*, in 1969, capitalizing on the popular resurgence of the genre on the heels of the late-'60s folk movement. He also rejoined Monroe's group for good, playing with the Blue Grass Boys through the 1980s. In 1989, he teamed with dobro king Josh Graves in a bluegrass supergroup called the Masters. Also featuring banjoist Eddie Adcock and mandolin virtuoso Jesse McReynolds, the Masters released two albums, including a Grammy-nominated, self-titled 1989 debut. Baker continued to perform throughout the 1990s, lodging a series of tours backed by the National Council on Traditional Arts. After an almost ten-year recording hiatus, Baker returned to wax in 2000 with *Cotton Baggin'*. The album included contributions from old friends Graves, McReynolds, and Blaine Sprouse. He returned in 2002 with the acclaimed *Spider Bit the Baby*. *—Johnny Loftus*

Baker's Dozen / May 1955-May 1957 / Dormouse ♦♦♦♦♦

This album is so straight to the point it reminds one of a roadside smokehouse that serves barbecued meat, and nothing but barbecued meat. And the back cover of the album actually looks like a menu from such a place. Fiddler Baker and his accomplices, including mandolinist Sam Bush when he was young enough to be called Sammy, whip through a dozen classic country fiddle tunes as if demonstrating that nothing else could possibly be as important. This is totally classic old-time music from the heart of the North Carolina Piedmont, but the musicologists can argue about whether Baker is going too far claiming authorship of some of these titles. The pickers constantly attempt to outdo each other, with some of the finest soloing coming from Butch Robins on banjo and the Greek-American flatpicker John Kaparakis. *—Eugene Chadbourne*

Farmyard Swing / 1979 / County ♦♦♦♦

This album is a swing through several different farmyards as a variety of different sessions with overlapping ensembles are mixed together for an ultimately satisfying listening experience. This was released at a time when many bluegrass groups were beginning to record rock and jazz-flavored experiments and longer pieces more in the style of jam sessions. This may have influenced the way this material is presented, but most of the eggs in the basket are traditional ones, the type of old-time instrumentals that have served as satisfying material for many a session. Fiddler Baker is in fine form, and it is nice to hear him play off against so many different hot pickers without having to change records. The Osborne Brothers are all on hand, as is hands-of-steel banjo picker Butch Robins. *—Eugene Chadbourne*

Indian Springs / 1989 / Rounder ♦♦♦

Kenny Baker's *Indian Springs* is an instrumental recording that encompasses several different styles of bluegrass and folk music and features stellar musicianship from Baker, co-leader Blaine Sprouse and their supporting band, which includes David Grier and Allen Shelton. Alternating between fast dance numbers and ballads, *Indian Springs* is a multi-layered and thoroughly entertaining bluegrass album that demonstrates how the music can progress without losing touch of its roots. *—Thom Owens*

Master Fiddler / 1993 / County ♦♦♦♦♦

Master Fiddler compiles the highlights of Kenny Baker's albums recorded between 1968 and 1983. Throughout that 15 year span, Baker turned out a number of wonderful recordings, alive with his distinctive, fluid technique. Every cut on *Master Fiddler* demonstrates Baker's unique style and prodigious talent—the record proves that the musician is indeed a *Master Fiddler*. *—Thom Owens*

● **Plays Bill Monroe** / Aug. 19, 1994 / County ♦♦♦♦♦

Is this the best bluegrass album ever made? No matter what choice might be made in this regard, it would surely inflame the passions of some picker who wouldn't agree. Nonetheless, consider some of the circumstances. The maestro Kenny Baker is one of the most straightforward, no-nonsense, clean and clear-cut players of bluegrass and old-time music. He has never been the slightest bit interested in any gimmicks or new trends, and in fact looks like he would be at a loss at what to do with hands were he not brandishing a fiddle. He always puts together fantastic bands, and in this case the musicians were paying tribute to one of the all-time fathers of bluegrass music, Bill Monroe. Anytime such a strong bearer of tradition is being saluted, one winds up with strongly felt, convincing playing. And then what happened... Monroe himself happened to come by the studio, was asked to play "a bit" by Baker, and wound up playing on the entire album. So, this is Kenny Baker plays Bill Monroe, with Bill Monroe, and it doesn't get much better than that. An effort was made to avoid warhorses and overly familiar material. This is a dozen (no, not 13; the label missed the opportunity to give listeners a Baker's dozen!) of Monroe's classic bluegrass constructions, although they come across more like freshly baked biscuits. Is that steam coming out of the speaker box? *—Eugene Chadbourne*

Puritan Sessions / Aug. 24, 1994 / Rebel ♦♦♦♦

Butch Baldassari

b. Dec. 11, 1952

Mandolin, Guitar (Electric) / Old-Timey, Classical, Swing, Classical Guitar, Traditional Bluegrass

The mandolin has been turned into an instrument of melodic brilliance by Butch Baldassari. A former member of Lonesome Standard Time, Baldassari has continued to explore his six-stringed instrument on his solo albums and recordings with the Nashville Mandolin Ensemble. In addition to working with Richard Greene's Grass Is Greener since 1995, Baldassari is the leader of his own group, the Butch Baldassari Trio, featuring guitarist Gene Ford and mandocello player John Hedgecoth. Influenced as much by the Beatles and Frank Sinatra as he is by Bill Monroe, Baldassari played guitar with his brother, Buster, in late-'60s garage bands. A trip to the 1972 Philadelphia Folk Festival proved to be the impetus for Baldassari's switch to the mandolin.

After earning a bachelor's degree in music from the University of Scranton, Baldassari moved to Las Vegas for post-graduate studies at the University of Nevada in Las Vegas. While there, he befriended three musicians who were forming a tradition-rooted bluegrass band, Weary Hearts, and he was invited to join. The group went on to win the International Band Competition held by the Society for the Preservation of Bluegrass Music in America in 1989. Their debut album, *By Heart*, was released shortly afterwards. Moving to Nashville in 1985, Baldassari continued to explore the possibilities of the mandolin. While attending the Classical Mandolin Society convention in 1990, he conceived the Nashville Mandolin Ensemble, an 11-piece group featuring mandola, mandocello, guitar, and bass. After four months of rehearsals, the band made its public debut at the Dark Horse Theater in Nashville in October 1991.

Baldassari has remained active with numerous outside projects. As a member of Lonesome Standard Time from 1992 to 1996, he recorded three albums—*Lonesome River Band*, *Mighty Lonesome*, and *Lonesome as It Gets*. Together with innovative bluegrass fiddler Richard Greene and his band, the Grass Is Greener, Baldassari recorded *Wolves A' Howlin'* in 1996 and *Sales Tax Toddle* in 1997. Baldassari's musical career has been balanced by his work as a teacher. In addition to conducting bluegrass mandolin workshops in Nashville, he became the adjunct associate professor of mandolin at Vanderbilt University's Blair School of Music in 1996. *—Craig Harris*

● **Old Town** / 1990 / Rebel ♦♦♦♦

Evergreen/Mandolin Music for Christmas / 1990 / Cactus ♦♦♦

Butch Baladassari's *Evergreen / Mandolin Music for Christmas* is a charming collection of folky Christmas carols—such as "Away in a Manger," "Little Drummer Boy," and "The First Noel"—recorded with a variety of stringed instruments, from mandolin and guitar to viola and violin. *—Stephen Thomas Erlewine*

Day in the Country / 1994 / Pinecastle ♦♦♦

Evergreen / Nov. 16, 1994 / CMH ♦♦♦

You'll probably find this filed with the country releases, ghettoized, which is a real shame. *Evergreen* is performed by mandolinist Butch Baldassari and a fairly large group of Tennessee musicians, all of whom turn in fine, gentle performances on 16 Christmas standards. The arrangements have been allowed to follow the spirit of the mandolin, rather than being pushed into the spirit of Nashville, which means that this is an album of gentle, sweet instrumental music. It's not just easy to listen to and enjoy, though; Baldassari's playing slips into the mind and stays there, unlike many a Christmas album. *—Steven McDonald*

The Balfa Brothers

f. 1967

Group / Traditional Cajun

The Balfa Brothers (Les Freres Balfas) helped keep traditional Cajun music alive in the 1960s, when it was in danger of disappearing. The sons, three of a family of six, were born to a poor southwest Louisiana sharecropper, from whom they learned about traditional Cajun lore and culture. Fiddler Dewey Balfa was heavily influenced by players such as J.B. Fusilier, Leo Soileau, Harry Choates and Bob Wills. He and his brothers—Rodney, who sang and played guitar and harmonica, Will, the second fiddler, Harry, the accordion player, and Burkeman, who played triangle and spoons—began playing informally at family parties and local gatherings during the '40s. They achieved enough local popularity to play up to eight dances a week at local dance halls. The Balfas were later joined by neighbor Hadley Fontenot on accordion. They made their recording debut in 1951 with "La Valse de Bon Baurche" and "Le Two Step de Ville Platte," which were captured on a home recorder and released as a 78-rpm single. Dewey Balfa went on to a solo career playing with numerous Cajun artists and recording on such labels as Khoury, Kajun, and Swallow.

In 1967, Dewey, Rodney, Will and his daughter Nelda, along with Fontenot formed the Balfa Brothers and began spreading the Cajun sound throughout Europe and at folk festivals across the U.S. In 1968, they played for the Olympics Festival in Mexico City. They made their first professional recording, "Le Valse de Bambocheurs/Indian on a Stomp," in 1967 for Swallow. This led to an album, *Balfa Brothers Play Traditional Cajun Music*, also on Swallow. After releasing another LP, the Balfas appeared in the 1972 Les Blank documentary *Spend It All*, which introduced a new generation to the lively Cajun sound. That year they also recorded *The Cajuns* on Sonet and another for Swallow, *The Good Times Are Killing Me*, which included the soundtrack for the documentary of the same name. Although most of their musical focus was on tradition, the Balfas were not averse to trying more modernized Cajun songs with a nightclub orchestra comprised of Dewey, Rodney, accordion player Nathan Menard, fiddler Dick Richard, J.W. Pelsia on steel guitar, Austin Broussard on drums and Rodney's son Tony on bass guitar.

Things went well for the band until February 1979, when Rodney and Will were killed in a car wreck. The next year, Dewey's wife died of trichinosis. Despite the tragedy, the Balfa Brothers continued (with a few personnel changes) even after Dewey's death in 1992. Through them, his rich and valuable legacy of Cajun music carries on. *—Sandra Brennan*

● **Play Trad. Cajun Music, Vols. 1 & 2** / 1987 / Swallow ♦♦♦♦♦
The Balfa Brothers Play Traditional Cajun Music, Vols. 1 & 2 combines both of the group's original *Play Traditional Cajun Music* albums onto one disc. The first volume was released on Swallow Records in 1965 and helped kick-start the Cajun revival of the '60s. It's an excellent album, featuring wonderful harmonies from Rodney, Will and Dewey, as well as stellar instrumental work. The second volume, recorded and released in 1974, isn't quite as strong as its predecessor, but it is still very good and is filled with terrific music. Both albums represent the Balfa Brothers at their peak. They may have a number of very good albums in their catalog, but *The Balfa Brothers Play Traditional Cajun Music, Vols. 1 & 2* effectively explains what they are all about. *—Thom Owens*

★ **J'ai Vu le Loup, Le Renard et la Belette** / 1988 / Rounder ♦♦♦♦♦
The Balfa Brothers are the real deal. They were recording Cajun music back before anyone outside of south-central Louisiana knew such a thing existed. This 13-track album, originally released on a tiny regional label in 1976 and reissued untouched by Rounder in 1989, is utterly authentic traditional Cajun music, performed on acoustic instruments with no drums (and only two tracks' worth of accordion, which may disappoint those who equate that instrument with Cajun music) and lyrics sung entirely in the regional Acadian French. (Even the liner notes are in this patois.) What matters is not how "authentic," this music is, however, but how good it is, and that's where this record shines. All 13 tracks (well, technically, track 11 is just a spoken-word introduction to the ballad "Mon N'Onc' Charlot") are utterly outstanding; as driving and rhythmic as music can get on an acoustic guitar and a pair of fiddles, with an unfettered joy in the vocals that comes across even to those listeners who don't understand the language. Those interested in traditional Cajun music would do well to start right here. *—Stewart Mason*

David Ball

b. Jul. 9, 1963, Rock Hill, SC
Guitar, Vocals / Contemporary Country
David Ball was born in Rock Hill, SC, on July 9, 1963. The son of a Baptist minister father and musician mother, Ball started playing the ukulele as a young boy, but by age 12 had switched to guitar. After high-school, he and hometown friends Walter Hyatt and Champ Hood moved to Nashville, where they scraped out a living as Uncle Walt's Band. The going was tough, and eventually the trio moved to Austin, TX, hoping to find greener pastures. There Ball and his friends matured as musicians, playing covers of popular folk and roots numbers, but also writing and performing their own compositions. Ball played bass, sang lead, and also contributed backup vocals. Uncle Walt's Band was a hit in Austin, where the music scene was more progressive and hungry young players like Lyle Lovett would pack the group's dancehall shows. The band released three successful albums before breaking up in 1983 as its members pursued solo careers.

Cut loose from Uncle Walt's Band, Ball returned to Nashville, where he gutted it out for most of the 1980s until landing a recording contract with Warner Bros. Success was quick. *Thinkin' Problem*, his 1994 release for the label, went double platinum and spawned three hit singles. The following year, Ball was nominated for a Male Vocalist of the Year Grammy. He returned in 1996 with *Starlite Lounge*, which continued to display his penchant for dressed-up honky tonk. While his 1999 effort, *Play*, was shellacked with a Music City sheen, Ball redeemed himself with the dust-caked traditional country of 2001's *Amigo*. *—Johnny Loftus*

● **Thinkin' Problem** / 1994 / Warner Bros. ♦♦♦♦♦
This hard-country album has a cerebral twist, as the title song suggests. Ball, 41 when this album came out, had a craggy Texas face and a voice to match. When he has material to match, such as "Thinkin' Problem" or the ballad "When the Thought of You Catches Up with Me," he's the kind of singer neo-traditional country fans dream about. *—Brian Mansfield*

David Ball / Nov. 22, 1994 / RCA ♦♦♦
This self-titled release repackages the best of David Ball's early material, originally released prior to his signing to Warner Bros.; even at the outset of his career, he's a gritty vocalist whose reverence for the classic honky tonk sound is obvious, and songs like "If She Were Mine," "Texas Echo" and "Smokin' Cigarettes and Drinkin' Coffee Blues" clearly anticipate the music still to come. *—Jason Ankeny*

Starlite Lounge / Jun. 25, 1996 / Warner Bros. ♦♦♦♦
Starlite Lounge is another set of gritty, contemporary honky tonk from David Ball, highlighted by his gutsy vocals and no-holds-barred approach. Ball doesn't treat honky tonk as a museum piece, but he has respect for its roots, as well—he just tears through the songs with energy and conviction, which means *Starlite Lounge* is simply an invigorating listen. *—Thom Owens*

Play / Jul. 13, 1999 / Warner Bros. ♦♦♦
For his third album, one-time traditionalist Ball trades in the honky tonk of his first two albums for more conventional contemporary country. And while he still has the barroom voice to make even the corniest of material sound soulful and authentic, there is an abundance of barely-average songs filling out *Play*'s songbook. Worse, the Nashville gloss is piled on heavy, turning Ball's strum and twang into just another outing from a probationary member of Music City's hat club. Still, there's an edge to several of the songs here that a bigger selling artist like Garth Brooks could never muster. A slight misstep. *—Michael Gallucci*

Super Hits / Jul. 18, 2000 / Warner Bros. ♦♦♦♦
Country singer David Ball was born in South Carolina. While still in school he learned to play the guitar, tried his hand at songwriting, started his own band, and began performing regularly. A few years later he moved to Texas and formed a new group, Uncle Walt's Band. After a couple of albums, Ball got the chance to go solo in 1994 with a self-titled offering that went gold. Three other full-length recordings followed during the '90s. It's from these that the tunes for *Super Hits* were selected. This best-of collection carries fan favorites like "Watching My Baby Not Coming Back," "Thinkin' Problem," "When the Thought of You Catches Up With Me," and "Look What Followed Me Home." All are songs that Ball either wrote or co-wrote. David Ball's music is country, even honky tonk and touching ballads, but many of his tunes are full of rock and pop flavor, paced out with snare drums and electric guitar. The mixture has been a successful one and gives him a chance to reach country music lovers from different generations. *—Charlotte Dillon*

Amigo / 2001 / Dual Tone ♦♦♦♦♦
When honky tonk singer/songwriter David Ball took country programmers (and hence country listeners) by surprise back in the late '90s—because unless the country programmers (Nash Vegas' fascist culture police) can unplug their payola-ed ears long enough for something to penetrate, no one *ever* gets to hear anything new—with "Thinkin' Problem," and got himself nominated for every single award a new artist can, he's since dropped off the screen. Why? *Amigo* may provide an answer. Rather than follow-up his hit with another track just like it and an album full of them, which is what the majors and country programming geeks want, Ball stayed true to his muse and his own idea of what country music was supposed to be. As a result, *Amigo* is the finest record he's ever done and the one least likely to get him anywhere out of Nash Vegas in terms of radio. However, the alt-country fans out there, and that guy Michael Elta who runs BikerBar Internet Radio, should get hip to him. If they did, Ball's record might get the hearing it truly deserves. This is real country music, full of honky tonk memories, easy Western swing blues, and tough, lean-hearted stories peopled with broken heroes, shattered love affairs, and the determination to never give up in the face of defeat. And what's weird, there isn't anything on this album that isn't "commercial" enough to connect with people if they ever had the opportunity to hear it. OK, enough of the manifesto—the songs on *Amigo* are stellar. There's the opening title track (written with country giant Kostas) with its fiddle lines, steel guitar wranglings, and slippery horns. Then there's the awesome "She Always Talked About Mexico," with its killer Buck Owens' melody and mariachi band backing. And then there's the solid Merle Haggard/Bob Wills-ish shimmy of "Swing Baby," one of the finest party songs of the last ten years with a gorgeous Andrews Sisters-styled chorus in the background. And as far as badass old Texas tunes, there's "New Shiner Polka," with the accordion blaring and the pedal steel whipping up a storm of atmosphere on an instrumental break in the midst of the carousing, heartbreak, and regret that is *Amigo*. There isn't a weak moment here, as Ball has given listeners one of the purest, most solid, and most accessible (largely because of his gorgeous, mellifluous tenor) country & *western* records in over a decade. And, as much as one might love the Hag, this disc blows his *If I Could Only Fly* away. *—Thom Jurek*

E.C. and Orna Ball

f. 1938, **db.** 1975
Group / Country Gospel, Field Recordings, Old-Timey
A fine old-time gospel singer and guitarist, Estil C. Ball (1913-1978) hailed from Rugby, VA, and performed with his wife Orna (b.1907) and the Friendly Gospel Singers. First recorded for the Library of Congress in 1938, Ball was recorded extensively in his later years by the County and Rounder labels. His lively, Travis-style guitar was an unusual element in traditional gospel singing. *—Mark A. Humphrey*

● **E.C. Ball with Orna Ball & the Friendly Gospel Singers** / 1996 / Rounder ♦♦♦♦♦
This is old-time mountain gospel as good as it gets. His guitar virtuosity and powerful baritone blend beautifully. *—David Vinopal*

Fathers Have a Home Sweet Home / Rounder ♦♦♦

The Band

f. 1967, Toronto, Ontario, Canada, **db.** Nov. 1976
Group / Rock & Roll, Country-Rock, Folk-Rock, Album Rock
For about six years, from 1968 through 1975, the Band was one of the most popular and influential rock groups in the world, their music embraced by critics (and, to a somewhat lesser degree, the public) as seriously as the music of the Beatles and the Rolling Stones. Their albums were analyzed and reviewed as intensely as any records by their one-time employer and sometime mentor Bob Dylan. And for a longtime, their personalities were as recognizable individually to the casual music public as the members of the Beatles. The group's history went back nearly as far as the Beatles, to 1958 (just about the time that the formative Beatles gave up skiffle for rock & roll). Ronnie Hawkins, an Arkansas-born rock & roller who aspired to a real career, put together a backing band that year that included his fellow Arkansan Levon Helm (born May 26, 1942), who played drums (as well as credible guitar) and had led his own band, the Jungle Bush Beaters. The new outfit, Ronnie Hawkins & the Hawks, was recording by the spring of 1958 and gigged throughout the south and also up in Ontario, Canada, where the money was better than in their native American south. It was the fact of being based in Canada late in 1959,

coupled with pianist Willard Jones leaving the lineup, that got Hawkins to start looking at some of the local music talent in Toronto; Hawkins approached a musician named Scott Cushnie about joining the Hawks on keyboards. Cushnie was already playing in a band with Robbie Robertson (born in 1944), however, and would only join Hawkins if he came along.

After some resistance from Hawkins, Robertson came into the lineup on bass, replacing a departing Jimmy Evans. More multiple lineup switches took place over the next few years, Robbie Robertson shifting to rhythm guitar behind Fred Carter's (and, briefly, Roy Buchanan's) lead playing. Rick Danko (born December 9, 1943) came in on bass in 1961, followed by Richard Manuel (born April 3, 1944) on piano and backing vocals. Around that same time, Garth Hudson (born August 2, 1937), a classically trained musician who could read music, became the last piece of the initial puzzle as organ player.

For four years, from 1959 through 1963, Ronnie Hawkins & the Hawks were one of the hottest rock & roll bands working, which was very special in a time when rock & roll had supposedly died. Hawkins himself was practically Toronto's answer to Elvis Presley, and he remained true to the music even as Presley himself softened and broadened his sound. The mix of personalities within the group meshed well, better than they did with Hawkins, who, unbeknownst to him, was soon the odd man out in his own group. As new members Danko, Manuel, and Hudson came aboard—all Canadian, and replacing Hawkins' fellow southerners—Hawkins lost control of the group, to some extent, as they began working together more closely.

Finally, the Hawks parted company with Ronnie Hawkins during the summer of 1963, the singer's at times overbearing personality and ego getting the better of the relationship. The Hawks decided to stay together with their oldest member, Levon Helm, out in front, variously renaming themselves Levon & the Hawks and the Canadian Squires and cutting records under both names. A hook-up with a young John Hammond Jr. for a series of recording sessions in New York led to the group's being introduced to Bob Dylan, who was then preparing to pump up his sound in concert. Robertson and Helm played behind Dylan at his Forest Hills concert in New York in 1965 (a bootleg tape of which survives, and can be heard), and he ultimately signed up the entire group. The hook-up with Dylan changed the Hawks, but it wasn't always an easy collaboration. In their five years backing Ronnie Hawkins, the group had played R&B-based rock & roll, heavily influenced by the sound of Chess Records in Chicago and Sun Records in Memphis. Additionally, they'd learned to play tightly and precisely and were accustomed to performing in front of audiences that were interested primarily in having a good-time and dancing. Now Dylan had them playing electric adaptations of folk music, with lots of strumming and lacking the kind of edge they were accustomed to putting on their work. His sound was traceable to the music of Big Bill Broonzy and Josh White, while they'd spent years playing the music of Jerry Lee Lewis, Chuck Berry, and Bo Diddley. As it happens, all of those influences are related, but not directly, and not in ways that were obvious to the players in 1964.

Ironically, in the spring of 1965, the group had just missed their chance at what could have been a legendary meeting on record with a musician they did understand. They'd met Arkansas-based blues legend Sonny Boy Williamson II, and jammed with the singer/blues harpist one day, hoping to cut some records with him. They hadn't realized it at the time, but Williamson was a dying man—by the time the Hawks were ready to return and try to cut some records with him, he had passed on. Another problem for the group about working with Dylan concerned his audience. The Hawks had played in front of a lot of different audiences in the previous four years, but almost all of them were people primarily interested in enjoying themselves and having a good-time. Dylan, however, was playing for crowds that seemed ready to reject him over principle. The Hawks weren't accustomed to confronting the kinds of passions that drove the folk audience, any more than they were initially prepared for the freewheeling nature of Dylan's performances—he liked to make changes in the way he did songs on the spot, and the group was often hard put to keep up with him, at least at first, although the experience did make them a more flexible ensemble on-stage.

Eventually the group did get together with Dylan as his backup band on his 1966 tour, although Levon Helm left soon after the tour began at the end of 1965. The group ultimately fell under the management orbit of Dylan's own manager, Albert Grossman, who persuaded the four core members (sans Helm) to join Dylan in Woodstock, NY, working on the sessions that ultimately became the *Basement Tapes* in their various configurations, none of which would be heard officially for almost a decade. (Indeed, up to this time, only a single song, "Just Like Tom Thumb's Blues," done live from the tour just ended, on a 45 B-side, had surfaced representing the group playing with Dylan).

Finally, a recording contract for the group—rechristened the Band—was secured by Grossman from Capitol Records. Levon Helm returned the fold, and the result was *Music From Big Pink*, an indirect outgrowth of the *Basement Tapes*. This album, enigmatically named and packaged, sounded like nothing else being done by anybody in music when it was released in July of 1968. It was as though psychedelia, and the so-called British Invasion, had never happened; the group played and sang like five distinct individuals working toward the same goal, not mixing together smoothly. There was a collective sound to "the band," but it made up five distinct individual voices and instruments mixing folk, blues, gospel, R&B, classical, and rock & roll.

The press latched on to the album before the public did, but over the next year, the Band became one of the most talked about phenomenon in rock music and *Music From Big Pink* acquired a mystique and significance akin to such albums as *Beggars Banquet*. The group and album ran counter to the so-called counterculture, and took a little getting used to, if only for their lack of a smooth, easily categorizable sound. Their music was steeped in Americana and historical and mythic American imagery, despite the fact that all of the members except Helm came from Canada (which, in fact, may have helped them appreciate the culture they were dealing with, as outsiders). Robertson, Manuel, and Danko all wrote, and everyone but Robertson and Hudson sang; their vocals didn't mesh sweetly but simply flowed together in an informal manner. Classical organ flourishes meshed with a big (yet lean), raw rock & roll sound and the whole was so far removed from the self-indulgent virtuosity and political and cultural posturing going on around them that the Band seemed to be operating in a different reality, to different rules.

During this same period, the group's past association with Bob Dylan—whose name at the time had an almost mystical resonance with audiences—was mentioned in the rock press and also put right in the faces of listeners through a new phenomenon. Only a single track from the group's 1966 tour with Dylan had ever surfaced, and that was an out-of-print B-side to an old single. But in 1969, the first widely distributed bootleg LP, *The Great White Wonder*, featuring the then-unreleased *Basement Tapes*, started turning up on college campuses and record collectors' outlets. The quality was limited, the labels were blank, and there was no "promotion" as such of this patently illegal release, but it got around to hundreds of thousands of listeners and only heightened the mystique surrounding the Band.

Music From Big Pink, which featured a painting by Bob Dylan on its cover, began selling—slowly at first and then better—and the group played a few select shows. A second album, simply titled *The Band*, was every bit as good as the first. Dominated by Robertson's writing, it was released in September of 1969, and with it, the group's reputation exploded; moreover, they began their climb out of the shadow of Bob Dylan with songwriting of their own that was every bit a match for anything he was releasing at the time. A pair of songs, "Up on Cripple Creek" and "The Night They Drove Ol' Dixie Down," captured the public imagination, the former getting them onto *the Ed Sullivan Show* in an appearance that's fascinating to watch on the official Ed Sullivan video release; the host comes out to embrace and congratulate them, obviously thrilled after the psychedelic and hard rock acts that he usually booked, to see a group whose words and music he understood. Meanwhile, "The Night They Drove Ol' Dixie Down" became a popular radio track and yielded a hit cover version in the guise of an unaccountably corrupted rendition by Joan Baez (in which, for reasons that only Baez may be able to explain, Robert E. Lee is transformed into a steamboat) that made the Top Five.

Following the release of the second album, things changed somewhat within the group. Partly owing to the pressures of touring and the public's expectations of "genius," and also to the growing press fixation on Robbie Robertson at the expense of the rest of the group, the other group members remained familiar enough that their names and personalities were well-known to the public. The Band was still a great working ensemble, as represented on their brilliant third album, *Stage Fright*, but gradually exhaustion and personal pressures took their toll. Additionally, the huge amounts of money that the members started collecting, against hundreds of thousands and ultimately millions of record sales, led to instances of irresponsible behavior by individual members and their spouses and raised the pressure on the group to perform. The members had always engaged in a certain amount of casual drug use, mostly involving marijuana, but now they had access to more serious and expensive chemical diversions. Some private resentments also began manifesting themselves about Robertson's dominance of the songwriting (some reality of which was questioned openly in Levon Helm's autobiography years later), and the fact that the group was now constantly in the public eye didn't help.

By the time of the fourth album, *Cahoots*, some of the glow of experimentation and easygoing comaraderie was gone, though ironically, the album was still one of the best released in 1971. The problem for the group became fulfilling all of the commitments involved in success, including touring and writing new material to record. By the end of 1971, they'd decided to take a break, cutting a live album, *Rock of Ages*, that was all fans had to content themselves with in 1972. The fact that their next album, issued in 1973, was a collection of studio versions of the oldies that the group used to do on-stage, and numbers that they knew from their days as the Hawks, should have been a warning sign that not everything was well within the group. More troubling still was the fact that the renditions were so plain and flat sounding compared to the music they'd cut on every prior album; it simply wasn't up to the standard that one expected of the group and the fact that they didn't tour behind the record seemed to indicate that they were marking time with *Moondog Matinee*. The group did play one major show that year, at the race track at Watkins Glen, NY, before the largest audience ever assembled for a rock concert—it was a demonstration of their place in the rock pantheon that the Band was booked alongside the Grateful Dead and the Allman Brothers Band.

The year 1973 was also where they let the other shoe drop on their association with Bob Dylan, cutting the *Planet Waves* album with him and preparing for a huge national tour together in 1974. That tour, in retrospect, seemed more a basis for cashing in on their association with Dylan than for any new music-making of any significance. In many critics' eyes, the Band was superior to Dylan in their performances, an idea borne out on much of the live LP *Before the Flood* that was distilled down from the two February 14, 1974, performances. Everyone made a fortune from it, but the tour with Dylan also thrust the group right into the middle of the most decadent part of the rock world. A lot of the simplicity and directness of their music and lives succumbed to the easy availability of sex, drugs, and other diversions and the expensive lifestyles they were all starting to maintain.

By the end of 1974, the Band had expended much of the good will they'd built up from their first four albums. Another album, *Northern Lights—Southern Cross* released in late 1975, was a major comeback and restored some of the group's reputation as a cutting-edge ensemble, even encompassing elements of synthesizer music into its writing and production. Around this same time, Levon Helm and Garth Hudson made a belated contribution to the history of Chess Records (in light of their near-miss with Sonny Boy Williamson a decade earlier) when they worked with Muddy Waters, cutting an entire album with the blues legend at Helm's studio in Woodstock, NY. The Muddy Waters *Woodstock Album*, although ignored at the time by everyone but the critics, was the last great album cut by the label or by Waters at the label, and his best album in at least five years. It was too late to save the Band as a working ensemble, however; the members were all involved in their own interests and lives and the group stopped touring. The inevitable best-of album in 1976, ahead of what proved to be their final tour, marked the unofficial end of the original lineup's history. One last new album, *Islands*, fulfilled the group's contract and had some fine moments, but they never toured behind it and it was clear to one and all that the Band was finished as a going concern. The group marked the end of their days as an active unit with the release of the film (and accompanying soundtrack LP set) *The Last Waltz*, directed by Martin Scorsese, of their farewell concert, which was an all-star performing affair pulling together the talents of Ronnie Hawkins,

Muddy Waters, Eric Clapton, Neil Young, Van Morrison, and a dozen other luminaries drawn from the ranks of old friends, admirers, and idols of theirs. Robertson and Helm pursued musical and film careers, while Danko tried to start a solo career of his own.

Capitol Records kept repackaging their music on vinyl with an *Anthology* collection and a second best-of LP, as well as a pair of CD recompilations, *To Kingdom Come* and *Across the Great Divide*, in the '90s. As it turned out the members, apart from Robertson, weren't quite as ready or willing to close the book on the group, in part because they saw no reason to and also because several of them proved unable to sustain profitable solo careers (Robertson, having written most of the songs, had a steady income from the publishing as well as the record sales). The other members of the group reunited at various times—in 1983, four members of the Band, with Robertson replaced by Earl Cate of the Cate Brothers on guitar, reunited for a tour that yielded a full-length concert video and a healthy audience response. The death of Richard Manuel in 1986 cast a dark pall on any future reunions, of which there were several—Robertson issued his first solo album a year later, which included a tribute to Manuel ("Fallen Angel").

This was as close as the guitarist would get to a Band reunion, however, which became a bone of contention among onlookers and the members. Robertson publicly questioned what the meaning of *The Last Waltz* had been and would never participate. And as the group's major songwriter and principal guitarist, he was their most famous member, but he almost never sang significant vocal parts on their recordings (indeed, it is said that one reason their set from *Woodstock* was never issued was because his mike was live and his voice too prominent). Other guitarists could build on his work well enough, and the rest of the group had made significant contributions to virtually every song they ever did, so the reunions made sense. In 1993, the Band released *Jericho*, their first new album in 16 years, which received surprisingly good reviews. *High on the Hog* followed in 1996 and two years later, they celebrated their 30th anniversary with *Jubilation*. The death of Rick Danko in his sleep at his home in Woodstock on December 10, 1999, the day after his 56th birthday, seemed to call an end to future activities by any version of the Band. *—Bruce Eder*

☆ **Music From Big Pink** / Jul. 1, 1968 / Capitol ♦♦♦♦♦

None of the Band's previous work gave much of a clue about how they would sound when they released their first album in July 1968. As it was, *Music From Big Pink* came as a surprise. At first blush, the group seemed to affect the sound of a loose jam session, alternating emphasis on different instruments, while the lead and harmony vocals passed back and forth as if the singers were making up their blend on the spot. In retrospect, especially as the lyrics sank in, the arrangements seemed far more considered and crafted to support a group of songs that took family, faith, and rural life as their subjects and proceeded to imbue their values with uncertainty. Some songs took on the theme of declining institutions less clearly than others, but the points were made musically as much as lyrically. Tenor Richard Manuel's haunting, lonely voice gave the album much of its frightening aspect, while Rick Danko and Levon Helm's rough-hewn styles reinforced the songs' rustic fervor. The dominant instrument was Garth Hudson's often icy and majestic organ, while Robbie Robertson's unusual guitar work further destabilized the sound. The result was an album that reflected the turmoil of the late '60s in a way that emphasized the tragedy inherent in the conflicts. *Music From Big Pink* came off as a shockingly divergent musical statement only a year after the ornate productions of *Sgt. Pepper*, and initially attracted attention because of the three songs Bob Dylan had either written or co-written. Soon, however, as "The Weight" became a minor singles chart entry, the album and the group made their own impact, influencing a movement toward roots styles and country elements in rock. Over time, *Music From Big Pink* came to be regarded as a watershed work in the history of rock, one that introduced new tones and approaches to the constantly evolving genre. *—William Ruhlmann*

★ **The Band** / Sep. 22, 1969 / Capitol ♦♦♦♦♦

The Band's first album, *Music From Big Pink*, seemed to come out of nowhere, with its ramshackle musical blend and songs of rural tragedy. *The Band*, the group's second album, was a more deliberate and even more accomplished effort, partially because the players had become a more cohesive unit and partially because guitarist Robbie Robertson had taken over the songwriting, writing or co-writing all 12 songs. Though a Canadian, Robertson focused on a series of American archetypes from the union worker in "King Harvest (Has Surely Come)" and the retired sailor in "Rockin' Chair" to, most famously, the Confederate Civil War observer Virgil Cane in "The Night They Drove Old' Dixie Down." The album effectively mixed the kind of mournful songs that had dominated *Music From Big Pink*, here including "Whispering Pines" and "When You Awake" (both co-written and sung by haunting tenor Richard Manuel), with rollicking uptempo numbers like "Rag Mama Rag" and "Up on Cripple Creek" (both sung by Levon Helm and released as singles, with "Up on Cripple Creek" making the Top 40). As had been true of the first album, it was the Band's sound that stood out the most, from Helm's (and occasionally Manuel's) propulsive drumming to Robertson's distinctive guitar fills and the endlessly inventive keyboard textures of Garth Hudson, all topped by the rough, expressive singing of Manuel, Helm, and Rick Danko that mixed leads with harmonies. The arrangements were simultaneously loose and assured, giving the songs a timeless appeal, while the lyrics continued to paint portraits of 19th century rural life (especially Southern life, as references to Tennessee and Virginia made clear), its sometimes less savory aspects treated with warmth and humor. [The 2000 CD reissue featured seven bonus tracks.] *—William Ruhlmann*

Stage Fright / Aug. 17, 1970 / Capitol ♦♦♦♦

Stage Fright, the Band's third album, sounded on its surface like the group's first two releases, *Music From Big Pink* and *The Band*, employing the same dense arrangements, with their mixture of a deep bottom formed by drummer Levon Helm and bassist Rick Danko, penetrating guitar work by Robbie Robertson, and the varied keyboard work of pianist Richard Manuel and organist Garth Hudson, with Helm, Danko, and Manuel's vocals on top. But the songs this time around were far more personal, and, despite a nominal complacency, quite troubling. Only "All La Glory," Robertson's song about the birth of his daughter, was fully positive. "Strawberry Wine" and "Sleeping" were celebrations of indolence, while "Time to Kill," as its title implied, revealed boredom while claiming romantic contentment. Several of the album's later songs seemed to be metaphors for trouble the group was encountering, with "The W.S. Walcott Medicine Show" commenting on the falseness of show business, "Daniel and the Sacred Harp" worrying about a loss of integrity, and the title song talking about the pitfalls of fortune and fame. "The Shape I'm In" was perhaps the album's most blatant statement of panic. The Band was widely acclaimed after its first two albums; *Stage Fright* seemed to be the group's alarmed response, which made it their most nakedly confessional. It was certainly different from their previous work, which had tended toward story songs set in earlier times, but it was hardly less compelling for that. [The 2000 expanded edition was the first CD reissue containing the mixes that had been used on the original LP.] *—William Ruhlmann*

Cahoots / Sep. 15, 1971 / Capitol ♦♦♦

In comparison to its predecessors, *Cahoots*, the Band's fourth album, may be characterized as an essentially minor effort that nevertheless contains a few small pleasures. These pleasures begin with the leadoff track "Life Is a Carnival," a song that continues the theme of *Stage Fright* by emphasizing the false nature of show business and its impact on reality. The song features a lively Dixieland horn chart courtesy of Allen Toussaint. "When I Paint My Masterpiece," a Bob Dylan song making its recorded debut here as the second selection, is another welcome track, buoyed by mandolin and accordion in a charming arrangement appropriate to its tale of an odd trip to Europe. "4% Pantomime" is a duet between the Band's Richard Manuel and Van Morrison that is entertaining to hear, even if the song itself is slight. Unfortunately, that just about completes the list of the album's attractions. Annotator Rob Bowman claims that the overriding theme of the songs is "extinction and the sadness that accompanies the passing of things that once were held to be of great value"; actually, there is no overriding theme to the minor songs written by Robbie Robertson. Several of the songs' lyrics come across as half-baked film scenarios, but they fail to be evocative, and they are paired to music lacking in structure. The failure is solely in the writing; the Band sounds as good as ever playing the songs, with singers Manuel, Levon Helm, and Rick Danko all performing effectively and primary instrumentalist Garth Hudson filling in the arrangements cleverly. It's just that the material is not strong enough, particularly in comparison to the three impressive albums the Band had released previously. [By adding four good bonus tracks, the 2000 reissue significantly strengthens the collection.] *—William Ruhlmann*

Rock of Ages / Aug. 15, 1972 / Capitol ♦♦♦♦♦

Recorded on New Year's Eve 1971/1972, this was the Band's last gig for a year and a half. Allen Toussaint was brought in again to write horn arrangements for many of their classics. The results were inspired. Highlights are many, but of particular note are a cover of Marvin Gaye's "Baby Don't Do It" and a live recording of a track that had earlier been relegated to B-side status only, "Get Up Jake." *—Rob Bowman*

Moondog Matinee / Oct. 15, 1973 / Capitol ♦♦

The Band essentially went back to being the Hawks of the late '50s and early '60s on this album of cover tunes. They demonstrated considerable expertise on their versions of rock & roll and R&B standards like Clarence "Frogman" Henry's "Ain't Got No Home," Chuck Berry's "The Promised Land," and Fats Domino's "I'm Ready," but of course that didn't do much to satisfy the audience they had established with their original material and that, two years after the disappointing *Cahoots*, was waiting for something in the same league with their first three albums. *—William Ruhlmann*

Northern Lights—Southern Cross / Nov. 1, 1975 / Capitol ♦♦♦♦

The first studio album of Band originals in four years, in many respects *Northern Lights—Southern Cross* was viewed as a comeback. It also can be seen as a swan song. The album was the Band's finest since their self-titled sophomore effort. Totaling eight songs in all, on this album the Band explores new timbres, utilizing for the first time 24 tracks and what was (then) new synthesizer technology. "Acadian Driftwood" stands out as one of Robertson's finest compositions, the equal to anything else the Band ever recorded. *—Rob Bowman*

Islands / Mar. 15, 1977 / Capitol ♦♦

Theoretically, even though the Band had given up touring as of Thanksgiving 1976, they were going to keep making records, and *Islands* was the first album released in the new era. Only it wasn't; it was the album they scraped together to complete their ten-LP contract with Capitol Records and the last new full-length album the original five members ever made. The playing, as ever, was impeccable, and the record had its moments, notably a Richard Manuel vocal on the chestnut "Georgia on My Mind" that had been released as a single in 1976 to boost Georgia governor Jimmy Carter's successful run for the presidency. But the songwriting quality was mediocre, and the Band had set such a standard for itself in that department that *Islands* couldn't help suffering enormously in comparison. *—William Ruhlmann*

The Last Waltz / Apr. 1978 / Warner Bros. ♦♦♦♦

As a film, *The Last Waltz* was a triumph—one of the first (and still one of the few) rock concert documentaries that was directed by a filmmaker who understood both the look and the sound of rock & roll, and executed with enough technical craft to capture all the nooks and crannies of a great live show. But as an album, *The Last Waltz* soundtrack had to compete with the Band's earlier live album, *Rock of Ages*, with which it bears a certain superficial resemblance—both found the group trying to create something grander than the standard-issue live double, and both featured the group beefed up by additional musicians. While *Rock of Ages* found the Band swinging along with the help of a horn section arranged by Allen Toussaint, *The Last Waltz* boasts a horn section (using Toussaint's earlier arrangements on a few cuts) *and* more than a baker's dozen guest stars, ranging from old cohorts Ronnie Hawkins and Bob Dylan to contemporaries Joni Mitchell, Neil Young, and Van Morrison. The Band are in fine if not exceptional form here; on most cuts, they don't sound quite as fiery as they did on *Rock of Ages*, though their performances are never less than expert, and the high points are dazzling, especially an impassioned version of "It Makes No Difference" and blazing readings of "Up on Cripple Creek" and "The Night They Drove Old Dixie Down" (Levon Helm has made no secret that he felt breaking up the Band was a bad idea, and here it sounds if he was determined to prove how much they still had to offer). Ultimately, it's the Band's "special guests" who really make this set stand out—Muddy Waters' ferocious version of "Mannish Boy" would have been a wonder from a man half his age, Van Morrison sounds positively joyous on "Caravan," Neil Young and Joni Mitchell do well for their Canadian brethren, and Bob Dylan's closing set finds him in admirably loose and rollicking form. (One question remains—what exactly is Neil Diamond doing here?) And while the closing studio-recorded "Last Waltz Suite" sounds like padding, the contributions from Emmylou Harris and the Staple Singers are beautiful indeed. It could be argued that you're better off watching *The Last Waltz* on video than listening to it on CD, but either way it's a show well worth checking out. *—Mark Deming*

To Kingdom Come / Sep. 1989 / Capitol ✦✦✦✦✦

Released in the fall of 1989, *To Kingdom Come* is a double-disc set that purports to be "The Definitive Collection" and, in a sense, it does provide a good overview of the band's career. Over the course of 31 songs, the collection works its way through the hits and album tracks, adding such rarities as "Get Up Jake," "Back to Memphis," and "Lovin' You Is Sweeter Than Ever," even if it never touches on *The Basement Tapes*. All the predictable items are here and the album tracks are well-chosen, and it is a good representation of the band, worth the time of listeners who want a smartly assembled anthology. The 2000 *Greatest Hits* gets the edge for casual fans, since it has 20 tracks on one disc, yet this remains worthwhile for listeners who want a fairly comprehensive, thorough anthology. *—Stephen Thomas Erlewine*

Jericho / Nov. 2, 1993 / Pyramid/Rhino ✦✦✦

A full 17 years after *The Last Waltz*, the Band re-formed without Robbie Robertson or the late Richard Manuel and recorded *Jericho*. Far from being an embarrassment, *Jericho* is their strongest record since *Northern Lights—Southern Cross* and arguably their best since *Stage Fright*. Without Robertson, the Band relies on a variety of sources for their material (including Bob Dylan, Bruce Springsteen, and Jules Shear) and prove that they can interpret nearly any song well. Musically, the Band can still juggle rock, folk, blues, and country effortlessly, producing a rootsy sound distinctly their own. It sounds like the heyday of the group, which is more than can be said of either of Robertson's solo albums. *—Stephen Thomas Erlewine*

Across the Great Divide / Nov. 15, 1994 / Capitol ✦✦✦

Capitol's 1989 Band compilation *To Kingdom Come* was subtitled "The Definitive Collection," so what is this? Well, the other one was only a two-disc set, and this is a three-disc set. As the CD reissue/box set boom goes on, record companies have taken to redoing acts they've already done once, so even though the Band has one classy CD anthology (and a few tacky ones), Capitol gives us another. In this case, they've divided it into two discs' worth of the greatest hits, followed by a disc of rarities (some not so rare) and unreleased tracks that includes pre-Band recordings by the Hawks, collaborations with Bob Dylan, live tracks from the *Woodstock* and *Watkins Glen* festivals, and the like. All of which pushes this set up a price point or two from the earlier one without adding anything substantial to the story. *—William Ruhlmann*

Live at Watkins Glen / Apr. 4, 1995 / Capitol ✦✦

High on the Hog / Feb. 27, 1996 / Rhino ✦✦

Jubilation / Sep. 15, 1998 / River North ✦✦✦

Jubilation, the tenth studio album by the Band, showcases a group that has aged better than the finest port wine. Yes, although the voices have aged noticeably (particularly in the cases of Rick Danko and Levon Helm), this fact only makes the record more charming. The songwriting is still spiritual and evocative, and all of the tunes are peppered with a Grant Wood-ish plain-spoken sensibility that are at once familiar and instantly engaging. The group (Danko, Helm, and resident keyboard genius Garth Hudson) are augmented by Richard Bell (keyboards), Randy Ciarlante (drums, vocals), and Jim Weider (guitar). The odd thing is that this version of the group has probably been together as long as the original Band. Guest appearances by Eric Clapton and John Hiatt are nice additions, but are not reasons to buy this album, as it holds up quite well on its own merits. *—Matthew Greenwald*

The Best of the Band, Vol. 2 / Oct. 5, 1999 / Rhino ✦✦✦

The name of the album is *The Best of the Band, Vol. 2*, the label is Rhino, the lauded reissue specialist—it would be easy to assume that the collection would fill in gaps left by Capitol's fine 1976 sampler, *The Best of the Band*. That train of logic forgets an important point. The Band, minus Robbie Robertson, reunited in 1993 and recorded *Jericho*, which was the first of three new albums by the group. *Jericho* and its successor, *High on the Hog*, happened to be released by Pyramid, Rhino's new music label; the third, 1998's *Jubilation*, appeared on River North. These three albums provide the basis for *The Best of the Band, Vol. 2*. Even hardcore fans would admit that these comeback albums did not match the original records, yet they could justifiably argue that the music wasn't bad, even quite good at times. And it was—none of the three albums were perfect, but they had strong moments, most of which are collected here. That's not to say this music is for everybody, or even for fans of the Band's prime years, since it does have the feel of a reunion and is a bit nostalgic-minded. However, it is a good summary of the Band's reunion, and listeners willing to take a chance may be surprised how strong they sound on "Atlantic City" and "Blind Willie McTell" or how loose they are on "Youngblood," the set's sole unreleased track. *—Stephen Thomas Erlewine*

Greatest Hits / Sep. 26, 2000 / Capitol ✦✦✦✦✦

The Band was a very album-oriented group, and only had two Top 40 hit singles. So one could argue that a single-disc greatest hits compilation, or best-of anthology as this might more properly be called, is not the optimum way to dig into their repertoire. But if you're limiting yourself to one Band collection and your budget or patience does not stretch for the two-CD *To Kingdom Come* set, this 18-song program hits all the famous buttons, including "The Weight," "Chest Fever," "Up on Cripple Creek," "The Night They Drove Old Dixie Down," "The Shape I'm In," "Stage Fright," and "When I Paint My Masterpiece." Naturally, it leans most heavily on their first two albums, which supply four songs each. Good, lengthy liner notes by Rob Bowman are a nice bonus, considering that single-disc career-spanning overviews often dispense with such frills. Strange, though, that "Don't Do It," their one Top 40 hit single other than "Up on Cripple Creek," isn't here; in fact, there's nothing from their live *Rock of Ages*. *—Richie Unterberger*

The Last Waltz [Box Set] / Apr. 16, 2002 / Rhino ✦✦✦✦

'The road was our school. It gave us a sense of survival; it taught us everything we know and out of respect, we don't want to drive it into the ground...or maybe it's just superstition but the road has taken a lot of the great ones. It's a goddam impossible way of life"—Robbie Robertson, from the movie *The Last Waltz*, quoted in the box set. Perhaps Robbie Robertson's greatest gift is how he can spin a myth, making the mundane into majestic fables. Outside of his songs, his greatest achievement in myth-making was *The Last Waltz*, where he doesn't necessarily overstate the amount of time the Band spent on the road, but he sure tried to make it all seem like something special, both in amount of time they spent on the road and what they've accomplished. And while he was right on the latter—the Band did change the course of music, leaving behind records that still sound gloriously rich and out of time—the former is a bit of a stretch since not only were the rest of the Band not exactly ready to stop touring (they would later reunite without him), it ignores the basic fact that touring is what working musicians do. They make music, they play for audiences, they keep rolling throughout the years, and many of the artists invited to participate in the Band's farewell concert—Ronnie Hawkins, Dr. John, Muddy Waters, Van Morrison, Neil Young, the Staple Singers, Emmylou Harris, Eric Clapton, and Bob Dylan, who legendarily launched a never-ending tour in the '80s—lived the life of a working musician, performing live well past age 50. The Band was cut from the same cloth as this, but Robertson realized that the group wasn't doing themselves any good by staying on the road—and the accompanying Martin Scorsese-directed film does suggest that the Band was indulging themselves way too much—and that it was the perfect time to draw the curtain on the Band with a lavish concert that turned their entire career into a burnished myth, nearly as ancient and romantic as photographs from the Civil War. Hence, *The Last Waltz*, a farewell concert on Thanksgiving 1976 promoted by Bill Graham and turned into a timeless documentary by Scorsese, was released as a triple-album set in 1978 and finally reissued as a four-disc box set by Rhino in 2002, on its near-25th Anniversary (it's somewhere between 24 and 26, depending if you're counting performance or release, so 25 is a good compromise). Many people call this the greatest rock movie and greatest live performance of all time. They're wrong. It could be argued that the film is among the greatest rock films—convincingly so, actually—but the music amplifies not just what was great about the Band, but also their greatest flaws. That is, their effortless virtuosity and wonderful organic sound is a joy to hear, yet it can be undercut by the literary pretensions of Robertson, which gives the songs and sometimes the performances an artificial, academic feel—something that is accentuated here, since the music is being presented in an artificially romantic setting, where everything was heightened for the cinema; the Band even gives the entire enterprise a theme straight out of *The Third Man*. This resulted in something equally wonderful and affected, with each track having portions of both in different proportions. On the whole, the sublime outweighs the missteps, particularly since the invited guests are by and large troubadours who enjoy playing—Dr. John hauling out "Such a Night" (such a standard practice, it was later parodied on SCTV), Bobby Charles turning in the happiest performance of the evening with "Down South in New Orleans," Muddy Waters roaring through "Mannish Boy," Paul Butterfield playing mean harp, Van Morrison's joyous set, Dylan performing with an authority that suggests that he always thought he owned the Band. Other good moments are here—Clapton croons his Band-supported album track "All Our Past Times" with appropriate melancholy; Neil Young turns out a sweet "Helpless"; Joni Mitchell's "Coyote" is alluringly allusive; even Neil Diamond's "Dry Your Eyes"; all are engaging—but it doesn't add up to something transcendent, either in its original triple-album set or in this quadruple-disc box. Part of the problem is that the concert is supplemented by a studio set—entitled "The Last Waltz Suite," expanded to a full disc here—that feels entirely out of place, even if it was designed to spotlight influences of the Band that weren't covered in the concert. Perhaps that's the reason why it feels so studied and affected, right down to the Staple Singers' celebrated version of "The Weight." This draws attention to one of the problems of the Band shining a spotlight on their influences—they are treating their influences with a respective distance, not as if something that is still vital to them, making even appearances by ruffians like Hawkins seem like museum pieces. Much of the Band absorbed these influences, so some of the spirit echoes throughout their own performances, but that distance is still evident—enough so that this music isn't transcendent, when it should be. This is all evident in spades within the box of *The Last Waltz*, which is an admittedly handsome, loving production. It's not necessarily historically accurate—the Band performed a full set before the guests show up, but here their songs are interspersed throughout the first three discs, a couple of songs are left off, and even "The Genetic Method/Chest Fever" doesn't have the latter part of the song. Still, this is as good as an historical release as imaginable, since it is expertly detailed, impeccably mastered, perfectly annotated, and filled with great liner notes and much unreleased material. None of the newly released material is revelatory—the jams are negligible (everybody sounds like they just ate a bunch of turkey before they played), the rehearsals confirm that Van the Man really clicked with the band, the studio ideas fall flat, "Don't Do It" is as great as ever, everything inserted into the proper concert is welcome, even if it varies in quality—but it's all good, all welcome for those that have bought the myth of the Band and, particularly, *The Last Waltz*. But the box proves that the myth, in regards to the final concert, is not accurate—for those listeners who didn't grow up with the music, or those that never thought this particular concert pulled the curtain down on a wonderful era, it's easy to wonder what all the fuss was about. Because the thing is, the people who sound the best here—Dylan, Van Morrison, Dr. John, Levon Helm himself—are the ones who didn't treat the road as a goddam impossible way of life, but as what a working musician *does*. *The Last Waltz* teeters between these two schools of thought, wanting to celebrate the end while blithely ignoring that musicians make music for a living—and that's what keeps the music from truly captivating, from being essential, even if this set is perfectly assembled. *—Stephen Thomas Erlewine*

Moe Bandy

b. Feb. 12, 1944, Meridian, MS

Vocals, Guitar / Traditional Country, Honky Tonk, Contemporary Country

Moe Bandy was one of the most popular country singers of the 1970s, turning out a series of hits in the latter half of the decade that made many fans and critics believe he was one of the great honky tonk singers. Bandy's songs never strayed far from the traditional barroom fare—delivered with a knowing sense of humor, loving, cheating, drinking, and patriotic songs form the core of his repertoire. Throughout the late '70s and early '80s, the singer racked up hits. His audience declined somewhat a decade after his career took off, yet he has remained a popular favorite through his theater in Branson, MO.

Bandy was born in Meridian, MS, the birthplace of Jimmie Rodgers. In fact, Bandy's grandfather worked with Rodgers on the railroad, so it's no surprise that the singer first fell in love with country music through the Jimmie Rodgers records that were around his house, as well as the Hank Williams albums. Bandy's family moved to San Antonio, TX, when he was six. During high-school, he was a rodeo rider, but his career came to a halt once he suffered too many injuries. Once he left school, Bandy was a sheet metal worker, singing in country nightclubs at night. He landed a one-record deal with Satin Records in 1964. The label released Bandy's original song "Lonely Lady," but the record made no impact. Nevertheless, he continued to perform at night in various Texas honky tonks.

In 1972, Bandy met record producer Ray Baker on a hunting trip and convinced him to listen to some demo tapes he had made. Provided that Moe could pay for the recording sessions, Baker agreed to produce the singer. Excited by his new prospect, Bandy pawned his furniture and financed a session. Once they were released, the records went nowhere. The following year, the singer took out a loan to pay for another recording date. "I Just Started Hatin' Cheatin' Songs Today" was the result of this session, and Baker released the single on Footprint Records, manufacturing only 500 copies. Unlike Bandy's previous records, the single began to sell. GRC acquired the rights to the record and released it nationally; it eventually became a Top 20 hit. Nevertheless, Bandy kept his job as a sheet metal worker, uncertain of the end result of his taste of success.

Bandy followed "I Just Started Hatin' Cheatin' Songs Today" with several singles on GRC, including the Top Ten hits "It Was Always So Easy (To Find an Unhappy Woman)" (1974) and "Bandy the Rodeo Clown" (1975), which was written by Lefty Frizzell and Sanger "Whitey" Shafer. Bandy signed with Columbia Records in 1975, keeping Baker as a producer. "Hank Williams You Changed My Life," his first single for the label, was an instant number-three hit, leading to his Most Promising Male Vocalist award from the Academy of Country Music. Bandy's string of hit singles in 1976—including "Here I Am Drunk Again" and "She Took More Than Her Share"—confirmed that he was one of the most popular singers of the latter half of the decade. The following two years were equally successful for the singer, as he had hits with "I'm Sorry for You My Friend," "Cowboys Aren't Supposed to Cry," "She Just Loved the Cheatin' Out of Me," "That's What Makes the Jukebox Play," and "Two Lonely People."

Bandy's career reached a peak in 1979. During that year, he teamed up with Janie Fricke in 1979 for "It's a Cheatin' Situation." The song became a number-three hit and won the Song of the Year award from the ACM. Bandy had another successful duet that year with Joe Stampley. The pair released *Just Good Ol' Boys*, which became one of the most popular albums of the year, spawning the number-one title track and the Top Ten "Holding the Bag." Like his pairing with Fricke, the duet with Stampley was an award-winning combination, as the duo won the Country Music Association's Duet of the Year and the ACM's Duo of the Year awards in 1980. Bandy also had a pair of major solo hits with the number one "I Cheated Me Right Out of Her" and the Top Ten "Barstool Mountain."

During 1980, Moe Bandy's winning streak continued with the Top Ten hits "Yesterday Once More" and "Following the Feeling," a duet with Judy Bailey. Bandy teamed up Stampley again in 1981, which proved as successful as the duo's first outing. The pair again reached the Top Ten with "Hey Moe Hey Joe" and charted with "Honky Tonk Queen." With "My Woman Loves the Devil Out of Me" and "Rodeo Romeo," Bandy had a pair of solo hits the same year. For the next two years, he regularly charted in the Top 20, both as a solo act and with various duet partners, including Becky Hobbs on the Top Ten 1983 hit "Let's Get Over Them Together." However, none of his songs caused the sensation of "Where's the Dress," a parody of Culture Club's Boy George recorded with Stampley. Although Boy George sued the duo, the song was a major hit, winning an award for Best Country Video from the America Video Awards and the New York Film Festival.

Moe Bandy switched record labels in 1986, signing with MCA/Curb. Not only did he change labels, he changed producers, abandoning his old collaborator, Ray Baker, for Jerry Kennedy. Appropriately, the sound of the singer's records changed as well. No longer were they modern-day honky tonk; they were slicker and more pop-oriented. Ironically, the change in sound didn't bring about more commercial success. For a brief time, Bandy continued to have Top Ten hits, including "Till I'm Too Old to Die Young" (1987) and "Americana" (1988), which became presidential candidate George Bush's campaign theme song; Bandy played Bush's Presidential Inauguration, as well as playing the White House twice in 1989. However, he wasn't faring as well on the country charts. His albums became increasingly safer and smoother, yet they failed to reach the peaks of his rowdier early material.

Bandy opened the Moe Bandy Americana Theatre in 1991, becoming one of many country performers to establish themselves in Branson, MO. Bandy frequently performs in the 900-seat venue with his Americana Band. His theater has been more popular than his records in the '90s and '00s, but for a time in the late '70s and early '80s he was one of the most popular and exciting singers recording. *—Stephen Thomas Erlewine*

☆ **I Just Started Hatin' Cheatin' Songs Today** / 1974 / GRC ✦✦✦✦✦

When Moe Bandy released his first album, *I Just Started Hatin' Cheatin' Songs Today*, on GRC Records in 1974, country music was immersed in one of its periodic infatuations with pop crossover. Bandy wasn't having any of that. He was based outside of Nashville and was a hardcore honky tonk singer who made no concessions to pop. In a way, he was a kindred spirit to the emerging outlaw country movement, since both disdained Nashville and were trying to get the music back to its roots, but Bandy had none of the rock or folk influences of outlaw; he was country, pure and simple, as his debut illustrates. This is direct, unadorned country music, with plenty of steel guitars and barroom weepers, all about heartache, drinking, and cheatin' women. If Bandy's voice is somewhat plain, lacking the rich resonance of George Jones, Johnny Paycheck, or Ray Price, he doesn't lack character; he's learned from the greats and his plaintive voice emphasizes the directness of his music. Plus, he knows how to deliver a line, knows how to wring emotion out of a great song. Fortunately, he has more than his share of great songs here. Not one of them is a cover of a well-known song. Instead, they're all newly written tunes, most by Whitey Shafer and A.L. Owens, which gives the album its own character, as if it was a collection of forgotten favorites. The title track and "Honky Tonk Amnesia" were the hits, breaking Bandy through to a wide audience, but they aren't the only highlights here. There isn't a weak song or a weak performance on *I Just Started Hatin' Cheatin' Songs Today*, and its strict adherence to the tenets of hardcore honky tonk resulted in one of the all-time great pure country records. *—Stephen Thomas Erlewine*

☆ **It Was Always So Easy (To Find An Unhappy Woman)** / 1975 / GRC ✦✦✦✦✦

Moe Bandy made quite a splash with his 1974 debut *I Just Started Hatin' Cheatin' Songs Today*, cracking the country Top 20 twice with its hits, but with his second album, *It Was Always So Easy (To Find an Unhappy Woman)*, he not only proved that the debut was no fluke, he wound equalling it. There isn't much difference in its sound or approach—the biggest change is that there is one well-known cover tune here, in the presence of a great version of the great Bob Wills song "Home in San Antone"—but that's hardly a detriment. Thankfully, there isn't a sense of complacency here, just the sense that producer Ray Baker, Bandy, and his band—featuring such stellar sidemen as Johnny Gimble, Pig Robbins, and Charlie McCoy—know better than to mess with something that they got right the first time around. If anything, the group stretches themselves a bit (the Western swing of "Home in San Antone" was not heard on the debut), giving rich, relaxed performances which Bandy complements with assured, confident singing. Then, there are the songs, which are as good as what came before, highlighted by three Dallas Frazier songs ("Don't Anyone Make Love at Home Anymore," "Loving You Was All I Ever Needed," "I'm Gonna Listen to Me"), as well as Owens/Shafer's great title track. If the debut edges this one slightly, it's partially because of the lack of the thrill of the new and partially because the mood on that first album is more intense, something that's appropriate for a record about drinking, jealousy, and cheating. This is a bit of a lighter affair, with sprightlier tempos and a more cheerful mood, even if the sound and topics are largely the same. In the end, it's merely the opposite of the same coin, really, and both records aren't just equally satisfying, they constitute a peerless pair of pure hardcore country. *—Stephen Thomas Erlewine*

Bandy, the Rodeo Clown / 1975 / GRC ✦✦✦✦

For *Bandy the Rodeo Clown*, his final record for GRC, Moe Bandy didn't depart from the musical template his first two albums created, but he did lighten the mood a little bit, beginning to hint at the good-natured persona that would dominate his Columbia Records. Much of this is, of course, telegraphed in the title track, written by Lefty Frizzell and Whitey Shafer, which literally casts Moe Bandy as a clown who laughs through the tears, but the music also reflects a shift toward lighter material. The beginnings of this were heard on his previous *It Was Always So Easy (To Find an Unhappy Woman)*, and this follows through on that move, boasting a set of songs that feel lighter than the late-night honky tonk of his debut. That's not to say that it's poppier, since it is still straight country, but it is hurt by a somewhat inconsistent set of songs; a flaw that is particularly striking considering how uniformly excellent his first two records were. Still, this is an enjoyable platter, particularly compared to some of the Columbia Records that followed. *—Stephen Thomas Erlewine*

Hank Williams, You Wrote My Life / 1976 / Columbia ✦✦✦

The urge to raise one's stature in the world of country music from that of a lowlife joker or clown to a serious, significant figure may, in many cases, lead to the ghost of Hank Williams being revived. In fact, it happens with the regularity of low-budget movie studios bringing their box-office bonanza monsters back from the grave. Moe Bandy is likable enough, and he comes from the generation of country singers that actually had to learn to sing, not just look studly. While he hardly looks the latter role, he was part of a duo with Joe Stampley, whose material can hardly be said to have been designed to cater to females, even female country & western music fans. In this solo outing, he attempts a combination of knockout punches by coming up with a Hank Williams tribute song, naming the album itself after the song, and then designing cover art in which Williams is seen only from the back, a technique which was devised by the stand-in for

Bela Lugosi on the film *Plan Nine From Outer Space*. The continuing comparison with low-budget horror films is not an attempt to divert attention from Moe Bandy; like these sorts of films, this singer and his duo partner create a style of rowdy country music that really does have its charms. Coming on more seriously does not elevate Bandy to a higher level; in fact, any comparison with Williams would not be sweet as candy for Bandy. There are several titles here; such as "I Think I Got a Love on You," that Williams would have gladly died young rather than record, as they represent the direct opposite of the type of heartfelt and straightforward country music that he was all about. There is almost nothing at all that's good on the first side other than the instrumental interjections of a typically stellar Nashville crew. "The Biggest Airport in the World" brings the record to life on the second side, Bandy brilliantly interpreting the lyrics with a production that has all the bustle of a busy airport itself. One or two decent songs follow until the production once again bottoms out. Considering that there are more tributes to Hank Williams then any other figure in country music, losing track of this particular one might not be such a bad idea. —*Eugene Chadbourne*

Here I Am Drunk Again / 1976 / Columbia ✦✦✦✦
I'm Sorry For You, My Friend / 1977 / Columbia ✦✦✦
Cowboys Ain't Supposed to Cry / 1977 / Columbia ✦✦✦
Soft Lights and Hard Country Music / 1978 / Columbia ✦✦✦✦
Love Is What Life's All About / 1978 / Columbia ✦✦✦
It's a Cheating Situation / 1979 / Columbia ✦✦✦
One of a Kind / 1980 / Columbia ✦✦✦
The Champ / 1980 / Columbia ✦✦✦
Hey Joe!/Hey Moe! / 1981 / Columbia ✦✦✦✦✦
She's Not Really Cheatin' (She's Just Gettin' Even) / 1982 / Columbia ✦✦✦
Devoted to Your Memory / 1983 / Columbia ✦✦✦
Motel Matches / 1984 / Columbia ✦✦
The Good Ol' Boys—Alive and Well / 1984 / Columbia ✦✦✦
Live from Bad Bob's, Memphis / 1985 / Columbia ✦✦✦✦✦
You Haven't Heard the Last of Me / 1987 / MCA ✦✦✦
Released nearly four years after his last previous Top Ten single, this album gave Bandy a brief return to the spotlight. Working with record-producer Jerry Kennedy for the first time, Bandy maintains more command of his delivery than in any previous album. —*Tom Roland*

No Regrets / 1988 / Curb ✦✦
Many Mansions / 1989 / Curb ✦✦✦
Greatest Hits / 1992 / Curb ✦✦✦✦✦
Moe Bandy's late-'80s hits for Curb records are collected on this brief album. By this time, he had tamed a lot of the rowdier aspects of his music, settling into a smoother rhythm. There are some genuine overlooked gems here—"Back in My Roarin' 20s" and "Till I'm Too Old to Die Young" are particularly noteworthy—but fans of his gut-level honky tonk might be disappointed. Nevertheless, it's a first-rate retrospective of a generally overlooked era. —*Stephen Thomas Erlewine*

★ **Honky Tonk Amnesia: The Hard Country Sound of Moe Bandy** / Feb. 20, 1996 / Razor & Tie ✦✦✦✦✦
Razor & Tie's 1996 collection *Honky Tonk Amnesia: The Hard Country Sound of Moe Bandy* is a superb summary of Bandy's peak as a hitmaker in the '70s and '80s, containing no less than 20 tracks, all of them major hits. Since his run at the top of the charts was lengthy, encompassing a number of big duets with both Janie Fricke and Joe Stampley, not everything is here. The biggest absences are these duets, with solo singles like "Here I Am Drunk Again" and "Cowboys Ain't Supposed to Cry" also being MIA, but these are minor grievances, particularly since the Stampley duets are available on other collections. What is here is the cream of the crop, the best songs from a series of generally satisfying albums that did tend to be a little uneven as his star got bigger. While his first two albums—*I Just Started Hatin' Cheatin' Songs Today* and *It Was Always So Easy (To Find an Unhappy Woman)*, both available as a two-fer from WestSide Records—are excellent albums in their own right, this is valuable in how it rounds up the rest of the best, including such great barroom anthems as "Hank Williams, You Wrote My Life," "Soft Lights and Hard Country Music," "It's a Cheating Situation," and "Barstool Mountain," along with a bunch of other pure country sides that are nearly their equal. During a time when country either tended toward pop or the unruly band of outlaws, Bandy kept country pure, and the best of it has stood the test of time, standing as fine hardcore country. Those first two albums are indeed classics, but there's no better proof of his enduring talents than *Honky Tonk Amnesia*, a flawless overview of Bandy at his best. —*Stephen Thomas Erlewine*

Once More / 1997 / Sony Special Products ✦✦✦
It may just be a budget-priced compilation, but Sony Music Special Products' *Once More* is actually a very good sampling of Moe Bandy's biggest hits. Sure, several big tunes are missing, but what's here—"Bandy the Rodeo Clown," "Barstool Mountain," "Hank Williams, You Wrote My Life," "Two Lonely People," "I'm Sorry for You, My Friend," "I Cheated Me Right Out of You," "It's a Cheating Situation," "It Was Always So Easy (To Find an Unhappy Woman)," "She's Not Really Cheatin' (She's Just Gettin' Even)," "Yesterday Once More"—are all hits, and most of them rank among his very best songs, making this budget-priced disc more than worthwhile. It's a bargain. —*Stephen Thomas Erlewine*

Crazy Cajun Recordings / Feb. 18, 1999 / Edsel ✦✦✦

Edsel's *Crazy Cajun Recordings* contains recordings Moe Bandy cut early in his career for Huey P. Meaux's regional independent labels. In other words, this is music from before Bandy started having hits, and it's very much in the Texas hard country tradition, with strong honky tonk and Western swing influences, every once and while tempered by some R&B and rock & roll. If anything, it cuts a larger stylistic path than Bandy's breakthrough albums on GRC, which were deliberately purist in the their honky tonk ideals. Much of this is somewhat generic, but in a good sense; the songs conform to honky tonk tradition, the performances are good, and the records sound like they were coming from a jukebox in a beer joint with saw dust on the floor after all the George Jones sides had already been played to death. Some of the tracks don't cut much of an impression, but there's enough good stuff—"As Long as There's a Chance," "Playboy," "You're Part of Me," and "Lonely Girl" among them—that makes it worthwhile for Bandy fanatics, as well as fans of '60s straight-ahead country with a Texas tilt. In fact, since this recalls '60s country in general more than it does Bandy's best, it very well be of *more* interest to that latter group. —*Stephen Thomas Erlewine*

Super Hits / Mar. 2, 1999 / Sony ✦✦✦
As a duo, Moe Bandy and Joe Stampley hit the country charts nine times between 1979 and 1985, usually with comic or novelty material, and they provoked enough laughs to be named the CMA Duo of the Year in 1980. But you will find only their four most successful collaborations here—"Just Good Ol' Boys," "Where's the Dress," "Holding the Bag," and "Hey Joe (Hey Moe)." The other six tracks on this budget-priced album are evenly divided, with three of each singer's solo Top Ten hits. While that's in keeping with the "super hits" logo (none of the other Joe & Moe singles made the Top Ten), it may not be what consumers expect when they see the two co-billed. Better to have given Bandy and Stampley their own separate *Super Hits* albums for their solo works and collected all the duo records here instead. —*William Ruhlmann*

Live at Billy Bob's Texas / Feb. 29, 2000 / Smith Music Group ✦✦✦
This live, circa the end of the 20th century show (no date is given in the liner notes) is billed to both Bandy and Stampley. However, it's not exactly a duet album. About one-third of it is Stampley solo, one-third of it is Bandy solo, and then they team together in a crowd-pleasing manner for the remaining third of the program. So you get to hear Stampley-associated numbers like "All These Things" and then Bandy going it solo for a while before they team up for numbers like "Roll on Big Mama," "Honky Tonk Queen," "Just Good Ol' Boys," and "Where's the Dress." The duo numbers do have a spark generated by repartee that's missing from the solo spots. It's another unsurprising-sounding document in the *Live at Billy Bob's Texas* series, capturing them and the crowd having fun, but hardly likely to challenge better, more definitive versions of these tunes in the listener's minds. That's certainly true of "All These Things," which has the kind of adult contemporary-friendly electric keyboards that should be banned from honky tonks on sight. —*Richie Unterberger*

★ **I Just Started Hatin' Cheatin' Songs Today/It Was Always So Easy (To Find An Unhappy Woman)** / Dec. 3, 2002 / WestSide ✦✦✦✦✦
WestSide released Moe Bandy's first two albums, *I Just Started Hatin' Cheatin' Songs Today* and *It Was Always So Easy (To Find an Unhappy Woman)*, as a two-fer CD toward the end of 2002, adding the single "Bandy the Rodeo Clown" as a bonus track. These are the highlights from Bandy's time at GRC Records, an independent label based in Atlanta, GA, and it's no coincidence that these two albums were released on a small, non-Nashville label, because Bandy was operating outside of what Music City U.S.A. was doing in the early '70s. Bandy was holding firm to hardcore honky tonk, which is precisely what these two records are. Lean, direct, and unadorned, they form the core of Bandy's musical identity, and since they never stray from the sound of classic honky tonk, they don't sound dated; either record would still sound right coming from a jukebox in a lonely barroom. Another key to their success is that the material is excellent, relying on new songs—one or two co-written by Bandy, but most written by some combination of A.L. Owens and Whitey Shafer, along with select moments by Dallas Frazier—that sound like timeless country classics. This is music that doesn't care about crossover: it's pure country music. Which is why this is a preferable introduction to Moe Bandy's music than the fine *Honky Tonk Amnesia* collection on Razor & Tie; if you want to hear what Moe Bandy was all about, this tells you everything you need to know. —*Stephen Thomas Erlewine*

Moe and Joe: The Ultimate Hits Collection / 2003 / Audium ✦✦✦✦✦
Carousing, drinking, and dodging wives are the order of the day here. "Holding the Bag" and "Tell Ole I Ain't Here, He Better Get on Home" are particularly amusing, but the biggest laughs come with the transvestite storyline of "Honky Tonk Queen." —*Tom Roland*

Glenn Barber

b. Feb. 2, 1935, Hollis, OK
Guitar, Vocals / Traditional Country
Country and rockabilly performer Glenn Barber was born in Hollis, OK, on February 2, 1935. From there, he and his family moved to Pasadena, TX, where the young Barber showed an early interest in music. Originally a guitar player, he also took up bass, drums, dobro, and mandolin. He first appeared on wax with the 1952 Stampede single "You Took the Twinkle Out of My Stars"; by 1954, he had a contract with the Starday label. Over the next few years, Barber would release numerous countrified rockabilly singles on the label, the last being issued in 1956, just as rock & roll was sweeping the country. From there, he and manager Pappy Dailey traveled to the D imprint, which issued four Barber singles during the remainder of the 1950s.

As the '60s arrived, Barber became a disc jockey and featured performer on Houston's KIKK. He and his band, the Western Swingmasters, appeared on the station five nights a week until 1968, when he signed with the Nashville outfit Hickory. There he made his full-length debut with 1970's *A New Star.* While with Hickory, Barber charted four times, taking songs like "Kissed By the Rain, Warmed By the Sun" (1969) and "Unexpected Goodbye" (1972) all the way to the Top 30. Another Hickory single, "She Cheats on Me," would later be recorded by Roy Orbison. Barber jumped to MMI in 1979, and penned the hit "Everyone Wants to Disco." It was his last charting single, and Barber turned to other interests in the 1980s and '90s, including painting and screenwriting. *—Johnny Loftus*

New Star / 1970 / Hickory ✦✦✦✦

● **The Best of Glenn Barber** / 1972 / Hickory ✦✦✦✦

Glenn Barber / 1974 / MGM/Hickory ✦✦✦

First Love Feelings / 1983 / Tudor ✦✦✦

Saturday's Heros Are Gone / 1984 / Tudor ✦✦✦

It's not a bad album. Many of the the songs are quite good, and on a couple, it's difficult imagining anyone but Barber performing them. He doesn't have a great voice, but overall each song is done well. *—Jim Worbois*

Close But No Cigar / Mar. 7, 2000 / Edsel ✦✦✦

Close But No Cigar spotlights Glenn Barber's Crazy Cajun recordings for Huey P. Meaux's Houston-based label. Among the ten tracks are honky tonk tunes "Cheating," "Warm All Over Feelin'," "I Created a Monster," and the Doug Sahm-penned "We'll Take Our Last Walk Tonight." While these tracks never made a dent on the country charts, they are still recommended for Barber fans, especially taking into account the lack of his music that remains in print. *—Al Campbell*

Bobby Bare

b. Apr. 7, 1935, Ironton, OH

Vocals, Guitar / Progressive Country, Country-Folk, Nashville Sound/Countrypolitan, Traditional Country, Outlaw Country

Bobby Bare's story is nearly as fascinating as his music. Bare's mother died when he was five. His father couldn't earn enough money to feed his children, forcing the family to split up. Bare was working on a farm by the time he was 15 years old, later working in factories and selling ice cream to support himself. Building his first guitar, he began playing music in his late teens, performing with a local Ohio band in Springfield. In the late '50s, he moved out to Los Angeles. Bare's first appearance on record was in 1958, as he recorded his own talking blues "The All American Boy," which was credited to Bill Parsons. A number of labels refused the record before the Ohio-based Fraternity Records bought it for $50; the fee also included the publishing rights. "The All American Boy" was released in 1959 and it surprisingly became the second-biggest single in the U.S. that December, crossing over to the pop charts and peaking at number three. The single was also a big hit in the U.K., reaching number 22.

Before Bare could capitalize on his success, he was drafted into the armed forces. While he was on duty, Fraternity hired another singer to become Bill Parsons and sent him out on tour. After Bare left the army, he became roommates with Willie Nelson. During this time, he decided to become a pop singer. Soon, he was touring with pop/rock stars like Roy Orbison and Bobby Darin, recording records for a number of California labels. Meanwhile, his songs were being recorded by a number of artists; three of his tunes were featured in the Chubby Checker movie *Teenage Millionaire.*

Even though he was having some modest success, Bare decided he wasn't fulfilled playing pop music. Instead, he turned back to country, developing a distinctive blend of country, folk, and pop. In 1962, Chet Atkins signed him to RCA Records. By the end of the year, he had a hit with "Shame on You," which was notable for being one of the first records out of Nashville to make concessions to the pop charts by featuring horns. The production worked, as the single broke into the pop charts. The following year, he recorded Mel Tillis and Danny Dill's "Detroit City," which became his second straight single to make both the country and pop charts. Bare followed up the single with a traditional folk song, "500 Miles from Home." It was another big hit for the singer, peaking in the Top Ten on both the country and pop charts. Bare continued to rack up hits in 1964 and 1965, as well as appearing in the Western movie *A Distant Trumpet.*

As the '60s progressed, Bare continued to blur the lines between country and folk, as he was influenced by songwriters like Bob Dylan, recording material by Dylan and several of his contemporaries. Not only did he explore American folk, but Bare traveled to England, where he was popular. In 1967, he recorded an album with a Liverpool country band called the Hillsiders (*The English Country Side*), which signaled his artistic drive. Bare switched record labels in 1970, signing with Mercury Records. He stayed at the label for two years, producing a string of Top Ten hits, including "How I Got to Memphis," "Please Don't Tell Me How the Story Ends," and "Come Sundown." Bare's tenure with Mercury was a busy one, releasing four albums with the label including *This is Bare Country* (1970), *Where Have All the Seasons Gone* (1970), *I Need Some Good News Bad* (1971), and *What Am I Gonna Do?* (1972). After leaving Mercury, he re-signed with RCA in 1973 with the condition that he be allowed to produce his own albums.

Later in 1973, Bare released a double album of Shel Silverstein songs, *Bobby Bare Sings Lullabys, Legends and Lies.* Not only did the album represent the beginning of a collaboration with Silverstein, it was arguably the first country concept album, adding fire to the outlaw movement of the '70s in the process. The record was a hit with country audiences as well as rock fans, gaining airplay on FM radio stations. The following year, he had his first number one single with "Marie Laveau." Bare released another record of Silverstein songs, *Bobby Bare and the Family Singin' in the Kitchen,* in 1975. Unfortunately, the singer's oldest daughter died shortly after recording the album; she was only 15. In 1977, Bare received a major publicity push from Bill Graham, the legendary rock concert promoter. Graham signed the singer to his management company, proclaiming that Bare was the "Springsteen of country music." Soon, the singer found new audiences at college campuses and in Canada. He switched record labels the same year, recording the self-produced *Bare* for Columbia. Two years later, he released *Sleeper Wherever I Fall,* which featured contributions from Rodney Crowell and rearranged rock & roll songs like the the Rolling Stones' "The Last Time" and the Byrds' "Feel a Whole Lot Better." Bare resumed his collaboration with Silverstein in 1980, releasing the live collection *Down & Dirty,* which spawned two humorous hits, "Numbers" and "Tequila Sheila." The following year, he released *As is,* which showed that he was continuing to record a diverse selection of songwriters, including Townes Van Zandt, J.J. Cale, and Guy Clark.

Despite the fact that his work was consistently critically acclaimed, Bare's record sales began to slip in the early '80s, as the 1982 Silverstein collaboration *Drinkin' From the Bottle, Singin' From the Heart* and his 1985 record for EMI failed to launch any major hit singles. Nevertheless, Bobby Bare continued to retain a devoted following in the U.S. and the U.K., and his influence on contemporary country music remains evident. *—Stephen Thomas Erlewine*

500 Miles Away from Home / 1963 / RCA ✦✦✦✦✦

Detroit City / 1963 / RCA ✦✦✦✦✦

Detroit City/500 Miles Away From Home / 1963 / RCA ✦✦✦✦✦

Bobby Bare's first two albums, *Detroit City* and *500 Miles Away From Home,* are combined on this single disc. Though there are some weak tracks on the disc, this is one of the strongest and most exciting collections of Bare's music, showcasing the songwriter in his earliest stages. He might not have perfected his sound, but it is thrilling to hear him sort it out. *—Stephen Thomas Erlewine*

The Travelin' Bare / 1964 / RCA ✦✦✦✦

Tunes for Two / 1965 / RCA ✦✦✦

Bobby Bare and Skeeter Davis recorded two duet albums, the first of which was 1965's *Tunes for Two.* The album's hit was a remake of Jean Shepard and Ferlin Husky's "A Dear John Letter," a song that seemed timely again in light of the conflict in Vietnam. One can't help but notice how homely Davis' vocals sometimes sound in this context, placed alongside Bare's assured performances instead of her own overdubbed harmonies. On "Let It Be Me," she also reinforces the country music stereotype that women can't do recitations. Songs include duet classics like "We Must Have Been Out of Our Minds" and excellent takes of Gale Garnett's "We'll Sing in the Sunshine" and Ned Miller's "Invisible Tears." In spite of a few minor shortcomings, *Tunes for Two* is a perfectly enjoyable album that deserved a sequel. *—Greg Adams*

Constant Sorrow / 1965 / RCA ✦✦✦✦

Talk Me Some Sense / 1966 / RCA ✦✦

The Streets of Baltimore / 1966 / RCA ✦✦✦✦✦

This I Believe / 1966 / RCA ✦✦✦

The Game of Triangles / 1967 / RCA ✦✦✦

A Bird Named Yesterday / 1967 / RCA ✦✦✦

Theme albums have always been a favorite of country music, with plenty of singers devoting themselves to the work of a particular songwriter, or songs about a particular subject, whether it's gunfighters, heartbreak, or drinking. However, concept albums are an entirely different animal than theme albums, since they tell a particular story. On their 2002 reissue of Bobby Bare's 1967 album *A Bird Named Yesterday,* Audium/Koch notes that this is "Nashville's VERY FIRST concept album"—a fact that may or may not be strictly true, but it is certainly one of the first story-oriented concept albums in country history. According to the original liner notes, Jack Clement is the one who conceived this nostalgic trip through a small town and how modernity has changed it, and he wrote six of the nine songs, crafting this evocation of a storybook Americana past. It's designed to be more about myth and memory than about an individual song, so each tune is open-ended, even if each is prefaced by lengthy, specific recitations by Bare. These recitations slow down the momentum of the album and give away the fact that it was recorded in the early days of concept albums, when musicians and producers thought it was necessary to state the story plainly in prose. Songwise, Clement's songs are typically sturdy, though he does veer into some pretty corny territory quite often over the course of the record, a sentiment that is emphasized by the incessant narration. There are no classics here, but there are highlights, including the sweet title track, "I've Got a Thing About Trains," "They Covered Up the Old Swimmin' Hole," and the Foster & Rice song "The Day the Saw Mill Closed Down," which captures the nostalgic vibe better than many of Clement's tunes. And while nostalgia is the impetus for the entire *A Bird Named Yesterday,* several decades after its release the album evokes not just the nostalgia it intends, but another wistful sentiment—they simply don't make records like this anymore. As a result, it's a time machine unlike what it was meant to convey, and while it's not a trip you'd want to take every day, it's nice to know you can, when you want to relive two eras at once. *—Stephen Thomas Erlewine*

The English Country Side / 1967 / RCA ✦✦✦

Folsom Prison Blues / 1968 / Camden ✦✦✦

Margie's at the Lincoln Park Inn / 1969 / RCA ✦✦✦✦✦

Your Husband, My Wife / 1970 / RCA ✦✦

Bobby Bare and Skeeter Davis' first duet album, *Tunes for Two,* was moderately successful in 1965, but it took five years for a follow-up to materialize. *Your Husband, My Wife* was one of the last albums Bare made for RCA before moving to Mercury, and the title track was his last RCA hit until he returned to the label a few years later. It makes one wonder whether the album was a rush job, because the performances are spotty and Davis sounds particularly wobbly. "Let's Make Love Not War" attempts to solve that problem by multi-tracking Davis' vocals, which makes the song sound like Bare singing along with one of her solo recordings. The material is more downcast and less satisfying on this outing, but the album is buoyed up a little by a lively rendition of "Jackson." *—Greg Adams*

Real Thing / 1970 / RCA ✦✦✦

This Is Bare Country / 1970 / Mercury ✦✦✦✦✦

Where Have All the Seasons Gone / 1970 / Mercury ✦✦✦✦

I Need Some Good News Bad / 1971 / Mercury ✦✦✦✦

What Am I Gonna Do? / 1972 / Mercury ✦✦✦✦

☆ **Bobby Bare Sings Lullabys, Legends and Lies** / 1973 / Bear Family ✦✦✦✦✦
Returning to RCA after a stint at Mercury records, Bobby Bare teamed up with songwriter Shel Silverstein for 1973's *Sings Lullabys, Legends and Lies*. The idea of the record is clearly laid out in the title—this album is a collection of American tall tales and myths, all filtered through Silverstein's signature humor (sometimes silly, sometimes clever, sometimes sentimental, sometimes slyly lewd) and delivered with Bare's signature warm, friendly manner. Bare had recorded a song or two of Shel's before, but this was the first time that he devoted a full album to his material, but more noteworthy is that this album finds the singer developing a loose, offhand way of performance that emphasizes both his character and the freewheeling eclecticism of his music. Musically, it's not far removed from his Mercury records, where his progressive country rubbed shoulders with pop, rock and folk, but his laid-back, open-ended performances let the music breathe while the Silverstein songs give the album cohesion and an overt, welcome sense of humor. All this helped reignite Bare's career, giving him a new signature sound that carried him through the next few years (until he left RCA for Columbia, where he just got rowdier), and it gave him the biggest album of his career, spending 30 weeks on the *Billboard* country charts where it peaked at number five and giving him a number-one hit in "Marie Laveau" and a number-two single with "Daddy What If." Years later, it still stands as one of his very best—maybe it didn't produce classics like "Detroit City," nor does it have as brilliant highs as some earlier and later records, but song for song, Bare was rarely this consistent or enjoyable. —*Stephen Thomas Erlewine*

I Hate Goodbyes/Ride Me Down Easy / 1973 / RCA ✦✦✦✦

Singin' in the Kitchen / 1974 / RCA ✦✦
Bobby Bare's 1973 album *Sings Lullabys, Legends and Lies*, yielded two major hits, so he repeated the formula the following year on *Singin' in the Kitchen*. Both albums are largely devoted to the songs of Shel Silverstein, but *Singin' in the Kitchen* takes the loose, live-in-the-studio vibe of its predecessor to an extreme, making the listener believe that they're really hearing the Bare family singing around the kitchen table. The singles "Where'd I Come From" and "Singin' in the Kitchen" became only minor hits, which isn't surprising because this album is less appealing overall. It's too casual, and the lightweight material coupled with the ragged chorus of kids makes it sound like a children's record. Bare's wife, Jeannie, is a competent vocalist, and Bare brings a measure of solid professionalism to the effort by performing a couple of songs solo, but the end result is a little like watching another family's home movies. *Singin' in the Kitchen* is a cute album as long as you don't expect too much from it. —*Greg Adams*

Cowboys and Daddys / 1975 / RCA ✦✦✦✦✦
Instead of singing about outlaws and rhinestone cowboys, Bare's songs speak of the struggles and joys of those who truly make their home on the range. —*Michael McCall*

Hard Time Hungrys / 1975 / Edsel ✦✦✦
Bobby Bare and Shel Silverstein struck a partnership in the '70s that yielded the number-one hit "Marie Laveau" and a few concept albums, of which *Hard Time Hungrys* is one. Created during the mid-'70s' economic recession, the album takes a hard look at poverty and unemployment, tempered with touches of world-weary humor. The songs are preceded by interview segments in which everyday people tell Bare of their plights, while the back cover photo shows a man picking through an alley trash can. "Alimony" and "Back Home in Huntsville Again" were the album's two hits, but both were only moderately successful, perhaps because the country audience preferred escapism to stark reality. Another explanation is that Silverstein's songs are not quite up to the level of those on his first collaboration with Bare, 1973's *Sings Lullabys, Legends and Lies*, although the powerful subject matter and the talent of the principals make this an admirable and rewarding album. —*Greg Adams*

The Winner and Other Losers / 1976 / RCA ✦✦✦

Me and McDill / 1977 / RCA ✦✦✦

Bare / 1978 / Columbia ✦✦✦✦✦
Bobby Bare's 1978 Columbia album *Bare* reveals in spades that the performer still had plenty to offer. He utilizes the talents of an army of Nash Vegas guitar pickers here. Steel boss Ben Keith (one of Neil Young's Stray Gators on *Harvest*) is here, along with Johnny Gimble on fiddle, Bobby Emmons on piano, and Larrie Londin and Buddy Harman on skins, as well as a host of backing vocalists, including Shel Silverstein and Willie Nelson. There are also a couple of folks with the names Waylon Jennings and Chet Atkins who fell by the studio to help on a couple tracks. But it isn't the players who made the record; it's Bare's inspirational performance on no less than eight songs by Silverstein, Larry Wilkerson's "Finger on the Button," and a better version of the "The Gambler" than Kenny Rogers could have ever dreamed of cutting. Why Bare didn't strike pay dirt with his version is beyond the point of reason, because in the grain of his voice it feels like a story being told almost in the present tense, and accurate as a reading by someone who believes he has received life-saving advice from a ghost. "Yard Full of Rusty Cars" is one of Silverstein's better songs, and contains the proverb "Show me a man with a yard full of rusty cars/And I'll show you a man with a 'frigerator full of beer that's nice and cold." Ditto the tracks such as "Too Many Nights Alone," "This Guitar Is for Sale," and "Sing for the Song." Bare's command of the humorous line equals Roger Miller's, his depth of emotion goes into the same well that Willie Nelson's does (albeit in a baritone fashion), and he reveals a gift for turning a phrase so it remains memorable in the mind of the listener. His duet with Jennings on "This Guitar Is for Sale" is one of the stellar broken ballads of Bare's career, reflecting on the shattered fortunes and wasted years in the life of a

singer/songwriter. Why hasn't Sony/Legacy reissued this fine platter? Sometimes life just ain't fair. —*Thom Jurek*

Sleeper Wherever I Fall / 1978 / Columbia ✦✦✦✦✦
Some of Bare's best albums barely registered on the radio charts, but they're rich in unusual songs and distinct performances. Selections here include a cover of the Rolling Stones' "The Last Time" and a Rodney Crowell gem, "On a Real Good Night." —*Michael McCall*

Down & Dirty / 1980 / Columbia ✦✦✦✦
This 1979 Columbia release is Bobby Bare in his element: live, rowdy, and dangerous. This is good-time outlaw country. Bare's band—which is uncredited—rocks and rolls, swings and strolls through 13 tracks (and none of them include "Detroit City," thank God) from a rejuvenated Bare. The humor is in large supply; the poignancy is spilling out of all corners. But it's the tune selection that makes this is such a killer record. The hysterical good-time country of "Numbers" and the sincerity and richness in Bare's voice on "Some Days Are Diamonds (Some Days Are Stone)" (and yeah, forget John Denver's version) are two sides of a multi-dimensional performer. Kris Kristofferson's "Good for Nothin' Blues" and Shel Silverstein and Mac Davis' "Pour Me Another Tequila, Sheila" take the good-times to absurd extremes, as does Silverstein's "Quaaludes Again." But on the other hand, there's Townes Van Zandt's devastatingly beautiful "Tecumseh Valley" and the morality tale of "Blind Willie Harper" before the rock & roll country swing anthem "Goin' Back to Texas." The set closes with "I Can't Watch the Movie Anymore," a busted-up love song, full of imagery that underlines the hollowness and emptiness of the song's protagonists—and this is the way it all ends! Thus, *Down & Dirty* reveals the complexity of Bare, one of the greatest performers in the music's history, and also one of the most misunderstood. This is certainly an album that belongs on compact disc. —*Thom Jurek*

Drunk and Crazy / 1980 / Columbia ✦✦✦

As Is / 1981 / Columbia ✦✦✦✦✦
Produced by Rodney Crowell, it's a solid collection of good songs in which Bare's sly, low-key charms shine. —*Michael McCall*

Ain't Got Nothin' To Lose / 1982 / Columbia ✦✦✦

Drinkin' From the Bottle, Singin' From the Heart / 1983 / Columbia ✦✦✦

★ **The Best of Bobby Bare** / 1994 / Razor & Tie ✦✦✦✦✦
Bobby Bare was a restless artist, pushing country music forward in the '60s by incorporating elements of folk and rock in equal measures on his recordings for RCA. His music could have an epic narrative sweep, or it could be intimate in its telling details. He could be a warm, sensitive singer and he also could be tougher than many other vocalists in the heyday of countrypolitan—and he also could be wickedly funny when given half a chance. He was a fine songwriter and an even better judge of material, championing songwriters like Tom T. Hall, Tompall Glaser, and Waylon Jennings before they became country legends, finding songs from folkies like Ian Tyson, while also cherry-picking great tunes from Nashville stalwarts like Hank Cochran, Lee Hazlewood, and Jack Clement. This resulted in one of the richest bodies of work in the '60s (not to mention his '70s and early-'80s highlights), but its diversity and unpredictability meant that he wasn't always at the top of the charts—instead, he continued to chart, occasionally finding the right tune to bring him back to the Top Ten. Nevertheless, his music stands as some of the finest of its time, and while Bear Family's comprehensive box set *All-American Boy* explores these '60s RCA recordings in thorough detail, Razor & Tie's 21-track *The Best of Bobby Bare* is the best summary of this time, functioning not only as a superb introduction, but as a great, compulsively listenable collection of highlights. This does not have all of his '60s hits—singles like "Shame on Me" and "It's Alright" are left behind—but it does have all the big tunes, along with a good cross-section of album tracks and B-sides that illustrate the range of his music. There's his first single, the Elvis send-up "The All-American Boy"; there's the heartbreaking lament "Detroit City," which proved he was no novelty; there's "500 Miles Away From Home" and "Miller's Cave"; one of the first versions of "Long Black Limousine"; excellent versions of Waylon Jennings' "Just to Satisfy You" and the Glaser Brothers' "The Streets of Baltimore"; a taboo-breaking tale of infidelity in Tom T. Hall's "(Margie's At) The Lincoln Park Inn." These are the major moments, but they certainly aren't the only highlights on this essential collection. Bare released music as good as this, but he never bettered it, and everything on *The Best of Bobby Bare* stands among the very best and most adventurous country of the '60s. —*Stephen Thomas Erlewine*

☆ **The Mercury Years 1970–1972, Vol. 1** / 1994 / Bear Family ✦✦✦✦✦
As the '60s gave way to the '70s, Bobby Bare left RCA Records for Mercury, beginning a two year stint that found him with mixed fortunes, as he scored Top Ten hits without making much headway on the album charts. Despite the uneven commercial fortunes, this was an exceedingly rich time for Bare if judged solely in terms of music. He picked up on the rolling blend of country, folk and rock & roll that marked his best '60s singles from "Detroit City" to "(Margie's At) The Lincoln Park Inn" and followed through on its promise, creating a layered, inventive body of work that stands as one of the peaks of progressive country and points the way toward the outlaw movement of the mid-'70s. Part of the reason that his recordings for Mercury worked so well is that Bare demonstrated exceptional taste in songwriters, covering new writers Tom T. Hall, Kris Kristofferson and Billy Joe Shaver regularly while relying on such Nashville stalwarts as Harlan Howard and Hank Cochran, as well as dipping into the pop charts on occasion crossover pop hits, such as John Denver's "Leaving on a Jet Plane," heard on this, the first of three volumes from Bear Family covering his complete work for Mercury. Bobby Bare always favored stories and character sketches, so these are all sharply-written, evocative tunes, sometimes moving, sometimes funny, and they're given layered, slyly adventurous productions that give his warm, nuanced voice support that hints at rolling folk, roadhouse country,

the introspectiveness singer/songwriters, sweet pop, the spirit of rock & roll and the professionalism of Nashville, without belonging to any particular style. It's a wonderful sound, and, as this extensive Bear Family set proves, it was one that offered plenty of possibilities, almost all of which were explored on Mercury, which resulted in a consistently fascinating and enjoyable body of work. Of the three volumes, the first is the best, because it has not only the most consistent selection of songs—from the hit "That's How I Got to Memphis," several Kristofferson classics (including "For the Good Times," "Help Me Make It Through the Night" and "Please Don't Tell Me How the Story Ends"), plus lesser-known gems like the genial, silly "I'm Her Hoss If I Never Wina Race" or the sweetly melancholy "The Fool"—but also because it has the excitement of discovery, as Bare finds his groove. All three volumes are necessary, but this first installment is the first among equals. *—Stephen Thomas Erlewine*

The Mercury Years 1970–1972, Vol. 2 / 1994 / Bear Family ✦✦✦✦✦
The second installment of Bear Family's three-volume retrospective of Bobby Bare's Mercury recordings covers 1971 and early 1972, and features the minor hit "Short and Sweet." Though there is a fair amount of mediocre material on *Vol. 2*, the best songs here—including "The World Is Weighing Heavy on My Mind," "Don't You Ever Get Tired of Hurting Me," "West Virginia Woman," "The Year That Clayton Delaney Died" and "Lonely Street"—rank among Bare's best. *—Stephen Thomas Erlewine*

The Mercury Years 1970–1972, Vol. 3 / 1994 / Bear Family ✦✦✦✦✦
The final volume of Bear Family's three-disc overview of Bobby Bare's Mercury Recordings includes the minor hits "What Am I Gonna Do" and "Sylvia's Mother," plus a number of good, but overlooked cuts, such as "Footprints in the Sand of Time," "Even the Bad Times Are Good," "Laying Here Lyin' in Bed," "Lorena" and "Music City, U.S.A." Though the overall quality of the disc isn't as strong as its two predecessors, *Vol. 3* remains a necessary purchase for Bobby Bare completists. *—Stephen Thomas Erlewine*

All-American Boy / 1994 / Bear Family ✦✦✦✦✦
The four-disc box set *All-American Boy* contains all of Bobby Bare's RCA recordings between 1962 and 1970, including the Top 10 hits "Detroit City," "500 Miles Away From Home," "Miller's Cave," "Four Strong Winds," "A Dear John Letter," "It's Alright," "The Streets of Baltimore," "The Game of Triangles" and "(Margie's At) The Lincoln Park Inn." In addition to all of the master recordings, the set also includes several alternate takes, unreleased tracks, incomplete takes, duets and rarities. Certainly, box sets that are this comprehensive only appeal to dedicated fans, yet *All-American Boy* is more listenable than the average all-encompassing Bear Family release because Bare's RCA recordings were of consistently high quality. Of course, that doesn't mean casual fans should purchase the set—it means that the set is worthwhile for serious fans. *—Thom Owens*

Essential / Jan. 28, 1997 / RCA ✦✦✦✦✦
Like all the other volumes of RCA's *Essential* series, *The Essential Bobby Bare* contains a cross-section of Bare's hits, lesser-known singles, rarities and album tracks. Though it is a useful and entertaining collection, Razor & Tie's compilation remains a more definitive retrospective. *—Thom Owens*

Pure Country / Aug. 25, 1998 / Sony Special Products ✦✦✦
Sony Music Special Products' *Pure Country* contains a selection of ten hits and miscellaneous tracks from Bobby Bare's late-'70s and early-'80s recordings for Columbia. Although Bare wasn't at the top of his game during this era, he still could turn out strong singles, as this collection occasionally proves. There are a few slow spots on the disc, which is standard for any budget-priced compilation, but there are many very good songs here, including "Tequila Sheila," "Willie Jones," "Learning to Live Again," "(I'm Not) A Candle in the Wind," "If You Ain't Got Nothin' (You Got Nothin' to Lose)," "New Cut Road," "Sleep Tight, Good Night Man," and "It's a Dirty Job," all of which were charting hits. In that sense, it's nearly a hits collection (at least of his Columbia years), and that makes it of considerable interest—and not just to fans on a tight budget. *—Stephen Thomas Erlewine*

Bare Tracks / Feb. 16, 1999 / Koch ✦✦✦✦✦
After some steady success on Mercury and RCA in the first half of the '70s, including the Top Ten hit *Sings Lullabys, Legends and Lies*, Bobby Bare seemed poised for a breakout crossover success, particularly because such colleagues as Waylon Jennings and Willie Nelson had become as popular as rock stars with the ascendancy of outlaw country in the mid-'70s. So, Bare signed with super-manager Bill Graham—better known for managing rock stars than country singers, possibly best-known as a self-promoter—rode out his second contract with RCA, and signed with Columbia... where he promptly flamed out on the charts, scoring just four Top 20 country singles over the course of seven LPs in six years, never once cracking the Top Ten. This lack of success may suggest that there was a dip in quality, which is hardly the case, since the Columbia albums were as consistently enjoyable and high-quality as his RCA and Mercury sides, as both Koch's 1999 compilation *Bare Tracks* and its unofficial companion, Edsel's 2000 *The Columbia Years: Bare's Picks*, prove. Although they cover the same ground and share seven songs, the two collections are quite different in character and intent, with Koch's sticking closer to the dictates of the charts and favoring his lighter, funnier material. Not that *Bare Tracks* has nothing but hits—11 of the 16 tracks charted, leaving room for a number of great album tracks, such as the surging "Appaloosa Rider," Shel Silverstein's "Rough on the Living," and a version of Don Schlitz's "The Gambler," which not only predates Kenny Rogers' hit version, it's weathered and knowing and much better. (None of these three songs made the Edsel collection.) Then, there are the singles, many of them very funny songs by Silverstein, who may never have had a better interpreter, because Bare brought a gravity to his silliness along with a wry, engaging delivery. "Numbers," where Bare gets subjected to a hilariously humiliating putdown by a woman he's trying to pick up, is perhaps the best example of this, but the rowdy "Tequila Sheila" (both taken from the wild live album *Down & Dirty*) is equally good, while the all-star goofy singalong "Greasy Grit Gravy" is as irresistible as "Food Blues" is clever. But it's not just silly songs—Bare turns in a great version of Guy Clark's raver "New Cut Road," finds the pathos in Boudleaux Bryant's "Take Me as I Am (Or Let Me Go)," and has a fine duet with Charlie Daniels' "Willie Jones." All of these are prime examples of Bare's knack for choosing the right material to match his gifts, something that didn't abandon him during his time at Columbia, no matter what the chart positions say. If anything, he started to know his gifts too well, choosing songs that fit him so comfortably, and delivering them so naturally, that only the already-converted appreciated them. Even so, the music has aged wonderfully and this, along with *The Columbia Years*, is well worth adding to any serious collection of '70s and early-'80s country music—and they're different enough that both are necessary. *—Stephen Thomas Erlewine*

Live at Gilley's / Jul. 27, 1999 / Atlantic ✦✦✦
Live at Gilley's captures a concert Bobby Bare gave in April 1984. Bare wasn't exactly at the height of his popularity at that time, but he was still a fine performer, as this 12-disc album proves. There are a few throwaways here, but the performances themselves are all top-notch; he sounds particularly good when tackling classics like "500 Miles Away From Home," "Ride Me Down Easy," "Tequila Sheila" and "Detroit City." Ultimately, a latter-day live recording isn't of interest for anyone outside of hardcore fans, but they'll likely be pleased by this solid live album. *—Stephen Thomas Erlewine*

☆ **The Columbia Years: Bare's Picks** / Jul. 11, 2000 / Edsel ✦✦✦✦✦
Released a year after Koch's *Bare Tracks*, Edsel's *The Columbia Years: Bare's Picks* covers the same ground—the six years Bobby Bare spent at Columbia between 1978 and 1983, and the seven albums he released during those years. The two collections share seven songs, including five hits—"Numbers," "Tequila Sheila," "Take Me as I Am (Or Let Me Go)," "New Cut Road," and the Rosanne Cash duet "No Memories Hangin' Round," all front-loaded here—but the two take very different approaches, with the selections on the Edsel disc being far less hits-driven and far more idiosyncratic than the Koch collection. Perhaps this is due to Bare's participation in the song selection, or perhaps his co-compiler John Lomax III was interested in digging up some hidden gems from these overlooked records, but either way they wound up with an album that's a perfect complement to the Koch disc. On the whole, it has a slightly quieter, introspective feel, with even Shel Silverstein songs like "The Jogger" feeling less rowdy than their counterparts on *Bare Tracks* and with a far heavier quotient of ballads and introspective midtempo numbers and narratives. This is an attribute, since the different emphasis offers proof that Bare's Columbia LPs were as deep as his RCA/Mercury recordings; sonically, they may have been a little streamlined, whether they were taking in rock guitars, folk styles, or singer/songwriter trappings, but the quality of the material remained very high, something this collection of largely reflective material illustrates. Sometimes, the good-natured rowdiness—which *is* apparent on the shared tracks, including the ridiculous closer "Greasy Grit Gravy"—is missed, but this quieter side is missed on *Bare Tracks*, which is why both collections are necessary. Taken together, they give a full picture of the range and quality of material Bare tackled on his unheralded Columbia albums, and both prove that, despite their lack of success on the charts, they easily hold their own among his finest work. Now, if only somebody would reissue the proper albums.... *—Stephen Thomas Erlewine*

★ **Singles: 1959–1969** / Mar. 13, 2001 / BMG International ✦✦✦✦✦
If BMG International's 2001 double-disc set *Singles: 1959-1969* looks and feels like a Bear Family release, there's good reason for it: The label's president and mastermind, Richard Weize, produced this reissue, and it bears that label's typeface and zeal for completion. Considering that Bear Family covered this era in depth on their four-disc 1994 box set *All-American Boy*, some might wonder whether a thorough, 47-song double-disc set like this is necessary, but it is, because it's the sharpest, savviest overview yet of this great body of work. Throughout his career, Bobby Bare produced surprising, unpredictable country music that mixed in elements of rock & roll, honky tonk, folk, and even a hint of pop—a sound that he etched out during those fruitful, successful years at RCA chronicled here. While not as concise as a single-disc collection, this not only offers more hits than any single CD, it also illustrates how far-reaching and imaginative the bulk of his RCA work is. True, this sprawls out over its two discs, and there are a couple of merely OK songs scattered throughout its running length (including two tracks in German), but there are so many great songs here—not just "All American Boy," "Detroit City," "The Streets of Baltimore," and "500 Miles Away From Home," either, but sides like "Just to Satisfy You" and "Times Are Gettin' Hard" that didn't climb so high on the charts—that such complaints seem churlish. Yes, completists will opt for the box set, and Razor & Tie's 1994 single-disc collection remains an excellent introduction, but those listeners that merely want a comprehensive look at Bare's most essential recordings should turn here. *—Stephen Thomas Erlewine*

Barefoot Jerry

f. 1971

Group / Country-Rock, Southern Rock

Guitarist Wayne Moss remained the one constant member of Barefoot Jerry on the band's recordings for Capitol, Warner Bros., and Monument during the '70s. Moss had played in several rock and R&B groups before he joined Brenda Lee's backing band in the early '60s. Session work in Nashville brought him a credit on Bob Dylan's *Blonde on Blonde* in 1966, and he also played with the Escorts during the late '60s before forming Area Code 615 with several other Dylan alumni. The group recorded a self-titled album in 1970 and *A Trip in the Country* the following year, but musical commitments prevented them from touring. Area Code 615 played its only live show in 1970 at *the Fillmore West*, and broke up soon after. Moss was back in action by 1971, though, forming Barefoot Jerry with two members of Area Code 615—vocalist/guitarist Mac Gayden and drummer Kenny Buttrey—plus keyboard player John Harris.

The group signed to Capitol and released *Southern Delight* in 1971. By the time of the following year's self-titled LP for Warner Bros., Russ Hicks and Kenny Malone had replaced Gayden and Buttrey. Another label change (to Monument) and additional lineup replacements (Si Edwards on drums, Dave Doran on bass, Fred Newell on vocals) characterized 1974's *Watchin' TV*, which featured Moss' friend Charlie McCoy. Barefoot Jerry returned the favor on McCoy's country hits "Boogie Woogie" and "Summit Ridge Drive." The following year, after Barefoot Jerry recorded *You Can't Get Off With Your Shoes On*, Monument re-released both the Capitol and Warner Bros. albums on a double-LP set titled *Grocery*.

Moss assembled yet another group for Barefoot Jerry's 1976 update, *Keys to the Country*. His band included bassist Terry Bearmore, guitarist Jim Colvard, Warren Hartman on various keyboards, and Charlie McCoy, who again made a guest appearance. The same members (sans McCoy) returned for a final album in 1977, *Barefootin'*. Wayne Moss has continued to play and produce, especially for his friend McCoy. —*John Bush*

Southern Delight / 1971 / Capitol ♦♦

Barefoot Jerry / 1972 / Warner Bros. ♦♦♦

Watchin' TV / 1974 / Monument ♦♦♦
The picking is hot but the songs leave something to be desired. For example: "Funky Lookin' Eyes" is based on the same lick as Cream's "Sunshine of Your Love" but isn't nearly as interesting. —*Jim Worbois*

You Can't Get Off With Your Shoes On / 1975 / Monument ♦♦

● **Grocery** / 1976 / Monument ♦♦♦♦

Keys to the Country / 1976 / Monument ♦♦♦
Somewhat an outgrowth of Area Code 615, it's more interesting. Instead of just doing jams, this group does proper songs which include vocals. While not great by any stretch of the imagination, it's a nice-sounding record. —*Jim Worbois*

Barefootin' / 1977 / Monument ♦♦♦

Watchin' TV/You Can't Get off With Your Shoes On / Apr. 8, 1997 / See For Miles ♦♦♦
See For Miles reissued Barefoot Jerry's third and fourth albums, *Watchin' TV* and *You Can't Get Off With Your Shoes On*, on a single CD in 1997. Both records are fairly uneven, but they have enough moments to make it of interest to hardcore collectors of early-'70s country-rock. —*Stephen Thomas Erlewine*

Keys to the Country/Barefootin' / Apr. 8, 1997 / See For Miles ♦♦♦
See For Miles reissued Barefoot Jerry's two Monument albums from 1976, *Keys to the Country* and *Barefootin'*, on a single CD in 1997. Both records are fairly uneven, but they have enough moments to make it of interest to hardcore collectors of early-'70s country-rock. —*Stephen Thomas Erlewine*

Southern Delight/Barefoot Jerry / Oct. 7, 1997 / See for Miles ♦♦♦
The impeccable steel guitar sound of the great Russ Hicks is the driving force behind Barefoot Jerry, whose 1971 debut *Southern Delight* and self-titled 1972 follow-up make up this welcome reissue. —*Jason Ankeny*

Russ Barenberg
b. Oct. 8, 1950
Guitar, Mandolin / Progressive Bluegrass, Traditional Bluegrass, String Bands, Contemporary Bluegrass
Russ Barenberg is one of the most melodic instrumentalists in contemporary bluegrass. Best known for his Clarence White-style flatpicking, Barenberg often uses his other three fingers to enhance rhythm and melody and create a more textural sensitivity. A former member of Country Cooking, Heartlands, Fiddle Fever, and Laughing Hands, Barenberg has remained active since moving to Nashville in 1986. Inspired by Doc Watson and Mississippi John Hurt, Barenberg began playing guitar at the age of 13. Along with his brother and sister, he took lessons from Alan Miller, the older brother of future bandmate John Miller. A turning point came in 1964, when Barenberg discovered the late Clarence White on an album by the Kentucky Colonels, *Appalachian Swing!*

While attending Cornell University in Ithaca, NY, in 1968, Barenberg met banjo whiz Pete Wernick. Two years later, the two instrumentalists joined with Tony Trischka, Kenny Kosek, and John Miller to form the seminal bluegrass band Country Cooking. During the four years that Country Cooking was together, the group recorded two influential albums, *Country Cooking* and *26 Bluegrass Instrumentals*, and accompanied mandolinist Frank Wakefield on a third album. After Country Cooking disbanded in 1975, Barenberg temporarily switched to electric guitar and performed with a jazz-rock band, Carried Away. Frustrated by the music business, however, he stopped playing from 1975 to 1977 when he moved to New York and, together with Trischka, Miller, and fiddler Matt Glaser, formed the innovative bluegrass band Heartlands. Although the band failed to record an album of its own, Heartlands backed Barenberg on his 1979 solo album, *Cowboy Calypso*.

Moving to Boston, Barenberg freelanced with several pickup bands and taught guitar and mandolin at the Music Emporium in Cambridge. In 1982, he joined Glaser and fiddler/mandolinist Jay Ungar in the eclectic string band Fiddle Fever, recording two albums with the group. In addition, Barenberg worked with Glaser and mandolinist Andy Statman in the short-lived experimental bluegrass-jazz band Laughing Hands. Since moving to Nashville, Barenberg has worked extensively with dobro player and record producer Jerry Douglas. In addition to accompanying Irish vocalist Maura O'Connell, the two musicians recorded a trio album, *Skip, Hop & Wobble*, with upright bassist Edgar Meyer.

As a session player, Barenberg has recorded on numerous demo tapes for Nashville publishing companies and appeared on albums by Béla Fleck, Hazel Dickens, Mel Tillis, and Randy Travis. Barenberg has also been featured on instructional tapes, including

How to Play Bluegrass Guitar and *Teach Yourself Bluegrass Guitar*, released by Homespun Tapes and Videos. —*Craig Harris*

Cowboy Calypso / 1979 / Rounder ♦♦♦

Behind the Melodies / 1983 / Rounder ♦♦♦♦

● **Halloween Rehearsal** / 1987 / Rounder ♦♦♦♦♦

Moving Pictures / 1988 / Rounder ♦♦♦♦

Randy Barlow
b. Mar. 29, 1943, Detroit, MI
Trumpet, Vocals / Country-Pop, Singer/Songwriter, Neo-Traditionalist Country
A singer/songwriter who reached his commercial peak in the late '70s, Randy Barlow was born in Detroit in 1943. By the age of ten, he was playing guitar with local R&B bands; at 14, he was performing professionally. After leaving college in 1965, he moved to California to become a Hollywood stuntman, but instead found work with Dick Clark's *Caravan of Stars*, serving as a promoter and emcee in addition to performing music and comedy.

In 1968, Barlow issued his first single, "Color Blind," which failed to chart. After years of struggle playing local clubs, he was awarded another shot at recording in 1974, making the best of it with the minor hit "Throw Away the Pages." After a string of other small successes, he reached the Top 20 in 1976 with a rendition of "Twenty Four Hours from Tulsa," which had been a Top Ten hit for Gene Pitney in 1963. From 1978 to 1979, Barlow issued four back-to-back number-ten singles—"Slow and Easy," "No Sleep Tonight," "Fall in Love With Me Tonight," and "Sweet Melinda"—and received notice for the 1977 album *Arrival*, its 1978 follow-up *Fall in Love With Me*, and a 1979 self-titled effort. However, subsequent singles and albums (like 1981's *Dimensions*) failed to garner much commercial or critical acclaim; in 1983, Barlow released his final chart single, "Don't Leave Me Lonely Loving You," which hit number 67. —*Jason Ankeny*

Arrival / 1977 / Republic ♦♦♦

Fall in Love With Me / 1978 / Republic ♦♦♦

● **Randy Barlow featuring Sweet Melinda** / 1979 / Republic ♦♦♦♦

Dimensions / 1981 / Paid ♦♦♦

Max D. Barnes
b. Jul. 24, 1936, Hardscratch, IA
Songwriter, Vocals / Contemporary Country, New Traditionalist
Max D. Barnes may not have released many records, but he left an important mark on contemporary country music. As a songwriter, Barnes composed many familiar songs of the '80s and '90s, receiving 42 songwriter awards in his career. Artists like George Jones ("Who's Gonna Fill Their Shoes"), Waylon Jennings ("Drinkin' and Dreamin'"), Conway Twitty ("Red Neckin' Love Makin' Night"), Keith Whitley ("Ten Feet Away"), Randy Travis ("I Won't Need You Anymore [Forever and Always]"), Vern Godsin ("Way Down Deep," "Slow Burnin' Memory"), Pam Tillis ("Don't Tell Me What to Do"), and Vince Gill ("Look at Us") have recorded his songs, as have many others. Although he has had a couple of minor hits himself (most notably "Allegheny Lady" in the mid-'70s), his true legacy lies in his songs, not his records.

Barnes grew up in Iowa, receiving his first guitar from his sister Ruthie Steele at age 11. Shortly afterward, his parents were divorced. He moved to Omaha, NE, with his mother and two younger brothers. At 16, he dropped out of school and began singing in a local nightclub. During this time, he formed a band called the Golden Rockets, which featured his future wife, Patsy, as lead singer. Max and Patsy quit playing clubs after the birth of their son, Patrick. At first, Max worked for an Omaha concrete company, but the family soon moved to Long Beach, CA, where he was the foreman at a lamp factory. After a while, he quit, spending his summers in Omaha and his winters singing in California. By 1962, he saved up enough money to buy a nightclub near Lake Okiboji, IA, but he sold it after eight months. Again, the Barnes family moved back to Omaha, where Max spent nine years driving as a truck driver.

Barnes' musical career didn't really begin until 1971, when he recorded a single for Jed, "Ribbons of Steel"/"Hello Honky Tonk." He followed it with "You Gotta Be Putting Me On"/"Growing Old With Grace," which was released on Willex. Following some words of encouragement from songwriter Kent Westberry, Barnes moved to Nashville in 1973. Barnes became a staff writer for Roz-Tense Music, which led to Charley Pride recording two of his songs. Soon, he moved to Gary S. Paxman Music, then to Danor Music. While he was with Danor, Barnes wrote nearly 30 songs recorded by other artists, including several hit singles; on one occasion, he had five of his songs on the charts simultaneously. He also co-wrote many songs with Troy Seals, one of the co-owners of the publishing company. Sadly, tragedy befell the Barnes family, as the eldest son, Patrick, died in a car accident in 1975. Max wrote about the incident on "Chiseled in Stone," which was co-written with Vern Gosdin, who had a hit with the song in 1989.

In 1976, Barnes signed a publishing deal with Screen Gems EMI, which helped him secure a recording contract with Polydor. Released the following year, *Rough Around the Edges* spawned the minor hit "Allegheny Lady," which scraped the bottom of the charts. If he didn't have hits with his own records, he did have hits with his songs, as Conway Twitty brought several of Barnes' songs to the charts, including the Loretta Lynn duets "I Can't Love You Enough" and "From Seven Till Ten," and the solo "Don't Take It Away," which hit number one. —*Stephen Thomas Erlewine*

● **Rough Around the Edges** / 1980 / Ovation ♦♦♦♦

Pieces of My Life / 1981 / Country Roads [UK] ♦♦♦

Bobby Barnett
b. Feb. 15, 1936, Cushing, OK
Vocals / Traditional Country, Country-Pop
Country singer Bobby Barnett was born in Cushing, OK, in 1936, and moved to El Paso after graduating from high-school in 1953. He'd long been interested in country music,

and his singing career took off in 1960 thanks to a cover of Eddie Miller's "This Old Heart" that made the national Top 30. He signed briefly with Republic, which dropped him after his next single flopped, but Reprise picked him up in 1962 and issued two singles, "Crazy Little Lover" and "Same Old Love." However, it wasn't until Barnett signed with Sims in 1963 that he scored his first Top Ten hit, "She Looks Good to the Crowd." He charted several more times over the next 15 years, and his biggest subsequent single, 1968's "Love Me, Love," narrowly missed the Top Ten. Barnett's final hit was the minor 1981 comeback single "Born in Country Music." *—Steve Huey*

At the World Famous Crystal Palace / 1964 / Sims ✦✦✦

Lyin', Lovin' and Leavin' / 1968 / Columbia ✦✦✦

● **American Heroes** / Apr. 22, 1997 / Bear Family ✦✦✦✦
Bear Family's 1997 release *American Heroes* contains the entirety of Bobby Barnett's two concept albums about the history of the American West: 1975's *Heroes, History and Heritage of Oklahoma* and its 1985 sequel, which cast its sights to the entire West, not settling for just Oklahoma. Unlike nearly every Bear Family set, this plays a little fast and loose with the historical facts (kind of ironic considering the nature of the set), sequencing the two albums nearly interchangeably and not giving indication of the original track order (the origin of the 27 tracks is delineated on the back cover, along with the supporting musicians); the booklet explains the stories of the songs and prints the lyrics, but gives little history on Barnett or these albums. So, the focus is on the history, the myths, and the heritage of the West and Oklahoma in particular, and while it may have been better to have the two albums presented as originally released, the fact of the matter is, these are cult items, and anybody who knows about these albums will likely just be happy that they're able to get them in any form. Also, the two records fit together remarkably well; not only do they share many of the same players, the sound on the 1985 LP isn't overly clean and processed, so it sounds much like those from 1975. Unlike some historical-oriented recordings—whether it's folk narratives or "The Battle of New Orleans"—Barnett's records wind up being as much about the sound and feel of the music as they are about the narrative, so this doesn't feel like a doggedly serious listen. In fact, even if the history here is pretty good—accurate and well-told—the albums often play like something heard on an Americana segment of the Disneyland TV show, where the myth and fantasia are more important than the particulars. This is not a bad thing by any means, but it does mean this is a corny curiosity more than a great lost album—but, as a curiosity, it's entertaining, since Barnett has a good batch of songs, a good voice, and a steady-rolling, varied traditional country style that fits the music right. It's easy to enjoy without listening to the lyrics, and if the lyrics are kind of silly, well, that's part of its charm. *—Stephen Thomas Erlewine*

Mandy Barnett

b. Sep. 28, 1975, Crossville, TN
Vocals / Neo-Traditionalist Country, Contemporary Country
Born Amanda Carol Barnett, Mandy Barnett began singing as a child, winning the Best Country Act at Dollywood when she was only ten, and her mother started bringing her on trips to Nashville. As a teenager, she was signed by renowned talent scout and producer Jimmy Bowen, and eventually Asylum Records. An uncompromising singer whose style was rooted in the classic country of Patsy Cline, Jim Reeves, Webb Pierce, and Brenda Lee, Barnett's keen interpretive sense enabled her to delve into a song, study the intricacies of its emotional content, and render a powerful performance through her full-bodied voice. Her torchy delivery on her contemporary yet retro-sounding country and pop-tinged material recalled Patsy Cline, so it's no wonder that, while waiting to record her self-titled debut, she paid her bills by playing the legendary singer four nights a week and 26 weeks a year in the musical production *Always... Patsy Cline* at the Ryman Auditorium. She left Asylum for Sire Records with 1999's *I've Got a Right to Cry*. *—Jack Leaver*

● **Mandy Barnett** / 1996 / Elektra ✦✦✦✦✦
Tennessee native Mandy Barnett had already been busy bringing Patsy Cline back to life by playing (and singing the songs of) the rowdy, legendary vocalist in the stage production *Always... Patsy Cline*. Then Barnett, not yet even 21 years old, took that experience and used it to power her self-titled debut album for Asylum Records. Cline's influence is out front on Barnett's handling of Willie Nelson's 1962 classic "Three Days" and the brand-new Kostas/Richard Bennett song "I'll Just Pretend." The downside of Barnett's album is that the production tends toward clean and safe territory (such as the over-abundance of strings on the syrupy "Rainy Days"). The upside is that, even during her album's most middle-of-the-road moments, Barnett's voice remains strong, smooth, and confident. And a few of the songs shine with real promise—Barnett's delicate handling of Jim Lauderdale's "Planet of Love," for example, and the traditional "Wayfaring Stranger," which closes the album on a comfortable, unhurried note. *—Kurt Wolff*

Traveller Songs / 1997 / Asylum ✦✦✦✦✦
While Mandy Barnett may not exactly be a household name, her Asylum Records debut is one of the finest country-pop records to come out of the 1990s. Producer Andy Paley (the Paley Brothers, Brian Wilson) frames Barnett's exquisite vocals with subtle and emotional backings that truly spotlight her wonderful, Patsy Cline-influenced vocals. The record contains an excellent cover of "Dream Lover," revisiting the classic with a new country dimension that sounds as if it was originally written for Barnett. *—Matthew Greenwald*

I've Got a Right to Cry / Apr. 13, 1999 / Sire ✦✦✦✦
If ever there was a singer who was born to sing the torch and twang style that Patsy Cline created, it is Mandy Barnett. A soft-spoken performer who belts 'em out with all the guts and grit of the founding mothers of traditional country music, Barnett is amazing. Producer Owen Bradley, a legend himself, is known for his classic production style for country music's true stars like Cline, Bill Monroe, Ernest Tubb, and Brenda Lee. Working at his studio, Barnett was given the kind of support an artist of her caliber deserves. However, Owen Bradley passed away suddenly during the course of production, leaving the project unfinished. Barnett, along with Owen's brother and longtime partner, Harold, as well as Harold's son, Bobby, forged ahead; the result is a lasting and honorable tribute to Owen Bradley's distinguished career, as well as the harbinger of a great career about to blossom. Songs as traditional as the title cut and as jazz-infused as "Who" show off Barnett's talents. Able to rip and roar with the boys, Barnett distinguishes herself on the pure honky tonk of "Trademark" while being very cool as she performs "Falling, Falling, Falling." Barnett pays homage to Cline on "Mistakes" and swings hard on "Don't Forget to Cry." A remarkable feat in the face of Owen Bradley's passing, Mandy Barnett is most certainly one of the few women recording as a country artist who can actually sing country music. She does so with flair and with a sense of history, while still being firmly grounded in who she is and the music she wants to make. *I've Got a Right to Cry* is lush and breathtaking, fulfilling the promise of the country & western genre and providing the listener great satisfaction. *—Jana Pendragon*

The Barrier Brothers

Group / Traditional Bluegrass
The Barrier Brothers were pioneers of bluegrass music. All three, Herman, Ernest and Henry were born in Hardin, Tennessee, where Herman and Ernest learned to play old-time music when they were young. They started out at a small radio station in Corinth, MS, during the early '50s. Later, the whole Barrier family moved to South Bend, IN, to find work. There, when not working, they honed their musical skills: Ernest mastered the 5-string banjo, while Herman became an adept bass player. The two taught young Henry to sing lead and play guitar. After Henry grew up, they formed a band that included fiddler Gene Dykes. The Barriers were a semi-professional weekend band and during the '50s mostly played at parks, fairs, and minor jamborees throughout the Midwest.

The brothers and their Ozark Mountain Boys finally cut their first record for Ray Earle's independent Armoneer label near the end of the decade. They had two singles and a gospel EP, which led to a major contract with Philips International, where they recorded three albums in as many years. The Barriers were a versatile band, but they didn't get to show it on these albums, as Philips executives insisted on their recording bluegrass standards. After their contract expired, Herman and Ernest returned to Tennessee and Henry remained in Indiana, where he continued to play in various bands. Following Herman's death in 1988, Ernest continued working in his welding business. He continued jamming with local musicians until his death in early 1994. *—Sandra Brennan*

Gospel Songs, Bluegrass Style / 1962 / Philips ✦✦✦

● **Golden Bluegrass Hits** / 1962 / Philips ✦✦✦✦

More Golden Bluegrass Hits / 1962 / Philips ✦✦✦✦

Pickin' and Singin' / 1977 / Old Homestead ✦✦✦

Bashful Brother Oswald (Beecher Ray Kirby)

b. Dec. 26, 1911, Sevier County, TN, **d.** Oct. 17, 2002, Madison, TN
Vocals, Banjo, Dobro, Guitar / Old-Timey, Traditional Country
For nearly 60 years, Bashful Brother Oswald was one of the most influential and talented dobro players in country music. For the majority of his career, he was the dobroist for Roy Acuff's Smoky Mountain Boys, becoming the leading dobroist in country as well as one of the most popular members of the band. Over the course of his career, Oswald released only a handful of solo recordings, but left behind enough music to illustrate why he was one of the most influential players of his era.

Bashful Brother Oswald (born Beecher Ray Kirby) was the son of an Appalachian musician. As a child, he learned how to play dobro and banjo, as well as sing gospel music. When he was a teenager, he began playing square dances with various country groups. In the late '20s, Oswald moved to Flint, MI, to work in a Buick factory. After the Great Depression hit, he lost his job and became a musician at the radio station WFDF. Because Hawaiian music was very popular, the station manager decided to feature it prominently during regular programming, thus inspiring Oswald to buy his first steel guitar. In 1933, he performed at the Chicago World's Fair and found himself greatly influenced by the wide variety of music he heard there. The following year, he went to Knoxville and began playing dobro with several different bands, including Acuff's Crazy Tennesseans. Oswald became a permanent member of Acuff's band after the singer was invited to join the *Grand Ole Opry* in the late '30s.

As a vocalist, Oswald gained recognition for singing a few lines on Acuff's classic "Precious Jewel" (1940) and on "Wreck on the Highway" (1942). Acuff named his sideman "Brother Oswald" in a ruse to convince audiences that he was the brother of the band's singer, Rachel Veach, to obscure the fact that Veach was an unmarried woman. The dobroist happily complied in creating the Oswald character, and began wearing a floppy mountain hat, tattered overalls, and enormous shoes while adopting a braying horse laugh. The cartoonish character became a favorite of audiences immediately, and it stayed popular throughout his career.

Oswald continued performing and recording with Acuff until the '80s, but began a solo career in the '60s. After working as a session musician, he released a few albums of his own, beginning with 1962's *Bashful Brother Oswald*. In the early '70s, the Nitty Gritty Dirt Band had Oswald perform on their 1972 hit album, *Will the Circle Be Unbroken*. Also in 1972, guitarist and dobro player Tut Taylor produced Oswald's *Brother Oswald* album. In the late '70s, he began playing in the Opryland theme park with former Smoky Mountain bandmate Charlie Collins. During the 1980s, Oswald continued performing with Collins at the Opryland and Acuff at the *Opry*. Following Acuff's death in 1992, he and Collins earned a regular slot on the *Opry*'s main stage. Oswald died ten years later. *—Sandra Brennan*

Bashful Brother Oswald / 1962 / Starday ✦✦✦✦

● **Brother Oswald** / 1972 / Rounder ✦✦✦
Pete "Bashful Brother Oswald" Kirby joined Roy Acuff's Smoky Mountain Boys in January of 1939. His dobro playing and comedic persona were staples of both Acuff's

band and the *Grand Ole Opry.* On this solo outing from 1972, Brother Oswald's comedic persona is nowhere to be found, it's just his first-rate dobro mastery on favorites including "Blue Eyes Crying in the Rain," "Wabash Cannonball," and "Tennessee Waltz." While this Rounder disc is highly recommended for fans, the novice may want to check out his classic recordings with Acuff before venturing here. *—Al Campbell*

That's Country / 1975 / Rounder ✦✦✦

Oz & Charlie / 1976 / Rounder ✦✦

Don't Say Aloha / 1998 / Rounder ✦✦✦✦
The term legend is tossed around quite a bit. But what qualifies one more than 38 years with Roy Acuff and the *Grand Ole Opry?* Oswald didn't just help develop the dobro sound, he is a master picker, and this set finds him in great form. Covering Hank Williams and Bob Wills, he also throws in a few nice originals for a swell batch of twang. *—Tim Sheridan*

Carry Me Back / Oct. 20, 1999 / RME ✦✦✦

All Instrumental / Rounder ✦✦✦✦

The Bastard Sons Of Johnny Cash

f. 1995
Group / New Traditionalist, Honky Tonk, Contemporary Country
The Bastard Sons of Johnny Cash, who came together in 1995, play modern country with an "outlaw" edginess, with some of the attitude and some of the swagger of artists we've come to expect from the man in black himself, Johnny Cash, or from Waylon Jennings, Merle Haggard, and Kris Kristofferson (to name a few others). Mark Stuart and his fellow Bastard Sons—Dean Cote (guitar), Clark Stacer (bass) and Joey Galvan (drums) (an early lineup included Buzz Campbell (lead guitar), Alex Watts (lead guitar) and Johnny D'Artenay (bass))—had been playing in blues and rock bar bands, along the lines of Blues Traveler and the Black Crowes in their native San Diego, but it was Stuart's love of country music that led him to putting together this outfit, even though his city had no country music scene whatsoever when we started out. Like his musical heroes, Stuart didn't change TBSoJC to fit contemporary in with country's heavily produced, pop-oriented Nashville-Branson sound.

The band saw their stock soar after opening for Haggard at the Coach House, in San Juan Capistrano. They recorded their own six-song EP and hit the road, playing gigs along the way with Willie Nelson, Joe Ely, Asleep at the Wheel, Billy Joe Shaver, Dale Watson, and the Derailers (to name a few), and received a lot of attention along the way from record label reps, including two former San Diegoans who both saw potential early on: Joe Rinaldi (A&R) and Lou Niles (VP) of Ultimatum (a record label started by the William Morris Agency), who signed the group in December of 1999. Another self-produced nine-song CD, *Lasso Motel*, garnered more attention (they were proclaimed one of the Top 100 Unsigned Bands last year by industry rag *Music Connection*) and in 1998, they received an invitation to perform for over 20,000 attendees of Willie Nelson's Annual 4th of July Picnic in Luchenbach, TX, a three decade old institution featuring today's rebel-artists of country music.

In case you are wondering, this band earned Cash's permission to use his name (who reportedly went against the advice of his own organization to give his blessing). "He's been very supportive over the years, and even helped us get a show at the House of Blues in Los Angeles, which really helped us get a lot of industry attention," said Stuart during one interview, "and that's just one more reason we'd really like to keep the name, and honor the man." After much recording, touring, and numerous personnel changes, *Walk Alone*, their full-length debut, was released in early 2001. *—Bryan Thomas*

● **Walk Alone** / Sep. 25, 2001 / Artemis ✦✦✦✦
Mark Stuart—sounding here like a younger Waylon Jennings—has the kind of dusky, throaty growl perfectly suited for singing this kind of Bakersfield honky tonk country-rock. As a songwriter, however, he's meandering down that same wagon wheel-worn path that his outlaw forebears have already tread down to the ground 'til there's nothing left but dust-filled ruts. While there's certainly nothing wrong for replicating the Telecaster-and-pedal steel twang of a much loved sub-genre (Dwight Yoakam and Chris Isaak, on occasion, have made attempts to keep it alive among younger listeners), there's nothing original being added here to it either. Stuart's lyrics cover much the same imagery and topical narrative; it must be a requirement for honky tonkers to write about trains, for instance, even though it's doubtful that many bands use them today as means of transportation. The Bastard Sons of Johnny Cash's cover of Merle Haggard's "Silver Wings" has a nice loping feel, and one of Stuart's own, "Texas Sun," rolls along like a semi with rambling guitars and a kicking drumbeat, but this has all been heard before. While he certainly can turn a phrase about "putting the hammer down" on the road ("Interstate Cannonball") or thinking about a woman he left behind but is still on his mind ("Memphis Woman"), the Bastards' next outing should find a way to say what hasn't been said before. [The 2001 reissue adds two bonus tracks: "Nowhere Town" and "Spanish Eyes"] *—Bryan Thomas*

Distance Between / 2002 / Ultimatum ✦✦✦
Given the fact that the Bastard Sons of Johnny Cash have one of the most superbly arrogant names any alt-country band could hope to dream up, it's a bit of a puzzler that they don't sound leaner and meaner than they do, and while the group's second album, *Distance Between*, is a solid collection of well-crafted country-rock, the fact is these guys hardly sound like outlaws in the manner of their hero, either musically, legally, or attitudinally. While there are a few potent twang-rock numbers on *Distance Between*—the two best being about cars, "Wind It Up" and "1970 Monte Carlo"—most of the album is dominated by languid midtempo numbers whose temperament seems influenced either by U2 during their "thinking about America" period (such as "Tears of Gold") or a slightly grittier take on '70s country-rock (typified by "Marfa Lights"). Mark Stuart is a dependable songwriter, and his voice makes him sound like Lyle Lovett's rough-and-tumble younger brother (or Bruce Springsteen's twangier cousin), while the band is tight and professional on all 12 songs here. But while the Bastard Sons of Johnny Cash's chops are just fine, their inspiration often sounds a bit forced, and there's very little here that sounds particularly passionate or strikingly original. There isn't a thing wrong with the craft or the execution of *Distance Between*, but it sounds a bit short on fire and feeling, and it's hard not to think that a little dose of their namesake's attitude and defiance would do them a world of good. *—Mark Deming*

The Beau Brummels

f. 1964, San Francisco, CA, **db.** 1968
Group / Country-Rock, Folk-Rock, Pop
While they only had two big hits, the Beau Brummels were one of the most important and underrated American groups of the 1960s. They were the first U.S. unit of any sort to successfully respond to the British Invasion. They were arguably the first folk-rock group, even predating the Byrds, and also anticipated some key elements of the San Francisco psychedelic sound with their soaring harmonies and exuberant melodies. Before they finally reached the end of the string, they were also among the first bands to record country-rock in the late '60s.

The key axis of the band was formed by guitarist/songwriter Ron Elliott, who penned most of the Brummels' moody and melodious material, and singer Sal Valentino, owner of one of the finest voices in mid-'60s rock. Spotted by local DJ Tom Donahue in a club in San Mateo (just south of San Francisco), the group was signed to Donahue's small San Francisco-based label, Autumn Records, in 1964. With Sly Stewart (later Sly Stone) in the producer's chair, they made the Top 20 right off the bat with "Laugh, Laugh." The melancholy, minor-key original sounded so much like the British bands inundating the airwaves that many listeners initially mistook the Brummels for an English act. The follow-up single, "Just a Little," was another excellent, melancholy number that became their biggest hit, making the Top Ten.

The Beau Brummels made a couple of fine albums in 1965, dominated by strong original material and featuring the band's ringing guitars and multi-part, mournful harmonies. The best of their early work is nearly as fine as the Byrds' first recordings, yet the band was losing ground commercially, partially because Autumn, being such a small label, lacked promotional muscle. "You Tell Me Why" was their only other Top 40 hit, though "Sad Little Girl" and the Byrds knock-off "Don't Talk to Strangers" were excellent singles. The band also shuffled personnel a few times, and Ron Elliott was unable to stay on the road because of diabetes. Autumn was sold in 1966 to Warners, who made the lunkheaded move of forcing the band to record an entire album of Top 40 covers—ignoring the fact that original material was one of the Brummels' primary fortes.

Regrouping as a trio, the group recorded a critically acclaimed, more experimental album in 1967, *Triangle.* Their last Warners LP, *Bradley's Barn*, found the group branching into country-rock, a year or so before it became trendy. The Beau Brummels did re-form for an unimpressive reunion album in 1975, and although Ron Elliott and Sal Valentino continued to make music and work on various low-profile projects of their own, they've never made records on par with the Brummels' vintage work. *—Richie Unterberger*

Introducing the Beau Brummels / Apr. 1965 / Sundazed ✦✦✦✦✦

The Beau Brummels, Vol. 2 / Aug. 1965 / Sundazed ✦✦✦

Beau Brummels '66 / Jul. 1966 / Warner Bros. ✦✦

Triangle / Jul. 1967 / Warner Bros. ✦✦✦✦✦
The jewel in the Beau Brummels' crown, *Triangle* was an unexpected departure from the band's earlier hit-making formula—and demonstrated Ron Elliott's growing maturation as a songwriter. All the band's signature styles (folk, country swing, and Brit-pop) are still heard in the mix, but the tunes here assume an added aura of mysticism. Buried commercially by the likes of *Sgt. Pepper, Triangle* shared its premise of songs loosely united by a common theme—in this case, a ruminative dream cycle (though to call *Triangle* a concept album might be overstating the case). The exquisite "Magic Hollow," graced by Van Dyke Parks' delicate harpsichord, was surely the LP's highlight. Plucked as a single, it barely dented the charts, yet remains one of the most beautiful tunes in the entire Brummels canon. The album's first five songs—"Are You Happy," "Only Dreaming Now," "Painter of Women," "Keeper of Time," and "It Won't Get Better"—form a surprisingly coherent and cohesive whole despite marked differences. "Dreaming"'s accordion transports the listener to Paris' Montmartre, while "Painter" suggests the shifting sands of the Middle East. Elliott's lyric imagery in these tunes and a third track—"The Wolf of Velvet Fortune"—is particularly striking, and Sal Valentino's richly expressive voice elevates all three to sublime heights. Too long ignored by rock cognoscenti, *Triangle* is (all hyperbole aside) a fine album that deserves to be heard by a wider audience. [In late 2002, Collector's Choice increased the odds of this occurring by reissuing the album on CD.] *—Stansted Montfichet*

Bradley's Barn / Oct. 1968 / Edsel ✦✦✦✦
After taking the Beau Brummels to the pop/folk psychedelic edge, producer Lenny Waronker took the band to Nashville, literally. Possibly influenced by the Byrds *Sweetheart* experiments, the group (now down to just Sal Valentino on vocals and Ron Elliott on guitars) wedded with Nashville's finest, including guitarist Jerry Reed and drummer Kenneth A. Buttrey, both veterans of Dylan's Nashville sessions. These players were not just good musicians, but *smart* musicians, easily embellishing the Elliott/Valentino duo as if they had been playing with the two for years, not days. The resulting masterpiece, no doubt due to the awesome Brummels original songs (especially "Cherokee Girl," "Turn Around," and "Deep Water"), is a virtual tapestry in country and rock. *—Matthew Greenwald*

The Beau Brummels / Apr. 1975 / Warner Bros. ✦✦✦✦
Revisiting their country & western roots, surviving Brummels Ron Elliott and Sal Valentino joined forces with a host of ace session men at Owen Bradley's Nashville

studios in 1968 and cut a clutch of tunes which included some of their finest work to date. From these sessions came "Deep Water" and the similarly constructed "Turn Around"—each a solid 24-carat gold specimen of a new musical hybrid: country-rock. Both tracks are distinguished by stellar Dobro guitar work (the instrument's distinctive twang is heard on several other cuts as well). Valentino's lush voice, alternately playful and plaintive, is on this LP at its absolute peak. Valentino's effortless readings of "Jessica" and "An Added Attraction (Come and See Me)" could charm birds out of trees, and his persuasive handling of the smoke-filled bar ballad "Love Can Fall a Long Way Down" should make a believer out of anyone who ever doubted his vocal gift. Like its predecessor, *Triangle*, *Bradley's Barn* failed to attract the attention that it so richly deserved, though many critics gave it high marks. The more accessible and mainstream of the two, *Bradley's Barn* ranks right up there with the Byrds' *Sweetheart of the Rodeo*, the International Submarine Band's *Safe at Home*, and the freshman efforts of Gene Clark, Steve Young, and the Flying Burrito Brothers as a milestone of early country-rock. Fans of the genre would do well to seek out its German or Japanese CD reissue. *—Stansted Montfichet*

● **The Best of the Beau Brummels: Golden Archive Series** / 1987 / Rhino ✦✦✦✦✦

This is probably the best (and best-sounding) anthology covering their golden years, although it lacks their brilliant, later country-based work at its best. *—Bruce Eder*

Autumn of Their Years / 1994 / Big Beat ✦✦✦

These underrated folk-rock pioneers cut a great number of unreleased outtakes/demos during their mid-'60s prime that didn't make it onto the albums they released for the tiny Autumn label during that period. Fourteen of those songs were released in the early 1980s by Rhino on the fine *From the Vaults* album. *Autumn of Their Years* reprises ten of those tunes and adds 16 previously unreleased cuts for a grand total of 26, all of which are group originals. There are a lot of fine moments here, but it's actually a bit much for all but hardcore fans. First off, the best cuts—ones like "She Sends Me," "Dream On," and "Love is Just a Game," which display their supremely haunting folk-rock melodicism and minor-key harmonies—were already available on *From the Vaults*. The 16 newly found demos aren't as good, production-wise (several are acoustic sketches) or material-wise. Earlier demos of their hits "Laugh Laugh," "Just a Little," and "Still in Love With You Baby" are interesting in comparison to the originals, but not as good. And some strong cuts from *From the Vaults* are inexplicably omitted. Of the new vault finds, the highlight is "Tomorrow Is Another Day," an acoustic ballad showcasing Sal Valentino's rich and moving vocals. *—Richie Unterberger*

San Fran Sessions / Jun. 11, 1996 / Sundazed ✦✦✦

Be clear from the get-go: this three-CD, 60-song set, which consists *solely* of rarities, demos, alternate takes, and unissued performances from 1964-1966, should only be acquired by serious fans of the band. It's not the place to start, and most listeners would be better served by picking up a greatest hits disc or the original Autumn albums. If you do love the band, though, it's an excellent journey through the back waters of their early repertoire. The Brummels rarely wrote or recorded anything lousy, and this presents interesting, substantially different versions of officially released songs like "Laugh, Laugh" and "Just a Little"; and quite a few demos that have never before seen the light. The beautifully sad harmonies and glittering guitar arrangements are usually present, and the compositions—even the totally unissued ones—are usually quite strong. From a historical viewpoint, it's interesting in that it presents a lot of previously unheard Sal Valentino-penned tunes (Ron Elliott wrote most of the songs that ended up on official releases). The sound is superb, as are the liner notes. *—Richie Unterberger*

From the Vaults / Jun. 29, 1999 / One Way ✦✦✦✦

No group ever straddled the gap between folk-rock and garage punk better than the Beau Brummels—and anyone who wants to take issue with that statement should give a listen to this CD. Rhino Records assembled and issued this 14-song collection in 1982 on vinyl, and it marked the first serious attempt to make sense of the Beau Brummels' large body of unissued recordings; since then, Sundazed has outdone them with a three-CD set covering the years 1964-1966, but most of those are here confined to around the time of their second album, later in 1965. It says something about the quality of the band's work that these 14 outtakes make one of the best albums of the period, rivaling the best contemporary work of the Byrds and nudging up alongside the likes of the Beatles, the Rolling Stones, and the Kinks for listening time. The funny thing is, the entire album plays like a specimen of the group's work from some alternate universe, even opening on an unexpected note with a lead vocal by Ron Meagher doing a beautiful punkish lament on "I Will Go," with chiming rhythm guitars and a lead guitar part laden with faux-Arab-esque flourishes. The rest is made up not just of leftovers, but rejected singles ("Gentle Wandering Ways"), songs ("She Loves Me") proposed but never recorded officially, a vocal version of a song ("Woman") originally issued as an instrumental, and an extended demo version of one key song ("Sad Little Girl") that was never otherwise issued complete, among other oddities. The latter is one of the best recordings in the group's entire output, and worth the price of the CD by itself; the Declan Mulligan-sung version of "Woman" (once only available as part of the movie *Village of the Giants*) isn't far behind on the harder, punkier side of the band's output. The whole disc is one of the best folk-rock and garage punk albums of the 1960s, and essential listening for anyone interested in those genres or that decade. *—Bruce Eder*

Live! / Aug. 29, 2000 / Dig ✦✦✦

Molly Bee (Molly Beechwood)

b. Aug. 18, 1939, Oklahoma City, OK

Vocals / Traditional Country, Country-Pop, Rockabilly, Country Boogie

Molly Bee had several hits in the early '60s, crafting a showy stage persona, ideal for clubs. Raised in Beltbuckle, TN, Bee didn't begin singing until her family moved to Tucson, AZ. Even then, she started her singing career much earlier than most—she was ten years old when she gained the attention of Rex Allen, the singing cowboy. Bee's mother took her to see the singer at a local concert, where she had her daughter sing for him. Impressed with her performance of "Lovesick Blues," Allen had the child sing on his radio show shortly afterward. A year later, her family moved to Hollywood, where she became a regular on *Hometown Jamboree*, a Los Angeles-based television show run by Cliffie Stone. Bee sang on the *Jamboree* throughout her teens, gaining a large following of fans; she was so popular, the program was occasionally called the "Molly Bee Show." During this time, she was also a regular on *The Pinky Lee Show*, appearing on the television program for three years.

When she was 13, Bee signed with Capitol Records, releasing her first single, "Tennessee Tango." However, it was "I Saw Mommy Kissing Santa Claus," released late in 1952, that was her first major success. In 1953, she recorded "Don't Start Courtin' in a Hot Rod Ford," a duet with Tennessee Ernie Ford. The following year, she left Pinky Lee's show for Ford's daytime television show. Bee's career continued to grow, as she had more hit singles—including "Young Romance," "Don't Look Back," and "5 Points of a Star"—and appeared on a variety of television shows. By the late '50s, her live shows were drawing large, record-breaking crowds.

In the early '60s, Bee began to move her talents to other areas, acting in several musical plays (*The Boy Friend*, *Finian's Rainbow*, *Paint Your Wagon*) and movies (*Chartreuse Caboose*, *The Young Swingers*), as well as becoming a fixture in Las Vegas. However, her recording career began to decline after she signed to Liberty Records in 1962. After two unsuccessful years there, she moved to MGM in 1965, releasing the *It's Great... It's Molly Bee* album. Bee found her greatest success at MGM the following year with "Losing You"/"Miserable Me." By the late '60s, Bee had fallen prey to drug addiction and had to take several years off the road as she rebuilt her life. She re-emerged in 1975 with *Good Golly Ms. Molly*, this time on Cliffie Stone's Granite record label. Her comeback was successful, producing two charting singles: "She Kept on Talking" and "Right or Left at Oak Street." In 1982, she released her final album, *Sounds Fine to Me*, which failed to match the performance of *Good Golly*, although she remained a popular concert draw. *—Stephen Thomas Erlewine*

Young Romance / 1958 / Capitol ✦✦✦

It's Great . . . It's Molly Bee / 1965 / MGM ✦✦✦✦

● **Swingin' Country** / 1967 / MGM ✦✦✦✦✦

Carl Belew

b. Apr. 21, 1931, Salina, OK, **d.** Oct. 31, 1990

Songwriter, Vocals / Nashville Sound/Countrypolitan

Despite recording eight albums between 1960 and 1972, Carl Belew is best remembered as a songwriter whose work was covered by an eclectic group of artists ranging from Patsy Cline to Gene Vincent to Andy Williams. Born in Oklahoma in 1931, Belew first entered the studio in 1955; by the following year, he gained his first widespread exposure thanks to appearances on a pair of California-based radio programs, *Town Hall Party* and *The Cliffie Stone Show*. In 1957, he performed on the *Louisiana Hayride*.

Belew's composition "Stop the World (And Let Me Off)" hit the Top Ten in 1958 in a rendition by Johnnie & Jack; the following year, Andy Williams hit the Top Five with "Lonely Street," a song which would become Belew's trademark tune thanks to subsequent covers by Cline, Vincent, and Rex Allen Jr. Later in 1959, the breakup of his marriage inspired Belew to write "Am I That Easy to Forget," a Top 40 pop hit for actress Debbie Reynolds which was later recorded by Engelbert Humperdinck, Skeeter Davis, Don Gibson, Jim Reeves, and Leon Russell. Belew's own rendition hit the Top Ten in 1959. In 1960, Belew released his self-titled debut LP; in the same year, he notched a Top 20 hit with the single "Too Much to Lose." Two years later, a label change prompted another eponymous effort; the single "Hello Out There" earned him another Top Ten hit, his last.

Between 1964 and 1968, Belew released an album a year, beginning with *Hello Out There* and continuing with *Am I That Easy to Forget*, *Country Songs*, *Lonely Street*, and finally *Twelve Shades of Belew*. His last studio album, *When My Baby Sings His Song*, a record of duets with Betty Jean Robinson, was issued in 1972, while one final single, "Welcome Back to My World," appeared in 1974. Throughout his career, Belew's songs continued to be popular with (and popularized by) other singers; Eddy Arnold hit number one in 1965 with "What's He Doing in My World," while Jim Reeves scored a posthumous success in 1968 with "That's When I See the Blues (In Your Pretty Brown Eyes)." "Stop the World (And Let Me Off)" also reached the Top 20 twice more thanks to a 1965 cover by Waylon Jennings and a 1974 version by Susan Raye. Carl Belew died of cancer on Halloween in 1990 at the age of 59. *—Jason Ankeny*

Carl Belew / 1960 / Decca ✦✦

Hello Out There / 1964 / RCA ✦✦✦

Am I That Easy to Forget? / 1965 / RCA ✦✦✦

Country Songs / 1966 / Vocalion ✦✦✦

Lonely Street / 1967 / Vocalion ✦✦✦

● **Twelve Shades of Belew** / 1968 / RCA ✦✦✦✦

When My Baby Sings His Song / 1972 / Decca ✦✦✦

The Bellamy Brothers

f. 1958, Darby, FL

Group / Country-Pop, Contemporary Country, Urban Cowboy, Country-Rock

Although the Bellamy Brothers are the most successful duo in country music history, they have never been favored by the critics. That doesn't mean their music was rote, by the book, and formulaic country-pop. More than most acts of the late '70s and '80s, the Bellamys pushed the borders of country music, adding strong elements of rock, reggae, and even rap. Nearly a decade after their first hit—the 1975 pop chart-topping, Southern rock-tinged "Let Your Love Flow"—the brothers had earned a stack of best-selling records, and critical respect came by the late '80s. By that time, they had firmly established themselves as the top duo of the '80s, both in terms of popularity and musical diversity. Howard and David Bellamy were raised in Florida. Their father, Homer, played traditional country music around the house and performed with a Western swing band on the weekends. In addition to the country music they heard in their house, the brothers were drawn to the calypso music of the neighboring Caribbean islands. However, nothing provided as much attraction as the rock & roll they heard on their sister's records and the radio. From the Everly Brothers to the Beatles, the Bellamy Brothers soaked up the sounds of contemporary pop and rock. In their late teens and early twenties, they once again became infatuated with country music, thanks to the music of George Jones and Merle Haggard.

Both Howard and David learned how to play a variety of instruments in their childhood. Neither child had any formal training, but Howard managed to learn the guitar, banjo, and mandolin, while David learned the piano, accordion, fiddle, banjo, organ, and mandolin. Both brothers went to college at the University of Florida. While they were students, they had their first paying gigs—playing fraternity parties. Howard and David both earned degrees at the University of Florida; Howard majored in veterinary medicine, while David earned one in psychology. During the late '60s, the two performed in a number of bands, both together and separately. In 1968, they moved to Atlanta, forming Jericho. Performing in such a large number of bands meant that the brothers perfected a number of different musical styles, since they were expected to please the tastes of many different club audiences. Playing in a never-ending series of bands and clubs proved tiring, and the brothers moved back home to work on their songwriting.

In a short time, the move paid off. In 1973, they met a friend of singer Jim Stafford, who directed the vocalist to David's "Spiders and Snakes." Stafford was immediately taken with the tune, releasing it as his next single; the humorous retelling of David's boyhood farm experiences would eventually sell over three-million copies. The success of "Spiders and Snakes" gave the Bellamy Brothers enough money to move out to Los Angeles, where they began to concentrate on a full-time musical career. In 1975, the brothers signed to Curb/Warner Bros., releasing their first single, David's "Nothin' Heavy." The song flopped. Dennis St. John, who was a friend of the Bellamys and Neil Diamond's drummer, suggested that the duo record a song written by Larry E. Williams, one of Diamond's roadies. After some encouragement, the Bellamy Brothers recorded and released Williams' song, "Let Your Love Flow." The song broke the doors wide open for the brothers, topping the pop charts and climbing into the country Top 30, as well as being a major hit in Britain, West Germany, and Scandinavia.

The Bellamy Brothers quickly released their debut album, also called *Let Your Love Flow*, which became nearly as successful as the single. Instead of concentrating on a domestic follow-up, the brothers spent their time in Europe, touring off and on for the next two years, which led to a great deal of financial success. Soon, they were able to pay off their debts and install their mother, Frances, as their financial manager. Their second album, 1977's *Plain & Fancy*, was a major success in Sweden and Norway, but it didn't make much of an impact in America. The following year, the Bellamy Brothers moved back to America and returned to the family farm in Darby, FL. Not only did they change their address, but they changed their musical direction, moving closer to a straight country sound. The shift in style paid off, even if "Slippin' Away," the second single they released after they returned to the U.S., only made it into the country Top 20.

The Bellamy Brothers' country breakthrough happened in 1979, with the tongue-in-cheek "If I Said You Had a Beautiful Body (Would You Hold It Against Me)." Initially, the song was a hit in Ireland, convincing the duo's American record company to release it as a single. The song rocketed to number one on the country charts, which led to the Top Five success of "You Ain't Just Whistlin' Dixie." The Bellamy Brothers' success continued to roll forward in 1980, as they scored two straight number-one hits, "Sugar Daddy" and "Dancin' Cowboys." They earned a Grammy nomination for Best Country Performance by a Duo or Group and the CMA named them the Most Promising Group of the Year. Throughout 1980 and 1981, the group continued to rack up the hits, including "Do You Love as Good as You Look" and "They Could Put Me in Jail."

Curb switched the Bellamy Brothers' distribution from Warner Bros. to Elektra at the end of 1981. Coincidentally, the change in distribution coincided with Howard and David's desire to experiment with their music. After they released the number one "For All the Wrong Reasons," the brothers followed with "Get into Reggae Cowboy," which was a groundbreaking country record that incorporated Jamaican rhythms. In 1982, the group was given a Lifetime Membership of the Federation of International Country Air Personalities, as well as being named the Top Country Duo by *Billboard*. Throughout 1983, the brothers logged a number of hits. The following year, Curb signed a distribution deal with MCA, which had no effect on the continuing success of the Bellamy Brothers. For the next three years, the brothers were at their peak, both popularly and artistically, scoring a number of hit singles that showcased their continuing musical development as well as their increasing lyrical sophistication, as indicated by the Vietnam vet anthem "Old Hippie" and "Kids of the Baby Boom." The Bellamy Brothers continued to have hits on Curb/MCA until the end of the '80s.

By the turn of the decade, their audience had begun to shrink, leading the duo to switch record labels to Atlantic. After one album with Atlantic, 1991's *Rollin' Thunder*, the Bellamys left the label, founding their own record company, Bellamy Brothers Records. *The Latest & the Greatest* (1992) was the first album released on the label. Although the independent record label meant that the group wasn't charting as frequently as it used to, that was also a reflection of the shift of the country audience's taste. The duo could still have minor hits, like the Top 25 "Cowboy Beat," which proved that the Bellamy Brothers continued to hold on to a dedicated group of fans in their second decade of performing. *Reggae Cowboys* followed in 1998, and a year later the duo resurfaced with *Lonely Planet*. —*Stephen Thomas Erlewine*

Let Your Love Flow / 1976 / Warner Bros. ✦✦✦✦✦

The Bellamy Brothers / 1976 / Warner Bros. ✦✦✦

Plain & Fancy / 1977 / Warner Bros. ✦✦

If you stumble onto this record expecting to hear the group who had all the country hits, you may be sadly surprised. Produced by Phil Gernhard (who produced Lobo), this record

has no direction, and probably wouldn't be mistaken as the same group that had a hit with "Let Your Love Flow" just a short time before. "Miss Misunderstood" was done again on *You Can Get Crazy* to much better effect. —*Jim Worbois*

Beautiful Friends / 1978 / Warner Bros. ✦✦✦

The Two and Only / 1979 / Warner Bros. ✦✦✦

The Bellamys explore a number of musical styles with success. In addition to the hits, check out "May You Never," written by the outstanding British folk artist John Martyn, the bluesy "Miss Misunderstood," or "Why Did We Die So Young?" with a strong early-'60s pop influence. —*Jim Worbois*

You Can Get Crazy / 1980 / Warner Bros. ✦✦✦

These prolific brothers turn in another fine batch of tunes (and one non-original) for this record. Their harmonies are appealing whether on the reggae-influenced "Dancin' Cowboys" or "Let Me Waltz Into Your Heart" with not a weak track here. It's not great, but highly enjoyable. —*Jim Worbois*

Sons of the Sun / 1980 / Warner Bros. ✦✦✦✦

When We Were Boys / 1982 / Elektra ✦✦✦✦✦

Michael Lloyd, probably best-known as the producer on Shaun Cassidy's "Da Doo Ron Ron," oversaw the brothers' cute, early country years. In this album, they were given the reins for the first time, leading to a more serious, reflective and simple approach. Also for the first time, they recorded the album at their own home studio, located on their farm in Darby, FL. —*Tom Roland*

Greatest Hits / 1982 / Curb ✦✦✦✦

This was the first in what would become a series of Bellamy Brothers greatest-hits compilations released over the years. These ten tracks are the original versions on Warner Bros. that were played to death on the radio at the beginning of the urban cowboy craze, including "Let Your Love Flow," "If I Said You Had a Beautiful Body (Would You Hold It Against Me)," "Redneck Girl," and "For All the Wrong Reasons." —*Al Campbell*

Strong Weakness / 1983 / Curb ✦✦✦

Restless / 1984 / Curb ✦✦

● **The Best of the Bellamy Brothers** / 1985 / Curb ✦✦✦✦✦

Best of the Bellamy Brothers is a ten-track budget-priced collection that features some of his biggest hits, including "Let Your Love Flow," "If I Said You Had a Beautiful Body (Would You Hold It Against Me)," "Kids of the Baby Boom," "Old Hippie," "Dancin' Cowboys," "Slippin' Away," "Ole Faithful" and "Satin Sheets." Although this isn't a bad budget-priced disc, there are better collections available, offering more songs and better sound for not much more money. —*Stephen Thomas Erlewine*

Howard & David / 1986 / Curb ✦✦✦

Country Rap / 1987 / Curb ✦✦✦

"Kids of the Baby Boom," encapsulating images from JFK to Third World abusiveness, speaks out for an entire generation. But the album is dominated by experimental and infectious "fun stuff," including "D-D-D-D-Divorcee," "Country Rap" and their bopping group effort with the Forester Sisters, "Too Much Is Not Enough." —*Tom Roland*

Greatest Hits, Vol. 3 / 1989 / Curb ✦✦✦✦✦

This member of the series contains "The Center of My Universe," "Big Love," "Hillbilly Hell," "Santa Fe," and other hits. —*AMG*

Reality Check / 1990 / Curb ✦✦

Crazy from the Heart / 1990 / Curb ✦✦✦

Rollin' Thunder / 1991 / Atlantic ✦✦✦

The Latest & The Greatest / 1992 / Bellamy Brothers ✦✦✦

Rip off the Knob / Aug. 1, 1993 / Bellamy Brothers ✦✦✦

Rip off the Knob is a combination of new material and older favorites from the Bellamy Brothers. The highlights include "Stayin' in Love," featuring Texas Tornados Freddy Fender on guitar and Flaco Jimenez on accordion; a call for simpler days long gone on "The Andy Griffith Show"; and the hits "Feelin' the Feelin'," "Crazy From the Heart," "I Need More of You," and "Sugar Daddy." The album concludes with a weak reworking of "Reggae Cowboy" as a "Special Bonus Dance Mix." —*Al Campbell*

Greatest Hits, Vol. 2 / Sep. 5, 1995 / Curb ✦✦✦✦✦

Picking up where the first installment left off, *Greatest Hits, Vol. 2* captures the Bellamy Brothers maturing, both in terms of music and message. *Greatest Hits, Vol. 2* collects ten of their biggest singles—including "Feelin' the Feelin'," "When I'm Away From You," "I Need More of You," "Old Hippie," "Lie to You for Your Love," and "Too Much Is Not Enough"—all of which hit the charts between 1982 and 1986. The production and arrangements on these songs borrow from soft rock and folk-rock, taking away most of the duo's country edge. Of course, this is what their fans wanted to hear and these singles dominated the charts during the '80s. —*Thom Owens*

Dancin' / Jul. 1996 / Intersound ✦✦✦

The Bellamy Brothers' *Dancin'* is a professional, immaculately produced latter-day album and that's part of its fault. It might sound high-tech, but it's high-class production makes it sound lifeless. The Bellamys perform with some conviction, but they lack the songs to make it worth the effort to listen to the stale sound of the record. —*Thom Owens*

At Their Best / Apr. 10, 1998 / Cema Special Markets ✦✦✦

At Their Best repackages the 1992 Bellamy Brothers collection *The Latest & the Greatest*, and in addition to the new title, the other changes are purely cosmetic, adding new cover art and shuffling the running order of the ten tracks. Needless to say, fans who have the earlier compilation don't really need this as well, but with the inclusion of Bellamys favorites like "Let Your Love Flow," "I'd Lie to You for Your Love" and "If I Said You Had a Beautiful Body (Would You Hold It Against Me)," it's a good introduction for new listeners. *—Jason Ankeny*

The 25 Year Collection, Vol. 1 / Mar. 27, 2001 / Delta Disc ✦✦✦
How do you sum up a quarter century of history making music? The Bellamy Brothers succeed in doing just that in a 25-year celebration of the hits they have given the world. *The 25 Year Collection, Vol. 1* is the first in a two-part release for Howard and David Bellamy. Listening to the album is a digitally enhanced stroll through the past. Modern recording and re-mastering technology is used to produce a crisper sound on Bellamy classics such as "Let Your Love Flow," "Old Hippie," "Crazy From the Heart," and "Sugar Daddy." In a refreshing change from many greatest-hits collections, the Bellamys include three live cuts: "If I Said You Had a Beautiful Body (Would You Hold It Against Me)," featuring an outstanding guitar solo; "I Could Be Persuaded"; and "Redneck Girl," which effectively closes the album on an upbeat note. With its retrospective photo montage insert, the Bellamy Brothers' *25 Year Collection, Vol. 1* is sure to stir memories from the days when traditional country music first began its merge with mainstream light rock. *—Rick Cohoon*

The 25 Year Collection, Vol. 2 / Jul. 31, 2001 / Delta Disc ✦✦✦

Redneck Girls Forever / Jul. 16, 2002 / Bellamy Brothers ✦✦✦
After reuniting with Curb Records late in their career, Howard and David Bellamy re-emerge with new material following a double greatest-hits collection. *Redneck Girls Forever* is typical of the Bellamy style, featuring a smattering of social commentary about how the world has left the over-40 crowd in the dust intermingled with steamy love songs. Most of the cuts are written by David Bellamy. The Bellamy Brothers can't seem to let go of the past, constantly bewailing the state of the modern world and the fact that the two siblings are just plain getting older. Most of the songs are curved around a seemingly catchy hook, such as "What I Used to Do All Night," a 60-something's lament on losing "intimate stamina." Sometimes the hook is effective, but other times ("The Andy Griffith Show") the nostalgia is stifling. A shining moment comes when the Bellamys recount the story of a marital infidelity and deliver the line, "After I go to hell can I come on home to you?" When you've recorded as many hits and albums as the Bellamys have, the pressure to continue the streak isn't as great; unfortunately, the trade-off can result in mediocrity. *—Rick Cohoon*

Boyd Bennett

b. Dec. 7, 1924, Muscle Shoals, AL
Bass, Vocals / Rockabilly, Rock & Roll
Boyd Bennett's music fell into the cracks between country and the early days of rock & roll. Boyd never received much recognition from country circles while he was performing, possibly because his music sounded more like the emerging rockabilly than hardcore honky tonk. Bennett was raised outside of Nashville, performing as a drummer and singer with a band led by Francis Craig. After a stint in the military at the end of World War II, he became a regular performer on a local radio station, assembling a band named the Southlanders. The Southlanders sounded similar to Western swing, with some additional honky tonk grit. Bennett signed with King Records in late 1952, recording his first single in December. The resulting record, "Time," became a minor country hit the following year.

Later in 1953, Bennett revamped the Southlanders, renaming them the Rockets and adding R&B and blues elements to his music with the intention of gaining a younger audience. Not coincidentally, this occurred at the same time Bill Haley was reworking his sound and renaming his backing band the Comets. Early in 1955, Bennett and the Rockets recorded the rock & roller "Seventeen." King Records was unsure of the record's commercial appeal, yet they eventually released it, which proved to be fortunate. "Seventeen" rocketed to number five on the pop charts, eventually becoming one of the best-selling records in the label's history. Not only was the original successful, but the song spawned several cover versions, making Bennett and his co-author John Young several million dollars.

The Rockets' next single, "My Boy Flat-Top," was sung by the group's Big Moe (aka James Muzey), and it also made it into the pop Top 40. In 1956, the Rockets supported Moon Mullican on the classic rockabilly single "Seven Nights to Rock." One more Rockets single—a 1956 cover of Carl Perkins' "Blue Suede Shoes"—was a minor pop success, but the Rockets couldn't replicate their success with "Seventeen" no matter how many times they tried. And throughout 1957 and 1958 they tried a lot, recording several regional hits ("Hit That Jive," "High School Hop") that never made it nationally. While all of these songs touched on rockabilly, they were significantly tamer than most of their contemporaries; consequentially, the Rockets never developed much of a cult following.

Boyd Bennett left King Records in 1959, signing with Mercury Records. Late in 1959, he had one minor hit on his new record label, "Boogie Bear." After a series of unsuccessful singles, Boyd realized that he was too old for the current rock & roll audience and decided to retire from performing. With the money he earned from "Seventeen," he had already bought three nightclubs and co-owned a television station. A decade after his retirement, he founded Hardcast Manufacturing, which primarily constructed parts for air conditioning. For most of his musical retirement, Bennett lived in Dallas. With the exception of the occasional charity concert with Ray Price, Boyd Bennett never reentered the music business. *—Stephen Thomas Erlewine*

Boyd Bennett / 1957 / King ✦✦✦✦

● **Tennessee Rock 'n' Roll** / 1991 / Charly ✦✦✦✦✦
Boyd Bennett turned to Bill Haley-style rock & roll when his country recordings failed, and immediately scored a major hit in 1955 with "Seventeen," one of the early rock hits. "My Boy Flat-Top" and a version of "Blue Suede Shoes" were Bennett's minor follow-up hits, and those three charters are included on *Tennessee Rock 'n' Roll*, an excellent 24-track anthology of Bennett's original King recordings from 1955-1956, including two previously unreleased tracks. The sound quality is great, and although Bennett's adherence to the Bill Haley sound makes for a bit of a monochromatic listening experience, lovers of '50s rock & roll—and Haley in particular—will love this collection. *—Greg Adams*

Stephanie Bentley

b. Georgia
Vocals / Contemporary Country
Georgia-born singer Stephanie Bentley earned her first taste of musical success at the age of nine, when she, her sister Camille, and a friend took top honors in a local talent contest. The young vocal trio's success won Bentley a slot in a music and drama troupe, where she remained for a number of years, singing everything from show tunes to modern dance-pop and even performing at the White House for then-President Jimmy Carter. In 1984, she formed her own band, Special Delivery, which specialized in Top 40 music and oldies.

After a stint in Georgia singing demos and advertising jingles, Bentley reunited with sister Camille and, as the Bentley Sisters, signed a Nashville production deal that failed to pan out. Discouraged, she eventually relocated to Nashville on a permanent basis and returned to recording demos; one, for a song called "Shake the Sugar Tree," was later used as a backing vocal when the tune was recut by Pam Tillis. Another developmental deal followed, but again proved fruitless. A third contract, however, resulted in a hit 1995 duet with Ty Herndon, "Heart Half Empty." Bentley's solo debut, *Hopechest*, followed in 1996. *—Jason Ankeny*

● **Hopechest** / 1996 / Columbia ✦✦✦✦

Matraca Berg

b. Feb. 3, 1964, Nashville, TN
Songwriter, Vocals / Country-Pop, Contemporary Country
Before she became a recording artist in her own right, Matraca Berg was a professional songwriter with a strong industry pedigree: her mother was songwriter and session vocalist Icee Berg, who helped get her daughter started in the music business as a teenager thanks to her contacts at several music-publishing companies. Berg scored her first success in 1983, teaming with Bobby Braddock to write "Faking Love," which became a number-one hit for T.G. Sheppard and Karen Brooks. Berg subsequently spent two years as the keyboardist for the Kevin Stewart Band, then returned to her Nashville songwriting career. She would go on to contribute material to Suzy Bogguss, Patty Loveless, Trisha Yearwood, Reba McEntire, Pam Tillis, Deana Carter, Martina McBride, and many others.

Eventually, Berg began to toy with the idea of recording her own compositions, and issued her debut album, *Lying to the Moon*, on RCA in 1990. The album won numerous critical accolades for its musical eclecticism, thoughtful lyrics, and rootsy, acoustic sound. However, it wasn't a blockbuster, and RCA tried to push Berg in a more contemporary, commercial direction—so much so that they rejected her proposed follow-up album. Berg switched from the label's Nashville division over to the pop side, and many critics felt that the resulting albums, 1991's *Bittersweet Surrender* and 1993's *The Speed of Grace*, failed to replicate the strengths of *Lying to the Moon*. Finally frustrated with RCA's interference, Berg left to sign with the indie label Rising Tide; her first effort, 1997's *Sunday Morning to Saturday Night*, returned to the style of her debut with (most critics agreed) resounding creative success. Since then, Berg has continued her successful songwriting career, also finding work as a backup session singer; meanwhile, RCA reissued her debut with some bonus tracks as *Lying to the Moon & Other Stories*. *—Steve Huey*

Lying to the Moon / 1990 / RCA ✦✦✦✦✦
This young Nashville singer/songwriter takes a sultry photo and sometimes delivers with brio. *—Mark A. Humphrey*

Bittersweet Surrender / 1991 / RCA ✦✦✦

The Speed of Grace / Nov. 1993 / RCA ✦✦✦
After RCA Nashville refused a second album, Berg moved to the label's pop division, recording an album primarily with such L.A. studio musicians as guitarist Michael Landau and drummer Jim Keltner. The results highlighted Berg's bluesy side, but, aside from a cover of Dolly Parton's "Jolene" recorded with her Nashville buddies, lacked the acoustic Southern mysticism of *Lying to the Moon*. *—Brian Mansfield*

Sunday Morning to Saturday Night / Sep. 23, 1997 / Rising Tide ✦✦✦✦✦
After spending several years fighting with RCA over how they should market her, Matraca Berg left the label and signed with the emerging indie Rising Tide. Her first effort for the label, *Sunday Morning to Saturday Night*, rivals her previous masterwork, *Lying to the Moon*. Between her debut and *Sunday Morning*, she had immense success as a songwriter, penning such hits as "Strawberry Wine" for the likes of Deana Carter. During that time, however, RCA was more concerned in trying to make Berg fit into conventional contemporary country musical styles, when her eclecticism is a large part of what makes her special. Rising Tide fortunately gave her an opportunity to reclaim that exciting eclecticism with *Sunday Morning to Saturday Night*. Nearly every song on the record either sparkles with wit or is impeccably observed and affecting. Similarly, the music is fresh and alive, ranging from hard-rocking honky tonk to country-folk to country-rock to moving ballads. It's a terrific, individual album that fully captures everything Berg is capable of achieving. *—Thom Owens*

● **Lying to the Moon & Other Stories** / Aug. 10, 1999 / RCA ✦✦✦✦✦
Joe Galante at RCA was the moving force behind this reissue of Berg's splendid RCA debut album *Lying to the Moon*, recorded in 1990. Berg has added several new tunes to the original tracks, resulting in a sort of hybrid re-release that recalls old favorites while introducing some outstanding new material. Berg is one of the premier tunesmiths in Nashville, having authored hits for the likes of Deana Carter, Reba McEntire, Pam Tillis, and Suzy Bogguss. Berg is, however, quite capable of delivering her own material in a convincing fashion. As the listener will hear, these aren't just cool tunes; they're cool tunes

performed by a pretty cool singer. Special moments include the elemental blues of "I Got It Bad," the melancholy, mountain soul of "Appalachian Rain," the marvelous rollercoaster metaphor of "Along for the Ride," the witty, easygoing groove of "Eat at Joe's," and the sexual semantics of "Back in the Saddle." This is a welcome reincarnation of an excellent album from an artist whose level of talent is way beyond her level of recognition. *—Philip Van Vleck*

Bering Strait

f. Obninsk, Russia

Group / Bluegrass, Traditional Bluegrass, Old-Timey

The country group Bering Strait took one of the more unusual paths to major-label status in Nashville. Natives of Obninsk, Russia, the group—consisting of Ilya Toshinsky (guitar, banjo, vocals; born November 28, 1977), Natasha Borzilova (vocals, guitar; born August 19, 1978), Sasha Ostrovsky (dobro, steel guitar, lap steel; born August 11, 1980), Lydia Salnikova (keyboards, vocals; born August 10, 1980), and Alexander Arzamastsev (drums; born September 15, 1973)—was organized by a bluegrass-loving music teacher. (Sergei "Spooky" Olkhovsky (born February 15, 1978) replaced an earlier bass player, and mandolin and fiddle player Sergei Passov, an original member, dropped out after participating on their debut album.) They began to play out as teenagers and earned opportunities to visit Nashville in the early '90s. Eventually, they attracted the attention of a Nashville-based manager, who brought them over the U.S. and sought a record deal for them. They signed to Arista Nashville, but that label shuttered before they could record an album. The former head of Arista moved on to Gaylord, a start-up label, and they followed him there, recording an album with producer Brent Maher. But that association fell through, too, and it was not until January 2002 that they followed the same record executive to his next berth with the newly formed Universal South imprint of Universal. Finally, in January 2003, their self-titled debut album was released, while their travails were detailed in the 90-minute documentary *The Ballad of Bering Strait.* *—William Ruhlmann*

Bering Strait / Jan. 14, 2003 / Universal ✦✦✦

For the benefit of the geographically challenged, the Bering Strait is the stretch of water, 55 miles across at its narrowest, between western Alaska and eastern Siberia, the place where the U.S. and Russia come the closest to connecting. In fact, since it is frozen over more than half the year, it's the point at which the two countries do connect. The name is an appropriate one, then, to be taken by a Russian group playing Western-style country music. The classically trained musicians certainly known their way around Nashville licks, and lead singer Natasha Borzilova has her accent under control to the extent of sounding American, if not actually southern. As a result, you could listen to most of the group's debut album without knowing that they come from Obninsk. But if the members transcend the novelty status of their origins, Bering Strait necessarily faces a second challenge: Is it a significant country act? And here the answer is more problematic. Producer Brent Maher has marshaled the usual songwriting pros in Music City and given the group a contemporary country (which is to say, pop/rock) sound that makes it possible to play them on country radio alongside Faith Hill and Shania Twain, but that means that, for the most part, *Bering Strait* is just another mediocre Nashville product. It isn't until near the end, with the instrumental "Bearing Straight," which is actually a medley of bluegrass and new age tunes, that the group's musicianship begins to have an individual flavor. This is followed by "Porushka-Paranya," a country hoedown with Russian lyrics. If the album contained more tracks like that, instead of being dominated by bland romantic ballads, Bering Strait might seem like an interesting new wrinkle in country music instead of another run-of-the-mill Nashville project with exotic origins. *—William Ruhlmann*

Byron Berline

b. 194?, Caldwell, KS

Fiddle, Mandolin, Violin / Progressive Bluegrass, Traditional Bluegrass, Bluegrass

Like his contemporary Vassar Clements, fiddler Byron Berline expanded the sonic possibilities of bluegrass, adding elements of jazz, pop, blues, rock and traditional country to the genre. In addition to being a popular solo act, he performed as a session musician on a number of albums, including records by the Flying Burrito Brothers, Stephen Stills, the Dillards, Gram Parsons, the Nitty Gritty Dirt Band, Emmylou Harris, Kris Kristofferson, and James Taylor.

Berline learned to play from his father, an old-time fiddler. After graduating from highschool, he attended the University of Oklahoma, where he played music with a campus folk group. In 1963, the Dillards played a concert on the University of Oklahoma campus. A friend of Berline's arranged an audition for him with Doug Dillard, who was so impressed he invited the young fiddler to join them for a number. Berline then joined the Cleveland Country Ramblers, and in 1964, he appeared on the Dillards' *Pickin' and Fiddlin'* and won the National Fiddle Championship in Missoula, MO. He played the Newport Folk Festival in 1965, where he met Bill Monroe, who told Berline that he wanted him to join the Blue Grass Boys in the future. In 1967, he graduated with a BA in education, but chose to join Monroe; his first appearance with the band was a show at the *Grand Ole Opry.* Six months after he joined the Blue Grass Boys, he was drafted into the U.S. Army.

Just before Berline was discharged from the Army in 1969, he was invited to join the Dillard & Clark Expedition. He remained with Dillard & Clark until 1971, when the group disbanded. While with them, he played sessions for a number of other artists, including the Flying Burrito Brothers' debut album, *The Gilded Palace of Sin.* Following the breakup of Dillard & Clark, Berline played with the Dillard Expedition. In 1970, Berline scored the ABC television movie, *Run Simon Run*, the first of many films he would score. In 1971, he toured with a revamped version of the Flying Burrito Brothers. Following the tour, Berline and fellow Burritos Roger Bush and Kenny Wertz formed the Country Gazette. During this time, he also continued with his session work, appearing on albums by Gram Parsons, Bert Jansch, Ian Matthews and Southern Comfort, and Bill Wyman.

In 1975, Berline left Country Gazette and moved to Los Angeles with his family, where he intended to concentrate on songwriting, session work, and scoring films. Later that year, he founded Sundance with Dan Crary, Jack Skinner, John Hickman, Allen Wald, and Skip Conover; the following year, Vince Gill and Mark Cohen joined the band. Sundance recorded one eponymous album in 1976 before disbanding. In the late '70s, Berline recruited Crary and Hickman for a tour of Japan. Following the tour, the trio recorded three albums for Sugar Hill; concurrently, Berline also founded the L.A. Fiddle Band.

In 1980, Berline founded the production company BCH with Crary and Hickman, and released a solo album, *Outrageous*, on Flying Fish. In 1981, the L.A. Fiddle Band released an eponymous solo album for Sugar Hill. Berline worked on Chris Hillman's 1984 album *Desert Rose* and also an album of duets with fiddler Hickman in 1986. Two years later, Berline, Crary, and Hickman changed the name of their trio to BCH and added bassist Steve Spurgin to their lineup. The new incarnation of BCH released *Now They Are Four* in 1989. The group added mandolinist/guitarist John Moore in 1990; following his addition, the group re-named itself California, and released their first album, *Traveler*, in 1992. Berline also continued releasing solo efforts.*—Sandra Brennan*

Dad's Favorites / 1977 / Rounder ✦✦✦✦

This heartfelt and powerhouse tribute to Byron Berline's father Luc Berline is a testimony to the family traditions of folk music and beyond that, it is quite a get-together of bluegrass greats with five—count 'em—five banjo players on board just because Dad liked the banjo so much. Vince Gill is also on hand in the rhythm section; this was back in the days before he left bluegrass for country & western stardom. The family concept also extends to featuring Bette Berline on piano. The music is well recorded although nit-pickers may balk at the too-meticulous nature of a typical Rounder production. The music could use a bit more of an edge to it, but it dances along with a tremendous lightness, the players sometimes presenting the traditional themes as if they were piling up shining gold coins. Berline's tribute is a treasure chest indeed. *—Eugene Chadbourne*

Live at McCabes / 1978 / Takoma ✦✦✦✦

This long-unavailable record features Byron Berline and Sundance in a delightful live set recorded at McCabe's Guitar Shop in the late '70s. The veteran fiddler is in terrific form, buoyed by a strong supporting cast that includes banjo player John Hickman, guitarists Dan Crary and Alan Wald, dobro player Skip Conover (who was a guest on the previous album), along with a young Vince Gill on mandolin, who was also a new addition to the group following their self-titled debut LP released the previous year. The sound of the band is considerably different from the previous year's disc, with a full drum kit being replaced by a snare drum, the omission of the pedal steel, and a concentration on a heavier mix of traditional bluegrass favorites, such as Rex Allen's "Tear Drops in My Eyes," Bill Monroe's "Can't You Hear Me Callin'" and "Molly and Tenbrooks," as well as Reno & Smiley's "Used to Be You" and their well-known "Dixie Breakdown" instead of the originals that dominated their first record. Sadly, this fine outing ended up being the band's swan song, as its members went their separate ways in 1979. *—Ken Dryden*

Byron Berline and the L.A. Fiddle Band / 1980 / Sugar Hill ✦✦✦✦

Outrageous / 1980 / Flying Fish ✦✦✦

Berline, Crary, Hickman / 1981 / Sugar Hill ✦✦✦✦✦

Night Run / 1984 / Sugar Hill ✦✦✦

B-C-H / 1986 / Sugar Hill ✦✦✦

● **Double Trouble** / 1986 / Sugar Hill ✦✦✦✦

Byron Berline is a fiddler whose talents have been employed by artists as diverse as Bill Monroe and the Rolling Stones; John Hickman has stayed closer to the bluegrass mainstream, but his playing is melodically adventurous and highly inventive. "Double Trouble" is a reissue of a 1986 session that finds Berline and Hickman playing a stripped-down, but still innovative, style of bluegrass that may come as a surprise to fans of the influential Berline/Crary/Hickman ensemble and of California, the band they formed in 1990. There are several Berline originals here as well as standards like "Blackberry Blossom" and "Sugar in the Gourd." Everywhere Hickman's picking is supple, slippery, and crystalline, and Berline shows more humor and intelligence in his playing than just about any ten other fiddlers you could think of. These guys have been playing together so long that they almost share a brain, and this disc is a pleasure. *—Rick Anderson*

Now They Are Four / 1989 / Sugar Hill ✦✦✦

Jumpin' the Strings / 1990 / Sugar Hill ✦✦✦

While the fiddle playing of Byron Berline sets him squarely within the realm of bluegrass, the melodic originality of his work seems to almost transcend the genre over the course of the 21 self-penned songs that make up *Jumpin' the Strings.* While Berline is the star attraction, a fine backing band comprised of banjoists Alan Munde and John Hickman, guitarists Howard Yearwood and Joe Carr and dobro player Skip Conover is also given the chance to cut loose on this fine release. *—Jason Ankeny*

Fiddle & a Song / 1995 / Sugar Hill ✦✦✦✦

Byron Berline's *Fiddle & a Song* is a star-studded affair with numerous guests, for the most part recorded in 1995. It's hard to beat "Sally Goodin," a traditional bluegrass favorite, with veterans Bill Monroe and Earl Scruggs prominently featured. But there are other worthwhile tracks as well; ex-Sundance member Vince Gill sings lead and plays guitar on "Rose of Old Kentucky" and "Sweet Memory Waltz," while Mason Williams wrote "Skippin' Along on Top" in honor of Berline and sings lead in this humorous ditty as well. Berline is even joined by the Sherman Oaks Presbyterian Church Quartet (where Berline and his wife are longtime members, with Bette Berline playing piano and singing soprano) for a heartfelt treatment of the hymn "Were You There?" Of course, the leader's magical fiddle is in the center of every track, and bluegrass fans should consider this one of Byron Berline's finest recordings. *—Ken Dryden*

Byron Berline with John Hickman & Vince Gill / Dec. 27, 1995 / Koch ✦✦✦✦

Byron Berline and Sundance / 2002 / MCA ✦✦

The debut recording by Byron Berline and Sundance focuses heavily on the writing and lead vocals of bassist Jack Skinner; unfortunately, neither his compositions nor his singing are especially remarkable. Sadly, Berline doesn't have as prominent a role as he did in his previous group, Country Gazette. The album is also a tad over-produced, with the unexpected inclusion of Bill Withers' quickly tiresome "Sweet Wanomi," which is a bit too repetitious (a common problem with Withers' songs) to work very well in a country-rock setting. It is not surprising that there was a major upheaval in personnel and instrumentation by the time the band's follow-up record (*Live at McCabes*) was recorded the following year, most notably with the departure of Skinner and a return to a more acoustic sound and traditional bluegrass play list. This long out-of-print disc will be of minimal interest to most fans of Byron Berline. —*Ken Dryden*

Crystal Bernard

Vocals / Contemporary Country, Adult Contemporary

Crystal Bernard is best known as an actress, particularly for her starring role on the sitcom *Wings*, but she also pursued a musical career as a songwriter. Several of her songs were recorded in the late '80s and '90s by adult contemporary artists like Paula Abdul, the Winans, Lisa Stansfield, and Tracie Spencer. After scoring an adult contemporary hit with "(I Wanna Take) Forever Tonight," a duet with Peter Cetera, she launched a recording career in 1996 with a country album, *Girl Next Door*. —*Stephen Thomas Erlewine*

Girl Next Door / Oct. 29, 1996 / A&M ✦✦✦

Girl Next Door is Crystal Bernard's first full-fledged country album. Prior to its release, Bernard had previously sung and wrote mainstream pop hits for the likes of Paula Abdul and Peter Cetera, so it isn't surprising that her take on country is filled with pop flourishes. Essentially, Bernard takes a simple song structure, arranges it as an adult contemporary song and adds country instruments. Though the results can occasionally be diverting—particularly on uptempo numbers—it isn't particularly country. Nevertheless, Bernard has a surprisingly strong voice and the album is well-produced. It just doesn't rise above background music. —*Thom Owens*

● **Don't Touch Me There** / Feb. 2, 1999 / Platinum ✦✦✦

OK, the real test on this one is whether ex-*Wings* star Crystal Bernard can bring the title track across in a manner that demands seriousness instead of obvious chuckles. The surprise is that it is actually a haunting, breathtaking ballad concerning an abused woman who is standing up for herself for the first time. Bernard has done a greater deal of writing on *Don't Touch Me There*, her sophomore album, and has improved in nearly every way over her first album, *Girl Next Door*. It is nearly impossible not to take to Bernard's gentle but assured voice, though up until now she hasn't had such strong material to work with. "Something to Go On" reveals that, although she has country roots, her pop is impeccable. In fact, it should be noted that Bernard walks a fine line between country and pop, and therefore the album will appeal to fans of both. There is a lot of past love reminiscing and there is no sparing the agony of abandonment and regret. Whether saying goodbye to her non-communicative lover on "Hey" (a beautiful opener) or listening to an elderly Hollywood star speak her last words on "Gardenia," she is bringing together memorable music that tells stories and brings us through twisted emotions and shattered love lives before closing to a duet with father Jerry Bernard on the Jesus praising "If You Need a Touch." The gospel song (despite her father's living as a minister) is one of the bravest feats a popular artist has accomplished in recent years. Making an outright call to the son of God for help on an otherwise worldly album would be enough to turn many nonbelievers in the other direction. But the song is earned, not only because of how good it is, but because the rest of *Don't Touch Me There* is so brutally honest and endearing. —*Peter Fawthrop*

Rod Bernard

b. Aug. 12, 1940, Opelousas, LA

Vocals, Guitar / Traditional Cajun, New Orleans R&B, Rock & Roll

Swamp pop musician Rod Bernard was born in Opelousas, LA, in the early '40s and made his professional debut on KSLO Opelousas when he was only ten. Two years later, Bernard was a DJ at the station, but in 1954, his family moved to Winnie, TX. There Bernard became acquainted with the town barber Huey Meaux, who later became a major producer of Cajun recordings. By the time he was a teenager, Bernard formed his first band (the Twisters) and cut two records on Jake Graffagnino's Carl label.

They then recorded King Karl's "This Should Go on Forever" for Floyd Soileau's Jin label (which eventually licensed the recording to Chicago's Argo label) and took the records to Huey Meaux—who was now hosting a French music show on KPAC Port Arthur. Meaux had the song played throughout East Texas and took a copy to the Big Bopper, who played it at KTRM Beaumont, TX. It took seven months, but eventually the record made it to the Top 20 on the pop charts. Bernard then appeared on Dick Clark's *American Bandstand* (where he had to sanitize some of the lyrics for mainstream audiences) and signed with Mercury Records. After recording over 40 songs for the label, Bernard watched as only four sides were released. One of them, "One More Chance," made it to the pop charts as a minor hit.

By 1962, Bernard's Mercury contract had run out. He began working for Hall-Way Records, where many of his sessions were backed by Johnny and Edgar Winter. He achieved small success with a rocked up version of the traditional Cajun song "Colinda," before Bernard became a DJ and musical director at KVOL, and later a sales executive at KLFY-TV, both Lafayette stations. He also performed on television with the Shondells, a group he had co-founded in 1963. In 1965, a compilation of 12 songs he and the Shondells sang on the show were released as *Saturday Hop* on the La Louisianne label. The group also released a single, "Our Teenage Love" for Teardrop. Bernard and Carol Ranchou of La Louisianne founded the Arbee label. Bernard released several albums

throughout the seventies and continued to work for KLFY-TV for years. In the late '90s, Rod Bernard returned to the studios and recorded *The Louisiana Tradition.* —*Sandra Brennan*

Rod Bernard / 1978 / Jin ✦✦✦✦

Boogie in Black & White / 1979 / Jin ✦✦✦

Country Lovin' / 1979 / Jin ✦✦✦

Nights Lights & Love Songs / 1979 / Jin ✦✦✦

This Should Go on Forever / 1985 / Ace ✦✦✦✦

Lot of Dominoes / 1992 / Jin ✦✦

● **Essential Collection** / Jan. 27, 1998 / Jin ✦✦✦✦✦

For a brief moment in the early 60s, Louisiana swamp pop singer Rod Bernard's tune "This Should Go On Forever," was so enormous that he was featured on American Bandstand, the only artist from that specific geographic region, playing that style of music, to ever appear on that TV show. Trivia aside, Bernard's R&B Cajun hybrid still holds up and is revisited on this 22 track compilation including two New Orleans R&B standards from the pen of Dave Bartholomew and Fats Domino "Good Hearted Man," and "Don't Blame It on Me," the traditional cajun tunes "Colinda," and "Big Mamou," and Bernard's biggest hits "Just One More Chance," and "This Should Go on Forever." —*Al Campbell*

Cajun Blue / Feb. 23, 1999 / Edsel ✦✦✦

The Louisiana Tradition / Jun. 29, 1999 / CSP ✦✦✦✦

Rod Bernard is one of the few Louisiana swamp pop musicians to have ever made the hit parade. His record, "This Should Go on Forever," made the Top 20 chart in 1959 and won the young musician an appearance on *American Bandstand*. Popular hits may come and go, but Bernard's position as one of the driving forces in the idiom has remained a constant. The man designated as a "living legend" in the Louisiana Music Hall of Fame has continued to perform his style of music at clubs and festivals and has recorded numerous CDs. *Louisiana Tradition* was made in 1999. As the name suggests, the CD is faithful to his Cajun roots, as well as to the R&B style in which he sings. The vocalist is backed by Rufus Thibodeaux on fiddle, Jimmy Breaux on accordion, Oran "Junior" Guidry on guitar, Warren Storm on drums and rub board, Richard Comeaux on steel guitar, John Kimbrough and Gene Romero on saxophones, and Gerald Melancon on drums. There is a scorching cover of Chuck Berry's "Maybelline"; most of the tunes are penned by Bernard himself. He starts right off in a Louisiana mode with "Backwater Bayou," sings in French on "Gardez Donc," describes the apprehension and camaraderie of a "Hurricane Watch," and gets melancholy with "When I Hold You in My Dreams" and "The Fantasy Is Over." The obligatory alligator song of the genre is the last on the album, with a cover of Guidry's "See You Later, Alligator." Thus do things go in the swamp. —*Rose of Sharon Witmer*

John Berry

b. Sep. 14, 1959, Aiken, SC

Vocals / Contemporary Country

John Berry began his musical journey by making a name for himself in the Georgia club scene. From 1979-1991, Berry recorded six independent albums before signing with Capitol Records in 1992. With his first major self-titled album on the shelves, Berry took to the road on a major concert tour opening for the likes of Reba McEntire, Aaron Tippin, and the Mavericks. The Georgia tenor has been recognized by the Grammy Association, the Academy of Country Music, and the Country Music Association as a nominee in the Best Male Vocalist category and has scored hits such as "Your Love Amazes Me," "Kiss Me in the Car," and "Standing on the Edge of Goodbye." *Songs & Stories* is a live, acoustic set released independently of any label and includes a mix of Berry favorites and the singer's choice cuts from previous albums. —*Rick Cohoon*

John Berry / Jun. 7, 1993 / Liberty ✦✦✦

Though his eponymous debut shows promise, only a few cuts on *John Berry*—most notably the hit single "Kiss Me in the Car"—are completely successful. —*Thom Owens*

Things Are Not the Same / Nov. 15, 1994 / Capitol Nashville ✦✦✦✦

Saddle the Wind / Nov. 15, 1994 / EMI-Capitol Special Markets ✦✦✦✦

Originally issued in 1990, *Saddle the Wind* was among John Berry's final independent releases before his leap to major label Liberty; although his skills as a songwriter had yet to reach the level of his later work, originals like "That Woman," "Here in My Heart," and "Is It Too Late" all show considerable promise, while covers of classics like "When a Man Loves a Woman" and Bruce Springsteen's "Thunder Road" spotlight his prowess as a vocalist. —*Jason Ankeny*

Standing on the Edge / 1995 / Patriot/Liberty ✦✦✦✦

O Holy Night / Sep. 26, 1995 / Capitol Nashville ✦✦✦

Faces / Sep. 17, 1996 / Capitol Nashville ✦✦✦

John Berry's fifth album finds the singer's formula beginning to wear a bit thin, as he turns out the same blend of countrified MOR ballads and slick, rock-injected uptempo numbers. Berry still has enough skills to make a handful of tracks worthwhile—check out the single "Change My Mind"—but much of the album is a little too bland and predictable for comfort. —*Thom Owens*

Better Than a Biscuit / Sep. 8, 1998 / Capitol Nashville ✦✦✦

Better Than a Biscuit is stylistically similar to *Faces*, finding John Berry moving ever closer to middle-of-the-road pop territory and leaving country behind. This isn't necessarily a bad thing, since Berry's voice is strong and charismatic, but the lack of strong country influences leaves the album somewhat homogenous—even the uptempo dance numbers sound a little too polished for their own good. Still, the best moments on the record—such as "The Stone" and his duet with Wynonna, "We Can't Unmake Love"—rank among the best contemporary country and make the album a worthwhile endeavor for fans. *—Thom Owens*

Wildest Dreams / Sep. 28, 1999 / Hollywood ♦♦♦♦
Listeners won't be able to notice it in the vocals on this 1999 album, *Wildest Dreams*, but only a short year before this recording was made, award-winning artist John Berry was facing one of the most horrible waking nightmares a singer can—the urgent need for throat surgery. If this offering is the end result, then he came through the operation in fine form. The songs on *Wildest Dreams* can lean a little more toward soft pop and rock than country at times. This includes a lot of guitar action on some numbers, but Berry's tenor voice is a powerful match. Both country and pop fans will find plenty to like here with tracks like "Rivers in the Clouds," "Love Is for Giving," "You'll Be in My Heart," "Where Would I Be," and "Salvation." *—Charlotte Dillon*

● **Greatest Hits** / Mar. 28, 2000 / Capitol Nashville ♦♦♦♦

My Heart Is Bethlehem / Oct. 3, 2000 / Ark 21 ♦♦♦♦

All the Way to There / Oct. 16, 2001 / Ark 21 ♦♦♦♦
Country singer and songwriter John Berry completed *All the Way to There* in 2001. With a dozen albums listed to his credit in less than ten years, Berry has had the chance to reach a wide audience and build a stable fan base with huge hits like "Your Love Amazes Me." Since his professional career began there have been many hardships to overcome, including a motorcycle accident and major health problem that caused the resilient country artist to undergo brain surgery and later throat surgery, and then find himself without a label. Somehow, Berry and his music have made it through. This release is a solid recording that carries excellent contemporary country songs like "How Much Do You Love Me," "Settle for Everything," "Let's Find Out," and "He Makes Me Want Her Again." The album was recorded in the basement of Berry's home. He easily proves once again that he has a way with delivering ballads with plenty of heart and soul. Without a major label backing this album it has kind of gone unnoticed, making a hidden treasure that many country fans might have overlooked. That's a shame, since John Berry is a talented singer and songwriter whose music is first-rate. *—Charlotte Dillon*

Certified Hits / Sep. 24, 2002 / Capitol Nashville ♦♦♦♦

Big Sandy & His Fly-Rite Boys

f. 1993

Group / Western Swing, Alternative Country-Rock, Americana, Rockabilly, Mariachi, Bluegrass

Authenticity is the key to the music of Rockabilly Hall of Fame members Big Sandy & His Fly-Rite Boys. Although they've moved from their rockabilly roots to a sound that encompasses folk, bluegrass, Western swing, Cajun, and mariachi influences, the six-piece Southern California-based band continues to be faithful to the music of the past. According to *CD Review*, "you'd swear that the sound's a match for any early Capitol album you have tucked away in your collection." Despite their connection with days gone by, Big Sandy & His Fly-Rite Boys maintain a foot in the present as well. Internet fanzine *Eatmag* claimed that the "music might remind you of yesteryear, but the stories about love, wanting to love, and wanting to be loved are timeless." *Metroactive Music* also commented on Big Sandy & His Fly-Rite Boys' ability to create their own niche when they wrote that the band "flies right by the poseur high-moussed hair and washable tattoos of such '80s rockabilly phenoms as the Stray Cats into an aerie all their own where the music is to dance to and the words can make you cry."

Big Sandy (born Robert "Rusty" Williams) grew up listening to his parents' collection of jump blues records. Inspired by the rockabilly revival of the early '80s, he began to perform with a variety of neo-rockabilly bands in Southern California. Formed as a trio, Big Sandy & His Fly-Rite Boys soon expanded to its lineup featuring Wally Hersom (bass), Lee Jeffriess (steel guitar), Ashley Kingman (guitar), and Bobby Trimble (drums). Big Sandy & His Fly-Rite Boys represent an international collaboration with Kingman and Jeffriess hailing from the U.K. Their debut album, *Jumping from 6 to 6*, was produced by ex-Blasters guitarist Dave Alvin. While their second album, *Swingin' West*, released in 1995, focused on the Western swing influences on their sound, Big Sandy & His Fly-Rite Boys took a more eclectic approach with their effort *Feelin' Kinda Lucky*, released in 1997.

The following year, Big Sandy and the group took a break from each other and recorded separately. Big Sandy's solo album, *Dedicated to You*, featured covers of R&B and doo wop oldies, while the band's album, *Big Sandy Presents His Fly-Rite Boys*, was an instrumental *tour de force*. Big Sandy and the band reunited during the recording of an EP, *Radio Favorites*, released in 1999. Although original plans called for three new tracks to be combined with three tunes available only on vinyl copies of the band's albums, the camaraderie in the recording studio was so strong that they decided to record six new songs instead. The EP introduced the piano playing of Carl "Sonny" Leyland, who joined shortly after the recording of *Feelin' Kinda Lucky*. *Night Tide* appeared in 2000, *It's Time* in 2003. *—Craig Harris*

● **Jumping from 6 to 6** / 1994 / Hightone ♦♦♦♦
While others may suggest that this Western swing/rockabilly outfit's second Hightone release, *Swingin' West*, is a more definitive representation of the band's potential and brilliance, it is more likely that those who have watched Big Sandy & His Fly-Rite Boys' development will stand by this debut project as the group's defining work. Much in the same way that *Guitars, Cadillacs, Etc., Etc.* gave Dwight Yoakam his calling card, *Jumping from 6 to 6* gives Big Sandy and the band their identity in the minds of listeners. On this outstanding freshman effort with energy to spare, Big Sandy's voice is phenomenal. The band is tight, especially the teamwork displayed by steel man Lee Jeffriess and lead picker Ashley Kingman. As always, the King of California, Dave Alvin, is an impeccable producer who knows how to get the very best from each artist. The additions of guests Brantley Kearns on fiddle and Bobby Mizzell's rockin' piano on "Juiced" make for a well-layered musical experience that is multidimensional. Their treatment of Hank Sr.'s "Weary Blues from Waitin'" is inspired, as is "Honky Tonk Queen," an E.G. Thornton tune. Jeffriess lends his skills as a songwriter with outstanding cuts like "Hi-Billy Music" and "This Ain't a Good Time." The significance of this debut was not lost on the many bands that followed in the wake of Sandy's success. A landmark recording that opened the floodgates for others seeking to bring Western swing back to prominence, *Jumping from 6 to 6* marks the birth a new era in country & western music. *—Jana Pendragon*

Swingin' West / Oct. 1995 / Hightone ♦♦♦♦
The follow-up to a strong 1994 debut, *Swingin' West* continues the Western swing and rockin' hillbilly assault that first endeared the California-based Big Sandy & His Fly-Rite Boys to fans and critics alike. While many rockabilly outfits derive their sound primarily from artists from the 1950s, Big Sandy & His Fly-Rite Boys are a more accurate take on the style, venturing back into the '30 and '40s to tap the influences for legends such as Elvis Presley and Gene Vincent. With the lead guitar/steel guitar combination of Ashley Kingman and Lee Jeffriess—both originally out of Britain's rockabilly scene—the five-piece band is fully empowered to explore Western swing, jump blues, and hillbilly boogie, while still injecting originality to make the sound unique. Big Sandy (aka Robert "Rusty" Williams) possesses a big rich, molasses-coated voice that is engaging throughout this 15-song set. Produced once again by Dave "Everything-I-Touch-Turns-into-Musical-Gold" Alvin, *Swingin' West* captures the energy of the band's live show intact. Highlights include the Latin-influenced rhythms of "Hey Muchachita" and the vintage dancehall-like call-and-response vocalizing on "We Tried to Tell You." *—Jack Leaver*

Feelin' Kinda Lucky / Jun. 10, 1997 / Hightone ♦♦♦♦
Big Sandy & His Fly-Rite Boys come from the Land of Retro, and it's a happening place. Their bag is small-combo Western swing, and the refreshing thing is their lack of irony, even with the matching yoke shirts, white scarves, and greasy kid stuff. The band's spartan instrumentation leaves nothing for a weak vocalist to hide behind; luckily, Big Sandy has a rich, cultivated tenor that harks back to the glory days of Tommy Duncan while also invoking some of Hank Williams' haunted edginess. He also has an amazing idiomatic facility—without looking at the liner notes, it's difficult to distinguish the oldies from the originals on any of the band's three albums. Their third release departs not at all from the band's winning signature style: steel player Lee Jeffriess carries on a constant good-natured duel with lead guitarist Ashley Kingman (whose bag of jazzy licks is seemingly bottomless), while Sandy croons above and the bull fiddle and drums hold things down gently below. The only letdown is a touch of fatigue that slips through Big Sandy's voice from time to time—it's as if he tires out as the album progresses. By the end of "Backdoor Dan," the album's closer, he sounds a little bit like Bootsy Collins. Which, actually, is kind of cool in a twisted sort of way. If you had to pick just one Big Sandy record, go with the debut—but there's no reason not to own 'em all. *—Rick Anderson*

Big Sandy Presents His Fly-Rite Boys / May 19, 1998 / Hightone ♦♦♦♦
Big Sandy's ace backup band steps up to the plate and delivers its first solo album—and it's a corker. Sort of like a Western swing version of a Buckaroos album, this record features the Fly-Rite Boys running through a set of originals, primarily showcasing their considerable instrumental chops with a few stray vocals from piano man Carl "Sonny" Leyland. The sound here is decidedly retro, sounding for all the world like it was cut in somebody's living room under a pile of blankets while the drummer bangs away in another room, which only enhances its 78 single authenticity. Highlights include Leyland's turn on the jazz-pop standard "Rosetta," steel man Lee Jeffriess' "Flyin' Rite," drummer Bobby Trimble's drum workout "Hit and Run," guitarist Ashley Kingman's "Straight-8 Boogie," and the atmospheric "Laguna Sunset." For lovers of true Western swing honky tonk with a slight jazz edge sounding like it was cut over 50 years ago, here's your album. *—Cub Koda*

Radio Favorites / Mar. 23, 1999 / HMG ♦♦♦
Rockabilly group Big Sandy & the Fly Rite Boys, who play a style of music popularized over four decades ago, certainly aren't trying to reinvent the wheel—they're just trying to help it keep rollin'. That having been said, the '90s revivals of genres such as swing and ska have taught us that it's one thing to approximate the sounds of a stylish era, but it's a whole different thing to play traditional music really well. This releases attests to the fact that Big Sandy and company do just that—in fact, they inhabit it, from Western swing to doo wop to R&B. And if that doesn't mean anything to you, no matter. On this six-song album, recorded after the members of the group came back from a sabbatical to explore other projects, all you have to do is listen to the big man sing. The velvet-throated Big Sandy is a vocalist and songwriter of the highest order. Highlights include "First and Last Blues," "Buddy I Ain't Buyin'," and "It's a Mystery to Me." *—Erik Hage*

Night Tide / Aug. 15, 2000 / Hightone ♦♦♦
On this, their fourth full-length album, Big Sandy & His Fly-Rite Boys continue to ply their unique brand of small-group rockabilly and western swing, and the combination of Sandy's sweet, rich baritone voice and his band's effortless and pitch-perfect vintage virtuosity continues to be a joy. But this time out there's a distinct lack of party anthems: no cute wordplay, no steel-guitar wolf whistles, no ebullient loverman lyrics. Instead, you have song titles like "In the Steel of the Night" and "Nothing to Lose" and couplets like "I wish I knew what to do/When sleep won't come" and "Heaven help a man like me who walks alone." Perhaps the strangest and most disconcerting song on this album is the almost creepily bouncy "Tequila Calling" on which the singer hears alcohol beckoning him into oblivion. Sandy is singing better than ever, and his band, even in this more subdued vein, is still the best thing on the retro-rock circuit; there's no questioning the musical and emotional power of this album. But *Night Tide* is a strikingly apt title; it sounds like it was recorded by a man who feels himself being pulled out to sea by dark forces. *—Rick Anderson*

It's Time! / Jun. 17, 2003 / Yep Roc ♦♦♦♦
Big Sandy & His Fly-Rite Boys have added a stronger dose of rockabilly rhythm to a few cuts on their seventh album, *It's Time!*, but otherwise they haven't changed much—and there's nothing wrong with that. Big Sandy and company have earned a richly deserved reputation as one of the best retro-country acts on the current scene, and *It's Time!* boasts 14 more examples of what makes them so much fun. Big Sandy has a big, warm voice that's well suited to vintage styles without ever sounding as if he's mired in the past, and his band understands that a light hand (which guitarist Ashley Kingman and pedal steel man Jimmy Roy have along with chops to spare) is what makes vintage country swing. And *It's Time!* gives the band a healthy variety of material to play with, including the Cajun-flavored "Bayou Blue," the jazzy "Money Tree," the rockin' "Chalk It Up to the Blues," and the swing-centric title cut, while the live-in-the-studio production by Joey Altruda captures the roomy but dynamic sound of a good live gig. In short, if you dig Big Sandy, *It's Time!* will chart high on your personal play list, and if you're not familiar with their uptown twang, this is a pretty good place to get started. *—Mark Deming*

Black Tie

Group / Country-Rock
Black Tie was a country-rock band that featured Billy Swan, Bread's Jimmy Griffith, and Randy Meisner, formerly of the Eagles, who was fresh off a failed reunion with his first band, Poco. Black Tie's lone release was a 1986 covers collection entitled *When the Night Falls*. While the project was quite brief, it did produce a minor charting hit in a country-fried cover of Buddy Holly's "Learning the Game." *—Johnny Loftus*

When the Night Falls / 1985 / Bench ♦♦♦♦

Clint Black

b. 1962, Long Branch, NJ
Guitar, Harmonica, Vocals / New Traditionalist, Contemporary Country
A country music traditionalist from Texas, Clint Black was one of the first artists to kick-start the mass-market popularity of country in the '90s. Black is also one of the first artists of a generation that was equally inspired by rock-oriented pop—like '70s singer/songwriters and '60s rock & roll—as well as country artists like Merle Haggard, Bob Wills, and George Jones. He offered a shiny, marketable version of traditional country, and in the process paved the way for a new generation of country artists, particularly Garth Brooks. After Brooks broke through into the pop mainstream, Black's career began to fade somewhat, but he remained one of the most popular and acclaimed vocalists of the '90s.

Clint Black was born in New Jersey but raised in Katy, TX, a suburb of Houston. As a child, he listened to both country and rock & roll, but he didn't begin playing guitar until the age of 13, when he started playing harmonica. Two years later, he began writing songs, as well as performing in his brother Kevin's band, where he played bass and sang. In the early '80s, he began busking on the streets of Katy, eventually working his way into coffeehouses, bars, and nightclubs. In 1987, Clint met Hayden Nicholas, a guitarist and songwriter who had a home studio. Nicholas and Black began collaborating, writing songs and recording demos; Nicholas would become the bandleader for Black, playing lead guitar and co-writing a large majority of his hit singles. A tape of their songs made its way to Bill Ham, the manager of ZZ Top. Impressed with the tape, Ham became Black's manager; the singer had a contract with RCA Nashville by the end of 1988.

"A Better Man," Black's first single, was released early in 1989 and it went to number one—he was the first new male country artist to have a number-one hit with his debut single in 15 years. Black was an immediate sensation throughout country music and he played the *Grand Ole Opry* in April, one month before his debut album, *Killin' Time*, was released. *Killin' Time* was an immediate hit, going gold within six months and spawning four other hit singles, including the number ones "Killin' Time," "Nobody's Home," and "Walkin' Away." At the end of 1989, he won the Country Music Association's Horizon Award, as well that organization's Best Male Vocalist Award. He also won Best Album, Best Single, Best Male Vocalist, and Best New Male Vocalist awards from the Academy of Country Music and the NSAI Songwriter/Artist of the Year Award. By the end of 1990, *Killin' Time* sold over two-million copies in America.

Black released his second album, *Put Yourself in My Shoes*, in 1990. Like the debut, *Put Yourself in My Shoes* was a major success, spawning four Top Ten hits ("Put Yourself in My Shoes," "One More Payment," and the number ones "Loving Blind" and "Where Are You Now"), selling over two-million copies, and peaking at number 18 on the pop charts. Even though it sold well, it didn't receive the same critical acclaim as the debut. Nevertheless, Black was named Best Male Vocalist that same year. Throughout 1990, Black was on tour with Alabama and appearing on television shows across the country. In 1991, several singles from *Put Yourself in My Shoes* charted and he was inducted into the *Grand Ole Opry*. On New Year's Eve of 1991, he married the television actress Lisa Hartman.

Clint Black began 1992 in a lawsuit with his manager Bill Ham. Black claimed that his original contract gave Ham too large of a percentage of the singer's royalties and publishing rights. For seven months he was embroiled in the lawsuit, during which he was recording his third album. By the summer, the suit was settled and his new album, *The Hard Way*, finally was released. *The Hard Way* received positive reviews and became an immediate hit, peaking at number two on the country charts and crossing over into the pop Top Ten. The first single from the album, "We Tell Ourselves," reached number one that summer. Black began a lengthy world tour in June of 1992 to support *The Hard Way*. Although it was a success, *The Hard Way* wasn't as popular as Black's first two records, selling no more than a million copies. Released in 1993, *No Time to Kill*, his fourth album, continued the stagnation in his record sales, even though its sales were more than respectable—the album went platinum and spawned the hit single "When My Ship Comes In." During the fall of 1994, Clint Black released his fifth album, *One Emotion*, followed a year later by the seasonal effort *Looking for Christmas*. *Nothin' But the Taillights* appeared after a two-year hiatus, and in 1999 Black celebrated a decade of recording with *D'Lectrified*. *—Stephen Thomas Erlewine*

☆ **Killin' Time** / 1989 / RCA ♦♦♦♦♦
Black's accessible brand of Texas country burned up the charts upon its release, selling two-million copies and yielding the hit singles "Better Man," "Killin' Time," "Nobody's Home," and "Walkin' Away," and "Nothing's News." *—Brian Mansfield*

Put Yourself in My Shoes / 1990 / RCA ♦♦♦
Put Yourself in My Shoes never approaches the perfection of Black's debut, but it still produced a number of singles, including "Put Yourself in My Shoes," "Loving Blind," "Where Are You Now," and "This Nightlife." *—Brian Mansfield*

The Hard Way / 1992 / RCA ♦♦♦♦♦
Back to form, Black put some of his most exciting singles on his third album. "We Tell Ourselves" rocked without resorting to Southern boogie, and "When My Ship Comes In" contained a masterful chorus. The album also included the hit "Burn One Down." *—Brian Mansfield*

Clint Black / Mar. 1993 / RCA ♦♦
Not a proper album nor a greatest-hits collection, the budget-priced *Clint Black* contains a selection of material from his first and second albums, *Killin' Time* and *Put Yourself in My Shoes*. Comprised entirely of album tracks, there are gems scattered throughout the record but there is simply no reason for this album to exist—*Killin' Time* should be heard in its entirety, while not all of the good songs from *Put Yourself in My Shoes* are included. There is good music on *Clint Black*, but it's hard to call the album anything but a rip-off. *—Stephen Thomas Erlewine*

No Time to Kill / Jul. 1993 / RCA ♦♦♦
Black's albums seems to alternate between the remarkable and the merely pretty good. *No Time to Kill*, which plays off the title of his first album, is one of the latter. All of this is acceptable, though little matches quality of the title track. Black does a duet with Wynonna Judd called "A Bad Goodbye." *—Brian Mansfield*

One Emotion / 1994 / RCA ♦♦♦
One Emotion continued Clint Black's streak of uneven albums, featuring a handful of exemplary tracks, including the Merle Haggard collaboration "Untanglin' My Mind," but just as many mediocre songs, like "You Made Me Feel," which was written with Michael McDonald. Nothing on *One Emotion* is particularly bad, but it doesn't sound like Black is pushing himself into new territories, either. *—Stephen Thomas Erlewine*

Looking for Christmas / Oct. 17, 1995 / RCA ♦♦♦
Clint Black's *Looking for Christmas* consists entirely of new seasonal songs that he wrote or co-wrote himself. This clearly breaks country music law, and the Nashville police must be in hot pursuit. Black often lets schmaltzy production overcome him, but the many fine songs include killer ballad "The Kid" (co-written with Merle Haggard) and the back-porch bluegrass of "The Coolest Pair." *—Roch Parisien*

★ **Greatest Hits** / Sep. 24, 1996 / RCA ♦♦♦♦♦
Clint Black's 16-song *Greatest Hits* is a comprehensive collection, featuring eight number-one hits—including "Killing Time," "Where Are You Now," and "Nobody's Home"—four additional hits, plus four new songs ("Like the Rain," "Half Way Up," "Cadillac Jack Favor," and a live version of the Eagles' "Desperado"). Though the collection is missing a handful of essential tracks, it still provides a convincing argument that Clint Black was one of the finest new traditionalist singers of the early '90s. *—Stephen Thomas Erlewine*

Nothin' But the Taillights / Jul. 29, 1997 / RCA ♦♦♦
Nothin' But the Taillights doesn't find Clint Black stretching himself too much—he's pretty much content to turn out workmanlike neo-traditionalist country. Black has less twang to his music than ever before, but he remains a charismatic vocalist and he's given generally sturdy songs on *Nothin' But the Taillights*, which makes the record worthwhile for dedicated fans. *—Thom Owens*

D'Lectrified / Sep. 28, 1999 / RCA ♦♦♦♦♦
Clint Black also produced *D'Lectrified*—his first time as producer—and it's probably a good thing, because this is easily the most eccentric and personal recording project he has ever released. The album opens with a jazzy cover of Toy Caldwell's "Bob Away My Blues," complete with horns. The sound is very uptown and snazzy, and Black sings the hell out of the song. This track may not exactly set the mood of the album, but it sure states the mindset. Black pulls tunes from all over the ballpark: Eric Idle's "Galaxy Song," Leon Russell's "Dixie Lullaby," and a slightly revised cover of Waylon Jennings' "Are You Sure Hank Done It This Way" (titled "Are You Sure Waylon Done It This Way"). Black also wrote/co-wrote several songs, including "Hand in the Fire" and "Been There." His wife, Lisa Hartman-Black, sings with him on "When I Said I Do," and she's believable. He also includes rearranged versions of his hit singles "Burn One Down" and "No Time to Kill." Guest players include Jennings, Bruce Hornsby, Jerry Douglas, Stuart Duncan, and Steve Wariner. Amid the welter of ideas, players, and influences at work here, Black's singing shines through. When it's all said and done, *D'lectrified* is a pretty wonderful album, easily the most musical record Black has ever done. *—Philip Van Vleck*

Greatest Hits, Vol. 2 / Oct. 30, 2001 / RCA ♦♦♦♦
This 16-track collection of bona fide hits picks up where the first greatest-hits album left off. Songs like "The Shoes You're Wearing," "When My Ship Comes In," and "Something That We Do" are just some of the kickers that grace this well-chosen package of songs. Added to the mix are three duets that remind us of Black's ability to play off other singers, including the emotionally charged "Still Holding On" with labelmate Martina McBride. Also included here are three new recordings, clearly reflective of Black's newfound fatherhood and his awe for his beautiful wife: "Little Pearl and Lily's Lullaby" expresses his joy at the birth of his daughter, "Money or Love" debates the pros and cons of both, and "Easy for Me to Say" is the sweet follow-up to last year's duet with Lisa, "When I Said

I Do." With over an hour of listening time, *Greatest Hits, Vol. 2* is worth every second. *—Maria Konicki Dinoia*

Super Hits / Jan. 21, 2003 / RCA ♦♦♦♦

BlackHawk

f. 1992

Group / Contemporary Country

Comprised of a trio of seasoned professional musicians, BlackHawk became one of the most successful new country groups of the mid-'90s, scoring a string of Top Ten hits from their first two albums. Featuring Henry Paul (lead vocals, mandolin), Van Stephenson (guitar, vocals), and Dave Robbins (keyboards, vocals), the band formed in the early '90s, releasing its first single, "Goodbye Says It All," on Arista Records in late 1993. "Goodbye Says It All" sailed to number one, quickly followed in 1994 by the number two "Every Once in a While," the number nine "I Sure Can Smell the Rain," the number ten "Wherever You Go," and the band's eponymous debut album, which would eventually go platinum. *Strong Enough*, BlackHawk's second album, was released in the fall of 1995 and was equally successful, spawning the hit singles "I'm Not Strong Enough to Say No," "Like There Ain't No Yesterday," "Almost a Memory Now," and "King of the World." *Love & Gravity* followed in 1997, with *The Sky's the Limit* appearing a year later. After just four albums, BlackHawk issued its first hits collection in mid-2000. *—Stephen Thomas Erlewine*

BlackHawk / 1994 / Arista ♦♦♦

Strong Enough / Sep. 12, 1995 / Arista ♦♦♦♦

After their debut album became a platinum success, BlackHawk decided to follow the same formula for their follow-up, *Strong Enough*. Not merely a reproduction of their self-titled debut, *Strong Enough* finds the group consolidating their strengths as songwriters and performers. Throughout the album, the group turns in first-rate songs and tight performances, distinguished by their strong harmonies. *—Stephen Thomas Erlewine*

Love & Gravity / Jul. 29, 1997 / Arista ♦♦♦

Love & Gravity finds BlackHawk breaking away from the standard slick contemporary country formula and attempting to deepen their musicality with layered harmonies and subtly structured songs. Although the results don't always work—several of the songs are simply unmemorable—its best moments demonstrate that BlackHawk is more talented and diverse than their previous two albums would suggest. *—Thom Owens*

The Sky's the Limit / Sep. 29, 1998 / Arista ♦♦♦♦

BlackHawk, like many of their contemporary country peers, struggle to have it both ways. They want to have the hits, but they also want to keep country. At times, the scales have tipped toward the pop end, but with *The Sky's the Limit*, they move back toward country, coming up with a record that harks back to their organic debut. There is a difference, however. Here, they have more confidence, not only in their performances but in the way they merge their pop songwriting instincts with more authentic country instrumentation. It's a combination that works terrifically, enlivening even the weaker songs. Unfortunately, there are a few of those here, but that's part and parcel for a contemporary country album. What counts are the moments that work, and there enough of those—"There You Have It," "Think Again," "Nobody Knows What to Say"—to make it rank as one of their better efforts. *—Thom Owens*

● **Greatest Hits** / May 16, 2000 / Arista ♦♦♦♦

How appropriate for a greatest-hits album to begin with a song that was such a huge hit that it made the band a household name. In this case, *Goodbye Says It All*, BlackHawk's very first release, lands at the top spot. This *Greatest Hits* album plays like a career retrospective and tribute to co-founder, collaborator, and friend, Van Stephenson who not only fought but won a battle against melanoma and decided to leave the road in favor of spending time with his family. Fans will go nuts for all the oldies but goodies on this fine compilation: "I'm Not Strong Enough to Say No," "Every Once in a While," "Almost a Memory Now," and eight memorable others. *Greatest Hits* introduces three new songs, including the very last song on the album, "Ships of Heaven," written by Stephenson while he was facing his continually declining health. Those songs represent more than just new music; they represent the future of BlackHawk without Stephenson. And the future looks pretty bright. *—Maria Konicki Dinoia*

Spirit Dancer / Aug. 27, 2002 / Sony ♦♦♦

BlackHawk's fifth album comes following many fundamental changes for the group. First and foremost, co-founder Van Stephenson died of cancer, leaving Henry Paul and Dave Robbins to carry on. The two were faced with further challenges. After a promising and successful beginning, the trio, all songwriters, had taken to putting out albums largely consisting of songs written by Nashville professionals that sold less and less well, to the point that Arista Records dropped them. So, Paul and Robbins signed to Columbia and tried to take back their music. The result is their most personal album. The title track, not surprisingly, is a tribute to Stephenson, and it's one of several earnest and sincere efforts, including "Days of America," a chart single ten months in advance of the album's release that unintentionally touched on the spirit of the country in the wake of September 11, 2001, and "Brothers of the Southland," Paul's attempt to honor the dead among his old Southern rock colleagues in the Allman Brothers Band, the Marshall Tucker Band, and Lynyrd Skynyrd. (He himself used to be in the Outlaws, another Southern rock outfit.) In other words, this is not your typical country album. The question is whether, for all its good intentions, it's any better. The music is defined by Paul's distinctively whiny voice, which cuts through the country-pop arrangements, and that voice is best put to use in the more introspective songs, such as "Forgiveness" and "Leavin' the Land of the Broken Hearted," which reflect on personal and professional mistakes. They may not be any more deeply felt than the other deeply felt songs on the album, but they're more revealing and touching. This is an album BlackHawk probably had to make. It's a risk, but at this point in the band's career, one worth taking. *—William Ruhlmann*

The Blacks

Group / Alternative Country-Rock

The Blacks, a Chicago-based insurgent country band, were formed in 1994 by singer/guitarist Danny McDonough, a former member of psychedelic hard rockers Cornmother, who quit the latter group after discovering the music of Hank Williams, Tom Waits, and Louis Armstrong. Teaching himself basic drumming and trumpeting skills, he began writing songs on a four-track recorder; after several months, he met DePaul University symphonic music student and bassist Gina Black at a local concert, and days later they played together for the first time.

Within weeks Black dropped out of DePaul, and after McDonough adopted the surname Black as well, the couple began performing as the Black Family, making their live debut in late 1995. After going through a series of drummers, the group (now shortened to simply the Blacks) recruited James Emmenegger, becoming a four-piece with the addition of guitarist Nora O'Connor; upon playing hundreds of live dates across the Midwest, the group signed with the Bloodshot label, issuing its Eric "Roscoe" Ambel-produced debut, *Dolly Horrorshow*, in 1998. *Just Like Home* followed two years later. *—Jason Ankeny*

● **Dolly Horrorshow** / Sep. 22, 1998 / Bloodshot ♦♦♦♦

With a power chord and a plaintive croon, this fine disc is off and running. From the barroom harmonies of "Dolly" to a riveting interplay of lounge smoothness and punk rage on "Horrorshow," this band proves to be one of the more interesting on the "insurgent country" scene. Leaders and multi-instrumentalists Gina and Danny Black create a fine dynamic, backed by Nora O'Connor on guitar and organ and James Emmenegger on drums. The blissfully sinful cover of Bill Monroe's "I'll Meet You in Church Sunday Morning" is perfect for a beer-stained singalong. *—Tim Sheridan*

Just Like Home / Jan. 1, 2000 / Bloodshot ♦♦♦♦

The Blacks deal in what might be described as country-goth, a rather spooky off-shoot of the alt-country movement. Their second offering is filled with the same moody, ramshackle sprit that made their first album so rewarding. While there is a bit too much reliance on the bull-horn distortion effect on vocals, it's a solid effort overall. Danny Black's impassioned voice helps drive home tunes like "Head on a String" and the clever "Fake Out Jesus." The dull cover of Tom Waits' "Goin' Out West," however, has nothing on the original. *—Tim Sheridan*

The Blackwood Brothers

f. 1934

Group / Southern Gospel, Country Gospel, Traditional Gospel

The Blackwood Brothers sang gospel for over 60 years, and from the 1950s to the '70s, they were one of the most popular gospel groups in the U.S. One of their biggest fans was a young Elvis Presley, who auditioned—and was turned down—for the group in 1953. The quartet was formed in 1934 by brothers Roy (b. December 24, 1900, Fentress, MS; d. March 21, 1971), Doyle (b. August 22, 1911, Ackerman, MS), and James Blackwood (b. August 4, 1919, Ackerman, MS; d. February 3, 2002, Memphis, TN), along with Roy's 13-year-old son R.W. Blackwood (b. October 23, 1921, Ackerman, MS; d. June 30, 1954, Clanton, AL). The Blackwoods sang at churches around their base of Ackerman, MS, during the mid-'30s. By 1937, however, they began working a radio show in Kosciusko, MS. The quartet moved to WJDX in Jackson later that year, singing pop and country in addition to gospel. After two years in Jackson, they were popular enough to move to KWKH in Shreveport, LA, a regional superstation that broadcast over much of the South.

While working in Shreveport, the Blackwood Brothers were signed by V.O. Stamps, the largest Southern gospel publisher of the 1930s. The group worked for Stamps during the late '30s and early '40s, but broke up during World War II. When they re-formed in 1946—without the Stamps affiliation—Doyle Blackwood had been replaced by Don Smith. The Blackwoods began their own record company, and became so popular that Doyle soon returned to start another group, the Blackwood Gospel Quartet.

By 1950, Roy had retired and was replaced by Bill Lyles. The Blackwoods then moved to Memphis and signed a contract with RCA Victor. They began recording in 1952, and the increased exposure led to national recognition and a spot on Arthur Godfrey's TV show in 1954. Less than a month later, however, R.W. Blackwood and Bill Lyles were killed in a plane crash. The Blackwoods immediately disbanded and vowed to never perform again. Fortunately, they returned several years later, gradually adding J.D. Sumner (as a replacement for Lyles) plus Roy's son Cecil Blackwood (b. October 28, 1934, Ackerman, MS; d. November 13, 2000) and James' son Jimmy Blackwood (b. July 31, 1943, San Diego). The Blackwoods entered the LP era during the mid-'50s and eventually recorded many albums for RCA and Skylite throughout the 1950s and '60s. They won the first of their eight Grammy Awards for Best Gospel Performance in 1966, and James Blackwood won seven Dove Awards for Male Vocalist of the Year during the '70s. He was inducted into the Gospel Music Hall of Fame in 1974 and was known as "Mr. Gospel Singer of America" for years thereafter. *—John Bush*

The Best of the Blackwood Brothers Quartet / 1992 / RCA ♦♦♦

● **Gospel Classics Series** / Apr. 7, 1998 / RCA ♦♦♦♦♦

Gospel Classic Series is a budget-line series from RCA that was designed to showcase great gospel recordings from individual artists that had yet to appear on compact disc. The Blackwood Brothers were one of the most popular gospel groups of the '50s and '60s, but their recordings were out of print for years. Although it isn't a perfect collection, this budget-line collection is a good overview of their most popular recordings, featuring such songs as "The Old Rugged Cross Made the Difference," "Because He Lives," "Just a Closer Walk With Thee," "How Great Thou Art," "Precious Memories" and "Amazing Grace." It's a nice introduction to the group, even if it is a little brief. *—Stephen Thomas Erlewine*

★ **Rock-A-My-Soul** / Aug. 13, 2002 / Bear Family ♦♦♦♦♦

Nancy Blake (Nancy Short)

b. Independence, MO

Cello, Vocals, Composer / Neo-Traditional Folk, Progressive Bluegrass, Traditional Bluegrass

Folk musician Nancy Blake was born Nancy Short in Independence, MO. She took up cello at 12 and moved to Nashville, where she performed on the instrument with the Nashville Youth Symphony. In 1972, Nancy and her band, Natchez Trace, opened a show for virtuosic acoustic picker Norman Blake, who had performed with such luminaries as Bob Dylan and Johnny Cash. The performance led to a partnership, which in turn led to marriage. Eventually, Nancy moved on from cello to instruments such as the fiddle, acoustic guitar, bass, and accordion. In 1986, Nancy's first solo recording, *Grand Junction*, was released on the Rounder imprint. Nancy went on to accompany Norman on many Grammy-nominated releases throughout the 1990s, such as *Just Gimme Somethin' I'm Used To* (1992) and *Hobo's Last Ride* (1996). In 2001, she performed with her husband at the landmark *O Brother Where Art Thou* concert at New York's *Carnegie Hall*. *—Johnny Loftus*

● **Grand Junction** / 1986 / Rounder ✦✦✦✦✦

Just Gimme Somethin' I'm Used To / 1992 / Shanachie ✦✦✦

More pleasant parlor traditionalist tunes by Norman and Nancy Blake. Fine guitar from both, plus Norman's fiddle and Nancy's cello. *—Mark A. Humphrey*

Norman Blake

b. Mar. 10, 1938, Chattanooga, TN

Dobro, Fiddle, Guitar, Mandolin, Vocals, Slide Guitar / Neo-Traditional Folk, Bluegrass, Traditional Bluegrass, Traditional Folk, Progressive Bluegrass

Although he is proficient with a variety of stringed instruments, Norman Blake is famous for his acoustic guitar skills—he was one of the major bluegrass guitarists of the '70s. Blake came into view in the late '60s, when he began performing as a sideman with artists as diverse as June Carter and Bob Dylan. During the '70s, he began a solo career that quickly became one of the most popular and musically adventurous within bluegrass. He continued recording and performing—occasionally with his wife, Nancy—well into the '90s. Blake began playing music professionally when he was 16 years old, joining the Dixieland Drifters as a mandolinist in 1954; the group debuted on *Tennessee Barn Dance*, a radio show based in Knoxville. After two years, he left the band and became a member of the Lonesome Travelers, which was led by banjoist Bob Johnson. By the end of the '50s, the Lonesome Travelers had added a second banjoist, Walter Forbes, and had made two records for RCA. Although he joined Hylo Brown & the Timberliners in 1959, Blake continued to perform with Johnson. The following year, he also became a member of June Carter's touring band.

In 1961, Blake was drafted into the Army, where he was stationed in Panama. While he was in the service, he was a radio operator on the Panama Canal and he formed a band called the Kobbe Mountaineers. The band became a popular attraction and was voted the best band in the Caribbean Command. In 1962, Blake recorded *12 Shades of Bluegrass* with the Lonesome Travelers while he was on leave. He was discharged from the Army the following year and moved to Nashville. Once he was in Nashville, Blake joined Johnny Cash's band. That same year, he married Nancy Short and settled in Chattanooga, TN. For the next few years he played with Cash, both on recordings and concerts. In 1969, Bob Dylan hired Blake to play on his country-rock album *Nashville Skyline*, providing the guitarist a whole new audience. That audience expanded even further when he became Cash's main guitarist on the singer's television show. Cash's program featured a wide array of musical guests, who were often impressed with Blake's talents. Kris Kristofferson asked him to join his touring band and Norman did so, playing both guitar and dobro; he also played on several of Kristofferson's records. Blake also played on several of Joan Baez's records, including her hit version of "The Night They Drove Old Dixie Down."

Following his folk and country-rock experiments, Blake returned to his bluegrass roots in 1971 when he joined John Hartford's band, Aeroplane, which also featured fiddler Vassar Clements. Aeroplane fell apart quickly, but Blake stayed with Hartford for a year and a half. In 1972, Norman recorded his first solo album, *Back Home in Sulphur Springs*, which began a long relationship with Rounder Records. This arrangement lasted through Blake's 1990 album, *Norman Blake & Tony Rice 2*, a follow-up to an earlier collaboration with Tony Rice. Most of Blake's output in the '90s was released on the equally venerable Shanachie label, including 1999's *Be Ready Boys: Appalachia to Abilene*. *—Kurt Wolff*

Back Home in Sulphur Springs / 1972 / Rounder ✦✦✦✦✦

Norman Blake had been a prominent performer and studio guitarist for over a decade before this solo debut was recorded, and although he had largely made his name playing backup to bigger stars, this is the first of a long string of albums that confirmed Blake's reputation as a master guitarist and songwriter. Joined by dobroist Tut Taylor, who had played with Blake on John Hartford's *Aereo-Plain* earlier in the year, the two run through a delightful mix of old-time songs and Blake originals, many of which show the progressive characteristics that would lead the guitarist to form the Rising Fawn String Ensemble to play what was called "hillbilly baroque." Although he only got better over time, this record is among Blake's best, demonstrating his nearly incomparable virtuosity, easygoing style, and broad repertoire, highlighted by "Cattle in the Cane," "Crossing No. 9," and the lovely closer "Spanish Fandango," which according to the notes is the first song he ever learned to play. *—Jim Smith*

The Fields of November / 1974 / Flying Fish ✦✦✦✦✦

Blake's second album is a thoroughly relaxed affair that did much to establish the sound he would follow throughout the rest of his career, mixing wistful ballads with controlled instrumental material. He demonstrates his musical prowess by playing fiddle, mandolin, and dobro, as well as composing all of the album's songs. His soon-to-be wife, cellist Nancy Short, makes her debut here, as does second guitarist/fiddler Charlie Collins, the partner with whom Blake would record most of his great early instrumentals. Later albums proved that he was one of the most electrifying guitar-pickers of his time, but *Fields* showed that Blake's overall muse was a gentle one. *—Jim Smith*

Going Places / 1974 / Flying Fish ✦✦✦

Norman Blake/Tut Taylor/Sam Bush/Butch Robins/Vassar Clements/David Holland . . . / 1975 / Flying Fish ✦✦✦✦

Although this 1974 Nashville recording session might at first glance seem to fall be a bluegrass date, it straddles jazz, Western swing, and folk as well, with a fair degree of spontaneity throughout. Norman Blake is primarily heard on guitar, though he dabbles with a bit of mandocello as well, the rest of the cast includes jazz bassist Dave Holland, the superb (and underrated) Jethro Burns on mandolin, Sam Bush on mandolin and mandola, fiddler Vassar Clements, banjo player Butch Robins, and dobro player Tut Taylor, who also doubles on mandolin. "Sauerkraut 'n Solar Energy," a swinging blues that was evidently written on the spot, defies being pigeonholed into any one category of music. Blake's original "The Old Brown Case" showcases the leader's hot picking in a solo setting. Clements and Burns (on guitar) combine forces for a lively interpretation of Antonín Dvořák's "Going Home," and both the full band version of "Sweet Georgia Brown" and the violin and guitar duet of Duke Ellington's theme song, "Take the 'A' Train," blur the imaginary lines between jazz and bluegrass even further; after all, a good musician in either field should be a great improviser. Due to the demise of Flying Fish, a great independent label that seemed to specialize in producing sessions such as this one, this disc will be somewhat difficult to acquire. *—Ken Dryden*

Old & New / 1975 / Flying Fish ✦✦✦✦✦

Originally released in 1975, *Old & New* follows the same muse as its predecessor, mixing traditional material with Blake originals. All of the musicians from *Fields of November* are present, but overall the energy is higher, especially on the instrumentals "Miller's Reel" and "Aljimina." "Sweet Heaven" is one of Blake's best performances, and it became one of his career touchstones. [In 1992, Flying Fish coupled this album with *Fields of November* as a single-disc release.] *—Jim Smith*

☆ **Whiskey Before Breakfast** / 1976 / Rounder ✦✦✦✦✦

Blake's best album, and one of the finest bluegrass albums of the '70s. "Church St. Blues" and "Slow Train Through Georgia" are great originals that demonstrate Blake's natural ease with a sung ballad, while the fabulous medleys "Sleepy Eyed Joe/Indian Creek" and "Fiddler's Dram/Whiskey Before Breakfast" show off the graceful flatpicking that made him famous. All told, there have been many albums in the folk idiom featuring many a guitar virtuoso, but very few achieve such a mix of relaxed subtlety and eye-popping virtuosity, and *Whiskey Before Breakfast* will perhaps stand as the greatest achievement by this master picker. *—Jim Smith*

Norman Blake and Red Rector / 1976 / County ✦✦✦

Live at McCabe's / 1976 / Takoma ✦✦✦✦✦

Long cherished by Norman Blake's fans as one of the greatest flatpicking albums of all time, *Live at McCabe's* isn't as essential as some of the guitarist's studio records of the time (see *Whiskey Before Breakfast*), but there's a warm, ramshackle beauty about this concert that is every bit as charming. Originally released on Takoma in 1976, it was out of print for years before an overwhelming fan petition prompted a reissue of the album in 1999. The sound is marvelous and, as one would expect, there's a ton of fine flatpicking here, as well as a rare chance to hear Blake live and in his prime. Joined by then-wife Nancy on three cuts, Blake switches to fiddle for a few tunes, including the lovely "Border Widow." His rendition of "Nine Pound Hammer" is one of the best on record, and equally great is a loose arrangement of "Arkansas Traveler" that finds a number of other half melodies and improvisations darting in and out. Some of these tunes turned up on previous and later studio albums; some he would never record again. *—Jim Smith*

Blackberry Blossom / 1977 / Flying Fish ✦✦✦✦✦

Norman Blake had barely begun his solo career in 1977 when he recorded *Blackberry Blossom*. This album finds Blake's artistry already fully developed, with the material divided between traditional songs and instrumentals. All nine cuts feature Blake's nifty guitar and mandolin work, with occasional back up from Nancy Blake on cello. The album gets started with a Tin Pan Alley tune, "Are You From Dixie?," an upbeat song that plays off the motif of the lonely Southerner away from his homeland and longing for a friendly face. On the oddly titled "The Rights of Man Hornpipe" Blake is backed by Nancy Blake on cello, creating something akin to flatpicking baroque. When the cello is combined with the fiddle on "D Medley," the sound comes much closer to a medium-paced Appalachian jig. The original "Lonesome Jenny" fits comfortably with the album's traditional material, drawing a portrait of the empty life of a woman who has been left a widow. This seven-minute portrait is filled with fascinating chord changes and tender lyrics. All of the songs on *Blackberry Blossom* are delivered in Blake's straightforward manner, both down-to-earth and emotive. It is perhaps easy to take an artist as uncomplicated as Blake for granted: he never seems to be going out of his way to impress the listener with fancy guitar licks or vocal hysterics. Instead, he imbeds himself in tradition, offering honest interpretations and fresh originals that are respectful of their roots. In this way, his true artistry grows each time the listener places a disc like *Blackberry Blossom* in the CD player. To those familiar with Blake, this re-issue will be warmly welcomed; for the unfamiliar, *Blackberry Blossom* is a great place to get started. *—Ronnie Lankford Jr.*

Directions / 1978 / Takoma ✦✦✦✦

Rising Fawn String Ensemble / 1979 / Rounder ✦✦✦

Full Moon on the Farm / 1981 / Rounder ✦✦✦

Original Underground Music / 1982 / Rounder ✦✦✦✦

Nashville Blues / 1984 / Rounder ✦✦✦

Lighthouse on the Shore / 1985 / Rounder ✦✦✦

The Norman & Nancy Blake Compact Disc / 1986 / Rounder ✦✦✦✦✦
The Norman & Nancy Blake Compact Disc combines Norman's *Lighthouse on the Shore* and Nancy's *Grand Junction* on one 21-track compact disc, offering neophytes a good introduction the duo's distinctive style of acoustic country and bluegrass. —*Thom Owens*

Blake & Rice / 1987 / Rounder ✦✦✦✦
Like consummate musicians, for their first album together Norman Blake and Tony Rice largely ignored flash and speed in favor of songs and mood. There is some exceptional flatpicking here, but even the more manic passages are tempered by a softness that is striking, and perhaps even a little disappointing, in its modesty. Once the listener gets past the desire to hear hardcore chops, though, the album reveals its full beauty, especially in Blake's gorgeous "Last Train From Poor Valley" and Rice's cover of Gordon Lightfoot's "I'm Not Sayin'." Perky fiddle tune medleys and bluegrass standards provide some balance, but this is gentle listening throughout. —*Jim Smith*

Slow Train through Georgia / 1987 / Rounder ✦✦✦✦✦
Slow Train Through Georgia collects 22 tracks from Norman Blake's early '70s albums, making it an excellent retrospective of the beginning of his solo career. —*Thom Owens*

Natasha's Waltz / 1987 / Rounder ✦✦✦✦✦
Natasha's Waltz is a compilation of highlights from the albums Norman and Nancy Blake recorded for Rounder during the '80s, giving an excellent overview of one of the finest bluegrass and new acoustic duos of the era. —*Thom Owens*

Blind Dog / 1988 / Rounder ✦✦✦✦
Blind Dog is a fine summation of bluegrass guitarist's Norman Blake's career and aesthetics, a largely- instrumental collection of favorites from his own catalog as well as from his influences. The covers include songs by A.P. Carter and Woody Guthrie, while Blake dips into his own back pages to re-do fan-favorite "Billy Gray." The focus of the record, however, is Blake's playing; a tasteful, economical picker, he shadows the melodies to allow the songs to speak for themselves. —*Jason Ankeny*

Norman Blake & Tony Rice 2 / 1990 / Rounder ✦✦✦✦
Blake & Rice #2 is every bit as enjoyable as the guitarists' first duets albums, featuring an astonishing array of flatpicking and harmonies. —*Thom Owens*

Just Gimme Somethin' I'm Used To / 1992 / Shanachie ✦✦✦
Just Gimme Somethin' I'm Used To is another charming album by Norman and Nancy Blake, featuring an excellent selection of old-timey country and traditional folk like "Wabash Cannonball" and "Georgia Railroad." There's not much that separates *Just Gimme Somethin' I'm Used To* from the rest of the duo's catalog, yet it remains a thoroughly enjoyable listen. —*Stephen Thomas Erlewine*

The Fields of November/Old and New / 1992 / Flying Fish ✦✦✦✦✦
This compact disc combines two of Norman Blake's finest mid-'70s albums for Flying Fish Records, *The Fields of November* (1974) and *Old and New* (1975). —*Thom Owens*

While Passing Along This Way / 1994 / Shanachie ✦✦✦
Following his highly prolific relationship with Rounder Records, multi-instrumentalist Norman Blake found an equally congenial home for his music at Shanachie. The first fruits of this new partnership were four collaborative albums with his wife, Nancy, all of which earned the duo Grammy nominations for Best Traditional Folk Album. A pair of folk music faithfuls, Norman and Nancy Blake balance the traditional material they love with original compositions in the old-timey vein on *While Passing Along This Way*. The Blakes cover a wide spectrum of traditional styles and themes from "He's Passing This Way," a hymn that recalls the Stanley Brothers and "Sweet Freedom" with its echoes of the Carter Family, to the bluegrass-tinged "Sweet Heaven" and the fiddle showcase "Old Mother Flanagan." Nancy Blake's harmony work and acoustic guitar playing mesh expertly with her husband's. For the most part her voice remains well in the background, but it's plainly obvious, listening to material like "The Grave of Bonaparte" and "Old Stepstone," how much it is enriching this music. The couple's two guitars sound like one instrument on the graceful, fingerpicked instrumental medley "Bonaparte Crossing the Rhine/Going Down the Valley." Adept at a number of string instruments, Norman Blake sticks largely to guitar, though he's also in fine form on fiddle, dobro, and mandolin. These are expert musicians who, through their loyalty to this rich tradition, have done a great deal to keep its spirit alive. —*Nathan Bush*

The Hobo's Last Ride / Aug. 20, 1996 / Shanachie ✦✦✦✦✦
This fine collection of tunes proves once again that no one can breathe life into a traditional number like the Blakes. Besides masterfully handling just about anything with strings, Norman and Nancy Blake's weathered vocals blend beautifully and are perfectly set in these obscure chestnuts. For a real wake-up call, listen to the chilling "Starving to Death on the Government Claim," a cry for help from the little guy. This disc is proof that some things never change, especially good songs. —*Tim Sheridan*

Chattanooga Sugar Babe / Jan. 20, 1998 / Shanachie ✦✦✦
Few musicians can breathe life into traditional tunes with the authenticity of Norman Blake, and even fewer can pen original songs that have the same timeless qualities as songs written 100 years ago. This is another fine collection by the master of American song. Indeed, Blake exudes an element of pure Americanism that spares us overt nationalism. And he's one hell of a picker, too. —*Tim Sheridan*

Be Ready Boys: Appalachia to Abilene / Jun. 22, 1999 / Shanachie ✦✦✦✦
Bringing together the musical traditions of the Appalachian Mountains and Texas, Norman Blake and Rich O'Brien convened in Denver, CO, in July of 1998 to collaborate on a beautiful recreation of traditional instrumentals and early country forms. A very loose and impromptu feel pervades the 16 tracks, as Blake provides guitar, six-string

banjo, mandolin, fiddle, and viola, with O'Brien adding guitar on both combining for classic country harmonies on tracks like "When It's Lamplighting Time in the Valley," A.P. Carter's "Homestead on the Farm," and the spiritual "Heavenly Sunlight." As is to be expected, the instrumentals are outstanding, incorporating rags, waltzes, and even Spanish elements. O'Brien's own "Grandpa's Barn" is guaranteed to be a tearjerker for anyone with rural roots. —*Matt Fink*

Far Away, Down on a Georgia Farm / Nov. 16, 1999 / Shanachie ✦✦✦
If you want to hear fingerpicked acoustic guitar played with delicacy and precision matched with a straight-ahead vocal delivery, then just start stacking up a pile of recordings by Norman Blake. The back cover of this new one quotes the *Oxford American* as saying, "Norman Blake is one of the most nuanced and quietly influential acoustic guitarists in this whole great land," and you're inclined to agree by the time he's finished the opening track. His playing—even when flailing on a six-string banjo, like he does on the title track—always displays a stateliness and gentility missing in most instrumentalists mining the same turf; it's ornate, yet drills to the heart of the song every time. Not that Blake is one to toot his own horn. Instead, in a move that spells out "let the music do the talking," there's not a smidgen of liner note hype on *Far Away, Down on a Georgia Farm*. There's no typewriter razzmatazz telling you some tortured artist story about how Blake holed up in a cave for two years to produce this little gem. Nope, just a printout of the lyrics to the songs—most of them penned by Blake—and a short list of what type of guitars he used on this session for the pegheads in the crowd who still cling to the belief that what you play is as important as how you play it. Although the guy plays old-time vintage acoustic guitars, mandolin, and dobros to die for, he could probably pick your cousin's 100-dollar cheapie and sound like God on it, he's *that* good. This is finger-style guitar music at its apex, music of substance and form. What makes *Far Away* stand out as a fine work is the wealth of original tunes aboard, arguably the strongest material on the album. There's a bone-chilling line in "Whiskey Deaf and Whiskey Blind" that goes, "Can't stand the government/can't stand the law/can't stand the dark days/a' comin' on us all," that sounds more like a prophecy of Y2K doom than a genteel folk ballad about the wickedness of the demon alcohol. Yet for all the surrealism, there's also a refreshing dosage of honesty running straight through all of Blake's work that ties all of these performances together beautifully, from the traditional instrumentals to Blake's heartfelt originals. This is music that works in a variety of listening settings, and let's face it, CDs like that are worth their weight in gold. Norman Blake shines like gold on this one. —*Cub Koda*

Flower From the Fields of Alabama / Jun. 12, 2001 / Shanachie ✦✦✦
While Norman Blake is far from a household name, the artists he has backed on record certainly are. As a guest musician, Blake has played behind legendary figures like Kris Kristofferson, Johnny Cash, and Bob Dylan. As the 20th century was drawing to a close however, Blake was still largely unrecognized beyond the confines of folk circles. Then Joel and Ethan Coen paid tribute to the founding fathers of Americana on the soundtrack to their 2000 film, *O Brother, Where Art Thou?* There, Blake's readings of "You Are My Sunshine" and "Man of Constant Sorrow" (instrumental), rested comfortably amongst contributions from folk's old and new guard. Though the film and its soundtrack drew near-universal acclaim from critics and moviegoers alike, on the evidence of *Flower From the Fields of Alabama*, little had changed in the heart and mind of Norman Blake. This is a fact longtime folk fans will no doubt find refreshing, betraying an "if it isn't broken …" philosophy that had served him well over a 28-year recording career. The lion's share of the material on *Flower* is drawn from the vast pool of traditional American material that Blake grew up with as a young mandolin player in Chattanooga, TN. As always, excellent musicianship is the focus with most of the tracks featuring stunning duets between Blake and guitarist Bill Chuckrow. Though Blake has always been praised more for his picking skills than his limited but steady tenor, he's particularly expressive on readings of "Sitting on Top of the World" and "Eastbound Freight Train." With *Flower*, Blake proves once again that, though fads may change, the quality of these songs remains the same. —*Nathan Bush*

Meeting on Southern Soil / Feb. 12, 2002 / Red House ✦✦✦✦
Neither Norman Blake nor Peter Ostroushko is well-known to the general public, but both are towering giants of American music, and this duet album plays to the strengths of both—the exquisite taste, brilliant playing, and choice of material that plays to their combined strengths. *Meeting on Southern Soil* really is a tour below the Mason-Dixon line. And so they offer their take on the venerable ballad "Oh, Death," the sentimental "I Cannot Call Her Mother," and many other traditional songs and instrumental pieces, as well as originals that fit both the tone and the spirit, including the wonderful "President Richard Milhous Nixon's Hornpipe," which actually brings in the only other performer on the disc, Nancy Blake, on cello. The pair draws from many sources for their older material—78s, books, even the oral tradition—keeping alive a style that's existed for many years, but in a refined way, thanks to the quality of performance. Albums like this renew the roots of American music, bringing new blood (tunes and songs) into what is really a flowing river of history. To hear these two together is a sheer joy and a triumph of musical skill and love. —*Chris Nickson*

★ **Old Ties** / Jun. 4, 2002 / Rounder ✦✦✦✦✦
Norman Blake will never be known as a revolutionary. His starkly honest guitar picking and gently lulling voice have sounded almost exactly the same for the 30-some years that the Rounder release *Old Ties* encompasses. Often performing solo, occasionally accompanied by his wife, Nancy, and any of a number of bluegrass and neo-traditional folk musicians (Tut Taylor, Charlie Collins, Doc Watson), Blake's summery, porch-swing ballads and blues are perfectly performed and humbly executed. Working with the traditional themes of old-timey folk music, Blake re-creates the earthy feel of a timeworn classic the

first time a song emerges from his guitar, and his unpretentious, reverent style delivers the music in an intimate environment. The compilation sticks to his more traditional-sounding compositions and interpretations, making for a wonderful afternoon listen and the perfect introduction to Blake's uniquely faithful style. Although his musical offerings may never be seen as revolutionary, his unwillingness to change to a more contemporary mode of folk music may be a kind of revolution... if anyone wanted to argue about it. Luckily, with music this pure, no one does. *—Zac Johnson*

Tommy Blake (Thomas Givens)

b. Shreveport, LA, **d.** 1985

Vocals / Rockabilly

Rockabilly artist Tommy Blake, like so many before him, started his career as a straight-ahead country singer before making the switch to the big beat. Born and raised in Shreveport, LA, Blake (born Thomas Givens) was already working in a teenage combo playing country music at station KTBS in the early '50s. By 1955, he had graduated to the Big D Jamboree in Dallas, TX, and Shreveport's junior version of the *Opry*, the *Louisiana Hayride*. A year later, he was a regular member of Johnny Horton's TV show out of Tyler, TX, and had cut his first record for the tiny Buddy label out of Marshall, TX. By 1957, Blake had put together his first great band, the Rhythm Rebels, featuring the red-hot guitar talents of one Carl Adams, who would later find fleeting fame with Dale Hawkins.

After a one-off session for RCA Victor, yielding a track called "All Night Long," Blake met Sam Phillips and re-recorded the same tune for Sun as "Lordy Hoody." By March of 1958, Blake was back at 706 Union recording more material, with another single seeing release and the rest finding its way into rockabilly history via reissues in the 1970s and '80s. Blake kept recording for smaller and smaller labels, pitching songs to anyone who had a ready advance, leaving "Story of a Broken Heart" for Johnny Cash to record after Blake had left Sun. He continued to write tunes, like "Cool Gator Shoes" with Carl Belew, and record a few stray 45s for Chancellor and Recco after his time with Sun, but Blake continued a downward spiral until he was killed by his wife in a domestic dispute during the Christmas holidays in 1985. *—Cub Koda*

Tommy Blake and Gene Wyatt / 1997 / White Label ♦♦♦

Not a collaborative effort, despite the plain-Jane title implications, but rather a compilation of rare sides by two of rockabilly's lesser lights who nonetheless made some great music. Tommy Blake is perhaps the better-known, at least to hardcore rockabilly fans, through the small handful of brilliant sides he cut for RCA Victor and Sun in the late '50s; he only clocks in with four sides of the 18 tracks collected here, but they make a nice addition to his meager discography. Gene Wyatt is as about as obscure as one or two collectible-record rockabillies get: almost nothing is known about his life, and his family has seemingly destroyed all records of his existence out of some personal pique. But his "Prettiest Girl at the Dance" is here, along with some demos cut in his native Shreveport with a very young James Burton on lead guitar. Here is the real motherlode of this compilation, as "Love Fever," "Campus Queen," and the Elvis-inspired "Boo Hoo" (a knockoff of "I'm Left, You're Right, She's Gone") feature Burton spraying licks all over the place. Another small cache of unissued demos with a different band also produces winners with "Rock and Roll Guitar," "Like Last Night," and the instrumental "One Love" leading the pack. If you can get past the sometimes-woeful audio deficiencies inherent in listening to beat-up 78 rpm acetates, there is some really extraordinary music to be enjoyed here. *—Cub Koda*

Clay Blaker

b. Houston, TX

Vocals, Guitar (Acoustic), Producer / Honky Tonk, New Traditionalist, Alternative Country

Clay Blaker is perhaps best known as the writer of half a dozen songs recorded by George Strait, but with his Texas Honky-Tonk Band he is also a popular regional entertainer and has released four albums of his own material. Blaker was born in Houston and raised in nearby Almeda, TX, to a father who loved big bands and a mother who listened to country music. Thus, his musical influences range from Glenn Miller to Ernest Tubb, and in a home movie, a five-year-old Blaker can be seen decked out in a green cowboy suit and singing Hank Williams' "Hey Good Lookin'" on a Roy Rogers model guitar.

In 1970 Blaker, an avid surfer, moved to Maui, but by 1973 music was becoming more important to him, and he moved to southern California to be near some friends who were in bands. Blaker started his own band in 1974 and played all along the California coast until December 1976, when he took the Texas Honky-Tonk Band to Houston for a week's vacation. They became so popular in Houston that they stayed. Blaker began recording songs in Houston studios and released his first album, *What a Way to Live*, in 1981. Also in that year George Strait, an old friend of Blaker's, hit the charts. Blaker and his band opened for Strait on many of his first tour dates, and Strait recorded Blaker's "The Only Thing That I Have Left" (later re-recorded by Tim McGraw) for his 1982 *Strait from the Heart* album.

Strait, along with LeAnn Rimes, Clay Walker, and Mark Chesnutt, recorded many more of Blaker's songs through the years, while Blaker remained a relatively unknown local performer. In 1998 he released his fourth album, *Rumor Town*. *Welcome to the Wasteland* followed three years later. *—Brian Wahlert*

What a Way to Live / 1981 / Texas Musik ♦♦♦

Sooner or Later / 1986 / Texas Musik ♦♦♦

Laying It All on the Line / 1993 / Neobilly ♦♦♦

● **Rumor Town** / 1998 / Neobilly ♦♦♦♦

On Clay Blaker's fourth album, he amply displays why he has been one of George Strait's favorite writers throughout Strait's recording career. Blaker wrote or co-wrote eight of the ten songs here, and nearly all of the songs meet the high standards of excellence and timelessness to which Strait has usually subscribed. Musically, Blaker's Texas Honky-Tonk Band is a crack country outfit that crosses stylistic boundaries. John Carroll plays a hot electric guitar on the title track, whose great groove and story of new love against the odds make it a likely hit for some savvy mainstream country artist. Tommy Detamore's crying steel guitar drives the traditional country ballad, Buck Owens' "Heart of Glass." And on the album's only throwaway song, the Tracy Byrd co-write "Livin' Every Day Like It's Saturday Night," the arrangement from producer and surfing enthusiast Blaker can only be described as surf country. So if Blaker has the songs and the band and the producer's ear to put it all together, what's missing? Unfortunately, it's the voice. Blaker's is smooth and pretty—it's pleasant enough, but lacks the distinctiveness of the singers who have had hits with his songs. Nowhere is this fault more apparent than on "I May Be a Fool." Mark Chesnutt's version of the song is dark and haunting, but try as he may to duplicate the arrangement, Blaker's voice just can't carry the song down to the depths of loneliness like Chesnutt's does. Nevertheless, the timeless quality of much of Blaker's music made this album a breath of fresh air in the tradition-deficient late-'90s country scene. *—Brian Wahlert*

Welcome to the Wasteland / Jan. 30, 2001 / Neobilly ♦♦♦

There is a theory that, whatever his or her vocal limitations, the songwriter brings a more effective interpretation to a song than any subsequent interpreter can. In country music, however, that theory can be turned on its head, since the formulaic nature of the songwriting often demands a distinctive interpreter to make the song sound like more than just a genre exercise. Clay Blaker is best known as a songwriter for George Strait among others, and his fifth album, *Welcome to the Wasteland*, makes it clear why his material benefits from the cover versions. Blaker has an adequate tenor voice, and his backup band plays his songs efficiently. But he and his co-writers, who contributed nine of the ten songs on the album, have a very strict sense of what constitutes a song. Their music is stylistically diverse, but generic. "Brown Eyes of Mexico" sounds like countless other Tex-Mex ballads, for example, and "Helpless Heart" like any other country-rock number. And like most country songwriters, Blaker seems to write by coming up with some simple metaphor ("This House Has No Doors") or fractured cliché ("A Day Late and a Darlin' Short") and constructing a lyric around it, so that his writing never achieves any real depth. What all this requires is a great singer, someone who can make you believe the reference in the opening line of "Helpless Heart" to "a wild one," for example, or a rough-edged vocalist like Joe Ely to put some grit in "Brown Eyes of Mexico." Blaker is not such a singer, and that means *Welcome to the Wasteland* is more likely to function as a well-realized publisher's demo than as an album unto itself. *—William Ruhlmann*

Ronee Blakley

b. Idaho

Songwriter, Vocals / Country-Rock, Singer/Songwriter

Ronee Blakley was a folky singer/songwriter who found critical acclaim with her self-titled 1972 debut. With the praise of such luminaries as Bob Dylan, Blakley was cast in the 1975 Robert Altman film *Nashville* as Barbara Jean, a victimized and ultimately doomed singer. While a follow-up LP that same year was generally strong, it went nowhere, and Blakley chose to concentrate on acting. She appeared in numerous films throughout the 1970s and '80s, including the original *Nightmare on Elm Street*. In 1985, she wrote, directed, and appeared in a psuedo docu-drama entitled *I Played It for You*. She was also briefly married to German filmmaker Wim Wenders. *—Johnny Loftus*

● **Ronee Blakley** / 1972 / Elektra ♦♦♦♦

A fine album by an often overlooked singer/songwriter, it was released three years before her appearance in Robert Altman's *Nashville*. All the validation one needs for her inclusion in the film, it's worth the effort to find.*—Jim Worbois*

Welcome / 1975 / Warner Bros. ♦♦♦

The songwriting on this album isn't as strong as on her self-titled album. Too bad, because the band fairly smokes. *—Jim Worbois*

Jack Blanchard & Misty Morgan

f. 1967, Florida

Group / Contemporary Country, Country-Pop

The country duo of songwriter/saxophonist/keyboardist Jack Blanchard and his wife, keyboardist Misty Morgan, placed 15 singles on the country charts between 1969-1975. The two were born (three years apart) in the same hospital in Buffalo, NY, and both moved to Ohio during childhood. But it wasn't until they both found work in the Florida club circuit that they finally met and fell in love. Misty was a piano player; Jack was scraping by as a musician and comedian. The two were married in 1967, and began writing and performing together soon after. Their first charting hit in 1969, "Big Black Bird," made its way into the Top 60. But it was 1970's "Tennessee Bird Walk" that would be their biggest and most memorable hit. The song hit the top of the country charts, did well on the pop charts, and even garnered a Grammy nomination.

The duo went on to release country-tinged, lighthearted singles like "Humphrey the Camel," "Fire Hydrant 79," and "The Legendary Chicken Fairy." Another Top 30 hit followed with "You've Got Your Troubles (I've Got Mine)." Jack and Misty moved to Mega in 1971 and scored such hits as "There Must Be More to Life (Than Growing Old)" and "The Legendary Chicken Fairy." In 1973, the two moved to Epic and had their last major hit, "Just One More Song," before moving on to subsequent record companies. Their career slowed in the 1980s and '90s, but Jack and Misty returned with a vengeance in the new millennium, establishing their own label to release such albums as *Jack and Misty Are Crazy!*, *Back From the Dead*, and *Masters of the Keyboards*. *—Johnny Loftus*

● **Birds of a Feather** / 1970 / Wayside ♦♦♦♦

Two Sides of Jack and Misty / 1972 / Mega ♦♦♦

The Blood Oranges

Group / Alternative Country-Rock, Alternative Country

An alternative country band with a strong bluegrass background, the Blood Oranges were fronted by Jim Ryan, a singer/songwriter who led the group on a custom-produced electric mandolin. Born in New York in 1957, Ryan was first introduced to traditional American bluegrass and folk as a child through the state university in his hometown of Binghamton, where a local country and blues organization sponsored shows highlighting the nation's musical roots. After spending his formative years attending bluegrass festivals, he began honing his own skills as a performer by playing with fiddlers and pickers of all ages and musical backgrounds.

Ryan formed the Blood Oranges in the late '80s with bassist/vocalist Cheri Knight, guitarist Mark Spencer, and drummer Ron Ward as a forum for fusing his love of traditional music along with his interest in rock & roll; while Ryan's twangy vocals and bluegrass background stood as the dominant elements of their sound, the Blood Oranges' experimental nature aligned their music more strongly with the Americana movement of the 1990s than with any stripe of straightforward country. In 1991, the band issued its debut album, *Corn River*, a collection of bluegrass originals combined with renditions of classics like "Dig a Hole" and "Shady Grove." Both 1992's *Lone Green Valley* and 1994's *The Crying Tree* continued to refine the quartet's distinctive sound. In 1995, Spencer left the group to tour with Lisa Loeb, and the Blood Oranges promptly disbanded; Knight continued as a solo performer, while Ryan and Spencer ultimately reunited in Wooden Leg. *—Jason Ankeny*

Corn River / 1990 / East Side Digital ♦♦♦♦♦

The Blood Oranges' debut offers both strong originals and well-chosen covers (including "Dig a Hole"), propelled by Jim Ryan's reedy twang and bassist Cheri Knight's impassioned backing vocals. *—Jason Ankeny*

Lone Green Valley / 1992 / East Side Digital ♦♦♦

In addition to a reprise of "Shady Grove" from their debut *Corn River*, this five-cut EP includes four original efforts, highlighted by the frenetic "Potters Field" and the mournful "All the Way Down." *—Jason Ankeny*

● **The Crying Tree** / 1994 / East Side Digital ♦♦♦♦♦

Before there was alt-country there were the Blood Oranges. Their three releases fell squarely in a genre that didn't even have a name yet; indeed, had it formed, they'd have been one of the leading names. Not only did they have a superb guitar player in Mark Spencer (check his jaw-droppingly good break on "Hell's Half Acre" if you need proof; they can't play that fast and cleanly outside of Nashville, can they?), but they had a wonderfully emotional writer and singer in Cheri Knight and Jimmy Ryan's mandolin, composing, and singing provided much of the country flavor. And with *The Crying Tree* they perhaps reached their zenith, firing on all cylinders with the slow crunch of the title track, the quiet desperation of "Shadow of You," and the loneliness of "This Old Town," which segues into the breakneck, guitar-driven "On the Run," with its breathless vocal and utterly wild guitar. They were never afraid to mix a bit of noise with their melody, with Spencer's solo edging out past the stratosphere in true guitar-hero fashion. Everything's helped by Eric Ambel's production, capturing lovely, raw harmonies and giving the band real musical freedom, as on "Hinges," which almost sounds like a Richard Thompson song gone below the Mason-Dixon line (ironic, given the fact the band was based in the Northeast). They had it all going and brought it all together in perfect fashion here. It's just a shame they were ahead of their time. *—Chris Nickson*

Blue Highway

Group / Progressive Bluegrass, Contemporary Bluegrass

The five experienced members of progressive bluegrass group Blue Highway have played in the bands of such notable artists as Alison Krauss & Union Station, Ricky Skaggs, Larry Sparks, and Doyle Lawson. Guitarist and vocalist Tim Stafford played on the Grammy-winning album *Every Time You Say Goodbye* by Alison Krauss & Union Station, while dobro player Rob Ickes earned one for his contribution to the various-artists project *The Great Dobro Sessions* and another for his playing on *I Know Who Holds Tomorrow*, the collaborative album project by Krauss and the Cox Family.

Other Blue Highway members include Shawn Lane on tenor vocals, mandolin, and fiddle; bassist, vocalist, and songwriter Wayne Taylor; and Jason Burleson on banjo, mandolin, and vocals. The Tennessee-based group has been nominated for four International Bluegrass Music Association Awards, including 1996 Album of the Year for its debut release, *It's a Long, Long Road*, with both the title track single and album staying at number one on the national bluegrass chart for five months. After 1996's *Wind to the West*, in 1998 Blue Highway issued *Midnight Storm*; the following year, the band's self-titled fourth album appeared. While most contemporary groups sail through musical peaks and valleys from album to album, Blue Highway continued to produce high quality material in the 00's with *Still Climbing Mountains* (2001) and *Wonderous Love* (2003). *—Jack Leaver*

It's a Long, Long Road / Jul. 4, 1995 / Blind Pig ♦♦♦♦

● **Wind to the West** / Jul. 1996 / Rebel ♦♦♦♦

Contemporary bluegrass at its best, this album contains masterful playing, inspired singing and memorable songwriting. Blue Highway turns in an affecting vocal and instrumental performance on guitarist Tim Stafford's haunting "The Rounder," and as well as ripping through a cover of Merle Haggard's "Huntsville," and showcasing their gospel side on a soul-stirring arrangement of the traditional "God Moves in a Windstorm." Shawn Lane's lonesome tenor is pleasing, as well as the harmony blend and the lead vocals of the rest of the band. Ace dobro player Rob Ickes—voted 1996 Dobro Player of the Year by the International Bluegrass Music Awards—shines throughout, rounding out this band's second effort and making it more than a worthwhile choice. *—Jack Leaver*

Midnight Storm / Jan. 27, 1998 / Rebel ♦♦♦

Blue Highway / Jul. 13, 1999 / Ceili Music ♦♦♦♦

This is Blue Highway's first album for the Ceili label and it's an auspicious piece of work. The group members are all reaching the peak of their musical powers, both in terms of their instrumental prowess and their vocal skill. Factor in the strong songwriting of Shawn Lane and Tim Stafford and it all adds up to one of the most polished acts in bluegrass. The album features not only fiery instrumental work, as in "Lonesome Hearted Blues," but also a wonderful a cappella, rhythmic gospel number, "I Am Near the Gate" (written by Lane), a couple of tunes that approximate country music rather well ("Lonely Old Town" and "That Could Be You"), an evocative folklike version of Stafford's "Clay and Ottie," and the Western-flavored bluegrass sound of "I Hung My Head," a song written by Sting. Dobro player Rob Ickes is the primary IBMA award winner in this group but, as this self-titled release indicates, Blue Highway is a versatile and creative outfit. This album clearly ups the ante, but there's reason to believe that Blue Highway will achieve results at this level for some time to come. *—Philip Van Vleck*

Still Climbing Mountains / Sep. 11, 2001 / Rounder ♦♦♦♦

Consistently turning in the best contemporary bluegrass performances on record, Blue Mountain continues their streak with *Still Climbing Mountains*. Vocalist Tim Stafford and the exceptional dobroist Rob Ickes are well-worth every IBMA award they've won, and the songs remain as strong as any the band has recorded before. An early highlight is the blistering instrumental "Monrobro," featuring some of the fastest dobro playing on record, and the rousing harmonies of "Danville Pike." Producer Jerry Douglas may have something to do with the dobro-centricity of the album, but the band is certainly playing to their strengths, and the help they get from Alison Krauss and legendary country drummer Kenny Malone on the spiritual "Seventh Angel" only makes their best qualities stronger. In a year of many terrific bluegrass releases, *Still Climbing Mountains* ranks among the best of them. *—Zac Johnson*

Wondrous Love / Jun. 24, 2003 / Rounder ♦♦♦♦

Contemporary bluegrass supergroup Blue Highway's gospel album *Wondrous Love* shines brightly with reverent harmonies and hard-earned precision. Expertly recorded and produced, each voice gets equal space and every instrument's strum is clean and warm, intimate and clear. Peppering their repertoire with a handful of a cappella spirituals, the band not only demonstrates their ability to harmonize like a choir, but when the music kicks back in after these vocals-only tracks it reminds the listener of Blue Highway's strong pickin' ability as well. Pure and honest, reverent and welcoming, bright and rollicking, clear and convicted, Blue Highway have continued their winning streak of terrific albums by picking a theme close to their hearts and making it available to everyone who will listen. Far beyond being just one of the best bluegrass-gospel albums of the year, *Wondrous Love* could easily stand on critics lists as one of the best albums of the year. *—Zac Johnson*

Blue Mountain

f. 1993, **db.** 2001

Group / Alternative Country-Rock

Blue Mountain is led by the husband and wife team of Cary Hudson and Laurie Stirratt; the roots rockers drew their name from a small town near their home base of Oxford, MS, where the bandmembers first began soaking up the country, blues, and rock influences that informed their distinctive sound. Blue Mountain was founded in 1993 by vocalist/guitarist Hudson and bassist Stirratt after their previous band, the Los Angeles-based, punk-inspired Hilltops (which also included Stirratt's twin brother, John, who would go on to join the band Wilco), dissolved following the release of a lone LP, *Big Black River*.

Returning to Mississippi, the couple hooked up with drummer Matt Brennan and began writing and performing live. After a self-titled album—recorded for about $1,000—issued on the band's own label, 4-Barrel Records, Blue Mountain was signed to indie label Roadrunner, and in 1995 released *Dog Days*, an album cut mostly live in the studio with new drummer Frank Coutch and producer Eric "Roscoe" Ambel. Reprising a number of songs from the first release, *Dog Days* ran the gamut of the group's influences, incorporating everything from country hoedowns to gentle acoustic numbers to a cover of the Skip James jam "Special Rider Blues." In 1997, Blue Mountain returned with the superb *Homegrown*; *Tales of a Traveler* followed two years later and *Roots* was issued in early 2001. Celebrating ten years together, the band released the live retrospective *Tonight It's Now or Never* in 2002. *—Jason Ankeny*

Blue Mountain / 1993 / 4-Barrel ♦♦♦

Blue Mountain's self-titled first album was released independently in 1993. Containing early versions of some songs that would appear on the subsequent *Dog Days*, it also contains otherwise unreleased tracks such as "Song Without a Name," "Westbound," and the sublime "In a Station." The raw blues concert favorite "Go 'Way Devil" is to be found here, as well as a more mandolin-heavy version of "Mountain Girl" than the one on *Dog Days*. Though the album is essential for any Blue Mountain fan, the group's later releases are of more consistent quality and reflect a more mature sound. *—Rob Caldwell*

● **Dog Days** / Jul. 25, 1995 / Roadrunner ♦♦♦♦

Once you hear the songs on *Dog Days*, you will want to hear them over and over and over again. Anyone who likes roots rock will feel right at home on Blue Moutain's turf. Great songs such as "Blue Canoe," "Soul Sister," "Eyes of a Child" and a cover of Skip James' "Special Rider Blues" sound familiar on first listening and soon grow to become good friends. This band has heart and is well worth your listening time. Enjoy! *—James Chrispell*

Homegrown / Jul. 15, 1997 / Roadrunner ♦♦♦♦

A worthy follow-up to the fine *Dog Days*, *Homegrown* continues Blue Mountain's exploration of the vast reserves of American roots music, resulting in an eclectic and gritty effort highlighted by Cary Hudson's increasingly strong songwriting skills. Shifting fluidly from blistering workouts like the opening "Bloody 98" and "Black Dog" to the lovely "Myrna Lee" and the catchy "Babe," *Homegrown* is informed by melodic smarts absent from so many contemporary alt-country records; Hudson's parched, Dylan-esque vocals remain wonderfully evocative as well, helping establish an authentic sense of time and place. *—Jason Ankeny*

Tales of a Traveler / Oct. 5, 1999 / Roadrunner ✦✦✦✦
This band's spirited roots rock take on country blues finally does justice to Cary Hudson's tough, well-crafted songs, recalling Neil Young and Crazy Horse back when they had a few things to prove. Only the cloying, sentimental "Comic Book Kid" rings false. Co-producer Dan Baird should be complimented for putting a burnished polish on this fine set of world weary (wary) tunes. *Brian Beatty*

Roots / Feb. 27, 2001 / Blue Mountain ✦✦✦
It seems every alt-country act must record an exploratory roots album at one point or another. Wilco and Dave Alvin have done it quite successfully. While the members of Blue Mountain grew up in the Mississippi hill country, the traditional music they explore on *Roots* is of Appalachian origin, not country blues. (Of course, Blue Mountain has never embraced the blues so why start now?) Choosing traditional public domain tunes of obvious Scots-Irish pedigree means we get plenty of songs about drinkin', sinnin', and murders of passion. Best of the set are the spare murder ballad "Rain and Snow" and the bittersweet "Banks of Lake Pontchartrain," the singer intoning pain and defeat with a knowing wistfullness. These sad but beautiful tunes are well balanced with uptempo versions of "That Nasty Swing" and "Little Stream of Whiskey." Haunting and timeless songs performed by one America's best alt-country groups. *—John Duffy*

Tonight It's Now or Never / Aug. 13, 2002 / DCN ✦✦✦✦
Serving as their last official release, their first live album, as well as something of a career retrospective, *Tonight It's Now or Never* is a fitting coda for one of alternative country's pioneering bands. With two discs and 21 tracks, the band delves into generous helpings of traditional folk tunes, cowpunk anthems, and bluesy, feedback-heavy rock with equal aplomb. Whether storming through the rollicking "Bloody 98" or dipping into the hypnotic English folk of "Young and Tender Ladies," Cary Hudson and Laurie Stirratt imbue songs of sadness and longing with the genuine spirit of the Appalachian folk and Delta blues from which they draw. Similarly, the Neil Young & Crazy Horse riff rock of "My Wicked, Wicked Ways" and the Celtic shades of "Rye Whiskey" show a band who was more than capable of moving past the commonplace strains of Americana, sounding as much like John Doe and Exene Cervenka on their harmonies as they do George Jones and Tammy Wynette. Sadly, the group would part ways shortly after the March 11, 2001, performance at Chicago's *Schuba's*, with both Hudson and Stirratt either releasing or readying solo albums within a year, making this an excellent document of one of the band's final moments. *—Matt Fink*

Blue Rodeo

f. 1985, Toronto, Canada
Group / Folk-Rock, Alternative Country-Rock, Americana, Heartland Rock
Blue Rodeo's style has drawn comparisons to a number of pop and rock icons, including the Beatles, Buffalo Springfield, the Band, and Bob Dylan. Formed in Toronto, Blue Rodeo is led by the songwriting team of vocalists/guitarists Jim Cuddy and Greg Keelor, and also features bassist Bazil Donovan, drummer Glenn Milchem, and keyboardist Bob Wiseman, who also plays harmonica and accordion. Their debut album, 1987's *Outskirts*, showcased the group's harmonies and musical interplay in a classic, rootsy folk-rock style. The punchier *Diamond Mine* (1989) covered more lyrical ground, bringing a bit of social commentary into Blue Rodeo's tales of loss and heartbreak, but the recording site (an empty hall in Toronto) dulled the songs' impact somewhat.

In 1990, Wiseman recorded his own solo album, *Bob Wiseman Sings Wrench Tuttle: In Her Dreams*. Producer Pete Anderson (Michelle Shocked, Dwight Yoakam) accentuated the group's vocal harmonies on the following year's *Casino*, which was well-received. Even higher praise was reserved for *Lost Together*, which synthesized the previous albums' stylistic changes into a cohesive whole. Wiseman left soon after the album's release, and was replaced on keyboards by James Gray. Also, Kim Deschamps joined the group on pedal steel. Blue Rodeo continued innovating throughout the '90s, releasing three more studio albums during the decade. *The Days in Between* followed in mid-2000. *—Steve Huey*

Outskirts / 1987 / Discovery ✦✦✦

Diamond Mine / 1989 / Discovery ✦✦✦

● **Casino** / 1991 / Discovery ✦✦✦✦

Lost Together / Aug. 4, 1992 / Discovery ✦✦✦✦
Lost Together is easily the best Blue Rodeo album to date. Hit the random button on the disc player and no matter where the laser touches down, you're assured a worthwhile listening experience. Blue Rodeo have built a fortress on the foundation of their previous three outings. The straight pop song "Flying" and ballads "Already Gone" and the epic title track offer added depth and maturity without rehashing previous successes. "Willin' Fool" and "Angels" tackle the progressive elements of Blue Rodeo's second album *Diamond Mine* and sharpen them to a manic, cutting edge. "Fools Like You" spits out a defense of native rights, Greg Keelor doing his best outraged-Bob Dylan impression. *—Roch Parisien*

Five Days in July / Sep. 27, 1994 / Discovery ✦✦✦✦
While the members of Blue Rodeo are stars in their native Canada, the roots-based band remains a brilliant, well-kept secret south of the border. Blue Rodeo's fifth album *Five Days in July* didn't heighten the band's profile, but it is another stellar entry into the sextet's catalog. The group continues to experiment with longer mood pieces like the sparse, gentle (save for some fierce, almost dissonant guitar from Greg Keelor) title track. Lead singer Jim Cuddy's warm vocals add to the compelling, emotional thrust of songs like the infectious "It Hasn't Hit Me Yet," the heartbreakingly honest "Bad Timing" (with some breathtaking harmonies between Cuddy and Keelor), and the plaintive "English Bay." Sarah McLachlan lends some vocals (and piano) to a couple tracks, including the solemn "Dark Angel." *Five Days in July* builds on Blue Rodeo's wonderful blend of melodic rock and Americana, while continuing to push out around the edges, and it does so in spectacular fashion. *—Tom Demalon*

Nowhere to Here / Sep. 5, 1995 / Discovery ✦✦✦
Blue Rodeo continues to experiment on this release. Opening and closing with expansive mood pieces, it takes a little bit of listening to get into this album. But sandwiched in between lies the real meat of this record. Bluesy ballads such as "Sky" and "Train" are balanced by upbeat poptunes like "What You Want" and "Better Off as We Are." The rockin' Beatles-esque "Get Through to You" shows them in top form. Every song here tends to evoke the pictoral majesty of the Canadian countryside while never sounding hokey. Once you let these tunes seep into your psyche, you'll find there isn't a bum tune in the bunch. Fantastic! *—James Chrispell*

Tremolo / Jul. 15, 1997 / Discovery ✦✦✦
The songs on *Tremolo* were deliberately sprung on Blue Rodeo on the day of recording, in order to ensure spontaneity—they spent a day working on each song, but not becoming overly familiar with any of it, in order to keep a fresh edge to their performances. And for the most part, it worked—the result is a technically polished album that retains a good deal of jam-type spontaneity and can rank up there with the very best work of Poco; indeed, this is sort of the studio analog to that group's most popular early-'70s album, *Deliverin'*, achieving similar results in the reverse manner. The sounds range from genial acoustic folk-rock ("Moon and Tree") to more reflective singer/songwriter-type pieces like "Falling Down Blue" to bluesier songs like "Fallen From Grace" and harder, heavier numbers like "No Miracle, No Dazzle," which could pass for Buffalo Springfield on a good day. Other numbers aren't quite as strong, and a few, like "Disappear," run a little too long for their own good; but then there are songs like "It Could Happen to You," with its dazzling wordplay and wonderfully fluid guitar work, which, in an alternate universe, would have been the greatest song ever written by Richie Furay. And "Brother Andre's Heart" bears a startling—but not unpleasant or excessive—resemblance to "Wild Horses" as the Flying Burrito Brothers did the song. One must conclude, a triumphant album. *—Bruce Eder*

Just Like a Vacation / 1999 / WEA ✦✦✦
Just Like a Vacation is a somewhat disappointing affair. Blue Rodeo have built their career on their live performances, and some fans might say that their albums (or CDs) have not done them justice. This live collection does not provide the evidence for such reputation. Recorded during their last Canadian tour, this CD (their first "live" release) is more or less a best-of compilation with extended solos and applause. The extended solos are quite long and drawn out, and songs that are brilliant in their original form sound boring here. Blue Rodeo might have been better served by either releasing a studio compilation CD or diving into their archive and releasing older live material which had more energy. Also, this is a two-CD set, which is far too long—a single CD of highlights might have been a better idea. Having said all that, there is some great music on this CD, as Blue Rodeo have written some incredible songs. They have always managed to blend country with rock to come up with their own unique sound. *Just Like a Vacation*, however, is not the best representation of their music. Fans will no doubt enjoy this, but others would be better served turning to their older, studio releases. *—Aaron Badgley*

The Days in Between / Jan. 11, 2000 / WEA ✦✦✦
On this, their eighth studio album, Blue Rodeo continues, quite frankly, pretty much as they always have. This is not necessarily a bad thing, as they produce fine country-rock music, but some new sounds would not be bad either. Principal writers Greg Keelor and Jim Cuddy both released solo efforts since the group's previous studio release (*Tremolo*, 1997), and while neither solo albums were classics, they did attempt new sounds, especially Keelor. However, they returned to their tried and trusted formula for *Days in Between*. The playing is tight and professional, and their remarkable harmonies and strong melodies are all present. The problem is that any one of these songs could be on any of their albums, and by the end of this CD all of the tracks begin to sound somewhat too familiar—no surprises. Fans will not be disappointed, and indeed enthusiasts of the country-rock genre will enjoy this release as well. Yet when all is said and done, one cannot help but feel somewhat disappointed, since the band fails to live up to the potential demonstrated on earlier releases. *—Aaron Badgley*

Greatest Hits / Oct. 2, 2001 / WEA/Warner Canada ✦✦✦✦
After 15 years as one of Canada's most lauded and consistently popular bands, Blue Rodeo offers their first hits package. A two-disc live album, *Just Like a Vacation*, released in 1999, covered a lot of ground but went a bit too deep for casual fans. Two extras are added, a far too sluggish version of the Bee Gee's "You Don't Know What It's Like" (borrowed via Gram Parsons' version, no doubt) and a demo fidelity recording of "After the Rain" from 1990's *Casino*. In between are the high points: the anthemic "Lost Together," their breakthrough single "Try," and "Side of the Road" from the group's psychedelic masterpiece *Nowhere to Here*. There are 12 hits in all, chosen from all but one of the group's eight albums (their studio effort *The Days in Between* is curiously bypassed), and they show that barring the sonically deficient *Diamond Mine*, Blue Rodeo's albums improve markedly with each passing effort. With the right attention, *Greatest Hits* could even turn on a few American listeners. Here's hoping. *—John Duffy*

Palace of Gold / Oct. 8, 2002 / Warner Bros. ✦✦✦
After having spent the last few years going over old ground on *Greatest Hits* and the double live *Just Like a Vacation*, as well as treading water with the less than stellar (but appropriately named) *Days in Between*, Blue Rodeo found its stride again with *Palace of Gold*. Having built their own studio, the bandmembers took the time to record in a comfortable, relaxed manner in which they could workshop tunes at their leisure. This newly found freedom allowed them to experiment with the addition of strings and horns on

several tracks, a move they had taken tentative stabs at before. On some tunes, the experiment clearly needed some fine tuning; the moody bossa nova of singer Jim Cuddy's "What a Surprise" borders on lounge, and the slight psychedelia of "Comet" seems half-baked, literally. But ballads like Greg Keelor's soulful "Find a Way to Say Goodbye" and the uptempo "Clearer View" both ring with added depth thanks to the new sonic touches. At their core, the songs on *Palace of Gold* (at least the best ones) remain close to the group's country-rock core; "Palace of Gold," "Glad to Be Alive," and "Tell Me Baby" all featuring heartfelt singing, jangling guitars, and soaring pedal steel. They could have dropped the gushing "Bulletproof" and still gained some ground as well. While many longtime fans insist the group reached its high watermark with the fruitful *Five Days in July* or *Lost Together* albums, Blue Rodeo's willingness to move forward while staying true to a good basic sound on *Palace of Gold* hinted that the group's best days may be yet to come. *—John Duffy*

Blue Rose

f. 1972, **db.** 1972

Group / Traditional Bluegrass

Blue Rose was a bluegrass combo that continued to break the traditional, male modes of the genre with its all-female lineup. The group was comprised of dobroist Sally Van Meter; renowned fiddler Laurie Lewis; banjoist Cathy Fink; the guitar and mandolin of Marcy Marxer; and bassist Molly Mason. Blue Rose's lone release was a self-titled affair on Sugar Hill in 1972; Fink and Lewis contributed lead vocals to the project, which included a swinging take on the obscure Hank Williams number "Blue Love." *—Johnny Loftus*

Blue Rose / 1972 / Sugar Hill ✦✦✦✦

The Blue Sky Boys

f. 1936, **db.** 1976

Group / Old-Timey, Traditional Country, Close Harmony

In the '30s, brother duets were common in country music: Among the better known were the Monroes, the Delmores, the Dixons, and the Carlisles. Bill and Earl Bolick, who in 1936 were ready to make their first recording, followed their producer's suggestion that they should be *different* by avoiding the word "brother." From "Blue Ridge Mountains, Land of the Sky" they took two words and named their act. But the Bolicks would have been different without the new name. Their intricate yet simple harmonies, their perfectly matching voices, and their unadorned mandolin and guitar instrumental backing set them off from the competition, so much so that two generations of subsequent duet singers echo them, some without realizing it. The Everly Brothers and the Louvin Brothers, themselves recognized as exceptional vocal duets, acknowledge the influence of the Blue Sky Boys. In the '50s, when tastes in country music changed drastically, the Blue Sky Boys retired from music rather than forsake their love of old mountain ballads for the uptempo popularity of electric instruments, drums, and honky tonk. In the '60s they were coaxed to come out of retirement, playing an occasional college date during the hootenanny phenomenon and recording albums in 1963, 1965, and 1976.

Born and raised in East Hickory, NC, Bill and Earl Bolick—the fourth and fifth of six children by deeply religious parents—learned how to harmonize by singing hymns and gospel songs at home. Bill learned how to play guitar and banjo from his neighbor, teaching Earl in the process. Earl had been given a mandolin, but he preferred guitar, so the two brothers switched instruments and began performing as a duo. Bill also performed with another local group, the Crazy Hickory Nuts, who happened to land a radio spot in Asheville, NC, in 1935. Shortly afterward, the siblings formed the JFG Coffee Boys with Homer Sherrill, a fiddler who played with the Crazy Hickory Nuts, and the new group also had a regular spot on Asheville radio. The group stayed in Asheville for a while, before moving to Atlanta to play as the Blue Ridge Hillbillies. While in Atlanta, the Bolicks split away from Sherrill and recorded several sides for RCA Victor, which were released under the name the Blue Sky Boys.

Over the next four years, the Blue Sky Boys made nearly 100 recordings for RCA that made them one of the more popular brother duos of the period. The Bolicks' career was sidetracked in 1941, when the brothers both entered the military to fight in World War II. Early in 1946, they were discharged, and they returned to playing radio in Atlanta and recording for RCA. Occasionally, the duo recorded with a fiddler, usually Sam "Curley" Parker, Joe Tyson, Leslie Keith, or Richard "Red" Hicks. Many of the records from 1946 and 1947, including "Kentucky," ranked among their biggest hits, but by the end of 1947 the duo was growing frustrated at the changing climates in country music and their record label as well. Honky tonk music was beginning to take over the country market, and the Bolicks refused to bend to fit into the new instrumental style. RCA asked them to add an electric guitar and try some newer songs, but they steadfastly refused and didn't even record until 1949. Over the course of the next year, they made a handful of recordings, performing their final sessions for RCA in the spring of 1950.

Given their frustrations about the changes in country music, the Blue Sky Boys disbanded and retired from music in 1951. For the next 11 years, they were silent, with Bill living and working for the post office in North Carolina and Earl making his residence in Georgia, working at Lockheed Aircraft. Starday Records released an album of Blue Sky Boys radio transcriptions in 1962. The following year, Bill convinced Earl to come out of retirement and record two albums, the secular *Together Again* and the inspirational *Precious Moments*, for Starday. Over the next few years, they played the occasional concert and appeared at folk festivals. In 1965, Capitol released a live album capturing the duo at the UCLA Folk Festival. By the end of the '60s, the Blue Sky Boys had retired again. In 1975, the Bolicks were coaxed out of retirement to record an album for Rounder and play several bluegrass and folk festivals. Shortly afterward, Bill retired and moved back to his hometown of East Hickory, while Earl settled in Tucker, GA.

No one in country music has done vocal duets better than the Blue Sky Boys. If your taste runs more to Conway and Loretta, George and Tammy, or Wynonna and Naomi, listen to the effortless, exquisite singing of Bill and Earl Bolick. See where it all started. *—David Vinopal*

★ **There'll Come a Time/Can't You Hear That Nightbird Crying?** / 1936 / Blue Tone ✦✦✦✦✦

The Blue Sky Boys' records are, to modern ears, among the most effortlessly listenable of the early country recordings because of the Bolick brothers' sublime close harmony singing. Their arresting style was cited as an influence by the Louvin Brothers and the Everly Brothers, and although they weren't as commercially successful, they certainly belong in the pantheon of '20s and '30s hillbilly stars with Jimmie Rodgers and the Carter Family. *There'll Come a Time/Can't You Hear That Nightbird Crying?* collects 21 sides from the duo's earliest Bluebird 78s, with track-by-track commentary by Bill Bolick in the liner notes. The sound quality is excellent, and the program seems to be a complete chronicle of the Blue Sky Boys' two 1936 recording sessions. The odd number of tracks is because one of their 78s from this period had a Dixon Brothers track on the flip side. *—Greg Adams*

☆ **Within the Circle/Who Wouldn't Be Lonely** / 1937 / Blue Tone ✦✦✦✦✦

Within the Circle/Who Wouldn't Be Lonely is the second and final volume in this reissue series devoted to the Blue Sky Boys' seminal Bluebird sides. The 24 tracks are drawn from two recording sessions held in 1937 and 1938, with a number of songs hailing from the repertoire of Karl and Harty. Some of the Blue Sky Boys' best-remembered performances are here, and the purity of their close harmony duet style is simply breathtaking. Despite the disc's enigmatic origins, the sound quality is very good, and the liner notes include extensive reminiscences by Bill Bolick, one of the two Blue Sky Boys. *—Greg Adams*

Presenting the Blue Sky Boys / 1966 / Capitol ✦✦✦✦✦

The original Capitol Records session that this re-release was drawn from was the result of a successful attempt to lure this brother duo back into performing in the early '60s, after Bill and Earl Bolick had been retired for almost a decade. They had lost none of their stunning ability to harmonize and create an instrumental sound with the impact of a full band out of basic guitar and mandolin. In fact, the improvements in recording technology make it even easier to hear all the small details, and thus to appreciate just how good the Blue Sky Boys were. This program has a fair share of perhaps overly familiar folk chestnuts, but the brothers could make an audience weep singing from a restaurant menu, so listeners shouldn't let the song list put them off. Kudos to the John Edwards Memorial Foundation, which created this reissue, and the National Endowment for the Arts, whose funding once supported a number of worthy projects such as this. It comes complete with a 31-page booklet that includes complete lyrics as well as music, and tons of information. *—Eugene Chadbourne*

Sunny Side of Life / 1973 / Rounder ✦✦✦

Most likely the best thing to ever come out of Hickory, NC, this brother duo comes across as somewhat reactionary in a quoted statement given prominent play on the back cover. (Certainly more prominent play than information on the recording sessions or who wrote the songs, which isn't supplied at all.) This gentle music, sometimes spirited, sometimes melancholy, is neither hillbilly music nor country & western, the brothers insist, not that most listeners would make the mistake of identifying it as such. It is more in the spirit of the American cowboy song or folk songs in general, although the high-end harmony and trinkling mandolin certainly sound like old-time music and may bring to mind the hillbilly label that is part of that particular sonic package. Yet brothers Bill and Earl Bolick remind listeners, "Hillbilly songs are usually the bum and hobo songs of the barroom and Honky Tonk nature and do not carry the quality and character that you will find in the songs handed down to us by our Pioneer Ancestors." (Their capitals.) A nice remastering job was done on these classic recordings from the old Bluebird archive. The singing is beautiful, truly ringing in the memory of an earlier, less-troubled age, unless one happened to be a bum or hobo hanging out in a honky tonk. *—Eugene Chadbourne*

The Blue Sky Boys / 1976 / Rounder ✦✦✦✦

The Blue Sky Boys—brothers Earl and Bill Bolick—sprang out of the same era of brother duets that produced the Monroe Brothers, the Delmore Brothers, and the Louvin Brothers, but their sound was entirely their own. Theirs was, in some respects, an earlier sound; it was also a quieter, slower, and more serious sound than that of their contemporaries. While the other brother acts veered toward and experimented with newer styles of bluegrass or electrified country boogie, the Bolicks held stubbornly to their roots; rather, in fact, than joining the trend toward electrification, they retired from recording altogether, performing only occasionally in the years following World War II. This 1976 recording, together with a 1964 live album and a couple other early-'60s offerings, represents their gradual return from retirement to the studio and shows the brothers in true form. The 14 guitar-mandolin duets here are mostly mournful songs of unrequited love, murder, and loss, all sung in close, aching harmonies; while the brothers sing often of violence or sorrow, though, they invest in their songs of tragedy the overarching peace of an unshaking religious faith, itself the subject of a few of the songs. More than most country duets, the Bolicks consciously created in their repertoire a sense of beauty, emotion, and tradition—you can sense in their performances not only their musical heritage, but also the spiritual traditions of the Holiness Church. While all the songs on this album had been popular among the Bolicks' earlier radio audiences, the brothers had never recorded any of them before, making them available here for the first time. The result is a compelling collection of rare and soulful recordings by this quietly enduring country act. *—Burgin Mathews*

The Blue Sky Boys (Bill and Earl Bolick) / 1976 / Bluebird ✦✦✦✦

The Bluebird recording catalog of this classic brother duo has been pillaged and scattered into the hinterlands as if it was a moonshine still left unguarded, and let's hope that brothers Earl and Bill Bolick will forgive such a sordid comparison. This out-of-print two-record set is one of the best collections that has been culled from this material. Unlike many "two-fers" of this marketing period, the display space is not wasted and there is an informative and well-written essay as well as full information on all the recording sessions. There are practically three dozen separate ditties here, some of them, such as "Paper Boy," expressing morbid sentimentality on a level that defies description. Musicianship is also at a high level. The smoothness with which the brothers negotiate both the sung harmony parts and picked instrumental passages on a gospel tune such as "When Heaven Comes Down" shows why they continue to be a favorite of many country and old-timey enthusiasts. —*Eugene Chadbourne*

In Concert, 1964 / 1989 / Rounder ✦✦✦✦✦
The Blue Sky Boys *In Concert, 1964* captures a reunion concert that Bill and Earl Bolick gave at the University of Illinois. The show was designed to be a mini-history of the group's career, since it was the first time the duo performed outside of the South. Consequently, the show features most of their biggest hits and functions as an excellent retrospective and introduction to their music, in addition to being a delight for dedicated fans, since the group sounds as good as they ever have. —*Stephen Thomas Erlewine*

Blue Sky Boys on Radio, Vol. 1 / Jan. 30, 1996 / Copper Creek ✦✦✦✦
Blue Sky Boys on Radio, Vol. 1 contains a selection of the group's radio transcriptions from 1946 and 1947, when the Blue Sky Boys were at the height of their career. Most of the group's most popular songs are included, as are some commercials, comedy routines, and instrumental solos, all of which help to effectively evoke the era. But the album is much more valuable than just a mere artifact—it also demonstrates what a tremendous duo Bill and Earl Bolick actually were, as well as how rich their music was. —*Thom Owens*

Blue Sky Boys on Radio, Vol. 2 / Jan. 30, 1996 / Copper Creek ✦✦✦
The *On Radio* series presents complete radio programs including themes, comedy skits and advertisements. The presentation is likely very similar to the Blue Sky Boys' live act of the time, and the song selections reflect a mix of popular and traditional tunes, some of which were never otherwise recorded by the duo. The songs are seldom over two minutes in length due to the time constraints of the programs. This volume collects transcriptions made between late 1946 and early 1947, including an abbreviated performance of "Turn Your Radio On." The *On Radio* series provides a valuable time capsule of rural radio of the early postwar era. —*Greg Adams*

Farm & Fun Time Favorites, Vol. 1 / Jan. 30, 1996 / Copper Creek ✦✦✦
Farm & Fun Time was the name of the radio program for which these transcriptions were recorded in 1949, and this series of CDs preserves the programs in their entirety. The songs are generally abbreviated versions, sometimes barely a minute in length, as necessitated by the format. Unlike the *On Radio* series, the *Farm & Fun Time* transcriptions include only brief spoken intros without comedy skits or advertisements. The songs covered range from parlor tunes and traditional folksongs to breakdowns and novelty material, all featuring the Blue Sky Boys' excellent close harmonies. —*Greg Adams*

Farm & Fun Time Favorites, Vol. 2 / Jan. 30, 1996 / Copper Creek ✦✦✦
This second volume of the *Farm & Funtime Favorites* series differs from the first in that Leslie Keith, one-time fiddler for the Stanley Brothers, appears on eight of the 22 tracks. The program, however, features a similar mix of sentimental songs, sacred and novelty material, including a nice version of "Nine Pound Hammer." Until the Blue Sky Boys' '40s recordings for Victor/Bluebird become available, the *Farm & Funtime* and *On Radio* series provide a fascinating glimpse of this duo at their peak. —*Greg Adams*

Blue Sky Boys on Radio, Vol. 3 / Nov. 4, 1997 / Copper Creek ✦✦✦✦

Blue Sky Boys on Radio, Vol. 4 / Nov. 4, 1997 / Copper Creek ✦✦✦
The fourth volume in a series of radio transcriptions, this installment collects 31 tracks from 1946-1947 including comedy skits, advertisements, themes and introductions. Excellent liner notes by the surviving Blue Sky Boy, Bill Bolick, comment track-by-track on the origins of the songs. A few fiddle breakdowns are included in addition to the usual vocal duos and trios on remakes of their RCA recordings as well as tunes they never otherwise recorded. The Blue Sky Boys were in their commercial prime around the time of these recordings and this disc is a must for fans of their influential close harmonies. —*Greg Adams*

The Bluegrass Album Band

f. 1980, **db.** 1989
Group / Bluegrass, Progressive Bluegrass
The Bluegrass Album Band was a bluegrass supergroup formed in 1980. Originally, the band featured J.D. Crowe, Doyle Lawson, Tony Rice, Bobby Hicks, and Todd Phillips. All of the members were known as progressive bluegrass musicians, but the Bluegrass Album Band was designed to showcase the traditional side of their talents. Their first album, *The Bluegrass Album*, was intended as a one-shot project, but it proved so successful that the group recorded four other albums over the course of the decade. Over the years, the lineup of the Bluegrass Album Band shifted, but Crowe, Lawson, and Rice remained its core members. The group's final album, *The Bluegrass Album, Vol. 5: Sweet Sunny South*, was released in 1989 and featured Crowe, Lawson, Rice, Vassar Clements, Jerry Douglas, and Mark Schatz. —*Stephen Thomas Erlewine*

The Bluegrass Album, Vol. 1 / 1981 / Rounder ✦✦✦✦✦

The Bluegrass Album, Vol. 2 / 1982 / Rounder ✦✦✦✦
The Bluegrass Album Band's second record reiterates all of the strong points of their debut—the group's interaction and harmonies are so natural, they're breathtaking. —*Thom Owens*

The Bluegrass Album, Vol. 3: California Connection / 1983 / Rounder ✦✦✦✦✦
On their third album, the Bluegrass Album Band adds some more country-rock to the mix, in the form of the Flying Burrito Brothers' "Devil In Disguise," but they largely stick to bluegrass classics from the likes of Bill Monroe and Flatt & Scruggs. Like the group's two previous albums, *California Connection* is filled with graceful, stunning musicianship that continues to astonish after several listens. —*Thom Owens*

The Bluegrass Compact Disc / 1986 / Rounder ✦✦✦✦✦

● **The Bluegrass Compact Disc, Vol. 2** / 1987 / Rounder ✦✦✦✦✦

The Bluegrass Album, Vol. 5: Sweet Sunny South / 1989 / Rounder ✦✦✦

Down the Road: Songs of Flatt and Scruggs / 2002 / Rounder ✦✦✦✦
The Bluegrass Album Band is a bluegrass supergroup consisting of A-list session players and established bandleaders who got together in the early '80s to record an album of straight-ahead bluegrass standards; the result was called simply *The Bluegrass Album*, and it was so popular that the same pickup group (in slightly changing configurations) made five more such recordings over the course of the next 15 years. This compilation focuses on their renditions of songs either written or made famous by the great Lester Flatt and Earl Scruggs, known to most Americans as the composers and performers of the theme from *The Beverly Hillbillies*. Led by the rich voice and powerful guitar playing of Tony Rice, the Bluegrass Album Band never sound less than completely tight and assured, and on timeless material like "The Old Home Town," "I'll Never Shed Another Tear," and the charming novelty tune "Head Over Heels," their affection for their illustrious musical forebears is both obvious and infectious. J.D. Crowe's banjo playing, which in other contexts can get a bit adventurous, here pays explicit tribute to the metronomic solidity of the classic Scruggs sound, and Bobby Hicks' fiddling is similarly old school. The Bluegrass Album Band's full-length albums are a better value for your money (this collection is offered at mid-price, but contains only a half-hour of music), but there's no denying the consistently high quality of the music on this one. —*Rick Anderson*

Lonesome Moonlight: Songs of Bill Monroe / 2002 / Rounder ✦✦✦✦✦
The all-star pickup group who calls themselves the Bluegrass Album Band (after their first album, which was called simply *The Bluegrass Album* and on which the band performed without a name) has hardly recorded a weak song in the course of their strangely ad hoc existence, but the group never sounds better than when they are playing the music of Bill Monroe, the man who is generally credited with having invented the genre and who coined the term "high lonesome" to describe his own vocal style and the essential character of his compositions. *Lonesome Moonlight* is culled from the Bluegrass Album Band's six albums and finds the group in a super-charged mode on almost every track, from the powerfully mournful "On My Way Back to the Old Home" that opens the program to the incongruously jaunty "River of Death" that closes it. In between are joyful and virtuosic renditions of the classic Monroe instrumentals "Cheyenne" and "Brown County Breakdown," as well as one of the tightest performances of "Molly and Tenbrooks" ever recorded. As always, Tony Rice's lead voice is a major highlight, but the presence of former Monroe sideman Vassar Clements on fiddle is another, and his twin fiddle work with Bobby Hicks on "Lonesome Moonlight Waltz" is brilliant. Highly recommended. —*Rick Anderson*

The Bluegrass Cardinals

f. 1974, Los Angeles, CA, **db.** 1997
Group / Bluegrass, Progressive Bluegrass, Traditional Bluegrass
The Bluegrass Cardinals came together in Los Angeles in 1974 when banjoist Don Parmley and mandolinist Randy Graham teamed up with Parmley's 15-year-old son, David, to form what was to become a successful bluegrass trio who wielded considerable influence from the latter half of the '70s through the early '90s. Don Parmley and Randy Graham's partnership had preceded the official start of the band by seven years when they started a musical friendship after the demise of Parmley's previous group, the Hillmen (whose leader, Chris Hillman, found success as a member of the Byrds), and so it seemed natural to grow into a trio with the addition of the younger Parmley. In 1976, the three moved from southern California to Virginia and cut their self-titled debut album for Sierra Records, followed by their 1977 Rounder offering, *Welcome to Virginia*. These two albums quickly cemented the oft-described "Cardinal sound," which dealt mainly with the intricate harmonies centered around David Parmley's lead vocal, his dad's baritone, and Graham's high tenor.

Almost off the bat, the Bluegrass Cardinals shuffled through countless lineups and proved a springboard for many bluegrass musicians, including fiddler Dennis Fetchet, bassist Bill Bryson, and mandolinist Larry Stephenson. They recorded several albums in the late '70s and early '80s for the CMH label with these and a slew of other fine musicians as well as making several appearances on the *Grand Ole Opry* before settling with Sugar Hill Records for three albums between 1983-1986. In 1991, Don and David took a short hiatus to record *Parmley and McCoury—Families of Tradition* with Del McCoury and his two sons, Ronnie and Rob McCoury, and by 1992, David chose to leave the Cardinals and pursue his own solo career. He recorded three albums under his own name and then reunited with original Bluegrass Cardinal fiddler Randy Graham in 1995 to form the Continental Divide. The Bluegrass Cardinals continued on until 1997, when Don Parmley announced his retirement from the music business. In late 2002, CMH Productions released a collection put together by David Parmley titled *The Essential Bluegrass Cardinals*. —*Gregory McIntosh*

The Bluegrass Cardinals / 1976 / Briar ✦✦✦✦

Welcome to Virginia / 1977 / Rounder ✦✦✦✦
The Bluegrass Cardinals' second album is as fine as their first, featuring wonderful, empathetic playing and pure, joyous vocals, as well as a good batch of originals and covers. —*Thom Owens*

Livin' in the Good Old Days / 1978 / CMH ✦✦✦

Cardinal Soul / 1979 / CMH ✦✦✦

Sunday Mornin' Singin' / 1980 / CMH ✦✦✦

The Bluegrass Cardinals put a little bit of church in their down-home picking and country harmonies. *Sunday Mornin' Singin'* is the group's 1980 album, a classic in the genre. Led by the father and son duo of Don and David Parmley, the Bluegrass Cardinals define bluegrass-gospel music with impassioned renditions of preacher tunes like "Crossing of Jordan," "Shine Hallelujah Shine," and "Touch of God's Hand." And, though the production is a little slicker, many of the numbers evoke the feeling of the Coen Brothers' old-timey *O Brother, Where Art Thou?* But the Bluegrass Cardinals prove they are just as devoted to gospel as to bluegrass and country; for example, their version of "He Is Near" is done a cappella, purely with vocal harmonies. This 2003 re-release of the album is the definitive version, with seven extra tracks, and even if it's not the number-one choice for hardcore bluegrass collectors, listeners who appreciate both gospel and bluegrass will be in heaven. *—Charles Spano*

Live & On Stage / 1980 / CMH ✦✦✦✦✦

Where Rainbows Touch / 1982 / CMH ✦✦✦

● **Cardinal Class** / 1983 / Sugar Hill ✦✦✦✦✦

Home Is Where the Heart Is / 1984 / Sugar Hill ✦✦✦

The Shining Path / 1986 / Sugar Hill ✦✦✦✦

Essential Bluegrass Cardinals / Nov. 5, 2002 / CMH ✦✦✦✦✦

This collection does a valuable service in remembering one of the most underappreciated bluegrass outfits of the '70s and '80s. The unit made its mark as a trio, but the list of alumni who have spent time as part of that triad is formidable, including Bill Bryson, Randy Graham, Ernie Sykes, Norman Wright, Mike Hartgrove, Ronnie Simpkins, Bobby Clark, Dale Perry, Greg Luck, and Larry Stephenson. The Bluegrass Cardinals came out of the Los Angeles scene in the mid-'70s led by the evocative vocals of David Parmley (later of Continental Divide) who was only a teenager at the time but sounded like he had lived a few lifetimes. They soon headed east, cutting an album for Rounder in 1976 and following that with their CMH debut. Through consistent lineup changes, the group continued to release strong albums full of strong musicianship and extraordinary vocal work. The group's canon is well-represented here, from ballads such as "Blue Is the Color of Lonesome" (a Cardinals original penned by the Parmleys), "Sweet Hour of Prayer," and a heart-piercing take on Merle Haggard's "Don't Give Up on Me" to more uptempo tracks, such as "I've Had a Time" and "Knee Deep in Lovin' You." This is not a comprehensive collection, but the selection is excellent, culling Cardinals originals as well as bluegrass, country, and gospel standards. The top-notch vocalizing is worth the price of admission alone. *—Erik Hage*

Ginger Boatwright (Ginger Kay Hammond)

b. Sep. 21, 1944, Columbus, MS

Rhythm, Guitar, Vocals / Traditional Bluegrass

Singer and bluegrass performer Ginger Boatwright was born Ginger Kay Hammond in Columbus, MS, on September 21, 1944. As a child, Ginger sang bluegrass tunes with her father, Hap Hammond, and his Magic Circle Ramblers. She grew up studying piano, but switched to guitar while studying history and sociology at the University of Alabama-Birmingham. At a 1966 Grant Boatwright concert, the guitarist invited Ginger on-stage to play. That impromptu performance led to a creative partnership, which in turn led to marriage.

By 1969, a cancer diagnosis had forced Ginger to quit the university. She focused instead on music, and made her duo with husband Grant a trio with the addition of cousin Dale Whitcomb. Christening themselves Red, White & Blue (Grass), the trio released *Pickin' Up!* in 1974 and a self-titled effort that same year. The group found some success outside of normal bluegrass circles, and even garnered a Grammy nomination for its debut album. Meanwhile, Ginger was also signed to the GRC imprint as a solo act, and had a hit single there in 1972 with "The Lovin's Over." (That year she also purchased The Pickin' Parlour, a Nashville club and gathering place for musician types, which she owned until 1981.) While both Ginger and Red, White & Blue (Grass) were signed to Mercury throughout the latter part of the 1970s, neither found very much success with the label. In 1979 Red, White & Blue (Grass) dissolved, and Ginger and Grant Boatwright divorced.

Ginger's next project was the Bushwhackers, an all-female countrified bluegrass band comprised of banjoist Susie Monick, bassist April Barrows, and Ingrid Reese on fiddle and guitar. The Bushwhackers' one album was issued in 1980 on Laser Lady, and they supported the record with a series of successful college tours. After the Bushwhackers broke up in 1981, Ginger joined up with banjoist Doug Dillard's backing band, where she stayed until the mid-'90s, appearing on most of the band's releases for Flying Fish. Her solo career flourished as well; 1991's *Fertile Ground* featured contributions from Dillard and bluegrass master Sam Bush. Boatwright also released an interesting bluegrass-jazz hybrid LP in 1994 entitled *Sentimental Journey*. The album featured her old pal Monick on banjo, the fiddle of Vassar Clements, and clarinetist Woody Herman. She returned in 2000 with the traditional bluegrass release *Sipsey*, and continued to perform sporadically with the Doug Dillard Band. *—Johnny Loftus*

● **Fertile Ground** / 1991 / Flying Fish ✦✦✦✦

With the right marketing, Ginger Boatwright could be huge in the country market. She certainly has the talent to become as successful as Loretta Lynn, Barbara Mandrell, or Tammy Wynette, but instead of having the support of a big Nashville promotional team, Boatwright has concentrated on the traditional bluegrass market. With its mandolin, banjo, fiddles, and heavy bluegrass elements, *Fertile Ground* is characterized by its earthiness and a definite lack of slickness. But make no mistake: "Nashville in the Rain," "Where Does All the Love Go (When It's Gone)," "City Ties," and other Boatwright originals are country-pop gems. Had any of these songs been recorded by Tanya Tucker or Emmylou Harris and enjoyed the support of a major label, they could have easily been huge country hits. Although *Fertile Ground* received most of its support from bluegrass audiences, Boatwright is someone country fans shouldn't ignore. And this fine CD wouldn't be a bad starting point. *—Alex Henderson*

Sentimental Journey: The Bluegrass-Jazz Experience / 1994 / Laserlight ✦✦✦

Dock Boggs (Moran Lee Boggs)

b. Feb. 7, 1898, West Norton, VA, **d.** 1971

Vocals, Banjo / Old-Timey, Traditional Folk, Country Blues, Appalachian Folk, Folk Revival

Dock Boggs was just one of the primeval hillbillies to record during the '20s, forgotten for decades until the folk revival of the '60s revived his career at the twilight of his life. Still, his dozen recordings from 1927 to 1929 are monuments of folk music, comprised of fatalistic hills ballads and blues like "Danville Girl," "Pretty Polly," and "Country Blues." Born near Norton, VA, in 1898, Boggs was the youngest of ten children. (He gained his nickname at an early age, since he was named after the doctor who delivered him.) Boggs began working in the mines at the age of 12. In what remained of his spare time, he began playing banjo, picking the instrument in the style of blues guitar instead of the widespread clawhammer technique. Boggs began picking up songs from family members and the radio. He married in 1918 and began subcontracting on a mine until his wife's illness forced him to move back to her home. He worked in the dangerous moonshining business and made a little money playing social dances.

His big break finally came in 1927, when executives from the Brunswick label arrived in Norton to audition talent. He passed (beating out none other than A.P. Carter), and recorded eight sides in New York City for the label. Though they didn't quite flop, the records sold mostly around Boggs' hometown. He signed a booking agent, and recorded four more sides for W.E. Myer's local Lonesome Ace label. The coming of the Great Depression in late 1929 put a hold on Boggs' recording career, as countless labels dried up. He continued to perform around the region until the early '30s, however, when his wife forced him to give up his music and go back into the mines. Boggs worked until 1954, when mechanical innovations forced him out of a job.

Almost a decade later, in 1963, folklorist Mike Seeger located Boggs in Norton and convinced him to resume his career. Just weeks after their meeting, Boggs played the American Folk Festival in Asheville, NC. He began recording again, and released his first LP, *Legendary Singer & Banjo Player*, later that year on Smithsonian/Folkways. Two more LPs followed during the '60s, although, like his original recordings, they too were out of print not long after his death in 1971. The revival of interest in early folk music occasioned by a digital reissue of Harry Smith's *Anthology of American Folk Music* finally brought Boggs' music back to the shelves. In 1997, John Fahey's Revenant label released *Complete Early Recordings (1927-1929)*, and one year later *His Folkways Years (1963-1968)* appeared. *—John Bush*

☆ **The Legendary Dock Boggs** / 1965 / Folkways ✦✦✦✦✦

Listeners would obviously miss out on a great deal of enjoyment if confined to only one artist in the genre of Appalachian old-timey music. But if that had to be the case, this particular production would be in the running for the honors, as it hits home with just about every swing. First and most important, it fits the criterion of a brilliant documentation of an artist whose playing in front of the microphones was refined to a high degree, having had plenty of time to be seasoned by years of playing music. Mike Seeger recorded the tracks with all the love in his heart, coming up with the warm, appealing sound that is ultimately desired from any analog recording of acoustic instruments. When one digs deep into the 15 songs, all featuring the artist's voice and banjo, a wealth of valuable information seems to be waiting there. There is the matter of Boggs' playing style, an approach to banjo which is quite different than many other players. The details are technical, and would be of interest mostly to banjo players, but the more important dimension to this is the way in which the technical aspects of a style actually dictate the flow of the music while also disappearing into the background. The latter aspect would have to be an essential in order for performances of this emotional quality to emerge. Each track draws the listener in, the bassline being played on the banjo's lowest strings having an effect that goes well beyond the hypnotic. The words are delivered like the mist coming off the French Broad river, the words always clear and a fascinating aspect of this recording in their own right. These are all considered traditional pieces, the type of material of which there are almost endless variations within the state of North Carolina alone. In some ways, these songs all blend together into some kind of bubbling stew of detail, ranging from the inspiration of animals to the cataloging of morbid atrocities. A lyric that is part of old-timey songs such as "Darling Corey" and "Dig a Hole in the Meadow" shows up casually in one of Boggs' other songs, and another corpse is buried in the holler. Verve was smart to nab this as one of the Folkways releases it licensed during the '60s folk revival. Pressings on the former label are pretty darn yummy. *—Eugene Chadbourne*

★ **Country Blues: Complete Early Recordings (1927–1929)** / Oct. 21, 1997 / Revenant ✦✦✦✦✦

Released on John Fahey's Revenant label, this Dock Boggs collection includes all 12 of his 1927-1929 recordings, plus five alternate takes and four cuts by Bill and Hayes Shepherd, friends and fellow players of Boggs. Included with the set is a 64-page book with essays by Greil Marcus, among others, and this is undoubtedly the best Dock Boggs collection ever assembled. *—John Bush*

His Folkways Years (1963–1968) / Sep. 15, 1998 / Smithsonian Folkways ✦✦✦✦✦

After Boggs, the Appalachian singer-banjoist who had released a dozen sides in the late 1920s, was rediscovered by Mike Seeger in 1963, he did some recording for Folkways Records. This double-CD, 50-song set contains the material from three Boggs LPs for Folkways: *Legendary Singer & Banjo Player* (1963), *Vol. 2* (1965), and *Vol. 3* (1970). The unearthly qualities of his '20s recordings that caused critics such as Greil Marcus to get wet were not in such exotic force on these later efforts; Boggs had only recently started playing music again after a gap of about 30 years. He's in fairly good form on this extensive compilation, dominated by old folk and blues tunes (some traditional, some learned from mundane sources such as commercial records and a Banker's Life Insurance ad). His singing and banjo playing are the definition of "stark," an overused adjective when applied to traditional Appalachian music. He's much easier to take than even starker proponents such as Roscoe Holcomb, however, with vocals that are effectively plaintive and rough-hewn without sounding unduly pinched, although they sometimes crack and strain. His best tunes are the ones with a spooky undercurrent, like "Danville Girl," which shares the same melody as the famous standard "St. James Infirmary," and "Oh Death." The reissue has excellent, lengthy historical liner notes from Barry O'Connell, and fascinating recollections of Boggs' rediscovery by Mike Seeger. *—Richie Unterberger*

Noel Boggs

b. Nov. 14, 1917, Oklahoma City, OK, **d.** Oct. 1974

Guitar (Steel) / Traditional Country, Western Swing

One of the finest steel guitarists in country music's history, Noel Boggs incorporated jazz influences—from his friend Charlie Christian—into Western swing on his over 1,000 sideman credits. Born in Oklahoma City on November 14, 1917, he began playing guitar as a teenager; by the time he had graduated from high-school, he was playing on three different radio stations around Oklahoma City. Boggs toured with Hank Penny's Radio Cowboys during 1936-1937, but was back in Oklahoma by 1937. He played with Wiley & Gene and Jimmy Wakely during the late '30s and formed his own band in 1941.

By 1944, Boggs joined the king of Western swing bands, Bob Wills & the Texas Playboys. He replaced Leon McAuliffe in Wills' band and played for two years, appearing on many of the *Tiffany Transcriptions* and several Columbia sessions. Boggs left in 1946 to join another Western swing giant, Spade Cooley. He played with Cooley's Dance Band until 1954, but suffered a heart attack just one year later. He couldn't play for three months, but formed the Noel Boggs Quintet in 1956. The band recorded several albums for Repeat during the '60s, but a series of heart attacks later limited Boggs' energy to record and tour. He died in 1974. *—John Bush*

● **The Very Best of Noel Boggs** / Jul. 25, 2000 / Varese ✦✦✦✦

The only extant collection of Boggs' solo career on CD, *The Very Best of Noel Boggs* is made up of a dozen recordings by his quintet from 1958, augmented by four performances by his trio six years later, all recorded for Jimmy Wakely's Shasta Records. Boggs' own "Steelin' Home" takes the greatest advantage of the steel guitar as a pure instrument, with a slashing sound that isn't exploited often elsewhere here. The rest is engaging enough, showing off his steel guitar (usually in tandem with Ivan Ditmars' organ, and lead guitarist Neil Levang) carrying melodies of such familiar tunes as "Beer Barrel Polka," "Coquette," "September Song," "The Birth of the Blues," and "Tenderly." The latter is the prettiest track in this collection and a great showcase for Paul Smith's piano; all of it is entertaining, although in at least one instance, the waltz "Lover" by Richard Rodgers, the underlying composition is sort of lost in the rendition. The music, much of it obviously drawn from the highlights of Boggs' stage act, all has the feel of stripped down, light jazz rather than country music, showing off the direction in which Boggs turned after the early '50s. Juan Tizol's "Caravan" is probably the best track here for sheer virtuosity, a scintillating high-speed workout for the two guitars and organ. *—Bruce Eder*

Suzy Bogguss

b. Dec. 30, 1956, Aledo, IL

Vocals / Contemporary Country, New Traditionalist, Country-Pop

One of the most acclaimed female country singers of the late '80s and '90s, Suzy Bogguss was able to balance country tradition with a contemporary mainstream sensibility, thereby satisfying both audiences and critics. Bogguss was born in Aledo, IL, in 1956, and began singing in her church choir at age five. Encouraged by her parents, she learned piano and drums as a child, and took up guitar as a teenager. While studying art at Illinois State University, she performed in local coffeehouses and clubs, and after graduating in 1980, she hit the road, playing wherever she could find a gig around the Midwest, Northeast, and even parts of Canada. She moved to Nashville in 1985 and worked as a demo singer while playing in clubs by night; she later took a job singing at the Dollywood theme park and sold tapes of her own music, one of which got her signed to Liberty/Capitol when a label executive heard it.

Bogguss released her first singles in 1987, and her debut album, *Somewhere Between*, appeared the following year. It received hugely positive reviews for blending country's past and present, and featured covers of Patsy Montana's "I Want to Be a Cowboy's Sweetheart" and Merle Haggard's "Somewhere Between," and also produced a decent-sized hit in "Cross My Broken Heart." The 1990 follow-up, *Moment of Truth*, took Bogguss in a more polished direction, but failed to break her to a wider audience.That all changed with 1991's gold-selling *Aces*, which spun off a total of four hit singles: "Someday Soon," "Letting Go," "Outbound Plane," and the title track (the latter three all made the country Top Ten).

Bogguss was now a star, and her 1992 follow-up, *Voices in the Wind*—a more pop-oriented effort—brought the highest-charting hit of her career in the number-two cover of John Hiatt's "Drive South"; it also became her second straight gold album. *Somethin' Up My Sleeve* (1993) gave her two additional Top Five hits in "Just Like the Weather" and "Hey Cinderella." For her next outing, 1994's *Simpatico*, Bogguss took something of a left turn, cutting a charmingly low-key album of duets with guitar legend Chet Atkins; she also released a greatest-hits collection that year.

Bogguss took a bit of time off to start a family with her husband and songwriting partner, Doug Crider, and returned in 1996 with *Give Me Some Wheels*, which proved a commercial disappointment. The same was true of 1998's *Nobody Love, Nobody Gets Hurt*, and Bogguss subsequently parted ways with Capitol and signed on with the smaller Platinum label. Her label debut, *Suzy Bogguss* (aka *It's a Perfect Day*), failed to reverse her downward sales spiral. *—Steve Huey*

★ **Somewhere Between** / 1988 / Liberty ✦✦✦✦✦

A fabulous, truly surprising debut, this album firmly plants one foot in the past and the other in the Nashville mainstream. The best songs here come from country legends. Merle Haggard penned the powerhouse title cut "My Sweet Love Ain't Around" came from Hank Williams, and "I Want to Be a Cowboy's Sweetheart" was an old Patsy Montana tune. The new stuff was pretty danged good, too: "Cross My Heart," written by Verlon Thompson and Kye Fleming, was the album's highest-charting single. *—Brian Mansfield*

Moment of Truth / 1990 / Liberty ✦✦✦

Under the wing of producer and new label-head Jimmy Bowen, Bogguss relinquished her cowboy's sweetheart role and began recording more polished records that often burnished singer/songwriter material. This album didn't do so well, though: it produced only two weakly performing singles, "Under the Gun" and "All Things Made New Again." *—Brian Mansfield*

Aces / 1991 / Liberty ✦✦✦✦✦

Employing such A-listers as Vince Gill, Beth Nielsen Chapman, and Mark O'Connor helped make this a strong outing, but Suzy Bogguss' appealing girl-next-door approach, her choice to straddle the fence between contemporary and traditional C&W and her perfectly pitched voice are what helped this album be the catalyst for making her a household name among country music fans. Whether she's handling the parting of mother and daughter in "Letting Go," the sorrowful heartbreak of "Part of Me," or the spunky "Outbound Plane," she expresses such sincerity you never doubt an emotion. Additionally, not many mainstream artists have the nerve to take on a subject that doesn't involve boy-girl love. But Bogguss' choice in the compelling title track shows just how savvy she is. Concerning envy of success between friends, Cheryl Wheeler's "Aces" is smart and hits just the right nuances without ever being as cloying or manipulative as many adult contemporary singles are in their need to be touching. Immediately following that emotional twister is the album's second strongest cut, "Someday Soon." A twangy, yearning tune of a girl longing for a boy who loves "his damned old rodeo" as much as he loves her, Bogguss elicits youthful hope that hasn't leaned toward jaded frustration quite yet. Not many singers can make riding the rodeo sound like the most romantic thing in the world, but that's what makes Bogguss an artist and not just a vocalist. *—Bryan Buss*

Voices in the Wind / 1992 / Liberty ✦✦✦

This sounded like one of those white-bread pop albums folks occasionally try to pawn off as country—until you started listening to the lyrics. *Voices in the Wind* may have been bigger on string sections than twin fiddlers, but Bogguss' choice in covers remained just off-center enough to be exciting, with Cheryl Wheeler's "Don't Wanna" and Lowell George's "Heartache." She revived John Hiatt's "Drive South" for a hit. The more risky material—especially the bleary-eyed blues of "Eat at Joe's" and the troubled alcoholic haze of Bogguss' own "In the Day"—shows why the Country Music Association gave her its Horizon Award just before the release of this album. *—Brian Mansfield*

Somethin' Up My Sleeve / Sep. 13, 1993 / Liberty ✦✦✦

Something Up My Sleeve is one of Suzy Bogguss' finest and most consistent albums. Exercising her crystal-clear vocals in ways she hadn't heretofore, she touches the heart in the most earnest way, whether it's the simplicity of "Diamonds and Tears," the skewering of America in "Souvenirs," or the hopelessness of "Something Up My Sleeve." Always a step ahead of her peers, Bogguss also always has a firm foot embedded in her roots, and she has a knack for straddling both contemporary and classic country so that they mesh seamlessly. She employs some A-list female writers and vocalists on this album; Matraca Berg, Martina McBride, and Beth Nielsen Chapman all make contributions, showing how respected she is as an artist. With a keen eye on contemporary society ("Hey Cinderella") or an accusing "You Wouldn't Say That to a Stranger," Bogguss puts young upstarts to shame. *—Bryan Buss*

Greatest Hits / Mar. 8, 1994 / Liberty ✦✦✦✦

Capping off the first wave of her career, this compilation spotlights Suzy Bogguss' clear, emotive voice on adult contemporary-flavored ballads ("Letting Go"), plucky country ("Outbound Plane"), and even yodeling odes to the rodeo ("I Want to Be a Cowboy's Sweetheart"). Her strengths have always been her consummate vocals and strong material, and this album shows both off to their fullest extent. "Aces" covers the dynamics of a friendship taxed by success; "Drive South" is sexy and carefree; and only Bogguss could make lyrics like "he loves his damned old rodeo/as much as he loves me" swooningly romantic in "Someday Soon." But as much territory as this covers, letting every facet of her talent shine, this is a compilation of a talent in growth, only hinting at what she has. *—Bryan Buss*

Simpatico / Oct. 1994 / Liberty ✦✦✦

Simpatico is a laid-back, charming duet album with Chet Atkins. The duo covers a lot of ground, beginning with Jimmie Rogers' "In the Jailhouse Now," and running through Elton John's "Sorry Seems to Be the Hardest Word," and playing a couple of nice, understated originals. Although it isn't a strict country record—there are quite a bit of pop flourishes scattered throughout the record—it's a charmingly low-key listen. *—Stephen Thomas Erlewine*

Give Me Some Wheels / Jul. 23, 1996 / Liberty ✦✦✦

In the three years between the release of Suzy Bogguss' fourth studio album of new material, *Something Up My Sleeve*, and her fifth, *Give Me Some Wheels*, she released a greatest-hits album and a duet album with Chet Atkins (*Simpatico*); her record company, Liberty, was reconfigured into Capitol Nashville; and she took time out to start a family. None of those factors may be as important as the sheer passage of time for an artist who had achieved a moderate level of success in a new traditionalist vein and now faces a tough post-Garth country music environment defined by a new crop of female singers. *Give Me Some Wheels* is a sturdy album of well-performed, consistently written country songs. The title track, which Bogguss co-wrote with Matraca Berg and Gary Harrison, is a satisfying statement of purpose, and the album's second single, "No Way Out," is a pleasing uptempo love song. But neither became hits ("She Said, He Heard" would have made a better single choice), and the album was a commercial disappointment. If it had been released two years earlier, it probably would have done better, but coming back to a new climate in Nashville, Bogguss needed to make a bolder or more accomplished album than this to keep from losing ground. *—William Ruhlmann*

Nobody Love, Nobody Gets Hurt / Jun. 2, 1998 / Liberty ✦✦✦
Suzy Bogguss runs the gambit as far as the material she elected to use on this project is concerned. From great tunes by Cheryl Wheeler, Bobbie Cryner, and Julie Miller to run-of-the mill country-pop songs that elicit a response of little more than a yawn, Bogguss does almost nothing to excite her listening audience either way. With a few exceptions, her little-girl voice is ineffectual and mild-mannered. However, Bogguss does seem to come to life on a tune she co-wrote with Matraca Berg and husband Doug Crider called "Somebody to Love." She also exhibits a little fire on "Take Me Back," the Julie Miller tune that stands out because of its bluegrass charm. Assisted along the way by friends Patty Loveless, Trisha Yearwood, Alison Krauss, Kathy Mattea, Harry Stinson, and guitarman Dan Dugmore, this should have been a landmark recording for the likable singer who thrilled fans when she worked with cowboy bard Michael Martin Murphy and Nashville legend Chet Atkins. *—Jana Pendragon*

Suzy Bogguss / Aug. 24, 1999 / Platinum ✦✦✦
Award-winning singer Suzy Bogguss has been gifted with a truly beautiful voice, just right for country music—or any kind of ballad, really. On this 1999 self-titled album that pristine voice of hers shines through with touching songs that are good for both the heart and soul, like "Love Is Stronger," "An Empty Heart and a Harvest Moon," "Goodnight," and "Look What Love Has Done to Me." On this emotional recording, Bogguss combines her vocal and songwriting talents to offer country fans an album that is sure to go on their keeper shelf, probably next to others by this artist. She also brought in some pretty impressive help for this recording, such as her husband, songwriter and producer Doug Crider, singer T. Graham Brown (who does a duet with her), Carolyn Dawn Johnson and Alison Krauss (who add a little sweet backing harmonies), and many other top musicians. If you really love this album, be sure to check out a few others by singers such as Alison Krauss, Martina McBride, Mary-Chapin Carpenter, and a new rising star compared to the others, Cyndi Thomson. *—Charlotte Dillon*

● **20 Greatest Hits** / Sep. 17, 2002 / Capitol ✦✦✦✦✦
Arguably, Suzy Bogguss did more than anybody to change the role of the female vocalist during then 1990s. Certainly she racked her share of hits—which are chronicled without fault on this collection. But more than that, she was a singer who weathered the Nash Vegas storms with grace, took control of her own career and became a producer of her own recordings. She selected material rather than having Jimmy Bowen—her cohort in the producer's chair—select it for her. Bogguss broke all the rules regarding genre from Western Swing yodels (Patsy Montana's "I Wanna Be a Cowboy's Sweetheart"), to cowboy songs (Ian Tyson's "Someday Soon"), to modern Americana (John Hiatt's "Drive South" and Nanci Griffiths' "Outbound Plane"). And that's only the start, she also recorded the work of cutting edge Nashville songwriters such as Matraca Berg and Gary Harrison ("Diamonds and Tears" and "Eat at Joe's") as well as Kim Richey ("From Where I Stand") and even added her own songwriting to the country music canon ("One More For the Road" and "Far and Way" with Doug Crider). Almost nothing was outside her reach and her interpretation of Jimmie Rodgers classic "In The Jailhouse Now" offered further proof. It's one thing to record songs of a different stripe and to break down the barriers between genres, it's quite another to make hit records while doing so, which is exactly what Bogguss did with Capitol in 1990s. She and Pam Tillis made it possible for singers like Martina McBride, Shania Twain, Bobbie Cryner, Deana Carter and others to arrive and even eventually eclipse them—due to the fickle nature of what Nashville's radio geeks' (yes, geeks) dictates what the populace wants rather than what might actually be the case. These 20 cuts offer a vivid and extremely pleasurable look at a run that has succeeded in making Suzy Bogguss one of the rare ones—an artist in full control of her destiny. When she walked away to concentrate on her family, she did so on top; now that she's back, and this collection serves as a guidepost to wherever she's moved to now musically. This is '90s country at its very best and the only thing that might be finer than this collection is to possess the actual albums these songs came from for the hidden gems. *—Thom Jurek*

Eddie Bond

b. Jul. 1, 1933, Memphis, TN
Guitar, Vocals / Traditional Country, Rockabilly
Despite never becoming a major national figure, Eddie Bond has carved out a place as a rockabilly and country star, as well as a radio personality, for 50 years. A contemporary of Elvis Presley and a fixture in Memphis and on the *Louisiana Hayride* in the mid-'50s, Bond was one of the best singers of the period. He led the Stompers, one of the hottest bands, but he never broke out the way Elvis did. His records, whether rockabilly, country, or gospel, however, were among the best to come from Memphis from the mid-'50s through the 1960s, and helped Bond remain a much loved country/rockabilly performer into the new millennium.

Born Eddie James Bond in Memphis, he was originally drawn into music by the work of Ernest Tubb and Roy Acuff. By age eight, Bond had saved enough to buy his first guitar, and as a teenager he played at beer joints around Memphis. He drifted through various jobs after finishing school, including furniture factory worker and truck driver, before serving an 18-month hitch in the Navy. After returning to civilian life, he began putting together his band, the Stompers, whose membership at various times in the years 1952-1954 included Jody Chastain and Curtis Lee Anderson. By 1955, the group's mainstays included Reggie Young on lead guitar, John Hughey on the pedal steel, and Johnny Fine at the drums. Bond led the Stompers on tours across the South and Southwest, billed alongside Roy Orbison, among other future country and rock & roll stars. They failed in auditions for Sam Phillips at Sun and the Bihari brothers' Meteor label, and in 1955 he signed with tiny Ekko Records, which resulted in a pair of singles issued late in the year, "Double Duty Lovin'"/"Talking Off the Wall" and "Love Makes a Fool (Everyday)"/"Your Eyes." These were pleasant, well-played country numbers, but they didn't include the band, only Bond as singer. With Hank Garland on lead guitar, Jerry Byrd on steel guitar, and Marvin Hughes at the ivories, they were OK records and then some, but not representative of Bond's real sound—"Talking Off the Wall" was a rocker, with a solid beat and lots of tension in the lead and rhythm guitar parts, but it was the B-side to the milder "Double Duty Lovin'." In any case, neither record attracted any notice from the public or the musical world.

Bond and his band managed to get signed to Mercury Records in 1956, and this was where they came into their own. From their first Mercury session in February of 1956, Eddie Bond & the Stompers cooked, with a lean, hard rockabilly sound that rocked with the best of them. The band in those days featured Young, Hughey, and Fine, with Bond playing rhythm. The single "I Got a Woman"/"Rockin' Daddy" from that session is testimony to the excitement they could generate. That Mercury debut sold well in the spring of 1956, and they were getting lots of gigs and broadcast exposure at the time. Bond played the *Louisiana Hayride* alongside Elvis Presley, Johnny Cash, and Johnny Horton, and it was around this time that he started his own radio show, an activity that was to loom ever larger in his career. His second Mercury session produced still more rockabilly gold, including "Slip, Slip, Slippin' In" and "Flip, Flop Mama," and they sold respectably, if not spectacularly.

Bond didn't stay with rockabilly music, however, and his later Mercury sessions produced country sides, although "Love Love Love" rocks pretty well. His Mercury contract ended in 1957, and for his next sessions, Bond was back doing rockabilly again, followed by more country music and even a foray into gospel in the early '60s. Bond's biggest success in the years that followed came on radio, where his show achieved huge ratings; this, in turn, helped sustain his record sales, as he recorded or licensed various songs to different labels, mostly in a country vein.

Eddie Bond was never going to be another Elvis Presley—he wasn't going to be turned into a movie star as easily, or branch into other, heavily produced sounds, and he was too successful early on as a radio personality to abandon that activity. But he made a more than fair rival to Conway Twitty (whom he played with around 1955, when the latter was still known as Harold Jenkins), with a pleasing tenor voice, understated in its sweetness and dramatic nuance, and a good sense of how to deliver a song, whether ballad, rocker, or gospel number. He continued performing through the 1990s and into the new century. His broadcasting career was especially successful and assured him a wide country audience, while his classic rockabilly sides from the '50s helped make him a living legend among enthusiasts, especially in Europe. Five decades into performing, he remains true to his country and rockabilly roots. *—Bruce Eder*

Rockin' Daddy / 1993 / Bear Family ✦✦✦✦✦
Rockin' Daddy presents two discs of Eddie Bond's complete recordings from 1955 through 1962. The first disc includes Bond's ten classic rockabilly numbers surrounded by his early country sides, and makes a great extended album, capturing both sides of his work in the first flourish of his youth. But it's the second disc, which covers Bond's 1962-vintage recordings released by Sun, that is the surprise. This should be the less interesting and important disc, because he's slowed down as a maturing artist in his late twenties, and is doing an album's worth of gospel numbers—but the music is as exciting as the earlier stuff, in a different way. His performances of the religious songs ("Just a Closer Walk With Thee," "Will I Be Lost or Will I Be Saved," etc.) are surprisingly straightforward and non-melodramatic, making it all exceptionally appealing when compared with the overwhelming seriousness of most country religious songs of the era. He does the most driving (really hard-rocking) version of "I Saw the Light" that anyone has ever heard, one that gets the listener not only wanting to singalong but tap his foot as well. Equally important, the playing on these numbers is as fresh as his best stuff from the '50s, only a little slower, which is why his remake of "Rockin' Daddy" is pretty cool, if not the groundbreaking effort that the 1956 version was. There are also surprises in the instrumentation throughout—the late-'50s country stuff on disc one features some of the best, most understated saxophone you'll ever hear on a country session, and organist Jimmy Smith, playing on the religious stuff, manages to be both reverent *and* lively. Cool all the way through. *—Bruce Eder*

Johnny Bond (Cyrus Whitfield Bond)

b. Jun. 1, 1915, Enville, OK, **d.** Jun. 12, 1978, Burbank, CA
Guitar, Vocals / Traditional Country, Cowboy, Country-Pop, Bakersfield Sound
Johnny Bond had several successful facets to a career that lasted over 30 years. As a member of the Jimmy Wakely Trio and as a session musician, he was an important support musician in dozens of B-Westerns, working alongside Wakely, Tex Ritter, and Johnny Mack Brown. As a songwriter, he was responsible for several compositions that became country standards, including "Cimarron," "I Wonder Where You Are Tonight," "Conversation With a Gun," "Tomorrow Never Comes," and "I'll Step Aside," which became hits for everyone from Billy Vaughn & His Orchestra to Johnny Rodriguez. He also contributed mightily to the recorded music of Wakely, Ritter, and other country stars of the 1940s and 1950s. And his own recordings—which included work with such luminaries as Merle Travis—were popular from the 1940s onward, and included several hits, but it wasn't until the 1960s that he had the biggest record of his career, "Ten Little Bottles."

Cyrus Whitfield Bond was born in Enville, OK, on June 1, 1915, to a poor farming family. His first instrument was the trumpet, but as a boy he also learned to play the guitar and the ukulele, and by the time he was a teenager he was entertaining at local dances—his main inspiration was the playing of Jimmie Rodgers and Milton Brown and the Light Crust Doughboys. After graduating from high-school in 1933, he headed for Oklahoma City to try for a career on radio, first broadcasting under the name Cyrus Whitfield, and later as Johnny Whitfield, before he settled on Johnny Bond. In Oklahoma City he also hooked up with Jimmy Wakely and Scotty Harrell (later replaced by Dick Reinhart), with whom he formed a group, originally known as the Singing Cowboy Trio and later the Bell Boys, in acknowledgment of their radio sponsorship from Bell Clothing. Their repertoire in those days was influenced heavily by the work of Gene Autry and the Sons of the Pioneers, and featured many cowboy songs. They did their broadcasting on radio station WKY, and cut transcription discs at KVOO in Tulsa. By then, Bond was already writing songs of his own, and in 1938 he wrote his first classic, "Cimarron." Gene Autry saw their work when he was on tour late in the 1930s and indicated his interest in using them on his *Melody Ranch* radio show, should they ever make it out to California.

By 1939, they were brought out to Hollywood for an appearance, under the name of the Jimmy Wakely Trio, in *The Saga of Death Valley*, starring Roy Rogers and produced by Republic Pictures. This taste of movie work registered with Wakely and Bond—there was more film work being offered by Republic, and Autry's offer was difficult to ignore. In May of 1940, Wakely, Bond, Reinhart, and their families headed west in Wakely's Dodge. They immediately became regulars on *Melody Ranch*, and Bond continued to play on the show for 16 years, until it was canceled in 1956. They also made their second film appearance, in *The Tulsa Kid*, starring Don "Red" Barry, with the group credited as "Jimmy Wakely & His Rough Riders." The group later moved to Universal, making its debut there in *Pony Post* (1940), starring Johnny Mack Brown. And they played the usual concerts, ballrooms, and clubs throughout southern California.

Bond, Wakely, and Reinhart—along with Scotty Harrell, who came out to Hollywood a little later and was welcomed back into the fold—continued to work together in the early '40s in various configurations, although the Wakely Trio had more or less ceased to exist officially after 1941. Curiously, it was Bond—and not Wakely—who was the first member of the trio to get a recording contract of his own. Art Satherly of Columbia Records, who'd previously signed Gene Autry, Tex Ritter, Leadbelly, and a dozen other music legends to recording contracts, got Bond under contract in 1941, and his first recording sessions were held in August of that year. The highlight of those sessions was "Those Gone and Left Me Blues."

In April of 1942, he cut four songs, covers of the recent Carson Robison hits "1942 Turkey in the Straw," "Mussolini's Letter to Hitler," and "Hitler's Reply to Mussolini," in an attempt to give Columbia covers of the Robison hits, but the company decided not to release them. Bond also began getting his own songs published during this period, most notably "I Wonder Where You Are Tonight" and "Cimarron." In July of 1942, he cut another four songs, among them "I'm a Pris'ner of War" and "Der Fuhrer's Face," as well as the originals "You Let Me Down" and "Love Gone Cold," backed by a band that included Spade Cooley on the violin. The wartime recording bans imposed by the Musicians' Union, coupled with the shellac shortages of the era, interrupted Bond's career on record until June of 1945, when he cut three originals, "Heart and Soul," "Gotta Make Up for Lost Time," and "Sad, Sad and Blue." In addition to his appearances on the Autry show and other radio programs, and performances on behalf of the war effort, Bond recorded many radio transcription discs, and also worked in 38 films, either as a musical sidekick to the hero, in the case of Jimmy Wakely or Tex Ritter, or in the musical sequences built around non-singing heroes such as Johnny Mack Brown or Ray "Crash" Corrigan, and even showed up with his group in non-Westerns such as the comedy *Six Lessons from Madame La Zonga* (1941), starring Leon Errol and Lupe Velez. He made a rare appearance in a major film, as a supporting player in David O. Selznick's *Duel in the Sun*, during 1946, and his last movie appearance took place a year later in Jimmy Wakely's final Western, *Song of the Wasteland* (1947).

Meanwhile, Bond was also a member and leader of Tex Ritter's studio band, the Red River Valley Boys, and was playing on his records as well as those of other West Coast country stars. The end of his movie career in 1947 was more than made up for by his burgeoning success as a recording artist. Bond had three Top Five country hits that year, "So Round, So Firm, So Fully Packed" (which sold well, though not quite as well as the version by his friend Merle Travis), "Divorce Me C.O.D.," and "The Daughter of Jole Blon." The next year, he had a Top Ten hit with "Oklahoma Waltz," and in 1949 he hit the charts in a big way twice with "Till the End of the World" and "Tennessee Saturday Night." He was back in the Top Ten again in 1950 with "Love Song in 32 Bars," and in 1951 he hit again with "Sick, Sober and Sorry."

By the end of 1957, Bond had written 123 songs, several of which—"Cimarron," "I'll Step Aside," "Tomorrow Never Comes," and "I Wonder Where You Are Tonight"—were very heavily covered by numerous other artists. The most successful version of "I Wonder Where You Are Tonight" was the cover by Johnny Rodriguez, but it was also recorded by Bobby Bare, Roy Clark, Flatt & Scruggs, Jerry Lee Lewis, Bill Monroe, the Louvin Brothers, Hank Snow, Red Allen & the Kentuckians, and even Arthur Alexander. "Cimarron" was not only a country standard, with versions by the Sons of the Pioneers, Foy Willing, Bob Wills, and Jimmy Dean, and concert renditions by Johnny Cash and Chet Atkins, but it was also recorded by Les Paul and Mary Ford and as an instrumental by Harry James and Neal Hefti, with Billy Vaughn & His Orchestra doing the biggest-selling version of them all. "Tomorrow Never Knows" was a hit for Glen Campbell, but was also covered by Lynn Anderson, Elvis Presley, Little Jimmy Dickens, Loretta Lynn, the Statler Brothers, and Ernest Tubb. "Conversations With a Gun" was recorded by Tex Ritter and Marty Robbins, among others, and "I'll Step Aside" done by Hank Thompson, Ernest Tubb, and Marty Robbins.

Bond played with Autry on his tours during the 1940s and 1950s, and his place in the band was later taken by Johnny Western, a younger singer with a surprisingly similar rich baritone voice. Unlike a lot of country artists of his generation, he wasn't too threatened by the coming of rock & roll, and even tried—in some cases successfully—to adapt his sound to the new beat, which, he was the first to recognize, wasn't too far from country music. Additionally, much of Bond's music had a rollicking sense of humor that made it closer in spirit to some early rock & roll than many other country artists of the day. Despite his acceptance of changing tastes and trends in music, however, Columbia Records declined to renew Bond's contract when it was up in 1957, at it seemed as though his career on records might be at an end.

He spent a brief time on Autry's Republic Records label, for which he recorded "Hot Rod Lincoln," a crossover record that did well and later became a rock & roll standard. Then, in 1960, Bond was signed to the Starday label, beginning an 11-year relationship with the company. In 1964, he recorded a new version of "Ten Little Bottles," a song that he'd previously done twice, as far back as 1954—this proved to be the biggest hit of Bond's career, rising into the Top Three and making it to number one on some charts. Unfortunately, none of Bond's follow-up records, including the comical "Morning After," sold nearly as well.

Part of Bond's problem may have been that either he or Starday evidently decided to continue trying to hit with more drinking songs—the majority of his songs and albums during the middle and late '60s were dominated by such songs, making him seem like a one-note performer and songwriter. Not even the presence, albeit uncredited, of Tex Ritter on a song like "New Year's Day," recorded in 1965, could coax some major chart action out of the public. His contract with Starday ended in 1969, and Bond immediately signed to Capitol—where Ritter had been trying to get him a contract for more than 20 years—and Bond recorded a Delmore Brothers tribute album with his longtime friend Merle Travis. It didn't sell, however, and by the end of the year both Bond and Travis were gone from Capitol. He resigned to Starday and remained there only for another two years before leaving permanently in 1971. He continued making records for the Lamb & Lion label, and then moved over to his old friend Jimmy Wakely's Shasta label in 1974, where he did one session, backed by James Burton and Red Rhodes, re-recording some of his best-known records out of the past, including his own "Cimarron" and "I'll Step Aside," as well as covers of Woody Guthrie's "Oklahoma Hills" and a reprise of "Hot Rod Lincoln."

There has been only one collection of Johnny Bond's Columbia recordings, the 25-track mid-priced *Johnny Bond & His Red River Valley Boys* CD import released by the British ASV label in 2001. As for Columbia itself, the company had issued a Bond EP in 1958 with "Sick, Sober and Sorry" and "Ten Little Bottles," but didn't release a full-length LP on him until 1965, eight years after he left the label. That same year, Gene Autry decided to revive his *Radio Ranch* series on his own station, and Bond renewed his weekly broadcasts on that show, as a musician, singer, and script writer, for another five years, until it was canceled once again. Starday, by contrast, released 14 Bond albums between 1960 and 1971, which included various collections of hits and recent singles as well as concept LPs (most of them after 1963 built around drinking songs), the best of which was 1961's *That Wild, Wicked But Wonderful West*. Additionally, in 1969, he recorded one album, *Great Songs of the Delmore Brothers*, with his old friend Merle Travis on Capitol, and cut individual albums for the Lamb & Lion and Shasta labels, which also issued radio performances by Bond from Wakely's radio show in the late '50s. *—Bruce Eder*

That Wild, Wicked, But Wonderful West / 1961 / Starday ✦✦✦✦✦
This is a jewel of an album, Bond's very first for the Starday label, and one that deserves to be at least as well-known as Marty Robbins' *Gunfighter Ballads*. The selection of material is rich and diverse, and the production is fairly elaborate. Bond is joined by the Sons of the Pioneers' Karl Farr on guitar, and his playing lives up to its extraordinary reputation on most of the songs. A churchy organ comes to the fore on "The Fool's Paradise," and a honky tonk piano carries the band on a jaunty performances of "The Bully" and "Sadie Was a Lady." Bond was one of the players on Tex Ritter's original recording of "High Noon," and he recorded that Western film classic himself for this album. His voice isn't as effective as Ritter's, but he puts a lot of feeling into the performance, his acoustic guitar backed by an ominous drumbeat and more of that church-style organ. "Wonders of the Wasteland" has an almost lyrical content, and Bond achieves an almost preternatural presence on the song, reveling in that imagery. There's also one stripped-down gem here, "Belle Starr," which sounds like a mid-'20s field recording, with all of the raw, direct power that implies. Bond's version of "Carry Me Back to the Lone Prairie" may be the best recording that this Western standard has ever received; this track and the soaring, romantic "Dusty Skies" by themselves make this record worth owning. Of the two narrative songs, "Conversation With a Gun" works and "The Deadwood Stage" doesn't, but overall this is a fine recording by an underappreciated country star of yesteryear. *—Bruce Eder*

Live It Up, Laugh It Up / 1962 / Starday ✦✦✦✦
Bond's second album, recorded live in the studio before an invited audience, with a backing group that included Grandpa Jones and Archie Campbell, includes "Ten Little Bottles," "Oklahoma Hills," "Tumbling Tumbleweeds," "You Are My Sunshine," and numerous other classics. (out of print) *—Bruce Eder*

Songs That Made Him Famous / 1963 / Starday ✦✦✦✦✦
Bond's new recordings of material that he'd previously been known either as a songwriter or recording artist, including "I Wonder Where You Are Tonight" and "Divorce Me C.O.D." The backing band includes Pete Drake on steel guitar, and the Anita Kerr Singers on some songs. (out of print) *—Bruce Eder*

Johnny Bond's Best / 1964 / Harmony ✦✦✦
This is Columbia's first LP on Johnny Bond, featuring 11 songs, among them the original 1954 "Ten Little Bottles," "Cimarron," "Smoke, Smoke, Smoke," "Barrel House Bessie," and "Oklahoma Waltz." Not yet on compact disc, for which one would hope more songs would be added. (out of print) *—Bruce Eder*

Hot Rod Lincoln / 1965 / Starday ✦✦✦✦
Here is "Hot Rod Lincoln" re-recorded from his Republic days, along with a lot of drinking songs and songs of bad men and bad women, and one satire of the prevailing styles of the era, "Hot Rod Surfin' Hootlebeatnanny." (out of print) *—Bruce Eder*

Ten Little Bottles / 1965 / Starday ✦✦✦
The chart-topping "Ten Little Bottles" led to the release of this compilation of recent Johnny Bond recordings, alas, a paltry nine songs, including a rendition of "New Years Day" on which he's backed by his old friend Tex Ritter. *—Bruce Eder*

Famous Hot Rodders I Have Known / 1966 / Starday ✦✦✦
"Hot Rod Lincoln" is brought out once again, in the same 1964 version, along with a bunch of other car songs that show off Bond's guitar skills and his rollicking sense of humor. (out of print) *—Bruce Eder*

Bottled in Bond / 1967 / Harmony ✦✦
This is another collection of Bond's pre-1957 Columbia sides, including, not surprisingly, more than a couple of drinking songs. (out of print) *—Bruce Eder*

The Man Who Comes Around / 1968 / Starday ♦♦♦♦

Bottles Up / 1968 / Starday ♦♦♦
Here is another collection of Johnny Bond drinking songs, cut in 1966, including a re-recording of "Love Song in 32 Bars." (out of print) *—Bruce Eder*

Great Songs of the Delmore Brothers / 1969 / Longhorn ♦♦♦♦♦
It's an essential recording, if only for the extended collaboration between Bond and guitar wizard Merle Travis, and the sheer beauty of the material. Unfortunately, Bond only stayed with Capitol for one year, despite his friend Tex Ritter's longtime efforts to get him on the label. (out of print) *—Bruce Eder*

Branded Stock of Johnny Bond / 1969 / Starday ♦♦♦
This is Bond's first collection of largely new songs in a year or two, cut a couple of years earlier, including "Invitation to the Blues," "The Ballad of Bugle Bill," "Hell's Angels," and "Ragged But Right." (out of print) *—Bruce Eder*

Ten Nights in a Barroom / 1970 / Starday ♦♦♦
It's another concept album, with Jerry Scoggins (the singer on the TV version of *the Beverly Hillbillies* theme) as "the bartender." Cheerful drinking songs, mostly originals, dating back to 1967. (out of print) *—Bruce Eder*

Drink up and Go Home / 1970 / Starday ♦♦♦
Another collection of mostly drinking songs, rounded out with a comic number or two ("Don't Squeeze My Sharmon"), this time mostly not Bond originals. (out of print) *—Bruce Eder*

Something Old, New, Patriotic and Blue / 1971 / Starday ♦♦♦
As the title suggests, this is a collection of patriotic songs, intermixed with nostalgic love songs and other numbers with a generally old time feel. (out of print) *—Bruce Eder*

● **The Best of Johnny Bond** / 1971 / Starday ♦♦♦♦♦

Here Come the Elephants / 1972 / Starday ♦♦♦
Close to the end of Bond's stay on Starday, and his last album, mixing country band sounds with songs cut with orchestra and a vocal backing group. (out of print) *—Bruce Eder*

How I Love Them Old Songs / 1974 / Lamb & Lion ♦♦
Here is a nostalgic look back at 1940's and 1950's material, from Bond's repertory and other popular standards of the day (including "Chattanooga Choo Choo"), including a duet with Tex Ritter on two western numbers. (out of print) *—Bruce Eder*

Johnny Bond Rides Again / 1975 / Shasta ♦♦♦♦
Johnny Bond back with his old stablemate Jimmy Wakely, recutting many of his best known songs ("I Wonder Where You Are Tonight," "Hot Rod Lincoln") with James Burton and other top 1970's country sessionmen. (out of print) *—Bruce Eder*

The Way They Were Back When / 1975 / Shasta ♦♦♦
This is valuable historical multi-artist document, containing radio performances by Bond and other performers from Jimmy Wakely's 1950's radio show. (out of print) *—Bruce Eder*

The Singing Cowboy Rides Again / 1992 / CMH ♦♦♦♦
This 18-song collection, recorded in July of 1976, features Johnny Bond backed up by the Willis Brothers, doing a superb series of songs mostly associated with the singing cowboys of B-Westerns, although several have since become country & western hits in their own right, separate from the movies. Bond's singing and enunciating are a bit stiffer than Gene Autry's on songs like "Back in the Saddle Again" and "South of the Border," although he also has a bit more grit in his presentation—the duet between Bond and the Willis Brothers on "Cool Water" makes for a compelling mix of voices. Their delightfully jaunty work on "One More Ride" and "Take Me Back to Tulsa" should also be heard, just for the sheer fun of their approach. The instrumentation is mostly guitars (acoustic, electric, dobro, and steel), with fiddle, accordion, piano, and some restrained brass on the numbers that call for it, such as the moody and atmospheric "Along the Navajo Trail." The attempt was to find a compromise between old and new electric sounds, and it mostly worked. Other songs include "Sky Ball Paint," "San Antonio Rose," "Streets of Laredo," "High Noon" (on the original recording, Bond played guitar behind Tex Ritter), and "Cimarron," the latter one of Bond's most beloved original songs, originally sung by the Jimmy Wakely Trio. Officially designated as the Red River Valley Boys, the group, in addition to Bond and Vic and Guy Willis, included Curtis Young on vocals, with Johnny Gimble and Pete Wade, among others, providing the instrumental support. *—Bruce Eder*

The Very Best of Johnny Bond / Sep. 22, 1998 / Varese ♦♦♦♦♦
Whether this 17-song compilation represents the very best of Johnny Bond is an arguable point, since it only includes material from 1955-1974, and none of his big hits from the late '40s and early '50s. For the period it covers, it does a decent job, emphasizing the rockabilly tinged material he did in the late '50s and early '60s (particularly "Hot Rod Lincoln," which opens up the collection). The Top 30 pop hit "Hot Rod Lincoln," actually a cover of a 1955 single by Charlie Ryan, was the best thing he did in this mold; other tracks from this period included novelties ("The Way a Star Is Born" is pretty close to Bobby Bare's "The All American Boy"), variations of "Hot Rod Lincoln" ("Side Car Cycle"), honky tonk-styled cuts that sounded close to Johnny Horton ("Wild Cat Baby"), country swing (Sheb Wooley's "Louisiana Swing"), even a bluesy cover of "The Tijuana Jail." There are some less distinguished, more mainstream country efforts from the 1960s and early '70s, including his tacky smash "Ten Little Bottles." *—Richie Unterberger*

Heart and Soul of the West / Jul. 11, 2000 / Jasmine ♦♦♦
The 26 vintage radio transcriptions on this import CD are predominantly in a Western vein, including such well-worn numbers as "Red River Valley," "Tumbling Tumbleweeds," and "The Last Round-Up." There are a few departures from the Western theme, a handful of guitar instrumentals and several original compositions, but the majority of the performances feature Bond in a vocal ensemble mining Sons of the Pioneers territory. Bond was a talented guitarist and songwriter but an average vocalist, which means that the renditions of Western favorites are accomplished but underwhelming. Johnny Bond deserves wider recognition, but this modestly entertaining collection doesn't adequately convey the scope of his talents. *—Greg Adams*

Country & Western / Jan. 16, 2001 / Bloodshot ♦♦♦♦
There is something pleasantly romantic about Johnny Bond's cowboy songs, perhaps because they capture the saga of the once untamed West. Who wouldn't feel a certain longing in the wake of starry nights, tumbling tumbleweeds, and riding one's horse on the open range? A number of classic songs fill this collection, including "Red River Valley," "Boots and Saddles," and "Mexicali Rose." Bond is joined by a few friends—the Red River Valley Boys—who sing harmony and offer tasteful support. The arrangements are spare, featuring little more than bass, accordion, and a guitar on most cuts. The group is clearly comfortable performing together and maintain the same intimacy as the Sons of the Pioneers on songs like "Saddle Serenade." Bond has written a number of these songs, including the memorable "Ten Years" and the instrumental "Ridin' Down to Santa Fe." There is a haunting version of "Empty Saddles," sort of an early, less dark version of "(Ghost Riders) in the Sky." Bond is perfectly capable of generating a cowboy version of honky tonk flavored songs like "Headin' Down the Wrong Highway," or a heartfelt rendition of pop ballads like "Have I Stayed Away Too Long." The sound quality of these transcriptions from 1944-1945 is very good, and the number of selections—31—is generous. This disc will sit comfortably beside the recordings of other singing cowboys like Gene Autry and Roy Rogers. Bloodshot has put together a fine collection that will be a real treat to lovers of swinging cowboy music. *—Ronnie Lankford Jr.*

Johnny Bond & His Red River Valley Boys / Mar. 27, 2001 / ASV ♦♦♦♦♦
Although reissues of Johnny Bond's radio transcriptions and late-career recordings had been available on CD for some time, his classic Columbia hits from the late '40s and early '50s remained uncollected until the appearance of this mid-priced import. Despite the omission of two of his eight Columbia hits, this is a welcome collection mastered from vintage 78s. The sound quality is better than some other country & western titles from ASV, and regarding the 25 hits, misses and flips encompass a range of excellent novelties and drinking songs from Bond's peak years. Bond was never the most exciting of singers, but the dynamic and energetic vocal performances here are among his best. Listen to Bond's two tracks on Columbia's *Hillbilly Boogie!* compilation to get an idea of how good this collection could have sounded if the original masters had been used. *—Greg Adams*

The Home Recordings / Sep. 17, 2002 / Varese ♦♦♦

I Like My Chicken Fryin' Size / Jan. 21, 2003 / Jasmine ♦♦♦♦♦

Bonnie Lou (Mary Jo Kath)

b. Oct. 27, 1924, Talawanda, IL
Vocals / Cowboy

Country and rockabilly performer Bonnie Lou was born Mary Jo Kath in Talawanda, IL, on October 27, 1924. The signal from Chicago's AM powerhouse WLS reached loud and clear into central Illinois, and Bonnie grew up listening to Prairie Ramblers recordings featuring the yodeling cowgirl vocals of Patsy Montana. Mary also learned to yodel, both through those old records and the influence of her Swiss grandmother. She also studied violin and guitar as a child. By 16, Mary was singing on a radio show in Bloomington, IL; two years later, she was performing as Sally Carson with the Brush Creek Follies radio variety show, airing each Saturday from KMBC in Kansas City. The Brush Creek Follies program was regularly broadcast nationwide through the Columbia radio network. This valuable exposure led Mary to WLW in Ohio, where station exec Bill McLuskey hired her as a singer and yodeler with his *Midwestern Hayride* country & western radio program. McLuskey also christened Mary with the Bonnie Lou moniker. While with the *Hayride*, Bonnie performed regularly with the Girls of the Golden West, a cowboy yodeling combo she used to hear on WLS as a child.

While a few of her radio performances were cut to acetate and eventually released, it wasn't until the 1950s that Bonnie had any real success as a recording artist. Signing with the local Cincinnati label King in 1953, Bonnie had hits with "Tennessee Wig Walk" and "Seven Lonely Days," which both broke the Top Ten on the country charts. When the rockabilly sound hit, Bonnie recorded "Daddy-O" for King; the single went to number 14 on the *Billboard* charts in 1955-1956. The Rusty York duet "La Dee Dah" followed in 1958. After another uneventful York duet, Bonnie left King for another Cinci local, Fraternity. There she released several singles, though none found the success her early work for King had. Bonnie also continued to work with the *Midwestern Hayride*, which by this point had spun off the television program *Louisiana Hayride*. She eventually retired from the business and settled in Cincinnati with her husband, Mort.

Bonnie's choice to work and live in Cincinnati prevented her from finding the nationwide fame that a contract with RCA or another big label would have. However, she was a prime mover in the first days of rockabilly, and has seen many of her early recordings reissued on niche labels like Bear Family and WestSide, which issued the definitive collection of her King years with 2000's *Doin' the Tennessee Wig Walk*. *—Johnny Loftus*

Bonnie Lou Sings / 1958 / King ♦♦♦♦

Daddy-O / 1958 / King ♦♦♦

● **Doin' the Tennessee Wig Walk** / Jun. 6, 2000 / WestSide ♦♦♦♦♦
Bonnie Lou's three major country and pop hits, "Seven Lonely Days," "Tennessee Wig Walk" and "Daddy-O," are collected on this superbly packaged CD with 23 of her other King recordings from the 1950s, including a couple of alternate takes. Bonnie Lou's music began as pop-oriented country with double-tracked vocals and later incorporated more and more R&B and rock & roll flourishes, until by the late '50s she was recording teen novelties

such as "Little Miss Bobby Sox" and "Teenage Wedding." "La Dee Dah" is a duet with labelmate Rusty York, while "Two Step, Side Step" is an attempt at repeating the "Tennessee Wig Walk" formula. Featuring extensive liner notes and interesting photos, *Doin' the Tennessee Wig Walk* is an excellent anthology of an artist whose genre-straddling recordings will appeal to '50s country, rock, and pop music lovers. *—Greg Adams*

Boone Creek

f. 1977, **db.** 1978

Group / Progressive Bluegrass, Traditional Bluegrass

Boone Creek was the first band Ricky Skaggs led after his apprenticeship with Ralph Stanley, Country Gentlemen, and J.D. Crowe & the New South. Skaggs formed the band in 1977, when he was only 23 years old. Even though he was quite young, he had already played with some of the most respected musicians in bluegrass, playing both traditional bluegrass with Stanley and progressive newgrass with the Country Gentlemen and Crowe. With Boone Creek, Skaggs wanted to create a music that approached traditional bluegrass with a progressive attitude. To achieve this sound, he added electric guitar, drums, and piano to the traditional bluegrass lineup.

Boone Creek released its eponymous debut in 1977. It was quickly followed by *One Way Track* in early 1978. After the release of *One Way Track*, Skaggs broke up the group and joined Emmylou Harris' Hot Band. Skaggs would achieve solo success after leaving Harris in the early '80s. *—Stephen Thomas Erlewine*

Boone Creek / 1977 / Rounder ✦✦✦

• **One Way Track** / 1978 / Sugar Hill ✦✦✦✦

Boone Creek's second album *One Way Track* showcases the stunning instrumental skills of a young Ricky Skaggs, as well as his compatriots Jerry Douglas and Terry Baucom. The three musicians blend on tight, thrilling harmonies, but where they really shine is on their rampaging instrumentals, where they demonstrate their virtuosity. The title track, a Skaggs original, sets the pace for the album: a warm but still disciplined collection showcasing not only the players' abilities, but also their passion for the traditional material they cover. The emphasis on playing makes *One Way Track* a little uneven, yet when digested in small, individual bits, the album is quite enjoyable. *—Thom Owens*

Larry Boone

b. Jun. 7, 1956, Cooper City, FL

Vocals / Contemporary Country, New Traditionalist

Larry Boone was born in Cooper City, FL, on June 7, 1956. He set off for Nashville in 1981, after financing a stint at Florida Atlantic University with singing gigs in local Florida honky tonks. At first, Music City was unkind to the young singer/songwriter. Boone busked on the city streets, substitute taught, and even worked as a sportswriter before finally landing a songwriting gig with MTM. In 1985, Marie Osmond charted with his song "Until I Fall in Love Again," and the exposure led to more of his songs finding singers. Nashville nice guy John Conlee would even perform Boone's "American Faces" on NBC during the 1988 Olympic Games.

In 1986, Boone signed with Mercury as a solo artist, but his initial singles didn't make much noise. Nevertheless, the label issued his full-length debut in 1988, hoping to chip some success off of the formula popularized by country hunks like Garth Brooks and Clint Black. Neither Boone nor his album found that level of fame, but the single "Don't Give Candy to a Stranger" did find the Top Ten in 1988. Meanwhile, Boone's songwriting career continued to flourish. That same year, Kathy Mattea took his "Burnin' Old Memories" to number one, and "Old Coyote Town" was a Top Ten hit for Don Williams. Boone recorded two more lukewarm LPs for Mercury before jumping to Columbia, where his 1993 album, *Get in Line*, was a minor chart hit. He continued to work as a songwriter, and in 1998, Lonestar hit number one with the Boone composition "Everything's Changed." *—Johnny Loftus*

One Way to Go / 1987 / Columbia ✦✦

This includes the singles "I Need a Miracle" and "To Be with You." *—Brian Mansfield*

Larry Boone / Dec. 1987 / Mercury ✦✦✦✦✦

Boone had had a number of small hits ("Stranger Things Have Happened," "Roses in December") when his debut album came out in the wake of such country hunks as Garth Brooks and Clint Black. Boone figured to tap into that market with his muscular voice, but didn't quite make it, though this album includes his biggest hit, "Don't Give Candy to a Stranger." *—Brian Mansfield*

Swingin' Doors, Sawdust Floors / 1988 / Mercury ✦✦✦

This album, currently out of print, contains three Top 40 hits: "I Just Called to Say Goodbye Again," "Wine Me Up" and "Fool's Paradise." *—Brian Mansfield*

Down That River Road / 1990 / Mercury ✦✦✦

"Everybody Wants to Be Hank Williams," a brutal song about the price singers pay for commercial success, is the best thing Boone has recorded. It's also the closest thing to a hit this now out-of-print album produced. *—Brian Mansfield*

• **Get in Line** / Mar. 23, 1993 / Columbia ✦✦✦✦✦

Working with producer Don Cook (Brooks & Dunn, Mark Collie), Boone tried to retool his image into a tougher, leaner figure. Musically, he was fairly successful with rockers like "Call Me When the Sun Goes Down" and "I Still Got (What You Got Over)." Commercial success was another matter: "Get in Line," the album's only charting single, peaked at 65 in *Billboard*. *—Brian Mansfield*

The Bottle Rockets

f. 1992

Group / Roots Rock, Alternative Country-Rock

Festus, MO's Bottle Rockets ranked as one of the leading lights of the 1990s roots rock revival, thanks to a sound that bypassed the punk heritage proudly upheld by most of the band's contemporaries in favor of a redneck fusion of Southern boogie, country-folk, and crunching rock & roll. The group was fronted by singer/guitarist Brian Henneman, a Missouri native who formed his first band, Waylon Van Halen & the Ernest Tubbadours, in 1977 with friends Tom and Bob Parr. After a succession of names and a steady rise in musical competence, the threesome began landing club dates both locally and in Illinois, where they became friends with the young Jay Farrar and Jeff Tweedy, who would later start Uncle Tupelo.

In 1985, the trio was playing straight-ahead honky tonk under the guise Chicken Truck (so named in honor of the John Anderson song) with a new drummer, Mark Ortmann. Instead of giving in to local crowds who wanted to hear covers rather than originals, the bandmembers focused solely on performing their own material, which they began roughing up with a Crazy Horse-like edge. Shortly after frequent tour mates Uncle Tupelo signed a 1990 record deal, however, internal problems led Chicken Truck to disband; while the Parrs returned to civilian jobs, Ortmann moved to Nashville to become a session player, and Henneman became a roadie with Uncle Tupelo, even playing on their *March 16-20, 1992* album.

During his roadie days, Henneman recorded a demo tape of new material, which Tupelo manager Tony Margherita began discreetly shopping around. After cutting a solo single backed by Farrar and Tweedy, he re-formed his old band, replaced Bob Parr with bassist Tom Ray, and renamed the outfit the Bottle Rockets. After a 1993 self-titled effort, a year later the band issued its second independent LP, *The Brooklyn Side*, named after a bowling term. A portrait of life in rural, blue-collar America, *The Brooklyn Side* was the subject of lavish critical praise, and the positive notices led to the band signing with a major label, Atlantic, which promptly reissued the album. Shakeups at the label led to delays in the release of their next album, 1997's *24 Hours a Day*, and when the album sold poorly, the Bottle Rockets were dropped. In 1998, they signed with the small Doolittle label and released an odds-and-ends EP, *Leftovers*; by the time they completed their next album, 1999's *Brand New Year*, the label had gained major label distribution, but that deal proved to be short-lived, and in 2000 the Bottle Rockets were once again without a label. In 2001, they signed a deal with alt-country trailblazers Bloodshot Records; their first album for the label, a tribute to Doug Sahm, was released early the following year. *—Jason Ankeny*

Bottle Rockets / Sep. 18, 1993 / East Side Digital ✦✦✦✦

If Neil Young had played guitar and written songs with Lynyrd Skynyrd, it might've come out something like the eponymous debut by Festus, MO's own Bottle Rockets. Raw and spirited, with a guitar attack that burns furiously, this record was recorded and mixed in a couple of days. And although it contains some strong material, overall it lacks the focus of the band's follow-up, *The Brooklyn Side*. That's not to say that this one should be passed over; there's a satisfying mix of rockers and country-tinged numbers. Frontman and principle songwriter Brian Henneman's keen observations on everyday rural life and characters are explored with insightful detail in songs about convenience store clerks and trailer inhabitants. In the Southern rock-sounding "Wave That Flag," he takes an angry shot at rebel flag-wavers, and the escape of a dead-end life in the ragged and breakneck-speed country-rocker "Rural Route." Before the Bottle Rockets, Henneman served a tenure as guitar technician and sometime instrumentalist for Uncle Tupelo, and both Jeff Tweedy and Jay Farrar make backup vocal appearances, with Farrar giving a particularly strong performance on the highlight ballad, "Kerosene." *—Jack Leaver*

• **The Brooklyn Side** / Sep. 19, 1995 / East Side Digital ✦✦✦✦✦

While the Bottle Rockets' brand of Skynyrd-esque raunch 'n' roll is considerably more good-timey than most of the band's roots rock brethren, their incisive, provocative songwriting skills set them squarely among the genre's elite. *The Brooklyn Side*, produced by Eric "Roscoe" Ambel, is fairly bursting with dead-on character studies exploring the realities and quiet desperation of rural Southern life, from the blackly humorous ("Sunday Sports," about a family man who finds that watching TV in his underwear is "the only way to get away from everything else" in his life) to the poignant ("Welfare Music," a depiction of the struggles facing a young single mother). The band also possesses a wickedly comic edge, as evidenced by "Idiot's Revenge" (a diatribe against alt-rock rhetoric), "1000 Dollar Car" (a eulogy for a used automobile), and the flamethrower single "Radar Gun" (the tale of a sadistic, ticket-happy traffic cop). *—Jason Ankeny*

24 Hours a Day / Aug. 12, 1997 / Atlantic ✦✦✦

The Bottle Rockets' first two albums were two of the most influential and popular records of the alternative country movement, setting the stage for their third album, *24 Hours a Day*, to be a popular breakthrough upon its 1997 release. After all, alt-country was beginning to emerge from the mainstream and establish itself as one of the cornerstones of adult alternative radio. It's too bad they dropped the ball with *24 Hours a Day*, then, since it could have been the one that made their career. It's not that the album is bad—it's just not great. There are a couple of good moments, such as the propulsive "Perfect Far Away," but much of it is simply solid, craftsmanlike country-rock that sounds like it could have been done by any alt-country band. While that means the album is listenable, it also means that it's a disappointment, since the Bottle Rockets have the potential to be much more than just another alt-country band. *—Stephen Thomas Erlewine*

Leftovers / Nov. 24, 1998 / Doolittle ✦✦✦

It's not too difficult to figure out why much of the material here was left in the vaults at the end of the *24 Hours a Day* sessions. "My Own Cadillac" makes a big, grinding racket, but goes nowhere. "Skip's Song," an uncharacteristically introspective, singer/songwriter tribute to Moby Grape madman Skip Spence, seems to drag in comparison to its more rollicking company. "Coffee Monkey" and the fake Irish ballad "Chattanooga" are both novelty songs that border on the daft. On the other hand, Bottle Rockets fans will find more than enough to love mixed in with the experimentation and monkey business. "Get Down River" is Brian Henneman and company at their best, telling the story of everyday folks whose lives are inextricably linked with the rise and fall of the

Mississippi. Like Bruce Springsteen with a broader sense of humor, Henneman gives a voice full of grace and grit to otherwise unsung Americans. "Financing His Romance" is another short story, this one the wry tale of a loser in love with a bar-owner's girlfriend. "If Walls Could Talk" swings like a lost country & western classic, and "Dinner Train to Dutchtown" matches its amusing lyrics to a pleasantly ramshackle blues groove. Throughout *Leftovers*, the band plays with its accustomed, no-fuss virtuosity. They manage to sound tight and loose at the same time. The lyrics are keen-eyed narratives at best, good, raucous fun at worst. When it comes to great, underappreciated artists like the Bottle Rockets, even a stopgap release like this one can yield some mighty fine rewards. *—Daniel Browne*

Brand New Year / Aug. 10, 1999 / Doolittle ♦♦♦

The '90s turned out to be a little tough for the Bottle Rockets. Upon the release of its eponymous debut in 1993, the Missouri quartet was almost universally hailed as one of the leaders of the post-Uncle Tupelo Americana movement, but the band lost momentum when trying to make it in the big leagues. It wasn't for lack of trying. They labored over their official Atlantic debut, *24 Hours a Day*, but when they were touring the album, the label pulled their support, leaving them to flounder. The Rockets regrouped and released a collection of outtakes, *Leftovers*, the following year, as they decided what to do next. Wisely, they seized an opportunity for a fresh start, which is what *Brand New Year*, their first studio album for Doolittle Records, is. They've decided to emphasize their roots as a bar band, cutting away their country tendencies and playing up their fondness for '70s hard rock. The twist is, Rockets leader Brian Henneman tries to inject some intelligence and self-aware humor into the lyrics. At times, it works, but it's just as frequently awkward or self-conscious, especially since it seems that the words have taken precedence over hooks or melodies. Even so, there's a sense of songwriterly craft, if not actual songs, that is welcome, and it's made all the more engaging by the earthy performances by what is, after all, a really good bar band. There's no question that *Brand New Year* is a proudly Luddite record, celebrating the virtues of loud guitars and living without computers (see "Helpless," as in "how come I don't feel helpless"), which naturally makes it feel like an album out of time, but that is its redeeming virtue—it might not have the hooks of a classic rock album, but it's a good, solid slice of organic hard rock. *—Stephen Thomas Erlewine*

Songs of Sahm / 2001 / Bloodshot ♦♦♦

If there's an artist who deserves a tribute album, it's Doug Sahm, the tireless Texas groover whose Lone Star state of mind encompassed roots rock, blues, country, garage rock, norteño, psychedelia, and a countless number of spots in between over the course of a career that spanned five decades. One might have figured some bunch of Austin all-stars would have been the most likely candidates to honor Sahm on disc after his untimely passing in the fall of 1999, but the responsibility has instead fallen to those proud sons of Festus, MO, the Bottle Rockets, who take a lively stab at 13 of Sahm's compositions on their first album for Bloodshot, *Songs of Sahm*. The Bottle Rockets have long proven themselves a superb straight-ahead rock & roll band with a deep feeling for rough-and-tumble roadhouse country, but while those are both paths Sahm traveled, that was hardly the sum total of his accomplishment, and while there's never a moment on *Songs of Sahm* where you doubt that the BoRox love these songs with all their heart and soul, on a few cuts they sound as if they're playing a bit out of their league—the easy shuffle of "Be Real" doesn't quite suit a band whose forte is stomp, the bluesy lament of "At the Crossroads" is a few notches too slow for comfort, and "Sunday Sunny Mill Valley Groove Day" sure sounds goofy coming from a band with no outwardly hippie-like tendencies. Also, producer Lou Whitney doesn't get this band's power on tape with the same élan as Eric "Roscoe" Ambel. But, for the most part, Sahm's tunes fit the Bottle Rockets better than you'd have any right to expect, and this album's best moments are superb, especially the hard rock groove of "Floatway," the manic rave-up on "I'm Not That Kat Anymore," and the deathless "Lawd, I'm Just a Country Boy in This Great Big Freaky City." One hopes that Brian Henneman has another batch of quality originals on deck for the Bottle Rockets' next album, but *Songs of Sahm* is not only a fitting tribute to one of alt-country's primal influences, it's a healthy dose of rockin' country and lots of fun. *—Mark Deming*

Jimmy Bowen

b. Nov. 30, 1937, Santa Rita, NM

Bass, Vocals, Producer / Rock & Roll, Rockabilly, Pop, Traditional Pop

Since the 1970s, Jimmy Bowen has been a powerful executive in the record industry; he's worked for several labels, but has stayed with MCA since 1986, and is acknowledged as one of the most influential figures in Nashville. He entered the business a longtime before that, though, as a teenage rockabilly singer, landing a Top 20 hit in 1957 with "I'm Stickin' With You." The song was basic in the extreme, built around a thwacking bass riff, a singsong melody, and Bowen's own nervous, boyish vocals, suggesting that it may have been intended as nothing more than a demo. That indeed may have been close to the truth, as it was first released as a B-side to a song that made number one, Buddy Knox's "Party Doll."

Bowen and Knox's careers were bound together in an unusually close fashion that makes thumbnail sketches of their recording activities rather cumbersome and tangled. Knox (guitar, vocals) and Bowen (bass, vocals) met in the '50s and became the frontmen of a rockabilly combo, the Orchids. They were directed to Norman Petty's studio in Clovis, NM, by Roy Orbison. There the Orchids cut "Party Doll" (with Knox on vocals) and "I'm Stickin' With You" (with Bowen on bass). The tracks, both co-written by Knox/Bowen, were issued on the small Triple D label, the top side billed to Buddy Knox & the Orchids, the other to Jimmy Bowen & the Orchids. When the single was leased to Roulette for nationwide distribution, the company shrewdly divided the product into two separate singles. When both became hits, it found itself with two separate new stars, although nominally they were still part of the same group (now renamed, to further confuse matters, the Rhythm Orchids).

Bowen and Knox embarked on simultaneous solo careers for Roulette, although each continued to use the Rhythm Orchids as his backup band for quite a while. That accounts for the similar mild rockabilly-pop sound of each artist, but Knox was a far better singer, songwriter, and instrumentalist than Bowen; for that matter, he was far more successful, landing a string of smaller follow-up hits to "Party Doll." Bowen never entered the Top 20 again, although he did quite a bit of recording for Roulette in the late '50s. He found it hard to recapture the unforced bounce of "I'm Stickin' With You," and indeed his Roulette sides rate as some of the tamest rockabilly of the '50s. Bowen was probably unsuited to be a frontman to begin with, despite his teen-idol looks; his range was narrow (sometimes he sounds like a gawky Johnny Cash), and his delivery was stiff and unsure of itself. His material was fairly slight as well, and at the end of his stay with Roulette, he'd abandoned rock for misguided and soggy attempts at orchestrated pop.

Bowen would make some more records, but it was really more the beginning than the end when he moved into production. In the mid-'60s he worked with Frank Sinatra, Sammy Davis Jr., and Dean Martin at Reprise; since then he's had high posts at Capitol, MGM, Elektra/Asylum, and MCA, concentrating mostly on country music in recent times. *—Richie Unterberger*

Best of Jimmy Bowen / Nov. 25, 1991 / Collectables ♦♦♦

Pleasant if unambitious midtempo rock & roll, very well-played (especially the guitar, played by Buddy Knox) by the Rhythm Orchids with something of a country flavor, although the best track here is the slow, Elvis-style ballad "Last Night." The name of the CD is a bit of a cheat—this is simply Bowen's first (and only) album for Roulette with a new title grafted on; it does include several of his modest chart successes following in the wake of "I'm Sticking With You," but doesn't include "By the Light of the Silvery Moon" (admittedly, not a high point of his career, but it did chart better than some of the singles that are here). The sound is decent, as the master was obtained from Capitol/EMI's Roulette holdings, and the interior of the insert reprints the original LP's jacket notes, which are surprisingly involved and thorough for their period. *—Bruce Eder*

● **The Complete Roulette Recordings** / 1996 / Sequel ♦♦♦♦♦

Bowen has only half of this double CD; the other disc consists of Buddy Knox's complete Roulette recordings, not Bowen's. It may be an unwieldy way to pick up Bowen's material, but his disc, with 30 tracks, presents a thorough retrospective of his late-'50s rockabilly and pop recordings, including all the singles, LP cuts, and two previously unreleased tracks. It's more than anyone but the collector needs to hear, despite the quality of the meticulous packaging. Nothing else Bowen did matched the leadoff song, "I'm Stickin' With You," which is better heard as a track on various-artist '50s compilations. The rest of this mild rockabilly is pretty trivial, and the pop sides (with orchestration) are exactly the kinds of things rockabilly was reacting *against*. Though he couldn't have been considered one of rockabilly's leading lights either, Knox's half of the program outshines Bowen's by a considerable margin. *—Richie Unterberger*

Bryan Bowers

b. Aug. 18, 1940, Yorktown, VA

Autoharp, Composer / Traditional Bluegrass, Old-Timey

Autoharpist Bryan Bowers was born in Yorktown, VA, on August 18, 1940. As a boy, he would often singalong with the call-and-response harmonies of the railroad workers. He enrolled at Randolph Macon College in Ashland, VA, where he eventually began playing the guitar. But an itinerant multi-instrumentalist turned him on to the autoharp, and he was immediately hooked. Bowers dropped out of school and in 1971 moved to Seattle. While in Washington, Bowers busked on street corners and in barrooms, honing his autoharp performance skills. Then he made his way to Washington, D.C., where he was noticed by the Dillards during a performance at that city's famed folk club The Cellar Door. He tagged along with the band to a bluegrass festival in Berryville, VA, and when they brought Bowers out for their final encore, he brought the house down. Bowers' five-fingered picking of the instrument (rather than the traditional strum) was unique, and added resonance to his already dynamic performances.

In 1977, Bowers signed with the Flying Fish label, which released his debut in 1977. *The View from Home* featured contributions from New Grass Revival members Sam Bush and Courtney Johnson. Released in 1980, *Home, Home on the Road* showcased not only Bowers' astonishing autoharp technique, but his easygoing wit as well. Bowers was always as much a singer and storyteller as he was an instrumental virtuoso; the rich vocals and Celtic arrangements on his 1982 LP, *For You*, speak to this. Despite these successful recordings, Bowers was always more comfortable as a live performer, and continued to appear at festivals and workshops throughout the 1980s and '90s. In 2000, Bowers returned to wax with *Friend for Life*. He also released an instructional autoharp video intended for intermediate players interested in taking the next step toward advanced songs and styles. *—Johnny Loftus*

● **The View from Home** / 1977 / Flying Fish ♦♦♦♦

This, the debut record of the autoharpist virtuoso, features backing from some of the country's best pickers. *—AMG*

Home, Home on the Road / 1980 / Flying Fish ♦♦♦

On this album, Bowers plays the autoharp and sings a mixture of serious and comic songs. *—AMG*

By Heart / 1982 / Flying Fish ♦♦♦

For You / 1982 / Flying Fish ♦♦♦♦

One of the things that frustrates folk lovers is the fact that Bryan Bowers doesn't have a larger catalog. In an ideal world, the veteran singer/harp player would have recorded at least 20-30 albums. But Bowers seems to think of himself as primarily a live attraction instead of a recording artist; consequently, he has only recorded sporadically. One of the pleasing CDs that Bowers provided for the Chicago-based Flying Fish label is *For You*, which favors an acoustic format. There is no folk-rock or folk-pop on this album; Bowers' style of folk is very old-time, and that is true whether he is singing or playing an instrumental on his harp. The charming instrumentals demonstrate Bowers' virtuosity as harp player, while vocal gems like "Rufus and Beverly" and "Festival Love" remind listeners how captivating a storyteller he can be. Listening to *For You*, one hears a variety of influences. Old-time country —the acoustic country that preceded the rise of Roy Acuff, Hank Williams, Ernest Tubb, and other honky tonk legends in the 1930s and 1940s—is an influence, and some of the material hints at Irish-Celtic folk. Bowers' thorough knowledge of Anglo storytelling traditions is impressive; when *For You* is playing, you can hear how the Celtic music that Irish and Scottish immigrants brought with them to the U.S. paved the way for bluegrass, country, and Anglo-American folk. Again, it's regrettable that an artist of Bowers' caliber doesn't have a larger catalog—especially when you consider how rewarding *For You* is. *—Alex Henderson*

Friend for Life / Jul. 11, 2000 / Flying Fish ✦✦✦
Autoharp virtuoso Bryan Bowers is known for his unique fingerpicking style attached to an instrument that is normally strummed. Bowers no doubt developed this style during his early proficiency on guitar as a kid. Bowers is primarily a live performer and storyteller, so his recorded works are few. *Friend for Life* is his first release on the Flying Fish label in over 18 years. He delivers an eclectic 21 tracks that cover traditional folk compositions as well as the blues of Howlin' Wolf, the traditional country of the Carter Family, the bluegrass of Jimmy Martin, and even lullabies ("Frere Jacques" and "Twinkle, Twinkle Little Star"). *—Al Campbell*

Boxcar Willie (Lecil Travis Martin)

b. Sep. 1, 1931, Sterret, TX, **d.** Apr. 12, 1999
Guitar, Vocals / Traditional Country, Country Comedy
Boxcar Willie was perhaps the most successful invented character in the history of country music. With his kitschy persona and stage act—highlighted by his amazingly accurate impersonation of a train whistle—Willie played into the stereotype of the lovable, good-natured hobo who spent his life riding the rails and singing songs. Since his popularity had more to do with his image than his music, it makes sense that he was massively successful in England, where he personified Americana. Willie's English success carried him over to American success in the early '80s, where he ironically was perceived as carrying the torch for traditional country, because he kept the stereotypes alive.

Born Lecil Travis Martin, Boxcar Willie never worked on the railroads—his father did. However, Willie loved the railroads and kept running away to ride the trains when he was a child. He also loved country music, particularly the songs of Jimmie Rodgers, Roy Acuff, and Ernest Tubb. As a teenager, Boxcar Willie would perform under his given name, eventually becoming a regular on the Big D Jamboree in Dallas, TX. In his early twenties, he served in the Air Force. After he left the service, he continued to sing in clubs and radio shows. In the late '50s, he began performing as Marty Martin, while working blue-collar jobs during the day. Marty Martin released an album, *Marty Martin Sings Country Music and Stuff Like That*, around 1958, but it was ignored.

In the mid-'60s, Martin wrote a song called "Boxcar Willie," based on a hobo he saw on a train. Martin continued to struggle in his musical career until the mid-'70s. By that time, he had become a DJ in Corpus Christi, TX. In 1975, he decided to risk everything he had on one final chance at stardom. He moved to Nashville and developed the Boxcar Willie character, using his song as the foundation.

Initially, Boxcar Willie wasn't very successful, but he had a lucky break in 1976 when he was called in to replace a sick George Jones at a Nashville club. During that performance, he was spotted by Drew Taylor, a Scottish booking agent. Taylor brought Boxcar Willie over to England for a tour, where he was enthusiastically received. Later that year, he released his first album, which was a moderate success in the U.K. Through the rest of the '70s, Willie toured Britain and every tour was more successful, culminating in a performance at the International Country Music Festival at Wembley in 1979. After his Wembley show was finished, he received a standing ovation—the performance established Boxcar Willie as a star. His next album, *King of the Road*, became a huge success in England, reaching number five on the album charts; the record was helped immeasurably by its accompanying television advertisements, which sold the record through the mail. By the end of 1980, Willie had become the most successful country artist in England, and his American success had just begun. *King of the Road* was available through an American television advertisement. "Train Medley" was a minor hit on the country charts, and he was becoming a popular attraction on U.S. concert circuits. In 1981, he received a spot on the Country Music Hall of Fame's Walkway of the Stars and became a member of the *Grand Ole Opry*.

Boxcar Willie enjoyed his time in the spotlight, becoming a regular on the television show *Hee Haw* in 1982 and turning out albums as fast as he could make them. "Bad News" became his only American country Top 40 hit in 1982. In 1985, he played a hobo in *Sweet Dreams*, a film about Patsy Cline. By the mid-'80s, his star had faded, but he remained a popular concert attraction, particularly in England, into the '90s. Boxcar Willie died in Branson, MO, on April 12, 1999, after a three-year battle with leukemia. *—Stephen Thomas Erlewine*

Marty Martin Sings Country Music / 1958 / AHMC ✦✦✦

Boxcar Willie / 1976 / MCA ✦✦✦✦✦
Never issued on compact disc, *Boxcar Willie* remains one of the hobo's best albums, highlighted by a guest appearance by Willie Nelson. *—Stephen Thomas Erlewine*

● **The Collection** / 1987 / Castle ✦✦✦✦✦
Castle's *The Collection* is the best Boxcar Willie compilation ever assembled, featuring his signature hit, "Train Medley," as well as several other songs in a similar vein. Appropriately, *The Collection* was only released in England, the country that made Boxcar Willie famous. *—Stephen Thomas Erlewine*

Best Loved Favorites / 1989 / Vanguard ✦✦✦✦
Best Loved Favorites is not a greatest-hits collection from Boxcar Willie. Instead, it's a a selection of some of the most popular and enduring country standards, performed by the

singing hobo. Willie is in good voice throughout and with songs like "In the Jailhouse Now" and "Blue Moon of Kentucky," it's an entertaining listen. *—Stephen Thomas Erlewine*

Truck Driving Favorites / 1991 / Madacy ✦✦✦

Rocky Box: Rockabilly / 1993 / K-Tel ✦✦✦
Country music's favorite fake hobo teams up with the Midwest's top roots music combo for a spirited, if at times surreal, outing. The Skeletons, featuring D. Clinton Thompson's excellent fretboard work, provides perfect retro backing on everything, while Boxcar is quite at home on traditional '50s boppers like "Mystery Train" and "Rockin' Bones." But the true candidate for the twilight zone is his version here of "Achy Breaky Heart," complete with his patented train whistle. It doesn't get much weirder than this in any style of music. *—Cub Koda*

King of the Road / 1997 / Planet Entertainment ✦✦✦✦✦
King of the Road is the album that made Boxcar Willie famous. Advertised on English television, the record wound up climbing to number five on the U.K. charts, setting the stage for his breakthrough success in the U.S. and Canada. *King of the Road* consists of a number of traditional country songs, including "Wabash Cannonball," "San Antonio Rose," "You Are My Sunshine," "Mule Train," "Rolling in My Sweet Baby's Arms," and three Hank Williams songs, with a couple of cute originals thrown in for good measure. Although it doesn't have his signature song, "Train Medley," it remains his best album. *—Stephen Thomas Erlewine*

Boy Howdy

f. 1990, Los Angeles, CA
Group / Country-Rock, Contemporary Country
Boy Howdy was a contemporary country-rock band who formed in Los Angeles in 1990. Their primary influence was Little Texas, though one could catch bits of the Eagles and CCR in their sound, and they frequently covered classic rock tunes as well. Vocalist/bassist Jeffrey Steele had previously recorded as a solo artist, and under the guidance of Dwight Yoakam producer Pete Anderson, he contributed the song "Driftin' Man" to the compilation *A Town South of Bakersfield, Vol. 2*. Brothers Cary (guitar, mandolin) and Larry Parks (guitar, fiddle) were the sons of bluegrass fiddler Ray Parks, and the former had played with Randy Meisner (Eagles) and Rick Roberts (Flying Burrito Brothers) before hooking up with Steele at an L.A. club. Also present at that gig was drummer Hugh Wright, who completed the lineup.

Their first single was 1991's independently released "When Johnny Comes Marchin' Home Again," which proved locally popular thanks to the Gulf War, and helped land Boy Howdy a deal with Curb. Their debut album, *Welcome to Howdywood*, was released in 1992, and the group went on to appear in George Strait's film *Pure Country* that year. Tragedy nearly struck when Wright was hit by a car and spent five months in a coma; fortunately, he recovered, and rejoined the band in time for their breakthrough, 1994's *She'd Give Anything*. Even though it was only a mini-album, it produced two Top Five country singles in the title track and "They Don't Make 'Em Like That Anymore." Their full-length, *Born That Way* (1995), didn't quite duplicate that success, however. *—Steve Huey*

Welcome to Howdywood / 1992 / Curb ✦✦✦

● **She'd Give Anything** / Jan. 11, 1994 / Curb ✦✦✦✦

Born That Way / 1995 / Curb ✦✦✦

Bill Boyd

b. Sep. 29, 1910, Fannin County, TX, **d.** Dec. 7, 1977, Dallas, TX
Guitar, Leader, Vocals / Western Swing
For true fans of Western swing music, Bill Boyd rates with his contemporary, Bob Wills, even though the two utilized very different styles; whereas Wills & His Playboys often used horns and recorded songs from a variety of genres, Boyd remained true to his western roots, using only a string band, the Cowboy Ramblers. Born on a ranch near Ladonia, TX, Boyd grew up as a working cowboy, learning the traditional songs from the impromptu campfire jam sessions of the ranch hands. Both he and his younger brother frequently sang with the cowboys, as did their parents. The boys got to be pretty good, and in 1926, made their debut on KFPM in Greenville. The family moved to Dallas in 1929, where Boyd played in a band that included fiddler Art Davis. By this time, Boyd knew he wanted a career in music, first joining a band on WFAA and then the first incarnation of the Cowboy Ramblers in 1932 on WRR. Included in Boyd's new band was his brother, Jim, on bass; Davis on fiddle; and Walter Kirkes on tenor banjo. When not actually performing, Boyd was out recruiting new sponsors and in this way managed to survive the Depression.

In 1934, he and the band moved to San Antonio to record for Bluebird, cutting hits including the standard "Under the Double Eagle" and "Going Back to My Texas Home." In the late '30s, their membership increased to ten; among their better-known members were fiddler Carroll Hubard, piano player Knocky Parker, and steel guitar player Wilson "Lefty" Perkins. During their long association with RCA, Boyd & the Ramblers recorded over 229 singles; in the early '40s, they appeared in six el cheapo Hollywood cowboy films, including *Raiders of the West* and *Prairie Pals*. Boyd's jaunt through Hollywood was interesting, as it overlapped with the career of cowboy actor William Boyd, famous for his portrayal of Hopalong Cassidy.

Boyd effectively retired from the music business in the early '50s, and began a second career as a radio DJ at Dallas' WRR. Upon his posthumous induction into the Texas Western Swing Hall of Fame, a bill was introduced into the Texas legislature to honor Boyd and his contributions to the state's cultural identity. *—Johnny Loftus*

● **Bill Boyd's Cowboy Ramblers** / Aug. 7, 1934-Feb. 7, 1950 / RCA Bluebird ✦✦✦✦✦
This two-LP set gives one a definitive look at the many versions of Bill Boyd's Cowboy Ramblers, one of the top Western swing groups of the 1930s. Boyd's band was a bit

unusual in that it rarely ever travelled, mostly performing in the recording studio and frequently on radio shows. The 32 selections on this two-fer date from 1934-1938 (with the exception of three later pieces) and help to define the Western swing sound, emphasizing the jazzier side of Boyd's music; 17 of the performances are instrumentals. Among the sidemen are the fiddles of Jesse Ashlock and Cecil Brower and pianist Knocky Parker. Highlights include "Under the Double Eagle," "Barn Dance Rag," "Goofus," "Fan It," "Beaumont Rag," "New Steel Guitar Rag," "Boyd's Tin Roof Blues," "New Spanish Two Step" and 1950's "Domino Rag." Well worth searching for. *—Scott Yanow*

With His Cowboy Ramblers 1943–1947 / 1943 / RCA Bluebird ✦✦✦✦

This features "On the Texas Plains," "You're Just About Right, " "Boyd's Blues, " and more. *—AMG*

BR5-49

f. 1993, Nashville, TN

Group / Alternative Country, Neo-Traditionalist Country, Americana

One of the most critically acclaimed alternative country bands of the '90s, BR5-49's sound, style, and even look were unabashedly retro. Dressing in old, budget-friendly clothes, the band played a mixture of classic '50s honky tonk, Western swing, boogie, Bakersfield country, rockabilly, and Gram Parsons-style country-rock. The group was founded by guitarists/vocalists Gary Bennett and Chuck Mead in early 1993, not long after they'd moved to Nashville from the Pacific Northwest and Kansas, respectively. Bennett led an informal band at Robert's Western Wear, a combination bar and clothing store on Lower Broadway in Nashville's old district, and Mead—an alumnus of roots rockers the Homestead Grays—worked at a nearby bar before joining up. They later added upright bassist Smilin' Jay McDowell, who'd previously been a guitarist in Hellbilly; drummer Shaw Wilson, a friend of Mead's from Kansas; and fiddle/steel guitar/mandolin/dobro player Don Herron, an old cohort of Bennett's.

The group took up residency at Robert's Western Wear, playing for tips three nights a week, and built a strong local following among both country and alternative rock fans, thanks to their eclectic repertoire and punkish, left-of-center attitude. They adopted the name BR5-49 from a phone number in a Junior Samples sketch on *Hee Haw*, and signed with Arista in 1995. BR5-49's first release was an EP, *Live at Robert's*, which appeared in early 1996 and featured both originals and vintage country covers. The group built up their following via tours with the Mavericks, Junior Brown, and rockers the Black Crowes, and also issued their self-titled debut album later in the year. *BR5-49* won rave reviews from both country and rock critics, and climbed into the country Top 40 with virtually no support from country radio. The same was true of the 1998 follow-up, *Big Backyard Beat Show*.

BR5-49 toured with Brian Setzer in 1999, during which time they recorded their first full-length live album, *Coast to Coast*; the record was released the following year, again to excellent reviews. Unfortunately, Arista's country division was swallowed up in a merger, leaving the band without a record deal for a short time. Sony subsidiary Lucky Dog picked them up, and their label debut, 2001's *This Is BR549*, found them making a decided move toward the contemporary country mainstream (as well as dropping the oddly placed hyphen from their name). In its wake, Bennett and McDowell both broke ties with the band, reportedly weary of touring; amidst rumors of the group's permanent breakup, they were replaced by Geoff Firebaugh and Chris Scruggs. *—Steve Huey*

Live at Robert's / 1996 / Arista ✦✦✦

BR5-49 know where the gems are found when it comes to digging out old material. They gained their street rep by transforming Nashville's downtown honky tonk scene into a hopping place that draws a blend of punks, hipsters, frat kids, tourists, and drunks; with *Live at Robert's*, the band make their first major national move by providing a glimpse of their vibrant, all-night live show. Anyone who has danced through one of the quintet's sets at Robert's Western Wear—where the band have played for tips for five hours a night, four nights a week for the last two years—will recognize the chilling version of the Stanley Brothers' "Knoxville Girl" and the go-for-broke take on Johnny Horton's "Ole Slewfoot." But the live, six-song EP also displays their knack for novel originals, including the rumbling boogie of "18 Wheels & a Crowbar," the soiled innocence of the Bettie Page tribute, "Bettie Bettie," and the crafty wit of the crowd favorite, "Me 'n' Opie (Down by the Duck Pond)," which finds Opie, Goober, Barney, and Otis hitting the homegrown while hiding out from Andy and Aunt Bea. It's the song that explains everything. *—Michael McCall*

● **BR5-49** / Sep. 17, 1996 / Arista ✦✦✦✦✦

BR5-49 was hardly the first retro-country act to emerge in the 1990s, but as one of the first trad-style C&W bands to gain a following (and a major label contract) in Nashville for nearly 20 years, they suggested that in the midst of Garth-mania there were still folks in Music City hungry for some down-home twang in the classic style, which made country music a phenomenon in the first place. BR5-49's self-titled debut album may lack a bit of the grit and high spirits of their live show (either as witnessed in person or as preserved on the *Live at Robert's* EP), but it does a great job of capturing this band's spunky attitude and superb chops, and makes clear they can write original songs just as well as they can give new life to classics by Moon Mullican and Ray Price. While a few tunes like "Little Ramona (Gone Hillbilly Nuts)" play to the slightly kitschy side of the group's collective personality, "Even if It's Wrong," "One Long Saturday Night," and "Lifetime to Prove" testify that BR5-49 truly respect classic country music, and write songs as smart and heartfelt as the classics they cover. And boy, can they play—Don Herron shines on every instrument he touches (including fiddle, steel guitar, and mandolin), Shaw "Hawk Shaw" Wilson and Smilin' Jay McDowell are a superbly uncluttered rhythm section, and Gary Bennett and Chuck Mead can pick just as well as they harmonize (and that's mighty fine indeed). Adding a here-and-now energy and drive to classic styles of the past, *BR5-49* proves you can not only have it both ways, but have a great time to boot. *—Mark Deming*

Bonus Beats / 1998 / Arista ✦✦✦✦

BR5-49 are a young band from Nashville who play country & western music as if they just stepped out of a honky tonk circa 1957, and whose fans include Ralph Stanley, Guy Clark, and Kay Adams. Steve Albini is a recording engineer who emerged from Chicago's volatile punk rock scene to oversee sessions with such advocates of the abrasive as Helmet, the Jesus Lizard, and Killdozer. So putting them together sounds like a marriage made in heaven, right? Well, it's a lot closer than you'd imagine; *BR5-49* rolled into Electrical Recording studio for a three-day session with Albini at the controls shortly after they wrapped up their second full-length album, *Big Backyard Beat Show*, and the jumpin' *Bonus Beats* EP was the result. While as a engineer Albini is best known for his work with punishingly loud rock bands, he's also shown a sure hand with quieter stuff (most notably on Robbie Fulks' Country Love Songs), and his dry but roomy sound, full of natural ambience, flatters BR5-49's live-in-the-studio performances; the result sounds like a higher-fi version of an old Bradley's Barn session, and captures the interplay of one of country's best live acts with greater accuracy than their more polished studio stuff. And while the group didn't bring any new material to these sessions, it's a solid collection of great songs, and the versions of "18 Wheels & a Crowbar" and "Seven Nights to Rock" easily outpace those on *Big Backyard Beat Show*. Unfortunately, *Bonus Beats* was only released as a promo item (it was included as a bonus disc with some copies of *Big Backyard Beat Show*), but it's well worth digging up for fans, and BR5-49 could do a lot worse than to give this successful experiment another try, as Steve Albini gets more of their live magic on tape than the Nashville studio hands they're accustomed to. *—Mark Deming*

Big Backyard Beat Show / Jul. 14, 1998 / Arista ✦✦✦✦

When BR5-49 was first signed by a Nashville major, eyebrows were raised on both sides of the country music border. Traditionalists wondered what it would cost the hillbilly boys who gained fame while playing in the window of Robert's Western Wear on Lower Broadway in Music City. On the other side of the fence, the cats in the suits were shaking their heads, predicting that BR5-49 would be a short-lived novelty act. With some moderate success, no thanks to country-pop radio, and several years on the road, BR5-49 endured. This, the band's third release, shows a maturing quintet ready to come into its own. With their integrity intact, the boys have learned a thing or two about writing songs, and display their own material proudly. Sandwiched between a Buck Owens cover, "There Goes My Love," and Billy Joe Shaver's forever powerful "Georgia on a Fast Train," Gary Bennett and Chuck Mead provide the band with some worthy tunes. "Storybook Endings (If You Stop Believin')," "My Name Is Mudd," "You Are Never Nice to Me," and "Change the Way I Look" all score big. "Goodbye, Maria" is the band's effective salute to the Tex-Mex sound of country & western music. They even present listeners with a fast-movin' truck-drivin' song, "18 Wheels & a Crowbar." With Don Herron's magnificent musicianship providing steel, fiddle, dobro, mandolin, and almost anything else that is required, BR5-49 deserves more than just a modicum of respect for hanging in there despite predictions. If the infinitely listenable *Big Backyard Beat Show* is any indication of their future, they should be around for a longtime. *—Jana Pendragon*

Coast to Coast / Apr. 2000 / Arista ✦✦✦✦

For all their acclaim and genuine talent, retro-country act BR5-49 struck some listeners the wrong way—namely, fans of the honky tonk, Bakersfield country, Western swing, country boogie, and rockabilly that BR5-49 revitalized with their studio records. To these listeners, the quintet may have had the chops, but they were just a bit too knowing—they weren't playing with a smile, but a smirk. Reasonable enthusiasts could disagree on this point, and they did, but there still remained a significant portion of would-be fans that couldn't get with the band, because what some perceived as good humor seemed like condescension to others. Those listeners may be surprised by the group's first live album, *Coast to Coast*. Recorded in the summer of 1999 (at five different locations), the album finds the group in their element, passionately knocking out tunes in front of an appreciative audience. They're tight, energetic, and musically deft, effortlessly switching genres and spitting out high-octane solos. It's pretty intoxicating, actually, especially since the band has great taste—not only do they revive Don Gibson's overlooked "Sweet Sweet Girl" and Bob Wills & Tommy Duncan's standard "Brain Cloudy Blues," but they are no elitists, choosing to cover Gram Parsons ("Big Mouth Blues") and the far less hip Charlie Daniels ("Uneasy Rider") as well. Some fans of pure country music may find Chuck Mead's voice just a little jive, but he's a hell of a guitar player in a crackerjack band, and if you only concentrate on that, *Coast to Coast* doesn't just come alive—it crackles. Not enough credit can be placed on the live setting; its kinetic excitement is the reason why *Coast to Coast* is the BR5-49 album for listeners who aren't already fans, while still being a delight for diehards. *—Stephen Thomas Erlewine*

This Is BR549 / Jun. 26, 2001 / Sony Nashville ✦✦

Nashville upstarts BR5-49 have become known for their hybrid of old-fashioned Western swing, slick country-pop, and punk-infused honky tonk, however, on their fourth release, *This Is BR549*, they start by straying closer to the young country side of the industry. The first half of the album seems to lag behind the beat, not in a lazy, porch-sittin' manner, but in a "prime for a slick CMT video" manner. The first single, "Too Lazy to Work, Too Nervous to Steal," chugs along passionlessly. Similarly, the distortion-laden and tremolo-heavy cover of the Everly Brothers' "The Price of Love" might work well in concert with some live energy behind it, but on CD it lumps along, in desperate need of a carrot held in front of the horse. The incorporation of pop culture references have worked in the band's favor on their previous albums ("Little Ramona," "Bettie Bettie"), but their social and political commentaries on "Psychic Lady" and "A Little Good News" would get 'em thrown offstage at both Gilley's and CBGB; not because their topics are controversial, but because they are boring. About midway through the album, starting with the Gary Bennett-penned "While You Were Gone" (the record's best cut), they start cookin'. Here, the record steps into the groove and focuses on their familiar pedal steel uptempo swing as opposed to the slicker sound dominating the first half. The barn dance toe-tapper "Fool of the Century" would do Bob Wills proud, and the upright bass-led "Look Me Up" is in line with the truly inspired stuff they recorded in their days at Robert's Western Wear. As unfortunate as the first half is, the flip side hides some true gems, making the more cynical country fans wonder if side A was engineered by Nashville suits and side B is more along the band's original vision. Either way, the album is a toss-up, with its share of unfortunate cuts and real winners. *—Zac Johnson*

Bobby Braddock

b. Aug. 5, 1940, Lakeland, FL

Songwriter, Piano, Vocals / Country-Pop, Nashville Sound/Countrypolitan

Country songwriter Bobby Braddock was one of the more prolific hitmakers of the '70s, and also made a few of his own recordings toward the end of the decade. Born in Lakeland, FL, in 1940, Braddock first entered the music industry as a keyboard player for Marty Robbins, whose backing band he joined in 1964. Two years later, Robbins recorded the Braddock-penned "While You're Dancing," and had a chart hit with it. Building on that foundation, Braddock joined the songwriting staff at Tree International Publishing, where he replaced Roger Miller. He also found work as a session musician, and began making his own recordings, charting with the 1967 single "I Know How to Do It." That same year, the Oak Ridge Boys had a Top Ten hit with Braddock's "Would They Love Him Down in Shreveport," and his career was on its way. He had two Top Tens for the Statler Brothers in 1968, plus Braddock's first number-one hit in Tammy Wynette's "D-I-V-O-R-C-E," which he co-wrote with Curly Putman.

Over the next ten years, Braddock kept cranking out hits for countless artists, the biggest of which included "I Believe the South's Gonna Rise Again" (Tanya Tucker), "Come on In" (Jerry Lee Lewis), "Womanhood" (Wynette again), and the duet "Something to Brag About" (recorded by Willie Nelson with Mary Kay Place, as well as Wynette and George Jones). Braddock landed a recording deal with Elektra in his own right in 1979, and scored a chart hit that year with the title track of his first full-length album, *Between the Lines*. The 1980 follow-up, *Love Bomb*, was a semi-concept album filled with witty, southern-fried social commentary, and was followed in 1983 by the mini-album *Harepore Cornography*. The same year, Braddock teamed with Matraca Berg to write T.G. Sheppard's number-one hit "Faking Love."

Braddock's songwriting career began to slow down a bit during the '80s, but he still came up with periodic successes, penning hits for Tracy Lawrence ("Time Marches On," "Texas Tornado") and Mark Chesnutt ("Old Flames Have New Names"), among others, during the '90s. *—Steve Huey*

Between the Lines / 1979 / Elektra ✦✦✦

● **Love Bomb** / 1980 / Elektra ✦✦✦✦

This is a wry look at social situations circa the late '70s done up southern style. Braddock touches on such topics as drugs, Madison Avenue advertisers, the Klu Klux Klan, failed marriages, and just about anything else that mattered in good ol' Harper Valley and all done with tongue firmly stuck in cheek. Braddock supplies appropriate melodies for each of these ten tunes and is backed by solid studio pros. A good-time for those seeking out little slice of humor along with a bit of message. *—James Chrispell*

Harold Bradley

b. Jan. 2, 1926, Nashville, TN

Guitar / Western Swing

The brother of country music legend Owen Bradley, Harold Ray Bradley is reportedly the most recorded guitar player in history. Not a ridiculous assumption considering Bradley has been a Nashville session musician for over 50 years. Born in Nashville, Bradley first became interested in the banjo, but switched over to the guitar after his older brother Owen convinced him that the banjo was going out of style. His first professional experience also came at the hands of his older brother who, by the early '40s, was already a respected bandleader on WLAC. The eldest Bradley arranged for Harold to tour with Ernest Tubb during the break between his junior and senior years in high-school. After graduating and spending a stint in the Navy, Harold enrolled at George Peabody College in Nashville, where he studied music and made extra money by backing singers at the *Opry*.

By the late '40s Owen was one of the most popular bandleaders in the country and, along with Harold, decided to build Nashville's first recording facility, Castle Recording Studio. The small studio lasted several years, until the Bradley brothers built a larger facility capable of making stereo recordings. Around the same time Harold's session career began taking off as well and, throughout the '50s and '60s, his reputation for dependability and excellence landed him session work with some of the best names in the business, including Patsy Cline, Willie Nelson, Roy Orbison, and Elvis. Playing bass guitar, Harold also invented the "tic-tac" style of muting the bass notes. Throughout his career, he has never strayed far from his brother Owen and, in a large way, the Bradleys were among the key architects of the Nashville sound and style of recording, helping to build a recording industry where previously there was none. *—Steve Kurutz*

Owen Bradley

b. Oct. 21, 1915, Westmoreland, TX, **d.** Jan. 7, 1998

Piano, Producer / Nashville Sound/Countrypolitan

As one of the architects of the Nashville sound, Owen Bradley was one of the most influential country music producers of the '50s and '60s. Along with his contemporary Chet Atkins, Bradley helped country music move away from its rootsy origins to a more accessible, radio-friendly format by blending pop production and songwriting techniques with country. Bradley's country-pop productions relied on non-traditional country instruments like light, easy listening piano, backup vocals, and strings, using steel guitars and fiddles as flourishes instead of a foundation. This smooth production style helped make Patsy Cline and Brenda Lee into stars during the '50s, and its success often overshadowed Bradley's other musical contributions. Bradley wasn't just capable of the lush, detailed Nashville sound—he could also produce bluegrass by Bill Monroe or hardcore honky tonk by Ernest Tubb and Loretta Lynn. In addition to producing, Bradley was vice president of Decca Records' Nashville Division, and in that position he was able to produce a huge variety of artists, including Conway Twitty, Kitty Wells, and Webb Pierce. With his work in country-pop, honky tonk, and bluegrass, Bradley left behind a large legacy that proved vastly influential on contemporary country music.

Born outside of Westmoreland, TN, and raised in Nashville, Owen Bradley began playing piano professionally when he was a teenager, playing in local juke joints, clubs, and roadhouses. When he turned 20, he began working at WSM radio, and within five years he had established himself as an integral part of the station. In 1940, he was hired full-time by WSM, working as an arranger and instrumentalist. Two years later, he was made the station's musical director, and started playing regularly on the programs *Noontime Neighbors* and *Sunday Down South*. During this time, Bradley was also leading his own dance band, which played parties throughout Nashville's high society. The group stayed together until 1964.

Bradley began working for Decca Records in 1947 as an assistant to producer Paul Cohen. By working at Cohen's side, Bradley learned to produce, and assisted in making records by Ernest Tubb and Red Foley, among many others. Eventually, Owen began producing records by himself, whenever his mentor couldn't travel to Nashville from New York. Owen and his brother Harold opened a film studio in 1951, moving its location to Hillsboro Village within a year. It stayed there for two years, before it was moved again, this time to a house on 16th Avenue South with a Quonset hut attached to the main building. The Quonset hut was converted into a studio in 1955—it was the first studio on the street that would become known as Music Row. Two years later, RCA built a studio a block away from the Bradley hut; in 1962, the brothers sold the studio to Columbia Records.

Cohen left Decca in 1958, and the label offered Bradley a position as vice president of the label's Nashville Division. At Decca, he began pioneering the Nashville sound, incorporating orchestration and pop production techniques into country music. Patsy Cline was Bradley's most successful country-pop production. He had worked with her when she was with Four Star, but when she signed with Decca, Cline's music shifted toward country-pop and she began a string of Top Ten hits. Following her success, other artists that he produced in that style, most notably Brenda Lee, became successful as well. During this time, Bradley also produced harder-edged hits by Webb Pierce and Kitty Wells. In addition to his record production, Owen released a handful of records by his instrumental quintet, including the minor 1958 hit "Big Guitar." With his brother Harold, Bradley produced a half-hour television series, *Country Style U.S.A.*, during the late '50s.

Bradley bought a farm outside of Nashville in 1961, converting a barn into a demo studio. Within a few years, the barn was upgraded to a first-class recording studio called Bradley's Barn, and over the next two decades it became one of the most popular and legendary studios in country music. In 1980, it burned down, yet it was rebuilt with a few years in the exact same spot. Throughout the '60s and '70s, Bradley worked with many of Decca's most famous artists, including Loretta Lynn and Conway Twitty. In 1974, Bradley was inducted into the Country Music Hall of Fame. In the early '80s, he retired from full-time producing, yet he continued to work on the occasional special project. His last major work was k.d. lang's 1988 album, *Shadowland*. Bradley died January 7, 1998. *—Stephen Thomas Erlewine*

Paul Brandt (Paul Rennee Belobersycky)

b. Jul. 21, 1972, Calgary, Alberta, Canada

Vocals / Country-Pop, Contemporary Country, Neo-Traditionalist Country

Paul Brandt was one of the Canadian country singers able to take advantage of the massive success of Shania Twain and parlay a successful career for himself in America. Brandt was born and raised Calgary, Alberta, where he sang gospel music and learned to play guitar as a child. During high-school, he began playing local talent contests, singing his own songs. Most of his original material was directly inspired by neo-traditionalists like Dwight Yoakam and George Strait. Instead of pursuing country music as a full-time career, he decided to attend college and study nursing. For two years, Brandt went to college and practiced as a pediatric nurse at Alberta's Children's Hospital. However, he continued to enter local talent contests and to place well in each event.

The turning point in Brandt's musical career came when he entered a national contest sponsored by the Canadian performance organization, SOCAN. At the contest, Brandt won first prize for Best Original Canadian Country Song with "Calm Before the Storm," and placed as the runner-up for Best Performance. The SOCAN competition was monitored by several insiders in the Nashville music community, and Warner Bros. expressed interest in signing the singer. A demo tape of Brandt's songs made its way to Reprise's Nashville office. Reprise arranged to see a showcase concert by Brandt and, following the show, the label signed the young singer. After signing the record contract, Brandt moved to Nashville, where he recorded his debut album with producer Josh Leo, who had previously worked with Kathy Mattea and Alabama. Brandt's debut, *Calm Before the Storm*, was released in June to critical acclaim and strong sales. *Outside the Frame* was released the next year, followed by both *That's the Truth* and *A Paul Brandt Christmas: Shall I Play For You* in 1999. *—Stephen Thomas Erlewine*

● **Calm Before the Storm** / Jun. 1996 / Reprise ✦✦✦✦

Paul Brandt's debut *Calm Before the Storm* introduces a neo-traditionalist singer/songwriter of considerable potential, with an ability to skillfully bridge vintage honky-tonk with a contemporary country sound; along with the chart-topping "I Do," the album also includes the much-acclaimed "My Heart Has a History," Brandt's first Top Five hit. *—Jason Ankeny*

Outside the Frame / Nov. 11, 1997 / Reprise ✦✦✦✦

Paul Brandt's second album, *Outside the Frame*, is a successful continuance of the neo-traditionalist formula that made his debut, *Calm Before the Storm*, such a success. Again working with producer Josh Leo, Brandt finds the middle ground between traditional honky tonk and contemporary country-pop and while the songwriting is occasionally uneven, the conviction and passion of the performances make the weaker moments glide by.

All in all, the album—from the ballad "What's Come Over You" and the rocker "Yeah!" to "A Little in Love"—proves that Brandt is one of the better mainstream contemporary country vocalists of the late '90s. —*Thom Owens*

That's the Truth / Jul. 13, 1999 / Reprise ♦♦♦

Reprise released the title track of Paul Brandt's third album as a single months before the full disc appeared, in an attempt to re-ignite radio interest in the singer. But like all his singles and radio tracks since the two country Top Tens that launched his career in 1996, "That's The Truth" was a disappointment, which did not help set up the subsequent album. The song, co-written by Brandt, is a lyrically confused effort that starts out excoriating politicians and lawyers before settling into romantic cliché. After it's out of the way, Brandt turns to simpler, more conventional country sentiments, from the wedding song "It's a Beautiful Thing" to the unrequited love of "That Hurts." "Scrap Piece of Paper" is an entertaining novelty in a honky-tonk style, but the big surprise is Brian Setzer's typically rockabilly/jump blues-tinged "Let's Live It Up," which is given a Western swing treatment and could be a left-field hit. Certainly, it's time to take chances in Brandt's faltering career. —*William Ruhlmann*

A Paul Brandt Christmas: Shall I Play For You / Aug. 10, 1999 / Reprise ♦♦♦♦

Walter Brennan

b. Jul. 25, 1894, Swampscott, MA, **d.** Sep. 21, 1974, Oxnard, CA

Actor / Country-Pop, Nashville Sound/Countrypolitan

Three-time Oscar winner and country musician Walter Brennan was born in Swampscott, MA, on July 25, 1894. A veteran of World War I, Brennan began acting professionally in 1929. He received his first Oscar for his supporting role in Howard Hawks' *Come and Get It*, and two more followed for 1938's *Kentucky* and 1940's *The Westerner*. By the time he took a popular role as Grampa Amos McCoy on the TV show *The McCoys* in the late '50s, he had over 100 film credits to his name. His recording career was at its most prolific during the early '60s. A duet with Billy Vaughn, "Dutchman's Gold," was his first chart hit. Three more—"Old Rivers," "Houdini," and "Mama Sang Me a Song"—registered two years later. He passed away in 1974, due to emphysema, on September 21. —*Andy Kellman*

Dutchman's Gold / 1960 / Dot ♦♦♦♦

Old Rivers / 1962 / Liberty ♦♦

● **Old Rivers/Twas the Night Before Christmas . . . Back Home** / Apr. 21, 1998 / Collectors' Choice Music ♦♦♦♦

Compiling two complete Walter Brennan LPs onto one disc, *Old Rivers/'Twas the Night Before Christmas . . . Back Home* is probably the best collection of the actor/singer's music on the market, although one can't help but wonder why a seasonal record was included in the package as opposed to one more easily enjoyed all yearlong. —*Jason Ankeny*

Old Shep / May 16, 2000 / Universal Special Products ♦♦♦♦

Character actor Walter Brennan's recordings are an acquired taste. Recognized for his many movie appearances and his role as Grandpa on the TV show *The Real Mccoys*, Brennan also recorded and made the music charts in the early '60s. This ten-song budget-line disc from Universal features "Old Shep," "Tribute to a Dog," "Suppertime," "Life Gets Tee-jus, Don't It," and the Top Ten hit "Dutchman's Gold." —*Al Campbell*

Brinsley Schwarz

f. Oct. 1969, England, **db.** 1975

Group / Rock & Roll, Country-Rock, Pub Rock

Pub rock, the English roots rock movement of the early '70s, would never have earned a cult following if it wasn't for Brinsley Schwarz. Initially, Brinsley Schwarz was a rambling, neo-psychedelic folk-rock band that borrowed heavily from Crosby, Stills & Nash and the Grateful Dead. Following a disastrous publicity stunt to promote its debut album, the band went into seclusion outside of London and developed a laid-back, rootsy sound inspired by Eggs Over Easy, an American band that had been playing a mixture of originals and covers in English pubs. Following their conversion to pub rock, the Brinsleys ditched their pretensions of stardom and became a down-to-earth, self-effacing rock & roll band. Between 1971 and 1974, Brinsley Schwarz toured England innumerable times, playing pubs across the country. Along the way, they established a circuit for similar bands like Dr. Feelgood and Ducks Deluxe to follow. Though the group was nominally guitarist Brinsley Schwarz's band, bassist/lead vocalist Nick Lowe provided the bulk of the group's songs. Lowe developed a distinctive songwriting voice—conversational, melodic, offbeat, and funny—and the band was infused with his skewed sense of humor. Despite strong reviews and a dedicated fan base, the Brinsleys never managed to escape cult status, yet they influenced a legion of other artists, creating an underground, back-to-basics movement that laid the foundation for punk rock.

Brinsley Schwarz didn't plan to start a grassroots movement—the bandmembers wanted to be stars. Lowe and Schwarz had already spent several years in Kippington Lodge, a Tunbridge Wells-based guitar pop group that released five singles on Parlophone during the mid-'60s to no success. By 1968, the members of Kippington Lodge were beginning to feel restless with their straight-ahead pop/rock and were eager to explore psychedelia. Keyboardist Bob Andrews joined the band later that year and drummer Billy Rankin came aboard in the fall of 1969. By that time, Kippington Lodge had completely revamped its musical style, evolving into a folk-rock band with psychedelic pretensions and appropriately changing its name to Brinsley Schwarz after the group's lead guitarist. Ironically, it was around this time that Lowe became the band's lead singer and primary songwriter.

Within a few months, Brinsley Schwarz had come to the attention of Dave Robinson, a fledgling rock & roll manager who had founded the Famepushers Agency. Robinson developed a complex scheme to elevate Brinsley Schwarz to stardom. According to his plan, the Brinsleys would play an opening set for Van Morrison at the Fillmore East in New York in the spring of 1970, and he would fly all of the leading rock journalists to America to review the show. Late in 1969, Brinsley Schwarz signed a record contract with United Artists, and the band financed the publicity stunt with its advance. The group planned to leave a few days before the show in order to rehearse, but the Brinsleys were denied visas on a technicality. They were finally given visas on the morning of the show, and arrived in New York hours before the concert. Back in Britain, the journalists ran into trouble, as their plane developed a mechanical fault, delaying the flight for four hours. When the journalists arrived at the Fillmore 18 hours later, they were either drunk or hung over. When Brinsley Schwarz finally hit the stage, the band gave a competent but underwhelming performance, setting the stage for a flood of scathing reviews for both the concert and the eponymously titled debut album, which appeared weeks after the showcase.

Reeling from the Fillmore fiasco, the group rented a house outside of London and spent days and nights playing music. By the end of 1970, the Brinsleys released a second album, *Despite It All*, which indicated that they were evolving into a country-rock outfit; guitarist/vocalist Ian Gomm joined the band at the end of the sessions for the record. For much of 1971, Brinsley Schwarz rehearsed, developing a blend of country, folk, R&B, and rock & roll that was largely inspired by the Byrds, Van Morrison, and the Band, as well as Eggs Over Easy, which the group met at the Tally Ho pub in Kentish Town. *Silver Pistol*, released early in 1972, demonstrated a new versatility, but the group truly flexed its muscles in concert, particularly during regular concerts at the Tally Ho. Soon, they had built a small but loyal following, and a number of likeminded bands began playing the same circuit. Eventually, this grassroots phenomenon came to the attention of the U.K. press, which dubbed the groups' style as "pub rock" and proclaimed Brinsley Schwarz as the style's leaders.

Nervous on the Road, released in the fall of 1972, was Brinsley Schwarz's best-reviewed album to date, and while it didn't chart, it helped the group land an opening slot for Paul McCartney. Throughout 1973, the Brinsleys toured constantly, not only playing pubs, but also colleges. As a result, they weren't able to record frequently, which hurt their already weak recording career. In an attempt to land a hit, the band released a series of non-album singles, none of which charted; they were compiled for the *Please Don't Ever Change* album, which was released in late 1973. Early the following year, the group cut its fifth album with producer Dave Edmunds. Released in the summer of 1974, *New Favourites of Brinsley Schwarz* was more polished than the band's previous albums, yet the record failed to generate any sales. The group continued for nearly another year, turning out a handful of singles under other names, before deciding to call it a day in the spring of 1975. Following the band's demise, Schwarz and Andrews became members of Graham Parker's backing band, the Rumour. Gomm pursued a solo career; Rankin played with Terraplane and Big Jim Sullivan's Tiger before retiring from music. Lowe became a successful solo artist and producer, scoring his biggest hit in 1980 with "Cruel to Be Kind," a Brinsley leftover that the band never recorded. —*Stephen Thomas Erlewine*

Brinsley Schwarz / 1970 / One Way ♦♦♦

Brinsley Schwarz's eponymous debut is the stuff of rock legend because it is the punch line to a great story. It arrived after a disastrous publicity blitz, where the band's management arranged for prominent British journalists to cross the ocean to hear the Brinsleys' showcase performance at the Fillmore East. In a series of mishaps that would shame Spinal Tap, the band arrived in New York hours before their show and the journalists, who dipped heavily into the courtesy bar when their plane nearly crashed, arrived minutes before the concert. The press was underwhelmed to say the least and savaged the band and the record. Listening to *Brinsley Schwarz*, it's easy to see why they weren't turned on by the Brinsleys: this is a bizarre, naïve blend of Crosby, Stills & Nash, Dylan & the Band, and Buffalo Springfield, with a heavy dose of early Yes. It's filled with awkward steps and bad judgments, fueled by the group's romanticized view of Californian hippies. Consequently, it's hard not to cringe or chuckle by their hippie affectations, whether it's the lyrics ("she was my lady/had no plans to make her my wife") or the a cappella folk-rock harmonies that come out of nowhere on "Lady Constant" (it doesn't help that they sing "colored serpent coiled around your waist") or the bongo solo that ends "Shining Brightly." But, amidst all this hippie posturing, there some weird touches, like the multi-octave chromatic guitar break on "Hymn to Me" or the heavy prog jam of "What Do You Suggest?" and "Ballad of a Has-Been Beauty Queen" that illustrate how English the Brinsleys still were at this stage. All of this adds up to a debut that's decidedly uneven and unsure, but in retrospect, it's easy for sympathetic listeners to be charmed by their eccentricities. —*Stephen Thomas Erlewine*

Despite It All / 1970 / Liberty ♦♦♦

Brinsley Schwarz was hit hard by the terrible performance of their debut, so they rented a communal house and concentrated on becoming a real, organic band. They also recorded a second album swiftly, releasing *Despite It All* by the end of 1970. As soon as the folksy, fiddle-driven "Country Girl" amiably ambles out of the gates, the difference between the two records is apparent. They tried this kind of rootsy country-rock before, but it sounded awkward. Here, it rings true, not just because the songwriting is stronger, but because the band knows what they're doing, adding real grit and passion to the performances. *Despite It All* benefits from this looser playing, and for a while, it sounds like the group accomplished everything it wanted to do, since the first three songs are all early Nick Lowe masterpieces—"Country Girl," the fine ballad "The Slow One" and the flat-out terrific "Funk Angel," which is the first real flowering of his gifts as a pop tunesmith and sly humorist. After this, the record doesn't go off the rails, but it slowly loses its momentum, deteriorating to pleasant aping of CSN and Band plus the prog-inflected jams that were the bane of their debut. Some of this works—"Love Song" is a sweet tune, "Ebury Down" has a campfire charm—but when it ends with the drawn-out "Old Jarrow" (which does boast the timeless question "why don't you financially back her?" in its refrain) it's clear that the group is still in the process of finding of its voice. Their stumbles are brought into perspective by those three wonderful songs that begin the album, which not only make the record, but prove that the group does indeed have greatness in them. —*Stephen Thomas Erlewine*

Silver Pistol / 1972 / Edsel ✦✦✦✦✦
Silver Pistol isn't the definitive pub rock album, but it is the first great record to surface from the scene. Like much of the first wave of pub rock, *Silver Pistol* is quiet, laid-back and low-key—with its warm, rustic sound and a gentleness that infuses even the rockers, this is the closest to the Band that the Brinsleys got. There are some major differences, most of them coming from Nick Lowe. That's not to denigrate new guitarist/songwriter Ian Gomm, since his four numbers (particularly "Dry Land" and "Range War") reveal a fine songwriter with a keen sense of melody and a knack for synthesizing country, rock, and folk into something distinctive, but Lowe really hits his stride with this record. This is in to some degree due to the influence of Jim Ford, a renegade American roots rocker who Brinsley Schwarz backed on an unreleased and subsequently lost 1971 album. The group covers two of his songs, "Niki Hoeke Speedway" and "Ju Ju Man," on *Silver Pistol*, and these numbers reveal the appealingly off-kilter sense of humor and pop hooks that would form the foundation of Lowe's style. Those sensibilities are just beginning to creep into his songwriting on *Silver Pistol*, on the Beatles-meets-Band "Unknown Number," the lovely "Nightingale," the wonderful pop tune "The Last Time I Was Fooled," and the epic "Silver Pistol." His other two songs are sturdy country-rock numbers a notch below Gomm's best on the record, but still very good, and it all adds up to an endearing low-key roots rock album that doesn't just find Brinsley Schwarz coming into their own, it stands as one of the most appealing records of its kind. *—Stephen Thomas Erlewine*

☆ **Nervous on the Road** / 1972 / United Artists ✦✦✦✦✦
Silver Pistol wrote the blueprint for Brinsley Schwarz's pub rock, but *Nervous on the Road* perfected the group's sound, helping Brinsley to become the definitive pub rock band in the process. *Nervous on the Road* has a fuller, more detailed production than its predecessor, as well as a looser feeling—even with the smooth production, it sounds like the band was captured on a good night at the Tally Ho. But what really makes the record is its excellent selection of songs, almost all of which were written by Nick Lowe. "Happy Doing What We're Doing," "Surrender to the Rhythm," and "Nervous on the Road" are all great rock & roll songs about rock & roll, spiked with an off-kilter sense of humor. "Don't Lose Your Grip on Love" is Lowe's first great ballad, while Ian Gomm's "It's Been So Long" is one of his best songs. And the covers of "I Like It Like That" and "Home in My Hand" are wonderful pub rockers, giving the album the feeling of an excellent concert. Nevertheless, what makes *Nervous on the Road* such a fine record is the combination of empathetic performances, unpredictable songwriting, and charming unpretentiousness, all of which help make the album one of the great forgotten rock & roll records. *—Stephen Thomas Erlewine*

Please Don't Ever Change / 1973 / Edsel ✦✦✦✦
Released in 1973 as Brinsley Schwarz was busy touring and recording the follow-up to *Nervous on the Road*, *Please Don't Ever Change* is a collection of singles, live cuts, and radio sessions from the early '70s. The odds-and-sods nature of the record actually works in its favor, since it accentuates the group's ramshackle nature. Sure, there's a fair amount of filler on the record—their ill-advised reggae excursion "The Version (Hypocrite)" is simply mystifying—but unevenness was part of the Brinsleys' charm, and the simply enjoyable cuts make the best tracks feel like classics. And some of them are definitive Brinsley cuts. "I Worry ('Bout You Baby)" is a revamped R&B number, the live "Home in My Hand" speeds along with a relentless energy, the cover of Goffin/King's "Don't Ever Change" indicates Nick Lowe's latent pop roots, "Down in Mexico" is a hysterical travelogue, and "Play That Fast Thing (One More Time)" is among the classic pub rock singles, distilling the essence of pub rock into one piledriving song. *—Stephen Thomas Erlewine*

New Favourites of Brinsley Schwarz / 1974 / United Artists ✦✦✦✦✦
With their final album, Brinsley Schwarz turn in their most pop-oriented record, filled with infectious gems like "The Ugly Things," "Trying to Live My Life Without You," and "(What's So Funny 'Bout) Peace, Love and Understanding." Lowe's songs were the best he had ever written and show that his ambitions were beginning to conflict with those of the rest of the band. Nevertheless, there isn't a weak song or uninspired performance on *New Favourites*, making it an excellent farewell album. *—Stephen Thomas Erlewine*

15 Thoughts of Brinsley Schwarz / 1978 / United Artists ✦✦✦✦
Released at the end of the band's career, *15 Thoughts of Brinsley Schwarz* has a few questionable oversights and inclusions, and it does take a couple of detours, but it contains the bulk of the group's best-known songs. Yes, some highlights are missing, and it does overlap with *Original Golden Greats*, but it's a stronger overall collection than its predecessor, capturing the Brinsleys at their best. [It was made even stronger in 2000, when BGO combined *15 Thoughts* and *Golden Greats* as a two-fer.] *—Stephen Thomas Erlewine*

★ **Surrender to the Rhythm** / 1991 / EMI ✦✦✦✦✦
The 20-track compilation *Surrender to the Rhythm* is an excellent retrospective of Brinsley Schwarz's career. The compilation is culled from each of the group's albums, touching lightly on their earlier records and drawing heavily from *Silver Pistol*, *Nervous on the Road*, and *The New Favourites*, which is appropriate, since they were the stronger records. Although *Nervous on the Road* remains a necessary album, *Surrender to the Rhythm* compiles nearly every one of the Brinsleys' greatest tracks, including "Country Girl," "Ju Ju Man," "Down in Mexico," "Play That Fast Thing (One More Time)," "Happy Doing What We're Doing," "Don't Lose Your Grip on Love," "The Ugly Things," a ripping live version of "Home in My Hand," and the original version of Nick Lowe's classic "(What's So Funny 'Bout) Peace, Love and Understanding." *Surrender to the Rhythm* offers convincing evidence that Brinsley Schwarz is one of the great underrated bands of the early '70s, while essentially summing up the spirit of pub rock. *—Stephen Thomas Erlewine*

Hen's Teeth / May 5, 1998 / Edsel ✦✦✦
Hen's Teeth is a bit of a godsend for longtime Brinsley Schwarz collectors, gathering all of the group's non-LP singles—including the first singles released when the band was a Swinging London pop combo called Kippington Lodge—plus singles the group released under aliases. As the Hitters, they released the reggae single "Hypocrite," complete with the dub "Version" on the flip. As the Knees and Limelight, they released 45s of Beatles covers. All this is interesting, fun trivia, but the true meat of the collection lies in the Kippington Lodge material and the official non-LP Brinsley tunes. Kippington Lodge may not be earth-shattering and the band is quite derivative, borrowing heavily from psychedelic British pop, in particular the Beatles and early Yes. This isn't bad, but it is silly, whether it's the cascading psychedelia of "Lady on a Bicycle," the exhortation to have a "peace-off" on "Tomorrow Today," or the Vanilla Fudge-styled, bombastic soul cover of "In My Life." All artifacts, of course, but they're pretty engaging artifacts all the same, and the last Kippington song, "I Can See Her Face," is notable as Nick Lowe's first recorded song. The Brinsley material stands the test of time, finding the group at its very poppiest, whether turning out spirited covers of Naomi Neville's "I've Cried My Last Tear" and Tommy Roe's stomping "Everybody," or on originals, divided equally between Lowe, Ian Gomm, and co-compositions between the two. These four songs—"(It's Gonna Be a) Bring Down," "I Like You, I Don't Love You," "There's a Cloud in My Heart," and "I Got the Real Thing"—are shiny, glittering pop, finding the group exercising its mainstream melodic muscle. The songs didn't land the band any hits, but they stand as terrific little gems that offer a nice conclusion to this terrific, necessary compilation. *—Stephen Thomas Erlewine*

What IS So Funny About Peace Love and Understanding? / Oct. 23, 2001 / Hux ✦✦✦✦✦
Although it doesn't top the peerless *Hen's Teeth*—which is about as perfect an archival release as any Brinsley fan could hope for—it's impossible not to delight in Hux's 2001 collection, *What IS So Funny About Peace Love and Understanding?* a collection of the band's Radio 1 sessions from 1972 and 1975. This is not the complete sessions, but the great thing is, these are sessions that haven't widely circulated on bootleg; there is some overlap with the relatively famous *Unknown Numbers* boot, but there are a number of delights here that didn't appear on that collection, including covers of "You Got Me Hummin'," "Mama Told Me Not to Come," and a storming "Everybody" which tears their already great studio version. Then, there's Sam Cooke's "Havin' a Party" and "She's Got to Be Real," which they never did anywhere else, plus ace versions of such Nick Lowe favorites as "Nervous on the Road," "Play That Fast Thing One More Time," and the fan favorites "I Worry ('Bout You Baby)" and "Small Town Big City." The capper is four cuts of Brinsley Schwarz backing Frankie Miller in dynamite versions of his own "Ann Eliza Jane," "In No Resistance," and "You Don't Need to Laugh," plus a lively cover of Van Morrison's "Wild Night," plus great notes from Mr. Schwarz himself. It all adds up to a first-rate archival release; one for the fans, to be sure, but it's hard to imagine that there isn't a single fan who wouldn't delight in this terrific addition to Brinsley Schwarz's catalog. *—Stephen Thomas Erlewine*

Elton Britt (James Britt Baker)

b. Jun. 27, 1913, Marshall, AR, **d.** Jun. 23, 1972
Vocals / Traditional Country, Honky Tonk, Yodeling
Elton Britt parlayed his Jimmie Rodgers imitation—with a yodeling ability and range that surpassed Rodgers'—into country's biggest hit of the World War II era, "There's a Star Spangled Banner Waving Somewhere," which sold four-million copies in the early '40s. He was born James Britt Baker in Marshall, AR, on June 27, 1913, and began playing guitar and singing around his hometown while in his mid-teens. Baker's career was made in 1930 when the Beverly Hill Billies returned from California to their Arkansas home to recruit a new vocalist. He won the talent search, and after being renamed Elton Britt, spent three years performing and recording with the Hill Billies. Britt moved to New York in 1933, initially playing in a quartet named Pappy, Zeke, Ezra & Elton. He recorded later in the '30s, as a solo act and also with the Wenatchee Mountaineers, Zeke Manners' Gang, and the Rustic Rhythm Trio.

Britt began his period of fame in 1939, thanks to two circumstances: his signature on a contract for the discount label RCA Bluebird and—most importantly—his friendship with songwriter/producer Bob Miller. Miller wrote all of Elton Britt's greatest early hits, including "Chime Bells," "Rocky Mountain Lullaby," "Buddy Boy," "Driftwood on the River," and in 1942, "There's a Star Spangled Banner Waving Somewhere." The latter was adopted as a symbol of the war effort by patriotic audiences—much as "Over There" had served World War I sympathizers. President Franklin Roosevelt even invited Britt—billed as "the World's Highest Yodeler"—to the White House in 1942 to perform the hit.

By the time the charts came into existence in 1944, though, Britt had peaked. He did hit the Country Top Ten 11 times during the last half of the '40s, but never topped the charts. "Someday" reached number two in 1946, and six other songs peaked in the Top Five, including the double-sided "Wave to Me, My Lady"/"Blueberry Lane," "Detour," "Gotta Get Together With My Gal," "Candy Kisses," and "Quicksilver." A re-recording of his early hit "Chime Bells" hit number six. Britt continued recording with RCA, eventually releasing over 50 albums until 1957, when he moved to ABC/Paramount. He made a brief bid for the presidency in 1960, and recorded the number 26 "Jimmie Rodgers Blues" eight years later, but retired soon after. *—John Bush*

16 Great Country Performances / 1971 / ABC ✦✦✦✦

The RCA Years / Apr. 21, 1998 / Collectors' Choice Music ✦✦✦✦

● **Ridin' with Elton** / Nov. 25, 2000 / Soundies ✦✦✦✦
Elton Britt is one of the true mystery men of country music; not much is known of his life and offstage he was described as a dull and colorless sort. But he left behind a brace of marvelous cowboy recordings in the Gene Autry style that have endured nicely and this set of transcription recordings enhances his rep just that much more. Nice transfers from the original lacquers yield top flight versions of "Pinto Pal," "Goodbye May God Take Care of You," "Trip to the Moon," "Some Time Sue," "Ain't You a Little Bit Sorry?," "Put Me in

Your Pocket," and "There's a Star Spangled Banner Waving Somewhere." Elton could sing a ballad and break your heart, yodel with the best of 'em, and dig right into an uptempo toe tapper with equal flair. Here's a nice introduction to his style. *—Cub Koda*

Chad Brock

b. Jul. 31, 1963, Ocala, FL

Vocals / Country-Pop, Contemporary Country, Honky Tonk, Neo-Traditionalist Country
Contemporary country singer/songwriter Chad Brock was born and raised in Ocala, FL; despite performing in the church choir throughout his youth, his initial love was athletics, and he was a highly touted high-school football player. After joining the school chorus, however, Brock also emerged as a star soloist, and became so enamored of music that he turned down a collegiate athletic scholarship to pursue a career as a performer. Relocating to Nashville to work as a songwriter, he initially struggled to get his foot in the music industry's door, and as a result spent three years touring as a member of the World Championship Wrestling organization.

Finally, in 1998, Brock signed with Warner Bros. and issued his self-titled debut later that year. The second single, "Ordinary Life," was a breakout hit, climbing into the country Top Five, and "Lightning Does the Work" was also moderately popular. Brock's follow-up was 2000's *Yes!*, and the title track—a story song about meeting and romancing his wife—became his first country chart-topper, nearly making the pop Top 20 as well. In 2001, *III* didn't quite duplicate that success. *—Jason Ankeny*

● **Chad Brock** / Oct. 20, 1998 / Warner Bros. ✦✦✦

Yes! / May 2, 2000 / Warner Bros. ✦✦

Chad Brock broke through with "Ordinary Life," the second single from his self-titled 1998 debut, and he returns with this follow-up, another agreeable collection of bland pop-country. It is some measure of the state of country music that a performer as faceless as this one can be thought of as sufficiently traditionalist to attract cameos from George Jones and Hank Williams Jr. on a boneheaded update of that boneheaded anthem "A Country Boy Can Survive," when the rest of his music adopts a crossover style that often makes it sound more appropriate for the adult contemporary rather than the country charts. But that remake did make the charts, and the title track, a Brock co-composition telling the story of how he met and married his wife, was a substantial hit by the time the album was released. The reason is that Brock is well-suited to the limited demands of country radio; on these sketchy songs, he references country music without really playing it. Somewhere in the mix a fiddle and steel guitar usually lurk, but not so you'd notice them, and the songs, two-verse specials with big choruses built on clichés ("You Had to Be There," "If I Were You"), outline the kind of sentimental, sometimes maudlin, common-man love stories typical of country lyrics, without ever getting specific enough to sound believable (and that includes the "true story" in "Yes!"). Brock sings in an artless, unaffected tenor that makes him seem more like an anonymous demo singer than a name recording artist. If this is the kind of harmless, homogenized music that country radio likes in 2000 (and it is), maybe that's just because it makes for little interruption in mood from the commercials that really pay the bills. *—William Ruhlmann*

III / Sep. 25, 2001 / Warner Bros. ✦✦✦

For Chad Brock, it looks like the third time's a charm. Brock has been making great music for quite some time, but up until now it seems that he has been shifting around musically, trying to find his niche in country music. It's like the old game of pegs where one tries to put the round peg in the round hole, the square peg in the square hole, and so on. With the release of *III*, Chad Brock seems to have all of his pegs in the right spot. Brock never abandons the fun country style, with songs like "Park the Pick-Up (Kiss the Girl)" and "Livin' in Las Vegas" running in a similar vein to past hits "Yes!" and "Lightning Does the Work." Some better-than-average ballads pop up on this CD, too; the best one is "The Lie," a song about a woman who pays the price of one infidelity with a permanent reminder. Brock takes a chance by including "Population Minus One," a song that features spoken verses and a singing chorus. That doesn't always work, but Brock manages to pull it off without leaving a cheesy residue on the CD. No doubt about it, Chad Brock is a vocalist who continues to entertain with his third album. *—Rick Cohoon*

Lane Brody

b. Racine, WI

Vocals / Country-Pop, Urban Cowboy
Lane Brody was born in Racine, WI, where her love of singing was established at a very early age. She wrote her first song, "Through the Darkness," at 12, founded an all-girl trio while still in high-school, and by age 18 had set out for New York, where she was discovered by vocalist Bobby Whiteside. Eventually, Brody moved to Chicago, where she sang commercial jingles and modeled in print for such products as Harley Davidson motorcycles and Pabst Blue Ribbon beer.

In 1976 she made her recording debut with the single "You're Gonna Make Love to Me" under the pseudonym Lynn Niles. Brody next moved to California, where she in 1981 signed with Liberty and debuted on the singles chart with the self-penned "He's Taken." Her next release, "More Nights," made it to the Top 60. Near the end of the year she had a minor-hit duet with Thom Bresh, "When It Comes to Love." That same year Brody made her television acting debut on the series *Taxi* and was nominated for an Emmy the following year for singing "Just a Little More Love" in the TV-movie *The Gift of Life*. Her next chart appearance came in 1983 with a song she co-wrote, the Oscar-nominated "Over You," which was featured in the film *Tender Mercies*. She scored a number-one hit with her 1984 duet with Johnny Lee, "The Yellow Rose," which she and John Weilder adapted from a Civil War standard for use as the theme song to a short-lived TV series.

Brody's self-titled 1985 debut album contained two hits, including Bobby Lee Springfield's "He Burns Me Up." The next year she and Lee recorded another popular

duet, "I Could Get Used to This." She then played a country singer on ABC's TV series *Heart of the City*. Brody continued to tour with Bresh following a joint appearance on a Lee Greenwood special for TNN and their own subsequent special. She also wrote and performed "All the Unsung Heroes" for a documentary on the Vietnam War Memorial in Washington, D.C. Throughout her career Brody was also a frequent performer with the USO, entertaining servicemen and veterans. She continued to perform throughout the late '90s and early 2000s, including appearances on Nashville's *Grand Ole Opry*. In 1996, she was honored by the Country Music Hall of Fame with her very own star on its famous walkway. Her album *Pieces of Life* appeared in 2002. *—Johnny Loftus*

● **Lane Brody** / 1985 / EMI America ✦✦✦✦

Pieces of Life / Apr. 9, 2002 / Scream Marketing ✦✦✦

Lisa Brokop

b. 1973, Surrey, B.C., Canada

Vocals / Contemporary Country
Lisa Brokop was born in Surrey, British Columbia, in 1973. Born into a musical family, Brokop was on-stage with her accordion-playing mother by age seven, performing polkas and popular country hits like "The Gambler." By 15, she was gigging throughout the thriving country music scene in Vancouver, both as a singer and guitar player, and soon began issuing her own singles. Her debut Canadian album appeared in 1991, when Brokop was only 17.

A year later, the young country singer headed for Nashville. Making it look easy, a 30-minute showcase at a local club and a performance on TNN's *Ralph Emory Show* was all it took to land Brokop a deal with Capitol-Nashville, and in 1994 the label issued her proper Nashville debut. *Every Little Girl's Dream* was produced by Jerry Crutchfield, and found moderate success with its singles *Give Me a Ring Sometime* and *Take That*. A self-titled effort followed in 1995, spawning the singles *Before He Kissed Me* and *She Can't Save Him*. There was no question that Brokop had already achieved more Nashville success than many who brought their dreams to the city. But at 22, she was burned out. Brokop ended her relationship with Capitol and took some time off to work on her own songwriting.

In 1998, Brokop returned to the spotlight. Now with Columbia, she issued the CD-5/EP *When You Get to Be You*. While the release did well in her native Canada, Columbia chose not to release it in the U.S. Evidently, the Columbia deal wasn't the right fit either, because when Brokop next surfaced, it was with the 2000 LP *Undeniable*, released through her own Cosmo label and available only in Canada or through her website. However, the record was a success in her home country, and Brokop continued to tour in support of it through 2003. *—Johnny Loftus*

● **Every Little Girl's Dream** / 1994 / Capitol ✦✦✦✦

Lisa Brokop / 1995 / Capitol ✦✦✦

David Bromberg

b. Sep. 19, 1945, Philadelphia, PA

Dobro, Guitar, Mandolin, Vocals, Session Musician, Fiddle / Singer/Songwriter, Contemporary Folk
Often referred to as a musician's musician throughout his career, Bromberg has spent almost as much time being a sideman to people like Bob Dylan and Jerry Jeff Walker as he has fronting his own band. Session credits for albums by Tom Paxton and Jerry Jeff Walker started getting Bromberg attention in the mid-'60s, and he began making the transition from sideman to frontman in the early '70s, when he was signed to record for Columbia records. The key to appreciating Bromberg is to realize he has an equal passion for blues, folk, country and western, bluegrass and rock & roll. This diverse range of influences is reflected on all his recordings for Columbia, Fantasy, and Rounder, and in his performances as well. His musical eclecticism over the years may have cost him some fans, but a typical Bromberg concert can be a musical education. *—Richard Skelly*

David Bromberg / 1971 / Columbia ✦✦✦✦✦

David Bromberg was already a well-known folk instrumentalist before this album proved he was also a top-notch songwriter and an appealing vocalist as well. The styles mix folk, blues, rock, and jug-band music, and the songs alternate from the painfully sensitive ("Sammy's Song") to the rib-tickling "The Holdup," which was cowritten by George Harrison. *—William Ruhlmann*

Demon in Disguise / 1972 / Columbia ✦✦✦

Wanted Dead or Alive / 1974 / Columbia ✦✦✦✦

Midnight on the Water / 1975 / Columbia ✦✦✦

A big-band blowout album with guest appearances by Bonnie Raitt, Linda Ronstadt, Emmylou Harris, it features "The Jokes on Me" and "Don't Put that Thing on Me." *—Richard Meyer*

How Late'll Ya Play 'Til? / 1976 / Fantasy ✦✦✦

Bromberg's band, with two horns and a fiddle player, is capable of playing just about any style of popular music, and most of them are here on a double album, half recorded in the studio and half live. (Fantasy has also issued the two discs separately.) The standout inclusion is Bromberg's "Will Not Be Your Fool," which became his on-stage showstopper from here on out. *—William Ruhlmann*

Hillbilly Jazz, Vol. 1 / 1977 / Sonet ✦✦✦

Hillbilly Jazz, Vol. 2 / 1977 / Sonet ✦✦✦

Reckless Abandon / 1977 / Fantasy ✦✦✦

By billing this album to the David Bromberg Band, Bromberg signals that the listener can expect to hear more than just his adenoidal voice and variety of acoustic instruments. But then, that just means it's as eclectic as most David Bromberg albums. The leadoff track "I Want to Go Home" has a blues-rock feel; horns wail into a Dixieland swarm during the old folk tune "Stealin'"; and then comes a medley of old-timey country tunes played on banjo, mandolin, and guitar. That's just the first three tracks, and before the album is over, one has been treated to melodic folk-rock ("Baby Breeze"), blues ("Nobody's Fault but Mine"), and jump blues with a touch of funk ("Beware Brother Beware"), not to mention a jazzy sequel to "Stagger Lee," "Mrs. Delion's Lament," in which Stagger Lee takes over hell, and a medley of Civil War songs. Not bad for a performer who tends to get categorized as a folksinger. *—William Ruhlmann*

Out of the Blues: Best of David Bromberg / 1977 / Columbia ✦✦✦

Out of the Blues: Best of David Bromberg is a solid ten-track collection that features many highlights from Bromberg's '70s recordings, including both originals ("The Holdup," "The Joke's on Me," "The New Lee Highway Blues," "Demon in Disguise," "Sharon") and covers ("Send Me to the 'Lectric Chair," "Mr. Bojangles," "Kansas City," "(What A) Wonderful World"). It's a good summation of his prime period and, therefore, a good introduction to his music. *—Stephen Thomas Erlewine*

Bandit in a Bathing Suit / 1978 / Fantasy ✦✦✦

Here's a lot of hot playing that includes Pink Anderson's "Travelin' Man" and "If You Don't Want Me Baby." *—Richard Meyer*

My Own House / 1978 / Fantasy ✦✦✦

You Should See the Rest of the Band / 1980 / Fantasy ✦✦

Sideman Serenade / 1990 / Rounder ✦✦

Bromberg's debut for Rounder included versions of traditional blues, country, folk and soul/R&B tunes. He sang them earnestly and backed himself tastefully while working with both large groups and small combos. The guest roster included everyone from Dr. John to Jackson Browne and David Lindley, as well as Chris Daniels and the Kings and some members of what was then Willie Nelson's traveling band. The only problem with this session was Bromberg, for all his knowledge and zeal, just wasn't that convincing or gripping a vocalist. Still, this is an instructive disc for those interested in hearing faithful recreations of various classic genres. *—Ron Wynn*

● **The Player: Retrospective** / May 5, 1998 / Columbia/Legacy ✦✦✦✦✦

The Player: A Retrospective is an incomplete but effective summary of David Bromberg's career, containing the majority of his best songs. It is true that some personal favorites such as "The New Lee Highway Blues" may be missing—and this may be a sticking point, since Bromberg fans are very dedicated—but most of the important songs—"Sharon," "The Hold Up," "Mr. Bojangles," "Sammy's Song," "The Joke's on Me," "Wallflower"—are here, making this a fine replacement for the earlier compilation, *Out of the Blues*, as well as a good introduction for the curious. *—Stephen Thomas Erlewine*

Reckless Abandon/Bandit in a Bathing Suit / Jun. 9, 1998 / Fantasy ✦✦✦

In 1998, Fantasy released *Reckless Abandon/Bandit in a Bathing Suit*, which contained two complete albums—*Reckless Abandon* (1977, originally released on Fantasy) and *Bandit in a Bathing Suit* (1978, originally released on Fantasy)—by David Bromberg on one compact disc. *—Tim Sendra*

My Own House/You Should See the Rest of the Band / 1999 / Fantasy ✦✦✦✦✦

As of the late '90s, guitarist and fiddler David Bromberg was in musical semi-retirement, supplementing his day job (making his living buying and selling American-made violins) with the odd club gig. But in the 1970s, he had a thriving career as both a bandleader and a sideman, having played on seminal recordings by Bob Dylan, the Eagles, and Jerry Jeff Walker, among others. This disc includes two of his early albums: first, the acoustic and largely solo *My Own House*, on which he plays a program that ranges from traditional Scottish and American fiddle tunes through Delta blues and songs by Hoagy Carmichael and Phil Spector. Talk about Americana. The second album included on this disc couldn't be more of a contrast: *You Should See the Rest of the Band* is a live recording with a large and very definitely electric band. David Bromberg the rock & roll bandleader is much more inclined toward horn-driven R&B ("Key to the Highway," "Sharon"), although he does pull out the fiddle for a high-octane romp through a medley of traditional tunes at the end of the show. His singing, while not bad, isn't really worth mentioning. What stand out are his wide-ranging tastes, his instrumental chops, and his skill as a bandleader, all of which combine to make this both a valuable piece of pop music history and a thrilling listening experience. *—Rick Anderson*

The Brooklyn Cowboys

f. 1996

Group / Roots Rock, Country-Rock

The Brooklyn Cowboys is the moniker of a group featuring several members of known bands, in-demand session players, and touring musicians. The group was formed in 1996 when singer/songwriter Walter Egan (well-known to pop fans and '70s enthusiasts for his Top Ten single "Magnet & Steel") was called upon by Fredrough Perry to work on some of Perry's sessions. The pair worked well together and an offhand remark by Perry led to the formation of the Brooklyn Cowboys. Bringing respected steel player Buddy Cage (the New Riders of the Purple Sage) into the fold, the group began to tour its brand of country-rock throughout the Northeast, building a live following. In 1997, Egan moved to Nashville and the band re-formed to include singer Brian Waldschlager, bass player Jeff "Stick" Davis (of the Amazing Rhythm Aces), and keyboard player Michael Webb. Entering the studio, the Brooklyn Cowboys were guided by producer Al Perkins (the Flying Burrito Brothers, Gram Parsons) and the sessions produced a debut, entitled *Doin' Time on Planet Earth*, which included a version of "Carolina Calypso" that Egan had co-written with Parsons, originally appearing on the latter's acclaimed *Grievous Angel* set. The release received high marks from critics and also managed to achieve commercial success in Europe, where the album made Top Ten placings on independent release charts. In early 2002, the Brooklyn Cowboys released a mini-album, *The Other Man in Black: Tribute to Dale Earnhardt*, and followed it with a sophomore full-length album, *Dodging Bullets*. *—Tom Demalon*

● **Doin' Time on Planet Earth** / Mar. 28, 2000 / Leap ✦✦✦✦

Raised in Washington, D.C., Walter Egan—best known for his '70s hit "Magnet & Steel"—returns to his East Coast honky tonk roots with the Brooklyn Cowboys, a pseudo-superband comprised of established country-rock vets. Bassist Michael Supa did time in the Ozark Mountain Daredevils, pedal steel-meister Buddy Cage was a major player in the New Riders of the Purple Sage, singer/songwriter Joy Lynn White maintains a substantial career as a solo artist, and the whole shebang is produced by Al Perkins who added authentic country twang to the Stones, Manassas, and most notably the Flying Burrito Brothers. It's the latter band whose ghost haunts this set, as Egan—writer of the beautiful "Hearts on Fire" that was recorded by Gram Parsons and Emmylou Harris on *Grievous Angel* and is reprised here—plays Parsons to White's Harris on many tracks. Egan shares the low-key plaintive vocal qualities of Parsons, and these songs—most co-written by Egan and drummer/co-founder Fredrough Perry—could easily have been included on either of Parsons' two Burrito or solo albums. "Californ'," "Juke Box Girl," and "Learn How to Love Me," while not as dramatic as Parsons' best work, echo with his sense of "cosmic American music" as bits of soul, Tex-Mex, and even zydeco pepper the hard-core honky tonk arrangements. Vassar Clements' rootsy fiddle adds even more authenticity, but it's on tracks like the yearning "Exquisite Torture" where the band sounds as authentic as if they were born and raised on a back road in the South. White, who provides only backing vocals, is sadly under-utilized here, yet it's her aching voice that provides the album's most heartbreaking sounds. Egan's singing is certainly respectful but lacks the effortless soul resonance of Parsons', and some of the tunes like the jaunty, enthusiastic, double-time "Burning Bridge" and the by-the-numbers country-rocking of "Wishful Drinking" sound a little forced, if not quite clichéd. Egan may not have the offhand charm or visionary genius of Gram Parsons, but with this sturdy debut the Brooklyn Cowboys prove they are talented and resourceful musicians, who, though they don't push the boundaries of the hardcore C&W music they so obviously love, work remarkably well within its confines. *—Hal Horowitz*

The Other Man in Black: Tribute to Dale Earnhardt / Feb. 12, 2002 / Leap ✦✦

Dodging Bullets / Sep. 10, 2002 / Leap ✦✦✦

Forget the seeming oxymoron in their name, the Brooklyn Cowboys deliver the real goods with no dispute. This is a group of veteran musicians that has done many one-nighters with a variety of bands: from the Amazing Rhythm Aces (Jeff "Stick" Davis) to New Riders of the Purple Sage and Bob Dylan (Buddy Cage), this band can walk that walk that only comes from experience. This veteran group has blended a sound that unites two strands of a musical juggernaut. This twangy and hard-driving band melded together 14 songs that are a product of the whole band. It seems to be a whole group effort this time out, and in that sense it is more cohesive as a disc. The songs rock when they rock ("I Was Wrong," written by Perry Egan), and when they are country, they have that hard twang of deep country ("Trick Ponies," written by Brian Waldschlager). It is taking this combination of two distinct styles and fusing them that carries it that one step further. Neither of the elements are missing from any song; however, the songs make a true amalgam of the two disparate styles, while remaining predominately in one of the frameworks. Walter Egan's vocals are in top form, and he is joined on several cuts by either Lona Heins (two cuts) or Joy Lynn White (two cuts), both of whom add a pleasant contrast in vocal styles. The playing by everyone is stellar throughout the disc. Jeff "Stick" Davis (bass) and Fredro Perry (drums and group founder) anchor the group with their tight rhythms, allowing the rest of the band to soar and explore, led by Buddy Cage's steel guitar. Though there is anomaly in the group's name, that is the only place where you will hear it. (Just for the record there are a few top-hand cowboys from Brooklyn hiding out in the Arizona and New Mexico hinterlands.) *—Bob Gottlieb*

Brooks & Dunn

f. 1988, Nashville, TN

Group / Country-Pop, Contemporary Country, New Traditionalist

The undisputed kings of the '90s' line-dancing craze, Brooks & Dunn are not only the biggest-selling duo in country music history, they've also sold more records than any other duo period, save for Simon & Garfunkel. Ronnie Dunn was the quietly intense singer with the soulful voice, while Kix Brooks played the part of the high-energy showman. Neither had been able to break through as a solo act, but together they hit upon a winning formula of rambunctious, rocked-up honky tonk with punchy, danceable beats, and alternated those cuts with smooth, pop-tinged ballads. The combination made them one of the most popular country artists of the '90s, and they were still going strong as the new millennium dawned.

Leon Eric "Kix" Brooks (born in Shreveport, LA) and Ronnie Gene Dunn (born in Coleman, TX) arrived in Nashville from very different backgrounds. Brooks was a neighbor of Johnny Horton and first began singing with the country legend's daughter at age 12; after a time working on the Alaskan oil pipeline, he moved to Maine and performed in ski resorts and other local venues. He went to Nashville in the early '80s and found success as a songwriter, penning hits for John Conlee, Highway 101, and the Nitty Gritty Dirt Band, among others; however, his solo recordings—a few small-label singles in 1983 and a self-titled album in 1989—failed to make any impact. Dunn, meanwhile, had been playing with traditional string bands since he was a teenager, but originally aspired to become a Baptist minister. He attended the highly conservative Abilene Christian University, but was kicked out for continuing to play music on the side in area bars. He decided to pursue music full-time and moved to Tulsa, where he led a house band and recorded for a local label from 1983-1984. In 1988, he won a songwriting contest whose prize included a recording session in Nashville; the producer, Scott Hendricks, was impressed enough to pass some of Dunn's material on to Arista executive Tim DuBois. DuBois had a hunch that Dunn and Brooks would complement each other well, and he introduced the two and encouraged them to try writing and recording some demo songs together. When he heard the results, DuBois signed the newly minted Brooks & Dunn duo to a contract.

Brooks & Dunn issued their debut album, *Brand New Man*, in 1991, and it was an out-of-the-box smash. The title track, "My Next Broken Heart," "Neon Moon," and "Boot Scootin' Boogie" all hit number one on the country charts, and the latter song in particular was an inescapable smash that helped kick-start the line-dancing fad that swept country bars across the nation. *Brand New Man* eventually went on to sell over five-million copies, and made the duo into country superstars; their supporting tour established their penchant for theatrical live shows as well. Their follow-up, *Hard Workin' Man*, consolidated their success with a string of five Top Five country hits: the title track, the number ones "She Used to Be Mine" and "That Ain't No Way to Go," and the number twos "We'll Burn That Bridge" and "Rock My World (Little Country Girl)." *Hard Workin' Man* sold over four-million copies, and by the time its run of singles was exhausted, the duo had already completed a follow-up in 1994's *Waitin' on Sundown*.

Five more Top Ten hits followed, including the number ones "She's Not the Cheatin' Kind," "Little Miss Honky Tonk," and "You're Gonna Miss Me When I'm Gone" (the others were "I'll Never Forgive My Heart" and "Whiskey Under the Bridge"). *Waitin' on Sundown* went double platinum, confirming Brooks & Dunn's status as a blockbuster success. Brooks & Dunn's commercial dominance continued apace with 1996's *Borderline*, another double-platinum success which produced two more chart-toppers in "My Maria" (a cover of the B.W. Stevenson pop hit from 1972) and "A Man This Lonely," and a number-two hit in "I Am That Man." In 1997, the duo issued *The Greatest Hits Collection*, whose new tracks, "Honky Tonk Truth" and "He's Got You," both reached the Top Five. And they weren't done as hitmakers by any means; despite failing to go platinum, 1998's *If You See Her* contained two number ones in "Husbands and Wives" (a Roger Miller cover) and "How Long Gone," and another Top Fiver in "I Can't Get Over You." With such a consistent track record, Brooks & Dunn were perhaps due for the inevitable slip, and 1999's *Tight Rope* was the closest thing to a commercial misstep they'd ever recorded. Despite some chance-taking in the production and the cover of rocker John Waite's ballad "Missing You," other parts of the album found their formula wearing thin. The record produced only one Top Ten hit in "You'll Always Be Loved by Me," and failed to even go gold. Faced with a downturn in their sales, Brooks & Dunn spent more time crafting their next album, 2001's *Steers and Stripes*. It helped restore their commercial fortunes with a trio of chart-topping singles: "Ain't Nothing 'Bout You," "Only in America," and "The Long Goodbye." The following year, the duo issued their first holiday album, *It Won't Be Christmas Without You.* —*Steve Huey*

Brand New Man / 1991 / Arista ✦✦✦✦

An impressive debut that proudly proclaims its country roots without being afraid to dip its toes into pop and rock, *Brand New Man* is an entertaining listen. Like most Nashville records from the early '90s, *Brand New Man* is short, barely clocking in over 30 minutes, but Brooks & Dunn have clearly brought their A material to the table. The voices of the leaders blend well, and they are backed by a crack Nashville band that handles the all-original material with ease. Highlights include the insanely catchy title track and the almost Springsteen-esque "Lost and Found." Fairly traditional country songs such as "Cheating on the Blues" cohabitate peacefully with more pop-oriented fare like "Neon Moon" and "Still in Love With You." Thankfully, these latter tracks do not follow in the all-too-common mold of over-production that would bury the charms of these songs beneath string orchestras, rock guitars, and huge drums. As individual vocalists, both Brooks and Dunn are competent and expressive, although they do lack something in originality and distinctiveness. Although it's probably too much to ask from this kind of record, it would still be great to hear this great band really letting loose in extended fashion; such small tastes as at the end of "Cool Drink of Water" make the listener thirsty for more. Occupying the middle ground between Johnny Cash and the Eagles, Brooks & Dunn have put together a terrific group of songs that are memorable, hummable, and, most importantly, fun. Despite the diversity in the material, the album works well as a coherent whole. All in all, *Brand New Man* is a fine, fine collection of pop-country songs, masterfully played. —*Daniel Gioffre*

Hard Workin' Man / 1993 / Arista ✦✦✦

As with most second albums, the successful traits started to isolate themselves on *Hard Workin' Man*: Macho stuff like "Hard Workin' Man" and "Rock My World (Little Country Girl)" rocked harder than anything on *Brand New Man*, though B&D made sure their women came off as good as they did (catch the "and women too" tag on "Hard Workin' Man"). The slower songs ("That Ain't No Way to Go," "She Used to Be Mine") tended toward the sort of evocative images that ran all through the debut. The pair never put all the elements together they way they did the first time, but they came close enough that few people noticed. —*Brian Mansfield*

Waitin' on Sundown / Sep. 27, 1994 / Arista ✦✦✦

Waitin' on Sundown didn't depart from Brooks & Dunn's formula much, but the fans didn't mind—it sold over three-million albums anyway. By this point, the duo's albums have become a handful of solid singles—this time out, they were "Little Miss Honky Tonk," "She's Not the Cheatin' Kind," and "You're Gonna Miss Me When I'm Gone"—surrounded by filler, but the hits will make the fans forgive the filler. —*Thom Owens*

Borderline / Apr. 1996 / Arista ✦✦

Brooks & Dunn get a lot of mileage out of two potent personalities. Ronnie Dunn's expressive voice, underrated even with the band's huge success, and Kix Brooks' energized stage presence gave their otherwise routine material enough of a spin to earn them their status as country music's leading duet team of the 1990s. With *Borderline*, their fourth and weakest album, they have to strain a bit too hard to give their songs weight. The primary exception is an outstanding cover of B.W. Stevenson's 1972 pop hit "My Maria," which Dunn elevates with an outstanding vocal performance that puts him in a league with the Mavericks' Raul Malo. Other than a powerful ballad or two and an

entertaining novelty number about a wife bluntly persuading her man that they are going out on the town that night, too much of *Borderline* relies on country clichés and formulaic arrangements. These two failed to make an artistic statement that went beyond light entertainment. —*Michael McCall*

● **The Greatest Hits Collection** / Sep. 16, 1997 / Arista ✦✦✦✦✦

The Greatest Hits Collection is a thorough overview of one of the most popular country acts of the '90s, containing 11 of Brooks & Dunn's biggest hits—including "Brand New Man," "My Next Broken Heart," "Boot Scootin' Boogie" and "She Used to Be Mine"—plus three new songs which are nearly as good as their older hits. It's an excellent summation of the first part of their career, and an ideal place to become acquainted with the duo. —*Thom Owens*

If You See Her / Jun. 2, 1998 / Arista ✦✦✦

The studio formula that melded vocalist Ronnie Dunn with Kix Brooks is still in effect on cuts like "Your Love Don't Take a Backseat to Nothing" and a duet with country-pop diva Reba McEntire ("If You See Him/If You See Her"); there are some good moments here. Dunn's cover of Roger Miller's "Husbands and Wives" displays his abilities nicely, while Brooks comes to life as a rock & roller on "Way Gone." Also good are "Brand New Whiskey" and "Born and Raised in Black and White." However, the final cut, a gospel-kissed tune ("You're My Angel") that shows just how strong Dunn's voice is, evokes the most emotion. Dunn, when allowed to free himself from trite material and heavy production practices, is amazing. —*Jana Pendragon*

Super Hits / Mar. 23, 1999 / Arista ✦✦✦

For most fans, it's inconceivable to have a Brooks & Dunn hits collection without "Boot Scootin' Boogie" or "Hard Workin' Man," neither of which are on the budget-line compilation *Super Hits*. And that, naturally, is a problem for the casual fan, the kind who would buy a budget-line disc expecting that their favorites would be present. That's not the case with *Super Hits*, which shares only three songs with the exhaustive 19-track *Greatest Hits*, released just a year and a half before this nine-cut sampler. Those songs—"Neon Moon," "Rock My World (Little Country Girl)," "You're Gonna Miss Me When I'm Gone"—are good, as are the remaining six songs (all album tracks), but this collection simply doesn't deliver the hits it promises. Taken on its own terms, as a random sampling of nine songs from Brooks & Dunn's catalog, it's entertaining and possibly even a bargain for listeners on a tight budget, but most fans are much better-served by the definitive *Greatest Hits.* —*Stephen Thomas Erlewine*

Tight Rope / Sep. 14, 1999 / Arista ✦✦✦

Seven is a lucky number for Brooks & Dunn. The seven-time winners of duo awards from the Country Music Association and the Academy of Country Music have bestowed on listeners their seventh album (including *The Greatest Hits Collection*). As always, 12 of *Tight Rope*'s 13 songs were written by the duo (six by Kix and six by Ronnie), but what adds to the mix this time is the addition of producer Byron Gallimore (Tim McGraw, Faith Hill, and Jodee Messina), who has stirred things up a bit with a more progressive, technical edge and new-sounding instrumentation to some of the songs. And love is the predominant theme of this album with the longing lyrics of "Goin' Under Gettin' Over You, the sorrowful "Too Far This Time," and the can't-go-wrong re-release of John Waite's 1984 "Missing You." —*Maria Konicki Dinoia*

Steers and Stripes / Apr. 17, 2001 / Arista ✦✦✦

Ronnie Dunn told *Country Weekly* magazine that "Country music is more diversified than ever, so you can really do more styles and different things." Lucky for Brooks & Dunn, who've obviously used the state of country music to their advantage, making album number nine something undoubtedly worth hearing. Or maybe it's the year they spent working on it. Whatever it is, *Steers & Stripes* is one of the finer albums from the eight-time winners of CMA's Vocal Duo of the Year. It seems to recapture everything likable about Brooks & Dunn that's been missing from the last few albums. The 14-track collection offers up a bevy of beauties from hardcore country to some penetrating rock. The slow, agonizing conviction in "The Long Goodbye," the Latin-flavored "My Heart Is Lost to You," the reassuring sentiment in "Unloved," and the rockabilly revelry of "See Jane Dance" are just a few tunes on this eminent song-packed album that really make a lasting impression. —*Maria Konicki Dinoia*

It Won't Be Christmas Without You / Sep. 10, 2002 / Arista ✦✦✦

Red Dirt Road / Jul. 15, 2003 / Arista ✦✦✦

Garth Brooks

b. Feb. 7, 1962, Tulsa, OK

Vocals, Guitar / Country-Pop, New Traditionalist, Contemporary Country

Garth Brooks is a pivotal figure in the history of country music, no matter how much some country purists would like to deny it. With his commercially savvy fusion of post-Merle Haggard country, honky tonk, post-folk-rock sensitive singer/songwriter sensibilities, and '70s arena rock dramatics, Brooks brought country music to a new audience in the '90s—namely, a mass audience. Before Brooks, it was inconceivable for a country artist to go multi-platinum. He shattered that barrier in 1991, when his second album, *No Fences*, began its chart domination, and its follow-up, *Ropin' the Wind*, became the first country album to debut at the top of the pop charts; *No Fences* would eventually sell a record-shattering 13-million copies. After Garth, country music had successfully carved a permanent place for itself on the pop charts. In the process, it lost a lot of the traditionalism that had always been its hallmark, but that is precisely why Brooks is important.

Garth Brooks is the son of Troyal and Colleen Carroll Brooks. Colleen was a country singer herself, recording a handful of records for Capitol in the mid-'50s that never experienced any chart success. As a child, Garth was interested in music and frequently sang at family gatherings, but he concentrated on athletics. He received a partial athletic scholarship at Oklahoma State University as a javelin tosser, but he wound up dropping the sport during his collegiate career. While he was at college, Brooks began singing in local Oklahoma clubs, often with lead guitarist Ty England. After he graduated with an advertising degree in December of 1984, Garth Brooks decided to try to forge out a career as a country singer. In 1985 he traveled to Nashville with hopes of being discovered by a record label. Just 23 hours after arriving in Nashville, he returned to Oklahoma, frustrated with the industry, his prospects, and his naïve dreams. Brooks continued to perform in Oklahoma clubs, and in 1986, he married his college girlfriend, Sandy Mahl.

The couple moved to Nashville in 1987, this time with a better idea of how the music industry operated. Brooks began making connections with various songwriters and producers, and he sang on a lot of songwriter's demo tapes. Although he had made several connections within the industry and had a powerful management team, every label in town was refusing to sign him. In 1988, six weeks after Capitol Records passed on his demo, one of the label's executives saw Brooks sing at a local club. Impressed with the performance, the executive convinced the label to sign Garth. Brooks recorded his first album with producer Allen Reynolds at the end of 1988; the self-titled debut appeared early in 1989. The album was an instant success, with its first single, "Much Too Young (To Feel This Damn Old)," climbing into the country Top Ten. Garth's debut was a success, crossing over into the pop album charts, but it was overshadowed by the blockbuster appeal of Clint Black, as well other similar new male vocalists like Travis Tritt and Alan Jackson. Within a year, Brooks would tower above them all with his surprise, widespread success.

Garth Brooks had three other hit singles—the number one "If Tomorrow Never Comes," the number two "Not Counting You," and the number one "The Dance"—but it was his second album, *No Fences*, that established him as a superstar. *No Fences* was released in the fall of 1990, preceded by the massive hit single "Friends in Low Places." *No Fences* spent 23 weeks at the top of the country charts and sold 700,000 copies within the first ten days of its release. Throughout 1990 and 1991, Brooks had a string of number-one country hits from the album, including "Unanswered Prayers," "Two of a Kind, Workin' on a Full House," and "The Thunder Rolls." By 1993, *No Fences* would sell over ten-million copies. Not only did his record sales break all the accepted country conventions, but so did Garth Brooks' concerts. By the end of 1990, he was selling out stadiums within minutes and was putting on stadium-sized shows, patterned after '70s rock extravaganzas. Brooks used a cordless, headset microphone so he could run around his large stage. He had an elaborate light show, explosions, and even a harness so he could swing out above the crowd and sing to them. It was the first time any country artist had incorporated such rock & roll techniques into stage shows.

Ropin' the Wind, Brooks' third album, was released in September of 1991 and became the first country record to debut at the top of the pop charts. *Ropin' the Wind* matched the success of *No Fences*, selling over ten-million copies within its first two years of release and spawning the number one hit singles "Shameless," "What She's Doing Now," and "The River." By the end of 1991, Brooks had become a genuine popular music phenomenon—even his 1992 Christmas album, *Beyond the Season*, went multi-platinum—and there were no signs of his momentum slowing down. Naturally, a backlash began to develop in the fall of 1992, beginning with the release of "We Shall Be Free," the first single from his fourth album. Featuring a strong gospel underpinning, the single stalled at number 12 and many radio stations refused to play it. It was indicative of the eclectic nature of his forthcoming album, *The Chase*, which pushed the boundaries of contemporary country. *The Chase* debuted at number one upon its October 1992 release and by the end of the year, it sold over five-million copies. Nevertheless, that number was half the size of the figures for his two previous albums and there was speculation in the media that Brooks' career had already peaked.

Sensing that he was in danger of losing his core audience, Brooks returned to straight country with 1993's *In Pieces*. The album was critically acclaimed and sold several million copies, though it was clear that Brooks would not reach the stratospheric commercial heights of *No Fences* and *Ropin' the Wind* again. Even so, he remained one of the most successful artists in popular music, one of the few guaranteed to sell millions of records with each new album, as well as sell out concerts around the world. *The Hits*, which was only available for a year, was released in the fall of 1994 and would eventually sell over eight-million albums. Brooks released *Fresh Horses*, his first album of new material in two years, in November of 1995; within six months of its release, it had sold over three-million copies. Despite its promising start, *Fresh Horses* plateaued quickly, topping out at quadruple platinum—a healthy number for any artist, but a little disappointing considering Brooks' superstar status. Brooks decided to push his seventh album, appropriately titled *Sevens*, very hard to confirm his superstar status. Originally, it was scheduled to be released in August of 1997, when he would promote it with a huge concert in Central Park. Plans went awry when Capitol Records experienced a huge management shakeup, leaving many of his contacts at the label out in the cold. Upset at the new management, Brooks held back the release of *Sevens* until he received commitment for a major marketing push for the album. He went ahead and performed the Central Park concert, which received major coverage in the media. On the strength of the concert, Capitol acquiesced to Brooks' demands, and *Sevens* was released in November of 1997. *Sevens* catapulted to number one upon its release and quickly went multi-platinum over the holiday season.

The following spring, Brooks pulled his first six albums out of print and issued *The Limited Series*, a box set that contained all six records plus bonus tracks. Once all two million copies of *The Limited Series* were sold, the individual albums would remain out of print until their tenth anniversary, when they would be released only on DVD audio. The *Double Live* set followed in late 1998, and its sales were brisk but not quite as heavy as projected. In the spring of 1998, Brooks unsuccessfully tried out for the San Diego Padres pro baseball team, a major indication of his growing desire to expand his success beyond country music.

Once it became clear that professional baseball wasn't in his future, he became fascinated with film, specifically starring in *The Lamb*, a supposed thriller about a conflicted, tortured rock star called Chris Gaines. He was determined to win the role, and he did after extensive lobbying. Sometime in the spring of 1999, the film was given the green light with Babyface as a producer and Brooks as the star. During pre-production, Brooks

decided the best way to prep for the role was to become Chris Gaines. He invented a brooding, leather-clad image and filled in holes in Gaines' back story by inventing biographies and a musical history. The most important piece in the puzzle was a collection of Gaines' "greatest hits," since it would prime audiences for the big-budget spectacular of *The Lamb*, scheduled for late 2000. So, Brooks jumped the gun, recording a set of 13 songs—as Chris Gaines—that would fill in the fictional singer's history.

As the Chris Gaines album was about to hit stores, Brooks' new persona was revealed to the public. Since the machinations of *The Lamb* were only known to music insiders and fans who religiously followed the trades, Brooks' sudden re-emergence as a slimmed-down, soul-patched, shaggy-haired soulful pop crooner was utterly bizarre to almost every observer. There was a massive PR campaign to shed light on Chris Gaines, complete with a TV special, but the details were so convoluted that it couldn't be explained easily. *In the Life of Chris Gaines* was released at the end of September 1999, and although it entered the charts at number two, it was a major commercial disappointment; by the time Christmas rolled around, some major stores were offering heavy discounts on the record in hopes of clearing out unsold stock. Fan bewilderment over the Gaines project also likely hurt sales of Brooks' second holiday record, *Garth Brooks & the Magic of Christmas*, a traditional pop-styled outing that appeared just two months later.

Brooks kept a low profile through most of 2000, as the disastrous marketplace showing of the Chris Gaines album effectively scuttled plans for *The Lamb*. Late in the year, it was announced that Brooks and his wife were getting a divorce; the rumors may have proven premature, though, as Brooks publicly speculated about preserving his family life by retiring after his next solo project. —*Stephen Thomas Erlewine*

Garth Brooks / Apr. 12, 1989 / Liberty ✦✦✦

On Garth Brooks' self-titled debut, his fusion of rock & roll and traditional country genres like honky tonk and Western swing was already fully formed, as was his gift for extended metaphors. One listen to his signature song and breakthrough hit, "The Dance," proves that, which is why he broke away from the hat acts that he was initially grouped with. Nevertheless, *Garth Brooks* is the most straightforward of all of his albums; Brooks sticks with neo-traditional country on about half of the tracks. He sings traditional country quite well—"Not Counting You" is a particularly effective honky tonk number, demonstrating a debt to both George Jones and George Strait—but what makes the album an exciting debut are songs like the genre-bending ballads "The Dance" and "If Tomorrow Never Comes"; and that is the style that brought him mass success with his next album, *No Fences*. —*Stephen Thomas Erlewine*

☆ No Fences / Aug. 27, 1990 / Liberty ✦✦✦✦✦

Essentially, Garth Brooks' second album *No Fences* follows the same pattern as his debut album, but it is a more assured and risky record. Brooks still performs neo-traditional country, such as the honky tonk hit "Friends in Low Places," but now he twists it around with clever pop hooks. Those pop/rock influences are most apparent on the ballads, which alternate between sensitive folk-rock and power-ballad bombast. But what made *No Fences* such a success is how seamlessly he blends the two seemingly opposing genres, and how he chose a set of material that makes his genre-bending sound subtle and natural. Of course, it doesn't hurt that the songs are consistently entertaining, either. —*Stephen Thomas Erlewine*

☆ Ropin' the Wind / Sep. 1991 / Liberty ✦✦✦✦✦

With *Ropin' the Wind*, Garth Brooks began to make his '70s rock influences more explicit. Naturally, that was most notable in his reworking of Billy Joel's "Shameless," which he transformed from a rock power ballad into contemporary country. But that influence is also evident on ambitious epics like "The River" and even the honky tonk ravers of "Papa Loved Mama" and "Rodeo." Some might say that those rock influences are what made Brooks a crossover success, but he wouldn't have been nearly as successful if he didn't have a tangible country foundation to his music—even when he comes close to standard arena rock bombast, there a gritty steel guitars or vocal inflections that prove he is trying to expand country's vocabulary, not trying to exploit it. —*Stephen Thomas Erlewine*

Beyond the Season / Aug. 17, 1992 / Liberty ✦✦✦

One of the most successful Christmas albums ever, *Beyond the Season* is a varied collection for a country star, even one as "progressive" as Brooks. The tunes range from a gospel version of "Go Tell It on the Mountain" to a song-play where Brooks' songwriters take the roles of animals in the manger. It's about half traditional and half original, with Brooks co-writing the hardest rocking tune, "The Old Man's Back in Town." —*Brian Mansfield*

The Chase / Oct. 1992 / Liberty ✦✦✦✦

The Chase is Garth Brooks' most ambitious and personal album. Not coincidentally, it is one of his least popular releases, selling about half of what the previous *Ropin' the Wind*. But in its own way, *The Chase* is more rewarding and deeper than *Ropin' the Wind*. That's partially due to Brooks' naked ambition; not only does he record "We Shall Be Free" with a gospel choir, but he tackles deeper social and personal issues than he has before. However, the true key to the album is Brooks' conviction; even when his musical experiments don't quite work, it's easy to admire and respect his ambition. Although there are light moments like "Night Rider's Lament" and a cover of Little Feat's "Dixie Chicken," *The Chase* is a more somber, reflective record than his previous three albums; but given a bit of a time, it's as satisfying as anything he's ever recorded. —*Stephen Thomas Erlewine*

In Pieces / Aug. 23, 1993 / Liberty ✦✦✦✦

After the relative commercial disappointment of *The Chase*, Garth Brooks toned down his experimental eclecticism on *In Pieces*. Alternating between heavily rock-influenced numbers, dramatic ballads, and revamped honky tonk, *In Pieces* appeals to the audience that found *The Chase* too pretentious and overly serious. That doesn't mean Brooks abandoned his desire to bend the rules—he's just masked his more ambitious material with crowd-pleasing uptempo numbers like "American Honky-Tonk Bar Association" and "Ain't Going Down (Til the Sun Comes Up)." *In Pieces* is an album that was made for the fans, and it shows—it is one of Brooks' most energetic and exciting collections. —*Stephen Thomas Erlewine*

★ **The Hits** / 1994 / Liberty ✦✦✦✦✦
The Hits is exactly what it says it is—18 of Garth Brooks' biggest hits, including his first 14 number-one singles. Although he has good album tracks on each of his records, this is the essential Garth Brooks album—it gives a good sense of the singer's talents, especially his under-appreciated eclecticism. *The Hits* was only in print for a year, but it sold in excess of eight-million copies, so it could hardly be called a limited edition. —*Stephen Thomas Erlewine*

Fresh Horses / Nov. 21, 1995 / Capitol ✦✦✦
Garth Brooks had to move forward in a dramatic way with *Fresh Horses*, his first new album since 1993. Following the massive successive of *The Hits*—which effectively recapped why the singer became the single most popular American performer of the '90s—Brooks positioned himself for a new direction with *Fresh Horses*. The problem is, he doesn't know which way he should go. Throughout the album, he swings back and forth between country and rock without any sense of purpose. Brooks tries to rework Aerosmith's "The Fever" into a rowdy rodeo country-rocker, but the end result is forced and half-hearted. The Aerosmith cover illustrates the problems of *Fresh Horses*: Brooks is trying too hard to cover new territory and restore hardcore honky tonk grit to his slick country-rock. When he lets his guard down—such as the melancholy ballad "The Beaches of Cheyenne" and the sassy, suggestive "It's Midnight Cinderella"—he can still come up with winners, but those moments don't come frequently on *Fresh Horses*. —*Stephen Thomas Erlewine*

Sevens / Nov. 25, 1997 / Capitol ✦✦✦
Despite a massive publicity campaign, *Fresh Horses* failed to match the success of its predecessors, which meant that its successor, *Sevens*, had to return Garth Brooks to his superstar status in order to be considered a hit. Part of the problem with *Fresh Horses* is that it embraced arena rock instead of merely flirting with it; as a result, large portions of his audience refused to follow him. *Sevens* corrects that misstep by retreating to traditional country territory and establishing a new, folky country-pop direction. Theoretically, it sounds like the perfect move, but *Sevens* doesn't quite play as smoothly as it should. The music never catches fire and often sounds weary instead of hushed and intimate. There are no sweeping epics, no rockers, no steps forward; there's none of the risk-taking that made his early albums so successful. Instead, *Sevens* is an album of small, subtle pleasures, whether it's the swinging "Longneck Bottle" or the moving ballad "She's Gonna Make It." These aren't great leaps forward, but they're well-written and performed, making for solid additions to his catalog. Unfortunately, there aren't enough of these moments on *Sevens*. Only a handful of songs match the level of those two, and since the filler itself lacks power, the end result is an album that is surprisingly lackluster. —*Stephen Thomas Erlewine*

The Limited Series / May 5, 1998 / Capitol ✦✦✦✦✦
Is Garth Brooks a musician or a businessman? From the looks of *The Limited Series*, the answer may be businessman. Under the guise of providing customers and independent retailers a bargain, Brooks repackaged his first six studio albums (Christmas albums not included) as a limited-edition box set, adding one bonus track to each album; the set also includes a photo booklet instead of liner notes. Ignoring the fact that this favors big chains instead of indie record stores, since they're able to purchase large quantities and then offer the set at an enormous discount, there's a major catch that may frustrate fans. Once the two-million copies of the box set are sold out, each of the individual titles will be taken off the market and placed on "moratorium" until their tenth anniversary. Evidently, Brooks has taken his cue from Disney, who pull their classic animated movies from the video market for several years, waiting for a new generation to come of age. It hasn't been proven that Brooks' tactic will work since music consumers are drastically different than movie buffs, but there's also the problem that once each of the records are reissued, they'll only be available in the DVD Audio form. In other words, *The Limited Series* is the last time these albums will be released on CD. That may not be a big deal, considering there are countless used copies of *No Fences* and *Ropin' the Wind* floating around, but it's still something to give even die-hard fans pause. So, if you haven't bought these albums on CD yet, this is an easy, affordable way to pick up all the records at once. But keep in mind that by picking this set up, you're implicitly endorsing Brooks' marketing scheme. —*Stephen Thomas Erlewine*

Double Live / Nov. 17, 1998 / Capitol ✦✦✦
Garth Brooks' first live album, the generically titled *Double Live*, is a professionally entertaining album with a few nice bonuses—including extra verses for "Friends in Low Places" and "The Thunder Rolls," plus three new songs: the dedicated-to-mama "It's Your Song," the Trisha Yearwood duet "Wild as the Wind," and the rocker "Tearin' It Up (And Burnin' It Down)"—but much of this record is either identical to the studio counterparts or offers nothing new. Brooks makes no attempt to camouflage his studio trickery—it's clear that the intros to "Two Pina Coladas," "The River" and "We Shall Be Free" are pasted on in the studio—and even when the crowd intrudes on "The Fever," it feels forced, not like the genuine kinetic energy that can be captured on a live recording. Part of the problem is that the album is a compilation, selecting 25 songs from 25 different dates. Even with studio polish (and there is quite a lot of that), an album culled from such a wide variety of sources can't help but feel patchwork, and *Double Live* does. The handful of new twists will surely satisfy diehards, yet *Double Live* simply isn't that interesting for the average Garth fan. It's the kind of record that's touted as an event

upon its original release, but years later, it seems like little more than a curio. —*Stephen Thomas Erlewine*

In the Life of Chris Gaines / Sep. 28, 1999 / Capitol ✦✦✦
When his popularity reached a plateau in the late '90s, Garth Brooks knew it was time to try something new, deciding to *become* somebody new: Chris Gaines, a brooding, leather-clad rock star. When Brooks' new persona and his album was revealed to the public, they were unforgiving—they didn't think that he was playing a role, they simply though he'd lost his mind. Granted, the story behind Chris Gaines—both the invented biography and the reasons why Brooks decided to become Gaines—is more interesting than the record itself. Instead encapsulating mainstream pop from the mid-'80s through the end of the '90s, thereby sounding like a true "greatest hits," it's basically the state of adult pop at the close of the '90s. Essentially, the record is anchored in the acoustic balladry Babyface constructed for Eric Clapton's "Change the World," with little touches of Mellencamp rock, lite Prince funk, and Beatles-esque pop-craft. While the tunes might not have much flair, they're all sturdy, whether it's the silky ballad "Lost in You," the self-conscious Beatles tribute "Maybe," the folky "It Don't Matter to the Sun," or the Wallflowers-styled "Unsigned Letter." Judged as Brooks' first pop album, it's pretty good, and if it had been released that way, it likely would have been embraced by a wide audience. As it stands, it's an album more fascinating for what it is than for the music itself. —*Stephen Thomas Erlewine*

Garth Brooks & the Magic of Christmas / Nov. 23, 1999 / Capitol ✦✦
Appearing two months after his much-hyped pop crossover move *In the Life of Chris Gaines*, *Garth Brooks & the Magic of Christmas* suffers from extraordinarily bad timing. When it was being recorded as the soundtrack for a television special, Chris Gaines had yet to be unveiled and, if anything had gone according to plan, *The Magic of Christmas* would have been the cherry on the top of a successful year for Brooks. Even the best-laid plans have a way of unravelling, however, and none unravelled more spectacularly than Brooks' hopes for the fourth quarter of 1999. It's likely that *The Magic of Christmas* was intended to reveal another layer of Brooks' musical talents, to complement Chris Gaines' mainstream pop by illustrating that Brooks can also sing Christmas standards like a big band crooner. That's right—*The Magic* is another stylistic departure for the most popular country artist of all time—this one finds him doing big band, swing, ballads, and even gospel. Certainly, he had to find a way to distinguish this album from 1992's *Beyond the Season*, especially since it shares a handful of songs with the previous holiday affair. Traditional pop may not have been the wise way to go, however. On paper, it's a bold, gutsy move, but the artist just doesn't have the voice to pull it off. Throughout the record, he's entirely too self-conscious, trying to keep the twang out of his voice while struggling to adhere to the textbook image of a classic pop crooner. His voice is way too flat for this predictable setting. In order to make such chestnuts as "It's the Most Wonderful Time of the Year," "Let It Snow," "Winter Wonderland," and "Sleigh Ride" sound fresh, particularly when they're given such predictable, brassy, post-Don Costas arrangements, a singer has to be both powerful and filled with charisma. Brooks is neither—swallowed up by his big band, he sounds meek on each track, no matter how hard he tries to make himself heard. An interesting stylistic experiment, perhaps, but one that doesn't work. Unfortunately, *The Magic of Christmas* appeared just weeks after another interesting stylistic experiment from Brooks, the instantly legendary Chris Gaines. Musically, Gaines worked, but Brooks' invention of a fictional alter-ego was just too plain weird for his entire audience. Usually, Brooks records went platinum within two weeks of their release dates; two months after its release, *In the Life of Chris Gaines* didn't even go gold. Clearly, this was not the time for yet another stylistic departure, even if it was in the guise of a holiday album, but Brooks and Capitol had already locked themselves into a November release for *The Magic of Christmas*, and they couldn't stop it. To make matters worse, the TV special for *The Magic* wasn't completed in time, so it was bumped to Christmas 2000, leaving the album stranded in 1999. To save face, Brooks and Capitol decided to have the original release of *The Magic of Christmas* be a "Christmas 1999—First Edition" limited edition, planning to reissue the album with a different cover in 2000, when the TV special actually aired. That still doesn't explain the bizarre cover shot of a possibly airbrushed Brooks, dressed in black and sucking in his cheeks, standing beneath a spooky moon, holding a crystal ball, staring demonically into the camera—it gives the impression that the album celebrates the black magic of Christmas. The picture doesn't ease the suspicions raised by Chris Gaines: the feeling that Brooks is retreating into his own insular world. From any other artist, such a wildly divergent sequence of albums would be seen as an attempt to alienate his audience, but Garth isn't Bob Dylan, who has been known to go out of his way to irritate his dedicated followers. Brooks wants to be all things to all people, but he not only can't pull everything off, he doesn't have an audience that will follow all of his detours. Consequently, the further away he goes from his standard sound, the smaller his audience becomes, and the more fascinating his recordings become. And, truth be told, few pairs of albums from a superstar have been quite so bizarrely fascinating as *Chris Gaines* and *The Magic of Christmas*. —*Stephen Thomas Erlewine*

Scarecrow / Nov. 13, 2001 / Capitol ✦✦✦✦
Garth Brooks had a real hard time in the latter half of the '90s, running through a couple of muddled near-crossover records before diving off the deep end with the extraordinary *In the Life of Chris Gaines*. Following that historic bellyflop—few albums in history have been as misconceived and as widely rejected—Brooks took some time off, retreating from the spotlight (which was particularly helpful when he divorced his high-school sweetheart) and laying low until late fall of 2001, when he returned with *Scarecrow*. The extended time off turned out to be a blessing, since it seemed to help him focus for *Scarecrow*, his strongest album since he delved into unabashed crossover with *Fresh Horses*. Sure, there's still a healthy dose of pop here—he does cover America's fine Californian folk-rock "Don't Cross the River," for instance—but this is a clean, spare record that never

overplays its hand and, in turn, it showcases Brooks' talent for synthesizing popular music styles particularly well. Really, there are no new twists here, but that's part of what's good about the record: He's returned to his strengths, whether it's boozy barroom ravers like the deliriously good George Jones duet "Beer Run" or the preponderance of dramatic, portentous ballads like "The Storm." On paper, this may sound like a retreat, but it plays like a revitalization since it plays to Brooks' strengths—a country boy raised on Eagles who likes country when it rocks, but pumps up power ballads with fiddles and twang. This is no surprise, of course, but it's refreshing to hear him in such a simple, unadorned context, performing good songs with conviction—performances good enough to prove that there's more soul here than on most alt-country records. The friskier songs, from "Beer Run" to "Big Money," fare better than the ballads, but those ballads still work, and overall *Scarecrow* proves that mainstream modern country doesn't have a better singer than Brooks at his best. And it's good to have him at his best again. —*Stephen Thomas Erlewine*

Karen Brooks

b. Apr. 29, 1954, Dallas, TX
Vocals / Progressive Country, Contemporary Country
Dallas-born Karen Brooks came up in Austin's country music scene. During the latter half of the '70s and the early half of the '80s, she leant her vocals to recordings by Jerry Jeff Walker, David Allan Coe, Steve Fromholtz, Gary P. Nunn, and Townes Van Zandt. She then headed to California to work alongside Rodney Crowell, where she eventually picked up a recording contract with Warner Bros. Both "New Way Out" and "Faking Love" hit the Top 20 of *Billboard*'s country singles chart, with the former—a duet with T.G. Sheppard—reaching the top position. Before leaving Warners, she released two mid-'80s albums, *Walk On* and *Hearts on Fire*. She was relatively quiet until 1992, when she released an album with Randy Sharp. The album, titled *That's Another Story*, was released on Mercury. —*Andy Kellman*

Walk On / 1982 / Warner Bros. ✦✦✦

Hearts on Fire / 1985 / Warner Bros. ✦✦✦✦

● **That's Another Story** / 1992 / Mercury ✦✦✦✦
While *That's Another Story* is credited to both Karen Brooks and Randy Sharp, it is not a collection of duets; only two of the tracks are shared collaborations, while the rest are solo efforts split between the two singers. Brooks' "Baby I'm the One" offers what is in all likelihood the first female rap ever to appear on a country record. —*Jason Ankeny*

Kix Brooks (Leon Erix Brooks)

b. May 12, 1955, Shreveport, LA
Songwriter, Vocals / Contemporary Country
Before he became one-half of Brooks & Dunn, the most popular country duo of the '90s, Kix Brooks cut an unsuccessful solo album on the basis of a much more productive songwriting career. Brooks was born in Shreveport, LA, in 1955, and discovered country music through his neighbor, Johnny Horton; he began performing with Horton's daughter as a youth, and spent his high-school years playing clubs and writing songs on the side. After graduation, he moved to Alaska to work on the oil pipeline, and then relocated to Maine, where he performed often at ski resorts and other venues. He moved to Nashville in the early '80s and landed a job as a staff songwriter with Tree Publishing, which resulted in his compositions being recorded by the likes of the Nitty Gritty Dirt Band, Highway 101, and John Conlee, among others.
Brooks recorded his first solo single, "Baby, When Your Heart Breaks Down," for Avion in 1983, but returned to songwriting when it barely made the charts. In 1989, he gave recording a second try, cutting an entire album for Liberty/Capitol; *Kix Brooks* failed to make the charts when it was released, but was reissued all the same in 1994, once Brooks & Dunn had hit the big time. Moreover, the track "Sacred Ground" was later covered by McBride & the Ride for a hit. —*Steve Huey*

Kix Brooks / Oct. 25, 1993 / Capitol ✦✦✦
A worthy addition to the collection of any Brooks & Dunn fan, the album was nevertheless widely ignored upon its release. ("Sacred Ground," the album's only charting single, would become McBride & the Ride's first big hit in 1992.) On his own, Brooks' bayou roots show through, and his music often sounds just as tough as Brooks & Dunn's. —*Brian Mansfield*

Brother Boys

f. 1988
Group / Neo-Traditional Folk, Progressive Bluegrass, Traditional Country, Rockabilly, Singer/Songwriter, Close Harmony
The heartfelt vocal harmonies of country music's brother duos are echoed by the Brother Boys. Although Tennessee-born vocalists Eugene Wolf and Eddie Lynn Snodderly are not related by blood, the harmonic blend of their vocals shows that they were born to sing together. Joined by Missy Raines (acoustic bass) and Roger Rasnake (acoustic guitar), Wolf and Snodderly have created the Brother Boys' unique hybrid of country, folk, pop, bluegrass, swing, and rockabilly that they've dubbed "new hillbilly music."
Wolf and Snodderly first sang together in a theatrical show, *Echoes and Postcards*, produced by the Road Company in 1986. Wolf's musical talents were obvious from the time that he first produced a musical tone. At the age of two, he won a talent contest at the Capital Theater in Greeneville, TN. Inspired by local variety television programs, he pursued a career in theater. He appeared in the film *The Curse* and with David Keith (*An Officer and a Gentleman*) in the stage production *Greater Tuna*. Snodderly, who plays guitar, dobro, fiddle, mandola, and harmonica as well as singing, was inspired as a youngster by country artists including Flatt & Scruggs and the Wilburn Brothers. Acquiring his first guitar in 1964, he formed a band with neighborhood friends and spent the next six years rehearsing; his professional debut came in 1970. A melodic songwriter, Snodderly recorded two solo albums—*Sidewalk Shoes* in 1977 and *Sweet Light* in 1980.

Following their success in *Echoes and Postcards*, Wolf and Snodderly agreed to make their musical partnership more permanent. Thus, the Brother Boys were born. After releasing a self-produced cassette album in 1990, they signed with Sugar Hill. While their debut CD, *Plow*, was produced by dobro wiz Jerry Douglas, Snodderly oversaw the recording of their second CD, *Presley's Grocery*. —*Craig Harris*

Plow / 1992 / Sugar Hill ✦✦✦

● **Presley's Grocery** / 1995 / Sugar Hill ✦✦✦✦
The Brother Boys sound like a modern combination of the Everly Brothers with Elvis' rockabilly drive. They offer up a jaunty mixture of old and new tunes distinct enough that any soundalike comparisons are academic. One low point is an attempt to recast "I Don't Care If the Sun Don't Shine"; the Elvis version is just too epochal to be outshined. The playing is hot, and the album sounds crisp and immediate. *Presley's Grocery* is a good album for fans of country vocals who need a break from bluegrass and the outlaws. —*Richard Meyer*

The Brother Boys / New Hillbilly Music ✦✦✦

Brother Phelps

f. 1992
Group / Contemporary Country
Singer/bassist Doug Phelps and singer/guitarist Ricky Lee Phelps first started performing together in their teens, learning to harmonize like the Everly Brothers. After leaving the Kentucky HeadHunters in 1992, they formed their own project, Brother Phelps, which contrary to appearances was actually their minister father's nickname. They quickly landed a deal with Asylum Records, and in 1993 they issued their debut album, *Let Go*, an unassuming record with a more traditional country bent than their often rock-flavored work with the HeadHunters. The title track made the country Top Ten, and several other singles made the lower reaches of the charts. The follow-up album, *Any Way the Wind Blows*, appeared in 1995 to positive reviews, but Brother Phelps decided to disband the following years, whereupon Doug rejoined the HeadHunters. —*Steve Huey*

Let Go / Aug. 3, 1993 / Asylum ✦✦✦
Much more low-key than most people expected, *Let Go* proves that the Phelps were the smarts behind the HeadHunters. The title cut was a breezy single that recalled Buddy Holly, and elsewhere on the album, the Phelps made judicious use of Southern boogie ("Were You Really Livin'") and strings ("What Goes Around"). Not a perfect album, and not as good as the HeadHunters at their peak, but *Let Go* still contains some mighty nice listening. —*Brian Mansfield*

● **Any Way the Wind Blows** / Mar. 7, 1995 / Asylum ✦✦✦✦
Any Way the Wind Blows doesn't stray from the laid-back, rootsy vibe of the Brother Phelps' debut, but it boasts a more assured performance and a stronger set of songs, making it a more engaging listen. —*Stephen Thomas Erlewine*

Alison Brown

Banjo / Progressive Bluegrass, Traditional Bluegrass
Progressive bluegrass banjoist Alison Brown made her name not only as a virtuosic instrumentalist, but as an accomplished, jazz-influenced composer, a combination that earned plenty of comparisons to Béla Fleck and David Grisman. Brown began playing the banjo before reaching her teens and developed quickly, winning numerous contests and even getting a chance to perform at the *Grand Ole Opry*. She was also an excellent student, and temporarily left music to attend Harvard University; following graduation, she worked as an investment banker for a couple of years, but quit to pursue music.
Brown gained her first wide exposure as a member of Alison Krauss' Union Station, covering the banjo slot from Krauss' 1987 debut album through 1990. That year, she departed to record her own debut, the entirely instrumental *Simple Pleasures*, for Vanguard, and also spent some time as the musical director for folkie Michelle Shocked. Brown's 1992 follow-up, *Twilight Motel*, was jazzier and more eclectic, and 1994's *Look Left* displayed her increasing interest in world and ethnic music. *The Alison Brown Quartet* (1996) refocused on her jazz sensibility and found her switching to guitar on a few tracks; it was also her last album before moving to the Compass imprint, for which she debuted in 1998 with *Out of the Blue*. *Fair Weather* (2000) featured a duet with Béla Fleck on "Leaving Cottondale," which won Brown a Grammy for Best Country Instrumental. Her follow-up album, *Replay*, was another of her jazzier outings. —*Steve Huey*

Simple Pleasures / 1990 / Vanguard ✦✦✦✦✦
Her all-instrumental debut instantly earned respect among progressive acoustic music fans. Produced by David Grisman, and featuring guests Mike Marshall and Alison Krauss, Brown weaves cello, flute and congas into her hybrid string sound, and she maintains an innate elegance amid the tricky arranging. —*Michael McCall*

● **Twilight Motel** / 1992 / Vanguard ✦✦✦✦✦
Produced by Mike Marshall, Brown moves in several new directions, showing off the breadth of her talent while keeping the composition at the center of her playing. Jazzier, yet also more relaxed, than her debut. Maura O'Connell provides vocals on a traditional Irish song. —*Michael McCall*

Look Left / 1994 / Vanguard ✦✦✦✦
Brown criss-crosses the globe sonically, taking on Cajun, Celtic, Native American and Australian Aboriginal music with characteristically relaxed proficiency. —*Michael McCall*

Alison Brown Quartet / 1996 / Vanguard ✦✦✦
Alison Brown, believe it or not, is a five-string banjo player. The rest of her quartet is a standard jazz ensemble consisting of piano, bass, and drums, and you can be confident that there's nary a bluegrass lick anywhere on this album. Like her compadre Béla Fleck (to whom she must be absolutely sick of being compared), Brown figured out some time ago that the banjo is a fully chromatic instrument with every bit as much melodic flexibility as a guitar, and that its clear, crisp tone is perfectly suited to jazz. It works especially

well as a bebop instrument, which Brown demonstrates on this album's opening track, the rollicking, Charlie Parker-ish "G Bop." It also works pretty well as a cool jazz instrument, which Brown demonstrates on the album's second track, the loping, Bill Evans-ish "Red Balloon." This sort of stylistic variety is grist for Brown's mill, but it doesn't always work in her favor: "My Favorite Marsha" (one of several tracks on which she switches to guitar) is nice but borders on new acoustic sappiness—her guitar playing is good but not exceptional. However, "Without Anastasia" draws nicely on classical influences without sounding pedantic, and "Banjo Mambo (Revisited)" is a very fun Latin romp. Strongly recommended overall. *—Rick Anderson*

Out of the Blue / Feb. 17, 1998 / Compass ✦✦✦

It's a long trip down the career path from a top investment banker to a bluegrass banjo picker. But that's the path this very talented lady chose to take. To be honest, she has kind of traveled that path backwards, and more than once. Even before her teens, Alison Brown was winning contests for her skills on the banjo. One of those landed her a chance to perform on the *Grand Ole Opry.* She even did some recording before heading off to college—to Harvard, no less. After finishing her schooling and spending a couple of years in the corporate world, she turned back to her music. Since then she has recorded a number of solo albums, including this 1998 one, *Out of the Blue.* Brown has won a number of much-deserved awards since the rebirth of her music career, such as the International Bluegrass Music Association's Banjo Player of the Year Award and even a nomination for a Grammy. The music on this album is bluegrass flavored with a little jazz. Fans won't notice anything untried or bold here from Alison Brown, but there are a number of good songs on this album, including "Mood Ring," "Rebel's Bolero," and "Four for Launch." *—Charlotte Dillon*

Fair Weather / May 9, 2000 / Compass ✦✦✦✦

Banjo virtuoso Alison Brown, whose primary group is a jazz quartet, returns to her bluegrass roots on this beautiful and exhilarating album. Well, sort of. The instrumental format is certainly bluegrass, given guest artists like Stuart Duncan and Darol Anger on fiddles, guitarists Mike Marshall and Tony Rice, and mandolinist Sam Bush, and with Brown's fiery five-string picking front and center. But much of this is bluegrass music of a type that Bill Monroe might not recognize; while "Late on Arrival" is a good old-fashioned Scruggs-style banjo showcase and "Fair Weather" a modern bluegrass song with all the standard accouterments, the twin mandolins and easy-swinging rhythm of "Poe's Pickin' Party" sound kind of like an old-time string band playing turn-of-the-century salon music. And then there are the cover tunes, which include a gently winning rendition of the old Elvis Costello hit "Everyday I Write the Book." The album's most thrilling moments come on the complex and exhilarating "Leaving Cottondale," which is both one of the prettiest and one of the most technically impressive of Brown's compositions. Here she's joined by fellow banjo maverick Béla Fleck for one of the most jaw-dropping passages of twin-banjo counterpoint ever put on tape. Call it bluegrass, call it newgrass, call it jazzgrass, whatever. This is one of the best albums of 2000 in any genre. *—Rick Anderson*

Replay / Jan. 8, 2002 / Compass ✦✦✦✦

While Alison Brown has received credit for her banjo innovations, she's often been crowded out by hotshot picker Béla Fleck. That's unfortunate, because there's more than enough room for two pioneering banjo players, and besides, both players have different gifts to offer. First of all, the Alison Brown Quartet approaches acoustic jazz from a different, perhaps more traditional, standpoint than Fleck & the Flecktones. Brown's banjo vies with John R. Burr's piano for fancy lead work, while both are superbly backed by bassist Garry West and drummer Kendrick Freeman. While the band doesn't mind playing lighter pieces like "The Wonderful Sea Voyage" and "My Favorite Marsha," they can also kick out the bluegrass jams on a cut like "Late on Arrival." This makes the unit more muscular than the Flecktones. Burr's piano also adds lots of energy, whether bopping along on "Etouffee Brutus?" or laying down bluesy ragtime on "Shoot the Dog." West and Freeman's ability to conquer every style from good old mountain music to Brazilian rhythms assures that the band moves forward with one voice. The band also displays a healthy sense of humor on "Spiderman Theme," a tune that'll have the listener climbing the walls, while a more serious side takes over on "Without Anastasia," a piece resembling a Bach fugue. It would be remiss to not mention "Daytime TV" and "The Inspector," two pieces jumping with spontaneous energy and featuring some great guitar work by Brown. One may not be able to please all of the fans all of the time, but *Replay* should please most of Alison Brown's fans most of the time. The Alison Brown Quartet distinguish themselves from competitors by building a solid musical framework and taking flight from there. *—Ronnie D. Lankford Jr.*

Best of the Vanguard Years / Feb. 5, 2002 / Vanguard ✦✦✦✦

Sometime back, Alison Brown established herself as an innovative banjo stylist and founded her own record label (Compass). It's easy to forget that she started off playing with another Alison, Alison Krauss that is, and recorded a number of solo albums for Vanguard. *Best of the Vanguard Years* draws from Brown's four Vanguard albums, recorded in the early to mid-'90s. As with her later recordings, she has composed material that stretches the limits of the banjo and traditional acoustic music: "Cara's Way (The Little People)" resembles an Irish jig, "Mambo Banjo" bossa nova, and "Wolf Moon" straight-ahead bluegrass. She also reveals that she's an accomplished guitarist on "The Inspector" and "Hello Mendocino!" There are differences, however, between *Best of the Vanguard Years* and her later recordings. Her writing and playing are more muscular and structured on this earlier set, meaning that even jazzy, open-ended pieces like "Deep North" never seem to drift into new acoustic vagueness. Straightforward arrangements of piano, banjo, bass, and drums on "Look Left" give Brown and company a more traditional sound than Béla Fleck & the Flecktones. It should also be noted that Brown surrounds herself with a number of great musicians, including Mike Marshall, Stuart Duncan, and Roy Huskey Jr. *Best of the Vanguard Years* offers a 65-plus minute intro to the pre-Compass years, and will please Brown's fans and anyone interested in original banjo music. *—Ronnie D. Lankford Jr.*

Hylo Brown (Frank Brown)

b. Apr. 20, 1922, River, KY, **d.** Jan. 17, 2003, Mechanicsville, OH

Vocals / Traditional Bluegrass

Bluegrass and country singer Frank Brown earned the nickname "Hylo" thanks to the considerable vocal range that became his trademark. Born in 1922 in Johnson County, KY—later the birthplace of Loretta Lynn—Brown had thoroughly absorbed the music indigenous to his Appalachian home before moving with his family to Ohio, where his career as a performer began to gather steam. There, he played on local radio broadcasts and began writing songs; one composition, a tribute to the *Grand Ole Opry,* was recorded by Jimmy Martin. In 1950, he sang harmony on a Bradley Kincaid session.

In 1954, a song titled "Lost to a Stranger" earned Brown a recording contract with Capitol Records; the subsequent single, along with follow-ups like "Lovesick and Sorrow" and "The Wrong Kind of Life," were minor hits. In 1957, Brown joined Lester Flatt and Earl Scruggs, becoming a featured vocalist with the duo's Foggy Mountain Boys. The group's increasing popularity prompted Flatt & Scruggs to form a second Foggy Mountain band, called the Timberliners, with Brown as the unit's frontman; the Timberliners were fleshed out by mandolin player Red Rector, fiddler Clarence "Tater" Tate, Jim Smoak on the banjo, and bassist Joe Phillips.

At their inception, the Timberliners performed on a circuit of television stations in Tennessee and Mississippi, later swapping schedules with Flatt & Scruggs in order to appear on West Virginia airwaves as well. In 1958, the group released Hylo Brown & the Timberliners, an LP that remains a traditional bluegrass classic. However, the advent of syndication and videotape allowed the original Flatt & Scruggs band to appear on any number of TV stations, effectively ending the Timberliners' career soon after, although Brown soldiered on for a time with a group including Norman Blake on Dobro and Billy Edwards on banjo. After the Timberliners' demise, Brown rejoined Flatt & Scruggs as a featured singer. In the early '60s, Brown cut a handful of solo records, including 1961's *Bluegrass Balladeer,* 1962's *Bluegrass Goes to College,* and the next year's *Hylo Brown Meets the Lonesome Pine Fiddlers.* Throughout the decade and into the first years of the '70s, he performed solo in clubs, releasing records infrequently on small labels. However, a gradual diminishment in his vocal range resulted in Brown's eventual retirement around the middle of the decade. Brown passed away January 17, 2003. *—Jason Ankeny*

Bluegrass Balladeer / 1962 / Starday ✦✦✦

Bluegrass Goes to College / 1962 / Starday ✦✦✦

Sing Me a Bluegrass Song / 1963 / Starday ✦✦✦

★ **1954–1960** / 1992 / Bear Family ✦✦✦✦✦

1954-60 is a double-disc collection that contains all 46 songs that Hylo Brown & the Timberliners recorded for Capitol Recordings during the late '50s. Many of these tracks feature stellar support from Clarence Tate, Merle Taylor and Dale Potter, and any serious bluegrass fan will find this expensive double-disc set worth the investment. *—Thom Owens*

20 Old-Time Favorites / Dec. 9, 1997 / Rural Rhythm ✦✦✦✦

These are late '60s recordings by this early bluegrass and country music institution, and although he had already been playing professionally for three decades, Hylo Brown sounds neither worn out nor unenthusiastic about doing things the old fashioned way. While the bluegrass world was going progressive all around them, Hylo and his Blue Ridge Mountain Boys stick to the basics, keep the tempos reasonable and the solos within the easily recognizable perimeters of the basic chords. Listeners who enjoy country music, old-time, or bluegrass should check out this artist if they haven't discovered him already. He combines some of the best aspects of all these musics into his own unique style. The rich sentimentality and ironic humor of country & western lyrics is blended with an instrumental sound that is heavy on the acoustic axes associated with bluegrass, such as banjo and dobro, handled with aplomb by Sid Campbell and Dale Brotherington, respectively. Two of the best tracks come right in a row, namely the abbreviated "Intoxicated Rat" and the profound "Ace in the Hole." *—Eugene Chadbourne*

Jim Ed Brown

b. Mar. 1, 1934, Sparkman, AR

Vocals / Traditional Country, Honky Tonk, Nashville Sound/Countrypolitan

Jim Ed Brown came to fame as a member of the '50s vocal group the Browns, where he was the band's lead male vocalist. In 1965, when the group was still together, he embarked on a solo career that would eventually eclipse the success of the Browns. Brown and his older sister, Maxine, began performing while he was still in high-school. In 1954, the duo signed a contract with Fabor, releasing five singles on the label. Later that year, their sister Bonnie joined the duo and they became the Browns. From 1956 until 1967, the Browns were signed to RCA Records, where they had a number of moderately successful hit singles, highlighted by the 1959 number one "The Three Bells."

Brown began his solo career in 1965, two years before the Browns disbanded. Initially, he didn't have much success and just scraped the bottom of the country Top 40. Once the Browns disbanded, Brown began to have more substantial hits, beginning with the number-18 single "You Can Have Her," which was a cover of the Roy Hamilton hit. That was followed by the beer-drinking anthem "Pop a Top," which climbed to number three. Although his next single, "Bottle, Bottle," reached number 13, Brown didn't have any major hits for the rest of the '60s. As his chart performance stagnated in 1968, he formed a backing group called the Gems and began a residency at the Sahara Tahoe's *Juniper Lounge.* In 1969, he hosted the syndicated television show *The Country Place,* which ran until 1970.

As *The Country Place* was ending its run, Brown had his first major hit since "Pop a Top" with the number-four single "Morning." Again, he wasn't able to immediately follow

"Morning" with another Top Ten hit, but he began charting more frequently. In 1973, he had two Top Ten hits, "Southern Loving" and "Sometime Sunshine," which were followed by the Top Ten "It's That Time of Night" in early 1974. Jim Ed Brown had his greatest success in the late '70s, when he regularly performed duets with Helen Cornelius. They had six Top Ten hits between 1976 and 1980, including their debut single, "I Don't Want to Have to Marry You," which went to number one in 1976. During this time, he had some solo hits, but only two of them broke the Top 40. Brown and Cornelius ended their partnership in 1981, following the number-13 hit "Don't Bother to Knock."

After the breakup of his duo with Helen Cornelius, Jim Ed Brown pretty much retired from recording. He made the occasional appearance on the *Grand Ole Opry*, and he sometimes reunited with Cornelius. Brown also hosted TV game shows and talent contests throughout the '80s. Toward the end of the decade, he opened the Jim Ed Brown Theater near Opryland in Nashville, TN, where he performed regularly for a number of years. — *Stephen Thomas Erlewine*

Alone With You / 1966 / RCA ✦✦✦
Just Jim / 1967 / RCA ✦✦✦✦
Gems By Jim / 1967 / RCA ✦✦✦
Bottle, Bottle / 1968 / RCA ✦✦✦✦✦
Country's Best on Record / 1968 / RCA ✦✦✦✦
This Is My Beat! / 1968 / RCA ✦✦✦✦
Remember Me / 1969 / RCA ✦✦✦
Going Up the Country / 1970 / RCA ✦✦✦
Just for You / 1970 / RCA ✦✦✦
Morning / 1971 / RCA ✦✦✦
Angel's Sunday / 1971 / RCA ✦✦✦✦

Following the success of Jim Ed Brown's biggest solo hit, "Morning," in 1970, he entered the Top 15 again a few months later with "Angel's Sunday," which brandishes a surprising vocal rhythm as a hook. Brown's albums are usually good, but *Angel's Sunday* is a little better than average thanks to the strong material and predominantly female background vocals, which re-create in spots the sound of his former trio, the Browns. Production touches add variety to what is mostly a platter of ballads, such as the Spanish guitar on "Four Seasons of Life," but the songs overall are so melodic that they require little more than Brown's honeyed voice to put them across. — *Greg Adams*

She's Leavin' / 1972 / RCA ✦✦✦✦

She's Leavin' is from Jim Ed Brown's solo period between the end of the Browns and the beginning of his successful partnership with Helen Cornelius. The title track, which borrows the "Auld Lang Syne" gimmick from the G-Clefs' 1961 hit "I Understand (Just How You Feel)," barely cracked the country Top 40 in 1971. The leadoff track, "Summerset," is a wistful beauty that should have been a hit and stands out as the album's highlight. The remainder is given over to love ballads old and new, from Cindy Walker's classic "Not As a Sweetheart (But Just As a Friend)" to Kris Kristofferson's "Help Me Make It Through the Night." Reinforcing the album's contemporary vibe, two songs come from Kristofferson's pen, and Freddie Hart's "Easy Lovin'"—which must have been recorded while it was still on the charts—closes the set. One might wish for more original material, but Brown has a beautiful voice that seldom disappoints. — *Greg Adams*

Evening / 1972 / RCA ✦✦✦
Brown Is Blue / 1972 / RCA ✦✦✦
Barrooms and Pop-A-Tops / 1973 / RCA ✦✦✦✦
It's That Time of Night / 1975 / RCA ✦✦✦
I Don't Want to Have to Marry You / 1977 / RCA ✦✦✦
Born Believer / 1977 / RCA ✦✦✦✦✦

The level of quality on *Born Believer* is so high that the album plays like a greatest hits collection. The title track and "If It Ain't Love By Now" didn't quite make the Top Ten, but Jim Ed Brown's golden baritone is as appealing as ever, and Helen Cornelius, whose frequently double-tracked voice adds a distinctive element, sounds quite a bit like Jeannie Kendall of the Kendalls. Practically every song is a potential hit, and the full production and excellent material throughout make not a minute of it seem like filler. The duo remakes the Browns' 1955 oldie "Here Today and Gone Tomorrow," Reba McEntire's early hit "(There's Nothing Like the Love) Between a Woman and a Man," and two songs are credited or co-credited to Cornelius. Anyone who listens to a lot of '60s and '70s country albums comes to expect uneven quality, but *Born Believer* is impressively consistent. — *Greg Adams*

Greatest Hits / Feb. 1992 / RCA ✦✦✦✦✦

Greatest Hits collects the biggest hits from Jim Ed Brown's duets with Helen Cornelius, including the Top Ten hits "I Don't Want to Have to Marry You," "Saying Hello, Saying I Love You, Saying Goodbye," "Lying in Love With You," "If the World Ran Out of Love Tonight," and "Fools," among several others. — *Stephen Thomas Erlewine*

● **The Essential Jim Ed Brown & the Browns** / Jan. 30, 1996 / RCA ✦✦✦✦
Since this set features none of Brown's duets with Cornelius, it must be assumed that there is a compilation in the works based solely on that aspect of his career. As for this set, it opens with three mellow Jim and Maxine Brown hits, including the 1956 smash "Looking Back to See." There are four songs by the Browns, including the dreamy ballad "Send Me the Pillow You Dream On." The remainder of the album is devoted to Brown's solo material. While he was smooth, Brown could lay down a good honky tonk, too, as on "Pop a Top," "Southern Loving," and "Barroom Pals and Goodtime Gals." Also included is his slick, finger-popping read of "You Can Have Her." "Bottle, Bottle" is an ode to drinking his pain away: "You give me the strength to go on day to day/You help keep the mem-

ories of a lost love away." After calling it his crutch, he asks: "Bottle, bottle why do I love you so much?" There are also plenty of pretty love ballads to go around, such as "Gently Comes Love" and "You're the Part of Me." — *Bil Carpenter*

Anthology / Apr. 4, 2000 / Renaissance ✦✦✦✦✦
Jim Ed Brown & Helen Cornelius' *Anthology* collects many of their most memorable duets, including "I Don't Want to Marry You," "Saying Hello, Saying I Love You, Saying Goodbye," "You Don't Bring Me Flowers," "Don't Bother to Knock," and "One Man Woman, One Woman Man." A welcome retrospective of one of the '70s most popular country duos. — *Heather Phares*

Junior Brown

b. 1953, Kirksville, IN

Guitar, Guitar (Steel), Vocals, Slide Guitar / Alternative Country, Neo-Traditionalist Country, Americana

A singer and demon guitarist whose raucous blend of country and rock & roll helped make him a successful crossover act, Junior Brown was born in 1953 and raised in the backwoods of Kirksville, IN. He first learned to play the piano from his father, and was exposed to country through radio and TV, becoming a fan of Ernest Tubb's music and television program. He became a professional musician at the tail end of the '60s, while still in his teens. After honing his guitar skills in relative anonymity throughout the '70s, Brown became an instructor at the Hank Thompson School of Country Music, an affiliate of Rogers State College in Oklahoma. There, while teaching under the auspices of steel guitar legend Leon McAuliffe, a onetime member of Bob Wills & His Texas Playboys, Brown met "the lovely Miss Tanya Rae," a student whom he would later marry in 1988 and who eventually joined his band as a rhythm guitarist and backing vocalist.

At the same time, a dream prompted him to set about creating an instrument fusing a six-string guitar with its steel counterpart. Contacting guitar maker Michael Stevens in 1985, he developed the "guit-steel," a double-necked guitar combining the standard instrument with the steel. (A decade later, the two men reunited to update the "guit-steel," and Brown's cherry axe, "Big Red," was born.) After moving to Austin, TX, Brown and his group became the house band at the city's *Continental Club*, where strong word-of-mouth eventually earned them a record deal. He made his long-awaited album debut in 1993 with *12 Shades of Brown*, which featured a tribute to his biggest influence, "My Baby Don't Dance to Nothing but Ernest Tubb." It also showcased his often-stunning instrumental work, and blended Western swing, honky tonk, and electrified Bakersfield country. *Guit With It* followed later in the year, and like its predecessor, was met with considerable critical acclaim. After a five-song stopgap EP, 1995's *Junior High*, Brown returned in 1996 with *Semi-Crazy*, which continued in the vein established on his previous recordings. *The Long Walk Back* followed two years later, and displayed a bit more rockabilly flavor. Brown issued his fifth album, *Mixed Bag*, in 2001. — *Jason Ankeny*

12 Shades of Brown / 1993 / Curb ✦✦✦✦✦
Brown's debut deck shines like gold with standout original material like "They Don't Choose to Live That Way," "My Hillbilly Hula Gal" and "My Baby Don't Dance to Nothing but Ernest Tubb" being particular noteworthy. Possessing a voice that will curl the hair on the back of your neck while picking both single-string picking and slide stylings on his twin neck "guit-steel," this is a mighty talented fella, neo-traditionalist or not. — *Cub Koda*

● **Guit with It** / Aug. 24, 1993 / Curb ✦✦✦✦✦
Junior Brown's rumbling, strikingly deep voice, tasty electric and steel guitar playing, and splendid honky-tonk and Western swing songs have made him a sensation in country circles. There's nothing phony or clichéd about Brown's music; this is the genuine, untutored, undiluted article. Brown can sing tunes requiring sincerity, ache or irony with equal flair. The CD's 12 cuts include the nearly 12-minute "Guit-Steel Blues," and a sharp cover of Hank Garland's "Sugarfoot Stomp," and the bittersweet "Doin' What Comes Easy to a Fool" and "Holding Pattern." Brown is as vital and refreshing as early John Anderson or Randy Travis. — *Ron Wynn*

Junior High / Jul. 18, 1995 / Curb ✦✦✦
Junior High is an EP that features re-recorded versions of "Highway Patrol," "Sugarfoot Rag," and "My Wife Thinks You're Dead," plus two new songs, "That's Easy for You to Say" and "Lovely Hula Hands." It's a minor entry in Brown's catalog, but it is an enjoyable one, even if it is only necessary for die-hard fans. — *Stephen Thomas Erlewine*

Semi-Crazy / May 1996 / Curb ✦✦✦✦
On *Semi-Crazy*, Junior Brown's third full-length album, the suit-and-tied Texas singer's clever lyrics, Ernest Tubb-like voice, and virtuoso guitar playing (on his custom-made, double-necked "guit-steel," which allows him to switch quickly between picking and steel playing) are once again intact and on the mark. *Semi-Crazy* may not bowl Brown fans over immediately—he offers no new twists as either a writer or player. On the other hand, because Brown is one of country music's most stunning guitarists (imagine Ornette Coleman crossed with Speedy West)—not to mention possessing a truly original sound—it's hard not to fall for the classic Brown sound of "I Hung It Up" (a standout for the guitar work), "Gotta Get Up Every Morning," and the fun-loving title track (his duet partner, Red Simpson, penned Brown's earlier song "Highway Patrol"). — *Kurt Wolff*

The Long Walk Back / Aug. 18, 1998 / Curb ✦✦✦✦
Just as much fun and as satisfying as he always is, Junior Brown once more gits gone with all the energy and punch that has come to be expected of this hardcore honky tonker. While the title cut is good, he really revs things up on the all-instrumental "Peelin' Taters" and "I'm All Fired Up." "Stupid Blues," "Just a Little Love" and "Read 'Em and Weep" display the interesting blend of Brown's own Texas swing/Bakersfield/honky tonk brand of country & western music. For a little spice, Junior adds a cover of the Elvis hit "Rock-A-Hula Baby" and the Hunter/Vincent tune "(I'm Just) Looking for Love." As always, Tanya Rae provides the complementary backing vocals that make the Brown sound so unique.

One of traditional country music's favorite good ol' boys, Junior Brown hits the nail directly on the head once again. —*Jana Pendragon*

Mixed Bag / Jul. 31, 2001 / Curb ✦✦✦
The quirky country and roots rocker with the self-fashioned "Big Red" double-necked steel guitar always seems like he's got his tongue in his cheek, whether he's doing a travelogue tale by Jerry Hubbard ("Guitar Man") or a hilarious spy romance fable ("Cagey Bea"). Brown and his extreme tenor have their sweeter, romantic side in full bloom here as well ("Our First Bluebonnet Spring"), and it's clear he has a penchant for classic Southern sounds like the ragtime tune "Riverboat Shuffle." He complements a mix of fast-paced and gently laconic originals with a folksy reading of a tune written by his idol, Ernest Tubb ("Kansas City Blues"). The listener might be so riveted by Brown's voice, attitude, and lyrical dramas that he or she might miss another of the album's consistent joys—his potent electric guitar jamming, used well as harmony and in solo spots. —*Jonathan Widran*

Marty Brown

b. 1965, Maceo, KY
Guitar, Vocals / Contemporary Country, New Traditionalist
Though he's never had a substantial hit, Marty Brown won a devoted following among hardcore country fans thanks to his twangy, classic-style honky tonk and a nasal delivery straight from the hills of Kentucky. Specifically, Brown was raised in the small tobacco-farming town of Maceo, and started playing the local honky tonks at age 14. He later recorded a demo tape and hitchhiked to Nashville, where he was profiled on the news magazine *48 Hours* and secured a contract with MCA. His debut album, *High and Dry*, was released in 1991 and won fierce praise for its raw energy, wide musical range, and unrepentant hillbilly attitude. Afraid of being pigeonholed because of the latter, Brown moved into a more commercial sound for the 1993 follow-up, *Wild Kentucky Skies*; though it wasn't a hit, it helped continue to build Brown's fan base, as did his tour with Jimmie Dale Gilmore. 1994's *Cryin', Lovin', Leavin'* also failed to bring Brown to a wider audience, despite continued acclaim, and MCA parted ways with him afterwards. Brown signed with the independent label Hightone and debuted for them in 1996 with *Here's to the Honky Tonks*, which again was released to favorable reviews. —*Steve Huey*

● **High & Dry** / 1991 / MCA ✦✦✦✦✦
If everything here were as pure a hillbilly distillation as the title track or the loopy "Old King Kong," Brown might come off like a simple hick with limited nostalgia appeal. But his range is surprisingly wide. Brown's ballads—"I'll Climb Any Mountain" and "Wildest Dreams"—though simple, build to stunning, emotional climaxes. "Every Now and Then" is the equal of many of the Everly Brothers' best. And "Nobody Knows" is surely one of the most lonesome wails in a long, longtime. —*Brian Mansfield*

Wild Kentucky Skies / 1993 / MCA ✦✦✦✦✦
One of the best things about Marty Brown's music is that it possesses the qualities that people both love and hate about country music. Brown takes a surefire hit song, "I Don't Wanna See You," then sings it in a voice that won't let folks forget just how backwoods country music can be. Songs like "It Must Be the Rain" and "Let's Begin Again" have soaring choruses that recall the Everlys at their best. On the other hand, "No Honky Tonkin' Tonight" and "I'd Rather Fish Than Fight" put to shame the lip service some singers pay to Hank Williams Sr. and Jimmie Rodgers. With the eerie "She's Gone," Brown takes the country death ballad into territory it's never seen before, and he follows it with the sentimental "Kentucky Skies." Brown is pure country without being purist. Flatly put, he's a hillbilly and proud of it. —*Brian Mansfield*

Cryin', Lovin', Leavin' / 1994 / MCA ✦✦✦✦
By his third album, Brown and producer Richard Bennett could be pretty confident they weren't going to get any radio play, so they just cut loose and made as pure an album as Brown was had in him. "You Must Be Mistakin' Me" and "Too Blue to Crow" possess a country sound so hard, they make most New Traditionalists sound like Muzak. Brown cuts Moon Mullican's "Cherokee Boogie," sings "Shameless Lies" with Melba Montgomery, shamelessly cops from Buddy Holly's "Crying, Waiting, Hoping" with the title cut, and finishes with a gorgeous duet with Joy Lynn White on "I Love Only You." —*Brian Mansfield*

Here's to the Honky Tonks / Sep. 17, 1996 / Hightone ✦✦✦
Here's to the Honky Tonks continues Marty Brown's streak of excellent hard country albums. Recording for an independent label, Brown sounds liberated, as if he can freely try out any number of different styles. Divided between driving bluegrass-styled picking and rollicking honky tonk, what makes *Here's to the Honky Tonks* particularly compelling is how Brown's songwriting continues to improve. —*Thom Owens*

Milton Brown

b. Sep. 8, 1903, Stephenville, TX, d. Apr. 13, 1936, Crystal Springs, TX
Leader, Vocals / Western Swing
One of the fathers of Western swing, Milton Brown was a vocalist and bandleader who was one of the first to fuse country, jazz, and pop together into a unique, distinctly American hybrid. Along with Bob Wills—who he performed with at the beginning of his career—Brown developed the sound and style of Western swing in the early '30s and for a while he and his band, the Musical Brownies, were just as popular as Bob Wills & His Texas Playboys. Tragically, Brown's career was cut short in 1936 when he died after a car accident, just as he was poised to break into national stardom. Born in Stephenville, TX, in 1903, Milton Brown moved to Fort Worth, TX, in 1918. After graduating from high-school in 1925, he worked as a cigar salesman, but he lost his job when the Great Depression hit in the late '20s. Brown began his musical career in 1930, when he happened to meet Bob Wills at a local Fort Worth dance. The Wills Fiddle Band was

performing at the dance and Brown joined the group on a chorus of "St. Louis Blues." Wills was impressed with Brown's voice and immediately asked him and his guitarist brother, Derwood, to join the band.

The Wills Fiddle Band played medicine shows around Texas and landed a regular radio spot on WBAP, where they played a show sponsored by the Aladdin Lamp Company, which had the band change its name to the Aladdin Laddies. In early 1931, the group was hired by the Light Crust Flour Company—which was run by Burrus Mill and Elevator Company—to appear daily on radio station KFJZ. The company, which was managed by W. Lee O'Daniel (who also hosted the radio shows) had the group rename itself as the Light Crust Doughboys. The Light Crust Doughboys were an instant success, and soon O'Daniel moved them to another radio station, then syndicated the program statewide. The Doughboys were playing cowboy songs, jazz, blues, and popular songs—a repertoire so diverse that the band's audience continued to expand. In February of 1932, they recorded a single for Victor under the name the Fort Worth Doughboys.

The band was playing dance music and wanted to play at dances, but O'Daniel was reluctant to let the group play outside of its radio shows. He also was hesitant to pay them much money, which greatly angered Milton Brown. In September of 1932, Brown left the band after he had an argument about money with O'Daniel. After leaving the Light Crust Doughboys, Brown formed the first Western swing band, the Musical Brownies. The first incarnation of the Brownies featured Brown, guitarist Derwood Brown, bassist Wanna Coffman, Ocie Stockard on tenor banjo, and fiddle player Jesse Ashlock. Shortly afterward, pianist Fred Calhoun and fiddle player Cecil Brower (who replaced Ashlock) joined the group. Like the Light Crust Doughboys, the Musical Brownies played a mixture of country, pop, and jazz, but the Brownies had a harder dance edge than their predecessors.

Almost immediately, Milton Brown & His Musical Brownies were a huge success. The group had a regular spot on radio station KTAT and drew large crowds at Texas dances. The band recorded eight songs for Bluebird in April of 1934, and another ten for the label in August of that year. Toward the end of 1934, the Brownies added electric steel guitarist Bob Dunn—the first musician to play an electric instrument in country music. In January of 1935, the band signed with Decca Records and recorded 36 songs for the label. Released as singles over the course of 1935, the songs helped establish the band as the most popular Western swing band in Texas. In March of 1936, the Brownies traveled to New Orleans to record its second set of sessions for Decca. By this time, fiddler Brower had been replaced by Cliff Bruner. At these sessions, the Brownies cut about 50 songs, which were issued throughout 1936 and 1937.

In April of 1936, Brown had a major car accident. Although he wasn't killed on impact, he died from pneumonia five days after the crash. Following Milton's death, Derwood Brown kept the Musical Brownies together for two years, recording a dozen sides for Decca in 1937. At the time of his death, Milton Brown rivaled Bob Wills in popularity. Although he never became as famous as Wills, he was equally important in the development of Western swing—without him, the genre as it is now known wouldn't exist. —*Stephen Thomas Erlewine*

★ **Pioneer Western Swing Band (1935–1936)** / Jan. 1935+Mar. 1936 / MCA ✦✦✦✦
This out-of-print LP from MCA's early-'80s *Collectables* series has been superceded by Texas Rose's complete reissuance of all of the recordings of Milton Brown & His Brownies on a five-CD set, but at the time it served as a good sampler of Brown's music. The singer, who led the first important Western swing band on record, heads an impressive octet (which also includes the fiddles of Cliff Bruner and Cecil Brower, the steel guitar of Bob Dunn, and banjoist Ocie Stockard) through a swing-oriented set. Two of the selections are from January 1935 while the other ten are taken from a marathon session in March 1936. Highlights of the spirited program include "The Sheik of Araby," "Yes Suh," "Hesitation Blues," "When I Take My Sugar to Tea," and "Easy Ridin' Papa." —*Scott Yanow*

Taking Off! / 1977 / String ✦✦✦✦✦
Here is more Decca material, it includes a couple of 1937 cuts recorded without Brown after he died. —*Dan Cooper*

Country & Western Dance-O-Rama / 1985 / Western ✦✦✦✦
Singer Milton Brown was one of the founders of western swing, actually predating Bob Wills & His Texas Playboys slightly. A complete set of all of Brown's recordings have been released, but this ten-inch Decca LP (reissued by the Mutual Music Corporation in the mid-'80s) is a fine best-of set. Unfortunately the personnel and dates are not given, but the eight numbers are all quite fun. Among the highlights are "St. Louis Blues," "Sweet Jennie Lee," "Brownie Special," and "Right or Wrong." —*Scott Yanow*

☆ **Complete Recordings of the Father of Western Swing: 1932–1937** / 1996 / Texas Rose ✦✦✦✦✦
Singer Milton Brown led the first Western swing band, beating Bob Wills on record as a bandleader by one year. Milton Brown's Musical Brownies, which consisted of the leader/vocalist, guitarist Derwood Brown, violinist Cecil Brower, pianist Fred Calhoun, bassist Wanna Coffman, banjoist Ocie Stockard, and, in its later period, the steel guitar of Bob Dunn and violinist Cliff Bruner, could play swing, sentimental waltzes, country stomps, and novelties with equal skill. Cary Ginell, who wrote a definitive book on Brown, produced this masterful five-CD set which contains not only all 102 recordings by the Brownies (seven marathon sessions held during 1934-1936) but Milton Brown's two numbers with the Fort Worth Doughboys in 1932 (a unit that includes Bob Wills on fiddle), Derwood Brown's 1937 session with the Brownies after his brother Milton's death, and a couple numbers by Roy Lee Brown (one with a reunion band) in 1984 and 1987. Add to that an extensive 40-page booklet and this is certainly the one Milton Brown set to get. Essential music, available from the small Texas Rose label. —*Scott Yanow*

Western Swing Chronicles, Vol. 1 / Aug. 21, 2001 / Original Jazz Library ✦✦✦✦✦
☆ **Daddy of Western Swing** / May 13, 2003 / Proper Box ✦✦✦✦✦

T. Graham Brown

b. Oct. 30, 1954, Arabi, GA

Vocals / Country-Pop, Country-Rock, Urban Cowboy

T. Graham Brown rose to country stardom through the uniquely Southern phenomenon of beach music, a party-ready mix of old-time rock & roll, R&B, country, and blues. Born in Arabi, GA (his real first name is Anthony), he got his start performing while attending the University of Georgia, as part of the beach-music duo Dirk & Tony. He then joined the outlaw country band Reo Diamond, and retooled his image as a hairy, tattooed wildman in a ten-gallon hat. Moving on in 1979, Brown formed his own R&B band, Rack of Spam, and officially settled on T. Graham Brown as his stage name. He moved to Nashville three years later, where with the help of Harlan Howard he found work singing demos and commercial jingles.

In 1983, he signed with CBS as a staff songwriter, and went on to join the Tree International publishing firm in the same capacity. Meanwhile, he also landed a deal as a recording artist with Capitol, and released his debut album, *I Tell It Like It Used to Be*, in 1986. Partly recorded at Alabama's legendary Muscle Shoals studios, the record spawned a number-one country single in "Hell or High Water," and both the title track and "I Wish That I Could Hurt That Way Again" went Top Ten. *Brilliant Conversationalist* (1987) gave Brown a second number one in "Don't Go to Strangers," and two more Top Tens with "She Couldn't Love Me Anymore" and the title cut. Meanwhile, he made appearances in the 1987 films *Greased Lightning* and *Cursed*, and the following year he and his backing group, the Hardtops, played Elvis' band in *Heartbreak Hotel*. *Come as You Were* (1988) continued Brown's success with the chart-topping "Darlene" and two further Top Tens in the title track and "The Last Resort."

Unfortunately, Brown was also battling alcoholism, and his problems began to take their toll on his career. He managed one further Top Ten country hit in 1990's "If You Could Only See Me Now," and also dueted with Tanya Tucker on the hit "Don't Go Out" that year. But after his 1991 album, *You Can't Take It With You*, missed the charts, he found himself dropped by Capitol, and spent most of the '90s sorting himself out. He finally returned in 1998 with the acclaimed comeback effort *Wine into Water*, which reaffirmed his roots rock leanings and marked his most personal effort to date. The concert album *T. Graham Brown Lives!* appeared in 2001. *—Steve Huey*

I Tell It Like It Used to Be / 1986 / Capitol ✦✦✦✦✦

With the sessions split between Nashville's Woodland Sound Studio and Muscle Shoals, T. Graham Brown's debut often sounds affectionately like the raw, impassioned work of a garage band. *—Tom Roland*

Brilliant Conversationalist / 1987 / Capitol ✦✦✦

With blaring horns and bluesy growled vocals, this record has more to do with Southside Johnny than any country band one could name. That aside, there are some nice songs on here. Not a great record but if this is your type of thing, you could do worse. *—Jim Worbois*

Come as You Were / 1988 / Capitol ✦✦✦✦

Bumper to Bumper / 1990 / Capitol ✦✦✦

This contains "I'm Sending One up for You," "If You Could Only See Me Now, " and more. *—AMG*

You Can't Take It with You / 1991 / Capitol ✦✦✦

● **The Best of T. Graham Brown** / 1992 / Curb ✦✦✦✦

This is an excellent single-disc compilation of T. Graham Brown's Capitol recordings from the mid- to late '80s. These ten tracks highlight the majority of his radio favorites, including "I Tell It Like It Use to Be," "I Wish I Could Hurt That Way Again," "She Couldn't Love Me Anymore," "Darlene," and his first number one from 1986, "Hell and High Water." This is a good place to get familiar with Brown's soulful vocals and R&B-inspired country. *—Al Campbell*

All-Time Greatest Hits / Aug. 24, 1993 / Curb ✦✦✦

All-Time Greatest Hits is a ten-track budget-priced collection that features some of T. Graham Brown's biggest hits, including "I Tell It Like It Used to Be," "Hell and High Water," "Brilliant Conversationalist," "Darlene," "Come as You Were," "Shakey Ground," "With This Ring" and "If You Could Only See Me Now." Although this isn't a bad budget-priced disc, there are better Brown collections available, offering more songs and better sound for not much more money. *—Stephen Thomas Erlewine*

Wine into Water / Aug. 25, 1998 / Intersound ✦✦✦✦✦

T. Graham Brown spent most of the '90s out of the spotlight and the reason why was alcoholism. As the title says, he spent many years trying to figure out how to turn the wine into water, and the record shows that there is indeed light at the end of the tunnel. *Wine into Water* is one of Brown's very best albums, not only because it finds him coming to terms with his own personal demons, but because it is so well-crafted. He's decided to pursue the gritty direction of Dan Penn, Spooner Oldham, and Delbert McClinton, creating a record that falls between country, soul, blues, and roots rock. Brown wrote all of the songs with Bruce "Troy Duke" Burch, and the results are alternately haunting and soul-affirming. It may have been painful to create, but this is the quality record that Brown has been promising he'd deliver for many years. *—Thom Owens*

Jann Browne

b. Mar. 14, 1954, Anderson, IN

Vocals / Contemporary Country, Singer/Songwriter, Roots Rock

A singer/songwriter whose eclectic body of work has embraced both retro-styled honky tonk and tough, bluesy lyrical introspections, Jann Browne is an artist with the talent to craft a mainstream success—and the guts and integrity to walk away from Nashville when she grew uncomfortable with the music industry.

Jann Browne was raised in Indiana and developed a taste for country music from her grandparents, who were members of a square dancing troupe that often performed at bluegrass festivals. However, Browne's own musical impulses leaned more toward rock & roll and blues, and as a teenager she began performing with local rock bands. In the late '70s, Browne pulled up stakes and moved to California, where she began writing and performing new songs with a stronger country influence. After a brief stint as a vocalist with Asleep at the Wheel, Browne moved to Nashville, and her material caught the ear of an A&R executive at Curb Records; in 1990, Browne was signed to the label and she released her debut album, *Tell Me Why*, that same year. *Tell Me Why* was a surprise success, spawning two hit singles, "Tell Me Why" and "You Ain't Down Home," and earned Browne a nomination as Female Vocalist of the Year by the Academy of Country Music.

However, Browne—a maverick who felt at home with such off-mainstream country & western artists as Emmylou Harris and Iris DeMent, both of whom have recorded with her—very soon discovered she had little taste for the politics of the major-label music industry. After her second album, 1991's *Only When I Laugh*, failed to sell as well as her debut, she opted out of her contract with Curb and moved back to California. Browne still had a substantial audience in Australia and Europe, and in 1995, she recorded her third album, *Count Me In*, for Red Moon Records, an independent label in Europe (it later received an American release from the independent Cross Three label). The album displayed a rawer sound that had more to do with blues and rock than mainstream country, and while it didn't find a large audience in the U.S., it won a number of enthusiastic reviews and reestablished Browne as a singer/songwriter with a sharp and distinctive vision. For her fourth album, 2001's *Missed Me by a Mile*, Browne continued to reassert her independence by co-producing the album herself, and releasing it in America on her own label, Plan B Records. *—Mark Deming*

● **Tell Me Why** / 1990 / Curb ✦✦✦✦✦

It Only Hurts When I Laugh / 1991 / Curb ✦✦✦✦✦

The backbeat rocks as well as swings this time. The song choices are supreme, as she covers everything from a Ray Price shuffle to progressive country by Jim Lauderdale and John Hiatt. *—Michael McCall*

Count Me In / Oct. 1995 / Cross Three ✦✦✦

Missed Me By a Mile / 2001 / Plan B Records ✦✦✦✦✦

There seems to be something about being bright, ambitious, and talented in Nashville that leads people to take a dramatic left turn, and that certainly seems to be the case with Jann Browne. A former vocalist with Asleep at the Wheel, Browne scored a couple of minor hits in an updated honky tonk style in the early '90s before she got lost in the shuffle of the Garth/Billy Ray boom. Browne's fourth album, *Missed Me By a Mile*, is a very different kettle of fish, and it happens to be a pretty tasty bouillabaisse; cut with a tight but soulful roots rock band (anchored by guitarist and co-producer Matt Barnes), Browne's voice is in great shape, but her music has gained some welcome grit and hard-won attitude since her brief brush with fame, and her songwriting has gotten tougher and smarter at the same time. "Cold Here in London" and "The Lucky Few" are witty character studies that really resonate; "Don't Worry About Tomorrow" and "Can't Build a Better Love" are songs about romance written by someone who happens to be living in the real world; and the title cut is as good a kiss-off to a former lover as you're likely to hear this year. Like Lucinda Williams and Shelby Lynne, Jann Browne has decided there's no room in her life for Nashville polish, and it's done her a world of good—anyone looking for a strong dose of root-conscious songwriting sung by someone with top-shelf country pipes would do well to give *Missed Me By a Mile* a spin. *—Mark Deming*

The Browns

f. 1955, **db.** 1967

Group / Traditional Country, Nashville Sound/Countrypolitan

During the '50s and '60s, the vocal harmonies of the Browns gave the lie to those who would stereotype country music as a raw product distinguished more by pure feeling than by art; perhaps the single word that best describes their music is "polished." The original brother-sister duo of Jim Ed Brown and Maxine Brown were joined by younger sister Bonnie in 1955, creating a trademark smooth trio sound that proved wonderfully adaptable to down-home harmony singing, to folk-pop arrangements that rode the crest of the hootenanny craze, and to lush Nashville sound extravaganzas. Bonnie and Jim were born in Sparkman, AR, where their father owned a sawmill and a large farm; older sister Maxine was born in Campti, LA. With the encouragement of their parents, the Brown children began singing and developing their characteristic close harmonies early on. In their teens they performed in school and began appearing at local events.

In 1952, Jim Ed placed second in a talent contest and won a slot on Little Rock's Barnyard Frolics radio program. Joined by Maxine, he was soon appearing on other local radio shows, which led to local TV appearances as well. The duo earned national recognition and a guest spot on Ernest Tubb's television show for their humorous song "Looking Back to See," which hit the Top Ten and stayed on the charts throughout the summer of 1954. The Browns were joined by recent high-school graduate Bonnie and began appearing on Shreveport's *Louisiana Hayride*. By the end of 1955, the trio had another Top Ten hit with "Here Today and Gone Tomorrow," which was given a boost by their national appearances on *the Ozark Jubilee*. The show's producer arranged for them to sign with RCA Victor in 1956, and soon afterward they had two major hits, "I Take the Chance" (a cover of a Louvin Brothers composition that showed how close the Browns remained to traditional harmony textures) and "I Heard the Bluebirds Sing." When Jim Ed was called to serve in the military, the group continued to record while he was on leave, and sister Norma filled in for him on tours.

By the late '50s, the Browns, now teamed with RCA's visionary producer Chet Atkins, had become one of the country acts that were most successful in exploiting the new national enthusiasm for folk music. On album covers they were pictured with a clean-cut, almost collegiate look that diverged sharply from country norms. The Nashville songwriters responsible for creating the sentimental, romantic world of Eddy Arnold's music contributed idealized visions of small-town life such as "The Old Village Choir" to the Browns' repertoire, but a song whose origin was not even American gave the trio its biggest hit. "The Three Bells," a translation of a hit song by hard-bitten French chanteuse Edith Piaf, not only spent ten weeks on top of the country charts in 1959, but also crossed over and spent four weeks at number one on the pop charts. As a result, the Browns appeared on *the Ed Sullivan Show, the Jimmy Dean Show,* and *American Bandstand.*

The Browns remained in the folk mode for their two follow-up hits, "Scarlet Ribbons" and "The Old Lamplighter," both of which did extremely well on both country and pop charts. Their string of hits continued until 1961, when the first phase of the folk boom died down. Two years later, after touring widely in the U.S. and Europe, the Browns joined the *Grand Ole Opry.* In late 1967, the Browns disbanded. Maxine and Bonnie went back to Arkansas to concentrate on their families, while Jim Ed focused on the successful solo career he had launched in 1965. An eight-disc retrospective of the Browns' music was released under the title *The Three Bells* on Germany's Bear Family label in 1993. *—Sandra Brennan & James Manheim*

Jim Edward, Maxine and Bonnie Brown / 1957 / RCA ✦✦✦✦

Sweet Sounds by the Browns / 1959 / RCA ✦✦✦

Town and Country / 1960 / BMG ✦✦✦

Town & Country is an uneven, but highly enjoyable, 1960 album from the Browns, featuring two of their signature hits: "Scarlet Ribbons (For Your Hair)" and "The Old Lamplighter." [The 1996 CD reissue includes four bonus tracks: "Love Me Tender," "The Three Bells," "Unchained Melody" and "Oh My Pa-Pa (O Mein Papa)."] *—Thom Owens*

Our Favorite Folk Songs / 1961 / RCA ✦✦✦✦

Songs from the Little Brown Church Hymnal / 1961 / RCA ✦✦✦

Grand Ole Opry Favorites / 1964 / RCA ✦✦✦

This Young Land / 1964 / RCA ✦✦✦

I Heard the Bluebirds Sing / 1965 / Camden ✦✦✦✦

Three Shades of Brown / 1965 / RCA ✦✦✦

When Love is Gone / 1965 / RCA ✦✦

Our Kind of Country / 1966 / RCA ✦✦✦

Alone With You / 1966 / RCA ✦✦✦

The Best of the Browns / 1966 / RCA ✦✦✦✦✦

The Old Country Church / 1967 / RCA ✦✦✦

Browns Sing the Big Ones From the Country / 1967 / RCA ✦✦✦

As the title suggests, this album is devoted to the Browns' renditions of recent country hits such as Buck Owens' "Where Does the Good Times Go"; Lynn Anderson's "Ride, Ride, Ride"; and Kenny Price's "Happy Tracks." It was conceived and executed for the album market in an era when many music buyers were happy to hear the current hits performed by their favorite artist rather than the original performers. "I'm a Lonesome Fugitive" might seem like an unlikely choice of material for the easygoing trio, but their version is haunting and quite enjoyable. The Browns were one of the smoothest and most pop-oriented harmony groups in the field of country music, and practically everything they recorded is worth hearing. *—Greg Adams*

Sugar Cane County / 1969 / Chart ✦✦✦

Rockin' Rollin' Browns / Sep. 1984 / Bear Family ✦✦✦

The Browns didn't really rock or roll, so the title refers to the fact that the album consists of the group's more pop-oriented material, like "The Three Bells," "Buttons and Bows," and "Tobacco Road." Several tracks on the record are previously unreleased and most are album cuts, making the collection necessary only for serious fans that would rather sample from the group's extensive back catalog instead of listening to all of it. Casual fans would be better served with a greatest-hits collection. *—Stephen Thomas Erlewine*

● **20 of the Best** / 1985 / RCA ✦✦✦✦✦

20 of the Best collects the great majority of the Browns' biggest hits. Even though it bypasses early hits like "Looking Back to See," "Here Today and Gone Tomorrow," "I Take the Chance," and "I Heard the Bluebirds Sing"—which were all recorded under the name Jim Edward, Maxine & Bonnie Brown (with the exception of "Looking Back to See," which was recorded without Bonnie)—the compilation is the only recent set to attempt a concise retrospective of the vocal group. *—Stephen Thomas Erlewine*

Looking Back to See / Sep. 1986 / Bear Family ✦✦✦

Looking Back to See collects some of the Browns' big hit singles, including the title track, but it mainly concentrates on obscurities and unreleased tracks from early in their career. Consequently, it's an album that would appeal only to collectors, even though there is some fine music on the record. *—Stephen Thomas Erlewine*

The Three Bells / 1993 / Bear Family ✦✦✦✦✦

Eight CDs and over 240 songs is overkill, except that there's a lot worth hearing here. Disc one opens in 1954 with Jim Ed and Maxine Brown's debut recordings for the Fabor label, including "Looking Back to See," which was successful enough to get them a touring slot with a young Elvis Presley. The sound, while primitive in comparison to their subsequent RCA recordings is very pleasing, with bright harmonies and simple, straightforward accompaniment. As soon as they got to RCA, their sound bloomed—the textures of the instruments became more vivid, with the "voices" of the guitars nearly as crisp as those of the singers themselves. By this time, they were one of country music's great mixed harmony groups, and were applying those vocal talents to bluesy numbers, as well as softer country and bluegrass material. "The Three Bells" was the massive hit that turned the trio toward pop material in 1959. Their repertory on disc three was broadening to include more folk material and pop standards. By the time of disc four, Hank Garland and John D. Loudermilk were playing most of the guitar, though Atkins was still producing, and the results remained impressive. Disc five is dominated by a brace of inspirational tunes cut for their *Little Brown Church Hymnal* album, and also includes

their cover of "They Call the Wind Maria," one of Jim Ed Brown's best performances. Disc six is probably the only 1964-vintage archive to feature songs by Hank Snow and Bob Dylan coming from the same outfit. Discs seven and eight leave the group at the end of their time as a trio, prior to Bonnie's retirement late in 1967—highlights include a ton of beautifully sung country, pop, and folk numbers. *—Bruce Eder*

Family Bible / Mar. 12, 1996 / Rock Bottom ✦✦

Notwithstanding the vintage photos that appear on the cover and in the booklet, please note the legend on the inlay card: "All new recordings." The ten gospel songs on *Family Bible* feature the original trio of Jim, Bonnie and Maxine, and despite being recent recordings, the old smooth harmony sound is still there. Better yet, the instrumentation is thankfully not of the synthesizer-and-drum-machine schlock that often taints these sorts of late-career projects. The Browns cover "Life's Railway to Heaven," "He'll Set Your Fields on Fire," "I'll Fly Away," and other gospel standards with such aplomb it makes one wonder at this trio's absence from today's country charts. Hey, why not? Jim Ed Brown, in particular, sounds as good as ever. *Family Bible* is an enjoyable gospel package that demonstrates that the Browns still have it. *—Greg Adams*

Sweet Sounds by the Browns/Grand Ole Opry Favorites / Sep. 12, 2000 / WestSide ✦✦✦✦

These two albums were originally released on RCA in 1959 and 1964, respectively, by the vocal group the Browns. Before Jim Ed Brown would receive substantial status on the country charts and as a *Grand Ole Opry* star, he recorded with his siblings Maxine Brown and Bonnie Brown. In 1959 they scored big on both the pop and country charts with "The Three Bells," included on the *Sweet Sounds* album. The remainder of that album contains 11 tracks that are mostly filler: "Love Me Tender," "Unchained Melody," and "Only the Lonely." *Grand Old Opry Favorites*, on the other hand, is the stronger session, keeping with pure country roots on "Sugar Foot Rag," "Wondering," "Mansion on the Hill," and "Four Walls." This disc is geared toward collectors, while casual listeners would do better with a greatest-hits package. *—Al Campbell*

Ed Bruce (William Edwin Bruce Jr.)

b. Dec. 29, 1939, Keiser, AR

Songwriter, Vocals / Traditional Country, Progressive Country, Rockabilly, Outlaw Country, Rock & Roll

Like so many other artists, singer Ed Bruce got his start as a rockabilly act for Memphis' famed Sun Records; however, he was probably best known for his songwriting acumen. Born William Edwin Bruce Jr. in Arkansas in 1939, he cut his first sides for Sun at the age of 17. His career as a frenetic rockabilly performer was largely unsuccessful, however, and by 1964 Bruce had moved to Nashville to become a member of the Marijohn Wilkins Singers. He also entered into a lucrative career singing advertising jingles; his best-known campaign cast him as a character called the Tennessean.

In 1966, Bruce signed with RCA, notching his first chart hit with the single "Walker's Woods." More singles and a change of labels followed, but the singer struggled until 1975, when he took his composition "Mammas Don't Let Your Babies Grow Up to Be Cowboys" into the Top 20. The song, Bruce's best-known, was later a monster hit when covered by the duo of Waylon Jennings and Willie Nelson in 1977. His songs have also been recorded by the likes of Charlie Louvin, Tex Ritter, Tanya Tucker, and Crystal Gayle.

After a brief tenure at Epic Records between 1977 and 1978, Bruce achieved his greatest commercial success with MCA in the 1980s. "The Last Cowboy Song," featuring guest vocals from Willie Nelson, hit number 12 in 1980; both "Girls, Women and Ladies" and "(When You Fall in Love) Everything's a Waltz" also fell just short of entering the Top Ten. In 1981, Bruce hit number one with "You're the Best Break This Heart Ever Had"; other Top Five singles included "Ever, Never Lovin' You" (number four, 1982), "After All" (number four, 1983), "You Turn Me On (Like a Radio)" (number three, 1984), and "Nights" (number four, 1986). After the 1986 album *Night Things* and a 1988 self-titled follow-up, Bruce made a conscious decision to cut back on his music to focus on his acting career, appearing in several made-for-TV films. *—Jason Ankeny*

If I Could Just Go Home / 1968 / RCA ✦✦✦✦

Shades of Ed Bruce / 1969 / Monument ✦✦✦

Mamas, Don't Let Your Babies Grow Up to Be Cowboys / 1976 / United Artists ✦✦✦✦✦

Ed Bruce / 1980 / MCA ✦✦✦

One to One / 1981 / MCA ✦✦✦

Last Train to Clarkesville / 1982 / RCA ✦✦✦

I Write It Down / 1982 / MCA ✦✦✦

You're Not Leaving Here Tonight / 1983 / MCA ✦✦✦✦

Rockin' and Boppin' Baby / 1986 / Bear Family ✦✦✦✦✦

Greatest Hits / 1986 / MCA ✦✦✦✦✦

This album documents the most rewarding period of Ed Bruce's recording career. Easygoing, midtempo love songs dominate, particularly with "You're the Best Break This Old Heart Ever Had," "Ever, Never Lovin' You" and "You're Leavin' Here Tonight." The reflective "After All" is permanently haunting. *—Tom Roland*

● **The Best of Ed Bruce** / 1995 / Varese ✦✦✦✦✦

After kicking around Nashville for a while—recording for RCA, UA, and Epic, all without success—Ed Bruce landed at MCA in 1980, where he finally managed to have success by positioning himself somewhere between the cowboy fantasies of outlaw and the commerciality of urban cowboy. He wound up sounding like a cross between a tamer Waylon Jennings and an adventurous Kenny Rogers, which wasn't a bad thing, and it led to several hits between 1980 and 1986, by which time he moved to RCA. All of them (with the mild exception of a few minor latter-day hits for RCA) are on Varese's 18-track 1995 collection *The Best of Ed Bruce*. This also features the first version of "Mamas Don't Let

Your Babies Grow Up to Be Cowboys," which he co-wrote with Patsy Bruce and had a hit with on United Artists in 1975, before Waylon and Willie brought it fame in 1978. It's the earthiest thing here and it's also the best, in no small measure due to that hint of earthiness, but his MCA material is also enjoyable. It is a little subdued and samey, with a production too polished for a real cowboy, but its gentleness suits Bruce's warm voice and he has a good taste in material, along with a knack for writing sturdy songs. This music is a little sleepy, but not in an unpleasant way, and it does capture the moment when outlaw was diluted with country-pop. Perhaps it's not Bruce's very best work, but it is his most popular, and it is good listening, even if it is a little dated. *—Stephen Thomas Erlewine*

Puzzles / 1995 / Bear Family ✦✦✦✦✦
The single-disc, 29-track compilation *Puzzles* collects all of Ed Bruce's RCA recordings from the late '60s, including "Blue Denim Eyes," "By Route of New Orleans," "Walker's Woods," "Last Train to Clarksville," "Painted Girls and Wine," "Memphis Morning," "Why Can't I Come Home," "Ninety Seven More to Go," "Give Me More Than You Can Take," "Something Else to Mess Your Mind" and no less than three versions of the title track. While this material is not among Bruce's best-known, it is among his best. Though the duplicate versions of some tracks can be tedious—"Puzzles" is presented in three versions, there are two takes of "I'd Be Best Leaving You," there are both dubbed and undubbed versions of "Painted Girls and Wine" and "Blue Bayou"—*Puzzles* nevertheless is an excellent way to become acquainted with a fine, underappreciated talent. *—Thom Owens*

This Old Hat / May 14, 2002 / Old Hat Productions ✦✦✦
Country singer and songwriter—and actor—Ed Bruce was a teenager when he started his musical career recording at the now-legendary Sun Records. He didn't have any success with his rockabilly tunes and eventually moved on. Years later he found an excellent job singing advertising jingles, then finally landed a contact with RCA. Bruce is probably best known by country fans for a catchy little song he penned and recorded in the '70s called "Mammas Don't Let Your Babies Grow Up to Be Cowboys." Though it made it onto the Top 20 charts for Bruce, two years later it became a huge hit when it was recorded as a duet by Waylon Jennings and Willie Nelson. A gifted songwriter who has written numbers for greats like Tanya Tucker and Tex Ritter, Bruce wrote or co-wrote most of the songs on this 2002 recording, *This Old Hat*. He lets his talents shine on songs like "You're the Best Break This Old Heart Ever Had," "My First Taste of Texas," "Did He Say It Better Than Me?," and "My Baby Don't Need No Polish to Shine." *—Charlotte Dillon*

12 Classics / Apr. 22, 2003 / Varese ✦✦✦
Varese Sarabande's *12 Classics* is not a collection of Ed Bruce's original hits. As explained in small type on the back cover, this collection "contains new recordings of Ed Bruce's greatest hits, recorded April 1997," so it's not really a good substitution for Varese's regrettably out of print 18-track 1995 collection *The Best of Ed Bruce*, although most of these 12 songs were on that collection of 1975-1986 material. These aren't bad recordings by any means. They're a little too laid-back, perhaps, and the arrangements are a little limp, but Bruce is in good voice and they're entirely pleasant. Although they're nice to hear, they're not the kind of recordings you'd seek out unless you were a hardcore fan who might like to have these mellow re-recordings as part of your collection. But anybody who thinks this is indeed a replacement for the previous Varese collection should stay away. *—Stephen Thomas Erlewine*

Vin Bruce (Ervin Bruce)

b. Apr. 25, 1932, Cut Off, LA
Guitar, Vocals / Zydeco, Swamp Blues, Traditional Cajun
Born Ervin Bruce in Cut Off, LA, on April 25, 1932, Cajun singer Vin Bruce grew up in the musical environment provided by his father, whose fiddle playing for the local Cajun dances influenced Bruce to take up the guitar and write music. He honed his smooth and gentle vocal style by playing with local groups, and by the age of 18, Bruce decided to take his career solo and caught the ears of Columbia Records. He recorded a number of 78s with Columbia between 1951-1956, scoring a hit with "Dans la Louisianne," which made him one of the first Cajun musicians to gain national attention, even landing him on the stage of the *Grand Ole Opry*, where he befriended Hank Williams, Chet Atkins, and others.

When the first wave of rock & roll devoured the industry, Bruce was dropped from Columbia, and while he maintained a much lower national profile, he was still lauded as among the best Cajun singers of all time by fans of the genre. Juggling a day job on an oil rig (he could no longer support himself on music alone) and a singing career, Bruce remained somewhat busy between the 1960s and the 1990s, releasing several albums and singles on various small labels. He continued to play regularly in and around Louisiana, and eventually he converted a barn into a recording studio and released the album *Carousel for Two* on the Louisiana Red record label in the fall of 2000. *—Jeff Hannusch & Mark A. Humph*

Cajun Country / 1979 / Swallow ✦✦✦

● **Greatest Hits** / 1979 / Swallow ✦✦✦✦
Recorded by one of the pioneers of Cajun music, these early-'60s sides are a mix of traditional songs and French interpretations of country hits. *—Jeff Hannusch*

The Essential Collection / Jun. 6, 2000 / Swallow ✦✦✦✦

Cliff Bruner

b. Apr. 25, 1915, Houston, TX, **d.** Aug. 25, 2000
Fiddle / Traditional Country, Western Swing, Honky Tonk
In the late '30s, during the classic era of Western swing, Cliff Bruner was one of the fiddlers who helped to create and develop that music by fusing country and jazz sounds. As the bandleader of his own Texas Wanderers, Bruner carved out a place in country music history by focusing on a new kind of song—not the smooth, heavily jazz-influenced arrangements to which other Texas bands of the day aspired, but simpler vocal pieces with lyrics that spoke of disillusionment and hard luck. Bruner is particularly noted for his recording of Ted Daffan's composition "Truck Driver's Blues"—the first trucker song ever committed to disc.

Born in Houston, TX, in 1915, Bruner was performing professionally and wandering around Texas in search of gigs by the late '20s. The medicine show provided him with early employment, as it did for many other early country stars; he had signed on with Dr. Scott's Medicine Show, a traveling caravan hawking a cure-all called Liquidine Tonic. In 1934, Bruner joined the pathbreaking Western swing band Milton Brown & His Musical Brownies, an act which billed itself as "The Greatest String Band on Earth." He cut close to 50 songs with the group before Brown was killed in an auto accident in April 1936; the twin fiddles often heard in the Brownies' music (setting a pattern that lasted for decades in country music) are those of Bruner and the classically trained violinist Cecil Brower.

After Brown's death, Bruner returned to Houston and formed a group called the Texas Wanderers (sometimes called Cliff Bruner & His Boys). The band settled into a slot on Beaumont radio station KDFM, whose listenership crossed the state line into heavily Cajun southwestern Louisiana. As did other Western swing bands, this one fused traditional fiddle-led country music with elements of 1920s and '30s pop and jazz. But Bruner, from the start, favored a strikingly contemporary sound. He brought the wildly experimental electric steel guitarist Bob Dunn on board from the Brownies and featured an electric mandolinist, Leo Raley, and an energetic barrelhouse pianist, Moon Mullican. The Texas Wanderers' recordings on the Decca label crowded jukeboxes along the oil-rich, heavily industrialized Texas Gulf Coast. Among the many songs featuring vocalist Dickie McBride were several that were recognized in retrospect as early classics of the honky tonk genre: the band had perhaps its biggest hit in 1938 with a recording of the Floyd Tillman composition "It Makes No Difference Now" and "Truck Driver's Blues" followed in 1939.

In the early '40s, Bruner dissolved the Texas Wanderers, but he continued to work with Mullican and with other musicians who were forging modern country music out of the forms of Western swing: he performed with former Texas governor W. Lee O'Daniel and with Louisiana governor-to-be Jimmie Davis. Bruner and Mullican headed a band called the Showboys, and he made some recordings for Mercury and for small Texas labels after World War II. Bruner largely dropped out of music in the early '50s in favor of an insurance-sales career. When the Western swing revival flowered in the 1970s, however, he gained proper recognition as an enormously influential figure. He appeared on Johnny Gimble's 1980 LP *Texas Swing Pioneers* and remained active as a performer well into his ninth decade. On August 25, 2000, Bruner's long lifetime of making music came to an end when he died of cancer at the age of 85. *—James Manheim*

★ **Cliff Bruner's Texas Wanderers** / 1983 / Texas Rose ✦✦✦✦✦
This is a fine compilation covering the years 1937-1944. Beaucoups chops from the aforementioned Bruner, Dunn and Mullican, as well as Leo Raley, the first Western swinger to "plug in" a mandolin. *—Dan Cooper*

Cliff Bruner & His Texas Wanderers / Mar. 18, 1997 / Bear Family ✦✦✦✦✦
This five-CD set is the only extant collection by this legendary Western swing outfit. At 140 dollar list, it's a hefty investment, but it's such solid music that it's difficult not to justify on the basis of quality. Disc one, covering sessions from 1937, is justified by the presence of the greatest version ever of "Milk Cow Blues," with a vocal by Leo Herbert Raley that will curl every hair you have; an awesome Western swing version of "You Got to Hi De Hi"; the bluesy, fiddle-driven "Can't Nobody Truck Like Me"; the smooth yet touching "Under the Silvery Moon"; and a trio of distinctive alternate takes of three of the best numbers here, only uncovered in 1997. Disc two has even more of a freewheeling feel to it, and some of the best rags and dances ever cut by anybody. By the late 1939 sessions that open disc three, the group isn't as much of a blues band, no less lively but playing more straight dance material. Disc four moves into the 1940s, and topicality is reflected by the presence of the rollicking "Draft Board Blues"; the disc also encompasses the extended periods of recording inactivity by the group, including a gap from 1941 and 1944, and then, again, until 1947. By this time, Bruner and his band were losing the edge that had made their earlier music such a delightfully intense listening experience. Their playing was as good as (and more polished than) ever, but as they moved into the late '40s and the dawn of the 1950s—covered on disc five—their overall sound lacked sharpness, although it was still eminently listenable. The notes and discography are both exceptionally detailed. *—Bruce Eder*

James Bryan

b. Mentone, AL
Fiddle / Traditional Bluegrass
James Bryan was born in Mentone, AL. A fiddler almost since birth, Bryan won his first competition at 12, apprenticed with bluegrass master Kenny Baker, and took the title of Tennessee Valley Fiddle King at 17. Bryan eventually joined Norman Blake's Rising Fawn String Ensemble, where his mastery of the fiddle and repertoire of old-timey songs was honed. He made his solo debut on Rounder with *Lookout Blues* in 1983; *The First of May* followed two years later. Both albums featured a mix of old-timey Southern tunes, many with twinges of their English and Scottish heritage intact. Bryan continued to perform throughout the 1980s, both solo and with Norman and Nancy Blake. In 1995, he released *Two Pictures*, a collaboration with guitarist Carl Jones. He continued to make regular appearances at bluegrass and folk festivals, often accompanied by his daughter Rachel Bryan on guitar. *—Johnny Loftus*

Lookout Blues / 1983 / Rounder ✦✦✦✦

● **The First of May** / 1986 / Rounder ✦✦✦✦
This set includes a variety of unusual local tunes and old favorites. *—Charles S. Wolfe*

Boudleaux Bryant

b. Feb. 13, 1920, Shellman, GA, **d.** Jun. 25, 1987, Knoxville, TN

Songwriter, Composer / Rock & Roll, Traditional Country, Nashville Sound/Countrypolitan

He became one of the greatest songwriters in country music history, but Boudleaux Bryant studied classical violin from the age of five and played with the Atlanta Philharmonic during its 1938 season. He joined a country band that same year when a friend needed help and toured with Hank Penny's Radio Cowboys in the early '40s, but had switched his allegiance to jazz music when in 1945 he met Felice Scaduto (b. August 7, 1925, Milwaukee, WI), his future wife and songwriting companion. They began writing songs together and sent "Country Boy" to Fred Rose, who bought the song and began Acuff-Rose Publishing's long association with the Bryants. Little Jimmy Dickens hit the country Top Ten with the song in June 1949. Carl Smith recorded the Bryants' "Hey Joe" in 1953 and it also became a hit; Frankie Laine's pop version the same year sold over a million copies. Later in the '50s, Felice and Boudleaux began to move into rock & roll as well, writing a song for Buddy Holly plus most of the Everly Brothers' big hits: "Bye Bye Love," "Problems," "All I Have to Do Is Dream," "Wake Up Little Susie," and "Bird Dog."

Though they had never completely deserted country, in the '60s the Bryants resumed their focus, writing hits for Jim Reeves and Sonny James, among others. In 1967, they left Acuff-Rose and formed their own House of Bryant publishing company. The classics continued to come during the '70s, and in 1979, Boudleaux produced the Bryants' first album as performers, *All I Have to Do Is Dream*—known in the U.S. as *A Touch of Bryant*. By the late '80s, it was estimated that Boudleaux and Felice's warehouse of 3,000 songs had sold over 300 million copies worldwide; that fact made them a shoo-in for the Nashville Songwriters Hall of Fame and even the Country Music Hall of Fame—a rare honor for strict songwriters. Boudleaux died in June 1987, and Felice continued to write occasionally until her April 2003 death at age 77 in Gatlinburg, TN. *—John Bush*

● **Boudleaux Bryant's Best Sellers** / 1963 / Monument ✦✦✦✦

Cody Bryant (Jeff Ruff)

Guitar, Banjo, Fiddle / Cowboy, Western Swing, Bluegrass, Bakersfield Sound

Born Jeff Ruff, Cody Bryant was raised in Whittier, CA. The son of Bob Ruff, a member of the Square Dance Hall of Fame, Cody grew up around the music business since his father also founded Wagon Wheel Records and Windsor Records, two California labels that not only provided square dancers with the calls and tunes they needed, but periodically recorded other artists as well.

Impressed at an early age by Jimmy Bryant, an early mentor rumored to be a relative of the Ruff family, the boy who would grow up to be Cody Bryant took to pickin'. Playing sometimes all through the night in his bedroom, the Ruffs' youngest child soon developed a style of his own. As high-school beckoned, so did more and more bluegrass festivals as well as playing in some heavy metal bands. Hitting the road after he finished school, Bryant spent some time in Colorado learning more about playing and songwriting from an old cowboy singer, J.B. Tankersley. Picking up the banjo and eventually the fiddle, Bryant's smooth and clean style of guitar playing became his calling card.

Moving back to California, he was befriended by Hank Cochran. Again, Bryant absorbed everything he could. Settling in, he put together two bands, the Caffeine Dream Bluegrass Band and the Cody Bryant Western Band. Playing coffeehouse and acoustic gigs with his bluegrass outfit allowed Cody to delve back into some of the old mountain and hillbilly tunes he was introduced to as a youngster. His Western band gave him the format to develop his singing style even further. Often compared to Marty Robbins, Bryant quickly became a known talent on the L.A. scene.

Working with greats Brantley Kearns, Rick Shea, Doug Livingston, and Rick Dunham encouraged him along. For a time he hosted a monthly honky tonk showcase in Hollywood that featured the Losin' Brothers, Shea, Kearns, Patty Booker, Barry Holdship and many other roots, bluegrass, and country & western artists. After putting out several indie cassettes, 1996 was the year Bryant pulled out all the stops, investing in himself and his career and putting out a CD. *Big Dose of Country* was launched with a celebration at *Jack's Sugar Shack* that included friends the Losin' Brothers, Barry Holdship, and the now-defunct Plowboys. Moving beyond Los Angeles, Bryant quickly made a place for himself in Bakersfield after attaining the approval and friendship of Red Simpson. Working at the Golden West Casino in Bakersfield and sitting in with Simpson gave Bryant the courage and the conviction to move forward with his career. *—Jana Pendragon*

Big Dose of Country / 1996 / Wagon Wheel ✦✦✦

Big Dose of Country should have been a reflection of Cody Bryant and not of someone else's idea of what would sell. Somewhere between the two concepts, Bryant got lost just enough to make this first CD outing a slight disappointment. While the artist is flawless, and Bryant's guitar and vocals are beyond reproach, there is still something a little too over-produced about *Big Dose* to adequately demonstrate the monster talent that Bryant is. His songs are strictly country & western, yet some of them come off a little too manufactured on this project. Still, the CD shows his strengths. Cuts like "I Don't Want to Go Home Tonight," "Good Ol' Boy," and "Haul Off and Love Me" scintillate. Rick Shea's "Bed of Roses" and Bryant's own "Tell Me I'm Not Losing You" demonstrate the softer side of this Hollywood cowboy. "Too Far Under" establishes Bryant as a romantic balladeer, while his love song to his Cadillac, "Big Iron" (not to be confused with the Marty Robbins hit), shows how much high speed and power there is in his singing and playing. Neither does the CD reflect his style and charisma with an audience. For serious students of country & western, the Bakersfield sound, and the West Coast country and roots music scene, this is a must. But be forewarned: The real Cody Bryant has yet to be revealed on CD. *—Jana Pendragon*

Felice Bryant (Matilda Genevieve Scaduto)

b. Aug. 7, 1925, Milwaukee, WI, **d.** Apr. 22, 2003, Gatlinburg, TN

Lyricist, Songwriter, Composer / Rock & Roll, Traditional Country, Nashville Sound/Countrypolitan

With her husband Boudleaux, Felice Bryant formed one of the most potent songwriting teams in country history, writing many songs that became hits. She had been performing and writing songs since she was a child, but her fame came after she met and married Boudleaux in 1945. They began writing together and sent "Country Boy" to Fred Rose, who bought the song and began Acuff-Rose Publishing's long association with the Bryants. Little Jimmy Dickens hit the country Top Ten with the song in June 1949. Carl Smith recorded the Bryants' "Hey Joe" in 1953 and it also became a hit; Frankie Laine's pop version the same year sold over a million copies. Later in the '50s, Felice and Boudleaux began to move into rock & roll as well, writing a song for Buddy Holly plus most of the Everly Brothers' big hits: "Bye Bye Love," "Problems," "All I Have to Do Is Dream," "Wake Up Little Susie," and "Bird Dog."

Though they had never deserted country, the Bryants resumed their focus in the '60s, writing hits for Jim Reeves and Sonny James, among others. In 1967, they left Acuff-Rose and formed their own House of Bryant publishing company. The classics continued to come during the '70s, and in 1979, Boudleaux produced the Bryants' first album as performers, *All I Have to Do Is Dream*—known in the U.S. as *A Touch of Bryant*.

By the late '80s, it was estimated that Boudleaux and Felice's warehouse of 3,000 songs had sold over 300 million copies worldwide; that fact made them a shoo-in for the Nashville Songwriters Hall of Fame and even the Country Music Hall of Fame—a rare honor for strict songwriters. Though Boudleaux died in June 1987, Felice Bryant continued to write occasionally. She was 77 when she passed away in her Gatlinburg home in April 2003. *—John Bush*

Jimmy Bryant

b. Mar. 5, 1925, Moultrie, GA, **d.** Sep. 22, 1980

Guitar / Traditional Country, Instrumental Country

With steel guitar wizard Speedy West, guitarist Jimmy Bryant formed half of the hottest country guitar duo of the 1950s. With lightning speed and a jazz-fueled taste for improvisation and adventure, Bryant's boogies, polkas, and Western swing—recorded with West and as a solo artist—remain among the most exciting instrumental country recordings of all time. Bryant also waxed major contributions to the early recordings of singers like Tennessee Ernie Ford, Merrill E. Moore, Kay Starr, Billy May, and Ella Mae Morse, and has influenced country guitarists like Buck Owens, James Burton, and Albert Lee. While he enjoyed a career that spanned several decades, it was his sessions with Capitol Records in the early '50s that allowed him his fullest freedom to strut his stuff. *—Richie Unterberger*

Two Guitars Country Style / 1954 / Capitol ✦✦✦✦

Country Cabin Jazz / 1960 / Capitol ✦✦✦✦

Along with his frequent partner, pedal steel guitarist Speedy West, Jimmy Bryant was one the most in-demand session players in country music. Recording mostly behind Capitol's considerable lineup of artists during the '50s and '60s, Bryant augmented his frequent work for the likes of Tennessee Ernie Ford, Kay Starr, and Buck Owens with a fair share of solo dates, often featuring West. This classic Capitol release from 1960 finds the two jazz-influenced players wending stealthily through 12 incredible instrumentals, most of which were penned by Bryant. Bryant and West turn in a bevy of complex, yet swinging solos over a mix of blues ("Whistle Stop"), country ballads ("Deep Water"), polkas ("Hometown Polka"), and bebop-country swingers ("Stratosphere Boogie"). Along with several exciting exchanges between Bryant and West, the whole band turns in a fine round of call-and-response solos on "Jammin' With Jimmy"; figuring prominently in the mix are guitarist Billie Strange, pianist Billy Liebert, bassist Cliffie Stone, and an unlisted violinist. While many of these tracks can be found on Razor & Tie's two fine Bryant and West collections, *Country Cabin Jazz* still qualifies as a very good first-disc choice for newcomers. *—Stephen Cook*

Bryant's Back in Town / 1966 / Longhorn ✦✦✦

Laughing Guitar, Crying Guitar / 1966 / Imperial ✦✦✦

We Are Young / 1966 / Imperial ✦✦✦

Play Country Guitar With Jimmy Bryant / 1967 / Dolton ✦✦✦

The Fastest Guitar in the Country / 1967 / Imperial ✦✦✦✦

● **Guitar Take-Off** / 1989 / See For Miles ✦✦✦✦✦

This is undisputably the best Bryant compilation with 20 tracks from 1951 to 1955, many taken from rare singles, and many also featuring Speedy West. Also includes cuts by Ella Mae Morse, Tennessee Ernie Ford, Merrill E. Moore, and Billy May that feature Jimmy as a sessionman. "Stratosphere Boogie" and "Catfish Boogie" are breathtaking Bryant/West duels. *—Richie Unterberger*

Richard Buckner

b. 1967

Guitar, Vocals / Singer/Songwriter, Country-Folk, Alternative Country, Americana

This husky-voiced country-folksinger/songwriter is very much in the mold of the Lubbock, TX, school of mavericks, including Butch Hancock, Terry Allen, and Jimmie Dale Gilmore. Richard Buckner is actually based in San Francisco, but the Lubbock connection is no accident. His debut album, *Bloomed*, was recorded in Lubbock, for one thing, with producer Lloyd Maines, who has also worked with Hancock, Allen, Joe Ely, and Uncle Tupelo. Maines himself plays several instruments on the record, and Buckner's band is fleshed out with several other Texas musicians, including Hancock (who adds a harmonica cameo) and accordion player Ponty Bone. Buckner's principal following, however, is not with the country audience, but the alternative rock one. Like Allen and Hancock, the guitarist's work is based in rootsy country traditions, but his lyrics are far too personal and ambitious for those who think of country music as virtually synonymous with Nashville. So, like those Lubbock musicians, he tends to appeal to open-minded rock fans, or adventurous general music fans, more than country ones. The alternative rock thread has been strengthened by Buckner's leadership of a San Francisco country-rock band, the Doubters (who do not appear on his album), and a support slot on a Son Volt tour in early 1996.

Appearing on a small Texas independent label, his album won good critical notices, and his signing to a major company for 1997's acclaimed *Devotion + Doubt* seemed to signal that both rock and country listeners would be much more widely exposed to him in the future. *Since* followed in 1998 and *The Hill*, an interpretation of Edgar Lee Masters' *Spoon River Anthology*, was issued two years later. Recorded at his home studio in Canada, 2002's *Impasse* was next, and was his first CD of all original music in over four years. The next year, Buckner returned with a self-titled release, a divine set of songs that was limited to 2,000 pressings and previously available only as a tour item. *—Richie Unterberger*

Bloomed / 1994 / Dejadics ✦✦✦

Buckner's debut is an accomplished but subdued affair with hardly a trace of rock in sight. The emphasis is on his rich-but-weary vocals and sober tales of romance and restlessness, with dignified Texas prairie backup by such esteemed regionals as Lloyd Maines (who produced) and Ponty Bon. Very much in the vein of Butch Hancock, but much more ordinary at this point, without the eccentricity and boisterousness that characterize much of Hancock and fellow Lubbockite Terry Allen's work. [The 1999 reissued of *Bloomed* contains five previously unreleased bonus tracks.] *—Richie Unterberger*

Unreleased / 1995 / Chelsea Music ✦✦✦

While on the road following the release of his debut album, *Bloomed*, Richard Buckner compiled and sold this cassette-only collection of early performances as a concert souvenir, and while it's hardly "the Great Lost Buckner Album," *Unreleased* is certainly an intriguing look at what this artist was up to before he gained a hearing outside San Francisco. While most of *Unreleased*'s ten songs would be re-recorded on Buckner's first three albums, this marks the only release to date for four of the tracks, the best being the tape's first two selections, "House of Rotten Timbers" and "Sister," both fine and intimate examinations of people on the emotional brink. (On the other end of the scale, "Tracy Truly" richly deserves its obscurity as the silliest thing Buckner has ever put to tape, if only for the line "Pull that truck around/Let's get the f—k out of this town.") The set also features three performances with Buckner's early band the Doubters, and if the version of "Gauzy Dress" pales compared to its re-recorded version (as "Gauzy Dress in the Sun" on *Bloomed*), the twangier take of "Jewelbomb" makes for an interesting companion to his later rendition on *Since*. Hard to find and not likely to receive greater circulation any time soon, *Unreleased* is nevertheless a compelling look at the formative years of one of the most gifted singer/songwriters to emerge in the 1990s, and fans will find it an entertaining bit of musical archeology. *—Mark Deming*

● **Devotion + Doubt** / Mar. 11, 1997 / MCA ✦✦✦✦✦

Buckner's second album of cross-country-folk is an exploration of love's paranoia and its resulting desperation and hopelessness. Stemming from the singer/songwriter's divorce, the 13 songs on *Devotion + Doubt* reflect and, to a lesser degree, celebrate both his new-found independence and loneliness. His road-weary voice (often calmed to a whisper here), coupled with the sparing strums of his acoustic guitar, strikes a point of intimacy within the songs, giving the best of them ("Pull," "4am") the feeling that they were reluctantly cribbed from personal diary entries. But Buckner never sounds defeated on *Devotion + Doubt*, only a bit haunted, as if he's convinced himself—based on past attempts at love and their eventual failures—that he's destined to make the same mistakes again and again, no matter how hard he tries to make the relationships work. *—Michael Gallucci*

Since / Aug. 11, 1998 / MCA ✦✦✦✦

Richard Buckner's follow-up to his 1997 divorce odyssey *Devotion + Doubt* is a more up-beat affair, with questions of faith and being tossed into the electric mix. Moving from contemplative singer/songwriter treks ("Once") to blurry guitar rave-ups ("Believer"), *Since* is the picking-up-and-getting-on antidote to *Devotion + Doubt's* downer trip. Buckner still seems troubled by life's little hang-ups, but instead of falling into an acoustic-drenched funk, he rages against his blues with his guitar. That doesn't mean *Since* isn't without its distressing moments; there are plenty of hushed and fragile songs here that recall the breaking tone of his previous two albums. Yet, for all of the creeping positivity going on within the grooves, Buckner sounds more weary than ever, his already delicate voice cracking under the pressure as he trudges his way through his own brand of electric folk music. *—Michael Gallucci*

Richard Buckner / 2000 / Overcoat ✦✦✦

Richard Buckner first pressed up this low-frills, self-titled item for sale at his concerts following the 2000 release of *The Hill*; the self-titled disc consists of Buckner performing 11 songs armed only with his acoustic guitar in a San Francisco studio in 1996. All these songs were later re-recorded on the albums *Devotion + Doubt* and *Since*, and while listening one gets the feeling that these were really just demos cleaned up for release. That said, that's not to say these performances don't offer some surprises for fans; this version of "Boys, the Night Will Bury You" has a very different arrangement and melodic sense than the one which would appear on *Since*, while the more straightforward take of "Pull" gives the song a very different spin than it had on *Devotion + Doubt*. And anyone who has ever seen one of Buckner's solo acoustic shows knows he's a compelling and charismatic performer, and this disc manages to capture a bit of that presence on a piece of aluminum and plastic. However, none of the performances on *Richard Buckner* can honestly be said to be better than the studio recordings which followed. [In 2003, Buckner reissued this disc in a widely available edition, which seems fitting—while this is music worth hearing, it's too slight to merit the three-figure prices it was fetching among collectors.] *—Mark Deming*

The Hill / Oct. 3, 2000 / Overcoat ✦✦✦

Edgar Lee Masters' *Spoon River Anthology*, a series of poems originally published in serial form in 1914-1915, provided the subject matter for nomadic troubadour Richard Buckner's 2000 release *The Hill*. In the poems, the dead in an Illinois graveyard relay details from their lives in matter-of-factly haunting tones. When originally published, Masters' believable characters tore away at the strict moral façade of small-town life through their tales of adultery, casual murder, and morphine addiction. Who better than Buckner to interpret these lost souls' voices in his growling, plaintive murmur, accompanied most often by sparse acoustic guitar and stark accompaniment. Through this earthy channeler, the names from ragged gravestones almost float in front of the listener while hollowed eyes reveal the details of their own deaths. Unfortunately, while the subject matter and the musician are an ideal match, the album as a whole falls short of Buckner's famous heartfelt intimacy and inventive songwriting. Fans who have come to appreciate his snapshot imagery and dark wordplay may be disappointed at this interpretation of someone else's work, as appropriate as it may be. The 18 individual poems are recorded as one continuous 34-minute track, making it difficult to tell when one woman's childbirth death travels into another man's drunken despair, and the warm acoustic guitar, mandolin, and violin are on occasion jarringly interrupted by misplaced electronic sweeps and buzzes. Still, the haunting charm of "Oscar Hummel" and "Emily Sparks" show the familiar passion and honesty the singer is known for. Buckner continues to distance himself from the limiting country-folk label with increasingly ambitious projects, all of which are interesting but some of which fail to fully utilize his talents. *—Zac Johnson*

Impasse / Oct. 8, 2002 / Overcoat ✦✦✦

Grizzled folkie Richard Buckner evokes more dark snapshots of life and the intricacies of relationships on his fifth release, *Impasse*. Similar in feel and texture to his previous releases, *Impasse* winds around the same moody corners, experimenting with the intimacy of the best singer/songwriters and the quirky fuzz and crunch of indie rock. The spirits of frequent collaborators Joey Burns and John Convertino linger large over this project, and after an initial listen it is surprising to find out that Buckner played all of the instruments this time around (with the exception of the drums, performed expertly by his wife, artist Penny Jo Buckner). Mellotron hums and vibraphone chimes back the singer's familiar growl and warm, nylon-stringed guitar, with textures floating past like faded slides bought from a garage sale. Landing somewhere between *Since*'s driving experimentation and the melancholy drones of *Devotion + Doubt*, the album fits squarely into Buckner's catalog, but may not push too far in either direction. While *Since* emphasized Buckner's grit with rocked-out guitar passages and wild sonic abandon and *Devotion + Doubt* pushed him nearly over the edge in its soul-crushing depression and beautifully haunting themes of loss and heartbreak, *Impasse* finds the author seemingly more comfortable with the cards in his hand. The tension between musicians on *Since* and the tensions between Buckner and himself on *Devotion + Doubt* are subtly missing on *Impasse*, but this wiser and gentler Richard Buckner seems to be embracing a more even keel. With no soul-baring a cappella tracks and no glitchy rave-ups, the album seems to be painted with the same brush from start to finish, which certainly makes for a more even listen, but there is something about the contrast in his previous works that is missing here. Listening to just the first few seconds of each track, there is a discomforting similarity in the way each song starts, almost as if Buckner has worked himself into a familiar pattern and is happy working within it time and time again. Still, every song on the album is fantastic—starkly beautiful and unusually comforting. While this collection of songs is not Buckner's best, it still is head and shoulders above 99 percent of the angst-fueled singer/songwriters out there. *—Zac Johnson*

Buffalo Springfield

f. 1966, Los Angeles, CA, **db.** 1968

Group / Rock & Roll, Country-Rock, Folk-Rock

Apart from the Byrds, no other American band had as great an impact on folk-rock and country-rock—really, the entire Californian rock sound—than Buffalo Springfield. The group's formation is the stuff of legend: driving on Sunset Boulevard in Los Angeles, Stephen Stills and Richie Furay spotted a hearse that Stills was sure belonged to Neil Young, a Canadian he had crossed paths with earlier. Indeed it was, and with the addition of fellow hearse passenger and Canadian Bruce Palmer on bass and ex-Dillard Dewey Martin on drums, the cluster of ex-folkys determined, as the Byrds had just done, to become a rock & roll band.

Buffalo Springfield wasn't together long—they were an active outfit for just over two years, between 1967 and 1968 —but every one of their three albums was noteworthy. Their debut, including their sole big hit (Stills' "For What It's Worth"), established them as the best folk-rock band in the land barring the Byrds, though Springfield was a bit more folk and country oriented. *Again*, their second album found the group expanding their folk-rock base into tough hard rock and psychedelic orchestration, resulting in their best record. The group was blessed with three idiosyncratic, talented songwriters in Stills, Young, and Furay (the last of whom didn't begin writing until the second LP) yet they also had strong and often conflicting egos, particularly Stills and Young. The group, who held almost infinite promise, rearranged their lineup several times, Young leaving the group for periods and Palmer fighting deportation, until disbanding in 1968. Their final album clearly shows the group fragmenting into solo directions.

Eventually, the interpersonal tensions and creative battles led to a perhaps inevitable split, starting with Young's departure for a solo career. He would later reunite with Stephen Stills in Crosby, Stills, & Nash, joining the trio once a decade for various projects. In addition to CSN, Stills released solo albums and worked with another band, Manassas. Initially, Jim Messina and Richie Furay stayed together, forming the country-rock group

Poco, but Messina left after three albums to team up in a duo with Kenny Loggins. Furay himself left Poco and teamed with Chris Hillman and JD Souther in the Souther Hillman Furay Band before pursuing a solo career. Rumors of a Buffalo Springfield reunion circulated for years—Young even hinted at it with the song "Buffalo Springfield Again"—but it never materialized. *—Richie Unterberger & Stephen Thomas Erlewine*

Buffalo Springfield / 1967 / Atco ♦♦♦♦

The band themselves were displeased with this record, feeling that the production did not capture their on-stage energy and excitement. Yet to most ears, this debut sounds pretty great, featuring some of their most melodic and accomplished songwriting and harmonies, delivered with a hard-rocking punch. "For What It's Worth" was the hit single, but there are several other equally stunning treasures. Stills' "Go and Say Goodbye" was a pioneering country-rock fusion; his "Sit Down I Think I Love You" was the band at their poppiest and most early Beatles-esque; and his "Everybody's Wrong" and "Pay the Price" were tough rockers. Although Neil Young has only two lead vocals on the record (Richie Furay sang three other Young compositions), he's already a songwriter of great talent and enigmatic lyricism, particularly on "Nowadays Clancy Can't Even Sing," "Out of My Mind," and "Flying on the Ground is Wrong." The entire album bursts with thrilling guitar and vocal interplay, with a bright exuberance that would tone down considerably by their second record. [A 1997 CD reissue presents both mono and stereo mixes of the album, and includes "Baby Don't Scold Me" (which was on the first pressing of the record, but soon replaced by "For What It's Worth").] *—Richie Unterberger*

☆ **Buffalo Springfield Again** / 1967 / Atco ♦♦♦♦♦

Due in part to personnel problems which saw Bruce Palmer and Neil Young in and out of the group, Buffalo Springfield's second album did not have as unified an approach as their debut. Yet it doesn't suffer for that in the least—indeed, the group continued to make major strides in both their songwriting and arranging, and this record stands as their greatest triumph. Stills' "Bluebird" and "Rock & Roll Woman" were masterful folk-rockers that should have been big hits (although they did manage to become small ones); his lesser-known contributions "Hung Upside Down" and the jazz-flavored "Everdays" were also first-rate. Young contributed the Rolling Stones-derived "Mr. Soul," as well as the brilliant "Expecting to Fly" and "Broken Arrow," both of which employed lush psychedelic textures and brooding, surrealistic lyrics that stretched rock conventions to their breaking point. Furay (who had not written any of the songs on the debut) takes tentative songwriting steps with three compositions, although only "A Child's Claim to Fame," with its memorable dobro hooks by James Burton, meets the standards of the material by Stills and Young; the cut also anticipates the country-rock direction of Furay's post-Springfield band, Poco. Although a slightly uneven record that did not feature the entire band on several cuts, the high points were so high and plentiful that its classic status cannot be denied. *—Richie Unterberger*

Last Time Around / 1968 / Atco ♦♦♦

The internal dissension that was already eating away at the group's dynamic on their second album came home to roost on their third and final effort. This was in some sense a Buffalo Springfield album in name but not in spirit, as the songwriters sometimes did not even play on cuts written by other members of the band. Young's relatively slight contribution was a particularly tough blow. He wrote only two of the songs (though he did help Furay write "It's So Hard to Wait"), both of which were outstanding: the plaintive "I Am a Child" and the bittersweet "On the Way Home" (sung by Furay, not Young, on the record). The rest of the ride was bumpier: Stills' material in particular was not as strong as it had been on the first two LPs, though the lovely Latin-flavored "Pretty Girl Why," with its gorgeous guitar work, is one of the group's best songs. Furay was developing into a quality songwriter with the orchestrated "The Hour of Not Quite Rain" and his best Springfield contribution, the beautiful ballad "Kind Woman," which became one of the first country-rock standards. But it was a case of not enough, too late, not only for Furay, but for the group as a whole. *—Richie Unterberger*

★ **The Best of Buffalo Springfield . . . Retrospective** / 1969 / Atco ♦♦♦♦♦

Best of Buffalo Springfield . . . Retrospective may not be definitive, but it's a good, basic overview of the group's career, containing most of the group's biggest hits and signature songs. Yes, several worthy album cuts are missing, but as a sampler, this works quite well, offering a nice introduction to the group. *—Stephen Thomas Erlewine*

Buffalo Springfield / 1973 / Atco ♦♦♦♦♦

Not to be confused with their self-titled debut album, this double LP, which can still be found without too much hassle, is clearly the best Springfield compilation, at least until the overdue day when a box set appears that includes everything recorded by this superb band. It does miss some good songs, especially from the first album, but zeroes in on their very best work, and includes a nine-minute version of "Bluebird" available nowhere else, as well as excellent liner notes. *—Richie Unterberger*

Box Set / Jul. 17, 2001 / Rhino ♦♦♦♦♦

The plainly named *Box Set*—that's the actual title—contains four CDs by a band that made only three albums in their brief lifetime. It goes without saying that this has a lot of great music, and is an essential purchase for fans of this phenomenal 1960s folk-rock-psychedelic band, containing no less than 36 previously unreleased demos, outtakes, and previously unissued mixes. It's the unreleased stuff that holds the most interest, especially since even on their outtakes, Buffalo Springfield were often superb. Songs like "Neighbor Don't You Worry," "Down Down Down" (which contains seeds of both "Broken Arrow" and the Neil Young solo standout "Country Girl"), "We'll See," and "My Kind of Love" are actually up to the standard of many of the songs that made it onto the official albums. Although acoustic demos of various Young, Stills, & Furay songs are not as strong, they are always at the least pleasant, and often show intriguing, unsuspected sentimental pop and folk leanings. Alternate versions of great songs, such as "Hung Upside Down" and a piano-only "Four Days Gone," are substantially different from the fully arranged familiar versions, yet worthwhile performances in their own right. At the same time, this box—which, other than the last disc, sequences the material in the chronological order it was recorded—is not all it could have been. First of all, for some reason, this does *not* have everything the band ever released. Not only are a few songs from *Last Time Around* missing (including one of Richie Furay's best moments, "In the Hour of Not Quite Rain"), but the nine-minute version of "Bluebird" (available on the two-LP *Buffalo Springfield* compilation) and the Neil Young-sung take of "Down to the Wire" (which came out on his *Decade* collection) are also absent. First-rate songs from *Last Time Around*, including "On the Way Home," "Pretty Girl Why," and "Four Days Gone," are represented by different demos and remixes, though it would have been easily possible to include the official final versions too. Worst of all, disc four is comprised solely of all the material from the group's brilliant first two albums—which would not be cause for criticism, except that identical versions of every one of them (except for "Mr. Soul" and "Baby Don't Scold Me") also appear at some point in the course of the preceding three discs. This bizarre repetition is doubly galling both because that space could have been used for remaining *Last Time Around* absentees, and because other quality unreleased material, both studio and live, is known to exist, and is far more hungrily desired by fans eager to purchase a box set in the first place. Fortunately you can still (almost) complete the Springfield discography by buying *Last Time Around* itself. The sound is very good, and on the rarities, notably superior to bootlegs (such as the famous *Stampede*) on which some of the songs have previously surfaced. The 82-page booklet, primarily comprised of vintage clippings, is nice too, even if specific details and anecdotes about the unreleased songs in particular would have been good. As good as it is, though, this could have been one of the greatest rock box sets of all time, if only a saner approach to presenting the band's complete official albums, and more rarities, in one place had been employed. *—Richie Unterberger*

Jimmy Buffett

b. Dec. 25, 1946, Pascagoula, MS

Guitar, Vocals / Country-Rock, Singer/Songwriter, Pop/Rock

Singer/songwriter Jimmy Buffett has translated his easygoing Gulf Coast persona into more than just a successful recording career—he has expanded into clothing, nightclubs, and literature. But the basis of the business empire that keeps him on the *Fortune* magazine list of highest-earning entertainers is his music. Buffett moved to Nashville to try to make it in country music in the late '60s. Signed to Barnaby, he released one album, *Down to Earth* (1970), from which the socially conscious single "The Christian?" suggested he might be more at home protesting in Greenwich Village. (Barnaby "lost" his second album, *High Cumberland Jubilee*, though they would find it and release it after he became successful.) Instead, he moved to Key West, FL, where he gradually evolved into the beach bum character and tropical folk-rock style that would endear him to millions.

Signing to ABC-Dunhill Records (later absorbed by MCA), Buffett achieved notoriety but not much else with his second (released) album, *White Sport Coat and a Pink Crustacean* (1973), which featured a song called "Why Don't We Get Drunk" ("... and screw?" goes the chorus). Buffett revealed a more thoughtful side on *Living and Dying in 3/4 Time* (1974), with its song of marital separation "Come Monday," his first singles-chart entry. But it took the Top Ten song "Margaritaville" and the album in which it was featured, *Changes in Latitudes, Changes in Attitudes* (1977), to capture Buffett's tropical world view and, for a while, turn him into a pop star.

By the start of the '80s, Buffett's yearly albums had stopped going gold, and he briefly tried the country market again. But by the middle of the decade, it was his yearly summer tours that were filling his bank account, as a steadily growing core of Sun Belt fans he dubbed "Parrotheads" made his concerts into Mardi Gras-like affairs. Buffett launched his Margaritaville line of clothes and opened the first of his Margaritaville clubs in Key West. He also turned to fiction writing, landing on the book bestseller lists.

His recording career, meanwhile, languished, though a hits compilation sold millions; a 1990 live album, *Feeding Frenzy*, went gold; and a 1992 box set retrospective, *Boats, Beaches, Bars, & Ballads*, became one of the best-selling box sets ever. Buffett finally got around to making a new album in 1994, when *Fruitcakes* became one of his fastest-selling records. It was followed in 1995 by *Barometer Soup* and *Banana Wind* in 1996. The following year, Buffett began working on a musical adaptation of Herman Wouk's novel *Don't Stop the Carnival* with the author himself. After Broadway producers expressed little interest, the production ran for six weeks in Miami during 1997. In spring of 1998, Buffett released a collection of songs from the production as he began mulling over the idea of taking the play on the road. In 1999 he released *Beach House on the Moon* as well as *Live: Tuesday/Thursday/Saturday*. *—William Ruhlmann*

Down to Earth / 1970 / Varese ♦♦

Yes, that smiling youth with a non-receding hairline pictured on the back cover is actually Jimmy Buffett, back in 1970 when this was a new album on a label that's long since stopped making phonograph records for the masses. In 1998, this finally came out on compact disc in its original form, with only "Richard Frost" as a bonus track to flesh it out. Instead, the focus stays right on Buffett's strong early writing and his almost organic empathy with his backing band. The results on tracks like "Truckstop Salvation," "Ellis Dee (He Ain't Free)," "The Christian?" and "Captain America" number among some of the best of his early recordings. *—Cub Koda*

A White Sport Coat and a Pink Crustacean / Jun. 1973 / MCA ♦♦♦

Buffett was beginning to put in place his folk/rock/country sound and his laid-back, humorous, hedonistic persona with this album, which features later concert favorites like "Why Don't We Get Drunk (and Screw)" and "Grapefruit—Juicy Fruit." *—William Ruhlmann*

Living and Dying in 3/4 Time / Feb. 1974 / MCA ✦✦✦
Jimmy Buffett was already on the second edition of his Coral Reefer Band by the time his third album rolled around. He had also firmly established his Gulf Coast beach-bum/poet persona, but he hadn't written a classic song until "Come Monday," which put him, and the album, on the map. *—William Ruhlmann*

A-1-A / Dec. 1974 / MCA ✦✦✦
Before Jimmy Buffett became a novelist, entrepreneur, and founder of a business empire, he was a prolific singer/songwriter and a great storyteller. In the song "Migration," which chronicles his failed first marriage and his subsequent move to Florida, he sings "I got a Caribbean soul I can barely control and some Texas hidden here in my heart." This perfectly describes the music of Jimmy Buffett, who incorporates steel drums, harmonica, and slide guitar to tell stories about life by the sea. While many of the songs for which he is famous involve a life of leisure told with a keen sense of humor, Buffett is more thoughtful than your average beachcomber. In fact, the best moments on this album are the slower tunes such as "A Pirate Looks at Forty" where a reflective Buffett looks back at his lifelong love of the ocean and his place in the universe. *A-1-A* may be Buffett's most autobiographical album, as he sings about making music on his own terms in the opening uptempo "Makin' Music for Money" and tells stories of his idyllic childhood in "Life Is Just a Tire Swing." As with most of Buffett's work, his stories convey the importance of enjoying life, living free, and doing as you please. This is one of Jimmy Buffett's classic '70s albums that established his persona, and it is a perfect introduction to his music. *—Vik Iyengar*

Rancho Deluxe / 1975 / Rykodisc ✦✦✦
This is the soundtrack to a movie written by Buffett's brother-in-law, novelist Thomas McGuane. Buffett appeared in the movie and sang "Livingston Saturday Night" with slightly more risqué lyrics than he would later in his career. *—William Ruhlmann*

High Cumberland Jubilee (1972) / 1976 / Varese ✦✦
Jimmy Buffett's second album for the now-defunct Barnaby label came out in 1976, but didn't see a compact disc reissue until 22 years later. It was worth the wait, as it features some of Buffett's best early recordings, including "Livingston's Gone to Texas," "God Don't Own a Car," "Rockefeller Square" and "High Cumberland Jubilee/Comin' Down Slow." Strong songwriting in tandem with Buzz Cason makes this an essential in building up the perfect Buffett collection. *—Cub Koda*

Havana Daydreamin' / Jan. 1976 / MCA ✦✦✦✦✦
Buffett's best overall collection of songs yet bears the influence of Steve Goodman, who wrote "This Hotel Room" and cowrote "Woman Goin' Crazy on Caroline Street." But a personal favorite is Buffett's own "My Head Hurts, My Feet Stink, and I Don't Love Jesus." *—William Ruhlmann*

Changes in Latitudes, Changes in Attitudes / Jan. 1977 / MCA ✦✦✦✦✦
Buffett's biggest-selling regular release contains his biggest hit single, "Margaritaville." It's also a peak in terms of songwriting, both for the artist himself and in his covers of the work of Steve Goodman and Jesse Winchester, among others. Funny, wistful, and celebratory, the album is the definitive statement of Buffett's worldview. *—William Ruhlmann*

Son of a Son of a Sailor / Mar. 1978 / MCA ✦✦✦✦✦
If this album was a slight step down from its predecessor, it was almost equally successful commercially, and it contained its share of terrific material, notably the uptempo hit "Cheeseburger in Paradise" and one of Buffett's older songs, "Livingston Saturday Night." *—William Ruhlmann*

You Had to Be There / Oct. 1978 / MCA ✦✦
Buffett has made most of his considerable fortune out of the following he's developed through his concerts, and this double-record live set recorded before an enthusiastic crowd at the Fox in Atlanta serves notice of what's to come. It also serves as a consistent best-of for the artist, most of whose albums are uneven. *—William Ruhlmann*

Volcano / Aug. 1979 / MCA ✦✦
After breaking into the mainstream with his hit "Margaritaville" two years earlier, Jimmy Buffett stuck to his formula of mixing fun, uptempo songs with slower, reflective ones. Although the album contains concert favorites including the playful "Fins" and the Caribbean-flavored title track, it seems as if Buffett doesn't have as many deep insights to share on this release. The vocal help from James Taylor on "Treat Her Like a Lady" adds to the singalong chorus, but overall the ballads are uninteresting. As a result, this album marks a low point for Jimmy Buffett in a decade in which he delivered one solid album after another. However, *Volcano* is notable for its inclusion of a wonderful children's song ("Chanson Por les Petits Enfantes"), complete with nursery rhyme lyrics. This album is for Parrotheads only, as most of the popular tracks are available on compilations like *Songs You Know By Heart*. *—Vik Iyengar*

Coconut Telegraph / Feb. 1981 / MCA ✦✦
Here are more Caribbean rhythms and weak jokes—"The Weather Is Here, Wish You Were Beautiful"—plus, in Mac McAnally's "It's My Job," a whiff of the elitism always implied in Buffett's stance. *—William Ruhlmann*

Somewhere over China / Jan. 1982 / MCA ✦✦
Perhaps inevitably, Buffett begins to descend from self-satisfaction to self-pity on tracks like "Where's the Party" and "I Heard I Was in Town." Here and on such tracks as "If I Could Just Get It on Paper," it's apparent that the fast life is losing its charm for the singer. *—William Ruhlmann*

One Particular Harbour / Sep. 1983 / MCA ✦✦✦
For many listeners, Jimmy Buffett's late-'70s work left something to be desired. The head parrot had gone domestic and albums like *Somewhere Over China* and *Coconut Telegraph* seemed more like afterthoughts than inspired artifacts. Against this backdrop, *One Particular Harbour* (1983) was something like a comeback, with Buffett's best batch of songs since *Son of a Son of a Sailor* in 1978. Mellow ballads with a soft rock production like "Stars on the Water," "California Promises," and "Twelve Volt Man" presented the former party animal as a thoughtful dreamer. There are also pleasant pieces like "Distantly in Love" and "Why You Wanna Hurt My Heart?," which find Buffett in a confessional singer/songwriter mode. Of course, it wouldn't be a typical Jimmy Buffett album without a couple of humorous songs. While "I Used to Have Money One Time" is a bit obnoxious, "Honey Do" and "We Are the People Our Parents Warned Us About" tell fun tales about being single and growing older. The album also has a bouncy version of "Brown Eyed Girl." *One Particular Harbour* may not qualify as classic Buffett, but it did prove that he still had a thing or two to say after the party was over. Like *Changes in Latitudes, Changes in Attitudes*, it's also the type of album that's perfect for a weekend getaway at the beach. *—Ronnie D. Lankford Jr.*

Riddles in the Sand / Sep. 1984 / MCA ✦✦
Buffett, who never cared for country music, hires Nashville insider Jimmy Bowen as his producer, goes to Fan Fair, puts on a cowboy hat on his album cover, and scores country hits with cheating songs like "Who's the Blonde Stranger?" Actually, things haven't changed that much, it's just a marketing move. *—William Ruhlmann*

Last Mango in Paris / Jun. 1985 / MCA ✦✦✦
Buffett's rapid recording schedule tended to outrun his muse in the late '70s and early '80s, resulting in some uneven albums with occasional good songs. This time he came up with a far more consistent collection, including three entries on the country charts: "Gypsies in the Palace," "If the Phone Doesn't Ring, It's Me," and "Please Bypass This Heart." *—William Ruhlmann*

● **Songs You Know By Heart** / Oct. 1985 / MCA ✦✦✦✦✦
Combining aloof humor with a laid-back, devil-may-care island attitude, Jimmy Buffet sang songs about alcohol consumption, lazing around in the sun, and the freedom of not having to work for a living. *Songs You Know By Heart* is a solid offering of Buffet's greatest hits, pulling together his truly strongest material and avoiding the unnecessary filler that appears on his albums. His claim to fame, "Margaritaville," is the jewel in the crown here, and still harbors that tropical feel thanks to its Caribbean-styled rhythm and relaxed flow. "Come Monday" picks up where "Margaritaville" leaves off, only this ballad plays out with subdued sincerity and has Buffet sounding strangely serious, and romantic. Most of the songs from Buffet are centered around his frolicking lifestyle, like the comical "Cheeseburger in Paradise" or the naughtiness of "Why Don't We Get Drunk," an ode to his party-filled outlook on life. Buffet's voice shines on the clever "Changes in Latitudes, Changes in Attitudes," which again spotlights his love of living without concern, especially in someplace warm. The catchy and whimsical "Fins" is lifted by a contagious pace with a smart chorus and serves as one of the highlights of this collection. As a compilation, this bunch of Jimmy Buffet's most famous tunes contains just the right amount of tracks. Any less would be inconsistent and any more would be deemed as overkill. *—Mike DeGagne*

Floridays / Jun. 1986 / MCA ✦✦
If *Last Mango in Paris* suggested a new interest in recording and a new care in songwriting, *Floridays* marked a scuttling of such efforts. The leadoff track, "I Love the Now," was co-written by Buffett and Carrie Fisher, which just goes to show that good novelists don't necessarily write good songs together. *—William Ruhlmann*

Hot Water / Jun. 1988 / MCA ✦✦
The best song is Jesse Winchester's oldie "L'Air De La Louisiane." "Smart Woman (In a Real Short Skirt)" did not restore Buffett to the favor of feminists. And you don't get on the radio by complaining that they don't play your "Homemade Music" because there's something wrong with them. *—William Ruhlmann*

Off to See the Lizard / Jun. 1989 / MCA ✦✦
By this point, record making was starting to become just a small part of Jimmy Buffett, Inc., and this is a piece of musical product, efficiently produced and highly consumable, but not very nourishing. Not surprisingly, Buffett didn't bother to make another studio album for five years. *—William Ruhlmann*

Feeding Frenzy / Oct. 1990 / MCA ✦✦
Buffett's real business is summer touring, and this second live outing was overdue. It also makes a good sampler of his work since his last one, but unfortunately even carefully selected, the later work is inferior to the early work. *—William Ruhlmann*

Boats, Beaches, Bars & Ballads / May 1992 / MCA ✦✦✦✦✦
Most listeners will be satisfied with the excellent Jimmy Buffett summary *Songs You Know By Heart*, but anyone that wants to dig deeper should bypass the albums (there are several that are first-rate, yet many are spotty) and pick up the four-disc, 72-track box set, *Boats, Beaches, Bars & Ballads*. Assembled thematically, with each disc devoted to one of the words in the title, this rounds up not just every Buffett hit, but pretty much every one of his noteworthy album tracks, plus a couple of rarities and unreleased cuts. For some, this much Buffett may cause sunstroke, yet this proves that he had some fine moments that weren't singles, and even those that aren't Parrotheads will be impressed by the consistency of his music—if you like Jimmy, he usually delivers what you like. *—Stephen Thomas Erlewine*

Before the Beach / May 25, 1993 / MCA ✦✦
This is yet another reissue of Buffett's first two Barnaby albums, this time released on his own record label, on one CD, and minus the controversial "The Christian?" *—William Ruhlmann*

Fruitcakes / May 24, 1994 / MCA ✦✦
On his first new studio album in five years, Buffett starts out talking about an investment banker, an appropriate concern for this sun-bleached entrepreneur. Soon enough, the

sprung calypso rhythms kick in, and you can imagine the Parrotheads swaying and chuckling along, especially when Buffett indulges in the kind of comic raps common to his stage shows. He also covers the Grateful Dead's "Uncle John's Band," one more appropriation in his careful observation of that band's marketing plan. There's also a cover of the Kinks' "Sunny Afternoon," a wealthy man's lament, which is uncomfortably on target. But even with half a decade to come up with original material, Buffett hasn't gotten much to add to his usual sun-and-sand philosophy, and for all his millions he remains a pleasant, but distinctly minor, singer/songwriter. *—William Ruhlmann*

Barometer Soup / Aug. 1, 1995 / Margaritaville ✦✦
Having gotten back the record-making habit with *Fruitcakes*, Jimmy Buffett repaired to the Monroe County Library in Key West during the winter of 1994-1995 with cohorts Russ Kunkel, Jay Oliver, Roger Guth, and Peter Mayer, where they read fiction and came up with most of the songs on this album. Hence, we have "Remittance Man," drawn from Mark Twain's *Following the Equator*, and "Diamond As Big As the Ritz," loosely adapted from F. Scott Fitzgerald's short story. Typically, there are also the comedy numbers "Bank of Bad Habits" and "Don't Chu-Know" and an appropriation consistent with Buffett's philosophy, James Taylor's "Mexico." Much of the music is low-key, though there are a couple of uptempo tunes to add to the concert repertoire. As Jimmy Buffett albums go, this is another one. *—William Ruhlmann*

Banana Wind / Jun. 1996 / Margaritaville ✦✦✦
Banana Wind is typical latter-day Jimmy Buffett. Over a laid-back, Caribbean-inflected folk-rock, Buffett waxes eloquent over boats, booze, sun, and women. Although the sound of the album certainly is pleasant, there's not a single distinctive song on the record, which means it's good for Parrotheads, but casual fans should let this *Banana Wind* sail on by. *—Stephen Thomas Erlewine*

Christmas Island / Oct. 8, 1996 / Margaritaville ✦✦
Largely comprised of original material, Jimmy Buffet's *Christmas Island* is a holiday album that only Parrotheads will need bother with. Though Buffet is relaxed and entertaining, few of his new Christmas songs are remarkable and his rearrangements of classic carols are rather forced. Still, *Christmas Island* remains a pleasant diversion for his dedicated fans, even if it isn't a particularly memorable one. *—Thom Owens*

Don't Stop the Carnival / Apr. 28, 1998 / Polygram ✦✦✦
Herman Wouk's novel *Don't Stop the Carnival*—a tale of a frustrated middle-aged man who dreams of escaping the city for tropical paradise—is the ideal literary vehicle for Jimmy Buffett, a man who made a living selling suburbanites the tropical dream. Buffett convinced Wouk to collaborate with him on a musical adaptation of the novel, which had a brief run in Miami in 1997. To stir up interest in the project, Buffett recorded 20 songs from the show with his Coral Reefer Band. Truth be told, there's little difference between these songs and any other Jimmy Buffett album, but it's actually heartening to hear him craft songs to fit a story. There are a few other vocalists, including narration from Wouk, sprinkled throughout the album, but *Don't Stop the Carnival* remains a Buffett album, filled with the breezy melodies and laid-back charm that distinguishes all of his work. If anything, the record holds together better than many of his latter-day efforts because he has something new to say, and he has written his strongest set of songs in many a moon. *—Stephen Thomas Erlewine*

Beach House on the Moon / May 18, 1999 / Polygram ✦✦✦
After 30 albums, it would seem as if Jimmy Buffett has said everything he's needed to say, and in a way, that's true. Every once in a while, he'll depart from his sun-kissed, mellow country-rock, such as he did with his music for the audio reading of Hunter S. Thompson's *Fear and Loathing in Las Vegas* or his musical adaptation of Herman Wouk's *Don't Stop the Carnival*, but for his regular albums, he hasn't varied his formula in two decades. That's the case with *Beach House on the Moon*, his 31st effort. Some may make a big deal about the presence of multimedia sections on the disc, but that's because it's the only thing that separates *Beach House* from *Banana Wind*, Buffett's last proper studio album. It's the same style of music, recorded in the same way as that 1996 effort, and to all but the dedicated fan, it could be the same record. There are slight difference, however, particularly in the quality of songs. Although some of *Beach House* seems a little too cutesy for comfort ("You Call It Joggin'," "I Will Play for Gumbo," etc.), it's by and large a stronger effort than *Banana Wind*, with more distinctive songs. It's still an album for Parrotheads, who will groove with the laid-back vibe and laugh at the silly jokes, and it's unlikely that it will convert any new fans. But it's a solid Buffett record, delivering everything a fan could want—it may not offer anything new, but it doesn't disappoint. *—Stephen Thomas Erlewine*

Far Side of the World / Mar. 19, 2002 / Mailboat ✦✦✦
It's easy to compare any singer to their best work, though not always very helpful. In fact, comparing *Far Side of the World* to *A-1-A* or *A White Sport Coat and a Pink Crustacean* is a little like comparing steak to seafood. They're simply two different entrées, and while someone may like steak and dislike seafood, a number of discerning individuals like both. Critics and certain fans may prefer Jimmy Buffett's 1970s output, but the head parrot has long ago sailed on to smoother waters. It's probably more helpful to compare *Far Side of the World* to albums like *Banana Wind* and *Fruitcakes*, where Buffett settled into his role as elder statesman of sun, surf, and sand fantasies. First of all, the arrangements and production on *Far Side of the World* vary quite a bit from these earlier 1990s efforts. The rich vocal harmony in "Blue Guitar" evokes Paul Simon's *Graceland*, while the dirty slide guitar of "Last Man Standing" casts a glance back at Little Feat. Still, the basic approach remains the same. Funny songs like "What if the Hokey-Pokey Is All It Really Is About?" remind one of "Vampires, Mummies and the Holy Ghost" (*Fruitcakes*), while self-referential pieces like "Altered Boy" recall "Only Time Will Tell" and "Cultural Infidel" (*Banana Wind*). Buffett talks his way through much of the eight-minute "Autour du Rocher," just as he talks his way through much of "Overkill" (*Banana Wind*) and "Fruitcakes" (*Fruitcakes*). There are tender moments and outrageous ones, all signifying that only one person could've made this album. *Far Side of the World* holds up well to *Fruitcakes* and *Banana Wind*, and more important still, Parrotheads will love it. *—Ronnie D. Lankford Jr.*

Meet Me in Margaritaville: The Ultimate Collection / Apr. 15, 2003 / MCA ✦✦✦✦
Meet Me in Margaritaville: The Ultimate Collection really *should* deliver on the promise of the title, considering that it has 38 songs over the course of two discs. Something that exhaustive would seem like the perfect compromise for the Parrothead who wants more than *Songs You Know By Heart* but doesn't want as much as the four-disc box set *Boats, Beaches, Bars & Ballads*, but the compilation is undone by a scattershot sequencing and the inclusion of *11* new recordings, nine of which are remakes (four of which are live). This is a problem on a collection that purports to be a career-spanning overview, particularly because such key Jimmy Buffett songs as "Son of a Son of a Sailor" and "A Pirate Looks at Forty" are here in new versions. These new recordings aren't *bad* by any means—they have a nice, breezy feel to them, and some of the cult favorites benefit from the reinterpretations (Buffett mentions in his track-by-track liner notes—which appear only for the new numbers, by the way—that "Saxophones" needed to be reworked, and he was right). But their quality isn't the issue; their presence is. They're perfectly fine new recordings, but they cut into *Meet Me in Margaritaville*'s effectiveness as a career-spanning compilation, since these are of interest primarily to those dedicated longtime fans who like to hear new versions of old favorites, whereas the target audience for this compilation is those listeners who want one Jimmy Buffett album with all of their favorites in the versions they know by heart. This doesn't deliver on that level because over a *quarter* of the collection consists of new versions. Considering that, it's not bad, since the actual key *songs* are here, and it's all pretty enjoyable, but the fact remains, if you just want one Jimmy Buffett album in your collection, *Songs You Know By Heart* has all the tunes you need. *—Stephen Thomas Erlewine*

Sonny Burgess

b. May 28, 1931, Newport, AR
Guitar, Vocals / Rockabilly
Sonny Burgess is one of the wildest rockers to record for the legendary Sun label in Memphis. He and his band the Pacers came out of Newport, AR, with a hard-rocking style that, unlike that of most rockabillies, owed little to nothing in the way of a stylistic debt to country music. With his red-dyed hair, matching stage suit and guitar, and wild stage performances, Burgess & the Pacers made mincemeat of the competition on many of the early-'50s rock & roll package tours. Though his Sun releases never brought him much in the way of commercial success, his recordings nonetheless remain landmarks of the early rockabilly style. Currently touring and recording with other Memphis alumni in the Sun Rhythm Section, the rockin' flame that is Sonny Burgess refuses to be snuffed out. *—Cub Koda*

We Wanna Boogie / 1990 / Rounder ✦✦✦✦✦
If you want a fairly definitive compilation of the Sun material by this minor rockabilly figure, but don't want to go the whole nine yards for the expensive import double CD on Bear Family, this domestic anthology is a recommended alternative. The 13 tracks contain six sides from his '50s singles (including the most noted, "Red Headed Woman" and "My Bucket's Got a Hole in It"), and seven other cuts from the '50s that were unissued at the time. *—Richie Unterberger*

The Classic Recordings 1956–1959 / Jul. 1991 / Bear Family ✦✦✦✦✦
This features Sonny's complete output for Sun spread over two CDs. Wild and crazed, featuring Burgess' spitfire guitar and booming vocals and the relentless drive of the Pacers in support. *—Cub Koda*

Tennessee Border / Feb. 1992 / Hightone ✦✦✦

● **Hittin' that Jug: Best of Sonny Burgess** / Jun. 20, 1995 / AVI ✦✦✦✦✦
Sonny Burgess is one of the most enduring wildmen of the '50s Sun Records rockabilly scene, and a half-century later his classic "We Wanna Boogie" is still about as exciting as a record can be. *Hittin' That Jug!* is a 26-track collection of Sun recordings, including several alternate takes. Burgess offered fun and excitement with his unique, horn-driven rockabilly sound and bluegrass-inflected vocals, but not a lot of variety. Consequently, casual listeners may opt for a well-packed anthology such as this, rather than Bear Family's two-disc set of Burgess' complete Sun recordings. *—Greg Adams*

Sonny Burgess / Jun. 18, 1996 / Rounder ✦✦✦✦
If trying to bring back an old artist from the '50s is an idea that seldom merits results that exceed "you can't go home again" or worse, here is an album that proves it *can* be done and done right. Producer Gary Tallent keeps Sonny Burgess focused with the lead vocal and blistering lead guitar duties squarely on his shoulders, gives him a pile of great songs from the likes of Radney Foster, Fred James, Dave Alvin, Steve Forbert, and Springsteen to interpret, then frames it all with a backing band that's the essence of drive and simplicity. The spotlight stays on Burgess throughout, just letting him do what he does best. While it all sounds simple enough, it seldom—if ever—happens on these kind of affairs, making the achievement of this record all that more astounding. A modern rockabilly classic, this also features wonderful guest appearance turns by Scotty Moore and the Jordanaires on Henry Gross' "Bigger Than Elvis." The tray card on this reads "Sonny Burgess has still got it." Believe it. *—Cub Koda*

● **The Very Best of Sonny Burgess: We Wanna Boogie** / Jan. 1, 1998 / Collectables ✦✦✦✦✦
Not everybody is a crazed rockabilly cat, needing everything that Sonny Burgess recorded for Sun. That's what the previous best collection of Burgess material, the 1991 Bear Family double-disc set *Classic Recordings* offered (like most Bear Family discs): a complete overview of the artist's work for a seminal label. Meanwhile, other good collections like

1995's *Hittin' That Jug* have gone out of print. So there certainly is a market for Collectables' 1998 collection, *The Very Best of Sonny Burgess: We Wanna Boogie*. This collection rounds up 21 tracks from his Sun recordings and, since he didn't really have big hits, the collection sinks or swims based on the song selection. Fortunately, it is first-rate, getting all the real big items—"We Wanna Boogie" and "Red-Headed Woman," most prominently—along with a consistently entertaining selection of Sun sides, meaning that if one wants only one Burgess collection and doesn't need to have the complete Sun sessions, this suits the bill very nicely. —*Stephen Thomas Erlewine*

Frenchie Burke (Leon Bourke)

b. Kaplan, LA
Fiddle, Vocals / Traditional Country
Referred to as "the Cajun Gentleman Fiddler," Frenchie Burke was born Leon Bourke in Kaplan, LA. While still a youngster, he received his first musical lesson from his grandfather. His teeth were cut playing in local bands, and it was during these performances that he began developing his flamboyant showmanship. Shortly after his family moved to Texas, he joined the U.S. Air Force and continued to play, taking first place in one of the U.S.A.F.'s annual talent contests. Following his stint of service, he took up a job as a machinist in Houston and played fiddle on the side, alongside the likes of Ray Price, Johnny Bush, and Jimmy Dickens. He finally began his professional recording career with Bush, and then a series of his own albums followed, beginning with 1974's *Fiddlin' Frenchie Burke & the Outlaws* (20th Century Fox). "Big Mamou," a Cajun waltz, gave him his most commercial success, reaching the top spot on the country chart. By the end of the '80s, he had several albums to his credit. After beating cancer, he continued to record and perform on throughout the early 2000s, including the albums *Fiddlehead* and *Frenchie Burke's Dance Album*. —*Andy Kellman*

Crazy Cajun Recordings / May 11, 1999 / Edsel ✦✦✦✦
● **Cajun Memories** / Jun. 18, 2002 / Fuel 2000 ✦✦✦✦

Ed Burleson

b. Jun. 10, 1969
Vocals, Guitar (Acoustic), Guitar (Electric) / Cowboy, Alternative Country, Americana, Honky Tonk
Ed Burleson is a baby-faced, sixth-generation Texan who works construction by day and crafts traditionally minded honky tonk by night. He has counted among his supporters the late Texas legend Doug Sahm, who served as Burleson's manager and co-produced his *My Perfect World* album. For that effort, Burleson was also joined by such elite Texas players as Bill Kirchen (Commander Cody) and Lloyd Maines, among others.

Burleson, a descendant of General Edward Burleson, a war hero from the Texas independence Battle of San Jacinto, was born on June 10, 1969. Burleson's father was a salesman, so Burleson grew up in various locales around Texas—Garland, Denison, Conroe, El Paso—as well as in Tulsa, OK. Burleson eventually settled in Lewisville, TX, where he was on the high-school rodeo team. It was traveling to rodeos and listening to small-town radio that introduced him to Texas music. Burleson won a rodeo scholarship to Hill College in Hillsboro, TX, and it was there that he first started learning guitar. Upon graduation, he acquired a knee injury that needed surgery. While recovering, his love for playing country music grew. He first started playing at a newcomer's showcase at the Three Teardrops Tavern in Dallas. The owner told Burleson if he could put a band together, he could play every Thursday night. (The drummer for that band was his father, Richard Burleson.) Burleson's first CD was 1997's *Comin' Around*. One night at the Broken Spoke Saloon in Austin, Burleson gave a copy of the album to Doug Sahm, who was so impressed that he became Burleson's manager. Sahm also polished up the CD and released it on his fledgling Tornado Records label. That effort, 1999's *My Perfect World*, hit number four on the Americana charts. —*Erik Hage*

My Perfect World / Sep. 21, 1999 / Tornado ✦✦✦✦
Ed Burleson's earthy country music is melodic and winning enough to please Nashville, but doesn't drip with any of that city's clichés. Burleson's country, here augmented by legends like producer Doug Sahm and pedal steel player Lloyd Maines, is straight-ahead, no-frills honky tonk, and his work shows enough reverence for classic country to ring authentic while avoiding the trap of sheer revivalism. Burleson is a great songwriter and singer, and the opener, "Wide Open Spaces," even shows shades of Texas predecessor Willie Nelson. Several tracks also find Burleson hunkering down into a beer-soaked ballad while avoiding any twangy, dramatic clichés. He can also slip into cruising Bakersfield-tinged honky tonk with nary a wrinkle ("No Closing Time"). This construction worker and former rodeo competitor has made a debut that puts a lot of platinum artists to shame. It's just plain old country music—not mainstream, not insurgent, not trad—that's done right. It's no small wonder that the late Doug Sahm picked Burleson as the flagship artist on his label, Tornado. —*Erik Hage*

T-Bone Burnett (Joseph Henry Burnett)

b. Jan. 14, 1948, St. Louis, MO
Guitar, Vocals, Producer / Singer/Songwriter, Roots Rock, College Rock, Heartland Rock
Despite critical acclaim as a performer, the rootsy singer/songwriter T-Bone Burnett earned his greatest renown as a producer, helming recording sessions for acts ranging from Roy Orbison and Elvis Costello to Counting Crows and Sam Phillips. Born Joseph Henry Burnett on January 14, 1948, in St. Louis, MO, he grew up in Fort Worth, TX, soaking in the area's indigenous blend of blues, R&B, and Tex-Mex sounds. Instead of attending college, he opted to open his own Fort Worth recording studio, while also performing in a series of blues bands; in the early '70s he relocated to Los Angeles, producing sessions for Glen Clark and Delbert McClinton.

After recording his own 1972 debut, *The B-52 Band & the Fabulous Skylarks*, Burnett toured with Delaney & Bonnie before befriending Bob Neuwirth, a singer/songwriter known for his ties to Bob Dylan. Three years later, Dylan invited Burnett to play guitar

on his *Rolling Thunder Revue* tour. After the *Revue* concluded, he and fellow *Rolling Thunder* alumni Dave Mansfield and Steve Soles founded the Alpha Band, releasing their eponymous debut in 1977. *Spark in the Dark* followed later that year, and like its predecessor failed to find commercial favor; when 1978's *Statue Makers of Hollywood* met a similar fate, the Alpha Band split, and Burnett returned to his solo career.

He resurfaced in 1980 with the acclaimed *Truth Decay*, which, like all of his solo work, found its lyrical center in his spiritual concerns. A move to Warner Bros. followed for 1982's *Trap Door* EP, and 1983's full-length *Proof Through the Night* featured guests Pete Townshend, Ry Cooder, and Richard Thompson. Still, commercial success eluded him, and so he continued working as a producer, overseeing highly regarded records like Los Lobos' *How Will the Wolf Survive?*, Marshall Crenshaw's *Downtown*, and the BoDeans' *Love & Hope & Sex & Dreams*.

After recording a self-titled 1986 solo effort, Burnett agreed to produce *The Turning*, an album for the successful Christian pop singer Leslie Phillips. The album won wide acclaim even from secular outposts, but it was to be Phillips' last overtly religious release; instead, she began performing under her nickname, Sam, and with Burnett's aid landed a deal with the Virgin label for 1987's acclaimed *The Indescribable Wow*. Prior to recording her 1991 LP, *Cruel Inventions*, Phillips and Burnett wed, and he remained in the producer's seat for her later efforts, including 1994's *Martinis & Bikinis* and 1996's *Omnipop*. Despite his additional success manning albums like Elvis Costello's masterful 1986 effort *King of America* as well as producing the star-studded 1987 Roy Orbison tribute *Black & White Night*, Burnett continued his solo career; like earlier efforts, 1988's *The Talking Animals* won raves from the press but failed to find an audience outside of his devoted cult following. His output dwindled as his production work increased, and only in 1992 did he release a follow-up, the spartan *Criminal Under My Own Hat*. Instead, Burnett remained one of the most prolific and distinctive producers of his day, crafting successes like Costello's *Spike*, Counting Crows' *August and Everything After*, the Wallflowers' *Bringing Down the Horse*, and Gillian Welch's *Revival*. —*Jason Ankeny*

The B-52 Band & the Fabulous Skylarks / 1972 / UNI ✦✦✦

Truth Decay / 1980 / Demon ✦✦✦✦✦
T-Bone Burnett released *Truth Decay* for John Fahey's Takoma Records, his first solo effort since 1972. Burnett delivers a collection of parables, tales, and personal struggles propelled by his strong beliefs and some captivating roots rock. "Quicksand," with a rhythm reminiscent of "Ring of Fire," opens the proceedings with a word of caution, and from there Burnett takes you through scenes of international affairs, betrayal, pure and untamed love, need, greed, and resolution. Songs such as "Talk Talk Talk Talk Talk," "Boomerang," and "Love at First Sight" couple sophisticated lyrical content with the simplest of materials (rockabilly, blues, folk, and country), as does the album's best cut, the bare-bones "House of Mirrors," a spoken, state-of-the-times parable in which the protagonist's fate is summed up in a wonderful historical reference. This, along with his passion and reverence for the music—as well as a willingness to subvert it if necessary—keeps him from coming across as retro or revivalist. Aside from the more complex material here, Burnett also proves to be equally adept at a more direct lyrical approach. Whereas in the past he would tend to lean toward the abstract, much of *Truth Decay*, with songs such as "Come Home," "Power of Love," and "Tears Tears Tears," owe as much to the eloquent simplicity of Hank Williams, Buddy Holly, and Willie Dixon as it does to Dylan. Removed from the big label, budget, and expectations of the Alpha Band, T-Bone Burnett produced a modest, passionate gem. —*Brett Hartenbach*

Trap Door / 1982 / Warner Bros. ✦✦✦✦✦
Following a short stint with Takoma Records, T-Bone Burnett moved back into the majors with a 1982 release for Warner Bros., the six-song EP *Trap Door*. Whereas his previous record, *Truth Decay*, had the feel of an early Sam Phillips recording for Sun Records, *Trap Door* is filled with tight, radiant folk-rock. Fronting the same basic lineup (Davids-Mansfield, Miner, and Kemper), Burnett adorns this batch of provocative tunes with shimmering guitar hooks, crafty rhythms, and an astute sense of detail and subtlety to create some of the most irresistible pop of his career (check out his terrific cover of the Marilyn Monroe standard "Diamonds Are a Girl's Best Friend"). "Hold on Tight," a message of love and mercy, is pure '60s pop, while "I Wish You Could've Seen Her Dance" opens with what could be a lyrical update of "I Saw Her Standing There" and then proceeds to recollect a conversation with a beautiful dancer set to a propulsive, shifting rhythm and an engaging melody. The title track closes the record with a half-spoken array of life's contradictions before an infectious chorus diverts your attention, only to arrive at the stark warning, "Watch out for the trap door." Intelligent and compelling, *Trap Door* is well worth hunting down. —*Brett Hartenbach*

Proof Through the Night / 1983 / Warner Bros. ✦✦✦✦
Proof Through the Night, T-Bone Burnett's first, and last, full-length release for Warner Bros., is an ambitious take on the state of the union and times, personified by various fallen characters. To some, his persistent morality may come across as being a bit cold or even self-righteous, but further investigation reveals an underlying empathy for the individuals, even if a cynicism for the times in which they live is expressed. And if Burnett may seem tough, don't think he excludes himself from the same scrutiny. In cuts such as "Pressure" and the record's best song, "Shut It Tight," he sees himself as "just an ordinary man," struggling with the same sorts of questions, temptations, and contradictions as, for instance, those of the protagonist in the record's centerpiece, "The Sixties." Musically, he serves his tales of "beautiful, wealthy, young divorcees," fallen women, and victims of times where we "keep all the bad, destroy all the good" on a bed of vibrant, guitar-driven rock & roll and folk, even lacing spoken parables such as "Fatally Beautiful," "The Sixties," and "Hefner and Disney" with subtle hooks and enticing nuances and choruses. Like T-Bone Burnett's other Warner Bros. release, *Trap Door*, *Proof Through the Night* is smart, tight, insightful, and unfortunately not yet available on CD. Guests include Pete

Townshend, Mick Ronson, Richard Thompson, the Williams Brothers, and Ry Cooder. —*Brett Hartenbach*

Behind the Trap Door / 1984 / Demon ✦✦✦

Behind the Trap Door, T-Bone Burnett's fourth recording (his second EP) following the breakup of the Alpha Band, is a varied collection of material that includes collaborations with Bono, Bob Neuwirth, and Richard Thompson. The record, with its stripped-down and decidedly uncommercial sound, along with the inclusion of a soundtrack instrumental and a cut recorded prior to 1980's *Truth Decay* sessions, has the feel of a career filler for Burnett (he was between major labels). This by no means suggests that *Behind the Trap Door* is without its charms. The opener, "Strange Combination," is pure Burnett, with its impressionistic spoken lyric over a chunky acoustic guitar and clanging percussion. "Amnesia and Jealousy (Oh! Lana)" and "The Law of Average" are infectious acoustic pop, while the winsome instrumental "Welcome Home, Mr. Lewis," written with Thompson, closes the record nicely. Fans of T-Bone Burnett's work will find pleasures throughout *Behind the Trap Door*, although it's by no means an essential piece of his catalog. —*Brett Hartenbach*

T-Bone Burnett / 1986 / Dot ✦✦✦

Released as a one-off project for MCA's briefly revived country subsidiary Dot Records, T-Bone Burnett's self-titled fourth album is the most austere and uncluttered project he's released to date, quite a switch from the high-concept folk-pop of his best-known work. Recorded and mixed live to two track in four days, *T-Bone Burnett* is subtle but strong, with a warm, natural acoustic sound that's gentle but surprisingly full-bodied, and the production is the perfect match for the songs, especially on the beautiful "River of Love," which is among Burnett's finest moments on record. Backed by a superb acoustic band (including David Hidalgo, Jerry Douglas, Byron Berline, and Jerry Scheff), Burnett's vocals are in superb form here, and while the album is a bit short on top-shelf T-Bone originals (half the album's songs are either covers or collaborations), what is here is compelling and listenable. *T-Bone Burnett* in many ways sounds like a casual project sandwiched between Burnett's "real" albums, but one listen confirms it's still the work of a major talent. —*Mark Deming*

The Talking Animals / 1988 / Acadia ✦✦✦

Following a brief brush with country music, T-Bone Burnett's seventh solo release, *The Talking Animals*, continues the studio rock he began in 1983 with *Proof Through the Night*. Burnett once again starts with basic rock, pop, and folk roots, which he wastes no time in subverting, adding assorted twists along the way. Along with co-producer and guitarist David Rhodes, he colors a foundation of steady rhythms driven by drummer Mickey Curry and bassist Tony Levin with affected and atmospheric guitars, as well as Mitchell Froom's various keyboards. One exception is the Van Dyke Parks-arranged "Image," with its swirling strings and one verse repeated in four different languages by Burnett and three guest vocalists (Cait O'Riordan, Rubén Blades, and Ludmilla). Here he sheds the bounds of the standard pop song format to create a piece that seems to have sprung from a Weill-Brecht musical. Lyrically, *The Talking Animals*, like his best work, can be scathing, searching, and surreal. Burnett explores uncertainty, longing, fear, lust, fantasy, greed, and eventually justice and mercy in his quest for "The Wild Truth" (the title of one of the album's best tracks). Often criticized for preaching, Burnett seems to ask as much of himself as he does of the cast of characters here, even allowing one of them to denounce him in the wonderful final cut, "The Strange Case of Frank Cash and the Morning Paper" (although it's T-Bone Burnett who gets the last word). Even with a few less than stellar songs, *The Talking Animals* is a strong, inspired record. Bono, Peter Case, and Tonio K. each co-write with Burnett, as well as lending support on vocals. —*Brett Hartenbach*

● The Criminal Under My Own Hat / Jul. 14, 1992 / Columbia ✦✦✦✦✦

On 1992's *The Criminal Under My Own Hat*, T-Bone Burnett seemed to be searching for a middle ground between his previous two albums, the bright, angular pop/rock of *The Talking Animals* and the spare, acoustic introspection of *T-Bone Burnett*. On this album, though, Burnett was willing to let these two sides of his musical personality display a greater influence upon one another; the acoustic numbers are more passionate and fuller sounding than on his previous efforts (often buoyed by Jerry Douglas on dobro and Mark O'Connor on violin), and the rockers have been peeled back a bit, giving the individual musicians a bit more room to move and letting the inner workings of the songs show. The operative philosophy appears to have been to allow the songs to shine though without excess gingerbread, and that's just what the material demanded; as always, Burnett's songs reveal his obsessions with the human failings of pride, fear, and greed, and he's willing to point the finger at himself as often as he finds shortcomings in others (though he saves his greatest wrath for the corrupt politicians and media savvy preachers attacked on "I Can Explain Everything," in which he suggests a little selective beheading might be a good idea—as Burnett puts it, "the French knew how to lynch"). But unless his subjects happen to be George Bush or Jimmy Swaggart, Burnett finds room for compassion in nearly all of these songs, once again proving he's one of the few avowed Christians in pop music who seems to understand how tricky the nature of sin and forgiveness can be. Thoughtful, often witty, and boasting a stellar cast of fine musicians, *The Criminal Under My Own Hat* was easily T-Bone Burnett's strongest album since *Proof Through the Night*, and a rare pleasure for thinking music fans. —*Mark Deming*

Billy Burnette

b. May 8, 1953, Memphis, TN

Guitar, Vocals / Country-Rock, Country-Pop, Contemporary Country

Born May 8, 1953, in Memphis, Billy Burnette began his career as a country performer at the tender age of seven. Due to his father Dorsey's fame as a rockabilly star (not to mention his uncle Johnny), Billy cut "Hey Daddy (I'm Gonna Tell Santa on You)" for Dot

Records with Ricky Nelson's band in 1960. Billy followed his recording debut with another session in 1964, and toured with Brenda Lee soon after. He moved to Memphis in 1969 to work as a guitarist and producer, and began his solo career three years later with a self-titled album for Entrance Records.

Billy Burnette led his father's backing band during the '70s, while his songwriting talent gradually came to the fore through covers by Dolly Parton and Kin Vassy. Burnette signed with Polydor in 1979, and recorded a second self-titled album. "What's a Little Love Between Friends" was a modest chart entry that year. *Between Friends* was released in 1980, and after Burnette signed with Columbia, he issued his third eponymous album. *Gimme You* followed in 1981.

In 1985, Eddy Raven and Ray Charles both charted Burnette songs, and Burnette himself charted with "Ain't It Just Like Love" and "Try Me." The action earned him honors as the ACM's Best New Male Vocalist, but he dropped out of country music for several years when Fleetwood Mac offered him a spot replacing Lindsay Buckingham. He appeared on Fleetwood Mac's *Greatest Hits* (1988) and *Behind the Mask* (1990), and toured with the band constantly. Billy Burnette returned to country music in 1992 with a contract from Warner Bros. and the charting single "Nothin' to Do (And All Night to Do It)." He moved to Capricorn later that year, and released *Coming Home*. After a long absence, Burnette resurfaced in the spring of 2000 with *Are You With Me Baby.* —*John Bush*

Billy Burnette / 1972 / Entrance ✦✦✦

Billy Burnette / 1980 / Columbia ✦✦✦

● **Gimme You** / 1981 / Columbia ✦✦✦✦

Coming Home / 1993 / Warner Bros. ✦✦✦

All Night Long / 1999 / Grand Avenue ✦✦✦

Are You With Me Baby / 2000 / FreeFalls ✦✦✦

Dorsey Burnette

b. Dec. 28, 1932, Memphis, TN, **d.** Aug. 19, 1979, Canoga Park, CA

Bass, Vocals / Country-Pop, Rockabilly

Dorsey Burnette is best remembered today as the brother of Johnny Burnette and a member of the Johnny Burnette Trio, and as the father of Billy Burnette. He had a solo career of his own, however, during the early '60s, and also wrote over 350 songs covered by the likes of Rick Nelson, Jerry Lee Lewis, Waylon Jennings, Glen Campbell, and Stevie Wonder, among many others.

Dorsey Burnette was born on December 28, 1932, in Memphis, the older of two sons of Dorsey Sr. and Willy May Burnette. He got his first guitar, a Gene Autry model, from his father at age six, at the same time that his father gave four-year-old Johnny a similar instrument—the two immediately smashed them. His father eventually convinced the pair that if they learned to play guitar, they could be like the players on the *Grand Ole Opry*. Dorsey was a tough kid with a violent temper and not a lot of smarts holding it in check, and he was constantly in trouble in school and spending time with the wrong crowd. By the time he was a young teenager, Dorsey was hanging out at the Poplar Street Mission with future recording artist Lee Denson, when he wasn't getting arrested for truancy or fighting. He competed in the Golden Gloves as an aspiring boxer, and it was at the 1949 championship that he met Paul Burlison, another aspiring fighter. They made note of their shared interest in music, but Burlison's induction into the Army in 1951 prevented him from hooking up just then with Dorsey and Johnny, who had begun playing together in the late '40s. They were good enough to get sponsored by a local appliance store on one of the Memphis radio stations, doing country music, and they played gigs throughout the Memphis area, principally for beer money, fun, and girls—he and his confederates worked hard and played hard, and music and the possibility of success that it offered probably kept Dorsey out of jail.

Dorsey, Johnny, and Burlison finally hooked up in mid-1952, working as a trio and within other, larger groups. They cut their first record, "Go Mule Go"/"You're Undecided," for the tiny Von label in 1954, their lineup augmented by a fourth member, fiddler Tommy Seeley. That record may have sold fewer than 200 copies, but Dorsey Burnette wasn't to be stopped—he claimed that the group auditioned for Sam Phillips at Sun, but was rejected. Dorsey worked his day jobs—picking cotton, deckhand on a riverboat, fisherman, carpet-layer, and electrician's apprentice at Crown Electric. While he was there, a day laborer a little younger than Dorsey who had grown up in the same housing project quit his job to try making it in music after cutting a couple of records. Elvis Presley's example, going off as part of a trio with Scotty Moore and Bill Black, brought the Burnette brothers and company to the decision to formalize their work together. Burlison and Burnette's subsequently layoff from Crown Electric made the decision a no-brainer.

As a result, in early 1956, they were off to New York, where Dorsey Burnette and Paul Burlison got jobs as electrician's assistants while Johnny Burnette went to work in the garment district in Manhattan's West 30s. They decided to try out for *Ted Mack's Amateur Hour*, which was one of the top new talent showcases in the country, just at the time when Elvis Presley—now signed to RCA Victor—was burning up the airwaves with "Heartbreak Hotel," and were picked to play on the program. The group, known as the Rock 'n Roll Trio, won three successive shows broadcast over the ABC network; by the time of the third they had professional management, and soon after that they were signed to the Coral label, part of the Decca Records (now MCA) family of labels.

The Rock 'n Roll Trio didn't last, either as a trio or a name, as they failed to find any hits—despite a killer version of "Train Kept A-Rollin'" to their credit—and by late 1957 they were getting billed as "Johnny Burnette & the Rock 'n Roll Trio." This was probably as much a marketing ploy as a reflection of the reality that a fourth member, in the person of a drummer, had joined the group—Johnny Burnette was a good rock & roll name to push in lieu of the group's moniker, although Dorsey was the one who did most of the songwriting and had also sung lead on some of their numbers. He couldn't stomach the change in billing or his younger brother's sudden push to the front, and finally quit the group and returned to Memphis just prior to the group's scheduled appearance in the Alan Freed jukebox movie *Rock Rock Rock*.

He tried assembling his own group, Dorsey Burnette & the Rock 'n Roll Trio, but they never caught on and disbanded before 1958 was over. He tried reconstituting himself as a solo act and got an offer to go out to California to appear on the *Town Hall Party* (the West Coast's leading country music showcase), rejecting the chance to work the *Louisiana Hayride.* He moved his whole family—including Johnny, who was no longer recording, under his name or any other—out with him and struggled to make ends meet, working as an electrician and writing songs in his spare time.

It was Burnette's brashness in walking up to the home of Ozzie and Harriet Nelson—famous from television and radio as entertainers, and the parents of Ricky and David Nelson—and asking to speak to Ricky that got him his break as a songwriter. Rick Nelson literally pulled up on his motorcycle, accepted Dorsey's introduction, and had him and Johnny audition right there. He ended up recording a dozen of their songs, most of them written by Dorsey Burnette, and his success with "Waitin' in School" got the Burnettes a new contract with Imperial Records and Dorsey a hookup with Imperial's publishing division, Commodore Music. Roy Brown later covered Dorsey and Johnny's "Hip Shakin' Baby," and Dorsey managed to get a solo hit in 1959 on the Era label with "Tall Oak Tree," a song that Rick Nelson had rejected. Ironically, given Johnny Burnette's prominence, Dorsey's first hit came five months before his brother finally reached the charts with "Dreamin'." The two successes led Coral Records to dig into their vaults and release a 1957-vintage single of "Blues Stay Away from Me."

The Burnettes never had another hit, although Dorsey kept writing and recording long after "Tall Oak Tree." His contract was sold to the Dot label (now owned by MCA), and he cut three singles and an album during the six months he was there. During this period, eight-year-old Billy Burnette made his recording debut on the maudlin "Little Child," which mercifully wasn't released until 1992. Dorsey Burnette's family life took a tragic turn from which he never fully recovered in 1964, when Johnny Burnette died in a drowning accident. The surviving brother, driven by guilt or depression and his self-destructive nature, became a chronic alcoholic and drug abuser, his musical abilities and reliability suffering in the process as he staggered from failure to failure across a dozen labels over the next 15 years. Dorsey found some belated comfort in Christianity, becoming "born again" in the 1970s and returning to where he started, in country music. His country recordings for Capitol Records got him pegged as "most promising newcomer" by one music organization that never recognized his earlier activity in rock & roll, and revitalized his career. By then, Burnette was appearing in small venues and playing to anyone who would pay him, getting into fights occasionally, and taking too many drinks and too many pills. In his shows, he would do his newer songs and a few of the old rockabilly numbers like "Tear It Up," which he counted as country music.

Somehow, he never found the right label once the Capitol contract was over. In 1979, however, he signed a contract with Elektra Records and began recording with fellow former rockabilly star Jimmy Bowen. Things looked promising, and Burnette, whose fame in England had never subsided (American rockabilly stars being treated like Olympian demigods anywhere but America), even supposedly did a recording session with Led Zeppelin (according to rumor). The first single by Burnette and Bowen had just been released when Burnette died of a heart attack on August 19, 1979. Among those who performed at the benefit concert organized on behalf of Burnette's widow by Delaney Bramlett were Kris Kristofferson, Tanya Tucker, Roger Miller, and Glen Campbell.

Dorsey Burnette will probably always be best remembered as a member of the Rock 'n Roll Trio in association with his brother Johnny, their work spread between the MCA and Capitol/EMI labels (which took over the Liberty catalog), but he spent most of his time in music as a solo act, whether he was recording or writing songs. Apart from "Tall Oak Tree" and "Hey Little One," he recorded an impressive array of soulful pop and rockabilly numbers, eerily recalling Elvis Presley's 1950s and early-'60s sound (only Burnette's songs are better), most of which are worth owning. —*Bruce Eder*

● **Great Shakin' Fever** / 1992 / Bear Family ◆◆◆◆◆
There isn't a chart record here, but this 25-song collection is still worth owning by any rock & roll fan worthy of the designation. The title tune, cut for Era Records, with its imitation Bo Diddley-style chorus, is a rockabilly classic, but there's a lot more here to recommend this collection—Burnette's cover of Jesse Stone's "Don't Let Go" and the slow "Rainin' in My Heart"; the soulful ballad "Sad Boy"; the stirring, religious-inspired "He Gave Me My Hands"; the Marty Robbins-style "A Full House"; and the Del Shannon-like "Feminine Touch." The pop stuff is a little sappy (though it's still better than Elvis' work of the same period), and the previously unissued cuts are not quite as strong as the Burnette sides that came out at the time—and "Little Child" is an embarrassment—but there's a lot here to love, and it makes a great adjunct to the best of the Rock 'n Roll Trio. —*Bruce Eder*

The Very Best of Dorsey Burnette / Oct. 23, 2001 / Collectables ◆◆◆◆
The Very Best of Dorsey Burnette gathers highlights from the rockabilly/country singer/songwriter's solo career with ERA Records, including his biggest hit, the self-penned "(There Was A) Tall Oak Tree." Other definitive singles range from rockabilly oriented material like "Great Shakin' Fever" to smooth pop songs such as "Hey Little One" and "That's Me Without You"; both styles complement Burnette's rich voice. The collection's tracklisting is virtually identical to the 1994 compilation *The Best of Dorsey Burnette*, and both of these albums are a solid overview of the high point of Burnette's career, but his fans might be better served by the Bear Family collection *Great Shakin' Fever.* —*Heather Phares*

Johnny Burnette
b. Mar. 28, 1934, Memphis, TN, **d.** Aug. 1, 1964, Clear Lake, CA
Guitar, Vocals, Songwriter / Rockabilly
A contemporary of Elvis Presley in the Memphis scene of the mid-'50s, Burnette played a similar brand of fiery, spare wildman rockabilly. With his brother Dorsey (on bass) and guitarist Paul Burlison forming his Rock 'n Roll Trio, he recorded a clutch of singles for Decca in 1956 and 1957 that achieved nothing more than regional success. Featuring the groundbreaking fuzzy tone of Burlison's guitar, Johnny's energetic vocals, and Dorsey's

slapping bass, these recordings—highlighted by the first rock & roll version of "Train Kept A-Rollin'"—compare well to the classic Sun rockabilly of the same era. The trio disbanded in 1957, and Johnny found pop success as a teen idol in the early '60s with hits like "You're Sixteen" and "Dreamin'." Burnette died in a boating accident in 1964. His brother, Dorsey, achieved modest success as a solo act in the early '60s, and Burlison recently resurfaced as a member of the Sun Rhythm Section. —*Richie Unterberger*

Johnny Burnette & The Rock 'n Roll Trio / 1957 / Coral ◆◆◆◆

● **Rockabilly Boogie** / 1989 / Bear Family ◆◆◆◆◆
All of the Johnny Burnette Trio's primal rockabilly records, including the blazing "Train Kept A-Rollin'," are collected on this single-disc compilation. The alternate takes might border on overkill, but the original takes remain powerful years after they were recorded. —*Stephen Thomas Erlewine*

The Best of Johnny Burnette: You're Sixteen / 1992 / EMI ◆◆◆◆
Burnette's best pop-oriented recordings are featured on this collection, including the classic "You're Sixteen." —*Stephen Thomas Erlewine*

Rock 'n Roll Trio/Tear It Up / Jan. 23, 1996 / BGO ◆◆◆◆◆
This two-fer assembles Johnny Burnette's 1956 debut LP along with the later *Tear It Up*, which offers highlights including "Train Kept A-Rollin'," "Rock Therapy," and "Honey Hush." —*Richie Unterberger*

Rock and Roll Tonight / 1999 / Hydra ◆◆◆
Rock and Roll Tonight is a German import collection of odds and ends that pairs Johnny and Dorsey Burnette. Sources include television performances, demos, and studio recordings, the latter of which are dubbed from vinyl. Some of the original vinyl records represented are extremely rare, such as "We're Having a Party," only 50 or so copies of which were pressed as an invitation to a friend's party. "Green Grass of Texas," released under the pseudonym The Texans, was a (barely) charting single. The 32-page full-color booklet and detailed notes are chock full of esoteric information for die-hard fans who will be the only ones dedicated enough to track down this collection. —*Greg Adams*

● **Dreamin': Very Best Of** / Jul. 27, 1999 / Collectables ◆◆◆◆◆
Collectables' *Dreamin': Very Best Of* does something many Johnny Burnette collections do not—captures both the sweet teen dreams of "Dreamin'" and "You're Sixteen" and the wildman rockabilly of "The Train Kept A-Rollin'." True, the collection leans a bit too much on the former in expense of the latter, but this is one of the rare CD collections to feature both sides of Burnette's personality and to do it quite well. —*Stephen Thomas Erlewine*

Dreamin'/Johnny Burnette / Mar. 13, 2002 / BGO ◆◆◆
In 2002, BGO released *Dreamin'/Johnny Burnette*, which contained two albums—*Dreamin'* (1960, originally released on Sunset) and *Johnny Burnette* (1962, originally on Liberty)—by rockabilly madman turned gentle pop crooner Johnny Burnette on one compact disc. —*Tim Sendra*

Train Kept A-Rollin'—Memphis to Hollywood: The Complete Recordings 1955–1964 / Feb. 2003 / Bear Family ◆◆◆◆

Johnny Burnette Sings/The Johnny Burnette Story / May 6, 2003 / BGO ◆◆◆
After Johnny Burnette broke up the legendary and revolutionary Rock 'n Roll Trio, he turned to songwriting, and after co-writing (with his brother, Dorsey) some great rockabilly songs like "Believe What You Say" for Rick Nelson, Burnette entered the world of pop music and the cloying sounds of cute lyrics, simple melodies, strings, and vocal choruses. On his first solo album, *Johnny Burnette Sings*, released in 1960 on Liberty, you'd never know he was the same guy responsible for some of the wildest rockabilly imaginable. Here Burnette totally immerses himself in the warm embrace of the easygoing pop sound of the toothless early '60s. Well, almost. If you stripped all the studio sweetness and gloss off one or two of the uptempo numbers, the songs still would be great rockabilly. On songs like "Mona Lisa" and "Little Boy Sad," Burnette sings and growls like a tamer version of the unhinged rockabilly maniac he so recently was and ex-Cricket Tommy Allsup makes a ruckus on guitar. Sadly, moments like this are few and far between. Most of the album is taken up with syrupy ballads like "In the Chapel in the Moonlight" and featherweight pop tunes like "Red Sails in the Sunset." *The Johnny Burnette Story* was released posthumously and the 12 songs include his big hits "Dreamin'" and "You're Sixteen," "You're Beautiful (And You're Mine)," and some of his more memorable tunes, like the tougher-than-his-usual-fare "Little Boy Sad" and the country tearjerker "Clown Shoes." The rest of the songs are the usual, over-orchestrated pop with smothering strings and choruses. The real Johnny Burnette story is a tragic tale of talent wasted. To go from king of the rockabilly hill to a mediocre crooner who makes Fabian look like a madman probably made financial sense, but to anyone who found his early sides life-changing, it is enough to make them cry. —*Tim Sendra*

Smiley Burnette
b. Mar. 11, 1911, Summum, IL, **d.** Feb. 17, 1967
Guitar, Accordion, Vocals, Saw / Traditional Country, Cowboy, Country Comedy
Based on his record sales, Smiley Burnette wasn't more than a footnote in the annals of recorded country music. However, thanks to his appearances as a sidekick to Gene Autry in dozens of Republic Pictures Westerns before World War II, and with Charles Starrett and Roy Rogers later on, he was one of the most familiar country & western performers in movies, and a beloved performer on-stage and radio. Burnette began his performing career at age nine, playing the musical saw. He organized and led his own band in high-school in the late '20s, and after graduation he set out on a performing career. Burnette became successful as a one-man band—he claimed proficiency on 100 instruments—and worked in vaudeville before becoming an announcer and performer on radio in Tuscola, IL. Autry discovered Burnette and hired him to appear on the WLS *Barn Dance* out of

Chicago, where Autry was already the top singing star. His recording career began around this time, centered around the Conqueror and American Record Company labels.

Autry went to Hollywood when producer Nat Levine at Mascot Pictures decided to put a professional country singer into the Ken Maynard film *In Old Santa Fe*, and he brought Burnette with him. The duo was established on the screen as a double act, one of the most popular in the history of B picture Westerns. With his portly physique, good-natured but slightly dim-witted persona, and trademark floppy hat, he became a familiar screen presence as Autry's sidekick Frog Milhouse, appearing in 55 Westerns alongside Autry between 1933 and 1942. In most of these, he was also called on to sing at least one number of his own, which he did in either his normal voice, which was funny enough, or a deep, frog-like croak.

As an actor, Burnette was one of B-Westerns' two "kings of the sidekicks" (the other was George "Gabby" Hayes, who didn't sing). His featured musical numbers, like his records ("Mama Don't Allow No Music" on ARC, reissued by Sony in 1995, is a good representative piece), were usually novelty songs with a strong comedic content, in contrast to the romantic ballads that Autry or Rogers would do in the same movies. He also made appearances in supporting roles in non-Westerns, including Republic's serials (*Dick Tracy*, etc.) in the 1930s. Burnette subsequently did dozens of films with Rogers and Starrett (*The Durango Kid*).

Burnette was a successful songwriter, and his music was recorded by the likes of Bing Crosby, Dean Martin, Red Foley, and Ferlin Husky, among others. He made appearances on his own, as a musical performer, on the Ozark Jubilee, Jubilee USA, the *Grand Ole Opry*, and the Louisiana Hayride, and played rodeos as well. In 1962, Starday Records released an album of Burnette's funniest songs under the title *Ole Frog*. From 1962 through 1967, he was a regular on the television series *Petticoat Junction*, playing railroad engineer Charlie Pratt. In 1971, four years after his death from leukemia, Burnette was inducted into the Nashville Songwriters Hall of Fame. —*Bruce Eder*

Ole Frog / 1962 / Starday ✦✦✦

This is the perfect companion to any volume of Gene Autry's movie songs, capturing Burnette's funny musical contribution to his early movies. —*Bruce Eder*

Is Frog Millhouse / May 6, 1997 / King ✦✦✦

● **Collectors Edition** / Feb. 24, 1998 / Simitar ✦✦✦

This budget CD reissue of Smiley Burnette's 1959 album *Smiley Burnette and His Rodeo Songeree* includes three previously unreleased recordings. Although originally conceived as an album for children, most of the songs are not children's songs per se, but novelty tunes with broad appeal, and some others are straight Western numbers. Befitting his silver screen image as a humorous cowboy sidekick, there is much comedy and light-heartedness in these songs, most of which were written by Smiley. Occasionally, as on the delightful "Deep Froggy Blues," Smiley makes use of the deep voice that inspired the name of his popular Frog Millhouse character. —*Greg Adams*

Jethro Burns (Kenneth C. Burns)

b. Mar. 10, 1920, Conasauga, TN, **d.** Feb. 4, 1989, Evanston, IL

Mandolin, Instrumental / Traditional Country, Country Comedy

As the mandolinist in the classic country comedy duo Homer & Jethro, Kenneth Burns was one of the finest instrumentalists of his generation, yet many people never realized that fact. Behind the country hayseed garb, the hick patter, and the outrageous parodies of popular songs, "Jethro" Burns and guitarist Henry "Homer" Haynes were expert jazz musicians whose exaggerated hillbilly appearance and zany sendups of songs belied the cleverness of their comedy and the extraordinarily high quality of their music. From the duo's formation in 1936 to Haynes' death in 1971, Homer & Jethro were immensely popular, selling many records and becoming a fixture at the *Grand Ole Opry*. After Haynes' death, Burns began a solo career that abandoned comedy in favor of jazzy bluegrass and country. Jethro's music was extremely melodic and graceful, combining elements of jazz, swing, country, folk, and bluegrass, resulting in one of the most distinctive and influential mandolin styles in country music history.

Born in Conasauga, TN, but raised in Knoxville, Jethro Burns began playing mandolin when he was a child, picking up his brother Aytchie's instrument. By the age of 11, he had grown into a skilled and accomplished instrumentalist, and he and his brothers frequently entered talent contests across Tennessee. At one of the concerts they lost, the sponsoring station, WNOX, asked the brothers to join a band called the String Dusters with another losing contestant, Henry Haynes. They accepted, and the group quickly earned a following; even at this stage, Jethro's playing demonstrated jazzy influences and inflections.

By 1936, Aytchie had left the group and Burns and Haynes had created the comedic Homer & Jethro characters that brought them to popularity. The duo made a good living from these rubes, winning a Grammy in 1959, starring in Las Vegas, and appearing regularly on TV, including *The Tonight Show*. Although they canned the country corn occasionally (as on *Playing It Straight*, a 1962 album), their on-stage wit and parodies of well-known songs ranging from the opera to the *Opry* made them famous. Regarding his "Jambalaya" being turned into "Jam Bowl Liar," Hank Williams said you know a song's good when it's been given the Homer & Jethro treatment. Other zingers include "She Was Bitten on the Udder by an Adder," "Mama, Get the Hammer (There's a Fly on Papa's Head)," and "I've Got Tears in My Ears from Lying on My Back in Bed While I Cry Over You."

Following Haynes' death in 1971, Burns continued to perform and teach the mandolin. During that decade, he wrote two instructional books on how to play the instrument with Ken Edison, which were published by Mel Bay. During the late '70s, Jethro played with the folksinger Steve Goodman, as well as the great country guitarist Chet Atkins. He also began recording a series of jazz albums during that era, many of which featured his son John on guitar. Jethro Burns continued to perform at string music festivals and concerts until his death in 1989. In the series of swing jazz albums he released during the last decade of his career, Burns demonstrated why he was considered the best

mandolin player of a generation and, in the opinion of many, the best who has ever lived. —*David Vinopal*

Back to Back / 1980 / Kaleidoscope ✦✦✦✦✦

The two modern giants of mandolin, Jethro Burns and Tiny Moore, are backed by guitar-great Eldon Shamblin of Bob Wills' Texas Playboys. —*David Vinopal*

● **Tea for One** / 1982 / Kaleidoscope ✦✦✦✦✦

Known for cornball comedy as half of Homer & Jethro, Burns was also a deft swing-style mandolinist. This album features Jethro Burns and his mandolin and no one else. —*Mark A. Humphrey*

Old Friends / 1983 / Rebel ✦✦✦

Jethro Live / 1990 / Flying Fish ✦✦✦✦

Bye Bye Blues / Oct. 21, 1997 / Acoustic Disc ✦✦✦✦

The recordings on this CD are among the last made by Jethro Burns prior to his death. Don Stiernberg, who studied with Burns, plays rhythm guitar accompanying his teacher's brilliant mandolin as they sail effortlessly through a mixture of standards ("Bye Bye Blues," "Idaho," and "I Can't Give You Anything but Love, Baby") and forgotten chestnuts ("Tuck Me to Sleep (In My Old 'Tucky Home)" and "Jeanine, I Dream of Lilac Time"), delving into jazz as well with a tantalizing take of Duke Ellington's "Mood Indigo." Burns, who is best remembered as a member of the musical comedy duo Homer & Jethro, is recognized by mandolin players as one of the greats; as he explains in an interview with Stiernberg (which is excerpted in the liner notes), he actually changed his approach to his instrument from single string to chord melody style following Homer's death. Burns' consistently inventive improvisations and Stiernberg's solid accompaniment make this swinging CD one that fans of string jazz (à la guitarist Django Reinhardt) will want to pick up; it is available directly from the label at www.dawgnet.com. —*Ken Dryden*

James Burton

b. Aug. 21, 1939, Shreveport, LA

Dobro, Guitar / Rock & Roll, Traditional Country, Rockabilly, Bakersfield Sound, Instrumental Country

Born in Shreveport, LA, on August 21, 1939, influential guitarist James Burton got his start in the 1950s as a backup musician on the radio show *Louisiana Hayride*, where he met Dale Hawkins. Hawkins' 1957 hit, "Suzie Q," was the first in a string of successes to feature the young Burton. A six-year stint (1958-1964) recording and touring in Ricky Nelson's band followed, subsequently landing him a couple of cameo bits on *Ozzie & Harriet*. Because of his brilliant and unique guitar skills—he perfected a style he dubbed "chicken pickin'"—Burton quickly landed jobs as a side musician for a diverse cast including: Buffalo Springfield, the Monkees, Elvis Presley's band (from 1969 until Presley's death in 1977), Gram Parsons, Joni Mitchell, Judy Collins, John Denver, Buck Owens, and Merle Haggard (with the latter two he was an important catalyst in the fine-tuning of the Bakersfield sound).

He later lent his talents to several Elvis Costello recordings as well as those by Gillian Welch, Jimmie Dale Gilmore, and countless others. With this schedule, it is no surprise that Burton has only cut two records of his own over a 40-year career; both his 1969 debut, *Corn Pickin' & Slick Slidin'*, and his 1971 offering, *The Guitar Sounds of James Burton*, provide spotlights on his legendary pickin'. —*Gregory McIntosh*

Corn Pickin' & Slick Slidin' / 1969 / See for Miles ✦✦✦

● **The Guitar Sounds of James Burton** / 1971 / A&M ✦✦✦

James Burton has a well-deserved reputation as one of the finest guitar pickers in either country or rock, having played subtly dazzling solos on sessions for everyone from Ricky Nelson and Dale Hawkins to Buffalo Springfield and Gram Parsons, and he's also played alongside both Elvises—Presley *and* Costello. However, Burton's virtuoso talent was not paired with a desire to either sing or take the spotlight (perhaps a blessing in disguise), and *The Guitar Sounds of James Burton* is something of a disappointment for longtime fans of the shy genius. Here, Burton and an (unfortunately uncredited) band of top-shelf studio musicians run through a set of pop and rock hits of the day (including a few that were mainstays of his sets with Presley during the Las Vegas years), with two loose-limbed originals thrown in for good measure (one of which, "Long Reach," is a none-too-subtle rewrite of Tommy Johnson's "Cool Drink of Water Blues"). The performances are solid and Burton is in typically impeccable form, but the arrangements aren't especially imaginative, so if you were hoping for a definitive musical statement from one of the best guitars players to ever touch a fretboard, you're out of luck. On the other hand, if you want to hear James Burton and some other fine players stretch out and play up a storm on a dozen tunes without a lead singer to get in the way, then *The Guitar Sounds of James Burton* is just what you've been looking for; it's hardly a masterwork, but anyone who loves Burton's picking will find it as refreshing as a cold drink on a hot day. —*Mark Deming*

Johnny Bush (John Bush Shin III)

b. Feb. 17, 1935, Houston, TX

Vocals / Traditional Country, Western Swing, Honky Tonk

Singer/songwriter/drummer Johnny Bush, born John Bush Shin III in Houston, began his country career as a vocalist and guitar player in 1952 at the Texas Star Inn in San Antonio. Eventually he switched to drums and in the early '60s began working in Willie Nelson's band, the Record Men. A year later, he joined Ray Price's Cherokee Cowboys. During his three years with the band, Bush tried to cut a record deal, but the labels felt he sounded too much like Price to be marketable. Nelson stepped in and paid for Bush to cut his first album, *The Sound of a Heartache*. After strong local response, he first hit the charts in 1967 with the minor hit "You Oughta Hear Me Cry." The next year he had three hits, including the Top Ten "Undo the Right."

In 1972, Bush had a Top 20 hit with "I'll Be There," which led to a deal with RCA and a Top Ten hit with his song "Whiskey River," which later became Willie Nelson's signature song. Just as Bush reached the brink of stardom, he started to lose his vocal range. Doctors were not able to diagnose the reason until 1978, when they found he had a rare neurological disorder, spastic dysphonia. This did not prevent his recording, but his career soon took a downturn. Working with "voice builder" Gary Catona in 1985, Bush was able to bring back about 70 percent of his original voice. The following year he and Darrell McCall teamed up to record the successful honky tonk album *Hot Texas Country.* He then assembled a large country band and began performing around San Antonio. In 1994, he and the band released *Time Changes Everything* and launched a major tour; RCA also released a greatest hits album. *—Sandra Brennan*

The Sound of a Heartache / 1968 / Stop ✦✦✦✦

Undo the Right / 1968 / Stop ✦✦✦

You Gave Me a Mountain / 1969 / Stop ✦✦✦

Johnny Bush / 1970 / Stop ✦✦✦

Here's Johnny Bush / 1972 / Starday ✦✦✦

Bush Country / 1972 / Stop ✦✦✦

Greatest Hits / 1972 / Stop ✦✦✦✦

Whiskey River / 1973 / Bellaire ✦✦✦

● **Greatest Hits 1968–1972** / 1993 / GH ✦✦✦✦✦

Greatest Hits / 1994 / RCA ✦✦✦✦

Johnny Bush is Back: Great Texas Honky Tonk Music / May 28, 1996 / Collectables ✦✦✦✦

Talk to My Heart / Mar. 10, 1998 / Watermelon ✦✦✦✦

Johnny Bush's second album after a 1994 comeback from an obscure neurological disorder that affected his voice finds the honky tonk singer challenging his voice with a set of uptempo, tenor-led songs. In the opener, a Ray Price nugget named "Please Talk to My Heart," Bush places his voice front-and-center, proving it's just as expressive as it ever was, and possibly a bit stronger. Originals like "The Cheatin' Line" and "It Sure Feels Good (Not to Feel So Bad)" show no concessions to contemporary country, and Bush's backing band—including Floyd Domino on piano, Jimmy Day on steel guitar, and Bobby Caldwell on electric guitar—forge a clean, crisp honky-tonk that accentuates every song. *Talk to My Heart* isn't just an excellent comeback album, it's a superb country album. *—Earl Simmons*

Lost Highway Saloon / Sep. 12, 2000 / Texas Music Group ✦✦✦

At age 65, a rejuvenated Johnny Bush continues to purvey styles of country music that had begun to go out of fashion before he was 25. He begins with "The Same Ole Me" (aka "The Same Old Me"), which was a number-one country hit for Ray Price in 1959, and which he no doubt played as part of Price's backup band in the early '60s. Going even further back, there is a version of the 1950 hit "I'll Never Be Free," originally sung as a duet by Kay Starr and Tennessee Ernie Ford, here performed by Bush with Leona Williams. (Just to reiterate the point, there is a second version of the song included as a hidden track, complete with scratchy sound as if transferred from an old single.) Bush isn't always reviving 1950s chestnuts, but his choices among more recent material reflect his vintage sensibilities, notably on the title song, a ghost story in which a man travels back to a barroom where Hank Williams and Bob Wills are holding forth on the bandstand. In the past or the present, Bush never gets too far away from a bar, and the songs are drenched in alcohol and tears, though they often proceed at a danceable pace. Despite the vocal problems of the past, Bush is in good voice here, especially for his years, and anyone with a taste for old-time honky tonk country is advised to have a listen. *—William Ruhlmann*

Sings Bob Wills / Sep. 12, 2000 / Texas Music Group ✦✦✦

This is a repackaged version of *Time Changes Everything*, an album with a curious history. It represented a comeback attempt for Johnny Bush after years of vocal problems. He organized a session in which his regular band, the Bandoleros, was augmented by a horn section to record a tribute to Bob Wills and cut it at Willie Nelson's studio in the early '90s. Unfortunately, that was just when Nelson experienced his troubles with the I.R.S., which seized all the tapes at the studio, Bush's included. It took two years to free the material for release, and then it was little heard. This is a second attempt to present it. After all that trouble, it turns out to be a brief, sturdy, minor effort, a welcome celebration of Wills that begins and ends with tributes to the great Western swing bandleader, leading off with Merle Haggard's "Don't Sing Me No Songs About Texas" and closing with "Bob Said It 'Aw' (And Called It Western Swing)." In between, Wills favorites such as "Time Changes Everything" (a duet with Nelson) and "South of the Border" are revived in appropriately lively fashion. The big-voiced Bush makes a good frontman for this music, and the performances are obviously heartfelt. There are many tributes to Wills, and this is not the best one, but it is good and enjoyable. *—William Ruhlmann*

Green Snakes / Nov. 13, 2001 / Texas Music Group ✦✦✦✦

Johnny Bush has been around Texas forever—or maybe it just seems that way. Certainly the man with the massive tenor has been a legend since he started up as a frontman in the '60s, and the renewed popularity of his 1972 song, "Green Snakes," about a man with the DTs has brought him back into the spotlight and pulled a new disc from him. He's re-recorded that classic and offers material both old—like "Driving Nails (In My Coffin)," which was a hit for Floyd Tillman—and much newer, like the very funny "Dos Tacos." Bush sticks to the straightforward Texas honky tonk style that's been his trademark throughout his career, even on the gospel tune "Glory Train" (which is followed, ironically, by the adultery ballad "Cheatin' Fire," a wonderful duet with Leona Williams). Particularly interesting are his spoken reminiscences of the late, great Moon Mullican, coming right between Bush's versions two songs associated with Mullican: "You Don't Have to Be a Baby to Cry," given a rocked-out Western swing treatment, and "The Pipeliner Blues," performed in neo-rockabilly fashion to round out the disc. But that's far from being all—a bonus EP contains nine songs demoed in 1965 by Bush (who was already 30 then), with friends Willie Nelson and steel guitarist Tommy Morrell. The sound quality's far from great—calling it muddy is kind—but the songs themselves are wonderful, especially "Between Heartbreak and Dawn." It's country music for a time before country was big, raw, heartfelt, and vibrant—like Bush himself. *—Chris Nickson*

Sam Bush

b. Apr. 15, 1952, Bowling Green, KY

Fiddle, Mandolin, Vocals / Progressive Bluegrass, Country-Folk, Contemporary Bluegrass, Instrumental Country

Sam Bush extended the musical capabilities of the mandolin and the fiddle to incorporate a seamless blend of bluegrass, rock, jazz, and reggae. As the founder and leader of the New Grass Revival, Bush pioneered and guided the evolution of modern hill country music. Together with the bluegrass supergroup Strength in Numbers, he pushed the traditions even further. During a five-year stint with the Nash Ramblers, he provided a diverse range of textures for the songs of Emmylou Harris. On his own, Bush has continued to explore an eclectic musical spectrum.

Bush was exposed to country music and bluegrass at an early age through his father's record collection and, later, by Flatt & Scruggs' television show. Buying his first mandolin at the age of 11, his musical interest was further piqued when he attended the Roanoke Bluegrass Festival in 1965. A child prodigy on the fiddle, he placed first at the national fiddle contest in Weister, ID, three times in a row. Together with childhood friends Wayne Stewart and Alan Munde, later of Country Gazette, he formed a band and recorded his first album, *Poor Richard's Almanac*, in 1969. The same year, he made his debut appearance on the *Grand Ole Opry*.

Attending the Fiddlers Convention at Union Grove, NC, in 1970, Bush overheard the pioneering progressive bluegrass band the New Deal String Band. Inspired by their rock-flavored approach to bluegrass, he formed the New Grass Revival in 1972. Over the next 17 years, Bush and the New Grass Revival revolutionized the music of the hill country, incorporating everything from gospel and reggae to rock and modern jazz into their tradition-rooted sound. The New Grass Revival went through numerous personnel changes, with Bush remaining as the sole original member. Bassist and vocalist John Cowan joined in 1973, with banjo ace Béla Fleck and acoustic guitarist Pat Flynn being enlisted in the early '80s. In 1980, the group toured with Leon Russell, opening the shows and backing Russell during his headlining set. A live performance at the Perkins Palace in Pasadena, CA, was released as *Leon Russell & the New Grass Revival: The Live Album* in 1981.

Beginning in 1980, Bush and Cowan periodically jammed with the Nashville-based Dockbusters Blues Band. Bush recorded his debut solo album, *Late as Usual*, four years later. In 1989, Bush and Fleck joined Mark O'Connor, Jerry Douglas, and Edgar Meyer in an all-star bluegrass band, Strength in Numbers, at the Telluride Bluegrass Festival in Colorado. When Fleck and Cowan elected to leave the New Grass Revival in 1989, Bush disbanded the group and joined Emmylou Harris' Nash Ramblers. He toured and recorded with Harris and the band for the next five years.

In 1995, Bush worked as a sideman with Lyle Lovett and Béla Fleck's Flecktones. He formed his own band, featuring Cowan and ex-Nash Ramblers Jon Randall and Larry Atamanuick, shortly before recording his second solo album, *Glamour & Grits*, in 1996. He released his next album, *Howlin' at the Moon*, in 1998, with many of the same players and special guests, including Harris, Fleck and J.D. Crowe. In the winter of 1997, Bush and the New Grass Revival reunited for an appearance on *The Conan O'Brien Show* as the backup band for Garth Brooks. On March 28, 1998, Bush's hometown of Bowling Green, KY, honored him with a special "Sam Bush Day" celebration. *—Craig Harris*

Late as Usual / 1985 / Rounder ✦✦✦✦

● **Glamour & Grits** / Apr. 1996 / Sugar Hill ✦✦✦✦

Sam Bush's newgrass mandolin playing is at its peak on the appropriately titled *Glamour & Grits*—solidly rooted with the traditional feel of the best contemporary bluegrass, but constantly pushing at the edges of composition and performance, giving each song a decidedly progressive feel. Surrounding himself with a blindingly talented list of supporting musicians (Béla Fleck, Jerry Douglas, Al Kooper, among others), Bush still manages to maintain his own presence on the mandolin and even with his own pleasantly everyman vocals. The instrumentals nudge themselves slightly ahead of the vocal tracks, not because Bush is an unpleasant singer, but because the instrumental passages allow the players to focus on the inventive changes and nuanced picking that the players in this group do so well. Fans of his work with New Grass Revival and Strength in Numbers would be remiss in not picking this one up. *—Zac Johnson*

Howlin' at the Moon / Apr. 21, 1998 / Sugar Hill ✦✦✦

A wildly talented multi-instrumentalist (mandolin, fiddle, banjo, guitar, pretty much anything with strings), Bush weaves an eclectic blend of bluegrass, country, folk and jazz on this solo release from Sugar Hill. With such gifted cohorts as Béla Fleck, Jerry Douglas and J.D. Crowe on hand, the musicianship here is frequently dazzling. The album is evenly split between instrumental and vocal numbers, with the instrumentals faring better. Bush and John Cowan handle the vocal duties, and while both are good enough singers, several of the songs tend lyrically toward a new-agey sort of earnestness. *—Joel Roberts*

Ice Caps: Peaks of Telluride / Jul. 25, 2000 / Sugar Hill ✦✦✦✦

With the release of *Ice Caps: Peaks of Telluride*, Bush pays tribute to the legendary music festival, pulling together some of his finest live performances from the event, all taped during the 1990s. Accompanied by longtime compatriot Jerry Douglas on Dobro, Bush turns in an unparalleled rendition of Bob Dylan's "Girl From the North Country" and the music just keeps flowing free and pure. Speaking of special guests, the album is chock full of them, from New Grass bandmates Béla Fleck and John Cowan, guitarists Darrell Scott and Jon Randall Stewart, bassist Byron House, drummer Larry Atamanuik, and Subdudes alumnus John Magnie. One of the album's finest moments—and there are many—comes at the end, as Bush joins John Cowan in a bass, mandolin, and vocal song on Lowell George's Little Feat staple, "Sailing Shoes." This one just has to be heard. It defies any journalistic description. If that isn't reason enough to check out *Ice Caps*, Sam Bush covers "Celebration" by Kool and the Gang on mandolin. Oddly enough, Bush pulls it off with his usual class and style, where many would fall flat on their face in a puddle of disco mud. *Ice Caps: Peaks of Telluride* is another stellar release from one of acoustic music's true innovators. *—Michael Smith*

Carl Butler

b. Jun. 2, 1927, Knoxville, TN, **d.** Sep. 4, 1992
Guitar, Vocals, Songwriter / Traditional Country, Honky Tonk
Born in Knoxville, TN, on June 2, 1927, Carl Butler blended the popular honky tonk style prevalent in the '50s with the mountain harmony of his Tennessee upbringing. Though his early recordings were as a solo act, most of his popular material was performed with his songwriting wife, Pearl. Carl grew up influenced by the *Opry*'s Roy Acuff as well as the old-timey music and bluegrass prevalent around his home. He began singing at amateur dances at the age of 12, and after service in World War II, he sang with bluegrass bands such as the Bailey Brothers and the Sauceman Brothers.

In 1950, Butler began singing as a solo act at a Knoxville radio station; he signed with Capitol and began recording in his bluegrass style, but later changed to a honky tonk sound inspired by Lefty Frizzell and Hank Williams, who were then tearing up the charts. Though the sides weren't successful, he did meet Pearl Dee Jones at the time; she shared composing credits on his "I Need You So," and the two were married by 1952. Carl moved to Columbia that same year, recording solo and with the Webster Brothers throughout the '50s.

By the end of the '50s, Carl Butler still hadn't produced a charting single, though he had recorded steadily for almost a decade. Finally, in late 1961, his single "Honky Tonkitis" made it to number 25 on the country charts. The Butlers joined the *Grand Ole Opry* the following year, and the exposure helped them push "Don't Let Me Cross Over" to number one. Their first single as a duo, it spent almost three months at the top of the charts, and led to an appearance in the film *Second Fiddle to a Steel Guitar* in 1963. Carl and Pearl continued to chart as a duo throughout the '60s, hitting the Top Ten with "Too Late to Try Again" and number 14 with both "Loving Arms" and "I'm Hanging Up the Phone." The Butlers had worked with Dolly Parton around Knoxville for quite a while beginning in the late '50s, and they were her biggest initial supporters when she became popular in 1967. They continued to release Columbia albums during the '70s and also recorded for Chart and CMH, but retired in the '80s. Carl Butler attempted something of a comeback in 1990, two years after Pearl's death, but it proved unsuccessful and he died in 1992. *—John Bush*

● **Don't Let Me Cross Over** / 1963 / Columbia ♦♦♦♦♦
Butler is best remembered for the title track (a country heartbreak style song) but this album is quite versatile and, in one instance, quite innovational (check out the "fuzz" guitar solo on "Wonder Drug"). Butler's wife, Pearl, also joins him on several of the songs including the title track. *—Jim Worbois*

Lovin' Arms / 1964 / Columbia ♦♦♦

The Old and the New / 1965 / Columbia ♦♦♦

Avenue of Prayer / 1967 / Columbia ♦♦♦

Our Country World / 1968 / Columbia ♦♦♦

Honky Tonkin' / 1969 / Columbia ♦♦♦

Cryin' My Heart out over You / 1994 / Bear Family ♦♦♦♦♦

Billy Byrd

b. Feb. 17, 1920, Nashville, TN, **d.** Aug. 7, 2001
Guitar / Honky Tonk, Nashville Sound/Countrypolitan
Billy Byrd was among the first musicians to make the electric guitar "sing" in a country voice, and make the public love it. He was also one of the first country players to make a name for himself with the electric guitar. He was also that rarity in country music, a bandmember who was allowed to "co-star" alongside the singer for whom he was working. As lead guitarist in Ernest Tubb's band from the end of 1949 until 1959, his playing was among the most widely heard in country music, and Tubb always made a point of featuring Byrd prominently in his stage act and on his records, and introducing him by name wherever possible.

William Lewis Byrd was born in Nashville. Whatever the city's musical inclinations, however, his family didn't want to see him become a country musician. A guitarist from age ten on, he displayed an impressive level of skill and technique, and his parents hoped he would pursue a career in classical music. He began playing with his older brother James, and made his radio debut on WLAC in Nashville in 1935. At age 18, he was hired as a backup musician on the *Grand Ole Opry*, and began working that same year with the Tennessee Valley Boys. Toward the end of the 1930s, he also worked in various dance bands in the Nashville area. Byrd served in the U.S. Navy as a cook on a destroyer escort. He resumed his career in Nashville after the war, initially as a member of Wally Fowler & His Georgia Clodhoppers, where he remained until 1948. That year he went to Louisiana, joining the *Louisiana Hayride* and playing with Curly Williams & the Georgia Peach Pickers.

During the fall of 1949, Byrd joined Ernest Tubb's Texas Troubadours, succeeding Tommy "Butterball" Page as lead guitarist on the single "Tennessee Border No. 2." It was as a member of the Texas Troubadours that Byrd became a star, Tubb mentioning Byrd by name ahead of each solo, and his solos were among the prettiest, most fluid, and memorable in country music. Byrd appeared on hundreds of songs, among them "Two Glasses Joe," "Jealous Loving Heart," "Answer the Phone," and "Letters Have No Arms," from 1949 until 1959, and was also prominently featured as part of Tubb's appearances on the *Grand Ole Opry* and other television shows. His playing made the electric guitar a popular instrument among country audiences, and in 1950 he collaborated with Hank Garland in the design of the Byrdland guitar for Gibson. While in Tubb's band, he played a customized instrument that included the name "Billy Byrd" prominently embossed on the neck.

Byrd also played a considerable number of sessions with other artists, including Tex Ritter, Webb Pierce, Burl Ives, Cowboy Copas, Little Jimmy Dickens, and Eddy Arnold, and shuttled between Tubb's and Red Foley's bands. In addition to the electric guitar, Byrd was also renowned for his skill on the mandolin, the banjo, and the bass. In 1959, Byrd, who didn't enjoy touring, left the Texas Troubadours to pursue a solo recording career with the newly formed Warner Bros. label—where he recorded three albums through 1964—and he moved to California to join fiddle player Gordon Terry. Byrd later moved back to Nashville to continue as a session musician, and was also featured throughout the early and mid-'60s as a guitarist on the local morning television program *the Eddie Hill Show*. He briefly rejoined the Texas Troubadours—who sorely missed his playing—at the end of the 1960s, but touring had never agreed with Byrd, and he left once again in 1970. He returned again in the early '70s, before leaving for the last time in 1973, although he played on one last single with Tubb in 1974. He also later participated on Pete Drake's Ernest Tubb tribute album, *The Legend and the Legacy*. Byrd's best work, apart from his solo albums, can be heard on any Ernest Tubb record cut between 1949 and 1959. The two Bear Family Ernest Tubb boxes covering this period are virtually a celebration of Billy Byrd's playing. *—Bruce Eder*

● **I Love a Guitar** / 1960 / Warner Bros. ♦♦♦♦
The first solo album by one of the most celebrated country guitarists this side of Merle Travis and Chet Atkins. Beautiful playing on a wide range of material. *—Bruce Eder*

Lonesome Country Songs / 1962 / Warner Bros. ♦♦♦

The Golden Guitar of Billy Byrd / 1964 / Warner Bros. ♦♦♦

Jerry Byrd

b. Mar. 9, 1920, Lima, OH
Guitar (Steel) / Steel Band, Tropical
Famed guitarist Jerry Byrd was born on March 9, 1920 in Lima, OH. As a child, he developed a passion for Hawaiian music, although he made his first inroads into performing by playing country on an area radio station between 1935 and 1937. After a stint on Cincinnati's WLW, he joined the *Renfro Valley Barn Dance* in 1941; a year later, he jumped to WJR in Detroit, and remained there until he signed on with Ernie Lee's Pleasant Valley Boys in 1944.

Byrd remained with Lee until 1946, when he formed his own group, the Jay-Bird Trio. Two years later, he joined Red Foley's band and became a session staple at King Records. Also in 1948, Byrd cut his first singles, "Mountain Mambo" and, under the name Jerry Robin, "Sun Shadows." Later in the year, he issued his first 78, "Steelin' the Blues." While at King, Byrd also recorded a handful of Hawaiian songs, and as the years wore on, the music became his primary focus. Still, Byrd remained an active figure on the country landscape; in 1950 he became a regular on Foley's NBC television program, and from 1954 to 1956 he was featured on the Nashville-based series *Home Folks*. An eight-year stint on the program *Country Junction* followed, and in 1964 he became a member of Bobby Lord's TV band. In 1968, Byrd left country for good, moving to Hawaii to focus exclusively on the state's native music. *—Jason Ankeny*

Byrd of Paradise / 1961 / Monument ♦♦♦
Byrd's stellar steel guitar is featured on tracks like "Hawaiian Wedding Song," "Evening in the Islands," "Beautiful Kahana" and "Tangi Tahiti." *—Keith Farley*

● **Man of Steel** / 1964 / Mercury ♦♦♦♦

Steel Guitar Hawaiian Style / Aug. 15, 1995 / Lehua ♦♦♦

Jerry Byrd: By Request / Jun. 12, 2002 / Mountain Apple ♦♦♦

Tracy Byrd

b. Dec. 18, 1966, Vidor, TX
Guitar, Vocals / Contemporary Country, New Traditionalist
Tracy Byrd's brand of new traditionalist country made him a star in the '90s, particularly his playful, good-time party singalongs (though he also turned in the occasional ballad success). Byrd was born in the small rural town of Vidor, TX, in 1966, and grew up listening to his family's extensive country record collection. When Byrd was 20 years old, he visited a novelty recording studio in a shopping mall and sang over a karaoke-style backing track of "Your Cheatin' Heart." Impressed, the saleswoman invited him to perform in an amateur talent show, and when Byrd was well-received, he decided to make country music his vocation. He dropped out of college and joined Mark Chesnutt's band, eventually replacing Chesnutt as the house headliner at a popular nightspot in Beaumont, TX. He made one unsuccessful trip to Nashville in search of a record deal, but his second time around, he landed a private audition with MCA executives, who signed him right away.

Byrd's self-titled debut album was released in 1993, and while it wasn't a blockbuster, it put the singer on the map in a big way with its third single, the number one smash "Holdin' Heaven." The follow-up album, 1994's *No Ordinary Man*, was Byrd's commercial breakthrough; it sold over two-million copies thanks to four Top Five hits: the dance tunes "Watermelon Crawl," "Lifestyles of the Not So Rich and Famous," and "The First Step," and the change-of-pace ballad "The Keeper of the Stars," which became a wedding favorite among country fans. Byrd followed his big success quickly with 1995's *Love Lessons*, and while singles like "Walking to Jerusalem" and "4 to 1 in Atlanta" didn't duplicate the massive popularity of their predecessors, they still helped the album sell at a respectable gold level. *Big Love* (1996) returned Byrd to the Top Five of the singles charts with the title track and "(Don't Take Her) She's All I Got," and the title track of 1998's *I'm From the Country* reached similar territory.

Byrd subsequently decided to leave MCA for RCA, and made his label debut with 1999's *It's About Time*, which featured a smoother, poppier production on tracks like the near-Top Ten "Put Your Hand in Mine" (the record's biggest single). However, Byrd returned to straight-ahead, good-time country for the follow-up, 2001's *Ten Rounds*; fans rewarded him by sending the single "Ten Rounds With Jose Cuervo" to the top of the charts, giving Byrd his second number one. The album also featured the Top Ten hit "Just Let Me Be in Love" and a duet with Mark Chesnutt on the playfully anti-pop "A Good Way to Get on My Bad Side." *—Steve Huey*

Tracy Byrd / Apr. 27, 1993 / MCA ✦✦✦

Tracy Byrd's self-titled debut is an uneven but appealing set of new traditionalist country, highlighted by the number-one hit, "Holdin' Heaven." On about half of the album's tracks, Byrd sounds confident and skillful, but on the other half, he sounds unsure and timid. Which just means that *Tracy Byrd* is a promising debut album, not a great one. *—Thom Owens*

No Ordinary Man / 1994 / MCA ✦✦✦✦✦

No Ordinary Man, Tracy Byrd's second album, was his breakthrough record and its easy to see why. While he was still sorting out the ins and outs of recording on his debut album, Byrd sounds raw, vibrant, and confident throughout *No Ordinary Man*, which is clear from the record's first single, "Lifestyles of the Not So Rich and Famous" and the first-rate weeper "The Keeper of the Stars." Byrd plays ballads and uptempo dance numbers equally well and his set of material on the album is fairly consistent, making the album his best to date. *—Thom Owens*

Love Lessons / 1995 / MCA ✦✦✦

On his third album *Love Lessons*, Tracy Byrd doesn't come up with quite as winning a collection as he did on *No Ordinary Man*, but he comes close enough to make the record a worthwhile purchase for fans. *—Thom Owens*

Big Love / Oct. 22, 1996 / MCA ✦✦✦✦

Tracy Byrd doesn't change his formula much with *Big Love*. He still works the same new traditionalist ground that he did with his debut album, only with more confidence—his voice is more assured and, more impressively, his selection of material is stronger and more adventurous. On the whole, *Big Love* is the equal to *No Ordinary Man*. *—Thom Owens*

I'm From the Country / May 12, 1998 / MCA ✦✦✦✦

With *I'm From the Country*, Tracy Byrd continues his streak of sturdy, well-crafted neo-traditionalist contemporary country. With each album, Byrd grows more confident in his delivery and choice of material, which naturally makes the albums stronger. There are still a couple of filler numbers on *I'm From the Country*, but the key to the record's success is that he takes pains in proving the title true—and by the end of the record, you have no questions that he is indeed country. *—Thom Owens*

● **Keepers: Greatest Hits** / Feb. 23, 1999 / MCA ✦✦✦✦

Keepers: Greatest Hits is an excellent summary of Tracy Byrd's first five albums, collecting the very best of his hits. Included are the radio version of "The Keeper of the Stars" (rather than the earlier recording that appeared on *No Ordinary Man*) and a new song, "When Mama Ain't Happy," neither of which appear on other Byrd albums. The collection makes plain that there are two sides to Byrd's career. The first, and most familiar, comprise the lighthearted staples of new country radio like "Lifestyles of the Not So Rich and Famous" and "Watermelon Crawl." These songs border on the formulaic, playing up the stereotypes of Southern culture. The other side of Byrd's musical personality is that of a neo-traditionalist balladeer. "Heaven in My Woman's Eyes" sounds like Merle Haggard singing to a Marty Robbins backing track, and both "Someone to Give My Love To" and "Don't Take Her She's All I Got" are stellar covers of early-'70s Johnny Paycheck hits. With these songs, Byrd's interpretive skills are given a chance to really shine. While his commercial successes have been the campy favorites, Tracy Byrd's lasting artistic triumphs are the ballads. *—Martin Monkman*

It's About Time / Nov. 2, 1999 / RCA ✦✦✦✦

On *It's About Time*, his first album for RCA Records, Tracy Byrd slyly adds some pop flourishes to his neo-traditionalist style. Some longtime followers may be surprised how smoothly the opening track "Put Your Hand in Mine" goes down, but Byrd straightens things out with the next two cuts, "It's About Time" and "Can't Have One Without the Other," which glide along with mildly twangy guitars and his rich baritone. From that point on, *It's About Time* follows a strange path, bouncing between good, neo-traditionalist country and music that seems a little too smooth for Byrd. That's not really a problem, since he's a very good singer and he sounds good no matter what he's singing, but the pace of the album nevertheless is a little awkward, mainly due to the fact that the pop-tinged material isn't quite as strong as the straight country. Still, Byrd is a classy, professional performer, which makes sorting through the chaff to find the wheat a worthwhile experience. *—Stephen Thomas Erlewine*

20th Century Masters—The Millennium Collection: The Best of Tracy Byrd / Nov. 20, 2001 / MCA ✦✦✦

One of the more current artists to have a *20th Century Masters—The Millennium Collection*, Tracy Byrd's volume in the best-of series compares favorably to his other career retrospective, *Keepers*. Indeed, the collections have very similar tracklistings, which is to be expected considering he's only been recording for eight years. Highlights include "Watermelon Crawl," "Heaven in My Woman's Eyes," and "Keeper of the Stars." While *Keepers* might still be the preferable Tracy Byrd best-of, *The Millennium Collection* does a better-than-average job of collecting his definitive tracks. *—Heather Phares*

The Truth About Men / Jul. 1, 2003 / RCA ✦✦✦

The Byrds

f. 1964, Los Angeles, CA, **db.** 1973

Group / Country-Rock, Psychedelic, Folk-Rock

Although they only attained the huge success of the Beatles, Rolling Stones, and the Beach Boys for a short time in the mid-'60s, time has judged the Byrds to be nearly as influential as those groups in the long run. They were not solely responsible for devising folk-rock, but they were certainly more responsible than any other single act (Dylan included) for melding the innovations and energy of the British Invasion with the best lyrical and musical elements of contemporary folk music. The jangling, 12-string guitar sound of leader Roger McGuinn's Rickenbacker was permanently absorbed into the vocabulary of rock. They also played a vital role in pioneering psychedelic rock and country-rock, the unifying element being their angelic harmonies and restless eclecticism. Often described in their early days as a hybrid of Dylan and the Beatles, the Byrds in turn influenced Dylan and the Beatles almost as much as Bob and the Fab Four had influenced the Byrds. The Byrds' innovations have echoed nearly as strongly through subsequent generations, in the work of Tom Petty, R.E.M., and innumerable alternative bands of the post-punk era that feature those jangling guitars and dense harmonies.

Although the Byrds had perfected their blend of folk and rock when their debut single, "Mr. Tambourine Man," topped the charts in mid-1965, it was something of a miracle that the group had managed to coalesce in the first place. Not a single member of the original quintet had extensive experience on electric instruments. Jim McGuinn (he'd change his first name to Roger a few years later), David Crosby, and Gene Clark were all young veterans of both commercial folk-pop troupes and the acoustic coffeehouse scene. They were inspired by the success of the Beatles to mix folk and rock; McGuinn had already been playing Beatles songs acoustically in Los Angeles folk clubs when Clark approached him to form an act, according to subsequent recollections, in the Peter & Gordon style. David Crosby soon joined to make them a trio, and they made a primitive demo as the Jet Set that was nonetheless bursting with promise. With the help of session musicians, they released a single on Elektra as the Beefeaters that, while a flop, showed them getting quite close to the folk-rock sound that would electrify the pop scene in a few months.

The Beefeaters, soon renamed the Byrds, were fleshed out to a quintet with the addition of drummer Michael Clarke and bluegrass mandolinist Chris Hillman, who was enlisted to play electric bass, although he had never played the instrument before. The band was so lacking in equipment in their early stages that Clarke played on cardboard boxes during their first rehearsals, but they determined to master their instruments and become a full-fledged rock band (many demos from this period would later surface for official release). They managed to procure a demo of a new Dylan song, "Mr. Tambourine Man"; by eliminating some verses and adding instantly memorable 12-string guitar leads and Beatles-esque harmonies, they came up with the first big folk-rock smash (though the Beau Brummels and others had begun exploring similar territory as well). For the "Mr. Tambourine Man" single, the band's vocals and McGuinn's inimitable Rickenbacker were backed by session musicians, although the band themselves (contrary to some widely circulated rumors) performed on their subsequent recordings.

The first long-haired American group to compete with the British Invasion bands visually as well as musically, the Byrds were soon anointed as the American counterpart to the Beatles by the press, legions of fans, and George Harrison himself. Their 1965 debut LP, *Mr. Tambourine Man*, was a fabulous album that mixed stellar interpretations of Dylan and Pete Seeger tunes with strong, more romantic and pop-based originals, usually written by Gene Clark in the band's early days. A few months later, their version of Seeger's "Turn! Turn! Turn!" became another number-one hit and instant classic, featuring more great chiming guitar lines and ethereal, interweaving harmonies. While their second LP (*Turn! Turn! Turn!*) wasn't as strong as their debut full-length, the band continued to move forward at a dizzying pace. In early 1966, the "Eight Miles High" single heralded the birth of psychedelia, with its drug-like (intentionally or otherwise) lyrical imagery, rumbling bassline, and a frenzied McGuinn guitar solo that took its inspiration from John Coltrane and Indian music.

The Byrds suffered a major loss right after "Eight Miles High" with the departure of Gene Clark, their primary songwriter and, along with McGuinn, chief lead vocalist. The reason for his resignation, ironically, was fear of flying, although other pressures were at work as well. "Eight Miles High," amazingly, would be their last Top 20 single; many radio stations banned the record for its alleged drug references, halting its progress at number 14. This ended the Byrds' brief period as commercial challengers to the Beatles, but they regrouped impressively in the face of the setbacks. Continuing as a quartet, McGuinn, Crosby, and Hillman would assume a much larger (actually, the entire) chunk of the songwriting responsibilities. The third album, *Fifth Dimension*, contained more groundbreaking folk-rock and psychedelia on tracks like "Fifth Dimension," "I See You," and "John Riley," although it (like several of their classic early albums) mixed sheer brilliance with tracks that were oddly half-baked or carelessly executed.

Younger Than Yesterday, (1967) which included the small hits "So You Want to Be a Rock 'n' Roll Star" and "My Back Pages" (another Dylan cover), was another high point, Hillman and Crosby in particular taking their writing to a new level. In 1967, Crosby would assert a much more prominent role in the band, singing and writing some of his best material. He wasn't getting along so well with McGuinn and Hillman, though, and was jettisoned from the Byrds partway into the recording of *The Notorious Byrd Brothers*. Gene Clark, drafted back into the band as a replacement, left after only a few weeks, and by the end of 1967, Michael Clarke was also gone. Remarkably, in the midst of this chaos (not to mention diminishing record sales), they continued to sound as good as ever on *Notorious*. This was another effort that mixed electronic experimentation and folk-rock mastery with aplomb, with hints of a growing interest in country music.

As McGuinn and Hillman rebuilt the group one more time in early 1968, McGuinn mused upon the exciting possibility of a double album that would play as nothing less than a history of contemporary music, evolving from traditional folk and country to jazz and electronic music. Toward this end, he hired Gram Parsons, he has since said, to play keyboards. Under Parsons' influence, however, the Byrds were soon going full blast into country music, with Parsons taking a large share of the guitar and vocal chores. In 1968,

McGuinn, Hillman, Parsons, and drummer Kevin Kelley recorded *Sweetheart of the Rodeo*, which was probably the first album to be widely labeled as country-rock.

Opinions as to the merits of *Rodeo* remain sharply divided among Byrds fans. Some see it as a natural continuation of the group's innovations; other bewail the loss of the band's trademark crystalline guitar jangle, and the short-circuited potential of McGuinn's most ambitious experiments. However one feels, there's no doubt that it marked the end, or at least a drastic revamping, of the "classic" Byrds sound of the 1965-1968 period (bookended by the *Tambourine Man* and *Notorious* albums). Parsons, the main catalyst for the metamorphosis, left the band after about six months, partially in objection to a 1968 Byrds tour of South Africa. It couldn't have helped, though, that McGuinn replaced several of Parsons' lead vocals on *Rodeo* with his own at the last minute, ostensibly due to contractual obstacles that prevented Parsons from singing on Columbia releases. (Some tracks with Parsons' lead vocals snuck on anyway, and a few others surfaced in the 1990s on the Byrds box set).

Chris Hillman left the Byrds by the end of 1968 to form the Flying Burrito Brothers with Parsons. Although McGuinn kept the Byrds going for about another five years with other musicians (most notably former country picker Clarence White), essentially the Byrds name was a front for Roger McGuinn and backing band. Opinions, again, remain sharply divided about the merits of latter-day Byrds albums. McGuinn was (and is) such an idiosyncratic and pleasurable talent that fans and critics are inclined to give him some slack; no one else plays the 12-string as well, he's a fine arranger, and his Lennon-meets-Dylan vocals are immediately distinctive. Yet aside from some good echoes of vintage Byrds like "Chestnut Mare," "Jesus Is Just Alright," and "Drug Store Truck Drivin' Man," nothing from the post-1968 Byrds albums resonates with nearly the same effervescent quality and authority of their classic 1965-1968 period. This is partly because McGuinn is an erratic (though occasionally fine) songwriter; it's also because the Byrds at their peak were very much a unit of diverse and considerable talents, not just a front for their leader's ideas. The Byrds' diminishing importance must have stung McGuinn doubly in light of the rising profiles of several Byrds alumni as the '60s turned into the '70s. David Crosby was a superstar with Crosby, Stills, Nash & Young; Hillman, Parsons, and (for a while) Michael Clarke were taking country-rock further with the Flying Burrito Brothers; even Gene Clark, though he'd dropped out of sight commercially, was recording some respected country-rock albums on his own. The original quintet actually got back together for a one-off reunion album in 1973; though it made the Top 20, it was the first, and one of the most flagrant, examples of the futility of a great band reuniting in an attempt to recapture the lightning one last time.

The original Byrds continued to pursue solo careers and outside projects throughout the 1970s and 1980s. McGuinn, Clark, and Hillman had some success at the end of the 1970s with an adult contemporary variation on the Byrds' sound; in the 1980s, Crosby battled drug problems while Hillman enjoyed mainstream country success with the Desert Rose Band. The Byrds' legend was tarnished by squabbles over which members of the original lineup had the rights to use the Byrds name; for quite a while, drummer Michael Clarke even toured with a "Byrds" that featured no other original members. The Byrds were inducted into the Rock & Roll Hall of Fame in 1991; Gene Clark died several months later, and Michael Clarke died in 1993, permanently scotching prospects of a reunion involving the original quintet. *—Richie Unterberger*

☆ **Mr. Tambourine Man** / Jun. 21, 1965 / Columbia/Legacy ♦♦♦♦♦

One of the greatest debuts in the history of rock, *Mr. Tambourine Man* was nothing less than a significant step in the evolution of rock & roll itself, demonstrating that intelligent lyrical content could be wedded to compelling electric guitar riffs and a solid backbeat. It was also the album that was most responsible for establishing folk-rock as a popular phenomenon, its most alluring traits being McGuinn's immediately distinctive 12-string Rickenbacker jangle and the band's beautiful harmonies. The material was uniformly strong, whether they were interpreting Dylan (on the title cut and three other songs, including the hit single "All I Really Want to Do"), Pete Seeger ("The Bells of Rhymney"), or Jackie DeShannon ("Don't Doubt Yourself, Babe"). The originals were lyrically less challenging, but equally powerful musically, especially Gene Clark's "I Knew I'd Want You," "I'll Feel a Whole Lot Better," and "Here Without You"; "It's No Use" showed a tougher, harder-rocking side and a guitar solo with hints of psychedelia. [The CD reissue adds six less impressive (but still satisfying) bonus tracks and alternate takes from the same era.] *—Richie Unterberger*

Turn! Turn! Turn! / Dec. 12, 1965 / Columbia/Legacy ♦♦♦♦♦

The group's second album was only a disappointment in comparison with *Mr. Tambourine Man*. They couldn't maintain such a level of consistent magnificence, and the follow-up was not quite as powerful or impressive. It was still quite good, however, particularly the ringing number-one title cut, a classic on par with the "Mr. Tambourine Man" single. Elsewhere they concentrated more on original material, Gene Clark in particular offering some strong compositions with "Set You Free This Time," "The World Turns All Around Her," and "If You're Gone." A couple more Dylan covers were included as well, and "Satisfied Mind" was their first foray into country-rock, a direction they would explore in much greater depth throughout the rest of the '60s. The CD adds seven decent alternate takes and bonus tracks, the most interesting being a version of Dylan's "It's All Over Now, Baby Blue," and an enigmatic Gene Clark song, "The Day Walk (Never Before)." *—Richie Unterberger*

Fifth Dimension / Jul. 18, 1966 / Columbia/Legacy ♦♦♦♦♦

Although *Fifth Dimension* was wildly uneven, its high points were as innovative as any rock music being recorded in 1966. Immaculate folk-rock was still present in their superb arrangements of the traditional songs "Wild Mountain Thyme" and "John Riley." For the originals, they devised some of the first and best psychedelic rock, often drawing from the influence of Indian raga in the guitar arrangements. "Eight Miles High," with its astral lyrics, pumping bassline, and fractured guitar solo, was a Top 20 hit, and one of the greatest singles of the '60s. The minor hit title track and the country-rock-tinged "Mr. Spaceman" are among their best songs; "I See You" has great 12-string psychedelic guitar solos; and "I Come and Stand at Every Door" is an unusual and moving update of a traditional rock tune, with new lyrics pleading for peace in the nuclear age. At the same time, the R&B instrumental "Captain Soul" was a throwaway, "Hey Joe" not nearly as good as the versions by the Leaves or Jimi Hendrix, and "What's Happening?!?!" the earliest example of David Crosby's disagreeably vapid hippie ethos. These weak spots keep *Fifth Dimension* from attaining truly classic status. [The CD reissue has six notable bonus tracks, including the single version of the early psychedelic cut "Why" (the B-side to "Eight Miles High"), a significantly different alternate take of "Eight Miles High," "I Know My Rider" (with some fine McGuinn 12-string workouts), and a much jazzier, faster instrumental version of "John Riley."] *—Richie Unterberger*

☆ **Younger Than Yesterday** / Feb. 6, 1967 / Columbia/Legacy ♦♦♦♦♦

Younger Than Yesterday was somewhat overlooked at the time of its release during an intensely competitive era that found the Byrds on a commercial downslide. However, time has shown it to be the most durable of the Byrds' albums, with the exception of *Mr. Tambourine Man*. Crosby, McGuinn, and especially Hillman come into their own as songwriters on an eclectic but focused set blending folk-rock, psychedelia, and early country-rock. The sardonic "So You Want to Be a Rock 'n' Roll Star" was a terrific single; "My Back Pages," also a small hit, was the last of their classic Dylan covers; "Thoughts and Words," the flower-power anthem "Renaissance Fair," "Have You Seen Her Face," and the bluegrass-tinged "Time Between" are all among their best songs. The jazzy "Everybody's Been Burned" may be David Crosby's best composition, although his "Mind Gardens" is one of his most excessive. [The CD reissue has six bonus tracks, including the fine Crosby-penned single "Lady Friend" and notably different alternate versions of "Mind Gardens" and "My Back Pages."] *—Richie Unterberger*

The Notorious Byrd Brothers / Jan. 3, 1968 / Columbia/Legacy ♦♦♦♦♦

The recording sessions for the Byrds' fifth album were conducted in the midst of internal turmoil that found them reduced to a duo by the time the record was completed. That wasn't evident from listening to the results, which showed the group continuing to expand the parameters of their eclecticism, while retaining their hallmark guitar jangle and harmonies. With assistance from producer Gary Usher, they took more chances in the studio, enhancing the spacy quality of tracks like "Natural Harmony" and Goffin-King's "Wasn't Born to Follow" with electronic phasing. Washes of Moog synthesizer formed the eerie backdrop for "Space Odyssey," and the songs were craftily and unobtrusively linked with segues and fades. But the Byrds did not bury the essential strengths of their tunes in effects: "Goin' Back" (also written by Goffin-King) was a magnificent and melodic cover, with the expected tasteful 12-string guitar runs, that should have been a big hit. "Tribal Gathering" has some of the band's most effervescent harmonies; "Draft Morning" is a subtle and effective reflection of the horrors of the Vietnam War; and "Old John Robertson" looks forward to the country-rock that would soon dominate their repertoire. The CD reissue adds six bonus tracks, including different versions of "Goin' Back" and "Draft Morning," a few instrumentals, and David Crosby's controversial "Triad"; unlisted on the sleeve is a rehearsal outtake which captures comically vitriolic arguments among the band. *—Richie Unterberger*

★ **Sweetheart of the Rodeo** / Aug. 30, 1968 / Columbia/Legacy ♦♦♦♦♦

The Byrds' *Sweetheart of the Rodeo* was not the first important country-rock album (Gram Parsons managed that feat with the International Submarine Band's debut *Safe at Home*), and the Byrds were hardly strangers to country music, dipping their toes in the twangy stuff as early as their second album. But no major band had gone so deep into the sound and feeling of classic country (without parody or condescension) as the Byrds did on *Sweetheart*; at a time when most rock fans viewed country as a musical "L'il Abner" routine, the Byrds dared to declare that C&W could be hip, cool, and heartfelt. Though Gram Parsons had joined the band as a pianist and lead guitarist, his deep love of C&W soon took hold, and Roger McGuinn and Chris Hillman followed his lead; significantly, the only two original songs on the album were both written by Parsons (the achingly beautiful "Hickory Wind" and "One Hundred Years from Now"), while on the rest of the set classic tunes by Merle Haggard, the Louvin Brothers, and Woody Guthrie were sandwiched between a pair of twanged-up Bob Dylan compositions. While many cite this as more of a Gram Parsons album than a Byrds set, given the strong country influence of McGuinn and Hillman's later work, it's obvious Parsons didn't impose a style upon this band so much as he tapped into a sound that was already there, waiting to be released. If the Byrds didn't do country-rock first, they did it brilliantly, and few albums in the style are as beautiful and emotionally effecting as this. [Columbia's 1997 CD reissue of the album improves on the masterpiece by adding eight strong bonus tracks, including four cuts with Gram Parsons singing lead trimmed from the original release for legal reasons.] *—Mark Deming*

Dr. Byrds & Mr. Hyde / Feb. 3, 1969 / Columbia/Legacy ♦♦♦

Chris Hillman, Gram Parsons, and Kevin Kelley all left the Byrds in wake of the release of *Sweetheart of the Rodeo*, leaving Roger McGuinn to assemble a new band from scratch. *Dr. Byrds & Mr. Hyde*, the first album with McGuinn as unquestioned leader (and sole founding member), was an interesting but uneven set that saw him attempting to bring together the psych-tinged rock of the group's early period with the pure country that Parsons had brought to *Sweetheart*. The new lineup on this album was as strong as any the band would ever have, with guitarist Clarence White sounding revelatory whenever he opens up, and Gene Parsons and John York comprising a strong and sympathetic rhythm section. But while everyone on board was a great musician, they don't always sound like a band just yet, and the strain to come up with new material seems to have let them down; McGuinn contributes a few strong originals (especially "King Apathy III" and "Drug Store Truck Drivin' Man," the latter written with Parsons before his departure from the group), but the two songs he penned for the movie *Candy* are just short of disastrous, and the closing medley of "My Back Pages" and "Baby What You Want Me to Do" sounds like padding. *Dr. Byrds & Mr. Hyde* proved there was still life left in the Byrds, but also suggested that they hadn't gotten back to full speed yet. —*Mark Deming*

Live at the Fillmore West February 1969 / Feb. 1969 / Columbia/Legacy ✦✦✦
Recorded by Columbia engineers in February 1969, this is an early show by the first Byrds lineup to feature only one original member: founding member Roger McGuinn and Clarence White on guitars, John York on bass, and Gene Parsons on drums. Despite the recent departures of Chris Hillman and Gram Parsons for the Flying Burrito Brothers, the sound and repertoire are still very much in the Byrds' country-rock phase, many of the 16 tracks coming from the *Sweetheart of the Rodeo* and *Dr. Byrds & Mr. Hyde* albums. The big mid-'60s hits are revisited in a medley, and a few other songs first recorded in the pre-White days—"So You Want to Be a Rock 'n' Roll Star" and "Chimes of Freedom" among them—also show up. There are also covers of Merle Haggard and Buck Owens tunes that would *not* show up on Byrds albums. It's a pleasant, but not outstanding, set, probably of most interest to those who enjoy White's guitar playing. He and McGuinn work pretty well together here, but the timing of the band as a whole is sometimes tenuous, and the vocal harmonies are not as full as those of other Byrds configurations. —*Richie Unterberger*

Ballad of Easy Rider / Oct. 29, 1969 / Columbia/Legacy ✦✦✦✦
If *Dr. Byrds & Mr. Hyde* found Roger McGuinn having to recreate the Byrds after massive personnel turnovers (and not having an easy time of it), *Ballad of Easy Rider* was the album where the new lineup really hit its stride. Gracefully moving back and forth between serene folk-rock (the title cut, still one of McGuinn's most beautiful melodies), sure-handed rock & roll ("Jesus Is Just Alright"), heartfelt country-rock ("Oil In My Lamp" and "Tulsa County"), and even a dash of R&B (the unexpectedly funky "Fido," which even features a percussion solo), *Ballad of Easy Rider* sounds confident and committed where *Dr. Byrds & Mr. Hyde* often seemed tentative. The band sounds tight, self-assured, and fully in touch with the music's emotional palate, and Clarence White's guitar work is truly a pleasure to hear (if Roger McGuinn's fabled 12-string work seems to take a back seat to White's superb string bends, it is doubtful that any but the most fanatical fans would think to object). While not generally regarded as one of the group's major works, in retrospect this release stands alongside *Untitled* as the finest work of the Byrds' final period. —*Mark Deming*

Untitled / Oct. 1970 / Columbia/Legacy ✦✦✦✦
This two-CD set contains the Byrds' 1970 *Untitled* album (originally a double LP) on disc one, and 14 previously unissued alternate versions, studio recordings, and live performances on disc two. This was not the Byrds' most exciting era, but a lot of extra material existed, and *Untitled* was going to be reissued either way. *Untitled* itself was one of the Byrds' better late efforts, with an album of live material (built around updates of their most famous tunes) sharing space with uneven new studio recordings in the expected country/folk-rock mode, highlighted by "Chestnut Mare" and "Just a Season." Listeners will be most interested in this expanded reissue for the disc of previously unreleased stuff, which is not remarkable, but is OK for those who enjoyed *Untitled*. There are alternate studio versions of two songs from *Untitled*'s studio portion ("Yesterday's Train" and a more jangly "All the Things"); a studio alternate of "Kathleen's Song," without the orchestration that would be added when it was redone for *Byrdmaniax*; a studio version of "Lover of the Bayou" (done live on *Untitled*); the instrumental "White's Lightning Pt. 2"; and Lowell George's "Willin'" (different from the version that appears on the Byrds' box set). Then you get eight previously unavailable 1970 live recordings, much in the style of what's heard on the live part of *Untitled*, and including such favorites as "It's Alright Ma (I'm Only Bleeding)," "Ballad of Easy Rider," "My Back Pages," and "Jesus Is Just Alright." An unindexed bonus track, an a cappella studio rendition of "Amazing Grace," ends the set. —*Richie Unterberger*

Byrdmaniax / Jun. 23, 1971 / Columbia/Legacy ✦✦
As legend has it, the Byrds wrapped up the basic tracks for *Byrdmaniax* in early 1971 and then hit the road for a concert tour, leaving producers Terry Melcher and Chris Hinshaw to polish the final mix. Melcher and Hinshaw then proceeded to add copious overdubs to what the group had set down, drowning the songs in a swampy morass of keyboards, horns, strings, and massed background singers in the misguided hope of making the album sound more "commercial" (even Clarence White's superb lead guitar often gets lost in the murk). The shame of it is that the aural gingerbread managed to spoil what might have been one of the Byrds' better albums; it's hard to imagine what Skip Battin's goofy "Citizen Kane" or Roger McGuinn's witty "I Wanna Grow Up to Be a Politician" were intended to sound like originally, but "I Trust" and "Kathleen's Song" are lovely if you can listen past the overproduction, and "Green Apple Quick Step" gives White and Gene Parsons plenty of room to show off their old-time country chops. Not an awful album, but *Byrdmaniax* is hardly the pleasure it could have been in the hands of a more tasteful production team. [The 1999 CD reissue adds three bonus tracks, including an un-overdubbed alternate take of "Pale Blue" that indicates how the album was originally intended to sound.] —*Mark Deming*

Farther Along / Dec. 29, 1971 / Columbia/Legacy ✦✦✦
One thing the Byrds had in common with most of their fans was that they weren't especially happy with the absurd overproduction that had been inflicted upon *Byrdmaniax* in their absence. As a response, the group quickly cut *Farther Along* in 1971, producing the sessions themselves and getting the album into stores a mere six months after its predecessor. It's certainly a significant improvement, but something short of a triumphant return; the band sounds a bit tired in spots, as if they were starting to run out of gas—which quickly proved to be the case as the Byrds split up a few months after the album's release. However, Roger McGuinn and Clarence White were nothing if not professionals, and if

Farther Along doesn't always sound inspired, it's never less than well-played, really connecting when the group can get their enthusiasm up; the tough rockin' "Tiffany Queen" and the pensive "Bugler" are the late-period Byrds at the top of their game, and "Bristol Steam Convention Blues" features some superb bluegrass picking from White. This is hardly the rousing conclusion the the Byrds' story that some fans might have hoped for, but it's a strong and well-crafted set from a band that inarguably gave it their all right up to the finish line. —*Mark Deming*

The Best of the Byrds: Greatest Hits, Vol. 2 / 1972 / Columbia ✦✦
It goes without saying that *The Best of the Byrds: Greatest Hits, Vol. 2* doesn't have as many classic singles as the group's first hits collection, since the Byrds stopped being a singles band shortly after the release of *Greatest Hits*. They never had another Top 40 hit after 1967's "My Back Pages," and between 1968 and 1970, they only had three charting singles. Instead of turning out hits, the band concentrated on albums, almost all of them (with the notable exception of *The Notorious Byrd Brothers*) explorations of country-rock, and that's what dominates *Greatest Hits, Vol. 2*. Two of their three charting singles, "You Ain't Going Nowhere" and "Ballad of Easy Rider," are present, as are staples like "He Was a Friend of Mine," "Wasn't Born to Follow," "Chestnut Mare," and "Drug Store Truck Drivin' Man." It's not a bad sampling of the Byrds' final years, but it's far from perfect; in fact, *Sweetheart of the Rodeo* itself offers a better summation of the musical direction the Byrds took after their classic period ended in 1967. —*Stephen Thomas Erlewine*

The Byrds / Feb. 1973 / Asylum ✦✦
In 1972, Roger McGuinn's final version of the Byrds unceremoniously broke up, but the following year the group briefly reunited—surprisingly enough, with the classic original lineup of McGuinn, Gene Clark, Michael Clarke, David Crosby, and Chris Hillman. However, if most of the participants meant for this to be anything more than a one-shot get-together, you couldn't tell from listening to the resulting album; *Byrds* never sounds much like a Byrds album, with McGuinn's chiming 12-string guitar and the group's striking harmonies (the Byrds' twin aural calling cards) largely absent, and much of the original material (especially David Crosby's) sounding like cast-offs from their other projects. And what sort of a Byrds album features two Neil Young covers and not a single Bob Dylan tune? In all fairness, *Byrds* has its moments: Gene Clark's "Full Circle" and "Changing Heart" are great songs from the group's least-appreciated member, and McGuinn's "Born to Rock 'n' Roll" is a top-notch rock anthem. But for the most part, *Byrds* sounds like a competent but unexciting country-rock band going through their paces, rather than the work of one of the best and most innovative American bands of the 1960s. —*Mark Deming*

☆ **The Byrds [Box Set]** / Oct. 1990 / Columbia/Legacy ✦✦✦✦✦
The value of the four-disc box set *The Byrds* as a rarities set has diminished somewhat, as much of the truly rare items later appeared on Columbia/Legacy's excellent reissues as bonus tracks, but this set remains a good overview of the group's career. Although the remastering and rarities are prominent enough to draw in the hardcore, the main strength of this compilation is that it tells the story exceedingly well, capturing the scope of their career. Very few (if any) great songs are missing, and if it dwells a little bit too long on the fourth disc, such is the nature of box sets. The rest of the record is remarkably well-balanced, containing all their hits and key album tracks, making it a nice, thorough retrospective. —*Stephen Thomas Erlewine*

20 Essential Tracks From the Boxed Set: 1965–90 / 1991 / Columbia/Legacy ✦✦✦
For those who don't want to invest the time or money in the full four-disc *The Byrds*, *20 Essential Tracks* is a decent sampler of the Byrds' better tracks throughout the years. If the collection has any faults, it's that only 12 of the 20 tracks come from the quintessential 1965-1968 period, and selections from the country-rock classic *Sweetheart of the Rodeo* have been omitted entirely. Instead, unnecessary tracks such as "I Wanna Grow Up to Be a Politician" and a few more obscure songs like the Beach Boys-esque "Lady Friend" are included. The low point of the collection is the inclusion of box set-only tracks like "Paths of Victory," "Love That Never Dies," and a maudlin "From a Distance"—while interesting, these cuts are definitely not essential. Still, as greatest-hits compilations go, this one does a fairly good job of showing quite a few different sides of the entire Byrds body of work. —*Matt Fink*

Byrd Parts / Sep. 15, 1998 / Raven ✦✦✦✦✦
Some of those involved with Columbia's Byrds box urged the producers to use tracks by the Jet Set, the Beefeaters, the pre-Byrds David Crosby, and the Hillmen; instead, they chose to weigh it down with a lot of later, Skip Battin-era tracks. So Raven Records has done the job instead, gathering together the major pre-Byrds and early Byrds-related tracks in one place: David Crosby's bluesy "Willie Gene" and "Come Back Baby"; the pre-Byrds Jet Set trio's Beatles-esque "The Only Girl I Adore" (complete with "yeah-yeah"'s) from the *Early L.A.* album; the Hillmen's bluegrass version of Dylan's "When the Ship Comes In"; and the Byrds/Beefeaters' "It Won't Be Wrong" from Elektra. But the producers haven't stopped with obvious stuff like that. They've also included David Hemmings' rendition of Gene Clark's "Backstreet Mirror" from the all-but-forgotten Jim Dickson-produced, Byrds-backed *David Hemmings Happens*; Jackie DeShannon's previously unissued demo recording of "Splendor in the Grass," backed by the Byrds; the Fred Neil-Gram Parsons "Ya Don't Miss Your Water" off of Neil's 1971 *Other Side of This Life* album; the International Submarine Band's lost Columbia single; rare single cuts by Dillard & Clark; and tracks by Clarence White, Skip Battin, Gene Parsons, and McGuinn, Clark & Hillman. Hemmings' "Anathea," even with his non-singing out in front, manages to achieve a trippy decadence through the Byrds playing and Dickson's production. Most of the rest gets far afield of the original Byrds, although "Ya Don't Miss Your Water" has a dark, brooding, ominous feel that makes it well worth owning, the Doug Dillard-Gene Clark stuff is always welcome, and the early International Submarine Band songs sound a lot

more Beatles-esque (and punkier) than anything on their subsequent *Safe at Home* album. —*Bruce Eder*

★ **The Byrds' Greatest Hits [Expanded Edition]** / Mar. 30, 1999 / Columbia/Legacy ◆◆◆◆◆

Without question, the Byrds were one of the great bands of the '60s and one of the few American bands of their time to continually turn out inventive, compelling albums. As they were recording a series of fine records, they released a number of classic singles that defined their era. *The Byrds' Greatest Hits* does an excellent job of chronicling the peak years of their popularity before they went country-rock on 1968's *Sweetheart of the Rodeo*. Columbia/Legacy's expanded 1999 reissue added the three minor hits missing from the original collection, which means that *Greatest Hits* now contains all of the group's hit singles—from 1965's "Mr. Tambourine Man" to 1967's "Have You Seen Her Face." That's an impressive collection indeed, and it also includes "All I Really Want to Do," "Turn! Turn! Turn! (To Everything There Is a Season)," "It Won't Be Wrong," "Set You Free This Time," "Eight Miles High," "5D (Fifth Dimension)," "Mr. Spaceman," "So You Want to Be a Rock 'n' Roll Star," and "My Back Pages." Yes, some great songs were left behind on the albums, but important cuts like "I'll Feel a Whole Lot Better," "The Bells of Rhymney," and "Chimes of Freedom" are included, making this pretty close to a definitive single-disc summary of the Byrds' prime. —*Stephen Thomas Erlewine*

The Preflyte Sessions / Nov. 2001 / Sundazed ◆◆◆◆

This double CD brings together all of the early Byrds rehearsals/demos found on the *Preflyte* and *In the Beginning* releases, and adds quite a bit more. As such, it stands as the definitive document of the birth of the group and how they sounded prior to recording the "Mr. Tambourine Man" single for Columbia at the beginning of 1965. For that reason alone it would be essential for any Byrds fan. But even for non-fanatics, there's a great deal of excellent music here to enjoy, even if the songwriting is more Beatles-like than it would be on the Byrds' early albums, and the performances more tentative. If you already have *Preflyte* and *In the Beginning*, what you really want to know is what's been added. To begin with, there are four pre-Byrds solo David Crosby electric rock cuts, also produced (as everything here was) by early Byrds manager Jim Dickson. Two of those, "Come Back Baby" and "Willie Jean," have shown up on other compilations, but "Jack of Diamonds" and Dino Valenti's "Get Together" have not. "Get Together" is particularly intriguing, kicking off with a weird "Twist and Shout"-like intro. Then there are no less than 14 additional previously unreleased alternate takes by the Byrds themselves, although unfortunately just one of these (an instrumental run-through of "The Times They Are a-Changin'") was not available in a different version, or different versions, on *Preflyte* or *In the Beginning*. None of these additional, multiple versions, alas, are as good as the ones that were first heard on those prior collections, though there are some interesting minor differences, like the bluegrass-type fractured guitar solo on a take of "You Movin'." Also, three of the new takes are just instrumental backing tracks without vocals. Still, it's great to have all of this material in one place, and the 50-page booklet of essays and photos is another major bonus. —*Richie Unterberger*

The Byrds Play Dylan / Jun. 11, 2002 / Columbia/Legacy ◆◆◆◆

Byrd Parts, Vol. 2 / Apr. 2003 / Raven ◆◆◆◆

Cache Valley Drifters

Group / Progressive Country, Traditional Bluegrass

An outgrowth of informal picking sessions, the Cache Valley Drifters continue to bring a modern outlook to bluegrass and country music. Although they disbanded for more than a decade, between 1979 and 1992, the group has been steadily making up for lost time. Their performances are as likely to include bluegrass-ized interpretations of songs by Paul Simon, Leon Russell, and Cream as they are to feature tunes by the late country folksinger Kate Wolf or traditional hill country material. The Cache Valley Drifters' association with Wolf is natural considering that the band's longest-standing member, Bill Griffin, toured with her backup band and produced her last recordings.

Griffin had previously been a sideman on albums by Earl Robinson, Pete Seeger, and Odetta and a series of national radio spots with the late Burl Ives. Mike Mullins was added to the Cache Valley Drifters in 1992 and plays guitar and mandolin and sings with the group. The brother of banjo player Tim Mullins, who played with the band from 1972 to 1973, Mike has been active in acoustic music since the 1980s when he played guitar in the Phil Salazar Band. In 1990, Mullins joined with ex-Cache Valley Drifters member Cyrus Clarke to form the Acousticats. Bassist/vocalist Wally Barnick, who played with the Cache Valley Drifters from 1975 until 1979, has worked with the group since their re-formation. Building an early reputation for their rich vocal harmonies and virtuosic musicianship, the Cache Valley Drifters were encouraged by the support they received from bluegrass guitarist Dan Crary, who helped them secure their first recording contract. Their self-titled debut album was released in 1978. —*Craig Harris*

New Cache Valley Drifters / 1979 / Flying Fish ✦✦✦

● **Step up to Big Pay** / 1980 / Flying Fish ✦✦✦✦

Tools of the Trade / 1983 / Flying Fish ✦✦✦✦

White Room / Apr. 16, 1996 / CMH ✦✦✦

This is an excellent and often amusing bluegrass set that goes around some unusual and fascinating corners, starting with the title track, an excellent rendition of the Cream song. The cover of Paul Simon's "The Boy in the Bubble" isn't quite as successful, but it's a noble attempt well in keeping with the superior performances to be found on this album. Definitely not your average bluegrass band, and definitely worth checking out. —*Steven McDonald*

The Cactus Brothers

f. 1991

Group / Contemporary Country, Alternative Country-Rock, Americana

Originally a side project for several members of Nashville's popular Walk the West, the Cactus Brothers eventually overshadowed their alter ego to take on a life of their own. After touring for the better part of a year in support of Walk the West's self-titled 1986 debut album, vocalist/guitarist Paul Kirby and bass player John Golemon joined with multi-instrumentalist Tramp to play at a friend's funeral. With Walk the West cohort Will Golemon (banjo/guitar) in tow, the four soon started gigging around Nashville and the Southeast, playing acoustic sets that offered more of a traditional country sound than the country-rock that Kirby et al. displayed on the album. It wasn't long before the popularity of the Cactus Brothers surpassed that of Walk the West, which was having trouble with the expectations of its West Coast label. Dropped from the Capital EMI roster, Walk the West subsequently morphed itself into the Cactus Brothers.

The trio of Paul Kirby and the Golemon brothers had been playing music together since grade school, Kirby the son of songwriter Dave Kirby (writer of "Is Anybody Goin' to San Antone") and the Golemons the sons of songwriter Guy Golemon. Tramp, equally adept at fiddle, mandolin, and guitar, earned his stripes as a member of the Kendalls' touring band. Manager John Lomax III brought in dulcimer master David Schnaufer and, adding drummer David Kennedy and steel guitar player Sam Poland, the Cactus Brothers hit the road. The band was signed to Jimmy Bowen's Liberty Records in 1992, the Nashville office of the same label that had dropped Walk the West, recording its self-titled debut album in 1993 with producers Allen Reynolds and Mark Miller. The band toured for almost two full years to support the album, performing in 38 states, Canada, Mexico, and six European countries.

The Cactus Brothers were one of the earliest country bands to embrace video and cable television as a way to reach an audience. Videos for "Fisher's Hornpipe" and "Crazy Heart," from the band's debut album, would go on to win Bronze Awards in the World-fest Competition in Houston in 1994. A video for the band's scorching cover of the country classic "Sixteen Tons" earned significant airtime on cable networks VH1 and CMT. The band performed in the film *Pure Country*, appearing alongside country star George Strait, and starred in a comic book illustrated by noted Austin, TX, artist Mack White. The Cactus Brothers returned to the studio in 1995 with producer Randy Scruggs to record *24 Hrs., 7 Days a Week* with the help of John Mellencamp drummer Kenny Aronoff and Double Trouble keyboard wizard Reese Wynans. By this time, Poland, Schnaufer, and

Kennedy had left the band, replaced by steel guitarist Jim Fungaroli and drummer Johnny Tulucci, who played in the theatrical presentation of *Always Patsy Cline*.

The bandmembers would make history later that year when they would become the first Nashville artists to travel to the former Soviet satellite state of Estonia, performing at the Baltic country's third annual *Country Picnic*, a show that was filmed for later broadcast on Estonian television. By this time, a familiar cycle was recurring, and changes in executives at the label left the band on the outside. By the end of 1995, the Cactus Brothers were out of a job at Capitol EMI and, one by one, the members drifted off to other gigs. The talented Tramp resurfaced in Bonepony, while former member David Schnaufer joined Nashville's prestigious Blair School of Music as a professor; he performs at mountain music and bluegrass festivals and markets his music online. —*Rev. Keith A. Gordon*

● **The Cactus Brothers** / Apr. 1993 / Capitol ✦✦✦✦

Originally formed as the twangier alter ego of popular Nashville cowpunks Walk the West, the Cactus Brothers soon took on an identity of their own, mixing weepy, pedal steel punctuated honky tonk country with Walk the West's edgier roots rock sound. By the time of this self-titled debut for Jimmy Bowen's short-lived Liberty Records, the band's original four members had grown into a powerful seven-piece band that built a loyal following by constant touring. With producers Allen Reynolds and Mark Miller at the helm, this solid collection of songs did a fair job of capturing the band's live dynamic on tape. The disc mixes traditional country gems like Tennessee Ernie Ford's classic "Sixteen Tons" and the Everly Brothers' "The Price of Love" with originals penned by vocalist Paul Kirby such as the precious "Sweet Old Fashioned Girl" or the rollicking "Swimmin' Hole." Although Kirby's distinctive nasal-inflected vocals do a fine job of caressing his lyrics (which tend to lean toward the typical romantic vein), the Cactus Brothers' strength was always in the band's skilled instrumentation. Few country bands in the '90s could boast of players such as pedal steel wizard Sam Poland, fiery fiddler Tramp, and mountain dulcimer master David Schnaufer. Along with Walk the West veterans and brothers Will Golemon (guitar, banjo) and John Golemon (bass) and drummer David Kennedy, the band's multi-talented multi-instrumentalists added complexity and depth to every song. When allowed to take a song and run with it, such as on instrumental tracks like "Blackberry Blossom" or their popular take on the traditional "Fisher's Hornpipe"—the accompanying video received constant airplay on several cable TV networks—the Cactus Brothers stood without peer. —*Rev. Keith A. Gordon*

24 Hrs., 7 Days a Week / Sep. 12, 1995 / Capitol ✦✦✦

The Cactus Brothers shook up their creative roster quite a bit for *24 Hrs., 7 Days a Week*, the band's sophomore album. Sam Poland and dulcimer wizard David Schnaufer were gone, as was drummer David Kennedy. The band added steel guitarist Jim Fungaroli and drummer Johnny Tulucci and carried on with pretty much the same sound that they had built their audience and reputation on, a high-energy blend of roots rock and traditional country. *24 Hrs., 7 Days a Week* benefits from the evenhanded production of fellow musician Randy Scruggs, who brought the band's natural rowdy inclinations to bear on both original material and covers alike while also managing to add a slight commercial sheen to the band's rough edges. Singer/songwriter Paul Kirby's original songs are stronger and more expressive than much of his previous material; cuts like "A Woman's Touch" and "Secret Language," a duet with Matraca Berg, mine a familiar romantic vein in a lively and lyrically intelligent fashion. The Cactus Brothers offer a pair of red-hot covers here, delivering a spirited performance of the Creedence Clearwater Revival favorite "Lodi" while the band's honky tonk roots shine brightly on a rave-up reading of Red Simpson's classic "Highway Patrol." Producer Scruggs adds some choice six-string work to fill out a handful of songs, assisted in the studio by drummer Kenny Aronoff and keyboard player Reese Wynans. However, it was multi-instrumentalist Tramp who was the band's secret weapon, his fiery fiddle elevating songs like "You're the Reason" and the title track above the generic country-rock finding favor in Nashville in 1995. When Tramp leads the entire band through the rocking instrumental "Redhead" you realize that, unlike many country bands during the mid-'90s, the Cactus Brothers were no studio creation, but rather a working band of talented musicians. *24 Hrs., 7 Days a Week* proved to be a swan song for the Cactus Brothers, a lack of commercial success and too many nights on the road taking its toll on the bandmembers. —*Rev. Keith A. Gordon*

Chris Cagle

b. Louisiana

Vocals / Contemporary Country

When he was four years old, Chris Cagle moved from Louisiana to the outskirts of Houston, where he grew up. He began taking guitar lessons at six, but gave them up after a year. He took piano lessons during high-school and returned to the guitar in his senior year. After high-school, he enrolled at the University of Texas at Arlington, but dropped out at 19 to pursue a musical career. He moved to Nashville in 1994 and struggled for five years. His earliest songs were published by famed Nashville songwriter Harlan Howard, after which he landed a publishing deal and placed some of his songs with David Kersh. He was discovered by the assistant to the president of Virgin Records Nashville, whom he met in a restaurant where he was working. Virgin signed him and released his debut single, "My Love Goes on and On," which reached the country charts in July 2000, eventually peaking in the Top 20. His first album, *Play It Loud*, followed in October. It reached the country charts, and its track "Laredo" made the country Top 40. In 2001, Cagle switched from Virgin to Capitol Records (both are subsidiaries of EMI), and his new label reissued *Play It Loud* in June 2001 with two bonus tracks. A self-titled album came in 2003. *—William Ruhlmann*

● **Play It Loud** / Oct. 24, 2000 / Virgin ✦✦✦✦
Like many young country music artists, Chris Cagle didn't grow up with country music so much as he did country-influenced pop and rock; his touchstones are the Eagles and Lynyrd Skynyrd, not Hank Williams and Merle Haggard. While his debut album *Play It Loud* unquestionably deserves to be filed under country, it's best to think of it just as much in the Southern rock category. Listening to it, music fans will be reminded most frequently of the Marshall Tucker Band and, especially, the Charlie Daniels Band. Cagle is most at home on uptempo tracks like "Country By the Grace of God," "Rock the Boat," and the title track, also showing an affinity for swamp rock on "Love Between a Woman and a Man." Hence the leadoff track, "My Love Goes on and On," released months ahead of the album as Cagle's first single, is a good representation of his style, since it is another driving country-rocker. Necessarily, Cagle mixes in a few ballads, but they are not among the album's most impressive tracks. It may be that, with slower tempos and more emphasis on lyrics, such songs reveal Cagle's formulaic songwriting approach less flatteringly. The cliché-ridden, stereotypical declarations of romantic devotion would require a more distinctive balladeer to put over successfully. The chief exception is the heartrending "I Breathe in, I Breathe Out," actually Cagle's first song to be recorded (David Kersh cut it in 1997), which was added to the album for its Capitol Records reissue on June 19, 2001, along with another bonus track, "Are You Ever Gonna Love Me," and some multi-media content including the video for "Laredo," the album's second emphasis track and second chart hit. Cagle is an enthusiastic and engaging performer on his first album, but not yet a fully developed talent. *—William Ruhlmann*

Chris Cagle / Apr. 1, 2003 / Capitol ✦✦✦
Though there are moments when he's clearly trying a little too hard, Chris Cagle delivers a generally agreeable set on his sophomore release. There are a few problems: the extremely crisp production has almost too much presence and the artist and his musicians seem to be emoting about an inch in front of the listener's nose. And Cagle's writing leans too often on the creaky formula of hanging the song on the hook of a knee-slap punch line. This can work as long as the language feels natural, like something someone in the country demographic might actually say—which is why "we're not growing old, we're growing love" misses the mark on "Growin' Love," for example. (Cagle's decision to rhyme "change" with "change" in the same song is even more awkward.) Elsewhere, though, his earnest, nasal singing and overall exuberance sell even the weaker material, and where he comes up with a writing gimmick that's actually fresh, such as the chronological breakdown of a happy relationship on "What a Beautiful Day," he hits a clean home run. *—Robert L. Doerschuk*

Camp Creek Boys

f. 193?
Group / Traditional Bluegrass, Old-Timey
The Camp Creek Boys formed in the 1930s, but didn't become influential in helping preserve and promote old-time string band music until the folk revival of the 1960s. All of the bandmembers hailed from Surrey county in North Carolina's Blue Ridge Mountains. Their leader was banjo picker Kyle Creed, who was accompanied by fiddler Fred Cockerham and guitarist Paul Sutphin. The other members were guitarist Ronald Collins, fiddler Ernest East, mandolin player Verlin Clifton and guitarist Roscoe Russel, making this string band considerably larger than traditional bands which featured a guitar, a fiddle, and vocalists. The band's name came from the community where Creed was raised. During the 1930s, the Camp Creek Boys started out playing at local social events ranging from dances to corn shuckings. They then began working on the radio and playing at old-time fiddle conventions. Even then the Camp Creek Boys were interested in preserving their musical heritage and the distinctive sound of string band music; after live radio performances became less common, they focused on performing at conventions and in fiddle contests. Eventually Creed became a key figure in the revival of his music. During their career, the Camp Creek Boys recorded four albums for the County and Mountain labels. Their best known songs include "Fortune," "Cider Mill," and the modern bluegrass favorite "Let Me Fall." *—Sandra Brennan*

June Apple / 1967 / Mountain ✦✦✦

Old-Time String Band: Traditional Dance Tunes / Jun. 3, 1997 / County ✦✦✦✦
Released on CD 30 years after their original recording in 1967, these 14 sides represent old-time mountain music at its most authentic. The Camp Creek Boys all hailed from North Carolina's Blue Ridge Mountain valley, and their playing on such standards as "Old Joe Clark," "Soldier's Joy," and "Cotton Eyed Joe" harked back to an era on the verge of dying out when these performances were captured on tape. The names Kyle Creed, Fred Cockerham, and Paul Sutphin have long since acquired an aura of the legendary about them in traditional music circles, based on these recordings and others the County label has made available in the name of preserving the mountain tradition. Justifiably so. Creed's banjo frailling and Cockerham's fiddling could jump start any number of revivals. This CD reissue includes two bonus cuts ("Breaking Up Christmas" and "Pretty Little Girl") that appeared as a 45 rpm single in 1967, too. If some of the band's song choices seem obvious or overdone in an era of nationwide festivals and younger revival bands like the Freight Hoppers, the spirited playing here makes this disc a highly recommended addition to all old-time collections. *—Brian Beatty*

● **Blue Ridge Square Dance** / Mountain ✦✦✦✦

The Camp Creek Boys / Mountain ✦✦✦

Shawn Camp

Fiddle, Guitar (Electric), Guitar (Acoustic), Vocals / Neo-Traditionalist Country, Contemporary Country
Country singer/songwriter Shawn Camp spent his early years on a farm outside of Perryville, AK. His father was an ironworker and his mother a beautician. Both sang and played guitar, infusing their child with a love of music; he began playing guitar himself at five. At the age of 20 in January 1987, he moved to Nashville to become a professional musician. He first found a berth as a fiddle player for the Osborne Brothers, and subsequently moved on to the backing bands for Jerry Reed, Alan Jackson, Suzy Boggus, Shelby Lynne, and Trisha Yearwood. In 1991, he left Yearwood to become a solo performer. He was signed to the Reprise division of Warner Bros. Records, which released his debut single, "Fallin' Never Felt So Good," in 1993. It entered the country charts that July and peaked in the Top 40 in October. That month, Reprise released Camp's first album, *Shawn Camp*, which spent several weeks in the country charts.

A second single, "Confessin' My Love," peaked in the country Top 40 in January 1994. Camp recorded a second album for Reprise, but the label rejected it and dropped him. He turned to working as a session musician, appearing on albums by John Prine, Garth Brooks, Nanci Griffith, and Guy Clark, among others, over the rest of the decade. At the same time, he co-wrote songs that were covered by many artists, including Diamond Rio, Tracy Byrd, Kenny Chesney, John Anderson, and Randy Travis. "Two Piña Coladas," which he co-wrote for Garth Brooks, appeared on Brooks' *Sevens* album and hit number one on the country charts in May 1998, and "How Long Gone," which he co-wrote for Brooks & Dunn, hit number one on the country charts in September 1998. Camp self-released his second album, *Lucky Silver Dollar*, in July 2001. *—William Ruhlmann*

Shawn Camp / 1993 / Reprise ✦✦✦

● **Lucky Silver Dollar** / Jun. 26, 2001 / Skeeterbit ✦✦✦✦
Shawn Camp's career as a country singer was derailed in 1994 when Reprise Records rejected his second album and dropped him. Happily, he was able to pick himself up and become a successful songwriter, scoring number one hits in 1998 with Garth Brooks' "Two Piña Coladas" and Brooks & Dunn's "How Long Gone." Conventional wisdom would suggest that his self-released disc, *Lucky Silver Dollar*, would be a glorified publishing demo, except that a guy with his success probably doesn't need to be passing his CD to potential clients. Rather, the album seems designed to demonstrate that Camp still has potential as a performer. He has gotten Allen Reynolds and Mark Miller, Garth Brooks' producers, to handle the board, which is pretty high-voltage help for a vanity release. But his performances justify the effort. Unlike a lot of Nashville's writers, he's a good singer with an elastic tenor and, having co-written all the material, he has a good interpretative handle on it. Still, it's that material that makes *Lucky Silver Dollar* a success. Good songs are always at a premium in Nashville, and it's hard to believe some of these titles (the ones that haven't already been cut by Tracy Byrd, John Anderson, or Brooks & Dunn) haven't been put on hold or on record by major stars. There are more strong ballads by Camp and John Scott Sherrill where "How Long Gone" came from (the Jimmy Buffett-styled "Middle of Nowhere" and "Lost at Sea"), a terrific Cajun story-song ("Tune of the Twenty Dollar Bill"), and a song Hank Williams could sing if he were around to do so ("Walkin' the Line," cut by Byrd in 1998). These compositions are a cut above what you usually hear on a country album, and Camp deserves to be back on a major label. *—William Ruhlmann*

Archie Campbell

b. Nov. 7, 1914, Bulls Gap, Greene County, TN, **d.** Aug. 29, 1987, Knoxville, TN
Guitar, Vocals / Country Comedy, Nashville Sound/Countrypolitan
Archie Campbell, a star and chief writer for *Hee Haw* beginning in 1968, also recorded several hits for RCA during the '60s. Born on November 7, 1914, in Bulls Gap, TN, Campbell studied art at Mars Hill College, NC, and in 1936 went to work for WNOX-Knoxville's *Mid-Day Merry Go Round*. He moved to WDOD-Chattanooga in 1937 and stayed until 1941, when he joined the Navy. Campbell returned to WNOX after World War II, and added a Knoxville TV show called *Country Playhouse* in 1952. The show ran for six years, after which he moved to Nashville to join the *Grand Ole Opry*.

Campbell signed to RCA Victor in 1959, just after his *Opry* debut. He reached the country Top 25 in 1960 with "Trouble in the Amen Corner," but later singles flopped. He moved to Starday in 1962, but found no success there either. Another stint with RCA beginning in 1966 brought the Top 20 entry "The Men in My Little Girl's Life." Two other singles—"The Dark End of the Street" and "Tell It like It Is"—hit the Top 30 in 1968, but Campbell's chart activity declined after he joined *Hee Haw* in 1968. He recorded several comedy/music albums, including *Bull Session at Bull's Creek* (with Junior Samples) and a self-titled album for Elektra in 1976. He also hosted the TNN interview show *Yesteryear* during 1984. *—John Bush*

● **The Best of Archie Campbell** / 1969 / RCA Victor ✦✦✦✦

Cecil Campbell

b. Mar. 22, 1911, Danbury, NC, **d.** Jun. 18, 1989
Guitar (Steel) / Traditional Country
Cecil Campbell was most famed as a steel guitarist for the Tennessee Ramblers during the 1930s and '40s, although he also played tenor banjo. Born March 22, 1911, in North Carolina, Campbell worked on his father's tobacco farm and played occasionally on WSJS in Winston-Salem. While visiting his brother in Pittsburgh in the early '30s, he met Dick Hartman and was asked to join Hartman's Tennessee Ramblers, a large group that played

both Western swing and old-time string music. Campbell played on radio broadcasts and Bluebird sessions with the band throughout the '30s, taking over the leadership of the Ramblers' by-then skeleton crew in 1945, when the only original member left was guitarist Harry Blair.

Cecil Campbell & the Tennessee Ramblers gained a contract with RCA Victor in 1946 and recorded throughout the late '40s. Campbell's steel guitar wizardry was emphasized, and the Ramblers gradually became more Campbell's backing group than an original entity themselves. During his RCA tenure, "Steel Guitar Ramble" became Campbell's only hit when it reached the country Top Ten in May 1949. Campbell also recorded for Disc and Palmetto Records during the early '50s, but signed with MGM in 1955, mixing some rockabilly material in with his traditional swing. He recorded in the '60s for Starday, and Campbell later founded his own label in North Carolina, occasionally playing shows and recording. He also appeared often at the Western Film Fair (held in Raleigh, NC) until his death in 1989. *—John Bush*

- **Steel Guitar Jamboree** / 1963 / Starday ✦✦✦✦

Greatest Hawaiian Instrumentals / 196 / Winston ✦✦✦

Glen Campbell

b. Apr. 22, 1936, Delight, AR

Guitar, Vocals, Banjo / Country-Pop, Pop, Soft Rock, Nashville Sound/Countrypolitan, Urban Cowboy

It isn't accurate to call Glen Campbell "pure country," but his smooth fusion of country mannerisms and pop melodies and production techniques made him one of the most popular country musicians of the late '60s and '70s. Campbell was one of the leading figures of country-pop during that era, racking up a steady stream of Top Ten singles, highlighted by classics like "By the Time I Get to Phoenix," "I Wanna Live," "Wichita Lineman," "Galveston," "Rhinestone Cowboy," and "Southern Nights." Boasting Campbell's smooth vocals and layered arrangements, where steel guitars bounced off sweeping strings, those songs not only became country hits, the crossed over to the pop charts as well, which was appropriate, since that is where he began his musical career. Originally, he was a Los Angeles session musician, playing on hits by the Monkees, Elvis Presley, Frank Sinatra, and Merle Haggard. By the end of the '60s, he had become a successful solo artist, and that success would not abate until the late '80s, when he stopped having radio hits and began concentrating on live performances at his theater in Branson.

Campbell was born and raised in Delight, AR, where he received his first guitar when he was four years old. Learning the instrument from various relatives, he played consistently throughout his childhood, eventually gravitating toward jazz players like Barney Kessel and Django Reinhardt. While he was learning guitar, he also sang in a local church, where he developed his vocal skills. By the time he was 14, he had begun performing with a number of country bands in the Arkansas, Texas, and New Mexico area, including his uncle's group, the Dick Bills Band. When he was 18, he formed his own country band, the Western Wranglers, and began touring the South with the group. Four years later, Campbell moved to Los Angeles, CA, where he became a session musician.

Shortly after arriving in California, Campbell earned the reputation of being an excellent guitarist, playing on records by Bobby Darin and Rick Nelson. In 1960, he briefly joined the instrumental rock & roll group the Champs, who had the hit single "Tequila" two years earlier. The following year, he released his debut single, "Turn Around, Look at Me," on the small Crest label; the single reached number 62 later in the year. By the summer of 1962, he had released "Too Late to Worry—Too Blue to Cry" on Capitol Records; the single only spent two weeks on the charts, peaking at 76. While he was tentatively pursuing a solo career, Campbell continued to play professionally, most notably for Elvis Presley and Dean Martin. Also in 1962, he played guitar and sang on "Kentucky Means Paradise," a single by the one-off group the Green River Boys, who released an album, *Big Bluegrass Special.* "Kentucky Means Paradise" became a hit on the country charts, climbing to number 20. Instead of pursuing a full-fledged country career after the single's release, Campbell returned to studio work, and over the next two years he played on sessions by Frank Sinatra ("Strangers in the Night"), Merle Haggard ("The Legend of Bonnie and Clyde"), the Monkees ("I'm a Believer"), the Association, and the Mamas & the Papas, among many others.

Following Brian Wilson's breakdown and retirement from the road in 1965, Glen Campbell became a touring member of the Beach Boys for several months. At the end of his tenure as the group's temporary bassist, the Beach Boys offered him a permanent spot in the band, but he turned them down when they wouldn't allow him to have an equal cut of the group's royalties. A few months after rejecting the band's offer, the Beach Boys' record label, Capitol, offered Campbell a full-fledged contract. His first release under his new long-term Capitol contract was a version of Buffy Sainte-Marie's "The Universal Soldier," which peaked at number 45. For much of 1966, he continued to pursue studio work, but he released "Burning Bridges" toward the end of the year, and it climbed to number 18 on the country charts early in 1967.

During 1967, Capitol pushed Campbell as a country recording artist, and their breakthrough arrived in the late summer when his folky country-pop rendition of John Hartford's "Gentle on My Mind" became a Top 40 hit on both the country and pop charts. By the end of the year, he had released a cover of Jimmy Webb's "By the Time I Get to Phoenix," which reached number two on the country charts, and number 26 on the pop charts. Early in 1968, "Gentle on My Mind" won the Grammy Award for Best Country & Western Recording of 1967. Campbell's success continued in 1968, as "I Wanna Live" became his first number-one hit and "Dreams of the Everyday Housewife" reached number three. The following year, CBS television hired him to host the variety show *The Glen Campbell Good Time Hour,* which became quite popular and helped establish him as not only a country star, but a pop music superstar.

Throughout the late '60s and early '70s, Campbell continued to rack up hit singles, including the number-one hits "Wichita Lineman" (1968) and "Galveston" (1969), plus the Top Ten singles "Try a Little Kindness" (1969), "Honey Come Back" (1970), "Everything a Man Could Ever Need" (1970), and "It's Only Make Believe" (1970). In 1968, he began recording duets with Bobbie Gentry, and they had hit singles with their versions of two Everly Brothers songs: "Let It Be Me," which reached 14 in 1969, and "All I Have to Do Is Dream," which peaked at number six in 1970. Also in 1969, he began a film career, appearing in the John Wayne movie *True Grit* that year and *Norwood* the following year. By 1972, Campbell's record sales started slipping. After "Manhattan Kansas" reached number six that year, he had trouble having Top 40 hits for the next two years. Furthermore, his television show was canceled. As his career slowed, he began sinking into drug and alcohol addiction, which continued even through his mid-'70s revival. In 1975, he returned to the Top Ten with "Rhinestone Cowboy," a huge hit that reached number one on both the country and pop charts. Over the next two years, he had a number of Top Ten country hits, including "Country Boy (You Got Your Feet in L.A.)" and "Don't Pull Your Love"/"Then You Can Tell Me Goodbye," which also reached the pop charts. In 1977, he had his final number-one hit with "Southern Nights," which topped both the country and pop charts.

Following the success of "Southern Nights" and its follow-up "Sunflower," Campbell stopped reaching the country Top Ten with regularity, yet he had a string of lesser hits and was an immensely popular performer in concert and television. During the mid-'80s, he experienced a brief commercial revival, as the singles "Faithless Love," "A Lady Like You," and "The Hand That Rocks the Cradle" all reached the country Top Ten. By that time, he had begun to clean up his act. Over the course of the mid-'80s, he kicked his addictions to drugs and alcohol and became a born-again Christian. Appropriately, he began recording inspirational albums, yet he didn't abandon country music. As late as 1989, Campbell's smooth, synth-laden contemporary country-pop was reaching the country Top Ten; his last two Top Ten country hits were "I Have You" (1988) and "She's Gone, Gone, Gone" (1989).

Campbell began recording less frequently in the early '90s, especially since he could no longer reach the charts and the radio, since they were dominated by new country artists. Over the course of the decade, he gradually moved into semi-retirement, concentrating on golf and performing at his Goodtime Theater in Branson, MO. In 1994, he published his autobiography, *Rhinestone Cowboy. —Stephen Thomas Erlewine*

Big Bluegrass Special / 1962 / Capitol ✦✦✦✦✦

Anyone who only knows Glen Campbell's country-pop hits like "Wichita Lineman" will find his first album a revelation. Recorded in the midst of the college folk boom, *Big Bluegrass Special* paired off Campbell with Dale Fitzsimmons and Carl Tanberg, aka the Green River Boys, doing songs by Merle Travis, Cliffie Stone, Bob Nolan, and the Delmore Brothers. A long way from Campbell's Jimmy Webb-authored pop hits, this earthy bluegrass weaves in and out of folk, blues, and traditional country, and casts a wonderful spell in the process. The sound is more robust than the Louvin Brothers and has more raw energy than the Kingston Trio or the Shilos, and the songs are played and sung with an infectious enthusiasm, although their playing is no match for the Kentucky Colonels. Among the surprises is the bluesiest version of "One Hundred Miles Away from Home" ever done. Nick Venet's production gave the acoustic trio a very "hot" sound, and the digital transfer brings out every detail in the playing and singing, all to the advantage of the participants. True, this album only sold a fraction of Campbell's later '60s efforts, but it's still a pity, musically speaking, that it was never followed up. [The CD contains two bonus cuts, covers of Travis' "Dark as a Dungeon" and "Divorce Me C.O.D.," both of which are worthwhile. *Big Bluegrass Special* was reissued in an upgraded, newly remastered edition in August of 2001 as part of Capitol-Nashville's *Cornerstones* series, eclipsing the earlier Capitol CD in terms of sound quality.] *—Bruce Eder*

Too Late to Worry, Too Blue To Cry / 1963 / Capitol ✦✦✦

Swingin' 12 String Guitar / 1963 / Index ✦✦✦

The Astounding 12-String Guitar / 1964 / Capitol ✦✦✦

There was a brief vogue for recording guitar-oriented instrumentals of folk songs for the pop and rock market just around the time the early-'60s folk boom started to taper off. Billy Strange's *Twelve String Guitar* was one of them, and so was *The Astounding 12-String Guitar.* And like that Strange LP, this was not so much a folk-rock precursor as an appropriation of folk melodies for Hollywood studio sessions that happened to use some bass and drums in addition to the guitar. If nothing else, this album is notable evidence of Campbell's considerable instrumental skills, which have generally been overlooked since his rise as a pop vocal star. But these readings of tunes like "Puff (The Magic Dragon)," "Blowin' in the Wind," "Green, Green," and "This Land Is Your Land" are rather perfunctory, as if they were laid down in an hour or two between the players' other session commitments (and it would be no surprise to learn that was the case). Campbell does take one vocal, on Bob Dylan's "Walkin' Down the Line" (which Dylan had yet to release at that point), which is probably the highlight of the album. He also wrote a couple of serviceable instrumental showcases for his 12-string, "12-String Special" and "Bull Durham." Notable session players on the record include drummers Hal Blaine and Earl Palmer, banjoist Roy Clark (who wrote one of the tracks, "Lonesome Twelve"), and Chip Douglas (later to produce the Monkees); noted pop and rock producer Nick Venet co-produced. Make sure you check the disc itself before you buy it, as a reissued version, unfortunately, deleted a couple of the dozen tracks from the already-short running time; those were "Wimoweh" and "The Ballad of Jed Clampett" (aka the theme to *The Beverly Hillbillies*). *—Richie Unterberger*

The Big Bad Rock Guitar of Glen Campbell / 1964 / Capitol ✦✦

Gentle on My Mind / 1967 / Capitol ✦✦✦✦✦

The best of Campbell's early albums, and also his first real commercial success. Ironically, the title track (written by John Hartford) which started Campbell on the road to stardom, was never intended for release—he had submitted it as a demo, and Capitol issued it, to everybody's profit. Campbell's cover of "Catch the Wind" is one of the finest covers of a Donovan song ever done, stripping away any hint of the composer's sub-Dylan pretensions and bringing out the song's genuine beauty—it's folk-pop, in the same manner that Peter, Paul & Mary's cover of Dylan's "Blowin' in the Wind" was, but excellent folk-pop.

This is Campbell's folksiest album, albeit with string orchestra accompaniment, as he covers "Bowling Green," "Mary in the Morning," and the title tune, and you get to hear him do a solo guitar and voice number, his own "Just Another Man." Even the most overproduced stuff here, "You're My World" and Rod McKuen's "The World I Used to Know," come off well, and Campbell is in excellent voice throughout, most especially on a wonderfully restrained and beautiful rendition of Roy Orbison's "Crying." [*Gentle on My Mind* was reissued in August of 2001 as part of Capitol-Nashville's "Cornerstones" series, in an upgraded, remastered edition with crisper sound than the 1996 Capitol CD.] *—Bruce Eder*

Burning Bridges / 1967 / Capitol ♦♦♦♦

By the Time I Get to Phoenix / 1968 / Capitol ♦♦♦♦
Glen Campbell's commercial breakthrough came by way of the title track, which was the direct precursor in production terms to "Wichita Lineman," and by the same writer. The cover of Paul Simon's "Homeward Bound" is sincere if a little perfunctory, but Campbell's rendition of Ernest Tubb's "Tomorrow Never Comes" is a bravura performance, rich and soulful, as well as recalling Rodgers & Hammerstein's "You'll Never Walk Alone" as done by Gerry & the Pacemakers. "Cold December in Your Heart" harks back to Campbell's country-folk material, a piece of midtempo country-pop. Material like that and the similar "Back in the Race," Dorsey Burnette's "Hey Little One," Jerry Reed's "You're Young and You'll Forget," and Bill Anderson's "Bad Seed" hold up better than more pop-focused numbers like "My Baby's Gone," though the string backings on most of these very much date them. The final number here, the touching "Love Is a Lonesome River," makes a brilliant coda. [*By the Time I Get to Phoenix* was reissued in August of 2001 in a newly remastered, upgraded edition, with somewhat crisper sound, as part of Capitol-Nashville's *Cornerstones* series.] *—Bruce Eder*

Hey, Little One / 1968 / Capitol ♦♦♦
Glen Campbell is richly brought into light here with a talented backup group and the enchanting power of a full string orchestra. His record, *Hey Little One,* was inspired with nine covers and one original, and though not a compelling work, his vocal style and his arrangements overshadow the record's list of covers. Enchanting in presence, Campbell sings with a sizzling flair for the romantic. Songs covered for the record include melodies about lost loves, break ups and getting back together. The title track, written originally by Dorsey Burnette and Barry De Vorzon, is a beautiful melody of solitude, loneliness, and one's initial experience of being far from home. "The Elusive Butterfly," a haunting and joyful statement of love written by Bob Lind, is played with great compassion. Campbell isn't afraid to explore the country genre as well, with a heartwarming rendition of John D. Loudermilk's "Break My Mind." He pays homage to the renowned poet Bob Dylan with his version of "I Don't Believe You." Thankfully, the record's form of originality is not lost, due to Campbell's original composition, "Turn Around and Look at Me," a charming and romantic tune later covered by the Beach Boys. The song was a remake of hit 1961 hit, and is presented here with full of emotion and endearing sentimental quality. It, like many of the tunes presented in this collection, radiates with a distinctive style Campbell can sincerely call his own. The orchestral arrangements are still necessary to carry the record, and they do so with a chilling degree of dynamics. *—Shawn Haney*

A New Place in the Sun / 1968 / Capitol ♦♦
The song selection is interesting (including songs by Merle Haggard, a bluegrass standard by two members of Paul Revere & the Raiders, and an early Mac Davis composition), but the production is Hollywood's version of country music. It's OK for Campbell fans, but not suggested for anyone interested in country music. *—Jim Worbois*

Wichita Lineman / 1968 / Capitol ♦♦♦♦
This disc, a certified double-platinum album, captures Campbell's appeal at his most mainstream, mixing midtempo country-pop, spiced by a smooth if unambitious cover of Otis Redding's "(Sittin' On) The Dock of the Bay" and the prettiest version of Tim Hardin's "Reason to Believe" ever done. The latter two make the album hipper than Campbell himself seemed at the time to most of us. On the other hand, there's ample romantic pop here, including his heartfelt, string-laden performance of the McKuen/Brel "If You Go Away" and "Words." Right there at the center of Campbell's appeal is the still-beautiful title track (for which he had composer Jimmy Webb's organ hauled to the studio to re-create its exact sound from the demo) and "Dreams of the Everyday Housewife," alongside midtempo country-pop like Billy Ed Wheeler's sprightly "Ann" and Campbell's own "Fate of Man." Sonny Curtis' "The Straight Life" is closer in spirit to the *Mary Tyler Moore* theme song (still a year or so away) than to the work of an ex-Buddy Holly compadre, and Sonny Bono's singsongy divorce ode, "You Better Sit Down Kids," did little to enhance the future congressman's musical credibility. He saves the best for last, "That's Not Home," the most heartfelt song here. The production is excellent throughout, if a little overly reliant on strings. [*Wichita Lineman* was reissued in an upgraded, remastered CD edition in August of 2001 as part of Capitol-Nashville's *Cornerstones* series, with somewhat crisper sound than the 1996 vintage Capitol CD.] *—Bruce Eder*

Galveston / 1969 / Capitol ♦♦♦♦♦
On Glen Campbell's albums—*By the Time I Get to Phoenix* and *Wichita Lineman*—the Jimmy Webb-authored title cuts tended to dominate the LP tracks somewhat; good as the album tracks were, they usually weren't quite up to the standard achieved by the AM-aimed title songs. On *Galveston*, Campbell and producer Al DeLory overcame that problem—the Jimmy Webb title tune is fine, to be sure, but this time out, Campbell and DeLory no longer felt the need for the singer to cover contemporary rock and soul hits like "Homeward Bound" and "Dock of the Bay," which he pulled off, but not as well as some other songs he might've sung on those earlier albums. On *Galveston*, he stuck closer to country with some pop embellishments and found a better fit. The result is a smooth, lively, sentimental, and occasionally even exciting album. Jimmy Webb's "Where's the Playground Susie" was the other hit off this album, but no one needed to think of skipping to it, around such heartfelt Campbell performances as "Gotta Have Tenderness" or "Time"; "Friends," built around the melody to "Danny Boy," may come dangerously close to sinking in mawkishness, but Campbell compensates for it with another co-authored effort, "If This Is Love," a stunning guitar workout with a haunting melody and sincere urgency in his singing; he also shows off his guitar prowess (and the harder side of his voice) on "Oh What a Woman," and to some extent on "Every Time I Itch I Wind Up Scratching You." And he wraps himself very neatly around the New Christy Minstrels' number, "Today," singing it with a directness and honesty that makes one forget the original. It's only 28 minutes long, but it shows off the romantic, the virtuoso, and the country sides of Campbell's persona about as well as any album he ever cut. [*Galveston* was finally reissued on CD in August of 2001 as part of Capitol-Nashville's *Cornerstones* series, remastered in state-of-the-art sound that is a wonder—on "Oh What a Woman," the hardest number here, you get the close thump of the bass, nice and upfront, and crisp guitars, and the rest of the album isn't far behind.] *—Bruce Eder*

True Grit / 1969 / Capitol ♦♦♦

Glen Campbell: Live / 1969 / Trace ♦♦♦
Recorded on July 4, 1969, at *the Garden State Arts Center,* this album is a good one—essentially a live greatest-hits album—but it isn't a completely fair representation of Campbell in concert, since it features an orchestra as well as a group of top L.A. session musicians who would normally not go on tour. Campbell himself was satisfied with the album, which contains all of his best-known numbers up to that point in his career (augmented by numbers like "The Impossible Dream" and "The Lord's Prayer"), except for the orchestra's playing—it seems the idea of orchestral accompaniment to a country-pop concert was new enough that the musicians weren't entirely comfortable at first with the idea. (Out of print.) *—Bruce Eder*

Try a Little Kindness / 1970 / Capitol ♦♦♦

Oh Happy Day / 1970 / Capitol ♦♦♦

The Glen Campbell Goodtime Album / 1970 / Capitol ♦♦♦
A spin-off of the TV show of the same name, this album is a nice representation of what Campbell was about at the time. In addition to the hit on the album (the cover of Conway Twitty's "It's Only Make Believe"), he dips into the Jimmy Webb songbook for two of the tracks. *—Jim Worbois*

Norwood / 1970 / Capitol ♦♦♦

The Last Time I Saw Her / 1971 / Capitol ♦♦♦

☆ **Glen Campbell's Greatest Hits** / 1971 / Capitol ♦♦♦♦♦
It covers the most productive period of his recording career, the years in which Al DeLory's soaring string arrangements, Jimmy Webb's snapshot songs, and the identifiable low-tuned guitars vaulted Campbell to the upper strata of both the country and pop charts. You simply weren't alive if you didn't hear "Wichita Lineman," "Galveston," or "Try a Little Kindness." *—Tom Roland*

Glen Travis Campbell / 1972 / Capitol ♦♦♦

I Knew Jesus (Before He Was a Star) / 1973 / Capitol ♦♦♦
On this album, Campbell became one of the first (and only) artists to cover, and give exposure to, the talents of Kinky Freidman. Overall, not a great album, but certainly an eclectic batch of songs, including songs that had been recent hits by Charlie Rich, Judy Collins, and Olivia Newton-John. *—Jim Worbois*

I Remember Hank Williams / 1973 / Capitol ♦♦
Good intentions should count for something, but the syrupy strings and background singer will make more than one fan comment, "I don't think Hank done it this way." *—Jim Worbois*

Reunion: The Songs Of Jimmy Webb / 1974 / Capitol ♦♦♦♦
It doesn't really matter if Glen Campbell was Jimmy Webb's best interpreter or if Webb gave Campbell his best songs—in other words, it doesn't matter who *helped* the other more—because it doesn't change the essential fact that the duo fit each other so naturally. Webb's intricate, idiosyncratic compositions sounded warm and accessible in Campbell's hands, while the songs revealed Campbell's musical range and ambition. Other singers had big hits with Webb's songs and Campbell made tremendous music with other people's songs, but there was something special about their collaboration that was evident on their big hits of the '60s: "By the Time I Get to Phoenix," "Wichita Lineman," "Galveston," "Where's the Playground, Suzie?" These songs provided the background for *Reunion*, the 1974 album where Campbell and Webb reunited for a set of Webb songs. Well, that's not exactly accurate, since Webb never produced or arranged the hits Campbell had in the '60s, and the record isn't entirely written by Webb, since it features Susan Webb's "About the Ocean" and Lowell George's "Roll Um Easy" (here retitled "Roll Me Easy"). So, this marks the first time that Webb arranged a full album of Campbell's, along with providing the majority of the songs, a move that in many ways made this closer to a Jimmy Webb record than a Glen Campbell LP. Certainly, it favored Webb's idiosyncrasies, particularly his elliptical songs with winding melodies and no straightforward songs. Not a song here outside of "Roll Me Easy" announces itself as a potential single (which very well may be why this tremendous song was added to the play list, particularly as the first single, since it might be the easiest way into the record for most listeners). Since most of the songs share a similar easy midtempo pace and have similar lushly interwoven arrangements, it's not necessarily the most accessible of Campbell's records; it doesn't set out to alienate, it's just that Webb's songs and arrangements call for close listening, which is precisely why it's an album beloved by Campbell/Webb connoisseurs. So, it's not entirely surprising that the record didn't make much of an impression, certainly nothing close to their big hits of the '60s, but rather that it's become a cult item, with some fans regarding it among Campbell's best work. And, in many ways, they're right. *Reunion*

has a quiet power that grows with repeated listenings since it does indeed showcase Webb at his best as songwriter/arranger and Campbell as an interpretive singer. But this is very much a record for the dedicated, those that are already convinced of the strengths of both men, because it reveals its gifts slowly, and even when they're out in the open, the songs are so delicately, if exquisitely, crafted they're best appreciated by listeners with an eye for detail. Those listeners will surely find *Reunion* among Campbell's best work, and it is certainly among his most consistent and ambitious records, but it's just a little too reserved to play to an audience outside of the already converted. —*Stephen Thomas Erlewine*

Houston (I'm Comin' to See You) / 1974 / Capitol ✦✦✦✦

Arkansas / 1975 / Capitol ✦✦✦

☆ **Rhinestone Cowboy** / 1975 / Capitol ✦✦✦✦✦

Early on in *Rhinestone Cowboy*, Glen Campbell sings that he's making his "comeback," a sentiment that can't help but seem to carry an autobiographical heft. While it is true that he was hardly off the charts in the early '70s, the quality of his music was a little inconsistent; the singles were often good, but his albums were burdened with schlock and erratic in quality. He started to break free with a pair of 1974 albums, *Houston (I'm Comin' to See You)* and the Jimmy Webb duet *Reunion*, but it wasn't until 1975's *Rhinestone Cowboy* that he seemed in full control of his talent, delivering a record that stands proudly next to his '60s peaks. Much credit is due to the presence of producers Dennis Lambert and Brian Potter, who help focus Campbell through their own tunes, their expert selection of songs, and their shimmering, high-gloss production that dazzles on the surface but also delivers considerable thematic and musical substance. Throughout the record, there are allusions to Campbell being a country boy stranded in the big city, where he's successful but emotionally adrift. This is most evident on the album's two big hits, "Country Boy (You Got Your Feet in L.A.)" and "Rhinestone Cowboy" itself, but his yearning is underpinned by sad songs like "I'd Build a Bridge," the despairing "We're Over," and a heartbreaking version of Randy Newman's "Marie." Among this, a cheerful cover of the Temptations' "My Girl" seems a little out of place, but this is the only outright misstep in an otherwise masterful album that manages to sound soothing even when it's sad. Even with its undercurrents of melancholy, *Rhinestone Cowboy* sounds and feels like a triumph because of the assured, layered lushness of the Lambert/Potter production and Campbell's fine performances. He sounds engaged by the material, bringing out nuances within the songs, and it's positively a joy to hear after several years of wandering. —*Stephen Thomas Erlewine*

I'll Paint You a Song / 1975 / Pickwick ✦✦✦

Bloodline / 1976 / Capitol ✦✦✦✦✦

Like its immediate predecessor, *Rhinestone Cowboy*, 1976's *Bloodline* is produced by Dennis Lambert and Brian Potter and is something of a very loose concept album, where about half the songs have distinct thematic undercurrents that help bring the record together as a whole. Here, many of the songs address familial situations, whether it's relations between a man and wife or a man and his child. So, the title *Bloodline* does indeed have significance; even if not every song here fits a particular theme, it certainly has an undercurrent of how a man is tied to his kin, his bloodline. While this record didn't produce crossover hits on the level of "Rhinestone Cowboy" or "Country Boy (You Got Your Feet in L.A.)"—only the deliberate pop crossover medley of "Don't Pull Your Love/Then You Can Tell Me Goodbye," easily the weakest moment on the record, reached the Top Ten on either the pop or country charts—*Bloodline* is in many ways stronger than the *Rhinestone Cowboy* album, because it follows through its themes better and has a slightly stronger, or at least more consistent, set of songs. Glen Campbell is at his most effective when he's singing songs that are at least tangentially related to the main theme. Take the two tales of fatherhood: The joint custody epic "See You on Sunday," where he says goodbye to his kid for the weekend, is as heart-wrenching as the fatherly advice in "Christiaan No" is moving. But it's not just the songs that flow into the "bloodline" theme that work—"Everytime I Sing a Love Song," is a lovely ballad and Lambert/Potter's opener, "Baby Don't Be Givin' Me Up," is deceptively cheerful and all the stronger for it. And the same could be said for the album—it's soothing on the surface, but dig deeper, and real pain can be heard, making *Bloodline* one of Campbell's most complex, and best, records. —*Stephen Thomas Erlewine*

The Best of Glen Campbell / 1976 / Capitol ✦✦✦✦✦

This record really does live up to the title. All killer and no filler, covering Campbell's career up through 1976. A nice selection of songs, and it's just right for people who know Campbell for the hits or for someone wanting to get into his music for the first time. —*Jim Worbois*

Southern Nights / 1977 / Capitol ✦✦✦✦

Basic / 1978 / Capitol ✦✦✦

Highwayman / 1979 / Capitol ✦✦

Something 'Bout You Baby I Like / 1980 / Capitol ✦✦

It's the World Gone Crazy / 1981 / Capitol ✦✦

Old Home Town / 1983 / Atlantic ✦✦✦

Letter to Home / 1984 / Atlantic ✦✦✦

Letter to Home features Campbell's hits "Faithless Love," "A Lady like You" and "(Love Always) Letter to Home." —*Jason Ankeny*

It's Just a Matter of Time / 1986 / Atlantic ✦✦

The Best of the Early Years / 1987 / Curb ✦✦✦✦

Best of the Early Years features Campbell staples like "Gentle on My Mind," "By the Time I Get to Phoenix," "Galveston" and "Wichita Lineman." —*Jason Ankeny*

The Very Best of Glen Campbell / Mar. 20, 1987 / Capitol ✦✦✦✦

The Very Best of Glen Campbell features 15 of his biggest hits, from "Gentle on My Mind" and "Wichita Lineman" to "Rhinestone Cowboy," making it the place to get acquainted with Campbell's career. —*Stephen Thomas Erlewine*

Light Years / 1988 / MCA ✦✦✦

The songs of Jimmy Webb constitute the majority of the material found on *Light Years*. —*Jason Ankeny*

Still Within the Sound of My Voice / Aug. 10, 1988 / MCA ✦✦✦

Still Within the Sound of My Voice features the chart hits "I Remember You" (a cover of the Frank Ifield hit), "The Hand That Rocks the Cradle" (a duet with Steve Wariner), and the title cut. —*Jason Ankeny*

Greatest Country Hits / 1990 / Curb ✦✦✦

A hodgepodge of material from the mid-'70s through 1989, this displays a variety of Glen Campbell approaches to country. "She's Gone, Gone, Gone" is twangy enough to do originator Lefty Frizzell justice. "Still Within the Sound of My Voice" catches Campbell at his most sensitive, and "Southern Nights" is just plain fun. —*Tom Roland*

Classics Collection / May 21, 1990 / Liberty ✦✦✦✦

Classics Collection is a comprehensive anthology of Campbell's biggest chart hits from the 1960s ("Wichita Lineman," "By the Time I Get to Houston," "Galveston," "Gentle on My Mind") and 1970s ("Rhinestone Cowboy," "Southern Nights"). —*Jason Ankeny*

Somebody Like That / 1993 / Capitol ✦✦✦

Hey, for a guy who's been around almost forever, Glen Campbell's *Somebody Like That* cooks nicely. Campbell has always has good taste in songwriters and sidemen and his latest upholds this tradition, recruiting material from Paul Overstreet, Naomi Martin, and Billy Burnette, among others. Only a couple of ballads are given schmaltzy arrangements; for the most part the tracks chug along in midtempo, semi-rockabilly fashion. Best bets here are "Swimming Upstream, Ain't It Just Like Love" and (especially) the chorus-kicking title track. For "Love's Old Song," Campbell indulges in some jazzy, country-swing. —*Roch Parisien*

Essential, Vol. 1 / 1995 / Capitol ✦✦✦✦

The first serious attempt to explore the full range of Glen Campbell's legacy on Capitol Records might have worked better in a more coherent and cohesive three- (or four-) CD box than in this strangely disorganized series of three separate CDs. *Vol. 1* of the *Essential* series sets the tone for all three CDs, beautiful remasterings of the hits, some excellent lesser-selling singles and outstanding album tracks, and a handful of unreleased cuts that are, by themselves, worth the price of the disc. There are relatively few major hits here, and one of them, "By the Time I Get to Phoenix," is represented paired with "I Say a Little Prayer for You" in a fine 1971 duet with Anne Murray, but that's what should have made this such a priceless collection—it works the breadth and depth of Campbell's catalog, going all the way back to 1962, and encompasses tracks that showcase both his vocal and instrumental prowess. Thus, in between glowing remasterings of his singles and some notable album tracks covering 17 years of work, you get a brilliant acoustic instrumental workout, "Twelve Blues," showing off Campbell's prodigious guitar skills and his too-little-explored appreciation of the blues, and a rendition of "I Walk the Line" from 1967, in which he handles the song Sinatra-style (and most effectively, one might add); his previously unissued live 1975 rendition of "My Way"; and his poignant, gently swinging version of "Blue Sky Shining," done with the Nelson Riddle Orchestra in 1979. Casual listeners will be surprised by Campbell's range as a singer, while serious fans will simply want to immerse themselves in the contents from the opening note. The only flaw, and it is a big one with this series, is the producers' failure to put the music together in any rational chronological order—a box set could have done it, but the jumping around, from decade to decade and between hits and unissued tracks, on each disc and between the three discs in this series will make some listeners dizzy just trying to decide whether or not to buy each. —*Bruce Eder*

Essential, Vol. 2 / 1995 / Capitol ✦✦✦✦

The track selection of the second in a three-volume series is a little less impressive than its predecessor, mostly because the previously unissued material is less intriguing—the 1971 version of Buddy Holly's "Oh Boy!" is the highlight, a surprisingly hot rendition of the rock & roll standard that shows another side of Campbell's virtuosity; his version of "The Last Thing on My Mind" wouldn't trouble anyone else who's covered the song, and "Don't It Make You Want to Go Home" is about on a par with his released material from 1971, a good but not exceptional or surprising cover of a Joe South song. The rest is an engaging mix of singles, important album cuts, and rarities, such as his version of "Greensleeves" from a limited-edition vinyl release; it's always good to hear Campbell do any Jimmy Webb song, but his live recording of "Macarthur Park" only really catches fire in the last two minutes, where the guitar comes in to provide something unique to the performance. This and the rest all sound very good, and the annotation, despite a few digressions, is fairly thorough—as with the previous volume in the series, however, the seemingly random order of the songs and the intermixing of multimillion-selling hits, album tracks, and outtakes is certain to confuse the casual listener. —*Bruce Eder*

Essential, Vol. 3 / Oct. 10, 1995 / Capitol ✦✦✦✦✦

The third installment of Glen Campbell's *Essential* series features his number-one hit "Wichita Lineman" among a handful of other hit singles and selected rarities. —*Thom Owens*

★ **Glen Campbell Collection (1962-1989): Gentle on My Mind** / Feb. 18, 1997 / Razor & Tie ✦✦✦✦✦

Glen Campbell not only had an enormous number of hit singles, he was also a staple of pop culture, appearing in films and hosting a TV show during the late '60s and early '70s.

Before that, he was a respected studio musician and performer in search of a hit in the early '60s, cutting great singles that nobody heard. All this makes his career difficult to compile, even on a double-disc set with 40 songs, so it shouldn't be a huge surprise that Razor & Tie's 1997 compilation *The Glen Campbell Collection (1962-1989)*, for all its attributes, is heavily flawed. Its biggest problem is its scope; by extending its reach to the end of the '80s, when Campbell was still having hits out of sheer inertia and was far past his peak, the listenability of the second disc nosedives about halfway through. Conversely, there's not enough of his earlier singles, such as his debut, "Universal Soldier," and, most egregiously, the Brian Wilson-written "Guess I'm Dumb," an achingly gorgeous song that is easily as good as any of the classic *Pet Sounds*-era Beach Boys singles. Of course, the heart of this—or any—Glen Campbell collection is the hits he had in the late '60s and early '70s on Capitol Records, when he was a fixture in the country and pop Top Ten with singles like "Wichita Lineman," "Galveston," and "By the Time I Get to Phoenix." They're all here, along with "I Wanna Live," "Dreams of the Everyday Housewife," "Gentle on My Mind," "True Grit," "Where's the Playground Susie," and, on the second disc, "Rhinestone Cowboy," "Country Boy (You Got Your Feet in L.A.)," "Southern Nights," and "Sunflower." At the time of its release in 1997, it was more hits than any other Campbell collection, and it still is a very good cross-section of basics. Where it stumbles is on the selection of smaller hits and album tracks, which are entirely too chart-bound (he had many songs better than some songs that reached the middle of the charts) and sometimes just plain silly and annoying, as in "The William Tell Overture" that closes the first disc. This, combined with the bland adult contemporary material that comprises the second half of the second disc (only "Bloodline" and perhaps "Can You Fool") make this an imperfect collection, but given that most Campbell collections have been a hodgepodge of hits, it's still one of the better discs to make sense of his entire career—especially because the dip in quality toward the end does mirror the arc of his career. But, if you want a two-disc collection of Glen Campbell at his peak, seek out the U.K. collection *Capitol Years: 1965-1977*, which is a much more consistent and pleasing retrospective, with a much better selection of songs. —*Stephen Thomas Erlewine*

Reunited With Jimmy Webb / 1999 / Raven ✦✦✦✦
Reunion With Jimmy Webb is an Australian import that pairs Campbell's complete 1974 album of Jimmy Webb compositions, *Reunion*, with 14 songs from later albums, all of which were also written by Webb. Webb was the songwriter behind some of Campbell's biggest hits, including "Galveston" and "Witchita Lineman," so their collaboration on *Reunion* would seem to have been a commercially promising move. As it turned out, the album wasn't a big seller, although it did spawn the Top 40 country single "It's a Sin (When You Love Somebody)." The liner notes suggest that *Reunion* may be Campbell's finest hour, and although that overstates its excellence, it is a very good, consistent album that sits somewhere between Elton John and John Denver in the country music spectrum. The additional tracks, some of which were recorded as late as 1988, are generally less good, sometimes much less. —*Greg Adams*

★ **Capitol Years: 1965–1977** / Dec. 14, 1999 / EMI ✦✦✦✦
There is no definitive Glen Campbell compilation, but this 130-minute, two-disc set from England comes very close to it, and also forms a perfect complement to Razor & Tie's *Glen Campbell Collection: 1962-1989* (which it overlaps amazingly little). With 46 songs, selected from various singles, starting with Campbell's first pop/rock hit "Universal Soldier" and rarities such as the beautiful flops "Guess I'm Dumb" (co-authored and produced by Brian Wilson) and "Less of Me," along with various album tracks and B-sides, it's as good a cross-section of his sound (including two duets with Bobbie Gentry) and his successes as you can find. What's more, by ranging freely through the hits and the album cuts, it shows off Campbell's strengths in various idioms, from the country-ish "Just Another Man" and the more pop-focused "It's Over," to the brilliant "Reason to Believe" and non-LP sides, such as "You're Young and You'll Forget" sandwiched in between "Wichita Lineman" and Campbell's own "Everytime I Itch I Wind Up Scratching You." "True Grit," the title song of the film in which he co-starred, is very much a piece with the best of his singles from that era, immersed in rich melodic textures, supported by moderately dense orchestration backing a superb vocal performance. Disc two is intriguing for its inclusion of the Jimmy Webb songs Campbell recorded during the early '70s (beginning with "Honey Come Back") that didn't become hits, and which haven't been heard often (if at all) on CD; they make a logical core for the second half of Campbell's Capitol history, and have generally been ignored along with most of that history (other than "Rhinestone Cowboy" and "Southern Nights"), and "As Far As I'm Concerned," "It's Only Make Believe," "Just Another Piece of Paper," "Last Time I Saw Her," and "Dream Sweet Dreams About Me" are among the best sides Campbell ever recorded, and are comparable to his finest work from the 1960s. The sound is crisp, state-of-the-art fidelity circa 1998, which makes it comparable (or superior) to most of the rival compilations out there from American Capitol. The annotation is also reasonably thorough, and the packaging is neat and unpretentious. This British release is worth tracking down, though its virtues are also both sad reflections of the lack of respect with which American Capitol has usually treated Campbell's catalog. —*Bruce Eder*

20 Greatest Hits / Feb. 29, 2000 / Capitol ✦✦✦
This isn't Campbell's greatest hits by any means, a definitive collection of which on one CD has so far eluded Capitol Records. On the other hand, it is a good selection of some of Campbell's most impressive cuts, singles, and album tracks alike, in a multitude of settings and genres: his own most durable hits ("By the Time I Get to Phoenix," "Galveston," "Wichita Lineman," "Rhinestone Cowboy," "Southern Nights"), outstanding covers of other artists' hits ("The Dock of the Bay," "He Ain't Heavy, He's My Brother"), good duets ("Scarborough Fair/Canticle"), and live cuts ("Classical Gas"), in country, pop, rock, and gospel. There's just enough here that will be familiar from the radio that casual fans won't be disappointed, and enough that they would only know from his albums (if they had

them) that it's also a voyage of discovery. This album is worthwhile even for those who already own one of his other compilations—the hard country-rock "Somebody Like That," from 1967, is a punchy, catchy performance that ought to have been a single and could've been another "Gentle on My Mind" with more of an edge, and might've made him a rival to the likes of Johnny Rivers; while his version of "If Not for You," if not as sweetly lyrical as George Harrison's cover, has a lean, easygoing quality and some superb playing on several guitars. The remastering, in high-definition digital audio, doesn't make a world of difference, though it does perhaps bring out details slightly more sharply. In all, this is a fair cross-section of Campbell's work—indeed, if there were, say, a complete Glen Campbell box on Capitol, this might be the perfect sampler for it, representing some of the best of it. —*Bruce Eder*

All-Time Greatest Hits / 2001 / CEMA ✦✦✦
The budget-priced, triple-disc, 35-song set *All-Time Greatest Hits* contains the bulk of Glen Campbell's biggest hits—"Rhinestone Cowboy," "Galveston," "By the Time I Get to Phoenix," "I Wanna Live," "Gentle on My Mind," "Wichita Lineman," "Country Boy (You Got Your Feet in L.A.)," "Southern Nights"—presented in a (non-chronological order and packaged without notes. For a budget-priced collection, *All-Time Greatest Hits* isn't bad—it has most of the hits in their original versions—but it isn't well thought-out. Razor & Tie's double-disc *The Glen Campbell Collection* remains a better overview of Campbell's career, but *All-Time Greatest Hits* is good on its own terms. —*Stephen Thomas Erlewine*

☆ **Rhinestone Cowboy/Bloodline** / Jul. 2, 2002 / Raven ✦✦✦✦✦
Raven's 2002 two-fer reissue of Glen Campbell's 1975 album *Rhinestone Cowboy* and 1976's *Bloodline* is given three bonus tracks and billed as "The Lambert & Potter Sessions 1975-1976," since these two albums were produced (and occasionally written) by Dennis Lambert and Brian Potter and have a distinctive sound unlike many other records in Campbell's catalog. It's not a coincidence that Campbell began working with Lambert and Potter after reuniting with Jimmy Webb for the understated *Reunion*, since this is a logical step forward from Webb's symphonic, intricate compositions. Lambert and Potter weren't as quirky as songwriters or producers, but they had an excellent ear for songs and had grand concepts, helping Campbell build on the excellent *Reunion*, as well as songs like "Houston (I'm Coming to See You)," with these two grandly polished, sweeping records. Sonically and thematically, there's not much separating the two records; they work as companion pieces, almost like two halves of a double album, so they work perfectly as a two-fer. Simply put, these two records are the best Campbell released since the late '60s, when he was delivering records like *Galveston* and *By the Time I Get to Phoenix*, because they work like those albums—they're commercial and catchy, but there is real emotion in their opulent arrangements, along with consistently strong songwriting that makes this music easily enjoyable and quietly moving. And also essential to any country-pop library. [In addition to the two proper albums, this two-fer contains three bonus tracks, two of which are not Lambert/Potter tracks. Of those, "Houston (I'm Comin' to See You)" is clearly a template for their productions, and if "Bonaparte's Retreat" doesn't quite fit sonically, it's still fun. Then, there's the one song they *did* produce, "Record Collector's Dream." It is the greatest song Nick Lowe never wrote, a surging, tongue-in-cheek ode to collecting singles that was tucked away on a B-side until its glorious appearance here—it's the icing on the cake for this great two-fer.] —*Stephen Thomas Erlewine*

All the Best / Jan. 28, 2003 / Capitol ✦✦✦✦
With 25 tracks and a running time of over 70 minutes, this Glen Campbell compilation lives up to its name, as long as you believe that Campbell's best consists of his pop singles hits. There are of the 21 recordings he placed in the *Billboard Hot* 100 for Capitol Records included. (The missing are "Can You Fool" (number 38) and "Oh Happy Day" (number 40).) Of course, Campbell was an even bigger country star than he was a pop star, but this collection focuses on the tracks that became pop crossover hits. Also included are of his 39 singles to reach the Top 40 on *Billboard*'s country chart. Among the 15 not included are such Top Ten entries as "Bonaparte's Retreat" and "Manhattan Kansas," which failed to cross over pop. The one track on the album that made neither chart is Campbell's version of Jimmy Webb's "Highwayman," cut before it became a number-one country hit for the quartet of Waylon Jennings, Willie Nelson, Johnny Cash, and Kris Kristofferson, later dubbed "the Highwaymen" after the record. The album's sequencing pushes Campbell's biggest hits and best-remembered recordings—"Rhinestone Cowboy," "Galveston," "Wichita Lineman," "By the Time I Get to Phoenix," "Gentle on My Mind," and "Southern Nights"—up to the front, thus satisfying the desires of more casual fans. Country fans and those who have a deeper interest in the singer may find the result inadequate, but if you only want to have one Glen Campbell album in your collection, this is it. —*William Ruhlmann*

Stacy Dean Campbell

b. Jul. 27, 1967, Carlsbad, NM
Vocals / Contemporary Country
Singer/songwriter Stacy Dean Campbell was first inspired to become a musician by his father Buddy, a gospel singer. Raised by his grandparents in Carlsbad, NM, he grew up enamored of the music of Marty Robbins, whose smooth crooning influenced Campbell's own vocal style. Encouraged by his brother Spencer, himself a professional musician, Campbell moved to Nashville to pursue a career in country, and soon earned a songwriting contract with Tree Music. In 1992, he released his debut solo record, *Lonesome Wins Again*; the follow-up, the eclectic *Hurt City*, appeared in 1995. —*Jason Ankeny*

● **Lonesome Wins Again** / Feb. 1992 / Columbia ✦✦✦✦✦
Sexy, low-key rockabilly (like Chris Isaak but not as spooky), this album includes the singles "Rosalee," "Baby Don't You Know," and "Poor Man's Rose." —*Brian Mansfield*

Hurt City / Jul. 25, 1995 / Sony ✦✦✦

Ashes of Old Love / Apr. 13, 1999 / Warner Bros. ♦♦♦
Stacy Dean Campbell's third album, *Ashes of Old Love*, reaffirms his position as a contemporary singer/songwriter in the classic American mold. "Makin' Good Time," "Gone by Now" and "All the Winters We've Known," along with eight other tracks, feature Campbell's working-class poetic lyrics, yearning voice and adept playing. His appeal may be subtle, but as *Ashes of Old Love* shows, his talent is obvious. *—Heather Phares*

Ray Campi

b. 1934, New York
Bass, Guitar, Vocals / Rock & Roll, Rockabilly, Rockabilly Revival
Rockabilly wildman Ray Campi recorded several classic singles during the music's prime era, and later staged a comeback that earned him a substantial cult audience over the '70s and '80s. Campi was born in New York in 1934 and moved with his family to Austin, TX, at age ten. He started listening to country music, learned the guitar, and formed his first band in high-school, which played on local radio stations. Campi made his first recordings in 1951, but it wasn't until 1956, when he cut the single "Caterpillar" b/w "Play It Cool" for the small TNT label, that any of them were released. He went on to record for Domino ("Screamin' Mimi") and Dot ("The Ballad of Donna & Peggy Sue"), and moved to Los Angeles in 1959, where he signed with Colpix and recorded "Hear What I Wanna Hear."

During the early '60s, Campi lived in New York and spent two and a half years as a staff writer at Aaron Schroeder's publishing firm, but was never allowed to record any of the songs he'd written. He returned to Austin in 1967 and recorded "Civil Disobedience" for the Sonobeat label, but nothing came of it, and he settled in Los Angeles and became a junior-high-school teacher. Around 1973, Campi hooked up with Ronny Weiser's revivalist Rollin' Rock label and started making new recordings in the classic, high-energy rockabilly style. A steady stream of albums followed into the '80s, which also brought a couple of sets for Rounder, 1980's *Rockin' at the Ritz* and 1986's *Gone, Gone, Gone!* Campi continued to record into the new millennium, releasing occasional albums on his own label. *—Steve Huey*

Rockabilly Rebellion / 1981 / Rollin' Rock ♦♦♦
Rockabilly Rebellion is an excellent summation of Ray Campi's latter-day recordings for Rollin' Rock in the late '70s, including such cuts as "Eager Boy" and "Tore Up." *—Thom Owens*

● **Gone, Gone, Gone!** / Oct. 1986 / Rounder ♦♦♦♦

Perpetual Stomp: 1951–1996 / Nov. 12, 1996 / Bacchus ♦♦♦
Perpetual Stomp: 1951-1996 combines 16 tracks that represent Ray Campi's honky tonk and rockabilly sound recorded throughout his career. While Campi has recorded way more material than this disc could possibly cover, this collection gives you a good idea of his overall sound. Along with Campi originals, his choice of covers penned by Chuck Berry, Richard M. Jones, Hank Ballard, and Floyd Tillman gives you a pretty good idea of where he is coming from musically. If you can find them, any of Campi's recordings for Rockin' Ronny Weiser's Rollin' Rock label from the '70s are definitely worth checking into. *—Al Campbell*

Train Rhythm Blue / Jan. 13, 1998 / Mouthpiece ♦♦♦
Ray Campi returns back to California, where he cut all those Rollin' Rock records in the '70s, gets together with a bunch of old friends, and seemingly picks up right where he left off with this spirited session. Everything is firmly in the rockabilly '50s country mold, and the core band of Campi on upright bass, Rip Masters on piano, D.J. Bonebrake on drums and producer Skip Heller on guitar provides a solid backdrop throughout. Guest turns from Dave Alvin, Stan Ridgway, Sheryl Farber, Tony Gilkyson, Greg Leisz, and Michael Dubin keep the proceedings full of surprises and fuel tracks like "Lorena," "The One Who Got Away," "Luther Plated Guitar," "Burning In Water, Drowning in Flame" and "Little Love Lies." A solid modern-day rockabilly and roots music session. *—Cub Koda*

Ace Cannon

b. May 5, 1934, Grenada, MS
Instrumental, Saxophone, Session Musician / Country-Pop, Nashville Sound/Countrypolitan, Memphis Soul, Soul, R&B
One of Nashville's premier session men from the late '50s through the early '70s, alto saxophonist Ace Cannon began playing at the age of ten and signed with Sun Records during the early days of rock & roll. He performed with Billy Lee Riley and Brad Suggs but then in 1959 joined the original Bill Black Combo, recording for the Hi label. He stayed with the band until 1961, when he made his solo chart debut with the instrumental "Tuff," which made it to the country Top 20. This in turn was followed by a Top 40 hit, "Blues (Stay Away From Me)," and a minor hit for the Santos label, "Sugar Blues." He had two more hits in the mid-'60s with "Cotton Fields" and "Searchin'," both recorded for Hi. A decade later, he became the subject of the 1974 documentary film, *Ace's High*. After moving to Nashville in the mid-'70s, Cannon's version of "Blue Eyes Crying in the Rain" became a minor hit and was nominated for the Best Country Instrumental Performance Grammy that year. Cannon continued to perform into the '90s and frequently toured with such legends of early rock & roll as Carl Perkins. *—Sandra Brennan*

Aces High/Plays the Great Show Tunes / Nov. 20, 1995 / Hi ♦♦♦♦
Two early albums from Ace Cannon, *Aces High* and *Plays the Great Show Tunes*, were reissued on one CD by HI Records in 1995. Although each record has its share of weak spots, they remain infectious and enjoyable, and this disc is worth seeking out for any hardcore fan of Cannon or early-'60s rock & roll and R&B. *—Stephen Thomas Erlewine*

Tuff Sax/Moanin' Sax / Nov. 20, 1995 / Hi ♦♦♦
An early album from Ace Cannon, *Moanin' Sax*, was reissued on the same CD with a latter-day record, *Ruff Sax*, by Hi Records in 1995. Although each record has its share of weak spots, they remain infectious and enjoyable, with the former leaning toward early-'60s rock & roll and R&B and the latter leaning toward '70s funk, disco and soul. The two musical styles on the disc don't necessarily sit well together, but both albums have been out of print for years, so their reappearance on disc is welcome. *—Stephen Thomas Erlewine*

Unsafe Sax / Jan. 1, 1996 / King ♦♦
Ace Cannon's *Unsafe Sax* contains several familiar sax hits—including "Tuff," "Fever," "Honky Tonk" and "Raunchy"—but at eight tracks, it's too skimpy even to justify its budget price. *—Stephen Thomas Erlewine*

The Best of Ace Cannon / Nov. 19, 1996 / Curb ♦♦♦
The Best of Ace Cannon contains pleasant but unexceptional '90s re-recordings of Ace Cannon's biggest hits, including "Tuff" and "Blue Eyes Crying in the Rain," plus versions of standards like "Tennessee Waltz" and "Georgia on My Mind." *—Stephen Thomas Erlewine*

● **The Best of Ace Cannon: The Hi Records Years** / Apr. 10, 2001 / Hi ♦♦♦♦
On this 18-song best-of, the chronological and stylistic breadth is a little—not much—greater than you'd suspect, starting with his biggest single, 1961's "Tuff," and going all the way up to 1971. Most of the time, the saxophonist was content to grind out slow to medium shuffles with repetitive riffs and simple R&B-pop hooks, occasionally using organ, much in the style of his labelmates Bill Black's Combo (with whom Cannon sometimes played sax). Like Black, Cannon's singles were good jukebox fare, sometimes selling a lot to the specific jukebox market even when they didn't chart. (And often they didn't chart; only three singles besides "Tuff" made the Top 100, all of them included here.) The formula was simplistic and sometimes monotonous, especially when piled right after the other. However, his grooves were tight, and in the unavoidable Cannon-Black comparisons, Cannon comes out on top, simply because his instrumentals were more soulful and just a bit grittier. Toward the end of the 1960s, too, he unexpectedly got into a tougher bag that was explicitly derivative of fellow Memphians Booker T. & the MG's, but was actually pretty well done. It made for an improved sound, anyway, on cuts like "Funny (How Time Slips Away)," the downright funky "Soul for Sale," and "If I Had a Hammer" (yes, the old Peter, Paul & Mary folk hit). The 1971 cover of Joe Liggins' "Drunk" is, again unexpectedly, quite creditable funk, and only number here to feature vocals, done in a suitably phlegmy manner. *—Richie Unterberger*

Judy Canova

b. 1916, Jacksonville, FL, **d.** 1983
Vocals / Yodeling, Novelty, Country-Pop, Pop, Vocal Pop, Americana, Western Swing
Judy Canova is best remembered today as a comic actress, but she cut her share of records from the early '30s and into the end of the '50s. As either actress or singer, however, she was a most unlikely success story. She was born Juliette Canova in Jacksonville, FL, in 1916. By the time she was 12, she and her sister, Diane, and brother, Leon, were performing together and she had adopted the stage name Judy. The trio, known as the Three Georgia Crackers, told jokes and sang songs on the radio in Jacksonville, which led to bookings for nightclub performances in New York. The trio was signed to the American Record Company in 1931, cutting hillbilly novelty songs, and later appeared in a Broadway revue entitled *Calling All Stars*.

Judy Canova always stood out; she was very tall, with a wide-eyed expression seemingly impressed upon her face. This made her ideal as a future foil in comedy sketches, but not attractive in the conventional sense. She tried studying classical singing only to discover that she lacked the fundamental vocal equipment needed for that repertory. She then decided to take advantage of the one gift she did have—a loud voice.

Following *Calling All Stars*, she made her debut onscreen as a Warner Bros. contract player, specializing in comedic material. The most notable of these early appearances was in the film *In Caliente*, doing a comical rendition of the then-current hit "The Lady in Red" under the direction of Busby Berkeley. Then it was back to Broadway to the *Ziegfeld Follies*, and then more work with her brother and sister. The trio even made it onto television before the decade was out. They were likely the first country group to perform in the new medium, courtesy of NBC's experimental broadcasting in 1939. Canova had played bit parts in movies like *Thrill of a Lifetime* (starring Betty Grable and Dorothy Lamour) and *Artists and Models* (with Jack Benny and Ida Lupino). These were walk-ons, however, and nothing better came along from the major studios. Then in 1940, she received an offer of a contract from Republic Pictures, the biggest of Hollywood's "B" movie studios. Republic specialized in producing high-quality serials and entertaining low-budget comedies, Westerns, and action films.

Her first film for Republic, *Scatterbrain*, gave Canova star billing, and this was her breakthrough. She proved a sympathetic figure on the screen, the kind of persona audiences loved to root for. *Sis Hopkins* followed and was the movie that cemented her image. Canova played an innocent good-natured country waif new to the big city, whose honesty and fortitude allowed her to triumph over the more sophisticated people around her. She made 13 movies for Republic in 15 years, never veering from the role of the corn-fed Cinderella. She often worked opposite the likes of such then-popular comedians as Jerry Colonna and Joe E. Brown, and her co-stars included up-and-coming players like Susan Hayward.

Canova also took advantage of her singing voice and her yodelling, both onscreen and in the recording studio. During the early '40s, she was signed to RCA/Victor and she later also cut sides for the OKeh, Mercury, and Varsity labels. She also got her own radio program, *the Judy Canova Show* on CBS, beginning in 1943, which proved even more successful than her movies. In 1945, the program moved to NBC and became one of the Top Ten most popular radio shows in the country, drawing 18-million listeners at the peak of her career. A mix of country comedy and music, Canova's program was the forerunner to television series such as *the Beverly Hillbillies*. There was a serious, patriotic side to her work during World War II, when one of her most popular numbers was her show-closer, a version of the Patsy Montana song "Good Night Soldier." She also sold a lot of War Bonds and entertained thousands of soldiers.

Canova's radio show ended in 1953 and she never made the jump to television. She preferred doing guest appearances in the new medium, in between engagements in Las Vegas and other personal appearances. Her last film performance was in the 1960 feature *Huckleberry Finn* and she was seldom seen after that, apart from rare guest spots on shows such as *Pistols 'N Petticoats* in the 1960s, in which she again exploited her hillbilly persona. Her daughter Diana, born in 1953, emerged as an actress in the late '70s with appearances on shows like *Happy Days*, before getting starring roles in *Soap* and *I'm a Big Girl Now.* Judy Canova died in 1983 after a long battle with cancer. Her movies aren't shown very much anymore, even on television, but there's no mistaking the tall, big-voiced country girl, a unique persona in movies and music for three decades. *—Bruce Eder*

● **Judy Canova** / 1958 / Simitar ♦♦♦
Canova's only full-length LP, reissued on CD in 1998, is an amazing musical document, not only for its quality but the range of styles that she embraces. One suspects that this must have been what her Las Vegas shows were like, covering a wide range of songs and styles. With guitar virtuoso Speedy West and master fiddler Harold Hensley in her backing band, she plays it straight, doing credible versions of "Wabash Cannon Ball," "Wabash Blues," "Just Because," "The Butcher's Boy," and "Ain't Gonna Grieve No More," but she also does a superb job with the torch song "I Don't Know Why (I Just Do)" and the lullaby "Go to Sleep Little Baby." Canova proves equally adept at the boisterous and the sultry, and the sound is quite fine, well-separated stereo that gives good detail to the playing without compromising on the singer's presence. *—Bruce Eder*

Collectors Edition / Feb. 24, 1998 / Simitar ♦♦♦

Laura Cantrell

b. Nashville, TN
Guitar, Vocals / Neo-Traditionalist Country
Possessing a bright clear voice that combines the vulnerability of a young girl with the intelligence and resilience of a grown woman, Laura Cantrell burst onto the international music scene in 2000 with a debut album that showcased her affecting vocals, literate songwriting, and superb taste in musicians and fellow songwriters. Cantrell, however, had followed a rather unusual path to become one of the new favorites of Americana—she moved from her home in Tennessee to New York City, studied law and accounting in college, and juggles a career in finance with her busy sidelines as a musician and disc jockey.

Laura Cantrell was born and raised in Nashville, TN; her father was a lawyer (in time, he earned a seat with the Tennessee Court of Appeals), and she initially intended to follow suit. However, as a teenager she developed a keen interest in music, and before leaving Tennessee at attend Columbia University, she landed a summer job as a tour guide at the Country Music Hall of Fame. The job sparked an interest in classic country sounds of the '30s, '40s, and '50s, and while at Columbia she became involved in student radio, hosting a show in which she spun country sounds both old and new, as well as immersing herself in the alternative rock scene. Cantrell discovered she liked to sing, and began making occasional club appearances with her many musically inclined friends; she also made her recording debut in 1990, singing backup on a single by Bricks, a lo-fi collaboration between Mac McCaughan of Superchunk and Andrew Webster of Tsunami. Cantrell's interest in radio led to her landing her own show on New Jersey's WFMU-FM, one of America's best regarded free-form radio stations, and on Radio Thrift Shop Cantrell won a large and loyal audience playing classic country, folk, and singer/songwriter recordings as well as her favorite artists from New York's burgeoning alt-country scene.

In 1996, Cantrell released her first solo recording, a locally distributed EP called *Hello*; by this time, Cantrell was supporting her enthusiasm for music by working in the New York offices of Bank of America, where she rose to the position of Vice President of Equity Research (making her that rare musician who can actually understand an accounting statement from her record company). In 1999, Cantrell recorded her first album, *Not the Tremblin' Kind*, which was produced by Jay Sherman-Godfrey, a former member of New York-based honky tonk rockers the World Famous Blue Jays (whose leader, Jeremy Tepper, is also Cantrell's husband). Released by a small Scottish label, Spit & Polish Records, *Not the Tremblin' Kind* soon received a stack of rave reviews, most notably from legendary British disc jockey John Peel, who called it "my favorite record from the last ten years, and possibly my life." Tepper's "rig rock" label Diesel Only Records released the album stateside in 2000, and Cantrell quickly began balancing tour dates and recording sessions with her careers in finance and radio. (Cantrell, describing music as "insanely expensive," has yet to quit her day job, despite her growing success in music.) Cantrell's second album, *When the Roses Bloom Again*, followed in 2002; to support its release, Cantrell toured Europe and the U.S. opening for another noted fan of her records, Elvis Costello. *—Mark Deming*

Not the Tremblin' Kind / Oct. 10, 2000 / Diesel Only ♦♦♦♦
Laura Cantrell's debut album, *Not the Tremblin' Kind*, is a mix of originals and covers by little known yet superb songwriters like George Usher, Joe Flood, Amy Allison, and the Volebeats' Bob McCreedy—resulting in an evocative blend of neo-traditionalist country. As a singer, Cantrell doesn't have the pipes of a someone like Lucinda Williams, but, like Merle Haggard, her clear and simple way with a tale or sentiment leaves the listener hanging on every word. Cantrell's own "Queen of the Coast" tells the story of a female country singer from a bygone era who stands toward the back of a stage while her man basks in the spotlight. (Think Bonnie Owens: The mandolin line even slyly echoes one-time husband Haggard's signature "I Am a Lonesome Fugitive.") The era the song nods to is also expressive of Cantrell's sound, which is of clearly different stock than the high drama of alt-country young lion Neko Case or the good-natured folkyness of predecessor Nanci Griffith. Rather, Cantrell's music echoes a truck-stop jukebox circa the 1950s or '60s and such woman pioneers as Kitty Wells. Also, Cantrell's work as a DJ at famed free-form station WFMU allowed her to cull the finest tracks that crossed her turntable, and her ear for the right tunes to cover is clearly evident. On her heart-piercing take on the Volebeats' "Two Seconds," her plaintive voice is used to excellent effect, driving home the primary sentiment, "Two seconds of your love is all I need of you/two seconds of your time, that's enough to say we're through/two beats of your heart is enough to know we'll never part." Another great cover is Amy Allison's "Whiskey Makes You Sweeter," which Cantrell delivers with the poise of a woman who won't make the same mistake twice—rather than the sloppy, temporary regret the song might suggest. Solid production by World Famous Blue Jays member Jay Sherman-Godfrey and strong musicianship make this first-class, enduring Americana—with one foot in the past and an eye towards the future. *—Erik Hage*

● **When the Roses Bloom Again** / 2002 / Diesel Only ♦♦♦♦♦
With her debut, *Not the Tremblin' Kind*, Brooklynite Laura Cantrell quietly made a great little Americana album that earned kudos across the board. The effort also found Cantrell, an award-winning DJ at New Jersey's famed WFMU who knows her way around a record collection, championing tracks by little-known yet top-notch songwriters. Expect more of the same from *When the Roses Bloom Again*; Cantrell has completely sidestepped the sophomore jinx with a wonderful album that builds upon the strengths of her debut. Listeners may be familiar with the title track (adapted from traditional lyrics) through the Wilco/Billy Bragg collaboration that finally surfaced on the *Chelsea Walls* soundtrack in early 2002. Cantrell steers away from the rolling drama of that rendering, however, opting instead for a more subtle approach that emphasizes her plaintive delivery and is bolstered by mandolin, fiddle, and stark percussion. And Cantrell's version is just as heart-rending. Cantrell is no vocal powerhouse, but she has found a way—much like Merle Haggard—to use her gifts to maximum effect. One hangs on every word and each phrase is a clarion call to sincerity. This album also finds Cantrell once again paying fine tribute to songwriter Joe Flood; the upbeat, Byrdsy performance of Flood's "All the Same to You" is one of the finest tracks here. Just as with her lauded radio show, the listener is in good hands with this album; Cantrell mixes classic country sensibility, pop chops, and a great taste in tunes to stirring effect. *—Erik Hage*

Henson Cargill

b. Feb. 5, 1941, Oklahoma City, OK
Vocals, Songwriter / Traditional Country, Nashville Sound/Countrypolitan
Henson Cargill had tried his hand at being a lawyer, rancher, and deputy sheriff before settling on country music as a career after returning to Oklahoma from Colorado State University. He began playing local bars and was asked to join the Kimberlys by their leader, Harold Gay. Cargill went to Nashville in the mid-'60s and, after auditioning for different labels, signed with Fred Foster at Monument in 1967. Foster teamed Henson with producer Don Law to record the Jack Moran song "Skip a Rope." The single was a tremendous success and not only topped the country charts for five weeks, but also crossed over to the Top 25 on the pop charts. During 1968-1969, Henson went on to have two more Top 20 country hits, including "None of My Business."

In 1969, he also began hosting Avco Broadcasting's syndicated show *Country Hayride* and recorded steadily for the next few years. In 1971, the single "The Most Uncomplicated Good-Bye I've Ever Heard" hit the Top 20, and two years later he recorded two Top 30 hits, including "Some Old California Memory." Cargill's next hit, however, was over six years in coming. Finally, in 1979, "Silence on the Line" made the Top 30. Cargill eventually left Nashville and returned to Oklahoma, but continued to perform sporadically. During the 1980s and '90s, Cargill was a fixture on the Las Vegas/Reno casino entertainment circuit. In 2003, he issued *All American Cowboy* through his website. The double album featured re-recorded versions of hits like "Skip a Rope," as well as new material. *—Johnny Loftus*

● **Skip a Rope** / 1968 / Monument ♦♦♦♦
The title song of this album is the only song this particular country artist is really known for, and anyone that has heard it will probably not forget it. It wouldn't have been possible as a radio hit in any other era but the '60s, the age of the cynical anti-hero. It was a bitter sounding, haunting country song about hypocrisy that was not written by Cargill, but suggested he might be a performer who would have an interesting career ahead of him. According to the liner notes, Cargill got the song from a batch available from the big country publisher Tree Music and financed the recording sessions himself. When the song took off and the label was ready to put out a whole album, the producer seems to have sandbagged Cargill right off the bat by having him cover three, and that is three too many, blockbuster hits of the day. The album needed better material than this to really standup and although there are a few pretty good tracks, nothing is anywhere near the level of the mighty "Skip a Rope." *—Eugene Chadbourne*

Coming on Strong / 1969 / Monument ♦♦♦

None of My Business / 1969 / Monument ♦♦♦♦
Henson Cargill's biggest hit was the gritty "Skip a Rope," which struck a socially conscious pose that seemed more activist in the context of 1960s country music than it actually was. The title track from *None of My Business* attempted to exploit the formula anew, but apparently the country audience found the pro-family and traditional morality message of "Skip a Rope" more appealing than the paean to political involvement in "None of My Business," since the song came nowhere close, sales-wise, to "Skip a Rope." Nevertheless, "None of My Business" reached the Top Ten and was Cargill's only other major hit. The corresponding album reinforces Cargill's soon-to-be-abandoned image as a maker of message-oriented country songs, with covers of Glen Campbell's self-improvement masterpiece "Less of Me" and Roger Miller's anti-divorce lament "Husbands and Wives." The anthemic "This Generation Shall Not Pass" was a minor hit for Cargill, and one of his last attempts at explicit message-oriented music. Elsewhere, the album aims for wide appeal with "Welcome to My World" and Kenny Price's "Walking on New Grass," but the semi-political songs are ultimately the most interesting ones. *—Greg Adams*

This Is Henson Cargill Country / 1974 / Atlantic ♦♦♦

Bob Carlin

b. Mar. 17, 1953, New York, NY

Banjo / Traditional Bluegrass, Old-Timey

Bob Carlin was one of the best old-time banjo pickers in country music, unique in that he played in the old clawhammer style with a few personalized twists. But Carlin was also a noted folk-music expert who coordinated numerous field recordings. He also wrote and produced respected documentary albums and radio programs on numerous subjects related to American roots music, and started his own label, CarTunes Records.

Carlin was born in New York City; growing up during the folk revival, he was inspired by the banjo at age five when he saw Pete Seeger in concert. Later he began studying blues guitar with other aspiring folk musicians, including Roy Book Binder. He took up the banjo at age 16 and eventually became the protégé of Hank Sapoznick, who in 1977 appeared with Carlin on his debut album, *Melodic Clawhammer Banjo.* Later he began studying music under two Appalachian masters, Tommy Jarrell and Fred Cockerham. He and Sapoznick then joined the Delaware Water Gap String Band and recorded a broad range of music that included reggae and swing.

In 1980, Carlin left the group to launch a solo career. He signed to Rounder in 1981 and released *Fiddle Tunes for Clawhammer Banjo.* He made two more albums for Rounder before moving to the Merrimac label, where he recorded *Take Me as I Am* (1990) and *Mr. Spaceman* (1992). An active participant in trying to save the oldest traditional songs, between 1983-1985 Carlin produced a 12-part documentary, *Our Musical Heritage,* for PBS radio. In 1988, Carlin recorded the *Library of Congress Banjo Collection* and later *The Banjo on Folkways, Vols. 1 & 2* (1992). He also lectured and offered workshops, spending much of the early '90s researching a comprehensive history of the banjo's place in American music. He continued to record, both as a solo artist and accomplished sideman, appearing with John Hartford and Dolly Parton, among others. In 2003 he compiled and produced *Songs and Ballads of the Bituminous Miners* for the Library of Congress. *—Johnny Loftus*

● **Fun of Open Discussion** / Jan. 17, 1995 / Rounder ✦✦✦✦

Bob Carlin plays banjo in the old-timey clawhammer style, and John Hartford has a scratchy, laconic fiddle technique that sounds like it was formed on the humid, mossy banks of the Mississippi River that he loves so much. The disc's title is apt: This album is the musical equivalent of two guys chatting over a beer. There are no rip-roaring displays of virtuosity in this collection; instead, Carlin and Hartford linger lovingly over a set of midtempo numbers, mostly traditional but some composed by Hartford and one an Irish tune by Turlough O'Carolan. Chestnuts like "Shortenin' Bread" and "Dry and Dusty" nestle next to such obscure fare as "Lantern in the Ditch" and "Bull at the Wagon." Carlin's playing is not quite as down-home traditional as you might expect—his strict melodic style is an old-sounding modern innovation. Banjo players who covet his licks will wish the banjo were more clearly recorded, but that's the only flaw on this wonderful record. *—Rick Anderson*

Banging and Sawing / 1996 / Rounder ✦✦✦

As melodic clawhammer banjo players go, Bob Carlin is certainly one of the most compulsive; it's hard to think of another banjoist who goes to such pains to make sure he plays every note in the melody. Sometimes groove gets sacrificed in the pursuit of that vision, and when you're playing with a fiddler you need to be able to groove—as neat as melodic-style banjo is, something sounds wrong if the banjo completely abdicates its percussive function. But Carlin does usually have fun, and he sounds like he's having a blast on this generously augmented reissue of his 1985 solo album. Most of the tracks are just banjo and fiddle, though a few feature guitarists as well (including the redoubtable Norman Blake). That leads to a certain sameness of texture, a sameness that Carlin and John Hartford overcame on their duo album, *The Fun of Open Discussion,* with sheer humor and good-naturedness; here that same personality comes through on tracks like "Big Footed Man in the Sandy Lot" and "Far in the Mountain," but on others, he settles for mere virtuosity. Recommended with reservations. *—Rick Anderson*

Bill Carlisle

b. Dec. 19, 1908, Wakefield, KY, **d.** Mar. 17, 2003

Guitar, Vocals / Traditional Country, Cowboy

Yodeling singer/songwriter/guitarist Bill Carlisle was the younger brother of popular 1930s country singer Cliff Carlisle. During the '30s, Bill established himself as an expert purveyor of racy, blues-tinged country songs, but during the '50s and '60s, he was best-known for his novelty songs as he and his family band, the Carlisles, became regulars on the *Grand Ole Opry.*

The brothers performed as part of a Carlisle family group on Louisville radio in the 1920s in an early manifestation of the barn-dance format. Brother Cliff gave Carlisle his start as a soloist in 1933 by letting him sit in on an audition at the ARC label. His first single, "Rattlesnake Daddy," became quite popular and later evolved into a bluegrass favorite. Dubbed "Smilin' Bill" by publicists, Carlisle was noted for his precise and extremely fast runs on the guitar. Eventually Bill became almost as popular as his older brother, with whom he shared a talent for yodeling and a tendency to sing songs filled with risqué double entendres, such as "Copper Head Mama" (1934) and "Jumpin' and Jerkin' Blues" (1935). The Carlisle brothers signed with Decca in 1938 and built outward from the blues/Hawaiian core they had established around Cliff Carlisle's pioneer dobro stylings. During a long stint on Knoxville radio station WNOX, they became stars of two barn-dance programs, and Bill continued to appear on other stations around the Southeast as a solo artist.

After World War II, the Carlisle brothers signed with the upstart King label, based in Cincinnati, scoring a giant hit with a cover of Ernest Tubb's wartime classic "Rainbow at Midnight" in 1946. Two years later, Bill had his own Top 15 hit with "Tramp on the Street." Cliff eventually retired around 1950, and Bill then organized the Carlisles, a group that despite its family moniker actually included a succession of unrelated individuals, gospel singer Martha Carson and songwriter Betty Amos among them. Carlisle also performed with several 1950s stars in the early stages of their careers—Don Gibson, Chet Atkins, and Homer & Jethro, among others. It was during these performances that he began to leap about on-stage and develop his comical alter ego, Hotshot Elmer, a character he had created earlier in his career. As Elmer, Carlisle would interrupt performances by jumping over chairs, falling off the stairs, and creating general mayhem on-stage. Carlisle's trademark athletic leaps earned him the nickname "Jumpin' Bill."

The scene was set for the recordings that brought Carlisle his greatest renown in the 1950s: a series of novelty songs, delightfully off-center gospel pieces like "Rusty Old Halo," and straight-country harmony numbers recorded for the Mercury label. The first, "Too Old to Cut the Mustard," hit the Top Ten in 1952 and was covered by Rosemary Clooney and other pop artists. The 1950s were much less friendly to lyrics of sexual tension than were the decades in which Carlisle began his career, but "Too Old to Cut the Mustard" was one of several of Carlisle's numbers (another was the "The Old Knot Hole") that evoked the styles of a more tolerant era. "No Help Wanted" climbed to number one the following year and stayed there five weeks. That year he had three more hits, all of which made it to the Top Ten, including the Ira Louvin song "Taint Nice (To Talk Like That)." Though seemingly striking an old-fashioned pose in their cornball humor, these recordings crackled with an energy in tune with the stirrings of what became rock & roll; they featured sharp electric guitar solos and such instrumental novelties as a bass saxophone. This string of successes led the *Opry* to invite the Carlisles aboard in 1953. Carlisle's children joined his band in the 1960s, and he had another hit in 1965 with "What Kind of Deal Is This." Carlisle was a fixture of the *Opry* in later years, performing there up until ten days before his death on March 17, 2003. *—James Manheim*

On Stage With the Carlisles / 1958 / Mercury ✦✦✦✦

Carlisle Family: Old Time Great Hymns / 1965 / Old Homestead ✦✦✦

● **The Best of Bill Carlisle** / 1966 / Hickory ✦✦✦✦✦

Jumpin' Bill Carlisle / 1983 / Brylen ✦✦✦

Cliff Carlisle

b. May 6, 1904, Taylorsville, KY, **d.** Apr. 2, 1983, Lexington, KY

Guitar, Vocals / Cowboy, Country Blues

White country bluesman Cliff Carlisle was among the most prolific recording artists of the 1930s; a blue yodeler in the tradition of Jimmie Rodgers, he helped pioneer the popularity of the Hawaiian steel guitar in country music, while the ribald imagery of his material established him among the wittiest and most reckless composers of his day. Born in Taylorsville, KY, on May 6, 1904, as a child Carlisle was enamored of the Hawaiian guitar recordings of Frank Ferera, and eventually placed a steel nut under the strings of his own guitar to achieve a similar sound. Rural blues was also an early influence, and while working on his family's farm he also absorbed the inspiration of old-time string bands and sacred songs; he began his performing career at the age of 16, performing socials and local talent contests alongside a cousin, Lillian Truax. After Truax's marriage disbanded the duo, in 1924 Carlisle began collaborating with Wilbur Ball, a construction worker who also played guitar and sang tenor harmony; over the course of the decade to follow, the duo regularly toured the vaudeville and tent show circuit, performing across the country as quite possibly the first blue yodeling duet team.

In 1930, Carlisle and Ball debuted on Louisville radio WHAS, a fledgling station their popularity helped establish; that same year Carlisle made his first recordings on the Gennett and Champion labels, virtually all of them firmly in the tradition of Jimmie Rodgers. In 1931, he and Ball actually recorded with the Singing Brakeman himself; that same year Carlisle also cut "Shanghai Rooster Yodel," the first in a series of ribald barnyard-themed outings that served him throughout his career, and might have influenced similar tracks by Charley Patton ("Banty Rooster Blues") and Howlin' Wolf ("Little Red Rooster"). Upon signing to ARC in late 1931, Carlisle's career truly took flight, as he landed a regular spot on Charlotte, NC, station WBT, followed by subsequent gigs at Chicago's WLS and Cincinnati's WLW. His younger brother, Bill, replaced Ball as rhythm guitarist circa 1934, and when Carlisle resumed recording in 1936 after a lengthy hiatus, his material became even saltier—"Get Her By the Tail on a Down Hill Drag" was a classic barroom boast, while "That Nasty Swing" employed metaphorical imagery of surprising explicitness. (He typically recorded his more blue material under a variety of pseudonyms, including Bob Clifford and Amos Greene.)

During the mid-'30s, Carlisle's son—billed as "Sonny Boy Tommy"—began regularly appearing on live dates and recording sessions, a situation that often ran afoul of individual states' child labor laws. The recordings Carlisle made with his son were typically mild and innocuous, but his solo sides continued to get down and dirty—"A Wild Cat Woman and a Tom Cat Man" offered a cartoonish portrait of domestic disputes, while the snarky "You'll Miss Me When I'm Gone" was later covered by Elvis Presley as "Just Because." In 1939, he recorded "Footprints in the Snow," later to become a bluegrass standard; the song offered clear proof that consumers' appetite for blue yodels was on the wane; in the years to follow, Carlisle was a regular on WMPS in Memphis, but by the early '50s he was essentially retired from the music industry, having recorded well over 300 sides during his heyday. He was rediscovered a decade later when the Rooftop Singers covered his "Tom Cat Blues," leading to a handful of reunion performances with Wilbur Ball and even the recording of new material for the Rem label. Cliff Carlisle died in Lexington, KY, on April 2, 1983; he was 78. *—Jason Ankeny*

● **Blues Yodeler and Steel Guitar Wizard** / 1996 / Arhoolie ✦✦✦✦✦

This excellent compilation of 24 sides from the 1930s presents Carlisle in a variety of settings, including tracks on which his steel guitar is the only accompaniment, and slightly fuller arrangements with Wilbur Ball on backup guitar and harmony. As a yodeler, Carlisle did not shy away from risqué lyrics, but that was only one facet of his repertoire, which also included hobo songs and standards. It's like hearing Jimmie Rodgers with first-rate steel guitar, and indeed this will probably appeal mightily to Rodgers fans, as well as some listeners who don't even have any Rodgers discs. *—Richie Unterberger*

• **Volume 1-2** / Old Timey ✦✦✦✦✦

Born in 1904 in Taylorsville, KY, Cliff Carlisle was raised in tobacco country. He drew on songs he heard growing up and wrote a number of his own incorporating themes of the old West. His style was uptempo with a lot of yodeling and Hawaiian guitar licks. He performed on the radio in the '30s and with his brother. These LPs collect his rare original recordings. *—Richard Meyer*

Thumbs Carllile (Kenneth Ray Carllile)

b. Apr. 2, 1931, St. Louis, MO, **d.** Jul. 31, 1987

Guitar, Songwriter / Traditional Country

Kenneth Ray "Thumbs" Carllile was an innovative guitar player and songwriter. The son of an impoverished Illinois tenant farmer, he began playing music at the age of eight after his sister Evelyn won a dobro for selling balm. He used the new instrument so much that his irritated sister hid the steel bar, but the resourceful young man began using his thumbs to practice. When his father gave him a Silvertone guitar, Carllile's thumbs were too short and fat to make it around the neck, so he began playing it on his lap like a dobro. Carllile's family moved to Granite City, MO, when he was ten. There he made his debut playing "Sweet Georgia Brown" during a Ferlin Husky performance. He was tossed out of high-school at age 16 for refusing to shave and then began performing regularly with Husky until being discovered by Little Jimmy Dickens during a performance in St. Louis. Dickens was impressed and gave Carllile the nickname "Thumbs," a moniker Carllile never really liked.

From 1949 to 1952, Thumbs played with Dickens' Country Boys. In 1952, he began a two-year stint in the Army's Special Services. He was stationed in Stuttgart, Germany when he met and married singer/songwriter Virginia Boyle in 1955. After his discharge, Carllile played with Bill Wimberley's Rhythm Boys and Red Foley's Troupe. As a soloist, he regularly appeared on the *Ozark Jubilee*. He met guitar great Les Paul, who was impressed by both Boyle's writing and Carllile's skill and took them to his home recording studio to lay down enough tracks for two albums. Later that year, Carllile sang a duet with Ginny O'Boyle, "Indian Girl, Indian Boy." Two years later he joined the Wade Ray Five and Ray's Las Vegas band. Carllile joined Roger Miller in 1964; later, Miller helped Carllile sign with Smash Records, where he released two albums, *Roger Miller Presents Thumbs Carllile* and *All Thumbs*, in 1965. During 1966, he released several singles, including "Let It Be Me," "Caravan," "Blue Skies," and "Hold It." In 1968, he made the album *Walking in Guitar Land*. Although no singles were released from it, three songs, "It's a Good Day," "Work Song" and "High Noon," found favor with the public.

In 1986, Carllile, whose daughter Virginia had a minor hit with "Stay Until the Rain Stops" in 1980, underwent surgery for colon cancer. After recovering, he began playing on *Sagebrush Boogie* in Atlanta. In 1987, Carllile was preparing to perform as the opening act for Michael Hedges when he suffered a massive coronary and died. *—Sandra Brennan*

• **Roger Miller Presents Thumbs Carllile** / 1965 / Smash ✦✦✦✦

All Thumbs / 1965 / Smash ✦✦✦

This guitarist came up with a style all his own, as a good musician should, but is mostly known through a lick here and there on various hits by his old boss, Roger Miller. One could keep worse company than Miller, who definitely helped Thumbs Carllile's recording career during the years with Smash. The gimmick with the Carllile style is that he mainly uses his thumb to pick with, hence the nickname he was given while a sideman for Little Jimmy Dickens (and apparently was not overly fond of). If one is going to use an appendage to play the guitar with, a thumb is a good choice because is fat, fleshy, and resonant. It is that all too rare combination of swing and country that makes Carllile enjoyable to listen to, although his recordings of this sort are similar to some of the work of Nashville session pro Chet Atkins: overly controlled, cheesy choice of tunes, and stodgy playing at times. But there are some great tracks, particularly the kickoffs to each side: one a funky original and the other a killer version of "On the Street Where You Live." *—Eugene Chadbourne*

Walking in Guitar Land / 1968 / Capitol ✦✦✦

Paulette Carlson

b. Oct. 11, 1953, Northfield, MN

Guitar, Vocals / Contemporary Country

Paulette Carlson was born October 11, 1953, in Northfield, MN. A talented singer and guitar player, Carlson built a large local following before heading to Nashville. Once in Music City, Carlson found work as a staff writer with the Oak Ridge Boys' Silverline/Goldmine music-publishing syndicate, and wrote songs for Tammy Wynette, among others. In early 1983, she secured a solo recording contract. But despite promising critical praise for her early singles, Carlson was back in Minnesota by 1985.

There she was rediscovered two years later by Nitty Gritty Dirt Band manager Chuck Morris, who promptly built a band around her that included guitarist Jack Daniels, drummer Cactus Moser, and bassist/mandolin player Curtis Stone. As Highway 101, the quartet debuted in 1987 with the Carlson-penned number four country single "The Bed You Made for Me." A self-titled LP was issued that same year, and the release spawned two more successful singles. In 1988, Carlson and Highway 101 released *Highway 101, Vol. 2*. The album was essentially a rewrite of their debut, with rollicking country-rock singles the order of the day. Nevertheless, the album was a hit. A year later, *Paint the Town* arrived. By now, the formula had become a bit tired, and the album didn't do as well on radio. Carlson parted ways with Highway 101 in 1990, embarking once again on a solo career. 1991 saw the release of *Love Goes On*, which contained the Top 20 smash "I'll Start With You." However, Carlson couldn't capitalize on her success, and in 1995 she rejoined Highway 101 for the band's ten-year reunion. A year later, *Reunited* appeared. Of its 12 tracks, four were re-recordings of the group's past hits. *Latest & Greatest* followed in 1997; both were issued through Kardina/Intersound. In 1998, Carlson exited Highway 101 yet again, but her star seemed to fade a bit, and her only credits through 2003 were as a backing vocalist for artists such as Michael Martin Murphey. *—Johnny Loftus*

• **Love Goes On** / Nov. 11, 1991 / Capitol ✦✦✦✦

Her best songs continue the feisty, I'm-not-gonna-take-it-anymore attitude she flashed so well in Highway 101. But the collection suffers from overly slick production and a handful of weak songs. *—Michael McCall*

Jenks "Tex" Carman

b. May 14, 1903, Hardinsburg, KY, **d.** Feb. 2, 1968

Guitar (Steel), Vocals / Traditional Country, Country Comedy, Country Boogie

Jenks Tex Carman was one of the more dubious but interesting talents ever to achieve stardom, however fleeting, in country music. A player of great dexterity but severely lacking in any sense of rhythm, and even more lacking in a voice, Carman succeeded on the basis of the sheer enthusiasm of his performances, achieving some respectable record sales and a national following based on his television appearances. Jenkins Carman was the seventh of eight children born to Alford Carman and his wife. They were a farm family with a great love of music—throughout his career, Carman also claimed part Cherokee ancestry, and tried to emphasize this by wearing Native American regalia in some of his public appearances and later album cover art. By age 12 he was on his way to becoming an accomplished guitarist, and he left home in his teens to pursue a career in music. He started out in vaudeville and playing Chautauqua shows, and by the end of the 1920s had emerged as a solo-guitar novelty act. He cut a pair of songs in late 1929 for the Gennett label in Indiana, but neither was ever issued.

In the early '30s, he hooked up with Hawaiian guitar virtuoso Frank Plada, who taught Carman the basics of Hawaiian guitar technique. This instrument became the core of Carman's music from the early '30s onward, and it was using the unamplified acoustic Hawaiian guitar, hung from his neck and fretted with a steel bar, that he began making a name for himself in country music. By the late '40s, he had signed to the Four Star label and begun recording under the name Jenks Tex Carman, "the Dixie Cowboy," as well as appearing on local radio. Soon after, he started to perform regularly on television on the country music showcase *Town Hall Party*, hosted by Tex Ritter and Johnny Bond, and later still became a regular on Cliffie Stone's *Hometown Jamboree*. His contract with Four Star ended, and Stone brought Carman to Capitol Records and producer Ken Nelson in 1951.

Carman's Capitol recording career lasted from April of 1951 until December of 1953, and despite some very uncomfortable moments in the studio, he generated some choice sides—"Hillbilly Hula" was his most famous and requested song, a number he featured on his television appearances, but other highlights included "The Caissons Go Rolling Along" and "Locust Hill Rag." The backing personnel on these cuts is not known, although essayist Cary Ginell believes that Joe Maphis was probably one of the participants on electric guitar or banjo. Carman never acquired much more than a cult following through his records, but on-stage or television he was a major attraction. The sheer wildness of his appearances and the unbridled enthusiasm of his work made him a continual showstopper, despite his inability to hold a beat or hit a cue.

The sales of Carman's singles were too low to justify the renewal of his Capitol contract, and after a lapse of several years, he signed to the small Sage & Sand label, even as he continued to work on television as a regular on locally produced variety series. His later albums tended to emphasize his unverified claims to Cherokee ancestry, which were reinforced by his unusual physiognomy—as one onlooker recalled, Carman dressed like a cowboy and looked like an Indian; occasionally, he even donned a feathered headdress. Carman's last album was called *The Ole Indian*, released by Sage & Sand in 1962. By the mid- to late '60s, he had retired after a 40-year career in music. Jenks Tex Carman was not in a league with the best steel or Hawaiian guitarists, and his vocal skills were even more limited. He was a master showman, however, and accomplished with sheer enthusiasm and reckless abandon what he couldn't do with technical skills or musical instincts. *—Bruce Eder*

Hillbilly Hula / 1991 / Bear Family ✦✦✦

Carman's 20 Capitol sides, which never appeared on LP. "Hillbilly Hula" is the best track here, both instrumentally and vocally, and no words can adequately describe its brittle textures and lunatic meter, or Carman's twangy hillbilly singing on this number. His singing is strictly backwoods primitive, and his playing is downright weird throughout—check out "Hilo March" and the ultra-strange "Samoa Stomp" (Pidgin Samoan words with a hillbilly twang and completely, delightfully off-kilter slide playing), which gets even stranger juxtaposed with "Dixie Cannon Ball." And maybe the most haywire stuff here is Carman's attempts at conventional country balladry, such as "My Lonely Heart and I," where his limited, nasal voice almost sounds like a parody of traditional country. The whole thing is like some eerie Hawaiian/country delirium, but also great fun, and the CD includes three songs that went unreleased until 1991. *—Bruce Eder*

• **Chippeha!: The Essential Dixie Cowboy (1947–1957)** / May 19, 1998 / Revenant ✦✦✦✦✦

Everything you'd ever want by Tex Carman is contained on this great reissue from John Fahey's wonderful indie label Revenant. There are 22 tracks (three versions of "Hillbilly Hula"), including an entire 15-minute radio show recorded for a program called *Country Music Time*, which was produced as an extended advertisement for the U.S. Air Force, make this a hoot and a half. Carman's guitar playing is not nearly as bad as many have said; in fact, he's a vernacular virtuoso, approaching the instrument with a completely original mindset, especially when it comes to tempo, phrasing, and soloing. His voice ain't much either, but none of these alleged shortcomings will deter from the total enjoyment of this wonderfully rambunctious music. Some might call this crude and unsophisticated music, but that's precisely part of its charm and greatness. None of the new breed of country performers coming out of Nashville are what Tex was: an American original. *—John Dougan*

Mary-Chapin Carpenter

b. Feb. 21, 1958, Princeton, NJ

Guitar, Songwriter, Vocals / Singer/Songwriter, Country-Folk, Contemporary Country

Mary-Chapin Carpenter was part of a small movement of folk-influenced country singer/songwriters of the late '80s. Although many of these performers never achieved commercial success, Carpenter was able to channel her anti-Nashville approach into chart success and industry awards by the early '90s.

Carpenter was born and raised in Princeton, NJ, the daughter of a *Life* magazine executive; she spent two years of her childhood in Japan, where her father was launching the Asian edition of *Life*. During the folk explosion of the early '60s, her mother had begun to play guitar. When Mary became interested in music as a child, her mother gave her a guitar. Carpenter played music during her high-school years, but she didn't actively pursue it as a career. In 1974, her family moved to Washington, D.C., where she became involved in the city's folk music scene. After graduating from high-school in the mid-'70s, she spent a year traveling Europe; when she was finished, she enrolled at Brown University, where she was an American civilization major.

Following her college graduation, she became deeply involved in the Washington-area folk scene, performing a mixture of originals, contemporary singer/songwriter material, and pop covers. Carpenter met guitarist John Jennings during the early '80s and the pair began performing together. Eventually, they made a demo tape of their songs, which they sold at their concerts. The tape wound up at Columbia Records, which offered Carpenter an audition. By early 1987, the label had signed her as a recording artist. Her first album, *Hometown Girl*, was released that year.

Hometown Girl and its follow-up, *State of the Heart* (1989), earned her a dedicated cult following, as well as two Top Ten singles, "Never Had It So Good" and "Quittin' Time." Country radio was hesitant to play her soft, folky, feminist material, but she received good reviews and airplay on more progressive country stations, as well as college radio. *Shooting Straight in the Dark*, released in 1990, managed to break down a lot of the barriers that stood in her way. "Down at the Twist and Shout" became a number-two single and the album sold well, setting the stage for her breakthrough album, 1992's *Come on Come On*. *Come on Come On* signaled a slight change in direction for Carpenter—although there were still folk songs, she felt freer to loosen up on honky tonk and country-rock songs, which resulted in several hit singles. Two of the singles from the album—"I Feel Lucky" and "Passionate Kisses"—hit number four, and "He Thinks He'll Keep Her" became her first number one. *Come on Come On* would eventually sell over two-million copies. *Stones in the Road*, her fifth album released in 1994, concentrated on the folkier material, but it was still a major success, selling over a million copies within the first six months of release. *A Place in the World* was released in October 1996. *Time* Sex* Love** appeared in spring 2001. *—Stephen Thomas Erlewine*

Hometown Girl / Feb. 1987 / Columbia ♦♦♦

Although she gained popularity and commercial success on country radio, New Jersey-born Mary-Chapin Carpenter owes as much to folk as she does to country. With the release of her debut album *Hometown Girl*, Carpenter emerged as a new strong voice in the folk revival of the late '80s. Her songwriting skills are apparent here, and her lyrics read like journal entries of a young musician on the road and trying to make it. She looks back at where she's been and honors her heroes ("Family Hands") while looking ahead at the adventures to come ("A Road Is Just a Road"). Her best songs are the romantic ballads such as "Just Because," the album's highlight, where the spare acoustic arrangements bring out her one of a kind voice. Carpenter also demonstrates the breadth of her musical influences by covering Tom Waits' "Downtown Train" years before Rod Stewart turned the song into a hit. *Hometown Girl* is an understated affair—there are not as many rollicking, fun tunes as on future efforts—but this album is worth checking out for fans familiar with her 1990s catalog. *—Vik Iyengar*

State of the Heart / 1989 / Columbia ♦♦♦

Carpenter, a folkie, eventually turned to the country market, especially on her third album, *Shooting Straight in the Dark*. On this, her second, she's still in transition, which makes her more thoughtful than the average country singer and catchier than the average folkie, especially on her breakthrough country hit, "Never Had It So Good." Also includes "Quittin' Time," "Something of a Dreamer," and "How Do." *—William Ruhlmann*

Shooting Straight in the Dark / 1990 / Columbia ♦♦♦♦♦

Although Mary-Chapin Carpenter's second album yielded two Top Ten hits, it was the release of 1990's *Shooting Straight in the Dark* that confirmed her talents as an artist who could easily stage a crossover without relinquishing her country roots. With an even stronger infusion of folk and pop, Carpenter opened herself up to a wider market, taking the Cajun-tinged "Down at the Twist and Shout" (with the help of Beausoleil) to number two on the country charts, a song that also netted her a Grammy for best country vocal performance by a female. Both "You Win Again" and Gene Vincent's "Right Now" were also released as singles, expanding Carpenter's exposure even more so, but the other tracks from the album also reveal her lyrical strength and attentive songwriting prowess. "Halley Came to Jackson" is a wonderful tale about a small town's fascination with and misconception about Halley's comet back in 1910, while tracks such as "What You Didn't Say" and "When She's Gone" are also fresh-sounding country efforts that shine a light on her delicate but hearty singing style. Carpenter gets some help from Shawn Colvin on a few of the cuts and, because their collaboration worked so well, she and a number of other artists appeared on her next album and on 1994's *Stones in the Road*, expanding her material to an even greater extent. *Shooting Straight in the Dark* was indeed a breakthrough album for Carpenter, not only in a commercial sense but at a personal level as well, and its progressive repercussions helped in making 1992's *Come on Come On* an even stronger effort, spawning a myriad of hit singles. *—Mike DeGagne*

● **Come on Come On** / 1992 / Columbia ♦♦♦♦♦

With an astounding seven hit singles, *Come on Come On* climbed all the way to number six on the country charts, fully revealing Carpenter's astuteness and magnitude as one of the decade's most illustrious country artists. With friends such as Rosanne Cash, Joe Diffie, Shawn Colvin, and the Indigo Girls lending a hand, there's a full range of country, folk, and pop-styled songs strewn across the album, helping it and Carpenter herself gain enormous recognition from other audiences outside of country music. "He Thinks He'll Keep Her," a title keeping with country music's tradition of double entendres, became Carpenter's first number-one hit, while the confident "I Feel Lucky" peaked at number four and netted her another Grammy. Lucinda Williams' "Passionate Kisses," with its beautiful guitar arrangements, also made it to number four, and Carpenter's vocal enthusiasm makes Dire Straits' "The Bug" one of the album's most spirited efforts. These songs, along with the title track's compelling folk essence, gave *Come on Come On* a well-rounded sound and exposed her talent for reaching slightly beyond the genre's long-established niches. Not only is Carpenter's music extendable, but her writing rescues country music from its familiar themes of "love 'em and leave 'em" conventionality while still managing to portray maturely the perils of romance and heartbreak from a female perspective. Carpenter repeated much of *Come on Come On*'s full-ranged charm for 1994's *Stones in the Road* release, which garnered her yet a third Grammy in as many albums. *—Mike DeGagne*

Stones in the Road / 1994 / Columbia ♦♦♦♦

With *Stones in the Road*, Mary-Chapin Carpenter stripped her sound down and returned to the core of her music—namely, her singer/songwriter roots. Although the lyrics are among her best, Carpenter unfortunately cut back the number of hooks and melodies in her songs. Previously, she found a nice balance between the two, but here, she concentrates on the lyrics to the detriment of the actual songs. The sound of *Stones in the Road* is pleasant, but there aren't any songs that stick in your head after the record is finished. *—Thom Owens*

A Place in the World / Oct. 22, 1996 / Columbia ♦♦♦

Mary-Chapin Carpenter's breakthrough to stardom occurred with *Stones in the Road*, one of her most introspective collections. In order to consolidate that success with her follow-up, *Place in the World*, Carpenter returned to the looser sounds of *Come on Come On*, turning in a collection of songs that still touches on reflective folk, but also catchy county-rock. On the whole, *Place in the World* doesn't offer the deeper rewards of *Stones in the Road*, nor is it quite as kinetic as *Come on Come On*. Still, the record is well-crafted and boasts several excellent songs, making it a worthwhile purchase. *—Thom Owens*

Party Doll & Other Favorites / May 25, 1999 / Columbia ♦♦♦♦

Mary-Chapin Carpenter has always eschewed the schlock material that often plagues country artists, avoiding the trappings of Nashville in favor of a more independent approach to her music. *Party Doll*, a greatest-hits collection, stays in line with Carpenter's approach of giving listeners substance rather than gloss. Instead of releasing the typical "best-of" collection that includes only the standard radio hits, Carpenter has put enough thought and imagination into *Party Doll* that even familiar fans will be surprised. Her career making hits are here, but often in an alternate form such as the live version of "Down at the Twist and Shout" recorded at Super Bowl XXXI or the version of "Quittin' Time" from the Ryman Auditorium. Also included are songs from soundtracks and tribute albums and an achingly beautiful cover of the Mick Jagger song that serves as the album's namesake. While some may be disappointed they can't buy one CD that includes all her hits the way they first heard them, Carpenter's true fans will appreciate the effort that went into this greatest-hits package. *—Steve Kurutz*

Time* Sex* Love* / May 29, 2001 / Columbia ♦♦♦♦

The asterisks following the words in the title to Mary-Chapin Carpenter's seventh album of new material, *Time* Sex* Love**, hide more words: the full title is "Time Is the Great Gift; Sex Is the Great Equalizer; Love Is the Great Mystery." If that sounds a bit overdone, it accurately introduces a collection given over to big statements. After four and a half years, Carpenter weighs in with a 73-plus-minute disc that thoughtfully examines important issues. Songs like "Simple Life" and "Maybe the World" take on the uncertainty of life at midstream, a subject also addressed in specifically careerist terms in "The Long Way Home" and philosophically in "Late for Your Life." But if that's the "time" part of the record, "sex" and "love" take primary place. Simply put, the better part of the album consists of torch songs that depict romantic and sexual obsession. Titles like "Swept Away" and "Slave to the Beauty" reveal the theme, and even attempted recoveries like "This Is Me Leaving You" reinforce it. The narrator of that song sounds like she'd be happier singing, "This is me crawling back to you." Working against the theme are the musical elements. Recording in Sir George Martin's Air Studios, Carpenter harks back to the Beatles' *Rubber Soul* for the album's sound, which lightens the mood. And her singing never supports the victimization in her lyrics, always maintaining its calm, murmuring tone. But the point is unmistakable. It's hard to see what any of this has to do with country radio, which, in any case, has been increasingly resistant to Carpenter. This album may not be a country blockbuster, ending the sleight of hand by which an artist who is essentially a folk-rock singer/songwriter has succeeded in Nashville, but it is a mature examination of life and love. *—William Ruhlmann*

The Carpetbaggers

f. 1991

Group / Alternative Country-Rock, Alternative Country, Americana

An alternative country trio from, of all places, the affluent Minneapolis suburb of Edina, the Carpetbaggers were formed in 1991 by guitarists Mike Crabtree and John Magnuson, along with upright bassist Rich Copley. Two well-received independent label releases, 1992's *Country Miles Apart* and 1993's *Nowhere to Go But Down*, helped earn the

Carpetbaggers a series of high-profile gigs opening for Son Volt. In 1996, the group issued *Sin Now ... Pray Later*. —*Jason Ankeny*

Country Miles Apart / Sep. 29, 1992 / Twin/Tone ✦✦✦

● **Nowhere to Go But Down** / 1993 / Clean ✦✦✦✦

Sin Now ... Pray Later / May 7, 1996 / Hightone ✦✦✦

Joe Carr

b. 1910

Guitar, Mandolin, Vocals / Bluegrass-Gospel, Contemporary Bluegrass, Bluegrass, Traditional Bluegrass, Progressive Bluegrass

Country guitarist Joe Carr has issued several solo releases over the years, in addition to being a one-time member of the bluegrass outfit Country Gazette, guesting on other artist's records, and issuing numerous instructional guitar videos. An entirely self-taught musician, Carr began playing guitar at the age of 13 (inspired by Doc Watson), which led to such other instruments as mandolin, fiddle, banjo, and ukulele. Carr joined the Country Gazette in the late '70s, appearing on 1978's *All This and Money Too* and 1981's *American & Clean*, before leaving the group in 1984 to play with others and pursue a solo career, as well as joining the music faculty in the "commercial music program" at South Plains College in Levelland, TX.

Carr has issued several solo releases over the years, including such titles as *Let's Go Dancing Down in Texas* and *Line Dance Party Texas Style*, has collaborated with ex-Country Gazette banjo player Alan Munde (on the album *Windy Days and Dusty Skies*, and the book *Prairie Nights to Neon Lights: The Story of Country Music in West Texas*), and issued numerous instructional videos for the acclaimed Mel Bay company covering a wide variety of playing styles (everything from Western swing and bluegrass to hard rock). —*Greg Prato*

Windy Days and Dusty Skies / Jun. 16, 1995 / Flying Fish ✦✦✦

With *Windy Days and Dusty Skies*, Joe Carr and Alan Munde have pulled off a tight and traditionally reverent bluegrass album. This is to be expected, however, for the two men aren't only great players—both are renowned musicians whose collective resumé boasts stints with the Country Gazette, Jimmy Martin, Sam Bush, and Roanoke—they are also scholars of the form. Both are professors of bluegrass music at South Plains College in Texas. And besides recording ventures, they have co-authored the book *Prairie Nights to Neon Lights: The Story of Country Music in West Texas*. For *Windy Days and Dusty Skies*, the two have brought along pickers such as Beppe Gambetta, David Grier, and Gerald Jones, as well as Ed Marsh, Roland White, and Randy Howard. Besides tracks by Carr and fiddler Marsh, the album boasts traditional numbers and a fine run-through "Texas Blues," which is well known as a standard for Texas swing pioneer Bob Wills. This album is an excellent showcase for Munde's vaunted banjo skills and the formidable flatpicking of Carr. Don't expect any front-porch looseness, however; this is tight and technical playing. —*Erik Hage*

Johnny Carroll

b. Oct. 23, 1937, d. Feb. 18, 1995

Piano, Keyboards, Vocals / Rockabilly, Rockabilly Revival, Rock & Roll

Part of the original rockabilly movement in the 1950s, singer/guitarist Johnny Carroll issued several oft-overlooked yet classic singles for the Decca label, including such titles as "Crazy, Crazy Lovin'," "Wild, Wild Women," and "Hot Rocks." Although he never truly obtained substantial success stateside, European rockabilly audiences revered Carroll. After falling off the rock & roll radar shortly after his '50s singles, Carroll emerged once again in 1974. He immediately recorded a tribute to Gene Vincent, "Gene Vincent Rock" (also issued under the title "The Black Leather Rebel"), following it up three years later with the full-length *Texabilly*, as well as a few other releases during the '80s. On January 13, 1995, Carroll passed away due to liver failure, but his classic early recordings were honored a year later in the form of the 33-track compilation *Rock Baby Rock It: 1955-1960*. —*Greg Prato*

Texabilly / 1980 / Rollin' Rock ✦✦✦✦

This 18-track collection brings together Johnny Carroll's entire output for collector Ronny Weiser's Rollin' Rock label, recorded between 1974 and 1977. Chronologically beginning with the tribute tip of the hat on "Gene Vincent Rock" from 1974 (although it's not sequenced that way on the disc), featuring original Fabulous Thunderbirds drummer Mike Buck, the bulk of this disc comprises the entire 1997 *Texabilly* album. This minor classic of the idiom was cut in Weiser's living room in one marathon 27-hour session and featured fellow Texan rocker Ray Campi on slappin' string bass. Carroll's voice is full of the same sore-throated hollering power that he possessed in his 1950s prime, and his guitar work is funky in tone and simplistic in derivation. The big surprise is the preponderance of original material, most of it coming from Carroll's pen, with "Who's to Say," "Is It Easy to Be Easy," "Her Throbbing Lips," and "Whatcha Gonna Do?" being particular standouts. The 1970s were barren years for the original rockers, and the rockabilly revival hadn't built up a full head of steam yet, but these recordings helped to show that there was still plenty of energy left in the genre and one of its original practitioners. —*Cub Koda*

● **Rock Baby Rock It: 1955–1960** / 1996 / Bear Family ✦✦✦✦✦

Johnny Carroll's 1956 recording of "Wild Wild Women," with its lean rockabilly arrangement and exciting vocal performance that owes little debt to Elvis Presley, is one of the greatest early rock & roll singles. Unfortunately, the record wasn't a hit and Carroll bounced from label to label without much success, making a little rockabilly and several Gene Vincent-style rockers along the way. *Rock Baby Rock It: 1955-1960* is a complete summary of Carroll's early career, beginning with a generous helping of hot but rough demos made in 1955 and continuing through his complete recordings for Decca, Warner Bros., and Sun Records. The collection wraps up with a novelty single recorded by his backing band, the Spinners; a pair of indie label waxings; and the four songs Carroll

performed in the 1957 film *Rock, Baby, Rock It*. The half-dozen Decca recordings, including "Wild Wild Women," are the essential cuts and have been anthologized elsewhere, but exemplary rockers are scattered throughout the track list. It is a shame that Decca didn't record Carroll more, but the work he did in those two days has given him a reputation among rockabilly aficionados that has only grown. —*Greg Adams*

Fiddlin' John Carson

b. Mar. 23, 1868, Fannin County, GA, d. Dec. 11, 1949, Atlanta, GA

Vocals, Fiddle / Old-Timey

Fiddlin' John Carson was already 55 when in 1923 the OKeh label released "Little Old Log Cabin in the Lane"/"The Old Hen Cackled"—the first recording by a strictly country artist and arguably the beginning of the country music recording industry. Carson was born in the Blue Ridge Mountains of Georgia in 1868, and worked in cotton mills for over 20 years until his fiddling talents won several contests. He began performing in minstrel shows, and came to be quite popular around the Georgia area—so much so that Atlanta furniture salesman Polk Brockman recommended Carson's name to OKeh field recorder Ralph Peer. Though Peer agreed to record the fiddler, he was disgusted with the results and sent only a few copies to the furniture store—then the only outlet for records. Brockman sold out of several pressings, convincing Peer that there was a market for hillbilly recordings.

Carson was brought to New York late in 1923 to begin recording the first of his over 150 sides for the label. The following year, Carson updated his old-timey sound by recording with a string band called the Virginia Reelers. He also recorded as a comedy duo with his daughter, Rosa Lee (known as Moonshine Kate). Carson's fortunes declined during the Depression, however; his final recordings were for Victor Bluebird in 1934. He later worked as an elevator operator at the Georgia State Capitol, a job he received from governor Eugene Talmadge in return for the popular musician's campaign help. Rounder has released a compilation of the fiddler's recordings with the Virginia Reelers and Moonshine Kate. —*John Bush*

The Old Hen Cackled / 1976 / Rounder ✦✦✦✦✦

● **Fiddlin' John C** / Oct. 17, 1990 / Rounder ✦✦✦✦✦

Complete Recorded Works, Vol. 1 (1923–1924) / Jan. 2, 1998 / Document ✦✦✦

Complete Recorded Works, Vol. 2 (1924–1925) / Jan. 2, 1998 / Document ✦✦✦

Complete Recorded Works, Vol. 3 (1925–1926) / Jan. 2, 1998 / Document ✦✦✦

Complete Recorded Works, Vol. 4 / Jan. 2, 1998 / Document ✦✦✦

Complete Recorded Works, Vol. 5 / Mar. 2, 1998 / Document ✦✦✦✦

Complete Recorded Works, Vol. 6 / Mar. 2, 1998 / Document ✦✦✦✦

Complete Recorded Works, Vol. 7 / Mar. 2, 1998 / Document ✦✦✦✦

A Fiddlers Convention in Mountain City, Tennessee / County ✦✦✦

Jeff Carson

b. Dec. 17, 1964, Tulsa, OK

Vocals / Contemporary Country

Jeff Carson was one of the new country singers who was able to parlay the mass success of country music in the early '90s to a massive hit with his eponymous first album. Carson was born in Tulsa, OK, but raised in the small Arkansas town of Gravette. As a child, he sang in church and played harmonica and guitar. While he was in high-school, he and his friends formed a band to play their school's talent show, performing the Eagles' "Seven Bridges Road." After the ad hoc group won second place, Carson was convinced to pursue a musical career. Following his high-school graduation, he entered a talent contest at an entertainment complex called Ozark Mountain Music in Rogers, AR. Although he didn't come in first, the winner asked Carson to play in his house band. For the next four years, he played with the outfit, until they finally disbanded.

Carson moved to Branson, MO, where he played bass in local bands and started writing his own songs. In Branson, he met and married his wife, Kim Cooper, who encouraged him to move to Nashville. Kim had a friend who played at the Opryland Hotel and his group Texana needed a bassist—hence, Carson moved to Music City in 1989. After some persuasion, he convinced the hotel to book him as a solo act. Around the same time, he signed a songwriting deal with Little Big Town Music and began singing on demo tapes for a variety of companies. Eventually, publisher/producer Chuck Howard heard Carson's original material and signed a publishing and development deal with him. By 1994, Jeff had signed with Curb Records. Jeff Carson's self-titled debut album was released in early 1995; the first single, "Yeah Buddy," went nowhere, but the second single, "Not on Your Love," rocketed to number one. It was followed by the Top Ten hit "The Car." —*Stephen Thomas Erlewine*

● **Jeff Carson** / 1995 / Curb ✦✦✦

Butterfly Kisses / Jun. 24, 1997 / Curb ✦✦✦

Real Life / Sep. 4, 2001 / Curb ✦✦✦

Fans haven't heard from Jeff Carson since 1995's mega-hits "Not on Your Love" and "The Car." Album number three reminds us of what we've been missing for the last six years. Carson has a way with a ballad, so *Real Life* is chock-full of them. He pours his heart and soul into "My One and Only Love" and the touching "What's Not to Love." Fans will be moved by the heartbreak of "Until We Fall Back in Love Again" and the failing relationship in "It Wouldn't Kill Me." But they'll also appreciate the feel-good beats and uplifting messages of "Where Did I Go So Right," "Shine On," and "Divine Intervention." *Real Life* is a nice re-introduction to this talented artist. —*Maria Konicki Dinoia*

Joe Carson

b. 1937, d. Feb. 1964

Vocals / Honky Tonk, Traditional Country

Born in 1937, this musician wasted little time beginning his professional singing career. By the age of 16, "Little" Joe Carson was performing and writing his own material. In

1956, he signed a recording contract with Capitol Records. Performing around Nashville and the southern U.S., Carson was known as a great yet classic country singer. In 1963, he released his biggest hit, "I Gotta Get Drunk," a song that was penned by a young and promising songwriter at the time named Willie Nelson. Tragically, Carson was killed in a car accident in 1964; he was 27. That same year, a memorial album was released. In 2002, a selection of songs from Carson's catalog was issued as a retrospective. *Hillbilly Band from Mars* was released on Bear Family Records. From 1953 to 1964, Carson worked with the Mercury, Capitol, Liberty, and D record labels. His other big hits were "I Don't Have a Contact With You" and "Helpless." *—Jason MacNeil*

- **Hillbilly Band from Mars** / Aug. 13, 2002 / Bear Family ✦✦✦✦

Martha Carson (Irene Ambergey)

b. Mar. 19, 1921, Neon, KY

Songwriter, Vocals / Traditional Country, Nashville Sound/Countrypolitan, Country Gospel, Country Boogie

During the 1950s, Martha Carson's rock & roll-flavored gospel tunes had a strong influence on her country peers, most notably Elvis Presley. She was also one of the first country artists to deliberately seek and find popularity on the pop charts. Carson was born Irene Ambergey in Neon, KY. She and her two sisters were spotted by radio barndance impresario John Lair and invited to join the cast of the WSB Barn Dance in Atlanta in 1938. The Ambergey sisters were given the fanciful hayseed names of Minnie, Marthie, and Mattie, and after Irene Ambergey left the group and teamed with her husband, mandolin player James Carson, in the 40s, the stage name stuck and she became Martha Carson. The duo performed (with Martha on guitar) as the Barn Dance Sweethearts. By the time of their divorce in 1950, Martha had begun making solo appearances on Knoxville's WNOX radio. Unfortunately, she couldn't record because the Barn Dance Sweethearts' label, Capitol, had them contracted through 1957 and refused to let her go solo, instead trying to pair her up with other male singers. She began doing session work instead, appearing on the Carlisles' "Too Old to Cut the Mustard" and other recordings by that group of unrelated performers headed by WNOX stalwart Bill Carlisle.

Things began to change after Carson met Fred Rose in Nashville. He helped convince Capitol to let her record alone, and in 1951 she made her solo-single debut with "Satisfied," a gospel song she had written in response to audience disapproval over her divorce. The combination of Carson's powerful alto voice and the song's propulsive handclap backbeat formed one of the blocks on which early rock & roll was built. The song featured backup by Carlisle, Chet Atkins, and Carson's sister, Opal, now known as Jean Chapel; it was, curiously, not a hit in its initial incarnation, but it gained momentum continuously over the next several years. By 1954, Carson had recorded more than 24 songs, become a member of the *Grand Ole Opry*, and done extensive tours with such stars as Jimmy Dickens, Ferlin Husky, and rising star Elvis Presley. After their performances, she and Presley sang gospel duets, and he later claimed that she had more influence on his stage style than anyone else.

Around 1954, Carson married Xavier Cosse, a pop promoter who had tried to learn more about the burgeoning phenomenon of country and gospel music by working with Hank Williams and Chet Atkins in Nashville. Carson seemed to be exactly what he was looking for, and he persuaded RCA producer Steve Sholes to sign her to that label and to whisk her off to Hollywood for a recording session. By 1955, Carson was living and recording all her work in New York. She had a series of minor hits that included "Journey to the Sky," "This Ole House," and "Saints and Chariot," a combination of two old favorites that Presley later covered in concert. After signing with the William Morris agency in 1957, Carson and Cosse became full-time residents of New York, and she gained national exposure by appearing on *the Steve Allen Show.*

She moved temporarily away from gospel-oriented music and toward citified country-pop, appearing on Tennessee Ernie Ford's television program and pursuing a style shaped in part by his big, low vocals and pop orchestral arrangements. It was a successful move for a time, but by the late '50s, her star began to wane. She continued periodically recording on labels such as Decca, Cadence, and Sims, but although she was a fixture of live venues in Las Vegas and in California for a time, chart success eluded her. Her rockabilly roots showed in a series of performances she gave on the riotous Los Angeles country television show *Town Hall Party* in the late '50s. By the 1980s, she was living in semi-retirement. *—Sandra Brennan & James Manheim*

Journey to the Sky / 1955 / RCA ✦✦✦

Rock-A My Soul / 1957 / RCA ✦✦✦✦

Satisfied / 1960 / Capitol ✦✦✦

Talk With the Lord / 1962 / Capitol ✦✦✦✦

Martha Carson / 1963 / Sims ✦✦✦

- **Martha Carson's Greatest Gospel Hits** / 1988 / Starday ✦✦✦✦

The Carter Family

f. 1926, Virginia, **db.** 1943

Group / Old-Timey, Traditional Country

The most influential group in country music history, the Carter Family switched the emphasis from hillbilly instrumentals to vocals, made scores of their songs part of the standard country music canon, and made a style of guitar playing, "Carter picking," the dominant technique for decades. Along with Jimmie Rodgers, the Carter Family were among the first country music stars. Comprised of a gaunt, shy gospel quartet member named Alvin P. Carter and two reserved country girls—his wife, Sara, and their sister-in-law, Maybelle—the Carter Family sang a pure, simple harmony that influenced not only the numerous other family groups of the '30s and the '40s, but folk, bluegrass, and rock musicians like Woody Guthrie, Bill Monroe, the Kingston Trio, Doc Watson, Bob Dylan, and Emmylou Harris, to mention just a few.

It's unlikely that bluegrass music would have existed without the Carter Family. A.P., the family patriarch, collected hundreds of British/Appalachian folk songs and, in arranging these for recording, enhanced the pure beauty of these "facts-of-life tunes" and at the same time saved them for future generations. Those hundreds of songs the trio members found around their Virginia and Tennessee homes, after being sung by A.P., Sara, and Maybelle, became *Carter* songs, even though these were folk songs and in the public domain. Among the more than 300 sides they recorded are "Worried Man Blues," "Wabash Cannonball," "Will the Circle Be Unbroken," "Wildwood Flower," and "Keep on the Sunny Side."

The Carter Family's instrumental backup, like their vocals, was unique. On her Gibson L-5 guitar, Maybelle played a bass-strings lead (the guitar being tuned down from the standard pitch) that is the mainstay of bluegrass guitarists to the present. Sara accompanied her on the autoharp or on a second guitar, while A.P. devoted his talent to singing in a haunting though idiosyncratic bass or baritone. Although the original Carter Family disbanded in 1943, enough of their recordings remained in the vaults to keep the group current through the '40s. Furthermore, their influence was evident through further generations of musicians, in all forms of popular music, through the end of the century.

Initially, the Carter Family consisted of just A.P. and Sara. Born and raised in the Clinch Mountains of Virginia, A.P. (b. Alvin Pleasant Delaney Carter, April 15, 1891; d. November 7, 1960) learned to play fiddle as a child, with his mother teaching him several traditional and old-time songs; his father had played violin as a young man, but abandoned the instrument once he married. Once he became an adult, he began singing with two uncles and his older sister in a gospel quartet, but he became restless and soon moved to Indiana, where he worked on the railroad. By 1911, he had returned to Virginia, where he sold fruit trees and wrote songs in his spare time.

While he was traveling and selling trees, he met Sara (b. Sara Dougherty, July 21, 1898; d. January 8, 1979). According to legend, she was on her porch playing the autoharp and singing "Engine 143" when he met her. Like A.P., Sara learned how to sing and play through her family. As a child, she learned a variety of instruments, including autoharp, guitar, and banjo, and she played with her friends and cousins. A.P. and Sara fell in love and married on June 18, 1915, settling in Maces Springs, where he worked various jobs while the two of them sang at local parties, socials, and gatherings. For the next 11 years, they played locally. During that time, the duo auditioned for Brunswick Records, but the label was only willing to sign A.P. and only if he recorded fiddle dance songs under the name Fiddlin' Doc; he rejected their offer, believing that it was against his parents' religious beliefs.

Eventually, Maybelle Carter (b. Maybelle Addington, May 10, 1909; d. October 23, 1978)—who had married A.P.'s brother Ezra—began singing and playing guitar with Sara and A.P. Following Maybelle's addition to the Carter Family in 1926, the group began auditioning at labels in earnest. In 1927, the group auditioned for Ralph Peer, a New York-based A&R man for Victor Records who was scouting for local talent in Bristol, TN. The Carters recorded six tracks, including "The Wandering Boy" and "Single Girl, Married Girl." Victor released several of the songs as singles, and when the records sold well, the label offered the group a long-range contract.

The Carter Family signed with Victor in 1928, and over the next seven years the group recorded most of its most famous songs, including "Wabash Cannonball," "I'm Thinking Tonight of My Blue Eyes," "John Hardy Was a Desperate Little Man," "Wildwood Flower," and "Keep on the Sunny Side," which became the Carters' signature song. By the end of the '20s, the group had become a well-known national act, but its income was hurt considerably by the Great Depression. Because of the financial crisis, the Carters were unable to play concerts in cities across the U.S. and were stuck playing schoolhouses in Virginia. Eventually, all of the members became so strapped for cash they had to move away from home to find work. In 1929, A.P. moved to Detroit temporarily while Maybelle and her husband relocated to Washington, D.C.

In addition to the stress of the Great Depression, A.P. and Sara's marriage began to fray, and the couple separated in 1932. For the next few years, the Carters only saw each other at recording sessions, partially because the Depression had cut into the country audience and partially because the women were raising their families. In 1935, the Carters left Victor for ARC, where they re-recorded their most famous songs. The following year, they signed to Decca. Eventually, the group signed a lucrative radio contract with XERF in Del Rio, TX, which led to contracts at a few other stations along the Mexican and Texas border. Because of their locations, these stations could broadcast at levels that were far stronger than other American radio stations, so the Carters' radio performances could be heard throughout the nation, either in their live form or as radio transcriptions. As a result, the band's popularity increased dramatically, and their Decca records became extremely popular.

Just as their career was back in full swing, Sara and A.P.'s marriage fell apart, with the couple divorcing in 1939. Nevertheless, the Carter Family continued to perform, remaining in Texas until 1941, when they moved to a radio station in Charlotte, NC. During the early '40s, the band briefly recorded for Columbia before re-signing with Victor in 1941. Two years later, Sara decided to retire and move out to California with her new husband, Coy Bayes (who was A.P.'s cousin), while A.P. moved back to Virginia, where he ran a country store. Maybelle Carter began recording and touring with her daughters, Helen, June, and Anita.

A.P. and Sara re-formed the Carter Family with their grown children in 1952, performing a concert in Maces Spring. Following the successful concert, the Kentucky-based Acme signed A.P., Sara, and their daughter Janette to a contract, and over the next four years they recorded nearly 100 songs that didn't gain much attention at the time. In 1956, the Carter Family disbanded for the second time. Four years later, A.P. died at his Maces Spring home. Following his death, the Carter Family's original recordings began to be reissued. In 1966, Maybelle persuaded Sara to reunite to play a number of folk festivals and record an album for Columbia. In 1970, the Carter Family became the first group to be elected into the Country Music Hall of Fame, which is a fitting tribute to their immense influence and legacy. *—David Vinopal*

Diamonds in the Rough / 1990 / Copper Creek ✦✦✦

Subtitled *Heart Songs, Hymns & Ballads as Featured on Border Radio in 1941,* this radio transcriptions reissue of the Carter Family's appearances on the legendary Del Rio border radio stations in 1938 is a fine representation of their repertoire of songs about home, hearth, and heartbreak. *—Mark A. Humphrey*

Clinch Mountain Treasures / 1991 / County ✦✦✦✦✦
As the title suggests, the songs are treasures, but they're not among the seminal group's best-known songs. Recorded for OKeh Records in Chicago in 1940, it captures the group's instrumentation and vocals at their most incisive. *—Michael McCall*

☆ **Country Music Hall of Fame** / 1991 / MCA ✦✦✦✦✦
After ending an eight-year association with Victor Records, the Carter Family recorded 60 sides for Decca between 1936 and 1938; 15 of those recordings are collected here. Decca wanted to emphasize new material; this posed no problem for A.P. Carter, who was long accustomed to taking copyright credit for minor rewrites of other people's songs. The Decca songs are less familiar than the recordings for Victor or, later, OKeh, but they're worth hearing. *—Brian Mansfield*

★ **Anchored in Love: Their Complete Victor Recordings (1927–28)** / 1993 / Rounder ✦✦✦✦✦
No American label (except perhaps Arhoolie) deserves a shot at reissuing the treasured Carter Family recordings more than Rounder. The Carter Family's sessions are seminal country music, raw and wonderfully unsophisticated with an emotional directness and honesty that makes a mockery of the slick, overproduced rock/folk now being marketed as country. Charles Wolfe's notes are an ideal combination of insight, historical overview, and musical examination. These are only the first 16 songs in the series, but they get things off to a rousing start. The menu is a sensational mix of originals, mountain and folk tunes, and old-timey hymns. *—Ron Wynn*

☆ **My Clinch Mountain Home: Their Complete Victor Recordings (1928–1929)** / Oct. 1, 1993 / Rounder ✦✦✦✦✦
The second volume in the Carter Family reissue series brings things forward to 1928 and 1929. The 16 selections provide family views of their life, home and background and include a rare topical number, "The Cyclone of Rye Cove," plus prophetic tunes like "The Grave on the Green Hillside" and the reflective selections "The Homestead on the Farm" and the title cut. Rounder plans nine volumes in the line; the first two only make you eager for more. *—Ron Wynn*

On Border Radio, Vol. 1 / 1995 / Arhoolie ✦✦✦✦✦
About an hour of material taken from transcription discs recorded for broadcast on XET in Monterrey, Mexico in 1939. This isn't extraneous stuff by any means, containing their characteristic harmonies and well-executed guitar arrangements. It's of special interest to Carter Family fans, however, for the inclusion of much material that the group never recorded in their original lineup (although six were recorded by Sara and A.P. Carter with two of their children in the 1950s). The demands of constant radio broadcasts necessitated a wide repertoire and varying approaches, and this collection also shows facets of the group that were underrepresented on record. These include instrumentals, several songs by A.P. on which he accompanies himself on guitar, and a few selections featuring the young daughters of various members of the Carter family (June Carter among them). *—Richie Unterberger*

☆ **When the Roses Bloom in Dixieland: Their Complete Victor Recordings (1929–30)** / Oct. 31, 1995 / Rounder ✦✦✦✦✦
The third volume in Rounder's projected eight-disc series of the Carter Family's 1927-1941 recordings for RCA Victor picks up in Atlanta in November 1929, where the family records ten tracks, including "Motherless Children," "Wabash Cannonball," and "Jimmy Brown the Newsboy," among other country classics, then travels to Memphis for six tracks from the Carters' fifth recording session in May 1930. *—William Ruhlmann*

☆ **Worried Man Blues: Their Complete Victor Recordings (1930)** / Oct. 31, 1995 / Rounder ✦✦✦✦✦
The fourth volume in Rounder's projected eight-disc series of the Carter Family's 1927-1941 recordings for RCA Victor picks up in Memphis in May 1930 and continues in the same city in November for 16 sides, including the title track and "Lonesome Valley." There are an unusually large number of three-part harmony vocals in this set, much of which is given over to gospel songs. The only complaints about this brilliant chronological series are that it could be accomplished faster: This disc runs less than 48 minutes, and Rounder seems to be doling out the albums at a rate of two every two years, which means that it could take until the end of 1999 to hear them all. (The fifth volume, *Sunshine in the Shadows: Their Complete Victor Recordings 1931-32* was scheduled for release June 18, 1996, speeding up the schedule somewhat.) *—William Ruhlmann*

Sunshine in the Shadows: Their Complete Victor Recordings (1931–32) / 1996 / Rounder ✦✦✦✦✦
These 16 tracks from 1931 and 1932, originally recorded for Victor, were mostly penned by A.P. Carter. It displays the Carters' usual unadorned consistency, moving harmonies, and accomplished picking; "Picture on the Wall," "Where We'll Never Grow Old," and "Lonesome for You" are just some of the more striking examples of their skill with material that is both humble and mournfully evocative. Of special interest are a few songs (and a couple corny sketches) on which the clan is joined by Jimmie Rodgers, the most influential country act of the day bar the Carters themselves. *—Richie Unterberger*

On Border Radio, Vol. 2: 1939 / 1997 / Arhoolie ✦✦✦
Another dip into the surviving transcription discs of their 1939 XET broadcasts, which like the first volume presents the family in various contexts. The best cuts are generally those on which Sara and Maybelle handle the vocals; there are also ones by the young Carter Sisters, and a couple of instrumentals. The content isn't quite as strong on this second installment, and some of the songs are extremely short, coming to an end just when they seem to be approaching the heart of the matter. Of course, fans will still want it, because the performances and harmonies are good, and the sound quality isn't much different from the standards of officially released 1930s sessions. *—Richie Unterberger*

Give Me the Roses While I Live: Their Complete Victor Recordings (1932–33) / Feb. 11, 1997 / Rounder ✦✦✦
Give Me Roses While I Live picks up where *Sunshine in the Shadows* left off, compiling several tracks from the Carter Family's classic early '30s recordings for Victor. This disc features 16 songs the group cut over the course of 1933. *—Thom Owens*

Country by the Carter Family / May 27, 1997 / Vanguard ✦✦✦
This compilation combines recordings from 1940 by the original Carter Family—A.P. Carter, his wife Sara, and his sister-in-law Maybelle—with recordings made by an extended family of Carter-related performers including: the group the Carter Sisters and Mother Maybelle (consisting of Maybelle and her daughters, Anita, Helen, and June Carter), who were sometimes billed as the Carter Family; Johnny Cash (whose second wife was June Carter); and Rosanne Cash (Cash's daughter by his first wife). All of these later performers wound up on Columbia Records in the 1960s and '70s, and they recorded together in various combinations so that, for example, "the Carter Family with Johnny Cash" made the country Top 40 in 1972 with "The World Needs a Melody," included here. Another country Top 40 hit was "A Song to Mama" from 1971, a narration by Cash with the Carters providing backup. Sara and Maybelle also got together for an album for Columbia, from which "The Ship That Never Returned" is excerpted. Of course, none of this material ranks with the handful of songs by the original Carters, and sometimes the segues can be jarring, as when the 1940 recording of "Behind Those Stone Walls" gives way to a Carter Sisters cover of Cash's "I Walk the Line." But the album gives a sense of the breadth of talent in the Carters, their progeny, and their in-laws and stepchildren. *—William Ruhlmann*

Best of the Best of the Original Carter Family / Jan. 6, 1998 / Koch ✦✦✦✦✦
There are better, more extensive Carter Family compilations available than *Best of the Best of the Carter Family*, but it does make a nice, budget-priced introductory sampler. *—Steve Huey*

On Border Radio, Vol. 3: 1939 / Mar. 23, 1999 / Arhoolie ✦✦✦
There's apparently a well-full of transcription discs of late-'30s Carter Family broadcasts on XET in Monterrey, Mexico, as this series enters its third volume with no drops in quality. Again it shows the Carters in various combinations, sometimes featuring Janette Carter, sometimes the then-young Carter children, sometimes A.P. There are a bunch of famed standards on board here, like "You Are My Sunshine," "Worried Man Blues," "Great Speckled Bird," "I Shall Not Be Moved," "Wade in the Water," "Something Got a Hold on Me," "I've Been Working on the Railroad" and "Oh, Susanna," though many of the 20-odd tracks are less familiar. It, and other discs in the series, are less recommended than their studio recordings because the songs (including some station IDs) are often extremely short and the presentation less consistent than on the average Carter Family compilation. For serious Carter Family fans, though, they're valuable additions to the act's discography. *—Richie Unterberger*

★ **Can the Circle Be Unbroken?: Country Music's First Family** / Jul. 4, 2000 / Columbia/Legacy ✦✦✦✦✦
The second half of the Carter Family's recorded output largely rests with the contents of this CD. It's their output for Columbia's OKeh and Conqueror labels, 17 of the 20 recorded over five days in May 1935 and the final three from an October 1940 session. In typical Carter Family fashion, the material is wide ranging and eclectic, running from British folk music ("Black Jack David," "Sinking in the Lonesome Sea") to gospel ("On the Rock Where Moses Stood," "River of Jordan") to blues ("Worried Man Blues") and beyond. Along the way we're treated to re-cuts of notable Carter "hits" like "Can the Circle Be Unbroken," "Wildwood Flower," and "Keep on the Sunny Side." After you collect all of their Victor recordings from the 1920s, here's your next stop, an indispensable addition to any basic country collection. *—Cub Koda*

Country Music Hall of Fame: 1970 / Jul. 11, 2000 / King ✦✦
A decent overview of "The First Family of Country Music," filled with excellent examples of why the Carter Family was so influential. Old-timey classics like "Can the Circle Be Unbroken" and "Wildwood Flower" are represented as familiar favorites, but "Black Jack David" stands out as a showcase of both Maybelle Carter's pervasive guitar picking and the family's haunting vocal harmonies, so much so that Harry Smith selected it to be included it on his *Anthology of American Folk Music, Vol. 4*. The recording is beautifully dotted with analog pops from the original masters, but the packaging is woefully lacking detail regarding the tracks and recording dates. *—Zac Johnson*

Wildwood Flower / Aug. 8, 2000 / ASV ✦✦✦✦✦
As a single-disc compilation of the Carter Family's peak years, *Wildwood Flower* is unbeatable. These 25 songs are the original hits recorded for RCA and Decca from 1927-1938, in the finest remastered sound possible. Mountains of praise have been written about the Carters over the years, from their wonderful harmony singing to Maybelle's influential guitar technique, and this is the place to go to hear why. *—Jim Smith*

☆ **In the Shadow of Clinch Mountain** / Sep. 12, 2000 / Bear Family ✦✦✦✦✦
It seems simple enough: Find every single recording by the first family of American country music and put 'em in a big box with a killer hardcover book full of essays and pictures and intricate track notation, right? Wrong. While it's true that Germany's Bear Family label produces box sets that virtually put every other company—especially those in America—to shame, it's the fanatical attention to detail and aesthetics that makes these sets so necessary. *In the Shadow of Clinch Mountain* is a case in point, for it contains virtually every recording done by the Carter Family for every label they recorded for. No one else, not even Rounder with its exhaustive but slipshod reissuing of the Victor recordings, has even come close. Contained on 12 CDs are the sides that the Carter Family recorded

for Victor, ARC, Decca, APS, Columbia, and even Bluebird. The sound sets a re-mastering standard for regaining fidelity from old masters without compromising integrity, and the package features photographs from the personal collections of Mother Maybelle and Janette Carter, as well as numerous publicity shots. There is a fine biographical essay by Charles Wolfe, and disc 12 is an interview conducted in 1963 by Mike Seeger and Ed Khan with Sara and Maybelle. The attention to detail on the track notation is frightening in its intricacy, and the book as a whole weighs more than the box with the CDs! Enough about the package; it's the music that counts. From the earliest days of the Bristol, TN, sessions recorded by Ralph Peer in 1927, the Carters are documented not only as a developing recording and touring act, but also as interpreters of virtually forgotten songs of every type: folk songs, child ballads, gospel songs, blues, primitive forms of bluegrass, adapted shapenote songs, etc. The beginnings are easy enough to hear as history, for they have been presented in numerous settings before. On those first two days of August in Bristol, the Carters—A.P., his wife Sara, and cousin Maybelle—cut six sides for Peer, who was on a mission not only as a talent scout searching for the best of the traditional music acts in the Clinch Mountain vicinity (the Stonemans were already recording by then), but was also hoping to find songs that had not been recorded before to bring them under a publishing umbrella. A.P., as is demonstrated on CD after CD, was an astute and crafty collector of old songs that he, Sara, and Maybelle remade in their own image. "Single Girl, Married Girl," from that first session, sticks out as something unmistakably and purely Carter, no matter how many times it was cut subsequently by other artists. The Victor period was certainly the freshest period for the group, as is evidenced here, but the Coral, Brunswick, Bluebird, and OKeh tenures, the final recordings by the original Carters made a scant 14 years later, are equally strong for their assurance and the haunting demeanor the songs and delivery had taken on. A.P.'s bass voice picked up the bottom end and fed it to Sara, who soared with Maybelle finding her way through the middle and playing some of the meanest slide guitar north of the Mississippi Delta. The now famous "No Depression" along with "In the Shadow of the Pines," "Answer to Weeping Willow," and "Dark Haired True Lover" from 1936 and 1937 were stellar in their delivery and in the lively harmony style A.P. developed around Sara's voice. But even at the very end, when the Carters recut "Keep on the Sunny Side" and "Single Girl, Married Girl," there were new gems in the form of Maybelle's "Lonesome Homesick Blues" and "You Tied a Love Knot in My Heart," as well as the final recording of A.P.'s "Wabash Cannonball." When A.P. walked away from music in 1941, it was Mother Maybelle, mother of June Carter Cash, and Janette Carter, A.P. and Sara's daughter, who kept the flame alive. That story, too, is told here. But in the pictures, the song lyrics (complete), and the music itself, a much broader story is told, not only of the Carters but of the entire history of country music in particular and American popular music in general. Here were ordinary people who made extraordinary music, and changed the face of everything forever. It's hard to say if Peer had any inkling of this when he signed the Carters, but he had the vision and crafty knowhow to get the records made, pressed, and delivered to the public. The Carters' legacy as documented here leaves behind far more than the story of the first family of country music; it documents the continuation of the folk song tradition as administered by the Carters. While it's true that A.P.'s name is on almost all of these songs, he didn't write them. They were old as the hills themselves and in some cases older. In many cases, when the roots of a particular song could not be found, A.P. would learn it, change some words or a harmony or a melody line, and call it his own. And it was far from unethical during that time. And thank God he did, for many of these treasures, so readily available to anyone who wants to seek them out, would no doubt have passed into antiquity unremembered. This is the box set of the year 2002. *—Thom Jurek*

☆ **The Decca Sessions, Vol. 1 (1936)** / May 22, 2001 / Catfish ✦✦✦✦✦

If there was a Mount Rushmore of country music, the Carter Family would be on it. That, however, doesn't mean that everyone listens to their music; their old-timey vocals strike many as out of tune, rough-hewn, and otherworldly. The recordings the Carter Family made for Decca between 1936 and 1938, however, are different. Some aficionados consider these to be the group's finest. *The Decca Sessions, Vol. 1* may also be one of their most assessable recordings. What's the difference? Mostly it comes down to the superb harmony that Maybelle and Sara Carter sang while working for Decca. Their close harmony on songs like "My Dixie Darling" and "Bonnie Blue Eyes" is similar to the type of harmony the Monroe Brothers and the Blue Sky Boys sang during the '30s. Sara Carter usually sings lead, as on "You've Been a Friend to Me," and is joined by Maybelle, and sometimes A.P. Carter, on the chorus. A.P. Carter brought new material to these sessions (at least new to their repertoire), and while only hardcore fans will be familiar with songs like "In the Shadow of the Pines," it is all excellent. *The Decca Sessions, Vol. 1* represent the groups first two recording dates for Decca on June 3rd and 9th of 1936. Catfish has put together a nice package and fans will know the value of these recordings. To the uninitiated, *The Decca Sessions, Vol. 1* offers an excellent chance to find out why the Carter Family have been long held in such high esteem. *—Ronnie D. Lankford Jr.*

The Carter Family: 1927–1934 / Apr. 30, 2002 / JSP ✦✦✦✦✦

Fans looking for more than ASV/Living Era's *Wildwood Flower* collection but scared off by Bear Family's massive 12-disc box could comfortably pick up this five-disc budget compilation. At 126 songs, it covers all of their RCA Victor recordings in chronological order, omitting only alternate takes. The remastering isn't necessarily better than other Carter Family issues—rather than clean up the crackle, the engineers have simply boosted the sound level, and while that does bring out some nuances, the ever-present hiss is louder than usual. That and the scanty liner notes mean that casual fans could probably do perfectly well with *Wildwood Flower*, but this music is going to be an outstanding addition to any collection, especially at a price this low. *—Jim Smith*

The Decca Sessions, Vol. 2 / May 21, 2002 / Catfish ✦✦✦

☆ **The Carter Family, Vol. 2: 1935–1941** / Apr. 8, 2003 / JSP ✦✦✦✦✦

British label JSP offers another of their fine budget collections on *The Carter Family, Vol. 2: 1935-1941*. On 129 songs collected on five CDs, this second volume in the series gives a complete overview of the first family of country music's later years. Legendary songs like "Can the Circle Be Unbroken," "Keep on the Sunny Side," "No Depression," "Single Girl, Married Girl," and "I'm Thinking Tonight of My Blue Eyes" are all represented, and the sound quality is slightly more even than on the first JSP box, *The Carter Family: 1927-1934*. Essentially, anyone who can pull together the 60 dollars or so that it would take to own both sets will have not only virtually every Carter Family studio recording, but also a valuable archive of the roots of American music. *—Zac Johnson*

Carter Sisters

f. 1943, **db.** 1960

Group / Old-Timey, Traditional Country

An offshoot of the legendary Carter Family, the Carter Sisters consisted of Helen, June, and Anita Carter, the three daughters of original Carter Family member Maybelle Carter (with whom they often performed) and Ezra Carter. Helen (accordion, guitar, autoharp; b. September 12, 1927), June (autoharp; b. June 23, 1929), and Anita (standup bass; b. March 31, 1933) all made their performing debuts with the Carter Family as young girls, with the elder two starting in the mid-'30s. When the original Carter Family lineup officially disbanded in 1943, Maybelle gathered her daughters into a new group dubbed Mother Maybelle & the Carter Sisters, built around Helen's musicianship, Anita's lead vocals, and June's gregarious, comic stage presence. They quickly became radio regulars in Richmond, VA, performing on two prominent stations through 1948. That year, they moved to a radio station in Knoxville, TN, where they found a brilliant accompanist in guitarist Chet Atkins, then a young virtuoso just beginning to make his mark. The year 1949 took the family to Springfield, MO, for another radio engagement, and in 1950 they moved to Nashville to join the *Grand Ole Opry*, where they remained regulars for the next decade. During that time, both Anita and June went off on occasional solo ventures, and also served as duet partners for singers like Hank Snow and Carl Smith, respectively. Over 1956-1957, the group toured as Elvis Presley's opening act.

When family patriarch A.P. Carter passed away in 1960, Mother Maybelle & the Carter Sisters took over the Carter Family name. Aside from their solo recordings, they spent much of the '60s backing Johnny Cash in various combinations, appearing on his 1963 hit "Busted"; June, of course, married him in 1968, and she and her sisters appeared regularly on his variety show during the next few years. As the Carter Family, the group also made several recordings, including a 1962 album for Decca, another for CBS in 1964 (*Keep on the Sunny Side*), and two for Columbia—*Travelin' Minstrel Band* and *Three Generations*—in 1972 and 1974, respectively. Mother Maybelle passed away in 1978. Ten years later, all three Carter Sisters reunited for the Mercury album *Wildwood Flower*, a collection of Carter Family standards that also featured June's daughter, country-rock singer Carlene Carter. Helen passed away on June 2, 1998; Anita followed her on July 29, 1999; and June succumbed to heart problems on May 15, 2003. *—Steve Huey*

● **Maybelle, Anita, June & Helen** / Bear Family ✦✦✦✦✦

Anita Carter

b. Mar. 31, 1933, Maces Springs, VA, **d.** Jul. 29, 1999, Goodletsville, TN

Vocals / Old-Timey, Traditional Country

A member of country music's most famous family, Anita Carter found success of her own as a folk solo act during the early '50s and late '60s. The Carter Family had ruled country music during the 1930s, but broke up in 1943 after patriarch A.P. Carter and his ex-wife Sara decided to retire. Sara's cousin Maybelle, the third member of the Carters, re-formed the group the same year—as Mother Maybelle & the Carter Sisters—with her daughters Helen, June, and Anita. The sisters had sung on Carter Family radio broadcasts in 1935, and the new group more than made up for the breakup of the originals. The Carters performed on radio from Virginia, Tennessee, and Missouri during the late '40s, but moved to the *Grand Ole Opry* in 1950.

In 1951, Anita stormed the charts with a one-off duet with Hank Snow; both "Bluebird Island" and its B-side, "Down the Trail of Achin' Hearts," reached the country Top Five. During the mid-'50s, she also performed with the teen trio 'Nita, Rita & Ruby, but spent most of her time with the Carters. The group continued to be popular on the *Opry*, and even opened for Elvis Presley in 1956-1957. After A.P. Carter's death in 1960, Mother Maybelle & the Carter Sisters became the Carter Family and performed more contemporary country than gospel.

In 1961, the Carters began a long-running association with Johnny Cash by appearing in his road show. They recorded the country Top 15 single "Busted" with Cash in 1963, and after June Carter married him in 1967, the Carters appeared on his ABC-TV show from 1969 to 1971. Though the Carter Family continued to record—usually with Cash—during the early '70s, they disbanded in 1969. Mother Maybelle became recognized as a major figure in the folk revival that year, appearing with Sara at the Newport Folk Festival and on the Rounder album *An Historic Reunion*.

Meanwhile, Anita had begun to record for RCA in 1966, hitting the country charts with "I'm Gonna Leave You." Another single charted in 1967, and her duet with Waylon Jennings on "I Got You" reached number four in March 1968. Later in 1968, Anita moved to United Artists, but several singles proved unsuccessful. She recorded for Capitol in the early '70s and almost hit the Top 40 with "Tulsa County." Her last chart appearance with the Carter Family, "Praise the Lord and Pass the Soup," was released in August 1973. In July of 1999, ten years after the release of the collection *Ring of Fire* on the Bear Family label, vocalist Anita Carter passed away in Tennessee. *—John Bush*

Folk Songs Old and New / 1963 / Mercury ✦✦✦✦

● **Ring of Fire** / 1989 / Bear Family ✦✦✦✦✦

It's been well documented that June Carter Cash and Merle Kilgore wrote the song "Ring of Fire," which is about her early relationship with Johnny Cash. What's less well known is that it was her youngest sister, Anita, not Johnny Cash, who cut it first, accompanied only by a pair of acoustic guitars. *Ring of Fire* is the German Bear Family label's presentation of Anita Carter's 1962-1964 Mercury recordings. While Carter is also a daughter of Mother Maybelle, country music, at least in the early '60s, was not her forte—folk music was. There are 25 tracks here, all of them stunning, some of them unknown, but all of them fine. Some of the cuts here are historic debuts of songs performed by folk and country artist later on. The initial recording of "Satan's Child," written by sister Helen and Danny Dill, Kilgore's "Sour Grapes," her own "All My Trials," and the cut she wrote with June and Kilgore, "As the Sparrow Goes," are all here, as well as readings of A.P. and Maybelle tunes such as her mother's "Fair and Tender Ladies" and "In the Highways," A.P.'s "John Hardy, Bury Me Beneath the Willow," and more. There are unreleased gems here too: a recording of Harlan Howard's "A Few Short Years Ago" and Irving Gordon's "The Kentuckian Song." But more than the cuts—produced in Nashville and New York by Jerry Kennedy, Shelby Singelton, and Milt Okun—this recording reveals that Carter's voice is one of the purest and most expressive vehicles either country or folk ever produced. Carter's own reticence is what held her back from superstardom. The music here, most of it with two acoustic guitars, some with a double bass, is simple, even ghostly in the way it frames a voice so seemingly plaintive, yet with a range that is awe-inspiring, given how pristine her singing was, and how she could take even the corniest song ("Voice of the Bayou") and make it a believable and true statement of passion, purpose, or poisonous emotion. By the time the record ends with "Wildwood Flower," the listener has been transported out of time and space and into the heart of Carter's mysterious, darkly inviting, and spiritually resilient vocal. This is one of the best single-volume compilations Bear Family has ever done. *—Thom Jurek*

Carlene Carter

b. Sep. 26, 1955, Nashville, TN

Guitar, Piano, Vocals / Contemporary Country, Roots Rock, New Wave, Neo-Traditionalist Country

Carlene Carter has always straddled the line between country and rock. Beginning her career as a rock singer in the mid-'70s, she became immersed in the new wave in the late '70s, before emerging as a new country singer in the late '80s, Throughout it all, her music has always infused roots music—whether country or rock & roll—with a nervy, edgy energy. Carlene is the daughter of June Carter and Carl Smith, who divorced when their daughter was just two. June would frequently take her daughter on Carter Family tours, which meant that Carlene developed a musical interest at an early age. When she was 12, her mother married Johnny Cash. Following the marriage, Carlene and her stepsister, Rosanne Cash, became backup singers in the Carter/Cash touring show. At the age of 15 she married Joe Simpkins and had a child; they were divorced within a few years. Carter enrolled in college as a piano major in her late teens, but she never graduated. At 19, she married Jack Routh and had another child; they were divorced within two years.

In 1978, she decided to pursue a musical career, heading to Los Angeles where she received a record contract with Warner Bros. Her debut album, *Carlene Carter*, was a rock & roll record recorded in London with Graham Parker's backing band, the Rumour. The following year, she released her second album, *Two Sides to Every Woman*, which featured support from the Doobie Brothers. That same year she married singer/songwriter/producer Nick Lowe, who was currently the co-leader of the new wave rock & roll revival band, Rockpile. Lowe helped Carter shape her musical direction in the early '80s, and her third album—the new wave-inflected country-rock record *Musical Shapes* (1980)—showed the influence of Lowe, Rockpile, and Dave Edmunds. Although the album was critically acclaimed, it was a commercial failure. She followed *Musical Shapes* in 1981 with *Blue Nun*, which continued to pursue a new wave-country direction; like its predecessor, it was ignored.

During the early '80s, Carter was shut off from the country community because she was living in England with Lowe. After *Blue Nun*, she stopped recording, choosing to perform solo shows instead; she also had a starring role in the theatrical production *Pump Boys and Dinettes*. Carter and Lowe's marriage collapsed in the mid-'80s and she returned to the States, where she became part of the touring Carter Family. In 1989, she began working on a comeback record with Howie Epstein, the bassist for Tom Petty & the Heartbreakers. That same year, she performed a duet with Southern Pacific on the Top 40 hit "Time's Up." Reprise signed Carter in 1990 and she released her overdue fifth album, *I Fell in Love*, later that year. *I Fell in Love* still had rock influences, but it was a more straightforward country record than her previous albums, and country radio paid attention. The album became a hit and two singles, "I Fell in Love" and "Come on Back," climbed all the way to number three. *Little Love Letters*, her 1993 follow-up (which was released on Giant Records), was equally successful; its first single, "Every Little Thing," was another number three hit. *Little Acts of Treason*, her 1995 album, wasn't as big a hit as its two predecessors, but it still enjoyed moderate success on the country charts. A hits collection, *Hindsight 20/20*, appeared in the fall of 1996. *—Stephen Thomas Erlewine*

Carlene Carter / 1978 / Warner Bros. ✦✦✦

By recording her debut album in England, Carlene Carter served notice that despite coming from a legendary American country music family, she intended to make her own way in the biz and establish her own musical identity. So while there's a strong country-rock vibe throughout *Carlene Carter*, it's filtered through the British pub rock sensibilities of the Rumour, whose members produce, arrange, and play on all of the tracks on this album (with occasional cameo appearances from pub rock icons Graham Parker, Terry Williams, and Nick Lowe). The results of this transatlantic crossbreeding are generally winning, if a little uneven; on a few tracks, it seems as if both Carter and the Rumour are keeping some of their energy in check as they try to feel each other out. For the most part, though, the performances on *Carlene Carter* are bright and enthusiastic, and the songwriting contributions of Alex Call, Graham Parker, and Carter herself are all quite good, even if their subject matter is generally nothing more complex than love gone wrong. To top it all off, Carter had the good sense to call in at least one family member to help out—and brother-in-law Rodney Crowell did not disappoint, contributing "Never Together But Close Sometimes," a bouncy rocker that's the album's clear highlight. *—K.A. Scott*

Two Sides to Every Woman / 1979 / Warner Bros. ✦✦✦

This is Carter's second album and not as interesting as the first. Some of the songs are a bit weak and the Rumour have been replaced with studio musicians. It's OK, but not for everyone. *—Jim Worbois*

Musical Shapes / 1980 / F Beat ✦✦✦✦✦

This is Carter's masterpiece to date. Great songs and production that could easily fit into today's climate of country radio. *—Cub Koda*

Blue Nun / 1981 / F Beat ✦✦✦

Carter's American label passed on this one, and it's too bad. While it's not one of her best albums, when she's on, she's dead on. It's interesting from a historical point because it somewhat chronicles her musical associations with former-husband Nick Lowe and Paul Carrack (ex-Ace, Squeeze, Mike + the Mechanics). *—Jim Worbois*

C'est C Bon / 1983 / Razor & Tie ✦✦

This not particularly interesting album suffers from lack of direction. It was the last album of her early period, before she re-created herself in 1990 as a country singer to be reckoned with. For die-hard fans only. *—Jim Worbois*

I Fell in Love / 1990 / Reprise ✦✦✦✦✦

This comeback album has a perfect mix of old (A. P. Carter's "My Dixie Darlin'") and new (guest spots from Dave Edmunds, David Lindley, and Albert Lee). If Carter hasn't come to terms with her love for rock and her duty to heritage, she's at least learned to balance them. *—Brian Mansfield*

Musical Shapes/Blue Nun / 1992 / Demon ✦✦✦✦✦

Demon Records reissued Carlene Carter's *Musical Shapes* and *Blue Nun* on one disc in 1992. Neither album is straight country—with their propulsive rhythms and jangling guitars, they exhibit the influence of her then-current husband Nick Lowe—but *Musical Shapes* is one of her best records, and worth getting in any form. *—Stephen Thomas Erlewine*

Little Love Letters / 1993 / Giant ✦✦✦✦✦

This is the album fans always dreamed she would make. While it shows off her love of, and ability to handle, various styles of music, she never loses her direction. *—Jim Worbois*

Little Acts of Treason / Oct. 1995 / Giant ✦✦✦

Carlene Carter's *Little Acts of Treason* doesn't break much new ground for the singer, but that's not necessarily a bad thing. While she continues in the same vein as *Little Love Letters*, the music is done well, even if the album isn't as infectious and catchy as her previous album. *—Stephen Thomas Erlewine*

★ **Hindsight 20/20** / Sep. 9, 1996 / Giant ✦✦✦✦✦

Hindsight 20/20 is a comprehensive overview of Carlene Carter's career, concentrating on country hits like "Every Little Thing" and "I Fell in Love," but also touching on her earlier recordings like "Never Together But Close Sometimes." The compilation offers an excellent introduction and encapsulation of one of the finest female country singers of the '80s and '90s. *—Stephen Thomas Erlewine*

Deana Carter

b. 1964

Vocals / Contemporary Country, Singer/Songwriter, Country-Folk, Neo-Traditionalist Country

Though she didn't begin her musical career until relatively late, Deana Carter managed to defy conventional expectations and unexpectedly shot to the top of the country charts upon the release of her 1996 debut, *Did I Shave My Legs for This?* Carter's success was equally unexpected considering that she didn't quite fit into the mold of a standard female contemporary country singer. Melding the popular appeal of country chanteuses with folky singer/songwriters like Mary-Chapin Carpenter, Carter racked up both positive reviews and healthy sales with *Did I Shave My Legs for This?*, becoming one of the most pleasant success stories of the post-Garth Brooks generation.

As the daughter of Nashville studio guitarist Fred Carter Jr., Deana Carter grew up in a musical environment, and was exposed to a wide variety of music. Fred played guitar for a wide variety of musicians, including Willie Nelson, Bob Dylan, Waylon Jennings, and Simon & Garfunkel. The music of those artists would eventually seep into Deana's own style, which she hadn't yet formed when she initially tried to land a record contract at the age of 17. Despite her efforts and her father's assistance, Carter wasn't able to secure a deal, so she abandoned music to study nursing at the University of Tennessee. While she was a student, she continued to sing for fun, yet she didn't devote much energy to music. After graduation, Carter worked in a few hospitals before deciding to pursue a musical career at the age of 23. Learning the guitar for the first time, Deana also began to write songs. For several years, she worked odd jobs as she continued to develop her songwriting skills and sing at Nashville nightclubs. Eventually, one of her demo tapes made its way to Willie Nelson, while another wound up in the offices of Capitol Nashville. Nelson, who remembered her from her childhood, was impressed with Carter's songs and asked her to perform at *Farm Aid VII* in 1994; she was the only female artist on the entire bill. Within a year, Capitol Nashville had signed Deana Carter to a contract.

Boasting six songs co-written by Carter, her debut album, *Did I Shave My Legs For This?*, was released to strong reviews in late summer of 1996. By the end of the year, the record had climbed to the upper reaches of the country charts and had made inroads on the pop charts, going gold in the process. *Everything's Gonna Be Alright* followed in late 1998. In 2001, Carter realized her dream of performing with her father on her holiday album, *Father Christmas*, which featured her dad on guitar. *I'm Just a Girl*, a recording that leans strongly toward adult pop, was released on Arista Nashville in 2003. *—Stephen Thomas Erlewine*

● **Did I Shave My Legs for This?** / 1995 / Capitol Nashville ✦✦✦✦✦
Deana Carter's debut album may have seemed like the arrival of an overnight sensation, but that was hardly the truth. Carter cracked it finally at 30, after trying since she was 17 as the daughter of kicking country guitar picker Fred Carter Jr. With its ironic odd title and its mix of singer/songwriter folk, new traditionalist country, and pop, Carter came up with a winner. Produced by Chris Farren and Jimmy Bowen, Carter's album features six originals, including the title track, "Count Me In," the amazing opener, "I've Loved Enough to Know," with its hooky guitars, shimmering fiddles, and cascading pianos, the gorgeous "Love Ain't Worth Making" and "Before We Ever Heard Goodbye," and "How Do I Get There." These are the album's strongest tunes, full of passion and sincerity regarding love, its fulfillment and impossibility, as well as its mystery. And the woman can write a hook. There's a radio-friendly rock and pop feel to tracks such as Mac Wiseman's hard country tonkin' "If This Is Love" and Matraca Berg's pedal steel-ringing "Strawberry Wine." That she sold a few million copies of this record to country fans is not surprising at all; that she sold a few million more to AAA radio fans and to those whose musical tastes are dictated by NPR is. Most of these folks bitch like crazy about "young country," and Carter defined it with her very first record in all the best ways: using the country tradition to make fine, well-crafted music that appeals to a broad range of tastes. *—Thom Jurek*

Everything's Gonna Be Alright / Oct. 20, 1998 / Capitol Nashville ✦✦✦✦
Deana Carter's debut album, *Did I Shave My Legs for This?*, was a surprise hit, considering that its grace, subtlety, and wit were largely qualities unheard of in contemporary country in 1996, the year it climbed up the charts. It immediately marked her as a major artist, placing great expectations on her second album, *Everything's Gonna Be Alright.* Lacking the surprise element of *Legs*, *Everything's* is nevertheless in many ways its equal, since Carter has chosen to expand its sound, not to replicate it. There are more laid-back rock and pop elements to her style this time around, which fits well with her folky, melodic country. Even the presence of Lynyrd Skynyrd as the support band for "The Train Song" (earthy, not rowdy), works better than it reads. Furthermore, her songwriting is melodic and memorable, and her choice of covers, including Melanie's "Brand New Key," is inspired. As long as Carter continues to deliver albums as enchanting as *Everything's Gonna Be Alright*, things are going to be just fine for her and her fans. *—Thom Owens*

The Deana Carter Collection / Aug. 13, 2002 / Capitol Nashville ✦✦
One can't call this collection a greatest-hits album because Deana Carter really only had two albums and five Top Ten hits from which she would be able to choose. So essentially what you have here is an obvious attempt by her record label to resurrect an ailing career from someone fans haven't heard from in more than four years. A few favorites like "Strawberry Wine," "Did I Shave My Legs for This," "How Do I Get There," and "We Danced Anyway" serve as a reminder to why this barefoot baroness was loved back in her day. She includes songs previously released on 1998's *Everything's Gonna Be Alright* but never released to radio. The one standout is "Rita Valentine," once available only in Europe, about a woman who blows throw people's lives. There's little that's new here, but if you're a fan of Carter's folksy style and melodic country-pop/rock, you could find something worthwhile here. *—Maria Konicki Dinoia*

I'm Just a Girl / Mar. 18, 2003 / Arista ✦✦✦✦
Deana Carter had a hard time following up her acclaimed debut, 1995's *Did I Shave My Legs For This?*, stumbling with 1998's *Everything's Gonna Be Alright* before leaving Capitol Records and re-emerging nearly four and a half years later on Arista Nashville with *I'm Just a Girl.* A lot had happened in country music in the years that Carter sat out, including shifts toward both pop (in Shania Twain and Faith Hill) and roots (the *O Brother Where Art Thou?* phenomenon), and Carter continues to run outside the path by not pursuing either direction. Instead, she aims straight toward the heart of adult pop (slightly ironic, given the album's title and its *17* magazine-styled artwork), which really isn't too far off from where she was with on her first record. Still, there are telling differences: The production, apart from the closing raver "Girls' Night," is all smooth and polished, sweetened with pop and lacking nearly any hint of country, as well as the clear sense of humor. There's a keener eye toward a broader audience, right down to the cheesecake photos inside the liner notes, and the product placement in "I'm Just a Girl" sits uneasily (particularly since closing the chorus with "I'm a Chevy girl" makes it sound like an unofficial commercial). Those may seem disarming to those looking for the organic feel of *Did I Shave My Legs*, but Carter does this pleasing adult pop better than nearly any of her peers, partially because her ambitions are modest and her songwriting is sturdy and tuneful. At times, the production is so even, the music simply flows out of the speaker without distinction between tracks, but the result is a record that holds together as a nice mood piece while holding up as individual songs. True, it doesn't deliver a knockout punch upon the first listen, but it wasn't designed to. It's a quiet grower, filled with easy listening and sunny vibes. It might not earn quite the same audience as her debut, but this is about as good as adult-oriented pop gets in 2003. *—Stephen Thomas Erlewine*

Mother Maybelle Carter (Maybelle Addington)

b. May 10, 1909, Nickelsville, VA, **d.** Oct. 23, 1978, Nashville, TN
Guitar, Autoharp, Vocals, Banjo / Old-Timey, Traditional Country
Affectionately and even reverently known as "Mother" Maybelle, Maybelle Carter was one-third of country music's original first family, the Carters. Born Maybelle Addington in May of 1909, she was related by marriage to A.P. and Sara Carter—she married A.P.'s brother Ezra. Maybelle Carter was the group's guitarist and also played autoharp and banjo; she created a unique sound for the group with her innovative bass tunings and played on all of their most famous recordings from 1928-1943, some 270 sides. After the Carters split as an act, Maybelle went on the road and into the recording studios with her daughters Helen, Anita, and June, all of whom achieved some degree of success in the country music field; June became a legend. Mother Maybelle enjoyed many milestones in her long career, and was sought out for counsel by two succeeding generations. Most notable was her reunion appearance with Sara at *the Newport Folk Festival*, which was released as *An Historic Reunion*, issued on CD first by the Bear Family label in Germany in 1991 and then by Koch International in 1997. Of her solo recordings, her eponymously titled debut issued on the Ambassador label in 1957 drew great acclaim, as did her *Queen of the Autoharp* album on Kapp in 1964. Mother Maybelle was prominently featured as a centerpiece on the 1971 Nitty Gritty Dirt Band classic, *Will the Circle Be Unbroken*, which introduced her to an entirely new generation of rock fans. She died in October of 1978. *—Thom Jurek*

● **Mother Maybelle Carter** / 195 / Ambassador ✦✦✦✦✦

Queen of the Autoharp / 1964 / Kapp ✦✦✦

Living Legend / 1965 / Columbia ✦✦✦

Wildwood Pickin' / Jan. 21, 1997 / Vanguard ✦✦✦✦

Sara & Maybelle Carter

Group / Old Timey, Traditional Country
Sara & Maybelle Carter are two-thirds of the Carter Family, the first family of country music. Sara (born Sara Dougherty) married A.P. Carter, and her cousin Maybelle Addington married A.P.'s brother Ezra. A.P., an avid song collector and writer, created a trio along with Sara and Maybelle, the prime vocalist of the trio. They recorded 270 songs between 1927 and 1943, when they officially split. Sara and A.P. divorced in 1939 and continued as an act until 1943. Sara moved west in 1945 with her new husband, Coy Bays (A.P.'s cousin). In 1952 Sara and A.P. were reunited professionally with their children and, between 1952-1956, recorded 90 more sides before disbanding permanently. Maybelle began to tour and record with her daughters June, Helen, and Anita as Mother Maybelle & the Carter Sisters. Sara retired from music entirely in 1956 and recorded just one more time in 1967 with Maybelle and a nephew (also named A.P. Carter) at *the Newport Folk Festival.* A documentary album from the concert was released as *An Historic Reunion* on LP. It was reissued on CD by the German Bear Family label in 1991 and in America by Koch International in 1997. Sara Carter died in 1979 and Maybelle continued to record solo with her daughters and granddaughters until her death in 1978. Her appearance on the Nitty Gritty Dirt Band's *Will the Circle Be Unbroken* album is the stuff of popular music legend. *—Thom Jurek*

● **Sara & Maybelle Carter** / 1991 / Bear Family ✦✦✦✦✦
Bear Family's *Sara & Maybelle Carter* compact disc combines the duo's 1966 album *An Historic Reunion* with Maybelle's solo record, *A Living Legend*, from that same year. *An Historic Reunion* was a moving final album from the duo, divided between gospel and traditional songs. Despite the fact that Sara and Maybelle hadn't sung together in over 20 years, the two sound like they never left; their harmonies, occasionally with Sara and Joe Carter's son A.P. providing a third part, are as spine-chillingly pure as ever. *A Living Legend* isn't quite as thrilling, but there are a handful of fine songs from the record and its inclusion is a nice way to round out the disc. *—Stephen Thomas Erlewine*

Wilf Carter

b. Dec. 18, 1904, Port Hilford, Nova Scotia, Canada, **d.** Dec. 5, 1996, Scottsdale, AZ
Guitar, Vocals / Traditional Country, Cowboy, Yodeling
Although he is largely forgotten today outside of Canada, where his commercial career lasted far longer than it did in the U.S., Wilf Carter was a unique presence in country music and cowboy music from the 1930s until the end of the 1950s. Rare is the mid-century yodeller whose background predates the start of Jimmie Rodgers' career—Carter represented one of the longest surviving links with country music before there was a recording industry. Although Canadian by birth, he was seduced by country music and, specifically, by the wonder of the American West, and created a body of work as unique and distinctive as any singer/guitarist of his era, romantic, playful, and upbeat.

He was born Wilfred Arthur Charles Carter, one of nine children. The family was poor, and by the time he was eight or nine, Carter was helping to support them by working in the fields in the nearby Annapolis Valley. By age 12, he was working away from home. It was a traveling show and the presence of a performer known as "The Yodeling Fool" introduced him to country music and inspired him to learn to yodel. Carter worked farms in central Nova Scotia during his early teens, and when he was 16, he left home in a dispute with his father, a strict Baptist and missionary, over attending prayer services. At age 17, he came to the U.S. to work in Massachusetts for a time, but he later returned to Nova Scotia. He later headed to western Canada to work the harvests out in Alberta, and he became adept at breaking horses. It was while in western Canada that Carter began singing at local dances, and he auditioned for a spot on the radio in 1925. At the time, he usually sang and yodeled without accompaniment, or occasionally added an autoharp.

By 1929, he'd moved to Calgary and competed in local rodeos. When he sang, it was mostly for money on the street. Finally, in 1930, he got a job with a Calgary radio station, CFCN ("The Voice of the Prairies"), singing one night each week. This led to a job offer from the CBC, and he also signed a contract as a songwriter with a Toronto publishing house. Carter had taken up the guitar by then, which he taught himself. Carter was hired as a trail hand and entertainer by the Canadian Pacific Railway, which ran tours for Easterners seeking a taste of the real West. Eventually he became the company's major entertainer. He had a chance to audition for RCA Records' Canadian branch in Montreal, but couldn't afford to lose the pay that it would cost him if he made the trip, even if passage was free (as the Canadian railway was offering). Finally, late in 1933, when the cruise ship on which he was singing was on the East Coast of Canada, he got to Montreal for a chance to audition for RCA, and this resulted in a contract early in 1934 and the release of his first record, "My Swiss Moonlight Lullaby" b/w "The Capture of Albert Johnson." The record went on to become a hit in Canada, and prospects were looking better for Carter. In those days, however, most record contracts—in the U.S. and even more so in Canada—were structured more as a means of getting the artist exposure, rather than a lucrative activity in their own right, and Carter continued living hand-to-mouth.

In 1935, while in New York, he began broadcasting on the CBS radio network as "Montana Slim," a name he picked up when the typist transcribing lyrics attached it to him. The name seemed to fit him, however, and from that time on, many of his records were issued in Canada credited to Wilf Carter, and American releases were credited to Montana Slim. In contrast to Canadian broadcasting, radio in New York during the 1930s was the big time—at the epicenter of the entertainment world in those days, in fact—and paid commensurately better; by 1937, his broadcasts out of New York had brought Carter (who was by then married to the former Bobbie Bryan, a Pennsylvania-born nurse) sufficient success to allow him to buy a ranch in Alberta in 1937. He moved between the CBC, NBC, and CBS over the next three years until CBS dropped him in 1940. An automobile accident around that time resulted in a period of nearly four years during which Carter didn't record at all and hardly performed.

In 1947, Carter began recording for RCA-Victor in America, and two years later, he and his family moved to New Jersey. That same year, Carter made his only appearance on the *Grand Ole Opry*. Despite his sporadic success, Carter still had a following sufficient in the postwar era to keep him busy performing on a regular basis, including at least one national tour, and he always had bookings in Canada, where he began touring with his daughters Sheila and Carol as backup singers in 1953. His first contractual relationship with RCA ended in 1952, and two years later, he signed with Decca Records. These sessions, done at Owen Bradley's studio in Nashville, featured a backing band that included Chet Atkins and Grady Martin. His record sales in America had dropped steadily and he left Decca in 1957. He was still popular enough in Canada to justify recording, however, and Carter simply financed the recordings himself and then leased them to one of the major Canadian labels, including RCA.

Carter lived a dual existence between Calgary and the American South for many years. He went into semi-retirement in the late '60s, although he continued to record and perform occasionally, and some of his later RCA sides, although they were intended for the Canadian market, did get released in America. He remained busy recording and writing through the 1960s—briefly for Starday Records but primarily for RCA—and into the 1980s. The death of his wife in 1989 and the ravages of age all served to take their toll, so that by the early '90s, Carter was considered retired, although he was planning another tour as of 1993, which never took place. Despite his sporadic career in the U.S., he made a sufficient impression on his peers to be elected to the Nashville Songwriters Hall of Fame in 1971. Carter died in early December of 1996, just a couple of weeks short of his 92nd birthday, two months after he was diagnosed with stomach cancer. —*Bruce Eder*

Montana Slim / Aug. 15, 1994 / Starday ✦✦✦

Wilf Carter made some overtly commercial music in the '50s but otherwise devoted his long career to traditional folk, cowboy songs, and old fashioned country music. *Montana Slim*, Carter's second Starday album from 1966, is an unrehearsed set of 12 songs that would be characterized as "old timey" today, performed with minimal accompaniment and no drums. There are traditional songs like "Frankie and Johnny" and "On Top of Old Smokey," but also modern topical songs ("A Mother's Son in Viet Nam"), yodeling songs ("I Love My Yodeling Man"), and old vaudeville numbers ("I'm Ragged but I'm Right," aka "Ragged but Right"). *Montana Slim* was created for folk revivalists and fans of early country music rather than the country charts, and is rooted in the sensibilities of an earlier era. —*Greg Adams*

● **The Golden Years** / 1996 / Collectors' Choice Music ✦✦✦✦✦

The Golden Years—a collection compiled by the mail-order record catalog, Collector's Choice—contains 24 of Wilf Carter's RCA Victor tracks from the '30s and '40s, capturing the essence of the Canadian singing cowboy on one disc. Included on the set are such classic western songs as "Goodnight Irene," "Blue Canadian Rockies," and "There's a Love Knot in My Lariat." —*Thom Owens*

A Prairie Legend / 1996 / Bear Family ✦✦✦✦

Four CDs containing more than 100 songs recorded by Wilf Carter (aka Montana Slim) between 1944 and 1952, and his self-produced sessions from 1959. Disc one features more than a dozen tracks with Carter accompanied primarily by his own acoustic guitar, and they're pretty fair cowboy songs. Carter's voice is a pleasing one, reminiscent at times of Gene Autry, but his repertory generally doesn't intersect much with Autry's—the early electric-accompanied sides from 1947 are also very spare and have more of a raw quality than one would expect from this era. Disc two captures Carter at the beginning of his most commercial period for RCA, doing romantic ballads as well as his usual cowboy songs. Disc three covers the tail end of his RCA period, when Carter was trying for more of a pop sound, in keeping with the declining public response to cowboy songs—the stuff is more sentimental, but Carter never strays too far from the playful mood of his best work. Disc four closes out the RCA years with numbers like the shockingly upbeat "Goodbye Maria (I'm Off to Korea)," probably the most cheerful song ever done about that war, and "Mockingbird Love," the song Carter believes helped cost him his RCA contract. The real highlight of this disc, however, is the stuff that Carter cut himself at the end of the 1950s, which mostly consists of really good cowboy material, all originals and all played in a spare, eloquent style with Carter's voice showing tremendous vigor. With his spoken introduction to the first of these numbers, these could have been the basis for a radio show, if only the time had been right, and they capture the spirit of Carter's earliest work in Alberta and on the CBC. —*Bruce Eder*

Cowboy Songs / Aug. 5, 1997 / Bear Family ✦✦✦✦✦

Lionel Cartwright

b. Feb. 10, 1960, Gallipolis, OH
Vocals / Contemporary Country

Lionel Cartwright was a multi-talented performer and songwriter whose career took off in the late '80s. Like his peers Garth Brooks, Travis Tritt, and Alan Jackson, Cartwright favored a contemporary country-pop sound. His love of music began during childhood

piano lessons; Cartwright also went on to master the guitar and eight other instruments. At age ten, he began performing at community gatherings in his hometown of Glendale, WV. While in high-school, he was a regular on a country radio show in Milton, WV, also appearing on Columbus, OH's Country Cavalcade. After joining the Wheeling Jamboree in West Virginia as a pianist, he was soon promoted to performer status, and from there became the show's musical director.

Cartwright started working on the Nashville Network music and comedy series *I-40 Paradise* in 1981 and later on the show's spinoff, *Pickin' at the Paradise*. On both shows he served as a performer, arranger, and musical director, also writing and performing the theme songs. While working on the show, he met Cindy Stewart, who went on to become his songwriting collaborator and wife. He also met Boudleaux and Felice Bryant, the two composers behind many of the Everly Brothers' greatest hits, who encouraged him to further develop his songwriting skills. While performing live in Knoxville, Cartwright was spotted by MCA producer Tony Brown, who was impressed but felt the young singer needed more experience before he could land a record contract.

In 1986, Cartwright went to Nashville with his best songs and had a formal audition with Brown, who signed him to MCA. In 1988, Cartwright released his debut single, "You're Gonna Make Her Mine," and scored a Top 50 hit. He also released a self-titled album in 1989, which contained the aforementioned single and three other Top 20 hits, including "Give Me His Last Chance," which made it to the Top Five. His next album, *I Watched It on the Radio* (1990), contained several hits. He scored his first chart-topper, "Leap of Faith," in 1991, from the album *Chasin' the Sun*. —*Sandra Brennan*

● **Lionel Cartwright** / 1989 / MCA ✦✦✦✦✦

Produced by Tony Brown and Steuart Smith (formerly Rodney Crowell's lead guitarist) Cartwright's debut disc is still his best. It includes the hits "Like Father, Like Son" and "Give Me His Last Chance." —*Dan Cooper*

I Watched It on the Radio / 1990 / MCA ✦✦✦

It features "My Heart Is Set on You," "Say It's Not True," "In the Long Run," and other hits. —*AMG*

Chasin' the Sun / 1991 / MCA ✦✦✦

Johnny Carver

b. Nov. 24, 1940, Jackson, MS
Vocals / Country-Pop

Country-pop singer Johnny Carver enjoyed his greatest popularity during the '70s, when he occasionally hit with countrified versions of soft pop smashes. Carver grew up in a rural area near Jackson, MS, and sang in a local country gospel quartet with his family. He went on to form his own band, the Capital Cowboys, which were sponsored by an ice-cream company. Carver embarked on his first national tour in 1959, playing at clubs and fairs, and moved to Los Angeles in 1965, where he made regular appearances on local television and led the house band at the Palomino club. His composition "New Lips" was recorded by Roy Drusky in 1967, and Carver landed his own record deal with Imperial.

His self-titled debut album was released later that year, and contained the minor hit "Your Lily White Hands"; he had a few more modest successes with country-pop offerings like 1968's "I Still Didn't Have the Sense to Go" and 1969's "That's Your Hang Up." In 1972, he moved to ABC and had a major country hit with a version of Tony Orlando & Dawn's "Tie a Yellow Ribbon Round the Ole Oak Tree." A string of Top 40 country hits followed over the next five years, including the Top Tens "You Really Haven't Changed" (1973), "Don't Tell (That Sweet Old Lady of Mine)" (1974), and another country cover of a pop hit, the Starland Vocal Band's "Afternoon Delight" (1976). Carver's last Top 40 hit was 1977's "Living Next Door to Alice," and his final charting single was a 1981 cover of ABBA's "S.O.S." He subsequently became a regular performer in Branson, MO. —*Steve Huey*

● **The Best of Johnny Carver** / 1977 / ABC/Dot ✦✦✦✦✦

Neko Case

b. Sep. 8, 1970, Alexandria, VA
Vocals / Alternative Country-Rock, Adult Alternative Pop/Rock, Americana, Alternative Pop/Rock, Indie Rock

Alternative country singer/songwriter Neko Case won a steadily growing cult audience for her smoky, sophisticated vocals and the downcast beauty of her music. Born in Alexandria, VA, Case moved around often as a child, spending the largest part of her youth in Tacoma, WA. She left her parents at age 15, and three years later she started playing drums for several bands around the Northwest's punk rock scene. In 1994, she moved to Vancouver to enter art school, and simultaneously joined the punk group Maow, who released a record on the Mint label. She also played with roots rockers the Weasles, and eventually formed her own backing band, the Boyfriends, which initially featured alumni of the Softies, Zumpano, and Shadowy Men on a Shadowy Planet.

Case released her solo debut, *The Virginian*, in 1997, delving wholeheartedly into traditional country via a mix of covers and originals. She went on to perform with Carolyn Mark in the old-timey side project the Corn Sisters, and recorded with the Vancouver indie supergroup the New Pornographers. In 1998, Case completed her studies, and with her student visa expired, she returned to Washington and began work on her second solo album. The lovely, melancholy *Furnace Room Lullaby* was released on Bloodshot Records in 2000 and won high praise from most critics. Case subsequently relocated to Chicago, home of a thriving alt-country scene, and released the home-recorded *Canadian Amp* EP in 2001. Its moody, late-night ambience carried over to 2002's *Blacklisted*, a darker yet more eclectic affair; it garnered Case her strongest reviews yet, making many year-end critics' polls, and landed her a tour slot opening for Nick Cave. —*Steve Huey*

The Virginian / Jul. 29, 1997 / Bloodshot ✦✦✦

Neko Case's solo debut is a delightful collection of heartfelt originals and vibrant covers ranging from traditional country fare (Ernest Tubb's "Thanks a Lot," Loretta Lynn's "Somebody Led Me Away") to more eclectic material (Scott Walker's "Duchess"); the highlight is a rip-snorting rendition of the Everly Brothers' "Bowling Green," a duet with Zumpano's Carl Newman. *—Jason Ankeny*

Furnace Room Lullaby / 2000 / Bloodshot ✦✦✦✦

It would be easy to call Neko Case alt-country's answer to k.d. lang; after all, they're both from Canada, both came into country music through artier pursuits, and both blend trad-style twang with a modernist lyrical perspective. But Case also has a couple more important things in common with lang—she has a superb voice that's as big as all outdoors, and there's nothing at all ironic about her love for the luxurious sadness of classic country & western. Case fronts a dramatically revamped lineup of Boyfriends on her second solo album, *Furnace Room Lullaby*, and it's even stronger and more impressive than her fine debut set, *The Virginian.* Case co-wrote all of the album's 12 songs, and the material strikes a more deeply personal note this time out, from the busted romance of "Set Out Running" and "We've Never Met" to the road-weary and unsentimental nostalgia of "Thrice All American" and "South Tacoma Way" (not many artists could put a lump in your throat at the notion of a Wal-Mart replacing the old downtown, but Case does it here). Case's vocals are superb from front to back, as smooth and fiery as good brandy, and her revolving circle of musicians (including Ron Sexsmith and Kelly Hogan on backing vocals) are subtle and beautifully evocative, balancing sorrow and good-times with an easy grace. Dozens of rock artists have wrung cheap laughs from the sound and feel of classic country, but Neko Case understands the honest emotions and working-class poetry Loretta Lynn and Dolly Parton brought to their best music, and if her own take on such things is a bit different, *Furnace Room Lullaby* makes clear how deeply she cares for this music, and confirms her status as one of alt-country's strongest artists. *—Mark Deming*

● **Blacklisted** / Aug. 20, 2002 / Bloodshot ✦✦✦✦✦

While the spare and often haunted sound of Neko Case's home-recorded *Canadian Amp* EP seemed at the time like a late-night detour from alt-country's leading songbird of the North, listening to Case's first full-length album following *Canadian Amp* suggests it may have been the first step along a new and different path for her. *Blacklisted* is a considerably darker and more understated affair than *The Virginian* or *Furnace Room Lullaby*, and its sometimes stark, sometimes elegant 3 a.m. sound is informed as much by pop, jazz, and blues flavors as the country & western-slanted melodies of her first two solo albums. Which isn't to say *Blacklisted* is a total departure for Neko Case; her big, bold, but silky smooth voice is still a thing of beauty, and if anything, she's still learning more remarkable things she can do with it, with the result being some of her finest and most insightful performances to date. And Case continues to grow as a songwriter; penning most of the album all by herself, Case is a lyricist willing to answer to both her heart and her head, and she had a fine ear for a melody to boot. With Joey Burns and John Convertino of Calexico, Howe Gelb of Giant Sand, Dallas Good of the Sadies, and Kelly Hogan all contributing to *Blacklisted*, Neko Case has crafted an album whose quiet drift only adds to its power; it's hard to say if hanging out with Nick Cave on tour had much of an influence on her, but this disc sounds a bit like Case's version of *The Boatman's Call*, a personal exploration of the heart and soul that proves sad and beautiful can often walk hand in hand. Highly recommended. *—Mark Deming*

The Cash Brothers

Group / Alternative Country-Rock

Brothers Andrew and Peter Cash have long individual musical histories, although they only came together musically in 1999 for the first time. They never played music together as children, but both are established figures in the Canadian music scene; Peter Cash was the principal songwriter for the Skydiggers, and Andrew Cash was a longtime solo artist who appeared in the bands L'Etranger and Ursula.

After ten years of touring, writing, and recording in these separate projects, the curious brothers decided to find out what sounds they could create if they joined musical forces. The result was 1999's *Raceway.* The first song that they recorded together, in 1997, was the title track on the album. "I remember going into the control room to hear what it sounded like," Andrew recalled. "We just looked at each other and said: 'Hey, this is going to work!'" The brothers' vocal harmonies on that first recording endeavor foreshadowed what was to come; between 1997 and 1999 the Cash Brothers built up a repertoire of over 40 songs spanning genres from moody pop to alternative country and guitar rock. *Raceway* features 12 of these songs; the album's musical journey showcases the differences and similarities of these talented brothers. *How Was Tomorrow* was issued in spring 2001. *—Linda Woods*

Raceway / 1999 / Cash Brothers ✦✦✦✦

The Cash Brothers are Andrew and Peter, and they're in the strange position of being a Canadian alt-country supergroup while at the same time most people can't place either of them. Andrew Cash released a string of widely released but mostly ignored solo albums for Island and Universal Canada, while brother Peter Cash was more anonymous as a member of acclaimed group The Skydiggers. With *Raceway*, they teamed up to create an album that's more accessible than either brother's past work, one that is unlikely to get a very wide audience because of its release on an indie label. It's a shame, because it is every bit as good as much of the material that clogged up the alt-country world at around the same time, if not better. Many of the songs are filled with melodic hooks that stick with you, and you may find yourself humming them later on in the day. *—Sean Carruthers*

● **How Was Tomorrow** / Apr. 17, 2001 / Rounder ✦✦✦✦

How Was Tomorrow is essentially the American-release version of the Cash Brothers' debut *Raceway*, which had hit record shelves in their native Canada two years earlier. The song lineup is slightly altered. It deletes four songs from *Raceway* and replaces them with three new tracks, among them the hushed, highly atmospheric gem "I Am Waiting." The album is, indeed, better than a great majority of the so-called alt-country and No Depression efforts that glutted the music industry in the 1990s, this side of Jayhawks and Wilco. In fact, the songs have all the best aspects of the music of Neil Young and Gram Parsons, the most oft-cited but rarely matched country-folk luminaries, while slyly referencing the folkiest side of Bruce Springsteen ("Nebraska") as well. And the duo easily equals the harmonies of Mark Olson and Gary Louris, occasionally even approaching the sweet tandem singing of the Everly Brothers ("Take a Little Time"). The hooks are consistently so gorgeous that you immediately want to wrap yourself in them, despite the sparseness of the music and mood. It is a bucolic, beautifully melancholy, and humble album, even when it turns up the amplifiers, and it deserves to win the brothers a lot of American converts. *—Stanton Swihart*

A Brand New Night / Jul. 2003 / Zoë ✦✦✦✦

American audiences got their first taste of the Cash Brothers with *How Was Tomorrow* in 2001. Andrew and Peter Cash combined acoustic and electric guitars, smart songwriting, and their distinct harmony on catchy, if depressing, songs like "Nebraska." On 2003's *A Brand New Night*, the brothers add a new touch here and there, but mostly echo the earlier album. In this sense, the Cash Brothers seem to be in a holding pattern, tentatively reaching out for new things, but mostly sticking to the familiar. The guitar work and overlapping harmony on tracks like "Shadow of Doubt" and "You're It" capture an appealing groove, and both "Fire Dying" and the title track are nice low-key ballads, taken at dreamy pace. The album gets more intriguing, though, when the brothers stretch out a bit on "Give Me Your Hips." Here, they trade their usual down-and-out lyrics for a scornful, funky track with a heavy dose of passion. Unfortunately, the song is an anomaly. While *A Brand New Night* is solid enough, there's nothing quite as captivating as "Guitar Strings and Foolish Things" or "Dream Awake" from *How Was Tomorrow.* Fans of the first album, though, will be glad to have a new Cash Brother's album in the stores. *—Ronnie D. Lankford Jr.*

Johnny Cash

b. Feb. 26, 1932, Kingsland, AR, **d.** Sept. 12, 2003, Nashville, TN

Guitar, Songwriter, Vocals / Traditional Country, Cowboy, Country-Pop, Rockabilly, Country Gospel, Rock & Roll

Johnny Cash was one of the most imposing and influential figures in post-World War II country music. With his deep, resonant baritone and spare, percussive guitar, he had a basic, distinctive sound. Cash didn't sound like Nashville, nor did he sound like honky tonk or rock & roll. He created his own sub-genre, falling halfway between the blunt emotional honesty of folk, the rebelliousness of rock & roll, and the world weariness of country. Cash's career coincided with the birth of rock & roll, and his rebellious attitude and simple, direct musical attack shared a lot of similarities with rock. However, there was a deep sense of history—as he would later illustrate with his series of historical albums—that kept him forever tied with country. And he was one of country music's biggest stars of the '50s and '60s, scoring well over 100 hit singles.

Johnny Cash was born and raised in Arkansas, moving to Dyess when he was three. By the time he was 12 years old, Cash had begun writing his own songs. Johnny was inspired by the country songs he had heard on the radio. While he was in high-school, he sang on the Arkansas radio station KLCN. Johnny Cash graduated from college in 1950, moving to Detroit to work in an auto factory for a brief while. With the outbreak of the Korean War, he enlisted in the Air Force. While he was in the Air Force, Cash bought his first guitar and taught himself to play. He began writing songs in earnest, including "Folsom Prison Blues." Cash left the Air Force in 1954, married a Texas woman named Vivian Liberto, and moved to Memphis, where he took a radio announcing course at a broadcasting school on the GI Bill. During the evenings, he played country music in a trio that also consisted of guitarist Luther Perkins and bassist Marshall Grant. The trio occasionally played for free on a local radio station, KWEM, and tried to secure gigs and an audition at Sun Records.

Cash finally landed an audition with Sun Records and its founder, Sam Phillips, in 1955. Initially, Cash presented himself as a gospel singer, but Phillips turned him down. Phillips asked him to come back with something more commercial. Cash returned with "Hey Porter," which immediately caught Phillips' ear. Soon, Cash released "Cry Cry Cry"/"Hey Porter" as his debut single for Sun. On the single, Phillips billed Cash as "Johnny" which upset the singer, because he felt it sounded too young; the record producer also dubbed Perkins and Grant the Tennessee Two. "Cry Cry Cry" became a success upon its release in 1955, entering the country charts at number 14 and leading to a spot on the *Louisiana Hayride*, where he stayed for nearly a year. A second single, "Folsom Prison Blues," reached the country Top Five in early 1956 and its follow-up, "I Walk the Line," was number one for six weeks and crossed over into the pop Top 20.

Johnny Cash had an equally successful year in 1957, scoring several country hits including the Top 15 "Give My Love to Rose." Cash also made his *Grand Ole Opry* debut that year, appearing all in black where the other performers were decked out in flamboyant, rhinestone-studded outfits. Eventually, he earned the nickname of "The Man in Black." Cash became the first Sun artist to release a long-playing album in November of 1957, when *Johnny Cash With His Hot & Blue Guitar* hit the stores. Cash's success continued to roll throughout 1958, as he earned his biggest hit, "Ballad of a Teenage Queen" (number one for ten weeks), as well another number-one single, "Guess Things Happen That Way." For most of 1958, Cash attempted to record a gospel album, but Sun refused to allow him to record one. Sun also was unwilling to increase Cash's record royalties. Both of these were deciding factors in the vocalist's decision to sign with Columbia Records in 1958. By the end of the year, he had released his first single for the label, "All Over Again," which became another Top Five success. Sun continued to release singles and albums of unissued Cash material into the '60s.

"Don't Take Your Guns to Town," Cash's second single for Columbia, was one of his biggest hits, reaching the top of the country charts and crossing over into the pop charts in the beginning of 1959. Throughout that year, Columbia and Sun singles vied for the top of the charts. Generally, the Columbia releases—"Frankie's Man Johnny," "I Got Stripes," and "Five Feet High and Rising"—fared better than the Sun singles, but "Luther Played the Boogie" did climb into the Top Ten. That same year, Cash had the chance to make his gospel record—*Hymns by Johnny Cash*—which kicked off a series of thematic albums that ran into the '70s.

The Tennessee Two became the Tennessee Three in 1960 with the addition of drummer W.S. Holland. Though he was continuing to have hits, the relentless pace of his career was beginning to take a toll on Cash. In 1959, he had begun taking amphetamines to help him get through his schedule of nearly 300 shows a year. By 1961, his drug intake had increased dramatically and his work was affected, which was reflected by a declining number of hit singles and albums. By 1963, he had moved to New York, leaving his family behind. He was running into trouble with the law, most notably for starting a forest fire out West.

June Carter—who was the wife of one of Cash's drinking buddies, Carl Smith—would provide Cash with his return to the top of the charts with "Ring of Fire," which she co-wrote with Merle Kilgore. "Ring of Fire" spent seven weeks on the top of the charts and was a Top 20 pop hit. Cash continued his success in 1964, as "Understand Your Man" became a number one hit. However, Cash's comeback was short-lived, as he sank further into addiction and his hit singles arrived sporadically. Cash was arrested in El Paso for attempting to smuggle amphetamines into the country through his guitar case in 1965. That same year, the *Grand Ole Opry* refused to have him perform and he wrecked the establishment's footlights. In 1966, his wife Vivian filed for divorce. After the divorce, Cash moved to Nashville. At first, he was as destructive as he ever had been, but he became close friends with June Carter, who had divorced Carl Smith. With Carter's help, he was able to shake his addictions; she also converted Cash to fundamentalist Christianity. His career began to bounce back as "Jackson" and "Rosanna's Going Wild" became Top Ten hits. Early in 1968, Cash proposed marriage to Carter during a concert; the pair were married in the spring of 1968.

In 1968, Johnny Cash recorded and released his most popular album, *Johnny Cash at Folsom Prison*. Recorded during a prison concert, the album spawned the number-one country hit "Folsom Prison Blues," which also crossed over into the pop charts. By the end of the year, the record had gone gold. The following year, he released a sequel, *Johnny Cash at San Quentin*, which had his only Top Ten pop single, "A Boy Named Sue," which peaked at number three; it also hit number one on the country charts. Johnny Cash guested on Bob Dylan's 1969 country-rock album, *Nashville Skyline*. Dylan returned the favor by appearing on the first episode of *The Johnny Cash Show*, the singer's television program for ABC. *The Johnny Cash Show* ran for two years, between 1969 and 1971. Johnny Cash was reaching a second peak of popularity in 1970. In addition to his television show, he performed for President Richard Nixon at the White House, acted with Kirk Douglas in *The Gunfight*, sang with John Willams and the Boston Pops Orchestra, and he was the subject of a documentary film. His record sales were equally healthy, as "Sunday Morning Coming Down" and "Flesh and Blood" were number-one hits. Throughout 1971, Cash continued to have hits, including the Top Three "Man in Black." Both Cash and Carter became more socially active in the early '70s, campaigning for the civic rights of Native-Americans and prisoners, as well as frequently working with Billy Graham.

In the mid-'70s, Cash's presence on the country charts began to decline, but he continued to have a series of minor hits and the occasional chart topper like 1976's "One Piece at a Time," or Top Ten hits like the Waylon Jennings duet "There Ain't No Good Chain Gang" and "(Ghost) Riders in the Sky." *Man in Black*, Johnny Cash's autobiography, was published in 1975. In 1980, Johnny Cash became the youngest inductee to the Country Music Hall of Fame. However, the '80s were a rough time for Cash, as his record sales continued to decline and he ran into trouble with Columbia. Cash, Carl Perkins, and Jerry Lee Lewis teamed up to record *The Survivors* in 1982, which was a mild success. The Highwaymen—a band featuring Cash, Waylon Jennings, Willie Nelson, and Kris Kristofferson—released their first album in 1985, which was also moderately successful. The following year, Cash and Columbia Records ended their relationship and he signed with Mercury Nashville. The new label didn't prove to be a success, as the company and the singer fought over stylistic direction. Furthermore, country radio had begun to favor more contemporary artists, and Cash soon found himself shut out of the charts. Nevertheless, he continued to be a popular concert performer.

The Highwaymen recorded a second album in 1992 and it was more commercially successful than any of Cash's Mercury records. Around that time, his contract with Mercury ended. In 1993, he signed a contract with American Records. His first album for the label, *American Recordings*, was produced by the label's founder, Rick Rubin, and was a stark, acoustic collection of songs. *American Recordings*, while not a blockbuster success, revived his career critically and brought him in touch with a younger, rock-oriented audience. In 1995, the Highwaymen released their third album, *The Road Goes on Forever*. The following year, Johnny Cash released his second album for American Records, *Unchained*, which featured support from Tom Petty & the Heartbreakers. His *VH-1 Storytellers* outing was released in 1998, and in the spring of 2000 Cash compiled *Love, God, Murder*, a three-disc retrospective focusing on the major songwriting themes dominant throughout his career. The new studio album *American III: Solitary Man* appeared later that year.

Health problems plagued Cash throughout the '90s and into the 2000s, but he continued to record with Rubin; their fourth collaboration, *American IV: The Man Comes Around*, was released in late 2002. The following year, the Mark Romanek-directed video for his cover of Nine Inch Nails' "Hurt" garnered considerable acclaim and media attention, culminating in an unexpected nomination for video of the year at the MTV Video Music Awards. Not long after the video sparked numerous stories, his beloved wife June Carter Cash died on May 15, 2003, of complications following heart surgery. Five months later, Johnny Cash died of complications from diabetes in Nashville, Tennessee. *—Stephen Thomas Erlewine*

Wanted Man / 1957 / Mercury ♦♦♦

Wanted Man is an uneven, but useful, sampler of Johnny Cash's brief, scattershot time at Mercury Records. For every strong track like "Wanted Man" or "The Night Hank Williams Came to Town," the ten-song collection has unnecessary items like a remake of "Ballad of a Teenage Queen" (featuring Rosanne Cash and the Everly Brothers) and "Beans for Breakfast." It rescues some songs from obscurity—after all, the Mercury years were Cash's most ignored period—but it doesn't present enough evidence that it was unjustly overlooked. *—Stephen Thomas Erlewine*

Johnny Cash With His Hot & Blue Guitar / 1957 / Sun ♦♦♦♦♦

Cash's first album, released on Sun in 1957, was a little more folkloric and traditional in bent than what he put on most of his singles, though not pronouncedly so. In fact, four of the tracks ("I Walk the Line," "Cry! Cry! Cry!," "So Doggone Lonesome," and "Folsom Prison Blues") had already been hit singles. For the rest of the set, Cash drew on some older folk ("Rock Island Line," "The Wreck of the Old '97"), country ("(I Heard That) Lonesome Whistle," "Remember Me (I'm the One Who Loves You)"), prison ("Doin' My Time"), and spiritual ("I Was There When It Happened") songs. Filling out the set was a good, rollicking Cash original, "Country Boy," and a rather sassy tune by the young Jerry Reed, "If the Good Lord's Willing." It's a good, solid record that's very much in the mold of his classic early Sun sound, with spare accompaniment that nevertheless often approaches a rockabilly-country bounce. The album's desirability's a little diminished by the presence of the material on numerous other compilations in the CD era, though it still stands well on its own. [The 2002 CD reissue on Varese Sarabande adds five bonus tracks: the fine, brisk B-sides "Hey, Porter!" and "Get Rhythm," as well as alternate versions of "I Was There When It Happened," "Folsom Prison Blues," and "I Walk the Line."] *—Richie Unterberger*

The Sings the Songs That Made Him Famous / 1958 / Sun ♦♦♦♦

These early Cash classics provided him with hits and many other artists with some great material, and the sparse sound of the Tennessee Two holds up well. *—Jim Worbois*

The Fabulous Johnny Cash / 1958 / Columbia ♦♦♦♦♦

The Fabulous Johnny Cash was Cash's first album for Columbia Records and one of his best for the label. Unlike some of his latter-day albums, there wasn't much filler on the record. At the time of its recording, Cash had just been freed from his contract with Sun. Instead of recording these songs for his last Sun sessions, he wound up saving much of his best material for his Columbia album, and that's what makes *The Fabulous* so consistent. The album builds on his basic, spare sound, but it is slightly more polished than his Sun records. But what makes it so entertaining are the songs themselves. From "Don't Take Your Guns to Town" and "Frankie's Man, Johnny" to "Pickin' Time" and "The Troubador," the album is filled with first-rate songs, with only a handful of mediocre songs like "Suppertime," which don't distract from the overall quality of the album at all. *—Stephen Thomas Erlewine*

Hymns by Johnny Cash / 1959 / Columbia ♦♦♦♦

Although Sam Phillips steered Cash away from gospel and sacred music in the mid-'50s at Sun Records, in fact much of what Cash recorded in his early career still had a devout tone, often with piety and imagery that wouldn't have sounded foreign in a gospel context. So although this 1959 album was entirely devoted to religious songs, it didn't really sound that different from his prior work, and remains accessible to Cash fans whether or not they're religious or have an interest in sacred song. The arrangements remain as sparse as most from his 1950s catalog, though stately backup vocals are often present. Too, these aren't strictly traditional numbers, as Cash writes or co-writes about half the tunes. Sure, "Are All the Children In" skirts bathos with its spoken sections, yet songs like "The Old Account" and "It Was Jesus" have the country-rockabilly bounce characteristic of much of his secular material. In fact, despite its specialized focus, it's somewhat generic 1950s Cash at a casual listen, though even generic 1950s Cash is good. The CD reissue adds just one bonus track, and a peripheral one at that: a "mono EP version" of "It Was Jesus," which is lacking the backup vocals found on the LP one. *—Richie Unterberger*

Songs of Our Soil / 1959 / Columbia ♦♦♦♦

One of Cash's earlier pseudo-concept albums, this doesn't exactly follow a specific theme like farming or hymns of the American land the whole way through. Rather, it's a collection of a dozen songs that generally are on the folkier and more Americana-centered side of Cash's repertoire, though of course such songs have always had a prominent place in his material. He bagged the songwriting credits for all but one of the songs on *Songs of Our Soil*, skillfully relaying tales of drinking, disastrous farm flooding ("Five Feet High and Rising"), the vicious circle of sharecropping ("The Man on the Hill"), death and burial ("The Caretaker"), Native Americana ("Old Apache Squaw"), and spiritual-like piety ("It Could Be You (Instead of Him)"). The death-in-the-desert tale of "Hank and Joe and Me" might get unintentionally camp with its rather jaunty depiction (complete with gospel-like backup choral vocals) of the narrator dying of thirst on a quest for gold. Although "J. Cash" gets the songwriting credit for "I Want to Go Home," in fact it's his version of the homesick sailor folk tale more commonly known as "Sloop John B," recorded elsewhere by the Weavers, the Kingston Trio, the Beach Boys, and others. It's a good set, though pretty short at 26 minutes, and lacking the hits or classics that decorate some of his other vaguely Americana concept albums. [The 2002 CD reissue peps things up a bit with two bonus tracks, the singles "I Got Stripes" and "You Dreamer You," both recorded at the same March 12, 1959, session that yielded most of the songs on the original LP.] *—Richie Unterberger*

Now, There Was a Song! / 1960 / Columbia/Legacy ♦♦♦♦♦

This is an outstanding album of covers of old country songs, from the familiar (Ernest Tubb, Hank Williams, George Jones) to lesser-known gems. *—Michael McCall*

Ride This Train / 1960 / Columbia ♦♦♦♦♦

Ride This Train was the first explicit Americana concept album that Johnny Cash recorded. As the title implies, the album is about railroads, how they developed and how they changed the land. Apart from a couple of songs, *Ride This Train* isn't comprised of traditional folk ballads—they are songs that tell the history of trains and rails, offering an educational lesson. Cash expounds on the songs with brief spoken narratives. Though it is hard to fault Cash's intentions, the songs aren't very good (although "The Shifting Whispering Sands" is a standout) and the history is a bit simplistic and silly. On the whole, *Ride This Train* sounds as if it is of a piece with the Walt Disney educational features produced at the same time, and like those films, it is more interesting as an historical artifact than a piece of art. *—Stephen Thomas Erlewine*

The Lure of the Grand Canyon / 1961 / Columbia ✦✦

Hymns from the Heart / 1962 / Columbia ✦✦✦

The Sound of Johnny Cash / 1962 / Columbia ✦✦✦

Ring of Fire: The Best of Johnny Cash / 1963 / Columbia ✦✦✦✦

Technically, *Ring of Fire/The Best of Johnny Cash* isn't a greatest-hits collection, but it does contain a number of his greatest performances and singles, including "Ring of Fire," "I Still Miss Someone" and "The Rebel—Johnny Yuma." These are supported by solid originals ("Forty Shades of Green," "I'd Still Be There," "Tennessee Flat-Top Box") and covers ("(There'll Be) Peace in the Valley," "Bonanza"), which help make the record one of Cash's best. *—Stephen Thomas Erlewine*

Blood Sweat & Tears / 1963 / Columbia/Legacy ✦✦✦

Where *Ride This Train* was about railroads and how they shaped America, *Blood, Sweat & Tears* is not only about the folklore of trains, it's about the fables of the American working man. That means there are classic ballads like "Casey Jones" and "The Legend of John Henry's Hammer," but also relatively recent blues like "Busted," the field song "Pick a Bale of Cotton" and the worker's lament "Tell Him I'm Gone." The delivery is plain, simple and never overly sentimental, but the thing that makes the record really work is the fact that the album consists almost entirely of first-rate material, without much of the unintentionally corny history lessons that weigh down most of Cash's Americana records. *—Stephen Thomas Erlewine*

Keep on the Sunnyside / 1964 / Columbia ✦✦

I Walk the Line / 1964 / Columbia ✦✦✦✦✦

Despite the title, this is practically a greatest-hits package. It's great stuff, it's not to be missed. *—Jim Worbois*

Bitter Tears (Ballads of the American Indian) / 1964 / Columbia/Legacy ✦✦✦✦✦

Though on the surface *Bitter Tears* is just another installment in the seemingly endless series of Americana albums that Johnny Cash released in the '60s, it was a more daring collection than any of its predecessors or successors. Where Cash's previous Americana albums had previously concentrated on cowboys and Western pioneers, *Bitter Tears* is all about Native Americans and their trials and tribulations. It isn't a crass move—it's a sensitive, clear-eyed take on the unfair treatment of the American Indian that uses traditional folk ballads and newly written songs in the same vein. It's stark and moving, his best Americana album of the '60s. *—Stephen Thomas Erlewine*

Orange Blossom Special / 1965 / Columbia ✦✦✦✦

Even if the best and most popular of the songs on this 1965 album are the ones most likely to show up on greatest-hits compilations ("The Long Black Veil, "Orange Blossom Special," "It Ain't Me Babe"), it certainly rates as one of Cash's finer non-greatest-hits releases. If for nothing else, it would have historical importance for the inclusion of three Bob Dylan covers, at a time when Dylan was just starting to get heavily covered by pop musicians (and not often covered by country ones). "It Ain't Me Babe," with duet vocals by June Carter, was the most notable of them, although hearing it these days, some may be taken aback by the mariachi horns. Ditto for "Mama, You Been on My Mind" (which Dylan himself had not released when Cash recorded it), where it's startling to hear Boots Randolph's yakety sax come in for a bit. "The Long Black Veil," though, is an ageless classic, and the title cut one of his best train-oriented songs. The rest of the album is respectable and diverse, if not as outstanding, including the stark Cash original "You Wild Colorado," more duet vocals from Carter on the Johnny Horton cover "When It's Springtime in Alaska," a bouncy rendition of the Carter Family's "Wildwood Flower," the spiritual "Amen," and, less successfully, a sentimental reading of "Danny Boy." [The 2002 CD reissue adds three bonus tracks that were previously unavailable in the United States (and had been included on the Bear Family box set *The Man in Black: 1963-1969*), among them an acoustic cover of A.P. Carter's "Engine 143" and a different version of "Mama, You Been on My Mind" (this time *with* mariachi horns!).] *—Richie Unterberger*

☆ **Sings the Ballads of the True West** / 1965 / DCC ✦✦✦✦✦

One of the projects Johnny Cash wanted to do when he was on Sun Records was to record an album of songs from the Old West. Of course, Sam Phillips wouldn't hear of it, but the idea—along with concept albums of gospel, train songs, and others—all came to fruition when he moved to Columbia Records. This concept album is a 20-track set that combines songs and narrations, the bulk of which were recorded in 1965 (the lone exception is Carl Perkins' "The Ballad of Boot Hill," which originates from a 1959 session). The booklet includes Johnny's original liner notes to the album, along with song-by-song comments. It's one of Cash's best concept albums. *—Cub Koda*

Mean As Hell / 1965 / Columbia ✦✦✦✦

Mean As Hell! Ballads From the True West is Johnny Cash's gunslinger album: a collection of songs about cowboys and their myths. That means there are classic Western ballads like "Bury Me Not on the Lone Prairie" and "The Shifting Whispering Sands," there are fables like "The Blizzard" and the title track, history lessons like "Remember the Alamo," and jokey satires like "25 Minutes to Go." *Mean As Hell* has a handful of good songs—usually the straight ballads, but some of the myths are fun too—but for the most part, there's too much unintentional kitsch on the record to make it necessary. *—Stephen Thomas Erlewine*

Happiness Is You / 1966 / Columbia ✦✦✦

Everybody Loves a Nut / 1966 / Columbia ✦✦✦✦

Supposedly at odds with this country artist's image as the somber Man in Black, this collection of humorous songs actually isn't that much of a departure for Johnny Cash. Listeners who may have grown up during his days as a Top Ten artist will recall his steady stream of singles that always seemed to have a clever gimmick or catchy twist; why, some of those aren't even on this collection, meaning there ought to be a second volume! More than three decades later, Cash would release concept CDs collecting songs based around particular themes—*Love, God,* and *Murder*—so perhaps this album is a thematic link, or a theme he could return to. The songs are just basically nutty. If one could imagine a project combining Cash with the cartoon character Screwy Squirrel, then this would be it, meaning not all the material is in good taste all the time. There are some real choice roasted nuts here, especially the duet with Ramblin' Jack Elliot, in which for once it is OK that the performers get drunk while playing. There is no credit for Elliot in the original liner notes. Some of these songs were favorites of Cash, including "Dirty Old Egg Sucking Dog," which, as a highlight of his career, he performed on *The Muppet Show.* Cash's sense of humor is really great, and although he certainly makes brilliant music when totally in a dark mood, there is something to be said for a project like this, where he gives free rein to that side of his personality that has always made him popular with children, for example. And incidentally, this album has proven to be a very popular item with younger listeners. Cash's romping, stomping buddy Jack Clement actually has a large hand in the proceedings, although one has to read the fine print on the label to know it. He wrote practically all the best songs, except for the hilarious "Please Don't Play Red River Valley," which is a request from the Man in Black himself. *—Eugene Chadbourne*

Carryin' On / 1967 / Columbia ✦✦✦

Johnny Cash has called June Carter-Cash one of the most neglected artists in country music, whose contributions will always be overlooked in the shadow of her husband's own success—his only regret, he says, in having married her. On the couple's 1967 release *Carryin' On With Johnny Cash and June Carter*—recorded a year before their marriage and while Cash was still officially, unhappily wed to his first wife Vivian—June emerges briefly not merely as a longtime backup singer or opening act, but as an equal and able performer and partner. Indeed, her gritty country voice is one of the album's greatest strengths, providing a nice complement and counter to Cash's famous, unadorned bass. *Carryin' On* contains the hit single "Jackson," along with "Long-Legged Guitar Pickin' Man," a boisterous, rocking and rolling minor hit featuring Johnny in the lead role and June as his lovably nagging "Big-Mouthed Woman." Other performances include less effective detours into folk-rockish and pseudo-soulful realms: They cut a fine cover of Richard & Mimi Farina's then-popular "Pack Up Your Sorrows" and wade a little awkwardly through Bob Dylan's "It Ain't Me, Babe," Johnny gracelessly spitting out the "babe" of the title against "Ring of Fire" mariachi horns. Both sides of the record end with versions of Ray Charles classics, "I Got a Woman" and an especially shaky "What'd I Say," which, like "Babe," may prove as endearing to Cash fans as irritating to less-dedicated listeners. While Cash seems a little uncomfortable, or at least out of place, on the Charles numbers, June sounds surprisingly at home and rescues the performances with her soulful, growling vocals. The album's lowest moment, meanwhile, is its second track, "Shantytown," in which syrupy female voices provide sentimental, *Hee Haw* routine choruses of "I live down in Shantytown/Where the chicken's 20 cents a pound." Despite such moments, though, the album manages to overcome its weaknesses by the strength of the couple's collaboration; Johnny and June, eternally genuine and altogether unembarrassed even in the midst of their worst or most ridiculous arrangements, can perform corny or ill-fitted material with such honesty and conviction that you have almost no choice but to believe and enjoy it. Along with the duo's unforgettable voices, the record's mix of harmonicas, banjo, dobro, and hot electric guitar licks lends a down-home, carefree spirit to the entire effort. This, on some level, is Johnny and June at home, or—as on the cover—kicked back in a grassy field, *Carryin' On*, and the world is better off for having witnessed the whole thing. *—Burgin Mathews*

Greatest Hits, Vol. 1 / 1967 / Columbia ✦✦✦✦✦

Released in 1967, *Greatest Hits, Vol. 1* chronicles Johnny Cash's first years at CBS/Columbia, presenting 11 of his biggest hits from 1959-1967. Of course, this couldn't include all of his charting hits from this era, but it does have the biggest and best singles from that time—"Jackson," "Ring of Fire," "Five Feet High and Rising," and "Don't Take Your Guns to Town" among them—as well as the timeless Sun side "I Walk the Line." At the time, this was a really good summation of his Columbia hits, and it remains a good listen, even though it has been supplanted by many more thorough collections that appeared later. *—Stephen Thomas Erlewine*

From Sea to Shining Sea / 1967 / Columbia ✦✦✦

From Sea to Shining Sea is an ambitious but brief attempt to cross the U.S. in song. Out of all his concept albums, *From Sea to Shining Sea* relies more on sailing songs than cowboy songs; those tunes that don't involve water are usually about mid-American events, whether its fairs, mines, prisons, or gas stations. Most of the songs rely on their themes, not lyrics or music, and they suffers accordingly: *From Sea to Shining Sea* is enjoyable as a campy snapshot of America, not as an album. *—Stephen Thomas Erlewine*

☆ **At Folsom Prison** / 1968 / Columbia/Legacy ✦✦✦✦✦

At Folsom Prison was one of two legendary live albums Johnny Cash recorded in front of a prison audience in the late '60s. Part of the appeal of the records is the way Cash plays to the audience, selecting a set of songs that are all about prison, crime, murder, regret, loss, mother, God, and loneliness. Cash stimulates the audience's emotions, which in turn stimulates his performance, especially since he delivers the songs with the conviction of someone who has lived through it. There aren't many hits on the record—"Folsom Prison Blues," "I Still Miss Someone," "Jackson," "Give My Love to Rose," and "I Got Stripes" are the familiar items—but few albums come as close to capturing the darkness and rage that lays deep in Cash's music, as well as the depth of his talent. [The 1999 CD reissue of *At Folsom Prison* presents the complete concert, including three previously unreleased tracks: "Busted," "Joe Bean," and "The Legend of John Henry's Hammer."] *—Stephen Thomas Erlewine*

Johnny Cash / 1969 / Columbia ✦✦✦

The Holy Land / 1969 / Columbia ✦✦

Johnny Cash's "The Holy Land" is such a personal recording that it should have stayed in his vaults. Cash mixes many self-penned country/gospel songs with a recorded narrative account of a trip he took with June Carter to the Holy Land. Cash's narration is passionate and personal, but ultimately it is uninteresting, because he ends up sounding more like a tour guide than a spiritually enlightened artist. As for the music, most of it is unsatisfactory. Songs like "Land of Israel" and "God Is Not Dead" have a really dated sound and a forced sense of religious politics. The two standout tracks on the album are the big hit "Daddy Sang Bass" (written by Carl Perkins) and "Nazarene," a religious song that could have fit next to "Greystone Chapel" on *Johnny Cash at Folsom Prison.* It should be noted that the original vinyl copies of *The Holy Land* included a really cool 3-D image on the cover, à la the Rolling Stones' *At Their Satanic Majesties Request.* *—Brian Flota*

Hello, I'm Johnny Cash / 1969 / Columbia ✦✦✦✦

The energy that Johnny Cash and the Tennessee Three captured on the legendary *Johnny Cash at Folsom Prison* live record can probably never be duplicated. That being said, *Hello, I'm Johnny Cash* comes very close, blending slow talking-blues songs with steam-engine-paced country-rockers. This forgotten album may be one of the five best in the Cash discography. It is fueled by great originals (like "Southwind" and "Route #1, Box 144") and well-executed covers (Kris Kristofferson's "To Beat the Devil" and Tim Hardin's "If I Were a Carpenter"). On top of that, those songs are upstaged by "See Ruby Fall" (co-written with Roy Orbison) and one of his best '70s hits, "Blistered." The lean, minimalist instrumentation of the Tennessee Three insures the album with great rhythm, and Johnny Cash's voice is as affecting as ever. [Note: this album, which is currently out of print, should not to be confused with the 1995 Sony Music Special Products compilation of the same name.] *—Brian Flota*

☆ **At San Quentin** / 1969 / Columbia ✦✦✦✦✦

To put the performance on *At San Quentin* in a bit of perspective: Johnny Cash's key partner in the Tennessee Two, guitarist Luther Perkins, died in August 1968, just seven months before this set was recorded in February 1969. In addition to that, Cash was nearing the peak of his popularity—his 1968 live album, *At Folsom Prison*, was a smash success—but he was nearly at his wildest in the personal life, which surely spilled over into his performance. All of this sets the stage for *At San Quentin*, a nominal sequel to *Folsom Prison* that surpasses its predecessor and captures Cash at his rawest and wildest. Part of this is due to how he feeds off of his captive audience, playing to the prisoners and seeming like one of them, but it's also due to the shifting dynamic within the band. Without Luther, Johnny isn't tied to the percolating two-step that defined his music to that point. Sure, it's still there, but it has a different feel coming from a different guitarist, and Cash sounds unhinged, careening through his jailhouse ballads, old hits, rockabilly-styled ravers and even covers of the Lovin' Spoonful ("Darlin' Companion"). No other Johnny Cash record sounds as wild as this. He sounds like an outlaw and renegade here, which is what gives it power—listen to "A Boy Named Sue," a Shel Silverstein composition that could have been too cute by half, but is rescued by the wild-eyed, committed performance by Cash, where it sounds like he really was set on murdering that son of a bitch that named him Sue. He sounds that way throughout the record, and while most of the best moments did make it to that original 1969 album, the 2000 Columbia/Legacy release eclipses it by presenting nine previously unreleased bonus tracks, doubling the album's length, and presenting such insanely wild numbers as "Big River," as well as sweeter selections like "Daddy Sang Bass." Now, that's the only way to get the record, and that's how it should be, because this extra material makes a legendary album all the greater—in fact, it helps make a case that this is the best Johnny Cash album ever cut. *—Stephen Thomas Erlewine*

Johnny Cash Show / 1970 / Columbia ✦✦✦✦

A Man in Black / 1971 / Columbia ✦✦✦✦

That this particular album was the source of the "Man in Black" image for country icon Johnny Cash is a good example of how the public remembers what it wants to and forgets the rest. Indeed, there are few experiences that one might desire being able to forget quicker than the slide show this artist used to present at his concerts, in which all musical action would grind to a dead halt while shots of the extended Cash and Carter families cavorting in the Holy Land flashed across the stage. This album was actually the musical equivalent of these born-again yearnings, not only featuring a cameo by the horrifying Billy Graham but also at least one or two more gospel numbers than are normally present on a Cash collection not devoted primarily to that genre. Admittedly, Graham is better off cutting country records than counseling American presidents on whom they ought to drop bombs on, but many younger country fans would probably be shocked to find any connection between the "Man in Black" concept and pretensions toward being some kind of country messiah. In reality, it seems the grueling schedule of a three-year stint in television had more of an effect on Cash than religious conversion, as the liner notes are signed with the intriguing initials "J.C.A.T."—for "Johnny Cash After Television." The sparse and subtle backup does indeed go a long way toward smoothing out the wrinkles in this project, while the song "Singing in Vietnam Talking Blues" is a fine example of the socially conscious material this artist was coming up with during the late '60s and early '70s. *—Eugene Chadbourne*

Johnny Cash and Jerry Lee Lewis Sing Hank Williams / 1971 / Sun ✦✦✦✦✦

It pretty much goes without saying that in the world of traditional country music, no one is more revered than the great Hank Williams, which is why it takes a special kind of artist to interpret his songs in the way they so richly deserve to be interpreted. Here, two artists combine their talents to breathe fresh country air into twelve of Williams' greatest hits, Johnny Cash and Jerry Lee Lewis. The Killer and the Man in Black were both schooled in rock & roll and traditional country, and that education pays off in spades with *Johnny Cash and Jerry Lee Lewis Sing Hank Williams.* Never has Williams' catalog been touched on with more emotion and inspiration. *—Michael B. Smith*

A Thing Called Love / 1972 / Columbia ✦✦✦

The title track from *Thing Called Love* was another country Top 40 ringer for the the legendary Johnny Cash, a man whose roots were nourished by the waters of country, rock & roll, folk ballads and gospel in equal doses. Unfortunately, the rest of the album is comprised mostly of throwaway filler. Still, the single and "Mississippi Sand" make this a record worthy of note. *—Michael B. Smith*

Any Old Wind That Blows / 1973 / Columbia ✦✦

Several years before Johnny Paycheck told his boss the "Take This Job and Shove It," Cash was getting his revenge in "Oney;" one of several good cuts on this record (and one of the two hits). While it's not great, it's a good sounding record. *—Jim Worbois*

Johnny Cash and His Woman / 1973 / Columbia ✦✦

America / 1973 / Columbia ✦✦

America: A 200-Year Salute In Story and Song is the culmination of all of Johnny Cash's Americana albums: An attempt to tell the entire history of America over the course of a 40 minute album. Of course, America's history is a bit too convoluted to be adequately told with one album, but there's no denying there's a certain kitsch value in hearing songs like "Come Take a Trip on My Airship" and "The Gettysburg Address." Cash doesn't just sing the history, he tells it with narratives that tie the tracks together. On the whole, the album doesn't amount to much more than a curiosity, but it is an entertaining—if campy—one. Just don't expect to learn anything from *America.* *—Stephen Thomas Erlewine*

Junkie and the Juicehead Minus Me / 1974 / Columbia ✦✦✦

Aside from some fine performances from Cash, this album also features solo tracks by two future country music stars: daughter Rosanne and step-daughter Carlene. *—Jim Worbois*

Ragged Old Flag / 1974 / Columbia ✦✦✦

It's a little hard to recover from the over-the-top patriotism of the opening title cut on this mid-'70s release, with its overbearing spoken narrative and shamelessly melodramatic orchestral production. Actually, however, that song is not typical of this release, which otherwise finds Cash backed only by the Tennessee Three (Carl Perkins, Larry McCoy, and Ray Edenton), with the Oak Ridge Boys singing backup on a couple of tracks. "Don't Go Near the Water" is, in contrast to the title song, rather radical for a country singer in its ecological protest, with its chorus: "Don't go near the water children/See the fish all dead upon the shore/Don't go near the water/'Cause the water isn't water anymore." The rest of the album is agreeable low-key Cash country, though with something of a more-of-the-same feeling that makes it a middle-of-the-pack Cash release at best; "All I Do Is Drive" sounds like a hybrid of old Sun singles like "Cry, Cry, Cry" and "Big River," for instance. The songs go over familiar Cash territory like drifting, loneliness, and the struggle to keep your head above water. But none of them rate among his best, though "Please Don't Let Me Out" puts a twist on his prison stories by taking the viewpoint of a prisoner who wants to stay put as he now considers jail his home. *—Richie Unterberger*

John R. Cash / 1974 / Columbia ✦✦✦✦

This album, mostly made up of covers, is one of Johnny Cash's most enjoyable albums of the '70s. Cash has long been recognized for his ability to pick great material by other writers, and this is a prime example of that talent. *—Jim Worbois*

At Osteraker Prison / 1974 / Columbia ✦✦

Look at Them Beans / 1975 / Columbia ✦✦

This record has the feeling of a project that never quite got off the ground. Songs like Guy Clark's "Texas-1947" is a song Cash could sink his teeth in and make his own. Yet it sounds as though he's just walking through it. Not a bad record, it still leaves one with the feeling that this record could really have been something. *—Jim Worbois*

Sings Precious Memories / 1975 / Epic ✦✦

Children's Album / 1975 / Columbia ✦✦

A very odd release from Cash, this 1975 album contains a series of novelty children's songs stands as one of the more perplexing releases of the artist's career. Certainly, the recordings seem good-intentioned, with Cash asserting his patriarchal role in the album's cover, and generally having fun on many of the tracks, albeit occasionally the humor is rather forced. Naturally, this is not one of Cash's great artistic triumphs, or even that much fun for the average listener—it's more an interesting curiosity. Having said that, it's hard to conceive even the biggest Cash fan (or their children) listening to the record more than once. *—Thomas Ward*

Precious Memories / 1976 / Columbia ✦✦✦

Destination Victoria Station / 1976 / Columbia ✦✦

Strawberry Cake / 1976 / Columbia ✦✦

This is a live history lesson hosted by Johnny Cash. Between many of the tracks are dialogs that give background on the upcoming song and on what Cash was up to at the time it was recorded. Unlike many live albums, the audience doesn't interfere with the music. Also, the dialogues are separate tracks so the album can be enjoyed as a whole or, by skipping around, for the music. *—Jim Worbois*

One Piece at a Time / 1976 / Columbia ✦✦✦
In the mid-'70s, Johnny Cash was holding his own against the onslaught of progressive rock, psychedelic rock, and intense funk that ruled the airwaves. The trademark shuffling twang of the Tennessee Three remained an attractive feel, unique and apparently impossible to copy, but there was more to it than that. His choice of subjects solidified the impression of him as an all-American mainstream type who happened to side with the hippies and hang out with Bob Dylan, a fact of great significance during this era, and which might have sustained Cash had he decided to begin performing on harpsichord. His radio hit "One Piece at a Time" detailed a small victory in the common man's battle over corporate greed, and it certainly wasn't the only great song on this overlooked album. "Committed to Parkview" belongs to the unfortunately tiny genre of country songs about mental institutions, and might be the best of them all, seriously rivaling Faron Young's "Rubber Room." "Love Has Lost Again" is one of his bittersweet ballads along the lines of "I Still Miss Someone," while unpretentious numbers such as "Go on Blues" represent the type of music that slips sneakily into a listener's consciousness, staying for days. There are uncomfortable duds, sure, but sometimes instrumental touches manage to bring a song to life, whether it is the loudly mixed jaw harp on "Sold Out of Flagpoles" or the rubato harmonica on the relatively corny "Let There Be Country." "One Piece at a Time" was the work of the fine country songwriter Wayne Kemp, but much of the other good material on this recording comes from Cash himself. *—Eugene Chadbourne*

Last Gunfighter Ballad / 1977 / Columbia ✦✦
This is an OK album with some nice moments such as the title track and "Silver Haired Daddy" on which John teams up with his brother Tommy. The liner notes, on the other hand, are interesting, and funny, and have a real personality. *—Jim Worbois*

The Rambler / 1977 / Columbia ✦✦
Out of all of Johnny Cash's Americana concept albums, *The Rambler* is by far the most forced and stilted. More of a radio play than an album, the record is about Cash's drive across America, where he picks up hitchhikers along the way. Every song on *The Rambler* is tied together by dialogues between Cash and the hitchhikers, which means the record never develops a sense of momentum. Furthermore, the songs themselves are slight, without much musically or lyrically to recommend them. In all, it's an ambitious, overwrought failure that is fascinating for one listen, but nearly impossible to sit through more than once. *—Stephen Thomas Erlewine*

I Would Like to See You Again / 1978 / Columbia ✦✦✦
As great as Columbia's *Essential Johnny Cash* box is, their decision to exclude this album's best songs prove that Cash's catalog needs more than three discs' worth of attention. The title track, "Who's Gene Autry?," and the humorous "After Taxes" are typical Cash classics, while the heartbreaking "Abner Brown" easily ranks among his best narrative ballads. Elsewhere the record's feel-good bounce and outlaw licks (provided by a pair of duets with Waylon Jennings) make it a fun listen, with Cash generally turning in better covers than originals. *—Jim Smith*

Gone Girl / 1978 / Columbia ✦✦
The liner notes describe a last-minute scramble to find songs for an upcoming session and, unfortunately, the record bears that out. Many of the tracks are covers which leave the listener wondering "Why?" *—Jim Worbois*

Silver / 1979 / Columbia ✦✦
Silver was a below-average Cash outing, due both to the routine material and the mixed attempt to update his sound with more modern production techniques. Brian Ahern, who produced Emmylou Harris, was at the helm of a set that often put a more contemporary sheen on the sound with filters and phase shifters. Plenty of session help was on hand as well, sometimes on trumpet and French horn, and it's usually not a great sign when the list of players on some tracks run to more than a dozen. The idea was probably to make Cash sound less old-fashioned; the ironic result was to make it sound more dated and flat than most of the rest of his catalog, without comparing to his better recordings in the quality of the content. Still, erratic production can't smother Cash's strengths, and the record's not terrible, just uninspired. Some of the better songs include his reading of Tom T. Hall's "The L&N Don't Stop Here Anymore"; a cover of "(Ghost) Riders in the Sky" (a song that's hard to ruin) with contributions from Ricky Skaggs, Wayne Jackson, and the Carter Family; and veteran cohort Jack Clement's memorably titled "West Canterbury Subdivision Blues." George Jones adds harmony vocals to "I'll Say It's True." [The 2002 CD reissue on Columbia/Legacy adds two previously unreleased duets with Jones on remakes of the late-'50s Cash recordings "I Still Miss Someone" and "I Got Stripes."] *—Richie Unterberger*

A Believer Sings the Truth / 1980 / Columbia ✦✦✦

Rockabilly Blues / 1980 / Koch ✦✦✦✦
While stepdaughter Carlene Carter was hanging out with then-husband Nick Lowe and his British roots rock mates Dave Edmunds, Martin Belmont, and Pete Thomas, Johnny Cash decided to see what they thought about the font they claimed for inspiration: rockabilly and roots country. Lowe got to produce one track on *Rockabilly Blues*, as did old pal and rockabilly co-conspirator Cowboy Jack Clement. Earl Pool Ball did the other eight, but Cash held the reins tight. *Rockabilly Blues*, along with *Johnny 99*—also reissued by Koch—is one of the great lost Cash records. Not only does it feature two of his finer songs from the period, the title track and the bitter love song "Cold Lonesome Morning," it features Cash singing a pair of gems by Billy Joe Shaver, "The Cowboy Who Started the Fight" and "It Ain't Nothing New Babe," as well as one by Cash acolyte Kris Kristofferson, "The Last Time" (which, incidentally, is one of the last times a new Kristofferson tune was recorded by anyone). Cash's "Rockabilly Blues (Texas 1955)" is not essentially a rockabilly tune, though Edmunds' guitar playing certainly embodies its feel—but then, Cash was never a rockabilly singer, either. "One Way Rider," with its horns and staccato pacing, is the perfect song for Lowe to produce. June Carter is wailing on the duet, and the slide guitar parts ring like jagged bells through the heart of the mix. The only problem with this set is how quickly it blazes by. Why Columbia wasn't interested in Cash in 1980 is as confusing now as it was then. All the kids they groomed to come up after him, including newbies Montgomery Gentry, would have killed to make a record this fine. *—Thom Jurek*

The Baron / 1981 / Columbia ✦✦

Adventures of Johnny Cash / 1982 / Columbia ✦✦✦

Survivors Live / 1982 / Razor & Tie ✦✦
In 1981, all three of these Sun Records alumni were touring Europe. Both with the night off, Lewis and Perkins attended a Johnny Cash concert in Stuttgart, West Germany. Called out onstage for the second half of the program, the three sang together on old gospel favorites, with each of them doing a turn singing one or two of their big hits. It's all very loose and much fun, with the grizzled vets going at it together on everything from "That Silver Haired Daddy of Mine" to the closing "I Saw the Light," with stops for "Blue Suede Shoes," "Whole Lotta Shakin' Going On," and "Get Rhythm" in between. A fun and spirited get-together. *—Cub Koda*

Johnny 99 / 1983 / Koch ✦✦✦✦
If the Springsteen tunes hadn't been included, this would still have been a good album. But Cash sinks his teeth into "Highway Patrolman" and the title tune and gives them the guts that Springsteen only dreamed of. *—Jim Worbois*

The Sun Years / 1985 / Charly ✦✦✦✦✦
Since this five-LP box set was issued, Bear Family has come out with an even more comprehensive box covering the same era (1954-1958) on CD. If you're determined to get a box set of his earliest work, you should probably spring for Bear Family's, but if you want to save some bucks and get Charly's vinyl production (though it may be hard to find these days, used or new), this is hardly an embarrassing substitute. It has virtually everything he did for Sun, including quite a few alternate takes, and versions of previously released recordings that remove the often-distracting additional instruments and voices that were dubbed onto some of his later Sun sides. Some of the alternate takes may be rough going for those whose devotion to Cash is less than fanatical, but otherwise it's surprisingly consistent listening. Almost every track is worth hearing, and much of it is excellent, demonstrating that he had a good deal of fine early material besides the well-known hits. Comes with a full-sized booklet with lots of photos and mountainous liner notes by Hank Davis, Colin Escott, and Martin Hawkins. Incidentally, this is an entirely different release than the 1990 Rhino single-disc CD, *The Sun Years*. *—Richie Unterberger*

Up Through the Years, 1955–1957 / 1986 / Bear Family ✦✦✦✦✦
Up Through the Years is the most comprehensive single-disc collection of Johnny Cash's Sun recordings. Featuring a total of 24 songs—including all the big hits, plus interesting minor ones like "Straight A's in Love"—the collection is preferable to Rhino's *The Sun Years* for fans that want to delve a little deeper into the Sun years, but don't want to invest in the massive *The Man in Black* set. *—Stephen Thomas Erlewine*

Classic Cash: Hall of Fame Series / 1987 / Mercury ✦
Johnny Cash's period with Mercury Records was not his finest. It wasn't that he recorded a batch poor records; it was the fact that those records were barely heard by anyone. However, *Classic Cash* isn't a compilation of those neglected gems—it's a collection of re-recordings of his biggest hits. As re-recordings go, these aren't particularly bad—Cash is in strong voice and his band is tight, professional and accomplished—but they aren't inspired and hardly are substitute for the original records. *—Stephen Thomas Erlewine*

Vintage Years: 1955–1963 / 1987 / Rhino ✦✦✦✦✦
To a large degree, this compilation of Cash's early work has been superseded by Rhino's own *Sun Years* (which goes into his '50s work in some greater depth), CBS' *Columbia Years 1958-1986* (which goes into his early Columbia work in much greater depth), and the Bear Family *1954-1958* box set (which goes into his early work with as much detail as anyone could ask for). Collectors care about these distinctions a great deal, but the average listener does not. If you just want some early Cash and come across this for a good price, there's no reason to feel ashamed for picking it up. It has all of the big Sun hits (which comprise over two-thirds of the record), a few of his early Columbia smashes ("I Still Miss Someone," "Ring of Fire"), and good liner notes. *—Richie Unterberger*

☆ **Columbia Records 1958–1986** / 1987 / Columbia ✦✦✦✦✦
Released in 1987, *Columbia Records 1958-1986* is an excellent summary of his two and a half decades at the label, even if it is not perfect. First of all, the title is slightly misleading, because this compilation stops roughly around 1986 and the one new track, the opener "Oh, What a Dream," is really an outtake from the early '60s. Appropriately, the set favors music made in the late '50s and '60s, since that was Cash's artistic and commercial peak; out of the 20 songs, only four are from the '70s and only three date from the '80s. This isn't really lopsided, since this is his most popular music released on Columbia and, even though he made interesting records throughout his time there, it's also his best. There are some notable omissions—"Daddy Sang Bass" isn't here, along with "The Rebel—Johnny Yuma" and "Understand Your Man," not to mention a number of smaller hits—but it hits most of the big songs ("I Still Miss Someone," "Don't Take Your Guns to Town," "Ring of Fire," "Boy Named Sue," "Sunday Morning Coming Down"), and overall provides a good, concise overview of his greatest hits for Columbia. This collection has since gone out of print, and while it hasn't been replaced by an equivalent Columbia-only collection, nearly all the tracks here are on the 1992 box set *The Essential Johnny Cash*. *—Stephen Thomas Erlewine*

Johnny Cash Is Coming to Town / Apr. 13, 1987 / Mercury ✦✦✦✦
Johnny Cash Is Coming to Town is one of Cash's criminally overlooked recordings from the 1980s. First, it's his debut for Mercury after almost 30 years with Columbia. Secondly,

it is produced by a Cash aficionado, the legendary Cowboy Jack Clement, who had worked with the Man in Black on such classics as "Ballad of a Teenage Queen," "Ring of Fire," and "Gone Girl," among others. Third, this is Cash taking what he started on *Rockabilly Blues* back in 1980 to a whole different level. Fourth, the two Cash originals on this set, "The Ballad of Barbara" and "I'd Rather Have You," are among the finest songs Cash has written—ever. If these reasons weren't enough for the attention this set never got, then the rest of the package—with Elvis Costello's "The Big Light," Guy Clark's "Let Him Roll," Merle Travis' "16 Tons" (which is every bit as great as Tennessee Ernie Ford's version), James Talley's "W. Lee O'Daniel (And the Light Crust Doughboys)," and Bobby Braddock's "The Night Hank Williams Came to Town"—should have been (there are a few more besides these, too!). What it does amount to is a scorching hard country/rockabilly set from Cash; this is not some revival work by a has-been, but a vital, transformational, and powerful work by a man in firm control of his vision, his talent, and his articulation. His reading of "Let Him Roll" is more believable than Clark's and the story becomes bigger than the tale of a broken wino jilted by a whore; it becomes the story of every jilted lover who felt his/her world has come to an end. This is "Long Black Veil"'s other side, a place where the man who dies protects no one but the beloved in his idealized vision of her, and she returns his love with her grief at his passing. In the grain of Cash's voice, "Sixteen Tons" sounds more like a union-organizing song than a novelty pop hit. The darkness in this song is pervasive and barely contains the rage at its core. Along with backing vocals by June, Anita, and Carlene Carter, Waylon Jennings, and Cash's own live band, this one is a bona fide classic. This set is offered as part of a two-fer on CD with another excellent set, *Boom Chicka Boom* from 1989. *—Thom Jurek*

1955–1958 Recordings / 1988 / Charly ♦♦♦♦

There are a lot of collections of Johnny Cash's classic Sun sides, but this 32-track compilation is certainly one of the best. The fidelity is absolutely top-notch, taken from first-generation tapes, and brings the sound of Sam Phillips' Sun studio to life, minus any later annoying overdubs. It's also a nice mix of a few hits, like "I Walk the Line," "Folsom Prison Blues," "Get Rhythm," and "Rock Island Line," with classic album tracks like "Luther Played the Boogie," "The Wreck of Old '97," and "Train of Love." Two versions of "Wide Open Road" are here, one from Cash's original Sun audition, featuring the halting steel guitar of original bandmember A.W. "Red" Kernodle. Most telling are the undubbed versions of later material, like "Thanks a Lot" and "Katy Too," which sound refreshingly free of useless background vocals, and keep the focus on Cash and Luther Perkins' elemental but very effective lead guitar. A single-disc set that packs a lot of wallop. *—Cub Koda*

Water from the Wells of Home / May 1988 / Mercury ♦♦

By 1988, neither Johnny Cash nor his label, Mercury, wanted much to do with each other, and it's easy to see why—Mercury was simply not supporting Cash, not letting him tackle challenging material, and Cash, in turn, wasn't delivering hits. Of course, making him re-record such classics as "Ballad of a Teenage Queen" was no guarantee of getting him back in the charts, but that's exactly how *Water from the Wells of Home* kicks off. It gets quite a bit better from there, as Cash sings a variety of material from Roy Acuff's "As Long as I Live" (also featuring Emmylou Harris) and Tom T. Hall's "The Last of the Drifters" to J.J. Cale's "Call Me the Breeze" and "New Moon Over Jamaica," which was co-written with Paul McCartney, who also appears on the song. In fact, the album is filled with guest appearances, including June Carter, Glen Campbell, Jessi Colter, the Everly Brothers, Waylon Jennings, Hank Williams Jr., Rosanne Cash, and John Carter Cash. It's almost too many cameos for one album—it might have garnered attention, which is exactly what Mercury would have wanted, but it tends to obscure Cash himself. Still, it makes for an interesting curio, and several cuts are strong enough to make the record worth a listen for hardcore fans. It's likely, however, that they'd rarely return to it after that initial listen. *—Stephen Thomas Erlewine*

Boom Chicka Boom / 1989 / Mercury ♦♦♦♦

Boom Chicka Boom is one of those Johnny Cash records that touches on everything, from the craziness of being backstage at a Willie Nelson gig to a stirring cover of "Family Bible" (with Cash's mom singing backing vocals) to Harry Chapin's "Cat's in the Cradle" (done Tennessee Three style) to the custom-fitted "Hidden Shame" (written for Cash by Elvis Costello). But it's Cash's own songs that give this record its merit: the funny and poignant "A Backstage Pass," the solid bluesy morality tale "Farmer's Almanac," the rollicking environmentalist anthem "Don't Go Near the Water," and "I Love You, Love You." "Harley," by Chick Rains and Michael Martin Murphey, is a vehicle made for a singer like Cash, written about a down and outer whose entire life consisted of working the assembly line—until one of those magic moments where a choice gets made, something gets traded in for something gained, and what's lost is its own gain. There's more rock than billy and more country than Willie here, and while the tracks add up to a fine record, it does lack the loose feel of *Johnny Cash Is Coming to Town*, in part because Bob Moore isn't Cowboy Jack Clement, and the other part is that the family, friends, and regular road band that made that earlier record feel so hand in glove are all absent here. The studio cats like Reggie Young, Hargus Robbins, and Roy Huskey Jr. are fine players and they work well with Cash, but they don't make him go as deep as he could with these songs. So it's a good record, but not a great one. *—Thom Jurek*

★ **The Sun Years** / 1990 / Rhino ♦♦♦♦♦

Rhino's single-disc compilation *The Sun Years* contains 18 highlights from Johnny Cash's early years, including nearly every one of his hits for the label (the only ones missing are minor singles or B-sides). During his time at Sun, Cash established his sound and these songs—"Cry! Cry! Cry!," "Folsom Prison Blues," "I Walk the Line"—remained the core of his repertoire throughout his entire career. Hit singles like "There You Go," "Guess Things Happen That Way," "Ballad of a Teenage Queen," and "Luther Played the Boogie" round out *The Sun Years* in an exemplary fashion. There might be more comprehensive collections of Cash's Sun recordings than *The Sun Years*, but this disc contains everything you need to know. *—Stephen Thomas Erlewine*

The Man in Black: 1954–1958 / Sep. 1990 / Bear Family ♦♦♦♦♦

The Man in Black: 1954-1958 is a five-disc box set that includes everything Johnny Cash recorded for Sun Records, plus the fruits of his first year with Columbia Records. In addition to all of the classic singles—from "Hey Porter" to "Don't Take Your Guns to Town," they're all here—there is a wealth of unreleased material and alternate takes, including a disc that captures an entire recording session from his early days with Columbia. The problem with the set is its very comprehensiveness—only dedicated fans or historians can listen to this much music, especially with all of the alternate takes mixed in with the official versions. And the disc with the recording session isn't interesting—it's a curiosity that makes for tedious listening. Certainly anyone who is willing to invest in this expensive box will find it rewarding, but only serious listeners should consider purchasing the set. *—Stephen Thomas Erlewine*

The Man in Black: 1959–1962 / 1991 / Bear Family ♦♦♦♦♦

Picking up where the previous set left off, *The Man in Black: 1959-1962* collects all of the recordings Johnny Cash made for Columbia between 1959 and 1962; the only music that was left off are his historical albums, which Bear Family had already released on *Come Along on Ride Train*. Like the other set, it has an abundance of alternate takes and outtakes, plus a disc that captures an actual recording sessions. Again, it is primarily of interest for historians and dedicated fans willing to take the time to delve deeply into this music—since the songs are presented in chronological order according to their session date, it doesn't make for casual listening. *—Stephen Thomas Erlewine*

Come Along and Ride This Train / 1991 / Bear Family ♦♦♦♦♦

It's a statement of Johnny Cash's longevity that the eight albums collected here—each one a concept collection devoted to American historical themes—were considered worthy and viable commercial releases back when, and that most were very successful. This four-CD set assembles *Ride This Train, Blood, Sweat and Tears, Bitter Tears, Ballads of the True West, Mean as Hell! (Johnny Cash Sings Ballads from the True West), America: A 200 Year Salute in Story and Song, From Sea to Shining Sea*, and *The Rambler*, all in one place. They fit together as a body of work, and he put a lot of heart into all of these songs individually. He also engendered a good deal of enmity from members of his core audience of white Southerners, for the sympathies he displayed for the plight of Native Americans on 1964's *Bitter Tears*. *America: A 200 Year Salute* is the strongest of the other albums, covering the widest scope and allowing Cash to tie together several singing and songwriting traditions. Cash's two Western-song albums make a natural pairing, as do his two albums of railroad-related songs. The last of the four discs, encompassing *From Sea to Shining Sea* and *The Rambler*, is a logical pairing, the latter album being the realistic, somewhat theatrical contemporary equivalent to the former's folk music/history travelogue. Most of the dialogue sequences don't work too well, but the best of the songs come up to Cash's highest standard. Unlike other Bear Family boxes, the book in this one forgoes a detailed sessionography in favor of reprinting original album jacket notes and a good essay by Bob Allen. *—Bruce Eder*

☆ **The Essential Johnny Cash 1955–1983** / 1992 / Columbia/Legacy ♦♦♦♦♦

Assembling a comprehensive multi-disc Johnny Cash collection is a difficult task for a variety of reasons, not the least of it being the sheer number of records Cash put out in the '60s and '70s. Counting duets, he had over 130 charting singles, which is far too much for the average box set, plus those singles don't necessarily tell the full story of Cash the recording artist, since he was a prolific album artist, as well. Then, there's the sheer variety of what he recorded—rockabilly, folk tunes, tales of gunslingers and Indians, scores of novelty numbers, gospel, Americana kitsch, train songs, pop, and straight-ahead country, he tried it all, giving it all his own unique stamp, distinguished by his booming voice and the distinctive two-step muted rhythm picked out by his guitarist, Luther Perkins. In other words, there is a lot of material to choose from, and while it all sounds similar—in that it all sounds like Johnny Cash music—there are so many themes and styles, it's difficult to distill it down to the essentials, as Columbia/Legacy's 1992 triple-disc box set *The Essential Johnny Cash 1955-1983* attempts to do. Spanning 75 tracks, this takes in nearly three decades of Cash's career, starting at Sun and ending when Cash left the label in the mid-'80s. It hits all the big, iconic hits—"Folsom Prison Blues," "I Walk the Line," "Ballad of a Teenage Queen," "Guess Things Happen That Way," "Don't Take Your Guns to Town," "I Got Stripes," "Ring of Fire," "Daddy Sang Bass," "A Boy Named Sue"—but makes no pretense of containing all the hits, and in fact leaves many other hit singles behind, not to mention album tracks. There really isn't anything big missing—after all, all but one song from the 1967 Columbia *Greatest Hits* is here—but what makes a box set great is the quality of the songs that aren't the hits, and here *Essential* is a bit wobbly. It's hurt by the compilers' desire to touch upon every style Cash performed, sometimes to the detriment of overall listenability—and that listenability is also hurt by the sequencing, which is just slightly non-chronological ("Don't Take Your Guns to Town," his first Columbia single, is saved for the second disc opener, long after we're already in Columbia territory; on the second disc, 1965's "Orange Blossom Special" is followed by 1963's "Ring of Fire"), which hampers the momentum in subtle, but noticeable ways. Then, there's the song selection. While there's nothing bad here (although the novelty numbers or topical songs may wear on some listener's nerves), apart from the aforementioned big hits—along with other iconic songs like "The Rebel—Johnny Yuma," "The Ballad of Ira Hayes," and "Cocaine Blues"—it's hard not to feel that for every merely good song here, there's something better that could have been included instead, particularly because there are indeed many great tracks left behind. These are the things that prevent this box from being one of the great country box sets—compare it to Merle Haggard's *Down Every Road*, for instance, a set that captures a complex figure in all of his glory—and keep it from being as definitive as it seems. As a basic library piece, it's pretty good—after all, it has all the basics from Sun and Columbia in one place—but given its idiosyncrasies, it's not an ideal introduction, and it also shouldn't be seen as a one-stop summary of everything worthy Johnny Cash did at Sun and Columbia. It is a good sampler of what he did at those two labels, but once you know the lay of the land, other compilations and proper albums are easier to listen to and more enjoyable. *—Stephen Thomas Erlewine*

American Recordings / 1994 / American/Sony ✦✦✦✦✦

There are few artists who possess the seemingly unlimited crossover appeal of Johnny Cash. With *American Recordings*, the country legend somehow introduced himself to a modern rock audience by releasing a folk record. Of course, the Man in Black isn't your typical country musician, and *American Recordings* encompasses several different genres, but the folk label was applied chiefly because the songs feature Cash's vocals, acoustic guitar, and nothing else. Universally acknowledged as a country music icon, Cash found himself struggling to get any sort of support from country radio in the '90s as it became dominated by younger, pop-influenced acts. Not one to be discouraged by being shunned by the industry he helped to create, Cash signed with Rick Rubin's American Recordings, which was known for its hard rock and rap acts. Rubin, who had cut his teeth as a producer by working with Run-DMC and the Beastie Boys, was at the controls for the *American Recordings* album and comes off looking like a genius for simply giving Cash a microphone and getting out of the way. The album opens with "Delia's Gone," a Cash original about murder that is both haunting and humorous. Several deftly chosen covers also appear, and Cash effortlessly makes each of them his own. One would be hard-pressed to think of a more perfect song for Cash to cover than Nick Lowe's "The Beast in Me." There is no one more qualified to perform a song asking God for salvation from one's inner demons than Johnny Cash. The diverse list of writers who also contribute songs includes Leonard Cohen, Kris Kristofferson, Glenn Danzig, and Tom Waits. Cash deftly applies his signature baritone and rhythmic guitar work to each track and creates what is ultimately a stark, foreboding, and supremely enjoyable album. For some reason, two tracks are live recordings from a performance at L.A.'s ultra-trendy *Viper Room.* The audience offers a few hoots and hollers, but it's unclear if it's because they're having a good-time or because they think that's what country audiences are supposed to do. Taking Cash to the hipsters ultimately worked, as *American Recordings* was embraced by the alternative rock audience. "Delia's Gone" popped up on MTV and college radio, and Cash was a hit with a generation of listeners who had yet to be born when he had his first hit. *American Recordings* also garnered the 1995 Grammy Award for Best Contemporary Folk Album. *—Mark Vanderhoff*

The Man in Black: 1963–1969 / Feb. 1996 / Bear Family ✦✦✦✦✦

The Man in Black: 1963-1969 is Bear Family's fourth box set of Johnny Cash recordings and the third in *The Man in Black* series. *1963-1969* picks up where the previous *Man in Black* box left off—in the beginning of the '60s, after Cash established himself as a hit-maker for Columbia. It collects all of the music Cash made for Columbia Records between 1963 and 1969, including outtakes and alternate versions but not the albums that were issued on the *Come Along and Ride This Train* set. Again, this collection is more for collectors and scholars than fans. There is terrific music here, but the strict chronological order—sequenced by the session date, not release date—makes listening to each disc somewhat tiring. *—Stephen Thomas Erlewine*

Unchained / Nov. 5, 1996 / Warner Bros. ✦✦✦

For all of its critical praise, the all-acoustic Rick Rubin-produced *American Recordings* was slightly listless. For the follow-up, Cash and Rubin wisely decided to ditch the minimalist approach of *American Recordings* and set the Man in Black in front of a full band—namely, Tom Petty & the Heartbreakers. The pairing is surprisingly inspired, as the Heartbreakers prove to be a loose and muscular supporting band, giving Cash the opportunity to invest himself completely in the songs. Cash is more than up to the task, bringing life not only to classic country songs from Jimmie Rodgers and the Louvin Brothers, but also classic pop by Dean Martin ("Memories Are Made of This"), alternative rockers (Soundgarden's "Rusty Cage," Beck's "Rowboat"), and several made-to-order songs from the likes of Petty himself. Occasionally, the pairings are a little forced, but more often than not *Unchained* consists of remarkably vibrant and inspired music that lives up to Cash's status as a legend. *—Stephen Thomas Erlewine*

Live and on the Air / 1997 / Double Gold ✦✦✦✦

Ideally, either Columbia Records or Cash himself would have put together a well-edited and fully balanced double-CD historical live set. This isn't it—there are shortcomings in the sound—but this double CD is an enjoyable footnote to Johnny Cash's history from the 1950s through the 1980s, and the second disc, containing late-'50s live radio broadcasts, included elements of Cash's live set that would otherwise be lost and forgotten. Disc one derives from television appearances dating from the late '80s that are of near state-of-the-art quality, at least as far as clarity is concerned, though the miking is not ideal. Cash's voice has greater presence than any element of the band. The repertory is a mixture of Cash classics such as "Folsom Prison Blues," "Ring of Fire," "Big River," and "Get Rhythm"; then recent additions to his set such as "City of New Orleans" and "Highwayman"; and gospel numbers like "Peace in the Valley" and "These Hands." Cash's performance is expressive and heartfelt, although "Get Rhythm" is a little loose-jointed as a performance. The audience presence in the recording is subdued, and overall this set reminds one of Cash's HBO special of the early '80s, performed in Washington, D.C., before a black-tie VIP audience including the then-Speaker of the House, Tip O'Neill. Disc two is the far more interesting of the two, made up of performances from the radio dating from the 1950s (some from a show called Ranch Party) and early '60s. The rendition of "Big River" by Cash and the Tennessee Two has a tension, forcefulness, and urgency that nothing on disc one displays—he goes through a jocular version of "I Got a Woman" amid the standard part of his set, which includes "I Walk the Line," "Hey, Porter," and "Luther Played the Boogie." Also included is a track called "Impersonations," which features Cash and his band doing impressions of then-popular hits in other genres, including calypso, and satirizing Ernest Tubb's late-'50s singing style and then-recent hits by Red Foley and Kitty Wells. From a slightly later show, Cash does a live version of Gene Autry's "Goodbye Little Darlin'" and covers his then-new single, "Bandana." And from 1964, Cash performs Pete LaFarge's "The Ballad of Ira Hayes," his most controversial recording up to that time in his career. In contrast to disc one, which is recorded very close, the sound on disc two reflects the ambience of the various halls in which the shows were done, some fairly cavernous, but the recording is always of a professional standard. The notes and credits give no indication of performance locations or specific dates. *—Bruce Eder*

VH-1 Storytellers / Jun. 9, 1998 / Sony ✦✦✦

Borrowing a concept from Ray Davies, who promoted his *X-Ray* autobiography with a series of intimate concerts where he read excerpts, told stories about his songs and played both familiar and obscure tunes, VH-1 designed their *Storytellers* show as a way for celebrated singer/songwriters to work their way through their back catalogs, adding some insights along the way. Johnny Cash and Willie Nelson's *VH-1 Storytellers* is one of the first records in the series and it's something of a minor gem. The two songwriters share the stage, telling brief stories about their work and exchanging compliments as they play a selection of both famous and relatively obscure tunes. Neither Cash nor Nelson reveals too much, but the relaxed atmosphere, wry anecdotes and warm versions of standards makes *VH-1 Storytellers* a welcome supplement to their catalogs. *—Stephen Thomas Erlewine*

16 Biggest Hits / Feb. 2, 1999 / Sony ✦✦✦

The titles in Legacy's *16 Biggest Hits* series have been so well done otherwise that it is surprising its Johnny Cash title is such a disappointment. While many of Cash's biggest hits, among them "Ring of Fire," "Understand Your Man," and "A Boy Named Sue," are included, so are minor hits and songs that were not hits at all. Not that there's anything wrong with tracks like "I Still Miss Someone" and "The Legend of John Henry's Hammer," it's just that they are not appropriate to an album of this name. Cash had 13 number-one country hits between 1956 and 1976; you'll only find eight of them here. *—William Ruhlmann*

★ **Man in Black: Greatest Hits** / Mar. 2, 1999 / Columbia/Legacy ✦✦✦✦✦

There have been no shortage of Johnny Cash compilations over the years, particularly of his classic Columbia recordings. There's something for whatever your taste—single-disc compilations with just the hits and extravagant multi-disc box sets tracing his entire career. *Man in Black: Greatest Hits* falls somewhere in between, presenting a comprehensive 30-song overview of (primarily) Cash's work for Columbia. That means the bulk of his groundbreaking Sun work is missing—"I Walk the Line," "Ballad of a Teenage Queen," and "Guess Things Happen That Way" are here, but classics such as "Get Rhythm," "Cry! Cry! Cry!," and "Folsom Prison Blues" (included in a later live version) aren't—but they're all available on Rhino's excellent *Sun Years* collection; this is notable for being an affordable and relatively exhaustive overview of the Columbia years, which is something that hasn't been attempted before this collection. There may be a few hits and cult favorites missing from this compilation, but it does a stellar job in featuring the best, most important cuts from Cash's prolific years with the label, and it makes an excellent companion to *The Sun Years* for the serious Cash fan on a budget. *—Stephen Thomas Erlewine*

Essential Sun Collection / Sep. 15, 1999 / Recall ✦✦✦✦✦

Never has a pile of recordings been so ruthlessly exploited and reissued time and time again like the ones Johnny Cash recorded for Sun Records in Memphis. He actually had more hits *on* the label after he actually *left* the label than during the time he was officially signed to the label, and the reissues have kept coming ever since. This two-disc set contains 36 tracks of what were primarily issued as singles during and after his tenure with the label, along with a few stray album tracks like "Wreck of the Old '97," "Rock Island Line," and "Country Boy" to fill things out. The overdubbed and sweetened single versions stand in place for the original undubbed masters, giving a clear idea of just how much Cash's music was tampered with after he left Sun, and Sam Phillips and company kept combing the vaults looking for more tracks to issue. This is not the only Cash Sun singles collection out there, but it's still a darn good one to have in the pile. *—Cub Koda*

☆ **The Complete Original Sun Singles** / Sep. 21, 1999 / Varese ✦✦✦✦✦

This is a two-CD, 40-song set with both sides of all 20 of the singles released by Johnny Cash on Sun through 1964. (Even though Cash left the label in 1958, Sun plundered its vaults for more Cash singles for about five years, with some of the 45s doing quite well on the country charts and denting the lower reaches of the pop ones.) This is really an excuse for a compilation that's more comprehensive than the usual greatest hits set, but more affordable and digestible than the box sets of his Sun stuff. There's nothing wrong with that, either. It's well-packaged, the music is good-to-classic, and it's an excellent compromise for listeners who want a lot of Johnny Cash at Sun, but not everything. *—Richie Unterberger*

I Walk the Line/Little Fauss and Big Halsey / Sep. 27, 1999 / Bear Family ✦✦✦✦

In 1999, Bear Family released *I Walk the Line/Little Fauss and Big Halsey*, which contained two complete albums—*I Walk the Line* (1964, originally released on Columbia) and *Little Fauss and Big Halsey* (1970, originally released on Columbia)—by Johnny Cash on one compact disc. *—Jason Birchmeier*

Original Golden Hits, Vol. 1-2 / Oct. 12, 1999 / Collectables ✦✦✦✦

Get Rhythm/Story Songs of the Trains and Rivers / Oct. 12, 1999 / Collectables ✦✦✦✦

Singing Story Teller/Rough Cut King of Country Music / Oct. 12, 1999 / Collectables ✦✦✦

Sunday Down South/Sings Hank Williams / Oct. 12, 1999 / Collectables ✦✦✦✦

Showtime/Original Golden Hits, Vol. 3 / Oct. 12, 1999 / Collectables ✦✦✦

Sings I Walk the Line/Sings Folsom Prison Blues / Oct. 12, 1999 / Collectables ✦✦✦✦

Sings the Greatest Hits/The Blue Train / Oct. 12, 1999 / Collectables ✦✦✦

Murder / May 23, 2000 / Columbia/Legacy ✦✦✦✦✦
Of the three thematic Cash CDs simultaneously released in the spring of 2000 (the others are *God* and *Love*), *Murder* is the most sensible. For one thing, there are actually far fewer Cash songs about murder than there are Cash songs about love or God, so this compilation is a more thorough retrospective of a niche in his repertoire. In addition, one has to admit that Cash's somber vocals and flair for storytelling are well-suited for tales of assassination. Also, this is a well-selected set of 16 tunes, spanning the mid-'50s to the mid-'90s. With the exception of the classics "Folsom Prison Blues" (the original Sun version), "The Long Black Veil," and "Don't Take Your Guns to Town," most of these will be unfamiliar to many Cash fans, taken as they are from LPs, B-sides, and live recordings. Most of them are moving, sometimes chilling performances, whether Cash takes on the role of the killer or an observer. Cool overlooked cuts include 1965's spare and spooky "Hardin Wouldn't Run," and "When It's Springtime in Alaska (It's Forty Below)," recorded with wife June Carter. Some of these are pretty oddball tunes, too, in the best sense of that adjective. "Mister Garfield" is a gung-ho tribute to the most obscure assassinated American president, and "Joe Bean" actually manages some wicked gallows (literally) humor, its concluding punch line the message from the governor from whom Bean is hoping to obtain pardon: a gaily sung "Happy birthday, Joe Bean." One track, a 1966 cover of Harlan Howard's "The Sound of Laughter," was previously unreleased in the U.S., although it doesn't rate as one of the more notable entries on the anthology. [*Murder* is also available as part of the three-CD box set *Love, God, Murder*, comprised of thematic discs that are available together or separately.] —*Richie Unterberger*

Love / May 23, 2000 / Columbia/Legacy ✦✦✦✦✦
After 16 songs, you're going to adequately sum up Johnny Cash's take on love, the most common element in his lyrics (as love is in the lyrics of most popular music performers). That's more of a sampler than a survey. Still, this is a decent compilation, spanning 1956-1996, and understandably most heavy on the earliest part of that period; only three of the songs postdate 1970. "I Walk the Line," "Ring of Fire," and "I Still Miss Someone" will be familiar to, and most likely already in the collection of, any Cash listener. To its credit though, the bulk of this disc spotlights LP tracks that are not all that well known, and are sometimes superb, such as "Oh, What a Dream." Also to its credit, this emphasizes the starker and less embellished of Cash's productions, with little in the way of gloppy supplements to the guitars and voices. Cash never sounded more like Leonard Cohen than he did on the brief "'Cause I Love You" (recorded 1969), though it's more likely that Cash influenced Cohen than it is the other way around. As bait to the completists, perhaps, there are two songs that were previously unreleased in the U.S.: the 1964 Cash-June Carter composition "My Old Faded Rose," whose jivey vocal does not sound altogether serious, and the 1967 cut "I Tremble for You" (co-penned by Cash and L.C. DeWitt Jr.), which has a satisfying acoustic demo ambience. June Carter contributes the liner notes. [*Love* is also available as part of the three-CD box set *Love, God, Murder*, comprised of thematic discs that are available together or separately.] —*Richie Unterberger*

God / May 23, 2000 / Columbia/Legacy ✦✦✦
God is the weakest of the thematic CD trilogy that Cash released simultaneously in the spring of 2000 (the others being *Love* and *Murder*). It's not that Cash himself necessarily feels less strongly about spiritual matters than he does about romance or violent death. Musically, however, Cash did not, generally speaking, paint as striking an oeuvre in the religious field as he did with those other subjects (not to mention with subjects other than love, god, or murder). The 16 songs, recorded between 1957 and 1996, are on the whole more glossily produced than those selected for the *Love* and *Murder* sets, and not as arresting. There are, of course, some excellent performances here, particularly the lone Sun track ("Belshazzar") and the 1962 LP cut "Were You There (When They Crucified My Lord)," sung with the Carter Family. There's also the chance to hear Cash cover songs not associated with his repertoire, such as "Swing Low, Sweet Chariot" and Kris Kristofferson's "Why Me." [*God* is also available as part of the three-CD box set *Love, God, Murder*, comprised of thematic discs that are available together or separately.] —*Richie Unterberger*

Love, God, Murder / May 23, 2000 / Columbia/Legacy ✦✦✦✦

☆ **At San Quentin (The Complete 1969 Concert)** / Jul. 4, 2000 / Columbia/Legacy ✦✦✦✦✦
To put the performance on *At San Quentin* in a bit of perspective: Johnny Cash's key partner in the Tennessee Two, guitarist Luther Perkins, died in August 1968, just seven months before this set was recorded in February 1969. In addition to that, Cash was nearing the peak of his popularity—his 1968 live album, *At Folsom Prison*, was a smash success—but he was nearly at his wildest in the personal life, which surely spilled over into his performance. All of this sets the stage for *At San Quentin*, a nominal sequel to *Folsom Prison* that surpasses its predecessor and captures Cash at his rawest and wildest. Part of this is due to how he feeds off of his captive audience, playing to the prisoners and seeming like one of them, but it's also due to the shifting dynamic within the band. Without Luther, Johnny isn't tied to the percolating two-step that defined his music to that point. Sure, it's still there, but it has a different feel coming from a different guitarist, and Cash sounds unhinged, careening through his jailhouse ballads, old hits, rockabilly-styled ravers and even covers of the Lovin' Spoonful ("Darlin' Companion"). No other Johnny Cash record sounds as wild as this. He sounds like an outlaw and renegade here, which

is what gives it power—listen to "A Boy Named Sue," a Shel Silverstein composition that could have been too cute by half, but is rescued by the wild-eyed, committed performance by Cash, where it sounds like he really was set on murdering that son of a bitch that named him Sue. He sounds that way throughout the record, and while most of the best moments did make it to that original 1969 album, the 2000 Columbia/Legacy release eclipses it by presenting nine previously unreleased bonus tracks, doubling the album's length, and presenting such insanely wild numbers as "Big River," as well as sweeter selections like "Daddy Sang Bass." Now, that's the only way to get the record, and that's how it should be, because this extra material makes a legendary album all the greater—in fact, it helps make a case that this is the best Johnny Cash album ever cut. —*Stephen Thomas Erlewine*

The Legend at His Best: Ultimate Box Set & Autobiography / Jul. 11, 2000 / Collectables ✦✦✦
With a title like *Ultimate Box Set* you may expect a complete overview of the several decades Johnny Cash made music, however this set only incorporates 30 of his early Sun sides spread out over two discs. This isn't a bad thing by any means, but omitted are many of the hits released on Columbia, Mercury Nashville, and his quick stint on American Records. If the Sun sessions are what you're looking for, this is a great start. Containing the original recordings of classics, including "I Walk the Line," "Folsom Prison Blues," "Get Rhythm," "Cry, Cry, Cry," and "Hey Porter." Also included in this package is a hardcover edition of Johnny Cash's 300-page autobiography, *Cash*, which doubles as the most extensive set of liner notes ever released in a box set. —*Al Campbell*

American III: Solitary Man / Oct. 17, 2000 / American ✦✦✦
The Man in Black shows hints of gray on *American III: Solitary Man*, his first studio album since being interrupted by a series of serious illnesses in 1997. While the inevitability of aging has been the downfall of many of his contemporaries, Johnny Cash's dark convictions and powerful presence have gone from rough hardwood to solid stone. The stark beauty of his 1994 release *American Recordings* and the warm, friendly collaborations on 1996's *Unchained* combine to create two distinct moods: one of living-room jam sessions with invited friends, and another of stark solo (and near-solo) songs highlighting Cash's years and stories. Partnering once again with Tom Petty, the two join together on Petty's own "I Won't Back Down" and the Neil Diamond-penned title track. Cash also lays his lonesome hands on U2's "One" and reunites with fellow outlaw Merle Haggard on the stubborn "I'm Leavin' Now." These duets and well-known covers show an inviting side of Johnny Cash. But the real highlights of the album are those reminiscent of his *American Recordings* songs; they feature just the man and his guitar, with nothing else to clutter the story. The creaks and despair of the vaudeville song "Nobody" tell of a man who has become hardened by his solitude, while the Palace hymn "I See a Darkness" soars with the passion of a thousand gospel choirs, even though there are only two men singing. Although at times it is difficult to hear past Tom Petty's growl or Sheryl Crow's young harmonies in the more popular songs Cash covers, these obscure prison songs and country ballads sound as honest and heartfelt as his own compositions. At age 68, his warm baritone may waver but his passion never does. —*Zac Johnson*

Roads Less Travelled: Sun Recordings / Mar. 13, 2001 / Varese ✦✦✦✦
Varese's *Roads Less Travelled* contains 18 hard-to-find Sun recordings from Johnny Cash and the Tennessee Two, songs that were either not released or weren't issued as A-sides or languished as album tracks. This is actually a bit of a godsend, since Cash and the Tennessee Two were at their peak at Sun and it's a little difficult to dig deep into their catalog for lost treasures, unless you're willing to delve into Bear Family's overly exhaustive *Man in Black* set. This culls many of the highlights from the set and while there are no revelations, there are finds the very best elements of that set, and while there's no revelations, there are plenty of small gems to enjoy and it's easily the best choice for serious listeners (who are not completists) after they've absorbed the very best of his Sun material. —*Stephen Thomas Erlewine*

The Essential Johnny Cash / Feb. 2002 / Columbia ✦✦✦✦✦
Issued in commemoration of Cash's 70th birthday, this double CD is a good survey of 1955-1993 career highlights (and a different release than the similarly titled three-CD *The Essential Johnny Cash 1955-1983*). Is it a good place to start? That depends on what you have or don't have already, considering that so many greatest-hits compilations containing some or much of this material appeared prior to this, yet another repackage. All of his very biggest hits are here, and it leans very heavily on his first 15 years of recordings, with just eight of the 36 tracks postdating 1970 (and only one of them, his 1993 U2 collaboration "The Wanderer," postdating 1986). For that reason some may complain that it doesn't give some phases of his career proper weight, and certainly not evenly distributed weight. But let's be cold about this: Cash's best records *were* between 1955 and 1970, and focusing on his early work, as this compilation does, means higher overall quality. It's too bad nothing is included from his acclaimed, unadorned 1994 album, *American Recordings*, but otherwise this will serve as a quite satisfactory best-of for those who want both the familiar hits and a few good, not-so-overplayed ones, like his versions of "It Ain't Me Babe," "Jackson," and "If I Were a Carpenter." —*Richie Unterberger*

The Man in Black: The International Johnny Cash / Mar. 12, 2002 / Bear Family ✦✦
Although this album features a photo of the Man in Black alone on the cover, Johnny Cash doesn't actually appear on half of *The International Johnny Cash*. Instead, the listener is treated to a disc of German translations of Cash's greatest hits performed by Gunter Gabriel, Jürgen Herbst, Ralf Bendix, and others. The other half of this compilation consists of Cash himself performing "Five Feet High and Rising," "Ring of Fire," and "I Got Stripes" in German. Cash first picked up the guitar while he was stationed in Germany after college, so his easy German isn't as awkward as many translated pop stars, and the recordings (mostly from the '60s and '70s) sound pretty good. Fans should

keep in mind that he only performs nine of the songs on this 26-track disc, but anyone who has "The Chicken in Black" on both vinyl *and* CD will get a kick out of this novelty. *—Zac Johnson*

The Essential Sun Singles / Apr. 2, 2002 / Varese ✦✦✦✦✦

As great as Cash's Sun catalog was, it's been reissued on so many compilations that one wonders whether the world needs any more. This 25-track single disc, after all, appears just three years after *The Complete Original Sun Singles*, also on the Varese Sarabande label, which covers much of the same territory, albeit with greater depth as it contains two discs and 40 songs. Should your budget or patience extend just to one CD, though, *The Essential Sun Singles* is about as good as any single-disc Sun-period Cash compilation likely to be assembled. The major hits "Cry Cry Cry," "Folsom Prison Blues," "I Walk the Line," "Ballad of a Teenage Queen," "Big River," "Guess Things Happen That Way," "Come in Stranger," "The Ways of a Woman in Love"—they're all here. So are pretty good smaller hits like "Straight A's in Love" and "Next in Line," the odd non-charting B-side like "Get Rhythm," and one song (a cover of "Rock Island Line") that was actually an album track, not a 45. It's all classic country music with liberal dips of rockabilly, pop, and folk, with enough historical liner notes to give novices a decent grounding in Cash's early career. *—Richie Unterberger*

20th Century Masters—The Millennium Collection: The Best of Johnny Cash / May 21, 2002 / Mercury ✦✦

When he was dropped by Columbia Records after 28 years in 1986, Johnny Cash immediately signed to Mercury Records, for whom he recorded with middling success over the next few years. There is a reasonable compilation to be constructed from this material, a collection that, for example, might include Cash's version of Elvis Costello's "The Big Light" (from 1987's *Is Coming to Town*) and the Paul McCartney collaboration "New Moon Over Jamaica" (from 1988's *Water From the Wells of Home*), but this isn't it. During the course of his tenure at Mercury, Cash made the mistake of agreeing to cut a low-budget quickie album for the European market on which he only covered a bunch of his old hits. You guessed it: *Classic Cash: Hall of Fame Series* (1988) was issued stateside, too, the excuse being a tie-in with a Cash exhibit at the Country Music Hall of Fame. The compilers of this discount-priced compilation have pulled nine of 12 tracks from that album. So, instead of being a collection that would accurately represent Cash's stint at Mercury, this is just an attempt to fool consumers into buying a bunch of re-recordings. Too bad. *—William Ruhlmann*

At Madison Square Garden / Aug. 27, 2002 / Columbia/Legacy ✦✦✦✦

Not released until 2002, all 26 of these songs—adding up to a generous 77 minutes—were recorded at Cash's successful show at Madison Square Garden in New York on December 5, 1969. Two best-selling live late-'60s Cash albums, *At Folsom Prison* and *At San Quentin*, have long been available, and it will be pretty difficult for this to dislodge those in prominence among those scouting for live material in the Cash catalog. Still, it's a good document of Cash as he reached the apex of his mainstream popularity. Also, its setting in a large, popular venue by itself guaranteed that the ambience would be somewhat different than it would be on the two aforementioned live albums, both recorded in prisons. While Cash has a full band (including Carl Perkins on electric guitar and his long-time associate Marshall Grant on bass), the sound, to its credit, remains spare. The sound is not amazingly top-of-the-line, but it's pretty good, and the repertoire is extremely varied, taking in oldies like "Big River," "I Still Miss Someone," "Long Black Veil," and "Folsom Prison"; his then-recent smashes "Boy Named Sue" and "Daddy Sang Bass"; the Americana and Native American advocacy of songs like "The Ballad of Ira Hayes" and "Remember the Alamo"; the spiritual "Were You There (When They Crucified My Lord)"; and Ed McCurdy's anti-war folk revival tune "Last Night I Had the Strangest Dream." There are also guest star turns for Carl Perkins (who does "Blue Suede Shoes"), the Statler Brothers (who do their hit "Flowers on the Wall"), and the Carter Family, whose two songs are actually vivacious highlights of the disc, and a good change of pace from Cash's customary low chug. Between-song raps on the Vietnam War, prison, and other topics testify to Cash's ability to reach out to all stripes of his constituency, though the finale medley (and the bits near the end announcing the renewal of his TV show and explaining pregnant June Carter's absence) are a tad showbizzy. *—Richie Unterberger*

American IV: The Man Comes Around / Nov. 5, 2002 / Universal ✦✦✦

Johnny Cash's fourth project with producer Rick Rubin continues on the same path as many of their previous releases: Cash's warm and rumbling baritone over minimal production and gentle duets with some surprising guests. One of the things that sets *American IV: The Man Comes Around* apart from the others is Cash's song selections. The success he experienced with his previous interpretations of contemporary songwriters (Soundgarden's "Rusty Cage," Nick Cave's "The Mercy Seat") is applied to this album with varying degrees of success. His throaty reading of Nine Inch Nails' "Hurt" easily fits into his "Man in Black" persona, and the spiritual conviction underlying Depeche Mode's "Personal Jesus" is certainly powerful. Unfortunately, the inclusion of "Bridge Over Troubled Water" (featuring a lost-sounding Fiona Apple) and a passionless snooze through the Beatles' "In My Life" should have been so much stronger (given the subject matter of both songs and Cash's prolific life story). One of the reasons his previous covers were so successful is that in the past he had chosen some pretty obscure songs (Bonnie Prince Billy's "I See a Darkness" and Beck's "Rowboat," to name a couple) and reinterpreted them with his unique perspective and unmistakable voice. However, there is really no need to hear his versions of the Irish standard "Danny Boy" or the clunky rendition of Sting's "I Hung My Head," since something about them just doesn't fit—either Cash wasn't entirely comfortable with the song or the performance was never fully realized. Luckily, the new songs Cash wrote for the album are pretty strong, and his cover of the standard "We'll Meet Again" is among the best versions of the song ever recorded. It is a relief to hear that although Cash's voice is clearly older and not the booming powerhouse it was in the earlier Sun and Columbia days, he's still got some punch left in him, and the wisdom he's gained in his later life seeps through between the grooves, revealing a man who has lived through it all and lived to tell the tale. *—Zac Johnson*

Rosanne Cash

b. May 24, 1955, Memphis, TN

Guitar, Vocals / Singer/Songwriter, Neo-Traditionalist Country, Contemporary Country

The history of popular music is littered with the careers of the children of famous artists, performers who manage to carve out some small measure of success based far less on talent than on the recognition that their famous names afford them. Perhaps no greater exception to this trend was Rosanne Cash, the daughter of Johnny Cash, whose idiosyncratic and innovative music made her one of the pre-eminent singer/songwriters of her day.

Born May 24, 1956, to her father and his first wife, Vivian Liberto, Rosanne was raised by her mother in Southern California after her parents separated in the early '60s. She was largely uninfluenced by her father's music until she joined his road show following her graduation from high-school; over a three-year period, she was promoted from handling the tour's laundry duties to performing, first as a backup singer and then as an infrequent soloist. Still, Cash remained unsure of choosing a career in music, and took some acting classes; not wishing to succeed solely on the basis of her family's influence, she also worked as a secretary in London and traveled extensively abroad.

After releasing an eponymously titled solo record—later disavowed—in Germany in 1978, Cash signed with Columbia Records, and began performing with Texas singer/songwriter Rodney Crowell, who produced three songs for her American debut, 1979's *Right or Wrong*. The record featured three Top 25 hits, including "No Memories Hangin' Round," a duet with Bobby Bare. The same year, she and Crowell also married. Cash issued her commercial breakthrough *Seven Year Ache* in 1981; not only did the album yield three number-one singles, the title track even crossed over into the Top 30 on *Billboard*'s pop chart. However, the follow-up, 1982's *Somewhere in the Stars*, was a rush job, recorded during Cash's pregnancy. While failing to repeat *Seven Year Ache*'s success, it did produce two more Top Ten singles, "Ain't No Money" and "I Wonder."

After a three-year hiatus, Cash returned with her most significant artistic statement yet in *Rhythm & Romance*, a deft fusion of country and pop that won wide acclaim from both camps. The record earned her two more number ones, "I Don't Know Why You Don't Want Me" (co-written with Crowell) and a cover of Tom Petty's "Never Be You." In 1987, she issued *King's Record Shop*, a meditation on country music traditions which generated four successive number-one hits in John Hiatt's "The Way We Make a Broken Heart," "Tennessee Flat Top Box" (a hit for her father in 1961), "If You Change Your Mind," and John Stewart's "Runaway Train." Also hitting number one was "It's Such a Small World," a duet with Crowell from his *Diamonds and Dirt* LP; not surprisingly, she was named *Billboard*'s Top Singles Artist in 1988.

The next year, Cash assembled the retrospective *Hits 1979-1989*; one of the record's few new songs, a cover of the Beatles' "I Don't Want to Spoil the Party," pushed the consecutive number ones streak to five. By 1990, her marriage to Crowell was beginning to dissolve; *Interiors*, an essay on the couple's relationship, was released the following year, and while the record was the subject of great critical acclaim, it was a commercial failure that generated only one Top 40 hit, "What We Really Want." In 1991, Cash and Crowell divorced; *The Wheel*, released in 1993, was an unflinchingly confessional examination of the marriage's failure that ranked as her most musically diverse effort to date. After a three-year hiatus, Cash returned with a vengeance in 1996; not only did she publish her first book, a short-story collection titled *Bodies of Water*, but she also issued her first release on Capitol Records *10 Song Demo*, an 11-cut collection of stark home recordings released with minimal studio gloss. In 2003, Cash returned with *Rules of Travel*, an album five hears in the making and her first full-fledged studio release since *The Wheel*. *—Jason Ankeny*

Right or Wrong / 1979 / Columbia ✦✦✦✦

On her debut American release (she'd done a record in Germany that she now disowns), Rosanne Cash may not have shaken the money tree or the *Billboard* charts, but she and husband/producer/collaborator Rodney Crowell began to change the face of contemporary country music forever. Recorded in L.A. and not Nash Vegas, *Right or Wrong* still utilized talent synonymous with Music City, but the sound that took country and merged it with the rock and pop styles of the day was a winning formula. Crowell and Cash made the song selections while Rodney called in Emmylou Harris' band (of which he was an alumnus) and some up and comers and created a sonic palette that accented the brave new world of stripped-down mixes and songs that came from the left field of country or pop (the European version of the album featured a Lennon/McCartney tune). Here are nods to the past and heritage in her father's "Big River," a couple of outlaw tunes from Keith Sykes (the title track and "Take Me, Take Me"), as well as the stunning ballad "Couldn't Do Nothing Right" by Karen Brooks and Gary P. Nunn. Jerry Jeff Walker recorded a hell of a version in the early '70s, but the crooning sorrow and ache in the grain of Cash's voice and the faux Caribbean rhythm behind a pedal steel-driven melody line make it an entirely different song. Speaking of voice, Cash is most comfortable singing her own searing ballads such as "This Has Happened Before," Crowell's "No Memories Hanging' Round," "Seeing's Believing," and "Anybody's Darlin'." But Crowell's "Baby, Start Turnin' Em Down" is perhaps the strongest track on the album as it combines a restless country shuffle, a rocker's minor key blues riff, and a deliberate nod to Marvin Gaye's "Heard It Through the Grapevine" and Motown. *Right or Wrong* only got to number 42 on the *Billboard* chart, but it did make radio take notice that something new was about to happen, and on *Seven Year Ache*, the follow-up to this fine album, the floodgates opened. *—Thom Jurek*

★ **Seven Year Ache** / 1981 / Columbia ✦✦✦✦✦

Blame whomever you want to for Garth Brooks and Shania Twain, but the bottom line is that Rosanne Cash's masterpiece *Seven Year Ache* paved the way for all of those folks as well as for Mary-Chapin Carpenter, Shawn Colvin, and then some. Proclaimed by Cash and her husband/producer/collaborator, Rodney Crowell, as "punktry," the album adds an entirely new twist on the Nashville sound. Perhaps it is because this is L.A. country and reflects the cocaine bliss sound of the era as well as Fleetwood Mac's *Tusk* does. Utilizing everything from synthesizers and rock arrangements to pop ballad-styled charts and plenty of attitude, *Seven Year Ache* yielded three number-one singles and songs by rock musicians such as Tom Petty and singer/songwriters like Keith Sykes and Steve Forbert. Of the singles, Cash penned two; the title track, which is a sorrowful indictment of her husband's philandering ways, and the shattering ballad "Blue Moon With Heartache." The third, the smash "My Baby Thinks He's a Train," was written by Asleep at the Wheel's Leroy Preston. Musically, the band included many of the same players from the *Right or Wrong* sessions, with the emerging vocal talent of former Pure Prairie League member Vince Gill. Forbert's "What Kinda Girl" is almost rockabilly in its shuffling intensity and punk bravado. It dares the listener to define the protagonist just to shatter the preconception. There's also a nod to tradition here in Cash's beautifully updated read of the Merle Haggard/Red Simpson nugget "You Don't Have Very Far to Go," complete with whinnying pedal steels and a honky tonk backbeat. In "My Baby Thinks He's a Train," Cash and Crowell very consciously offer a new generation interpretation of dad Johnny's sound. This rocks harder yet is smooth as silk and full of that desolate want Johnny offered in his delivery. But unlike her father's, this isn't a forlorn yearning want, it's a pissed off anthemic want. For the ambulance chasers, this record with its songs of infidelity and broken promises may indeed be the first crack in a marriage and collaboration that ended a decade later. The tempo borrows the old Tennessee Three rhythm, but sped up into the stratosphere, with a shifting Western swing line near the refrain. Over 20 years after it was first issued, *Seven Year Ache* sounds as fresh and revolutionary as it did when it was issued. Any album that stands that test of time in a field like country deserves to be regarded as a classic. Yes, this is the one that changed everything. *—Thom Jurek*

Somewhere in the Stars / 1982 / Columbia ♦♦♦♦

Somewhere in the Stars followed by one year the wildly successful *Seven Year Ache*, Rosanne Cash's breakthrough record. Once again with husband Rodney Crowell in the producer's chair and acting as a full collaborator, Cash pushed the Nash Vegas envelope to the breaking point for the time. A listen to Shania Twain's *Come on Over* and *Up!* will point, in a winding manner, back to *Somewhere in the Stars*. Here are guitars ringing through with influences from Dire Straits to Graham Parker & the Rumour. Give a listen to Susanna Clark's "Oh, Yes I Can," and listen to Albert Lee's Mark Knopfler cop. Interestingly, Cash, while writing a great deal during this period, only recorded one of her own songs and co-wrote another with Crowell. The feel has British new wave, country, and L.A. rock blended into a seamless whole. Listen to the chug and tug of "Ain't No Money," written by Crowell, that opens the album. Linda Ronstadt in her prime could have cut this, but only Cash could bring the solid country gutbucket pout in her delivery. The horn charts on "It Hasn't Happened Yet," a John Hiatt composition, are deep rooted in the Memphis soul tradition of Stax. Given Cash's voice, though, the track comes off at odds with traditions that have little in common except for being heartfelt articulations of the unspeakable. But the longing in Cash's voice stands at odds with the normally reserved slickness of Nash Vegas productions. Tom T. Hall's "That's How I Got to Memphis" feels out of place here, with its slim production and relatively straight country feel, but Cash doesn't skimp on her vocal; it's believable if not overly inspired, and her read of the song is true to Hall's—and the appearance of Johnny Cash on the last verse adds depth and mystery. The most angular track on the album is "I Look for Love," also by Hiatt, which seems like it was written after hearing Joe Jackson for the first time. With its odd lead line and funked-up bass, it feels like the track from outer space here, but in the grain of Cash's deeply passionate delivery it fits right in. The set closes with the title track. In its intimacy and shimmering surfaces, it points directly at records like *Interiors* and *The Wheel* that would come a decade later, though it's a love song, not a dark paean to something lost. As a follow-up to a smash album, *Somewhere in the Stars* was more than worthy and stands the test of time as a pillar in Cash's catalog. *—Thom Jurek*

Rhythm & Romance / 1985 / Columbia ♦♦♦♦♦

Rhythm & Romance was recorded in 1984 and issued in 1985, almost three years after *Somewhere in the Stars*. *Rhythm & Romance* is significant in a number of ways—besides its obvious quality as a piece of popular art. Foremost, it's the first recording that really showcases Rosanne Cash as a songwriter. Of the ten tracks here, she wrote six and co-wrote two others. This is the beginning of a new path in her career, which remains to this day, where she writes all of her own material. Secondly, it's the first record she made without producer/husband/songwriting partner Rodney Crowell (who was busy making his own breakthrough record, *Diamonds & Dirt*), David Molloy, and David Thoener. Thirdly, even after a nearly three-year absence and with a radical—by country standards—cover, the album topped the charts and charted two singles (in those days almost a unheard of). Lastly, she used musicians who were from the L.A. studio scene rather than Nash Vegas stalwarts, guitarist Waddy Wachtel and keyboard ace Benmont Tench from Tom Petty's Heartbreakers among them. Vince Gill also began to emerge from the shadows on this set as a solid singer and guitarist in his own right. But it's the material that makes any record. First there's Cash's sultry, sexual "Hold On" (which hit the number-one spot) with its loping vocal and wanton ache, then there's "Second to No One," with its gorgeous melody, scathing autobiographical lyric, and shimmering acoustic guitars. The keyboard-driven "Halfway House," with its '50s rock melody filtered through '80s new wave riffing, where the guitars move into overdrive on the refrains, is a startling exercise in pushing the envelope. The stunning "Never Gonna Hurt," all hard rock guitars playing a Warren Zevon-esque "Werewolves of London"-type riff, is remarkable in how tough and snotty it is. A cover of John Fogerty's classic "Feelin' Blue" closes the album. It's Memphis funky and full of jagged angles where soul meets the blues meets rock & roll, in a context that is pure modern country. Cash's vocal is thoroughly convincing. Where the original is full of fear and spooky realization, Cash's is full of bravado and resignation to meet the rough stuff on the horizon head-on. Remarkable in every way, *Rhythm & Romance* stands the test of time as an expertly conceived and executed collection of songs that reveals a songwriter in full command of her talent and a singer at the peak of her powers—for whom the restraints of Nashville had become to tenuous to contend with for much longer. *—Thom Jurek*

King's Record Shop / 1987 / Columbia ♦♦♦

King's Record Shop takes Rosanne Cash closer to rock and pop than any of her past albums, but she still manages to infuse enough of her country charm in a few of the tracks to keep it from evolving into a complete crossover. Both her and Rodney Crowell fall precisely into place as a team even though their relationship was suffering. Cash's proficiency can be heard best on the exuberant "Rosie Strikes Back" and to a bit of lesser extent on "The Real Me." The album itself reached the number-six spot, and once again the hits just kept on coming. Four number-one singles emerged from the album, with the two best being a cover of John Hiatt's "The Way We Make a Broken Heart" and a jangly rendition of her father's "Tennessee Flat Top Box." John Stewart's "Runaway Train" is yet another standout, as is the earnest "If You Change Your Mind." Cash's sound is at its fullest, and even on the slower tracks she has more focus and appetence than ever before. She's also a bit more revealing and personal, especially on "I Don't Have to Crawl," where the lyrics she sings are deep-cutting and foretelling. Not only do the songs sound strong on their own, but the entire album exudes a pinpointed direction and a "complete package" feel which enabled fans to feel closer to Cash and her work than ever before. In 1990, Cash released *Interiors*, an album in which she exposed all of her feelings and pains about her relationship (which had just deteriorated) with Rodney Crowell. *King's Record Shop* isn't exactly a full-fledged precursor to their breakup, but there are enough hints between the lines to indicate their marital troubles. *—Mike DeGagne*

Hits 1979–1989 / 1989 / Columbia ♦♦♦

Rosanne Cash recorded many worthwhile albums in the years after *Hits 1979-1989* was released, but this compilation covers the time when Cash was a country star and reliable hitmaker—namely, the '80s. At only 12 tracks, the collection doesn't feature all of her hits, but it does contain what are arguably the cream of the crop—"No Memories Hangin' Around," "Seven Year Ache," "My Baby Thinks He's a Train," "Blue Moon With Heartache," "I Wonder," "I Don' t Know Why You Don't Want Me," "Never Be You," "Hold On," "The Way We Make a Broken Heart," "Tennessee Flat Top Box" and "I Don't Want to Spoil the Party." With a catalog as rich as Cash's, a compilation this brief can only skim the surface, but the end result is a terrifically engaging listen for the devoted and the curious alike. *—Stephen Thomas Erlewine*

★ **Interiors** / 1990 / Columbia ♦♦♦♦♦

On Rosanne Cash's final recording for Columbia's Nashville division she pulled out all the stops. Already known for her unflinching honesty, she took it to its most poignant and searing extreme on *Interiors*. Cash produced the record herself and wrote or co-wrote all the material here. A country record it's not, but that hardly matters. This is a pop record with teeth and ache and broken hearts strewn all over the place. In fact, *Interiors* has the feel of a battlefield emptied of everything but its ghosts. The album is a collection of ten songs linked thematically by the chronicling of the tension, dysfunction, and ultimate dissolution of Cash's marriage to Rodney Crowell caused by dishonesty, infidelity, substance abuse, and physical distance; and she owns her side of the street with courage without laying blame. Carefully wrought with subtle instrumentation surrounding her fearless yet wavering vocals. Acoustic guitars, pianos, brushed drums, an occasional organ, a bass almost hidden under layers of ethereal grace—these are the musical trappings that frame Cash's voice as she sets about a task so seemingly painful it's almost uncomfortable to listen to. It's as if the listener is granted a private audience with her heart and innermost thoughts. Everything is here: the disillusionment, the anger, the vain hope of reconciliation, and finally the acceptance and resignation that endings are a part of life and serve their purpose. While these ten tracks are virtually inseparable from one another, there are standouts such as "Dance With the Tiger" written with John Stewart, "Real Woman" written with Crowell, "Mirror Image," "I Want a Cure," and the harrowing closer, "Paralyzed," where Cash is accompanied only by a piano. Here she lets her current position be known, that seeing the end of this relationship leaves her in the clutches of being unable to move from the emotional space she is in. This album is full of a truth that most would rather not acknowledge, but it is morally and spiritually instructive in terms of its lyrical content, and musically it is her masterpiece. In fact, it's proof that art can redeem what cannot be in human terms. *—Thom Jurek*

The Wheel / Jan. 19, 1993 / Columbia ♦♦♦♦♦

Like the dark, cathartic *Interiors*, *The Wheel* is an introspective, soul-searching set of confessional songs revolving around love and relationships. While many of the themes and emotions of *Interiors* are repeated on *The Wheel*, Roseanne Cash hasn't repeated herself, either lyrically or musically. Working from the same combination of folk and country that has fueled her songwriting throughout her career, she has created an album of subtle, melodic grace that helps convey the deep feelings of her lyrics. It's an immaculately-produced album, but that never detracts from the emotional core of Cash's music. *—Stephen Thomas Erlewine*

Retrospective / Nov. 7, 1995 / Columbia ♦♦♦

Retrospective is an odd overview of Rosanne Cash's later recordings for Columbia, featuring a combination of hits, album tracks, rarities, and new songs. Which means, the album does contain hits like the number one "Runaway Train," but it concentrates on the lesser-known material, whether it was the minor hit "On the Surface" or Elvis Costello's "Our Little Angel." It's a good compilation, but it's a little unnecessary, since the albums it is culled from—*Interiors, The Wheel*—function better as individual albums, and don't lend themselves well to collections. *—Thom Owens*

10 Song Demo / Apr. 2, 1996 / Capitol ✦✦✦✦

Despite its title, *10 Song Demo* isn't really a demo tape, but it is what the title suggests—a stripped-down, direct collection of songs (for the record, there are 11 songs, not ten). Conceptually, it is a brilliant way to signal that Rosanne Cash has severed ties with Nashville, as well as begun her contract with Capitol Records. However, the album doesn't completely work. Essentially, *10 Song Demo* is an official statement from Cash that she is no longer strictly a country singer, but an all-around singer/songwriter. Of course, she has always bent the rules of country music, so this isn't a big departure as far as songwriting goes. Musically, however, the spare, simple arrangements lack all of the country and pop production flourishes that marked her last two albums. Though it initially sounds fine, there isn't much variation to the music, and her melodies are frequently uncompelling. That can't be said of her lyrics—they are as cutting, emotional, and affecting as they have been, and they are the main reason for listening to *10 Song Demo*. *—Stephen Thomas Erlewine*

Right or Wrong/Seven Year Ache / Nov. 13, 2001 / Raven ✦✦✦✦

The issue of Rosanne Cash's first two Columbia albums in a single package is not only a listening delight, it's more importantly a historical document. In the same way archivists go back to finds the roots of certain evolutions in earlier strains of country music, these two records will be marked undoubtedly as the turning point from the countrypolitan and outlaw sounds of the late '70s to the fusion of country music with modern pop styles that could crossover and reach audiences on both sides of the country music divide. It also marked the resurgence of the female singer/songwriter that the music hadn't seen since the late '50s through the mid-'60s. *Right or Wrong* is Cash's first collaboration with her husband and producer, Rodney Crowell. Formerly a member of Emmylou Harris' Hot Band, he recruited Emmylou's crew for this project and picked Los Angeles as the site; Cash chose songs based on their merit as songs rather than as country-potential country records. Consequently, writers such as Keith Sykes, Karen Brookes, Gary P. Nunn, and (at least on the British version) Lennon and McCartney got shots at the mainstream country charts. In addition, Cash and Crowell both honed their songwriting skills specific to her voice and delivery style, to the point where on *Seven Year Ache* they scored with three number-one singles and a Top Ten album. Two of those singles, the title track and "Blue Moon With Heartache," were Cash compositions. The third single, Leroy Preston's "My Baby Thinks He's a Train," was covered by virtually every major female country performer in its wake. Add covers of Tom Petty and Steve Forbert songs and the appearance of the queen herself, Emmylou Harris, and you have a dynamite recording. These sides hold up well over two decades later—especially after what happened to country in the '90s (yeccccchhhhhh!!!!). The sound is pristine, the package has extensive liner notes, and there are bonus tracks to boot. Necessary. *—Thom Jurek*

Somewhere in the Stars/Rhythm & Romance / Mar. 18, 2003 / Raven ✦✦✦✦✦

Even more so than its predecessor, the Raven two-fer *Right or Wrong/Seven Year Ache*, this pair of albums on one CD shows the depth and breadth of how far Rosanne Cash was willing to go in order to remake modern country music into something she considered not only interesting but also valid for the time period. *Somewhere in the Stars* and *Rhythm & Romance* are exercises in making seamless all the music that she and Rodney Crowell, her then husband, producer, and collaborator, had absorbed in London, Los Angeles, and New York. On these two records, particularly on the latter, Cash utilized the sounds of British new wave and the L.A. studio sound as a bottom for her lyrical and melodic explorations. The two discs are sharply contrasted by two things: On *Somewhere in the Stars*, Cash and producer Crowell chose mainly material by other songwriters, and on *Rhythm & Romance*, Crowell departed as producer and Cash wrote nearly everything on the record. Both records charted and did very well, but *Rhythm & Romance* went to number one, garnering a pair of singles in that spot as well as a Grammy for Cash's "I Don't Know Why You Don't Want Me." Sonically, they dovetail one another. Whereas on *Stars*, Cash and Crowell experiment with textures and riffs from various other types of pop music, on *Rhythm & Romance* there is no holding back, from the tough guitars to Benmont Tench's keyboards to the album's more rock and soul feeling overall. Each album stands on its own, and as a pair they are an amazing whole and deeply satisfying listening experience, standing the test of time exceedingly well. *—Thom Jurek*

Rules of Travel / Mar. 25, 2003 / Capitol ✦✦✦✦

At every level, *Rules of Travel* distinguishes itself. A latecomer to songwriting, Rosanne Cash delivers plenty of compelling material, fully comparable in quality to the album's two non-original cuts. She comes up with fresh and intriguing chord changes to end verses and choruses on the title track, and images whose rugged eloquence perfectly fits the early-morning mumble of Steve Earle on "I'll Change for You." On "September When It Comes," she switches to a more homespun, folkloric imagery that suits her father's weathered, timeless rumble. The production values change very subtly according to what best suits each song, from the Wallflowers-oriented roots rock saunter of "Hope Against Hope" to the shadowy urban swing of "Will You Remember Me" to the stark acoustic setting of "Western Wall." Though her voice is hardly the most impressive instrument in country music, Cash knows how to compensate by using an understated approach to more quietly highlight the essence of a song. Given the quality of what she gives herself to work with on *Rules of Travel*, it's a method that can't miss. *—Robert L. Doerschuk*

Tommy Cash

b. Apr. 5, 1940, Dyess, AR

Vocals, Guitar / Traditional Country, Country-Pop

Younger brother of the Man in Black, Tommy Cash enjoyed some chart success in his own right. Born April 5, 1940, in Dyess, AR, Tommy was eight years younger than big brother Johnny. He formed his first band in high-school, but enlisted in the Army soon after graduation. While serving in Germany during 1958, he was a DJ for Armed Services Radio—perhaps contributing in some part to the incredible success of Johnny's hit of that year, "Ballad of a Teenage Queen."

After resuming civilian life in the early '60s, Tommy played with Hank Williams Jr. and gained his own recording contract from Musicor by 1967. After a move to United Artists, he just missed the country Top 40 in 1968 with "The Sounds of Goodbye." Transferred yet again, to Epic Records, Tommy delivered his biggest hit—"Six White Horses," a tribute to JFK, RFK, and Martin Luther King Jr.—in late 1969. The single hit number four and was followed by two Top Ten singles in 1970, "Rise and Shine" and "One Song Away." During the '70s, Cash continued to tour and record—for Epic, Elektra, 20th Century, and Monument—but his only Top 20 entry occurred when "I Recall a Gypsy Woman" made number 16 in 1973. *—John Bush*

● **The Very Best of Tommy Cash** / Aug. 24, 1999 / Collectables ✦✦✦✦✦

The Very Best of Tommy Cash is a nearly complete summation of the chart career of Tommy Cash, whose remarkable similarity to his famous older brother makes this quite a find for fans of the Man in Black. Cash had three Top Ten country hits in 1969-1970, the biggest of which was "Six White Horses," a powerful tribute to John F. Kennedy, Robert Kennedy, and Martin Luther King Jr. that crossed over to the lower reaches of the pop chart. "Rise and Shine" and "One Song Away" were Cash's only other major hits, but his material was consistently good and generally upbeat, so it's surprising that he didn't fare better with music buyers. All of Cash's hits for Epic and Monument are included on this 16-track anthology. *—Greg Adams*

Pete Cassell

b. Aug. 27, 1917, Cobb County, GA, **d.** Jul. 29, 1954

Guitar, Vocals / Old-Timey, Traditional Country

A blind country minstrel content to perform on radio broadcasts rather than record his material, Pete Cassell impressed many listeners with his near-perfect pitch and self-taught musicianship. Born in Georgia on August 27, 1917, Cassell was blinded in his infancy, and received his education at special schools in Georgia. He specialized in law, but turned to performing after teaching himself to play guitar and sing.

He first appeared on radio in the late '30s for WSB-Atlanta, and spent the rest of his life in roughly yearlong stints for stations in Georgia, West Virginia, Virginia, Pennsylvania, Missouri, and Wisconsin. Between the migrations, Cassell recorded sporadically for Decca, Mercury, and Majestic, from March 1941 to 1949. None of his sides became popular, though Cassell was a hit for nearly every station he performed with, including Wheeling, WV's talent-packed WWVA. He died of coronary thrombosis in 1954. In 1993, Old Homestead released a collection entitled *Pete Cassell, Blind Minstrel*. *—John Bush*

● **The Legend** / 1965 / Hilltop ✦✦✦✦

Joey Castle (Joseph Fohn Castaldo)

b. Jun. 24, 1942, New York, NY [The Bronx], **d.** Dec. 15, 1978

Vocals / Rock & Roll, Rockabilly

Joey Castle was like a lot of the kids who came up in the wake of Elvis Presley, trying to sound like him and not making it, but with a difference—Castle left behind a dozen or so records that are well worth hearing. Among the ranks of Elvis Presley sound-alikes, there are the imitators who came along in the wake of his death in 1977 and then there are those who came to the sound a little more honestly, back in the formative days of rock & roll. Joey Castle, aka Cliff Rivers, real name Joseph Fohn Castaldo, fits into the latter category—he was even signed to RCA. And he never had the chance to cash in on Elvis' death as a sound-alike artist, succumbing to brain cancer less than 18 months after the demise of his onetime idol.

Joseph Castaldo was born in the Bronx, NY, in 1942, and was 13 years old when rock & roll broke nationally—the family was a musical one, his uncle Lee Castle having become famous as a bandleader in the 1940s, but Joey took to the new music. By the end of 1957, at 15, he was ready to take the plunge, and a year later his demo tapes landed him a contract with RCA. His first and only RCA release, "Come a Little Bit Close Baby" b/w "That Ain't Nothing But Right," failed to chart, and he was dropped from the label at the end of the year. He next turned up on the Headline label with a rockabilly screamer, "Rock & Roll Daddy-O," backed with the brooding "Wild Love," both extraordinarily effective rockabilly tunes to come out of New York City—it didn't sell, but it did become a highly prized collector's item.

Castle kept performing locally but didn't record again until 1963, when he hooked up with entrepreneur Sid Prosen, who had previously recorded the teenaged Simon & Garfunkel as Tom & Jerry. Castle cut a series of sessions that yielded one single, "Marsha" b/w "True Lips," on Prosen's Thanks label, credited to "Cliff Rivers"—intentional or not, it was an Elvis homage, recalling the latter's performance as "Deke Rivers" in the best of his early movies, *Loving You*, as well as alluding to English rock & roller Cliff Richard. The A-side sounded like Elvis Presley crossed with Del Shannon, while the B-side recalled the Elvis of 1956 in a softer moment. Ironically, it was his best-selling record, although it never moved more than a few thousand copies, and most of those in England—too far away to do Joey Castle/Cliff Rivers any good.

Apart from a handful of unreleased tracks that year and the demos that got him signed to RCA in the first place, much of Castle's work consisted of cutting demos for publisher Hill & Range. He made his last single in the late '60s, still true to his rock & roll roots even amid the changing tastes of the era. During the 1970s, he re-emerged in a rock & roll/variety act featuring music and comedy, and put out an album of his own—Castle evidently had enough of a following locally to perform at least part-time and sell the album after his shows. He died of cancer in December of 1978. *—Bruce Eder*

Rock & Roll Daddy-O / 1991 / Bear Family ♦♦♦♦♦

Joey Castle's claim to fame, aside from some non-hit singles for RCA and various indies, is that he was a demo singer for the Hill & Range publishing company on songs earmarked for Elvis Presley. Two of those demos appear on this 16 song package, as well as his complete known recordings (Castle may have recorded additional material under pseudonyms). The early singles are mostly straight Elvis-style rockers and ballads, the highlights of which are the title track and the uptempo "True Lips." The gem of this collection, though, may be "(I'm the) Phantom Lover," a self-financed single Castle released in the late '60s as a last stab at commercial success; the song is a minor masterpiece that sounds like a product of the previous decade. Three of the tracks on this collection are alternate takes, and the sound quality on the demos is a bit rough. The notes attempt to piece together as much of the Joey Castle story as is known (which isn't much). *Rock & Roll Daddy-O* has its minor charms for fanatics, and this collection was made for them. *—Greg Adams*

Kasey Chambers

b. Jun. 4, 1976, Australia

Lyricist, Leader, Guitar / Country-Rock, Singer/Songwriter, Country-Folk

In 2000, Kasey Chambers emerged as Australia's first successful country-to-rock crossover female singer. It was just the latest chapter in a unique 25-year life journey. In 1976, hoping to earn a living hunting foxes, Bill and Diane Chambers took their two-year-old son Nash and newborn daughter Kasey into the 100,000 square mile (260,000 square km) sparsely vegetated and generally flat plateau called the Nullarbor Plain. The family would spend seven or eight months of the year on the Nullarbor, resupplying themselves from the world's longest stretch of straight railroad track, 330 miles (530 km), running through the Nullarbor. The rest of the year, the hot months, the family spent at a small South Australian fishing village. Each night out on the Nullarbor, after a day's hunting, the family would camp in a different spot on that vast Australian landmark and, grabbing his guitar, Bill Chambers and his wife Diane passed on their love of country music, by the glow of the campfire, under the stars. This is how Kasey Chambers spent the first nine years of her life.

In 1986, the family returned to "civilization" so that Bill and Diane could pick up interrupted music careers. First, Kasey joined them as lead singer, then brother Nash, and they became known as the Dead Ringer Band. By 1992, the family had become full-time musicians, playing to city audiences as well as heading back out into the countryside, pulling a small trailer behind their Toyota Land Cruiser.

During the '90s, the Dead Ringer Band members, known as performers of quality country music, released seven CDs and collectively earned two ARIA's (Australian Grammys) and seven Gold Guitars at the annual Australian Country Music awards in Tamworth. Kasey was the face of the new generation in Australian country. She appeared at Tamworth dressed as a spice girl, wearing a nose ring, and posed nude for a country music magazine (walking down the streets of a deserted country town with brother Nash). In 1998, Chamber's world was turned upside down with the separation of her parents, with mother Diane choosing to go and live in distant Norfolk Island, two-and-a-half hours by plane off the Australian coast. Chambers started putting her feelings into songs, and over a few weeks during July and August 1998, Kasey Chambers recorded her solo album *The Captain* on Norfolk Island. With brother Nash Chambers acting as producer, Kasey and her musicians set up in an old homestead on the island and practically recorded the album live. Father Bill was on hand to play guitar. Country legends Buddy and Julie Miller added voices and guitar to four tracks afterwards in Nashville.

Released in May 1999, the album *The Captain* initially won Kasey the 1999 ARIA award for Best Country album and at the 2000 awards named her Best Female Artist. With double-platinum sales at home in Australia, Kasey spent the latter part of 2000 following up enthusiastic reviews for her album internationally. She also spent time touring the U.S. with Lucinda Williams and playing gigs in her native land with Emmylou Harris. She was in the studio as well. With her brother Nash at the production board, Kasey Chambers delivered another sonic beauty with 2002's *Barricades & Brick Walls*. *—Ed Nimmervoll*

● **The Captain** / Jun. 5, 2000 / Virgin ♦♦♦♦

In "Southern Kind of Life," a song on her debut album, *The Captain*, Kasey Chambers convincingly describes a rural Southern upbringing—poverty stricken and Bible dominated—and since she performs in a style associated with the Appalachians as developed into commercial country music, it's easy to assume she's singing about the American South. But she isn't; she's singing about the Nullarbor Plain in South-Central Australia, where she grew up, apparently listening to a lot of country records. The result is a style that will remind some listeners of Dolly Parton and others of Lucinda Williams, as Chambers, backed by her father and produced by her brother, both of them members of the family's Dead Ringer Band, sings in a breathy voice that breaks expressively. Her tunes tend to be either "I am" songs of self-description like "Southern Kind of Life" and "Cry Like a Baby," accounts of romantic difficulties, or celebrations of life on the road. Though she has a gift for wordplay that favors internal rhyme, her imagery can be trite ("You got the car and I got the break"), and her compositions are less interesting in themselves than in the performances she gives them. Like many young artists, she is still a compendium of her influences rather than a distinct figure unto herself, but *The Captain* is a sincere effort steeped in the kind of country/folk/rock style that made Lucinda Williams a critical success in the late '90s, and it is likely to attract similar attention. *—William Ruhlmann*

Barricades & Brickwalls / Oct. 23, 2001 / EMI ♦♦♦

On *Barricades & Brickwalls*, Chambers exceeds the high standards that critics had already attached to her even at age 25. The instrumental tracks, raw and unpretentious, provide an ideal setting for her vocals, whose hint of world-weary reflection suggests significant growth even in the brief span of time since her American debut, *The Captain*. The material is presented concisely, never so much as a verse too long; from the title track, a menacing meditation on obsession, to gentler and more traditional reflections such as "On a Bad Day," Chambers delivers each lyric with disarming artlessness, after which the music simply stops or fades without flourish. Images of restless and rootless wandering crop up repeatedly, appropriate in different ways to a variety of settings: A "lonesome whistle cries" like a promise of danger in "Barricades & Brickwalls," while "the railway line" points toward a chaos of ecstasy on "Runaway Train" and "the whistle blows" rumors of faraway wonders through the desolation of her homeland on "Nullabor Song." Chambers is strongest when evoking these metaphors of distance, isolation, and redemption; on harder-edged material, such as the rock-oriented "Crossfire," she seems, by comparison, a step or two outside of her comfort zone. The replication of a Patsy Cline vibe on "A Little Bit Lonesome," complete with vintage production and bouncy fiddle fills, clarifies that Chambers draws from the most vital currents that feed the body of her chosen tradition. Guest appearances by Lucinda Williams, Buddy Miller, and Matthew Ryan further authenticate *Barricades & Brickwalls* as prime-cut Americana—an ironic appellation, perhaps, given Chambers' Australian roots, but appropriate nonetheless. *—Robert L. Doerschuk*

Beth Nielsen Chapman

b. Harlington, TX

Vocals / Singer/Songwriter, Country-Folk, Contemporary Country

A talented artist in her own right, scoring a number of adult contemporary radio hits, Beth Nielsen Chapman rose to prominence as a successful songwriter, penning a string of songs that would earn their performers hits on both pop and country radio. Born in Harlington, TX, Chapman spent her youth moving frequently due to her father's Air Force career. Teaching herself to play guitar on an instrument that was intended as a gift for her father, Chapman wrote her first song at age 11. While singing in clubs in Mobile, AL, she met Beach Boy Bruce Johnston, who encouraged her to move to Nashville to pursue her career. The move proved to be a wise decision as Chapman became an in-demand songwriter and session vocalist. Among the hits to her credit were number ones by Willie Nelson ("Nothing I Can Do About It Now") and Lorrie Morgan ("Five Minutes").

Her numerous writing credits also included tracks by Alabama, Kathy Mattea, Trisha Yearwood, and Pam Tillis. Chapman's own recording career began in earnest with the release of an eponymous album in 1990, although she had recorded an earlier effort, *Hearing It First*, a decade before. *Beth Nielsen Chapman* and 1993's *You Hold the Key* were warmly received by critics and she garnered radio play with songs like "All I Have" and "You Hold the Key." It was with the release of *Sand and Water* in 1997 that Chapman gained the most attention as an artist when Elton John, moved by the title song inspired by her husband's death from cancer, began performing the song in concert.

In 1998, Chapman saw Faith Hill's "This Kiss," which she had co-written, become one of her biggest successes yet, dominating the airwaves by reaching number one on the country charts and the Top Five on the pop charts. Her continued efforts in the latter half of the decade included contributions to films (*Prince of Egypt, Message in a Bottle*), session work, and the release of *Deeper Still* in 2002, which Chapman also produced. *—Tom Demalon*

Hearing It First / 1980 / Capitol ♦♦♦

● **Beth Nielsen Chapman** / Sep. 25, 1990 / Reprise ♦♦♦♦♦

Beth Nielsen Chapman had established herself as a Nashville-based songwriter and session vocalist by the time of her self-titled debut in 1990. Although much of her previous work was more country oriented, *Beth Nielsen Chapman* reveals more pop-minded sensibilities and she is backed by an array of top session players from Nashville and L.A. "Life Holds On" is a wide-eyed affirmation of life graced by Mark Casstevens mandolin playing. The scope of most of the album is more focused on relationships, and Chapman delivers songs like "All I Have," "Avalanche," and "Down on My Knees" with a beautiful, crystal-clear voice. Intelligent and mature, she is a gifted artist who comfortably fits alongside '70s singer/songwriters like Carole King and Carly Simon. *—Tom Demalon*

You Hold the Key / 1993 / Reprise ♦♦♦♦

The arrangements are peppier, but the subject matter is as intensely internal as on her previous album. *—Michael McCall*

Sand and Water / Jul. 15, 1997 / Reprise ♦♦♦♦

Although the arrangements on *Sand and Water* are slicker than anything on Beth Nielsen Chapman's previous albums, boasting everything from country to pop influences, her songwriting remains incisive, melodic and altogether striking, resulting in another stunningly accomplished record. *—Thom Owens*

Greatest Hits / Mar. 23, 1999 / Reprise ♦♦♦♦♦

While the variety of producers and production styles makes for a rather choppy flow, this disc offers excellent proof of Beth Nielsen Chapman's considerable talents as both a singer and songwriter. While she is often associated with country-pop, her stylistic approach is closer to adult-oriented rockers like Sheryl Crow or Joan Armatrading. Indeed, tunes like "Life Holds On" and "Beyond the Blue" are emotionally resonant without slipping into pure sentimentality or cliché. It's a strong collection from an honest artist. *—Tim Sheridan*

Deeper Still / Mar. 26, 2002 / Artemis ♦♦♦

Biblical imagery mixes with down-home poetics on *Deeper Still*. With a sound stripped of studio tinsel, Chapman delivers her material in earnest understatement over crisp, if antiseptic, accompaniment. When supporting her own vocals on piano during tracks like "Every December Sky," she achieves a special intimacy; the band's entry, though discrete, somewhat dilutes the effect. No such diminution mars her performance of the Celtic-flavored "Feathers Bones and Shells," largely a piano and vocal piece with touches of cello, or "Deeper Still," on which the absence of drums allows Chapman to ride a delicate rubato, with a subtle but electrifying acceleration when Vince Gill enters with harmony on the chorus. On uptempo numbers she allows herself less elasticity in both phrasing and writing; "Shake My Soul," with beat pumping and Bonnie Raitt joining in on backup vocals, locks the lyric into a choppy pattern that emphasizes rhythm more than shaded meaning ("Gonna shake my soul/And release my hold/Givin' up control/And let the rest unfold"). At its best moments, *Deeper Still* displays a strong confessional perspective, plenty of sensitive arrangement, and the occasional surprise; there are moments in "All Comes Down to Love" that even recall the Beatles, from the pinched production in one short segment to a "yeah, yeah, yeah" riff on the fade. On every cut she maintains the high level of craftsmanship that has long made her a hometown heroine in Nashville; her match of lyric to rhythm in "World of Hurt" has an especially Music Row resonance. Nothing, however, seriously challenges any commercial conventions. *Deeper Still* is in fact more broad than deep, polished and pleasing but a step shy of profound. *—Robert L. Doerschuk*

The Chapmans

Group / Contemporary Country, Contemporary Bluegrass

The Chapmans don't quite fit the profile of the usual family bluegrass band. Unlike the Renos, the McCourys, and others, there are no ancestors with years of musical experience lurking in the Chapmans' background, nor does the obvious talent stretch back generation after generation. They are the first of the family to carve out a career in music, but they aren't going at it alone. All the members of the Chapman family—father Bill; mother Patti; and sons Jason, Jeremy, and John—were big fans of Denver-based bluegrass bands Hot Rize and Front Range long before they formed friendships with bandmembers or went on to form their own bluegrass unit. Despite the family's lack of a professional background in music, they formed strong alliances through frequent attendance at bluegrass shows in the region. When they were ready to strike out and make their mark, musicians such as Front Range's Bob Amos stepped in to lend a hand. In fact, the Chapmans recorded their first release at Amos' home studio.

Encouraged by recording sessions that turned into an enjoyable learning experience, Bill Chapman installed a studio of his own at home, which enabled his three boys to gain valuable industry skills. During his early years, the Chapman patriarch played the piano and organ before taking up the banjo. John Chapman, who evolved into the band's centerpiece with his guitar and lead vocals, started early in life on the fiddle. Patti Chapman took up the bass when son Jeremy became interested in the mandolin. When his mom opted out of performing, son Jason stepped in on bass, even though he had only recently begun playing the instrument. John Chapman took home a junior division fiddling championship as a young teenager in his home state of Colorado. At the dawn of the 1990s, the family started playing local fairs and other smaller venues, and they went on to put out several recordings on their own.

The Chapmans settled in Missouri in 1998, the same year they took home the International Bluegrass Band Championship, a title conferred by the Society for the Preservation of Bluegrass Music in America (SPBGMA). The year continued to bring good fortune to the family, starting with the release of their debut, *Love's Gonna Live Here*, and the offer of a contract from Pinecastle Records. The following year, the record company released *Notes From Home*. The CD garnered glowing reviews, as well as a nomination for Album of the Year from the SPBGMA. In the same awards competition, the society also honored the Chapmans with a Vocal Group of the Year nomination, while John Chapman took home the title of Guitar Player of the Year in 2002. The bluegrass family band spent 2000 on the road at a variety of prestigious festivals. Among the stops were the Louisville, KY, stage of Fan Fest run by the International Bluegrass Music Association (IBMA), Indiana's Bean Blossom, and Kentucky's Poppy Mountain, as well as a number of performances at Tennessee's Dollywood. The following year, Pinecastle put out *Follow Me*, while the Chapmans played festivals throughout the south and enjoyed an IBMA nomination in the category of Emerging Artists of the Year. *—Linda Seida*

Notes From Home / Jan. 1, 1999 / Pinecastle ✦✦✦

● **Follow Me** / 2001 / Pinecastle ✦✦✦

One sign of maturity in a bluegrass band is the willingness to play at a moderate tempo. One sign of virtuosity in a bluegrass band is the ability to play at a moderate tempo with driving intensity. So when the Chapman's open their second album (and Pinecastle debut) with the muscular but restrained "Losing Again," it grabs your attention. That they follow it up with the overly sweet "My Heart's Bouquet" is a minor misstep, but things pick up again quickly: "Follow Me to Tennessee" strikes a perfect balance between sugar and vinegar, while the swinging "Candy Kisses" harks back more to Bob Wills than to Flatt & Scruggs and the juxtaposition of Bill Monroe's "I'm Going Back to Old Kentucky" with the Sam Cook hit "You Send Me" bespeaks both musical depth and a sense of humor. And the harmonies on the latter—which features only bass and voices—are nothing short of angelic. What looks on the cover like just one more traditional bluegrass album by one more family band turns out to involve layers of musicianship that you wouldn't necessarily anticipate. That's another sign of virtuosity. *—Rick Anderson*

Chesapeake

Group / Neo-Traditional Folk, Country-Pop, Singer/Songwriter, Country-Folk, Contemporary Folk, Neo-Traditionalist Country

Dobro whiz Mike Auldridge, bassist T. Michael Coleman, and lead vocalist and guitarist Lawrence "Moondi" Klein started Chesapeake to fill in their schedule between gigs with the Seldom Scene. But, when they were joined by mandolinist Jimmy Gaudreau, formerly of the Tony Rice Unit, the result was so successful that they agreed to make it a more permanent unit. The decision proved to be one of the best they'd ever made. Taking a more serious approach than they did with the Seldom Scene, they created one of the most innovative sounds in contemporary bluegrass. While the group's ties to the hill country tradition remains as solid as its past efforts, Chesapeake takes things a step further with well-conceived arrangements, pure-as-honey vocal harmonies, and masterful instrumentation.

Chesapeake represents a natural evolution for Auldridge. A founding member of the Seldom Scene, he had grown frustrated by the band's lackadaisical attitude toward rehearsing. Although banjo player Ben Eldridge, who worked as a mathematician during the week, and the late mandolinist/vocalist John Duffey, who worked as a guitar repairman, rarely played their instruments outside of performances, Auldridge lived and breathed music. Coleman, a former sideman for Doc and Merle Watson who joined the Seldom Scene in 1988, was the same way. The two musicians had previously recorded a trio album with former Seldom Scene lead singer Lou Reid.

Their disenchantment with the Seldom Scene's light touring schedule intensified when Reid left the band and the group's original lead singer, John Starling, who worked as a medical doctor, returned. Starling only remained for a little over a year. Although Moondi Klein, formerly of Rock Creek, replaced him, Auldridge and Coleman continued to seek other outlets. When Guadreau became equally frustrated with the schedule slowing down of the Tony Rice Unit, the final pieces of Chesapeake were assembled. After rehearsing for several months in Auldridge's basement, the group gave its first performance. While Auldridge, Coleman, and Klein worked with both the Seldom Scene and Chesapeake for a while, they gave their notice in 1995.

A wide range of material has been incorporated into Chesapeake's repertoire. While country songs by the Carter Family, Norman Blake, and Bill Emerson have been treated to modern interpretations, the band has been as effective with its renditions of tunes by folksinger/songwriters, including Tom Paxton and Steve Gillette, and rock performers such as Van Morrison and Little Feat. *—Craig Harris*

Rising Tide / 1994 / Sugar Hill ✦✦✦

● **Full Sail** / Feb. 1996 / Sugar Hill ✦✦✦✦

On their second record *Full Sail*, Chesapeake combine elements of folk, country and pop music. Their diverse influences are reflected in their choice of cover material, which includes Little Feat's "Let It Roll," Ricky Skaggs' "One Way Track," Tom Paxton's "The Last Thing on My Mind" and Steve Gillette's "Sweet Melinda." *—Jason Ankeny*

Pier Pressure / Oct. 21, 1997 / Sugar Hill ✦✦✦✦

If you want the key to Chesapeake, the outfit formed by three ex-Seldom Sceners and Tony Rice's mandolinist, you'll find it in T. Michael Coleman's "Rockin' Hillbilly," the tale of a man who just loves bluegrass, country, and R&B. And that neatly sums up this band; they don't put up any barriers between the styles (and why should they, since they complement each other?). So they're equally comfortable with the bluegrass/gospel standard "Working on a Building," their tribute to the late, great Bill Monroe, the country gospel of "White Pilgrim," and the fabulous country of "Bed of Roses," where guest Linda Ronstadt adds sublime harmonies behind the lead voice of Moondi Klein. With their pedigrees, it goes without saying that these are real pickers, but they give their fingers a workout on "Sleepwaking(ing) at the Drive-In," where Jimmy Gaudreau shines on mandolin. Truthfully, it's an album of highlights, and Coleman proves to be a far-above average songwriter on all his contributions. The covers are tasteful (an excellent version of Van Morrison's "Full Force Gale," for example), and there's a general sense of about pleasure about the disc. Call it newgrass, country, whatever you like, but make sure you call it superior. *—Chris Nickson*

Kenny Chesney

b. Mar. 26, 1968, Knoxville, TN

Guitar, Vocals / Contemporary Country, Neo-Traditionalist Country

Contemporary country star Kenny Chesney didn't have the immediate breakout success that many of his peers enjoyed upon signing with major labels, but gradually built up a significant following via hard work, pop-friendly ballads, and a likable, average-guy persona. Chesney was born in Knoxville, TN, in 1968 and raised in the nearby small town of Luttrell, better-known as the home of Chet Atkins. He grew up listening to both country and rock & roll, but didn't get serious about music until college, when he studied marketing at East Tennessee State University. He received a guitar as a Christmas present and set about practicing, and was soon performing with the college bluegrass band. He soon started writing songs as well and played for tips in local venues—most often a Mexican restaurant—every night he could; additionally, he managed to sell 1,000 copies of a self-released demo album.

After graduation in 1991, he moved to Nashville and became the resident performer at *the Turf*, a rougher honky tonk in the city's rundown historic district. While he gained experience, it wasn't the sort of place where he'd be discovered, and in 1992 he moved onto a publishing deal with Acuff-Rose. From there he landed a record contract with Capricorn, and released his debut album, *In My Wildest Dreams*, in late 1993. Unfortunately for Chesney, Capricorn wasn't much of a country label; not only was the album underpromoted, but the label's country division shut down completely not long after its release. Still, it sold 100,000 copies and caught the attention of several big-time major labels. Chesney ended up signing with RCA subsidiary BNA, where he released *All I Need to Know* in 1995. The album gave him his first two Top Ten hits in the title track and "Fall in Love." His follow-up, 1996's *Me & You*, became his first album to go gold, thanks to two number-two singles in the title track and "When I Close My Eyes."

I Will Stand (1997) was another gold-selling effort that gave Chesney his first-ever number one hit in "She's Got It All," plus another number two with "That's Why I'm Here." His big-time breakthrough, however, came with 1999's *Everywhere We Go*, which sold over two-million copies and spawned two number-one hits with "You Had Me From Hello" and "How Forever Feels"; it also featured another Top Ten single in "What I Need to Do," and another, "She Thinks My Tractor's Sexy," that just missed. In 2000, Chesney issued his first *Greatest Hits* compilation, and two newly recorded songs—"I Lost It" and "Don't Happen Twice"—went to number three and number one, respectively. *Greatest Hits* became Chesney's second straight double-platinum release, and topped the country LP charts. He followed it with the all-new *No Shirt, No Shoes, No Problems* in early 2002, which gave him his strongest commercial performance yet. It, too, hit number one on the country album charts, and spun off four Top Ten singles in "Young," the number one "The

Good Stuff," the Bill Anderson co-write "A Lot of Things Different," and "Big Star."
—*Steve Huey*

In My Wildest Dreams / 1994 / Capricorn ✦✦✦

All I Need to Know / Jun. 13, 1995 / BNA ✦✦✦✦

Kenny Chesney was working parking cars when he got his first songwriting contract. In less than two years he had another contract, this one as a singer. His debut album hit the shelves in 1993. After a couple more years he was signed under a new label and had completed a noteworthy sophomore offering. This is that album, *All I Need to Know*. The tunes on this recording earned the artist three hit singles. Chesney has been overlooked many times by some of the big players in the world of country music, but that doesn't lessen his ability to please country music fans. He is a gifted singer, performer, and songwriter. In fact, he helped write four of the songs on *All I Need to Know*. Other numbers were written by talents like Skip Ewing and Bob McDill. You'll find some touching ballads on this album, such as "Grandpa Told Me So," "Me and You," and "The Tin Man." There are also feel-good tunes to pick up the pace, including "The Bigger the Fool (The Harder the Fall)," "Someone Else's Hog," and "Paris, Tennessee." This is a great one to add to your country stockpile. —*Charlotte Dillon*

Me & You / 1996 / BNA ✦✦✦

Me & You finds Kenny Chesney breaking free from his standard ballad formula and loosening up, revealing that he is a richer, better musician than he had previously demonstrated. Not only does he try out some cracking country-rockers (which he pulls off with flair), but he contributes some remarkably accomplished narrative ballads. The range and depth of the material suggests that Kenny Chesney is only beginning to come into his own on *Me & You*. —*Thom Owens*

I Will Stand / Jul. 15, 1997 / BNA ✦✦✦✦✦

I Will Stand is Kenny Chesney's best, most assured record to date. Balancing his smooth contemporary country with rootsy, bluegrass-inflected numbers and muscular country-rockers, Chesney has created a record that is eclectic and accessible, filled with catchy, professional songs and tight performances. Chesney has never sung better and he's never had a collection of songs as consistent as those on *I Will Stand*, his best record to date. —*Thom Owens*

Everywhere We Go / Mar. 2, 1999 / BNA ✦✦

Kenny Chesney's voice has always been a remarkable instrument, capable of a wide range of emotional expression, despite Chesney's subtle approach and laid-back delivery. On *Everywhere We Go*, however, this unique talent seems wasted on too many cookie-cutter ballads and country-rock numbers that don't even pretend to rock. Chesney is at his best on songs like "What I Need to Do," a Don Henley-like midtempo pop song. The song's quietly desperate, regular-guy lyrics fit Chesney like a glove, and consequently make ridiculous country stud muffin filler like "She Thinks My Tractor's Sexy" sound completely out of place. In its finest moments, this album recalls the work of Don Williams. Unfortunately, these moments are rare; unlike Williams, Chesney seems afraid to explore the darker areas of his psyche and is content to wallow in Hallmark card emotional territory. The musicianship on *Everywhere We Go* is superb (typical for Nashville studio cats), yet the players here—like Chesney—have little meat in which to sink their teeth and, thus, sound a bit sleepy. —*Pemberton Roach*

● **Greatest Hits** / Sep. 26, 2000 / BNA ✦✦✦✦

The culmination of seven years' work, Kenny Chesney's *Greatest Hits* CD is a good overview of his career and also throws in four unreleased tracks and a live version of "Back Where I Come From." His unique blend of traditional country vocal stylings and contemporary, slick pop orchestration is showcased on songs like "She's Got It All" and "All I Need to Know." Among these songs of heartache and loss, there hides a little sunny gem of a song in "She Thinks My Tractor's Sexy," in which Chesney reveals that his girl is kinda crazy about his farmer's tan and how she brings him a "basket 'a chicken and a big cold jug 'a sweet tea." *Greatest Hits* stands as a good introduction to one of the most popular country artists of the '90s or a worthwhile addition to the die-hard fan's collection. —*Zac Johnson*

No Shoes, No Shirt, No Problems / Apr. 23, 2002 / BNA ✦✦✦✦

Kenny Chesney has a voice that'd be perfect for hard country, but he just doesn't have his heart in it. He likes the sweet melodies and smooth production that come with crossover country-pop, and while that may have been a frustration at one point, at least for those who consider pure country as the only guideline for quality in country, but by his sixth album, 2002's *No Shoes, No Shirt, No Problems*, he's landed upon an effortless blend of pop and twang, something that is undeniable in its crossover intentions but rather charming all the same. Perhaps Chesney relies a bit too much on ballads and midtempo numbers throughout this album, but even the sprightlier numbers here—the terrific opener "Young," "Big Star"—are not honky tonk ravers, but heartland-styled rockers that gently rock and keep the melody in the forefront. So, all of *No Shoes* flows smoothly, and little of it could be called pure country—the most down-home thing about the entire enterprise is the rounded twang in his voice—but as a mature, even-handed country-pop album, it doesn't get much better than this in 2002, since it's melodic, well-produced, strong on solid material and, most of all, very well-sung. It's one of the highlights in his catalog. —*Stephen Thomas Erlewine*

Mark Chesnutt

b. Sep. 6, 1963, Beaumont, TX

Vocals / Contemporary Country, New Traditionalist

Neo-honky tonker Mark Chesnutt parlayed a solid grounding in classic country into chart-topping stardom during the '90s. Born in Beaumont, TX, in 1963, Chesnutt grew up listening to his father's extensive country-record collection (Bob Chesnutt had been a locally popular singer who never hit it big, and thus worked as a used-car salesman). Chesnutt

learned both guitar and drums, and made his professional singing debut with his father's band at age 15 on the local club scene. He even dropped out of high-school for a time to pursue music, but later reconsidered and got his diploma; meanwhile, his father began taking him to Nashville for recording sessions. During the '80s, Chesnutt released singles on local labels like the San Antonio-based Axbar (where he also issued a full album, *Doing My Country Thing*) and the Houston-based Cherry. He also served as the house headliner at the Beaumont club *Cutter's*, where his band often featured future star Tracy Byrd.

After around a decade of dues-paying, positive word-of-mouth finally helped Chesnutt land a record deal with MCA. Chesnutt's debut album, *Too Cold at Home*, was released in 1990, and the title track became his first hit, climbing into the country Top Five. With a style that blended George Jones, Merle Haggard, and Bob Wills, Chesnutt went on to score four more Top Ten hits from the album: the number one "Brother Jukebox," "Blame It on Texas," "Your Love Is a Miracle," and "Broken Promise Land." By the time that string ran out, Chesnutt had finished his follow-up, 1992's *Longnecks & Short Stories*. It gave him four more Top Five singles in "Bubba Shot the Jukebox" (one of Chesnutt's signature songs), "Old Flames Have New Names," the chart-topping "I'll Think of Something," and "Ol' Country." Chesnutt kept his hit-machine status going on 1993's *Almost Goodbye*, which gave him three more chart-toppers in the title track, "It Sure Is Monday," and "I Just Wanted You to Know." *What a Way to Live* (1994) offered the number one "Gonna Get a Life" and the number two "Goin' Through the Big D."

For 1995's *Wings*, MCA briefly resurrected its Decca country imprint and made Chesnutt the flagship artist; while the album wasn't the hit factory of its predecessors, many critics dubbed it one of Chesnutt's most eclectic and consistent sets. Seeking to restore his commercial momentum, MCA issued *Greatest Hits* in 1996, and the new song "It's a Little Too Late" went all the way to number one. *Thank God for Believers* (1997) found Chesnutt back on MCA Nashville, and produced a number-two hit in the title cut. For 1999's *I Don't Want to Miss a Thing*, Chesnutt flirted with crossover material, namely the titular Diane Warren ballad that became a big hit for Aerosmith. Praised by many critics for its relative subtlety, Chesnutt's version topped the country charts for a month, and even reached the pop Top 20. Despite that success, the album's other singles didn't perform as well, and his 2000 follow-up album *Lost in the Feeling* was something of a flop in comparison to his past work. Chesnutt and MCA subsequently parted ways, and he signed with Columbia for 2002's *Mark Chesnutt*, which sold decently but didn't quite mark a return to past glories. —*Steve Huey*

Too Cold at Home / 1990 / MCA ✦✦✦✦✦

An impressive traditional country debut that often drew on George Jones and Texas swing, *Too Cold at Home* started Chesnutt off strong with the hits "Too Cold at Home," "Brother Jukebox," "Blame It on Texas," and "Your Love Is a Miracle." It also included a version of "Friends in Low Places" that came out at almost exactly the same time Garth Brooks' did. —*Brian Mansfield*

Longnecks & Short Stories / 1992 / MCA ✦✦✦✦

Longnecks heralded the emergence of a Texas voice that contained both the knack for humor ("Old Flames Have New Names," "Bubba Shot the Jukebox"), and the depth for heartache ("I'll Think of Something"). —*Brian Mansfield*

Almost Goodbye / Jun. 22, 1993 / MCA ✦✦✦

Weak material weighs down Chesnutt's third release, though he still sings them like the most romantic western swinger since George Strait. "Almost Goodbye" is backed by a string arrangement as powerful as the one on "I'll Think of Something," but songs like "Texas Is Bigger" and "My Heart's Too Broke" aren't the attention-grabbers "Old Flames Have New Names" and "Bubba Shot the Jukebox" were. One of Chesnutt's biggest strengths is his casual delivery, but *Almost Goodbye* sounds too easy. "Almost Goodbye" and "It Sure Is Monday" both topped the singles charts. —*Brian Mansfield*

What a Way to Live / 1994 / MCA ✦✦✦

Like its predecessor *Almost Goodbye*, *What A Way To Live* is dogged by inconsistent material, but Chesnutt's fine singing manages to save most of the weaker material from being a bore. —*Stephen Thomas Erlewine*

Wings / Oct. 3, 1995 / MCA ✦✦✦✦✦

Mark Chesnutt's *Wings* is one of his most impressive efforts, showing the singer expanding his sonic template by stepping away from the commercial leanings of his recent material, yet leaving a slight pop and rock influence to his straightforward traditional country. What really makes the album rank among his best is the consistent quality of songwriting. Featuring songwriters like Jim Lauderdale and Todd Snider, *Wings* is filled with first-rate material that pushes at the borders of contemporary country while preserving its heritage. Ranging from romantic ballads to Bakersfield-type raveups, the record showcases Chesnutt at his finest. —*Stephen Thomas Erlewine*

● **Greatest Hits** / Nov. 19, 1996 / MCA ✦✦✦✦

Mark Chesnutt's *Greatest Hits* does a fair job of summing up the neo-traditionalist's biggest hits, adding two new songs—"It's A Little Too Late" and "Let It Rain"—to the collection. Though his biggest hits are showcased on the album, many of his proper albums offer a better representation of his talent. —*Thom Owens*

Thank God for Believers / Sep. 23, 1997 / MCA ✦✦✦✦

Thank God for Believers continues Mark Chesnutt's streak of winning albums, confirming his status as one of the finest neo-honky tonkers of '90s contemporary country. What sets Chesnutt apart is his passion—he genuinely believes in this music, and he delivers it with conviction. That passion makes the occasional weak song forgivable, but fortunately, there aren't many weak moments on *Thank God for Believers*—it's just strong, thoroughly enjoyable modern country. —*Thom Owens*

I Don't Want to Miss a Thing / Feb. 9, 1999 / MCA ✦✦✦✦

What do we make of Mark Chesnutt's foray into crossover territory? The bulk of *I Don't Want to Miss a Thing* is smooth new country, retaining the elements of neo-traditionalism that characterize the best of Chesnutt's earlier albums. There's a nice mix of material, ranging from the tender "Tonight I'll Let My Memories Take Me Home" to the honky tonk of "That's the Way You Make an Ex," which seems to be an homage to George Strait's "All My Ex's Live in Texas." There's also the witty "My Way Back Home," the tale of a man who returns back to "home sweet mobile home" to find that his woman has left him, literally, homeless, and the vaguely Cajun "Jolie." If *I Don't Want to Miss a Thing* ended there, this would be another good, but not necessarily great, Mark Chesnutt album. But overshadowing the other nine songs on the album is the title track. "I Don't Want to Miss a Thing" was penned by Diane Warren, best known for writing hit adult contemporary ballads for the likes of Cher and Celine Dion. The song's first appearance was on the *Armageddon* movie soundtrack, where it became a major hit for Aerosmith in 1998. While Aerosmith's rendition was over the top, Chesnutt tames the beast, even as the arrangement builds to a dangerously bombastic climax toward the end. On "I Don't Want to Miss a Thing," Chesnutt proves he can sing power ballads with the best of them. But that one of the best honky tonk singers of his generation starts tackling this sort of material says a lot about the state of traditional country in Nashville, none of it good. —*Martin Monkman*

Top Marks: His First 20 Hits / May 16, 2000 / Edsel ✦✦✦✦
Despite his rather lengthy major label recording career, Mark Chesnutt has never quite become a country superstar. His 20-track greatest-hits collection *Top Marks* acts more like a reminder of what his hits were rather than a compilation of his best work. These tracks show him at his best with traditional country tunes like "Too Cold at Home" and "Old Flames Have New Names" and at his blandest with suburban country-pop songs like "She Dreams." It is evident when listening to these songs (which are in chronological order) that Chesnutt never quite found his sound. He appears to be struggling for an identity between the music of artists like George Strait and Tim McGraw. Still with 20 songs this compilation is ideal for casual fans of his music. Those who already have his albums might want to skip this one because it contains no new material. —*Curtis Zimmermann*

Lost in the Feeling / Oct. 17, 2000 / MCA ✦✦✦
Album number ten is a good, solid effort from Mark Chesnutt. From songs one to ten, *Lost in the Feeling* is symbolic of the old days, pure tradition and lots of honky tonk. Chesnutt, sounding very Haggard-esque says he picks songs simply because he likes them and they'll work well in his live show. From the toe-tapping "Angelina" to the provocative "Love in the Hot Afternoon," it's clear what works well for him. He takes a stab at the old Conway Twitty hit, the album's title track, "Lost in the Feeling"and sings it with the finesse of an artist who has been doing this for a longtime. Worth mentioning also are two of the album's ballads, "Try Being Me" and "Somewhere out There Tonight." *Lost in the Feeling* works as a must-have for Chesnutt fans. —*Maria Konicki Dinoia*

20th Century Masters—The Millennium Collection: The Best of Mark Chesnutt / Nov. 20, 2001 / MCA ✦✦✦
Although both compilations contain 12 tracks, the mid-priced *20th Century Masters—The Millennium Collection: The Best of Mark Chesnutt* is actually a bit longer than the full-priced *Greatest Hits* from 1996 and more current, containing Chesnutt's 1997 hit "Thank God for Believers" and his 1999 hit "I Don't Want to Miss a Thing." But neither collection is complete. Chesnutt scored 21 Top Ten country hits during the 1990s, and each album inevitably misses some of them. The major omissions from this one are "Blame It on Texas," "Old Flames Have New Names," "Old Country," "Almost Goodbye," and "Goin' Through the Big D," each of which hit the Top Five, with "Almost Goodbye" going all the way to number one. Four of these five are on *Greatest Hits*, which otherwise has an overlap of seven tracks with *The Best of.* That means a Chesnutt fan is likely to be somewhat dissatisfied with either one and may be forced to buy both to have a reasonable collection of hits. (And even then, there are some missing from both collections.) At least this one costs a few bucks less. —*William Ruhlmann*

Mark Chesnutt / May 21, 2002 / Columbia ✦✦✦
Mark Chesnutt was one of country music's top stars in 1991-1994, a period when he scored five number-one hits. In the subsequent five years, he cooled slightly, but still scattered eight Top Ten hits, the last of them being a chart-topping country version of the Diane Warren-penned Aerosmith hit, "I Don't Want to Miss a Thing," in 1999. He has struggled since then, and the failure of his 2000 album *Lost in the Feeling* led to the severing of a decade-long relationship with MCA Records. As the eponymous title of his Columbia Records debut indicates, he is attempting to start afresh, but he is doing so without changing much other than his label affiliation. He has picked 11 entries from the Nashville songwriting combine, hired the usual Nashville sidemen, and made an average country album. The release was preceded by several months by a single, "She Was," a sentimental ballad about a saintly mother, that hadn't made a lot of headway on the charts by the time the album was released. Its one-dimensional idea is fairly typical of mediocre country songwriting, and there's more of the same on the full-length disc, including "I'm in Love With a Married Woman" (the twist, of course, being that the married woman is the singer's own wife). Chesnutt turns comic on the album-opening litany of screwups, "Don't Know Why I Do It," and "My Dreams." But just as the sentimental songs aren't really that moving, the humorous ones aren't that funny. There are potential singles that turn up late on the disc, particularly the country-pop "I Want My Baby Back" and the romantic "I Drew Me." But *Mark Chesnutt* is a just-OK collection appearing at a time when the singer really needs to shake things up to get his career back on track. —*William Ruhlmann*

Charlie Chesterman
Guitar, Vocals / Roots Rock, Alternative Country, Americana
Charlie Chesterman was a Boston-area bandleader who first found fame with the slap-dash punk outfit Scruffy the Cat. The band gigged throughout Boston and made some headway nationally but was finished by 1990 or so. Chesterman's next project was the Harmony Rockets, which released exactly one EP. In 1994, he embarked on a decidedly

twangier solo career with *From the Book of Flames*, which appeared on the Slow River imprint. The similar sounds of *Studabakersfield* followed two years later; in 1997, Ryko released *Hit This & Kick That*, a Europe-only LP compiling tracks from his two solo albums. The self-released *Ham Radio* followed in 2000. —*Johnny Loftus*

● **From the Book of Flames** / 1994 / Slow River ✦✦✦✦
Studabakersfield / Jan. 30, 1996 / Slow River ✦✦✦
Hit This & Kick That / 1997 / Rykodisc ✦✦✦
Dynamite Music Machine / Sep. 9, 1997 / Slow River ✦✦✦

The Chicken Chokers
f. Boston, MA
Group / Neo-Traditional Folk, Progressive Bluegrass, Old-Timey, Alternative Country
The Chicken Chokers were an old-timey string band from the Boston area who intersected their roots influences with reggae, punk, and rap. Fiddler Chad Crumm and multi-instrumentalists Paul Strother, Taylor Smith, and Jim Reidy released two albums on Rounder, 1987's *Shoot Your Radio* and *Old Time Music* in 1990. But when Crumm departed for New York City, the group fizzled. The remaining Chokers went on to form Primitive Characters, a more tradition-oriented fiddle band. Together with fiddler Sandy Stark, the band issued *The Leavin's* in 1997. However, PC fizzled too, since the rigid song structure didn't allow for the kind of creativity Strother, Smith, and Reidy craved. This led to the formation of Twang with bassist Robbie Phillips. Twang's debut, *Second Slam*, appeared in 2000. —*Johnny Loftus*

● **Shoot Your Radio** / 1987 / Rounder ✦✦✦✦
Old-time instrumentation, a pseudo-punk bad attitude, and a hilarious title-track rap from this short-lived but fun band from Boston. —*Mark A. Humphrey*

Old Time Music / Oct. 17, 1990 / Rounder ✦✦✦
On this album, two avant-garde/old-time bands, The Chicken Chokers and the Horseflies, pushed the envelope of the new/old-time styles. —*Mark A. Humphrey*

Lew Childre
b. Nov. 1, 1901, Opp, AL, **d.** Dec. 3, 1961
Producer, Guitar, Guitar (Steel), Vocals / Old-Timey, Traditional Country
One of the holdovers from the early days of vaudeville shows and one-man bands, Lew Childre managed a successful career during the 1930s and '40s playing radio broadcasts and doing his own advertising transcriptions. Born in Opp, AL, in 1901, he played trombone, trumpet, and drums in high-school before being persuaded to attend the University of Alabama by his parents. Childre finished school, but in 1923 joined a tent show as a singer/performer.
He then formed a jazz band called the Alabama Cotton Pickers—which also included Lawrence Welk—and recorded several sides before becoming fascinated with country music, then in its commercial infancy. Childre learned to play guitar and then returned to the tent shows until joining broadcast radio in Texas in 1930. After recording several sides for Gannett Records during September 1930, he toured the state with Wiley Walker (later of Wiley & Gene fame) as the Alabama Boys. Lew Childre moved to New Orleans in 1934, broadcasting over WWL and recording for ARC. He spent the late '30s working the Texas border station XERA with the Carter Family, but moved to West Virginia's *Wheeling Jamboree* by the early '40s. Childre's talent for ad-libbing comedy and songs made him a natural for advertising, and after he joined the *Grand Ole Opry* in 1945, he began producing transcriptions for General Foods and Pepsi, among other companies. He recorded an LP for Starday in the mid-'50s, but retired from music in 1959 and died two years later. —*John Bush*

● **Old Time Get Together** / 1961 / Starday ✦✦✦✦

Chilli Willi & the Red Hot Peppers
f. 1971, **db.** Feb. 1975
Group / Pub Rock, Country-Rock, Rock & Roll
Chilli Willi & the Red Hot Peppers were one of the main British pub rock groups of the early '70s, playing a laid-back yet rocking mixture of rock & roll, R&B, country, and folk. The band has its origins in a folk-rock duo formed by ex-Junior's Blues Band members Martin Stone (vocals, guitar, mandolin) and Phil "Snakefinger" Lithman (vocals, guitar, piano, lap steel, fiddle). Lithman moved to San Francisco in the late '60s, leaving Stone to play with Savoy Brown and Mighty Baby. The duo reunited in the early '70s, recording *Kings of Robot Rhythm* with vocalist Jo-Ann Kelly and various members of Brinsley Schwarz.
Kings was released in 1972; that same year, the duo expanded to a band, adding Paul "Dice Man" Bailey (guitar, banjo, saxophone), Paul Riley (bass), and drummer Pete Thomas. During the next two years, Chilli Willi & the Red Hot Peppers became a popular live act in Britain. The full band released *Bongos Over Balham* in 1974, yet the record sold poorly and the band split in February 1975. Thomas became the drummer for Elvis Costello's backing band, the Attractions, Riley played with Graham Parker, Bailey formed Bontemps Roulez, and Stone played with the Pink Fairies before quitting the music business. Lithman moved back to San Francisco where he began to work with his former associates, the Residents, under the name Snakefinger. —*Stephen Thomas Erlewine*

Kings of the Robot Rhythm / 1972 / Revelations ✦✦✦
● **Bongos over Balham** / 1974 / Mooncrest ✦✦✦✦✦
I'll Be Home / Oct. 12, 1999 / Proper ✦✦✦✦

Harry Choates
b. Dec. 26, 1922, Rayne, LA, **d.** Jul. 17, 1951, Austin, TX
Fiddle / Western Swing, Traditional Cajun
Harry Choates was not only one of the most influential musicians in the history of Cajun music, but one of its most tragic figures. A wild and imaginative fiddler, Choates wrote such classic tunes as the Cajun national anthem, "Jole Blon," and popularized such songs as "Allons à Lafayette." Recording for Gold Star, DeLuxe, D.O.T., Allied, Cajun Classics,

Macy's, and Humming Bird, Choates introduced Western swing, blues, jazz, and country music to the two-steps and waltzes of southwest Louisiana's bayous, influencing nearly every Cajun musician who followed in his footsteps.

Like Hank Williams, Choates balanced his musical talents with painful struggle in his real life. An acute alcoholic, he sold the rights to "Jole Blon" for $100 and a bottle of whiskey. His habit of missing concerts led him to be blacklisted by the musicians union in San Antonio and resulted in his band breaking up. His death was equally tragic. Failing to make support payments of $20 a week for his son and daughter following his divorce, he was jailed by a judge who found him in contempt of court. After three days of being forced to curtail his drinking habit, he began beating his head against the cell bars and fell into a coma. He died a few days later on July 17, 1951.

Born in Rayne, LA, Choates moved to Port Arthur, TX, with his mother in the 1930s. Rather than going to school, Choates spent much of his childhood in bars and taverns, listening to honky tonk and blues records on the jukebox. By the age of 12, Choates was playing fiddle in barbershops for tips. Launching his professional music career in Cajun bands led by Leo Soileau and Leroy "Happy Fats" LeBlanc, Choates formed his own group, the Melody Boys, in 1946. The same year, he rewrote the classic Cajun tune, "Jolie Blonde," for his daughter, Linda, and recorded it for the Gold Star label. Although the tune became a country hit when covered by Aubrey "Moon" Mullican, Choates had given up all rights to the song and received no further compensation for his composition. Choates & the Melody Boys continued to record at a prolific rate, releasing more than two dozen songs for Gold Star in 1946 and 1947. Adapting the Western swing of Bob Wills & His Texas Playboys to Cajun music, Choates became known as "the fiddle king of Cajun swing."

Although he performed with Jesse James & His Gang on radio station KTBC after the disbanding of the Melody Boys in 1951, Choates suffering ended a few months later. His grave was left unmarked until 1980, when money was raised for a gravestone with the bilingual inscription, "Purrain de la Musique Cajun—The Godfather of Cajun Music." In the mid-'60s, Cajun musician Rufus Thibodeaux was one of the first to pay homage to Choates' influence when he recorded an album of Choates' songs, *A Tribute to Harry Choates.* —*Craig Harris*

Jole Blon / 1979 / D ♦♦♦♦♦
The title cut has become the "Cajun national anthem," plus many other great fiddle-led Cajun tunes. —*Jeff Hannusch*

★ **Fiddle King of Cajun Swing** / 1982 / Arhoolie ♦♦♦♦♦
Fiddle King of Cajun Swing is a 26-track collection featuring most of Harry Choates' finest recordings. All of the material on this compilation was recorded for Gold Star Records between 1946 and 1950. Though his biggest hit, "Jole Blon," is inexplicably missing, the music on this disc demonstrates Choates talent for blurring the lines between Western swing and Cajun music. It's an excellent introduction to one of the finest Cajun fiddlers of the '40s and '50s. —*Thom Owens*

Five-Time Loser 1940-1951 / 1990 / Krazy Kat ♦♦♦
A follow-up to "Jole Blon" and thirteen other performances, it includes the Hank Williams-inspired "Cat 'n Around." It has a rough sound but great music, blending Cajun, swing, and honky tonk. —*Mark A. Humphrey*

Cajun Fiddle King / Oct. 26, 1999 / Aim ♦♦♦♦

Devil in the Bayou—The Gold Star Recordings / Nov. 12, 2002 / Bear Family ♦♦♦♦♦

Original Cajun Fiddle of Harry Chotes / D ♦♦♦

His Original 1946–1949 Recordings / Arhoolie ♦♦♦♦
Here are 16 performances by the man dubbed "The Godfather of Cajun Music," including his swingin' takes on such standards as "Allons à Lafayette" and "Grand Mamou." —*Mark A. Humphrey*

Chuck Wagon Gang

f. 1936
Group / Traditional Country, Southern Gospel, Country Gospel
Although the Chuck Wagon Gang has been around since 1936—undergoing many personnel changes over the years—its sound and devotion to old-fashioned gospel has remained much the same. Their greatest significance is that the band provides an important link between country music and traditional sacred songs of the South.

The original incarnation of the Chuck Wagon Gang was made up of four members of the Carter family—no relation to *the* Carter Family. They were Dad Carter (David Parker Carter), his son Jim (born Ernest), daughter Rose (born Rosa Lola), and his daughter Effie. Dad Carter was born in Kentucky, but was raised in Clay County, TX. He was enrolled in a singing school there when he met Carrie Brooks, whom he married in 1909. They had eight children, and to support them, Carter worked for the Rock Island Railroad in 1927. At other times, he and the family also picked cotton. The band formed around 1935 after one of the children became deathly ill and the family was left destitute; for additional income, Dad Carter talked the management at station KFYO Lubbock into hiring him as a host for a daily radio program. The original group was called the Carter Quartet, in which Dad sang tenor, Jim sang bass and played guitar, while Rose and Effie sang soprano and alto. They became popular and soon began earning $15 per week. The following year, the Carters moved to WBAP and billed themselves as the Chuck Wagon Gang; they sang a variety of secular and sometimes sacred songs. Their earliest recording session for ARC produced country singles, rather than gospel. As the years passed, they gradually became more gospel-oriented, and by the early '40s had switched over completely. In 1942, they spent a few months at a Tulsa radio station.

The Chucks broke up for the duration of World War II. Afterward, they reunited and returned to WBAP, remaining primarily a radio band. They began recording again in 1948 for Columbia. Two years later, Wally Fowler had them perform at one of his All-Night Singing Conventions in Augusta, Georgia; they then became a full-time touring band. In 1953, they underwent the first of many subsequent membership changes when Jim left and was replaced by Howard Gordon; he remained with the Chucks until his death in 1967. Another brother, Roy, also joined and sang bass in Jim's stead. Dad Carter

retired in 1955 and was at first replaced by Eddie Carter. In the late '50s, non-family members such as Alynn Billodeau, Patrick McKeehan, Ronnie Page, and Ronnie Crittenden spent time with the Chuck Wagon Gang. Through it all, the band kept touring part-time and making records—408 masters by 1975. After three years of inactivity, the group began recording for the Copperfield label.

The Chuck Wagon Gang continued on in a similar vein until 1987, when they once again became a full-time band with new members joining the last of the Carters, Roy and his sister Ruth Ellen Yates. In 1984, Dad Carter (who had died in 1963) was posthumously inducted into the Gospel Music Hall of Fame. By the late '80s, the Chuck Wagon Gang had been named Gospel Artist or Group of the Year by *Music City News* five years in a row. In 1990, Bob Terrell published an authorized history of the group, *The Chuck Wagon Gang: A Legend Lives On.* —*Sandra Brennan*

Family Tradition / 1973 / MCA ♦♦♦
It contains "Standing on the Promises" and other performances that show that throughout the many lineup changes this group has experienced, their sound remains a constant. —*AMG*

Looking Away to Heaven / 1976 / Columbia ♦♦♦
This is one of the best of the more recent Columbia sets. —*Charles S. Wolfe*

American Tradition / 1986 / MCA ♦♦
The Chuck Wagon Gang has existed in one incarnation or another for the better part of a century, selling millions of records along the way. Their later efforts, as represented on this 18-track CD from 1989, are far removed from their country gospel roots and adhere to the kind of white gospel style that is frequently heard on television evangelists' programs. The sterile arrangements and characterless performances are technically accomplished but nearly devoid of uniqueness or novelty. Perhaps with these recordings the focus should be on the songs rather than the presentation, in which case the effort is a rousing success and probably thoroughly palatable to its devout audience, few of whom are likely to review music criticism. More critical-minded music lovers, on the other hand, will find the latter-day Chuck Wagon Gang to be bland in the extreme. —*Greg Adams*

★ **Columbia Historic Edition** / 1990 / Columbia ♦♦♦♦♦
Columbia Historic Edition compiles highlights from the Chuck Wagon Gang's Columbia recordings between 1936 and 1960. Many of their greatest songs—including "After the Sunrise," "He Set Me Free," "We Are Climbing," and "I Want to See My Jesus"—are featured on this 16-track collection, making it a terrific introduction to this influential country gospel group. —*Thom Owens*

Chuck Wagon Gang's Greatest Hits, Vol. 1 / 1990 / MCA ♦♦♦
Featuring sixteen tracks, *Greatest Hits* is a solid compilation of some of the Chuck Wagon Gang's best tracks and offers a good introduction to this contemporary country-gospel vocal group. —*Stephen Thomas Erlewine*

Old Time Hymns, Vol. 2 / 1991 / MCA ♦♦♦
The Chuck Wagon Gang's heartfelt renditions of some well-known traditional hymns are somewhat hampered by the sterile production, but their strong performances carry the disc. —*Stephen Thomas Erlewine*

In Harmony / Jun. 7, 1994 / Copperfield ♦♦♦

Headed for the Promised Land / Dec. 1, 1995 / Sony Special Products ♦♦

The Church Brothers

f. Wilkes County, NC
Group / Traditional Bluegrass
Bluegrass group the Church Brothers, often billed as the Church Brothers & Their Blue Ridge Ramblers, featured brothers Bill (guitar), Edwin (fiddle), and Ralph (mandolin). The Wilkes County, NC-born siblings began performing together as the Wilkes County Entertainers, after Bill (already an established performer from his time with Roy Hall & His Blue Ridge Entertainers) returned from his duty during World War II. This group also included cousin Ward Eller and neighbor Drake Walsh. After some lineup changes, the group changed names to become the Church Brothers & Their Blue Ridge Ramblers. They made their first recording in 1950 and cut several more songs that remained unissued until Blue Ridge Records' Noah Adams came along; Adams bought the unreleased material and also funded new studio sessions, which featured help from songwriter Drusilla Adams. However, by the middle of the decade, the group was no more. GHP and Rounder have since made efforts to keep the group's recorded legacy in circulation. —*Andy Kellman*

The Church Brothers, Traditional Bluegrass / 1969 / GHP ♦♦♦

The Church Brothers / 1978 / Rounder ♦♦♦

● **Early Days of Bluegrass, Vol. 8** / 1981 / Rounder ♦♦♦♦

Claudia Church

b. Lenoir, NC
Vocals / Country-Pop, Contemporary Country
Claudia Church's story is a clichéd country music fairy tale. She grew up in fairly humble surroundings in North Carolina, with dreams of becoming a country music star. Her good looks landed her work as a model (including a stint in Paris) and she performed on local radio programs, including the legendary *Louisiana Hayride.* In 1988, she moved to Nashville to realize her dreams of becoming a star. Once there, Church found work, and gained valuable singing experience recording songwriter's demos.

She also garnered roles in various music videos, including those by Ricky Van Shelton, Steve Wariner, and most significantly, Rodney Crowell. Church met Crowell on the set of his "Lovin' All Night" video in 1992, and the pair married in 1998. Crowell went on to produce Church's debut album, *Claudia Church,* released by Reprise in 1999. The album features her debut single, "What's the Matter With You Baby." Stylistically, Church is squarely in the country-pop vein that has followed in the wake of Reba McEntire's success. —*Martin Monkman*

Claudia Church / Mar. 9, 1999 / Warner Bros. ✦✦
Claudia Church's self-titled debut is an example of run-of-the-mill Nashville musical product of the late '90s. That the album is so bland is something of a shock, given that producer (and Church's husband) Rodney Crowell distinguished himself with over 20 years of work on a series of first-rate albums. Here, though, Crowell's production never rises above the ordinary, in spite of the presence of some of Nashville's best session players. In some spots, Crowell embraces some of the worst aspects of the country-pop sound that he was previously immune from. The songs on the album never rise above the commonplace. "The Man I Love," penned by Crowell, contains his trademark musical elements but lacks the lyrical punch of his finest compositions. "Lost in a Feeling" is pure country-pop: middle-of-the-road pop with syrupy strings, with some "small-town-girl" references, a bit of vocal twang, and occasional steel guitar to make it seem "country." And no new country album would be complete without a cover of a '60s or '70s pop classic; here, it's the Gerry Goffin/Carole King song "Will You Still Love Me Tomorrow," made country by simply adding some steel guitar flourishes. Most importantly, Church never distinguishes herself as a vocalist, lacking the interpretive power of country-pop stars such as Reba McEntire and Pam Tillis, or the character of a neo-traditionalist like Carlene Carter. *—Martin Monkman*

Cigar Store Indians

f. 1993, Atlanta, GA
Group / Alternative Country-Rock, Rockabilly Revival
The Atlanta-based rockabilly combo Cigar Store Indians formed in 1993 after the breakup of frontman Ben Friedman's previous band, the alternative rockers IBM. After enlisting Jim "Low Note" Lavender on guitar, Keith Perissi on bass, and Francis "Fast Pedal" Ferran on drums, the band grew quickly from an underground sensation to one of the Atlanta club scene's most popular acts. After releasing a cassette on a local label in 1994, the Cigar Store Indians made their formal bow with a 1995 self-titled LP. *—Jason Ankeny*

• **Cigar Store Indians** / Feb. 1996 / Landslide ✦✦✦✦

El Baile de la Cobra / Jul. 7, 1998 / Deep South ✦✦✦

Guest List / May 2002 / Overall ✦✦✦
After a handful of releases that toed the line of straightforward rockabilly, eschewing the foreboding punker stuff for something more genteel and congenial (you could say they got Stray Cat style), *Guest List* sees Cigar Store Indians branching out to hit upon all manner of nostalgic niceties on live material culled from two Georgia tour stops. The result is an homage to the era of poodle skirts and liking Ike, from the country-fried "Eagles Need a Push" to the Alan Freed-approved "Arms Around Me" to "Get on the Throttle," a track as thoroughly good as Thorogood's similar overtures. That said, there's still plenty of classic rockabilly to go around; disc finale "Ring of Fire" (featuring a Ramones snippet) shows that the y'alternative crowd can still champion the band as one of its own. *—Brian O'Neill*

The Clark Family Experience

f. 1993, Rocky Mount, Virginia
Group / Neo-Traditionalist Country, Country-Pop, Contemporary Country
The brotherhood behind the Clark Family Experience shook up country music during 2001 with the hot single "Meanwhile Back at the Ranch." The six brothers, who were between the ages of 18 and 28, made history with the song—it became the 13th best selling single in country music and pushed the Clark Family Experience into the spotlight. The Clark Family Experience is comprised of the six eldest children of traveling ministers Freddy and Sylvia Clark. Alan (guitar/vocals), Aaron (electric bass/vocals), Adam (mandolin/vocals), Ashley (fiddle), Andrew (drums), and Austin (lap slide guitar/keyboards) were born and raised in Virginia. The Clark's 11 children were surrounded by music from an early age, but the boys started performing professionally in 1993.

Nearly a decade later, Curb Records inked the Clark Family Experience a deal. They went on to perform on TNN's weekly special *The Oak Ridge Boys: Live from Las Vegas* and appeared on *Prime Time Country* on several occasions. Opening slots for Faith Hill, Martina McBride, AC/DC, Charlie Daniels, the Dixie Chicks, and Tim McGraw allowed them to grow in a live setting; two summers with the George Strait festival tour also proved golden. The Clark Family Experience gained momentum in the new millennium, and Tim McGraw joined them in the production of their first studio album. *The Clark Family Experience* was released in August 2002. *—MacKenzie Wilson*

The Clark Family Experience / Aug. 20, 2002 / Curb ✦✦✦

Gene Clark

b. Nov. 17, 1944, Tipton, MO, **d.** May 24, 1991, Sherman Oaks, CA
Guitar, Vocals, Songwriter / Progressive Bluegrass, Country-Rock, Singer/Songwriter, Folk-Rock
Gene Clark will always be best remembered for his two-year stint as a vocalist with the Byrds between 1964 and 1966. A fine legacy to be sure, but the shame of it is that there was far more to Clark's body of work than that; he was a superb songwriter, one of the founding fathers of country-rock, and recorded a number of fine albums with an impressive array of collaborators whose quality far outstripped their modest sales figures. Gene Clark was born in Tipton, MO, in 1944. Clark's father was an amateur musician with a passion for country music that rubbed off on young Gene; he began learning the guitar at age nine and was soon picking out Hank Williams tunes, as well as material by early rockers such as Elvis Presley and the Everly Brothers. Before long, Clark started writing his own songs, and at 13, he cut his first record with a local rock & roll combo, Joe Meyers & the Sharks, but Clark developed an interest in folk music after the Kingston Trio rose to popularity. Clark began performing with several folk groups working out of Kansas City which led to a more lucrative position with the New Christy Minstrels, a well-scrubbed folk-pop ensemble who scored a hit single with "Green Green." However, Clark longed to perform his own songs and didn't care for life on the road; after hearing the Beatles for the first time, Clark decided he wanted to form a rock band and he quit the NCM and moved to Los Angeles. There, he met a fellow folky who had his head turned around by the Beatles, Jim McGuinn (he would later change his name to Roger) and in 1964 they started assembling a band that would, in time, come to be known as the Byrds.

Gene Clark quickly became the Byrds' dominant songwriter, penning most of their best-known originals, including "Feel a Whole Lot Better," "Here Without You," and "Eight Miles High," and was one of the group's strongest vocal presences. However, Clark's less-than-impressive skills as a guitarist often made him look like a backing vocalist on-stage and the combination of Clark's dislike of traveling (including a fear of flying) and resentment that his songwriting income made him the best-paid member of the group led to tensions within the Byrds, and in 1966, Clark opted to leave the group. Columbia Records, the label the Byrds recorded for, signed Clark as a solo artist, and in 1967, he released his first solo set, *Gene Clark With the Gosdin Brothers*, a pioneering fusion of country and rock. However, Clark's album was released almost simultaneously with the Byrds' *Younger Than Yesterday*, and Clark's set was a commercial bust. With the future of his solo career in doubt, Clark briefly rejoined the Byrds in 1967, but by the end of the year, he once again parted ways with the group.

In 1968, Clark signed with A&M Records and, once again following his interest in blending country with rock, he began a collaboration with virtuoso multi-instrumentalist Doug Dillard. Dillard & Clark recorded a pair of fine albums for A&M, but they fared no better at the marketplace than Clark's efforts with the Gosdin Brothers, and in 1969, Clark began work on his first proper solo album, recording a pair of tracks with several members of the Byrds. However, legal problems prevented their release at the time, and it wasn't until 1971 that a Gene Clark solo set finally emerged, entitled *White Light*. A strong, primarily acoustic set, *White Light* sold poorly in America but was an unexpected hit in the Netherlands. Clark's next album, *Roadmaster*, combined new material with the unreleased 1969 tracks cut with the Byrds; while it was a strong album, A&M chose not to release it and it was initially released only in Holland. Clark left A&M just in time for the Byrds to cut a reunion album with their original lineup; Clark contributed a pair of fine songs to the project, "Full Circle" and "Changing Heart," but most of the album sounded uninspired and the reunion quickly splintered.

In 1974, Clark signed to Asylum Records and cut the polished but heartfelt *No Other*. Clark, however, had hoped to release the set as a double album, which did not please labelhead David Geffen, and the album stalled in the marketplace without promotion. In 1977, Clark returned with a new album, *Two Sides to Every Story*, and put his fear of flying on hold to mount an international tour to promote it. For his British dates, Clark found himself booked on a tour with ex-Byrds Roger McGuinn and Chris Hillman; audiences were clearly hoping for a Byrds reunion and while the three men had planned nothing of the sort, they didn't want to let down their fans and played a short set of Byrds hits as an encore for several dates on the tour. This led the three men to begin working up new material together once they returned to America, and in 1978, they began touring as McGuinn, Clark, & Hillman. After a well-received acoustic tour, the trio signed a major deal with Capitol Records and released their self-titled debut in 1979. However, the slick production (designed to make sure the group didn't sound too much like the Byrds) didn't flatter the group, and the album was a critical and commercial disappointment. Clark soon became disenchanted with the project, and on their second album, 1980s *City*, the billing had changed to Roger McGuinn and Chris Hillman, with Gene Clark. By 1981, Clark had left and the group briefly continued on as McGuinn/Hillman.

After splitting with McGuinn and Hillman, Clark stayed on the sidelines of music for several years, assembling a band called Flyte that failed to score a record deal. Clark finally re-emerged in 1984 with a new band and album called *Firebyrd*; the rising popularity of jangle-rockers R.E.M. sparked a new interest in the Byrds, and Clark began developing new fans among L.A.'s roots-conscious paisley underground scene. Clark appeared as a guest on an album by the Long Ryders, and in 1987, he cut a duo album with Carla Olson of the Textones called *So Rebellious a Lover*. *So Rebellious* was well-received and became a modest commercial success (it was the biggest selling album of Clark's solo career), but Clark began to develop serious health problems around this time; he had ulcers, aggravated by years of heavy drinking, and in 1988, he underwent surgery, during which much of his stomach and intestines had to be removed. Clark also lost a certain amount of goodwill among longtime Byrds fans when he joined drummer Michael Clarke for a series of shows billed *A 20th Anniversary Celebration of the Byrds*. Many clubs simply shortened the billing to the Byrds, and Clarke and Clark soon found themselves in an ugly legal battle with Roger McGuinn, David Crosby, and Chris Hillman over use of the group's name. The Byrds set aside their differences long enough to appear together at their induction into the Rock & Roll Hall of Fame in January of 1991, where the original lineup played a few songs together, including Clark's "Feel a Whole Lot Better." However, Clark's health continued to decline as his drinking accelerated, and on May 24, 1991, not long after he had begun work on a second album with Carla Olson, Gene Clark died, with the coroner declaring he succumbed as a result of "natural causes" brought on by a bleeding ulcer. *—Mark Deming*

Gene Clark With the Gosdin Brothers / 1967 / Edsel ✦✦✦✦
The first album that Gene Clark released after his departure from the Byrds followed very closely on the model of his earlier efforts on the Byrds' first two albums. His backing musicians included ex-bandmates Chris Hillman and Michael Clarke, as well as future Byrd Clarence White and Clark collaborator Doug Dillard; not to mention the Gosdin brothers, whose harmonies resembled a rockier Everly Brothers and brought the sound very close to the Byrds'. The album contains a number of fine pop-oriented tunes and stellar folk-rock/country-rock numbers (a year before the Byrds' *Sweetheart of the Rodeo*, which employed both White and Dillard) and established Gene Clark as a major songwriter, rivaling his old band and often coming close to the fabness of the Beatles. Still, despite such solid songs and backing musicians, *Gene Clark With the Gosdin Brothers* failed to make much of an impact, perhaps due to its being released in the same week as the Byrds' *Younger Than Yesterday*, itself a *tour de force* that cemented their influence.

However, in the realm of Clark's recorded output, this album stands as the one of the best, if not the best, example of how powerful a singer, writer, and bandleader Gene Clark was. *—Alex Stimmel*

Echoes / 1967 / Columbia/Legacy ✦✦✦✦✦
This is Gene Clark's debut album, *Gene Clark With the Gosdin Brothers.* The Byrds comparison is really unavoidable: it's both Clark's best solo work, and not coincidentally, the one which resembles the Byrds most strongly. Indeed, this could easily pass for a somewhat less-than-average vintage Byrds album, with actual Byrds Chris Hillman and Michael Clarke forming the rhythm section, and Vern and Rex Gosdin on guitar (hence the title). To be brutal, it doesn't measure up to Clark's best songs from his Byrds days, but it's fairly strong, melodic '60s folk-rock nonetheless, perhaps with a bit of a more countrified, laid-back, generic feel. "So You Say You Lost Your Baby," "Echoes," and especially "Tried So Hard" are standouts. [The CD adds three interesting previously unreleased outtakes from the era, as well as six of the best early Byrds songs graced by Clark's songwriting and vocals.] *—Richie Unterberger*

Fantastic Expedition / 1969 / A&M ✦✦✦

Through the Morning / 1969 / A&M ✦✦✦

Gene Clark / 1969 / Together ✦✦✦✦
Easily one of Gene Clark's finest outings ever. This, his first solo album for A&M (after the wonderfully ahead of its time Dillard & Clark), was an album that should have put Gene Clark in the same league as Neil Young. Aside from Clark's incredible eight originals (as well as a great cover of "Tears of Rage"), one reason this record succeeds is the pairing of Clark and producer/guitarist Jesse Ed Davis. Davis' guitar accompaniment has all of the subtlety of Robbie Robertson, and he framed the songs perfectly, especially the expansive set closer, "1975." As for the songs themselves, Clark rarely bettered himself. "Spanish Guitar" is easily one of Clark's most intense and arresting compositions, with lines like "from deep in my soul to my brain to a Spanish guitar . . ."; it's no wonder Bob Dylan claims that he wished he'd written the song. The whole album, frankly, is that good, and is a must for anyone interested in the most criminally underrated singer/songwriter of his era. *—Matthew Greenwald*

American Flyer / 1971 / MediaArts ✦✦

White Light / 1971 / A&M ✦✦✦✦✦
If one wanted to start listening to Gene Clark as a solo artist, this is the place to start. Variously titled *Gene Clark* (thanks to an art error) or *White Light*, this album never attracted quite as much attention as Clark's work as part of Dillard & Clark, but it shows the ex-Byrd in the best voice of his whole career. By 1971, Clark had evolved out of his '60s folk-rock sound and into country-based singer/songwriter territory. In tandem with producer Jesse Ed Davis, he gave it a roaring start with his greatest body of songs ever, all of it romantic with a somewhat downbeat cast, similar to "Feel a Whole Lot Better" and "Tried So Hard"—"White Light," the intended title track, is the best of a brace of superb songs, interweaving the folksiest of melodies with a sophisticated lyric that carries meanings on several levels. The emphasis is on acoustic guitars (and harmonica) with a tiny bit of amplification, and organ accompaniment on one cut, and Clark singing in the most relaxed and richest voice of his life. The sessions for the album yielded five outtakes that proved worthy of release in 2002, including a truly rare moment, of Clark recording a pop song by another composer, Ben E. King's "Stand By Me." *—Bruce Eder*

Roadmaster / 1972 / Demon ✦✦✦✦✦
Gene Clark, record business equals bad news. Case in point, this album. Or masterpiece, you could say. After two brilliant Dillard & Clark albums, A&M signed Clark to a solo deal. OK, fair enough—so far. In 1972, he delivered perhaps the finest album of his career, *Gene Clark* (also known as *White Light*). Excellent reviews in all the top magazines, including *Rolling Stone.* Guess what? Almost zero sales. Now, here's the follow-up, almost—if not more—brilliant. Released only in Holland. Aside from containing some of Clark's finest tracks like "In a Misty Morning" and "Full Circle Song," this record contains two gems recorded with the willing participation of the other original Byrds. "One in a Hundred" and "She's the Kind of Girl" are so good that they would have easily stood out on *The Byrds* box set, had McGuinn elected to include them. Oh well, the music is still here—an example of an artist who couldn't quite get in on with commerce. What a disaster. The man should be mentioned in the same breath as Neil Young. *Roadmaster* is one of the many reasons why. *—Matthew Greenwald*

No Other / 1974 / Line ✦✦✦✦✦
This album is easily Gene Clark's most misunderstood and strangest project that he ever involved himself with. By turns described as Clark's "*Sgt. Pepper,*" and "one of the greatest albums of the '70s" to "largely un-listenable in certain places . . ." well, you get the idea. With a monumental budget at Asylum Records, and Thomas Jefferson Kaye in the producers chair, it was one wild ride, and that is certainly reflected in the grooves. Clark's songwriting rarely needed more than a four-piece backing band at any stage of his career. Granted Leon Russell used strings and horns on the epic *Echoes* album to great effect, but these arrangements are just over the top, and Clark's songs and vocals are clearly weak under the weight. And there are some fine songs. "No Other" is a wondrous composition, showing Clark exploring the metaphysical. "Lady of the North" (co-written by Doug Dillard) is a beautiful song, and fortunately escaped Kaye's overindulgence with a fine, restrained arrangement by Richard Greene. Overall though, it's indulgent and the *sound* of the record says more about the '70s than the songs do. You can almost *taste* the cocaine. *—Matthew Greenwald*

Two Sides to Every Story / 1977 / RSO ✦✦
Two Sides was Gene Clark's last solo album for a major label. Signed to RSO Records shortly after his wildly experimental (and occasionally engaging) 1974 Elektra album, *No Other,* which is often cited as his masterpiece, Clark and producer Thomas Jefferson Kaye released this. *Two Sides* is a much lower-key affair, and it succeeds on many more levels than the more heralded *No Other.* Clark's explorations into country music are much more at home on this album, as tracks such as "Mary Lou" and "Kansas City Southern" demonstrate. Oddly, one of the highlights of this record is a non-Clark composition, the traditional "In the Pines," which showcases Clark's brilliant (and underrated) vocal ability. The following year would see Clark team up with ex-Byrd mates Roger McGuinn and Chris Hillman on the forgettable McGuinn, Clark & Hillman project. *Two Sides* shows Clark in full command of his awesome gifts. Essential for Gene Clark enthusiasts. *—Matthew Greenwald*

Firebyrd / 1984 / Takoma ✦✦✦
Gene Clark's post-Byrds solo career was as fraught with false starts and unmet promises as his two years with the Byrds were filled with fame, fulfillment, and recognition. *Firebyrd* was an artistic triumph and a commercial disaster—released to rave reviews and an enthusiastic response as one of the finest solo projects ever to come from an ex-Byrd, it was killed by poor distribution (demand in Europe, especially Germany and Italy, where fan interest in Clark and the Byrds was very high, resulted in high premiums being paid for used copies). "Rain Song," "Rodeo Rider," and "Something About You" were some of Clark's best songs in years, and his covers of two old Byrds numbers, "Mr. Tambourine Man" and "Feel a Whole Lot Better," are perfectly credible reinterpretations, and he even does justice to Gordon Lightfoot's "If You Could Read My Mind." Not a "lost Byrds album" by any means, but a must-own for any serious Byrds fan. [In 1995, an expanded version of *Firebyrd* was released in Great Britain with the title *This Byrd Has Flown.*] *—Bruce Eder*

So Rebellious a Lover / 1987 / Razor & Tie ✦✦✦✦
An exquisite pairing of talent, the duo of Carla Olson and Gene Clark apparently came out of casual living room sessions while Clark was preparing for another project. The feeling of spontaneity and closeness of spirit engulfs all of the cuts here. Olson's strident and powerful vocals mesh beautifully with Clark's slightly world-weary, soulful performances. As for the material, both songwriters obviously put their best foot forward here. Olson's "The Drifter" and "Are We Still Making Love" are excellent country-folk outings. Clark contributes one of his finest later compositions, "Gypsy Rider," a multi-leveled song that can easily be viewed as autobiographical. Excellent support is provided by an array of backing musicians, especially Stephen McCarthy (lap steel and dobro) and guest Chris Hillman (mandolin). Chemistry is the operative word here. The only sad thing is that *So Rebellious a Lover* was to be the only studio effort by the duo before Clark passed away in 1991. This record is important not only for what it is, but for what it could have become. *—Matthew Greenwald*

Silhouetted in Light / 1992 / Edsel ✦✦✦

This Byrd Has Flown / Oct. 1995 / Edsel ✦✦✦✦✦
This Byrd Has Flown is an expanded British import CD of *Firebyrd,* with extra tracks added from later recording sessions. The songs add a considerable amount to the original album: "C'est La Bonne Rue" is a hot little rocker, and "All I Want" is one of Clark's most poignant and impassioned love songs, and by itself is worth the price of the album. The notes by drummer/singer/composer Andy Kandanes add considerably to the information about the circumstances behind the recording of *Firebyrd* and Clark's later career, up until his death in May of 1991. *—Bruce Eder*

American Dreamer / Feb. 11, 1997 / Raven ✦✦✦✦✦
Kudos to Australia's Raven for assembling this fine 24-track overview of Gene's most fertile period. Included are three Clark-penned Byrds stunners, two of the best from his first solo album, six from the Dillard & Clark albums (the Velvet Crush-covered "Why Not Your Baby" is unfortunately overlooked), a Flying Burritos-backed gem, two ersatz Byrds-reunion cuts from *Roadmaster,* a whopping six from *White Light,* "Full Circle" from the otherwise tepid 1973 Byrds reunion, and two selections from *No Other* (though not the This Mortal Coil-covered "Strength of Strings"). An interesting early mix of "Full Circle" is included as a bonus. For the uninitiated, this is a great place to start, but even a fanatic will be pleased by the inclusion of the hard-to-find *White Light* cuts and Sid Griffin's fannish liner notes. *—Michael Ribas*

● **Flying High** / 1998 / A&M ✦✦✦✦✦
When someone mentions the Byrds in conversation, the names of McGuinn, Crosby, and maybe Hillman pop up, but hardly anyone mentions Gene Clark, the Byrds' first original songwriter and lead singer until a fear of flying caused him to leave the band and strike out on his own. With *Flying High,* all of that should be put to rest, because the spotlight is finally on Clark and his many contributions to both rock and country. Starting with Byrds cuts like "Feel a Whole Lot Better" and "She Don't Care About Time," this two-disc set moves through Clark's early solo career into his fine collaboration with Doug Dillard and onto more mature solo work while attempting to reunite the Byrds on "One in a Million" and "She's the Kind of Girl," which never quite got off the ground. Added here are some otherwise unreleased cuts, such as "Winter In," "That's Alright by Me," and Dylan's "I Pity the Poor Immigrant," which show that Clark had more talent than was released to the public in his lifetime. And while disc two does have waning interest and fewer cuts, it does show that Clark never gave up on trying to restart his career, even if the chips appeared to be down; of special note is his sensitive cover of Phil Ochs' "Changes." Compiled and re-produced for disc by Sid Griffin, *Flying High* is a fine spotlight on an underappreciated artist. With liner notes by Griffin and Chris Hillman, this has just about everything one needs to know about Gene Clark. *—James Chrispell*

Gypsy Angel: The Gene Clark Demos 1983–1990 / Jul. 2001 / Evangeline ✦✦✦
In 1990, Gene Clark was blocking out plans for a second album with Carla Olson after their 1987 duo set, *So Rebellious a Lover,* became the most popular work of his career

after leaving the Byrds, and he recorded a batch of acoustic demos that year in preparation for the project. However, Clark died in the spring of 1991 before he could take any of the songs into the studio. *Gypsy Angel: The Gene Clark Demos 1983-1990* compiles eight songs from the casually recorded 1990 sessions, with four tunes Clark demoed in the mid-'80s. The biggest problem with the material on *Gypsy Angel* is that these recordings were clearly demos (the fidelity isn't especially good, and except for one song, these demos feature just Clark and his rudimentary acoustic guitar), and one wonders if some of these songs were in their finished form yet; the songs are quite long (the eight 1990 cuts clock in at over 53 minutes), and while they boast the sort of lovely melodies that were second nature to Clark, nearly all of them would have benefited from some judicious editing. In the last years of his life, Gene Clark's health was in serious decline, and it's hard not to tell on this album; his voice is not in especially good shape (especially on "Rock of Ages"), and even on the selections where his pipes rise to the occasion, he sounds a bit tired, as if he's not running at full-strength (and he almost certainly wasn't). By comparison, the four 1983 recordings find Clark in much stronger form, with his voice sounding strong and sure and the songs better-crafted and more concise. To say that Gene Clark deserved a better shake from his career is an understatement, and by all accounts he left behind a treasure trove of unreleased material that deserves to be heard. *Gypsy Angel*, however, is hardly the best place to start exploring the work he left behind; fans may find it intriguing, but it's by no means an essential listen. *—Mark Deming*

Guy Clark

b. Nov. 6, 1941, Monahans, TX

Guitar, Songwriter, Vocals / Progressive Country, Singer/Songwriter, Country-Folk, Outlaw Country, Alternative Country

Guy Clark doesn't just write songs, he crafts them with the kind of hands-on care and respect that a master carpenter (a favorite image of his) would have when faced with a stack of rare hardwood. Clark works slowly and with strict attention to detail—his output has been sparse since he first signed to RCA in the early '70s—but he has produced an impressive collection of timeless gems, leaving very little waste behind. His albums have never met with much commercial success, but the emotional level of his work consistently transcends sales figures and musical genres. He remains the kind of songwriter whom young artists study and seasoned writers (and listeners) admire.

Clark was born in the West Texas town of Monahans, where he was raised mostly by his grandmother (his mother worked and his father was in the Army) who ran the town hotel. One of her residents was an oil-well driller who would later end up the subject of one of Clark's most moving and stunningly beautiful songs, "Desperados Waiting for a Train." Many of Clark's songs, in fact, have centered around his days growing up in West Texas, including "Texas 1947" (from his debut album) and the 1992 song "Boats to Build," which hearkened back to a summer job he once had as a teenager on the Gulf Coast. The first songs Clark learned were mostly in Spanish. Later, when he moved to Houston and began working the folk-music circuit, he met fellow songwriter Townes Van Zandt (the two often toured together until Van Zandt's death in 1997) and blues singers Lightnin' Hopkins and Mance Lipscomb. It was here that Clark began playing and writing his sturdy brand of folk- and blues-influenced country music.

In the late '60s, Clark moved to California, living first in San Francisco (where he met and married his wife Susanna, a painter and songwriter) and then in Los Angeles, where he worked in the Dopera Brothers' dobro factory. Tiring quickly of Southern California (sentiments he expressed in another of his classics, "L.A. Freeway"), he and Susanna packed up and headed for Nashville in 1971, where he picked up work as a writer with publishing companies and, eventually, a recording contract with RCA. Clark's first album, *Old No. 1*, came out in 1975, a few years after Jerry Jeff Walker had turned "L.A. Freeway" into a minor hit. By this time Clark was considered one of the most promising young writers in country music, and while he didn't live in Texas anymore, the state's influence still ran thick in his blood.

Clark recorded one more album for RCA, *Texas Cookin'*, in 1976 before switching to Warner Bros. for his next three albums, released between 1978 and 1983. Three of his songs from these albums cracked the Top 100. By the mid-'80s, however, a number of his songs had been made into hits by country stars such as Johnny Cash, David Allen Coe, Ricky Skaggs (who took "Heartbroke" to number one), George Strait, Vince Gill, and the Highwaymen. Clark continued to work as a writer but didn't record again until 1988's *Old Friends*, released by Sugar Hill. He then switched labels once more, this time to Asylum, who released his 1992 album *Boats to Build* as part of their acclaimed American Explorer series. His eighth album, *Dublin Blues*, came out in 1995, and among its finely crafted moments is a re-reading of one of his most enduring songs, "Randall Knife," about the death of his father. *Cold Dog Soup* followed in 1999. *—Kurt Wolff*

★ **Old #1** / 1975 / RCA ✦✦✦✦✦

Though Guy Clark recorded only two albums for RCA, the label was fortunate to have him at all at the beginning of his career. If only every country songwriter could release a debut album as auspicious and fine as this one. Houston's Guy Clark, well known to the outlaw movement for his poetic, stripped-to-the-truth songs about ramblers, history, the aged and infirm, the drunken, the lost, and the simple dignity of working people who confront the darkness and joy of life quietly, issued *Old #1* when his compadres had already been making waves with his songs. Jerry Jeff Walker had already cut "L.A. Freeway" and other tunes by Clark, as had Gary Stewart, Billy Joe Shaver, and others. But the definitive versions come from Clark himself. On this disc with help from Emmylou Harris, fellow Houstoners (a young) Steve Earle and Rodney Crowell, guitar wizards Chip and Reggie Young, Mickey Raphael on harp, pianist David Briggs, fiddle boss Johnny Gimble, and the angel-voiced Sammi Smith, Clark executed a song cycle that is as intimate and immediate as it is quietly devastating with its vision of brokenness and melancholy, loose wild times, and unforgettable characters. The opener is the uptempo Texas swing of "Rita Ballou," a woman out for all she can get and then some; the outlaw's statement of love's determination on "L.A. Freeway" to not get killed or caught; and the summation of so much of what is contained here and on the follow-up to this album, *Texas Cookin'*, "That Old Time Feelin'," which should be the new "Auld Lang Syne." Acoustic guitars dominate everything here. *Old #1* is a quiet record because its songs don't need to be amplified; they speak for themselves in a straight, poetic, and powerful way. In addition to the above, two Clark classics are here as well, the amazing recollection "Desperadoes Waiting for a Train" and one of the most beautiful and confessional love songs ever written in any genre, "Like a Coat From the Cold." The most underrated track is an aural movie called "Instant Coffee Blues," where Clark's protagonist is a lonesome rambler, aimlessly hitchhiking his way to who knows where. He is picked up by a single working woman who is also on the wrong side of alone; they have an evening of companionship that has its share of intimacy and passion—until morning when, "she just had to go to work/and he just had to go." The disc closes with "Let Him Roll," a snappy, laid-back observation about destiny having its own way at staying out of its way. *Old #1* was unequaled in 1975 for the depth of its vision and the largeness of its artistic and empathetic heart; only Bruce Springsteen's *Born to Run* came close to it in terms of aesthetic merit. *—Thom Jurek*

Texas Cookin' / 1976 / RCA ✦✦✦✦

Guy Clark's sophomore effort sounds more like a party of friends who got together to pick together on a Saturday night that it does a sensitive singer/songwriter outing. Essentially that's what it is, coming as it did in 1975 at the height of the outlaw movement fever. Recorded at Chips Moman's American Studios in Nash Vegas, there is no producer listed on the set, so you can assume Clark did it himself with the aid of his many compadres here, who include but are not limited to Emmylou Harris, Susanna Clark, Johnny Gimble, Jerry Jeff Walker, Hoyt Axton, Waylon Jennings, Tracy Nelson, Brian Ahern, Mickey Raphael, Rodney Crowell, David Briggs, and Chip Young. Songwise, Clark's on a roll here; first there's the woolly party tune, "Texas Cookin'," that celebrates the Lone Star State's particular ability to make their food taste good with beer, and then there's the stunning "Anyhow I Love You," with Emmylou, Waylon, and Crowell accompanying Clark as a chorus. Jennings' harmony singing here is the best he did in his career. There's the midtempo "Good to Love You Lady" with Walker, Axton, Crowell, and Harris singing in a smoky contralto, an honest-to-goodness country song, baring its fiddles, pedal steel, and a trio of acoustic guitars to carry those rough and sweet voices through the story. And while the uptempo tunes here are wondrously raucous fare, Clark's strength as a ballad writer is almost unequaled among his peers. Nowhere is this more evident than on "Broken Hearted People" (since retitled for the refrain, "Take Me to a Barroom"). Clark's version of the song lacks any sentimentality. He is one of the tune's subjects; his resignation is to spend his mourning days on a barstool after discovering a lover's faithlessness, but he's already wasted and can't even get there under his own power. His devastation is only eclipsed by his desperation: "Take me to a barroom driver/Set me on a stool/If I can't be her man, I'm damned/If I'll be her fool." In addition, Clark's "The Last Gunfighter Ballad" is a signature song, like his "Randall Knife" or "Desperadoes Waiting for a Train." It's a song; it's a story; it's a movie with acoustic guitars a bass, a cello, finger cymbals, and Waylon. Chilling, stirring, and unforgettable, just like the album itself. *—Thom Jurek*

Guy Clark / 1978 / Warner Bros. ✦✦✦

On his Warner Bros. debut and third album overall, Guy Clark made a hard turn to a more polished country sound—though it was hardly the "hard" country of Conway Twitty. It was also the most experimental record he'd released to date, cello, clavinet, and harpsichord gracing some of the tunes, and a backing band that included Albert Lee, Buddy Emmons, and Mickey Raphael, among others. Backing vocalists, always a part of Clark's recordings, included Don Everly, the Whites, and Rodney Crowell as well as a young, previously unrecorded Kay Oslin (later K.T. Oslin). Rather than pen everything himself, Clark wrote only half the tunes on the record; the others came from Townes Van Zandt ("Don't You Take It Too Bad"), Rodney Crowell ("Voila, an American Dream"), and Jimmie Rodgers ("In the Jailhouse Now"), among others. Clark's touch was at once more pastoral and more honky tonk, the folky traces of the RCA albums vanished inside tracks like "Houston Kid," the Van Zandt tune, and "Comfort and Crazy." It's only in the open-wound "Fool on the Roof Blues" that Clark allows himself the same lightheartedness he did on the earlier records. This is a fine label debut, and if Clark hadn't recorded those two albums for RCA, it might have sounded like a great one. The end result, however, is an artist trying new things and trying to grow, coming up with a handful of real gems in the process. *—Thom Jurek*

The South Coast of Texas / 1981 / Warner Bros. ✦✦✦

Guy Clark's Warner Bros. album *The South Coast of Texas* was issued in 1981. Rodney Crowell, Clark's Houston running partner, produced. It was before Crowell struck pay dirt producing his then wife Rosanne Cash or landing his own platinum records, which made this a big record for both men. Recorded in Los Angeles instead of Nash Vegas, Crowell was trying something that would affect his career in a very positive way when handling the production duties on Rosanne's records. *The South Coast of Texas* boasted a new slew of studio masters including Emory Gordy, Richard Bennett, Hank DeVito, Glen D. Hardin, the late drummer Larrie Londin, Rosanne Cash, Ricky Skaggs, and Pure Prairie League frontman and guitarist Vince Gill—completely unknown in Nash Vegas. Moving toward a more basic but electric approach, Crowell and Clark ran through a deck of songs that reflected Clark's attention to minute, even painstaking detail. The pair recut "Rita Ballou" from Clark's first album, making it sizzle and pop with a run of guitars and pedal steel. In addition, Clark's version of his own "Heartbroke" appeared here. While it received airplay, it wasn't until Ricky Skaggs recorded it a year later (he sang backup on the original) that it was a hit, going to the top of the country charts. The Clark/Crowell co-write, "She's Crazy for Leavin'," was among the most commercial songs Clark ever wrote, but it was also one of the most poignant. (Crowell hit pay dirt with it in 1988 on his own record.) "Crystelle" with Rosanne Cash is a stunner with its cascading chorus and haunting refrain, and "New Cut Road" is classic Clark, all masculine and unsentimental yet nonetheless reflecting a kind of folky tenderness that lies at the heart of his best work. *The South Coast of Texas* was a transition album toward the mature Clark style, one that was first to emerge on his next album, *Better Days*. It's not a landmark in his catalog, but neither is it anything that could remotely be considered a failure. —*Thom Jurek*

Better Days / 1983 / Warner Bros. ◆◆◆◆
No one can accuse Guy Clark of rushing. In 1983, he released of his fifth album since 1975 and his first in two years. Not exactly cranking them out at Waylon's and Willie's pace, Clark is far more concerned with his conception of quality. And *Better Days* proved two things: not only that Clark was a writer of fine songs that other people had hits with, but that he was a viable commercial entity on his own. Once again produced by Rodney Crowell, who had struck pay dirt with his productions of Rosanne Cash's hit records and his own *Diamonds & Dirt*, *Better Days* was a Clark record that set and broke the mold simultaneously. Back in Nashville after recording *The South Coast of Texas* in L.A., Crowell assembled a crack team for the set, including Vince Gill, who not only was making his name as a vocalist but also as a fine guitarist. Gill holds down the lead chair on this set by himself. Crowell, Johnny Gimble, Emory Gordy, Hank DeVito, and Reggie Young also helped out as did the late Larrie Londin on drums. Clark scored his first hit single with "Homegrown Tomatoes," a radio-friendly, easy-drawling, silly little catchy tune that Clark liked despite its relatively light weight. But it was enough. Like "Rita Ballou" in second gear, the plucked steel strings, the muted percussion, and Clark's elegant phrasing make it the most summery tune he's ever written. But there are better songs here such as his cover of Townes Van Zandt's "No Deal," the title track, "Supply and Demand," and the chilling, deeply moving, hunted "Randall Knife," an elegy for Clark's father. The song had been part of his live repertoire for some time but until now hadn't been recorded. It closes the record with the most astonishing silence, one that roars in the listener's ears long after the record is over and haunts her for the rest of the day. By *Better Days*, Clark, who was already a fine and polished songwriter, had arrived at the full possession of his power as a storyteller, ironist, and musing philosopher of song. —*Thom Jurek*

Old Friends / 1989 / Sugar Hill ◆◆◆
One would think that coming off what amounted to the closest thing to a hit Guy Clark ever had—with "Homegrown Tomatoes" off his Warner album *Better Days*—he'd want to follow it up with something. Not so, for Guy Clark is the king of anti-ambition. While an RCA greatest-hits package had appeared in the interim, Clark had not made a new record in five years and had left Warner. With 1988's *Old Friends*, Clark teamed with eccentric producer Miles Wilkinson for the first time and recorded his debut album for Sugar Hill. In many ways this set feels like nostalgia. There are familiar faces (Rodney Crowell, Vince Gill, Emmylou Harris, Rosanne Cash) and sounds from the days of yore—meaning his 1970s records—but there are some new ones too (Verlon Thompson, Sam Bush, and slide boss Mike Henderson to name three). What is new is Clark's willingness to cover songs and co-write. There are only two songs he penned solo—"Watermelon Dream" and "Doctor Good Doctor," two of the finest things on the record—and there are three covers, including a stunning read of Townes Van Zandt's "To Live Is to Fly" and Joe Ely's "The Indian Cowboy" as well as a cover of wife Susanna's collaboration with Richard Leigh entitled "Come From the Heart." The rest are co-writes with Susanna, Jim McBride, Joe Henry, Richard Leigh, Thompson, and Jim Murraugh. Sonically Wilkinson keeps everything restrained and held in check. For others this would be a travesty, but for Clark it's the right touch. The singing is inspired and the playing more so. It's the way the material is carried off that doesn't work as well. The feeling here on all but the Van Zandt track and the opening title track is that Clark was looking for the feel of "Texas Cookin'" with a producer whose very nuances are proscribed and elegant. While the material is good and the performances are as well, the sound feels flat, two-dimensional. It's not disappointing, but it is the least memorable of his recordings. It's as if there isn't enough Clark in the mix, personality-wise anyway. —*Thom Jurek*

Boats to Build / 1992 / Elektra/Nonesuch ◆◆◆◆
Four years after the release of the tepid *Old Friends*, Guy Clark signed to the newly revitalized Elektra Asylum label seemingly dedicated to recording and marketing American roots music. Teaming once again with producer Miles Wilkinson, Clark delivered an ambitious, soulful, and state-of-the-art batch of songs. There is an all-star cast here, as per usual. Nonetheless Clark and Wilkinson solidified their vision, and here it works seamlessly, and virtually all of the musical arrangements and sounds serve the songs. Players and singers included Jerry Douglas, Sam Bush, Verlon Thompson, Foster & Lloyd, Marty Stuart, Emmylou Harris, Rodney Crowell, Suzy Ragsdale, Brian Ahern, and drummer Kenny Malone. The opener, a light country shuffle flavored with the blues entitled "Baton Rouge," is catchy in the same way that "Homegrown Tomatoes" was nine years earlier. The title track, written with Thompson, is an intimate look at what goes on inside a man's mind when he works with his hands and the universe he encounters there. Douglas' slide guitar solo and the gorgeous Thompson harmonies deepen the impact. "Picasso's Mandolin," co-authored with Foster & Lloyd, is a lilting number with hand percussion, Bush's mandolin playing sad and sweet, and three-part harmonies by Clark with Foster & Lloyd. What strikes the listener in the first five tracks is how spare everything is, no matter how many or few instruments are on a given cut. Wilkinson sculpts the sound around Clark's stiletto-fine lyrics. Perhaps this is best encountered on "Hey, Where'd You Get This Number." It's a humorous funky country tune with a quartet and no backing vocals, and Clark's wit sizzles in the mix, full of cruelty and irony. But it also comes through in the tender and moving "I Don't Love You Much, I Do." Stuart's mandolin and Thompson's guitar wind around one another, framing Clark's creaking and elegant lyrics as he sings them in his usual slow, deliberate manner, getting every ounce of insight and emotion from the syllables. It took three more years to get another record out of Clark, but it's a winner all the way around. —*Thom Jurek*

Craftsman / 1995 / Philo ◆◆◆◆◆
This double-CD collection issued by Rounder's Philo imprint contains on a double CD all three of Guy Clark's late-'70s and '80s recordings for Warner Bros.: *Guy Clark*, *The South Coast of Texas*, and *Better Days*. Clark's Warner period was one of intense self-scrutiny and exploration, not only with the way songs are written, but also in the way they are recorded. In terms of experiment and adventure, these are the most sonically interesting of Clark's records. While some of these titles seemed odd at the time, particularly the self-titled album, in retrospect they more than hold their own and prove to be ahead of what some are doing even now. As for the tracks themselves, this was a fruitful, if difficult, period for Clark. While his biggest hit, "Homegrown Tomatoes," is here, so is the redo of "Rita Ballou," "New Cut Road," and the original recorded version of "Randall Knife," far spookier and more haunted than the redo on *Dublin Blues*. In addition, there are a few covers here that Clark had been loathe to cut while on RCA, and these include Townes Van Zandt's "Don't You Take It Too Bad" and "No Deal," as well as a stellar modern version of Jimmie Rodgers' "In the Jailhouse Now." Also there are a pair of collaborations with fellow Houstonian Rodney Crowell in "The Partner Nobody Chose" and "She's Crazy for Leavin'." Clark always surrounded himself with fine musicians and this trio of albums was no exception—everyone from Emmylou Harris and Rosanne Cash to Crowell, Verlon Thompson, Kenny Malone, David Briggs, and dozens more appear on them. In many ways, because of the heady work Clark had issued before and after these Warner recordings, this trio has become somewhat of a cipher in his catalog, as part of some misguided apocrypha. This impression is simply erroneous and can be proven so with even the most casual listen. These 30 songs are as integral to Guy Clark's body of work than anything else he has ever issued. —*Thom Jurek*

Dublin Blues / Apr. 4, 1995 / Elektra ◆◆◆◆◆
A mere three years after *Boats to Build*, Guy Clark offered *Dublin Blues*, a record filled with sizzle, inspiration, and his best batch of songs in years. Teaming with Miles Wilkinson for the third time and using in the studio for the first time his road band—which includes über guitarist and singer Darrell Scott—Clark delivers a batch of searing portraits, intimate observations, first-person narratives, and one dumb throwaway cut ("Baby Went to Memphis in a Limo"). As usual, some old friends return to the fold—Rodney Crowell, Emmylou Harris, Sam Bush, Verlon Thompson, Kenny Malone, and Suzy Ragsdale—but there are new faces as well like Ramblin' Jack Elliott, Nanci Griffith, and Kathy Mattea. The magic begins with the title track. Haunted Celtic melodies played on the fiddle and a mandolin with an acoustic guitar usher in a country song that could be from the countryside of Ireland. With Mattea on the backing vocals, the listener is transported between worlds in time and space. "Black Diamond Strings" is a friendly little number about what else: guitar strings! Its catchy hook and singalong chorus make it a Clark winner. "Shut Up and Talk to Me" features Scott playing the swinging blues as Clark counts off the music like a fierce memory. "Stuff That Works" is another of Clark's quiet observation tunes, where his words speak volumes and the instruments underline their meanings. It's a workingman's anthem sung seemingly from the workshop bench. But "Hank Williams Said It Best," "Tryin' to Try," "Cape," and "Hangin' Your Life on the Wall" are all tremendous in their scope and intimacy. They are full of dimension and depth, and Wilkinson gives them textures. The set ends with a re-recording of the spooky yet shattering elegy "The Randall Knife" Clark cut on *Better Days*. The difference here is age. The view Clark sings from is one of distance and age. "The Randall Knife" doesn't feel quite so spooky this time out, but it does resonate with empathy and even tenderness. As it winds to a close, the listener is left not in bewildered silence but in awe that such a bond exists at all. —*Thom Jurek*

Keepers / 1997 / Sugar Hill ◆◆◆◆
Keepers is the first live album Guy Clark has ever released. Recorded in 1996 in front of a small audience in an intimate venue (Daniel's Corner in Nash Vegas), it showcases Clark with a full band playing his best-loved songs. While that might seem like an easy way out for some, it's not for Clark, who pushes these songs—despite his easy, laid-back demeanor—to the breaking point in terms of meaning and emotional truth. With a band consisting of Verlon Thompson and Darrell Scott on guitars (Scott also plays virtually everything with strings except fiddle), Suzy Ragsdale (not only singing backup, but playing accordion), Kenny Malone, and bassist Travis Clark, Guy uses his material as a way of communicating something quite mercurial yet universally felt with his audience. Opening with a fine, drinking song rendition of "L.A. Freeway," Clark pulls out the stops from the word "go" and travels all over his career map, from "Texas, 1947," "Like a Coat From the Cold" (which is chilling in its amorous simplicity), "Heartbroke," "Last Gunfighter Ballad," "Better Days," and "Homegrown Tomatoes," before catching a breath—though none of these songs seem rushed. Miles Wilkinson's live mix is spot-on and flat, allowing for the natural dynamics in the music to come across, and it translates well to CD. The second half of the program features "She Ain't Goin Nowhere," "South Coast of Texas," "Let Him Roll," "Texas Cookin'," a new track called "Out in the Parking Lot," and a few others, including a rousing, deeply moving rendition of "Desperados Waiting for a Train." In sum, it's a better greatest-hits record than any available, since all the songs come from one source, and it's a fine example of how live records should be made. —*Thom Jurek*

Essential / Jan. 28, 1997 / RCA ◆◆◆
It took all the way until 1997 for RCA to get it together to replace their *Best of Guy Clark* with this package. The major differences: all 20 tracks Clark cut for RCA on two separate albums—*Old No. 1* and *Texas Cookin'*—are included here; the best-of-contained only 16. Secondly, this set is represented by an adequate set of liner notes that give all the credits and production information. Lastly, with recordings this important, they are given first-rate sound treatment. All of the cuts on this set have been remastered in 20-bit sound from the original source tapes. Therefore, the original versions of tracks like "Rita Ballou,"

"The Last Gunfighter Ballad," "Desperados Waiting for a Train," and "That Old Time Feelin'" as well as many others sound better here than they do on any import recordings that are known of. The only complaint is that using the term "essential" in the title instead of just straight reissues of the albums as two-fers with their given titles (this is part of a series RCA has going) makes it confusing for both the fan and the casual listener. Given this, neither of these records are actually out of print, except under their own names, which is ridiculous. *—Thom Jurek*

Cold Dog Soup / Oct. 26, 1999 / Sugar Hill ♦♦♦♦
Cold Dog Soup follows *Dublin Blues* in its poignant observations of life, love, death, and all the states in between. Clark's voice may be a little worn, but his songwriting skills are sharper than ever here. He uses a group of musicians that revolve around longtime collaborators Verlon Thompson and Darrell Scott and the backing vocals of Emmylou Harris. Clark has become comfortable with co-writing in recent years and *Cold Dog Soup*'s no exception. Three of the cuts were penned with Verlon Thompson, a pair with Jon Randall Stewart, and one with Shawn Camp, who is also part of his band. In addition, there are two new Clark songs and a trio of covers that are awesome and very different interpretations of the originals. There's Steve Earle's "Fort Worth Blues," written as an elegy for their late friend, songwriter Townes Van Zandt; there's a gorgeous read of Richard Dobson's "Forever, for Always, for Certain"; and the album closes with the old-time folk song "Be Gone Forever," written by Anna McGarrigle and Keith Sykes. Performed as a duet, it is one of the most traditional pieces of music Clark has ever recorded. The tragedy "Water Under the Bridge" feels a lot like the folk-blues of Bob Dylan's "Ballad of Hollis Brown," and in its own way is just as harrowing, with the mandolin fills floating around the guitar lines. "Bunkhouse Blues" is a cowboy blues complete with yodels that gets to the high and lonesome better than most bluegrass. "Men Will Be Boys" is a good-time anthem that could have been written and recorded during the Austin era with Jerry Jeff Walker and the rest. Ultimately, *Cold Dog Soup* is another fine Guy Clark album. He's been on a roll for nearly three decades and shows no sign of resting on his considerable laurels. *—Thom Jurek*

Old No. 1/Texas Cookin' / May 29, 2001 / Camden ♦♦♦♦♦
The master songwriter's first two long-players have been released on a single import CD that is more than worth searching out for listeners with a thing for impressionistic story-songs delivered in a voice as dry and true as the dust of West Texas. These classic recordings, including "She Ain't Goin' Nowhere" and "Desperados Waiting for the Train," may date back to the mid-'70s, but their production holds up decades later. None of that horrible Nashville spit and polish of the era distracts from Clark's fine songs. Essential listening for fans of today's alternative country and folksinger/songwriters. *—Brian Beatty*

The Dark / 2002 / Sugar Hill ♦♦♦♦
Clark's easygoing, front-porch delivery benefits from the intimate setting provided throughout *The Dark.* With plenty of space around the instruments and no production clutter in the way, the essence of each song conveys clearly as well. Surprises are few, and perhaps the least-surprising aspect of this set is that it is as well-crafted as one has a right to expect from Clark. (Only one track, by Townes Van Zandt, is a cover.) Subjects range from the historical, in the gruesome yet stoic "Soldier's Joy, 1864," to reflections on more modern tragedies; in the spoken verses and weary-sung choruses of "Homeless," Clark captures the fatalism of living on the streets with vernacular eloquence. Clark turns the death of a beloved dog into a mordant lament on "Queenie's Song" and ruminates on simple, visceral pleasures on "Mud." In truth, no one track stands out; each reflects the care of a writer (or, on these songs, co-writer) and singer—more than that, an actor for whom music is his stage, and whose high standards seem likely to persist for a long, longtime. *—Robert L. Doerschuk*

Roy Clark

b. Apr. 15, 1933, Meherrin, VA

Guitar, Vocals, Banjo, Fiddle / Country-Pop, Instrumental Country, Traditional Country, Nashville Sound/Countrypolitan

In the '70s, Roy Clark symbolized country music in the U.S. and abroad. Between guest-hosting for Johnny Carson on *the Tonight Show* and performing to packed houses in the former Soviet Union on a tour that sold out all 18 concerts, he used his musical talent and his entertaining personality to bring country music into homes across the world. As one of the hosts of TV's *Hee Haw* (Buck Owens was the other) for more than 20 years, Clark picked and sang and offered country corn to 30 million people weekly. He is first and foremost an entertainer, drawing crowds at venues as different as Las Vegas, Atlantic City, and the *Opry.* His middle-of-the-road approach has filled a national void, with Clark offering country that was harder-edged than Kenny Rogers but softer and more accessible than Waylon Jennings. Among his numerous vocal hits are "Yesterday, When I Was Young" and "Thank God and Greyhound." Instrumentally he has won awards, for both guitar and banjo. Clark has also co-starred on the silver screen with Mel Tillis, in the comedy *Uphill All the Way.*

The son of two amateur musicians, Roy Clark began playing banjo, guitar, and mandolin at an early age. By the time he was 14, he was playing guitar behind his father at local dances. Within a few years, he had won two National Banjo Championships, with his second win earning him an appearance at the *Grand Ole Opry.* Despite his success as a musician, Clark decided to pursue an athletic career, rejecting baseball for boxing. At the age of 17, he won 15 fights in a row before deciding that he would rather be a musician than a fighter.

Clark found work at local clubs, radio stations, and television shows. By 1955, he was a regular on Jimmy Dean's D.C.-based television show, *Country Style.* Once Dean left Washington for New York, Clark took over the show, and over the next few years he earned a reputation as an excellent musician and entertainer. In 1960, he decided to leave the East Coast to pursue his fame and fortune out West. That year, he became the leader of Wanda Jackson's band, playing on her hit singles like "Let's Have a Party," as well as touring with the singer and playing concerts with her in Las Vegas. Once Jackson decided to break up her band, Clark continued to play regularly at the Frontier Hotel in Vegas and through his new manager, Jackson's ex-manager Jim Halsey, he landed spots on *the Tonight Show* and the sitcom *the Beverly Hillbillies*, where he played both Cousin Roy and Big Mama Halsey.

In 1963, Clark signed to Capitol Records, and his first single for the label, "Tips of My Fingers," became a Top Ten hit. Over the next two years, he had a handful of minor hits for Capitol before he switched labels, signing with Dot in 1968. At Dot, his career took off again, through covers of pop songs like Charles Aznavour's "Yesterday, When I Was Young" (number nine, 1969). However, what really turned Clark's career around was not records, but rather a television show called *Hee Haw.* Conceived as a country version of *Laugh-In, Hee Haw* began its run in 1969 on CBS. Roy Clark and Bakersfield country pioneer Buck Owens were picked as co-hosts. Over the next two years, it was one of the most popular shows on television. In 1971, CBS dropped the show because its corny country humor didn't fit the network's new, urban image, but *Hee Haw* quickly moved into syndication, where it continued to thrive throughout the decade.

While *Hee Haw* was at the height of its popularity, Clark had a string of country hits that ranged from Top Ten singles like "I Never Picked Cotton" (1970), "Thank God and Greyhound" (1970), "The Lawrence Welk—Hee Haw Counter-Revolution Polka" (1972), "Come Live With Me" (1973), "Somewhere Between Love and Tomorrow" (1973), "Honeymoon Feelin'" (1974), and "If I Had It to Do All Over Again" (1976) to a multitude of minor hits. Though he didn't consistently top the country charts, Clark became one of the most recognizable faces in country music, appearing on television commercials, *Hee Haw,* and touring not only the United States but a number of other countries, including a groundbreaking sojourn to the then Soviet Union in 1976. Frequently, he played concerts and recorded albums with a wide variety of musicians from other genres, including the Boston Pops Orchestra and Clarence "Gatemouth" Brown.

In 1979, the momentum of his career began to slow down, as he left his longtime label ABC/Dot for MCA. Over the next two years, he had a number of minor hits before leaving the label. He recorded one inspirational album for Songbird in 1981 before signing to Churchill in 1982. *Hee Haw*'s audience was beginning to decline in the early '80s, but Clark diversified his interests by investing in property, minor-league baseball teams, cattle, publishing, and advertising. None of Clark's recordings for Churchill were big hits, and his brief stays at Silver Dollar in 1986 and Hallmark in 1989 also resulted in no hits. Nevertheless, Clark had become a country icon by the mid-'80s, so his lack of sales didn't matter—he continued to sell out concerts and win awards; he even made the comedy Western *Uphill All the Way* in 1986 with Mel Tillis. In 1987, he was belatedly made a member of the *Grand Ole Opry.* During the '90s, Clark concentrated on performing at his theater in Branson, MO, sporadically releasing re-recordings of his big hits on a variety of small labels, though 2000's *Live at Billy Bob's Texas* marked his first live release in nearly a decade. *Christmas Memories* followed that same year. *—David Vinopal*

The Tip of My Fingers / 1963 / Capitol ♦♦♦
This album features "My Baby's Gone," "Silver Threads & Golden Needles," "Faded Love," and "Take Me As I Am," among others. *—AMG*

The Lightning Fingers of Roy Clark / 1963 / Razor & Tie ♦♦♦♦
Originally recorded for Capitol Records in his pre-*Hee-Haw* days (1963), this is Roy's instrumental album, an all-guitar fest that showcases the country artist's amazing chops. Kicking off with a warp-speed version of "Twelfth Street Rag" that actually gets doubles in tempo by the final chorus, this album features a brace of generic "twistin'" instrumentals (read: public domain tunes given a twist beat) like "Texas Twist," "Weeping Willow Twist," "Wildwood Twist" ("Wildwood Flower"), "Golden Slippers" and "Over the Waves," rocked up cha cha's like "Pink Velvet Swing" and Bob Wills' "A Maiden's Prayer," and boogies like the closing "Chicken Wire." Produced by Ken Nelson and sounding for all the world like it was cut in a single afternoon session, this should open up anyone's eyes and ears who think of Roy Clark only as a belly scratchin' fool, telling corny jokes and singing sappy love ballads. *—Cub Koda*

Roy Clark Guitar Spectacular / 1965 / Capitol ♦♦♦♦

Roy Clark Sings Lonesome Love Ballads / 1966 / Capitol ♦♦♦

Do You Believe This Roy Clark / 1968 / Dot ♦♦♦

Yesterday, When I Was Young / 1969 / Dot ♦♦♦
"Yesterday, When I Was Young" was Roy Clark's biggest crossover hit, an easy listening ballad by Charles Aznavour that made a strong showing on the country, pop, and adult contemporary charts in 1969. Clark was riding high from his exposure on CBS' country music variety show *Hee Haw,* but "Yesterday, When I Was Young" and the album that accompanies it are pure pop. The closest the album comes to country music is "When a Man Becomes a Man," which sounds like John Denver, and John Hartford's "A Simple Thing as Love," which—surprise!—sounds like Glen Campbell. The album yielded two other minor hits, "Love Is Just a State of Mind" and an appealing arrangement of Kurt Weill's "September Song." MOR pop ballads comprise only a small part of what Clark can do, but he does it well and—in the case of *Yesterday, When I Was Young*—he does it exclusively. *—Greg Adams*

The Everlovin' Soul of Roy Clark / 1969 / Dot ♦♦
What do you make of a completely serious, string-laden version of "Me and Bobby McGee" that ends with a kazoo solo? That is by far the biggest surprise on *The Everlovin' Soul of Roy Clark*, a 1969 album of pop ballads on which Clark makes even Rex Griffin's country classic "The Last Letter" sound like a lounge singer's torch song. "Right or Left at Oak Street," a melancholy piece about an ambivalent family man, was a minor hit, as was the conversational "Then She's a Lover." Clark delivers a contemplative reading of Paul Weston's 1951 hit "Morningside of the Mountain" years before Donny & Marie Osmond made it a hit again, and "Unchained Melody" is well suited to Clark's style. A

gospel song, "Say Amen," wraps up an album that tries, in the grand MOR tradition, to offer something for everyone while offending no one. — *Greg Adams*

Honky Tonk / 1969 / Pickwick ♦♦
Honky Tonk reissues nine of Roy Clark's Capitol recordings from the early '60s. Clark made a few hits during this period, but none are included; guitar instrumentals dominate the program, and the only vocal track is "Spooky Movies," a rock & roll novelty. Clark's instrumentals from this period sound more like rock with a slight jazz influence than country—"Hold It," for example, strikes a guitar-and-organ groove that is closer to John Patton than *Hee Haw*. Many of the songs are traditional or country oldies such as "Worried Mind," "Frankie and Johnny Blues," and "Blues Stay Away From Me," but Clark also tackles Bill Doggett's instrumental R&B classic "Honky Tonk." Interesting but uncharacteristic. — *Greg Adams*

I Never Picked Cotton / 1970 / Dot ♦♦♦
Unlike Eddy Arnold, Roy Clark's crossover success as an MOR vocalist and television personality didn't compromise his identity as a country artist. The hit title track of this 1970 LP, for example, features a banjo, and Clark almost always included some straight country alongside his pop ballads. That said, pop ballads comprise a substantial portion of *I Never Picked Cotton*, the cover of which portrays Clark as an affluent sophisticate. The album's other hit single, "Thank God and Greyhound," made the country Top Five and became a minor crossover hit, while the obligatory covers of recent hits include "Sunday Morning Comin' Down" and a facsimile rendition of "(Is Anybody Going To) San Antone." "You Gotta Love People" is a ringer for a Jerry Reed composition, and the album ends on an ambiguous note with "Middle of the Road," a mild jab at those who choose the path of least resistance, written by Clark's *Hee Haw* co-star Kenny Price. — *Greg Adams*

Roy Clark in Concert / 1976 / MCA ♦♦♦♦♦
It's a nice sampling of Clark's stage show, great guitar playing, corny jokes and all. —*Cub Koda*

Banjo Bandits / 1978 / ABC ♦♦♦

Makin' Music / Dec. 1979 / One Way ♦♦♦
Surround two of the most versatile guitar pickers on the planet in a studio with a cadre of world-class sidemen and what do you get? This irresistible duet album by Gate and Roy Clark, first out on MCA. Good vibes abound as the fun-loving pair blast out "Caldonia," "Take the 'A' Train," "The Drifter," "Justice Blues," and more, trading licks, vocals, and quips with a jam session-oriented looseness. — *Bill Dahl*

• **Greatest Hits** / Sep. 12, 1995 / Varese Vintage ♦♦♦♦
By concentrating on his biggest straight country hits for Capitol and Dot Records ("Tips of My Fingers," "Yesterday, When I Was Young," "I Never Picked Greyhound," "Thank God and Greyhound," "Come Live With Me") and sidestepping many of the novelty numbers that were associated with *Hee-Haw*, the 14-song *Greatest Hits* makes a case for Roy Clark's talents as songwriter and performer, providing a good introduction to his career. —*Stephen Thomas Erlewine*

Roy Clark & Joe Pass Play Hank Williams / Nov. 1995 / Buster Ann Music ♦♦♦♦
At first glance, this project, which would be Joe Pass' final recording, might seem a bit unlikely. Pass is teamed up with country guitarist Roy Clark to play a set of Hank Williams tunes, but the date is actually quite successful. Clark has long been a closet jazz player; many of Williams' tunes have attractive chord changes, and Pass had his longtime rhythm section (rhythm guitarist John Pisano, bassist Jim Hughart and drummer Colin Bailey) serving as a solid foundation. Such songs as "Hey, Good Lookin'," "Your Cheatin' Heart," "Long Gone Lonesome Blues" and "There'll Be No Teardrops Tonight" work quite well in this setting. Since Clark (a brilliant guitarist himself) had long been a Joe Pass fan, the results are both competitive and complementary. Recommended. — *Scott Yanow*

Greatest Hits, Vol. 2 / Oct. 7, 1997 / Varese Vintage ♦♦♦♦
Roy Clark had his first brace of hits for the Capitol label in the mid- to late '60s. But his second batch came with a brace of hit singles and charting albums for the Dot label the following decade with charters on the small Churchill label into the 1980s. This 15-track compilation gives the rest of the story of Roy's country charting hits, including "The Great Divide," "Then She's a Lover," "I Have a Dream, I Have a Dream," "September Song" and "Do You Believe This Town." And Roy's famous guitar chops are well highlighted on "Wildwood Flower" and "Alabama Jubilee." — *Cub Koda*

Live at Billy Bob's Texas / Feb. 29, 2000 / Smith Music Group ♦♦♦
Like all of the entries in the *Live at Billy Bob's Texas* series, this does not divulge the date of recording, but one can reasonably assume it's from a show not long before the CD's mid-2000 release. Clark is still an excellent, fast-as-anyone guitar picker, as heard on this set's instrumentals. Those instrumentals cover a lot of ground, too: the jazz standard "Caravan," "Riders in the Sky," the bluegrass perennials "Foggy Mountain Breakdown" and "Dueling Banjos," "Malaguena," "El Cumbanchero," and (least successfully) "Lara's Theme." He still sings, too—unfortunately, one could say, given both the lesser material he applies his vocals to and the good-natured but limited, gruff tone of his voice. The overall effect is a bit schizophrenic, if fairly typical of all-around shows that some country stars like to give. Pretty hillbilly sounding instrumentals are interspersed with sentimental, drippy MOR country ballads like "Love Takes Two" and "Yesterday When I Was Young," though the corny, satirical "Thank God and Greyhound" breaks up that mood a bit. The audience eats it up, though, and also responds favorably to his mildly amusing stage announcements. Too bad the band, which plays pretty well, includes an ill-chosen synthesizer (though that instrument isn't extremely prominent). — *Richie Unterberger*

Absolutely the Best, Vol. 1 / Feb. 25, 2003 / Fuel 2000 ♦♦♦
Roy Clark is known mostly as the grinning co-host of *Hee Haw*, but like fellow *Hee Haw* host Buck Owens, there is much more to Roy Clark than that. He made his name as a

lightning-fast guitar picker and spent time playing with lots of great country artists like Hank Thompson, Bob Wills, and Wanda Jackson before he got his big break and signed with Capitol as a solo artist. This best-of collection compiles tracks recorded during Clark's seven-year stay with Capitol between 1961-1967. It includes a couple of his instrumental songs (the rip-roaring "Chicken Wire," "South," and "Alabama Jubilee"), but otherwise focuses on vocal tracks he cut. Apart from the live take of his first vocal single, "Talk About a Party"; the other side of that 1962 single, a burning take on Ruth Brown's "As Long as I'm Moving"; and the fun novelty song "Spooky Movies," Clark is flanked by vocal choirs, orchestras, and unfortunate arrangements. His serviceable voice isn't strong enough to overcome these obstacles and the disc is soon mired in Nashville mush. What Clark does to Faron Young's honky tonk classic "Live Fast, Love Hard, Die Young" (buries it in strings and silly background chirping) is criminal. The only track that isn't swamped by the backing is "Turn Around and Look Again," a surprising blend of country-pop and uptown soul that has Clark turning in his best vocal effort. This is a very uneven collection that races through seven years of Clark's career in an exceedingly brief 32 minutes. Fuel 2000 could have doubled the running time, fleshed out the different aspects of Clark's music, and given more room to his flying fingers. Roy Clark deserves to have a solid retrospective that truly does show off his very best work. This isn't it. — *Tim Sendra*

Sanford Clark

b. 1935, Tulsa, OK
Vocals / Traditional Country, Rockabilly, Rock & Roll
Sanford Clark found fleeting fame with his rendition of the Lee Hazlewood song "The Fool." With a vocal style that blended elements of Johnny Cash with Ricky Nelson, Clark released the song in 1956, and it eventually peaked in the Top Ten of the pop charts and in the Top 15 of the country charts—his first and only hit. Clark was born in Tulsa, OK, and raised in Phoenix, AZ. A guitar player from childhood, he was influenced by both early rock & roll music and by country music. He got his start in the early '50s playing in Phoenix clubs. While stationed in the South Pacific during his stint in the Air Force, he formed a band and won a talent contest in Hawaii. Eventually, the Air Force stationed him back in Phoenix, where he met his old friend Al Casey, who introduced Clark to Hazlewood, who was still working as a local DJ and hadn't yet made his mark as a songwriter. Soon afterward, Clark recorded "The Fool" with Casey on guitar. The song was released on MCI and went nowhere until a Philadelphia DJ heard it and took the song to Dot Records' Randy Wood, who liked it and had Hazlewood license the song to his label. Afterward, Clark and Casey began a promotional tour opening for such stars as Ray Price and Roy Orbison. In 1957, Clark returned to the studio to record another Hazlewood song, "The Cheat." It only became a minor hit. At this time, Clark was having trouble with Wood who wanted him to become a virtual clone of Dot's most popular artist, Pat Boone. The label sent Clark to Hollywood to continue recording, but many of the songs were not released until much later. Those that were released did little or nothing on the charts.
In 1958, Clark signed to Jamie Records. Casey and Hazlewood joined him and began working with Duane Eddy. They also worked with Clark, who recorded "Still as the Night," featuring Eddy on guitar. Nothing happened on the charts and he began recording on other independent labels. He eventually landed in Hollywood where he hooked up with songwriter/aspiring performer Roger Miller, who was playing the Palomino Club. Miller wanted him to record a few of his songs, but Clark wasn't interested. Sanford almost had a hit in 1964 when he recorded Hazlewood's "Houston" for Warner. Unfortunately, Dean Martin also recorded it on Reprise and his version became the hit. The following year, Clark returned to Ramsey's label and created a new version of "The Fool" featuring Waylon Jennings on guitar. By this time Hazlewood had become a prominent producer and signed Clark to his LHI label. He made an album there, *Return of the Fool*, but it went nowhere and by the early '70s Clark had finally had enough and joined the construction industry, where he found success at last. He continues to record sometimes on his Desert Sun label. — *Sandra Brennan*

The Fool / 1983 / Ace ♦♦♦♦

• **Rockin' Rollin'** / 1986 / Bear Family ♦♦♦♦♦

Rockin' Rollin' 2 / 1986 / Bear Family ♦♦♦♦♦

Shades / 1994 / Bear Family ♦♦♦♦♦
Shades contains all of Sanford Clark's classic early recordings for MCI and Dot, including "The Fool," "(They Call Me) Country," "Pledging My Love" and "Black Jack County Chain." In addition to the studio masters, *Shades* features a handful of rarities and demos, making the compilation both the perfect introduction and the definitive retrospective. —*Thom Owens*

Terri Clark

b. Aug. 5, 1968, Montreal, Canada
Vocals / Contemporary Country, Neo-Traditionalist Country
Like her contemporary, Shania Twain, Terri Clark came storming out of Canada and captured the attention of America's country music industry in the mid-'90s. Where Twain incorporated more rock & roll into her music, Clark pretty much stayed close to her country roots, even if those roots were more new country than hardcore honky tonk. Raised in Medicine Hat, Alberta, Canada, Terri Clark was born into a musical family. Her grandparents, Ray and Betty Gauthier, were country stars in Canada, opening shows for stars like George Jones and Little Jimmy Dickens, while her mother sang folk songs in local coffeehouses. As a child, Terri listened to her grandparents' country records and taught herself how to play guitar. Throughout her adolescence, Clark sang, played, and listened to country music; she was particularly inspired by female artists like Reba McEntire, the Judds, and Linda Ronstadt.
Following her high-school graduation in 1987, she moved to Nashville. Upon her arrival, she wandered into *Tootsie's Orchid Lounge* unannounced and asked if she could sing. Surprisingly, she impressed the management and landed a job as the club's house

singer. Though her initial arrival in Nashville was successful, it took Clark quite a longtime to work her way into the actual industry. For the next seven years, she sang at clubs and worked odd jobs, all the while trying to land a record contract. During this time, she met and married a fiddler named Ted Stevenson. In 1994, she landed an audition for Mercury Records. After seeing a live performance by Clark, the label's president signed the singer. Clark's eponymous debut album was released in the summer of 1995. *Terri Clark* was a hit upon its release, spawning the Top Ten hits "Better Things to Do," "When Boy Meets Girl," and "If I Were You," as well as going gold. Clark supported the album with a tour opening for George Strait.

In 1996, she was nominated for the Country Music Association's Horizon Award, as well as the Academy of Country Music Awards' Best New Female Vocalist. She won a bevy of Canadian Country Music Awards in 1996, including Album of the Year and Single of the Year; she was also named the Top New Female Country Artist of 1995 by *Billboard* magazine. Her second album, *Just the Same*, was released in the fall of 1996, preceded by the hit single "Poor Poor Pitiful Me." *How I Feel* followed in 1998. *Fearless* brought the country chart single "A Little Gasoline" in fall 2000, and *Pain to Kill* was released in 2003. *—Stephen Thomas Erlewine*

● **Terri Clark** / 1995 / Mercury Nashville ✦✦✦✦
Terri Clark's self-titled debut established the vocalist as a promising singer and songwriter. Working from a basic, traditional country foundation, Clark adds in slight elements of pop and rock, making her music more immediately accessible. Though there are some flaws in the songs—occasionally, the melodies fail to stick—her impassioned, powerful singing make the album consistently entertaining. *—Stephen Thomas Erlewine*

Just the Same / Nov. 5, 1996 / Mercury Nashville ✦✦✦
Terri Clark may be a glamour queen, with lots of high style and flash. But then so is Dwight Yoakam, and he's a hell of a singer and songwriter, right? Clark is a honky angel singer with ambition, taste, looks, and a voice that's as big as a canyon. Oh yeah, and she's a fine songwriter as well. So bring on the glamour if it brings out the music. Luke Lewis over at Mercury has got to believe in this woman—she gets a producer's credit alongside Keith Stegall! Not every country singer or songwriter gets a production say on her second record. And this one develops the strengths that made her debut so compelling, even if it was flawed. Choosing to cover Warren Zevon's "Poor, Poor Pitiful Me" after the Linda Ronstadt version takes guts. But Clark has more than that; her version is as valid as her predecessor's and as full of rock & roll heart as the songwriter's own version. Other than this, Clark, Chris Waters, and Tom Shapiro wrote the majority of this album. They're a decent team, though the fullness of Clark's potential as an emotive artist—without sentimentality—is not exploited in these songs. They are solid, they belong here, and they're good listening, but given what she is obviously capable of, they are workmanlike. Other than the aforementioned, the best two tracks on the set are "Something in the Water," where Clark gets her blues growl out into the mix, "Twang Thang," which is as tough as anything Alan Jackson ever wrote and sung with twice the verve and grit, and the ballad "Keeper of the Flame," which Clark wrote on her own. In this song, the protagonist's hope is what keeps a relationship together, and in the grain of her voice one can hear both weariness and determination; when she gets to the top of her contralto in the refrain, chills run down the listener's spine and recall the fine songs of Lacy J. Dalton, Trisha Yearwood when she was a singer instead of a status symbol, and Loretta Lynn when trying to deliver a countrypolitan song with Kentucky grit. She's not there yet, but so close you can hear the train coming all the way round the bend. Pick it up. *—Thom Jurek*

How I Feel / May 19, 1998 / Mercury Nashville ✦✦✦✦
With *Just the Same*, Terri Clark proved she was going to be around for a while, and that the impression her self-titled debut made was no fluke. And like most acts Luke Lewis oversees, she's been allowed to grow with each release. *How I Feel* opens with one of the best songs written in the country genre in the preceding decade or so, Kim Richey's testimonial anthem "I'm Alright" from her own *Bitter Sweet* album. In Clark's interpretation, the song is less Americana and more mainstream pop-country, but Clark's voice is no ordinary instrument. She delivers both the humor and the pathos in the tune without forcing the issue. Produced by Keith Stegall, Clark is allowed to let her natural voice more fully into the mix. Her inflections are her own, and the songs are well suited to her forthright style of delivery. To say that Clark is emotive is one thing, to say that her voice is the sound of emotion itself is another, and it is the latter that's true—take a listen to "Everytime I Cry" or Clark's own "Not Getting Over You," a ballad ruled by her throaty contralto, gorgeous pedal steel fills, and synth strings that sound natural. "Till I Get There" displays just how comfortable Clark is with traditional country music. Despite the presence of a B-3 in the mix, the tune itself comes right out of the early '70s. Further, there is Melba Montgomery's classic "Cure for the Common Heartache," a honky tonk pearl handled expertly with the righteous brokenhearted Western swing blues bustin' out all over it. The sum total of these 12 songs is Clark's restlessness as a vocalist and as a songwriter. Her attempt to be true to country's traditions while riding the pop-country wave of the present creates a wonderful tension that never seems resolved. In addition, Clark's songwriting is stronger, more assured, and as recognizable as her voice. A fine effort. *—Thom Jurek*

Fearless / Sep. 19, 2000 / Mercury Nashville ✦✦✦✦✦
Fearless is the most accurately titled album in Terri Clark's catalog. It's an attempt at breaking out of the bonds of contemporary country without leaving the music entirely behind. She's since distanced herself from it because Nash Vegas—in its typical, screwed-up intolerant way—disowned it as not format friendly. Her label, thanks to visionary Luke Lewis and Keith Stegall, encouraged her to make the record she wanted to make, and promoted the hell out of it. But country radio balked. Nashville critics, and the country music press in general, didn't know what to make of it and consequently it was a

commercial failure. The bottom line is her songwriting collaborations with Mary-Chapin Carpenter, Beth Nielsen Chapman, Angelo, and Gary Burr are all dead-on. Her own songs, a killer cover of Carlene Carter and Susanna Clark's "Easy from Now On," one from Tammy Rodgers, another from Jann Arden, as well as a Carpenter and Kim Richey collaboration prove one thing: This woman knew how to pick songs that fit around a theme, taking chances and moving toward destiny. The opener, "No Fear," penned with Carpenter and featuring Steuart Smith's trademark electric guitar slashing, is sung with resolve yet without hysteria or false bravado. And along with a statement of purpose like this in life comes one in love as well. "Empty," written with Burr, is the most poetic and naked she's ever written. In the refrain, her voice begins to crack as she sings: "I want to call out for love 'til I can't breathe/I want to stare at the truth until I can't see/I want to pour out my soul 'til I'm empty. Empty, until only the flesh and bones remain...." On another of their co-writes, "Getting There," Benmont Tench drives the track as Stuart Duncan's fiddle paints the backdrop and Smith's guitars crunch the entire middle into a solid country-rocker. With its mandolin, banjos, and gentle drum loop, "Sometimes Goodbye" is one of the freshest sounding tracks to come out of Music City in 20 years. Listening to it years later, it's so obvious that Clark is not only a bright talent, but an original one. Never has a statement of broken love and a personal decision to end it sounded so affirmative. Covering "Easy from Now On" after Emmylou Harris' definitive version took guts, but in keeping with the previous track it made sense. And it's an absolutely chilling version with Harris providing the backing vocal. Like the aforementioned, it's a strong statement of determination, of affirmation, and of feminist principle in defining oneself in one's own terms. Certainly one can read plenty of autobiographical interpretations into songs like this and examine Clark's personal life, but it's irrelevant to the work of art in the disc player as it affects the listener. "The Real Thing" is a kicking bit of country-rock with a riff that comes out of Prince's "When You Were Mine." The album closes quietly with Jann Arden's "Good Mother," dedicated to the woman who raised her, and a hymn to personal transformation from the ruin and waste of past mistakes to a future uncertain but supported by the maternal connection to unconditional love. It whispers to a close with acoustic guitars and Jonathan Yudkin's cello, and in the silence, the listener feels empowered, emboldened, and just a bit wiser. Screw Nashville; this record will be regarded as a classic one day. One can only hope that Clark will reconsider one day that what she made here wasn't a mistake, but a real work of popular art. If Shania Twain displayed on her records an ounce of the integrity delivered here in full, she'd be a recording artist instead of a pop star. *—Thom Jurek*

Pain to Kill / Jan. 14, 2003 / Mercury Nashville ✦✦✦✦
Pain to Kill is Terri Clark's pop-country release after the artistic triumph—yet commercial failure—of *Fearless*. There are many things on *Pain to Kill* that are different. For one, like *Fearless*, this is the work of a mature, fully realized artist. She's well aware of her strengths and uses them to her advantage in every song on the set. Second, veteran producer Keith Stegall worked on only half this record—the latter half. Byron Gallimore produced the first half, including the first single, "I Just Wanna Be Mad." Third, none of Clark's songwriting contributions to the project appear until the second half of the record. One has to ask why. Clark is a fine songwriter, either alone or in collaboration with others. Gallimore likes country music, he likes lots of guitars (layers and layers of them), and he likes very slick production styles. His drum loops and compression on the guitars squeeze everything so tight that Clark's voice is so far out front she no longer feels as if she's part of the musical accompaniment. It's not bad; it's just very different, jarring even for someone who's been listening to her records for a while. "I Just Wanna Be Mad" was an obvious choice to open the record with a grab-you hook and tough-woman stance. But this is a tough woman who believes in standing by her man even though she's pissed. The title track is a rock & roll prime mover with Skynyrd-styled slide guitar, with about a million fiddles sawing through the mix. Clark growls her way through the lyric like she's in Black Oak Arkansas—yes, that is a compliment. The Stegall half of the record begins with a Clark and Gary Burr ballad, with a lilting piano, shimmering acoustic, and glistening pedal steel carrying the message about those who love self-destructive people. It's devastatingly real and there's no false solemnity in the body of the tune. "Almost Gone," written with Stephony Smith and Lisa Scott, is an exhortation—prodded by rows of acoustic guitars and a B-3—for a man to get his act together because the woman is on her way. The disc closes with "God and Me," written by Clark and Carol Ann Brown. Once again, here is self-determination, as well as absolute and relative truth, all considered on Sunday morning while watching preachers on television. It's simple affirmation and acknowledgment. Stegall surrounds Clark's vocal with Brent Mason playing Mark Knopfler-styled electric guitar, mandolins, acoustic guitars, and rim shots on top of floor toms. The effect is inspirational without being dogmatic—easy, light, and free with a beautiful coda. As a new chapter in the catalog of an artist who will be with listeners for a longtime, it's a fine one. *—Thom Jurek*

Joe Clay (Claiborne Joseph Cheramie)

b. 1939, Gretna, LA
Vocals (Background), Guitar, Vocals / Rockabilly
Rockabilly singer/guitarist Joe Clay was on the cusp of stardom in 1956, when he appeared on *the Ed Sullivan Show* at 17 and won a contract with RCA Records. But Sullivan, in typical repressive fashion, told the young singer to play the Platters subdued "Only You" instead of his rollicking "Duck Tail," and Clay's domineering manager refused to allow him to play outside New Orleans and eventually drove RCA away. But it wasn't the last the world would hear from Joe Clay. Born in Louisiana's Cajun territory as Claiborne Joseph Cheramie, Clay began playing in a country band at 12 which went on to get a gig on WWEZ radio. RCA created a subsidiary called Vik Records, which called the station looking for talent. The label then offered Clay a contract, to which Clay replied, "Hell yes!" Clay, who had already recorded *Sixteen Chicks*, *Goodbye Goodbye*, and *You*

Look That Good to Me in Houston, was flown to New York, where he recorded with some of the finest black rhythm musicians of the time (guitarist Mickey Baker, guitarist Skeeter Best, bassist Leonard Gaskin, and drummers Bobby Donaldson and Joe Marshall) in one of the earlier integrated studio sessions.

But the raucous music went nowhere. Clay played like Carl Perkins and Elvis Presley, and appeared on *Sullivan* months earlier than Presley, but only succeeded in playing backup on some Elvis recordings. Clay spent the next 30 years singing in the Bourbon Street lounges of New Orleans, eventually driving a bus to support himself. By the 1980s, after he'd given up performing, Clay was becoming a star in Europe, unbeknownst to him. A West German label issued a '50s revival album featuring Clay that took off, and a die-hard English promoter spent years trying to track Clay down, placing classified ads, calling DJs, and working contacts. Willie Jeffrey finally found Clay and arranged a tour of England in 1986. —*Ron DePasquale*

Ducktail / 1986 / Bear Family ✦✦✦
Collectors who cherish obscure also-rans worship Clay as a gawky godhead; his psuedo-tough cover of Rudy Grayzell's greasy "Ducktail" (a "Blue Suede Shoes" knockoff) is deemed a sublime rockabilly ruckus. —*AMG*

Philip Claypool
b. Memphis, TN
Vocals, Vocals (Background) / Contemporary Country, Country-Folk
Memphis-born country-folk performer Philip Claypool began writing songs and leading his first band while in high-school. While in college, he became a regular on the university circuit before releasing his debut, *A Circus Leaving Town*, in 1995. *Perfect World* followed four years later. —*Jason Ankeny*

● **A Circus Leaving Town** / Nov. 21, 1995 / Curb ✦✦✦
Philip Claypool's debut album *A Circus Leaving Town* is a diverse collection. Building on a solid contemporary country base, Claypool adds elements of blues, gospel, and folk, making the record a thoroughly southern affair. Much of the music and production is intriguing, saving even the weakest songs on the record. It has a slightly uneven selection of material, but *A Circus Leaving Town* remains a promising debut. —*Stephen Thomas Erlewine*

Perfect World / Jul. 6, 1999 / Curb ✦✦

Lee Clayton
b. Oct. 29, 1942, Russellville, AL
Guitar, Songwriter, Vocals, Guitar (Steel) / Progressive Country, Singer/Songwriter, Outlaw Country
Best-known for penning the outlaw country anthem "Ladies Love Outlaws," singer/songwriter Lee Clayton never achieved the same level of notoriety as some of the artists who recorded his songs. Yet in spite of a limited singing voice, he crafted some expressive, highly personal music in his own right. Clayton grew up in Oak Ridge, TN, and took up the steel guitar at age nine; after just a year and a half, he was good enough to perform on local radio. After a stint in the Air Force, Clayton moved to Nashville in 1969 to make it in the music business, and scored his first big success when Waylon Jennings turned "Ladies Love Outlaws" into a hit anthem in 1972. Clayton recorded his own self-titled debut album for MCA the following year, but despite critical praise, it wasn't commercially successful.

Clayton left Nashville for Joshua Springs, CA, but continued to pen songs for other artists; among his most notable contributions were Jerry Jeff Walker's "Lone Wolf" and Willie Nelson's "If You Could Touch Her at All." His success as a songwriter encouraged him to return to Nashville, and he signed a solo deal with Capitol in 1977. Two acclaimed albums—1978's *Border Affair* and 1979's *Naked Child*—followed, and Clayton embarked on his first world tour. However, immediately following the release of 1981's *The Dream Goes On*, he abruptly quit the music business, instead devoting his energies to writing; the '80s produced two autobiographical books and a play, *Little Boy Blue*. Clayton did eventually return to recording with 1990's *Another Night*, a live album recorded in Oslo, Norway; the same year, the Highwaymen recorded his "Silver Stallion." However, little has been heard from him since. —*Steve Huey*

Lee Clayton / 1973 / MCA ✦✦✦✦

Border Affair / 1978 / Capitol ✦✦✦✦
Undeserving of his relative obscurity, Lee Clayton belongs in the company of Waylon Jennings and other elite outlaw country-rockers. His defiance and independence are plain when he sings "Tequila Is Addictive," but he doesn't seem to give a damn, sticking to his own fiercely personal material. The album was cut in Nashville, but hot lead guitar/Memphis Horns mainstays Andrew Love and Wayne Jackson separate this from the establishment by a country mile. Sincerity makes up for any deficiencies in singing range. —*Mark Allan*

Naked Child / 1979 / Capitol ✦✦✦
Neil Wilburn, who also produced the excellent *Border Affair* the year before, casts the intensely personal outlaw manifestos on this third album much more in rock than country. By simultaneously mixing down Clayton's admittedly limited voice, the producer loses more than he gains in spite of assistance from Carlene Carter, Tracy Nelson and J.J. Cale. —*Mark Allan*

The Dream Goes On / 1981 / Capitol ✦✦✦

Another Night / 1990 / Provogue ✦✦✦

● **Border Affair/Naked Child** / Nov. 21, 1995 / Edsel ✦✦✦✦✦
In 1995, Edsel released *Border Affair/Naked Child*, which contained two complete albums—*Border Affair* (1978) and *Naked Child* (1979), both originally released on Capitol—by outlaw country singer Lee Clayton on one compact disc. —*Tim Sendra*

The Essential Lee Clayton 1978 / Nov. 15, 2002 / Repertoire ✦✦✦✦

Vassar Clements
b. Apr. 25, 1928, Kinard, SC
Fiddle, Violin / Bluegrass, Traditional Bluegrass
Combining jazz with country, Vassar Clements became one of the most distinctive, inventive, and popular fiddlers in bluegrass music. Clements first came to prominence as a member of Bill Monroe's band in the early '50s, but he never limited himself to traditional bluegrass. Over the next four decades, he distinguished himself by incorporating a number of different genres into his style. In the process, he became not only one of the most respected fiddlers in bluegrass, he also became a sought-after session musician, playing with artists as diverse as the Monkees, Hank Williams, Paul McCartney, Michelle Shocked, Vince Gill, and Bonnie Raitt. Clements taught himself to play fiddle at the age of seven. Soon afterward, he formed a band with two of his cousins. By the time he was 21, Clements' skills were impressive enough to attract the attention of Bill Monroe. Monroe hired the young fiddler and Clements appeared on the *Grand Ole Opry* with the mandolinist in 1949. The following year, the fiddler recorded his first session with Monroe.

For the next six years, Clements stayed with Monroe's band, occasionally leaving for brief periods of time. In 1957 he joined Jim & Jesse's Virginia Boys, and stayed with the band for the next four years. In the early '60s Clements was sidelined for a while as he suffered from alcoholism. By the end of the '60s he had rehabilitated, and he returned to playing in 1967. That year he moved to Nashville and began playing the tenor banjo at a residency at the Dixieland Landing Club. In 1969 he toured with Faron Young and joined John Hartford's Dobrolic Pictorial Society. The band only lasted ten months, and after its breakup Clements joined the Earl Scruggs Revue; he stayed with that band for a year. Clements began playing sessions in 1971, appearing on albums by Steve Goodman, Gordon Lightfoot, David Bromberg, J.J. Cale, and Mike Auldridge over the next two years.

In 1972 he was featured on the Nitty Gritty Dirt Band's hit album *Will the Circle Be Unbroken*, which helped establish him as a country and bluegrass star. Clements capitalized on the record's popularity in 1973, when he released his first solo album, *Crossing the Catskills*, on Rounder Records and began touring the festival and college circuits. That same year, he appeared on a number of albums, including the Grateful Dead's *Wake of the Flood*, Jimmy Buffett's *A White Sport Coat and a Pink Crustacean*, and Mickey Newbury's *Heaven Help the Child*. In 1974, Clements signed a record contract with Mercury Records, releasing two albums for the label—*Vassar Clements* and *Superbow*—the following year. That same year, he appeared in the bluegrass supergroup Old & In the Way, which also featured Jerry Garcia, David Grisman, Peter Rowan, and John Kahn. He also had a cameo role in Robert Altman's film *Nashville* in 1975. In 1977, Clements released two albums for two different labels—*The Vassar Clements Band* on MCA Records and *The Bluegrass Sessions* on Flying Fish.

It would be four years before he released another solo album. During that time, he toured constantly and appeared on numerous albums. Clements reappeared in 1981 with *Hillbilly Rides Again* and *Vassar*, which were both released on Flying Fish. During the '80s and '90s, Clements continued to record sporadically, but he cut numerous sessions for other artists and played numerous concerts every year. In 1995, Clements reunited with Old & In the Way, which released *That High Lonesome Sound* in 1996. The solo *Back Porch Swing* followed three years later; *Full Circle* appeared in spring 2001. —*Stephen Thomas Erlewine*

Crossing the Catskills / 1973 / Rounder ✦✦✦✦✦

☆ **Hillbilly Jazz** / 1975 / Flying Fish ✦✦✦✦✦
The name *Hillbilly Jazz* might sound like an oxymoron to some, but when you think about it, jazz and "hillbilly music" have made for a healthy combination from time to time. The seminal country singer Jimmie Rodgers featured Louis Armstrong as a vocalist on some of his classic 1920s recordings, and Western swing came about when, in the 1930s, Bob Wills and others combined jazz with country and bluegrass. Then, in the 1950s and early '60s, jazz and pre-rock pop influenced country-pop stars like Patsy Cline and Willie Nelson. *Hillbilly Jazz* was a project that, in 1991, drew on jazz, bluegrass, Western swing, blues, and country. With such talented players as fiddle great Vassar Clements, guitarist David Bromberg, drummer D.J. Fontana, and singer Gordon Terry on board, *Hillbilly Jazz* successfully turns its attention to everything from Wills' "San Antonio Rose" (a natural choice) to Duke Ellington's "'C' Jam Blues," Benny Goodman's "Breakfast Feud," and Les Brown's "Sentimental Journey." Improvisation is a high priority on *Hillbilly Jazz*, and a love of improvisation is one thing that jazz, bluegrass, and Western swing players have in common. This rewarding but little-known CD reminds listeners that jazz and "hillbilly music" can fit together quite nicely. —*Alex Henderson*

Vassar Clements / Sep. 1975 / Mercury ✦✦✦

Superbow / 1976 / Mercury ✦✦✦

The Bluegrass Sessions / 1977 / Flying Fish ✦✦✦✦✦

Nashville Jam / 1979 / Flying Fish ✦✦✦
As you may guess from the title, this album features a lively jam session with many greats in bluegrass music. —*AMG*

Vassar / 1980 / Flying Fish ✦✦✦
This album features Clements strutting his stuff on jazz fiddle with sympathetic backing from his band. Clements is one of the very best on his instrument, and the album showcases his talent. —*AMG*

Westport Drive / 1984 / Mind Dust Music ✦✦✦

Hillbilly Jazz Rides Again / 1987 / Flying Fish ✦✦✦
Hillbilly Jazz Rides Again is a collection of Western swing revival by Vassar Clements, a former sideman for Bill Monroe. With pianist Bob Hoban and guitarists Dave Salyer and Doug Jemigan in tow, the album actually veers closer to swing than Western, which isn't necessarily a bad thing. However, the performances aren't always inspired, which

becomes even more noticeable on the numerous mediocre original songs by Hoban. —*Stephen Thomas Erlewine*

Vassar Clements, John Hartford, Dave Holland / 1988 / Rounder ✦✦✦✦
Vassar Clements is the star here, but John Hartford and Dave Holland hold their own. Besides each contributing tunes, Hartford and Holland combine on the wonderful "Till Something Better Comes Along." Hartford's singing is almost comic relief, but nobody's really going to sweat it on this charming little gem. Put it on and let your mind roam to the hills and the streams and the simple life. —*Mark Allan*

Grass Routes / 1991 / Rounder ✦✦✦
This recent album shows why Clements is one of the greatest fiddlers in modern country music. —*Mark A. Humphrey*

Once in a While / 1993 / Flying Fish ✦✦✦
Violinist Vassar Clements has demonstrated the improvisatory link between bluegrass and jazz, and this was another example of the two styles' affinity. Clements' soaring phrases and adept solos were right at home on such standard jazz tunes as "Perdido," "Cherokee" and "Sonnymoon For Two," but he didn't stray far from his favorite breakdown riffs or signature country sound. The results were the kind of loose, joyous jam date where labels meant nothing, and musicianship rather than genre ruled. —*Ron Wynn*

Vassar's Jazz / 1996 / Winter Harvest ✦✦✦✦
Best known as a country fiddler, veteran Vassar Clements has occasionally recorded in jazz settings through the years. On this set, he is joined by a guitar/piano/bass/drums rhythm section with pianist Stephen Davidowski occasionally contributing a tenor solo. With the exception of one song written by bassist Gene Watson and one co-written by Clements and Jake Landers, all 11 numbers on this set were co-written by Clements and his wife, Millie Clements, although several sound as if they could have been standards in the 1930s. Clements' violin playing hints at times at Stephane Grappelli and Bob Wills, but is fairly original. This is one of his best jazz-oriented sets. —*Scott Yanow*

20 Fiddle Tunes & Waltz Favorites / Oct. 27, 1998 / Rural Rhythm ✦✦✦

Bottom Line Encore Collection / Apr. 27, 1999 / Bottom Line ✦✦✦

● **Back Porch Swing** / Nov. 30, 1999 / Cedar Glen ✦✦✦✦
Vassar Clements has always been one of the most recognizable fiddlers in bluegrass. When he steps to the mike to take a solo, the most foursquare traditional breakdown or reel takes on a jazzy, swinging flavor—one that generally disappears as soon as his solo ends. On this album, he moves well away from the whole bluegrass genre, opting instead for the accompaniment of a jazz band and a program of undiluted swing, jazz, and R&B. Opening with a burning rendition of Jelly Roll Morton's "King Porter Stomp," Clements delivers one original (the thoroughly charming "Hillbilly Jazz"), several standards ("That Old Black Magic," "String of Pearls") and a handful of numbers by his pianist, Fred Bogert. Bogert's "If That's Love" sounds like it came straight out of Muscle Shoals, with Clements' slinky fiddle weaving in, out, and around the sturdy drumming and funky bass. "Ezra's Holler" is a sort of modified bossa nova on which Clements plays the head in unison with sax player Paul Martin Zonn, to very fine effect. Just about everything on this album is both musically interesting and lots of fun. Highly recommended. —*Rick Anderson*

Full Circle / Jun. 12, 2001 / Oms ✦✦✦
Except for Bill Monroe, there is probably no figure in bluegrass music who commands as much respect across so many musical boundaries as fiddler Vassar Clements. Having fiddled not only with such bluegrass eminences as Monroe and Jim & Jesse, but also for the Grateful Dead and Dickey Betts, among many others, his name is spoken with reverence in just about every circle of American music. But his most famous recording is the one he made with the Nitty Gritty Dirt Band and a host of other bluegrass and country music stars, the now-legendary *Will the Circle Be Unbroken*. This album's title makes reference to that release and employs a similar (if much more restricted) approach to studio personnel—he's joined here by Jim & Jesse (on the standard "Hard Hearted"), Ricky Skaggs (on the lovely "Your Love Is Like a Flower"), banjoist J.D. Crowe, mandolinist Sam Bush, and many others. The result is mostly very good, but occasionally disappointing. Interestingly, the least interesting songs are the ones that cross genre boundaries most boldly—a muscular take on Cream's "White Room" (sung by the insufferable John Cowan) and a really awful instrumental rendition of "Yesterday." However, the group's cover of the Beatles' "I've Just Seen a Face" works very nicely, and the more traditional material is uniformly excellent. Clements leads the band through a barn-burning performance of the Monroe instrumental "Tall Timber," and Peter Rowan makes a nice appearance on "When the Golden Leaves Begin to Fall." Fans will love this album, and newcomers will find plenty to enjoy as well. —*Rick Anderson*

Bill Clifton (William Marburg)

b. 1931, Riderwood, MD
Piano, Guitar, Autoharp, Vocals / Traditional Bluegrass, Traditional Country
If you attend a bluegrass festival, thank Bill Clifton for having the idea to present the very first one. Clifton was not the most famous of the first generation of bluegrass artists, but he did much to establish the idea of bluegrass as a preserver of half-forgotten songs and styles. Clifton's background was hardly a typical one for bluegrass—although the players who would populate the distinctive Washington, D.C., bluegrass scene often shared Clifton's professional background. He was born William Marburg to a wealthy family in Riderwood, MD, in suburban Baltimore County. As a child, he became fascinated by country music he heard on the radio. A folk-music enthusiast, he made the obligatory trip to New York to visit Woody Guthrie. Attending graduate school in business at the University of Virginia, he formed a trio called the Dixie Mountain Boys with folksingers

Paul Clayton and Dave Sadler, adopting the stage name Bill Clifton because his family objected to his musical activities.

In 1952, the group made their first recordings and enjoyed some regional success. The trio then added banjoist Johnny Clark and began playing more traditional bluegrass music. After signing with Blue Ridge Records, they appeared on the *Wheeling Jamboree* radio barn-dance program. While there, Clifton made the acquaintance of the Stanley Brothers and A.P. Carter. In 1955 he published a songbook, *150 Old-Time Folk and Gospel Songs*, which circulated widely among bluegrass musicians. After a stint in the military, he began recording in the late '50s, releasing five albums over the next seven years. They were suffused with the sentimental imagery of old-time songs, and several singles, including "Little Whitewashed Chimney," became bona fide hits and bluegrass standards.

On July 4, 1961, Clifton organized an outdoor "Bluegrass Day" concert at Oak Leaf Park in Luray, VA, featuring a reunion of Bill Monroe's original bluegrass boys, the Stanley Brothers, the Country Gentlemen, Jim & Jesse, and several other top bluegrass acts. Although it was only an all-day rather than weekend-long event, the concert is generally recognized as the first bluegrass festival, as the progenitor of the hundreds of grassroots campground gatherings that flourish annually all over the U.S. and Canada. Clifton's concert didn't make much of a splash with the general public at the time, but key figures in the folk-music world were paying close attention. Clifton himself was hired as one of the organizers of the Newport Folk Festival in 1963, and Carlton Haney, one of the attendees at Clifton's Luray concert, went on to organize a larger event in Roanoke in 1965. From that point on, the modern bluegrass-festival movement grew rapidly.

In 1963, Clifton and his family moved to England; he played in local clubs and other small venues around Europe. In 1967 he joined the Peace Corps and spent three years in the Philippines. While there, he visited New Zealand, recording an album with the Hamilton County Bluegrass Band. Clifton occasionally returned to the U.S. to record, and also kept recording in Europe. In 1972, he returned briefly to America to play his first bluegrass festival circuit. Encouraged by the experience, he began visiting the U.S. more frequently and recorded more regularly, signing with County Records. For his third album on the label, he formed the First Generation with mandolinist Red Rector and banjoist Don Stover. After the album's release, the trio toured the bluegrass circuit for the remainder of the 1970s. In the early '80s, Clifton and his family moved to Virginia, where he worked as a businessman. However, Clifton continued to perform at bluegrass festivals and occasional concerts into the 21st century. —*Sandra Brennan & James Manheim*

Are You From Dixie / 1971 / Bear Family ✦✦✦
Since both the artists involved in this collaboration are top-flight bluegrass musicians, the inevitable question concerning this recording is: Why it is so dull? Mandolinist Red Rector, known for hard-driving and technically intricate soloing, seems to be having a bad day in the studio, or else was attempting to see how many times he could use the same licks on one record, a musical contest that he neither invented nor should have participated in. A guitar and mandolin album could and should be a beautiful thing, as these lovely sounding instruments have the ability to create their own world in which a listener would not miss the other instruments in a bluegrass band, such as banjo or fiddle. But with Rector turning in such an uninspired performance, the onus is really on his partner to save the day, and again the Mighty Mouse outfit must have been at the dry cleaner's. Clifton drives the rhythm along nicely, and he better since his axe is the whole rhythm section here. But his vocals miss the mark completely, not technically problematic but lacking any sort of motivation. Sally Feldman said it best when she wrote in 1971 that "Clifton's voice is so bland that it could make a Sex Pistols song sound like a campfire favorite." This must have been the only time the name of this British band appeared in an old-time music journal, by the way, and how was the reviewer to know that by the year 2000, Sex Pistols songs would have actually become campfire favorites? The comment still applies, however. The best parts of the album are the instrumental numbers, which might lead a listener to surmise that it was the vocals that were wearing Rector down. —*Eugene Chadbourne*

Getting Folk / 1972 / Bear Family ✦✦✦✦✦

★ **The Early Years (1957–1958)** / Jun. 15, 1992 / Rounder ✦✦✦✦✦
Bill Clifton was one of bluegrass's finest guitarists and also an underrated vocalist. He was especially gripping on slow, aching tunes like "Lonely Heart Blues" or gospel numbers like "I'm Living the Right Life Now" and "When You Kneel at Your Mother's Grave." Clifton's late-'50s singles were collected on this CD, featuring him working alongside such musicians as Curley Lambert on mandolin and Johnny Clark on banjo, as well as fiddler Tommy Jackson, Ralph Stanley on banjo and Gordon Terry on fiddle. These songs are light-years away from the polished, intricate newgrass and contemporary bluegrass sounds of the 1980s and '90s. The harmonies, leads, solos and arrangements reflect simpler, more innocent times, but don't lack intensity or musical quality. —*Ron Wynn*

Beatle Crazy / Dec. 25, 1999 / Bear Family ✦✦✦✦

Around the World to Poor Valley / Jun. 13, 2001 / Bear Family ✦✦✦✦

Patsy Cline

b. Sep. 8, 1932, Gore, VA, **d.** Mar. 5, 1963, Camden, TN
Vocals, Piano / Traditional Country, Rockabilly, Nashville Sound/Countrypolitan
One of the greatest singers in the history of country music, Patsy Cline also helped blaze a trail for female singers to assert themselves as an integral part of the Nashville-dominated country music industry. She was not alone in this regard; Kitty Wells had become a star several years before Cline's big hits in the early '60s. Brenda Lee, who shared Cline's producer, did just as much to create a country-pop crossover during the same era; Skeeter Davis briefly enjoyed similar success. Cline has the most legendary aura of any female country singer, however, perhaps due to an early death that cut her off just after she had entered her prime.

Cline began recording in the mid-'50s, and although she recorded quite a bit of material between 1955 and 1960 (17 singles in all), only one of them was a hit. That song,

"Walkin' After Midnight," was both a classic and a Top 20 pop smash. Those who are accustomed to Cline's famous early-'60s hits are in for a bit of a shock when surveying her '50s sessions (which have been reissued on several Rhino compilations). At times she sang flat-out rockabilly; she also tried some churchy tear-weepers. She couldn't follow-up "Walkin' After Midnight," however, in part because of an exploitative deal that limited her to songs from one publishing company. Circumstances were not wholly to blame for Cline's commercial failures. She would have never made it as a rockabilly singer, lacking the conviction of Wanda Jackson or the spunk of Brenda Lee. In fact, in comparison with her best work, she sounds rather stiff and ill-at-ease on most of her early singles. Things took a radical turn for the better on all fronts in 1960, when her initial contract expired. With the help of producer Owen Bradley (who had worked on her sessions all along), Cline began selecting material that was both more suitable and of a higher quality than her previous outings.

"I Fall to Pieces," cut at the very first session where Cline was at liberty to record what she wanted, was the turning point in her career. Reaching number one in the country charts and number-12 pop, it was the first of several country-pop crossovers she was to enjoy over the next couple of years. More important, it set a prototype for commercial Nashville country at its best. Owen Bradley crafted lush orchestral arrangements, with weeping strings and backup vocals by the Jordanaires, that owed more to pop (in the best sense) than country. The country elements were provided by the cream of Nashville's session musicians, including guitarist Hank Garland, pianist Floyd Cramer, and drummer Buddy Harmon. Cline's voice sounded richer, more confident, and more mature, with ageless wise and vulnerable qualities that have enabled her records to maintain their appeal with subsequent generations. When k.d. lang recorded her 1988 album *Shadowland* with Owen Bradley, it was this phase of Cline's career that she was specifically attempting to emulate.

It's arguable that too much has been made of Cline's crossover appeal to the pop market. Brenda Lee, whose records were graced with similar Bradley productions, was actually more successful in this area (although her records were likely targeted toward a younger audience). Cline's appeal was undeniably more adult, but she was always more successful with country listeners. Her final four Top Ten country singles, in fact, didn't make the pop Top 40. Despite a severe auto accident in 1961, Cline remained hot through 1961 and 1962, with "Crazy" and "She's Got You" both becoming big country and pop hits. Much of her achingly romantic material was supplied by fresh talent like Hank Cochran, Harlan Howard, and Willie Nelson (who penned "Crazy").

Although her commercial momentum had faded slightly, she was still at the top of her game when she died in a plane crash in March of 1963, at the age of 30. She was only a big star for a couple of years, but her influence was and remains huge. While the standards of professionalism on her recordings have been emulated ever since, they've rarely been complemented by as much palpable, at times heartbreaking emotion in the performances. For those who could do without some of more elaborate arrangements of her later years, many of her relatively unadorned appearances on radio broadcasts have been thankfully preserved and issued. *—Richie Unterberger*

Patsy Cline Showcase / 1961 / MCA ✦✦✦
One of only three albums released in her lifetime, *Showcase* was the first set of sessions after her near-death in a car crash in 1961. The recordings teamed her up with the Jordanaires and produced the hits "Crazy" and "I Fall to Pieces" as well as new, more stylized versions of "Walkin' After Midnight" and that single's original flip, "A Poor Man's Roses (Or a Rich Man's Gold)." This release features the second cover photo that was issued after her death, replacing the original cover art. *—Cub Koda*

Sentimentally Yours / 1962 / MCA ✦✦✦✦
There is an exact blend of country and pop that went into the classic albums by this enchanting country songstress. Anyone capable of reproducing this formula would be followed everywhere by country artists and pop stars. Unfortunately, what actually happened in the era of this music's first wave of popularity was that everyone cooked up an individual recipe. And many of these productions had as much good taste as spaghetti sauce does after someone stirs in the burned bits from the bottom of the pan. Producer Owen Bradley's approach to Patsy Cline does have its moments of bad taste as well, and even the biggest fans of these albums will have moments when they will wish the male vocal chorus had gotten caught in traffic somewhere in the pretzel of Nashville's freeway system. Air and forget these complaints, because what is here is a rare type of country music that maintains its identity without marching forward with the usual troops of pedal steel and twangy guitars. The combo sound that is created has an incredibly light swing—the drummer is often using brushes—and there is an effortless sense of propulsion through rhythm arrangements both catchy and intelligent. What she and the musicians do with the numbers by Hank Williams is nothing short of a revelation, while the ballads such as "Lonely Street" are done with a moody flair that has never quite been matched. *—Eugene Chadbourne*

The Patsy Cline Story / 1963 / MCA ✦✦✦
The Patsy Cline Story is a double-record, 24-track collection that Decca released in 1963, shortly after her tragic death. The compilation remains one of the strongest and most thorough retrospectives ever assembled, featuring most of her biggest hits—"Walking After Midnight," "She's Got You," "Crazy," "I Fall to Pieces," "Sweet Dreams"—plus a number of lesser-known gems like "Why Can't He Be You" and "Leavin' on Your Mind." The presence of these relatively unfamiliar tracks means that the album gives a more rounded and complete picture of Cline's career than *12 Greatest Hits*, even if it isn't as thorough as the subsequent four-disc box set *The Patsy Cline Collection*. In short, *The Patsy Cline Story* is the ideal introduction for a listener who wants a little more than the basics, but doesn't want to invest in a box set. *—Stephen Thomas Erlewine*

That's How a Heartache Begins / 1964 / Decca ✦✦✦
A certain level of consistency marks all the Patsy Cline recordings for Decca, many of which were recycled in their entirety by MCA when it bought out the older company's catalog. This is business as usual for the supreme country songstress, mixing up some Tin Pan Alley material with hardcore country and a few choices out of left field, some of which are a bit unfortunate, such as "Bill Bailey, Won't You Please Come Home." It is true that this is a singer who could rend emotion from the label under a sofa, but these albums go by quickly and the best of the bunch are the ones with the highest quotient of classic songs. The high point here has to be her version of "Lovesick Blues," in which the supposedly carved-in-stone association with Hank Williams quickly crumbles as the sassy, honky tonk-with-class arrangement sets in. There's also some good material from Harlan Howard and Hank Cochran, but in summation there are other albums in this series that Cline collectors might want to grab first. *—Eugene Chadbourne*

☆ **Patsy Cline's Greatest Hits** / 1967 / Decca ✦✦✦✦✦
This is the standard collection of Patsy Cline's most successful singles, containing among its 12 tracks seven of her eight Top Ten country hits, 1957-1963. *—William Ruhlmann*

Country Great / 1969 / Universal Special Products ✦✦✦✦
Country Great is essentially a retitled re-release of Patsy Cline's eponymous first album for Decca. Working with Owen Bradley, Cline tackles a number of different styles, from straight-ahead country to swinging blues, dazzling at each step of the way. There may not be any huge hits that jump out to the casual listener, but discerning fans will realize that any album containing "That Wonderful Someone," "Too Many Secrets," "Then You'll Know" and "Three Cigarettes (In an Ashtray)" is essential listening. *—Stephen Thomas Erlewine*

Last Sessions / 1985 / MCA ✦✦✦

Sweet Dreams / 1985 / MCA ✦✦✦✦✦

★ **12 Greatest Hits** / 1988 / MCA ✦✦✦✦✦
12 Greatest Hits is exactly what it says it is—12 of Patsy Cline's biggest hits, including all of her classic singles: "Walkin' After Midnight," "I Fall to Pieces," "Sweet Dreams," "Crazy," "She's Got You," "Faded Love," and "Leavin' on Your Mind." There's also a number of lesser-known gems like "Why Can't He Be You," which are as good as the big hits. *12 Greatest Hits* may be brief, but it contains absolutely no filler and leaves no gaps, making it the perfect introduction to one of the greatest singers in country music history. *—Stephen Thomas Erlewine*

Live at the Opry / 1988 / MCA ✦✦✦

Her First Recordings, Vol. 1: Walkin' Dreams / 1989 / Rhino ✦✦✦✦✦
Although Cline recorded quite a bit during the last half of the 1950s, it was a frustrating period for her, both commercially and artistically. Commercially, there was only one hit; artistically, she had yet to perfect her delivery, and didn't have access to nearly as much first-rate material as she would later on. Rhino's three-part *Her First Recordings* series presents a few dozen sides from this era. While they aren't as impressive as her more widely known '60s recordings, they're worthwhile both for the occasional first-rate performance and the illustration of the various approaches Cline and producer Owen Bradley attempted in her formative days. *Vol. 1,* focusing on recordings from 1955-1957, is variable in both style and quality, as Cline tries out spirituals, melodramatic ballads, and upbeat country-pop. Includes "Walkin' After Midnight," which is the original pop Top 20 version, not the later re-recording that is featured on many compilations. *—Richie Unterberger*

Her First Recordings, Vol. 2: Hungry for Love / 1989 / Rhino ✦✦✦✦✦
The second installment of *Her First Recordings*, with 14 tracks from 1957-1959, is more pop-oriented than *Vol. 1,* and perhaps less interesting because of that. It does show Cline and producer Owen Bradley beginning to develop the Nashville sound that would serve her well in the '60s, with contributions from such regulars as the Anita Kerr Singers, the Jordanaires, Floyd Cramer, Grady Martin, and Hank Garland. With some more work and better material, the prototype would pay big dividends just a year or two down the road. *—Richie Unterberger*

Her First Recordings, Vol. 3: Rockin' Side / 1989 / Rhino ✦✦✦✦✦
Patsy Cline—rocker? Well, sort of. At the outset of her recording career in the late '50s, Cline tried a variety of approaches, including rockabilly and uptempo hillbilly. This disc assembles 13 of her rockabilly flavored recordings from 1956-1959. It's not bad, but rockabilly was not Cline's forte—she was much more at ease with ballads and midtempo numbers with a heavier pop/country feel. In comparison with '50s female rockabilly singers like Brenda Lee (who shared Cline's producer), Patsy comes off as rather stiff and inhibited. "Stop, Look and Listen" (1956) is the clear highlight here, with a natural snare-paced groove absent from the other tracks. *—Richie Unterberger*

Live, Vol. 2 / 1989 / MCA ✦✦✦✦✦
A sequel to *Live at the Opry*, it's not called *Live at the Opry, Vol. 2* because it wasn't taken from *Opry* broadcasts, but from radio shows produced for the U.S. Navy and Armed Forces. The 12 performances date from 1956 to 1962, and are of special interest in that they include five songs that she never recorded in the studio for commercial release, including numbers by Roger Miller, Webb Pierce, and Sonny James. Cline's in good form throughout, the fidelity is very good, and the arrangements are on the whole considerably sparer than her studio recordings were wont to employ. The straight-ahead reading of "Strange," a top-notch 1962 Mel Tillis composition that went on the B-side of "She's Got You," is a particular highlight. A good album that will appeal to most country fans, not just Cline collectors. *—Richie Unterberger*

☆ **The Patsy Cline Collection** / 1991 / MCA ✦✦✦✦✦
If an artist ever deserved a box set chronicling her entire career, it is Patsy Cline. Having recorded 102 sides between 1955 and her death at the age of 30 in 1963, Cline changed not only country music forever, but affected the world of pop as well. Over four CDs, arranged chronologically, the listener gets treated to a story in the development and maturation of a cultural icon who was at least, in terms of her gift, the equal of her legend.

Discs one and two document the recordings Cline made for the 4-Star label between 1955 and 1960. Here are not only the roots and branches of Cline as a song stylist, but also the full arrival of the artist. Cline recorded honky tonk, gospel, some bluegrass, and country standards as well as some awe-inspiring rockabilly. Her voice takes the heart of each song, bends it to her emotional will, and transforms it into a vehicle for the listener to carry within herself. Some of the songs here are radio transcriptions that were tacked onto singles as B-sides, while others are alternate takes, but the vast majority were officially released tracks. Along with a 1954 radio transcription of Cliff Grimsley's honky tonk boogie number "Walking the Dog" is a live version of J.D. Miller's classic "It Wasn't God Who Made Honky Tonk Angels" from the same program. But the rockabilly of Sammy Masters' "Turn the Cards Slowly" from 1955 is a woolly departure. In early 1956, Cline scored "I Don't Wanna," with her mature style making its first impression on wax. "Stop Look & Listen" was another venture into rockabilly that would not have been out of place on a Johnny Burnette or Gene Vincent record. But only a few months later Cline was in the studio recording the definitive version of Webb Pierce's "Yes, I Know Why." The initial version of "Walking After Midnight" with its lazy, swinging Western stroll that shuffled slowly enough for a Bob Wills tune and was gutsy enough to be a slow rockabilly number was recorded the same year. From here to end of disc one, the tracks become more and more consistent while the voice takes more and more chances with its prowess and emotional range. "Try Again," from April of 1957, is so lush it could have been rearranged by Nelson Riddle. So smooth and beautiful is the tune, it left a lot of country fans at the time scratching their heads. Disc two, which documents 1958-1960, offers the listener Cline completing her restless transition from a country singer who experimented with different styles to a vocalist who mastered any type of music she set her voice to sing. Here are the tracks like "Crazy Dreams," "Loose Talk," "I Fall to Pieces," "San Antonio Rose," "Lovesick Blues," "Gotta Lotta Rhythm in My Soul," and the amazingly unheard "How Can I Face Tomorrow." The third disc, which charts her transition to Decca Records, is comprised of some of the greatest torch songs released between 1961 and 1962, among them "Crazy," "Have You Ever Been Lonely," "You Made Me Love You," the single version of "Walkin' After Midnight" that became an international smash, and the haunting "That's My Desire." Finally, in the last year and a half of her life, Cline had become a singer that other writers sought out. There are the single and radio transcription versions of "Leavin' on Your Mind," a rollicking read of "Blue Moon of Kentucky" (that blows Elvis' away), "Always," "Crazy Arms," "He Called Me Baby," "Sweet Dreams (Of You)," and the last track she ever cut, "Just a Closer Walk With Thee." Eerie, isn't it? In addition to the 102 tracks here is a booklet packed with photos, complete session notes, interviews with surviving *Grand Ole Opry* members, a reprint of the *Nashville Banner*'s front page reporting the fatal crash that killed Cline, Cowboy Copas, Hawkshaw Hawkins, and others, and excellent liner notes by Paul Kingsbury of the Country Music Foundation. It's indispensable, comprehensive, and not nearly enough. *—Thom Jurek*

At Her Best / Aug. 29, 1992 / International Marketing Group ♦♦♦

Not strictly a hits collection, *At Her Best* is an excellent but brief, nine-track album that features several of Patsy's most familiar songs ("Walkin' After Midnight," "Just Out of Reach"), plus many wonderful lesser-known gems, like "Stop the World," "Too Many Secrets," and "Life's Railway to Heaven." *—Stephen Thomas Erlewine*

Today, Tomorrow and Forever / 1993 / Sony Special Products ♦♦♦

Today, Tomorrow and Forever is easily one of the most popular titles in Patsy Cline's catalog—and, in this case, the word "title" refers to the *name* of the record, not the record itself. This title has been recycled numerous times since her tragic death, presumably because it offers a fitting tribute to her legacy. Each collection that sports the name is considerably different, usually sharing only the title track, but sometimes more than one. Sony Music Special Products—who licensed all of the material from Masters International—turns out one of the better *Today, Tomorrow and Forever* albums with their ten-track disc. Apart from "Walkin' After Midnight," there aren't too many crossover hits here, but each track is very good, with the quality often—in the case of "Three Cigarettes in an Ashtray," "Stop the World (And Let Me Off)," and "Walking Dream"—verging on the excellent. True, most collectors will have these songs on better, more coherent compilations, but this isn't a bad choice for listeners on a budget. *—Stephen Thomas Erlewine*

Classics Collection: Patsy Cline / May 3, 1994 / Curb ♦♦♦

Classics Collection has a weird cross-section of songs from Patsy Cline, featuring hits ("Lonely Street," "Lovesick Blues"), lesser-known singles, and B-sides. Most of the material here is very, very good, but listeners looking for a hits collection should go elsewhere. *—Stephen Thomas Erlewine*

Crazy Dreams / Dec. 12, 1995 / Sundown ♦♦♦

Patsy Cline's early recordings for the 4-Star label show that this country music legend was far from infallible. Her musical instincts weren't always good, as evidenced by her penchant for ending nearly every song on a bombastic high note, and, of course, her personal tastes ran to hard country rather than the crossover material that made her famous (and was arguably better-suited to her talents). Cline's early recordings appear on countless budget discs, but *Crazy Dreams* collects them all in one place. Besides the original hit version of "Walkin' After Midnight," this two-disc set covers an assortment of gospel, rockabilly, and country recordings that are in many cases quite different from her more soulful and pop-oriented Decca hits. These sides are worth hearing for their historical value, and there are several songs and performances here of high quality, but there is also a shortage of good material. Most of these tracks are duplicated on the *Patsy Cline Collection* box set, but completists will want *Crazy Dreams* for the handful that are omitted. *—Greg Adams*

The Birth of a Star / 1996 / Razor & Tie ♦♦♦

Although Cline only had one hit in the late '50s ("Walking After Midnight"), she managed to appear on Arthur Godfrey's popular network television show several times in 1957-1958. This disc presents 17 performances that she delivered on these programs (including two versions of "Walking After Midnight"), accompanied by Godfrey's house band. In truth, this isn't the best context in which to hear Cline. It's far more pop than country in orientation, especially given the mainstream flavor of her accompanists, whose arrangements were far from rootsy and could be downright square, especially with the frequent interjections of brass and clarinet. Cline herself had yet to reach her vocal peak, but she does project with assurance on this material, most of which was issued in the late '50s on her official (and better) studio recordings. It's not one of the first Cline albums that should be added to your collection, but it's certainly of considerable interest to serious Cline fans, with versions of "Your Cheatin' Heart" and the spirituals "Down By the Riverside" and "The Man Upstairs" rating as the most unusual items. *—Richie Unterberger*

Crazy Dreams: The Four Star Years / 1996 / Magnum ♦♦♦♦♦

The Four Star Years is a double-disc set that contains all 50 recordings that Patsy Cline made for the Four Star record label in the mid-'50s. Recorded before she signed to Decca, these recordings represent Cline at her rawest and roughest—there are none of the string arrangements that graced many of her biggest Decca hits. Since Four Star forced her to sing songs that their company published, the quality of the material is somewhat uneven, but the performances are all first-rate and the set is essential for any serious Patsy Cline fan. *—Stephen Thomas Erlewine*

Crazy Dreams: The Classic Early Years / May 20, 1997 / Music Club ♦♦♦

Patsy Cline's early recordings for Bill McCall's Four Star label were a mixed batch. Tied to his restrictive production practices of only letting her record songs he held the copyrights to for the first five years of her recording career, Patsy was often stuck doing substandard material. She would never record a bluesier, more back-shack number like her first hit, "Walking After Midnight" (not even coming close on the later re-recording of it for Decca), but like a street toughie facing impossible odds, she gave as good as she got, injecting her already evolving stylistic flair into slight offerings like "Hungry for Love," "I Cried All the Way to the Altar," and "Three Cigarettes in an Ashtray." Early sides like "Hidin' Out," "A Church, a Courtroom and Then Goodbye," "I Go to Church on Sunday," and "Pick Me Up on Your Way Down" are all songs far better-suited to Kitty Wells, but Cline's approach is both musical and varied, given the sawing fiddles and paint-by-numbers backing. A hint of her style to come surfaces on the bluesy "There He Goes," the rocking "Stop Look and Listen," the brassy take on "Lovesick Blues," and the orchestrated "A Poor Man's Roses or a Rich Man's Gold," country with a strong vein of pop ballad running through it. This material has been repackaged countless times, and all 51 tracks she cut for McCall are available on a double-disc set, but this 18-track collection cherry-picks through most of the dross and makes for better overall listening. While most of this pales in comparison to her later hits, it's nonetheless a fine collection showing that a star was already in the making, emerging from the cookie-cutter material she was saddled with. *—Cub Koda*

Live at the Cimarron Ballroom / Jul. 29, 1997 / MCA ♦♦♦♦♦

Recorded at a Tulsa, OK, show on July 29, 1961, this newly released concert performance captures Patsy Cline at what was then a new peak in her professional career, enjoying her first number-one country hit at the time with "I Fall to Pieces." The set she does on this disc includes that song, along with "Walking After Midnight," "Bill Bailey, Won't You Please Come Home," "Stupid Cupid," "Shake, Rattle & Roll," "Lovesick Blues," "When My Dreamboat Comes Home," and "A Poor Man's Roses or a Rich Man's Gold." She's in good form, although, alas, hardly at the peak of her powers—the singer had barely survived an automobile accident 15 days earlier, and was on crutches and still bore scars on her face. She talks rather freely about the accident at one point and seems to be in good spirits, and this is, in many ways, a typical show of hers (although many numbers she did haven't survived on the tape), but probably not the one that she would have wanted to represent her concert work to posterity. Her raspy enthusiasm on "Shake, Rattle & Roll" is effective, and everything here works, especially the eight-piece band backing her up, although they're somewhat under-recorded. Still, any newly discovered Patsy Cline performances are worth hearing, and this one especially, as the closest thing to an official live album that we'll ever see. *—Bruce Eder*

Live Broadcasts / Apr. 10, 1997 / Razor & Tie ♦♦♦

EMI/Capitol Special Markets and Razor & Tie released *Live Broadcasts* in 1997. The disc was a distilled ten-track version of Razor & Tie's *The Birth of a Star*, which featured 17 songs she performed on *the Arthur Godfrey Show* between 1957-1958. That compilation was a boon for collectors, but the purpose of *Live Broadcasts* is a little puzzling. Surely any serious Cline fan who wants these rare broadcasts would only buy them on *The Birth of a Star*, since it is a comprehensive overview, complete with liner notes and dialogue from the program. Casual fans of Cline will not be interested in this material, not only because it is live, but because there aren't many hits and the arrangements are more pop than country. There certainly is some good (or at least interesting) music on *Live Broadcasts*, but truth be told, it's better-heard on *The Birth of a Star*, even if this budget-price disc is considerably cheaper than its parent. *—Stephen Thomas Erlewine*

Walkin' After Midnight: The Very Best of Patsy Cline / Jul. 28, 1998 / Collectables ♦♦♦♦

Don't take the title of *Walkin' After Midnight: The Very Best of Patsy Cline* too literally, because the disc is not a hits compilation. Instead, it's a collection of 24 songs she recorded for the Four Star label before she had her breakthrough hit, "Walkin' After Midnight." That single is included here, along with covers of familiar country hits from that era, plus a number of lesser-known country tunes. The material may be a little uneven, but throughout it all, Cline's voice shines. Furthermore, the collection earns points for offering a generous number of lesser-known recordings which aren't always that easy to acquire on CD. As long as you're not expecting a hits package and you're a dedicated fan, *Walkin' After Midnight* is a good disc to have. *—Stephen Thomas Erlewine*

20th Century Masters—The Millennium Collection: The Best of Patsy Cline / Jul. 20, 1999 / MCA ✦✦✦

Patsy Cline's *20th Century Masters—The Millennium Collection* gathers some of her better-known songs, including "Your Cheatin' Heart," "Crazy Arms," "I Love You So Much," and "Always." Yet the collection fails to include definitive Cline tracks such as "Crazy," "Walkin' After Midnight," or "I Fall to Pieces," to name a few. Whether or not this has to do with the licensing or publishing rights to her best-known singles, this compilation doesn't really work as either a career overview or a concise best-of package. Still, the songs included here are more than worthwhile, so this album may please fans looking for a collection of her slightly lesser-known singles. *—Heather Phares*

Duets, Vol. 1 / Sep. 14, 1999 / Crash ✦✦

Maybe *Patsy Cline: Duets* was conceived as a way to bring Cline's classic music to a new generation, maybe the artists involved with the record have genuine love and respect for Cline plus the desire to duet with one of the greatest vocalists of the 20th century, but it's still hard to imagine why the record of electronic duets was made. There is no interaction on electronic duets and it often sounds very, very creepy. Sure, a few tracks work fairly well—Glen Campbell, Willie Nelson, and Waylon Jennings are such seasoned professionals that it almost seems like they are singing with Cline instead of a tape—but most of this is awkward or stilted, such as Bob Carlisle's mis-matched opening, "That Wonderful Someone." Perhaps fans of the duet partners or Cline will find this to be a curiosity, but they'd be better off with the original Cline classics or covers. *—Stephen Thomas Erlewine*

True Love: A Standards Collection / Apr. 25, 2000 / MCA ✦✦✦✦

True Love: A Standards Collection presents Patsy Cline's pop side with a variety of classic songs like "I Love You So Much It Hurts," "You Belong to Me," "Bill Bailey, Won't You Please Come Home," and "Always," which was a Top 20 country hit. All of the tracks, recorded between 1961 and 1963, feature Owen Bradley's lush arrangements and have been digitally remastered. Though Cline's best work always had a strong pop element to it anyway, *True Love: A Standards Collection* is another welcome reminder that her voice still transcends musical genres. *—Heather Phares*

25 All-Time Greatest Recordings: The 4-Star Sessions 1955-1960 / Sep. 12, 2000 / Varese ✦✦✦✦

Varese's 2000 collection is billed as *25 All-Time Greatest Recordings* but pay attention to the subtitle—it makes clear that this is "The 4-Star Sessions 1955-1960," recordings made before Patsy Cline signed to Decca and started to have big hits. So, this does not live up to its billing as her "greatest recordings," but that doesn't mean it doesn't serve a purpose. As a matter of fact, it's very useful in collecting the best moments of her early 4-Star recordings, when Cline not only cut pure country but also sides that bordered on rockabilly. This has been released in many different forms before, including complete sets that will appeal to the serious collectors, but those who just want a well-produced sampling of this era won't go wrong with this. *—Stephen Thomas Erlewine*

★ **The Ultimate Collection** / Oct. 17, 2000 / UTV ✦✦✦✦✦

UTV's 2000 release *The Ultimate Collection* spans two discs and 32 songs, considerably more than the *12 Greatest Hits* that previously stood as the best, most concise overview of her career, yet more manageable than the 1991 box set, *The Patsy Cline Collection*, whose four discs do not lend themselves to an easy introduction. This two-disc set, however, does work as both a concise summary and good introduction, naturally containing all the classic hits, but digging deep enough into other areas—smaller hits, album tracks, and earlier sessions—to demonstrate the range and depth of her music. Serious fans will still want the box, and *12 Greatest Hits* remains as perfect as greatest-hits albums get, but anybody who wants a more thorough selection of Patsy Cline's best should turn here. *—Stephen Thomas Erlewine*

Jerry Clower

b. Sep. 28, 1926, Liberty, MS, **d.** Aug. 24, 1998, Jackson, MS

Vocals / Country Comedy

One of the most popular country comedians of all time, Jerry Clower's down-home, folksy Southern humor might never have become a mainstream phenomenon, but it's resulted in a lengthy career and an enormous catalog of recordings. A country boy born in the rural Mississippi town of Liberty in 1926, Clower was an excellent football player and an active member of the 4-H club as a youth. He served in the Navy after graduating from high-school, and went on to study agriculture at Southwest Mississippi Junior College and Mississippi State University (the latter on a football scholarship). After completing his studies, he took a job as a fertilizer salesman. In 1970, Clower had a speaking engagement before a farm group in Lubbock, TX, and a local DJ who was present encouraged him to take up comedy as a profession. The DJ recorded Clower's next speech and sent it to MCA, who offered Clower a recording contract.

Clower's first comedy album, *Jerry Clower From Yazoo City (Mississippi Talkin')*, was released in 1971. It wasn't distributed nationally at first, but it became a word-of-mouth hit, and eventually climbed into the Top 20 of the country album chart. A string of hit albums followed, most notably *Clower Power* (1973, a Top Ten hit), *Country Ham* (1974), *Live in Picayune* (1975, also a Top Ten seller), and *The Ambassador of Goodwill* (1976). His single most famous routine was "Coon Huntin' Story," but he was also known for his tales about the colorful characters in the fictional Ledbetter family. His last album to chart in the Top 50 was 1981's *More Good 'Uns*, but he remained a popular presence on the country comedy circuit, and he continued to record new material at a steady pace. He appeared often on country-themed television shows, especially on the then-Nashville Network, and hosted his own syndicated show for a time, not to mention his own national radio show. He also wrote three books—*Ain't God Good*, *Let the Hammer Down*, and *Life Everlaughter*—and the first lent its title to a documentary film of the same name about his life. MCA has kept a boatload of Clower albums on the market, and he continued to record and perform up until his passing in 1998. *—Steve Huey*

More Good 'Uns / 1981 / MCA ✦✦✦

Starke Raving! / 1984 / MCA ✦✦✦

Clower Power / 1992 / MCA Special Products ✦✦✦

Jerry Clower is one of those comedians you either get or you hate. Generally, there's no explaining *why* you dislike a particular comedian, you just know that he or she grates on your nerves. Clower, however, pushes those buttons more than most, possibly because his country cornball act is often either too obvious or too backwoods for city dwellers. *Clower Power*, with cuts like "Ole Brumey Wasn't Runnin' a Coon" and "The Ole Timey Ice Box," will undoubtedly make Clower fans chuckle heartily. *—Stephen Thomas Erlewine*

● **Jerry Clower's Greatest Hits** / 1994 / MCA ✦✦✦✦✦

Country Ham / 1995 / MCA ✦✦✦✦

Country Ham is guaranteed to make you happier than a pig in slop—although the record was originally issued in 1974, routines like "The She Coon of Women's Lib," "Ole Slantface" and "The Young People of Today" sound even fresher decades later, proof positive that Jerry Clower's genius is truly timeless. *—Chuck Donkers*

Live at Dollywood / May 13, 1997 / MCA ✦✦✦✦

Peaches & Possums / Oct. 6, 1998 / MCA ✦✦✦

Coal Porters

f. Los Angeles, CA

Group / Roots Rock, Cowpunk, Progressive Bluegrass, Americana, Alternative Country-Rock

After the dissolution of the Long Ryders, Sid Griffin (who is also a music journalist and author of *Gram Parsons: A Music Biography*) formed the Coal Porters in Los Angeles with Long Ryders drummer Greg Sowders and English bassist Ian Thomson. The group, which would soon relocate to England, debuted with *Rebels Without Applause* (originally an Australian 12-inch EP), following that in 1994 with the band's first LP, *Land of Hope and Crosby*. The effort featured such guests as ex-Green on Red organist Chris Cacavas and ex-Rockpile member Billy Bremner. Griffin continued to use a revolving cast of musicians on the follow-up, *Los London*.

The Gram Parsons Tribute Concert, a recording of a concert at the Garage in London in September of 1998, would prove to be the Coal Porters' last electric effort before Griffin took the group in an acoustic direction. Griffin was producing *Here Comes the Neighbourhood* by Lindisfarne when he found himself inspired by that group's acoustic sound. Subsequently, the Coal Porters re-emerged as an acoustic bluegrass project, with Griffin on mandolin, Pat McGarvey on banjo, Neil Robert Herd on guitar, Alan Bisset on bass, and Ivor Ottley on fiddle. In 2001, that version of the Coal Porters released the all-acoustic bluegrass album *The Chris Hillman Tribute Concerts*, which explored the career of the ex-Byrds and Flying Burrito Brothers member. *—Erik Hage*

Land of Hope and Crosby / 1994 / Prima ✦✦✦✦✦

Los London / Oct. 1995 / Prima ✦✦✦

After the breakup of the Long Ryders, Sid Griffin packed up his bags and moved to England, forming the Coal Porters with a revolving cast of British musicians. The typically punning title for the band's second full-length album, *Los London*, reflected the push and pull between Griffin's California heritage and his new surroundings in the U.K. The album finds Griffin not straying far from the path of his previous work; it's a set of strong roots-oriented rock tunes with a decided country influence (though the twang is a bit less pronounced than in the Long Ryders' best-known stuff) and witty/intelligent lyrics that betray an interest in progressive politics (especially "A Jacobite at Heart" and "It Happened to Me"). Griffin's longstanding fascination with Gram Parsons also makes its presence known with a graceful cover of "Apple Tree," a rare Parsons copyright that was previously recorded by Johnny Rivers, of all people. But the biggest difference between *Los London* and Griffin's best work is that, quite frankly, the band working with Griffin just isn't as strong. While Griffin himself is as sound as ever, the assorted backing musicians (bassist Pat McGarvey is one of the few constants throughout this set) generally sound competent but uninspired, and the album's slightly flat, generic-sounding production doesn't help matters much; while there's nothing strikingly wrong with the album, most of the time it fails to connect the way it should. *Los London* leaves little doubt that Sid Griffin's talents as a singer and songwriter followed him as he crossed the pond, but it also suggests that the talent pool available to him isn't what it once was; it would be nice to hear these songs with a better (and more passionate) set of players than those who populate *Los London*. *—Mark Deming*

EP Roulette / 1998 / Prima ✦✦✦✦

This six-song odds-and-ends EP from Sid Griffin's post-Long Ryders project turned out to be the Coal Porters' last studio release before they retooled themselves into an acoustic group, and it sends this edition of the band off into the sunset on a high note. The leadoff tune, "Everything," is a winning bit of country-pop with the sort of anthemic chorus Griffin was born to write, while the live at the BBC version of "Me, Here at Your Door" that closes out the disc beats the studio take on *Los London* hands down. In between, you get a tasty preview of Griffin's subsequent band, Western Electric ("Emily in Ginger"), a remastered (and audibly improved) cut from *Los London* ("Help Me"), a cool Creedence Clearwater Revival cover ("Who'll Stop the Rain," appropriately mournful), and a tribute to that other Cole Porter ("Don't Fence Me In"), which swings nicely. It's no masterpiece, but *EP Roulette* is a fine pocket-sized picture of what Sid Griffin does best, and captures the Coal Porters in much stronger form than on the disappointing *Los London*. *—Mark Deming*

- **The Gram Parsons Tribute Concert** / Jun. 8, 1999 / Prima ✦✦✦✦
Although the Gram Parsons tribute CD on Almo Records may seem like the last word on the matter, it really isn't. Country music, in its purest form, is road music, meant to be played by and for the people. Like the blues, it comes alive on the stage. Gram Parsons—one of the most revolutionary practitioners of the form—knew this intrinsically, and to that end, the Coal Porters disc *The Gram Parsons Tribute Concert* accomplishes this simple but necessary phenomenon with grace and style. Led by Sid Griffin, who was the founder of the Long Ryders—one of the most influential roots-based bands performing in Los Angeles in the 1980s—the Coal Porters are a band who are not only trying to emulate Parsons' freewheeling spirit, but are also emulating what quite simply can be called a friggin' great evening on a Saturday night in a club in north London. This factor is important, because Parsons' music is neither heavy-handed nor ponderous. Spontaneous soul, direct and to-the-heart, is the agenda here, and the Coal Porters (aka "the Bootleg Burritos," for this evening) deliver that on this recording. And how. The liner notes on this CD explain that certain tunes were lost due to curfew, technical difficulties, and the like. "Wires went unplugged due to stage diving. The heat was affecting everyone." No matter; in the end, you have a recording that captures the ambience and spirit of the evening perfectly. Of course, the music deserves it—so do you. —*Matthew Greenwald*

The Chris Hillman Tribute Concerts / Jul. 10, 2001 / Prima ✦✦✦✦
Given his enthusiasm for both the Byrds and the Flying Burrito Brothers, it's no wonder that author and musician Sid Griffin is a big fan of Chris Hillman, who was a major figure in both groups; Hillman was also the leader of the Desert Rose Band and is a superb bluegrass instrumentalist, not to mention a sideman who's worked with more fine musicians than you can shake a stick at. Given his background, it wouldn't be hard at all to put together an album's worth of great tunes Mr. Hillman has been involved with in some way, and Sid Griffin has capably proved it with this disc, which compiles performances from several Hillman tribute concerts Griffin has staged (he traditionally plays one every year on Hillman's birthday). *The Chris Hillman Tribute Concerts* features Griffin and the latest lineup of his band the Coal Porters playing in acoustic, bluegrass-influenced style, and given Hillman's sympathies for acoustic music, it makes sense that these songs all work quite well in that format, even the one that was originally written and performed by electric rock bands ("Draft Morning" and "Time Between," both written by Hillman during his tenure in the Byrds, sound especially strong in this context). And if the bluegrass edition of the Coal Porters isn't quite up to the level of, say, the Del McCoury Band, they play with a skill and conviction that outstrips the vast majority of rock bands who've decided to pick up acoustic instruments, and the arrangements at once honor their sources and put a distinctive spin on the Porters' approach. *The Chris Hillman Tribute Concerts* is a thoroughly enjoyable disc that presents 17 great songs played with heart, soul, and skill; it's a fan's gesture in the best sense of the word. —*Mark Deming*

Anita Cochran

b. Feb. 6, 1967, South Lyon, MI
Guitar, Vocals / Contemporary Country, Neo-Traditionalist Country
Born into a family obsessed with country music (who named her after one member of the Carter Family, and her brother after Faron Young), Anita Cochran began playing guitar at the age of four. Though she was born and raised in suburban Detroit, her parents were both originally from Kentucky. Her father was a local country performer who encouraged his daughter by bringing her to countless country music festivals. Although she spent time working for an insurance firm, she continued to perform in bands and as a solo act, and she caught her first break by being hired to manage a local recording studio. She sang backing vocals and engineered many sessions, recording on her own when she had time.
Although she lacked confidence in her abilities, Anita Cochran and her manager sent off several demos to the Warner Bros. label. One week later, she was called to Nashville, where she met with executives and later signed a contract. For her debut album, *Back to You*, Cochran wrote or co-wrote all but one of the songs and played guitar, dobro, banjo, and mandolin on the sessions. The album was released in April 1997 and spawned four country chart entries, including the number-one hit "What if I Said," a duet with Steve Wariner. *Anita* followed three years later. —*John Bush*

- **Back to You** / Apr. 22, 1997 / Warner Bros. ✦✦✦✦
Anita Cochran's debut album *Back to You* is an audacious statement of purpose, or at least a thrilling display of talent. Cochran wrote or co-wrote all but one of the album's ten songs and played lead guitar, along with contributing banjo, dobro and mandolin on other songs. Those instruments alone give a good idea of what kind of music she makes—it's contemporary country with roots not only in honky tonk, but also in bluegrass. At times, the fusions are a little unfocused—after all, this is a debut—but for most of *Back to You*, Cochran's music is unpredictable and exciting, as her songwriting is inspired and her musicianship is fresh. It's a first-rate debut. —*Thom Owens*

Anita / Oct. 5, 1999 / Warner Bros. ✦✦✦✦
Anita Cochran let a dangerously long three years slide by before the release of a follow-up to her debut, but though the album is a somewhat more compromised effort than her first album, raves are once again in order. Cochran is a triple threat: she writes songs steeped in country tradition yet distinctly individual, sings them in a throaty voice that sounds alternately like Mary-Chapin Carpenter and Wynonna (who guests on the characteristically sassy "God Created Woman"), and plays her own lead guitar breaks. That probably seemed like a more commercial proposition in 1997, when traditionalists like Deana Carter and Trisha Yearwood were the reigning queens of country, but in the late '90s, when the crossover dreams of Shania Twain and Faith Hill were the rule, a straight-ahead country performer like Cochran must seem a dicier proposition. So Warner Bros. Nashville hedged its bets by imposing some outside songwriting, including an inevitable

Diane Warren ballad. At least in a couple of cases, that's all the better: The uptempo "For Crying Out Loud" sounds like a potential hit; and "Let the Guitar Do the Talkin'" gives Cochran the opportunity to trade licks with Kenny Wayne Shepherd. But all the other best songs are Cochran's own compositions, especially the ballad "You With Me" and "Every Time It Rains." All of which is to say that *Anita* is a consistent straight country album that sounds like it has three or four hits on it. But it is also a risky effort because it sounds like the kind of record Nashville wanted in the early '90s. Maybe Anita Cochran can turn things around. If not, she can still make a living playing guitar. —*William Ruhlmann*

Eddie Cochran

b. Oct. 3, 1938, Albert Lea, Minnesota, **d.** Apr. 17, 1960, Wiltshire, England
Bass, Guitar, Drums, Guitar (Electric), Vocals / Rock & Roll, Rockabilly
Somehow, time has not accorded Eddie Cochran quite the same respect as other early rockabilly pioneers like Buddy Holly, or even Ricky Nelson or Gene Vincent. This is partially attributable to his very brief lifespan as a star: he only had a couple of big hits before dying in a car crash during a British tour in 1960. He was in the same league as the best rockabilly stars, though, with a brash, fat guitar sound that helped lay the groundwork for the power chord. He was also a good songwriter and singer, celebrating the joys of teenage life—the parties, the music, the adolescent rebellion—with an economic wit that bore some similarities to Chuck Berry. Cochran was more lighthearted and less ironic than Berry, though, and if his work was less consistent and not as penetrating, it was almost always exuberant.
Cochran's mid-'50s beginnings in the record industry are a bit confusing. His family had moved to Southern California around 1950, and in 1955 he made his first recordings as half of the Cochran Brothers. Here's the confusing part: although the other half of the act was really named Hank Cochran, he was *not* Eddie's brother. (Hank Cochran would become a noted country songwriter in the 1960s.) Eddie was already an accomplished rockabilly guitarist and singer on these early sides, and he started picking up some session work as well, also finding time to make demos and write songs with Jerry Capehart, who became his manager. Cochran's big break came about in a novel fashion. In mid-1956, while Cochran and Capehart were recording some music for low-budget films, Boris Petroff asked Eddie if he'd be interested in appearing in a movie that a friend was directing. The film was *The Girl Can't Help It*, and the song he would sing in it was "Twenty-Flight Rock." This is the same song that Paul McCartney would use to impress John Lennon upon their first meeting in 1957 (Paul could not only play it, but knew all of the lyrics).
Cochran had his first Top 20 hit in early 1957, "Sittin' in the Balcony," with an echo-chambered vocal reminiscent of Elvis. That single was written by John D. Loudermilk, but Eddie would write much of his material, including his only Top Ten hit, "Summertime Blues." A definitive teenage anthem with hints of the overt protest that would seep into rock music in the 1960s, it was also a technical *tour de force* for the time: Cochran overdubbed himself on guitar to create an especially thick sound. One of the classic early rock singles, "Summertime Blues" was revived a decade later by proto-metal group Blue Cheer, and was a concert staple for the Who, who had a small American hit with a cover version. (Let's not mention Alan Jackson's country rendition in the 1990s.)
That, disappointingly, was the extent of Cochran's major commercial success in the U.S. "C'mon Everybody," a chugging rocker that was almost as good as "Summertime Blues," made the Top 40 in 1959, and also gave Eddie his first British Top Tenner. As is the case with his buddy Gene Vincent, though, you can't judge his importance by mere chart statistics. Cochran was very active in the studio, and while his output wasn't nearly as consistent as Buddy Holly's (another good friend of Eddie's), he laid down a few classic or near-classic cuts that are just as worthy as his hits. "Somethin' Else," "My Way" (which the Who played in concert at the peak of psychedelia), "Weekend" (covered by the Move), and "Nervous Breakdown" are some of the best of these, and belong in the collection of every rockabilly fan. He was also (like Holly) an innovator in the studio, using overdubbing at a time when that practice was barely known on rock recordings.
Cochran is more revered today in Britain than the U.S., due in part to the tragic circumstances of his death. In the spring of 1960, he toured the U.K. with Vincent, to a wild reception, in a country that had rarely had the opportunity to see American rock & roll stars in the flesh. En route to London to fly back to the States for a break, the car Cochran was riding in, with his girlfriend (and songwriter) Sharon Sheeley and Gene Vincent, had a severe accident. Vincent and Sheeley survived, but Cochran died less than a day later, at the age of 21. —*Richie Unterberger*

Singin' to My Baby / 1958 / EMI ✦✦✦
While Eddie Cochran was one of the greatest early rock performers, a genius at overdubbing guitar parts, and the mastermind behind some of the most intoxicating rhythms and enjoyable songs in the genre, very little of that finds its way onto this early effort. It took Cochran a little while to really find his footing as a recording artist, and while completists inevitably acquire the early material, having quickly run out of everything else in the relatively small Cochran discography, listeners who are looking for a small, solid dose of his best material would be advised to look elsewhere. There is nothing that wrong with any of the songs here, most of which are in the kind of slightly or more than slightly corny '50s rock mode with plenty of echoes of R&B and doo wop. Reverb and slapback are piled on as if it was a submarine sandwich parlor, and Cochran's voice is never less than pleasant to listen to, whether he is pretending to be "Mean When I'm Mad," begging for "One Kiss," or fussing lecherously about "Stockings and Shoes." What is really missing is an emphasis on his guitar playing. Instead of a good small combo, he is backed up by the Johnny Mann Orchestra and Chorus, which is kind of like inviting the Air Force to a knife fight. Reissues of this material add some B-sides, none of which are of much interest. —*Eugene Chadbourne*

Legend in Our Own Time / 1972 / Union Pacific ✦✦✦
This Dutch album provides a generous portion of side dishes by rockabilly all-star Eddie Cochran. It is more a history than a legend, as we have actual milestones in his career

such as first recordings, air shots from the big British tour, tunes grabbed off Mamie Van Doren film soundtracks, and so forth. Cochran enthusiasts will want to hear this stuff, but should be alert to find it scattered around on various other issues and repackagings, the legal confusion around the Cochran estate resulting in a supply of his material too big to fit into Imelda Marcos' shoe closet. The first side finds us in a straight country & western groove, with Eddie Cochran fronting a group with his twin in last name only, Hank Cochran. Though not technically a "brother" duet because they are not really related, the Cochrans present tracks of authentic country music, each one slanting a bit more toward rockabilly. After these recordings were done, Cochran got to see Elvis Presley live and was never the same. The music is immediately affected by Presley's model, but listeners unswayed by the lure of the King may prefer what Cochran does with this type of material. He certainly is way ahead of Presley as a guitarist, and just about anybody else for that matter. He is already playing great guitar solos on the 1956 "Tired and Sleepy." Fans of creative guitar will definitely want to check out the instrumentals. The blues and rhythm & blues material doesn't have the kick of his best rockabilly numbers, but does show his sure command of the roots music on guitar. Only one of his really famous songs is here, an airshot version of "C'mon Everybody" that is a lot of fun. There are 16 other tracks leading up to this, some of it first-class Cochran and some on the middling side. —*Eugene Chadbourne*

Legendary Masters / 1972 / Capitol ✦✦✦✦✦
Perhaps if Eddie Cochran had died a more spectacular death than a car crash during a tour of Europe in 1960, he'd be better remembered today; while he doesn't always get his due as one of the best of the first wave of rock & rollers to emerge in the 1950s, few performers of the era can match the body of work he left behind for consistent quality. Cochran's best (and best-known) songs were tough, guitar-based rockers that proved he'd forgotten little about life in the teenage nation after leaving high-school to go pro ("Summertime Blues," "C'mon Everybody," "Something Else"). Dig a little deeper into his catalog, and you'll discover Cochran was a great guitar player (check out the instrumental fretboard workout "Eddie's Blues"), had a real knack for country-flavored material ("Pretty Little Devil" and "Thinkin' About You" suggest he would have been a natural for the C&W charts if his hitmaking days in rock & roll dried up), and could work well in other pop formats—"Opportunity" sounds like one of the best Everly Brothers tunes Don and Phil never cut and, while "Three Stars," a weepy tribute to Buddy Holly, Ritchie Valens, and the Big Bopper, would have sounded like pure treacle in the hands of most singers, Cochran's take is dignified and genuinely moving (owing perhaps to the fact that he and Holly had been good friends). Given the brevity of his recording career, a 30-track two-LP set might give you a bit more Eddie Cochran than you actually need, and *Legendary Masters* does have a certain amount of filler, most notably "Let's Get Together" (actually an alternate take of "C'mon Everybody") and "Cotton Picker" (a throwaway tune he cut for the movie *Untamed Youth*). But the vast majority of this set is great vintage rock, with Cochran always sounding tough and committed, even on the most suspect material. Add a superb liner essay from Lenny Kaye and you get one of the finest Eddie Cochran collections your money can buy—and no record collection is truly complete without "Summertime Blues," right? —*Mark Deming*

Portrait of a Legend / 1985 / Rockstar ✦✦✦
Fine-looking and fine-sounding collection of unreleased stereo versions and alternate takes, this is nonetheless unnecessary for all but Cochran completists. In the spirit of numerous Beatles bootlegs (though this LP is quite official), these are in the main studio recordings with small (sometimes minute) differences in the mixing, or stereo versions which are not easy to come by on official releases, although mono versions of the exact same takes are plentiful. There are plenty of fine songs here ("Weekend," "Summertime Blues," "C'mon Everybody," "Three Steps to Heaven"), but they're better heard both in their more common versions, and in the context of a coherent anthology. And if you need to settle for just one version of "Summertime Blues" or "C'mon Everybody," why spring for the "Summertime Blues" *without* the echoed vocal, or "C'mon Everybody" *missing* a guitar overdub? —*Richie Unterberger*

The Early Years / 1988 / Ace ✦✦✦
Compilation of 16 tracks from the mid-'50s, most or all dating from before Cochran's breakthrough to national recognition with "Twenty-Flight Rock." Some were recorded when Eddie was half of the Cochran Brothers, with (the unrelated) Hank Cochran; there are also tracks credited to Jerry Capehart and Albert Stone, which Eddie most likely had a prominent role on, as session man or producer (the liner notes are resolutely unhelpful on providing exact details). Most of this is pretty solid rockabilly, not much below the standards of Cochran's best releases. There are also a couple of hot instrumentals, and ballad-type numbers on which Eddie employs a husky, echoed Elvis-esque delivery. A decent release, but assembled in a scattershot fashion. Also, if you're interested enough in Cochran to want to track this down, you may well also be interested enough in him to spring for a box set, and most or all of these are also contained on whatever box set you manage to locate. —*Richie Unterberger*

Box Set / 1988 / Liberty ✦✦✦
This six-LP import—which still, somehow, manages not to include every track Cochran recorded—is excessive for the non-fanatic. Nevertheless, it does include quite a few obscure, interesting pre-fame performances from the mid-'50s (some as part of the Cochran Brothers). Other bonuses include a live 1960 British TV broadcast, an album's worth of sessions and his work as a producer, and entire sides of instrumentals and stereo versions, as well as a 32-page booklet. —*Richie Unterberger*

Legendary Masters / Jan. 29, 1990 / EMI America ✦✦✦✦✦
EMI did a bit of adjusting to their excellent 1971 Eddie Cochran collection for CD release in 1990, and that wasn't necessarily a bad idea—losing a few of the lesser tracks on that

slightly overstuffed two-LP set wouldn't have hurt the disc in the least. While that album's most obvious filler got the axe, so did a few obscurities that added a lot of flavor to a superb collection (especially Cochran's early country-influenced material), and adding "Drive-in Show" and "Three Steps to Heaven" hardly make up for deleting the guitar showcase "Eddie's Blues" or the Everly Brothers-style pop tune "Opportunity." And shame on whoever decided to scrap Lenny Kaye's brilliant liner notes from the LP edition. But if you want most of Eddie Cochran's best stuff on one disc, this set more than fits the bill, and the truth is if you hadn't heard the earlier version of this compilation, you'd never know what you were missing. The *Legendary Masters* CD is all choice cuts and no filler, and a fine introduction from one of the finest artists of the first rock & roll era—if you don't know Cochran's music, this will get you started right, and if you know and love his work, you'll find this disc a joy from start to finish—it's as good a cure for the "Summertime Blues" as you'll ever find. —*Mark Deming*

EP Collection / 1991 / See for Miles ✦✦✦✦
Look at the title—it's an *EP Collection*, not a greatest-hits collection, or a best-of retrospective. That means that it is not comprehensive, nor should it be seen as an introduction, since it doesn't contain all of Eddie Cochran's great songs. After all, not only does it lack nifty obscurities like "Cut Across Shorty," it doesn't have such monumental efforts as "Somethin' Else," one of the greatest rock & roll songs ever recorded. So, this shouldn't be seen as a way to pick up the hits, but rather a way for collectors to pick up a handful of songs that are hard to find on other collections—and, in that respect, it works pretty well. It still would have been better if it had the hits, plus the rarities, but it's a pretty fun listen as it is. —*Stephen Thomas Erlewine*

Singin' to My Baby/Never to Be Forgotten / Feb. 23, 1993 / Capitol ✦✦✦✦✦
Two original albums on one compact disc, with only two hits between the two—"Sittin' in the Balcony" and "Twenty-Flight Rock." But for devoted fans of Eddie Cochran, this lovingly packaged CD is worth their time, even if some of the material is slightly weak. *Singin' to My Baby* concentrates on ballad material; the posthumously released *Never to Be Forgotten* has more rockers. —*Stephen Thomas Erlewine*

Rare 'n' Rockin' / 1998 / Music Club ✦✦✦

★ **Somethin' Else: The Fine Lookin' Hits of Eddie Cochran** / Feb. 24, 1998 / Razor & Tie ✦✦✦✦✦
Eddie Cochran hasn't been unaccounted for in the reissue sweepstakes since the rockabilly revival of the late '70s/early '80s—quite the contrary. His greatest hits have been around the block a few times, and his voluminous amount of session work has all resurfaced on myriads of foreign collector labels. This 1998 best-of on Razor & Tie duplicates 15 of the 20 tracks on EMI's *Legendary Masters Series* compilation from 1990. Hits *are* hits, after all, and Cochran's best is hardly open to debate. What distinguishes this package is the inclusion of "Tired and Sleepy" from the Cochran Brothers, an early swipe at "Long Tall Sally," the instrumental "Guybo," "Cherished Memories," and the almost pop-folk "Boll Weevil." Great liner notes from Colin Escott and top-flight sound also make this disc highly recommended. If you're looking to start your Eddie Cochran collection, this makes an excellent first purchase. —*Cub Koda*

12 of His Biggest Hits/Never to Be Forgotten / Jul. 17, 2001 / EMI ✦✦✦✦
This two-fer from EMI features a pair of out-of-print Eddie Cochran LP's: *12 of His Biggest Hits* and *Never to Be Forgotten* both issued after Cochran's death in 1960. Highlights among the 24 tracks include the original hit recordings of "C'mon Everybody," "Summertime Blues,"and "Sittin' in the Balcony." —*Al Campbell*

Hank Cochran

b. Aug. 2, 1935, Isola, MS
Composer / Traditional Country, Country-Pop, Honky Tonk
Nashville songwriter Hank Cochran penned dozens of country hits during the 1960s, '70s, and '80s, including "I Fall to Pieces" (Patsy Cline), "The Chair" (George Strait), "Don't Touch Me" (Jeannie Seely), "Don't You Ever Get Tired of Hurtin' Me?" (Ray Price and Ronnie Milsap), "It's Not Love (But It's Not Bad)" (Merle Haggard), "Make the World Go Away" (Eddy Arnold), and "She's Got You" (Cline again). Cochran balanced music and lyric chores evenly when writing co-compositions with Nashville legends like Harlan Howard, Vern Gosdin, and Dean Dillon. —*John Bush*

● **Make the World Go Away** / 1980 / Elektra ✦✦✦
The music scene is full of composers or songwriters whose creations are better-known than they are. If Hank Cochran has been frustrated in his attempts to launch a career as a performer, he has certainly kept quiet about it, as he is a country artist who has mostly remained in the background, recording only about a half-dozen complete albums under his own name. He has made up for that with a legacy of classic country songs recorded by other artists, some of which are included on this collection. Cochran is a likable character whose songwriting talents are not to be disputed. He is not an especially charismatic vocalist, however, and listeners will no doubt want to return, for example, to Johnny Paycheck's take on "A-11" which is simply a lot more lively. The underrated and largely unknown Tuscaloosa-based country artist Rock Killough was involved in the production, as was super country session bassist Michael Rhodes. Listen for a guest appearance by Cochran pal Willie Nelson, credited only in the fine print. —*Eugene Chadbourne*

Jackie Lee Cochran

b. Dalton, GA, d. Mar. 15, 1998, Burbank, CA
Vocals / Rockabilly, Roots Rock, Rockabilly Revival, Rock & Roll
Although not as instantly recognizable as certain other rockabilly artists, vocalist Jackie Lee Cochran was one of the genre's earliest supporters, issuing several overlooked singles in the late '50s. Born in Dalton, GA, in the early '30s, Cochran was raised in both Louisiana and Texas. He was attracted to music and singing via country artists he heard

on local radio, and decided to relocate to Los Angeles in the mid-'50s, where he soon became a featured artist on Cliffie Stone's Hometown Jamboree. This eventually led to a contract with Decca Records, for whom Cochran cut several singles for. When rockabilly's popularity began to dwindle in the early '60s, Cochran continued to perform, as his live shows showcased a wide variety of musical styles: country, pop, blues, rockabilly, and rock & roll. During the '70s, Cochran adopted the nickname "Waukeen" (as a tribute to his American-Indian heritage), and continued to tour. Come the '80s, Cochran began issuing full-length albums on a somewhat regular basis: 1980's *Swamp Fox*, 1985's *Fiddle Fit Man*, and 1987's *Jack the Cat*. In 1997, a 20-track compilation of songs that Cochran recorded with renowned rockabilly producer Ronny Weiser back in the '70s was issued, titled *Rockabilly Music*. On March 15, 1998, Jack "Waukeen" Cochran died in his sleep in his Burbank, CA, apartment, at the age of 64. —*Greg Prato*

Rockabilly Music / Nov. 4, 1997 / HMG ✦✦✦✦

After cutting a handful of brilliant singles for Decca in the mid-'50s, Jackie Lee Cochran became the King of Rockabilly, West Coast Division, with a decade's worth of performances in barrooms up and down the West Coast. Producer/rockabilly fanatic Ronny Weiser recorded Cochran in the 1970s for his Rollin' Rock label, and the best of those sides are collected here on this 20-track compilation. Cochran still had a lot of gas left in the tank when these sides were cut, and Weiser wisely kept the production simple and spartan. Highlights include a snappy recut of "Mama, Doncha Think I Know," "Hell to Pay," "Hip Shakin' Mama" and "Hug 'N' Kiss Me." —*Cub Koda*

Tammy Cochran

b. Austinburg, OH

Vocals / Country-Pop, Contemporary Country

Singer Tammy Cochran was born and raised in Ohio, in a little rural town called Austinburg. Its tranquil setting would be just right for a country song. She knew all of her neighbors and people smiled and waved when someone walked by. There was also enough sadness and pain in Cochran's life to write a country song about. She was the last born of three children, the only daughter of Mabel and Delmar Cochran. Cochran had two older brothers, Shawn and Alan, both tragically born with cystic fibrosis. Shawn was only 14 when he lost his battle with the disease in 1980. Alan made it to 1991, to the age of 23. Her brothers' lives, illness, and deaths touched Cochran in a way that shows in her music, especially in a touching song she co-wrote, called "Angels in Waiting."

Cochran's father taught her the words to her first song, "Heartaches by the Numbers," when she was around eight years old. A short time later she was given a child's record player that came with a microphone and that was that. Her favorite pastime instantly became singing along with country tunes by artists like Barbara Mandrell and Loretta Lynn. She preferably sang in front of an audience, with her brothers' help. The story is that they charged their parents a whole 50 cents to attend each of those early performances. Over the next few years young Cochran gained experience singing at her family's church. By the time she was 12 she entered her first talent contest, a local one, that she won. With a newfound confidence, she entered more contests, winning over and over. The next step was to join a band, and she did, a number of them. While still in her teens, she put together a band of her own called TC Country. The group appeared at fairs, weddings, and clubs.

Planning for a future that might never live up to her dreams of musical fame, Cochran finished high-school and took vocational training so she could be a secretary. That responsible thing done, she went right on struggling to reach that dream. In 1991, full of determination, she picked up and moved to Nashville, TN, with her supportive parents as well. For years Cochran tried to make a name for herself, to find a label that would back her. In 1996 she married, and mostly gave up her hopes of making a living with her voice and songs. The marriage only lasted a couple of years, and so did her time away from singing.

In 1998 all of the years of hard work began to pay off at last. It started when she was introduced to Shane Decker after one of her performances. Decker worked for Warner-Chappell Music as a songwriter. He offered to help her get a demo ready. He also helped her land a job writing songs at Warner-Chappell. Good things seemed to happen quickly after that. In no time Cochran's music was being showcased for labels, and when the dust settled, she had a signed contract with the major label Sony. In May of 2001, Tammy Cochran's self-titled debut album hit the stores. Her first single was already burning up the airwaves, and its music video appearing on CMT to rave reviews. Suddenly Cochran was one of those overnight success stories you hear about—that was only years of hard work in the making. —*Charlotte Dillon*

● **Tammy Cochran** / May 1, 2001 / Epic ✦✦✦

Tammy Cochran kicked around Nashville for almost a decade before she gained a hearing on Music Row, which says more about the goals of the country music establishment in the 1990s than it does about her. Cochran is a heartthrob singer in the tradition of Loretta Lynn and Tammy Wynette, which is not what Nashville was looking for in the Garth Brooks crossover days of the '90s, and not even what much of Nashville has been looking for in the Faith Hill crossover days of the '00s. But Sony producer Blake Chancey has been bucking that trend with the Dixie Chicks, among others, and he finally gave Cochran her chance with the May 2000 single "If You Can." Chancey understood that Cochran's strength was ballads, and though "If You Can" wasn't a hit, it displayed her talent well. Her debut album seems to have been delayed several times, until a second single, "So What," released in October 2000, got some traction. It fulfills the promise of those songs by sticking mostly with ballads, on which Cochran emotes most effectively. It's not that she can't handle uptempo material such as "Better Off Broken" and her own co-composition "When Love Was Enough," it's that she isn't able to put as personal a stamp on those songs, which sound like they could be by any competent female vocalist. But when she gets hold of a slow one with a bitterly romantic edge like "Say Goodbye," she reminds you of generations of great country women. *Tammy Cochran* may be too country for country radio (it always feels funny to say that), but it should attract fans of dyed-in-the-wool country who have been waiting for an artist not so concerned with crossing over to the pop charts. —*William Ruhlmann*

Life Happened / Sep. 17, 2002 / Sony ✦✦✦

There's a sadness to Tammy Cochran's music that's hard to put a finger on. Perhaps it's simply in her voice—that delicious Midwestern intonation—or perhaps it's just a direct reflection of the sorrow she's had to overcome in her personal life. Whatever it is, it works with the songs she's chosen for this satisfying sophomore album. "White Lies and Picket Fences," about promising to be together forever and having it go wrong; "I Used to Be That Woman," about a cheating husband; and "If You Can," the first single she ever released about questioning the end of a relationship, all remind listeners about the sometimes gritty realities of existence. Cochran says she tries to keep things real in her music, so she does manage to also give listeners hope in songs like "I'm Getting There," "Life Happened," and "All in How You Look at Things." Cochran's unarguable second effort is a steadfast lesson in determination. —*Maria Konicki Dinoia*

David Allan Coe

b. Sep. 6, 1939, Akron, OH

Guitar, Songwriter, Vocals / Progressive Country, Outlaw Country, Country-Folk, Traditional Country

A life-long renegade, singer/songwriter David Allan Coe is one of the most colorful and unpredictable characters in country music history. One of the pioneering artists of the outlaw country movement of the '70s, he didn't have many big hits—only three of his singles hit the Top Ten—but he was among the biggest cult figures in country music throughout his career. Born in Akron, OH, Coe first got into trouble with the law at age nine. As a result, he was sent to reform school. For the next 20 years, he never spent more than a handful of months outside of a correctional facility—he spent much of his 20s in the Ohio State Penitentiary. Released from prison in 1967, the wild-haired, earring wearing, heavily tattooed Coe went straight for Nashville, where he lived in a hearse that he parked in front of the old Ryman Auditorium, the home of the Grand Ole Opry. Although he didn't conform to Nashville's professional standards, he soon gained the attention of the independent label, Plantation Records, which released Coe's debut album *Penitentiary Blues* in 1968. Followed within a year by a second volume, all of the songs on these albums were based on his prison experiences.

Coe then toured with Grand Funk Railroad, a signal that he drew as much from rock's traditions as he did from country. Soon, he began performing in a rhinestone suit given to him by Mel Tillis, as well as a Lone Ranger mask, and began calling himself the "Masked Rhinestone Cowboy." Coe's concerts became notorious for their unpredictability—frequently he would roar up on-stage astride his enormous Harley, swearing at the audience. He cultivated a large cult following with his act, but he couldn't break into the main stream. However, other artists found success with his songs—in 1972, Billie Jo Spears had a minor hit with his "Souvenirs & California Mem'rys," and in 1973, Tanya Tucker had a number-one hit with Coe's "Would You Lay with Me (in a Field of Stone)." After Tucker's hit, David Allan Coe suddenly became one of Nashville's hottest songwriters; some of the biggest country artists—including Willie Nelson, George Jones and Tammy Wynette—recorded his tunes, leading to his own contract with Columbia Records.

Coe's first two singles for Columbia didn't come close to the country Top 40, but his 1975 cover of Steve Goodman's "You Never Even Called Me By My Name" cracked the Top Ten. Although a string of moderate hits followed, he rarely cracked the country Top 40, although in 1977 Johnny Paycheck took Coe's "Take This Job and Shove It" to number one. During his 13-year association with Columbia, Coe released 26 albums, including the double album set *For the Record: The First 10 Years* (1985), 1986's *Son of the South* (featuring Willie, Waylon, Jessi Colter and other "outlaws"), and the highly regarded *Matter of Life and Death* (1987).

Although Coe had a successful career, it was one plagued with many setbacks. The conservative Nashville music industry frequently snubbed him and he had tax problems with the IRS; at one time, they seized his Key West home, and he went to live in a Tennessee cave until he got back on his feet. Towards the end of the '80s, Coe remarried and began to settle down. Throughout the '90s, he was a popular concert attraction in America and Europe. In addition to his musical career, he also acted in a few movies including *The Last Days of Frank and Jesse James*. He also published a novel, *Psychopath*, and an autobiography. The LP *Recommended for Airplay* was issued in 1999. The new millennium saw the release of *Long Haired Country Boy* in 2000; *Songwriter of the Tear* appeared on Cleveland the following year. —*Sandra Brennan*

Penitentiary Blues / 1968 / SSS ✦✦✦

David Allan Coe's debut album, released in 1969 shortly after his release from prison, is in its way a wonder. *Penitentiary Blues* is far more a blues album than it is a country record, musically styled after the dark, loungy blues of Charlie Rich and Jerry Lee Lewis in his Mercury period as well as the rawer mercurial blues of Bo Diddley, Lightnin' Hopkins, and Tony Joe White. The subject matter is far darker and foreshadows the subjects and themes of Coe's later country records. The title cut mentions everything from working for the first time to taking blood tests in his heroin veins. "Cell 33" is a wide-open rocking shuffle with Jerry Lee Lewis piano coming out of the backdrop of a muddy mix and playing solo after choogling guitar riff over lines like: "They'll find me hangin' here tomorrow/If they don't come with the key." Musically, Coe was wrapped in the blues, particularly the barroom tradition. At the time, his band was clearly not capable of handling the more sophisticated honky tonk songs he would be writing shortly thereafter, some appearing on his next recording, *Requiem for a Harlequin*. This is redneck music, pure and simple, fresh out of hell and trying to communicate the giddiness of reprieve as well as its horrors to the listener. There's an obsession with hoodoo imagery and death, with self-loathing and boasting, and the contradictions in a man who doesn't want to go back to prison but who seems resigned to the fact he will because he's been inside so long (for Coe it was almost 20 years), he has no idea how to live on the outside. There are hints and traces of the lyrical genius Coe would display later, but taken as a whole,

Penitentiary is thoroughly enjoyable as a rowdy, funky, and crude blues record full of out-of-tune guitars, slippery performances, and an attitude of "f*%$ it, let's get it done and get it out." *Penitentiary Blues* is a set of voodoo blues from a future country legend and pariah. *—Thom Jurek*

Requiem for a Harlequin / 1970 / SSS ✦✦✦

The Mysterious Rhinestone Cowboy / 1974 / Columbia ✦✦✦✦✦

David Allan Coe's debut album for Columbia proves beyond the shadow of doubt that he was the original alt-country antihero. Released in 1974, Coe revealed an adopted persona: *The Mysterious Rhinestone Cowboy.* He was equal parts hell-raising biker ex-con (this aspect was accurate); a pre-punk badass full of piss and vinegar, spewing vitriol (and bad humor) at the Nash Vegas establishment (and anyone who didn't like his music); a hillbilly version of Marc Bolan's glitz and glitter; and a sensitive country singer and songwriter heavily influenced by Merle Haggard, as good as anybody at his best—and that includes Willie Nelson, Waylon Jennings, Billy Joe Shaver, and Kris Kristofferson, to name but a few. Opening with "A Sad Country Song," Coe displays his lyrical and melodic gift that comes out of the great Texas and Bakersfield traditions. Amid a whining pedal steel, shimmery fiddle, and a waltz tempo heard above the guitars, Coe sings to the lonely and alone and offers his brand of empathy this way: "Just look for my name on a jukebox/When you're tired of being alone/Put in a dime and I'll take the time/ To sing you a sad country song." On the very next track, producer Ron Bledsoe borrows textural ideas from Mickey Newbury's recordings and Scott Walker's delivery on Michael Smith's folk classic "Crazy Mary." And speaking of Newbury, Coe's reading of his "33rd of August" is reverential but not to the point of mere imitation. The rain and thunder sounds are kept as essential elements of the song's composition. Coe understates his beautiful baritone in homage to Newbury's own considerable gift for understatement. Other Coe signature tunes like "I Still Sing the Old Songs" and "Atlanta Song" are recorded here for the first time, along with a killer cover of Guy Clark's "Desperadoes Waiting for a Train." Unlike later Coe recordings, there are no novelty tracks here, and as a label debut this is as auspicious as it gets. *—Thom Jurek*

☆ **Once Upon a Rhyme** / 1975 / Columbia ✦✦✦✦✦

In 1973, Tanya Tucker went to the top of the country charts with David Allan Coe's "Would You Lay With Me (In a Field of Stone)," turning a lot of singers and Nash Vegas executives' heads in his direction. Coe opens 1975's *Once Upon a Rhyme* with his own version of the song—a gutsy thing to do for anybody, but then, Coe was always equal parts talent and raw nerve. The amazing thing is that both versions are definitive. But that first track is only the beginning of a truly wondrous journey through the mysterious and poetic sound world of David Allan Coe as both a singer and a songwriter. Produced by Ron Bledsoe and accompanied by some of Music City's finest new-generation session players—like Charlie McCoy, Buddy Spicher, Reggie Young, and Pete Drake—Coe follows his opener with another of his inimitable classics, "Jody Like a Melody," with its winding, lilting choruses and ethereal couplets. After the emotional impact of the first two tracks, add two self-penned masterpieces—"Loneliness in Ruby's Eyes" and "Would You Be My Lady"—and the listener is left nearly breathless. But with Coe, that's not enough, and he digs deeper emotionally with "Sweet Vibrations" and "Another Pretty Country Song." And brilliantly but inexplicably, he closes the set with three songs that either were, or became part of, the country canon as a result of this recording: Lawton Williams' "Fraulein," Richard Dobson's "Piece of Wood and Steel," and Steve Goodman's "You Never Even Called Me By My Name." The last of these is the only version most people know; it was as if the late Goodman had written it for Coe. His voice wraps itself so completely around the melody that the lyrics run like a river from his mouth, and he becomes the song's protagonist, supported in the weight of his grief by an electric guitar, a fiddle, and a pedal steel slipping in and out of an airy mix that is punctuated by a rhythm section that only underlines the truth in every line. This album and its predecessor, *The Mysterious Rhinestone Cowboy,* established Coe as a major songwriting force; they remain enduring testaments to his songwriting brilliance as a criminally under-examined talent in the country tradition. *—Thom Jurek*

Longhaired Redneck / 1976 / Columbia ✦✦✦✦

By 1976, singer and songwriter David Allan Coe had grown tired of being ignored by the Nash Vegas DJs and promotion men. His wild, long hair; multiple earrings; flashy, glitzy rhinestone suits; Harley Davidson biker boots; and football-sized belt buckles had become obstacles to getting people to take him seriously as a recording artist. Other singers continued to record and succeed with his material, but the author himself—who was as good a singer as almost anyone and better than most—languished in obscurity. Rather than tone it down, Coe characteristically shoved the stereotypes in their faces. He retired the *Mysterious Rhinestone Cowboy* persona and billed his new album as "David Allan Coe Rides Again as the Longhaired Redneck," something equally off-putting to institution types. The album is composed entirely of self-penned tunes and co-writes. It begins with the title track, an outlaw anthem akin to Ray Wylie Hubbard's "Up Against the Wall Redneck Mother." But the album also includes some of Coe's most enduring material: "Revenge," "When She's Got Me Where She Wants Me," "Texas Lullaby," "Family Reunion," and "Livin' on the Run." The two hinge tracks on the album come near its end. "Free Born Rambling Man," with its Allman Brothers guitar lines, is a nod to Coe's friend Dickey Betts' hit, "Ramblin' Man," full of early country melody and first-class storytelling. "Spotlight," however, is where Coe sums up the way he views his life at this particular juncture, and given the lyrics, his mind couldn't have been a nice place to live. The simple three-chord waltz sets a backdrop for songs that strip the issues to the bone: "All of my music is lonely/Yea, all of my heartaches were free/Don't waste your time or your flashbulbs/Too many heroes are dead/You like to live in the city/I like to live in my head . . . I spend my nighttimes in mournin'/I spend my mornings alone/You spent your money to see me tonight/Yea, I spent all mine getting stoned . . . Everyone's lyin' about livin'/ I'm tired of livin' a lie." Like most of Coe's '70s material, this one's essential outlaw country that stands the test of time. *—Thom Jurek*

Rides Again / 1977 / Columbia ✦✦✦

Even though *Rides Again* marks the first time David Allan Coe was allowed to use his own band on half of the album—a major concession on the part of Columbia Records because he hit pay dirt a couple of times—this stands as his most disappointingly inconsistent record of the 1970s. The last track on his previous album, "Dakota the Dancing Bear, Part II," was an exercise in cynical, pointless counterculture idiocy and, unfortunately, was the first of Coe's "novelty" songs. On *Rides Again*, by trying to make a conscious outlaw record and aligning himself with the movement's two progenitors on the opening track, "Willie, Waylon, and Me" (and equating himself with not only the Flying Burrito Brothers and the Eagles, but the Beatles as well!), Coe already set up self-parody unintentionally—something that continued to curse him. There are fine moments as well, such as "Under Rachel's Wings," "The House That We Call Home" (though it is the first of Coe's songs about polygamy), the plaintively moving "A Sense of Humor," the passionate and poetic "Greener Than the Grass We Laid On," and a killer cover of Dale Murphy's "Laid Back and Wasted." And while not without merit, the opening track—with its reprise halfway through the album—"Young Dallas Cowboy," and the infamous "If That Ain't Country (You Can kiss My Ass)" mar what might have been an exceptional album if Coe could only have contained his anger at the musical establishment in Nash Vegas, and not begun caricaturing himself—which added credibility to critics. This is not the place to start with Coe, but fans will most certainly want at least half of the tracks on this album. *—Thom Jurek*

Tattoo / 1977 / Columbia ✦✦✦✦✦

Tattoo was David Allan Coe's fifth Columbia album and displayed a return to form after the disappointing *Rides Again.* (There was also a return to plantation for an album called *Texas Moon* that's long been out of print and was most notable for its cover of Billy Joe Shaver's "Ride Me Down Easy.") Issued in 1977, it shows Coe sticking hard and fast to his traditional country roots just as the music began to mutate into urban cowboy-ism. Ron Bledsoe and Coe chose ten tunes, eight of which Coe either composed or co-wrote, as well as a cover of Mickey Newbury's classic "Frisco Mabel Joy." This is one of Coe's finest recordings—it's full of love songs, divorce tunes, cheating songs, and rootsy, gutsy honky tonk playing by a stellar cast of musicians. Opening with the stomping honky tonk love paean "Just to Prove My Love for You," with echoes of Bill Monroe and Ralph Stanley haunting the fringes, and "Face to Face," one would be hard-pressed to find two tougher love songs stacked back to back on any country album. But he even moves toward the cheating breakup tune with a gorgeous Johnny Gimble-styled fiddle on "You'll Always Live Inside of Me." "Maria Is a Mystery" features some of the most haunting imagery in any Coe song, and he follows it with the amazing "Just in Time to Watch Love Die," before a deeply moving read of "Frisco Mabel Joy." The album closes with "Hey Gypsy," a dramatic, fully orchestrated plea for wanderers to return to a place of solace. It sounds like Coe is so haunted by these songs that he's looking directly into the depths of the mirror of his own soul. He probably was. This is easily one of the finest country records issued in the 1970s. *—Thom Jurek*

Texas Moon / 1977 / Plantation ✦✦✦

Family Album / 1978 / Columbia ✦✦✦

Family Album (1978) features one of the most bizarre covers in David Allan Coe's—hell, anybody's—catalog. He is dressed in a minister's black, flowing robe with an Amish hat, a little blonde girl in his lap, his two—yes, two (of three at one time)—wives standing behind him, and behind them, a black Lincoln Town Car and Coe's Silver Eagle tour bus. The album is dedicated to his two mothers—he's apparently from a Mormon family—and stipulates how difficult it is for a child to have two mothers. It's so surreal one is almost afraid to play the recording. *Family Album* marks the first time Coe worked with Billy Sherrill as well as his regular producer, Ron Bledsoe. It begins with the title track, dedicated to those mothers, and you never know which one he is speaking of—though it hardly makes a difference, it's a beautiful country song. "Million Dollar Memories," co-written with Carol Anderson, is a honky tonk piano number stylistically reminiscent of Jerry Lee Lewis' Mercury years and of his cousin, Mickey Gilley's piano work, played wonderfully by Hargus "Pig" Robbins. The album also features Coe's first attempt at emulating Jimmy Buffett with "Divers Do It Deeper," an excellent choice for the guy in a minister's robe on the cover. This song belongs somewhere, but not on this recording. Other worthy honky tonk numbers here include "Guilty Footsteps," "Bad Impressions," and "Whole Lot of Lonesome," co-written with George Jones. But the album's high point is Coe's version of "Take This Job and Shove It," a song he authored that Johnny Paycheck took into the stratosphere. Coe's own version is more than credible. It lacks the outlaw swagger and big production of Paycheck's version, but none of its conviction. *Family Album* is a fine album except for the strange look and feel of its cover and the aforementioned Buffett rip-off, but it's not the place to start if you are seeking an introduction to Coe. *—Thom Jurek*

Human Emotions / 1978 / Columbia ✦✦✦✦

By the end of 1978, outlaw singer/songwriter David Allan Coe had gone through another divorce—one that was apparently very difficult, because he recorded this entire album around the topic. The subtitle of *Human Emotions* is "Happy Side/Suicide." Side one is comprised of songs composed—and some recorded—before his wife left; side two is the aftermath. At this time, producer Billy Sherrill had really begun to make his presence felt on David Allan Coe's records. Ron Bledsoe is still here with his patented honky tonk production style, but the Sherrill ambience creeps in here and gives everything a certain commercial-sounding fullness rather than the space of his earlier records. *Human Emotions* is a very commercial record that might have done well with radio and in stores had it not been for the positively menacing cover of an aviator-shaded Coe in full biker attire holding an acoustic guitar, next to the skull of an antelope. The album opens with a re-recording of "Would You Lay With Me (In a Field of Stone)," a track Sherrill convinced Coe to redo. This version is not as strong, perhaps because it comes from a place of brokenness rather than the ecstatic font of new love, but it is still an elegant and powerful tome. *Human Emotions* has plenty of standouts, however, like "You Can Count on Me," with its irrepressible chorus and phase-shifting guitars, and "Mississippi River Queen," a country-rocker that sounds as if it were written for Hank Williams Jr. The title track is a masterpiece, with its syncopated vocal lead lines, country-waltz tempo, and huge backing chorus. There are also the outlaw anthems "Whiskey and Women" (with Janie Fricke on backing vocals) and one of the greatest drinking songs of all time, "Jack Daniels if You Please." The album finishes on a downer note with the track "Suicide," but despite its dark theme, *Human Emotions* is one of Coe's better efforts in the 1970s. *—Thom Jurek*

Buckstone County Prison / 1978 / COE ✦✦✦

Nothing Sacred / 1978 / COE ✦✦✦

Greatest Hits / 1978 / Columbia ✦✦✦✦✦

Featuring the hits "You Never Even Called Me By My Name," "Longhaired Redneck" and "Willie, Waylon and Me," this ten-track compilation of mid-'70s material from David Allan Coe is all you need to know about the ex-con turned country con-man/songwriter. He was one of country's more intriguing egos from the '70s. *—Mark A. Humphrey*

Spectrum VII / 1979 / Columbia ✦✦✦✦✦

Spectrum VII (1979) is one of the lighter recordings in David Allan Coe's storied career; not in the sense of lightweight, but in spirit, all things being relative. This is a reflective album from the first two tracks. "Rollin' With the Punches" is a rollicking country-rocker with choogling guitars and whinnying steel guitars; Billy Sherrill and Ron Bledsoe loaded the deck to make this an anthem. "On My Feet Again" is a 3/4-time honky tonk testament to Coe's ability to survive everything from prison to broken marriages to Nashville's indifference to a burst appendix and come out on the other side—free as a bird, just like a child left to play. "Fall in Love With You" sounds like a cross between something from the Allman Brothers' *Brothers and Sisters* album and Jimmy Buffett's *Changes in Latitudes, Changes in Attitudes*. There's a stellar hard rock tune called "Sudden Death" dedicated to Meat Loaf (!) "for believing in rock & roll and Ohio Boys." Another of Coe's most beautiful love songs reveals itself in "Fairytale Morning," a song that could have been written by Harlan Howard, it's so damn classy. The album closes with the definitive version of Dave Loggins' hit "Please Come to Boston." Coe's conviction as a singer and the washes of instruments with his acoustic guitar in the foreground are pure impressionistic production artistry. With the exception of "Love Is Just a Porpoise" (one of Coe's better novelty songs), every performance on *Spectrum VII* is stellar, and this is among Coe's finest records. *—Thom Jurek*

Compass Point / 1979 / Columbia ✦✦✦✦

David Allan Coe was prolific in the 1970s; he released nine albums between 1974-1979 on the Columbia label alone, along with some self-released albums of questionable taste for fan-club members and *Texas Moon* on the Plantation label. *Compass Point* is a solid outing from top to bottom. Coe goes to the well once more for respect, with a cast of killer studio musicians—some of whom were members of his road band—and the combined production talents of Billy Sherrill and Ron Bledsoe, who had come to work together seamlessly. With Bledsoe's gritty, in-your-face, performance-based approach and Sherrill's polish and sense of space and texture, they were able to balance all of the inherent contradictions in Coe's music, from the gorgeous balladry of "Gone," "Heads or Tails," and the elaborately arranged dark honky tonk of "Merle and Me" (not Haggard) to the rocking bluegrass stomp of "Honey Don't" and the boozy Tex-Mex swagger of "Lost." The album's classic has to be "Loving Her (Will Make You Lose Your Mind)." Here, hard country instrumentation meets Tejano melody and Caribbean backbeats in an easy, shuffling breeze of a dark song of regret and warning. As a coda to a decade that went by in a blur of fame, success, madness, tragedy, and disappointment, Coe left it on a very high note with an album that looked brightly to the future. *—Thom Jurek*

☆ **Invictus Means Unconquered** / 1980 / Columbia ✦✦✦✦✦

After the bleak, showbiz disappointment of *I've Got Something to Say*, David Allan Coe showed his eternal penchant for rebounding by releasing what is arguably the finest album of his career. *Invictus Means Unconquered* is a solid collection of originals, co-writes, and a cover or two that is so emotionally riveting, gorgeously played and sung, and tastefully produced it's a shame it was released at the height of urban cowboy-ism and sank without a trace. This time out, Coe really did have something to say, evidenced by the poem "Invictus" that appears as an epigraph for the album. Billy Sherrill took a front production seat and Ron Bledsoe concentrated on the instrumentation and the mix. The opening cut, "Rose Knows," by the seasoned songwriting team of Goodman, Kennedy, and Rose, featured a shimmering B-3, a staccato Telecaster, and a chugging pedal steel just under Coe's effortless vocal. True to form, Coe has always been underrated as a singer, and nowhere is this more evident than on *Invictus*. His co-write with Guy and Susanna Clark on "Ain't It Funny How Love'll Do Ya" is one of the most convincing vocal performances Coe ever recorded, ranking with "Mona Lisa Lost Her Smile" and "Would You Lay With Me (In a Field of Stone)." As if this weren't enough for a one-two punch, there's also the Coe-Shel Silverstein collaboration with its ethereal backing vocals and echo-plexed pedal steel. The conviction in his voice is so present, it almost cracks, but he never quite allows himself to lose control. These are the words of a man who has stared into the face of broken love's void and lived to tell about it. And yet, Coe just goes deeper with Ray Kennedy and Bobby David's "Purple Heart" ("I should get the Purple Heart for loving you"). Whoever she (referred to as "shortcake" in the previous track) is, Coe is not letting her—or himself—off the hook (he dedicates this one to his former alter ego, the Mysterious Rhinestone Cowboy, for keeping David Allan Coe alive). The album moves toward lighter territory with a killer reading of Gary P. Nunn's "London Homesick Blues" that rivals Jerry Jeff Walker's easily, and this writer would argue it is superior. Coe's reading of "Stand By Your Man" is heartfelt and moving, and takes on a new meaning in a man's voice. It's a plea, not a declaration. The band is crack on *Invictus*; Bledsoe held the reins tight and let Sherrill create an atmosphere that was both immediate and dreamy. While there isn't a weak second on this disc, two other tracks stand out above the rest: Coe's version of Silverstein's "Someplace to Come to When It Rains" and he and Clark's outlaw anthem dedicated to John Dillinger, "I Love Robbin' Banks." From top to bottom, *Invictus Means Unconquered* towers above most country records not only of the era, but of all time. It's a quintessential example of everything country music can achieve when it is honest, true, and from the center of a broken heart. *—Thom Jurek*

Tennessee Whiskey / 1981 / Columbia ✦✦✦✦

Coming on the heels of the brilliant *Invictus Means Unconquered* in 1980, *Tennessee Whiskey* from 1981 is another strong David Allan Coe outing, full of interesting song choices and hard country performances à la Merle Haggard and George Jones. Refusing to give into the flavor-of-the-month generic country "talent," Coe stuck to what he knew and sharpened the edges. Opening with the Dean Dillon/Linda Hargrove classic title track, with a honky tonk performance that is softened only by the swell of backing vocals, it sets a high standard for the rest of the album to follow, which it does. Coe's own folk-country nugget, "If I Knew," softened the electric guitars in favor of a 12-string and a honky tonk piano with a slippery steel in the distance to color his vocal before a banjo arrives on the final two choruses and transforms them into something akin to a bluegrass stomp. The most eclectic and risky track on the set is a cover of Otis Redding's "Dock of the Bay." Many have tried and almost no one has succeeded with this one, but Coe's read is immediate, deep, and soulful in a restless country way. Anyone who ever doubted his ability to interpret a classic tune should give this one a listen because, frankly, it'll blow your mind. The band puts in a credible performance as well, with its funky, dirty groove. Shel Silverstein and Fred Koller's lovely "Juanita" is given the *Volcano*-era Jimmy Buffett treatment. The blues-ed-out "We Got a Bad Thing Goin'" with Terry McMillan is a greasy little number that gives the album something edgy. The honky tonk standard "D-R-U-N-K" is given fine treatment here by Coe and guest the late John Hartford, and Coe's own "Little Orphan Annie" is a ballad-turned-bluegrass orgy. In all, *Tennessee Whiskey* proved once again that no matter what the critics and programmers said or didn't, when he made records, he always showed up to play. *—Thom Jurek*

D A C / 1982 / Columbia ✦✦

Rough Rider / 1982 / Columbia ✦✦✦

Underground Album / 1982 / D.A.C. Records/*Easy Rider* Magazine ✦✦✦

Castles in the Sand / 1983 / Columbia ✦✦✦✦

Castles in the Sand is one of David Allan Coe's most underrated and consistent—if extraordinarily haunted and strange—recordings. Coming well after his glory—and scandal—years in the 1970s, Coe and producer Billy Sherrill integrated their partnership into a seamless whole. Over their years of working together, Sherrill was increasingly able to consistently rein in Coe's excesses, while giving him enough freedom to explore whatever directions in country and rock & roll he needed to in order to grow as a singer. Coe wrote only three tracks on the album, and co-wrote another with Karen Brooks. Sherrill showcases Coe as a fine, understated, interpretive singer. And there is a reason, however odd—the secret lies in the middle of the album. Coe wrote the title track as an autobiographical tribute to Bob Dylan as one of the two most misunderstood artists of his generation—Coe being the other one. Coe emulates Dylan's voice throughout the verses and sings in his own on the refrains. Whether the information in the tune is literally true is of no consequence, as it is one of the more poetically beautiful songs in his catalog. This is followed by a funky country read of Dylan's own "Gotta Serve Somebody" with Lacy J. Dalton, who adds a certain depth and wildness to the mix. This pair of tunes eases into one of the eeriest covers of the Detterline/Gentry classic "The Ride," about the ghost of Hank Williams making an appearance to offer advice to a young Turk. Coming at the place it does in Coe's career—on the downside, but certainly not out—its irony is particularly poignant. Sonically, *Castles in the Sand* is closer to the radio country of the early 1980s than any of his other records, except for the horrible *I've Got Something to Say*, but given Sherrill's way with getting the emotion from a song in the mix, it is still a fine of example of Coe's hard country records. No matter how much he rocks, rolls, or plays the blues, Coe remains a honky tonk singer of the highest order. "Missin' the Kid" is a self-penned waltz that is sad and hunted, full of regret and remorse over the loss of his daughter when his second marriage broke up, something he never got over. It's also one of the most sensitive things he's ever written, as it is full of empathy for a daughter he hasn't seen in over ten years. The album closes with two love songs, the bittersweet Brook/Coe tune "Don't Be a Stranger," a duet with Eve Shapiro, and Coe's own "For Lovers Only (Part 1)." Like a Tom Waits ballad, the keyboard whispers as Coe begins to sing from a barstool, offering a portrayal of himself trying to write the song in some gin mill—asking an imaginary waitress for a Jack Daniels and water, and a pencil with an eraser on it. He stumbles, flubs, and finds his way through a fond wish for those who dare to love not to give up, no matter how rough the breaks can be. The band kicks in after a minute with a Caribbean rhythm over a country shuffle and a pair of lead guitars next to steel drums and synths, evoking the sounds of the Florida Keys. The saxophone fills are a bit startling, but they work beautifully and the album comes to a very upbeat close, marking the end of Coe's most creative and prolific period, which began in 1969. *—Thom Jurek*

Hello in There / 1983 / Columbia ✦✦

Just Divorced / 1984 / Columbia ✦✦✦

Unchained / 1985 / Columbia ✦✦

Darlin', Darlin' / 1985 / Columbia ✦✦✦

17 Greatest Hits / 1985 / Columbia ✦✦✦✦✦
17 Greatest Hits is the most thorough retrospective assembled of David Alan Coe's outlaw heyday, containing every one of his biggest hits—including "You Never Even Called Me By My Name," "The Ride," "Mona Lisa Lost Her Smile," "Willie, Waylon and Me," "Longhaired Redneck," and "She Used to Love Me a Lot"—plus a wealth of minor hits and lesser-known album tracks. The result is a comprehensive overview of one of the most respected and admired, if not necessarily popular, country singers of the late '70s and early '80s. *—Thom Owens*

● **For the Record: The First 10 Years** / 1985 / Columbia ✦✦✦✦✦
For the Record: The First 10 Years gets a slight edge over its counterpart *17 Greatest Hits*, not just because it contains three more songs, but because it gives a greater context for David Allan Coe's achievements. Yes, his redneck tendencies sound a little disturbing to PC-leaning ears, but Coe was a great, unashamed country singer, singing the purest honky-tonk and hardest country of his era, making even Waylon and Willie seem a little conventional. There is an undeniable reactionary streak to his music yet, especially in retrospect, this makes it stronger, since he seems like one of the lone voices fighting for traditional country values. Did he win the fight? Well, in a way, he did, since he created pure, hardcore country, as this set of songs proves. This is Coe at his very best, from covers of "Please Come to Boston" to his trademarks "Longhaired Country," "Willie, Waylon and Me," "Jack Daniels, if You Please," and "Mona Lisa Lost Her Smile." He winds up relying on covers a bit much, but his attitude makes him stand apart from his brethren. He may not be the most original outlaw, but there's none more outlaw than him. *—Stephen Thomas Erlewine*

Son of the South / 1986 / Columbia ✦✦✦

I Love Country / 1987 / Columbia ✦✦

A Matter of Life and Death / 1987 / Columbia ✦✦✦✦
In 1987 the David Allan Coe/Bill Sherrill partnership was still running strong as evidence by *A matter of Life and Death.* Like many of Coe's recordings, this one is a concept record, full of "dedications and meditations." The inspiration behind its making was the passing of Coe's father Donald Mahan Coe, and the return home (on the day of his father's funeral) of his 16-year old daughter from living with her mother for the majority of her life, and the birth of his and Jody Lynn's two children Tyler and Tanya Montana. Coe and Sherrill are particularly suited to each other on recordings like this. They serve to curb each other's excesses and rely on making sure the right songs come out of the mix, representing the emotional intention of the set rather than burying those songs under production or hyperbole. This set yielded some of the strongest Coe songs of the 1980s—and that's saying something: "Jody like a Melody," If Your Eyes Could Only Lie," and "The Ten Commandments of Love." And "Southern Star," with its searing lyric and screaming guitar solos, is among his most under-noticed, poetic tomes worthy of being recorded by .38 Special or Lynyrd Skynyrd. Sherrill's sequencing is brilliant and each song seems to segue into another creating a kind of impressionistic narrative. Interestingly this record sounds so outside the new traditionalist mould that dominated Nash Vegas at the time it was quickly lost to oblivion—despite the fact that it's a true traditional country record in the most strident use of the word. This is a fine if forgotten album. Coe may have had some hits, but it's records like this one that make one wonder if there wasn't a conspiracy to marginalize him and make him fail. Coe is a brilliant songwriter well into the 21st century and deserves to be lauded with the Nelson's and Jenning's and Kristofferson's and Newbury's and even Cash's. *—Thom Jurek*

Crazy Daddy / 1989 / Columbia ✦✦✦

18 X-Rated Hits / 1990 / D.A.C. Records ✦✦✦

☆ **Mysterious Rhinestone Cowboy/Once Upon a Time** / 1993 / Bear Family ✦✦✦✦✦
The first volume in Bear Family's excellent David Allan Coe reissue series pairs 1974's raucous breakthrough album with its follow-up, which garnered him his first Top Ten single ("Jody Like a Melody"). Despite the error in the title of the second album (which is actually *Once Upon a Rhyme*), this nearly flawless collection of original and well-covered songs gives the listener an idea of just how fully Coe had developed by the time he signed to Columbia. On the former recording, some of Coe's early classics, such as "A Sad Country Song" and "I Still Sing the Old Songs," are featured, with truly brilliant interpretations of Mickey Newbury's "33rd of August" and Guy Clark's "Desperadoes Waiting for a Train." On the latter, Coe's brilliant songwriting is fully on display with "Would You Lay With Me (In a Field of Stone)," a number one for Tanya Tucker a year earlier; "Jody . . ."; "Loneliness in Ruby's Eyes"; and "Sweet Vibrations (Some Folks Call It Love)." These originals are accompanied by inspiring and even definitive reads of Steve Goodman's "You Never Even Called Me By My Name" and Richard Dobson's "Piece of Wood and Steel." This two-fer features excellent remastering and a deluxe package with a full liner-note essay and the lyrics to all tracks, as well as photos. *—Thom Jurek*

Super Hits / Mar. 8, 1993 / Columbia ✦✦✦✦✦
Yet another repackaging of Coe's handful of successful radio songs; these hits barely hint at the more outrageous material featured on the albums from which they're drawn. *—Michael McCall*

Longhaired Redneck/Rides Again / 1994 / Bear Family ✦✦✦✦
Long Haired Redneck/Rides Again is the second volume in Bear Family's David Allan Coe two-fer series of his work at Columbia Records from 1974-1981. This pair of albums, released in 1976 and 1977, respectively—his third and fourth albums for the label—find Coe aligning himself completely with the Willie, Waylon, and Billy Joe Shaver "outlaw" movement—as if he ever had to try. Coming on the heels of his first Top Ten hit, a cover of Steve Goodman's "You Never Even Called Me By My Name" from *Once Upon a Rhyme, Longhaired Redneck* is one of Coe's finest records. He either wrote or co-wrote every song on the album, and the title track became his anthem. In addition, the haunting ballad "Revenge," "Free Born Rambling Man," and "Living on the Run" are hallmarks of his best work as a songwriter and as a performer. *Rides Again* is an altogether different affair. While Coe once again wrote or co-wrote all but one of the album's ten tracks, it is also the beginning of a darkly cynical period in his work, featuring such tracks as the conceited "Willie, Waylon, and Me" (complete with a reprise six tracks later); "If That Ain't Country (You Can Kiss My Ass)"; his paean to his polygamy, "The House We've Been Calling a Home"; and the bitter "Sense of Humor." There are also excellent songs here, such as "Under Rachel's Wings," "Greener Than the Grass We Laid On," and a cover of Dale Murphy's "Laid Back and Wasted." *—Thom Jurek*

Best of the Best / 1995 / Federal ✦✦✦✦✦

Tattoo/Family Album / 1995 / Bear Family ✦✦✦✦✦
Tattoo and *Family Album* mark singer/songwriter David Allan Coe's fifth and sixth albums for Columbia, respectively, issued in 1977 and 1978. They also make up the third volume of Bear Family's Columbia Records retrospective covering the years 1974-1981. The issue of *Tattoo* marked the third album Coe issued in 1977. First there was the often-angry *Rides Again*, where the "Mysterious Rhinestone Cowboy" made his final recorded appearance; then the self-released *Texas Moon*, recorded on the road; and finally *Tattoo. Tattoo* also marks the beginning of Coe's association with Billy Sherrill (though Ron Bledsoe would remain with him until 1980's *Invictus Means Unconcquered*). *Tattoo* and *Family Album* mark a far more sensitive side of Coe. *Tattoo* features more love songs than most Coe records, and there are some fine ones, such as "Just to Prove My Love for You," "Face to Face," "You'll Always Live Inside of Me," and "Just in Time (To Watch Love Die)." *Family Album* centers more on the connection to one's roots and connections not only between Coe and his family of origin (raised a Mormon, he was the son of polygamy), but his progeny and the concept of family as a universal concept. Inexplicably, in keeping with his contradictory nature, *Family Album* also contains the classic "Take This Job and Shove It," which Johnny Paycheck took to number one, and the tasteless "Divers Do It Deeper," which sounds more like Jimmy Buffett than Coe. These albums are generally overlooked in Coe's catalog and shouldn't be; they are consistent, literate, and represent the other side of the outlaw persona Coe worked so hard to create. *—Thom Jurek*

Human Emotions/Spectrum VII / 1995 / Bear Family ✦✦✦✦
David Allan Coe's seventh and eighth albums for Columbia (documented here on CD by the illustrious Bear Family label from Germany as the fourth issue in their Coe retrospective series) reveal just how influential producer Billy Sherrill became on Coe's sound, and how completely he trusted Sherrill's instincts. *Human Emotions*, written and recorded after being left by his wife of two years, had Coe offering two sides of his complex feelings of despondency. There is the "Happy Side," comprised of songs written and recorded before his wife left, and in some cases before they even met. The other side is entitled "Suicide" (also the name of the album's final track, the definitive black metal country song), which is a painful examination of one's shortcomings and bitterness after the divorce. Most notable is the re-recording of "Would You Lay With Me (In a Field of Stone)," which is perhaps even more powerful than the original, done four years earlier. *Spectrum VII*, issued in 1979, barely a year later, is full of beautiful honky tonk songs and whining pedal steel guitars as well as folky country waltzes and progressive country tunes that have as much in common with songwriters such as Jesse Colin Young and Jimmy Buffett as they do with Nash Vegas' finest. There is a corny track—characteristic of all Coe outings—as well as the truly definitive version of Dave Loggins' unintentional pop hit "Please Come to Boston." As with all the Coe reissues, this one is chock-full of session photographs and the sound is spectacular. The liner-note essays—which ceased to be a part of the packaging after the second Bear Family volume—are missed, though. *—Thom Jurek*

Compass Point/I've Got Something to Say / 1995 / Bear Family ✦✦✦
The pairing of *Compass Point* and *I've Got Something to Say* is the oddest of the two-fers issued by Bear Family as volume five in their David Allan Coe Columbia retrospective. On his ninth and tenth albums for Columbia, Coe was still looking for respect from radio program directors in Nash Vegas and nationwide—and wasn't getting it, despite the ace production team of Billy Sherrill and Ron Bledsoe. *Compass Point* is the most reflective of Coe's albums in the sense that it seemingly constantly looks back to the previous, and most of that isn't pretty; in fact, it's full of regret and remorse, but the determination to transcend as well. The percussion tracks are straight out of Jimmy Buffett's classic records and the atmospherics are pure Sherrill—phased guitars and accordions and fiddles shimmering in and out of the mix. Two of the finest songs on the album are "Gone (Like)" and "Loving Her (Will Make You Lose Your Mind)." *I've Got Something to Say* is Coe's star-guest album—a blatant attempt for radio airplay (it says so in the liner notes) that doesn't work at all. From the re-recording of "This Bottle (In My Hand)," with George Jones (given that this was recorded in 1980, when Jones was a recently recovering alcoholic, it's tasteless) to the re-recording of "Take This Job and Shove It," done as a reaction to the film of the same name, the songs are more boisterous than inspired. "Take It Easy Rider," with Guy Clark, sounds more confused and lost than anything else, and "Hank Williams Junior-Junior" with the Allman Brothers' Dickey Betts and Kris Kristofferson is a bad—no, make that terrible—novelty song. This is the only case in which it is too bad that a very decent outing like *Compass Point* was paired with such a poor one. *—Thom Jurek*

☆ **Invictus Means Unconquered/Tennessee Waltz** / 1995 / Bear Family ✦✦✦✦✦
The sixth and final volume of Bear Family's David Allan Coe two-fer series ends on a high note with his final albums for Columbia, the gorgeous *Invictus Means Unconquered* and the gutsy, rootsy *Tennessee Whiskey.* Both of these records represent a return to form for

Coe, who had hit a career and creative low with his first attempt at a commercial album, *I've Got Something to Say*, complete with "special guests." No one was really paying attention to Coe when he recorded *Invictus*; he and producer Billy Sherrill had nothing to lose, so they put together a collection of ten very strong songs that are, for the very first time, comprised entirely of either co-writes or covers. The covers include Gary P. Nunn's "London Home Sick Blues," "Stand By Your Man," and Bobby David and Ray Kennedy's "The Purple Heart," among others. Among the co-writes are two by Coe and Guy and Susanna Clark, "Ain't It Funny the Way Love'll Do Ya" and "I Love Robbin' Banks," and the Coe/Shel Silverstein classic "If You Ever Think of Me at All." The album flows from beginning to end and never slacks, even for a moment. It is Coe's most criminally ignored record and may be his very best. *Tennessee Whiskey*, by contrast, is a record that seeks to expand on the vision created with *Invictus*. Sherrill's influence in helping to choose material is evident in the title track, Larry Kingston's "Bright Morning Light," and the Shel Silverstein/Fred Koller nugget "Juanita," among others. The rest features new Coe material, songs that are tight, hooky, and downright country—which might have been a problem in 1981 when Karen Brooks, Janie Fricke, David Frizzell, Eddie Rabbit, Rosanne Cash, and Lacy J. Dalton were topping the charts. The huge surprise is Coe's odd, funky, but very credible reading of "Dock of the Bay." The singing on both of these records is amazing; Coe was never in better voice. Anyone interested in finding out about Coe's work apart from his myth would do well to actually begin with these records. *—Thom Jurek*

Super Hits, Vol. 2 / Mar. 19, 1996 / Columbia ✦✦✦

This ten-song compilation is *Vol. 2* in the sense that it contains David Allen Coe's less successful "super hits." For "Mona Lisa Lost Her Smile" and "The Ride," look for *Super Hits* (Columbia 53311). The biggest hits here are "Long Haired Redneck" and "She Used to Love Me a Lot," both of which made the Country Top 40. The rest are minor chart entries or worse. But that's not to say there isn't some characteristically provocative material here, including the Willie Nelson duet "I've Already Cheated on You" and "Now I Lay Me Down to Cheat," a song that manages to mix infidelity with prayer. Coe was always a near-parody of a country singer, and the humor content is high, but so is the fun. And if you want to hear strange, wait for the duet with Lacy J. Dalton on Bob Dylan's "Gotta Serve Somebody" that closes the album. *—William Ruhlmann*

David Allan Coe Live: If That Ain't Country . . . / Jul. 15, 1997 / Sony ✦✦✦✦

Live: If That Ain't Country... captures David Allan Coe in concert in the mid-'90s, running through most of his best-known songs ("Would You Lay With Me In a Field of Stone," "Take This Job and Shove It," "Willie Waylon and Me"), illustrating that he delivers them nearly as well—and often a whole lot more country—than the artists that made them famous. Although the sound is a little ragged at times, *If That Ain't Country . . .* is a great, bracing listen, full of rowdy spirit and rollicking energy. It's yet another album from Coe that suggests he should have been a star, even though his cult audience has allowed him to flourish and make records as fine as this. *—Thom Owens*

Johnny Cash Is a Friend of Mine / Jun. 9, 1998 / King ✦✦

Recommended for Airplay / Mar. 30, 1999 / Columbia ✦✦✦✦

Following his 1997 live album, David Allan Coe releases a new studio album on Sony Music's Lucky Dog imprint, and not much has changed since the 1970s and '80s, when he was putting albums out on sister label Columbia. The songs, all written by Coe, are still full of references to drinking ("Drink Canada Dry"), riding motorcycles ("A Harley Someday") and having trouble maintaining romantic relationships ("Drink My Wife Away," "She's Already Gone"). Coe's throaty baritone is more effective, if anything, and the music still veers between honky tonk country and blues-rock. Alternately humorous, sentimental and belligerent, the 59-year-old outlaw continues to pursue his own peculiar muse even if, despite the hopeful album title, he is unlikely to get the kind of notice he did 20 years earlier. *—William Ruhlmann*

16 Biggest Hits / Aug. 10, 1999 / Sony ✦✦✦✦

16 Biggest Hits may be missing some noteworthy songs, but it does provide an excellent summary of his Columbia recordings between 1974 and 1996. Since it does contain the majority of his best-known songs—"You Never Even Called Me By My Name," "Would You Lay With Me (In a Field of Stone)," "Longhaired Redneck," "Willie, Waylon and Me," "Now I Lay Me Down to Cheat," "The Ride"—at a mid-line price, it's an excellent introductory collection. *—Stephen Thomas Erlewine*

Castles in the Sand/Once Upon a Rhyme / Nov. 9, 1999 / Collectables ✦✦✦✦

This set is typical of the Collectables label's bizarre and unexplainable pairing strategies. This two-fer repackages outlaw country singer/songwriter David Allan Coe's 1983 *Castles in the Sand* and 1975's *Once Upon a Rhyme*. The former record scored on the charts a pair of singles ("Cheap Thrills," "The Ride"), neither of which Coe wrote. Along with these cuts is the strange title track, which is a backwards tribute to Bob Dylan followed by a cover of his "Gotta Serve Somebody" with Lacy J. Dalton. This very modern-sounding album is contrasted with the 1975 classic *Once Upon a Rhyme*, produced by Ron Bledsoe, which featured the timeless "Would You Lay With Me (In a Field of Stone)," "Jody Like a Memory," and a definitive cover of Steve Goodman's "You Never Even Called Me By My Name." The latter, despite its age, is the superior recording in that it features Coe's strongest songs, less-intrusive production, and a conscious sense of itself as part of a new kind of country music. The problem is that for true core collectors and fans of the later material, this is the only way to get *Castles in the Sand* on CD. For those who can live without everything after *Invictus Means Unconquered*, the Bear Family coupling of *Once Upon a Rhyme* with *The Mysterious Rhinestone Cowboy* is a better fit, despite the higher price. As usual, there are no production or musician credits in Collectables' package, which is always a disappointment. *—Thom Jurek*

Songwriter of the Tear / Mar. 20, 2001 / Cleveland Int'l ✦✦✦

Kellie Coffey

b. Moore, OK

Vocals / Contemporary Country, Country-Pop

Growing up in Moore, OK, Kellie Coffey made her stage debut at the age of nine when she sang at *the Oklahoma Opry*. Her interest in music continued and Coffey attended the same high-school that country star Toby Keith had attended. Her involvement in music took on a more serious course while attending the University of Oklahoma, where she participated in musicals and other performance activities. Relocating to Los Angeles to pursue a career as a singer, Coffey soon found work singing on demos, as well as doing sessions for television, film, and audio tracks used by Disney in their theme parks. She began making trips to Nashville to write and signed a publishing deal with Warner Chappell, followed by a record deal with BNA. Her first single, "When You Lie Next to Me," was released at the end of 2001, heralding her Dan Huff-produced debut, which was released the following summer. *—Tom Demalon*

When You Lie Next to Me / May 7, 2002 / BNA ✦✦✦

On her debut album, *When You Lie Next to Me*, vocalist Kellie Coffey comes across like a more approachable Faith Hill—her polished country-pop is every bit as urbane, yet it doesn't feel as glamorous, a little more down to earth. It's an appealing sound, especially since her voice is warm and friendly, and this is produced as professionally as it can be from Dann Huff, who keeps Coffey's voice at the forefront, letting certain flourishes—the occasional steel guitar run, a little bit of keyboards and guitars—peep out from the warm wash of the instrumental backdrop. With repeated plays, the best of these songs—whether they're pleasant midtempo numbers like "At the End of the Day," ballads like the title track, or light rockers like "Love's Funny That Way"—sound like they could be staples on adult contemporary radio, which is what they were designed to do, after all. *—Stephen Thomas Erlewine*

Ben Colder

b. Apr. 10, 1921, Erick, OK

Vocals / Novelty, Country Comedy

Ben Colder was the alter ego of singer Sheb Wooley (of "Purple People Eater" fame), which he used specifically for recording parodies of country hits. Due to various acting commitments, Wooley had been unable to record the song "Don't Go Near the Indians," which was instead cut by Rex Allen for a significant hit in 1962. Wooley recorded a drunken-sounding parody called "Don't Go Near the Eskimos" and released it under the pseudonym Ben Colder (other choices reportedly included Ben Freezin and Klon Dyke). "Eskimos" was a Top 20 hit on the country charts, and Wooley decided to keep returning to his new comic persona on a regular basis. "Hello Wall No. 2" went Top 30 in 1963, and "Almost Persuaded No. 2" went all the way to number six in 1966, giving Wooley the second-biggest country hit of his career.

Ben Colder had a few more chart singles through the '60s, including "Harper Valley P.T.A. (Later That Same Day)" and "Little Green Apples No. 2," and continued to release albums on MGM through the '70s. Thanks to his penchant for comedy, Wooley was tapped as a staff songwriter for the television series *Hee Haw* when it debuted in 1969. Colder made a comeback in 1996 thanks in part to Billy Ray Cyrus, who inspired the title track of *Shakey Breaky Car*. *—Steve Huey*

Spoofing the Big Ones / 1962 / MGM ✦✦✦

Ben Colder / 1963 / MGM ✦✦✦✦

Big Ben Strikes Again / 1966 / MGM ✦✦

Wine, Women and Song / 1967 / MGM ✦✦✦

Wacky World of Ben Colder / 1973 / MGM ✦

Sheb Wooley's long association with MGM ended in 1973, and *The Wacky World of Ben Colder* is the last album he recorded for the label under his comedy pseudonym, Ben Colder. All of Wooley's hits as Colder were song parodies, but this album concentrates on silly original songs written by Wooley and such paragons of comedy as Bobby Braddock and Eddy Raven. In other words, it isn't very funny, and the voice Wooley affects for his Colder efforts quickly wears thin. The title of "The Unhappiest Squirrel in the U.S.A.," a parody of Donna Fargo's "The Happiest Girl in the U.S.A.," gives an indication of the level of wit on display. *The Wacky World of Ben Colder* has the power to make even devoted fans of Wooley feel a little embarrassed on his behalf. *—Greg Adams*

Golden Hits / 1979 / Hollywood ✦✦✦✦

Ben Colder was the humorous alter ego/wise guy of singer Sheb Wooley. This Hollywood compilation includes the corny classics "Don't Go Near the Eskimos" and "Little Bottles," with parodies of country-pop hits of the era: "Sunday Morning Fallin' Down," "Detroit City," "Little Green Apples," "Games People Play," and "Almost Persuaded." If you need to hear Colder's parodies next to the originals he pokes fun at, pick up *Eskimos, Mean Old Queens and Little Bitty Steers* on Bear Family. *—Al Campbell*

Shakey Breaky Car / Nov. 1, 1996 / Koch ✦✦✦✦

● **Eskimos, Mean Old Queens and Little Bitty Steers** / May 21, 2002 / Bear Family ✦✦✦✦

Eskimos, Mean Old Queens and Little Bitty Steers is a collection of Ben Colder parodies paired up with the original songs he's lambasting. Whether it's Johnny Cash's "Ballad of a Teenage Queen" transformed into "Ballad of a Mean Old Queen" or Johnny Preston's "Running Bear" tweaked into "Running Bare," Colder's humor translates quite well when compared to the original songs. *—Bradley Torreano*

B.J. Cole

b. Jun. 17, 1946, London, England

Guitar (Steel) / Rock & Roll, Traditional Country, Nashville Sound/Countrypolitan

Born on June 17, 1946, in London, B.J. Cole was inspired by the instrumental work of the Shadows' Hank Marvin, and picked up a guitar. He worked his way through various versions of the instrument, eventually settling on pedal steel guitar. During the 1970s, Cole was a sought-after session man, playing alongside Elton John, Scott Walker, T. Rex, and Nazareth, among others. He also founded the post-psychedelic, country-influenced combo Cochise in 1970, and released three albums with the group. Cole issued the solo effort *New Hovering Dog* upon the dissolution of the band, and went on to work with David Sylvian (1986's ambient piece *Gone to Earth*), and vocalist Hank Wangford. The ambient country piece *Transparent Music* appeared in 1989. Cole continued to work as a session man throughout the 1990s, contributing to the work of the Verve, Björk, and Beck, among others. In 2000 he collaborated with electronica experimentalist and producer Luke Vibert on *Stop the Panic*, which intersected his shimmering guitar lines with the squelch and bop of Vibert's electronics. —*Johnny Loftus*

Swallow Tails / 1971 / United Artists ✦✦✦

So Far / 1972 / United Artists ✦✦✦

New Hovering Dog / 1973 / United Artists ✦✦✦

● **Transparent Music** / 1989 / Hannibal ✦✦✦✦

Heart of the Moment / 1995 / Resurgence ✦✦✦✦
Performed with the help of the Transparent Music Ensemble, featuring keyboardist/collaborator Guy Jackson and so named because of previous work on B.J. Cole's album of that name, *Heart of the Moment* shows Cole creating a fine recording as noteworthy as his many session appearances. Unlike any number of studio musician projects that consist of little more than cold, clean, and cloying results, Cole actually sounds like he has something to perform that isn't motivated by a paycheck. The majority of pieces are written by Cole and Jackson together, and the two make for an excellent team, the former's exquisite steel guitar lines blending well with the latter's piano and synth work. As a whole, the album is relaxing mood music but not simply background new age—sleepy smooth jazz this isn't, though on "Eastern Cool" Jackson's keyboard sounds are inexplicably cheap and cheesy. Though having said that, it might be Cole feeding his guitar through the MIDI controller listed in the credits—too bad the end result doesn't succeed as it should. The core country element of Cole's playing always lends a subtle bite to the proceedings, while the equally prevalent hints of Hawaiian guitar and other influences add to the overall effect. The sense is always of a thorough student of the instrument who wants to do much more than simply make "that" sound when needed. One of the early highlights is "Icarus Enigma," a guitar/piano duet that adds enough understated touches in the mix to make it seem like something David Sylvian could have done on *Gone to Earth*. Cellist Ben Davies adds lovely work throughout the album—"Indian Willow" is a fine example of how he can add to the proceedings—while guest performers on percussion, further strings, and (on "Forever Amber") Chinese flute all make their mark well. —*Ned Raggett*

Mark Collie

b. Jan. 18, 1956, Waynesboro, TN
Guitar, Vocals / Contemporary Country, New Traditionalist
Mark Collie made a splash on the '90s country scene by blending traditional honky tonk with raw rockabilly energy. Born in Waynesboro, TN, he grew up a fan of the Sun Records stable and later discovered progressive country songwriters like Willie Nelson and Kris Kristofferson. He took up both guitar and piano, and joined his first band at the age of 12. He worked part-time as a local radio DJ while in high-school, and toured the Southwest with several different bands after graduation. In 1982, he moved to Nashville to pursue a songwriting career, but failed to make the grade at any of the city's publishing houses. Instead, he started performing his own material, and took up a monthly residency at the Douglas Corner Cafe, which helped earn him a following. MCA's country division signed Collie after witnessing a 1989 showcase performance, and his debut album, *Hardin County Line*, was released the following year. Despite critical acclaim, the album wasn't a huge seller, and of its singles—"Something With a Ring to It," the title track, "Looks Aren't Everything," and "Let Her Go"—only the latter managed to make the Top 20.

The 1991 follow-up, *Born & Raised in Black & White*, was a more polished effort that featured the minor hits "She's Never Comin' Back" and "Calloused Hands," but some felt it backed off the strengths of his debut. That changed on his 1993 breakthrough effort, *Mark Collie*, which returned to the rowdier, harder-rocking style of his debut and produced his first Top Ten country hits with "Even the Man in the Moon Is Cryin'" and "Born to Love You." He also had some success with "Shame Shame Shame Shame" and "Something's Gonna Change Her Mind," and he kept going strong with the stripped-down 1994 follow-up, *Unleashed*, which spawned the hit "Hard Lovin' Woman." Collie subsequently moved to Warner subsidiary Giant for 1995's *Tennessee Plates*, which slowed his career momentum somewhat. The only other Collie release that has appeared to date is the budget-priced greatest-hits-live set *Even the Man in the Moon Is Cryin'* (1998). —*Steve Huey*

Hardin County Line / 1990 / MCA ✦✦✦✦✦
This honky tonk rebel's debut evokes the heart of '50s country, with detailed and compassionate songwriting, wildcat vocals, and guitar by James Burton. One song, "Looks Aren't Everything," hit the Top 40, while two others, "Hardin County Line" and "Something With a Ring to It," didn't fare quite so well. —*John Floyd & Brian Mansfield*

Born & Raised in Black & White / 1991 / MCA ✦✦✦
The first half of Collie's second album contained some smartly written songs, including "She's Never Coming Back" and "Calloused Hands," but some of the first album's edge had been smoothed off. —*Brian Mansfield*

● **Mark Collie** / 1993 / MCA ✦✦✦✦✦
At once a move to the mainstream and a return to Collie's West Tennessee rockabilly roots, the album worked fairly well. "Even the Man in the Moon Is Crying" and "Born to Love You" were Collie's first Top Ten hits, and "Shame Shame Shame Shame" rocked as hard as anything he'd done. —*Brian Mansfield*

Unleashed / 1994 / MCA ✦✦✦
In the same vein as *Mark Collie*, this album is more aggressive. "It Is No Secret" followed in Collie's tradition of midtempo romantic singles, while he rocks it up elsewhere. —*Brian Mansfield*

Tennessee Plates / Jul. 18, 1995 / Giant ✦✦✦
Tennessee Plates delivers the edgy rockabilly punch that fans have come to expect from Mark Collie, but not in quite as a consistent fashion as some of his earlier records. Although it has its share of love songs, the album does continue the stripped-down, direct approach of *Unleashed*—it just doesn't have the same amount of high-quality songs. That said, the best songs on the record are very good indeed, and make the album a fun, entertaining listen. —*Thom Owens*

Even the Man in the Moon Is Cryin' / Jan. 13, 1998 / Universal Special Products ✦✦✦
Even the Man in the Moon Is Cryin' is a budget-line collection that features ten of Mark Collie's biggest hits as performed live in concert. It's an enjoyable record showcasing Collie at his most energetic, running through such songs as "It Don't Take a Lot," "Calloused Hands," "Looks Aren't Everything," "Shame Shame Shame Shame" and "Even the Man in the Moon is Crying." Hardcore fans will definitely enjoy this record, but casual fans will want to wait for a collection of the original hit versions of these songs. —*Stephen Thomas Erlewine*

The Collins Kids

f. 1954, California, **db.** 1962
Group / Rockabilly
By the time Lawrence (b. 1944) and Lawrencine Collins (b. 1942) were 11 and 13, respectively, they were already tearing it up on country package shows, recording for Columbia Records, and performing on national TV almost weekly. Older sister Lorrie held up the cowgirl fringe-rustling-against-nylons teenage sensuality department; kid brother Larry was a bundle of hyperkinetic energy, bopping all over the place while laying down exciting, twangy guitar breaks learned firsthand from the King of the Doubleneck Mosrite, Joe Maphis. As time went on, the Collins' recordings veered from mawkish brother/sister country-style duets to white-hot rockabilly, and they were just reaching their peak when Lorrie eloped, effectively breaking up the act. Revered by rockabilly collectors the world over, their filmed television appearances and recordings are testimony to the fact that the Collins Kids weren't just "good for their age," they were just plain good, period. —*Cub Koda*

Introducing Larry and Lorrie / 1958 / Columbia ✦✦✦✦✦
For those who don't want to spring for the lengthy and expensive Bear Family box, this is an excellent distillation of 12 of their best late-'50s rockabilly sides. "Hoy Hoy," "Whistle Bait," "Mercy," "Just Because," and "Party" rank among the most smokin' rockabilly sides ever waxed. —*Richie Unterberger*

Rockin' Rollin Collins Kids / 1983 / Bear Family ✦✦✦

Rockin' Rollin Collins Kids, Vol. 2 / 1983 / Bear Family ✦✦✦
There's some good stuff on this 16-track anthology, though it's not nearly as good as the domestic Columbia compilation *Introducing Larry and Lorrie*. But with the appearance in 1991 of Bear Family's *Hop Skip & Jump* box set, there's no reason to hunt this (or *Vol. 1*) down anymore. —*Richie Unterberger*

Television Party / 1989 / TV ✦✦✦
Here are 14 lo-fi songs from vintage television broadcasts, on a label of questionable legitimacy. There's a 31-song compilation of this stuff on a 1993 Krazy Kat album; hold out for that one instead. —*Richie Unterberger*

Hop, Skip & Jump / Aug. 1991 / Bear Family ✦✦✦✦✦
The Collins Kids were a brother-and-sister act that got real good real young and made it out of their native Oklahoma, settling out in California, where they landed a radio/TV hookup with Tex Ritter's *Town Hall Party* out of Compton. Older sister Lorrie handled the teenage-sensuality department with nylons rustling against cowgirl fringe, while little brother Larry was a hot-as-a-firecracker bundle of energy, bopping all over the place while laying down excitable, twangy guitar breaks learned first-hand from another *Town Hall Party* regular, the King of the Doubleneck Mosrite, Joe Maphis. With all that in mind, what we have here is another excellent CD box set from Bear Family, two discs with a booklet in an album-size format. Everything's here, from the great early sides like "Beetle Bug Bop," "The Cuckoo Rock," "I'm in My Teens," and "The Rockaway Rock" to the rockabilly classics "Just Because," "Hoy Hoy," "Mercy," "Sweet Talk," and "Party," through the Maphis/Collins guitar instrumentals to Larry and Lorrie's solo sides from the end of the trail. Joe Maphis' great guitar is sprayed all over the place and the master-tape transfer is as clear as you expect stuff out of the Columbia vaults produced by Don Law to be. A booklet crammed full of great live photos and excellent liners by Colin Escott rounds out the package. —*Cub Koda*

Rockin' on T.V. / 1993 / Krazy Kat ✦✦✦✦
Larry and Lorrie, the Collins Kids, were a live act to be savored. In their early days, they were cute without being cloying and highly energetic without being annoying. As they moved into their teens by the late '50s, Larry had developed into a phenomenal guitarist while Lorrie had bloomed into a beautiful teenager with a voice that could belt out both rock & roll and sensual ballads. The recordings contained on this CD stem from live television appearances on the *Town Hall Party* television show, culled mostly from shows in February and May of 1959 and January 1960. Tex Ritter and Jay Stewart were the hosts of this West Coast version of the *Grand Ole Opry*, and some of their introductions and interview chat has been left in between numbers. Larry and Lorrie were the nominal rock & roll act on the show; their appearances would always give a show a quick shot of much-needed energy between the staid and traditional country acts, and that energy and

youthful passion literally leaps off this disc. The Kids clock in with aces-up versions of "Kokomo," "Hoy Hoy," "Hot Rod," "Chantilly Lace," a blistering "Way Down Yonder in New Orleans," and "Dance to the Bop," while Larry and Joe Maphis' duets on "Feisty," "Under the Double Eagle," "Wildcat," and "Hurricane" are guitar showcases with the accent on show. Lorrie's sultry voice is heard to great effect on "Waiting Just for You," an original they never got around to recording. Perhaps the most intriguing tunes here are a trio of Buddy Holly numbers ("That'll Be the Day," "Peggy Sue," and "Oh Boy!") rearranged to fit Larry and Lorrie, in completely different keys and with completely different guitar breaks than the original versions. There's not a lot of Collins Kids material available, and this collection makes a wonderful addition to their small but rocking discography. —*Cub Koda*

● **Rockin'est** / Feb. 11, 1998 / Bear Family ✦✦✦✦✦
If Larry and Lorrie, the Collins Kids, were denied their rightful place at the hitmaking table during the 1950s, then the music some 40 years later poises them as the very energetic embodiment of ground-floor rockabilly music. Lorrie's sexy vocals and Larry's twangy guitar breaks fused to his hyperkinetic little-brother stance make for some pretty exciting music on this collection; performances like "Hoy Hoy," "I'm in My Teens," "Whistle Bait," "Party," "Hot Rod," and the flame-throwing "Mercy" show the kids at their rocking best. The collection is also sprinkled with their country big-sister/cute-but-pesky-little-brother novelties ("Make Him Behave," "Hush Money") and early country-approved rockers ("Shortnin' Bread Rock," "Beetle Bug Bop") to give a more complete picture of the duo's recorded oeuvre. If springing for their deluxe box set is too much for your wallet to handle, then this 22-track single-disc collection is absolutely the way to go. —*Cub Koda*

Larry Collins

b. 1944, Tulsa, OK
Guitar, Vocals / Traditional Country, Rockabilly
With his sister Lorrie, guitarist and singer Larry Collins was part of the brother-sister duo the Collins Kids, who cut some of the best rockabilly of the 1950s. Playing a double-neck guitar, Collins was a brilliant guitar prodigy, and took time to cut some hot instrumental duets with mentor Joe Maphis, a country guitarist 20 years his senior. The Collins Kids broke up when Lorrie married, and Larry cut some undistinguished diluted rockabilly-pop before drifting back, like so many early rockabilly singers, to country music. As a songwriter, his most famous credit is co-penning "Delta Dawn." —*Richie Unterberger*

Rockin Rollin / 1983 / Bear Family ✦✦✦
In the mid-'50s, country picker Joe Maphis and early rockabilly guitarist Larry Collins (one-half of the Collins Kids) were both members of the *Town Hall Party*, a barn dance show broadcast from the Los Angeles area. This LP gathers odds and ends from both artists, starting with the four songs the guitarists recorded together on a rare 1957 EP. Both Maphis and Collins (then just 13) smoke on their respective double-necked axes on these instrumentals, which bisect country boogie and rockabilly. Side one closes with four instrumentals Maphis cut on his own between 1955 and 1957; more country-oriented than his sides with Collins, they are respectable country boogie, the standout being "Flying Fingers," which features some of the most blindingly fast guitar work recorded in any genre. The eight songs on side two are entirely given over to solo numbers that Collins cut in the early '60s, a few previously unreleased, a few from rare Columbia singles. Mostly soft rockabilly pop with unexceptional lead vocals (by Collins) and female harmonies, it totally lacks the fire of Larry's '50s work; even the two concluding instrumentals are insubstantial, one a Duane Eddy ripoff, one slightly anticipating the sound of surf music. Side one has some pretty hot country-cum-rockabilly, but the flip side weighs this production down into "collectors only" territory. —*Richie Unterberger*

Tommy Collins (Leonard Raymond Sipes)

b. Sep. 28, 1930, Bethany, OK, **d.** Mar. 14, 2000, Ashland City, TN
Vocals, Guitar, Songwriter / Traditional Country, Bakersfield Sound, Honky Tonk
Along with his contemporary Wynn Stewart, Tommy Collins was one of the first country musicians to establish a distinctive Bakersfield, CA, sound. During the course of the '50s, he released a series of hit singles that lightened up the tone of honky tonk with bouncing backbeats, novelty lyrics, and electric guitars. Collins explored a more serious side with his ballads, yet they continued to sound slightly different than his peers—though they weren't as polished as the countrypolitan coming out of Nashville, they didn't have the grit of honky tonk. Legions of West Coast country performers—most notably Buck Owens, who played guitar on several of Collins' hit singles, and Merle Haggard—built on the sound that Collins established in the early '50s. Collins wasn't able to cash in on the Bakersfield craze of the '60s. By then, he had already quit the music business once, and was mounting a marginally successful comeback. Nevertheless, his influence loomed large, particularly on Haggard, who took Collins' "Carolyn" and "The Roots of My Raising" to the top of the charts in the early '70s.

Collins (b. Leonard Raymond Sipes) was born just outside of Oklahoma City, spending his entire childhood in Oklahoma, where his father worked for the county. As a child, he began to sing and write songs, eventually appearing on local radio shows. Following his high-school graduation in 1948, he attended Edmond State Teachers College while he continued to perform music. During this time, he made a handful of singles for the California-based record label Morgan. In the early '50s, he was in the Army for a brief time, before he moved to Bakersfield with his friend Wanda Jackson and her family. Shortly afterward, the Jackson family moved back to Oklahoma, leaving Collins alone in Bakersfield.

In a short time, Collins had begun to make friends and contacts within the city, eventually becoming friends with Ferlin Husky, and the pair roomed together. After recording a handful of Collins' songs, Husky convinced his record company, Capitol, to offer Collins a record contract, and the fledgling singer/songwriter signed to the label in June of 1953; at the time of signing, he adopted his stage name of Tommy Collins, since it sounded more commercial than Leonard Sipes. Capitol and Collins immediately assembled a backing band, which featured a then-unknown Buck Owens on lead guitar. Following one unsuccessful single, Collins released the jaunty "You Better Not Do That," which became a huge hit in early 1954, spending seven weeks at number two on the country charts. Since the song was a success, Collins continued to pursue a lighthearted, near-novelty direction with his subsequent hits, and the formula initially worked. Between the fall of 1954 and the spring of 1955, he had three Top Ten hits—"Whatcha Gonna Do Now," "Untied," and "It Tickles"—and in the fall of 1955, the double A-sided single "I Guess I'm Crazy" and "You Oughta See Pickles Now," which both reached the Top 15. In addition to these hit singles, Faron Young had a huge hit with Collins' "If You Ain't Lovin'," which was one of many songs that Collins wrote but didn't record that became hits.

Collins was on the fast road to major success, but it stopped just as soon as it began. Collins had a religious conversion in early 1956, and much of the material he recorded that year was sacred music; occasionally, he recorded duets with his wife Wanda Lucille Shahan as well. In 1957, Collins enrolled in the Golden Gate Baptist Seminary with the intention of becoming a minister. Two years later, he became a pastor. During all of his religious teachings, Collins continued to record for Capitol, but neither he nor the label was much interested in promoting his records, and he had no hits. When his contract with the label expired in 1960, he stopped recording and enrolled as a student at Sacramento State College. For the next two years, he studied at the university. In early 1963, Collins decided he was unfulfilled by the ministry, so he left the church and headed back to Bakersfield with the intention of reentering the music business. Capitol agreed to re-sign him, and in 1964 he returned to the lower reaches of the charts with "I Can Do That," a duet with his wife, Wanda.

With the help of Johnny Cash, Collins switched labels and signed with Columbia in 1965; the following year, he had a Top Ten hit with "I Can't Bite, Don't Growl." For the next few years, he had a string of minor hit singles, none of which cracked the country Top 40. During this time, he also toured with his protégés, Buck Owens and Merle Haggard, acting as their opening act. By the early '70s, both Collins' professional and personal lives were on the verge of collapse, due to his increasing dependency on drugs and alcohol. In 1971, Wanda filed for divorce, sending Collins into a deep depression.

Collins began to recover by continuing to write songs, many of which were recorded by Merle Haggard, including the 1972 number-one hit single "Carolyn." In 1976, Collins moved to Nashville, where he was able to secure a contract with Starday Records. Later that year, he released *Tommy Collins Callin'*, a collection of his own versions of songs he had provided for other artists. Following the album's release, Collins turned almost entirely to professional songwriting. In 1981, Merle Haggard had a hit single with "Leonard," his tribute to Collins. After the release of "Leonard," the spotlight again turned to Collins, who was now sober. Collins signed a songwriting contract with Sawgrass Music, where his most notable success was Mel Tillis' Top Ten 1984 hit, "New Patches." Throughout the '80s, Collins kept a low profile, though his songs continued to be recorded. George Strait recorded some Collins compositions during the decade, taking a new version of "If You Ain't Lovin'" to number one on the country charts. European record companies like Bear Family began reissuing his recordings, which led to an appearance at the 1988 *Wembley Country Music Festival* in England. In 1993, Collins signed a new publishing contract with Ricky Skaggs Music and continued to write songs professionally throughout the mid-'90s, dying at his home in Ashland City, TN, on March 14, 2000. —*Stephen Thomas Erlewine*

Words and Music Country Style / 1957 / Capitol ✦✦✦✦✦

Light of the Lord / 1959 / Capitol ✦✦✦

This Is Tommy Collins / 1959 / Capitol ✦✦✦

Songs I Love to Sing / 1961 / Capitol ✦✦✦

Let's Live a Little / 1966 / Tower ✦✦

The Dynamic Tommy Collins / 1966 / Columbia ✦✦✦
Songwriter and country music legend Tommy Collins performs some of his own material. (For more background on Collins, check out Merle Haggard's record, "Leonard.") It's not necessarily some of his best work but it is fun to hear how the songwriter interprets his own stuff. —*Jim Worbois*

Shindig / 1966 / Tower ✦✦✦✦
Shindig, Tommy Collins' second album for Tower, includes his minor comeback hit from 1964, "I Can Do That," performed as a duet with his wife, Wanda. The title of the album comes from the leadoff track, "Shindig in the Barn," one of several buoyant throwbacks to the '50s on this entertaining and anachronistic album. Collins' novelties sound a bit like Little Jimmy Dickens, but with crisp electric guitar leads that keep the corn planted firmly in Bakersfield. The songs on *Shindig* aren't entirely humorous—a few oldies such as "Wreck of the Old '97" (for which Collins takes songwriting credit!) and "Oklahoma Hills" add a measure of seriousness while maintaining the retro feel, which is just fine. —*Greg Adams*

Tommy Collins on Tour / 1968 / Columbia ✦✦

Tommy Collins Callin' / 1972 / Starday ✦✦✦✦✦
Featured are "Cigarette Milnar," "I Could Sing All Night," "You Gotta Have a License," and others. —*AMG*

● **Leonard** / 1992 / Bear Family ✦✦✦✦✦
Spanning five discs and well over one hundred tracks—featuring all of the songs he cut for Capitol in the late '50s and early '60s, including alternate takes and unreleased material—*Leonard* contains too much Tommy Collins for anyone but completists and historians. Nevertheless, it is the only collection of Collins' prime material to appear on CD. Collins was very influential and he deserves this deluxe box set treatment, but a single disc collection is needed—it would make his music available to country fans that simply can't afford a box set of this magnitude, but still want to hear the singer. If you can afford *Leonard*, it's a worthwhile investment for dedicated country music fans, but there

isn't enough first-rate material on the box to justify the expense for listeners that want to explore the roots of the Bakersfield sound. *—Thom Owens*

Jessi Colter (Miriam Johnson Eddy)

b. May 25, 1947, Phoenix, AZ

Keyboards, Vocals, Piano / Traditional Country, Country-Pop, Outlaw Country

Perhaps best known in conjunction with her husband Waylon Jennings, Jessi Colter was the only significant female singer/songwriter to emerge from the mid-'70s "outlaw" movement. Born Miriam Johnson on May 25, 1943, in Phoenix, AZ, Colter in fact affiliated herself with outlaw imagery long before the musical movement blossomed, adopting her stage name in honor of ancestor Jess Colter, a real-life train robber and counterfeiter who rode with Frank and Jesse James.

Raised in a strict Pentecostal home, Colter was just a teenager when she left Phoenix to tour as a vocalist with twang-guitar innovator Duane Eddy, whom she met through her sister Sharon, the wife of producer "Cowboy" Jack Clement. In 1962, she and Eddy married, and after several years of extensive touring (mostly throughout Europe), the couple settled in Los Angeles in 1966. Under the name Miriam Eddy, she wrote songs for Don Gibson, Dottie West, and Nancy Sinatra.

In 1968, she and Eddy divorced, and Colter returned to Phoenix. There she met Waylon Jennings, who was so taken with her voice that he invited her to record a duet with him. After helping secure Colter a record deal with his label, RCA, Jennings co-produced the tracks that would make up her 1970 debut *A Country Star Is Born*; by the time of the record's release, the couple was already married. Under the name Waylon and Jessi, they also issued two Top 40 singles, a 1970 cover of the Elvis Presley hit "Suspicious Minds" and 1971's "Under Your Spell Again." Colter's commercial breakthrough came in 1975 when her composition "I'm Not Lisa," a single from the LP *I'm Jessi Colter*, hit number one on *Billboard*'s country charts while also making the Top Five on the pop charts; the album spawned another hit in "What's Happened to Blue Eyes." In 1976, she released two more highly successful albums, *Jessi* and *Diamond in the Rough*.

Also in 1976, Colter teamed with Jennings, Willie Nelson, and Tompall Glaser for the album *Wanted! The Outlaws*, which at the time of its release was the biggest-selling album in country history, and the first country album certified platinum in sales. In between spending much of the remainder of the decade on tour with her husband and Nelson, she also released the albums *Miriam* in 1977 and *That's the Way a Cowboy Rocks* in 1978. Colter and Jennings re-teamed in 1981 for *Leather and Lace*, an album of duets featuring the hits "Storms Never Last" and the medley "Wild Side of Life/It Wasn't God Who Made Honky Tonk Angels." In the same year, she released the solo album *Ridin' Shotgun*, which produced her final chart hit in 1982's "Holdin' On." As the 1980s progressed, Colter's success tapered off; 1985's *Rock 'n' Roll Lullaby*, produced by Chips Moman, was released only on a small label. By the early '90s, she began directing her energies toward performing children's music, and starred in the home video *Jessi Colter Sings Songs From Around the World Just for Kids*, which featured a guest appearance by Jennings, who recited some of his poetry. *—Jason Ankeny*

A Country Star Is Born / 1970 / RCA ✦✦✦

I'm Jessi Colter / 1975 / Capitol ✦✦✦✦

● **Jessi** / 1976 / Capitol ✦✦✦✦✦

After the success of "I'm Not Lisa" it's surprising that this record wasn't more popular than it was. Many of these songs are better than her big hit. *—Jim Worbois*

Diamond in the Rough / 1976 / Capitol ✦✦✦✦

Mirriam / 1977 / Capitol ✦✦✦

That's the Way a Cowboy Rocks / 1978 / Capitol ✦✦✦

Ridin' Shotgun / 1981 / Capitol ✦✦✦

Rock 'n' Roll Lullaby / 1985 / Triad ✦✦

Collection / Apr. 4, 1995 / Capitol ✦✦✦✦

Collection is a brief ten-song compilation of Jessi Colter's hits for Capitol, including her number-one hit "I'm Not Lisa" and number-five hit "What's Happened to Blue Eyes." Her remaining two Top 40 hits on Capitol are included in addition to other select tracks. Colter was often associated with the outlaw movement because of her marriage to Waylon Jennings and her appearance on *Wanted! The Outlaws*, but none of her music here fits with the image. The tempos are generally slow and Colter's music is more reminiscent of Crystal Gayle than Waylon Jennings. *—Greg Adams*

Commander Cody (George Frayne IV)

b. Jul. 19, 1944, Ann Arbor, MI

Piano, Vocals, Producer / Rock & Roll, Country-Rock, Western Swing Revival

Commander Cody & His Lost Planet Airmen were equally adept at stripped-down basic rock & roll, R&B, and gritty country-rock. Commander Cody's country-rock rocked harder than the Eagles or Poco—essentially, the group was a bar band. Much like English pub rock bands like Brinsley Schwarz and Ducks Deluxe, Commander Cody resisted the overblown and bombastic trends of early-'70s rock, preferring a basic, no-frills approach. Commander Cody & His Lost Planet Airmen never had the impact of the British pub rockers, yet their straightforward energy gave their records a distinguishing drive; they could play country, western swing, rockabilly, and R&B, and it all sounded convincing.

The group originally formed in 1967 in Ann Arbor, MI; Commander Cody (born George Frayne IV; piano), John Tichy (lead guitar), Steve Schwartz (guitar), Don Davis (bass), Don Bolton (aka the West Virginia Creeper; pedal steel guitar), and Ralph Mallory (drums) formed the original lineup. When the group relocated to San Francisco the following year, only Frayne, Bolton, and Tichy made the move; the group's membership included Billy C. Farlow (vocals, harp), Andy Stein (fiddle, saxophone), guitarist Billy Kirchen, bassist "Buffalo" Bruce Barlow, and drummer Lance Dickerson at the time of their 1971 debut album, *Lost in the Ozone*. The following year the group scored a fluke Top Ten hit with "Hot Rod Lincoln," taken from their first album, *Lost in the Ozone*. Commander Cody was never able to capitalize on the single's success, partially because their albums never completely captured their live energy. They continued to release albums until Tichy left the band in 1976. Commander Cody released his first solo album, *Midnight Man*, in 1977, then he re-formed the group as the Commander Cody Band. The group recorded three albums between 1977 and 1980. *—Stephen Thomas Erlewine*

Lost in the Ozone / 1971 / MCA ✦✦✦

This is the monumental debut by one of insurgent country's pioneer bands. Playing with electric instruments, including the all important steel and fiddle, and a good dose of irreverence allowed the band to adhere to their own agenda. This first release was only a taste of the things to come. A combination of original tunes and some dusty covers, Cody & His Lost Planet Airmen were at the head of a parade that continued on through the '90s. Songs by Billy C. Farlow like "Daddy's Gonna Treat You Right" and the ever-popular "Lost in the Ozone" were instant hits with the country-rock and hippie crowds. But, the rednecks loved them, too, and this was an amazing social phenomenon. Cody, whose real name is George Frayne, partnered with Farlow on a number of songs from this first collection that still pack a wallop. "Wine Do Yer Stuff" and the tearful "Seeds and Stems (Again)" left no doubt where these boys were coming from. A strong honky tonk album that swings, *Lost in the Ozone* is a viable recording. Cover tunes performed with energy and humor won crowds over everywhere. "Hot Rod Lincoln" is still played on outlaw country radio stations, as is "20 Flight Rock," a boogie number that lets everything hang out. With not a single cut wasted, this is one of the buried gems of modern country music that displays guitarman Bill Kirchen at his wildest and Bruce Barlow, Lance Dickerson, Andy Stein, John Tichy, Bobby Black, West Virginia Creeper, Farlow, and Commander Cody comin' out of the shoot ready to change the world for the better. *—Jana Pendragon*

Hot Licks, Cold Steel & Truckers' Favorites / 1972 / MCA ✦✦✦

Again, a groundbreaking release from the wildest band in country music (during the '70s). This time around they are honoring the American trucker. A part of society few see into, the music that keeps the big rigs running is something else again. With originals and some oldies, the Commander and his band make a big sound that is still reverberating through time. With their own trucker tunes, "Truck Stop Rock" and "Semi Truck," leading the way, this LP includes some classics like "Looking' at the World Through a Windshield," "Mama Hated Diesels," and the granddaddy of the bunch, "Truck Drivin' Man," a performance hit for Rick Nelson and the New Riders of the Purple Sage as well. Other high-powered covers include Little Richard's "Tutti Frutti" done up in a way no one will forget. The Cajun "Diggy Liggy Lo" is given a workout as is "Rip It Up," and the Commander's class-A performance of "It Should've Been Me" leaves no doubt as to the punch this outfit gives to everything they do. From the band comes "Cravin' Your Love," "Watch My .38," and "Kentucky Hills of Tennessee." Again, every cut counts. As with *Lost in the Ozone*, this is top-flight music in every regard that shows another side to this great band. *—Jana Pendragon*

Country Casanova / 1973 / MCA ✦✦✦

Live From Deep in the Heart of Texas / 1974 / MCA ✦✦✦✦✦

This is Commander Cody & His Lost Planet Airmen at their best, live on-stage and out on the road with the New Riders of the Purple Sage. What a bill and what a grand time for a live album. This is how it really was—wild, loud, and fun. Again, they intersperse their own songs with old favorites. "Armadillo Stomp" was penned for this event, and a woolly version of "Down to Seeds and Stems Again Blues" has the crowd on its feet. Their "Oh Momma Momma" and "Too Much Fun" become legendary during this performance. But, it is their reworking of Buck Owens' "Crying Time" that makes them such a wonderful country band. Johnny Horton's "I'm Comin' Home" is also masterful, as is their take on a favorite cowboy tune, "Sunset on the Sage." "Mean Woman Blues" is another highlight. As for the Commander, his wanton style is perfectly at home when he takes the Leiber & Stoller tune "Riot in Cell Block #9" and makes it his own vehicle for a musical theatrical performance. Every cut is perfection, every cut is substantial. This 1973 performance, captured here for posterity, is evidence enough to suggest that Commander Cody & His Lost Planet Airmen were one fine honky tonk band, perhaps one of the finest. *—Jana Pendragon*

Commander Cody & His Lost Planet Airmen / 1975 / Warner Bros. ✦✦✦✦

This was their first recording for Warner Bros. after leaving Paramount. With songs by Hoyt Axton, Lowell George, as well as plenty of contributions from Farlow, Tichy, Barlow, and all the rest, this is another good outing for the wild boys. The Tower of Power horn section lends a hand, making their big sound even bigger. Their cover of "Don't Let Go" is outstanding and "House of Blue Lights" never rocked or shuffled and twanged the way the Airmen do it. With plenty of hillbilly stuff to go around, "California Okie" stands proud. A tip of the hat to the South is found on "That's What I Like About the South." "Keep on Lovin' Her," "Hawaii Blues," and "Four or Five Times" are also wonders to behold. "Willin'," done up right here, fits the band perfectly. This Lowell George tune is a standard, and when the Airmen did it their way they gave a whole new meaning to the song. One more time, this band holds all the aces and plays every hand with a poker face that just won't quit. Commander Cody & His Lost Planet Airmen knew exactly what they were doing. *—Jana Pendragon*

Tales From the Ozone / 1975 / Warner Bros. ✦✦✦✦✦

Tales From the Ozone was the second album Commander Cody & His Lost Planet Airmen cut for Warner Bros. in 1975. It was to be their last studio effort with the label, but what a way to go out. Like their eponymously titled set earlier in 1975, *Tales From the Ozone* featured a plethora of great songs, from writers as diverse as Cab Calloway ("Minnie the Moocher," which opens the set) to Billy Joe Shaver ("I Been to Georgia on a Fast Train") to Hoyt Axton ("Lightning Bar Blues" and "Paid in Advance"), who produced the band here, to Leiber & Stoller ("The Shadow Knows") to Blackie Farrell ("Tina Louise"), Mel McDaniel ("Roll Your Own"), George Hawke ("Honky Tonk Music"), and Hank Williams

("Cajun Baby"). There was also room for a couple of group originals, the swinging rock-abilly of "It's Gonna Be One of Those Nights" and the stomping "Gypsy Fiddle." Critics have been critical of the production on this set in the past, but Axton knew exactly what he was doing in the studio. The "flat" sound is the dynamic the band had live, with everything up in the mix. Check out the country subtleties in "Connie," where the story comes across full and plain despite the outrageous chops of this very large-voiced octet. The Shaver tune rocks far harder than it ever did in either its original or Waylon Jennings' versions, especially with the Commander (George Frayne) riding the upper register with Bobby Black's steel and Billy Kirchen's Telecaster struggling for dominance against the horn section—provided courtesy of Tower of Power. There is care and delicacy put into country songs like "Honky Tonk Music" and "Lightning Bar Blues." The latter is one of the great party songs ever put on wax, and equals Jerry Jeff Walker's "Pick Up the Tempo" in singalong quotient. The Williams tune, "Roll Your Own," and "Tina Louise" are equally driven country gems, rounding out one of the most consistent and live sounding records the Lost Planet Airmen ever cut. —*Thom Jurek*

We've Got a Live One Here / 1976 / Warner Bros. ✦✦✦
This is really the final hurrah for the band, in spite of the fact that there were more recordings to follow. This is a two-record set from their 1976 tour of Europe with most of the original members still onboard. After this tour, George Frayne (aka Commander Cody) broke up the band, which now included Norton Buffalo. While this live recording is just as powerful as the preceding *Live Deep in the Heart of Texas*, it is obvious that some of their fire is burning mighty low. Still, this bunch always did their best work on-stage and they never failed to satisfy. Full of old standards, some new favorites, and plenty of wattage to make it all work just right, the standout tunes here are the Commander Cody classics like "Seeds and Stems," "Too Much Fun," and "Lost in the Ozone." Other numbers that bring back the good old days include the Airmen's version of "Milkcow Blues" and "San Antonio Rose." Trucker songs, big with the Continental crowd, are "Semi Truck," "Lookin' at the World Through a Windshield," and "18 Wheels." Other numbers of note are "One of Those Nights," written by Farlow, Frayne, and Kirchen, as well as the Commander's send-ups of "Smoke! Smoke! Smoke!," "Riot in Cell Block #9," and "Hot Rod Lincoln." Always extraordinary, the era of Commander Cody & His Lost Planet Airmen was a special moment in time that created a place for hipsters, cosmic cowboys, rednecks, and the working class to all come together and enjoy some real American music. Never will there be another band like this one or recordings like the ones they made between 1971-1976. They ended this project with "Lost in the Ozone," bringing the band and its audience full circle. —*Jana Pendragon*

Midnight Man [Solo] / 1977 / Arista ✦✦

Rock 'n' Roll Again / 1977 / Arista ✦✦

Flying Dreams / 1978 / Arista ✦✦

Lose It Tonight / 1980 / Line ✦✦

Let's Rock / 1986 / Blind Pig ✦✦✦

The Very Best of . . . Plus / 1986 / See for Miles ✦✦✦✦✦
Containing 22 tracks, all pulled from the group's first three albums, *The Very Best of . . . Plus* condenses the best of Commander Cody & His Lost Planet Airmen to a single disc, making it an excellent introduction to one of the finest American country-rock bands of the early '70s. —*Stephen Thomas Erlewine*

Returns From Outer Space / 1987 / Edsel ✦✦✦

Sleazy Roadside Stories / 1988 / Relix ✦✦✦

Aces High / 1990 / Relix ✦✦✦

● **Too Much Fun: Best of Commander Cody** / Oct. 1990 / MCA ✦✦✦✦✦
Commander Cody & His Lost Planet Airmen were a long-haired, flannel-wearing, good-time party band that got started in the late '60s. What set them apart from the majority of other bands at the time was they had more in common with old Bob Wills records than anything Jimi Hendrix ever recorded. They were a damn good bar band and one of the few from that era who could play at both political rallies and the honky tonk down the street. These 15 tunes include cover versions of Western swing classics like "Hot Rod Lincoln," "Smoke, Smoke, Smoke (That Cigarette)," and "Beat Me Daddy, Eight to the Bar," along with countryfied originals that hippies loved like "Stems and Seeds." The music Commander Cody and his boys recorded during the hippie era remains timeless, unlike, say, the first Country Joe & the Fish record. —*Al Campbell*

Bar Room Classics / Sep. 6, 1994 / Aim ✦✦✦

Worst Case Scenario / Sep. 13, 1994 / Aim ✦✦✦

The Best of Commander Cody & His Lost Planet Airmen / Aug. 8, 1995 / Relix ✦✦✦✦✦
This brings together 14 of the group's biggest successes in one collection. Commander Cody & His Lost Planet Airmen were one of the very first country-rock groups, with guitarist Bill Kirchen who later moved on to a successful solo career of his own. Although much of the material consists of retreads of old and sometimes obscure country standards, the group handles the material with a tongue-in-cheek attitude, tempering that with a heartfelt understanding of it at the same time. A marvelous document of one of the more unique groups of the '70s. —*Cub Koda*

Tour From Hell (1973) / Nov. 5, 1996 / Aim ✦✦✦

Live at Gilley's / Feb. 15, 2000 / Atlantic ✦✦
Q/Atlantic's *Live at Gilley's* captures a 1982 concert given by a latter-day lineup of the Commander Cody Band. The liner notes indicate that it was recorded in the summer of 1982 with the Commander's current lineup, but they never say who's in the band, which is frustrating, because this is the kind of release that will appeal only to hardcore collectors, who need to know this kind of information. After all, *Live at Gilley's* hardly captures

the band at their peak—instead, it's a snapshot of a touring band in the middle of their tour. They play their best-known songs ("Hot Rod Lincoln," "Down to Seeds and Stems," "Beat Me Daddy, Eight to the Bar," among others) professionally and competently, but never quite excitedly. That's not to say this is a bad listen, particularly if you're a dedicated fan. But it's not an inspired, kinetic performance—it's the work of journeymen, banging out the sounds they know by heart for a mildly appreciative crowd. Not a disaster, by any stretch, but nothing to attract the attention of the average fan, either. —*Stephen Thomas Erlewine*

Best Of / Mar. 12, 2002 / Akarma ✦✦✦✦
Long before country acquired an "alt" to distinguish the roots material from the product of Nashville, there was Commander Cody & His Lost Planet Airmen. Long before it became fashionable, they were a bunch of hippies rocking up the honky tonk music. While their audience was mostly the longhair crowd, as evidenced by the pot anthem "Down to Seeds and Stems Again Blues," they could also create some mass appeal, and even scored a hit single with their souped-up version of "Hot Rod Lincoln." Mostly, though, it was about the boogie, whether covering some old jive like "Beat Me Daddy, Eight to the Bar" or their own "Truck Stop Rock." Moreover, they could pick like the best players on the country scene, as they show on "Rock That Boogie," or make the tears flow into the beer, as on a wonderful cover of Lowell George's trucking anthem, "Willin'." Successful as they were—and they were a major draw live, able to whip up a fever in an audience—they were ahead of their time. Had they arrived in the '90s as fully formed as they were at the beginning of the '70s, they'd have ruled the alt-country scene. This compilation draws from their most glorious years, 1971-1975, and there's simply not a dud to be found here—no filler, not a second wasted. If you're at all curious as to what the fuss was about and where the hippies and Buck Owens intersected, start here. —*Chris Nickson*

Confederate Railroad

f. 1987, Atlanta, GA
Group / Contemporary Country, Southern Rock, Neo-Traditionalist Country
Often described as a cross between Alabama and Lynyrd Skynyrd, Confederate Railroad made their name with a party-ready hybrid of modern country and Southern rock, which also earned them comparisons to Charlie Daniels and Hank Williams Jr. Their trashy, roughneck wardrobe was a good indicator of their rowdy, tongue-in-cheek sense of humor, but they were also able to balance that with a sincere sentimental streak. Singer/guitarist Danny Shirley, lead guitarist Michael Lamb, steel guitarist Gates Nichols, keyboardist Chris McDaniel, bassist Wayne Secrest, and drummer Mark Dufresne got together in the early '80s and spent years playing the Atlanta bar scene, eventually merging into a tight unit with original material. They served as the house band at Miss Kitty's in Marietta, GA, for several years, and also worked as a backing band on the road behind Johnny Paycheck and David Allan Coe.

After around a decade of dues-paying, Confederate Railroad finally earned a shot with Atlantic, and released their self-titled debut album in 1992. The lead single "She Took It Like a Man" inched into the Top 40, but the record really took off with the next two singles; "Jesus and Mama" and "Queen of Memphis" both shot into the country Top Five. Fan favorite "Trashy Women" also made the Top Ten, and two additional singles—"When You Leave That Way You Can Never Go Back" and "She Never Cried"—hit the Top 40. With such a large store of hits, *Confederate Railroad* went double platinum. The band's 1994 follow-up, *Notorious*, also sold over a million copies, and spawned another Top Ten hit with "Daddy Never Was the Cadillac Kind"; another concert favorite, "Elvis and Andy," made the Top 20. The title track of 1995's *When and Where* proved to be their last significant hit for a while, and guitarist Lamb left the band, to be replaced by Jimmy Dormire. *Keep on Rockin'* (1998) confirmed the band's downward commercial slide, and keyboardist McDaniel eventually left as well; his replacement was Cody McCarver. Confederate Railroad parted ways with Atlantic and signed with the smaller Audium label for their next album, 2001's *Unleashed*. —*Steve Huey*

Confederate Railroad / 1992 / Atlantic ✦✦✦
Featured are "Queen of Memphis," "Time Off for Bad Behavior," and "She Took It like a Man," among other hits. —*AMG*

Notorious / 1994 / Atlantic ✦✦✦✦✦
Despite its unkempt, biker image, Confederate Railroad is a country band in the tradition of Alabama. Rooted in traditional country sounds and values, both bands also have the breadth to appeal to those outside the genre (in CR's case, Southern rockers). The group rocks hardest on the funny stuff ("Elvis & Andy," "Move over Madonna") but gets serious with some impressive ballads ("Daddy Never Was the Cadillac Kind," "Summer in Dixie," "Three Verses"). —*Brian Mansfield*

When and Where / 1995 / Atlantic ✦✦✦✦✦
By their third album, Confederate Railroad had established their fusion of Lynyrd Skynyrd and Alabama and knew what worked and what didn't. In other words, *When and Where* offers nothing new from the band, but it is far from a bad record. The group has gotten predictable, but they continue to shine, whether it's on the rowdy rockers or the surprisingly smooth, radio-ready ballads. They do have a problem coming up with a batch of consistent material, but the album is as enjoyable as its predecessor and nearly as solid. —*Thom Owens*

● **Greatest Hits** / Jun. 18, 1996 / Atlantic ✦✦✦✦✦
Greatest Hits compiles Confederate Railroad's biggest hits, including all of their Top Ten singles, as well as several singles that never made it quite as far up the charts. As an added bonus, the group has added two new songs—which aren't particularly noteworthy—to lure fans that already own all the band's albums to the new collection. Even with the addition of the new songs, *Greatest Hits* remains the province of casual fans—it's a serves up all the hits in an engaging, concise manner. —*Stephen Thomas Erlewine*

Keep on Rockin' / Oct. 20, 1998 / Atlantic ✦✦✦

Rockin' Country Party Pack / Aug. 22, 2000 / Atlantic ✦✦
Rockin' Country Party Pack isn't quite a hits collection and it isn't quite a rarities collection, either. It's a combination of singles, album tracks, and "club" remixes, all adding up to an album that's designed to be a good-time record—a party album, as it were. It succeeds on that count, and even if the lack of a handful of hits may irritate a casual fan or two, this comes pretty close to summarizing the group's strengths. Anyone looking for a strong, entertaining Confederate Railroad album should turn here. *—Stephen Thomas Erlewine*

Unleashed / Aug. 28, 2001 / Audium ✦✦✦✦
In some parts of the world, it's always 1974. The deaths of Berry Oakley and Duane Allman still sting, Waylon Jennings and Jerry Jeff Walker are revered, shouts of "Free Bird"!!! at concerts aren't meant ironically, and people still remember who the Marshall Tucker Band were. It's a simpler, better place, and there, Confederate Railroad are superstars. On their fifth album, the unreconstructed country-rockers plow through songs like the sassy "She Treats Her Body Like a Temple" ("and I treat mine like a honky-tonk," continues lead singer Danny Shirley) and the self-explanatory story-song "White Trash With Money," with all the twangy guitars, honky tonk piano, and keening steel guitar that are required for a good country-rockin' time. David Allan Coe and George Jones drop by to lend a further air of outlaw country bad-assedness, and the group even throws in an honest to goodness ballad, the touching "Between the Rainbows and the Rain," to prove that it's not just a bunch of retro-macho poseurs. Good stuff. *—Stewart Mason*

The Essentials / Jun. 4, 2002 / Rhino ✦✦✦✦

John Conlee

b. Aug. 11, 1946, Versailles, KY
Vocals, Guitar / Country-Pop, Neo-Traditionalist Country
One of the most respected vocalists to emerge during the urban cowboy era, John Conlee was known for his superb taste in material and his distinctively melancholy voice. Conlee was born and raised on a tobacco farm in Versailles, KY, in 1946, and took up the guitar as a child, performing on local radio at age ten. He went on to sing with the town barbershop chorus, but didn't initially pursue music as a career, instead becoming a licensed mortician. He also worked as a disc jockey at numerous area radio stations, and made important industry connections via that area when he moved to Nashville in 1971. Five years later, Conlee's demo tape got him a contract with ABC. He released a few singles, but didn't find acceptance until 1978's "Rose Colored Glasses," a song he'd co-written with a newsman at his radio station, rocketed into the country Top Five.

Conlee spent the next decade or so scoring hit after hit, nearly all of them helmed by producer Bud Logan. He had two number ones in 1979 alone—"Lady Lay Down" and "Backside of Thirty"—and four number-two hits through 1981, which included "Before My Time," "Friday Night Blues," "She Can't Say That Anymore," and "Miss Emily's Picture." Conlee returned to the top of the charts three times over 1983-1984 with "Common Man," "I'm Only in It for the Love," and "In My Eyes," and had his last number one in 1986 with "Got My Heart Set on You." All told, Conlee made the Top Ten 19 times through 1987, when he moved from MCA to Columbia and reached the Top Five with "Domestic Life." Never much for touring, Conlee subsequently curtailed his recording activities as well, instead devoting his time to charity work (often on behalf of American farmers), raising his family, and running his own farm outside Nashville. *—Steve Huey*

Rose Colored Glasses / 1978 / MCA ✦✦✦

Forever / 1979 / MCA ✦✦✦

Friday Night Blues / 1980 / MCA ✦✦✦

With Love / 1981 / MCA ✦✦✦✦
Nine of the ten cuts in this package came from Tree Publishing, meaning that Conlee and producer Bud Logan limited themselves unnecessarily. But Conlee is extremely convincing on "Only Oklahoma Away" and "What's Forever For," not to mention the mysterious "Miss Emily's Picture." *—Tom Roland*

Busted / 1982 / MCA ✦✦

In My Eyes / 1983 / MCA ✦✦✦

John Conlee's Greatest Hits / 1983 / MCA ✦✦✦✦✦
With simple, slice-of-life statements about the real world, the songs cover (in)fidelity ("She Can't Say That Anymore," "Baby, You're Something"), relationship issues ("Friday Night Blues"), and personal finance ("Busted," "Common Man"). The asylum piece, "I Don't Remember Loving You," is eternally vivid. *—Tom Roland*

Greatest Hits, Vol. 2 / 1985 / MCA ✦✦✦✦

Songs for the Working Man / 1986 / MCA ✦✦✦

Conley Country / 1986 / MCA ✦✦✦✦

American Faces / 1987 / Columbia ✦✦

Harmony / 1987 / Columbia ✦✦

● **20 Greatest Hits** / 1987 / MCA ✦✦✦✦✦
20 Greatest Hits combines material from Conlee's *Greatest Hits* and *Greatest Hits, Vol. 2*, leaving off one track from each record ("Baby, you're Someting" and "Lifetime Guarantee," respectively). As such, it offers a perfect retrospective of his career. *—Stephen Thomas Erlewine*

Fellow Travelers / 1989 / 16th Avenue ✦✦✦

The Best of John Conlee / 1991 / Curb ✦✦✦
The Best of John Conlee is a 12-track budget-priced collection that features some of his biggest hits, including "Common Man," "I'm Only in It for the Love," "In My Eyes," "Where Are the Pieces of My Heart," "River of Time," "Hit the Ground Runnin'" and "Till You Were Gone." Although this isn't a bad budget-priced disc, there are far better collections available, offering more songs and better sound for not much more money. *—Stephen Thomas Erlewine*

Live at Billy Bob's Texas / Apr. 27, 1999 / Live at Billy Bob's Texas ✦✦✦✦
It's been far too long since a new John Conlee studio album, but in the meantime this concert date recorded at *Billy Bob's Texas* is more than an acceptable substitute. The 18 tracks included here feature almost all of the singer's biggest hits, from "Rose Colored Glasses" to "Lady Lay Down" to "Common Man," each crisply rendered by a fine backing band; Conlee himself is in excellent form throughout—if anything, the passage of time has made his vocals even more affecting. *—Hank Small*

Earl Thomas Conley

b. Oct. 17, 1941, Portsmouth, OH
Vocals / Country-Pop, Neo-Traditionalist Country, Urban Cowboy
Early in his career, Earl Thomas Conley's music picked up the label "thinking man's country." An accurate description—Conley looks into the heart and soul of his characters, finding the motivations for their actions and beliefs. In the process, the astute listener can find fragments of himself/herself in nearly any Conley creation. Born into poverty in Portsmouth, OH, Conley struggled with the limits of his social class. He aspired to be a painter or actor, but found that his aspirations for music lingered after the other interests died down. Influenced by everyone from Hank Williams to the Eagles, Conley delved into the details of writing, trying to learn the craft by following the rules and regulations of the Music Row songwriting community. Eventually, torn by the limits of the "law," he found his own niche by breaking many of those same rules. His public self-analysis—in both his songs and his interviews—has proven inspirational to some, bothersome to others, but Conley has evolved stylistically, even though the "thinking man" label continues to follow him. He's admittedly chased a more commercial sound, with a certain degree of success, but the run for the dollars also put him into a financial bind. He spent part of the late '80s and early '90s overworking himself to pay off his debts. Although he has been a hitmaker for more than a decade, his contributions to country have often gone almost unnoticed.

The son a railroad man, Conley left his Portsmouth home at the age of 14, once his father lost his job. After living with his older sister in Ohio, he rejected a scholarship to art school, deciding to join the Army instead. While he was in the military, he fell in love with country music. Following his discharge, he worked a number of blue-collar jobs while he played Nashville clubs at night. Conley wasn't making any headway, so he relocated to Huntsville, AL, where he worked in a steel mill. While in Huntsville, he met Nelson Larkin, a producer who helped the fledgling singer sign to the independent label GRT in 1974. Over the next two years, he released four singles on the label—which were all credited to "Earl Conley"—and each one scraped the lower regions of the country charts. While his chart success was respectable for a developing artist, he was soon eclipsed by other artists who were having hits with his songs. Nelson Larkin gave his brother Billy "Leave It Up to Me," which became the first Earl Thomas Conley song to reach the Top 20. It was followed shortly afterward by Mel Street's number-13 hit "Smokey Mountain Memories" and Conway Twitty's version of "This Time I've Hurt Her More (Than She Loves Me)," which reached number one in early 1976. By that time, he had moved to Nashville, where he was writing for Nelson Larkin's publishing house.

In 1977, Conley signed with Warner Bros., and in early 1979 he had his first Top 40 hit, "Dreamin's All I Do." By the end of the year, he had begun performing and releasing records under his full name, Earl Thomas Conley. None of his Warner singles became big hits, and he left the label at the end of 1979. After spending six months reassessing his career and musical direction, he signed to Sunbird Records and began working with Nelson Larkin again. Conley's first single for Sunbird, "Silent Treatment," was an immediate Top Ten hit late in 1980, and it was quickly followed by the number one "Fire and Smoke" early in 1981. Following his breakthrough success, RCA signed Conley to a long-term deal. "Tell Me Why," his first single for the label, reached number ten in late 1981, followed shortly afterward by the number 16 "After the Love Slips Away." In the summer of 1982, "Heavenly Bodies" kicked off a string of 21 straight Top Ten hits that ran for seven years. During that time, he had a remarkable 17 number-one hits, including a record-setting four number one singles from 1983's *Don't Make It Easy for Me*—it was the first time any artist in any genre had four number-one hits from the same album. Though he had some financial and vocal problems during the mid-'80s, the hits never stopped coming during the entire decade.

By the end of the '80s, he had stopped working with Nelson Larkin, preferring to collaborate with Randy Scruggs, which brought his music back to his country and R&B roots. His sales took a dramatic dip during 1990 due to the rise of contemporary country, but he had two new Top Ten hits, "Shadow of a Doubt" and the Keith Whitley duet "Brotherly Love." The singles set the stage for the harder-edged country of his 1991 album, *Yours Truly*. Despite receiving some of the best reviews of Conley's career, the record was a commercial failure, and RCA dropped him shortly after its release. For much of the '90s, he was without a record label, yet he continued to give concerts and to tour, finally landing on Intersound for 1998's *Perpetual Emotion*. *—Tom Roland*

Blue Pearl / 1980 / Sunbird ✦✦✦
This is the album that earned Conley the thinking-man label. "Middle-Age Madness" and "Blue and Green" stand out as classically written profiles of people in pain. "Silent Treatment," "Fire and Smoke," and "You Don't Have to Go Too Far" possess a captivating, slick sheen that belies their raw approach. *—Tom Roland*

Fire & Smoke / 1981 / RCA ✦✦✦

Somewhere Between Right & Wrong / 1982 / RCA ✦✦✦

Don't Make It Easy for Me / 1983 / RCA ✦✦✦✦✦
Conley speaks of "programming" himself to write, and in setting the tone for this album—as well as the follow-up, *Treadin' Water*—he programmed "radio records" into his consciousness. The result: a driving, rock-inflected package that yielded four number one singles—the first time an album did that in any format. The title track and "Your Love's on the Line" are particularly listenable, but there's not a bad cut on it. *—Tom Roland*

Treadin' Water / 1984 / RCA ✦✦

Greatest Hits / 1985 / RCA ✦✦✦✦
Some of his biggest songs are here, including "Angel in Disguise," "Silent Treatment," "Holding Her and Loving You," "Once in a Blue Moon," and others. *—AMG*

The Heart of It All / 1988 / RCA ✦✦✦
This album contains "What I'd Say," "What She Is," "We Believe in Happy Endings," "You Must Not Be Drinking Enough," and other hits. *—AMG*

The Best of Earl Thomas Conley, Vol. 1 / 1988 / RCA ✦✦✦✦✦
As much as any of his '80s peers, Conley might have benefited from moving his sound toward harder country. The hits he did score ("Fire & Smoke," "Somewhere Between Right and Wrong," among the ones on this album) projected a voice ideally suited to a more Whitley-esque setting. *—Dan Cooper*

Greatest Hits, Vol. 2 / 1990 / RCA ✦✦✦✦
Conley was one of the hottest recording artists of the '80s. While this album isn't quite as strong as the first hits package, it shouldn't be ignored. It also features two new tracks. *—Jim Worbois*

Yours Truly / 1991 / RCA ✦✦✦✦
Yours Truly is one of Earl Thomas Conley's finest efforts, boasting a consistently impressive set of songs and wonderful vocals from Conley. *—Thom Owens*

● **The Essential** / Apr. 1996 / RCA ✦✦✦✦✦
The Essential by Earl Thomas Conley highlights the gruff-voiced country singer's 20 chart-topping entries from the late '70s and early '80s. These original RCA recordings include "Holding Her and Loving You," "Angel in Disguise," "Chance of Loving You," and his first number-one single, "Fire and Smoke." The only complaint about this set is the omission of Conley's duets with Emmylou Harris ("We Believe in Happy Endings," number one in 1988) and Anita Pointer ("Too Many Times"). *—Al Campbell*

Love out Loud / Sep. 8, 1998 / BMG Special Products ✦✦✦
BMG Special Products' *The Encore Collection: Love Out Loud* is a good sampling of Earl Thomas Conley's smooth country-pop hits. With only a handful of exceptions, everything on the budget-priced collection was a Top Ten country hit, including "Silent Treatment," "Holding Her and Loving You," "What She Is (Is a Woman in Love)," "Once in a Blue Moon" and the title track. There are more comprehensive Conley collections on the market, but this is a good choice for listeners on a budget. *—Stephen Thomas Erlewine*

Super Hits / Sep. 29, 1998 / RCA ✦✦✦

Contenders

f. Nashville, TN

Group / Country-Rock, Country-Folk, Progressive Country, Alternative Country, Western Swing Revival, Honky Tonk, Ragtime

The Contenders are considered one of the great "could have been" bands from the progressive country scene, featuring several of the brilliant players associated with Uncle Walt's Band in combination with a pair of North Carolina pickers and songwriters. It wasn't the quality of music that kept this group from ever hitting it big, despite the adage "the worse the music, the more the people." But it very well could have been the group's name, since a band that calls itself the Contenders is going to have to compete with a religious cult, a Kinks album, a television series, a film, and an eight-piece Minneapolis ska band, not to mention the category of shreeves running for public office that refer to themselves as "contenders" as well. The Contenders under discussion here originally formed in Nashville in the early '70s. Singer and guitarist Walter Hyatt and Champ Hood, a pro on fiddle as well as guitar and vocals, joined up with Steve Runkle and Tommy Goldsmith. Hyatt and Hood were two of the three members of Uncle Walt's Band, a group that had formed while still in high-school in Spartanburg, SC. Drummer Jimbeau Walsh consolidated the Contenders lineup, which boasted a whopping (or horrifying, depending on one's point of view and band politics) four songwriters and lead vocalists.

Fans of the band tend to feel the wonderful harmonies and ace picking was severely overlooked by the country-rock audience. The success of groups in this genre, such as the Eagles, could have been the Contenders'. Yet not a single recording made by the Eagles had the complexity or musical interest of the Contenders, which goes a long way toward explaining one group's popularity and the other's lack of it. Ragtime and swing influences came into the band via Hyatt and Hood, while Goldsmith brought in an authentic old-time country-rock sound that is completely out of the Glenn Frey universe. Runkle's lovely ballad "Snowing Me Under" revealed another side to the group. As much praise as it received from critics, *Light From Carolina, Vol. 1* was unable to do much for the group's career, because unfortunately, the Contenders had broken up and were no longer in the contending when the album was released. Hyatt and Hood continued on with a re-formed Uncle Walt's Band into the early '80s, followed by solo careers for both and a busy schedule as a fiddle session man for Hood.

In 1997, Hyatt died in the awful ValuJet crash in the Everglades. Runkle remained in Nashville as a writer and player, working and recording with artists such as David Olney and Tom House. Goldsmith, on the other hand, became a journalist while Walsh is supposedly in Hawaii doing who knows what. Of interest to song collectors obsessed with American cities would be Runkle's "Greensboro Blues," supposedly inspired by Olney's "Original Greensboro Blues." Other songs about Greensboro include "Greensboro Woman" by Townes Van Zandt and yet another "Greensboro Blues," this one by Bruce Piephoff, the only one of these jokers who actually lives in Greensboro. The Contenders, minus Goldsmith, who was recovering from an operation, backed Olney up on short tours in the late '70s. *—Eugene Chadbourne*

Light From Carolina, Vol. 1 / Aug. 1, 2000 / Moonlight ✦✦✦✦
If there is more inauspicious use of "*Vol. 1*" in an album title, the record would still probably not be as much fun to listen to as this one. It is the only album ever released by the Contenders, so there was never a second volume, nor any material available to put on one barring some kind of major find in the future. Furthermore, the group itself even broke up before the debut album came out in 1977. Two reissues of the material came about a bit less than a quarter of a century later. The 2002 Gadfly set entitled *The Contenders* folded in three more songs the group worked on for the never-to-follow album. In a perfect world, one of those additional songs would be on this album, as the other two aren't really that great. Of course, in a perfect world a band such as the Contenders would not have broken up after one album. This neglected band was not only a combination of five great talents, it was a combination of talents who were basically neglected by the music business as individuals as well. This at least establishes some consistency in the universe. "Light From Carolina" is perhaps the best title for the small treasure trove of Contenders documentation, at least in terms of a title representing a group putting its best collective feet forward. This haunting song by Steve Runkle, sung in his trademark Appalachian falsetto, closes out the album so wonderfully that a hole seems to appear in the musical universe, that of course being all the other possible material a group as talented as this could have recorded. At least Walter Hyatt's "Lean on Your Mind" was set down for posterity. It, along with the title track, establish that these were musical thinkers who had their heads on straight, who had the right priorities, and whose music was thus engraved with absolutely sincere emotion. No surprise, then, that the Contenders band was such a flop in the music business! Other great tracks include the lively "Silver Cup," which rushes forward rhythmically like a crowd greeting a train. *—Eugene Chadbourne*

● **The Contenders** / 2002 / Gadfly ✦✦✦✦✦
First off, this collection is highly recommended to fans of country, rock, or any type of American roots music. It is a musical dish with genuine flavors baked in time, the '70s, as well as place, the South. If one were to lapse into native North Carolina dialect, any discussion of the Contenders leads to "coulda woulda shoulda" sort of speculation. Anyone who wasn't around to catch the band during its live touring days might wonder what all the hubbub is about, but the head-scratching will halt by the end of the first verse of "Lean on Your Mind," the Walter Hyatt original that kicks things off. This low-key rocker, which like many Contenders numbers features a rootsy rave-up in the middle, is on par with the songwriting of Mose Allison, putting forward an intellectual point of view during an era when most music was fascinated with cute butts. From there on in, listeners can prepare to be underwhelmed as well as overwhelmed, to continually wrap enjoyment of the recordings in conditional greeting wrap. Sometimes something that sounds bad approaching the band from one perspective winds up sounding good from another, and there is no doubt this will happen since few people are willing to listen to this recording only once. There are bound to be somersaults involving aesthetic judgment when dealing with one of the few professionally recorded documents of a group whose membership's musical creativity was vital down to the man, and which apparently had a fairly full repertoire of diverse material worked out and ready to go. This disc contains the group's one and only release, a 1977 vinyl side, in its entirety. Three tracks recorded by producer Don Dixon for a follow-up finish out the collection, a programming decision that means the band sort of limps off into the sunset, since this trio of pieces can't possibly have the coherence of the complete album that is heard first. Not that the latter was any kind of lavish production in the first place. To the song, these are totally simple productions that could pass for board tapes made at a club soundcheck. From the perspective of a 2002 listener, the idea of a band combining elements of rock, country, reggae, beach music, rockabilly, and Western swing, even within one song, is not as far out as it was in the '70s. Most listeners have become used to more refined production touches with material such as this, especially country, and may wince at the harmonies on numbers such as "The Lack of Love." On the first listen, the thought occurs that if this were recorded by a major label in Nashville, many hours would have been spent refining the complicated vocal arrangement so even the most fleeting moment of pitch discomfort would be glossed over. Would all this effort be worth the trouble? David Ball, a later associate of some of the Contenders' members, had a huge hit with the song "Riding With Private Malone," a country & western ghost story that is a good example of music that would have been much more atmospheric and effective if the harmony singing had been a bit more out of tune. On the second listen, several songs haunted by such harmonic horror are reminiscent of a delightful documentary on garage bands presented by a Midwest public television station in the same year this reissue came out. The vocal sound of the Contenders can seem like the harmony singing of a typical garage band—and not one that has been slicked up with studio reverb, either. It is a charming, essential sound, one of those elements at the heart of rock & roll. Great, but on the third listen, "The Lack of Love" sounds completely different. Although still a bit rough, an element that ought to be overlooked anyway because it is such an ambitious song, it now sounds like an amalgam of gospel music and the '60s rock vocal sound of groups such as the Association. So it goes with the Contenders. Each song has layer upon layer of interest. Points of reference are paradoxes—for example, the garage band analogy. No garage bands could play songs such as Tommy Goldsmith's "Dim the Light," in which the chords move so brilliantly, or "Smokey Night Life," a classic songwriting collaboration between Hyatt and bassist and vocalist Steve Runkle that is genuine and over the top. It is Runkle's falsetto vocals, each lyric he sings seeming to float in from the Blue Ridge Mountains, that give some of these songs such a distinctive sound. Material and lead vocals are provided by all members, however, and the overall impression of a somewhat fractured band personality comes above all from having to make such judgments based on only 14 songs. Of the three tracks from the second unfinished album, only "Volcano" really erupts. "The Last of Me" is a collaboration between Champ Hood and Hyatt that utilizes part of the riff from "The Pusher," among other things. The Goldsmith song "Lelah" is uneven, really ending things on an unsatisfactory note. But perhaps that is appropriate, since just about everything involving this band is soaked with regret. Lyrics are provided for the 11 songs from the 1977 album, but not the extra material. *—Eugene Chadbourne*

Elizabeth Cook

b. 1972

Vocals / Neo-Traditionalist Country

Country singer/songwriter Elizabeth Cook made her *Grand Ole Opry* debut on March 17, 2000, appearing repeatedly thereafter—a remarkable achievement considering that, at the time, she was an indie artist with no radio airplay. But such was the excitement generated by her clear, beautiful voice, strong songwriting ability, and live performances, all of which have drawn comparisons to younger, critically respected artists like Kelly Willis and legends such as Dolly Parton.

Cook was born in Wildwood, FL. Her West Virginia-born mother played guitar and mandolin and sang on local radio shows. Her father, a Georgia native, also performed country music and served jail time for running moonshine. Upon his release, he and Elizabeth's mother played in local bands together, eventually marrying. Elizabeth, born in 1972, moved to Nashville in her 20's and quickly got a publishing deal. Demos recorded between 1997 and 2000 comprised her self-titled, independently released debut album, which showcased her formidable songwriting ability and featured such well-known Music City musicians as Tim Carroll, Kenny Vaughan, and Rick Schell. Atlantic Records signed Cook soon after its release, and she began working on her major-label debut. *Hey Y'All* appeared in summer 2002. *—Erik Hage*

Hey, Y'all / Aug. 27, 2002 / Warner Bros. ✦✦✦✦

Through more than 100 appearances on the *Grand Ole Opry*, Elizabeth Cook built strong ties to the audience most likely to respond to her debut album. Her voice throughout *Hey Y'all* begs comparison to classic country divas such as Loretta Lynn and especially Dolly Parton, to whom Cook pays good-humored tribute on "Dolly." Her nasal intonation and Southern lilt bear the ring of authenticity and her writing bypasses contemporary distractions in order to connect directly to a more conservative aesthetic. The results, always agreeable, can be startling when Cook throws a lyrical curve: The word "virginity" clangs like a dinner bell on the last line of "Demon," a finger-wag warning set to a honky tonk saunter. The classic old-time harmonies and medium-tempo rockabilly sway of "Blue Shades," the cameo monologue by Bill Anderson on the barroom lament "Don't Bother Me," the steel guitars that slither through several tracks, the unabashed if predictable gospel hand-clapper "God's Got a Plan," the infectious barn-dance hook of "Stupid Things," and above all her thrilling rendition of Jessi Colter's "I'm Not Lisa" all affirm the power of unadulterated old-time country and Cook's complete command of this idiom. *—Robert L. Doerschuk*

Spade Cooley (Donell C. Cooley)

b. Feb. 22, 1910, Grand, OK, **d.** Nov. 23, 1969, Vacaville, CA

Fiddle, Cello / Western Swing

A musician and actor whose often sordid private life tended to overshadow his career as an entertainer, Spade Cooley was the self-proclaimed King of Western Swing, an innovator who at his peak led the largest band ever assembled in the annals of country music. The product of a multi-generational family of fiddle players, Donnell Clyde Cooley was born in Oklahoma in 1910, and at the age of four, his family moved to Oregon. Despite his impoverished background, Cooley was a classically trained fiddler, and by the time he was eight years old, he was performing professionally at square dances with his father John. In 1930, Cooley (who received his nickname thanks to his poker skills) moved to Los Angeles, playing with a number of western-oriented acts. By the mid-'30s, he was working as an actor, with bit parts in several Westerns; for Republic Studios, he served as Roy Rogers' stand-in. He also toured with Rogers as a fiddle player, and handled vocal duties with the Riders of the Purple Sage.

Cooley did not begin a recording career until 1941, when he entered the studio while a member of Cal Shrum's band. A year later, he took control of bandleader Jimmy Wakely's group, the house band at Santa Monica, CA's Venice Pier Ballroom, and their Western swing music began attracting thousands of fans each Saturday night. The densely populated band, home to as many as three vocalists and fiddlers at a time, featured singer Tex Williams and guitarists Joaquin Murphey and John O. Weis. In 1945, Spade Cooley & His Orchestra's first single, "Shame on You," lasted nine weeks atop *Billboard*'s country charts. The first in an unbroken string of six Top Ten singles (including "Detour" and "You Can't Break My Heart"), "Shame on You" would remain Cooley's theme song for years to come. Also in 1945, he married his second wife, Orchestra backup singer Ella Mae Evans.

Ultimately, the Orchestra's success led to the dissolution of its most popular lineup; by 1946, Williams, the vocalist on all of the group's hits, was demanding more money, and Cooley refused to pay it. As a result, Williams quit, taking much of the Orchestra with him to form the Western Caravan. In 1947, Cooley began a career in television, hosting a program in Los Angeles titled *The Hoffman Hayride*. The show's popularity grew quickly, and within months an estimated 75 percent of all televisions in the L.A. area tuned into the show each Saturday night. He also resumed his film career, this time with much higher visibility; in addition to significant roles in a number of Westerns, he also starred in two 1949 short subjects, *King of Western Swing* and *Spade Cooley & His Orchestra*.

Throughout the early '50s, Cooley continued to record, but the group's popularity waned as public tastes changed; after a time, he even fired the Orchestra to replace its members with an all-female band. A heavy drinker, Cooley descended into alcoholism as his career declined, and he suffered a series of minor heart attacks. Furthermore, he was facing financial ruin as a result of problems with a planned water theme park to be located in the Mojave Desert. In 1961, his wife Ella Mae left him; after an argument on April 3, he stomped her to death while the couple's 14-year-old daughter Melody looked on in horror. The resulting trial, a media circus during which Cooley suffered another heart attack, culminated in a sentence of life imprisonment. Throughout his term, he was a model prisoner, and thus was allowed to perform at a sheriff's benefit in Oakland, CA, on November 23, 1969. After playing in front of a crowd of over 3,000, Cooley returned to his dressing room, suffered yet another heart attack, and died. *—Jason Ankeny*

★ **Spadella: The Essential** / 1994 / Columbia/Legacy ✦✦✦✦✦

Spadella: The Essential Spade Cooley collects 20 highlights from Cooley's stint as one of the most popular Western swing bandleaders in America. All of the selections on the album were recorded between 1945 and 1946, when Cooley and his group scored six straight Top Ten singles, all of which are included here ("You Can't Break My Heart" is in an alternate version). This is when the group was at its peak, and vocalist Tex Williams was always in stellar form. Although it doesn't cover his entire career, *Spadella* remains the one essential Cooley compilation. *—Stephen Thomas Erlewine*

King of Western Swing / 1997 / Collectors' Choice Music ✦✦✦

There's not a lot of Spade Cooley available—only a fraction of what one can find on Bob Wills—so this live performance from his first radio show, on July 21, 1951, is a welcome release. This was done five years or more after the contents of Sony's collection, after Cooley had become a major media star on television. The music includes solo spots for steel guitarist Noel Boggs and vocalists Becky Barfield, Ginny Jackson, and Phil Gray. Unfortunately, in contrast to Bob Wills' work, the performances and arrangements are more swing than Western, and they don't really swing that well—the resident bands on television shows such as *the Old American Barn Dance* did better. It's fun, but clunky, lacking the smoothness one expects and remembers. Luckily, the special guest is Jimmy Wakely, who performs three numbers including his then new release, "The Solid South," and it's amazing to hear the band come to life on his numbers. The disc includes three comedy routines from the show—luckily, they're indexed and can be bypassed on repeated listening (the jokes were old then, and haven't aged well). The sound is fair, without the crisp resolution of the best radio transcriptions. *—Bruce Eder*

Radio Broadcasts 1945 / May 5, 1998 / Country Routes ✦✦✦✦

Shame on You: The Western Swing Dance Gang / Apr. 20, 1999 / Bloodshot ✦✦✦✦

Shame on You collects 25 previously unreleased radio transcriptions recorded in 1944-1945, nine of which feature Tex Williams on vocals. The title track is a version of Cooley's number-one hit from 1945, and the other material runs the gamut from polkas ("Cowbell Polka," "Yodeling Polka") and hillbilly hoe-downs ("Down Home Rag") to tunes that have become instrumental standards ("Steel Guitar Rag," "Silver Bell.") The sound quality is excellent, and *Shame on You* is a fine companion piece to *Spadella*, Columbia's collection of Cooley's classic OKeh sides. *—Greg Adams*

Big Band 1950–1952 / Oct. 12, 1999 / Harlequin ✦✦✦✦

1941–1947 / Apr. 11, 2000 / Country Routes ✦✦✦

This collection straddles several different eras and facets of Cooley's career, from his pre-bandleader days working with Cal Shrum to mid-'40s transcriptions featuring his regular band to some 1947 sides. Cooley's fiddle work is showcased nicely on tunes like "MacGregor Swing" and "MacGregor Blues" while Tex Williams does the vocal honors on classics like "Sweethearts or Strangers." The 1947 tracks feature stalwarts like Noel Boggs and Jimmy Wyble along with vocalists Ginny Jackson, Red Egner, and even ex-Spike Jones City Slicker Del Porter. The quality of these transcription discs is pretty decent, taking into factor their age and rarity, and this is a delightful set that showcases the talents of one of Western swing's best. *—Cub Koda*

A Western Swing Dance Date with Spade & Tex / Jul. 11, 2000 / Jasmine ✦✦✦

While the title implies that this is a joint CD of Spade Cooley and Tex Williams' music, it actually focuses more on Cooley's repertoire. Tex Williams & His Western Caravan have eight tracks, while Cooley's band has 19, although four of them do feature Williams who was part of his band for a time. In fact, when Williams was offered a solo recording deal and broke off ties with Cooley he took most of the group with him. Even with all the backstage shenanigans and ego bouts, this budget CD, containing all original recordings, is hardly a comprehensive example of either of the artists work. Cooley's biggest hit, "Shame on Me," is absent, as well as Williams biggest, "Smoke! Smoke! Smoke!" Still, for those looking to save a few bucks this is a good introduction to the sounds of '40s and '50s Western swing, even if there are better compilations available. *—Curtis Zimmermann*

Rita Coolidge

b. May 1, 1944, Lafayette, TN

Vocals / Country-Rock, Pop, Soft Rock

A versatile singer blessed with a clear, pure voice, Rita Coolidge was a capable stylist in rock, pop, R&B, country, and folk, and was a hugely in-demand session vocalist outside of her own solo recording career. Born near Nashville, TN, in the town of Lafayette in 1944, Coolidge was part Cherokee and first sang in the church where her father was a minister. She studied art at Florida State University, but also sang and wrote songs on the side, and decided to give music a shot before settling into teaching. She moved to Memphis after graduation and worked singing commercial jingles, sometimes with her sister, Priscilla, and soon landed a job touring with Delaney & Bonnie as a backup vocalist. She subsequently relocated to Los Angeles, where she sang on recording sessions by the likes of Eric Clapton, Stephen Stills, Leon Russell, and Joe Cocker, among others. After returning from the supporting tour for Cocker's *Mad Dogs & Englishmen*, Coolidge landed her own solo contract with A&M.

Coolidge's self-titled debut album was released in 1971, but despite critical acclaim for it and the follow-up, *Nice Feelin'*, she failed to break through commercially. Over the course of the next few years, she moved into country-rock and Southern California soft rock, working territory not too dissimilar from Linda Ronstadt. She also married progressive country singer/songwriter Kris Kristofferson in 1973; the same year she recorded a duet album with him titled *Full Moon*. *Full Moon* topped the country charts, and "From the Bottle to the Bottom" won a Grammy for Best Country Vocal by a Duo or Group. The following year, the couple released a follow-up, *Breakaway*, whose "Lover Please" won them another Grammy in the same category. Coolidge finally broke through in her own right with 1977's *Anytime, Anywhere*, a collection of well-chosen covers with a strong R&B bent. Paced by the hit singles "(Your Love Has Lifted Me) Higher and Higher" (a Jackie Wilson cover that went to number-two pop), "We're All Alone" (Top Ten), and "The Way You Do the Things You Do" (a Top 20 Temptations cover), *Anytime, Anywhere* climbed into the Top Ten and sold over a million copies. Coolidge and Kristofferson released one final duet album, *Natural Act*, in 1979, but their marriage was on the rocks, and they separated by the end of the year.

Coolidge never repeated the pop success of *Anytime, Anywhere*, but she did continue to land hits on the adult contemporary charts through the early '80s, including "You," "I'd Rather Leave While I'm in Love," and "All Time High" (the theme for the James Bond flick *Octopussy*). She parted ways with A&M after 1984's *Inside the Fire*, and spent some time away from the music business to devote herself to various social causes. She returned to recording with 1992's *Love Lessons*, on Critique, and went on to cut several albums for other small labels during the latter half of the '90s. *Cherokee* (1995), in particular, signaled a renewed interest in her Native American musical heritage, and she teamed up with her sister, Priscilla, and her niece, Laura Satterfield, to form Walela, which explored those roots in greater detail over two albums in 1997 and 2000, respectively. *—Steve Huey*

Rita Coolidge / Feb. 1971 / A&M ✦✦✦✦✦

Nice Feelin' / Nov. 1971 / A&M ✦✦✦✦

It is amazing given the exposure Rita Coolidge obtained through the *Mad Dogs & Englishmen* soundtrack that her second album for A&M is such a cult item. Covers of songs by Bob Dylan, Neil Young, Graham Nash, and participation by names like Al Kooper, Glyn Johns, Bruce Botnick, and Marc Benno should have made this record her breakthrough. Instead, it took quite a few more discs before she would hit the Top 40 on her own with her eighth solo album, *Anytime, Anywhere*. Asylum Choir member Marc Benno's "Family Full of Soul" opens the album with wonderful bluesy pop resplendent in guitars, vibes, and Coolidge's distinctive voice. As guitarist Benno gets two compositions on this album, so does keyboardist Mike Utley, and his co-write "You Touched Me in the Morning" is a far cry from the slick, similarly titled Diana Ross hit. These authentic tunes and performances are so soulful and moving it is stunning to think that it takes a bright and intelligent audience to seek out and find music this important, music this good. Parallel to the sounds generated by Bonnie Bramlett's various ensembles, the title track by Marc Benno is sheer brilliance; but then again, so is "I'll Be Here," which leads off side two, the swelling organ raising Coolidge's voice into the space where angels dwell on this Jimmy Lewis tune. Graham Nash's "Better Days" works so well in this company as the band changes their approach to the music, David Anderle's production brimming with deep drumbeats and a more majestic go at the sound created by labelmate Joe Cocker and his Grease Band. "Lay My Burden Down" is laced with gospel, and you can hear the future hit sound as Coolidge takes Dylan's "'Most Likely You'll Go Your Way" and makes it her own. Neil Young's "Journey Through the Past" also is transformed by this band, producer, and singer, creating an atmosphere that demands attention. A pity that the radio-listening public doesn't have the opportunity to hear what is inside this beautifully packaged and well-crafted set of recordings. *—Joe Viglione*

The Lady's Not for Sale / Oct. 1972 / A&M ✦✦✦

Rita Coolidge's third album is a fine mixture of covers and originals that manages to showcase her fine vocal abilities as well as show off an impressive array of friends. Booker T. Jones contributes not only his fine flute skills, but also two songs. Noted guitarist and songwriter Marc Benno also lends his impressive, laid-back guitar work all throughout the album. His "Donut Man" adds an air of lazy funk to the proceedings. Bob Dylan's "I'll Be Your Baby Tonight" probably gets the most soulful reading, with Coolidge's take on Leonard Cohen's "Bird on a Wire" following close behind. Kris Kristofferson is represented at the tail end of the album with the title track. She may not have had the most distinctive of voices, but Coolidge definitely captured the sort of laid-back energy and approach associated with early-'70s country-rock. If Rita Coolidge's voice and stellar class of backing musicians aren't enough to sway you, consider the cover that shows her bedecked in what looks to be several pounds of turquoise, or the gatefold in which she appears pensive, with Stonehenge not too far in the background. *—Jon Pruett*

Fall into Spring / Apr. 1974 / A&M ✦✦✦

It's Only Love / Nov. 1975 / A&M ✦✦

Anytime, Anywhere / Mar. 1977 / A&M ✦✦✦

Love Me Again / May 1978 / A&M ✦✦✦

Satisfied / Sep. 1979 / A&M ✦✦✦

With Steve Cropper recording Mitch Ryder and Yvonne Elliman, the great Booker T. Jones and A&M exec David Anderle counter with a shimmering production for Rita Coolidge, emerging from her underground status with Mad Dogs & Englishmen to unleash her fifth Top 40 hit here: Peter Allen and Carole Bayer Sager's "I'd Rather Leave While I'm in Love." With an array of fine players, the Delta Lady weaves an album that is up there with *Dusty in Memphis*, though it never got the similar acclaim, with the stigma of adult contemporary pop not giving this wonderful effort the hip luster it deserves. A breathy and seductive cover of "One Fine Day" is another gem; it was being released by Jimmy & Kristy McNichol and Jane Oliver as well, with songwriter Carole King winning the race in 1980, going Top 15 with the 1963 Chiffons hit she composed. That's OK, titles like Dave Loggins' co-write, "The Fool in Me," and Donna Weiss/Lenny Macaluso's "Trust It All to Somebody" are perfectly structured adult contemporary with more than a touch of the Philly sound created by Gamble & Huff; indeed, "Trust It All to Somebody" could have fit on an album by the O'Jays or the Three Degrees, the strings just needed to be brought up a notch. Donna Weiss, of course, was riding high, having co-written the biggest hit of 1980 with Jackie DeShannon, "Bette Davis Eyes," the inner circle that Yvonne Elliman, Kim Carnes, and Coolidge walked so obvious when one looks at the same players showing up on their respective discs: Mike Utley on keyboards and Jim Keltner on drums (Keltner and Anderle are on 1975's *Kim Carnes*, Keltner is also on 1977's *Night Flight* by Elliman). What all this work comprises are the girl groups of the '70s, and it is remarkable stuff. The quasi-disco of Booker T. Jones' "Let's Go Dancin' is acceptable years later as a classy slice of pop that qualifies as art, beyond the trendy K.C. & the Sunshine Band sign of the times it might appear to be on lesser albums. Johnny Bristol's "Pain of Love" is a dramatic departure from his Supremes hit, "Someday We'll Be Together," for this album contains a more subtle intensity, best displayed in the gorgeous hit. "I'd Rather Leave While I'm in Love" was not her biggest chart record, but it is one of her most triumphant performances. The way Rita Coolidge takes Priscilla Jones' "Sweet Emotion" to a funky, laid-back groove is the genius of the matchup of Booker T. Jones producing Rita Coolidge. It's more of an album for the ages than people realize; "Crime of Passion" and "Can She Keep You Satisfied" are rich with the unique voice of Coolidge and the blend of these first-rate musicians. *—Joe Viglione*

Greatest Hits / Dec. 1980 / A&M ✦✦✦✦✦

Heartbreak Radio / Aug. 1981 / A&M ✦✦✦

Never Let You Go / 1983 / A&M ✦✦✦

Inside the Fire / 1984 / A&M ✦✦

● **Classics, Vol. 5** / 1987 / A&M ✦✦✦✦✦

Out of the Blues / 1996 / Varese ✦✦✦

Even though the duo-tone cover looks new and jazzy, most of this cozy set was recorded over 20 years ago. Primarily working with bass, drum and piano, the smoky-voiced chanteuse delivers these 11 songs with her own inimitably laid-back vigor, performing best on moody ballads such as "Am I Blue," "Mean to Me" and "The Man I Love." Some of these tracks have appeared on Rita's albums during her A&M Records tenure in the 1970s, but most of them remained in the vault until now. It's a fine set with simple arrangements of chestnuts such as "Bring It on Home to Me" and the blues staple "Stormy Monday." Rounding the set out are two recent cuts, the Top 40-ish "When the Night Rolls In" and the bluesy "Out of the Blues." *—Bill Carpenter*

Collection / Nov. 3, 1998 / Spectrum ✦✦✦✦

A solid CD featuring many of Rita Coolidge's most stirring performances. Casual fans with a limited knowledge of Coolidge's discography won't quibble with these selections, consisting mainly of close-to-definitive remakes of familiar rock/soul classics. She dazzles on Jackie Wilson's "(Your Love Has Lifted Me) Higher and Higher," the Bee Gees' "Words," Boz Scaggs' "Slow Dancer," the Sweet Inspirations' "Sweet Inspiration," a hot rendition of the Falcons' "Your So Fine," and others, like "All Time High" from the movie *Octopussy*. Some worthy tracks didn't make the cut, which will irk long-standing fans, but *Collection* will please most. *—Andrew Hamilton*

20th Century Masters—The Millennium Collection: The Best of Rita Coolidge / Feb. 8, 2000 / Interscope ✦✦✦✦

Part of Universal's massive *20th Century Masters/The Millennium Collection*, this 11-song budget set draws on a dozen of Coolidge's best-known tunes. Highlights include "Higher and Higher," "Superstar," "Fever," "You," and "One Fine Day." It's a solid introduction to this artist. *—Cub Koda*

Coon Creek Girls

f. 1937, Kentucky, **db.** 1957

Group / Old-Timey, Traditional Bluegrass

One of the most famous all-female string bands in country, the Coon Creek Girls were also among the first female groups to play their own instruments and focus on authentic mountain music, instead of sentimental and cowboy songs.The founding member of the long-lived group was Lily May Ledford. Born in Pilot, KY, she was the daughter of poor tenant farmers who frequently played string band music; consequently, Lily May learned how to play guitar and fiddle as a child. By the time she was an adolescent, she had formed the Red River Ramblers with her sister, Rose, and her brother, Cayen, and the group began playing local square dances. The Ramblers auditioned for talent scouts in 1935, and Lily May was chosen to appear on WLS Chicago's *Barn Dance*. During her performance, she caught the attention of announcer John Lair, who became her manager; in the process, he landed her a regular spot on the *Barn Dance*, where she became so popular that the station's magazine based a comic strip on her.

Following its success in Chicago, Lair moved the show to Cincinnati and then to Renfro Valley, were he decided to base an all-female string band around Lily May. The original Coon Creek Girls were comprised of Lily May, her sister Rosie, Evelyn "Daisy" Lange, and Ester "Violet" Koehler. On October 9, 1937, they made their live radio debut from *Cincinnati Music Hall*. Shortly after their debut, the group began appearing on the Renfro Valley Barn Dance; they would sing on the program for the next 15 years. In 1938, the Coon Creek Girls cut their first session, although their records, which featured traditional mountain songs, never proved as popular as their radio performances.

In 1939, the original group disbanded when Koehler and Lange left to go work with the Callahan Brothers' Blue Ridge Mountain Folk in Dallas. Lily May and Rosie were then joined by their younger sister, Minnie. The Coon Creek Girls kept performing together in various incarnations until 1957. After the group broke up, Lily May launched her own solo career. In 1980 she published her autobiography, *Coon Creek Girl*. In 1985, Ledford died. Ester Koehler spent time in the Boone County Jamboree and eventually married one of Lily May's brothers. Evelyn Lange married and moved to Indiana, where she sometimes competed in fiddle contests. During the 1980s, John Lair created the New Coon Creek Girls to appear on a revival of his old radio show. The group included the banjo of Vicki Simmons, guitarist/vocalist Dale Ann Bradley, banjoist Ramona Church Taylor, and fiddler Katy Kinn. Simmons actually learned her instrument from original Coon Creek Girl Lily May, linking the two groups' fine tradition of breaking down gender barriers while bringing up listeners' spirits. *—Johnny Loftus*

Lily May, Rosie and Susie / 1967 / County ✦✦✦

● **Early Radio Favorites** / 1982 / Old Homestead ✦✦✦✦✦

Early Radio Favorites contains all of the music that the Coon Creek Girls recorded during the '30s, including "Banjo Picking Girl" and "How Many Biscuits Can You Eat?" Not only were the Coon Creek Girls one of the last mountain string bands of their era, they were the only female old-timey group, which made them unique. If they were just unique, the band would simply be a historical curiosity, but the girls also made good music, as evidenced by this stellar collection. For fans of string bands, *Early Radio Favorites* is an essential addition to their record collections. *—Stephen Thomas Erlewine*

Roger Cooper

Fiddle, Guitar / Neo-Traditional Folk, Traditional Bluegrass, Old-Timey
Roger Cooper was raised in Kentucky, where the fiddle music tradition of such greats as Buddy Thomas inspired him to pick up the instrument himself. In addition to his 1996 Rounder release *Going Back to Old Kentucky*, Cooper has performed with the Bing Brothers, a rapid-fire bluegrass combo from West Virginia. *—Johnny Loftus*

Going Back to Old Kentucky / Oct. 8, 1996 / Rounder ✦✦✦✦
Going Back to Old Kentucky is essentially a showcase for the instrumental skills of Roger Cooper, one of the best old-timey fiddlers of the '90s. As a result, there's might be a lack of full-fledged songs here—nearly every song is arranged as a vehicle for Cooper's fiddling—but it stands unparalleled as a fiddle record. There is zest and vigor within in his playing, which elevates him from the category of a mere technical wonder and into a fully rounded musician. *—Stephen Thomas Erlewine*

Stoney Cooper

b. Oct. 16, 1918, Harman, WV, **d.** Mar. 22, 1977
Fiddle, Vocals / Traditional Bluegrass, Old-Timey, Traditional Country
Dale Troy "Stoney" Cooper and his wife Wilma Lee were one of the premier husband-and-wife duos in country music. Staples of the *Grand Ole Opry* for twenty years, they performed together for close to four decades, and helped old-time music evolve into modern country music. They were born four years apart on opposite ends of Randolph County, West Virginia. Cooper came from a family of fiddle players, while Wilma's family loved performing sacred songs, billing themselves as the Singing Leary Family. Following his high-school graduation, Cooper began fiddling for Rusty Hiser's Green Valley Boys at a radio station in West Virginia; Wilma's family was singing on the air in Virginia. Following the breakup of his band, Stoney joined the Learys as a sideman. He and Wilma began singing together and were married in 1941. The couple began their career together singing at various radio stations around the country, ending up on the *Wheeling Jamboree* and staying there for the next ten years as one of the show's most enduringly popular acts.

The duo signed to Columbia in 1949 and remained for five years, releasing several classic singles, including "Sunny Side of the Mountain" and the devotional "Walking My Lord Up Calvary Hill." Stoney and Wilma formed a backing acoustic band called the Clinch Mountain Clan, which featured several dobro, fiddle, and mandolin players over the years. They moved to Hickory Records in 1955 and the following year had two small hits. In 1957, the Coopers joined the *Opry*. Their most successful year was 1959, when they released three Top Five hits: "Come Walk With Me," "Big Midnight Special," and "There's a Big Wheel." They had two Top 20 hits in 1960 and scored their last chart appearance in 1961 with the Top Ten hit *Wreck on the Highway*. Stoney suffered a heart attack in 1963 and was forced to slow down considerably. The two moved to Decca in 1965 and tried to update their sound, without much success. In 1977, Stoney finally succumbed to his health problems; Wilma Lee continued to tour and play the banjo in a more bluegrass-oriented style. *—Sandra Brennan*

There's a Big Wheel / 1960 / Hickory ✦✦✦

Sacred Songs / 1960 / Harmony ✦✦✦

Family Favorites / 1962 / Hickory ✦✦✦

Songs of Inspiration / 1963 / Hickory ✦✦✦

Sunny Side of the Mountain / 1966 / Harmony ✦✦✦✦

A Tribute to Roy Acuff / 1970 / Skylite ✦✦✦

Wilma Lee & Stoney Cooper / 1976 / Starday ✦✦✦✦✦

● **The Very Best of Wilma Lee and Stoney Cooper & The Clinch Mountain Clan** / 2002 / Varese ✦✦✦✦

● **Classic Early Recordings** / County ✦✦✦✦✦
Originally recorded between 1949 and 1953, the wife-and-husband duo let it fly with passionate zeal on these old-time mountain and gospel songs. Wilma Lee could shake the coal out of the hills with her raw and full-throated voice, and she didn't bother with nuance. *—Michael McCall*

Wilma Lee Cooper

b. Feb. 7, 1921, Valley Head, WV
Vocals / Old-Timey, Traditional Bluegrass, Traditional Country, Country-Pop
Born Wilma Lee Leary, songwriter and singer Wilma Cooper was raised in a well-known musical group that sang at local churches and festivals, billing themselves as the Leary Family. At one point, the Leary's were even invited by Eleanor Roosevelt to perform at a national folk festival. Upon graduating high-school Wilma obtained a degree in banking at Davis and Elkins College. Near the same time she met and married guitarist Stoney Cooper. For the next 40 years the two performed as one of country music's most popular duos. Their performances, including a ten year stint on Wheeling West Virginia's *Jamboree* and another decade performing at the *Grand Ole Opry*, led to recording contracts with both Columbia and Decca. Wilma, who is a skillful banjoist, guitarist and organist, wrote or co-wrote several of their most successful compositions including "Cheated Too," "Loving You," "I Tell My Heart," and "Heartbreak Street." After Stoney's death in the mid-'70s Wilma continued to perform, once again joining the cast of the *Opry*. She is featured among the Smithsonian Institute's collection of great singers. *—Steve Kurutz*

● **The Very Best of Wilma Lee & Stoney Cooper & the Clinch Mountain Clan** / Mar. 19, 2002 / Varese Vintage ✦✦✦✦✦
As a 19-track CD that covers the duo's most commercially successful period, this should be considered the best compilation of Wilma Lee & Stoney Cooper's work as a duo. Devoted to their Hickory material from 1956-1963, it features seven Top 20 hits: "Come Walk With Me," "Cheated Too," "Big Midnight Special," "The Wreck on the Highway," "There's a Big Wheel," "Johnny, My Love (Grandma's Diary)," and "This Ole House." That's less than half of the anthology; more importantly, it captures them in their artistic prime too, at a good midpoint between their Appalachian old-time country music and the more modern commercial Nashville sound (including some drums and electric instruments). Wilma Lee Cooper's vocals still jump out with an exuberance that marks her as one of the most emotional, expressive, and downright extroverted country singers of the time. The material selected for this comp is a good and diverse mix, including the near-gospel boogie of the Louvin Brothers' "There's a Higher Power," Woody Guthrie's "Philadelphia Lawyer," "The Tramp on the Street" (Wilma Lee Cooper's singing reaches sublime heights of yearning on that cut), some originals from the pen of Wilma Lee Cooper, and a reworking of the folk standard "Midnight Special" into "Big Midnight Special." "Johnny, My Love (Grandma's Diary)," one of their best hits, was written by Boudleaux Bryant and Felice Bryant, the same team responsible for many early Everly Brothers classics. There's some real hot country and rockabilly picking, too, on songs like "Cheated Too," the rollicking "I Tell My Heart," and "There's a Higher Power." *—Richie Unterberger*

Cowboy Copas (Lloyd Estel Copas)

b. Jul. 15, 1913, Adams County, OH, **d.** Mar. 5, 1963, Camden, TN
Vocals, Fiddle, Guitar / Traditional Country, Honky Tonk
A honky tonk singer popular in the late '40s, Cowboy Copas made something of a comeback in the early '60s before he died in the air crash that also killed Patsy Cline and Hawkshaw Hawkins. Born Lloyd Estel Copas on July 15, 1913, he dropped out of school at the age of 14 and began playing fiddle in several string bands around his Ohio home. On a dare, Copas traveled to Cincinnati to enter a contest, and wound up performing on radio shows for Cincinnati's WLW and later WKRC. By 1940, Copas moved to WNOX-Knoxville with a band called the Gold Star Rangers.

Three years later, Cowboy Copas got his big break: He was tapped to replace Eddy Arnold as the vocalist for *Pee Wee King's Golden West Cowboys* on WSM-Nashville and the *Grand Ole Opry*. He signed with King Records in 1946, and his debut single, "Filipino Baby," hit number four on the country charts that August. Two years later, Copas was back in the Top Ten with "Signed, Sealed and Delivered" (number two), "Tennessee Waltz" (number three), and "Tennessee Moon" (number seven). He also continued to perform with Pee Wee King on the *Opry*, recording a hit version of "Tennessee Waltz." After the Top 20 singles "Breeze" and "I'm Waltzing With Tears in My Eyes," Copas hit the Top Ten again in early 1949. "Candy Kisses" peaked at number five, "Hangman's Boogie" reached number 14, and "The Strange Little Girl" hit number five. His next single, 1952's "'Tis Sweet to Be Remembered," hit number eight, but it was his last chart entry for more than eight years. His King contract expired in 1955, and a brief time with the Dot label also failed.

During the late '50s, Copas bided his time on the *Opry*, and he finally signed to Starday in 1960. His first single for the label, "Alabam," became the biggest of his career when it captured country's pole position for three months during the last half of 1960. "Flat Top" hit the Top Ten in April 1961, and a remake of his early hit "Signed, Sealed and Delivered" also reached the Top Ten in September. A year and a half later, Copas was returning to Nashville from a benefit show in Kansas City when his private plane went down, killing him, Patsy Cline, Hawkshaw Hawkins, and Copas' son-in-law, pilot Randy Hughes. Cowboy Copas' last single, "Goodbye Kisses," hit the Top 15 one month after his death. *—John Bush*

Favorite Scared Songs / 1957 / King ✦✦✦✦✦

Broken Hearted Melodies / 1960 / King ✦✦✦

● **Tragic Tales of Love and Life** / 1960 / King ✦✦✦✦✦
A collection of recordings cut between 1946 and 1955, *Tragic Songs of Love and Life* includes Copas' renditions of "Tragic Romance," "Old Farm for Sale," and the 1949 hit "Hangman's Boogie." *—Jason Ankeny*

Mister Country Music / 1962 / Starday ✦✦✦
There is an especially grim irony in the final track of this album (Copas' last), "I Dreamed of a Hillbilly Heaven," where Copas mentions himself alongside the likes of such deceased country stars as Jimmie Rodgers, Hank Williams, etc.— in March of 1963, he died in the same plane crash that killed Patsy Cline and Hawkshaw Hawkins. Otherwise, the material is a mix of uptempo numbers ("Sal," "You Are the One," "Black Eyed Susan") and, more often, romantic ballads ("Louisiana," "A Thousand Miles of Ocean," "A Penny For Your Thoughts"), some of which is delightful, some of it less than memorable. As with many stereo recordings of this era, the sharp separation is unnatural and leaves the overall recording without some body and depth. And as usual with King and Starday reissues, there is no information on the date, circumstances, or personnel on the original release. *—Bruce Eder*

Opry Star Spotlight / 1962 / Starday ✦✦✦
A pretty fair album, showing off Cowboy Copas' more jaunty sound ("Sixteen Fathoms") as well as his softer romantic ballads ("Now That You're Gone"). The best song here is Copas' version of Porter Wagoner's "A Satisfied Mind," as are covers of Ferlin Husky's "Wings of a Dove" and Carl Smith's "Loose Talk," but there's a lot more to recommend this disc. Copas also turns in a cover of the television theme song "Johnny Yuma," where he sounds more thoughtful than Johnny Cash, with some really sweet male harmony singing behind him. The two duets with Copas' daughter Kathy (whose husband died in the same crash that killed her father) are also quite lovely. Another surprise is the instrumental "Flat Top Pickin'," a bluegrass-style piece featuring some fine fiddle playing (probably by Tommy Jackson). And some of it is just plain fun, like "Sleepy Eyed John." *—Bruce Eder & Jason Ankeny*

Country Music Entertainer #1 / 1963 / Starday ♦♦♦
The Nashville sound is rarely heard on Cowboy Copas' records as prominently as it is on *Country Music Entertainer #1.* Copas died in 1963, so this is also one of his last albums, featuring a vocal chorus and very commercial production. Copas covers two Webb Pierce songs ("Cow Town" and "Alla My Love"), Claude King's "Wolverton Mountain," and Burl Ives' "Call Me Mr. In-Between." "The Ballad of Frank Clement" is a biographical song about the former Tennessee governor, and "Bury Me Face Down" ("so I'll see where I'm a-goin'") is a good cut that failed as a single. The vocal chorus isn't as tight as would be expected from a major label, but it is interesting to hear an old-timer like Copas take a swipe at newer country music styles. *—Greg Adams*

The Legend of Cowboy Copas and Hawkshaw Hawkins / 1964 / King ♦♦♦♦♦

The Late and Great Cowboy Copas / 1966 / Nashville ♦♦♦
King/Starday has reissued a few of Cowboy Copas' original LPs on CD, but *The Late and Great Cowboy Copas* has yet to resurface. Although it includes no hits, this posthumous album reveals the variety of Copas' talents, from flat-top picking ("Pickin' the Blues," "Cope's Wildwood Flower") to inspirational tunes ("Wherever He Leads I'll Go") and popular songs. "Sal," an example of the latter, sounds like a viable commercial counterpart to Copas' smash hit "Alabam," and Copas' daughter, Cathy, adds duet vocals on two others. Copas recorded several sea-faring songs, and two of them ("South Pacific Shore" and "A Thousand Miles of Ocean") are here. With liner notes by Don Pierce and a dozen uncommon selections from Copas' later period, *The Late and Great Cowboy Copas* is a worthwhile addition to his album catalog. *—Greg Adams*

Late Great Cowboy Copas: Star of the Opry / 1970 / Guest Star ♦♦♦
The recording industry may seem like a corrupt old whore at times, but a cursory glance at this album would lead even the worst pessimist to the conclusion that at least a few things have improved. Namely, no company would release a package such as this anymore. The layers of manure are piled so high in this barn that it would require a few months' residency on the part of several cows in order to produce a matching amount. Cowboy Copas, a sentimental favorite among old-timey country fans, although hardly a genius as a recording artist, is played up as the headline star on a recording on which he actually appears on less than half the tracks. Most of the album actually features Johnny Colmus, described as an "up and coming artist," which must mean the typeface used to print his name is up-and-coming, stopping at about 16-point type, whereas Copas is just plain "up," at about 78-point type. The front cover of the album is a drawing so bad that neither of the artists would want to shout out "That's me!," suggesting that perhaps it is a portrait of the unknown country singer. As for the back cover, the subject of the music at hand is dismissed as quickly as possible so that the record label can get on to printing more important things. "Fine Records Need Not Be Expensive" is a sophisticated and useful philosophy, printed expansively across the middle of the back cover, a big clue that this record was some kind of low-budget number, meaning customers maybe would feel like they had no right to complain about being improperly Copas-ated. Then there is a long list of other ways in which "Diplomat and Guest Star Recordings offer many additional hours of listening pleasure," including a record by Borah Minnevitch & His Harmonica Playboys. The music on the Copas/Colmus album is not bad—it's a pretty straightforward style of small-combo country music in which the vocal is placed front and center like a behemoth. The Colmus vocals are brought back a notch, and he seems to be a bit into a Western swing feel, although at languid tempos with none of the crackpot hysteria of a Bob Wills side. "No Sad Songs to Sing" has a nice, relaxing feel to it, the singer stepping back to leave room for a series of fiddle and guitar exchanges which are polite, but groovy. "Satisfied Mind" works well for Copas, as it does for most masculine singers, and "Flattop Pickin'" is an enjoyable cop at a "Tennessee Flat-top Box" matcher. No information about songwriters is provided. *—Eugene Chadbourne*

● **Copasetic** / Oct. 9, 2001 / WestSide ♦♦♦♦♦
Copasetic earns a lot of points for being the best-mastered Cowboy Copas CD yet, and for including the mammoth number one hit "Alabam," which did not appear on any of King/Starday's Copas reissues. Copas was an important artist who nearly single-handedly kept King Records afloat in its early years, but today he is most often remembered for having died in that fateful plane crash with Patsy Cline and Hawkshaw Hawkins. The mix of hits and rarities on *Copasetic* does a good job of demonstrating what Copas was all about: tight, Western swing-influenced hillbilly music with mellow vocals, like a deeper-voiced Floyd Tillman minus the honky tonk lyrics. Copas was often joined by premier guitarists such as Roy Lanham and Merle Travis (his artistry is impressively heard on two takes of "Hangman's Boogie"), and Copas turns in some accomplished flat-top picking himself on "Tennessee Flat Guitar." Lengthy notes by Dave Sax add to the historical value of this set, as do the handful of truly rare sides. *Copasetic* emphasizes Copas' early years and misses fully half of his hits, so buyers can hope for a second volume to wrap up the story of this great but underappreciated country artist. *—Greg Adams*

Tennessee Waltz / Nov. 26, 2002 / ASV ♦♦♦♦♦

Corbin/Hanner

f. 1980
Group / Contemporary Country
Bob Corbin and David Hanner met in high-school, and began writing songs together after seeing the Beatles on *the Ed Sullivan Show.* The young musicians cut an album for Jubilee, but it went nowhere. It wasn't until college that the duo began to have some real success. Corbin and Hanner formed the rock band Gravel, and began gigging throughout Pennsylvania, Ohio, and West Virginia. But while the successful bar band recorded a few singles for Columbia, Gravel was never more than a regional phenomenon. In 1979, Gravel became the Corbin/Hanner Band and began to focus on a country-rock sound. They also added keyboardist Al Snyder, bassist Kip Paxton, and drummer Dave Freeland to the lineup. Over the next two years, the band scored four hits, including "Time Has Treated You Well," and recorded two albums for the Alfa label, *Son of America* (1980) and *For the Sake of the Song* (1981). But after touring through 1984, Corbin and Hanner decided a hiatus was in order and parted ways.

The duo regrouped in 1990 at the urging of Mercury Nashville president Harold Shedd, became simply Corbin/Hanner, and were soon at work on new material for the label. *Black & White Photograph* appeared in 1990; the release included five songs from each songwriter, with Corbin leaning more toward rootsy rock and Hanner on the 1960s pop of his youth. *Just Another Hill* appeared two years later and featured numerous songs co-written by the duo. They returned in 1997 with a live recording of a 1982 concert, and in 1998 dropped *Every Stranger Has a Story,* the first release on their new Liddl' Red Hen imprint. The album produced the title cut to Kenny Rogers' 1999 comeback album, and featured a few minor hits for Corbin and Hanner themselves. The songwriting team next focused on a few fan-friendly releases. 2000's *By Request* featured re-recorded versions of 20 of the duo's songs; 2002 saw the release of *The Corbin/Hanner Band,* which contained all 40 songs from the Alfa years, as well as both of the Mercury releases in their entirety. *—Johnny Loftus*

For the Sake of the Song / 1981 / Alfa ♦♦♦

Black & White Photograph / Apr. 1990 / Mercury ♦♦♦♦
Black & White Photograph offers five compositions apiece from the harmony duo of Bob Corbin and Dave Hanner; while Corbin's material leans toward roots rock, Hanner's work bears the stamp of '60s pop. *—Jason Ankeny*

● **Just Another Hill** / Nov. 1992 / Mercury ♦♦♦♦
Just Another Hill ups the ante on Corbin/Hanner's debut by offering a number of songs—the title cut, "I Could Be the One" and "Any Road" among them—co-written by both vocalists. *—Jason Ankeny*

Silver Eagle Cross Country Presents Live: Corbin/Hanner / Apr. 15, 1997 / Silver Eagle ♦♦♦
Silver Eagle Cross Country Presents Live captures a 1982 concert Corbin—Hanner gave in Los Angeles. Over the course of the show, they ran through their best-known material—including "Lord, I Hope This Day Is Good" and "Oklahoma Crude"—and while these versions aren't particularly inspired, they are enjoyable, making it a worthwhile purchase for dedicated fans. *—Thom Owens*

Larry Cordle

Composer, Guitar, Vocals / Honky Tonk, Traditional Bluegrass, Traditional Country, Progressive Bluegrass
Songwriter Larry Cordle has numerous hits to his credit, including three that went to the top of the charts. His awards include the 1992 Song of the Year, which Cordle received from the International Bluegrass Music Association for his "Lonesome Standard Time." The song also garnered a Grammy nomination. Despite these high points that mark a successful career in the music business, Cordle later made news with a song that some listeners thought might be biting the hand that fed the songwriter. "Murder on Music Row," a song Cordle co-wrote with Larry Shell, makes no bones about criticizing Nashville for drifting away from the roots of country music. Plenty of people in the industry were aghast and angry over the song's condemnation of the town and of the turn country music had taken in recent years. Probably just as many cheered it. The song wasn't released to radio as a single, at least not officially, and there wasn't even any real promotion to speak of. But the duet by George Strait and Alan Jackson raised the song's profile. It hit a nerve and it hit deep. The song made it onto the airwaves, landed in the Top 40, and made a lot of people sit up and take notice of the things Cordle had to say about the state of country music. The ripples that spread from the song's impact even led the very industry that the song condemns to acknowledge and honor its honesty.

The Country Music Association bestowed a pair of nominations in 2000, one for Vocal Event of the Year and another for Song of the Year. Other artists who have recorded Cordle's songs include Diamond Rio, Ricky Skaggs, Garth Brooks, Trisha Yearwood, George Jones, Loretta Lynn, Alison Krauss, John Michael Montgomery, and John Anderson, among others. Shell Point Records of Nashville issued the album *Murder on Music Row,* while Sugar Hill Records released three other Cordle albums. His band, Lonesome Standard Time, includes Terry Eldredge on upright bass, lead acoustic guitarist Booie Beech, fiddler Fred Carpenter, mandolinist David Harvey, and banjo player David Talbot. *—Linda Seida*

Lonesome Standard Time / 1992 / Sugar Hill ♦♦

● **Murder on Music Row** / Dec. 15, 1999 / Shell Point ♦♦♦
From the album title and the cover, which depicts a hearse picking up a pedal steel guitar in a crosswalk on 16th Avenue South in Nashville, you might assume this is a country comedy album. But singer/songwriter Larry Cordle and his cohorts in *Lonesome Standard Time* are deadly serious when they get around to performing the title song at the end of the record, lamenting a country music scene in which "The almighty dollar, and the lust for worldwide fame / Slowly killed tradition." "Old Hank wouldn't have a chance on today's radio," the song notes, and that's probably also true for this aggregation, which is a traditional bluegrass outfit of lead guitar, rhythm guitar, banjo, mandolin, fiddle, and "doghouse" bass, with three-part harmonies. Cordle's songs examine familiar country themes, from love to drinking and religion, and he gives over a couple of instrumentals to pure picking. A successful country songwriter, Cordle is not quite as traditional as he claims, but on this independent label release he can pose as the last of the great real country artists, even as the people who he claims murdered country music record his songs and pay his rent. *—William Ruhlmann*

Songs from the Workbench / Sep. 10, 2002 / Shell Point ♦♦♦

Helen Cornelius (Helen Lorene Johnson)

b. Dec. 6, 1950, Hannibal, MO

Choir, Chorus, Songwriter, Vocals / Country-Pop

Helen Cornelius was known to country music fans as a singer/songwriter, but she also danced, acted, and played several instruments. She was born Helen Lorene Johnson in Monroe City, MO, and grew up on a farm with older brothers who played in bands. She and her sisters Judy and Sharon formed a trio, and their supportive father took the girls to their gigs. Eventually Cornelius left her sisters and began touring with her backup band, the Crossroads. After graduating from high-school, Cornelius married and worked as a secretary. She returned to touring during the '60s and became a songwriter, gaining recognition in 1970 when she was signed as a writer to Columbia/Screen Gems Music after submitting a demo tape. After the company folded, Cornelius sent a tape to Jerry Crutchfield and began working for MCA Music; he later helped her sign with Columbia Records. In 1973, she came to Nashville and recorded two unsuccessful singles, later signing to RCA. She released her first single for the label in 1975; neither it nor its follow-up charted.

The key to success proved to be Ferguson's pairing of Cornelius with Jim Ed Brown. The duo debuted in 1976 with "I Don't Want to Have to Marry You," which soon became a major hit. She again tried a solo single, "There's Always a Goodbye," but it did nothing. She had no other hits until her duet with Brown on "Saying Hello, Saying I Love You, Saying Goodbye" became a Top Three success. Later in 1976, the two began appearing regularly on the TV series *Nashville on the Road*. Cornelius went out on tour with Brown's road show and also made her debut on the *Grand Ole Opry*.

In 1978, she and Brown had more chart success with two Top 15 duet singles, "I'll Never Be Free" and "If the World Ran Out of Love Tonight," and Cornelius scored a solo hit with "What Cha Doin' After Midnight Baby." The Cornelius/Brown hit streak continued until 1981, when Cornelius, feeling as though she was losing her identity as a performer, decided to break up the duo. She then released "Love Never Comes Easy," which made it to the Top 50. Her next hit came in 1983, the year she also worked as a spokesperson for the Cystic Fibrosis Foundation. In 1984, Cornelius changed directions and joined the road revival of *Annie Get Your Gun*, also touring with the Statler Brothers. She released a self-titled album in 1985, and three years later, she joined Brown for *the Reunited Tour '88*. The 1990s saw the grand opening of Helen Cornelius' Nashville South, located in the thick of Gatlinburg, TN, a thriving entertainment district. The facility featured live country entertainment by Cornelius and her band nightly, and saddles for stools in the cocktail lounge. In 2002 and 2003, Cornelius performed at the Jim Stafford theater in Branson, MO, as a rotating part of the women-in-country entertainment production *Us Girls!* —*Johnny Loftus*

● **Helen Cornelius** / 1975 / Dot ♦♦♦♦

The Country Gazette

f. 1971, USA, **db.** 1988

Group / Progressive Bluegrass

One of the most influential bluegrass acts of the '70s—as well as one of that decade's most popular country artists in Europe—Country Gazette blended bluegrass with country-rock and, in the process, sowed the seeds for the newgrass movement of the '80s. The Los Angeles-based band was originally formed in 1971 by fiddler Byron Berline, bassist Roger Bush, and banjoist Billy Ray Latham, who had all played with Dillard & Clark. The trio added guitarist Herb Pedersen, who was quickly replaced by Alan Munde. Shortly after the band's formation, Berline and Bush played on the Flying Burrito Brothers' *Last of the Red Hot Burritos* album, which turned out to be the last album the group would release before breaking up; they would reunite later in the decade. Berline and Bush convinced guitarist Kenny Wertz to join Country Gazette during the Burrito sessions and, following the Burritos' dissolution, the trio returned to Country Gazette and finished recording the band's debut, *A Traitor in Our Midst*.

A Traitor in Our Midst was released on United Artists in 1972. During the summer of that year, Country Gazette played gigs at *Disneyland* and soon landed opening spots for Steve Miller, Crosby & Nash, and Don McLean, which indicated that the group was aiming for a more rock-oriented audience. Later that year, they recorded and released the *Live in Amsterdam* album. Their second studio album, *Don't Give Up Your Day Job*, appeared in 1973. Following its release, the band switched labels, signing with the European-based Ariola, which released *Bluegrass Special* later in 1973. As the location of their record label indicated, the band was more popular in Europe than America.

In 1975, Byron Berline left the band and formed Sundance; Roger Bush left that same year. The following year, Country Gazette added guitarist/mandolinist/vocalist Roland White to its lineup and released *Live*. After its release, the band added fiddler Dave Ferguson and released *Out to Lunch* on the American independent label Flying Fish; in Europe, the album was called *Sunny Side of the Mountain*. Following the recording of *Out to Lunch*, Wertz left the band. Two albums—1977's *What a Way to Earn a Living*, which was recorded with Berline, not Ferguson, and 1979's *All This, and Money, Too*—followed on Ridge Runner.

American and Clean and *America's Bluegrass Band* appeared on Flying Fish in 1981 and 1982, respectively. The group disbanded after the release of *America's Bluegrass Band*, but re-formed in 1983. The reunited lineup featured Roland White, banjoist Alan Munde, bassist Mike Anderson, and dobroist Gene Wooten. For the next five years, the band toured America and Europe. Country Gazette broke up for a second and final time in 1988. Roland White joined the Nashville Bluegrass Band after the group's split. —*Stephen Thomas Erlewine*

A Traitor in Our Midst / 1972 / United Artists ♦♦♦♦

The Country Gazette evolved as a sort of spin-off from the first edition of the Flying Burrito Brothers, with fiddler Byron Berline (doubling on mandolin), bassist Roger Bush, guitarist Kenny Wertz, and banjo player Alan Munde. Their debut record for United Artists mixed traditional bluegrass and country songs ("Lost Indian" and the Louvin Brothers' "I Wish You Knew"), a pair of rocker Gene Clark's songs ("Keep on Pushin'" and "Tried So Hard"), and original material. On a few tracks the group is augmented by the presence of guitarist Herb Pedersen, guitarist Chris Smith, and dobro player Skip Conover. The colorful album packaging is rather campy, but the music has held up very well in the decades which have followed, though the instrumentals are more memorable than the vocal numbers. —*Ken Dryden*

Don't Give Up Your Day Job / 1973 / United Artists ♦♦♦♦♦

Country Gazette's second studio album is a stunner. Highlighted by the likes of such great songwriters as Stephen Stills, whose "The Fallen Eagle" is on a par with Manassas' Graham Nash, whose "Teach Your Children" gets a great bluegrass treatment here, and Elton John, whose "Honky Cat" finds a home where it belongs, everything seems to work on *Don't Give Up Your Day Job*. Original tunes, the likes of "Deputy Dalton" and "Huckleberry Hornpipe," only add to this fine disc. With the help of such friends as Herb Pedersen, Clarence White, and Leland Sklar, Country Gazette puts on an amazing array of music that tickles you in all the right places. It's no wonder these guys were looked upon as stars by bluegrass-crazy Europeans. *Don't Give Up Your Day Job* is as wonderful as it gets. —*James Chrispell*

Bluegrass Special / 1973 / Ariola ♦♦♦

Banjo Sandwich / 1974 / Ariola ♦♦♦

Live / 1975 / Transatlantic ♦♦♦

Live was released after Byron Berline had left Country Gazette, but that shouldn't deter music fans from seeking out this fine bluegrass disc. From the opener, "Black Mountain Rag" on through to "Down In the Bluegrass" there is much for listeners to sink their teeth into. Highlights also include "Never Ending Song of Love" courtesy of Delaney & Bonnie, along with such bluegrass staples as "Sally Goodin" and the Louvin Bros.' "My Baby's Gone" are all aided in the club atmosphere which helps *Live* show off Country Gazette's charm. It's hard to find, but well worth seeking out. —*James Chrispell*

What a Way to Earn a Living / 1977 / Ridge ♦♦♦♦

It was difficult to think of the Country Gazette as an actual working band by the time *What a Way to Earn a Living* was recorded. There were only two regular members left: guitarist and banjo player Alan Munde and guitarist/mandolin player Roland White. They relied on an auxiliary of supporting guest musicians on selected tracks, including founding member Byron Berline or Richard Greene on fiddle, bassist Bill Bryson, guitarist Mike Richey, and dobro player Skip Conover. Fortunately, the turmoil in the band's shifting roster doesn't affect the music, as they interpret timeless pieces such as "Dark Hollow," "Last Letter," and the traditional bluegrass favorite "Don't Let Your Deal Go Down" with spirited vocals and tremendous picking. Munde and White also co-composed a pair of first-rate instrumentals, "Goodbye Mitchell Jayne" and "Nantyglo R.F.C." An obscure release that is definitely worth searching for by progressive bluegrass fans. —*Ken Dryden*

Out to Lunch / 1977 / Flying Fish ♦♦♦♦

Out to Lunch marked the return of founding member Kenny Wertz on guitar. Fiddler Dave Ferguson and pedal steel guitarist Al Perkins (a veteran of Stephen Stills' Manassas and the Flying Burrito Brothers) are listed as contributing musicians rather than working members of the group. Even without the presence of the outgoing Berline, the Country Gazette still succeed in delivering their unique brand of progressive bluegrass, mixing favorites from classic country and bluegrass ("Why You Been Gone So Long" and "Sunny Side of the Mountain"), along with relatively modern material by rocker Gram Parsons ("Still Feeling Blue") and Waylon Jennings ("Sure Didn't Take Him Long"). Banjo player Alan Munde is featured prominently in his lively instrumental "Uncle Cloony Played the Banjo (But Mostly out of Tune)." The group is in great form, though the gastric distress suggested by a photo of the band on this LP's back cover proved to be an omen; both Kenny Wertz and bassist Roger Bush departed for good following the making of this release. —*Ken Dryden*

All This, and Money, Too! / 1978 / Ridge Runner ♦♦♦

The Country Gazette produced one of its most wide-ranging albums with the making of *All This, and Money, Too!* At this point, the group featured Roland White and Alan Munde with new members Michael Anderson on bass and guitarist Joe Carr, as well as perennial guest fiddler Dave Ferguson, jazz guitarist Slim Richey, pedal steel guitarist Tommy Spurlock, and drummer Michael J. Dohoney, so it was clear the group was expanding its scope. In addition to traditional bluegrass and country favorites (for example, "Cotton Eyed Joe," "Gone, Gone, Gone," and "Why Don't You Tell Me So?"), the band detours into the realm of rock with the Beatles' "Eleanor Rigby" and Western swing with "Old Fashioned Love," and also revisits earlier pieces by one of the pioneers in country-rock, the Flying Burrito Brothers, performing both "I'm Your Boy" (also known as "Hot Burrito No. 2") and "Devil in Disguise" (originally titled "Christine's Tune"). With White, Anderson, and Carr rotating the lead vocals and superb playing throughout the session, this somewhat obscure LP is well worth searching for. —*Ken Dryden*

Strictly Instrumental / 1981 / Flying Fish ♦♦♦♦♦

The Country Gazette's impassioned bluegrass goes instrumental on this release, with assistance from fiddler Billy Joe Foster, guitarist David Grier and bassist Kathy Chiavola. Still, the show belongs to Alan Munde's banjo work, which articulately navigates the rest of the group through the dozen traditional tunes contained here. —*Jason Ankeny*

● **Hello Operator . . . This Is Country Gazzette** / 1991 / Flying Fish ♦♦♦♦♦

Hello Operator . . . This Is Country Gazette covers the group's five Flying Fish records, which were made between 1976 and 1987. During that time, a number of excellent musicians made their way through the band, but Country Gazette retained a distinctive progressive bluegrass style, as this compilation demonstrates. Certainly, anyone wanting an idea of what the group achieved during the height of their career should pick up *Hello Operator*, since it sums up their music succinctly and effectively. —*Thom Owens*

Keep on Pushing / 1991 / Flying Fish ♦♦♦

The Country Gentlemen

f. Jul. 4, 1957, Washington, D.C.

Group / Bluegrass, Progressive Bluegrass, Traditional Bluegrass, Contemporary Bluegrass
The Country Gentlemen expanded the definition of "bluegrass"—they were progressive bluegrass before the term existed. The Gentlemen came along with the first wave of the folk music revival in the late '50s and quickly made a name for themselves as a band that could not only play traditional material straight, but also brought Bob Dylan and contemporary country material into the genre. Because of their exceptional singing and virtuoso instrumentals, the Gentlemen attracted a broad audience, ranging from traditional country/bluegrass fans to folk and soft rock lovers.

Formed in Washington, D.C., on July 4, 1957, the original lineup of the Country Gentlemen featured guitarist/vocalist Charlie Waller—who has led the band through all of its numerous incarnations—mandolinist/vocalist John Duffey, banjoist Bill Emerson, and bassist Tom Morgan. Waller had spent time with a number of country string bands in the early '50s, most notably Buzz Busby's band, the Bayou Boys, which also featured Emerson. After the Bayou Boys suffered a car crash in early 1957, Waller and Emerson put together a group to fulfill the band's regular spot at a Virginia venue while various members were recovering. That replacement band evolved into the County Gentlemen. For the first two years of their existence, the Country Gentlemen went through numerous lineup changes.

In 1959, they finally landed on a permanent lineup, with banjoist Eddie Adcock and bassist Tom Gray joining a band that already included Waller and Duffey. This lineup secured a contract with Starday Records and released a handful of singles, as well as one album, *Traveling Dobro Blues*. Following their Starday recordings, the group moved to Folkways, where they released three albums, including their breakthrough, *Country Songs Old & New*. After their stint at Folkways, the group moved to Mercury in 1963, where they released *Folk Session Inside*. The following year, they began a long association with Rebel Records. During the '60s, the Country Gentlemen built up a dedicated fan base in America through constant touring. Although their lineup shifted rapidly—following Gray's 1964 departure, they went through several of bassists before settling on Ed McGlothlin—their sound pretty much stayed the same.

At the end of the '60s, the core lineup began to splinter as Duffey left in 1969; he was replaced by Jimmy Gaudreau. In the following year, both Adcock and McGlothlin left the lineup. In 1971, the second classic lineup of the Country Gentlemen—featuring Waller, a re-joined Bill Emerson, mandolinist Doyle Lawson, and bassist Bill Yates—fell into place and stayed together for two years. For the next 20 years, various lineups of the Country Gentlemen, which were all led by Waller, remained popular on the bluegrass festival circuit. —*Stephen Thomas Erlewine & David Vinopal*

Traveling Dobro Blues / 1959 / Starday ✦✦✦✦

★ **Country Songs Old & New** / 1960 / Smithsonian Folkways ✦✦✦✦✦

Return Engagement / 1963 / Rebel ✦✦✦
First issued in 1963, *Return Engagement* features the Gentlemen tackling songs like "Miner's Life," "Lonely Child" and "Lonesome Highway." —*Jason Ankeny*

On the Road / 1963 / Folkways ✦✦✦
Side one of this live LP was recorded at Antioch College on April 13, 1962, and side two done on January 6, 1963, at the Sacred Mushroom coffeehouse in Columbus, OH. This is a good representation of what the group's classic quartet lineup—Eddie Adcock, Charlie Waller, John Duffey, and Tom Gray—sounded like in the early '60s. The 13 songs include an assortment of country, folk, and gospel material, as well as the popular music standard "Heartaches" and the unexpected cover of Clarence "Frogman" Henry's 1950s rock & roll hit "Ain't Got No Home." Waller did Donald Duck vocals for part of this, and perhaps the mikes didn't pick it up, but the absence of laughter from the audience indicates that this grating routine didn't go down that well. As for a quality pop-crossover cover, better was their cover of the country music hit "The Long Black Veil." [The entire album is included on the 2001 Smithsonian Folkways CD reissue *On the Road (and More)*, which adds six bonus tracks that are believed to have been recorded at *Carnegie Hall* on September 16, 1961.] —*Richie Unterberger*

Nashville Jail / 1964 / Copper Creek ✦✦✦
In 1964, the Country Gentlemen were one of very few bluegrass acts on a major label (Mercury, in this case). *Nashville Jail* is a complete unreleased album that fell by the wayside when, soon after its completion, Mercury dropped the group. Copper Creek's 1990 reissue contains the ten original tracks slated for the album plus, on CD only, a version of Ernest Tubb's "Are You Waiting Just for Me" from the same sessions. The material gives only a little indication of the Gentlemen's aptitude for converting pop and straight country material to bluegrass (a surprising version of "Theme From 'Exodus'"; Jimmie Rodgers' "Blue Yodel #3"), but covers Jimmie Murphy and Scotty Wiseman while providing an occasional showcase for banjo ace Eddie Adcock ("Uncle Joe"). *Nashville Jail* is well-recorded, thanks to its major label funding, and is a significant missing chapter in the Country Gentlemen story. —*Greg Adams*

Live in Japan / 1970 / Rebel ✦✦✦✦
Live in Japan captures a strong early '70s concert from the Country Gentlemen, spotlighting much of their best-known material, as well as their excellent harmony and instrumental skills. —*Thom Owens*

☆ **Award Winning Country Gentlemen** / 1972 / Rebel ✦✦✦✦✦
Not only does *Award Winning Country Gentlemen* culminate a major shift in direction for the Country Gentlemen, it is also quite possibly their finest album. Charlie Waller had to re-assemble the group in the early '70s, bringing in a new lineup—including mandolinist Doyle Lawson, bassist Bill Yates and banjoist Bill Emerson—that helped move the Country Gentlemen even further into contemporary music. On *Award Winning*, the band covers songs by rock and folk songwriters like Bob Dylan and Gordon Lightfoot, bringing a bluegrass attitude and instrumentation to the contemporary num-

bers. The result is a stunning record, with a great selection of songs and simply stunning musicianship. —*Thom Owens*

Remembrances & Forecasts / 1974 / Vanguard ✦✦✦✦
This is an aptly titled set of traditional and progressive bluegrass songs and instrumentals from the band that practically invented the genre. The Country Gentlemen only recorded two albums for the Vanguard label, but both featured the band in its prime, showcasing two of its strongest post-John Duffey lineups. On *Remembrances and Forecasts*, singer and multi-instrumentalist Ricky Skaggs has become a formal member of the group, spending most of his time on fiddle and contributing a charming Celtic-flavored instrumental called "Irish Spring"; Doyle Lawson and Jerry Douglas are both still aboard as well, making this one of the most powerful versions of the group in both vocal and instrumental terms. Highlights here include the Bill Monroe gospel number "Lord Protect My Soul" (on which Skaggs' high harmony is hair-raisingly otherworldly) and an acerbic modern bluegrass song called "Willow Creek Dam." [In 2002, *Remembrances & Forecasts* was reissued on a single CD with the Country Gentlemen's other, eponymously titled Vanguard album.] —*Rick Anderson*

Calling My Children Home / 1978 / Rebel ✦✦✦
Thanks to the superb direction of mandolinist Doyle Lawson, *Calling My Children Home* is an excellent bluegrass-gospel album, highlighted by a handful of tremendous a cappella quartets. —*Thom Owens*

☆ **25 Years** / 1980 / Rebel ✦✦✦✦✦
25 Years was released in 1980, when the Country Gentlemen were celebrating their 25th anniversary. The compilation covers the group's recordings for Rebel Records, which began in the mid-'60s. Over the course of *25 Years*, various incarnations of the Country Gentlemen are displayed. Each one has its own merits, but the the classic lineup of Eddie Adcock, John Duffey, Tom Gray, and Charlie Waller does stand out in particular. Though the other incarnations aren't quite as accomplished as this lineup, the compilation nevertheless remains an excellent purchase and introduction, since it gives a fine overview of the group's career. —*Thom Owens*

Good as Gold / 1981 / Sugar Hill ✦✦✦

One Wide River / 1987 / Rebel ✦✦✦

The Country Gentlemen Featuring Ricky Skaggs on Fiddle / 1987 / Vanguard ✦✦✦
Featuring Ricky Skaggs on Fiddle collects material drawn from Skaggs' early-'70s tenure with the band, and features "House of the Rising Sun," "The City of New Orleans," and "Catfish John." —*Jason Ankeny*

Folk Songs & Bluegrass / 1988 / Smithsonian Folkways ✦✦✦✦✦
Folk Songs & Bluegrass is one of the Country Gentlemen's best releases, featuring the classic lineup of Eddie Adcock, John Duffey, Tom Gray, and Charlie Waller at the height of their power. Both the songs—which are divided between standards and newer folk numbers—and the performances are first-rate, making *Folk Songs & Bluegrass* an essential purchase for any bluegrass collection. —*Thom Owens*

Sit Down Young Stranger / 1988 / Sugar Hill ✦✦✦✦✦

Bluegrass at Carnegie Hall / 1988 / Hollywood ✦✦✦✦✦
Originally released on Starday in 1962, *Bluegrass at Carnegie Hall* isn't a live album, even though the title suggests that it is. Instead, it is a collection of excellent studio recordings made around the same time as their 1961 appearance at Carnegie Hall, that rank among their finest early recordings. —*Thom Owens*

River Bottom / 1989 / Sugar Hill ✦✦✦✦✦

Classic Country Gentlemen: Nashville Jail / 1990 / Copper Creek ✦✦✦

Let the Light Shine Down / 1991 / Rebel ✦✦✦
Let the Light Shine Down is a fine compilation of gospel and inspirational songs the Country Gentlemen recorded between 1962 and 1976, including several tracks that have never been available before on compact disc. —*Thom Owens*

Sugar Hill Collection / 1995 / Sugar Hill ✦✦✦✦✦
As the title suggests, *Sugar Hill Collection* compiles the highlights from the Country Gentlemen's recordings for the independent label Sugar Hill. Although these were made later in their career, the group sounds as good as they ever have. —*Thom Owens*

Souvenirs / Apr. 7, 1995 / Rebel ✦✦✦

☆ **The Early Rebel Recordings 1962–1971** / 1998 / Rebel ✦✦✦✦✦
This is an especially pleasing four-CD set, comprising most of the Country Gentlemen's recordings for the Rebel label over a period of nine years, when they used bluegrass music as a vehicle for innovation by way of country, folk, and rock. The influence of the Osborne Brothers can be heard throughout their early work (along with more mainstream country sources), but then they start cutting Dylan and Tom Paxton songs. The odd early individual tracks lead into the contents of the *Bringing Mary Home* album, which established their reputation nationally as a bluegrass act to be reckoned with. Disc one ends with the controversial "Big Bruce," a gay parody of Jimmy Dean's "Big Bad John" that skirts a fine line between satire, burlesque, and slur. Disc two features several previously unissued songs, and also shows the group growing artistically amid a flurry of concert activity—a surprising number of songs from this period were cut on the fly at semi-pro and improvised studios, as the band fit recording in anywhere they could. Disc three picks up in 1969—the group by this time was freely adapting popular as well as folk tunes, thus the presence of "Mrs. Robinson" amid the bluegrass standards. By Disc four, the group was nearing a summit of popularity and creativity. The irony was that, even as they were achieving success, the group was nearing a decision to leave Rebel. This collection isn't quite ideal, since it is missing a key mid-'60s live recording; the booklet

and annotation are very thorough, as is the session information, all of it pitched at the Bear Family level. —*Bruce Eder*

High Lonesome: Complete Starday Recordings / 1998 / Starday ✦✦✦✦✦
Since the group's founding in 1957, the Country Gentlemen have had a more or less constantly revolving roster of members, some of whom (John Duffey, Tom Gray, Eddie Adcock) have gone on to significant fame on their own and in other bands, while others (John Hall, Ed Ferris) did not. The lineup shown on the cover—guitarist and bandleader Charlie Waller, mandolinist John Duffey, banjo player Eddie Adcock, and bassist Tom Gray—is generally considered the "classic" Country Gentlemen configuration; however, on these early recordings, the personnel rotates around that lineup more than it settles there. There are many tracks featuring the equally fine banjo player Bill Emerson, some early contributions from fiddlers John Hall and Carl Nelson, and a number of songs featuring dobro player Kenny Haddock. But the distinctive voices of Charlie Waller and John Duffey are the dominating flavors throughout, and on songs like "Nobody's Business," "Blue Man," and "Long Journey Home," the band's future sound is almost fully realized. This two-disc, 51-track set includes a number of previously unreleased songs and alternate takes (several of which, it must be said, were probably unissued because of terrible sound quality), and all in all it provides a unique and enjoyable window on the earliest days of one of bluegrass music's most influential ensembles. Recommended. —*Rick Anderson*

On the Road (And More) / Apr. 24, 2001 / Smithsonian Folkways ✦✦✦✦✦
Continuing in their now feverish quest to reissue every single thing Moses Asch ever released on CD, the folks at Smithsonian have pulled from the catalog a true gem, added six more tracks, and given it to listeners to marvel over. The Country Gentlemen were the inspiration for pickers from Norman Blake to Clarence White to Tony Rice and every third-generation member in Del McCoury's band—not to mention the New Grass Revival and David Grisman. The original album was a compilation of the best moments of two concerts in 1962 and 1963, respectively; the Smithsonian added six tracks from a third concert in 1963 to round out the time and offer a further glimpse into the mysterious, passionate musicality of the band. This is a live document of the band at the beginning of their maturity, with a style already etched in stone. Here is the perfect blending of folk music, country music, and bluegrass, all offered to an American public who was rediscovering its own folk traditions musically. This obviously knocked out a young Bob Dylan who continues to cover the Gentlemen's version of "Handsome Molly." Banjoist Eddie Adcock, guitarist and lead vocalist Charlie Waller, mandolin player John Duffey, and bassist Tom Gray worked through folk songs like a bluegrass band and bluegrass tunes like an old-timey string band full of ballad singers. Their version of "Long Black Veil" on this record is what made Johnny Cash decide to cut it for himself. The instrumental "Heartaches" is literally a fusion of bluegrass and gypsy swing reads through a blues idiom, and their reading of their "I Am a Pilgrim" is the most bluesed-out reading that worn hymn will ever get. It is also the finest example of the gorgeous vocal harmony between Duffey and Waller. There are no sharp spots in their midst, just pure vocal consonance. This record is an awesome example of the radical yet beautiful and respectful shift of Bill Monroe's bluegrass creation to a more expansive view of the same tradition that was just as soulful, just as pure. —*Thom Jurek*

The Complete Vanguard Recordings / Feb. 5, 2002 / Vanguard ✦✦✦✦
Hearing a title like *The Complete Vanguard Recordings* sounds a little daunting, like some of the 12-disc Bear Family boxed sets. Fortunately (or unfortunately, as a matter of fact), the Country Gentlemen only released two LPs for the Vanguard label in the early '70s, so their complete output fit neatly on CD for this 2002 reissue. In this era, the group featured future bluegrass luminaries Doyle Lawson, Ricky Skaggs, Mike Auldridge, and Jerry Douglas alongside the established legends guitarist/vocalist Charlie Waller and banjo player Bill Emerson. With talented artists like these, it comes as no surprise that the music is top-notch—the thing that really sets these recordings apart is the fact that the band was choosing to perform songs by decidedly non-bluegrass musicians such as John Prine, Gordon Lightfoot, Paul Simon, and Kris Kristofferson, and still managing to transform these progressive songwriters' works into down-home stomps. Another interesting hindsight is to hear the emerging voices of Skaggs and Lawson harmonizing with Waller, progressively getting bolder and finding their own sound. While the songs on 1973's *The Country Gentlemen* are the most traditional-sounding on the disc, the later material from 1974's *Remembrances & Forecasts* best-illustrates the group's push into increasingly progressive material like the vaudevillian "Heartaches" and Skaggs' own split-stereo "Irish Spring." While this album could be seen as an archival document, it works best as a living and breathing work to be listened to and enjoyed 30 years later, even more so than when the music originally was released. —*Zac Johnson*

The Country Rockers

f. 1986, Memphis, TN
Group / Roots Rock, Alternative Country-Rock
The Country Rockers' name alone was a wholly accurate gauge of their sound and aesthetics. A somewhat obscure trio based in Memphis, TN, the group was led by Durand Easley, an accomplished producer and session musician. While drinking in a Mississippi roadhouse in 1986, Easley hooked up with Sam Baird, a singer and guitarist he recognized from the latter's long tenure as a staple of the Memphis club circuit. Though Baird was in his mid 60's at the time, he and the 35-year-old Easley decided to form a band, enlisting Gaius L. "Ringo" Farnham, a then 73-year-old drummer, to fill out their sound.

After developing a repertoire of country standards and eclectic obscurities, the trio cut a demo with Easley's brother Doug, a prominent indie rock producer. After the session, Easley left for Europe to tour with his old friend Alex Chilton; after shopping the Country Rockers' demo to New Rose Records, Chilton's label, a deal was struck. In 1989, the group issued its debut LP, *Free Range Chicken*, a varied collection of rockabilly, country, and novelty tunes featuring the original demo tracks along with newly recorded material; while the vocal chores were split mainly between Easley and Baird, Ringo Farnham—just like his namesake in the Beatles—was allowed to sing on one cut. The Country Rockers' second effort, *Cypress Room*, appeared in 1991. —*Jason Ankeny*

● **Free Range Chicken** / 1989 / New Rose ✦✦✦✦
Split between demos and more polished material, *Free Range Chicken* is a wildly eclectic and raucous debut, offering forays into rockabilly ("Rockin' Daddy"), surf ("Wipe Out"), straightforward country ("There Stands the Glass") and the self-explanatory ("Guitar Polka"). —*Jason Ankeny*

Cypress Room / 1991 / New Rose ✦✦✦
Continuing the formula (or lack thereof) established on the Country Rockers' first effort, *Cypress Room* is another diverse affair, this time dabbling in honky-tonk, calypso, and lewd R&B. —*Jason Ankeny*

John Cowan

b. Aug. 24, 1952, Evansville, IN
Bass, Vocals / Contemporary Bluegrass, Americana
John Cowan got his start in Louisville, where he played in scrappy rock outfits like Everyday People and Louisville Sound Department. In 1974, he auditioned as a bassist and vocalist for New Grass Revival, and together with Sam Bush and later bandmates Béla Fleck and Pat Flynn, led the charge of the 1980s' bluegrass revival. New Grass Revival disbanded in 1990 when Fleck departed for a solo career, but Cowan didn't slow down. He did distance himself a bit from NGR's acoustic foundation, however, choosing to tour as a solo rock act as well as front the country-rock band Sky Kings (with Poco's Rusty Young). But despite writing an album, arranging the artwork, releasing a single, and setting a release date (March 27, 1997), the Sky Kings' full-length sat on a shelf.

Cowan next busied himself with solo work for the Sugar Hill label. His releases there included an ambitious self-titled effort in 2000, as well as the lower-key *Always Take Me Back* in 2002. The final release of the Sky Kings album *From Out of the Blue* took place in 2000; the set included the entire original LP, as well as demos and songs that were subsequently completed for the project. —*Johnny Loftus*

● **Soul'd Out** / 1990 / Sugar Hill ✦✦✦✦✦
Former New Grass Revival member John Cowan adds his own twist to some solid soul tunes. A strong vocalist with an amazing amount of control, Cowan continues to be one of the unsung heroes of American music. Certainly his work with the New Grass Revival throughout the latter part of the '70s to the final release by the band in 1989 places him in an interesting position. A progressive bluegrasser with some strong leanings, this native of Evansville, IN, has all the chops to cross genres without blinking an eye. Here he wails Wilson Pickett's "634-5789 (Soulsville, U.S.A.)," a recognizable radio hit, just as he does another Pickett tune, "99½," with plenty of heart and soul. "I Was Made to Love Her," penned by Stevie Wonder, is given life through Cowan's treatment. Just as good are his versions of the classics "Mustang Sally" and "Groove Me." However, it is Cowan's rendition of the Percy Sledge Muscle Shoals standard "When a Man Loves a Woman" that takes him (and his listeners) over the top. With as much sensuality and raw emotion as any singer has ever mustered up for a single performance, Cowan takes the reins of blue-eyed soul firmly in hand and flies. Cowan's already significant talent is enhanced by backing from the likes of the Ken Smith Band, Sam Bush, Paul Worley, and Grooveyard, as well as the harmony vocals of Jonell Mosser and Maura O'Connell. His magnificent version of the bluesy "Two Steps from the Blues" takes him into new territory that could very easily be termed "bluesgrass." While he may have made his name in bluegrass, he is certainly an artist who defies definition. This a wonderful introduction to the solo career of John Cowan and to the revival of blue-eyed soul music, a close cousin to country & western, bluegrass, and many other types of American music. And seemingly, Cowan can handily cover all of them with spirit. —*Jana Pendragon*

John Cowan / Apr. 18, 2000 / Sugar Hill ✦✦✦
Forget the New Grass Revival connections, the bluegrass and country hooks, and let go of expectations—John Cowan opens this album up with a defiant roar of a tune driven by electronic drums and batteries of guitars, as well as bass tracks that will make some subwoofers quit under the strain. There are bluegrass and country elements to be had throughout, but Cowan isn't constrained by them—or constricted by a need to overcome the connections. What has come out of this is a collection of songs steeped in Americana that leaves the listener's head spinning with the changes in direction. It's good work, but not so easy to get used to. —*Steven E. McDonald*

Always Take Me Back / Apr. 2, 2002 / Sugar Hill ✦✦
John Cowan's *Always Take Me Back* is layered with the slick sheen of production. The former New Grass Revival bassist/vocalist is in fine form vocally, though the material feels, if not contrived, then at least cluttered. The emotionally raw "18 Years," for example, is covered by a thick gloss. What should be snapping drums and penetrating acoustic guitars are filtered through a variety of shiny doublings. It sounds false. When Cowan's voice comes in on top, the listener just doesn't want to believe his angst, even as he lets loose with several long and well-sustained screams during the outro of the song. The same problems plague the bulk of the album. A basic tastelessness pervades the arrangements throughout. It would be a little more tolerable if the songs were better. On *Always Take Me Back*, Cowan sinks to cliché quickly and never really rises. —*Jesse Jarnow*

Cowboy Junkies

f. 1985, Toronto, Ontario, Canada
Group / Alternative Pop/Rock, Alternative Country-Rock, Adult Alternative Pop/Rock, College Rock
Although it didn't originally have anything to do with their sound, the Cowboy Junkies' name wound up seeming pretty accurate: their music was grounded in traditional country, blues, and folk, yet drifted along in a sleepy, narcotic haze that clearly bore the stamp

of the Velvet Underground. The vast majority of their songs were spare and quiet, taken at lethargic tempos and filled with languid guitars and detached, ethereal vocals courtesy of Margo Timmins. Over the late '80s and '90s, the group recorded a succession of critically acclaimed albums that found favor in the alternative rock community.

The Cowboy Junkies were founded by guitarist/songwriter Michael Timmins and bassist Alan Anton (born Alan Alizojvodic), who first played together in a Toronto-based band called the Hunger Project in 1979. They later moved to the U.K. and played with an avant-garde instrumental outfit called Germinal, but eventually grew weary of the group's style and returned to Toronto in 1984. They started jamming with Timmins' brother, Peter, on drums, and in 1985 they recruited a vocalist in sister Margo, at the time a social worker who'd never sung publicly before. Dubbing themselves the Cowboy Junkies simply because the name had a ring to it, they formed their own independent label, Lament, and released their debut album, *Whites Off Earth Now!!*, in 1986. Featuring only one original song, the album was recorded using only one microphone, and although it was initially available only in Canada, it helped them land a major-label deal with RCA. Their first widespread release was 1988's *The Trinity Session*, which was recorded inside Toronto's Holy Trinity church in the span of one night—again using only one microphone. *The Trinity Session* became a cult hit, earning rave reviews from critics and substantial college-radio airplay for tracks like "Misguided Angel" and their cover of "Sweet Jane."

Now an underground sensation, the Cowboy Junkies decided to concentrate more on Michael Timmins' original material for the bigger-budget follow-up, 1990's *The Caution Horses*. The album didn't cause quite as much of a stir, although it helped maintain their cult fan base. The even more countrified *Black-Eyed Man* found Timmins settling more comfortably into his songwriting voice, which set the stage for 1993's *Pale Sun, Crescent Moon*. Hailed as their finest effort since *The Trinity Session*, the record bore more influence from rock and blues, and returned the Junkies to critics'-darling status. However, it also proved to be their final album of new material for RCA. As the band left for Geffen, RCA issued the two-disc live compilation *200 More Miles* and the best-of *Studio*.

Meanwhile, the Junkies debuted for Geffen in 1996 with *Lay It Down*, a relatively high-volume effort compared to their shimmering early work. Following 1998's *Miles From Our Home*, the group parted ways with Geffen and revived their own Latent label. Their first release was the 2000 live album *Waltz Across America*, which was initially available only through the band's website. They followed it a year later with an album of all-new material, *Open*. *—Steve Huey*

Whites Off Earth Now!! / 1986 / RCA ♦♦♦

Featuring only one original song, the Cowboy Junkies' debut *Whites Off Earth Now!!* captures the band forming their own sound through covers, including songs by Robert Johnson and Bruce Springsteen. It's not as captivating as their later releases, but it's fascinating to hear their signature country-on-valium sound develop. Margo Timmins sings beautifully. *—Stephen Thomas Erlewine*

● **The Trinity Session** / 1988 / RCA ♦♦♦♦♦

Who says you can't make a great record in one day—or night, as the case may be? *The Trinity Session* was recorded in one night using one microphone, a DAT recorder, and the wonderful acoustics of the Holy Trinity in Toronto. Interestingly, it's the album that broke the Cowboy Junkies in the U.S. for their version of "Sweet Jane," which included the lost verse. It's far from the best cut here, though. There are other covers, such as Margo Timmins' a cappella read of the traditional "Mining for Gold," a heroin-slow version of Hank Williams' classic "I'm So Lonesome I Could Cry," "Dreaming My Dreams With You" (canonized by Waylon Jennings), and a radical take of the Patsy Cline classic "Walkin' After Midnight" that closes the disc. Those few who had heard the band's previous album, *Whites Off Earth Now!!*, were aware that, along with Low, the Cowboy Junkies were the only band at the time capable of playing slower than Neil Young and Crazy Horse—and without the ear-threatening volume. The Timmins family—Margo, guitarist and songwriter Michael, drummer Peter, and backing vocalist and guitarist John—along with bassist Alan Anton and a few pals playing pedal steel, accordion, and harmonica, paced everything to crawl. That said, it works in that every song has its own texture, slowly and deliberately unfolding from blues and country and drones. An example is the Michael and Margo song "I Don't Get It," ushered in with a few drawling guitar lines, a spooky harmonica, and brushed drums. Margo Timmins doesn't have a large range and doesn't need it as she scratches each song's surface like an itch until it bleeds its truth. This is also true on "Misguided Angel," another original where the verses become nearly a round alternating between her voice and Michael's snaky spare guitar lines to fill an almost unimaginable space. The Williams tune becomes a dirge in the Cowboys' hands. It's a funeral song, or an elegy for one who has dragged herself so far into the oblivion of isolation that there is no place left to go but home. Michael's guitar moves around the changes as bassist Anton plays them; he colors the space allowing for Margo to fill the melodic space spot-on, yet stretching each syllable out to the breaking point. For most, this *was* the Cowboy Junkies debut—*Whites Off Earth Now!!* was re-released in the States a few years later—and it established them firmly in the forefront of the "alternative" scene with radio and MTV. As an album, it's still remarkable at how timeless it sounds, and its beauty is—in stark contrast to its presentation—voluminous and rich, perhaps even eternal. *—Thom Jurek*

The Caution Horses / Feb. 1990 / RCA ♦♦

With the ethereal voice of Margo Timmins gleaning the lyrics "The phone rings, but I don't answer it/Good news always sleeps till noon" on the opener ("Sun Comes Up, It's Tuesday Morning), listeners rest assured—the Junkies haven't compromised their comfortable, country-twanged, folk-rock style to cater more to the trends of the masses. Mellow, honest, and provocatively reticent at points, their melancholic tone might seem bland to those with more aggressive tastes, or to simply more mainstream palettes, but for those whose tastes float serenely upstream, and for Junkies fans in general, this album is a treat. As usual, brother and lead guitarist Michael Timmins has created narratives that make poetry of everyday observations and anecdotes. Not as rocking as later releases, but offering more originals than earlier ones, this, their third full-length, brings back the mandolin and fiddle playing of Jeff Bird, the accordion stylings of Jaro Czerwinec, and pedal & lap steel guitar from Kim Deschamps—all of which gracefully complemented the *Trinity Sessions* recordings. Their arrangements seem simply planned, and it's the combination of such a consistently minimalist quality with Michael Timmins' delicate songwriting that evokes ghost-story moods ("Witches") and sunset-beyond-the-porch-swing moments. Aside from the Neil Young cover "Powderfinger," *The Caution Horses* marks the Junkies' gradual shift toward more original work, and stands as the calm before the more rocking, commercially successful storm of material that followed. Highlights include "'Cause Cheap Is How I Feel," "Rock and Bird," and "Escape Is Simple." *—Deanne Briggs*

Black-Eyed Man / Feb. 11, 1992 / RCA ♦♦♦

The Cowboy Junkies' *Black-Eyed Man* is an excellent return to form following their disappointing third LP, *The Caution Horses*. Where Michael Timmins' songwriting was stilted and overly self-conscious on the previous record, here his character studies are literate and finely-etched; like Robbie Robertson before him, Timmins' Canadian roots allow him to view the rural American experience with unique objectivity, and narratives like the opening "Southern Rain" and "Murder, Tonight, in the Trailer Park" are told with compassion and cinematic detail. *Black-Eyed Man* also broadens the Junkies' musical horizons: "If You Were the Woman and I Was the Man," a duet with John Prine, is like a '50s-era love song intercepted from an alternate reality; while tracks like the lilting "A Horse in the Country" push the group closer to the folk-pop territory of 10,000 Maniacs. At the same time, their country roots are further reinforced by a pair of outstanding Townes Van Zandt covers, "Cowboy Junkies Lament" and "To Live Is to Fly"; sandwiched between them is Timmins' own tribute, "Townes' Blues." *—Jason Ankeny*

Pale Sun, Crescent Moon / Nov. 23, 1993 / RCA ♦♦♦♦♦

A refreshed, revitalized sound that doesn't sacrifice the delicate touches that first made them unique; rugged, but still pristine. Much of the new spark emanates from the strings of honorary Junkie Ken Myhr, who peals out intense, biting lead guitar throughout. Especially prominent is his incendiary slide work on "Seven Years" and a spectacular cover of Dinosaur Jr.'s "The Post." Still, it's hard to imagine a ballad instrument more haunting and ethereal than Margo Timmins' voice. *—Roch Parisien*

200 More Miles, Live Performances 1985-1994 / Oct. 10, 1995 / RCA ♦♦♦

Subtitled, "Live Performances 1985-1994" (though the earliest track comes from Halloween 1986), *200 More Miles*, which concluded the Cowboy Junkies' contract with RCA, was a 17-track compilation of concert recordings. Its five and a half cover songs spanned the group's influences: "Blue Moon Revisited (A Song for Elvis)" drew upon the Rodgers & Hart song (that's the half) as interpreted by the King of Rock & Roll; "Me and the Devil Blues" came from the King of the Delta Blues Singers, Robert Johnson; "I'm So Lonesome I Could Cry" was by the King of Country Music, Hank Williams, "Walking After Midnight" by the Queen, Patsy Cline, and "State Trooper" and "Sweet Jane" came from a couple of Rock's Crown Princes, Bruce Springsteen and Lou Reed. Of course, this was for the most part downbeat material, and the Cowboy Junkies rendered it in their usual transfixing, if soporific style. They did the same on a set of Michael Timmins originals such as "Sun Comes Up, It's Tuesday Morning" and "Murder, Tonight, in the Trailer Park." (John Prine guests on "If You Were the Woman and I Was the Man.") "Before I do some rock & roll I always like to sit down," Margo Timmins noted at the outset, and she wasn't kidding. *— William Ruhlmann*

Lay It Down / Feb. 27, 1996 / Geffen ♦♦♦

Released in 1996, this CD definitively answers a question that has occasionally plagued the Cowboy Junkies—"yes, they sound good, but can they rock?" Though still laden with the melancholia that has marked previous efforts, this CD is sonically dense, guitar-drenched, and good at high volume levels. Margo Timmins' voice has never been more expressive, and the lyrics shimmer with intensity. Although the band has occasionally touched on quiet moments reminiscent of fellow Canadian Neil Young, little they have done before this album approached the emotive wail of his louder efforts. The Cowboy Junkies have proven their versatility while retaining their unique sound. *—Jeff Crooke*

Miles From Our Home / Jun. 30, 1998 / Geffen ♦♦♦

Working with producer John Leckie on *Miles From Our Home* has enlivened the Cowboy Junkies' trademark lackadaisical style somewhat. Replacing the group's calm, minimalist sound with a polished production, Leckie manages to make the record sound unlike anything else in the band's catalog. That's not to say that there's no trace of the old style—he has simply updated their sound, bringing it in line with adult alternative pop that they played a part in establishing in the late '80s. If the results aren't as magical as *The Trinity Sessions*, they're far from disappointing. Margo Timmins' voice remains as enchanting as ever and her brother Michael Timmins' songs are sturdy. There might not be any masterpieces on *Miles From Our Home*, but there aren't any misfires, either—it's simply a solid album from a reliable band. *—Stephen Thomas Erlewine*

Rarities, B-Sides and Slow, Sad Waltzes / Oct. 12, 1999 / Valley ♦♦♦

Rarities, B-sides and Slow, Sad Waltzes offers exactly what the liner notes promise: a hodgepodge of songs that were written and recorded for various albums and projects but that somehow ended up on soundtracks, tribute albums, or simply on demos that never left their rehearsal room before this release. Echoing the driving tone of more recent albums, the opener, "I Saw Your Shoes," establishes an electric, fast-paced beginning to the album—appropriate for a song about desire, but something of a non sequitur given the track that follows, "Five Room Love Story." A Junkies fan will likely be able to distinguish certain other tracks as if they were intended for specific albums. "Leaving Normal," for example (written as a theme song for a film by the same name, but never used), lyrically recalls *Pale Sun Crescent Moon*'s spoken-word "Floorboard Blues." "To Lay Me Down," a beautiful cover, compelling and moving in its stillness, was included on *Deadicated: A Tribute to the Grateful Dead.* The final, bonus (hidden) track, Bruce Springsteen's "My Father's House," offers listeners a peak into a rehearsal/soundcheck which turns into an a cappella, impromptu performance, capturing the band's characteristic sense of family and humor better than any of the other official tracks here. The album is, by definition, a brief jumble of contrasting periods in the band's evolution. As such, however, these "orphan" tracks are a treat to Junkies fans—such a quantity of rarities and B-sides being put out during a band's active years, rather than posthumously, is a delightful rarity. *—Deanne Briggs*

Waltz Across America / 2000 / Latent ✦✦✦
With a roster of songs that highlights some of their best-loved work, *Waltz Across America* has the feel of an intimate evening spent in private concert with Cowboy Junkies, a feat made possible by a combination of seamless production design, carefully chosen music, and singer Margo Timmins' quiet, heartfelt rapport with her audience. The second release on the band's own Latent Recordings label, the album is a live compilation of 12 of the 60 songs played on the Junkies' end-of-the-millennium tour of the U.S. and Canada. Thanks to the band's ability to put a fresh spin on time-honored favorites, *Waltz* is one of those rare albums equally well-suited to both first-time listeners and loyal fans. All of the band's hallmark songs are here—"Misguided Angel," "Sweet Jane," and "Blue Guitar," to name a few—but none of them take their listener's familiarity for granted: hearing them on *Waltz* is a bit like re-reading an old bedtime story and finding that the ending has been subtly changed. Perhaps one of the album's most gratifying surprises comes from the completely rewritten "Hollow As a Bone": Originally performed as an angry, hard-driving rock anthem, it plays here as a plaintive love song laced with wistful poignancy. Similarly, the 11-minute version of "Blue Guitar," the Junkies' elegy to friend, inspiration, and fellow musician Townes Van Zandt, is a brooding work of haunting and unexpectedly taut beauty. All of the songs on *Waltz* illustrate the Junkies' continued evolution as a band, and as a whole the album's rich, often hypnotic sound flows with an ease and depth that will reassure longtime listeners even as it entrances new ones. *—Rebecca Flint*

Open / May 15, 2001 / Zoë ✦✦✦
Cowboy Junkies have a sound, a vibe. There's no denying it. You can tell it's them within a few notes and each successive record seems to pick up right where the last one left off. Some, like *The Trinity Sessions*, are dark, moody, and mellow, like being coated in honey and draped in velvet. Others, take *Pale Sun, Crescent Moon* for example, seem downright energetic in comparison. *Open* is more in line with the first batch, though it has moments of near-enthusiastic revelry. With Alan Anton's plump (rather than phat) basslines, Peter Timmins' laid-back drumming, and Michael Timmins' dirty guitars to ride on, Margo Timmins contributes her trademark sensual, yet understated vocal performances. The whole gang sounds as good as ever. And, although he may be called a songwriter, Michael Timmins is more a true poet with musical inclinations. Full of wonder and romance, fear and passion, *Open* is simply the next chapter in his sublime book of heartfelt verse. The compassionate tenderness of "Thousand Year Prayer" contrasts nicely with the harmonica and feedback duel of "Dragging Hooks." And darn if "I'm So Open" doesn't bounce right along on a little groove. They've got it all here. If nothing else, this band is one of the most consistent around. Though album sales may not always reflect it, they continually deliver strong records that refuse to be faulted for anything other than being non-mainstream. *—Kelly McCartney*

Best of Cowboy Junkies / Aug. 21, 2001 / RCA ✦✦✦✦
Like so many of their '80s contemporaries, Cowboy Junkies have never quite broken into the mainstream, yet their music has seeped into movies, television, and alternative radio. Despite their lack of fame, they still made great music that persevered through trends and imitators, and the best of that music is found on this compilation. Their early covers of "Sweet Jane" and "I'm So Lonesome I Could Cry" highlight the first third of the album, featuring Margo Timmons' whispered vocals over the lazy shuffle pumped out by the rest of the band. The uptempo country lament "Sun Comes Up, It's Tuesday Morning" and the cheery "To Live Is to Fly" show Timmons' vocals shaping into a strong croon reminiscent of Natalie Merchant. Even their '90s work, which critics were never very kind to, still has strong representation with "Anniversary Song" and "Hard to Explain." Fans may wonder why no songs from any album past *Pale Sun, Crescent Moon* are included, as so many great songs—from "Common Disaster" to "Dragging Hooks"—could have rounded out the album. Although these albums may have been financial disappointments, they still could have included some of the stronger tracks. As it is, this is still a good retrospective of the strongest years of a band who made good albums long after the compilation's cutoff date. *—Bradley Torreano*

Radio 1 Sessions / Jul. 29, 2002 / Strange Fruit ✦✦✦

Cowboy Nation

f. 1996

Group / Traditional Country, Cowboy, Alternative Pop/Rock

Formed by Chip and Tony Kinman in 1996 after the demise of their infinitely successful cowpunk band, Rank & File, Cowboy Nation is an outfit dedicated to keeping real cowboy and Western music alive and vital. The Kinmans began doing an acoustic gig around L.A. before adding the unique talents of percussionist Jamie Spidle to their live performances. Combining well-known cowboy standards with certain country classics and their original tunes allowed them to appeal to a broad audience. With as much support from the honky tonk crowd as from cowboy festival-goers, by 1997 Cowboy Nation had created a specific niche for itself.

They recorded their first self-titled project with "Taco" John Norman on drums. Released in Europe and Australia in 1997 on Shock Records, it was only available in the U.S. as an import on the Demon label. Still, Cowboy Nation was immediately a hit, and garnered a Gavin Pick in August of 1997. Rave reviews mounted up before an American label decided to take a chance on the neo-traditionalist cowboy band in 1998, when the group's project was finally released in the U.S. The early success of this cowboy band is a tribute to the talent of the Kinmans and their ability to see beyond the musical present. *A Journey Out of Time* followed in mid-2000. *—Jana Pendragon*

Cowboy Nation / May 20, 1997 / Coconut Grove ✦✦✦✦✦
A wonderful blend of old-time cowboy songs, country classics, and new tunes, this debut from L.A.'s top cowboy band is exceptional and highlights the talented Kinman brothers. With a bare-bones style that allows the heart and soul of the music to shine, Cowboy Nation brings "Old Paint" and "Cowboy's Lament" to a whole new audience. Harlan Howard's "The Blizzard" is a standout, as is the movie tune "My Rifle, My Pony and Me," originally sung by everyone's favorite cowboy, Dean Martin. Of their new material, "Cowboy Nation," a theme song of sorts, is satisfying, as is "Way Out West" and "Cowboy Way." For listeners who have never been exposed to cowboy music, this is a tremendous opportunity to learn all about it at the feet of a trio of fine players. Just as important is the fact that Cowboy Nation knows the history of cowboy music and can talk about it just as intelligently as the band plays it. *—Jana Pendragon*

A Journey Out of Time / Jun. 13, 2000 / Shanachie ✦✦✦
This is indeed cowboy music done in a spare style that puts it within the country and cowboy tradition, with harmony brother duet Tony Kinman and Chip Kinman joined on drums by Jamie Spidle. What's not so easy to determine is exactly how squarely in the tradition this falls. Certainly the low lead vocals have an almost deadpan quality that makes you occasionally wonder if they're playing this entirely straight. There are also some lyrics that might pass for deadpan humor or satire of the genre, as on "Blood on the Saddle": "Oh pity the cowboy all gory and red, a bronco fell on him and mashed in his head." It's well-executed, and has a broader musical and thematic range than much pure cowboy music has. Still, given the long and colorful resumés of the Kinmans, you also wonder whether the fellows are stretching their talents as much as they can. Cowboy music *does* have limits to what it can cover, certainly lyrically and to some extent musically, and there's a curious sense of the musicians coasting a bit here. It's best when they apply their harmonies to give the generally dolorous tunes a lift, as on "Cut Above." *—Richie Unterberger*

● **We Do as We Please** / Aug. 21, 2001 / Paras Recording ✦✦✦✦✦
It should be noted upfront that *We Do as We Please* is a repacking of Cowboy Nation's first, self-titled album, re-released and retitled for a new label, Real West. This is a good thing, because regardless of the name, it's a keeper. There's a somber, hypnotic quality about Cowboy Nation's approach to Western music and mythology. Each time the listener places *We Do as We Please* in the disc player, the intertwining voices of Tony and Chip Kinman create an enigmatic mix that pulls him or her deeper into the music. Their stripped-down arrangements and stylized synthesis draw from the past while adding newfangled nuances, dragging the cowboy song—kicking and whooping—into the 21st century. "Rifle, Pony, and Me" begins simply, with no more than a guitar and bass to support Tony Kinman's deep vocal. When his brother adds his voice to the chorus the song achieves a beautiful austerity. A list of worthy songs—"Remember the Alamo," "Big Train," and "Old Paint"—is really arbitrary, because there aren't any bad cuts. Purists may question whether the Kinman brothers have succeeded at preserving the cowboy song; they sure don't sound like Gene Autry, Roy Rodgers, or even Marty Robbins. But so what? Like the Western hero of old, they've found themselves a piece of land and staked their claim. So curious listeners should just say no to nitpicking and go out and get a copy. *We Do as We Please* is a contemporary country classic. *—Ronnie D. Lankford Jr.*

Cowgirl A-Go-Go / Oct. 1, 2002 / Paras Recording ✦✦✦✦
Although Cowboy Nation has received good press, it isn't the type of band that calls a lot of attention to itself. Instead, Chip and Tony Kinman have followed their low-key muse, singing old cowboy songs with spare accompaniment, crafting a sound that evokes the past without seeming passé. Like the band's first two albums, *Cowgirl A-Go-Go* features Tony Kinman's deep, straightforward lead supported by a steady bass and mostly acoustic guitars. Chip Kinman adds harmony and lead guitar work. The slow, steady pulse of "Dollar a Day" and "Good Old Days" is mesmerizing, while shifting tempos fill "Paniolo" with pleasant surprises. A couple of things separate *Cowgirl A-Go-Go* from the group's previous albums. First, the Kinmans have written all of the material this time, meaning that while they're still evoking the West, they're putting a contemporary spin on it. On the title track, for instance, the cowgirl is described as a cross between a sexpot and independent woman. "She don't want you to think that you're the only/man she wants around/she'll take her pick, she gets away quick/she don't stop messing around." In other words, she's not Dale Evans. *Cowgirl A-Go-Go* also varies its instrumental formula more often than its predecessors, adding fancy electric guitar fills and slide guitar on a piece like "Full Fathom 5." The album's cover art is quite a curiosity. The front displays a scantily clad cowgirl with a pistol, recently fired, in hand; on the back, a jackrabbit takes aim with a rifle. It isn't clear if the rabbit is aiming at something in the desert or at the poster of a cowgirl on a horse. The inside lyric sheet also folds out into a calendar/poster of the 1930s cowgirl on the cover. This is hardly the kind of cover art that would receive Gloria Steinem's stamp of approval, but it certainly captures one's attention. The music on *Cowgirl A-Go-Go* will likewise capture one's attention. Cowboy Nation has once again crafted a fine album by combining spare arrangements with the myths of the American West. *—Ronnie D. Lankford Jr.*

The Cox Family

f. 1976, Cotton Valley, LA

Group / Neo-Traditional Folk, Progressive Bluegrass, Traditional Bluegrass

The singing Cox Family from Cotton Valley, LA, is comprised of father Willard, son Sidney, and daughters Evelyn and Suzanne, who derive their sound from combining country, bluegrass, and gospel styles. They first began performing together in 1976 and were a popular draw at fairs and festivals, but their career was given a big boost when in the early '90s they met Alison Krauss, who brought them to the attention of Rounder Records. They also gained massive exposure when in 1994 they caught the ear of Adam Duritz, frontman of the multi-platinum-selling Counting Crows, who was so impressed with the Cox Family that he invited them to open for the band during its North American tour.

Krauss—who produced all but the family's very first release, *Quiet Storm* on Wilcox Records—recorded several of Sidney's songs, which appeared on both of her Grammy-winning albums, including the title track of *I've Got That Old Feeling*. The Cox Family recorded two records of their own on Rounder Records: *Everybody's Reaching Out for Someone* (1993) and *Beyond the City* (1995), which earned them a Grammy nomination for Best Bluegrass Album. They also collaborated with Krauss on an album entitled *I Know Who Holds Tomorrow*, which won a Grammy in 1994 for Best Country/Gospel/ Bluegrass Album. The Cox Family also shared a Grammy for their participation in the various-artists project *Amazing Grace: A Country Salute to Gospel*. Their major-label debut, *Just When We're Thinking It's Over*, was released on Asylum Records in 1996. *—Jack Leaver*

Everybody's Reaching Out for Someone / Apr. 1, 1993 / Rounder ✦✦✦

Beyond the City / 1995 / Rounder ✦✦✦✦✦

● **Just When We're Thinking It's Over** / Jul. 1996 / Elektra ✦✦✦✦✦
The smooth and effortless vocal blend of the Cox Family make this a pleasurable experience throughout. And although their angelic four-part harmonies are based in bluegrass, to categorize the family in that genre solely, would be to pigeonhole them. The performances here also mix in country, gospel and a touch of blues, with top-notch session players providing a sound foundation that employs electric, as well as acoustic instruments and includes producer Alison Krauss' fiddle and viola playing on a couple of cuts. All four family members take turns singing lead, and there isn't a weak link in the group, nor a weak song on the album. Highlights include a great bluegrass reworking of Del Shannon's 1961 hit "Runaway" and the beautiful ballad "Nothing Else I Can Do," penned by Sidney and Suzanne Cox. *—Jack Leaver*

Quiet Storm / Wilcox ✦✦✦

Billy "Crash" Craddock

b. Jun. 16, 1939, Greensboro, NC
Guitar, Vocals / Traditional Country, Rockabilly, Honky Tonk
After an aborted career as a '50s teen idol, Billy "Crash" Craddock returned to his first love, country music, and earned the nickname "Mr. Country Rock" with a string of popular hits during the '70s. Born in Greensboro, NC, in 1939, Craddock earned his nickname as a running back on his high-school football team, and grew up a huge fan of the *Grand Ole Opry*. He signed with Columbia in the late '50s, but instead of marketing him as a country singer, the label tried to make him a teen idol, and had him record a mix of Elvis-style rockabilly tunes and pop ballads. Craddock did manage to land three hit singles in Australia, but none in his home country, and aside from a lone album for King in 1964 (*I'm Tore Up*), he was largely missing-in-action afterwards. That all changed in 1971, when Craddock signed with Cartwheel Records—this time as a country artist. His first five singles—a remake of "Knock Three Times," "Dream Lover," "You Better Move On," "Ain't Nothin' Shakin' (But the Leaves on The Trees)," and "I'm Gonna Knock on Your Door"—all made the country Top Ten over 1971-1972.

He subsequently moved to ABC and scored his first chart-topper with 1974's "Rub It In," which also crossed over to the pop Top 20. More hits followed, including a second number one in 1975 with a remake of the Drifters' "Ruby Baby," and a third in 1977's "Broken Down in Tiny Pieces." All told, Craddock landed in the country Top Ten a total of 18 times from 1971-1979, with his final entry being "If I Could Write a Song as Beautiful as You." He recorded for Capitol during the late '70s and early '80s, by which time his commercial momentum had finally slowed. *—Steve Huey*

Sings His Greatest Hits / 1978 / MCA ✦✦✦✦✦
A good summation of his peak years, it includes the ballads "Easy as Pie" and "Broken Down in Tiny Pieces." But Craddock's at his best when he's "in the groove," as in "Ruby Baby," "Still Thinkin' 'Bout You," and his staple, "Rub It In." *—Tom Roland*

Boom Boom Baby / 1992 / Bear Family ✦✦✦✦✦
Although Billy "Crash" Craddock claims that he's "always" been country, there's no evidence of it on these late-'50s rock & roll recordings. Sounding very much like Elvis, Craddock tackles 21 rockers, novelties and teen ballads on this collection of his complete Columbia recordings. A few of these tracks charted in Australia, but Craddock's success in the U.S. was limited. Some of these songs, including "Blabbermouth," "Sweetie Pie" and "Ah, Poor Little Baby," seem to have had hit potential, but it wasn't to be. Fans of Elvis and '50s rock in general should check this one out. *—Greg Adams*

● **Crash's Smashes: The Hits of Billy "Crash" Craddock** / Feb. 20, 1996 / Razor & Tie ✦✦✦✦✦
Drawing from three different labels—Cartwheel, ABC, and Capitol—*Crash's Smashes: The Hits of Billy "Crash" Craddock* is the definitive compilation of Craddock's career. All of his biggest hits—from "Knock Three Times" and "Dream Lover" through "Rub it In," "Easy as Pie" and "Broken Down in Tiny Pieces" to "If I Could Write A Song As Beautiful As You"—are included on the 19-track single disc, making it both a perfect introduction and retrospective. *—Stephen Thomas Erlewine*

Floyd Cramer

b. Oct. 27, 1933, Samti, LA, **d.** Dec. 31, 1997
Piano, Session Musician / Country-Pop, Instrumental Pop, Nashville Sound/ Countrypolitan
A distinctive pianist whose unique, slip-note playing style came to typify the pop-oriented Nashville sound of the late '50s and early '60s, session and solo musician Floyd Cramer was born October 27, 1933, in Louisiana. After a childhood spent largely in Arkansas, he returned to his home state in 1951 and began appearing on the radio program *the Louisiana Hayride*, where he performed with the likes of Jim Reeves, Faron Young, Webb Pierce, and, in his debut, Elvis Presley. While Cramer cut a few solo sides in 1953, his most important work in the early '50s was as a session musician, where he first met Chet Atkins, who encouraged the pianist to move to Nashville. He did in 1955, rejoining Atkins as the house pianist at RCA Records to begin developing what would ultimately be recognized as the Nashville sound, a style shorn of the elements associated with traditional country and honky tonk instead favoring a more polished, progressive sheen. With Atkins behind the production boards, Cramer began to perfect his unique style of playing, a method not dissimilar to guitar-picking in that he would hit one key and then slide his finger onto the next, creating a blue, lonesome sound. Under Atkins' guidance, Cramer played on hundreds of sessions, including many for Presley, among them "Heartbreak Hotel."

In 1957, Cramer released his own solo debut, *That Honky-Tonk Piano*, and in the next year scored a minor pop hit with the single "Flip, Flop and Bop." As his solo career was largely secondary in relation to his session work, he recorded his own music sporadically, but in 1960 notched a significant country and pop hit with the self-penned instrumental "Last Date." The follow-up, a cover of Bob Wills' "San Antonio Rose," reached the Top Ten of both charts. He also released an LP a year between 1960 and 1962, starting with *Hello Blues* and followed by *Last Date* and *I Remember Hank Williams*.

From 1965 to 1974, Cramer annually released a *Class Of...* album, a collection of the year's top hits done in his own inimitable style. In 1971, he also teamed with Atkins and saxophonist Boots Randolph for the album *Chet, Floyd and Boots*. By 1977, Cramer was exploring modern technology, and on the LP *Keyboard Kick Band*, he played a number of instruments, including a synthesizer. In 1980, he released his last significant hit, a recording of the theme from the hit TV drama *Dallas*. Though largely quiet for most of the decade, in 1988 Cramer released three separate albums—*Country Gold, Just Me and My Piano!*, and *Special Songs of Love*. He died December 31, 1997. *—Jason Ankeny*

That Honky-Tonk Piano / 1957 / MGM ✦✦✦

Hello Blues / 1960 / RCA ✦✦✦✦
Hello Blues is Floyd Cramer's attempt to play the blues in his own distinctive, "slip-note," style. Of course, the laid-back tempos and gentle arrangements of all the music on the album mean that it never sounds as gritty or down-home as the best country blues, but that isn't the point of the record—*Hello Blues* is a pleasant collection of bluesy easy listening, not a blues record, and taken on its own terms, it's entertaining. [The CD reissue includes four bonus tracks that are not necessarily "blues:" "Sentimental Journey," "Red Roses for a Blue Lady," "Mr. Lonely," and "Love Letters." *—Thom Owens*

Last Date / 1961 / RCA ✦✦✦✦✦

On the Rebound / 1961 / RCA ✦✦✦

Floyd Cramer Gets Organ-Ized / 1962 / RCA ✦✦✦

I Remember Hank Williams / 1962 / RCA ✦✦✦

Comin' On / 1963 / RCA ✦✦✦
Upon first hearing the album's title one might conjure up a Nashville rife with hallucinogens; but after glimpsing a crew cut adorned Floyd Cramer and dancing model teens on the cover, one can only fathom the reverie of wholesome moves and fruity punch. Thankfully, while Cramer's easy listening style oozes with glee-club innocence, it also, unwittingly, contains some strains of psychedelia—ghostly sweet choruses, tinker-toy piano, space-age pedal steel, and the occasional variety show trumpet break—Muzak to many; a needed break from being a Nashville-sound sideman for Cramer. After plying his unique slip-note technique on recordings by Jim Reeves and Elvis Presley, the pianist found time to record a slew of solo discs, including this 1963 release featuring the pianist's usual genre-busting program and countrypolitan sound. The mix roams from fairly substantial versions of Ray Charles' "Drown in My Own Tears" and something called "The Huckle Buck," to the strangely noirish "Satan's Doll" and an overwrought "Green Door." More novel than interesting—with pearly-white versions of "Ol' Man River" and "Back in the Saddle Again" sealing the deal—Floyd Cramer's *Comin' On* is tailored made for diehards of kitsch country. *—Stephen Cook*

Super Hits / 1979 / RCA ✦✦✦
One of thousands of cheapy hits collections put out by RCA, Floyd Cramer's *Super Hits* delivers only in the flimsiest ways with a mere ten tracks. But, in the case of perennial lounge pianist Cramer, this small dose might be all one needs. And while Cramer certainly made mighty contributions to myriad Nashville sessions in the '50s and '60s, his contemporary solo turns often meant some romper room-issue covers and the most clean-cut playing. Covering his almost two-decade stay at RCA, the collection's latter-day cuts ("Dallas," "Help Me Make It Through the Night") thankfully balance out the pap with some semblance of country grit. It's better, though, to pick up a cheap copy of the pianist's earlier RCA hits album, *The Best of Floyd Cramer*. *—Stephen Cook*

Collector's Series / May 23, 1995 / RCA ✦✦✦✦✦
Collector's Seres is a reasonably thorough overview of Floyd Cramer's career, offering nearly every one of his hits ("Last Date," "Tennessee Waltz," "For the Good Times") in its original version. *—Stephen Thomas Erlewine*

★ **The Essential Floyd Cramer** / Aug. 1, 1995 / RCA ✦✦✦✦✦
Although it isn't necessarily a definitive retrospective, *Essential* is the best CD compilation of Floyd Cramer's solo recordings yet assembled. Containing 20 tracks, including his hits "Last Date," "San Antonio Rose" and "Stood Up," the disc captures Cramer's signature stride piano style in all of its glory on a variety of country, pop and R&B numbers. Cramer was as well-known as a sideman as he was a solo artist, and even if *Essential* contains none of his session work, it contains a good portion of his very best recordings, making it a fine introduction to one of the most influential pianists in country and pop history. *—Stephen Thomas Erlewine*

Favorite Country Hits / Oct. 1995 / Ranwood ✦✦✦✦
Favorite Country Hits is a condensed, 18-track single disc of Floyd Cramer's mid-'90s double-disc set, which was only sold through television. On the album, Cramer runs through a number of country classics, including his trademark "Last Date." Though Cramer's talent hasn't diminished over the years, *Favorite Country Hits* is largely best used as easy listening background music, since it rarely hits any peaks or valleys—it just is pleasant, low-key country-pop. *—Thom Owens*

Last Date/On the Rebound / Apr. 7, 1998 / Collectables ✦✦✦✦
Two of pianist Floyd Cramer's early-'60s albums on RCA, *Last Date* and *On the Rebound*, are combined on this single compact disc. Although many of the best songs—including "Last Date," "On the Rebound," "Flip Flop and Bop," and "Fancy Pants"—have been featured on various greatest-hits packages, these albums work well as individual records and are worth acquiring for any Floyd Cramer fan. *—Al Campbell*

RCA Country Legends / Feb. 20, 2001 / Buddha ✦✦✦✦✦
This release highlights one of the most noted keyboard influences in pop music—Floyd Cramer. His laid-back and non-threatening demeanor garnered him a reputation as an MOR artist although the influence he had on rock & roll is also duly noted. This 16-track career retrospective presents many of Cramer's best-loved and remembered pieces in the highest sonic quality available on a domestic CD release. However, the collection does seem a bit less definitive considering that under half of the compact discs' maximum playing time—80 minutes—is utilized on this package. Before Cramer became a solo artist, he spent his formidable years as a session pianist performing first on the *Louisiana Hayride* radio program, accompanying the likes of Webb Pierce, Jim Reeves, and even a fledgling Elvis Presley. After signing with RCA Records in Nashville, TN, the sides he cut for the label in the mid- to late '50s and early '60s became international hits synonymous with the full-bodied timbre and laid-back style known as "the Nashville sound." Every track on this compilation reveals Cramer's ability to take the piano—which was becoming increasingly replaced by the electric guitar in pop music—to a new strata as a lead instrument. His abilities ranging from the jazzy pop music standards such as "Stormy Weather" to the chicken shack rockabilly of "Flip Flop Bop" to the haunting cover of "Rhythm of the Rain"—which includes an effective false ending. Cramer's influence spread to wherever there was a turntable. The effect that songs such as "Stormy Weather" and "Tricky" would have on the burgeoning West Coast "Bakersfield sound" is evident. What lies just below the surface however, is the persuasion that this music would admittedly have on artists such as Keith Emerson and Elton John—both of whom cite Cramer's sound as paramount among their inspirations. *—Lindsay Planer*

Dan Crary

b. Kansas
Guitar, Composer / Progressive Bluegrass, Traditional Bluegrass
Flatpicking guitarist Dan Crary was born and raised in Kansas. It was there that he first developed an interest in guitar, particularly the steel-string, flat-top version favored by artists like Doc Watson. In 1968, Crary helped found the Bluegrass Alliance, and used Watson's influence as a jumping-off point for innovation in the genre. Throughout the 1970s, Crary appeared with the group Sundance, which included fiddler Byron Berline and banjoist John Hickman. He also developed his reputation as a master interpreter of traditional music (like that written for the fiddle) for six- and 12-string guitars. His albums include 1983's *Guitar*, which was a who's who in the new bluegrass scene of the time. Béla Fleck, Sam Bush, and Mark O'Connor all contributed to the record, which included modern bluegrass interpretations of classical music pieces. California was established in 1990 with Berline and Hickman; the combo experimented even further with bluegrass' intersections into other genres, and stayed active even as Crary appeared with his other projects, including Men of Steel with Genovese flatpicking master Beppe Gambetta. MOS released a live recording in spring 2003. *—Johnny Loftus*

Sweet Southern Girl / 1969 / Sugar Hill ✦✦✦

Bluegrass Guitar / 1970 / Sugar Hill ✦✦✦✦
There really were no solo guitar heroes in bluegrass music (unless you count Clarence White, who never made a solo album before his tragically young death) until Dan Crary made this record back in 1970. Up to that point, the guitar had been almost exclusively a rhythm instrument, and even then its function often appeared to the casual observer to be limited to giving the singer something to do with his hands. This record was a fiery declaration of independence for bluegrass guitarists; it showed that the guitar could compete very well with the mandolin, banjo, and fiddle as a solo instrument in traditional music. Crary's fleet fingers make deceptively easy work of such classic fiddle tunes as "Devil's Dream," "Forked Deer," and "Salt Creek," and his rendition of "Black Mountain Rag" has probably been as influential as Doc Watson's—perhaps even more so. His backing band is outstanding. This reissue was long overdue when it was released in 1992, and its only drawback is its 30-minute length. *—Rick Anderson*

Thunderation / 1981 / Pamlico Sound ✦✦✦✦✦

● **Guitar** / 1983 / Sugar Hill ✦✦✦✦✦
The title leaves the erroneous impression that this is a solo set. Instead, it's an exciting blowing session featuring the cream of the new generation of bluegrass players who emerged in the '80s—Sam Bush, Mark O'Connor, and Béla Fleck. But on selections ranging from a "Bill Monroe Medley" to a transcribed Mozart piano sonata, Crary and his guitar more than hold their own. *— William Ruhlmann*

Take a Step over / Oct. 19, 1993 / Sugar Hill ✦✦✦
On *Take a Step Over*, Dan Crary once again demonstrates that he is one of the most talented bluegrass acoustic guitarists of his generation. Crary has a knack for interpreting fiddle tunes for the guitar, playing them with a nimble grace and effortless musicality. As long as he sticks to instrumentals, Crary is fine—after all he, has some great duels with Béla Fleck, Sam Bush, John Hickman and Byron Berline—but when he sings, the album becomes a little tedious; he simply doesn't have the vocal skills to match his instrumental acumen. However, the guitar showcases are strong enough to make the album worthwhile for any fans of bluegrass guitar. *—Stephen Thomas Erlewine*

Lady's Fancy / 1994 / Rounder ✦✦✦✦✦

Jammed If I Do / May 24, 1994 / Koch ✦✦✦

Holiday Guitar / Oct. 14, 1997 / Sugar Hill ✦✦✦

Dan Crary & Lonnie Hoppers / Sep. 26, 2000 / Pinecastle ✦✦✦

Red Cravens

Vocals, Guitar / Traditional Bluegrass, Bluegrass-Gospel
Red Cravens & the Bray Brothers consisted of Red Cravens (guitar, tenor vocals), Nate Bray (mandolin, lead vocals), Harley Bray (banjo, baritone), and Francis Bray (bass). They were one of the first bluegrass outfits to master the full capabilities of the recording studio in bringing out the full range of their singing and playing. Nate Bray first began building his reputation as a wizard on the mandolin while in high-school in Clinton, IL. He began playing with guitarist Red Cravens around 1956, informally in the company of Bill Monroe, with Harley Bray. Where Nate Bray's influence was Bill Monroe, Harley practically slept with his banjo and lived and breathed Earl Scruggs' playing. Later on, Francis Bray picked up the cello, later switched to bass, and an act was formed. The group improvised a great deal, especially with regard to the tuning of their instruments, but they developed a coherent sound and began playing fairly steady gigs, and a knack for adapting non-bluegrass material, including classic pop tunes, to their style.

For years they were a fixture on WHOW in Clinton on a show hosted by Uncle Johnny Barton, and they left behind a large body of tapes done for radio. The quartet, whose lineup sometimes expanded to include a fiddle player (John Hartford was one, appearing on some of their recordings), became very skilled at recording themselves in the studio—they learned the best way to get the cleanest possible sound, and also understood the virtues of singing softly on their recordings, which gave them a lyricism that many other bluegrass outfits of the era lacked. Eventually, they landed a contract (as the Bluegrass Gentlemen) with Liberty Records, for which they recorded a series of instrumental tunes.

Ironically, it was the Liberty contract that led to the breakup of the group in the early '60s. Faced with the pressure of becoming a popular recording act and catering to other peoples' tastes, and the pressure of having to produce seriously popular records, the group decided that the original reason for their getting together—to have fun—was being threatened, and they stopped working together. All they wanted to do was play square dances, and Liberty wanted them to do much more than that. *—Bruce Eder*

419 West Main / 1997 / Rounder ✦✦
Assembled by John Hartford from radio tapes left behind by the group, and named for the house where they lived, this 40-minute disc showcases the group's sound better than their official Liberty recordings. There are some instrumentals here, but also lots of songs, showing off their originals, covers of numbers by Bill Monroe and A. P. Carter, and arrangements of traditional tunes ("Our Darling's Gone," etc.). The sound is exceptionally good for early-'60s radio sources, and shows off the degree of sophistication that this group achieved experimenting on their own. *—Bruce Eder*

Slim Critchlow

d. Oct. 31, 1969
Vocals / Irish Folk, British Folk, Folksongs, Traditional Scottish Folk, Traditional Folk, Cowboy
A guitarist and singer of old-time cowboy songs, Slim Critchlow became known as a performer in the early '30s, when he sang on radio and became a friend of folklorist John A. Lomax. Critchlow, in his early 20's, was working as a national park ranger in Utah when he began doing live radio on a Salt Lake City radio station, with a repertoire and style that were more traditional and authentic than the cowboy music popularized via movies and records. In the early '60s he garnered some acclaim in the folk revival, performing at festivals and doing some recording. He played an eight-string guitar (the two top strings were doubled) and, when recorded in the late '50s and early '60s, sang in a warm, vibrant, relaxed voice, drawing mostly from tunes originating during the late 19th century. He died at the age of 60 in 1969, shortly before the release of an album of his recordings on Arhoolie; that album, with the addition of unreleased material, was issued on CD in 1999. *—Richie Unterberger*

Cowboy Songs: Crooked Trail Holbrook / May 18, 1999 / Arhoolie ✦✦✦
These 27 songs were recorded between 1959 and 1963, although all but six were done on the evening of April 13, 1963, taped by Barry Olivier at Olivier's Berkeley, CA home. It's just Slim and his guitar, singing a wide variety of songs he learned, mostly about cowboy life as described in song prior to the advent of motion pictures. He's got a low-key, even-tempered voice, and the ambience is that of a singer entertaining friends, which was exactly the set-up at Olivier's house. Exciting? No, but it's a good representation of cowboy music in its unadorned, traditional state. *—Richie Unterberger*

J.D. Crowe

b. Aug. 27, 1937, Lexington, KY
Banjo, Vocals / Progressive Bluegrass, Traditional Bluegrass
Banjoist J.D. Crowe was one of the most influential progressive bluegrass musicians of the '70s. Initially influenced by Earl Scruggs, as well as rock & roll and the blues, Crowe worked his way through several bands during the '60s, developing a distinctive instrumental style that melded country, bluegrass, rock, and blues. Crowe didn't receive national exposure until the early '70s when he formed the New South, but after the release

of the band's eponymous debut in 1972 he became a fixture on the bluegrass scene for the next 20 years.

Born and raised in Lexington, KY, Crowe picked up the banjo when he was 13 years old, inspired by one of Flatt & Scruggs' performances on *the Kentucky Barn Dance*. After that show, he regularly attended the duo's performances, sitting down in the front row to study Scruggs' revolutionary picking. Soon, Crowe was playing with various groups in Kentucky, including an outfit that also featured Curley Parker and Pee Wee Lambert. The young banjo player frequently played on local radio stations, and that is where he got his first major break in 1956. Jimmy Martin was driving through Lexington when he heard Crowe on the radio station, and was so impressed with what he heard that he drove to the station and asked him to join his band, the Sunny Mountain Boys. Crowe immediately accepted and began touring with Martin. While he was in the Sunny Mountain Boys, Crowe didn't stick to a strict bluegrass set list—he often added rock & roll songs to his repertoire.

After spending six years with Martin, Crowe left the Sunny Mountain Boys in 1962 to pursue a solo career. For a while, he played Lexington bars and hotels, developing a new, progressive direction for bluegrass which incorporated stronger elements of folk, blues, and rock. In the mid-'60s, he formed the Kentucky Mountain Boys with Red Allen and Doyle Lawson; they released their first album, *Bluegrass Holiday*, in 1968 on Lemco Records. The Kentucky Mountain Boys had a varied repertoire, but played solely acoustic instruments. Two other records followed—*Ramblin' Boy* and *The Model Church*—before the group broke up in the early '70s.

Following the disbandment of the Kentucky Mountain Boys, Crowe formed the New South, which was the most revolutionary bluegrass outfit of its time. Originally, the band consisted of guitarist Tony Rice, mandolinist Ricky Skaggs, dobroist Jerry Douglas, and fiddler/bassist Bobby Sloan, and they played a wildly eclectic brand of bluegrass on electric instruments. When they released their debut, *J.D. Crowe & the New South* in 1975 on Rounder Records, it caused an instant sensation—it marked a genuine turning point in the sound of the genre. All of the musicians in the original lineup of the New South were acclaimed and would later go on to popular solo careers—in fact, most of them had left within a few years of the debut. By the end of the decade, the band featured guitarist/vocalist Keith Whitley, mandolinist Jimmy Gaudreau, fiddler Bobby Slone, and bassist Steve Bryant.

During the '80s, the New South featured an ever-revolving lineup, as former members came back for guest appearances and Crowe discovered fresh, developing talents—the group became known as a source for new musicians who would later go on to individual success. In 1980, Crowe formed the Bluegrass Album Band with Tony Rice, Bobby Hicks, Doyle Lawson, and Todd Phillips. The Bluegrass Album Band toured and recorded sporadically throughout the course of the decade, always to great critical and popular acclaim. J.D. Crowe continued with the New South until 1988, when he decided to retire from the road. Following his decision, he appeared at special, one-shot concerts—including a tour with Tony Rice—but concentrated on studio work, particularly producing records for developing bands. —*Stephen Thomas Erlewine*

Bluegrass Holiday / 1968 / Lemco ♦♦♦

☆ **The Model Church** / 1969 / Rebel ♦♦♦♦♦

This gospel album was recorded and originally released in the early '70s on the Lemco label. When Rebel acquired the rights to Lemco's catalog several years later, it reissued this and two other J.D. Crowe albums (*Bluegrass Holiday* and *Ramblin' Boy*, retitled *Blackjack*). What may be most noteworthy about *The Model Church* is the fact that it's the first gospel album to feature singer Doyle Lawson, who would later make some of the best bluegrass-gospel recordings to date at the head of his own band Quicksilver. With J.D. Crowe on banjo and vocals, Larry Rice on mandolin and vocals, and Bobby Slone on bass, this quartet delivers a lovely set of gospel songs, some of which have since become standards. Highlights include the hauntingly beautiful title track "Goin' Up," a the Gosdin Brothers classic, and a fine version of Jim & Jesse's "Look for Me." The echoey production is a little bit strange for a bluegrass album; it won't satisfy everyone's tastes, but there's no denying the power of these performances. —*Rick Anderson*

Bluegrass Evolution / 1973 / Starday ♦♦♦♦♦

J.D. Crowe and the New South's *Bluegrass Evolution* is not only a sturdy collection of tunes, but a piece of important history as well. The album caused a stir when it was released in the early '70s, as Crowe and company spearheaded the fusion of traditional bluegrass elements with such electric country instruments as steel guitar, piano, and drums. This was certainly not viewed as a scandalous approach later on—except in fiercely traditional bluegrass circles—but consider that *Bluegrass Evolution* is no less pioneering an effort than the Byrds' *Sweetheart of the Rodeo*, the effort that spearheaded country-rock and introduced the larger public to Gram Parsons. Along with albums by folks such as New Grass Revival (among others), *Bluegrass Evolution* paved the way for progressive bluegrass. Despite the pioneering bent, Tony and Larry Rice give remarkably tight and trad-minded vocal performances. The album was re-released on CD in the late '90s. —*Erik Hage*

☆ **J.D. Crowe & the New South** / 1975 / Rounder ♦♦♦♦♦

J.D. Crowe & the New South's eponymous debut album is one of the most influential and pioneering records in the history of bluegrass. For the first edition of the New South, Crowe assembled a stellar group of musicians—including Ricky Skaggs (fiddle, mandolin, vocals), Tony Rice (lead vocals, guitar), and Jerry Douglas (dobro)—and gave them each equal weight. Consequently, this is vibrant collaborative music, not just a leader with some faceless studio hacks. Furthermore, Crowe pushed the music in new direction with his section of material, taking songs from contemporary singer/songwriters like Gordon Lightfoot, adding a couple of originals, as well as standards. With such an eclectic selection of songs, plus the band's trailblazing instrumental style, *The New South* did indeed offer a new kind of bluegrass and its impact could still be felt years after its release. —*Thom Owens*

You Can Share My Blanket / 1977 / Rounder ♦♦♦

My Home Ain't in the Hall of Fame / 1978 / Rounder ♦♦♦

In the late '70s, banjo virtuoso and bandleader J.D. Crowe was one of several forward-looking bluegrass artists looking to expand the music's stylistic boundaries. Bands like the Country Gentlemen and the Seldom Scene did so by taking rock & roll songs and giving them relatively traditional bluegrass settings; Crowe's approach, at least temporarily, was to bring steel guitar, electric bass, and drums to bear on bluegrass material. The resulting sound on this 1978 recording was completely different from most of what was then being called "progressive bluegrass," and in fact, to call this album "progressive bluegrass" would be rather misleading. Basically, this is a honky tonk album with a banjo and a few bluegrass numbers thrown in. On "(I'll Be Your) Stepping Stone," singer Keith Whitley sounds like he's building an altar to George Jones, and the band's version of "Lady" sounds like a Bellamy Brothers outtake. Even the relatively straightforward bluegrass number "She's Gone, Gone, Gone" and the heavily bluegrassified arrangement of the old Flying Burrito Brothers number "Sin City" prominently feature pedal steel and drums. None of this is a criticism; in fact, many of these arrangements work beautifully, and the combination of Crowe's brilliant banjo picking (listen to his backup work on "Will You Be Lonesome Too?") and Whitley's even more brilliant singing is pretty much unbeatable. But bluegrass purists should consider themselves duly warned. —*Rick Anderson*

Somewhere Between / 1981 / Rounder ♦♦♦♦♦

A hard-country album with lovely ballads, it features Lefty Frizzell-style vocals from Keith Whitley. —*Mark A. Humphrey*

Live in Japan / 1982 / Rounder ♦♦♦

J.D. Crowe & the New South were perhaps the finest purveyors of bluegrass in the '70s, and this live recording from 1979 documents all their glory. Lead vocalist Keith Whitley is in fine form throughout, but the band really shakes the rafters when J.D. Crowe lets loose with his lightning banjo work. Highlights include a lovely "Don't Give Your Heart to a Rambler" and a bluegrass version of Chuck Berry's "Memphis." This is traditional music expertly executed. —*Tim Sheridan*

Straight Ahead / 1986 / Rounder ♦♦♦

This is more or less traditional bluegrass, with Sam Bush on mandolin and Jerry Douglas on dobro. —*Mark A. Humphrey*

Blackjack / 1987 / Rebel ♦♦♦

Blackjack is one of J.D. Crowe & the New South's best albums, featuring a mixture of bluegrass standards and contemporary country-rock and folk songs, like the Flying Burrito Brothers' "Sin City." It's a stunning display of ambition, progression and heritage, highlighted by Crowe's excellent instrumental work and Doyle Lawson's wonderful lead vocals. —*Thom Owens*

★ **Flashback** / 1994 / Rounder ♦♦♦♦♦

Flashback is a first-rate retrospective of banjo player J.D. Crowe. Originally released on the Rounder label in 1994, Flashback traces Crowe's formative years with the Osborne Brothers, Jimmy Martin and as leader of the New South. The album was embraced by bluegrass fans and was nominated for a Grammy for Best Bluegrass Album upon release. Among the 12 tracks include "Nashville Skyline Rag," "Long Journey Home," "When the Angels Carry Me Home," and "Waiting for You." FlashBack is an excellent way to get acquainted with all aspects of J.D. Crowe's music. —*Al Campbell*

Come on Down to My World / Jan. 12, 1999 / Rounder ♦♦♦♦

This 1998 release found J.D. Crowe and his band, the New South, at their creative best and definitely at the top of their game. Always skirting the fine line between what is traditional bluegrass and what is country, Crowe and his band stick close to tradition while alternately blazing new trails in the genre. That said, this album probably has a higher quotient of straight country done up Crowe style than any previous outing. From its remake of Charley Pride's "(I'm So) Afraid of Losing You Again" to Merle Haggard's "Back to the Barrooms" to Townes Van Zandt's "White Freight Liner Blues," the band takes on this type of material with considerable élan, imparting a fresh slant to everything. The more traditional instrumentals, "J's Tune" and "Careless Love," individually call to mind the work of Bill Monroe and Earl Scruggs, respectively. Mandolinist and lead singer Dwight McCall's original "I Don't Know" is another highlight falling into that nether region between bluegrass and country. "Come Back Sweetheart" and "You Didn't Say Goodbye" are more traditional pieces and serve as musical anchors to *Come on Down to My World*, an album that shows the wide range of Crowe's music and his unbelievable facility on his instrument. —*Cub Koda*

My Home Ain't in the Hall of Fame [Reissue] / 2002 / Rounder ♦♦♦

Rodney Crowell

b. Aug. 7, 1950, Houston, TX

Guitar, Songwriter, Vocals / Contemporary Country, Singer/Songwriter, New Traditionalist, Country-Rock, Neo-Traditionalist Country, Progressive Country

While Rodney Crowell first gained widespread recognition as a leader of the new traditionalist movement of the mid-'80s, he in fact was a singer, songwriter, and producer with roots and ambitions extending far beyond the movement's parameters. Born to a musical family on August 7, 1950, in Houston, TX, Crowell formed his first band, the Arbitrators, while in high-school, and in 1972 moved to Nashville to become a professional musician. There, he struck up friendships with singer/songwriters Townes Van Zandt and Guy Clark. Crowell's first big break came while he was performing as a lounge singer, where one of his acoustic sets was heard by Jerry Reed. Crowell's own "You Can't Keep Me Here in Tennessee" caught the ear of Reed and his manager, and two days later Reed recorded the song after signing Crowell to his publishing company.

In 1975, Crowell moved to Los Angeles to join Emmylou Harris' Hot Band as a guitarist, and soon became one of her primary songwriters; among the Crowell compositions Harris first popularized were "Till I Gain Control Again," "Ain't Livin' Long Like This," "Leaving Louisiana in the Broad Daylight," and "Bluebird Wine." In 1977, Crowell exited the Hot Band to form his own group, the Cherry Bombs, and in 1978 released his first album, *Ain't Living Long Like This*; surprisingly, given that he had built his growing reputation as a songwriter, his first two minor hits—"Elvira" and "(Now and Then, There's) A Fool Such As I"—were both covers. Also in 1978, Crowell began producing tracks for the album *Right or Wrong*, the American debut from singer/songwriter Rosanne Cash; around the time of the record's 1979 release, he and Cash married. In between recording his own 1980 sophomore record, *But What Will the Neighbors Think*, and producing Cash's commercial breakthrough *Seven Year Ache*, Crowell's songwriting career took full flight when "Leavin' Louisiana in the Broad Daylight" hit number one for the Oak Ridge Boys in 1980.

Among his other significant compositions were "Till I Gain Control Again" (a number one for Crystal Gayle in 1983); "Shame on the Moon" (a Top Five pop hit for Bob Seger in 1982); "Long Hard Road (The Sharecropper's Dream)" (a 1984 number one for the Nitty Gritty Dirt Band); and "Somewhere Tonight" (a number one in 1987 for Highway 101). In 1980, Crowell issued his own first hit, "Ashes by Now," which was a Top 40 pop crossover success; the follow-up, "Stars on the Water," was popular with both pop and country listeners. In 1981, he issued his third LP, a self-titled effort which was not commercially successful; when a fourth effort was rejected by his label, he turned his energies to writing and producing, most significantly helming Cash's 1985 masterpiece *Rhythm and Romance*. At Cash's urging, Crowell re-ignited his performing career in 1986 with the acclaimed *Street Language*, an eclectic effort co-produced by Memphis soul legend Booker T. Jones.

In 1988, Crowell finally broke through commercially with *Diamonds & Dirt*, a record which generated an unbroken string of five number-one singles with "It's Such a Small World" (a duet with Cash), "I Couldn't Leave You If I Tried," "She's Crazy for Leavin'" (co-written by Guy Clark), "After All This Time," and "Above and Beyond." *Keys to the Highway* was also highly successful. Crowell and Cash divorced in 1991, prompting both artists to document their marriage's dissolution with starkly confessional albums; Crowell's 1992 *Life Is Messy* featured guests Steve Winwood and Linda Ronstadt. Switching to MCA Records for *Let the Picture Paint Itself* in 1994, he followed with *Jewel of the South* the next year. In 1997, he formed the Cicadas with longtime backup musicians Steuart Smith, Michael Rhodes, and Vince Santoro. He married singer Claudia Church in 1998, and in 1999 wrote her country chart debut, "What's the Matter With You Baby." Crowell issued his first album since 1995, 2001's *Houston Kid*. *—Jason Ankeny*

☆ **Ain't Living Long Like This** / 1978 / Warner Bros. ✦✦✦✦✦

Rodney Crowell's auspicious 1978 debut, *Ain't Living Long Like This*, not only showcases his songwriting prowess, but also his ability to deliver a song, whether it's one of his own or the work of another writer. Crowell possesses a sort of Everly Brothers, Nashville soul in his strong, emotive tenor, that's equally effective on the country blues of Dallas Frazier's "Elvira," as it is on the rocking title cut or a country-folk ballad such as the self-penned "Song for the Life." Along with producer Brian Ahern (Emmylou Harris), Crowell employs a who's who of country and rock & roll session players, including James Burton and Glen D. Hardin, both of whom played with Elvis Presley and Gram Parsons, as well as enlisting the aid of artists such as Dr. John, Ry Cooder, Nicolette Larson, Emmylou Harris, Ricky Skaggs and Willie Nelson. As a writer, Crowell, who chose to include three terrific covers over any of his backlog of excellent original material, has the knack for mixing a pop sensibility and rock & roll vitality, with the heart and reverence of a traditionalist. A song such as "California Earthquake (A Whole Lotta Shakin' Goin' On)," sounds as if it could've been written decades before, while "Voila, An American Dream" hit the pop charts the following year for *the Dirt Band*. *Ain't Living Long Like This* became a mining-ground of material for others. Nearly every one of Crowell's tunes from the album was covered within the next few years, spawning at least a couple of major hits. Even "Elvira," which he had resurrected, became an early-'80's smash for the Oak Ridge Boys . *—Brett Hartenbach*

But What Will the Neighbors Think / 1980 / Warner Bros. ✦✦

On his second album, Rodney Crowell demonstrates slight new wave influences, which is evident from his "Here Come the '80s" and a cover of "Queen of Hearts," which demonstrates a debt to Rockpile, as well as his choice of Ramones producer Craig Leon as a collaborator. The problem is, Crowell doesn't quite have the skills or the heart to pull off a country-new wave fusion, as Carlene Carter did successfully around the same time. There are several fine songs on the record, but they are better heard on *The Rodney Crowell Collection*. *—Thom Owens*

Rodney Crowell / 1981 / Warner Bros. ✦✦✦

Crowell plays down his performance on this album. Yes, he's a bit cool toward the material vocally on occasion, but the overall effect is raw, energetic, and natural, in the best garage-band tradition. A good mix of club rock & roll and country-rock, with, incidentally, his own renditions of "Till I Gain Control Again" and "Shame on the Moon." *—Tom Roland*

Street Language / 1986 / Columbia ✦✦

With *Street Language* Rodney Crowell created an awkward country-soul hybrid. Working with organist Booker T. Jones, Billy Joe Walker, and John Hiatt—who he also covers—Crowell doesn't quite realize his concept. Although the songs are usually quite good, the sound of the record is forced and hamfisted. At the very least, the album suggested that Crowell was at his best when he was at his most direct. And he became direct on his next album, *Diamonds & Dirt*. *—Thom Owens*

☆ **Diamonds & Dirt** / 1989 / Columbia/Legacy ✦✦✦✦✦

This reissue adds three previously unreleased bonus tracks to Crowell's watershed 1988 album, which produced five chart-topping country hits. The songs range from soft acoustic ballads to twangy, uptempo slices of neo-rockabilly. *Diamonds & Dirt* functions as a song cycle of romantic relationships, from the bliss of "I Couldn't Leave You If I Tried" to the regret of "I Didn't Know I Could Lose You." The three added tracks were recorded during a demo session for the album. The best of the bonus tracks, "Lies Don't Lie" and the Buck Owens-styled "I've Got My Pride But I've Got My Kids to Feed" would have fit in perfectly on the original album line-up. *—Mary Grady*

Keys to the Highway / 1989 / Columbia ✦✦✦

The success of Rodney Crowell's *Diamonds & Dirt* was a surprise, if only because Crowell had been making records for ten years with only modest sales. It was more country-oriented and less challenging than his previous recordings, but the album threw off a record-setting five number one country hits while remaining in the charts more than two years. *Keys to the Highway*, therefore, should have consolidated Crowell's status as a major country star; instead, it was a commercial disappointment from which he did not recover. Though Crowell had bowed to a traditional approach somewhat on *Diamonds & Dirt*, he remained essentially a stylist as interested in folk, rock, and R&B as he was in country. At the same time, emboldened by his success, Crowell apparently wanted to try to recover some of his critical standing, and he also seems to have been influenced by the death of his father to be true to himself. Momentum pushed the leadoff single, the slow, thoughtful folk-rock ballad "Many a Long and Lonesome Highway," into the country Top Five, but it was not what fans of *Diamonds & Dirt* were expecting, and despite the neo-Nashville sound of second single "If Looks Could Kill," which reached the country Top Ten, *Keys to the Highway* failed to make the country Top Ten or go gold. It's a much better album than that history suggests, however, carefully balanced between exercises in early rock & roll and rockabilly, country-soul, mainstream '60s-style rock, and even dyed-in-the-wool country. *Keys to the Highway* didn't have the songwriting depth of Crowell's early albums, but it was more substantial and more varied than *Diamonds & Dirt*, and if handled well, it might have been even more successful. Instead, it remains an album yet to be really discovered. *—William Ruhlmann*

The Rodney Crowell Collection / 1989 / Warner Bros. ✦✦✦✦✦

Rodney Crowell was one of the premier songwriters of the 1980s. Although his albums were not commercially successful, the high quality of Crowell's songs did not escape the attention of the music community. This compilation collects the best moments from his early albums, and most of these songs will sound instantly familiar to people who listened to country radio in the 1980s. Many of the songs featured on this album were made into hits, including "Queen of Hearts" (Juice Newton), "Stars on the Water" (Jimmy Buffett), "I Ain't Living Long Like This" (Waylon Jennings), and "Shame on the Moon" (Bob Seger). As is often the case when songwriters sing their own material, the songs carry more emotional weight under the care of the original author. Although Rodney Crowell does not have a powerful or distinctive voice, he has a genuine warmth in his delivery and a lyrical directness that gives his songs universal appeal. The finest tracks are the relationship songs, whether it's rising above the pain of heartbreak ("Ashes By Now") or finding romance in the simple pleasures of everyday life ("An American Dream"). Given the uneven nature of his solo albums, this album is a terrific introduction to a respected songwriter. *—Vik Iyengar*

Life Is Messy / May 12, 1992 / Columbia ✦✦✦✦

After the commercial fall-off of *Keys to the Highway*, Rodney Crowell took two-and-a-half years crafting his seventh album, *Life Is Messy*, in the interim going through a divorce from his wife Rosanne Cash. The most notable characteristic of *Life Is Messy* was that it marked a complete return to his original style. With nary a steel guitar or fiddle to be heard, and featuring top pop session musicians as well as a slew of pop guest stars (Linda Ronstadt, Don Henley, Steve Winwood, etc.), *Life Is Messy* wasn't really a country record at all. A couple of songs had a country-rock, honky tonk feel, but the dominant musical style was a pastiche of late-'50s/early-'60s pop. The title song was a somewhat abstract meditation on romantic discord and career disappointment that was followed by the equally despairing "I Hardly Know How to Be Myself," which actually had been co-written with Cash. These songs sounded so pained and deeply felt that some of the more uptempo songs came off as trivial, even if they made for a change of pace. But other songs came up to their standard without being quite so low in mood. "Alone But Not Alone" found the singer beginning to find his way, and "It's Not for Me to Judge" revealed the non-committal feelings one can have when emotional certainties are uprooted. Taken together, the songs on *Life Is Messy* made for a fascinating portrait of an artist at a personal and professional crossroad—but it didn't have much to do with commercial country music circa 1992, which is what it was primarily marketed as. After a few months, Columbia Records pulled the plug on promotion and parted ways with Crowell, who moved on to MCA Records. *—William Ruhlmann*

● **Greatest Hits** / 1993 / Columbia ✦✦✦✦✦

The music on *Greatest Hits* is taken from an era when Rodney Crowell actually had hits, including the number ones "I Couldn't Leave You If I Tried," "She's Crazy for Leavin'," and "After All This Time." Those songs and several more are collected on *Greatest Hits*, making it a fine introduction to the singer/songwriter. *—Stephen Thomas Erlewine*

Let the Picture Paint Itself / 1994 / MCA ✦✦✦

So much of Crowell's best work has been co-produced by MCA executive Tony Brown, it seemed inevitable he would wind up at MCA himself. This, his first release for his new label, emphasizes Crowell, the thoughtful songwriter, over Crowell the neo-honky tonk bandleader. It's a fair trade, but requires repeat listening to fully appreciate. *—Dan Cooper*

Jewel of the South / 1995 / MCA ✦✦✦

Crowell tries to stretch out a bit too much on *Jewel of the South*, but it remains a fine album, nonetheless. Featuring guest performances by the Mavericks' Raul Malo, Béla Fleck, Vince Gill, Kim Richey, and Billy Joe Walker Jr. among others, the album tries to do too many thing, but it does enough of them well enough to make it an entertaining listen. *—Thom Owens*

The Houston Kid / Feb. 13, 2001 / Sugar Hill ✦✦✦✦✦

At least impressionistically, this is a soundtrack to a documentary about the life of Rodney Crowell, who grew up in East Houston (the same neighborhood as the Ghetto Boys, but 25 years earlier), a rough and rumble neighborhood lying in the shadows of downtown Houston. It also happens to be the finest record Crowell has recorded since *Diamonds & Dirt*, and it's better than that one by a mile. After being tossed off by the major labels, it took a big-time indie like Sugar Hill—a label founded to showcase bluegrass artists (but also home to many fine singer/songwriters including Crowell's running mate and inspiration Guy Clark)—to release *The Houston Kid*. The album comes off as a song cycle; first, in "Telephone Road," the atmosphere is painted onto a backdrop. Showcasing the dark underbelly's finest sights, smells, sounds, and tastes, it's a country shuffle that moves ahead straightforwardly offering the stage for the creation of a rounder. On "The Rock of My Soul," Crowell tells all about the boy growing up in such circumstances. Fact and fiction are interwoven in a moving narrative that has plenty of twang and punch. Steel guitars and acoustic Fenders carry the melody along until the story reaches its nadir. "Why Don't We Talk About It" is Crowell's "accept me as I am because this is the real me" narrative. The band sounds like Rockpile playing country music. Truly, the backing vocals and the mix could be pure Dave Edmunds and Nick Lowe. Crowell has always hidden his brashness under a sheen of Nashville style, which is why his songs always sounded truer coming out of other people's mouths. But that's not the case here. It feels raw and immediate, full of something he's never revealed before. "I Wish It Would Rain" is a folk/country song so down and out that it could have been written by deceased writers Townes Van Zandt or Blaze Foley (both Texans and both friends of Crowell). It's a confessional. There is no braggadocio, no posturing. It's a song of regret but not remorse. The guitars are spare, just enough of a skeleton to hang the lyric on, and as he spills his tale of woe, the listener becomes as haunted as the protagonist is hunted. The craziest moment is Crowell's rewiring of Johnny Cash's "I Walk the Line." With an electric country blues shuffle (à la Merle Haggard), Crowell tells the story of how he first heard the song, and then Cash himself comes in on a completely rewritten narrative and chorus! Cash reportedly told Crowell he had a lot of nerve to rewrite his classic song, to which Crowell brazenly replied, "Yes sir." Though the record closes two songs later, "Banks of the Old Bandera" is where it could have—and maybe should have—the first song Crowell ever wrote. Author Tom Robbins told him he should write a bunch more songs and tour them in art galleries! Thank God he didn't. *The Houston Kid* offers listeners Rodney Crowell the performer in a way they've never heard before; the songwriter who has been been missing in Nashville for quite some time is back. *—Thom Jurek*

● **Small Worlds: The Crowell Collection 1978–1995** / 2002 / Raven ✦✦✦✦✦

Small Worlds: The Crowell Collection 1978-1995 epitomizes why Rodney Crowell is a perfect example of the "new" country, a combination of styles creating slick pop music that would have had a tougher time in the '60s garnering the country & western play many of these songs achieved. There are lots of names lending their talents on these 21 tracks: Vince Gill, Dr. John, Emmylou Harris, Nicolette Larson, Booker T. Jones, Hal Blaine, and Russ Kunkel, among many others. "Let the Picture Paint Itself" borrows more from Elton John/Bernie Taupin's "Country Comforts" than it does from Jeannie C. Riley's "Harper Valley P.T.A.," though you can hear nicks of both melodies in this song, which is very different from both those tunes, and Roy Orbison lives again on Crowell's duet with former wife Rosanne Cash on the title track, "It's Such a Small World," as well as on "I Couldn't Leave You if I Tried" and "If Looks Could Kill." "If Looks Could Kill" is certainly not the song by Heart, but when Crowell references the Beatles and quotes their lyrics in "Lovin' All Night," one has to consider if the inspiration is coming from the land of Hank Williams or the realm where the sisters Wilson ruled. These influences seem to be co-writing with Rodney Crowell when he reads a brilliant lyric like, "What kind of love hears you when you pray?" in "What Kind of Love," composed by Crowell with Will Jennings and Roy Orbison, additional voices courtesy of Linda Ronstadt and Don Henley. Emulating Orbison by having his voice go into that texture is a tribute to his hero indeed, and very present on this "first multi-label career overview." Tracks were culled from releases on Warner Bros., Columbia, and MCA, making for another excellent collection from Australia's Raven Records with 21 tracks, over 77 minutes of music, all on one disc. And like 7-N/BMG's meticulous re-releases, Raven's come spilling over with definite and comprehensive liner notes, 16 pages here, making this repackaged music all the more vital for longtime fans as well as a great primer for the uninitiated. *—Joe Viglione*

Fate's Right Hand / Jul. 29, 2003 / DMZ / Columbia ✦✦✦✦✦

Fate's Right Hand is one of those albums that couldn't have been written or recorded at any other time in Rodney Crowell's career. Two years after his monumentally acclaimed *The Houston Kid*, Crowell has laid out his autobiography in sight and sound. His track record of hits—written for himself as well as for other artists—could have just gone on untarnished. But *Fate's Right Hand* is the flip side of *The Houston Kid*. Whereas the latter album is about the past, the former is about the present, not only in the artist's life, but in the lives of those around him, and in the question of life itself: why is it worth living and how can suffering be alleviated? While many will think this is blasphemy, *Fate's Right Hand* is the finest record Crowell has issued since *Diamonds & Dirt* and may turn out to be the finest of his entire career—and that's saying a lot considering his first few albums. Crowell and Pete Coleman produced this outing and enlisted the help of friends old and new: Steuart Smith, Pat Buchanan, Michael Rhodes, Gillian Welch, David Rawlings, Richard Bennett, Béla Fleck, Carl Jackson, Marcia Ramirez, Charlie McCoy, Kim Richey, and Will Kimbrough, to name a few. From the opening track, "Still Learning How to Fly" (not the Daniel Lanois track; Crowell wrote the entire record himself), Crowell digs deep inside for the ugly stuff in order to uncover what shines beneath it. "Still Learning How to Fly" is a song about living in the moment because the moment is all you have. Crowell claims he wrote it based on conversations he had with a friend dying of terminal cancer; about what comes in the afterlife. With dobros, electric guitars, and acoustic six-strings wrapping around each other in a big, airy mix painted with a Hammond B-3, it is one of Crowell's transcendent moments. Remember *Diamonds & Dirt*? Yeah—like that. The title track ushers itself in around some warm, rounded bass tones, an organ, and maracas, as Crowell begins a series of seemingly unrelated non sequiturs. It's a pissed-off song that is as close to punk as Crowell will ever write. The notion of the transcendent is again present as it drenches Fleck's banjo riff in "Earthbound." Crowell makes the argument for living day-to-day in a world full of death and cynicism: where surrender is not an option until its time. All of this points to the most naked song Crowell has ever written: "Time to Go Inward," with both spoken word and sung refrains over fingerpicked acoustic guitars and electric dobros. It's a folk song about seeing; a country song about acceptance; a human song about the fear of what you might find when you look so deeply inside yourself. "The Man in Me" is about the negativity found there. It's a country-rock song that looks deeply into the mirror, doesn't like what it sees, and can't escape. Crowell wrote "Preaching to the Choir" as an answer to "Time to Go Inward," but it's another mirror he sees: it's a bluesy rock tune touched by country gospel and bluegrass, and it smokes. There are a couple of other thoughtful moments here, cuts where Crowell is trying to make sense rather than preach—which is what this album is all about: making sense of things rather than preaching about them. But it all comes to a head in "This Too Will Pass," a country song with a rockabilly shuffle that expresses the wisdom of those who believe and practice what Buddhism's Four Noble Truths and the 12 Steps of Alcoholics Anonymous teach (*no* claim is made or intended for Crowell being part of either): impermanence, suffering, and joy—and everything in between—are merely the stages of cyclical existence. Happiness *is* possible. There *is* a way out, but you have it discover it for yourself. *—Thom Jurek*

Bobbie Cryner

b. Sep. 13, 1961, Woodland, CA

Vocals / Country-Pop, Contemporary Country

Country-pop singer/songwriter Bobbie Cryner issued her honky tonk-flavored self-titled debut LP in 1993 to widespread critical acclaim, but when the record failed commercially, she was dropped by her label. Following a divorce and a battle with alcoholism, she returned in 1996 with *Girl of Your Dreams*, a smoother, more sophisticated effort spotlighting Cryner's gift for singing—and writing—ballads. *—Jason Ankeny*

● **Bobbie Cryner** / 1993 / Epic ✦✦✦✦

Girl of Your Dreams / Feb. 1996 / MCA Nashville ✦✦✦✦

When Bobbie Cryner introduced her sultry voice in 1993, critics lined up to commend her. In a field where most performers come sweet and innocent, whether they are or not, Cryner wasn't afraid to drip an adult sensuality. She doesn't exploit her inherent sexuality, but she doesn't attempt to hide her obvious carnality, either. Unfortunately, her debut proved too distinctive for the conformists who run country radio and never got a fair shake. *Girl of Your Dreams* is another strong offering by the bold redhead. She opens with Dusty Springfield's "Son of a Preacher Man," a gutsy move that works. No one else in country music would put across the line, "being good ain't always easy," with such believable forwardness; rather than apologizing, she sounds like she's celebrating her lack of virtue. She employs the same stunning directness when she asks, in another song, "If you want me to stay/just say so." Elsewhere, she confronts her own weaknesses while finding the inner fortitude to overcome them ("I Didn't Know My Own Strength"), and, in the album's most unusual song ("You'd Think He'd Know Me Better"), takes on the role of a mean-spirited spouse who treats her husband with dismissive spite then wonders why he's cheating on her. Cryner sounds too good to ignore and her rare qualities are her greatest strengths. *—Michael McCall*

Dick Curless

b. Mar. 17, 1932, Fort Fairfield, ME, **d.** May 25, 1995

Vocals / Bakersfield Sound, Truck Driving Country

Dick Curless was best known for singing truck-drivin' songs such as "Drag 'Em Off the Interstate, Sock It to 'Em J. P. Blues"; a tall man with an eye-patch and rich baritone voice, Curless was often called the "Baron of Country Music," after one of his popular songs, "The Baron." He was born in Fort Fairfield, ME, and started out professionally in 1948 with the Trail Blazers at a radio station in Ware, MA. While with the group, Curless was billed as the "Tumbleweed Kid." In 1951, he was drafted, and while stationed in the Far East frequently appeared on the Armed Forces Network, where he was known as "The Rice Paddy Ranger." He returned to Maine three years later and began singing in Bangor clubs. He got his big break when he won on *Arthur Godfrey Talent Scouts*. Afterward Curless began performing in Las Vegas and Hollywood; a record contract followed, but his budding career was interrupted by an illness.

He then returned to Maine, and soon was working with such stars as Gene Hooper and Lone Pine and Betty Cody. He finally reached the country charts in 1965 with the Top Five hit "A Tombstone Every Mile," followed by nine more chart hits including the highly successful "Six Times a Day (the Trains Came Down)." In 1970, Curless signed to Capitol and scored a Top 30 hit based on the classic "Wabash Cannonball," titled "Big Wheel Cannonball." The follow-up "Hard, Hard Traveling Man," (1970) made it to the Top 40. During his career, he had a total of 22 hits. During '60s, Curless was a member of the *Wheeling Jamboree*, and from 1966-1968 he toured with the Buck Owens show. During the '70s and '80s, Curless recorded infrequently, and eventually became a born-again Christian. He recorded an album in Norway in 1987, and by 1992 was a regular at the Cristy Lane Theater in Branson, MO. Curless died in 1995. *—Sandra Brennan*

Songs of the Open Country / 1958 / Tiffany ✦✦✦

Singing Just for Fun / 1959 / Tiffany ✦✦✦

I Love to Tell a Story / 1960 / Tiffany ✦✦✦

Hymns / 1965 / Tower ✦✦✦

A Tombstone Every Mile / 1965 / Tower ✦✦✦✦✦

A Devil Like Me Needs an Angel Like You / 1966 / Tower ✦✦✦

The Soul of Dick Curless / 1966 / Tower ✦✦✦

Travelin' Man / 1966 / Tower ✦✦✦✦

At Home with Dick Curless / 1967 / Tower ✦✦✦✦

All of Me Belongs to You / 1967 / Tower ✦✦✦✦

All of Me Belongs to You takes its name from Dick Curless' moderate 1967 hit, which was nonetheless one of the biggest of his career. Curless is associated with truck-driving songs and novelties, but *All of Me Belongs to You* concentrates on straight country with only a couple instances of humor. "A Good Job—Huntin' and Fishin'" will please fans of the latter, and a different kind of novelty is found in the bizarre distorted guitar runs on the otherwise straightforward "Try and Leave Me." The minor hits "The Baron" (which gave Curless one of his nicknames) and "House of Memories" round out this respectable if slight long-player. —*Greg Adams*

Ramblin' Country / 1967 / Tower ✦✦✦

Some of Dick Curless' most appealing songs are tall tales set to music, like *Ramblin' Country*'s "Tornado Tillie" and the minor hit "Big Foot." The latter, about a Paul Bunyan-like character who saves his town from a flood, matches Curless' flair for storytelling with wryly humorous and inventive material, and makes one wonder why he never saw greater success. Curless also deals in conventional country music, like the mournful "Life Goes On," and, in fact, most of *Ramblin' Country* falls into that category. But the story songs are the ones that really stand out, and Curless deserves praise for preserving the narrative tradition in country music and making prominent use of his acoustic guitar (check out *Ramblin' Country*'s guitar instrumental, "Mumble Boogie," for evidence of his ability). —*Greg Adams*

The Long Lonesome Road / 1968 / Tower ✦✦✦

The Wild Side of Town / 1968 / Tower ✦✦✦✦

Hard Hard Traveling Man / 1970 / Capitol ✦✦✦✦✦

Doggin' It / 1971 / Capitol ✦✦✦✦

Comin' on Country / 1971 / Capitol ✦✦✦✦✦

Stonin' Around / 1972 / Capitol ✦✦✦

A Tombstone Every Mile / 1973 / Capitol ✦✦✦✦✦

Live at the Wheeling Truck Driver's Jamboree / 1973 / Capitol ✦✦✦✦

The Last Blues Song / 1973 / Capitol ✦✦✦

Traveling Through / 1995 / Rounder ✦✦✦✦✦

Traveling Through was the last record Dick Curless ever made, and it's a winner. Recorded in 1994, in Brookfield, MA, the album is a rootsy, stripped-down collection of country, blues and gospel tunes. Throughout the album, Curless is in fine voice, wrenching out emotion from each of the songs. —*Stephen Thomas Erlewine*

A Tombstone Every Mile / Mar. 19, 1996 / Bear Family ✦✦✦✦✦

For a man who was regarded as a cult artist for most of his career, Dick Curless was certainly able to surround himself with the cream of the crop when it came to producers and sidemen, among whom are listed Buck Owens, Tommy Collins, James Burton, Ralph Mooney, Harold Bradley, Pete Drake, David Duke (not that one), and a slew of others. *Tombstone Every Mile*, the name of Curless' first bona fide hit in 1964, is a Bear Family collection that compiles 191 tracks over seven CDs. It is an exhaustive collection of everything Curless recorded for Tower, Event, Alagash, Standard, and Tiffany from 1950 through 1969. He signed with Capitol in 1970, and there's another box covering that period. Curless recorded until finishing his last album literally days before his death in 1995. While this set documents the singer/songwriter's first forays into Ernest Tubb-style honky tonk, it spends a great deal of time displaying his roots in the Bakersfield sound pioneered by Buck Owens, Merle Haggard, and others and his transition into making "truck driver's music"—mostly because his cult was made of truckers, not because he wrote for them exclusively. Virtually every kind of country music is documented here, from honky tonk barnburners to gospel tunes to love ballads to novelty tunes to cowboy songs and classic ballads. There are train songs and pain songs, truck songs and mama songs. His readings of tunes by Lefty Frizzell, Red Simpson, Merle Travis, Don Gibson, Billy Mize, Buck Owens, Johnny Cash, Haggard, Collins, public domain tunes such as "Streets of Laredo," and his own early efforts established him as a great stylist and singer as well as a keen interpreter—his version of Cash's "I Walk the Line" is only eclipsed by the master's. Curless' repertoire covered the entire history of the music as it came down from the Carter Family. There are over a dozen complementary unreleased masters here, making this a must for the country collector, and to have the material organized in such painstaking chronologically recorded fashion adds depth and dimension to Curless' development as an artist. Ultimately, if you are at all a fan, this set and his final album, *Traveling Through* on the Rounder label, are the things to have. The Capitol period is good, it's just not revelatory like this stuff is. —*Thom Jurek*

★ **Drag 'Em off the Interstate, Sock It to 'Em: The Hits of Dick Curless** / May 19, 1998 / Razor & Tie ✦✦✦✦✦

Dick Curless cut an imposing figure. Tall, lanky, and weathered, with a battered cowboy hat and an eye patch slung over his right eye, Curless possessed a booming baritone voice so powerful, he could seem like the toughest singer in country during the '60s and '70s. Perhaps that's why he was so perfectly suited for truck driving country—he sounded and

looked like a trucker. But Curless couldn't be reduced to an equation as simple as that, and he was one of the most interesting figures in '60s/early-'70s country music, since he was producing music that was traditionalist yet modern, music that was more versatile than it seemed on the surface, touching on folk ballads, Western swing, blues, and even rock. Best of all, this pure country singer was from Maine, not the South, which may be the reason he was so individual: He existed outside of the country mainstream, so he had his own distinctive voice in his words and music, which can be best heard on Razor & Tie's excellent 1998 collection, *Drag 'Em off the Interstate, Sock It to 'Em: The Hits of Dick Curless*. He had enough depth to his music to make his two Bear Family boxes compelling—and that's where his surprising sensitive side is revealed—but that's far too much information for an introduction. Here, his work is boiled down to 16 charting hits, a couple of lesser-known singles and a couple of excerpts from his great 1973 album *Live at the Wheeling Truck Drivers Jamboree*. Curless started out with songs of the road and songs of main, coming out of folk tradition but with a Johnny Cash spin, with the wonderfully ominous "A Tombstone Every Mile" making him a star and a favorite with truck drivers. This side of Curless—including other great hits like "Travelin' Man," "Nine Pound Hammer," "Tater Raisin' Man," "Bury the Bottle With Me," and "The Baron"—accounts for the first half of the disc, with the second given over to wild, woolly songs of the road, truck stops, drink, loose women, and heartache. Topically, it's all over the place and the music is, too, as he croons ballads and swing tunes, rocks out on the lewd "Chick Inspector (That's Where My Money Goes)," and acts out as the bartender on "Loser's Cocktail," one of the greatest unheralded barroom songs in country history. Though this roughly divides into two halves, both serve up some of the finest hardcore country of the '60s and early '70s—the kind that true connoisseurs adore. And, for those listeners, Curless is a necessary listen, with this standing as the best overview and summary of his extraordinary music. —*Stephen Thomas Erlewine*

Hard Hard Traveling Man / Sep. 12, 2000 / Bear Family ✦✦✦✦✦

Sonny Curtis

b. May 9, 1937, Meadow, TX

Guitar, Songwriter, Vocals / Traditional Country, Nashville Sound/Countrypolitan

Sonny Curtis was involved in country music for over 40 years, composing songs recorded by numerous stars, among them the Everly Brothers, Hank Williams Jr., and even Bing Crosby. He was born and raised near Lubbock, Texas, and began performing as a teen on local radio, playing fiddle on the popular *Buddy and Bob* show, featuring an up-and-coming Buddy Holly. Waylon Jennings was also a DJ at the station, and together they all performed at the town movie theater during intermissions. Curtis joined Holly's band, the Three Tunes, in 1956 as a fiddler, guitar player and back-up singer; when the group went to Nashville to record with famed producer Owen Bradley, they recorded one of Curtis's songs, "Rock Around with Ollie Vee." Eventually Curtis amicably left Holly and began touring with Slim Whitman before making his solo debut in 1958 with the single "Wrong Again."

In 1959, after Holly's tragic death, his band, the Crickets, asked Curtis to become their lead guitarist and singer. He was drafted in 1960 and stationed in Fort Ord, where he penned the song "Walk Right Back," a major hit for the Everly Brothers in 1961 later popularized by Andy Williams, Perry Como and Anne Murray. Despite a string of mid-range hits including "My Way of Life," "Atlanta Georgia Stray," and "The Straight Life," Curtis had his greatest success as a songwriter. One of his best known and most recorded songs was "I Fought the Law," which has been done by artists like the Bobby Fuller Four, the Clash and Lou Reed. He also wrote the theme song for *the Mary Tyler Moore Show*, "Love Is All Around," which became a Top 30 hit on the country charts. In the early '90s, Curtis also wrote the theme song to the TV show *Evening Shade*.

In the early '80s, he and two former Crickets, Joe B. Maudlin and Jerry Allison, reunited and performed with Waylon Jennings' show. He had a Top 15 single with "Good Ole' Girls" for Elektra in 1981, followed by "Married Women," which made it to the Top 40. He made his final chart entry in 1986 with the minor hit "Now I've Got a Heart of Gold." Curtis also made a name for himself as a commercial jingle singer/songwriter, and continued writing country songs for artists such as Keith Whitley, Ricky Skaggs, and John Schneider. In 1991 he was inducted into the Songwriters Hall of Fame by the Nashville Songwriters Association International. —*Sandra Brennan*

Beatle Hits Flamenco Style Guitar / 1964 / Imperial ✦✦

● **First of Sonny Curtis** / 1968 / Viva ✦✦

The Sonny Curtis Style / 1969 / Elektra ✦✦✦

Love Is All Around / 1980 / Elektra ✦✦✦

Curtis has been performing since the '50s and writing nearly as long. This album reprises two of the songs he wrote that were hits for someone else. Additionally, the title song was the theme for the *Mary Tyler Moore Show* which Curtis wrote (he also sang it the first season). But the real gem on this record is Curtis' rebuttal in song to the film *the Buddy Holly Story*. Curtis knew, and played with Buddy, long before his rise to stardom, and as he says in the song, this is his attempt to set straight some things that weren't right in the film. —*Jim Worbois*

Rollin' / 1981 / Elektra ✦✦✦

Spectrum / 1987 / Nightlite ✦✦

Billy Ray Cyrus

b. Aug. 25, 1961, Flatwoods, KY

Vocals, Guitar / Contemporary Country

Billy Ray Cyrus will forever be known for the catchy, lightweight single "Achy, Breaky Heart," which became a line-dancing anthem upon its 1992 release. "Achy, Breaky Heart" made Cyrus famous, but it also proved to be his undoing. No matter how he tried, he could not escape the song, nor could he replicate the success. Cyrus' music was never particularly innovative—it owed as much to the country-rock of the Eagles as it did to the new traditionalism of George Strait and the new country of Clint Black and Garth Brooks—but his musical worth became irrelevant in the wake of the success of "Achy, Breaky Heart," and its accompanying album, *Some Gave All*. The album became a crossover success after the single became a hit, spending 17 weeks on the top of the album charts. Part of Cyrus' success was due to his handsome, hunky good looks, and part of it was due to the catchiness of "Achy, Breaky Heart." However, both his good looks and the single were soon forgotten, and just two years after *Some Gave All* ruled the charts, Cyrus virtually disappeared from both the pop and country charts and became part of the long history one-hit wonders.

Enamored of baseball, Cyrus intended to become another Johnny Bench as he grew up in Flatwoods, KY. While attending Georgetown College on a baseball scholarship, he bought a guitar and decided immediately that athletics wasn't the proper direction for his life. Instead, he formed a band called Sly Dog with his brother and gave himself a ten-month deadline for finding a place to play. One week prior to that cutoff date, the group went to work as the house band for a club in Ironton, OH, where they remained for two years. When a 1984 fire destroyed the bar—and Cyrus' equipment—he moved to Los Angeles to pursue his career. Eventually, he decided to return to Kentucky and commuted regularly from there to Nashville in search of a record deal. *Grand Ole Opry* star Del Reeves got Mercury Records to take a look, and division head Harold Shedd signed him in the summer of 1990. When his first album came out in mid-1992, Cyrus—with his good looks, sculpted body, and groundbreaking single "Achy, Breaky Heart"—became an instant groundbreaking sensation. Spending five weeks at the top of the country charts, "Achy, Breaky Heart" made his debut album, *Some Gave All*, a blockbuster success. By the time it fell off the charts, it had sold over nine million copies and spent 17 weeks on the top of the pop charts.

Despite his attempts, Cyrus wasn't able to replicate the success of *Some Gave All*. He quickly followed the album with *It Won't Be the Last* in the summer of 1993. Initially, the album sold well, entering the pop charts at number three, but it fell far short of expectations by only reaching platinum status. *Storm in the Heartland*, delivered in the fall of 1994, managed to go gold, even though it was ignored by country radio. However, by the time it finished its chart run, Cyrus had slipped from the public's eye. When he returned with the harder-edged, introspective *Trail of Tears* in 1996, his audience had virtually disappeared—the album only spent four weeks on the charts and didn't even go gold. *Shot Full of Love* followed in 1998 and *Southern Rain* was issued two years later. In March 2001, Cyrus hit TV screens in the role of a country doctor moved to Manhattan in the sitcom *Doc*. *—Tom Roland & Stephen Thomas Erlewine*

Some Gave All / 1992 / Mercury ✦✦✦✦

Some Gave All became the first debut album by a country artist to enter the pop charts at number one (it hit number one on the country charts as well). The album's sales were fueled by the breakout single "Achy, Breaky Heart," which offered Southern-fried Rolling Stones rhythms and a goofy chorus with a hook so big it demanded a reaction. Not one to eschew the obvious, Cyrus pumped his songs full of as much rock & roll as the market would bear, so songs like "Could've Been Me" and "Never Thought I'd Fall in Love with You" appealed to young fans who had just discovered the possibilities (both musical and sexual) of country music. *—Brian Mansfield*

It Won't Be the Last / Jun. 22, 1993 / Mercury ✦✦

Cyrus' follow-up to his smash debut, *Some Gave All*, offers more of the same—country injected with a healthy dose of rock & roll. It won't win him any new fans, but those who loved *Some Gave All* will enjoy *It Won't Be the Last*. *—AMG*

Storm in the Heartland / 1994 / Mercury ✦✦✦

Although it didn't win him any new fans, *Storm in the Heartland* delivered what Billy Ray Cyrus' fans wanted to hear—good-humored rockers and powerful ballads. In fact, it

was a stronger, more assured effort than *It Won't Be the Last*, offering a catchier batch of songs, even though it doesn't have the goofy charm of *Some Gave All*. *—Stephen Thomas Erlewine*

Trail of Tears / 1996 / Mercury ✦✦✦✦

Trail of Tears is the most personal and most accomplished album Billy Ray Cyrus has recorded to date. Cyrus' elaborates his pop-oriented country with some rootsy production flourishes—the album sounds edgier and grittier than any of his previous records. Furthermore, Cyrus delivers both his originals and the covers with conviction, far more conviction than could have been believed possible from his first two albums. In fact, *Trail of Tears* suggests that he may be able to carve out a successful career for himself, after all. *—Thom Owens*

● The Best of Billy Ray Cyrus: Cover To Cover / Jun. 24, 1997 / Mercury ✦✦✦✦

Billy Ray Cyrus recorded only four albums before releasing *The Best of Billy Ray Cyrus*, which indicates his status as a one-hit wonder. "Achy, Breaky Heart" was the hit that made his career, but it also ruined it, since its jokey refrain and his good looks meant that no one took him seriously. There's not much evidence on *The Best of Billy Ray Cyrus* that those critics were wrong, but there are more enjoyable songs here than you might expect, especially since it whittles all four albums down to just the highlights. For every casual fan, this is the one Cyrus disc they'll want to own, even if *Some Gave All* functions fairly well as an album itself. *—Thom Owens*

Shot Full of Love / Nov. 3, 1998 / Mercury ✦✦✦

Southern Rain / Oct. 17, 2000 / Monument ✦✦

Hooking up with Dixie Chicks producer Blake Chancey and with producer Dann Huff, Billy Ray Cyrus made a label debut that showed off his country-rock abilities well. The single, "You Won't Be Lonely Now," which was rising in the country Top 40 and the pop charts at the time of the album's release, properly displayed the artist's sense of determination against adversity, cloaked in the terms of a love song. Similarly, the title song (co-written by Cyrus), which followed on the album, spoke of perseverance despite lean times. The rest of the record was more varied, including heartfelt ballads ("I Will," "Everywhere I Wanna Be") and uptempo novelties ("Burn Down the Trailer Park," "Hey Elvis"), but the point had been made. Chancey and Huff helped Cyrus pick material that suited his country-rock style. "Southern Rain," for example, sounded like Bob Dylan's "Knockin' on Heaven's Door" as it might sound played by Lynyrd Skynyrd, while "Love You Back" recalled Little Feat's "Willin'." The result was a sturdy collection of average country songs effectively performed by a minor country talent. All of which was fine, unless you were hoping for an album that measured up to Cyrus' early sales figures, which, of course, Monument was. *—William Ruhlmann*

20th Century Masters—The Millennium Collection: The Best of Billy Ray Cyrus / Mar. 25, 2003 / Universal ✦✦✦✦

To some, Billy Ray Cyrus is merely a one-hit wonder, scoring nothing of note after "Achy, Breaky Heart" ruled the airwaves. That, of course, is not true, and he continued to have hits throughout the '90s—nothing as big as "Achy, Breaky Heart," to be sure, but he had 14 other charting country singles that decade before leaving Mercury. His installment of *20th Century Masters—The Millennium Collection* doesn't have all those hits, but neither did the previous Cyrus collection, 1997's *The Best of Billy Ray Cyrus: Cover to Cover*. In fact, even though this has only ten songs compared to that collection's 12, this has more hits. Every track here was a hit, and there's not a major tune missing, which makes this a far better bargain than the previous Cyrus collection, and one that's not likely to be bettered anytime soon. *—Stephen Thomas Erlewine*

Pappy Daily (Harold W. Daily)

b. Feb. 8, 1902, Yoakum, TX, **d.** Dec. 5, 1987, Houston, TX

Producer / Traditional Country, Honky Tonk, Nashville Sound/Countrypolitan

Pappy Daily was one of the most important record executives and producers of the post-war era. He didn't have a distinctive production style, nor was he much of a musician, yet he had an ear for talent and was instrumental in cultivating the careers of George Jones and Gene Pitney, among others. Along with his partner, Jack Starnes, Daily established Starday Records, which was one of the most successful Texas independent labels of the '50s. During the '60s, he founded Musicor with Art Talmadge. Throughout both labels, Daily's fortunes were forever tied to those of Jones. Daily's career was strong as long as he had an association with Jones, and when the singer left the producer and Musicor in 1971 for Billy Sherrill and Epic Records, Musicor and Daily quickly faded from view.

After returning from fighting in the Marine Corps during World War I, Daily (born Harold W. Daily) was voted the Commander of the American Legion during 1931 and 1932. Following his service in the American Legion, he began working in the country music industry in the early '30s, but he didn't have much of an impact until 1953, when he founded Starday Records with his partner, Starnes. Based in Beaumont, TX, all of Starday's records were originally made at Starnes' house. Early in 1954, the label had its first hit, when their fourth single, Arlie Duff's "You All Come," climbed to number seven. The following year, Starday signed a young singer named George Jones, whose "Why Baby Why" reached number four in the fall of the year.

Shortly before Jones joined the label, Starnes left Starday and was replaced by Don Pierce. Daily and Pierce concentrated on cultivating the career of Jones, and by 1957, Mercury Records was interested in the singer and the duo's production talents. That year, Jones signed to Mercury, and the production team of Daily and Pierce joined the label; their agreement allowed them to continue to run Starday. For the next four years, they worked with Mercury, producing a respectable string of hits that were mostly by Jones. During this time, Daily began a new label called D, which concentrated on releasing music by local Texas artists. Over the next few years, D had a few minor hit singles, including songs by Claude Gray, James O'Gwynn, and Eddie Noack.

In late 1961, Daily and Pierce ended their relationship and split Starday's assets between the two of them. Pierce took the label itself, while Daily received the publishing division; both received half of the label's master recordings and catalog. At the end of the year, Daily moved from Starday and Mercury to United Artists, where he became the label's country & western director. Jones, who had come to consider Daily as a father figure and professional advisor, followed him to the label. While at United Artists, Jones continued to have a number of Top Ten hits, but Daily didn't cultivate the careers of many other artists. A notable exception was Melba Montgomery, whom he signed upon George's insistence.

Daily ended his relationship with United Artists in 1965, the same year he folded D Records. He turned his attention to Musicor, the label he founded with Talmadge in 1961. Musicor was a bigger venture than either Starday or D, signing established artists like Jones, Floyd Tillman, and Pitney. Though Daily and Talmadge had set their goals high, they weren't equipped to run the label in any sensible fashion and flooded the market with records, which usually competed with other Musicor releases. Nevertheless, Jones had a number of hits during that time, as did Pitney, but they weren't able to make any of the label's other artists into stars. By 1971, Pitney was no longer actively recording, and Jones had grown frustrated with his Musicor contract, deciding that he wanted to sign to Epic Records. After some prolonged negotiations, Jones left the label that year, leaving Musicor without a star. Daily struggled on with Musicor for the next few years, reissuing a lot of Jones material and licensing other Jones tracks to RCA. By the mid-'70s, Daily quietly retired from the music industry, and Musicor disappeared along with him. *—Stephen Thomas Erlewine*

Vernon Dalhart (Marion Try Slaughter)

b. Apr. 6, 1883, Jefferson, TX, **d.** Sep. 14, 1948, Bridgeport, CN

Vocals / Old-Timey, Traditional Country, Cowboy

Vernon Dalhart came to country music from outside the tradition, becoming a national star in the years just before more indigenous kinds of country music found their place in the machinery of the music industry. A 1924 recording by Dalhart became country music's first million-selling record; pairing a train song ("Wreck of the Old 97") with a sentimental ballad ("The Prisoner's Song"), the release set patterns for two key genres of early country music on record. Dalhart was born Marion Try Slaughter in Jefferson, TX; the stage name Vernon Dalhart, like Conway Twitty, was a combination of the names of two Texas towns. Dalhart's grandfather was a rancher, a former Confederate soldier who became a member of the Ku Klux Klan; he was killed in a knife fight while Dalhart was a boy. Though Dalhart's classical-music background is often emphasized in accounts of his life, he did actually work for a time as a cowboy while in his teens. Dalhart sang at community gatherings, where he also played the harmonica and the jew's-harp. He studied music at the Dallas Conservatory, married, and moved to New York in 1910. Dreaming of an operatic career, he worked in a music store and earned extra cash singing for

funerals. He appeared in his first opera two years later and in 1913 appeared in Puccini's *Madame Butterfly* and Gilbert & Sullivan's *H.M.S. Pinafore*. Light opera and operetta remained his specialties.

Dalhart was a keen observer of the early power of the phonograph industry and jumped at the chance to record. His first releases, made around 1916, fell into various pop styles; one of them, "Can't You Heah Me Callin', Caroline," was a blackface minstrel song, a genre that never disappeared completely from his repertoire. Dalhart was an eclectic urban singer who recorded whatever might sell: comic songs (sometimes featuring the sprightly tenor banjo of John Cali), Hawaiian pieces, sentimental numbers, and much more. When he turned to country music it may have been simply a way of capitalizing on a song type that his competitors had neglected, but he immediately showed a flair for story songs. He tightened his operatic voice slightly, producing a distinctive, reedy vibrato that signaled his rural roots but appealed to mainstream record buyers. After "The Wreck of the Old 97" became a smash hit, Dalhart was a national star of sorts—he was never a really recognizable figure, but he could sell records in the millions.

During the '20s and '30s, he used over 100 pseudonyms to record over 5,000 78 rpm singles for a variety of labels; among the names he adopted were Frank Evans, Vernon Dale, Tobe Little, Bob White, Hugh Lattimer, Sid Turner, and Al Craver. Dalhart scored successes with a series of topical songs based on current events such as the death of a Kentucky spelunker and the notorious Scopes trial, selling enough copies to firmly establish the Columbia label's 15,000-numbered country series as a force in the industry. He was often teamed with guitarist and songwriter Carson Robison, who composed some of his material and went on to a long career of his own. Dalhart continued on with recording through the late '30s, at which time his rather formal interpretation of down-home music fell out of favor as record buyers became more familiar with "authentic" country singers such as the Carter Family and turned to hip new genres such as Western swing.

Dalhart, despite persistent efforts to interest record labels in his work, was largely forgotten later in life. In the 1940s he eked out a living giving voice lessons and working as a night watchman in Bridgeport, CT, realizing no royalties from his earlier million-sellers. He died of heart failure in 1948. One of the achievements of the first stirrings of country music scholarship in the 1960s and 1970s was a new appreciation of his importance, and in 1981 Dalhart's contribution was finally given its due recognition when he was inducted into the Country Music Hall of Fame. *—James Manheim*

Vernon Dalhart (First Recorded Railroad Songs) / 1978 / Mark 56 ✦✦✦✦

● **Ballads & Railroad Songs** / 1980 / Old Homestead ✦✦✦✦✦

Wreck of the Old 97 / 1985 / Old Homestead ✦✦✦✦✦

Inducted into the Hall of Fame, 1981 / Nov. 9, 1999 / King ✦✦✦✦

At the time of its release in the fall of 1999 as part of a series devoted to members of the Country Music Hall of Fame, this ten-song, discount-priced album was the only collection in print in the U.S. devoted to 1920s country star Vernon Dalhart. Dalhart was an opera singer who found pop success in his early '40s as a singer of what was then called hillbilly music. In 1925, he hooked up with Victor Records for the single "The Prisoner's Song"/"The Wreck of the Old 97" (he also recorded under pseudonyms for many other labels). It became the biggest hit of the year and reportedly is second only to Bing Crosby's "White Christmas" as the best-selling record of the first half of the 20th century in the U.S. The two songs set a pattern Dalhart followed for the next few years; they were sad story songs of people in tragic circumstances. With his clearly articulated yet slightly accented voice (he was from Texas) singing over simple guitar or piano accompaniment, plus occasional whistling and jew's-harp among other spare effects, Dalhart became the king of sentimental and maudlin music, singing about "The Death of Floyd Collins" (in a cave collapse), "The Governor's Pardon" (which comes just in time to save a condemned man), "The Wreck of the Shenandoah" (a dirigible), and "A Memory That Time Cannot Erase" (for a deceased loved one), and declaring "There's a New Star in Heaven To-Night" (recently deceased silent-film star Rudolf Valentino). All of these are found on this collection, along with a few more pleasant tunes that were also hits and a cover of the 1910 song "Casey Jones" (about a train wreck). On several tracks, Dalhart is accompanied by his partner Carson Robison, who wrote a number of the songs. Unusual for recordings of this vintage, no noise-reduction process has been employed, and while that preserves the dynamic range, it also means that these are very noisy tracks. Listening to the album is exactly like playing a bunch of original 78s on a record player, with their excessive hiss and crackles. Still, this is a reasonably priced collection of some of the biggest hits by one of the biggest hitmakers of the second half of the 1920s and a clear influence on country progenitors like Jimmie Rodgers. *—William Ruhlmann*

On the Lighter Side / Old Homestead ✦✦✦

That Good Old Country Town, Vol. 4 / Old Homestead ✦✦✦✦

Lacy J. Dalton (Jill Byrem)

b. Oct. 13, 1948, Bloomsburg, PA

Guitar, Vocals / Country-Pop, Neo-Traditionalist Country, Contemporary Country

Eclectic and bluesy, Lacy J. Dalton was one of the most distinctive female country singers of the '80s, landing a few hits on the strength of her gritty, nuanced vocals. Dalton was born Jill Byrem in Bloomsburg, PA, in 1948, and grew up in a highly musical family; her first loves were folkies like Bob Dylan and Joan Baez, but she also soaked up country music through her father. She briefly attended Brigham Young University, but dropped out and drifted around the country for a time; she eventually went to Los Angeles, then migrated to Santa Cruz, where she performed as a protest-oriented folksinger. During the late '60s, she sang with a Bay Area psychedelic rock band called Office; she also became Jill Croston when she married the group's manager, though, sadly, he died in a swimming pool accident.

She went on to reinvent herself as a country performer, adopting the stage name Lacy J. Dalton, and landed a deal with CBS when producer Billy Sherrill heard her demo tape in 1979. Her Top 20 debut single, "Crazy Blue Eyes," helped her win the CMA's Best New Artist Award, and she scored an impressive run of hits over the next three years, highlighted by "Hard Times," "Tennessee Waltz," "Hillbilly Girl With the Blues," the number-two smash "Takin' It Easy," "16th Avenue," and "Everybody Makes Mistakes" (all but "Tennessee Waltz" made the Top Ten). Dalton's albums also received strong reviews for their adventurous, borderless taste in material, particularly her self-titled debut. A 1983 cover of Roy Orbison's "Dream Baby (How Long Must I Dream)" was her final Top Ten entry, but she continued to record for CBS through 1987; part of her commercial slide was due to her ambitious stylistic shifts, as she devoted attention to rock-oriented material (1986's *Highway Diner*, whose "Working Class Man" was a decent-sized hit), blues, and bluegrass. She subsequently departed for Capitol, where she recorded four albums through 1992. In 1999, she assembled the *Wild Horse Crossing* compilation, which featured several new tracks of her own and was released by her own Let 'Em Run foundation, which worked to preserve the wild horses of the west. *—Steve Huey*

Jill Croston / 1978 / Harbor ◆◆

Lacy J. Dalton / 1979 / Columbia ◆◆◆

Hard Times / 1980 / Columbia ◆◆◆

Takin' It Easy / 1981 / Columbia ◆◆◆

16th Avenue / Mar. 1982 / Columbia ◆◆◆◆

Dream Baby / 1983 / Columbia ◆◆◆◆

● **Greatest Hits** / 1983 / Columbia ◆◆◆◆◆

Dalton's best songs weren't always her hits, but *Greatest Hits* is still a good sampler, including "Crazy Blue Eyes," her first hit; "Hard Times"; remakes of "Tennessee Waltz" and "Dream Baby"; and the music-biz anthem "16th Avenue." *—Brian Mansfield*

Can't Run Away From Your Heart / 1985 / Columbia ◆◆◆

Highway Diner / 1986 / Columbia ◆◆◆

I Love Country / 1986 / Columbia ◆◆◆

Blue-Eyed Blues / 1987 / Columbia ◆◆◆

Survivor / 1989 / Capitol ◆◆

Lacy J. / Apr. 9, 1990 / Capitol ◆◆◆

Crazy Love / 1991 / Capitol ◆◆◆

The title song is by Van Morrison, and if Dalton is not the vocalist Morrison is, she still may be the best female soul singer country offers, and she's a better one than Michael Bolton, whose "Walk Away" she also covers. *Crazy Love* is an appropriate title because Dalton seems genuinely bewildered by the vagaries of the emotion—why her lover loves her ("Crazy Love"), why he leaves her ("Forever in My Heart"), and why sometimes neither marriage nor divorce makes sense. But she's a great singer, not God. *—Brian Mansfield*

Chains on the Wind / Apr. 13, 1992 / Liberty ◆◆

The Best of Lacy J. Dalton / Mar. 29, 1993 / Liberty ◆◆◆◆◆

The Best of Lacy J. Dalton collects many of the highlights from Dalton's late-'80s and early-'90s albums for Liberty Records. It's a good sampler of Dalton's sound and offers a nice introduction to her work. *—Stephen Thomas Erlewine*

Pure Country / Aug. 25, 1998 / Sony ◆◆◆◆

Sony Special Products' *Pure Country* is an effective sampler of Lacy J. Dalton's country-pop work for Columbia Records in the '70s and '80s. In fact, in many ways it works as a hits compilation, since seven of the featured songs—"Takin' It Easy," "Hillbilly Girl With the Blues," "Hard Times," "Whisper," "Everybody Makes Mistakes," "Dream Baby (How Long Must I Dream)," "16th Avenue"—were Top Ten country hits, while the remaining three ("Slow Down," "Size Seven Round (Made of Gold)," "Working Class Man") charted in the Top 20. Because of that, *Pure Country* is more than just a good bargain for a budget-line collection—it's a good bargain in general. *—Stephen Thomas Erlewine*

Anthology / May 16, 2000 / Renaissance ◆◆◆◆

Anthology collects Lacy J. Dalton's biggest hits and most important tracks, including "Crazy Blue Eyes," "Hillbilly Girl With the Blues," "16th Avenue," "Working Class Man," and "Don't Fall in Love With Me." There are 15 other tracks, making this collection the most complete overview of Dalton's gritty yet sensual work available. *—Heather Phares*

Country Classics / May 29, 2001 / EMI ◆◆◆◆◆

Davis Daniel (Robert Andrykowski)

b. Mar. 1, 1961, Arlington Heights, IL

Vocals / Contemporary Country, Singer/Songwriter

Inspired by the songs of late country singer/songwriter Keith Whitley, Davis Daniel (born Robert Andrykowski) continues to build on his own legacy as a top-notch performer. One

of nine children born to impoverished parents in Arlington Heights, IL, he moved to Nebraska as a youngster. Poverty continued to plague his family, who were forced to live in a three-room shack without heat. Moving with his mother and siblings to Denver, at the age of 14, following his father's death, Daniel continued to be drawn to music. Before his 18th birthday, he had begun performing in Denver nightclubs. Moving to Nashville, in the late '80s, Daniel spent several years honing his craft at songwriter showcases before signing his first record contract. His debut album, *Fighting Fire With Fire*, released in 1991 on Mercury/Polygram, yielded three Top Ten hits—"Picture Me," "Still Got a Crush on You," and the title track—and a Top Five smash, "For Crying Out Loud." He followed with an equally impressive album, *Undeniable*, in 1993. *People* magazine called him "country's most plaintive voice since Eddy Arnold."

Daniel's subsequent career, however, was an uphill battle. Moved to Polygram's Polydor subsidiary, he had to wait three years for his third album, *Davis Daniel*, to be released in 1994. By then, the label was struggling financially and unable to adequately promote the album. Transferred to A&M after Polydor declared bankruptcy in early 1996, he released his first album for the label in August 1996, *I Know a Place*. Daniel's problems were far from over. One week after he released a single, "I'm Not Listening Anymore," A&M announced that it was folding. Beginning in the late '90s, Daniel resided in Atlanta, GA. *—Craig Harris*

Fighting Fire With Fire / 1991 / Mercury ◆◆◆

Davis Daniel / 1994 / Polydor ◆◆◆

In the crowded field of young, good-looking country singers, add Davis Daniel's name to the list of new hopefuls. He debuts here with a solid ten-song outing chock-full of radio-ready country-lite tunes, any one of which could easily fit a "young country" station's play list. With top-notch writing contributions from Paul Overstreet ("She Could Make a Freight Train Take a Dirt Road"), George McCorkle ("William and Mary"), and Mark Sherrill ("Somebody's Gonna Lose"), there's certainly no shortage of well-crafted Nashville ready-mades aboard, and the session playing is equally modern country, assembly-line perfect. Daniel, for his part, contributes two fine songwriting efforts, "Out Here Sits the King" and "Tyler," and while his looks outweigh the relative thinness of his voice, there's enough good stuff here to make you think that he might develop into something more than a one-shot artist. If you heard music this good in a bar, you'd be thrilled, and you'd buy his CD or tape right off the bandstand. *—Cub Koda*

Undeniable / 1994 / Mercury ◆◆◆

● **I Know a Place** / Jun. 18, 1996 / A&M ◆◆◆◆

Daniel Davis' third album, *I Know A Place*, is a breakthrough. For the first time, he's been able to convey the raw energy of his concerts on a recording and that frisky spark gives more dimension to his music. The material on the album remains inconsistent, however. Even though he has written several of the record's songs, Davis hasn't assembled a thoroughly winning collection of songs—he's merely chosen a few enjoyable numbers. Nevertheless, *I Know A Place* is his best album because the quality of the performance makes the weakness of the material less noticeable. And when he does have a good song, the music is simply top-drawer contemporary honky tonk. *—Thom Owens*

Charlie Daniels

b. Wilmington, NC

Fiddle, Guitar, Violin, Vocals / Southern Rock, Country Gospel, Urban Cowboy, Traditional Country, Country-Rock

A talented and showy fiddler, Charlie Daniels and his band fuse hardcore country with a hard-edged Southern rock boogie and blues. The group—which has had a rotating cast of musicians over the years—has always been known for their instrumental dexterity, but they were also notorious for their down-home, good-old boy attitude; in the early '80s they became a virtual symbol of conservative country values. Daniels and his band experienced the height of their popularity at the end of the '70s and early '80s, but they remained a popular concert attraction well into the '90s.

Daniels was born and raised in North Carolina, playing fiddle and guitar in several bands during his teenage years. At the age of 21, he decided become a professional musician, assembling an instrumental rock & roll combo called the Jaguars. The group landed a recording session for Epic Records in 1959 with Bob Johnson, who would later become Columbia Records' leading folk and country producer. The record didn't receive much attention, but the band continued to play and Daniels continued to write songs. One of his originals, "It Hurts Me," was recorded by Elvis Presley in 1963. By the late '60s, it had become clear that the Jaguars weren't going to hit the big time, so Johnson recommended to Daniels that he move to Nashville to become a session musician. Daniels followed the advice and became one of the most popular fiddlers in Nashville. He played on several Bob Dylan albums—*Nashville Skyline, Self Portrait, New Morning,* and *Dylan*—as well as Ringo Starr's 1970 record *Beaucoups of Blues*. He also became part of Leonard Cohen's touring band in the late '60s and produced the Youngbloods' *Elephant Mountain* album around the same time.

Daniels cut an album for Capitol Records in the early '70s which was ignored. In 1972, he formed the Charlie Daniels Band, using the Southern rock of the Allman Brothers as a blueprint. The band comprised Daniels (lead guitar, vocals, fiddle), lead guitarist Don Murray, bassist Charlie Hayward, drummer James W. Marshal, and keyboardist Joe DiGregorio. The formula worked, and in 1973 they had a minor hit with "Uneasy Rider," which was released on Kama Sutra Records. In 1974, they released *Fire on the Mountain*, which became a gold record within months of its release; the album would eventually go platinum. Its successor, 1975's *Nightrider*, did even better, thanks to the Top 40 country hit "Texas." *Saddle Tramp*, released in 1976, became his first country Top Ten album, going gold.

Throughout the mid-'70s, the Charlie Daniels Band pursued a Southern rock direction. They were moderately successful, but they never had a breakthrough hit either on the pop or country charts. By the late '70s, Daniels sensed that the audience for Southern rock was evaporating, so he refashioned the band as a more straightforward country band. The change paid off in 1979 when the single "The Devil Went Down to Georgia" became a number-one hit, crossing over into the pop charts, where it hit number three. The song was named the Country Music Association's Single of the Year and helped its accompanying album, *Million Mile Reflections*, become a multi-platinum success. Daniels wasn't able to follow "The Devil Went Down to Georgia" with another blockbuster single on the country charts, ironically, but he had several rock crossover successes in the years following the success of *Million Mile Reflections*, *Full Moon* (1980) went platinum and *Windows* (1982) went gold. Although he continued to sell respectably throughout the '80s, he didn't have a big hit until 1989's *Simple Man*, which went gold. In the '90s, his records failed to chart well, although he remained a popular concert draw. *—Stephen Thomas Erlewine*

☆ **Charlie Daniels** / 1970 / Capitol ✦✦✦✦✦

When Charlie Daniels released his eponymous debut in 1970, Southern rock was in its nascent stages. It had been a year since the Allman Brothers Band released their debut and Lynyrd Skynyrd wouldn't unleash its first record for another three years, so the genre was in the process of being born, and Charlie Daniels' debut plays a pivotal role in the genre—not so much because it was directly influential, but because it points the way to how the genre could and would sound, and how country music could retain its hillbilly spirit and rock like a mother. Where the Allmans were firmly grounded in the blues, especially on the first two records, Daniels was a redneck from the start, and all ten songs on his debut were country at their foundation, even if some of it is country via the Band (as Rich Kienzle points out in his brief liner notes to Koch's 2001 reissue of the album). The Band connections derive from Daniels' time as a session musician for Columbia in Nashville, where he played on many country-rock albums, including Dylan's *Nashville Skyline*, but there's a heavy dose of hard rock, often via the Allmans' extended jams, on this record. Daniels simply wails on his guitar here, most notably on the six-minute closer "Thirty Nine Miles From Mobile," but, apart from the ballads, he doesn't miss a chance to solo. The heavy guitars give Charlie Daniels a real rock feel, and that vibe is continued through the loose rhythm section and a strong dose of counterculture humor, heard strongest on "The Pope and the Dope." That song also shows signs of Daniels' redneck sensibilities, which also surface in unpredictable ways throughout this wild, woolly album. He makes crude jokes, celebrates the South (particularly his home, "Georgia"), spits out bluesy leads, exaggerates his vocals, croons sweetly, and steals women. He's a redneck rebel, not fitting into either the country or the rock & roll of 1970 with this record, but, in retrospect, he sounds like a visionary, pointing the way to the future when southern rockers saw no dividing lines between rock, country, and blues, and only saw it all as sons of the south. That's what he achieves with *Charlie Daniels*—a unique Southern sound that's quintessentially American, sounding at once new and timeless. Once he formed the Charlie Daniels Band, he became a star and with *Fire on the Mountain*, he had another classic, but he would never sound as wild, unpredictable, or as much like a maverick as he does on this superb album. *—Stephen Thomas Erlewine*

John, Grease & Wolfman / 1972 / Epic ✦✦✦

On this, Charlie Daniels' second release, there are obvious signs of a bright future for the guitar- and fiddle-playing hillbilly rocker. Along for the ride is Joel "Taz" DiGregorio, Charlie's longtime bandmate and keyboard wizard. Taz even takes lead vocal duties on one song, "Billy Joe Young," and his ivory tickling is a highlight of this historical Southern-rock document. Daniels rocks with the intensity of a downbound train on "Great Big Bunches of Love," and on his cover of the Jerry Lee Lewis chestnut "Drinkin' Wine, Spo-Dee-O-Dee." A true Southern poet, Charlie Daniels is seen here in the infancy of his artistic development, but even at this early stage, the poet is alive and well. *—Michael B. Smith*

Honey in the Rock / 1973 / Kama Sutra ✦✦✦

☆ **Fire on the Mountain** / 1975 / Epic ✦✦✦✦✦

Four albums in, Charlie Daniels—now fronting the Charlie Daniels Band—finally found a way to not just synthesize his various influences, he found a way to streamline them and polish them, turning them into something proudly Southern and redneck yet commercial with *Fire on the Mountain*. This means that he's toned down the wild, messy eclecticism that he displayed on his ignored debut in favor of a bluesy, jam-oriented country-rock owing a great deal to the Allman Brothers. The change is brought into sharp relief because he revives two of the best songs from *Charlie Daniels*—the rampaging rocker "Trudy" and the sweet ballad "Georgia," both given more direct arrangements here; the originals were ragged and right, but these have more of a rock feel, even if they're not as loose as those on the debut. And that pretty much sums up the difference with *Fire on the Mountain*—here, Charlie Daniels and his band have fused their Southern-fried country to a rollicking, jam-intensive blues-rock, where it plays like rock but feels like redneck country. It's a rather brilliant move, because it's every bit as jam-oriented as Capricorn bands like the Allmans or the Marshall Tucker Band (the latter are thanked in the liner notes, while Dickey Betts of the former cameos on this record), but the CDB have yet to give themselves over to playing for the sake of playing (which they soon would with *Saddle Tramp*). Instead, they focus that energy into the songs, which are all top-notch, and the result is probably the best balance of songs and performances that the Charlie Daniels Band ever did. They would wander into longer jams and Daniels would become unapologetically redneck later, but here the mix is just right, which is why this is the quintessential Charlie Daniels Band album. *—Stephen Thomas Erlewine*

Nightrider / 1975 / Epic/Legacy ✦✦✦✦✦

Charlie Daniels found his sound on 1974's *Fire on the Mountain*, but with its 1975 follow-up, *Nightrider*, he found the definitive lineup of the Charlie Daniels Band and, with it, crystallized the group's sound and entered into his golden era. Guitarist Barry Barnes and drummer Gary Allen are replaced by Tom Crain and Don Murray, respectively, and the result is a band that sounds fuller and more adventurous than before, capable of following all the paths that the country and blues-rock fusion on *Fire on the Mountain* suggested. As such, *Nightrider* focuses much more on the playing as opposed to the songs—which is kind of ironic, considering that this brought Daniels his first big hit in "Texas." Then again, the jamming, while heavy, never overwhelms the songs. In fact, it enhances the songs, opening them up to new vistas in how rock, blues, hillbilly country, and bluegrass sit next to each other, and when the group just lays back and plays, there's the kinetic excitement of hearing these musicians learn how they interact together. *Fire on the Mountain* remains the Charlie Daniels Band's classic album, but this damn fine album comes in as a close second. *—Stephen Thomas Erlewine*

Saddle Tramp / 1976 / Epic ✦✦✦✦

Around the time the Charlie Daniels Band recorded the music that became 1976's *Saddle Tramp*, the group was experiencing its first wave of success, as both *Fire on the Mountain* and *Nightrider* found an audience, and the group became known for their live performances, particularly through Daniels' *Volunteer Jams* concerts. *Saddle Tramp* rode this momentum into the country Top Ten and a gold album—all without a Top Ten country single, it should be noted. That's because the Charlie Daniels Band turned into the country equivalent of a radio-oriented rock band, where singles were less important than a unified whole of an album, which sought to replicate the feel of live performances. Since the CDB was a country band, that meant that they had less of a theme to tie together their records—not even to the extent that the Grateful Dead did on *Workingman's Dead* and *American Beauty*, two records whose influence is felt on *Saddle Tramp*. Instead, the band cut seven songs, sometimes stretching out and jamming for a long, longtime, other times focusing that energy into a three- or four-minute song. So, *Saddle Tramp* becomes about the texture and feel of the performances more than the songs, which makes it a quintessential jam record, complete with the flaw of putting a ten-minute title track as the second song, thereby killing any forward momentum the album had. It's a good jam, and it shows that the CDB was a vigorous, muscular band capable of shifting styles and tones easily and gracefully; it would have worked better at the end of the album, where it would have summarized the rest of the record and how it touches on cowboy music, bluegrass, blues, hillbilly, and swinging jazz in equal measure. Arriving so early in the record signals that this is a jam record for jam fans, and on that level, it works very well, since it does showcase the band at a near-peak of its talents. But, like many other jam records, *Saddle Tramp* winds up not being about the songs (which, apart from the single "Wichita Jail," aren't particularly memorable), but being about the feel of the music and the sound of the band, which can make for good listening, provided that's what you're looking to hear. *—Stephen Thomas Erlewine*

High Lonesome / 1976 / Epic ✦✦✦✦

Following *Saddle Tramp* by a matter of months, *High Lonesome* finds the Charlie Daniels Band retaining their focus on jamming—meaning not just long solos and improvisations, but a loose feel that brings in elements of a number of different Southern styles, blurring the line between country, rock, blues, and bluegrass. Compared to *Saddle Tramp*, which felt as wide-open and sunny as the plains or desert, *High Lonesome* is a little darker and denser, a byproduct of the Charlie Daniels Band playing harder as they up the rock quotient while simultaneously playing up cowboy myths. There are strong elements of the Allmans throughout the record, particularly when Charlie Daniels and Tom Crain trade off electric guitar leads and double-up on harmonies, and there's a harder backbeat. Even better, there's more of an emphasis on songwriting and tighter arrangements, which means that the Band's improvisatory fire is distilled into tight, concise four-minute bursts, which makes the record as a whole a more infectious, invigorating listen. Also, with Crain singing on "Tennessee" and a pianist taking lead on "Roll Mississippi," this not only feels more like a band album, it has a welcome, loose, anything-goes feel, actually sounding like the work of a bunch of Southern renegades. If there are no true CDB classics outside of the title track and arguably "Carolina," there are no bum songs, either, and the whole thing holds together well, perhaps because, unlike its predecessor, it plays as if it has a theme, thanks to the songs about cowboys and the Southern mythology, not to mention its focused arrangements and the muscular blues-rock guitar that ties it all together. All this makes *High Lonesome* a highlight in Charlie Daniels' discography. *—Stephen Thomas Erlewine*

Uneasy Rider / 1976 / Epic ✦✦✦✦

The Essential Charlie Daniels / 1976 / Kama Sutra ✦✦✦✦

Volunteer Jam / 1976 / Capricorn ✦✦✦

When Charlie Daniels held his first-ever Volunteer Jam in his home state of Tennessee, the tapes were rolling and the cameras were as well. Sections of the jam were filmed and released theatrically in 1975. The Volunteer Jam was scheduled to go on the road in 1999, with the film being screened prior to each show. This live recording serves as a good cross section of the music that was created on-stage that day; there is also an EP included in Daniels' *Fire on the Mountain* album, taken from the same show. The Charlie Daniels Band burn white-hot on the first three numbers before turning the show over to the Marshall Tucker Band for a smoking version of "The Thrill Is Gone." The CDB backs Dickey Betts of the Allman Brothers Band on the J.J. Cale tune "Sweet Mama," and the stage fills for the finale, "Mountain Dew," with Betts, Mylon LeFevre, Jimmy Hall of Wet Willie, and Ronnie Stoneman on banjo—a down-home hoedown. This album serves as a landmark, the beginning of a Charlie Daniels tradition that would continue into the 21st century. *—Michael B. Smith*

Midnight Wind / 1977 / Epic ✦✦✦

The song "Heaven Can Be Anywhere" and, to a lesser extent "Sugar Hill Saturday Night," save this from being just another Charlie Daniels record. No great shakes but fans won't be disappointed. *—Jim Worbois*

Whiskey / 1977 / Epic ◆◆◆

A whole album of Daniels' brand of Southern boogie may be a bit much for the average listener but his fans will eat it up. This isn't a bad record but there isn't anything here to recommend it either. —*Jim Worbois*

Volunteer Jam, Vol. 3-4 / 1978 / Epic ◆◆◆

Apart from the third side (featuring Willie Nelson), this record may not appeal to the average country fan. Still, there is some fine music on this record featuring many of the artists who were signed to Capricorn in the '70s. —*Jim Worbois*

Million Mile Reflections / 1979 / Epic ◆◆◆

Despite the inclusion of the hit "Devil Went Down to Georgia," this is, at best, a mediocre record. Certainly not for everyone, Daniels' fans will still enjoy it. —*Jim Worbois*

Full Moon / 1980 / Epic ◆◆◆

Volunteer Jam, Vol. 6 / 1980 / Epic ◆◆◆

The Volunteer Jams have always resulted in some of Charlie Daniels' most interesting albums and this one fits the bill. There is something for everyone—from the country of Crystal Gayle and the blues of Papa John Creach to funk of Rufus and the rock of the "Motor City Madman," Ted Nugent and others. —*Jim Worbois*

Christmas Time Down South / 1980 / Epic ◆◆

Windows / 1982 / Epic ◆◆◆

● **A Decade of Hits** / 1983 / Epic/Legacy ◆◆◆◆◆

More than half of the songs from the Charlie Daniels Band's compilation *A Decade of Hits* were chart successes, especially the fiery "Devil Went Down to Georgia," a boot-kickin' mix of rock and country fiddle that proved to be this group's biggest hit. Played on both country and rock radio, it hit number three on *Billboard*'s Top 40 in 1979 thanks to its hard-based rhythm and entertaining narrative. *A Decade of Hits* puts together ten of the band's most solid songs that integrate both a country and rock feel. "The South's Gonna Rise Again" unleashes Daniels' pride of being from North Carolina and the attributes of being a good ol' boy. "Long Haired Country Boy" does much of the same, but with a more generous amount of countrified fervor. "Still in Saigon" leans on a more rock-oriented style, and loosely deals with one veteran's flashbacks to the Vietnam War. As a story song, "The Legend of Wooley Swamp" basks in the Southern slang of Daniels drawl, which contributes to its bayou campiness. The most delightful aspect of the Charlie Daniels Band's music is the way in which Daniels uses his fiddle to liven up his music, customizing it to the drums and guitar. Most of the tunes on this album contain a feisty mix of instruments that gives the band a different feel and a slightly unique sound. Not the typical country norm, this collection of the Charlie Daniels Band's best songs will satisfy anyone who is interested. —*Mike DeGagne*

Me & the Boys / 1985 / Epic ◆◆

Powder Keg / 1987 / Epic ◆◆◆

Charlie Daniels does it all, from dead-on country ballads to bluegrass to gospel to rock & roll. In this collection, Daniels puts on his rock & roll hat and delivers another winning set. From "Bogged Down in Love With You" to "Powder Keg," Charlie, Taz, and the rest of the band stand and deliver. It's a great album by one of the best. —*Michael B. Smith*

Homesick Heroes / 1988 / Epic ◆◆◆

Simple Man / 1989 / Epic ◆◆◆◆

This album features the title track plus "Play Me Some Fiddle," "Saturday Night Down South," and other hits. —*AMG*

Renegade / 1991 / Epic ◆◆◆◆

This strong collection of Daniels songs rocks harder than usual, despite showing his soft side on "Little Folks" and "Fathers and Sons." Daniels practically gives a cultural history of the violin on "Talk to Me Fiddle," the album's most unusual song, and continues to extol the virtues of country living ("The Twang Factor") and patriotism ("Let Freedom Ring.") —*Brian Mansfield*

All-Time Greatest Hits / 1993 / Epic ◆◆◆◆◆

This traces his career from early high points—"Long Haired Country Boy," "The South's Gonna Do It," "The Devil Went Down to Georgia"—to the desperate attempts to revive his late career with self-referential updates ("Uneasy Rider '88") and jingoistic, red-baiting blather ("Simple Man") that was out of date before he released it. —*Michael McCall*

America, I Believe In You / 1993 / Capitol ◆◆

Super Hits / 1994 / Epic ◆◆◆◆◆

Super Hits is a budget-priced collection that features a handful of Charlie Daniels Band's biggest hits, but it doesn't provide a definitive retrospective, nor does it have every hit that a casual fan could want. It's entertaining, but it leaves you wanting more. —*Stephen Thomas Erlewine*

The Door / 1994 / Sparrow ◆◆

Same Ol' Me / Sep. 12, 1995 / Capitol ◆◆◆

On *Same Ol' Me*, Charlie Daniels returned to the country and rock hybrid that sent him to the top of the charts in the late '70s and early '80s. As always, the album is a bit inconsistent, featuring too much filler, but the best moments on the record are some of the best music he has recorded in the '90s. —*Stephen Thomas Erlewine*

Steel Witness / Aug. 1996 / Chordant ◆◆

Daniels' second gospel set finds him firmly fixed in his comfort zone of country-rock with strong hooks. Whether he's condemning hypocrites on "New Pharisees," acknowledging someone's prayers on the bouncy "Somebody Was Prayin' For Me" or the revival-styled "Jesus," all the songs exude a sinuous melody and catchy hook. The prettiest song was the bluesy ballad "Heart of My Heart," which Daniels endows with a soulful rhapsody. It wasn't as coherent and satisfying as his first gospel set, but it was still good. —*Bill Carpenter*

Roots Remain / Oct. 29, 1996 / Epic/Legacy ◆◆◆◆◆

Roots Remain is a three-disc box set covering the Charlie Daniels Band's entire career. Over the course of 45 songs, the box touches upon all of his hits—including "The Devil Went Down to Georgia," "Long-Haired Country Boy," and "Uneasy Rider"—plus key album tracks, B-sides, and several unreleased and rare gems, such as his take on Eric Clapton's "Layla." *Roots Remain* is the most comprehensive compilation of Charlie Daniels recordings ever assembled and it misses very few important tracks, making it the one definitive retrospective. —*Stephen Thomas Erlewine*

Volunteer Jam, Vol. 7 / May 5, 1997 / Sony ◆◆◆

By the Light of the Moon: Campfire Songs & Cowboy Tunes / Aug. 12, 1997 / Sony Wonder ◆◆◆

Blues Hat / Dec. 23, 1997 / Blue Hat ◆◆◆

Fiddle Fire: 25 Years of the Charlie Daniels Band / Aug. 18, 1998 / Blue Hat ◆◆◆◆

Charlie Daniels displays his exceptional fiddle playing in this compilation of his best fiddle songs. From the obvious inclusions, like "The Devil Went Down to Georgia" and "The South's Gonna Do It Again," to lesser-known romps like "Texas" and "Talk to Me Fiddle," there isn't a bad track on the disc. Daniels delivers perhaps the definitive version of the country-bluegrass "Orange Blossom Special" and downright rocks the log cabin with "Drinkin' My Baby Goodbye." An excellent collection of Tennessee mountain-inspired fiddle-sawing. —*Michael B. Smith*

Tailgate Party / Mar. 9, 1999 / Blue Hat ◆◆◆◆

Charlie Daniels' *Tailgate Party* serves as his tribute to the great bands of the South. The CD itself rocks from beginning to end, kicking things off with a retelling of his Southern rock & roll call, "The South's Gonna Do It Again." Next up, Daniels pays homage to Stevie Ray Vaughan, ripping through "Pride and Joy," before tipping his substantial hat to Toy Caldwell and the Marshall Tucker Band with "Can't You See." Perhaps the biggest surprise of the set comes when Charlie Daniels covers Hootie & the Blowfish, the pride of Columbia, SC. His rendition of "Let Her Cry" is genuinely nice, and Daniels' cover of Atlanta Rhythm Section's "Homesick" is a brilliant reminder of the power and hard-rocking energy that Atlanta Rhythm Section possessed. "Keep Your Hands to Yourself" is filled with a maximum dose of good humor, and lots of good old-fashioned Charlie Daniels Band guitar work. The Georgia Satellites would be proud. "Statesborro Blues" serves as Daniels' tribute to the Allman Brothers Band, and the Charlie Daniels Band delivers a rousing rendition of the Grinderswitch hit "Peach County Jamboree." Covering all the Southern bases, ZZ Top's "Sharp Dressed Man" follows, leading into a tender and emotionally charged cover of Lynyrd Skynyrd's own tribute to Duane Allman, "Freebird." Following this outstanding salute to the South's greatest players, Daniels and the boys in the band smoke a trio of their own, delivering red-hot versions of their "Legend of Wooley Swamp," "El Toreador," and "The Devil Went Down to Georgia." —*Michael B. Smith*

Road Dogs / May 30, 2000 / Blue Hat ◆◆◆◆

Not since *Fire on the Mountain* has the Charlie Daniels Band delivered a record so emotionally charged with screaming guitars and honest, to goodness Southern-style rock & roll. From the opening chords of the ultimate rock-band-on-the-road tune, "Road Dogs," it is obvious that this release is neither a straight gospel recording like *Steel Witness* nor a country flavored album like *Same Old Me*. This is Charlie's hottest rocking recording in many years and a breath of clear, fresh air. Not that there was anything wrong with his previous endeavors. Each had its own set of high points and bits of musical genius, but *Road Dogs* rocks. "Ain't No Law in California" is an especially memorable rebel yell of a song, with Charlie belting out "Welcome to the wild wild west." "Sidewinder" is more than a little reminiscent of the very best Allman Brothers Band instrumental, featuring triple-lead guitars, overlapping in smooth, tight harmony with all the flavor of a Mexicali road trip. At the age of 63, Charlie Daniels has returned to his Southern rock roots and sounds as good as ever. This is one old road dog who isn't even considering curling up on the porch and letting life pass him by. He's rockin,' but it's not in a rocking chair, it's behind a Gibson guitar. —*Michael Smith*

How Sweet the Sound: 25 Favorite Hymns and Gospel Greats / 2001 / Sparrow ◆◆

Country-rock fiddler Charlie Daniels leads his band through two CDs of religious music on *How Sweet the Sound: 25 Favorite Hymns and Gospel Greats*. Backed by a full choir, Daniels' gruff road dog image is nowhere to be found on this collection, but stripped-down gems like "Softly and Tenderly" or the bluegrass infused "I'll Fly Away" are tucked in among the big production numbers. —*Zac Johnson*

The Live Record / Oct. 9, 2001 / Koch ◆◆◆◆◆

Making music involves two very separate but integral worlds: the electronic environment of the studio and the high-octane world of the stage. Even though Charlie Daniels and his band have proven that they can move recorded merchandise, it has been the group's energetic live performances that have marketed them as one of country-rock's hottest commodities. The two musical worlds unite to spawn the digitally mastered adrenaline rush that is *The Live Record*. Recorded live in Florida, North Carolina, and Virginia, the extended play truly captures both the energy and musical genius of a live Charlie Daniels concert, at least as close as humanly possible without the huddle of bodies dancing in their seats. Perhaps best of all is the chance to enjoy over an hour of Daniels favorites, such as "In America," "Still in Saigon," and "The Devil Went Down to Georgia" without the muffle that might occur at a large outdoor venue. Each guitar lick and fiddle assault is crystal clear and is especially laudable on Daniels' seven-minute instrumental, "Sidewinder." Lynyrd Skynyrd's Southern classic, "Freebird," is another set-list sizzler, featuring the electronic wail of the lead guitar. As live albums go, this one deserves kudos. The added bonus is that the listener gets not only a rousing good-time, but a greatest-hits collection of one of country's greatest entertainers. —*Rick Cohoon*

★ **The Ultimate Charlie Daniels Band** / May 12, 2002 / Epic/Legacy ✦✦✦✦✦

It could be argued that Epic/Legacy's 2002 double-disc compilation *The Ultimate Charlie Daniels Band* falls a little short of the title's claim, but then you'd have to realize that they're being literal with the title—Daniels' first album may not be represented here, but it was a solo affair, not a band effort. This 30-track collection covers only recordings from the Charlie Daniels Band, then, and it does an expert job of selecting the best, from the biggest hits to album tracks and concert favorites. Perhaps it would have been better if the selections were presented in chronological order instead of jumping all over the place—it starts in the '90s, heads into the '70s, goes into the '80s a while later before winding back in the '70s just on the first disc—but the music here is proof positive that rowdy, Southern-fried, redneck rocking country had few better bands than this. And that does make it *The Ultimate Charlie Daniels Band* compilation. *—Stephen Thomas Erlewine*

Redneck Fiddlin' Man / Jul. 23, 2002 / Audium ✦✦✦

No surprises here—but the Charlie Daniels Band is never about surprise. As with most artists who define themselves according to established musical traditions, their goal is to conform to audience expectations. In fact, there's something almost un-American about surprise, according to Daniels: On an album dripping with patriotic affirmation, the terrorists who felled the World Trade Center are reviled as "cowards" who "attacked without a warning" ("The Last Fallen Hero"), and the most familiar melody in America, "The Star Spangled Banner," closes things on a comforting note. Other hallmarks of Dixie life, nearly as important as xenophobia, receive attention elsewhere on *Redneck Fiddlin' Man*: drinkin', oglin', and fightin' on "Southern Boy," the same stuff plus eatin' on "Little Joe and Big Bill," dancin', lovin', and fishin' on "My Baby Plays Me Just Like a Fiddle," NASCAR machismo and the sainthood of Dale Earnhardt on "High Speed Heroes." Daniels isn't the most nuanced singer out there, nor the smoothest fiddler—but within the confines of the style, which means the span from squint-eyed menace to keg-popping jocularity, no one matches his vocal expressiveness. And let it be said that he unleashes some sizzling fiddle licks on the title track and the jazz-inflected instrumental "Crosstown Traffic," and his rendition of "The Star Spangled Banner" conveys the rugged eloquence that marks his style at its best. *—Robert L. Doerschuk*

In America / Jul. 8, 2003 / Audium ✦✦

Clint Daniels

b. Aug. 24, 1974, Panama City, FL

Guitar / Traditional Country, Singer/Songwriter, Bakersfield Sound

Clint Daniels was born in Panama City, FL, on August 24, 1974. He grew up in Lynn Haven, a suburb of Panama City, where he learned to ride horses. His father was a painter and played guitar, and his mother worked at home. Recalling those early years, Daniels remembers singing with his sister and in church. He also claims to have been influenced by bluegrass music. At the age of 12 he began to teach himself guitar. Locked in his room with Haggard and Jones, he began to figure out the chords and notes he needed to play the songs he loved so much. Like many future honky tonkers, Daniels played in a number of bands and found his way into a good many dives. Being underage was not keeping him from his dreams, and after he graduated from high-school, he set off for Nashville, something he would do several times before finding his way through the Music City system. Discovered by a member of Arista's A&R staff while rehearsing a song he wrote in a Nashville studio, Daniels was soon signed.

Releasing his self-titled debut project on September 15, 1998, placed Daniels on the rising tide that seemed to indicate a return to more traditional forms of country music. With a strong baritone voice and some hearty honky tonk songwriting skills, Daniels appeared to be in the right place at the right time. *—Jana Pendragon*

● **Clint Daniels** / Sep. 15, 1998 / Arista ✦✦✦✦✦

Clint Daniels is a Merle Haggard fan and finds inspiration in his work, admitting that *Big City* is his favorite album. Now, for a kid trying to make an impression on Music City, that could be a problem. But if Arista lets him follow his heart, Daniels might have more than a snowball's chance in hell of building himself a career. And the fact remains that as he was releasing his debut project, there was a growing interest in the more traditional forms of country & western music. With a good voice reminiscent of a young Haggard and some phrasing that sounds surprisingly old-timey, Daniels comes out of the gate full force. While he had a hand at writing many of the songs, he also chose a few that he didn't write but which show off his talent. The leadoff cut is one of his with co-writer Tony Martin, "A Fool's Progress," and it sets up the rest of the project. Hardcore with what could be honed into a nice edge, Daniels also shines on "Wish It Was Easy," "Another Me for You," and a cut that should even get radio's attention, "When I Grow Up." Just as good is "Swing Through Dallas" and the moody "Long Way Down." The Dean Dillon-Larry Bastian tune "If I Stay" is a nice ending to what turns out to be a very impressive introduction to an extremely promising artist. *—Jana Pendragon*

Darby & Tarlton

f. 1920

Group / Old-Timey, Traditional Country

Singer Tom Darby and slide guitarist Jimmie Tarlton were not only legendary bluesmen, but also pioneers of country music. Although they were only together for a brief time during the late '20s and early '30s, they popularized the steel slide guitar in the genre and exerted a heavy influence on the Allen Brothers and the Delmore Brothers. Tarlton was born in Chesterfield County, SC, the son of sharecroppers. His parents taught him traditional songs and the fretless banjo, and by age 12, he was learning to play the slide guitar from the black musicians he encountered in his family's numerous travels. As a young man he became a traveling street musician living off tips. His travels led him across the country, and everywhere he went, he added local songs to his expanding repertoire. On the West Coast in the early '20s, he met Frank Ferera, who taught him how to use the steel slide to play the more free-flowing Hawaiian guitar.

When Tarlton settled down in Columbus, GA, he met a guitarist and extraordinary blues singer named Tom Darby, a Columbus native who learned his vocal stylings from local black singers. Darby was related to Riley Puckett, star of the Skillet Lickers. A local talent scout convinced the two to team up and landed them an audition with Columbia Records. Their first recorded single made fun of Florida land speculators and was titled "Down in Florida on a Hog." Their next two songs, "Birmingham Jail"—a song Tarlton claimed sprang from his experience there after being incarcerated for moonshining—and "Columbus Stockade Blues," were enormously successful and have since become country standards. Audiences were impressed as well—the record sold close to 200,000 copies. Despite the profits reaped from their records, Darby & Tarlton received only a flat 75 dollar fee.

The duo scored their second major hit in 1928 with "Birmingham Jail, #2" and "Lonesome Railroad"; among their other hits were the straight-ahead blues tunes "Traveling Yodel Blues" and "Heavy Hearted Blues." The two experienced contract difficulties with Columbia in late 1929 and finally recorded their last session the following year. They went their separate ways, occasionally reuniting without much success. By 1935, both men gave up and left the music business. They remained largely forgotten until the folk revival of the 1960s, which allowed Tarlton to record an album, appear at folk clubs, and sit for interviews with a number of folklorists. Darby also did a few performances and even reunited briefly with Tarlton, but at their age, neither particularly enjoyed performing. *—Sandra Brennan*

Complete Recordings / 1995 / Bear Family ✦✦✦✦

Let's start by saying that there aren't any other collections of Darby and Tarlton's work currently available, so if you want any of it, you've got to take it all. Having said that, one should add that there isn't a bad song among the 70 surviving tracks (among 84 recorded) included on these three CDs, and anyone who enjoys white country blues should seriously consider saving up for it. The duo's first recording features the kind of spirited vocal and guitar interplay that would characterize their subsequent work together. The appeal of the double-barrel hit "Columbus Stockade Blues"/"Birmingham Jail" is obvious—drawing on several strands of Kentucky-based folk material that will be familiar even to casual listeners, but the harmonizing and the distinctive sound of Jimmie Tarlton's steel guitar give it several fresh twists. By the end of the disc, the duo and their recording managers had enough expertise at capturing their sound in the studio that their harmonies and paired guitars were outstanding on record, and they were transcending the work that made them famous. Disc two shows off generally better sound and better blues. The duo returned to more pop and country-oriented material in the sessions that followed these, as though searching for the formula that would bring them new success. The sound quality of all three discs is generally very good, although a few tracks, where surviving source material is limited, retain considerable surface noise. Disc three's real highlights are the straight blues, though pop music also makes its influence felt. By the dawn of the 1930s, the duo—who never really liked each other personally—began working independently of each other, and this part of their careers make up a section of the third disc. This is followed by a series of Jimmie Tarlton solo numbers that are almost all stunners—listening to these songs, it becomes clear that the playing of either of these men was good enough that their vocal harmonies were almost distractions. Tom Darby and Jesse Pitts' jaunty recordings under the name of the Georgia Wildcats, are among the best numbers here. The booklet is, as usual, very thorough, although as there is astonishingly little known about Darby & Tarlton, much of the booklet is given over to Tarlton's career revival in the 1960s and to a song-by-song analysis. *—Bruce Eder*

Helen Darling

b. Louisiana

Vocals (Background), Vocals / Country-Pop, Contemporary Country

A former commercial jingle singer, Helen Darling found open arms in Nashville after her country backup vocals impressed hillbilly heavyweight Garth Brooks. Born in Louisiana and raised in Houston, Darling sang from an early age and first recorded with her University of Texas choir. She moved to Chicago after graduation and sang radio jingles during the early '90s, but moved again to Nashville when a friend encouraged her. After making the rounds in Music City and getting occasional work, Darling impressed Garth Brooks enough for him to use her vocals on "The Red Strokes" (from *In Pieces*). Signed to a contract herself in 1994, Helen Darling released an eponymous album—with vocal backup from Brooks himself—for Decca in 1995. *—John Bush*

Helen Darling / 1995 / Decca ✦✦✦✦✦

Helen Darling began her recording career with the encouragement of Garth Brooks and the music on her self-titled debut recalls his rock-inflected country. The first single pulled from the album, "Jenny Come Back," was a straightforward country number, but it was "I Haven't Found It Yet" that brought her to the attention of many country fans. *—Stephen Thomas Erlewine*

Johnny Darrell

b. Jul. 23, 1940, Hopewell, AL, **d.** 1997

Vocals / Progressive Country, Traditional Country, Nashville Sound/Countrypolitan

Johnny Darrell was born on July 23, 1940, in Hopewell, AL, but grew up in Marietta, outside of Atlanta. After a stint in the Army, he moved to Nashville to manage a Holiday Inn. It was in this way that he made a few music-business contacts. Darrell came to the attention of United Artists producer Kelso Herston through Bobby Bare, who had heard about Darrell's curious brand of songwriting through one such contact. Darrell signed with UA, and issued his first single, "Green Green Grass of Home," in 1965. A year later, "As Long as the Wind Blows" made it into the Top 30. "Ruby Don't Take Your Love to Town," from 1967, found the Top Ten. The song, written by Mel Tillis, would later be a hit for Kenny Rogers, establishing a trend of songs Darrell performed later becoming country standards recorded by others. "The Son of Hickory Holler's Tramp" charted in 1968, and Darrell crossed over to the pop charts with "Pen in Hand." The latter song would eventually be a hit for Vicki Carr.

It's unclear how it happened (his early encounters with Bobby Bare?), but by the 1970s Darrell had been lumped in with the outlaw country movement. He joined Hank Snow, Willie Nelson, Nat Stuckey, and Wes Buchanan at *Opry's Party Night*, an English concert celebrating the birthday of the now-defunct *Opry* magazine. Darrell charted with a few more singles, including "Dakota the Dancing Bear" and "Orange Blossom Special," but his career continued to wane. Despite a brief comeback, little was heard from him during the 1980s. Darrell passed away in 1997. Three years later, the European indie Raven issued the Darrell retrospective *Singin' It Lonesome*; the release included all of Darrell's charting singles. *—Johnny Loftus*

- **Singin' It Lonesome: The Very Best . . . 1965-1970** / 2000 / Raven ✦✦✦✦✦

The Australia's Raven has issued a number of discs oriented toward Byrds collectors. Presumably, this explains the label's reissue of this relatively obscure country hitmaker's '60s hits and 1969 album *California Stop-Over*, since Clarence White plays on the latter. Johnny Darrell may not be a household name, but he displayed a remarkably consistent knack for being the first to record songs that—in the hands of others—soon became hits known by all, including "Ruby, Don't Take Your Love to Town" (a number-nine hit for Darrell) and "Green Green Grass of Home." Darrell also enjoyed the hits "With Pen in Hand" (his biggest at number three), "The Son of Hickory Holler's Tramp" (which soon became a smash for O.C. Smith), and "Why You Been Gone So Long" (with a giant, driving hook that should have propelled it to number one). The *California Stop-Over* album is an all-star affair as far as the songwriting is concerned, featuring compositions by Kris Kristofferson, Johnny Cash, Hoyt Axton, Jackson Browne, and others. Although he made the Top 40 nine times in the late '60s, Darrell never caught on the way he should have, and now he's undeservedly a mere footnote for Byrdmaniax. *—Greg Adams*

The Complete Gusto/Starday/King Recordings / Aug. 20, 2002 / King ✦✦✦✦

Chris Darrow

b. July 30, 1944, Sioux Falls, SD

Guitar, Mandolin, Violin, Vocals / Country-Rock, Folk-Rock

Chris Darrow was born on July 30, 1944, in Sioux Falls, SD, to a military dad who soon afterward moved his family to Southern California where Darrow still makes his home. Darrow began learning to play anything he could get his hands on that had strings, and over the course of the next 30-plus years, became one of the most sought after multi-instrumentalists in professional music. Shortly after high-school graduation, Darrow put together a bluegrass band called the Dry City Scat Band with David Lindley, Steve Cahill, Richard Greene, and Pete Madlem. Within a couple of years, the Scat Band would become one of the hottest bluegrass ensembles in Southern California. During the summer of 1964, the Scat Band got a gig at Disneyland which was steady work and Darrow was able to support his new bride. During this period, signs were starting to appear indicating imminent changes in the hearts of some of the most pure of bluegrass musicians. Bandmate Richard Greene introduced Darrow to a friend of his who played in the Chad Mitchell Trio and who had just returned from England raving about the British music scene. Darrow had never before seen anyone with Beatle boots and long hair. The gentleman happened to be future Byrds founder Jim McGuinn. Later that summer, the Scat Band was replaced by the Scottsville Squirrel Barkers and mandolinist Chris Hillman, a hardcore bluegrass purist who quietly and sheepishly said to Darrow, "I joined a rock & roll band. I need the money. They're called the Byrds."

In the latter part of the '60s, Darrow had his first major breakthrough by putting a band together, called Kaleidoscope, with David Lindley, Solomon Feldthouse, and Max Buda. American folk, Middle Eastern, country & western, and blues, which would have seemed an unlikely combination of musical flavors, proved to mix very well and ultimately became successful. Led Zeppelin's Jimmy Page was quoted as saying that, "Kaleidoscope was his favorite band of all time." Kaleidoscope went on to release several albums in the late '60s with no hit singles, but with a large cult following that is still growing.

In late 1967, Darrow was asked to join the Nitty Gritty Dirt Band as a fiddle player/singer replacing predecessors Jackson Browne, who left to embark upon a solo career, and Bruce Kunkel, who left the band because of philosophical differences. As it turned out, the Dirt Band abruptly adopted a more electric sound anyway, which is what Kunkel had been campaigning for, but was resigned to defeat. In the meantime, Darrow's presence gave the Nitty Gritty Dirt Band some glory by virtue of their performance in the smash musical comedy flick *Paint Your Wagon*. The Dirt Band's short-lived and waning success would soon cause a breakup, but it would later reorganize with different personnel. Darrow, on the other hand, who has more sides to him than a mirror ball, hung out his shingle attracting a great number of new opportunities.

One of these opportunities was in the form of an intermittent working relationship with Linda Ronstadt that came as the result of an introduction by a primate. Former Monkee Michael Nesmith produced a couple of singles for a band called, the Corvettes, founded by Darrow and former Dirt Band mate Jeff Hanna. The Corvettes would soon become Ronstadt's backup band. She had heard about them through Nesmith, who was the writer of her hit song "Different Drum." Darrow stayed with Ronstadt's band off and on for a number of years, witnessing a personnel change whereby Bernie Leadon came in to replace Hanna, who had decided to make his exit and re-form the Dirt Band. Darrow was offered a recording contract by United Artists Records in 1972. He recorded the albums *Chris Darrow*, followed up by *Under My Own Disguise* the following year. "Whipping Boy," from the former, received critical acclaim and is still viewed as an attractive "cover" prospect. Over the years, he has continued to be called upon by other artists who wanted his multifaceted musical influence on their albums. Artists such as James Taylor, Sonny & Cher, Gene Vincent, Helen Reddy, and John Fahey are only a few examples.

In the mid-'90s, Darrow started recording for the Taxim label of Germany. In 2000, the label released a two-CD set, called *Coyote/Straight From the Heart*. It includes a 40-minute instrumental suite and 20 original songs. Taxim also released *Fretless*, *Southern California Drive*, *Los Chumps* with Max Buda, and *Mojave*, a Darrow-produced album featuring members of Emmylou Harris' band, Lone Justice, and the Byrds. In early 2001, BGO Records in England released Darrow's second and third albums, *Chris Darrow* and *Under My Own Disguise*, as a two for one package. All of Kaleidoscope's early records have been re-released on Demon Records in England and Sony/Legacy in the U.S. Darrow's fabulous slide guitar work is featured on a compilation album called *Everybody Slides, Vol. 2*. The album features cuts by such slide greats as Lowell George, John Hammond, David Lindley, and Rory Block. It is on Sky Ranch Records in France with Virgin distribution, as well as Rykodisc in the U.S. Darrow also appears on two Takoma Records compilations, *Takoma Slides* and *Takoma Eclectic Sampler, Vol. 2*.

Other sides of this mirror ball (metaphorically speaking) lay in business and photography. Darrow plans to publish a book containing photographs he has taken over the last 35 years, many of which appear on album covers. By his own admission, Darrow said he decided to take his photojournalism to a professional level after he learned that the man with whom his wife ran off was a photographer. In retrospect, during the late '60s and through the '70s, there seemed to be a delicate balance of relationships that would influence the evolution of country-rock music (as it would come to be known) for the remainder of the 1900s and beyond. Chris Darrow was right in the middle of all of this and played an integral part of the formation and ultimate success of more than just a handful of his contemporaries. *—Tom Kealey*

- **Chris Darrow/Under My Own Disguise** / Feb. 14, 2001 / BGO ✦✦✦✦

This two-fer from Beat Goes On features a pair of out-of-print Chris Darrow LP's: *Chris Darrow* and *Under My Own Disguise* both originally issued on United Artists in 1973 and 1974. Highlights among the 22 tracks include "Don't Let Your Deal Go Down," "Hong Kong Blues," "Livin' Like a Fool," and "Live or Die Rag," which provide an interesting combination of country and folk-rock. *—Al Campbell*

The Dave & Deke Combo

f. 1990

Group / Alternative Country, Neo-Traditionalist Country

The Dave & Deke Combo, a band of Los Angeles country rockabillies, consist of three Midwest transplants—leaders Dave Dickerson and Deke Stuckey, plus drummer Lance—and only one West Coast native, bassist Shorty. After releasing several seven-inch singles and an EP, the group's album debut, *Moonshine Melodies*, appeared in 1993 on the British label No Hit Records. After moving to Heyday in 1995, the Dave & Deke Combo released *Hollywood Barn Dance* the following year. *—John Bush*

- **Hollywood Barn Dance** / 1996 / Heyday ✦✦✦✦✦

Hollywood Barn Dance, the Dave & Deke Combo's second album (their debut was a British release in 1993), is full of sharp harmony singing, Dickerson's excellent guitar leads, and solid rhythms as the combo jumps from one dance-friendly cut to another, most of them (such as "Henpecked Peckerwood" and "Chrome Dome") originals written by Dickerson and Stuckey. These guys aren't just paying tribute to the past, they're having a blast. *—Kurt Wolff*

Gail Davies (Patricia Gail Dickerson)

b. Sep. 1, 1948, Broken Bow, OK

Vocals, Guitar / Singer/Songwriter, Country-Folk, Neo-Traditionalist Country, Country-Pop

The daughter of country singer Tex Dickerson, Gail Davies (born Patricia Gail Dickerson) is one of country music's most influential female artists. One of the first women to produce her own records, Davies was a major inspiration to such country music performers as Kathy Mattea, Suzy Bogguss, and Pam Tillis. In addition to composing and recording such country hits as "Grandma's Song" and "Someone Is Looking for Someone Like You," Davies has written hit tunes for the Whites, Jann Browne, and Wild Rose. Her songs have been covered by Susan McCann, Mari Nagatomi, George Hamilton IV, and Nana Mouskori.

Born in Broken Bow, a small town in Oklahoma's McCurtain County, Davies grew up in Washington state, where she moved after her mother remarried. Graduating from high-school, she relocated to Los Angeles, where she met and married a jazz musician. Although she briefly flirted with jazz, she returned to country music following her divorce. A session singer for A&M, Davies recorded with Neil Young, Hoyt Axton, and Tom Pacheco. Befriended by Joni Mitchell, she was taught the art of record producing by Mitchell's engineer, Henry Lewy. Although she was invited to tour Europe with Frank Zappa's band, Davies chose to work with witty country singer Roger Miller instead. Inspired by her older brother, Ron Davies, whose song, "It Ain't Easy," was covered by David Bowie and Three Dog Night, Davies bought a guitar and began writing songs. Signed by EMI Publishing, she moved to Nashville to write songs. One of her first efforts, "Bucket to the South," became a hit for Ava Barber and was later recorded by Lynn Anderson and Mitzi Gaynor.

Determined to stake her claim as a performer, Davies signed with CBS/Lifesong in 1978. Her self-titled debut album included two hit singles. "No Love Here I" reached the 26th slot on the *Billboard* charts, while her second single, "Someone Is Looking for Someone Like You," barely missed the Top Ten and was translated and recorded in seven languages. Producing her second album, *The Game*, in 1979, Davies continued to bring a new perspective to country music. Her third album, *Giving Herself Away*, released in 1982, included the single "'Round the Clock Lovin'." Penned by K.T. Oslin, the single reached the ninth position on the charts. The year proved monumental. In addition to giving birth to a son, Christopher Scruggs, the son of Gary Scruggs and the grandson of influential bluegrass banjo player Earl Scruggs, she released her second album of 1982, *What Can I Say*. Produced by James Taylor's bass player, Leland Sklar, Davies' fifth album, *Where Is a Woman to Go*, released in 1984, climaxed with a rendition of John Prine and Bobby Braddock's tune "Unwed Fathers," featuring harmony vocals by Dolly Parton. Performing at the Wembley Festival in London in 1985, Davies was inspired by British singer Hank Wangford to form her own country-rock band, Wild Choir. *—Craig Harris*

Gail Davies / 1978 / Lifesong ✦✦✦

The Game / 1979 / Warner Bros. ✦✦✦
Her second album was the first in which she displayed her commanding vocals on a blend of folk-influenced ballads and punchy, melodic pop-country. *—Michael McCall*

I'll Be There / 1980 / Warner Bros. ✦✦✦✦✦
Here's another consistently strong album. At a time when Barbara Mandrell and Crystal Gayle were country's biggest female stars, Davies was creating albums as distinctive and progressive as Rosanne Cash. *—Michael McCall*

Giving Herself Away / 1982 / Warner Bros. ✦✦✦✦✦
Davies brought in such outside of Nashville help as guitarist Albert Lee, bassist Leland Sklar and pianist Bill Payne of Little Feat to create an excellent album that blends Southern California folk-pop with the cutting edge of modern country. Includes the hit "Hold On" as well as a popular version of Joni Mitchell's "You Turn Me On (I'm a Radio)" and "'Round the Clock Lovin'," written by a then-unknown K.T. Oslin. *—Michael McCall*

What Can I Say / 1983 / Warner Bros. ✦✦✦
It's lighter-hearted than her others, but even when in a playful mood Davies sounds feisty, as on "Boys like You" and "You're a Hard Dog (To Keep Under the Porch)." Covers come from Rodney Crowell, Harlan Howard, Mark Knopfler and Ray Charles. *—Michael McCall*

Where Is a Woman to Go / 1984 / RCA ✦✦✦✦✦
This is her fiercest album, as far as emotional content, and her most consistently forceful, as far as musical arrangements. It's an unheralded classic. *—Michael McCall*

Wild Choir / 1986 / RCA ✦✦✦
Billed as a band, Wild Choir's songs and spirit were pure Davies, but the arrangements took on mild new wave/rock tendencies. The record proved to be too progressive at the time, and it still sounds fresher than most Nashville bands of the 1990s. "Walls" and "Never Cross That Line" rank with Davies' best compositions. *—Michael McCall*

Pretty Words / 1989 / MCA ✦✦✦
A touching combination of songs, some seeking spiritual strength, others drenched in melancholy without sinking into bathos. *—Michael McCall*

● **The Best of Gail Davies** / Jan. 21, 1991 / Liberty ✦✦✦✦✦
A substantial collection of radio hits and crowd favorites, including the poignant "Grandma's Song," "I'll Be There (If You Ever Want Me)," "'Round the Clock Lovin'" and "It's A Lovely, Lovely World." *—Michael McCall*

Greatest Hits / Jun. 16, 1998 / Koch ✦✦✦
At the close of the outlaw era in country music, a true outsider emerged on the scene who embodied all that the original cats, Waylon, Willie, Kristofferson, etc., stood for: control of their recordings, from choice of material to production. That person was Gail Davies who, on her sophomore effort for Warner Bros. in 1979, wrote, arranged, and produced all of the material on the album, becoming the first—and still one of the only—women in the history of country music to do so. This collection is a handpicked set of Davies' greatest hits from 1979-1990, re-recorded in 1997 for her Little Chickadee label. Along the way she had help from backing vocalists like Kevin Welch, Emmylou Harris, Kathy Mattea, Michelle Wright, and Ricky Skaggs. Usually efforts like this are a mixed bag. Some songs are improved upon in this process, while others pale in comparison. While none of the tunes here pale in comparison to the originals, given that they are re-recorded, they have a consistency of production that leaves out an important ambience—Davies' development as a recording artist as evidenced by the originals, which came from different albums. All the greats are here, such as "Jagged Edge With a Broken Heart," "Tell Me Why," "Blue Heartache," "Bucket to the South," and, of course, "Grandma's Song," which should never have been touched let alone redone—yes, it does contain the original fragment of her grandmother singing an old Irish folk song. "I'm Hungry, I'm Tired" is here, as is "Not a Day Goes By." Also included are some more unusual covers, like her read of Joni Mitchell's "You Turn Me On (I'm a Radio)," which actually blows away her first version, and the stomping cover of Susanna Clark and Harlan Howard's "You're a Hard Dog," which is in a dead heat with its predecessor. Of course the ballads, such as "What Can I Say" and "Not a Day Goes By," are here, and they are beautiful, but perhaps not as shockingly stunning as on their first appearances. But the big plus is that on any given day, any track on this album can still inspire, awe, and satisfy in a way few country records can anymore. And that alone is worth the cover price. *—Thom Jurek*

Live & Unplugged at the Station Inn / Sep. 25, 2001 / Valley ✦✦✦

The Davis Sisters

f. 1949, Lexington, KY, **db.** 1953
Group / Traditional Country
Known to country fans mainly as the act in which Skeeter Davis originally rose to fame, the Davis Sisters' career would have surely been much more influential and successful if tragedy hadn't derailed them just after their first hit. Although they only had one big single ("I Forgot More Than You'll Ever Know," in 1953), their outstanding close dual harmonies helped link the Appalachian harmonies of the Delmore Brothers with the more modern ones of subsequent acts like the Everlys. They were also among the earliest female country singing stars of the post-World War II era, and occasionally went into a boogie mode that foreshadowed the rockabilly movement by a year or two.

The Davis Sisters were in fact not sisters at all. Betty Jack Davis and Mary Frances Penick met in high-school in Kentucky in the late '40s, soon forming a close friendship and musical partnership. Penick changed her name to Skeeter Davis for professional purposes, so that the duo could be billed as a sister combination. By the early '50s they'd performed regularly on radio shows in Cincinnati and Detroit and made their first studio recordings in Detroit. By 1953 they were recording for RCA, backed by Nashville session players such as Chet Atkins. The mournful "I Forgot More Than You'll Ever Know" was a big hit that made them immediate stars; just as interesting, in retrospect, was the flip side, "Rock-A-Bye Boogie," which anticipated the rockabilly revolution with its frenetic rhythms and Les Paul-influenced electric guitar runs.

That first RCA session was to be Betty Jack's last, as the pair were involved in a serious auto accident in August 1953; Betty Jack died instantly, though Skeeter would recover. With the support of the Davis family, Skeeter continued the act with Betty Jack's older sister, Georgie. The reconstituted Davis Sisters continued to record through 1956, performing in the same harmony style that Skeeter had formulated with Betty Jack. These outings were quite respectable mixes of traditional country ballads with slicker, more uptempo fare, but there were no more hits, and Skeeter couldn't fully re-create the artistic and personal spark she had enjoyed with Betty Jack. While Georgie retired from music, Skeeter would by the 1960s become one of the most successful woman singers in the country-pop field. *—Richie Unterberger*

★ **Memories** / 1993 / Bear Family ✦✦✦✦✦
Bear Family does its usual astonishingly thorough job on this double-CD compilation, which has no less than 59 tracks recorded by both incarnations of the Davis sisters between 1952 and 1956 (as well as a brief 1957 Skeeter Davis solo take on "It Wasn't God Who Made Honky Tonk Angels)." The RCA singles are embellished by numerous outtakes, alternates, pre-RCA acetates of radio broadcasts, an unreleased tape of spirituals at a Kentucky Baptist Church, and their rare pre-RCA singles for the Fortune label; in fact, half of this collection was previously unreleased. The fidelity isn't always stellar on the non-RCA tracks, but most of the material is strong, and the harmonies always affecting, whether on the sad ballads, spirituals, or the occasional proto-rockabilly outings ("Rock-A-Bye Boogie," "Rag Mop," "Gotta Git A-Goin'"). While Skeeter understandably bemoaned the loss of original partner Betty Jack Davis, the sides with her replacement Georgie Davis (which actually comprise over half the package) are on about the same level as the earlier ones. Chet Atkins' guitar can be heard on most of the tracks. *—Richie Unterberger*

Danny Davis (George Nowlan)

b. Apr. 29, 1925, Dorchester, MA
Trumpet, Session Musician / Bakersfield Sound, Nashville Sound/Countrypolitan
Popularizing the use of brass instruments in the string-dominated world of country music, Danny Davis' work with his Nashville Brass inspired Buck Owens to form the Bakersfield Brass and also influenced the music of Ray Pennington, Buddy Emmons, and Merle Haggard. Born George Nowlan in Dorchester, MA, he aspired to be a horn player while in high-school. He attended the New England Conservatory of Music and at age 14 became a soloist with the Massachusetts All State Symphony Orchestra. The next year in 1940, he joined jazz drummer Gene Krupa's band and played with some of the greatest musicians of the jazz and swing era, including Bobby Byrne, Bob Crosby, and Art Mooney. After leaving Krupa, he joined Vincent Lopez's band at the Astor Hotel in New York. He remained with Lopez for many years, also working with Blue Barron and Sammy Kay.

Davis became a record producer in 1958 for Joy and MGM, producing six number one singles for Connie Francis at the latter. While on a trip to Nashville, Davis met Fred Rose and Chet Atkins; Atkins invited Davis to become a production assistant in Nashville and in 1965, Davis became an executive A&R producer (with Atkins) for several years. Near the end of the decade, Davis approached Atkins with the idea of adding brass to country music. Atkins gave the go-ahead, and the Nashville Brass was born. Their first album, *The Nashville Brass Featuring Danny Davis Play Nashville Sounds*, came out in 1968 with little fanfare. The following year, they released *More Nashville Sounds*, and people began to take notice. A new Grammy category, Best Country Instrumental Performance, was created to accommodate them, and the CMA voted them Instrumental Group or Band of the Year for five years in a row.

Since 1969, they have continued to record steadily. Davis has also collaborated with other country stars; Davis, Atkins, and Floyd Cramer made *Chet, Floyd and Danny* in 1977, and 1980 witnessed a Nashville Brass/Willie Nelson collaboration album which contained two Top 50 hits, "Night Life" and "Funny How Time Slips Away." Soon afterwards, Davis left RCA and began recording on Wartrace, his own label. The Nashville Brass continues to play in Las Vegas, in Branson, MO, and on television. *—Sandra Brennan*

● **The Best of Danny Davis & the Nashville Brass** / 1974 / Curb ✦✦✦✦✦
Fans of trumpeter and bandleader Danny Davis will have to search the used record stores to obtain any of his numerous titles recorded for RCA, since they haven't made the switch from vinyl to CD. Unfortunately, *The Best of Danny Davis & the Nashville Brass* is a shoddy and haphazard collection of nine instrumental versions of tried and true country hits, including "Make the World Go Away," "San Antonio Rose," and "Wabash Cannonball." Until the RCA material is reissued, fans will have to settle for this poor-excuse best-of CD. *—Al Campbell*

Jimmie Davis (James Houston Davis)

b. Sep. 11, 1899, Quitman, LA, **d.** Nov. 5, 2000, Baton Rouge, LA
Songwriter, Vocals, Guitar / Traditional Country
In a performing career spanning eight decades of the 20th century, Jimmie Davis embraced both risqué country blues and later traditional gospel, meanwhile maintaining a concurrent public-service career that saw him twice elected governor of Louisiana. In fact, his greatest musical successes came during his two terms as governor, once in the mid-'40s and again in the early '60s.

Born James Houston Davis in Quitman, LA, on September 11, 1899 (he would later report it as 1902, then switch back to the earlier date), Davis was the son of a poor sharecropper, but nevertheless he earned a bachelor's degree from Louisiana College–Pineville and in 1927 a masters degree from Louisiana State University. The following year, he began teaching history at a small college in Shreveport. Davis began singing occasionally for a local radio station and first recorded in 1928. One year later, he signed with Victor and began recording; these initial releases reflect a style devoted to Jimmie Rodgers, emphasizing Rodgers' penchant for double entendre. Over five years he recorded almost 70 sides for the label, and though none of the singles sold well, Davis was probably less to blame than the Depression-era economy. He moved to Decca in 1934 and gained his first major hit, "Nobody's Darlin' but Mine." Another hit, "It Makes No Difference Now," was bought from Floyd Tillman, but Davis' biggest success came from his own copyright, "You Are My Sunshine." First recorded by Davis in 1940, the song quickly entered the first rank of popular and country music standards, covered many times over by artists from both genres.

Meanwhile, Davis had quit teaching and accepted a position at the Criminal Court in Shreveport. He became the chief of police in 1938 and moved to state government four years later by being elected Louisiana Public Service Commissioner. He even found time to add another career to his resumé: Davis appeared in three film Westerns from 1942-1944 and in 1947 starred in the somewhat autobiographical *Louisiana*. Elected governor of Louisiana in 1944, he continued to record and scored five Top Five singles during his first term, including the double-sided hit "Is It Too Late Now"/"There's a Chill on the Hill Tonight" in 1944 and the number one "There's a New Moon Over My Shoulder" the following year.

Davis moved back to full-time recording in 1948, and after a stint with Capitol, he returned to Decca. Some of his country singles such as "Suppertime" began to please gospel listeners as well, and Davis gradually moved to a more sacred style. He returned to the governorship in 1960 on a segregationist platform, but to his credit, he prevented much of the unrest apparent in the South through his moderate position. Though he hadn't recorded a hit since his first term, Davis reached the Top 20 in 1962 with "Where the Old Red River Flows." By 1964, he was back to gospel music, and he recorded heavily throughout the late '60s and early '70s. Decca ended his contract in the 1975, but Davis continued to perform and record even into the 1990s. He was elected to the Country Music Hall of Fame in 1971 and lived for nearly 30 years after his election, dying at the age of 101 on November 5, 2000. *—John Bush*

Louisiana / 1947 / Daywind ✦✦✦
Louisiana is billed as "the first commercial release of the first country & western soundtrack." The 12 songs are drawn from a promotional record sent out in conjunction with the release of Jimmie Davis' 1947 bio-pic *Louisiana*. Four songs appear in instrumental and vocal versions, including Davis' super-smash "You Are My Sunshine." "Bang Bang" and "There's a New Moon Over My Shoulder," both big hits for Davis, are likewise included, although it should be emphasized that these are transcription recordings and not the original hit versions. The playing time, at just over 21 minutes, is too brief, but these sessions have historical value and at the very least provide a remedy to the dearth of Davis' music available domestically. *—Greg Adams*

● **Country Music Hall of Fame** / 1991 / MCA ✦✦✦✦✦
Country Music Hall of Fame contains 16 tracks Jimmie Davis recorded between 1934 and 1954 for Decca Records. The material ranges from country blues and novelties to gospel, Western swing, and honky tonk with a few pop crossovers like his signature hit "You Are My Sunshine" and "Nobody's Darling but Mine" thrown in for good measure. Though some of his biggest hits are missing—including "Is It Too Late Now," "Bang Bang," and "There's a Chill on the Hill Tonight"—the collection nevertheless draws a representative portrait of Davis and his career, making it a nearly definitive retrospective. *—Stephen Thomas Erlewine*

Greatest Hits: Finest Performances / Jul. 11, 1995 / Sun ✦✦✦

Nobody's Darling But Mine: 1928–1937 / May 20, 1998 / Bear Family ✦✦✦✦✦
Jimmie Davis' music is a strange mix of sentimentality and double entendre, serious devotional songs juxtaposed with utterly raunchy (and playful) blues and novelty tunes. This five-CD box consists of Davis' sides for Doggone, Victor and American Decca between July 1928 and December 9, 1937. Few performers, especially in prewar country music, could have juggled the range of repertory here for very long without offending someone and killing a chunk of their careers; instead, Davis used his music to get to the Louisiana governor's mansion twice, once in 1944 and again in 1960. Disc one opens with Davis' earliest sides for Victor in 1929, which were heavily influenced by the work of Jimmie Rodgers. Disc one ends with Davis' four 1928 sides for Doggone. The sides show serious wear and surface noise, but their main drawback is that Davis is trying to sound like Bing Crosby as he covers a quartet of then-contemporary hits. Disc two opens with a trio of hobo songs. In content and delivery, Davis' blues sound uncannily like contemporaries such as Furry Lewis, especially on this session, where most of what follows the hobo material is straight blues or novelty tunes with a risque edge. Disc three opens with a pair of the most sexually explicit songs never to make the cut on any "risqué blues" collection. The pairing of pieces like this with sentimental numbers is downright mind-boggling, yet Davis pulled it off. Discs four and five comprise the first three years of his career with Decca Records, which produced his biggest hit of the early '30s, "Nobody's Darlin' but Mine." The booklet isn't as full or detailed as one might wish, and it's sad to know that some session information on these 1920s and '30s numbers is lost to fading memories. *—Bruce Eder*

You Are My Sunshine: 1937–1948 / May 20, 1998 / Bear Family ✦✦✦✦✦
The second volume of Bear Family's retrospective on Jimmie Davis' recorded output carries listeners from 1937 through 1948, across five CDs. By this time, Davis had developed a smooth, quietly elegant yet stripped down sound, not too different from that of his slightly younger contemporary Gene Autry, with a virtuoso band behind him. Many of Davis' romantic ballads have a certain hint of jauntiness about them that prevents them from ever seeming overly sentimental. He intersperses them with the occasional jaunty country blues like "Hard Hearted Mama," and it's that balance—the bouncing between the risqué, honky tonk style numbers, the romantic ballads, the Western trail ballads, and the gospel-themed numbers—that make Davis' music early in this set very easy to take *en masse*. As time went by, however, he tended to emphasize the ballads more, partly out of the feeling that a man holding public office, as he did at different times from 1938 onward, shouldn't sing about certain subjects. Discs three and four show Davis becoming downright sophisticated by country standards, his intonation far more subtle and his backing group evoking Hollywood as well as the South, and freely incorporating elements of swing and popular music. And then, suddenly, in 1942, the blues returns, albeit dressed up a little, in the guise of "Columbus Stockade Blues" and "Walkin' My Blues Away," surrounding a fast-paced "Plant Some Flowers By My Grave." And disc five ties up loose ends between the two sets, closing out this phase of Davis' career with the recordings that he did with the Lawrence Welk Orchestra during the late '40s, which work astonishingly well, but also featuring his hard blues and stripped-down country from the early '30s. *—Bruce Eder*

Linda Davis

b. Nov. 26, 1962, Dodson, TX
Vocals / Country-Pop, Contemporary Country
A protégée of Reba McEntire, Linda Davis is best-known for a Grammy-winning duet with her mentor, "Does He Love You." Davis grew up in Texas and was singing on local radio by the age of six. She moved to Nashville in 1982 and teamed up with Skip Eaton as the duo Skip & Linda; together they had three minor hit singles, the biggest of which was "If You Could See You Through My Eyes." Davis subsequently worked as a commercial-jingle singer before catching on as a backup vocalist with Reba McEntire. Davis had a minor chart single in 1988 with "All the Good Ones Are Taken," but didn't record her debut album until 1991, when she signed with Liberty. *In a Different Light* produced two more minor hits in the title track and "Some Kinda Woman," but it wasn't a big seller; nor was the self-titled follow-up, which appeared in 1992. However, 1993 brought Davis (and McEntire) to the top of the country charts thanks to "Does He Love You," which won a Grammy for Best Country Vocal Collaboration.

With the newfound exposure and a deal with Arista, Davis' next album, 1994's McEntire-esque *Shoot for the Moon*, charted in the country Top 30, as did its follow-up, 1996's poppier *Some Things Are Meant to Be*. She switched to DreamWorks for 1998's *I'm Yours*, which featured new tracks and some previously released material, like the *Prince of Egypt* soundtrack offering "Make It Through." *—Steve Huey*

In a Different Light / 1991 / Liberty ✦✦✦✦✦
Working with producer Jimmy Bowen, Davis created lush, MOR country rife with emotional drama. *—Michael McCall*

Linda Davis / Apr. 13, 1992 / Liberty ✦✦✦

● **Shoot for the Moon** / Apr. 26, 1994 / Arista ✦✦✦✦✦
Her post-duet follow-up, the style is steamier and bluesier than her previous work, and it sounds somewhat forced. Her vocals work best on the ballads. The album does not include her duet with McEntire. *—Michael McCall*

Some Things Are Meant to Be / Jan. 30, 1996 / Arista ✦✦✦✦✦
Linda Davis is another singer who suffered through struggles to get heard. In her case, however, she tended to release formula-heavy albums empty of much character or individuality. Always an obvious talent, she bounced between record companies, all of which tried to force her into one ill-fitting trend or another. Davis finally enjoyed some exposure through a hit duet with her co-manager, Reba McEntire. Their song, "Does He Love You," won several awards and gained Davis another record contract, this time with Arista Records. Still, her 1994 album with the company had little impact. This time, she attempted to come across as a steamy chanteuse. She danced through several lame swamp-pop songs, a style that proved as unconvincing as her previous guises. However, on each of her albums, she would display her possibilities when given a chance to sing a grown-up love song. Finally, on her *Some Things Are Meant to Be*, she didn't have to try to sing two-steppers or novelties or country-rock or traditional tear-jerkers. Instead, the strong-voiced singer takes on straight-ahead, middle-of-the-road, pop-country songs, and she lives up to her promise. The songs are about women in their 30s and 40s facing up to the trouble or the joy in their lives. They're about finding strength through acknowledgment, or how sometimes perseverance is the only reward we have. They're good songs, devoid of gimmickry. And Davis brings them to life with a subtle, intelligent power. Perseverance, it seems, indeed has its rewards. *—Michael McCall*

I'm Yours / Nov. 3, 1998 / DreamWorks ✦✦✦✦
Many country fans first took notice of singer Linda Davis when she did the hit song "Does He Love You" as a duet with well-known music star Reba McEntire. That little tune became a number-one single and earned Davis a Grammy Award for Best County Vocal Collaboration in 1994. Even before then she had been touring and performing with McEntire. Four years after that huge hit single, Davis is on her own with a new label where she completed a solo offering titled *I'm Yours*. This album holds 14 tracks, all worth a listen. Seven of them have been previously released, including "Three Way Tie," "Some Things Are Meant to Be," "Love Story in the Making," and "Company Time." The other seven songs are new. One of the tracks, "Make It Through," was recorded for the *Prince of Egypt* soundtrack. It's an impressive duet done with Randy Travis. "I Wanna Remember This" was also selected to be including in a movie soundtrack *Black Dog*. *—Charlotte Dillon*

Link Davis

b. Jul. 8, 1914, Wills Point, TX, **d.** Feb. 5, 1972
Saxophone, Vocals, Session Musician / Western Swing, Rockabilly, Traditional Cajun, Rock & Roll
Link Davis was born in 1914 in Wills Point, Van Zandt County, TX, near Dallas. One of eight children, he formed a trio with two of his brothers during the late '20s, playing local

dances. A natural musician, Davis started out playing the fiddle and later took up the saxophone. He gravitated toward Western swing music when he turned professional and one of his earliest known steady gigs was as a member of the Crystal Springs Ramblers, a Fort Worth-based outfit with which he cut his first record in 1937. It was after passing through several other local bands that Davis became a member of Cliff Bruner & the Texas Wanderers, playing fiddle or saxophone on a number of their records during the early '40s. He tried forming his own band—later known as the Blue Bonnet Playboys—in 1945, and cut his first solo sides in 1948. Davis moved to the Gold Star label the following year for one release, which included his version of "Good Rockin' Tonight," retitled "Have You Heard the News."

Davis spent the 1950s working under a variety of names, as well as backing various other musicians, including bandleader Benny Leaders, Floyd Tillman, and Smith Spadacene (working as "the Harmonica Kid") on fiddle or saxophone, occasionally singing with them, and making music in a variety of idioms and styles, ranging from country blues and Cajun music to rockabilly. He was equally capable in all of these areas—as far back as 1949, he'd cut a hot adaptation of "Good Rockin' Tonight" under the title "Have You Heard the News"—and could easily have been a competitor in the new field of rock & roll when it began breaking out in the middle of the decade. Some of the flavor of his stuff, such as "Grasshopper," was a little too Southern to ever find favor outside of the region, but he was better suited in style to the new music than many other country music veterans who tried it on for size. Moving between the Starday, OKeh, Columbia, Nucraft, Sarg, and Allstar labels, and his own Western and Tanker labels, among many others, he left behind a significant legacy spread among all of those variant styles, which may be one reason Davis isn't better known. A fixture in the industry, he was too good at too many different kinds of sounds and not great enough in any one of them to make a deep impression with the public. He did earn a spot in the footnotes of rock & roll history by accompanying the Big Bopper's "Chantilly Lace" and Johnny Preston on "Running Bear," but most of Davis' recognition would reside in the country field.

Even into the 1960s, he occasionally made a foray into rock & roll with songs like "Rice and Gravy," but he failed to make a lasting impression in the field. He continued to be a top session musician and cut records in Western swing, Cajun, and blues style throughout the decade for different labels, mostly based in Houston, TX, until he was sidelined by a stroke late in the decade. After that, Davis' activities were far more limited, until his death in 1972 at age 57. It's only in the 1990s, some 20 years after his death, with the deep reissues of music by Cliff Bruner and Floyd Tillman, that Davis' wide-ranging contributions to country music, Western swing, and rock & roll fully began to be acknowledged. His son, Link Davis Jr., also a multi-instrumentalist, has similarly worked in a multitude of musical idioms, including recordings with Asleep at the Wheel and one of the latterday incarnations of the 13th Floor Elevators. —*Bruce Eder*

Cajun Crawdaddy / 1969 / Mercury ✦✦✦

● **Big Mamou Boogie** / 1989 / Edsel ✦✦✦✦
Here are 16 tracks recorded for OKeh from 1952-1954. A standout among these waltzing numbers is "Falling For You," a riveting call-and-response boogie with a great steel guitar solo. —*Richie Unterberger*

Let the Good Times Roll, 1948–1963 / Mar. 18, 1997 / Krazy Kat ✦✦✦✦
Given the sheer length of Link Davis' career, it's surprising that this 20-track CD, covering highlights across 15 years of recording, is the only compilation out on him—on the other hand, the diversity of his music also makes it difficult to quantify in a single survey. The selection covers Davis' own recordings, done for Gold Star, Nucraft, Starday, and Allstar, as well as records on which he played and sang, either backup behind Floyd Tillman or lead with Benny Leaders & the Western Rangers, or was working under the pseudonym of "the Harmonica Kid." The sound is a mix of Cajun and honky tonk, leaning toward rockabilly as the '50s sides advance, intermingled with elements of country blues—"O.P.S. Blues," credited to the 102 Ranch Boys, is an extraordinary piece of topical white blues that's almost a throwback to the Depression-era in purpose and style; it's juxtaposed with the jaunty, Cajun-flavored "Coo-Coo-Coo," which contains a gorgeous fiddle workout. The real treat for rock & roll historians, however, will be "Grasshopper," a 1955 piece of Cajun-style rockabilly that was probably a little too deep Southern to have caught on more than regionally, but would delight any fan of Sun-era Elvis Presley or Carl Perkins. Much of what Davis did over the next few years, as represented here, moved between blues, rockabilly, and country, culminating with "Beatle Bug," a 1962 instrumental credited to "The Man With the Buzzin' Sax." The makers of this collection have done their best to be comprehensive, but as this is not an authorized release (coming out of the Czech Republic by way of England), there is a mild deficiency in the sound; the sources for the early material were clearly discs—clean ones to be sure, but definitely not studio master quality. The notes are thorough enough to make up for some of the sonic drawbacks, and one shouldn't question the quality of releases like this too extensively—rather, we should be glad to have it. —*Bruce Eder*

Mac Davis (Scott Davis)

b. Jan. 21, 1942, Lubbock, TX
Vocals, Guitar / Country-Pop, Soft Rock, Nashville Sound/Countrypolitan
At his commercial peak in the mid-'70s, Mac Davis was one of America's most popular entertainers, a countrypolitan-styled singer and actor who found considerable success in both fields. Born Scott Davis on January 21, 1942, in Buddy Holly's hometown of Lubbock, TX, he began performing in local rock groups while still in his teens. After moving to Georgia, Davis first broke into the music business in 1962, when he was hired by the Chicago-based record label Vee-Jay as their Atlanta-based regional manager. After joining the Liberty label three years later, in 1967 he moved to Los Angeles to head the company's publishing arm, Metric Music; in addition to running Metric's day-to-day operations, he also began composing his own songs, with Glen Campbell, Bobby Goldsboro, Lou Rawls, and Kenny Rogers & the First Edition among the artists recording his work.

In 1968, Elvis Presley recorded Davis' "A Little Less Conversation," and soon after the King was requesting more of his work. After notching a Top 40 hit with Davis' "Memories," Presley reached the Top Five in 1969 with the songwriter's "In the Ghetto," a single from the landmark *From Elvis in Memphis* LP. Davis also arranged the music for Presley's first television special before signing his own recording contract in 1970. In that year, he released his first chart single, "Whoever Finds This, I Love You," from his debut album, *Song Painter.*

In 1972, Davis scored a number one pop hit with "Baby, Don't Get Hooked on Me," which also reached the country Top 20. His crossover success continued throughout the decade, with singles like 1974's "Stop and Smell the Roses," 1975's "Burnin' Thing," and the following year's "Forever Lovers" scoring with listeners in both camps. Between 1974 and 1976, Davis hosted a musical variety show for NBC television, followed by a string of specials; in 1979, he also starred in the film *North Dallas Forty* with Nick Nolte. Davis' success continued in the early '80s; "It's Hard to Be Humble," the title track of his 1980 album, was the first of four consecutive Top Ten country hits that culminated with his biggest country single, "Hooked on Music," the next year.

In 1980, he also starred in a TV movie, *Cheaper to Keep Her.* However, a co-starring role opposite Jackie Gleason and Karl Malden in 1983's disastrous *The Sting II* effectively ended Davis' career in Hollywood, and by 1985, he had recorded his last Top Ten hit, "I Never Made Love (Till I Made Love With You)." In 1990, Davis made a comeback as a songwriter, co-authoring Dolly Parton's hit "White Limozeen"; that same year, he also took over the title role in the Broadway hit *the Will Rogers Follies. Will Write Songs for Food*, his first LP in nearly a decade, appeared in 1994. —*Jason Ankeny*

Song Painter / 1971 / Columbia ✦✦✦

I Believe in Music / 1972 / Columbia ✦✦✦✦
I Believe in Music is partly a journey through Mac Davis' songwriting past in that he revisits a few of his songs that were hits for other artists, like "Watching Scotty Grow" (a hit for Bobby Goldsboro) and "A Little Less Conversation" (a hit for Elvis Presley). The anthemic title track became a hit for the pop group Gallery in 1972, and received wider exposure than its modest chart placement suggests. The aggressive electric guitar leads and classic rock attack of "Something's Burning" illustrate Davis' uneasy alliance with country music; his country-soul style is comparable to that of Charlie Rich, another '70s superstar who was far from traditional in his approach to the genre. *I Believe in Music* was Davis' second album for Columbia, delivered a year before his commercial breakthrough with "Baby Don't Get Hooked on Me." Columbia was pushing Davis as the "Song Painter" (the title of his Columbia debut, and the subtitle of this album) on the basis of his songwriting success, but in short order Davis would become a name performer as well. —*Greg Adams*

Baby Don't Get Hooked on Me / 1972 / Columbia ✦✦✦✦✦
Mac Davis' breakthrough album and the bearer of his biggest hit, *Baby Don't Get Hooked on Me* established Davis as a major performer as well as a songwriter. "Baby Don't Get Hooked on Me" topped the pop chart for three weeks and set the tone for this accomplished singer/songwriter album that straddles the lines between commercial pop, folk, and country. "Singer/songwriter" became a genre rather than a descriptor in the early '70s when artists like Davis, Jonathan Edwards, and James Taylor began mixing styles into a cohesive but hard-to-classify blend. Davis had less of a folk orientation than Edwards or Taylor, which may be why his music has a more period-specific sound, but he remains one of the most multi-talented artists of his day. —*Greg Adams*

Mac Davis / 1973 / Columbia ✦✦✦✦

Stop & Smell the Roses / 1974 / Columbia ✦✦✦✦

All the Love in The World / 1974 / Columbia ✦✦✦

Burnin' Thing / 1975 / Columbia ✦✦✦
The title track from *Burnin' Thing* wasn't a very big hit for Mac Davis, but the album—helped along by exposure from Davis' television program, *the Mac Davis Show*—made the charts. It's a wild assortment of songs, from glossy pop to Elvis Presley-style country-rock. "The Hits Just Keep on Coming," an ode to rock & roll radio, is the best cut, and the award for most unusual goes to Davis' own "Rufus Was a Redneck," a Hoyt Axton soundalike about a racist who gets his due. "The Jimmy Brown Song" is better known as "The Three Bells," and "I Still Love You (You Still Love Me)" made an even weaker chart showing than "Burnin' Thing." Davis' fans may enjoy the full range of offerings on *Burnin' Thing*, but most listeners will find only a few cuts that strike their fancy. —*Greg Adams*

Forever Lovers / 1976 / Columbia ✦✦✦

Thunder in the Afternoon / 1977 / Columbia ✦✦✦

Fantasy / 1978 / Columbia ✦✦✦

Greatest Hits / 1979 / Columbia ✦✦✦✦✦
In addition to '70s smashes like "Baby Don't Get Hooked on Me" and "Stop and Smell the Roses," *Greatest Hits* also includes the Davis-penned "In the Ghetto," a major hit for Elvis Presley. —*Jason Ankeny*

It's Hard to Be Humble / 1980 / Casablanca ✦✦✦

Texas in My Rear View Mirror / 1980 / Casablanca ✦✦✦✦
Boasting hits like "Hooked on Music," "Me 'N Fat Boy," and the title track, *Texas in My Rear View Mirror* returned Mac Davis to the top of the charts. Consistently solid songwriting and production help to make this release a worthy effort. —*James Chrispell*

Midnight Crazy / 1981 / Casablanca ✦✦✦

Forty 82 / 1982 / Casablanca ✦
You have to wonder if Mac Davis knew that when he signed to Casablanca Records there was a subliminal message in every contract that somehow every record on the label except for Kiss albums had to have disco elements—even after disco was dead. After all, if they did it to T. Rex with *Light of Love*, why wouldn't they do it to the "I Believe in Music"

man. This record is so bad it's almost surreal. Rick Hall should have had his producer's license taken away just for the opening cut, "Lying Here Lying," with its swirling strings, synthesizers, and funky drum machines popping off those ping sounds in the background. Even on the "country" songs such as "Late at Night," the guitars are so compressed they sound like thin spaghetti played through a Fender amplifier, and the keyboards can't make up their minds whether to sound like pianos or synths. Ugh. "The Beer Drinkin' Song," a self-penned, hedonistic racist anthem, is embarrassing in its blatant rip-off of Ray Wylie Hubbard and Jimmy Buffett. OK, that's just side one, and side two is worse. Enough said; hopefully all the remaining copies of this record in the warehouse—and surely there were plenty—were melted down and used for something constructive. —*Thom Jurek*

Soft Talk / 1984 / Casablanca ✦✦✦

Very Best & More . . . / 1984 / Casablanca ✦✦✦✦

All of Davis's hits from his 1980-1984 tenure at Casablanca Records are included in the collection *Very Best & More . . .* In addition to "Hooked on Music," and his biggest-seller, the album includes "You're My Bestest Friend," "Texas in My Rear View Mirror," "Let's Keep It That Way," and "It's Hard to Be Humble." —*Jason Ankeny*

I Sing the Hits / Dec. 1, 1995 / Sony Special Products ✦✦✦

Baby Don't Get Hooked on Me/Stop & Smell the Roses / Jul. 1, 1997 / Collectables ✦✦✦✦

Two of Mac Davis' most popular albums from the early '70s, *Baby Don't Get Hooked on Me* and *Stop & Smell the Roses*, were combined on this single-CD reissue by Collectables. Although the sound and the packaging could be a little better, this still is a fine way for collectors to pick up these two records on disc. —*Stephen Thomas Erlewine*

● **The Best of Mac Davis** / Oct. 24, 2000 / Razor & Tie ✦✦✦✦✦

Razor & Tie's *The Very Best of Mac Davis* overlooks some late-'70s and early-'80s hits, but they're not missed, since this winds up as a first-rate chronicle of Davis at his peak. Davis walked the thin line between country and AM pop with his lavishly produced, sweet soft rock, delivering the melodies with just a hint of twang. This is unabashedly mainstream stuff, but it's so well done that it's hard to resist, especially since Davis' warm baritone is the perfect foil for his evocatively corny tales. This concentrates on his late-'60s/early-'70s material, when he was at the peak of his powers. The compilers were savvy, and this doesn't slow as it winds through his biggest hits of the time, along with a couple lesser-known hits. It's an excellent compilation, and even if it doesn't have "I Believe in Music," it will make you a believer. —*Stephen Thomas Erlewine*

Skeeter Davis (Mary Frances Penick)

b. Dec. 30, 1931, Dry Ridge, KY

Vocals / Country-Pop, Pop, Nashville Sound/Countrypolitan, Traditional Country, Country-Rock

Skeeter Davis has never gotten a lot of critical attention, but in the '50s and '60s, she recorded some of the most accessible crossover country music, occasionally skirting rock & roll. Born Mary Frances Penick, Davis took her last name after forming a duo with Betty Jack Davis, the Davis Sisters. Their 1953 single "I Forgot More Than You'll Ever Know" was a big country hit; its B-side, the remarkable "Rock-A-Bye Boogie," foreshadowed rockabilly. That same year, however, the duo's career was cut short by a tragic car accident in which Betty Jack was killed and Skeeter was severely injured. Skeeter did attempt to revive the Davis Sisters with Betty Jack's sister but was soon working as a solo artist.

In the early '60s, Davis followed the heels of Brenda Lee and Patsy Cline to become one of the first big-selling female country crossover acts, although her pop success was pretty short-lived. The weepy ballad "The End of the World," though, was a massive hit, reaching number two in 1963. "I Can't Stay Mad at You," a Top Ten hit the same year, was downright rock & roll; penned by Gerry Goffin & Carole King, it sounded like (and was) an authentic Brill Building girl group-styled classic. Goffin/King also wrote another successful girl group knockoff for her, "Let Me Get Close to You," although such efforts were the exception rather than the rule. Usually she sang sentimental, country-oriented tunes with enough pop hooks to catch the ears of a wider audience, such as "I Will."

Davis concentrated on the country market after the early '60s, although she never seemed too comfortable limiting herself to the Nashville crowd. She recorded a Buddy Holly tribute album in 1967, when Holly wasn't a hot ticket with either the country or the rock audience. But she certainly didn't reject country conventions either: She performed on the *Grand Ole Opry* and recorded duets with Bobby Bare, Porter Wagoner, and George Hamilton IV. In the 1980s, she had a mild comeback with the rock crowd after recording an album with NRBQ; she also married NRBQ's bass player, Joey Spampinato. —*Richie Unterberger*

I'll Sing You a Song and Harmonize, Too / 1960 / RCA ✦✦✦✦

Here's the Answer / 1960 / RCA ✦✦

Country's never been afraid to lay on the corn, but even by its own standards, the concept driving this 1960 album was hokey. Davis sings "answer" songs to hits by Jim Reeves, Hank Locklin, Eddy Arnold, Jim Reeves, and Ray Peterson—"I Really Want You to Know," for instance, in response to Arnold's "I Really Don't Want to Know." As all of those singers happened to be contracted to Davis' label, RCA, the original versions were available for inclusion/instant comparison. That means that half of this album isn't Davis at all; you'll hear, for instance, Jim Reeves singing "He'll Have to Go," followed immediately by Davis' "He'll Have to Stay"; Ray Peterson's "Tell Laura I Love Her" is countered with Davis' "Tell Tommy I Miss Him"; and so on. It gets really ridiculous when Davis sings an answer song ("My Last Date") to Floyd Cramer's *instrumental* hit "Last Date." Davis' songs are OK mainstream country/pop; a couple of them ("(I Can't Help You) I'm Falling Too" and "My Last Date") were even Top 40 pop hits. But alternating her tracks bang-bang with hits by various other male country stars makes for a rather herky-jerky listening experience.

[A mid-'90s European CD reissue of the album adds four bonus tracks from a 1962 duet single with Porter Wagoner and a 1964 duet single with Bobby Bare (including a cover of "We'll Sing in the Sunshine"), none of which rate among the better performances of either Davis or her partners.] —*Richie Unterberger*

Cloudy, With Occasional Tears / 1963 / RCA ✦✦✦

End of the World / 1963 / RCA ✦✦✦✦

Let Me Get Close to You / 1964 / RCA ✦✦

I Forgot More Than You'll Ever Know / 1964 / Camden ✦✦✦

I Forgot More Than You'll Ever Know is a budget album on RCA's Camden imprint that compiles an assortment of material, from the Davis Sisters' 1953 number-one hit "I Forgot More Than You'll Ever Know" to various Skeeter Davis non-hits and B-sides going back at least as far as 1960. "I'm Going Steady With a Heartache" cleverly melds country with teen pop, and the solo tracks feature the trademark double-tracked vocals that later put Davis in a position to exploit the girl group craze from the direction of country music. The recordings are presented in reprocessed rather than true stereo, and there isn't even a minor hit in the bunch besides the Davis Sisters' track, but *I Forgot More Than You'll Ever Know* gives true fans an opportunity to obtain some good-to-excellent stray tracks in a single package. —*Greg Adams*

Written by the Stars / 1965 / RCA ✦✦

Skeeter Sings Standards / 1965 / RCA ✦✦✦✦✦

The Best of Skeeter Davis / 1965 / RCA ✦✦✦✦✦

Skeeter fused country, pop, and even occasional girl group sounds during her commercial peak in the early '60s, which found her at her most fetching and tuneful. This has 12 of her most successful recordings of the era, including the huge ballad "The End of the World," which hit number two on the pop charts in 1963, and Goffin/King's irresistible girl group composition "I Can't Stay Mad At You," which reached the Top Ten the same year. —*Richie Unterberger*

My Heart's in the Country / 1966 / RCA ✦✦✦

The cover art, with Davis fondling farm animals in front of the barn and extolling the rural life in the liner notes, makes a pretty determined effort at presenting Davis in as much of a pure country light as possible. The actual music, by and large, follows suit. Produced by Felton Jarvis in Nashville, it's plainer and more traditional in mood than her work with Chet Atkins and Anita Kerr. The strings are banished and the guitar picking and fiddles are at the forefront, although the vocals are still double-tracked. It's kind of an average effort, without any particular flaws or standout material. Includes compositions by Dolly Parton and Loretta Lynn, as well as Davis' rendition of the traditional "Goin' Down the Road (Feelin' Bad)." —*Richie Unterberger*

Skeeter Davis Sings Buddy Holly / 1967 / RCA ✦✦✦

Here are 12 Holly covers, produced by Felton Jarvis in Nashville and featuring Waylon Jennings on guitar, at a time when neither Davis nor Holly were exactly in the forefront of pop's collective consciousness. A modest accomplishment, this LP is nevertheless fairly worthwhile, with a much more upbeat sound than Davis' early-'60s recordings. The arrangements are pretty straightforward and close to the originals, with solid country-rock backing and occasional light, tasteful strings. —*Richie Unterberger*

Why So Lonely? / 1968 / RCA ✦✦✦

What Does It Take (To Keep a Man Like You Satisfied) / 1968 / RCA Victor ✦✦✦

I Love Flatt & Scruggs / 1968 / RCA ✦✦✦

Closest Thing to Love / 1969 / RCA ✦✦✦

Foggy Mountain Top / 1971 / Camden ✦✦✦

Love Takes a Lot of My Time / 1971 / RCA ✦✦✦

The End of the World / 1972 / Capitol ✦✦✦

Recorded at the peak of Davis' brief stardom, this emphasizes the weepy country-pop that gave her a number-two pop hit with the title track. Nothing here measures up to that wonderful smash, but it's tasteful enough period Nashville country, with producers Anita Kerr and Chet Atkins ensuring that the LP measured up to state-of-the-art country-pop production by double-tracking Davis' vocals against a background of strings and lazy barroom piano runs. They did let her loose on Little Eva's "Keep Your Hands off My Baby," which is replete with primitive fuzz guitar. Though it may sound enticing, the result is actually kind of lousy and ill-fitting. —*Richie Unterberger*

The Best of Skeeter Davis, Vol. 2 / 1973 / RCA ✦✦✦

A ridiculously uneven collection, veering between solid country uptempo numbers to pathetic weepers (which could be either effective or embarrassing), a fine girl group pastiche, a stupid courtroom divorce song, and a couple lousy covers of early-'70s pop hits ("One Tin Soldier"?!). By far the best cut is her girl group take on Goffin-King's "Let Me Get Close to You," which is in the same class as her similar 1963 Top Ten pop hit "I Can't Stay Mad at You" (also written by Goffin/King). "Sunglasses" is an out-of-character pop number by John D. Loudermilk, and a couple of the straight country tunes are decent, but this is a very scattershot compilation; surely Skeeter recorded enough decent material to warrant a better selection. —*Richie Unterberger*

● **The Essential Skeeter Davis** / 1996 / RCA ✦✦✦✦✦

Featuring 20 tracks, *The Essential Skeeter Davis* collects all of her big hits from both the country and pop charts, making it the one definitive compilation. —*Stephen Thomas Erlewine*

RCA Country Legends / Sep. 25, 2001 / Buddha ✦✦✦✦✦

As part of RCA's *Country Legends* series, this set highlights Skeeter Davis' earliest records as one part of the Davis Sisters, along with her solo outings. Among the 16 tracks are the hit singles "Rock-A-Bye Boogie," "I Forgot More Than You'll Ever Know," and her signature song, "The End of the World." With the exception of omitting "I Can't Stay Mad at You," this collection serves as an excellent career overview. —*Al Campbell*

Julian Dawson

Guitar, Harmonica, Vocals / Alternative Country, Americana
Combining British pop and American roots rock, Julian Dawson first gained prominence in Europe with a single on Rough Trade Records in the mid-'80s. He then released two albums on Polydor Records. He also recorded two albums with Ian Matthews' band, Plainsong. His first domestic release, *Live on the Radio*, appeared in 1990 on Watermelon Records. Dawson then recorded *Fragile as China* the following year for BMG/Ariola. The first single, "How Can I Sleep Without You," reached the charts. 1994 brought a greatest-hits album, *How Human Hearts Behave*, which included a re-recording of "How Can I Sleep Without You" with Lucinda Williams. The next year, *Travel On* was issued, again on Watermelon Records. It featured collaborations with Nicky Hopkins, Jules Shear, and Willie Nile; the Roches and Curtis Stigers contributed vocals. *Move Over Darling* followed in 1997, and two years later Dawson returned with both *Spark* and *Under the Sun.* —*John Bush*

Live on the Radio / 1990 / Watermelon ◆◆◆
Dawson—the only Brit on the label, recorded the engaging, thought-provoking *Live on the Radio* before an audience of 500 in a radio station studio in Cologne, Germany. —*Roch Parisien*

Fragile as China / Mar. 17, 1991 / Ariola ◆◆◆

● **Travel On** / 1995 / Watermelon ◆◆◆◆

Move Over Darling / Jun. 24, 1997 / Compas ◆◆◆

Spark / Mar. 23, 1999 / Gadfly ◆◆◆◆◆
What do Richard Thompson, Steve Forbert, the Roches, and Lucinda Williams know that most Americans don't? They know about the brilliant singer/songwriter Julian Dawson, who has released numerous albums in Europe while experiencing an unfortunate lack of distribution in the U.S. Not only do they know about him, but they think enough of him to have been guest artists on those obscure European albums. *Spark* is a superb compilation that brings together 14 of his best songs, including "How Can I Sleep Without You" (an acoustic-based duet with Lucinda Williams), the rocking "Fragile as China" (which features E Street Band bassist Garry Tallent) and "Two Shots of Jealousy" (with Richard Thompson), and the whimsical "I Like Your Absence" (with the equally whimsical Roches on backing vocals). The songs and performances are of consistently top quality, muscular and solid and bright and poppy by turns. Dawson sings in an unaffected baritone voice that cuts through the mix but never draws attention to itself. —*Rick Anderson*

Under the Sun / Oct. 12, 1999 / Gadfly ◆◆◆

Hillbilly Zen / Jul. 9, 2002 / Fledg'ling ◆◆◆

Ronnie Dawson

b. Aug. 11, 1939, Waxahachie, TX
Guitar, Vocals / Rockabilly
The son of a swing bandleader, Ronnie Dawson came close to achieving success as a rockabilly guitarist/singer. An only child, born in Waxahachie, TX, Dawson launched his musical career while still in his teens. Forming a band, Ronnie Dee and the D Men, he won a talent contest at the Big D Jamboree in Dallas ten weeks in a row. He signed with Gene Vincent's manager, Ed MacLemore. His first two singles, "Action Packed" b/w "I Make the Love" and "Rockin' Bones," sold well regionally and resulted in a contract with Dick Clark's label, Swan, and an appearance on *National Bandstand*. Dawson's success came to a halt when the payola scandal forced Clark to close the record company, leaving Dawson without a label. Limited to a sideman position, Dawson toured with the Light Crust Doughboys and played rums on Paul & Paula's "Hey Paula" and Bruce Chanel's "Hey Baby."

A member of the Dallas-based Levee Singers in the 1960s, he performed with a country-rock band, Steelrail, in the 1970s and '80s and recorded commercial jingles for Hungry Jack pancakes, Jax beer, and Cici's pizza. Although he remained little-known in his native country, Dawson was hailed as a rock pioneer in England. Signing with the British No Hit label in 1986, he recorded three impressive albums: *Monkey Beat!!*, *Rockinitis*, and *Just Rockin' & Rollin'*. The label also released a compilation of his earlier recordings, *Rockin' Bones*. Dawson recorded a live album, *Live! at the Continental Club*, in Austin, TX, in January 1998. In October 1998, he returned to the recording studio to record *More Bad Habits*, his first studio recording in the U.S. in nearly three decades.

Dawson's song "Yum, Yum, Yum" was featured in Mike Nichols' film *Primary Colors*. Izzy Stradlin of Guns n' Roses recorded his tune "Up Jump the Devil." Two songs from *More Bad Habits* were included in the December 1999 film *Simpatico*. In addition to recording under his own name, Dawson credited a 1961 single, "Do Do Do" b/w "Jump and Run," to the fictional character Commonwealth Jones. —*Craig Harris*

Still a Lot of Rhythm / 1988 / No Hit ◆◆◆
Dawson's first comeback effort was impressive in that it found him in good (if noticeably lower) voice, though the material was average and the performances a bit restrained. No need to look for the hard-to-find British import; it's been reissued domestically, in its entirety, as bonus material on Crystal Clear's *Monkey Beat!!* CD. —*Richie Unterberger*

Rockinitis / 1989 / Crystal Clear ◆◆◆
Dawson's second album since his mid-'80s rediscovery is an above-average latter-day rockabilly effort, sensibly avoiding temptations to modernize the sound with too much clutter. Dawson's voice has lowered considerably since his early days, meaning that instead of sounding like a little kid, he sounds like a young man (although he was about 50 when this was recorded). [The American CD reissue adds a bonus cut, "Sloppy Drunk," not on the original British release.] —*Richie Unterberger*

● **Rockin' Bones** / 1990 / No Hit ◆◆◆◆◆
This 20-track CD has all his essential early recordings, with both sides of five singles (the Swan teen idol efforts aren't included). Besides "Action Packed," highlights are the subsequent A-sides "Do Do Do" and "Rockin' Bones," as well as a spooky rendering of "Riders in the Sky." The unreleased tracks include several raw demos he cut prior to his first single, as well as a few outtakes from his Columbia session that feature some harmonica work by Delbert McClinton. —*Richie Unterberger*

Monkey Beat!! / Oct. 1994 / Crystal Clear ◆◆◆◆◆
Monkey Beat!! confirmed Dawson's status as the most vital of the middle-aged rockabilly singers who was still performing and recording in the 1990s. It's actually rawer (in the positive sense of the term) than the two previous comeback albums he recorded for No Hit in the late '80s. He's in fine, spontaneous voice, and the material (including a few originals), as always, avoids overdone standards. As a significant bonus, the CD tacks on the entirety of his 1988 album, *Still a Lot of Rhythm*, originally released on the British No Hit label; it's a respectable but tamer effort than the first half of the program. —*Richie Unterberger*

Just Rockin' & Rollin' / Jun. 1996 / Upstart ◆◆◆
A more easygoing effort than *Monkey Beat!!*, with a decidedly more countrified influence. Echoes of Tex-Mex creep in here and there as well, and a few tracks have a horn section. A lot of Dawson fans will prefer Ronnie's wilder latter-day releases, where he lets go more, and where singing and playing skirt a more reckless, dangerous edge. Rockabilly's a limited form, though, and he should get some credit for playing around with the format mildly, instead of just serving up more of the same. It's still a solid, crisp record of reasonably strong material, though Dawson himself wrote little of it. —*Richie Unterberger*

● **Rockin' Bones: The Legendary Masters** / Sep. 17, 1996 / Crystal Clear ◆◆◆◆◆
This is a two-CD, 34-song overview of Dawson's early recordings, spanning 1957 to 1962. It includes most of his singles from the era, and a tall heap of acetates, demos, and alternate takes; in fact, over half of the material was unreleased at the time. The stylistic variety is a little manic, moving from raw home demo rockabilly-blues to straight studio rockabilly (including the classic "Action Packed") to teen idol pop to country arrangements that prominently feature banjo. It's the definitive compilation, though, of the early work of this one-of-a-kind rockabilly singer. It has almost all of the tracks of the previous collection of his early sides (on No Hit), and replaces that disc as the anthology of choice. —*Richie Unterberger*

More Bad Habits / Aug. 31, 1999 / Yep Rock ◆◆◆◆
At age 60, and with a lifetime of rock & roll behind him and accounted for, Ronnie Dawson could still bring the heat, as exemplified by this inspired session. Recording for the first time in America in a couple of decades, Dawson turned in a plate of originals, co-written with manager/producer Barney Koumis, that tell the tale of what happens when a rockabilly wildcat reaches middle age. Tunes like "Good at Being Bad," "Mac Attack," "Toe Up from the Flo Up," and "Bad Habit or Two" address rebel concerns in an age of political correctness, seeing life for what it is while defiantly refusing to equate getting older with *getting old*. Sharing the lead guitar duties with Mike Molnar and Matt Robbins (on "Party Slab"), Dawson rocks just as hard as ever and his material has never been better. This record puts the lie to most any "too old to rock & roll" myth you'd care to encounter. —*Cub Koda*

Jimmy Day

b. Jan. 9, 1934, Tuscaloosa, AL, d. Jan. 22, 1999
Guitar (Steel) / Traditional Country, Western Swing, Honky Tonk, Instrumental Country
Along with Shot Jackson and Buddy Emmons, legendary sideman Jimmy Day stood among the finest steel guitarists ever to grace country music; "Mr. Country Soul," he and his guitar, the legendary Blue Darlin', lent their artistry to records from performers ranging from Webb Pierce to Ray Price to Willie Nelson. Born January 9, 1934, in Tuscaloosa, AL, Day harbored dreams of a career in country music from childhood onward; his initial attempts to learn guitar proved frustrating, however, when he faced considerable difficulty with his fret work. His problems were solved in 1949, when he saw Jackson providing steel support for the Bailes Brothers; that Christmas, Day received his first steel guitar, and by the age of 16 he was regularly performing at area honky tonk shows.

After graduating high-school, in 1951 Day successfully auditioned for the *Louisiana Hayride* radio program; he soon began working with Pierce, with whom he recorded his first sessions. He soon introduced Pierce to pianist Floyd Cramer, whom Day had known since junior high; these sessions produced the Pierce smash "This Heart Belongs to Me," which hit number one just prior to Day's 18th birthday. In the spring of 1952, he also began a six-month stint backing Hank Williams; in November—less than two months before his tragic death—Williams asked Day to join a new band he planned to assemble in the year to follow. In the wake of the tragedy, Day worked with Red Sovine and Jim Reeves, and overdubbed a handful of posthumous Williams recordings. He also appeared on Mitchell Torok's 1953 hit "Caribbean."

With the advent of pedal steel guitar in 1954, Day began moving away from lap steel during a tenure with Lefty Frizzell; among his final sessions playing lap steel was a *Louisiana Hayride* date backing Elvis Presley. In early 1955 Presley assembled a backing band comprised of Day, Cramer, guitarist Scotty Moore, bassist Bill Black, and drummer D.J. Fontana that remained his supporting unit for much of the year; when Presley relocated to Hollywood he invited the band to join him, but both Day and Cramer declined in order to pursue careers with the *Grand Ole Opry*. In 1956 Day switched permanently to pedal steel and appeared on Ray Price's "Crazy Arms"; he soon relocated to Nashville to join Price's band, the Cherokee Cowboys, and by extension became a member of the Opry. He also convinced Jackson to begin manufacturing his own pedal steel guitars, and soon the Sho-Bud, the first classic electric pedal steel, hit the market; with it came Day's first steel to bear the Blue Darlin' name.

In 1955 Day cut his first instrumental single, "Rippin' Out"; over the next two years he toured extensively with Pierce and also appeared infrequently with the Cherokee Cowboys, Ernest Tubb's Texas Troubadors, and Jim Reeves' Blue Boys. In 1959, Day rejoined Price, where he was teamed with a young bassist named Willie Nelson; when Nelson broke from Price three years later, he took Day with him. By 1963 Day also began performing with George Jones, and released his debut solo LP, *Steel & Strings*. In the years to follow he tenured with the likes of Ferlin Husky, Leon Russell, Clay Baker, Charlie Louvin, and Don Walser, and also cut a number of records, including *All Those Years, For Jimmy Day Fans Only*, and *Jimmy Day and the Texas Outlaw Jam Band*. He was inducted into the International Steel Guitar Hall of Fame in 1982. *—Jason Ankeny*

Golden Steel Guitar Hits / 1962 / Philips ♦♦♦

Steel and Strings / 1963 / Philips ♦♦♦

Day with Remington / 1992 / Glad Music ♦♦♦

● **Golden Steel Guitar Hits/Steel and Strings** / 1992 / Bear Family ♦♦♦
Jimmy Day's talent as a steel guitarist is indisputable, and this import two-fer reissues his 1962 instrumental albums *Golden Steel Guitar Hits* and *Steel & Strings* on one disc. The albums were recorded under the direction of Shelby Singleton and Jerry Kennedy and feature an all-star cast of Nashville A-team accompanists. Like fellow steel guitarist Noel Boggs, Day could venture into easy listening territory as evidenced on the *Steel & Strings* album, which is indistinguishable from the music of 101 Strings. The mellow mood is exacerbated by the use a vocal chorus on both albums (which isn't necessarily bad, but isn't what many buyers would expect). The fluid steel guitar solos make it all worthwhile, though, and Day certainly deserves the spotlight. *—Greg Adams*

Jesse Dayton

Guitar / Alternative Country
Raised in Beaumont, TX, near the childhood home of George Jones, Jesse Dayton grew up on the hardcore honky tonk of Jones, Hank Williams Sr., and Lefty Frizzell, but also blues artists such as Lightnin' Hopkins and Mance Lipscomb. During the late '80s and early '90s Dayton fronted two rockabilly bands, the Roadkings and the Alamo Jets, playing around the state in honky tonks and dives. After beginning a solo career, he played support slots at shows by Willie Nelson, Merle Haggard, and Waylon Jennings, and even appeared as the bandleader in a Pam Tillis video. Signed to Justice Records in 1995, he released *Raisin' Cain* that same year and also appeared on the Willie Nelson tribute record, *Twisted Willie*. Dayton's songs have also appeared in the FOX-TV series *Melrose Place* and in the film *Curse of the Starving Class*. In fall 2000, Dayton issued *Tall Texas Tales*. *—John Bush*

Raisin' Cain / Jul. 25, 1995 / Justice ♦♦♦

Tall Texas Tales / Oct. 24, 2000 / Bullet Records ♦♦♦

● **Hey Nashvegas** / Sep. 25, 2001 / Stag ♦♦♦♦
Formerly leader of the Road Kings, the second solo album from Jesse Dayton offers up a healthy dose of personal stories and melodies that fall even further into pure country than any previous record. Perhaps with more vocal character than the mainstream would cater to, Dayton nonetheless embraces a slicker, more Nashville-like production on *Hey Nashvegas* (hence the poking comparison in the title). Songs such as "Never Started Living" and "One Life Stand" have his trademark clever wordiness over his always top-notch musicians and guitar playing, while "Date With the Angels" is an example of Dayton's ability to evoke imagery with solid, enthusiastic lyrics (though bordering on over-singing at times). His voice is especially kind when coupled with others, and he gets some help from Mandy Barnett on "Hey Nashvegas" and "Don't Take Yesterday." Even the Dixie Chicks stop by to sing backups on the most fun song of the lot, "Panhandle Jane." The bittersweet longing of "Letter to Home" is good as any Merle Haggard song, and the south of the border stylings of "Heartbreak California" is a welcome and successful change of pace. What makes this album impressive is Dayton's insightful take on everyday heartbreaks, as told through a classic formula of country and with just the right amount of personality. *—Ian Trumbull*

Billy Dean

b. Apr. 1, 1962, Quincy, FL
Vocals, Guitar / Country-Pop, Neo-Traditionalist Country, Contemporary Country
Billy Dean received a basketball scholarship to attend East Central Junior College in Decatur, MS, where he majored in physical education, but instead of wearing a whistle around his neck, he opted for a guitar strap. Inspired by Merle Haggard, Marty Robbins, and Dean Martin, he played the club circuit along the Gulf Coast in Florida and used national talent contests as a vehicle for his music. He made the finals of the Wrangler Country Star Search in 1982, then won as a Male Vocalist champ on Ed McMahon's *Star Search* program in 1988. Even before the release of his debut album, *Young Man*, he'd already gone on tour as an opening act for Mel Tillis, Gary Morris, and Ronnie Milsap. In the midst of recording, Dean also dabbled in television. He contributed to commercials for Valvoline, McDonald's, and Chevrolet, and had an acting role in the brief *Elvis* series on ABC-TV in 1990. He landed bit parts on soap operas and dramas, and even hosted the 1994 season of *ABC in Concert Country*.

Dean followed up his debut with a self-titled 1991 effort for EMI; *Fire in the Dark* appeared two years later. A 1994 greatest-hits package included the song "Once in a While," written for the soundtrack to the Luke Perry rodeo vehicle *8 Seconds*. A greatest-hits collection so early in an artist's career might seem strange, but considering that Dean had already charted seven singles, the release was easy money for Capitol. However, Dean's reign at the top of the charts was short-lived. Despite frequent releases throughout the rest of the 1990s, Dean wasn't able to crack the charts again. After three studio records and a live, fan-club-only disc, Dean issued *Love Songs* through Capitol in 2000. The collection of previously released material was followed by another, similar collection for Capitol/EMI in 2002. Dean continued to tour through 2003. *—Johnny Loftus*

Young Man / 1990 / Liberty ♦♦♦♦♦
Nashville launched so many new acts from 1989-1992 that many who deserved a shot went overlooked. Thanks in part to his own songwriting skills, and to signing with SBK Records, which had just one country act to push, he got a good listen and was able to capitalize with a strong debut. His vocals aren't unique, but he sings with strength and conviction, regardless of the style. You can't go wrong with "Somewhere in My Broken Heart." *—Tom Roland*

Billy Dean / 1991 / Liberty ♦♦♦♦♦
Billy Dean's second album follows the same pattern that made his first so popular: a strong emphasis on the ballads on which his supple baritone thrives. The rollicking "Hammer Down" flies in the face of everything else, but even there the message remains the same: obvious but effective. *—Brian Mansfield*

Fire in the Dark / 1993 / Liberty ♦♦♦
Like *Billy Dean* before it, *Fire in the Dark* doesn't stray from the pattern Dean established on *Young Man*, which might not necessarily be a bad thing. However, there is the problem of diminishing returns—each time he goes back to the well, he's coming back with a lesser number of first-rate songs. There are highlights on *Fire in the Dark*, but nothing on the album represents a progress from his first two albums. *—Thom Owens*

Men'll Be Boys / 1994 / Liberty ♦♦♦
With *Men'll Be Boys*, Billy Dean's formula began to wear thin. Although he was still in good voice and he had a handful of good songs, the calculation behind the album's sound is apparent—the filler isn't as enjoyable as it was on his first three records. *—Thom Owens*

● **Greatest Hits** / Mar. 8, 1994 / Liberty ♦♦♦♦♦
As the title implies, the ten-track *Greatest Hits* collects Billy Dean's biggest hit singles, which usually happen to be the best parts of his albums. Consequently, *Greatest Hits* is Dean's most consistent and enjoyable album. *—Thom Owens*

It's What I Do / Apr. 1996 / Capitol ♦♦
Billy Dean mixes thoughtful ballads with brisk rockers. But after a couple of memorable early hits, he has settled for songs that carry no distinctive passion or energy. *It's What I Do* follows an extensive lay-off from the road, but the introspective period has done little to improve his work. Mistaking tender sincerity for genuine emotion is an error many acoustic-based artists make. Unfortunately, the more Dean attempts to add tension or drama to his work, the tamer his performances become. With this album, it's hard to delineate exactly what it is that Dean does well. *—Michael McCall*

Real Man / Aug. 25, 1998 / Capitol ♦♦♦♦
Award-winning country singer Billy Dean grew a huge fan base in the early '90s with hit songs like "A Fire in the Dark," "Billy the Kid," and "Somewhere in My Broken Heart," and then he kind of slipped from the spotlight. Then he put his best foot forward again with the release of this emotional and thought-provoking 1998 album, *Real Man*. The acoustic-based tunes on this recording leave a little of the pop flavor behind and lean more comfortably on the simple country he is so good at offering fans. The ballads really let his vocal talents shine. Dean's father was a guitar player and singer and part of a group called the Country Rocks. Working with his band, young Dean grew up under influences like Marty Robbins, Charley Pride, Hank Williams, Jim Reeves, and even Chuck Berry and Elvis. Many of these early influences show on Dean's music. When he started working on this album, Dean took time to rediscover the songwriter within him. The result is that most of the songs on *Real Man* were written by him, or co-written with longtime friend and former frontman of the group Bread, David Gates. Other songwriters lent some talent to this album also, including Richard Leigh. On this album, you'll find great songs like "Voices Singing," which was done with the backing help of the St. Nicholas School Children's Choir of Chattanooga and Dean's son, Eli. Singer Gina Jefferys duets with Dean for the tune "If I Can Find the Heart." *—Charlotte Dillon*

Love Songs / Apr. 11, 2000 / Capitol ♦♦♦

Certified Hits / Sep. 24, 2002 / Capitol ♦♦♦

Eddie Dean (Edgar Dean Glosup)

b. Jul. 9, 1907, Posey, TX, **d.** Mar. 4, 1999, Los Angeles, CA
Vocals / Cowboy
Singer/songwriter/musician and B-movie cowboy Eddie Dean (born Edgar Dean Glosup) appeared in Hollywood westerns of the late '30s through the late '40s and also had a modest career in country music. He was born in Posey, TX, to a farmer and a singing school teacher, who taught her son to harmonize. In 1926, Dean moved to Chicago to see if he could make it on the radio, but was only able to obtain a few guest spots. He shortened his name to Eddie Dean and the following year was hired in Shenandoah, IA.

In 1929, Dean and his older brother Jimmy (not the sausage magnate) began singing together. By late 1933, they were appearing on an early morning Chicago show and the prestigious *National Barn Dance*. Through 1935, they recorded duets for the ARC label under the direction of Art Satherley, plus some gospel tunes for Decca. After the Deans separated, Jimmy moved to a new station and appeared on a network daytime show, *Modern Cinderella*. Eddie decided to try his luck in Hollywood in 1936 and began playing minor roles in Westerns. He also appeared regularly on Judy Canova's network radio show and released eight singles between 1941 and 1942, including "On the Banks of the Sunny San Juan." As an actor, Dean got his big break in 1944 when he starred in the musical Western *The Harmony Trail*. After that, he went on to star in 19 more Westerns; at the apex of his film career, Dean was listed among the top ten cowboy stars of the 1940s.

After 1948, Dean retired from films and focused on using his movie fame to promote his singing career. Although a talented vocalist with a remarkably strong, clear voice, Dean never made it big. He did have a few hits and wrote some excellent songs, including "One Has My Name (The Other Has My Heart)," co-written by his wife and recorded by Jimmy Wakely and Jerry Lee Lewis in 1961 and 1969, respectively. As a songwriter, his best-known hit remains 1955's "I Dreamed of a Hillbilly Heaven," a country music classic. Dean continued recording on low-budget labels through the 1970s. Through the 1980s, Dean continued to sing and share anecdotes at Western film fairs. In 1993 he was inducted into the Cowboy Hall of Fame. Dean passed away six years later in Los Angeles. *—Sandra Brennan*

Collectors Edition / Feb. 24, 1998 / Simitar ✦✦✦✦✦

This 12-song collection cut between 1958 and 1960 for Pickwich International is a good, basic representation of Eddie Dean's work. His rich, baritone voice was still very good at age 51, and stylistically he was equally adept at honky tonk ("Hey Good Lookin'"), cowboy ("The Streets of Laredo"), and straight country ("Half as Much," "Teardrops in My Heart"), though his ballad interpretations are a bit schmaltzy. The backing band includes a surprisingly unobtrusive organ with the standard contingents such as fiddles and acoustic guitar. The sound is very clean, and the producers have included one previously unissued cut, the gently jaunty "Ain't No Gal Got a Brand on Me." One surprise here is a rocking version of "Boogie Woogie Cowboy" which, with a different mix or a little more amplification, might've found chart action as a single in 1958. *—Bruce Eder*

● **The Very Best of Eddie Dean** / Jul. 25, 2000 / Varese ✦✦✦✦

This is a "very best" compilation in the Varese *Shasta Masters* series that can live up to its name. Eddie Dean recorded 14 of the 16 tracks on this CD for Jimmy Wakely's Shasta Records label during the mid-'70s—that date may shock listeners, for it places Dean in his sixties but sounding at least 25 years younger than that, and performing as a contemporary country artist of the era, not a nostalgia act or a latter-day singing cowboy, though he does do some of that repertory. The mix of songs includes the hits that Dean authored ("One Has My Name (The Other Has My Heart)," "I Dreamed of a Hillbilly Heaven"), plus a brace of songs associated with people that Dean worked with or traditions with which he was connected, among them Gene Autry's "That Silver Haired Daddy of Mine," Bob Nolan's "Cool Water," and "Tumbling Tumbleweeds." Interspersed among them is a selection of country standards, such as "The Green, Green Grass of Home," and traditional numbers, including "Shenandoah." There is also one cover of a song associated with Elvis Presley, "I Can't Help Falling in Love With You," which, with its engaging guitar flourishes and gentle accompanying chorus, could make you forget Presley's version. Dean's rich baritone is startlingly good, and sufficiently expressive to carry a country-waltz version of "Somewhere, My Love (Lara's Theme)" from *Doctor Zhivago* that ought not to be as appealing as it is. As a special bonus, the disc also includes a mid-'50s radio performance of "On the Banks of the Sunny San Juan" (which Dean co-authored in his singing cowboy days with his fellow actor Glenn Strange) and a demo of "My Whole Life Was You." *—Bruce Eder*

1501 Miles of Heaven / May 1, 2001 / Roots of Country ✦✦✦

It's ironic that Texas native Eddie Dean moved to Chicago in the '30s. Many of his cowboy songs painted such vivid pictures of life in rural, small-town America, and Chicago is about as urban as it gets. But even when Dean was living in the Windy City, he was still a Texan to the core—and his Texas roots assert themselves in a major way on *1501 Miles of Heaven.* This two-CD collection, which Allegro assembled for its Roots of Country label in 2001, is full of gems that are the essence of '40s and '50s cowboy music—it doesn't get much more Western than "Rose of Santa Fe," "Red Sails in the Sunset," "Whoopie Ti Yi Yo," and "Oregon Trail." And Dean wasn't strictly a cowboy singer; he handles honky tonk impressively well on the tear-jerker "I'm a Stranger in My Home" and Ernest Tubb's "Walking the Floor Over You," while the 1948 classic "One Has My Name (The Other Has My Heart)" successfully combines country and pre-rock pop sensibilities. But as captivating as *1501 Miles of Heaven* is, the collection isn't without its problems. Roots of Country fails to list either personnel or recording dates, and for serious collectors that type of laziness is infuriating. Further, many of Dean's definitive recordings are missing, including "On the Banks of the Old San Juan" and his most famous song, "I Dreamed of a Hillbilly Heaven." But while *1501 Miles of Heaven* is far from ideal, it does have a lot of good points and is worth acquiring for those interested in hearing more than Dean's most basic and essential work. *—Alex Henderson*

● **Dean of the West** / WFC ✦✦✦✦✦

Dean of the West is a ten-track collection featuring songs from Eddie Dean's most popular films, including "Black Hills," "Wagon Wheels," "Tumbleweed Trail," and "Banks of the Sunny San Juan." Neither of his big hits—"One Has My Name (The Other Has My Heart)" and "I Dreamed of a Hillbilly Heaven"—are included on this LP, but it remains a fine collection of cowboy songs, delivered by one of the most theatrical of all the screen cowboys. *—Thom Owens*

Jimmy Dean (Seth Ward)

b. Aug. 10, 1928, Plainview, TX

Vocals, Guitar, Piano, Accordion / Country-Pop, Nashville Sound/Countrypolitan, Traditional Country

The average man on the street is most likely to recognize Jimmy Dean from the line of smoked sausage that bears his name, but prior to becoming a spokesman for pork products, Dean was a successful television personality and a country hitmaker noted for his half-spoken narrative songs. Dean was born Seth Ward in Plainview, TX, in 1928, and grew up poor, often working on farms as a boy to help make ends meet. His mother taught him piano starting at age ten, and he went on to pick up guitar, harmonica, and accordion. He joined the Merchant Marines at age 16, and after two years he enlisted in the Air Force, where he first performed publicly with a band called the Tennessee Haymakers. The Haymakers played venues near the Washington, D.C., base at which Dean was stationed, and when he left the service in 1948, he remained in the area and formed a new group called the Texas Wildcats.

He eventually scored a record deal with Four Star, and his first hit, "Bummin' Around," reached the country Top Ten in 1953. During the mid-'50s, Dean hosted a local television show devoted to country music, giving important early exposure to regulars Patsy Cline and Roy Clark. The show proved popular enough that CBS offered him his own national program in 1957, though it wasn't as successful. In the meantime, Dean signed with Columbia, and when his show was canceled, he recorded a series of singles for the label that didn't get much attention. That all changed when he recorded the self-penned "Big Bad John" in 1961. Establishing Dean's flair for spoken narratives, the song went to number one on both the pop and country charts. He followed it with a string of popular singles in 1962: "Dear Ivan," "Little Black Book," and "P.T. 109" (the latter about John F. Kennedy's war exploits in the South Pacific) all made the country Top Ten, and the latter also made the pop Top Ten. Meanwhile, "To a Sleeping Beauty" and "The Cajun Queen" reached the country Top 20; all of Dean's hits from this hot streak charted at least in the pop Top 40.

In 1963, Dean returned to television as the host of his own daily variety show on ABC. Roger Miller became a regular, helping to jump-start his career, and the show also helped introduce America to another talent: puppeteer Jim Henson, whose regular appearances made Rowlf the piano-playing dog the first Muppet to become a household name. *The Jimmy Dean Show* ran until 1966, by which point Dean had switched labels to RCA; he returned to the country Top Ten that year with "Stand Beside Me," and placed several more minor chart entries through 1971, leaving off with "Slowly," a Top 40 duet with Dottie West. In the meantime, he developed an acting career, appearing as a regular on the TV series *Daniel Boone* during the late '60s, and landing the part of reclusive billionaire Willard Whyte in the 1971 James Bond flick *Diamonds Are Forever.*

Dean had invested most of his showbiz earnings in hog-farming concerns, and founded the Jimmy Dean Meat Company in the late '60s. His sausage recipes soon turned into a popular mass-market product, and while he accepted the occasional guest acting role on TV during the '70s and '80s, he spent most of his time focusing on his burgeoning business. He recorded a bit more for Casino in 1976, landing a final Top Ten country hit that year with "I.O.U.," a narrative tribute to his mother. Dean eventually sold his meat company to Sara Lee Foods, but remained its chairman and TV spokesman, which kept him active and visible into the new millennium. *—Steve Huey*

His Television Favorites / 1957 / Mercury ✦✦✦

Hour of Prayer / 1957 / Columbia ✦✦✦

Big Bad John and Other Fabulous Songs and Tales / 1961 / Columbia ✦✦✦✦

This was the album that established Jimmy Dean as a hitmaker in the early '60s, switching from mainly gospel material to country/pop. Along with his biggest hit, "Big Bad John," the other ten tracks include "Sixteen Tons" and the light country swing of "Night Train to Memphis" and "Smoke, Smoke, Smoke That Cigarette." This particular album was reissued by Sony Special Products with the same songs but different cover art. *—Al Campbell*

Featuring the Country Singing of Jimmy Dean / 1961 / Spin-O-Rama ✦✦✦

This record is half a Jimmy Dean album and half Luke Gordon. The Dean side really is a pleasure, with some excellent country-pop novelties like "You Little Devil" and "I'll Always Love You" sung with Dean's impossibly funny and engaging nasal whine. The Gordon side is almost as good, although Gordon does not have the personality or warmth of Dean. There is, though, some excellent (and uncredited) mandolin playing on the Gordon material, which helps make this collection worthwhile. *—Matthew Greenwald*

Everybody's Favorite / 1963 / Columbia ✦✦✦

Songs We All Love Best / 1964 / Columbia ✦✦✦

Jimmy Dean's Golden Favorites / 1964 / Hilltop ✦✦

The Hilltop label cashed in on Jimmy Dean's popularity with this budget reissue of recordings he made for 4 Star Records in the early '50s. The dozen tracks probably comprise nearly everything he cut for 4 Star, including his first hit, "Bumming Around" from 1953. That song was a major hit for Dean, but is out of print today, which makes this album a good anthology of his early recordings. Dean's ballad style on these cuts is nearly the same as on his Columbia recordings from ten years later, although in places he tries to approximate the sound of Webb Pierce, who was very popular at the time. The repertoire is mostly weepers, but "Why Don't You Shut Your Mouth" ("and open up your heart") is an atypical hillbilly rave-up. The sound quality is good considering that many of the 4 Star 78s sounded rough even in their day, and the content has not been otherwise reissued. *—Greg Adams*

The First Thing Ev'ry Morning / 1965 / Columbia ✦✦✦

The most successful in a string of pop-oriented albums Jimmy Dean released during the early to mid-'60s, *The First Thing Ev'ry Morning* is perhaps the finest example of Dean's super-smooth, Hank Williams-by-way-of-Lawrence Welk hybrid country style. At times sounding like Frank Sinatra's backwoods cousin, Dean combines full-throated crooning, lush orchestral arrangements, and an oohing/aahing chorus with a fairly straight two-step beat. The material consists of both pop standards (by the likes of Irving Berlin and Henry Mancini) and Nashville fare, which, given the Jimmy Dean treatment, all sound as if they could've been written by the same person. Music this slick is obviously a love-it-or-hate-it affair, but Dean's genius was that he could inject just the right amount of honky tonk raw edge into even the sappiest surroundings. Of course, if one were to take away the glockenspiel and oboes, Dean's voice would still be a thing of supple beauty, the equal of any of his contemporaries. The string-laden title track was a number one record, but the best tunes are the ones where the real Jimmy Dean can step out a little. On "Shutters and Boards," the lyrics' rural imagery seems to be pulling out his country roots despite the producers' efforts to keep them in check. Dean invests the song with a pathos worthy of George Jones, which is no mean feat considering the backing singers sound like they just stepped out of the Mormon Tabernacle. On the album's last song, "Harvest of Sunshine," which gets the Hollywood-style Dixieland treatment (think *Apple Dumpling Gang*), Dean goes so far over the top that it's almost subversive. Considering his ever-present fake smile and later success in the sausage business, it just may be. *—Pemberton Roach*

Jimmy Dean's Greatest Hits / 1966 / Legacy/Columbia ✦✦✦✦✦
Jimmy Dean's Greatest Hits remains an excellent summation of his years at Columbia Records, containing the hit singles "Big Bad John," "The Cajun Queen," "To a Sleeping Beauty," "P.T. 109," "Little Black Book," "The First Thing Ev'ry Morning (And the Last Thing Ev'ry Night)" and "Harvest of Sunshine." [For the 1998 CD reissue, Columbia/Legacy added the 1962 Top Ten hit "Dear Ivan," making the record a near-definitive overview of Dean's peak years.] *—Stephen Thomas Erlewine*

Jimmy Dean Show / 1967 / RCA Victor ✦✦✦

Dean's List / 1968 / Columbia ✦✦✦

Speaker of the House / 1968 / RCA Victor ✦✦✦

Dean of Country Music / 1970 / RCA Victor ✦✦✦

Everybody Knows / 1971 / RCA ✦✦
Eventually, everyone would know Jimmy Dean as a maker of sausages, but once upon a time this journeyman country singer had his own television show and a string of chart hits. Although competent to a fault, his efforts in the country genre probably rank about as high in the overall scheme of things as his sausages. Nobody will get seriously poisoned through exposure to Dean's products, but one could no doubt do a whole lot better in terms of something to listen to or eat for breakfast. His voice is good, but he puts it to use presenting cornball, or over-exposed material. Here we have "Rocky Top," for example. It isn't totally tasteless, though, as he has the good sense to do songs by Merle Haggard, Tammy Wynette, Charlie Rich, and Buddy Mize, and the backing from a typical Chet Atkins-produced session band is professional but not memorable. *—Eugene Chadbourne*

These Hands / 1972 / RCA ✦
These Hands was Jimmy Dean's final album for RCA, and it's easy to see why the label didn't keep him on. Even though "The One You Say Good Mornin' To" inched into the country Top 40, nothing on the album works very well, from Dean's homely ballad efforts to the forced humor of "(The Ballad Of) Big Ole Sam" and the execrable "Aunt Maudie's Fun Garden." Jerry Bradley and Felton Jarvis split the production chores 50/50, and Jarvis seemed more driven to experiment with Dean and push him in different directions, resulting in the aforementioned novelties and "Love Looks Good on You," on which Dean croons in an affected Eddy Arnold voice. Aside from the hit, which isn't particularly memorable, *These Hands* will be of interest only to completists. *—Greg Adams*

American Originals / 1989 / Columbia ✦✦✦
American Originals collects ten of Jimmy Dean's biggest hits from Columbia Records, featuring everything from "Big Bad John" to "The First Thing Ev'ry Morning (And the Last Thing Ev'ry Night)." It only covers five years—between 1961 and 1965—but it offers the best introduction to his sound. *—Stephen Thomas Erlewine*

Country Spotlight / 1991 / Dominion ✦
The cover may lead you to believe that this is a collection of Dean's hits in their original versions, but *Country Spotlight* features ten dreadful rerecordings of Dean's hits. *—Stephen Thomas Erlewine*

Big Bad John / 1993 / Bear Family ✦✦✦✦✦
This 26-song single disc collection covers the highlights of Jimmy Dean's 1961-1962 recordings for Columbia Records; not everything, but most everything that counts. The sheer diversity of material demonstrates some of the problems that Dean had finding and following up on hits; he was a passable singer and likable personality, but he would follow-up a pop/rock piece like "Little Black Book" with a blues piece such as "Gonna Raise a Ruckus Tonight." But apart from the hokiest of these tracks ("A Day That Changed the World"), it all holds up, including the title track; the freewheeling "Smoke, Smoke, Smoke That Cigarette"; the weirdly topical "Dear Ivan"; his cover of Merle Travis' "Sixteen Tons"; the sentimental father-to-daughter soliloquy "To a Sleeping Beauty"; the rough-hewn "Big Bad John" follow-up "The Cajun Queen"; the delightful sequel to both songs, "Little Bitty Big John"; "P.T. 109," a tribute to John Kennedy's World War II exploits written in the same vein as Johnny Horton's "Sink the Bismarck"; the wryly cynical "Walk on Boy"; the workers' anthem "Steel Men"; the pop/rock ballad "Little Black Book"; the old Texas blues "Gonna Raise a Ruckus Tonight"; the strange D-day remembrance "A Day That Changed the World"; the breezily folky "Gotta Travel On"; the sad dog (and war) song "Oklahoma Bill"; the effective sub-Elvis "Night Train to Memphis"; and two previously unissued numbers, the slow blues "Lonesome Road" and the swamp ballad "Cajun Joe." *—Bruce Eder*

● **Greatest Hits** / Jan. 27, 1998 / Columbia ✦✦✦✦✦
Jimmy Dean's Greatest Hits remains an excellent summation of his years at Columbia Records, containing the hit singles "Big Bad John," "The Cajun Queen," "To a Sleeping Beauty," "P.T. 109," "Little Black Book," "The First Thing Ev'ry Morning (And the Last Thing Ev'ry Night)" and "Harvest of Sunshine." [For the 1998 CD reissue, Columbia/Legacy added the 1962 Top Ten hit "Dear Ivan," making the record a near-definitive overview of Dean's peak years.] *—Stephen Thomas Erlewine*

Larry Dean

b. Texas

Vocals / Cowboy, Bakersfield Sound

Larry Dean was one of the chief proponents of the Bakersfield sound and a strong presence within the West Coast country music scene. Born in Texas and raised in Oklahoma and Idaho, Dean came from a strict religious background that forbade dancing and secular music. As the oldest of two boys, Dean was expected to help out on the family farm, where he spent long hours alone working the fields. It was here that he began writing songs in his head. A self-taught musician, as a teenager he played with various bands in the Middleton, ID, area. In 1980 he packed up and moved to Los Angeles. By 1981 he had formed his own band, Larry Dean and the Shooters. Awarded numerous honors by ASCAP and the California Country Music Association for his skills as a songwriter and a performer, Dean caught the attention of Nashville in 1985. He spent the next two years as a Nashville songwriter honing his craft. In 1989 Dean moved back on the West Coast, but not before accepting an invitation to appear on Ralph Emery's morning television show on TNN. Working with famed songwriter Wayne Carson, Dean penned tunes for his first CD. This 1989 release entitled *Outside Chance* included the title cut, written with Carson, as well as "Old Time Movies." Both singles charted. 1995 saw the release of Dean's second disc, *From a Distance.* This project was critically acclaimed even though country radio failed to take notice.

As a prominent member of the Bakersfield revolution, Dean garnered the respect and friendship of the legendary Roy Nichols, famed guitar player for Wynn Stewart, Lefty Frizzell, and Merle Haggard. Nichols, who acted as a mentor to Dean, instilled the importance of passing on the heritage of Bakersfield and the West Coast to the next generation in his student. Dean acted as mentor to several young artists, including California native and Merle Haggard disciple Michael Dart. Constantly on the move, Dean performed all across the West, where he was a favorite with the honky tonk crowd as well as with ranchers, rodeo stars, and cowgirls. As a songwriter, he composed in the Bakersfield style as well as paid tribute to the cowboy culture he was so much a part of. As a producer of note, Dean worked both in L.A. and Nashville and was often sought out to help develop several younger artists. *—Jana Pendragon*

Outside Chance / 1989 / USA Music Group ✦✦✦✦
This debut from one of the West Coast's finest should have brought Larry Dean the attention someone of his caliber deserves. With as much finesse as George Strait and as much gumption as fellow West Coaster Dwight Yoakam, this release represents Dean's evolution into the ranks of country music's elite. Starting out with his paean to roots rock & roll, "It All Started 30 Years Ago" (written with Bill Graham), this cowboy kicks up some dust and never lets up. Even when he is crooning a touching ballad, as he does on the Dean/Rocky Burnette/Ron Coleman tune "Whispering Wind," this artist is not afraid to expose true emotions. And, as a cowboy singer, Dean can stand side by side with Don Edwards and Michael Martin Murphey. Dean's charting hits include "Old Time Cowboy Movies," a slice of the Americana pie that documents a time and place long gone. Still, it is his ability to honky tonk that gives Dean his edge and allows him to roam wide and free. "Tramp," "Good Lookin' Liar," and his version of the very classic "There Stands the Glass" all suggest an artist whose talent is elevated above the common and mundane. *—Jana Pendragon*

● **From a Distance** / 1995 / Boulevard ✦✦✦✦
Critically acclaimed, this is Larry Dean's second release. Pure, unadulterated, and true to the Bakersfield sound, Dean shows himself to be a solid country traditionalist with a definite style all his own. A bit of a rebel, Dean has refused to mold himself to the marketing schemes that so often go with a major label deal in Music City. Writing about what he knows allows Dean to tap into the universal appeal that made country & western music from decades past so alluring to a wide variety of listeners. Honky tonkin' once again, "I'm Gettin' Known (For All the Wrong Reasons)" sets the stage for this accomplished project. With other outstanding selections such as "Things Are Lookin' Up," "It Must Be Angel Day," and the Kostas song "Brown Paper Bag," this a lively, provocative release. More thoughtful are Dean's "Sweet Magnolia," which demonstrates his skill with a ballad, and the haunting title track. The musicianship here is quality all the way. Using his own band, the Shooters, as well as some of L.A.'s top players like Taras Prodaniuk, Skip Edwards, and Harry Orlove gives Dean the support his songwriting and vocal skills deserve. *From a Distance* stood as one of 1995's outstanding true country releases and a signpost marking the continuation of an exceptional talent. *—Jana Pendragon*

Delevantes

Group / Country-Rock, Roots Rock

With Everly Brothers-like vocal harmonies set to hard-edged, roots-oriented arrangements, the Delevantes created some of the most exciting music of the late '90s. Their second album, *Postcards From Along the Way*, was produced by E Street Band bassist Gary Tallant, who joined the Delevantes on tour, and featured Benmont Tench of Tom Petty & the Heartbreakers on keyboards. The sons and grandsons of General Motors workers, Bob and Mike Delevante created a formidable collaboration. Playing guitars since childhood, the brothers made their stage debut as members of Wreckless Abandon, a band formed at Rutherford High School who specialized in bluegrass versions of Top 40 hits.

Although the brothers briefly separated to attend art school, they reunited to form Who's Your Daddy? in the mid-'80s, and became fixtures on the Hoboken, NJ, circuit. While attending a new music seminar in New York, the Delevante brothers were encouraged to bring their music to Nashville. They made several trips over four years before moving permanently to Tennessee's music city in 1992. Signing with Rounder, the Delevantes released their debut album, *Long About That Time*, in 1995. An immediate hit, the album reached the sixth slot on the Gavin Americana charts, thus making them the first alt-country act to reach the Top Ten. Nominated for a Nashville Music Award, *Long About That Time* was named Pop Album of the Year by NAIRD (the National Association of Independent Records and Distributors).

Switching to the larger Capitol label, the Delevantes continued their success with their sophomore effort, *Postcards From Along the Way*, which spent four weeks at the top of the Gavin Americana chart. Pursuing their own respective directions, the Delevante brothers separated in the late '90s. While Bob released a solo album, *Porchlight*, Mike worked with Jeff Black's band. *—Craig Harris*

● **Long About That Time** / 1995 / Rounder ✦✦✦✦
As it turns out, New Jersey working-class angst doesn't have to come out sounding like Bruce Springsteen; not only do Bob and Mike Delevante look like genuine Middle

American heartland country-rockers (what with Mike's Danelectro and Bob's bowling shirt), they sound like the genuine article, too (what with Mike's pedal steel licks and Bob's overpronounced Rs). Maybe you think boys from a nice Italian family have no business writing songs with titles like "I Wish I Were a Cowboy" and "Pocketful of Diamonds." If so, here are two words for you: Joe Val. If not, then you'll have no problem with the fact that this album was recorded in Nashville with E Street Band bassist Garry Tallent behind the board, and you'll be prepared for some truly winsome songwriting and singing from a musical team whose sweet harmonies and better than average lyrics will make you feel like you're 20 years old, unemployed, and in love all over again. At their best, the Delevantes tap into themes that are stereotypical not because they're easy, but because they're timeless: "Big Love" is a perfect song, an ode to a happy marriage embedded in roots-country fusion with just the right boogie inflection. "It's a Living" is a classic 12-bar blue-collar anthem that achieves effortlessly what Huey Lewis never did in all his years of trying. And even if "A Little Bit of Heaven" errs on the side of obviousness (first two lines: "Don't you know that life/Can be very hard"), "I Wish I Were a Cowboy" hits the target perfectly with the pitch-perfect plaint of a restless urbanite whose grammar is better than his girlfriend's ("I wish I were a cowboy/She says I wish you was one too"). This disc is a perfectly fine debut album from an impressive young band. *—Rick Anderson*

Postcards From Along the Way / Jul. 15, 1997 / Capitol ♦♦♦

The Delmore Brothers

f. 1926, Elkmont, AL, **db.** 1952

Group / Country Boogie, Old-Timey, Honky Tonk, Close Harmony, Traditional Country

The Delmore Brothers are not nearly as well-known as such early country giants as the Carter Family, Jimmie Rodgers, Bob Wills, and Hank Williams. The reasons for this, upon close inspection of their work, are not readily apparent. They were one of the greatest early country harmonizers, drawing from both gospel and Appalachian folk. They were skilled songwriters, penning literally hundreds of songs, many of which have proven to be durable. Most important, they were among the few early traditional country acts to change with the times, and pioneer some of those changes. Their recordings from the latter half of the 1940s married traditional country to boogie beats and bluesy riffs. In this respect they laid a foundation for rockabilly and early rock & roll, and rate among the most important white progenitors of those forms.

The Delmores were born into poverty in Elkmont, AL, as the sons of tenant farmers. Alton (b. December 25, 1908) would write most of the duo's original material, although his younger brother Rabon (b. December 3, 1916) was also a competent writer. Performing on guitar and vocals from early ages, they were playing as a pair by the time Rabon was ten years old. In the early '30s, they were confident enough to enter professional music, auditioning for Columbia in 1931 and successfully auditioning for Nashville radio station WSM the following year.

Throughout the 1930s, the Delmore Brothers recorded often, as well as performing on several radio stations. They probably gained their most early fame, however, from their long-running stint with the *Grand Ole Opry* between 1932 and 1938. The music emphasized their beautiful soft harmonies, accomplished guitar picking, and strong original compositions. Unusually for that time (or any other), the Delmores would switch high and low harmony parts from song to song (or even within the same song), although Alton would usually sing lead. Whether performing their own songs, traditional ones, or gospel, they brought a strong bluesy feeling to both their music and their vocals. It's that element, perhaps, that enables the Delmores, more than many other acts of the time, to speak to listeners of subsequent generations. Not to be underestimated either are their down-to-earth lyrical concerns, which address commonplace struggles and lost love with grace and redeeming, good-natured humor, rarely resorting to cornball tears.

In 1944, the Delmores signed with King, inaugurating an era which found them delving into and innovating more modern forms of country. Although their first sides for the label stuck to a traditional mold, in 1946 they expanded from their acoustic two-piece arrangements into full-band backup, with bass, mandolin, steel guitar, fiddle, harmonica, and additional guitars. Some of those additional guitars were supplied by Merle Travis, who credited Alton Delmore as a key influence.

In retrospect, however, the most important backup musician on these sides was Wayne Raney, who played a "choke" style of harmonica that was heavily influenced by the blues. The Delmores were also leaning increasingly toward uptempo material that reflected the upsurge in Western swing and boogie-woogie. By the end of 1947, they were also using electric guitar and drums. Raney (who also sang) in effect acted as a third member of the Delmores in the late '40s and early '50s, when they plunged full-tilt into hillbilly boogie. These are the most widely available and, in some ways, best Delmore Brothers sides. They were also the most successful, and in the late '40s the brothers reached their commercial peak, releasing a series of hard-driving boogies with thumping backbeats and bluesy structures. Arguably they milked the cow dry, recording "Hillbilly Boogie," "Steamboat Bill Boogie," "Barnyard Boogie," "Mobile Boogie," "Freight Train Boogie," and even "Pan American Boogie."

These were usually exciting performances, though, featuring extended guitar solos that clearly looked forward to the rock era. Listen, for instance, to the lengthy guitar breaks of "Beale Street Boogies" (unreleased at the time)—very few, if any, white or black artists were riffing so extensively in 1947. And of course "Beale Street" itself was a tribute to the most famous musical street in Memphis, the city that did so much to cross-fertilize black and white roots music into what became rock & roll.

The Delmores didn't stick entirely to boogies during the King era, also releasing some slower bluesy material. One of these, the original "Blues Stay Away From Me," became their biggest hit, and indeed the most famous Delmore Brothers song of all, often covered by subsequent country and pop artists. Interestingly, the Delmores continued to record gospel on the side, as part of the Brown's Ferry Four, a quartet which also included (at various points) Grandpa Jones, Merle Travis, and Red Foley.

As influential as the Delmores' King sides may have been on the future of American pop, the Delmores themselves would not be able to capitalize on that future. By the early '50s, their commercial success was fading. After the death of his young daughter, Alton drank heavily; worse, Rabon died of lung cancer on December 4, 1952. Alton (like longtime accompanist Wayne Raney) did record some material as a solo act, in both the gospel and rockabilly fields. Alton was way too old to begin a new career as a rockabilly singer, though, and he didn't record much for the last decade of his life. He wrote the autobiography *Truth Is Stranger Than Publicity* (published posthumously in 1977 by CMF) before dying on June 9, 1964. By that time the Delmore Brothers' work had already proven extremely influential, particularly on the harmonies of fellow sibling acts the Louvin Brothers and the Everly Brothers. They left behind an extraordinary lengthy and consistent body of recorded work—virtually none of their sides are lousy, at least the ones which have been reissued. Much of the Delmores' early material, unfortunately, can be hard to locate, although many of the King sides have been reissued on CD. *—Richie Unterberger*

The Best of the Delmore Brothers / 1970 / Starday ♦♦♦♦♦

Terrific nasal vocal harmonies, their brisk, bubblin' tenor, and six-string guitars and Wayne Raney's wailin' locomotive harmonica make The Delmores' late-'40s King label hits the most accessible of their early brother-duo material. Sounding a mite like the amiable smalltown uncles of Elvis and the Everly Brothers, the chooglin' "hillbilly boogie" of the Delmores was just a hairpin curve away from rockabilly. *—Mark A. Humphrey*

Brown's Ferry Blues / 1971 / County ♦♦♦♦

One has to separate the confusion created by various packagings and repackagings of this material from the simple beauty of this classic music, which continues to hold up decades after it was recorded. It is a coming together of so many American streams, including folk songs, cowboy songs, blues, and, of course, country & western. The format couldn't be simpler, vocal solos and harmonies with backup guitar, and the delivery couldn't be clearer. This particular disc differs in both content and order from a disc released later by the same label; the later issue had a color cover while the earlier version was in the more typically Country black-and-white text, and is sometimes referred to as *Early Original Recordings* because it is subtitled thusly on the back cover. That's also a warning as to sound quality. Many of these tracks come from old 78s, so listeners should expect sound quality of a certain vintage. *—Eugene Chadbourne*

Weary Lonesome Blues / 1983 / Old Homestead ♦♦♦♦♦

Unfortunately, there's no documentation on this 18-song set, but it's a safe guess that the tracks date from the 1930s and early '40s. It's another strong and varied set of blues, ballads, and spirituals, duplicating virtually nothing from the other Delmore Brothers reissues that have been compiled. *—Richie Unterberger*

Singing My Troubles Away / 1984 / Old Homestead ♦♦♦

The Delmores recorded over 200 sides, many of which have been reissued by Old Homestead. The quality is so consistently high and the material so similar in focus, that there's really little to differentiate them; if you like their sound, you'll like any given album. This one focuses mostly on their early days in the '30s, reaching back as far as 1933 (a couple of previously unissued cuts in a much more boogie-oriented style from 1946 and 1947 are also included). Perhaps more traditional in focus than some of their other compilations, it includes a fair number of blues-derived tunes. The harmonies and guitar playing are consistently fine. *—Richie Unterberger*

When They Let the Hammer Fall / 1984 / Bear Family ♦♦♦♦♦

Contains 18 of the boogie sides this great country duo cut (with harmonica player Wayne Raney) between 1945 and 1952, though it inexplicably fails to include their biggest hit from this time, "Blues Stay Away From Me" (later recorded by Johnny Burnette and Gene Vincent). This is the bluesiest and most raucous material cut by the harmonizing siblings. These tunes sound about as close to rock & roll as any other music recorded by white musicians prior to the 1950s, and still makes fine party music today, with its thumping shuffle beats, bluesy solos, and loose abandon. The great "Beale Street Boogie," cut in 1947 (and unissued at the time), is one of the dozens of songs which could make a strong case for being the first rock & roll record. There's a classic opening bluesy call-and-response riff, a long electric guitar solo duel, and appropriate homage to Memphis' famed Beale Street, certainly one of the locales most responsible for brewing together the basic ingredients of rock & roll—"the Beale Street Boogie is eight beats to the bar," they sing in unison, just in case you don't get the point. Compared to their early recordings, the Delmores seem less pious and devout on these sessions and more concerned with celebration than lamentation. *—Richie Unterberger*

Lonesome Yodel Blues / 1985 / Old Homestead ♦♦♦♦♦

Here are 18 of their early sides, recorded between 1933 and 1940, focusing on the more traditional elements of their repertoire. As the title implies, the brothers do often actually yodel throughout the proceedings, although in a more restrained fashioned than many of their peers. Remastered nicely from original copies of these rare singles, though some unavoidable surface noise is evident. *—Richie Unterberger*

Early Sacred Songs / 1985 / Old Homestead ♦♦♦♦♦

This features 14 of their more spiritually inclined tracks, mostly cut between 1935 and 1940. Those who favor secular material over gospel or traditional spirituals shouldn't be wary of this release because of its lyrical content. If you enjoy early country harmonizing, or any of the other material the Delmores cut in their early days, you'll like this as well. Aside from the nominally different lyrical concerns (presented here with humility and without preaching), the basic strengths of the pair remain intact: peerless close harmonizing, fine acoustic guitar playing, and strong songs that can be enjoyed regardless of what your faith (or lack thereof) may be. *—Richie Unterberger*

Sand Mountain Blues / 1986 / County ♦♦♦♦♦

The Delmores' recordings for King in the mid-'40s found them shifting away from traditional sounds into more energetic boogies that foreshadowed—however faintly—the blend of R&B and country that would give birth to rock & roll. This has 14 sides from

1944-1949, some of which feature such stellar sidemen as guitarist Merle Travis, mandolinist Jethro Burns, and harmonica player Wayne Raney. *—Richie Unterberger*

★ **Freight Train Boogie** / 1993 / Ace ✦✦✦✦✦

It's kind of a toss-up as to whether this or the German *When They Let the Hammer Down* is the best compilation of the Delmores' best work from the late '40s and early '50s. *When They Let the Hammer Down* is more raucous and uptempo; the 20-track *Freight Train Boogie*, though, has more variety. *Freight Train Boogie* is much easier to locate in the U.S. than *When They Let the Hammer Down*. In addition, there's a fair amount of duplication between the anthologies, though each includes several noteworthy songs not on the other. In any case, you won't be disappointed by *Freight Train Boogie*, whether it's your first exposure to the Delmores or not. Featuring King material from 1946-1951, it has plenty of high-spirited country boogies, balanced by more traditionally folk-oriented material ("Sand Mountain Blues," "Weary Day") and bluesy, slower numbers, including their biggest hit (and one of their best), "Blues Stay Away From Me." These sides were not only some of the finest country music of the era, but important building blocks of rockabilly and early rock & roll. *—Richie Unterberger*

Iris DeMent

b. Jan. 5, 1961, Paragould, AR

Guitar, Songwriter, Vocals / Neo-Traditional Folk, Singer/Songwriter, Country-Folk, Alternative Country, Contemporary Folk, Neo-Traditionalist Country, Americana

One of the most celebrated country-folk performers of her day, singer/songwriter Iris DeMent was born on January 5, 1961, in rural Paragould, AR, the youngest of 14 children. At the age of three, her devoutly religious family moved to California, where she grew up singing gospel music; during her teenaged years, however, she was first exposed to country, folk, and R&B, drawing influence from Loretta Lynn, Johnny Cash, Bob Dylan, and Joni Mitchell. Upon graduating high-school, she relocated to Kansas City to attend college. After a series of jobs waitressing and typing, DeMent first began composing songs at the age of 25. Honing her skills at open-mike nights, in 1988 she moved to Nashville, where she contacted producer Jim Rooney, who helped her land a record contract. DeMent did not make her recording debut until 1992, when her independent label offering, *Infamous Angel*, won almost universal acclaim thanks to her pure, evocative vocal style and spare, heartfelt songcraft.

Despite a complete lack of support from country radio, the record's word-of-mouth praise earned her a deal with Warner Bros., which reissued *Infamous Angel* in 1993 as well as its follow-up, 1994's stunning *My Life*. Her third LP, 1996's eclectic *The Way I Should*, marked a dramatic change not only in its more rock-influenced sound but also in its subject matter; where DeMent's prior work was introspective and deeply personal, *The Way I Should* was fiercely political, tackling topics like sexual abuse, religion, government policy, and Vietnam. In 1999, she collaborated with country man John Prine on his album, *In Spite of Ourselves*. DeMent recorded four duets with Prine that earned her a Grammy nod the following year. *—Jason Ankeny*

● **Infamous Angel** / 1992 / Warner Bros. ✦✦✦✦✦

A remarkable debut, *Infamous Angel* established Iris DeMent as one of the greatest artists of her generation. With her gift for poignant, confessional songwriting and a voice that makes raw beauty seem like a brand new thing, she invokes the elemental magic of the Carter Family while sounding as fresh and modern as John Prine (who, not surprisingly, is one of her biggest champions). DeMent's concerns are largely family and tradition, and many of these songs deal with memories of life and love. Her Carter influence is revealed in a spirited cover of the classic "Fifty Miles of Elbow Room" as well as "Mama's Opry," a tribute to her mother, who also sings lead on "Higher Ground." These are wonderful, but DeMent's greater talent is the ballad, and she delivers an astonishing handful, including "When Love Was Young," "Sweet Forgiveness," and "After You're Gone," a tribute to her dying father that is so profoundly affecting that one is rendered nearly helpless listening to it. In the end, one finishes this record somber but refreshed by DeMent's charming, almost naïve, outlook on life. That naïveté isn't an act, either—DeMent claims in her liner notes that she's never thought of herself as a great singer. She couldn't be more wrong, and listeners can thank heaven that she changed her mind, for this is an album to be cherished and played as long as one has life to listen. *—Jim Smith*

My Life / 1993 / Warner Bros. ✦✦✦✦

Like *Infamous Angel*, *My Life* opens on a light note, which is hardly adequate preparation for the emotional turbulence that follows. The album is dedicated to Iris DeMent's father, who passed away prior to its release, and although there are some scattered moments of joy here, they are largely absorbed by a collection of songs dealing with primal anguish and longing. DeMent's writing has hardened a bit, producing her most mature and encompassing song in "No Time to Cry," which serves as an anchor for the album's rich sentimentality and is also an indication, in its social obsessions, of the direction her next album would take. Elsewhere, DeMent's songcraft remains exceptional but, as before, the true magic is in her voice, which imbues even the simplest songs with perfect, pure emotion. Highlights include Maybelle Carter's "Troublesome Waters," "Easy's Gettin' Harder Every Day," and a terrific rendition of Lefty Frizzell's "Mom and Dad's Waltz." The gorgeous title track closes the album, a piano-cello duet that is one of her most moving performances. For those who appreciate DeMent's rough-hewn voice, it is nearly impossible to exaggerate the beauty of these recordings. *—Jim Smith*

The Way I Should / Oct. 8, 1996 / Warner Bros. ✦✦✦

The introspective scope of DeMent's first two records expands to tackle global topics like religion, sexual abuse and war on the tough-talking *The Way I Should Be*, a more rock-influenced offering including cameo appearances from Mark Knopfler, Lonnie Mack, and Delbert McClinton (who duets on "Trouble"). *—Jason Ankeny*

Derailers

f. 1994, Austin, TX

Group / Country-Rock, Honky Tonk, Alternative Country, Bakersfield Sound

A honky tonk band following the tradition set by Buck Owens, Austin, TX's Derailers were led by vocalist/rhythm guitarist Tony O. Villanueva and lead guitarist Brian Hofeldt, long-time friends who grew up together in Oregon. After playing in various Portland-area rockabilly outfits, Villanueva relocated to Texas at the age of 19, and Hofeldt soon tagged along; after settling in Austin, the duo joined forces with Vic Gerard Ziolkowski, the bassist in a band called Two Hoots & a Holler, and began focusing on playing straightforward honky tonk music. In 1995, the Derailers issued their first LP, *Live Tracks*; following their second release, 1996's *Jackpot*, Terry Kirkendall became the group's permanent drummer.

Reverb Deluxe appeared in 1997, and two years later the Derailers returned with *Full Western Dress*. By this point the lineup had shifted to include drummer Scott Matthews and bassist Ed Adkins. *Here Come the Derailers* appeared in 2001; it was the band's first for Sony's Lucky Dog imprint, and featured a slicker version of their signature sound, designed for larger exposure. *Genuine*, their second effort for the major label, appeared in March 2003. It included songwriting contributions from Jim Lauderdale and Al Anderson. *—Johnny Loftus*

Jackpot / Feb. 27, 1996 / Watermelon ✦✦✦

There's good news for lovers of genuine country music: Texas Music Group is reissuing a number of recordings originally released by Watermelon. In this particular case, that means the Derailers' 1996 release, *Jackpot*, will be available again. Stated briefly, the Derailers play honest-to-God honky tonk, just like Buck Owens did way back in the '60s. Of course, vocalist Tony O. Villanueva, guitarist Brian Hofeldt, and bassist Vic Gerard only use the old Bakersfield sound as a blueprint. They're perfectly capable of writing good songs like "My Heart's Ready" and "Tarnished Love," which bring honky tonk kicking and screaming into the contemporary world. The age-old country themes, however, remain the same. There's love lost and found, the joys of clean rural living, and the pie-in-the-sky dream of hitting the jackpot. In "This Big City," a country boy feels at home among the bright lights... until his girl leaves him, while "Vision to Dream On" extols the right of a man to dream even when he knows better. To keep things interesting, the boys even throw in a little rockabilly on "She Left Me Cold." The Derailers may not be the saviors of country music, but compared to their Top 40 Nashville colleagues, these guys are a fresh breeze from Texas. Direct in its execution and results, *Jackpot* succeeds by offering a bit of red meat to old-time honky tonkers and the alternative country crowd. *—Ronnie D. Lankford Jr.*

Live Tracks / Jun. 10, 1995 / Freedom ✦✦✦

Reverb Deluxe / Jul. 1, 1997 / Watermelon ✦✦✦

As FM country gets safer and safer, turning into mere confection, there is a rising tide of "insurgent country" and other hardcore twangers, a band of ruffian camp followers raising their heads from all corners. Claiming allegiance to the tougher Bakersfield sound exhibited by Merle Haggard, Buck Owens, and more during the '50s and '60s, the Derailers are a shiny rhinestone in the country & western belt. Listeners are taken into a rowdy honky tonk with the Derailers' male harmonies and strong upright bass. This disc also features plenty of steel guitar from guest musician Scott Walls, who should be signed on as a permanent member. His contributions add the necessary validity and melodic commentary to make this recording classic-sounding and worth obtaining. There are only three covers present, "I Don't Believe I'll Fall in Love Today," "No One to Talk To (But the Blues)," and a cleverly countrified "Raspberry Beret," but any one of their swinging originals holds up as well as a tried traditional. *—Thomas Schulte*

● **Full Western Dress** / Jul. 13, 1999 / Sire ✦✦✦✦

For their first full-fledged major-label album, the Derailers teamed with producer Dave Alvin—a legend in Americana circles—and crafted another fine, straight-ahead country record in *Full Western Dress*. The group never makes any apologies about being an unabashed traditionalist honky tonk group, equally comfortable with twangy Bakersfield, gritty honky tonk, and western swing. It's easy to spot the group's influences, from Buck Owens to Dwight Yoakam (or even the Beatles on the Merseybeat singalong of "Just to Spend the Night With You"), but the key to the record's success is that the Derailers never become mired in tradition, they simply play the music as if it was still vital and relevant, which is exactly what makes it vital and relevant. Of course, it doesn't hurt that the 12 songs are all very strong, whether they're covers or new originals that sound as if they're classics. It's a classy, inspired release that is much stronger and more charming than the average Americana release. *—Stephen Thomas Erlewine*

Here Come the Derailers / 2001 / Lucky Dog ✦✦✦

It says a lot about the current state of affairs in Nashville that the Derailers, one of the finest retro-style country acts around, are able to make better and more purely C&W-oriented albums recording for a Texas-based indie label than for one of the Big Boys on Music Row. *Here Come the Derailers*, the group's fourth studio album, is their first for Lucky Dog, a Sony imprint, and the idea seems to have been to create an album that rides a middle ground between the spunky Buck Owens-style honky tonk of their earlier albums and something that might find airplay on contemporary country radio. Unfortunately, the formula turns out to have been a little off, and producer Kyle Lehning has added enough polish to the Derailers' sound that a large percentage of the group's personality has been buffed away in the process. While Brian Hofeldt's picking is as stellar as always and Tony Villanueva's vocals are in fine form, the energetic snap of the band's best work is considerably muted here, and the glossy keyboard and steel overdubs generally don't add to the songs, but take away from them. While there's some great material on board—the honky tonkin' wit of "Bar Exam," the spunky "There Goes the Bride," and the Orbison-esque "I See My Baby"—there's an uncomfortable amount of filler, especially the failed weepers "All the Rage in Paris" and "My Angel's Getting Tired." And while covering "Mohair Sam" sure sounds like a good idea, the results are disappointing, though their take on Arthur Alexander's "If It's Really Got to Be This Way" is terrific. *Here Come the Derailers* isn't a bad album—this band is far too talented for their virtues not to shine through—but it's a far cry from the high-spirited retro-twang of their earlier albums, and while a lot more people are likely to hear this record, it's not an introduction that flatters the group. *—Mark Deming*

Genuine / Mar. 18, 2003 / Lucky Dog ✦✦✦

The Derailers' second album since moving up to a major label, 2003's *Genuine* sounds like a genuine improvement over their previous release, 2001's *Here Come the Derailers*; while it still suffers from the excess of slickness that's been heaped upon one of the finest honky tonk acts in the land, this time around the bandmembers sound as if they've been able to work through Kyle Lehning's production instead of being completely buried by it. Which isn't to say this album wouldn't be better sounding a bit leaner—do you really need 11 additional musicians to accompany a four-piece band, especially one this tight?—and with some of the lesser material clipped away (most notable offender being the faux-nostalgic "Whole Other World"). But at least vocalist Tony Villanueva and guitarist Brian Hofeldt get their fair chance to strut their stuff on *Genuine*, and with Jim Lauderdale and Al Anderson pitching in on the songwriting, the material manages a higher batting average this time around. Sure, most of *Genuine* sounds as if it were crafted in hopes of landing on country radio, but "The Way to My Heart," "Take It Back," and "Boomerang Heart" would class up any play list they were added to, and show these guys haven't completely lost touch with their Buck Owens-loving souls (they also toss in a vintage Owens and Don Rich instrumental for good measure, which Hofeldt plays the hell out of). If *Here Come the Derailers* found the band losing round one of the battle against the corporate ogre, *Genuine* at least finds the Derailers fighting to a draw, and that's good news. *—Mark Deming*

Desert Rose Band

f. 1985, Southern California

Group / Country-Rock, Contemporary Country

A contemporary vehicle for country-rock pioneer Chris Hillman (ex-Byrds and Flying Burrito Brothers), the Desert Rose Band formed in 1985 with primary songwriter Hillman on lead vocals, guitar, and mandolin. Other members, culled mainly from southern California session players, included banjoist/guitarist Herb Pedersen, guitarist John Jorgenson, steel guitarist Jay Dee Maness, bassist Bill Bryson, and drummer Steve Duncan. Their first single was a 1986 cover of Johnnie & Jack's "Ashes of Love," which climbed into the country Top 30. Their self-titled debut album followed in 1987 and spawned a number-one hit in "He's Back and I'm Blue," plus two more Top Tens in "Love Reunited" and "One Step Forward." *Running* (1988) produced the number-one smash "I Still Believe in You," the number two "Summer Wind," and the number three "She Don't Love Nobody." *Pages of Life* (1990) brought their final Top Ten hits in "Story of Love" and "Start All Over Again."

Major personnel turnover followed; Maness was replaced by steel guitarist Tom Brumley, Jorgenson by guitarist Jeff Ross, and Duncan by drummer Tim Grogan. This lineup recorded three albums—1991's *True Love* and two in 1993, *Traditional* and *Life Goes On*—but failed to duplicate the success of the band's first incarnation. After the Desert Rose Band broke up, Hillman and Herb Pedersen continued to work together on a sporadic basis. *—Steve Huey*

The Desert Rose Band / 1987 / Curb ✦✦✦✦

The Desert Rose Band's eponymous debut demonstrated that Chris Hillman's new band could continue his country-rock tradition effortlessly. Throughout the record, the Desert Rose Band turns in tight performances, highlighted by brief, tasteful instrumental solos and yearning vocals. *—Thom Owens*

Running / 1988 / Curb ✦✦✦✦✦

This is certainly a good representation of the work the Desert Rose Band did in their prime and a project that remains a favorite. With some solid songwriting by Chris Hillman and a cover of Buck Owens' "Hello Trouble," this second release is a definitive work. With hits like "I Still Believe in You," "Summer Wind," and John Hiatt's "She Don't Love Nobody," there is nothing lacking in either performance, production, or material. Like their first release, 1987's *Desert Rose Band*, *Running* was based upon the experience of the bandmembers as musicians, songwriters, and singers who were (and continue to be) an important part of the Bakersfield-Los Angeles music community. Both Hillman and Herb Pedersen have impressive resumés that include working with the Byrds, Gram Parsons, Buck Owens, and Emmylou Harris. As for Steve Duncan, Bill Bryson, Jay Dee Maness, and John Jorgenson, each had equally brilliant backgrounds as California musicians and were recognized as such. Be it Bakersfield honky tonk, love songs, or bluegrass, the Desert Rose Band delivered. *—Jana Pendragon*

She Don't Love Nobody / 1989 / Curb ✦✦✦

Pages of Life / 1990 / Curb ✦✦✦

This contains "In Another Lifetime," "Time Passes Me By," "Start All Over Again," and other favorites. *—AMG*

● **A Dozen Roses: Greatest Hits** / 1991 / Curb ✦✦✦✦✦

A showcase for Hillman's pop-country vocals and the considerable chops of bandmembers such as Herb Pedersen. Together they made some of the best country singles of the late '80s, all collected here. *—William Ruhlmann*

True Love / 1991 / Curb ✦✦✦

True Love proves that the Desert Rose Band has a knack for mixing a country-pop attack with pure bluegrass harmonies, making music that is accessible to both mainstream country fans and hardcore bluegrass fanatics. Though *True Love* has too much mediocre material to make it rank among their best, it is nevertheless a very good collection, featuring a wonderful version of Peter Rowan's "Undying Love" that features gorgeous duet vocals between Chris Hillman and Alison Krauss. *—Stephen Thomas Erlewine*

Traditional / 1993 / Curb ✦✦

Life Goes On / Sep. 21, 1993 / Curb ✦✦✦✦✦

Al Dexter (Clarence Albert Poindexter)

b. May 4, 1902, Jacksonville, TX, d. Jan. 28, 1984, Lewisville, TX

Guitar, Songwriter, Vocals, Violin / Country Boogie, Traditional Country, Cowboy, Honky Tonk, Nashville Sound/Countrypolitan

Al Dexter earned a spot in the popular music canon when he wrote "Pistol Packin' Mama" in 1942. Recorded by him a year later, the single sold three-million copies—not counting sheet music—in less than two years and was ranked the third most popular song of the war years. Both Bing Crosby (with the Andrews Sisters) and Frank Sinatra recorded "Pistol Packin' Mama" for hits, and the song influenced country's pop-influenced Nashville sound of the '50s. It's difficult to believe, but Dexter also managed to influence the honky tonk style that later proved a vivid counterpoint to the Nashville sound. He owned a bar for a time during the '30s and popularized the term honky tonk—slang for both rowdy bars and later the music that emerged from their jukeboxes—on his 1937 recording "Honky Tonk Blues." However, the popular theory that Dexter actually coined the term can be blown full of holes; he had never heard of honky tonk before his songwriting partner James B. Paris suggested it as a title in 1936.

Born Clarence Albert Poindexter in Jacksonville, TX, on May 4, 1902, Dexter began playing square dances around oil-rich eastern Texas during the 1920s. The Depression forced him to work as a house painter, but Dexter began moonlighting after he formed the Texas Troopers in the early '30s. The group recorded for OKeh and Vocalion during the rest of the '30s and into the '40s. In 1944—the first year when charts can be accurately predicted—Dexter scored four number ones on the country chart. "Pistol Packin' Mama" was re-released on the B-side of "Rosalita," and both songs hit number one in January 1944. His biggest hit of the year came in March, though, when "So Long Pal" spent 13 weeks at number one on the country chart—its B-side, "Too Late to Worry, Too Blue to Cry," stayed at the top for two weeks.

The last of the war years were also successful for Dexter: "I'm Losing My Mind Over You"/"I'll Wait for You Dear," hit number one and number two, respectively, in January 1945, with the former spending seven weeks at number one. His second double-sided hit of the year, "Triflin' Gal"/"I'm Lost Without You," both hit the Top Five in August. In February 1946, Dexter's "Guitar Polka" spent almost four months at number one; it was his biggest country hit and managed the Top 20 on the pop charts (also producing the number two B-side "Honey Do You Think It's Wrong"). After "Wine, Women and Song" also hit number one later in 1946, Dexter recorded three more Top Five singles during 1946-1947, "It's Up to You," "Kokomo Island," and "Down at the Roadside Inn." His final chart singles were the 1948 Top 15 singles "Rock and Rye Rag" and "Calico Rag."

All told, Dexter received 12 gold records for million-sellers in the five-year period from 1943 to 1948. He won an Oscar for "Guitar Polka" and was voted the Leading Artist of 1946 by the Jukebox Operators Association. In the late '40s, Dexter opened his own club in Dallas; he performed there until his retirement. Dexter was inducted into the Nashville Songwriters Hall of Fame in 1971. *—John Bush*

● **Pistol Packin' Mama** / Oct. 19, 1999 / ASV ✦✦✦✦✦

Pistol Packin' Mama is a long-overdue collection of Al Dexter's classic recordings, including all but one of his Top 40 hits, seven of which reached number one. The 25 tracks span the years 1942-1949 and run the gamut from honky tonk to instrumental polkas to boogies. Although this generous anthology offers nearly 80 minutes of music, the disc was mastered from commercial 78s, and as a result the sound is sometimes crackly and thin. Perhaps Columbia will someday release a better-mastered Al Dexter collection of their own, but until then *Pistol Packin' Mama* has nearly all of the essential sides and then some. *—Greg Adams*

Pistol Packin' Mama / Aug. 7, 2001 / Roots of Country ✦✦✦

By the early '50s, Al Dexter's popularity had faded—his last major hits were in 1948. But when the Texas singer was still on top, he was among country's more progressive and cutting-edge artists. Dexter, who favored an unassuming, easygoing style of singing, managed to influence hardcore honky tonk and Nashville country-pop at the same time, and he also demonstrated that a country artist could successfully incorporate swing, classic jazz, and jump blues elements. Assembled in 2001, this two-CD set boasts many of Dexter's definitive '40s hits, including "Rosalita," "So Long Pal," "Triflin' Gal," "Wine, Women and Song," "Too Late to Worry, Too Blue to Cry," "Kokomo Island," and "I'm Losing My Mind Over You." The title track, of course, became Dexter's signature tune—and the fact that "Pistol Packin' Mama" was covered by Bing Crosby and Frank Sinatra illustrates his crossover appeal. Although Dexter was admired by hardcore honky tonkers, he wasn't a country purist. Again, jazz and blues were strong influences, and many of the 28 songs on this double CD are full of jazz-minded horn arrangements. Dexter, like fellow Texan Bob Wills, could make a fiddle and a twangy steel guitar sound perfectly natural alongside a Louis Armstrong-influenced trumpet. As much as *Pistol Packin' Mama* has going for it, the collection isn't without its shortcomings. A few essential recordings are missing, including "Guitar Polka" and 1937's "Honky Tonk Blues" (the single that popularized the term honky tonk). And regrettably, Roots of Country doesn't bother to provide recording dates, which is the type of laziness that frustrates collectors to no end. But all things considered, *Pistol Packin' Mama* is a rewarding collection by one of the most important country stars of the '30s and '40s. *—Alex Henderson*

Diamond Rio

f. 1984

Group / Contemporary Country, Neo-Traditionalist Country

Diamond Rio found major commercial success in the '90s by playing an eclectic hybrid of modern country, traditional bluegrass (especially in their harmony singing), and a hint of rock & roll. The band was composed of Marty Roe (lead vocals, guitar), Jimmy Olander (guitar, banjo), Gene Johnson (mandolin, vocals), Dan Truman (keyboards), Dana

Williams (bass), and Brian Prout (drums). Roe had already been touring professionally since age 12, when he was a member of Windsong, and Olander had previously worked with the Nitty Gritty Dirt Band and Foster & Lloyd. The band first got together at Nashville's Opryland theme park, and spent the first part of the '80s performing bluegrass music there under the name the Tennessee River Boys. The future members of Diamond Rio joined one by one, and in 1986, they left Opryland to try their luck as a touring band. Dana Williams was the last official member to join in 1989, upon which point the band changed their name to Diamond Rio (taken from the side of a truck) and landed a contract with Arista.

Diamond Rio's self-titled debut album was released in 1991 and quickly became a platinum-selling smash. Its lead single, "Meet Me in the Middle," went all the way to number one on the country charts, and it also spun off a stunning four additional Top Ten hits—"Mirror Mirror," "Mama Don't Forget to Pray for Me," "Norma Jean Riley," and "Nowhere Bound." By the time that run ended, the group had already recorded a follow-up, *Close to the Edge*, which appeared in late 1992. The Top Tens "In a Week or Two" and "Oh Me, Oh My, Sweet Baby" continued the group's incredible run of success, helping the album go gold, while "This Romeo Ain't Got Julie Yet" just missed the Top Ten, their first single to do so. *Love a Little Stronger* (1994) produced a number-two hit in its title track, but since the album was more of a showcase for the group's musicianship and eclectic tastes, it wasn't as commercially successful as its predecessors. The group took a similar approach for 1996's *IV*, but this time it slowly caught fire; "That's What I Get for Lovin' You" and "Walkin' Away" both went Top Five, and a re-release of the album's first single, "Holdin'," did likewise.

With their commercial momentum restored, Diamond Rio issued *Greatest Hits* in 1997; both of the compilation's two new songs—"How Your Love Makes Me Feel" and "Imagine That"—went Top Five, and the former became their second number-one hit. The all-new *Unbelievable* followed in 1998, and landed two more Top Five hits in "You're Gone" and the title cut, the latter of which inched into the pop Top 40 as well. The group kept going strong on their sixth album, 2001's *One More Day*, whose title song gave them a third number one. *Completely* (2002) ran that total to four with the chart-topping "Beautiful Mess," and added another Top Ten hit in "I Believe." —*Steve Huey*

Diamond Rio / 1991 / Arista ✦✦✦✦✦
One of the most successful debut albums in country music, *Diamond Rio* sparked plenty of hits—"Meet in the Middle," "Mama Don't Forget to Pray for Me," "Nowhere Bound," "Norma Jean Riley"—by combining bluegrass harmonies, old-fashioned country virtues, and just enough rock to keep things moving. —*Brian Mansfield*

Close to the Edge / 1992 / Arista ✦✦✦
On *Close to the Edge*, Diamond Rio took the cue of the debut's best songs and created an entire album cut from the same cloth. Diamond Rio's strongest material emphasizes the virtues of God, family and honest living—traditional stuff, no doubt influenced by the members' bluegrass background. But while most folks who'd claim divine intervention in their relationship sound sappy at best, Marty Roe comes off earnest and convincing. Unfortunately, amid hits like "In a Week or Two" and "Oh Me, Oh My, Sweet Baby," *Close to the Edge* reveals such weaknesses as a penchant for bad puns ("This Romeo ain't got Julie yet"—ouch!). —*Brian Mansfield*

Love a Little Stronger / 1994 / Arista ✦✦✦✦
Spurred by the relatively lackluster performance of *Close to the Edge* (it barely went gold compared to the debut's platinum), Diamond Rio explored the musical possibilities of its talents rather than digging for easy commercial success. The instrumentalists, particularly Jimmy Olander and mandolinist Gene Johnson, assume larger roles on songs like "Love a Little Stronger" and the instrumental "Appalachian Dream," but they rarely show off. The bandmembers even tap into an acoustic jazz-rock mode for "Kentucky Mine," one of the best songs they've ever recorded. —*Brian Mansfield*

IV / Feb. 27, 1996 / Arista ✦✦✦✦
Though the group wasn't able to regain its commercial status with *Love A Little Stronger*, Diamond Rio decided not to play things safe with *IV*. Taking its cue from its predecessor, *IV* explores a number of different country subgenres, thereby demonstrating the versatility and depth of its musicians. However, there's a problem when musicians are this talented—the music is impressive on the surface, but it rarely gels into something memorable. —*Thom Owens*

● **Greatest Hits** / Jul. 15, 1997 / Arista ✦✦✦✦
Greatest Hits is a fine collection of the hit singles from Diamond Rio's first four albums, featuring such hits as "Meet in the Middle," "Mirror Mirror," "Norma Jean Riley," "In a Week or Two," "Oh Me, Oh My, Sweet Baby," "Love a Little Stronger," "Night Is Fallin' in My Heart," "Walkin' Away," "That's What I Get for Lovin' You," "Holdin'," and two new songs, including the single "How Your Love Makes Me Feel." —*Thom Owens*

Unbelievable / Jul. 28, 1998 / Arista ✦✦✦
Unbelievable finds Diamond Rio extending the stylistic diversity that marked *IV*, but this time around, they have a better, more memorable set of songs that makes it their best album in a longtime. Diamond Rio are professionals, and that's part of their charm. They can deliver any song smoothly, and make their musical eclecticism easy to swallow. Also, Marty Roe's rich, nuanced vocals make the mediocre material (and there are a couple of weak cuts here and there) sound sweet. It's not perfect, but *Unbelievable* nevertheless offers proof that Diamond Rio has found a near-irresistible mix of contemporary country and bluegrass. —*Thom Owens*

One More Day / Feb. 6, 2001 / Arista ✦✦✦
The key word with Arista Nashville's Diamond Rio is "consistent." This band is probably one of the finest in the business when it comes to developing a sound all its own and maintaining that sound over time. When the sound is as harmonious as Diamond Rio's, a solid album is a given. *One More Day* remains in the thread of its predecessors; the incredible lead vocals of Marty Roe still float on the breeze of Gene Johnson's mandolin and Jimmy Olander's guitar. The Sunday morning choir harmonies are there too. The title cut,

clearly the album's powerhouse cut, has the distinction of occupying the *Billboard* Hot Country Singles chart more than once. "Stuff" is a fun yet insightful tune about how we tend to measure our success in life by how many material things we accumulate. "Sweet Summer" is the epitome of what songwriting is all about. The essence of time is captured here in reminiscences of running home and getting your money before the ice cream man was gone. Chely Wright appears on the CD as well, sharing vocals on the ballad "I'm Trying." If any flaw can be found here it would be the band's choice not to experiment with new sound, but then again, why tamper with a good thing? —*Rick Cohoon*

Completely / Jul. 23, 2002 / Arista ✦✦✦
The material on *Completely* by Diamond Rio has two powerful qualities behind it: individuality and positive outlook. With artists as well anchored in the business as Diamond Rio, the musical quality is a given. The real challenge is outdoing yourself and coming up with fresh concepts. The selections on this album seem to be the fruition of that search for musical renewal with unique cuts such as "Wrinkles," co-written by Ronny Scaife and Neil Thrasher. The age-conscious will find this song especially appealing with its fun, hopeful message. Even the pain of "I Believe" is alleviated with spiritual guidance, while "You'll Find Me" reunites a husband and wife on the verge of good-bye. On the instrumental side, Diamond Rio offers "Rural Philharmonic," a fast-paced composition by group member Jimmy Olander. If that Diamond Rio harmony is what you're after, it's here too and is especially powerful on the oxymoronic "Beautiful Mess," though it overpowers some of the lyrics in "The Box." On the whole, *Completely* marks another musical revival for Diamond Rio. —*Rick Cohoon*

Hazel Dickens

b. Jun. 1, 1935, Mercer County, WV
Vocals / Neo-Traditional Folk, Old-Timey, Traditional Folk, Political Folk
Protest and folksinger Hazel Dickens grew up the eighth of 11 children in a large, poor mining family in West Virginia, and she has since used elements of country and bluegrass to spread truth about two causes close to her heart: the plight of non-unionized mineworkers and feminism, born not of the '60s movement but traditional values. Born June 1, 1935, in Mercer County, WV, Dickens learned about music from her father, an occasional banjo player and Baptist minister who drove trucks for a mining company to make a living. She was early influenced by country traditionalists such as Uncle Dave Macon, the Monroe Brothers, and the Carter Family. When she was 19, her family's dire poverty forced Dickens to move to Baltimore, where she worked in factories with her sister and two brothers.

The four displaced siblings often attended old-timey festivals and gatherings, watching others and performing themselves. At one of these festivals, Hazel Dickens met Mike Seeger (younger brother of folk legend Pete Seeger), and the two formed a band with her brothers. Over the ensuing decade, Dickens became active in the folk/bluegrass movement around the Baltimore/Washington, D.C., area, playing bass and singing with several bands, including the Greenbriar Boys, who toured with Joan Baez in the '60s. Around this time she met Mike Seeger's wife, Alice Gerrard, a classically trained singer also interested in old-timey music. At the nearby Library of Congress, the two began researching early feminist songs and then incorporated them into their own repertoire. The duo performed throughout the country—particularly the South—and recorded two albums for Folkways, *Who's That Knocking (And Other Bluegrass Country Music)* (1965) and *Won't You Come & Sing for Me* (1973).

The two separated in 1973—two later albums were compiled from previous recordings—and Dickens began her solo career with a flourish. She recorded four songs for the soundtrack to the Academy Award-winning documentary about coalmining, *Harlan County, USA*. Three years later, she contributed to the soundtrack for *With Babies and Banners* and began a solo career five years later. Her three solo albums for Rounder, *Hard Hitting Songs for Hard Hit People* (1980), *By the Sweat of My Brow* (1983), and *It's Hard to Tell the Singer From the Song* (1986), include old-timey country alongside protest songs and songs in a more contemporary country style. Rounder's *A Few Old Memories* distills the best of the three albums onto one disc. —*John Bush*

Won't You Come & Sing for Me / 1973 / Smithsonian Folkways ✦✦✦✦

Hazel & Alice / May 1973 / Rounder ✦✦✦✦✦
Although Dickens and Gerrard had recorded a couple of albums as a duo in the mid-1960s, those were more traditional-minded bluegrass recordings than this 1973 effort. Several of the songs documented women's experiences in personal terms that struck a chord in many listeners involved in the women's movement, a constituency that the performers were not consciously addressing and somewhat surprised (though pleased) to reach. In fact, about half of this was devoted to traditional numbers by the likes of the Carter Family and Wilma Lee Cooper, but the original numbers brought a still-rare feminist viewpoint to folk and bluegrass music, particularly Dickens' "Don't Put Her Down, You Helped Put Her There." The songs make their points about women's struggles without being doctrinaire; the vocals (both solo and harmony) are impassioned, particularly on the Dickens a cappella showcase "Pretty Bird," and the musicianship appropriately spare. [The CD reissue features extensive historical liner notes and track-by-track commentary by country music authority Charles Wolfe.] —*Richie Unterberger*

Hard Hitting Songs for Hard Hit People / 1980 / Rounder ✦✦✦

★ **By the Sweat of My Brow** / 1983 / Rounder ✦✦✦✦✦
On *By the Sweat of My Brow*, the "First Lady of Bluegrass" strays from her familiar protest songs and focuses on traditionally themed orphan ballads and tormented love songs, many of which were penned by Dickens herself. Her gruff West Virginia voice stomps its way through the rough-and-tumble "Are They Gonna Make Us Outlaws Again," but still gently croons during the tender "Scars of an Old Love." Although she certainly paved the way for female neo-traditional folk artists like Gillian Welch and Iris DeMent, no other artist in the latter half of the 20th century really captured the hardship and struggle of

rural coal-town living like Hazel Dickens did in every syllable, and this album represents the high point of an artist at the high point of her career. —*Zac Johnson*

It's Hard to Tell the Singer From the Song / 1986 / Rounder ✦✦✦✦✦

It's Hard to Tell the Singer From the Song is a beautiful, emotionally raw album from start to finish. Throughout, Dickens creates a music that's traditional and timeless, while also having her feet firmly planted in the here and now. Traditional country songs like "California Cottonfields" clearly share an affinity for the working person, while Dylan's "Only a Hobo" reveals the sacredness of even the "lowliest" life. Dickens also enjoys singing feminist-tinged songs like "You'll Get No More of Me" and the anti-war anthem "Will Jesus Wash the Bloodstains From Your Hands?" Dickens seems to enjoy updating tradition, drawing from her West Virginia background while adding political touches usually absent from folk and country music. Part of the success of this project is that excellent musicians like Jerry Douglas, Russ Barenberg, and Blaine Sprouse offer tasteful support throughout. Dickens' voice also proves a perfect instrument to communicate the stark lyrics of songs like "Hills of Home." Her delivery has more in common with the Carter Family than contemporary bluegrass and country singing, and her old-time vocals add to the emotional impact of this material. Songs like "Hills of Home" and "A Few Old Memories" deal with the sense of loss that comes from leaving behind familiar places like a childhood home. "Play Us a Waltz" sketches a portrait from inside a nursing home, "where there's no one to love, and nothing to do." The characters that inhabit *It's Hard to Tell the Singer From the Song* long for a sense of place in the modern world and cry out for compassion and understanding. This is powerful album and a mature artistic statement. —*Ronnie Lankford Jr.*

Hard to Tell the Singer from the Song / 1987 / Rounder ✦✦✦✦

Few singers in the last 30 years evoke the essence of bluegrass twang as does Hazel Dickens. And this platter from 1987 is one of her strongest, with a fine band backing her and a superior batch of songs. Listening to weepers like "A Few Old Memories" and "Do Memories Haunt You," it is clear just where a host of recent alt-country artists such as Freakwater and Sally Timms got their inspiration. —*Tim Sheridan*

A Few Old Memories / 1987 / Rounder ✦✦✦

Few Old Memories collects highlights from Hazel Dickens' early '80s albums for Rounder Records. Like the original studio albums, the compilation balances excellent renditions of standards with new songs written in the same vein. Consequently, *A Few Old Memories* is a terrific overview of Dickens' old-timey revival and a good introduction to her surprisingly influential career. —*Thom Owens*

Pioneering Women of Bluegrass / May 21, 1996 / Smithsonian Folkways ✦✦✦✦✦

Dickens and Gerrard recorded a couple of albums in the mid-'60s that are now acknowledged as groundbreakers in demonstrating that women could play and record quality bluegrass. This collection remasters and resequences 26 tracks from the sessions, as well as adding lengthy historical liner notes, much of them contributed by the performers themselves. Historical significance aside, it's pretty good bluegrass, the two singers and instrumentals supported by other good musicians, including a young David Grisman. Their set leaned heavily on covers of tunes by the Carter Family and Bill Monroe (who specifically gave "I Hear a Sweet Voice Calling" to the duo), with additional items by the Delmore Brothers, the Stanley Brothers, and the like. Alice Gerrard's low vocals give this a greater gravity than much bluegrass. A special highlight is the cover of the magnificently mournful "The One I Love Is Gone," another tune that Monroe donated to the pair. Inverting the usual bluegrass cliché, one might call it an example of the *low* and lonesome sound. —*Richie Unterberger*

Little Jimmy Dickens

b. Dec. 19, 1925, Bolt, WV

Guitar, Vocals / Novelty, Traditional Country, Nashville Sound/Countrypolitan

Little Jimmy Dickens is the master of the country novelty song, as well as a renowned ballad singer. He also known for his diminutive stature—he's less than five feet tall—and his affection for flamboyant, rhinestone-studded outfits and country humor. Although he never had a consistent presence on the charts, he managed to have hits in every decade between the 1940s and the 1970s, and he became one of the *Grand Ole Opry*'s most popular performers.

Dickens was the 13th child of a West Virginian farmer. During his childhood, he fell in love with music and had a dream of performing on the *Grand Ole Opry*. He began performing professionally while he was a student at the University of West Virginia in the late '30s, singing on a local radio station. Dickens left school shortly after he received his regular radio job. He began traveling around the country, singing on radio shows in Indiana, Ohio, and Michigan under the name Jimmy the Kid. Roy Acuff heard Dickens sing on a radio show in Saginaw, MI, and invited him to sing on the *Grand Ole Opry*. In 1949, Dickens—who was now using the name Little Jimmy Dickens—became a permanent member of the *Grand Ole Opry*. That year, he also signed a record contract with Columbia Records, releasing his first single, "Take an Old Cold Tater and Wait," in the spring of 1949. The song became a Top Ten hit and launched a string of hit novelty, ballad, and honky tonk singles that lasted for a year, including "Country Boy," "A-Sleeping at the Foot of the Bed," "Hillbilly Fever," and "My Heart's Bouquet."

Early in the '50s, he formed a band called the Country Boys, which featured a steel guitar, two lead guitars, and drums. With their spirited traditional country approach and vague rockabilly inflections, the band didn't sound like their Nashville contemporaries. Perhaps that's why Dickens only had one hit between 1950 and 1962: 1954's "Out Behind the Barn." Dickens bounced back to the Top Ten with the ballad "The Violet and the Rose" in 1962. Three years later, he had his biggest hit, "May the Bird of Paradise Fly up Your Nose." The single topped the country charts and crossed over to number 15 on the pop charts.

Although his next single, "When the Ship Hit the Sand," was moderately successful, Dickens wasn't able to replicate the success of "May the Bird of Paradise Fly up Your

Nose." In 1968, he stopped recording for Columbia, signing with Decca Records, where he had three minor hits in the late '60s and early '70s. In 1971, he moved to United Artists, which resulted in two more small hits, but by that time he had begun to concentrate on performing as his main creative outlet. Dickens continued to tour and perform at the *Grand Ole Opry* into the '90s, becoming one of the most beloved characters in country music. —*Stephen Thomas Erlewine*

Old Country Church / 1954 / Columbia ✦✦✦

Raisin' the Dickens / 1957 / Columbia ✦✦✦

Aside from the fact that this contains a couple of Dickens' hits, the album is just OK. It relies a little too much on his gimmick of being the little guy with a lot of energy and not enough on the songs. —*Jim Worbois*

Big Country Songs By Little Jimmy Dickens / 1960 / Columbia ✦✦✦✦

Out Behind the Barn / 1962 / Columbia ✦✦✦

Handle With Care / 1965 / Columbia ✦✦✦

May the Bird of Paradise Fly Up Your Nose / 1965 / Columbia ✦✦✦

The Big Man in Country Music / 1968 / Columbia ✦✦✦

Columbia Historic Edition / 1991 / Columbia ✦✦✦✦✦

The 11-track *Columbia Historic Edition* gathers together a selection of Little Jimmy Dickens' most popular novelties, plus several straightforward honky tonk cuts, all of which were recorded for Columbia Records during the late '40s and '50s. Only a handful of hits are included—"Take An Old Cold 'Tater (And Wait)," "Out Behind the Barn"—but the inclusion of offbeat honky tonk songs and forgotten novelties makes it a useful compilation. —*Thom Owens*

● **I'm Little But I'm Loud: The Little Jimmy Dickens Collection** / May 21, 1996 / Razor & Tie ✦✦✦✦✦

Razor & Tie's 1996 compilation *I'm Little But I'm Loud: The Jimmy Dickens Collection* is the first comprehensive collection assembled on the diminutive Nashville legend, and it's also a collection that takes his frequently silly music seriously. While it hardly digs as deep as the two Bear Family boxes that followed this in 1997 and 1998, it covers the same period with the same purpose: Namely, it goes through his Columbia recordings of 1949 through 1967 with the intention of not just serving up the hits, but illustrating that Dickens was a first-rate country singer and not just a purveyor of novelties. Although it may get a little too silly at times for some listeners, it nevertheless does its job well, because it does show that Dickens' high, plaintive, nasal voice was quite versatile, and that he could tackle heartbreak ballads, hillbilly boogie, and honky tonk as well as his goofy novelties. Of course, those silly songs are what he was known for, and they're all here, from "Take an Old Cold Tater (And Wait)" in 1949 to "May the Bird of Paradise Fly Up Your Nose." If this collection was just 22 tracks of novelties, it would wear thin quickly (and, truth be told, the nasal qualities of Dickens' voice may make this a bit much for some listeners, even those who like hillbilly music), but instead the compilers vary the material, sometimes leaving hits behind—it's missing the 1965 cut "He Stands Real Tall," plus two pure novelties from 1966 in "When the Ship Hit the Sand" and "Who Licked the Red Off Your Candy"—in favor for stronger material. It's a gambit that works, because it reveals that Little Jimmy Dickens was a first-rate pure country singer, filled with all the corn and heartbreak that made the *Grand Ole Opry* great in the late '40s and '50s. While the Bear Family boxes will be for those who really want to dig deep, most listeners will be more than satisfied with this first-rate collection that explains exactly why Little Jimmy Dickens is a country legend. —*Stephen Thomas Erlewine*

Country Boy / Dec. 24, 1997 / Bear Family ✦✦✦✦

Country Boy is a four-disc import box set that collects Little Jimmy Dickens' complete Columbia recordings from 1949-1957 including most of his biggest hits, several sacred recordings, a handful of instrumentals, and much more. Dickens' music from this era vacillated between silly hillbilly novelties and maudlin weepers, which might sound like a jarring mix but actually makes for a more engaging listening experience when digesting a huge set of this sort. Dickens was an adept ballad singer but, because of his physical appearance, wasn't taken as seriously as he might have been. On the novelties, with his trademark twin electric guitar sound and humorous rural sensibility, Dickens made some of the most fun and funny music of the '50s. *Country Boy* unearths a number of excellent unreleased performances and stands as a well-deserved tribute to a beloved figure of country music. —*Greg Adams*

Out Behind the Barn / Feb. 11, 1998 / Bear Family ✦✦✦✦

Joe Diffie

b. Dec. 28, 1958, Tulsa, OK

Vocals / Contemporary Country, New Traditionalist

Joe Diffie was regarded by many of his peers as one of the better vocalists in contemporary country, and lent his traditional sensibilities to humorous, rock-tinged novelties and plaintive ballads. Diffie was born in Tulsa, OK, in 1958 and grew up in a musical family, first performing in public at age four with his aunt's country band. He played in a rock band during high-school, and later moved on to a gospel quartet and, during college, a bluegrass band called the Special Edition. He worked on his songwriting and singing over the next few years while working in a foundry, and caught a break when his "Love on the Rocks" was recorded by Hank Thompson. When Randy Travis nearly recorded another of his songs, Diffie was convinced he had a shot in the business, and moved to Nashville in 1986. He took a job at the Gibson guitar plant while continuing to write songs, and became an in-demand demo singer as well. Holly Dunn's 1989 recording of a Diffie collaboration, "There Goes My Heart Again," proved a major hit, and Diffie found himself a hot commodity.

He signed with Epic and released his debut album, *A Thousand Winding Roads*, in 1990. His first single, "Home," went all the way to number one on the country charts, and

"If the Devil Danced (In Empty Pockets)" duplicated that feat; meanwhile, two more singles from the album, "If You Want Me To" and "New Way (To Light Up an Old Flame)," reached number two. Diffie became a regular hitmaker over the rest of the '90s, and scored again with his sophomore LP, 1992's *Regular Joe*; "Is It Cold in Here" and "Ships That Don't Come In" both made the Top Five. Known primarily for his ballads at this point in his career, Diffie switched things up with 1993's *Honky Tonk Attitude*, which emphasized his rambunctious, rocking side and sense of humor, and proved to be his biggest-selling album yet. The title track, "Prop Me Up Beside the Jukebox (If I Die)," and "John Deere Green" all went Top Five.

Sticking with engaging humor as the selling point of his hugely popular follow-up, 1994's *Third Rock From the Sun*, Diffie scored two number ones with the title track and "Pickup Man," plus a Top Fiver in "So Help Me Girl." A holiday album, *Mr. Christmas* hit in 1995 as well as a proper release in *Life's So Funny*, which gave Diffie his fifth number-one hit in "Bigger Than the Beatles." *Twice Upon a Time* (1997) saw his commercial momentum slipping a bit, and so Epic issued a *Greatest Hits* compilation the following year; its new song, "Texas Sized Heartache," returned Diffie to the Top Five. *A Night to Remember* (1999) was the most straight-ahead, traditional country record Diffie had yet recorded, and it gave him two Top Ten hits in the title cut and "It's Always Somethin'." He returned to his more established style for 2001's *In Another World*, which found him transferred to Sony's reactivated Monument subsidiary; its title track went Top Ten early the next year. *—Steve Huey*

A Thousand Winding Roads / 1990 / Epic ✦✦✦✦✦

Regular Joe / Jan. 14, 1992 / Epic ✦✦✦✦✦
Diffie's second album has all the cliches of country music, and all the good stuff too. If "Ain't That Bad Enough" is a run-of-the-mill song, Diffie rescues it by tearing the melody loose from its mooring. He's also willing to push the line: of all Diffie's country heroes—and you'll be able to name them after one listen—maybe only Merle Haggard would rock out as hard as Diffie does on the title track. *—Brian Mansfield*

Honky Tonk Attitude / Apr. 20, 1993 / Epic ✦✦✦
Taking a cue from some of his peers, balladeer Diffie makes a point to get rowdy on this, his most commercially successful album to date. Besides the title track, it includes the hits "Prop Me Up Beside the Jukebox (If I Die)" and "John Deere Green." *—Dan Cooper*

Third Rock From the Sun / Jul. 26, 1994 / Epic ✦✦✦✦✦
Third Rock From the Sun represents a bit of a musical departure for Joe Diffie. Though he keeps his basic honky tonk roots, he experiments more, adding more rock flourishes to his sound. Not all of his attempts are successful, but his ballads are frequently compelling. Nevertheless, it's a little distressing that he has only written one song on the album—there's no reason for his well to dry up by only his fourth record. *—Thom Owens*

Life's So Funny / Dec. 5, 1995 / Epic ✦✦✦
Led by the tongue-in-cheek single "Bigger Than the Beatles," Joe Diffie's fifth album *Life's So Funny* delivers the relaxed, funny contemporary country that fans have come to expect from the singer. *Life's So Funny* isn't as consistently engaging as his previous *Third Rock From the Sun*, yet its warm sense of humor and varied collection of ballads and midtempo rockers makes it a worthy follow-up to the most popular record Diffie ever released. *—Thom Owens*

Twice Upon a Time / Apr. 22, 1997 / Epic ✦✦✦
Like *Life's So Funny*, *Twice Upon a Time* doesn't offer anything new or especially remarkable from Joe Diffie, yet it's a charmingly relaxed and entertaining album that confirms his place as one of the better mainstream contemporary country singers of the late '90s. *—Thom Owens*

Greatest Hits / Jun. 9, 1998 / Epic ✦✦✦✦
Greatest Hits is an excellent summation of Joe Diffie's first six albums, offering 12 of his biggest hit singles, including "Third Rock From the Sun," "John Deere Green," "Texas Size Heartache," "Prop Me Up Beside the Jukebox (If I Die)," "Honky Tonk Attitude" and "Bigger Than the Beatles." It's ideal for casual fans and neophytes, but even hardcore fans may want the collection, since it's the most consistently enjoyable record in his catalog. *—Stephen Thomas Erlewine*

A Night to Remember / Jun. 1, 1999 / Epic ✦✦✦✦
Throughout his career, Joe Diffie was known as a reliable recordmaker, the kind of country musician that could always turn out a hit single or two on a solid album. It's easy to take an artist like that for granted, and it's also easy to not notice when there's a subtle change in his style, as there is on *A Night to Remember*, his seventh album and first since the career-capping 1998 *Greatest Hits* collection. It's not that *A Night to Remember* radically redefines Diffie's music, but it does find him supremely confident—confident enough to create the purest country album he's ever made. With just ten songs, he has made the tightest album of his career, one that features no novelties or pop trifles. With the assistance of producers Don Cook and Lonnie Wilson, Diffie has stripped back his music to the bare essentials, yet retained the easygoing charm and clean, melodic appeal that has made him a dependable chart-topper. The combination is quite enjoyable, especially since the ten songs are all very strong, whether they're originals (including his own version of his co-written "You Can't Go Home," originally recorded by Conway Twitty) or covers (such as the title song, "The Quittin' Kind," and "Don't Our Love Look Natural"). The best country artists don't lose their gifts as they age, their talents deepen. And from the basis of *A Night to Remember*, Diffie was one of the few artists of the '90s whose talents were deepening. *—Stephen Thomas Erlewine*

In Another World / Oct. 30, 2001 / Monument ✦✦✦
Country is more a music of songs than albums, as its practitioners scour Nashville publishers for ten good compositions in the established style, then hope one or two of them will connect with fans. Joe Diffie has put together a decade-plus career in country largely on his ability to succeed in this quest. An adequate but undistinguished singer, he has proven versatile enough to score with a variety of material, and if he has never ascended to superstar status, that he is still going after ten years is a considerable accomplishment. His albums as albums tend to suffer from the typical country flaw: They sound like ten separate songs instead of coherent collections. That's true of *In Another World*, too, but, as usual, there seem to be enough potential singles to keep him going. The title song, which, typical of the current market, was on country radio for months prior to the album's release, isn't really one of the stronger tracks; it's a wistful reflection on lost love, but a bit sketchy. Far better is the second track, the raucous kiss-off song "My Give a Damn's Busted." Diffie has made a small specialty of such novelties, and he gives a letter-perfect reading to this one, which sounds like a hit waiting to happen if country fans don't find it a tad too sarcastic. Typically, though, it's a one-off; nothing else on the record sounds remotely like it. "If I Lost Her" is the best ballad, while "This Pretender" sounds like something the Eagles could have done. The rest of the tracks are sturdy formula country with their twisted clichés, sentimental messages, and instrumentation. The producers have achieved a remarkably high-tech sound for a country disc, even if the result comes off as freeze-dried on occasion, especially in the harmony vocals. *—William Ruhlmann*

● **16 Biggest Hits** / Feb. 19, 2002 / Epic ✦✦✦✦✦
16 Biggest Hits does an effective job of chronicling the majority of Joe Diffie's biggest hits from the '90s. Most of his Top Ten hits are featured, including the number-one singles "Home," "If the Devil Danced (In Empty Pockets)," and "Ships That Don't Come In." This single disc is the perfect introduction to the singer who successfully mixed traditional country with rock-oriented pop. *—Al Campbell*

The Essential Joe Diffie / Apr. 1, 2003 / Epic ✦✦✦✦
Epic/Legacy's 2003 collection *The Essential Joe Diffie* weighs in at 14 tracks, just two less than the 2002 collection *16 Biggest Hits*, with which it shares a whopping 12 tracks. Given that considerable overlap, it's not surprising that the two collections are essentially interchangeable, but *16 Biggest Hits* has the edge, not just because it has two more tracks, but because the four songs unique to that collection are stronger than the two unique songs here (for the record, they are the Mary-Chapin Carpenter duet "Not Too Much to Ask," which has never appeared on a Joe Diffie album, and the modest hit "This Is Your Brain"). That said, *The Essential Joe Diffie* is hardly a bad album—after, it's pretty much the same album, down to identical sequencing for the first three cuts—and it is also an effective overview of the peak of Diffie's career. *16 Biggest Hits* may be slightly stronger, but that's all it is: a slight difference. On its own terms, *The Essential Joe Diffie* is a first-rate collection. *—Stephen Thomas Erlewine*

Johnny Dilks

b. San Mateo, CA

Guitar, Vocals / Rockabilly, Country Boogie, Western Swing, Honky Tonk

Born and raised in San Mateo, CA, rockabilly and Western swing was hardly the choice of music for Johnny Dilks until he was a young teenager. It was then that his aunt gave him her record collection, which contained albums by Carl Perkins, Jerry Lee Lewis, and other artists. It was Dilks intention to sell the records and make some money, but instead, the proprietor of the store where he had taken them turned him on to Western swing and honky tonk country. Although he continued to play in local punk bands during his high-school years, Dilks joined a rockabilly band when he was 18, and a year later formed the Rhythm Wranglers, a Western swing act that managed to garner a following in the Bay Area. He was concurrently playing in the original version of the Visitacion Valley Boys, named after an area south of San Francisco that had been a hotbed for the country music of the '40s that had inspired Dilks.

In 1998, the Visitacion Valley Boys, whose lineup included Dilks as lead singer and guitarist Paul Wooton, fiddle player Brian Godchaux, steel guitarist Billy Wilson, stand-up bassist Brendan Ryan, and drummer Pat Campbell, were invited to back hero Charlie Louvin on a string of West Coast dates. The following year, now signed to Hightone, Dilks released his debut, *Acres of Heartache*, to enthusiastic reviews praising the manner in which he had captured the spirit of the music he had embraced. In 2002, Dilks' band consisted of bass player Marc Bernasconi, guitarist Hank Maninger, steel player Les Jeffriess, and drummer Leor Beary. *—Tom Demalon*

Acres of Heartache / May 25, 1999 / HMG ✦✦✦✦
If you're wondering where the return-to-roots movement that happened in country music in the mid-'80s went, it's alive and well in bands like Johnny Dilks & His Visitacion Valley Boys. They play true country & western music with a distinct West Coast edge, à la *Town Hall Party* in the early to mid-'50s. Dilks' voice is raw hillbilly, with an unrepentant redneck tone. He's not even above yodeling, as he does to great effect on "Lose That Woman Blues." His band, the Visitacion Valley Boys, is a sturdy combo of lead guitar, string bass, fiddle, steel guitar, and drums that keeps it simple and swinging throughout. They tackle a number of grooves from roadhouse rock to Latin rhumba and still keep it in the vintage pocket with a solid ensemble sound and Sons of the Pioneers harmonies that are a fine bonus on the acoustic-based "Close But So Far Away." If Garth Brooks and Shania Twain are supposed to represent all the progress country music has made from its older hillbilly beginnings, *Acres of Heartache* turns the tables and honors those beginnings by celebrating them, warts and all. This is one great little album of hillbilly music. *—Cub Koda*

Dillard & Clark

f. 1968

Group / Progressive Bluegrass, Country-Rock

Dillard & Clark, a duo featuring former Byrd Gene Clark and Doug Dillard of the Dillards, was one of the first country-rock groups to form in the late '60s. The group formed in 1968 and became one of pioneers of country-rock, releasing two albums before dissolving after releasing only two albums. In 1968, Dillard recorded his first solo album, *The Banjo*

Album, which featured such rock musicians as Clark and Bernie Leadon. In the spring of 1968, Dillard toured England as a member of the Byrds, which led to the duo of Dillard & Clark, which officially formed later that summer. The duo secured a record contract with A&M and released their debut album, *The Fantastic Expedition of Dillard & Clark*, late in 1968. The record was recorded with Bernie Leadon (guitar), Don Beck (dobro, mandolin), and David Jackson (bass). Dillard & Clark toured following the release of the album; their supporting band featured former Byrd Michael Clarke on drums.

Dillard & Clark began recording a second album early in 1969 with a new supporting band. The new lineup featured Leadon, fiddler Byron Berline, drummer Jon Corneal, and guitarist Donna Washburn; steel guitarist Sneaky Pete Kleinow and Chris Hillman, who were both members of the Flying Burrito Brothers, also guested on the album. The resulting record, *Through the Morning, Through the Night*, appeared later in the year. After its release, Leadon left the duo; he would join the Eagles soon after his departure. Clark decided to pursue a solo career in early 1970. Dillard continued his solo career, using the remaining members of the duo's backing band as the core of his new outfit, the Expedition. Dillard & Clark continued to pursue solo careers throughout the '80s and '90s, with Dillard garnering more success and critical acclaim than Clark. Clark died in 1991 at the age of 46. *—Stephen Thomas Erlewine*

☆ **The Fantastic Expedition of Dillard & Clark** / 1968 / Edsel ✦✦✦✦✦

Gene Clark was the greatest underrated singer/songwriter to emerge from the '60s rock explosion, and deserves to be mentioned in the same breath as Neil Young. This album, his debut as a duo with virtuoso banjoist/guitarist Doug Dillard, is perhaps his most brilliant recording. Out of the ashes of the Byrds and a brilliant false start of a solo career (the excellent *Echoes* album), the 1968 Dillard & Clark project found Clark collecting some of his finest material (basically the entire album) and putting it in the familiar context of bluegrass and country, a good year before these elements became vogue in the pop world. But Gene Clark was always ahead of his time. Bookended by two exquisite autobiographical explorations into consciousness—"Out on the Side" and "Something's Wrong"—the album's other tracks run from mournful ballad statements such as "Radio Song" to joyous celebrations like "With Care from Someone." There is also a very hot cover of the gospel number "Git It on Brother," which features Chris Hillman on mandolin. Doug Dillard's playing on the record is uniformly excellent. Not only a virtuoso musician, Dillard is a truly *smart* player who never gets in the way of the songs. Graceful, spellbinding, and tasteful all at the same time. Absolutely essential. *—Matthew Greenwald*

Through the Morning, Through the Night / 1969 / Edsel ✦✦✦

Dillard & Clark's second outing was a disappointment in relation to their far more eclectic and original prior effort, *The Fantastic Expedition of Dillard & Clark*. The primary difference is that whereas the earlier record had leaned on Gene Clark's original compositions, and a reasonably adventurous attitude toward country-rock fusion in general, the follow-up saw them turning into a much more traditional folk/bluegrass act. In part this was due to the addition of guitarist Donna Washburn on harmony and occasional lead vocal, and the departure of Bernie Leadon. But in the main, it was because Clark wrote just four of the tracks, surrounded by covers of songs by Reno and Smiley, Bill Monroe, the Everly Brothers, and even the Beatles' "Don't Let Me Down" (which is actually one of the better songs on the album). Taken on its own, it's a fair, pleasant heavily bluegrass-flavored outing with few surprises. The Clark originals sound considerably more personal and contemporary than the more traditional tunes, though Clark's "Corner Street Bar" was a surprisingly dreadful comic barroom lament. Either the band didn't realize that Clark's voice and compositions were their greatest potential assets, or Clark himself was not assertive enough in pushing himself to the forefront. *—Richie Unterberger*

Grass Roots (Half LP + Half Burritoes) / 1972 / Mayfair ✦✦✦

Kansas City Southern / 1975 / Ariola ✦✦✦

Gene Clark & Doug Dillard / 1975 / Ariola ✦✦✦✦✦

★ **The Fantastic Expedition of Dillard & Clark/Through the Morning, Through the Night** / 1989 / Mobile Fidelity ✦✦✦✦✦

The duo's two albums are combined on one CD, making for more than an hour of great listening. Mastered in state-of-the-art sound that still holds up years later, this is the version of the two albums to get. The Dillard & Clark duo was Gene Clark's most artistically successful post-Byrds collaboration, and his best venture into country-rock as well. With Chris Hillman and Bernie Leadon playing behind the duo throughout the first album, in many ways it is as much an offshoot of the Flying Burrito Brothers' work as it is of the Byrds, with more of the Burritos' feel. The standard of playing and singing on both albums is extremely high, but the ten songs on *The Fantastic Expedition of Dillard & Clark* are more impressive, both as recordings and compositions. The ten songs from *Through the Morning, Through the Night* fail to match the joyous quality or the originality of their predecessors and the sound is less unified, mostly due to the presence of a third singer in the guise of Donna Washburn. The mix of rollicking bluegrass (such as "Rocky Top" which is sung by Washburn) and covers like the Beatles' "Don't Let Me Down" and the Everly Brothers' "So Sad" is also less successful. But combined together, these 20 songs are an essential addition to any country-rock collection and are also indispensible to fans of the Byrds or the Flying Burrito Brothers. *—Bruce Eder*

☆ **The Fantastic Expedition of Dillard and Clark Plus** / Aug. 14, 2001 / Edsel ✦✦✦✦✦

Doug Dillard

b. Mar. 6, 1937, Salem, MO

Banjo, Guitar, Vocals / Progressive Bluegrass, Traditional Bluegrass, Country-Rock

Doug Dillard was one of the pre-eminent ambassadors of bluegrass banjo during the '60s and '70s, incorporating pop, folk, and country-rock material into his repertoire and supporting a wide variety of artists with those sensibilities. Born in Salem, MO, in 1937, Dillard started playing bluegrass early on, eventually teaming with his younger brother,

Rodney. The duo made their first recordings in 1958, then played with several bands before forming their own group, the Dillards. In 1962, the Dillards relocated to Los Angeles, where they quickly landed a deal with Elektra and issued a string of groundbreaking albums over the rest of the '60s. The Dillards were among the first bluegrass groups to use amplified instruments, and they also had highly eclectic taste in covers, drawing from pop and rock as well as traditional material. Dillard was active outside the group as well, working with a side project called the Folkswingers, backing ex-Byrd Gene Clark with the Gosdin Brothers, and collaborating with Rodney on material for the *Bonnie & Clyde* soundtrack in 1967.

Later in 1967, Dillard left the band he'd co-founded to pursue new projects. He recorded a solo LP, *The Banjo Album*, in 1968, which featured backing by several rock musicians, including Gene Clark and Bernie Leadon. Dillard soon formed a partnership with Clark, and recording with a backing band as Dillard & Clark, the two cut some of the earliest country-rock material in existence. Two groundbreaking albums followed before Clark went solo in 1970, and Dillard briefly reorganized the remaining band as the Doug Dillard Expedition, which contributed a song to the soundtrack of 1971's *Vanishing Point*. Dillard soon resumed his solo career, however, taking occasional session gigs and signing with 20th Century. He released two solo albums—*Duelin' Banjo* and *Douglas Flint Dillard—You Don't Need a Reason to Sing*—in 1973 and 1974, respectively. In 1977, he re-teamed with brother Rodney and John Hartford in Dillard-Hartford-Dillard, who recorded two albums for Flying Fish in 1977 and 1980. Dillard himself released two LPs on the same label: the 1979 gospel effort *Heaven* and the concert set *Jackrabbit* in 1980. During the '80s, he performed regularly with the Doug Dillard Band and also recorded sporadically; Flying Fish released *What's That?* in 1986 and *Heartbreak Hotel* three years later. *—Steve Huey*

● **The Banjo Album** / 1968 / Together ✦✦✦✦✦

The Banjo Album is first, and foremost, an album of traditional bluegrass played by musicians firmly rooted in the work of pioneers like Flatt and Scruggs, the Stanley Brothers and Bill Monroe. These same musicians, however, are all top-notch, second generation players influenced by the rock scene. Consequently, Dillard and crew manage to breathe genuine new life into many standards without sacrificing the integrity of the originals. In fact, the musicians not only play ferociously, but often completely reinterpret the old chestnuts, occasionally making them sound even better. In many cases, Dillard employs droning harmonic tonalities characteristic of Indian music and Indian-influenced psychedelic rock guitar. The record also features atypical bluegrass instruments such as harpsichord, harmonica, drums, dembek, and tablas. Rather than coming off as gimmicky, though, the use of exotic instrumentation serves to add exciting new textures and moods to music which, during this pre-"Newgrass" period, rarely deviated from very strict stylistic guidelines. Plus, nearly every performance here is simply an all-out jam, with Dillard playing particularly explosively. Special mention should be made of his fantastic version of "Clinch Mountain Backstep," which shows a confidence, boldness and energy that rivals even the definitive version by Clarence White's Kentucky Colonels. *—Pemberton Roach*

Duelin' Banjo / 1973 / 20th Century ✦✦✦✦✦

Douglas Flint Dillard—You Don't Need a Reason to Sing / 1974 / 20th Century ✦✦✦

You Don't Need a Reason to Sing / 1974 / 20th Century ✦✦

Heaven / 1979 / Flying Fish ✦✦✦

Jackrabbit / 1980 / Flying Fish ✦✦✦✦

What's That? / 1986 / Flying Fish ✦✦✦

Heartbreak Hotel / 1989 / Flying Fish ✦✦

The Dillards

f. 1962, Missouri, db. 1980

Group / Bluegrass, Progressive Bluegrass, Traditional Bluegrass, Country-Rock

One of the leading lights of progressive bluegrass in the '60s, the Dillards played a major part in modernizing and popularizing the sound of bluegrass, and were also an underappreciated influence on country-rock. The group was founded by brothers Doug (banjo) and Rodney Dillard (guitar), who grew up in Salem, MO, playing music together. During the late '50s, they appeared often on local radio and performed with several different area bands, including the Hawthorn Brothers, the Lewis Brothers, and the Dixie Ramblers; they also recorded a couple of singles for the St. Louis-based K-Ark label as the Dillard Brothers in 1958. In 1960, they decided to form their own group, recruiting DJ pal Mitch Jayne on bass, as well as mandolin player Dean Webb. Christening themselves the Dillards, the quartet decided to move to Los Angeles in 1962, and were quickly signed to Elektra after being discovered at a gig with the Greenbriar Boys.

Not long after, the group landed a recurring role on *the Andy Griffith Show*, appearing in several episodes over the next few years as a musically inclined hillbilly family called the Darlings. Meanwhile, the Dillards released their debut album, *Back Porch Bluegrass*, in 1963, and also teamed up with Glen Campbell and Tut Taylor for the side project the Folkswingers, who went on to release two albums. The Dillards' second album, 1964's concert set *Live! Almost!*, captured their controversial move into amplified electric instruments, which was considered heresy by many bluegrass purists; they also began to tour with rock groups, most notably the Byrds. In response to purist criticism, the group followed *Live! Almost!* in 1965 with the more traditional *Pickin' & Fiddlin'*, which featured co-billing for fiddler Byron Berline. Dissatisfied with the way Elektra was marketing them, the Dillards switched labels to Capitol, but found a similar lack of kindred spirits in the producers they worked with there, and wound up returning to Elektra without releasing an album.

Meanwhile, Doug and Rodney were increasingly at odds over the group's creative direction, with Rodney pursuing a more radical break with tradition than Doug. Doug moonlighted in the backing band for ex-Byrd Gene Clark's groundbreaking collaboration with the Gosdin Brothers, and after he and Rodney recorded some material for the

Bonnie & Clyde film soundtrack in 1967, he decided to leave the Dillards and strike out on his own. Doug soon teamed up with Gene Clark as Dillard & Clark and recorded some highly regarded material before starting a solo career that remained productive through the '70s. Rodney, meanwhile, replaced his brother with banjoist Herb Pedersen, and the Dillards recorded what many critics regard as their masterwork, *Wheatstraw Suite*. Released in 1968, the album displayed Rodney's progressive eclecticism in full cry, featuring fuller instrumentation and covers of the Beatles' "I've Just Seen a Face" and Tim Hardin's "Reason to Believe." Though it wasn't a hit, critics and musicians praised its unpredictable mix of bluegrass, country, folk, rock, and pop. *Copperfields* (1970) took a similarly adventurous approach, and drummer Paul York became an official member of the group. Unfortunately, Elektra was still somewhat mystified by their music, and they parted ways again. Pedersen departed in 1972 to join Byron Berline's band, Country Gazette, and was replaced by Billy Ray Latham; by this time, the Dillards had signed with the smaller Anthem label, where they landed their only charting pop hit, "It's About Time," in 1971.

An opening slot on tour with Elton John in 1972 helped *Roots & Branches* become their biggest-selling album to date, but the group subsequently switched over to the Poppy label for their follow-up, 1973's country-rock effort *Tribute to the American Duck*. Mitch Jayne left the group in 1974, partly due to hearing loss, and was replaced by new bassist Jeff Gilkinson. It took several years to reconvene for their next album, 1977's *The Dillards vs. the Incredible L.A. Time Machine*, which was released on Flying Fish. Latham subsequently departed and was replaced by Doug Bounsall, and Herb Pedersen also returned for the group's next two albums, 1978's *Mountain Rock* (after which Paul York retired) and 1979's *Decade Waltz*. Also in 1979, the group reunited with Doug Dillard and other past members (and relatives) for the Salem, MO, concert celebration *Homecoming & Family Reunion*. Following that performance, most of the Dillards left the group.

Rodney Dillard and Dean Webb briefly organized a new lineup that featured Joe Villegas, Eddie Ponder, and Peter Grant, but it proved short-lived; Rodney subsequently formed the Rodney Dillard Band and settled in Branson, MO. In 1988, the original Dillards lineup reunited for a series of performances, and interest in the group was rekindled thanks to the publicity surrounding *the Andy Griffith Show*'s 30th anniversary. With new member Steve Cooley later taking Doug Dillard's place, the group cut two new albums for Vanguard, 1990's *Let It Fly* and 1992's *Take Me Along for the Ride*. The group reunited several times throughout the '90s for concert performances, and both Doug and Rodney continued to pursue their own ventures. *—Steve Huey*

Back Porch Blue Grass / 1963 / Elektra ✦✦✦✦✦

The Dillards Live! Almost! / 1964 / Elektra ✦✦✦✦✦

Pickin' and Fiddlin' With Byron Berline / 1965 / Elektra ✦✦✦✦

Wheatstraw Suite / 1968 / Elektra ✦✦✦✦✦

It never got any better than this. In 1968, as the Byrds were making valiant (if unappreciated) efforts to bring rock and country music closer together, the Dillards were trying to do some of the same for bluegrass and rock. The result was 13 all-but-perfect tracks mixing some pretty laid-back topicality ("Hey Boys") and humor ("The Biggest Whatever"), cowboy songs ("Single Saddle," which Gene Autry should have covered), just plain gorgeous poetry ("Lemon Chimes"), and a couple of unexpected covers ("I've Just Seen a Face," "Reason to Believe"), with arrangements that exude a delicate, subdued lushness ("Listen to the Sound") and an element of electric rock (courtesy of Joe Osborn on electric bass and Jim Gordon on drums) that worked perfectly. In many ways, this is a finer rural/rock fusion album than *Sweetheart of the Rodeo*, the first Flying Burrito Brothers album, or the Beau Brummels' efforts during this same period, and an indispensable part of any collection of '60s music. *—Bruce Eder*

Copperfields / 1970 / Elektra ✦✦✦✦

The Dillards' second album with rock-influenced arrangements was not as barrier-busting as 1968's *Wheatstraw Suite*, and further removed from their bluegrass roots. However, it was a similarly eclectic and, for the most part, joyous romp through a fusion of bluegrass, rock, folk, and country, with a bit of pop and orchestration along the ride, and the group's superb vocal harmonies being the main constant. "Touch Her If You Can" was the number with the most pop and orchestration, and worked extremely well, with its achingly sad melody. If anything the Dillards did on Elektra could have been a hit single, this would have been a likely candidate. Their unusual a cappella arrangement of the Beatles' "Yesterday" caught some attention, and "Brother John" is another simultaneous detour and highlight, with its Dave Brubeck-influenced jazzy rhythms and guitar picking that recalled the Byrds' psychedelic era. While other tracks, like the bluegrass tune "Old Man at the Mill" and Eric Andersen's "Close the Door Lightly," were more in the standard country-rock mode, they're also good, with the musicians applying care and creative production to the material throughout the disc. *—Richie Unterberger*

Roots and Branches / 1972 / Anthem ✦✦

Tribute to the American Duck / 1973 / Poppy ✦✦

Really, it should have been "the Dillard," because banjo hotshot Doug Dillard had left the band, leaving the direction up to Rodney Dillard and holdovers from previous groupings, such as mandolinist Dean Webb. An incident in Las Vegas in the '80s involving the latter player is a good illustration of why expanding the bluegrass audience during the late '60s and early '70s might not have been such a good idea. An audience waiting for Webb to sit in and play bluegrass was horrified when the mandolinist instead launched into an extended version of the song "Cocaine." There was none of the fleet, light-fingered beauty associated with bluegrass, and it was all about thudding old-school rock vibes. And that, to a large extent, describes what happens on this record, as well as what often happened when the Dillards played to a rock audience. It wasn't really the bluegrass audience that got expanded—the ranks of the bluegrass-playing musicians actually shrank, since the music being played bore less and less resemblance to bluegrass. Often, as in the case of that version of "Cocaine" and many of the tracks on this album, it was just out and out rock or, even worse, wimpy country-rock. It is really unfortunate, because an album dedicated to the duck, one of the greatest animals to ever waddle the earth's muck, should be better than this. Ducks Unlimited should really sue, since a color photograph of a duck is prominently featured on the front. It is an exploitation of the duck's image in order for the group to appear arty and whimsical. If "art" is defined by effort, then this album is indeed quite an artistic project for this group. Each song is like a flower arrangement in which a nice-looking tulip is twisted, turned, and buried with soils and rocks until the flower shreds beyond recognition. The tulip in this case isn't so much the traditional sound of the bluegrass band, which some reactionaries think is lost simply by adding drums. Really, drums are the least of the problems here, as Paul York is a capable player who shines in the rare instances when a bluegrass beat actually emerges. There are touches of nice playing here and there from everyone, including banjoist Billy Ray Latham, and the ensemble passages are tweaked to an impressive level. Some listeners may enjoy the way songs evolve into harmonies that sound more like the Beatles than the Monroe Brothers. It is the songwriting and arrangements that cover the joy of old-time music with a smothering layer of rock and pop influence, and what is really dangerous is that this is referencing the music of the '70s, a time when artificially "down-home" and "funky" foot soldiers were limping through the work of artists such as J. J. Cale, Elton John, the Average White Band, and so on. To hint that these are the influences that take over on this record is a polite way of waving a large red flag. Perhaps the bird of the title is part of a pun, and it is the listener who should "duck" when this particular album flies by. *—Eugene Chadbourne*

Decade Waltz / 1979 / Flying Fish ✦✦✦

On this album one of the most important bands in the development of country-rock returns to its beginnings. *—AMG*

Homecoming & Family Reunion / 1979 / Flying Fish ✦✦✦

This is a pleasant album of several Dillard generations live at a picnic. *—Mark A. Humphrey*

Let It Fly / 1990 / Vanguard ✦✦✦✦

Over the years, the Dillards have had their share of personnel changes. When they recorded *Let It Fly* for Vanguard in 1990, the main participants were founding member Rodney Dillard (lead vocals), Steve Cooley (acoustic guitar, banjo), Dean Webb (mandolin), and Mitch Jayne (who co-wrote a few of the tunes). Produced by the Desert Rose Band's Herb Pedersen, *Let It Fly* is really more country-rock than bluegrass—no one will mistake this CD for a collection of Bill Monroe recordings from the '40s. *Let It Fly*, which favors a blend of acoustic and electric instruments, doesn't cater to bluegrass purists. But then, the Dillards quit catering to bluegrass purists in the '60s when they started using electric instruments. *Let It Fly* should be judged by country-rock standards—not traditional bluegrass standards—and when country-rock standards are applied, one realizes that the album is excellent. Although bluegrass purists will be disappointed to learn that *Let It Fly* is far from a carbon copy of the Dillards' earliest recordings, country-rock items like "Out on a Limb," "Livin' in the House," and "Close the Door Lightly" have more heart than most of the slick, contrived stuff that country radio was playing in the early '90s. Rodney Dillard is expressive and convincing throughout the album, and in a perfect world, *Let It Fly* would have received a lot of airplay on country radio. But country radio didn't give this release the time of day. And while that was regrettable, it certainly wasn't the end of the world. The Dillards still had plenty of hardcore fans, and those are the people who bought *Let It Fly*. Arguably, *Let It Fly* is the best album that the Dillards provided in the '90s. *—Alex Henderson*

★ **There Is a Time (1963–70)** / 1991 / Vanguard ✦✦✦✦✦

This features 29 tracks drawn from the Dillards' first five albums (originally on Elektra), which are otherwise unavailable. The CD is assembled not in chronological order, but with musical coherence as the main determining factor, so tracks from different albums get juxtaposed together. From *Back Porch Bluegrass* we get five songs, including "Banjo in the Hollow" and "Dooley" (another version of which they performed with Andy Griffith on his TV show), while *Pickin' and Fiddlin'* is represented by the bracing "Hamilton County Breakdown" and "Sally Johnson." *Live!! Almost!!* gets six tracks, including the group's version of Dylan's "Walkin' Down the Line." There are five numbers (including the title track and the Beatles' "Yesterday") off of their 1970 release, *Copperfields*, and the legendary *Wheatstraw Suite*, from two years earlier, has nine songs, among them the group's loving covers of the Beatles' "I've Just Seen a Face" and Tim Hardin's "Reason to Believe." *—Bruce Eder*

Take Me Along for the Ride / 1992 / Vanguard ✦✦✦

The Dillards' Rodney Dillard/Dean Webb/Mitch Jayne/Steve Cooley lineup recorded two albums for Vanguard in the early '90s. While 1990's excellent *Let It Fly* was primarily a country-rock effort, their next album, *Take Me Along for the Ride*, had more of a folk-rock outlook. That isn't to say that everything on this CD falls into the folk-rock category. "Food on the Table" and "Against the Grain" are among the country-rock offerings, and the lively instrumental "Wide Wide Dixie Highway" is a perfect example of the type of straight-ahead bluegrass that the Dillards became famous for in the early '60s. But if any style is ultimately dominant, it is folk-rock—and those who enjoy hearing the Dillards as folk-rockers will find a lot to admire about tracks like "Banks of the Rouge Bayou," "Move On (Life of the Common Man)," and the sociopolitical title song (which is about those who feel like they are on the outside of the American dream looking in). One of the most interesting tracks is a cover of the Beatles' "In My Life," which receives an unlikely folk-rock makeover. Of course, there are still some bluegrass purists who resent the fact that the Dillards have recorded anything other than traditional straight-ahead bluegrass—people who have that mindset wish they would stay away from folk-rock and country-rock. They would lament the fact that "Wide Wide Dixie Highway" isn't typical of the album on the whole. But then, Rodney Dillard probably would have become bored if he had to play traditional acoustic bluegrass 100 percent of the time. And for those who have eclectic tastes, the Dillards' versatility is a plus. Although not quite essential, *Take Me Along for the Ride* was a solid and rewarding addition to the Dillards' catalog. *—Alex Henderson*

Roots and Branches/Tribute to the American Duck / Mar. 19, 1996 / BGO ✦✦✦✦
After leaving Elektra Records in the early '70s, but before signing with Flying Fish, the Dillards released two albums, *Roots and Branches* and *Tribute to the American Duck*, on independent labels. Neither was particularly remarkable, but they're of interest to hard-core fans. Beat Goes On reissued the pair on one CD in 1996. *—Stephen Thomas Erlewine*

Best of the Darlin' Boys / Sep. 30, 1997 / Vanguard ✦✦✦✦

A Long Time Ago / 1999 / Varese ✦✦✦✦
According to Mitch Jayne's brief liner notes, this was the Dillards' very first concert, from the summer of 1962 (although the wording is such that it's a little vague). If this was their first concert, it's an amazingly accomplished outing for a debut. The playing and harmonies are tight and exuberant, and the repertoire diverse, from familiar tunes like "John Hardy" and "Cumberland Gap" to "Cannonball Blues" and Woody Guthrie's arrangement of "Hard, Ain't It Hard." The tempos are lightning and the picking breathlessly fast on "Katie Cline," "Banjo in the Hollow," "Buckin Mule," and the instrumentals "Cripple Creek" and "Watermelon on the Vine." In fact, they're incredibly rapid in a lot of places, but not gratuitously flash. The documentation on this set isn't the greatest; the notes offer that nine of the 16 songs are previously unreleased performances, but they don't explain where the other seven songs were issued. The important thing, though, is that the album is a good, historically valuable set of music, solid on its own merits as well. *—Richie Unterberger*

The First Time Live / Nov. 2, 1999 / Varese ✦✦✦✦
Varese's *First Time Live* compiles 16 live performances recorded in 1962 by the original lineup of the seminal bluegrass band. As should be expected, this is a gem in the rough, capturing the band as they're finding their distinctive voice. Even though this music was recorded within the band's first year of existence, the band is still surprisingly assured, yet their very newness keeps this fresh, vital, and exciting. A priceless dip into the vaults that's sure to thrill die-hard Dillards fans. *—Stephen Thomas Erlewine*

Dean Dillon

b. Mar. 26, 1955, Lake City, TN
Songwriter, Vocals / Contemporary Country, Neo-Traditionalist Country
Dean Dillon was born on March 26, 1955, in Lake City, TN, and learned to play guitar at a young age. At 15, he appeared in a local Knoxville variety show as a songwriter and performer; by the end of high-school, Dillon had his mind set on Nashville. Almost as soon as he arrived in Music City, Dillon was on his way. He met songwriter Frank Dycus, who introduced him to idol and honky tonk legend Merle Haggard. He also worked with ex-Porter Wagoner fiddler Mac McGahey's combo at the Opryland theme park. In 1976, he landed the role of Hank Williams in the Country Music Show at Opryland. While there, a friend introduced him to songwriter John Schweers, who became Dillon's mentor. Three weeks later, Barbara Mandrell recorded three of Dillon's songs. In 1979, Jim Ed Brown and Helen Cornelius had a number one hit with his "Lying Here in Love with You."

Between 1979-1983, Dillon charted eight times, and broke the Top 30 with "I'm into the Bottle (To Get You Out of My Mind)." He also wrote hits for other country stars, like the 1983 George Jones hit "Tennessee Whiskey." These successes established Dillon as a performer and songwriter; however, they were also a telling reminder of his bouts with drug and alcohol abuse. In late 1983, a freshly rehabbed Dillon was paired by new label RCA with Gary Stewart, the "King of the Honky Tonkers." The two mens' vices fed off of one another, and while their two bleary, good-timing albums were successful (especially 1982's *Brotherly Love*), the partnership had little use for the straight and narrow. After *Those Were the Days*, Dillon took a five-year hiatus from recording, cleaned up his personal life, and concentrated on songwriting. He wrote or co-wrote a number of hits during this period, and had considerable success with George Strait, who took five of his songs to the charts between 1985-1988.

The exposure landed Dillon a new contract with Capitol, who released two Ricky Scruggs-produced albums, *Slick Nickel* and *I've Learned to Live*. The latter featured the Tanya Tucker duet "Don't You Even Think About Leaving." Dillon next signed with Atlantic, where he issued his most successful album. *Out of Your Ever-Lovin' Mind* (1991) referenced the hard country of Dillon's heroes, but it also flirted with pop. The LP was lauded as a throwback, an answer to Nashville's penchant for vapidity. While he stopped performing, Dillon's songwriting career thrived for the rest of the 1990s, as he continued to work with Strait and newer faces like Kenny Chesney. In 2002, he was inducted into the Nashville Songwriters Hall of Fame (along with Bob Dylan and Shel Silverstein). Early the following year, Dillon signed a songwriting contract with Sony/ATV Tree, which came after his 15-year relationship with Acuff Rose, a smaller publishing company Sony acquired in July 2002. *—Johnny Loftus*

Brotherly Love / 1982 / RCA ✦✦✦

Those Were the Days / 1982 / RCA ✦✦✦

I've Learned to Live / 1989 / Capitol ✦✦✦

● **Out of Your Ever-Lovin' Mind** / 1991 / Atlantic ✦✦✦✦✦
In the early '90s, Dean Dillon was exalted as a representative of neo-traditionalism in country, meaning that he was one of the artists allegedly fighting to return country to its down-home, honky tonk roots after so many years of Nashville making the pop market a high priority. However, Dillon's best-selling album, *Out of Your Ever-Lovin' Mind*, isn't devoid of pop considerations by any means. Rather, he balances honky tonk and pop elements on this CD, which ranges from hardcore country like "Holed Up in Some Honky Tonk" to such pop-flavored offerings as "Holding My Own," "Friday Night's Woman" (a poignant tearjerker describing a single mother's loneliness), and Dillon's heartfelt ode to Buddy Holly, "A Country Boy (Who Rolled the Rock Away)." On the whole, the album (which came out when the singer/composer was 36) isn't magnificent, although most of the songs are likable and decent. And, to be sure, *Ever-Lovin' Mind* has more soul and integrity than a lot of the contrived, homogenized music that had been coming out of Nashville in the 1980s. *—Alex Henderson*

Hot, Country, & Single / 1991 / Atlantic ✦✦✦✦
Dillon's second album features "Holed Up in Some Honky Tonk," recut from his *Out of Your Ever-Lovin Mind* LP. More serious fare can be found in "Everybody Knows," the latest in a long line of country portraits of hard-drinking loners. *—Jason Ankeny*

Dixiana

f. 1986
Group / Contemporary Country
Dixiana was a country band formed in 1986 by brothers Mark (bass/vocals) and Phil Lister (string instruments/vocals), along with keyboardist Randall Griffith and drummer Colonel Shuford. The group was scheduled to appear on *Nashville Now* when they suddenly lost their original lead singer; fortunately, the Listers' childhood friend, Cindy Murphy, formerly a member of the bluegrass Wooden Nickel Band, agreed to be their primary vocalist. The group signed to Epic in 1992 and released their first self-titled album, which contained two Top 40 singles, "Waitin' for the Deal to Go Down" and "That's What I'm Working on Tonight." Dixiana followed up their debut with *The Gospel Truth*, an album of standards. Phil and Mark Lister then issued *Classic Gospel Instrumentals*, and later, *Classic Country Instrumentals*. The two also worked with the Nashville indie Red Horse as producers and A&R specialists. *—Johnny Loftus*

● **Dixiana** / Aug. 1991 / Epic ✦✦✦✦
This album contains "Are You over Her?," "Waitin' for the Deal to Go Down," and "A Little in Love," among other favorites. *—AMG*

Dixie Chicks

f. Maryland
Group / Country-Pop, Contemporary Country, Neo-Traditionalist Country, Progressive Bluegrass
The Dixie Chicks rose from relative obscurity in 1998 to become one of the most popular acts in contemporary country music. Their origins date back nearly a decade earlier, to 1989, when fiddler Martie Seidel and her banjo-playing sister Emily Erwin formed the group in Dallas with bassist Laura Lynch and guitarist Robin Lynn Macy; after getting their start on local street corners, the quartet soon graduated to clubs, receiving an enormous boost when Seidel earned third place honors at the National Fiddle Championships. Originally, the Dixie Chicks (their name inspired by the Little Feat song "Dixie Chickens") promoted a classic cowgirl image, complete with a sound inspired by traditional country, folk, and bluegrass; they even titled their 1990 indie-label debut *Thank Heavens for Dale Evans*.

With 1992's *Little Ol' Cowgirl*, the Chicks began slowly moving toward a more contemporary sound, a transformation which in part resulted in the exit of Macy; with Lynch assuming lead vocal duties, the remaining trio resurfaced in 1993 with *Shouldn't a Told You That*. Shortly after the Chicks signed with Sony's newly revived Monument imprint in 1995, Lynch left the group as well—according to a December 10, 1998, feature in the *Dallas Observer*, both she and Macy were likely victims of Seidel and Erwin's desire to foster a more youthful image; the magazine goes on to call the group "the country version of Menudo, hiring and firing based on age." Soon named as Lynch's replacement was then-21-year-old lead vocalist Natalie Maines, the daughter of steel guitar legend Lloyd Maines.

The lineup switch brought with it a new contemporary wardrobe and an equally modernized country sound; still, few predicted the enormous success of the Dixie Chicks' 1998 major-label debut *Wide Open Spaces*. After the album's advance first single, "I Can Love You Better," became the group's first Top Ten hit, both "There's Your Trouble" and the title track went on to top the country charts. Within a year of *Wide Open Spaces*' release, the record had gone quadruple platinum, and the Dixie Chicks had become superstars—not only did they take home Best Vocal Group honors and the Horizon Award from the Country Music Association, but they were also named Favorite New Country Artist at the American Music Awards. *Wide Open Spaces* additionally earned a Grammy for Best Country Album on its way to becoming the best-selling duo or group album in country music history.

Fly followed in 1999, immediately returning the Dixie Chicks to the upper reaches of the country charts with the lead single, "Ready to Run." "Goodbye Earl" was also a smash single for the group and a guarantee in star power. In May 2002, the Dixie Chicks joined Shakira, Mary J. Blige, Cher, and Celine Dion for the Fifth Annual VH1 *Divas* Show in Las Vegas. Three months later, the girls were back in the game with release of their sixth album, *Home*, their first for their own Sony imprint, Open Wide Records. *—Jason Ankeny*

Thank Heavens for Dale Evans / 1992 / Crystal Clear ✦✦✦
Their first album captures their charm and eclectic tastes in its early, amateurish stages. Ragged in spots, but gloriously enthusiastic. *—Michael McCall*

Little Ol' Cowgirl / 1992 / Crystal Clear ✦✦✦
Their non-stop performance schedule quickly tightened the band's sound, and their musical ability leaps forward in confidence and flair. They're still willing to try anything, at least once, which results in a collection that's uneven but entertaining. *—Michael McCall*

Shouldn't a Told You That / 1993 / Crystal Clear ✦✦✦
Down to a trio, the sound is more focused now, but only slightly less varied. With Laura Lynch taking lead vocals, and with help from producer Steve Fishell, the band sounds more professional and as delightful as ever. *—Michael McCall*

★ **Wide Open Spaces** / Jan. 27, 1998 / Monument ✦✦✦✦✦
When sisters Martie Seidel and Emily Erwin founded the Dixie Chicks in 1989, could they have possibly known the success that would someday be theirs? After three independent records and several lineup changes, the group was re-energized by new lead singer Natalie Maines and the support of a major label, and exploded onto the contemporary

country scene with the release of *Wide Open Spaces*. As always, their strengths lie in their honey-sweet harmonies and superb musicianship, now topped off by the sassy power of Maines' lead vocals. Apparently, they know how to pick songs as well, with "I Can Love You Better," "Wide Open Spaces," and "There's Your Trouble" all breaking into the Top Ten and pushing album sales into the multi-platinum category. *Wide Open Spaces* is a wonderful blend of traditional elements such as banjo, fiddle, and steel guitar, and contemporary attitude, most notably a strong female perspective. As far as subject matter goes, they cover all the bases by tossing in a great honky tonk/bar/broken-heart song with "Tonight the Heartache's on Me," several touching ballads including "I'll Take Care of You," "Loving Arms," and "You Were Mine," and an in your face, unapologetic breakup anthem ("Let 'Er Rip"). When choosing tunes to cover, they tip their hat to some great, though perhaps surprising, women songwriters in Maria McKee and Bonnie Raitt with the last two tracks on the record. The charm and talent of the Dixie Chicks earned them well-deserved popularity across genre borders, and rightly so. *Wide Open Spaces* is a highly enjoyable listen. *—Kelly McCartney*

Fly / Aug. 31, 1999 / Monument ✦✦✦✦

With more than six-million copies of the Chicks' first album *Wide Open Spaces* sold, the highest ever by a country group, it's reasonable to have pretty imposing expectations of their sophomore album. But *Fly* delivers. When you watch Natalie, Martie, and Emily being interviewed on TV or performing in front of an audience, they always look they are having a blast. And that fun shines through in their songs, particularly in "Goodbye Earl," a song about spousal abuse and getting even. If someone like Patty Loveless or Faith Hill sang it, it'd seem silly, but with Natalie's sassy vocals and Emily and Martie's spirited harmonies, it's just good, plain, ol' fun. From the first track, the ebullient "Ready to Run," to the final track, the wistful "Let Him Fly," the Chicks know how to belt out a tune with confidence and flair and have a good-time doing it. *—Maria Konicki Dinoia*

Home / Aug. 27, 2002 / Open Wide/Sony ✦✦✦✦✦

Delivering a successor to their breakthrough smash *Wide Open Spaces* was easy—*Fly* followed a year afterward, sounding sleek and satisfying. Following that album turned out to be a little more difficult for the Dixie Chicks, not least because they were involved in an ugly battle with their record company over royalties. While they were away, country radio grew stricter, but there were undercurrents of change, particularly in the grassroots success of the *O Brother, Where Art Thou?* soundtrack. Dixie Chicks always had deep country roots, but it was entirely conceivable that they could have chosen the pop route, since it's always the safest bet for established stars to follow the mainstream—especially after they have been away for a while. Fortunately, one thing this trio has never been is predictable, and they were emboldened by their successful battle with the label, along with the *O Brother*, leading to the stunner that is *Home*, their sixth album. There may be a Stevie Nicks cover here, but there are no concessions to pop anywhere; there are hardly any electric guitars, actually. This is a pure country album, loaded with fiddles, acoustic guitars, and close harmonies, but retaining the Chicks' signature flair, sense of humor, and personality. It's a vibrant, quirky, heartfelt record that finds the group investing as much in a funny, rollicking number like "White Trash Wedding" or something as sadly sweet as "Godspeed (Sweet Dreams)." But the key to the album is that, as they so brilliantly put it on the wonderful opener "Long Time Gone," they recognize many modern country singers "sound tired but they don't sound Haggard," and "have money but they don't have Cash"—and this is a sentiment that doesn't just apply to those riding the charts, but to the po-faced alt-country contenders who are too serious to have fun. They deftly balance modern attitudes with classic instrumentation, all built on terrific songwriting, winding up with an album that feels purer than anything on the charts, yet much livelier and genuine than alt-country. This is what country music in 2002 should sound like. With *Home*, Dixie Chicks illustrate that country music should be simple but adventurous, sincere but fun. In doing so, they've delivered not just their best album, but what's arguably the best country album yet released in the 2000s. Needless to say, an instant classic. *—Stephen Thomas Erlewine*

Dixie Gentlemen

f. 1956, Alabama, **db.** 1966

Group / Bluegrass, Progressive Bluegrass, Traditional Bluegrass

The Dixie Gentlemen were a bluegrass group from Alabama who were active during the early-'60s folk revival. Herschel Sizemore (mandolin) and Rual Yarbrough (banjo) first met in 1956 playing in a group called the Alabamians, and joined up with Sizemore's friend, Jake Landers (guitar, lead vocals), in 1957 after Landers was discharged from the service. They first called themselves the Country Gentlemen, but quickly changed it to Dixie when they discovered another group who already had that name. They toured in and near their home state for the next few years, making appearances on local radio and television. They cut their first record, "Pray for Me" b/w "Three Steps," in 1959 for the small Blue Sky label, and soon went on to back fiddler Tommy Jackson on an album for Dot.

Under the alias the Blue Ridge Mountain Boys, the Gentlemen recorded two albums for another small label, Time, and wound up scoring a deal with United Artists. Their lone album to find wide release, *The Country Style of the Dixie Gentlemen*, appeared in 1963 and contained all-original material, mostly written by Landers. The group's last recording session during their initial lifespan took place in 1966, with backing by fiddler Vassar Clements (a sometime cohort) and dobro player Tut Taylor; Yarbrough later released it on his own label. After the group's breakup, Sizemore and Yarbrough both worked as sidemen with artists both prominent and local, and later reunited briefly as the Dixiemen. All three Gentlemen reunited with Clements in 1972 and recorded an album for Old Homestead; they would reconvene again toward the dawn of the '90s for another record on Rutabaga. *—Steve Huey*

● **The Country Style of the Dixie Gentlemen** / 1963 / United Artists ✦✦✦✦✦

Deryl Dodd

b. Apr. 12, 1964

Vocals / Contemporary Country, Honky Tonk, Neo-Traditionalist Country

Honky tonker Deryl Dodd grew up in Dallas, TX, where he favored football over music throughout his formative years. When an injury permanently derailed his athletic career, his fellow students at Baylor University encouraged him to begin performing his music in public, and soon, he was one of the biggest attractions on the Waco club circuit. After graduating in 1987, he pursued music full-time, moving in 1991 to Nashville to form a band with his friend Brett Beavers. After supporting Martina McBride during her 1992 tour opening for Garth Brooks, Dodd sang backing vocals on McBride's second LP before embarking on a solo career. He also played in Tracy Lawrence's band and sang harmony on records by Radney Foster and George Ducas. After a 1994 demo deal fell through, Dodd issued his debut album, *One Ride in Vegas*, in 1996. A self-titled effort followed two years later. *—Jason Ankeny*

One Ride in Vegas / Oct. 8, 1996 / Sony ✦✦✦

● **Deryl Dodd** / Nov. 24, 1998 / Sony ✦✦✦✦

This is Dodd's second release, and it is by far a better showing than his first CD, *One Ride in Vegas*, which was too slick and too pop-radio-ready. Produced again by Blake Chancey and Chip Young, Dodd's sophomore effort displays a young man who obviously has some honk and twang he wants to share with the world. Chancey, whose affinity for traditional country & western music makes him a more knowledgeable producer in this arena, allows Dodd to honky tonk with the best of them. Hitting the nail on the head right from the start, Dodd covers a distinctive Jim Lauderdale number, a co-written with Clay Blaker, "It's Only 'Cause You're Lonely." Dodd's own "30-30," "Best I Ever Had," and the Troy Jones tune "John Roland Wood" all show Dodd's talent as something of more substance. This release places Dodd beyond the pop-schlock country world and gives him entrance into the real world of country & western music. This could be the start of something good. *—Jana Pendragon*

Pearl Snaps / Jan. 29, 2002 / Lucky Dog ✦✦✦

Continuing with the success of his honky tonk-fueled second album, Nashville recording artist Deryl Dodd plays up his Texas roots on *Pearl Snaps*. The opening title track is a barroom romp about how his girl loves the pearl snaps on his country-western-style shirts, and the follow-up, "She'll Have You Back," is complete with Bob Wills-style "aww-hawws." Well-placed covers by Tom T. Hall ("That's How I Got to Memphis") and Gordon Lightfoot ("Sundown") offer familiar reference points among these originals, most of which were co-written by the performer himself (a fact which is an increasing rarity on music row). Unfortunately, many of the songs begin to sound like a lot of the product in heavy rotation on CMT, despite Dodd's willingness to mix up styles somewhat, and the words "honky" and "tonk" show up in two song titles and at least three songs, demonstrating almost an overeagerness to repeat what has worked in the past. Still, Dodd's winning personality and his likable voice make for an enjoyable listen, and those who have picked up his previous releases will be more than pleased with *Pearl Snaps*. *—Zac Johnson*

John Doe

b. 1954, Decatur, IL

Bass, Vocals / Roots Rock, Alternative Country-Rock

As one of the founding members of the Los Angeles punk band X, John Doe was one of the most influential figures in American alternative rock during the early '80s, but when he launched a solo career in the early '90s, he decided to pursue a rootsy, country-rock direction instead of continue with punk. X's latter-day albums exhibited a rockabilly and country influence, but it wasn't until Doe's 1990 debut, *Meet John Doe*, that he recorded a pure country album. *Meet John Doe* was recorded during a hiatus in X's career. Following the release of the 1988 live album *Live at the Whiskey A Go-Go* the band went on hiatus. Initially, Doe concentrated on the acting career he began in 1986 with Oliver Stone's *Salvador*, appearing in *Road House* and the Jerry Lee Lewis biopic *Great Balls of Fire* in 1989. The following year, *Meet John Doe* was released on DGC to positive reviews, yet it didn't appeal to an audience outside of X's cult, peaking at 193 on the pop charts.

Later in 1990, X began playing live again and Doe's solo musical career went on hiatus, although he continued to act in movies like *Pure Country*, *Liquid Dreams*, *Roadside Prophets*, *Wyatt Earp*, and *Georgia*. Following X's 1993 reunion album *Hey Zeus!*, Doe signed a solo contract with Rhino/Forward. In the summer of 1995, Doe released *Kissingsohard*, a punkier album than his debut. A few months after its release, X released the live *Unclogged*, which would turn out to be its final album. In early 1996, X broke up, with John Doe turning his attention to his musical and acting career. His solo efforts resurfaced in mid-2000 with the release of *Freedom Is...* on the SpinART label. *—Stephen Thomas Erlewine*

● **Meet John Doe** / 1990 / Geffen ✦✦✦✦

"Raw" and "honest" tend to be vastly overused words when it comes to rock music of any stripe, but they may just apply to John Doe's solo debut on the DGC label (spun off from Geffen). In some respects, this was always something of a trademark with Doe's former band, X, but there was always the whirlwind of Exene Cervenka carrying most of the weight of the vocals, and the frontline immediate image, while Doe was always just slightly back in the shadows, seemingly as anonymous as his name. Now he's out front, and the impact is quite immediate—*Meet John Doe* roars into action with a blaze of Texas-styled rhythm guitar and a gorgeously weathered voice that's a sheer delight to listen to, even though the thrust of the song is, essentially, love and anger: "Let's Be Mad." There's a quite deliberate irony in the song and in the performance, and one can sometimes hear an undercurrent of bitter laughter in it all. The band backing Doe up is unpretentious, to say the least—two guitarists, bass, and drums, with visits from piano and organ here and there, and scatterings of backing vocals. There's no effort to deliberately go after a certain style, though; this all has the feeling of falling together naturally, the way the best albums often do. Get a bunch of guys into the studio and let the music find its own direction. Doe is to be commended for this—he could as easily have utterly cloned X, which would have provided him with a solid holding pattern but nothing more. There's a sadness pervading the selection of songs, though, but it's not depressing; instead, it's more like the earmark of some of the best country material, and the album's theme of personal expression could as easily been seen as an act of personal therapy—a cleansing of the system. The final track, "My Offering," admits to a universal truth as the narrator, exhausted in an Atlanta hotel room, admits how much turns out badly, sees how people can be hurtful, comes to understand that he can do nothing to stop it—and yet still has something to offer to someone, despite it all. Many of the lyrics here verge on raw poetry and carry a breathtaking force, partly because of the way they're delivered. Doe's worn voice is one of his greatest assets; the expansive sound of his music fits right in with that. All told, an excellent solo debut. *—Steven McDonald*

Kissingsohard / 1995 / Forward/Rhino ✦✦✦

A better showcase for Doe's songwriting than the first solo album, *Kissingsohard* isn't completely successful, since he's never found the right players to back him up. This time he pulls in real L.A. working musicians; however, no one seems to understand Doe's music like his old bandmates in X, and his strong vocals and lyrics just can't carry the record on their own. He reprises the X song "My Goodness" in a space-jam/hip-hop (!) arrangement, with Exene singing along. *—Denise Sullivan*

For the Rest of Us EP / Jan. 27, 1998 / Kill Rock Stars ✦✦✦

On *For the Rest of Us*, Doe works with members of Beck's backing band to successfully revitalize his sound; among the highlights of this five-track EP is "This Loving Thing," co-written by the Foo Fighters' Dave Grohl. *—Jason Ankeny*

Freedom Is . . . / Jul. 18, 2000 / spinART ✦✦✦✦

Arriving on the heels of 1998's EP for Kill Rock Stars indie, John Doe's third full album for his third label, this time on spinART, finds him sounding more natural and comfortable than in past, post-X, efforts. He's left the spunky, poetic crash and burn of his old band and the country-tinged rock of his previous solo works behind, opting instead for a homey singer/songwriter approach, which fits his leathery vocals and unusual song structures just fine. Exene Cervenka, his ex-wife and vocal foil in X, makes a brief appearance, but Doe's new songs don't sound much like the hyperactive tunes of his Hollywood punk days. On sublime, world-weary, predominantly acoustic songs like "No One Cares," "A Picture of This," and "Beat Up World," Doe seems relaxed and under no pressure to push these low-key tunes in any particular direction. Only the insistent "Smile and Wave" and the angry, self-explanatory "Too Many Goddamn Bands" up the volume and intensity to X levels. Doe's voice has mellowed, but not softened, which works well with twisting, often off-beat lyrics like "somebody's mumbling in someone else's dream." The album unwinds slowly and gradually, without catchy choruses, instantly memorable hooks, or slick production, making it more difficult to quickly absorb. But after a few spins, Doe's meandering tunes find a focus as they wrap around the listener like a favorite pair of worn jeans. It's still not his most impressive set of songs, and nothing jumps out with the nervy impetuousness of his work with X, but after some disappointing tries, *Freedom Is . . .* finally demonstrates that John Doe's best years might still be ahead of him. *—Hal Horowitz*

Dim Stars, Bright Sky / Sep. 10, 2002 / Artist Direct BMG ✦✦✦✦

If the Los Angeles punk scene produced a better or more passionate singer than John Doe, it would be nice to know who it is, but while he knew how to belt it out over the gale-force blast of X, in his work with the Knitters (and on X's late-period acoustic album *Unclogged*), Doe proved he also knew how to communicate just as well in a quieter and more intimate setting. *Dim Stars, Bright Sky*, Doe's fourth solo album, is being billed as his first acoustic solo LP, but that bends the boundaries of truth in advertising just a bit; while several of the songs are built around low-key non-amplified arrangements (most notably "Seven Holes," "Faraway (From the North Country)," and "Always), most of the album's tunes feature electronic keyboards, drum loops, electric guitars, or some combination thereof. Not that that's bad; the blend of the acoustic rhythm guitar and fuzzy leads on "This Far" (not to mention the old-school electric piano sound) makes the most of a solid song, and the splashing drums and Rickenbacker leads on "Backroom" give the tune a Byrds-ian undertow that's superb. However, if you were hoping for "John Doe Unplugged," that's not quite what you get. Also, while the cover promises duets with a number of notables, including Aimee Mann, Jakob Dylan, Jane Wiedlin, and Rhett Miller, most of Doe's co-vocalists are little more than glorified backup singers, lending fine harmonies but little personality of their own (faring best are Mann, whose sweet-and-sour harmony on "This Far" suggests a smoother version of Doe's vocal byplay with Exene Cervenka, and Juliana Hatfield, who proves to be a superb accompanist on her two tracks). *Dim Stars, Bright Sky* isn't the "just John with his guitar" album one might be expecting (and hoping for), but with John Doe writing great songs and singing them very well with a top-notch band, only a fool would complain. It's a great album from a great artist, but hopefully he'll take another stab at a *real* acoustic album one of these days. *—Mark Deming*

Johnny Dollar

b. Mar. 8, 1933, Kilgore, TX, **d.** Apr. 13, 1986

Vocals / Traditional Country, Nashville Sound/Countrypolitan

Country and rockabilly vocalist Johnny Dollar was born in Kilgore, TX, on March 8, 1933. Arriving in Dallas in the early '50s, Dollar worked a series of odd jobs, including roughneck, truck driver, and lumber-yard foreman. He cut a record with Shelby Singleton's D Records around 1952, but it went nowhere fast. Dollar then became a DJ in Louisiana and New Mexico, while also leading the Texas Sons, who played regularly on *Louisiana Hayride*, the Shreveport-based variety show broadcast on KWKH. He then left the Sons to join Martin McCullough's Light Crust Doughboys, but by the late '50s was back in Dallas, feeling out the new rockabilly sounds made famous by Elvis Presley. Dollar fell in with promoter Ed McLemore and songwriter Jack Rhodes. The combination yielded some fiery rockabilly gems like "Action Packed," later popularized by Ronnie Dawson and an eventual standard of the rockabilly genre.

However, despite his fiery performances, darkly handsome looks, and powerful voice, Dollar's rockabilly sides were never released. Disenfranchised once again, a disgusted Dollar left the music industry and sold insurance in Oklahoma. There, a chance run-in with country star Ray Price led Dollar to a contract with Columbia, who signed him in 1964. Dollar—now occasionally billed as Johnny $ Dollar or "Mr. Personality"—scored a Top 50 hit with 1966's "Tear-Talk," and cracked the Top 15 with "Stop the Start (Of Tears in My Heart)" a year later. He moved from Dot Records to Date Records, and finally to Chart Records, where he landed in 1968. There he scored again with the truck-driving country hits "Big Big Rollin' Man" and "Big Wheels Sing for Me." In 1970, he returned to the Johnny Dollar moniker and scored his final hit for Chart with "Truck Driver's Lament."

This was the apex of Dollar's chart success, and for the rest of the decade he focused on producing. Based in Nashville, Dollar worked with the New Coon Creek Girls, Jimmy Dickens, and Teddy Nelson. But Dollar's personal life was a shambles. After the divorce of his fourth wife, Dollar battled alcoholism and depression. He was diagnosed with throat cancer, and a subsequent operation caused him to lose his voice. This plunged the singer into further depths of depression, and on April 13th, 1986, he took his own life. *—Johnny Loftus*

Johnny Dollar / 1967 / Date ✦✦✦

Big Rig Rollin' Man / 1969 / Chart ✦✦✦✦

Country Hit Parade / 1969 / Chart ✦✦✦

● **Mr. Action Packed** / May 18, 1999 / Dragon Street ✦✦✦✦

Mr. Action Packed presents an incredible missing chapter in the Johnny Dollar story. The 20 songs here, all rockabilly classics from 1957-1958, were lost for 40 years until the tapes were discovered in a closet. Dollar recorded country before and after these sessions and had some chart success in the late '60s, but these tracks really rock, including smoking versions of "Rockin' Bones" and "Action Packed." Two live performances from *the Big 'D' Jamboree*, "Great Balls of Fire" and "Jailhouse Rock," show that Dollar was serious about being a rock & roller during this period, and the collection is rounded out with a few alternate mixes, attractive packaging, and excellent notes. *—Greg Adams*

Florence Dore

Vocals / Singer/Songwriter, Alternative Country-Rock

Nashville native Florence Dore played with various punk, rock and country bands for 15 years before cutting her first LP *Perfect City*. An academic by day, Dore pursued her music career while earning a doctoral degree in American literature. Her dissertation was on modernism in the American novel and emphasized the work of William Faulkner, whom she's been known to reference in her literary, emotionally articulate songwriting. At the time of the release of *Perfect City*, Dore was working on a tenure track at Kent State, while holding residence in New York City due to a post doctoral fellowship at N.Y.U. Before that, she absorbed the musical climates of Boston, where she taught eighth grade while moonlighting with the Myrtles; Berkeley, where she played with San Francisco band the Mudsills; and Wesleyan College in Connecticut, where she performed alongside Matt Ashare in renowned punk band Puse Escalator.

On-stage, Dore's academia goes out the window, and she can rock with the best of them. The band, which consists of Chris Erikson (lead guitar), who's been playing with Dore for over a decade; Scott Yoder (Mojo Dixon) on bass; and Dennis Diken (the Smithereens) on drums, holds its own on Dore's brand of poetically economical, Lucinda Williams-inspired country-rock. *—Travis Drageset*

Perfect City / Apr. 23, 2002 / Slewfoot ✦✦✦✦

Like that of Liz Phair or Laura Cantrell, Florence Dore's music is literate and personal and uses its chosen genre—folk/pop/rock with a twang—as a vehicle for an immersion in intellect and emotion. *Perfect City* was produced by guitarist Eric Ambel (Steve Earle, Blood Oranges, Bottle Rockets), and features references to William Faulkner's *The Sound and the Fury* ("Perfect City") and Kent, OH ("Wintertown"), where, at the time of its recording, she was a professor of American literature at Kent State. Her stylistically informed background—punk, folk, country—allows for a diversity of styles within the album, which achieves cohesion within its own feverish and soothing permutations. The album speaks of dignified love and embraces the fact that it rarely ever is ("Postcard"), of the leaps that can be achieved by doing nothing ("Early World"), and of the beauties in life that can only be seen in reference to one's own immortality ("Say the Thing"), where she plaintively asks the song's recipient to "Say the thing that keeps the plaster from peeling/Say the thing that keeps the stairway from reeling." "Christmas," which first received notoriety in a version by the Posies, is a dirge about spending the holiday alone, dealing with a breakup, and questioning everything, wherein she sings, "I'm holding onto you and I don't know why/I don't have faith in what's supposed to be," and pours into the chorus, "You made me cry for the last time/That's OK Christmas means little to me." The album's other slow, bittersweet ballad, "No Nashville," which reflects on the ambiguities felt when returning to one's hometown, is simply a classic in waiting. *—Travis Drageset*

Jerry Douglas

b. 1955, Columbus, OH

Dobro, Slide Guitar / Progressive Bluegrass, Contemporary Bluegrass

Jerry Douglas is widely renowned as perhaps the finest dobro player in contemporary acoustic music. His main foundation is bluegrass, but Douglas is an eclectic whose tastes run toward jazz, blues, folk, and straight-ahead country as well, and he's equally capable of appealing to bluegrass aficionados or new agers with a taste for instrumental roots music. What's more, his progressive sensibility as a composer has earned him comparisons to likeminded virtuosos Béla Fleck and David Grisman. Douglas was born in Columbus, OH, in 1955, and began playing the dobro at age eight with encouragement from his father, who was also a bluegrass musician. By his teen years, Douglas was already a member of his father's band, and his playing was especially influenced by Josh Graves of Flatt & Scruggs' Foggy Mountain Boys. Douglas was discovered at a festival by the Country Gentlemen, who took him on tour with them for the rest of the summer and later brought him into the recording studio. From there, Douglas established himself as a hugely in-demand session musician; during the latter half of the '70s, he worked with the likes of J.D. Crowe & the New South, David Grisman, Ricky Skaggs, Doyle Lawson, and Tony Rice. Additionally, Douglas released his debut album, *Fluxology*, on Rounder in 1979; he followed it three years later with *Fluxedo*, which like its predecessor stuck relatively close to traditional (albeit sometimes jazzy) bluegrass.

During the early '80s, Douglas continued his session career with even greater success, adding Emmylou Harris, Béla Fleck, the Whites, and Peter Rowan to his list of credits. He returned to his solo career with 1986's *Under the Wire* on Sugar Hill, which reflected his interest in the progressive new-acoustic (or "newgrass") movement. He subsequently signed with MCA, where he issued *Changing Channels* (1987) and the smoother, strongly jazz-influenced *Plant Early* (1989). More session work for increasingly prominent artists brought him into the '90s, with names like Alison Krauss, Del McCoury, Garth Brooks, Trisha Yearwood, Randy Travis, Clint Black, Patty Loveless, Suzy Bogguss, Reba McEntire, Kathy Mattea, and Dolly Parton on his resumé. In 1992, he returned to Sugar Hill for the more traditional bluegrass outing *Slide Rule*, which many critics ranked among his finest recordings. The following year brought the all-instrumental *Skip, Hop & Wobble*, a trio recording with Russ Barenberg and Edgar Meyer. In 1994, Douglas contributed to the Grammy-winning compilation *Great Dobro Sessions*, and cut a duo album with Peter Rowan, *Yonder*, in 1996. *Restless on the Farm* (1998), true to its title, was a return to Douglas' freewheeling eclecticism, which continued on 2002's *Lookout for Hope*. *—Steve Huey*

Fluxology / 1979 / Rounder ✦✦✦✦

Fluxedo / 1982 / Rounder ✦✦✦

Under the Wire / 1986 / Sugar Hill ✦✦✦

Though all of his releases are dobro *tour de forces*, this is a highly sophisticated ensemble album with some of the best players in the new- acoustic realm, including Mark O'Connor, Russ Barenberg, Béla Fleck, and Sam Bush. With seven of the ten tracks written by Douglas, the album is also a tribute to his inventive compositional style. *—Linda Kohanov*

Changing Channels / 1987 / MCA ✦✦✦

Everything Is Gonna Work out Fine / 1987 / Rounder ✦✦✦✦

Everything Is Gonna Work Out features Jerry Douglas' first two albums—*Fluxology* and *Fluxedo*—on one compact disc. The two records showcase the dobroist at his rootiest, and contain some wonderful traditional bluegrass, which is occasionally spiked by jazzy flourishes. *—Thom Owens*

Plant Early / 1989 / MCA ✦✦

● **Slide Rule** / 1992 / Sugar Hill ✦✦✦✦✦

On *Slide Rule*, Jerry Douglas moves away from the the jazz experiments of *Plant Early*, returning to the straightforward bluegrass of his early work. The result is a stunner, featuring not only a remarkable performance from Douglas, but also from an impressive list of guest musicians, including Alison Krauss, Sam Bush, Maura O'Connell, Stuart Duncan, and Tim O'Brien. *—Thom Owens*

Skip, Hop & Wobble / 1993 / Sugar Hill ✦✦✦✦

This excellent 1993 Sugar Hill CD features three of the top artists playing newgrass today. Entirely instrumental, entirely enjoyable, the tracks on this CD run the gamut of musical expression from the humorous play of "Why Don't You Go Back to the Woods" to the slow, beautiful "Hymn to Ordinary Motion." The liner notes discuss the creative process around each song, as well as the group's union and the challenges/rewards of playing as a trio. Sam Bush does a couple of very nice guest spots on mandolin. If you are tired of the musical simplicity and inane lyrics of much of today's music, this CD cleanses the palate. *—Jeff Crooke*

Yonder / 1996 / Sugar Hill ✦✦

The CD case defines *Yonder*: within sight, but not near, further. That might define the music on this disc as well. Whatever they were trying to get on tape here, it is still up "yonder." It isn't that the music is lousy, any collaboration between bluegrass favorites Peter Rowan and Jerry Douglas couldn't be lousy, it is just that the music never seems to really heat up. Almost all of the tunes here are midtempo songs, and there aren't any brilliant solos, mostly just competent, communicative playing between the two. The music is nice, the playing is nice, the singing is nice. The album is disappointing because of the sense that these two could have stepped it up a notch. Why aren't they having more fun? The album is about one-third traditional arrangements, one-third covers, and one-third original Rowan tunes. The most interesting of the Peter Rowan compositions is "You Taught Me How to Lose," which is reminiscent of a Hank Williams song, fitting in well with these traditional songs. *—David Lavin*

Restless on the Farm / May 19, 1998 / Sugar Hill ✦✦✦

Dobro master Jerry Douglas steps out of his usual sideman's role (he has appeared on over 1,000 albums) on this excellent solo effort. He shows off his instrumental virtuosity and versatility on a mix of bluegrass, hard country, jazz (covering an old Erroll Garner tune), blues, and even traditional Irish music. Guest vocalists include Maura O'Connell, Tim O'Brien, John Cowan and Steve Earle, who offers a gritty reading of Johnny Cash's "Don't Take your Guns to Town." Among the standout instrumentalists joining Douglas are Béla Fleck, Sam Bush and Sonny Landreth, who delivers some remarkable work on metal-body dobro. *—Joel Roberts*

Lookout for Hope / May 7, 2002 / Sugar Hill ✦✦✦✦

Jerry Douglas sure can play the dobro. As the world's undisputed premier dobro player, Douglas has played with just about everybody. And, as would befit somebody with that kind of distinction, his playing is utterly virtuosic. The only question left, then, is what he wants to do with it. On *Lookout for Hope*, Douglas' fifth release for Sugar Hill, Douglas delivers up his usual newgrass, accompanied by some of the usual newgrass heavyweights, including Sam Bush, Stuart Duncan, and Jeff Coffin. Maura O'Connell, James Taylor, and Phish guitarist Trey Anastasio turn in appearances as well. Douglas tries to do a lot. "Patrick Meets the Brickbats" and "Cave Bop," for example, show off his lightning-fast playing. They are dazzling displays, but ultimately none too satisfying. Douglas does far better in milking the slow, bittersweet tones of the instrument, such as he does on a cover of Duane Allman's "Little Martha." The ten-minute title track (and album centerpiece), penned by jazz guitarist Bill Frisell, is most intriguing, combining Middle Eastern-sounding scales (such as on David Grisman's "Arabia" opus) with resonant and percussive acoustic sounds. As the master of the instrument, Douglas can do pretty much whatever he wants. *Lookout for Hope* does not find him resting on his laurels. Instead, he explores a variety of settings and moods, all bound together with the distinctive sound of his instrument. *—Jesse Jarnow*

Ronnie Dove

b. Sep. 7, 1940, Herndon, VA

Vocals / Pop, Soft Rock, Nashville Sound/Countrypolitan

Ronnie Dove was born in Herndon, VA, but the pubs of Baltimore were his performance training ground. After a stint in the Coast Guard, he formed Ronnie Dove & the Belltones, and the group gigged throughout Baltimore and the East Coast for the next four years. In 1959, the band cut the single "Lover Boy" as its debut release; their only other recorded output was a rendition of Buddy Knox's "Party Doll" for Decca in 1963. Dove left the Belltones soon after, and landed in Nashville. There he singed a contract with the Diamond label and released his first solo single, "Sweeter Than Sugar." But it was 1964's "Say You" that really established Dove. The cut broke into the Top 20 and began a series of major pop hits. In 1965 alone, Dove scored five hits, with all but one cracking the Top 20 or higher. He repeated this feat in 1965, but by a 1967 *Ed Sullivan Show* appearance, Dove's star was beginning to fall.

He took a break, but returned in 1971 with a new deal on Decca. This time around, Dove scored two minor hits on the country charts with "Kiss the Hurt Away" (1972) and "Lilacs in Winter" (1973). He then signed to Melodyland Records in 1975, and had two more hits. With the advent of oldies radio in the 1980s, Dove's star rose again, and the vocalist toured consistently. He even re-signed with Diamond in 1987 and had one final entry on the charts with "Rise and Shine." Dove continued to perform in the Baltimore area and nationwide throughout the 1990s and early 2000s. Numerous collections of his past hits were released, and Dove offered a collection of Christmas tunes through his detailed website. *—Johnny Loftus*

● **Golden Classics** / Jun. 25, 1994 / Collectables ✦✦✦✦✦

Ronnie Dove should have been as big as Bobby Vinton. Both artists were seemingly untouched by the British Invasion and continued creating excellent retro-sounding pop/rock into the 1970s, but Dove never cracked the Top Ten despite placing nearly a dozen singles in the Top 40 between 1964-1966. *Golden Classics* contains most of Dove's '60s hits, a few non-hits, and the country charter "Rise and Shine" from 1987—Dove's final hit. Dove is an expressive balladeer whose distinctive and slightly country-sounding voice resembles Bobby Helms, and his updates of classic material like Johnnie Ray's "Cry" and Harold Dorman's "Mountain of Love" are simultaneously fresh and familiar. Chronological sequencing would have worked better, and more substantial liner notes wouldn't have hurt, but *Golden Classics* is a fine anthology of a major talent who enjoyed only moderate success. *—Greg Adams*

For Collectors Only / Feb. 1996 / Collectables ✦✦✦

For Collectors Only is an extensive three-disc set that contains all of his biggest hits, as well as a wealth of rarities. As the title suggests, it is only for dedicated fans and collectors, and even they may be dismayed by the haphazard packaging and production on the set. Nevertheless, they'll find a number of hidden gems among the numerous cuts on the collection, making its purchase worthwhile. *—Thom Owens*

The Love Album / Sep. 10, 2002 / Collectables ✦✦✦

Having previously issued *Golden Classics*, three volumes of *The Collection*, and a *Rarities* album on Ronnie Dove, reissue label Collectables Records has covered Dove's Diamond Records recordings thoroughly. A common reissue concept not yet mined is found on *The Love Album*, in which an artist's romantic ballads are collected. The concept is always a bit of a conceit, since popular singers sing about love in nearly all their performances. In Dove's case, Collectables has decided there must be at least a smattering of the singer's hits, so his two biggest ones, "One Kiss for Old Times Sake" and "Right or Wrong," leadoff the set, and also included are his chart remake of "Mountain of Love" and the Top 20 hit "When Liking Turns to Loving." As the inclusion of the uptempo "Mountain of Love" suggests, the collection is not restricted to ballads, but also includes several rhythm numbers, notably the rollicking "That New Old Fashioned Love." Dove is an emotive singer in the Johnnie Ray mold, employing a similar adenoidal tenor, so his performances have an urgency and intensity that takes them beyond the usual warmth and affection of the "love album" concept. In his hands, standards like "You Made Me Love You" and "I Can Stop Loving You" shake off their dust and become passionate statements. And the love Dove has in mind is not always above-board; on the country song "Lovin' on Backstreets," it is illicit. The Ronnie Dove version of a "love album" thus offers more varieties of love than most, and is better for it. *— William Ruhlmann*

Johnny Dowd

b. 1948

Guitar / Alternative Country-Rock, Alternative Country, Americana

Johnny Dowd was almost 50 when *Wrong Side of Memphis*, his record of wracked country-folk-rock tunes, drew comparisons to Nick Cave in the alternative press. To a degree, the parallel is justified. *Wrong Side of Memphis*, after all, is devoted in large part to murder songs and tales of doomed sinners, and suffused with outlaw paranoia. Yet Dowd is—as someone who grew up in Texas, Memphis, and Oklahoma, and now runs a trucking business in upstate New York—someone who's genuinely closer to the source of American creepiness. He's also not so damn serious about it all; aside from the gallows humor permeating much of his work, his crackly voice tends to undercut any traces of self-importance. Dowd's sound is dominated by his singing and guitar, yet spooky dabs of organ and synthesizer place him outside of the rootsy Americana camp. His debut immediately established him as an important cult figure whose weirdness seemed to be wrought from true experience, and not the result of some phony pose. On his second album, 1999's *Pictures From Life's Other Side*, Dowd edged slightly away from the edge, using a full band of musicians and a female backup singer to craft a punchier and less folk-rooted sound. His singing and lyrics, however, remained nearly as disquieting as they were the first time around. *Temporary Shelter* was issued in early 2001. *—Richie Unterberger*

Wrong Side of Memphis / Jan. 20, 1998 / Checkered Past ✦✦✦✦

"I won't say that I'm lonely, 'cause there's too many voices in my head," sings Dowd in "Ft. Worth, Texas." Fair enough warning that this is not your average singer/songwriter; lines like "be content with your life, it may not get any better" and a preoccupation with murder, death, and evil also make it clear that this is not jovial schizophrenia, on the order of Syd Barrett or Roky Erickson. One hopes for Dowd's sake that the unrelenting tales of madness-fueled evil are not wholly based in real-life experience; otherwise, this is not the guy to meet at the end of a dark alley. It's compellingly creepy, though, if hard to take entirely seriously, and the inventive, unsettling washes of church-organ-from-hell synthesizer make it clear that it's someone who knows what he's doing in a studio, not a Daniel Johnston-type whose childlike dementia is being captured in spite of itself. They're calling this "country" in some circles, but songs like "Welcome Jesus," with its transistor-radio-from-the-foxhole vocals and opening line "welcome Jesus to this dismal swamp," all but ensure that Dowd won't be welcome in Nashville. If Dowd does not become widely known (and, frankly, it would be surprising if he even broke out on a college radio level), this is guaranteed to be hailed as a cult classic 20 years down the line. Adding to the mystique is the lack of a label or catalog number on the CD, though you can get it through Checkered Past Records (3940 N. Francisco, Chicago, IL 60618) if your hip local indie store isn't carrying it. *—Richie Unterberger*

● **Pictures From Life's Other Side** / Aug. 17, 1999 / Koch ✦✦✦✦

If there was even the tiniest bit of comfort to be wrung from Johnny Dowd's singularly disturbing debut album, *Wrong Side of Memphis*, it was that the record's stark, homespun tales of murder, misery, and malice seemed light years removed from reality, evoking a backwoods dementia so completely over the top it often threatened to veer into the ridiculous. *Pictures From Life's Other Side* ups the ante considerably: Complete with full-band backing, crisp production, and a broader musical spectrum, the effect is much more chilling, as within this more conventional framework, Dowd's obsessions manifest themselves in new and sinister ways, cloaking his fixations and fetishes behind the subterfuge of a suspiciously listenable blend of country, blues, and pop. Where *Wrong Side of Memphis* immediately revealed itself as the ravings of a madman, *Pictures From Life's Other Side* is much sneakier—at first glance, "Hope You Don't Mind" appears to be a heart-wrenching ballad of unrequited love, but on closer inspection the object of the middle-aged Dowd's affection is a schoolgirl; likewise, the hauntingly atmospheric "No Woman's Flesh But Hers" is a testament to undying love, in this case a husband's pledge to his comatose wife. Sick, twisted, and undeniably compelling, *Pictures From Life's Other Side* delivers where countless shock rock and gangsta rap records fall short, capturing a musical vision that's genuinely disquieting. *—Jason Ankeny*

Temporary Shelter / Feb. 13, 2001 / Koch ✦✦✦✦

If there are any contemporary songwriters who look deeper into the dark and troubling underside American life than Johnny Dowd, I'm not sure anyone has the courage to listen to their work. Dowd's music comes from a place that's at once singularly disturbing and easy to recognize, charting a landscape of murder, obsession, misguided love, guilt, fear, and betrayal that's as common, as violent, and as familiar as the morning newspaper. Dowd's first album, *Wrong Side of Memphis*, was a stark, blunt homemade affair, while the follow-up, *Pictures From Life's Other Side*, was a (relatively) high-fidelity companion piece that captured the Dock Boggs-meets-Pere Ubu sound of Dowd's touring band (Justin Asher on keyboards, Brian Wilson on drums and bass pedals, and Kim Sherwood-Caso on vocals). *Temporary Shelter*, however, finds Johnny Dowd displaying his surest hand in the record-making process to date; while Dowd's production is simple and uncluttered, he and his band have also learned how to layer their sheets of sound in the studio, and while the album still possesses the jarring intimacy of Dowd's live shows, there's also a subtlety and broader sonic palette that brings the details of this music into sharper and more telling focus. And while Dowd is obviously in charge, *Temporary Shelter* makes it clear this is the work of a real band; here, Johnny is willing to ease back his sturdy blues-based guitar leads to make more room for Asher and Wilson, and he even turns the lead vocal on "Death Comes Knocking" over to Sherwood-Caso. The sinister, dreamlike sound of *Temporary Shelter* provides the perfect backdrop for this cycle of songs about the troubling legacies of childhood and (dysfunctional) family life; it sounds like Dowd's most personal collection to date, and while the images are often disturbing, the effect isn't morbid—these songs are not about wallowing in the dark side of life, but about one man's struggle through his heart and soul to escape the demons that have crippled him. As you've surely guessed by now, *Temporary Shelter* isn't for everyone, but while it's strong meat, it's also rich and deeply satisfying if you have an adventurous taste. *—Mark Deming*

The Pawnbroker's Wife / 2002 / Munich ✦✦✦✦

Critics have been calling this Johnny Dowd's "most accessible" album—but that's all relative, isn't it? For even among iconoclasts, the fiercely independent Johnny Dowd sets high-water marks for originality. Like previous efforts, *The Pawnbroker's Wife* still finds Dowd wallowing in the dredges of his psyche while somehow avoiding the flip into bloated drama that has dogged such would-be spooksters as 16 Horsepower or even Nick Cave. Dowd's music is stridently slippery—punk and rock & roll are the foundation here (and Dowd and Justin Asher are remarkable rock guitarists), but there's something vaguely techno about some of his music as well. And then there's Kim Sherwood-Caso, whose disconcertingly sweet yet detached vocals can raise the hair on the back of your arms just as effectively as Dowd's foreboding drawl. This effort is top-notch Dowd, however, and if you allow yourself into Dowd's world through this album, you'll find he's actually a somewhat benign host. He even unfurls the Christmas classic "Jingle Bells" for your listening pleasure. Elsewhere, on the campily euphonious "I Love You," Dowd is in a romantic mood . . . yet "desperately" so. (And Dowd knows desperation.) This fine effort may move Dowd and company in the direction of pop accessibility, but it's still a long way off and Dowd's charming morbidity is still fully intact. *—Erik Hage*

Big Al Downing

b. Jan. 9, 1940, Centralia, OK

Vocals / R&B, Rock & Roll, Traditional Country, Rockabilly

An unsung figure of early black rock & roll, Big Al Downing had a series of enjoyable if derivative singles in the late '50s and early '60s for a several small labels that didn't achieve anything other than regional success. Downing was an eclectic pianist/singer who did not owe his allegiance to pure R&B, but also had a taste for rockabilly, country & western, and occasional hints of New Orleans music, hewing closer to white rock & roll than most African-American performers of his era. On some of his early sides, in fact, Downing sounds like a black Jerry Lee Lewis, with impressively hyper piano runs and slicing electric guitar breaks; at other points, he landed closer to Little Richard or Fats Domino territory. His material and production wasn't strong enough to place him in the major leagues, but his early work has an engaging looseness (sometimes verging on sloppiness). Long active, he started to focus on country & western in the late '70s, although he still played some rock & roll in his live shows. *—Richie Unterberger*

● **Rockin' & Rollin'** / Mar. 19, 1996 / Rollercoaster ✦✦✦✦✦

Two of the greatest rock & roll records ever have to be "Down on the Farm" and "Georgia Slop" by Big Al Downing. For ice-pick-in-the-ear rockabilly lead guitar, you have to go some distance to burn "Down on the Farm," and "Georgia Slop" is one of those absolutely perfect, not-a-wasted-note-on-it-anywhere records that comes along once in a very blue moon. To have both discs on this collection is the main incentive for purchasing it. This 18-tracker collects up just about everything you'll ever need on this underrated performer. Downing was versatile; he could do voices from Fats Domino to Little Richard and pound one very cool piano in the bargain. All the essentials are here plus some very hip bonuses, including his midsong Little Richard entrance with a chorus of "Good Golly Miss Molly" on Bobby Poe's white white white refrigerator-white "Rock & Roll Record Girl." *—Cub Koda*

Pete Drake

b. Aug. 8, 1932, Atlanta, GA, **d.** Jul. 29, 1988, Nashville, TN

Guitar (Steel) / Traditional Country, Country-Rock, Nashville Sound/Countrypolitan

When rock artists, including Bob Dylan and members of the Beatles, began to record in Nashville, Pete Drake (born Franklin Drake) was the natural choice as steel guitarist. Although he had a Top 30 hit, "Talking Steel," in 1964, Drake recorded very little on his own. Instead, he used the trademark mellow tone of his steel guitar to strengthen albums by other artists. In addition to working with country artists, including Marty Robbins, Bobby Bare, Johnny Cash, the Louvin Brothers, Dolly Parton, and Ernest Tubb, he pioneered the use of the steel guitar in rock, performing on recordings by Buddy Holly, the Everly Brothers, Carl Perkins, Jerry Lee Lewis, and Elvis Presley. He played on such seminal recordings as Lynn Anderson's "(I Never Promised You A) Rose Garden," Charlie Rich's "Behind Closed Doors," and Tammy Wynette's "Stand By Your Man." Featured on Dylan's albums *John Wesley Harding*, *Nashville Skyline*, and *Self Portrait*, Drake also produced and assembled the band for Ringo Starr's country album, *Beaucoups of Blues*, and played on George Harrison's solo debut, *All Things Must Pass*.

The son of a Pentecostal minister, Drake began his career with a group, the Drake Brothers, that he shared with his brothers, one of whom, Jack, went on to play with Ernest Tubb's Texas Troubadors for nearly a quarter of a century. Drake's melodic steel guitar playing made him one of Atlanta's top young instrumentalists. He joined with future country music superstars Jerry Reed, Doug Kershaw, Roger Miller, and Joe South in a mid-'50s band. Although this group failed to record, it provided Drake with the impetus to move to Nashville in 1959. Drake's involvement with Elvis Presley, which began in May 1966 when he played on Presley's *How Great Thou Art* album, lasted for more than a year and included appearances on the soundtracks of Presley's films *Double Trouble*, *Clambake*, and *Speedway*.

Launching his own record label, First Generation, in the late '70s, Drake signed Ernest Tubb, who had left MCA after 35 years, and released an album, *The Legend and the Legacy*, in 1977. Comprised of reworkings of Tubb's greatest hits, the album included guest appearances by Willie Nelson, Waylon Jennings, Johnny Paycheck, Charlie Daniels, Conway Twitty, Marty Robbins, Loretta Lynn, Vern Gosdin, George Jones, Merle Haggard, and Johnny Cash. Drake occasionally stepped into the spotlight, releasing solo album of pop-gospel standards, *Steel Away*, and a eponymously titled album that included steel guitar interpretations of Dylan and Beatles tunes. *—Craig Harris*

● **Fabulous Steel Guitar** / 1962 / Starday ◆◆◆◆◆

Country Steel Guitar / 1963 / Cumberland ◆◆◆

Forever / 1964 / Smash ◆◆◆

Pete Drake's "talking steel guitar" effect was created when he sang through the pickup on his pedal steel, making a robotic sound that anticipated "Freak-A-Zoid" and vocoders by decades. On *Forever*, Drake uses the effect most extensively on "I'm Just a Guitar (Everybody Picks on Me)," but otherwise delivers more predictable fare on the order of an instrumental rendition of Bill Anderson's "Still," an entrancing steel guitar arrangement of Santo & Johnny's "Sleep Walk," and an occasional original. A vocal chorus chimes in wordlessly or, as on "Sleep Walk," by dreamily intoning the song title. Drake was a virtuoso and a sought-after sideman who deserved to step forward as a soloist. *Forever* is a treat for enthusiasts of the steel guitar and Drake's ability, but only ones who also have a liking or tolerance for easy listening—the country music content on *Forever* is very low.
—*Greg Adams*

Talking Steel Guitar / 1965 / Smash ◆◆◆

Talking Steel and Singing Strings / 1965 / Smash ◆◆◆

Pete Drake / Oct. 12, 1999 / First Generation ◆◆◆

For Pete's Sake / Nov. 21, 2000 / King ◆◆◆

Jimmie Driftwood (James Corbett Morris)

b. Jun. 17, 1917, Mountain View, AR, **d.** Jul. 12, 1998
Guitar, Vocals / Traditional Country, Folksongs, Traditional Folk

Jimmie Driftwood was almost an anachronism in the years he was at his commercial peak, from 1957 through 1961. A schoolteacher by training, he originally started writing songs as a way of helping his students learn about history, and subsequently composed (or collected and re-composed) over 5,000 songs, many of them dealing with some element of America's past and its history, telling old folk tales, or preserving some aspect of the daily lives of the people who sang them. Only one modern figure in folk music remotely approaches his contribution to American song and the popular understanding of its roots, and that is Lee Hayes of the Weavers—Driftwood was never the activist that Hayes was, however, being more concerned with teaching than political causes and, thus, never engendered either the blacklisting or the subsequent canonization by the Left that Hayes received. And Hayes, for all of his leftist sympathies, was never invited to sing before Soviet Premier Nikita Khrushchev on the occasion of the first visit of any Soviet leader to the United Nations, as Driftwood was.

In September of 1959, in the midst of the rock & roll era and the burgeoning boom in folk music, Driftwood had half a dozen of his songs somewhere on the American charts, pop or country. The best known of these was "The Battle of New Orleans," which managed to top both the country and pop charts in a version recorded by Johnny Horton, but also charting in September of 1959 were "Tennessee Stud," as recorded by country giant Eddy Arnold, Hawkshaw Hawkins' version of "Soldier's Joy," Johnny & Jack's "Sailor Man," Horton's recording of "Sal's Got a Sugar Lip," and Homer & Jethro's parody "The Battle of Kookamonga." Moreso than Hayes, Pete Seeger, or Woody Guthrie, Driftwood helped pull together elements of folk, pop, and country music and gave the mass public some sense of the history of all of it in the bargain.

James Corbett Morris' father was a singer who was well-known locally and who had been recorded by several folk song collectors in the early decades of the 20th century. He learned traditional folk songs from his mother and grandmother, while his father and grandfather taught him old-style fiddle tunes. And he grew up seemingly knowing every folk tale that there was to learn from the Ozarks, from whites and Native Americans (of whom there were many, including his future wife, who was one-quarter Cherokee) alike. It was his grandfather on his father's side, a fiddle maker, who built him the unique guitar that he used throughout his career, the neck made from a fence rail, the sides from an ox yoke, and the head and bottom from the headboard of a bed.

He began writing poetry at an early age, encouraged by a teacher. After graduating high-school, he attended John Brown College and later qualified as a teacher, eventually earning a proper education degree from Arkansas Teachers College. During the late '20s and early '30s, when he was still trying to earn some college credits, he headed west to Arizona, driving in an old Model A Ford that made it as far as Texas and hitchhiking the rest of the way. There wasn't much work to be found there in the midst of the Great Depression, but then an opportunity arose through a singing contest sponsored by a local radio station—he had his guitar with him and had written a song called "Arizona." He won the contest, which got him a spot on the station in the early morning hours, if he could find a sponsor. He eventually found one, in the guise of the grocery store chain that was willing to hire him as a worker and back his show. He was later taken in by an older couple who had heard him through the contest and not only gave him a place to live, but brought his mother—who, as it turned out, was dying from secondhand smoke from his father's cigarette habit—out to Arizona. She died in Arizona, and eventually his father died of cancer as well, by which time Driftwood was back in Arkansas teaching.

It was while teaching history in elementary school that he discovered the positive influence of music in presenting the panorama of American history. He wrote "The Battle of New Orleans," drawing his melody from the traditional fiddle tune "The Eighth of January," in order to help his students distinguish between the events of the Revolutionary War, the Civil War, and the War of 1812. All of the songs and stories that he'd heard during his childhood now stood him in good stead, as he was able to draw on a multitude of tales and traditional melodies, as well as devise his own traditional-sounding melodies, to deliver up songs as needed for his students or anyone else who would listen.

Driftwood married a former student of his, Cleda Azalea Johnson, in 1936, and the couple moved into a home that they built together, where they later raised their family. For the next 20 years, his life was concerned almost exclusively with teaching and his family, and during that time he wrote thousands of songs, almost all having to do with some aspects of American history. By the 1940s, he had his college degree and proper teaching credentials and was becoming a well-known local figure. That might have been

as far as the music took James Corbett Morris, as he was still known, but for several cultural changes that were taking place far from his home.

The late '40s had seen the beginnings of a revival of interest in folk music, with the success of the Almanac Singers and their successors, the Weavers, who transformed an activist songwriting process into popular success. Although their careers were interrupted by a political backlash against their activist roots, the 1950s saw a spread of interest in folk music and the roots and stories behind it to the college campuses, newly swelling with the ranks of middle-class students. By the mid-'50s, Driftwood suddenly found himself being sought after by scholars and folk song collectors, and he also began receiving invitations to speak at colleges and universities throughout the South and beyond. In 1957, a friend of Driftwood's, Hugh Ashley, told a friend of his, Don Warden, a steel guitar player in Porter Wagoner's band who had just started up a new publishing company and was looking for material, about a schoolteacher who'd written a huge number of songs that seemed to be pretty catchy, at least among the local school children.

At that time, he was still legally James Morris. The name Jimmie Driftwood was the outcome of a joke played on his grandmother when he was born—his grandfather had handed his wife a bundle that was supposed to be Jimmie, but proved to be a piece of wood, to which his grandmother exclaimed, "It's just a piece of driftwood." Morris liked the "Driftwood" name and picked it up and used it, both publicly and legally, from the late '50s onward. Warden signed Driftwood up as a songwriter after hearing him run-through 100 songs, of which "The Battle of New Orleans" was the last. The folk boom was in full swing, and he was signed soon after to RCA Victor, which was looking for folksingers. Driftwood's first recording session was held on October 27, 1957, the same month he signed with the label, and the first song he cut—to his own guitar accompaniment with backing from Chet Atkins on guitar and Bob L. Moore on bass—was "The Battle of New Orleans." There were 11 songs cut that day, all of which ended up on his first album, the rather awkwardly titled *Newly Discovered Early American Folk Songs*, issued in the summer of 1958. That album sold in small but respectable numbers, and received good reviews, but there was no hit single from it, principally because "The Battle of New Orleans" didn't get much airplay, a result of the use of the words "hell" and "damn" in the lyrics.

A second set of sessions was scheduled for November of 1958, but in the meantime, Warden's work as Driftwood's publisher was about to pay off in a totally unexpected way. Wagoner had toured with Horton late in 1958, and in the course of their work together, Warden had pitched "The Battle of New Orleans" to Horton by way of his manager, Tillman Franks. Horton immediately wanted to record the song, and after a few cuts that reduced its length—and an appearance on the *Louisiana Hayride*, where Driftwood sang "The Battle of New Orleans"—Horton cut the song on January 27, 1959, in Nashville. Released early the following spring, Horton's single eventually rose to the number-one spot on the country charts, which it held for ten weeks out of a 21-week run. Better yet, it crossed over onto the pop charts for a 21-week stay in that much bigger arena, holding the top spot there for six weeks out of that time. Horton helped the song's cause and its exposure by performing it live on *the Ed Sullivan Show* in June of that year.

Suddenly, everybody wanted to record Driftwood's songs, even as his own second album, *The Wilderness Road*, was being released. That record, in the wake of the exposure from Horton's single, sold considerably better than his first. By mid-1959, Driftwood's success was confirmed with dozens of recordings of his songs either out or in the works, and then there came the moment in September of that year when six of those records were on the *Billboard* chart simultaneously. "The Battle of New Orleans" earned him a Grammy Award, and *The Wilderness Road* not only sold well but yielded an additional Grammy, followed three years later by another award for *Songs of Billy Yank and Johnny Reb*.

The unusual nature of his success at first confused Driftwood, who originally thought of the publishing contract as a vehicle by which to get his songs heard, that he might succeed as a recording artist. His records did sell, but never in numbers resembling Horton's recording of "The Battle of New Orleans," which easily became a gold record and sold in huge numbers around the world—it can safely be considered the model upon which not only direct successors such as Horton's "Sink the Bismarck" were built, but also the impetus behind the willingness of labels like Columbia Records to record such more topical-historical songs as Pete Le Farge's "Ballad of Ira Hayes," in both its original form and the version by Johnny Cash, and even extending to England, where American-born skiffle/country star Johnny Duncan recorded "The Legend of Gunga Din."

He expected lots of money from RCA, and there was some, to be sure. But the checks he got from Warden's publishing company were enormous, in the five-figure range, which, by the standards of Timbo, AR, in 1959, was about as much money as anyone had ever seen. It set Driftwood and his wife and family up comfortably for years to come, and allowed them to buy all of the land they wanted for themselves. "The Battle of New Orleans" was recut by Driftwood in a slightly more commercial arrangement, and in stereo, and it had a short run of its own on the country charts in mid-1959, its sales only a pale shadow of Horton's record, which was still riding the charts. Driftwood was still a star, however, and in April of that year performed at Carnegie Hall in New York, made the folk festivals in Berkeley and Newport, received an honorary doctorate in American folklore from Peabody College in Nashville, TN, sang before the United Nations for Soviet leader Nikita Khrushchev's visit, appeared on network television game shows (*To Tell the Truth*, etc.), and got regular spots on the *Grand Ole Opry*, the *Louisiana Hayride*, and the *Ozark Jubilee*.

Amid all of this activity, Driftwood was forced to end his teaching career, which didn't sit well with him. He continued to educate audiences, most notably those consisting of other teachers, about the power of songs as a teaching tool, and was an invited lecturer before many national teachers meetings and organizations throughout the early '60s. Finally, in the early '60s, Driftwood found a cause closer to home that he could devote himself to, the Arkansas Folk Festival, which eventually attracted 100,000 people every year to hear the musicians that performed there. That led to the formation of the Rackansack Folklore Society, which led to the building of the Ozark Folk Center in the early '70s. His next endeavor was the Jimmie Driftwood Barn, which became a major performing showcase for players from the Rackansack Folklore Society. Driftwood's other concerns included environmental issues, among them the preservation of the Blanchard Caverns in Arkansas, and the Buffalo River. He served as head of the Arkansas Parks and Tourism Commission and was named to the Advisory Committee of the Kennedy Center for the Performing Arts in Washington, D.C., and worked as a musicologist for the National Geographic Society. During the 1960s and 1970s, in the course of this work, he appeared before audiences at hundreds of colleges and universities.

Driftwood's recording career ended in 1961, but his six albums for RCA remain a compelling country-folk legacy. Artists from Bob Dylan to Bruce Springsteen can trace some elements of their repertory and success to his unique brand of songwriting, and even '80s roots rock outfits like the Del-Lords have performed his songs with the kind of fervor that most acts usually reserve for songs by Dylan and Guthrie. Driftwood died on July 12, 1998, in Fayetteville AR; he was 91. —*Bruce Eder*

Newly Discovered Early American Folk Songs / 1958 / RCA Victor ♦♦♦♦

Wilderness Road / 1959 / RCA Victor ♦♦♦♦♦

Wilderness Road is Jimmie Driftwood's second album, and it has the simple, folk-based sound that typified the recordings he made before producer Chet Atkins began to pile on glossy production flourishes. Acoustic guitar, string bass, and an occasional jew's-harp are the only instrumental ingredients, and except for three traditional songs, the album was authored by Driftwood. Many country fans will be immediately interested in Driftwood's original recording of "Tennessee Stud," which Eddy Arnold remade into a sizable hit the same year. Driftwood exercises his penchant for historical songs on "Bunker Hill" and otherwise delivers another excellent platter of songs about pioneers, cowboys, and rustics. —*Greg Adams*

The Westward Movement / 1959 / RCA Victor ♦♦♦♦

The title of *Westward Movement* suggests that Jimmie Driftwood's third album is a collection of western or pioneer songs, but in reality it covers a variety of topics similar to his previous efforts. The nearly all-original album has a vague thematic drift, from Kentucky in "The Land Where the Blue Grass Grows" and "The Widders of Bowling Green" to traveling songs to evocations of the West, but there is no overarching concept besides Driftwood's superlative storytelling ability. The instrumental palette is a little broader this time around with the addition of banjo and subtle percussion, but does not approach the commercial orientation of Driftwood's last two albums for RCA Victor. —*Greg Adams*

● **Tall Tales in Song** / 1960 / RCA Victor ♦♦♦♦♦

Songs of Billy Yank and Johnny Reb / 1961 / RCA Victor ♦♦♦♦

Songs of Billy Yank and Johnny Reb is an unusual Civil War album in that Jimmie Driftwood wrote all of the material himself, although some of the songs were based on snatches of other songs or stories from Civil War days. The songs represent a wide range of perspectives, from the black slave whose bride is taken away to the German-Americans in "Oh Florie." A few songs contain martial drumbeats and "hup-two-three-four" choruses, as you would expect from the author of "The Ballad of New Orleans." Purists may object to the production values, which are understandably pop-oriented given the participation of Chet Atkins, John D. Loudermilk, and Anita Kerr. On the other hand, enthusiasts of Johnny Horton's so-called historical folk music will find nothing to complain about. —*Greg Adams*

Driftwood at Sea / 1962 / RCA Victor ♦♦♦♦

Voice of the People / 1963 / Monument ♦♦♦

Down in the Arkansas / 1965 / Monument ♦♦♦

The Best of Jimmie Driftwood / 1966 / Monument ♦♦♦♦

● **Americana** / 1991 / Bear Family ♦♦♦♦♦

Comprising Jimmie Driftwood's complete recordings for RCA, cut between 1957 and 1961, this three-CD set opens with Driftwood's most famous song, "The Battle of New Orleans," and the ten other songs that comprised the classic country-folk collection *Newly Discovered Early American Folk Songs*. The material here, when compared to the music of the Weavers or the Kingston Trio, seems like a field recording from 100 years earlier, with Driftwood's rural Arkansas pronunciation, twangy intonation, and spare backing. *The Wilderness Road* is every bit as good and even more entertaining, since Driftwood seems even more comfortable with the recording process. Disc two opens with Driftwood's September 1959 sessions for *The Westward Movement*, a series of songs about the beginnings of the great American migration west, which features a somewhat more sophisticated sound. The second half of the disc is made up of *Tall Tales in Song*, Driftwood's series of songs about myths and tall tales from history and local legend. The last five songs come from a Time-Life LP, *How the West Was Won*, and deal with such figures as General Custer, Jesse James, and Billy the Kid. Disc three opens with the Grammy-winning album *Billy Yank and Johnny Reb*, which returns Driftwood to his more familiar backing band (including John D. Loudermilk), accompanied in surprisingly restrained manner by the Anita Kerr singers. The last half of the disc includes *Sea Shanties*, Driftwood's final album from 1961. The sound throughout is excellent, and the music is all priceless, whether one's taste runs toward country or folk. The booklet transcends Bear Family's usual standard, with extremely detailed notes and essays (some by the man himself), as well as the usual full sessionography. —*Bruce Eder*

Roy Drusky

b. Jun. 22, 1930, Atlanta, GA

Vocals, Guitar / Nashville Sound/Countrypolitan

A singer/songwriter often called "the Perry Como of country music," Roy Drusky enjoyed success throughout the 1960s as a performer in the Nashville sound vein. Born June 22, 1930, in Atlanta, GA, Drusky's mother, a church organist, tried for years to interest her son in music, but throughout his childhood he focused the majority of his energies on sports. It was not until during a two-year stint in the U.S. Navy that he bought his first

guitar, and soon after began performing for his fellow crew members. After leaving the Navy, Drusky returned to college, and unsuccessfully tried out for baseball's Cleveland Indians. In 1951, he started his first band, the Southern Ranch Boys; the group's success on a Decatur, GA–radio talent show landed Drusky work as a DJ, where he attracted a substantial following among listeners. He also continued to perform in local clubs after the Southern Ranch Boys called it quits, and on the strength of a 1953 single, "Such a Fool," he was signed to Columbia Records in 1955.

After moving to Minneapolis to continue his work in radio, Drusky began headlining at the Twin Cities' prestigious Flame Club, where word of his talents began spreading to Nashville. As a result, Faron Young recorded Drusky's "Alone With You" in 1958; the single was the biggest of Young's career, topping the charts for 13 weeks. Soon after, Drusky moved to Nashville, and in 1960 released back-to-back Top Five hits, the honky tonk ballads "Another" and "Anymore," which led to an invitation to join the *Grand Ole Opry*. In the same year, he also released a hit duet with Kitty Wells, "I Can't Tell My Heart That."

In 1961, Drusky released the double-sided hit "I'd Rather Loan You Out"/"Three Hearts in a Tangle," and also issued his first LP, *Anymore With Roy Drusky*. The next year, he reached the Top Ten again with "Second Hand Rose," from the album *It's My Way*. Throughout the first half of the decade, he continued to release chart hits, peaking in 1965 with his lone number one, "Yes, Mr. Peters." He also issued two separate albums in 1964, *Songs of the Cities* and *Yesterday's Gone*. In 1965, Drusky appeared in his first film, *White Lightnin' Express*, and also sang the feature's title song; he later appeared in two other films, *The Golden Guitar* and *Forty Acre Feud*. In the middle of the decade, he also began recording with singer Priscilla Mitchell, and with her released two albums of duets, 1965's *Love's Eternal Triangle* and *Together Again* in 1966. In addition, Drusky began a career as a producer for acts like Pete Sayers and Brenda Byers.

As a recording artist, Drusky's success tapered off after 1965; although he released 11 chart hits between 1966 and 1969, only two, "Where the Blue and Lonely Go" and "Such a Fool," reached the Top Ten. However, in the early years of the next decade he made a comeback: 1970's "Long Long Texas Road," from the album *All My Hard Times*, was his first Top Five hit in six years. It was also his last, however, and as Drusky's brand of country fell victim to changing tastes, his singles and albums were less and less successful; after releasing two LPs in 1976, *This Life of Mine* and *Night Flying*, he returned to writing and producing. After remaining silent throughout the 1980s, he began a new sideline as a country-influenced gospel balladeer in the early 1990s. —*Jason Ankeny*

Songs of the Cities / 1964 / Mercury ♦♦♦♦

● **The Pick of the Country** / 1964 / Mercury ♦♦♦♦♦

Love's Eternal Triangle / 1965 / Mercury ♦♦♦

Together Again / 1966 / Mercury ♦♦

Roy Drusky's duets with Priscilla Mitchell accounted for three of his hits in the mid-'60s, including the chart-topper "Yes, Mr. Peters." *Together Again* is the duo's second album together, and it is a mediocre effort that tellingly contains no hits. Tony Hatch's "My Love" (a full four years before Sonny James took it to number one on the country charts) and Cole Porter's "True Love" are given middle-of-the-road treatments, and their very presence shows that producer Jerry Kennedy was probably casting too wide a net. Even Buck Owens' "Together Again" is given a bland, uninspired arrangement. There is one Roy Drusky co-composition ("Alone With You") and Harlan Howard's "Above and Beyond" (another great song associated with Buck Owens), but Drusky and Mitchell's voices don't create an especially appealing blend. The two vocalists alternated lines on "Yes, Mr. Peters," so perhaps that approach would have yielded a superior product here. Drusky and Mitchell are talented artists, but *Together Again* is an entire album of filler. —*Greg Adams*

Roy Drusky's Greatest Hits / 1966 / Mercury ♦♦♦♦

Roy Drusky's Greatest Hits, Vol. 2 / 1968 / Mercury ♦♦♦

Country Special / 1970 / Vocalion ♦♦♦

New Lips / 1976 / Hilltop ♦♦♦

Country Sunshine / 1983 / CBS ♦♦♦

Roy Drusky had been off the charts for over five years when he made *Country Sunshine*, and had not had a major hit in over a decade. Who would have predicted, then, that the commercially dubious enterprise of bringing back this aged country crooner from the Nashville sound era would yield such a rewarding and poignant album? *Country Sunshine*'s "Blue Skies" and "September Song" convey the same end-of-life melancholy and optimism as Louis Armstrong's "What a Wonderful World" or Jimmy Durante's 1963 album, *September Song*. "Room Full of Roses" and "You Are My Sunshine" pay tribute to country music history, and even the Oak Ridge Boys' "Sail Away" strikes just the right note as the album's closer. *Country Sunshine* is very much like a vocal pop album in places, which is fitting considering Drusky's appellation as the Perry Como of country music, and the country tracks don't strain to be very commercial. Unfortunately, the album was a flop and will never be widely heard unless an astute Hollywood music producer someday puts Drusky's "Blue Skies" over the end credits of a motion picture. —*Greg Adams*

Songs of Love and Life / 1995 / Mercury Nashville ♦♦♦

Songs of Love and Life features Roy Drusky's versions of country classics like "Tip of My Fingers" and "Make the World Go Away," but the album doesn't contain enough songs to make it a bargain. —*Stephen Thomas Erlewine*

Dry Branch Fire Squad

f. 1976

Group / Neo-Traditional Folk, Progressive Bluegrass, Traditional Bluegrass, Bluegrass-Gospel

Dry Branch Fire Squad was a modern bluegrass band dedicated to bluegrass, old-timey, and Southern gospel music traditions. Mandolin player and comedian Ron Thomason founded the Fire Squad in 1976. The earliest incarnation the group included guitarist John Baker, banjo player Robert Leach, and bass player John Carpenter. Two years later, Mary Jo Leet became the group's vocalist. The group released a series of independent releases before signing with Rounder in 1978; they would stay with the venerable roots label for the rest of their career.

The Fire Squad continued to release albums on Rounder throughout the 1980s; standouts included *Good Neighbours & Friends* (1985) and the gospel-flavored *Golgotha* from a year later. By 1996's *Live! At Last*, the group included Thomason, guitarist Adam McIntosh, and banjoist Dan Russell; Mary Jo Leet was joined by her husband, Charlie, on harmonies and acoustic bass. The live album displayed the Fire Squad's penchant not only for traditional bluegrass and other Americana styles, but uproarious comedy as well. *Memories That Bless & Burn* appeared in 1999. The record mixed older material with new, and featured vocalist Suzanne Thomas. The band followed with 2001's *Hand Hewn*, and continued to be a favorite on the bluegrass and folk festival circuit. *—Johnny Loftus*

Spiritual Songs From Dry Branch / 1977 / RT ✦✦✦

Born to Be Lonesome / 1978 / Rounder ✦✦✦

Dry Branch Fire Squad / 1978 / RT ✦✦✦

Dry Branch Fire Squad on Tour / 1979 / Gordo ✦✦✦

Antiques & Inventions / 1981 / Rounder ✦✦

Fannin' the Flames / 1982 / Rounder ✦✦✦

Fertile Ground / 1983 / Rounder ✦✦✦✦

● **Good Neighbours & Friends** / 1985 / Rounder ✦✦✦✦✦

Golgotha / 1986 / Rounder ✦✦✦

Tried & True / 1988 / Rounder ✦✦

Long Journey / 1991 / Rounder ✦✦✦✦

Just for the Record / 1993 / Rounder ✦✦✦

Live! At Last / Oct. 8, 1996 / Rounder ✦✦✦✦

It's worth pointing out that while many bluegrass bands become more modern and forward-looking as they continue along their career paths, experimenting with Bob Dylan and Eric Clapton songs or throwing in the odd pedal steel guitar, the Dry Branch Fire Squad has, if anything, drifted back in the other direction. There are several bluegrass standards ("Late Last Night," "Bluegrass Breakdown," "John Henry") on this live album, but the program ranges widely and tends to look more backward than forward. A cowboy song rubs shoulders with the old-timey "Red Rocking Chair" (sung and played on clawhammer banjo by Suzanne Thomas); Stephen Foster's "Hard Times" is followed by a pair of traditional gospel numbers. What all of this adds up to is the fact that the Dry Branch Fire Squad isn't really a bluegrass band, and hasn't been for some years—the group is sort of a tour-bus version of the Smithsonian Institution, lovingly displaying a rotating exhibit of traditional mountain music. What makes this album particularly special is the fact that it allows those who have never experienced one of the band's live performances to hear bandleader Ron Thomason expound at hilarious length in his exaggerated hillbilly accent about North-South culture clashes, the War on Poverty, and the finer points of knife fighting. His bad puns ("J.D. Crowe Magnon," indeed) and slyly left-of-center social commentary are at least as much fun as the music. Highly recommended, and not just to bluegrass fans. *—Rick Anderson*

Memories That Bless & Burn / Oct. 26, 1999 / Rounder ✦✦✦✦✦

With *Memories that Bless and Burn* Dry Branch Fire Squad has made the kind of music that the alt-country-folks are copying, but a few steps closer to the real thing. Sweet gospel harmonies exist side-by-side with episodes of banjo madness and the vocalists, especially Mary Jo Leet and Ron Thomason, sometimes sound like they are singing right on top of their last raw nerve. This is not to say that the members of Dry Branch Fire Squad lack talent—rather their sound is stripped down to a kind of pure mirror of the music of their grandparents, something which helps make their faith-driven lyrics sound sincere and evokes the sound of the church itself, with its shouting preachers and passionate bursts of praise. This album functions as sort of a greatest-hits album—the first three songs are new material—including the excellent title track, which features the sweet singing of Suzanne Thomas and helps set the mood for the rest of the album. Tracks 4-10 are from previous Rounder recordings and provide a profile of the band's earlier work. Tracks 4 and 5 are two versions of the same song, interesting because they show the evolution of both the band's technique and the quality of the equipment that they recorded on (the second version is amazingly clearer, as well as featuring a more powerful vocal). Tracks 11-13 are songs that had been featured on other albums but were re-recorded for this one, and 14-16 are songs that have long been a part of their gospel shows but are being recorded for the first time. "Touch the Hem of His Garment," provides a beautiful closing to this album, evoking the gentle despair and hope that echo all throughout this fine work. *—Stacia Proefrock*

Hand Hewn / Apr. 24, 2001 / Rounder ✦✦✦✦

Great albums from Dry Branch Fire Squad are nothing new. The band's lineup has changed slowly but fairly constantly over its 25-year history, but the commitment of its leader, mandolinist, and singer Ron Thomason to the various strains and traditions of old-time and bluegrass music has never flagged. Nor has his sense of humor, which is legendary. His voice, on the other hand, is aging somewhat, not that that really detracts from the pleasure of his singing on traditional favorites like "While Roving on Last Winter's Night" and the Ralph Stanley gospel rave-up "Two Coats." He sounds best of all here on "Black Lung," a hair-raising miner's lament that he sings in a spare, stark arrangement in duet with Hazel Dickens. The whole quartet kicks in for the rollicking gospel number "I'll Live Again," and there are a couple of great instrumentals as well, including Thomason's mandolin showcase, a Bill Monroe tribute titled "Nazeer, Nazeer (Nazeer, Nazeer)." The program's only misstep is a rather dull and overlong rendition of "Midnight, the Unconquered Outlaw." It's highly recommended overall. *—Rick Anderson*

George Ducas

b. Aug. 1, 1966, Texas City, TX

Vocals / Contemporary Country

Singer/songwriter George Ducas was born on August 1, 1966, in Texas City, TX, but was raised in San Diego, where he received his first guitar at the age of ten. Growing up on a steady diet of Willie Nelson records, Ducas spent much of his high-school years privately writing songs for his girlfriends and did not perform professionally until he attended college at Nashville's Vanderbilt University. After graduation, he accepted a banking job in Atlanta but returned to Nashville in 1990 to pursue music on a full-time basis. There a mutual friend introduced him to Radney Foster, and a songwriting partnership was forged; Ducas eventually co-wrote Foster's first solo hit, "Just Call Me Lonesome." A growing reputation as a live performer helped earn Ducas his own recording contract, and in 1994 he issued his self-titled debut LP, which generated the Top Ten hit "Lipstick Promises." In 1997, he released his second effort, *Where I Stand*. *—Jason Ankeny*

George Ducas / 1995 / Liberty ✦✦✦

● **Where I Stand** / Jan. 14, 1997 / Liberty ✦✦✦✦

Dave Dudley (David Darwin Pedruska)

b. May 3, 1928, Spencer, WI

Vocals, Guitar / Honky Tonk, Bakersfield Sound, Truck Driving Country, Traditional Country

Dave Dudley is the father of truck driving country music. With his 1963 song "Six Days on the Road," he founded a new genre of country music—a variation of honky tonk and rock-inflected country that concentrated lyrically on the lifestyles of truck drivers. Dudley had a string of Top 15 singles that ran through the '60s, while he continued to have Top 40 hits well into the '70s, establishing himself as one of the most popular singers of his era. At the age of 11, Dudley's father gave him a guitar, but he had his heart set on being a baseball player. Throughout his teenage years he played ball, becoming a member of the Gainesville Owls as a young adult. However, his career was cut short by an arm injury. Following his retirement from baseball, he became a DJ at a local Texas station, where he would sometimes play along with the songs on the air. The station owner encouraged to become a performer, and Dudley followed the advice.

Dudley moved to Idaho in the early '50s, where he formed the Dave Dudley Trio, which didn't have much success in its seven years together. In 1960, following the breakup of the trio, he moved to Minneapolis, where formed a group called the Country Gentlemen, which quickly built up a dedicated following. His career was thrown off track in December of 1960, when he was struck by a hit-and-run driver as he was packing his guitar into his car. After several months, he was recovered and managed to secure a record deal with Vee Records. His first single, "Maybe I Do," was minor hit in the fall of 1961 and was followed by another minor hit, "Under Cover of the Night," the following year on Jubilee Records.

In the summer of 1963, he had his breakthrough hit, "Six Days on the Road," which was released on Golden Wing. The song became a massive success, peaking at number two on the country charts and making the pop Top 40. That same year, he signed with Mercury Records, releasing his first single for the label, "Last Day in the Mines," by the end of the year. Throughout the '60s, he had a long string of truck driving singles, including "Truck Drivin' Son-of-a-Gun," "Trucker's Prayer," "Anything Leaving Town Today," "There Ain't No Easy Run," and "Two Six Packs Away." By the end of the decade, he was also making conservative, good-old-boy anthems as well. During the early '70s, he had several hits—notably the 1971 Top Ten singles "Comin' Down" and "Fly Away Again"—but by the beginning of the '80s, he was no longer a presence on the charts. His last hit single was 1980's "Rolaids, Doan's Pills and Preparation H." During the '80s and '90s, Dudley didn't record much, but he remained a popular concert draw. And truck drivers still loved him—the Teamsters Union awarded him an honorary, solid-gold membership card. *—Stephen Thomas Erlewine*

Songs About the Working Man / 1964 / Mercury ✦✦✦✦✦

Travelin' With Dave Dudley / 1964 / Mercury ✦✦✦✦✦

Talk of the Town / 1964 / Mercury ✦✦✦✦

Rural Route #1 / 1965 / Mercury ✦✦✦✦✦

Rural Route #1 was Dave Dudley's fourth album for Mercury and reflects his growing confidence in his medium—Dudley was the voice of the working man, the traveling man, and the decent folks who liked their music snappy, energetic, and with a sense of humor. There are two bona fide Dudley-penned classics here, the enigmatic "Big Country" and a song that has become part of country music's canon, "Sleepy-Eyed John." In addition, there is a far more authentic reading of Red Foley's "Old Shep" than the cornpone one done by Elvis eight years earlier. In the grain of Dudley's voice the song becomes a believable story—despite the cheesy lyrics—of conflict between a man and his lifelong best friend, his dog. A couple of other standouts on the set are a pair of Tom T. Hall covers, the rowdy, Saturday night celebration of "Pretty Weather" and the poignant ballad "The Drought," one of Hall's reflection songs about a farmer who's lost everything and everyone due to a drought and his stubbornness. It's the most poignant and painful song on the album and would not have been out of place in the repertoire of George Jones (in his Pappy Dailey years) or Merle Haggard. Above all, what carries *Rural Route #1* is Dudley's *basso profundo* charm. He hadn't yet become the trucker's songwriter, but he nonetheless had all the elements in place in his honky tonk tunes such as Don Dreyer's "Honey Babe." There's also a fine spoken word remake of "Old Rivers," but it's not the definitive one—Walter Brennan's is. Perhaps the finest moment on the album is in Dudley's version of the Harry Beasley Smith-Haven Gillespie classic "Lucky Old Sun."

Unlike Willie Nelson's crooning version of a decade later, Dudley's read comes from the voice of a man sweating over his plough, and the yearning in his voice comes from more than a turn of lyric, but rather from a genuine empathy with the song's protagonist. *Rural Route #1* may not be Dudley's most well-known album, but it is certainly one of his finest. *—Thom Jurek*

Truck Drivin' Son-of-a-Gun / 1965 / Mercury ♦♦♦

Mercury should release a compilation of Dave Dudley's prime truck-drivin' songs. He started the country subgenre and produced many fine singles that extolled the 18-wheeler lifestyle throughout the '60s. Save for the EMI import *20 Great Truck Hits*, there are hardly any decent Dudley reissues or collections available. So it's worth looking for the excellent Dudley album *Truck Drivin' Son-of-a-Gun*, which features two of the singer's biggest hits, "Two Six Packs Away" and the title track. Dudley's gravelly, vibrato-inflected voice and thick, reverb-drenched guitar lines (his own rough-hewn version of the Nashville sound) were perfect for songs detailing the perils of white line fever. Songs like "Jack Knife" and "Speed Traps, Weigh Stations & Detour Signs," which chronicle the hurdles of the highway, and "Two Six Packs Away," which—in very un-PC, yet hilarious fashion—reveals the dangers of a trucker's little helper (the liner notes include a friendly disclaimer: "A drinkin' and a drivin', here Dave's singing and guitar are much more compatible than alcohol and gas"). The out of print *Truck Drivin' Son-of-a-Gun* is a title definitely worth seeking out. If you don't mind import prices, though, get the EMI collection. *—Stephen Cook*

There's a Star Spangled Banner Waving Somewhere / 1966 / Mercury ♦♦♦

Lonelyville / 1966 / Mercury ♦♦♦

There is a concept—or at least a theme—behind *Lonelyville*: all the songs are in one way or another about loneliness, and most contain the word "lonely" or some variation thereof. "Have You Ever Been Lonely," "Lonely Street," "Oh Lonesome Me," and "Seven Lonely Days" are obvious choices once the idea presents itself, but Dudley himself contributes "Lonely Corner," and Tom T. Hall's name appears on four others (the only ones, incidentally, that don't contain the magic word, suggesting that they weren't made to order for the album). The songs are slow and somber—quite a departure from the good-time trucking songs for which Dudley is remembered. The title track was a respectable hit, showing that Dudley could attempt other kinds of material and performing styles (ballad singing in particular) without completely losing his audience. *—Greg Adams*

Free and Easy / 1966 / Mercury ♦♦♦

My Kind of Love / 1967 / Mercury ♦♦♦

Dave Dudley Country / 1967 / Mercury ♦♦♦♦

Thanks for All the Miles / 1968 / Mercury ♦♦♦♦♦

One More Mile / 1969 / Mercury ♦♦♦♦

It's My Lazy Day / 1969 / Mountain Dew ♦♦♦

It is hard to determine where this album fits into the recording career of this journeyman country singer and songwriter. He made most of his records in a 15-year span between the early '60s and the late '70s, developing a style so clearly his own, and so completely unchanged over the course of his career, that each of his albums has a sense of timelessness to it. Although only one of Dudley's songs was a number one hit, he recorded much music of comparable quality to the famous "Six Days on the Road," handling the lyrics gingerly with a voice that many a male country singer would gladly trade their soul for. A majority of the songs here deal with life in the country, with only "Old Shep" tilting the sentimentality meter. The best part of Dudley's music is, of course, the lead guitar sound, which sounds like the instrument is being picked with a wet oil can spout. The fly-by-night company that released this must have thought the song "It's My Lazy Day" was for them, and didn't bother to identify any of the songwriters, musicians, or year of release. *—Eugene Chadbourne*

The Pool Shark / 1970 / Mercury ♦♦♦♦♦

Dave Dudley Sings "Listen Betty, I'm Singing Your Song" / 1971 / Mercury ♦♦♦

"The highway is a part of hell that never caught on fire," sings Dave Dudley in the title track of this 1970 album. Memorable lyrics notwithstanding, the song barely cracked the Top 15, while the comparatively bland "Comin' Down" made the Top Ten. The album is otherwise full of fun material like the rocking "Six-O-One" and Shel Silverstein's "The Rollin's All Gone Out of This Rollin' Stone," and even a trucking song in deference to Dudley's musical past. Kris Kristofferson's "For the Good Times" is a little too treacly in Dudley's rendering, and in general the faster and funnier material is more successful than the ballads. One exception is the poignant "I Cry a Lot," in the tradition of—if not quite on par with—"I Guess Things Happen That Way" and "Funny How Time Slips Away." Dudley doesn't often get much recognition for his songwriting, but he wrote half of this album, a minor feat in the days when artists often released three or four albums a year. *—Greg Adams*

Will the Real Dave Dudley Please Sing / 1971 / Mercury ♦♦

Will the Real Dave Dudley Please Sing is supposed to show the many sides of Dudley's artistry, and the cover sports photos of Dudley in three personas: the city sophisticate, the country gentleman, and the truck-driving son-of-a-gun. The truck-driver image fittingly appears last in the order, since only two songs, "Through Hell and Half of Georgia" and "I Can See You in the Windshield," concern trucks. Apparently, the "real" Dave Dudley is a country crooner, if the preponderance of such material on the album is any indication. One of these songs, "Fly Away Again," became Dudley's last major hit, but he is remembered mainly for his truck driving country songs, and few listeners will care to hear his renditions of pop songs like "Fools Rush In." The one hidden gem is Tom T. Hall's humorous "Tulsa Telephone Book," on which Dudley's swaggering vocal performance sounds like a cross between Elvis Presley and John Wayne. *—Greg Adams*

The Original Traveling Man / 1972 / Mercury ♦♦♦

Keep on Truckin' / 1973 / Mercury ♦♦♦

1776 / 1976 / United Artists ♦♦♦

● **20 Great Truck Hits: Dave Dudley** / 1983 / EMI ♦♦♦♦♦

● **20th Century Masters—The Millennium Collection: The Best of Dave Dudley** / Sep. 10, 2002 / Universal ♦♦♦♦♦

Dave Dudley is one of the kings of truck-driving country, but his recorded legacy has been neglected in terms of CD reissues. That's why 2002's 12-track *20th Century Masters* is such a welcome release. It may have some flaws—chief among them, it contains the Mercury re-recording of his signature anthem, "Six Days on the Road," not the original Golden Wing version of the song; this is good all the same, but it would have been nicer to have the classic original—but the utter lack of Dudley on CD makes it easy to accept with open arms. The biggest flaw, of course, is the lack of the original "Six Days on the Road," as well as the presence of a re-recording of "Cowboy Boots," which was also released on the independent label (only then it was called Golden Ring, not Golden Wing). The other flaw is that it's a little bit short at 12 tracks, but given the utter lack of classic Dudley on CD, it seems a little churlish to complain, particularly because this contains the majority of his big Mercury hits: the story-song "Last Day in the Mines," the tough-as-nails "Mad," the deliriously funny drunk-driving tale "Two Six Packs Away," "Truck Drivin' Son of a Gun," his pro-Vietnam tune "What We're Fighting For," the travelogue "There Ain't No Easy Run," and the character sketch "The Pool Shark." All these pretty much stick to his signature, Bakersfield-styled truck-driving sound—filled with twangy Telecasters and rolling, two-step rhythms—but there are also hits that show how Dudley could stretch: the ballad "Please Let Me Prove (My Love for You)," along with the 1971 "Comin' Down" and "Fly Away Again," which both bear the hallmarks of post-Glen Campbell, post-psychedelia country-pop (check out the extremely flanged guitars on the latter!). This is just enough variety and just enough hits to make you hunger for more classic '60s Dave Dudley, but this is all that's easily available. So, until a more thorough compilation comes along—one that rounds up such missing singles as "Under Cover of the Night," "Vietnam Blues," "Lonelyville," "Trucker's Prayer," and "Anything Leaving Town Today" along with album tracks—this stands as the best Dudley collection on the market, and it's a necessary purchase for anybody who loves truck-driving country. *—Stephen Thomas Erlewine*

Johnny Duncan

b. Oct. 5, 1938, Dublin, TX

Guitar, Vocals / Urban Cowboy, Neo-Traditionalist Country

Not to be confused with the American expatriate and British skiffle star of the same name, Johnny Duncan is a country-pop singer best-known for a string of hits with producer Billy Sherrill in the late '70s. Born in the farm town of Dublin, TX, in 1938, Duncan learned guitar from his mother as a child, and also had two future performers in his family in the person of cousins Dan and Jimmy Seals (of England Dan & John Ford Coley and Seals & Crofts, respectively). All four family members, plus Duncan's fiddle-playing uncle, Ben Moroney, played together in a local dance band. Duncan took up singing in his late teens, and moved to Clovis, NM, in 1959, where he recorded some pop-oriented demos under producer Norman Petty. Nothing came of them, and he spent several years working as a DJ.

He moved to Nashville in 1964 and worked odd jobs before landing a guest spot on Ralph Emery's television show in 1966. That led to a deal with Columbia Records, which released his debut single "Hard Luck Joe," in 1967. Duncan had a few minor chart entries over the next few years, including two duets with June Stearns, but nothing that could be considered a breakout hit. That all changed when Duncan hooked up with the famed Nashville sound producer Billy Sherrill. Singles like 1972's "Baby's Smile, Woman's Kiss" and 1973's Top Ten "Sweet Country Woman" started to establish him as a hitmaker. However, his marriage subsequently broke up, and the distraught Duncan returned to Texas. He was talked back into the music business for the single "Jo and the Cowboy," which paired him with a then-unknown Janie Fricke, and the song was successful enough that Sherrill decided to feature her on some of Duncan's subsequent recordings. Sordid barroom sagas like "Stranger" and "Thinkin' of a Rendezvous" made Duncan a star, with the former becoming his first Top Five hit and the latter his first-ever number one in 1976.

"It Couldn't Have Been Any Better" (1977) was his second chart-topper, and his first credited duet with Fricke, "Come a Little Bit Closer," went Top Five the following year. Duncan also scored two big hits of his own in 1978 with the Top Five "Hello Mexico (And Adios Baby to You)" and the number one "She Can Put Her Shoes Under My Bed (Anytime)." His last Top Ten appearances came in 1979 with "Slow Dancing" and "The Lady in the Blue Mercedes," after which his commercial momentum abruptly halted. He and Columbia parted ways in the early '80s, and he subsequently remarried and returned to Texas. He recorded a bit for small labels during the '80s and '90s, cutting a couple of singles in 1986. *—Steve Huey*

Johnny One Time / 1969 / Columbia ♦♦♦

Sweet Country Woman / 1973 / Columbia ♦♦♦

The Best of Johnny Duncan / 1976 / Columbia ♦♦♦♦

Come a Little Bit Closer / 1977 / Columbia ♦♦♦

Johnny Duncan / 1977 / Columbia ♦♦♦♦

The Best Is Yet to Come / 1978 / Columbia ♦♦♦♦

See You When the Sun Goes Down / 1979 / Columbia ♦♦♦♦

Straight From Texas / 1979 / Columbia ♦♦♦

Johnny Duncan's slick, sometimes Caribbean-flavored country music is heard on his 1979 album *Straight From Texas*, including the hit "The Lady in the Blue Mercedes" and a cover of "If I Said You Had a Beautiful Body Would You Hold It Against Me." Elsewhere, Duncan adopts a somewhat harder country sound that is significantly less dated and more appealing. "My Woman's Good to Me" and "Runaway Housewife" are examples of the latter, and are reminiscent of Bob Luman's Epic recordings. Duncan has a great voice, but isn't as well remembered today as might be expected for an artist who charted nearly 40 hits; the reason might have something to do with the dated production style on many of his big hits. "Would You Like to Spend the Night (With a Memory)" is an example of a quality album track with a strong hook that keeps the pop gloss in check, and is one of a few such recordings that redeem an otherwise lukewarm album. *—Greg Adams*

In My Dreams / 1980 / Columbia ✦✦✦

Nice 'n' Easy / 1980 / Columbia ✦✦✦

● **Greatest Hits** / 1989 / Columbia ✦✦✦✦✦

Pure Country / Aug. 25, 1998 / Sony ✦✦✦✦
Sony Special Products' *Pure Country* is an effective sampler of Johnny Duncan's work for Columbia Records in the '70s. In fact, in many ways it works as a hits compilation, since every one of the featured songs—"Sweet Country Woman," "Stranger," "Thinkin' of a Rendezvous," "It Couldn't Have Been Any Better," "Come a Little Bit Closer," "A Song in the Night," "She Can Put Her Shoes Under My Bed (Anytime)," "Hello Mexico (And Adios Baby to You)," "Slow Dancing," "The Lady in the Blue Mercedes"—were Top Ten country hits for Duncan. Because of that, *Pure Country* is more than just a good bargain for a budget-line collection—it's a good bargain in general. *—Stephen Thomas Erlewine*

Classic Country / Sep. 1, 1998 / Simitar ✦✦✦✦✦
Classic Country collects 14 of Johnny Duncan's Columbia hits from 1971 to 1980, including three number-one hits, "Thinkin' of a Rendezvous," "It Couldn't Have Been Any Better," and "She Can Put Her Shoes Under My Bed (Anytime)." Four songs are duets with Janie Fricke, and a number of tracks adopt a Caribbean feel that suggests what Jimmy Buffet might sound like as a country singer. Every track here cracked the country Top 20, and the bulk of Duncan's hits are represented. *—Greg Adams*

● **It Couldn't Have Been Any Better** / Mar. 11, 2003 / Collectors' Choice Music ✦✦✦✦✦
Johnny Duncan cut an imposing figure: a tall, bearded Texan who seemed like he would bash out barroom ravers instead of crooning sweet country tunes and ballads. Which, of course, is what he did, producing a series of easy-rolling hits—including several duets with Janie Fricke—that kept him in the country Top Ten during the second half of the '70s. As his career rolled on, he moved further away from straightforward country and toward poppy, good-time country, slickly produced by Billy Sherrill and sung warmly by Duncan. In retrospect, his hits pointed toward the pop-country crossover of urban cowboy that followed just a few years later, particularly in how it covered '60s pop hits, appropriated breezy mariachi horns, and had a general sunny, party-ready disposition. Collectors' Choice 2003 collection *It Couldn't Have Been Any Better* captures all of this and, years after Duncan ruled the charts and became something of a forgotten name, this music is still easy to enjoy. All of his country Top 40 hits from his hitmaking streak are here—including the number-one hits "It Couldn't Have Been Any Better" and "She Can Put Her Shoes Under My Bed (Anytime)" and four duets with Fricke, highlighted by "Thinkin' of a Rendezvous"—and if the music does indeed sound a bit tied to the '70s, it nevertheless is enjoyable period-piece music with a warm feeling and nicely sung by Duncan who has a friendly, laid-back persona. Not essential, then, but worth seeking out for listeners who like their '70s country kind of traditional but with a notable pop bent. *—Stephen Thomas Erlewine*

Tommy Duncan

b. Jan. 11, 1911, Hillsboro, TX, **d.** Jul. 25, 1967, Tulsa, OK
Vocals / Traditional Country, Western Swing

As the lead singer for the classic lineup of Bob Wills' Texas Playboys, Tommy Duncan was the definitive Western swing vocalist. Crossing the smooth croon of Bing Crosby with the twang of Jimmie Rodgers and the bluesy inclinations of Emmett Miller, Duncan had a warm, distinctive, and welcoming voice that helped the Playboys cross over to a wider audience. Not only was he a wonderful, trendsetting vocalist, Duncan also wrote many of the Texas Playboys' biggest hits, including "Time Changes Everything," "Stay a Little Longer," "Take Me Back to Tulsa," "New Spanish Two Step," and "Bubbles in My Beer." Throughout the '30s and '40s, he was remained with Wills, leaving in 1948 when tensions between the two musicians became too great. Following his departure, Duncan launched a solo career that resulted in one major hit single, "Gamblin' Polka Dot Blues." Throughout the '50s, he sang both as a solo artist and a member of the Miller Brothers Band. In 1960, he and Wills patched up their differences and recorded several albums. Following his reunion with Wills, he began touring as a solo artist, and he remained on the road until his death in 1967.

Duncan was hired by Wills in 1933 to fill the vacant spot left in the Light Crust Doughboys by vocalist/pianist Milton Brown, who had left the band when W. Lee O'Daniel, the sponsor of the group's radio show, refused to let the band play dances. Wills auditioned a total of 67 singers before hiring Duncan. Later that year, Wills was fired from the radio station by O'Daniel for showing up drunk, Duncan chose to join Bob's new band, the Texas Playboys, instead of staying with the Lightcrust Doughboys. Once the Texas Playboys settled in Tulsa in 1934, Duncan moved to permanent lead vocalist, leaving the piano to Alton Stricklin. Over the next eight years, the group had a regular show on Tulsa's KVOO and recorded a number of hit singles for the American Recording Company, including "Right or Wrong" and "New San Antonio Rose."

In 1942, Duncan left the band to join the Army and fight in World War II. His departure began a wave of defections from the Playboys, as many of the members enlisted in the service. The Playboys' popularity crumbled with the absence of so many key musicians, yet they bounced back up the charts once Duncan and several other members rejoined following the end of the war. Duncan stayed with Wills until 1948, when the fiddler fired the singer, believing that Tommy was commanding too much attention. Upon leaving the Playboys, Duncan formed a Western swing band with several former members of the Texas Playboys and signed to Capitol Records. "Gamblin' Polka Dot Blues," his debut single, was a hit upon its summer release in 1949, peaking at number eight on the charts.

After touring with the band during 1948 and 1949, Duncan joined the Miller Brothers Band in the early '50s. Over the course of the early '50s, he recorded with the Miller Brothers on Intro Records, as well as solo for Coral. During the latter half of the decade, Duncan recorded for a variety of small labels, including Cheyenne, Fire, and Award. Despite his constant touring and recording, Duncan failed to have much success, primarily because Western swing had fallen out of favor with many contemporary country fans. Wills and Duncan patched up their differences and reunited in 1960, recording a number of sessions that were released as albums and singles over the next two years. One single, "The Image of Me," became a minor Top 40 country hit in early 1961. Following his brief reunion with Wills, Duncan continued to tour as a solo artist throughout the rest of the decade, usually employing a house band as his supporting group. In 1966, Duncan released his last single, "I Brought It on Myself"/"Let Me Take You Out," on Smash Records. The following year, he suffered a major heart attack and died in July, leaving behind a legacy of classic recordings and songs. *—Stephen Thomas Erlewine*

● **Texas Moon** / 1996 / Bear Family ✦✦✦✦
The 24-track compilation *Texas Moon* contains every song that Tommy Duncan recorded for Capitol Records in 1959, including the Top Ten hit "Gambling Polka Dot Blues," as well as his lone single on Natural, his first two sessions for Intro, and two singles that his brother Glynn recorded with Tommy's band, the Western All-Stars. Much of this material is in the vein of Duncan's classic work with Bob Wills, though the quality of the music is slightly inconsistent. Nevertheless, *Texas Moon* and its companion volume *Beneath a Neon Star in a Honk Tonk*, are necessary for hardcore collectors of Western swing in general and Duncan in particular. *—Thom Owens*

Beneath a Neon Star in Honky Tonk / 1996 / Bear Family ✦✦✦✦
The 27-track compilation *Beneath a Neon Star in a Honky Tonk* contains every song Tommy Duncan recorded for Intro Records between 1951 and 1953, as well as his lone single for Fire Records, which featured Buck Owens on guitar. The music on this disc is slightly more straightforward than conventional Western swing, yet it should appeal to fans of Duncan's classic recordings with Bob Wills, even with the slightly inconsistent musical quality. Nevertheless, *Beneath a Neon Star in a Honky Tonk* and its companion volume *Texas Moon*, are necessary for hardcore collectors of Western swing in general and Duncan in particular. *—Thom Owens*

Holly Dunn

b. Aug. 22, 1957, San Antonio, TX
Vocals / Contemporary Country

One of the most popular female country singers of the late '80s, Holly Dunn was born in San Antonio in 1957 and was the sister of future country songwriting pro Chris Waters. In high-school, she performed with a group called the Freedom Folk, which toured the South and performed at the White House bicentennial celebration. While attending Abilene Christian University, she sang with the school's Hilltop Singers touring choir, and also co-wrote a song with her brother called "Out of Sight, Not Out of Mind." It was recorded by Cristy Lane, which convinced Dunn to try her luck in Nashville after graduation. She worked as a demo singer for a time before joining her brother as a staff songwriter at CBS. In 1984, she moved over to MTM and penned material for several different singers, including Louise Mandrell, who made "I'm Not Through Loving You Yet" a Top Ten hit.

In the wake of its success, Dunn landed a record contract in her own right, and released her first single in 1985. Her self-titled debut album appeared the following year and produced her first Top Ten hit, "Daddy's Hands." *Cornerstone* (1987) contained two Top Five singles in "Love Someone Like Me" and "Only When I Love," and Dunn produced the 1988 follow-up, *Across the Rio Grande*, herself, resulting in the hits "Strangers Again" and "(It's Always Gonna Be) Someday." MTM subsequently went bankrupt, and Dunn signed with Warner Bros. for 1989's *The Blue Rose of Texas*, which produced her first-ever number-one single, "Are You Ever Gonna Love Me," as well as the Top Five "There Goes My Heart Again." *Heart Full of Love* (1990) spawned another chart-topper, "You Really Had Me Going," and Warner followed it with the hits compilation *Milestones* in 1991. One of the new tracks, "Maybe I Mean Yes," sparked controversy over its lyrical content, which some interpreted as an apology for date rape. Dunn's popularity took a hit with 1992's *Getting It Dunn*, and she subsequently parted ways with Warner. She resurfaced in 1995 on the smaller River North label with *Life and Love and All the Stages*, and was back on a major (A&M) for 1997's *Leave One Bridge Standing*, which failed to revive her commercial standing. *—Steve Huey*

Holly Dunn / 1986 / MTM ✦✦✦

Cornerstone / 1987 / MTM ✦✦✦
Dunn's second effort includes the hits "Love Someone like Me" and "Only When I Love." *—Jason Ankeny*

Across the Rio Grande / 1988 / MTM ✦✦✦✦✦
Dunn took over the production reins for her third album, which features the hits "That's What Your Love Does to Me" and "(It's Always Gonna Be) Someday." *—Jason Ankeny*

The Blue Rose of Texas / 1989 / Warner Bros. ✦✦✦
This "nu-country/pop" belter has an occasional rock punch and a Western swing and sway. *—Mark A. Humphrey*

Heart Full of Love / 1990 / Warner Bros. ✦✦✦

● **Milestones: Greatest Hits** / 1991 / Warner Bros. ✦✦✦✦✦
Holly Dunn was an important contributor to contemporary country in the mid- to late '80s. Similar to Kathy Mattea and Rosanne Cash, Dunn brought elements of modern

folk, bluegrass and pop to country music with the knack for writing engaging narrative songs. These 11 tracks include chart toppers "Stranger's Again," "Only When I Love," "A Face in the Crowd," and her debut number-one hit from 1985, "Daddy's Hands."
—Al Campbell

Getting It Dunn / 1992 / Warner Bros. ✦✦✦✦✦
It contains the hits "You Say You Will," "A Simple I Love You," "No Love Have," and others.
—AMG

Life and Love and All the Stages / Apr. 18, 1995 / River North Nashville ✦✦✦

Leave One Bridge Standing / Apr. 8, 1997 / A&M ✦✦✦

Slim Dusty (David Gordon Kirpatrick)
· ·
b. Jun. 1927, Kempsey, New Wales, Australia
Guitar, Composer, Vocals / Traditional Country
Slim Dusty is the most prolific and biggest-selling recording artist in Australia, with more than five million of his recordings sold on the domestic market of 20 million people and a status akin to the all-time greats in country music. In 2000, the 73-year-old Australian music legend released his 100th album. He was born David Gordon Kirpatrick in Kempsey, NSW, Australia, and spent most of his younger days at a dairy farm. The first major influence on his career in music was his father, who liked to vocalize to the accompaniment of his fiddle playing when Kirpatrick was still a toddler. The event that changed his life forever took place when he was ten and heard an aborigine sing a song called "The Drunkard's Child." He was so fascinated, that same year he wrote his first song, "The Way the Cowboy Died." At age 11, he decided to rename himself Slim Dusty.

In 1942, as a "seasoned performer" of 15, Slim talked his way into the studios of the local radio station, and at his own expense recorded two songs: "Song for the Aussies" and "My Final Song." He became a regular performer and in 1945 wrote his first classic, "When the Rain Tumbles Down in July." In November 1946, the singer hit the big smoke and in a Sydney studio recorded the six tracks which would be released as his first three 78 rpm singles, starting with "When the Rain Tumbles Down in July." By now, he had a part-time career in show business as an intermittent radio performer playing in music halls and tent shows. In 1952, he married country performer and songwriter Joy McKean.

By April 1957, Slim Dusty already had a recording career of ten-plus years behind him when he was scheduled to record four more songs, but only three had been chosen. At the time, Slim was traveling with Gordon Parsons, who was singing a song he'd written based on a poem by Dan Shean. Needing that extra song, Slim asked Parsons if he could record his song, thinking it would make a good B-side for a song called "Saddle Boy." Parsons had no problem with that as to him, "A Pub With No Beer" was just a novelty song. Months later, while Slim was working in outback Queensland, he was told that the B-side of his latest single had made the pop charts in Brisbane, and as the months rolled on "A Pub With No Beer" became the first-ever Australian-made single to reach the national number one spot. The record went on to reach number three in England, and also sold well in the U.S. For a longtime, it was the biggest selling single in Australian music history.

From then on, the Slim Dusty career was assured. Unmistakable in his workman's hat with the turned down brim, Slim remains the kind of country music performer America laments having lost. He's someone who, throughout his 100-album career, continues to sing songs about the Australian landscape and the people who occupy it, someone who continues to tour the length and breadth of the land as he's always done. The cream of Australian songwriters line up to offer him songs. Over the years, Slim has won every accolade possible, from Tamworth Music Awards Golden Guitars to his Member of the British Empire medal. In September 2000, he was one of the Australian performers featured in the closing ceremony of the Sydney Olympic Games. Slim was given the job of singing Australia's unofficial national anthem, "Waltzin' Matilda." No one else would have been as appropriate. —Ed Nimmervoll

• **Regal Zonophone Collection** / 1995 / EMI ✦✦✦✦✦
Slim Dusty's long recording career, which began in the '40s, has given him a stature in Australia similar to that which George Jones enjoys in America. *Regal Zonophone Collection* is one in an excellent series of multi-disc anthologies devoted to early Australian country artists. Slim Dusty's volume is a three-disc set that covers his early recordings for the Regal Zonophone label from 1947-1958. Dusty says in the liner notes that the label was unwilling to pay for accompanists, so most of these performances feature Dusty alone with his acoustic guitar, yodeling and singing Western-style songs about the Australian outback. "A Pub With No Beer," Dusty's signature song, is presented here in its early rendition from the late '50s, which is also the version that Capitol released in the U.S. at the same time. "Rusty It's Goodbye," co-written with Thel Carey, is a real classic and one of a handful that feature duet vocals by Dusty's wife, Joy McKean. Dusty himself wrote the liner notes, and although they are interesting it would have been nice to have a historical perspective as well. Encompassing 68 slices of vintage Australiana, *Regal Zonophone Collection* offers a definitive look at the early years of Australia's most prominent country singer. —Greg Adams

Huelyn Duvall
· ·
Guitar, Vocals / Rock & Roll, Rockabilly
This Texas rockabilly dude got his first guitar when he was 14. It was the early '50s, and most of the songs on local radio were country music. Duvall graduated from high-school in the exciting town of Huckabay, his rank among the school's total population of 300 unknown. What Huckabay might have lacked in exciting musical prospects was more than made up for in nearby Stephenville, a dairy town of about 10,000 people at the time, and the unlikely location of a tape recorder that would be used to record primitive examples of rockabilly and rock & roll. By the mid-'50s, Duvall was feeling the influence of new artists such as Carl Perkins, Elvis Presley, Buddy Holly, and others. He met older lead guitarist Lonnie Thompson in 1956; they started playing together, a classic case of the older, college kid leading the high-school lad astray. They began recording at the facilities of a

local radio station, the goal being to record enough songs on a given weekend to have a new song for the station to play on each day of the following week. They liked doing it, and each weekend would start the whole process over again. It was a demonstration of productivity that has been matched only by perhaps the pop group They Might Be Giants with their "Dial-A-Song" project, or the efforts of studio musicians who cook up tracks based on poetry submitted by mail-order customers.

There was also a similarity with the early recordings of fellow Texan Ernest Tubb, who had also started out backed by only lead guitar. It was one of Duvall's bosses at the dairy farm where he worked that suggested a slap bass would improve the duo's sound, and a drummer joined shortly thereafter. Anyone who couldn't get enough of Lonnie Thompson soon found to their unbridled delight that his twin brother Johnny Thompson had further filled out the instrumental lineup by coming on rhythm guitar. In 1957, the group did a full round of high-schools, colleges, radio stations, theaters, and sock hops. Gigs at the Majestic Theatre in Ft. Worth or the Cowtown Hoedown in Dallas are legendary; one can't even imagine how raucous these places must have been without possibly corrupting the imagination permanently. It was literally an open battle to play forbidden rock & roll at the Cowtown Hoedown, although, of course, country was OK. As the legend goes, one packed night, Duvall told the band to rock the house. Luckily, the enthusiastic crowd response prevented the management from taking reprisals.

Danny Wolfe came on the scene as a collaborating singer and songwriter in the summer of 1957, helping to put together material for recording session with Challenge. The label's name sounds like the ultimate summation of the indie record business, but it was actually owned by mild-mannered cowboy star Gene Autry. Duvall's sessions were taped at the wonderful studio of Owen Bradley in Nashville, meaning he was benefiting from the same recording genius behind the classic Patsy Cline sides. Tracks cut included the under-developed "Teen Queen," the indecisive "Comin' or Goin'," the explosive "Boom Boom Baby," and "Pucker Paint," an ode to lipstick whose title is best announced through a serious windscreen. Duvall could also brag about the session players on board, including lead guitarist Grady Martin, pianist Floyd Cramer, and Buddy Harmon. Like most country artists of that era, he also turned around in the studio at one point to see the Jordanaires preparing for their background vocal entrance. Yet, he was actually totally peeved that he was not allowed to use his own band, and thereby prevented from rocking out. This was a major disappointment for Duvall's combo, the Troublesome Three, who never played together again after that.

The following year, he again took the recording Challenge, this time at Goldstar Studios in Hollywood, quite a rockabilly haunt. He cut a classic version of "Fools Hall of Fame," a song that was also recorded by Johnny Paycheck and George Jones, as well as the economic "Friday Night on a Dollar Bill." It was during this period that Duvall claims to have sat in on sessions for the instrumental "Tequila!," and claims to have provided some of the vocal "oohs" and "ahs." It was this record that was a huge hit, not Duvall's releases. His career went into a weird stalemate, Challenge not only refusing to promote his records, but barring him from taking other recording offers. He was allowed to sign an acting contract with Republic, but the low-budget studio never actually asked him to appear in a picture. By the early '60s, Duvall and Thompson were still playing regularly, but only regionally. From 1962 through 1969, Duvall worked with computers in Houston and also attended the university there. He named his daughter Leah after a Roy Orbison song. He continued in the computer field, until the mid-'80s with the resurgence in original rockabilly artists. Duvall began performing again in 1985, with a gig in Eindoven, Holland, followed by an extremely successful show at the Mean Fiddler in London. —Eugene Chadbourne

Is You is or is You Ain't? / 1996 / Sundazed ✦✦✦
If borderline "should have made it big" 1950s rockabilly artists seemed to have been a mucho plentiful breed back in that decade, then add Huelyn Duvall's name to the list with an asterisk. He was, as they say, the complete package; the right name, the right look and the right sound. He only had one chart entry with "Little Boy Blue," but his handful of singles for Gene Autry's Challenge label have long been considered some of the shakin' music's finer moments. Everything Duvall recorded during that two-year period of rock & roll activity shows up on this 13-track compilation, including two takes of the unreleased "Fool's Hall of Fame" featuring the Jordanaires on backing vocals. The perfect one to pop in the player after you've spun every version of "Baby, Let's Play House" you own. —Cub Koda

Bob Dylan (Robert Allen Zimmerman)
· ·
b. May 24, 1941, Duluth, MN
Guitar, Harmonica, Songwriter, Vocals, Piano, Keyboards / Political Folk, Rock & Roll, Country-Rock, Singer/Songwriter, Folk-Rock, Album Rock
Bob Dylan's influence on popular music is incalculable. As a songwriter, he pioneered several different schools of pop songwriting, from confessional singer/songwriter to winding, hallucinatory, stream-of-conscious narratives. As a vocalist, he broke down the notions that in order to perform, a singer had to have a conventionally good voice, thereby redefining the role of vocalist in popular music. As a musician, he sparked several genres of pop music, including electrified folk-rock and country-rock. And that just touches on the tip of his achievements. Dylan's force was evident during his height of popularity in the '60s—the Beatles' shift toward introspective songwriting in the mid-'60s never would have happened without him—but his influence echoed throughout several subsequent generations. Many of his songs became popular standards, and his best albums were undisputed classics of the rock & roll canon. Dylan's influence throughout folk music was equally powerful, and he marks a pivotal turning point in its 20th century evolution, signifying when the genre moved away from traditional songs and toward personal songwriting. Even when his sales declined in the '80s and '90s, Dylan's presence was calculable.

For a figure of such substantial influence, Dylan came from humble beginnings. Born in Duluth, MN, Bob Dylan was raised in Hibbing, MN, from the age of six. As a child he learned how to play guitar and harmonica, forming a rock & roll band called the Golden Chords when he was in high-school. Following his graduation in 1959, he began studying art at the University of Minnesota in Minneapolis. While at college, he began performing folk songs at coffeehouses under the name Bob Dylan, taking his last name from the poet Dylan Thomas. Already inspired by Hank Williams and Woody Guthrie, Dylan began listening to blues while at college, and the genre weaved its way into his music. Dylan spent the summer of 1960 in Denver, where he met bluesman Jesse Fuller, the inspiration behind the songwriter's signature harmonica rack and guitar. By the time he returned to Minneapolis in the fall, he had grown substantially as a performer and was determined to become a professional musician.

Dylan made his way to New York City in January of 1961, immediately making a substantial impression on the folk community of Greenwich Village. He began visiting his idol Guthrie in the hospital, where he was slowly dying from Huntington's chorea. Dylan also began performing in coffeehouses, and his rough charisma won him a significant following. In April, he opened for John Lee Hooker at Gerde's Folk City. Five months later, Dylan performed another concert at the venue, which was reviewed positively by Robert Shelton in *The New York Times*. Columbia A&R man John Hammond sought out Dylan on the strength of the review, and signed the songwriter in the fall of 1961. Hammond produced Dylan's eponymous debut album (released in March 1962), a collection of folk and blues standards that boasted only two original songs. Over the course of 1962, Dylan began to write a large batch of original songs, many of which were political protest songs in the vein of his Greenwich contemporaries. These songs were showcased on his second album, *The Freewheelin' Bob Dylan*. Before its release, *Freewheelin'* went through several incarnations. Dylan had recorded a rock & roll single, "Mixed Up Confusion," at the end of 1962, but his manager, Albert Grossman, made sure the record was deleted because he wanted to present Dylan as an acoustic folky. Similarly, several tracks with a full backing band that were recorded for *Freewheelin'* were scrapped before the album's release. Furthermore, several tracks recorded for the album—including "Talking John Birch Society Blues"—were eliminated from the album before its release.

Comprised entirely of original songs, *The Freewheelin' Bob Dylan* made a huge impact in the U.S. folk community, and many performers began covering songs from the album. Of these, the most significant were Peter, Paul & Mary, who made "Blowin' in the Wind" into a huge pop hit in the summer of 1963 and thereby made Bob Dylan into a recognizable household name. On the strength of Peter, Paul & Mary's cover and his opening gigs for popular folky Joan Baez, *Freewheelin'* became a hit in the fall of 1963, climbing to number 23 on the charts. By that point, Baez and Dylan had become romantically involved, and she was beginning to record his songs frequently. Dylan was writing just as fast, and was performing hundreds of concerts a year.

By the time *The Times They Are A-Changin'* was released in early 1964, Dylan's songwriting had developed far beyond that of his New York peers. Heavily inspired by poets like Arthur Rimbaud and John Keats, his writing took on a more literate and evocative quality. Around the same time, he began to expand his musical boundaries, adding more blues and R&B influences to his songs. Released in the summer of 1964, *Another Side of Bob Dylan* made these changes evident. However, Dylan was moving faster than his records could indicate. By the end of 1964, he had ended his romantic relationship with Baez and had begun dating a former model named Sara Lowndes, whom he subsequently married. Simultaneously, he gave the Byrds "Mr. Tambourine Man" to record for their debut album. The Byrds gave the song a ringing, electric arrangement, but by the time the single became a hit, Dylan was already exploring his own brand of folk-rock. Inspired by the British Invasion, particularly the Animals' version of "House of the Rising Sun," Dylan recorded a set of original songs backed by a loud rock & roll band for his next album. While *Bringing It All Back Home* (March 1965) still had a side of acoustic material, it made clear that Dylan had turned his back on folk music. For the folk audience, the true breaking point arrived a few months after the album's release, when he played the Newport Folk Festival supported by the Paul Butterfield Blues Band. The audience greeted him with vicious derision, but he had already been accepted by the growing rock & roll community. Dylan's spring tour of Britain was the basis for D.A. Pennebaker's documentary *Don't Look Back*, a film that captures the songwriter's edgy charisma and charm.

Dylan made his breakthrough to the pop audience in the summer of 1965, when "Like a Rolling Stone" became a number-two hit. Driven by a circular organ riff and a steady beat, the six-minute single broke the barrier of the three-minute pop single. Dylan became the subject of innumerable articles, and his lyrics became the subject of literary analyses across the U.S. and U.K. Well over 100 artists covered his songs between 1964 and 1966; the Byrds and the Turtles, in particular, had big hits with his compositions. *Highway 61 Revisited*, his first full-fledged rock & roll album, became a Top Ten hit shortly after its summer 1965 release. "Positively 4th Street" and "Rainy Day Women #12 & 35" became Top Ten hits in the fall of 1965 and spring of 1966, respectively. Following the May 1966 release of the double-album *Blonde on Blonde*, he had sold over ten-million records around the world.

During the fall of 1965, Dylan hired the Hawks, formerly Ronnie Hawkins' backing group, as his touring band. The Hawks, who changed their name to the Band in 1968, would become Dylan's most famous backing band, primarily because of their intuitive chemistry and "wild, thin mercury sound," but also because of their British tour in the spring of 1966. The tour was the first time Britain had heard the electric Dylan, and their reaction was disagreeable and violent. At the tour's Royal Albert Hall concert, generally acknowledged to have occurred in Manchester, an audience member called Dylan "Judas," inspiring a positively vicious version of "Like a Rolling Stone" from the Band. The performance was immortalized on countless bootleg albums (an official release finally surfaced in 1998) and it indicates the intensity of Dylan in the middle of 1966. He had assumed control of Pennebaker's second Dylan documentary, *Eat the Document*, and was under deadline to complete his book *Tarantula*, as well as record a new record. Following the British tour, he returned to America.

On July 29, 1966, he was injured in a motorcycle accident outside of his home in Woodstock, NY, suffering injuries to his neck vertebrae and a concussion. Details of the accident remain elusive—he was reportedly in critical condition for a week and had amnesia—and some biographers have questioned its severity, but the event was a pivotal

turning point in his career. After the accident, Dylan became a recluse, disappearing into his home in Woodstock and raising his family with his wife, Sara. After a few months, he retreated with the Band to a rented house, subsequently dubbed Big Pink, in West Saugerties to record a number of demos. For several months, Dylan and the Band recorded an enormous amount of material, ranging from old folk, country, and blues songs to newly written originals. The songs indicated that Dylan's songwriting had undergone a metamorphosis, becoming streamlined and more direct. Similarly, his music had changed, owing less to traditional rock & roll, and demonstrating heavy country, blues, and traditional folk influences. None of the Big Pink recordings were intended to be released, but tapes from the sessions were circulated by Dylan's music publisher with the intent of generating cover versions. Copies of these tapes, as well as other songs, were available on illegal bootleg albums by the end of the '60s; it was the first time that bootleg copies of unreleased recordings became widely circulated. Portions of the tapes were officially released in 1975 as the double-album *The Basement Tapes*.

While Dylan was in seclusion, rock & roll had become heavier and artier in the wake of the psychedelic revolution. When Dylan returned with *John Wesley Harding* in December of 1967, its quiet, country ambience was a surprise to the general public, but it was a significant hit, peaking at number two in the U.S. and number one in the U.K. Furthermore, the record arguably became the first significant country-rock record to be released, setting the stage for efforts by the Byrds and the Flying Burrito Brothers later in 1969. Dylan followed his country inclinations on his next album, 1969's *Nashville Skyline*, which was recorded in Nashville with several of the country industry's top session men. While the album was a hit, spawning the Top Ten single "Lay Lady Lay," it was criticized in some quarters for uneven material. The mixed reception was the beginning of a full-blown backlash that arrived with the double-album *Self Portrait*. Released early in June of 1970, the album was a hodgepodge of covers, live tracks, re-interpretations, and new songs greeted with negative reviews from all quarters of the press. Dylan followed the album quickly with *New Morning*, which was hailed as a comeback.

Following the release of *New Morning*, Dylan began to wander restlessly. In 1969 or 1970, he moved back to Greenwich Village, published *Tarantula* for the first time in November of 1970, and performed at the Concert for Bangladesh. During 1972, he began his acting career by playing Alias in Sam Peckinpah's *Pat Garrett and Billy the Kid*, which was released in 1973. He also wrote the soundtrack for the film, which featured "Knockin' on Heaven's Door," his biggest hit since "Lay Lady Lay." The *Pat Garrett* soundtrack was the final record released under his Columbia contract before he moved to David Geffen's fledgling Asylum Records. As retaliation, Columbia assembled *Dylan*, a collection of *Self Portrait* outtakes, for release at the end of 1973. Dylan only recorded two albums—including 1974's *Planet Waves*, coincidentally his first number-one album—before he moved back to Columbia. The Band supported Dylan on *Planet Waves* and its accompanying tour, which became the most successful tour in rock & roll history; it was captured on 1974's double-live album *Before the Flood*.

Dylan's 1974 tour was the beginning of a comeback culminated by 1975's *Blood on the Tracks*. Largely inspired by the disintegration of his marriage, *Blood on the Tracks* was hailed as a return to form by critics and it became his second number-one album. After jamming with folkies in Greenwich Village, Dylan decided to launch a gigantic tour, loosely based on traveling medicine shows. Lining up an extensive list of supporting musicians—including Joan Baez, Joni Mitchell, Rambling Jack Elliott, Arlo Guthrie, Mick Ronson, Roger McGuinn, and poet Allen Ginsberg—Dylan dubbed the tour the Rolling Thunder Revue and set out on the road in the fall of 1975. For the next year, the Rolling Thunder Revue toured on and off, with Dylan filming many of the concerts for a future film. During the tour, *Desire* was released to considerable acclaim and success, spending five weeks on the top of the charts. Throughout the Rolling Thunder Revue, Dylan showcased "Hurricane," a protest song he had written about boxer Rubin Carter, who had been unjustly imprisoned for murder. The live album *Hard Rain* was released at the end of the tour. Dylan released *Renaldo and Clara*, a four-hour film based on the Rolling Thunder tour, to poor reviews in early 1978.

Early in 1978, Dylan set out on another extensive tour, this time backed by a band that resembled a Las Vegas lounge band. The group was featured on the 1978 album *Street Legal* and the 1979 live album *At Budokan*. At the conclusion of the tour in late 1978, Dylan announced that he was a born-again Christian, and he launched a series of Christian albums that following summer with *Slow Train Coming*. Though the reviews were mixed, the album was a success, peaking at number three and going platinum. His supporting tour for *Slow Train Coming* featured only his new religious material, much to the bafflement of his long-term fans. Two other religious albums—*Saved* (1980) and *Shot of Love* (1981)—followed, both to poor reviews. In 1982, Dylan traveled to Israel, sparking rumors that his conversion to Christianity was short-lived. He returned to secular recording with 1983's *Infidels*, which was greeted with favorable reviews.

Dylan returned to performing in 1984, releasing the live album *Real Live* at the end of the year. *Empire Burlesque* followed in 1985, but its odd mix of dance tracks and rock & roll won few fans. However, the five-album/triple-disc retrospective box set *Biograph* appeared that same year to great acclaim. In 1986, Dylan hit the road with Tom Petty & the Heartbreakers for a successful and acclaimed tour, but his album that year, *Knocked Out Loaded*, was received poorly. The following year, he toured with the Grateful Dead as his backing band; two years later, the souvenir album *Dylan & the Dead* appeared. In 1988, Dylan embarked on what became known as "The Never-Ending Tour"—a constant stream of shows that ran on and off into the late '90s. That same year, he released *Down in the Groove*, an album largely comprised of covers. The Never-Ending Tour received far stronger reviews than *Down in the Groove*, but 1989's *Oh Mercy* was his most acclaimed album since 1974's *Blood on the Tracks*. However, his 1990 follow-up, *Under the Red Sky*, was received poorly, especially when compared to the enthusiastic reception for the 1991 box set *The Bootleg Series, Vols. 1-3 (Rare & Unreleased)*, a collection of previously unreleased outtakes and rarities.

For the remainder of the '90s, Dylan divided his time between live concerts and painting. In 1992, he returned to recording with *Good As I Been to You*, an acoustic collection of traditional folk songs. It was followed in 1993 by another folk album, *World Gone Wrong*, which won the Grammy for Best Traditional Folk Album. After the release of

World Gone Wrong, Dylan released a greatest-hits album and a live record. Dylan released *Time Out of Mind*, his first album of original material in seven years, in the fall of 1997. *Time Out of Mind* received his strongest reviews in years and unexpectedly debuted in the Top Ten. Its success sparked a revival of interest in Dylan—he appeared on the cover of *Newsweek* and his concerts became sell-outs. Early in 1998, *Time Out of Mind* received three Grammy Awards—Album of the Year, Best Contemporary Folk Album and Best Male Rock Vocal. —*Stephen Thomas Erlewine*

★ **Bob Dylan's Greatest Hits** / Mar. 27, 1967 / Columbia ✦✦✦✦✦
Arriving in 1967, *Greatest Hits* does an excellent job of summarizing Dylan's best-known songs from his first seven albums. At just ten songs, it's a little brief, and the song selection may be a little predictable, but that's actually not a bad thing, since this provides a nice sampler for the curious and casual listener, as it boasts standards from "Blowin' in the Wind" to "Like a Rolling Stone." And, for collectors, the brilliant non-LP single "Positively Fourth Street" was added, which provided reason enough for anybody that already owned the original records to pick this up. This has since been supplanted by more exhaustive collections, but as a sampler of Dylan at his absolute peak, this is first-rate. —*Stephen Thomas Erlewine*

☆ **John Wesley Harding** / Dec. 27, 1967 / Columbia ✦✦✦✦
Bob Dylan returned from exile with *John Wesley Harding*, a quiet, country-tinged album that split dramatically from his previous three albums. A calm, reflective album, *John Wesley Harding* strips away all of the wilder tendencies of Dylan's rock albums—even the then-unreleased *Basement Tapes* he made the previous year—but it isn't a return to his folk roots. If anything, the album is his first serious foray into country, but only a handful of songs, such as "I'll Be Your Baby Tonight," are straight country songs. Instead, *John Wesley Harding* is informed by the rustic sound of country, as well as many rural myths, with seemingly simple songs like "All Along the Watchtower," "I Dreamed I Saw St. Augustine," and "The Wicked Messenger" revealing several layers of meaning with repeated plays. Although the lyrics are somewhat enigmatic, the music is simple, direct, and melodic, providing a touchstone for the country-rock revolution that swept through rock in the late '60s. —*Stephen Thomas Erlewine*

☆ **Nashville Skyline** / Apr. 9, 1969 / Columbia ✦✦✦✦✦
John Wesley Harding suggested country with its textures and structures, but *Nashville Skyline* was a full-fledged country album, complete with steel guitars and simple, direct songs. It's a warm, friendly album, particularly since Dylan is singing in a previously unheard gentle croon—the sound of his voice is so different it may be disarming upon first listen, but it suits the songs. While there are a handful of lightweight numbers on the record, at its core are several excellent songs—"Lay Lady Lay," "To Be Alone With You," "I Threw It All Away," "Tonight I'll Be Staying Here With You," as well as a duet with Johnny Cash on "Girl from the North Country"—that have become country-rock standards. And there's no discounting that *Nashville Skyline*, arriving in the spring of 1969, established country-rock as a vital force in pop music, as well as a commercially viable genre. —*Stephen Thomas Erlewine*

New Morning / Oct. 21, 1970 / Columbia ✦✦✦✦✦
Dylan rushed out *New Morning* in the wake of the commercial and critical disaster *Self Portrait*, and the difference between the two albums suggests that its legendary failed predecessor was intentionally flawed. *New Morning* expands on the laid-back country-rock of *John Wesley Harding* and *Nashville Skyline* by adding a more pronounced rock & roll edge. While there are only a couple of genuine classics on the record ("If Not for You," "One More Weekend"), the overall quality is quite high, and many of the songs explore idiosyncratic routes Dylan had previously left untouched, whether it's the jazzy experiments ("Sign on the Window" and "Winterlude," the rambling spoken-word piece "If Dogs Run Free" or the Elvis parable "Went to See the Gypsy." Such offbeat songs make *New Morning* a charming, endearing record. —*Stephen Thomas Erlewine*

☆ **Bob Dylan's Greatest Hits, Vol. 2** / Nov. 17, 1971 / Columbia ✦✦✦✦✦
Where Dylan's first *Greatest Hits* took its title literally, *Greatest Hits, Vol. 2* is a greatest-hits album only in the loosest sense of the term. While the double album does contain several genuine hits—"Lay Lady Lay," "Tonight I'll Be Staying Here With You," the non-LP "Watching the River Flow"—it is largely comprised of album tracks which became classics, either through Dylan's own version or through covers. These include "Don't Think Twice, It's All Right," "All I Really Want to Do," "My Back Pages," "Maggie's Farm," "She Belongs to Me," "If Not for You," and "Just Like Tom Thumb's Blues," among many others. There are also a number of rarities scattered throughout the 21 songs, including a live version of "Tomorrow Is a Long Time" from 1963, a live take of "The Mighty Quinn

(Quinn, the Eskimo)," and the *Basement Tapes* songs "I Shall Be Released," "Down in the Flood," and "You Ain't Goin' Nowhere." While some of the cuts may not be immediately familiar to some listeners, *Greatest Hits, Vol. 2* in many ways is a more accurate picture of the depth and breadth of Dylan's talents, making it an excellent introduction. And it's not just for casual fans, because the rarities and sequencing are revealing for even devoted Dylan fans. [*Greatest Hits, Vol. 2* was reissued with 24-bit remastering in the summer of 1999.] —*Stephen Thomas Erlewine*

☆ **The Basement Tapes** / Jun. 26, 1975 / Columbia ✦✦✦✦✦
The official release of *The Basement Tapes*—which were first heard on a 1968 bootleg called *The Great White Wonder*—plays with history somewhat, as Robbie Robertson overemphasizes the Band's status in the sessions, making them out to be equally active to Dylan, adding in demos not cut at the sessions and overdubbing their recordings to flesh them out. As many bootlegs (most notably the complete five-disc series) reveal, this isn't entirely true and that the Band were nowhere near as active as Dylan, but that ultimately is a bit like nitpicking, since the music here (including the Band's) is astonishingly good. The party line on *The Basement Tapes* is that it is Americana, as Dylan and the Band pick up the weirdness inherent in old folk, country, and blues tunes, but it transcends mere historical arcana by being lively, humorous, full-bodied performances. Dylan never sounded as loose, nor was he ever as funny as he is here, and this positively revels in its weird, wild character. For all the apparent antecedents—and the allusions are sly and obvious in equal measures—this is truly Dylan's show, as he majestically evokes old myths and creates new ones, resulting in a crazy quilt of blues, humor, folk, tall tales, inside jokes, and rock. The Band pretty much pick up where Dylan left off, even singing a couple of his tunes, but they play it a little straight, on both their rockers and ballads. Not a bad thing at all, since this actually winds up providing context for the wild, mercurial brilliance of Dylan's work—and, taken together, the results (especially in this judiciously compiled form; expert song selection, even if there's a bit too much Band) rank among the greatest American music ever made. —*Stephen Thomas Erlewine*

☆ **Biograph** / Oct. 28, 1985 / Columbia ✦✦✦✦✦
Historically, *Biograph* is significant not for what it did for Dylan's career, but for establishing the box set, complete with hits and rarities, as a viable part of rock history. Following *Biograph*, multi-disc box sets for veteran rockers became accepted and almost the norm, but that doesn't discount this set's strengths as a summary of Dylan's career, using the familiar and the rare to draw a fully rounded portrait of his strengths as a songwriter, musician, and record-maker in a way that conventional choices alone couldn't achieve. Certainly, the chief attraction of this set, even years after its initial release, is its smattering of rarities that aren't just rare, but revealing—ranging from forgotten rock B-sides and singles to demos, alternate takes, and unreleased songs that rival official releases. But *Biograph* is really remarkable for weaving these songs into a fabric that reveals the true trajectory of Dylan's career, offering as much to the curious as it does to the dedicated. That sets a standard for box sets that have rarely been matched, making *Biograph* all the more impressive in retrospect. [In 1997, Columbia Records issued an upgraded, reconfigured version of *Biograph*, with a new catalog number (65298), a lower list price, and with its packaging and booklet reduced from an LP-size box to a CD-size slipcase. The original 1985 set in the large-size box, which marked the first time that the label had gone back to original first-generation tapes on a Dylan CD, was pretty impressive; but the 1997 CD-size box version, remastered in Sony's Super Bit Mapping process, is a significant improvement over that, and is to be preferred.] —*Stephen Thomas Erlewine*

Bootleg Series, Vols. 1-3 (Rare & Unreleased) 1961–1991 / Mar. 26, 1991 / Columbia ✦✦✦✦✦
This three-disc box set is what Dylanphiles have been waiting for, sitting patiently for years, even decades. And, even after its 1991 release, it retains the feeling of being a special, shared secret among the hardcore, since—no matter the acclaim—it's the kind of record that only the hardcore will seek out. Of course, the great irony is that even casual Dylan fans will find much to treasure in this three-disc set of unreleased material. They'll find songs as good as anything that made the records (sometimes surpassing the official releases, especially on the last disc), plus alternate versions (including original versions of songs on *Blood on the Tracks*) and long-fabled songs, from the incomplete "She's Your Lover Now" to songs cut from *The Freewheelin' Bob Dylan*. This doesn't just function as an alternate history of Dylan, but as an expansion of Dylan's history, enriching what is already known about the greatest songwriter of his era—after all, every song here would qualify as the best song on anybody else's album. And that's no exaggeration. —*Stephen Thomas Erlewine*

The Eagles

f. 1971, Los Angeles, CA, **db.** 1982

Group / Country-Rock, Soft Rock, Folk-Rock, Pop/Rock, Album Rock

With five number-one singles and four number-one albums, the Eagles were among the most successful recording artists of the 1970s; at the end of the 20th century, two of those albums, *Eagles: Their Greatest Hits 1971-1975* and *Hotel California*, ranked among the ten best-selling albums ever, according to the certifications of the Record Industry Association of America. Though most of its members came from outside California, the group was closely identified with a country- and folk-tinged sound that initially found favor in and around Los Angeles in the late '60s, as played by such bands as the Flying Burrito Brothers and Poco, both of which contributed members to the Eagles. But the band also drew upon traditional rock & roll styles and, in their later work, helped define the broadly popular rock sound eventually referred to as classic rock. That helped the Eagles to achieve a perennial appeal among generations of music fans who continued to buy their records many years after they had split up, which inspired the reunion they mounted in the mid-'90s.

The band was formed by four Los Angeles-based musicians who had come to the West Coast from other parts of the U.S. Singer/bassist Randy Meisner (born in Scottsbluff, NE, on March 8, 1946) moved to L.A. in 1964 as part of a band originally called the Soul Survivors (not to be confused with the East Coast-based Soul Survivors, who scored a Top Five hit with "Expressway to Your Heart" in 1967) and later renamed the Poor. In 1968, he was a founding member of Poco, but left the band prior to the release of its debut album, joining the Stone Canyon Band, the backup group for Rick Nelson. Singer/guitarist/banjoist/mandolinist Bernie Leadon (born in Minneapolis, MN, on July 19, 1947) arrived in L.A. in 1967 as a member of Hearts & Flowers before joining Dillard & Clark and then the Flying Burrito Brothers. Singer/drummer Don Henley (born in Gilmer, TX, on July 22, 1947) moved to L.A. in June 1970 with his band Shiloh, which made one self-titled album for Amos Records before breaking up. Glenn Frey (born in Detroit, MI, on November 6, 1948) performed in his hometown and served as a backup musician to Bob Seger before moving to L.A. in the summer of 1968. He formed the duo Longbranch Pennywhistle with J.D. Souther, and they signed to Amos Records, which released their self-titled album in 1969.

In the spring of 1971, Frey and Henley were hired to play in Linda Ronstadt's backup band. Meisner and Leadon also played backup to Ronstadt during her summer tour, though the four only did one gig together, at Disneyland in July. They did, however, all appear on Ronstadt's next album, *Linda Ronstadt*, released in early 1972. In September 1971, Frey, Henley, Leadon, and Meisner signed with manager David Geffen, agreeing to record for his soon-to-be-launched label, Asylum Records; soon after, they adopted the name the Eagles. In February 1972, they flew to England and spent two weeks recording their debut album, *The Eagles*, with producer Glyn Johns. It was released in June, reaching the Top 20 and going gold in a little over a year and a half, following the release of two Top Ten hits, "Take It Easy" and "Witchy Woman," and one Top 20 hit, "Peaceful Easy Feeling."

The Eagles toured as an opening act throughout 1972 and into early 1973, when they returned to England and Glyn Johns to record their second LP, *Desperado*, a concept album about outlaws. Released in April 1973, it reached the Top 40 and went gold in a little less than a year and a half, spawning the Top 40 single "Tequila Sunrise." The title track, though never released as a single, became one of the band's better-known songs and was included on its first hits collection. After touring to support *Desperado*, the Eagles again convened a recording session with Glyn Johns for their third album. But their desire to make harder rock music clashed with Johns' sense of them as a country-rock band, and they split from the producer after recording two tracks, "You Never Cry Like a Lover" and "The Best of My Love." After an early 1974 tour opened by singer/guitarist Joe Walsh, they hired Walsh's producer, Bill Szymczyk, who handled the rest of *On the Border*. Szymczyk brought in a session guitarist, Don Felder (born in Gainesville, FL, on September 21, 1947), an old friend of Bernie Leadon's who so impressed the rest of the band that he was recruited to join the group.

On the Border was released in March 1974. It went gold and reached the Top Ten in June, the Eagles' fastest selling album yet. The first single, "Already Gone," reached the Top 20 the same month. But the most successful song on the LP, the one that broke them through to a much larger audience, was "The Best of My Love," released as a single in November. It hit number one on the easy listening charts in February 1975 and topped the pop charts a month later. The Eagles' fourth album, *One of These Nights*, was an out-of-the-box smash. Released in June 1975, it went gold the same month and hit number one in July. It featured three singles that hit the Top Five: the chart-topping title song, "Lyin' Eyes," and "Take It to the Limit." "Lyin' Eyes" won the 1975 Grammy Award for Best Pop Vocal Performance by a Duo, Group, or Chorus, and the Eagles also earned Grammy nominations for Album of the Year (*One of These Nights*) and Record of the Year ("Lyin' Eyes"). The group went on a headlining world tour, beginning with the U.S. and Europe. But on December 20, 1975, it was announced that Bernie Leadon had quit the band. Joe Walsh (born in Wichita, KS, on November 20, 1947) was brought in as his

replacement. He immediately joined the tour, which continued to the Far East in early 1976. The Eagles' extensive touring kept them out of the studio, and with no immediate plans for a new album, they agreed to the release of a compilation, *Eagles: Their Greatest Hits 1971-1975*, in February 1976. The first album certified platinum for sales of one-million copies, it topped the charts and became a phenomenal success, eventually selling upwards of 25,000,000 copies and dueling with Michael Jackson's *Thriller* for the title of the best-selling album of all time in the U.S.

It took the Eagles 18 months to follow *One of These Nights* with their fifth album, *Hotel California*. Released in December 1976, it was certified platinum in one week, hit number one in January 1977, and eventually sold over 10,000,000 copies. The singles "New Kid in Town" and "Hotel California" hit number one, and "Life in the Fast Lane" made the Top 20. "Hotel California" won the 1977 Grammy for Record of the Year and was nominated for Song of the Year; the album was nominated for Album of the Year and for Best Pop Vocal Performance by a Duo, Group, or Chorus. The Eagles embarked on a world tour in March 1977 that began with a month in the U.S., followed by a month in Europe and the Far East, then returned to the U.S. in May for stadium dates. At the end of the tour in September, Randy Meisner left the band; he was replaced by Timothy B. Schmit (born in Sacramento, CA, November 20, 1947), formerly of Poco, in which he also had replaced Meisner.

The Eagles began working on a new album in March 1978 and took nearly a year and a half to complete it. *The Long Run* was released in September 1979. It hit number one and was certified platinum after four months, eventually earning multi-platinum certifications. "Heartache Tonight," its leadoff single, hit number one, and "I Can't Tell You Why" and "The Long Run" became Top Ten hits. "Heartache Tonight" won the 1979 Grammy for Best Rock Performance by a Duo or Group with Vocal. The Eagles toured the U.S. in 1980, and at a week-long series of shows at the Santa Monica Civic Auditorium, they recorded *Eagles Live*. (Also included were some tracks recorded in 1976.) Released in November 1980, the double-LP (since reissued as a single CD) reached the Top Five and went multi-platinum, with the single "Seven Bridges Road" reaching the Top 40.

The Eagles were inactive after the end of their 1980 tour, but their breakup was not officially announced until May 1982. All five released solo recordings. (Walsh, of course, maintained a solo career before, during, and after the Eagles.) During the rest of the 1980s, the bandmembers received several lucrative offers to reunite, but they declined. In 1990, Frey and Henley began writing together again, and they performed along with Schmit and Walsh at benefit concerts that spring. A full-scale reunion was rumored, but did not take place. Four years later, however, the Eagles did reunite. In the spring of 1994, they taped an MTV concert special and then launched a tour that ended up running through August 1996. The MTV show aired in October, followed in November by an audio version of it, the album *Hell Freezes Over*, which topped the charts and became a multi-million seller, spawning the Top 40 pop hit "Get Over It" and the number-one adult contemporary hit "Love Will Keep Us Alive." The Eagles next appeared together in January 1998 for their induction into the Rock & Roll Hall of Fame, when the five present members performed alongside past members Leadon and Meisner. On December 31, 1999, they played a millennium concert at the Staples Center in Los Angeles that was recorded and included on the box set retrospective *Selected Works 1972-1999* in November 2000. — *William Ruhlmann*

The Eagles / Jun. 1, 1972 / Asylum ✦✦✦

Balance is the key element of the Eagles' self-titled debut album, a collection that contains elements of rock & roll, folk, and country, overlaid by vocal harmonies alternately suggestive of doo wop, the Beach Boys, and the Everly Brothers. If the group kicks up its heels on rockers like "Chug All Night," "Nightingale," and "Tryin'," it is equally convincing on ballads like "Most of Us Are Sad" and "Train Leaves Here This Morning." The album is also balanced among its members, who trade off on lead vocal chores and divide the songwriting such that Glenn Frey, Bernie Leadon, and Randy Meisner all get three writing or co-writing credit and two lead vocals, falls a little behind, while Jackson Browne, Gene Clark, and Jack Tempchin also figure in the writing credits.) The album's overall balance is worth keeping in mind because it produced three Top 40 hit singles (all of which turned up on the massively popular *Eagles: Their Greatest Hits 1971-1975*) that do not reflect that balance. "Take It Easy" and "Peaceful Easy Feeling" are similar-sounding midtempo folk-rock tunes sung by Frey that express the same sort of laid-back philosophy, as indicated by the word "easy" in both titles, while "Witchy Woman," a Henley vocal and co-composition, initiates the band's career-long examination of supernaturally evil females. These are the songs one remembers from *Eagles*, and they look forward to the eventual dominance of the band by Frey and Henley. But the complete album from which they come belongs as much to Leadon's country-steeped playing and singing and to Meisner's melodic rock & roll feel, which, on the release date, made it seem a more varied and consistent effort than it did later, when the singles had become overly familiar. — *William Ruhlmann*

Desperado / Apr. 17, 1973 / Asylum ✦✦✦
If Don Henley was the sole member of the Eagles under-represented on their debut album, *Eagles*, with only two lead vocals and one co-songwriting credit, he made up for it on their follow-up, the "concept" album *Desperado*. The concept had to do with Old West outlaws, but it had no specific narrative. On *Eagles*, the group had already begun to marry itself to a Southwest sound and lyrical references, from the Indian-style introduction of "Witchy Woman" to the Winslow, AZ, address in "Take It Easy." All of this became more overt on *Desperado*, and it may be that Henley, who hailed from northeast Texas, had the greatest affinity for the subject matter. In any case, he had co-writing credits on eight of the 11 selections and sang such key tracks as "Doolin-Dalton" and the title song. What would become recognizable as Henley's lyrical touch was apparent on those songs, which bore a serious, world-weary tone. Henley had begun co-writing with Glenn Frey, and they contributed the album's strongest material, which included the first single, "Tequila Sunrise," and "Desperado" (strangely never released as a single). But where *Eagles* seemed deliberately to balance the band's many musical styles and the talents of the band's members, *Desperado*, despite its overarching theme, often seemed a collection of disparate tracks—"Out of Control" was a raucous rocker, while "Desperado" was a painfully slow ballad backed by strings—with other bandmembers' contributions tacked on rather than integrated. Randy Meisner was down to two co-writing credits and one lead vocal ("Certain Kind of Fool"), while Bernie Leadon's two songs, "Twenty-One" and "Bitter Creek," seemed to come from a different record entirely. The result was an album that was simultaneously more ambitious and serious-minded than its predecessor and also slighter and less consistent. *—William Ruhlmann*

On the Border / Mar. 22, 1974 / Asylum ✦✦✦
The Eagles began recording their third album in England with producer Glyn Johns, as they had their first two albums, but abandoned the sessions after completing two acceptable tracks. Johns, it is said, tended to emphasize the group's country elements and its harmonies, while the band, in particular Glenn Frey and Don Henley, wanted to take more of a hard rock direction. They reconvened with a new producer, Bill Szymczyk, who had produced artists like B. B. King and, more significantly, Joe Walsh. But the resulting album is not an outright rock effort by any means. Certainly, Frey and Henley got what they wanted with "Already Gone," the leadoff track, which introduces new bandmember Don Felder as one part of the twin guitar solo that recalls the Allman Brothers Band; "James Dean," a rock & roll song on the order of "Your Mama Don't Dance"; and "Good Day in Hell," which is strongly reminiscent of Joe Walsh songs like "Rocky Mountain Way." But the album also features the usual mixture of styles typical of an Eagles album. For example, "Midnight Flyer," sung by Randy Meisner, is modern bluegrass; "My Man" is Bernie Leadon's country-rock tribute to the recently deceased Gram Parsons; and "Ol' 55" is one of the group's well-done covers of a tune by a singer/songwriter labelmate, in this case Tom Waits. The title track, meanwhile, points the band in a new R&B direction that was later pursued more fully. Like most successful groups, the Eagles combined many different elements, and their third album, which looked back to their earlier work and anticipated their later work, was a transitional effort that combined even more styles than most of their records did. *—William Ruhlmann*

One of These Nights / Jun. 10, 1975 / Asylum ✦✦✦✦
The Eagles recorded their albums relatively quickly in their first years of existence, their albums succeeding each other by less than a year. *One of These Nights*, their fourth album, was released in June 1975, more than 14 months after its predecessor. Anticipation had been heightened by the belated chart-topping success of the third album's "The Best of My Love"; taking a little more time, the band generated more original material, and that material was more polished. More than ever, the Eagles seemed to be a vehicle for Don Henley (six co-writing credits) and Glenn Frey (five), but at the same time Randy Meisner was more audible than ever, his two lead vocals including one of the album's three hit singles, "Take It to the Limit," and Bernie Leadon had two showcases, among them the cosmic-cowboy instrumental "Journey of the Sorcerer" (later used as the theme music for the British television series *The Hitchhiker's Guide to the Galaxy*). Nevertheless, it was the team of Henley and Frey that stood out, starting with the title track, a number one single, which had more of an R&B—even disco—sound than anything the band had attempted previously, and continuing through the ersatz Western swing of "Hollywood Waltz" to "Lyin' Eyes," one of Frey's patented folk-rock shuffles, which became another major hit. *One of These Nights* was the culmination of the blend of rock, country, and folk styles the Eagles had been making since their start; there wasn't much that was new, just the same sorts of things done better than they had been before. In particular, a lyrical stance—knowing and disillusioned, but desperately hopeful—had evolved, and the musical arrangements were tighter and more purposeful. The result was the Eagles' best-realized and most popular album so far. *—William Ruhlmann*

★ **Their Greatest Hits (1971–1975)** / Feb. 17, 1976 / Asylum ✦✦✦✦✦
On their first four albums, the Eagles were at pains to demonstrate that they were a group of at least near-equals, each getting a share of the songwriting credits and lead vocals. But this compilation drawn from those albums, comprising the group's nine Top 40 hits plus "Desperado," demonstrates that this evenhandedness did not extend to singles—as far as those go, the Eagles belong to Glenn Frey and Don Henley. The tunes are melodic, and the arrangements—full of strummed acoustic guitars over a rock rhythm section often playing a shuffle beat, topped by tenor-dominated harmonies—are immediately engaging. There is also a lyrical consistency to the songs, which often concern romantic uncertainties in an atmosphere soaked in intoxicants. The narrators of the songs usually seem exhausted, if not satiated, and the loping rhythms are appropriate to these impressions. All of which means that, unlike the albums from which they come, these songs make up a collection consistent in mood and identity, which may help explain why *Eagles: Their Greatest Hits 1971-1975* works so much better than the band's previous discs and practically makes them redundant. No wonder it was such a big hit out of the box, topping the charts and becoming the first album ever certified platinum. Still, there must be more to it, since the album wasn't just a big hit, but one of the biggest ever, becoming one of the very few discs to cross the threshold of 20 million copies and competing for the title of best-selling album of all time. There may be no explaining that, really, except to note that this was the pervasive music of the first half of the 1970s, and somehow it never went away. *—William Ruhlmann*

☆ **Hotel California** / Dec. 8, 1976 / Asylum ✦✦✦✦✦
The Eagles took 18 months between their fourth and fifth albums, reportedly spending eight months in the studio recording *Hotel California*. The album was also their first to be made without Bernie Leadon, who had given the band much of its country flavor, and with rock guitarist Joe Walsh. As a result, the album marks a major leap for the Eagles from their earlier work, as well as a stylistic shift toward mainstream rock. An even more important aspect, however, is the emergence of Don Henley as the band's dominant voice, both as a singer and a lyricist. On the six songs to which he contributes, Henley sketches a thematic statement that begins by using California as a metaphor for a dark, surreal world of dissipation; comments on the ephemeral nature of success and the attraction of excess; branches out into romantic disappointment; and finally sketches a broad, pessimistic history of America that borders on nihilism. Of course, the lyrics kick in some time after one has appreciated the album's music, which marks a peak in the Eagles' playing. Early on, the group couldn't rock convincingly, but the rhythm section of Henley and Meisner has finally solidified, and the electric guitar work of Don Felder and Joe Walsh has arena-rock heft. In the early part of their career, the Eagles never seemed to get a sound big enough for their ambitions; after changes in producer and personnel, as well as a noticeable growth in creativity, *Hotel California* unveiled what seemed almost like a whole new band. It was a band that could be bombastic, but also one that made music worthy of the later tag of "classic rock," music appropriate for the arenas and stadiums the band was playing. The result was the Eagles' biggest-selling regular album release, and one of the most successful rock albums ever. *—William Ruhlmann*

The Long Run / Sep. 24, 1979 / Asylum ✦✦✦
Three years in the making (which was considered an eternity in the '70s), the Eagles' follow-up to the massively successful, critically acclaimed *Hotel California* was a major disappointment, even though it sold several million copies and threw off three hit singles. Those singles, in fact, provide some insight into the record. "Heartache Tonight" was an old-fashioned rock & roll song sung by Glenn Frey, while "I Can't Tell You Why" was a delicate ballad by Timothy B. Schmit, the band's newest member. Only "The Long Run," a conventional pop/rock tune with a Stax Records R&B flavor, bore the stamp and vocal signature of Don Henley, who had largely taken the reins of the band on *Hotel California*. Henley also dominated *The Long Run*, getting co-writing credits on nine of the ten songs, singing five lead vocals, and sharing another two with Frey. This time around, however, Henley's contributions were for the most part painfully slight. Only "The Long Run" and the regret-filled closing song, "The Sad Café," showed any of his usual craftsmanship. The album was dominated by second-rank songs like "The Disco Strangler," "King of Hollywood," and "Teenage Jail" that sounded like they couldn't have taken three hours much less three years to come up with. (Joe Walsh's "In the City" was up to his usual standard, but it may not even have been an Eagles recording, having appeared months earlier on the soundtrack to *The Warriors* where it was credited as a Walsh solo track.) Amazingly, *The Long Run* reportedly was planned as a double album before being truncated to a single disc. If these were the keepers, what can the rejects have sounded like? *—William Ruhlmann*

Eagles Live / Nov. 7, 1980 / Asylum ✦✦✦
Although *Eagles Live* includes four tracks recorded in the fall of 1976 (thus allowing for the inclusion of departed singer Randy Meisner on "Take It to the Limit"), the bulk of the album comes from the end of the Eagles' 1980 tour, just before they broke up, and it reflects their late concert repertoire, largely drawn from *Hotel California* and *The Long Run*. The occasional early song such as "Desperado" and "Take It Easy" turn up, but many of the major hits from the middle of the band's career—"The Best of My Love," "One of These Nights," "Lyin' Eyes"—are missing, replaced by such curiosities as two extended selections from Joe Walsh's solo career, "Life's Been Good" and "All Night Long." At least Walsh introduces some live variations to his material; the rest of the Eagles seem determined to recreate the studio versions of their songs in concert, which may work for them live but almost makes a live recording superfluous. The previously unrecorded rendition of Steve Young's "Seven Bridges Road" is welcome, and the album would have benefited from more surprises as well as a livelier approach to a live recording. *—William Ruhlmann*

The Eagles Greatest Hits, Vol. 2 / Oct. 1982 / Asylum ✦✦✦✦
With the Eagles having officially disbanded in May 1982, leaving behind eight Top 40 hits that followed the release of the spectacularly successful *Eagles: Their Greatest Hits (1971-1975)*, Asylum Records naturally compiled a second hits collection for fall 1982 release. Seven of those hits were included (the exception being the seasonal "Please Come Home for Christmas"), along with three LP tracks, one each from *One of These Nights*, *Hotel California*, and *The Long Run*. Disdained by longtime fans and by the Eagles themselves, the collection was perfect for listeners who knew the band through number-one radio hits like "New Kid in Town," "Hotel California," and "Heartache Tonight." It also spared them having to buy mediocre albums like *The Long Run* and *Eagles Live* just to have copies of the best-known songs from those releases. No wonder, then, that over the years *Eagles Greatest Hits, Vol. 2* achieved multi-platinum status. *—William Ruhlmann*

Hell Freezes Over / Nov. 8, 1994 / Geffen ✦✦✦

The Eagles' first newly recorded album in 14 years gets off to a good start with the rocker "Get Over It," a timely piece of advice about accepting responsibility, followed by the tender ballad "Love Will Keep Us Alive," the country-styled "The Girl From Yesterday," and "Learn to Be Still," one of Don Henley's more thoughtful statements. Unfortunately, that's it. *Hell Freezes Over* contains an EP's worth of new material followed by a live album. The Eagles, known for meticulously recreating their studio recordings in concert, nevertheless released *Eagles Live* in 1980. Six songs from that set reappear here, and only one is in a noticeably different arrangement, "Hotel California," which gets an acoustic treatment. As was true on *Eagles Live*, the group remains most interested in their later material, redoing five songs from the *Hotel California* LP and two from its follow-up, *The Long Run*, but finding space for only three songs from their early days, "Tequila Sunrise," "Take It Easy," and "Desperado," the last two of which were also on *Eagles Live*. As such, *Hell Freezes Over* is hard to justify as anything other than a souvenir for the Eagles' reunion tour. That, however, did not keep it from topping the charts and selling in the millions. *—William Ruhlmann*

Selected Works: 1972-1999 / Nov. 14, 2000 / Elektra ✦✦✦✦

The relative sonic neglect suffered by the Eagles' catalog was the fault of the band's consistent success—with the original albums and hits collections still selling year after year, why bother to upgrade? Finally, however, longtime Eagles producer Bill Szymczyk remastered their albums in 1999, and the band put together a box set. Including most of their hits (the exception is "Seven Bridges Road") and lots of album tracks, the four CD set regroups the Eagles' material into three categories: "The Early Days," which consists of 13 tracks from their first four albums; "The Ballads"; and "The Fast Lane," i.e., rhythm songs. The fourth disc is drawn from their millennium concert at the Staples Center in Los Angeles. While their early albums balanced the contributions of their members, "The Early Days" is dominated by Glenn Frey and Don Henley; that means a few worthy efforts are missing, but the selection is generally good. "The Ballads" is a straightforward collection of popular slow songs. Along with their more uptempo hits, "The Fast Lane" contains what little unreleased material there is, but anyone hoping for greatness is going to be disappointed. The Eagles have gone out of their way in "The Millennium Concert" to perform songs out of their usual repertoire, including several solo hits and both sides of their 1978 seasonal single, "Please Come Home for Christmas" and "Funky New Year." Much of this is minor or atypical material, but at least the unusually animated bandmembers were trying (though it sounds like there was plenty of studio overdubbing). The overall result is a nearly four-hour collection that is something of a hodgepodge. There are enough rarities to bait the hook for hardcore Eagles fans, but not really satisfy them, and casual fans will probably be better off with the two single-disc hits collections. *—William Ruhlmann*

Fred Eaglesmith

b. Ontario, Canada

Vocals / Singer/Songwriter, Country-Folk, Americana

Country-folksinger/songwriter Fred J. Eaglesmith was one of nine children born to a farming family in rural southern Ontario. Often employing his difficult upbringing as raw material for his heartland narratives, he issued his self-titled debut LP in 1980. He recorded infrequently throughout the remainder of the decade, releasing only two more albums, *The Boy That Just Went Wrong* and *Indiana Road*. However, Eaglesmith gradually became an underground favorite in his native Canada, thanks largely to a relentless touring schedule in tandem with bassist Ralph Schipper and mandolinist Willie P. Bennett. In 1991, he released the double live collection *There Ain't No Easy Road*, followed two years later by *Things Is Changin'*. Another live set, *Paradise Motel*, appeared in 1994, and in 1995 Eaglesmith returned with *Drive-In Movie*. *50-Odd Dollars* was released in 1999. The double-disc *Live: Ralph's Last Show* was issued in Spring 2001. *—Jason Ankeny*

From the Paradise Motel / Oct. 1995 / Barbed Wire ✦✦✦

Drive-In Movie / 1996 / Vertical ✦✦✦✦✦

It's no big surprise that the majority of Canadian songwriters don't get their due in the U.S., but listening to *Drive-In Movie* from Ontario native Fred Eaglesmith, you have to wonder just how much we're missing. Eaglesmith's vivid lyrics, simple arrangements, and plaintive but sturdy voice echo the rural landscape and the wide, clear, Northern skies he grew up with. In the tradition of Texas songwriters such as Guy Clark and Robert Earl Keen—who evoke images of their home state with masterful clarity—he sings with the honest and sometimes mournful tone of a man who recognizes that the lifestyle he grew up with and loved is now drifting into the past. *—Kurt Wolff*

● **Lipstick, Lies & Gasoline** / Oct. 21, 1997 / Razor & Tie ✦✦✦✦✦

Eaglesmith strips the sound down for this one, building a lot out of relentless rhythm tracks that beat at the frontal lobes until things give way. Eaglesmith's songs have an intimate relationship with force and fury, all carried through in the arrangement and delivery, providing a sense of menace to each tune. This is album noir from end to end. Great stuff. *—Steven McDonald*

50-Odd Dollars / Jun. 15, 1999 / Razor & Tie ✦✦✦

Anyone who's come to know Fred Eaglesmith as one of the most brilliant folk-rock songwriters of the '90s can't help but be disappointed by *50-Odd Dollars'* middle-of-the-road country-rock crunch. Then again, it depends on what you like to hear. Fans of his trailer-trash tales of fast trains and drunken nights will probably enjoy this album's loud guitars and pounding beat, whereas folks who live for his wistful early work will be disappointed in its lack of clemency. The lone ballad flits by so unremarkably that it feels like a weak link, which is sad because Eaglesmith's sentimental poetry, like Dylan's, has always been a strong anchor for his records and the perfect foil for his folky comedy. Without it, songs like "Mighty Big Car" just sound tired. *—Jim Smith*

Live: Ralph's Last Show / May 8, 2001 / Signature ✦✦✦

Fred Eaglesmith may sound like another hardened Texas singer/songwriter, but he originally hails from Ontario, Canada. *Ralph's Last Show* finds him performing a live, two-disc set, featuring both old and new material, in Santa Cruz, CA. Things get started with "Freight Train" and "105," two hard-driving acoustic numbers, featuring Eaglesmith's rough-hewed vocals and down-to-earth lyrics. The poignant "Alcohol and Pills" takes a straight-ahead look at the substance abuse of performers like Hank Williams and Elvis Presley. The song wryly notes, "Fame doesn't take away the pain, it just pays the bills, and you wind up on alcohol and pills." The day-to-day life of migrant workers is explored in "Carmelita," a song once covered by the Cowboy Junkies. With his angry voice and driving sound, Eaglesmith's music might be described as aggressive acoustic. He nonetheless aptly handles more sensitive material like "Livin' on the Road," a poignant portrait of a lonely life, and "Carter," a heartfelt tribute to bluegrass legend Carter Stanley. The small backing band, while mostly acoustic, makes a big sound. Willie P. Bennett adds tasteful flourishes of dobro and mandolin on cuts like "He's a Good Dog" and "I Like Trains." Bennett, Washboard Hank, and Ralph Schipper (the "Ralph" who is playing his last show) also fill out the sound with some fine harmony. Of course one wouldn't want to miss Eaglesmith's humorous side, finely displayed on "White Trash," a song that ponders the joys of downward mobility. *Ralph's Last Show* finds Eaglesmith in his element, and will be appreciated by fans and anyone who enjoys literate singer/songwriters. *—Ronnie D. Lankford Jr.*

Falling Stars and Broken Hearts / Mar. 26, 2002 / MAPL ✦✦✦

After a few brilliant early records, Eaglesmith decided to more or less coast on the formula he had perfected with *Lipstick, Lies, and Gasoline*. *50-Odd Dollars* showed, however, that the trailer-trash shtick had already worn thin, which makes the improved *Falling Stars and Broken Hearts* all the more welcome. Wisely, Eaglesmith has chosen to alter his sound a bit, and although it takes awhile for the album to pick up, the loping country ballad "Ordinary Guy" touches off a string of winners that include the retro-rocker "Cumberland County," the atmospheric "Soft on the Shoulder," and "Cold War." In general, the country elements of this album are more traditional than Eaglesmith's past efforts, and while the substance may not be new, the fresh surroundings give a second chance to some of his more tired obsessions. *—Jim Smith*

Jim Eanes (Homer Robert Eanes Jr.)

b. Dec. 6, 1923, Mountain Valley, VA

Guitar, Vocals / Traditional Bluegrass

Though never considered a major star, Smilin' Jim Eanes was an influential figure in both bluegrass and country music for over five decades. He was born Homer Robert Eanes Jr., in Mountain Valley, VA, and received his first guitar at age nine from his banjo-picking father. While young, Eanes suffered an injury to his left hand; despite the difficulty and pain, he still managed to master rhythm guitar. He spent his early teen years playing square dances with his father's informal string band, and at age 16 joined Roy Hall's Blue Ridge Entertainers at a Roanoke radio station, and remained with the band until Hall died in 1943. Following World War II, Eanes joined Uncle Joe & the Blue Mountain Boys. He also worked briefly with Bill Monroe in 1948.

Eanes made his recording debut in 1949 under his given name, backed by fiddler Homer Sherrill and banjo player Snuffy Jenkins. Eanes organized the Shenandoah Valley Boys in 1951 after getting a radio gig in Virginia; the band cut a few singles on the tiny Blue Ridge label before signing with Decca. Until then, Eanes' music was heavily slanted towards bluegrass, but Decca groomed him to play country music. The singles he released sold well enough, but they didn't make the charts. His contract with Decca expired in 1955 and Eanes, now billing the band as Smilin' Jim & His Boys, began recording with Starday. His debut single, "Your Old Standby," became one of his signature songs. Over the next five years, he and the Shenandoah Valley Boys recorded albums on both Starday and Blue Ridge. Eanes wrote many of his own songs, and one of his best from this period was "I Wouldn't Change You If I Could," which became a number one hit for Ricky Skaggs in 1982.

During the 1960s, Eanes worked as a DJ on different Virginia radio stations; he also occasionally performed, and recorded songs on small independent labels. Eanes recorded his first bluegrass album, *Your Old Standby*, in 1967. His next two albums, *Jim Eanes* and *Rural Rhythms Present Jim Eanes*, featured backing by Red Smiley's Bluegrass Cut-Ups. Smiley and his band appeared regularly on WWVA's *Wheeling Jamboree* and when Red decided to retire, Eanes took over the band, and renamed it the Shenandoah Cutups. The band cut an album in 1970 and shortly after broke up.

Eanes began hosting festivals and recording bluegrass albums for smaller labels; among them was the excellent *Cool Waters Flow*. His heavy touring schedule was interrupted in 1978 when he suffered a heart attack. He recovered by the next year and launched a tour of Western Europe, which he repeated in 1980 and 1982; while visiting Belgium, he cut an album with a local band, Smoketown Strut. During the rest of the 1980s, Eanes cut back on his touring, but continued recording. In 1990, he celebrated his five decades in the industry with the album *50th Anniversary*. *—Sandra Brennan*

Early Days of Bluegrass, Vol. 4 / 1979 / Rounder ✦✦✦

Classic Bluegrass / 1992 / Rebel ✦✦✦✦

● **Your Old Standby** / Jun. 30, 1998 / Starday ✦✦✦✦✦

Despite Jim Eanes' identification with bluegrass, much of his music sounds like straight country performed on bluegrass instruments. As late as the early '60s, he was bucking trends by recording with acoustic instruments (including a banjo) but no drums and making constant use of the percussive "chop" rhythm. Eanes' midrange voice had none of the "high lonesome" character associated with bluegrass, and his willingness to experiment resulted in tracks like "Louise," a studio demo that Eanes wrote as a rock & roll song. That demo and 34 other studio recordings are included on this two-disc collection of Eanes' complete Starday sessions, considered by many fans to be Eanes' finest work. "Celebration," with its echoey shout-along chorus, hints at rockabilly and "Christmas Doll" is a novelty-flavored holiday number, but many other songs are more traditional. "Your Old Standby" is Eanes' most famous composition, having been recorded by George Jones more than once. Bluegrass purists may be left scratching their heads at times, but Allen Shelton's innovative banjo picking and Eanes' distinctive blend of bluegrass and country make for a unique listening experience. *—Greg Adams*

Complete Decca Recordings / Sep. 27, 1999 / Bear Family ✦✦✦✦✦

Stacey Earle

b. San Antonio, TX

Guitar (Acoustic), Vocals (Background), Producer, Guitar, Vocals / Country-Folk, Americana, Alternative Country, Singer/Songwriter

The younger sister of country renegade Steve Earle and a gifted singer/songwriter in her own right, Stacey Earle was born and raised in San Antonio, TX; she began playing music at 15, picking up a guitar Steve left behind at the family's home, but after marrying two years later and giving birth to her first child she seemed fated to a domestic life far removed from show business. In 1990 Earle divorced her husband and moved with her kids to Nashville, where they took up residence in Steve's home; after he heard her singing in the kitchen, she was recruited to lend backing vocals to his 1991 LP *The Hard Way.*

A world tour followed, and Earle soon began writing her own songs; she became a fixture at writers' showcases across Nashville, eventually agreeing to host a weekly showcase of her own at *Jack's Guitar Bar.* There she met another aspiring singer/songwriter, Mark Stuart, whom she married in 1994; Stuart later joined Steve's band the Dukes, appearing in Stacey's group the Jewels (named in honor of her grandmother) as well. After signing with the Nashville publishing company Ten Ten Music Group, Earle garnered attention when her song "For Years" was recorded by Sammy Kershaw on his 1996 LP *Politics, Religion and Her*; when no record deals were forthcoming, however, she instead released her superb debut *Simple Gearle* on her own Gearle Records label in 1998. *Dancin' With Them That Brung Me* followed two years later. A follow-up with husband Mark Stuart, *Never Gonna Let You Go*, appeared in June and captured Earle's most dynamic work yet. *—Jason Ankeny*

Simple Gearle / Feb. 9, 1998 / Gearle Records ✦✦✦✦

On her auspicious debut album, Stacey Earle, younger sister of country-rock icon Steve Earle, comes across as a rough-hewn blend of Emmylou Harris and Nanci Griffith. Her music is a folk-country hybrid, and is just the sort of thing that label executives in Nashville don't want to acknowledge exists in their vicinity. Her songs are exclusively about the relationships between women and men. These aren't narratives so much as finely drawn descriptions of emotional responses to situations. The emotions seem real, and drawn from experience, perhaps because they are ambiguous enough to sound like honest attempts to describe the indescribable. The sparse instrumentation aids Earle's knowing vocals in getting the emotions across. One of the most immediately appealing songs on the album is "Cried My Heart Out," a smart song about lost love. Driven by a steady groove and some nifty lead guitar work, this could conceivably get slicked up and become a hit for one of the pretty girls who populate Nashville these days. *Simple Gearle* has an immediacy and an honesty that is rare these days; Stacey Earle is a real treasure. *—Martin Monkman*

● **Dancin' With Them That Brung Me** / May 9, 2000 / E Squared ✦✦✦✦✦

The younger sister of rebel legend Steve Earle, Stacey Earle's latest effort, *Dancin' With Them That Brung Me*, is full of insightful lyrics and Nanci Griffith-like haunting vocals. Pointing out specific songs seems unnecessary, but suffice it to say that all the songs were written by Earle except for "Promise You Anything," which was penned by her brother, and that Sheryl Crow guests on the beautiful "Kiss Her Goodnight." *Dancin' With Them That Brung Me* is one of those independent gems that the listener must find. It will not hold a premier position in the record store or on the charts. It will not find its audience through glamorous videos or corporately sponsored arena tours. It is the kind of record the listener needs to take a chance on prompted by critical advice or intrigue while browsing the latest releases. In a time when many country records are poured from a similar mold, this record stands out as an awkward achievement. It might as well be packaged differently from the rest so it interrupts the flow of all the other releases leaning against each other in the country section. That way the unsuspecting shopper could not avoid its ungainly frame crammed amongst Nashville's latest productions. If you find Stacey Earle's *Dancin' With Them That Brung Me*, you deserve it because it probably was not easy. *—Michael Cusanelli*

Must Be Live / 2001 / Gearle ✦✦✦✦✦

Stacey Earle whispered onto the scene after singing backup for her brother, the notoriously cranky yet kindhearted, politically incorrect outlaw poet Steve Earle. She released two solo records, both produced by husband and musical compatriot Mark Stuart. And while those records were both charming and revealed Earle's natural talent as a songwriter, they felt just a tiny bit stiff in execution. Here is the remedy. *Must Be Live* is a double album of Stacey Earle and Mark Stuart recorded from some 40 or 50 concerts, with the tracks chosen by Stuart for musical spirit rather than musical perfection. The end result is an accurate—more or less—portrait of the depth, dimension, and charm of this pair working their magic in front of audiences. There is a real depth of commitment the listener can feel—not only to the material, but also from the performers to one another. If their marriage works as wonderfully as their musical partnership, it must have been made in heaven. Listen to the ache of longing in Earle's voice on "Is It Enough," or the depth of hurt in "White Lies," or Stuart's ringing, supportive guitar lines on "Gonna Love Me Someday." In fact, this may be the first time most folks will ever get to experience Stacey Earle's quirky, infectious musical personality on a recording. With Stuart playing solidly behind her and shoring up her gorgeous, reedy vocals with his own slightly raspy harmonies, Earle opens the floodgates of the burning, bleeding heart in her songs. While there isn't a weak moment on either disc, it's important for the sake of esthetics to play the thing—at least the first time—in sequence, to get the full picture of a pair of singer/songwriters whom everybody knew was gifted, but few knew how much. *—Thom Jurek*

Never Gonna Let You Go / Jun. 3, 2003 / Evolver ✦✦✦✦✦

On the four records Stacey Earle issued up to this point, only the last two feature companion and musical collaborator Mark Stuart's name as a co-leader. His presence is felt on every record, and the increasing sophistication of the pair's collaboration is best evidenced by *Never Gonna Let You Go.* Sharing songwriting credits, lead vocals, and a band between them, this is easily the finest effort Earle and Stuart have ever issued. Here are 13 tight songs that grace along topics of love and its loss, melancholy, desire, tenderness, sadness, and delight. No, it's not an alt-country record. No. No. No. Get over it. What it is, is a stellar exploration of the many varied styles country music and blues have touched upon and drawn from over the previous 50 years. Here are the gorgeous ragtime blues "Spread Your Wings" and the West Texas-drenched folk of "Me and the Man in the Moon," which is dusted with the fairy dust of 1940s pop. Stuart's "If You Want My Love" moves through the kind of swing Darrell Scott first evoked on his solo recordings, but is far more effective than Lyle Lovett's attempt at the same thing—especially with Earle's wonderfully unusual voice and a kazoo riding just above a thumping double bass in harmony. The swing band/jug ensemble feel that comes spilling from the record may seem an unlikely one, but it works like carrots in beef stew. The blues make an appearance on "Fishbowl," and the lyrics hark back to an earlier time, though the sound on the recording is anything but. There's even bona fide rock & roll on this set in the form of an Earle/Doug Gill composition called "Our World." Electric guitars fill up the center of the mix and a Hammond B-3 shimmies in from the edges. The dark folky minimalism of "Lay Down" is in stark contrast to its simple haunted beauty. Earle's singing seems to caress the lyrics with the bass to shore her up, and the Tony Joe White swamp blues of "Lookin' for Fool's Gold" offers Stuart a chance to play his slide guitar—dirty, spare, and funky. The truth of the matter is, there isn't a weak link in this chain. If you think you've heard Earle or this duo, it's time to think again. This is the first singer/songwriter record of 2003 that makes a listener take notice of all the elements with its gorgeous production (courtesy of Michael Webb with the duo) that is nonetheless unobtrusive when it comes to the sonic architecture of the songs themselves. In addition, its ambition is in proportionate scale to the quality of the writing. As if this weren't evidence enough, one need only to listen to the bonus disc, which includes working versions of all the tracks here. These too stand on their own, but the finished versions are simply so elegant and graceful, you'll only listen to disc two once or twice. This is how it used to be, an artist hit her stride three, four, or five records in and record companies nurtured that. In Earle's case, she may have had to do it herself, but this is easily the finest moment to date for either Stacey Earle or the incomparable Mark Stuart. *—Thom Jurek*

Steve Earle

b. Jan. 17, 1955, Fort Monroe, VA

Guitar, Vocals / Singer/Songwriter, Roots Rock, New Traditionalist, Alternative Country, Americana, Heartland Rock

In the strictest sense, Steve Earle isn't a country artist, he's a roots rocker. Earle emerged in the mid-'80s, after Bruce Springsteen had popularized populist rock & roll and Dwight Yoakam had kick-started the neo-traditionalist movement in country music. At first, Earle appeared to be more toward the rock side than the country. He played a stripped-down neo-rockabilly that occasionally verged on outlaw country. His unwillingness to conform to the rules of Nashville or to rock & roll meant that he never broke through into the mainstream. Instead, he cultivated a dedicated cult following, drawing from both the country and rock audiences. Toward the early '90s, his career was thrown off track by personal problems and substance abuse, but in the mid-'90s he reemerged stronger and healthier, producing two of his most critically acclaimed albums ever.

Born in Fort Monroe, VA, but raised near San Antonio, TX, Steve Earle is the son of an air-traffic controller. At the age of 11, he received his first guitar and, by the time he was 13, he had become proficient enough to win a talent contest at his school. Though he showed a talent for music, he was a wild child, often getting in trouble with local authorities. Furthermore, his rebellious, long-haired appearance and anti-Vietnam war stance was scorned by local country fans. After completing the eighth grade, Earle dropped out school and, at the age of 16, he left home with his uncle Nick Fain, and began traveling across the state. Eventually, he settled in Houston at the age of 18, where he married his first wife Sandie and began working odd jobs. While he was in Houston, he met singer/songwriter Townes Van Zandt and Jerry Jeff Walker, who would become Earle's foremost role model and inspiration. A year later, Earle moved to Nashville.

While he was in Nashville, Earle worked blue-collar jobs during the day; during the night, he wrote songs and played bass in Guy Clark's backing band, appearing on a cut on Clark's 1975 album *Old No. 1.* Steve stayed in Nashville for several years, making connections within the industry and eventually landing a job as a staff writer for the publisher Sunbury Dunbar. Patty Loveless and Johnny Lee recorded Earle's songs and Elvis Presley was scheduled to cut one of Steve's songs, but he never showed up at the session; Earle also appeared in Robert Altman's 1975 film, *Nashville.* After staying in Nashville for a few years, he grew tired of the city and returned back to Texas.

Back in Texas, he assembled a backing band called the Dukes and began playing local clubs. A year later, he returned to Nashville, where he married his second wife, a local cocaine dealer named Cynthia. The marriage to Cynthia was short-lived and he quickly married Carol, who gave birth to Earle's first child, a son named Justin Townes. Carol helped straighten Earle out, at least temporarily; for a while, he cut back on substances and concentrated on music. Publishers Roy Dea and Pat Clark signed Earle as a songwriter in the early '80s. Dea & Clark brought "When You Fall in Love" to Johnny Lee, who took the song to number 14 on the country charts in 1982; shortly before the success of "When You Fall In Love," Carl Perkins cut Steve's "Mustang Wine," and Zella Lehr recorded two of his songs. With his reputation as a songwriter growing, Earle wanted to become a recording artist in his own right. Dea & Clark had recently formed an independent record label called LSI and the pair signed Earle.

Earle's first release was an EP called *Pink & Black* in 1982. The record featured a formative version of the Dukes and earned good reviews. One writer, John Lomax, sent the EP to Epic Records who were impressed enough by the record to sign Earle in 1983. Shortly, before the signing of the contract, Lomax became Earle's manager. Although the prospect of being signed to a major label seemed promising, relationships between Epic and Earle quickly soured. After releasing the *Pink & Black* track "Nothin' But You" as a single, Epic sat on the song, refusing to promote the record; instead, they concentrated on their new signing. Earle entered the studio and cut an album of neo-rockabilly songs that the label was reluctant to send to radio and, therefore, they refused to release the record. Epic suggested Earle re-enter the studio with a new, more commercially oriented producer, Emory Gordy Jr. The pair cut four more songs which were released as two singles, but the records failed.

With his recording career going nowhere, Earle lost his publishing contract with Dea & Clark. He moved over to Silverline Goldline, where he met Tony Brown, a producer at MCA Records. At the end of 1984, Epic dropped Earle from their roster. In early 1985, Brown persuaded MCA to sign Earle and Lomax was fired as Earle's manager. In 1986, Steve Earle's debut album, *Guitar Town*, was released. Upon its appearance, Earle was grouped into the new traditionalist movement begun by Dwight Yoakam and Randy Travis, but he also gained the attention of rock critics and fans who saw similarities between Earle's populist sentiments and the heartland rock of Bruce Springsteen and John Mellencamp. *Guitar Town* became a hit, with its title track becoming a Top Ten single in the summer of 1986 and "Goodbyes All We've Got Left" reaching the Top Ten in early 1987. Following the album's success, Epic quickly assembled a compilation of previously unreleased Earle tracks, entitling it *The Early Years* and releasing it in early 1987. Later that year, he released his second album, *Exit O*, which bore a shared credit for his backing band the Dukes, which signalled the more rock-oriented direction on the album. Like the debut, *Exit O* was critically acclaimed and it sold well, even if it didn't match the levels of the debut.

Though his career was taking off, Earle's personal life was becoming a wreck. He had divorced his third wife, married a fourth named Lou who he quickly divorced, and then he married a sixth wife named Teresa Ensenat, who worked for MCA. He was also delving deeper and deeper into drug and alcohol abuse. With his third album, 1988's *Copperhead Road*, Earle's rock & roll flirtations came to the forefront and country radio responded in kind; none of the songs from the album charted or received much airplay. However, album rock radio embraced him, sending the album's title track into the album rock Top Ten, which helped make the album his highest charting effort, peaking at number 56. Not only had *Copperhead Road* been accepted by AOR, but it established him as a star in Europe; the duet with the Irish punk-folk group the Pogues on *Copperhead Road* signalled he had an affection for the area. In the late '80s, Earle frequently toured England and Europe and even produced the alternative rock band the Bible.

Earle's acceptance by the rock community didn't please the country establishment in Nashville. Although it seemed for a time that Earle wouldn't need Nashville anymore, his newfound success quickly began to collapse. Uni, a division of MCA Records, had released *Copperhead Road* instead of MCA proper and just before the album went gold, Uni went bankrupt, taking *Copperhead Road* along with it. Meanwhile, Earle's addictions and fondness for breaking rules began spinning out of control. On New Years' Eve, he was arrested in Dallas for assaulting a security guard at his own concert; he was charged with aggravated assault, fined 500 dollars, and given a year's unsupervised probation. Sandie, his first wife, sued for more alimony and he was served with a paternity suit by a woman in Tennessee. The title of his 1990 album, *The Hard Way*, reflected his problems, as did the record's tough, dark sound. Though the record was critically acclaimed and spawned a minor AOR hit with "The Other Kind," it received no support from the country market and quickly fell off the charts.

The commercial failure of *The Hard Way* was just the beginning of a round of serious setbacks for Earle. Later in 1990, he recorded an album of material that MCA refused to release. Instead, the label decided to release the live album *Shut Up and Die Like an Aviator* in 1991. At the end of the year, MCA decided not to renew Earle's record contract. For the next several years, Earle was severely addicted to cocaine and heroin and had several run-ins with the law. In 1994, he was arrested in Nashville for possession of heroin and was sentenced to a year in jail. He served in a rehab center instead of jail. This time, the treatment worked.

Late in 1994, he was released from the rehab center and he began working again. In 1995, he signed to Winter Harvest and released the acoustic *Train a Comin'*, his first studio album in five years. *Train a Comin'* received terrific reviews and strong sales, despite Earle's claim that the label botched the album's song sequence. The attention led to a new record contract with Warner Bros., who released *I Feel Alright* in early 1996, again to strong reviews and respectable sales. Steve Earle had returned from the brink and re-established himself as a vital artist. In the process, he won back the country audience he had abandoned in the late '80s. *The Mountain*, a bluegrass record cut with the Del McCoury Band, followed in 1999, and a year later Earle returned with *Transcendental Blues*. —*Stephen Thomas Erlewine*

★ **Guitar Town** / 1986 / MCA ✦✦✦✦✦

On Steve Earle's first major American tour following the release of his debut album, *Guitar Town*, Earle found himself sharing a bill with Dwight Yoakam one night and the Replacements another, and one listen to the album explains why—while the music was country through and through, Earle showed off enough swagger and attitude to intimidate anyone short of Keith Richards. While Earle's songs bore a certain resemblance to the Texas Outlaw ethos (think Waylon Jennings in "Lonesome, Orn'ry and Mean" mode),

they displayed a literate anger and street-smart snarl that set him apart from the typical Music Row hack, and no one in Nashville in 1986 was able (or willing) to write anything like the title song, a hilarious and harrowing tale of life on the road ("Well, I gotta keep rockin' while I still can/Got a two pack habit and motel tan") or the bitterly unsentimental account of small town life "Someday" ("You got to school where you learn to read and write/so you can walk into the county bank and sign away your life"), the latter of which may be the best Bruce Springsteen song the Boss didn't write. And even when Earle gets a bit teary-eyed on "My Old Friend the Blues" and "Little Rock 'n' Roller," he showed off a battle-scarred heart that was tougher and harder-edged than most of his competition. *Guitar Town* is slightly flawed by an overly tidy production from Emory Gordy Jr. and Tony Brown as well as a band that never hit quite as hard as Earle's voice, and Earle would make many stronger and more ambitious records in the future, but *Guitar Town* was his first shot at showing a major audience what he could do, and he hit a bull's-eye—it's perhaps the strongest and most confident debut album any country act released in the 1980s. —*Mark Deming*

Early Tracks / 1987 / Koch ✦✦✦

In the wake of *Guitar Town*'s success, Epic rushed out this collection of early Earle tracks recorded from 1982 to 1985, including songs from 1982's *Pink & Black* EP. While much of this is by-the-book rockabilly fare, it provides a good look at his formative years. [The CD reissue on Koch adds four tracks from Epic singles, including covers of tunes by John Hiatt and Dennis Linde.] —*Chris Woodstra*

Exit O / 1987 / MCA ✦✦✦

Exit O essentially follows the same formula as *Guitar Town*, and while it isn't as uniformly excellent as his debut, Steve Earle has come up with a couple of his best songs, including the yearning "I Ain't Ever Satisfied." The major difference between the two albums is the fact that Earle insisted on working with his road band the Dukes, which gives *Exit O* a tougher sound. If the material had matched the sound of the album, the record would have surpassed *Guitar Town*, but since the songs are uneven, it's just a respectable follow-up. —*Thom Owens*

Copperhead Road / 1988 / MCA ✦✦✦

Steve Earle always played hard country music with the swagger of a rock & roll star, so it made sense that he would take a detour out of Nashville, both literally and figuratively. On *Copperhead Road*, Earle opted to record in Memphis and veered away from mainstream country in several directions at once—into potent hard rock (most notably on the superb title song, which became his first rock radio hit), as well as Irish folk (with the Pogues backing Earle on "Johnny Come Lately"), and even bluegrass (virtuoso acoustic pickers Sam Bush and Jerry Douglas sit in on "Nothing But a Child"). If *Copperhead Road* lacked a bit of the tight focus of his acclaimed debut *Guitar Town*, it had energy, firepower, and smart-ass humor to spare (along with Earle's always-superb songs), and it made clear that Steve Earle had the stuff to be a contender in rock & roll, if that was what he wanted. —*Mark Deming*

The Hard Way / 1990 / MCA ✦✦✦

"I defend *The Hard Way* to the death, because I almost died in the process of making it," Steve Earle told a reporter in 2000, and he wasn't just being melodramatic. Earle's well-documented addiction to heroin and cocaine was spiraling out of control in 1990 while he was holed up in Memphis recording *The Hard Way*. And while his 1988 album *Copperhead Road* showed him moving away from country and more toward hard rock—and earned him a minor crossover hit in the process—his record label was hoping for a major commercial breakthrough so that his sales might begin to match his good press. The resulting album is a bit of a mess, often sloppy and overbearing where his country sides had been dynamic and precise, and Earle's voice was starting to show the strain of his lifestyle. Even his songwriting, usually peerless, wasn't at its best here, with "When the People Find Out," "Regular Guy," and "Justice in Ontario" sounding like they were tossed together fast to round out the album (the latter sounds like a transparent stroke to his Canadian fan base, where *Copperhead Road* went multi-platinum). But even his weakest studio album has plenty to recommend it, especially the swaggering title cut, the all-too-biographical "Have Mercy" and "West Nashville Boogie," and "Billy Austin," a deeply moving ballad about a man on death row. *The Hard Way* isn't much of an album by Earle's standards, but it's still got enough heart, soul, and fire to prove Earle couldn't throw away his talent, no matter how hard he tried. —*Mark Deming*

Shut Up and Die Like an Aviator / 1991 / MCA ✦✦✦✦

Released on MCA in 1991, *Shut Up and Die Like an Aviator* was recorded live in Ontario, Canada, in October of 1990. The live hits collection was the last for Earle on MCA, as the songwriter was released after his contract with the label ran out despite having issued a string of critically acclaimed, Grammy-nominated records. Shortly afterward, the singer's addictions got the best of him and he ended up in prison for a while and out of the music scene completely for four years. So this live collection could be considered the last of Earle's pre-prison and personally dark years. Culled from the track lists of the songwriter's seminal MCA catalog, which includes monumental releases like *Guitar Town* and *Copperhead Road*, the songs on this live effort are unrepentant, almost effusive odes to hard-living, blue-collar American life, rich with their perfectly drawn characters and tragic narratives. Along with his band the Dukes, Earle blasts through country-rock (in the greatest sense of the term) anthems and heartbreakers like "Devil's Right Hand" and "Copperhead Road." A couple upbeat rockabilly numbers like "Snake Oil," twangy ballads like "Billy Austin," and nice covers (most notably the Jagger/Richards-penned "Dead Flowers") get tossed in to add to the live show's dynamic, making the whole thing one big rootsy riot that's just about as good as contemporary American music can get. —*Vincent Jeffries*

The Essential Steve Earle / 1993 / MCA ✦✦✦✦✦
Steve Earle lives up to the title billing here. While some of Earle's recent work (and live shows) have inclined to excess, this disc collects lean, mean and vital material from Earle's first three outings—the country-rock masterpiece *Guitar Town*, the inward-looking *Exit O*, and the angry lashing out of *Copperhead Road*. *Essential* is topped off by "Continental Trailways Blues," previously available only on a 1987 compilation. These 13 tracks are a little skimpy; some rarities from the vaults would have been a nice touch. *—Roch Parisien*

● **Train a Comin'** / 1995 / Warner Bros. ✦✦✦✦✦
Released in 1995, *Train a Comin'* signaled Steve Earle's final declaration of independence from the Nashville assembly line. At last liberated from his personal demons, Earle found himself exiled from mainstream Nashville. So instead of releasing an album designed to appeal to honchos in Nashville or L.A., Earle released an album that appealed first and foremost to Earle. The result was a stupendous album, a foreshadowing of the renaissance of his career. The disc has the air of a "lost album" that somehow found its way to market. A crack band of Nashville string kings (Peter Rowan, Norman Blake, and Roy Huskey Jr., with Emmylou Harris singing harmony) tears into quasi-legendary tunes that had been lying around Earle's repertoire, neglected for years. Earle's narrative genius is showcased on three numbers—"The Mercenary Song," the Civil War ballad "Ben McCulloch," and the classic outlaw tune "Tom Ames' Prayer," all of which sound as if they were branded into leather rather than written on paper. "Tom Ames' Prayer" especially takes the breath away with its killer final stanza: "And then he cocked both his pistols/Spit in the dirt/And walked out in the street." The album is not all a history lesson, of course. The semi-autobiographical "South Nashville Blues" alarms with its deadpan musings from his self-described two-year "vacation in the ghetto," while "Goodbye" ranks with "My Old Friend the Blues" as one of his teariest weepers. *Train a Comin'* has proven to be just that—the locomotive that Earle drove through some dark tunnels, pulling behind it a boxcar or two of the finest music of his career. *—John Lomax*

I Feel Alright / Mar. 5, 1996 / Warner Bros. ✦✦✦✦
"Be careful what you wish for friends/I've been to hell and now I'm back again," Earle sings on the title track of *I Feel Alright*, immediately drawing us into one of the finest albums of his career. This is the Steve Earle we've been waiting for, as unadorned, unashamed, and plain-faced honest about his roots, dreams, and dirty past lives as any of country music's most heralded singers From the drifting, hard-loving woman in "Now She's Gone" to withdrawn junkie in the ghostly "CCKMP" ("cocaine cannot kill my pain") to the teenage outlaw in "Billy and Bonnie," Earle's characters are a string of loners, often down and out but, at the same time loyal, self-aware, and romantics right to the bitter end. Few artists can give us a picture of life's other side with such electrifying clarity. But despite its subject matter, "I Feel Alright" is imbued with true moments of hope. The closing duet with Lucinda Williams, "You're Still Standin' There," for example, is as strong a statement of faith as any Earle has written. *—Kurt Wolff*

Ain't Ever Satisfied: The Steve Earle Collection / Jul. 1996 / Hip-O ✦✦✦✦✦
Although his personal life was plagued with troubles during the late '80s, Steve Earle wrote a wealth of first-rate songs during that time and the majority of those tunes are collected on the double-disc set, *Ain't Ever Satisfied*. Spanning his career from 1985's *Guitar Town* to 1991's *The Hard Way*, *Ain't Ever Satisfied* hits nearly every high point from his studio albums and throws in a handful of rarities, including live covers of the Rolling Stones and Bruce Springsteen, for good measure. It's an excellent retrospective, illustrating exactly why Earle was one of the most acclaimed country singer/songwriters of the latter half of the '80s. *—Thom Owens*

Johnny Too Bad EP / Apr. 8, 1997 / E-Squared ✦✦✦
Johnny Too Bad is a four-song EP Steve Earle recorded with the reggae band the V-Roys. Running through both Earle originals and reggae classics, the group sounds ragged but right, and while there are no classics here—"Ellis Unit One" does come close, however—it's nevertheless a hell of a good-time. *—Thom Owens*

El Corazon / Oct. 7, 1997 / Warner Bros. ✦✦✦✦✦
I Feel Alright capped off Steve Earle's comeback, restoring his position as one of the most critically acclaimed roots songwriters of the '80s and '90s. *El Corazon*, the follow-up to *I Feel Alright*, doesn't stray far from its predecessor's formula, offering a blend of introspective folk, gritty country, and piledriving rock & roll. If anything, Earle sounds looser than he did before, tearing into these songs with pure passion. He may be surrounded by guest artists—Emmylou Harris offers harmonies on "Taneytown," the Fairfield Four are on "Telephone Road," the Del McCoury Band supports him on "I Still Carry You Around," and the Supersuckers kick him in the ass on "N.Y.C."—but he remains the focal point of the music. While *El Corazon* isn't quite as consistent as *I Feel Alright*, it nevertheless confirms Earle's status as one of the finest roots songwriters of the '80s and '90s. *—Stephen Thomas Erlewine*

The Mountain / Feb. 23, 1999 / E-Squared ✦✦✦✦
On *The Mountain*, Steve Earle has teamed up with one of the very finest bluegrass ensembles around, the Del McCoury Band. All 14 of the songs here were written by Earle, who confesses in the liner notes that his dream is to create a timeless bluegrass classic that will live on like Bill Monroe's "Uncle Pen." Well, he might very well have attained his dream. Each of the songs on *The Mountain* holds their own particular charm, and there isn't a loser in the bunch. "Carrie Brown" could have come from the very pen of "the father of bluegrass" himself, Monroe, and "Connemara Breakdown" has plenty enough fury to carve its own niche in the bluegrass tree. Outstanding performances from talented artists abound: there are the vocals of Emmylou Harris and Iris DeMent, the dobros of Jerry Douglas and Gene Wooten, some smoking Sam Bush mandolin, and the fiddle fire of Stuart Duncan, all wrapped around these instant classics and played straight from the heart. Marty Stuart, Gillian Welch, and John Hartford all drop in to embellish the sound as well. Anyone who saw Earle perform with the McCoury Band was anxiously awaiting a CD, and with *The Mountain*, the wait is over. The smooth strains of "Pilgrim," with its unparalleled roster of guest artists, fills the room, and everything in the world seems just a little bit happier. Steve Earle has truly gone to the mountain and had his vision quest answered in the unmistakable tones of a dobro, a banjo, and a guitar. Some good ol' American music, right from the peak of the mountain. *—Michael B. Smith*

Transcendental Blues / Jun. 6, 2000 / Artemis ✦✦✦✦
Steve Earle is a rebel. Not in the Hollywood/James Dean/*Easy Rider*/rebel-against-society sense but rather in a real and personal way. Throughout his life and career he has rebelled against the very industry that surrounded him and did not find the freedom he sought until he started his own label (E-Squared). He rebelled against his common sense and his health in search of true American artistry and did not find the freedom he sought until he hit the bottom of addiction, and he continues to rebel against mainstream American culture and politics with his attitudes and songs; *Transcendental Blues* is no exception. *Transcendental Blues* walks the line between Steve Earle the country-rock rebel who gave the world *Copperhead Road* and *Guitar Town* and Steve Earle the traditionalist who opened a new chapter in bluegrass with his last release *The Mountain*. This album rocks with songs like "Everyone's in Love With You" and "All My Life." It soothes with "The Boy Who Never Cried" and "Lonelier Than This" and it two-steps with new country like "The Galway Girl" and "Until the Day I Die." Fans of alternative country music sing the praises of artists like Charlie Robison, Jack Ingram, and Robert Earl Keen Jr., but Steve Earle proves again and again that he is the original alternative to the glossy side of Nashville. Steve Earle cut the path that all his followers thankfully hike along avoiding the weeds and branches that made him what he is today. *—Michael Cusanelli*

An Introduction to Steve Earle / May 8, 2001 / Universal International ✦✦✦

Together at the Bluebird Café / Oct. 9, 2001 / American Originals ✦✦✦✦
Steve Earle, Townes Van Zandt, and Guy Clark had a lot in common as revered Nashville singer/songwriters on the fringes of the country music industry, which made this gig at the famed Bluebird Café in Nashville, a benefit for the Interfaith Dental Clinic, an impressive lineup. Recorded September 13, 1995, it was an old-fashioned guitar pull, with each performer alternating as his fellows pitched in with a little guitar playing and encouragement. That's as much as they got together, however; there are no actual duos or trios on the disc. It does seem that Clark is singing along a little bit on Earle's "Mercenary Song," though, and an unidentified voice that sounds a lot like Emmylou Harris applies some harmony on Clark's "Immigrant Song" and Earle's "Copperhead Road." The performances are off the cuff to the point of being more like a casual get-together than an actual concert. Van Zandt, whose songs are the most depressing (and that's saying a lot), is the funniest, especially discussing his own dental needs in the light of losing a tooth in a dice game. He also goes up on the lyrics to "Pancho and Lefty," which doesn't keep it from being as amazing a song as ever. In fact, the songs just seem to get better and better as these three rough-hewn craftsmen demonstrate their remarkable abilities. Those who know their work will delight in hearing favorite songs in an intimate live setting; those who do not may be introduced to a world of great songwriting. *—William Ruhlmann*

Sidetracks / Apr. 9, 2002 / Artemis ✦✦✦✦
In his liner notes to *Sidetracks*, Steve Earle writes the following: "With the exception of the instrumentals . . . these (songs) are not outtakes. They are, rather, stray tracks, recorded at different times for different reasons that I am very proud of and are either unreleased or underexposed." In other words, Earle would appreciate it if you didn't call this another odds-and-sods collection and, given the consistent strength of his post-recovery body of work, he has every right to feel that way about this material. *Sidetracks* doesn't hold together with the cohesion of albums like *I Feel Alright* or *The Mountain*, but nothing here sounds like a leftover or something salvaged from the reject bin, either; these are solid and committed performances of good to very good songs, and they do indeed deserve wider circulation. *Sidetracks* also serves as a nice showcase for Steve Earle the Interpretive Singer. Since only six of the 13 tracks were written by Earle and two of those are instrumentals, for the most part you get to hear Earle try his hand at other people's songs, and for the most part he sounds great, bringing his own feisty stamp to tunes as diverse as the Flying Burrito Brothers' ode to draft dodging, "My Uncle," the reggae chestnut "Johnny Too Bad" (with Earle sounding like the first rude boy from Texas), the Chambers Brothers' psych-soul protest anthem, "Time Has Come Today" (featuring guest vocals from Sheryl Crow and ghostly samples from Abbie Hoffman; it was recorded for the soundtrack to *Steal This Movie*), and Nirvana's angst-fest "Breed" (actually the most faithful cover on this disc). Beyond a couple of minor quibbles (as much as one might enjoy "Creepy Jackalope Eye," the real keeper from Earle's EP with the Supersuckers was his high-attitude version of "Before They Make Me Run," which didn't make the cut here), *Sidetracks* is an impressive collection that makes clear Steve Earle's leftovers make for a better album than most songwriters could construct from their top-shelf work—and that he can get over as a singer and not just as a songwriter performing his own work. *—Mark Deming*

The Collection / May 21, 2002 / Spectrum Music ✦✦✦
While Steve Earle reached his commercial peak with the 1988 album *Copperhead Road*, his reputation with critics and discriminating music fans has grown steadily since his 1996 "comeback" album, *I Feel Alright*, and since then the material from his first five albums—*Guitar Town*, *Exit O*, *Copperhead Road*, *The Hard Way*, and *Shut up and Die Like an Aviator*—has been recycled on a number of different compilations aimed at new fans looking to catch up with his earlier stuff. *The Collection* is the fifth such album to be

released since 1993, and it's neither the best nor the worst of the lot; the track selection focuses on the usual suspects from the first three albums, shortchanges the uneven but interesting *The Hard Way* (how come "Justice in Ontario" made the cut instead of the superb "Billy Austin"?), and gives you more than you really need from the road-weary *Shut Up and Die Like an Aviator*. *The Collection* does tack on two hard-to-find live cuts for completists, "Little Sister" and a cover of Bruce Springsteen's "Nebraska" (another Springsteen cover on this disc, "State Trooper," popped up on an edition of *Guitar Town*), and the mastering and liner notes are fine, but someone looking for an overview of Steve Earle's years at MCA would be better served by picking up *Ain't Ever Satisfied: The Steve Earle Collection*. —*Mark Deming*

Jerusalem / Sep. 24, 2002 / Artemis ✦✦✦

Say what you will about him, but Steve Earle has never been afraid of getting people mad at him if he thought it was the right thing to do, and since his mid-'90s career rebirth after overcoming multiple drug addictions, Earle seems far more interested in stirring people up with a productive purpose in mind rather than cheesing folks off just for the hell of it. Like nearly everyone in the U.S., Earle was struck with anger and confusion following the events of September 11, 2001, and his thoughts on the subject form the backbone of his album *Jerusalem*. But instead of an appeal to patriotism or a tribute to the fallen, Earle has crafted a vision of America thrown into chaos, where the falling of the World Trade Center towers is just another symbol of a larger malaise which surrounds us. Before its release, *Jerusalem* already generated no small controversy over the song "John Walker's Blues," which tells the tale of "American taliban" John Walker Lindh as seen through his own eyes. While "John Walker's Blues" is no more an endorsement of Lindh's actions than Bruce Springsteen's "Nebraska" was a tribute to mass-murderer Charles Starkweather, even though it's one of the album's strongest songs, if anything, it doesn't go quite far enough. While Earle's thumbnail sketch of how an American boy could find a truth in the words of Mohammad rings true, it never quite explains making the leap from studying Islam to taking up arms thousands of miles from home. Still, it's makes the point that the issues of our new "war on terrorism" are as relevant to our own backyards as the Middle East. As Earle tries to sort out the hows and whys of our news fears in "Ashes to Ashes" and "Conspiracy Theory," he can't help but think of other evidence of the erosion of the American dreams—the growing gulf between the rich and the poor ("Amerika V. 6.0 (The Best We Can Do)"), the flaws of our judicial system ("The Truth"), illegal aliens chasing their own bit of an increasing elusive prosperity ("What's a Simple Man to Do"). Earle asks a lot of questions on *Jerusalem* for which no one has the answers, but for all the rage, puzzlement, and remorse of these songs, the title track closes the album with a message of fervent hope—that the answers can't be found in hate or violence, but peace and forgiveness. *Jerusalem* is the work of a thinking troublemaker with a loving heart, and while more than a few people will be angered by some of his views, Earle asks too many important questions to ignore, and the album is a brave and thought-provoking work of political art. —*Mark Deming*

Jack Earls

b. Aug. 23, 1932, Woodbury, TN
Vocals / Rock & Roll, Rockabilly

Jack Earls' early career is proof that Sam Phillips and Sun Records had a much deeper and wider talent pool than "just" Elvis Presley, Carl Perkins, Johnny Cash, and Jerry Lee Lewis to draw on. His sides, all but two unreleased, are as good as anything the label ever issued and Jack Earls' later career is proof that there is occasionally justice in the cosmos—25 years after Elvis Presley was put in the ground, Earls was playing Las Vegas. One of Sun Records' first wave of rockabilly artists, Earls was there when Elvis Presley was writing the book on how to meld hillbilly music with rock & roll, though his own impact on the music was more subtle. In contrast to Elvis, Earls only lasted at Sun for one single, "Slow Down," though that record did do well. By most accounts, he was also present in the studio the day that Elvis cut "Mystery Train," and ran home to get his copy of the single so that the Hillbilly Cat could learn the words.

Earls was born on August 23, 1932, in Woodbury, TN. One of seven children, he spent most of his childhood living on a farm in Manchester. He developed a taste for country music and a desire to make his own music, listening to the two owners of the farm play their instruments and sing. Already encouraged by his mother to sing, at 16 he also took up the guitar and by 17 he was living in Memphis. As early as 1949, he formed his first band, but pursuing music full-time had to wait behind other of life's considerations—he was married in 1950 and by the mid-'50s already had a growing family to feed. Still, he loved country music and thought he could make a living at it and in 1954, Earls formed a group that included Johnny Black, brother of music legend Bill Black, on guitar. This was a country band that played local bars and roadhouses, doing hillbilly music, one of hundreds in the Memphis area. The band's decision to spend ten dollars to cut a demo at Sam Phillips' Memphis Recording Services during the summer of 1955 put Earls into Phillips' orbit—the producer liked the song, an original by Earls called "A Fool For Lovin' You," and enjoyed Earls' singing, but told him he'd need a new band if they were to record anything.

Earls and Johnny Black stayed together, Black switching from guitar to upright bass, while Warren Gregory joined on lead guitar and Danny Wahlquist came in on drums. Their first recording session yielded a finished version of "Lovin' You" but also introduced a new original, called "Hey Jim," that Phillips liked even better for the A-side. Then Earls brought in yet another original song that Phillips liked even better than "Hey Jim" for his debut. "Slow Down" reportedly had the legendary producer jumping up and down with excitement when it was cut at Sun, and it became the A-side even though Phillips had already renamed Earls' band the Jimbos to capitalize on the expected popularity of "Hey Jim." "Slow Down" sold somewhere between 40,000 and 50,000 copies without ever charting, getting enough exposure in and around Memphis to perform respectably as a local and regional release. It might've done better but for the fact that Earls, who held down a job at a bakery to feed his family, couldn't really tour and stuck to playing venues close

to Memphis. "Slow Down" elicited interest from DJs from as far away as Texas, who played the record on their air and would happily have put Earls & the Jimbos on live, had they made the trip to the Lone Star State.

The $2,500 that Earls received for the sales that "Slow Down" did enjoy would have to suffice in lieu of a recording career, especially when Phillips declined to issue any further records—he was around the studio enough, including the date when Elvis was trying to cut "Mystery Train," and he cut enough sides to make a full LP, but Sun never issued any of them, possibly a result of Phillips' awareness that Earls couldn't do much to support their release with more than a few local gigs. It would have taken a truly exceptional record to overcome that handicap and Phillips evidently just never heard it in any of the sides that the man cut. Listening to those sides 40 plus years later, one's jaw drops at the stuff that was left on the shelf. Loose, hot rocking versions of "Crawdad Hole" that ought to have had teenagers bouncing off the walls and slow romantic laments like "If You Don't Mind" that were perfect for slow dancing and would've won over country listeners as well; ballads such as "A Fool for Lovin' You," frenetic rhythm numbers like "Let's Bop" that…well, the title tells it; and Warren Gregory's lead guitar underlines the key points with the kind of dexterity you usually got from the likes of Karl Farr, exceeded only by Earls' frantic vocal vamping. "Sign on the Dotted Line," a slow, burning country rocker sounds like Gene Vincent on a trip through rural Tennessee; "When I Dream," a slowie with elegant guitar and drum accompaniment that could've been part of Elvis' repertory and ought to have gotten a try from Tony Bennett or maybe Bobby Darin; the ominous, raw "Take Me to That Place," based on Earls' observation of the inmates at an institution for the insane he used to drive by in his truck while making deliveries, that ought to have found its way into the repertory of the Stray Cats 30 years later. And finally, the minimalist "My Gal Mary Ann," where the hottest guitar and drum work is all muted behind Earls' frantic, powerful countrified tenor, sounding like Carl Perkins with some loco-weed in his feed. They were all originals and one would've thought the publishing alone might amount to something serious for all concerned—the man was a natural musician and songwriter and deserved a lot more recognition than he got.

By January of 1957, Earls' contract with Sun was over and so was his recording career, despite offers from Meteor Records and King Records. He kept performing as his time and energy allowed until 1963, when he moved to Detroit. For the next few decades, he made his living exclusively on an assembly line at Chrysler, raising his family and living the life of a responsible middle-class citizen, while Elvis Presley's star rose, fell, and rose again, Jerry Lee Lewis and Carl Perkins got in and out of dire straits, and Johnny Cash became the musical conscience of the working man. He made a few attempts at recording in the 1970s, resulting in singles of "Take Me to That Place" b/w "Mississippi Man," "She Sure Can Rock Me" b/w "Crawdad Hole," and "Flip Flop and Fly" b/w "Rock Bop." Finally, in the 1990s, after 40 years of pursuing music in his spare time, Earls began to realize some of the glory that might've been due him. The burgeoning interest in American rock & roll and rockabilly music in Europe in general and England in particular drew Earls over to Great Britain, where he was greeted like a superstar. His Sun sides were compiled, first on LP by Bear Family Records and later in the 1990s on a CD from Charly Records entitled *Hey Slim, Let's Bop*, which is only slightly less essential listening than Elvis Presley's Sun recordings. In the years since, Jack Earls has played concerts in America as well played Las Vegas in tandem with Janis Martin and other survivors from rockabilly's first generation. —*Bruce Eder*

Let's Bop / 1990 / Bear Family ✦✦✦✦✦
● **Hey Slim, Let's Bop** / Jul. 1, 1999 / Charly ✦✦✦✦✦

Don Edwards

b. Mar. 30, 1939, Boonton, NJ
Vocals / Cowboy, Americana

Singer/songwriter Don Edwards has dedicated his musical career to recapturing and preserving the spirit of the Old West by recording old and new cowboy songs. Almost alone in his enthusiasm when he took up the cowboy genre, Edwards by the 1990s reigned as the pre-eminent specialist in a field that had attracted many other musicians. Edwards was born and raised in Boonton, a New Jersey farming community. Inspired by the books of cowboy author Will James (such as *The Lone Cowboy*), he took up the guitar at age ten. He learned his first Western songs from the films of cowboy crooners Gene Autry and Tex Ritter, later discovering Jimmie Rodgers. At age 16, Edwards left home to work in the oil fields and ranches of Texas and New Mexico in order to experience the Western life and landscape firsthand.

Edwards made his professional debut in 1961 after he was hired as a singer, actor, and stuntman at the newly opened amusement park Six Flags Over Texas. He worked there for five years before moving to Nashville to seek a recording contract. Although the folk revival was in full swing, no one was much interested in Western music at the time. Edwards eventually recorded an album combining classic Western numbers with some of his own compositions on the independent Stop label. Some of the songs were played on the radio, but they never hit the charts, and Edwards returned to Texas and settled in the Fort Worth area. In 1980, Larry Scott, a Los Angeles DJ, helped Edwards record the *Happy Cowboy* album, which featured backup musicians from Gene Autry's band and the Sons of the Pioneers. Edwards released the album on his own Sevenshoux label.

A visit to the Cowboy Poetry Gathering in Elko, NV, in the early '80s inspired him to create a 24-song tribute to Jack Thorp, the cowboy musician who first began collecting traditional cowboy songs, on a cassette packaged with a book entitled *Songs of the Cowboy*. He then released a second book/cassette anthology, *Guitars and Saddle Songs*, and in 1990 released the album *Desert Nights and Cowtown Blues*. In 1992 Edwards signed with the new Warner Western label helmed by Michael Martin Murphey and released *Songs of the Trail*, a spare album of traditional songs that gave the dry, melancholy, sometimes-violent narratives of the cowboy a startling immediacy. Edwards gained exposure from his major-label association and became a fixture at clubs and events with any kind of Western theme throughout Texas and the Southwest. He followed up *Songs of the Trail* with *Goin' Back to Texas* (1993), an album containing new Western songs by some of the best writers in Nashville. After *West of Yesterday* (1996), Edwards moved to the folk-oriented Shanachie label and continued to dip into his vast song bag of traditional Western material with the double CD *Saddle Songs: Vols. 1 & 2* of 1997. Subsequent Shanachie releases saw Edwards branching out musically even as he stuck with Western songs. *My Hero, Gene Autry: A Tribute* (1998) was recorded at a live appearance honoring Autry on his 90th birthday, and two years later Edwards resurfaced with *Prairie Portrait*, a project recorded with cowboy poet Waddie Mitchell and the Fort Worth Symphony Orchestra. *Kin to the Wind*, a tribute to Marty Robbins, was issued in early 2001. The 2002 project *High Lonesome Cowboy* teamed Edwards with folk-bluegrass singer Peter Rowan and several other acoustic-music luminaries, putting a new twist on Edwards' cowboy material. *—Sandra Brennan & James Manheim*

Happy Cowboy / 1980 / Sevenshoux ✦✦✦

Desert Nights and Cowtown Blues / 1990 / Sevenshoux ✦✦✦✦

● **Songs of the Trail** / Jan. 1992 / Warner Bros. ✦✦✦✦✦
Texas rancher Don Edwards spent several years researching and compiling the songs that comprise the excellent *Songs of the Trail*. Each tune on the album is an old cowboy song that well-known at the turn of the century. Edwards' delivery is spare, emotional and powerful—these songs don't sound like artifacts, they sound alive. It's one of the rare historical releases that is entertaining as it is educational. *—Thom Owens*

Goin' Back to Texas / Feb. 1993 / Warner Bros. ✦✦✦✦

West of Yesterday / Mar. 19, 1996 / Warner Western ✦✦✦

Saddle Songs, Vol. 1 & 2 / Sep. 16, 1997 / Shanachie ✦✦✦✦

Best of Don Edwards / May 12, 1998 / Warner Bros. ✦✦✦✦

My Hero, Gene Autry: A Tribute / May 19, 1998 / Shanachie ✦✦✦✦
This tribute, recorded live for Autrey's ninetieth birthday, is truly a labor of love. Edwards and company do a fine job of recreating the spirit of Autrey's cowboy persona: a mixture of lonesome innocence and true grit. *—Tim Sheridan*

Prairie Portrait / Jan. 11, 2000 / Shanachie ✦✦✦
This unusual project pairs the cowboy voices of Don Edwards and Waddie Mitchell with the stylish musical support of the Fort Worth Symphony Orchestra. Both dramatic and touching, the album manages to dramatize in music the spirit of the American West. *—Stacia Proefrock*

Kin to the Wind / Jan. 9, 2001 / Shanachie ✦✦✦✦
Don Edwards has dedicated his musical career to preserving Western songs, and the lovely *Kin to the Wind* follows this inclination. Here, he adds a special twist by concentrating on songs sung or appreciated by Marty Robbins. A number of things seem to make this album a success, including nice arrangements, intricate acoustic guitar, good song choice, and Edwards' vocals. Things get started with "Saddle Tramp," an ode to the freedom of roaming the range, while "San Angelo," an epic narrative of love and death, explores the pleasures and perils of the Western landscape. "I'm Kin to the Wind" is filled with evocative lyrics, painting such an idyllic portrait of Western life that the listener may be tempted to saddle up and hit the trail. Even on tragic ballads like "Old Red," this western landscape is tinged with romanticism; love may not work out in "I'll Step Aside" or "Is There Anything Left I Can Say," but the sadness is laced with beautiful melancholy. Edwards is in good voice, and his plaintive vocals are very reminiscent of Robbins. The arrangements are fairly simple, dominated by exquisite guitar fills, quiet steel guitar, and occasionally trumpets. Each of the 12 songs is a keeper, and it is refreshing that better-known songs (and perhaps overplayed ones) like "El Paso" were bypassed. It is unfortunate that this music will never end up on the country hit parade, but such is life. Edwards has made a great album that should be warmly appreciated by his fans, Robbins' fans, and lovers of good Western music. *—Ronnie Lankford Jr.*

Jonathan Edwards

b. Jul. 28, 1946, Aitkin, MN
Guitar, Harmonica, Vocals / Progressive Bluegrass, Singer/Songwriter, Folk-Rock
Best remembered for his crossover hit "Sunshine," country and folksinger/songwriter Jonathan Edwards was born July 28, 1946, in Aitkin, MN, and grew up in Virginia. While attending military school, he began playing guitar and composing his own songs. After moving to Ohio to study art, he became a fixture on local club stages, playing with a variety of rock, folk, and blues outfits, often in tandem with fellow students Malcolm McKinney and Joe Dolce. In 1967, Edwards and his bandmates relocated to Boston, where they permanently changed their name to Sugar Creek and became a full-time blues act, issuing the 1969 LP *Please Tell a Friend*. Wanting to return to acoustic performing, he left the group to record a solo album. Near the end of the 1970 sessions, one of the finished tracks, "Please Find Me," was accidentally erased, forcing Edwards to instead record a brand new composition. The song was "Sunshine," and when it was released as a single the following year, it quickly became a Top Five pop hit.

With the release of 1972's *Honky-Tonk Stardust Cowboy*, Edwards' music began gravitating toward straight-ahead country; his label was at a loss as to how to market the record, however, and over the course of two more albums, 1973's *Have a Good Time for Me* and the following year's live *Lucky Day*, his sales sharply declined. Soon, Edwards dropped out of music, buying a farm in Nova Scotia. In 1976, Edwards' friend Emmylou Harris enlisted him to sing backup on her sophomore record, *Elite Hotel*; the cameo resulted in a new record deal and the LP *Rockin' Chair*, recorded with Harris' Hot Band. *Sail Boat*, cut with most of the same personnel, appeared a year later. Another layoff followed, however, and when Edwards resurfaced—with an eponymous 1982 live record—it was on his own label, Chronic.

After touring the nation with a production of the musical *Pumping Boys and Dinettes*, Edwards joined the bluegrass group the Seldom Scene, issuing the 1983 LP *Blue Ridge*. After a 1987 solo children's record, *Little Hands*, Edwards moved to Nashville; his 1989 album *The Natural Thing* generated his biggest country hit, "We Need to Be Locked Away." A follow-up, *One Day Closer*, appeared in 1994. *—Jason Ankeny*

● **Jonathan Edwards** / 1971 / Atco ✦✦✦✦✦
This album is best known for Edwards' hit, "Sunshine" and the song "Shanty," which radio stations around the country call "The Friday Song." If either of these songs is as far as you've gotten with this album, you are missing a great deal. Edwards has a great sense of melody, which means there is not a weak track on this record. Aside from the previously mentioned numbers, one or two of the songs on the record have taken on a life of their own. "Don't Cry Blue," for instance, has been knocking around bluegrass circles for some years. One listen and you'll know why this album has never gone out of print. *—Jim Worbois*

Honky-Tonk Stardust Cowboy / 1972 / Atco ✦✦✦✦
Honky-Tonk Stardust Cowboy—singer/songwriter Jonathan Edwards' follow-up to his self-titled debut—was not as much of a commercial success as its predecessor. However, it is just as strong musically and features a few new twists and an increasingly countrified flavor, which Edwards himself attributes to a renewed interest in country & western artists such as George Jones and Merle Haggard. Combined with some tasty down-home contributions from occasional Stray Gator Ben Keith (pedal steel guitar), the somewhat schizophrenic nature of the album may very well have confused those looking and listening for the next "Sunshine"—which was more akin to the pop radio-friendly acoustic folk sound of America or James Taylor. *Honky-Tonk Stardust Cowboy* does have a few pop-oriented moments, however. Primary among them is the opening track, "Stop and Start It All Again," a spry rocker that could easily have fit onto the first album. "It's a Beautiful Day" likewise continues much in the standard of the first album. Those notable exceptions aside, *Honky-Tonk Stardust Cowboy* is more laid-back, with a sound and delivery reminiscent of the well-crafted material on Dillard & Clark's *The Fantastic Expedition of Dillard & Clark* and *Through the Morning, Through the Night*. Tracks such as "Everything," "Dues Days Bar," and "Ballad of Upsy Daisy" are noticeably influenced by the concurrently popular Bakersfield sound of artists such as Buck Owens & His Buckeroos. There are a few notable cover tunes included as well. The title track is perhaps best remembered as an early hit for Lefty Frizzell. "Paper Doll"—which was recorded live at A&R Studios in N.Y.C.—became a signature tune for the Mills Brothers as far back as the '40s. Folks who enjoyed the *Jonathan Edwards* disc will also find much to visit and revisit on *Honky-Tonk Stardust Cowboy*. *—Lindsay Planer*

Have a Good Time for Me / 1973 / Atco ✦✦✦
Jonathan Edwards is not considered a "country" artist per se, probably due to the success of "Sunshine" from his 1971 self-titled debut, but on his follow-up to the *Jonathan Edwards* album, *Honky-Tonk Stardust Cowboy*, and some of his discs on Reprise, most notably *Sailboat* and *Rockin' Chair*, he is indeed that. *Have a Good Time for Me* is a departure from *Honky-Tonk Stardust Cowboy* in that the artist is covering music by three of the songwriters from the Castle Hill Publishing group, a company owned by co-producer Peter Casperson, who also managed Edwards. Without the original compositions that were the bulk of the previous release, Edwards has an opportunity to put his stamp on outside material, which he does so well. There's an excellent cover of Jimmie Rodgers' "Travelin' Blues," along with a lively, almost gospel rendition of the traditional "When the Roll Is Called Up Yonder." The album starts off with longtime collaborator Eric Lilljequist's "Have Yourself a Good Time for Me," which would appear in a different form on Lilljequist's *More Orphan Than Not* album a year later. On that album, Edwards was pretty much a bandmember, his photo on the cover with the other musicians. Here, "Have a Good Time" is lighter and more introspective, a forlorn statement to a significant other who can't stay true, a perfect sentiment for country radio. "My Home Ain't in the Hall of Fame" sounds like Bostonian John Lincoln Wright, and one wonders had the two teamed up, how they might have decimated the country charts with hits. David Bromberg shows up on electric guitar, and the tune reappeared on Edwards' next album, the live *Lucky Day*, which actually has Orphan backing him up nine months after the recording of this LP. But it is in this context on *Have a Good Time for Me* where Edwards excels as an interpreter: "Something borrowed from the friends of gold" the singer writes in his poem inside the gatefold of an album. If you've had it in your collection for years, you may find strange white blotches appearing on the front and back cover; the singer explained that he demanded and got it released on recycled materials. Along with the poem, it is his calligraphy lettering inside and out, making for a very personal collection of material that didn't come from his pen, but does! Interesting indeed how he takes Malcolm McKinney's "Thirty Miles to Go" and makes it his own. McKinney contributes two titles here; Joe Dolce is represented with three; and Eric Lilljequist has four, including the title song. Dolce's "King of Hearts" has more of the pop flavor Edwards' fans from radio expect, the album working because the musicianship from Al Anderson, Bromberg, Stuart Schulman, Bill Keith, Lilljequist, Bill Elliot, and others blends in perfectly behind the singer. With the success of the Eagles at this point in time, one wonders why this album didn't do much much more. Perhaps it was too pure in its approach. It remains a very listenable and courageous work by an artist not content to clone past success but willing to follow his instincts. *—Joe Viglione*

Lucky Day / 1974 / Atco ✦✦✦
Lucky Day is an important 15-song live document of Jonathan Edwards' music, recorded at what was a wonderfully intimate little venue in Harvard Square, Cambridge, MA, the late, lamented Performance Center. This perfect live show is enhanced by the presence of Orphan members Eric Lilljequist, Dean Adrien, Dave Conrad, and Bobby Chouinard, along with friends like NRBQ's Al Anderson, pianist Bill Elliot, violinist/pianist Stuart Schulman, and Lynnie Dall. Though some of the material would naturally show up on other live discs by Edwards—"Shanty" appearing on 1980's *Live* and "Lucky Day" on 2000's *Cruising America's Waterways*—these takes have staying power, making this one of Edwards' most satisfying releases. The title track, "Lucky Day," works so much better

with Orphan backing him, and the violins on Malcolm McKinney's "Sometimes" flow beautifully next to Edwards' soulful voice. "Hit Parade of Love" is a hootenanny, while "Stop and Start It All Again" is one of the singer's best country-pop numbers. There is country-rock all over this folksinger's repertoire, and "That's What Our Life Is" deserved to be a country & western hit. The covers of "My Home Ain't in the Hall of Fame" and Merle Haggard's "Today I Started Loving You Again" give a glimpse of the range of Edwards' artistry. It's interesting to note that Orphan labelmates the Poppy Family covered this same Merle Haggard tune on *Poppy Seeds*, along with an Al Anderson number a couple of years before this release. At the time that Terry Jacks of the Poppy Family was riding the airwaves with "Seasons in the Sun," Orphan and Jonathan Edwards recorded this album (on March 22 and 23 of 1974). The medley of "You Are My Sunshine" into Edwards' own smash "Sunshine"—including the lyrics he brought on-stage during this era ("Nixon's got cards he ain't showing")—turned out to be a good bit of prophecy. Half the album contains covers and half is comprised of Jonathan Edwards originals, like the country-folk "Give Us a Song," which begins the disc, and the short and lively "Everybody Knows Her," which ends side one. The cover of the Chi-Lites' 1971 hit "Have You Seen Her" is complete parody, and that's the one downside—a soulful reading of the tune by Jonathan Edwards might have had chart potential. "Don't Cry Blue," the other McKinney title, brings the energy level up, while Dall's "Nova Scotia" shows Edwards in that sincere light his fans adore. Reopening these tapes recorded by legendary engineer Jay Messina (who worked with Aerosmith, among others) to expand this album and create a double CD of the performances would be a treasure. Not only is this a great moment in time for Jonathan Edwards, it displays the many talents of the hugely underrated Orphan and captures an important period in Boston music history at a fun venue which no longer exists. —*Joe Viglione*

Rockin' Chair / 1976 / Reprise ✦✦
Edwards, in 1976, had a new label, new backing musicians, and a new producer, the then very hot Brian Ahern. Unfortunately, change is not always a good thing. The songs and the band are both very good, but the intimate feel of the early albums is missing here and that was one of the things that always made Edwards' records so appealing. That lack of intimacy seems to fall on the producer's shoulders and should not be held against the artist. Despite the flaws in production, this is still a fine collection of songs and performances from a regrettably overlooked artist. —*Jim Worbois*

Sail Boat / 1977 / Reprise ✦✦
This just doesn't have the feel of a Jonathan Edwards album. It could be blamed on the relatively few Edwards originals, which leave the feeling that the creation of this record was more or less removed from the artist's hands. It's a pleasant enough collection, especially if you ever wondered what Jonathan Edwards would sound like singing other songwriters' songs. (His version of "Never Together" predates Carlene Carter's near hit by a year.) Still, if this is your first exposure to this artist, you may be tempted to skip the rest of his work and that would be a major mistake. —*Jim Worbois*

Live / 1980 / Chronic ✦✦✦

Blue Ridge / 1985 / Sugar Hill ✦✦✦

Natural Thing / Feb. 4, 1997 / MCA/Curb ✦✦✦

Man in the Moon / Sep. 9, 1997 / Rising ✦✦✦
Man in the Moon is one of the most satisfying and beautiful discs by singer/songwriter Jonathan Edwards in a history filled with such work. The title track is simply amazing in its subtlety, but every track on this disc has a presence and deep emotion. The opening track, "Stay Down," is like an uptempo take on Simon & Garfunkel's "The Boxer," and it drives with Gary Burke from the Joe Jackson Group on drums and Duke Levine on guitar. The song was used for the credit roll of the film *The Mouse*, for which Edwards did the soundtrack. The singer/songwriter has anecdotes about each tune printed beneath the lyrics in the generous ten-page booklet that comes with the CD and, historically, those liner notes are almost as important as the music. "Slave for Love" is a tune Willie Dixon co-wrote and wanted Edwards to cover—they performed on a show together in Boston during the late '60s, and three decades later the song finds its release here. It is tremendous, but so is Edwards' own "Whatever Gets You Through the Night" and keyboardist Kenny White's "To Me," which sounds like an Edwards original. Burke's drums are as lovely as ever, Hugh McDonald's bass is right on, and—with Levine, Michael Aharon, and Al Pettiway—the band combines to forge a really impressive sound, a natural progression from what Edwards was doing with Orphan years earlier. Monica Cohen's cover art matches the music inside, and though label Rising Records seems to have gone the way of all flesh, the material can still be found at www.jonathanedwards.net. Cheryl Wheeler's "Howl at the Moon" is covered here, and Edwards' own "Break Out of the Blue" is just stunning. Some great artists put out albums with highs and lows; songwriter David Pomeranz's *It's in Everyone of Us* comes to mind as a work of genius with inevitable filler. Edwards' *Man in the Moon* contains no flaws, and must be viewed as a favorite among his many discs even if not considered his best album by the general record-buying public. *Man in the Moon* is a major effort that deserves massive exposure. —*Joe Viglione*

Kathleen Edwards

b. 1979, Ottawa, Ontario, Canada
Guitar, Composer, Vocals, Fiddle / Singer/Songwriter, Alternative Country-Rock
Kathleen Edwards was born in Ottawa, Canada, in 1979, the daughter of foreign service parents who played piano and guitar in their spare time. At five, Edwards began to study classical violin, which continued through her early teens. At that point, the Edwards family moved overseas. Removed from the influence of mainstream North American pop music, Edwards delved into her older brother's collection of Bob Dylan, Neil Young, and early Tom Petty records. After high-school, Edwards landed back in Ottawa, singing and playing her guitar in local clubs and networking with other musicians in the scene.

In 1999, Edwards recorded her debut EP, *Building 55*, and toured throughout Canada to support it, busking and opening for acts like Hayden and Jane Siberry. A bad breakup led to more songwriting, much of which took place after Edwards moved out of Ottawa and into rural Quebec. Those songs became the basis of *Failer*, her debut full-length, which she recorded in Ottawa in late 2001. The album was a heartfelt mixture of folk and country, and drew upon influences like Whiskeytown and Gillian Welch. A major critical buzz began then, and gigs at the 2002 South by Southwest and opening for Richard Buckner led to a deal with Zoe/Rounder, which released *Failer* on January 14, 2003. —*Johnny Loftus*

● **Failer** / Jan. 14, 2003 / Zoë ✦✦✦✦
Teeming with roots and with alternative country oozing from every note, Kathleen Edwards could easily be compared to fellow Canadian Sarah Harmer, but there is a natural difference in their approaches. With songs such as "One More Song the Radio Won't Like," the singer tends to stand outside the conventional box, but her voice easily recalls Lucinda Williams at her most vulnerable. "I'm so tired of playing defense/And I don't even have hockey skates," she sings during "Hockey Skates," which straddles the country/pop line to perfection. "The Lone Wolf" is another strong nugget, demonstrating an earthy, Neil Young quality. There is also an adventurous side to the album, with saxophones and an edgier, tougher sound on "12 Bellvue." Possessing a lyrical cynicism far beyond her tender 23 years, Edwards seems best at her most melancholic, particularly during "National Steel" and relating the problems of addiction in "Mercury." But the prettiest number is the closing "Sweet Lil' Duck," whose overtones evoke "Here Comes a Regular" from the Replacements. Far from a failure, *Failer* is as gorgeous as it is flawless. —*Jason MacNeil*

Meredith Edwards

Vocals (Background), Vocals / Country-Pop, Contemporary Country
Country songster Meredith Edwards, at the tender age of 16, made many in Nashville's music business sit up and take notice with the release of her first single "A Rose Is a Rose." The love story video, poor girl meets rich boy, caused even more of a stir. It was the perfect vehicle to showcase her powerful and beautiful voice. Edwards, a native of Clinton, MS, began singing for family—and impressing family friends—when she wasn't even old enough for school. By the time she was five, she was a member of an impressive traveling choir called the Mississippi Showstoppers. One of her friends in the children's choir was none other than the future *NSYNC heartthrob Lance Bass, who just happened to also be from Clinton. A few years later the pair would be fellow members in another choir, Attaché.

After Bass hit the big time with *NSYNC, Edwards toured with the group and opened for them. When Bass started his own management company, it was little surprise that he picked the talented Edwards to be his debut artist. In 2001, Edwards finished working on her debut full-length album *Reach*. It was released under the major record label Mercury. "Places in Your Heart," "You Get to Me," and "In Any Given Moment" are some of the songs on the album. The music is country, but some of the numbers are what some call new country or today country, the kind that feels a little like pop/rock, but keeps its country flavoring. —*Charlotte Dillon*

Reach / 2001 / Mercury ✦✦✦
The strongest component of Meredith Edwards' debut album, *Reach*, is the young artist's vocal interpretation of her material. For those who are looking for extremely memorable, stellar songs, you may be disappointed by the general mediocrity of the cuts. On the other hand, for those who love a powerful vocalist, Edwards will definitely grab your attention. Embracing the country-pop sound, Edwards will have your toes tapping throughout "In Any Given Moment" and "The Bird Song," the cleverest of the cuts, told from the perspective of a feathered people-watcher. Shifting gears on songs like "This Is the Heartache" and "You," the teen shapes an even package of uptempo and ballad tunes. After a modern, pop vocal performance that suits someone of Edwards' age, along comes the twang of "Slow Learner," almost as if the speed of an old-fashioned long-play record got cranked up on a turntable. Edwards has some big names behind her in her career, including former pop singer/songwriter Richard Marx and *NSYNC's Lance Bass serving as her personal manager. That kind of musical talent can only mean that the talent of Meredith Edwards will continue to blossom. —*Rick Cohoon*

Stoney Edwards

b. Dec. 24, 1937, Seminole, OK, **d.** Apr. 5, 1997
Vocals / Traditional Country, Honky Tonk, Progressive Country
Stoney Edwards never made it to the big time, yet he and his soulful honky-tonk sound had a devoted following, and he was one of the few African-American performers to try his hand in the genre. He was born Frenchy Edwards in rural Oklahoma, one of seven children. Even as a boy, Edwards dreamed of playing on the *Grand Ole Opry* like his hero, Bob Wills. By the time he was 13, he had mastered several instruments and frequently jammed with his uncles. After leaving home as a teen, in 1954 he married and moved to San Francisco to settle down for the next 15 years. When not working, he played music. After breaking his back in a job-related mishap, Edwards was ordered to avoid heavy work by his doctors. Without an income, he seriously thought of leaving his family so they could receive welfare, but just as he was leaving his daughter came forth with the gift of wind-up toy. Deeply moved, Edwards was inspired to write his first song, "A Two Dollar Toy," and began focusing his energy on a music career.

In 1970, he was invited to play at a benefit for Bob Wills in Oakland, and his performance led to a contract with Capitol Records. The following year, he released his first album, *Stoney Edwards, A Country Singer*, and made his single debut with "A Two Dollar Toy," which made the Top 70. In 1972, Edwards released his second album, *Down Home in the Country*, and began to attract a following. "He's My Rock" came out in 1973 and stayed in the Top 20 for almost four months. Although his subsequent releases were generally minor hits, some have become regarded as country classics, such as his version of the Frazier & Owens song "Hank and Lefty Raised My Country Soul." He continued recording and appearing on the charts through the early '80s, when his career and his health began to wane. Eventually he had part of his right leg amputated due to problems with diabetes. In 1986, Edwards returned to make an album with Johnny Gimble, Ray Benson, Floyd Domino, Jimmy Day, Leon Rausch and Ralph Mooney. *—Sandra Brennan*

Stoney Edwards / 1971 / Capitol ♦♦♦♦

She's My Rock / 1973 / Capitol ♦♦♦♦

Mississippi, You're on My Mind / 1975 / Capitol ♦♦♦♦

Mississippi, You're on My Mind looks like a straight album, but is a collection of cuts from Stoney Edwards' previous three albums, including his two biggest hits (the title track and "She's My Rock") and arguably his greatest song, the self-penned "Two Dollar Toy." Like Charley Pride, Edwards recorded a number of hard country songs like "Hank & Lefty Raised My Country Soul" that helped the overwhelmingly white country audience accept a black country singer, but Edwards' musical outlook was pure country, and he must have found such material to his liking anyway. Unlike Pride, Edwards composed a number of his songs and proved himself to be a respectable songsmith. All but a few selections on *Mississippi, You're on My Mind* are duplicated on Razor & Tie's greatest-hits anthology, which is the recommended sampler for inquisitive listeners. *—Greg Adams*

Blackbird / 1976 / Capitol ♦♦♦♦♦

No Way to Back Down a Memory / 1981 / MCA ♦♦♦

● **Poor Folks Stick Together: The Best of Stoney Edwards** / May 19, 1998 / Razor & Tie ♦♦♦♦♦

Stoney Edwards is probably the best hardcore country singer of the '70s that never got the attention he deserved. He never had a big hit—two songs, "She's My Rock" and "Mississippi, You're on My Mind," peaked at 20 and he never got any higher than that—and after releasing four albums in five years, he was dropped by Capitol Nashville, with his recordings remaining out of print until Razor & Tie released this 20-track retrospective in 1998. Even this reissue didn't get the attention it deserved and was discontinued less than three years after its release, once again consigning Edwards to the status of a cult item among serious country fans, when he deserves much more. Why was it so difficult for Edwards to be heard? Most answers would likely say that it was because he was a black country singer, but Charley Pride was a fixture at the top of the country charts throughout Stoney's time on Capitol (indeed, his success was a significant factor in the label's decision to sign Edwards). Surely his race was likely a factor in his lack of success, but it's also true that he simply was not singing music that was fashionable at the time. Edwards was a pure country singer, in the vein of Lefty Frizzell and Merle Haggard, and his music was firmly in the hardcore honky tonk tradition, which was not exactly burning up the charts in the early '70s. Ironically, he didn't always stick to the tried-and-true honky tonk themes of drinking, cheating, love, and loss; he certainly sang his fair share of those songs, but he often sang about the pains of poverty, growing up country, trying to find work, and thinking about leaving his family behind. It was a sharp mix of expertly chosen covers and wonderful originals that revealed Edwards was as strong and imaginative a writer as he was a singer. Also, his productions and performances subtly stretched the boundaries of his beloved honky tonk, as he injected hints of the blues to his phrasing while the music occasionally flirted with modern and traditional folk. It was a rich blend and it has weathered the test of time, standing as some of the best hardcore country cut in the '70s, regardless of its status on the charts. It's the kind of music any true country lover will treasure, so even if it is difficult to find, it's worth seeking out because it's music that gets better with each listen. Sure, it would be nice to have actual albums on CD released eventually, but *Poor Folks Stick Together: The Best of Stoney Edwards* is such a perfectly assembled collection—containing all of his modest hits, terrific album tracks, and even the previously unreleased "Jimmie Rodgers Blues"—that after listening to it, it's hard to imagine that Edwards isn't better known. Too bad it's so hard to find. *—Stephen Thomas Erlewine*

Eggs Over Easy

Group / Pub Rock, Country-Rock

Historically renowned as the band that launched the entire British pub rock scene, the all-American Eggs Over Easy originally arrived in the U.K. to cut a record with producer Chas Chandler in 1970. Sessions at Olympic Studios went well, but escalating problems with the group's American backers, Cannon Films, saw the project run aground in the new year and the group moved onto the live circuit while they sought a new deal. They played a number of college gigs around the country, but it was at the Tally Ho pub in London's Kentish Town neighborhood, just around the corner from the band's communal home, that they made their reputation—and forged an entire new musical movement. Originally booked to play the traditionally slack Monday night at a venue which had hitherto favored jazz performers, Eggs Over Easy's reputation quickly spread, not only to the public but also among other bands. The members of Brinsley Schwarz were early admirers, frequently attending the band's *Tally Ho* dates and often joining them on-stage—before long, Brinsley Schwarz, too, was concentrating their attention on the pub circuit. With other bands hastening to join them, by early fall 1971, interest and enthusiasm was so high that Eggs Over Easy was able to organize a city-wide tour of Inde Coope brewery pubs. They followed through with a 12-date U.K. tour supporting John Mayall, Eggs Over Easy's country-rock-flavored repertoire offering a fascinating counterpoint to Mayall's then rampant jazz-blues fixation.

The group's U.K. sojourn was coming to an end, however. Despite having recorded an album, a record deal remained elusive, while the band's work permits were also expiring. On November 7, 1971, Eggs Over Easy played their final Tally Ho show, then returned to the U.S. They would disband shortly after, but before they did, they signed with A&M and finally consigned a fraction of their repertoire to vinyl—according to Brinsley Schwarz's Nick Lowe, the band had over 100 songs at their fingertips. Just one-tenth of that catalog appeared on *Good 'n' Cheap*; the band has also been enshrined on EMI's *Naughty Rhythms: The Best of Pub Rock* CD anthology. *—Dave Thompson*

● **Good 'n' Cheap** / 1972 / A&M ♦♦♦♦♦

In some quarters, Eggs Over Easy and their lone album, *Good 'n' Cheap*, are legendary. They are the band that kickstarted the entire pub rock movement of the early '70s—not just by sketching out the initial circuit of pubs throughout England, but by developing the signature blend of laid-back country-rock and straight-ahead, driving rock & roll that served as the template for the entire movement, heard most strongly in the work of Eggs Over Easy's biggest fans, Brinsley Schwarz. Unfortunately for them, they had worse luck than the Brinsleys, recording only a fraction of their reported 100 songs (which included covers), and that record was cut a short after they left the U.K. for their native America. They broke up not much later, and their lone album was never easy to find—in fact, it didn't appear on CD until the summer of 2002, and that was in a Japan-only release. Prior to that, their only song in print was "The Factory," a hard-rocking number anthologized on the classic *Naughty Rhythms* collection. That tune, combined with the presence of Link Wray as a co-producer, suggests that *Good 'n' Cheap* would be an entirely hard-rocking affair, but it's much more laid-back, capturing the genial, rootsy flavor that was heard so effectively on such records as the Brinsleys' *Silver Pistol*, and this record is just as good, a definition of a lost classic. It's a relaxed affair, even when it rocks, but that's the appeal—this is the sound of a great neighborhood roots band that can sing sweetly but also adds some real grit to their late-night laments or weekend party anthems. True, this is not the kind of record that will take anybody by surprise, but it's a quiet triumph all the same, and, for those pub rock fanatics who have waited many years to hear this full album, it's everything they wanted it to be: a record that not only sounds like the foundation for the music (whose influences become immediately apparent when heard in whole), but an album that's a hell of a lot of fun, that immediately sounds like an old favorite. *—Stephen Thomas Erlewine*

Tony Ellis

b. 1939

Banjo, Fiddle, Vocals / Old-Timey

Bluegrass and old-timey string band traditions are fused into the deeply personal solo banjo and fiddle style of Tony Ellis. A five-time recipient of composition awards from the ASCAP (American Society of Composers and Publishers), Ellis was featured during a national Masters of the Banjo tour, sponsored by the National Folk Council for the Traditional Arts, in 1997. Ellis was taught the two-finger style of playing banjo by his grandmother, an old-time fiddler. Upon hearing a radio broadcast by Flatt & Scruggs in the mid-'50s, Ellis sold his high-school trumpet and bought a resonator banjo. After studying with Swanson Walker and Don Reno, Ellis joined Bill Monroe & His Bluegrass Boys in 1960, recording 22 tracks during the two and a half years that he played with the influential group. In 1962, Ellis performed with Mac Wiseman at Carnegie Hall in New York.

Although he left full-time performing shortly afterwards, he continued to develop his unique sound. Temporarily living in the Bristol, TN, area, he performed old-timey music with Bruce Mongle, George Pegram, and Tommy Jarrell. After relocating to south central Ohio, he played with several bluegrass and old-timey bands. Ellis' two albums, produced by Stephen Wade, were critical successes. *Dixie Banner*, released in 1987, was named one of the five best albums of the year by National Public Radio. *Farewell My Home*, released in 1993, was included on the annual Top Ten list compiled by the *Washington Post*. Ellis was accompanied on both albums by his son, Bill Ellis, a graduate of the Cincinnati Conservatory of Music with a degree in classical guitar. In 1993, Ellis played banjo and fiddle in the People's Light and Theater Company's production *John Brown's Body* in Malvern, PA. The album *Quaker Girl* was released in June 1999, followed three months later by *Sounds Like Bluegrass to Me*. *—Craig Harris*

Dixie Banner / 1988 / Flying Fish ♦♦

Tony Ellis' *Dixie Banner* is closer to traditional, 19th century string music than 20th century bluegrass, and it's all the more distinctive and worthwhile as a result. Ellis' three-finger style enlivens the old-timey aspects of these original songs, creating an exceptionally musical blend of different traditional musics. In addition to being a fine banjoist, Ellis is also an accomplished fiddle player, and several tracks here demonstrate his skills, and help give the album added weight. *—Stephen Thomas Erlewine*

● **Farewell My Home** / Feb. 1993 / Flying Fish ♦♦♦♦

Like bebop and Dixieland, bluegrass often functions as repertory music. Straight-ahead jazz is full of artists who insist on playing the same beaten-to-death standards over and over, and there are many bluegrass musicians who have a similar mindset—only they'll give you yet another version of "Rocky Top" instead of yet another version of "Giant Steps." But Tony Ellis was never the sort of bluegrass musician who had a "warhorses only" policy. He's a prolific composer—in addition to being an excellent banjo player/fiddler—and he does almost all of the writing on *Farewell My Home*. The only song on this 23-track CD that Ellis didn't write is the traditional hymn "Come Thy Fount of Every Blessing; the other 22 tracks are all Ellis originals. Produced by Stephen Wade in 1991, *Farewell My Home* finds Ellis forming a duo with his son, Bill Ellis (who is heard on acoustic guitar). And this father-and-son team enjoys a strong rapport on tunes that range from fast and exuberant ("Wild Fox," "T Model Ford," "Red Dog") to contemplative and wistful ("Kate, Bride of Matt," "Straw Dolls"). One of the CD's most lyrical offerings is the title track, which Ellis wrote in memory of America's early Irish immigrants as well as those who starved during Ireland's tragic potato famine. The piece has a strong Irish/Celtic flavor, which makes perfect sense because bluegrass (like country and Anglo-American folk) is a descendent of the jigs, reels, and airs that Irish and Scottish immigrants brought with them when they moved to the U.S. in the 19th and 20th centuries. From the exhilarating to the reflective, *Farewell My Home* paints a consistently attractive picture of both Ellis the musician and Ellis the composer. *—Alex Henderson*

Sounds Like Bluegrass to Me / 1999 / Copper Creek ✦✦✦

Although banjoist Tony Ellis got his start as one of Bill Monroe's Blue Grass Boys, in his subsequent solo work he has often explored quieter terrain, as he did on the sweet and lovely *Farewell My Home*, an album he made with his son Bill, and which stayed about as far away from the driving sounds of bluegrass as you can get while still playing three-finger style banjo. On this album Ellis is back in the bluegrass fold, working through a program of potboiler material with an all-star band featuring Dudley Connell on guitar, Lester Woodie on fiddle, and Tom Gray on bass. The playing and the songs are all great; it's always fun to hear tunes like "Long Journey Home" and "Nine Pound Hammer," even if they have been done to death, and the group harmonizes convincingly on "The Old Cross Road" and "Man of Constant Sorrow." The problem is the production, which is muffled and flat throughout the album—it sounds as if these performances were recorded in someone's living room on a four-track cassette recorder. That's too bad; the performances are lots of fun. —*Rick Anderson*

Quaker Girl / Jun. 1, 1999 / County ✦✦

Joe Ely

b. Feb. 9, 1947, Amarillo, TX

Guitar, Vocals / Progressive Country, Country-Rock, Outlaw Country, Americana
In the '70s, country & western was full of artists referred to as outlaws, mavericks who bucked the stodgy Nashville music establishment by writing their own songs, recording with their road bands, and producing their own records. The genre produced a slew of acts, but Amarillo, TX, native Joe Ely epitomized the form. Unlike most of that era's big names, Ely remained a viable artist. He got his start back in the early '70s, working with Butch Hancock and Jimmie Dale Gilmore in a group called the Flatlanders. Their only album didn't go far, and the group broke up. (Rounder reissued the album in 1990.) Around the mid-'70s, Ely formed an eclectic group who were able to swing from Cajun and western to honky tonk stomps and rockabilly; they were signed to MCA in 1977. Ely released an eponymous debut that year, using songs written by ex-Flatlanders Gilmore and Butch Hancock and throwing in some of his own road-worn, oddly poetic originals.

The next year brought *Honky Tonk Masquerade*, the cornerstone of Ely's legacy and one of modern country's most ambitious albums. Further albums (especially *Live Shots*, recorded during his European tour with the Clash) brought Ely to the attention of rock fans and netted ecstatic reviews in country and pop magazines (but, mysteriously, produced no hits). MCA dropped Ely in 1983, and he woodshedded until 1987, when the independent Hightone label signed him and released *Lord of the Highway*. Another Hightone album followed before Ely (whose influence was being felt by the new breed of country neo-traditionalists) re-signed with MCA, releasing another live set and *Love and Danger*. *Twistin' in the Wind* followed in 1998, and *Live at Antone's* arrived two years later along with MCA-Nashville's *Best Of* collection. Ely remained an energetic and passionate live performer and an occasionally inspired songwriter. —*John Floyd*

Joe Ely / 1977 / MCA ✦✦✦✦

Ely's first album came out while country's outlaw movement was in full swing, but *Joe Ely* took it one better. This is a roots-rocking country album with tunes by Jimmie Dale Gilmore ("Treat Me Like a Saturday Night") and Butch Hancock ("She Never Spoke Spanish to Me," "If You Were a Bluebird") that deserve the near-classic status their cult of fans has bestowed on them. —*Brian Mansfield*

☆ **Honky Tonk Masquerade** / 1978 / MCA ✦✦✦✦✦

As strong as Joe Ely's self-titled solo debut was, his second album, 1978's *Honky Tonk Masquerade*, actually managed to top it, and the album remains one of the great creative triumphs of the Texas singer/songwriter community, as well as a high-water mark in Ely's career. Displaying a very Texan sense of eclecticism, *Honky Tonk Masquerade*'s ten tunes run the gamut from beer-stained weepers (the title cut) and late-night declarations of loneliness ("Tonight I Think I'm Gonna Go Downtown") to barrelhouse rock & roll ("Fingernails") and honky tonk dance numbers ("West Texas Waltz" and "Cornbread Moon"), and Ely's simple but expressive delivery makes the most of every song he sings. Ely's band deserves a special nod as well, especially steel guitarist Lloyd Maines and Ponty Bone on accordion, who can seemingly conjure up an orchestra or a horn section at will. And as strong as Ely's songs are, he has the good sense to also accept contributions from fellow ex-Flatlanders Butch Hancock and Jimmie Dale Gilmore, whose more introspective lyrical approach makes for a satisfying contrast to Ely's more down to earth style. Smart without sounding pretentious, and musically ambitious without losing focus or drive, *Honky Tonk Masquerade* is a superb album that captures Ely and his band at their best. —*Mark Deming*

Down on the Drag / 1979 / MCA ✦✦✦

Simply another set of decent country songs. Ely's momentum was gone: his band, for the first time, sounded like tired and bored pros. —*John Floyd*

Live Shots / 1980 / MCA ✦✦✦✦✦

Ely partakes of the musical diversity of his hometown, Lubbock, TX, freely mixing country, rock, Tex-Mex, and hard honky tonk music in excellent songs he writes himself or borrows from his friend Butch Hancock. This is a live best-of covering his first three albums, recorded on tour in England. —*William Ruhlmann*

Musta Notta Gotta Lotta / 1981 / MCA ✦✦✦

If you're making a tape of Ely's greatest hits, *Musta Notta Gotta Lotta* is a must—"Dallas" and "Wishin' for You" ensure its necessity. But anyone who has shed tears (and danced them away) to *Honky Tonk Masquerade* will feel cheated by such obvious covers as Roy Brown's "Good Rockin' Tonight" and Buddy Holly's "Rock Me My Baby." —*John Floyd*

Hi-Res / 1984 / MCA ✦✦

The only one of Ely's MCA albums the label hasn't issued on CD, *Hi-Res* is a synthesizer-heavy record that came after Ely learned about Apple computers. Preferable versions of

"Cool Rockin' Loretta" and "She Gotta Get the Gettin'" appear on *Live at Liberty Lunch*. —*Brian Mansfield*

Lord of the Highway / 1987 / Hightone ✦✦✦

After a long recording layoff, Ely picked up where he'd left off in 1984 with this typical collection, whose best songs—"Me and Billy the Kid" and "Are You Listenin' Lucky?"—were Ely originals. —*William Ruhlmann*

Dig All Night / 1988 / Hightone ✦✦✦

Dig All Night follows in the direction of *Lord of the Highway*, finding Joe Ely concentrating on hard-kicking roots rock and rockabilly. The country influences are now just flavoring, not the focal point, and that's not a bad thing, since *Dig All Night* is a lean, mean record that rocks harder than nearly any roots record of its era. —*Thom Owens*

Milkshakes & Malts / 1988 / Sunstorm ✦✦✦

Live at Liberty Lunch / Sep. 1990 / MCA ✦✦✦

This live album was recorded over two days at *Liberty Lunch* in Austin, TX. Ely's band has evolved from a country band with Tejano roots to a hard-rocking Texas ensemble highlighted by guitarist David Grissom, who later defected to John Cougar Mellencamp. —*Brian Mansfield*

Love & Danger / Sep. 29, 1992 / MCA ✦✦✦✦✦

Ely is stark and restless. His muse still roams the highways in search of whatever, his romance doomed by a twist of fate. He's a more objective observer; a storyteller who captures the tragic side to the well-defined characters of "The Road Goes on Forever" and "Every Night About This Time." Ely conveys much—if not most—of a song's emotion through his inspired electric guitar playing. The string-bending is at high-pressure intensity for "Love Is the Beating of Hearts," then drops deep, sonorous and echoed for "Slow You Down." —*Roch Parisien*

No Bad Talk or Loud Talk 1977–'81 / Apr. 25, 1995 / Edsel ✦✦✦✦

Edsel's *No Bad Talk or Loud Talk 1977-'81* is an exhaustive, 18-track collection that culls many highlights from his first five albums, including "Honky Tonk Masquerade," "Fingernails," "Tonight I Think I'm Gonna Go Downtown," "Treat Me Like a Saturday Night," "Maria," "Musta Notta Gotta Lotta," "Suckin' a Big Bottle of Gin," and "She Never Spoke Spanish to Me." While *Honky Tonk Masquerade* and *Live Shots* remain excellent albums in their own right, this is a superb collection, capturing the excitement of Ely's music and offering a definitive introduction to his peak years. —*Stephen Thomas Erlewine*

Letter to Laredo / Aug. 29, 1995 / MCA ✦✦✦✦✦

Flamenco guitarist Teye is the dominant instrumentalist on a Joe Ely album that fits the "unplugged" tag—drums, electric bass, and various, mostly acoustic guitars and occasional accordion and harmonica—and that could be played without complaint in any cantina along the Rio Grande. Ely is joined in his story songs about Southwest life and romantic devotion by Raul Malo, Jimmie Dale Gilmore, and Bruce Springsteen, while Butch Hancock and Tom Russell contribute the strongest material; Hancock's is a sequel, "She Finally Spoke Spanish to Me," and Russell's is the tragic story of a man who bets his future on a cock fight. *Letter to Laredo* is a mood piece with less of the raw energy of many of Ely's albums, but the singer is in his element and his mastery of the form is obvious. —*William Ruhlmann*

Time for Travellin': The Best of Joe Ely, Vol. 2 / Aug. 6, 1996 / Edsel ✦✦✦✦

Time for Travellin': The Best of Joe Ely, Vol. 2 fills the gaps left by Edsel's previous Ely compilation, *No Bad Talk or Loud Talk*, offering 19 tracks from Ely's first four albums that weren't featured on that collection. It's a testament to Ely's talent and the quality of the records that these aren't lesser songs—they're just a little less celebrated. Just a cursory listen to "Tennessee's Not the State I'm In," "Jericho (Your Walls Must Come Tumbling Down)," "I'll Be Your Fool," "She Leaves You Where You Are," "Wishin' for You," and "I Keep Gettin' Paid the Same" reveals that these songs are every bit as good as those on the first volume. In many ways, it makes more sense to acquire the original albums, since the songs that didn't make these collections are also quite good, but if you want to take the compilation route, neither *Time for Travellin'* or *No Bad Talk or Loud Talk* will disappoint. —*Stephen Thomas Erlewine*

Twistin' in the Wind / May 12, 1998 / MCA ✦✦✦✦

Joe Ely, like fellow Texans Billy Joe Shaver, Guy Clark, and Townes Van Zandt, is pure originality. An artist whom other artist seek to emulate, he never disappoints. With this release, Ely continues his wild ride into the heart and soul of a man and the landscape he inhabits. Effective as a songwriter and performer, Joe Ely became more potent with each passing year. His diversity buoys him up as he works his way through both the dark and the light. The title cut, "Up on the Ridge," and "You're Workin' for the Man" display his ability to cast a deep shadow upon life's more rugged passages. "Sister Soak the Beans" and "If I Could Teach My Chihuahua to Sing" are light and humorous, reflective of Ely's geography, Texas, and create a balance that too few artists ever find. With "Gulf Coast Blues" and a wonderful honky tonk concerto, "I Will Lose My Life," Ely proves to be a master painter who creates his songs from a vast palette of colors, textures, and experiences. —*Jana Pendragon*

Live at the Cambridge Folk Festival / May 16, 2000 / Strange Fruit ✦✦✦

Live at Antone's / Jun. 6, 2000 / Rounder ✦✦✦✦

Live at Antone's is Joe Ely's third release mixing his rock, country, folk, and Tex-Mex-fueled live show for an appreciative Texas audience. This retrospective was recorded by the Rounder label January 22 and 23, 1999, and showcases the heartfelt romanticism and storytelling on compositions by Jimmie Dale Gilmore, Tom Russell, Butch Hancock, Robert Earl Keen, Utah Phillips, and Ely. Pedal steel guitarist Lloyd Maines and the accordion of Joel Guzman add extra spice to this already high-energy performance. Favorites like "The Road Goes on Forever," "Me and Billy the Kid," "Dallas," "Road Hawg," and the obligatory Buddy Holly cover "Oh! Boy" are featured on another recommended Joe Ely live set. —*Al Campbell*

★ **The Best of Joe Ely** / Nov. 21, 2000 / MCA ✦✦✦✦✦
For all his critical hosannas, Joe Ely is something of an acquired taste, since his rebellious neo-traditionalist country fluctuates between heartfelt honky tonk evocations, self-conscious modern-day mocking, and material that falls somewhere in between. He did cut a series of albums that were acclaimed and influential, including the rollicking *Live Shots*, one the great country live albums of its time, but MCA Nashville's 2000 *The Best of Joe Ely* is the best introduction to his sound and aesthetic. Spanning his career from his 1977 debut to 1995's *Letter to Laredo*, this touches on every defining moment Ely had, including songs that he initially cut with the Flatlanders. In this setting, his blend of honky tonk, folk, and rock & roll is remarkably effective and consistent, with "She Never Spoke Spanish to Me," "Tonight I Think I'm Gonna Go Downtown," "Musta Notta Gotta Lotta," and "Letter to Laredo" all standing out as progressive/alternative country classics. Given his cult status—the kind of cult where all his recordings are acclaimed equally—this is the best way for outsiders to fall in love with Ely. —*Stephen Thomas Erlewine*

From Lubbock to Laredo: Best Of / May 21, 2002 / MCA ✦✦✦✦

Streets of Sin / Jul. 15, 2003 / Rounder ✦✦✦

Emerson Drive

f. Grande Prairie, Alberta, Canada
Group / Contemporary Country, Country-Pop
Emerson Drive began in the western Alberta town of Grande Prairie, where singer Brad Mates, bassist Jeff Loberg, fiddler Pat Allingham, and keyboardist Chris Hartman began honing their sound as high-school talent-show competitors. After everyone came on board, they chose the name 12 Gauge, refurbished a rickety old school bus, and began gigging throughout Canada. Eventually guitarist Danick Dupelle and drummer Mike Melocon joined up, and new manager Gerry Leiske sent the young sextet out on the road yet again. The six hard years of touring paid off when a Nashville showcase impressed industry powerhouse Dreamworks into offering a contract in 2001. The band's self-titled debut arrived in May of the following year. Produced by Richard Marx, the album was a slick pop-country affair that had as much in common with boy bands like BBMak as it did with country new traditionalists such as Mark Wills. —*Johnny Loftus*

Bill Emerson

b. Washington, D.C.
Organ, Banjo, Guitar, Piano, Vocals / Rock & Roll, Electric Memphis Blues
Bill Emerson is one of the most influential musicians in bluegrass. He began playing guitar in 1955 and banjo the following year, which was when he heard a performance by Uncle Bob & the Blue Ridge Partners on a Rockville, Maryland, radio station. He was so captivated by their sound that he went to the station to meet them, and was asked to join them. A few months later, Emerson joined Buzz Busby & the Bayou Boys. When an auto accident put Busby and some of the bandmembers out of commission, Emerson and bandmate Charlie Waller assembled a new band, the Country Gentlemen, to keep their booking at the Admiral Grill in Bailey's Cross Roads, Virginia. They recorded three singles for Dixie and Starday, including "High Lonesome"/"Hey Little Girl."
In 1958, Emerson left the Gentlemen to play live gigs with the Stonemans, later playing with Bill Harrell, Jimmy Martin & the Sunny Mountain Boys, and Red Allen & the Kentuckians. In 1963, he released the album *This World is Not My Home*. While playing with Allen, he recorded a few albums as Bill Emerson & His Virginia Mountaineers, including *Banjo Pickin' n Hot Fiddlin' Country Style*. In 1965, he left Allen's band and rejoined Jimmy Martin's for two albums. Emerson left again in 1967 and teamed up with Cliff Waldron to form Emerson & Waldron and the Lee Highway Boys. On Rebel, the group recorded three albums, including *Bluegrass Country*. He returned to the Country Gentlemen in 1970, playing club dates and recording with them until 1972, when he was hit in the arm during a drive-by shooting as he and the band were leaving the Red Fox Inn in Bethesda, Maryland. He recovered fully and joined the U.S. Navy Band the next year.
Emerson's 20-year military stint was spent playing music in Washington, D.C., doing outside session work, and performing with his country/bluegrass band, the Country Current. Beginning in 1988, Emerson recorded two solo albums for Rebel, *Home of the Red Fox* and *Gold Plated Banjo* (1991). The previous year, he was honored by Sterling Banjo Works, who issued a Signature Series of banjos ("Bill Emerson Red Fox Model") and gear after him. Emerson released his *Reunion* album in 1992, which features various lead singers he has worked with over the years, including Jimmy Martin, Charlie Waller, and Tony Rice. He finally left the Navy in 1993 and has since released a duet album with protégé Wayne Taylor. Occasionally, Emerson plays reunion concerts with some of the groups he belonged to, but has declined to rejoin them full-time. —*Sandra Brennan*

Home of the Red Fox / 1990 / Rebel ✦✦✦

Gold Plated Banjo / 1990 / Rebel ✦✦

Reunion / Sep. 1991 / Webco ✦✦✦✦

● **Webco Classic Series** / Sep. 5, 1995 / Webco ✦✦✦✦

Banjo Man / 1996 / Webco ✦✦✦

Buddy Emmons

b. Jan. 27, 1937, Mishawaka, IN
Guitar (Steel), Vocals, Bass, Piano / Traditional Country, Instrumental Country
Buddy Emmons earned a place among Nashville's elite as one of the finest steel guitar players in the business. Born in Mishawaka, IN, he first fell in love with the instrument at age 11 when he received a 6-string lap steel guitar as a gift. As a teen, he enrolled at the Hawaiian Conservatory of Music in South Bend, IN, and began playing professionally in Calumet City and Chicago at age 16. In 1956, Emmons went to Detroit to fill in for

Walter Haynes during a performance with Little Jimmy Dickens; soon afterward he was invited to join Dickens' Country Boys. He appeared with them a few times on the *Grand Ole Opry* and recorded with them on a few singles, including "Buddy's Boogie" (1957). He also recorded a pair of solo singles for Columbia, "Cold Rolled Steel" (1956) and "Silver Bells" (1957).
In the late '50s, Emmons began playing occasionally with Ernest Tubb's band on *Midnight Jamboree*. In 1963, he began a five year stint with Ray Price & His Cherokee Cowboys, and in 1965 teamed up with fellow steel player Shot Jackson to record the LP *Singing Strings of Steel and Dobro*. This led the two to create the Sho-Bud Company, which sold an innovative steel guitar that used push-rod pedals. In 1969, Emmons joined Roger Miller's Los Angeles-based band as a bass player. When not touring with Miller, he did session work for a variety of artists. He quit Miller's band in 1973 and signed a solo contract, releasing several albums in the late '70s. After 1978, Emmons began playing for a number of small labels, where he and Ray Pennington occasionally collaborated with some of Nashville's finest side men as the Swing Shift Band. In 1993, Emmons began touring with the Everly Brothers. Throughout the '90s, he continued to do session work. —*Sandra Brennan*

● **Steel Guitar Jazz** / Sep. 1963 / Mercury ✦✦✦✦✦
Buddy Emmons wasn't the first musician to be featured playing a pedal steel guitar in a jazz setting, but it is unlikely that anyone else recorded an entire date playing one prior to this 1963 session. Although both he and the instrument are indelibly associated with country music, Emmons makes it work for several reasons. He's surrounded by some top players, including Bobby Scott, Jerome Richardson, Art Davis, and Charlie Persip; he also interacts with the band rather than overdoing the special effects available to him, especially the horn-like sounds obtained from his use of the slide. Emmons also chose an intriguing mix of material. Obvious highlights are the loping treatment of "Where or When," featuring Richardson's delicious soprano sax trading off with the leader, and Emmons' hot playing of "(Back Home Again In) Indiana." Equally rewarding are the jazz classics: Ray Brown's soulful "Gravy Waltz," an intricate romp through Sonny Rollins' "Oleo," and Horace Silver's toe-tapping "The Preacher." This was pretty much a one-time affair for Emmons, who returned to country music, though he did record some additional jazz with guitarist Lenny Breau during the 1970s. [Although the instrument never really caught on in jazz, this highly recommended album, which was finally reissued on CD in 2003, is well worth checking out.] —*Ken Dryden*

Singing Strings of Steel and Dobro / 1965 / Starday ✦✦✦✦

The Best of Western Swing / 1967 / Cumberland ✦✦✦✦

Two Aces: Sho-Budding Again / 1971 / K-Ark ✦✦✦✦
It is hard to say exactly when this album was recorded and released. The producers provide no exact details, but do offer up a few clues. For example, Buddy Emmons' hair is black. And the phone number listed on the back does not work, although the area code is valid for the city of Nashville. For the most part, this is music that is timeless. Generally, country & western is not a music in which instrumental albums are that important. A funny thing, considering the musical talents of many of the participants. Kept on a tight rein and limited to short solos, the country picker sometimes spends an entire career without ever letting loose. Thankfully, the steel guitar tradition has pushed the idea of instrumental albums in which the pedal steel moves to the front, taking over the role of lead vocal. Listeners that like the groove and sound of country music but can't stand the lyrics might really like an album such as this, as should anyone who has ever had to listen to the lyrics of the maudlin "Footprints in the Snow." Fans of pedal steel and dobro should go wild. Emmons is joined by Shot Jackson, who gets a vivid sound out of his dobro that brings to mind flocks of geese and slices of chocolate cake, among many other things. A crack band is on hand to boister the two pickers, although only fiddler Vassar Clements is identified. The uptempo "Red Wing" is really great, and there is also a very moving version of the Bob Wills anthem "Maiden's Prayer." —*Eugene Chadbourne*

Steel Guitar / 1975 / Flying Fish ✦✦✦✦
The versatility of Buddy Emmons would never be questioned. Given the opportunity to do whatever he wanted on an album in a period when many listeners were waiting, their tongues hanging out, for the next bold innovation in country-flavored instrumental music, he convened two completely different groups to back him up. With one, he established his abilities to play traditional country and Western swing material as if he was regaining the heavyweight championship; each of his solos on these pieces is delivered with that type of combination of punches, and it is a good thing he hired a bona fide genius, guitarist Leon Rhodes, to play with him on these tracks since there are few other players who would be able to follow him up. If this album consisted totally of pieces such as the wonderful "Medley" of steel guitar favorites or the work-up of "Orange Blossom Special" on which Emmons is endlessly inventive, then it would receive the highest rating. On the second side there is the equivalent of rocks in bags of potatoes, however, a band who goes for a somewhat more contemporary feel, coming across like some kind of wedding band in the process. Sure, this is the type of wedding band where some of the music types in attendance would be commenting on how good the pedal steel player is, and the drumming of Kenny Malone is crisp-sounding and effective. Something about this music just grates, however, and yes, there are wedding bands who play "Nothing Is Delivered" by Bob Dylan, and better than on this record to boot. Still, everything described up until now was still not quite enough for the maestro, who chose to bring the album to an unforgettable conclusion by overdubbing himself to create a version of "Canon in D Major" by Johann Pachelbel that rectifies the situation, makes one restore the check next to the album's name that might have been angrily erased while listening to "Top Heavy." In fact, it could be said that this wonderful classical performance is one of the truly liberating moments in music from the perspective of any possible triumph over genre fascism. Here there is a so-called lowbrow country & western musician

playing European art music on an electric instrument, no less. The results are sheer genius, a contemplative and almost spiritual performance in which there is as much exquisitely small detail as any of the classics of minimalism. That the same person can be responsible for all the tracks on this record is one of the mysteries of the universe—but hey, that's Nashville. *—Eugene Chadbourne*

Sings Bob Wills / 1976 / Flying Fish ♦♦♦♦
This album features some of the best pickers in Nashville, with Pig Robbins and Johnny Gimble. *—AMG*

Buddies / 1977 / Flying Fish ♦♦♦

Live From Austin City Limits / 1979 / Flying Fish ♦♦♦

Minors Aloud / 1979 / Flying Fish ♦♦♦
In this second meeting between pedal steel guitarist Buddy Emmons and jazz guitarist Lenny Breau, they find common ground as they venture through a session mixing jazz standards and original compositions, accompanied by keyboardist Randy Goodrum, bassist Charles Dungey, and drummer Kenny Malone. "Minors Aloud" is a midtempo blues jointly written by Emmons and Breau, though all of the individual solos are rather perfunctory. Breau's salute to Johann Sebastian Bach, "Bach's Bouree," opens with his gorgeous unaccompanied solo; after the band is added, it maintains its magic with understated brushwork by Malone. The interpretation of "Scrapple From the Apple" has a bizarre quiet introduction, but quickly transforms into a cooker. The pedal steel definitely gives a rather unique sound to Benny Golson's "Killer Joe," though Breau is clearly the more interesting soloist. "Compared to What," which was a huge hit for Les McCann and Eddie Harris, is an unqualified dud, with a completely forgettable vocal by Emmons. Flying Fish was always interested in mixing musicians from country and jazz; this somewhat uneven date should be considered at least a partial success. *—Ken Dryden*

Emmons Live, Vol. 1 / 197 / Midland Int. ♦♦

Emmons Live, Vol. 2 / 197 / Midland Int. ♦♦

Christmas Sounds of the Steel Guitar / 1987 / Step One ♦♦♦

Swingin' By Request / 1992 / Step 1 ♦♦♦

● **Amazing Steel Guitar: The Buddy Emmons Collection** / May 20, 1997 / Razor & Tie ♦♦♦♦♦
Amazing Steel Guitar: The Collection is a terrific 16-track collection that covers Buddy Emmons' entire career. A couple of strong songs might be missing, but all the necessary items—including "Raisin' the Dickens," "Country Boy Bounce," "Four Wheel Drive," "Where or When," "Cherokee (Indian Love Song)," "Witchcraft," "There Will Never Be Another You"—are here, making it a definitive single-disc overview and introduction. *—Stephen Thomas Erlewine*

Buddy & Lenny / Flying Fish ♦♦♦♦♦

Melvin Endsley

b. Jan. 30, 1934, Drasco, AR
Guitar, Songwriter, Vocals / Traditional Country, Rockabilly, Country Blues
By rights, Melvin Endsley should have been a major country artist of the late '50s—he had the talent, and the songs, and the drive, but not the luck to become as well known as, say, Marty Robbins. But he provided Robbins with one of the biggest hits of his career, "Singin' the Blues," and became a popular artist on the *Grand Ole Opry* and the *Louisiana Hayride,* performing from a wheelchair. Endsley was born in the town of Drasco, AR, and at age three he contracted polio, which cost him the use of his legs but only gave him the motivation to pursue life with even greater drive. It was while at the Crippled Children's Hospital in Memphis, from ages 13 to 15, that he started listening to Wayne Raney, the Delmore Brothers, and other country acts of the era and began learning guitar as a way to break up the loneliness that he felt from his parents' infrequent visits. The major influences on his singing and later composing were the artists he discovered in his teen years, including Hank Williams, Ernest Tubb, and Lefty Frizzell.

It was while attending high-school in Drasco that he began writing songs, and before he was 20 he'd already written a song called "It Happens Everytime" that would find its way to Don Gibson and Dorsey Burnette. He began appearing on a local Arkansas radio station while he was attending a local teachers' college, but before he had finished there, he was a regular on KWCB out of Searcy, AR, chosen from the pack of aspiring artists by his longtime idol Raney. Endsley introduced the biggest hit song he ever wrote, "Singin' the Blues," on KWCB, and it was well enough received that he began looking into getting it copyrighted and published, along with "It Happens Everytime" and four other songs he'd written. He went to Nashville to try and sell the songs and impressed Robbins with "Singin' the Blues" enough that he brought Endsley to Wesley Rose, of Acuff-Rose; suddenly, Endsley had a publisher.

Robbins cut "Singin' the Blues" for Columbia in November of 1955, and the single was issued nine months later. It rode the number-one spot on the country charts from November of 1956 until February of 1957. The way the record business was set up in those days, Endsley was due for multi-layered success, as Columbia Records gave "Singin' the Blues" to pop vocalist Guy Mitchell, whose version, issued simultaneously with Robbins', got to number one on the pop charts. The combined sales of the two versions were over two and a half million copies, and while they were flying out the doors of record stores, Endsley's other songs were being cut by Gibson ("It Happens Everytime"), Billy Worth ("Too Many Times"), and Janis Martin ("Love Me to Pieces").

During this same era, Endsley toured with the *Grand Ole Opry* and the *Louisiana Hayride.* Endsley got a recording contract of his own with RCA and cut 15 songs for the label between 1956 and 1958, but none of these sold well. He revealed himself an expressive singer and an effective guitarist, leading the band in his own sessions and coming up with embellishments that producer Chet Atkins encouraged and utilized in the final versions—Endsley's sides had a brisk tempo and a good beat, and a few could even have qualified as rockabilly. In his own estimation, however, Endsley believed he was allowed the recording contract as a way of keeping him happy but was only really of interest to the label as a source of songs for other artists. He left RCA in 1958 for a contract with MGM, and later recorded for Acuff-Rose's own Hickory label. Endsley later left Acuff-Rose and briefly had his own record label, Mel-Ark, based in Drasco, but he didn't pursue recording seriously after the early '60s. His last hit as a songwriter came from Stonewall Jackson, whose "Why I'm Walkin'" charted in 1960, but he's best remembered as the writer of "Singin' the Blues" and a half-dozen other late-'50s country classics. *—Bruce Eder*

● **I Like Your Kind of Love** / 1992 / Bear Family ♦♦♦♦♦
These 29 songs, cut for RCA, MGM, and Hickory, represent a formidable body of work, as solid as any early collection of Marty Robbins or Carl Perkins, and not just as compositions—Endsley had a pleasing and powerful voice, easily and convincingly expressing heartache, frustration, or anger, and the hooks are all there in the songs. The title tune, "Keep A-Lovin' Me, Baby," "Gettin' Used to the Blues," the rockabilly-like "Lovin' on My Mind," "Hungry Eyes," the hard-rocking, guitar-driven "Let's Fall Out of Love," and "I Got a Feelin'" were all superb, along with the rest of the RCA sides. The later sides, produced at MGM and Hickory, don't match the smooth commercial edge that Chet Atkins gave the RCA stuff, but they're worthwhile listening as well, some with rougher, slightly bluesier edges (check out "Ain't It Fine," "Oh, Yeah Baby," and "Started Out A-Walkin'"), with a few surprising later forays into a near-rockabilly sound ("For My Baby"). Strangely enough, Endsley didn't cut "Singin' the Blues," "Knee Deep in the Blues," or his other early hit songs, which may partly explain his lack of success as a recording artist, but there are still a couple dozen inspired songs here, some of them just as good as the hits he provided to Robbins and company. *—Bruce Eder*

Ty England

b. Dec. 5, 1963
Guitar, Vocals, Session Musician / Contemporary Country
Ty England may have struck out on a solo career in 1995 to some success, but to most new country fans he was most recognizable as Garth Brooks' touring guitarist during the height of Brooks' stardom. Raised in Oklahoma, England began playing guitar as a child, teaching himself the instrument on his grandfather's guitar. Over the course of his childhood and adolescence, he delved deeply into country, learning the work of classic singers like Roy Acuff and Hank Williams, as well as contemporary stylists like Don Williams and Keith Whitley. While he was in high-school, England sang with a number of bands in addition to the school choir. Following graduation, he attended college at Oklahoma State. During the night, he sang at a campus coffeeshop. One night, he met a fellow student by the name of Garth Brooks. The two became roommates and began playing music together. Eventually, England's grades began to slip, so his parents took him out of school and got him a job back at home.

Working at night, he finished his marketing degree, but instead of pursuing that degree, he had a job as an auto plant representative. As he was working at the auto plant, he received a call from Brooks, who had just signed a record contract in Nashville. England immediately moved to Nashville and became Brooks' guitarist, backup vocalist, and on-stage comedic foil. After six years, he sought out his own record contract with the assistance of Garth Fundis, a record producer for RCA. Fundis helped England sign a solo deal with RCA and the guitarist released his eponymous debut album in the summer of 1995. The first single from the record, "Should've Asked Her Faster," peaked at number three, while the second single, "Smoke in Her Eyes," became a lesser hit. He followed with *Two Ways to Fall* in 1996, resurfacing three years later with *Highways & Dance Halls.* *—Stephen Thomas Erlewine*

● **Ty England** / 1995 / RCA ♦♦♦♦♦
While his voice hearkens back to classic honky tonk singers like Lefty Frizzell, Ty England's music falls halfway between Garth Brooks and Randy Travis, ranging from uptempo stomps to heartfelt ballads. *—Stephen Thomas Erlewine*

Two Ways to Fall / Sep. 17, 1996 / RCA ♦♦♦♦
Ty England's second album, *Two Ways To Fall*, is nearly as strong as his debut album, boasting an excellent selection of ballads and honky tonk ravers that establish him as one of the finest mainstream country singers of the mid-'90s. *—Thom Owens*

Highways & Dance Halls / Nov. 23, 1999 / Capitol ♦♦♦
England's first album in four years is a leap of faith. For one, he's gone from Ty to Tyler because he says, "this is a more grownup record, with a more mature sound and subject matter." Second, there isn't a song on this 12-track collection that sounds anything like the contemporary country-pop that radio favors. But he's true to his traditional roots and provides ear candy for the honky tonk soul with songs like the uptempo "My Baby No Esta Aqui," the moving story-song of the "Travelin' Soldier," or the eclectic remake of his only Top Five hit "Should've Asked Her Faster," with the guitar-lovin' Steve Wariner. What England does lack is vocal enthusiasm, but he makes up for it in originality. Produced by his college buddy Garth Brooks, *Highways & Dancehalls* is a verifiable reprieve from the bubblegum music we've gotten used to hearing on radio. Country music fans will welcome England back with open arms. *—Maria Konicki Dinoia*

Bill Engvall

b. 1957, Galveston, TX
Executive Producer / Standup Comedy, Country Comedy
Born in Galveston, TX, Bill Engvall was a nightclub DJ in Dallas until the call to comedy became too strong to deny. After startling amateur-night audiences at several local clubs and a brief stint in St. Louis, Engvall arrived in Los Angeles in 1990. He hosted the *Pair of Jokers* cable special with Rosie O'Donnell and also appeared on *Evening at the Improv* and *The Tonight Show With Jay Leno.* In 1992, he was awarded Best Male Standup at the American Comedy Awards, and moved into sitcom TV with an appearance on *Designing Women* and a regular role on the short-lived *Delta.* Signed to Warner Bros. in 1996,

Engvall released his countrified debut album, *Here's Your Sign*—also the title of his most famed bit—in 1996. A tour with likeminded everyman comic Jeff Foxworthy was next; that in turn led to a part on Foxworthy's sitcom that was as brief as the show itself. The *Dorkfish* LP followed in 1998, and Engvall saw both it and his debut achieve gold-record status. His seasonal effort, *Here's Your Christmas Album*, appeared the following year. In mid-2000, Engvall released *Now That's Awesome* and embarked on *the Blue Collar Comedy Tour*, again with Foxworthy. The tour continued through 2003. *—Johnny Loftus*

Here's Your Sign / 1996 / Warner Bros. ✦✦✦

Bill Engvall's debut album *Here's Your Sign* is a reasonably funny collection of country-oriented standup comedy. Engvall is certainly more urbane than the cornball comedians that formed the backbone of the *Grand Ole Opry*'s comedic contingent, yet much of his humor won't play well with those accustomed to, say, Jerry Seinfeld. Nevertheless, Engvall is sharper and more clever than, say, Jeff Foxworthy, even if he doesn't have a gimmick as catchy as "you know you're a redneck." Instead, Engvall is simply a solid journeyman comedian, and if *Here's Your Sign* isn't consistently hilarious, it at least offers enough good jokes to make it worth a listen. *—Thom Owens*

Dorkfish / Oct. 13, 1998 / Warner Bros. ✦✦

Here's Your Christmas Album / Sep. 28, 1999 / Warner Bros. ✦✦

For his follow-up to the masterful *Dorkfish*, country comedian Bill Engvall examines one of our great cultural unifiers: Christmas. Featuring a play on the title of his first album and hit single "Here's Your Sign," *Here's Your Christmas Album* consists of almost all new material, with the sole exception of the *Dorkfish* cut "Here's Your Sign Christmas," which definitely fits the theme of the album. Engvall has a knack for taking commonly accepted customs and turning them inside out, so that you can see their darker sides, that they can be irritating rather than cheerful. That's what he does on album highlights like "I'm Getting Sued by Santa Claus," "Rudolph Got a DUI," "That's What's Wrong With Christmas," and *two* versions of "Fruitcake Makes Me Puke." And who can't relate to "Gift Emergency"? More funny stuff from a funny, funny guy. *—Chuck Donkers*

Now That's Awesome / Aug. 22, 2000 / BNA ✦✦

Depending on who you talk to, Bill Engvall has made a lucrative career of either delivering a much needed dose of traditional values to comedy, or shamelessly sucking up to society's lowest common denominator. Even more than Jeff Foxworthy, Engvall has positioned himself as the anti-Seinfeld; just a regular good ol' boy trying to make it through this crazy ol' world with pickup truck and cold can of Pabst Blue Ribbon intact. He, however, is no throwback to *Hee Haw* and *The Dukes of Hazzard*. He represents a new breed of middle American populist: the financially stable, goateed Republican businessman who dresses casually in well pressed late '80s fashions and whose truck may just be a Toyota. In other words, Engvall is the perfect comedy equivalent of the Nashville new country "hat acts," with whom he shares a record label. These artists use the most basic soundbite style trappings of a disappearing rural America, buff them to a sickening sheen, and serve them up to a public that, while still conservative, desperately wants to distance itself from the hick image of old. In this, he succeeds. On *Now That's Awesome*, he performs before a large and enthusiastic crowd who is just waiting to cheer his every affirmation of their lifestyle. Unfortunately, although the party atmosphere is palpable, this kind of setting does not often make for good comedy. Like Steve Martin on his *Wild and Crazy Guy* album, Engvall is forced to rely on overused catch phrases and a sort of social equivalent to the worst kind of pavlovian political rhetoric. To his credit, he avoids using profanity to get easy laughs. Unfortunately, however, he instead relies on a Budweiser commercial vision of sexual politics, one minute telling his audience how he'd love to find a naked Shania Twain waiting in his room, and the next admitting that men are dumb. In the end, however, *Now That's Awesome* fails not because it doesn't aspire to something better, but because it's simply un-funny. *—Pemberton Roach*

● **Cheap Drunk: An Autobiography** / Sep. 24, 2002 / Warner Bros. ✦✦✦

Alejandro Escovedo

Guitar, Vocals / Singer/Songwriter, Roots Rock, Americana, Progressive Country, Alternative Country-Rock

Alejandro Escovedo's family tree includes former Santana percussionist Pete Escovedo and Pete's daughter, Sheila E (also Prince's former drummer and later a pop star). He began his music career with the Nuns, a mid-'70s punk band based in San Francisco. He co-founded the cowpunk band Rank & File in 1979, which moved to Austin, TX, in 1981 after a stint in New York City. The band released *Sundown* on Slash Records; shortly after, Escovedo left to form the True Believers with brother Javier. The band recorded two albums for EMI (the second was never released, a fact that eventually caused the band to break up in 1988) and toured the country, often as an opening act for Los Lobos. Escovedo released a solo album in 1992 on Watermelon Records, *Gravity*, uniting his wide variety of styles; the album was produced by Stephen Bruton of Bonnie Raitt's band. After 1996's *With These Hands*, he also began recording with the group Buick MacKane. The solo *Bourbonitis Blues* followed in 1999. *—John Bush*

● **Gravity** / 1992 / Watermelon ✦✦✦✦✦

While Alejandro Escovedo had shown plenty of versatility over the first 15 years of his career in music—playing with early punk ravers the Nuns, prescient alt-country upstarts Rank & File, and roots rock firebrands the True Believers, among many others—it wasn't until the Believers took shape that he began to display his formidable gifts as a songwriter, and with his first solo album, *Gravity*, Escovedo belatedly made it clear that he possessed one of the strongest and most distinctive lyrical voices of his generation. Opening with "Paradise," a haunting first-person narrative of a man about to be hanged, *Gravity* is a strikingly accomplished set of songs that deal with love ("Broken Bottle," "Five Hearts Breaking"), death ("She Doesn't Live Here Anymore"), and loss ("The Last to Know," the title song) in deeply personal terms, and Escovedo tells his stories with a talent for finely woven detail that would be the envy of a first-rate novelist. And the diversity of Escovedo's years of musical experience shows in the album's arrangements, which range from quiet, contemplative pieces structured around cello and piano ("Broken Bottle," "She Doesn't Live Here Anymore") to full-on, amped-up barrelhouse rock & roll ("Oxford," "One More Time"); Turner Stephen Bruton's clean, unobtrusive production gets all the details on tape with admirable clarity. Not every songwriter has the luxury of spending a decade and a half on the sidelines honing his craft before making a solo bow, but even with that advantage, there are few people who have the talent and vision to create an album as strong and moving as *Gravity*; to call it an "auspicious debut" is to risk understatement. [*Gravity* was re-issued in 2002 with a bonus disc of live material recorded at McCabe's Guitar Shop in 1993.] *—Mark Deming*

Thirteen Years / 1994 / Watermelon ✦✦✦✦

The Austin singer/songwriter reaches deep once again, adding triple violins, harp, and cello to his palette of movingly introspective material. Overall, the expanded lineup provides for plenty of tonal space. Before the mood ever gets maudlin, Escovedo cranks up the volume with guest guitarist Charlie Sexton for "Losing Your Touch," and a playful rocker that could have come from the Replacements/Paul Westerberg camp. With the exception of this track, "Mountain of Mud," and the John Cougar-ish "The End," *Thirteen Years* keeps to fragile, graceful interiors. *—Roch Parisien*

The End/Losing Your Touch / 1994 / Watermelon ✦✦✦

With These Hands / Jun. 18, 1996 / Rykodisc ✦✦✦✦

After recording two superb albums for the tiny independent label Watermelon Records, Alejandro Escovedo moved up, if not to the big leagues, then at least to AAA ball, when he signed with Rykodisc for his third solo set, *With These Hands*. While Escovedo's arrangements (he calls his band an orchestra without exaggeration) and Turner Stephen Bruton's production on *Gravity* and *Thirteen Years* were strikingly ambitious given their tiny budgets, *With These Hands* found them with a bit more money at their disposal, and if their approach wasn't remarkably different, the results display more polish and audibly greater depth than before, and Escovedo was able to bring along a few celebrity guests—among them Willie Nelson, Jennifer Warnes, and his cousin Sheila Escovedo (aka Sheila E)—who add to the music without calling undue attention to themselves. Lyrically, after the deeply (and sometimes painfully) personal material of *Gravity* and *Thirteen Years*, *With These Hands* found Escovedo stepping a bit outside himself to tell stories less obviously based on his own life, though the results are as compelling (and ring as true) as his more autobiographical material, especially the failed rock star's lament of "Pissed Off 2 A.M.," the dead of night heartache of "Sometimes," and "Nickel and a Spoon"'s story of a devastated family. If *With These Hands* seems less immediately striking than the two albums that preceded it, that's only because it's less surprising—with his first two solo albums, Alejandro Escovedo announced himself as a world class talent with a singular style, and if *With These Hands* doesn't break much new ground for him, it shows he's still in full command of his considerable gifts as a musician, and it's an impressive achievement. *—Mark Deming*

More Miles Than Money: Live 1994–1996 / Feb. 24, 1998 / Bloodshot ✦✦✦✦

If this disc is representative of Escovedo's live performance, he puts on one hell of a low-key show. Culled from gigs over a two year period, these renditions of his solo canon are so spare, so harrowing, you can hear the rattling of bones. The result ranks along side Frank Sinatra's *In the Wee Small Hours* and Tom Waits' *Closing Time* as one of the all-time great late-night LPs. *—Tim Sheridan*

Bourbonitis Blues / May 14, 1999 / Bloodshot ✦✦✦

After Alejandro Escovedo's relationship with Rykodisc came to a sudden halt following the release of an album by his glam punk side project Buick MacKane, he released two stopgap albums while writing the material for 2001's masterful *A Man Under the Influence*. *More Miles Than Money: Live 1994-1996* was a superb document of Escovedo's startlingly intimate live shows, but *Bourbonitis Blues* sounds like an odds-and-ends EP of covers, live tracks, and a few token new cuts that was somehow stretched to a 38-minute LP. The disc only features four original songs (one of which, "Guilty," is a remake of a tune from *With These Hands*), and while "I Was Drunk" is excellent, "Sacramento and Polk" and "Everybody Loves Me" suggest he was saving most of his A-list material for his next proper album. The rest of *Bourbonitis Blues* is filled up with covers, most of which are well worth hearing, especially his heart-rendering reading of Ian Hunter's "Irene Wilde," and a slow, ominous take on the Gun Club's "Sex Beat." But since Jon Langford happens to be singing lead on the take of "California Blues" featured here, it's not certain just what it's doing on an Alejandro Escovedo record. There isn't anything bad on *Bourbonitis Blues*, but there isn't a lot that's truly distinguished, either, and it's something of disappointment coming from one of the best singer/songwriters to emerge in the 1990s. *—Mark Deming*

A Man Under the Influence / Apr. 24, 2001 / Bloodshot ✦✦✦✦

"It's all about this love/It's all about this pain/It's all about the loss/We take to live again." Those lines hardly tell you everything there is to know about Alejandro Escovedo's songwriting, but he's rarely expressed his key themes with such strength and concision as he does in the first verse of "About This Love," and while Escovedo's fifth studio album, *A Man Under the Influence*, doesn't stray far from the musical and lyrical themes that have dominated his previous work, he's rarely (if ever) put the pieces together quite as well as he does here. Escovedo's latest lineup of his orchestra—anchored by Brian Standefer on cello, Eric Heywood on pedal steel, Mike Daly on keyboards and guitar, Hector Munoz on drums, and Cornbread on bass—sounds like his strongest and best controlled to date, as comfortable with the subtleties of "Wave" as the full-on rock of "Castanets." Quite simply, Escovedo has never sung better than he does on this set, running the emotional spectrum from plaintive longing to swaggering contempt and never sounding less than convincing at any stop along the way. And while Turner Stephen Bruton's production on Escovedo's first three studio albums was intelligent and intuitive, Chris Stamey's work on *A Man Under the Influence* suits him just as well while sounding clearer, sharper, and better focused; the sound catches the full range of Escovedo's personality while adding the sonic details that sometimes got lost on his previous records. And if love and loss still remain Escovedo's favorite themes, like Hank Williams or Leonard Cohen he seems to have something new and telling to say about them each time out; each of this album's 11 songs is worth hearing, and the cumulative effect is nothing less than stunning. No one who's heard Escovedo's work doubts his status as one of the finest singer/songwriters of his day, and he's never been heard to better advantage on disc than on *A Man Under the Influence*. *—Mark Deming*

By the Hand of the Father / May 14, 2002 / Texas Music Group ✦✦✦✦
The depth and feeling of *By the Hand of the Father* is a bit shocking. The project began as a play that premiered in Los Angeles in 2000 and has been stripped down to a handful of songs accompanied by voice-over texts. These songs and voice-overs weave a complex tapestry that explores the Mexican-American experience in the 20th century. Individuals leave their homeland, search for the American Dream, and attempt to hold on to their heritage. Alejandro Escovedo, who has written most of the lyrics and sings most of the vocals, stands at the center of this multi-faceted venture. "Rosalie" tells the tale of two lovers separated by "An ocean of powder and dust," who finally marry after a seven-year courtship punctuated by only seven visits. At the beginning of "Mexico Americano," the narrator recalls how his father always felt more Mexican than American until he joined the U.S. Army to defend a country "that was barely even his." These songs move forward in time, from the early 1900s to World War II to the Vietnam War. Heavy drums and a galloping guitar punctuate "Hard Road," a series of vignettes about the working lives of Mexican-Americans. Like other Americans, they hope their sons and daughters will be able to do better than them. *By the Hand of the Father* is a contemplative work of rare depth. By attempting to find meaning in the lives and stories of those who have come before them, Escovedo and friends have crafted a penetrating work of art that's also a joy to listen to. *—Ronnie D. Lankford Jr.*

Gravity [Bonus Disc] / May 14, 2002 / Texas Music Group ✦✦✦✦✦

Sara Evans

b. Feb. 5, 1971
Vocals / Country-Pop, Contemporary Country, Neo-Traditionalist Country
A female country traditionalist during a time when they were quite rare around Nashville, Sara Evans gained her RCA contract in 1996 after her rendition of Buck Owens' perennial chestnut "I've Got a Tiger by the Tail" impressed its songwriter, Harlan Howard, so much he considered it his bound duty to help her. While growing up poor in rural Missouri, Evans performed with her family's band—at the age of four—and even recorded in Nashville several years later. She eventually married and moved to Oregon in 1992, but continued to perform, as Sara Evans & North Santiam. The group opened for Willie Nelson and Tim McGraw, among others, but Evans eventually returned to Nashville to try to remake her career. There she impressed Howard enough to recommend her to RCA executives, who connected her with producer Pete Anderson (a veteran of many albums by Dwight Yoakam). After her debut album, *Three Chords & the Truth*, was released in July 1997, Evans earned a special honor by being hand-picked by George Jones to open a special show in Nashville. *No Place That Far* followed a year later, and in 1999 she resurfaced with *Girls' Night Out*; *Born to Fly* was issued the next year. *—John Bush*

Three Chords & the Truth / Jul. 1, 1997 / RCA ✦✦✦✦
Coming on like an up-to-date version of Patsy Cline, Sara Evans tosses her hat into the ring for best new female country artist of 1998. Surprisingly, with *Three Chords & the Truth*, she just may win. This disc rings out with an air of originality helped along by great tunes and solid backup musicianship. Producer Pete Anderson (of Dwight Yoakam fame) helps keep things pared down and centered, giving Evans the opportunity to shine. The title cut is a must for new country fans, while "Imagine That" calls to mind Billie Holiday. All in all, the title of this disc says it all. *—James Chrispell*

No Place That Far / Oct. 27, 1998 / RCA ✦✦✦✦
Country singer/songwriter Sara Evans gives fans another sample of her marvelous vocal talents on this 1998 recording, *No Place That Far*. With songs like "The Great Unknown," "I Thought I'd See Your Face Again," "Fool, I'm a Woman," "Love, Don't Be a Stranger," and "Cupid," country music lovers can sample both standard traditional styles and today's rocking country-pop on the same album. *No Place That Far* was recorded in Nashville, with harmonies added by country music stars such as Vince Gill, Martina McBride, George Jones, and Alison Krauss. If one had to pick one standout tune on this release, without a doubt it would be the wonderfully romantic title track, "No Place That Far." This is the kind of country album that goes well with good wine, low lights, and that special someone. *—Charlotte Dillon*

Girls' Night Out / Mar. 2, 1999 / BMG Special Products ✦✦✦
Unlike other country & western, diva collaborations, no one or two women outshine or overshadow the others on this harmless recording. While Lorrie Morgan ("Heart That Jack Broke," "Good As I Was to You") demonstrates the most thigh-slappin' chutzpah of the crowd, Martina McBride is the best and most authentic sounding singer, unafraid to belt those salutes to feminine freedom with the catchy "Independence Day" and promise-filled "'Til I Can Make It on My Own." Radio dial darlings Mindy McCready ("Ten Thousand Angels," "Over and Over") and her pal Sara Evans ("Three Chords and the Truth," "Almost New") have clear, competent voices but lack the subtle (or unsubtle) winning-ticket surprises that Morgan and McCready whip out occasionally. McBride's "Happy Girl" is a great, wonderfully written ode to sexual shyness with a fun melody: "I'm standin in a corner/with my concrete shoes/With my frozen smile/And a lighted fuse." But someone needs to sit Evans down for a real talking-to on the matter of song selection, since "Cryin' Game" is the most dismally cliché-clogged tune to drip out of the pipe in a longtime: "Bring me your love/Don't bring me pain/I've had enough of the crying game/Give me love/Don't tell me lies/I've had enough of your alibis." No, no, no! Get someone to keep an eye on these gals while they put these ambitious records together. Still, a good country, clear record for a good country, clear day. *—Becky Byrkit*

● **Born to Fly** / Oct. 10, 2000 / RCA ✦✦✦✦✦
The third time's a charm for the delightful Sara Evans. Bound to make her a household name, *Born to Fly* is, simply put, a great album. Whether it's her new mom status, or the fact that she co-produced for the first time and had a hand in writing six of the album's 11 enjoyable songs, Evans' confidence radiates in each and every song, from the playful title track "Born to Fly" to the unbreakable spirit of "I Learned That From You" about a love gone wrong even though they tried to make it work. She puts her own spin on distinguished renditions of Edwin McCain's "I Could Not Ask for More" and Bruce Hornsby's "Every Little Kiss." What must have added to her confidence was having her family (sister Ashley, sister Lesley, sister-in-law Melody) sing background vocals on some songs and brother Matt playing bass. Sara Evans has found herself musically and entertains country fans with an album they can be proud of. *—Maria Konicki Dinoia*

Leon Everette

b. Jun. 21, 1948, Aiken, SC
Vocals / Country-Pop, Urban Cowboy
Leon Everette was born June 21, 1948, in Aiken, SC. He joined the Navy after high-school, and while on leave in the Philippines bought a guitar and learned how to play. Encouraged by Navy talent-contest victories, he issued a series of singles once he was discharged and back in South Carolina. Unfortunately, the records went nowhere. Eventually, he got a job in the mailroom of True Records in Nashville. He then signed with the label, and in 1977 True assigned Everette to do a tribute to Elvis, *Goodbye King of Rock and Roll*. He was less than thrilled at the prospect and ripped up his contract. True released an Everette single anyway, and "I Love That Woman (Like the Devil Loves Sin)" became a minor hit. Toward the late '70s Everette signed with the Orlando imprint, which issued *Over* (1980).

The success of the album's singles led RCA to sign Everette the following year, and the partnership proved fruitful. He recorded five albums for the label between 1981-1984, and had several major hits, among them the label's reissue of the single "Giving Up Easy." His string of Top 20 hits continued with "Just Give Me What You Think is Fair" and "Soul Searching," both from 1982. But Everette became unhappy with RCA's promotion of his work and switched to Mercury Records, where he had three minor hits in 1985, including "Till a Tear Becomes a Rose." By the end of that year, he had moved back to the revitalized Orlando and in 1986 hit the charts with three singles, including "Still in the Picture." In 1988, he left country music to open an imported wicker shop with his wife in Ward, SC. *—Johnny Loftus*

● **The Best of Leon Everette** / 1985 / RCA ✦✦✦✦

The Everly Brothers

f. 1954, **db.** 1973
Group / Rock & Roll, Country-Rock, Rockabilly, Folk-Rock, Close Harmony, Pop
The Everly Brothers were not only among the most important and best early rock & roll stars, but also among the most influential rockers of any era. They set unmatched standards for close, two-part harmonies and infused early rock & roll with some of the best elements of country and pop music. Their legacy was and is felt enormously in all rock acts that employ harmonies as prime features, from the Beatles, Simon & Garfunkel, and legions of country-rockers to modern-day roots rockers like Dave Edmunds and Nick Lowe (who once recorded an EP of Everlys songs together). Don (born February 1, 1937) and Phil (born January 19, 1939) were professionals way before their teens, schooled by their accomplished guitarist father Ike, and singing with their family on radio broadcasts in Iowa. In the mid-'50s, they made a brief stab at conventional Nashville country with Columbia. When their single flopped, they were cast adrift for quite a while until they latched onto Cadence. Don invested their first single for the label, "Bye Bye Love," with a Bo Diddley beat that helped lift the song to number two in 1957.

"Bye Bye Love" began a phenomenal three-year string of classic hit singles for Cadence, including "Wake Up Little Susie," "All I Have to Do Is Dream," "Bird Dog," "('Til) I Kissed You," and "When Will I Be Loved." The Everlys sang of young love with a heart-rending yearning and compelling melodies. The harmonies owed audible debts to Appalachian country music, but were imbued with a keen modern pop sensibility that made them more accessible without sacrificing any power or beauty. They were not as raw as the wild rockabilly men from Sun Records, but they could rock hard when they wanted. Even their midtempo numbers and ballads were executed with a force missing in the straight country and pop tunes of the era. The duo enjoyed a top-notch support team of producer Archie Bleyer, great Nashville session players like Chet Atkins, and the brilliant songwriting team of Boudleaux and Felice Bryant. Don, and occasionally Phil, wrote excellent songs of their own as well.

In 1960, the Everlys left Cadence for a lucrative contract with the then-young Warner Bros. label (though it's not often noted, the Everlys would do a lot to establish Warners as a major force in the record business). It's sometimes been written that the duo never recaptured the magic of their Cadence recordings, but actually Phil and Don peaked both commercially and artistically with their first Warners releases. "Cathy's Clown," their first Warners single, was one of their greatest songs and a number-one hit. Their first two Warners LPs, employing a fuller and brasher production than their Cadence work, were not just among their best work, but two of the best rock albums of the early '60s. The hits kept coming for a couple of years, some great ("Walk Right Back," "Temptation"), some displaying a distressing, increasing tendency toward soft pop and maudlin sentiments ("Ebony Eyes," "That's Old Fashioned").

Don and Phil's personal lives came under a lot of stress in the early '60s: They were drafted into the Army (together), and studied acting for six months, but never made a motion picture. More seriously, Don developed an addiction to speed and almost died of an overdose in late 1962. By that time, their career as chart titans in the U.S. had ended; "That's Old Fashioned" (1962) was their last Top Ten hit. Their albums became careless, erratic affairs, which was all the more frustrating because many of their flop singles of the time were fine, even near-classic efforts that demonstrated they could still deliver the goods.

Virtually alone among first-generation rock & roll superstars, the Everlys stuck with no-nonsense rock & roll and remained determined to keep their sound contemporary, rather than drifting toward soft pop or country like so many others. Although their mid-'60s recordings were largely ignored in America, they contained some of their finest work, including a ferocious Top 40 single in 1964 ("Gone, Gone, Gone"). They remained big stars overseas—in 1965, "Price of Love" went to number two in the U.K. at the height of the British Invasion. They incorporated jangling Beatle/Byrds-esque guitars into some of their songs, and recorded a fine album with the Hollies (who were probably more blatantly influenced by the Everlys than any other British band of the time). In the late '60s, they helped pioneer country-rock with the 1968 album *Roots*, their most sophisticated and unified full-length statement. None of this revived their career as hit-makers, though they could always command huge audiences on international tours, and hosted a network TV variety show in 1970.

The decades of enforced professional togetherness finally took their toll on the pair in the early '70s, which saw a few dispirited albums and, finally, an acrimonious breakup in 1973. They spent the next decade performing solo, which only proved—as is so often the case in close-knit artistic partnerships—how much each brother needed the other to sound his best. In 1983, enough water had flowed under the bridge for the two to resume performing and recording together. The tours, with a backup band led by guitarist Albert Lee, proved they could still sing well. The records (both live and studio) were fair efforts that, in the final estimation, were not in nearly the same league as their '50s and '60s classics, although Paul McCartney penned a small hit single for them ("On the Wings of a Nightingale"). One of the more successful and dignified reunions in the rock annals, the Everlys continued to perform live, although they have not recorded an album since the late '80s. *—Richie Unterberger*

☆ **The Everly Brothers** / 1958 / Rhino ♦♦♦♦♦

Although the Everlys hadn't quite fully matured as artists, their debut is a fine, consistent effort divided between original material and respectably energetic covers of early rockers by Little Richard, Gene Vincent, and Ray Charles. Besides their first few hits, it includes some superb, underappreciated tracks that are nearly as good, like "Should We Tell Him" and "I Wonder if I Cared as Much." *—Richie Unterberger*

Songs Our Daddy Taught Us / 1959 / Cadence ♦♦♦

The Everlys had reached their commercial peak when they made this album of sparsely arranged traditional songs, a concept that was quite a surprise from a top rock & roll act, and considerably ahead of its time. It's actually not as enduring as their early rockers and pop ballads, but the singing is superb on their interpretations of standards like "Barbara Allen" and "Kentucky." *—Richie Unterberger*

☆ **The Fabulous Style of the Everly Brothers** / 1960 / Rhino ♦♦♦♦♦

The best of their original Cadence albums, packed with hits ("Bird Dog," "All I Have to Do Is Dream," "When Will I Be Loved," "'Til I Kissed You") and other classic tracks ("Devoted to You," "Let It Be Me," "Since You Broke My Heart," "Like Strangers"). Almost all of the songs show up on their greatest hits collections, so it might be a superfluous purchase for all but serious fans, despite its top-drawer quality. *—Richie Unterberger*

☆ **It's Everly Time** / 1960 / Warner Bros. ♦♦♦♦♦

While the Everlys' sound was diluted by more elaborate production in the '60s, that's not at all true on this LP, which is one of their very best. Not a stiff among the 12 tracks, most of which are barely known outside of serious Everly fans. Includes six stellar contributions by Boudleaux and Felice Bryant, one of Don Everly's best compositions ("So Sad"), and incredible harmony singing throughout. *—Richie Unterberger*

A Date with the Everly Bros. / 1961 / Warner Bros. ♦♦♦♦♦

Although the material is not on the killer level of *It's Everly Time*, there are some very fine songs on their second Warner LP. Includes "Cathy's Clown," their raucous cover of Little Richard's "Lucille," "Love Hurts" (which preceded Roy Orbison's hit version), and "So How Come" (covered by the Beatles in 1963 on the BBC). *—Richie Unterberger*

Both Sides of an Evening / 1961 / Warner Bros. ♦♦

Instant Party / 1962 / Warner Bros. ♦♦

The Golden Hits of the Everly Brothers / 1962 / Warner Bros. ♦♦♦♦

The Very Best of the Everly Brothers / Aug. 1964 / Warner Bros. ♦

The operative word here is: beware. This does indeed have 12 of their biggest hits, but half of them are re-recorded versions of Cadence-era material. It's not that they're bad or radically different (after all, they were recorded only a few years later). But why settle for these when only the originals will do? *—Richie Unterberger*

Rock N' Soul / 1965 / Warner Bros. ♦♦

A whole LP of oldies covers with guitar-heavy '60s arrangements, including such standards as "That'll Be the Day," "Kansas City," "Hound Dog," "Lonely Weekends, "I Got a Woman," and the then-recent "Dancin' in the Streets." It's decently played and sung, but not among the Everlys' most creative work, or even among their most interesting material of the mid-'60s. It's also not quite as good as the similar album they would release later in 1965, *Beat & Soul*. The version of "Love Hurts," incidentally, is a different, more rock-oriented version than the ballad arrangement they had recorded a few years previously. *—Richie Unterberger*

Gone, Gone, Gone / 1965 / Warner Bros. ♦♦

A jumble of tracks from varying sessions that, despite some excellent moments, were indicative of the general directionlessness of the Everlys' career at this point. The title song was their final Top 40 single of the '60s, and indeed one of their greatest performances. "The Ferris Wheel," also a 1964 single, was a decent, moody ballad that was a minor hit in both America and the U.K.; for some reason, it was excluded from the double-CD compilation of their best '60s work, *Walk Right Back*. Otherwise, the album contains a few other songs cut in 1964, and some odds and ends from sessions in the early '60s. The Everlys, John D. Loudermilk, and the great Boudleaux/Felice Bryant songwriting team wrote almost all of the material on this album, but unfortunately it was not up to the standards of either the writers or the performers. *—Richie Unterberger*

Beat & Soul / 1965 / Warner Bros. ♦♦♦

For the second album in a row, the Everlys presented an entire LP of rock & roll covers (and one original), most of which had originally been hits in the 1950s—"Love Is Strange," "Money," "Hi Heel Sneakers," "My Babe," "The Girl Can't Help It," "Lonely Avenue," and so on. While the performances are pretty good—and the vocals perennially better than good—it also seemed to be an indication that the pair were unwilling or unable to write or procure a decent supply of new material. Because of the over-familiarity of most of the songs, it has to rate as one of the brothers' less interesting efforts, regardless of the high level of execution. Nevertheless, "Love Is Strange" almost made the Top Ten in the U.K., and the sole original, "Man With Money," was a quality effort that was covered by several British groups including, unexpectedly, the Who (though their version was not released until the 1990s). *—Richie Unterberger*

In Our Image / 1966 / Warner Bros. ♦♦♦

The Everly Brothers were still in the game in 1966, and still capable of producing good tracks that didn't sound like anachronistic 1950s throwbacks. At the same time they were erratic, and their material wasn't nearly as consistent as what they procured in their heyday. This album very much reflects the Everlys' strengths and problems in the era. Overall, it's decent, yet it lacks anything on the killer level of their best vintage hits, with the arguable exception of "The Price of Love" (which *was* a big hit in Britain). The production is for the most part good, managing to incorporate the jangly full electric guitars coming to the forefront all over rock in the mid-'60s without diluting the Everlys' strongest assets: their harmonies. There was also access to some fine outside songwriters, such as Barry Mann-Cynthia Weil, who as a team contributed one of the best tracks, "Glitter and Gold." Still, the songs were just kinda good, not excellent, and occasionally they were below average or inappropriately cute, as in "Lovey Kravezit" especially. Still, all things considered, it's one of their better 1960s LPs, one worth finding by Everly Brothers fans, especially as most of the tracks have not been reissued on CD. Incidentally, Don Everly's ballad "It's All Over" would be covered for a Top Ten British hit the following year by Cliff Richard. *—Richie Unterberger*

Two Yanks in England / 1966 / Demon ♦♦♦♦

At first glance, this seems like a cash-in on the British Invasion. Recorded in London in 1966, no less than eight of the 12 songs were written by the Hollies (who released their own versions of many of the tunes). There are also covers of hits by the Spencer Davis Group and Manfred Mann. With a harder rock guitar sound (though not overdone or inappropriate) than previous Everlys discs, the duo's interpretations are actually worth hearing in their own right. The harmonies are fabulous, and indeed, the Everlys improve a few of the Hollies' songs substantially. "So Lonely" and "Hard Hard Year," in particular, have a lot more force, transforming the tunes from decent Hollies album tracks to excellence. Because so much of the material is non-original, this couldn't be placed in the top rank of Everly Brothers recordings. But it is a good effort that shows them, almost ten years after "Bye Bye Love," still at the top of their game and still heavily committed to a rock & roll sound. This was a bold contrast to other '50s white rock & rollers with roots in country, most of who had retreated to tamer country-oriented sounds by the mid-'60s. *—Richie Unterberger*

Roots / 1968 / Warner Bros. ♦♦♦♦♦

Considered one of the finest early country-rock albums, this showed the Everlys, unlike virtually every other top rock & roll act of the '50s, keeping abreast of contemporary rock and pop trends. In the manner of their 1958 LP *Songs Our Daddy Taught Us*, the concept was to cover songs by performers and composers that had been influential on the duo, including Jimmie Rodgers, Merle Haggard, traditional standards, and a couple of numbers by Ron Elliott of the Beau Brummels. Although this laid-back, tasteful, acoustic-oriented recording isn't as outstanding as their classic early hits, the vocals are superb, conveying qualities of innocence tempered by experience. *—Richie Unterberger*

Chained to a Memory / 1970 / Harmony ♦♦

An odd, what-were-they-thinking-when-they-put-this-out reissue of the Everly Brothers' 1966 LP *In Our Image*, minus three songs ("Glitter and Gold," "Lovey Kravezit," and "I Used to Love You"). So although the music's not bad, you really should try to track down *In Our Image* itself, particularly as the Barry Mann-Cynthia Weil song "Glitter and Gold" is one of their better obscure recordings. Who knows how this ended up on a Columbia subsidiary (Harmony) just four years after the material came out on Warner Bros., and here's betting the dumb liner note was dashed off in less than an hour. Unfortunately, most of *In Our Image* has not come out on CD, and the original *In Our Image* is not easy to find, which means that the inferior *Chained to a Memory* dilution might be about as easy a place to find some of the tracks as any. *—Richie Unterberger*

EB 84 / 1984 / Razor & Tie ♦♦♦

After their televised reunion concert, the Everlys made a commercial and artistic comeback with *EB 84*. With Dave Edmunds producing, Phil and Don brought their sound into the '80s while maintaining their trademark harmonies. Lifted by Paul McCartney's "Wings of a Nightingale" and Jeff Lynne's ethereal "The Story of Me," this record has more to offer than simply nostalgia. *—J.P. Ollio*

The Reunion Concert / 1984 / Mercury ♦♦♦

Lively, if ultimately too slick, this concert recording ties up a few loose ends. *—Bruce Eder*

All They Had to Do Was Dream / 1985 / Rhino ♦♦♦
Alternate takes of much of their strongest material from the Cadence era, cut between 1957 and 1960. A bit more tentative than the familiar renditions, these aren't as good as the versions that ended up on official releases, but are enjoyable and fascinating glimpses of works in progress, and the singing is excellent throughout. Includes different versions of hits like "Wake Up Little Susie," "All I Have to Do Is Dream," "'Til I Kissed You," and "When Will I Be Loved." *—Richie Unterberger*

Born Yesterday / 1986 / Mercury ♦♦
Born Yesterday was something of a disappointment following *EB 84*. Whatever spark the Everlys had on their earlier record is lost here. "Always Drive a Cadillac" and a version of Dire Straits' "Why Worry" are worthwhile, but it's easy to hear why this record quickly landed in the bargain bin. *—J.P. Ollio*

★ **Cadence Classics: Their 20 Greatest Hits** / 1986 / Rhino ♦♦♦♦♦
The single-disc collection *Cadence Classics: Their 20 Greatest Hits* compiles all of the Everly Brothers' hits, plus many terrific album tracks, from the duo's recordings for Cadence Records in the late '50s. Every one of the Everlys' biggest hits, including "Bye Bye Love," "I Wonder If I Care As Much," "Wake Up, Little Susie," "This Little Girl of Mine," "All I Have to Do Is Dream," "Claudette," "Bird Dog," "Devoted to You," "Problems," "Message to Mary," "('Til) I Kissed You," "Let It Be Me," and "When Will I Be Loved." *Cadence Classics* misses no essential track, making it a definitive collection and the perfect introduction to the duo's sound. *—Stephen Thomas Erlewine*

Hidden Gems from the Warner Years / 1989 / Ace ♦♦♦♦♦
This collects 14 songs that originally appeared on non-hit singles between 1962 and 1965; many of them had never been on LP. This material strongly counters the view that the Everlys faded artistically after "Cathy's Clown." The writing credits for these strong compositions read a bit like a who's who of early-'60s pop/rock, with contributions from Gerry Goffin, Mann/Weil, Doc Pomus and Mort Shuman, Sonny Curtis, Boudleaux and Felice Bryant, and the Everlys themselves. The singing is fabulous, and the arrangements still strong, rock-oriented, and tastefully produced. Tracks like "Nancy's Minuet" (1963), a great Don Everly original and one of their best paeans to lovelorn melancholia, and "You're the One I Love" (1964), a fine, brooding midtempo rocker, stand with their very best work. Only three of these appear on the '60s Everlys anthology *Walk Right Back*, making this a necessary purchase for Everlys fans. *—Richie Unterberger*

Best of the Everly Brothers: Rare Solo Classics / 1991 / Curb ♦♦♦
Between their breakup in 1973 and their reunion in 1983, Don and Phil Everly did a lot of recording on their own without achieving much in the way of commercial success, though Phil did reach the U.K. Top Ten in a duet with Cliff Richard on the excellent "She Means Nothing to Me" in 1983. You won't find that song here, but you will find 18 performances in 50 minutes of songs mostly released on singles—by Don on Hickory Records in 1976-1977, by Phil on Curb Records in 1980-1981. There's more of Don (who made the 1977 *Brother Juke-Box* album for Hickory) than there is of Phil, but the tracks are all mixed up, the singers are not identified on the jacket, and we bet you'll have trouble telling them apart. One hint: Don, freed of the brotherly harmonies, usually likes to sing solo lead against backup choruses, while Phil often recreates brother-like duo vocals. In either case, the brothers separately pursued a country-rock-pop style similar to what they did together. There are some good performances here, but as you might expect, this is a record more for Everly fans than first-time listeners. *—William Ruhlmann*

Classic Everly Brothers / 1992 / Bear Family ♦♦♦♦♦
The three-disc box set *Classic Everly Brothers* collects all of their Cadence recordings, including alternate takes, as well as several early radio shows and the four tracks the duo recorded for Columbia in 1955. While this music is the most essential the brothers ever made, the disc of rarities is only of interest to devoted fans. Nevertheless, the sound on the box is stellar, the liner notes are excellent, and the whole package is wonderful; for hardcore fans, the set is worth the money. *—Stephen Thomas Erlewine*

The Mercury Years / Jul. 20, 1993 / Mercury ♦♦♦♦
Mercury Years collects all of the finest moments from their two 1980s albums; its best moments, like "On the Wings of a Nightingale," are surprisingly strong. *—Stephen Thomas Erlewine*

☆ **Walk Right Back: The Everly Brothers on Warner Bros.** / Sep. 14, 1993 / Warner Archive ♦♦♦♦♦
This two-CD, 50-track compilation assembles the Everly Brothers' most memorable recordings of the 1960s. Although their work from this period has sometimes been criticized as inferior to their classic '50s recordings for Cadence, the best of these songs are a match for anything the duo recorded. As it happens, the strongest of these tunes are drawn from their first two albums for Warners in the 1960s, including the hits "Cathy's Clown" and "So Sad." In the following years, their material suffered from increasing inconsistency and ill-suited production. Yet the Brothers continued to intermittently hit the mark squarely—not only with early-'60s hits like "Crying in the Rain" and "Temptation," but neglected flop singles like "Nancy's Minuet" and "You're the One I Love," as well as the hard-rocking minor 1964 hit "Gone Gone Gone" (their last Top 40 single). They also showed a willingness to incorporate the hard-rocking beat of the British Invasion into their work that was not shared by any of the other major stars of the '50s. This compilation misses a number of fine B-sides and non-hit singles from the early and mid-'60s (check the Ace import collection *Hidden Gems* for those) and perhaps leans too heavily on their tepid late-'60s country-rock. But it's a good overview of a body of work that is often unfairly overlooked. *—Richie Unterberger*

☆ **Heartaches & Harmonies** / Oct. 18, 1994 / Rhino ♦♦♦♦♦
This four-CD, 102-song set includes all of their key performances, as well as many overlooked ones, dating from a previously unreleased 1951 radio performance of "Don't Let Our Love Die" to a 1990 live rendition of the very same tune. Opening with a disc's worth of classic Cadence performances, most of the next three CDs are given over to their largely overlooked Warner Bros. '60s output, including many interesting flop singles and album tracks, as well as top-notch rarities like an alternate version of the supremely moody "Nancy's Minuet" and the mid-'60s outtake "And I'll Go." Fine liner notes with detailed comments from the Everlys themselves, but it still manages to miss some great tunes (like the 1964 single "You're the One I Love" and various tracks from their late-'50s and early-'60s LPs), and shouldn't be considered a definitive collection of all their great performances. And the hard fact is, a lot of their post-1966 material (which comprises some of disc three and all of disc four) is kind of boring. *—Richie Unterberger*

● **All-Time Original Hits** / Nov. 2, 1999 / Rhino ♦♦♦♦♦
Rhino's 16-track collection *All-Time Original Hits* provides a useful service by compiling the Everly Brothers' greatest hits from both Cadence and Warner onto one disc. This, of course, means that many great songs are missing, particularly from the Cadence era, since only the A-sides of Top Ten singles were chosen for inclusion (which means such classics as "I Wonder if I Care As Much," "This Little Girl of Mine," "Claudette," "Poor Jenny," and "Like Strangers" are absent). Still, it's nice to have "Bye Bye Love," "Wake Up Little Susie," "Bird Dog," "('Til) I Kissed You," "When Will I be Loved," "Cathy's Clown," "Ebony Eyes," "Walk Right Back," and "Crying in the Rain" on one disc, which may make it preferable to *Cadence Classics* and *Walk Right Back: The Everly Brothers on Warner Bros.* for some casual fans. One caveat: the mixes on *All-Time Original Hits* sound wrong, with the voices pushed too far up in the mix and the instruments a little bit muted. At times, these mixes are disarming enough to distract from the actual music, at least to listeners well-acquainted with other mixes that are closer to the originals. *—Stephen Thomas Erlewine*

Devoted To You: Love Songs / Feb. 8, 2000 / Varese ♦♦♦♦
Another recycling of the original Cadence catalog, this rounds up 16 of the dreamy ones for a smoothie session that really hits the spot. Smashes like "All I Have to Do Is Dream," "Let It Be Me," and the title track are here, alongside obscure gems like "Oh True Love," the demo for "Life Ain't Worth Living" (both previously only available on a Bear Family box set), and the EP only track, "Oh, So Many Tears." Just so things don't get too draggy, "When Will I Be Loved" and "('Til) I Kissed You" are aboard to break things up. Even with a good cadence compilation, you have everything that's on here, making it worth adding to the collection if you haven't popped for one (or more) of the box sets yet. *—Cub Koda*

Both Sides of an Evening/Instant Party / 2001 / Warner Bros. ♦♦♦♦♦
Rock & roll legends the Everly Brothers get the two-fer treatment from Warner Bros. on this CD, released in 2001. It contains two of their original LP releases (from 1960 and 1961, respectively). *—Chris True*

☆ **It's Everly Time/A Date With the Everly Brothers** / 2001 / Warner Bros. ♦♦♦♦♦
It's Everly Time and *A Date With the Everly Brothers*, both from 1960, were excellent albums, a match for any other albums they did (including their earlier ones on Cadence). It's a shame that this CD, which combines both of the albums onto one disc and adds a few bonus tracks, was released for territories outside of the U.S. But it's not that hard to find in the U.S. as an import, and is about the best Everly Brothers release you'll come across outside of best-of compilations. There's not a stiff among the 12 tracks on *It's Everly Time*, though most of them are barely known outside of serious Everly fans. They include six stellar contributions by Boudleaux Bryant and Felice Bryant (particularly "Some Sweet Day," "Sleepless Nights," and "You Thrill Me (Through and Through)"), one of Don Everly's best compositions ("So Sad"), and incredible harmony singing throughout. Although the material on *A Date With the Everly Brothers* is not on quite the same killer level of *It's Everly Time*, there are some very fine songs. Particularly good are the smash hit "Cathy's Clown," their raucous cover of Little Richard's "Lucille," "Love Hurts" (which preceded Roy Orbison's hit version), and "So How Come" (covered by the Beatles in 1963 on the BBC). The five bonus tracks include the 1961 double-sided hit single "Walk Right Back"/"Ebony Eyes"; the less popular 1961 hit single "Temptation"; alternate takes of "Temptation" (this one previously unissued) and "Stick With Me Baby"; and the 1960 recordings "Why Not" and "The Silent Treatment," both released on the 1977 rarities compilation *New Album*, though neither of them are memorable. *—Richie Unterberger*

The Complete Cadence Recordings: 1957–1960 / Apr. 3, 2001 / Varese ♦♦♦♦♦
Strictly speaking, the title of this two-CD, 47-song collection is not accurate. This does have every recording the Everly Brothers released while they were on the Cadence label in 1957-1960, and does also include at least one version (always the more familiar one, in case only one is used) of every *song* the pair recorded for the label. However, it does not include most of the alternate versions that were released on the Rhino collection *All They Had to Do Was Dream*. That technicality out of the way, this is a very good collection for those who want more early Everly Brothers than a Cadence best-of disc, but may not want to have every last thing (and you can always pick up *All They Had to Do Was Dream* as a supplement), though it does have everything from their Cadence singles and LPs. Serious fans and collectors, however, are going to be tempted to fork out for this even if they have all that stuff already, since this has four previously unreleased demos, all Phil Everly songs, none dated, but almost certainly recorded in the late '50s. These are just OK, not great, and sound like Phil Everly solo acoustic numbers rather than full duo performances, but they're certainly worth having if you love your Everlys. Also of value are a couple of demos of Don Everly originals, "Give Me a Future" and "Life Ain't Worth

Living," that aren't that easy to come by either, although they've been previously released on Bear Family's *Classic Everly Brothers* box set; "Give Me a Future" uses, according to Varese Sarabande, an improved source from the one used on the Bear Family collection. *—Richie Unterberger*

A Night at the Royal Albert Hall / Aug. 13, 2002 / Cleopatra ✦✦✦✦
The Everly Brothers' September 23, 1983, reunion concert at Royal Albert Hall has been kicking around for so long that this double-CD European import has probably been ignored by most listeners. At the time of its release in 1984, there wasn't a huge amount of Everly Brothers material out there, and no truly comprehensive hits collection (apart from a strange but excellent Arista Records double LP that never got picked up as a CD); since then, however, virtually their entire Cadence Records catalog and much (though not all) of the best of their Warner Bros. recordings have been made available at various times. Thus, part of the imperative behind this release has sort of dissolved over time, but that doesn't mean this album doesn't have value—Don and Phil Everly are a little bit less spirited here than they were on the better parts of their Warner Bros. live album, recorded 13 years earlier, and the show is a little slicker than any they might've put on when they were an active, ongoing performing unit, but they can still rock out and their harmonizing was as fine as ever. Additionally, they had the advantage of doing all of this as a fresh start; the whole event was intrinsically special to the participants. It was soon after this performance that they proved they were something more than a pure "oldies" act by charting a number-four hit in England with "Wings of a Nightingale." Recording technology had improved significantly from 1969, even if the Everlys were older, so what was recorded was recorded better, and the remastering job on this CD is excellent, with a much louder, closer sound. There's about 40 minutes more music on this boxed double-CD set than there is on Mercury's single CD of the same concert, and the song order has also been restored to the actual sequence in which everything was played—the additional songs, including some medleys restored to their original order, and "Barbara Allen," "Lightning Express," "Put My Little Shoes Away," "Down in the Willow Garden," "Long Time Gone," Sam Cooke's "You Send Me" (which they make over completely in their own style), "Blues (Stay Away From Me)," and "Step It up and Go" make this show much more than the live greatest-hits performance that it seemed to be in the original release, and present the duo as more ambitious than listeners were led to believe they had been. There's also some very thorough annotation by Dave Thompson, but on the minus side, the track numbers don't match up with the listing on the box or in the enclosed booklet; each medley's individual section has been given an index number, so none of the index points on the first disc after track five correspond to the numbers listed. *—Bruce Eder*

Skip Ewing (Donald Ralph Ewing)

b. Mar. 6, 1964, Redlands, CA
Songwriter, Vocals / Contemporary Country, New Traditionalist, Country-Pop
An accomplished songwriter who supplied material for some of country's biggest names, Skip Ewing also made his own records and scored a few major hits during the late '80s. Born Donald Ralph Ewing in Redlands, CA, Skip grew up in a military family and moved around often as a child. He discovered country music through Merle Haggard and Lefty Frizzell and took up guitar at a young age; he began writing songs as a teenager, and also learned the banjo, which he played at bluegrass festivals. He took a job performing in a country show at the Busch Gardens theme park in Virginia, and from there moved to Nashville at age 19 to take a similar job at the Opryland theme park. He also branched out into demo and commercial singing, and worked at his songwriting enough to land a staff job with the famed Acuff-Rose music-publishing house. Some of his early compositions were recorded by the likes of George Jones, George Strait, and Charley Pride, among others.

In 1987, he landed a deal of his own with MCA, and recorded his breakthrough album, *The Coast of Colorado*, the following year. It gave him two Top Ten hits in "I Don't Have Far to Fall" and the number three "Burnin' a Hole in My Heart," and two additional minor hits in "Your Memory Wins Again" and the title track. *The Will to Love* (1989) produced another Top Five hit in "It's You Again" and a Top Ten in "The Gospel According to Luke." *Naturally* (1991) failed to keep his momentum going, however, and he returned to songwriting as his primary career. By the close of the '90s, his compositions had been recorded by stars like Clint Black, Randy Travis, Collin Raye, Lorrie Morgan, Kenny Rogers, Willie Nelson, Suzy Bogguss, Diamond Rio, and many others; he also occasionally worked as a session guitarist and made sporadic recordings like 1997's *Until I Found You* (for Word) and the holiday album *Following Yonder Star*. *—Steve Huey*

Dad / 1986 / MCA ✦✦✦✦

The Coast of Colorado / Apr. 4, 1988 / MCA ✦✦✦✦
The Coast of Colorado stands as Ewing's most consistently strong collection of songs; the highlights include the Top Ten hits "Burnin' a Hole in My Heart" and "I Don't Have Far to Fall." *—Jason Ankeny*

The Will to Love / 1989 / MCA ✦✦✦
The Top Five hit "It's You Again" is the centerpiece of Ewing's third LP. *—Jason Ankeny*

Healin' Fire / 1990 / MCA ✦✦✦
Here are such Ewing favorites as "I'm OK (And Gettin' Better)," "The Dotted Line," and "I'm Your Man." *—AMG*

● **Greatest Hits** / 1991 / MCA ✦✦✦✦✦
This collection of Ewing's hits includes "Your Memory Wins Again," "If a Man Could Live on Love Alone" and "Burnin' a Hole in My Heart." *—Jason Ankeny*

Naturally / Jun. 10, 1991 / Capitol ✦✦✦
Naturally features a pair of minor chart entries, "I Get the Picture" and the title song. *—Jason Ankeny*

Exile

f. 1963, Lexington, KY
Group / Contemporary Country, Country-Pop, Soft Rock, Urban Cowboy
Among rock listeners, Exile is remembered as the one-hit wonder responsible for 1978's number one smash "Kiss You All Over." However, in the early '80s, the Kentucky-bred band reinvented itself as a country outfit—and a hugely successful one at that. Exile was actually formed all the way back in 1963 in Berea, KY, by singer/guitarist J. P. Pennington, the son of onetime Coon Creek Girl Lily May Ledford. At that time, they were a rock & roll combo known as the Exiles, and got their first exposure by playing some Kentucky dates during 1965-1966 with the Dick Clark Caravan of Stars package tour, which featured pop stars like Brian Hyland, Tommy Roe, and Freddy Cannon. The group relocated to Lexington, KY, in 1968 and switched musical styles several times, also recording singles for labels ranging from Columbia to smaller local imprints.

Their name was shortened to Exile in 1973, at which point the group featured leader/guitarist Pennington, lead singer Jimmy Stokley, keyboardist Buzz Cornelison, bassist Kenny Weir, and drummer Bob Jones. That same year, they issued a self-titled album on Wooden Nickel, and their strong regional popularity eventually led to a deal with Atco in 1977, when they scored their first pop-chart entry with the minor hit "Try It On." Exile subsequently switched to Warner Bros., with a lineup that now featured Pennington, Stokley, Cornelison, second keyboardist Marlon Hargis, bassist Sonny LeMaire, and drummer Steve Goetzman. Their 1978 label debut, *Mixed Emotions*, produced an enormous hit in the disco-tinged pop number "Kiss You All Over," which topped the charts and also proved to be their only major success. After a few follow-up singles flopped, Exile returned to the clubs of Kentucky and completely revamped their sound, especially when lead singer Stokley departed in 1980. He was replaced by singer/guitarist Les Taylor, who helped spearhead the group's transformation into a country band with a strong Southern rock flavor.

In the meantime, some of their songs were covered for hits by major country artists like Janie Fricke ("It Ain't Easy Being Easy") and Alabama ("The Closer You Get," "Take Me Down"). Helped by this exposure, the new Exile signed with Epic in 1983, and soon notched their first Top 40 hit on the country charts with "High Cost of Leaving." By this time, Cornelison had left the group. Over the next few years, Exile tore off an astounding streak of chart-topping country hits. 1984 brought "Woke Up in Love," "I Don't Wanna Be a Memory," and "Give Me One More Chance"; 1985 duplicated that success with "Crazy for Your Love," "Hang on to Your Heart," and "She's a Miracle," with Lee Carroll now in place of Hargis. Though the next three years didn't find the band topping the charts with such regularity, they did score several more number ones: 1986's "I Could Get Used to You" and "It'll Be Me," 1987's "She's Too Good to Be True," and 1988's "I Can't Get Close Enough."

Les Taylor subsequently left the group for a solo career (replaced by Mark Jones) and had a couple of minor hits on Epic; Pennington fared much the same on MCA when he also departed in 1990. The remainder of Exile replaced him with Paul Martin and attempted to soldier on with Arista. They actually did land a couple of Top Ten hits in 1990 with "Nobody's Talking" and "Yet," both co-written by Sonny LeMaire and producer Randy Sharp. However, their success was fleeting, and Arista dropped them after their second album. The group disbanded in 1993, playing a farewell concert in Lexington with numerous past members rejoining. By 1996, Pennington and Taylor had reunited to tour the nostalgia circuit with a new Exile lineup. *—Steve Huey*

Exile / 1973 / Wooden Nickel ✦✦✦

Mixed Emotions / 1978 / Warner Bros. ✦✦✦

All There Is / 1979 / Warner Bros. ✦✦✦

Don't Leave Me This Way / 1980 / Warner Bros. ✦✦✦

Heart & Soul / 1981 / Warner Bros. ✦✦✦

Kentucky Hearts / 1984 / Epic ✦✦✦

● **Greatest Hits** / 1986 / Epic ✦✦✦✦✦
Exile—Greatest Hits offers a good cross-section of the band's late-'70s and early-'80s country-rock hits, including "Kiss You All Over" and "Woke Up in Love." *—Stephen Thomas Erlewine*

Shelter From the Night / 1987 / Epic ✦✦✦
It's astonishing to think that *Shelter From the Night* came at the end of what would prove a downward arc in Exile's history. About half of this album, including the title track (briefly a number-one hit), is comprised of country-rock ballads of tremendous beauty, power, and impact, mixing haunting melodies and solid electric guitar sound. From the opening number, "Just One Kiss," the band luxuriates in lush melodies and high-wattage, like England Dan & John Ford Coley with a major voltage boost, and the effect is most compelling. The whole album isn't up to the standard of the best half of the music, but it is all eminently listenable. Actually, much of *Shelter From the Night* (and this is not meant as an insult) should have rated a place as film music; J. P. Pennington hits the bull's-eye often as a songwriter here and it's all executed so smoothly and memorably, except music this good wouldn't be lucky enough to be used in a movie of equal quality. *—Bruce Eder*

I Love Country / 1988 / Epic ✦✦✦

Keeping It Country / 1990 / Curb ✦✦✦

Still Standing / 1990 / Arista ✦✦✦✦

The Complete Collection / 1991 / Curb ✦✦✦✦✦
The Complete Collection is a good summation of Exile's '80s career, concentrating on lesser-known tracks, not chart-toppers. For the big hits, stick with *Greatest Hits*, but if you want to dig a little deeper, start with *The Complete Collection*. *—Stephen Thomas Erlewine*

Super Hits / Mar. 9, 1993 / Epic ✦✦✦✦
Super Hits is a budget-priced ten-track collection that contains a selection of Exile's greatest hits ("Kiss You All Over," "I Got Love," "Just One Kiss," "Woke Up in Love," "Feel Like

Foolin' Around") which are padded by covers and album tracks. It's not bad for a budget-priced collection, but it's far from definitive. —*Stephen Thomas Erlewine*

Kentucky Hearts/Shelter From the Night / Nov. 9, 1999 / Collectables ◆◆◆

In 1999, Collectables released *Kentucky Hearts/Shelter From the Night*, which contained two complete albums—*Kentucky Hearts* (1984, originally released on Epic) and *Shelter From the Night* (1987, originally released on Epic)—by Exile on one compact disc. —*Jason Birchmeier*

Hang on to Your Heart/Exile / Nov. 9, 1999 / Collectables ◆◆◆◆◆

The group's best album of the 1980s (and one of the best country albums of that decade) paired with a record representing one of the key phases in getting them there. The mix of sounds is strange, since the band seems to "devolve" in harmonies and sophistication, as well as originality, between the first ten cuts here (from the later album) and the second. But any CD with "Hang on to Your Heart" on it is worth owning, and it's interesting and entertaining to compare those cuts with the less-developed work on *Exile*. The sound is excellent, and the annotation is thorough. —*Bruce Eder*

All the No. 1 Hits / Jun. 18, 2002 / Intercontinental ◆◆◆◆

All the No. 1 Hits collects 11 Exile tracks, mainly from the mid- to late '80s, that achieved number-one status at the time of their release. Many of these songs appealed to both the pop and country audiences, achieving crossover popularity. Some of the highlights from this budget-priced collection include "Woke Up in Love," "Kiss You All Over," "She's a Miracle," and "Hang on to Your Heart." —*Al Campbell*

Werly Fairburn

b. 1924, Louisiana, **d.** 1985

Guitar, Vocals / Rock & Roll, Country-Rock, Rockabilly

Werly Fairburn is remembered today as one of the lost legends of rockabilly, but in his own time, his music had a direct influence on country legend Jim Reeves, and he was sufficiently popular to earn his living as a country performer, without ever generating a national hit record. Fairburn recorded for four labels—Trumpet, Capitol, Columbia, and Savoy—during the '50s, but his earliest (and always principal) fame came from the radio, where he was both a DJ and a performer. Known as "the Singing Deejay" (and, before that, as "the Singing Barber") on New Orleans radio in the late '40s, he put together his own group, the Delta Boys, with whom he recorded during the '50s.

Fairburn was born in 1924 near Folsom, LA, the son of a farmer of Cherokee, Scots, Irish, and English ancestry. He grew up listening to the *Grand Ole Opry* on radio on Saturday nights with the family, and his father (who died in 1937, when Werly was 13) bought a guitar for his sons. Werly showed the greatest interest and competed with his older brothers to learn the instrument. He and his brothers learned to play from an elderly black man who lived nearby, teaching them blues licks, which they adapted to the hillbilly sounds they heard on the radio.

With the outbreak of World War II, 17-year-old Fairburn—who was married by then—left the family farm to take a job in New Orleans at the Higgins Shipyard. He enlisted in the Navy and joined its maintenance division in 1943, spending the war serving in Honolulu, HI. It was while in the service that Fairburn began thinking about trying music as a career, but as a precaution, he also got training as a barber when he returned to New Orleans. Music became an avocation, something he did in his spare time, but his style—heavily influence by both Jimmie Rodgers and Hank Williams, but also by New Orleans-style R&B—was attractive enough to get him a spot on WJBW radio broadcasting from his own barber shop.

Thus, in 1948, Fairburn first became known to the local public as the Singing Barber. His broadcasting career continued on WWEZ in New Orleans, and he became the Singing DJ. Subsequently, he enrolled in a local music school to formalize his playing and understanding of music. During the early '50s, he also made his recording debut on Lillian McMurry's Trumpet Records, best known as the early home of Sonny Boy Williamson II. The highlight of his association with the legendary blues label was "Camping With Marie," an upbeat proto-rockabilly-style number that later became regarded as a classic of the music's formative years.

His music was basically country but was done with a beat that made it accessible and even pleasing to younger rockabilly and rock 'n roll fans. His 1956 Columbia single "Everybody's Rockin'" is considered a quintessential example of rockabilly music. Fairburn was a favorite performer locally in New Orleans and had an audience as far away as Dallas, where he appeared at the *Big D Jamboree*, even without a hit record of his own. His music was heavily influenced by New Orleans R&B, and his stage repertory included pieces like Fats Domino's "All By Myself." Fairburn's openness to those sounds—coupled with his professional flexibility—may have helped him adapt when rock & roll hit in the mid-'50s. Unlike a lot of post-20 year old country artists, who sounded awkward trying to reach out to the youth market, Fairburn took naturally to rockabilly.

In 1964, he was performing one of his own songs, "I Guess I'm Crazy," on the *Louisiana Hayride* when it was heard by his friend Jim Reeves. Reeves decided to record the song himself, and "I Guess I'm Crazy" was the single that was in release when Reeves' plane went down on July 31, 1964. Reeves' success in the Southeast didn't follow him when he moved to California in the '60s, but he kept performing steadily, almost up until his death from lung cancer in 1985. In 1994, Bear Family Records released a CD assembling Fairburn's classic sides entitled *Everybody's Rockin'* and a live performance of Fairburn doing "All By Myself" at the *Big D Jamboree* in the mid-'50s surfaced on CD in 2000. —*Bruce Eder*

Everybody's Rockin' / 1994 / Bear Family ✦✦✦✦

Barbara Fairchild

b. Nov. 12, 1950, Knobel, AR

Vocals, Composer / Country-Pop, Country Gospel, CCM

Country and gospel singer/songwriter Barbara Fairchild recorded her first single when she was just 15 years old. She secured a songwriting contract with MCA right out high-school, but continued to perform. She soon had a recording contract with Columbia Nashville and delivered the single "Love Is a Gentle Thing" in 1969. She issued seven albums on Columbia during the 1970s, and scored charting singles like the 1970 Top 30 hit "A Girl Who'll Satisfy Her Man," 1972's Top 40 cut "Color My World," and "Teddy Bear Song" from that same year. The latter song slotted at number one for two weeks and even crossed over to the pop charts. It garnered Fairchild a Grammy nomination, and would go on to become her signature tune. She continued to enjoy chart success through the latter part of the '70s, hitting the Top 15 with "Cheatin' Is." In 1982, Fairchild married evangelical singer/songwriter Milton Carroll in San Antonio, TX. Later, a brief attempt at a Nashville comeback failed.

In 1989, Fairchild joined the gospel group Heirloom, which released a few albums in the early '90s. 1991 saw the release of Fairchild's first solo gospel album, *The Light*. It produced the hits "Turn Right and Then Go Straight" and "Mary Washed His Feet." By this point, her first marriage had failed. Fairchild did a few shows in the country/gospel entertainment haven of Branson, MO. The performances were well-received, and Fairchild moved to the city, landing a permanent gig with the Mel Tillis show. She remarried and began singing and performing with new husband Roy Morris. The duo released inspirational albums together, including 2001's *For God & Country* (which featured the song "Burning Bush (God Used a Burning Bush Before)") and 2002's *Wings of a Dove*. Fairchild and Morris had their own Branson production during the Christmas months, and continued to tour the U.S. —*Johnny Loftus*

Classic Country / Sep. 1, 1998 / Simitar ✦✦✦✦

Among female hitmakers of '70s country, Barbara Fairchild may not be remembered as fondly as Dolly Parton or Tanya Tucker, but this highly enjoyable anthology shows that the quality of her music certainly is not to blame. In fact, fans of those two artists would likely appreciate Fairchild's recordings. In addition to her 1973 number one hit "Teddy Bear," *Classic Country* collects all of Fairchild's Top 40 chart entries, which range from straight-ahead country to a few countrified covers of pop hits. Feminists may be put off by the number of songs describing worshipful submission to men, but such concerns shouldn't diminish the enjoyment to be had from this disc. —*Greg Adams*

Donna Fargo

b. Nov. 10, 1949, Mount Airy, NC

Vocals, Guitar / Country-Pop, Nashville Sound/Countrypolitan

In the early '70s, Donna Fargo was an unusual country star for a couple of reasons. She was one of the few female country singers to write her own material, and one of the few country singers of any sort to cross over to the pop charts in a big way, which she did in 1972 with "The Happiest Girl in the Whole U.S.A." (number 11) and "Funny Face" (number five). She never made the pop Top 40 again, but placed over a dozen more singles in the country Top Ten in the '70s, most written by herself. As an artist, she was squarely in the mainstream, her slightly lisping voice delivering upbeat, sweetly produced homilies to romance, home, and America. She faded after developing multiple sclerosis in 1979, although she continued writing and performing. —*Richie Unterberger*

The Happiest Girl in the Whole U.S.A. / 1972 / MCA ✦✦✦✦✦

My Second Album / 1973 / Dot ✦✦✦✦

All About a Feeling / 1974 / Dot ✦✦✦

"It Do Feel Good" was the last of Donna Fargo's big hits for Dot Records, reaching the Top Ten in 1975 (she would later make a commercial comeback on Warner Bros.). That song is included on *All About a Feeling*, which is comprised entirely of Fargo's original songs. Fargo was an excellent songwriter with a pop sensibility whose feel-good concerns skirted the hard country themes of cheating and abject misery, although some of her songs have a melancholy disposition. "Rotten Little Song," with it's "la la" chorus and Shirley Temple vocal performance, might seem terminally cute, but Fargo's brand of upbeat and accessible country is the sort of music that brought the genre such tremendous mainstream success from the '70s onward. —*Greg Adams*

Miss Donna Fargo / 1975 / ABC/Dot ✦✦✦

Whatever I Say Means I Love You / 1975 / ABC/Dot ✦✦✦

On the Move / 1976 / Warner Bros. ✦✦✦

Shame on Me / 1977 / Warner Bros. ✦✦✦

Fargo Country / 1977 / Warner Bros. ✦✦✦

Encore / 1990 / Bear Family ✦✦✦✦

This features "Great Balls of Fire," "Y'all Come Back Soon," and "I Know a Heartache," among other songs. —*AMG*

Country Spotlight / 1992 / Dominion ✦

Fargo's hits are here, but not in the original versions; instead, they're in new stereo re-recordings, which pale next to the originals. Leave this one on the shelf. —*Stephen Thomas Erlewine*

● **The Best of Donna Fargo** / 1995 / Varese ✦✦✦✦✦

18 songs, all but one from dating from her 1972-1975 prime, when she recorded for Dot. Contains ten Top Ten country hits, including of course "Funny Face" and "The Happiest Girl in the Whole U.S.A." —*Richie Unterberger*

20th Century Masters—The Millennium Collection: The Best of Donna Fargo / Jan. 8, 2002 / MCA ✦✦✦✦

Since Varese's 18-track 1995 collection *The Best of Donna Fargo* has gone out of print, MCA's *20th Century Masters* from 2002 stands as the best collection of her classic Dot material currently on the market. At 11 tracks, it's considerably shorter than that collection, but it does hit all of her big hits on ABC/Dot, including all of her Top Ten hits: "The Happiest Girl in the Whole U.S.A.," "Funny Face," "Superman," "You Were Always There," "Little Girl Gone," "I'll Try a Little Bit Harder," "You Can't Be a Beacon (If Your Light Don't Shine)," "U.S. of A.," "It Do Feel Good," and "Don't Be Angry." Of course, all these are on the Varese disc, along with seven other tracks, which makes it the preferable option, but it's much harder to find these days, so in lieu of that, *20th Century Masters* suits the bill of a concise overview of Fargo's peak period quite nicely. *—Stephen Thomas Erlewine*

Farm Dogs

f. 1996

Group / Country-Rock, Americana, American Trad Rock

Assembled and led by Bernie Taupin, known best for being the lyrical half of an extremely successful and long-running songwriting collaboration with Elton John, Farm Dogs is a labor of love for the storyteller, who has always been infatuated with American roots music. It was his intention to make a record that captured that simple uncluttered sound. Therefore the idea behind the Farm Dogs' project was to use only acoustic instruments, which the band stuck to except for the use of percussion and some sparse electric guitar for effect. The album was recorded at Taupin's home studio in the Santa Ynez Valley, where he runs a ranch with his wife.

Since his childhood, Taupin has been fascinated by American culture and the wild, wild West, so it's not surprising that the John album *Tumbleweed Connection* was Taupin's vision and that the Farm Dogs project brings him full circle. For Taupin, *Last Stand in Open Country* picks up where *Tumbleweed Connection* left off, with the new songs bringing to life a string of colorful characters that include fast women, drunkards, misfits, and movie stars. *Immigrant Sons* followed in 1998. Along with Taupin, Farm Dogs is comprised of guitarist Jim Cregan and guitarist/dobro player Robin LeMesurier, both of whom have served long tenures as sideman for Rod Stewart. Rounding out the group is Dennis Tufano, former lead singer for the '60s group the Buckinghams. Tufano also worked on Taupin's second solo album, *He Who Rides the Tiger*. Taupin's other efforts include an early-'70s, self-titled spoken word album, as well as his third solo project, *Tribe*. *—Jack Leaver*

● **Last Stand in Open Country** / 1996 / Discovery ♦♦♦♦

Best known for his work as lyricist with Elton John, Farm Dogs is the dream band Bernie Taupin always wanted to form. Collaborating with veteran musicians Jim Cregan, Dennis Tufano, and Robin LeMesurier, Taupin made a fine acoustic-oriented record that combines rootsy country, blues, and folk music with his immense talent as a storyteller. Much of this record recalls some of the early and more countrified work with Elton during the *Tumbleweed Connection* period, and lyrically it stands up to his best efforts. The songs are steeped with Americana and come alive with colorful and humorously twisted wordplay, while the folky instrumental backing and three- and four-part harmonies give the record a homey, front-porch quality. While there might not be anything as awe-inspiring as "Your Song," or "Goodbye Yellow Brick Road," *Last Stand in Open Country* has plenty of highlights. Taupin and company pull out the stops on songs such as the clever-talking blues of "Ballad of Dennis Hopper and Harry Dean," and the vivid imagery of "Burn This Bed" and "Barstool." *—Jack Leaver*

Immigrant Sons / Feb. 3, 1998 / Sire ♦♦♦

Led by famed lyricist Bernie Taupin, this predominately English quintet returns to the rootsy American styles which inspired Elton John's silent partner as a youngster. From the light ballad "This Face," the whispery lament "Aimless Driving," the spiritual "Stars & Seeds," and the truly immigrant-inspired "Workin' in the Fields" to chunkier drivers like "Bird of Prey," "America on Trial," and the lame clunky drawl of "Nothing Gonna Kill the Kid" (a biographical Superman song along the lines of Spin Doctors' "Pocket Full of Kryptonite"), the music is consistently well-orchestrated, clean, and convincing, evoking the stereotypical American garage band and even a porch-front play-along. However, the cynical and snide lyrics often go awry. Though Taupin and his experienced musical mates (including ex-Baby drummer Tony Brock, Rod Stewart collaborators Jim Cregan and Robin LeMesurier, and Sheryl Crow bassist Tad Wadhams) try to come to grips with folky blues, love, football and other distinctly colonial customs, there appears to be more than a bit of material lost in translation. For example, while Taupin is savvy enough to know the futile state of the gridiron game in Buffalo, he considers "3rd down and 3 to go" to be a metaphor for impending doom (which, in Buffalo, it may be). It is also surprising that the man who came up with the words to "Levon" and "Candle in the Wind" (i.e., the original version) has fallen back to such borderline offensive lines as "In Ho Chi Minh City/there's a new Pizza Hut./There's American dollars/up Columbia's butt." Is this Taupin's true vision of the land which helped make him a millionaire? I would hope that he has not become selfish in his middle age. Fortunately, his authentic musical tribute to this same land (which Taupin now calls home) quickly dispel any countercultural inklings. *—Matthew Robinson*

The Farmer Boys

db. 1964

Group / Western Swing, Rockabilly, Honky Tonk, Bakersfield Sound

From the early '50s until 1964, the Farmer Boys tried hard to make it as a national recording act, mixing Western swing with honky tonk, and in the process, helping to found the Bakersfield sound. Bobby Adamson (born September 20, 1933) and his fellow Arkansan Woody Murray (born September 11, 1933) were transplanted Southerners living in California and met when a teenage Adamson started singing along to a record on a jukebox and was joined by Murray. They started singing together informally at dances around 1952, with Adamson on lead and Murray handling harmonies and playing rhythm guitar. After appearing at the Happy-Go-Lucky Club in Tulare, they were invited by Cousin Herb Henson to appear on his nightly television show on KERO out out of Bakersfield, CA, where they became regulars, performing five nights a week. Henson dubbed the duo the Farmer Boys, due to their both having lived in Farmersville, CA, and the name stuck.

The duo had auditioned without success for MGM Records, then a major country label. At the end of 1954, however, they auditioned for Ken Nelson at Capitol Records, and their first recording session followed on January 12, 1955. Nelson intended to make them Capitol's answer to Homer & Jethro, and their first session resounded with these influences in songs like "You're a Humdinger" and "Onions, Onions," of which the latter became their most requested song and something of a signature tune. Novelty songs became their mainstay, with numbers like "Flip Flop" becoming successful singles. The Farmer Boys began playing the *Grand Ole Opry* and touring with Webb Pierce, Hank Locklin, and Carl Smith, as well as Elvis Presley. It was the effect that Elvis was having on music that resulted in the Farmer Boys cutting their own rockabilly sides at the behest of Nelson, who wanted to try to compete for the youth market. In May of 1956, they recorded a pair of near-classics, "Cool Down Mame" and "My Baby Done Left Me."

Their real sound was country, however, and they quickly returned to their roots. The duo's lead guitarist on most of their sessions was Merle Haggard alumnus Roy Nichols, whose lean, crisp playing helped give their records a special impact. By their last session for Capitol, in early 1957, their backing group was the Desert Stars, whose members included lead guitarist Gene Breedon and pedal steel player Norman Hamlet, as well a young Buck Owens, who wrote or co-wrote all four songs from the session, on rhythm guitar. By that time, Adamson and Murray had tired of doing nothing but silly novelty numbers and wanted to add more ballads to their repertory. The Capitol contract ended in 1957, and the group never did release another record. They tried working with Breedon in a session, and Buck Owens remained enough of a fan to attend their performances, even as his own career was taking off. The Farmer Boys called it quits in 1964, leaving behind a fascinating and varied body of work, including honky tonk numbers, novelty tunes, a smattering of rockabilly (which has gotten them pegged in that category by faulty rock & roll historians), all representing some of the prime early examples of the Bakersfield sound. *—Bruce Eder*

Flash, Crash and Thunder / 1991 / Bear Family ♦♦♦♦

The Farmer Boys' complete 16 sides for Capitol, cut between January of 1955 and February of 1957, represent about as varied a body of music as one could squeeze into just four sessions in three years. The order isn't chronological, as the producers have put the rockabilly numbers up first, even though they came later, while their first, traditional-sounding records (complete with fiddle and mandolin, the latter played by Bill Woods) come last. Taken in totality, one gets several beautiful harmony-based ballads ("No One"), Lonzo & Oscar-type novelty tunes ("Flip Flop," "Onions, Onions"), and high-energy near-rockers ("My Baby Done Left Me," "Cool Down Mame," "Flash, Crash and Thunder"). These 16 songs make a fair album, with no one side of the duo's sound dominating; apart from the vocals, which are equally effective on ballads or silly singalongs ("You're a Humdinger"), the music is worth owning for Roy Nichols' playing. It's hard to say where the duo would have gone had it recorded any further, but the material the Farmer Boys left behind is exceptionally appealing musically, as well as great fun. *—Bruce Eder*

Hugh & Karl Farr

Group / Cowboy, Western Swing

Hugh & Karl Farr were the most important fiddle-and-guitar duo in the history of country & western music, a team of brother virtuosos who brought the vocabulary and dexterity of the best jazz into the confines of country and cowboy songs for more than 25 years. That they aren't better known as a duo stems from the fact that their work from the mid-'30s onward was largely confined to membership in the Sons of the Pioneers.

Hugh was born in Llano, TX, on December 6, 1903. Karl was born April 25, 1909, in Rochele, TX. Their father and mother were both part-time musicians, when he wasn't working as a building contractor and she wasn't raising a family, playing local dances as a fiddle-and-guitar duo. Hugh took up the guitar at age seven, mastered it quickly, and within a year was playing local dances as part of a duet with his father, playing songs like "Texas Crapshooter," "The Arkansas Traveler," and "Fire in the Mountain." His father wanted a fiddle player, however, and by age nine Hugh had not only learned the instrument but also knew how to play every song in their repertory. By 1916 Karl was playing with Hugh and their brother Glen on the mandolin. Hugh's fiddle style, as it developed in the late teens and early '20s, was influenced heavily by the jazz of the era, especially the work of the Kansas City Nite Hawks. Karl had started out learning the mandolin and then picked up the banjo and finally the guitar.

The three Farr brothers continued to play together after their father moved the family to California in early 1925. Hugh had landed a gig with a local combo at a place called Mammy's Shack, and by 1928, when the group broke up, he was ready to pursue music as a permanent career. Karl later followed suit, after he and his brothers made their first appearance on radio in Los Angeles. Hugh & Karl joined Len Nash & His Country Boys, a Los Angeles country music group which hosted the program *Len Nash & His Country Boys' Barn Dance*. The program lasted from 1929 until 1933, during which time Hugh appeared on several Len Nash records, among them "On the Road to California," "Going Down to Town," and "Kelly Waltz." In 1933, the group moved to a new dancehall in Anaheim, which was unsuccessful, and they broke up. Hugh & Karl then formed a group, the Haywire Trio, with fellow bandmember Ira McCullough.

Hugh joined Jack LeFevre & His Texas Outlaws, while Karl worked as a staff musician at radio station KFOX. It was while playing with LeFevre's group on Los Angeles radio station KFWB that Hugh made the acquaintance of a group of musicians called the Pioneer Trio. Sometime in late 1933 or early 1934, Hugh was asked by Pioneers Leonard Slye, Bob Nolan, and Tim Spencer to join, and the quartet was renamed the Sons of the Pioneers. In addition to playing the fiddle, Hugh also sang the bass parts on their records. Meanwhile, Karl continued playing with different groups around Los Angeles. The Pioneers, however, knew that they needed a proper guitar player who could handle lead parts; Hugh proposed his brother, and in 1935 Karl joined the group. While Nolan and Spencer were brilliant songwriters and Slye was a great performing talent, the Farrs brought an instrumental dexterity that was extraordinary. The brothers were also improvisers capable of coming up with material to fill time on radio shows on a moment's notice.

The Farr brothers remained with the Pioneers for more than 20 years, sacrificing some of the recognition that they might've received on behalf of the group. Karl could easily have been another Merle Travis or Chet Atkins—he was that good—and was sufficiently well-known within professional music circles to have been given one of Fender's very first Telecasters in 1949. For Hugh, however, the lack of recognition created tension, particularly as its membership went through massive line-up changes during the mid-'50s, and he left the group late in 1957. Karl remained with the Sons of the Pioneers until a show in Massachusetts on September 20, 1961, when a string broke on his guitar in the middle of a solo and, while struggling to change it, he collapsed and died of a heart attack.

After leaving the Pioneers, Hugh tried for a time to lead his own version of the Sons of the Pioneers, claiming ownership of the name as the last active member of the original quartet. Farr's group failed to find an audience, however, and disbanded soon after it was organized. He played with singing cowboy star Jimmy Wakely and later co-founded the Country Gentlemen with Pat Patterson, Kenny Baker, and Jimmie Widener, who broke up after a short but successful performing career and recording one album. Farr spent the 1960s playing with different groups and passed away on April 17, 1980. *—Bruce Eder*

★ **Texas Stomp 1934–1944** / 1993 / Country Routes ♦♦♦♦♦

Even though a lot of the material here is jazzier than anything the Sons of the Pioneers ever did, no Pioneers collection can be considered complete without this 26-track CD. Not only is there work here by Hugh & Karl Farr together, but also Hugh playing guitar/fiddle duets with Leonard Slye (aka Roy Rogers)—who proved an able jazz-style guitarist—in 1934, and playing with Slye and Bob Nolan in 1935, and the two Farrs (with Karl on electric guitar) playing with fellow Pioneers Lloyd Perryman and Shug Fisher in 1940. The stuff shows off the Farr brothers' debt to jazz (especially Eddie Lang and Joe Venuti) and blues as well as country influences. As part of the Pioneers' contract with Decca Records, the group recorded for the label's radio transcription service—this music was licensed directly to radio stations for use over the air and was intended to fit into specific timings. Hugh & Karl were separated off from the Pioneers and billed as the Cornhuskers, and they made hundreds of instrumental transcription discs. Still later, they made discs for NBC radio's Thesaurus Electronic Transcription service. Hugh Farr's violin is a spellbinding and humbling thing to hear, while Karl plays like Charlie Christian crossed with Chet Atkins, especially on the dozen electric sides included here. Even subsumed into the identity of the Pioneers, Hugh was one of the most acclaimed violinists of his era among his fellow musicians (once compared to Fritz Kreisler), and Karl was one of the most respected guitarists—this disc shows how fine they were even when they weren't playing for posterity, just a paycheck. There's some surface noise on the tracks off of the 78-rpm radio-transcription discs, but it is never obtrusive, and the session information is a nice bonus. *—Bruce Eder*

Jay Farrar

b. Belleville, IL

Guitar, Vocals / Adult Alternative Pop/Rock, Alternative Country-Rock, Singer/Songwriter

One of the founding fathers of the 1990s alt-country movement, Jay Farrar was a founding member of two of the genre's key bands, Uncle Tupelo and Son Volt, though his solo career has made it plain that his musical ambitions stretch far beyond the retro-leaning twang of many of his contemporaries. Farrar was born and raised in Belleville, IL, a small town not far from the Illinois/Missouri border. Farrar was 12 when he first began leaning to play the guitar, and in high-school he made friends with a fellow musically inclined student named Jeff Tweedy. Farrar and Tweedy formed a garage rock band called the Primitives, but after a few years (and the arrival of drummer Mike Heidorn), Farrar and Tweedy would begin incorporating the influence of the country music they had grown up with and the traditional folk sounds that had struck their fancy. Renaming themselves Uncle Tupelo, they forged a sound that fused the ferocity of punk rock with the melodic structures and lyrical intimacy of country, and while they weren't the first to combine punk and country, their formula was unusual enough to spawn a whole new musical subgenre, with literally dozens of likeminded bands soon following in their wake. Uncle Tupelo would release four highly acclaimed albums between 1989 and 1993, but Farrar and Tweedy had a falling out while touring in support of their first major-label release, *Anodyne*, and in the summer of 1994, Farrar announced his resignation from Uncle Tupelo, effectively ending the group.

While Tweedy and several members of the expanded version of Uncle Tupelo from the *Anodyne* tour soon formed Wilco, Farrar teamed up with drummer Heidorn (who had left Uncle Tupelo in 1992), bassist Jim Boquist, and multi-instrumentalist Dave Boquist to comprise the band Son Volt. Alternating between quiet and contemplative ballads and Neil Young-influenced rockers, Son Volt's 1995 debut album, *Trace*, musically picked up where Uncle Tupelo left off, and the follow-up, *Straightaways*, followed a similar path. With Son Volt's third album, 1998's *Wide Swing Tremolo*, Farrar began exploring more adventurous musical textures and instrumental avenues, but while the album signaled a new direction for Farrar, it marked at least a temporary conclusion to the Son Volt story; while Farrar never formally folded the group, Son Volt did go on hiatus while Farrar began exploring solo projects.

After a layoff of nearly two years, Farrar returned with his first album under his own name, *Sebastopol*, in 2001; the disc found Farrar expanding on the sonic innovations of *Wide Swing Tremolo* while also maintaining clear ties to the melodic tenor of his best work; guest artists on the album included neo-traditionalists Gillian Welch and David Rawlings as well as Jon Wurster from Superchunk and Matt Pence from Centro-Matic. Farrar raised even more eyebrows in 2002 with a follow-up EP, *ThirdShiftGrottoSlack*, which included a dance-friendly remix of *Sebastopol*'s "Damn Shame" along with four unreleased songs. In 2003, Farrar tried his hand at film scoring by composing incidental music for the acclaimed independent film *The Slaughter Rule* (Bloodshot Records released a soundtrack album, featuring Farrar's score as well as source music used in the film), and he launched his own independent record label, Act/Resist (distributed by Artemis), with the release of his second full-length solo set, *Terroir Blues*. *—Mark Deming*

● **Sebastopol** / Sep. 25, 2001 / Artemis ♦♦♦♦

After the breakup of Uncle Tupelo, most fans would have guessed that Jay Farrar was a cinch for a brilliant solo career, but that hasn't quite been the case. While *Trace*, the first album from Farrar's post-Uncle Tupelo group, Son Volt, was a low-key masterpiece, the follow-up, *Straightaways*, sounded like he was treading water, offering up more of the same but without the same level of quality, and the songs simply weren't as interesting. Son Volt's third album, *Wide Swing Tremolo*, was a conscious effort to bring new colors to the band's sound, and while it was a decided improvement over *Straightaways*, it still paled in comparison to *Trace* or his better Uncle Tupelo work. In 2001, with Son Volt on hiatus (widespread rumor had it that the band had split up, though the group's representatives denied this), Jay Farrar cut his first proper solo album, *Sebastopol*, which seems to pick up where *Wide Swing Tremolo* left off. The arrangements move much of the focus away from Farrar's Neil Young-styled electric guitar, with keyboards and sampled horns and strings taking a prominent role in many of the tunes (though don't worry, Farrar's big fuzzy leads are still very much in evidence on "Clear Day Thunder," while "Outside the Door" shows he's still in touch with his acoustic, introspective side). The melodies are often brighter than on the Son Volt albums, and the blend of keyboards and acoustic guitars give the songs a more buoyant quality than one might expect ("Directions" sounds downright poppy), and Farrar injects a welcome sense of humor on "Barstow" and "Damn Shame." But, while Farrar has streamlined the chassis and thrown a new coat of paint on his music, *Sebastopol* proves the engine that drives his songwriting is still the same, and that's part of the problem. Without a strong collaborator, Farrar seems to have trouble finding new and different things to say, even while he's finding new and interesting ways to say them; *Sebastopol* sounds like a variation on the same themes he's been pursuing since *Trace*, and while it's probably his strongest album since Son Volt's debut, it also suggests he still isn't living up to his potential. *—Mark Deming*

ThirdShiftGrottoSlack / 2002 / Artemis ♦♦♦

Jay Farrar gets funky? Hard to imagine, but it actually happens on *ThirdShiftGrottoSlack*, an EP of unreleased material the Son Volt and Uncle Tupelo alumnus has released, presumably while he contemplates his next move. On this EP, Farrar's increased funk quotient comes courtesy of producer Tom Rothrock, who adds a good and greasy backbeat to a remix of "Damn Shame," which originally appeared on Farrar's solo debut, *Sebastopol*; having performed similar duties for R.L. Burnside on the *Come on In* album, Rothrock knows how to add a groove without getting in the way, and his "Memphis Mix" of "Damn Shame" gives the tune unexpected shake appeal while respecting the bluesy undertow of Farrar's original take. The EP's other four tracks feature Farrar more or less as we've come to know him, though he's in solid form; the stark voice-and-guitar surfaces of "Greenwich Time" suggest the track is a demo, but the song is served well by the simple presentation, while the other three tunes sound like outtakes from *Sebastopol*, though they're certainly up to that album's level of quality, especially the piano-driven "Station to Station." *ThirdShiftGrottoSlack* isn't a major work from Jay Farrar, but in many ways that's to its benefit; short and sweet, it doesn't wear out its welcome and suggest Farrar's songs work well in small portions, while the "Damn Shame" remix suggests this guy should get his groove on more often. *—Mark Deming*

Terroir Blues / Jun. 24, 2003 / Artemis ♦♦♦♦

Jay Farrar's music since leaving behind Uncle Tupelo had suggested the work of a man who has little desire to be hemmed in by the sounds he created in the past (not unlike the attitude of his former musical partner, Jeff Tweedy). However, Farrar's progress from the bracing country punk fusion of his early UT sides has been at once gradual and full of uncertain steps, as if he knew where he wanted to go but seemed a bit fuzzy about just how to get there. After putting Son Volt on the back burner, Farrar seemed to have gained a clearer perspective on his creative directions with his first solo album, *Sebastopol*, but paradoxically his second solo set, *Terroir Blues* finds him continuing to stake out new musical and sonic territory while stripping his sound down to its framework. The album's production is at once adventurous and spare; the distorted blues structures of "Fool King's Crown," the multiple sonic layers of "Hard Is The Fall," and the abstract "Space Junk" pieces scattered throughout the sequence make it clear Farrar has taken the more adventurous textures of *Sebastopol* and run with them. However, at the same time *Terroir Blues* (named for a French word which describes the way soil and environment affects the grapes used to make wine) is the most purposefully stark album Farrar has made since Uncle Tupelo's *March 16-20, 1992*, with the silences carrying as much weight as the sounds. The album's musical core lies in the guitars of Farrar and Mark Spencer, and many of the album's most striking tracks feature only one or two other instruments, such as the dark cello-infused "Cahokian," and "Out On The Road," which suggests Tim Buckley's jazzier moments with the addition of Lew Winer III's flute. *Terroir Blues* also finds Farrar embracing the more cryptic corners of his lyrical conceits; these songs seem to have far more to do with mood than literal meanings, though the warm but often downbeat mood and the bookending versions of "No Rolling Back" (which begins with the questions "Who do you know/ Who do you trust/ Who keeps you sane/ Who cleans off the dust") embrace personal and worldly concerns in a manner that registers emotionally even when it remains murky at face value. *Terroir Blues* is a significantly more ambitious and confident work from Jay Farrar than *Sebastopol*, but it's also more elusive, and ultimately this is the sort of record fans will love, but the unfamiliar will have a hard time embracing. *—Mark Deming*

Charlie Feathers

b. Jun. 12, 1932, Holly Springs, MS, **d.** Aug. 29, 1998

Guitar, Songwriter, Vocals / Traditional Country, Rockabilly

Charlie Feathers was many things to many fans of rock and country music. To some, he was a superb country stylist who could take almost any piece of material and stamp it with the full force of his personality. To others, he was one of rockabilly's great pioneers, there at the dawn of Sun Records. And Feathers' stubborn insistence on combining elements of country, raw blues, and bluegrass to make his own version of the rockabilly experience showed him to be one of the genre's most original and enduring artists.

Feathers was born in Holly Springs, MS, with music all around the sharecropping community he grew up in. After day jobs in Illinois and Texas, Feathers moved to Memphis in 1950, working for a box manufacturer until a bout with spinal meningitis left him hospitalized. Listening to the radio there on a daily basis, he emerged from his stay determined to become a professional singer. By 1954, Feathers was working his way into the confines of Sam Phillips' Memphis Recording Service, with an eye toward getting something released on Sun Records. He filled in whenever and wherever he could, helping with arrangement ideas, even playing spoons on a Miller Sisters session. Demoing songs for steel guitarist Stan Kesler found him getting half credit on the Elvis Sun side "I Forgot to Remember to Forget." Phillips decided to start a local non-union label called Flip to test out new artists, and after pairing Feathers with country session songwriter-musicians Bill Cantrell and Quinton Claunch, released Charlie's first single on that label, the classic "Peepin' Eyes" coupled with "I've Been Deceived." The record kicked enough noise locally to get Feathers transferred to Sun for a second single, but the artist had bigger visions. Although Phillips saw him as "a superb country stylist," Feathers wanted to rock and cut many Sun demo sessions in that style.

When Phillips turned a deaf ear to it all, Feathers' impatience led him to Memphis rival Meteor Records, where he waxed the two-sided rockabilly classic "Tongue-Tied Jill" and "Get With It." This single garnered enough Memphis airplay to cement him a deal with King Records, and it is here that the Charlie Feathers as rockabilly legend story begins in earnest. The dozen or so sides he cut as singles for King are the greatest '50s rockabilly tracks to escape the hegemony of the Sun studios, with "One Hand Loose," "Bottle to the Baby," "Everybody's Lovin' My Baby," and "I Can't Hardly Stand It" all becoming classics of the genre. Their territorial success got Feathers on numerous package tours and multiple appearances on Dallas' Big D Jamboree. When the King contract ran out, Feathers continued to record one-off singles of very high musical quality, for a variety of Memphis labels, while stubbornly playing his music for whatever local audience cared to listen.

When the rockabilly revival started up in Europe in the early '70s, Feathers became the first living artist up for deification by collectors. His old 45s suddenly became worth hundreds of dollars, and every interviewer wanted to know why he never really made it big and what his true involvement with Sun consisted of. Feathers embroidered the story with a skewed view of rock & roll history with each retelling, to be sure, but once he picked up his guitar and sang to reinforce his point, the truth came out in his music. Never mind why he didn't make it back in the '50s; he could still deliver the goods *now.* With health problems plaguing him from his diabetes and a surgically removed lung, Feathers continued on his own irascible course, recording his first album for a major label in 1991 (Elektra's American Masters series) and continuing to perform and record for his wide European fan base. Truly an American music original, Feathers died August 29, 1998, of complications following a stroke; he was 66. *—Cub Koda*

That Rockabilly Cat! / 1979 / Edsel ✦✦✦✦

This more-than-slightly eccentric Memphis-based artist may have turned off concert audiences with his penchant for telling long, boring stories when he should be rocking, but his recording sessions tend to be good stuff. First things first, he knows how to put a good groove together, with the music ranging from brisk rockabilly to slower country numbers. It is the type of playing where not a note is wasted, not a single unnecessary lick played. Everything is cut down to the basics. Floating over the top of this are his vocals, which are completely unique. There is no one singing rock, rockabilly, or country with a voice like this, although many mouths have opened in attempt. He can sound sinister, romantic, or funny. The vocal effects he uses run the full range of what works for communication in rockabilly music—hiccups, whines, muffled burps, and mumbling included. One of the great things that happens is the transformation of well-known country material into music that is totally Feathers' own. He is certainly one of the most original interpreters of the songs he chooses. The sessions were recorded by Tom Phillips and are a re-creation of the vintage Sun sound. Players are all part of the regular Feathers gang, including Bubba Fuller on drums. *—Eugene Chadbourne*

Live in Memphis / 1979 / Barrelhouse ✦✦✦

Rockabilly Rhythm! / 1981 / Cowboy Carl ✦✦✦✦

The career of this top-notch rockabilly artist certainly had its downs and downs, as one can ascertain from the fact that it is a rare Charlie Feathers session that was released anytime near the date it was recorded. These sides languished for nearly a decade, although the playing is great and Feathers is in fine vocal form. He assembled a minimalist group—no drums, although it is a rare listener that even notices this because the rhythm sound is so happening thanks to popping bass playing from both Charlie and Bubba Feathers. The program is mostly cover versions, which was an area where this artist really shone. Very few recording artists could take something such as "Roll Over Beethoven" and make something personal out of it, but this is just what Feathers does in his jaunty, medium-tempo version complete with goofy background singers. Some of these tunes are ones Feather recorded over and over, such as "I'm Movin' On" by Hank Snow, perversely done at a tempo slow enough to suggest a broken-down truck rather than a smoothly running eight-wheeler. Other song transformations are done with such simplicity of technique that it is remarkable, such as the laid-back but still threatening cover of Johnny Cash's "Folsom Prison Blues." *—Eugene Chadbourne*

Jungle Fever / 1987 / Kay ✦✦✦✦✦

Boasting a generous 20 tracks, *Jungle Fever* is the best available compilation of Charlie Feathers' original rockabilly recordings; all of his best-known songs are collected here, including "Get With It" and "Tongue-Tied Jill." *—Stephen Thomas Erlewine*

Charlie Feathers / 1991 / Elektra/Nonesuch ✦✦✦✦✦

In its short-lived "American Explorer" series, Nonesuch Records issued a quartet of records by artists they considered seminal yet ignored. Of the four, the furthest out-to-lunch choice was '50s Sun rockabilly hero Charlie Feathers. Feathers was always a fringe player. He claims to have arranged all of the Elvis Presley Sun material, and though he recorded for Sam Phillips' label a full eight months before Presley, Feathers scored only marginal hits and became a shadowy figure almost as soon as the '50s ended, surfacing now and again in country and roots rock circles to make an odd record for King, Meteor, Flip, and other small labels. Feathers is the man who first brought the late bluesman Junior Kimbrough to Robert Palmer and did some recording with him (see the Revenant compilation *Get With It* for these). This disc, recorded in 1990 and produced by Ben Vaughn, features Feathers doing a number of his own truly eccentric and brilliant songs accompanied by former Sun Studios musicians guitarist Roland James, drummer James Van Eaton, and bassist Stan Kesler, and an alternate rhythm section on a few other cuts provided by bassist Terry Bailey and drummer (as well as cardboard-box percussionist) Perry York. Of the Feathers "classics" that appear here are "Pardon Me Mister," "A Man in Love," "A Long Time Ago," and a rewrite of "I Can't Remember to Forget," dedicated to Presley, who first cut the song as "We Can't Seem to Remember to Forget." Other material includes rockabilly nuggets like "Fraulein," "Mean Woman Blues," "Uh Huh Honey," and Stan Kesler's true gem, "You're Right, I'm Left, She's Gone." Instrumentation aside—all the playing here is expert, authentic, and full of raw immediacy—it's Feathers' voice that is the spark and spook of these proceedings. He is a man haunted by the past eternally, trying to make it a renewable present, and offering the truth in how forgotten it all is in his delivery (check out "Defrost Your Heart," in which Feathers moans, growls, does the hillbilly wail, and sings a blues that is truly unearthly in that same way that Hank Williams and Roscoe Holcomb's are). Feathers died in the late '90s, but he leaves behind an enduring testament to his particular brilliance as a frighteningly intense singer and canny songwriter. This album is near the pinnacle of that legacy. *—Thom Jurek*

Uh Huh Honey / Nov. 16, 1993 / Norton ✦✦✦

An important part of any Charlie Feathers or rockabilly collection, this brings together all of his late-'60s recordings for the Memphis-based Philwood label, along with some fascinating live TV recordings from 1978. Charlie is in rare form on these explosive sides, turning in the best version of "Tear It Up" ever recorded, with its legendary B-side, "Stutterin' Cindy." The television broadcast from Houston finds Charlie in a drummer-less trio format—as real as rockabilly gets—running through an inspired set that covers everything from the ballad "We're Getting Closer to Being Apart" to his classic "Get With It." Even if you already have the double set of Feathers classics on Revenant, here's the companion volume. *—Cub Koda*

Tip Top Daddy / 1995 / Norton ✦✦✦

Call this one "Charlie Feathers Unplugged" if you want to, but what we have here is a bushelbasket of unissued acoustic demos from 1958 to 1973 from the King of Rockabilly. It doesn't much matter when Feathers cut something as long as he was into it when the tape was rollin' and here's 23 tracks that bear that simple fact out. It also doesn't seem to matter much if Feathers wrote the tune or not, because everything he puts his pipes to—along with his consummate arranging talents—stamps it with the crazed redneck mark of hizzown personality. Electric guitar fleshes out a couple of tracks here and there, but in the main it's pure, unvarnished Charlie Feathers and that's worth more than the next dozen hat hunk albums that come down the pike. *—Cub Koda*

Rock-a-Billy / 1998 / Bear Family ✦✦✦✦✦

This 1998 Bear Family reissue of a CD originally issued in 1990 on Colin Escott's Zu-Zazz imprint gathers together the absolute cream of Charlie Feathers' unreleased and alternate recordings. Usually an album of outtakes would infer a compilation of less than releasable material. But Charlie Feathers' unreleased demos and outtakes are every bit as illuminating and wonderful as his better-known singles, making this just as good as any Feathers collection out there, save for the two-disc Revenant anthology, which contains all of his '50s recordings intact. Here are 1954 living room rehearsals for his first Sun session ("Defrost Your Heart," "Runnin' Around," "I've Been Deceived"), outtakes from his second ("Wedding Gown of White," "Defrost Your Heart"), the 1956 Sun demo session ("Corrine, Corrina," "Frankie & Johnny," "So Ashamed," "Honky Tonk Kind," and an early stab at "Bottle to the Baby" with different lyrics), rowdier and looser King outtakes ("Bottle to the Baby," "One Hand Loose," "Everybody's Lovin' My Baby," and "I Can't Hardly Stand It"), and rare singles for local labels like Wal-May, Memphis, and Kay ("Dinky John," "Today and Tomorrow," and "Wild, Wild Party"), rounded out by some great '60s and early-'70s sides cut at the Sun and Select-O-Hits studios (a recut of "Tongue-Tied Jill," "Gone! Gone! Gone!," "Where's She at Tonight," and "Wild Side of Life"). Some—but not all—of this also appears on Revenant's *The Essential Recordings* two-disc set. This particular edition, however, sports superior sound and mastering. *—Cub Koda*

● **Get With It: The Essential Recordings (1954–1969)** / Jul. 21, 1998 / Revenant ✦✦✦✦✦

John Fahey and Richard K. Spottswood's Revenant label has done some pretty audacious things since it began issuing recordings. The label released everything from the earliest Dock Boggs material to primal material from the Stanley Brothers, a collection of (very) raw American pre-World War II gospel music, and even Cecil Taylor's *Nefertiti, the Beautiful One Has Come.* But nothing could have prepared the public for this deluxe double-CD issue of the work of rockabilly legend and music biz phantom Charlie Feathers. Feathers was an enigma, a man who claimed to have shown Jerry Lee Lewis how to play his "pumping" style of piano and arranged Elvis' Sun material. He co-wrote Elvis' first number-one hit, "I Forgot to Remember to Forget," and spouted off about why music sucks and the secrets of the Sun sound ad nauseum for close to four decades. But in this collection, none of that matters—it does not prove or disprove his claims, but certainly testifies that it is possible that what he boasted was true, because the truth is in the grooves. The package is deluxe as hell: long essays by Peter Guralnick, Jim Dickinson, and Colin Escott accompany two CDs broken down into issued and unissued material. The released material features all the masters of his singles for Sun, Meteor, King, Kay, Wal-May, and Holiday Inn. There are a couple of missing sides, such as the Memphis label single "Wild, Wild Party," covered by Link Wray in the 1980s, and a Philwood single of Feathers' cover of "Tear It Up." There is something in the grain of Feathers' voice on his issued singles that is off-kilter or off the rails. It stutters, sputters, spits, and stings, while slipping and blurring and rolling through lyrics as if they are dialogue from outer space being dictated to him on the spot. From "I've Been Deceived"; "Defrost Your Heart," with its ghostly, voodoo lyrics; to the King "Can't Hardly Stand It," with its sidewinder guitar; to Meteor's "Get With It" and RCA's "When You Decide," the effect is the same. This is a cat who knows just what he's about, even if nobody else does. And he doesn't try too hard to get it across, he just lets it all happen, like a flood on a suburban street—the sewer blocks up and all sorts of crazy sh*t pours out into the gutter. Disc two is where the revelation and science-fiction show really happens, though. All of it is unissued demos. Feathers accompanies himself on a guitar, or someone else helps him out and remains uncredited; his son plays lead. Feathers changes words mid-sentence, figures out a new bridge as the tape is rolling and the song is unfolding from the confines of his spooked-out mind—and then there are the recordings Feathers did in Mississippi with Junior Kimbrough. Feathers celebrated Kimbrough as the greatest musician alive long before the late Bob Palmer ever heard of him. These 21 tracks (including three takes of "Bottle to the Baby") offer a view of an artist whose time never came, whose dreams simply will not give way to reality, and whose amazing merit as a creative force will not let him rest. It's too much and not nearly enough; it's full of questions with only ciphers for answers. For any fan of primitive, pure American roots music, *Get With It* is indispensable. —*Thom Jurek*

Rock-A-Billy: Rare & Unissued Recordings / Nov. 25, 1998 / Bear Family ✦✦✦✦
Spanning 26 tracks, Bear Family's *Rock-A-Billy: Rare & Unissued Recordings* has a wealth of little-heard Charlie Feathers songs from his prime. This may not contain anything that qualifies as a flat-out classic, but for rockabilly fanatics—the people who will be buying this set—this is an engaging, even exciting, collection of tunes that lives up to Feather's reputation as the rockabilly cat's rockabilly cat. —*Stephen Thomas Erlewine*

His Complete King Recordings / Mar. 9, 1999 / King ✦✦✦

Terry Fell

b. May 13, 1921, Dora, AL
Songwriter, Vocals / Traditional Country, Honky Tonk, Truck Driving Country
Known for his one big hit, 1954's "Truck Driving Man," Terry Fell is but a footnote in country history, but an important one nonetheless. His hit literally spawned the whole truck driving saga that is still a major part of country music's lyrical pool. He was also the first to see the promise in a young Buck Owens, signing him to a manager's contract and using him as a lead guitarist on his sessions.
Fell started his recording career around 1945 as a member of Billy Hughes' group for Fargo Records. After the lone Fargo release, Fell recorded for Courtney and 4-Star, kicking up enough noise and sales with the 4-Star singles to get signed to RCA Victor's new "X" subsidiary in 1954. It was at his first RCA session held in Hollywood that Fell waxed his first, and biggest, hit, the two-sided smash "Don't Drop It" and the immortal "Truck Drivin' Man." At first, "Don't Drop It" was the side to watch, spawning no less than five different cover versions for two different marketplaces. But it was the flip side that became the classic, spawning innumerable cover versions and hitting again on the country charts as late as 1976 for Red Steagall. Fell stayed with RCA and show business for the next five or six years, seeing no more hits but making serious inroads into the behind-the-scenes side of Nashville. Although he continued to record sporadically for Crest, Lode, and even RCA again, he had made the successful move into songwriting and music publishing, earning far more than he ever had as a performer. —*Cub Koda*

● **Truck Drivin' Man** / 1993 / Bear Family ✦✦✦
Terry Fell's legacy consists almost entirely of the song "Truck Driving Man," a standard that has been recorded by countless country artists after being revived by Buck Owens in the '60s. Fell's original 1954 RCA version is a harmonica-driven stomper with all-star accompanists. The other 23 tracks on this collection of Fell's '50s recordings are mostly hillbilly novelties, including his sole hit, "Don't Drop It," which features the sort of nonsense vocalizing that later became Del Reeves' trademark. Terry Fell was a capable but not particularly distinctive vocalist who is remembered more for his songwriting than his recordings, but if you're crazy about '50s country you'll enjoy almost everything on *Truck Driving Man*. —*Greg Adams*

Dick Feller

b. Jan. 2, 1943, Bronaugh, MO
Guitar, Songwriter, Vocals / Novelty, Country-Pop, Country Comedy
Best-known for a brief run of country novelty hits in the mid-'70s, Dick Feller was also a songwriter responsible for several hits by other artists, most notably his oftentime writing partner, Jerry Reed. Feller was born in Bronaugh, MO, in 1943, and started performing and writing in his late teens; he moved to Nashville for a brief period, then went to Los Angeles, where he played in a band and made some demos of his songs. He returned to Nashville in 1966, where he worked as a session musician and in touring bands behind Mel Tillis, Skeeter Davis, and others. Eventually, he landed a songwriting contract with Johnny Cash's publishing company, and wrote the singer's 1972 Top Five hit "Any

Old Wind That Blows." The following year, Feller's "Lord Mr. Ford"—originally written for Jimmy Dean—became a number-one hit for Jerry Reed, who quickly signed Feller to his own publishing staff; Reed went on to record numerous Feller compositions, among them "East Bound and Down" and "I'm Just a Redneck in a Rock and Roll Bar."
Meanwhile, Feller also landed a record deal of his own with United Artists, and released his debut single, "Biff, the Friendly Purple Bear," in 1973. His best year as a solo artist was 1974, bringing two hits in "Makin' the Best of a Bad Situation" and the Top Ten "The Credit Card Song"; his final chart entry came with 1975's "Uncle Hiram and the Homemade Beer." Even if Feller had an obvious penchant for novelty humor, he could also play it straight, as evidenced by John Denver's 1981 hit version of the ballad "Some Days Are Diamonds (Some Days Are Stone)." In 1977, Feller and Reed collaborated on material for the hit film *Smokey and the Bandit*, which gave Feller his biggest exposure ever. He recorded only sporadically after that, drifting out of the music business after a self-titled 1984 album on the small Audiograph label. —*Steve Huey*

Dick Feller Wrote... / 1973 / United Artists ✦✦✦✦
Dick Feller was more successful as a songwriter than a singer, although he charted a few respectable hits in his career. One of them was "Biff, the Friendly Purple Bear," which is included on *Dick Feller Wrote...*, his first United Artists album. The album also contains Feller's recording of "Lord Mr. Ford," an original composition that became a number-one hit for Jerry Reed in 1973. Feller's homely voice and the acoustic-sounding folk-country instrumentation recalls Bob Dylan, and his tendency toward novelty material invites comparisons to John Hartford's RCA recordings. Feller's music ties in with country music's singer/songwriter movement of the late '60s and early '70s, but even in that context he sounds offbeat, despite the contributions of well-known country session players. Considering the limitations of his voice, it isn't surprising that Feller didn't fare better as a performer, but his funny and poignant songs are well worth hearing. —*Greg Adams*

● **No Words on Me** / 1975 / Asylum ✦✦✦✦✦
Some Days Are Diamonds / 1975 / Asylum ✦✦✦✦
Although *Some Days Are Diamonds* doesn't contain any big hit songs like 1973's *Dick Feller Wrote...* ("Lord Mr. Ford," "Biff the Friendly Purple Bear"), it contains examples of the country songwriter's craft as perfect as one is likely to find. For inventiveness, skill with rhyme, and attention to detail, Dick Feller had few equals in the '70s (Roger Miller and Tom T. Hall come to mind), and *Some Days Are Diamonds* contains some of his choicest material. In addition, the crack Nashville session cats who play on the record are given a chance to stretch out on some fun, quirky songs. On "More or Less," legendary picker Reggie Young plays an amazingly "out" fuzz guitar solo which has more in common with John McLaughlin than it does with Chet Atkins or Jerry Reed. The stripped-down, funky arrangements are always interesting, and Feller's nasal voice rides atop the music like an old man shouting hilarious comments from the peanut gallery. While Feller occasionally dips into drippiness ("Louie/Don't Give Up on Me"), his lyrics are so well crafted that even his missteps read like poetry. Although he is perhaps an acquired taste, much the same way as Warren Zevon, Randy Newman or the aforementioned Roger Miller, Dick Feller is certainly one of the most underrated and creative writers/performers of his time, and *Some Days Are Diamonds* is one of his best efforts. —*Pemberton Roach*

Then I Wrote / 1976 / United Artists ✦✦✦

Narvel Felts

b. Nov. 11, 1938, Bernie, MO
Songwriter, Vocals, Guitar / Rockabilly, Memphis Soul, Country-Soul, Traditional Country
Singer/songwriter Narvel Felts was in the country music business for over 30 years. Born in Bernie, MO, he was a self-taught guitar player inspired by the country music of such performers as Ernest Tubb and Floyd Tillman. Felts started out in 1956 when he won his high-school talent contest with a rousing rendition of "Blue Suede Shoes." A DJ from Dexter, MO, was in the audience, and was so impressed that the next day he announced over the air that his station, KDEX, wanted to get in touch with Narvel Felts. The excited teen and his father drove eight miles to the nearest phone, and soon Felts was appearing at the station for his own Saturday afternoon show.
He got his real break when he asked Jerry Mercer if he could jam with the latter's band during a performance. Soon Felts was a member and when Mercer left in 1956, 17-year-old Felts became the new frontman for the Rockets. His first manager was a record shop owner who arranged for the group to audition for Sun Records in Nashville. Felts and one band member attended the first tryout in front of Jack Clement, who suggested they return home, write a few more songs and return with the whole band; they did, but these first sessions were not released until much later. The Rockets returned to performing, and while opening for the film *Rock, Pretty Baby*, at a theater in St. Louis, a regional promoter from Mercury heard them and eventually signed them to his label. They cut five singles with Mercury but were released in 1959.
Felts continued recording some of the band's songs on independent labels and in 1960 had minor chart success with a cover of the Drifters' "Honey Love." This success led him to sign with MGM; he remained with them for two years and released nothing. Through the '60s, Felts continued performing and recording, but concentrated much of his energy on his wife and kids. In 1973, he finally got a big break in music when he signed to the Cinnamon label. His second single, "Drift Away," provided Felts with his first Top Ten record. He followed it with a string of hits including "All in the Name of Love" (1973), and "I Want to Stay" (1974). The label folded in 1975 and Felts then signed with ABC/Dot where he continued having chart success. It was about this time that Felts scored his biggest hit, "Reconsider Me." The song made it to number three and received accolades from industry magazines. Again, a string of hits such as "Lonely Teardrops" followed. Another smash was the 1978 song "Run for the Roses."
Felts lost his contract with ABC when it was purchased by MCA. It was during the mid-'70s that his road manager fired the Rockets and began booking Felts as a solo act backed by the band Wild Country. After a while he and the band went their separate

ways and the band went on to become the supergroup Alabama. Later Felts formed a new band, the Driftaways and in the late '70s became a favorite performer at England's Wembley Festival. In the '80s, he found religion and turned toward gospel music on the albums *On the Wings of a Song* and *Seasons Greetings*, a Christmas record. *—Sandra Brennan*

Reconsider Me / 1975 / Dot ♦♦♦

Narvel Felts / 1975 / Dot ♦♦♦♦

This Time / 1976 / Hi ♦♦♦

Another pleasant record from Felts that doesn't quite deliver the goods. There are some nice interpretations here but this isn't "The Record" he was meant to make. *—Jim Worbois*

Narvel the Marvel / 1976 / Dot ♦♦♦

Felts has an incredible voice (comparable to the late Jackie Wilson) and is able to handle most any style of music. The problem is, not many of these songs are up to his voice. Not a bad record, but something is missing that keeps it from being really good. *—Jim Worbois*

Narvel Felts Greatest Hits, Vol. 1 / 1976 / Dot ♦♦♦♦

Touch of Felts / 1977 / Dot ♦♦

Memphis Days / 1990 / Bear Family ♦♦♦♦♦

● **Drift Away** / 1996 / Bear Family ♦♦♦♦♦

Drift Away is a 28-track compilation of all of Narvel Felts' '70s country hits for ABC/Dot and Cinnamon, including "Lonely Teardrops," "Funny How Time Slips Away," "Reconsider Me" and "Drift Away." The single-disc compilation is the most complete collection ever assembled on Felts, and it stands as the definitive retrospective of this underrated roots musician. *—Thom Owens*

Did You Tell Me / Nov. 5, 1997 / Bear Family ♦♦♦♦

At Rolling Rock: Those Pink And Black Days / Aug. 3, 1999 / Goofin ♦♦♦

Hi Records Era: 1959–1973 / Jan. 1, 2002 / Hi ♦♦♦

Freddy Fender (Baldemar Huerta)

b. Jun. 4, 1937, San Benito, TX

Guitar, Vocals / Tex-Mex, Rock & Roll, Traditional Country, Country-Pop

Freddy Fender was one of the few Hispanic stars in country music, a singer and songwriter whose work was defined largely by its strong Latin sensibility. Born Baldemar Huerta to a family of migrant laborers in San Benito, TX, on June 4, 1937, Fender began playing guitar early in his childhood. After dropping out of school at the age of 16 to join the Marine Corps, he released his first Spanish-language recordings under his given name in 1958.

While his initial sides were successful with listeners in Texas and Mexico, in 1959 he decided to adopt his stage name, along with a stronger rockabilly feel, in order to attract "gringo" audiences. The following year, he released the self-penned "Wasted Days & Wasted Nights," his most successful single yet. But in May of 1960, Fender was convicted of marijuana possession, and was sentenced to five years in Louisiana's notorious Angola State Prison (the same correctional facility which once held blues legend Leadbelly). After serving three years, he was paroled thanks to the efforts of Louisiana governor Jimmie Davis, on the condition that upon Fender's release he stay away from the corruptive influences of the music scene. After his parole ended, Fender tried to re-ignite his career, but with the exception of a few scattered nightclub gigs in the New Orleans area, he found little success, and ultimately returned to San Benito.

In Texas, he spent several years working as an auto mechanic, and even returned to school to pursue a degree in sociology. In 1974, he met Huey P. Meaux, the owner of the Houston-based Crazy Cajun label; after agreeing on a recording deal, it was Meaux who convinced Fender to steer in the direction of country & western while maintaining his music's Hispanic roots. After Fender's first Meaux-produced single, "Before the Next Teardrop Falls," failed to attract the attention of a major label, it was released on Crazy Cajun; in the first weeks of 1975, the song hit the top of both the country and pop charts, and Fender became an overnight star. For the follow-up, he re-recorded his early single, "Wasted Days & Wasted Nights," and notched his second straight number-one country hit. Before the year ended, he had released yet another chart-topper in "Secret Love," and also issued two LPs, *Since I Met You Baby* and a self-titled effort.

Throughout the remainder of the '70s, Fender's success continued, most notably with the number two single "Living It Down" in 1976. That same year, he released two more albums, *Your Cheatin' Heart* and *Rock 'N' Country*. In 1977, he also issued a holiday record, *Merry Christmas/Feliz Navidad*. As the 1980s dawned, however, his popularity began slipping; after his final chart hit, 1983's "Chokin' Kind," he focused on an acting career, highlighted by an appearance in the 1988 Robert Redford film *The Milagro Beanfield War*. He remained largely silent as a musician until 1990, when he formed the Tex-Mex supergroup Texas Tornados with Doug Sahm, Flaco Jimenez, and Augie Meyers. After three albums, the group disbanded, and Fender again resumed his solo career. *—Jason Ankeny*

Are You Ready for Freddy? / 1975 / Dot ♦♦♦♦

The esteemed Freddie Fender, he of perfect voice and total confidence, shows he can take on elements as disparate as Doris Day and Ray Charles and make a listener forget either of these icons even exist. Fender has an edge on just about any other recording artist, in certain ways. For example, let's see Charles modulate up a key and start singing in Spanish. With some of the material on this record, it is almost as if somebody had hired an incredibly, hip, funky Tex-Mex band to play at a wedding. The completely revised "What'd I Say," complete with Cajun fiddling, has to be heard to be believed. The ultimate version of "How Much Is That Doggie in the Window," complete with bluesy guitar licks and, of course, Spanish verses, resides within these disc if such a thing sounds appealing. Like much of Fender's finest work, this is a collaboration with producer Huey P. Meaux, who also contributes one of the best songs, the rollicking "Loving Cajun Style." Vocally, Fender was enjoying his new success and pulling off mighty feats for country music, including actually creating a pleasing blend with background singers. *—Eugene Chadbourne*

Before the Next Teardrop Falls / 1975 / Dot ♦♦♦♦♦

Before the next teardrop falls, one thing is for sure: Another Freddy Fender collection will be issued with the same title as this one, the original blockbuster album that made him a household name among an audience that extended well beyond country fans, at least for a few years. "Before the Next Teardrop Falls" was such a smash hit that record companies cashing in on Fender's popularity just had to use it on their releases. The concept of calling these packages "greatest hits" never occurred to anybody, apparently. Thus the consumer might think they are buying this particular album when they are not, so careful. Although the later "Before" albums are perfectly good records, like most Fender productions, he really struck a tasty groove on the original 1974 session, done with a small band of his usual bandmates and studio accomplices. Obviously the same players are featured on all the tracks, creating great continuity and a pleasing flow to the light country-rock sound. Of course, there is the surprise appearance of a harpsichord but that hardly shakes the Tex-Mex foundation. The group's success was not just limited to the album's big hit. Even better tracks are here, such as Fender's own hilarious song "I Love My Rancho Grande," a few covers of great country songs such as "Wild Side of Life," and the obligatory Fender "fool" song (this time it's "I'm Not a Fool Anymore"). And to no surprise, he pulls off an effective version of the weepy "Roses Are Red" to kick things off. Maybe best of all is the fantastic honky tonk song "You Can't Get There From Here." This is surely the must-have Fender album in a country fan's collection. *—Eugene Chadbourne*

If You Don't Love Me / 1977 / ABC ♦♦

Yes, one gets a full meal at this particular buffet, but it is one of those steam-table affairs where some of the dishes give off the aroma of having sat out too long. Producer Huey P. Meaux, certainly not a slouch, works up a frenzy here with a half-dozen keyboard players, several choirs, and even an early appearance of synthesizers on a country album. Fender's voice is gorgeous and the choice of the material runs the gamut from righteous to sentimentality on a level that only a select few artists in this genre can pull off. Fortunately, Fender is among this group, but unfortunately even he gets pushed over the edge by oohs and aahs that would be more in place as a background to a romantic scene featuring Mickey and Minnie Mouse. The sublime production touches and cooking playing share space with the aforementioned spoiled food, often during the same song. The opening track is a cover of Doug Sahm's "We'll Take Our Last Walk Tonight" and features a groove that combines psychedelic and Cajun with so little clutter that there is still room for the inevitable choir to come stumbling in. Meaux seems to have forgotten that earlier Fender efforts of much better overall quality had been done with smaller, more focused groups and less show-offy production. Fans of picker Sonny Landreth can count him amongst this studio riff-raff, contributing some nice dobro licks. *—Eugene Chadbourne*

The Best of Freddy Fender / 1977 / MCA ♦♦♦♦♦

The Best of Freddie Fender collects all of his biggest hits from the early '70s, making it an excellent introduction to the singer. *—Thom Owens*

Swamp Gold / 1978 / ABC ♦♦♦♦

It's certainly not a country record; more like a roots record. These are the songs that Fender, the struggling performer, used to do; a little Tex-Mex, a little New Orleans, a little soul, a little.... It's obvious from the performance that these songs mean a lot to Fender. *—Jim Worbois*

Early Years: 1959–1963 / 1986 / Krazy Kat ♦♦♦

These 16 sides are taken from rare regional singles that were cut for tiny labels in the days when Fender was only known in Texas and Louisiana. While Fender's earliest recordings were in Spanish, he only sings in English on these cuts of decent, though not thrilling, early swamp pop. Fender takes his inspiration from rockabilly, doo wop, Tex-Mex, and smoldering R&B ballads on these singles, which include his first (and possibly best) version of "Wasted Days & Wasted Nights." One of the relatively few early rock performers to flavor his sound with Texas border music, these sides were most likely influential on Doug Sahm, although they were unheard by a national audience. *—Richie Unterberger*

Collection / 1991 / Reprise ♦♦♦♦♦

The Freddy Fender Collection is a ten-track compilation that contains his biggest hits, from the country-pop crossovers "Wasted Days & Wasted Nights" and "Before the Next Teardrop Falls" to country chart-toppers "Secret Love" and "You'll Lose a Good Thing." It's a brief but consistent collection, featuring nearly every one of his best singles from the mid-'70s, making it an excellent introduction to his long, prolific career, even if isn't as comprehensive as it could have been. *—Stephen Thomas Erlewine*

Canciones de Mi Barrio: The Roots of Tejano Rock / 1993 / Arhoolie ♦♦♦

Fender's earliest Tejano rock recordings are compiled on *Canciones de Mi Barrio*, a fine collection of singles first issued between 1959 and 1964 on the tiny San Benito, Texas label Ideal. Sung mostly in Spanish, these "canciones" bear a large debt to Elvis Presley's hits—there's even a cover of "Devil in Disguise"—although Fender's clear, sweet voice and the music's strong Latin roots combine to give his formative efforts their own distinct identity. *—Jason Ankeny*

The Best of Freddy Fender / Jul. 15, 1996 / MCA ♦♦♦♦♦

The Best of Freddy Fender contains the bulk of Fender's '70s hits, including the Top 10 hits "Wasted Days & Wasted Nights" and "Until the Next Teardrop Falls." Although it is missing a couple of key tracks, this single-disc collection remains a good introduction—in fact, it's nearly a definitive retrospective. *—Thom Owens*

El Mejor de Freddy Fender, Vol. 1 / 1999 / MCA ✦✦
El Mejor de Freddy Fender, Vol. 2 / 1999 / MCA ✦✦✦
El Mejor de Freddy Fender, Vol. 2, like its predecessor, collects some of Fender's best and most popular Spanish-language songs, as well as the major portion of the disc, re-recordings of some of his English-language hits in Spanish. It's an affordable, budget-priced way for Spanish-speaking listeners to have more accessible versions of some of his best material, even if the production sounds rather cheap and the performances not quite as inspired as on the original versions. —*Steve Huey*

● **Greatest Hits** / Apr. 20, 1999 / Edsel ✦✦✦✦✦
Freddy Fender's *Greatest Hits* collects 25 recordings made for Crazy Cajun Records in the mid-'70s. Taking the advice of Huey P. Meaux, the owner of the Houston-based Crazy Cajun label, Fender recorded country material that maintained a slight Tex-Mex feel. The winning combination resulted in many of the memorable crossover country-pop tunes of the era, including the hit singles "Before the Next Teardrop Falls" and "Wasted Days and Wasted Nights." They still sound fresh today. —*Al Campbell*

Lone Star: The Best of Freddy Fender / Oct. 19, 1999 / Music Club ✦✦✦✦
After serving time in Louisiana's Angola Prison on a trumped-up marijuana charge, Freddy Fender hit his stride with a spate of recordings for Cajun producer Huey P. Meaux, molder of hits for the Sir Douglas Quintet, Barbara Lynn, Roy Head, and others. Although he had recorded rock & roll for Imperial Records and Spanish-language versions of rock hits for Falcon Records in McAllen, TX (and the absence of those marvelous sides brings our rating for this set down a point), Fender found the right fit with Meaux's stripped-down approach. The dual-language version of his biggest hit, "Before the Next Teardrop Falls," kicks things off, with "Vaya Con Dios," "Wasted Days & Wasted Nights," and a country version of the Who's "Squeeze Box" also being counted up in the hits category. But this 16-tracker also features the swamp pop that Meaux could produce so well, and tracks like "Just a Moment of Your Time," "Breaking Up Is Hard to Do," and a re-cut of "Oh Holy One" (a regional hit for him back in his Imperial rocker days) shine as brightly as the hits. There's also strong R&B along with the country-oriented sides, with covers of Johnny Ace's "The Clock," Otis Redding's "These Arms of Mine," and a duet with Tommy McLain on Buster Brown's "Fannie Mae" being three more highlights of the set. Freddy Fender may have been an unlikely country star, but these are sides with a strong identity and a wonderful reminder of what great crossover music can accomplish in the marketplace. —*Cub Koda*

Live at Gilley's / Oct. 19, 1999 / Atlantic ✦✦✦
Freddy Fender's volume of *Live at Gilley's* captures a 1986 performance by the singer at the legendary Texas club. Fender isn't in exceptional form, but he acquits himself well, turning in an enjoyable, albeit unremarkable, performance. The typical hits are here, of course ("Wasted Days & Wasted Nights," "Before the Next Teardrop Falls"), but there are also a couple of nice twists (such as a cover of "Whiskey River") that'll keep hardcore fans interested. Not a necessary addition to a Fender library, but for dedicated fans, it's still enjoyable. —*Stephen Thomas Erlewine*

Crazy Cajun's Cosmic Cowboys / Oct. 26, 1999 / Edsel ✦✦✦✦
Digging deeply into Huey Meaux's vaults, we come up with the geographically linked (everybody's from Texas) compilation, largely centered around six live duets between Sahm and Fender. Fender checks in with six other sides, mostly R&B covers; Sahm also contributes two more tracks of his own in addition to his duet work. The collection closes with five sides by Floyd Tillman, a true honky-tonker to the bone. His takes on "Slippin' Around" and "I Love You So Much It Hurts" are Texas country frozen in time, classic in their execution. It's a quirky but very interesting collection. —*Cub Koda*

Tell It Like It Is: Best of Crazy Cajun Recordings / Oct. 26, 1999 / Edsel ✦✦✦✦
Edsel's version of a trip through Huey P. Meaux's Crazy Cajun yields a different bumper crop than Music Club's release, with no clear-cut winner. The version of "Wasted Days & Wasted Nights" here is different from the take on Music Club's, though both comps share the same tracks of "Before the Next Teardrop Falls," "Cowboy Peyton Place," and "Vaya Con Dios." This one, however, ropes in 11 different sides than its reissue cousin. Final verdict: well worth picking up as companion to the Music Club set—either one gets the basic job done right, yet both complement each other well. —*Cub Koda*

20th Century Masters—The Millennium Collection: The Best of Freddy Fender / Apr. 24, 2001 / MCA ✦✦✦✦
Freddy Fender's *20th Century Masters—The Millennium Collection* isn't particularly exhaustive, weighing in at only 12 tracks, but that's not necessarily a bad thing, since these songs provide a nice snapshot of the vocalist at his peak. His very biggest songs, including "Before the Next Teardrop Falls" and "Wasted Days & Wasted Nights," are here, along with several country Top Tens that crossed over into the pop charts—namely "Secret Love," "You'll Lose a Good Thing," "Vaya Con Dios," and "Livin' It Down." Though Fender did record other noteworthy material, much of it is noteworthy only after you've become a fan, and the conciseness of this collection makes it preferable for most listeners that just want the hits. —*Stephen Thomas Erlewine*

La Musica de Baldemar Huerta / Feb. 12, 2002 / Back Porch ✦✦✦
La Musica de Baldemar Huerta is comprised mostly of Mexican and South American songs that Fender heard while growing up in Texas, sung in Spanish, though there are English-language remakes of his hits "Before the Next Teardrop Falls" and "Secret Love." While this is too unassuming to count as a major career milepost, it's refreshingly basic in production and sincere in execution. The arrangements are low-key and acoustic-oriented, and though some sweeping strings are employed, they're pretty graceful and tasteful. It's optimum background music for romantic candlelit dinners in the Southwest; in the better sense of that description, it's romantic, but not unduly schmaltzy. —*Richie Unterberger*

Cathy Fink

b. Aug. 9, 1953, Baltimore, MD

Banjo, Guitar, Vocals, Dulcimer, Composer / Traditional Bluegrass, Contemporary Folk, Children's Folk
Cathy Fink may be best-known for the many children's albums she has recorded over the years, but she is also a key figure in feminist-oriented folk and country music. Born and raised in Baltimore, she got her professional start in 1973 at the Yellow Door coffeehouse in Montreal, at the height of the folk revival. There she became well-known for her excellent banjo and guitar playing, as well as her yodeling. The following year she debuted on CBC Canada and has since played in every major North American folk festival. She and Duck Donald teamed up that year and stayed together until the end of the decade. Fink made her recording debut in 1975 with *Kissing Is a Crime* for Likeable Records. Three years later, she and Duck released a self-titled album on Flying Fish; the two released their first children's album, *I'm Gonna Tell*, in 1980.

Following the breakup with Duck, she moved to Takoma Park, MD, and has immersed herself in the folk, bluegrass and old-time music scene, playing over 5,000 concerts. In 1983, she teamed up with Marcie Marxer. In 1985, she recorded *The Leading Role* for Rounder (her first "adult" album in several years) and began producing other artists a year later. In 1988, she moved to Sugar Hill and recorded *Blue Rose*; the next year, Fink and Marxer released a self-titled album. She also produced an album for Great Dreams and, along with Marxer and Si Kahn, released cassette tapes of the best-selling children's books *The Runaway Bunny/Goodnight Moon* for Harper & Row. In 1991, she released a solo album on Sugar Hill and then put together 80 songs to contribute to the Macmillan/McGraw-Hill reading curriculum, a project entitled *A New View* (1992). In 1993 she produced Si Kahn's children's album *Goodtimes and Bedtimes*. Fink returned in 1995 with *A Parent's Home Companion*. Two years later, she released *Voice on the Wind*. —*Sandra Brennan*

Grandma Slid Down the Mountain / 1984 / Rounder ✦✦✦✦

● **The Leading Role** / 1985 / Rounder ✦✦✦✦✦
This album is a bravura performance in which Cathy Fink, something of a country and old-time music historian, pays tribute not just to women in country music, but to the whole idea of women in country music. And, let's face it, the music would have been pretty boring without the women, no matter how many Hanks are tossed at the audience. Fink has been praised as both a women's artist and a children's performer, yet to some listeners her best attribute will be her banjo playing. She simply excels at the five-string, getting more of a sound with her fingers than many macho bluegrass dudes manage to get with a whole mitt full of brass finger picks. The material here is first-class, drawing on the work of several generations of country ladies, from Ola Belle Reed to Hazel Dickens to Ferron. Fink herself contributes "Little Darlin's Not My Name," a number that manages to be as tough as Johnny Paycheck's "Colorado Kool Aid" without anyone getting their ear cut off. A bit more care could have been taken with the packaging. —*Eugene Chadbourne*

When the Rain Comes Down / 1987 / Rounder ✦✦✦✦

Doggone My Time / 1990 / Sugar Hill ✦✦✦

Banjo Haiku / 1992 / Community Music ✦✦✦✦

Air Guitar / 1993 / High Windy ✦✦✦

Cathy Fink & Duck Donald / Flying Fish ✦✦✦
This album features skillful performances of old-timey and hillbilly music, some of it comic, all of it sprightly. —*AMG*

Firefall

f. 1975, Boulder, CO, db. 1983

Group / Country-Rock, Soft Rock, Pop/Rock
The mellow, easy country-rock sounds of Firefall, coupled with the group's penchant for pop melodies and high-pitched harmonies, produced a series of successful LPs in the late '70s and a series of chart singles, including the Top Ten hit "You Are the Woman." The group was formed by former Flying Burrito Brother Rick Roberts, who handled vocals, guitar, and most of the songwriting duties; he was joined by fellow ex-Burrito and Byrd Michael Clarke on drums, ex-Spirit and Jo Jo Gunne bassist Mark Andes, guitarist/vocalist Jock Bartley, guitarist/vocalist/songwriter Larry Burnett, and keyboardist/woodwind player David Muse, who joined in 1977. The group recorded its self-titled debut in 1976; it and its follow-up, *Luna Sea*, both went gold, and their third album, *Elan*, went platinum. However, the group's commercial fortunes began to decline, and even though Muse experimented with adding different instruments to the overall sound, Firefall's relaxed, toned-down approach simply wore out its welcome as pop trends moved elsewhere. Jock Bartley reformed the group in 1994 for the album *Messenger*. —*Steve Huey*

Firefall / 1976 / Rhino ✦✦✦✦✦
Given Firefall's pedigree of former Spirit and Flying Burrito Brothers members, it may seem that the group would have been a little more adventurous than the band that gave us the soft rock classic "You Are the Woman." Thing is, they were—the song was just so successful, it's overshadowed the fact that their 1976's eponymous debut was a varied, satisfying record. Yes, most of it was within the province of mellow Californian soft rock, but they do display their country-rock roots, along with some searching musicality throughout the record. And while a couple of the songs coast by on sound, they could also craft a good tune, with the singles "Livin' Ain't Livin'" and "Cinderella" standing proudly alongside "You Are the Woman." It's a fine, understated country-rock debut that remains one of the more underrated items of its kind—it holds its own next to Poco, Pure Prairie League, and the Eagles. —*Stephen Thomas Erlewine*

Luna Sea / 1977 / Atlantic ✦✦✦✦
After introducing their mild, country-rock charm with 1976's *Firefall*, Rick Roberts and the band were right back at it a year later with *Luna Sea*. Following in the footsteps of

their debut release, *Luna Sea* attached the same type of silky harmonies to light, breezy acoustics which confirmed the band's comfortable residence in their genre. Although Firefall's first album contained three hit singles (two of them making the Top 40), *Luna Sea* has Roberts fully revealing the influences that the Flying Burrito Brothers had on him during his stint with the group. Like their first album, *Luna Sea* went gold, and it netted them a number-11 hit with the glistening "Just Remember I Love You," with Timothy B. Schmit helping out on background vocals. "So Long" was also a minor hit, while the rest of the tracks are made up of typical love song material that draws more attention from their smooth AM sound than their actual lyrics. Firefall continued their success with 1978's *Elan*, which also sported a hit in "Strange Way," while the album itself went platinum. *—Mike DeGagne*

Elan / 1978 / Atlantic ✦✦✦✦

Firefall crested with its third album, *Elan*, which was prefaced by "Strange Way," an unusually vituperative leadoff single from the group who had broken through with songs of romantic devotion like "You Are the Woman" and "Just Remember I Love You." This time, lead singer and songwriter Rick Roberts was unmoved by a weepy lover, calling her emotional outbursts, "a strange way to tell me you love me," and adding that, if she wanted to cry to somebody, "don't cry to me." The single, which peaked just outside the Top Ten, introduced a somewhat more aggressive album from Firefall that rocked a bit harder, notably on such tracks as "Anymore," and added a horn chart to the closing track, "Winds of Change." For the most part, however, the album's dominant tone was determined by Roberts' romantic anguish, further expressed on the second single, "Goodbye, I Love You," which scraped into the Top 40 on the pop charts and made the Top Ten on the adult contemporary charts. *Elan* itself enjoyed about the same chart success as its predecessor, *Luna Sea*, but ultimately sold a little better, reaching a million-seller certification and marking Firefall's commercial peak. *—William Ruhlmann*

Undertow / 1980 / Rhino ✦✦✦

The fourth album from this country-rock semi-supergroup, *Undertow* failed to yield any major hit songs like the band's first three releases, yet is, in some ways, Firefall's most interesting and consistently pleasing effort. Released a year and a half after *Elan*, the group's first platinum album, *Undertow* was recorded at a time when the members of Firefall were beginning to succumb to infighting, drug and alcohol addiction, and the omnipresent "creative differences." Of course, these differences were an essential part of the Firefall sound, as the group's two principal songwriters, Rick Roberts and Larry Burnett, had very distinct styles. On *Undertow*, there is a greater stylistic variety than ever and the record is infused with a desperate intensity (perhaps caused by the tension resulting from the members' personal problems) not apparent on other Firefall albums. Highlights include "Headed for a Fall," a melancholy, Fleetwood Mac-esque, slow rocker; and "Business Is Business," a Burnett solo acoustic effort. Another standout is "Leave It Alone," a very un-Firefall power-pop song which sounds more like the Shoes than the Byrds. [The CD reissue of *Undertow* includes three bonus tracks, all of which (especially "Crying in the Night," a Stevie Nicks cover) are as good as anything on the original album.] *—Pemberton Roach*

Clouds Across the Sun / 1981 / Atlantic ✦✦

Break of Dawn / 1982 / Atlantic ✦✦

Although Firefall never achieved the soaring success of the Eagles or the national impact of America, the Boulder, CO, sextet should definitely be proud of its first four records. Things began to slide, however, by the early '80s and *Break of Dawn*. On the sixth Firefall spinner, Jock Bartley is the only original remaining, having retained the rights to the name. One-time Flying Burrito Brother Rick Roberts once ran the show, and now merely makes a guest appearance. None of this woefully wavy West Coast wussiness is bad, but nothing sticks to the ribs either. The title track, borne from a line out of "Just Remember I Love You," features Stephen Stills and conjures some cool Colorado imagery. More top-notch support (including ace saxman David Sanborn) helps the best bits float by like clouds across the sun, but the album didn't break anywhere. *—Doug Stone*

Mirror of the World / 1983 / Atlantic ✦✦

● **Greatest Hits** / Sep. 1, 1992 / Rhino ✦✦✦✦

Sharing a light, lush airiness with bands like Poco, America, and Air Supply, Firefall sang fluffy love songs that were weak in lyrical nutrients but abundant with softened chords and harmonies. When radio was saturated with light rock in the mid- to late '70s, they were right in the heart of it, reaching number nine on *Billboard*'s Top 40 with the gentle "You Are the Woman," which remained on the charts for a startling 15 weeks. Firefall's greatest hits collects all of their mellow rock favorites in one place, presenting some thin but not unlistenable soft rock tunes. Lead singer Rick Roberts pours his heart out but still manages to stir up a decent tempo with "Just Remember I Love You," their second biggest single. The blue of the Colorado skyline, the band's home state, is visioned on the soothing flow of "Break of Dawn," and a slight attractiveness is felt throughout "Strange Way," another chart single in 1978. Roberts, who replaced Gram Parsons in the Flying Burrito Brothers, and drummer Michael Clarke, a onetime Byrds member, did give Firefall a talented history within its lineup, but the music being produced contained ample amounts of schlock that soon faded as radio became tired of this shallow drivel. Sometimes harboring a country feel à la Michael Martin Murphey best heard in songs like "Someday Soon" and "It Doesn't Matter," it was evident that the band had only one direction, which was that of a folk-rock sound. Since their material never strayed from this subtle easiness, Firefall's greatest hits is their most worthwhile offering. *—Mike DeGagne*

The Essentials / Jun. 18, 2002 / Rhino ✦✦✦✦

This release is geared toward the average listener who only wants Firefall's mid- to late '70s hits. As part of Rhino's *Essentials* series, this collection of 12 tracks includes the undisputed country-rock classics "You Are the Woman," "Just Remember I Love You," and "Strange Way." This is a perfect summary of the band's '70s heyday that will appeal to fans who can't get enough of America, Poco, and the Eagles. *—Al Campbell*

The Flatlanders

Group / Progressive Country, Country-Folk, Alternative Country, Outlaw Country

The 1990 Rounder CD collecting the Flatlanders' entire recorded history wasn't called *More a Legend Than a Band* for nothing; although this Lubbock, TX, group had the worst business luck this side of Badfinger and never did manage a full-fledged release of their unique and challenging take on traditional country music during their early-'70s existence, the three key members—Jimmie Dale Gilmore, Joe Ely, and Butch Hancock—went on to become three of Texas' most respected singer/songwriters.

Lubbock, a smallish college town in the middle of the cotton-growing flatlands of the west Texas panhandle, is both a fiercely traditional bastion of conservative values and, thanks to the surprisingly good liberal arts departments at Texas Tech University and a relative lack of outside artistic influences, a place where creatively minded people can develop a unique and original style all their own. The Flatlanders embody both sides of this dichotomy, which is what makes their music so endlessly fascinating. The group began in 1970, when school friends Hancock, Ely, and Gilmore all found themselves back in Lubbock after having spent time in San Francisco, Europe, and Austin, respectively. The three musicians roomed together and began playing together, with various other local musicians drifting in and out of the lineup until the group solidified with Gilmore on lead vocals, Ely and Hancock on guitar, non-musician buddy Steve Wesson on autoharp and musical saw (both of which he learned for the express purpose of joining the group), Tommy Hancock (no relation) on fiddle, Sylvester Rice on upright bass, and Tony Pearson on mandolin.

The Flatlanders' manager, Lou Driver, met with another Lubbock boy, Royce Clark, a freelance producer who worked for Shelby Singleton, who at the time owned Sun Records. Far removed from its Sam Phillips glory days, Sun was at this time little more than a catalog which Singleton regularly plundered for his other labels, which included the bargain basement reissue label Share and the barely more mainstream Plantation Records, whose colorful logo was a fixture in the cheap bins at variety stores and truck stops throughout the South. Clark convinced Singleton to try the Lubbock boys out, and they arrived in Nashville in March 1972, where they recorded enough material for a full album. Singleton released a promo single of the group's strongest cut, "Dallas," in late April of that year. The single attracted absolutely no radio attention, and although the album had been mastered and artwork prepared, Singleton scrubbed the release.

In 1973, *Jimmie Dale & the Flatlanders* was just barely released—on 8-track only. Although the tape showed up in the aforementioned Southern variety stores and truck stops, a release on 8-track on a barely extant budget label with no distribution to speak of is the next thing to no release at all. The group returned to Lubbock and played a few more gigs, but Wesson, Pearson, and Tommy Hancock all left the group by the end of 1972. The core trio played a few more gigs and drifted apart more than definitively breaking up. Normally, that would have been that, but by the end of the '70s, Ely and Hancock were cult heroes, thanks to their respective solo albums, and Gilmore, who had written several songs for both of them but had retired from performing while he was studying with the guru Maharaji, was one of the hippest names for Texas music fans to drop.

In the mid-'80s, Gilmore returned to performing in his adopted hometown of Austin, and there was even a brief Flatlanders reunion at the Kerrville Folk Festival in the late '80s. In 1990, after a couple of partial reissues of the Flatlanders' material, Rounder Records released *More a Legend Than a Band*, which reissued the original *Jimmie Dale & the Flatlanders* album, minus the covers "Hello Stranger" and "Waiting for a Train," replacing them with four previously unreleased tracks recorded during the same sessions. Almost ten years later, the group reunited to perform a track for *The Horse Whisperer* soundtrack album. They enjoyed their reunion so much that they continued to perform together, eventually putting the *Now Again* album together in 2002. *—Stewart Mason*

One More Road (1972 Recording) / 1980 / Charly ✦✦✦

One More Road (1972 Recording) is a vinyl collection of the Flatlanders' only recording session that has since been supplanted by several CD issues of the same material. *—Thom Owens*

★ **More a Legend Than a Band** / 1990 / Rounder ✦✦✦✦✦

In any other circumstance, that title would be hyperbole, but in the case of the Flatlanders, it's the simple truth. Although their only commercial release during their nearly four-year existence was an eight track on the tacky Plantation label, bandleaders Jimmie Dale Gilmore, Joe Ely, and Butch Hancock went on to become pioneers in alternative country, directly influencing bands ranging from Uncle Tupelo to Ely disciples the Clash. This 1990 reissue gives that eight track a proper CD release for the first time ever (minus two weaker tracks, covers of the country standards "Hello Stranger" and "Waiting for a Train"), plus four previously unreleased tracks recorded during the same March 1972 sessions. The Flatlanders didn't fit in the least in early-'70s Nashville, both because their music is too weird (Gilmore, a devout Hindu, contributes a song of devotion called "Bhagavan Decreed," and non-musician Steve Wesson contributes musical saw to the proceedings) and, frankly, too country. Tunes like the heartbreaking "Tonight I'm Gonna Go Downtown" have much more in common with Lefty Frizzell and Jimmie Rodgers than the countrypolitan glop of the era. The percussionless, all-acoustic instrumentation is akin to traditional bluegrass, but the gentle, easygoing vibe (tempos barely even break into a trot on the entire album) are much more akin to mellow hippie folk-rock à la Pearls Before Swine. Every song is a small gem, with "Downtown" and Gilmore's career highlight, "Dallas," being the very best of a uniformly fabulous lot. The entire '90s alt-country movement can trace its genesis to these powerful and underappreciated songs. *—Stewart Mason*

Now Again / 2002 / New West ✦✦✦✦✦

When the Flatlanders' first (and for many years only) album finally received a proper release in America in 1990, 18 years after it was recorded, it was called *More a Legend Than a Band.* Three decades after those first sessions, Joe Ely, Jimmie Dale Gilmore, and Butch Hancock, three of Texas' most celebrated singer/songwriters, finally made it back into the studio to cut a second album, and on *Now Again* the Flatlanders finally sound like an honest-to-goodness band—or at least full collaborators—in a way they never did before. While Gilmore tended to dominate the songs on *More a Legend Than a Band* (not surprising, since the band was often billed as Jimmie Dale Gilmore & the Flatlanders), *Now Again* sounds a lot more democratic; the glorious waver of Gilmore's tenor is still the band's strongest vocal presence, but the bluesy bite of Joe Ely's voice and Butch Hancock's homey storyteller's twang get a much bigger share of the spotlight, and their harmonies have both the good humor and the Friday-night enthusiasm of a barroom singalong (though with a good bit more precision). With two exceptions, all the songs for *Now Again* were written collectively by the trio, and the material honors the three distinctive but complementary personalities on board, from the easygoing roadhouse stomp of "Wavin' My Heart Goodbye" and the down-home metaphysics of "Down in the Light of the Melon Moon" to the bluesy lope of "Right Where I Belong" and the joyously goofy neo-rockabilly of "Pay the Alligator." Rather than sounding like a reunion of some aging cosmic cowboys, *Now Again* is the work of three singular talents who are also good friends, and the give and take of their musical personalities speaks both for their respect for one another and the understanding of their abilities; in short, this time out the Flatlanders really are a band, and *Now Again* is an album from them that's strong enough to honor their long-simmering legend. *—Mark Deming*

Flatt & Scruggs

f. 1948, **db.** 1969

Group / Bluegrass, Traditional Bluegrass

Probably the most famous bluegrass band of all time was Flatt & Scruggs & the Foggy Mountain Boys. They made the genre famous in ways that not even Bill Monroe, who pretty much invented the sound, ever could. Because of a guitar player and vocalist from Tennessee named Lester Flatt and an extraordinary banjo player from North Carolina named Earl Scruggs, bluegrass music has become popular the world over and has entered the mainstream in the world of music. Like so many other bluegrass legends, Flatt & Scruggs' were graduates of Bill Monroe's Blue Grass Boys. Because of the unique sound they added ("overdrive," one critic called it), Monroe felt let down after Flatt's quality vocals and Scruggs' banjo leads left in 1948. Quickly the two assembled a band that in the opinion of many was among the best ever, with Chubby Wise on fiddle and Jody Rainwater on bass; a later band, with Paul Warren on fiddle and Josh Graves on dobro, was equally superb. With so many extraordinary musicians and the solid, controlled vocals of Flatt, it's no wonder the Foggy Mountain Boys were the band that brought bluegrass to international prominence. From 1948 until 1969, when Flatt & Scruggs split up to pursue different musical directions, they were *the* bluegrass band, due to their Martha White Flour segment at the *Opry* and, especially, their tremendous exposure from TV and movies.

Flatt and Scruggs were originally brought together by Monroe in 1945, when they joined a band that also featured fiddler Chubby Wise and bassist Cedric Rainwater. This quintet created the sound of bluegrass and helped bring it to national recognition through radio shows, records, and concerts. After three years with Monroe, Flatt left the mandolinist behind in 1948, and Scruggs followed his lead shortly afterward. The duo formed their own band, the Foggy Mountain Boys. Within a few months, they recruited ex-Blue Grass Boy Rainwater, fiddler Jim Shumate and guitarist/vocalist Mac Wiseman. Initially, the band played on radio stations across the South, landing a record contract with Mercury Records in late 1948. Over the next two years, they toured the U.S. constantly, played many radio shows, and recorded several sessions for Mercury. One of the sessions produced the original version of "Foggy Mountain Breakdown," which would become a bluegrass standard. In 1951, Flatt & Scruggs switched record labels, signing with Columbia Records. By this point, the band now featured mandolinist/vocalist Curly Seckler, fiddler Paul Warren, and bassist Jake Tullock. Where the careers of other bluegrass and hard country acts stalled in the early and mid-'50s, the Foggy Mountain Boys flourished. One of their first singles for Columbia, "'Tis Sweet to Be Remembered," reached the Top Ten in 1952, and in 1953, the Martha White Flour company sponsored a regular radio show for the group on WSM in Nashville. In 1955, the band joined the *Grand Ole Opry.* The following year, they added a dobro player called Buck Graves to the lineup.

Flatt & Scruggs reached a new audience in the late '50s, when the folk music revival sparked the interest of a younger generation of listeners. The duo played a number of festivals targeted at the new breed of bluegrass and folk fans. At the same time, country music television programs went into syndication, and the duo became regulars on these shows. In the summer of 1959, Flatt & Scruggs began a streak of Top 40 country singles that ran into 1968—their chart performance was directly tied to their increased exposure. The duo's popularity peaked in 1962, when they recorded the theme song to the television sitcom *the Beverly Hillbillies.* The theme, called "The Ballad of Jed Clampett," became the first number-one bluegrass single in early 1963, and the duo made a number of cameos on the show.

The Beverly Hillbillies began a streak of cameo appearances and soundtrack work for Flatt & Scruggs in television and film, most notably with the appearance of "Foggy Mountain Breakdown" in Arthur Penn's 1968 film *Bonnie & Clyde.* With all of their TV, film, and festival appearances, Flatt & Scruggs popularized bluegrass music more than any artist, even Monroe. Ironically, that popularity helped drive the duo apart. Scruggs wanted to expand their sound and pushed Flatt to cover Bob Dylan's "Like a Rolling Stone" in 1968 as well as land concert appearances in venues that normally booked rock & roll acts. Flatt wanted to continue in a traditional bluegrass vein. Inevitably, the opposing forces came to a head in 1969, and the duo parted ways. Appropriately, Flatt formed a traditional bluegrass band, the Nashville Grass, while Scruggs assembled a more progressive outfit, the Earl Scruggs Revue. Throughout the '70s, both Flatt and Scruggs enjoyed successful solo careers. In 1979, the duo began ironing out the details of a proposed reunion album, but they were scrapped upon Flatt's death on May 11, 1979. Scruggs retired in the '80s. In 1985, Flatt & Scruggs were inducted into the Country Music Hall of Fame. *—Stephen Thomas Erlewine & David Vinopal*

Foggy Mountain Jamboree / 1957 / Columbia ✦✦✦✦

Songs of the Famous Carter Family / 1961 / Columbia/Legacy ✦✦✦

On this album, Flatt & Scruggs cool their famous "overdrive" to turn in a collection of relaxed, almost dreamy adaptations of Carter tunes. Maybelle herself plays autoharp on the sessions, although it would have been nice if she had sung too, especially since the cover prominently displays her name and picture. This is a pleasant record, though, highlighted by the duo's original recording of "You Are My Flower," a song which they played throughout their career. *—Jim Smith*

☆ **Foggy Mountain Banjo** / 1961 / Columbia ✦✦✦✦✦

The album that secured their standing among folk music enthusiasts in the 1960s, it focuses on Scruggs' instrumental prowess as well as his sharp interplay with dobroist Josh Graves, fiddler Paul Warren and Flatt's flatpicking guitar. The album also features drummer Buddy Harman, whose appearance shocked purists. *—Michael McCall*

Flatt & Scruggs at Carnegie Hall! / 1962 / Columbia ✦✦✦

Live at Vanderbilt University / 1964 / Columbia ✦✦✦

Although not as famous as their *Carnegie Hall!* concert release, *Live at Vanderbilt University* was almost as significant an event at the time. The academic community in the South had always kept country music at arm's length—the antipathy was centered in both intellectual and class snobbery, as well as the notion of this music as "hillbilly" music. The wall began breaking down in the early '60s as the folk revival reached the Southern campuses, and recording a live album at Vanderbilt was Flatt & Scruggs' way of announcing that bluegrass had arrived academically and then some. The selection of songs here is more low-key than the *Carnegie Hall* show, and the displays of instrumental and vocal prowess somewhat more restrained—there's no "Ballad of Jed Clampett," but there is an achingly beautiful "You Are My Flower" and "Across the Blue Ridge Mountains," the exquisite Earl Scruggs-featured instrumental "Old Folks," and rippling versions of "Cannonball Blues" and "Shady Grove" (titled "Going Back to Harlan" here), among other folkier parts of the Flatt & Scruggs repertory. The crowd is sympathetic, the acoustics are fine, and this record is worth tracking down on CD or LP. *—Bruce Eder*

Greatest Hits / 1966 / Columbia ✦✦✦

This is a concise sampler for those who don't want their *20 All-Time Great Recordings* album. *—Mark A. Humphrey*

Strictly Instrumental / 1967 / Columbia ✦✦✦✦

Strictly Instrumental is a delightful duet album between Flatt & Scruggs and Doc Watson, giving the three musicians an opportunity to flaunt their exceptional instrumental talents. Sticking to a selection of songs that is traditional in approach, but are not played frequently ("John Hardy Was a Desperate Little Man," "Pick Along," "Spanish Two-Step"), Flatt & Scruggs and Watson play with a startling fluidity—these instrumentals are so rich and skillful that vocals would have been superfluous. For lovers of instrumental bluegrass, this album is a must-hear. *—Thom Owens*

Nashville Airplane / 1968 / Columbia ✦✦✦

Flatt & Scruggs came to a parting of the ways at the end of the 1960s, and it started with the opening cut on this album, a version of "Like a Rolling Stone." In a sense, it was the illustration of the same spirit that got them to record "The Times They Are a Changin'" on the album. Scruggs recognized this fact and embraced it, while Flatt resisted it to the point that their 20-year partnership was split up as a result. The irony is that "Like a Rolling Stone" is transformed into something so close to bluegrass music that it's a minor revelation hearing it done this way—it's that good, despite some awkward transitions. Among the rest of the songs, the other Dylan songs ("Rainy Day Women #12 & 35," "I'll Be Your Baby Tonight") come off beautifully, as do "Folsom Prison Blues," "Gentle on My Mind," and "Catch the Wind"; "If I Were a Carpenter" and "Universal Soldier" are less so. *—Bruce Eder*

Blue Ridge Cabin Home / 1979 / County ✦✦✦✦

Blue Ridge Cabin Home contains a selection of Flatt & Scruggs' finest recordings from the '50s, material that demonstrates why they had to leave Bill Monroe's band. Where Monroe wanted to keep the music pure, Flatt & Scruggs were constantly pushing the boundaries of what bluegrass could do, bringing in heavy elements of country, folk, gospel and even pop. The recordings on this compilation helped popularize bluegrass, and while it is available on more comprehensive collections, *Blue Ridge Cabin Home* remains a terrific single-disc sampler of their sound. *—Thom Owens*

Columbia Historic Edition / 1982 / Columbia ✦✦✦

20 All Time Great Recordings / 1983 / Columbia ✦✦✦✦

This 20-track overview of Lester Flatt and Earl Scruggs' defining brand of traditional bluegrass features many of their best-loved stomps from the mid- to late '60s, and also highlights some lesser-known gems. Any self-respecting Flatt & Scruggs collection is bound to have "The Ballad of Jed Clampett," "Foggy Mountain Breakdown," and "Salty Dog Blues." *20 All Time Great Recordings* goes a little bit further to include deeper cuts like "Detroit City," "When Papa Played the Dobro," and the mournful "Soldier's Return." While their material from the '40s and '50s was certainly more genre-defining, their music from this era is just as fun. *—Zac Johnson*

Mercury Sessions, Vol. 1 / 1987 / Rounder ✦✦✦✦✦

Mercury Sessions, Vol. 1 collects the first 14 tracks that Flatt & Scruggs recorded for Mercury Records between 1948 and 1950. The duo made these recordings after they broke away from Bill Monroe, and the adventurous qualities of the music demonstrates why they had to split away from the father of bluegrass—they were expanding the boundaries of the music. Consequently, these song are rightly regarded as Flatt & Scruggs' best and most influential recordings, and the duo's instrumental skills and harmonies are still breathtaking several decades after they were recorded. Any serious bluegrass collection isn't complete without Flatt & Scruggs' Mercury Recordings, either in this format or in Mercury's single-disc *The Complete Mercury Sessions.* — *Thom Owens*

Mercury Sessions, Vol. 2 / 1987 / Rounder ✦✦✦✦✦
Mercury Sessions, Vol. 2 collects the remaining 14 tracks that Flatt & Scruggs recorded for Mercury Records between 1948 and 1950, including the original version of their classic song, "Foggy Mountain Breakdown." This music is generally considered the finest that the duo ever recorded, and a simple cursory listen will reveal why—the duo's harmonies and instrumental interplay are simply astounding. Any serious bluegrass collection needs Flatt & Scruggs' Mercury Recordings, either in this format or in Mercury's single-disc *The Complete Mercury Sessions.* — *Thom Owens*

You Can Feel It in Your Soul / 1988 / County ✦✦✦✦✦
You Can Feel It in Your Soul contains 13 gospel songs that Flatt & Scruggs recorded during the '50s. Though it is brief, the compilation acts as a nice complement to the numerous collections of the duo's secular material, and the group sounds fantastic on each track here. Several cuts also benefit from the appearance of guitarist Chet Atkins. — *Thom Owens*

☆ **1948–1959** / 1992 / Bear Family ✦✦✦✦✦
The first of four box sets documenting the complete recordings of Flatt & Scruggs as a working band, this one detailing the group's first 11 years is generally considered the most essential. These 113 tracks represent the duo's complete Mercury recordings on disc one and the beginning of their Columbia sides on discs two through four. There is one completely unissued cut, and the entire package has been remastered and contains copious liner notes. Contained here are the 1949 recordings of their classic "Foggy Mountain Breakdown" and 1950's "Rollin' in My Sweet Baby's Arms," and also mid-'50s stompers such as "Dim Lights, Thick Smoke," "Flint Hill Special," and "You're Not a Drop in the Bucket"; gospel tunes such as "Give My Mother My Crown," "A Million Years in Glory," "Jesus Savior Pilot Me"; and hot singles such as "Cabin on the Hill," "Foggy Mountain Rock," and "Crying My Heart Out Over You." Beginning with the Bill Monroe band where Flatt's voice first countered Monroe's high lonesome, Flatt & Scruggs made that low, clear bell of a sound into a trademark—as they did with Scruggs' unique banjo styles. While the music on later collections is fine and rousing, this is truly exciting with all the hope and trepidation of discovery and walking the high wire in search of something original. These four CDs are essential for every serious fan of bluegrass music. — *Thom Jurek*

1959–1963 / 1992 / Bear Family ✦✦✦✦✦
While the first Flatt & Scruggs box on Bear Family documented the band's development over its first 11 years—1948-1959—this set captures the band at the height of its meteoric rise to fame into the stuff of legend. First and foremost, Flatt & Scruggs eclipsed the fame of their mentor, Bill Monroe by having six charting singles in *Billboard* between the mid-'50s and 1960. They also got reviewed in *Playboy* and *Downbeat* magazines and began to play the Newport Folk Festival and appear on-stages with Joan Baez, Cisco Houston, the Kingston Trio, New Christy Minstrels, Woody Guthrie, John Jacob Niles, and many others. Things began to heat up for Flatt & Scruggs in 1963, when they debuted the "Theme of Jed Clampett" for the new television comedy series *the Beverly Hillbillies.* This box contains six complete LPs recorded during those years, the complete edition of their concert at Carnegie Hall, and an album of square dancing fiddle tunes for which guitarist Merle Travis and fiddler Gordon Terry were added to the band. Over five CDs and 139 selections, the Flatt & Scruggs trek to superstardom is well documented. Their names became household for appearances on everything from the Ed Sullivan show to *the Price Is Right.* But most importantly, what Flatt & Scruggs accomplished during this period was extraordinary: They not only brought the American public at large to traditional country and bluegrass music from the Southern mountains; they also pushed the envelope on the bluegrass to places it literally would never have gone. Take a listen to their version of Doc Watson's "I'm Troubled" from 1963, recorded just four days after the assassination of John F. Kennedy, the use of Buddy Harman's drums on Guthrie's "Hard Travelin'" and "This Land Is Your Land," or Maybelle Carter's lead guitar on an entire program of Carter Family classics recorded in 1961. This is the sound of history in the making, of mountain music coming down from the mountain as the rest of the country opens to it in all of its raw, heartfelt glory. This is breathtaking material and is the most mainstream of the three sets devoted to Flatt & Scruggs—there is one devoted to Lester's music after the band's demise—and it is the most exciting. — *Thom Jurek*

1964–1969, Plus / 1992 / Bear Family ✦✦✦✦✦
The final five years of the team of Flatt & Scruggs is documented on the six-CD Bear Family set *1964-1969, Plus.* Their final six recordings together are on a Lester Flatt box set on the same label (*Flatt on Victor Plus More*). Though the pair never referred to themselves as bluegrass musicians—because of its association with their mentor, Bill Monroe—they had a difficult time telling the ever-increasing flood of international fans just what it was they did. Certainly it was folk music, but not the folk music of the folk revival of the late '50s and early '60s, and it was country music, though not what Owen Bradley and Chet Atkins was pushing through Nashville at the time, and while a lot of the music was rooted in blues and gospel, it couldn't be called that either. Flatt & Scruggs were the progenitors of what later pioneers like Tony Trischka, Randy Scruggs, Béla Fleck, and others would call "newgrass"—the pair wouldn't have liked that either. What this set documents is how the musical styles emerging in the 1960s were explored by Flatt & Scruggs, were turned inside out, were popularized, and put enough pressure on the duo, musically and professionally because of increased fame, to tear them apart. Here are the recordings of Waylon Jennings' "I'm a Man of Constant Sorrow" (before Ralph Stanley cut it), Bob Dylan's "It Ain't Me Babe," Tom Paxton's "The Last Thing on My Mind," Chuck Berry's "Memphis," "Foggy Mountain Breakdown" done for the film *Bonnie & Clyde,* traditional songs like

"Sally Goodin," Mel Tillis and Danny Dill's "Detroit City," Tom T. Hall's "I'm Gonna Ride That Steamboat," John Sebastian's "Nashville Cats," Doc and Merle Watson's "Southbound," and Flatt & Scruggs' amazing instrumental "Jazzing." But before the reader looks away in disgust, muttering "sellout," perhaps the music itself should be taken as an example of its own merit. Flatt & Scruggs stood outside of tradition from the beginning by breaking with standard vocal and instrumentation regimens. Using four-part harmonies, drums, and harmonica on a Dylan song, the duo were merely doing what they had done throughout their careers—they explored the roots of a song and discovered where it took them. Recording Buffy Sainte-Marie's "Universal Soldier," Donovan's "Catch the Wind," Dylan's "Wanted Man" and "Like a Rolling Stone," the Hall songs for the *Bonnie & Clyde* soundtrack, and Bobbie Gentry's "Ode to Billie Joe" were high-wire acts, cliff edges both men were looking over into an abyss that refused to stare back at them, and finally it separated them. But it was never for lack of an adventurous spirit of laziness or lack of respect. What is documented here may be the sound of disintegration, but it is also the sound of courage and preservation that brought the heart and soul of country music to popular music, not the other way around. — *Thom Jurek*

The Complete Mercury Sessions / Aug. 4, 1992 / Mercury ✦✦✦✦✦
The integral early recordings of this seminal bluegrass band. Included is their classic "Foggy Mountain Breakdown," "Roll in My Sweet Baby's Arms," "Old Salty Dog Blues" and others. It's indispensable for bluegrass fans. — *Michael McCall*

★ **The 'Tis Sweet to Be Remembered: Essential Flatt & Scruggs** / Jan. 28, 1997 / Columbia/Legacy ✦✦✦✦✦
Excepting a few years with Mercury at the beginning of their career, Flatt & Scruggs made all of their studio recordings for Columbia. This double-disc set is the most useful survey of their work for the label, spanning 1950 to 1969, and throwing in three unreleased tracks along the way. In addition to the expected sterling bluegrass, it has their occasional commercial breakthroughs ("The Ballad of Jed Clampett," "Petticoat Junction," and the version of "Foggy Mountain Breakdown" that was used as the theme to *Bonnie & Clyde*). Curiosity seekers will also be impressed by their cover of Bob Dylan's "Down in the Flood," recorded in late 1967, and unreleased by Dylan himself until *The Basement Tapes.* — *Richie Unterberger*

Flatt & Scruggs at Carnegie Hall!: The Complete Concert / 1998 / Koch ✦✦✦
When Flatt & Scruggs appeared on the Carnegie Hall stage in December of 1962, it was proof that bluegrass music had hit the big time. Guitarist and singer Lester Flatt and banjo god Earl Scruggs (who has been credited, not entirely accurately, with inventing the three-fingerpicking style that distinguishes bluegrass banjo playing from its old-time antecedents) had fully emerged from the shadow of Bill Monroe, their former boss, and made a national name for themselves. Columbia released an album that included 13 songs from that performance, and this CD reissue adds the rest of the set for a total of 32 tracks. The uncut version of the concert makes a couple of things clear. First, that we really were missing some fine moments, including a gorgeous version of "He Will Set Your Fields on Fire" and a couple of fun bass-and-banjo duets. Second, that we weren't missing more than a few. The 13 songs on the original LP, which included a roaring rendition of the Earl Scruggs composition "Flint Hill Special," the surprisingly lovely (given the subject matter) "Hot Corn, Cold Corn," and one of the best performances of "Take This Hammer" ever recorded, did indeed constitute the best of the *Carnegie Hall!* concert. Apart from the highlights noted above, the rest of it was good, but rarely transcendent—though it does end with fireworks when Merle Travis joins the band for a two-song encore. — *Rick Anderson*

Town and Country/Changin' Times / Nov. 14, 2000 / Collectables ✦✦✦
This two-fer from Collectables features a pair of out of print Flatt & Scruggs LPs: *Town and Country* and *Changin' Times.* Originally issued in 1966 and 1968, these 23 tracks are quite different in tone; however, funneling the songs through their arrangements, Flatt & Scruggs managed to combine traditional bluegrass with modern folk and make the songs their own. *Town and Country* is a loose concept album, a thematic musical journey featuring "Houston," "Memphis," and "Detroit City," while *Changin' Times* mixes popular songs of the late '60s written by Bobbie Gentry and Bob Dylan with the traditional "This Land Is Your Land" and "Foggy Mountain Breakdown." — *Al Campbell*

Hard Travelin' Featuring the Ballad of Jed Clampett/Final Fling / Nov. 14, 2000 / Collectables ✦✦✦
This two-fer from Collectables features a pair of out-of-print Flatt & Scruggs LPs: *Hard Travelin' Featuring the Ballad of Jed Clampett* and *Final Fling.* Originally issued in 1963 and 1970, these 23 tracks are quite different in tone, but funneled through Flatt & Scruggs' arrangements they manage to combine traditional bluegrass and modern folk and make them their own. This is especially the case with the seven Bob Dylan tunes from *Final Fling.* By the way, "The Ballad of Jed Clampett" would end up as a number-one hit as well as the theme song for *the Beverly Hillbillies* TV show. — *Al Campbell*

Earl Scruggs: His Family and Friends/Nashville Airplane / Nov. 14, 2000 / Collectables ✦✦✦✦✦
One of Scruggs' best solo albums paired with one of the duo's late LPs, on which Scruggs was the dominant personality. On *Nashville Airplane,* he got the duo doing four Bob Dylan songs and on *Earl Scruggs: His Family & Friends* he worked with Dylan himself, as well as the Byrds, Joan Baez, and Doc Watson. Neither album was ever on CD by itself, and the Earl Scruggs album is worth the cost of the disc by itself, for the outstanding performances by Baez, the Byrds, Watson, and, of course, Scruggs himself. — *Bruce Eder*

20th Century Masters—The Millennium Collection: The Best of Flatt & Scruggs / Apr. 24, 2001 / Mercury ✦✦✦✦
Flatt & Scruggs' volume of Mercury/Universal's *20th Century Masters—The Millennium Collection* is an excellent, basic collection of 12 of the duo's finest recordings for Mercury.

Many, though not all, of their signature tunes are here, including "Foggy Mountain Breakdown," "Roll in My Sweet Baby's Arms," "I'll Just Pretend," and "Pike County Break- down." This certainly can't be called definitive, even as a retrospective of just their Mercury recordings, but as a sampler for the curious or budget-minded listener, this is a strong choice. —*Stephen Thomas Erlewine*

16 Biggest Hits / Jan. 29, 2002 / Columbia ✦✦✦✦
This isn't the definitive Flatt & Scruggs collection, but it does contain a majority of the duo's best Columbia sides, including "'Tis Sweet to Be Remembered," "The Ballad of Jed Clampett," "Pearl Pearl Pearl," and the hit version of "Foggy Mountain Breakdown" from *Bonnie & Clyde*. It nicely encapsulates the two-disc *'Tis Sweet to Be Remembered* collection, and is surprisingly good considering the spotty nature of the overall series. —*Jim Smith*

★ **The Complete Mercury Recordings** / Apr. 22, 2003 / Mercury ✦✦✦✦✦
In what basically amounts to a re-issue of 1992's similarly titled *Complete Mercury Sessions*, Universal has improved upon the original by putting the songs in chronologi- cal order and including terrific liner notes by folk historian Mary Katherine Aldin. While both releases include the early classics "Foggy Mountain Breakdown," "Roll in My Sweet Baby's Arms," and "Salty Dog Blues," the extras on this release make it the one to own. —*Zac Johnson*

Lester Flatt

b. Jun. 19, 1914, Overton County, TN, d. May 11, 1979, Nashville, TN
Guitar, Vocals, Mandolin / Traditional Bluegrass
After Lester Flatt and Earl Scruggs parted ways in 1969, Flatt reassembled many of the Foggy Mountain Boys, renamed the group Nashville Grass, and toured very successfully until his death in 1979. Unlike Scruggs, who with his sons moved on to music that was only marginally country, Flatt and the Grass stuck to traditional bluegrass material. Even without Scruggs, the band shone, and Flatt's vocals, musical direction, and taste received the credit they had so long deserved. —*David Vinopal*

Changin' Times / 1969 / CBS ✦✦✦
In the mid- to late '60s, Bob Johnston was not just producing leading edge folk-rockers, like Bob Dylan and Simon & Garfunkel. He was also leading some old-school folk leg- ends, willing or unwilling, into little-remembered LPs with folk-rock-contemporary-pop arrangements. Among those were records by Pete Seeger, Burl Ives, and this one with Lester Flatt and Earl Scruggs. This is actually not bad, though, and while it does feature a repertoire fairly far from the bluegrass norm, Flatt & Scruggs do acquit themselves with dignity. Bob Dylan covers (five of them) figure heavily, and they also take cracks at "Where Have All the Flowers Gone," "Ode to Billie Joe," and "Four Strong Winds." It's most notable, however, for the Dylan composition "Down in the Flood," which the duo recorded in late 1967, but which Dylan himself wouldn't release until the 1970s. Perhaps to pick up some casual consumers, the record also includes "Foggy Mountain Breakdown," which had recently been featured in the movie *Bonnie & Clyde*. In the actual arrangements, the folk-rock influence is light, and the result isn't that much different from how Flatt & Scruggs usually sounded on record. —*Richie Unterberger*

Nashville Grass: Fantastic Pickin' / 1978 / CMH ✦✦✦

● **Greatest Bluegrass Hits, Vol. 1** / 1982 / CMH ✦✦✦✦✦
Lester Flatt & the Nashville Grass never attained the level of popularity that Flatt's work with banjo legend Earl Scruggs did, but his late-'60s and mid-'70s work with the youth- ful Grass still produced some of the finest traditional (and even slightly progressive) blue- grass of that era. Assisted by a youthful mandolin player named Marty Stuart, Flatt demonstrates his genial voice and fine guitar pickin' on these ten tracks, highlighted by revisions of old favorites "Foggy Mountain Special," "All the Good Times Are Past and Gone," and "Roll in My Sweet Baby's Arms." —*Zac Johnson*

Live at the Bluegrass Festival / 1986 / CMH ✦✦✦

Lester Raymond Flatt / 1989 / Flying Fish ✦✦✦

Lester Flatt's Greatest Performance / 1989 / CMH ✦✦✦✦✦

Flatt on Victor Plus More / Dec. 14, 1999 / Bear Family ✦✦✦
It started as early as 1966, when Earl Scruggs convinced his partner, Lester Flatt, to record some songs outside of the bluegrass tradition. Among them were some Bobby Bare cuts: "Passing Through," "Shut Your Face, I'm Talking to Your Head," "Before You Die," and "Take Me Home to Mama." In the same year there was the song that Ralph Stanley would make his signature, Waylon Jennings' "Man of Constant Sorrow." In 1967 it was Bob Dylan's "Girl from the North Country," and in 1968 it was Dylan's "Rainy Day Women #12 & 35," produced by Bob Johnston, Dylan's producer. And in 1969, amid the ringing electric guitars of Randy Scruggs, Charlie McCoy's harmonica, Charlie Daniels' rhythm guitar, and others bluegrass "innovations," it was over. Arguably the most famous duo in the history of bluegrass—eclipsing even the profile of the music's founders, Bill Monroe (their former employer) and Ralph Stanley in the early '60s—Flatt & Scruggs had a bitter parting of ways that would not be mended until Flatt was on his deathbed ten years later. This Bear Family set compiles the aforementioned tracks and five and a half more CDs, including Flatt's last live date, all recorded for RCA between 1969 and 1978. Flatt, by far the more traditional of the two men, and ten years Scruggs' senior, went to record with Mac Wiseman, Josh Graves, Marty Stuart, and a host of other traditional musicians— including Bill Monroe—on over ten albums' worth of material both original and from the bluegrass canon. None of it matches the majesty of Flatt & Scruggs at their peak—and neither does Scruggs'—but it is all worthwhile as a way of looking at how bluegrass mu- sic survived a particularly tumultuous era. Certainly, collectors will find the most use for these recordings, but their appeal cannot be denied because Flatt was the most original singer in the history of the music and remains so. His voice was far deeper than most,

and his phrasing reflected the same mountains he grew up in until the end, no matter what he was singing. This set may not be for everyone, but for those who sprung for the other Flatt & Scruggs boxes, or have found them to be irresistible, this is fine traditional country music. —*Thom Jurek*

Live at Vanderbilt / May 21, 2002 / Bear Family ✦✦✦
Legendary vocalist and guitarist Lester Flatt shares the bill with his former bandleader, Bill Monroe, on this live set from Vanderbilt's Neely Auditorium in 1974. Flatt & Scruggs had split from Bill Monroe & His Blue Grass Boys some 20 years earlier, and Lester Flatt's reconciliation at an early-'70s Bean Blossom Festival seemed to pave the way for Monroe's guest appearances on this live album. Although the headliners are nearing the far edge of their prime (in the '40s, '50s, and '60s, first Monroe, then Flatt & Scruggs were virtu- ally untouchable as leaders of the bluegrass movement), they still surrounded themselves with the best bands around. Curly Seckler, Charles Nixon, Kenny Baker, and even a 15-year-old Marty Stuart back the gentle-voiced Flatt and the always-energetic Monroe on a whole series of traditional standards. The college crowd (fresh from the radio popu- larity of "Duelin' Banjos") actively seems to enjoy the performances, and both bands feed off of that energy. Although Lester Flatt's performances with the Nashville Grass were never as strong as the Flatt & Scruggs recordings (as their *Flatt & Scruggs at Carnegie Hall!: The Complete Concert* showcases wonderfully), this live document captures the meeting of two bluegrass legends and old friends performing the music they love for a crowd who loves them. —*Zac Johnson*

Essential Lester Flatt and the Nashville Grass / Jan. 14, 2003 / CMH ✦✦✦✦

RCA Country Legends / Mar. 4, 2003 / RCA/BMG Heritage ✦✦✦✦✦

Béla Fleck

b. 1958, New York, NY
Banjo, Leader / Contemporary Bluegrass, Progressive Bluegrass, Fusion, Post-Bop
Premier banjo player Béla Fleck is considered one of the most innovative pickers in the world and has done much to demonstrate the versatility of his instrument, which he uses to play everything from traditional bluegrass to progressive jazz. He was named after composer Béla Bartok and was born in New York City. Around age 15, Fleck became fascinated with the banjo after hearing Flatt & Scruggs' "Ballad of Jed Clampett" and Weissberg & Mandell's "Dueling Banjos," and his grandfather soon gave him one. While attending the High School of Music and Art in New York, Fleck worked on adapting bebop music for the banjo. Fleck always had diverse musical interests, and his own style was influenced by Tony Trischka, Earl Scruggs, Chick Corea, Charlie Parker, John Coltrane, the Allman Brothers, Aretha Franklin, the Byrds, and Little Feat.

After graduation, he joined the Tasty Licks, a group from Boston. They recorded two albums and dissolved in 1979. Afterwards, Fleck joined the Kentucky band Spectrum. That year, only five years after he took up the instrument, he made his solo recording debut with *Crossing the Tracks*, which the "Readers' Poll" in *Frets* magazine named Best Overall Album. In 1982, he joined New Grass Revival and stayed with them until the end of the decade. During this time, his reputation continued to grow and in 1990, *Frets* magazine added his name to their Hall of Greats. In 1988, one of his compositions, "Drive" (from the album *New Grass Revival*), was nominated for a Grammy. Fleck, mandolin player Sam Bush, fiddler Mark O'Connor, bassist Edgar Meyer, and dobro player Jerry Douglas teamed up in 1989 to form Strength in Numbers and record *The Telluride Sessions*.

Late that year, Fleck was asked by PBS television to play on the upcoming *Lonesome Pine Special*; in response he gathered together a veritable "dream team" of musicians to form the Flecktones. The original members included Howard Levy, who played piano, harmonica, and ocarina, among other instruments; bass guitarist Victor Lemonte Wooten, and his brother Roy "Future Man" Wooten on the drumitar, an electronic drum shaped like a guitar. Though the special wasn't aired until 1992, the Flecktones recorded their eponymous debut album in 1990 and followed it up with *Flight of the Cosmic Hippo* (1991). In 1992, they released their fourth album, *UFO Tofu*, which featured music blend- ing different genres ranging from bluegrass to R&B to worldbeat. In 1995, they released *Tales From an Acoustic Planet*; *Left of Cool* followed in 1998, and *Tales From an Acoustic Planet 2: The Bluegrass Sessions* was released a year later. *Outbound* followed in mid- 2000. —*Sandra Brennan*

Crossing the Tracks / 1979 / Rounder ✦✦✦✦

Natural Bridge / 1982 / Rounder ✦✦✦
Before he single-handedly invented jazz-fusion five-string banjo, Béla Fleck was a young bluegrass player whose work with such bands as Spectrum and the New Grass Revival pushed the envelope of bluegrass tradition and contributed to the development of the New Acoustic movement spearheaded by mandolinist David Grisman, guitarist Tony Rice, and others. Fleck's playing was based on the melodic Keith/Trischka style along with the single-string technique of Don Reno, but his sound was all his own and as time went on his ideas became increasingly jazz-based. His second album finds him straddling the fence between bluegrass and jazz: "Punchdrunk" is a quirky romp built on an explicitly bluegrassy foundation, while "Flexibility" almost sounds like 1940s bebop. Other com- positions fall somewhere in between, such as the beautiful and gentle duet between banjo and dobro, "Daybreak" and the highly chromatic but traditionally textured "Applebutter." Guests include all the usual suspects: Grisman, guitarist/fiddler Mark O'Connor, fiddlers Darol Anger and Sam Bush, bassist Mark Schatz, and dobro fiend Jerry Douglas, among others. Great stuff. —*Rick Anderson*

Double Time / 1984 / Rounder ✦✦✦
Double Time may be among Béla Fleck's least ambitious solo projects, although it proves an easily digestible introduction to his wildly eclectic banjo forays. After all, Fleck is a true pioneer of the five-string, an artist who has not only pushed the stylistic bounds of the in- strument itself, but also established it as a stage centerpiece with his effortless rolls, subtle

use of harmonics, and single-string runs. Suffice it to say, this 13-track compilation of acoustic duets features all of the above—and in abundance. Fleck is the lone constant; the rotating cast he enlists is the variable that leads him into untrodden turf on each successive track. Perhaps the album's greatest strength is the ever-morphing musical landscape in which Fleck so easily adapts. The billing includes Mark O'Connor, Sam Bush, David Grisman, Pat Flynn, Tony Rice, and Jerry Douglas, among others. So, would this make *Double Time* a straight bluegrass album? Well, not exactly. Despite his relative newcomer status at the time of the recording, Fleck was already well-entrenched in jazzgrass explorations. As a result, *Double Time* nearly evades categorization. Two of the selections are particularly unconventional: "Lowdown," a plodding, walk of a tune—featuring the unique bowed bass work of Edgar Meyer—which builds to a frenzied crescendo, and "Light Speed," a spacy, improvisational jam recorded at half speed with Mike Marshall on octave mandolin. Otherwise, the program features a dozen or so warm, homegrown finger exercises that dot the music map everywhere between bluegrass and jazz fusion. If you happen to prefer a less adulterated Fleck, you won't be disappointed. If you're interested in discovering new pickers, *Double Time* is a ten-point intersection. —*Brian Kelly*

Deviation / 1984 / Rounder ✦✦✦

Inroads / 1986 / Rounder ✦✦✦

Daybreak / 1988 / Rounder ✦✦✦✦✦

Drive / 1988 / Rounder ✦✦✦

Béla Fleck & The Flecktones / 1990 / Warner Bros. ✦✦✦✦✦

After disbanding New Grass Revival, Béla Fleck began re-creating the role of the banjo in the same way Charlie Parker redefined the role of the saxophone. But Fleck may be the least-innovative member of this quartet: Howard Levy gets chromatics from his blues harp, Victor Wooten picks banjo rolls on his bass, and Roy "Future Man" Wooten plays a Frankenstein-monster drum-machine/guitar synthesizer. For all the flash, there's little pretense; the group's astonishing musicianship keeps an "aw-shucks" accessibility that lets everybody follow the melody while they marvel. —*Brian Mansfield*

● **Flight of the Cosmic Hippo** / 1991 / Warner Bros. ✦✦✦✦✦

The Flecktones owe more to bebop than bluegrass, and here the group finally names their style "blu-bop." That's why *Flight of the Cosmic Hippo* topped the jazz, not the country, chart. The Flecktones continue to make it look easy, adding banjo power chords to "Turtle Rock" and reworking Lennon/McCartney's "Michelle." —*Brian Mansfield*

Live Art / 1991-1995 / Warner Bros. ✦✦✦

Live Art is a double-disc, 20-track anthology of live performances by Béla Fleck & the Flecktones, spanning four years in the mid-'90s. The song selections cover the group's entire career, ranging from new arrangements of several of classics to covers and seven previously unrecorded originals. There are a couple of vocals on the record, but the core of the album is Fleck & the Flecktones' dynamite instrumental improvisations, where they can demonstrate the true range of their eclecticism and talent. Of special note are the songs that feature jams with Branford Marsalis, Chick Corea and Bruce Hornsby, who help spur the Flecktones to new heights. —*Thom Owens*

UFO Tofu / 1992 / Warner Bros. ✦✦✦

Though the Flecktones didn't change their formula with their third album, *UFO Tofu*, they did manage to craft one of their more consistent and impressive efforts. The band's fusion of jazz, bluegrass and funk gels quite well on *UFO Tofu*—not only does Béla Fleck turn in a rich, eclectic performance, but pianist Howard Levy's deft lines and inventive phrasing dominates the album. Occasionally, the material is lightweight, functioning only as vehicle for the group's solos. Then again, the whole point of Fleck's music *is* the solos, so that shouldn't upset his fans too much. Of course, it doesn't help him win new ones, either. —*Thom Owens*

Three Flew Over the Cuckoo's Nest / 1993 / Warner Bros. ✦✦✦

Those who have enjoyed earlier Flecktones recordings will not be disappointed with *Three Flew Over the Cuckoo's Nest*. Béla Fleck has stuck with the formula that made their previous records successful: complex, tight grooves wrapped in a very musical, user-friendly package. The Flecktones still suffer from the departure of keyboardist/chromatic harmonica player Howard Levy, who provided the band with needed additional musical colors and textures. Guest appearances by Bruce Hornsby (no vocals) and Branford Marsalis help fill this void. As always, the musicianship is excellent, and all players involved have ample space with which to display their virtuosity. —*Dan Cross*

Tales From the Acoustic Planet / Jan. 1994-Mar. 1994 / Warner Bros. ✦✦✦✦

Whether this exceptional album is jazz with its roots in bluegrass or vice versa doesn't matter, because whatever it is, it works—wonderfully. Fleck is joined by his jazz friends (Chick Corea and Branford Marsalis) as well as his progressive bluegrass pals (Sam Bush, Tony Rice, and Jerry Douglas), plus members of his usual backing band, the Flecktones (Victor Wooten and Future Man). The resulting performances should pique the interest of curious listeners across any number of genres. —*Brian Beatty*

Left of Cool / Jun. 9, 1998 / Warner Bros. ✦✦✦

By the release of 1998's *Left of Cool*, Béla Fleck & the Flecktones' once-startling blend of fusion, jazz, and bluegrass had lost its ability to surprise. That didn't necessarily mean that they had run out of ideas, but it does mean that *Left of Cool* simply isn't as captivating as earlier efforts by Fleck. For most fans, the pleasure will be finding the little details within the solos, and there's no denying that the group—which now boasted Jeff Coffin in addition to Fleck, Victor Wooten, and Roy "Future Man" Wooten—can play. Often, it's enjoyable to just hear them jam, but the problem is often the songs lack any substance beneath the playing. Only a handful of cuts, such as the opener, "Throwdown at the Hoedown," really make a lasting impression, but the fact that *Left of Cool* sounds good as it is playing may be enough for many fans. —*Stephen Thomas Erlewine*

The Bluegrass Sessions: Tales from the Acoustic Planet, Vol. 2 / Jun. 22, 1999 / Warner Bros. ✦✦✦✦

As it turns out, the *Tales From the Acoustic Planet* albums are where Béla Fleck sounds the most comfortable in the '90s. As his jazz fusion records begin to sound played out, his acoustic experimentation and returns to straight-ahead bluegrass sound lively, vibrant, and fresh. As a matter of fact, *The Bluegrass Sessions: Tales From the Acoustic Planet, Vol. 2* feels like one of his finest albums, due in no small part to the caliber of supporting musicians. The core band consists of Fleck, Sam Bush, Jerry Douglas, Stuart Duncan, Tony Rice, and Mark Schatz, while Vassar Clements, John Hartford, and Earl Scruggs all guest; it's a veritable who's-who of bluegrass. Fleck's idea was to record everything from the purest bluegrass to modern newgrass, giving his talented musicians the opportunity to explore every facet of their musical personality. Much of the album is devoted to Fleck originals, complemented by a handful of covers, none of which are predictable. The same can be said for the music: Even seasoned newgrass listeners will probably be surprised by some of the twists and turns here, while the sheer commitment and astonishing musicianship will win over traditionalists. But the true key to *The Bluegrass Sessions* is that even when it gets technical, it feels heartfelt, and the textures keep changing from song to song, enough to keep it interesting, even captivating, throughout 18 songs and 70 minutes. It had been easy to take Fleck for granted, but this record is a welcome reminder of what a talented and unique musician he is. —*Stephen Thomas Erlewine*

Greatest Hits of the 20th Century / Nov. 16, 1999 / Warner Bros. ✦✦✦✦

Whenever a group with the stature and critical reputation of Béla Fleck & the Flecktones issues a career-spanning collection, the quality of the work is not measured in the same way that an original album would be. The question isn't so much whether or not Béla Fleck & the Flecktones are talented musicians capable of producing worthwhile songs, but whether or not the editor of the collection has chosen wisely from their repertoire. On the satirically titled *Greatest Hits of the 20th Century*, someone has done a good job. In roughly chronological order (with the exception of the last song, "Sunset Road," from very early in the band's history), the collection presents a mixture of live and studio tracks and previously released and unreleased material, each song showing off a different facet of the band's style and abilities. There is the tight, funky quartet sounds of their first hit, "The Sinister Minister," the strong bluegrass influence on "The Yee-Haw Factor," the pleasant guest appearance by Dave Matthews on "Communication," and the sweetly minimal "Sunset Road." There isn't a dud in the bunch of this concise history of the Flecktones. An inventive blend of a world of influences, this collection offers an extremely pleasant listening experience. —*Stacia Proefrock*

Outbound / Jul. 25, 2000 / Columbia ✦✦✦

After a decade with Warner Bros., Béla Fleck jumped to Sony's Columbia Records, signing a five-record deal that called for two releases on Sony Classical, a solo album, and two discs with his band the Flecktones of which *Outbound* is the first. It is a typically eclectic effort. For example, the Fleck original "Shuba Yatra" (its title, he explains in the press materials, "is an Indian term that means taking a journey with a safe return") features a tabla player and Fleck on a "sitar banjo," an electrified instrument with a banjo head and a sitar bridge. Such instruments give the tune something of an Indian flavor, except that much of it is borrowed from traditional Irish music with a touch of South African rhythm. Such odd juxtapositions of instrumentation and style are typical not only from track to track but also within tracks. Fleck and his bandmates seem to view all styles of music as readily and randomly interchangeable, but sometimes, as with a colorblind person picking out clothes, the results clash or otherwise disturb, and the rest of the time they come off as flashy and insubstantial. Fleck really offers no defense to the charge of being a musical dilettante, he simply celebrates the surface pleasures of different varieties of music, offering an overlapping series of appetizers. A fan of any particular style is liable to feel that it has been trivialized, but Fleck doesn't mean any harm. His music represents the pursuit of facileness as a musical goal, one that he and his band achieve with alacrity. —*William Ruhlmann*

Perpetual Motion / Oct. 2, 2001 / Sony ✦✦✦

Banjo virtuoso Béla Fleck has certainly broken more boundaries than any other picker in recent memory, from his early days performing bluegrass-inspired folk compositions on Rounder in the late '70s to his quirky jazz freak-outs with the Flecktones throughout the '90s. In late 2001, this peculiar innovator released an album of banjo interpretations of classical works by Bach, Chopin, and Scarlatti. Before classical purists roll their eyes, they must remember that the banjo hasn't always been seen as the instrument of choice of backwoods musicians in the Appalachian mountains, but as recently as the 1940s was used as a primary rhythm instrument in all manner of parlor music. That being said, *Perpetual Motion* is a bright and unique take on several well-known classical pieces (Moonlight Sonata, Bach's Cello Suite No. 1) as well as a number of interpretations of Bach's two-part and three-part inventions. These light and brief inventions act as buffers between the longer, more dramatic pieces, but end up serving as some of the highlights of the album. With Fleck often accompanied by Evelyn Glennie on marimba and *Appalachia Waltz* musicians Joshua Bell and Edgar Meyer on violin and bass, these short, delicate pieces weave in and out of the album, proving that the banjo can be seen in a different light altogether. Fleck's picking is uniquely unparalleled in that he can so easily dip his feet into so many different genres with an instrument that is so quickly pigeonholed. The album drifts easily into the background, which is not necessarily a detraction but, knowing the fire that Fleck can unleash from his fingertips, it would have been nice to have a few more impassioned numbers on the album. The closest the ensemble comes to really making some noise is the final track, Paganini's Moto Perpetuo (arranged in a bluegrass style), which is not necessarily more forceful, but is certainly faster and louder. —*Zac Johnson*

Live at the Quick / Feb. 26, 2002 / Columbia ◆◆◆

Anyone who saw the Flecktones in their early days probably told you that it was an amazing experience, and a big part of that praise undoubtedly focused on the group's improvised jams. With Victor Wooten sometimes playing two basses simultaneously and Fleck wandering through the audience picking cosmic banjo lines, their shows were spectacles to be enjoyed for the simple thrill of hearing virtuosos play music that was mind-boggling but somehow utterly accessible. It's sad, then, that the group's live albums, while preserving the energy, have never quite captured the humor of those early shows. Many fans could relay stories of Fleck and Wooten's astounding call-and-response duels, which could incorporate anything from Tchaikovsky to full-throttle bluegrass breakdowns. The rapport was hilarious, and it endeared people to a group who might otherwise go down as whimsical showoffs. However, while the old shows may be legendary, the new ones aren't bad either, and the above isn't meant to say that *Live at the Quick* is a bad album; actually, there's plenty of stuff that Flecktones fans love, including Wooten's now-trademark arrangement of "Amazing Grace" and a Bach "Prelude" from Fleck's classical music projects. The concert was recorded with the Flecktone Big Band and features guest appearances from Paul McCandless, Andy Narell, Paul Hansen, tabla player Sandip Burman, and Tuvan throat singer Congar ol'Ondar. All that makes *Live at the Quick* the band's most diverse record yet, and fans of Fleck's post-*Acoustic Planet* work will be amply rewarded. —*Jim Smith*

Rosie Flores

b. Sep. 10, 1950, San Antonio, TX

Guitar, Vocals / Alternative Country, Neo-Traditionalist Country, Americana, Rockabilly Revival

Alternative country meets the rockabilly revival meets California guitar virtuosity in the music of Rosie Flores. Since the late '70s, guitarist, singer, and songwriter Rosie Flores has been an important figure on the alternative country scene in both Austin, TX, and Los Angeles. She's a hard-working, independently minded artist who's well-respected for her gritty, energetic vocals and fiery guitar solos. A native of San Antonio, Flores moved to San Diego with her family when she was 12. Her family encouraged her singing and guitar playing, and as a girl she soaked up the sounds of southern California—surf guitar, country and country-rock, blues, and rockabilly-flavored garage rock. By the time she was in her teens, Flores was playing in a band called Penelope's Children. During the first explosion of punk rock in the late '70s Flores formed Rosie & the Screamers, an otherwise all-male band that played hard country and rockabilly material, much of it written by Flores herself. She worked as a solo acoustic artist for a time but then formed an all-female punk band, the Screaming Sirens, who recorded the album *Fiesta* in 1984.

In 1987, Flores recorded her first solo album, *Rosie Flores*, produced by Pete Anderson (Dwight Yoakam's producer and guitarist) and released by Reprise. The album gained critical acclaim, and among music-industry folk a Flores concert remains a strong draw to this day. But it was only modestly successful commercially, and Flores was dropped by Warner Bros. She signed with the California independent label Hightone and in 1992 she released her second solo album, *After the Farm*, followed by *Once More With Feeling* a year later. These albums featured original songs by Flores, her own sharp guitar leads, and crackerjack session work from a variety of Los Angeles veterans. Flores then spent the better part of 1994 playing lead guitar in Butch Hancock's band.

In 1995, Flores recorded *Rockabilly Filly*, a spirited tribute to the music she grew up with. The album featured duets with her longtime idols Wanda Jackson and Janis Martin, both of whom Flores brought out of retirement for the project. The album led to a cross-country tour with Jackson, who hadn't played in nightclubs in over 20 years. In 1996, Rounder re-released her Warner Bros. debut along with six new bonus tracks under the title *Honky Tonk Reprise*, helping to sustain the momentum of her career. That same year, the Austin label Watermelon released her duet project with Ray Campi, entitled *A Little Bit of Heartache*. In the late '90s, Flores moved to the folk-oriented Massachusetts label Rounder, pushing the stylistic mix of her music slightly in the direction of rockabilly but not really changing course. The 1999 live album *Dance Hall Dreams* was recorded at a San Antonio country club and featured several of the top session players Flores has always been able to attract, among them Texas steel guitar stalwart Cyndi Cashdollar. Flores released *Speed of Sound* on the Eminent label two years later, offering yet more original songs as well as a scorching cover of Buck Owens' rockabilly classic "Hot Dog." Prolifically creative, Rosie Flores deserves to be numbered among the creators of the alternative country movement. Her career, never really flagging, has outlasted those of a host of other acts in that fast-moving genre. —*James Manheim*

● **Rosie Flores** / 1987 / Reprise ◆◆◆◆◆

Produced by Pete Anderson, Rosie Flores' debut made her out to be the female answer to Dwight Yoakam. Flores probably felt like that image straitjacketed her, but from a musical standpoint, it worked beautifully, incorporating Flores' San Antonio roots into Anderson's California country vision. Includes "Crying over You," "Somebody Loses, Somebody Wins," and "Blue Side of Town," which Patty Loveless wouldn't do nearly as well the following year. —*Brian Mansfield*

After the Farm / 1992 / Hightone ◆◆◆◆

Once More with Feeling / 1993 / Hightone ◆◆◆

Closer to modern commercial country than *After the Farm*, *Once More With Feeling* doesn't have the sleekly professional touch of *Rosie Flores*, but it's not without its charms. It includes a duet with Joe Ely ("Love and Danger," which Flores wrote with Jason & the Scorchers' Jason Ringenberg). Other songs contributed by Wendy Waldman ("Ruin This Romance") and Katy Moffatt ("Real Man"). —*Brian Mansfield*

Rockabilly Filly / Oct. 1995 / Hightone ◆◆◆◆

As the title indicates, *Rockabilly Filly* is Rosie Flores' first album that consists entirely of rockabilly tunes. Of course, she has always flirted with the genre, but it is refreshing to hear her take a full-fledged plunge. It's all the more impressive when you consider that it

was recorded after she recovered from a wrist-shattering accident—she plays with the vitality of a wild, young rockabilly cat throughout the album. —*Sara Sytsma*

Honky Tonk Reprise / Jun. 4, 1996 / Rounder ◆◆◆

Rounder repackaged a late-'80s major-label recording by this Austin-based artist and topped it up to CD length with a half-dozen unreleased tracks done around the same time. Make no bones about it, Flores is a better-than-good singer and definitely feels her honky tonk music in her heart. But when one looks at her picture on the cover in a cowboy outfit, one sees someone dressing up to play a part, and unfortunately there are plenty of moments on the album when a similar lack of sincerity can be detected. That is, if the listener is still awake after some of the more lifeless country ballads, one of which eventually became a hit for country crooner Patty Loveless. Is the Flores version better? It is like comparing food from two different Waffle Houses. The meat of the material is produced by Pete Anderson, and he seems to have overdone it a bit, as the unreleased numbers done with a smaller group actually have somewhat more bite, partially due to the better pickers on board, such as guitarist Albert Lee. For Flores, going back to her roots was obviously a move that paid off artistically, but in retrospect the results aren't going to make anyone give away their Patsy Cline or Kitty Wells records. —*Eugene Chadbourne*

A Little Bit of Heartache / Jan. 21, 1997 / Watermelon ◆◆◆◆◆

A Little Bit of Heartache, Rosie Flores' duet album with Ray Campi, is an engaging collection of originals written in the style of '50s country, complete with pedal steels, dobros, fiddles and close harmonies. It's a charming, delightful album, filled with lovely songs which are made indelible by Flores and Campi's pure harmonies. —*Thom Owens*

Dance Hall Dreams / Mar. 2, 1999 / Rounder ◆◆◆

Cut from the same mold as Rose Maddox and Wanda Jackson, Rosie Flores is a 100-percent-for-real honky tonk gal and this album brings it out every bit as well as her '80s debut, reissued with bonus tracks on Rounder as *Honky Tonk Reprise*. Partially recorded live at Cibolo Creek Country Club in San Antonio, TX, Flores brings a batch of great originals to the mix with a band featuring Cindy Cashdollar on steel guitar and slide, drummer Donald Lindley, keyboardist Justin Reinhardt, and the estimable Sarah Brown on bass, highlighted by her own spot-on-the-money lead guitar work. This is no retro paint-by-numbers album, although tracks like the opening "Little Bit More," "59 Tweedle Dee," and "It Came From Memphis" summon up that traditional vibe nicely. But in the main, Flores' well-crafted originals carry the day and her sound right into the new millennium nicely, with "We'll Survive," "From Where I Stand," "Tremolo," and her heartfelt tribute to her father, "Who's Gonna Fix It Now," being every bit as fine as any contemporary country that makes the airwaves. Her duet with Radney Foster on "Bring It On" and her version of Jackson's "Funnel of Love" (the only cover tune on here, by the way) are two more solid reasons to add this one to the collection. As nice of a contemporary traditionalist country album as you'll likely to find. —*Cub Koda*

Speed of Sound / May 8, 2001 / Eminent ◆◆◆◆

Rosie Flores reaffirms her rockabilly roots by leading off her fifth studio album, *Speed of Sound*, with "Rock-A-Bye Boogie," originally heard as the B-side of the Davis Sisters' number one country single of 1953, "I Forgot More Than You'll Ever Know," and closing it with Johnny Cash's "Country Boy." But in between, she tries out a number of other musical styles and succeeds mightily with them. The diversity begins with the second track, "Don't Know If I'm Comin' or Goin'," a little-known number from Billie Holiday's catalog. Then it's back to rockabilly for Buck Owen's "Hot Dog." Co-producer Rick Vito's "Devil Love," which follows, may sound like another oldie, with its sinuous samba rhythm, but it is actually a 2001 copyright. Flores puts her three co-compositions, "Don't Take It Away," "Speed of Sound," and "Somebody's Someone," in the middle of the disc. The first uses a Bo Diddley beat to make a romantic plea, while the title track demonstrates that Flores can write a contemporary-sounding song when she wants to. This one would make a good addition to the repertoire of Bonnie Raitt or Emmylou Harris. "Somebody's Someone" is another genre exercise, a relaxed Western swing number Flores might have played on her tour with Asleep at the Wheel in 1997. She takes her own stab at Marshall Crenshaw's "Somewhere Down the Line," having had her duet vocals mysteriously uncredited when she sang the song on Crenshaw's *Life's Too Short* album, and makes a point of crediting her own harmony partner, Terry McBride. "I Push Right Over" is an attractive two-step and the album's most likely candidate for a country radio single. Add it up, and *Speed of Sound* is a varied collection that addresses Rosie Flores' traditional strengths and also shows her capable of making good music in many styles. —*William Ruhlmann*

The Flying Burrito Brothers

f. 1969, Los Angeles, CA

Group / Country-Rock

The Flying Burrito Brothers helped forge the connection between rock and country, and with their 1969 debut album, *The Gilded Palace of Sin*, they virtually invented the blueprint for country-rock. Though the band's glory days were brief, they left behind a small body of work that proved vastly influential both in rock and country. The Flying Burrito Brothers reunited later in the '70s, albeit without their founding members Gram Parsons and Chris Hillman, and continued performing and recording in a variety of incarnations into the '80s. Originally, the Flying Burrito Brothers were a group of Los Angeles musicians who gathered together to jam. Gram Parsons and Chris Hillman took the band's name when they were forming their own band after leaving the Byrds. Parsons had helped steer the Byrds toward a country direction during his brief stint with the band, as captured on the 1968 album *Sweetheart of the Rodeo*. Following the release of *Sweetheart*, he left the Byrds, followed shortly afterward by Hillman. The duo added pedal steel guitarist "Sneaky" Pete Kleinow and bassist Chris Ethridge to the band and set about recording their debut album with a variety of session drummers.

The Gilded Palace of Sin, the Flying Burrito Brothers' debut album, was released in the spring of 1969. Although the album only sold 40,000 copies, the band developed a devoted following, which happened to include many prominent musicians in Los Angeles, Bob Dylan, and the Rolling Stones. Around this time, Parsons and Stones guitarist Keith Richards became good friends, which led to Parsons losing interest in the Burritos. Before the band recorded their second album, Ethridge left the band and was replaced by Bernie Leadon, and the group hired ex-Byrd Michael Clarke as their permanent drummer.

Burrito Deluxe, the group's second album, was released in the spring of 1970. After its release, Gram Parsons left the group and was replaced by Rick Roberts, a local Californian songwriter. Roberts' first album with the band, *The Flying Burrito Brothers*, was released in 1971. After its release, Kleinow left the band to become a session musician and Leadon departed to join the Eagles. The Burritos hired pedal steel guitarist Al Perkins and bassist Roger Bush to replace them, as well as adding guitarist Kenny Wertz and fiddler Byron Berline to the lineup. This new version of the group recorded the live album *The Last of the Red Hot Burritos*, which was released in 1972. Before its release, the band splintered apart. Berline, Bush, and Wertz all left to form Country Gazette, while Hillman and Perkins joined Manassas. Roberts assembled a new band to tour Europe in 1973 and then dissolved the group, choosing to pursue a solo career. Roberts would later form Firefall with Michael Clarke.

Close Up the Honky-Tonks, a double-album Flying Burrito Brothers compilation, was released in 1974 because of the burgeoning interest in Gram Parsons. Capitalizing on the collection and the cult forming around Parsons, Kleinow and Ethridge formed a new version of the Flying Burrito Brothers in 1975. The duo recruited Floyd "Gib" Guilbeau (vocals, guitar, fiddle), bassist Joel Scott Hill, and drummer Gene Parsons and recorded *Flying Again*, which was released on Columbia Records in 1975. Ethridge left the band after the release of *Flying Again*; he was replaced by Skip Battin, who appeared on the 1976 album *Airborne*. Also in 1976, a collection of Gram Parsons-era outtakes entitled *Sleepless Nights* was released on A&M Records.

For the two decades following their 1975 reunion, the Flying Burrito Brothers performed and recorded sporadically, undergoing the occasional lineup change. In 1979, the group released *Live From Tokyo* on Regency Records; the album spawned their first country hit, a cover of Merle Haggard's "White Line Fever," which hit the charts in 1980. Also in 1980, the group abbreviated its name to the Burrito Brothers when they signed a contract with Curb Records. The Burrito Brothers' *Hearts on the Line* spawned three minor country chart hits in 1981. *Sunset Sundown*, the Brothers second Curb album, appeared in 1982 and like its predecessor, it produced three minor hits. Following the release of *Sunset Sundown*, Kleinow left the band to become an animator and special-effects creator in Hollywood. The group carried on without him, led by Gib Guilbeau and John Beland. That incarnation of the band fell apart in 1985, the same year that Kleinow assembled yet another version of the band. For the next three years, this incarnation of the Flying Burrito Brothers toured America and Europe. In 1988, the group split apart again, although it did occasionally reunite for further tours and recordings in the '90s, including 1999's *Sons of the Golden West*. —*Stephen Thomas Erlewine*

☆ **The Gilded Palace of Sin** / Feb. 1969 / Edsel ✦✦✦✦✦

By 1969, Gram Parsons had already built the foundation of the country-rock movement through his work with the International Submarine Band and the Byrds, but his first album with the Flying Burrito Brothers, *The Gilded Palace of Sin*, was where he revealed the full extent of his talents, and it ranks among the finest and most influential albums the genre would ever produce. As a songwriter, Parsons delivered some of his finest work on this set; "Hot Burrito #1" and "Hot Burrito #2" both blend the hurt of classic country weepers with a contemporary sense of anger, jealousy, and confusion, and "Sin City" can either be seen as a parody or a sincere meditation on a city gone mad, and it hits home in both contexts. Parsons was rarely as strong as a vocalist as he was here, and his covers of "Dark End of the Street" and "Do Right Woman" prove just how much he had been learning from R&B as well as C&W. And Parsons was fortunate enough to be working with a band who truly added to his vision, rather than simply backing him up; the distorted swoops of Sneaky Pete Kleinow's fuzztone steel guitar provides a perfect bridge between country and psychedelic rock, and Chris Hillman's strong and supportive harmony vocals blend flawlessly with Parsons' (and he also proved to be a valuable songwriting partner, collaborating on a number of great tunes with Gram). While *The Gilded Palace of Sin* barely registered on the pop-culture radar in 1969, literally dozens of bands (the Eagles most notable among them) would find inspiration in this music and enjoy far greater success. But no one ever brought rock and country together quite like the Flying Burrito Brothers, and this album remains their greatest accomplishment. —*Mark Deming*

Burrito Deluxe / Apr. 1970 / Edsel ✦✦✦✦✦

Gram Parsons had a habit of taking over whatever band he happened to be working with, and on the first three albums on which he appeared—the International Submarine Band's *Safe at Home*, the Byrds' *Sweetheart of the Rodeo*, and the Flying Burrito Brothers' *The Gilded Palace of Sin*—he became the focal point, regardless of the talent of his compatriots. *Burrito Deluxe*, the Burritos' second album, is unique in Parsons' repertoire in that it's the only album where he seems to have deliberately stepped back to make more room for others; whether this was due to Gram's disinterest in a band he was soon to leave, or if he was simply in an unusually democratic frame of mind is a matter of debate. But while it is hardly a bad album, it's not nearly as striking as *The Gilded Palace of Sin*. Parsons didn't deliver many noteworthy originals for this set, with "Cody Cody" and "Older Guys" faring best but paling next to the highlights from the previous album (though he was able to wrangle the song "Wild Horses" away from his buddy Keith Richards and record it a year before the Rolling Stones' version would surface). And while the band sounds tight and they play with genuine enthusiasm, there's a certain lack of focus in these performances; the band's frontman sounds as if his thoughts are often elsewhere, and the other players can't quite compensate for him, though on tunes like "God's Own Singer" and a cover of Bob Dylan's "If You Gotta Go (Go Now)," they gamely give it the old college try. *Burrito Deluxe* is certainly a better than average country-rock album, but coming from the band who made the genre's most strongly defining music, it's something of a disappointment. —*Mark Deming*

The Flying Burrito Brothers / May 1971 / A&M ✦✦✦✦

On their first post-Parsons album, the Burritos (now led by Hillman and Rick Roberts, and with future Eagle Bernie Leadon replacing Ethridge) make an honest step forward in country-rock. It includes the Roberts song "Colorado." —*William Ruhlmann*

The Last of the Red Hot Burritos / Apr. 1972 / A&M ✦✦

Last of the Red Hot Burritos, the fourth Flying Burrito Brothers album, was a live recording by the current lineup led by sole original member Chris Hillman, billed as the group's swan song and released after their breakup. By now, the Burritos had evolved into a competent country-rock band with a repertoire of country standards such as "Orange Blossom Special" (featuring Byron Berline on fiddle), but few of the originals by Gram Parsons and Hillman. *Last of the Red Hot Burritos* would have been a respectable, if unexceptional, way to go out, if in fact this had been the end of the group. But three years later, Kleinow and original bass player Chris Ethridge would resurrect the name, and there would be editions of the Burritos performing and recording, with legal, if not moral, legitimacy, long into the future. —*William Ruhlmann*

Honky Tonk Heaven / 1973 / Ariola ✦✦✦

This two-record anthology of the Flying Burrito Brothers featured 22 as-yet-unreleased tracks when it was released in 1973 by the Dutch label Ariola, a year prior to the A&M collection *Close Up the Honky-Tonks* and three years before another A&M anthology, *Sleepless Nights*, became available. Even though it overlaps both of these American LPs, there are several tracks that seem to be unique to this release. Gram Parsons' vocal on "Just Because" sounds a bit under-rehearsed and as if it was recorded at a completely different session than its instrumental backing. Parsons fares better on a studio version of "Six Days on the Road," a track that the band would record in concert after his departure. Bernie Leadon has a rare lead vocal on John Fogarty's "Lodi," though this experiment was evidently a one-shot deal while he was with the group. Chris Hillman's strong vocals on the traditional country song "Pick Me Up on Your Way Down" and Jesse Winchester's "Payday" make it puzzling why they didn't merit release while the group was still intact. Rick Roberts, who came on board to replace Gram Parsons, both wrote and sang the upbeat ballad "In My Own Small Way" and the less successful "Feel Good Music." Since this long out of print two-LP set is likely to fetch a premium price, fans of the Flying Burrito Brothers may hesitate to acquire it for only six new tracks. —*Ken Dryden*

Live in Amsterdam / 1973 / Bumble ✦✦✦

After Chris Hillman disbanded the Burritos to join up with Stephen Stills in Manassas, Rick Roberts decided that the Burrito Brothers weren't a dead issue, especially in Europe, where country-rock was taking off in a big way. So, he decided to raid Country Gazette and added a few friends along for the ride. *Live in Amsterdam* shows their country, bluegrass and rock & roll roots to great effect. All the songs one associates with the Burrito Brothers are here, along with such surprises as "Foggy Mountain Breakdown" and "Roll Over Beethoven." Byron Berline and Roger Bush add much to the bluegrass outings and blend in well elsewhere as well. A fine testament to the Rick Roberts-led version of the Flying Burrito Brothers. —*James Chrispell*

Bluegrass Special / 1974 / Ariola ✦✦✦

This single LP released by the Dutch Ariola label followed the earlier double-LP *Live in Amsterdam*, but it was evidently recorded at the same concert because there is an overlap of five songs heard in identical performances on both albums. That doesn't mean that this hard to find import isn't worth a search; there are excellent renditions of bluegrass favorites such as "Orange Blossom Special," "Bugle Call Rag," plus Bill Monroe's songs "Uncle Penn" and "Shenandoah Valley Breakdown." By the time of this European tour in 1972, Rick Roberts had taken over from Chris Hillman as the leader, but fiddler Byron Berline and banjo player Alan Munde tend to attract the most attention. Particularly amusing is the brief three-banjo version of "Foggy Mountain Breakdown," though unlike the earlier Ariola release, this one was remixed a bit more cleanly. This is an essential LP for fans of the Flying Burrito Brothers. —*Ken Dryden*

Close Up the Honky-Tonks / Jun. 1974 / A&M ✦✦✦✦✦

A&M Records seemed to close the book on the Flying Burrito Brothers with *Close Up the Honky-Tonks*, a 23-track, double-LP compilation. A combination best-of and odds-and-sods career wrap-up, the album contained one LP given over to tracks from the Burritos' first two records, *The Gilded Palace of Sin* and *Burrito Deluxe*, plus the non-LP single "The Train Song." The second disc presented 11 previously unreleased tracks, most of them cover songs, ranging from the Bee Gees' "To Love Somebody" to the Everly Brothers' "Wake Up, Little Susie." Co-founder Gram Parsons was featured on the five songs on side three, while side four came from the Rick Roberts era of the band. The Burritos would lack a one-disc best-of until A&M came up with the CD/cassette release *Farther Along* in 1988. So, for more than a decade, *Close Up the Honky-Tonks* was the definitive Burritos compilation and contains some excellent performances available nowhere else. —*William Ruhlmann*

Flying Again / Sep. 1975 / Columbia ✦✦

The last that had been heard of the Flying Burrito Brothers was a 1973 European tour organized by Rick Roberts, replacement for founding member Gram Parsons, with a few hired guns. But with Parsons' growing posthumous legend, the band's name retained currency, and former bassist Chris Ethridge and former pedal steel guitarist "Sneaky" Pete Kleinow retained legal rights to that name. They brought in guitarist/fiddle player Floyd "Gib" Guilbeau, guitarist Joel Scott Hill, and former Byrds drummer Gene Parsons, and relaunched the Burritos with this album of competently played country-rock. Words like "travesty" and "insult" have been used to describe it, on the grounds that Ethridge and

Kleinow were trading on Parsons' reputation, but on its own, the album is an adequate, if unremarkable set. Just don't pick it up looking for the old glory. (Out of print.) *—William Ruhlmann*

Airborne / May 1976 / Columbia ✦✦

After the demise of the Flying Burrito Brothers, a new edition was formed in 1975 with original members Sneaky Pete Kleinow on pedal steel guitar and Chris Ethridge on bass, along with Cajun fiddler Gib Guilbeau, drummer and string player Gene Parsons (formerly of the Byrds), and guitarist Joel Scott Hill as the primary lead vocalist. The group was unstable from the start, with Ethridge departing after the first LP and another ex-Byrd, Skip Battin, replacing him. Compared to the earlier groups that recorded under the same name featuring Gram Parsons, Chris Hillman, and later, Rick Roberts, this reincarnation never seemed to find a focus, relying on too many lackluster originals composed by the group and uninspired covers of others' works. Guilbeau and Parsons also get their opportunities to sing lead, though no one is particularly impressive. A couple of curiosities include an almost-reggae-like take of John Prine's "Quiet Man" and a guest appearance by Stevie Wonder on his "She's a Sailor." Long out of print, it is a safe bet that this disappointing release will remain out of print. *—Ken Dryden*

Live From Tokyo / 1978 / Regency ✦✦

The second edition of the Flying Burrito Brothers, launched by "Sneaky" Pete Kleinow in 1975, turned out to have as many personnel shifts as the first edition put together by Gram Parsons in 1968. This lineup played familiar Burrito songs such as "Hot Burrito #2" and "Colorado," as well as a selection of honky tonk country standards. Far from the greatest of Burrito Brothers bands, this one nevertheless was superior to later versions, and the music was efficiently played before an enthusiastic audience. As the group's live albums go, however, the one to get is still *Last of the Red Hot Burritos*. [*Live From Tokyo* was reissued by Relix Records in 1991 under the title *Close Encounters to the West Coast*.] *—William Ruhlmann*

Hearts on the Line / Jan. 1981 / Curb ✦✦

This release continues the checkered history of the various groups that followed the revival of the Flying Burrito Brothers in the mid-'70s. By the time of this 1981 LP for Curb, only Sneaky Pete Kleinow and Gib Guilbeau remained from the first reincarnation of the dormant group, with bassist Skip Battin still on hand and guitarist John Beland fronting the band, which now sported a slightly shorter name. This studio date comes off badly over-produced due to the excess reverb used on many of the vocals (since producer Michael Lloyd's earlier credits included albums by Leif Garrett, the Osmonds, and Shaun Cassidy, this isn't surprising); neither did the weak material help matters. This is a record that clearly deserves to be left to collect dust in a used record store. *—Ken Dryden*

Cabin Fever / 1985 / Relix ✦

This 1985 live album chronicles a Burritos lineup anchored by original member "Sneaky" Pete Kleinow and singer/guitarist Skip Battin, who first joined the band in 1976. It is in essence a Gram Parsons/Burritos/Byrds tribute album on which the band tries unsuccessfully to address Parsons classics like "Wheels" and "Hickory Wind" as well as the Byrds' "Mr. Spaceman." The sound quality is low and the performances substandard. Skimpy packaging fails to tell you where it was recorded or even who the other members of the band are. *—William Ruhlmann*

Live From Amsterdam 1985 / 1985 / Relix ✦✦

Live From Europe / 1986 / Relix ✦✦

Relix Records, which has curious ideas about marketing, released a second Flying Burrito Brothers live album in 1986, the year after it released the live *Cabin Fever*. The same lineup of original member "Sneaky" Pete Kleinow, guitarist Skip Battin and the previously uncredited rhythm section of bassist Greg Harris and Jim Goodall once again came off as a Burritos/Gram Parsons/Byrds tribute band, with a few of its own new originals thrown in. It was a reasonable enough concept for a live show, but back home on the record player versions of songs like "Christine's Tune (Devil in Disguise)" and "Citizen Kane" didn't hold a candle to the original recordings. Maybe to Relix and its Dead Head fans, who hew to the notion that all live shows should be taped and disseminated, this sort of release made sense, but not to average fans. *—William Ruhlmann*

Dim Lights, Thick Smoke and Loud, Loud Music / Mar. 1987 / Edsel ✦✦✦

The British Edsel label's *Dim Lights, Thick Smoke and Loud, Loud Music*, the first try at a Flying Burrito Brothers compilation in a decade, is not a best-of. Because the label had recently reissued the Burritos' first two albums, *The Gilded Palace of Sin* and *Burrito Deluxe*, this 13-song collection is drawn from the rarities and outtakes first released on the A&M albums *Close Up the Honky-Tonks* and *Sleepless Nights* after the original group's (and Gram Parsons') demise. Specifically, as the album notes report, "... [I]t brings together for the first time on one record all the Burritos' material that features Gram Parsons and that wasn't on those first two LPs." The songs are for the most part covers of country music standards presented as demos or working versions that probably never would have been released if it were not for Parsons' death. Parsons, of course, is the reason the Burritos continue to interest fans, and he sings well here, but this half-finished material does not compare to the first two albums. *—William Ruhlmann*

★ **Farther Along: The Best Of** / 1988 / A&M ✦✦✦✦✦

Farther Along: The Best of the Flying Burrito Brothers is a nearly flawless compilation, containing a full 21 tracks of the pioneering group's best material. All but two of the songs from *The Gilded Palace of Sin* are included on the collection, as are all of the highlights from *Burrito Deluxe* and a handful of rarities and outtakes. In short, it's a definitive collection containing all of the Burrito Brothers' finest moments. It's indispensable to any rock or country collection. *—Stephen Thomas Erlewine*

Back to Sweethearts of the Rodeo / 1990 / Disky ✦✦✦

This 28-song double-CD set, intended as a farewell album to the Burrito Brothers' legions of European fans, consists of songs recorded in Sheffield, AL, in 1986 and 1987 by the final incarnation of the Burritos: John Beland and Gib Guilbeau (vocals, guitars), James Hooker (piano), Alan Jones (bass), Roger Clark (drums), Wayne Bridge (steel guitar), Steve Nathan (synthesizer), and Butch Johnson (harmonies). Most of the tunes are originals by Beland and Guilbeau, which are above average midtempo country-rock with some pleasant hooks and catchy choruses and harmonies—most are fairly romantic and some of it is very beautiful, especially tracks like "Shoot for the Moon" and "Baby Won't You Let Me Be the One." Interspersed are a few more ambitious story-songs, such as "Moonlight Rider," a few rockers like "Gold Guitar," and covers of stuff by Buck Owens and Felice and Boudleaux Bryant ("Take a Message to Mary"). Ironically, to most listeners the group here will sound very similar to the Eagles, one of the bands formed in the wake of the original Flying Burrito Brothers—but there is also a strong resemblance to circa 1970 Swampwater (Beland and Guilbeau's first band), a near contemporary of the original Burritos. Whatever one's reference point, they're worth checking out. *—Bruce Eder*

From Another Time / Apr. 1991 / Magnum ✦✦

This outstanding live recording from the mid-'70s features original Flying Burrito Brothers Chris Ethridge (bass, vocals) and Sneaky Pete Kleinow (pedal steel) with ex-Swampwater member Gib Guilbeau (fiddle, guitar, vocals), ex-Canned Heat alumnus Joel Scott Hill (guitar), and ex-Byrd Gene Parsons (drums, vocals). This disc bridged the gap between the original Flying Burrito Brothers and their 1980s successors (known simply as the Burrito Brothers). The repertory, recorded along the group's European tour, both covers old group standards ("White Line Fever," "Sin City," "Devil in Disguise," "Wheels," "Close Up the Honky-Tonks") and anticipates the songs that would comprise the later group's concerts. The performance is as spirited and inspired as any by the original group, even if the harmonies don't soar quite so easily—Hill's colorful though restrained guitar pyrotechnics are a particular treat. Good live recordings by different incarnations of the Burritos aren't much less common than live Dead recordings, but this one makes an excellent companion/follow-up to A&M's *Last of the Red Hot Burritos*. *—Bruce Eder*

Close Encounters to the West Coast / Jul. 1, 1991 / Relix ✦✦

The second edition of the Flying Burrito Brothers, launched by "Sneaky" Pete Kleinow in 1975, turned out to have as many personnel shifts as the first edition put together by Gram Parsons in 1968. This lineup played familiar Burrito songs such as "Hot Burrito #2" and "Colorado," as well as a selection of honky-tonk country standards. Far from the greatest of Burrito Brothers bands, this one nevertheless was superior to later versions, and the music is efficiently played before an enthusiastic audience. As the group's live albums go, however, the one to get is still *Last of the Red Hot Burritos*. [*Close Encounters to the West Coast* is a 1991 reissue of the 1978 Regency Records album *Live From Tokyo*.] *—William Ruhlmann*

California Jukebox / Jul. 8, 1997 / American Harvest ✦✦✦

Sons of the Golden West / May 18, 1999 / Arista ✦✦✦

Getting a handle on the ever-changing lineup of the Flying Burrito Brothers is more difficult than naming the musicians on-stage at a Lynyrd Skynyrd concert—at one point in the '80s, the Burritos contained no original members. On *Sons*, original pedal steel player Sneaky Pete Kleinow teamed with country songwriter John Beland to create an unassuming collection of country-rock tunes. By eschewing the slickness of modern Nashville in favor of a rootsier sound, the Burritos have the right idea, but country songs about UFOs ("Area 51") hardly do justice to the great body of work the group amassed in the late '60s and early '70s. The lyrics to "Ode to Gram," a tale about a spurned fan who came to a live show hoping to see the legendary singer, speak all too clearly about the Burritos' post-'70s career and its lack of direction. *—Steve Kurutz*

☆ **Hot Burritos! The Flying Burrito Brothers Anthology: 1969–1972** / Apr. 18, 2000 / A&M ✦✦✦✦✦

There's little question that the double-disc collection *Hot Burritos! The Flying Burrito Brothers Anthology: 1969-1972* is comprehensive, since it contains the entirety of the band's first three albums plus a bevy of rarities, including six songs from *Close Up the Honky-Tonks*, two cuts from *Sleepless Nights*, two tracks from *The Last of the Red Hot Burritos*, the non-LP single "The Train Song," and "Six Days on the Road," originally released on the 1988 collection, *Farther Along: The Best of the Flying Burrito Brothers*. That pretty much covers *everything* they cut during those four years. Since the Burritos were truly great while Gram Parsons was in the band—once he left, they were still solid, thanks to Chris Hillman—this may border on overkill for some listeners, especially since the Parsons years are covered expertly by *Farther Along*, which contained all but one song from *The Gilded Palace of Sin*, plus the best songs from *Deluxe* and rarities and highlights from posthumous releases. For neophytes, that's a better bet, yet the converted will find this quite nice. Apart from "The Train Song," which rarely shows up on collections, there aren't any revelations or even new songs, but there are nice liner notes, great outtakes from the photo shoot for *Gilded Palace*, and exquisite remastered sound. And, for Parsons fanatics, the Hillman-led *Flying Burrito Brothers* may seem like a new record, too, since they may have previously overlooked it. So, diehards get all the Parsons material in one place, while neophytes with a serious attention span will be introduced to one of the great bands of the last 25 years of the 20th century—and, yes, that means it qualifies as definitive. *—Stephen Thomas Erlewine*

20th Century Masters—The Millennium Collection: The Best of the Flying Burrito Brothe / Jun. 19, 2001 / A&M ✦✦✦✦

Since the Flying Burrito Brothers really didn't record that much material during their prime period, and since all of their recordings from this period are uniformly great (not just good, great), they're an exceptionally easy band to anthologize. So, it's possible to find songs that really should have been here—"Hot Burrito #1" (or, "I'm Your Toy," as Elvis Costello retitled it on reissues of *Almost Blue*) and "Farther Along" for starters, along with such fine moments as "To Love Somebody"—but when you're listening to this, it's hard to notice that they're missing simply because these 12 songs are so good. Also, they emphasize the barroom roots of the band—each song here would sound great on a payday Friday night, whether they're rockers or weepers. And, it's a rather inventive selection, since it does contain "Hot Burrito #2" instead of "#1," plus such rarities as "Lazy Day" and "Break My Mind," plus "Train Song," which was one of the carrots on the double-disc set *Hot Burritos!* for collectors. So, it's a little more than you'd expect for a collection aimed at casual fans, which makes it interesting even for the converted, but it has so much terrific music here that it's bound to convert the curious. After all, once you fall in love with a little of the Burrito Brothers or Gram Parsons, you're bound to want to hear it all. *—Stephen Thomas Erlewine*

Honky Tonkin' / Feb. 12, 2002 / One Way ✦✦✦
One Way's *Honky Tonkin'* is, in effect, an unacknowledged reissue of Arista Records' 1999 Flying Burrito Brothers album *Sons of the Golden West.* That album's 14th and final track, "Ode to Gram," has been replaced by "Wheel of Love," and two bonus tracks, live performances of Little Feat's "Willin'" and George Jones' "You're Still on My Mind" from a 1998 show in Norway, have been added. Otherwise, this is *Sons of the Golden West*, an album that unveiled yet another amended lineup of the Flying Burritos, with Sneaky Pete Kleinow once more departed and replaced by steel guitarist Wayne Bridge, such that the group became a unit led by John Beland, a Burrito since the early '80s, although there were no longer any original members. As on 1997's *California Jukebox*, the Burritos loaded up on guest stars, including Ricky Skaggs, Sam Bush, Alison Krauss, the Oak Ridge Boys, Delbert McClinton, and Merle Haggard, and employed plenty of covers: Mel Tillis' "Honky Tonkin'," Ricky Nelson's "Never Be Anyone Else but You," Hank Williams' "Honky Tonk Blues," and Keith Richards' "Locked Away." On his originals, Beland often reminisced about the early L.A. days that gave birth to the original band ("Down at the Palomino," "Up on Sycamore"), which only served to emphasize the oddity of a Burritos band made up entirely of replacements. By now, the group was basically a country-rock franchise, and all those guests and cover songs made it difficult to draw a bead on what this edition really sounded like. Maybe that was the idea. *—William Ruhlmann*

★ **Sin City: The Very Best of the Flying Burrito Brothers** / Jul. 16, 2002 / Universal ✦✦✦✦✦
This 25-song, single-CD anthology collects the cream of the recordings the Flying Burrito Brothers made while Gram Parsons was in the band. Since their career has taken in many more years and recordings than that relatively brief juncture, some might question whether it's a comprehensive or balanced overview. On the other hand, the majority of listeners would agree that the Parsons era of the Burritos was by far the most significant and best phase of the band. *Sin City* has everything from the first two Burritos albums, *The Gilded Palace of Sin* and *Burrito Deluxe*, as well as the single "Train Song" and a couple of other stray Parsons-era cuts, "Six Days on the Road" and "Close Up the Honky-Tonks." All 25 of these songs, plus 18 others (including a few on which Parsons plays that don't show up on *Sin City*), are on the more comprehensive two-CD set *Hot Burritos! The Flying Burrito Brothers Anthology 1969-1972.* That two-CD set thus still gets the nod for the best Flying Burrito Brothers comp. But for those looking for the core Parsons-Burritos tracks, or a more concise and consistent collection, *Sin City* serves its purpose well, with decent annotation (though likewise condensed in quantity from what you'll read in the *Hot Burritos!* booklet). *—Richie Unterberger*

Red Foley (Clyde Julian Foley)

b. Jun. 17, 1910, Blue Lick, KY, **d.** Sep. 19, 1968, Fort Wayne, IN
Vocals, Guitar / Traditional Country, Honky Tonk, Country Gospel
Red Foley was one of the biggest stars in country during the postwar era, a silky-voiced singer who sold some 25-million records between 1944 and 1965 and whose popularity went far in making country music a viable mainstream commodity. Born Clyde Julian Foley on June 17, 1910, in Blue Lick, KY, he began playing guitar and harmonica at a young age, and by the time he was 17 had taken first prize in a statewide talent competition. While attending college in 1930, he was spotted by a talent scout from Chicago's WLS radio and was tapped to sing with producer John Lair's Cumberland Ridge Runners, the house band on the program *National Barn Dance.*

After seven years with the Ridge Runners, Lair created a new show, *Renfro Valley Barn Dance,* especially to showcase Foley's talents. The singer remained with the program until late 1939, performing everything from ballads to boogie to blues. At the same time, he became the first country artist to host his own network radio program, *Avalon Time* (co-hosted by comedian Red Skelton), and performed extensively in theaters and clubs and at fairs. After exiting the *Renfro Valley Barn Dance,* Foley returned for another seven-year stint at the *National Barn Dance* show. In 1941, the same year he made his film debut with Tex Ritter in the Western *The Pioneers*, he signed a lifetime contract with Decca Records. His first chart single, 1944's "Smoke on the Water," topped the charts for 13 consecutive weeks; in 1945, he was the first major performer to record in Nashville.

In 1946, Foley signed on to emcee and perform on *the Prince Albert Show,* a segment of the *Grand Ole Opry* program broadcast on NBC; his popularity with listeners is often credited with establishing the *Opry* as country's pre-eminent radio show. Beginning in 1947, he began recording with his backing band, the Cumberland Valley Boys, earning another number-one single with "New Jolie Blonde (New Pretty Blonde)." With the group, he recorded seven Top Five hits between 1947 and 1949, including "Tennessee Saturday Night," a chart-topper in 1948. Again recording solo in 1950, he issued the song that would become his trademark tune, "Chattanoogie Shoe Shine Boy," which stayed in the number-one position for 13 weeks.

In 1951, Foley's second wife, Judy Martin (born Eva Overstake), committed suicide, reportedly over the singer's affair with another woman. In order to devote the majority of his time to raising a family, he cut back considerably on his performing commitments, although he continued to release hit after hit in a variety of musical styles, including rockabilly and R&B; "(There'll Be) Peace in the Valley (For Me)," a 1951 smash, was the first record ever to sell one million copies on the gospel charts. In the same year, he also released his first LP, *Red Foley Souvenir Album.* After several years spent in virtual retirement, in 1954 Foley was named to host *the Ozark Jubilee,* a country showcase for ABC television; the show was a hit, and ran through 1960. Also in 1954, he recorded the chart-topping "One By One," the first of many duets with Kitty Wells.

After *the Ozark Jubilee* went off the air, he spent one season co-starring with Fess Parker in the program *Mr. Smith Goes to Washington.* Although Foley continued recording throughout most of the 1960s, his hit-making days were largely behind him. In 1967, he was elected to the Country Music Hall of Fame. After a performance in Fort Wayne, IN, on September 19, 1968, Foley died of a heart attack. Among the survivors were his daughter Betty, a popular country vocalist in her own right, and another daughter Shirley, the wife of pop crooner Pat Boone. *—Jason Ankeny*

Red and Ernie / 1954 / Longhorn ✦✦✦✦✦
This is one of Ernest Tubb's and Red Foley's best albums, built around songs cut between 1949 and 1953. Jimmy Work's "Tennessee Border No. 2," and Leadbelly's "Goodnight Irene," and Bill Monroe's "Kentucky Waltz" are among the standards covered by the duo (Foley had previously cut "Tennessee Border" as a solo number). The shared vocals mesh together very well, Tubb's twangy tenor perfectly balancing Foley's throatier, more laconic singing; the stripped accompaniment also works well, although they might have left the organ out of the session in favor of the hot guitars. Worthwhile just for their version of George Vaughn's "Hillbilly Fever," which features one or two "in" references to the two men's careers, and their sprightly, playful cover of Cindy Walker's "Don't Be Ashamed of Your Age." *—Bruce Eder*

Souvenir Album / 1958 / Decca ✦✦✦✦

Beyond the Sunset / 1958 / Decca ✦✦✦✦✦
Foley's gospel albums ranked with Tennessee Ernie Ford's as the most popular of the era among country fans. This is his best. *—Michael McCall*

He Walks With Thee / 1958 / Decca ✦✦✦

Let's All Sing to Him / 1959 / Decca ✦✦
While Red Foley ruled the white gospel market during the 1950s, this 1959 effort is not one of his best. The key to Foley's most successful records was a sparse, restrained set of production values. This one epitomizes the saccharine strain of gospel production featuring an overdone backing choir and wailing organ. Probably intended to "evoke" being in church, the instrumentation and production add little emotional value. In terms of songs, you get plenty of bang—no less that 16 classic gospel numbers. Foley gives a decent treatment to songs such as "Rock of Ages" and "Sweet By-and-By," but neither his considerable gravitas, nor the material itself, can overcome the fetid production. *—Brian Whitener*

Let's All Sing With Red Foley / 1959 / Decca ✦✦✦

Songs of Devotion / 1961 / Decca ✦✦✦✦✦
If you were ever to own just one country gospel album, *Songs of Devotion* wouldn't be a bad choice. Unquestionably one of the greatest gospel albums ever, it stands as a pure hallelujah to Protestant religiosity in song and to Foley's strength as an interpreter. One of the keys to the album's success is it's carefully considered arrangements. With only a guitar and bass as accompaniment, Foley slows these gospel numbers to an almost complete halt. His deep, affecting voice resonates eerily in the long silences between lines. The backing group, the Jordanaires, are considered one of the finest vocal groups ever and are used here as a sparing counterpoint. The version of "I'll Fly Away" that opens the album does not transcend—it virtually breaks back in upon itself with sorrow. Another beautifully done number, "Life's Railway to Heaven" closes out the record. With a gesture of ironic homage, Smog's *Dongs of Sevotion* (1999) acknowledged the album's continuing significance and its still potent yearning for a better world. *—Brian Whitener*

Red Foley's Golden Favorites / 1961 / Decca ✦✦✦✦✦

Dear Hearts and Gentle People / 1962 / Decca ✦✦✦✦
Dear Hearts and Gentle People is a laid-back, pleasant album highlighted by "Down Yonder," "The Happy Song," and "River, Stay 'Way from My Door." *—Thom Owens*

Songs Everybody Knows / 1965 / Decca ✦✦

Red Foley / 1966 / Vocalion ✦✦✦
Country star Red Foley had great success on Decca Records during the '40s and '50s, selling close to 25 million records. *Red Foley* contains songs recorded during the first years of this fruitful period (1946-1952); it was released as a reissue compilation in 1966 on the Decca subsidiary Vocalion, but is unfortunately out of print. Still, there is a fine cross section of Foley material here, including the 1951 hit "Have I Told You Lately That I Love You," a duet with then-wife Judy Martin (born Eva Overstake). (Ironically, Martin committed suicide reportedly upon hearing of Foley's infidelity shortly after this single came out.) Other selections feature Foley with performers who appeared on his famous *Ozark Jubilee* show, like the Cumberland Valley Boys ("New Pretty Blonde") and his daughter and a country star in her own right, Betty Foley ("Cross of Gold"). To complete the "variety show" feel the album has, there are the comedic numbers "Playin' Dominoes and Shootin' Dice" and "Cincinnati Dancing Pig," which comes complete with hog grunts. Overall, though, the mood of *Red Foley* is low-key and the sound superb: Accordion, violin, and pedal steel all blend in nicely with Foley's commanding, honeyed baritone. Beyond MCA's *Country Music Hall of Fame* hits package, there are not many Foley titles in print. So, if you find this one at your local used record store, make sure to pick it up to hear some prime and very enjoyable Foley sides. *—Stephen Cook*

Songs for the Soul / 1967 / Decca ✦✦✦

Old Master / 196 / Decca ✦✦✦
The Old Master was Red Foley's last solo album before his death. None of the songs were hits and, in fact, Foley hadn't had a solo hit in nearly a decade at the time the album was made. The songs are a mixture of old and new, from classics like "South" and "Hang Your Head in Shame" to a pair of good Mel Tillis/Wayne P. Walker compositions. The second side of the album is heavy on ballads that allow Foley to exercise his ability as a country crooner with a Bing Crosby influence. In the late '60s, Foley, like his label-mate Webb Pierce, sounded like he was stuck in a time warp where his music would always sound the same no matter what was happening around him, but his ability and familiarity ensured a reliable product. *—Greg Adams*

Memories / 1971 / Vocalion ✦✦
Memories is a budget reissue of recordings Red Foley made in the late '40s and early '50s, and includes a few big hits. Foley's version of Slim Willet's "Don't Let the Stars Get in Your Eyes" was one of several renditions that reached the country and pop Top Ten in 1953. "Sunday Down in Tennessee" was a sizable hit, as was "As Far as I'm Concerned." The non-hits are sacred, traditional, and sentimental songs, from "Will the Circle Be Unbroken" to the tragic "Don't Make Me Go to Bed and I'll Be Good." Foley recorded numerous boogies, but only one—"Pin Ball Boogie"—is represented. Considering the scarcity of Red Foley reissues in the last twenty years, *Memories*—and practically any Foley LP, for that matter—is a valuable document of this Country Music Hall of Famer's exceptional music. *—Greg Adams*

★ **Country Music Hall of Fame** / 1991 / MCA ✦✦✦✦✦
Country Music Hall of Fame contains a good cross-section of Red Foley's heyday in the late '40s and early '50s. All of the selections of this 16-track, single-disc compilation were recorded for Decca Records. While not all of his hits are present—even some of his biggest singles, including "Smoke on the Water," are missing—but most of the essential items ("Chattanoogie Shoe Shine Boy," "Tennessee Saturday Night," "Peace in the Valley") are here, making it an essential introduction to one of country's biggest stars. *—Stephen Thomas Erlewine*

Stay a Little Longer / Nov. 14, 2000 / Jasmine ✦✦✦
Stay a Little Longer is packed with 26 radio transcription performances from the '50s, including remakes of hits, traditional songs, and other favorites. Because so little of his music is available on CD, *Stay a Little Longer* offers a valuable glimpse at the music of Country Music Hall of Famer Red Foley. This disc concentrates on boogies and uptempo novelties, with a couple of tracks exhibiting an awareness of rock & roll ("Rockin' Chair Money" and a version of his hit "Hearts of Stone"). The sound quality is good enough for easy enjoyment, but this CD was mastered from vinyl transcription discs and is noticeably rough in spots. *—Greg Adams*

Chattanoogie Shoeshine Boy / Feb. 26, 2002 / ASV ✦✦✦✦✦
At 25 tracks, this is the most complete package of Foley's Decca hits from 1944-1951; it is also arguably the best overview of his work yet assembled in the CD era. One marvels at how many personalities Foley had—the patriot of "Smoke on the Water," the Crosby-esque crooner of "Harriet," the humorous talking bluesman of "Never Trust a Woman"—and how he could pull them all off with inherent, uncontrived ease. "As Far As I'm Concerned" has sadly strayed from the compilers' list, but the original versions of "Old Shep," "Tennessee Saturday Night," and the title track assure this issue a top-shelf standing in any country collection. *—Jim Smith*

☆ **Tennessee Saturday Night** / Aug. 9, 2002 / Proper ✦✦✦✦✦
Yet another overview of Red Foley's Decca years (1944-1951), this two-disc Proper "pair" set is the clear first choice, chronicling all of the singer's biggest hits of the era. "Smoke on the Water," "Old Shep," "New Pretty Blonde (Jolie Blon)," "Tennessee Saturday Night," "Chattanoogie Shoe Shine Boy," and "Peace in the Valley" are all here, as well as "Freight Train Boogie," "Sugarfoot Rag," "Birmingham Bounce," "Hillbilly Fever," and many others. At 52 tracks, there's a lot of non-essential material here, but then, Foley's average stuff was still excellent, and the detailed liner notes (and low price!) make this a sweet deal. *—Jim Smith*

1937-39, Vol. 1 / Document ✦✦✦✦✦

The Forbes Family

f. 1977
Group / Traditional Bluegrass, Country Gospel, Bluegrass-Gospel
The traditional sounds of bluegrass-gospel are resurrected through the performances and recordings of the Forbes Family. In the two decades since they recorded their debut album, the two brothers (Homer and Jay) and two sisters (Lori and Lisa) have used their vocal harmonies to proclaim their faith and religious convictions. Although they took a hiatus from music from 1988 until 1994, the Forbes Family have produced some of the most powerful recordings in the years since their reorganization. The Forbes Family remains a family effort. Homer Forbes (born 1961) is the band's leader, playing banjo and singing lead and harmony vocals; Jay Forbes (born 1963) plays mandolin and guitar and sings bass; Lori Forbes Slate (born 1962) plays acoustic bass and sings vocal harmonies; and Lisa Forbes Roberts (born 1965) is the group's lead singer.

Born in the southeastern Pennsylvania city of New Oxford, the Forbes Family cut their first album in a local recording studio in 1977. Rehearsing after school, the four siblings continued to develop their soul-inspiring sound. Moving briefly with their parents to Greenville, TN, in 1979, they returned to Littletown, PA, a year later. After recording four more albums for a local recording studio, they signed with bluegrass label Rebel Records in 1984. Their first album for the label, *Gleams of That Golden Morning*, was released shortly after they relocated, on their own, to Mt. Airy, NC. They recorded two more albums for Rebel in the 1980s: *Outside the Gates* in 1986 and *Farewell* in 1988. Forced by family obligations to return to Pennsylvania, the group disbanded.

Performing again at local churches and community concerts, the Forbes Family reunited in 1994. The same year, Rebel Records released a compilation of their early recordings, *The Best of the Early Forbes Family*. The Forbes Family recorded their first studio album in six years, *I'll Look to Him*, in 1995. They followed it with *In the Shadow of Your Wings*, which was produced by Ron Block, a songwriter, arranger, and banjo player, and featured musical accompaniment by Alison Krauss' band, Union Station. *—Craig Harris*

● **The Best of the Early Forbes Family** / Nov. 30, 1994 / Rebel ✦✦✦

Brownie Ford (Thomas Edison Ford)

b. 1904, Gum Springs, OK
Vocals / Cowboy
Thomas Edison "Brownie" Ford was more than just a country singer, he was a cowboy balladeer with a vast repertoire based on his personal experience as a ranch hand and rodeo rider. He was born on 1904 in Gum Springs, OK, of Comanche and Anglo-American ancestry. He spent most of his life in Baton Rouge and later settled in the countryside of Hebert in Caldwell Parish. Ford practiced folk craft traditions like making cinches and bridles, and was well-known for his engaging storytelling ability, which earned him a National Heritage Fellowship in 1987. His legacy has been preserved on the lone album *Stories From Mountains, Swamps & Honky-Tonks*. Released in 1990 on Flying Fish Records, it was a combination of primitive field recordings and professional studio recording accompanied by D.L. Menard and David Doucet. *—Al Campbell*

Stories from Mountains, Swamps & Honky-Tonks / 1990 / Flying Fish ✦✦✦✦✦
He's a delightful geezer; he recalls skinny-dippin' in Oklahoma. He wails wizened folk and country to the guitar accompaniment of Dave Doucet and D. L. Menard. *—Mark A. Humphrey*

Jim Ford

Vocals / Singer/Songwriter, Country-Rock
Originally from New Orleans, Jim Ford lost interest in his academic pursuits and, in 1966, drifted out to California. He was passing through L.A., on his way to the Haight-Ashbury district in San Francisco, when he met two session musicians, Pat and Lolly Vegas. The Native American rockers—who later formed the commercially successful Redbone—had worked on the *Shindig* television show at the time, and had already recorded their *Pat and Lolly Vegas at the Haunted House* album for Mercury. After hearing his songwriting talent first-hand, the Vegas brothers brought Ford to the attention of Del-Fi Records' honcho Bob Keane, known around the L.A. music scene for his "open door policy." Keane released a couple of Ford's singles on Del-Fi's Mustang label, both of which sank without a trace. Del-Fi/Bronco recording artist Viola Wills also recorded one of his songs. Along with Pat and Lolly Vegas, Ford wrote the P. J. Proby hit "Niki Hoeke" (it peaked at number 23 on *Billboard*'s pop charts in January 1967), which Ford's former girlfriend Bobbie Gentry also sang on one of her later albums. In 1969, Ford got the opportunity to record his debut album. *Harlan County* (released on the Sundown label, a small subsidiary of White Whale) featured funky, midtempo country, and R&B-flavored rockers with a driving Muscle Shoals-style rhythm section, with backing and arrangements by the Vegas brothers and Gene Page.

Most of Ford's original songs had a lyrical narrative recalling the hardship of growing up in the coal-mining country of Harlan County, KY. Among the various highlights are his fuzz-drenched cover version of Willie Dixon's "Spoonful," his take on Delaney & Bonnie's hip-shake boogie "Long Road Ahead," and a remake of the swampy classic "I'm Gonna Make Her Love Me ('Til the Cows Come Home)." In 1971, Ford's manager, Si Waronker (founder of Liberty Records), flew his artist to London, where he was booked into Olympic Studios to record a follow-up album. This time he was backed by pub rockers Brinsley Schwarz (they later recorded "Niki Hoeke Speedway" and Ford's "JuJu Man"; Nick Lowe also recorded Ford's "36 Inches High" for his *Jesus of Cool* album). After three days of sessions, the band failed to keep up to the challenge of backing Ford, so Waronker brought in Joe Cocker's Grease Band, but they too didn't work out. As the project never did quite meet up to everyone's expectations, it was eventually aborted. The tapes for these sessions have reportedly disappeared.

Ford returned to the U.S. and his career never really took off as expected. He wrote songs for Bobby Womack in 1972 (including the wonderful "Harry Hippie"), and later worked with friend Sly Stone (he even moved into Stone's Holmby Hills home for awhile), but since the early '70s, Ford has slipped out of sight. *Harlan County* was reissued on the British Edsel label in 1997. *—Bryan Thomas*

Harlan County / 1969 / Edsel ✦✦✦
At his best, Jim Ford was a clever songwriter, capable of reworking rock & roll, R&B, and country clichés into fresh, funny roots rock. At his worst, Ford was cutesy and unfocused, pulling good songs into awkward detours. *Harlan County*, the only album he ever completed, captures Ford at both extremes. The laid-back, rootsy sound of *Harlan County*—equal parts country-rock, soul, and pop—provided a touchstone for British pub rock, especially for Brinsley Schwarz, which covered Ford's "JuJu Man" and "Niki Hoeke Speedway" (Brinsley's chief songwriter, Nick Lowe, later recorded "36 Inches High"). Those songs aren't on 1969's *Harlan County*; they're from an aborted 1971 record that was to feature the Brinsleys as Ford's backing band. Instead, *Harlan County* is filled with unassuming, midtempo rockers and ballads, which are either songs about love or driving. Ford has a pleasant, unremarkable white soul voice that, when combined with the mannered production, tends to undersell the songs, which would have benefited from grittier, committed performances. Then again, these songs aren't as good as "JuJu Man" and "Niki Hoeke," which deservedly became pub rock staples. Many of these songs are well-written, particularly the off-kilter title track and "I'm Gonna Make Her Love Me," but they lack the sharp humor and hooks of the previously mentioned songs. They are of interest as a curiosity, especially for pub rock fanatics, but *Harlan County* illustrates why Jim Ford never became a cult artist in his own right. *—Stephen Thomas Erlewine*

Tennessee Ernie Ford

b. Feb. 13, 1919, Bristol, TN, **d.** Oct. 17, 1991, Los Angeles, CA

Vocals / Traditional Country, Country-Folk, Nashville Sound/Countrypolitan, Country Gospel, Country Boogie

The booming baritone voice of Tennessee Ernie Ford was best known for his 1955 cover of Merle Travis' grim coal-mining song "Sixteen Tons," watered down by the dulcet strains of a Hollywood studio orchestra but retaining its innate seriousness thanks to the sheer power of Ford's singing. But there was more to Tennessee Ernie Ford than that. Over his long career, Ford sang everything from proto-rock & roll to gospel, recorded over 100 albums, and earned numerous honors and awards, including the Medal of Freedom. A native of Bristol, TN, he began his career a DJ on local radio station WOAI. He sang in high-school choirs, and in the late '30s he left to study voice at the Cincinnati Conservatory of Music. He held radio jobs in Atlanta and Knoxville between 1939 and 1941 and then joined the U.S. Air Force during World War II. After the war, Ford moved his family to San Bernardino, CA, and took a DJ job on a local radio station. It was there that he first took on the name "Tennessee Ernie."

Ford later moved to Pasadena's KXLA, where Los Angeles producer and media host Cliffie Stone heard his jocular "bless your little pea-pickin' hearts" routine and was impressed by his voice. Stone paved the way increasingly frequent appearances by Ford on Los Angeles radio and television. He was signed to Capitol Records in 1948. Five singles had been released by late 1949, including "Tennessee Border" and "Smokey Mountain Boogie" (both Top Ten) and his first number-one single, "Mule Train." On both Western songs and boogie-flavored numbers that in their energy and sexual suggestiveness were really rock & roll in all but name, Ford's recordings featured the fabulous instrumental talents of Travis on guitar and Speedy West on pedal steel. Early in 1951, "Shotgun Boogie" became his second number one, spending 14 weeks at the top of the country charts. By the beginning of 1953, although Ford wasn't having as many hits, he remained popular in America and also in England. He became a television quizmaster in 1954, hosting NBC's *Kollege of Musical Knowledge*. He also had his own daily show and continued recording.

Ford had two Top Ten country hits in 1955 with "The Ballad of Davy Crockett" and his biggest success, "Sixteen Tons," which spent ten weeks at number one on the country charts and eight weeks at number one on the pop charts. From 1956 to 1965 he was a prime-time network television host, making "Bless your little pea-pickin' hearts" a household catchphrase and providing powerful exposure for Ford's increasingly middle-of-the-road music. His voice was ideally suited to big arrangements of traditional hymns, and his first gospel album, *Hymns* (1956), became the first religious album to go gold. Ford's second gospel album, *Great Gospel Songs*, earned him a Grammy. In 1965, he had his last chart entry with the Top Ten single "Hicktown," but he continued to record gospel music; his large catalog of LPs on Capitol remained in print and sold well. Ford joined the ranks of the Country Music Hall of Fame in 1990, a year before he died of liver failure. *—James Manheim*

This Lusty Land! / 1956 / Capitol ✦✦

This Lusty Land! isn't very lusty, particularly if you're expecting rousing historical songs in the vein of "Ballad of Davy Crockett." The album places new and traditional songs in a subdued, jazzy setting in which Ford is accompanied by the orchestra from his '50s television show. The Delmore Brothers' "False Hearted Girl" sounds odd performed in this manner, but the stripped-down renditions of traditional and modern work songs like "John Henry," "Dark As a Dungeon," and "Nine Pound Hammer" are dramatic and appealing. Elsewhere, Ford's highbrow interpretations of old English ballads and early country songs seem condescending, or like an experiment that doesn't work. The album was nevertheless a strong seller, and Capitol kept it in print for many years. *—Greg Adams*

Spirituals / 1957 / Capitol ✦✦✦✦✦

Ol' Rockin' Ern' / 1957 / Capitol ✦✦✦

Gather 'Round / 1959 / Capitol ✦✦✦

Gather 'Round is similar to Tennessee Ernie Ford's 1955 album, *This Lusty Land!*, in that both contain mostly traditional songs. Unlike its predecessor, *Gather 'Round* is not arranged strictly as a pop album and offers a greater variety of moods. The Delmore Brothers' "Brown's Ferry Blues" is unwittingly transformed into a vocal jazz piece, and "Black Is the Color of My True Love's Hair" is slowed down to dirge speed and performed by Ford in the lower reaches of his vocal range. "Old Blue" is a teary dog story along the lines of "Old Shep," and is the album's highlight. Ford wasn't making any country hits at this point, but directed his efforts toward the pop charts, where he received a lukewarm reception. Accordingly, *Gather 'Round* is very pop-oriented in its approach to country repertoire, and proffers a nostalgic but surprisingly inauthentic trip through the folk canon. *—Greg Adams*

Come to the Fair / 1960 / Capitol ✦✦

Come to the Fair captures Tennessee Ernie Ford live at the Indiana State Fair during a 1960 performance that reportedly broke attendance records for that fair or any other. Made several months earlier than Hank Thompson's *At the Golden Nugget*, which is sometimes said to be the first commercially released live country album, *Come to the Fair* is musically slight but historically interesting. Singing along with an ensemble of local musicians that sounds like a Salvation Army band, Ford intros with "Back Home Again in Indiana" before touching upon sacred, pop, and country favorites aimed at the broadest possible demographic. Between songs he tells stories and jokes at a relaxed pace, and fully half of the album's content is spoken word. Ford even reads an inspirational poem after an electric performance of "Sixteen Tons," the only song in the program with which he is strongly identified. Like the whole-hog sandwiches and lemon shake-ups you'd find at the fair, this album is not fit for frequent consumption. *—Greg Adams*

Hymns at Home / 1961 / Capitol ✦✦

Here Comes the Mississippi Showboat / 1962 / Capitol ✦✦

I Love to Tell the Story / 1962 / Capitol ✦✦

Long, Long Ago / 1963 / Capitol ✦✦

Tennessee Ernie Ford's connection to country music was mostly tangential in 1963 because of his shift toward pop music and, in particular, pop interpretations of traditional folk songs. Ford had previously explored the latter territory on the albums *This Lusty Land!* (1956) and *Gather 'Round* (1959), but exploited the formula again on *Long, Long Ago*. The dozen somnolent renditions of sentimental standards like "Flow Gently, Sweet Afton" and "In the Gloaming" would pass by like a continuous, lulling tone if not for the perkiness of "When You and I Were Young, Maggie" in the middle of the album. Recommended for insomniacs and enthusiasts of parlor music. *—Greg Adams*

My Favorite Things / 1966 / Capitol ✦✦

My Favorite Things reflects Tennessee Ernie Ford's status as a popular television host with a broad audience. The album offers a little of everything, from Broadway show tunes ("Hello, Dolly!," "My Favorite Things") to recent pop hits ("Turn Around"). Throw in some pop standards like "Red Roses for a Blue Lady" and a dab of country ("I Can't Stop Loving You"), and there's the album. The problem is that *My Favorite Things* is spread too thin—all but the most accepting listeners will find too little of what they want in the try-to-please-everybody track list. Ford's performances are solid but his interpretations are not particularly inspired, and the songs are mostly ones we've heard a million times. Leave this one in the middle of the road from whence it came. *—Greg Adams*

Bless Your Pea Pickin' Heart! / 1966 / Pickwick ✦✦✦

One of Tennessee Ernie Ford's signature phrases is used as the title of this budget collection of stray Capitol recordings from the late '50s. The album begins with an agreeable song written around the aforementioned saying, and thereafter contains three of Ford's minor pop hits from the period: "Ivy League" is a cloying bit of collegiate humor, and "Sunday Barbecue" is a vocal version of the Sauter-Finegan Orchestra's "Doodletown Fifers." Add "Glad Rags," which scraped the bottom of the charts in 1959, and you have a fair collection of Ford's last few pop hits. Unfortunately , none of them are very good. The mild rock & roll of "She's My Baby" and "Kiss Me Big" (a re-recording from the *Ol' Rockin' Ern* 'EP) are more appealing, but—quality control issues notwithstanding—*Bless Your Pea Pickin' Heart* is a decent compendium of minor hits and oddities for collectors. *—Greg Adams*

I Love You So Much It Hurts Me / 1966 / Pickwick ✦✦

I Love You So Much It Hurts Me is a budget reissue of Capitol recordings from the '50s and '60s, a hodgepodge of B-sides and album tracks that vary wildly in production and orchestration. There are jazzy readings of Hank Williams songs ("Half as Much," "Cold, Cold Heart"), densely produced '60s pop songs ("Now It's All Over," "Since You've Been Gone"), grim story songs ("Code of the Mountains"), and pop treatments of traditional folk songs ("Black-Eyed Susie"). None of it is Ford at his best, and the seemingly random sequencing makes for a distracting listen. *I Love You So Much It Hurts Me* is of primary value to collectors looking for sundry single sides. *—Greg Adams*

Aloha From Tennessee Ernie Ford / 1967 / Capitol ✦✦✦

Aloha From Tennessee Ernie Ford was recorded in Hawaii with native accompanists for that authentic touch, and Ford sounds perfectly at ease warbling along with the steel guitar and ukulele on these 11 Hawaiian classics. He takes "Pearly Shells" at a brisk pace while singing in both English and Hawaiian, and exercises his basso profundo with particular profundity on the Jimmy Dorsey/Frank Ifield hit "I Remember You." The island vocalist known only as Lani duets with Ford on the ever-popular "Hawaiian Wedding Song," which joins "Aloha Oe" and "Beyond the Reef" as the best known tunes in the bunch. There was a time when the Hawaiian album, like the Christmas album and the sacred album, was a ready-made concept awaiting any popular entertainer, but Ford's genuine enthusiasm for Hawaiian music gives his entry into the Hawaiian album sweeps an easy charm with practically zero schmaltz. *—Greg Adams*

Tennessee Ernie Ford Deluxe Set / 1968 / Capitol ✦✦✦✦

Ernie Sings & Glen Picks / 1975 / Capitol ✦✦✦

In a different reality, a good alternate title for this jewel of a disc might have been "Tennessee Ernie Ford and Glen Campbell Unplugged." The idea behind it was a natural, teaming two of Capitol Records' biggest-selling country artists together. This album was actually a distant follow-up to a 1965 recording by Ford entitled *Country Hits... Feelin' Blue*, which had featured the singer in a back-to-basics musical setting. At the time, in 1975, Ford was 19 years from his last big hit, while Campbell was still near the top of his commercial form, having outsold the Beatles as recently as the end of the 1960s. There isn't a weak track here, as Ford, backed by Campbell on acoustic guitar and bassist Chuck Domonico, renews his approach to old standards like "Trouble in Mind" and covers songs associated with Dottie West ("Here Comes My Baby"), Patsy Cline ("She Called Me Baby"), and classics like Floyd Tillman's "I Gotta Have My Baby Back." There are only 30 minutes of music here, but the album is one of the high points of Ford's career; cut loose in a simple, all-acoustic setting, Ford's elegant baritone has tremendous expressive power, which it brings completely to the fore, and Campbell's playing is extraordinarily sensitive and articulate, even for him. His playing on the break of "I Gotta Have My Baby Back" is one of the best solos of his career, and is matched by Ford's magnificent, towering-yet-despairing vocal. If you only own one album by either Ford or Campbell, this should be the one. *—Bruce Eder*

For The 83rd Time / 1976 / Capitol ✦✦✦

As titles go, *For the 83rd Time* conveys a certain weariness, but it supposedly refers to the number of Capitol albums Tennessee Ernie Ford had made up to that point. Ford's final album for Capitol after a nearly 30-year association with the label, *For the 83rd Time* produced his last chart hit, "I Been to Georgia on a Fast Train." Ford all but abandoned country music for MOR pop through the '60s, but *For the 83rd Time* is a straight country album with entertaining songs and a sense of humor that harks back to his early days. "Daddy What's a Tree" is one of very few environmental country songs of its time, and the overall vibe is upbeat and optimistic. This is one of Ford's better albums from the second half of his career. —*Greg Adams*

☆ **16 Tons of Boogie: The Best of Tennessee Ernie Ford** / 1990 / Rhino ✦✦✦✦✦
In his later years, Ford's little pea-pickin' heart was closely associated with gospel and patriotic music, but in earlier years he knew how to—as the album title says—boogie. This includes all the essential material from that period: "Sixteen Tons," "The Shot Gun Boogie," "Mule Train," and "Blackberry Boogie," for starters. —*Tom Roland*

All-Time Greatest Hymns / 1990 / Curb ✦✦✦✦

Country Gospel Classics, Vol. 1 & 2 / 1991 / Capitol ✦✦✦✦✦
The '60s follow-up to the previous decade's *All-Time Greatest Hymns* wasn't as overwhelmingly successful, but it holds up better. The interplay between Ford's baritone and The Jordanaires harmony support is beautiful. —*Michael McCall*

Sings Songs of the Civil War / Feb. 4, 1991 / Capitol ✦✦✦
The 1991 release combines two evocative albums of Civil War-era songs Ford recorded for that conflict's centennial remembrance in 1961. His somber style perfectly fits the subject matter. —*Michael McCall*

Country Gospel Classics, Vol. 2 / Jun. 10, 1991 / Capitol ✦✦✦✦✦
The Jordanaires join Ford on many of these spiritual songs, including "How Great Thou Art," "Just a Closer Walk With Thee," and the standard "Peace in the Valley." —*Jason Ankeny*

Red, White & Blue / Jun. 24, 1991 / Capitol ✦✦✦
This gathers together his patriotic songs, including the complete *America the Beautiful* LP from 1970. —*Michael McCall*

Capitol Collectors Series / Jul. 8, 1991 / Capitol ✦✦✦✦✦
Tennessee Ernie Ford's *Capitol Collectors Series* contains 29 of his biggest hits and best-known songs, including "Sixteen Tons," "The Shot-Gun Boogie," "Mule Train," "The Cry of the Wild Goose," and "I'll Never Be Free," as well as a handful of lesser-known gems, making it the perfect single-disc introduction to one of the most popular country singers of the early '50s. —*Stephen Thomas Erlewine*

Best Sacred Memories / May 18, 1993 / Curb ✦✦
Best Sacred Memories is a ten-track budget-priced collection of Ford's versions of such classic hymns and gospel songs as "Sweet Hour of Prayer," "Old Time Religion," "I Love to Tell the Story," "I Need Thee Every Hour," "Where Could I Go" and "Nearer My God to Thee." Although this isn't a bad budget-priced disc, there are better collections available, offering more songs and better sound for not much more money. —*Stephen Thomas Erlewine*

Greatest Hits / Jul. 13, 1993 / Curb ✦✦✦
Greatest Hits is a budget-priced, ten-track selection of some of Tennessee Ernie Ford's hits, and while there are plenty of essential items missing, it still functions as a good, affordable sampler, featuring such hits as "Sixteen Tons," "The Ballad of Davy Crockett," "Mule Train," "The Shot-Gun Boogie" and "The Rovin' Gambler." —*Stephen Thomas Erlewine*

Sixteen Tons / Jun. 27, 1994 / Bear Family ✦✦✦✦
Tennessee Ernie Ford was one of the biggest singing stars in the '50s. After an Air Force stint during World War II, Ford left his Southern roots for the proto-fame of several radio jobs in Los Angeles. He soon met bassist and Capitol A&R man Cliffie Stone and proceeded to cut a slew of hit sides for the label. The country bumpkin character Ford had developed in radio was put in front of the mike and surrounded by some of Capitol's top country session men. Along with Stone, Ford's band included the likes of guitarist Jimmy Bryant, pedal-steel wizard Speedy West, drummer Roy Harte, and pianist Billy Liebert. This generous Bear Family disc rounds up 25 of Ford's prime Capitol sides, including the hit title track and sides bearing both his Ma & Pa Kettle persona and more straightforward honky tonk in the Hank Williams mode. Beyond Ford's incredibly varied singing, there's a wealth of stellar contributions from his cohorts—Bryant and Liebman are particularly impressive. As usual, Bear Family provides excellent notes and very thorough discography details. A must for fans of vintage country music. —*Stephen Cook*

Sixteen Tons / Oct. 10, 1995 / Capitol ✦✦✦✦✦
Though named after Tennessee Ernie Ford's biggest hit, *Sixteen Tons* was released five years after the single was a hit. The large gap of time between the release of the single and album is inconsequential—in essence, the album is a compilation of Ford's greatest hits of the '50s, containing not only the title track, but also "Mule Train," "The Cry of the Wild Goose," and "The Shot-Gun Boogie." Though more comprehensive compilations of Ford's work were later released, *Sixteen Tons* remains an entertaining listen from start to finish; in fact, in terms of sheer listenability, it rivals any of the latter-day collections. —*Stephen Thomas Erlewine*

Vintage Collections Series / Mar. 11, 1997 / Capitol ✦✦✦✦✦
Capitol's stellar *Vintage Collections Series* continues with this excellent overview of Tennessee Ernie Ford's far-ranging 27-year tenure with the label. Along with the singer's hits, the 20-track collection also includes a number of rare performances; featured are "Sixteen Tons," "Smokey Mountain Boogie," "I'll Never Be Free" (with Kay Starr) and "Hey, Good Lookin'" (with Helen O'Connell). —*Jason Ankeny*

★ **The Ultimate Collection (1949-1965)** / Mar. 18, 1997 / Razor & Tie ✦✦✦✦✦
As Rhino's excellent *16 Tons of Boogie* compilation went out of print once Capitol was no longer their distributor, this 1997 40-track, two-disc collection takes its place and picks up the slack admirably. Covering the prime years of Ford's recording tenure with Capitol

(1949-1965), it contains all of his biggest hits, including "Sixteen Tons," "Hicktown," "Tennessee Border," "Mule Train," and "The Shot-Gun Boogie." Keeping things in a fairly chronological order (with the lone exception of a 1975 duet with Glen Campbell), it begins with a nice cross-section of his early hillbilly boogie hits, including "Smokey Mountain Boogie" and "Blues Stay Away From Me," a duet with Merle Travis. Ford was also one of the first country artists to be mated with pop performers for country-crossover duet work, and his pairings with the brassy Kay Starr ("I'll Never Be Free" and "Ain't Nobody's Business but My Own"), the Dinning Sisters ("Rock City Boogie"), movie star Betty Hutton ("This Must Be the Place"), ragtime pianist Joe "Fingers" Carr ("Tailor Made Woman"), and big band singer Helen O'Connell ("Hey Good Lookin'") are largely successful for what he brings to the proceedings. The pop crossover years, starting with the 1950s success of "Sixteen Tons," is well-represented by tracks like "You Don't Have to Be a Baby to Cry" (later a pop hit for the Caravelles), and his many fine gospel recordings from the early '60s also come in for a fine selection, with the Jordanaires featured on most tracks. Until a multi-disc box set retrospective of Ford's complete Capitol recordings gets issued (and with 83 LPs and a pile of singles, this would be bordering on unwieldy), this is the best—and most digestible—cross-section of his work available, accessible to both fans and historians alike. —*Cub Koda*

The Real Thing! / Apr. 18, 2000 / Jasmine ✦✦
The Real Thing! consists of an entire Tennessee Ernie Ford radio program from the 1950s, and the 31 tracks include the opening and closing theme, comedy sequences, Speedy West steel guitar instrumentals, and many solo and ensemble vocal tracks featuring Ford's character-laden baritone. The program bypasses his hits in favor of other popular and traditional songs such as "Pliney Jane," "John Henry," and "When the Red, Red Robin (Comes Bob, Bob Bobbin' Along)." A couple of western songs are included and the novelty "They Were Doin' the Mambo." The sound quality is very good and the selections unfailingly entertaining, which makes *The Real Thing!* a real find for those who want more Tennessee Ernie than is offered by the various greatest-hits packages. —*Greg Adams*

Tennessee Ernie Meets the Girls / Nov. 28, 2000 / Jasmine ✦✦✦
Although credited to Tennessee Ernie Ford, the emphasis here is on "the girls." Lou Dinning of the Dinning Sisters, Helen Forrest, Helen O'Connell, and other female pop singers perform with and without Ford on these recordings from his 1950s radio program. About a third of the 27 tracks are duets with Ford, and he sings solo on only one track ("Sleepy Time Gal"). The real thrill is the opportunity to hear these pop vocalists perform country material: Helen O'Connell does the Pee Wee King hit "Slow Poke," Lou Dinning covers the folk classic "In the Pines," etc. While Ford at least introduces all of these tracks, buyers looking for a straight collection of his recordings may be disappointed by the peripheral role he plays on *Tennessee Ernie Meets the Girls.* —*Greg Adams*

The EP Collection . . . Plus / Oct. 9, 2001 / See for Miles ✦✦✦
Tennessee Ernie Ford's *EP Collection...Plus* is a boon to collectors since most of the songs appear on CD for the first time. Potential buyers might not realize it by reading the track list, though, because of the numerous familiar titles. With only a few exceptions, the apparently common tracks are actually re-recordings from the late '50s, many of which were given rock & roll overhauls. "Sixteen Tons '65" is the most dramatic example, featuring an energetic vocal performance over a "Peter Gunn Theme" guitar riff. The material isn't entirely—or even mostly—rock-oriented; there are gospel songs, a jazzy version of the Delmore Brothers' "Browns Ferry Blues," and acoustic treatments of "Born to Lose" and "There'll Be No Teardrops Tonight" in the style to which Ford returned with the *Ernie Sings & Glen Picks* album in 1975. The four bonus tracks have been reissued elsewhere with the exception of the hilarious "Fatback, Louisiana." —*Greg Adams*

Absolutely the Best / Mar. 12, 2002 / Fuel 2000 ✦✦✦✦✦

The Forester Sisters

f. 1982, Lookout Mountain, GA
Group / Contemporary Country, Neo-Traditionalist Country
Vocal quartet the Forester Sisters enjoyed a strong run of success on the country singles charts during the latter half of the '80s. Kathy, June, Kim, and Christy grew up in Lookout Mountain, GA, and got their initial singing experience in their church choir. Kathy and June, the two eldest, both took jobs as teachers after graduating from college, and sang together in a local band by night. Kim joined in 1978, and the sisters soon hit on the idea of forming their own group; after Christy finished college, Kathy and June quit their day jobs, and the foursome soon began to perform on a regular basis. They were discovered at an arts festival by songwriters Bobby Keel and Billy Stone, who helped them record a demo that got the group signed to Warner Bros. in 1984; Keel and Stone also contributed "Yankee Go Home" to their self-titled debut album, which appeared the following year.
   Their first single, "That's What You Do (When You're in Love)," reached the Top Ten, and their next two—"I Fell in Love Again Last Night" and "Just in Case"—went all the way to number one in 1985 and 1986, respectively. Follow-up "Lonely Alone" stalled at number two, but "Mama's Never Seen Those Eyes" brought the Forester Sisters back to the top of the charts for a third time. While the group would never equal that incredible run of success, they went on to score eight more Top Ten hits—all consecutively—through 1991, when their run came to a close with the humorous number eight hit "Men." They recorded occasionally during the '90s, cutting the gospel album *Sunday Meetin'* in 1993 and returning to country with 1996's *More Than I Am.* —*Steve Huey*

The Forester Sisters / 1985 / Warner Bros. ✦✦✦✦✦
Rock music had the Go-Gos, Motown had the Supremes, and the standard pop era had the Andrews Sisters and the McGuire Sisters. Country music finally got an all-girl vocal group with the advent of the Foresters, and their debut is surprisingly uptempo and energetic. This is a first album that should have received more attention. —*Tom Roland*

I'd Choose You Again / 1987 / Warner Bros. ✦✦✦

You Again / 1987 / Warner Bros. ♦♦♦

Christmas Card / 1987 / Warner Bros. ♦♦♦

Sincerely / 1988 / Warner Bros. ♦♦♦♦♦

Already the possessors of a wonderful vocal harmony style, The Foresters hit a peak when they hooked up with writer/producer Wendy Waldman for this album, cutting her "Letter Home" and other strong material (note especially the shoulda-been-a-single "You Love Me," co-written by Matraca Berg). *—William Ruhlmann*

All I Need / 1989 / Warner Bros. ♦♦♦♦

All I Need is a collection of gospel staples and latter-day Christian songs. *—Jason Ankeny*

● **Greatest Hits** / 1989 / Warner Bros. ♦♦♦♦♦

A good selection of Forester singles presents the various stylistic approaches they've taken with country material, which range from good to terrific. *—William Ruhlmann*

Talkin' 'Bout Men / 1991 / Warner Bros. ♦♦♦

Love songs, love-gone-wrong songs, a little bit of swing, a little bit of reggae and, oh yeah, some country, too are included. The novelty hit "Men" (with lines like "You can't beat 'em up, 'cause they're bigger than you/You can't live with 'em and you just can't shoot 'em") was written by two guys. *—Brian Mansfield*

I Got a Date / 1992 / Warner Bros. ♦♦♦♦

Somewhere along the line, some executive got the idea that this Lookout Mountain group should concentrate primarily on ballads. As a result, their non-ballad material could've been better, but that's rectified in this collection, an excellent portrayal of the humor and heartaches faced by women in modern relationships. It's wide-ranging stylistically, with a strong dose of wit, particularly in the title track and "Redneck Romeo." *—Tom Roland*

More Than I Am / Aug. 27, 1996 / Warner Bros. ♦♦♦

More Than I Am is a diverse blend of adult pop and country styles, giving the Forester Sisters a wider array of sounds than they have ever previously displayed before on record. It's not wildly eclectic—all of the styles are fused into one sound. Unfortunately, it's not all entirely successful either. Roughly half the tracks are worthwhile, while the others rank as failed experiments. *—Thom Owens*

Greatest Gospel Hits / May 20, 1997 / Warner Bros. ♦♦♦♦

Peggy Forman

b. Centerville, LA

Songwriter, Vocals / Country-Pop

Peggy Forman was a well-known Nashville songwriter. The daughter of an oilfield worker and a homemaker, she hailed from Centerville, LA. A music lover and singer since childhood, young Peggy met her husband Wayne Forman while still in high-school. After their marriage, they began performing together in a band with Wayne singing leads and playing guitar and Peggy on harmonies. Later, she became the lead singer. At the time, she was also writing songs, and one of them was recorded by Joe Lewis. Not long after, her "Out of My Head and Back in My Bed" became a chart-topping hit for Loretta Lynn. In 1978, Conway Twitty, an early supporter, recorded her "Yours to Hurt Tomorrow," and helped Forman sign a recording contract with MCA in the mid-'70s. He and Snuffy Miller then became the producers of her debut single "The Danger Zone," which became a minor hit.

She recorded several other singles, but they never made it to the charts. Around 1980, she signed to Dimension Records and had a small string of hits beginning with "There Ain't Nothing like a Rainy Night" and ending in 1982 with "That's What Your Lovin' Does to Me." Forman has had considerably more success as a writer; many prominent artists such as Bill Anderson, Jean Shepard and George Strait recorded her songs. *—Sandra Brennan*

● **Presenting Peggy Forman** / Dimension ♦♦♦♦

Foster & Lloyd

f. 1987, **db.** 1990

Group / Contemporary Country, New Traditionalist

Foster & Lloyd stood out from the contemporary country pack in the late '80s thanks to Radney Foster's intelligent, literate lyrics; Bill Lloyd's flair for memorable pop melodies; and the duo's Everly Brothers-style close harmony singing. It was an influential mix that, in its own way, helped pave the way for country's crossover success of the '90s. Foster & Lloyd met in 1985 while working as staff songwriters for the MTM publishing firm. Foster had grown up in Del Rio, TX, and attended the University of the South, a liberal arts college in Sewanee, TN, before moving to Nashville to make it in the music business. Lloyd, meanwhile, was a native of Bowling Green, KY, who loved the chiming, Beatlesesque sound of power pop nearly as much as country music. When their composition "Since I Found You" became a hit for the Sweethearts of the Rodeo, Foster & Lloyd managed to score a record deal of their own with RCA on the strength of the demo tape they'd recorded together.

Their self-titled 1987 debut was a hit, paced by the Top Ten singles "Crazy Over You," "Sure Thing," and "What Do You Want From Me This Time"; a fourth single, "Texas in 1880," made the Top 20. Their 1989 follow-up album, *Faster & Llouder*, received equally complimentary reviews from critics and sold fairly well, but didn't spin off hit singles in quite the same way. *Version of the Truth* (1990) confirmed their commercial downturn, and the duo subsequently split up to pursue solo careers. Foster recorded several solo albums during the '90s, veering between neo-traditional country and roots rock, while Lloyd returned to his power pop roots on two '90s albums of his own, also working often as a session guitarist. *—Steve Huey*

Foster & Lloyd / 1987 / RCA ♦♦♦

Faster & Llouder / 1989 / RCA ♦♦♦♦♦

The follow-up to Foster & Lloyd's hit-packed debut only spun off one country Top Ten entry ("Fair Shake"), but don't be fooled—the overall quality of the songs on *Faster & Llouder* is just as good, if not better, than that of the songs on the first album. The relatively low chart placings for follow-up singles "Before the Heartache Rolls In" and the Lloyd-sung "Suzette," therefore, were a bit of a puzzle at the time, and seem even odder in retrospect. The Foster & Lloyd formula of two parts country to one part power pop still works well, and if Foster (who takes most of the lead vocals) tends to dominate a little more of the group's sound than Lloyd, it's still Bill Lloyd's subtle pop/rock touches that end up allowing this record to transcend the duo's origins as Nashville songmill peddlers. Years after its release, *Faster & Llouder* still holds up as a superior example of "new country"—one that just happened to be recorded a few years before the term "new country" was invented. *—Rudyard Kennedy*

Version of the Truth / 1990 / RCA ♦♦♦

● **The Essential Foster and Lloyd** / Apr. 1996 / RCA ♦♦♦♦♦

The Essential Foster & Lloyd groups together 19 tracks by this influential duo who scored several hits in the 1980s. The two merged Lloyd's melodic pop smarts with Foster's Texas literary soul, giving them catchiness and substance in the same package. They also could rock out, leaning toward a rockabilly energy that didn't carry a trace of the redneck swagger of Southern rock. Instead, this was solid, clean-rocking fun with brains. The duo split in 1990 after three albums, but this collection is a good reminder that they anticipated the country youth movement that followed them. *—Michael McCall*

Radney Foster

b. Jul. 20, 1959, Del Rio, TX

Guitar, Vocals / Contemporary Country, New Traditionalist

Radney Foster started his career as a songwriter, then found commercial success and critical acclaim as part of the duo Foster & Lloyd, and finally embarked on a solo career in 1991 that centered on his literate approach to country songwriting. Foster was born in Del Rio, TX, and took up the guitar at age 12. He began performing small-club gigs while attending the University of the South, a liberal arts college in Sewanee, TN, and took leave from school to try his luck in Nashville. In 1985, he signed with the MTM publishing firm as a staff songwriter, and soon struck up a partnership with Bill Lloyd, who joined the company two months later. Their "Since I Found You" became a Top Ten hit for the Sweethearts of the Rodeo, and on the strength of their demo tape RCA signed them as recording artists.

Foster & Lloyd recorded three albums from 1987-1990, and landed a series of Top Ten singles in addition to complimentary reviews. When their third album tanked, the duo amicably disbanded and Foster pursued a solo career. His debut, *Del Rio, Texas, 1959*, appeared in 1992 and proved a commercial as well as critical success; four of its singles hit the Top 40, and of those, "Just Call Me Lonesome" made the Top Ten, while "Nobody Wins" fell one spot short of the top of the country charts. However, the 1995 follow-up, *Labor of Love*, wasn't quite as popular with audiences as it was with critics. Foster revamped his approach on his third solo effort, 1999's *See What You Want to See*, which was more influenced by pop and rock. He subsequently parted ways with his label, Arista, and signed with the smaller Dualtone, which issued the live album *Are You Ready for the Big Show?*, a more traditional country outing, in 2001. The studio follow-up, 2002's *Another Way to Go*, found Foster exploring classic-style R&B in addition to country. *—Steve Huey*

● **Del Rio, Texas, 1959** / 1992 / Arista ♦♦♦♦♦

Radney Foster's first album since dissolving the much-missed Foster & Lloyd duo is a tribute to the songwriter's coming of age in small-town Texas and all the musical baggage that stowed aboard for the ride. On many of the tracks, Foster seems a little too conscious of wanting to deliver a pure country effort. The songs are solid, but there's a slight archival feel to the result. The disc's best moments are the more contemporary hybrids. The gutsy "A Fine Line," the infectious "Nobody Wins" (with Mary-Chapin Carpenter on background vocals,) and the gospelly country-rocker "Hammer and Nails" are worth the price of admission alone. *—Roch Parisien*

Labor of Love / 1995 / Arista ♦♦♦

See What You Want to See / May 18, 1999 / Arista ♦♦♦♦

For Radney Foster, country music stopped reaping dividends after his second solo album, *Labor of Love*. Although it had its moments, it sounded a little tired, compared to his work with Bill Lloyd and his debut *Del Rio, Texas, 1959*. Sensing that the time was right for a change, Foster made a pop move with his third record, *See What You Want to See*. Where his former partner decided to return to his power-pop roots, thereby confining himself to a niche audience, Foster decided to shoot for a larger audience, redefining his music as rootsy, adult pop. The presence of Emmylou Harris, Abra Moore, Darius Rucker, and Patrice Pike of Sister 7 telegraphs Foster's intentions—he still has a bit of a twang, but this is classy, mature pop music, not contemporary country. By and large, his gambit works. At times, *See What You Want to See* sounds a little bit too mannered and considered, which means the hooks never quite take off, but it all sounds pleasant, and the best moments—"Folding Money," "Angry Heart," "I'm In"—showcase him at his best as a songwriter while successfully delivering a fresh, updated sound. It may not feel as weighty as *Del Rio, Texas*, but in its own way, it's every bit as successful and introspective as that album, while occasionally matching Foster & Lloyd at their best. *—Stephen Thomas Erlewine*

Are You Ready for the Big Show? / May 15, 2001 / Dualtone ♦♦♦♦

Few contemporary country artists deliver a live performance distinctively unique from the formulaic recordings processed by Music Row; one artist who does this is Radney Foster. *Are You Ready for the Big Show?* released on Dualtone Music Group, takes various live performances from September 21st and 22nd, 2000, at the Continental Club in Austin, TX, of Fosters' new material as well as his standards. The album captures the basic artistry of Radney Fosters' songwriting repertoire as well as a back-porch jam session featuring mandolin protégé Chris Thile (Nickel Creek), and Nashville's best kept secret, guitarist Mike McAdam (Steve Earle, Mary-Chapin Carpenter, Jack Ingram). For fans of Fosters' earlier solo work, *Are You Ready for the Big Show?* includes a Cajun rearrangement of "Just Call Me Lonesome" (*Del Rio, Texas, 1959*) and a slimmed-down acoustic version of "Nobody Wins" (*Del Rio, Texas, 1959*). The album's single is the unearthed Foster & Lloyd classic "Texas in 1880," unlisted as hidden track 16. On *Are You Ready for the Big Show?* Radney Foster returns full circle to his neo-traditionalist roots, which separated him from the droves of aspiring Nashville singer/songwriters early in his career. —*Matt Reasor*

Another Way to Go / 2002 / Dualtone ✦✦✦
Backed by a band of Nashville stalwarts, Foster ends a four-year studio layoff with this set. There's nearly as much R&B as country here, with echoes of Van Morrison in the full organ chords, soulful guitar licks, and idiomatic chord progressions; all this, along with certain aspects of Foster's timbre, nods toward *Moondance* on "Again" and "Sure Feels Right," and especially in the sax harmonies of "What It Is That You Do." References to the Twin Towers disaster were practically mandatory in 2002, and Foster delivers his on "Everyday Angel," though by restricting it to the last verse he emphasizes that goodness needn't wait for tragedy to come knocking. Less-specific references to timely terrors crop up in "Scary Old World," whose rugged eloquence betrays the influence of co-writer Harlan Howard. The rest of the album generally shuffles through the heartbreak deck and comes up with a good but less-than-unbeatable hand. ("If love is what you want, I got what you need," Foster declaims on "I Got What You Need," as if this line could actually get results.) Three tracks do break from the norm: "Tired of Pretending," which argues that pretense is bad; "What Are We Doing Here Tonight," whose rhetorical structure follows a similar theme in a more thoughtful way (at least until the anticlimactic admission, "I guess what I'm saying is, I really like your style"); and "Just Sit Still," a rumination on the virtues of slowing down, taking a deep breath, and not getting upset over money, traffic jams, pop album reviews, and other nitpickeries. —*Robert L. Doerschuk*

Kevin Fowler
b. Amarillo, TX
Guitar, Vocals / Contemporary Country, Honky Tonk
Country-pop may have ruled the charts, but Kevin Fowler established himself impressively throughout Texas by making modest honky tonk-style country for regular folks. Raised in the West Texas town of Amarillo, the guitarist began his musical career on both drums and piano. He left Texas at age 20 for the bright lights of Los Angeles, where he studied music at the Guitar Institute of Technology. He returned to Texas soon after and settled in Austin, where he joined the hard rock band Dangerous Toys. Following this eyeopening stint, Fowler started his own Southern hard rock band, Thunderfoot. He soon came to the realization, however, that he couldn't shake his West Texas roots and gave up hard rock for country, the style of music he grew up with.

Fowler put together a country band in 1998 and began playing Tuesday nights at Babe's on Sixth Street in Austin. Within two years, he'd begun recording albums and struck big with his self-released *Beer, Bait and Ammo* (2000). The album sold around 30,000 copies in the Texas area and garnered an impressive amount of airplay, particularly for the album's title track. The song became somewhat of a Texas anthem; Mark Chesnutt made the song part of his live show, and Sammy Kershaw recorded it. Fowler returned in 2002 with his third album, *High on the Hog*, and boasted some impressive guests, including Willie Nelson and David Lee Garza. —*Jason Birchmeier*

One for the Road / 2000 / ✦✦

Beer, Bait and Ammo / Nov. 21, 2000 / Tin Roof ✦✦✦

High on the Hog / Aug. 6, 2002 / Tin Roof ✦✦✦

● **Live at Billy Bob's Texas** / Nov. 5, 2002 / Smith Music Group ✦✦✦✦

Curly Fox (Arnim LeRoy Fox)
b. Nov. 9, 1910, Graysville, TN, d. Nov. 10, 1995
Fiddle / Traditional Country
During the '40s and '50s, Curly Fox and Texas Ruby were the preeminent husband and wife team in country music. Fox remains one of the great hillbilly fiddlers, while Ruby was one of the first female singers to become a major star. Curly was born Arnim LeRoy Fox in Graysville, TN. His father, a barber, taught him to play the fiddle, with help from James McCarroll of the Roane Country Ramblers. He began his professional career playing and traveling with Chief White Owl's "Indian" medicine show. Fox soon began working with Claude Davis and the Carolina Tar Heels in Atlanta and founded the Tennessee Firecrackers. He played and recorded with the Shelton Brothers in New Orleans from 1934 to 1936, also recording three singles himself. In 1937, Fox met Texas Ruby (born Ruby Agnes Owens in Wise County, TX) at the Texas centennial celebration. Ruby, a true cowgirl and sister of radio cowboy Tex Owens, had sung several times on the *Grand Ole Opry* and various radio stations with Zeke Clements & His Bronco Busters. Soon after meeting Fox, the two married and began appearing on the *Opry* from 1937-1939 and again from 1944-1948. In between, they worked in Cincinnati and at other major stations as well.

The duo did make some recordings, but according to Fox, Ruby's throaty contralto didn't sound as good on records as it did on the radio. Her best recordings were made for King in 1947. In 1948 the couple moved to Houston, where they lived and worked for ten years bringing country music to local television. In 1960, they returned to the *Grand Ole Opry*. Unfortunately, Ruby's health was failing, so Fox often played alone. They did manage to record an album for Starday in 1963, but shortly thereafter, Ruby burned to death in a mobile home fire while her husband was playing on the *Opry*. Fox continued his solo career for a while after her death, but then left for Chicago to live with one of his daughters. Though he too suffered ill health, he made some albums and occasionally appeared live. He returned to his hometown in the mid-'70s and worked with a local

bluegrass band before retiring to live with an older sister. Fox died in 1995 at the age of 85. —*Sandra Brennan*

Curly Fox & Texas Ruby / 1963 / Starday ✦✦✦

● **Champion Fiddler Curly Fox, Vol. 1** / 1972 / Rural Rhythm ✦✦✦✦

Champion Fiddler Curly Fox, Vol. 2 / 1972 / Rural Rhythm ✦✦✦✦

Jeff Foxworthy
b. Sep. 6, 1958
Speech/Speaker/Speaking Part / Contemporary Country, Country Comedy, Standup Comedy
Jeff Foxworthy's wry Southern humor made him one of the most popular standup comedians of the '90s. Foxworthy grew up in Atlanta and was working for IBM when he tried standup on a dare. Before long, he'd quit his job to pursue comedy full-time. His material concentrated mainly on family situations, but it was his affectionate jabs at Southern rednecks (or the "gloriously unsophisticated") that catapulted him to stardom. Originally released on Laughing Hyena in 1993, *You Might Be a Redneck If...* became a word-of-mouth hit, and Warner Bros. bought his contract in 1994. With their added promotional muscle, *You Might Be a Redneck If...* climbed to number three on the country album charts in 1995, and eventually sold over four-million copies, making it the biggest-selling comedy album of all time. His follow-up album, *Games Rednecks Play*, appeared later in 1995 and went to number two on the country charts, also crossing over to the pop Top Ten; it sold over two-million copies.

Foxworthy was an undeniably hot commodity, and ABC offered him his own sitcom in 1995. Ratings for *The Jeff Foxworthy Show* were disappointing, but when ABC took a pass, NBC picked up the show for an additional season; it was canceled in 1997. Meanwhile, Foxworthy branched out into musical satire on 1996's *Crank It Up: The Music Album*, which went gold and once again made the country Top Five. He returned to standup on the 1998 live album *Totally Committed*, another country Top Ten hit. Foxworthy subsequently moved over to DreamWorks, where he debuted with 2000's *Big Funny*. That same year, he teamed up with Bill Engvall, Ron White, and Larry the Cable Guy for the hugely popular *Blue Collar Comedy Tour*, which spawned an album of highlights and, in 2003, an accompanying concert film. —*Steve Huey*

● **You Might Be a Redneck If...** / 1994 / Warner Bros. ✦✦✦✦✦
You Might Be A Redneck If... encapsulates the humor of Jeff Foxworthy on a single disc. Essentially variations on the title phrase "You Might Be a Redneck," Foxworthy's jokes are simple but never crude. Like any comedy album, it appeals to a specific taste. If you find Foxworthy's repetitive jokes hilarious, you might be a fan. If you don't find him funny, you might be better off leaving the album in the store. —*Sara Sytsma*

Redneck Test, Vol. 11 / Aug. 26, 1994 / Laughing Hyena ✦✦
Jeff Foxworthy's line of *Redneck Test* collection contains some good comedy, but by and large they are poorly packaged and produced; stick with his Warner records. —*Stephen Thomas Erlewine*

Redneck Test, Vol. 43 / 1995 / Laughing Hyena ✦✦

The Original / 1995 / Laughing Hyena ✦✦
The Original is a collection of early Jeff Foxworthy performances. While his humor is often as good as his better-known albums, the album isn't as consistent as his two major label albums. —*Sara Sytsma*

Sold Out / 1995 / Laughing Hyena ✦✦✦
Sold Out is a live concert featuring Jeff Foxworthy's trademark "redneck" humour. The crowd interacts well with the comedian and his performance is consistently funny, even if it isn't particularly special. —*Sara Sytsma*

Games Rednecks Play / Jul. 18, 1995 / Warner Bros. ✦✦✦✦✦
Games Rednecks Play was Jeff Foxworthy's follow-up to his breakthrough major-label debut, *You Might Be A Redneck If...* Like its predecessor, the album is basically variations on his down-home humor, which does show a genuine affection for the "rednecks" he jokes about. *Games Rednecks Play* is as funny as *You Might Be A Redneck*, but if you don't like that kind of humor, it's certainly not going to convince you that you were wrong. —*Sara Sytsma*

Crank It Up: The Music Album / Aug. 27, 1996 / Warner Bros. ✦✦✦
Jeff Foxworthy attempted to expand his recorded repertoire with *Crank It Up: Music Album*. The record was the first time he tried to make an album that didn't rely on redneck jokes. Don't worry, though—there's still plenty of humor here. It's just mixed in with competent neo-traditional honky tonk and slick new country. Though there's nothing particularly promising about the music, it isn't bad and *Crank It Up: Music Album* is far from the disaster it could have been. —*Thom Owens*

Totally Committed / May 19, 1998 / Warner Bros. ✦✦✦
To no one's surprise, *Totally Committed* is not a radical departure from Jeff Foxworthy's other albums. He's still cracking wise about rednecks—i.e., "You Can't Give Rednecks Money" and "Sophisticated People Vs. Rednecks"—plus marriage ("I Don't Want to Be Single Again," "The Rules of Marriage") and his general ignorance ("I Still Don't Know..."). Again, for fans of this style, *Totally Committed* delivers the goods, but if you don't like Foxworthy's down-home humor, stay clear. —*Stephen Thomas Erlewine*

Greatest Bits / Oct. 12, 1999 / Warner Bros. ✦✦✦✦

Big Funny / Apr. 25, 2000 / DreamWorks ✦✦✦
Jeff Foxworthy's first album for DreamWorks, *Big Funny*, is also his first standup record not to rely heavily on redneck-themed material. Of course, Foxworthy doesn't completely abandon it, although he does seem to acknowledge that it's time to move on in the title of the bit "I Thought I'd Heard Every Redneck Thing"; there's also a hilarious, well-done impression of stock car driver Jeff Gordon, mimicking how difficult it is to understand

any comments given in post-race interviews. But for the most part, Foxworthy concentrates on family life, gently and good-naturedly poking fun at gender differences in marriage and the pitfalls of child-rearing. It's subject matter that's been covered many a time, but Foxworthy's droll delivery will make *Big Funny* well worth the time of his fans. *—Steve Huey*

J.P. Fraley

Fiddle / Traditional Folk, Traditional Bluegrass, Old-Timey, Bluegrass

Considered one of the deans of Kentucky country fiddling, this musician has managed to keep busy well into his senior years, keeping up a schedule of bluegrass festivals, fiddle conventions, and traditional music workshops that might wear out a younger man. He learned music from his father and passed it on to his daughter Danielle Fraley, who has backed him up both on-stage and in the studio as a member of the Fraley Band. Although he started working in the Kentucky mines as a young man, he managed to be promoted well above the level of a miner of the type whose hard life frequently smears the pages of many an old-time musician's life story with coal dust. Fraley became a salesman for coal mining equipment, a job which took him not only all over Appalachia but throughout the world, to countries such as Italy, Brazil, and Norway. It sparked an interest in many different types of musical cultures which has expressed itself in the diversity of his fiddling as well as in actual meetings with players such as the Irish fiddler Ali Bain.

Fraley began playing as a young boy, and remembers that his first gig was sometime in the early '30s. Senior player Mark Dixon carried him through the woods to play music in exchange for a pie supper. Despite these early beginnings, he didn't really perform on a professional basis or begin recording until the '70s. Since that time he has been a huge influence on fiddlers as a teacher as well as player. Several published collections of fiddle pieces and instruction manuals have a strong focus on the Fraley style. He also works hard to provide opportunities for his genre of musicians, organizing a regular series of festivals such as J. P. Fraley's Mountain Music Festival in Olive Hill, KY. His 1974 album *Wild Rose of the Mountain* was released on Rounder and was greeted with rave reviews. It featured him in fiddle duets with his wife Annadeene, who passed away in the '90s. The recording was re-released 26 years later as a compact disc with additional tracks featuring Fraley in duo with his daughter on guitar. Another of Fraley's albums with Annadeene was entitled *Maysville*.

In 2000 he released a recording of twin fiddling with Betty Vornbrock, entitled *Side By Side* and featuring a familiar Fraley frolic of waltzes, two-steps, and other old-time numbers. With banjoist Bert Gavin, Fraley was featured on the Rounder anthology of *Kentucky Old Time Banjo*. He also accompanies cowboy singer Glenn Ohrin at concerts and on the album *A Cowboy's Life*, also released on Rounder. Fraley received the Appalachian Treasure Award from Morehead State University in 1998. His other talents include a legendary status as a teller of tall tales, leading most musicians to add "He's a heckuva storyteller!" to whatever florid praise has already been lavished on the man's fiddling. He also performs on cello in the Fraley Band, which performs country numbers and originals influenced by songwriters such as Bob Dylan. *—Eugene Chadbourne*

● **Maysville** / Oct. 17, 1995 / Rounder ✦✦✦

Wild Rose of the Mountain / Sep. 12, 2000 / Rounder ✦✦✦

Cleve Francis

b. Apr. 22, 1945, Jennings, LA

Vocals / Contemporary Country

While he dreamed of a career in country music as a boy and even learned guitar as a youth, performing seemed destined to became only a hobby when Cleve Francis obtained his degree from the Medical College of Virginia in 1973. Francis moved to Washington, D.C., and established himself as a cardiologist. However, he was soon moonlighting in local clubs as a singer, and even self-released three albums on his own label. Francis' real break came through heart-attack patient Olaf Hall, whose brother was "Big John" Garfield Hall, a member of the R&B band the Heartbeats. Big John helped Francis get an audition with Playback Records, who signed him and released an album; while it didn't sell well, his debut single and video, "Love Light," released in 1990, both won critical acclaim.

The widespread attention led to a deal with Liberty, who released Francis' *Tourist in Paradise* in 1992, when he was 48. It marked the first prominent contract for a black country artist since Charley Pride. The album featured a re-recorded version of "Love Light"; it and two other cuts from the record became minor chart hits. The next year Francis returned with *Walkin'*, which appeared on Capitol. Its title track made a few waves, but failed to make him a household name. *You've Got Me Now* appeared in 1994 on Liberty, but by 1995 Francis had left the industry and returned to his medical career. In 1998, he was one of the motivational forces behind Warner's *From Where I Stand: The Black Experience in Country Music*. *—Johnny Loftus*

● **Tourist in Paradise** / Mar. 16, 1992 / Liberty ✦✦✦✦

Tourist in Paradise highlights Francis' engaging tenor on songs like "You Do My Heart Good" and "Love Light." *—Jason Ankeny*

Walkin' / May 10, 1993 / Liberty ✦✦✦✦

Francis' second effort is a more wide-ranging affair featuring the ballads "I Won't Let You Walk Away" and "Your Love Stays With Me." *—Jason Ankeny*

You've Got Me Now / 1994 / Liberty ✦✦✦

Dallas Frazier

b. Oct. 27, 1939, Spiro, OK

Songwriter, Composer, Vocals / Rock & Roll, Traditional Country, Honky Tonk, Bakersfield Sound, Nashville Sound/Countrypolitan

One of country's most enduring songwriters, Dallas Frazier was born on October 27, 1939, in Spiro, OK. Raised in Bakersfield, CA, he was skilled on a number of musical instruments by the age of 12; while still in his teens, he became a featured member of Ferlin Husky's band, cutting his first solo single, "Space Command," in 1954. Soon after, he was named a regular on the *Hometown Jamboree* program, where he was often paired with fellow teen star Molly Bee. In 1957, Frazier scored a hit with a cover of the Hollywood Argyles' "Alley Oop." When *Hometown Jamboree* was canceled at the end of the decade, he moved to Nashville to work as a songwriter, composing Husky's 1964 hit "Timber I'm Falling." Two years later, his career caught fire; in addition to releasing his own debut album, *Elvira*, he penned three huge hits—Jack Greene's "There Goes My Everything," Connie Smith's "Ain't Had No Lovin'," and George Jones' "I'm a People." In 1967, Frazier released *Tell It Like It Is*, although his biggest success came on the pop charts, via Engelbert Humperdinck's rendition of "There Goes My Everything."

As the decade drew to a close, Frazier's songs remained popular fodder for other artists; in addition to supplying more hits for Jones, Greene, and Smith, his compositions were recorded by the likes of Willie Nelson, Brenda Lee, Charley Pride, and Merle Haggard, who included three Frazier songs on his 1968 LP *The Legend of Bonnie & Clyde*. His success only increased in the 1970s; in addition to generating a pair of solo records—1970's *Singing My Songs* and the following year's *My Baby Packed Up My Mind and Left Me*—Frazier became one of Nashville's most sought-after writers, composing hits for Elvis Presley, Moe Bandy, Roy Head, Rodney Crowell, and Ronnie Hawkins as well as frequent collaborators like Husky, Pride, and Greene. In 1972, he joined Smith for three cuts on her LP *If It Ain't Love (& Other Great Dallas Frazier Songs)*.

Frazier's songs continued to hit the charts well into the 1980s; his "Elvira" was a tremendous crossover smash for the Oak Ridge Boys, while Emmylou Harris topped the charts with "Beneath Still Waters." Even younger artists like George Strait, Randy Travis, and Patty Loveless found success with his compositions. In 1988, however, Frazier retired from songwriting, leaving Nashville to pursue a career in the ministry. *—Jason Ankeny*

● **Elvira** / 1966 / Capitol ✦✦✦✦

After penning hits for both R&B and country artists, Frazier decided to take a stab at performing his own songs for this album in 1966. The material chosen focuses on his more playful novelty numbers like "Alley Oop," "She's A Yum Yum," and "Whoop it on 'Um" and includes other hits such as the title track and "Mohair Sam." The arrangements are by-the-numbers pop R&B and while he's clearly a capable singer, his voice lacks the grit to make these songs as bluesy as he'd obviously like them to be. *—Chris Woodstra*

Freakwater

f. 1987, Louisville, KY

Group / Neo-Traditional Folk, Alternative Country-Rock, Traditional Country, Alternative Country

Despite their alternative rock pedigree and their home on a label better known for experimental music, Freakwater was one of the most traditionally grounded bands on the alternative country scene. Singers/guitarists/songwriters Janet Beveridge Bean and Catherine Ann Irwin mix original material (with a contemporary lyrical perspective) and traditional covers, all done in a spare, acoustic country-folk style with close vocal harmonies. Their instrumentation often features string band staples like steel guitar, fiddle, mandolin, and dobro, and the strong Appalachian overtones that result have often drawn the duo comparisons to the Carter Family. Freakwater originally formed in Louisville, KY, as an informal partnership; both Irwin and Bean had played in local punk bands, became roommates in 1982, and first performed together publicly the year afterward. Meanwhile, Bean co-founded the noisy, Neil Young-influenced alt-rock band Eleventh Dream Day with boyfriend and future husband Rick Rizzo, serving as the group's drummer; they soon moved to Chicago, and spent the late '80s and early '90s crafting a series of underappreciated, critically acclaimed albums.

Bean and Irwin continued to perform together, however, on an informal basis, and in 1988 were approached by Amoeba label head Keith Holland about recording. Choosing the name Freakwater—a term for moonshine—the duo cut a self-titled, EP-length record, which was released by Amoeba in 1989 (a year before Uncle Tupelo's seminal *No Depression* kick-started the alt-country movement). Upright bassist David Gay became the anchor of the duo's instrumental support team and remained with the group for the next decade. Their first true full-length, *Dancing Under Water*, was completed in 1991, but disagreements with Holland led to Amoeba seizing control of the masters and denying the duo any royalties. With Bean still heavily involved in Eleventh Dream Day, Freakwater completed *Feels Like the Third Time* in 1993, and finally found a home on the Thrill Jockey label, an independent more noted for its avant-garde, often electronic artist roster. Thrill Jockey finally released *Feels Like the Third Time* in 1995, the same year of the group's critical breakthrough, *Old Paint*. Benefiting from increased attention due to Eleventh Dream Day's hiatus, *Old Paint* led many critics to hail Freakwater as one of the best, most authentic-sounding alt-country artists around. They were offered a deal with Steve Earle's Warner-associated label, but ultimately turned it down to remain with Thrill Jockey.

Bean and Irwin consolidated their reputation on 1998's *Springtime*, which featured multi-instrumentalist Max Konrad Johnston of Wilco lending support. Sessions for 1999's *End Time* were reportedly difficult, but the record was yet another acclaimed outing, and featured all original material for the first time. Freakwater remained quiet for a few years, and 2002 found both Bean and Irwin working on solo albums for Thrill Jockey. Irwin's *Cut Yourself a Switch* appeared in late 2002, while Bean and her backing band, the Concertina Wire, issued *Dragging Wonder Lake* in early 2003. *—Steve Huey*

Freakwater / 1989 / Amoeba ✦✦✦

Their debut, a short LP or a long EP, depending on how you look at it, presents plaintive, raw country-folk in a modern context without sounding forced. *—Richie Unterberger*

● **Dancing Under Water** / 1991 / Thrill Jockey ✦✦✦✦

Dancing Under Water, Freakwater's first long-player, is insurgent country music for people who believe that the film *Deliverance* says more about the true nature of rural folks than it does about the fears and prejudices of city dwellers. The songs, just under half of which are original, fixate on the folk traditions of murder ballads and "dead child" songs, performed simply with ragged duet harmonies in a modern approximation of the Carter Family. The difference between Freakwater and the early country artists who performed similar material is that Freakwater approaches (and, in some cases, writes) these songs from an ironic distance with an indie rock perspective. Some listeners may wish that Catherine Irwin and Janet Beveridge Bean had practiced their vocal parts a few more times before committing them to tape, but the general audience for this music will relish its naïve primitivism. The pedal steel and dobro, contributed by John Spiegel and John Rice, add a professional touch, although the cover of George Jones' minor hit "You're Still on My Mind" shows that the group is better off when they avoid straight country. Other covers include Jon Anderson's number-one hit "Wild and Blue" (also recorded by the Mekons around this time) and Bill Monroe's "Little Girl and the Dreadful Snake." *Dancing Under Water* was originally paired with Freakwater's self-titled debut mini-album for CD release, but was reissued by Thrill Jockey in 1997 without the bonus. *—Greg Adams*

Feels Like the Third Time / May 23, 1995 / Thrill Jockey ✦✦✦✦

Freakwater's third album finds them treading similar ground to their first two albums, but since no one else really does what they do, more of the same is welcome. The beautiful harmonies of Catherine Irwin and Janet Bean remain the focus, and Dave Gay, as always, provides solid support on the upright bass; this time out augmented by Brian Dunn on guitar and Lisa Marsicek on fiddle and mandolin. Cathy Irwin's songwriting continues to progress, as this time she accounts for half of the album's tunes. Janet Bean contributes one song with choice covers by the likes of Woody Guthrie, Conway Twitty, and Nick Lowe. Similar in sound to the Carter Family and Gillian Welch, Freakwater stands apart because their lyrics are so firmly rooted in the modern world; no dustbowl ballads here. Sounding more traditional than most neo-traditional country acts with lyrics that have a more modern bite than most contemporary country, it's Freakwater's ability to effortlessly straddle these two worlds that makes them such a special band. *—Sean Westergaard*

● **Old Paint** / Oct. 10, 1995 / Thrill Jockey ✦✦✦✦✦

After a four-year gap since their second album, Freakwater returned with another solid effort that's not as bare-bones as their debut, but a little earthier than *Dancing Under Water.* Not a lot of new ground is broken, yet it somehow doesn't sound at all tiresome. All of their strengths remain in place: fine, mournful harmonies, good original songs, some well-chosen covers (Loudon Wainwright's "Out of This World" is a particular highlight), and nice unobtrusive touches of pedal steel and fiddle embellishing the acoustic guitars. This is modern country-folk at its best, and in fact would really be more suitable for the roots-country audience, except that the execution is too direct, the production too basic, and the songwriting too heartfelt for the contemporary country marketplace. Thus it is that the group's primary listenership is the alternative rock community, which is country's loss: Few performers today are performing roots music so convincingly, without sounding forced or dated. *—Richie Unterberger*

Springtime / Jan. 20, 1998 / Thrill Jockey ✦✦✦✦✦

A consolidation of Freakwater's status as one of the best—perhaps *the* best—1990s exponents of the folk-country tradition. The Appalachian flavor is, if anything, a little more pronounced than usual, but the songwriting is utterly contemporary, and the Irwin-Bean harmonies among their best. "Binding Twine," with its delectably sad melody and vocals, has the makings of a modern classic; "Jesus Year" has some great trembling harmonies; and "Slowride," more unexpectedly, has the country-rock punch of the late-'60s Byrds in that group's better moments. Most unusual lyrical twist: "Louisville Lip," inspired by Muhammad Ali's toss of his gold medal into the Ohio River after getting denied service at a restaurant. Max Konrad Johnston, formerly of Wilco, helps out on guitar, fiddle, banjo, dobro, mandolin, and vocals, helping devise a sound that is both spare and textured. *—Richie Unterberger*

End Time / Sep. 7, 1999 / Thrill Jockey ✦✦✦✦✦

With Freakwater records, continuity is a far greater trait than change or innovation. Yet this album does represent a significant advancement for the group, without altering the sound in any way that would alienate fans of their previous discs. The arrangements are fuller than ever before, without sounding overproduced—it's the first Freakwater record to have a full drum kit, and a three-piece string section appears on some tracks. This is also the first Freakwater album consisting entirely of compositions by the core duo of Catherine Irwin and Janet Bean. More noteworthy than any of these details, however, is the sheer level of vocal, musical, and lyrical accomplishment throughout, as well as the attention to diversity and nuance within their country/folk/alt-rock niche. At times this sounds like a pure country record (with lots of pedal steel) that's too country for Nashville; on "Good for Nothing" there's a Band-like organ that puts this in an early-'70s mood; "Sick, Sick, Sick" is just voice and what sounds like dobro, getting close to country blues territory; "Dog Gone Wrong" has a honky tonk feel; and "All Life Long" is nearly Appalachian folk. It makes a reasonable contender for the best Freakwater release to date, as Bean and Irwin also maintain their high standard of moving vocal harmonies and clever, emotionally complex lyrics. *—Richie Unterberger*

The Freight Hoppers

Group / Neo-Traditional Folk, Old-Timey

The Freight Hoppers, led by the distinctive vocals of Cary Fridley (who is also a solo artist), came together in the mid-'90s, inspired by 1920s and 1930s old-time music. The group's roots lie in the early '90s, when banjo player and Atlanta native Frank Lee was playing for the Great Smokey Mountain Railway in Bryson City, NC. He called upon his friend, fiddler David Bass, a Cleveland native who had been busking in N.Y.C. and New Orleans, to come to Bryson City to help him entertain disembarking passengers. Vocalist/guitarist Cary Fridley, a Kentucky native, was teaching school in Mocksville, NC, and had met Lee at a party. She soon gave up teaching to join the group. Acoustic bass player Jim O'Keefe (from upstate NY) met the group at Merlefest in North Carolina.

Now a full-fledged group, the Freight Hoppers played Bryson City railway from Memorial Day through October. In March 1996, they received national exposure when they played Garrison Keillor's acclaimed National Public Radio show *A Prairie Home Companion,* having won the Talent From Towns Under 2,000 contest out of nearly 500 entrants. Drawing on traditional standards from the 1920s and 1930s, the group released its debut, *Where'd You Come From, Where'd You Go?,* in 1996 on Rounder Records. The similarly minded *Waiting on the Gravy Train* emerged in 1998. Fridley released a solo album, *Neighbor Girl,* in 2001. *—Erik Hage*

Where'd You Come From Where'd You Go? / Oct. 15, 1996 / Rounder ✦✦✦✦

The title of this foursome's fine debut for the Rounder label comes from a lyric of the disc's second song—the old-timey warhorse "Cotton Eyed Joe." Nearly all of the songs here will be just as familiar to fans of traditional old-timey music and bluegrass, but that's OK. These relative youngsters pay homage to tradition by performing with a joy that all but leaps at the listener from the speakers. Their love for the music of Gid Tanner, Tommy Jarrell, and Uncle Dave Macon is apparent in every note the Freight Hoppers play. The CD's booklet includes fiddle and banjo tunings to help out listeners interested in playing along. *—Brian Beatty*

● **Waiting on the Gravy Train** / Aug. 18, 1998 / Rounder ✦✦✦✦

Carrying on the tradition of the hobo lament into the new millennium, this quartet spins some fine old-timey music. Utilizing a guitar/bass/fiddle/banjo configuration, they wonderfully execute a host of traditional tunes. Particularly beautiful are a baleful "We Shall All Be Reunited" and a chilling "Warfare." While banjo picker Cary Fridley's vocals sound self-consciously nasal at times, her harmonies with banjoist Frank Lee are strong. This is earthy music carried out with genuine loving care. *—Tim Sheridan*

Janie Fricke

b. Dec. 19, 1952, South Whitney, IN

Vocals, Guitar / Country-Pop, New Traditionalist, Contemporary Country

Janie Fricke was one of the most popular female country singers of the '80s, racking up an enviable string of hits and proving herself a versatile vocalist with a particular flair for ballads. Fricke was born in South Whitney, IN, in 1952 and learned piano and guitar as a child; her first vocal influences were folkies like Joan Baez and Judy Collins, but she fell in love with country music as well. During college, she sang commercial jingles for a Memphis radio station, and moved to Nashville in 1975, where she quickly became an in-demand session vocalist. She got her first major exposure in 1976, when producer Billy Sherrill teamed her with Johnny Duncan for a set of duets that included "Joe and the Cowboy," "Stranger," and "Thinkin' of a Rendezvous," the latter of which went to number one on the country charts. Sherrill signed Fricke as a solo act, and produced her 1977 debut single, "What're You Doing Tonight," which just missed the Top 20.

Collaborations with Charlie Rich (the number-one hit "On My Knees") and Duncan again (the Top Five "Come a Little Bit Closer") kept Fricke going strong through 1978, but her solo singles over the next couple of years had a hard time taking off. Sherrill advised her to establish an identity by focusing on one style, and Fricke began to record a generous selection of ballads. As a result, Fricke had a breakout year in 1981, when she landed two Top Five hits with "Down to My Last Broken Heart" and "I'll Need Someone to Hold Me (When I Cry)." That only set the stage for her smashing success over 1982-1984, when she scored an amazing six number-one hits—"Don't Worry 'Bout Me Baby," "It Ain't Easy Bein' Easy," "Tell Me a Lie," "He's a Heartache (Looking for a Place to Happen)," "Let's Stop Talkin' About It," and "Your Heart's Not in It." Plus, the three singles she released during that time period that didn't top the charts all made the Top Ten.

By this time, she'd broadened her style to include more uptempo tracks as well. Fricke landed five more Top Ten hits from 1985-1986, including another number one in "Always Have, Always Will" and a number two in "She's Single Again." However, her commercial momentum slowed abruptly afterwards, and following 1989's *Labor of Love* album, she and CBS Records parted ways. She recorded two albums for the small Branson label in 1992 and 1993, and issued the gospel record *Hymns of Faith* on Intersound in 1996. In 2000, she mounted a comeback tour behind the album *Bouncin' Back,* and two years later issued the concert set *Live at Billy Bob's Texas,* which featured many of her old hits. *—Steve Huey*

Singer of Songs / 1978 / Columbia ✦✦✦

Fricke has a big voice and gives the impression she can do a lot with it. She just never gets around to it on this record. Maybe it's the songs or maybe the arrangements, but she never seems to get into these songs or comes close to putting any emotion in her performances. *—Jim Worbois*

Love Notes / 1979 / Columbia ✦✦✦

From the Heart / 1980 / Columbia ✦✦✦✦

I'll Need Someone to Hold Me When I Cry / 1981 / Columbia ✦✦✦✦

Sleeping With Your Memory / 1981 / Columbia ✦✦✦

Sleeping With Your Memory is an impressively consistent album that matches its hits with material nearly as good. Fricke enjoyed two successful singles from the album, the mildly risqué "Do Me With Love," and "Don't Worry 'Bout Me Baby," a country chart-topper that by all rights should have landed on the pop chart too. An inspired country version of Simon & Garfunkel's "Homeward Bound" uses a spot of banjo to make the song sound like it could have come from the country canon, and the title track is a wistful song of heartbreak that shows that contemporary country ballads don't have to succumb to schmaltz. The album's second side isn't as strong as its first, but ends on a high note with "Midnight Words." Ricky Skaggs plays and sings on several songs, and Deborah Allen's songwriting husband, Rafe Van Hoy, appears as a guitarist. *—Greg Adams*

It Ain't Easy / 1982 / Columbia ✦✦✦

The versatility that made Fricke a jingles success might have been a liability as a solo performer. She's so adaptable that her voice might not have been distinctive enough. Here she sounds like a strong woman who's very familiar with heartache, and producer Bob Montgomery gives her some rockin' material to shout on. *—Tom Roland*

Greatest Hits / 1982 / Columbia ✦✦✦✦
While by no means a comprehensive collection of Fricke's hits, this anthology does offer the chart-topping "Don't Worry 'Bout Me Baby" along with "Pass Me By (If You're Only Passing Through," "Down to My Last Broken Heart," and "Please Help Me, I'm Falling (In Love with You)." *—Jason Ankeny*

Love Lies / 1983 / Columbia ✦✦✦

First Word in Memory / 1984 / Columbia ✦✦✦

Somebody Else's Fire / 1985 / Columbia ✦✦✦
Somebody Else's Fire is a typically fine collection of tunes from one of the finest contemporary country singers of the '80s. The upbeat "Party Shoes," "Single Again," "Somebody Else's Fire," and the great tearjerker "Easy to Please" are among the album's highlights. *—James Chrispell*

The Very Best of Janie Fricke / 1986 / Columbia ✦✦✦✦✦
The Very Best of Janie Fricke offers many of the singer's biggest hits, including "He's a Heartache (Looking for a Place to Happen)," "Tell Me a Lie," "Your Heart's Not in It" and "It Ain't Easy Bein' Easy"; while not all-encompassing, it's one of the best anthologies of her work to date. *—Jason Ankeny*

17 Greatest Hits / 1986 / Columbia ✦✦✦✦✦
Just like the title says—17 of Fricke's biggest hits from the early '80s, including the number ones "He's a Heartache (Looking for a Place to Happen)," "It Ain't Easy Bein' Easy," "Don' Worry 'Bout Me Baby," and "Your Heart's Not In It." *—Thom Owens*

Celebration / 1987 / Columbia ✦✦✦

Saddle the Wind / 1988 / Columbia ✦✦✦
Saddle the Wind includes the minor hits "Where Does Love Go (When It's Gone)," "I'll Walk Before I'll Crawl" and "Heart." *—Jason Ankeny*

Labor of Love / 1989 / Columbia ✦✦✦
Fricke tackles songs by Steve Earle ("My Old Friend the Blues") and Katy Moffatt and Tom Russell ("Walking on the Moon") on *Labor of Love*. *—Jason Ankeny*

Pure Country / Aug. 25, 1998 / Sony ✦✦✦✦
Sony Special Products' *Pure Country* is an effective sampler of Janie Fricke's country-pop work for Columbia Records in the '80s. In fact, in many ways it works as a hits compilation, since every one of the featured songs—"Down to My Last Broken Heart," "I'll Need Someone to Hold Me (When I Cry)," "Do Me With Love," "You Don't Know Love," "It Ain't Easy Bein' Easy," "He's a Heartache (Looking for a Place to Happen)," "Tell Me a Lie," "Let's Stop Talkin' About It," "Your Heart's Not In It"—were Top Ten country hits for Fricke. Because of that, *Pure Country* is more than just a good bargain for a budget-line collection—it's a good bargain in general. *—Stephen Thomas Erlewine*

Super Hits / Mar. 2, 1999 / Sony ✦✦✦
While it is hardly definitive, *Super Hits* is a solid compilation featuring ten of Janie Fricke's biggest hit singles. Usually, these kinds of collection skimp on actual hits, but that's not the case here, since the featured songs—"Down to My Last Broken Heart," "Don't Worry 'Bout Me Baby," "It Ain't Easy Bein' Easy," "He's a Heartache (Looking for a Place to Happen)," "Tell Me a Lie," "Let's Stop Talkin' About It," "Your Heart's Not In It," "You Don't Know Love," "She's Single Again" and "Always Have Always Will"—are all Top Five hits. That means this is a very useful compilation, since it offers most of the hits for a very affordable price. *—Stephen Thomas Erlewine*

● **Anthology** / Mar. 16, 1999 / Renaissance ✦✦✦✦✦
The most generous single-disc collection of Janie Fricke's late-'70s and 1980s chart hits, *Anthology* offers eight number-one country hits and 14 others. Fricke was a background vocalist on hundreds of sessions before becoming a solo artist, and her success as a background vocalist might explain her weakness as a lead singer: her voice is very professional, precise, and generic, lacking the character that makes so many great vocalists immediately identifiable, although she does have a slight Southern accent. Her music is slick and smooth pop-oriented country that recalls both Barbara Mandrell and Juice Newton. Certainly Fricke is a talented vocalist who has sold many records, but she has not forged a unique identity with her music, and consequently the real allure of these singles is in the songwriting rather than the uniqueness of the performances. *—Greg Adams*

Black & White/First Word in Memory / Nov. 9, 1999 / Collectables ✦✦✦✦
In 1999, Collectables released *Black & White/First Word in Memory*, which contained two complete albums—*Black & White* (1986, originally released on CBS) and *First Word in Memory* (1984, originally released on CBS)—by Janie Fricke on one compact disc. *—Jason Birchmeier*

Live at Billy Bob's Texas / Apr. 2, 2002 / Smith Music ✦✦✦

Kinky Friedman (Richard F. Friedman)

b. Oct. 31, 1944, Rio Duckworth, Palestine, TX
Songwriter, Vocals / Country Comedy, Outlaw Country
Who else could have written a country song about the Holocaust ("Ride 'Em Jewboy" about a human being kept in a cage as part of a circus ("Wild Man From Borneo"))? Outrageous and irreverent but nearly always thought-provoking, Kinky Friedman wrote and performed satirical country songs during the 1970s and has been hailed the Frank Zappa of country music. The son of a University of Texas professor who raised his children on the family ranch, Rio Duckworth, he was born Richard F. Friedman. He studied psychology in Texas and founded his first band while there. However, King Arthur & the Carrots—a group that poked fun at surf music—recorded only one single, in 1966. After graduation, Friedman served three years in the Peace Corps; he was stationed in Borneo, where he worked as an agricultural extension worker.

By 1971, he had founded his second band, Kinky Friedman & the Texas Jewboys. In keeping with the group's satirical songs, each member had a deliberately politically incorrect name: they called themselves Little Jewford, Big Nig, Panama Red, Rainbow Colors, and Snakebite Jacobs. Friedman got his break in 1973 thanks to Commander Cody, who contacted Vanguard Music on behalf of the acerbic young performer. That was the year he and his group made their debut album, *Sold American*, featuring John Hartford and Tompall Glaser. The title track, a bitter tale of a forgotten country singer dying an alcoholic death, barely made it onto the charts, but Friedman did attract enough attention to be invited to the *Grand Ole Opry*.

In 1974, he recorded an eponymously titled album for ABC Records. Produced by Los Angeles pop helmsman Steve Barri, the album dissolved whatever pure country listenership Friedman might have had but delighted his growing hardcore of fans with satirical pieces such as his response to anti-Semitism, "They Ain't Making Jews like Jesus Anymore." Along with the satires Friedman offered quieter sketches of American hard luck such as "Rapid City, South Dakota." In the mid-'70s, Friedman and his band began touring with Bob Dylan & the Rolling Thunder Revue. In 1976 he made his third album, *Lasso From El Paso*, featuring Dylan and Eric Clapton. The Texas Jewboys disbanded three years later, and Friedman moved to New York, where he often appeared at the Lone Star Cafe. In 1983, he released *Under the Double Ego* for Sunrise Records.

After that, Friedman turned primarily toward writing, although he continued to make occasional nightclub appearances. He has written for *Rolling Stone* and *Texas Monthly* magazines and, most famously, has become a writer of unique and outrageous mystery novels such as *Greenwich Killing Time*, *A Case of Lone Star*, and *The Mile High Club*. Equal parts whimsy and metaphysics, the books blur fiction and reality. They feature a Jewish country singer turned Greenwich Village private eye named Kinky Friedman, who sometimes returns to his native Texas; other characters are drawn from Friedman's circle of friends in both New York and Texas. Many of Friedman's songs of the 1970s and early '80s were collected on two CD compilations, *Old Testaments & New Revelations* (1992) and *From One Good American to Another* (1995). In 1999, the likes of Willie Nelson, Tom Waits, and Lyle Lovett covered Friedman's music on the tribute album *Pearls in the Snow: The Songs of Kinky Friedman*, and a second tribute volume was planned. In 2003, Friedman appeared in a nude, cigar-smoking triplicate on the cover of *the Dallas Observer* magazine, in a parody of the Dixie Chicks' nude *Entertainment Weekly* pose of that year. *—Sandra Brennan & James Manheim*

Sold American / 1973 / Vanguard ✦✦✦✦✦
Although Kinky Friedman has become better-known for his best-selling mystery novels than for his music, the country music renegade and self-proclaimed "Texas Jewboy" was one of the '70s' most iconoclastic and memorable performers. A singer/songwriter with a degree in psychology, a Peace Corps stint on his resumé, and a wicked sense of humor, Friedman was adept at raising either eyebrows or hackles with songs like "High on Jesus" and "Get Your Biscuits in the Oven and Your Buns in the Bed," but songs like "We Reserve the Right to Refuse Service to You" and "The Ballad of Charles Whitman" (about the military-trained sniper who shot and killed several people from the clock tower at the University of Texas while Friedman was a student there) show that he was more interested in smart alecky social commentary than cheap shocks and sensationalism. Indeed, the provocatively titled "Ride 'Em Jewboy" is actually a moving statement of Friedman's religious and cultural faith. The album's highlight, however, is the aching title track, the high point of Friedman's entire musical career. A sympathetic portrait of a down-and-out former country star dying on skid row, "Sold American" is a sad and lovely tune with an indelible chorus. Chuck Glaser's production throughout is low-key traditional (largely acoustic) country with a few folk and even fewer rock influences; Billy Swan, Norman Blake, and John Hartford are among the guests. This is by far Friedman's best album and a classic of '70s outlaw country. *—Stewart Mason*

Kinky Friedman / 1974 / Varese ✦✦✦
Willie Nelson, an inspired choice, was originally supposed to produce Kinky Friedman's second album, but after some unproductive sessions in Nashville, ABC-Dunhill pulled the plug and sent Friedman into a Los Angeles session with Steve Barri, a Dunhill staff producer whose history ran more toward the Grassroots, the Mamas & the Papas, and Tommy Roe. As Friedman writes in the liner notes of the 20th anniversary reissue on Varese Sarabande, he knew the album was in trouble when he looked up to the control room from the studio and saw Barri disinterestedly painting his fingernails during a vocal take. Obviously, Barri and Friedman were not meant to work together, and frankly, this album suffers as a consequence. Friedman's witty country songs too often end up, in Barri's hands, sounding like Three Dog Night. If one can ignore the poorly chosen and terribly dated production style, Friedman's songs this time out nearly equal those on his far superior debut, 1973's *Sold American*. Besides the usual satiric jibes, like "Before All Hell Breaks Loose" and "Somethin's Wrong With the Beaver," Friedman essays some gentler character sketches, like "Rapid City, South Dakota" and "Autograph." Friedman also honors his buddy and occasional bandmate Billy Swan by resurrecting Swan's "Lover Please," an early rock & roll hit for Clyde McPhatter. The album's two most famous tracks, though, are "Wild Man From Borneo," a sly tune inspired by Friedman's days in the Peace Corps in that country, and the anthemic "They Ain't Makin' Jews Like Jesus Anymore," a shaggy-dog story about a barroom encounter with a drunken racist. It's a shame about the production, but otherwise this is a classic of '70s outlaw country. *—Stewart Mason*

● **Lasso From El Paso** / 1976 / Varese ✦✦✦✦✦
Of the many albums that grew out of Bob Dylan's *Rolling Thunder Revue*, this must be the strangest. Friedman has a husky voice and an off-kilter sense of humor best captured on the live-from-the-revue track, "Sold American." Also notable for a version of the Bob Dylan outtake, "Catfish." *—William Ruhlmann*

Under the Double Ego / 1983 / Sunrise ♦♦♦

Old Testaments & New Revelations / 1992 / Fruit of the Tune ♦♦♦

Kinky Friedman, backed by his faithful combo the Texas Jewboys, bring old-time swing to Hollywood with plenty of satire on *Old Testaments & New Revelations*. Social satire from a Jewish perspective is Friedman's forte, and this generous live recording blends classics like "We Refuse the Right to Refuse Service to You" with a whole new set of barbed hooks. *—Roch Parisien*

From One Good American to Another / Oct. 1995 / Fruit of the Tune ♦♦♦

David Frizzell

b. Sep. 26, 1941, El Dorado, AR

Vocals / Traditional Country, Honky Tonk

Just like Hank Williams Jr. he's standing in the shadows of a very famous man, but David Frizzell became a country star in his own right during the '80s. The younger brother of country legend Lefty Frizzell, David was born September 26, 1941, in El Dorado, AR. At the age of 12, he hitchhiked to California to join Lefty, who added the youth to his show and persuaded Columbia to sign him in 1958. Nothing came of the deal, however, and David spent the '60s touring with his brother, recording for several minor labels and spending time in the Air Force. He returned to Columbia in 1970 and placed two singles on the country charts, including the Top 40 entry "I Just Can't Help Believing." (B. J. Thomas took it to the pop Top Ten the same year.)

Frizzell moved to Nashville a year later and recorded for the Cartwheel label. Just after he joined Buck Owens' *All American TV Show* in 1973, Frizzell signed a contract with Capitol and recorded two modest hits, "Words Don't Come Easy" and "Take Me One More Ride." After some mid-'70s recordings for RSO and MCA, he joined his younger brother Allen and Allen's wife Shelly West on a tour around the Southwest. David and West recorded some material, and their single "You're the Reason God Made Oklahoma" was included on Clint Eastwood's 1981 film *Any Which Way You Can*; it topped the country chart early that year. "A Texas State of Mind" hit number nine in June, and the duo closed out 1981 with "Husbands and Wives," a Top 20 hit.

The following year, Frizzell and West hit the Top Ten again on the strength of "Another Honky-Tonk Night on Broadway" and "I Just Came Here to Dance." They won numerous Duo of the Year awards beginning that year. Jump started by his duet success, Frizzell hit number one as a solo act in 1982 with "I'm Gonna Hire a Wino to Decorate Our Home," from *Family's Fine, But This One's All Mine*. His next two singles, "Lost My Baby Blues" and "Where Are You Spending Your Nights These Days," hit the Top Ten during 1982-1983. He recorded only one more Top 40 single, "A Million Light Beers Ago," but Frizzell and West had back-to-back hits in 1984: "Silent Partners" and "It's a Be Together Night." Frizzell continued to record during the '80s, for Nashville America, Compleat, and BFE. *—John Bush*

Carryin' on the Family Name / 1981 / Warner Bros. ♦♦♦

Family's Fine, But This One's All Mine / 1982 / Warner Bros. ♦♦♦

Featured is "I'm Gonna Hire a Wino to Decorate Our Home," a number-one country novelty that's made an even bigger splash in oldies rotation. *—Dan Cooper*

Our Best to You / 1982 / Viva ♦♦♦

On My Own Again / 1983 / Viva ♦♦♦♦

In Session / 1983 / Viva ♦♦♦

● **Golden Duets (W/Shelly West)** / 1984 / Viva ♦♦♦♦♦

"You're the Reason God Made Oklahoma" (the most majestic component of the Clint Eastwood movie *Any Which Way You Can*) spawned a run of duet hits by Frizzell and West. The significant ones, including "You're the Reason...," are all here. *—Dan Cooper*

My Life Is Just a Bridge / 1993 / RCA ♦♦♦

Best of the Best / Jan. 25, 2000 / Federal ♦♦♦

Best of the Best features a handful of David Frizzell's hits, including the duets he recorded with Shelly West, in the early to mid-'80s. "You're the Reason God Made Oklahoma," "I Just Came Here to Dance," and "I'm Gonna Hire a Wino to Decorate Our Home" are included along with a cover of his brother Lefty's signature tune, "Saginaw, Michigan." Even though this is a budget set, it's a bit skimpy at only ten tracks and does not include every hit that a casual fan would want. Until a proper Frizzell hits package is released, this will have to do. *—Al Campbell*

David Frizzell Sings Lefty's Greatest Hits / Aug. 8, 2000 / King ♦♦♦

Although the songs are very close to the originals, the bulk of the interpretations on *David Frizzell Sings Lefty's Greatest Hits* are enjoyable, but ultimately unnecessary. The ten tracks include "Saginaw, Michigan," "Always Late (With Your Kisses)," "If You've Got the Money I've Got the Time," "Long Black Veil," and an original composition written by Frizzell, the Lefty tribute "Lefty's Star." *—Al Campbell*

2001 / Apr. 17, 2001 / Nashville America ♦♦

2001 is the first major record release in a number of years from Lefty Frizzell's little brother. David Frizzell was actively involved from start to finish on this album, producing and writing or co-writing ten of the album's particularly traditional 12 tracks. He shares four convincing duets with partner Peggy Rains from Pryor, OK, including the customary but inviting "A Love That Might Have Been," one of the album's two songs not written by Frizzell. He sings mostly ballads, but a standout of this collection is the uptempo "I Ain't Going If There Ain't No Hank," about a guy who won't go dancing, to dinner, or even up to heaven if they "don't have Hank and Lefty too." With his own distinctive brand of country tradition, Frizzell rounds out the album with the song that made him a household name in the '80s—the seemly remake of the venomous "I'm Gonna Hire a Wino to Decorate Our Home." *—Maria Konicki Dinoia*

Lefty Frizzell (William Orville Frizzell)

b. Mar. 31, 1928, Corsicana, TX, **d.** Jul. 19, 1975, Nashville, TN

Guitar, Songwriter, Vocals / Traditional Country, Honky Tonk

Lefty Frizzell was the definitive honky tonk singer, the vocalist that set the style for generations of vocalists that followed him. Frizzell smoothed out the rough edges of honky tonk by singing longer, flowing phrases—essentially, he made honky tonk more acceptable for the mainstream without losing its gritty, barroom roots. In the process, he changed the way country vocalists sang forever. From George Jones, Merle Haggard, and Willie Nelson to George Strait, John Anderson, Randy Travis, and Keith Whitley, hundreds of artists have emulated and expanded Lefty's innovations. Frizzell's singing became the foundation of how hard country should be sung.

Despite his influence, there was a time when Lefty wasn't regarded as one of country's definitive artists. Unlike Hank Williams—the only contemporary of Lefty that had greater influence—he didn't die young, leaving behind a romantic legend. After his popularity peaked in the early and mid-'50s, Frizzell continued to record, without having much success. However, his recordings continued to reach new listeners and his reputation was restored by the new traditionalists of the '80s, nearly ten years after Lefty's death. Lefty (born William Orville Frizzell) was born in Corsicana, TX, in 1928, a son of an oiler; he was the first of eight children. During his childhood, his family moved to El Dorado, AR. As a child he was called Sonny, but his nickname changed to Lefty when he was 14, because he won a schoolyard fight; it was later suggested that he earned his nickname after winning a Golden Gloves boxing match, but that was eventually proven to be a hatched publicity stunt by his record company. Initially, Lefty was attracted to music through his parents' Jimmie Rodgers records. He began singing professionally before he was a teenager, landing a regular spot on KELD El Dorado.

Frizzell spent his teenage years playing throughout the region, singing on radio shows, in nightclubs, for dances, and in talent contests. He traveled throughout the South, playing in Arkansas, Texas, New Mexico, and even Las Vegas. During this time, he was refining his style, drawing from influences like Rodgers, Ernest Tubb, and Ted Daffan. Lefty's career was going fine until he was arrested in the mid-'40s, serving a jail sentence for statutory rape. Frizzell's run-in with the law led him away from music, as he temporarily worked in the oil fields with his father. However, his time as an oiler was brief and he was soon performing in clubs again. By 1950, he had landed a regular job at the Texas club Ace of Clubs, where he developed a dedicated following of fans. At one of his concerts at the Ace of Clubs he caught the attention of Jim Beck, the owner of a local recording studio. Beck recorded music for several major record labels, and he also had connections within the publishing industry. Impressed with Lefty's performance, he invited the singer to make some demos at the studio.

In April of 1950, Frizzell cut several demos of his original songs, including a new song called "If You've Got the Money, I've Got the Time," which Beck took to Nashville. Beck intended to pitch the song to Little Jimmy Dickens, but Dickens disliked the song. However, Columbia record producer Don Law heard the tape and liked Frizzell's voice. After hearing Lefty live in concert, Law signed the singer to Columbia; within a few months, he had his first recording session. "If You've Got the Money, I've Got the Time," Lefty's first single, climbed to number one upon its release. It was a huge hit—its B-side, "I Love You a Thousand Ways," even hit number one—with other artists hurrying into the studio to cut their own versions; over 40 performers wound up recording the song. Within 17 days of the single's release, Columbia had Frizzell record another single. The result, "Look What Thoughts Will Do"/"Shine, Shave, Shower (It's Saturday)," wasn't as big a hit, but it did reach the Top Ten.

By now, the Lefty Frizzell sound was being perfected by the vocalist and Law. Frizzell was working with a core group of Dallas-based studio musicians, highlighted by pianist Madge Sutee. In the beginning of 1951, he formed the Western Cherokees, which was led by Blackie Crawford. Soon, the Western Cherokees became his primary band for both live and recording situations. Lefty was in the studio frequently, recording singles. His third single, "I Want to Be With You Always," was number one for 11 weeks, and its follow-up, "Always Late (With Your Kisses)," spent 12 weeks at number one. At one point in early 1951, he had a total of four songs in the country Top Ten, setting a record that was never broken. Frizzell was a popular concert attraction, playing shows with the *Louisiana Hayride* and the *Grand Ole Opry*. He had three more Top Ten hits in 1951—"Mom and Dad's Waltz," "Travelin' Blues," and the number one "Give Me More, More, More (Of Your Kisses)."

The hits continued throughout 1952, as "How Long Will It Take (To Stop Loving You)," "Don't Stay Away (Till Love Grows Cold)," "Forever (And Always)," and "I'm an Old, Old Man (Tryin' to Live While I Can)" all went to the Top Ten. Even though he was at the peak of his popularity, things began to unravel for Lefty behind the scenes. Frizzell fired both his manager and his band. He joined the *Grand Ole Opry*, but he decided he didn't like it and left almost immediately. Lefty was earning a lot of money but was spending nearly all of it. He worked with Wayne Raney, but the sessions were a failure. In early 1953, he moved from Texas to Los Angeles, where he got a regular job on *Town Hall Party*. That year, he had only one hit, the Top Ten "(Honey, Baby, Hurry!) Bring Your Sweet Self Back to Me."

Early in 1954, he reached the Top Ten with "Run 'Em Off," but it would be his last Top Ten record for five years. During the mid-'50s, Frizzell felt burned out and didn't have the energy to invest in his career. He had a total of two hits between 1954 and 1959—"I Love You Mostly" in 1955, "Cigarettes and Coffee Blues"—because he decided to stop recording. Lefty was frustrated that Columbia wasn't releasing what he believed to be his best material, so he simply stopped writing and recording songs. However, he did tour sporadically, occasionally with his brother, David Frizzell. Deciding it was time for a change, he began working with Jim Denny's Nashville-based Cedarwood publishing company in 1959. Cedarwood gave him "The Long Black Veil," a song written by Danny Dill and Marijohn Wilkin that had overt folk music influences. Lefty recorded the song, and it became a surprise Top Ten hit in the summer of 1959. Encouraged by its success, Frizzell moved to Nashville in 1961, after *Town Hall Party* closed in 1960. He began touring and recording at a more rapid rate, although it only resulted in a couple of minor hits. Lefty's last big hit arrived early in 1964, when "Saginaw, Michigan" climbed to number one and spent four weeks on the top of the charts. After that, he came close to the Top Ten with 1965's "She's Gone Gone Gone," but he usually struggled to have any of his songs break the Top 20 for the next decade.

Frizzell didn't stop recording, but he did develop a debilitating alcohol problem that came to plague him throughout the late '60s and '70s. However, alcohol wasn't the only thing holding his career back—Columbia was only releasing handfuls of albums and singles, though Lefty was recording an abundance of material. Since his records weren't as successful, he drastically cut back the number of concerts he performed. In 1968, he cut some songs with June Stearns under the name Agnes & Orville, but none of the tracks became hits. The lack of success helped him sink deeper into alcoholism. In 1972, Lefty left Columbia, signing with ABC Records. Though the change in labels helped revitalize him artistically, he didn't sell that many more records. However, he did have the enthusiasm to record albums, as well as play concerts and television shows.

Frizzell's alcohol addiction worsened and he developed high blood pressure, but he wouldn't take the medication because he thought it would interfere with his drinking. As a result, he looked older than his 47 years when he died of a stroke in 1975. Years of mediocre and mis-marketed records had diminished Lefty's reputation, but after his death, a new generation of artists hailed him as an influence and an idol. Merle Haggard, Willie Nelson, and George Jones had all sung his praises before, but in the mid '80s, the kind words of George Strait and Randy Travis were supported by a series of reissues, beginning with Bear Family's 14-LP set, *His Life His Music* (later replaced by the 12-CD *Life's Like Poetry*). In 1982, he was inducted into the Country Music Hall of Fame, but the greatest testament to his music remains the fact that his voice can be heard in every hard country singer that followed. —*Stephen Thomas Erlewine*

Songs of Jimmie Rodgers / 1960 / Koch ♦♦♦♦♦

Originally, albums were nothing more than collections of 78-rpm singles, and Lefty cut eight sides for this Columbia-issued Jimmie Rodgers tribute album, one of the first of its kind. Those eight sides, plus four bonus sides, make up this reissue, which sports the original ten-inch LP's cover art and back cover. Though Lefty was in top form back in 1951, the later tracks from 1953 are no less terrific. Another chunk of the man's greatness. —*Cub Koda*

Saginaw, Michigan / 1964 / Columbia ♦♦♦♦

The career of this great country singer in some ways went in the opposite manner of other performers who came out of the honky tonk tradition. Usually the earlier recordings of this genre of country singers are the really good ones, with later productions tending to be saturated with the background choruses, string sections, and downplayed picking which passed for fancy productions once Nashville started going Pop like the weasel. However, in the case of Frizzell, this earlier album is one of the ones with somewhat excessive production, and the later recordings sport a more toned-down bar band sound, heavy on the barrelhouse piano. Not that the production here is really that obtrusive. Certainly other country singers have fallen much more the victim to their background singers than this man, who would sound good with a steam hammer and the entire roller-skating staff of a drive-in diner trying to back him up. The title song was of course a huge hit, and if there was ever a town that is too dull to deserve such a great song, "Saginaw, Michigan" would be it. "There's No Food in This House" is a chillingly understated Merle Kilgore number, the singer admitting that he "used to ask what there was for supper, now I don't ask anymore." The conclusion of the song involving a delivery of food from the good-hearted folks at a nearby church may rub some cynical listeners the wrong way. "Hello to Him" is an out and out classic, one of the best songs the artist ever recorded, while the jumping "James River" even sports a banjo in the arrangement, despite this instrument having been practically banned from Nashville recording studios. The best of this material is typical Lefty Frizzell—in other words, some of the best country music around. —*Eugene Chadbourne*

Lefty Frizzell's Country Favorites / 1966 / Columbia ♦♦♦♦

With a title such as this, the listener might expect a greatest-hits collection, and several repackagings emphasizing that kind of look hasn't helped clear up the confusion. Any collection by this uniquely smooth and expressive country singer will usually contain a few songs that developed into hits and/or country standards, such is the majesty of Frizzell, and this album is no exception. Beginning with a gorgeous vocal on "A King Without a Queen," the program continues through the rollicking "My Baby's Just Like Money," fat with honky tonk piano, and even counting in with a riff that Nina Simone also put to good use, among others. Other great numbers include "Run 'Em Off" and "Give Me More, More, More," which is a love song and not a description of merger and sell-off business tactics in the '80s. Although this is a singer who could easily hold interest without any backup musicians, it would have been nice to at least credit the session players who add so many nice touches, especially the lead guitar and somewhat underrecorded steel guitar. The abbreviated playing time might not strike buyers as much of a bargain, as the entire album could have fit on one side of the vinyl. —*Eugene Chadbourne*

Lefty Frizzell's Greatest Hits / 1966 / Columbia ♦♦

Lefty Frizzell's Greatest Hits presents a selection of Frizzell's best-known songs in re-recorded or overdubbed versions, which are decidedly inferior to the originals. Stick with Rhino's *The Best of Lefty Frizzell*. —*Stephen Thomas Erlewine*

The Legendary Last Sessions / 1986 / MCA ♦♦♦♦

Lefty Frizzell seemed poised for a lasting commercial resurgence after his 1964 hit "Saginaw, Michigan," but he spent the remainder of the '60s re-recording many of his early hits and watching single after single peak before reaching the country Top 40. By 1973, his 20-year association with Columbia records was finished and ABC-Paramount, a label that gave a number of aging legends second chances, signed Lefty and provided him with the opportunity to continue cranking out minor hits. "Lucky Arms" and "I Never Go

Around Mirrors" became his biggest hits in nearly a decade, but neither made the Top 20. Frizzell's ABC sides are fine recordings; Lefty sounds great, and there is a contemplative quality to some of these songs and performances that is deeply satisfying. *Legendary Last Sessions*, a mid-'80s LP, boasts three more tracks than *That's the Way Love Goes: The Final Recordings of Lefty Frizzell*, a 1996 CD that covers the same territory, and is in fact only a few songs shy of offering his complete ABC recordings. While they are not his most essential or representative, the twilight recordings of Lefty Frizzell are well worth hearing. —*Greg Adams*

Lefty's 20 Golden Hits / 1988 / TeeVee ♦♦

A curious collection of Lefty from his early Columbia period all the way into later Nashville recordings, literally swamped in Nashville production. On the early honky tonkers like "Give Me More, More, More of Your Kisses," "How Long Will It Take to Stop Loving You," "Look What Thoughts Will Do," and "Don't Stay Away," his message comes through loud and clear. The later tracks range from reflective acoustic turns to lighter fare and recuts of early hits drenched in the Nashville trappings of the time. If you already have a *real* Lefty best-of, this is an OK addition, but it's sure no first-time/one-time purchase, not by a long shot. —*Cub Koda*

American Originals / 1990 / Columbia ♦♦♦♦♦

Released in 1990, the Lefty Frizzell installment of *American Originals* is, like other editions in the series, far too short at only ten songs, and it makes that tight running time by leaving behind such major items as "If You've Got the Money, I've Got the Time." There are some major songs here—"Saginaw, Michigan," "The Long Black Veil," "Always Late (With Your Kisses)," "Look What Thoughts Will Do"—enough to make it a good sampler, but it shouldn't by any means be thought of as a perfect introduction, particularly since only a year later it was trumped by Rhino's excellent 18-track collection *The Best of Lefty Frizzell*, which remains the best concise overview and introduction to this country giant. —*Stephen Thomas Erlewine*

★ The Best of Lefty Frizzell / 1991 / Rhino ♦♦♦♦♦

Rhino's 18-track compilation *The Best of Lefty Frizzell* set the gold standard for Frizzell collections upon its release in 1991 and remains an excellent, succinct summary of his prime. It has since been surpassed in terms of comprehensiveness by Columbia/Legacy's 1997 double-disc set *Look What Thoughts Will Do*, which contained 34 songs, including every one that's on this disc, so the serious listener may prefer that to this relatively shorter collection, simply because it digs deeper into one of the richest catalogs in country music. Nevertheless, the Rhino disc may be a more effective introduction for neophytes, since it boils down his catalog to the 18 essentials, offering ample proof of Frizzell's genius as a songwriter and singer, including such classics as "If You've Got the Money I've Got the Time," "Look What Thoughts Will Do," "Always Late (With Your Kisses)," "The Long Black Veil," and "Saginaw, Michigan." Frizzell has often been imitated as a singer but never quite duplicated, and the music here is at the heart of his legend. It's necessary for any country collection. —*Stephen Thomas Erlewine*

Life's Like Poetry / 1992 / Bear Family ♦♦♦♦♦

Life's Like Poetry is a gigantic, 12-disc box set that includes all of Lefty Frizzell's recordings for Columbia and ABC, plus early demos, a session with Jay Miller, and several radio transcriptions—everything he recorded between 1950 and 1975. Certainly, the box is designed for collectors—no one but the most devoted fan could listen to all 330 tracks. Though all of his classic material is included, there is also a fair share of mediocre material, including some ill-advised attempts at country-pop. Nevertheless, there are gems sprinkled throughout the collection and it offers proof of his far-reaching talents and influence, as well as demonstrating that several of Lefty's later recordings were as worthwhile as his early singles. For any serious fan, it is an indispensible collection. —*Stephen Thomas Erlewine*

☆ That's the Way Love Goes: The Final Recordings of Lefty Frizzell / Oct. 22, 1996 / Varese ♦♦♦♦♦

After two decades, Columbia Records dropped Lefty Frizzell in 1972, a move that, according to all reports, hit the singer very hard. He signed with ABC by the end of the year, and, over the next two years cut 23 songs with producer Don Gant, enough material for two albums. Varese's 1996 compilation *That's the Way Love Goes: The Final Recordings of Lefty Frizzell* offers a 16-track overview of those ABC recordings, including the six minor hits he had for the label. By this point, Frizzell had gone nearly a decade without a major hit; his last was "Saginaw, Michigan" in early 1964, and he was best-known among country fans as a legend, one who was particularly influential on Merle Haggard (who used Frizzell's singing as the template for his own style). Frizzell had fallen on hard times; in addition to being dropped from his longtime home, he had descended into alcoholism and was divorcing his wife. Such sorrow makes for great country music, and the music he made for ABC was indeed great. It's not fair to compare it to his classic Columbia hits from the '50s—after all, that was groundbreaking work, and it's hard to break ground again—but as latter-day recordings go, it's not just good work, it's often great, standing proudly alongside the work of a younger Frizzell. What makes this music especially compelling is that it is indeed the work of an older Frizzell and all of the sorrow and loss is etched on his voice, giving this music depth even on numbers that don't necessarily have it on their own. Fortunately, he recorded excellent material throughout his time at ABC, highlighted by "That's the Way Love Goes" and the heartbreaking "I Never Go Around Mirrors" (both co-written by Frizzell with Sanger D. Schafer), Jerry Jeff Walker and Jimmy Buffett's "Railroad Lady," a revival of his old hit "I Love You a Thousand Ways," and Merle Haggard's moving "Life's Like Poetry." Gant's production is warm, relaxed, and mellow, faithful to Frizzell's pure country sound but slyly updated for '70s country radio, and it suits Frizzell's weary, introspective readings. It is music that has aged very well indeed, and while this may leave seven songs behind on LP, they can be heard on Bear Family's complete *Life's Like Poetry* set. This distills these recordings to the 16 best and provides a wonderful, near essential overview of the final days of a legend. *—Stephen Thomas Erlewine*

★ **Look What Thoughts Will Do** / Jan. 28, 1997 / Columbia/Legacy ♦♦♦♦♦
Look What Thoughts Will Do is a double-disc set covering all of Lefty's biggest hits ("If You've Got the Money I've Got the Time," "I Love You a Thousand Ways," "I Want to Be With You Always," "Always Late (With Your Kisses)," "Give Me More, More More (Of Your Kisses)," "Run 'Em Off," "The Long Black Veil," "Saginaw, Michigan"), plus several lesser-known singles, B-sides, and album tracks. Essentially, the compilation is an expanded version of Rhino's excellent single-disc *The Best of Lefty Frizzell*, featuring all of that disc's 18 tracks. What makes *Look What Thoughts Will Do* exciting for fans who already have the older compilation is the wealth of gems that haven't made it to compact disc in the past. For neophytes, the double disc is an excellent introduction, since it draws a full portrait of one of the greatest honky tonk singers to ever live. Casual listeners will want to stick with the Rhino compilation, but *Look What Thoughts Will Do* is the definitive overview of Frizzell's heyday, making it an essential addition to any serious country collection. *—Stephen Thomas Erlewine*

Steven Fromholz

b. Jun. 8, 1945, Temple, TX
Guitar, Vocals / Country-Rock, Folk-Rock, Singer/Songwriter
Though he's not widely known outside of a small cult audience, Steven Fromholz is an enormously respected songwriter among fans of progressive Texas country. Fromholz has cut his own records and appeared several times on *Austin City Limits*, but chiefly made his name by supplying other artists with material—artists such as Willie Nelson, John Denver, Jerry Jeff Walker, Michael Martin Murphey, and Hoyt Axton. Plus, later in the '90s, Lyle Lovett recorded two of Fromholz' best-loved songs, "Bears" and "Texas Trilogy," on his all-covers album *Step Inside This House*. Born in Temple, TX, on June 8, 1945, Fromholz's family frequently moved around during his childhood. During his first year at North Texas State University, he met Michael Martin Murphey and the two formed the Dallas County Jug Band; Fromholz later became a member of the Michael Murphey Trio before drifting out of school. He joined the Navy for a spell and upon his release in 1968, he moved to Colorado, where he met singer/songwriter Dan McCrimmon. They teamed up as the Western folk duo Frummox and recorded an album called *Here to There* for the Probe subsidiary of then major label ABC. It went nowhere at the time, although it gradually became something of a legend around the Texas/Colorado area and remains a highly prized (and pricey) collector's item on vinyl.

Frummox disbanded in 1971 over differences in musical direction and Fromholz was invited out on the road by his friend Stephen Stills, who was touring with his enormously eclectic all-star outfit Manassas. After about six months, however, Fromholz quit and returned home in poor health and tired of the tour's rampant ego battles and cocaine use. He had another connection, however, in former Monkee Michael Nesmith, who had become fascinated with country-rock and was busy scouting artists for his progressive-minded Countryside label. Fromholz recorded the single "Sweet Janey" for Countryside and also completed the full-length *How Long Is the Road to Kentucky* in 1973; unfortunately, two days before its scheduled release, Countryside lost its distribution arrangement with Elektra and the record remains in the vaults to this day. Frustrated with his run of bad luck, Fromholz moved from Colorado to Austin, hoping to find regular gigs on the developing progressive country.

Fromholz made a name for himself around Austin with his witty, engaging live performances and eventually landed a major-label deal with Capitol. His first solo album to see the light of day, wryly titled *A Rumor in My Own Time*, appeared in 1976 featuring backing musicians like John Sebastian, Doug Dillard, and members of Jerry Jeff Walker's Lost Gonzo Band. The LP probably best represents Fromholz' aesthetic and also supplied his only major hit—not for himself, but for Willie Nelson, who recorded the *Rumor* track "I'd Have to Be Crazy" on *The Sound in Your Mind*, the follow-up to his star-making *The Red Headed Stranger*. Featuring Fromholz on backing vocals, "I'd Have to Be Crazy" nearly topped the country charts, marking the only true commercial success of Fromholz's career. Hoping to give Fromholz's own career a similar breakthrough, Capitol sent him to L.A. to record the mellow, slicker-sounding follow-up *Frolicking in the Myth* in 1977. That same year, Fromholz appeared in the film *Outlaw Blues*, a depiction of the Austin scene starring Peter Fonda and Susan St. James. None of it helped his record sales and after Capitol dropped him, Fromholz cut *Jus' Playin' Along* in 1978 on Willie Nelson's own Lone Star label.

Frustrated with the music business, Fromholz formed his own Felicity Records label to give himself a musical outlet free from outside pressures; its inaugural release was *Fromholz Live!* in 1979. To pay the bills, Fromholz became the featured entertainer on several three-day white-water rafting trips in 1980 and liked it so much that he trained to become a guide, a side career he still holds. Sporadic releases on Felicity followed 1982's *Frummox II*, 1986's *Love Songs*, and 1991's *Everybody's Goin' on the Road* (the latter cut with the Almost Brothers). In the meantime, Fromholz was also bitten by the acting bug and became a regular featured player at Austin's local Live Oak theater; in 1992, the theater also staged Fromholz's original play *Bosque County, Texas*, based on his classic three-song suite "Texas Trilogy" (which dated all the way back to his Frummox days). In 1995, Fromholz cut an album for Jerry Jeff Walker's Tried and True label, titled *The Old Fart in the Mirror*. Three years later, he reunited with Frummox partner McCrimmon at the Kerrville Folk Festival and Lyle Lovett recorded "Bears" (from *A Rumor in My Own Time*) and the entirety of "Texas Trilogy" on his double-disc *Step Inside This House* album. Two new releases were issued in 2001 on Felicity: *A Guest in Your Heart* and *Live at Anderson Fair*, the latter recorded at the legendary Houston folk club. In addition to acting and white-water rafting, Fromholz continues to perform as often as possible around Texas and the Southwest. *—Steve Huey*

● **Frommox** / 1969 / Probe ♦♦♦♦♦

A Rumor in My Own Time / 1976 / Capitol ♦♦♦

Frolicking in the Myth / 1977 / Capitol ♦♦♦

Outlaw Blues / 1977 / Capitol ♦♦♦

● **Come on Down to Texas for Awhile: The Anthology 1969–1991** / Aug. 14, 2001 / Raven ♦♦♦♦♦
Steven Fromholz is one of Texas' most beloved songwriters whose career now spans four decades. Australia's Raven label specializes in re-issuing American music either in anthology or two-fer form with nice booklets, new liner notes, and photos. *Come on Down to Texas for Awhile* covers Fromholz's material from 1969 through his 1991 album *Everybody's Goin' on the Road*—though he continued to write and record in the 21st century. The songwriter is best known for his most often covered suite, "Texas Triology," and it opens the set here, sweeping to "Man With the Big Hat" and "Song for Stephen Stills," from his debut album *Here to There*. The next couple of tracks, "Blue Lines on White Linen" and the hilarious "Bears," come from his most consistent album, *A Rumor in My Own Time*. But in a sense, that's it. Admittedly, Fromholz is an acquired taste and fans of his will find their own reasons for liking or disliking this compilation based on what was left off in favor of something else. But for the rest—including those who became aware of him in the book *The Improbable Rise of Redneck Rock*, there is nothing but mystery. Fromholz does not have the storytelling ability of a Hoyt Axton, Tom T. Hall, or fellow Texans such as Guy Clark (at his best, anyway), Billy Joe Shaver, or Townes Van Zandt. He's not a great singer and many of his lyrics are, well, corny. These songs begin to resonate as one overly long chapter in a novel that never reveals its characters; and after a while, it becomes revealing that unlike other artists, Fromholz never developed his craft beyond a certain level. Certainly, as witnessed with Lyle Lovett and Robert Earl Keen, this isn't a problem for some people who want their heroes never to change. That's what you get here from the first track to the last, a songwriter with a particular gift who has chosen for whatever reason not to expand its context. *—Thom Jurek*

Robbie Fulks

b. Mar. 25, 1963
Guitar, Vocals / Singer/Songwriter, Alternative Country, Neo-Traditionalist Country, Roots Rock, Neo-Traditional Folk, Adult Alternative Pop/Rock
Singer/songwriter Robbie Fulks was one of the more heralded talents in the alternative country movement, displaying an offbeat, sometimes dark sense of humor in many of his best moments. As time passed, Fulks moved away from the country twang of his early work and into a crunchier roots rock hybrid. Fulks divided his childhood between Pennsylvania, Virginia, and North Carolina, and received his schooling at Columbia University. He moved to Chicago in 1983, and first served as vocalist and guitarist in bluegrass band the Special Consensus, appearing on their Grammy-nominated 1989 album *A Hole in My Heart*. He later performed in the musical revue *Woody Guthrie's American Song*, and formed his own rock band, the Trailer Trash Revue, with whom he cut a locally popular single, "Little King" b/w "Jean Arthur."

Fulks got his first significant exposure via Bloodshot Records' 1994 compilation *Insurgent Country, Vol. 1: For a Life of Sin*, which included his track "Cigarette State"; the 1995 follow-up, *Insurgent Country, Vol. 2: Hell Bent*, featured Fulks' "She Took a Lot of Pills (And Died)." Both cuts were produced by Steve Albini, who also helmed Fulks' Bloodshot debut, *Country Love Songs*, in 1996. The album received highly positive reviews, and featured backing from roots rockers the Skeletons, as well as former Buck Owens steel guitarist Tom Brumley. The follow-up, *South Mouth*, took a similarly retro-minded approach, drawing from classic honky tonk and Bakersfield country. With a growing cult reputation, Fulks earned a major-label shot with Geffen, but many critics felt that his 1998 label debut, *Let's Kill Saturday Night*, undermined the organic strengths of his previous work with overly slick roots rock production. Fulks returned to Bloodshot for the bleak follow-up, 2001's *Couples in Trouble*, a more creatively successful foray into roots rock. He followed it up later that year with *13 Hillbilly Giants*, a covers collection that spotlighted lesser-known songs from country's earlier days. *—Steve Huey*

● **Country Love Songs** / 1996 / Bloodshot ♦♦♦♦
Robbie Fulks is cleverly twisted, deliciously irreverent, and one of the best of the new country singer/songwriters. Musically, *Country Love Songs* supplies plenty of hardcore, bottle-tippin', honky tonk country, with a '50s production that sounds like it's supposed to be there. Fulks writes and sings country music that bears little or no resemblance to what dominates the airwaves; rather, his material harks back to an era when humor and dark subject matter shared the same page of a writer's composition book. Paying homage to the classic Bakersfield sound, with former Buckeroo Tom Brumley shining on pedal steel, Fulks delivers "The Buck Starts Here," which just might be the best country song since "He Stopped Loving Her Today." Lyrically, Fulks can travel some pretty spooky highways, as in the descriptive ballad "Barely Human," a drinking song that's as tortured as they get, with the song's character "barely human from twilight till dawn." Other strong tracks include the saga of an aging movie starlet who loses it in "She Took a Lot of Pills (And Died)"—which first appeared on the second volume of the label's *Insurgent Country* compilations—and the swingin' "Every Kind of Music But Country." *—Jack Leaver*

South Mouth / Oct. 7, 1997 / Bloodshot ♦♦♦
Fulks uses a backing musician cavalcade on each track in this exploration of "the dark side of country music." Not strictly downbeat, there is plenty of humor here, too ("I Told Her Lies," etc.). Especially noteworthy are the steel guitar players (Steve Byam and Buck Owens' Tom Brumley) and the solid bass guitar from Lou Whitney of the Skeletons. These arrangements, bolstered by a mob of electric and acoustic guitarists, make for the salient entertainment on this disc. Fulks is no Hank Williams, in that Fulks can't often hold your attention with merely his material, voice, and guitar. However, the variety on this disc, from ballads like "Forgotten but Not Gone" to real insurgency like "F*ck This Town," and the rich instrumentation make it a fine contribution to alternative country music. *—Thomas Schulte*

Let's Kill Saturday Night / Sep. 15, 1998 / Geffen ✦✦✦
Anyone who heard Robbie Fulks' first two independent albums, *Country Love Songs* and *South Mouth*, would doubtless have agreed he deserved wider exposure than he'd received. But while his first (and only) album for Geffen, *Let's Kill Saturday Night*, is hardly the most egregious example of the Major Label Debut Gone Wrong, at very least it sounds like a large-scale miscalculation that doesn't play to Fulks' strengths. Much of *Let's Kill Saturday Night* downplays his country influences in favor of a harder, rock-styled approach, but while it's easy to imagine Fulks making a good roots rock album (his work with the Skeletons on his pervious discs point the way), Rick Will's production here is intrusively slick and bombastic most of the time; the crashing guitars and booming drums on "Caroline" and "She Must Think I Like Poetry" have been processed within an inch of their lives and all but drown out the artist's vocals, and the guitar/keyboard arrangement of the title cut turns a charging rocker into a cut-rate Bruce Springsteen parody. Far more surprisingly, some of the his material is not up to his usual standards; "God Isn't Real" is smug and self-satisfied when it means to be bitterly witty, and "Take Me to the Paradise" is a neo-Mark Eitzel character study that ultimately goes nowhere. The shame of it is there are a few cuts on *Let's Kill Saturday Night* that suggest how good the album could have been in more sympathetic hands; the spare and understated "Night Accident" and "Bethelridge" are both subtle and superb, and "Can't Win for Losing You" is a top-shelf Buck Owens-style twanger. Geffen was swallowed up in a corporate merger shortly after *Let's Kill Saturday Night* was released, which put paid to the album's commercial prospects and sent Fulks back to the indies, which may have been just as well—it's hardly the sort of calling card Robbie Fulks deserved, and his 2001 album *Couples in Trouble* proved he had far better ideas of his own about how to direct his rock influences. *—Mark Deming*

The Very Best of Robbie Fulks / Jan. 18, 2000 / Bloodshot ✦✦✦✦
Indicative of Fulks' sly sense of humor, *The Very Best of Robbie Fulks* is nothing of the sort, but a collection of tracks culled from EPs, promos, limited release 45s, soundtracks, and various obscure compilations. While much of the material is probably meant to be a little more fun than serious, with Fulks adding humorous self-effacing humor in the liner notes, there is some truly first-rate material here. The very strong country ballad "I Just Want to Meet the Man," and the frantic mock rockabilly of "Roots Rock Weirdoes" make for very entertaining listening. "Parallel Bars," a nice duet with Kelly Willis, and the catchy straightforward rock of "Wedding of the Bugs" also should not be missed. "That Bangle Girl," which Fulks mentions as being a personal favorite, is an absolutely essential piece of sharp country-rock bliss that ranks well with anything he's ever written. While everything here may not always be in the best taste, the rather low-brow "White Man's Bourbon" comes to mind, the material is generally consistent enough for it to be possible that a few first-time listeners could mistake this for an actual greatest hits collection. *—Matt Fink*

Couples in Trouble / Aug. 21, 2001 / Bloodshot ✦✦✦✦
Robbie Fulks is certainly one of the best songwriters to emerge from the fertile Chicago alt-country scene, but it didn't take long for Fulks to make clear that his creative ambitions went far beyond the clever and cynical retro-twang of his debut album *Country Love Songs*. Fulks' first (and only) album for Geffen, *Let's Kill Saturday Night*, found him moving away from explicitly country-accented material in favor of high-bombast roots rock that unfortunately sounded like a deliberate effort to dumb down his material in hopes of scoring a hit. *Let's Kill Saturday Night* was released shortly before Geffen was swallowed up in a corporate merger, and the album died before it ever had a real chance in the marketplace. Left to his own devices (and recording for his own label), *Couples in Trouble* was Robbie Fulks' first album of new material since that last failed attempt, and while fans hoping for more stuff like "Tears Only Run One Way" or "She Took a Lot of Pills (And Died)" will be disappointed to learn this album offers practically nothing in the way of a straight (or twisted) country song, it's a far stronger, more ambitious, and more satisfying exploration of the rock and pop sides of Fulks' musical mind than anything he's released to date. *Couples in Trouble* also offers little in the way of laughs, presenting a fascinating but unrelentingly grim series of vignettes about human relationships gone wrong in a variety of ugly ways; "Real Money" and "Anything for Love" pack the edgy menace of a Jim Thompson novel set to music, "Brenda's New Stepfather" is a truly creepy tale of a teenage girl at the mercy of her mom's lecherous new husband (made all the more troubling by the jazzy swagger of the music), "My Tormentor" is a quietly desperate story of a marriage falling to pieces, and the closest thing to a cheerful uptempo number, "Mad at a Girl," is an old-school R&B throwback about a guy who, at least for the moment, has decided no one is going to let him forget he hates his significant other. Fulks produced this set himself, and the results are far more adventurous and sonically diverse than *Let's Kill Saturday Night* at a fraction of the budget; this is the most impressive bit of record-making Fulks has managed to date, and suggests he could have a solid career as a producer if he wants (he's also at the top of his game as a vocalist, never overplaying his hand on material that could easily seem melodramatic). If there's a criticism to be made of *Couples in Trouble*, it's that the album is a bit cold around the heart, but that's also probably the point; it's been said that the heart goes where it will, and on this album the human heart follows a dozen blind alleys into dangerous places. It ain't always pretty, but it's compelling listening and truly fine music. *—Mark Deming*

13 Hillbilly Giants / Nov. 6, 2001 / Bloodshot ✦✦✦
Many will interpret *13 Hillbilly Giants* as Robbie Fulks' return to the alternative country fold after an experiment or two in pop and rock. And what better way to return than to record 13 classic, if lesser-known, country music songs? The simple arrangements, straight from a two-track tape, give songs like Frankie Miller's "Family Man" a natural feel. Equally uncomplicated is Fulks' production, mixing fiddles, mandolins, and dobros to the left and right channels and leaving his voice front and center. The material runs the gauntlet, from drinking songs like Bill Anderson's "Cocktails" to heart-wrenching weepers like Dolly Parton's "Jeannie's Afraid of the Dark." Fulks proves quite versatile vocally, though he perhaps gets carried away with a crying jag in "I Want to Be Mama'D" and the comic histrionics in "Knot Hole." There's a lovely, sad version of "Bury the Bottle With Me," the story of a man who recounts his hell-bent tale as he looks over his own grave, and a marvelous take on the lust-driven ballad "Burn on Love Fire." It should also be mentioned that Donna Fulks offers fine harmony and background vocals on songs like "Cocktails." Fulks says in the liner notes that he wanted to introduce his audience to older country music on *13 Hillbilly Giants*. Toward this goal he succeeds, offering a piece of hillbilly history tailor-made for the alternative country crowd. *—Ronnie D. Lankford Jr.*

Fuller & Kaz

f. 1978

Group / Country-Rock, Soft Rock, Folk-Rock, Singer/Songwriter
Craig Fuller and Eric Kaz teamed up for this one-off project following the breakup of their previous band American Flyer. The band split up after two pleasant but commercially disappointing efforts for United Artists in the mid-'70s. As a member of Pure Prairie League for two albums, Fuller scored a hit with *Amie*; while Kaz was a successful songwriter, with tunes covered by the likes of Linda Ronstadt, Bonnie Raitt, and the Nitty Gritty Dirt Band, as well as being a member of the Children of Paradise and the Blues Magoos. *—Brett Hartenbach*

● **Craig Fuller & Eric Kaz** / 1978 / Columbia ✦✦✦✦
With producer/engineer Val Garay (Eric Carmen, Pablo Cruise, Linda Ronstadt), Craig Fuller & Eric Kaz found a sympathetic ear for their romantic, acoustic-based pop-rock. Garay's production, for the most part, stays out of the way of the material, which with Fuller's throaty tenor, carries the record. A handful of ordinary songs and Kaz's less than commanding vocal occasionally drag the album down, but cuts such as Fuller's "Feel That Way Again," the Kaz standard "Cry Like a Rainstorm" and their collaboration, "Annabella" make *Fuller/Kaz* worthwhile for anyone interested in the genre. *—Brett Hartenbach*

Tony Furtado

Banjo / Progressive Bluegrass, Jazz Blues, Celtic Folk, Bluegrass, Traditional Bluegrass, Americana
Before Tony Furtado became a highly-regarded slide guitarist/banjo player, he studied art and music at Cal State Hayward. It was during that time that he went on a whim to Kansas and entered and the Grand National Banjo Championship and won. It was then that Furtado's solid musical potential soared into the bluegrass ranks and led him on the road with Laurie Lewis and Grant Street, playing bluegrass and old-time music. This musical trail led him to ink a deal with Rounder Records to record his debut solo record, *Swamped*, which was released in 1990. Furtado continued recording music, playing into some of his favorite artists such as Béla Fleck and Earl Scruggs. He released *Within Reach* in 1992 with the help of luminaries Jerry Douglas, Alison Krauss, Stuart Duncan, and David Grier and headed out on the road in support of both records, as well as picking up Sugarbeat, a folk-funk-acoustic-bluegrass band. Furtado and Sugarbeat have supported each other since 1993.

His eclectic approach in playing swing, jazz style, Celtic-folk, and old-timey music has shaped Furtado's musical maturations to the point that they are compared to Ry Cooder's early '70s recordings. *Full Circle* (1994) marked Furtado's third album and a discovery of his passion for acoustic blues and slide guitar, citing musical influences like Cooder and Blind Willie Johnson. He continued to draw upon his own musical influences while in search for his own personal sound during the recording of 1997's *Roll My Blues Away*, a power hungry, blues driven record produced by Cookie Marenco (Ladysmith Black Mambazo, Charlie Haden, Oregon). He jammed with country alternative rock fiddler/accordion player Dirk Powell for their self-titled collaboration two years later, as well as a rock-intensive album that offered a full band including Buckethead. But the next true solo album, *American Gypsy*, appeared on the What Are Records? label in 2002. *—MacKenzie Wilson*

Swamped / 1990 / Rounder ✦✦✦✦✦

● **Within Reach** / 1992 / Rounder ✦✦✦✦✦
Tony Furtado's banjo shines throughout *Within Reach*, yet uneven material prevents the album from being truly captivating. Of special interest is Alison Krauss' gorgeous vocals on a version of the Beatles' "I Will." *—Thom Owens*

Full Circle / 1994 / Rounder ✦✦✦

Roll My Blues Away / Feb. 11, 1997 / Rounder ✦✦✦✦
Bluegrass banjo and slide guitar master Tony Furtado's 1997 album *Roll My Blues Away* is another remarkable set of performances. It features outstanding acoustic instrumentals, from "The Stark Raven" to the laid-back "Crow Canyon." Furtado, a Grand National Banjo Championship winner, offers ten original compositions on this release, as well as vocal arrangements of two traditional songs, "Willow Tree" and "Boat's Up the River." There's skillful accompanying fiddle on "Waterslide" and tambourine accents "The Ghost of Blind Willie Johnson," while "The Knave's Bane" will definitely have listeners reaching for repeat play. Highly recommended for everyone who likes acoustic banjo, slide guitar, and progressive bluegrass. *—Murrday Fisher*

Tony Furtado & Dirk Powell / Mar. 23, 1999 / Rounder ✦✦✦✦
A fine album of traditional music, expertly played by these multi-instrumentalists. While they touch on many styles here, their acoustic blues are particularly superb, with Furtado's slide guitar work nicely set against Powell's understated banjo. If their take on "The Sloes of the Penybanc" doesn't bring a lump to your throat, you have no heart. *—Tim Sheridan*

Tony Furtado Band / Jul. 4, 2000 / Cojema Music ✦✦✦✦

Mixing elements of Ry Cooder's American R&B pickin', Béla Fleck's bluegrass-jazz fusion, and Kelly Joe Phelps' dusty folk-Delta blues (Phelps also contributes high-profile vocals to three tracks), accomplished banjo player and guitarist Tony Furtado pushes all sorts of stylistic envelopes on this indie release. From the moody Americana of a rearranged "Raleigh and Spencer" to an album-closing version of Woody Guthrie's "I Ain't Got No Home," Furtado's vision stays focused as he peels off intricate and often lightning-fast riffs, yet never lets his obvious technical excellence overwhelm a song's melodic structure. Also impressive is the crystal-clear sound of this album, featuring an airy, uncluttered mix where all the unplugged instruments (including Darrel Anger's fiddle, tablas, Uilleann pipes, accordion, and sax) sound like they're in your room playing simultaneously. Furtado shifts from jazzy interludes to Celtic, bluegrass, and C&W styles with effortless poise, never needlessly grandstanding but keeping the spotlight on his immaculate picking and phenomenal backing musicians. As accomplished on guitar as on banjo (his primary instrument), the picker adds only what is needed to the songs, keeping them sparse yet filled with interesting twists and angles. The upbeat Leo Kottke-styled instrumental "Fat Fry on the Hog Farm" and the beautifully languid ballad "O Amante" are two of the album's six original compositions that show Furtado is as accomplished a songwriter as musician and arranger. Unpretentious and classy as its low-key cover art, this is a consistently winning album that shows off Tony Furtado's eclectic talents as master string picker, bandleader, vocalist, and composer. —*Hal Horowitz*

American Gypsy / Jul. 30, 2002 / What Are Records? ✦✦✦✦

American Gypsy introduces itself with about 15 seconds of rumbling instrumental noise, the equivalent of an outsider orchestra tuning, before the opening blues figure of "Oh Berta, Berta" falls down from Tony Furtado's guitar. In those early moments, a new direction is named for Furtado, a bluegrass virtuoso and genre-bending master whose 1997 release, *Roll My Blues Away*, introduced his perfection of the slide guitar and move away from traditional roots-style composition. Loved by jam band enthusiasts, Furtado's improvisational picking takes the fore in "The Angry Monk," "Hartford," and the funk-tinged "Rising Fog." The epic tradition of "Staggerlee" is continued, with Furtado's steel guitar and multi-guitared pop rendition recalling electric Bob Dylan. "Tinker's Fancy" integrates Celtic melodies for the oddest instrumental moment, combining squeeze box, banjo, and hand percussion. The banjo-led cover of Mike Nesmith's "Some of Shelley's Blues" tones down the album's flashy soloing for a moment of reverie. That said, songs like "Rove Riley Rove" detract from Furtado's charm by proving overly sentimental, hugging the notes a little too long for critical ears. Elsewhere on the album, modern country elements mix with almost ambient warbling guitar, proving Furtado a capable and even-handed stylist. His "gypsy" tendencies have left the hills, taking tales into the big city with modern inflections and a serious mind to bringing out the greatest melodies of all time. —*Daphne Carr*

Fuzzy Mountain String Band

Group / Traditional Bluegrass, String Bands

This larger than usual, and even larger than life, string band was one of several ensembles that came together out of informal music-making events at the Durham, NC, home of Tommy and Bobbie Thompson. Some of these musicians, including banjoist and playwright Tommy Thompson, would go on to form the Red Clay Ramblers, which would become the most successful of the old-time string band revival bands. The mid-'60s was a time of great interest in traditional American folk music, and not only were young musicians busy performing and learning about this music, many of them were wandering the hills, looking for the original performers for the purpose of music lessons, recording, and interviews. The new generation of old-time players came from completely different backgrounds than the originators they were seeking out. While early pioneers of this music who recorded in the '20s and '30s were from dirt-poor farming or mining backgrounds, players such as the members of this ensemble had college educations, indeed some of them even held master's degrees. A married couple that was part of the original formation of this group, Malcolm and Vickie Owen, are good examples.

In 1972, when the band's first album was released on Rounder, Malcom was a candidate for Ph.D. in romance philology at the University of North Carolina in Chapel Hill, while Vickie held a master's degree in French from the same campus. They were both introduced to old-time music when they moved to the Chapel Hill area in the mid-'60s. Banjo player Bertram Levy was their guide into this new world. Malcolm's brother Blanton picked up the banjo around the same time, at first imitating the styles of country players such as Stringbean and Grandpa Jones, gravitating toward string band music during

his late-'60s years in the Navy. Like many players at this time, he spent time studying and playing with influential old-time heroes, in his case, the banjoist Fred Cockerham and Kyle Creed. The group's first appearance was at the Union Grove Fiddler's Convention in 1968, but they were passed over for the recording compilation of that event. Band membership then shifted, with Bobbie Thompson joining as guitarist. The dulcimer style of Vickie Owen basically summed up the group's approach. She played a traditional instrument and a traditional repertoire, but did not attempt to create a carbon copy or even play her instrument in an acknowledged folk style. Her use of the instrument to accompany the fiddle on fiddle tunes was innovative and unusual.

The group would often play an old-time string band number, but in a subtly altered instrumentation. The most striking characteristic was of course the size of the group, by the end involving triple banjos and always a pair of fiddles doubling up on the melody. Bill Hicks joined the group as fiddler in 1970; he would later become one of the original Red Clay Ramblers. Most of the group's jobs were private parties and get-togethers, with the occasional festival or fiddler's convention thrown in. The group's size and the full-time jobs of various members made larger-scale touring enterprises unwieldy. They were pegged for a Rounder release in 1970, and this debut self-titled LP finally saw the light of day two years later, following appearances by the group on several compilations from the annual Union Grove event, as well as the Galax Festival.

After the release of the album, various members began moving away, and guitarist Thompson was killed in an auto accident. New members were added and an improved version of the band appeared again at Union Grove, this time placing first in the Old Time Band competition. A second album was released on Rounder in 1972. The band's final performance was at National Folk Festival in Washington, D.C., in the summer of 1973, by which time most of the members were scattered hither and yon, and Hicks and Tommy Thompson were becoming busy with the newly formed Red Clay Ramblers.

The Fuzzy Mountain String Band repertoire contained a great number of tunes by obscure but great old time players such as southwest Virginia fiddler Henry Reed, Taylor Kimble, or Gaither Carlton. The folk music tradition of passing music on from generation to generation certainly has no better example. As a result of the group's performances and recordings, this repertoire of tunes passed on to many new string bands around the world. This group was never really concerned with becoming ultra-professional or a full-time performing unit. It was more about social gatherings, family involvement with music, and the good times to be had when likeminded musicians get together. This vibration definitely soaked into the band's recordings and has made them classics. A CD reissue consisting of the entire first album and a big chunk of the second was released by Rounder in 1995, and some members of the group reunited under the original name for a performance that year at Merlefest in the Smoky Mountains. —*Eugene Chadbourne*

● **Summer Oaks and Porch** / 1973 / Rounder ✦✦✦✦

This Durham-based old-time string revival group lost guitarist Bobbie Thompson prior to recording this second Rounder album, superior to the first in terms of professional polish. Still, neither album really captures the epic majesty of this group in a live setting. A third banjo player had also been added to the group at this point—what, three banjos in a group?—which kind of has to be heard to be believed. The large group breaks down into various smaller combinations for some of the tracks, all of which are traditional numbers as learned from various old-time legends such as Henry Reed and Frank George. One of the best aspects of this group was its archival nature, as it didn't like to stick to tried and true numbers. Quite a bit of dust must have been cleaned off old 78s to have come up with some of this material. The group was also not known for wasting time, as many numbers clock in at under two minutes. [Some of these tracks, but not all, were combined with the group's entire first album for Rounder to make up a CD reissue in 1995. Unfortunately that selection omitted some of the best tracks such as the medley of Tommy Jarrell fiddle tunes.] —*Eugene Chadbourne*

Fuzzy Mountain String Band / 1995 / Rounder ✦✦✦

This was the first full-length album appearance for this large-scale old-time string, based out of Durham, NC, and featuring, for the most part, well-educated college graduates playing music that generations prior had been performed by farmers and laborers. It was also quite an early release in the Rounder legacy; in fact, it was the first double-digit number in the label's catalog. The musicians are wonderful and bring their great love of the genre to the performances without fail, and it is without question a lively sound with double fiddles, double banjos, and the interesting dulcimer style of Vickie Owen. The original LP presents 20 different traditional pieces, each of which is explained and documented as to source in the extensive liner notes. [A later CD reissue folded in most of the group's second LP, *Summer Oaks and Porch*.] —*Eugene Chadbourne*

Chris Gaffney

Guitar, Accordion, Vocals / Tex-Mex, Conjunto, Americana, Progressive Country
Chris Gaffney grew up in Arizona, where he learned to play the accordion as a young child. The instrument would later influence the performer's mix of norteño with country and rock & roll. Gaffney eventually mastered guitar as well and spent his teen years gigging in cover and house bands. In 1977, he formed a partnership with keyboardist Wyman Reese, who also produced Gaffney's initial solo efforts. *Road to Indio* appeared in 1986; it featured 1950s rock, soul, and dusty Bakersfield honky tonk. *Chris Gaffney & the Cold Hard Facts* followed in 1990, and delved into Gaffney's Hispanic heritage. His third solo effort, *Mi Vida Loca*, was issued in 1992. *Loser's Paradise* appeared in 1995. The album was produced by blue-collar stalwart Dave Alvin and featured contributions from Lucinda Williams and Jim Lauderdale. —*Johnny Loftus*

Road to Indio / 1986 / Cactus Club ✦✦✦✦
Chris Gaffney's *Road to India* is an excellent fusion of '50s rock & roll, Bakersfield country, and careening Tex-Mex. With the assistance of a top-flight backing band, Gaffney has made a rocking, rootsy record that effortlessly recreates not only the sound, but the ambience, of '60s roadhouse country and rock. —*Thom Owens*

Chris Gaffney & the Cold Hard Facts / 1990 / ROM ✦✦✦
Los Angeles dock-worker, singer, songwriter, and accordionist reflects Hispanic influences and working-class themes in songs of steely poetry. —*Mark A. Humphrey*

● **Mi Vida Loca** / 1992 / Hightone ✦✦✦✦✦
Gaffney infuses hard country with elements of Tex-Mex and pure rock & roll, coming off like a cross between Merle Haggard and the Blasters. Gaffney has a dusty voice with perfect country phrasing for ballads like "Quiet Desperation" and "Waltz for Minnie," but he's at his peak with rockers like "'68," a powerful song about a man who lost his best friend in Vietnam, and "Silent Partner," which sounds like souped-up George Jones. —*Brian Mansfield*

Loser's Paradise / 1995 / Hightone ✦✦✦✦
Although not quite the standout album that *Mi Vida Loca* is, *Loser's Paradise* is another consistent effort, serving up the same winning mix of country, roots rock, soul, and norteño. This time around, friend Dave Alvin handles the production, as well as providing some inspired six-string work, and contributes a couple of gems with the Cajun-flavored "East of Houston, West of Baton Rouge" and the honky tonkin' "Help You Dream." As with his other records, Gaffney's songwriting is superb, bringing hard-luck tales and characters to life with his weathered voice and keen roots sensibility. For instance, check out his George Jones-like ballad "Glasshouse," the melancholy "My Baby's Got a Dead Man's Number," and the lovely norteño number "Azulito." His cover choices also rule: Lucinda Williams duets on a wonderful version of the Intruders' 1968 soul chestnut "Cowboys to Girls," and Gaffney thoughtfully rediscovers the Ed Bruce-penned, 1964 Charlie Louvin hit "See the Big Man Cry." Gaffney plays guitar, accordion, and piano, while enlisting instrumental backing from a standout band that includes longtime Rod Stewart sideman Ian McLagan on Hammond organ and pedal steel guitarist Scott Wells. And the vocal help reads like an alternative country who's who, featuring Rosie Flores, Jim Lauderdale, Dale Watson, and Tony Villanueva (lead singer of the Derailers). A must-have for Gaffney fans, and a good introduction for new ones as well. —*Jack Leaver*

Jerry Garcia

b. Aug. 1, 1942, San Francisco, CA, d. Aug. 9, 1995, San Francisco, CA
Guitar, Guitar (Electric), Vocals / Rock & Roll, Country-Rock, Folk-Rock
Jerry Garcia was the lead guitarist, vocalist, and spokesman for the seminal '60s rock & roll band the Grateful Dead. Throughout his career, he led the Dead through numerous changes, becoming one of the most famous figures in the history of rock & roll. Simultaneously, Garcia pursued an eclectic array of side projects, ranging from the bluegrass group Old & in the Way to his folky solo recordings. Garcia stayed active as a member of the Grateful Dead and as a solo performer until his death in 1995. Garcia learned to play guitar when he was 15 years old, originally playing folk and rock & roll. In 1959, when he was 17 years old, he spent a brief time in the army. When he left the military after a matter of months, he moved to Palo Alto, CA, where he met and became friends with Robert Hunter, who would later become his lyricist. Garcia bought a banjo in 1962 and began playing in local bluegrass bands. Within a few years, he was a member of Mother McCree's Uptown Jug Champions, a popular local bluegrass and folk band whose membership also included Bob Weir and Pigpen. In 1965, this group evolved into the Warlocks, which would in turn become the Grateful Dead in 1966.

Over the course of the next five years, the Grateful Dead began building a reputation as a mesmerizing live act. During this time, Garcia guested with a number of bands, both in concert and in the studio; among the artists he appeared with are the New Riders of the Purple Sage (a band which he helped form), Jefferson Starship, and Crosby, Stills,

Nash & Young. In 1970, the Grateful Dead began to shift their music back toward their folk, country, and bluegrass roots with the albums *Workingman's Dead* and *American Beauty*. The following year, Garcia began a solo career with *Hooteroll?*, which was released on Douglas Records. For the next few years, Garcia recorded solo albums frequently, often with keyboardist Merl Saunders. In 1973, he was one of the founding members of the bluegrass supergroup Old & in the Way, which also featured David Grisman, Vassar Clements, and John Kahn.

Garcia's solo efforts slowed in the early '80s, as he battled heroin addiction and diabetes. After the Grateful Dead scored their first hit album in 1987 with *In the Dark*, Garcia pursued a number of solo projects, including several acoustic duet records with David Grisman and a handful of live tours and albums with the Jerry Garcia Acoustic Band. For the first half of the '90s, Garcia concentrated on Grateful Dead tours and albums, as the band confirmed their status as one of the most popular concert acts in America. However, the guitarist slowly sank back into heroin addiction. Late in the summer of 1995, he entered Serenity Knolls, a drug rehabilitation facility in Forest Knolls, CA. While he was attempting to recover, Garcia died in his sleep of a heart attack on August 9, 1995. Several months after his death, the Grateful Dead announced their disbandment. —*Stephen Thomas Erlewine*

● **Garcia** / Jan. 1972 / Grateful Dead ✦✦✦✦✦

Garcia (Compliments) / 1974 / Grateful Dead ✦✦

Reflections / Jan. 1976 / Grateful Dead ✦✦✦✦

Cats Under the Stars / 1978 / Arista ✦✦✦✦

Run for the Roses / 1982 / Arista ✦✦

Almost Acoustic / Dec. 1988 / Grateful Dead ✦✦✦✦✦
In the fall of 1987, Jerry Garcia (guitar/vocals) hit the Lunt Fontanne Theatre on the proverbial "Great White Way" for a series of 18 performances. The shows were additionally notable for the aggregate of musicians whom the guitarist gathered under the moniker of the Jerry Garcia Acoustic Band. The sextet included David Nelson (guitar/vocals), with whom Garcia had shared many a stage as a member of the pre-Grateful Dead Wildwood Boys, and again in 1969 as founding members of New Riders of the Purple Sage. Another longtime acquaintance was Sandy Rothman (mandolin/dobro/vocals), who crossed paths with Garcia in the early '60s as well as during a short-lived pairing as the Black Mountain Boys. While his association had lasted less than two decades, John Kahn (acoustic bass) had also been involved with Garcia as his solo bassist and primary non-Dead collaborator. David Kemper (snare drum) had been working as the drummer for the Jerry Garcia Band since the summer of 1983, when he inherited the position from former Sly & the Family Stone and Santana percussionist Greg Errico. The most recent addition to Garcia's band is Kenny Kosek (fiddle), who is perhaps best-known for his studio work with artists as far afield as Rory Block and Laurie Anderson. As a cohesive unit, this band provides a comfortable backdrop for Garcia to wind through a selection of traditional favorites ("I'm Troubled"), bluegrass ("Girl at the Crossroads Bar"), folk ("Casey Jones") [note: this should not be confused with the Grateful Dead song of the same name], and blues ("Spike Driver Blues") covers. Keen-eyed Deadheads will undoubtedly notice several tunes that the band had worked up during their various "unplugged" outings. Among them are "Deep Elem Blues," "I've Been All Around This World," "Oh, Babe, It Ain't No Lie," and the sole Garcia and Robert Hunter inclusion, "Ripple." As opposed to Garcia's electric fretwork—which had seemingly been steadily deteriorating since the late '70s—there is a sparkle and eternally youthful sound to his playing here. When coupled with his ragged but right vocals, the effect reveals the guitarist's organic infatuation with this music. Both the structured melodic lines as well as freewheeling solos hold his attention with a craftsman-like singularity and focus. Sadly, *Almost Acoustic* was the only release from this combo to have been issued prior to Garcia's death in 1995. It is highly recommended for all enthusiasts of "wooden music" and is a brilliant insight into Jerry Garcia's uncanny abilities as a guitarist of remarkable breadth. —*Lindsay Planer*

Jerry Garcia/David Grisman / 1991 / Acoustic Disc ✦✦✦✦✦
This Grammy-nominated disc heralds the origins of the highly acclaimed acoustic duo of Jerry Garcia (guitar/vocals) and David "Dawg" Grisman (mandolin). They had been chums for years by the time they began their direct partnership in earnest on December 7, 1990, with a nine-song set at the Sweetwater in Mill Valley, CA. Over half of that material would be reworked the following spring—for inclusion on this disc—at Grisman's newly appointed, plush, and well-lit Dawg Studios. Along with David Grisman Quintet members Jim Kerwin (bass) and Joe Craven (percussion/fiddle), Garcia and Grisman revive a few familiar tunes covering every dimension of popular music, ranging from the blues ("The Thrill Is Gone") to folk-rock ("Friend of the Devil"), as well as pop music standards such as Irving Berlin's "Russian Lullaby"—which Garcia had previously covered on his 1974 *Garcia (Compliments)* album—and Hoagy Carmichael's "Rockin' Chair." They

also examined the origins of authentic traditional folk ("Walkin' Boss"/"Two Soldiers"). Additionally, the pair collaborated on the original instrumental "Grateful Dawg," which coalesces the distinct styles of Grisman's "Dawg Music" with Garcia's Grateful Dead intonations. The results are categorically brilliant and undoubtedly helped usher in the contemporary bluegrass and progressive bluegrass movements. Grisman's sonically perfected studio coupled with his decades of hands-on engineering and producing expertise helped immensely in capturing and accurately reproducing their unaffected acoustic intimacy. Nowhere is this more evident than the 16-plus minute "Arabia"—which would become a showstopper once they hit the road in the early '90s. The sound quite literally envelopes the listener, who autonomically becomes drawn into the track as it twists and slithers through several different movements—including the central theme, credited in the liner notes as being based on the traditional Cuban melody "Hasta Siempre." All dimensions of "unplugged" enthusiasts who have not already made *Jerry Garcia/David Grisman* a top priority are strongly encouraged to do so. —*Lindsay Planer*

Jerry Garcia Band / Aug. 27, 1991 / Arista ✦✦✦✦
A double live album recorded in 1990 and featuring extended versions of songs by Bruce Cockburn, Bob Dylan, Smokey Robinson, the Beatles, the Band, Los Lobos, and others. The Garcia Band serves a kind of songbook function for its listeners (as, indeed, does the Dead), which may mean that its chief virtue is as instruction: if you're familiar with the originals, you don't really need to hear Garcia's covers, but if, like many Deadheads, you don't hear much music outside the band's orbit, this may help lead you to other good music. —*William Ruhlmann*

Bluegrass Reunion / 1992 / Acoustic Disc ✦✦✦✦✦
This is the fourth release on David "Dawg" Grisman's (mandolin/vocals) highly respected Acoustic Disc record label. While Dawg's multifarious talents in front of the microphone are undeniably brilliant, it is his lesser-lauded behind the scenes work as a conduit for equally skilled sonic craftsmen that is most prominently displayed here. This release gathers a quintet of musicians who at one time or another have crossed paths with Dawg. These range from bluegrass legend Red Allen (guitar/vocal), for whom Grisman cut his teeth as a producer as well as mandolin player in the early '60s, to Jerry Garcia (guitar/vocals), with whom he shared the stage on several occasions—including the all-star bluegrass revivalist combo Old & in the Way. The pinpoint accuracy and opulent soundscape are practically tangible, again thanks to Dawg's self-taught and seemingly innate acoustic recording techniques. *Bluegrass Reunion* features 20 standards and traditional adaptations by a revolving cast that also includes Herb Pedersen (banjo/vocals), Jim Buchanan (fiddles/vocals), and Jim Kerwin (bass). While there is no surprise that the track list is heavy on the Acuff-Rose catalog, the tastes of the musicians refreshingly delve into some lesser-heard deep cuts. Likewise, these interpretations literally redefine the "high and lonesome sound" with eerie authenticity. This is true of both the pensively emotive reading of Helen Carter's "Is This My Destiny?" to the hot-skillet and high-steppin' instrumental "Pigeon Roost"—the album's sole original composition. Garcia's poignant vocals and lead guitar reinvent the Stanley Brothers' classic "The Fields Have Turned Brown" into a minor noir masterpiece. His loose and throaty reading of "Ashes of Love" is equally inspired as it recalls Johnnie & Jack's classic reading. While there is nary a subpar performance on *Bluegrass Reunion*, there are several that are explicitly recommended to enthusiasts, including "She's No Angel," "Little Maggie," and "To Love and Live Together." —*Lindsay Planer*

Not for Kids Only / Oct. 1993 / Acoustic Disc ✦✦✦✦✦

Shady Grove / 1996 / Acoustic Disc ✦✦✦
In the last five years of his life, Jerry Garcia frequently dropped in on his old friend, mandolin player David Grisman, to play and record the kind of folk, bluegrass, and old-time music they had both begun their careers with in the early 1960s. Grisman released two Garcia/Grisman albums on his Acoustic Disc label during Garcia's lifetime, and this is the first to be compiled since his death. In a note, Grisman writes, "I decided to organize this material by genre; this first volume is comprised of traditional folk songs and ballads." Indeed, among the 13 tracks here are versions of child ballads and other ancient songs that formed the repertoire of some of the folk groups that both players belonged to. Grisman has included a lavish CD booklet containing thorough annotations by New Lost City Ramblers member John Cohen that trace the origins of each of the songs and detail Garcia and Grisman's backgrounds. One gets the sense that Cohen and Grisman are trying to provide a tutorial to Deadheads who may be puzzled. The effect of all the scholarship is to imply that the sessions are more deliberate than a hearing suggests, however. The playing is loose and spontaneous, and Garcia is not always in the best voice. Nevertheless, Grisman is right to begin his documentation of Garcia's last sessions with an album that ties directly into the guitarist's initial musical passions. —*William Ruhlmann*

How Sweet It Is / Apr. 15, 1997 / Arista ✦✦✦
Recorded at San Francisco's Warfield Theatre during 1990, *How Sweet It Is* captures the Jerry Garcia Band running through a selection of originals and covers. While it isn't as fluid or surprising as the double-disc 1991 set *Jerry Garcia Band*, which was culled from the same shows, it's nevertheless an entertaining set, especially for devoted fans, who will cherish previously unheard Garcia covers of songs like "Think" and the title track. —*Stephen Thomas Erlewine*

So What / Aug. 18, 1998 / Acoustic Disc ✦✦✦✦
Jerry Garcia of the Grateful Dead and David Grisman were friends for over 30 years. On an occasional basis they would get together and jam, and Grisman would tape the results. Sometimes they would play rock, folk music, country, or free improvisation, but the music on this CD put out by Grisman's Acoustic Disc label is strictly straight-ahead jazz. Joined by two (or sometimes three) sidemen from the mandolinist's regular band (bassist

Jim Kerwin, Joe Craven on percussion, and, on two numbers, flutist Matt Eakle), the co-leaders perform three versions of "So What," two apiece of "Bag's Groove" and "Milestones," and one of Grisman's "16/16." Garcia is quite credible as a jazz improviser without attempting to be a virtuoso; he apparently loved the music and does not sound at all like a rock player. The versatile Grisman effectively updates his swing style, and the rhythm section is driving and supportive despite being quite light in volume. Even with the repetition of titles (only the last version of "So What" sounds like a rehearsal rather than a regular recording session), the music holds one's interest throughout. A nice surprise that is well worth checking out. —*Scott Yanow*

The Pizza Tapes / Apr. 25, 2000 / Acoustic Disc ✦✦✦
Jerry Garcia and David Grisman released two albums on the latter's Acoustic Disc label during the last years of Garcia's life, and since his death in 1995, Grisman has culled a series of albums from other sessions the two recorded together. *Shady Grove* (1996) presented traditional folk and country material, while *So What* (1998) contained jazz compositions. *The Pizza Tapes* (so named because Garcia's cassette of the sessions supposedly was stolen by a pizza delivery boy and circulated clandestinely) chronicles two nights worth of sessions that Garcia and Grisman shared with guitarist Tony Rice. The Grisman albums with Garcia have become increasingly informal as he has delved into picking dates that may have been intended as rehearsals or just get-togethers, and *The Pizza Tapes* carries that trend further. There's lots of conversation (delineated by the five "Appetizer" titles), along with false starts, mistakes, and fragments of songs, and there is some repetition of tunes (though not performances) from previous albums. "Shady Grove" and "Louis Collins" from *Shady Grove* are here, as is "So What" from *So What*. But the two guitarists show a genuine rapport as they range from pop/jazz standards like "Summertime" to folk songs like "Man of Constant Sorrow" and folk-rock fare like "Knockin' on Heaven's Door." "I'm having a great time," declares Garcia enthusiastically, and his pleasure comes across. Deadheads long ago found that Garcia was at his best away from the formal restrictions and pressures of recording, and the same thing seems to hold for the Garcia/Grisman albums. Rice, meanwhile, more than holds his own. —*William Ruhlmann*

Don't Let Go / Jan. 23, 2001 / Arista ✦✦✦✦

Shining Star / Mar. 20, 2001 / Arista ✦✦✦✦

Brother Dave Gardner

b. Jun. 11, 1926, Jackson, TN, d. Sep. 22, 1983
Drums, Vocals / Country Comedy
Next to Homer & Jethro, the most successful Southern-derived comedian was undoubtedly Brother Dave Gardner. In the late '50s and into the mid-'60s, Gardner's albums found themselves ensconced in record collections in far more urbane and Northerly locales than one would suspect, and his style was instantly influential and widely imitated. Variously described as a "Southern Lenny Bruce" or "Billy Graham with a sense of humor," Gardner's best routines still sound fresh and original today, a testament to his off-kilter genius. There was much, much more to this small-statured standup comic than your average hillbilly plowboy set of wheezy jokes; Gardner may just very well have been the true innovative genius of classy Southern humor.

After recording a handful of semisuccessful singles as a drummer/vocalist in and around his native Memphis (he had the original hit of "White Silver Sands," Gardner found his true calling when Chet Atkins discovered him in Nashville doing comedy routines between drum solos. His on-stage character (and by most accounts, off-stage as well) was one part hipster, one part Sunday-morning preacher, peppered with off-the-wall observations about history and life, all of it barely concealing a personality that was as convention shattering as the times would barely allow. His debut album on RCA, *Rejoice, Dear Hearts!*, was released at the height of the comedy-album craze in 1960, and his follow-up, *Kick Thy Own Self*, was even more successful. Gardner's act played well on national TV, so well, in fact, that a young Ray Stevens took whole Gardner routines, set them to music, and scored big with most of them well into the late '60s ("Ahab, the Arab," "Speedball," etc.). In the late '60s, a Memphis rock & roll band—the Hombres—took one line from a Gardner routine and fleshed it out into a hit song, "Let It All Hang Out."

On-stage, Gardner was a law and entity unto himself. Although his original ascension to stardom was made, not unlike Bruce, with carefully constructed "bits," as time went on these gave way more and more to off-the-wall but trenchant observations. But unlike Bruce, Gardner never totally abandoned these staples of his nightclub act and his records. Instead, the nightly grind in clubs caused him to expand on them, and true fans of his fertile comic imagination can compare his telling of "The Motorcycle Story" (from one of his early albums) with the full-blown treatment it receives—almost covering an entire side of an album—on his second-to-last LP, *Out Front*. Rather than sounding like a comedian giving a perfunctory reading of a well-known (and well-worn) routine, he sounds as if he just concocted it moments ago, his enthusiasm in telling the tale literally bounding off the grooves. His sense of timing was unerring, and his ability to respond to his surroundings would often send him into a free association rant that would spawn an ad-lib passage that would stretch over several minutes. One of his greatest personal quirks on-stage was that he never timed his act in the conventional sense, and although he wore an expensive watch on-stage, he never bothered to look at it. Generally credited (oddly enough) with the invention of the 100 millimeter cigarette, Gardner had them custom-made for him in quantity starting in the early '60s. Once he had pulled three of them from his similarly custom-made cigarette case, fired them up, and disposed of them in rapid, chain-smoking succession, he knew he had filled his time on-stage.

Gardner's involvement with drugs somewhat derailed his career after a bust for marijuana possession in 1962. Although he never wore it on his sleeve the way Bruce did, Gardner—by all accounts—had a voracious and most experimental appetite for them and was not above sneaking in veiled references in one of his routines. He was cleared, but the resulting publicity flap closed off the big television shows and forced him out of the big rooms up North and into the small-time Southern club circuit. After a small prison stint for tax evasion in the early '70s (his defense at his trial was to tell the judge, "I didn't know how much money I made, so I figured it was a fraud to fill out one of them things"), Gardner's career was pretty much dead in the water, having gone from RCA Victor to Capitol to their budget label, Tower, to no deal at all. Working small clubs, his humorous and skewered outlook nonetheless stayed intact, a true rebel spirit that refused to be brought down, even though he was now under the "management" of a racist billionaire who was trying to remold him for the "good ol' boy" *Hee Haw* crowd. He recorded for a spate of small labels right up to the end, including one-offs for Four Star (his last, where he asks a stunned Nashville crowd, "I wonder if Johnny Cash turned Billy Graham on?") and another for the short-lived record division of the Tonka toy company. At the time of his death in 1983, he was working on a low-budget motion picture called, ironically enough, *Chain Gang*. Although he is seldom remembered today—except by old timers who smile when you mention his name—Gardner's influence on all branches of comedy continues to be writ large. *—Cub Koda*

Ain't That Weird? / 1961 / RCA ✦✦✦✦

On *Ain't That Weird?* Brother Dave Gardner takes his act on the road, appropriately enough to the Will Rogers Memorial Auditorium in Fort Worth, TX. As keen-eared enthusiasts will note, Gardner has somewhat restructured his performance style. Dispensing with the vaudeville song and joke man persona, Gardner now focuses his unique stream-of-consciousness dialogue into some socially advanced topics for the early '60s, including drugs, ecology, vegetarianism, and Beatniks. As Gardner proudly affirmed on a previous long-player, "the onlyest (sic) difference 'tween me and those other preachers, dear hearts, is that I'm preachin' *for* it." To that end, the antidotes and yarns fly in the face of political correctness as well as the conventions of the time. Using his admittedly underprivileged and relatively uneducated beginnings as a milieu, Brother Dave Gardner is able to adorn serious issues within the context of humor in such an innocuous way that issues such as "raw vegetarianism" (aka veganism) or the concept of higher learning—which involves, according to Gardener, the ability to "get high and learn"—seem almost ludicrous enough to be sensible. Additional fodder for Gardner's antics include some highly entertaining and non-PC views on hunting as well as the necessity for population control. Politically, observations on Nikita Sergeyevich Khrushchev, the Cuban Missile crisis, as well as the status of governing bodies in the state of Alabama tend to antiquate the remainder of the album. Of course in hindsight, it is startling just how accurate many of Gardner's predictions actually were. *Ain't That Weird* features a few stories that became legendary within Brother Dave Gardner's canon of work; these include "Promoter's Story" and the story of "Two Cows," as well as the tale of "The Preacher and the Drunk." Since the original record album was not banded and there are no names given to any of his fables, the exact titles may vary. Regardless, this is a touchstone release as it hones in on Gardner's strengths as a storyteller as well as a self-proclaimed "free thinkin' and swingin' cat." *—Lindsay Planer*

Did You Ever? / 1962 / RCA ✦✦✦

Brother Dave Gardner's fourth long-player is in many ways his most acerbic and direct. The performance captured on *Did You Ever?* comes from an appearance in the heart of Dixie and the proverbial buckle of the Bible belt, upon the campus of the University of Alabama. While this could be misconstrued as literally "preaching to the converted," in reality Gardner is once again manipulating the medium in order to make the most of his message. As with his previous album, *Ain't That Weird?*, Gardner sheds the image as a song and dance man, choosing instead to focus his satiric weaponry to those sitting right in front of him. Politics and history dominate the first side of the album. The subject matter revolves around John F. Kennedy's Cold War space race, as well as some very non PC—albeit particularly amusing—interpretations of the lives and contributions from such patriots as: Benjamin Franklin, Robert E. Lee, and one of Gardner's favorite targets, Abraham Lincoln. As his audience primarily consists of college students, naturally the topics of sex and drugs are never too far behind—usually insinuated, but rarely forgotten. The second side of the disc continues with Gardner's free-form stream of conscious dialogue with a revisitation of a subject which has popped up on numerous occasions—the senselessness of hunting animals for sport. The tale revolves around two cows and their outlook upon fate. While giving hunters a hard time, Gardner also speaks in favor of vegetarianism and gives an insane recipe for a carrot-based alcoholic beverage. The final segment of the album is devoted to a one-man routine featuring Brother Dave Gardner as a late-night radio evangelist. Ironically, this lengthy piece is not very well executed and confuses the listener as to Gardner's true meta-message. Is he making fun of himself or those who use the airways to beg for their week-to-week sustenance? The ambiguity makes for poor comedy in this case. *—Lindsay Planer*

● **Rejoice, Dear Hearts!/Kick Thy Own Self** / Apr. 21, 1998 / Collectors' Choice Music ✦✦✦✦✦

This two-fer CD contains Brother Dave Gardner's debut (*Rejoice, Dear Hearts!*) and follow-up (*Kick Thy Own Self*) long-players for RCA Records. Gardner's impact as a social and political humorist has been largely obscured by time as well as the reality that a majority of his seminal recordings remained out of print for over 30 years. Although considered "regional humor," the impact of these recordings is confirmed, as each disc attained an unprecedented number five on the *Billboard* album charts during the months of June and August of 1960, respectively. Gardner's Southern drawl and common-sense tales and fables first garnered him several appearances on the Jack Paar *Tonight Show* beginning in 1957. So by the time that Chet Atkins—then RCA's head of A&R in Nashville, TN—commissioned these discs, Brother Dave Gardner was a nationally known figure. Both albums are structured to mirror Gardner's live sets as well as television appearances. So in addition to the various yarns and fables, there are also a few musical numbers—most notably a percussion and vocal piece that Gardner calls "space music." This particular bit of improvisation had an incalculably profound influence on a young Andy Kaufman, according to Kaufman himself. In fact, his initial forays into standup comedy incorporated variations of this silly shtick. Although Gardner's more traditional comedy (i.e., jokes, fables, and stories) has been considered within the same subgenre as Andy Griffith and Jerry Clower, Gardner's tales are actually more cerebral. His unique retelling of William Shakespeare's *Julius Caesar* and the Biblical epic of *David and Goliath* are punctuated with anachronisms such as rock & roll and motorcycles, as well as a few sly references to social drug use—all while keeping true to the story from his own inimitable perspective. There are quite a few of Gardner's classic yarns spread throughout these two LPs. Among them are: "The Motorcycle Story," "L.C. and the Governor's Car," "Hainted House" (aka, "Is you gonna be here when John gets here?"), and "The Northern Cat and the Southern Cat." As was the nature of his early performances, the two albums are accented with brief musical interludes. This two-fer also features his only Top 40 hit, "White Silver Sands." *—Lindsay Planer*

Hank Garland

b. Nov. 11, 1930, Cowpens, SC

Guitar, Session Musician / Bop, Nashville Sound/Countrypolitan, Traditional Country

Nothing upsets preconceived minds like someone who successfully crosses over to another genre after he has been thoroughly pigeonholed by experts in a previous one. Such was Hank Garland, Nashville's busiest country guitar picker who, with little warning, made a superb jazz album in mid-career and seemed headed for jazz stardom until an auto accident left him unable to perform. As a jazz performer, Garland had a fertile melodic and harmonic imagination and a sound that had apparently honed to the gospel of tone and attack according to Charlie Christian—with some Les Paul mixed in and more than a touch of Bud Powell's influence as well. But even on his country records (check out Red Foley's sublime "Midnight" and "Hearts of Stone"), Garland's urbane jazz and blues sensibilities can be felt.

Cowpens is a rural suburb of Spartanburg, SC, and while growing up there, Garland absorbed country music from Arthur "Guitar Boogie" Smith and Mother Maybelle Carter on the radio, eventually switching from banjo to guitar. He joined the *Grand Ole Opry* at 15 in 1945, signed with Decca in 1949 as a solo artist, and appeared on innumerable Nashville recording sessions while jamming privately in local clubs. In July 1960, Garland came forward as a jazz musician, organizing a combo that was scheduled to play the Newport Jazz Festival but found itself on the sidelines after riots closed the festival. The following year, Garland's jazz debut on record, *Jazz Winds From a New Direction*, astonished both jazz and country circles, and a follow-up album, *The Unforgettable Guitar of Hank Garland*, was issued. But in September 1961, a near fatal auto accident robbed Garland of a good deal of his coordination and memory. Although he made attempts to perform again, he has been in retirement in South Carolina ever since. *—Richard S. Ginell*

Jazz Winds From a New Direction / 1961 / Columbia Special Products ✦✦✦✦✦

Lots of folks in the country music streets of Nashville and the jazz canyons of New York were shaken up by this release, for country supersession man Hank Garland demonstrated that he could be just as persuasive rattling off swift, sophisticated bebop as he was playing thousands of country licks on the jukeboxes. Nothing fazes him, not even the tricky "Move," for Garland had technique to burn and a thoroughly modern harmonic approach. Not only that, a 17-year-old Boston kid named Gary Burton makes an astonishingly brash and assured recorded debut on vibes on this record, and bassist Joe Benjamin and the Dave Brubeck Quartet's unquenchably swinging drummer Joe Morello (who had toured with Garland when Garland was a teenager) are on hand from New York. This record seemed to promise great things ahead for Garland in the jazz world, a prospect cut sadly short later in 1961 by a crippling auto accident. Originally recorded in Nashville by Columbia and country & western producer Don Law (another shock to the purists' systems), *Jazz Winds* has been in print in some form almost continuously. *—Richard S. Ginell*

★ **Hank Garland & His Sugar Footers** / 1992 / Bear Family ✦✦✦✦✦

The best of Hank Garland's solo sides from the late '40s and early '50s, featuring his signature tune, "Sugarfoot Rag," and 19 others equally abounding with hot guitar passages. Highlights also include the Red Foley-sung version of "Sugarfoot Rag" (on which Garland played lead guitar), cut some three months after his own version; a half-dozen selections sung with varying degrees of success by Garland (among them Hank Snow's "I'm Movin' On"), who primarily imitated established vocalists like Hank Snow and Floyd Tillman; and a surprisingly lively and bold version of the bluegrass instrumental "Billy in the Low Ground" (issued as "Lowdown Billy") for electric guitar. The set is rounded out with two never-issued solo sides cut in 1957 for the tiny Chic label. Some of country's best guitar work, and Garland's all too rare solo outings, are right here for the listening. *—Cub Koda & Bruce Eder*

Move! The Guitar Artistry of Hank Garland / Nov. 13, 2001 / Sundazed ✦✦✦✦✦

This long-awaited two-disc set features all of Garland's jazz sides for Columbia Records between 1959-1960, including the complete albums *Velvet Guitar*, *The Unforgettable Guitar of Hank Garland*, and *Jazz Winds From a New Direction*. Although it may seem a bit quaint, in its time *Jazz Winds* was a revelatory performance; previously, it was almost impossible to believe that a country guitarist could attack jazz lines with this much imagination and finesse, even taking into account what Chet Atkins had already accomplished. Also surprising was the fact that *Jazz Winds* wasn't commercial or countrified in any way; it was marketed as a straight jazz album, played by a real jazz quartet that included Joe Morello (drums), Joe Benjamin (bass), and vibraphonist Gary Burton in his debut recording. However, even if that album caused all the fuss, there's terrific playing scattered throughout the other two, whether it's the cleverly titled "Call D. Law," the hard-swinging Garland original "Why Not?," or lovely takes on "Scarlet Ribbons" and "Polka Dots and Moonbeams." These sessions have become legendary in guitar circles, and the fact that most of them have been out of print for decades makes this reissue a real treasure for Garland fans. —*Jim Smith*

Marvin Gaster

Banjo / Contemporary Bluegrass, Traditional Bluegrass
North Carolina's Marvin Gaster is a rare individual who has been part of two vastly different scenes in the ongoing drama of Appalachian music. He plowed behind a mule, and played music as entertainment at parties or other social events that allowed the hard working folk to unwind. He also studied for a history degree at UNC-Chapel Hill in the '70s, when there was more old-time music being played on that campus than anywhere back in the hills. And in his middle ages he has taken part in such modern day cultural phenomena as folk festivals and recording sessions in pristine studios. He is a living bit of banjo history, "the last in a line of Lee County two finger banjo pickers" to quote no less a banjo expert than Winston-Salem's Bob Carlin. Carlin is best known as a sidekick to the late John Hartford, but lovingly produced a superb CD of Gaster's music that was released on Rounder in 1995.

Gaster was not the first musician in his family. For all anyone knows the lineage of musicians might go back even further, but there was definitely Fiddlin' John Morris Francis Gaster, who died in 1942. But this was not a family that cherished and loved old-time music as a unified entity. In reality, John's father Big John Gaster detested music. He hated music so much that the fiddlin' son had to sneak up to the roof of one of the farm buildings to his sounds out of earshot. Marvin's father played guitar, but his main musical influence growing up became his Uncle Henry when his parents took off looking for work elsewhere, leaving the boy in the care of the childless relatives. During his time living with them, Gaster recalls that musical events were integrated into the scheme of work that needed to be done. Dances that were known as "frolics" were scheduled to take place alongside jobs such as corn shuckings or land clearings. Participants would literally dance all night, then head off to the fields when the sun came up. From these events Gaster remembers a fiddler named John Williams who used to pack his instrument inside a flour sack.

Speaking of casual instrument cases, Gaster also recalls that when he finally got the 36 dollars together that he needed to buy his first banjo, the storeowner put it in a bag from the dry cleaners. As soon as he got this instrument home, he noticed a change in his Uncle Henry. He hadn't realized that his uncle played the banjo. It turned out that Henry Perry had been a professional musician up until the '20s, alongside his brother Lacy Perry and cousin Everton Spivey, fiddlers the both of them. Perry's style of banjo playing had been learned from local musicians such as Abner Crutchfield and Bascom Caviness, the latter man a Civil War veteran. The uncle delighted in having the new interest in common with his nephew. Switching back and forth between banjo and fiddle and with some other local musicians putting in their two cents, Gaster learned both banjo and fiddle while the traditional ways of life began to change radically all around him. New things kept coming along, such as electricity. And some things seemed to be gone for good, like the frolics, replaced by dances held at public halls in town. The music itself was changing as players put on fingerpicks in order to be heard in the larger, noisier venues, and none of them were playing in the style of Uncle Henry anymore. A fiddler named W. Earl Wicker became Gaster's guide into a new level of professionalism. Wicker and Gaster began winning fiddle and banjo contests and played many weekend music events, many of them fundraisers.

By the '40s he was playing on two Sanford radio stations. He started trying to modernize his style at this time, but quickly dropped the use of the third finger, going back to the old ways. Still in high-school, he was playing with musicians such as Alton Williams, making about 12 dollars a gig. He pretty much sat out the '50s musically, as in between raising a new family and the changing times there didn't seem to be either interest or time for playing. In the late '60s he got back into it again, full steam ahead, with fiddler Lauchlin Shaw and guitarist and harmonica player Wade Yates. Gigs tended to be weekend dances in the Chapel Hill area. This was a good locale at the next decade began to unfold, because it turned out a resurgence in interest in old-time music was about to take place. Several different homes in the community were focal points for regular musical sessions, out of which a variety of old-time music bands were formed. Shaw's home was one of these hot spots, and this is where Gaster first came in contact with one of his regular collaborators, fiddler Norm Boggs.

The '80s were a good decade for Gaster's musical activities. With his children leaving home and his time his own, he became completely devoted to the fiddle and showed up at all the fiddler's gatherings, music festivals, contests, and jam sessions that would have him. When he retired from his job as a schoolteacher in 1993, he had even more hours to devote to music. It must have started looking like fun to his brother Harry Gaster, who learned bass and began to travel along providing backup. In the mid-'90s Gaster was presented the opportunity to record a full CD of his music for Rounder, an occasion to bring together many of his friends such as Boggs, Yates, and brother Harry. This disc, dedicated to and named after Uncle Henry, was greeted with rave reviews. Gaster continues to be a regular participant at southern fiddler's conventions, playing most often with fiddler J.P. Fraley or banjoist Will Keys, who plays in a similar style to Gaster. He is particularly fond of playing with younger musicians, passing the old music along to another generation. —*Eugene Chadbourne*

Uncle Henry's Favorites / Mar. 19, 1996 / Rounder ✦✦✦✦✦
North Carolina has always been a hub of old-time musical activity, although over the years the action has switched from the hills to the campuses back to the hills again. Banjo and fiddle player Marvin Gaster has been around the whole time, and plays in a historic style that largely vanished once players started sticking picks on their fingers and going progressive in the '50s. There have been many productions of this nature that have come out of this part of the country, all attempting to create high quality historical documents of old time music. From the Red Clay Ramblers to the Hollow Rock String Band, this is certainly one of the best. Every aspect of this production is top-notch. The packaging includes a wonderful booklet that includes a short-story length biography, as well as really extensive information on each track. Musically, Gaster is a gas, and he certainly was in

good hands here. Producer Bob Carlin is also one of the great old time banjo players of the new generation. He treats this project with love and respect, also playing guitar on some of the tracks. It was a wise decision to mix the band up. There are some of Gaster's senior cohorts, such as harmonica player Wade Yates, who passed on shortly after these sessions. The younger crowd is also on hand, with players such as guitarist Beth Hartness and guitarist and fiddler Robert Mitchener making nice contributions. A hefty two dozen tracks are presented, meaning, on top of everything else that is grand about this collection, it also serves as a one-stop archive of a particular type of material. Bravo, bravo to everyone involved. —*Eugene Chadbourne*

Gatlin Brothers

Group / Country-Pop, Neo-Traditionalist Country, Urban Cowboy
Led by Larry Gatlin, the Gatlin Brothers are one of the most popular country groups in the music's history. Adopting the close harmony vocal techniques of the Louvins and the Everlys to the highly polished country-pop era, Larry and the Gatlin Brothers scored a number of hits during the '70s and '80s. Often, the group walked the line between intricate, inventive country and pure commercial material, which resulted in strong sales but occasionally poor reviews. Nevertheless, they remained near the top of the charts until the late '80s, when the new traditionalists began to gain popularity. Following their decline in popularity, Gatlin and the Gatlin Brothers went into semiretirement during the early '90s, which resulted in the group relocating to Branson, MO, where they ran their own theater.

The Gatlin Brothers didn't officially form until 1979, when Larry began crediting them as a supporting band on his solo singles, but the three brothers—Larry, Steve, and Rudy—had been performing together since childhood, when they sang in church and on several local Texas television shows. While they were still in their teens, they recorded a religious album for the independent Sword & Shield label. Following high-school graduation, Larry, who was the eldest of the brothers, headed off to the University of Houston, where he briefly joined the gospel group the Imperials. Larry performed with the Imperials in Las Vegas, where he met Dottie West, who was impressed enough by his songwriting talents to record two of his songs, "You're the Other Half of Me" and "Once You Were Mine," and pay for him to move to Nashville. Once he arrived in Nashville, he found that West had been circulating his demo tapes, which led to Kris Kristofferson playing Larry's demo for Monument Records executive Fred Foster. Impressed by the tape, Foster offered Gatlin a contract in 1972. By that time, Larry had already invited his brothers to Nashville to form a backing group, and they wound up singing on his debut album, *The Pilgrim,* which featured his first country hit, "Sweet Becky Walker."

Gatlin's second album, *Rain Rainbow,* also featured support from his brothers and contained "Delta Dirt," which climbed to number 14. The third Gatlin album was officially credited to Gatlin With Family and Friends, and contained his first Top Ten hit, "Broken Lady," which peaked at number five in early 1976. Later that year, the Gatlin Brothers were made members of the *Grand Ole Opry.* In 1976, Gatlin's fourth album, *High Time,* was credited to Larry With Brothers and Friends and contained his first number-one hit, "I Just Wish You Were Someone I Love." After releasing one more solo album, the Gatlin Brothers were officially credited as Larry's backing band as of 1979, just as he signed to Columbia Records. The first hit single to bear this name was the number one "All the Gold in California."

Throughout the '80s, the Gatlin Brothers ran up a string of 15 Top 40 hits, including "Houston (Means I'm One Day Closer to You)," "Denver," "The Lady Takes the Cowboy Everytime," and "She Used to Be Somebody's Baby." All of their recordings during this time were released under a variety of names, including Larry & the Gatlin Brothers Band, Larry & the Gatlin Brothers, and Larry, Steve, Rudy: The Gatlin Brothers. By the end of the decade, the group's popularity began to decline, due to the popularity of new traditionalist performers. In 1991, the group decided to retire after they performed a farewell tour. Larry appeared in the lead role in the Broadway musical *the Will Rogers Follies* the following year, while Steve recorded an inspirational album and Rudy opened two Gatlin Brothers Music City Grilles. In 1993, the group opened their own theater in Branson, MO, where they began performing regularly; they also sang frequently in Las Vegas. That same year, the group signed to the small label Branson Entertainment and released *Moments to Remember,* which was followed by *Cool Water* the next year. —*Stephen Thomas Erlewine*

● **The Best of the Gatlins: All the Gold in California** / 1996 / Columbia/Legacy ✦✦✦✦
This 18-track compilation traces the work of Larry Gatlin, his brothers, family, and friends (as the various billings on the records had it) from 1975 to 1988. A greatest-hits collection, it slightly favors Gatlin's early work, including "Sweet Becky Walker" and "Delta Dirt," which were among his first chart singles, while skipping "Night Time Magic" and "Nothing But Your Love Matters," which were bigger hits. Otherwise, it's all country Top Ten singles, including the number ones "I've Done Enough Dyin' Today," "All the Gold in California," and "Houston (Means I'm One Day Closer to You)." Gatlin, who wrote all the songs and sings all the lead vocals, has a traditionalist bent, though the productions are not as lush as the '60s Nashville sound, the romantic lyrics are more erotic (it was the '70s, after all), and the best songs, such as "All the Gold in California," are unique efforts thematically and musically. [The unnecessarily brief 55-minute CD running time probably is due to song publishing royalties: all the albums in Columbia/Legacy's Country Classics series have only 18 tracks.] —*William Ruhlmann*

Larry Gatlin

b. May 28, 1948, Seminole, TX
Guitar, Vocals / Neo-Traditionalist Country, Urban Cowboy, Country-Pop
Larry Gatlin is best-known for his '80s hits with the Gatlin Brothers, but prior to forming and leading that family trio, he enjoyed a successful solo career with occasional support from his brothers. Gatlin was born in Seminole, TX, in 1948, and raised on country gospel music. He and his brothers, Steve and Rudy, often sang together in church, as well as on local radio and television every once in a while; they also recorded an album for

the small gospel label Sword & Shield. After high-school, Gatlin enrolled at the University of Houston, where he joined a gospel group called the Imperials. The Imperials went on to perform in Jimmy Dean's Las Vegas revue, where Gatlin met Dottie West. Impressed by his songwriting, West recorded two of his compositions, "You're the Other Half of Me" and "Once You Were Mine"; not only that, she passed his demo tape around Nashville, and even paid for him to relocate there. Gatlin quickly found work as a backup singer for Kris Kristofferson, and not long after, he landed a solo deal with Monument in 1973. Gatlin issued his debut album, *The Pilgrim*, later that year, and it produced his first charting country single, "Sweet Becky Walker," which inched into the Top 40. 1974's "Delta Dirt" was his first Top 20 hit, taken from the album *Rain Rainbow*. Gatlin's brothers first made their presence felt on his third album, 1976's *Larry Gatlin With Family & Friends*, which gave him his first Top Five hit in "Broken Lady." Sometimes accompanied by his brothers, Gatlin scored three more Top Five singles in 1977 ("I Don't Wanna Cry," "Love Is Just a Game," and "Statues Without Hearts"), and in 1978 scored his first number one, "I Just Wish You Were Someone I Love." When Gatlin left Monument for Columbia in 1979, he started crediting the Gatlin Brothers Band on all of his recordings, starting with that year's number-one smash "All the Gold in California." Although the group's subsequent releases had several variations on the Gatlin Brothers name, and often billed Larry out front, it was all essentially Gatlin Brothers music from then on.

The Gatlin Brothers' success continued for much of the '80s, bringing them nine more Top Ten hits and another number one with 1983's "Houston (Means I'm One Day Closer to You)." Their last big hit came in 1987 with the Top Five "Talkin' to the Moon," but their brand of smooth country-pop was soon eclipsed by the new traditionalist movement. After a commercial decline of several years, the group decided to retire in 1991 and embarked on a successful farewell tour. Larry Gatlin starred in the Broadway production of *The Will Rogers Follies*, and in 1993 the group opened their own theater in Branson, MO. In 1998, Gatlin released the solo gospel album *In My Life*. —*Steve Huey*

The Pilgrim / 1973 / Monument ✦✦✦

Rain Rainbow / 1974 / Monument ✦✦✦

Larry Gatlin With Family & Friends / 1976 / Monument ✦✦✦✦

High Time / 1976 / Monument ✦✦✦

Love Is Just a Game / 1977 / Monument ✦✦✦✦

Night Time Magic / 1978 / Sony Special Products ✦✦✦

Oh! Brother / 1978 / Monument ✦✦✦

Straight Ahead / 1979 / Columbia ✦✦✦✦✦

Occasionally overstated but predominantly satisfying, it's got a little jazz, a little gospel, a little pop, and a little country. Every country fan knows "All the Gold in California," but the best cuts are the controversial "Midnight Choir (Mogen David)" and a sweet little piece of ear candy: "Taking Somebody With Me When I Fall." —*Tom Roland*

Help Yourself / 1980 / Columbia ✦✦✦

Heavy on ballads that effectively show off the Gatlins' trademark genetic harmony. As always, all ten cuts are written by Larry; "Daytime Heroes," a nod to Prince Valium and the soaps, is most inspired. The Gatlin Brothers recorded "Songwriter's Trilogy" live—whether insightful or self-indulgent depends on the listener's viewpoint. —*Tom Roland*

Greatest Hits / 1980 / Columbia ✦✦✦✦✦

As the title suggests, *Larry Gatlin's Greatest Hits* features the biggest hits from both his pre-Gatlin Brothers solo career, as well as his late '70s solo hits. —*Thom Owens*

Sure Feels Like Love / 1982 / Columbia ✦✦✦

Greatest Hits, Vol. 2 / 1983 / Columbia ✦✦✦✦

17 Greatest Hits / 1985 / Columbia ✦✦✦

Despite the omission of a couple of Larry Gatlin's best-known songs like "I've Done Enough Dyin' Today," *17 Greatest Hits* rounds up the majority of Gatlin and the Gatlin Brothers biggest hits from the '70s and early '80s, including "Broken Lady," "Statues Without Hearts," "I Don't Wanna Cry," "I Just Wish You Were Someone I Love," "Sure Feels Like Love," "What Are We Doin' Lonesome," "Denver," and "Houston (Means I'm One Day Closer to You)." *17 Greatest Hits* balances Gatlin's best songs with his most popular (and often more commercial) hits, making it an excellent retrospective and introduction. —*Stephen Thomas Erlewine*

Biggest Hits / 1988 / Columbia ✦✦✦

The Gatlins' *Biggest Hits* these aren't; while songs like "She Used to Be Somebody's Baby," "The Lady Takes the Cowboy Everytime" and "Denver" achieved significant chart success, neither of the trio's number-one singles, "All the Gold in California" and "Houston (Means That I'm One Day Closer to You)," are included. —*Jason Ankeny*

Pure 'n Simple / 1989 / Capitol ✦✦✦

Larry Gatlin has an almost flawless voice that is one of the most soulful in country music. He also is a great songwriter, and he penned all the tunes on *Pure 'n Simple*. The songs are almost instantly accessible. As the album's title suggests, the tracks are simple with stripped-down accompaniment. The album does include a few sappy string arrangements, but they are low in the mix. Clocking in at 32 minutes, *Pure 'n Simple* is a little on the short side but, then again, there's no filler—every song is a winner. —*Tim Griggs*

Adios / 1991 / Liberty ✦✦✦

This album features such Gatlin favorites as "Half Moon Hotel," "Pretty Woman Have Mercy," and "Already on Fire," among others. —*AMG*

Super Hits / Feb. 17, 1998 / Sony ✦✦✦✦

Included are ten of the Gatlin Brothers' biggest hits, such as "Broken Lady," "She Used to Be Somebody's Baby," "I Don't Wanna Cry" and "Take Me to Your Lovin' Place." Though there would've been plenty of room for additional hits, this disc isn't bad value for money at a cheap price. —*John Bush*

Houston to Denver/Not Guilty / Jun. 6, 2000 / Collectables ✦✦✦

Two of Larry Gatlin's excellent early-'80s albums, *Houston to Denver* and *Not Guilty*, are combined on this single compact disc. Although many of the best songs, including "She Used to Sing on Sunday," "Houston (Means I'm One Day Closer to You)," "The Lady Takes the Cowboy Everytime," and "Denver," have been featured on various greatest-hits packages, these albums work well as individual records and are worth acquiring for any Larry Gatlin fan. —*Al Campbell*

● **16 Biggest Hits** / Jun. 13, 2000 / Columbia/Legacy ✦✦✦✦✦

There's only one thing wrong with this album, but it's a big thing. The title notwithstanding, Larry Gatlin & the Gatlin Brothers' *16 Biggest Hits* actually contains 16 of their 17 biggest hits, with one important omission: the number-one hit "I Just Wish You Were Someone I Love." It's hard to think of any excuse other than an error on the part of somebody at Columbia/Legacy to explain why one of the Gatlins' three biggest hits isn't on this collection. Certainly, Larry Gatlin and company were way overdue for a compilation of this sort, not having had any hits albums on the market since a series of three inadequate LPs in the late 1970s and early '80s. (The 1996 collection *The Best of the Gatlins: All the Gold in California* excludes Larry Gatlin's most successful solo recordings, making it another flawed compilation, and more expensive.) The Gatlin discography was subject to a dizzying series of varied billings, with different singles variously credited to: Larry Gatlin; Larry Gatlin With Family & Friends; Larry Gatlin With Brothers and Friends; Larry Gatlin & the Gatlin Brothers Band; Larry Gatlin & the Gatlin Brothers; Larry, Steve, Rudy: the Gatlin Brothers; and the Gatlin Brothers. But no matter what the credit, all of the major Gatlin country hits from 1975's "Broken Lady" to 1988's "Love of a Lifetime" are here, all except "I Just Wish You Were Someone I Love," that is. At a midline price, and containing more of the Gatlins' hits than any other disc, this album must be rated their first pick. But somebody at the record company should correct the obvious mistake and then reissue this reissue. —*William Ruhlmann*

Greatest Hits/Straight Ahead / Jan. 16, 2001 / Collectables ✦✦✦

Larry Gatlin and the Gatlin Brothers had several country hits in the late '70s and early '80s on Columbia records. Quite a few of those are collected on this two-fer reissue from Collectables. *Greatest Hits* contains original versions of "Broken Lady," "Night Time Magic," and "I Just Wish You Were Someone I Love," while Larry Gatlin's solo outing, *Straight Ahead*, contains "Taking Somebody With Me When I Fall," "All the Gold in California," and "Midnight Choir" (Mogan David). Fans of Larry Gatlin will be pleased to have this material combined on one disc. —*Al Campbell*

Danny Gatton

b. Sep. 4, 1945, Washington, D.C., d. Oct. 4, 1994, Newburg, MD

Guitar / Rock & Roll, Country-Rock, Neo-Traditionalist Country, Rockabilly Revival
Guitar virtuoso Danny Gatton was known for the incredibly wide stylistic range of his playing; based in rockabilly, Gatton's musical vocabulary included R&B, pop, country, rock, and jazz, all of which he could play effectively. Gatton began playing at age nine, joining his first band, the Lancers, three years later. In 1960, Gatton pursued a jazz direction when he joined the Offbeats, where pianist/organist Dick Heintze proved to be one of Gatton's biggest influences. The band broke up four years later, and Gatton moved to Nashville to get into session work; there he met Roy Buchanan, who briefly became his roommate and taught him more about his instrument of choice. Eventually, Gatton built a reputation as a top-notch guitarist around his native Washington, D.C., area through his club performances. He recorded an album with his backing band the Fat Boys titled *American Music* in 1975 and followed it with *Redneck Jazz* in 1978. The band on the latter featured steel guitarist Buddy Emmons, drummer Dave Elliott, and eventual longtime cohorts Evan Johns on vocals and rhythm guitar and John Previti on bass.

Gatton's albums led to offers from other musicians to join their bands. Lowell George extended an invitation after leaving Little Feat, but was found dead two days later. Gatton wound up touring with country singer Roger Miller and rockabilly artist Robert Gordon, giving him national exposure and a growing cult among guitar fans, who traded bootlegs of Gatton concerts. Gatton returned to Washington, D.C., to be near his friends and family while playing up and down the East Coast with several bands and doing session work. When Gatton purchased an old farmhouse in need of expensive renovations in 1988, he decided to pursue his music career more seriously. He released his first solo album since 1978 the next year, *Unfinished Business*, which drew notices from several guitar-oriented magazines as well as *Rolling Stone*.

Elektra Records signed him during the summer, and he made his major-label debut in 1991 with the tremendously varied instrumental album *88 Elmira St.* Gatton's first straight-ahead jazz album, *New York Stories*, recorded for none other than Blue Note came out in 1992. Gatton toured the nation solo for the first time in 1993 in support of *Cruisin' Deuces*, but its lack of success, coupled with the departure of A&R man Howard Thompson from Elektra, spelled the end of Gatton's association with the label. Gatton returned to session work to pay the bills, but sustained a further blow when rhythm guitarist Billy Windsor died of a heart attack early in 1994. Gatton collaborated with organ virtuoso Joey DeFrancesco on *Relentless* in May and toured Europe during the summer. Sadly, on October 4, 1994, Gatton locked himself in his garage and shot himself. He left behind no explanation. —*Steve Huey*

American Music / 1975 / NRG ✦✦✦✦

Danny Gatton's debut as a bandleader proved notable for its celebration of neglected idioms like rockabilly, which energized roots music advocates around his native Washington, D.C. Bassist Billy Hancock's uptempo title track comes across as a rallying cry of sorts, an impression underscored by the Clovers' presence on backup vocals. That's not the only unique thing happening here, however. *American Music* outlines the blueprint for Gatton's future development, where he covered whatever territory took his fancy. Whatever you want, it's all here, including Gatton's affinity for country surfaces on "Hauled off and Loved Her," which features a classic Hancock sung-spoken monologue.

Gatton and pianist Dick Heintze—an important collaborator in this era—let their bluesier side fly on "After Hours" and "TV Mama." The band's rockabilly is present and correct on "Ubangi Stomp," as are nods to R&B ("Memphis Disco Funk") and even reggae (Hancock's resigned "Move on Down the Line"). Naturally, there's also plenty of the swing and jazz that Gatton played so fearsomely well. Hard-bopping versions of Benny Goodman's "Good Enough to Keep" naturally coexist with "Harlem Nocturne," which is far more laid-back here than the biting live show piece it would later become. Gatton would famously dismiss the album as "so many different things with different guys who didn't play with us." That's true as far as the credits go, but it's also the diversity which makes this album such a fascinating listen. Five years before roots music became hip to explore, Gatton and friends knew the secret, as Hancock's title song so eloquently states ("never could I find such good American music and it's mine"). The thrill starts here for Gatton fans. —*Ralph Heibutzki*

Redneck Jazz / 1978 / NRG ✦✦✦✦✦
The guitar album of the '70s and the '90s worth unparalleled praise is Danny Gatton's 1978 release *Redneck Jazz*. This album showcases Danny on guitar and banjo, with such stellar talent as Buddy Emmons on pedal steel, pianist Dick Heintze and guitar/vocal support from Evan Johns. This was the work that earned Gatton the title World's Greatest Unknown Guitarist by the *Guitar World* Magazine. —*Thomas Schulte*

Unfinished Business / 1987 / NRG ✦✦✦✦✦
Danny Gatton's album *Unfinished Business* rated number ten of the Top 100 albums of the '80s by *Guitar World* Magazine. On that album, he uses six different Fender and Gibson guitars and amps of 1963 vintage and earlier. The material is very diverse. Included is the Les Paul tribute "Cherokee," an eerie version of the Jackie Gleason theme "Melancholy Serenade" and an intricate construction around the Santo and Johnny standard "Sleepwalk," this album deserves the accolades it has received. —*Thomas Schulte*

● **88 Elmira St.** / 1991 / Elektra ✦✦✦✦✦
After years of knocking around the Washington, D.C.-area circuit, local guitar legend Danny Gatton finally got to cut his first album for a major label. It was indeed worth the wait, spot-welding blinding speed and immaculate chops that went in a million different directions (jazz, country, rockabilly, blues, you name it) to a musical sensibility that made this all-instrumental album a whole lot more than just yer average fretboard wanking jam-fest. Gatton's Telecaster really shines on diverse material ranging from Martin Denny's "Quiet Village" to the roadhouse shuffle "Funky Mama" to the off-the-wall rendition of the theme to *the Simpsons*. Kudos to Elektra for having the corporate balls to put this out; short, chunky, and middle-aged, Danny Gatton was a bona fide guitar hero for the '90s, putting the lie to the hard canard that only speedburner metal mega-hair dudes can make the front covers of the guitar mags. —*Cub Koda*

Danny Gatton / 1993 / Asylum ✦✦✦✦
Cruisin' Deuces / May 18, 1993 / Elektra ✦✦
Following the brief jazz departure of *New York Stories*, Danny Gatton returned to his blues and rock & roll roots with 1993's *Cruisin' Deuces*, which was essentially the follow-up to 1991's *88 Elmira St.* Like that album, *Cruisin' Deuces* is peppered with stinging rockabilly leads and amazing country and blues licks. Gatton's skill was tasteful and lightning fast—he could sound like two guitars playing simultaneously, but he never sounded cluttered or heavy-handed. And his guitar playing is the reason why you listen to a Danny Gatton—the occasional appearance of guest vocalists like Delbert McClinton and Rodney Crowell is just an annoyance. With its reliance on country-oriented material, *Cruisin' Deuces* isn't as diverse as his previous efforts, but it is no less impressive than its predecessors. —*Thom Owens*

Relentless / 1994 / Big Mo ✦✦✦✦
This was a logical matchup. Danny Gatton was a high-powered and very versatile guitarist who could play virtually any modern style. His tonal distortions and use of feedback were impressive but he could also swing as hard as anyone around. The same could be said of organist Joey DeFrancesco and, together with bassist John Previti and drummer Timm Biery, the lead voices romp on a variety of fairly basic material with lots of blues and a few standards. Although no new revelations are offered, the joyful chancetaking of Danny Gatton kept the music from ever becoming predictable or too relaxed; he certainly challenges DeFrancesco throughout this set. —*Scott Yanow*

Humbler: Live / Sep. 17, 1996 / NRG ✦✦✦
This album's title derives from a famous Washington, D.C., music scene in-joke from when aspiring guitar players would play the original bootleg tape for their peers: "You think you're pretty good? Listen to this." Before long, the featured player, Danny Gatton, would be nicknamed "the Humbler" for his fearsome combination of technique and finesse. The nickname came from fellow guitarist Amos Garrett, who was in the audience for this performance with frenetic rockabilly frontman Robert Gordon. In keeping with Gordon's '50s and '60s stance, uptempo early rock & roll is the game here, with Gatton supplying the finger-popping coloration that the music demands. Even as a sideman, he knew the secret of backing a singer: play only what the song requires. Gatton reaches some inspired lickety-split peaks on "You Got Heart Like a Rock" and "Cruisin'." On other tracks—like the smoldering R&B territory of "Fire" or the fatalistic weeper "There Stands the Glass"—he simply drops terse atmospheric fills to bolster the mood. Guitar freaks will also enjoy the bonus soundcheck romp with drummer Shannon Ford through the echo-laden "Fingers on Fire," which starts slowly and builds to a frenzied climax. The liner notes provide a vivid description of the gig (although the date is curiously omitted). This album's more of a diversion to Gatton's back catalog, but stands up as an unpretentious snapshot of guys having fun before an audience who appreciates the goods being delivered. That's enough reason to listen, whether you're a Gatton or Gordon fan. —*Ralph Heibutzki*

In Concert 9/9/94 / Apr. 15, 1997 / Big Mo ✦✦✦
The performance captured on *In Concert 9/9/94* happened less than a month before Danny Gatton's death, and from the sound of the album, it's hard to believe he was in a deep depression. Gatton's playing is incendiary and fiery, an extended display of sheer virtuosity, and the songs are consistently better than his studio albums, which were hampered by filler. Similarly, the studio polish of his albums tended to obscure how dazzling Gatton's pure, unvarnished talent was. That's not the case with *In Concert 9/9/94*, which positively sizzles. It might not be the best way to become acquainted with the guitarist—after all, it doesn't show all of his versatility (the jazzier numbers are noticeably missing)—but for fans, it's one to cherish. —*Thom Owens*

Untouchable / Aug. 11, 1998 / NRG ✦✦✦
This album documents another fascinating, if overlooked aspect of Danny Gatton's musical career: Funhouse, his mid- to late-'80s sextet which also included trumpeter Chris Battistone and tenor saxophonists Phil Berlin and Bruce Swaim, rounded off by drummer Barry Hart and longtime bassist John Previti. The tapes had remained unmixed after the guitarist signed to Elektra Records, according to his mother, Norma, who released them on her NRG label after her son's 1994 death. Other Gatton albums may be more cohesive, but *Untouchable* actually works nicely as a companion to the *Portraits* collection. The result is a typically diverting Gatton free-for-all; the first three tracks alone steer the listener through moody bop ("Poinciana," "One for Lenny's"), a tribute to late jazz guitarist Lenny Breau and a storming R&B tune ("Ain't That Peculiar," which features a rousing Tommy Lepson vocal). The anything-goes atmosphere continues with "Stand By My Side," a soul rave-up written with longtime friend and vocalist Billy Windsor; a typically fleet-fingered rave-up on "Stumblin'"; and a shuffle through "Sweet Georgia Brown" (recorded live and slower than the uptempo Harlem Globetrotters theme rendition). For good measure, there's "Deep Purple," a souvenir from Gatton's famous December 31, 1978, Washington, D.C., gig with his Redneck Jazz Explosion ensemble—although "Gold Rush"'s swing from country to pure guitar pyrotechnic fury and back again is the undoubted highlight, if you could choose just one. But that's hardly possible with Danny Gatton, as the inspired interplay with his hornmen on Nelson Riddle's "Untouchables" theme shows. Trends be damned: wherever his fingers flew, he expected his listeners to follow. If nothing else, this release shows why the major-label world had difficulty containing that vision, but their loss is the listener's gain. —*Ralph Heibutzki*

Portraits / Oct. 27, 1998 / Big Mo ✦✦✦✦
One wonders when getting something that is done posthumously, why wasn't it released before? Is it of inferior quality? Is there something the artist didn't like about it? Is it just to make a buck on the death of the artist? Rest assured, in this case, this is not done just to cash in on the name—this work will stand with the music he produced while he was alive. These cuts were taken from various studio sessions over a 12-year stretch; the last three songs are taken from a live television special from 1989. The songs cover a variety of the flavors of guitar work that Gatton enjoyed playing and experimenting with. It is hung together with his phenomenal guitar work—it's a wonder that anyone could be doing what he is doing with only two hands—but, interestingly, since his death his legend has grown within the circles in which he was already known and has not spread a great deal further. Listen to the incredible work he does on "Pretty Blue." Before you get settled into a groove, he hits you with three rockabilly tunes that he loved to do, including "Dancin' Shoes," which he wrote with Billy Windsor (who did the vocals on this disc). If you happen to be into speed, see if your favorite guitar picker can play as fast and clean as Gatton. This man, though little-known, deserves some recognition for his blending and fusing of jazz, country, R&B, and rockabilly; for his mind-bending technique; and for the beautiful music that he produced. This is a disc that has something for any lover of music without bowing down to the common goal. It is superb. —*Bob Gottlieb*

● **Hot Rod Guitar: The Danny Gatton Anthology** / Apr. 20, 1999 / Rhino ✦✦✦✦✦
It's hard to look at Danny Gatton's career and not feel melancholy. As one of the most gifted guitarists of his generation, he always commanded the respect of his peers and critics, but he never was widely celebrated during his life. Nobody will ever know exactly why he chose to take his life at age 49, but there's little question that he left behind some impressive work—even if it is difficult to listen to his joyous, lively playing and not ponder why he chose suicide. Nevertheless, *Hot Rod Guitar: The Danny Gatton Anthology* is a glorious tribute to the unsung guitar hero, boasting 30 tracks that vividly illustrate why he was always considered a guitarist's guitarist. The compilers reach back to *American Music*, his 1975 indie debut with the Fat Boys, then touch on every phase of his career, including such rarities as a live cut with Robert Gordon. Even with such obscurities gracing the collection, *Hot Rod Guitar* is not a rarities compilation, it's a career history that traces the progression of Gatton's music quite gracefully. Die-hard fans may find a track or two missing, but most of the major pieces are here and all 30 tracks add up to a definitive portrait of a prodigiously talented, boundlessly inventive, and unfortunately tragic guitarist. —*Stephen Thomas Erlewine*

Crystal Gayle (Brenda Gail Webb)

b. Jan. 9, 1951, Paintsville, KY
Vocals / Country-Pop, Urban Cowboy, Soft Rock, Adult Contemporary
One of the most popular and widely recognized female country singers of her era, Crystal Gayle supported her trademark, nearly floor-length hair with a supple voice, a flair for ballads, and a crossover-friendly country-pop style that netted her the occasional mainstream hit. Gayle was born Brenda Gail Webb in Paintsville, KY, in 1951; her older sister was future superstar Loretta Lynn, though Lynn had already left home by the time Brenda was born. The family moved to Wabash, IN, when Brenda was four, and she started singing along with country and pop songs on the radio at a young age. Inspired in part by Lynn's success, Brenda learned guitar and started performing folk songs in high-school,

also singing backing vocals in her brother's band. Lynn encouraged her younger sister, and started bringing her out on tour for a few weeks each summer. Lynn's label, Decca, signed the young singer as soon as she was done with high-school, but suggested a name change so as to avoid confusion with labelmate Brenda Lee. Lynn suggested the name Crystal, inspired by the Krystal hamburger chain, and Brenda adopted her middle name to come up with Crystal Gayle.

Gayle's debut single was 1970's "I've Cried (The Blues Right Out of My Eyes)"; done in a style very similar to Lynn's, it reached the country Top 40. Far from encouraging Gayle to develop her own style, Decca pushed for more "little Loretta" records, and Lynn actually wrote some of her early singles. Unfortunately, this approach failed to establish Gayle in her own right, even with regular appearances on Jim Ed Brown's television show *The Country Place.* Frustrated, she parted ways with Decca and signed with United Artists in 1974, where she was teamed with producer Allen Reynolds. Reynolds offered Gayle the creative freedom she wanted, and she began to experiment with her style and phrasing en route to her own distinctive approach. Her first-ever album, titled simply *Crystal Gayle,* was released in 1974, and the following year she landed her first Top Ten country hit, "Wrong Road Again." In 1976, "I'll Get Over You" became the first of her 17 number-one country singles.

Reynolds, feeling that Gayle was poised for a larger breakthrough, encouraged her to record the jazz-flavored pop ballad "Don't It Make My Brown Eyes Blue," which he felt sure had crossover potential. He was right—not only did the song hit number one on the country charts in 1977, it also climbed to number two on the pop side, garnered substantial international airplay, and won Gayle a Grammy for Best Female Country Vocal. Plus, the accompanying album, *We Must Believe in Magic,* became the first by a female country artist ever to go platinum. Now a bona fide star, Gayle followed her breakthrough success with a string of hits that lasted for approximately the next decade. Before the '70s closed, she scored several more number-one country hits: "You Never Miss a Real Good Thing (Till He Says Goodbye)" (1977), "Ready for the Times to Get Better" (1978), "Talking in Your Sleep" (1978; also a pop Top 20 hit), and "Why Have You Left the One You Left Me For" (1979); plus, 1979's "Half the Way," her first single for new label Columbia, was a number-two country hit and also reached the pop Top 20. She kept on scoring as the '80s dawned; 1980 brought two chart-toppers in "If You Ever Change Your Mind" and "It's Like We Never Said Goodbye," 1981 another in "Too Many Lovers," and 1982 her first number-one duet, "You and I," which was recorded with Eddie Rabbitt and became her second Top Ten pop hit (it also inaugurated her tenure with Elektra/Warner).

Gayle hit number one three times in 1983 ("Baby, What About You," Rodney Crowell's "Till I Gain Control Again," "Our Love Is on the Faultline") and twice more in 1984 ("The Sound of Goodbye," "Turning Away"), and began to cross over to the adult contemporary charts with regularity as well. Gayle's last country number ones came in 1986 with "Cry" and the smooth Gary Morris duet "Makin' Up for Lost Time," after which she—rather abruptly—all but disappeared from the charts. She did continue to record, reuniting with Allen Reynolds for the 1990 Capitol set *Ain't Gonna Worry,* and cutting specialty projects for smaller labels thereafter. She recorded two gospel albums during the '90s, *Someday* (1995) and *He Is Beautiful,* and in 1999 completed a tribute project, *Crystal Gayle Sings the Heart & Soul of Hoagy Carmichael.* In the meantime, she ran a shop in Nashville devoted to fine jewelry and (naturally) crystal. Gayle opened the new millennium with 2000's *In My Arms,* an album of children's songs. —*Steve Huey*

Crystal Gayle / 1974 / EMI America ✦✦✦✦

Somebody Loves You / 1975 / EMI America ✦✦✦✦

Crystal / 1976 / EMI America ✦✦✦✦

We Must Believe in Magic / 1977 / Razor & Tie ✦✦✦

I've Cried the Blue Right Out of My Eyes / 1978 / MCA ✦✦✦

When I Dream / 1978 / Razor & Tie ✦✦✦

Miss the Mississippi / 1979 / Capitol ✦✦✦
Gayle's first LP for Columbia, *Miss the Mississippi* contains the hits "It's Like We Never Said Goodbye," "The Blue Side" and "Half the Way." —*Jason Ankeny*

• **Classic Crystal** / 1979 / EMI ✦✦✦✦✦
Of Gayle's many overlapping hits collections, this one's the best. Given her crossover success ("Don't It Make My Brown Eyes Blue," included here, hit number-two pop) it's interesting to note that all of these tracks were produced by Allen Reynolds, known these days for his work with Garth Brooks. —*Dan Cooper*

These Days / 1980 / Columbia ✦✦✦
These Days earned Gayle two more number-one hits, "Too Many Lovers" and "If You Ever Change Your Mind." —*Jason Ankeny*

Hollywood, Tennessee / 1981 / Capitol ✦✦✦
Hollywood, Tennessee features the Top Ten hits "You Never Gave Up on Me," "Livin' in These Troubled Times" and "The Woman in Me," as well as a cover of the Bill Withers classic "Ain't No Sunshine." —*Jason Ankeny*

True Love / 1982 / Elektra ✦✦✦✦✦
When Gayle delivered the album to then-Elektra-division-head Jimmy Bowen, he complained that it rocked too much. Producer Allen Reynolds refused to make changes, so Bowen produced three new tracks that seem out of place. Yeah, the Reynolds tracks do rock. So what? Gayle gives some of her best performances ever on "Our Love Is on the Faultline" and "Deeper in the Fire." —*Tom Roland*

Crystal Gayle's Greatest Hits / 1983 / Columbia ✦✦✦✦✦
Always greatly influenced by pop sounds, Gayle embraced that aspect of her musical heritage more in the late '70s and early '80s than any other period. This set covers it well ("Half the Way" is classic), and provides a nice cover photo too. —*Tom Roland*

Crystal Gayle / 1986 / Capitol ✦✦✦

What If We Fall in Love / 1987 / Warner Bros. ✦✦✦

Nobody's Angel / 1988 / Warner Bros. ✦✦
Nobody's Angel, Gayle's final album for Warner Bros., features the title cut and the minor hit "Tennessee Nights." —*Jason Ankeny*

All-Time Greatest Hits / 1990 / Curb ✦✦✦✦
Curb's *All-Time Greatest Hits* may be a budget-line collection, but there has been a dearth of collections of Crystal Gayle's '70s recordings for Decca as well as United Artists/EMI, which is arguably her best work. So, this 12-track collection is worthwhile because it contains some of the best of those recordings, including her Decca debut single, "I've Cried (The Blue Right Out of My Eyes)," and the big hits "Don't It Make My Brown Eyes Blue" and "You'll Never Miss a Real Good Thing ('Till He Says Goodbye)." This could have been presented with more care, and have more tracks, but it's as effective a sampler as any Gayle collection currently on the market—which is a bit of a shame, because this should be replaced by a nice, thorough collection spanning her Decca, UA, Elektra, and Warner Bros. recordings. —*Stephen Thomas Erlewine*

50 Original Tracks / 1993 / EMI Country ✦✦✦✦
50 Original Tracks is a two-CD import that offers every Top 40 country hit Gayle recorded for United Artists in the '70s, including "Don't It Make My Brown Eyes Blue" and several other number ones. She signed with Capitol Nashville in 1990, and a sampling of tracks from that period are collected as well. The quality is high throughout this very listenable anthology, and many of the non-hits and album tracks are nearly the equal of the better-known hits. Given the quantity of material, there is inevitably a bum track here and there (most notably the bizarre futuristic fantasy of "We Must Believe in Magic"), but in terms of sheer length, this generous import compilation far surpasses anything available domestically. Gayle's music during this era hovers somewhere between the pop-country of, say, Glen Campbell, and the smooth easy listening of the Carpenters, but an occasional strain of pure(r) country sometimes emerges, along with a faint echo of Gayle's hard country sibling, Loretta Lynn. —*Greg Adams*

Super Hits / Feb. 17, 1998 / Sony ✦✦✦
Included are ten of Crystal Gayle's biggest hits, like "Half the Way," "Too Many Lovers," "The Blue Side" and "It's Like We Never Said Goodbye." Though there would've been plenty of room for additional hits, this disc isn't bad value for money at a cheap price. —*John Bush*

The Best of Crystal Gayle / Mar. 19, 2002 / Rhino ✦✦✦
Rhino's 2002 release *The Very Best of Crystal Gayle* has many of her biggest hits, but it's not necessarily a representative collection. That's because the 19-track compilation concentrates on recordings that WEA, Rhino's parent company, owns—so after the first two songs, including her defining moment "Don't It Make My Brown Eyes Blue," it moves into her recordings for Elektra in the early '80s. Some of these were big country hits, some, like her Eddie Rabbitt duet "You and I," were even crossover hits, but they weren't as definitive as those she made for United Artists and Columbia, nor were they as good. They tend to be a little homogenized, even when they're good, which means this collection is a little too even-keeled for those that are expecting more of "Don't It Make My Brown Eyes Blue." Which means that even if this summarizes Gayle's '80s recordings well, it's not really the very best she ever recorded. —*Stephen Thomas Erlewine*

The Geezinslaws

f. 1960, Austin, TX
Group / Country Comedy, Nashville Sound/Countrypolitan
As you might expect from their name, the Geezinslaws were a musical comedy outfit who based their recording career on barroom-friendly parodies of popular country songs. They were originally known as the Geezinslaw Brothers, but actually consisted of singer/mandolin player Sammy Allred and singer/guitarist Raymond "Son" Smith, who attended high-school together in Austin, TX. They began performing locally, and in 1961 caught their big break when they were invited to appear on Arthur Godfrey's hit variety show. That helped lead to a record deal with Columbia, which issued their first album, *The Kooky World of the Geezinslaw Brothers,* in 1963; by this time, they'd relocated to New York permanently. They subsequently moved over to Capitol and recorded four albums for the label between 1966-1969, scoring minor hit singles with songs like "Chubby (Please Take Your Love to Town)" and "You Wouldn't Put the Shuck on Me." They continued to appear on TV variety shows, including those of Johnny Carson, Ed Sullivan, and Jackie Gleason, and became regulars on Ralph Emery's radio program *Pop Goes the Country.*

The Geezinslaw Brothers all but disappeared during the '70s, but suddenly returned—with their name shortened to the Geezinslaws—in 1986, when they appeared on the Emery-hosted *Nashville Now* TV show. They returned to recording in 1989 with *The Geezinslaws,* released on the Step One label, which mixed song parodies with more straight-ahead country. *World Tour* (1990) followed a similar pattern, and 1992's *Feelin' Good, Gittin' Up, Gittin' Down* gave them their first chart single in over two decades with "Help, I'm White and I Can't Get Down." They toured a bit more frequently during the early '90s, and issued a full-on comedy record in 1994 with *I Wish I Had a Job to Shove.* Another effort, *Blah...Blah...Blah,* followed in 1997, and remains the duo's final album to date. —*Steve Huey*

The Kooky World of the Geezinslaw Brothers / 1963 / Columbia ✦✦✦✦

Can You Believe / 1966 / Capitol ✦✦✦✦

My Dirty, Lowdown, Rotten, Cotton-Pickin' Little Darlin' / 1967 / Capitol ✦✦✦✦
It's too bad that the Geezinslaw Brothers didn't have any major hits, because their lack of chart success might prevent their fine and funny late-'60s Capitol recordings from being reissued. The duo made the country Top 100 three times during their stint with Capitol, but never cracked the Top 40. *My Dirty, Lowdown, Rotten, Cotton-Pickin' Little Darlin'* is their second album for the label and contains the hit "Change of Wife," which

is the only original composition on the album. The other songs are novelties written by assorted country greats such as Bill Anderson, George Jones, and Roger Miller. The excellent title track, from the pen of Jack Clement, apparently was never released as a single. Less hokey than Pinkard & Bowden and less hillbilly than Homer & Jethro, the sometimes serious Geezinslaws nonetheless belong within the pantheon of great country comedy duos. *—Greg Adams*

Chubby (Please Take Your Love to Town) / 1968 / Capitol ✦✦✦

The Geezinslaws Are Alive (And Well) / 1969 / Capitol ✦✦✦

If You Think I'm Crazy Now / 1979 / Lone Star ✦✦✦

The Geezinslaws / 1989 / Step One ✦✦✦✦
In addition to a frenetic take on "Over the Rainbow" and the tongue-in-cheek "Hank Williams Led a Happy Life," the Geezinslaws offer more straightforward covers of ace songwriters John Prine ("Fryin' Pan") and Robert Earl Keen Jr. ("Swervin' in My Lane"). *—Jason Ankeny*

● **World Tour** / 1990 / Step One ✦✦✦✦✦
Though the best of the Geezinslaws' earlier tracks have yet to be anthologized, this album comes the closest to capturing their peculiar brand of country mayhem. *—Cub Koda*

Feelin' Good, Gittin' Up, Gittin' Down / 1992 / Step One ✦✦
While *Feelin' Good* is made up of the usual Geezinslaws fare (the original "Help... I'm White and I Can't Get Down," a cover of Shel Silverstein's "Diet Song"), for some inexplicable reason the duo decided to add canned laughter between cuts, which makes their humor seem forced and uninspired. *—Jason Ankeny*

Bobbie Gentry (Roberta Streeter)

b. Jul. 27, 1944, Chickasaw County, MS

Vocals, Guitar / Country-Pop, Nashville Sound/Countrypolitan, Blue-Eyed Soul, Soft Rock, Pop

Bobbie Gentry remains one of the most interesting and underappreciated artists to emerge out of Nashville during the late '60s. Best-known for her crossover smash "Ode to Billie Joe," she was one of the first female country artists to write and produce much of her own material, forging an idiosyncratic, pop-inspired sound that, in tandem with her glamorous, bombshell image, anticipated the rise of latter-day superstars like Shania Twain and Faith Hill. Of Portuguese descent, Gentry was born Roberta Streeter in Chickasaw County, MS, on July 27, 1944; her parents divorced shortly after her birth and she was raised in poverty on her grandparents' farm. After her grandmother traded one of the family's milk cows for a neighbor's piano, seven-year-old Bobbie composed her first song, "My Dog Sergeant Is a Good Dog," years later self-deprecatingly reprised in her nightclub act; at 13, she moved to Arcadia, CA, to live with her mother, soon beginning her performing career in local country clubs. The 1952 film *Ruby Gentry* lent the singer her stage surname.

After graduating high-school, Gentry settled in Las Vegas, where she appeared in the Les Folies Bergère nightclub revue; she soon returned to California, studying philosophy at U.C.L.A. before transferring to the Los Angeles Conservatory of Music. In 1964, she made her recorded debut, cutting a pair of duets—"Ode to Love" and "Stranger in the Mirror"—with rockabilly singer Jody Reynolds. Gentry continued performing in clubs in the years to follow before an early 1967 recording a demo found its way to Capitol Records producer Kelly Gordon; upon signing to the label, she issued her debut single, "Mississippi Delta." However, disc jockeys began spinning the B-side, the self-penned "Ode to Billie Joe"—with its eerily spare production and enigmatic narrative detailing the suicide of Billie Joe McAllister, who flings himself off the Tallahatchie Bridge, the single struck a chord on country and pop radio alike, topping the pop charts for four weeks in August 1967 and selling three-million copies. Although the follow-up, "I Saw an Angel Die," failed to chart, Gentry nevertheless won three Grammy awards, including Best New Artist and Best Female Vocal. She was also named the Academy of Country Music's Best New Female Vocalist.

With her second album, 1968's *The Delta Sweete*, Gentry returned to the country charts with the minor hit "Okolona River Bottom Band." Although her recordings were typically credited to Capitol staff producers, she later maintained she helmed the sessions herself and also wrote much of her own material, drawing on her Mississippi roots to compose revealing vignettes that typically explored the lifestyles, values, and even hypocrisies of the Southern culture. Favoring more soulful and rootsy arrangements over the lavish countrypolitan style in vogue in Nashville at the time, Gentry's records sound quite unlike anything on either the country or pop charts at the time and her smoky, sensuous voice adapted easily to a variety of musical contexts. But to many listeners, she remained a one-hit wonder and her excellent third album, 1968's *Local Gentry*, received little notice. That same year, Gentry issued a duet album with Glen Campbell, returning to the country Top 20 with "Let It Be Me"; the duo regularly collaborated throughout the 1970s, scoring their biggest hit with a reading of "All I Really Want to Do."

In 1969, Gentry reached her creative zenith with *Touch 'Em With Love*—though cut in Nashville, the record owed far more to the gritty R&B sounds emanating across the state in Memphis and generated her first U.K. number one, a smoldering rendition of the Burt Bacharach/Hal David perennial "I'll Never Fall in Love Again." The single's success also earned Gentry her own short-lived BBC television variety series. However, as her star diminished stateside, she became a fixture of the Las Vegas circuit, mounting an elaborate nightclub revue that she not only headlined but also wrote and produced, even overseeing the choreography and costuming. Gentry's 1969 marriage to Desert Inn Hotel manager Bill Harrah ended after only three months, but the following year she returned to the country and pop Top 40 with the title cut from her fifth album *Fancy*. In 1971, she issued her final Capitol effort, *Patchwork*, primarily confining her performing to her nightclub act for the next several years. A CBS summer replacement series, *The Bobbie Gentry Happiness Hour*, aired for four episodes in 1974; Gentry next surfaced on the big screen, credited as co-writer for a 1976 film adaptation of *Ode to Billie Joe*. After a second marriage, to fellow singer/songwriter Jim Stafford, ended in 1979 after only 11 months, Gentry gradually receded from public view, retiring from performing and eventually settling in Los Angeles. *—Jason Ankeny*

Ode to Billie Joe / 1967 / Capitol ✦✦✦✦✦
Gentry's debut LP, which went to number one on the pop charts, was a promising but not wholly satisfying disc, with the singer penning all but one of the songs. Inevitably, the title track dwarfed everything else by comparison, but a greater problem was that several of the other tunes recycled variations of the "Ode to Billie Joe" riff. On the other hand, "Mississippi Delta" is gloriously tough, throaty swamp rock; few other women pop singers have sounded as raw. Other good cuts were "I Saw an Angel Die," an effective mating of Gentry's country blues guitar riffs and low-key orchestration, and the jazz waltz-timed "Papa, Woncha Let Me Go to Town With You." Her vocals are poised and husky throughout the record, on which she was definitely on the right track—one that she was quickly diverted from, into more MOR-oriented sounds. *—Richie Unterberger*

The Delta Sweete / 1968 / Capitol ✦✦✦✦✦
Delta Sweete was Bobbie Gentry's 1968 follow-up to her hugely popular *Ode to Billie Joe* record—the title track topped the pop charts and made the country Top 20. Although it doesn't quite match the quality of *Ode*, *Delta Sweete* does contain a good selection of Gentry originals and some fine covers. The "Sweete" in the title refers to both Gentry's southern-belle good looks (her publishing company was called Super Darlin') and the album's suite structure. The 12 segued songs detail Gentry's idyllic Mississippi childhood and include portraits of home and church life ("Reunion," "Sermon"), as well as recollections of blues and country hits she certainly heard as a youngster ("Big Boss Man," "Tobacco Road"). In fact, the prevailing sound on both *Delta Sweete* and *Ode to Billy Joe* is a swampy, folk-tinged combination of blues and country, with uptown touches like strings and horns seemingly added to reflect the then modern styles of soul and the Nashville sound. Gentry also includes some dreamy, pastoral originals like "Morning Glory" and "Courtyard," songs that could've been written by melancholy folkster Nick Drake. In light of all the album's good qualities, then, it's a shame it's out of print. [Collectables' *The Golden Classics of Bobbie Gentry* combines the *Ode to Billie Joe* album with a few tracks from *Delta Sweete*, including the hits "Okolona River Bottom Band" and "Louisiana Man."] *—Stephen Cook*

Bobbie Gentry & Glen Campbell / 1968 / Capitol ✦✦✦✦
Bobbie Gentry would soon become a regular guest on Glen Campbell's genial television variety show, where her pantsuited, beehived country-pop bombshell image belied her delicate, sweet voice and smart, blues-tinged songwriting. Sadly, the latter is underrepresented here, as only her minor "Mornin' Glory" makes the cut (compared to two of Campbell's own songs and a sweet but slight duet remake of his signature song, John Hartford's "Gentle on My Mind"), but Gentry's special vocal blend with Campbell—the pair's voices harmonize utterly delightfully—is the real highlight of this set. The song selection is pop-oriented, featuring surprising cover choices like Simon & Garfunkel's "Scarborough Fair/Canticle" and, even better, a winning version of Margo Guryan's "Sunday Morning" that's surprisingly well-suited to Kelly Gordon and Al DeLory's countrypolitan production. However, Bob Russell's "Little Green Apples" is smarmy mush no matter who records it. This album is well worth seeking out for fans of both singers. *—Stewart Mason*

Local Gentry / 1968 / Capitol ✦✦✦✦
Local Gentry is an exquisitely wrought collection of character studies steeped in the myth and lore of Southern culture—from the funeral parlor director portrayed in "Casket Vignette" to the titular "Ace Insurance Man," Bobbie Gentry etches a series of revealing, well-observed narratives populated by folks both larger-than-life and small-time, adding up to something not unlike a country-pop *Spoon River Anthology*. A subtle, primarily acoustic effort, the record's sound and sensibility are steeped in Gentry's Mississippi upbringing, but despite the music's warmth and humanity, the effect is neither nostalgic nor saccharine—instead, Gentry wistfully and wryly evokes a colorful rural culture populated by soldiers, widows, and traveling medicine shows. The five original compositions here rank among her most literate and personal, while covers like the Beatles' "Fool on the Hill" and "Eleanor Rigby" add to the roll call of misfits, eccentrics, and beautiful losers. Like all of Gentry's efforts, it's ripe for reissue. *—Jason Ankeny*

Touch 'Em With Love / 1969 / Capitol ✦✦✦✦✦
Touch 'Em With Love is Bobbie Gentry's finest studio effort, a fascinatingly eclectic and genuinely affecting record that broadened her musical horizons far beyond the limitations of the Nashville sound. Its unexpectedly gritty, soulful production makes it something of a spiritual twin to Dusty Springfield's *Dusty in Memphis*, also released in 1969 (both even feature renditions of "Son of a Preacher Man"): Gentry's husky, sensual delivery proves as ideally suited for the Southern-fried funk of the opening title track as it does for the bluegrass-flavored "Natural to Be Gone," deftly moving from genre to genre to encompass everything from faux-gospel ("Glory Hallelujah, How They'll Sing") to lushly orchestrated pop ("I Wouldn't Be Surprised," the disc's centerpiece). Even more eye-opening is that Gentry's originals stand tall alongside material from composers including Burt Bacharach ("I'll Never Fall in Love Again," which earned her a chart-topping single in the U.K.) and Jimmy Webb ("Where's the Playground, Johnny")—her folky "Seasons Come, Seasons Go," an acute tale of lost love, offers *Touch 'Em With Love*'s most profoundly beautiful moment. A truly great and tragically under-recognized album. *—Jason Ankeny*

Fancy / 1970 / Capitol ✦✦✦
Fancy is a wild ride through all the contradictions that are Bobbie Gentry. After her breakthrough smash, "Ode to Billy Joe," with its haunted guitar figure and cipher meaning, the Mississippi singer/songwriter became the embodiment of backwoods in the eyes of the American public. But on *Fancy*, Gentry told the truth of what she aspired to. The title track is a "Billie Joe"-type story with a similar guitar figure; it also has a host of West Coast horns telling an unapologetic rags-to-riches story without regrets that mirrors Gentry's

own. But it only begins here. From here, Gentry, assisted or perhaps directed by producer Rich Hall, cuts a pair of Bacharach/David numbers ("Raindrops Keep Fallin' on My Head" and "I'll Never Fall in Love Again"), James Taylor's "Something in the Way He (sic) Moves," Leon Russell's "Delta Man" (sic), Nilsson's "Rainmaker," Rudy Clark's "If You Gotta Make a Fool of Somebody," Laura Nyro's "Wedding Bell Blues," and a few others with full strings, horns, orchestras, and glockenspiels for accompaniment—along with a honky tonk piano, drum kit, and electric bass. What it makes for is even more of a mystery than "Ode to Billie Joe." Gentry's voice, with its smoke-tinged husky contralto, is ill-suited to this material. But that in itself is what makes this such a fascinating listen. None of it works, yet as a result, it's kind of a shambolic masterpiece. Not for the weak, but a compelling experience if you can make it through. —*Thom Jurek*

Bobbie Gentry's Greatest! / 1970 / Capitol ✦✦✦
A too-brief ten-song collection that does have, in addition to "Ode to Billie Joe," some of her best post-debut LP original material, like "Okolona River Bottom Band" and "Sweet Peony." However, there's not enough from the first album, and there's too much silly pop tripe on side two. A much better job could and should be done. —*Richie Unterberger*

Sittin' Pretty/Tobacco Road / 1971 / Capitol ✦✦✦✦

Patchwork / 1971 / Capitol ✦✦✦✦

Greatest Hits / 1990 / Curb ✦✦✦✦✦
Here are Bobbie Gentry's biggest hits from the late '60s including "Ode to Billie Joe," "Louisiana Man," "Fancy," plus her hit duets with Glen Campbell, "Let It Be Me" and "All I Have To Do Is Dream." —*Thom Owens*

The Golden Classics of Bobbie Gentry / Jan. 5, 1998 / Collectables ✦✦✦✦
Collectables' *The Golden Classics of Bobbie Gentry* is an expanded edition of her debut album *Ode to Billie Joe*, featuring all the songs from the original album plus eight bonus tracks, all of which were hits: "Louisiana Man," "Okolona River Bottom Band," "He Made a Woman Out of Me," "Fancy," "Apartment," plus the Glen Campbell duets "All I Have to Do Is Dream," "Let It Be Me" and "Mornin' Glory." The presence of the album tracks from *Ode to Billie Joe* prevents it from being a straight-ahead greatest-hits album, but *The Golden Classics* comes closer to filling that bill than any other disc on the market. —*Stephen Thomas Erlewine*

★ **The Capitol Years: Ode to Bobbie Gentry** / Nov. 28, 2000 / EMI ✦✦✦✦✦
EMI/Zonophone's 2000 release *The Capitol Years: Ode to Bobbie Gentry* was the first CD-era compilation to make a serious attempt at summarizing Bobbie Gentry's remarkable recordings for Capitol during the late '60s and early '70s. Gentry didn't quite fit into any category. She was a singer/songwriter with a strong talent for folk narratives, but she had a husky, sexy voice and a predilection for blues and R&B. Her productions were slick and bright, perfect for AM pop radio, but she was pitched in a country direction. She wound up having success in many of these markets—most notably with the Grammy-winning number one single "Ode to Billy Joe"—but her music got increasingly idiosyncratic and her sales got increasingly smaller. Years later, her legacy seemed down to "Ode to Billy Joe," particularly since her Capitol catalog wasn't widely available, but *The Capitol Years* went a long way to restoring that reputation. It's not perfect by any means, however. It has a weird duality in that it favors her pop side yet leaves off many of her American chart singles: "Okolona River Bottom Band," "Louisiana Man," "Mornin' Glory," and the Glen Campbell duets "Let It Be Me" and "All I Have to Do Is Dream" are all missing. Yet it also tends to bypass stark, eerie mood pieces like "Casket Vignette" that are at the core of her cult legend in some quarters, since these prove how deeply her work could cut. So, this compilation winds up following compiler Dean Rudland's whims, which means it emphasizes material that plays up her pop and soul sides, including covers of "You've Made Me So Very Happy," "Son of a Preacher Man," "In the Ghetto," "I'll Never Fall in Love Again," and "Big Boss Man." This may not be the most unique of Gentry's work, even if it still bears her unique vocal style, and given the lack of compilations on the market, it's hard not to wish that these were left behind for some original work. Still, *The Capitol Years* has considerable merit, particularly in light of Raven's subsequent *An American Quilt* compilation. Where that disc focused on her quirkier material—exactly the songs missing from here—this is pitched at the mainstream that she most certainly played a part in during her peak. So, even though there's overlap with the Raven title, *The Capitol Years* certainly has its own character, one that's lighter and fluffier, but still quite appealing; for those who like the *sound* of Gentry's records, this is the preferable introduction (those who want her riskier material should turn to *An American Quilt*), but most listeners will need both. —*Stephen Thomas Erlewine*

★ **An American Quilt: 1967–1974** / Aug. 13, 2002 / Raven ✦✦✦✦✦
Released two years after EMI/Zonophone's *The Capitol Years: Ode to Bobbie Gentry*, Raven's 26-track, single-disc collection *An American Quilt: 1967-1974*, intentionally or not, serves as a counterpoint to that pop-oriented compilation. Where that collection left off many charting hits, it did have an MOR, mainstream pop bent, particularly through its inclusion of many covers. This contains the missing hits—"Okolona River Bottom Band," "Louisiana Man," "Mornin' Glory," although "He Made a Woman Out of Me" and the Glen Campbell duets "Let It Be Me" and "All I Have to Do Is Dream" are missing—along with the hits and usual suspects from *The Capitol Years* ("Ode to Billie Joe," "Mississippi Delta," "Touch 'Em With Love," "Fancy," "Apartment 21"). *An American Quilt* excels in its non-hit song selection, in how it emphasizes Gentry's skill in creating evocative small-town narratives and eerie, low-key mood pieces like "Casket Vignette." Compiler John Dowler relies heavily on this material, which is good not only because *The Capitol Years* avoided it, but it also enhances Gentry's legacy as a songwriter and performer with a unique style and vision that could not be easily pigeonholed into country, pop, or soul. In its own way, however, it is just as skewed a compilation as *The Capitol Years*, since it does focus on one side of her musical personality over another, when what was so

fascinating about Bobbie Gentry is how she contained both sides, often on one album. Still, that's a minor point—this is a superb compilation of a neglected artist, and while both this and its *Capitol Years* companion are necessary, those more interested in her idiosyncratic side should turn here. —*Stephen Thomas Erlewine*

Mark Germino

Guitar, Vocals / Country-Rock, Singer/Songwriter, Americana
Originally a poet, Mark Germino eventually became a folk-rock artist as a means of furthering his literary aspirations. Born in North Carolina, he moved to Nashville in 1974; although he never intended to become a musician, he bought a guitar a few months later after reasoning that performing songs would be easier than reciting poetry. A trucker by day, Germino began performing in area clubs at night and signed a music publishing deal in 1981. After working as a songwriter for much of the decade, in the late '80s and early '90s Germino issued three major-label albums in a vein of heartland rock much like the work of Steve Earle, including 1990's *Radartown* (recorded with a backing band called the Sluggers) and *London Moon and Barnyard Remedies*. In 1995, he issued the folkier *Rank & File*. —*Jason Ankeny*

London Moon and Barnyard Remedies / 1986 / RCA ✦✦✦

Radartown (Mark Germino & The Sluggers?) / 1990 / Zoo ✦✦✦✦

● **Rank & File** / May 15, 1995 / Winter Harvest ✦✦✦✦
More proof that there are still plenty of decent writers in Nashville, ones who can write songs that tell a story and have some meat to them. Germino's clever songs have popped up on other artist's records, including Confederate Railroad. But Germino is a poet at heart, and this record is far from a commercial country album. Rather, *Rank & File* is a folk-oriented record, giving Germino the room to stretch with literary detail. Armed with a gravelly voice, and working within an acoustic setting, he falls somewhere between John Prine and Steve Earle; Germino's songs are also similar to both of these artists in the way he can weave a yarn, bringing characters to life through his biting wit and un-compromising sincerity. There's plenty of humor, but by no means is it all lighter fare; there are also serious songs, and they cut deep. —*Jack Leaver*

Alice Gerrard

Banjo, Fiddle, Guitar, Vocals, Singer / Neo-Traditional Folk, Old-Timey, String Bands, Contemporary Folk, Appalachian Folk
The daughter of trained classical musicians, Alice Gerrard didn't grow up with bluegrass or folk music. Her earliest musical memories are of singing along with family members and friends around the living room piano. Gerrard's albums with West Virginia-born folksinger Hazel Dickens, however, rank among the most influential recordings in folk music history. Gerrard's first exposure to folk music came while she was attending Antioch College in Ohio. Inspired by the folk songs played by dorm-mates, Gerrard abandoned the piano and became absorbed with the more rural sounds that she heard on such albums as *The Anthology of American Folk Music*.

Moving to Washington, D.C., to complete her college co-op experience, Gerrard encountered a thriving bluegrass scene. Hanging out in her spare time at the Famous Restaurant in Washington, D.C., Gerrard met numerous bluegrass and old-timey musicians, including Mike Seeger of the New Lost City Ramblers, who introduced her to Dickens. With their mutual love of traditional American music, Gerrard and Dickens became close friends. Developing a unique harmony style that combined the alto-below-lead of the Carter Family and the tenor-above-lead of Bill Monroe, the two vocalists soon became frequent performers in the folk clubs and coffeehouses of the Capitol region. Their repertoire continued to expand as they studied sheet music at the Library of Congress and taped old-timey musicians at folk festivals.

Gerrard and Dickens' debut album, *Who's That Knocking*, released in 1965, was recorded for 75 dollars at the First Unitarian Church in Washington and featured accompaniment by David Grisman (mandolin), Lamar Grier (banjo), and Chubby Wise and Billy Baker (fiddles). Although their second album, *Won't You Come and Sing?*, featuring the same musicians, was recorded the same year, it wasn't released until 1973. Gerrard and Dickens' first two albums were later combined and released as *Pioneering Women of Bluegrass* in 1996. The 26 tunes on the reissued album include six Carter Family songs, five Monroe tunes, three original songs by Dickens, and Gerrard's hard-hitting satire of sexist attitudes towards women, "Custom Made Woman Blues."

Gerrard and Dickens' *Get Acquainted Waltz* was released in 1975 and featured accompaniment by Seeger, who was at the time Gerrard's husband, and his New Lost City Ramblers bandmate Tracy Schwartz. Gerrard subsequently recorded two albums with Seeger—*Mike and Alice Seeger in Concert* in 1970 and *Mike Seeger and Alice Gerrard* in 1980—and one solo collection, *Pieces of My Heart* in 1994. Since 1987, Gerrard has published *The Old Time Herald*, a quarterly magazine devoted to the preservation of old-timey music. —*Craig Harris*

● **Pioneering Women of Bluegrass** / 1996 / Smithsonian Folkways ✦✦✦✦✦
Dickens and Gerrard recorded a couple of albums in the mid-'60s that are now acknowledged as groundbreakers in demonstrating that women could play and record quality bluegrass. This collection remasters and re-sequences 26 tracks from the sessions, as well as adding lengthy historical liner notes, much of them contributed by the performers themselves. Historical significance aside, it's pretty good bluegrass, the two singers and instrumentals supported by other good musicians, including a young David Grisman. Their set leaned heavily on covers of tunes by the Carter Family and Bill Monroe (who specifically gave "I Hear a Sweet Voice Calling" to the duo), with additional items by the Delmore Brothers, the Stanley Brothers, and the like. Alice Gerrard's low vocals give this a greater gravity than much bluegrass. A special highlight is the cover of the magnificently mournful "The One I Love Is Gone," another tune that Monroe donated to the pair. Inverting the usual bluegrass cliché, one might call it an example of the low and lonesome sound. —*Richie Unterberger*

Terri Gibbs

b. Jun. 15, 1954, Augusta, GA

Vocals / Country-Pop, CCM, Adult Contemporary, Country Gospel, Urban Cowboy, Soft Rock

Country-pop singer/songwriter/keyboardist Terri Gibbs enjoyed some success in the early '80s before returning to the gospel music she grew up with. Gibbs was born in Augusta, GA, in 1954; blind from birth, she turned to music at an early age, first playing the piano at only three years old. In addition to gospel music, she listened to early rock & roll, pop, and soul (particularly Ray Charles), and loved the *Grand Ole Opry* radio show. She sang in choirs and talent contests while growing up, and met Chet Atkins backstage at one show. At his request, she sent him a demo tape, and at 18 followed his advice to try her luck in Nashville. She didn't have much luck attracting record companies, and instead moved to Miami, where she played keyboards in a band called Sound Dimension. In 1973, she quit the band to attend college, but dropped out after a year to focus on songwriting. She returned to Augusta, formed her own band in 1975, and played locally for the next several years. Her demo tape found its way into the hands of producer/songwriter Ed Penney, who signed her to MCA in 1980.

The title cut of Gibbs' Top Ten debut album, *Somebody's Knockin'*, was a major crossover hit in 1981; not only did it reach the country Top Ten, it also just missed similar territory on the pop side, and climbed into the Top Five on the adult contemporary charts. The follow-up, "Rich Man," was a Top 20 country hit, and Gibbs was named the ACM's Best New Female Vocalist, also winning the CMA's inaugural Horizon Award (for artists rising to new levels of prominence). However, while Gibbs charted with two more albums (1981's *I'm a Lady* and 1983's *Over Easy*), neither matched the success of her debut. Likewise, she managed two more Top 20 country hits in 1982's "Ashes to Ashes" and 1983's "Anybody Else's Heart but Mine," but nothing on the level of "Somebody's Knockin'." Still, she embarked on a high-profile tour with George Jones over 1981-1982, often duetting on-stage with him. Gibbs spent several years off-record, then switched to the kind of country gospel music she'd started out singing. She returned in 1987 with the Grammy-nominated *Turn Around*; "Unconditional Love," "Comfort the People," and "Promised Land" were all successful on the CCM charts. After 1990's *Great Day*, on the small Morning Gate label, Gibbs left music to concentrate on her family. *—Steve Huey*

Somebody's Knockin' / 1981 / MCA ✦✦✦✦

Country singer and songwriter Terri Gibbs earned a lot of fans with her single, "Somebody's Knockin'," which quickly became a surprise nationwide country hit. It was also used as the first track for this debut album of the same name, released under the MCA Records label in 1980. A year later her songs landed her an Academy of Country Music's Best New Female Vocalist Award and the Country Music Association's Horizon Award. The album brought her a much-deserved Grammy Award nomination the following year, and a chance to appear on the *Grand Ole Opry*. This first full-length offering from the singer is a pleasant addition to any country music album collection. The title track, "Somebody's Knockin'" will probably be the favorite for many, but there are other gems to be sampled as well on this ten-track recording by Gibbs. *—Charlotte Dillon*

I'm a Lady / 1981 / MCA ✦✦✦

You Can't Run Away / 1982 / MCA ✦✦✦

Over Easy / 1983 / MCA ✦✦✦

Turn Around / 1987 / Canaan ✦✦✦✦

Singer, songwriter, and pianist Terri Gibbs first caught the public's attention in 1981 with her major hit, "Somebody's Knockin'," which brought her spots on the music charts in both country and pop. Gibbs completed a few other country albums over the next few years, but in the latter half of the '80s she took her talents in a gospel direction with the appropriately titled *Turn Around*. Since she was raised on Southern gospel music, it was a natural move for her, and fans responded. Just as listeners can hear gospel influences on Gibbs' country albums, you'll find the country influences come through on this gospel recording. The songs on *Turn Around* earned Gibbs a few more hits to add to her resumé, including "Unconditional Love," "Promised Land," and "Comfort the People." It also gained her a Grammy nomination in 1988. If you can locate this hard to find album, it is well worth a listen. *—Charlotte Dillon*

● **The Best of Terri Gibbs** / Oct. 22, 1996 / Varese Vintage ✦✦✦✦✦

All of Terri Gibbs' biggest hits from the early '80s—including "Somebody's Knockin'," "Rich Man," "Mis'ry River," "Ashes to Ashes," and "Anybody Else's Heart But Mine"—are included on this comprehensive, definitive collection. *—Thom Owens*

Don Gibson

b. Apr. 3, 1928, Shelby, NC

Guitar, Songwriter, Vocals / Traditional Country, Country-Pop, Nashville Sound/Countrypolitan

Singer/songwriter Don Gibson was one of the most popular and influential forces in '50s and '60s country, scoring numerous hit singles as a performer and a songwriter. Gibson's music touched on both traditional country and highly-produced country-pop, which is part of the reason he had such a broad audience. For nearly a decade after his first hit single, "Sweet Dreams," in 1956, he was a reliable hitmaker, and his songs have become country classics—they have been covered by a wide range of artists, including Patsy Cline, Ray Charles, Kitty Wells, Emmylou Harris, Neil Young, and Ronnie Milsap.

Gibson began playing guitar while he was a high-school student in North Carolina, playing local radio stations and dances. In 1946, he became a regular with the Tennessee Barn Dance in Knoxville. Around the same time, he began recording Western songs with the Sons of the Soil, both on Mercury and RCA Victor Records. In 1950, Gibson assumed control of the band, renaming them Don Gibson & His King Cotton Kinfolks and switching their musical direction to honky tonk. Although their sound was more focused, they remained unsuccessful. Gibson continued to perform on the radio, as well as at Esslinger's Club in Tennessee. At the nightclub, Wesley Rose saw Gibson perform and offered him a writing contract. Gibson would only accept the deal if he was allowed to record. Rose managed to get Gibson a contract with Columbia, which proved unsuccessful. Again, Rose secured him another contract, this time with MGM. Gibson's first single for the label, "Sweet Dreams," became a Top Ten hit and was covered by Faron Young, who took it to number three. Following the success of "Sweet Dreams," Gibson was signed to RCA in 1957 by Chet Atkins, who would become his producer for the next seven years. Released early in 1958, Gibson's first RCA single, "Oh Lonesome Me," was a blockbuster, spending eight weeks at the top of the country charts and crossing over into the pop Top Ten. Gibson and Atkins developed a pop-friendly style which featured rock & roll flourishes that brought him to a larger audience. In the course of 1958-1961, Gibson had a total of 11 Top Ten singles, including "I Can't Stop Lovin' You," "Blue Blue Day," "Who Cares," "Don't Tell Me Your Troubles," "Just One Time," "Sea of Heartbreak," and "Lonesome Number One."

Although his career wasn't as successful in the latter half of the '60s, he still had the occasional Top Ten single, including "(Yes) I'm Hurting" (1966), "Funny, Familiar, Forgotten, Feelings" (1966), "Rings of Gold" (1969), and "There's a Story (Goin' Round)" (1969). During the late '60s, he suffered from alcoholism and drug addiction, but he cleaned up in the early '70s, which led to a comeback in 1971. Switching record labels from RCA to Hickory, Gibson had a Top Ten hit with "Country Green" in 1972. The following summer, he had his last number-one single, "Woman (Sensuous Woman)." He also had a series of duets with Sue Thompson between 1971 and 1976, which were all moderately successful. After two Top Ten hits in 1974—"One Day at a Time" and "Bring Back Your Love to Me"—he settled into a string of minor hits that ran until 1980's "Love Fires." During the '80s and '90s, he continued to tour and perform at the *Grand Ole Opry*. *—Stephen Thomas Erlewine*

Oh Lonesome Me / 1958 / RCA Victor ✦✦✦✦

No One Stands Alone / 1959 / RCA Victor ✦✦✦

No One Stands Alone was recorded shortly after Don Gibson established himself as a popular recording artist as well as a successful songwriter. It was his first gospel album and it balanced traditional songs with a handful of original cuts. Gibson is in good voice throughout the record and the production is typical of late '50s country-pop records, featuring choirs and strings. Though it isn't a major album for Gibson, it is enjoyable and the best gospel record he recorded. The CD reissue includes four bonus tracks. *—Stephen Thomas Erlewine*

That Gibson Boy / 1959 / RCA Victor ✦✦✦✦

Gibson covers tunes from some of the best country songwriters of the period (himself included) to make this record, one of the finest examples of Gibson as an artist. Atkins' production, The Jordanaires' background vocals and Gibson's performances are all right on. *—Jim Worbois*

Look Who's Blue / 1960 / RCA Victor ✦✦✦

Look Who's Blue dates from Don Gibson's '70s tenure with Hickory Records, a time which saw him make something of a comeback. He had recently rejoined the *Grand Old Opry* and become sober, and his recordings were consequently of consistently high quality. This album is no exception and finds Gibson effectively maintaining his pop instincts while, for the most part, returning to a straight country format. There aren't a lot of surprises here—just quality songs (written by Gibson, Eddy Raven, Lorrie Morgan, and others), expertly sung and played. Truly the king of the crossover country singers, Gibson makes it all sound so easy. Whereas followers like Ronnie Milsap and Kenny Rogers are pop or country singers depending on the particular song being sung, Don Gibson has a voice that sounds inherently stone-cold country, but is just smooth and unaffected enough to appeal to a wider audience. At times sounding like a subtler combination of George Jones and country-era Jerry Lee Lewis, he attacks each song on the album with sincerity and flawless phrasing throughout. As always, the joys of Don Gibson come from repeated listenings—his artistry, like that of Waylon Jennings, is of the kind that speaks not just to drunken nights and hung-over mornings, but to a deeper existential loneliness only fully comprehended in quieter moments. Not surprisingly, the only misstep here is the one pure pop song, the Burt Bacharach standard "Any Day Now," which was later an international smash for Milsap. While Gibson's performance is beautifully and darkly bitter, the Nashville session cats (Grady Martin, Buddy Emmons) are unusually stilted, which causes the song to stick out like a sore thumb among the other, more relaxed tracks. *—Pemberton Roach*

Sweet Dreams / 1960 / RCA Victor ✦✦✦

This is a nice collection of some of Gibson's classic compositions and some fine covers. In addition to the title track, which was a hit for Patsy Cline, several of these songs became hits by other artists. *—Jim Worbois*

Girls, Guitars and Gibson / 1961 / RCA Victor ✦✦✦

This record features some odd song selections that equal mixed results. While standards like "Born to Lose" and "Beautiful Dreamer" sound as if they were written for Gibson, the inclusion of "Camptown Races" and a throw away version of "Above and Beyond" leave the listener asking why. *—Jim Worbois*

Some Favorites of Mine / 1962 / RCA Victor ✦✦✦

Gibson covers songs from four of country music's greatest songwriters. An interesting album, it doesn't work quite as well as one would hope. *—Jim Worbois*

I Wrote a Song / 1963 / RCA Victor ✦✦✦✦

God Walks These Hills With Me / 1964 / RCA Victor ✦✦✦

The Fabulous Don Gibson / 1965 / Harmony ✦✦✦

The Fabulous Don Gibson is an LP released on Columbia's subsidiary Harmony. While it contains several good songs, like "Ice Cold Heart," it also has its share of filler, making it just an average piece of product for the country audience of the mid-'60s. *—Thom Owens*

Too Much Hurt / 1965 / RCA Victor ✦✦✦✦
By the standards of Don Gibson, this is a pretty good album and one that should satisfy listeners who like their country with a bit of folk-rock mixed in. There are country artists who sing much better than Gibson, however, so his limitations should be taken into account. It isn't that he sings off key, since many country stars can get by simply talking their way through a song, even if they can't talk their way out of drunk driving convictions. Gibson just doesn't express a whole lot of personality through his voice no matter what the subject or setting of the song, usually sounding like some friendly truck driver singing along with the radio. The arrangements and playing were really totally with it in terms of what was going on musically in the first half of the '60s, and these carefully played tracks, heavy on acoustic guitar and harmonica, have an authentic Nashville groove and roots that go deep into the earth. Some unidentified wizard comes up with good pedal steel breaks, usually timed in such a way to balance out the folk element with a traditional country signature. It is a winning combination that has stood the test of time. The songs include some quite popular standards, whose presence in the title list was probably sales insurance; in fact, between the song selection and Gibson's voice, in some ways the second side is like hanging out in a country karaoke bar. But, as usual for his projects, lesser-known yet quality material by interesting country songwriters is tucked in the folds here and there. In this album's case, the highlight is a Roger Miller cover, and there is also a good version of a typically maudlin Mel Foree number. The Jordanaires don't get in the way that much. *—Eugene Chadbourne*

Don Gibson with Spanish Guitars / 1966 / RCA Victor ✦✦

Great Country Songs / 1966 / RCA Victor ✦✦✦✦
This record focuses more on Gibson the performer and less on his work as a songwriter. Gibson certainly has a way with a song, even one he didn't write. Just listen to how much he gets out of Jeannie Seely's 1966 hit, "Don't Touch Me" as he bends and weaves his way through the melody. *—Jim Worbois*

All My Love / 1967 / RCA Victor ✦✦✦

The King of Country Soul / 1968 / RCA Victor ✦✦✦

More Country Soul / 1968 / RCA Victor ✦✦✦

Rings of Gold / 1969 / RCA Victor ✦✦✦

★ **A Legend in My Time** / 1988 / Bear Family ✦✦✦✦✦
A Legend In My Time contains 26 tracks from Don Gibson's peak years of 1957-1965, including all of his country Top Ten hits ("Oh Lonesome Me," "I Can't Stop Loving You," "Blue Blue Day," "Sweet Dreams," and several others), as well as a selection of lesser-known material that is all first-rate. It's the definitive retrospective. Although hardcore fans will want Bear Family's box sets and casual fans might want a collection that's a little more concise, *A Legend in My Time* has every essential item from the classic singer/songwriter. *—Stephen Thomas Erlewine*

All-Time Greatest Hits / 1990 / RCA ✦✦✦✦✦
Released in 1990, *All-Time Greatest Hits* remains one of the best CD-era overviews of Don Gibson's classic RCA recordings. It not only had all the big hits—"Oh, Lonesome Me," "Sweet Dreams," "Blue Blue Day," "I Can't Stop Loving You," "Sweet Sweet Girl," "(I'd Be) A Legend in My Time," "Sea of Heartbreak"—but a generous song selection of 20 tracks, all containing some of the very best lesser-known sides and hits he had during his peak. The collection has since gone out of print and has been replaced by the excellent *RCA Country Legends* domestically, but, along with Bear Family's *A Legend in My Time*, it remains among the very best single-disc collections of Don Gibson's material assembled. *—Stephen Thomas Erlewine*

18 Greatest Hits / 1991 / Curb ✦✦✦
Gibson's best-known hits were recorded in the late '50s and early '60s for RCA with Chet Atkins producing. This recording are drawn from his work for Hickory Records in the early '70s. They include "Woman, Sensuous Woman," "Country Green" and several remakes of his earlier hits. *—Michael McCall*

The Singer, The Songwriter (1949–1960) / 1991 / Bear Family ✦✦✦✦✦
The 11 years covered in this first of two Don Gibson retrospectives by the German Bear Family label are the most captivating in his career. Beginning in 1949, Gibson began recording as part of the Sons of the Soil for Mercury, a hillbilly jump band. From the moment Gibson's lead vocal comes through the mix for the very first time, it is evident that even if he wasn't writing a lot of songs at the time, he was performing them as if they were his. His four early issued tracks from this period include the underground classic "Automatic Mama," a pre-rockabilly prototype. A year later Gibson & His King Cotton Kinfolks were at RCA working with Stephen Sholes, issuing eight sides that offered a more complex version of the Sons style of country, bluegrass, pop with just a shade of jump thrown in. In 1952, Gibson moved to Columbia as a solo artist recording with Don Law and Troy Martin, and guitarist Chet Atkins, which is where his mature voice began to take shape, as evidenced by "his first songwriting credit, No Shoulder to Cry On," and smoking version of Johnny Masters' "Walkin' in the Moonlight." His chart success was evident too, placing tracks steadily in the Top 40 of *Billboard's* country chart. In 1955, Gibson moved again to MGM where he recorded his first true smash and a bona fide country music classic, "Sweet Dreams." Yet, even here, it wasn't until he returned to RCA in 1957 that Gibson made of himself a living legend in recording arguably the greatest two-sided single ever issued in the history of the genre: "Oh, Lonesome Me," b/w "I Can't Stop Loving You," that sold not only for him, but was redefined by Ray Charles on his legendary *New Sounds in Country and Western Music* album. The late MGM period and his reunion with RCA is documented here, with alternate and unissued takes as well as unreleased tracks. Gibson was fortunate enough to be a big enough star when players like Floyd Cramer, Atkins, Rusty Kershaw, Buddy Harman, and Bob Moore were redefining the Nashville studio sound. The gospel tracks here, from the albums *No One Stands Alone*, and *That Gibson Boy* as well as *Sweet Dreams*—which he re-recorded three more times before the end of 1960, were all so far above the bar artistically, it was difficult for critics to define Gibson, hence his crossover into the pop world, influencing a young Gram Parsons among many others. In all there are 122 tracks on this four-CD set, a booklet that offers exhaustive and accurate track information, and a fine biographical essay. The sound is Bear Family fine, and the packaging—like all of their boxes—is exquisite. But it's in the music that the truth of Gibson's legend is borne out. On CDs two and three the songwriter finally eclipses the singer, though the singer remains a force of nature, capable of interpreting any song in a personal and original way—just check out Gibson's read of Hank Snow's "I'm Movin' On." This is essential for serious fans of the legendary music and for any Gibson collector because of its wealth of previously uncollected material. Volume two focuses on the years 1961 to 1968 and contains more gems, but this is the defining one. *—Thom Jurek*

Singer Songwriter, 1961–1966 / Jun. 28, 1994 / Bear Family ✦✦✦✦✦

Oh Lonesome Me / Jan. 5, 1998 / Collectables ✦✦✦✦
Collectables' reissue of *Oh Lonesome Me* contains the original track listening, which boasts hits like "Oh Lonesome Me," "Bad, Bad Day" and "I Can't Stop Loving You," and it adds several singles as bonus tracks, which only enhances a collection that was pretty great to begin with. There's some filler on the record, but it contains a number of gems among its lesser-known songs. *—Stephen Thomas Erlewine*

20 Greatest Songs / Mar. 13, 2001 / Varese ✦✦✦
Since Varese's 2001 collection *20 Greatest Hits* starts like so many other Don Gibson collections with "Sweet Dreams," "Oh, Lonesome Me," and "I Can't Stop Loving You," it's easy to assume that it's another collection of his RCA recordings. It's not. It's a collection of material he cut for Hickory Records in the first half of the '70s. He happened to re-record his big RCA hits for the label and, since those are the songs most identified with Gibson (and properly so), they are here, placed in the front to lure in listeners. These re-recordings aren't bad, but they aren't as good as the originals, and they taint a collection that's otherwise a good summary of his underappreciated Hickory recordings. While these don't match his RCA work—which were, after all, recorded at his peak as a writer and performer—they're good country-pop material of the early '70s, targeted at an older audience and sung nicely by Gibson. The big hits from his time at Hickory are here—"Woman (Sensuous Woman)," "Touch the Morning," "One Day at a Time," "Bring Back Your Love to Me," the Dottie West duet "Rings of Gold"—and they're good enough to make you wish the entire collection were devoted to Hickory sides that weren't remakes. Considering how hard these are to find on CD, it's easy to suck up the re-recordings and get this just for those latter-day singles—after all, it's the only way to get them—but it doesn't make that wish go away. *—Stephen Thomas Erlewine*

★ **RCA Country Legends** / May 15, 2001 / Buddha ✦✦✦✦✦
This may not be as comprehensive a compilation as Bear Family's terrific *A Legend in My Time*, but in its own way, it's just as definitive. First of all, it's available domestically, which means far more listeners will be willing to give a listen to the genius of Gibson, but more importantly, it really does offer a concise, exceptional overview of his career. All of his hits are here, and it's possible to hear his pure, unadulterated brilliance here—how he was as melodic as the best pop, yet was unassailably country at the same time. Several of these songs are indisputable classics—"Oh Lonesome Me," "Blue Blue Day," "I Can't Stop Loving You," "Sweet Dreams," and "(I'd Be) A Legend in My Time" are all timeless, and while others may have defined these songs, these are all classics in their own right, and they define what is so wonderful about Gibson. He was a classic songwriter—these are timeless, wonderful songs, and it's hard not to hear them and fall in love with his talents, how he was melodic as a Tin Pan Alley songwriter but was completely country. This is where to hear his greatness, and even if it may not be as sublime as *A Legend in My Time*, it's wonderful—nay, essential—all the same. *—Stephen Thomas Erlewine*

Oh Boy Classics Presents Don Gibson / Jul. 9, 2002 / Oh Boy ✦✦
Issued in 2002, *Oh Boy Classics Presents Don Gibson* offers 12 Don Gibson hits, including the ubiquitous "Oh, Lonesome Me," "(I'd Be) A Legend in My Time," "Sweet Dreams," "Blue Blue Day," and "I Can't Stop Loving You." However, these are not the versions that were big hits at RCA. They are re-recordings Gibson made for Hickory in the early '70s. Varese covered this same territory with a little more honesty and a lot more of his actual hits for Hickory on 2001's *20 Greatest Songs*, which is far preferable due to its ten or so songs that are not re-recordings. This tries to pass off the re-recordings as hits, sprinkling some of those latter-day sides along the way, and by doing so it's very unsatisfying. *—Stephen Thomas Erlewine*

Gibson/Miller Band

f. 1990

Group / Country-Rock, Contemporary Country, New Traditionalist
The hard-driving Gibson/Miller Band was one of many country-rock groups to spring up in the wake of the honky-tonk revival of the early 1990s. Frontmen Dave Gibson and Bill "Blue" Miller were guitarists from very different backgrounds. Gibson was born and raised in Arkansas surrounded by the music of Eddy Arnold, Hank Williams and Elvis Presley. As a young man, he worked with John Prine and Steve Goodman before becoming a well-known songwriter in Nashville. Miller hailed from Detroit and played on recordings by Bob Seger & the Silver Bullet Band; he also sang jingles, traveled with Isaac Hayes, and even won an Emmy for providing the theme of an ABC documentary. After living in various cities, he eventually settled in Nashville, despite having never before played country music.

Gibson and Miller were introduced by Epic Records Vice President Doug Johnson, who thought they might make a good writing team. They put together a band, made a demo and sent it back to Johnson, who was impressed enough to sign them. The other band-members were bassist Bryan Grassmeyer, who had previously played with Vince Gill and Suzy Bogguss; drummer Steve Grossman, who had worked closely with Grassmeyer; and steel guitarist Mike Daly, who had worked with Gibson for several years and played on all of his demos. The Gibson/Miller Band debuted in 1992 with the single "Big Heart," which, along with its video, was well-received and landed them in the Top 40 the following year. Their second single, "High Rollin'," made the Top 20, and their third, "Texas Tattoo," created quite a stir with its provocative video. This led to their first album, *Where There's Smoke* (1993). In 1994, their single "Stone Cold Country" reached the Top 40, followed by the album *Red, White & Blue Collar. —Sandra Brennan*

● **Where There's Smoke** / 1993 / Epic ✦✦✦✦
Gibson/Miller's Southern boogie debut features the hits "Big Heart," "Texas Tattoo," and "Stone Cold Country." *—Jason Ankeny*

Red, White & Blue Collar / 1994 / Epic ✦✦✦

Vince Gill

b. Apr. 12, 1957, Norman, OK
Guitar, Vocals / Bluegrass, Progressive Bluegrass, New Traditionalist, Contemporary Country
Vince Gill paid nearly a decade and a half of dues en route to becoming one of the most popular country stars of the '90s. Starting out as a bluegrass singer and multi-instrumentalist, he initially made his name with country-rockers Pure Prairie League, and spent the '80s as part of country's new traditionalist wing before finding massive success as a contemporary country hitmaker. Gill had strong mainstream appeal, yet enough songwriting chops and grounding in tradition that he could maintain his artistic credibility without being branded a crossover-happy hack. That balance made him the kind of performer that awards ceremonies can feel good about honoring, and honor him they did—Gill has won more CMA awards than any performer in history, and his 14 Grammys tie him with Chet Atkins for the most ever by a country artist.

Vincent Grant Gill was born April 12, 1957, in Norman, OK. His father, a judge, played banjo and guitar, and Vince picked up both by his teen years; he later added fiddle, do-bro, mandolin, and bass to his repertoire. In high-school, Gill played in the bluegrass band Mountain Smoke, which gained enough of a local reputation to open a concert for Pure Prairie League. Gill graduated in 1975 and moved to Louisville to join the band Bluegrass Alliance, with whom he stayed for a year. He then briefly played with Ricky Skaggs' Boone Creek outfit before setting out for Los Angeles, where he joined fiddler Byron Berline's group Sundance. In 1979, he accompanied a friend to audition for Pure Prairie League, mostly out of curiosity as to whether they remembered his high-school band, and they wound up hiring him as their lead singer.

Gill recorded three albums with the band, helping them land a Top Ten pop hit with "Let Me Love You Tonight," and also began writing songs for them. He departed in 1981 to join Rodney Crowell's backing band, the Cherry Bombs, where he met Emory Gordy Jr. and Tony Brown, both of whom would later produce his solo records. In 1982, he appeared on the David Grisman album *Here Today*, and the following year he landed a solo deal with RCA thanks to his connection with Brown. Gill, his wife Janis (née Oliver, a member of the Sweethearts of the Rodeo), and their young daughter moved to Nashville. With Gordy producing, Gill issued his debut mini-album, *Turn Me Loose*, in 1984, with a style in keeping with his recent country-rock past. He notched his first charting country single with the minor Top 40 entry "Victim of Life's Circumstance," and the following year completed his follow-up, *The Things That Matter*. A duet with Rosanne Cash, "If It Weren't for Him," gave Gill his first Top Ten hit, and his next single, "Oklahoma Border-line," duplicated its predecessor's success. *The Way Back Home* (1987) gave Gill his biggest RCA hit in the Top Five "Cinderella."

In the meantime, he also worked as a session guitarist, wrote songs for other artists, and toured with Emmylou Harris. In 1989, Gill left RCA to sign with MCA, where he re-united with Tony Brown, now a successful producer. Though he'd enjoyed some success in his own right, Gill wasn't really a star. That all changed with the release of his label debut, 1989's *When I Call Your Name*. A duet with Reba McEntire, "Oklahoma Swing," made the Top 20, but the title track was the true breakout hit, climbing to number two and winning Gill his first Grammy. Its follow-up, "Never Knew Lonely," hit number three, and the album went on to sell over a million copies. Perhaps partly as a result, Gill declined an offer from Mark Knopfler to become a full-time member of Dire Straits. Gill's follow-up album, 1991's *Pocket Full of Gold*, was another platinum smash, giving him four Top Ten singles in "Liza Jane," the title track, "Look at Us," and the number-two smash "Take Your Memory With You." *I Still Believe in You* (1992) made Gill an outright superstar; the title ballad was an enormous hit that became his first number-one single, and its follow-up, "Don't Let Our Love Start Slippin' Away," also topped the charts. The album took only a few months to go platinum, and still spun off more hits: two more number ones in "One More Last Chance" and "Tryin' to Get Over You," and the number three "No Future in the Past."

Additionally, "The Heart Won't Lie," another duet with McEntire from her *It's Your Call* album, went to number one in 1993. Over the next few years, *I Still Believe in You* would sell over four-million copies. Gill issued the stopgap holiday album *Let There Be Peace on Earth* in late 1993, and returned with *When Love Finds You* in 1994, which became his first album to break the pop Top Ten. It, too, sold over four-million copies, and gave him five Top Five country hits: "What the Cowgirls Do," the title track, "Whenever You Come Around," "Which Bridge to Cross (Which Bridge to Burn)," and "You Better Think Twice." Gill was clearly a country hit factory by this point, but instead of coasting into the inevitable decline, he got more ambitious with his next project, 1996's *High Lonesome Sound*. Returning to his bluegrass roots, Gill crafted a tour of American roots-music styles that earned him some positive critical attention, even if overall reviews were mixed. It proved commercially potent as well, giving him several more hits, including the Top Fivers "Worlds Apart," "Pretty Little Adriana," and "A Little More Love."

In 1998, Gill released his most universally acclaimed album, *The Key*, which was both a return to hardcore country and a chronicle of the breakup of his marriage to Janis

Oliver. Although country radio shied away from its more traditional approach (save for the Top Five hit "If You Ever Have Forever in Mind"), it sold well, going platinum and becoming Gill's first album—surprisingly—to top the country charts. Rumors about Gill's relationship with pop singer and onetime Christian star Amy Grant proved to be true, and the couple married in early 2000. Gill's next album, *Let's Make Sure We Kiss Goodbye*, was largely a tribute to his new romance that many critics found overly sentimental. It gave him another Top Ten hit in "Feels Like Love," but it was uncharacteristically snubbed come Grammy time, despite securing four nominations. Gill returned to critical favor with his next outing, 2003's *Next Big Thing*, which marked the first time he produced an entire album on his own. *—Steve Huey*

Turn Me Loose / 1983 / RCA ✦✦✦
This is one of the mini-LPs RCA, and several other labels, experimented with in the '80s. While Gill had been on the musical scene for several years, including a stint with Pure Prairie League, this is a nice sampler to display Gill's skills as both a performer and a writer. *—Jim Worbois*

The Things That Matter / 1984 / Buddha ✦✦✦

The Way Back Home / 1987 / Buddha ✦✦✦
For the most part this record doesn't sound much different than Gill's work with Pure Prairie League or, for that matter, the average Eagles album. Which isn't to say it's bad. Just that, except for the title song, nothing really stands out here. *—Jim Worbois*

When I Call Your Name / 1989 / MCA ✦✦✦✦✦
"Oklahoma Swing," Gill's duet with Reba McEntire, announced his return to a rootsier sound after leaving RCA. But it was the title cut, with Patty Loveless providing the harmonies, that soared highest from car radios and announced the arrival of a major star. *—Dan Cooper*

Pocket Full of Gold / 1991 / MCA ✦✦✦✦
This is a hit album with high bluegrass vocals, traditional country arrangement, and contemporary production. *—Mark A. Humphrey*

I Still Believe in You / 1992 / MCA ✦✦✦✦✦
Lots of folks inject a shot of R&B cliches into their honky-tonk and call it country-soul. Vince Gill is country's real soul man, and not because of a familiarity with black artists' catalogs (though "Nothin' Like a Woman" comes close to sounding what lovers imagine Percy Sledge's "When a Man Loves a Woman" to be). It's because Gill's voice captures pain and promise, love and loneliness—all in a distillation so smooth that you don't even notice it sneaking up to blindside you. With his high tenor harmonies on songs like "Tryin' to Get Over You" and "No Future in the Past," you might even call this bluegrass soul—and you know that's gotta be lonesome. *—Brian Mansfield*

I Never Knew Lonely / Mar. 1992 / RCA ✦✦✦
One of Gill's more pop-oriented efforts, *I Never Knew Lonely* features the title tune, "Everybody's Sweetheart" and "True Love." *—Jason Ankeny*

Let There Be Peace on Earth / 1993 / MCA ✦✦
Christmas music releases have become a country music tradition, but the result is often generic mushy background instrumentation on the same moldy standards. Guilty of this is Vince Gill, whose *Let There Be Peace on Earth* is as cliché-ridden as they come. *—Roch Parisien*

When Love Finds You / 1994 / MCA ✦✦✦
That Vince Gill—he sure is a nice guy. But at this point, we sure would welcome some serious nastiness from him to keep us awake. *—Dan Cooper*

Vince Gill & Friends / Aug. 16, 1994 / RCA ✦✦
Even for a budget-price collection, *Vince Gill & Friends* feels a little skimpy. Clocking in at only eight tracks where most budget-line comps feature ten, the collection sports a title that suggest it's a duet album. It's not. It's a collection of eight tracks that happen to have *backing* vocals by the likes of Emmylou Harris, Rodney Crowell, Bonnie Raitt, Carl Jackson, Janis Oliver, and the Sweethearts of the Rodeo. Of course, there are some very good songs here—"Turn Me Loose," "What If I Say Goodbye," "Oklahoma Borderline," "Oh Carolina," "Everybody's Sweetheart"—but the brevity of the disc, plus the misleading title, makes it appear something less than a bargain. *—Stephen Thomas Erlewine*

● **The Essential Vince Gill** / 1995 / RCA ✦✦✦✦✦
The Essential Vince Gill collects highlights from the singer's pop-inflected material for RCA in the early '80s. While Gill didn't have as many hits during this era, the best songs standup well next to his better-known songs. *—Thom Owens*

● **Souvenirs** / Nov. 21, 1995 / MCA Nashville ✦✦✦✦✦
Souvenirs collects the greatest hits from Vince Gill's most popular period—his recordings for MCA in the late '80s and early '90s. As such, it contains a wealth of first-rate songs and hits—including the number ones "I Still Believe In You" and "Don't Let Our Love Start Slippin' Away"—and functions as a good introduction to his music. *—Thom Owens*

High Lonesome Sound / Jun. 1996 / MCA ✦✦✦
Vince Gill takes off on a tour of American music on *High Lonesome Sound*. The title cut steps back to a time he hasn't visited in a while, drawing on his days as a bluegrass singer and guitarist to create a soaring, harmony-driven sound that applies Appalachian drive to modern country rhythms. Most of the rest of the album's journey treks in new directions. The aggressive guitar riff that opens "One Dance With You" is straight Chicago blues, while the jaunty feel that enlivens "Down to New Orleans" draws on that city's funky polyrhythms with a deft touch worthy of Little Feat. "Tell Me Lover," also bearing the toe print of Little Feat, dances through a swampy groove. The problem isn't with the arrangements; Gill and producer Tony Brown give traditional sounds a modern shine while maintaining a distinct regional flavor. Gill gets much more room to show off his impressive guitar prowess than on past albums. But the lyrics too often deaden the excitement; he over-sweetens the blues with a corny chorus, then drags every Cajun cliché

imaginable into his Louisiana homage. The album works best when he's not straining for authenticity: "Worlds Apart," "Given More Time" and "Pretty Little Adriana" leaven his tried-and-true formula into arrangements that are more progressively atmospheric than his past hits. Gill owns too many strengths to need to transform himself into Lowell George or Bonnie Raitt at this point in his career. *—Michael McCall*

Super Hits / Oct. 15, 1996 / RCA ✦✦✦

Super Hits is a budget-priced compilation that features ten of Vince Gill's biggest hits for RCA Records, including "I Never Knew Lonely," "The Radio," and "Oklahoma Borderline." Though the album isn't comprehensive, it nevertheless is an excellent collection by budget-line standards. *—Stephen Thomas Erlewine*

The Key / Aug. 11, 1998 / MCA ✦✦✦✦✦

This is perhaps the most distinctive and artistic project Vince Gill has released to date, an amazing array of traditional styles displaying his versatile talent. Going back to his roots as he has not done in too many years, Gill shines like God's brightest penny, and even Tony Brown's usual heavy-handed production style seems to be as light as an angel's feather this time around. Gill is in fine voice throughout, joining with a colorful cast of backup singers to create music that modern mainstream country radio has not played in well over a decade. With 13 tracks, Gill eases gracefully from one style to another. From a classic hillbilly waltz to the edgy Bakersfield sound. He even skillfully tips his hat to guitar great Roy Nichols on the soon-to-be-classic "There's Not Much Love Here Anymore." A duet with honky tonk songbird Patty Loveless, "My Kind of Woman/My Kind of Man," stands proudly next to the best country duets by George and Tammy or Merle and Bonnie Owens. Most impressive is "Kindly Keep It Country," a stone-cold country hit that details one man's heartbreak and the soothing effects of a jukebox and a bar stool. As heartbreaking as any song ever written is "Let Her In," told from the perspective of a divorced father who is trying to rebuild his life and still retain his relationship with his daughter. Just as effective is "The Hills of Caroline," a mountain tune with a strong melody and story that is enhanced by the beautiful backing vocals of Alison Krauss. The title cut, which is also the final cut, is endearing and comes directly from Gill's relationship with his late father. For emotional depth, honesty, and musical accomplishment, this is certainly Gill's crowning achievement to date. *—Jana Pendragon*

Let's Make Sure We Kiss Goodbye / Apr. 18, 2000 / MCA ✦✦✦✦

Written in the months before his marriage to Amy Grant, the songs on *Let's Make Sure We Kiss Goodbye* exemplify the words of a man who has been transcended by the power of love. Twelve of the album's 13 tracks, all written or co-written by Gill, relay the romance that has filled Gill's life, from illustrating ultimate sacrifices to showing heartwarming declarations of love, including the euphoric "When I Look Into Your Heart," a duet with his new bride and co-written by her. Gill is "The Luckiest Guy in the World," known lonely "For the Last Time," and wants to share the "Little Things." Enough said. If you're curious about the 13th track, "Hey God" is a moving tribute to honor his friend, the late golfer Payne Stewart. A must-have album for Gill fans (his daughter Jenny is a delight on harmony vocals for "That Friend of Mine") and anyone else who is at the height of a new romance. *—Maria Konicki Dinoia*

Next Big Thing / Feb. 11, 2003 / MCA ✦✦✦✦

Vince Gill's studio offering following his paean to his new bride, *Let's Make Sure We Kiss When We Say Goodbye*, is one of the strongest recordings in a decade. Perhaps it's the freedom from the usual Nashville production bullsh*t—Gill produced the album himself. His cast of players and singers is a veritable list of stars, including Emmylou Harris, Lee Ann Womack, the Doobie Brothers' Michael McDonald, life partner Amy Grant, Kim Keyes, Andrea Zonn, and Leslie Satcher. Famed producer and engineer Justin Niebank is at the mixing desk, and Gill's regular band propels a mixed bag of pop, boogie, swing, and neo-trad country tunes—and odd for a Nash Vegas album, there are 17 of them, not ten or 12. Standout tracks are the rollicking title with its booming guitars; the mariachi-tinged "We Had It All"; the slow country stroll of "Young Man's Town," despite its sweeping strings and electric violin moan; and the stunning ballad "These Broken Hearts," with McDonald adding a depth of emotion rarely matched on Gill's records. There is also the Merle Haggard tribute "Real Mean Bottle" that features the opening guitar lines to "Mama Tried." But it's far from syrupy—it's a tough song about a tougher, more visionary man than the singer could ever hope to be, sung in an unflinching manner. All of this said, there are the now-requisite Gill saccharine tracks such as "Whippoorwill River," an insufferable homage to his father that drowns in syrup. The hardcore honky tonk rock of "The Sun's Gonna Shine on You" is one of the strongest cuts on any Gill album, full of shuffling blues and rockabilly swagger. "Old Time Fiddle" is a cross-pollination of Cajun music and bluegrass that works surprisingly well considering how slick it is—perhaps it's the layered accordions and the organic-sounding percussion. The album closes with "In These Last Few Days," another ballad; Gill always makes records that are at least 60/40 ballads to uptempo tunes, and this track is that forlorn, bittersweet ballad that seems to close every record of his. But lyrically it's so strong and vulnerable that it works, leaving the listener haunted with the notion that something special has occurred, that he or she has born witness to a man becoming aware of the preciousness of his own life. In all, it's a strong effort. It's nice to see established artists reclaim control of their careers—especially when the results are so rewarding. *—Thom Jurek*

Mickey Gilley

b. Mar. 9, 1937, Ferriday, LA

Piano, Vocals / Traditional Country, Country-Pop, Honky Tonk, Urban Cowboy

For most of his career, pianist/vocalist Mickey Gilley lived in the shadow of his cousin, Jerry Lee Lewis, playing a similar fusion of country, rock, blues, and R&B. In the early '70s, he managed to breakthrough into country stardom, but it wasn't until the late '70s, when he became associated with the urban cowboy movement, that he became a superstar. Gilley, like Lewis, was raised in Ferriday, LA. It wasn't until Jerry Lee had a hit with his first Sun single, "Crazy Arms," that Mickey decided he wanted to pursue a musical career. Gilley began recording for a number of independent Texas labels without much success in the late '50s. In the early '60s, he became a local favorite by playing a never-ending series of bars and clubs. A few of singles became Texas hits, but he didn't have a national hit until 1968 with minor hit "Now I Can Live Again" on Paula Records.

In 1970, he opened Gilley's Club in Pasadena; the honky tonk had previously been known as Sherry's Club, and its owner, Sherwood Cryer, asked Mickey to re-open the bar with him. In 1974, Gilley had another local hit with "Room Full of Roses," which was released on Astro Records. Playboy Records, which was distributed by Epic, heard the record and acquired national distribution for the single. It became a number-one country hit, crossing over to number 50 on the pop charts. "Room Full of Roses" launched a string of updated, countrypolitan-inflected honky tonk hits for Gilley that ran for just over a decade. Gilley racked up 16 number one hits besides "Room Full of Roses," including "I Overlooked an Orchid," "City Lights," "She's Pulling Me Back Again," "True Love Ways," "Stand by Me," "That's All That Matters," and "A Headache Tomorrow (Or a Heartache Tonight)."

Gilley signed with Epic Records after Playboy folded in 1978. The following year, the film *Urban Cowboy*—which was based on Gilley's Club and featured a cameo by Mickey, as well as several of his songs—brought him to national attention, which resulted in a string of six straight number-one singles. He continued to have Top Ten hits until 1986, when his career began to slip. The late '80s were plagued with problems for Gilley. Not only had a new generation of country singers replaced him on the charts, he had financial problems which culminated in the closing of Gilley's Club. He turned his career around in the early '90s, when he became one of the first country stars to open a permanent theater in Branson, MO. Although Gilley recorded some albums in the '90s—which were primarily available through television advertisements—he focused his career on the theater. *—Stephen Thomas Erlewine*

Lonely Wine / 1964 / Astro ✦✦✦

Room Full of Roses / 1974 / Playboy ✦✦✦✦✦

Mickey Gilley's recording debut for then short-lived Playboy label proved to be a case of being in the right place at the right time. The label formed to be able to issue country records and get a piece of the biz pie, and Gilley was looking for a major label, or at least a label with major label distribution to get his music over to the public at large. As a single, "Room Full of Roses" sold well regionally and when Playboy issued it and got behind it, all of those A&R men who turned Gilley down must have been turning green, it was the first if no less than 16 number-one hits. Backed by an ace session band that included Bobby Dyson on bass, guitarists Dave Kirby, Bobby Thompson (both of whom worked with Waylon Jennings), and Jimmy Colvard, as well as fiddle whiz Buddy Spicher, drummer Larry London and steel boss Russ Hicks, Gilley delivered a program that was rock solid country that included: "Swinging Doors," Wade Jackson's "Don't Be Angry," Harlan Howard's "She Called Me Baby," and Bob Wills', "Faded Love." *Room Full of Roses* was pure, elegant honky tonk country done Gilley-style, with that smooth voice, slippery fingers and empathic attitude. Women and men dug him in equal measures. And with a recording as full of the country spirit and pathos as this one is, what's not to? Highly recommended. [This album has been issued on CD finally with *Gilley's Smokin'* on the Audium label with brilliantly reproduced sound.] *—Thom Jurek*

City Lights / 1974 / Playboy ✦✦✦✦

Mickey's Movin' On / 1975 / Playboy ✦✦✦✦

☆ **Gilley's Smokin'** / 1976 / Playboy ✦✦✦✦✦

It was 1976 and Mickey Gilley was still kickin' it for Playboy Records. And *Gilley's Smokin'* is kickin' it, period. Produced by Eddie Kilroy—the only man who ever got Gilley's piano sound right—and Gilley, the recording lays out ten tracks of piano-pumpin' rock & roll, honky tonk tunes, barroom weepers, and an R&B tune or two. Opening with his "Don't the Girls All Get Prettier at Closin' Time," the tone is set for a classic. Moving into Billy Sherrill's "There's a Song on the Jukebox" and tinkling the ivories from honky tonk to cocktail lounge on Bert Kaempfert's "L-O-V-E," and with that pedal steel whining in the background, it doesn't sound a damn thing like Wayne Newton. If there was any doubt at all, Bert was probably rolling in his grave when he heard it on the country airwaves. Side two is the real shiner, though, with tunes by Sam Cooke and Lloyd Price alongside Larry Gatlin, Vic McAlpin, and Gilley and Kilroy themselves. The country fiddle string section and Gilley laying into the right-hand runs on his piano for full soul effect make the reading of "Bring It on Home to Me" astonishing. The honky tonk classic "How's My Ex Treating You" is smooth as silk, with Gilley's vocal slipping through the dense mix to deliver a sad song in a good-time style. But it's "Lawdy Miss Clawdy" that hammers as hard as the opener. Gilley's pullin' Jerry Lee piano runs on this mother and striding the hell out of that boogie-woogie like Albert Ammons. The set ends with the classic "I'll Fly Away," a country gospel tune that feels like a sinner's barroom anthem and rocks like one, too. In all, this is the Gilley set to find. Now available on CD as part of a twofer on Audium (with the disc *Room Full of Roses*, another classic) in gorgeously remastered sound. the new issue includes one bonus track, the single version of "Roll You LIke a Wheel." This is a country afficionado's two-fer, but is also the only place to start when it comes to Gilley. *—Thom Jurek*

Overnight Sensation / 1976 / Playboy ✦✦✦✦

First Class / 1977 / Playboy ✦✦✦

Flyin' High / 1978 / Playboy ✦✦✦

The Songs We Made Love To / 1979 / Epic ✦✦✦✦

In 1979, Mickey Gilley's final album for Playboy was folded into Epic, who manufactured and distributed the label. Produced by Foster & Rice, *The Songs We Made Love To* was produced in Pasadena, TX, at Gilley's home studio, and feels so far out of Nash Vegas that it's a real country honky tonk record (only Vern Gosdin was making them in Tennessee). The title track opens the set with a beautiful midtempo country ballad before being rocked into "Bye Bye Baby," with Gilley pumpin' the box against a backdrop of pedal steel, a telecaster, and the Jordanaires singing doo wop in the background. And the Texas swing barroom twist of "Jr. P Jones" is a story Merle Haggard could've written, but with Gilley's amazing baritone wrapped around it, it feels like a cross between Jerry Lee and Bob Wills. But even on the string-laden ballads like "Lonely Wine," the R&B influence seeps into the mix and country and soul dance close and sexy. "Just Long Enough to Say Goodbye" is one of Gilley's wonderful theatrical songs, beginning soft and simple and slowly transforming itself into a large orchestrated torch song felt best by barroom light before shifting into overdrive for "Tonight I'll Help You Say Goodbye Again," all torched out with full-on rockabilly swagger and honky tonk blues criss-crossing in the refrain. Nobody but nobody, not even Ray Price in all his genius, can put together a full body of diverse material like Mickey Gilley can, and in 1979 he was still at the height of his powers. Between his smooth style and his complete immersion in all styles of country, blues, early rock & roll, and R&B, he could meld smooth and sweet or sweaty and sassy and still make a listener feel they were at the center of whatever party or tearfest was being thrown—usually on the same album; and this one is just an outing. *—Thom Jurek*

Down the Line / 1980 / Charly ♦♦♦

That's All That Matters to Me / 1980 / Epic ♦♦♦

This is the album that benefited most from Gilley's *Urban Cowboy* associations, and there's a perfunctory back-cover shot of some cowboy riding a mechanical bull at Gilley's nightclub. Though Gilley the Balladeer became pretty formulaic during the progression of the '80s, it was a new wrinkle with this album, and he delivers it convincingly. Gilley says the title track is his best performance ever. *—Tom Roland*

You Don't Know Me / 1981 / Epic ♦♦♦

Mickey Gilley was on a hot streak from the mid-'70s through the mid-'80s, and *You Don't Know Me*, produced by Jim Ed Norman for Epic Records, is another chapter in the Gilley odyssey that ends triumphantly despite the fact that the piano sound isn't as badass on this set, because Gilley only kicks on two cuts. But it's a small annoyance. Beginning with the crazy boogie rockabilly "Ladies Night," this is a set of pure inspiration, even though Norman tries to make it sound like it was recorded at Gilley's—dumb, but the feel is live, as the tracks were cut live on the floor of the studio with some overdubs being done later. "My Affection" continues the stomping rockabilly of the opener, with Gilley actually hammering the hell out of the ivories on this one before a slow honky tonk drinking song called "Drinking Old Memories Down," the other track with the inimitable Gilley "spider-on-the-keys" sound. Side two opens with Gilley's lovely and moving version of the Eddy Arnold classic that is the title cut. And the rest of the album is on the ballad side, which is fine since Gilley's singing is down in the groove with the darkest of emotions when necessary. "Lonely Nights," the Keith Stegall nugget, brings it all home and sets up a beautifully rendered version of Carl Rains' "Clinging to a Memory." If the first two tracks feel misleading, they're not; they're just one part of the good-time man's mystique and character. This is a fine set. *—Thom Jurek*

Put Your Dreams Away / 1982 / Epic ♦♦♦

You've Really Got a Hold on Me / 1983 / Epic ♦♦♦

Fool for Your Love / 1983 / Epic ♦♦♦

Too Good to Stop Now / 1984 / Epic ♦♦♦♦

Mickey Gilley / 1984 / Audio Fidelity ♦♦♦

Alternating between country tearjerker ballads and more mainstream pop tunes, *Mickey Gilley* shows off the pianist's flair for both genres. Although somewhat of a transitional album, nothing here is out of place in Gilley's vast catalog of music. It's good listening, but not the best way to enjoy the talents of Mickey Gilley. *—James Chrispell*

It Takes Believers / 1984 / Epic ♦♦♦

● **Ten Years of Hits** / 1984 / Epic ♦♦♦♦♦

Mickey Gilley may have been indebted to Jerry Lee Lewis, or it could be that the two cousins shared the same influences as well as bloodline, so they came out as near mirror images, right down to the way Gilley delivers a lascivious chuckle at the end of a verse in "Don't the Girls All Get Prettier at Closing Time." Mickey followed in Jerry Lee's country footsteps, never rocking as hard as the Killer did at Sun, but playing a blend of rock, gospel, pop, and country that strongly recalled Lewis' hits on Smash and Mercury. He finally had his breakthrough in 1974, after Playboy/Epic signed him and brought his Texas hit cover of George Morgan's "Room Full of Roses" to a national audience that sent it to number one. For the next ten years, he was a constant presence at the top of the country charts, scoring 17 number ones and becoming a pop culture touchstone when his bar, Gilley's, was used as a key location in the era-defining John Travolta film *Urban Cowboy*. Released in 1984, the two-LP (now one-CD), 20-track *Ten Years of Hits* chronicles this time expertly, containing all those number one hits along with three other Top Ten hits. The biggest flaw in the collection is that it isn't sequenced chronologically, which is only a problem because as the years wore on, Gilley turned increasingly to slick, sentimental ballads and oldies covers designed for the pop crossover audience that he stumbled upon. A few of these go a long way and, fortunately, only a few of them are here, with the great majority of this collection devoted to tear-in-your-beer ballads like "Room Full of Roses" and "I Overlooked an Orchid" or juke-joint ravers like "Don't the Girls All Get Prettier at Closing Time" and "The Power of Positive Drinkin'." These do recall Lewis—one that still delivers the musical goods, but isn't as fiery or wild, even on the slower numbers. But, if you want that crazed excitement, you go to the Killer. If you want to hear good, pure country music, Gilley (usually) served it up straight during his ten years on Playboy/Epic and the music still sounds just as good years later. *—Stephen Thomas Erlewine*

Live at Gilley's / 1985 / Epic ♦♦♦♦

This is a curious item in the sense that only part of it was previously available on the box set of various artists entitled *Live at Gilley's*. This is the entire set recorded sometime before the club closed in 1986 and does not have an exact date attached to it, but it hardly matters. This is one stompin' piano-pumpin' rock-a-rolla country set with Mickey Gilley revisiting his entire career in song, from 1974's "Room Full of Roses" (his first number one) and "She Called Me Baby" (the B-side), to the Jerry Foster classic "Here Comes the Hurt Again" and "A Headache Tomorrow or a Heartache Tonight," to Hank Cochran's classic "That's All That Matters" with many more. And, yes, "Don't the Girls All Get Prettier at Closin' Time" is here in the most over-the-top rock version ever recorded. It's fast, furious, exuberant, and hedonistic. But with ballads such as the Keith Stegall/Stewart Harris tearjerker "Lonely Nights," Gilley's deeply emotional and sensitive side comes across in spades. As a singer, Gilley was always underrated, and that's a shame because, as he proves in front of an audience, he is a monster of an interpretive vocalist. Another winner is "The Blues Don't Care Who's Got 'Em," a tune associated very closely associated with Charlie Rich. Gilley's version is a raw honky tonker with gorgeous piano runs and backing vocalists sweetly singing a doo wop chorus in the background. One of the true stunners on the set is Gilley's version of the Ben E. King/Leiber/Stoller classic "Stand by Me." His live version rivals King's and John Lennon's for pure emotional honesty and searing commitment. There are some limitations in the source tape on this set, but they do absolutely nothing to detract from the power of this 12-track set. For Gilley fans this is essential, as it may be his best live document. For roots rock and honky tonk fans, this is revelatory. *—Thom Jurek*

Live! At Gilleys / 1985 / Epic ♦♦♦

Live! At Gilleys is the second live album to be recorded in 1985. The other, released later, was on Atlantic's Q subsidiary, but this one was released during Mickey Gilley's heyday. Interestingly, even though they both open with Gilley's classic "Don't the Girls All Get Prettier at Closin' Time," they are entirely different in presentation. Immediately following here is the Kenny Rogers monster "Blaze of Glory," but Gilley's version is a honky tonk stomper. In typical fashion, Gilley tempers these two jumpin' numbers with a ballad, and this one, "I Was Born a Dreamer," showcases his gift of a voice in a way few of his records do. He goes for the upper range of his register and delivers it all clear as a bell and dripping with emotion. The end of side one closes with a version of cousin Jerry Lee Lewis' signature hit, "Great Balls of Fire," and Gilley wails through it in just over two minutes—and he's not foolin' around. It's rock & roll burning with honky tonk fever. The second half of the set is marked by three things: first is the smokin' rendition of "My Affection" with Gilley kicking ass all over the piano, criss-crossing left and right hands complemented by a horn section. The next is a medley of Gilley singles for theater—all ballads done in a dramatic fashion that is almost overpowering. Again, Gilley the singer is devastating with a love song; he's smooth and unhurried, pronouncing each syllable as if it is the only one left in his world. "Your Love Shines Through," "Tears of the Lonely," "Lonely Nights," and "Put Your Dreams Away" stand together as one of the finest centerpieces of any Gilley record, and here the way he says "thank you" at the end of each song as it segues into the next—as if it's a surprise he'd be acknowledged—is part of his humanity as well as his charm. Finally, the entire album ends with a Cajun anthem that echoes Gilley's Louisiana roots. This version of "Diggy Diggy Lo" (complete with Fats Domino-style sax break) may not be as consciously emotional as Doug Kershaw's, but it rocks one hell of a lot harder, leaving the audience—and the listener—wanting more. *—Thom Jurek*

Crazy Cajun Recordings / Feb. 18, 1999 / Edsel ♦♦♦

Although the liner notes say that the recording dates of Mickey Gilley's sessions for the Crazy Cajun label are unknown, the presence of a twist song, "Whole Lot of Twistin' Going On," puts them in the ballpark of the early '60s. Gilley sounds more like his cousin Jerry Lee Lewis on these tracks than he would later, and many of the songs were recorded Jerry Lee/Sun Records style with just piano, drums, and vocals. *The Crazy Cajun Recordings* sound like demos, but 18 tracks of early rockin' Gilley is a rare and welcome thing. *—Greg Adams*

Absolutely The Best, Vol. 1 / Mar. 4, 2003 / Fuel 2000 ♦♦♦♦♦

Fuel 2000's 2003 release *Absolutely the Best, Vol. 1* contains 18 tracks Mickey Gilley cut in the '60s for Paula Records, including the entirety of his 1967 album, *Down the Line*, where he pretty much split the difference between country and rock & roll. It also contains several singles he cut with Jack Clement after that album, where he settled on a barroom-ready, hardcore country style, as well as a version of Charlie Rich's "Mohair Sam," complete with compressed fuzz tones, wah-wah guitars, and a heavy four-four beat that suggest it was recorded *much* later than the rest of the music on this collection. To figure out which track came from where, you'd need to read Bill Dahl's excellent liner notes very closely; his work here, as a writer and compiler, is very good, but a track-by-track information breakdown is sorely needed. That said, *Absolutely the Best, Vol. 1* is a welcome addition to Gilley's catalog, since there not only isn't much out on the market, but because the music here is very, very good. While the *Down the Line* does find him in full-on Jerry Lee Lewis mode, even covering "Down the Line," "I'll Make It Up to You," and "Breathless," but he does also dabble in country and even if the performances are occasionally derivative, they're well-done and quite enjoyable. The real heart of the collection is at the end with the Clement-produced singles. This is where Gilley finds the sound that would lead him to the top of the country charts in 1974, and the songs—"A World of My Own," "Love in the Want Ads," "She's Still Got a Hold on You," and his first national hit, "Now I Can Live Again"—are expert honky tonk and barroom ballads that perhaps should have been bigger hits but stand as very fine unheralded country from the late '60s. So, there's more than enough high-quality material here to make *Absolutely the Best, Vol. 1* a necessary addition to any Gilley collection, but it's good enough to make it of interest to any fan of good, solid pure country and no-nonsense '50s-styled rock & roll. —*Stephen Thomas Erlewine*

16 Biggest Hits / Mar. 11, 2003 / Sony ◆◆◆◆◆

The title of Epic/Legacy's *16 Biggest Hits* is slightly misleading—not because the collection doesn't contain big hits, but because there's really 17 songs on this collection, with the last cut a bonus track on the CD only. This doesn't really matter, since it doesn't really effect the tenor and purpose of the collection, which is to serve up 16/17 of Mickey Gilley's biggest hits for Playboy/Epic from the '70s and early '80s. Of course, this was done very effectively with the definitive *Ten Years of Hits* in 1984, and this collection cribs heavily from that two-LP/single-disc set, sharing no less than 15 songs with that previous collection. This does have the advantage of chronological sequencing—something that helps Gilley more than some other artists, since he shifted toward slicker material as his career rolled on and it's nice to hear the purer stuff grouped together—along with better sound. However, as a representation of his best, *Ten Years of Hits* edges out this set because it captures his prime better; the two songs on *16 Biggest Hits* not on *Ten Years*—"Fool for Your Love" and "Paradise Tonight"—are from 1983 and aren't among his best, while everything, even the sappy stuff, on *Ten Years of Hits* showcases Gilley at his best. That said, this still has more than enough of his best to make it worthwhile, especially if it's found at a reasonable price. —*Stephen Thomas Erlewine*

Invitation Only / May 20, 2003 / Varese ◆◆◆

Mickey Gilley recorded the ten songs that comprise *Invitation Only* in 1991, a few years after he left Epic and about ten years after his commercial peak, but the sessions stayed on the shelf until Varese's release of the album in the spring of 2003. It wasn't just that this particular album was left behind; Gilley effectively abandoned the idea of being an active recording artist during the '90s, and he didn't cut another album during the decade. So, this album, which would have followed his last proper studio album by only three years, now appears 15 years later, re-produced by Matthew Miles to make it a little more modern...but only a little, since this record is firmly within the post-urban cowboy, mature country-pop tradition; it would have sounded dated if it appeared in 1991 or 1992. All this means is that *Invitation Only* is ballad-heavy—in the liner notes, Gilley recalls that "Conway Twitty once told me to find tunes the ladies love," and he takes that advice to heart—and the production is soft and hazy, playing up Gilley's considerable abilities as a crooner. If the production is a little too clean and the song selection a little unadventurous, it's nevertheless professionally done and appealing in its own MOR way, and when the tempo is varied a little—when he treads into mild Jerry Lee territory on "Sadly Ever After" or goes mildly tropical on "I Didn't Know Your Memory Loved Jamaica"—it's a nice change of pace. All in all, it's a good, solid listen. Not a lost classic by any means, but after years without any new Gilley whatsoever, it's good to hear him again. —*Stephen Thomas Erlewine*

★ Room Full of Roses/Gilley's Smokin' / Jun. 24, 2003 / Audium ◆◆◆◆◆

Audium does it again, issuing the first and third Playboy Records albums by Mickey Gilley from 1974 and 1976. *Room Full of Roses*, notable for its use of Gilley's patented swinging honky tonk style, is the album on which his first number-one single—the title cut—appeared. This pair of discs was among the three that introduced producer Eddie Kilroy's live-sounding style to audiences across the country music spectrum, with stellar results. Gilley scored 16 number ones during his career—and a band that was as fine as any ever assembled in Nash Vegas. Guitarist Dave Kirby was fresh off his stint with Waylon Jennings, Bobby Dyson brought electricity to the country bass, Buddy Spicher was already a living legend on the fiddle, drummer Larrie London (a veteran of so many sessions) was anchored in with Gilley until he passed away, and Bobby Thompson (who defined the actual sound of the acoustic guitar on so many records in the 1970s) also helped out. In terms of material, the title track, the Carl Smith nugget "I Overlooked an Orchid," Merle Haggard's "Swinging Doors," "Don't the Girls All Get Prettier at Closing Time," Bert Kaempfert's "L-O-V-E," Willie Dixon's blues stomper "My Babe," Lloyd Price's "Lawdy Miss Clawdy," and Sam Cooke's "Bring It on Home" offer a new perspective on R&B in the same way that Ray Charles offered it on country a decade and a half earlier. These sides offer Gilley as an ivory-tinkling honky tonk player and a piano-pumpin' R&B wild man, and both have enough high lonesome soul to be fantastic country records. As a package, this is damn near unbeatable. —*Thom Jurek*

Billy Gilman

b. May 24, 1988, Westerly, RI

Vocals / Contemporary Country

Only 11 years old when he notched his first hit single, Billy Gilman was the youngest performer ever to reach the *Billboard* country charts, breaking a record held by Brenda Lee since 1957. Gilman was born in Westerly, RI, on May 24, 1988, and grew up in nearby Hope Valley. He was singing before he started school, and developed rapidly enough to start performing publicly at age seven. He was booked as an opening act at several county fairs, including one with headliner Jo Dee Messina. Gilman caught his big break when Asleep at the Wheel leader Ray Benson heard him sing and was impressed by the precocious power behind his vocals. Benson had Gilman make a demo tape, which wound up landing the young singer a deal with Epic.

Backed by seasoned Nashville studio pros, Gilman completed his debut album, *One Voice*, in 2000. Its title song, a spiritual plea against school violence, climbed into the Top 20 of the country charts, and the album itself hit number two and quickly went gold. The follow-up single, "Oklahoma," was also a Top 40 hit, and the holiday album *Classic Christmas* was rushed out by the end of 2000; it reached number four on the country charts, and featured a duet with fellow vocal prodigy Charlotte Church. Gilman's proper second album, *Dare to Dream*, appeared in 2001 and hit number six; it also spawned two minor chart hits in "She's My Girl" and "Elisabeth," the latter a sentimental ballad about a girl battling a terminal illness. That theme became the basis for Gilman's third album

when he met young poet and best-selling author Mattie Stepanek—a muscular dystrophy sufferer—during a TV appearance with Larry King. Gilman decided to record Stepanek's poems in song form, and several Nashville pros were commissioned to set them to music. The result, *Music Through Heartsongs: Songs Based on the Poems of Mattie J.T. Stepanek*, was released in the spring of 2003. —*Steve Huey*

● One Voice / Jun. 20, 2000 / Sony ◆◆◆

Since "One Voice" made Billy Gilman the youngest person ever to place a song in the country singles charts, his pre-pubescent age is the unavoidable subtext of his debut album. Certainly, he's not the first pre-teen to make popular music, but the same problem always has to be faced: the usual subject of pop lyrics is romantic love, and what does that mean when the words are being sung by an 11 year old? At very least, there's a certain awkwardness, and the implications can be even more objectionable depending on the song. The producers of *One Voice* have mostly obviated this difficulty by choosing or writing harmless material. For example, the album begins with a rousing remake of Bobby Goldsboro's "Little Things," which perhaps can be viewed as a song being sung by a boy to his mother in this context. But what is one to make of the "bonus track" that closes the album, Tammy Wynette's "'Til I Can Make It on My Own"? The song's point, which in Wynette's version was that a woman might not be able to make a complete break with her romantic partner all at once, is out the window, but it would be a stretch to apply any other reading to those words, especially when Gilman, a sort of country-style choir boy, is singing it androgynously in Wynette's register. He is on much safer ground with the novelty "The Snake Song" and even the title track, which addresses grade school violence with religious platitudes. From LeAnn Rimes to Britney Spears, youth has been a major trend in popular music of the last few years, and Billy Gilman represents a new extreme, at least as far as country music goes. He can certainly carry a tune, and you can only hope that he won't be a has-been by the time his voice changes. —*William Ruhlmann*

Classic Christmas / Oct. 17, 2000 / Epic ◆◆◆

Dare to Dream / May 8, 2001 / Epic ◆◆◆

If you didn't know Billy Gilman was 12 years old, you certainly would know it after listening to this middle-of-the-road sophomore effort. His voice, although capable and gifted, is so innocent and child-like, it's hard to appreciate *Dare to Dream* as an adult album, and sounds more like something a ten year old would be listening too. At least he's not singing about broken hearts or love that lasts forever, but about the sweet things a preteen would know about: first kisses, summertime, and Mom. *Dare to Dream* does offer up some touching ballads, including "Elisabeth" about a young girl's battle with a life threatening disease and some appealing, animated melodies like "She's My Girl." The album certainly does demonstrate new artistic maturity and Gilman is definitely a talent to be reckoned with, but he's still quite a ways away from being "the huge country artist" that the industry has labeled him. —*Maria Konicki Dinoia*

Music Through Heartsongs: Songs Based on the Poems of Mattie J.T. Stepanek / Apr. 15, 2003 / Sony ◆◆◆

Although much was made of Billy Gilman's age when he hit the country charts just after his 12th birthday in 2000, his appeal to listeners was a combination of his youth and his first hit, "One Voice," a child's lament about school violence couched in religious terms. Gilman returned to such unabashedly sentimental material with "Elisabeth" on his second regular album in 2001, and after a two-year break, possibly to let his voice change (it has settled into a slightly lower tenor), the about-to-be-15 year old expands on the theme of that song, which was about a seriously ill girl, by commissioning musical settings for some of the poems of Mattie J.T. Stepanek, another young teenager suffering from muscular dystrophy whose series of life-affirming "heartsongs" books (*Heartsongs*, *Journey Through Heartsongs*, etc.) have made him a best-selling author. Stepanek's poems were not intended to be song lyrics, and the various composers, all Nashville pros, have been forced to write around the words, which nevertheless suffer stretching and enjambment here and there. Gilman offers up his "One Voice" innocent take on the simple-minded, repetitious sentiments ("We must celebrate the gift of life," "The gift of color is so beautiful," "Memories are a great gift"), adding depth with songs that turn maudlin ("It Happened Anyway," about the death of one of Stepanek's brothers) and plaintive ("I Could...if They Would," about Stepanek's hopes for a cure). Of course, the overhanging threat of death is what it takes to give this material substance; otherwise, it is revealed for what it really is, the vague musings of a not-particularly talented child. You can see why Gilman was attracted to the project, but he might be better off taking on lighter subject matter next time, lest he be typed as the voice of the unbearably earnest. —*William Ruhlmann*

Jimmie Dale Gilmore

b. May 6, 1945, Tulia, TX

Guitar, Songwriter, Vocals / Progressive Country, Singer/Songwriter, Country-Folk, Alternative Country

With his warm, warbling tenor voice and folksy, friendly approach to both his music and his audiences, Jimmie Dale Gilmore is an easy guy to like. His music is a rich blend of traditional country, folk, blues, and rock styles, and his lyrics reflect both his philosophical interests and his inherent down-home nature. Since moving to Austin, TX, and reviving his career in the 1980s, Gilmore has in many ways come to represent the current Austin music scene—its rootsy mix of country, rock, and folk music—the way Willie Nelson once reigned as king of the town's cosmic cowboys in the 1970s. Gilmore's roots go back to Tulia, a small West Texas town where his father played lead guitar in a country band. When Gilmore was in grade school the family moved to Lubbock, a Panhandle town known for being the starting point for a surprising number of musicians (including Buddy Holly, Waylon Jennings, Terry Allen, and Gilmore's onetime singing partners Butch Hancock and Joe Ely). Growing up in Lubbock, Gilmore met Hancock when they were both 12, and they remained friends and frequent musical collaborators ever since. Gilmore later met Allen, who he says inspired him to write his own songs. One of the first songs Gilmore wrote, in fact—when he was around 20—was "Treat Me Like a Saturday Night," which is today one of his most enduring pieces. Later, another casual friend of Gilmore's, Ely, turned him on to the music of Townes Van Zandt, which Gilmore says was a revelation for the way Van Zandt integrated the worlds of folk and country music.

Gilmore and Ely began playing music together around Lubbock as the T. Nickel House Band. Later, after a brief stint in Austin, Gilmore hooked up again back in Lubbock with Ely and Hancock and formed the Flatlanders, a now-legendary band that also included Steve Wesson, Tony Pearson, and several peripheral members. The group recorded an album in Nashville in 1972, but it was only ever released at the time on eight-track tape. (Long a collector's item, it was finally re-released by Rounder Records in 1990 under the title *More a Legend Than a Band*). A mix of acoustic folk, string band country, and country blues, the album included another of Gilmore's best-known songs, "Dallas," which was actually released as a promo single at the time but generated little interest. By the end of the year the band had split up.

Gilmore moved to Denver, playing music only as a hobby. Ely, meanwhile, had won a record contract and had recorded some of Gilmore's songs. In 1980, Gilmore moved back to Austin, where he began playing regular gigs in local clubs. Finally, in 1988, Gilmore released his debut solo album, *Fair and Square*, on Hightone, Ely's label at the time. This and his 1989 follow-up, *Jimmie Dale Gilmore*, featured songs by Gilmore as well as Hancock and Ely played in a more straightforward honky tonk style than anything Gilmore had done previously or since. These two albums gained Gilmore newfound acclaim just as Austin itself was becoming a musical hot spot again. In 1990, the Flatlanders album was re-released, and Virgin Australia put out *Two Roads*, a duet album with Hancock that was recorded live during the pair's Australian tour. Gilmore was soon signed to Elektra, which released *After Awhile* in 1991 as part of the label's American Explorer series. The album retained a country feeling but was less honky tonk in nature, and it attracted Gilmore even more acclaim. Nashville showed little interest in Gilmore's brand of country music, but he earned the praise of many critics. His next album, *Spinning Around the Sun*, came out in 1993 and again featured a mix of contemporary and traditional country-flavored songs and a fuller instrumental sound fronted by Gilmore's rich, warm voice. In 1996 he released *Braver Newer World*, produced by T-Bone Burnett; *One Endless Night* followed in early 2000. *—Kurt Wolff*

Fair and Square / 1988 / Hightone ♦♦♦

Jimmie Dale Gilmore's debut album, *Fair and Square*, established him out of the box as a major talent in the Texas country music scene, but in retrospect the record seems like a rather odd representation of his talents. With longtime friend and collaborator Joe Ely in the producer's chair, *Fair and Square* is for the most part a solid honky tonk session, with Gilmore's gloriously wobbly tenor sounding strong and clear over a band that's not afraid to turn up the gas on numbers like "White Freight Liner Blues" and the proto-rockabilly "All Grown Up." (Actually, Gilmore and Ely seem to have been in a rocking mood when they cut this album, given the presence of enthusiastic renditions of "Trying to Get to You" and "Singing the Blues.") However, given his strength as a songwriter, it seems curious that Gilmore only wrote two of the album's ten songs, though with Butch Hancock, Townes Van Zandt, and David Halley all willing to contribute tunes, it's not as if anyone was forcing him to cut second-rate material. More significantly, the subtle undercurrents of Gilmore's best material seem to have been left by the wayside, as if a coffeehouse singer/songwriter had been thrown into a dance hall and was trying to avoid getting the hook. *Fair and Square* is a fun album, but it's hardly the best place to start exploring Gilmore's brand of music. *—Mark Deming*

Jimmie Dale Gilmore / 1989 / Hightone ♦♦♦♦♦

Jimmie Dale Gilmore's self-titled sophomore effort boasted a less aggressive sound than his Joe Ely-produced debut, and that suited Gilmore's wavering tenor and impressionistic lyrical style just fine, though the album also sounds like an attempt to blend a traditional country approach with Gilmore's rather individualistic style. This time out, Gilmore wrote (or co-wrote half) of the album's ten songs, while old friend Butch Hancock ponied up two tunes of his own, and the production (by Bruce Bromberg and Lloyd Maines) generates a laid-back honky tonk vibe that recalls the feel of a Texas dancehall without forcing the issue. The album rescues one classic tune from the long-lost Flatlanders album ("Dallas"), and "Deep Eddy Blues" and "Beautiful Rose" prove he had plenty of other great songs at his disposal, which marks a major improvement over the covers-heavy debut. Sometimes, however, the spunky tempo and precise accompaniment of the music seem to be working against the grain of Gilmore's often world-weary songs, though Jimmie Dale himself accompanies these arrangements with grace and confidence. *Jimmie Dale Gilmore* is a fine album and a step up from *Fair and Square*, but in retrospect it sounds most like a stepping stone on the way to his definitive recording, *After Awhile*. *—Mark Deming*

● **After Awhile** / 1991 / Elektra/Nonesuch ♦♦♦♦♦

While Jimmie Dale Gilmore's first two solo albums presented him as an enlightened honky tonk cowboy, 1991's *After Awhile*, his first set for Elektra, was less stylistically bound to country music, and approached Gilmore as a singer/songwriter, albeit one with a decided West Texas sensibility. The result was a considerably more subdued and personal set than Gilmore had offered in the past; Gilmore wrote all of the album's 12 songs (except for Butch Hancock's "My Mind's Got a Mind of Its Own," which fits Gilmore like a glove), and the quieter, often acoustic-based arrangements provide a more sympathetic backdrop for the more cerebral corners of his songs than the spunky old-school country frameworks of his work for Hightone (Gilmore discusses his interest in Buddhist and Hindu teachings in the liner notes, which would have seemed a bit odd on *Fair and Square* or *Jimmie Dale Gilmore*). While the bluesy wail of "Midnight Train" and the uptempo shuffle of "My Mind's Got a Mind of Its Own" proved Gilmore hadn't turned his back on the rootsier side of his musical vocabulary, the more languid tracks reflect a high and lonesome mood that's solely Gilmore's province, and "Tonight I Think I'm Gonna Go Downtown," "Treat Me Like a Saturday Night," and "Blue Moon Waltz" are simply beautiful performances of remarkable songs that could have come from no one else. *After Awhile* is a subtle, unforced masterpiece that captures Gilmore at the subtle peak of his abilities. *—Mark Deming*

Spinning Around the Sun / 1993 / Elektra ♦♦♦

Released in 1991, *After Awhile* stripped back the traditional country backings from Jimmie Dale Gilmore's music and let the subtle textures of his lyrics shine through, and the result was one of Gilmore's finest recordings. After the critical success of *After Awhile*, Emory Gordy Jr., a top-shelf Nashville producer and session musician, was assigned to work on Gilmore's follow-up, *Spinning Around the Sun*, and his approach seemed to be to follow the subtle and scaled-back sound of *After Awhile*, but make it more polished and listener-friendly at the same time. If that seems a little confusing, *Spinning Around the Sun* for the most part sounds like a labor of love to honor Gilmore's work while making it more accessible (especially to the country marketplace). While the cover of "I Was the One" and "Reunion," a duet with Lucinda Williams, sound as if they were crafted with country radio in mind, most of the album mimics *After Awhile*'s relaxed but thoughtful sound, though the surfaces shine with Music City perfection rather than the more intimate and soulful attack of Gilmore's Austin, TX, compatriots. Ultimately, the bigger problem is that the material on *Spinning Around the Sun* just isn't as interesting; Gilmore only penned four of the album's songs, and while the rest of the material is solid, there are too many tunes that are beautiful but unremarkable, and beyond a near-definitive reworking of Butch Hancock's "Just a Wave, Not the Water," very little of this connects with the force of Gilmore's best work. *Spinning Around the Sun* is an album of many beautiful moments that never quite coheres into a fully satisfying whole. *—Mark Deming*

Braver Newer World / Jun. 25, 1996 / Elektra ♦♦♦♦♦

Although Jimmie Dale Gilmore has never been what one would call prolific—his recording career is characterized by lengthy gaps in between albums, seemingly for no reason other than he doesn't particularly feel like recording—his albums are among the finest in country music. The aptly-titled *Braver Newer World* (1996) finds the Lubbock native moving away from the staunch musical traditionalism that characterized his earlier releases, into a brilliant fusion of pure country, mystical explorations, and sonic experimentation that foreshadows the psychedelic tilt of nominally alt-country albums like Wilco's *Summer Teeth* or the Jayhawks' *Smile*. Produced by T-Bone Burnett and featuring the gifted multi-instrumentalist Jon Brion on guitars and keyboards, *Braver Newer World* places Gilmore's characteristically spiritual lyrics in vivid musical settings that complement but never obscure his singular worldview and magnificent high lonesome voice. The glorious title track, one of the most achingly beautiful songs of its time, is only the first of many highlights; the resigned "Headed for a Fall" and the uplifting "Come Fly Away" are nearly as brilliant, and a quirky but successful reimagination of Blind Lemon Jefferson's blues standard "Black Snake Moan" is one of the most musically daring tracks of Gilmore's career. Pure country traditionalists may blanch, but Gilmore's never been one to do the expected at any point in his career, and *Braver Newer World* is arguably his finest work. *—Stewart Mason*

One Endless Night / Feb. 29, 2000 / Rounder ♦♦♦

After two critically acclaimed albums on Hightone Records in the 1980s, Jimmie Dale Gilmore moved up to major label Elektra in the '90s. But the kudos did not translate into sales—only one of his three Elektra albums scraped into the bottom reaches of the country charts—and by the turn of the century he was back on an independent: the folkie label Rounder (distributing his own Windcharger imprint). Three and a half years separated *Braver New World*, the last Elektra album, from *One Endless Night*, his Rounder debut, but Gilmore apparently hadn't spent much time writing in the interim. Of the 12 listed songs (there was also a bonus track, the rockabilly "DFW," referring to Fort Worth and Dallas), only two are co-written by the singer. *One Endless Night* is a compendium of Texas songwriting, including the work of Gilmore cronies and mentors Butch Hancock, Townes Van Zandt, Willis Alan Ramsey, and Walter Hyatt, as well as such familiar names as John Hiatt, Jesse Winchester, Jerry Garcia and Robert Hunter, and Steve Gillette. Though Gilmore had always mixed his own compositions with covers, this album presents him basically as an interpretive singer, and you have to wonder what it was that he is bringing to the Grateful Dead's "Ripple" or the standard "Mack the Knife" that is all that special. The answer is, not much. Gilmore's voice had become less pinched and more confident in the course of his belated solo recording career but not enough so that he could be recommended as a singer rather than as a singer/songwriter. *—William Ruhlmann*

Johnny Gimble

b. May 30, 1926, Tyler, TX

Fiddle, Mandolin, Violin / Traditional Bluegrass, Western Swing, Instrumental Country

One of the most impressive fiddle players in country music's history, Johnny Gimble confounded most of his rivals by using a five-string fiddle. He gained most of his early success with Bob Wills' Texas Playboys, but Gimble has also recorded over ten albums of his own and picked up awards as Instrumentalist of the Year (CMA) and Best Fiddle Player (ACM). John Paul Gimble was born on May 30, 1926, in Tyler, TX. At the age of 12, he played in a band with his four brothers, and in the early '30s formed the Rose City Swingsters with brothers Gene and Jerry. The band played on local radio, but Gimble soon moved to Louisiana to play with Jimmie Davis. In the late '40s he joined Wills, playing fiddle and electric mandolin with the Texas Playboys. From 1951-1953, Gimble led his own group, which played as house band at Wills' club. He then returned to the

Playboys, but the decline of Western swing in the late '50s and early '60s forced him out of the business.

Gimble worked as a barber and a hospital worker during the '60s, but returned to record with Wills in 1969. The experience primed him for heavy session work during the early '70s, including Merle Haggard's 1970 Wills tribute album and Wills' final appearance on LP, *For the Last Time* (1974). That same year, he recorded the first of his many solo albums, *Fiddlin' Around*. Gimble gained the first of his five Best Instrumentalist and eight Best Fiddle Player awards in the late '70s, and performed with Willie Nelson's touring band from 1979-1981. Gimble finally hit the charts in 1983 with his Texas swing group and the added attraction of Ray Price on vocals. The single "One Fiddle, Two Fiddle" was taken from the Clint Eastwood film *Honkytonk Man*, and it reached number 70. The B-side, Wills' famous standard "San Antonio Rose," also charted. The sideman credits also continued to add up, and in 1993, Gimble was nominated for a Grammy award in the Best Country Instrumental Performance category, for his work on Mark O'Connor's fiddler tribute album, *Heroes*. Also, Gimble is often seen playing on *Austin City Limits* and Garrison Keillor's TV programs. *—John Bush*

Fiddlin' Around / 1974 / Capitol ✦✦✦

Johnny Gimble, Texas Dance Party / 1975 / Lone Star ✦✦✦✦

Still Swingin': Johnny Gimble and the Texas Swing Pioneers / 1976 / CMH ✦✦✦✦✦

Johnny Gimble's Texas Dance Party / 1976 / Columbia/Lone Star ✦✦✦

Recorded live in Austin in 1975, *Johnny Gimble's Texas Dance Party* is a reunion of Gimble and several of his colleagues and former bandmates, including pianist Curly Hollingsworth. It's an affectionate, fun tribute to the golden age of Western swing, even though none of the genre's standards are included on the album. Instead, the album does something more important—it captures the spirit of the genre. *—Thom Owens*

● **The Texas Fiddle Collection** / 1981 / CMH ✦✦✦✦✦

Texas Fiddle Collection was recorded in the mid-'70s featuring former Texas Playboys fiddler extraordinaire Johnny Gimble. These 28 tunes are timeless in both style and execution especially with a band consisting of the finest calibre Western swing musicians including former Texas Playboys guitarist Eldon Shamblin and from the Texas Wanderers, Cliff Bruner on electric fiddle! Among the highlights include "Sally Gooden," "Goodnight Waltz," "Redwing," "Lime Rock," "Draggin' the Bow," "Beaumont Roag," "Fat Boy Rag," and "Dreamy Eyes Waltz." One thing to keep in mind regarding this collection is some of these tunes are not full performances; a few clock in under two minutes. *—Al Campbell*

Texas Honky-Tonk Hits / 1988 / CMH ✦✦✦

Johnny Gimble recorded *Texas Honky-Tonk Hits* with a stable of guest artists, including Mac Wiseman and Merle Travis. The combination never quite gels, but Gimble plays well throughout the album. *—Stephen Thomas Erlewine*

Still Fiddlin' Around / Jun. 13, 1988 / MCA ✦✦✦

Although the production on *Still Fiddlin' Around* is a little too slick for most Western swing aficionados, Gimble and his band play very well and it is recommended for any serious fan of the genre. *—Thom Owens*

The Girls of the Golden West

Group / Traditional Country, Cowboy

The opening round of biographical details in the story of the Girls of the Golden West sets the tone with names that seem properly ironic. Sisters Mildred and Dorothy "Dolly" Good were born in Muleshoe, TX, in 1913 and 1915, respectively. They grew up listening to cowboy songs from the Southwest, and wound up getting the credit for spreading this regional influence into the blend of what developed into country & western music. The sisters began their duo the way many talented children do—by entertaining family and friends in the comfort of their home. And although this audience preferred the girls' versions of cowboy and western material, the sisters themselves personally preferred pop music. When Dolly was only 14, they made their professional debut on radio station WIL in St. Louis. Making their home near Chicago, the Girls of the Golden West appeared regularly on a variety of radio shows heard from Northern Canada to south of the Mexican border. Regular appearances on the Chicago radio station WLS' *National Barn Dance* began in 1933 and led to guest spots on Rudy Vallee's syndicated NBC show.

The sisters were such a hit on the Vallee program that it led to them being offered their own weekly NBC program, and a recording contract followed posthaste. Dorothy Good took the lead on most of the solo passages and played guitar in a basic manner that worked suitably as an accompanying instrument. She did not try to play lead fills in the manner of Maybelle Carter, instead specializing in top-quality harmony parts and catchy yodelling. In the recording studio, the girls created a repertoire that consisted of about half newly composed ditties based on Western themes. Then, there was a certain number of traditional cowboy songs from the realm of orally passed-on folk music, and the sessions were filled out with cover versions of pop standards they liked. What had always been a strong interest of the girls increased as their career went on, until the pop material started to take over more territory during their recording sessions. The Girls of the Golden West performed and recorded sporadically until Dorothy Good's death in 1967. Their discography includes three albums for the Fort Worth Bluebonnet label. In 1978, Sonyatone released a collection of their cowboy- and Western-orientated material. *—Eugene Chadbourne*

Selected Recordings, 1933–1938 / 1978 / Sonyatone ✦✦✦✦

Almost from the time they could walk, the sisters Dorothy and Mildred Good were entertaining family and friends with their versions of cowboy songs, sung as vocal duets with spare guitar backgrounds from Dorothy. The girls actually liked pop music better, and got into recording more and more of it as their career went on. This collection focuses on their cowboy songs, and it is delightful. A listener who wants to own only one album of this type of material may want to choose this one. One thing the Good girls bring to the mix is lively tempos, not at all a surprise considering their interest in pop music. Their songs move almost as if someone is giving the rhythm a gentle prod with a stirrup from time to time. The magic of siblings singing together has never been disputed and, indeed, is the stuff of an important genre of old-time and bluegrass music. These sisters can hold their own with any of the other brother-and-sister duets, and they look a darn sight better in their cowgirl outfits than the Delmore Brothers would have. *—Eugene Chadbourne*

Jim Glaser

b. Dec. 16, 1937, Spalding, NE

Vocals / Traditional Country, Country-Pop, Singer/Songwriter, Urban Cowboy

Jim Glaser has spent much of his professional career working within the context of his family's group, Tompall & the Glaser Brothers. As a member of that trio, which was celebrated for its singing, he also worked with Marty Robbins on several important projects as a session musician, playing guitar and mouth harp and singing backup on songs (most notably "El Paso" from the sessions that yielded the first two *Gunfighter Ballads* albums), and toured as well as recorded for years with Robbins and Johnny Cash; and he has written hits for performers as diverse as Warner Mack and Gary Puckett & the Union Gap. Jim and his brothers Tompall and Chuck were born in Nebraska, the sons of guitarist Louis, who taught his children music in the course of raising them on a ranch. They former Tompall & the Glaser Brothers in the mid-'50s and made it onto radio in Nebraska while playing dances and other local events. They met Robbins at one of his concerts, and impressed with their harmony singing, he signed them to his own label, making their debut with a Chuck song, "Five Penny Nickel."

An appearance on *Arthur Godfrey's Talent Scouts* helped break them nationally, and they signed with Decca Records in 1959, after moving to Nashville. They never had a hit for Decca, but their session work made their singing and playing very visible—it was Jim, along with guitarist-singer Bobby Sykes (a member of Robbins' band), that suggested Marty record an entire album of Western songs, which resulted in *Gunfighter Ballads and Trail Songs*, an album that was an immense hit at the time and still sells well several decades later, and which helped start a whole revival of interest in cowboy songs. The Glasers also played and sang on Claude King's *The Comancheros*, toured with Robbins, and ascended to the highest venue ever achieved by country music when they appeared with Johnny Cash at his Carnegie Hall performance.

Tompall & the Glaser Brothers enjoyed hits on MGM Records with "Gone, on the Other Hand" and "Through the Eyes of Love" in 1966 and 1967, and followed those up the next year with "The Moods of Mary" and "One of These Days" before they finally soared into the upper reaches of the charts with "California Girl (And Tennessee Square)" in 1969. During this period, Jim remained active as a songwriter, enjoying a Top Five hit for his "Sittin' in an All Nite Cafe" courtesy of Warner Mack; a huge pop hit, courtesy of Gary Puckett & the Union Gap, with "Woman Woman," which he'd co-authored with Jimmy Payne; and chart action from Liz Anderson's recording of "Thanks a Lot for Trying." The Glaser brothers opened their own studio in Nashville, which became a locus for the "outlaw" movement in country music, a favorite hangout for Waylon Jennings, Bobby Bare, and Billy Joe Shaver. They placed a song into the underrated topical dramatic film *Tick, Tick, Tick*, starring Jim Brown and George Kennedy, and scored a big hit in 1971 with "Gone Girl." They won the Vocal Group of the Year Award from the Country Music Association in 1970 and enjoyed their first Top Ten single, "Rings," in 1971. The group only enjoyed two more years together, scoring two more hits, one of them—"Ain't It All Worth Living For"—backed by the London Symphony Orchestra.

After the brothers split up to work on their own projects, Jim emerged as a solo artist at MGM, charting minor hits with "Forgettin' 'Bout You" and "Woman Woman" in 1974 and 1975. Unfortunately, MGM Records had entered a period of steep decline from which it would never recover, and he had to wait until 1982, after signing with Noble Vision, to recapture momentum to his recording career. During the interim period, he was reunited with his brothers in Nebraska—Chuck, who had suffered a stroke and temporarily lost his voice, had become a talent manager, handling singer/songwriter (and sometime novelist) Kinky Friedman, and Tompall managed the studio he'd founded. They were initially brought back together by the illness of their father, and they later had a musical reunion, which yielded a number-three hit with their version of Kris Kristofferson's "Lovin' Her Was Easier (Than Anything I'll Ever Do Again)" and a Top 20 single with "Just One Time." The brothers split up again professionally in 1982. That year Jim hit the Top 20 country listings with "When You're Not a Lady" for Noble Vision, and he had similar success a year later with "The Man in the Mirror," which became the title track of his first album for the label. "If I Could Only Dance With You" also made the Top Ten, and Glaser had his first number-one hit in 1984 with "You're Gettin' to Me Again," which rode the charts for half a year.

Everything looked promising for Glaser's future, but the merger of Noble Vision with MCA in 1984 seemed a harbinger of bad times ahead. Glaser continued with the label, but enjoyed relatively little success from 1984 onward, and he was dropped by the company in 1985, despite his past success. More recently, Glaser has continued performing his own songs and also includes a "Tribute to Marty Robbins" (who passed on in 1982) in his concert set, a recognition of the years that he and his brothers put in working with the country music legend. *—Bruce Eder*

● **Man in the Mirror** / 1983 / Noble Vision ✦✦✦✦

Everybody Knows I'm Yours / 1984 / Noble Vision ✦✦

Past the Point of No Return / 1985 / Noble Vision ✦✦✦

The Very Best of Jim Glaser / 1985 / Country Store [UK] ✦✦✦✦

Tompall Glaser

b. Sep. 3, 1933, Spalding, NE

Vocals / Traditional Country, Outlaw Country

Of all the "outlaw" singers of the mid-'70s, Tompall Glaser was the one who most exploited his newfound moniker. He even titled one album *The Great Tompall and His Outlaw Band*, which brazenly featured a huge picture of him, shirt unbuttoned halfway down his chest, on the cover. It's ironic, then, that even though he had numerous chart records alone and with his brothers, Chuck and Jim, into the 1980s, he's the least remembered of the four artists—Willie Nelson, Waylon Jennings, Jessi Colter, and himself—who were packaged together on the immensely popular 1976 album *Wanted! The Outlaws.* Tompall, however, deserves far more recognition for his achievements. Over the course of four decades he wrote and recorded a wealth of excellent folk- and rock-influenced country songs, and his rich, husky-sweet tenor voice is immediately distinct. He's at home with a tender love ballad or a playful novelty number as he is with a bottomed-out cowboy lament like the Kinky Friedman classic "Sold American."

Tompall and his brothers, Chuck and Jim, hailed from Spaulding, NE, and started singing together as the folk trio Tompall & the Glaser Brothers in the late '50s. Their tight harmony singing impressed Marty Robbins, who signed them to his label. Their debut single was "Five Penny Nickel." They then moved to Nashville in 1958 and signed with Decca in 1959, worked also as session players, toured with Johnny Cash, and then joined the *Grand Ole Opry* in 1962. In 1965 they hooked up with producer Jack Clement and a year later signed with MGM, which released several excellent albums. Songs like "Gone, on the Other Hand," "Through the Eyes of Love," and "California Girl (And the Tennessee Square)" made the charts, and the brothers remained a popular group throughout the decade. Tompall's "Streets of Baltimore" (co-written with Harlan Howard) also became a hit for Bobby Bare in 1966.

In 1969 the brothers opened their own recording studio in Nashville, which soon became known as Hillbilly Central and a focal point of the burgeoning outlaw movement. By this time they also had their own group of music publishing companies; Nashville's old-boy network was shaken up when one of their discoveries, John Hartford's "Gentle on My Mind"—which had been turned down by nearly every publishing house in town—became a smash hit for Glen Campbell. In 1973 the group split up, Tompall began recording as a solo artist, and outlaw became his badge of honor. But his intentions were true, and his 1973 album, *Charlie*, stands as one of the finest of that genre. It includes a stunning version of "Sold American" as well as the Tompall originals "Big Jim Colson" (about an unwed mother) and the excellent title track. The novelty song "Put Another Log on the Fire," from his 1975 album *Tompall (Sings the Songs of Shel Silverstein)*, became a chart hit, and it was one of Tompall songs included on *The Outlaws* two year later. Further Tompall's hits from that decade include "T for Texas" and "Drinking Them Beers," though these are by no means his best material. Tompall had also become a close friend and business associate with Jennings, but the two eventually had a major falling out.

The brothers reunited and signed with Elektra Records in 1980, and again they met success, especially with the Kris Kristofferson song "Lovin' Her Was Easier (Than Anything I'll Ever Do Again)." The group split again in 1983, and Tompall returned to his Nashville recording studio. He released the solo album *Nights on the Borderline* for MCA Dot in 1986. *—Kurt Wolff*

This Land-Folk Songs / 1960 / Decca ✦✦✦

Just Looking for a Home / 1961 / Starday ✦✦✦✦

The Ballad of Namu the Killer Whale / 1966 / United Artists ✦✦✦

Tompall & The Glaser Brothers / 1967 / MGM ✦✦✦

The debut album from Tompall Glaser & the Glaser Brothers for MGM was a huge step up from the crap they'd been recording at Vocalion. With Cowboy Jack Clement introducing elements of Western swing and Marty Robbins' brand of cowboy balladry into their sound, they were beginning their transformation from being a pop-folk act into a country band. And while it's a far-from-perfect album, it does have one genuine classic on it—the album's closer is one of Tompall's greatest songs, "The Streets of Baltimore," which charted for Bobby Bare in 1966 and would be covered by Gram Parsons and Emmylou Harris a few years later. (Interestingly, in 1967, the year this album was released, Parsons was trying to turn the Byrds into a genuine country-rock band.) Also notable is the appearance of John Hartford's "Gentle on My Mind," which was released and charted a week after Glen Campbell's version. Finally, acknowledging his debt to Marty Robbins, Tompall and family recorded a fine version of "El Paso," with full mariachi accompaniment. Hartford contributed another song to this set, "No End of Lover," and Clement and his songwriting partners wrote half the record, making Glaser with two and two others. This album is actually better because of the material than its subsequent follow-up in 1968, *Through the Eyes of Love.* It is worth it for the version of the Hartford hit alone, because the Glaser Brothers' version is every bit as authentic and moving as Campbell's. *—Thom Jurek*

Through the Eyes of Love / 1968 / MGM ✦✦✦

In late 1967, the Glaser Brothers left Vocalion—who thought they were a white version the Mills Brothers from Nashville—and signed with MGM. Once they got to MGM, the label hooked them up with producer Cowboy Jack Clement, who brought them along and turned them into an honest to goodness country act. This was their second album for the label and Clement. *Through the Eyes of Love* still has a touch or two of the Glaser Brothers' awful pop sound, but much of it had been bred out by then. Tompall Glaser's voice was beginning to take on that individualistic character of his and was moving away from that Pat Boone warble. Tompall only wrote three of the album's ten tracks, while four were written by Clement, and John D. Loudermilk and others filled the rest. This is countrypolitan mixed with elements of folk and pop, but the high lonesome in Glaser's tenor is what makes it country; his phrasing and delivery are moving toward a style that would become inimitable. "The Moods of Mary," "You Only Pass This Way One Time," the title track, as well as the Loudermilk classic "I Chose You" are the standout tracks. *—Thom Jurek*

Tompall (Of Tompall and the Glaser Brothers) / 1972 / MGM ✦✦✦

Rings and Things / 1972 / MGM ✦✦✦

★ **Charlie** / 1973 / MGM ✦✦✦✦✦

By 1973, Tompall Glaser had established a reputation for being a mean sumbitch, a wild and woolly drunk, a man of uncommon generosity and moodiness given to prolonged bouts of solitude, and the wild animal of the party. In other words, he was "complicated." *Charlie* is the final album by Tompall & the Glaser Brothers and is a fitting send-off and the beginning of earnest outlaw music. The 11 tracks here are 11 chapters in Glaser's life and experience, and they range from the tough yet misunderstood cowboy of "An Ode to My Notorious Youth," a honky tonk song about being barred from honky tonks, to the tenderness of "The Loneliest Man," to the repentant medley of Mickey Gilley's rendition of "I'll Fly Away" combined with Hank Williams' "I Saw the Light." And then there's the mysterious title track, a thinly veiled composite of Glaser and his friends. Side two is seamlessly fine, but the two most outstanding cuts are Glaser's own funky honky tonker "Bad, Bad, Bad Cowboy" and his cover of Kinky Friedman's "Sold American," which has a different accent than the original but is as deeply felt and emoted. On this cut, Glaser looks into the mirror and stares at a reflection that no longer looks him in the eye, but past him as if he were a ghost. The effect is chilling, haunting, and some strange kind of beginning where a man leaves the security of his past behind, but not his demons. Along with *The Outlaw Band*, this is one of Glaser's greats and should be sought out by anyone interested in 1970s outlaw music. *—Thom Jurek*

☆ **Tompall (Sings the Songs of Shel Silverstein)** / 1975 / MGM ✦✦✦✦✦

Tompall Glaser may have hoped to jump-start his solo career with *Tompall*, an album of songs written by Shel Silverstein. Bobby Bare cut a few albums of Silverstein's songs in the mid-'70s with varying degrees of success, and Glaser had yet to crack the Top 40 since the Glaser Brothers disbanded in 1973. The plan worked to the extent that Silverstein provided Glaser with his biggest solo hit, "Put Another Log on the Fire" (the parenthetical title "Male Chauvinist National Anthem" was added for the single). That song and "Musical Chairs," the album's other minor hit, offer the wry humor you'd expect from Silverstein, but the rest of the album is more serious and melancholy. The unadorned backing and Glaser's average-Joe delivery are superficially similar to Bare, but Glaser's voice has its own character. *Tompall* is Glaser's finest solo album and another excellent collection of songs by the late Shel Silverstein. *—Greg Adams*

☆ **Great Tompall and His Outlaw Band** / 1976 / MGM ✦✦✦✦✦

The year 1977 was the height of country outlaw fever, and Tompall Glaser was digging deeper into the blues than any of his contemporaries, with the possible exception of Mickey Newbury, who had influenced him profoundly when it came to production, texture, dynamics, and arrangement. Though not as well-known as his pals Willie and Waylon, Glaser had a style and a band that were second to none. With Mel Brown on lead guitar, Glaser and Fred Newell on rhythm, and Ben Keith of the Stray Gators (from Neil Young's backing band on *Harvest*) on dobro and pedal steel, anchored by Red Young on keys, Charlie Polk on drums, and bassist Teddy Reynolds, they were unbeatable. But it's the smooth swamp glide of Glaser's voice that is the key to his best records, and this is his classic. Sounding alternately wasted and worn, yet full of a slow-burning fire that comes from down in the belly like the best blues singers, Glaser delivers every time with electricity and rough-hewn elegance. This ABC album features one of the best openers to appear on any outlaw country record: "You Can Have Her" is a slow-building brush fire that is rooted in the same Southern-fried soul and rock that Delaney & Bonnie put across. The band, which erects a towering wall of dirty, greasy country-rocking blues and funk, is accompanied by a chorus of female backing vocalists that gives the record a real Muscle Shoals feel. At over five minutes, it has the time to develop into the bumping and grinding anthem it is. But what follows is so strange it's hard to believe it's on the same record. It's a version of the Miller/Stevenson classic "Please Release Me." Glaser sings it through the first half accompanied by only a piano in slow, pained fashion, creating an almost unbearable tension before opening it all up in the last two choruses. But it just gets better with "Tennessee Blues" and "Come Back Shane," two of the most gorgeous country ballads he ever cut, and the honky tonker "It'll Be Her," all rounding out the first side. Side two kicks it with the infamous "It's a Ain't Fair Medley" of "Look What Thoughts Will Do," "Pretty Words," and "It Ain't Fair," all waltzing in the grand bass-thumping outlaw fashion. While "Sweethearts or Strangers" is a fine song, it pales in comparison to the two closers, the redneck lovers' anthem "Let My Fingers Do the Walkin'" and Glaser's signature tune, the countrypolitan blues-rocker "I Just Want to Hear the Music," with its stuttering guitars, sweetly fingerpicked acoustics, mandolins, sweeping strings, pumpin' Jerry Lee-styled piano, and fiddles bleating in the best R&B sweatbox fashion. *Great Tompall and His Outlaw Band* is *the* Glaser record to own. *—Thom Jurek*

The Outlaw / 1977 / Bear Family ✦✦✦✦✦

Tompall Glaser is the great, unsung hero of the outlaw movement in country music that lasted from the middle '70s and into the 1980s. An interpretive singer of rare ability and great taste, he spent much of his time playing with his brothers in the Glaser Brothers before hanging out with Willie and Waylon and the boys. And as is typical of great American artists who have had some commercial success but overwhelming critical acclaim, there is no collection available stateside that does the man's contribution to country music justice. Leave to the folks at Bear Family in Germany to provide one that contains just about every major song the cat performed. There are 21 selections in all, ranging from Bill Chappell's "The Bad Times" and "It Never Crossed My Mind" to his definitive read of Mickey Newbury's "How I Love Them Old Songs." But there's more than the honky tonk stomp of those tracks here with their chunky rock & roll guitars, there's also the barroom blues of Jessi Colter's "Storms Never Last" and the drop-dead drunken heartache of "Release Me" (it may have been a respectable ballad, but Tompall turned it into a guttersnipe player's anthem). In the grain of Tompall's voice was the everyman that Waylon was too tough to be and Willie was too tender to be. Tompall could wring the truth from a song by the sheer power of his ordinary voice. He knew he had nothing special to work with as a singer, so transferring emotion from the song to the listener became everything. And it worked time and again, as he sounded like the good-time party buddy who is either up for raining hell or ready to break down and cry at the first bars of a sad song on the jukebox when drunk. There isn't an emotionally dishonest moment in any of these tracks, and they stack up to any string by the aforementioned artists and lay waste to some those by David Allan Coe or Hank Jr., even though Tompall didn't write the songs. *—Thom Jurek*

Tompall Glaser and His Outlaw Band / 1977 / ABC ♦♦♦♦♦

Wonder of It All / 1977 / ABC ♦♦♦♦♦

Tick Tick Tick / 1977 / MGM ♦♦♦

Nights on the Borderline / 1986 / Dot ♦♦♦

The Rogue / 1992 / Bear Family ♦♦♦

The Rogue is a companion disc to Bear Family's first Tompall Glaser CD, *The Outlaw*. That disc collected his two late-'70s albums for ABC, and *The Rogue* adds a third, previously unreleased album recorded for ABC before the label folded, and an album's worth of covers of classic country songs made circa 1990. Unlike most of Bear Family's CDs, *The Rogue* does not include session info so dates are a little hazy. The new recordings are melancholy and mellow renditions of such favorites as Eddy Arnold's "I'll Hold You in My Heart" and the musty traditional tune "My Pretty Quadroon," while the "lost" ABC album is much better and progresses logically from his previous two "outlaw" albums from this period. Despite the rarities and promise of lost treasure, *The Rogue* is merely pleasant and inessential for all but the most devoted followers of Tompall Glaser. *—Greg Adams*

★ **The Best of Tompall Glaser & the Glaser Brothers** / 2001 / Collectors' Choice Music ♦♦♦♦♦

Tompall Glaser was one of the leading lights of outlaw country, and before he struck out on a solo career, he made a name for himself with his brothers, who had several country hits in the early '70s. Though they rarely cracked the Top Ten—only "Rings" went into the upper reaches of the country charts—they made some of the best music of the era, turning out music that sounded country but had distinct elements of rock and pop and even post-Dylan singer/songwriterism. Clearly, they laid the groundwork for outlaw with this music and Glaser, along with Waylon and Willie, was one of the key figures of the movement, but for some reason he never became a legend and he and his brothers kind of faded into the history books by the late '80s. No good collection of their music existed for years, not until Collector's Choice Music issued *The Best of Tompall Glaser & the Glaser Brothers* late in 2001. Though it spins heavily toward the brothers' recordings—a full 18 or the 24 tracks are Glaser Brothers sides—that's fine, because that's where the great majority of the charting hits and great music was made. Perhaps the collection could have been a double-disc set, giving both sides of Glaser's career equal time, but what's here is tremendous, offering proof that Tompall and his brothers did indeed deserve to stand alongside Waylon, Willie, and Kris Kristofferson as one of the great progressive country icons of the '70s. Few reissues in 2001 were as essential and as necessary as this. *—Stephen Thomas Erlewine*

Golden Smog

f. 1989

Group / Alternative Country-Rock

A boozy, side-project covers band which gradually evolved into a kind of roots rock supergroup, Golden Smog was a loosely affiliated unit comprised, at various times, of members of Soul Asylum, the Replacements, Wilco, the Jayhawks, Run Westy Run, and the Honeydogs. The group first came together in the Minneapolis area in the late '80s as a country-rock reaction to the punk and hardcore sounds that dominated the Twin Cities' musical scene at the time; eventually Golden Smog became something of a fixture at local clubs, where they played a handful of shows annually. From the onset, the lineup was mercurial, although Run Westy Run vocalist Kraig Johnson as well as guitarists Dan Murphy (Soul Asylum) and Gary Louris (the Jayhawks) were relative constants. Smog shows were usually thematically based, in keeping with the tongue-in-cheek nature of the project; one performance was devoted exclusively to Eagles covers, while another paid homage to the Rolling Stones and was billed "Her Satanic Majesty's Paycheck."

Somewhat unexpectedly, a five-cut covers EP, *On Golden Smog*, appeared in 1992. While the closing track, a rendition of Thin Lizzy's "Cowboy Song" sung by Soul Asylum roadie Bill Sullivan, followed in the project's original devil-may-care spirit, the remainder of the record was considerably more focused, keeping in line with the primary musical work of the bandmembers—who, this time out, were essentially Johnson, Murphy, Louris, Jayhawks bassist Marc Perlman, and ex-Replacements drummer Chris Mars, along with Soul Asylum vocalist Dave Pirner (on a cover of Bad Company's "Shooting Star"). Even more unexpectedly, the next Golden Smog effort—1996's full-length *Down by the Old Mainstream*—was made up largely of original material composed strictly for the project. With a lineup that included Johnson, Murphy, Louris, Perlman, Wilco frontman Jeff Tweedy, and Honeydogs drummer Noah Levy (all of whom recorded under pseudonyms as a result of contractual obligations), the record bore few reminders of Smog's beer-soaked origins, instead revealing a more mature and thoughtful band breaking free of the restraints of their day jobs and having some serious fun in the process. *Weird Tales* followed in 1998. *—Jason Ankeny*

On Golden Smog / Dec. 11, 1992 / Rykodisc ♦♦♦

After a few years of haphazard shows in and about their native Minneapolis, the members of Golden Smog were approached by a small local label to put out a record; many, many beers later, *On Golden Smog* appeared. Complete with sleeve art by then-drummer Chris Mars, the five-song EP is comprised entirely of covers, including *Hair*'s "Easy to Be Hard," the obscure '60s band Michelangelo's "Son," Bad Company's "Shooting Star" (sung by Soul Asylum's Dave Pirner), and Thin Lizzy's "Cowboy Song," fronted by Soul Asylum roadie Bill Sullivan. *—Jason Ankeny*

● **Down By the Old Mainstream** / 1996 / Rykodisc ♦♦♦♦

Like most supergroup projects, Golden Smog's *Down By the Old Mainstream* is a loose, relaxed affair that sounds like it was a lot of fun to record. Unlike most supergroups, the members of Golden Smog improve on their regular bands. Comprised of a number of alternative country-rock stars—including Wilco's Jeff Tweedy, the Jayhawks' Gary Louris, and Soul Asylum's Dan Murphy—the musicians are relaxed and loose, giving the songs a raw, rootsy kick. Since the album wasn't carefully considered, it has an offhand, relaxed charm that is sometimes lacking from Jayhawks and Soul Asylum albums. Not all of the songs are first-rate—"Pecan Pie" and "Red Headed Stepchild" are a bit too cute to be effective—but the performances are full of grit and fire, which is what makes *Down By the Old Mainstream* such an engaging listen. *—Stephen Thomas Erlewine*

Weird Tales / Oct. 13, 1998 / Rykodisc ♦♦♦

Weird Tales, the second full length album from alt-country supergroup Golden Smog, while in theory a collective banging of the guitars, basses, and drums of its principal players, is actually a series of solo tunes by those artists fleshed out by a backing band consisting of likeminded, and extremely capable, performers. That doesn't make it any less a fine or well-intentioned album, it's just not the one-for-all, all-for-one group project that it's built up to be. Think of it as the *White Album* process: everyone (including members of Run Westy Run, the Jayhawks, Soul Asylum, Big Star, and Wilco) gets a chance to toss a tune or two into the consolidated song bin and let the gang go at it. And as expected, the best songwriters here (Gary Louris of the Jayhawks and Wilco's Jeff Tweedy) contribute *Weird Tales*' most solid tracks. A pet project aimed more toward fans of the genre than the casual listener, Golden Smog nonetheless deliver the goods with a good deal of twangy heart and soul. *—Michael Gallucci*

William Lee Golden

b. Jan. 12, 1939, Brewton, AL

Vocals / Country-Pop, Urban Cowboy

After more than two decades with the Oak Ridge Boys, baritone vocalist William Lee Golden was fired in 1986 when the other members wished to change the country band's image. He had joined the group in 1964, when the Oaks were a gospel/folk group, and he accompanied their rise through the country charts during the '70s. In 1985, Golden recorded the solo album *American Vagabond* for MCA with help from Booker T. Jones and Joe Walsh. Two singles, "Love Is the Only Way Out" and "You Can't Take It With You," appeared on the country charts, but then the Oak Ridge Boys let him go. He filed a 40 million dollar lawsuit, which was settled out of court, and then began to record with his sons Rusty and Chris. They moved to Mercury in 1990 and recorded the single "Louisiana Red Dirt Highway." Four years later, Golden released an album for North/South, a division of Atlantic. *—John Bush*

American Vagabond / 1986 / MCA ♦♦♦

The Goldens

f. 1987, Brewton, AL

Group / Country-Pop, Contemporary Country, Country Gospel

The Goldens were brothers Rusty and Chris, the sons of longtime Oak Ridge Boys singer William Lee Golden (he of the wild-haired mountain-man persona). Both Rusty and Chris were born in Brewton, AL, and grew up singing Southern gospel music; both went on to learn several instruments apiece. Chris played drums, keyboards, guitar, and mandolin, while Rusty took up the drums at age eight, and four years later learned piano upon discovering Elton John. Chris went on to play piano in the gospel group the Telestials at 15; at 18, he joined a band called Cedar Creek, and a year later sang on the TV show *Hee Haw*. Rusty, meanwhile, played occasionally with his father's backing band at age 15, and at 18 he joined Larry Gatlin's backing band. He recorded and toured with Gatlin for several years, working on his songwriting all the while, and left to start a pop-oriented group called the Boys Band, which recorded a self-titled album for Asylum in 1982. Chris played with the band as he was finishing up high-school, but it didn't last much longer. The brothers teamed up with friend Marc Speer in 1984 as Golden Speer, but a recording session went nowhere.

In 1987, Rusty and Chris formed their own group, the Goldens, and handled keyboards and lead vocals, respectively; supporting musicians included guitarist Skip Mitchell, fiddler/steel guitarist Bobby Randall, bassist Don Breland, and drummer Buster Phillips. They recorded a self-titled debut album for Epic, which produced the singles "Put Us Together Again" and "Sorry Girls." Neither broke them to the country audience, and they moved over to Capitol in 1989, issuing *Rush for Gold* the following year. Several more singles proved minor hits, but failed to establish the group commercially, and they disbanded soon after. Both Rusty and Chris continued to work as session musicians; most notably, Rusty played with Dallas County Line, while Chris was hired as the Oak Ridge Boys' drummer in 1998. *—Steve Huey*

The Goldens / 1982 / Epic ♦♦♦

● **Rush for Gold** / Sep. 10, 1990 / Capitol ♦♦♦♦

Curtis Gordon

Vocals, Guitar / Rock & Roll, Rockabilly, Honky Tonk

One of the most enduring and beloved rockabilly artists of the '50s, Curtis Gordon has never gotten the recognition he deserves as a true crossover artist between country, Western swing, and rockabilly. A devotee of both Ernest Tubb and Bob Wills as a boy, it's possible to hear echoes of Tubb's "Walkin' the Floor Over You" in his best sides, including "Play the Music Louder," "Caffeine and Nicotine," and "Baby, Please Come Home," indeed, the steel player in his '50s band, Freddie Calhoun, played for all the world like Tubb's steel guitarist Jerry Byrd. Gordon grew up listening to Tubb and Wills on the radio, as well as old records by Jimmie Rodgers and quickly developed his own aspirations as a singer, winning a local radio talent show. He left school as a teenager to front a band—whose membership included a young Jimmy Bryant, then a fiddle-player using the moniker Ivy J. Bryant—until his parents insisted he give it up. Being stuck in school didn't dampen Gordon's enthusiasm for music or a performing career, however, and he continued working with a Gulfport, MS, outfit called Pee Wee Mills & the Twilight Cowboys. At the age of 21, he put together his own Western swing band and worked the area around the

Georgia-Florida border. The band was good enough to earn a living of sorts, and in June of 1952, they entered a contest in Atlanta and ended up catching the ear of a local RCA Victor executive, who brought them to the attention of Steve Sholes, the head of A&R for the label's country division. They were signed that summer and had their first recording session in the fall of 1952, which focused principally on ballads.

By 1953, however, Gordon was recording a few swinging, harder numbers such as "Rompin' & Stompin,'" interspersed between the ballads and novelty tunes. His sound was a unique amalgam of styles like honky tonk and Western swing—equal parts Hank Thompson and Ernest Tubb—all grafted to a freer, looser, more vibrant singing style, a decade more youthful than Tubb's style. Gordon got steady work touring the *Grand Ole Opry*, playing support to Ernest Tubb or Hank Snow, and he was making a living, if not setting the world on fire. His RCA sides sold just well enough to keep him with the label for two full years, generating new records every few months, but music was changing around Gordon and Sholes faster than either could keep up with it, and none of his country-style singles generated enough interest or sales to chart. Gordon's potential seemed solid enough, however, that immediately upon parting company with RCA Victor, he was signed up by Mercury Records. Gordon's Mercury recordings were very different from his RCA sides, principally because the label let him cut a large number of originals, and because his Mercury contract coincided with rock & roll's rise to national prominence—the latter event was heralded, ironically enough, by a subsequent Steve Sholes signing to RCA, one Elvis Presley, with whom Gordon had shared the bill several times while playing shows in the South during 1954 and 1955.

Gordon's March 1956 sessions showed just how much the excitement surrounding Presley in the South, even before he'd broken nationally, had opened the way for him. Those recording dates, and the ones that followed in December of that year and October of 1957, showed Gordon plunging into the new music with total abandon and astonishing results. His country ballads were good enough, well-written, and performed with passion, and in another reality he might've been a serious rival to Lefty Frizzell. But when he turned to what they used to call "rhythm numbers," Gordon was spellbinding—his youthful, exciting and engaging singing style, and the tightness of his band's playing all combined to generate brilliant records that seemed to straddle the gap between rock & roll, Western swing, and country music, without treading on the essentials of any of them. He should have been huge, appealing across generational lines to country listeners and their children and to the Ernest Tubb crowd, and to the kids listening to Elvis Presley and Carl Perkins.

Alas, he never charted a record, despite a lot of tries working with producer Pappy Daily and some of the best session musicians in the business working behind him and his band. A stint in the Army (during which he crossed paths with a young would-be singer/songwriter named Roger Miller, whom he later helped get a contract) probably didn't help, but more broadly, Gordon never managed to be in the right place with the right record at the right moment. Gordon made a decent living playing locally in Mobile, where he had a solid and very loyal audience and where he also owned a very popular club. He also toured occasionally around the Southern and border states. His last long-term recording contract was with Dollie Records in the late '50s, but he never stopped performing and he made a good living, even if he didn't get rich doing it. Gordon saw some of his songs do well, particularly "I've Aged Twenty Years in Five," which was recorded by George Jones. He was concentrating mainly on running his successful dance club in Georgia, but resumed performing in the '80s largely as a result of his discovery of new demand out of Europe for his classic songs, where rockabilly music had acquired a large and fiercely devoted audience. He remains a revered figure in rockabilly as one of its great elder statesmen, and his music still appeals just as easily to fans of honky tonk and Western swing. —*Bruce Eder*

● **Play the Music Louder** / May 20, 1998 / Bear Family ✦✦✦✦
Curtis Gordon was a hitless major label country artist of the '50s whose music is so much fun it's hard to believe he isn't better known. "Mobile, Alabama" and "Rompin' and Stompin'" are only two of the many lost classics that appear among the 34 tracks on *Play the Music Louder*, which draws from Gordon's vintage recordings for RCA, Mercury, and Dollie. The music ranges from proto-rock and rockabilly to teen-oriented ballads and hillbilly novelties, most of which are good and some of which are great. As Gordon fished around for a hit he tried a myriad of different approaches and singing styles, which makes for fascinating variety but not a very identifiable sound. If you count yourself among the cult of '50s country fanatics you can't go wrong with this one. —*Greg Adams*

Gosdin Brothers

f. 1961, Woodland, AL, db. 1973
Group / Bluegrass, Progressive Bluegrass, Neo-Traditionalist Country
Despite a strong association with the Byrds, the Gosdin Brothers' progressive blend of bluegrass and country-rock never found its way to a popular audience, though Vern Gosdin would later become one of country's more acclaimed vocalists. Vern and Rex Gosdin grew up on a farm in Woodland, AL—two of nine children—and started singing together after discovering the Louvin Brothers. They performed regularly on local radio as teenagers, and moved to the Los Angeles area in 1961, where they joined a bluegrass group called the Golden State Boys. Chris Hillman was a member prior to joining the Byrds, and the group later changed its name to the Hillmen. When Hillman departed, the Gosdin Brothers teamed up to form their own outfit, and sometimes served as the Byrds' opening act. Additionally, when Gene Clark left the Byrds for a solo career, he teamed up with Vern and Rex to record the 1966 album *Gene Clark With the Gosdin Brothers*, an influential proto-country-rock effort.

The Gosdin Brothers subsequently scored a deal with Capitol, and had their only chart single with 1967's "Hangin' On." Their first and only album, *Sounds of Goodbye*, was released in 1968, and its brand of country owed much to Clark and the Byrds' influence. The Gosdins opened for Merle Haggard on tour, and the Byrds recorded Vern's "Someone to Turn To" for the soundtrack of *Easy Rider* in 1969, but the overall lack of exposure proved too frustrating, and the brothers disbanded in 1970. Vern moved to Atlanta and ran a glass business before returning to music in 1976; this time the charts were kinder,

and he ran off a string of country hits that lasted into the early '90s, when health problems curtailed his performing activities. Rex, too, mounted a solo career, but was less successful, and passed away in 1983. —*Steve Huey*

Sounds of Goodbye / 1968 / Capitol ✦✦✦✦
The Gosdin Brothers' obscure 1968 LP *Sounds of Goodbye* is an overlooked country-rock milestone, and one that owes as much to the sound of the Byrds 1966-1967 era as it does to country music. That's unsurprising, perhaps, given that the Gosdins helped out a lot on Gene Clark's debut solo album in 1967, and sometimes shared bills with the early Byrds, as they shared the same management. In truth, this will appeal far more to the early Byrds fan than to the straight country fan. That's not damning with faint praise, far from it; it's actually high praise. It's a fair guess, too, that anyone who likes Gene Clark's early work will enjoy this record, as it has a similar low-key, hurt, vulnerable mystique to the melodies, vocals, and harmonies. The material, though sometimes average, is also sometimes outstanding, as on "Love at First Sight," which actually comes quite close to the classic 1966 Byrds jangle rock sound; the melancholy, graceful "She's Gone," with the kind of unexpected compelling chord changes you'd expect from the Gene Clark songwriting school; and "The Victim," with its pungent burned-by-love lyrics, and an odd (though not displeasing) dash of psychedelic echo on the chorus. The covers cast an eclectic net ("Catch the Wind," "Let It Be Me," the Everly Brothers' "Bowling Green") and are not as distinctive as the originals, but even so there's an excellent reading of Ewan MacColl's "The First Time Ever I Saw Your Face." As the new millennium begins, it's very hard to find, and is of a high enough caliber to demand CD reissue. —*Richie Unterberger*

● **Greatest Hits** / 1986 / Compleat ✦✦✦✦

Vern Gosdin

b. Aug. 5, 1934, Woodland, AL
Guitar, Vocals / Progressive Bluegrass, Traditional Bluegrass, Traditional Country
As country music swung back toward traditional styles in the 1980s, an inheritor of the soulful honky tonk style of Lefty Frizzell and Merle Haggard rose to the top of the business and notched hit after barroom hit. Sometimes he was known simply as "The Voice." Born in Woodland, AL, Vern Gosdin idolized the Louvin Brothers and the Blue Sky Boys as a young man and sang in a gospel quartet called the Gosdin Brothers. When he was in his late teens, his family moved to Birmingham and began hosting the *Gosdin Family Gospel Show* on a local radio station. Gosdin and his brother, Rex, moved to Long Beach, CA, in 1961. They began performing bluegrass music in the milieu that gave birth to country-rock, joining a group called the Golden State Boys that evolved into the Hillmen, featuring future Byrds member Chris Hillman. Vern and Rex teamed up to sing country music as the Gosdin Brothers once again, had a Top 40 country hit in 1967 with "Hangin' On," and opened for the Byrds on occasion.

Gosdin moved to Atlanta in 1972, raising a family and running a retail shop. But he never gave up on music completely. He performed at local clubs and began to gravitate toward Nashville, where Emmylou Harris, a friend of Gosdin's from his California days, was laying the foundation for a neo-traditionalist style of country music. Around 1976 Gosdin and Harris cut a demo single consisting of "Hangin' On" backed with a newly written song, "Yesterday's Gone." The demo got Gosdin signed to the Elektra label, and both songs cracked the country Top 20. In the late '70s he notched several major hits, including "Till the End" (with Janie Fricke), "Mother Country Music," and a remake of the Association's "Never My Love."

In 1980, after the demise of Elektra's country division, Gosdin quickly moved through several contracts and landed with the independent Nashville label Compleat. He made the Top Ten consistently in the early '80s, really hitting his stride when he teamed with Max D. Barnes as a songwriting collaborator. The pair specialized in songs of cheating and barroom romance, often delivering an over-the-top emotionalism that got Gosdin compared to the ultimate legend of honky tonk vocals, George Jones. In 1983, Gosdin had two Top Five hits—"If You're Gonna Do Me Wrong (Do It Right)" and "Way Down Deep." The following year he had his first number-one single with "I Can Tell by the Way You Dance (You're Gonna Love Me Tonight)" and had two additional Top Ten hits. His career hit a lull in the mid-'80s, but in 1987, with the traditionalist movement in full swing and Warner Bros. artist Randy Travis roosting at the top of the charts, he was tapped by the Columbia label. He bounced back into the Top Ten that year with the tortured "Do You Believe Me Now," and in 1988 he hit number one once again with the perennially popular Ernest Tubb tribute "Set 'Em Up Joe." Gosdin's "Chiseled in Stone," co-written with Barnes, won the Country Music Association's Song of the Year award in 1989. His 1989 album, *Alone*, was a rarity: a concept album in a traditional country style. It chronicled the dissolution of Gosdin's marriage. Gosdin's popularity declined as rock-influenced country styles surged forward in the 1990s, but he continued to record on small labels and never abandoned the pure country vocalism he had cultivated for so long. —*James Manheim*

Till the End / 1977 / Elektra ✦✦✦✦✦
This is probably one of Gosdin's strongest records overall. Additionally, it netted him four hits. —*Jim Worbois*

Never My Love / 1978 / Elektra ✦✦
In the mid-'70s Vern Gosdin was approaching the height of his popularity, recording for Elektra with Gary S. Paxton handling the production duties. He was tricked out in a wide lapel suit that approached the perfect disco outfit, with lots of gold jewelry hanging about his neck, and singing a song—the title track—more closely associated with Robert Goulet than Hank Williams, with Janie Fricke lilting on the backing vocals and chorus. But it gets weirder: The very next track after "Never My Love" is an overblown, string-laden version of Donovan's "Catch the Wind." Forget countrypolitan, this is schlockopolitan. Even classics like Waylon Jennings' "Anita, You're Dreaming" and John D. Loudermilk's "Break My Mind" are unsalvageable—which is a real tragedy considering Gosdin's amazing baritone and his ability to move his voice around a song like George Jones can. This recording is an awful mistake in a stellar career from Gosdin. If the listener needs any

more proof, have a listen to the country-fried version of Carole Bayer Sager's "When I Need You" as one of the most horrific, overdressed representations of sedate senility ever recorded. *—Thom Jurek*

Today My World Slipped Away / 1983 / A&M ♦♦♦

There Is a Season / 1984 / American Harvest ♦♦♦♦

Now here's an oddity if there ever was one, but it also proves that Vern Gosdin is capable of anything if he sets his mind to it. *There Is a Season* is a direct quote from the Byrds' version of Pete Seeger's "Turn, Turn, Turn," which is also the first track on the album. In addition, there is a familiar 12-string and vocal on the set that belongs to none other than Roger McGuinn. Issued on the short-lived Compleat (sic) label, which was distributed by Polygram, the set dates from 1984, when country music was looking for itself again after the fade of the outlaws and just before Dwight Yoakam changed everything again with his return to Bakersfield honky tonk. This is a curiosity in Gosdin's catalog in that it openly reveals his restlessness in seeking a new direction. Gosdin seemed to be revisiting many of the moments in his past rambling days from California to Chicago to Nash Vegas to Texas, from street to honky tonk to concert hall and recording studio. He is accompanied by Emmylou Harris in a very prominent backing-vocalist role. Gosdin takes "Turn, Turn, Turn" and transforms it into a song that looks forward; it doesn't sit in the present tense, a reflection on the changing nature of the times. But in tracks like "How Can I Believe You (When You'll Be Leavin' Me)," Jim Rushing's "Slow Healing Heart," and Hank Cochran and Dean Dillon's "What Would Your Memories Do," Gosdin reaches deep into that golden throat of his to pull out every conflicting emotion that presents itself in the lyrics. Whether it is a ballad or a honky tonk waltz or a pop song, Gosdin holds them all in equanimity and delivers them as if they are the only songs in the world. In addition to his literally stunning performances here, Gosdin co-wrote over half of the record, making it one of his most inspired efforts. It's a crime this isn't available on CD. *—Thom Jurek*

Too Far Gone / 1984 / RCA ♦♦♦

If Jesus Comes Tomorrow / 1984 / Compleat ♦♦♦

If Jesus Comes Tomorrow (What Then) is part gospel standards, part complementary originals, all sung by a honky tonk voice hoping for heaven. *—Brian Mansfield*

★ **Chiseled in Stone** / 1988 / Columbia ♦♦♦♦♦

The 1980s were the beginning of a run of fine albums for Vern Gosdin that continued into the 21st century. It's true that he wasn't always as popular as he was in the late '60s and mid-'70s, but from his period on Compleat through his signing with Columbia and on into American Harvest Recordings in the late '90s, Gosdin has made solid, tough, and aesthetically beautiful country records. The new traditionalists, led by Dwight Yoakam, were the very movement that helped Gosdin regain popular acceptance for a time from the mid-'80s through 1993. *Chiseled in Stone* ranks as arguably his finest moment of that period. Produced by Bob Montgomery, the album features a deck of tunes from Gosdin and co-writers Hank Cochran and Dean Dillon; if Gosdin didn't co-write, Dillon and Cochran did. What's more, these songs were all written for Gosdin's wonderfully worn yet astonishingly versatile voice. "Do You Believe Me Now," the darkest and most wrenching song on the album, opens it. It's the story of a man on skid row who is suddenly and unexpectedly visited by his ex, and he convinces her by his very ravaged existence that he cannot live without her and asks the question in the title. As Sonny Garrish's steel winds out underneath Gosdin's vocal, all of the pain and pathos in the song comes at the listener full force, yet with the softness of Gosdin's voice, it is believable as a tender revelation as well as a song of unremitting darkness and surrender to the "road of no return." He is punishing no one but himself, but it's important she knows he wasn't lying when he said he was nothing without her. But the very next cut is one of those that Gosdin owns. With the fiddles and steel shuffling along in dance time, "Tight as Twin Fiddles" is a solid, authentic update on the Texas Playboys' sound. The truth is, there isn't a weak track here, from the honky tonk blues of "Set 'Em Up Joe" to the lonesome ache of "I Guess I Had Your Leavin' Comin'" and "Is It Raining at Your House" or the title track. For fans of George Jones' *I Am What I Am* and Merle Haggard's "Going Where the Lonely Go," this is a reward in and of itself. *—Thom Jurek*

Rough Around the Edges / 1989 / RCA ♦♦♦

Rough Around the Edges is a brief, eight-song collection of songs Vern Gosdin recorded in the early '80s for A.M.I. that concentrates on ballads like "When Love Was All We Had" and "Lovin' You is Music to My Mind." Since it only contains eight songs, the album can't be anything more than a sampler, yet it showcases his vocal skills quite effectively. *—Thom Owens*

Alone / 1989 / Columbia ♦♦♦

Written and released directly after a painful divorce, *Alone* is a moving set of honky tonk that works better in theory than it does in practice. Though Gosdin's performance is frequently sublime, his songs aren't always strong. However, when he has a good song at his disposal—such as "Right in the Wrong Direction," "I'm Only Going Crazy," "That Just About Does It" and "I'm Still Crazy"—his heart-felt delivery and tortured lyrics makes for some truly memorable music. *—Thom Owens*

● **The Best of Vern Gosdin** / 1989 / Warner Bros. ♦♦♦♦♦

The Best of Vern Gosdin contains ten of his his late '70s hits, which were originally released in the '70s. Although they bear all the hallmarks of the era—these are slick, string-laden productions—they remain pure, impressive country. Gosdin sounds especially good when Emmylou Harris or Janie Fricke provide harmonies. *—Thom Owens*

10 Years of Hits—Newly Recorded / 1990 / Columbia ♦♦♦♦

As the title says, *10 Years of Hits—Newly Recorded* has seven of Gosdin's Compleat hits—like "I Can Tell By the Way You Dance (You're Gonna Love Me Tonight)"—from the early '80s re-recorded for his new label, Columbia, as well as four new tracks. Although they aren't the originals, Gosdin is in good voice and the new versions nearly equal to the hit singles. *—Stephen Thomas Erlewine*

Out of My Heart / 1991 / Columbia ♦♦♦♦

Out of My Heart is a typically excellent album from Vern Gosdin, yet the power of his vocals—he's singing his heart out throughout the record—and the quiet grace of the music make this one to treasure. *—Thom Owens*

Nickels & Dimes & Love / Mar. 9, 1993 / Columbia ♦♦♦

Produced by Rick Hall in 1993, *Nickels & Dimes & Love* was recorded outside of Nash Vegas at Muscle Shoals in Alabama. It was also the last time Gosdin nailed the charts, with Hugh Prestwood's "Back When," a mid- to uptempo burner with gorgeous acoustic guitars, a lilting fiddle, and pedal steel that jumps in texture and phrasing from verse to refrain. It's a love song that verges on a breakup tune. But in the grain of Gosdin's voice, the track becomes a song of hope and redemption. One of Gosdin's five contributions is a solid honky tonk number, "Bury Me in a Jukebox." In that George Jones croon of his, Gosdin sounds like he's having a good-time even when he's broken—as long as the Telecasters and steel guitars are ringing out in the heart of the mix. And they certainly do here. Uncharacteristically, Gosdin travels deep into outlaw terrain with the pumping "I Like My Country Music Kinda Rock." Here a funky backbeat frames a razor-wire guitar and rounded high-pitched pedal steel, as a bluegrass fiddle anchors the tune in the country camp. The high point on the album, however, is a duet with Janie Fricke entitled "Two People With a Love Gone Bad," another Gosdin number. If there were ever a song written too late, this one was. It should have been written for George Jones and Tammy Wynette. In the voices of this pair, it's still a devastatingly beautiful country weeper that transcends the country genre and becomes simply a beautiful song. Gosdin was focused here on writing for the charts, and it is reflected in the production, but nonetheless he remains completely true to the tradition in his execution. Gosdin would remain with Columbia for another four years, but this was the beginning of a transformation in country music that would leave him out, as it had others in his generation. It was too bad for country, because Gosdin is the real thing. *—Thom Jurek*

Super Hits / 1994 / Columbia ♦♦♦♦♦

Super Hits collects all of the biggest hits Vern Gosdin had on Columbia Records in the late '80s, including all of his Top Ten hits and the number ones "I'm Still Crazy" and "Set 'Em Up Joe." *—Thom Owens*

Silver Eagle Cross Country Presents Live: Vern Gosdin / Apr. 15, 1997 / Silver Eagle ♦♦♦

Silver Eagle Cross Country Presents Live captures a concert Vern Gosdin gave in Colmesneil, TX, in 1983, when he was at the height of his popularity. Gosdin is in fine voice and the set is thoroughly entertaining, featuring such staples as "Way Down Deep," "Today My World Slipped Way," "Til the End" and "If You're Gonna Do Me Wrong (Do It Right)," making it a small gem for devoted Gosdin fans. *—Thom Owens*

Billy Grammer

b. Sep. 28, 1925, Benton, IL

Guitar, Vocals / Traditional Country, Nashville Sound/Countrypolitan

Longtime *Grand Ole Opry* member Billy Grammer was one of the great guitar players of country music; he even had a flat-top guitar named after him and installed in the Country Music Hall of Fame in 1969. He was one of 13 children born to a coal-mining family in downstate Benton, IL. Despite a youthful interest in science and engineering, the young Grammer often played fiddle, guitar, or mandolin at local gatherings, accompanying his father or performing solo. He served in the U.S. Army during World War II, and worked as an apprentice toolmaker. But after discharge, work was scarce for an eager young musician. When Grammer heard about an opportunity with Connie Gay's Radio Ranch, he hitchhiked to Arlington, VA; auditioned; and made the cut. Two years later, he made his recording debut. In 1955, Gay suggested to Jimmy Dean that Grammer join his television show. During his years on *the Jimmy Dean Show*, Grammer was a sideman in several bands, including those of Clyde Moody, Grandpa Jones, and Hawkshaw Hawkins.

He founded his own band in 1958 and also began recording as a solo act. In 1959, he had his first hit with "Gotta Travel On," which peaked in the Top Five on the country charts and did well on the pop charts. That same year, he became a regular cast member of the *Opry*. Grammer went on to release instrument-centric albums such as 1962's *Gospel Guitar* and 1967's *Sunday Guitar*. He also had some chart success during the 1960s with cuts like "I Wanna Go Home," "I'll Leave the Porch Lights a-Burning," and "Bottles." In the 1970s, Grammer recorded two final solo albums and continued to do session work. He later retired from the studio, but continued to perform regularly on-stage at the *Opry*. Grammer was also the namesake of the Grammer guitar, a flat-top model built to his specifications. The instrument enjoyed some success in the 1960s and '70s, but was later undercut by cheap imports and industry consolidation. *—Johnny Loftus*

Gotta Travel On: The Very Best of Billy Grammer / 1998 / Collectables ♦♦♦♦♦

Billy Grammer is remembered for his big crossover hit, "Gotta Travel On," which reached the Top Five on the pop and country charts in 1959. He scored only two other hits on the Monument label: "The Kissin' Tree" and "Bonaparte's Retreat," neither of which made the country chart even though the latter is a tune by Pee Wee King. This 21-track anthology reissues Grammer's 1959 LP *Travelin' On* and adds the aforementioned pair of hits plus a half-dozen commercially unsuccessful tracks recorded in the mid-'70s when Grammer returned to Monument after years of label-hopping. *Gotta Travel On: The Very Best of Billy Grammer* might have been wiser to stick with early recordings, but is a very thorough anthology considering Grammer's paucity of hits during this period. *—Greg Adams*

The Grateful Dead

f. 1965, San Francisco, CA, **db.** 1995

Group / Jam Bands, Country-Rock, Psychedelic, Folk-Rock, Album Rock

Rock's longest, strangest trip, the Grateful Dead were the psychedelic era's most beloved musical ambassadors as well as its most enduring survivors, spreading their message of peace, love, and mind-expansion across the globe throughout the better part of three decades. The object of adoration for popular music's most fervent and celebrated fan following—the Deadheads, their numbers and devotion legendary in their own right—they were the ultimate cult band, creating a self-styled universe all their own; for the better part of their career orbiting well outside of the mainstream, the Dead became superstars solely on their own terms, tie-dyed pied pipers whose epic, free-form live shows were rites of passage for an extended family of listeners who knew no cultural boundaries.

The roots of the Grateful Dead lie with singer/songwriter Jerry Garcia, a longtime bluegrass enthusiast who began playing the guitar at age 15. Upon relocating to Palo Alto, CA, in 1960, he soon befriended Robert Hunter, whose lyrics later graced many of Garcia's most famous melodies; in time, he also came into contact with aspiring electronic music composer Phil Lesh. By 1962, Garcia was playing banjo in a variety of local folk and bluegrass outfits, two years later forming Mother McCree's Uptown Jug Champions with guitarist Bob Weir and keyboardist Ron "Pigpen" McKernan; in 1965, the group was renamed the Warlocks, their lineup now additionally including Lesh on bass as well as Bill Kreutzmann on drums.

The Warlocks made their electric debut that July; Ken Kesey soon tapped them to become the house band at his notorious Acid Tests, a series of now-legendary public LSD parties and multimedia "happenings" mounted prior to the drug's criminalization. As 1965 drew to its close, the Warlocks rechristened themselves the Grateful Dead, the name taken from an Egyptian prayer discovered in a dictionary by Garcia; bankrolled by chemist/LSD manufacturer Owsley Stanley, the bandmembers soon moved into a communal house situated at 710 Ashbury Street in San Francisco, becoming a fixture on the local music scene and building a large fan base on the strength of their many free concerts. Signing to MGM, in 1966 the Dead also recorded their first demos; the sessions proved disastrous, and the label dropped the group a short time later.

As 1967 mutated into the Summer of Love, the Dead emerged as one of the top draws on the Bay Area music scene, honing an eclectic repertoire influenced by folk, country, and the blues while regularly appearing at top local venues including the Fillmore Auditorium, the Avalon Ballroom, and the Carousel. In March of 1967 the Dead issued their self-titled Warner Bros. debut LP, a disappointing effort which failed to recapture the cosmic sprawl of their live appearances; after performing at the Monterey Pop Festival, the group expanded to a six-piece with the addition of second drummer Mickey Hart. Their follow-up, 1968's *Anthem of the Sun*, fared better in documenting the free-form jam aesthetic of their concerts, but after completing 1969's *Aoxomoxoa*, their penchant for time-consuming studio experimentation left them over 100,000 dollars in debt to the label.

The Dead's response to the situation was to bow to the demands of fans and record their first live album, 1969's *Live/Dead*; highlighted by a rendition of Garcia's "Dark Star" clocking in at over 23 minutes, the LP succeeded where its studio predecessors failed in capturing the true essence of the group in all of their improvisational, psychedelicized glory. It was followed by a pair of classic 1970 studio efforts, *Workingman's Dead* and *American Beauty*; recorded in homage to the group's country and folk roots, the two albums remained the cornerstone of the Dead's live repertoire for years to follow, with its most popular songs—"Uncle John's Band," "Casey Jones," "Sugar Magnolia," and "Truckin'" among them—becoming major favorites on FM radio. Despite increasing radio airplay and respectable album sales, the Dead remained first and foremost a live act, and as their popularity grew across the world they expanded their touring schedule, taking to the road for much of each year. As more and more of their psychedelic-era contemporaries ceased to exist, the group continued attracting greater numbers of fans to their shows, many of them following the Dead across the country; dubbed "Deadheads," these fans became notorious for their adherence to tie-dyed fashions and excessive drug use, their traveling circus ultimately becoming as much the focal point of concert dates as the music itself. Shows were also extensively bootlegged, and not surprisingly the Dead closed out their Warners contract with back-to-back concert LPs—a 1971 eponymous effort and 1972's *Europe '72*.

The latter release was the final Dead album to feature Pigpen McKernan, a heavy drinker who died of liver failure on March 8, 1973; his replacement was keyboardist Keith Godchaux, who brought with him wife Donna Jean to sing backing vocals. *Wake of the Flood* (1973) was the first release on the new Grateful Dead Records imprint; around the time of its follow-up, 1974's *Grateful Dead From the Mars Hotel*, the group took a hiatus from the road to allow its members the opportunity to pursue solo projects. After returning to the live arena with a 1976 tour, the Dead signed to Arista to release *Terrapin Station*, the first in a series of misguided studio efforts that culminated in 1980's *Go to Heaven*, widely considered the weakest record in the group's catalog—so weak, in fact, that they did not re-enter the studio for another seven years. The early '80s was a time of considerable upheaval for the Dead—the Godchauxs had been dismissed from the lineup in 1979, with Keith dying in a car crash on July 23, 1980. (His replacement was keyboardist Brent Mydland.) After a pair of 1981 live LPs, *Reckoning* and *Dead Set*, the group released no new recordings until 1987, focusing instead on their touring schedule—despite the dearth of new releases, the Dead continued selling out live dates, now playing to audiences which spanned generations. As much a cottage industry as a band, they traveled not only with an enormous road crew but also dozens of friends and family members, many of them Dead staffers complete with health insurance and other benefits.

Still, the Dead were widely regarded as little more than an enduring cult phenomenon prior to the release of 1987's *In the Dark*; their first studio LP since *Go to Heaven*, it became the year's most unlikely hit when the single "Touch of Grey" became the first-ever Dead track to reach the Top Ten on the pop charts. Suddenly their videos were in regular rotation on MTV, and virtually overnight the ranks of the Deadheads grew exponentially, with countless new fans flocking to the group's shows. Not only did concert

tickets become increasingly tough to come by for longtime followers, but there were also more serious repercussions—the influx of new fans shifted the crowd dynamic considerably, and once-mellow audiences became infamous not only for their excessive drug habits but also for their violent encounters with police. Other troubles plagued the Dead as well: in July 1986, Garcia—a year removed from a drug treatment program—lapsed into near-fatal diabetic coma brought on by his continued substance abuse problems, regaining consciousness five days later. His health remained an issue in the years which followed, but the Dead spent more time on tour than ever, with a series of dates with Bob Dylan yielding the live album *Dylan & the Dead*. Their final studio effort, *Built to Last*, followed in 1989. Tragedy struck in October of that year when a fan died after breaking his neck outside of a show at the New Jersey Meadowlands; two months later, a 19-year-old fan on LSD also died while in police custody at the Los Angeles Forum.

As ever, the Dead themselves were also not immune to tragedy—on July 26, 1990, Mydland suffered a fatal drug overdose, the third keyboardist in group history to perish; he was replaced not only by ex-Tubes keyboardist Vince Welnick but also by satellite member Bruce Hornsby, a longtime fan who frequently toured with the group. In the autumn of 1992 Garcia was again hospitalized with diabetes and an enlarged heart, forcing the Dead to postpone their upcoming tour until the year's end; he eventually returned to action looking more fit than he had in years. Still, few were surprised when it was announced on August 9, 1995, that Garcia had been found dead in his room at a substance abuse treatment facility in Forest Knolls, CA; the 53 year old's death was attributed to a heart attack.

While Garcia's death spelled the end of the Dead as a continuing creative entity, the story was far from over. As the surviving members disbanded to plot their next move, the band's merchandising arm went into overdrive—in addition to *Dick's Picks*, a series of archival releases of classic live material, licensed products ranging from Dead T-shirts to sporting goods to toys flooded the market. Plans were also announced to build Terrapin Station, an interactive museum site. In 1996, Weir and Hart mounted the first Furthur Festival, a summer tour headlined by their respective bands RatDog and Mystery Box; in 1998, they also reunited with Lesh and Hornsby to tour as the Other Ones. In spirit if not in name, the Grateful Dead's trip continued on. —*Jason Ankeny*

☆ **Workingman's Dead** / Jun. 14, 1970 / Warner Bros. ✦✦✦✦✦

The Grateful Dead were already established as paragons of the free-form, improvisational San Francisco psychedelic sound when they abruptly shifted gears for the acoustic *Workingman's Dead*, a lovely exploration of American roots music illuminating the group's country, blues, and folk influences. The lilting "Uncle John's Band," their first radio hit, opens the record and perfectly summarizes its subtle, spare beauty; complete with a new focus on more concise songs and tighter arrangements, the approach works brilliantly. Despite its sharp contrast to the epic live space jams on which the group's legend primarily rests, *Workingman's Dead* nonetheless spotlights the Dead at their most engaging, stripped of all excess to reveal the true essence of their craft. —*Jason Ankeny*

☆ **American Beauty** / Nov. 1970 / Warner Bros. ✦✦✦✦✦

A companion piece to the luminous *Workingman's Dead*, *American Beauty* is an even stronger document of the Grateful Dead's return to their musical roots. Sporting a more full-bodied and intricate sound than its predecessor thanks to the addition of subtle electric textures, the record is also more representative of the group as a collective unit, allowing for stunning contributions from Phil Lesh (the poignant opener "Box of Rain") and Bob Weir ("Sugar Magnolia"); at the top of his game as well is Jerry Garcia, who delivers the superb "Friend of the Devil," "Candyman," and "Ripple." Climaxing with the perennial "Truckin'," *American Beauty* remains the Dead's studio masterpiece—never again would they be so musically focused or so emotionally direct. —*Jason Ankeny*

The Grateful Dead / Oct. 1971 / Warner Bros. ✦✦✦✦

The Grateful Dead's second live release was an eponymously titled double LP whose cover bears the striking skull-and-roses visual motif that would become instantly recognizable and an indelibly linked trademark of the band. As opposed to their debut concert recording, *Live/Dead* (1969), this hour and ten minutes concentrates on newer material, which consisted of shorter self-contained originals and covers. Coming off of the quantum-leap success of the studio country-rock efforts *Workingman's Dead* (1970) and *American Beauty*, *Grateful Dead* offers up a pair of new Jerry Garcia/Robert Hunter compositions—"Bertha" and "Wharf Rat"—both of which garnered a permanent place within the band's live catalog. However, "The Other One"—joined in progress just as Billy Kreutzmann fires up a blazing percussion solo—sprawls as the album's centerpiece. The Dead also begin incorporating several traditional folk, blues, and R&B cover tunes, such as Merle Haggard's "Mama Tried," Kris Kristofferson's "Me & Bobby McGee," as well as a few that had been in their songbook for several years, including John Phillips' "Me & My Uncle" and "Big Boss Man," a blues standard popularized by Jimmy Reed. Their formidable improvisational chops have begun to take on new facets of lean intricacy as Mickey Hart (percussion) and Tom Constanten (keyboards) were no longer in the band. Additionally, the arrival of Keith Godchaux (organ) and his wife, Donna Godchaux (vocals), had yet to occur. As such, the Grateful Dead spent the spring and summer of 1971 in their original five-piece configuration—which is when these recordings were documented. [The *Golden Road (1965-1973)* (2001) box set features a remastered version of *Grateful Dead* and includes two additional covers—Buddy Holly's "Oh, Boy!" as well as Leiber & Stoller's "(I'm A) Hog for You"—plus an unmarked vintage radio spot for the album. Enthusiasts should note that this era is likewise represented on the four-CD *Ladies and Gentlemen…The Grateful Dead* (2000) archival release.] —*Lindsay Planer*

Europe '72 / Nov. 1972 / Warner Bros. ✦✦✦✦

The Grateful Dead commemorated their first extended European tour with an extravagant triple-LP set appropriately enough titled *Europe '72*. This collection is fashioned in much the same way as their previous release—which had also been a live multi-disc affair. The band mixes a bevy of new material—such as "Ramble on Rose," "Jack Straw,"

"Tennessee Jed," "Brown-Eyed Woman," and "He's Gone"—with revisitations of back-catalog favorites. Among them are "China Cat Sunflower"—which was now indelibly linked to the longtime Dead cover "I Know You Rider"—as well as "Cumberland Blues," "Truckin'," "Sugar Magnolia," and "Morning Dew." With the additional album the band was able to again incorporate some of their exceedingly stretched-out instrumental improvisations—titled "Epilogue" and "Prelude" here. Since their last outing, the group had expanded to include the husband-and-wife team of Keith Godchaux (keyboards) and Donna Jean Godchaux (vocals). Sadly, this European jaunt would be the last of its kind to include the formidable talents and soul of founding member Ron "Pigpen" McKernan (organ/mouth harp/vocals), who was in increasingly fragile health. Although few in number, his contributions to *Europe '72* are among the most commanding not only of this release, but of his career. *—Lindsay Planer*

History of the Grateful Dead, Vol. 1 (Bear's Choice) / Jul. 13, 1973 / Warner Bros. ♦♦♦♦
This 1973 release was the very last collection that the Grateful Dead authorized during their tenure with Warner Bros. in the late '60s and early '70s. However, this live disc was a sort of melancholy affair, as it centered on material featuring Ron "Pigpen" McKernan (guitar/vocals/mouth harp), who had left the band due to illness in June of the previous year. *History of the Grateful Dead, Vol. 1 (Bear's Choice)* is somewhat misleading, as a follow-up never came to pass. Band historians, however, claim that this release was optimistically titled because the label had *hoped* to issue a series of live recordings (à la *Dick's Picks*) containing highlights from a variety of vintage Dead performances. Alas, with the formation of the group's own label it was not to be. The single disc includes performances from a highly touted series of shows held over two nights (February 13-14, 1970) at the Fillmore East in New York City. While most assuredly not the finest example of the Dead's formidable acoustic sets, the platter opens with a quartet of cover tunes—many of which had been entries in Jerry Garcia (guitar/vocals) and McKernan's folky jug band repertoire prior to ultimately forming the electric, psychedelic Grateful Dead. McKernan's playful cover of Lightnin' Hopkins' "Katie Mae" is a somewhat lightweight affair. He counterbalances ad-libbed lyrics with his own very sparse solo guitar picking, which is in perfect keeping with the lonesome nature of this blues. Garcia and Bob Weir (guitar/vocals) join in on the remaining "unplugged" tracks. Both the affective and noir "Dark Hollow" and "I've Been All Around This World" reveal the command of this highly under-utilized subdivision of the Dead. Clocking in at seven-plus minutes, the album's sole original composition, "Black Peter," is masterfully executed. It ultimately bests the original *Workingman's Dead* (1969) version in sheer emotive realization. The two electric offerings—a cover of Howlin' Wolf's "Smokestack Lightnin'" and Otis Redding's "Hard to Handle"—are full-blown rave-ups allowing the entire band to weave their collective R&B-influenced psychedelia, unedited and in real time. Both tracks had become assertive vehicles for McKernan's no-nonsense R&B sensibilities. [In 2001, *History of the Grateful Dead, Vol. 1 (Bear's Choice)* was included in the 12-disc *Golden Road (1965-1973)* box set. The remastered edition comes replete with a newly inked 16-page liner notes insert containing an essay from the "Bear" (aka Owsley Stanley) himself. The expanded track list yields four additional performances from the same cache of shows: the McKernan-led "Good Lovin'," "Big Boss Man," a second and equally scintillating version of "Smokestack Lightnin'," as well as an uptempo "Sitting on Top of the World," the latter of which keeps the frenetic spirit of the reading from the Dead's self-titled debut firmly intact.] *—Lindsay Planer*

Wake of the Flood / Nov. 15, 1973 / Grateful Dead ♦♦♦♦
After satisfying their nine-title/dozen-disc deal with Warner Bros., the Dead began their own record labels—Grateful Dead Records (for group releases) and Round Records (for solo projects). *Wake of the Flood* was the first Dead disc issued entirely under the band's supervision—which also included manufacturing and marketing. Additionally, the personnel had been altered as Ron "Pigpen" McKernan had passed away. The keyboard responsibilities were now in the capable hands of Keith Godchaux—whose wife Donna Jean Godchaux also provided backing vocals. It had been nearly three years since *American Beauty*—their previous and most successful studio album to date—and, as always, the Dead had been honing the material in concert. A majority of the tracks had been incorporated into their live sets—some for nearly six months—prior to entering the recording studio. This gave the band a unique perspective on the material, much of which remained for the next 20-plus years as staples of their concert performances. However, the inspiration and magic of the Grateful Dead's music has always been a challenge to capture in the non-reciprocal confines of a studio. Therefore, while *Wake of the Flood* was certainly as good—if not arguably better than—most of their previous non-live efforts, it falls far short of the incendiary performances the band were giving during this era. There are a few tracks that do tap into some of the Dead's jazzier and exceedingly improvisational nature. "Eyes of the World" contains some brilliant ensemble playing—although the time limitations inherent in the playback medium result in the track fading out just as the Dead start to really cook. Another highlight is Bob Weir's "Weather Report Suite," which foreshadows the epic proportions that the song would ultimately reach. In later years, the band dropped the opening instrumental "Prelude," as well as "Part One," choosing to pick it up for the extended "Let It Grow" section. The lilting Jerry Garcia ballad "Stella Blue" is another track that works well in this incarnation and remained in the Dead's rotating set list for the remainder of their touring careers. *—Lindsay Planer*

Skeletons From the Closet: The Best of the Grateful Dead / 1974 / Warner Bros. ♦♦♦
This is an 11-song compilation, five of whose songs come from *Workingman's Dead* or *American Beauty*. It presents a sampling of the Dead's 1967-1972 period, focusing on their more accessible material. In that sense, it is recommended to the uninitiated who want to get a feel for the group; not surprisingly, it is a perennial seller, turning up week after week on *Billboard* magazine's Top Pop Catalog chart. The initiated, however, despise it: In a survey of Deadheads conducted by DeadBase, it was rated above only *Dylan & the Dead* as the worst Grateful Dead album. *—William Ruhlmann*

The Grateful Dead From the Mars Hotel / Jun. 27, 1974 / Grateful Dead ♦♦♦
The Grateful Dead made their reputation on the road with their live shows, and they have always struggled to capture that magic in the studio. *From the Mars Hotel*, while not a classic, represents one of their better studio albums. Jerry Garcia sounds engaged throughout and takes the vocal reigns for most of the songs on the album—although he's not the most gifted vocalist, he proves himself able and versatile. He sings the rollicking opener "U.S. Blues" with a tongue-in-cheek seriousness that gives the political song an edge, and he lends emotional sincerity to the atmospheric ballad "China Doll." Garcia shines on guitar during the funk workout "Scarlet Begonias," but the ensemble work is best displayed on the album's centerpiece, "Unbroken Chain." During this song, all the musicians are allowed to shine: Phil Lesh, the bassist and songwriter, provides tender vocals over a piano-based arrangement while the bridge allows the guitars and drums to stretch out in classic Grateful Dead style. This album is highly recommended for fans, but casual listeners should start with *American Beauty* or *Workingman's Dead*. *—Vik Iyengar*

Blues for Allah / Sep. 1, 1975 / Grateful Dead ♦♦♦♦♦
The Grateful Dead went into a state of latent activity in the fall of 1974 that lasted until the spring of the following year when the band reconvened at guitarist/vocalist Bob Weir's *Ace Studios* to record *Blues for Allah*. The disc was likewise the third to be issued on their own Grateful Dead Records label. When the LP hit shelves in September of 1975, the Dead were *still* not back on the road—although they had played a few gigs throughout San Francisco. Obviously, the time off had done the band worlds of good, as *Blues for Allah*—more than any past or future studio album—captures the Dead at their most natural and inspired. The opening combo of "Help on the Way," "Slipknot!," and "Franklin's Tower" is a multi-faceted suite, owing as much to Miles Davis circa the *E.S.P.* album as to anything the Grateful Dead had been associated with. "Slipknot!" contains chord changes, progressions, and time signatures which become musical riddles for the band to solve—which they do in the form of "Franklin's Tower." Another highly evolved piece is the rarely performed "King Solomon's Marbles," an instrumental that spotlights, among other things, Keith Godchaux's tastefully unrestrained Fender Rhodes finger work displaying more than just a tinge of Herbie Hancock inspiration. These more aggressive works contrast the delicate musical and lyrical haiku on "Crazy Fingers" containing some of lyricist Robert Hunter's finest and most beautifully arranged verbal images for the band. Weir's guitar solo in "Sage & Spirit" is based on one of his warm-up fingering exercises. Without a doubt, this is one of Weir's finest moments. The light acoustic melody is tinged with an equally beautiful arrangement. While there is definite merit in *Blues for Allah*'s title suite, the subdued chant-like vocals and meandering melody seems incongruous when compared to the remainder of this thoroughly solid effort. *—Lindsay Planer*

Steal Your Face / Jun. 26, 1976 / Grateful Dead ♦♦
Some Deadheads and enthusiasts have dismissed this two-disc live set as being foul-sounding and wholly unrepresentative of a typical Grateful Dead show circa 1974. These are undeniably accurate thumbnail assessments. However, somewhat obscured beneath what is not on this collection are a few salvageable performances. The story of why the Dead would contribute to such substandard workmanship [note: at least the audio quality on the CD edition is infinitely improved] has long been grist for the rumor mill. The evidence, however, speaks in the package's indescribably poor song selection and complete lack of cohesion. *Steal Your Face* is compiled from the same four-night stand (October 16 through October 20, 1974) at Winterland Arena that the Dead filmed for the *Grateful Dead Movie* (1976). Because the band had announced their decision to cease their incessant touring and essentially go on sabbatical, these concerts were being touted at the time as the "final four." By all accounts there was plenty of inspired musical interaction during the course of the run. So, why weren't those tracks accessed for this release? In essence this boils down to two factors: the absence of quality control at the time the recordings were made, as well as some decidedly unsavory and unethical conduct by the band's concurrent management. What listeners are left with is a loose assortment of shorter tracks and self-contained performances. This was written off by the band as an attempt not to duplicate the style of their previous concert releases *Live/Dead* (1969), *Grateful Dead* (1971), and *Europe '72* (1972)—all of which were infinitely more realistic and warmly received. There are a few throwaways, such as the Chuck Berry covers "Promised Land" and "Around and Around" as well as Bob Weir's cowboy tunes "Big River" and "El Paso." It should be noted that these particular cuts are not all that bad. However, none of the songs have much room for any ensemble work or extended improvisation—key elements when capturing the essence of the Grateful Dead live. Conversely, newer originals such as the Jerry Garcia/Robert Hunter ballads "Ship of Fools," "It Must Have Been the Roses," and the album's unmitigated gem, "Stella Blue," rate among the package's most thoughtful and lyrical moments. *—Lindsay Planer*

● **What a Long Strange Trip It's Been** / 1977 / Warner Bros. ♦♦♦♦♦
This is a two-disc compilation of the Grateful Dead covering its tenure at Warner Bros., 1967-1972, and as such the most extensive sampler of their work in existence. Well-chosen, it contains many of their best songs from the period and is notable for giving album release to the studio-recorded single version of "Dark Star," the Dead's most requested song. Relative newcomers to the band (those who bought *Skeletons From the Closet* and liked it) can get a stronger dose here, and then perhaps go on to the individual albums. Of course, Deadheads hate this record. *—William Ruhlmann*

Terrapin Station / Jul. 27, 1977 / Arista ♦♦
It is generally agreed that the Grateful Dead's late-'70s studio releases left even the most enthusiastic Deadheads longing for something more. The theory being that the band's momentum is best experienced during the ebb and flow of a live performance rather than

the somewhat clinical tedium of a recording studio. *Terrapin Station* marks several milestones for the Grateful Dead: It was the band's first studio album in two years, as well as their return to a major label—in this case Arista Records. More significant however is the use of an outside (read: non-Grateful Dead) producer. This was only the second time in which the Dead did not seize complete control. And the first time in a decade that they would relinquish their production reigns. They chose Keith Olson—a former member of the '60s garage rock band Music Machine—whose production roster also included other Bay Area notables including the Sons of Champlin and Santana. Musically, *Terrapin Station* offers a few choice glimpses of the band doing what they do best. While the most prominent example is the album's extended title suite, there are a few others such as the cover of the Rev. Gary Davis gospel-blues "Samson and Delilah" and a resurrection of the Martha & the Vandellas hit "Dancin' in the Streets." The latter tune was originally performed by the Dead in their mid-'60s repertoire. What was once a garage rock and psychedelic reading has evolved into a 4/4-time, brass-influenced disco arrangement. Luckily, their extended versions during concert performances were infinitely more tolerable. Parties interested in examining the contrast between the studio and live performance versions of *Terrapin Station* material should seek the archival concert release *Dick's Picks, Vol. 3.* This two-disc set not only captures the band exactly two months and two days prior to the release of *Terrapin Station*, it also features stellar performances of every track from the album sans the uptempo rocker "Passenger." *—Lindsay Planer*

Shakedown Street / Nov. 15, 1978 / Arista ✦✦

Using Little Feat leader Lowell George as producer should have been a great idea, but somehow it didn't work out. The Dead have salvaged "Fire on the Mountain" and "I Need a Miracle" for live work from this collection, but it's one of their least satisfactory studio ventures. *—William Ruhlmann*

Reckoning / Apr. 1, 1981 / Arista ✦✦✦

Having given up on studio work after the disaster of *Go to Heaven*, the Dead recorded a series of concerts in New York and San Francisco in October 1980 for two live albums. This is the first, a set of acoustic material that will remind many listeners of the rustic feel of the classic *Workingman's Dead* and *American Beauty* albums, although much of it consists of traditional and bluegrass material favored by Jerry Garcia. [The original two-LP set was fit onto one CD in 1987 by eliminating the Dead's cover of Elizabeth Cotten's "Oh Babe It Ain't No Lie."] *—William Ruhlmann*

In the Dark / Jul. 6, 1987 / Arista ✦✦✦✦

The Grateful Dead's last lineup returned intact for *In the Dark*, an album that ironically thrust the band back into the spotlight on the strength of the band's lone Top 40 single, "Touch of Grey." Fans had long mused that the Dead's studio albums lacked the easygoing energy and natural flow of their live performances, and *In the Dark* does come close to capturing that lightning in a bottle. Jerry Garcia, who apparently had to re-learn the guitar after a near-fatal illness, approaches his instrument recharged, while his voice (a beneficiary of the extended hiatus?) shows some of its original smoothness. Of his four songwriting collaborations with long-standing lyricist Robert Hunter, "Touch of Grey" is far and away the best. "When Push Comes to Shove" and "West L.A. Fadeaway" use familiar blues-based riffs that lack the pair's often-contagious chemistry, and "Black Muddy River" has one foot firmly stuck in mawkish MOR terrain (although Garcia can be dealt a free pass here in light of the song's real-life implications as an attempt to make his peace with the world). What pushes *In the Dark* past the band's also-rans are two terrific songs from Bob Weir and John Barlow, the cheerfully cranky "Hell in a Bucket" (co-written with Brent Mydland) and the cautionary tale "Throwing Stones." Rarely have Weir's songs sounded so effortless; punctuated by Garcia's guitar, they have more in common with the upbeat, flavorful sound of past Garcia/Hunter compositions than the pair's own work this time out (a rare case of role reversal). In the middle of it all is a country-rock song from Mydland, "Tons of Steel," that sounds oddly out of place. Although the album is unmistakable as the work of the Dead, much of it recalls the punchy, pungent production of Dire Straits' recent work. It's not the second coming of the Dead, but a more entertaining epilogue you couldn't ask for. *—David Connolly*

Built to Last / Oct. 31, 1989 / Arista ✦✦

Supposedly, the Dead had broken their studio jinx with *In the Dark* and finally learned how to make good albums without an audience in front of them. So why was this follow-up such a letdown? Perhaps because they hadn't taken seven years to write and perfect new material as they had with the previous album. The dominant songwriter here was keyboard player Brent Mydland (who died the following year), while the crucial songwriting team of Garcia and Hunter contributed only minor efforts. Chastened, the Dead once again retreated from studio work. *—William Ruhlmann*

Josh Graves (Burkett Graves)

b. Sep. 27, 1925, Tellico Plains, TN

Dobro, Slide Guitar / Progressive Bluegrass, Traditional Bluegrass, Contemporary Bluegrass

Josh Graves (born Burkett Graves) was one of the major forces keeping the unique sounds of the dobro alive in both country and bluegrass music. Born and raised in Tellico Plains, TN, he was only nine when he heard Cliff Carlisle of the Carlisle Brothers performing a few Jimmie Rodgers tunes on the dobro. Though he would spend the early part of his career as a bassist, Graves loved the sound of the dobro and would eventually become one of its greatest supporters and innovators. In 1942, Graves joined the Pierce Brothers. Later he played with Esco Hankins and Mac Wiseman before becoming a member of the Wheeling Jamboree with Wilma Lee and Stoney Cooper, where he remained through the mid-'50s. During a performance with the Coopers at the *Grand Ole Opry*, Graves made a big impression upon Lester Flatt and Earl Scruggs, who invited him to join their Foggy Mountain Boys.

In the late '50s, acoustic instruments were out of favor due to the popularity of rock & roll; the survival of the dobro as an important instrument in country can largely be attributed to Graves, who electrified audiences with a red-hot picking style and then cooled them down with bluesy, sweet mellowness. An essential part of his technique was a three-finger banjo-roll move, adapted from Scruggs himself. Graves remained a primary member of the Foggy Mountain Boys until the group disbanded in 1969. Afterward, he joined Flatt's Nashville Grass and did session work on the side. In 1971, he began playing with the Earl Scruggs Review; three years later, he went solo with the LP *Alone at Last*. He also continued session work, playing with artists like Charlie McCoy, J.J. Cale, Steve Young, and Kris Kristofferson, and collaborating with other musicians. He continued in a similar vein through the 1980s and '90s, teaming with such greats as Kenny Baker, Eddie Adcock, and Jesse McReynolds in 1989 to form the Masters. He also released a series of masterful dobro recordings, including *King of the Dobro* (1996), *Sultan of Slide* (2000), and the poignant *Memories of Foggy Mountain* (2002). The Gibson Corporation also developed a Graves signature-model dobro, built to his specifications. *—Johnny Loftus*

Alone at Last / 1974 / Epic ✦✦✦✦

Sweet Sunny South / 1976 / CMH ✦✦✦

Same Old Blues / 1979 / CMH ✦✦✦

The Puritan Sessions / 1989 / Rebel ✦✦✦✦

Longtime fiddler Kenny Baker appears in an uncharacteristic role as a fingerstyle guitarist in a delightfully low-key set of tunes and songs with dobroist (and sometime-singer) Graves. *—Mark A. Humphrey*

King of the Dobro / 1996 / CMH ✦✦✦

This "musical documentary" is sort of the audio equivalent of a PBS special about the legendary dobro player Josh Graves. Narrator Bob O'Donnell walks the listener through stories and historical accounts from Bill Monroe, Marty Stuart, Mac Wiseman, Jerry Douglas, and others, as well as presenting musical examples of Graves' crisp playing. While informative and well-produced, it serves more as an instructional historical document rather than a solid listen from beginning to end. Still, anyone interested in an in-depth study of the man and his music would be hard-pressed to find a more educational place to begin. *—Zac Johnson*

● **Josh Graves** / Sep. 29, 1998 / Rebel ✦✦✦✦

On this album of mostly traditional bluegrass, split evenly between instrumental and vocal numbers (nicely handled by Terry Eldredge), Graves proves he is still one of the world's great dobro masters. The set includes familiar tunes from the catalogs of the Carter Family, Bill Monroe, the Delmore Brothers, and Flatt & Scruggs, plus a handful of Graves originals. Occasionally, Graves and fellow septuagenarians Kenny Baker (long-time fiddler with Monroe) and Curly Seckler (former mandolinist and vocalist with Graves in the Foggy Mountain Boys) push things into overdrive, embarking on some blazing runs that would challenge players of any age. Who says old dudes can't rock? *—Joel Roberts*

Billy Gray

b. Dec. 29, 1924, Paris, TX, **d.** Mar. 27, 1975

Guitar, Vocals / Western Swing

Western swing guitarist Billy Gray was born in 1924 in Paris, TX, and raised in a poor family. As a boy, he worked in the fields to earn money for his first guitar, which he purchased from a local pawnshop. At 19, he organized a band and hosted his own radio show in Paris. For the next few years, he logged a series of tours around Texas and the Southwest, eventually landing in Dallas. There he became the leader of Hank Thompson & His Brazos Valley Boys. He and Thompson eventually founded the Texoma Music Publishing Company and the Brazos Valley Publishing Company, and the two co-wrote some of Thompson's greatest hits, including "Waiting in the Lobby of Your Heart," "The New Wears off Too Fast," and "A Fool, a Faker." In 1954, Gray's lone charting hit was issued. "You Can't Have My Love" was a duet with rockabilly screamer Wanda Jackson.

The following year, he and his band, the Western Oakies, released *Dance-O-Rama*, but the album failed at charting any singles. Gray went on to work as a sideman for other bands, including the Nuggets and the Cowtowners, and also appeared on the syndicated TV show *Music Country Style*. He recorded one more album in 1965 on Longhorn Records, but faded from the public eye soon after. Billy Gray died in 1975 while undergoing heart surgery. *—Johnny Loftus*

Dance-O-Rama / 1955 / Decca ✦✦✦

● **Billy Gray** / 1965 / Longhorn ✦✦✦✦

Grayson & Whitter

f. 1927, **db.** 1930

Group / Old-Timey, Traditional Country

G.B. Grayson and Henry Whitter sang together for only three years during the late '20s and early '30s, but they had a tremendous effect on country music; even contemporary performers continue to cover their songs, which include "Handsome Molly" (recorded by Bob Dylan and Mick Jagger), "Cluck Old Hen," "Tom Dooley," "Rose Conley" and "Lee Highway Blues (Going Down the Lee Highway)." Fiddler/singer Gilliam Banmon Grayson was born in Ashe Country, NC. As a young man, he made his living as a minstrel, traveling through mountain towns playing at fairs and dances. He eventually settled near the Tennessee-Virginia border, where he played with such noted musicians as Clarence Tom Ashley and Doc Walsh. An excellent fiddler, Grayson was also an exceptional singer, and after teaming up with Whitter frequently sang lead vocals on their recordings.

Guitarist/singer Henry Whitter was born in Fries, VA; while not an exceptional musician or singer, he was devoted to promoting old-time music and was able to arrange many recording sessions. Whitter & Grayson met at a fiddlers' convention in Mountain City, Tennessee in 1927. They teamed up, and by autumn of that year, Whitter had gotten them two record deals. They recorded eight songs for the Gennet label and six for Victor, among them the classic "Handsome Molly," which sold over 50,000 copies. In total, the two recorded 40 songs in three years. Grayson was killed in an auto accident in August, 1930 while hitchhiking; Whitter was devastated, but continued performing and occasionally recording until his 1941 death from diabetes. —*Sandra Brennan*

The Recordings of Grayson & Whitter: Recorded 1928–1930 / Apr. 6, 1999 / County ✦✦✦✦

This duo recorded the original versions of quite a few songs that went on to become folk chestnuts. Tracing the source of a folk song might seem a confusing task, but it is simple compared to sorting out the various recordings, re-recordings, reissues, and repackagings of reissues that have come out on Grayson & Whitter. Old-time music experts can argue over which is the better recording of "Handsome Molly," but no one will argue that this particular County product is handsomely packaged. The front cover is a ghastly green sketch of a mill: reference? More than half the back cover is a list of other records on the label, but with the quality of music County has released this actually might be more valuable than more informative liner notes might have been. G.B. Grayson was mostly known as a singer, although he accompanies himself simply and effectively on fiddle. His partner accompanies him on guitar, sticking mostly to rhythm chording pattern. Sound quality obviously varies, with some of the source 78s' sound rather clean and rich while others provide a fair impression of what a stereo might sound like if it was able to play from inside a washing machine on the rinse cycle. It is lovely country-flavored folk music, always more about the songs than any flashy picking. —*Eugene Chadbourne*

- **Complete Recorded Works in Chronological Order, Vol. 1: 1927–1928** / Jan. 25, 2000 / Document ✦✦✦✦✦

The recorded performances of G.B. Grayson & Henry Whitter are among the most evocative and the most influential in early country music, providing a major source for the styles and repertoires of the Stanley Brothers, Doc Watson, and other later performers. These recordings remain forceful and immensely enjoyable decades after they were originally made, and Document must be commended for finally making available to the public the complete works of the duo, issued in two essential volumes. An unprecedented number of Grayson & Whitter's songs grew into the standards of old-time, bluegrass, and country music, though the power of the originals has seldom been surpassed in subsequent efforts. This disc contains versions of "Train 45," "Don't Go Out Tonight, My Darling," "Ommie Wise," "Handsome Molly," and several other staples in their earliest recorded forms. Overall, the work of Grayson & Whitter is full of lonesome roads and false-hearted lovers, remorseful ditties, and moralizing tales with endless admonitions of "Take warning, boys," juggling themes of love, death, and reckless abandonment in masterful waltzes, ballads, and breakdown dirges. The vocal interjections of the duo only enhance the songs, with Grayson or Whitter occasionally musing, "I don't know where I'm going, but I'm on my way," or weirdly philosophizing, "Why is a man born to die, anyhow?" in the middle of an otherwise festive dance tune. *Vol. 1* begins with the team's first recording session for Gennett in 1927, moving chronologically toward a Victor date in July of 1928. The sound quality is consistently good, despite the age of the original 78s and Document's typically unreliable remastering. Together with its companion disc, this set belongs—prominently—in any old-time collection. —*Burgin Mathews*

Complete Recorded Works in Chronological Order, Vol. 2: 1928–1929 / Jan. 25, 2000 / Document ✦✦✦✦✦

The second volume of Grayson & Whitter's complete works contains 14 more classic recordings by the duo, as well as seven tracks by another guitar and fiddle duo, Robinette & Moore. If the accomplishments of the latter pair are overshadowed by the towering figures of Grayson & Whitter, fiddler Melvin Robinette and guitarist Byrd Moore nonetheless perform some excellent sides of their own and conclude the collection very nicely. Their waltzing "Birmingham Jail" is fueled by the insistent rhythm of Moore's thumping bass notes and Robinette's nasally tenor harmony; on fiddle tunes such as "That Old Tiger Rag," Robinette demonstrates the remarkable prowess that made him one of the most expert, if under-recorded, players of his day. Despite these fine performances, though, the work of Grayson & Whitter will necessarily remain the disc's chief attraction for most listeners. As in their earlier sessions, fiddler Grayson and guitarist Whitter perform numerous latter-day standards for the first time on record, including "Tom Dooley," "Little Maggie With a Dram Glass in Her Hand," "The Nine-Pound Hammer," and the instrumental "Going Down the Lee Highway." The sound quality is thankfully very good throughout this set, and each recording is undertaken with considerable skill and care, resulting consistently in some of the finest pieces of their kind. The playing and singing of Grayson & Whitter is direct, honest, and timeless, akin to the duets of the Mississippi Sheiks in their combination of raw emotional depth and expert musical control. Along with Document's *Vol. 1*, this collection is highly and unreservedly recommended. —*Burgin Mathews*

The Great Plains

f. 1991

Group / Country-Rock, Contemporary Country

Great Plains came together in the late '80s around vocalist/guitarist Jack Sundrud, bassist Denny Dadmun-Bixby, drummer Michael Young, and pedal-steel player Russ Pahl. While touring as the backing band for Michael Johnson, the band came onto producer Brent Maher's radar, who promptly signed them to a deal with his publishing company. Great Plains' self-titled debut was issued on Columbia in 1991; it featured the hit singles "A Picture of You" and "Faster Gun." GP also got a boost with a high-profile opening slot for Garth Brooks. After Pahl and Young departed in 1993, Columbia dropped the band. However, Sundrud rallied the remaining Plainsmen and released *Homeland* (Magnatone) in 1996, upon which he wrote or co-wrote all 12 songs. Great Plains faded from view soon

after, but Sundrud stayed active, touring as a bassist with Poco and appearing on the country-rock veterans' 2002 comeback album, *Running Horse.* —*Johnny Loftus*

- **Great Plains** / Apr. 1991 / Columbia ✦✦✦✦

Great Plains' country-rock debut includes the hits "Iola" (a nod to the struggles of farmers) and the outlaw ode "Faster Gun." —*Jason Ankeny*

Homeland / Jun. 4, 1996 / Magnatone ✦✦✦

Lloyd Green

b. Oct. 4, 1937, Leaf, MS

Dobro, Guitar, Guitar (Steel), Session Musician / Country-Pop, Honky Tonk, Nashville Sound/Countrypolitan

Lloyd Green was born on October 4, 1937, in Leaf, MS, but moved to Mobile as a young boy and began taking music lessons there. He graduated from high-school in 1955 and went on to attend the University of Southern Mississippi. Green landed in Nashville after college and soon found steady work as a road musician supporting artists like Ferlin Husky and Faron Young. He stayed with Young's band for 18 months and then left to be with his new wife in Mobile. During those months, he appeared on one George Jones side, "Too Much Water Runs Under the Bridge" (1957). While in Mobile, Green played in numerous clubs and managed to save enough money to return to Nashville nine months later. But the touring life wasn't for him, and neither was the low pay or the lack of steady gigs.

He left the music business for a job in retail, but returned when Fred Rose's wife paid his union dues and secured him work as a supporting musician at the *Grand Ole Opry*. In 1964 he began working as a part-time assistant at the SESAC office for Roy Drusky. Although the pay was low, the gig was steady and did give Green the opportunity to make his own demos. He remained with SESAC for three years, and soon was earning good money from his session work. Green worked with pop musicians as well, including Vera Lynn, Paul McCartney, and Ringo Starr, as well as on the Byrds' seminal *Sweetheart of the Rodeo*. He had just a handful of solo chart hits, including instrumental versions of the pop tunes "I Can See Clearly Now" and "Here Comes the Sun" in the early '70s. He also made the charts singing "You and Me." During the 1980s an ear infection forced him to stop working, but Green eventually returned to session work, and did perform the occasional concert on dobro or steel guitar. —*Johnny Loftus*

Big Steel Guitar / 1964 / Time ✦✦✦✦✦

Day for Decision / 1966 / Little Darlin' ✦✦✦✦

Mr. Nashville Sound / 1968 / Chart ✦✦✦✦

- **Green Country** / 1969 / Little Darlin' ✦✦✦✦✦

Shades of Steel / 1973 / Monument ✦✦✦

Steel Rides / 1976 / Monument ✦✦✦

The Greenbriar Boys

f. 1958, db. 1967

Group / Progressive Bluegrass, Traditional Bluegrass, Old-Timey, String Bands, Folk Revival, Bluegrass-Gospel

One of the first urban bands to play bluegrass, the Greenbriar Boys were instrumental in transforming the sounds of the hill country from a Southern music to an international phenomenon. The Greenbriar Boys first came together during informal Sunday afternoon jam sessions at New York's Washington Square Park. The impetus for the group, however, had been conceived a few years before, when New York-born John Herald met banjo ace Eric Weissberg at the University of Wisconsin. Inspired by Weissberg's repertoire of Bill Monroe, Flatt & Scruggs, and Don Reno tunes, Herald acquired an acoustic guitar and, with help from Weissberg, taught himself to play.

After leaving the school, Herald and Weissberg moved to New York, where they were soon joined by Bob Yellin. Yellin had studied classical violin, piano, and vocal harmony as a child and trumpet at the High School of Music and Art. After listening to a recording of Flatt & Scruggs, Yellin had been converted to bluegrass and bought himself a banjo. Using Pete Seeger's instructional record *How to Play the 5 String Banjo*, Yellin mastered the three-finger Scruggs style of banjo picking. In 1958, Yellin and Mike Seeger (of the New Lost City Ramblers) attended the Old Time Fiddlers Convention in Galax, VA, and received a second prize for their double banjo rendition of the traditional folk tune "Old Joe Clark." Herald, Weissberg, and Yellin had few commercial aspirations when they formed the Greenbriar Boys, and their performances were limited to concerts at American Youth Hostels and the Sunday sessions at Washington Square Park. When Gerde's Folk City opened, the Greenbriar Boys were one of the first acts to play the club.

The Greenbriar Boys became more serious after Weissberg left to join the Tarriers and was replaced by Paul Prestopino and then Ralph Rinzler. A mandolin player and folklorist, Rinzler owned a large collection of tapes that included recordings by Riley Puckett, Charlie Poole, and Uncle Dave Macon. Rinzler encouraged the Greenbriar Boys to rehearse on a regular basis, and the group's sound began to meld. In 1960, the Greenbriar Boys traveled to Union Grove, NC, where they became the first Northern group to win the band competition at the Old Time Fiddlers Convention. A year later, Yellin returned to the festival and became the first northerner to win first prize in the banjo competition. A pivotal year for the Greenbriar Boys was 1962. In addition to accompanying Joan Baez on two songs—"Pal of Mine" and "The Banks of the Ohio"—on her second album, the group was signed by Vanguard Records. After being featured along with Jackie Washington, Bob Gude, and Hedy West on a multi-artist sampler, *New Folks*, the Greenbriar Boys released a self-titled debut album. They subsequently released three other albums—*Ragged but Right!* in 1964, *Dian & the Greenbriar Boys* in 1965, and *Better Late Than Never!* in 1966. With Rinzler leaving the group to accept a job as director of the folk department at the Smithsonian Institute, the Greenbriar Boys were joined by bluegrass mandolinist and vocalist Frank Wakefield and fiddler Jim Buchanan on *Better Late Than Never*. The Greenbriar Boys' arrangement of "Different Drum," by Mike Nesmith (later of the Monkees), was re-recorded and turned into a pop hit by Linda Ronstadt and the Stone

Poneys in 1967. However, the Greenbriar Boys disbanded in 1967, although they have occasionally reunited in the years since. —*Craig Harris*

● **Best of the Vanguard Years** / Aug. 13, 2002 / Vanguard ✦✦✦✦✦
This two-CD, 35-song compilation could probably hardly be bettered as a summation of this band's best-recorded work. Disc one focuses on tracks from 1961-1962, including four songs from the 1961 *New Folks* various-artists compilation, two songs from *Joan Baez, Vol. 2*, on which they played backup, and eight songs from their proper full-length debut, 1962's *The Greenbriar Boys*. Though their accent at this time was on traditional songs and covers of bluegrass tunes by the likes of Bill Monroe, this does include "Stewball" (here crediting the band as authors, though different writing credits were used when Peter, Paul & Mary covered it slightly later) and Wayne Raney's sly "We Need a Lot More of Jesus" ("and a lot less rock & roll," goes the end of the couplet when the title is sung on the refrain). Disc two contains 21 songs from their mid-'60s albums *Ragged but Right!* (1964) and *Better Late Than Never!* (1966). The first of these was the last to feature the trio lineup of John Herald, Bob Yellin, and Ralph Rinzler. Frank Wakefield replaced Rinzler for *Better Late Than Never!*, the record that was by far their most contemporary Vanguard effort, with more original material and some very interesting covers, like Floyd Chance's Cajun-flavored "Alligator Man." Far more familiar to rock and pop fans, though, is the original version of Mike Nesmith's "Different Drum," a slower and more whimsical arrangement than that used by the Stone Poneys on their 1967 hit cover of the tune. Linda Ronstadt also covered the Greenbriar Boys' best original song, "Up to My Neck in High Muddy Waters," also originally on *Better Late Than Never!* (and included on this compilation). As a whole, this is a good survey of a band who did a lot to popularize and preserve traditional bluegrass with skill, as well as take some occasional ventures into progressive directions, not only on the above-mentioned songs, but also on unusual (for bluegrass) Bob Yellin-penned instrumentals like "A Minor Breakdown" and "Russian Around." —*Richie Unterberger*

Jack Greene
b. Jan. 7, 1930, Maryville, TN
Vocals, Guitar, Drums / Traditional Country, Nashville Sound/Countrypolitan
Hailing from Maryville, TN, Greene got his start in the record business as a vocalist in Ernest Tubb's band, but he hardly had the same almost-on-key "twang" as his boss. In fact, Greene's smooth, pleasant sound contrasted a great deal with Tubb's blue-collar intonation. Nicknamed "the Jolly Green Giant," Greene learned guitar and drums but mined his vocal chords for a solid string of hit records from 1966-1969, including one with Jeannie Seeley, who joined his road show and recorded duets with him for several years. A bit of trivia: In 1967, Greene became the first country artist ever to appear in the Macy's Thanksgiving Day Parade. —*Tom Roland*

Greatest Hits / 1986 / Gusto ✦✦✦✦
This set spotlights the smooth, dynamic voice of Jack Greene during his heyday with Decca Records in the mid- to late '60s. These ten tracks include his number-one singles "There Goes My Everything" and "All the Time." Also included are several duets recorded with Jeannie Seeley that standup alongside the best of George Jones & Tammy Wynette or Porter Wagoner & Dolly Parton. While this CD has a shorter than usual running time, it will have to suffice until Greene's material is reissued properly. —*Al Campbell*

● **Jolly Green Giant** / Mar. 25, 1997 / Edsel ✦✦✦✦✦
Jack Greene's MOR country ballads brought him several years of chart success, but today he is not as well-remembered as one might expect considering his 36 charting country singles, five of which were number-one hits. "There Goes My Everything" was his career hit, spending seven weeks at number one and crossing over to the pop charts. Greene stuck with the style of that single for the rest of his years on Decca and MCA, during which he made a few hit duets with Jeannie Seeley (another maker of slick, easy-listening country). Pleasant and flawlessly executed, Greene's recordings are comparable to the late-'60s sounds of Eddy Arnold, or Roy Drusky's "croonier" moments. Greene's voice has character—he isn't a bland smoothie—and many of his songs ("Statue of a Fool," for one) are quite effective, but heard all at once they are so gentle as to recede into the background. *Jolly Green Giant* has the vast majority of Greene's big hits, but mysteriously omits his number-one hit "Until My Dreams Come True" in favor of a couple of minor hits. —*Greg Adams*

Lorne Greene
b. 1915, Ottawa, Ontario, Canada, **d.** Sep. 11, 1987, Santa Monica, CA
Vocals, Celebrity, Voices / Country-Pop, Celebrity
Actor Lorne Greene enjoyed a brief recording career in the mid-'60s, when he was at the height of his popularity thanks to his role as Ben Cartwright on the long-running Western series *Bonanza*. Greene was born in 1915 in Ottawa, Ontario, and went to college to study chemical engineering. He wound up discovering theater instead, and opted for a career in the performing arts. He worked in radio for a time, working his way up to become Canada's best-known newscaster. He left for New York in 1950, and soon appeared in Broadway productions and several films. He won the role of Ben Cartwright in 1959, playing the Ponderosa Ranch's patriarch until *Bonanza* finally went off the air in 1973.
In the meantime, NBC, hoping to capitalize on the series' popularity, brought several cast members into the recording studio. Greene released his first album in 1963, and the following year he scored a surprise number one smash with "Ringo," a Western story song he narrated rather than sang. Greene charted a couple more times with 1965's "The Man" and 1966's "Waco," and released a total of five albums on RCA Victor from 1963-1966. Afterwards, he returned to acting full-time, most notably appearing in the TV miniseries *Roots* and starring in the sci-fi series *Battlestar Galactica*, as well as narrating numerous documentaries. Just before he was scheduled to reprise his *Bonanza* role for a TV-movie reunion, Greene died of complications from surgery on September 11, 1987. —*Steve Huey*

● **R On the Ponderosa: Lorne Greene & His Western Classics** / Sep. 16, 1997 / Razor & Tie ✦✦✦✦
Lorne Greene, though primarily an actor, secured his place in music history by topping the *Billboard* pop chart in 1964 with the recitation "Ringo." *On the Ponderosa* collects that song and Greene's handful of lesser hits, along with a number of album tracks and noncharting singles. Greene had a deep, characteristic baritone that didn't always hit the note, but these sagas of the West are full of personality and drama. When not putting his stamp on such favorites as "Riders in the Sky" and "Sixteen Tons," Greene turns to more unique numbers like the should-have-been hit "An Ol' Tin Cup (And a Battered Ol' Coffee Pot)." "Skip to My Lou" showcases the vocal "talents" of Greene's fellow *Bonanza* cast members, and "Saga of the Ponderosa" is a long, tedious recitation performed in the character of Ben Cartwright. *On the Ponderosa* is the perfect solution for those who want to sample Greene's singing career without investing in Bear Family's *Bonanza* box set. —*Greg Adams*

Richard Greene
b. Nov. 9, 1942, Los Angeles, CA
Fiddle, Session Musician / Traditional Bluegrass, Country-Rock, Country-Pop, Folk-Pop, Folk-Rock
A session fiddler with hundreds of credits—and dozens of bands in which he has performed—Richard Greene's most famous period was the 1960s, when he played with both Bill Monroe's Blue Grass Boys and Seatrain. He was born November 9, 1942, in Los Angeles, where he studied classical violin beginning at the age of five. By the time he entered high-school, though, Greene switched his focus to folk music. He entered the University of California-Berkeley in 1960, and began playing in the Coast Mountain Ramblers and later the Dry City Scat Band. After college, Greene took a job in real estate, but also played with the Pine Valley Boys in San Francisco. On a trip to New York in 1964, he met Bill Keith of the Blue Grass Boys, and the association influenced Monroe's decision to hire the youngster two years later. Greene played at the *Grand Ole Opry* with Monroe and appeared on his Decca album *Bluegrass Time*.
After only one year with the Blue Grass Boys, Greene joined the Jim Kweskin Jug Band—which also included Keith plus Geoff and Maria Muldaur—and played on that band's 1968 album *Garden of Joy*. Not content to stay in one place, he split for California after one year and joined the Blues Project, which then evolved into Seatrain. Greene stayed for over three years, playing on the band's self-titled 1969 album for A&M, another self-titled LP for Capitol two years later, and 1972's *Marblehead Messenger*. With Eric Weissberg, Jim Rooney, and old friend Keith, he then formed the Blue Velvet Band, which recorded only one album, *Sweet Moments*. Greene spent the rest of the '70s playing with James Taylor, Emmylou Harris, Rod Stewart, Muleskinner, Taj Mahal, David Grisman, and Loggins & Messina, in addition to recording three albums as a solo act with his backing band, the Zone. The first two, *Duets* (1977) and *Ramblin'* (1979), appeared on Rounder, while 1980's *Blue Rondo* was released on the Sierra label. An early-'80s tour of Japan with Tony Trischka and Peter Rowan was documented on the Japanese Nippon label by *Bluegrass Album* and *Hiroshima Mon-Amour* (both 1980). —*John Bush*

Marblehead Messenger / 1972 / Capitol ✦✦✦

Duets / 1977 / Rounder ✦✦✦✦

Ramblin' / 1979 / Rounder ✦✦✦

Bluegrass Album / 1980 / Nippon Columbia ✦✦✦

● **Molly on the Shore** / 1988 / Hannibal ✦✦✦✦

Greene Fiddler / Oct. 17, 1995 / Sierra ✦✦✦

Sales Tax Toddle / Mar. 25, 1997 / Rebel ✦✦✦

Hands Across The Pond / Dec. 4, 2001 / Richard Greene ✦✦✦

Lee Greenwood
b. Oct. 17, 1942, Los Angeles, CA
Vocals, Banjo, Bass, Guitar, Piano, Saxophone / Adult Contemporary, Urban Cowboy, Contemporary Country, Country-Pop
Born with a good voice and a wide range, Lee Greenwood turned it into a unique voice accidentally, by overworking it in a less-than-healthy setting. Hailing from Sacramento, he used his musical training on the casino circuit, working in the green-felt jungles of Reno and Las Vegas, where he dealt cards by day and sang in dark lounges by night. The physical toll of two jobs, the vocal strain of performing six nights a week, and the damaging endeavor to sing in smoky nightclubs before the advent of smoking ordinances brought Greenwood a permanent hoarseness. He's used it to his advantage, becoming one of country music's premier balladeers. Discovered by Mel Tillis' road manager, Larry McFaden, Greenwood paid for his own ticket to fly to Nashville and cut a few demos, and it took more than a year for that effort to pay off. When it finally did, Greenwood broke through in late 1981 with "It Turns Me Inside Out," in which his exaggerated vibrato brought frequent comparisons to Kenny Rogers. In short order, Greenwood disposed of the "Kenny clone" image, but he continued to mine romantic material for the bulk of his hits. Occasional exceptions include "Touch and Go Crazy" and "Mornin' Ride," but the biggest exception is also his signature song, the self-written "God Bless the U.S.A.," which earned Song of the Year honors from the Country Music Association.
Growing up on a Sacramento farm, Greenwood was musical at a very early age, teaching himself how to play saxophone when he was nine years old. In his preadolescence, he played in a Western dance band called My Moondreams. At the age of 13, he moved with his recently remarried mother to Anaheim, CA, but three years later he returned to Sacramento to live with his grandparents. Between the two moves, he played in a variety of country and Dixieland bands. Upon his return to Sacramento, Greenwood joined Chester Smith's band, which raised his profile within California. Soon, Del Reeves hired Greenwood to play saxophone, and while he was with the singer, Lee learned how to become a showman. In 1962, he formed his own band, a pop combo named Apollo, and the

group moved to Las Vegas. Within five years, the group was renamed the Lee Greenwood Affair and relocated to Los Angeles, where they made a handful of records for Paramount. Once the record label went out of business, Greenwood was asked to join the fledgling Rascals by Felix Cavaliere and Dino Danelli, but he declined. Instead, he moved back to Las Vegas, where he worked as an arranger, backup vocalist, and lounge pianist, as well accompanied strippers by playing organ. By 1973, he became the lead singer and bassist in the Bare Touch of Vegas revue, while he continued to work as a blackjack dealer at the Tropicana. He held down both jobs for much of the mid-'70s.

By the end of the '70s, he was singing in lounges in Reno, which is where he met Larry McFaden, who was then leading Mel Tillis' touring band. Greenwood was initially reluctant to record, but he eventually travelled to Nashville, where he recorded a set of demos. Shortly afterward, McFaden became his manager and helped the singer sign a deal with MCA Records in June of 1981. Four months later, his first single, "It Turns Me Inside Out," climbed into the country Top 20. Greenwood's initial success was helped enormously by the similarity between his husky voice—toughened up by years of working in smoky casinos—and that of Kenny Rogers. In March of 1982, his second single, "Ring on Her Finger, Time on Her Hands," climbed into the Top Ten, beginning a streak of 19 Top Ten singles that ran virtually uninterrupted for the next six years. During that time, he racked up no less than seven number-one hits: "Somebody's Gonna Love You" (1983), "Going, Going, Gone" (1984), "Dixie Road" (1985), "I Don't Mind the Thorns (If You're the Rose)" (1985), "Don't Underestimate My Love for You" (1986), "Hearts Aren't Made to Break (They're Made to Love)" (1986), and "Mornin' Ride" (1986). In addition to his solo hits, Greenwood had a number of hit duets with Barbara Mandrell, including the number-three hit "To Me" (1984).

None of Greenwood's music was close to pure country—it was adult contemporary country pop, in the vein of Rogers. Unlike Rogers, however, Greenwood rarely crossed over into the pop charts, and when he did, it was only in 1983, when slickly produced country-pop could make inroads on adult contemporary radio. His popularity was at its peak during the mid-'80s, when his conservative music and neo-conservative lyrics managed to capture the imagination of the nation; though "God Bless the U.S.A." only peaked at number seven on the country charts in 1984, it became a recurring theme song for several Republican political campaigns during the Reagan and Bush administrations. Furthermore, Greenwood won many popularity polls and awards from various country music magazines and associations.

Greenwood switched labels in 1990, signing to Capitol Records. His initial singles for the label, "Holdin' a Good Hand" and "We've Got It Made," were successful, but his audience steadily declined during the first half of the decade. Though he tried to retain his audience through patriotic work during the 1991 Gulf War—even earning the Congressional Medal of Honor Society's Patriot Award and a Points of Light Foundation Award—he couldn't successfully battle the onslaught of harder-edged, contemporary country artists that overtook country radio in the early '90s. By the middle of the decade, he was no longer charting singles, and he had begun re-recording his biggest hits for a variety of labels; he also continued to tour and give concerts. In 2000 he attempted a comeback with his new album, *Same River...Different Bridge*. —*Tom Roland*

Inside Out / 1982 / MCA ✦✦✦✦

Inside Out features "It Turns Me Inside Out," the confessional hit which made Greenwood a star, as well as the as the Top Ten singles "Ring on Her Finger, Time on Her Hands," "She's Lying" and "Ain't No Trick (It Takes Magic)." —*Jason Ankeny*

If There's Any Justice / 1983 / MCA ✦✦✦✦

Somebody's Gonna Love You / 1983 / MCA ✦✦✦

Greenwood's sophomore effort includes the back-to-back chart-toppers "Somebody's Gonna Love You" and "Going, Going, Gone." —*Jason Ankeny*

The Wind Beneath My Wings / 1984 / MCA ✦✦✦

You've Got a Good Love Comin' / 1985 / MCA ✦✦✦

Greatest Hits / 1985 / MCA ✦✦✦✦

The extent to which Greenwood relies on ballads is fully evident here, although his departures—"Dixie Road" and "Ain't No Trick"—are most memorable. "God Bless the U.S.A." is the last track; if you're not inclined to ultra-patriotism, you can simply lift the needle or push "Stop." —*Tom Roland*

Streamline / 1986 / MCA ✦✦✦

If Only for One Night / 1988 / MCA ✦✦✦

Love Will Find It's Way to You / 1988 / MCA ✦✦✦

Greatest Hits, Vol. 2 / 1989 / MCA ✦✦✦

God Bless the U.S.A. / 1990 / MCA ✦✦✦

God Bless the USA is a budget-line collection that alternates between Lee Greenwood's slick country-pop hits and his inspirational works. Several of his biggest country hits—including the title track, "Ring on Her Finger, Time on Her Hands," "Dixie Road," "Somebody's Gonna Love You," and "Hearts Aren't Made to Break (They're Made to Love)"—are included on the collection, as well as recent recordings of standards like "Amazing Grace" and "O Holy Night." It's not a perfect collection, but Greenwood's biggest hits are present and accounted for and the album gives a good idea of his sound, making it a nice introduction for the budget-conscious. —*Rodney Batdorf*

Holdin' a Good Hand / 1991 / Capitol ✦✦✦

When You're in Love / 1991 / Capitol ✦✦✦

American Patriot / 1992 / Liberty ✦✦✦

Spurred on by George Bush's unofficial adoption of "God Bless the U.S.A." as the new American anthem, Lee Greenwood recorded *American Patriot* in the midst of the president's (ultimately unsuccessful) re-election campaign in 1992. *American Patriot* sealed Greenwood's stance as American songteller extraordinaire. Every song on the album is, unsurprisingly, about America, from "The Pledge of Allegiance" and "The Star Spangled

Banner" to "God Bless America" and "God Bless the U.S.A." Of course, Woody Guthrie's populist anthem "This Land Is Your Land" takes on a different meaning in this context, but that's not surprising—*American Patriot* is a slick, satisfied album designed for the modern-day patriot and conservative, not for dustbowl activists or smugly sophisticated liberals. In other words, if you've been a fan of "God Bless the U.S.A." since its first incarnation in the early '80s, you'll be happy with this full-blown sequel. —*Stephen Thomas Erlewine*

The Best of Lee Greenwood / 1992 / Curb ✦✦

The Best of Lee Greenwood is a ten-track budget-priced collection that features some of his biggest hits from the mid-'80s, including "Dixie Road," "I Don't Mind the Thorns (If You're the Rose)," "Mornin' Ride," "Hearts Aren't Made to Break (They're Made to Love)" and "Don't Underestimate My Love for You." Although this isn't a bad budget-priced disc, there are better collections available, offering more songs (including "God Bless the U.S.A.") and better sound for not much more money. —*Stephen Thomas Erlewine*

God Bless the U.S.A.: The Best of Lee Greenwood / 1996 / Curb ✦✦

God Bless the U.S.A.: The Best of Lee Greenwood is a ten-track budget-priced collection that features some of his biggest hits, including "Dixie Road," "Hearts Aren't Made to Break," "Ring on Her Finger, Time on Her Hands," "Touch and Go Crazy" and "God Bless the U.S.A." Although this isn't a bad budget-priced disc, there are better collections available, especially since the latter half of the disc bypasses hits and concentrates on gospel material. There are other discs that offer more songs, more hits and better sound for not much more money. —*Stephen Thomas Erlewine*

Super Hits / Mar. 19, 1996 / Epic ✦✦

Consumer advisory: In small print on the back of this record are the words: "All songs recorded 1994." This ten-track album contains Lee Greenwood's re-recordings of some of his biggest MCA Records hits of the 1980s, such as "Dixie Road" and "Hearts Aren't Made to Break (They're Made to Love)," along with several gospel tunes. —*William Ruhlmann*

● **20th Century Masters—The Millennium Collection: The Best of Lee Greenwood** / Jan. 15, 2002 / MCA Nashville ✦✦✦✦

Lee Greenwood scored 19 Top Ten country hits on the *Billboard* charts between 1982 and 1988 while contracted to MCA Records, and 12 of them are included on this midline-priced best-of, including ten of his 12 Top Five hits, among them all seven of his chart-toppers. Especially because country albums tend to be on the skimpy side (Greenwood's 1985 *Greatest Hits* LP had only ten tracks), this is an unusually good selection for a discount record. Of course, it includes Greenwood's signature song, "God Bless the U.S.A.," which was given a renewed burst of popularity in the wake of the September 11, 2001, terrorist attacks. This is not a complete collection of all of Greenwood's hits or even all of his MCA hits, but it presents most of his best-known material at a reasonable price. —*William Ruhlmann*

Clinton Gregory

b. Mar. 1, 1966, Martinsville, VA

Fiddle, Vocals / Contemporary Country

Born in Martinville, VA, Clinton Gregory came from a long line of fiddle players. He picked up the fiddle at five years old and made his performing debut at bluegrass festivals within a year. He came to Nashville at age 12, where his father, Willie Gregory, was playing at the *Grand Ole Opry*. When word of Clinton's fiddle prowess got around in Nashville, he was rarely without a steady gig and played on numerous studio sessions that included Dennis Robbins, the McCarters, and Suzy Bogguss. In 1990, Step One Records signed him to their label. His debut single, a rendition of the Jimmie Davis classic "Nobody's Darlin' But Mine," was followed by a string of country singles, including "Couldn't Love Have Picked a Better Place to Die," "One Shot at a Time," and the Top 20 hit "Play Ruby Play," which was also a video hit on both CMT and TNN. —*Al Campbell*

Music 'n Me / 1990 / Step One ✦✦✦

He reveals his influences by tapping them for material, recording Merle Haggard's "I Can't Be Myself," and Mel Street's "Loving on Backstreets," and Jimmie Davis' 1935 hit, "Nobody's Darlin." He also included "Made for Loving You," later a hit for Doug Stone. —*Michael McCall*

● **I'd Go Crazy If It Weren't for Country Music** / 1991 / Step One ✦✦✦✦

His commercial breakthrough came with "If It Weren't for Country Music (I'd Go Crazy)." His confidence and vocal range shows growth, and the album features "One Shot at a Time," a memorable song about the devastation drinking can cause. —*Michael McCall*

Freeborn Man / Dec. 1991 / Step One ✦✦✦

Gregory kicks a bit harder, as displayed on the hit "Play Ruby Play," but he still leans more on honky tonk than country-rock. —*Michael McCall*

Clinton Gregory / 1995 / Polydor Nashville ✦✦✦

Play Ruby Play / Jul. 28, 2000 / Step One ✦✦✦

Grievous Angels

Group / Progressive Bluegrass, Country-Folk, Alternative Country-Rock, Alternative Country, Americana

The Grievous Angels are an alternative country band from Tempe, AZ, that recorded albums for Bloodshot Records. Like the Old 97's, Grievous blends country, rock, and bluegrass into a hard-driving, frenetic sound. At concerts they'll play the Sex Pistols' "Bodies," yet they also have a more acoustic alter ego band called Ned Beatty and the Inbreds that plays bluegrass and folk. The band was named after Gram Parsons' 1973 seminal country-rock album *Grievous Angel*. Earl C. Whitehead (aka Russell Sepulveda) fronts the group, singing lead, playing acoustic guitar, and writing many of the band's songs. Dan Henzerling co-produced the band's 1998 album, *Miles on the Rail*, and plays guitar and sings. He worked with Robin Wilson in some bands in the '80s, including the

Gin Blossoms for a short time in 1988. Micky Ferrell played in Los Angeles for years before joining the Grievous Angels on bass, and Jesus H. Navarro plays drums. Jon Rauhouse is the newest member, playing everything from steel, banjo, and mandolin to Hawaiian guitar. The band released its debut album, *Angels and Inbreds*, on Bloodshot Records in 1995, followed by *New City of Sin* in 1997 and *Miles on the Rail* in 1998. *—Brian Wahlert*

New City of Sin / May 20, 1997 / Bloodshot ✦✦✦

● **Miles on the Rail** / Sep. 8, 1998 / Bloodshot ✦✦✦
The Grievous Angels' third album finds them playing their own hard-driving brand of country-rock on nine original tracks and two covers. Instrumentally, the music is driven by the chugging beat of Jesus Navarro's snare drum and a mix of acoustic and electric guitars. But the real instrumental genius is Jon Rauhouse, whose steel guitar, mandolin, and banjo flourishes add spice to the Angels' musical concoction. The lead vocals of Earl C. Whitehead (aka Russell Sepulveda) are not particularly remarkable, but fit the frenzied pace of much of the band's music well. Listening to this album, one realizes that Grievous must be a great barroom band. Their music is brisk and entertaining—in short, easy to dance to. Little of the songwriting carries much weight, but maybe that's the point. Part of the purpose of music is escapism, and Grievous provides that on this album with its fun, upbeat style. *—Brian Wahlert*

Buck Griffin

b. Feb. 23, 1923, Corsicana, TX
Guitar, Vocals / Rock & Roll, Traditional Country, Rockabilly
Buck Griffin has never made it as a star in country music, but not for lack of ability or talent. Described in his prime as a cross between Hank Williams and Red Foley, he was a charismatic performer and a prodigious songwriter who has simply failed to get the right breaks or the right contract at the right time. Albert C. Griffin was born on February 23, 1923, in Corsicana, TX, and raised in Oklahoma and Missouri; he inherited the nickname Buck from his father. He took up the guitar around age 12 and formed his first band with three other boys a couple of years later, with Griffin singing most of the lead parts at dances and school assemblies. Music had to take second place to earning a living, and Griffin made his digging pipeline ditches in Kansas. Eventually he made his way to the oil fields and became a driller, and it was life in the oil fields and time spent at the surrounding honky tonks that pulled Griffin back into music. He began playing nightly and eventually got a program of his own (as Chuck Wyman, a name owned by the station) on WKY.

The early '50s looked like a promising period for a new generation of country singers—what's more, the death of Hank Williams on New Year's Day 1953 had left a huge gap in country music that was waiting to be filled. Griffin looked like the man to fill it. He came out of the honky tonks much as Williams had, and his songs had a direct simplicity of expression and a complexity in their execution that recalled Williams at his best. He had a strong voice and a charismatic persona, wrote songs, was building a serious local following, and seemed to be haunted by none of the personal demons that had blighted Williams' later life. Griffin came to the attention of Joe Leonard, the owner of a radio station in Gainesville, TX, who had acquired the Lin Records label and saw an opportunity to make the singer/songwriter a star and both of them some money. He signed Griffin and recorded him at Dallas radio station WFAA in early 1954. His earliest sides, "It Don't Make No Nevermind" and "Meadowlark Boogie," were both hybrids of hillbilly and Western swing that failed to click. A series of follow-up sessions in September of that year yielded some more advanced sides and sounds that fell, similarly, on deaf ears as far as radio stations were concerned. On-stage, by contrast, he was as popular as ever and appeared on the same bills with the likes of Red Foley and Marty Robbins.

There were some great records, too. "Bawlin' and Squallin'" mixed the best elements of honky tonk and Western swing effortlessly (members of Bob Wills' band played on this side and the rest of that session), with a breezy delivery that rural rock & roll fans, at least, should have loved. And "Let's Elope Baby" should have been a mainstream country classic. What success Griffin found during this period was as a songwriter. His records may not have been getting played, but the songs on them, most notably "Goin' Home All Alone" and "Let's Elope Baby," got covered by Wade Ray and Janis Martin ("The Female Elvis") respectively; she turned "Let's Elope Baby" into a harder-rocking side, which was more commercial than Griffin's decidedly backwoods approach. Meanwhile, in early 1956, Griffin was signed to the Big D Jamboree in Dallas, a major showcase for country talent, and MGM Records picked up the distribution of his Lin Records sides.

MGM was looking to get in on the rock & roll boom and apparently saw Griffin as a potential rockabilly crossover star, in the manner of his Lin Records stablemate Andy Starr or future MGM rock & roller/country star Conway Twitty. Some of Griffin's songs did, indeed, have a hard, almost rockabilly-type edge. But he was too Southern in his sound and the sensibilities of his lyrics to find much appeal outside of the rural South, and many of the songs he was doing during this period were too serious for the kids he was supposed to be aiming at. The MGM deal ended in the early '60s, after which Griffin cut songs for the Holiday Inn label, none of which sold. He was almost out of the music business by 1963, making ends meet by selling Bibles. He continued to write and publish songs into the late '60s, and recorded occasionally. The onset of chronic asthma sidelined him as a performer, and since the 1970s, he's been content to sit of the sidelines, savoring his early success as a songwriter and hoping for more interest in his newer numbers. *—Bruce Eder*

Let's Elope Baby / 1995 / Bear Family ✦✦✦✦✦
There's stuff on this 28-song CD that would be loved by fans of Hank Williams, Bob Wills, Elvis Presley, Red Foley, and even Benny Goodman, and most of it should've been hits for Buck Griffin 40-some years ago. He runs the gamut from hard country to Western swing to a restrained but valid form of rockabilly, and he's good at all of it. "It Don't Make No Nevermind," "Meadowlark Boogie," "Bawlin' and Squallin'," "Let's Elope Baby," "Stutterin' Papa," and "One Day After Payday" are worth the price of admission, and all of it is eminently listenable. Some of this stuff, like "One Day After Payday," with Merle Shelton on steel guitar, Sonny James on fiddle, and Bill Simmons on piano, is striking for its sophistication—produced by Joe Leonard in Dallas, it's proof that Chet Atkins had no copyright on the Nashville countrypolitan sound, even back in 1954. Other tracks show a daring that is amazing to savor—the honking trumpet on "Meadowlark Boogie" and the romping clarinet on "It Don't Make No Nevermind." And then there's the harder country of "Lookin' for the Green." The disc is rounded out with four beautifully sung, utterly sincere and compelling religious numbers, of which "Next to Mine" is as fine as any of the country numbers here. The sound is excellent throughout, and the notes are well-written and informative. *—Bruce Eder*

Rex Griffin

b. Aug. 12, 1912, Gasden, AL, **d.** Oct. 11, 1959
Songwriter, Vocals / Traditional Country, Honky Tonk
As a songwriter, performer, and recording artist, Rex Griffin bridged the gap between Jimmie Rodgers and Hank Williams—indeed, it can be said that he bridged the gap between Rodgers and Buddy Holly, and between Rodgers and the Beatles. Griffin was among the first country music stars to record using his own material almost exclusively, and among the least of his accomplishments, one of his songs was covered (albeit without proper credit) by the Beatles. Griffin is the author of the original version of "Everybody's Tryin' to Be My Baby," which Carl Perkins later adapted into his own song, and the Beatles subsequently covered to the profit of all except Griffin, who'd been dead about six years when all of this happened.

Griffin is one of those prewar figures in country music whose legacy has been unjustly overlooked. He had no hits of his own after 1939, although his biggest hit from that year—"The Last Letter"—continues to get recorded at the end of the century. He was also a direct inspiration to both Hank Williams (whose recording of "Lovesick Blues" was virtually a copy of Griffin's from ten years earlier) and Lefty Frizzell. One of country music's first singer/songwriters, Griffin was the model for figures including Floyd Tillman, Willie Nelson, and Merle Haggard (and one could even throw Buddy Holly in there). And, like Williams, his personal demons in love and substance abuse brought a premature end—albeit not as suddenly as Williams'—to Griffin's performing career and his life. He was born Alsie Griffin, second of seven children of Marion Oliver Griffin and the former Selma Bradshaw. He grew up without much formal education and spent most of his early childhood on the farm that his family owned in Sand Valley. By the 1920s, Ollie Griffin was working in Gasden at the Agricola Foundry, and Alsie followed his father there. The family regarded music as a pastime to be pursued after finishing one's real work.

Alsie felt differently, however, wanting no part of farm life or the factory if there was any way of helping it. His first instrument was a harmonica, but it wasn't long before he picked up the guitar. Gasden didn't offer a big future in music, but Griffin took advantage of what was there, playing local parties and dances. If the guitar was the first instrument that Griffin felt strongly about, his first love was the music of Jimmie Rodgers. He quickly adopted Rodgers' style as his own and never entirely abandoned elements of his music—especially the yodeling—even once he had his own style nailed down. Griffin made his first professional appearance on a bill at the Gasden Theater in 1930, and not long after he moved to Birmingham, where better opportunities awaited. He joined the Smokey Mountaineers, and it was there that he got his new first name—the group's announcer had difficulty pronouncing Alsie, and simply renamed him Rex. The name stayed with him and he moved from city to city across the South, appearing on radio stations in Chattanooga, Atlanta, and New Orleans, among other cities.

His recording career began in 1935, when Griffin was signed to the newly formed Decca Record company, which already had the Sons of the Pioneers, Tex Ritter, Jimmie Davis, and Milton Brown in their roster of country artists. His first recording sessions were held in Chicago on March 25 and 26 of that year, during which he recorded ten songs, accompanied by his own guitar and Johnny Motlow on tenor banjo. All ten number were originals by Griffin, itself an astonishing achievement in those days. All of the material, both in its style and performance, recalled Rodgers—Griffin's yodeling never let one forget who his inspiration was, although the songs hold up well on their own terms. Also striking about the recordings is Motlow's banjo playing which, with its trilling, sounds almost like a mandolin.

Griffin's first releases were successful enough to justify another session for Decca nearly a year later in New Orleans. This time he provided the only accompaniment on ten of the songs and did two additional songs backed by an amplified steel guitar. Among the songs that came out of those sessions was "Everybody's Tryin' to Be My Baby," which in this context sounds almost like a blues composition, recalling works such as Tampa Red's "Tight Like That." The piece was also a dazzling guitar showcase for Griffin, whose prowess on the instrument was considerable. This blues influence was no fluke—"I'm Ready to Reform" from the same session is a superb piece of white blues that can fool listeners as to its origins as easily as Autry's or Rodgers' best blues sides.

Griffin's records continued to sell well, and in May of 1937, this time in New York, he cut two more sides, including his most famous number. "The Last Letter" became his biggest hit, a suicide note set to music. Stories vary as to its origins, the most commonly circulated one being that Griffin, who had a taste for alcohol that would later blight his life, was in a drunken depression over his failing first marriage when he wrote the note, and later set it to music as sobering up. Whatever the circumstances of its composition, the record caught on and became a hit throughout the South, and also brought Griffin the adulation of many of his colleagues, most notably Ernest Tubb, whose 20-year friendship with Griffin began over "The Last Letter." The song was covered by other artists, including Jimmie Davis, soon after its release. Gene Sullivan also covered three Griffin songs, including "Everybody's Tryin' to Be My Baby," in the late '30s, and even bandleader Bob Crosby cut Griffin's "I Told You So." Griffin's own career kept moving forward, with concerts and radio performances throughout the South that made him one of the more popular performers of the era.

Griffin's next recording sessions in September of 1939 yielded a dozen songs, including the follow-up to his biggest hit, "Answer to the Last Letter," and his recording of "Lovesick Blues," which was to be the model for Williams' recording nearly a decade later that made Hank a star. Also recorded at the session was "Nobody Wants to Be My Baby," a fast, breezy honky tonk-style number and one of several songs on which Griffin was backed by guitarist Ted Brooks and bassist Smitty Smith. The latter is also a beautiful piece of bluesy honky tonk and deserves to be better known. Despite the success of "The Last Letter," Griffin's record sales were too poor overall to justify the label keeping him, and he was dropped by Decca after 1939. In the mid-'30s, he had played with Billie Walker & Her Texas Cowboys in New Orleans, and in 1940 he rejoined her band in Memphis. He later moved back to Alabama to spend more time with his ailing mother and appeared locally for the next few years. Among the places he played often was the notorious crime-ridden Alabama town of Phenix City, which would later become the subject of two feature films. In Gasden, he performed with a group called the Melody Boys, which included two future members of Tubb's Texas Troubadours.

In 1941, following the death of his mother, Griffin moved to Dallas, where he had a regular spot on KRLD's *Texas Round-Up*. His popularity from these broadcasts made Griffin a natural to take over the *Texas Round-Up*. This was to be his best broadcast showcase, and had it not been for the war, Griffin might've become a major star from his work on KRLD. As it was, the show ended in 1943 as the available talent dwindled amid continued military call-ups. Griffin moved to Chicago in 1944, and it was there that he made his next batch of recordings. These 16 sides—recorded with a band that may have included Red Foley on guitar—were not intended for commercial release. Rather, they were made for Decca Records' World Transcription Services, for broadcast over the air by radio stations that licensed them. Despite these recordings for the company's transcription division, there was no interest at the time in trying to release new commercial sides by Griffin. To hear the material today is to glimpse some of the best honky tonk-style music of the era—by that time, Griffin had taken on a more modern style, and he had even cut his Rodgers-inspired yodeling to a minimum. In addition to capturing Griffin performing "live" in the studio, these are among the few sides he left that feature him working with a band and, thus, show something of the sound he must've had during that early-'40s Dallas period.

The oversight by the record company, in terms of offering him a new contract, is difficult to explain. It is possible, however, that the wartime rationing of shellac (a key ingredient in 78 rpm records) had so dampened interest in any risky new ventures (the record business at one point seemed doomed to shut down) that Griffin never had a chance with his old label. He made his last recordings in 1946 for Cincinnati-based King Records, which had previously recorded Grandpa Jones, the Delmore Brothers, and Merle Travis, among others. Griffin cut eight sides for King, backed by Homer & Jethro on guitars and mandolin. The sides showed Griffin in decent form, an easygoing honky tonk singer with a smooth style and a good voice, but lacking the sharp edge to his singing and playing that sparked his earlier work, clearly on the decline by this time.

These proved to be his last recording sessions. His worsening diabetic condition, complicated by drinking and other dietary abuses, forced an end to Griffin's career, and the collapse of his second marriage late in the 1940s sent him into a personal tailspin. He moved to Dallas and still wrote songs, and when his health allowed (he was hospitalized several times), he pitched them actively to singers who had recording contracts, including Ray Price, who cut "Answer to the Last Letter," "Beyond the Last Mile," and "I Saw My Castles Fall Today." His friendship with Tubb blossomed into a profitable professional relationship for both, as Tubb recorded many of Griffin's songs, and Griffin also became close to Tubb's nephew, Douglas Glenn Tubb. Their interest, coupled with the quality of his work, sustained Griffin during the 1950s, and in 1955 he wrote "Just Call Me Lonesome," his last hit, recorded by Eddy Arnold and Red Foley. His last years were blighted by further ill health, as Griffin was diagnosed with tuberculosis. He was confined to a New Orleans hospital for what proved to be the final months of his life, and died in October of 1959.

Griffin's death at the age of 47 was a great loss to country music. Moreover, his lack of any hit recordings of his own after 1939 resulted in there never being an LP release of his songs—there was no impetus on the part of Decca Records to explore his recording history, and he was left in limbo as a recording artist, a distant memory to older listeners. The possibility of Decca's successor, MCA Records, doing anything with Griffin's music in the 1990s or beyond seems even more remote. The songs he wrote, however, have endured over the 40 years since. Hank Thompson recorded "An Old Faded Photograph" in 1960, and "The Last Letter" was re-recorded by Jack Greene in 1964 and became a hit once again. Soon after, Tubb cut an entire album of Griffin songs, and other artists who have covered "The Last Letter" include Willie Nelson, Asleep at the Wheel, Waylon Jennings, and Merle Haggard.

At the time of his death, Griffin's quarterly royalty statement from the publisher of his newest songs was 18 dollars and change, a situation that had changed drastically by the 1960s. Additionally, his song "Everybody's Tryin' to Be My Baby," as appropriated by Carl Perkins—the inability of the family to protect the copyright probably cost his daughters millions in royalties—and later covered by the Beatles, has become a rock & roll standard only slightly less familiar than "Blue Suede Shoes" or "Maybelline." And then there was his version of "Lovesick Blues," which Williams freely admitted to having learned from Griffin, even though Hank was also familiar with the Emmett Miller original—Griffin did make changes in the lyrics and structure of the song that Williams kept in his version. In 1970, in recognition of his achievements as a composer, Griffin was among the very first composers inducted into the newly founded National Songwriters' Hall of Fame in Nashville. In 1996, Bear Family Records of Germany released a long overdue triple-CD career retrospective on Griffin entitled *The Last Letter*. —*Bruce Eder*

☆ Last Letter / 1996 / Bear Family ✦✦✦✦✦
Many Bear Family releases seem like overkill, but this one is easy to justify. This triple CD is a truly wonderful collection, including every one of the 64 sides that Rex Griffin recorded between 1935 and 1946, and also 16 songs recorded as demos by his brother Buddy between 1948 and 1955. The repertory runs the gamut from Jimmie Rodgers-style yodel pieces to highly effective white blues ("I'm Ready to Reform"), and even the future rock & roll standard "Everybody's Tryin' to Be My Baby." Griffin only had six series

recording sessions in his whole career, none lasting more than a day or two, and he recorded as many as ten songs at a time, in effect creating an album's worth of songs, more than 90 percent of it original material. The strange thing is that, despite the fact that each of these sessions pretty much meant using the same backgrounds on each song, they would work as albums—the material is so strong that it didn't have to be trickled out as singles. The other thing that one notices about these sides is that, along with the quality of the material, the playing is also first-rate. The 1944 sides, radio transcription discs recorded with a band that may have included Red Foley on guitar, intended for broadcast, capture some of the excitement of a Griffin stage performance with his own early-'40s band. These are brisk, rippling, immediate live-in-the-studio honky tonk-style renditions of "Everybody's Tryin' to Be My Baby," "An Old Faded Photograph," "Mean Woman Blues," and other 1930s vintage songs, as well as newer material. The set is worth the investment, even if that means saving up for it. —*Bruce Eder*

Nanci Griffith
b. Jul. 6, 1953, Austin, TX
Guitar, Songwriter, Vocals / Progressive Country, Singer/Songwriter, Country-Folk, Contemporary Folk, Contemporary Country

Striding the fine line between folk and country music, Nanci Griffith has become as well-known for her brilliant confessional songwriting as her beautiful voice. A self-styled "folkabilly" singer, Griffith began as a kindergarten teacher and occasional folksinger. The country scene took her to heart in the mid-'80s, giving her a reputation as a quality songwriter through hit covers of Griffith's songs by Kathy Mattea and Suzy Bogguss. Finding no luck with commercial country radio however, Griffith recorded several pop-oriented albums and then returned to her folk roots by the mid-'90s. Griffith was the daughter of musical parents, and she spent her childhood involved with theater and literature as well as music. She began playing clubs around Austin at the tender age of 14 and continued to perform during her college years at the University of Texas and even while she taught kindergarten in the mid-'70s. Griffith finally decided to make music her full-time ambition in 1977. Her songwriting won an award at the Kerrville Folk Festival, prompting the local label BF Deal to record Griffith for a compilation and later for her debut album, *There's a Light Beyond These Woods* (1978). Griffith's hectic touring schedule took her all over North America, playing festivals and TV shows in addition to the small clubs in which she had begun. Meanwhile, she recorded albums in 1982 (*Poet in My Window*) and 1984 (*Once in a Very Blue Moon*).

Finally, in 1986, Griffith got her big break after moving to Nashville. The title song from *Once in a Very Blue Moon* placed modestly on the country charts, she released the acclaimed *Last of the True Believers* on Philo (the label that later reissued her first three albums), and—most importantly—Mattea's cover of "Love at the Five & Dime" reached number three in the country charts. Though *Last of the True Believers* was nominated for a Grammy as Best Contemporary Folk Recording—perhaps because of the fact—commercial country radio still found it difficult to accept Griffith. Griffith signed with MCA and released her major-label debut, *Lone Star State of Mind*, in 1987. With it, she popularized the Julie Gold song "From a Distance"—later covered by Bette Midler—but also gave Griffith her first country Top 40 hit, the title song. Two other singles from the album, "Trouble in the Fields" and "Cold Hearts/Closed Minds," also grazed the country charts. *Little Love Affairs* and the live album *One Fair Summer Evening* (both 1988) were slight disappointments, though "I Knew Love" became Griffith's second country Top 40 hit.

Disappointed by lack of support from the country music scene, Griffith moved from Nashville to MCA's pop division in Los Angeles and paired with noted rock producer Glyn Johns for 1989's *Storms*. The album included guest stars Phil Everly, Albert Lee, and former Eagle Bernie Leadon and became her best-seller, though it featured no successful singles. A move from rock to pop—helped by producers Rod Argent and Peter Van Hook—characterized *Late Night Grande Hotel* (1991); it was clear by then that Griffith's move away from Nashville was also compromising her folk and country roots. A move to Elektra in 1992 marked a return to form for Griffith; her 1993 LP *Other Voices, Other Rooms* was a tribute to her influences, and several of them—including Emmylou Harris, Chet Atkins, and John Prine—made appearances. A compilation release of her best from the MCA years also appeared in 1993. The following year, Griffith's tenth studio album, *Flyer*, continued her dedication to folk. In March of 1997, Griffith released *Blue Roses From the Moons*; *Other Voices, Too (A Trip Back to Bountiful)* followed a year later, trailed in 1999 by *The Dust Bowl Symphony*. —*John Bush*

There's a Light Beyond These Woods / 1978 / Philo ✦✦✦
Returning to Nanci Griffith's first album, cut in 1978-1979, provides an interesting backdrop to view her work in the latter part of the '90s. Clearly, the singer/songwriter fans' love hasn't arrived yet, but one catches glimpses of future greatness on songs like "I Remember Joe" and "Song for Remembered Heroes." Call Griffith a songwriter-in-training on *There's a Light Beyond These Woods*, learning how to shape a melody, pitch her voice, and surround herself with the right musicians. Even on weaker pieces, like the title cut and "Michael's Song," Griffith attempts to write a strong melody, giving each piece a distinctive flavor. She doesn't take a lot of chances vocally though, and many of the songs could've used a more robust approach. Still, her voice is already singular, and she delivers lots of emotion on pieces like "John Philip Griffith." Most of the accompaniment is simple, as in the guitar and cello that underline her voice in "West Texas Sun." Lyrically, songs like "Montana Backroads" rely on uncomplicated imagery—pickup trucks, feed stores, and bars—to paint a lonely portrait of a washed-up rodeo rider. This integrated, low-key approach contrasts sharply with Griffith's later albums, like 2001's *Clock Without Hands*. While she exudes much more confidence on the latter effort, she forgets many of the basics of songcraft, overreaching lyrically and adding an overly bright production. In retrospect, *There's a Light Beyond These Woods* sounds better because it sticks closer its folk roots. Fans only familiar with Griffith's later work will enjoy watching a young poet find her muse. —*Ronnie D. Lankford Jr.*

Poet in My Window / 1982 / Philo ♦♦♦
While *Poet in My Window* is only a small step up from Nanci Griffith's debut, the album finds her inching toward the mature art of *Once in a Very Blue Moon.* While guitars and an occasional mandolin embellished *There's a Light Beyond These Woods*, a fuller country sound graces its follow-up. Pedal steel and multiple acoustic guitars fill out "Can't Love Wrong" and "Heart of a Miner," giving them lots of body. While Griffith's vocals sometimes bordered on timid on her first album, the bigger country-folk sound inspires a more vigorous approach here. Indeed, on "Wheels" and "October Reasons," she shows herself capable of belting out a phrase or two without losing the vulnerable underside of the song. Evelyn Taylor offers a bit of harmony here and there, adding to the "bigger" sound of the album and pleasantly complementing Griffith's voice. Lyrically, *A Poet in My Window* offers sharp observations and memorable lines on pieces like "Workin' These Corners." When Griffith sings "She's just a hill country girl home from the city/Her pockets full of plenty of those neon lights" on "Waltzing With the Angels," she manages to be both clever and insightful. While all of these elements work together to create a strong impression on *Poet in My Window*, the songs lack the standout quality that would mark a half-dozen cuts on *Once in a Very Blue Moon.* The earlier album is nonetheless easy on the ears, and fans unfamiliar with it will appreciate watching a young poet find her bearings. *—Ronnie D. Lankford Jr.*

Once in a Very Blue Moon / 1984 / Philo ♦♦♦♦♦
Nanci Griffith finds her voice on her third studio album, *Once in a Very Blue Moon.* This is the album where she established her musical identity—she is at home in many genres (which perhaps explains why she never gets played on formatted radio stations), and seamlessly blends folk, bluegrass, and country with a group of stellar musicians, including guitarist Pat Alger and a young banjo player named Béla Fleck. While the music is well-textured with cello, mandolin, dobro, and fiddle, it is Griffith's lyrics that distinguish her from her peers. Although not a concept album, the main theme explored is travel. She sings about the joys and excitement of the road as well as the longing that comes with extended periods away from home. Nanci Griffith is an excellent storyteller, with detailed, insightful lyrics that vividly portray the hopes and dreams of her characters ("Mary and Omie"). She sprinkles the album with songs of others, as she pays homage to folk veterans such as Bill Staines ("Roseville Fair") and sings a tune by newcomer Lyle Lovett ("If I Were the Woman You Wanted"). This album marks the emergence of a major talent. *—Vik Iyengar*

● **The Last of the True Believers** / 1986 / Philo ♦♦♦♦♦
This is Nanci Griffith's fourth and final release on Rounder Records' folk subsidiary, Philo. At the time Griffith relocated to Nashville, TN, her decidedly Texan sense of musicality had already begun developing subtle hues of Appalachia as well as the cosmopolitan country that would inform her mid- to late-'80s stint on MCA. However, it is the overwhelming strength and conviction in the singer/songwriter's original material on *The Last of the True Believers* that remain indelibly impressed upon enthusiasts and critics alike. As such, Griffith has retained a copious sampling from the disc in her subsequent live performance repertoire. Griffith's crystalline vocals are well matched to the warm, earthy acoustic instrumentation on the intimate "More Than a Whisper" and "The Wing and the Wheel." At times, the delicate interplay creates a mutual envelopment of the human vocal instrument with that of the stringed nature—most notably on the heartfelt "Love at the Five and Dime." By way of contrast, Griffith defies her somewhat introverted image on the tongue-in-cheek (no pun!) love song "Looking for the Time (Workin' Girl)" and the effervescent waltz "Love's Found a Shoulder." Lying nestled between are spry melodies such as "Banks of the Pontchartrain," featuring some nice picking from Béla Fleck (banjo), and "Goin' Gone," which perfectly captures some of Lloyd Green's finest pedal steel work on the disc. Griffith's pure and otherwise unaffected performance style would continue to carry through her subsequent efforts, most notably *Lone Star State of Mind* (1987), which in many ways is a companion, rather than simply the follow-up, to *The Last of the True Believers. —Lindsay Planer*

Lone Star State of Mind / 1987 / MCA ♦♦♦
Lone Star State of Mind was Nanci Griffith's commercial breakthrough, largely because it was her first step directly toward mainstream contemporary country. Instead of diluting her introspective folk songs, the full-fledged production actually enhances her music, as the steel guitars and dobros add body to her songs. Griffith responds in kind, delivering the most textured and nuanced vocal performance of her career, as evidenced by her version of "From a Distance." Of course, her songwriting is as good as it ever was; "Ford Econoline," "Sing One for Sister," "Beacon Street" and a revamped version of "Mary Margaret" called "There's a Light Beyond These Woods," are all terrific, ranking among her best songs. *Lone Star State of Mind* is one of the rare commercial moves that actually improves and artist's music instead of compromising it. *—Thom Owens*

Little Love Affairs / Feb. 1988 / MCA ♦♦♦♦♦
Little Love Affairs, Nanci Griffith's second MCA Records album and sixth album overall, was the crucial release in her attempt to achieve success as a Nashville-based country artist, and in that context it was a failure. But it was also an artistic success, containing 11 well-written and well-performed songs in the reflective style that the singer/songwriter had established previously. Griffith's first MCA album, *Lone Star State of Mind*, had been a moderate seller, reaching the Top 40 and spawning two country chart singles. MCA prefaced *Little Love Affairs* with perhaps its most overtly country song, "Never Mind," written by veteran songwriter Harlan Howard and prominently featuring a pedal steel guitar in its arrangement, but the single's failure to crack the country Top 40 suggested trouble confirmed when the album peaked lower than *Lone Star State of Mind.* "Never Mind" gave a good indication of the album's theme, embodied in its title, of carefully examining the romantic lives of common people. Howard's lovers were itinerant laborers who seemed out of the Depression, and other songs also looked back in stories of romance past such as Griffith's compositions "Love Wore a Halo (Back Before the War)" and "So Long Ago." The music, supplied by Griffith's backup band and New Grass Revival, was in her familiar country-folk style, and her vocals, with their ringing, aching tone, conveyed the songs' sense of longing and regret effectively. Country critics and radio programmers complained that, if anything, she was *too* country, her voice having an off-putting twang and nasality, but that was just an excuse for rejecting her literate lyrics and sophistication. At 33, she wasn't about to become some empty-headed Nashville bimbo willing to mouth romantic clichés, and for that she paid the price of being denied country stardom. Her fans breathed a sigh of relief. *—William Ruhlmann*

One Fair Summer Evening / Nov. 1988 / MCA ♦♦♦♦♦
This is singer/songwriter Nanci Griffith's first live album, and it captures the essence of what has endeared Griffith to fans of both folk and cosmopolitan country. Although *One Fair Summer Evening* was not an immediate phenomenon at the cash registers, the revealing nature of the performance has secured it a place in the hearts of enthusiasts since its release in 1988. In addition to highlights from her six previous long-players, she also adds a few new tracks—including her own composition "I Would Bring You Ireland" as well as "Deadwood, South Dakota" by her ex-husband, Eric Taylor—both of which became standards in her live performance canon. Her backing band, the Blue Moon Orchestra, is known for both its instrumental prowess and its keen knack for subtlety. Examples of this delicate balance range from the intimacy of "More Than a Whisper" and "Love at the Five and Dime" to the boot-scootin' fury of "Spin on a Red Brick Floor" and "Looking for the Time (Workin' Girl)." In between is a sampling of Griffith's organic folky roots ("Trouble in the Fields") as well as her pensive ballads ("Once in a Blue Moon"), which have become standards for the legions of would-be singer/songwriters who followed. Also included are stunning readings of Julie Gold's "From a Distance" and Bill Staines' (whom Griffith rightfully compares to a neo-Woody Guthrie) "Roseville Fair." There is also a 45-minute home video companion to *One Fair Summer Evening* that includes most of the music from this CD; missing are "The Wing and the Wheel," "Trouble in the Fields," and "Roseville Fair," while a whimsical version of "There's a Light Beyond the Woods (Mary Margaret)" has been added. *—Lindsay Planer*

Storms / Aug. 1989 / MCA ♦♦♦
Though it suffers somewhat from inconsistent material, *Storms* is a gorgeous collection of ballads and gentle observational country-rockers, highlighted by "It's a Hard Life Wherever You Go" and "Drive-In Movies and Dashboard Lights." *—Thom Owen*

Late Night Grande Hotel / 1991 / MCA ♦♦♦♦
Featuring some of Nanci Griffith's best and most original material—as well as a few equally brilliant cover songs—*Late Night Grande Hotel* blurs the lines between the singer/songwriter's Texas-rooted folk and the Nashville urban cosmopolitan country scene. Griffith has once again expanded her arrangements to include the five-piece Blue Moon Orchestra and also a few well-placed guest spots from Phil Everly (vocals), Mo Foster (electric bass), Tanita Tikaram (vocals), and Rod Argent (string arrangements/producer). The album's darker pop-oriented material can arguably be attributed to Argent's involvement. Of the 11 tracks, all but three are Griffith originals. Among them are some of the album's best material. As she had done with her crossover hit "From a Distance," Griffith beautifully interprets another Julie Gold composition, "Heaven." The cover of Vince Bell's introspective masterpiece "Sun & Moon & Stars" is not only one of this album's finest tracks, but it is also among the highlights of all the material during her five-year tenure with MCA. The remarkable intimacy she brings to the piece recalls her days on Philo and songs such as "Love at the Five and Dime" and "There's a Light Beyond These Woods." The third cover is of Tom Waits' somber "San Diego Serenade." While Griffith's vocals don't contain the huskiness and tragedy of the author, they add an even more distressing facet to the lyrics—perhaps coming from a deeper place within the artist. There are a few all-stars among Griffith's compositions as well. "One Blade Shy of a Sharp Edge" continues the overtly political messages that she often credits to the enormous influence that Lyndon B. Johnson and Pete Seeger have had on her life and work. "It's Just Another Morning Here" is full of the wit and innocuous charm that have continued to make Griffith such an endearing composer and performer. While not her best disc during the late '80s/early '90s, *Late Night Grande Hotel* is a solid effort with some of her most mature material to date. *—Lindsay Planer*

Other Voices, Other Rooms / 1993 / Elektra ♦♦♦♦♦
Griffith pays homage to a wide cut of folk music heroes, from Woody Guthrie to Townes Van Zandt, from Bob Dylan to Kate Wolf, from Malvina Reynolds to John Prine. She sounds looser and more spirited than usual, and her earnest adoration for the songs shines through in these compelling remakes. *—Michael McCall*

The MCA Years: A Retrospective / 1993 / MCA ♦♦♦♦♦

Flyer / 1994 / Elektra ♦♦♦♦
After getting increased exposure with her exquisite cover album *Other Voices, Other Rooms*, Nanci Griffith emerged with an album of originals that demonstrated to her new fans that she was more than just an interpreter of songs. She has always been a gifted and versatile songwriter with a knack for stepping inside her characters in story songs, but she writes from a more personal perspective on this album. With the help of high-profile friends from U2, Dire Straits, Indigo Girls, and Counting Crows, she incorporates more rock & roll instrumentation (electric guitar, piano, drums) into her acoustically based music. In fact, many of the highlights of this album involve collaborations. Mark Knopfler (Dire Straits) adds his usual tasteful guitar work in "Don't Forget About Me," and Adam Duritz of Counting Crows delivers perhaps his best vocal performance in the playful duet "Going Back to Georgia." As in previous releases, she wrestles with issues of love and loss; however, the songs resonate on a deeper level as she writes from the

perspective of someone who has seen and done a lot but still longs to connect souls with one special person ("Southbound Train," "On Grafton Street"). Although she falters a bit when choosing to tackle politics ("Time of Inconvenience"), this is her most consistent album of original songs in almost a decade. *—Vik Iyengar*

Blue Roses From the Moons / Mar. 25, 1997 / Elektra ♦♦♦

Blue Roses From the Moons expands the smoother sounds of *Flyer* by bringing Nanci Griffith firmly into the adult alternative playing field—not only does Don Gehman, the producer behind Hootie & the Blowfish, produce the record, but Darius Rucker has a vocal cameo, as well. Though the slick sound is a little disarming for longtime fans, Griffith's songwriting remains skilled and assured, and while there aren't as many as standout numbers as before, her graceful melodicism and lyricism and the professional production makes *Blue Roses From the Moons* a very pleasant listen. *—Thom Owens*

Other Voices, Too (A Trip Back to Bountiful) / Jul. 21, 1998 / Elektra ♦♦♦♦♦

Trailing five years behind the release of *Other Voices, Other Rooms*, Nanci Griffith's second collection of covers is that rare sequel which actually surpasses its predecessor. Boasting an even stronger and wide-ranging set of songs, *Other Voices, Too (A Trip Back to Bountiful)* captures the singer at her most radiant and expressive—moving easily from the Stephen Foster perennial "Hard Times Come Again No More" to '60s-pop hits like "You Were on My Mind" to British folk-rock chestnuts like Richard Thompson's "Wall of Death" and Sandy Denny's "Who Knows Where the Time Goes"—Griffith stamps each of these 19 tracks with her own indelible signature, revitalizing not only her material but herself in the process. *—Jason Ankeny*

The Dust Bowl Symphony / Sep. 14, 1999 / Elektra ♦♦

To say the least, *The Dust Bowl Symphony* is an ambitious effort on Nanci Griffith's behalf, an attempt to recast several of her songs in the context of a suite, complete with backing from the London Symphony Orchestra. Intriguing idea, but one that doesn't really quite work. Griffith sounds her best in intimate surroundings, which this album clearly illustrates; often, the songs themselves are lost in the swirl of strings, and it's hard to find their emotional core. It's not a complete disaster and there are some moments that work (surprisingly, duets with Beth Nielsen Chapman and Darius Rucker feel more successful than the cuts that just feature Griffith), but ultimately this is a curious, unfruitful detour in an adventurous career. When you take as many risks as Griffith does, it's inevitable that some projects won't work out as well as others. *—Stephen Thomas Erlewine*

20th Century Masters—The Millennium Collection: The Best of Nanci Griffith / Feb. 27, 2001 / MCA ♦♦♦♦♦

One of the strongest volumes in the *20th Century Masters—The Millennium Collection* series, *The Best of Nanci Griffith* does collect many of her career highlights, including "Trouble in the Fields," "Love at the Five and Dime," "From a Distance," and "It's a Hard Life Wherever You Go." Other highlights include "Once in a Very Blue Moon," "Lone Star State of Mind," and "Outbound Plane." Essentially a trimmed-down version of *The MCA Years: A Retrospective*, this collection is a wonderfully concise introduction to Griffith's radiant, earnest singing and songwriting. *—Heather Phares*

Wings to Fly & a Place to Be: An Introduction / Apr. 10, 2001 / MCA ♦♦♦

This European import provides an adequate introduction to singer/songwriter Nanci Griffith's first four albums on MCA. Oddly, there is no material from *Late Night Grande Hotel*—one of her best efforts during her run on the label. However, what *is* included represents an even-handed assortment of some of her best-known works from the late '80s. Griffith's first long-player for MCA was *Lone Star State of Mind* (1987)—from which "Trouble in the Fields," "From a Distance," "Ford Econoline," and the title track are derived. *Storms* (1987) was a rapidly issued follow-up and was likewise Griffith's breakout release. The tracks "Listen to the Radio," "I Don't Wanna Talk About Love," and her international hit "It's a Hard Life Wherever You Go" are all featured here. Unfortunately, a few of Griffith's signature pieces—such as "If Wishes Were Changes," "You Made This Love a Teardrop," and "Drive-In Movie and Dashboard Lights"—are not included. This is really in error, as they have become enthusiast favorites as well as concert staples. The uniformly brilliant *One Fair Summer Evening* is Griffith's first live album. The disc's track list includes many of her best-loved and most inspired performances, such as "Deadwood, South Dakota" and the achingly beautiful "More Than a Whisper"—neither of which are on this collection. However, the intimate "Love at the Five and Dime" and the uptempo toe-tapper "Spin on a Red Brick Floor" are featured on this anthology. By contrast, almost half of her next disc, *Little Love Affairs*, is here, including deep cuts such as "Sweet Dreams Will Come," "I Knew Love" and the better-known "Outbound Plane," "I Wish It Would Rain," and "Gulf Coast Highway." As there are two domestic best-of discs—*MCA Years: A Retrospective* and *From a Distance: The Very Best of Nanci Griffith*—that practically double this collection's track list and running time, it is difficult to recommend this title more on what is excluded, rather than what is included. *—Lindsay Planer*

Clock Without Hands / Jul. 31, 2001 / Elektra ♦♦♦

Clock Without Hands is Nanci Griffith's first recording of original material since 1997's *Blue Roses From the Moon*, leading to high expectations by fans and critics. These expectations, however, are also tinged by the disappointment—by many—of 1999's *The Dust Bowl Symphony*, a pseudo-best-of backed by an orchestra's strings. *Clock Without Hands*' catchy title track, propelled forward by steady percussion and insistent acoustic guitar, seems, on the surface, to get things off to a good start. But something isn't quite right. The production is a bit too bright and the lyric's metaphor is overextended. "Traveling Through This Part of You," the second cut, sends out other mixed signals: the production, with background strings, varies greatly from the first track. In fact, the changing production from track to track reminds one of a greatest-hits package. This song, along with "Roses on the 4th of July," also attempts to come to grips with the sacrifices that Vietnam War veterans made for their country. While this impulse is admirable, lines like "He still sends her roses on the Fourth of July," combining love with patriotic sacrifice, come across as cloying. Two other tunes should be mentioned. On "Shaking Out the Snow" Griffith delivers an agonized vocal, and one's response to it—that she overreaches or perfectly captures the mood—will depend on whether one buys the tortured lyric. The album ends with a cover of—don't even try to guess—"In the Wee Small Hours," complete with a syrupy string arrangement, once again recalling *The Dust Bowl Symphonies*. There are a number of things to like about *Clock Without Hands*, and the album will undoubtedly grow on listeners, but the album lacks the consistency of even a less than great album like *Flyer*. Fans will definitely want to pay the ticket for admission to find out what Griffith's been up to lately; the unfamiliar, few though they be, should turn to older titles like *Once in a Very Blue Moon* and *Last of the True Believers*. *—Ronnie D. Lankford Jr.*

From a Distance: The Very Best of Nanci Griffith / Jun. 25, 2002 / MCA ♦♦♦♦♦

MCA Nashville's 2002 release *From a Distance: The Very Best of Nanci Griffith* is a 22-track collection that covers the singer/songwriter's popular—and arguably creative—peak at MCA Records during the late '80s and early '90s. During this time she released five albums, each getting ample space on this collection. Since it concentrates just on MCA tracks, the four songs from her early records on Philo—"Once in a Very Blue Moon," "Lookin' for the Time (Workin' Girl)," "Love at the Five and Dime," and "The Wing and the Wheel"—are all live versions, cut during her time at MCA, but they're all good renditions, and they help make this a nice summary of Griffith's '80s peak. *—Stephen Thomas Erlewine*

Winter Marquee / Sep. 24, 2002 / Rounder ♦♦♦

Artistically speaking, Nanci Griffith has been in somewhat of a funk since 1998's *Other Voices, Too. The Dust Bowl Symphony* (1999) offered a syrupy greatest-hits package and 2001's *Clock Without Hands*, her first new material in several years, seemed both overproduced and overwrought. To further muddy the picture, Rounder released three early Griffith albums in 2002, reminding listeners how well she could write. Also released by Rounder, the live *Winter Marquee* is the first new album Griffith has released on the label since the mid-'80s. Following the reissues, it seems like something of a homecoming. The straightforward, hour-long set is made up of old favorites, a couple recent pieces, and a few covers. Accompanied by a country-folk band, Griffith's vocals take center stage to offer fine versions of "I'm Not Drivin' These Wheels" and "The Flyer." She's in great voice, and one of the pleasures of her music has always been the way she lovingly lingers over phrases for emphasis. She's joined by a couple of special guests, including Emmylou Harris on "Good Night, New York" and Tom Russell on "What's that I Hear" and "White Freight Liner." The set is also strengthened by the inclusion of less-frequently covered pieces like "There's a Light Beyond These Woods." While *Winter Marquee* may lack the spark of an early album like *Once in a Very Blue Moon*, fans will enjoy this live set. *—Ronnie D. Lankford Jr.*

Complete MCA Studio Recordings / Jun. 17, 2003 / MCA ♦♦♦♦♦

The standard line on Nanci Griffith's five-year sojourn at MCA Records is that Griffith, a Texas-born singer/songwriter, earned a major-label Nashville contract after four independent folkie releases on the basis of Kathy Mattea's Top Ten country recording of her song "Love at the Five and Dime," at a time when country music seemed more open to new sounds and MCA's Tony Brown was also signing such mavericks as Steve Earle and Lyle Lovett. But after two albums, *Lone Star State of Mind* (1987) and *Little Love Affairs* (1988), met resistance, failing to produce a major country hit, Griffith was transferred to the label's pop division, where *Storms* (1989) showed promise but *Late Night Grande Hotel* (1991) turned out to be too much of a pop move and turned off her existing fan base without attracting a new one. Then MCA dropped her. After a sojourn at Elektra Records, Griffith returned to indie status with Rounder in 2002, which oddly landed her back at MCA, since the major had a distribution deal with Rounder. MCA has also reissued Griffith's early albums, which gives the label a considerable stake in her catalog. So, there is a full-priced one-disc compilation of her actual MCA recordings (*From a Distance: The Very Best of Nanci Griffith*), a discount-priced *Millennium Collection* best-of, and now this two-disc package combining all four MCA albums with a few rarities. And when you listen to it from beginning to end, the standard line no longer seems to hold. The first two albums are no more country than Griffith's early "folk" albums, and the last two are not so "pop." The distinctions have more to do with production approaches, which pale before the dominant aspects of the music—Griffith's sweet and sour voice with its distinctive twang and the terrific songs. Maybe there was something to the notion that Griffith, who delighted in showing listeners what novel she was reading on her album covers, was a bit too erudite for a Nashville thrush, but the result is a set of songs, written by her and some well-chosen others, that standup well a decade later and are likely to sound just as good many decades hence. *—William Ruhlmann*

David Grisman

b. 1945, Hackensack, NJ

Mandolin, Leader / Bluegrass, Progressive Bluegrass

David Grisman is normally associated with the bluegrass wing of country music, but his music owes almost as much to jazz as it does to traditional American folk influences. Because he couldn't think of what to call his unique, highly intricate, harmonically advanced hybrid of acoustic bluegrass, folk, and jazz without leaning toward one idiom or another, he offhandedly decided to call it "dawg music"—a name which, curiously enough, has stuck. A brilliant mandolinist, with roots deep in the Quintet of the Hot Club of France, Grisman's jazz sensibilities were strong enough to attract the admiration of the HCQ's Stephane Grappelli, who has toured and recorded with Grisman on occasion. Grisman was already playing the piano, saxophone, and mandolin by the time he was a teenager, taking up the latter at age 16. While attending New York University in 1963, he began playing with the Even Dozen Jug Band, which at one time included Maria Muldaur and John Sebastian.

In 1966, bluegrass bandleader Red Allen invited Grisman to join his Kentuckians, and the following year Grisman joined Peter Rowan in the progressive-minded Earth Opera, which blended folk, country, rock, pop, and jazz. After two albums, he moved to San Francisco and hooked up with Jerry Garcia, playing on the Grateful Dead's classic *American Beauty*. He went on to play in Garcia's bluegrass side project, Old & In the Way, along with Peter Rowan, who also re-teamed with him in the loose all-star group Muleskinner. In 1974, Grisman co-founded the Great American String Band with Muleskinner fiddler Richard Greene, which first allowed him to explore the lengthy instrumental improvisations that would become his trademark.

Greene didn't stick around for too long, and in 1976 Grisman assembled a new group dubbed the David Grisman Quintet, which featured guitarist Tony Rice, fiddler Darol Anger, bassist Joe Carroll, and mandolinist/bassist Todd Phillips. The Quintet's self-titled debut was released in 1977 on Kaleidoscope, and proved a seminal influence on the so-called "newgrass" or "new acoustic" movements, thanks to its progressive, jazz-fueled harmonies and improvisations. The follow-up, 1979's *Hot Dawg*, was Grisman's breakthrough album; it was released on A&M's jazz imprint, Horizon, and featured guest work by jazz violin legend Stephane Grappelli. By this time, there was already personnel turnover in the Quintet; mandolinist Mike Marshall joined up, and by the time Grisman moved to Warner and recorded *Mondo Mando* in 1981, bassist Rob Wasserman and violinist Mark O'Connor joined Rice, Anger, and Marshall. In all, Grisman recorded four albums for Warner over 1980-1983; 1982's *Dawg Jazz/Dawg Grass* was another notable outing with Grappelli that, true to its title, split its repertoire between swing and bluegrass.

By 1984, the original "dawg music" lineup had largely broken up, with most of the members moving on to productive solo and/or collaborative projects (Anger notably joined the Turtle Island String Quartet). Grisman played on a number of sessions in the meantime, including with jazz-minded banjo virtuoso Béla Fleck, who claimed Grisman as a major influence. In 1985, Grisman organized a new group with seasoned jazz musicians: bassist Jim Kerwin, guitarist Dimitri Vandellos, and drummer George Marsh, who backed him on a 1987 duet album with jazz violinist Svend Asmussen, *Svingin' With Svend*. The more traditional bluegrass outing *Home Is Where the Heart Is* followed in 1988, before Grisman formed his own Acoustic Disc label in 1990 and got much more prolific.

A steady stream of releases appeared on Acoustic Disc during the first half of the '90s, starting with *Dawg '90*, which debuted a new core group that included Kerwin, fiddler/drummer Joe Craven, and flutist Matt Eakle, as well as returning alum Mark O'Connor, guitarist John Carlini, and fiddler Matt Glaser. Other notable releases included a 1991 reteaming with Jerry Garcia and two albums of *Tone Poems* (i.e., duets with Tony Rice and Martin Taylor, respectively). Argentinean guitarist Enrique Coria joined the lineup of Grisman, Kerwin, Craven, and Eakle for 1995's Latin-flavored *Dawganova*. Grisman entered another productive period in 1999, issuing several widely varied projects, and reconvened that quintet for 2002's *Dawgnation*. *—Richard S. Ginell & Steve Hue*

David Grisman Quintet / 1977 / Rhino ♦♦♦
The David Grisman Quintet's eponymous debut was a stunning achievement, capturing a pivotal point in newgrass history. It was a record that opened up new rhythmic textures and instrumental textures, specifically new, jazzier ways to solo. Grisman—who wrote the majority of the compositions—arranged each number as a way for his quintet to shine instrumentally, as a way for each musician to demonstrate their innovative skills. It's not traditional bluegrass—these instrumental recordings draw as equally from folk, rock, and country as they do from bluegrass—but it was a thrilling new variation on the form that broke down countless doors for the genre. *—Thom Owens*

Hot Dawg / 1979 / A&M ♦♦♦♦♦

Early Dawg / 1980 / Sugar Hill ♦♦♦

Quintet '80 / 1980 / Warner Bros. ♦♦
Throughout his career, mandolinist David Grisman has performed music that crosses between many boundaries, from "new acoustic" folk to bluegrass and swing-oriented jazz. This set features Grisman's string group (which also includes violinist Darol Anger, Mike Marshall on mandolin, guitar and violin, Mark O'Connor on violin and guitar, and bassist Rob Wasserman) playing six of Grisman's diverse originals, an obscure tune, and a brief rendition of John Coltrane's "Naima." The music is excellent, but Grisman's more jazz-oriented projects would be in the future. *—Scott Yanow*

Mondo Mando / Jul. 7, 1981-Jul. 16, 1981 / Warner Bros. ♦♦♦♦♦
David Grisman's desire to break or extend the boundaries of string music, folk, and bluegrass resulted in recordings that are also of interest to jazz listeners. The mandolinist performs seven colorful originals (including "Dawg Funk"), plus Django Reinhardt's lesser-known "Anouman" with various string players, including Mike Marshall on mandolin, violinists Darol Anger and Mark O'Connor, guitarist Tony Rice, and bassist Rob Wasserman; the Kronos String Quartet helps out on "Mando Mando." Unpredictable and fairly unique music. *—Scott Yanow*

Dawg Jazz/Dawg Grass / 1982 / Warner Bros. ♦♦♦♦♦
After several projects that hinted at his interest in jazz, David Grisman split this album between swing and bluegrass. The four jazz numbers include a big-band outing on "Dawg Jazz," and a guest appearance by violinist Stephane Grappelli on "Steppin' With Stephane," an appearance by violinist Darol Anger on "Fumblebee," and a version of "In a Sentimental Mood" with both Grappelli and Anger. The flip side of the LP (not yet issued on CD) finds Grisman's string group, Mike Marshall, Tony Rice, Rob Wasserman plus guest banjoist Earl Scruggs, stretching the boundaries of the bluegrass idiom on tunes such as "Swamp Dawg," "Dawggy Mountain Breakdown," and "Happy Birthday, Bill Monroe." A diverse and continually interesting set. *—Scott Yanow*

Here Today / 1982 / Rounder ♦♦
When this album was released in 1982, a number of interesting things were happening or were about to happen to the core members of Here Today. Mandolinist David Grisman had already defined his own style of bluegrass-inflected acoustic jazz that he had dubbed Dawg Music (after his own nickname). He was also on the verge of releasing several increasingly experimental albums. Guitarist and singer Vince Gill had not yet become one of the most popular traditional country singers in the business, but he was about to. Banjoist Herb Pedersen was soon to help found the commercially successful Desert Rose Band with former Byrd Chris Hillman. In short, this album was something of a last fling with traditional bluegrass for all three. They play and sing as if they know this, covering all the bases: vocal and instrumental barnburners ("I'll Love Nobody but You," "Foggy Mountain Chimes"), lovelorn country weepers ("The Children Are Crying," "Lonesome River"), and gospel ("Going Up Home to Live in Green Pastures"). Every song is a chestnut, and of all the members only Vince Gill has a singing voice really worth hearing, but the raw energy and instrumental prowess each musician brings to the music makes this album a genuine delight from beginning to end. *—Rick Anderson*

David Grisman's Acoustic Christmas / 1983 / Rounder ♦♦♦♦
Sticking to traditional Christmas songs, mandolinist David Grisman and his impressive string group, plus a few guests (including recorder players on two brief songs and banjoist Béla Fleck), alternate swinging renditions of familiar melodies with ballads. Highlights include "Santa Claus Is Coming to Town," "God Rest Ye Merry Gentlemen," and "Winter Wonderland." *—Scott Yanow*

Mandolin Abstractions / 1983 / Rounder ♦♦♦
Despite the musicianship and some colorful moments, this duo set by mandolinists David Grisman and Andy Statman (essentially melodic free improvisations) misses a rhythm section. The song titles (which include "Two White Boys Watching James Brown at the Apollo," "Journey to the Center of Twang" and the two-part "March of the Mandolas") are more colorful than the music, and although not without interest, this is one of David Grisman's least memorable recordings. *—Scott Yanow*

Acousticity / Jun. 5, 1984-Jun. 7, 1984 / Zebra ♦♦
By 1984, David Grisman's "Dawg Jazz" concept was at its prime. Grisman's string group (comprised of the leader's mandolin, violinist Jim Buchanan, guitarist Jon Sholle and bassist Rob Wasserman, plus guest drummer Hal Blaine) was flexible enough to play anything from bluegrass and folk music to swing; the latter is emphasized on this spirited set during such numbers as "Acousticity," "Blue Sky Bop," "Dawgalypso," and "Tango for Django." Recommended. *—Scott Yanow*

Svingin' With Svend / Nov. 5, 1986-May 21, 1987 / Zebra ♦♦♦♦♦
Despite his popularity, mandolinist David Grisman has made relatively few recordings since this CD. Matched with the great veteran swing violinist Svend Asmussen, Grisman holds his own on one of his most jazz-oriented dates. With guitarist Dimitri Vandellos, bassist James Kerwin and drummer George Marsh completing the quintet, Grisman and Asmussen jam on the title cut, two of the violinist's originals, "It Don't Mean a Thing," "Jitterbug Waltz," Milt Jackson's "The Spirit Feel," and a pair of Django Reinhardt-Stephane Grappelli tunes. Highly recommended. *—Scott Yanow*

Home Is Where the Heart Is / 1988 / Rounder ♦♦♦
A more traditional country and bluegrass album than his "dawg" sessions, Rounder issued this Grisman session in 1988. He's playing with J.D. Crowe, Ricky Skaggs, and Doc Watson, among others. There's little jazz here, but there are some superb bluegrass, country, and folk selections, plus marvelous playing. *—Ron Wynn*

● **Dawg '90** / 1990 / Acoustic Disc ♦♦♦♦♦
This CD marked the beginning of mandolin master David Grisman's own label, giving him the complete freedom he had sought so long to record as he wished. His continuously fascinating blend of elements of jazz, gypsy music, and bluegrass with additional influences help all ten compositions remain fresh after numerous hearings. The campy "Learned Pigs" and the delightful "Hot Club Swing" (with the obvious flavor of Django Reinhardt & Stephane Grappelli) are among the many strong tracks. The supporting cast includes guitarist John Carlini, fiddlers Mark O'Connor and Matt Glaser, and a trio of incredible musicians who continued to make a number of great recordings with Grisman after this gem: flutist Matt Eakle, bassist Jim Kerwin, and the unbelievably talented Joe Craven, who is not only the perfect percussionist for Grisman's "Dawg" music, but is also an outstanding fiddler as well. Anyone who enjoys masterful music should forget about trying to pigeonhole Grisman into any preconceived category and just go out and buy this incredible release. *—Ken Dryden*

Garcia/Grisman / 1991 / ♦♦♦♦♦

Dawgwood / 1993 / Acoustic Disc ♦♦♦

David Grisman Rounder Compact Disc / 1993 / Rounder ♦♦♦♦
David Grisman is primarily known as a (perhaps even *the*) pioneer integrator of jazz into the prog-bluegrass/newgrass/whatever-you-call-it ("Dawg Music" to Grisman) branch of the bluegrass family tree. And with a number of other suspect jazz dabblers (fiddler Vassar Clements, guitarist Tony Rice, and banjo picker Tony Trischka, for instance) on hand, one might expect *The Rounder Compact Disc* (originally released as *The Rounder Record*) to be a Grappelli-sounding crossbreed experiment in line with Grisman's longstanding quintet. Yet, despite some string-slingin', fancy-licked solos, *The Rounder Compact Disc* is really a true blue bluegrass record. Why, this record has enough gospel harmonies, Bill Monroe songs, stories of money lost on spend-thriftin' women, string sawin', and other neat-sounding contractions to keep even your most die-hard hillbilly warm as a mug of Grandpappy's moonshine on a cold Kentucky night. The tricky thing, the "how'd he do that?" part, is that in addition to (in spite of?) it's unabashed down-home country feel, this album is anything but traditional. Instrumentals like "Waiting on Vassar," "Op. 38," and "Boston Boy" integrate a complex network of orchestral voicings, solos, and interactive group play, and throughout the album solos by hotshots like Clements, Rice,

Jerry Douglas, and Grisman himself betray more than a passing interest in other styles of improvisation. In the coming years, the experimental wings of bluegrass would begin to incorporate electric instruments and more overtly bear the influence of jazz and rock. But *The Rounder Compact Disc* is some of the earliest evidence that bluegrass can be progressive without sacrificing any of its institutional twang. —*John Uhl*

Common Chord / 1993 / Cymekob ✦✦✦✦
One hears so many different musical influences within David Grisman's self-described "dawg" music that it wasn't surprising that he joined a number of excellent musicians from the fields of classical, bluegrass, rock, and jazz for this somewhat obscure date recorded for the tiny (and likely, now defunct) Cymekob. The music within this disc includes traditional American songs, country, and Texas swing. Classical violinist Daniel Kobialka (at the time of recording principal second violinist with the San Francisco Symphony) is as much at home with this music as former Grisman fiddler Mark O'Connor (who is not present on these sessions). The guests include Grisman's longtime bassist, Jim Kerwin, and guitarist Enrique Coria, son Monroe Grisman on guitar, bassist Edgar Meyer, banjo player Tony Trischka, and Jerry Garcia, to name just a few. The touching interpretation of Benny Thomasson's "Midnight on the Water" and traditional favorites like "Barbara Allen" and "Wayfaring Stranger" are just a few of the many high points of this CD. —*Ken Dryden*

Tone Poems / 1994 / Acoustic Disc ✦✦✦✦✦
While mandolin master David Grisman and the equally talented guitarist Tony Rice may be better known in the world of bluegrass, jazz fans need to check out this excellent collection of mandolin/guitar duets, performed with different vintage instruments on each track. The improvising by both men is never less than brilliant, transforming traditional folk tunes like "Grandfather's Clock" and "I Am a Pilgrim," plus the unlikely "O Sole Mio," into masterpieces. The lone track that's very familiar to jazz listeners is "Swing '42," played very convincingly by two men who are well versed in jazz even if they don't play it exclusively. —*Ken Dryden*

Dawganova / 1995 / Acoustic Disc ✦✦✦
On *Dawganova*, Grisman and his quintet add Latin and bossa nova rhythms and melodies to their distinctive blend of bluegrass, folk, and jazz; the results are energetic, and usually quite successful. —*Stephen Thomas Erlewine*

Tone Poems 2 / Oct. 31, 1995 / Acoustic Disc ✦✦✦✦✦
David Grisman doesn't stick exclusively to mandolin on this top-notch duo date with guitarist Martin Taylor, playing mandola, mandocello, tenor guitar, and guitar as well. As on this album's predecessor, the two artists play a different vintage instrument on each track, though the music this time is much more familiar to jazz fans. The interpretations of such classics as "Swanee," "Anything Goes," "Blue Moon," and "Over the Rainbow" are consistently both stunning and fresh. The gems among the jazz compositions include Django Reinhardt's "Tears" and a *tour de force* arrangement of Chick Corea's "Crystal Silence." Two surprising tracks are the usually trite "Mairzy Doats" (an irritating song that was a huge hit in the '40s) and the very snappy take of the often tedious "Besame Mucho"; when musicians the caliber of Grisman and Taylor can make something out of unpromising songs like these, it demonstrates how gifted they are. Highly recommended. —*Ken Dryden*

DGQ-20 / 1996 / Acoustic Disc ✦✦✦✦
Back in 1976, mandolinist David Grisman was one of the pioneers of what would come to be called "new acoustic music," a groovy, swinging fusion of bluegrass, hot jazz, and pop played primarily by young virtuosos from California. It was a scene that gave rise to such giants as Tony Rice, Béla Fleck, Sam Bush, and Mark O'Connor, and brought established artists like fiddler Vassar Clements and French jazz violinist Stephane Grappelli to new prominence. But David Grisman's mandolin was the signature sound of the genre, and still is—that's him you hear picking away between NPR news segments, and you've heard him in movie soundtracks and on hundreds of other people's records over the last twenty years. Of all the musicians who emerged from the new acoustic music scene, only Grisman had a subgenre named after him: "Dawg Music." This three-disc set brings together live recordings, alternate takes, and previously unreleased compositions from Grisman's tape vault. It charts the changes in his quintet from the earliest days, when it nurtured the fiery talents of the young guitarist Tony Rice and fiddler Darol Anger, to its modern incarnation, which features a percussionist and flutist. Some of the titles—"Swing '39," "Ricochet," "Rattlesnake"—will be familiar to new acoustic music aficionados, as will Grisman's penchant for punning titles based on his nickname ("Dawgma," "Dawggy Mountain Breakdown"). Others are more obscure, some of them deservedly so, as in the case of "Shasta Bull," an ill-conceived soda jingle. But most of these 39 tracks are delightful; among them are the two numbers the DGQ performed with Stephane Grappelli on the *Tonight Show* in 1979, a beautiful three-mandolin arrangement of "Ricochet," and a live version of "Mondo Mando" that features Jethro Burns and the young Kronos Quartet. It is highly recommended. —*Rick Anderson*

Retrograss / Sep. 21, 1999 / Acoustic Disc ✦✦✦✦
On the album cover, *Retrograss* is defined as "music shifted back in time," a direction that—while not impossible to conceive—is mildly shocking considering David Grisman's relentlessly progressive approach toward traditional styles. Alas, democracy still rules at Dawg Studios, and with John Hartford and Mike Seeger signing on, it comes as no surprise that this collection is a step back in time—old time, that is. The album features nearly one hour of 20th century classics "retrograssed" to achieve a rustic, jug band feel. From the opening banjo rolls of "My Walking Shoes," it's pretty obvious what you're getting into, and there are no quantum leaps thematically, tonally, or otherwise from that point on. However, *Retrograss* does explore a very fecund and diverse American musical fabric, which has threads of country, blues, bluegrass, folk, rock & roll, etc. Songs like

Dylan's "Maggie's Farm" or the Osborne Brothers' "Rocky Top" adapt quite naturally in this landscape, but Chuck Berry's "Maybelline" sounds like a '57 Chevy running on four cylinders. Simply stated, the bluegrass cuts that were born out of old time music—songs like "Airmail Special," "Jerusalem Ridge," and "Rocky Road Blues"—are the most appealing to the auditory senses. Oddly enough, Lennon & McCartney's vaudevillian "When I'm Sixty Four" is also a delightful moment. All in all, these live, in-studio recordings are mirthful, rocking chair adaptations of American music history. Seeger and Grisman's honeyed tenors conflict well with Hartford's quirky baritone. There are no breakneck solos, and the whole effort achieves more than the sum of its parts—which was enough to draw a 2000 Grammy nomination in the Traditional Folk Album category. —*Brian Kelly*

Dawg Duos / Oct. 19, 1999 / Acoustic Disc ✦✦✦
With *Dawg Duos*, David Grisman presents an album of duos with a variety of acclaimed musicians, including Indian classical percussionist Zakir Hussain, the New Lost City Ramblers' Mike Seeger, and Edgar Meyer and Béla Fleck, genre-crossers who are nonetheless well-known to modern bluegrass fans. These accomplished musicians bring complex techniques and impressive virtuosity, and turn it all into enjoyable bluegrass music with a simple, relaxed feel. The music is pretty, in much the same way that Bill Frisell's *Good Dog, Happy Man* is. There are tunes that pour world music into the bluegrass vocabulary, such as "New Deli Duo," a tune Grisman describes as the closest he'll probably come to playing a raga; the duo with Bob Brozman, "Trinidadian Rag"; and the somewhat gypsy feel and klezmer moments in "Clinch Mountain Windmills," a piece melding Ralph Stanley's "Clinch Mountain Backstep" and Michel Legrand's "Windmills of Your Mind" (from *The Thomas Crown Affair*). There are moments of liteness—such as with the mall-music-like quietude of Grisman's duo with Denny Zeitlin—but too few to detract from the fact that this is an album modern bluegrass fans will find well worth having. Overall, it's an airy, light-pickin' album with a peaceful center. —*Joslyn Layne*

Tone Poems 3: The Sounds of the Great Slide & Resophonic Instruments / Aug. 22, 2000 / Acoustic Disc ✦✦✦✦
Tone Poems 3 follows in the tradition of David Grisman's two previous *Tone Poems* albums, featuring vintage instruments and the musical styles for which they were designed. As this project was designed to show off slide and resophonic instruments, Grisman doesn't stick to just the mandolin. In addition to various steel and slide mandolins, the session leader plays tenor guitar and guitar with Mike Auldridge and Bob Brozman, two of the resophonic guitar's most eminent players. A different set of antique instruments is used for each song, and the vintage of the instruments progresses in roughly chronological order. The type of music, then, also develops from track to track. Initially, the album features Hawaiian-style songs like "Moonlight Bay" or once popular Tin Pan Alley tunes like "Whispering" that may have been played in a Hawaiian manner in the '20s. But as the trio starts working with post-Depression era instruments, songs such as "Limehouse Blues" and "Just Joshin'" show the influence of the blues and country genres that eventually began to employ steel-slide sounds. By the end of the record, the band plays some quite modern material, like the original "New Steal," a dirty, blues-heavy stomp. Indeed, one of the greatest perks of these *Tone Poems* sets is their educational value, and, like the others, this one comes with a 40-plus page booklet featuring descriptions and color photos of the instruments played on each song. Some of the album's best moments spring from the group's historical re-creations. The standard "Crazy Rhythm," for instance, is expanded into a sort of duet suite with quirky, out-of-time intros by Brozman on ukulele and Grisman on mandolin (not to mention some blistering solo work). Yet, this album isn't just a history project; it's sprinkled with several original compositions, including two gritty blues numbers, that are at least as appealing as the older tunes and raise hopes that these three masters will record together again. —*John Uhl*

New River / Jun. 26, 2001 / Acoustic Disc ✦✦✦✦
Many of the projects chosen for David Grisman's Acoustic Disc label are beautifully simple. On *New River* mandolinist Grisman and jazz pianist Denny Zeitlin have arrived at the studio with no more than their instruments, four self-penned pieces each, and the desire to cut an album of intimate duets. They have also co-authored a ninth tune titled "DG/DZ Blues," a piece that they successfully extend for over ten minutes, giving the listener an inkling of their daring on this album. The loose structure of "Brazilian Street Dance," followed by the progressive jazzgrass of "Dawg Funk," also notifies the listener that this will be a stylistically varied set. It should be mentioned that the piano and mandolin, two instruments seldom paired, work quite nicely here. The overall approach is fairly abstract, creating music that is more thoughtful than emotive. This tendency is perhaps most evident on Zeitlin's compositions like "Moving Parts" and the title track. Grisman also shows a knack for writing expansive tunes with "Waltz for Gigi," a piece that may remind some listeners of modal jazz. Its elastic structure provides an evocative mesh for both players to improvise against. The success of this project derives from the players' ability to understand one another and offer engaging support. This intuitive approach also synthesizes the variety of styles—Latin, swing, and modern—to give the album an integrated unity. Since there isn't a category for good acoustic music, it's difficult to know where this album will be shelved at the local record store. It will, nonetheless, be worth tracking down. *New River* is a lovely undertaking, fresh and in a category by itself. —*Ronnie D. Lankford Jr.*

Traversata / Nov. 6, 2001 / Acoustic Disc ✦✦✦✦
David Grisman has a habit of bringing likeminded musicians into his Acoustic Disc studio and recording eclectic, intelligent music. While noted for his skilled mandolin playing, he has also shown an interest in musical history. Like the *Tone Poems* series, *Traversata* travels into the past to re-introduce lost treasures. This time he's joined by fellow mandolinist Carlo Aonzo and guitarist Beppe Gambetta for 15 Italian-American instrumentals from the early 20th century. Also similar to the *Tone Poems* series, a

straightforward mix produces a clean sound and makes it easy to keep tabs on the players. There's a bouncy version of Nick Lucas' "Pickin' the Guitar" that reminds one of a tasty tune by Norman Blake or Doc Watson. Grisman and Aonzo quietly complement one another on the melancholy "Study for Two Mandolins," while Gambetta offers nice lead work on Eddie Lang's "April Kisses." *Traversata* flows with ease from track to track, creating a rich tapestry of acoustic music. Detailed liner notes give information on musicians, composers, and the music itself. *Traversata* was a term used by turn-of-the-century Italians to describe their journey to the U.S., and this album represents a similar musical journey shared by these three artists. This is a lovely recording, respectful of its source material and inspiring in its execution. *—Ronnie D. Lankford Jr.*

Dawgnation / Jun. 25, 2002 / Acoustic Disc ✦✦✦
David Grisman returns in fine, if standard, form on *Dawgnation*, the first record of new material produced by his David Grisman Quintet since 1995's *Dawganova*. The material on *Dawgnation* doesn't break any new ground particularly, though Grisman's so-called "dawg" music—a mix of bluegrass, hot jazz, Latin grooves, klezmer, and world rhythms—can still be exhilarating, especially if one has never heard it before. The band manages to keep the energy high and the music fresh-sounding, making this as fine a starting point into the quintet as any. Each of the tracks is a tribute to one of Grisman's extended musical family—such as "Slade" (for the late Charles Sawtelle), "Why Did the Mouse Marry the Elephant?" (for bassist Edgar Meyer), and the title track for "Spudboy" (aka Jerry Garcia). Still, the pastoral mix of Matt Eakle's flute, Enrique Coria's flamenco jazz guitar, and Joe Craven's fiddle and percussion with Grisman's mandolin melodies doesn't break any new boundaries. It is calming, pretty, well-executed music that is unlikely to offend anyone, but is ultimately (perhaps) slightly too lite to be considered ballsy and a touch too syncopated and strange to find acceptance among any mainstream audience. *—Jesse Jarnow*

Life of Sorrow / 2003 / Acoustic Disc ✦✦✦
David Grisman has never denied his roots in bluegrass, as it has always been an important ingredient in his self-described "Dawg Music." On this compilation, recorded over a three-decade stretch, the mandolin master sticks exclusively to bluegrass as he collaborates with a host of friends and influences interpreting various sorrow-laden melodies that have became staples within the genre. Every track packs an emotional punch, especially the intimate duets ("Doin' My Time" with the late John Hartford on banjo and vocals, "When You and I Were Young, Maggie" with guitarist/singer Mac Wiseman, "Tragic Romance" with banjo player Alan O'Bryant singing a duet with Grisman, and guitarist/singer Del McCoury performing the old chestnut "Tennessee Waltz"). It's also hard to overlook the contributions of veteran singer Ralph Stanley (belatedly discovered by many music fans following the revival of his early hit, "Man of Constant Sorrow," sung by Dan Tyminski for the soundtrack to the blockbuster movie *O, Brother Where Art Thou?*), whose still potent tenor vocal accompanies Grisman's vocal in a much more subdued interpretation of this landmark piece composed by his late brother, Carter Stanley. Perhaps the most unusual selection is "Pretty Saro," a 1969 recording by guitarist and singer John Nagy of an old English folk tune, backed by his orchestrations and Grisman's mandolin. As usual, Grisman sneaks in a bonus hidden track (the Carter Family's "Keep on the Sunny Side of Life," performed with Wiseman) following the last selection. Grisman's detailed liner notes, the inclusion of complete lyrics for every song and the treasure trove of photographs also help to make this an essential purchase for every bluegrass fan. *—Ken Dryden*

Sarah Ogan Gunning

b. Jun. 28, 1910, **d.** Oct. 14, 1983
Vocals / Political Folk, Folksongs, Appalachian Folk, Traditional Folk, Old-Timey
Sarah Ogan Gunning of the singing Gunning clan was the tenth of 11 children in a dirt-poor Kentucky mining family. Her father, Jim Garland, joined the Knights of Labor, who became the United Mine Workers of America in 1884. At that time, conditions for miners were atrocious, with the average worker bringing home a dollar and 44 cents for a ten-hour day. Garland became an outspoken representative for the miners, pressuring the mine-owners into coughing up a more decent wage. He was quickly blacklisted and the only way he could continue working was to go down into the mines under aliases. Much time passed before the plight of the Kentucky miners became a matter of national attention. In 1931, a group of Northerners called the Dreiser Committee came to Kentucky to investigate atrocities that had been committed against the miners. By this time, Sarah Garland and her sister, Molly (later known professionally as Aunt Molly Jackson), had literally brought their voices to the family struggle by singing at various events. Their songs often included lyrics of their own creation, or sometimes they would take an existing song and change the words to create a message about the labor struggle. These songs were a powerful tool for forging an emotional bond with crowds at labor rallies.

The members of the Dreiser Committee included authors John Dos Passos and Theodore Dreiser, who took the sisters back to New York City to help raise money for the miners' cause. By this time, Sarah Garland was already suffering from brown lung disease. She befriended folk artists such as Woody Guthrie, Pete Seeger, Lee Hays, and Burl Ives in New York City, and they would go on to record her songs, such as "I Hate the Capitalist System," "Dreadful Memories," "Let's Go Down on the Picket Line," "I Am Going to Organize," and "Babe of Mine." At the start of World War II, she moved with her husband to Vancouver, where she worked in the Kaiser shipyards. She returned to Kentucky for tuberculosis treatment, when a hole the size of a silver dollar was found in her lungs. In the years following these successful treatments she retired from performing, but was brought back into the public arena by folklorist Archie Green in the '60s, performing at several major folk festivals before fading out again. Her songs regularly turn up in documentaries or compilations focusing on the labor movement. *—Eugene Chadbourne*

The Silver Dagger / 1976 / Rounder ✦✦✦✦✦
Two sisters from a down and out Kentucky mining family, Aunt Molly Jackson and Sarah Ogan Gunning were each the subject of reissues and new recording projects in the '70s. This album was a new recording of Gunning, advanced in years but still the owner of a powerhouse voice, and also features some harmony vocals from her father Jim Garland, a lovely touch. It is kind of a retrospective look at many different types of songs and singing she recalled from her childhood and, for a record of a capella singing, the variety is tremendous. There is the tale of "Davy Crockett," almost side by side with the devastating "I Hate the Capitalist System," one of the best protest songs ever recorded. The enclosed booklet on her family's background and struggles is really superb, but could have used a few staples to keep it together. *—Eugene Chadbourne*

Hardrock Gunter (Sidney Louis Gunter Jr.)

b. Feb. 27, 1925, Birmingham, AL
Songwriter, Vocals / Rockabilly, Country Boogie, Rock & Roll
Though he doesn't get the same attention as other rock & roll pioneers, Hardrock Gunter was one of the earliest country boogie artists to start shifting the music into full-fledged rockabilly. A native of Birmingham, AL, he was born Sidney Louis Gunter Jr. in 1925, and earned his nickname when a car hood fell on his head with no noticeable effect, leading to the observation that it was as hard as a rock. An admirer of Hank Penny, Gunter formed his first band, the Hoot Owl Ramblers, at age 13, and also played talent shows under the name Goofy Sid. In 1939, he joined Happy Wilson's Golden River Boys, with whom he remained for several years; after Gunter and the other members served in World War II, they reorganized the band in 1946. Gunter began appearing on a local children's television show in 1949, and the following year he got a chance to record for the Bama label. His first release, 1950's "Birmingham Bounce," was tabbed by a small minority of critics as the first (or one of the first) rock & roll records, even prior to Jackie Brenston's "Rocket 88." It was covered by Red Foley for a hit, and recorded by the likes of Amos Milburn and Lionel Hampton as well.

Gunter signed with Foley's label, Decca, and his 1951 duet with Roberta Lee, "Sixty Minute Man," was one of the first country records to cross over to R&B audiences. He released several more singles on Decca through 1953, also working a couple of years as a DJ in Wheeling, WV. He went on to cut some material for MGM and Sun, the latter of which included some of his best-known singles—"Gonna Dance All Night" b/w "Fallen Angel" (1954) and "Juke Box Help Me Find My Baby" (1956). The latter song originally appeared on a smaller label, but was leased and re-edited by Sam Phillips without success. Gunter recorded for several other labels during the late '50s and early '60s, including King, Emperor, Island, Starday, and Seeco, without much commercial success. He quit the music business in 1964 to run an insurance agency, but occasionally performed into the 1980s. *—Steve Huey*

Boogie Woogie on a Saturday Night / 1984 / Charly ✦✦✦✦

● **I'll Give 'Em Rhythm** / Aug. 3, 1999 / Hydra ✦✦✦✦✦
I'll Give 'Em Rhythm is a 29-track German import containing mostly Decca and King sides from the 1950s plus a few other independent label and previously unreleased recordings. Many of the tracks were dubbed from vinyl so the sound quality isn't as good as it could be, but the music is excellent. Gunter's hillbilly boogies and novelties didn't land him on the charts, but he is respected for his talent and pioneering proto-rock (his "Birmingham Bounce," not included here, is sometimes said to be the first rock & roll song). This package is a perfect companion to the Hardrock Gunter anthology on England's Rollercoaster label; with *I'll Give 'Em Rhythm*'s generous program and thick photo- and text-packed booklet, it's a needed primer of rare recordings from a lesser-known but significant artist. *—Greg Adams*

Gonna Rock 'n' Roll, Gonna Dance All Night / Dec. 5, 2000 / Roller Coaster ✦✦✦
Hardrock Gunter played a brand of hillbilly boogie that was a definite precursor to rockabilly and rock & roll. He recorded quite extensively in the 1950s, jumping from straight country tunes to his own unique rhythmic experimentations. This 31-track collection brings together almost every tune Gunter recorded for a wide variety of labels, both big and small, ranging from his first and biggest hit, "Birmingham Bounce," to his sides for Sun like "Fallen Angel" and the title track, heard here in two versions. Also included is the Sun single issued as the Rhythm Rockers ("Fiddle Bop" and "Jukebox Help Me Find My Baby") and his various country novelties ("Dad Gave My Hog Away," "My Bucket's Been Fixed"), making this the most complete package on this unique and interesting artist. A chapter from Nick Tosches' book, *Unsung Heroes of Rock & Roll* truly come to life. *—Cub Koda*

Jack Guthrie

b. Nov. 13, 1915, Olive, OK, **d.** Jan. 15, 1948
Vocals / Traditional Country
If Jack Guthrie is remembered at all today, it is as the cousin of Woody Guthrie, but in his own lifetime, Jack was far more commercially successful than Woody ever was while he was alive. He was one of the most important and influential country singers of the mid-'40s, and only his early death from tuberculosis prevented his legacy from being better known to the generations since. Guthrie was born in Olive, OK, in 1915, the son of a blacksmith who also played the fiddle in his spare time. The family led a somewhat mobile existence in the area around Texas and Oklahoma, and Guthrie had little chance to put down deep roots. His main interests as a boy included roping and trick riding, at which he became very good. He also listened to his father's playing and the music of Jimmie Rodgers, and some sources indicate that he was taught guitar by Gene Autry in the years before Autry became a recording star.

The family had little to hold them in Oklahoma during the Dust Bowl era and eventually migrated to California, where they settled in the area around Sacramento. He performed in rodeos and was employed by the National Forest Service through the Works Progress Administration. In 1934, he married Ruth Henderson, and the two worked together for a time in an act together, in which he would use his skills with a bullwhip to snap cigarettes out of her mouth. By most accounts, the marriage was a lasting one, though not always happy, and the two spent a fair amount of time living apart from one another. Woody's arrival in California three years later gave the cousins the opportunity to team up. Their act was heard on radio during the summer of 1937, under the name *the Oklahoman and Woody Show*. It was a success in terms of listener response and fan mail, but it paid no money, and the boost it generated for their club performances wasn't sufficient to provide either man with a living. The partnership broke up when Jack took a job in construction to earn more money and Woody found a new partner, Maxine ("Lefty Lou") Crissman, although Jack continued to appear occasionally with the duo. By 1939, Woody had headed to New York, where he first hooked up with the organized Left and political singers like Pete Seeger, and began the main body of his musical career. Jack stayed in California and continued to play before live audiences in bars and other local venues whenever he could, and one of the songs that he picked up was a Woody original, "Oklahoma Hills." Jack made some changes and refinements in his cousin's song, effectively earning a co-authorship credit. At that time, California was populated by many thousands of transplanted Oklahomans, and Jack became well known for his version of "Oklahoma Hills."

Guthrie became a well-known figure in the clubs around Los Angeles, where his brand of dance music was extremely popular and his flamboyance made him a memorable figure—at rodeos, he was known for leaving the band and doing some trick riding during a set. By 1944, he was more than ready to begin recording. With the encouragement of Maxine Crissman's sister Mary Ruth, he approached Capitol Records, and she also put up the money for the demo record that he used to get in the door, "Oklahoma Hills." He recruited a band from among acquaintances, did the demo, and went to Capitol. In 1944, Capitol Records—which had only been founded four years earlier—had begun a new cycle of signing country and blues artists, which included Leadbelly and Merle Travis. Jack Guthrie was one of the new signings, in what turned out to be a seven-year contract. He made his Capitol recording debut in October of 1944 with "Oklahoma Hills," with a backing band called the Oklahomans, consisting of Porky Freedman (lead guitar), Red Murrell (rhythm guitar), Cliffie Stone (bass), and Billy Hughes (fiddle)—he cut the B-side "I'm Brandin My Darlin' With My Heart" and a cover of an Ernest Tubb number, "Careless Darlin'," at the same session on October 16, 1944. Nine days later, Guthrie had a second recording session that yielded four more songs, including his version of Jimmie Rodgers' "When the Cactus Is in Bloom," a number that highlighted Guthrie's yodeling ability. "Oklahoma Hills" was released early in 1945 and rose to number one on the country charts, spending six weeks in that spot.

Before the song was even released, however, Guthrie had been drafted and was serving in the Pacific, stationed as an entertainer in Special Services on Iwo Jima. He was unable to do anything about his record's success, and this led to decisions that would ultimately have tragic consequences. Desperate to return to the U.S. so he could resume recording, Guthrie signed up for an additional year's enlistment in Special Services in exchange to being sent stateside. He returned to the U.S. in the first days of 1946 and tried to resume his performing career while still in uniform. He was stationed at Fort Lewis, WA, began playing with Buck Ritchey & His K-6 Wranglers in Tacoma, and returned to Capitol on January 29, 1946, for his first recording sessions since October of 1944. His personal appearances were so popular that a publisher felt confident enough to issue a Guthrie songbook that proved very popular locally.

In early 1946, just as he was resuming his career, Guthrie's weight began dropping rapidly, and a civilian doctor diagnosed his problem as tuberculosis. He was immediately released from the army, and had he used this chance to convalesce, it is possible that Guthrie might have made a full recovery. Instead, never believing his ailment to be a serious case of the disease, he kept working, organizing a new band and going out of the road. And the irony was that he was on his way to stardom. "Oklahoma Hills" brought Guthrie to the attention of Ernest Tubb, who got Guthrie a gig on the *Grand Ole Opry* and toured with him for two weeks, during which they became good friends. Guthrie's band, which was later inherited by T. Texas Tyler, was a success, though by the time they were back in California in the spring of 1946, his health had begun to deteriorate further. Advised to lay off for a year and go into a sanitarium, he instead insisted on pushing himself to take advantage of the success he had found. Moreover, he never gave up the smoking or drinking that further taxed his system. Guthrie continued recording and performing every chance that he could, and he even turned up in the movie *Hollywood Barn Dance*, singing "Okie Boogie." He signed a contract that summer to do a movie with cowboy B-movie star Russell Hayden, but it never happened. By the spring of 1947, he weighed less than a hundred pounds, and that summer he entered a veterans hospital near Sacramento and was informed by the doctors that the prognosis was terminal.

This did nothing to slow him down. In fact, the result was the opposite—as all of Guthrie's records were selling and Capitol wanted every side that they could get out of him, he became a willing participant in this musical death march, seeing this as his best chance to leave a lasting legacy. Guthrie's attitude had always been that if he was going to die anyway, that he should make the most of the time he did have. Additionally, although it sounds grisly in retrospect, the dedication was justified. Even in the songs from Guthrie's later sessions, there is a compelling quality to the music. His easygoing manner, his way with a phrase, and his studio band's virtuosity leave the listener wanting to hear more. The play of the words and music are startling in their attractiveness, and there's hardly a weak number in his output, despite the conditions under which most of it was recorded.

Guthrie continued to record, despite being so weak that his wife had to set up a bed for him in the back of their car when he traveled anywhere. At his final sessions, he had to be transported in an ambulance, and he had to lie down and sleep between songs to regain what strength he still had. He finally amassed a body of more than 30 songs, in addition to radio transcription discs intended for broadcast. Guthrie lingered into the first weeks of 1948 and finally died in a sanitarium on January 15 of that year. Ironically, his records continued to sell for years after his death and remained in print, sometimes in redubbed form with extra instruments added. Meanwhile, Woody's reputation as an author of topical and political songs grew in the folk community; the folk music boom of the late '50s and early '60s and the rise of such figures as Bob Dylan, who freely traded on Woody's image and legacy in his early days, eventually eclipsed the memory and reputation of his cousin, at least in the popular culture.

In 1966, Capitol rather belatedly released an LP collection, *Jack Guthrie's Greatest Songs*. It helped keep Guthrie's legacy before the public, but it was Arlo Guthrie, Woody's son and Jack's nephew—and the first member of the Guthrie family since Jack to achieve mass popularity and sell large numbers of records to the public in his own musical prime—who played just as large a role, continuing to perform and record his uncle's music into the 1970s. *—Bruce Eder*

Jack Guthrie's Greatest Songs / 1966 / Capitol ♦♦♦♦

● **Oklahoma Hills** / 1991 / Bear Family ♦♦♦♦♦
This features 77 minutes of music, 29 of the songs that Jack Guthrie left behind, and damn if this isn't as good as it gets. Guthrie had an ear for good hooks, a memorable phrase, and a pleasing, twangy voice that recalled his one-time idol, Woody Guthrie, as well as his friend Ernest Tubb. The music here is among the finest country that Capitol recorded in the mid-'40s, and that's saying something, considering that the competition included Tex Ritter, Merle Travis, and Hank Thompson. "Oklahoma Hills" is really good, but there's better here, and even the little throwaway dance numbers like "Okie Boogie" are such fun that they bear repeated listening. Guthrie's music embraced country-folk and Western swing with equal aplomb, and virtually every word and note is memorable. A necessary part of any collection—and Bear Family's best single-CD release—as well as a reminder that the musical talent in the Guthrie family flowed equally rich through several branches. *—Bruce Eder*

Milk Cow Blues / May 8, 2001 / Bear Family ♦♦♦♦

When the World Has Turned You Down / May 8, 2001 / Bear Family ♦♦♦♦

Woody Guthrie

b. Jul. 14, 1912, Okemah, OK, **d.** Oct. 3, 1967, Queens, NY
Guitar, Harmonica, Vocals / Traditional Folk, Political Folk, Field Recordings
Woody Guthrie was the most important American folk music artist of the first half of the 20th century. Coming out of Oklahoma, Guthrie had firsthand knowledge of the dust-bowl diaspora chronicled in John Steinbeck's novel, *The Grapes of Wrath*. In fact, Guthrie wrote his own version of the story in a song called "Tom Joad." By the time he gained recognition in the '40s, Guthrie had written hundreds of songs, many of which remain folk standards to this day. When he was interviewed by Alan Lomax for the Library of Congress in March 1940, Guthrie punctuated his reminiscences by singing "So Long, It's Been Good to Know You," "Dust Bowl Blues," "Do-Re-Mi," "Pretty Boy Floyd," "I Ain't Got No Home," and other songs. He later wrote "Pastures of Plenty," "The Grand Coulee Dam," and his masterpiece, "This Land Is Your Land." He was also an author (*Bound for Glory*) and a newspaper columnist.

Guthrie made some recordings for RCA in 1940, but much of his work was issued on the small Folkways label. Meanwhile, in the late '40s and early '50s, versions of his songs became hits for such artists as the Weavers. By then, Guthrie himself was in physical decline, suffering from Huntington's chorea, a hereditary neurological disorder. But during his long illness, Guthrie's influence spread to the next generation, fostering the folk boom of the late '50s and early '60s. Not only is Bob Dylan unimaginable without him, but large segments of popular music are permanently affected by his concerns as a songwriter and his approach to the form. Guthrie also composed a body of children's music toward the end of his performing career in the early '50s, when he was raising a family with his wife Marjorie. The songs, many sung from a child's point of view, have been covered and performed extensively since. *—William Ruhlmann*

Nursery Days / 1958 / Smithsonian Folkways ♦♦♦♦♦
In *Songs to Grow On—Vol. 1 (Nursery Days)*, Guthrie effectively evokes the child's point of view with such simple, yet exciting songs as "Car Song" (with its chorus "Goin' for a ride in the car car") and "Put Your Finger in the Air." For ages 3-5. *—William Ruhlmann*

Woody Guthrie Sings Folk Songs / 1962 / Smithsonian Folkways ♦♦♦♦♦

☆ **Library of Congress Recordings, Vol. 1** / 1964 / Rounder ♦♦♦♦♦
Woody, the singer and storyteller, in his historic recordings from 1940 for Alan Lomax, explains the origins of many of his tunes including "Pretty Boy Floyd," "Goin' Down that Road Feelin' Bad," and "So Long it's Been Good to Know You." These are wonderfully relaxed sessions, just Woody and his guitar. *—Richard Meyer*

★ **Dust Bowl Ballads** / 1964 / Buddha ♦♦♦♦♦
Woody Guthrie's powerful, evocative, insightful narratives about the life and trials of Southwestern migrant workers battling the Dust Bowl were initially issued on two six-song albums in 1940. Later, the entire 14-song session was released on a 1964 album. It includes some of Guthrie's finest, most memorable prose, coupled with poignant vocals and sparse, effective harmonica accompaniment. The resiliency, spirit, and memories of both his early life and people he'd known are presented on such cuts as "I Ain't Got No Home," "Dust Pneumonia Blues," and "Dust Bowl Blues." Guthrie was a master storyteller, and his semi-autobiographical accounts remain among American music's most striking some 54 years after their original issue. The 2000 reissue CD on Buddha adds an alternate version of "Talking Dust Bowl Blues" and the original liner notes written by Guthrie himself. *—Ron Wynn*

Woody Guthrie Sings Folk Songs, Vol .2 / 1964 / Folkways ♦♦♦♦
The material this great folksinger recorded for the Folkways archive has since the time of its initial release been re-released in so many forms that it could almost have been scattered to the wind, probably appropriate for folk music if not so darn confusing. The '60s folk revival saw a series of Guthrie album releases, of which this one, known sometimes as "the green Guthrie album" was the second volume in one particular concept of a collection. Folk songs or not, Guthrie takes writing and publishing credit for all the titles, a very nice set of tunes indeed. Part of the fun is the accompaniment, if one can call it that, from two equally brilliant folk artists, the charismatic Cisco Houston, who perhaps

had a better singing voice than Guthrie, and the harmonica whiz Sonny Terry. This is one of the rare combinations of white folk and black blues artists, and it comes across extremely well. Highlights are the cowboy classic "Whoopee Ti Yi Yo, Get Along Little Doggies" and the lyrical "Danville Girl." This release came originally with a pamphlet of lyrics and music. —*Eugene Chadbourne*

The Early Years / 1964 / Legacy/Columbia ✦✦✦✦✦

The Early Years is one of the more lasting of Guthrie's compilations, being released for the first time in 1964 and re-released on a number of occasions. And though the title *The Early Years* is not totally correct, the songs offered give a good overview over Guthrie's early production, even if the space offered on a double album (or a CD) of course isn't enough. Original protest songs like "Pretty Boy Floyd" (covered up in an outlaw story) share the space with re-workings of folk songs like "Gypsy Davy," and even a few religious songs make it in. Guthrie has been vastly influential, and this album is packed with songs that already were or were later to become classics. Of course they have also been covered innumerable times, by artists as different as Lonnie Donegan and Nick Cave. The most obvious follower is Bob Dylan, who it is hard to figure without the influence of Guthrie. Not only the fake accent from Dylan's first record is taken from Guthrie, but also the guitar playing, and especially the singing. Listen to "Buffalo Skinners" for proof. The reissues of this album are often cheap, making them a good deal since there are 20 tracks included, but also meaning a lack of cover notes and sloppy credit lists. The CMD version, for example, labels all songs as traditional, even though many are written by Guthrie or other well-known artists. —*Lars Lovén*

☆ **Library of Congress Recordings, Vols. 1–3** / 1964 / Rounder ✦✦✦✦✦

Not so much an album as a historical aural document, this nearly three-hour, three-CD set chronicles three days of interviews and songs featuring a 27-year-old Woody Guthrie on March 21, 22 and 27, 1940. Alan Lomax and his wife, Elizbeth, take Guthrie through his autobiography and his reflections on the Dust Bowl, and he proves a witty, rustic raconteur who is even more impressive when he picks up the guitar and performs such original songs as "So Long, It's Been Good to Know You," "Talking Dust Bowl Blues," "Do-Re-Mi," and "Pretty Boy Floyd," as well as traditional material. Guthrie did not make his first studio recordings until later in 1940, but his repertoire and performance style were clearly long-established by this time. It is easy to hear why he was such a revelation to the folk world of the '40s, especially because his influence has been so pervasive: much of the next 20 years in folk music derives from these sessions, even though they were not commercially released until 1964, as a box set on Elektra Records. Rounder reissued the album on LP in the 1988 and on CD in the 1997. —*William Ruhlmann*

The Greatest Songs of Woody Guthrie / 1972 / Vanguard ✦✦✦✦

A two-record set reissued on one CD, this collection of great Woody Guthrie songs performed by some of Guthrie's apostles, as well as by Guthrie himself, serves as a nice overview of his music. From the opening notes of "This Land Is Your Land" and a composite arrangement that starts with Guthrie and his guitar, then folds into the Weavers completing the song, this is very special music. With the mix of performers, it's like a hootenanny featuring some of the top American folk music artists who had fallen under Guthrie's spell. In addition to Pete Seeger's Weavers, longtime Guthrie cronies Cisco Houston and Ramblin' Jack Elliot are featured, along with the next generation's Joan Baez and Country Joe McDonald. Deep-throated Odetta delivers the definitive version of "Pastures of Plenty," and Guthrie is spotlighted solo and with pals Sonny Terry and Houston. A folk-music delight from beginning to end. —*Jim Newsom*

Struggle / 1976 / Smithsonian Folkways ✦✦✦

This album was originally released by Moses Asch, founder of the Folkways label, on Asch Records in 1941 as *Struggle: Documentary No. 1*. It was released by him in 1976 to commemorate the bicentennial of the American Revolution with a special series of liner notes by Asch explaining the importance of Woody Guthrie's history of the working class through song. Both Guthrie's songs and the liner notes are stuff of supreme cultural importance. In the notes, Asch lays out a theory that the American Revolution has not yet been completed and there is a need for a "continuing struggle for human rights and equality." As a collection of songs, this is surely one of the best Guthrie collections, especially once it's known how important it was to him personally. In many ways, it seems as if this album was the fulfillment of a very personal vision, which starts with the songs but is only realized in their collectivity. Included here are such excellent songs as the unsettling "Hang Knot," the elliptic "Union Burying Ground," and the finely spun "Pretty Boy Floyd." These songs define Guthrie at his best, never didactic in tone but supreme in import. The album also features the Cisco Houston (Guthrie's sometime tramping companion) number "Get Along Little Doggies," as well as his vocal accompaniment on several tracks. Sonny Terry guests on "Lost John," lending his harmonica to Guthrie's tale of a chain gang escapee. Both as a historical artifact and as an amazing Guthrie album, this is required listening. —*Brian Whitener*

Columbia River Collection / 1988 / Rounder ✦✦✦✦

In May 1941, Woody Guthrie began working for the Bonneville Power Administration (BPA), a job that required him to write songs to promote development (dams) on the Columbia River. He would later claim that he wrote a song per day during his month-long association with the BPA, making it one of the most productive periods of his life. Several of his best-loved songs came from this period, including "Ramblin' Round," "Hard Travlin'," and "Pastures of Plenty." *Columbia River Collection* has two strong points to recommend it. First, it collects all of the available material that Guthrie wrote during this time in one place, giving the collection a thematic unity similar to *Dust Bowl Ballads*. Next, it includes 11 versions of the songs originally recorded in Portland, OR, in 1941, and never before released. This latter quality is *Columbia River Collection*'s strongest point, which makes it seem odd that the liner notes aren't more helpful with sorting out

which of the 17 tracks are from these early sessions. It is clear, however, that versions of "Roll on Columbia" and "Roll Columbia, Roll," two favorites, are new. It's also clear that Rounder borrowed the other six songs, including "Pastures of Plenty," from Smithsonian Folkways. The important thing, though, is that the listener can now gain a better view of Guthrie's artistic vision at this important juncture in his career. It also doesn't hurt that *Columbia River Collection* is a strong group of songs that capture the Dust Bowl Balladeer in top form. —*Ronnie D. Lankford Jr.*

☆ **Songs to Grow on for Mother and Child** / 1991 / Smithsonian Folkways ✦✦✦✦✦

Some of the last songs written and recorded by Woody Guthrie were his children's songs. Their strength, shown in *Songs to Grow on for Mother and Child*, is an unusually strong identification with actually being a child, in all its simplicity and charm, along with the ability to win over listeners. Good examples on here are "Rattle My Rattle" and "I Want My Milk." Guthrie is an acquired sonic taste worth acquiring. For ages 3-5. —*William Ruhlmann & Bob Hinkle*

Long Ways to Travel: The Unreleased Folkways Masters, 1944–1949 / 1994 / Smithsonian Folkways ✦✦✦

An odds-and-ends collection spanning 17 unreleased tracks recorded from 1944 to 1949, most being originals and not just alternate takes, *Long Ways to Travel* is a fine addition to any Guthrie fan's collection. Started as a project in 1991 to wade through Guthrie's unreleased catalog, this undertaking was no minor feat, seeing that Moses Asch kept sketchy records at best, and it is obvious that considerable work has gone into this collection. As such, not every track is note-perfect, with Guthrie occasionally stumbling over lines, but it does offer a very well-rounded picture of who Guthrie was as an artist. Though it might not be the best place to start for the uninitiated, there is some seriously interesting music here, from harmonica workouts on "Rain Crow Bill" with Sonny Terry to fiddle tunes like "Girl I Left Behind Me" and the bluesy "Long Ways to Travel." Many tracks focus on Guthrie's love of riding the rails with train narratives like "Seattle to Chicago" and "Train Ride Medley (part 2)," as well as a dialogue he delivered as an emcee at a concert. A wide variety is represented with "Wiggledy Giggledy," a song of mostly nonsense rhyming, while the strange mock radio show performance of "Rocky Mountain Slim and Desert Rat Shorty," one of the many featuring Cisco Houston, seems to be some sort of off-the-cuff comedy skit. In addition, the haunting autobiographical narrative of "Along in the Sun and the Rain" and the eloquent tribute "Harriet Tubman's Ballad" are tracks that no Guthrie enthusiast should be without. Interesting historical references such as "Warden in the Sky," written while Guthrie was briefly in jail, and the topical "Farmer-Labor Train," which was written for presidential candidate Henry Wallace's rallies, are a few of the more political pieces here, considering that the majority of the tracks are more autobiographical in nature. An excellent extensive transcription of an interview of Moses Asch, detailing his relationship with Guthrie is also of note. No doubt, when taken in addition to Guthrie's more quintessential work, this is a pretty substantial collection. —*Matt Fink*

Ballads of Sacco & Vanzetti / 1996 / Smithsonian Folkways ✦✦✦

Recorded between 1946 and 1947, Woody Guthrie crafted a truly fascinating historical document that serves as something of a prototype for a concept album. The trial of Italian-born radicals Nicola Sacco and Bartolomeo Vanzetti, which culminated in their execution in 1927, is one of the most controversial murder trials in the history of the American justice system; it remains to this day clouded with inconclusive findings. It was this trial that inspired Woody Guthrie to devote an entire album of songs in their defense, and in the process create some of the most fiery and impassioned verse in his recorded catalog. Guthrie is known to have considered these songs among the most important that he'd ever written, and he is said to have thought the project to be one of his most significant. Many of the pieces have a strong sense of immediacy in them, with Guthrie stumbling over lines and missing chord changes, seemingly racing to get the message out. Some might not particularly agree with his clearly one-sided view of the entire trial, though the way in which he eloquently presents the facts of the case to the listener is a powerful statement for their defense. Still, Guthrie paints a picture of Sacco and Vanzetti that almost seems too good to be true, leaving them as martyrs for American freedom and legends of the progressive movement, calling them Boston's "most noble sons." This might be Guthrie at his most openly radical, with semi-revolutionary lyrics in "Red Wine" recounting the scene in Boston after the execution: "I thought those crowds would pull the town down./ I was hoping they'd do it and change things around." The songs themselves are in the classic Guthrie vein, in that they're all solo acoustic tracks, with the exception of "Sacco's Letter to His Son," which is a letter Sacco wrote on the eve of his execution, set to music by Pete Seeger. Though the material seems a little biased, and maybe rightly so, this is Woody Guthrie at his most sincere and inspired, and no matter where you stand on the vagaries of the trial, you can't argue with the way he honestly presents the humanity of the condemned. While an album completely devoted to a trial that took place over 75 years ago might not be everyone's ideal Guthrie album, it's a fascinating historical snapshot in time, when the Red Scare was a real threat—when folksingers saw injustice and tried to do something about it. —*Matt Fink*

Early Masters / Apr. 1996 / Rykodisc/Tradition ✦✦✦

The 12 tracks on this mid-priced reissue were recorded by Moses Asch of Folkways Records in 1944, but issued several times by Stinson Records, notably on the album *Woody Guthrie* (SLP 44). Accompanied by Cisco Houston and Sonny Terry, Guthrie performs a series of traditional folk songs in his own adaptations, which went on to become folk and pop standards, including such songs as "Worried Man Blues," "Going Down the Road," and "Pretty Boy Floyd." Despite sonic cleansing, the recordings are sometimes of marginal sound quality, but the historic nature of the work overcomes such limitations. This is not as impressive a collection as some of the Smithsonian Folkways reissues of material from the same sessions, but it is also less expensive. —*William Ruhlmann*

★ **This Land Is Your Land: The Asch Recordings, Vol. 1** / Feb. 18, 1997 / Smithsonian Folkways ♦♦♦♦♦

You'd think the last word in Woody Guthrie reissues would have appeared before this. After all, the legendary folksinger recorded most of his best work nearly 60 years before this was released, and the bulk of it has been regularly reissued in fine collections on Folkways, Rounder, and other labels. So this CD is as surprising as it is welcome. What makes it probably the single best Guthrie disc you can own? For one thing, the compilers had total access to the archives of Folkways Records founder Moses Asch, for whom the singer made the lion's share of his most important recordings. And they picked for this package 27 songs that showcase the incredible range of his writing and performing talent—everything from children's ditties ("Car Song") to social commentary ("Do-Re-Mi") to historical tales ("End of the Line"). Then there's the title track—Guthrie's most famous tune—which was only sporadically available until this CD. It's here in two versions, including one that features the famous yet previously unreleased "private property" verses. The sound quality is as notable as the program. The compilers went back to the master recordings and did a magnificent job of cleaning things up without altering what Guthrie waxed. The result sounds pure and intimate—as if the singer were right there in the room with you. Finally, there's a superb 36-page book with all sorts of fascinating detail on Asch, Guthrie, and every track. The best news: This is only the first volume in a four-CD series. *—Jeff Burger*

This Land Is Your Land / Mar. 25, 1997 / Rounder ♦♦♦

In the early '90s, the remaining Guthrie children and producer Frank Fuchs were lamenting the fact that there were generations of kids growing up without the benefit of Woody Guthrie's goofy wordplay and sly education so perfectly combined in his more playful songs. Inspired, they decided to re-record or add to existing recordings of Woody's music and set this new collaboration to animation for *This Land Is Your Land: The Animated Kids' Songs of Woody Guthrie*. The result is a mixed bag of musical ideas—since the production team augmented recordings from the '40s and '50s with super-clean acoustic guitar and accordion/flute/saxophone and even Native American percussion, it is clearly evident where the archival recordings end and the new ones begin. This juxtaposition probably won't make a lick of difference to the kids who the recording is intended for, but any folk purists out there will certainly cringe at the syrupy-sweet production layered atop these beautifully gritty old recordings. While there is nothing really wrong with the record, listeners who want to expose their children to the wonder of either performer's music might be better off with Woody's *Nursery Days* on Smithsonian/Folkways Records, or Arlo's *Precious Friend* collaborations with Pete Seeger. *—Zac Johnson*

Muleskinner Blues: The Asch Recordings, Vol. 2 / Sep. 16, 1997 / Smithsonian Folkways ♦♦♦♦♦

Nearly 60 years after Woody Guthrie recorded most of his best work comes a series that finally does it total justice. The music all issues from the master tapes of Folkways Records founder Moses Asch, for whom Guthrie made his most important recordings. Sound quality is uniformly pristine, the liner notes are extensive and exceptional, and the gritty, direct, idiosyncratic performances leave no doubt why Guthrie is considered a giant of American folk. This second in a series of four CDs focuses on 25 examples of Guthrie's interpretive work—classic folk and country songs, most of which he learned on the road in Oklahoma, Texas, and California. The uninitiated should start with *Vol. 1*, which contains mostly original compositions, but the present set proves that Guthrie was almost as interesting a performer as he was a writer. And he had great taste in material. Among the many highlights, some of which feature accompaniment by Cisco Houston, Sonny Terry, and Pete Seeger, are Jimmie Rodgers' "Muleskinner Blues" and

traditional numbers like "Stackolee," "Danville Girl," and A.P. Carter's "Worried Man Blues." *—Jeff Burger*

☆ **Hard Travelin': The Asch Recordings, Vol. 3** / May 19, 1998 / Smithsonian Folkways ♦♦♦♦♦

This 27-song collection focuses on Guthrie's topical songs, though not all of the topics are political; there is, for instance, a "Hanukkah Dance" and an excerpt from his variation on the "Rubaiyat of Omar Khayyam," the children's song "Howdjadoo," and the gospel number "I Ain't Got No Home in This World Anymore." Progressives will find plenty to cheer along with here, though, whether it's a labor anthem like "Farmer-Labor Train" or "Ladies Auxiliary"; there are also a few tunes specifically directed toward the anti-fascism war effort in World War II. Despite the nominal topical anthology theme, this is really just a decent sampling of Guthrie's 1940s recordings (most done for Moe Asch), some of it socially conscious, some not. Some of these are among his better-known songs ("1913 Massacre," "Hard Travelin'," "So Long It's Been Good to Know You"); major folkies like Cisco Houston, Sonny Terry, and Pete Seeger help out occasionally, though it's usually just Guthrie alone with his guitar. The sound quality is good (especially considering that some of these have been transferred from fragile acetates), and the quality of the material and performance is strong; a few of the performances were previously unreleased. *—Richie Unterberger*

Buffalo Skinners: The Asch Recordings, Vol. 4 / Apr. 20, 1999 / Smithsonian Folkways ♦♦♦♦♦

This fourth and final volume of recordings Woody Guthrie made for Folkways and other small independent labels is just as remarkable as its predecessors. This time around, the focus is primarily on cowboy/Western music, and Guthrie—who is accompanied by Cisco Houston on many of the 26 tracks—proves himself a master of the genre. The program mixes well-known traditional material ("Go Tell Aunt Rhody," "Whoopie Ti Yi Yo," "Get Along Little Doggies," "Red River Valley," and "Chisholm Trail") with equally strong Guthrie originals ("Little Darling (At My Window Sad and Lonely)," "Ranger's Command," and "Dead or Alive (Poor Lazarus)." About a third of the tracks have never previously been released, among them the charming "Return of Rocky Mountain Slim and Desert Rat Shorty," a home recording on which Woody and Cisco make fun of radio ads for music songbooks. The sound quality is first-rate, particularly considering the acetate-disc sources of this material. Also excellent is the 36-page accompanying booklet, which completes the biographical sketch started on *Vols. 1-3* and includes extensive notes on each track. *—Jeff Burger*

The Asch Recordings, Vol. 1–4 / Aug. 17, 1999 / Smithsonian Folkways ♦♦♦♦♦

Woody Guthrie's *Asch Recordings, Vol. 1-4* is another shining example of Smithsonian/Folkways' ability to create a historically important document that is both fun and enriching. Combining four separate compilations (*This Land Is Your Land: The Asch Recordings, Vol. 1, Muleskinner Blues: The Asch Recordings, Vol. 2, Hard Travelin': The Asch Recordings, Vol. 3,* and *Buffalo Skinners: The Asch Recordings, Vol. 4*) into one box, Smithsonian/Folkways presents a fairly complete overview of Guthrie's career. The collection features deep forays into his union songs, political and social issue songs, cowboy and outlaw songs, and early country and frontier ballads, with each CD separated into specific themes. The liner notes are intelligently written but never dry, going through track by track, bringing to light Guthrie's warm contributions to American folksongs. In listening to the set as a whole, the only question left is "where is Guthrie's comedy album?" His biting humor on songs like "Talking Hard Work," "Ladies Auxiliary," "Howdjadoo," and "Mean Talking Blues" tell of a wry and witty side of the activist that would fit alongside his topical children's albums nicely. Each of these CDs are available individually, but purchasing the box set gives the listener a more well-rounded experience and makes more sense economically. *—Zac Johnson*

Hackberry Ramblers

f. 1933, Hackberry, LA

Group / String Bands, Traditional Cajun

The most important Cajun band of the 1930s, the Hackberry Ramblers—also known as the Riverside Ramblers—were formed in 1933 by fiddler Luderin Darbone (born January 14, 1913, Evangeline, LA). Darbone spent much of his early life in Texas, listening to—and becoming influenced by—Western swing as well as Cajun music. He studied at a business college in the early '30s but formed the Hackberry Ramblers soon after and found work at KFDM Lake Charles, LA.

The Ramblers soon became the best-known band around the area, and they began recording for RCA Bluebird in 1935 with a lineup including Darbone, vocalist Lennis Sonnier, guitarists Glenn Croker, Lonnie Rainwater, Floyd Shreve, and Joe Werner, bassist Johnnie Parket, and occasional accordion player Edwin Duhon. The initial sides were recorded in French, but a partnership with Montgomery Ward to perform on KVOL Lafayette prompted the Ramblers to record in English as the Riverside Ramblers—after Ward's brand of tires. Joe Werner provided most of the English vocals, and 1936's "Wondering" became a modest hit, sparking his brief solo contract with Decca.

The band broke up early in the World War II years but re-formed in 1946, recording for Deluxe and establishing a Saturday-night residency at a Lake Charles club that lasted ten years. The part-time band recorded an album for Arhoolie in 1963 and a few titles for Old Gold, and remained together, playing the occasional festival or event. In 1988, the Old Timey label released the best of the Bluebird and Deluxe material as *Early Recordings: 1935-1948.* —*John Bush*

Early Recordings: 1935–1948 / 1988 / Old Timey ♦♦♦♦♦

The Hackberry Ramblers were arguably the most influential Cajun string band from Louisiana, creating a raw fusion of Western swing, old-timey string bands, and Cajun. The Ramblers never used accordions—they were a pure string band, creating a distinctly New Orleans brand of country music. *Early Recordings, 1935-1948* collects highlights from the group's Bluebird and Deluxe material and offers a perfect distillation of why the Ramblers were important. —*Thom Owens*

● **Cajun Boogie** / Jun. 1992 / Flying Fish ♦♦♦♦♦

As they sing on the theme song that opens this CD, the Hackberry Ramblers "play you some music and try to make you smile" with their infectious brand of hoedown music. By and large the Hackberry, LA, band succeeds on this album, which features original members Glenn Croker (guitar) and Luderin Darbone (fiddle). Since 1933, they've been blending Cajun, country, and Western swing music with touches of blues and pop. Croker and Darbone haven't lost their manic energy and taste for get-down party sounds. Besides presenting several of their own compositions, they cover tunes by Bob Wills, Ray Price, and Howlin' Wolf. This CD features guest fiddle by zydeco star Michael Doucet on four tracks, as well as a guest vocal by country star Rodney Crowell on "Old Pipeliner." —*Richie Unterberger*

Jolie Blonde / 1993 / Arhoolie ♦♦♦♦

These 1960s recordings came about as a result of Chris Strachwitz tracking down fiddler Luderin Darbone in Louisiana in 1963. The Ramblers had not recorded for years, but assembled again for some sessions in both the Goldband Studio and Darbone's home. Two other Ramblers from the 1930s-era lineup, Edwin Duhon and Lennis Sonnier, were also on board, with the personnel filled out by some younger musicians. Old-timey purists will probably still prefer their 1930s and 1940s sides; this collection has the advantages of clearer fidelity and easier availability. The CD adds nine previously unreleased bonus cuts, most taken from their appearance at the 1995 UC-Berkeley Folk Festival. —*Richie Unterberger*

Deep Water / May 13, 1997 / Hot Biscuits ♦♦♦♦♦

The Hackberry Ramblers are among the very few popular musicians who seem to be reaching their peak well past Social Security age. Ramblers mainstay Luderin Darbone was in his early 80s when this was recorded, and the rest of the six-piece group (except for youthful drummer Ben Sandmel) doesn't look much younger, yet they continue to play with more exuberance than almost any act of any style or age. Buying this disc is not, as is often the case when buying recent efforts by old-time legends, an act of charity. It's a good set that encompasses Western swing, boogie, blues, French Cajun, and even a bit of rock (in the cover of "Proud Mary"), performed with a spontaneity that veers toward sloppiness without falling into carelessness. This stuff has diversity and eclecticism, two qualities which are often underemployed, even ignored, by Cajun musicians in the studio. There are guest shots by Jimmie Dale Gilmore, Rodney Crowell, Marcia Ball, and Michael Doucet, but they really don't add or subtract anything of note. The main show is the Ramblers themselves, playing with an utter lack of self-consciousness, as if they're performing at the neighborhood barbecue, not in front of studio mikes. —*Richie Unterberger*

First Recordings 1935–1947 / Feb. 25, 2003 / Arhoolie ♦♦♦♦♦

Despite the relatively wide time span indicated by the title, actually all but two of these cuts were recorded in a short period of time, from 1935 to 1937 (the remaining pair were done in 1950). For the mid-'30s sessions, the only constant in the Hackberry Ramblers' lineup was violinist and singer Luderin Darbone (who was still in the group when this CD was issued in 2003). Half a dozen different guys take lead vocals (in both English and French) at various points, and three of the tracks were actually issued under the name the Riverside Ramblers. Original guitarist Edwin Duhon was still in the lineup in 2003 too, but actually he doesn't appear on any of the mid-'30s sides, although he's on the 1950 cuts. Not that it matters that much—this is important early Cajun music, somewhat modernized by 1930s standards in how it's influenced by then-current American popular music, particularly Bob Wills' Western swing. They play with some real high-stepping jazz ragtime feel on the instrumental "Vinton High Society," while their version of the Cajun standard "Jolie Blonde" was the first time the song (previously recorded by Amédé Breaux under the title "Ma Blonde Est Partie") had been issued under that name. The sound quality is uneven, as is unavoidable given the age of the source material and original recording conditions, but is overall quite acceptable. A slightly more conventional country feel comes into play on the 1950 tracks. The package includes good liner notes by Ben Sandmel, who as of its 2003 release was drummer with the still-active band. —*Richie Unterberger*

Hagers

f. Park Ridge, IL

Group / Country-Pop, Country Comedy

Country music has produced countless brother acts, but the Hagers offered a new twist: They were identical twins. Best known for their long stint on the TV show *Hee Haw*, Jon and Jim Hager were adopted by a minister as infants, and as they grew up in Park Ridge, IL, their new parents passed along their love of country music. The brothers began performing together as teenagers, appearing at local venues and on a Saturday morning TV show aimed at other teens. After college, they served in Vietnam, primarily as entertainers for their fellow soldiers. Upon returning home, they spent a year and a half performing around Chicago, then moved to Los Angeles. There they were hired by Randy Sparks of the New Christy Minstrels to appear regularly at his Ledbetter's club. A performance at Disneyland won them a fan in Buck Owens, who became their manager and added them to his touring revue for two years. Signed to Capitol, the Hagers released their debut single, "Gotta Get to Oklahoma (Cause California's Gettin' to Me)," in 1969, and followed it with their self-titled debut album the next year.

What started as an engagement to perform two songs on *Hee Haw* in 1970 turned into an 18-year association; the Hagers became regulars both as musicians and comedians. They released three albums total for Capitol, as well as minor hit singles like "Silver Wings" and "I'm Miles Away," but television proved to be their primary medium. They cut an album for Barnaby in 1972, and another self-titled effort for Elektra in 1974, without much commercial success. Settled into their roles, the Hagers began moonlighting in other acting roles, including the 1976 TV movie *Twin Detectives*, with Lillian Gish; they also worked as standup comics for a time. In 1987, they left *Hee Haw* and co-hosted the TNN show *Country Kitchen* with Florence Henderson; a proposed comedy show never got off the ground. In 1990, they filmed their first music video for the single "I'm Wishin' I Could Go Fishin'" Forever." —*Steve Huey*

● **The Hagers** / 1970 / Capitol ♦♦♦♦

Two Hagers Are Better Than One / 1970 / Capitol ♦♦♦

Motherhood, Apple Pie and the Flag / 1971 / Capitol ♦♦♦

Countryside / 1972 / Barnaby ♦♦♦

The Hagers / 1974 / Elektra ♦♦♦

Merle Haggard

b. Apr. 6, 1937, Bakersfield, CA

Guitar, Songwriter, Vocals, Fiddle / Traditional Country, Honky Tonk, Bakersfield Sound, Western Swing Revival

As a performer and a songwriter, Merle Haggard was the most important country artist to emerge in the 1960s. Haggard became one of the leading figures of the Bakersfield country scene in the '60s. While his music remained hardcore country, he pushed the boundaries of the music quite far. Like his idol Bob Wills, his music was a melting pot that drew from all forms of traditional American music—country, jazz, blues, and folk—and in the process, developed a distinctive style of his own. As a performer, singer, and musician, he was one of the best, influencing countless other artists. Not coincidentally, he was the best singer/songwriter in country music since Hank Williams, writing a body of songs that became classics. Throughout his career, Haggard has been a champion of the working man, largely due to his rough and tumble history.

It's impossible to separate Haggard's music from his life. Haggard was born to James and Flossie Haggard on April 6, 1937. His parents moved from Oklahoma to California during the Great Depression, converting an old boxcar into a home. Before their marriage, James played fiddle in local honky tonk bars. Flossie was a member of the Church of Christ, which led to her forcing her husband to stop playing the honky tonks. James died from a brain tumor when Merle was nine years old. After his father's death, Merle became rebellious. In an attempt to straighten her son out, his mother put him in several juvenile detention centers, but it had little effect on Merle's behavior. As a teenager, he fell in love with country music, particularly Bob Wills, Lefty Frizzell, and Hank Williams. When he was 12 years old, Haggard was given his first guitar by his older brother; Merle taught himself how to play by listening to records that were lying around the house. Even though he had begun to pursue music, Haggard continued to rebel, running away with his friend Bob Teague to Texas when he was 14 years old. A few months later, the pair returned to California, where they were arrested as robbery suspects. After the real thieves were caught, Haggard was sent back to juvenile hall, but he and Teague took off to Modesto, CA. For a brief time, he did manual labor, was a short-order cook, drove a truck, and committed a series of small crimes. Soon after he moved to Modesto, Haggard made his performing debut with Teague at a bar named the *Fun Center*; the two were paid five dollars and given all the beer that they could drink.

By the end of 1951, Haggard had returned home and he was again arrested for truancy, as well as petty larceny. In the beginning of 1952, he was sent to Fred C. Nelles School for Boys in Whittier, CA; again, he ran away. This time, the courts decided he was incorrigible and sent him to the high-security Preston School of Industry; he was released after 15 months. Shortly after his release, he and a boy he met at PSI beat up a local boy during an attempted robbery, and Haggard was sent back to PSI. After getting out of PSI for the second time, Merle Haggard had the first major event in his musical career. Haggard went with Teague to see Lefty Frizzell in concert in Bakersfield. Before the show, he went backstage with several friends and he sang a couple songs for Frizzell. Lefty was so impressed he refused to go on-stage until Haggard was allowed to sing a song. Merle went out and sang a few songs to an enthusiastic response from the audience.

The reception persuaded Haggard to actively pursue a musical career. While he was working during the day in oil fields and farms, he performed local Bakersfield clubs. His performances led to a spot on a local television show, *Chuck Wagon*. In 1956, he married Leona Hobbs; the couple moved into his family's old converted boxcar. Throughout 1957, Haggard was plagued by financial problems, which made him turn to robbery. At the end of the year, he attempted to rob a restaurant along with two other burglars; the three were drunk at the time. Believing it was three o'clock in the morning, the trio tried to open up the backdoor of the restaurant. However, it was 10:30 and the establishment was still open. Although the trio fled the scene, Haggard was arrested that day. The following day, he escaped from prison in order to make peace with his wife and family; later that day, he was recaptured. Haggard was sentenced to a 15-year term and sent to San Quentin prison.

Prison didn't immediately lead Merle into rehabilitation. He was fired from a series of prison jobs and planned an escape from the jail, but was talked out of it by fellow inmates. Nearly two years into his sentence, Haggard discovered that his wife was pregnant with another man's child. The news sent Haggard over the edge. Soon, he and his cellmate began a gambling racket and brewing beer in their cell. Before long, Haggard was caught drunk and was placed in isolation for a week. During his time in isolation, he had several conversations with Caryl Chessman, an author and a member of death row. The conversations and the time in isolation convinced Haggard to turn his life around. After he left isolation, he began working in the prison's textile plant and took some high-school equivalency courses; he was also allowed to play in the prison's country band. At his second parole hearing in 1960, Haggard was given a five-year sentence—two years and nine months in jail, two years and three months on parole; he left prison 90 days later.

Merle moved back in with Leona and returned to manual labor. In the meantime, he sang at local clubs at night. After taking second place at a local talent contest, Haggard was asked to become a relief singer for a band led by Johnny Barnett at one of the most popular Bakersfield clubs, Lucky Spot. Soon, Merle was making enough money playing music he could quit his ditch-digging job. While he singing with Barnett, he gained the attention of Fuzzy Owen, who owned the small record label Tally Records. Owen and his cousin Lewis Talley were instrumental in establishing Haggard's musical career. Owen made the first recording of Haggard, cutting a demo version of one of the singer's first songs, "Skid Row." Shortly after the recording, Haggard called Talley, who had praised him earlier in his career. Talley was able to land Haggard a job at Paul's Cocktail Lounge, which led to a slot on a local music television show.

During this time, Bakersfield country was beginning to become a national scene, largely due to the hit singles of Buck Owens. At a time when mainstream country was dominated by the lush, smooth countrypolitan sound of Nashville, Bakersfield country grew out of hardcore honky tonk, adding elements of Western swing. Bakersfield country also relied on electric instruments and amplification more than other subgenres of country, giving the music hard, driving, edgy flavor. During the late '50s, Tommy Collins and Wynn Stewart were two of the Bakersfield artists to have hits, and both were influential on Merle Haggard's career, musically as well as professionally. Haggard had admired Stewart's vocal style, and it helped shape his phrasing.

Early in 1962, Haggard traveled to Las Vegas to see Wynn Stewart's club show. Stewart was not at the club, having left to find a replacement bass player. During the show, one of Stewart's guitarists remembered Haggard and invited him to sing a couple of songs on-stage. Stewart walked in while Haggard was singing and was impressed, asking him to join his band as a bassist. For six months in 1962 and 1963, Merle performed with Stewart's band. During this time, Haggard heard Wynn's song "Sing a Sad Song" and asked the star if he could record it. Stewart gave him the song and Merle recorded it for Tally Records in 1963. Although Tally had minimal distribution, the record became a national hit, climbing to number 19 on the country charts early in 1964. "Sam Hill," Haggard's second single, wasn't as successful, but a duet with Bonnie Owens, the former wife of Buck Owens, called "Just Between the Two of Us" broke into the Top 40. The next year, his version of Liz Anderson's "(My Friends Are Gonna Be) Strangers" broke him into the Top Ten and established him as a budding star. Capitol Records bought out his contract with Tally and Merle released "I'm Gonna Break Every Heart I Can," his first single for Capitol, in the fall of 1965. The single wasn't a success, scratching into the Top 50, but his next single, "Swinging Doors," was a smash hit, rocketing to number five in the spring of 1966. Late in 1965, Haggard began recruiting a backing band and named them the Strangers.

Merle Haggard became a genuine country superstar in 1966, with three Top Ten hits, including "Swinging Doors." "The Bottle Let Me Down" climbed to number three and "The Fugitive" (later retitled "I'm a Lonesome Fugitive") became his first number one. He was voted the Top Male Vocalist by the Academy of Country Music Awards, while he and Bonnie were named the Top Vocal Group for the second year in a row. Haggard's songwriting was beginning to blossom and audiences embraced his music, sending his "I Threw Away the Rose" to number three early in 1967, beginning a remarkable streak of 37 straight Top Ten hits, including 23 number one singles. "I Threw Away the Rose" was followed by four straight number-one hits—"Branded Man," "Sing Me Back Home," "The Legend of Bonnie and Clyde," and "Mama Tried," which was heard in *Killers Three*, a movie that featured Haggard's debut as an actor. With the exception of "Bonnie and Clyde," the songs represented a change in Haggard's songwriting, as he began to directly address his troubled history. By 1970, he was talking about his time in San Quentin in the press, yet these songs represented the first time he had mentioned his past directly. Each single was a bigger hit than the previous song, which encouraged Haggard to continue writing in a more personal style.

Throughout 1968, Haggard's star continued to rise, with two number-one hits ("Bonnie and Clyde," "Mama Tried") and the number three "I Take a Lot of Pride in What I Am," as well as four albums. Later that year, he recorded his first conceptual album, *Same Train, Different Train: A Tribute to Jimmie Rodgers*. Released in early 1969, the record was not only an affectionate salute to one of Haggard's heroes, it reflected a fascination with American history and a desire to expand his music by adding stronger elements of Western swing, jazz, and blues. Merle released three singles in 1969—"Hungry Eyes," "Workin' Man Blues," and "Okie From Muskogee"—and all three reached number one. In particular, "Okie From Muskogee" sparked a tremendous amount of attention. An attack on the liberal hippies that represented American pop culture in the late '60s, the song struck a chord in audiences across the country, just missing the pop Top 40. Because of the song, Haggard was asked to endorse George Wallace, but he refused. "Okie From Muskogee" cemented the singer's stardom, and he won a large amount of awards in 1969 and 1970. In both years, he was named the Top Male Vocalist by the ACM and the Strangers were voted the best band, while the new Country Music Association voted him Entertainer of the Year and Top Male Vocalist in 1970.

Haggard released a sequel to "Okie" called "The Fightin' Side of Me" at the beginning of 1970, and it also shot to number one. That year, he released *A Tribute to the Best Damn Fiddle Player in the World (Or My Salute to Bob Wills)*, which helped spark a revival of Western swing in the '70s. Throughout 1971 and 1972, the hits kept coming, including "Soldier's Last Letter," "Someday We'll Look Back," "Daddy Frank (The Guitar Man)," "Carolyn," "Grandma Harp," "It's Not Love (But It's Not Bad)," and "I Wonder If They Ever Think of Me." In 1972, the governor of California, Ronald Reagan, granted Haggard a full pardon. The following year, his hit streak continued, and he scored his biggest hit, "If We Make It Through December," which peaked at number 28 on the pop charts. As his reign on the top of the country charts continued in 1974, he played on Bob Wills' last album, *For the Last Time*. Wills died in 1975, leaving Merle his fiddle.

Haggard stayed with Capitol Records until 1977, and never once did his grip on the American audience slip during his tenure there. During his time on MCA, he continued to have a number of hits, but his work was becoming slightly inconsistent. His first two singles for the record label, "If We're Not Back in Love by Monday" and "Ramblin' Fever," hit number two and he continued to have hits with the label throughout the end of the decade and the first part of the '80s. "I'm Always on a Mountain When I Fall" and "It's Been a Great Afternoon" were number-two hits in 1978. In 1979, he only had two hits, while in 1980, two selections from the Clint Eastwood movie *Bronco Billy* reached the Top Three, "The Way I Am" and "Misery and Gin"; Haggard also appeared in the film. The two hits paved the way for his two biggest singles with MCA, the number-one duet with Eastwood, "Bar Room Buddies," and the number one "I Think I'll Just Stay Here and Drink." Early in 1981, Haggard had a Top Ten hit with "Leonard," a tribute to his old friend Tommy Collins.

Later that year, Haggard published his autobiography, *Sing Me Back Home*; he also left MCA and signed with Epic Records. Once he began recording for Epic, he began producing his own records, which gave the music a leaner sound. His first two singles for the label, "My Favorite Memory" and "Big City," were number-one hits. The following year, he released a duet album with George Jones, called *A Taste of Yesterday's Wine*, which featured the number-one single "Yesterday's Wine" and the Top Ten "C.C. Waterback." From 1983 until the beginning of 1985, Haggard continued to score number-one hits, including the number-one duet with Willie Nelson, "Pancho and Lefty." Merle's chart fortunes began to change in 1985, as a new breed of singers began to dominate the chart. Nearly every one of the artists, from George Strait to Randy Travis, was greatly influenced by Haggard, but their idol's new singles now had a tough time reaching the top of the charts. He had two Top Ten hits in 1986, and 1987's *Chill Factor* was a success, spawning the Top Ten title track and "Twinkle, Twinkle Lucky Star," which would prove to be his last number-one hit. In 1990, he signed with Curb Records, but he continued to have trouble reaching the charts; *1994* spawned his last modest hit, "In My Next Life," which reached the Top 60. When his contract with Curb ran out, Haggard, hoping for better promotion and greater artistic freedom, signed with Anti, a subsidiary of the Epitaph punk-pop label. His first effort for Anti was released in late 2000; titled *If I Could Only Fly*, the gentle acoustic album was greeted with strong reviews.

Even when success eluded him, Merle Haggard's music remained some of the most consistently interesting and inventive in country music. Not only have his recordings remained fresh, but each subsequent generation of country singers show a great debt to his work. That fact stands as a testament to his great talent even more than his induction to the Country Music Hall of Fame. *—Stephen Thomas Erlewine*

Strangers / 1965 / Koch ♦♦♦♦
Merle Haggard's first album *Strangers* was an impressive debut. Apart from the classic singles "(My Friends Are Gonna Be) Strangers," "Sam Hill," "Sing a Sad Song," and "I'm Gonna Break Every Heart I Can," there's a number of fine album cuts, including "I'd Trade All of My Tomorrows," "If I Had Left It Up to You," and "You Don't Even Try." Granted, there is some filler on *Strangers*, but that was the case for nearly every country album recorded in the '60s. What counts is the good stuff and the best songs on the record richly illustrate Haggard's talent and his potential. *—Stephen Thomas Erlewine*

Just Between the Two of Us / 1966 / Capitol ♦♦♦
Within the California country music community, there's no arguing that Bonnie Owens married well; her first husband was Buck Owens, whom she married in 1948, and in 1965 she tied the knot again with Merle Haggard. Bonnie performed in the same band with Buck for a brief period while they were first married, and she later enjoyed a few hits as Haggard's duet partner; when *Just Between the Two of Us* was released, Hag's career as one of country's most dependable hitmakers was only just getting off the ground. However, while Bonnie Owens was a good honky tonk singer, she was hardly a great one like Haggard, who seems to be holding himself back a bit musically as he defers to his spouse. And while Hag and his band the Strangers are in typically strong form, this set of love songs (and the occasional cheatin' weeper) lacks the flinty power of Haggard's classic outlaw ballads. It's good to have *Just Between the Two of Us* available again, but only Haggard completists will really feel obligated to own it. *—Mark Deming*

☆ **Swinging Doors** / 1966 / Koch ♦♦♦♦♦
Merle Haggard's third album, *Swinging Doors*, was assembled from a variety of singles and session like its two predecessors, but it contained a stronger overall selection of material than either album. In addition to the two masterpieces from which the album took its name, the record included a terrific version of Tommy Collins' "High on a Hilltop," and plus excellent songs like "The Girl Turned Ripe," "If I Could Be Him," and "Someone Else You've Known." There's a few weak tracks, but Haggard and his band are in fine form, making the filler enjoyable. *—Stephen Thomas Erlewine*

I'm a Lonesome Fugitive / 1967 / Capitol ♦♦♦

Branded Man / 1967 / Capitol ♦♦♦♦
Like *Swinging Doors* before it, *Branded Man* is merely a collection of songs pieced together to cash in on a couple of hit singles. Nevertheless, the intent of an album such as this doesn't really matter when the songs are this fine. In addition to the two title tracks, Haggard co-writes "You Don't Have Very Far to Go" and "Somewhere Between" (with Red Simpson and Bonnie Owens, respectively). While the latter isn't as good as his three other original songs ("Branded Man," "I Threw Away the Rose," "You Don't Have Very Far to Go"), the remainder of the album is comprised of outside material that ranks among some of Haggard's finest performances ("Go Home," "Long Black Limousine," "I Made the Prison Band," "Don't Get Married," "Loneliness Is Eating Me Alive"). *—Stephen Thomas Erlewine*

Sing Me Back Home / 1968 / Koch ♦♦♦♦♦
Sing Me Back Home follows the blueprint of Merle Haggard's first three albums, balancing a hit single with album tracks and a couple of covers, but there is a difference. Where the previous album *Branded Man* was a transitional album, hinting that Haggard's talents were deepening substantially, *Sing Me Back Home* is the result of the flowering of his talent. Like any '60s country album, there are a couple of throwaways (like "The Bottle Let Me Down" rewrite "I'll Leave the Bottle on the Bar"), but the majority of the album is full of rich material, from "The Son of Hickory Holler's Tramp," "Good Times," and "Wine Take Me Away." *—Stephen Thomas Erlewine*

Legend of Bonnie & Clyde / 1968 / Capitol ♦♦♦♦
Seven albums in, Merle Haggard began to reach out a little further than his trademark Bakersfield country with *The Legend of Bonnie & Clyde*. While the title may imply that this record is a concept album, Haggard's celebration of the legendary outlaws—inspired by Arthur Penn's 1967 film starring Warren Beatty and Faye Dunaway in the title roles—doesn't extend past the opening title track, nor does the ramped-up, neo-bluegrass of that song (featuring banjo by no less than Glen Campbell) echo throughout the record. Instead, it settles into a nice, mellow groove, building on the Bakersfield ballad style patented by such artists as Wynn Stewart and Tommy Collins (whose "Fool's Castle" is covered here), adding slightly stronger folk influences and maintaining a reflective mood. Haggard relies on material from several different writers here, recording three songs by Dallas Frazier—"Love Has a Mind of Its Own," "The Train Never Stops (At Our Town)," "Will You Visit Me on Sundays?"—the Leon Payne tune "You Still Have a Place in My Heart," plus "Money Tree," originally recorded by Lefty Frizzell. None of these are conventional choices, and they're given fine interpretations by Haggard, who also contributes two solid songs in "My Ramona" and "Because You Can't Be Mine." However, they're all overshadowed by "I Started Loving You Again," the timeless ballad Haggard co-wrote with Bonnie Owens that stands as one of his greatest moments. Its presence along with the terrific title track and Haggard & the Strangers' restless but quiet musical exploration make *The Legend of Bonnie & Clyde* another typically excellent album from Hag, who was on a hell of a hot streak late in the '60s, which this simply continues. *—Stephen Thomas Erlewine*

☆ **Mama Tried** / 1968 / Capitol ♦♦♦♦♦
Mama Tried is a typically fine late-'60s LP from Merle Haggard, comprised of a number of strong originals and several excellent covers. While "Mama Tried" stands out among Haggard's original material, "I'll Always Know" and "You'll Never Love Me Now" are both solid songs. Still, those two tracks pale next to the best covers on the record. Merle delivers "Little Ole Wine Drinker Me," "In the Good Old Days (When Times Were Bad)," "Teach Me to Forget," "Run 'Em Off" and "Too Many Bridges to Cross Over" with grit and an open, affecting honesty that makes *Mama Tried* one of Hag's best records. *—Stephen Thomas Erlewine*

The Best of Merle Haggard / 1968 / Capitol ♦♦♦♦
As the first Haggard greatest hits collection ever released, *The Best of Merle Haggard* is quite good, hitting all the major points ("I'm a Lonesome Fugitive," "I Threw Away the Rose," "Swinging Doors," "(My Friends Are Gonna Be) Strangers," "Sing Me Back Home," "Branded Man," "The Bottle Let Me Down," "Sam Hill"), but it does leave off a few hits for album cuts like "House of Memories," "Shade Tree (Fix-It Man)," and "High on a Hilltop," which are all good but not quite as strong as the singles. Nevertheless, the LP functions as a fine introduction to Hag's early career. However, it has been replaced by better, more thorough compilations. *—Stephen Thomas Erlewine*

Pride in What I Am / 1969 / Capitol ♦♦♦♦
Continuing with the subtle folk streak running beneath *The Legend of Bonnie & Clyde* and *Mama Tried*, Merle Haggard turned in one of his finest efforts to date in 1969's *Pride in What I Am*. While there are no flat-out classics outside of "I Take a Lot of Pride in What I Am"—it's the only track on the album here that was a hit—the album is certainly not lacking in strong material. In fact, it gains considerable strength from a diversity of material, where the rolling, folk-tinged sound epitomized by the title song is balanced by twangy, spare country and bits of hard honky tonk, blues, and cowboy, not to mention the slyly inventive arrangement on his version of Lefty Frizzell's "It Meant Goodbye to Me When You Said Hello to Him." There are also hints of the direction Hag would take in the near future, including a Jimmie Rodgers song (his tribute to the singing brakeman, *Same Train, Different Time*, would follow next), and the encroaching celebration of a time passed, though his cover of Red Simpson's "I Think We're Livin' in the Good Old Days." There is another Simpson cover in "Somewhere on Skid Row," but what fuels *Pride in What I Am* is a selection of graceful, low-key minor masterworks from Haggard himself, who explores gentler territory with "The Day the Rains Came" and "I Can't Hold Myself in Line," while kicking up the tempo with the delightful "I'm Bringin' Home Good News" and laying back with the steady-rolling "I Just Want to Look at You One More Time." None of these may be among his most celebrated songs, but they're all small gems that illustrate what a fine songwriter he is. They also help form the core of this subtly adventurous, rich album that may not be among his flashiest, but is another excellent record by one of the most reliable recording artists in country history. *—Stephen Thomas Erlewine*

☆ **Same Train, Different Time** / 1969 / Bear Family ♦♦♦♦♦
Same Train, Different Time is Merle Haggard's affectionate tribute to Jimmie Rodgers. Haggard provides narration between the songs, offering tales of Rodgers' life and music. While the album is rooted in the past, the key to its success is how Haggard updates these traditional songs without losing sight of their roots. There are contemporary folk, country and blues influences scattered throughout the record, adding depth to the music and proving that Rodgers' music is indeed timeless. *—Stephen Thomas Erlewine*

Okie From Muskogee / 1969 / Capitol ♦♦♦♦
Okie From Muskogee was quickly recorded to cash in on the success of the title song, which became a pop music sensation upon its release in the fall of 1969. Haggard and the Strangers went to Muskogee, OK, where they ran through a number of their hits and working class anthems. The first side is devoted to classics like "Mama Tried," "Swinging Doors," "Sing Me Back Home," and "Workin' Man Blues," while the first part of the second side is devoted to songs about the mythological "Hobo Bill," before it concludes with rousing versions of "White Line Fever" and "Okie from Muskogee." While the record isn't necessary, it is a hell of a lot of fun and not bad evidence of why Hag was the most popular figure in country music at the end of the '60s. *—Stephen Thomas Erlewine*

The Instrumental Sounds of Merle Haggard's Strangers / 1969 / Capitol ♦♦♦♦
The instrumental debut album by Merle Haggard's backing band, the Strangers, opens with the familiar riff from his hit "Mama Tried" before Roy Nichols' single-string electric guitar lead pops up to carry the melody in place of Haggard's vocal. Nichols' energetic and surprising guitar work dominates the album, which is similar in style and execution to the 1965 LP *The Instrumental Hits of Buck Owens & His Buckaroos*. Rather than rework Haggard's hits into instrumentals, the Strangers go on to cover Johnny Cash's "Tennessee Flat Top Box" and offer up a batch of originals with whimsical titles such as "Whooper Snooper" and "A Hop and a Skip." This charming album will certainly appeal to Haggard's fans, but enthusiasts of instrumental guitar albums will enjoy the confidence and sense of fun in Nichols' playing. *—Greg Adams*

Introducing My Friends, the Strangers / 1970 / Capitol ♦♦♦
The second all-instrumental effort by Merle Haggard and the Strangers is as enjoyable as the first, featuring a selection of Western swing, honky tonk, and Bakersfield instruments that both swing and rock with ease. Though lead guitarist Roy Nichols and steel guitarist Norm Hamlet remain from the classic incarnation of the Strangers, the rhythm section has been reworked; it now features drummer Biff Adam, bassist Dennis Hromek and rhythm guitarist Bobby Wayner, all excellent musicians in their own right. Most of the album is comprised of Nichols and Hamlet collaborations, but the songs that truly stand out are Nichols' jaunty instrumental "Street Singer" and Haggard's "Workin' Man Blues," which also happens to be the only vocal on the LP. *—Stephen Thomas Erlewine*

Gettin' to Know Merle Haggard's Strangers / 1970 / Capitol ♦♦♦♦

The Fightin' Side of Me / 1970 / King Special ♦♦♦
Like its predecessor, *Okie From Muskogee*, *The Fightin' Side of Me* was a rush-released live album designed to cash in on the success of his ultra-patriotic hit single of the same name. *The Fightin' Side of Me* was recorded live in Philadelphia, where Haggard drew a capacity crowd. The songs are a good representation of a typical Haggard concert from the early '70s: A classic hit opens the record ("I Take a Lot of Pride in What I Am"), followed by some selections from his recent records, a couple of songs from Bonnie

Owens and the Strangers, a medley of other singers performed as imitations, and, finally, three recent hits—including "Okie From Muskogee" and "The Fightin' Side of Me"—to close the show. It's a fun record, and one that gives a better indication of what a typical Haggard concert was like in the early '70s, but it's ultimately a minor entry in his catalog. *—Stephen Thomas Erlewine*

☆ **A Tribute to the Best Damn Fiddle Player in the World (Or My Salute to Bob Wills)** / 1970 / Koch ✦✦✦✦✦

After releasing his tribute to Jimmie Rodgers, Merle Haggard immediately set about working on a tribute to his other major musical idol, Bob Wills. Haggard learned how to play fiddle and, within a month, he recruited many of the original Playboys to augment the Strangers and began recording the album that became *A Tribute to the Best Damn Fiddle Player (Or My Salute to Bob Wills).* Where *Same Train, Different Time* was a measured, heartfelt tribute, *Best Damn Fiddle Player* is a ragged, enthusiastic good-time. Haggard, the Strangers, and the Playboys play their hearts out, breathing life into Wills warhorses like "Right or Wrong," "Stay a Little Longer," "Time Changes Everything," and "San Antonio Rose," while bringing attention to lesser-known songs like "Brain Cloudy Blues," "I Knew the Moment I Lost You," and "Old-Fashioned Love." The fact that Western swing re-established itself as a viable country genre after the release of *A Tribute to the Best Damn Fiddle Player* is a testament to the power and charm of this record. *—Stephen Thomas Erlewine*

Honky Tonkin' / 1971 / Capitol ✦✦✦✦✦

☆ **Hag** / 1971 / Capitol ✦✦✦✦✦

Arriving after the superb Bob Wills salute *A Tribute to the Best Damn Fiddle Player in the World*, 1971's *Hag* was Merle Haggard's first collection of largely original songs in two years, since 1969's *Portrait.* Since that album, Haggard experienced great success with "Okie from Muskogee," which launched two quick live albums (one bearing the name of the song, the other being *The Fightin' Side of Me*), plus an instrumental album by the Strangers, before the labor of love of the Wills album. Perhaps Haggard had a great stock of songs saved up during those two years, because *Hag* is one of his absolute best albums—which means a lot, because he recorded no shortage of great records. In contrast to the rowdy live albums and the raucous Western swing that preceded it, *Hag* is quite quiet and reflective, sometimes referencing the turmoil within America at the end of the '60s, but more often finding Haggard turning inward. This album turned out no less than four hits, with three of them addressing larger issues: the revival of Ernest Tubb's WWII hit "Soldier's Last Letter" is now cast in the shadow of Vietnam, Haggard's original "Jesus, Take a Hold" ponders the state of the world, while Dave Kirby's "Sidewalks of Chicago" is about homelessness. The other hit was "I Can't Be Myself," a haunting admission that the singer "can't be myself when I'm with you," and it's only one of many great originals on *Hag.* The tempo picks up twice, each time at the end of the side, when he kicks out the self-deprecating "I'm a Good Loser" and the nostalgic rave-up "I've Done It All," but the heart of this is in the gentler material, such as the melancholic elegy of "Shelly's Winter Love," the sighing heartbreak ballad "If You've Got Time," and "The Farmer's Daughter," an affecting tale of a father giving away his daughter in marriage. Each is an expertly observed, richly textured gem, and taken together they add up to one of Haggard's best albums, and one of his most moving. *—Stephen Thomas Erlewine*

☆ **Someday We'll Look Back** / 1971 / Capitol ✦✦✦✦✦

Someday We'll Look Back is a terrific early-'70s LP from Merle Haggard, one that showcases not only his exceptional songwriting skills, but also his rich, subtle electicism. Much of the album is given over to ballads, including both lush, string-laden country-pop crossovers and simple, folky tunes, but there are also hints of twangy Bakersfield honky tonk and blues, as well as Western swing. But what really makes the record so distinctive is the quality of the material. Haggard's original songs—including "Someday We'll Look Back," "Tulare Dust," "I'd Rather Be Gone," "One Sweet Hello"—are uniformly excellent, while he invests considerable emotion into covers of Tommy Collins' "Carolyn," Dallas Frazier and Elizabeth Montgomery's "California Cottonfields," and Roger Miller's "Train of Life." The result is one of the finest albums he ever recorded. *—Stephen Thomas Erlewine*

The Land of Many Churches / 1971 / Razor & Tie ✦✦✦✦

Released in 1971, *The Land of Many Churches* is similar to other Merle Haggard tribute albums released in the same era, including *Same Train, Different Time* and *I Love Dixie Blues.* To his credit, Haggard had a greater need to shine light on the music that influenced him, more so than the need to release material that guaranteed a surefire hit. These 24 tracks include gospel chestnuts "Precious Memories," "Turn Your Radio On," "Amazing Grace," and a great version of the Hank Williams composition "I Saw the Light." Recorded live at the Nashville Union Rescue Mission and several rural churches across the country, Haggard is joined by guests Bonnie Owens and the Carter Family. Highly recommended to traditional country fans. *—Al Campbell*

High on a Hilltop / 1971 / Capitol ✦✦✦

Sing a Sad Song / 1971 / Capitol ✦✦✦

Let Me Tell You About a Song / 1972 / Capitol ✦✦✦✦✦

Merle Haggard designed 1972's *Let Me Tell You About a Song* as a kind of musical autobiography, crafted in equal parts from personal reminiscence and from songs that formed the core of Hag the musician. So, in a way, the album brings together two big themes within Haggard's recording career—tribute albums and a rose-colored, nostalgic view of the past—and it does so smashingly. A project like this can't help but succumb to corniness on occasion, which this certainly does, particularly in the spoken recitations that pepper the album (he is, after all, telling you about a song on this record) and on the hit opening track, "Daddy Frank (The Guitar Man)," a tale about a traveling family band with a blind father and a deaf mother who "read our lips and helped the family sing," a story that Haggard says explains itself but only gets more mystifying with each listen. Some could also argue that his tribute to his recently deceased grandmother, "Grandma Harp," is also a little corny, but it gets through on its heart, and the rest of the album is so remarkably clear-eyed, even with those spoken introductions, that it makes up for the slight silliness. The album is pretty evenly divided between originals and covers, and the two hits—the aforementioned "Daddy Frank" and "Grandma Harp"—are actually the slightest numbers here, since they sit next to the stark autobiographical "They're Tearing the Labor Camps Down," the beautiful barroom ballad "Turnin' Off a Memory," and "Irma Jackson," a song about an interracial romance that Haggard was finally able to release on this record. These songs are contrasted by the covers: one song by Red Simpson, one by Red Foley, and two each by his heroes Tommy Collins and Bob Wills. None of these songs were hits and, in fact, apart from Wills' "A Maiden's Prayer," they're not particularly well-known, which only emphasizes Haggard's connection to the music, and helps ties together the album into the musical biography that was intended. It's quite a journey, and it's yet another excellent record from an artist who at this time in his career seemed capable of delivering nothing less. *—Stephen Thomas Erlewine*

It's Not Love (But It's Not Bad) / 1972 / Capitol ✦✦✦

Despite the presence of the excellent title track, *It's Not Love (But It's Not Bad)* is only a fitfully entertaining album, equally divided between the excellent and the mediocre. A few of the throwaways are entertaining, particularly the rolling "New York City Blues," but songs like "Dad's Old Fiddle" and "My Woman Keeps Lovin' Her Man" fail to make an impression. There are a handful of hidden gems ("I Wonder Where I'll Find You At Tonight," "I Wonder What She'll Think About Me Leaving," "Goodbye Comes Hard for Me"), but the record remains a frustrating listen. *—Stephen Thomas Erlewine*

The Best of the Best of Merle Haggard / 1972 / Capitol ✦✦✦✦✦

Totally Instrumental . . . With One Exception / 1973 / Capitol ✦✦✦

Designed as a showcase for Haggard's backing band the Strangers, *Totally Instrumental . . . With One Exception* is a thoroughly enjoyable set of relaxed, jazzy Western swing and honky tonk that illustrates the depths of instrumental talent in the group. In this incarnation, the Strangers featured lead guitarist Roy Nichols, rhythm guitarists Bobby Wayne and Marcia Nichols, steel guitarist Norm Hamlet, bassist Dennis Hromek and drummer Biff Adam. While this isn't the classic '60s incarnation of the Strangers, it is still a tight, exceptional group and they make this set of short instrumentals (only "Cotton Picker" features Merle's vocals) into a fun record. *—Stephen Thomas Erlewine*

I Love Dixie Blues . . . So I Recorded Live in New Orleans / 1973 / Capitol ✦✦✦

I Love Dixie Blues was recorded live in New Orleans, not only with the Strangers but with a brass section to give the music the feel of authentic Dixieland jazz. Haggard's gamble works quite well, since the brass section never feels like it's grafted onto the core band—they sound integrated, unlike his previous experiments with Dixieland horns. Of course, it helps that Hag has picked a selection of songs that emphasizes these strengths, such as his own anthem "Everybody's Had the Blues," "Way Down Yonder in New Orleans," "Lovesick Blues," and "The Emptiest Arms in the World." The only thing that slows the album's momentum is Merle's insistence in providing narration between the songs in an attempt to tell the history of Dixie blues. He should have known that the music itself tells the story well enough. *—Stephen Thomas Erlewine*

If We Make It through December / 1974 / Capitol ✦✦✦

Usually, Merle Haggard's musical eclecticism is a virtue, but on *If We Make It Through December*, it hurts the overall impact of the album. Many of the individual tracks—particularly the gentle, yearning title track and good versions of Lefty Frizzell's "I'm An Old, Old Man (Tryin' to Live While I Can)" and the country standard "To Each His Own"—work well on their own, but often the straight-up country, Western swing, Dixieland experiments and pop-tinged ballads seem at odds with each other. As a result, the LP never quite gels, yet there are enough fine moments to make it a worthwhile purchase. *—Stephen Thomas Erlewine*

Merle Haggard Presents His 30th Album / 1974 / Capitol ✦✦✦

The fact that Merle Haggard released 30 albums in less than ten years says as much about the country music industry's insatiable need for product as it does about Hag's own prolific creativity. Unfortunately, *His 30th Album* leans more to the industry side of the equation than Merle's artistic side, yet it still remains an enjoyable listen. There is a fair share of filler on the record, including a song sung by the Strangers' rhythm guitarist Ronnie Reno ("Travelin'"), but "Old Man from the Mountain," "White Man Singin' the Blues," "Holding Things Together" and "It Don't Bother Me" make the LP worthwhile for fans. *—Stephen Thomas Erlewine*

Keep Movin' On / 1975 / Capitol ✦✦✦

It's All in the Movies / 1975 / Capitol ✦✦✦

While the title track is a gentle, affecting ballad, *It's All in the Movies* doesn't contain enough similarly engaging material to make the record successful. The album is at its best when Haggard delves into Western swing, such as "Living With the Shades Pulled Down," or when he delivers straightforward ballads like "Nothin's Worse Than Losing" and "I Know An Ending When It Comes, " but too many of the songs on the LP are pleasant, but inconsequential, filler. *—Stephen Thomas Erlewine*

My Love Affair With Trains / 1976 / Capitol ✦✦✦✦

For anyone who has followed Merle Haggard's career over the decades, train and hobo songs seem to be recurrent in his work, no matter which decade—or century—he recorded in. *My Love Affair With Trains* is one of the last two records Haggard cut for Capitol in 1975. It is also is one of Haggard's trademark concept albums, upon which he pays tribute to and laments the railroads' decline as a centerpiece of American life. Haggard has made a life in music of charting the previous and its decline in the present.

In between each track, Hag introduces the next, as these songs cover different historical eras. There's the stunning title track written by Dolly Parton; Stephen H. Lemberg's corny but nonetheless compelling "Here Comes the Freedom Train"; Mark Yeary's "I Won't Give Up My Train," which he re-recorded later for MCA; Dave Kirby's "So Long Train Whistle" and "Where Have All the Hobos Gone"; as well as "The Hobo." It isn't only in the songs that Haggard chronicles the romance and decline of the American railroad; the grain of his voice is a lament, full of mourning and a genuine bittersweet grief—Haggard grew up on the rail lines as his father worked them. Interestingly enough, the tune of Haggard's to appear here is "No More Trains to Ride"; he introduces it with a short reflection on how it had become damn near impossible to hop a freight to ride coast to coast. The oddest inclusion here is the Jerry Jeff Walker/Jimmy Buffett collaboration "Railroad Lady." Hag justifies its inclusion by saying it was stories like this that helped further the legend of the great Black Iron Horse. As Haggard's records go, *My Love Affair With Trains* may seem a bit quaint in retrospect, but its soul and emotion don't date. There is great truth in his performances of these songs, and like virtually everything he records, he tells the truth through these songs as he sees it. —*Thom Jurek*

☆ **Songs I'll Always Sing** / 1976 / Capitol ✦✦✦✦✦
Though many compilations have followed it since it was first released in 1976, *Songs I'll Always Sing* remains one of the definitive Merle Haggard compilations. Relying not only on hit singles, the 20-track double-album set features a number of album tracks and obscurities—such as "Love and Honor," "Silver Wings," "Honky Tonk Night Time Man," "Things Aren't Funny Anymore," and "I Forget You Every Day"—which give a more rounded and accurate picture of Hag's classic Capitol recordings. After all, there were always a handful of killer songs on his individual albums that rivaled his hits singles in terms of quality. In terms of comprehensiveness, both the four-disc box *Down Every Road* and the double-disc *The Lonesome Fugitive* have superceded *Songs I'll Always Sing*, but the double album set will always remain an excellent summation of his heyday. —*Stephen Thomas Erlewine*

My Farewell to Elvis / 1977 / MCA ✦✦
Like much of America, Haggard was touched by the death of Elvis. And Haggard, like many of us, enjoys singing Elvis' tunes. Fortunately, most of us don't record and release those impressions. Sadly, Merle did. —*Jim Worbois*

Walking the Line / 1977 / Epic ✦✦

A Working Man Can't Get Nowhere Today / 1977 / Capitol ✦✦✦✦
One can quibble about packaging and marketing decisions regarding this music, but not the music itself. Sure, it is a little phony to see Merle Haggard dressed up like a hard-hat worker on the front, and making a joke about him leaving his lunchbox behind on the back certainly will bring to mind the line about someone being a couple of sandwiches short of a box lunch. And then there's the stupid note about the problems of the working man signed by "the girls at the office." The country fan would have been much better served by a list of the pickers on the album, because the playing is simply impeccable. This is one of this country legend's well thought-out combinations of hardcore traditional material from Hank Williams and the Delmore Brothers, combined with his own brilliant songwriting from some of his tried and true perspectives, such as the lonely loser of "The Running Kind" or the bittersweet, moderate beer drinking narrator of the title tune. Riding high on the success of the tongue-in-cheek "Okie From Muskogee," Haggard appears comfortable in his role as a philosopher, going way out on a limb on "I'm a White Boy," but, surprisingly enough, the limb doesn't break and he is home free. The hard to count highlights include the charming tribute to Lefty Frizzell, made up almost entirely of lines from his songs, "Blues for Lefty." Backup is simply credited to the Strangers, and it sounds like a well-recorded distillation of one of their typical sets, plenty of twangy picking with a bit of jazzy horns thrown in. There's a cliché about music being so good it goes by really quickly, but in this case not only sheer genius but a total running length of about 24 minutes contribute to this phenomenon. —*Eugene Chadbourne*

I'm Always on a Mountain When I Fall / 1978 / MCA ✦✦✦

The Way It Was in '51 / 1978 / Capitol ✦✦✦
There just doesn't seem to be any winning with record companies sometimes. Merle Haggard no doubt had to fight tooth and nail to get his tributes to Jimmie Rodgers and Bob Wills recorded and released in an era when traditional country music was falling by the wayside. Then, a few years later, Capitol must have decided these records were good ideas after all and wanted a few more of them. Not content to actually let the artist create a new tribute, the label glued together their own two-sided concept album by selecting previously recorded covers of Hank Williams and Lefty Frizzell songs that Haggard had done. These were then slapped on side A and B of this album, united under the theme of that's "The Way it Was in '51," an opening track that Haggard presumably composed and recorded in order to justify this album's reason for existence. What a great example of his vocal prowess, however, when Haggard enters with the song's very first line: "66 was just a narrow two lane highway...." The listener will feel like they have gone back in time a few decades and are tooling down just such a back road. Everything that is on this record was good material to begin with, and even though the concept is a bit bogus from the record buyer's standpoint, philosophically it joins a long list of similar projects as country artists always seem happy to pay tribute to each other. Haggard has a heck of a flair for Williams and Frizzell, draining every possible drop of drama and emotion out of the songs while letting his sidemen (credited? are you kidding?) pick away to their hearts' content. If the listener's country collection if small, this could definitely be an album to add. On the other hand, those who already own a few Haggard albums might want to be careful in case of duplicating too many tracks. —*Eugene Chadbourne*

Country Boy / 1978 / Pair ✦✦✦
Haggard's early years on Capitol are recalled on *Country Boy*, which includes "Everybody's Had the Blues," "Carolyn," and "Things Aren't Funny Anymore." —*Jason Ankeny*

Serving 190 Proof / 1979 / MCA ✦✦✦✦
Haggard appears here in the midst of what he admitted was a mid-life crisis. That's no reason to dismiss this record, however, as crisis introspection served him well. Possibly the best of his MCA albums, it includes "Red Bandana," "My Own Kind of a Hat," and a brooding meditation on the emptiness of stardom called "Footlights." —*Dan Cooper*

Back to the Barrooms / 1980 / MCA ✦✦✦✦✦
"Memories and drinks don't mix too well/Jukebox records don't play those wedding bells." So begins "Misery and Gin," the opening track on Merle Haggard's strongest—and second from last—outing for MCA. While this album is deservedly known for its four classic drinking songs—the aforementioned cut, "Back to the Barrooms," "I Don't Want to Sober Up Tonight," and "I Think I'll Just Stay Here and Drink"—what *Back to the Barrooms* is really about is the wreckage caused by broken amorous relationships and boozy escape as the only way to cope. Produced by Jimmy Bowen with his progressive country style, he understood Haggard's wish to utilize horns and strings in ways not necessarily in concert with traditional country music—à la Bob Wills—yet to write and perform in grand honky tonk fashion. Other than Haggard's relationship with Lewis Talley at Columbia, the Bowen-Hag collaboration was his most successful of the 1970s. Haggard wrote or co-wrote the majority of the album, and, whether intentionally or not, it coincides with the beginnings of his troubles with his then-wife, songwriter Leona Williams (whose co-write with Haggard, "Can't Break the Habit," appears here) as chronicled in his autobiography, *Sing Me Back Home*. The swinging barroom stomp of "Make-up and Faded Blue Jeans" reveals the kind of trouble a man can get into when he loses his focus and his inherent distrust in relationships based on "100 reasons for lookin' away one more time." The contradictions in love are revealed in how we love those who can hurt us the most in Curly Putman's "Ever Changing Woman," with its gorgeous low-end piano lines and Travis-style fingerpicked guitars. Like his best theme records, Haggard reveals all sides of the conflict and its paradoxical nature, showing that nobody ever wins when love ends. The drinking songs here also document Haggard's beginning of a long descent into chronic substance abuse, something he didn't pull out of until the 1990s. Even "Leonard," the seeming oddball track on the record, deals with the meteoric rise to country music fame and fortune to ruin and redemption of a close friend (Tommy Overstreet); it is fraught with the loss of relationships and resultant substance abuse as if it were an equation. This is underlined on the album's closer, "Think I'll Just Stay Here and Drink," which both Wills would have and Ernest Tubb did love. Hardcore honky tonk and swinging Western jazz meet head-on in a tale of romantic loss and alcoholic oblivion: "I could be holdin' you tonight/I could quit doin' wrong and start doin' right/But you don't care about what I think/I think I'll just stay here and drink." This album features Haggard's most consistent, inspiring performance since he left Capitol, and was the beginning of a creative renaissance, though the personal toll it took on him would prove considerable. Why this record has not been remastered for CD is a mystery. —*Thom Jurek*

The Way I Am / 1980 / MCA ✦✦✦
The Way I Am shares many of the same qualities of its predecessor (*Serving 190 Proof*) and successor (*Back to the Barrooms*) albums. That is, it's pretty much a straight-ahead honky tonk album that pays little mind to the contemporary trends of the day. Where it differs from *Serving 190 Proof* or *Back to the Barrooms* is that the performances are a little inconsistent, as is the material. Still, Hag is a reliable performer in that he always delivers a couple of gems. Here, it's in the form of the title track, Floyd Tillman's "It Makes No Difference Now," and three Ernest Tubb covers ("Take Me Back and Try Me One More Time," "I'll Always Be Glad to Take You Back," and "It's Been So Long, Darlin'"). It's enough to make it worth a listen for hardcore Hag followers, but all others may find it a little bit too uneven. —*Stephen Thomas Erlewine*

Rainbow Stew: Live at Anaheim Stadium / 1981 / MCA ✦✦✦
Rainbow Stew: Live at Anaheim boasts an augmented Strangers, with former Texas Playboys Eldon Shamblin, Tiny Moore, and Gordon Terry, and a horn section filling out the band's sound. The result is a wonderful, swinging album, that brings a new spin not only to classics like "I'm a Lonesome Fugitive" and "Sing Me Back Home," but also to Hag's newer songs, "Misery and Gin," "I Think I'll Just Stay Here and Drink" and the title track. —*Stephen Thomas Erlewine*

☆ **Big City** / 1981 / Epic/Legacy ✦✦✦✦✦
When Merle Haggard & the Strangers, along with producer Lewis Talley, entered a recording studio in July of 1981 to make his debut album for Epic—after leaving his long association with MCA—he had no idea that just 48 hours later he and the band would leave, having recorded enough material for two albums, *Big City* and its follow-up, *Going Where the Lonely Go*. *Big City* is a collection of songs focused on the themes of freedom from urban life. Haggard wrote or co-wrote almost every song on the record—except "Texas Fiddle Song," written by his then-wife, Leona Williams—and the free abandon the band plays with here stands in sharp contrast to the material featured on the latter album. *Big City*, both the cut and the album, revisits the seemingly eternal themes in Haggard's best work—the plight of the honest, decent working man amid the squalor, complication, and contradiction of urban life. Besides the title cut, there are bona fide Haggard classics here—and some that aren't but should be. The obvious ones were part of his shows in his fourth decade as a bona fide country legend: "My Favorite Memory" (one of the most beautifully sung and arranged moments of his long career), "Stop the World and Let Me Off," and "Are the Good Times Really Over for Good (I Wish a Buck Was Still Silver)" (an elegiac tome that reveals with resignation and disappointment—as well as some enlightenment—what was spouted off anthemically in "The Fightin' Side of Me" or

"Rainbow Stew" nearly 20 years earlier). For those who see Haggard as an unthinking, reactionary redneck, this song—with its waltz time and striking metaphors—is a prayer for a restoration not only to simplicity, but for those who make decisions to be held accountable for them: "I wish coke was still cola and a joint was a bad place to be/Back before Nixon lied to us all on TV," along with the complexities of his other side: "I wish a man could still work and still wood/I wish a girl could still cook and still would." And while most of the song is an elegy, it ends with Haggard pronouncing hope: "Stop rollin' downhill like a snowball that's headed for hell/Standup for the flag and the Liberty Bell/Let's make a Ford and a Chevy last ten years like they should/The best of the free life is still yet to come/And the good times ain't over for good." The album closes with a Hag stunner, one of his most beautiful and jazzy love songs, "I Always Get Lucky With You." In all, *Big City* and its companion were staggering, auspicious beginnings for Epic, and stand among his finest—and most lasting—recordings. [The CD contains two bonus tracks, an unreleased duet version of "I Won't Give up My Train," with Roger Miller (a solo version appeared on *Going Where the Lonely Go*), and the uncredited "Call Me," a simple ballad with an odd percussion signature that was best left on the cutting-room floor.] *—Thom Jurek*

Going Where the Lonely Go / 1982 / Epic ♦♦♦♦♦

Recorded after his Columbia hit *Big City, Going Where the Lonely Go* is one of Merle Haggard's most criminally overlooked recordings. Recorded in 1982, the vibe is one of Haggard's most laid-back albums, co-produced with Lewis Talley, one of Nashville's kings of understatement (not that there are many). Haggard wrote over half the album, the rest comprised of two songs by his then-wife, Leona Williams; a co-write with Little Jimmy Dickens; Willie Nelson's "Half a Man"; and Jimmy Davis' "Nobody's Darlin' but Mine." But it is Haggard's songs that make this a stellar outing. The title track is a piece of pure country poetry. A painfully slow 4/4 time signature fronted by a bassline, adorned by a three-chord pattern, and filled by slippery piano lines, Haggard sings, "Rollin' with the flow/Goin' where the lonely go/Anywhere the lights are low/Goin' where the lonely go/Makin' up things to do/Not runnin' in all directions tryin' to find you/I'm just rollin' with the flow/Goin' where the lonely go/And I've got to keep goin'/I can't lay down/Sleep won't hardly come/Where there's loneliness all around/I've got to keep goin'/Travellin' down this lonesome road/I'll be rollin' with the flow/Goin' where the lonely go." As Haggard gets to the bridge, a steel guitar and lead guitar trade lines as strings fall in from the edges and cascade around his gorgeous, bluesy voice. The next track, "Why Am I Drinkin'?," is pure honky tonk blues, full of heartbreak and resignation when he asks the question, "Is love just another word for memory?/And is love just another word for pain?/The question is love really the answer/And if so why is love so much to blame/If love is what we're really after, then why am I runnin' away?/And why am I drinkin'/Why am I hurtin' this way?" The guitars and fiddles wend their way around Norm Hamlett's gorgeous pedal steel and drive home the desolate edge in the song. "I Won't Give Up My Train," another country ballad, is particularly poignant, as Haggard addresses the metaphor of his life in music via a brakeman who is married and probably won't be for long, because his wife is tired of always waiting for him. Hargus "Pig" Robbins' piano is unmistakable as it ushers in the a narrative of paradox, contradiction, and loss. When Hag sings, "The baby came in April in Chicago in the pourin' rain/With 12 black cars and empty tank/With three box cars and an empty sack of mail," we can hear Jimmie Rodgers in the grain of his voice, calling from out in the freight yards of history. Other notables are the truly moving "Shopping for Dresses (With No One to Wear Them)," written with Dickens, and "For All I Know," another broken-love song from the other side of love's great divide. Haggard and the Strangers were one of the tightest and most sophisticated bands in country music, inspired by the elaborate arrangements of Bob Wills' band, to the point where Haggard's music from this period transcends country music in its appeal and elegance. It's a pity this one didn't get the notice it deserved—it's a masterpiece. *—Thom Jurek*

A Taste of Yesterday's Wine / 1982 / Epic ♦♦♦

That's the Way Love Goes / 1983 / DCC ♦♦♦

That's the Way Love Goes is another decent collection of laid-back ballads that lets Haggard display some of the full range of his vocal talents, from the jazzy pop of "The Last Boat of the Day" to the poignant lyric of "What Am I Gonna Do (With the Rest of My Life)." A cover of Lefty Frizzell's "That's the Way Love Goes" ranks among the great Haggard ballads. *—Matt Fink*

Pancho & Lefty / 1983 / Epic ♦♦♦♦

On *Pancho & Lefty*, their first album together, Merle Haggard and Willie Nelson managed a rare feat: an album by two legends that lives up to, and at one point exceeds, expectations. In 1982, both artists were at the top of their game, Haggard just having released a great comeback album in *Big City*, and Nelson in the midst of a creative and commercial peak. The centerpiece of the album is the title track. Penned by Texas songwriter Townes Van Zandt, the ballad of two renegades and the respect they earned from the law is the perfect vehicle for Haggard and Nelson, both of whom managed to achieve legendary status in spite of being outsiders to the Nashville establishment. The song's production enhances its power; it is polished without becoming slick (note Nelson's double-tracked guitar solo), and there's power in reserve—in the wrong hands, this could easily have become a bombastic, over the top performance. Nothing else on the album comes close to the majesty of "Pancho and Lefty." That's not to say that the rest is not good, though. The other songs are all relaxed ruminations on life, from the joys of taking it easy on the throwaway "It's My Lazy Day" to the pain of love lost on Nelson's chestnut "Half a Man." Throughout, Haggard and Nelson duet in equal measure; one gets the sense that this is a collaboration in every sense. The sequence of "Reasons to Quit" and "No Reason to Quit" is an inspired bit of programming, both honky tonk songs of the first rank. *Pancho & Lefty* was followed in 1987 by *Seashores of Old Mexico*, a far less successful collaboration. *—Martin Monkman*

Epic Collection (Recorded Live) / 1983 / Epic ♦♦♦

This live album (Haggard's fourth, dates and personnel not indicated) showed up during his stay at Epic Records, allowing the new label to market its own versions of some of his established hits. The '60s material includes Liz Anderson's "(My Friends Are Gonna Be) Strangers" and Haggard's own "Workin' Man Blues," while the '70s are represented by "Trouble in Mind" and "Things Aren't Funny Anymore," and Haggard also gives a fine, loose rendition of "Blue Yodel #2." All of it is well played, though there isn't nearly as much energy here as there is on Capitol's *I Love Dixie Blues*. A good mid-priced mid-career document. *—Bruce Eder*

It's All in the Game / 1984 / Epic ♦♦

His Epic Hits: First Eleven to Be Continued / 1984 / Epic ♦♦♦

As the title implies, *His Epic Hits: First Eleven* covers the first 11 hits Merle Haggard had on Epic Records, including "Are the Good Times Really Over (I Wish a Buck Was Still Silver)," "Pancho & Lefty," "Reasons to Quit," "That's the Way Love Goes," "My Favorite Memory," "What Am I Gonna Do (With the Rest of My Life)," and "You Take Me for Granted." Since most of his early Epic albums were uneven, *His Epic Hits* is especially useful, gathering his best material onto one disc. It should be supplemented by *Greatest Hits of the '80s*, which covers his mid-'80s hits for Epic, as well as a few fine cuts that didn't make this collection. *—Stephen Thomas Erlewine*

Kern River / 1985 / Epic ♦♦♦♦

Amber Waves of Grain / 1985 / Epic ♦♦

His Greatest & His Best / 1985 / MCA ♦♦♦♦♦

Haggard's tenure on MCA was brief but productive. Highlights, all included here, were "If We're Not Back in Love by Monday," "Leonard" (a tribute to songwriter Tommy Collins), and "Misery and Gin." *—Dan Cooper*

Friend in California / 1986 / Epic ♦♦

Out Among the Stars / 1986 / Epic ♦♦♦

On his '90s comeback album, *If I Could Only Fly*, this country legend makes a reference to the "roaring '80s." Listeners familiar with the Merle Haggard output during that decade, however, will know that for Hag it was more like the snoring '80s, at least musically. This is a typical album from this period, and although a low point on a Haggard album might be better than entire records by some country artists, there is still plenty of room for criticism. What he does emotionally with his lyrics is so ripe with sentimentality that with the wrong kind of production it can quickly evolve into just plain rotten. The liquor store robbery that forms the narrative line for the opening track, "Out Among the Stars," might be perfect fodder for a Haggard album of another time and another place, and in fact he makes reference to this type of lawless violence in the lyrics to the much later "Wishing All These Old Things Were New," one of the finest songs he has ever written. But here the result is just overblown, a potboiler on the level of the worst Bruce Springsteen material. Haggard looks exhausted on the cover—it looks like an airbrush was used to remove lines from his face—and perhaps the picture is a reaction shot to the playing of the session guys here. The swinging "Pennies From Heaven," the kind of material Haggard does really well, is a welcome relief from the dirge of over-processed country music, '80s style, but even on this song we have a drummer with feet of lead. The turgid "My Life's Been Grand" is pretty good proof that country music is better when the artist is complaining about things and not indulging in a pastime best described by the Yiddish word "kvelling." *—Eugene Chadbourne*

Chill Factor / 1987 / Epic ♦♦♦♦

Merle Haggard's *Chill Factor* is one of his best efforts of the 1980s, marked by passionate singing and some of his strongest writing of the decade. The songs on the album, most of them written by Haggard, survey his usual concerns: love lost, love found, growing older, and the state of the world. Throughout, Haggard exhibits wisdom in his writing, a wisdom that is also evident in his singing. He's never really resigned to his fate, but he's not railing against it, either. The love songs are varied. "Chill Factor" is a ballad in which Haggard equates the cold outside with the cold he feels inside himself at losing a love, while "Twinkle, Twinkle Lucky Star" picks up the tempo and gives a hint that his lost love may indeed return to him. At the other extreme, "Thanking the Good Lord" finds Haggard singing to a woman with whom he has found love. Haggard's songs of growing older include "Man from Another Time," which eloquently considers a May-December romance, and "Thirty Again," in which he pines for the days when he was 30, delivering the killer line, "They say life starts at fifty/ We've been lied to again my friend." In "1929," Haggard lists problems in the world—hunger lines, skid-row life, inflation—and asks, "Is it the eighties now or 1929?" *Chill Factor* is a solid collection of songs that ranks as one of Merle Haggard's most consistent albums. *—Martin Monkman*

Seashores of Old Mexico / 1987 / Epic ♦♦

Five years after the triumph of *Pancho & Lefty*, Merle Haggard and Willie Nelson recorded the follow-up, *Seashores of Old Mexico*. Alas, little of what made the earlier album so great is in evidence. At times the album sounds like a Merle Haggard record with Willie Nelson on hand as support. "Without You on My Side" reveals no evidence of Nelson and his guitar at all; it sounds like a castoff from Haggard's 1987 *Chill Factor* album. More importantly, the song selection is a mixed bag, with a few top-notch songs mixed with many second-rate ones. The title track and "Jimmy the Broom," both by Haggard, don't match his best writing of the period, and sound stilted and forced. A cover of the Beatles' "Yesterday" doesn't really work either, although they give it a good try. The best tracks on the album are the last two: Nelson's "Why Do I Have to Choose" and Haggard's "Silver Wings," both from the artists' back catalogs. These mark the only times on the album when it sounds like they are really working together. Having achieved a masterpiece on their first outing together, Haggard and Nelson may have set a standard impossible to match; *Seashores of Old Mexico* certainly doesn't come close. *—Martin Monkman*

5:01 Blues / 1989 / Epic ✦✦✦

Though it is a bit uneven, *5:01 Blues* is a mature, subtle and often engaging latter-day release from Merle Haggard. Hag's voice has become jazzier and more nuanced with age, which helps give weight to the lesser material on the album. When he's matched with a terrific song, such as "Sea of Heartbreak," the results are magnificent. *—Stephen Thomas Erlewine*

Blue Jungle / 1990 / Curb ✦✦✦

Greatest Hits of the '80s / 1990 / Epic ✦✦✦

Greatest Hits of the '80s is a nice ten-track collection that covers many of Merle Haggard's biggest hits for Epic Records, including "Chill Factor," "Natural High," "Twinkle, Twinkle Lucky Star," "Let's Chase Each Other Around the Room," and "I Had a Beautiful Time." The rest of the songs are album tracks and concert favorites like "Yesterday's Wine." Though it isn't a comprehensive retrospective of his Epic work, *Greatest Hits of the '80s* remains a good overview and introduction of his latter-day career. *—Stephen Thomas Erlewine*

The Best of Country Blues / 1990 / Curb ✦✦✦

A worthwhile, ten-track budget-line collection, *The Best of Country Blues* includes his treatments of Bob Wills and Jimmie Rodgers, plus original material, all taken from his heyday at Capitol Records. *—Richard Lieberson*

Capitol Collectors Series / Jan. 29, 1990 / Capitol ✦✦✦✦✦

Like any *Capitol Collectors Series*, Merle Haggard's compilation contains an odd mix of classic and lesser-known hits, with a couple of obscurities thrown in for good measure. Though many of his very best songs—"Swinging Doors," "The Bottle Let Me Down," "Sing Me Back Home," "Hungry Eyes," "Okie from Muskogee"—are featured, classics like "Mama Tried," "Sing a Sad Song," "Branded Man," "Carolyn," "If We Make It Through December," and "Kentucky Gambler" aren't included. Which means that *Capitol Collectors Series* is a good sampler of Haggard's classic work and, therefore a good introduction to his sound, even if it isn't a definitive retrospective. At the time of its release, some of the gaps *Capitol Collectors Series* left were filled by *More of the Best*. Both discs have since been supersceded by the comprehensive double-disc *The Lonesome Fugitive*. *—Stephen Thomas Erlewine*

More of the Best / Feb. 1990 / Rhino ✦✦✦✦✦

Rhino's *More of the Best* was designed to complement the hits compilation *Capitol Collectors Series* that was released concurrently, and the single-disc collection certainly does cover many of the songs that failed to make Capitol's cut. Not only does it have hits like "Sing a Sad Song," "Branded Man," "Mama Tried," "Someday We'll Look Back," and "If We Make It Through December," it also has a couple of terrific Capitol-era album tracks ("Silver Wings," "White Line Fever") and MCA hits like "If We're Not Back in Love By Monday," "Ramblin' Fever," "Red Bandana," "I Think I'll Just Stay Here and Drink," and "Rainbow Stew." The MCA hits make *More of the Best* valuable not only as a supplement to *Capitol Collectors Series*, but as a portrait of his late-'70s work. Of course, the four-disc box set *Down Every Road* has superseded *Capitol Collectors Series* and *More of the Best* in terms of comprehensiveness, but the pair of discs is useful for beginners looking for a broad overview of Hag's career, not just the Capitol hits covered by the double-disc *The Lonesome Fugitive*. *—Stephen Thomas Erlewine*

18 Rare Classics / 1991 / Curb ✦✦✦

18 Rare Classics haphazardly compiles number-one hits like "Kentucky Gambler" and "Grandma Harp" alongside obscure material like "Silver Wings" and "Here in Frisco." *—Jason Ankeny*

The Best of the Early Years / 1991 / Curb ✦✦✦

The Best of the Early Years is a fine budget-priced collection of 12 songs Merle Haggard recorded in the late '60s and early '70s, including classics like "Mama Tried," "Today, I Started Loving You Again," "(My Friends Are Gonna Be) Strangers" and "Sam Hill." Though it isn't a comprehensive overview, and it is missing several key track, it is a fine mid-line compilation. *—Stephen Thomas Erlewine*

Super Hits / Mar. 8, 1993 / Epic ✦✦✦

Super Hits offers an overview of Haggard's early-'80s tenure at Epic, and includes the hits "That's the Way Love Goes," "Are the Good Times Really Over (I Wish a Buck Was Still Silver)," and "Going Where the Lonely Go." *—Jason Ankeny*

1994 / Mar. 22, 1994 / Curb ✦✦✦

After a four-year recording silence, he returns with his strongest record since 1981's *Big City*. The first single, "In My Next Life" (written by Max D. Barnes), is the latest entry in Haggard's incomparable registry of the unfulfilled dreams of the salt of the bitter earth. *—Dan Cooper*

★ **Lonesome Fugitive: The Merle Haggard Anthology (1963–1977)** / 1995 / Razor & Tie ✦✦✦✦✦

Razor & Tie's 1995 collection *The Lonesome Fugitive: The Merle Haggard Anthology (1963-1977)* is the gold-standard among Hag collections, containing 40 songs from his classic years at Capitol Records (plus a couple of early singles originally released on Tally, later acquired by Capitol). While there are two box sets—Capitol's essential *Down Every Road* and Bear Family's excellent complete recordings, *Untamed Hawk*—this is the only hits collection to be both comprehensive and concise, containing all the big hits and major songs on one compulsively listenable collection. It's not just that this has all the hits, since it does, it's that the collection chronologically follows his charting singles from 1963's "Sing a Sad Song" to 1977's "A Working Man Can't Get Nowhere Today," skipping only a couple of mid-'70s hits toward the end, adding the timeless "Today I Started Loving You Again" on the first disc, thereby offering a streamlined summary of his period of greatest creativity and commercial success. While Haggard certainly has many terrific, even classic, songs from the 15 years covered here that didn't make the cut, the hits—and every song outside of "Today I Started Loving You Again" charted, including a staggering *22* country number ones—illustrate his growth as both a songwriter and musician and constitute one of the greatest bodies of work in American popular music. It's possible to dig deeper—and most serious listeners owe it to themselves to dig deeper, acquiring either or both of the aforementioned boxes, along with proper albums—but this not only serves as an ideal introduction, it's a perfect summary of Haggard's work and a necessary cornerstone of any country collection. *—Stephen Thomas Erlewine*

☆ **Untamed Hawk: The Early Recordings of Merle Haggard** / 1995 / Bear Family ✦✦✦✦✦

The thing that makes Bear Family's *Untamed Hawk* a little difficult to listen to for pleasure is the very reason it's necessary for serious Merle Haggard fans and collectors: over the course of five discs, it contains all of the Capitol recordings (plus his early work for Talley) between 1962 and 1968, including alternate takes and unreleased cuts. This is a bonanza, since from the outset, Haggard was one of the most reliable of all country singers, turning out consistently enjoyable work, due to his terrific ear for material, excellent songwriting, and performances. He certainly did record a few duds, or at least unrealized tracks, during this time, but those are fascinating in context (either on the original albums or on this box set), but the consistency is rather remarkable; the singles are usually the standouts, but there are many tracks nearly as compelling, as well. This is all apparent on the original albums as well as *Untamed Hawk*, but the box set may not be the best way to hear this music, largely because of the sequencing. Like many Bear Family boxes (or at least their sets from the '80s through the mid-'90s), this places chronological order before listenability, as it presents everything in session order—which means that the alternate takes and false starts slow the momentum of the sessions. This is a problem, but it is one that can be avoided through judicious use of CD programming (or at least the fast forward button), but it does also point out that this set is more for the historian than the casual listener. That said, those listeners that want a complete set of Merle Haggard's groundbreaking '60s recordings will certainly not be disappointed with this, particularly because many of these songs are not easily available on CD, even with the straightup reissues of his '60s albums. And, frankly, if you love Merle Haggard, it is worth investing in this set. His music may have grown richer in the years after this set, but even at the outset, he was one of the most inventive, interesting, enjoyable and flat-out wonderful country artists of his time, and it's all worth hearing, from the singles to the album tracks to the cuts that never were aired before this set. Even if not everything here is perfect, the overall effect is pretty awe inspiring all the same. *—Stephen Thomas Erlewine*

Super Hits, Vol. 3 / Sep. 5, 1995 / Epic ✦✦✦

As part of the Sony *Super Hits* series, these ten tracks provide only adequate representation, at best, of Merle Haggard's mid- to late-'80s hits for that label. Original Epic material—including "Big City," "Twinkle, Twinkle Lucky Star," and "Chill Factor"—is programmed with re-recorded tracks from Haggard's Capitol years: "Workin' Man Blues," "Sing Me Back Home," "Branded Man," and "Carolyn." The disappointment isn't with Haggard's voice as much as his need to revamp his back catalog. For completists only. *—Al Campbell*

I'm a Lonesome Fugitive/Mama Tried / 1996 / BGO ✦✦✦✦✦

I'm A Lonesome Fugitive and *Mama Tried*, two of Merle Haggard's classic late-'60s albums for Capitol Records, are included on this single disc. Though there is a handful of filler on each of the albums, the overall quality of the music on both records is very high—not only are classic singles like "Mama Tried," "I'm a Lonesome Fugitive," and "Someone Told My Story" present, but so are excellent album tracks like "Little Ole Wine Drinker Me," "In the Good Old Days (When Times Were Bad)," "Run 'Em Off," "Skid Row," and "Mary's Mine." *—Stephen Thomas Erlewine*

Vintage Collections Series / Jan. 23, 1996 / Capitol ✦✦✦✦✦

Merle Haggard may be the most over-compiled country artist of his generation, with more than half a dozen different collections over the last few years. This 20-song single disc overlaps several of the others, but will prove of interest even to owners of Capitol's four-CD box, for its inclusion—amid numerous expected hits—of a pair of superb previously unreleased cuts ("Worried, Unhappy, Lonesome and Sorry," "Streets of Berlin"), and a quartet of otherwise unavailable live tracks, including "White Line Fever," "Family Bible," "Okie From Muskogee," etc., from various concert albums. The sound is fine and the notes are fair, though overwritten. *—Bruce Eder*

1996 / Jan. 23, 1996 / Curb ✦✦✦✦

In late 1995, Merle Haggard stood on the stage of the Grand Ole Opry House, acknowledging the music industry's ovation as he accepted his induction into the Country Music Hall of Fame. A few months later, however, his next album came out with no fanfare at all. His record company didn't send promotional copies to reviewers until the album had been out for nearly a month, and no advertising or promotion has been devoted to the music. The album artwork and cover reflect this lack of care: the title, *1996*, is boxed on the cover like a tomb, exactly like Hag's last set, *1994*. What's inside deserves more attention. Recorded in Bakersfield, Haggard's album takes a jaunty yet melancholy look at a middle-aged man's concerns. Not everything works; "Kids Get Lonesome Too" has a grandfatherly sentimentality, but it's not very substantial. The rest carries plenty of meat: "Sin City Blues" bemoans the temptations of New Orleans with Dixieland verve; "Beer Can Hill" is a humorous reminiscence about honky tonkin' in Bakersfield; and "Untanglin' My Mind" (a hit for co-writer Clint Black) is a textbook example of the difference between the stiff perfection of Nashville over-production and the loose, life-affirming musicianship that Haggard prefers. The album's standout is a cover of Iris DeMent's great "No Time to Cry," which Haggard fills with aged, tired wisdom. *—Michael McCall*

★ **Down Every Road** / Apr. 1996 / Capitol ✦✦✦✦✦
Merle Haggard is a rarity: a complex artist, whose rich scope can accurately be summarized through singles, but has far more great material than can be fit on one or two discs. Which, of course, makes him the perfect candidate for a box set, and Capitol released the first comprehensive Hag retrospective in 1996 with the four-disc set, *Down Every Road*. Since Haggard has such a rich, consistent body of his work—the best of his MCA and Epic work, two eras which are covered here, hold their own next to his seminal Capitol material—even four discs leaves behind many a great song, yet only those who would already own all the albums would argue about omissions, because this offers a generous 100 songs, spanning from his earliest work for Talley in the early '60s to his Epic sides of the late '80s, containing all of his big hits and an expert selection of album tracks, such as "Tulare Dust," "Holding Things Together" and "Living With the Shades Pulled Down," that reveal the depth of his music. This is a body of work with few peers in all of popular music—the variety of styles and sounds, his ease on freewheeling Western swing and plaintive ballads, his inventive, nuanced originals and expert ear for material, his supple voice and underrated guitar playing, the support from his brilliant band the Strangers, all add up to one of the greatest catalogs in 20th century music. And while you can get the basics from Razor & Tie's excellent double-disc set *The Lonesome Fugitive*, only *Down Every Road* captures the full extent of his gifts, in a way that is compulsively listenable as well. It's not just the perfect Merle Haggard box set, it's one of the greatest box sets ever released, as well, since it truly presents all sides of its subject, while offering nothing but sheer pleasure in terms of mere listening. (Plus, this is the only place to find some of these great songs, including the aforementioned trio of album tracks, on CD, which makes it necessary for those that already own the albums.) *—Stephen Thomas Erlewine*

16 Biggest Hits / Jul. 14, 1998 / Legacy/Epic ✦✦
One could easily get the impression, just perusing the front and back covers of this album, that it contains the original recordings of some of Merle Haggard's most popular recordings—this is, as a sleeve note puts it, a "unique, chronological collection." In fact, 13 of the 16 tracks are rerecordings made by Haggard in October 1994; only "Big City," "Are the Good Times Really Over (I Wish a Buck Was Still Silver)" and "Going Where the Lonely Go," three of the 12 number-one country hits Haggard recorded for Epic Records in the 1980s, are the original recordings. Don't be fooled. *—William Ruhlmann*

I'm a Lonesome Fugitive/Branded Man / Nov. 3, 1998 / EMI ✦✦✦✦
In 1998, EMI released *I'm a Lonesome Fugitive/Branded Man*, which contained two complete albums—*I'm a Lonesome Fugitive* (1967, originally released on Capitol) and *Branded Man* (1967, originally released on Capitol)—by Merle Haggard on one compact disc. *—Jason Birchmeier*

Strangers/Swinging Doors / Nov. 3, 1998 / EMI ✦✦✦✦✦
In 1998, EMI released *Strangers/Swinging Doors*, which contained two complete albums—*Strangers* (1965, originally released on Capitol) and *Swinging Doors* (1966, originally released on Capitol)—by Merle Haggard on one compact disc. *—Jason Birchmeier*

Yesterday's Wine 1981-1988 / Nov. 15, 1998 / Edsel ✦✦✦✦✦
After a nearly five-year stint at MCA, Merle Haggard left the label for Epic in 1981, where he continued his remarkable string of number-one country singles and chart-topping albums. Even though he had no less than nine number-one hits for the label—and he had nary a one for MCA, although he reached number two often—this time is often overlooked in the history of Hag, because it didn't produce many flat-out classics, which were not running short on MCA (where he did record "I'm Always on a Mountain When I Fall," "Misery and Gin," and "I Think I'll Just Stay Here and Drink"). That's not to say that the Epic recordings were without classics—"Big City," "Are the Good Times Really Over (I Wish a Buck Was Still Silver)," "Let's Chase Each Other Around the Room," and "Twinkle, Twinkle Lucky Star," along with the Willie Nelson duet "Pancho and Lefty," are all firmly part of his canon. But they were a little quieter, a little more laid-back, the sound of a middle-aged man entering a reflective period of his life and career, which is why, even when they were uneven, they made for a fascinating listen. However, as Edsel's 23-track collection *Yesterday's Wine 1981-1988* (billed as 24 on the back cover, but due to running time, a live version of "Workin' Man Blues" was cut) proves, Haggard was hardly erratic during his time at Epic. His first two records, *Big City* and *Going Where the Lonely Go*, were masterpieces, and he constantly delivered good music, which is effectively summarized on this necessary collection. This contains all of his Top Ten hits for Epic, along with a couple of smaller singles and a few live versions of classic oldies (which instead of functioning as filler or bait for the general audience, give the rest of the music here context, especially since his weathered voice gives these readings a different feel), and in their own quiet way they're as solid a body of work as the MCA or Capitol recordings—not as groundbreaking or influential, but they have a deep emotional resonance and are among the finest straight-ahead country of the '80s. The biggest songs here are included at the end of the absolutely essential four-disc retrospective *Down Every Road*, but Haggard certainly had more to offer on Epic, and this necessary collection is as excellent a summary as could be assembled on this phase in Hag's career. *—Stephen Thomas Erlewine*

For the Record: 43 Legendary Hits / Aug. 24, 1999 / BNA ✦✦✦
Released to coincide with the publication of Hag's autobiography, *My House of Memories*, *For the Record: 43 Legendary Hits* is a lavish double-disc set of re-recordings of his biggest hits. With co-producer Lou Bradley, Haggard wisely keeps things spare, simple, and direct, letting the 1999 version of the Strangers, along with a number of studio musicians, treat these songs gracefully. Haggard's voice isn't what it used to be, but it's not bad, either, and he turns in respectable, enjoyable renditions throughout the album. Some listeners may find it to be a little disappointing that there are no real revelations here, but the music is always entertaining, and the duets—with Willie Nelson, Alabama, Brooks & Dunn, and Jewel, whose inclusion may be surprising, but she acquits herself nicely—are all strong. Of course, it doesn't function as a substitute for Haggard's classic original recordings, but longtime fans will likely find this to be a warm, enjoyable stroll through the past with one of country's all-time greats. *—Stephen Thomas Erlewine*

20th Century Masters—The Millennium Collection: The Best of Merle Haggard / Feb. 8, 2000 / MCA ✦✦✦
Part of Universal's massive *20th Century Masters/The Millennium Collection*, this 12-song budget set draws on songs from Haggard's tenure with MCA. Highlights include "I Think I'll Just Stay Here and Drink," "From Graceland to the Promised Land," "If We're Not Back in Love By Monday," and "Misery and Gin." A nice little chunk of another interesting part of Hag's career. *—Cub Koda*

The Ultimate Collection / May 16, 2000 / Hip-O ✦✦✦
If Hip-O's *The Ultimate Collection* doesn't come close to fulfilling the promise of its title, it's because Hip-O is a division of Universal, which also owns MCA. That means that this 20-track collection leans heavily on Merle Haggard's late-'70s recordings for MCA, containing only four singles from his classic '60s stint at Capitol, plus three cuts from his time at Epic in the '80s. In other words, a huge portion of his greatest music is missing. Still, this is Hag that we're talking about, and even if his MCA work pales in comparison to his Capitol recordings, it's still very good to great, and when it's presented in a compilation like this, it seems particularly good. That's because the compilers did an excellent job of picking the highlights from Haggard's time at MCA; even if they did tend to lean on his biggest hits, that still results in a good listen. In fact, it's a bit of a shame that there are Capitol and Epic selections here; since so much of this is devoted to MCA, it's hard not to think *The Ultimate Collection* would be stronger (and more necessary to some Haggard collectors) if it just was devoted to that label. Still, what's here is really good, making *The Ultimate Collection* a good sampler of his mid-period work, even if it falls short of its title promise. *—Stephen Thomas Erlewine*

20 Number One Hits / Sep. 12, 2000 / Varese ✦✦
As the title suggests, *20 Number One Hits* collects a fistful of Merle Haggard's best-loved (and highest charting) hits in this compilation released by Varese Sarabande. Arranged chronologically from his outlaw hit "I'm a Lonesome Fugitive" in 1967 through 1981's "I Think I'll Just Stay Here and Drink," this would seem like the ultimate collection for Haggard fans, but alas this is not the case. Due to rough and reckless livin', the singer was forced to file for bankruptcy in December of 1992 and in order to balance his debts Haggard sold his publishing rights to Sony/Tree. He spent a large portion of time in the mid- to late '90s re-recording his biggest songs, many of which ended up here. The liner notes infer that the tracks appearing on this collection are improvements over the original singles because the wisdom of the years adds a worldly knowledge to the songs. Unfortunately, what this maturity replaces is the fire and guts that made Haggard one of the most rebellious members of the Bakersfield scene. The man who once professed to be proud to be an "Okie From Muskogee" now sounds like he would be quite at home in a slick Nashville studio. A mediocre release, only because the gritty words of a man who turned 21 in prison are saturated in bland young country style. Better compilations exist, notably the Razor & Tie double-disc set *Lonesome Fugitive: The Merle Haggard Anthology (1963-1977)*, which delivers the original recordings of these classic country songs. *—Zac Johnson*

New Light Through Old Windows / Oct. 10, 2000 / 7-N Music ✦✦
Colin Escott's essay in the eight-page booklet accompanying *New Light Through Old Windows* explains that after Merle Haggard sold his publishing to Sony/ATV/Tree Music, the artist re-recorded "his greatest hits for Tree and over the course of several sessions in 1993, 1994, and 1995, put a new spin on some of the most timeless songs in country music." For those not familiar with the originals, these are smooth and flawless renditions released with the care that compilation producer Paul Williams of House of Hits Productions and Digital Sound and Picture's Bill Lacey are known for. Artists from Skeeter Davis to the Grass Roots and girl group faves the Crystals and the Chiffons have updated their repertoire in this fashion, and no matter where a fan falls in the argument for or against, it's as good a thing to have multiple versions as it is to have multiple formats. Who knows how this will pan out hundreds of years into the future, but to have Merle Haggard actually producing the new versions and singing them with an older and wiser voice and perspective is as essential as any random live recording of a vital artist. Nine originals, one co-write—the classic "Okie From Muskogee"—and five cover songs, including a wonderful update of Snuff Garrett and John Durrill's "Misery and Gin," make for an important and enjoyable journey through Haggard's past. *—Joe Viglione*

If I Could Only Fly / Oct. 10, 2000 / Epitaph ✦✦✦✦
For all the '90s, Merle Haggard was stuck in a kind of exile, recording albums that were strangely perched between familiar Haggard material and futile compromises to a modern country radio that would never play material from veterans. Hag knew that he hadn't lost it, so when he finally ran out his contract for Curb, he smartly signed to Anti, a subsidiary of the indie punk label Epitaph. Finally at a label that would let him record a traditional Haggard album, he seized the opportunity with *If I Could Only Fly*, a gentle, understated, largely acoustic album that's easily his best in over a decade. It's easy to draw comparisons to Johnny Cash's Rick Rubin-produced *American Music*, but this is actually a better fit, since nothing here is forced. There's no mention of his wild ways or outlaw posturing; instead he, dwells on being old, not wanting to leave home, and writes frequently about his family. This is not sad and melancholy, it's a sweet, soothing record, filled with intimately autobiographical songs, delivered with ease and subtle shading

through Haggard's always superb vocalizing. *If I Could Fly* benefits considerably from its sheer, warm musicality, and it's easy to be charmed by its stripped-back, organic sound. It sounds so good that it's also easy to overlook that the album is shy a couple of great songs it needed to be an unqualified triumph. Only the sublime "Wishing All These Old Things Were New," "If I Could Only Fly," and "Listening (To the Wind)" are truly significant additions to Haggard's canon. Ultimately, that may be a bit of nitpicking—*If I Could Only Fly* is the first album in years that deserves to be compared to Haggard's classic work. —*Stephen Thomas Erlewine*

Roots, Vol. 1 / Nov. 6, 2001 / Epitaph ✦✦✦✦✦
If I Could Only Fly, Merle Haggard's first album for the indie label Anti, was deservedly hailed as his finest record in decades, as audiences and critics recognized a revitalized Hag. It wasn't just that his songwriting was stronger than it had been, but it was also the unhurried grace of the performances that recalled his peaks with the Strangers in the '60s and '70s. *If I Could Only Fly* set the bar so high that it would have been easy to assume that Haggard couldn't match it with his next album for Anti but, remarkably, *Roots, Vol. 1* surpasses its predecessor, ranking among the very best albums of his long, storied career. The title implies that the record is a return to the beginnings for Haggard, and that's true to a certain extent, but *Roots, Vol. 1* is hardly a studied, self-conscious tribute. Instead, it's an unexpected return to how country records used to be made, inspired largely by Haggard's teaming with Norman Stephens, Lefty Frizzell's longtime guitarist. Stephens and Hag started playing and not long afterward, they decided to make a record, comprised largely of Lefty songs, but also some Hank Thompson and Hank Williams, along with three tunes from Haggard. There are no surprises here—if you know country music, you know these songs—but that's the beauty of the record; since you know these songs so well, it's possible to hear the joy, the elegance, and the brilliance of the performances. And, make no mistake about it, this is a brilliant record, the equal of his legendary Bob Wills tribute, but where that had the spirit of a punk record—Merle learned how to play fiddle weeks before recording—this is the sound of a veteran relaxing, playing the music he loves, but personalizing it through his years of experience, both personal and professional. So, it's an album filled with small gems, but they add up to a large triumph—a rich, masterful album that's not just the best country album of 2001, but one of Haggard's finest moments. —*Stephen Thomas Erlewine*

My Love Affair With Trains/The Roots of My Raising / May 21, 2002 / BGO ✦✦✦✦
This import BGO two-fer combines Merle Haggard's last two records for Capitol, both of them from 1976. *My Love Affair With Trains* harkens back to Haggard's tribute album to Jimmie Rodgers in spirit. It is narrated between cuts, offering different facts, from the history of the railroads to Haggard's personal observations. While he only contributes one original to the set ("No More Trains to Ride"), it nonetheless bears a deeply personal and heartfelt stamp with cuts by Mark Yeary, the title by Dolly Parton, Dave Kirby, and Red Lane. Haggard weaves an iconographic history of the rails—from past to present to uncertain future—seamlessly and with great taste. Likewise, *The Roots of My Raising* is also a deep and moving personal statement. Again, there is only one original on the set ("Am I Standing in Your Way"), but it is no less symbolic an album than *My Love Affair With Trains*. *The Roots of My Raising* garnered Haggard two number-one singles in the title track and Cindy Walker's classic "Cherokee Maiden," which had been a hit for Bob Wills in 1941—Haggard's version uses the same melody. These "roots" Haggard is referring to are loose and slippery; some of them are stylistic and musical roots, hence Jimmie Rodgers' "Delta Blues" and "Gamblin' Polka Dot Blues" as well as Lefty Frizzell's "I Never Go Around Mirrors," while others seem episodically biographical, such as Dave Kirby's "Walk on the Outside," Norm Hamlet's "The Waltz You Saved for Me," and the mythical but symbolic "What Have You Got Planned Tonight Diana?" Together they mark an excellent bookend to the Capitol period, but both albums standup just as well on their own. —*Thom Jurek*

☆ **Hag/Let Me Tell You About a Song** / Jul. 2, 2002 / BGO ✦✦✦✦✦
In 2002, BGO released Merle Haggard's 1971 album *Hag* and 1972 effort *Let Me Tell You About a Song* on a single CD. These two albums were separated by two other records: *Land of Many Churches* and *Someday We'll Look Back*, both from 1971. If *Someday We'll Look Back* would have fit better with *Hag* on a two-fer since it shares a similar sound and sentiment, it's still hard to complain about this disc, since neither album has been released on CD before and they're both among Haggard's best. Which, of course, means this is a necessary purchase for any serious fan of either Hag or country music. —*Stephen Thomas Erlewine*

The Legend of Bonnie & Clyde/Pride in What I Am / Jul. 23, 2002 / BGO ✦✦✦✦
BGO released two of Merle Haggard's late '60s albums, 1968's *The Legend of Bonnie & Clyde* and 1969's *Pride in What I Am*. Two records separated these two albums—the collection *The Best of Merle Haggard* and *Mama Tried*, both released in 1968—and while *Mama Tried* might have made more chronological sense when paired with either, it has frequently been released on CD, whereas these two albums have not. Plus, they fit well together, both sharing folk overtones and complementing each other well in how the first boasts more covers than originals while the latter is the reverse. Furthermore, both are first-rate records, with much more to offer than their respective hit singles, which is why this is a necessary purchase for any serious Haggard fan. —*Stephen Thomas Erlewine*

Bill Haley

b. Jul. 6, 1925, Highland Park, MI, d. Feb. 9, 1981, Harlingen, TX
Guitar, Vocals / Rock & Roll, Western Swing, Rockabilly
Bill Haley is the neglected hero of early rock & roll. Elvis Presley and Buddy Holly are ensconced in the heavens, transformed into veritable constellations in the rock music firmament, their music respected by writers and scholars as well as the record-buying

public, virtually every note of music they ever recorded theoretically eligible for release. And among the living rock & roll pioneers, Chuck Berry is given his due in the music marketplace and by the history books, and Bo Diddley is acknowledged appropriately in the latter, even if his music doesn't sell the way it should. Yet Bill Haley—who was there before any of them, playing rock & roll before it even had a name, and selling it in sufficient quantities out of a small Pennsylvania label to attract attention from the major labels before Presley was even recording in Memphis—is barely represented by more than a dozen of his early singles, and recognized by the average listener for exactly two songs among the hundreds that he recorded; and he's often treated as little more than a glorified footnote, an anomaly that came and went very quickly, in most histories of the music. The truth is, Bill Haley came along a lot earlier than most people realize and the histories usually acknowledge, and he went on making good music for years longer than is usually recognized.

The central event in Haley's career was the single "Rock Around the Clock" topping the charts for eight weeks in the spring and summer of 1955, an event that most music historians identify as the dawn of the rock & roll era. Getting the song there, however, took more than a year, a period in which the band had already done unique and essential service in the cause of bringing rock & roll into the world, with the million-selling single "Shake, Rattle and Roll" to their credit; equally important, in the three years before that, Haley and his band had already broken new ground with the singles of "Rocket 88," "Rock the Joint," and "Crazy, Man, Crazy."

Born in Highland Park, MI, in 1925, Haley was blind in one eye from birth, and, as a consequence, suffered from terrible shyness as a boy. The family moved to Boothwyn, PA, during the mid-'30s, where Haley developed a strong love for country music and began playing guitar and singing; by 14, he had left school in the hope of pursuing a career in music. He bounced through a few country bands based in the Middle Atlantic states and also tried to establish himself as a singing and yodeling cowboy. His first big break came in 1944, when he replaced Kenny Roberts—who was being drafted—in the Downhomers, with whom Haley made his first appearance on records. Haley left the group in 1946 and went through several other bands before returning to his home in Chester, PA, where he initially hoped to get some work as a DJ. Instead, he formed a new band, the Four Aces of Western Swing, with keyboardman Johnny Grande, bassist Al Rex, and steel guitar player Billy Williamson, and signed a contract with Cowboy Records, a new label formed by James Myers, a composer, musician, and publisher, and his partner, Jack Howard.

Their first record was released in 1948, a version of "Candy Kisses"; by 1949, the group had changed its name to the Saddlemen and began moving between labels, including liaisons with the fledgling Atlantic Records, Ivin Ballen's Gotham Records, and Ed Wilson's Keystone Records, before finally settling at Holiday Records, a small label owned by David Miller, in 1951. Their first release, done at Miller's insistence, was a cover of "Rocket 88," a song that originated out of Sam Phillips' fledgling recording operation in Memphis, courtesy of Jackie Brenston. It was a pumping piece of sexually suggestive, rollicking R&B, and Haley and the Saddlemen simply put a broader, slightly loping country boogie sound onto it and boosted the rhythm section, while a lead guitar (probably played by Danny Cedrone) noodled some blues licks on the break. Haley hadn't liked the idea of doing the song, but Miller wanted it, and the result—though no one knew it at the time—was the first white-band cover of what is now regarded by many scholars as the first real rock & roll song.

Just to put this in perspective, rock & roll is usually written about as a phenomenon (and a reaction to) the complacency of the Eisenhower era. But Haley had released what amounted to a rock & roll single in 1951, when "Ike" wasn't even yet running to be president, the country was still mired in Korea, and John Kennedy not yet even a senator. Howlin' Wolf was still based in Memphis and cutting sides for Sam Phillips, while a 15-year-old Elvis Presley was in tenth grade. The members of the Beatles and the Rolling Stones were still in grammar school; Lonnie Donegan was still known as Anthony Donegan and thinking of becoming an entertainer; and Alexis Korner and Cyril Davies had not yet even met. And Big Bill Broonzy was about to introduce American blues to England.

At the time, "Rocket 88" didn't seem to matter too much in terms of sales, as it was neither fish nor fowl; not good enough R&B to eclipse Brenston's original among black record buyers, nor sufficiently a country record the way white audiences or the radio stations that catered to them wanted. No one even had a name for what it was; a "race record" as the trades called discs done in a style that seemed aimed at black listeners, but one done by a white band in a kind of country style. Indeed, the band itself remained strangely anonymous; Miller had seen to it that there were no publicity photos of Bill Haley & the Saddlemen, a calculated effort to obscure their race, though the band's name and the country ballad B-sides to those early singles pretty much told who they really were. That debut single sold just a few thousand copies regionally, as did its follow-up, "Green Tree Boogie." Meanwhile, when Haley and his band played, they and their business manager, Jim Ferguson, began to notice that it was the younger audience members who responded best to the R&B-style songs that Miller had them doing. They also saw all around them that enthusiasm for country music was flat, and that if they were looking for a hit, it likely wasn't going to come from this new direction.

They were trying all kinds of permutations of country and R&B and getting some response, but they didn't know what it exactly was that they were doing musically. Then came "Rock the Joint," their first release on Miller's new Essex Records label; it had a beat, it had a memorable catch phrase, and it had a great performance at its core (including the very same solo that Danny Cedrone would later use on "Rock Around the Clock"), and it sold well enough that the band had to go on tour promoting it. One of the places where it sold well was Cleveland, where DJ Alan Freed picked up on the song; it was immediately after this that Freed began referring to the music embodied by "Rock the Joint," music that he played every night on his show, as "rock & roll," thus giving Haley a good deal of justification for his later claim to have been in on the birth of the music before anyone ever knew it. [Note: Marshall Lyttle remembers "Rock the Joint" as the song Freed was playing during an appearance by the band on his radio show, when he began using the phrase "rock & roll"—scholars who agree with the Haley connection also often attribute Freed's inspiration to the later single "Crazy, Man, Crazy," while other historians say that Freed appropriated the phrase from Wild Bill Moore's "We're Gonna Rock, We're Gonna Roll".]

By this time, the bandmembers, all well into their 30s and long past being teenagers, were taking what amounted to a crash course in what that audience wanted; at Ferguson's suggestion, they played hundreds of high-school dances, not normally a venue that a professional country band would bother with. In the process, they also changed their image and name. By 1952, Bill Haley & the Saddlemen were history; instead, playing off of their leader's name and the celestial phenomenon called Halley's Comet, they became Bill Haley & His Comets. The cowboy hats and other country paraphernalia were junked as well. And they took a close look at the successful R&B stage acts of the time, especially the Treniers, and began working out wild quasi-acrobatic moves by their bass player and saxman, in particular, stuff that was unthinkable for a country band but seemingly what the kids devoured at dances.

Most important, they would try out material, phrases, and stage moves, seeing what worked and what didn't, in front of the teenage audiences they found in Pennsylvania; and they listened to the way that this teenaged audience talked. Haley tried to use phrases that he heard, and put them into this musical stew; some of what they came up with was pleasantly silly material like "Dance With a Dolly" and "Stop Beatin' Round the Mulberry Bush" (though even the latter had a guitar solo worth hearing more than once). But some of it, like "Rockin' Chair on the Moon," was years ahead of its time; and some of it, like "Crazy, Man, Crazy"—a Haley original whose title came from a piece of teen slang that he'd heard—did exactly what was intended, hitting the Top 20 on the pop charts in 1953, a first for a white band playing an R&B-style song. Late that year, James Myers offered Haley and Miller a song that he had published (and, on paper, at least, co-authored as Jimmy De Knight) entitled "Rock Around the Clock." Written almost as a parody of R&B conventions, its principal composer was Max C. Freedman, a songwriter best remembered up to that time for his 1946 hit "Sioux City Sue," and also responsible for such songs as "Do You Believe in Dreams" and "Her Beaus Were Only Rainbows." Miller either genuinely didn't see the potential of the song, or else he didn't like the business arrangement that Myers had with Haley, because he refused to record it. After a few more attempts at cutting other songs for the teen market that simply didn't work, Haley and the band and their manager were ready to leave Miller and Essex Records. A meeting was set up with Milt Gabler, a producer at Decca Records, who not only liked the song and had no problem cutting it, but saw some serious potential in Bill Haley & His Comets, based on what Essex had done with them on "Rock the Joint" and "Crazy, Man, Crazy." A contract was signed, and on April 12, 1954, the band, with Danny Cedrone on lead guitar, did a two-song session in New York that yielded "Thirteen Women"—a post-nuclear holocaust sex fantasy worthy of Hugh Hefner (who had only started up *Playboy* magazine a year earlier)—and "Rock Around the Clock." It was released a month later and made the charts for one week at number 23, selling 75,000 copies, not bad but not very significant either.

It was enough, however, for Gabler to schedule another session in early June, where the band recorded "Shake, Rattle and Roll." That was the record that broke the band nationally on Decca, reaching number seven and selling over a million copies between late 1954 and early 1955. They followed it up quickly with "Dim, Dim the Lights (I Want Some Atmosphere)," a jaunty piece that reached number 11 nationally and actually made the R&B charts for Haley, a first for him. Then, in early 1955, James Myers managed to get "Rock Around the Clock" placed in the juvenile delinquency drama *The Blackboard Jungle*, playing over the credits. The movie was a huge hit, and in its wake Decca re-released the song that spring. "Rock Around the Clock" shot up the charts this time, and the result was an eight-week run in the number-one spot; by some estimates, it became the second biggest worldwide-selling single after Bing Crosby's "White Christmas" (oddly enough, also a Decca release), 25-million copies sold worldwide.

The success of "Rock Around the Clock" took place while Elvis Presley had yet to chart a record nationally; at a point when Chuck Berry's very first single for Chess had barely been recorded; and when Roy Orbison and Buddy Holly weren't even close to auditioning for recording contracts. One has to visualize a reality in which Bill Haley & His Comets were the only established white rock & roll band, and the only white rock & roll stars in the world. Within a year, that would all change, but it was long enough for Haley and his band to become stars, with appearances on national television and a movie deal of their own. From the end of 1954 until the end of 1956, they would place nine singles into the Top 20, one of those at number one and three more in the Top Ten.

The Comets were one of the best rock & roll bands of their era, with a mostly sax-driven sound ornamented with heavy rhythm guitar from Haley, a slap-bass, and drumming with lots of rim-shots; they had the "blackest" sound of any white band working in 1953-1955. It wasn't always obvious then, and has been forgotten today, precisely how fluid their membership was, for all of the consistency of that sound. Haley's two original bandmates from his Four Aces days, Johnny Grande and Billy Williamson, were formal partners, joined to him at the hip legally, with fixed shares in the group's earnings; tenor saxman Joey D'Ambrosio, bassist Marshall Lytle, and drummer Dick Richards, by contrast, were hired employees earning 150 dollars a week plus expenses—a respectable living for most working musicians in 1955—when "Rock Around the Clock" hit the top of the charts. Ironically, Danny Cedrone, whose guitar dominated that song and the key Essex hits "Rock the Joint" and "Crazy, Man, Crazy," died in an accident in July of 1954, and his successor, Franny Beecher, was earning 150 dollars a week when he worked with the band. In the late summer of 1955, with a number-one single to their credit and lots of work in front of them, D'Ambrosio, Lytle, and Richards all demanded raises, which Haley refused to grant them. They quit that month and formed a short-lived Comets soundalike unit called the Jodimars (taken from parts of their first names), who recorded for Capitol Records. Beecher was taken into the group as a full-time member (though not a partner) and remained with them until 1961, while D'Ambrosio's successor, Rudy Pompilli, became a core member of the band, working with them virtually without interruption for the next 19 years, until his death in 1975.

In the late spring of 1956, rock & roll changed again as Elvis Presley, who was younger, leaner, and a more fiercely sexual presence, emerged as a star; he not only made music that was as good as Haley's but he looked the role of a rock & roll star. The differences in their respective images could be summed up by examining the truest scenes in the movies that each did. *Rock Around the Clock*, starring Bill Haley & His Comets, was a highly fictionalized account of the band and its success, but it did capture something of the spirit of the early days of rock & roll, with some good performance clips; the comparable Elvis Presley movie was *Loving You*, in which the singer played a fictionalized version of himself, named Deke Rivers. In *Loving You*, when Deke Rivers performs in front of an audience and sets the girls screaming and swooning, his would-be manager comments, "If he'd gone on any longer, they'd be giving him their door keys." In *Rock Around the Clock*, by contrast, the single truest scene depicts a would-be promoter driving through rural Pennsylvania and chancing upon a dance where Haley and company are playing; he enters, sees hundreds of kids dancing to the band's music, and asks a woman being lifted up over the head of her partner, "Hey sister, what's that exercise you're getting?" She answers, exuberantly, legs in the air, "It's rock & roll!"

Haley's music was the soundtrack to a good-time, whether dancing or more private recreation; Presley's music, at least where women were concerned, was an invitation to sexual fantasy about the singer. Nobody except the three Mrs. Haleys could have had sexual fantasies about pudgy, balding, dorky-looking Bill Haley. And, yet, Haley was every bit as outrageous and daring in what he got away with in his music as the worst accusations ever leveled against Presley; even Haley's bowdlerized version of "Shake, Rattle and Roll" was the most overtly sexual song ever to reach the American Top Ten up to that time, and "Rock Around the Clock" wasn't very far behind. Though Max C. Freedman might've meant his song differently, taken literally in the true meaning of the word "rock" as it was used in 1953-1954, "Rock Around the Clock" was a bouncing, beguiling musical account of 24 hours of sexual activity, and the precursor to such numbers as "Reelin' & Rockin'" by Chuck Berry. Haley might've looked the part of the square trying to be cool once Presley came along, but on those two songs he was as culturally and morally subversive as the worst warnings of the anti-rock & roll zealots intimated.

Haley may not have seemed a cutting-edge artist after mid-1956, but he remained a force to be reckoned with in music for another year, cutting good singles—including "Razzle-Dazzle," "Burn That Candle," and "See You Later Alligator"—and several surprisingly strong albums. He did gradually lose touch with the teenage audience, and his square persona couldn't possibly compete with the likes of Presley, Jerry Lee Lewis, and Chuck Berry, though the group always put on a good show. Additionally, overseas, where any visiting American artist was treated well, Haley was greeted like visiting royalty; he always had large and fiercely loyal audiences in England, France, and Germany, which would turn out in huge numbers to see him.

By 1959, Haley was no longer placing either singles or albums anywhere near the top of the charts. His brand of rock & roll, made up of R&B crossed with country boogie and honky tonk, was passé, and a switch to instrumentals didn't solve the problem of falling sales. None of this would have been so bad, except that Haley—mostly through the horrendous job done by his business manager Jim Ferguson—had managed to squander most of what he'd earned during the good years, and owed a crippling tax liability to the government as well. Contrary to the popular perception, he remained an active musician throughout the 1960s, recording for Warner Bros. and a brace of other U.S. labels, and he also found a lucrative performing and recording career in Mexico (where Haley, not Chubby Checker or Hank Ballard, started the "twist" craze). He pursued a music career while avoiding tax liens, and trying to keep a marriage and a collapsing publishing business together. Haley managed to pull it off, getting through the decade with some possessions still in his hands, mostly by juggling a lot of gigs in Mexico and Europe and taking lots of payments in cash. Curiously, during this period Haley himself became something of a rock & roll historian in interviews; perhaps sensitive to his own experience of being shunted aside, when he talked about the twist phenomenon, he went out of his way to credit Hank Ballard as the originator of the song, and always acknowledged his debt to Big Joe Turner for "Shake, Rattle and Roll."

By the late '60s, with the advent of the rock & roll revival, Haley suddenly found himself faced for the first time in a decade with major demand for his work in America. It couldn't have happened at a better time, because that same year, for the first time in more than ten years, he didn't owe anything to the government. The Internal Revenue Service had been seizing all of his royalties from Decca Records for a decade, and luckily for him, Decca (possibly thanks to Milt Gabler) had been honest in its accounting; in that time, sales of "Rock Around the Clock" and his other Decca hits, mostly overseas, had wiped out Haley's entire six-figure tax debt. And to top off the good news, Haley not only had a full concert schedule in front of him in the U.S., but major record labels interested in recording him; he ended up signing with Buddha/Kama Sutra Records for a pair of live albums. The next few years showed Haley in a triumphant comeback around the world. To top it all off, "Rock Around the Clock" even charted anew in the Top 40 during 1974 when it turned up as the theme music for the hit television series *Happy Days* during its first season.

By the 1970s, however, age and the ravages of time were starting to catch up on all concerned. Saxman Rudy Pompilli, who'd been with him since 1955, died in 1975, and Haley eventually retired from performing. During his final years, Haley developed severe psychological problems that left him delusional at least part of the time. By the time of his death in 1981, the process of reducing his role in the history of rock & roll had already begun, partly a result of ignorance on the part of the writers handling the histories by then, and also, to a degree, as a result of political correctness; he was white, and was perceived as having exploited R&B, and there were enough people like that in the early history who had to be written about but were easier to cast as "rebels."

In the years since his death, the surviving members of the Comets, including pianist Johnny Grande, guitarist Franny Beecher, saxman Joey D'Ambrosio, bassist Marshall Lytle, and drummer Dick Richards, all in their 70s and 80s, have continued to work together and were still able to perform to sell-out crowds in Europe during the 1990s and early 2000s, doing Haley's classic repertory. Haley's own reputation has increased somewhat, particularly in the wake of Bear Family Records' release of two boxes covering his career from 1954 through 1969, and Roller Coaster Records' issuing of Haley's Essex Records sides. True, there are perhaps 45 songs on those 12 CDs of material that Haley should not have bothered recording, but there are hundreds more in those same collections, some of it dazzling and all of it constituting a serious body of solid, often inspired rock & roll, interspersed here and there with some good country sides. Perhaps little of the post-1957 stuff could set the whole world on fire, but Haley had already been there and done that, and still had a lot of good music to play. *—Bruce Eder*

Greatest Hits / 1969 / MCA ✦✦✦
The mini-skirted go-go dancers pictured on the cover reveal the year of release, a considerable distance from Haley's classic period, and it is amazing that Decca didn't have a hits compilation out earlier. The songs speak for themselves, and loudly, however—apart from "Rock Around the Clock" and "Shake Rattle and Roll," the highlights include "Thirteen Women," a delightfully surreal end-of-the-world rockabilly fantasy about a man on a post-nuclear world who finds himself the only male to service 13 fertile female survivors. *—Bruce Eder*

★ **From the Original Master Tapes** / 1985 / MCA ✦✦✦✦✦
This is it—the Bill Haley record to own! Compiled by producer Steve Hoffman from the original session masters (you even get studio chatter ahead of "Rock Around the Clock"), this 20-song collection is the definitive Haley hits collection, with every song of consequence that he recorded for Decca Records during the years 1954-1956. The sound is extraordinary—you haven't really heard Haley's music till you've heard this disc—and the sessionography adds a great deal to our knowledge of the players. From "Rock Around the Clock" and "Thirteen Women" to "Don't Knock the Rock," this is the best representation of Haley's peak years. *—Bruce Eder*

The Decca Years & More / 1991 / Bear Family ✦✦✦✦
Any casual listener looking over this 132-track five-CD set would probably conclude that it was far more Bill Haley than they need bite off in one gulp—and they'd be right, as casual listeners. For the serious rock & roll enthusiast, as well as the hardcore Bill Haley fan, however, there's a wealth of worthwhile material to be found here, some of which will amaze even those fans: a dozen great songs and 55 or so more that are good, and another 20 that are fascinating mistakes, and that's a good average for an artist who is generally thought of as having generated just a handful of important records. What Haley had most of all was a distinctive sound—between the backbeat, the country boogie roots, and the R&B sources—that pretty much defined white rock & roll for almost its first two years (until Elvis Presley and Carl Perkins emerged in the spring of 1956); the first two CDs here offer that sound in abundance. They offer Haley's complete recordings from April 12, 1954 (the session that yielded "Rock Around the Clock"), until July 15, 1957, capturing an urgent, creative, and exciting era in the music and the band's output, when they seemingly couldn't help but make good records. The first 40 songs in the box are a reminder of a time when Haley and company were still very much in the game, with Elvis Presley, Carl Perkins, and more in the front ranks of rock & roll (although, to be fair, the later sides on the second disc show them losing that game). Discs three and four's chronology cover the group's decline in 1958-1959, as they careened from one especially disastrous idea (the *Rockin' Around the World* album) through some good, thumping rock & roll that just happened to be out of date in 1958 (in the guise of "Skinny Minnie"), then into a movie-related musical liaison with Caterina Valente, and to their final sessions for Decca. That was a point where Haley and his band got back some of their vitality and creativity and cut some better-than-decent rock & roll, tagging on his good 1964 single "Green Door" and a pair of 1958 vintage demos. Disc five is a fascinating bonus, a 62-minute assembly of excerpts from two complete recording sessions in January 1959 working their way back to a body of musically (if not commercially) viable, solid rock & roll on numbers like "A Fool Such As I" and "I Got a Woman." In addition to the usual excellent Bear Family mastering job, the box offers a very nicely designed booklet by rockabilly scholar Colin Escott, and one of the better accounts of Haley's overall career up through 1964. The price may be steep, but most of what's here—and most of it isn't easily found anywhere else, or organized as neatly where it does show up—will appeal to anyone who ever took a closer listen on their own to "Rock Around the Clock," just to pick up on what's going on inside of it between the boogie-woogie beat and the string-bending by Danny Cedrone. The total immersion that it allows in the work of Haley, Cedrone's successor, Frannie Beecher, and saxman Rudy Pompilli will delight those listeners who have the budget to afford it. *—Bruce Eder*

Best of Bill Haley / 1995 / Castle Communication ✦✦✦
There are no liner notes to speak of on Castle's 1995 compilation *The Best of Bill Haley*, outside of a list of other titles available form the label's MAC series, and while there may be a perfectly innocent explanation for this, it's hard not to think that whoever released this album wanted to make sure that listeners didn't realize that these were '60s re-recordings by Haley and his latter-day Comets until the last possible minute. Unlike some re-recordings, these aren't horrible—sometimes, they're sorta fun, like with the slow swaggering groove of "See You Later Alligator"—but they sure ain't what you want to hear if you're looking for the original versions of "Rock Around the Clock" and "Shake, Rattle and Roll," among other hits. Not a bad overview of the re-cuts and also-rans from the '60s for Haley, but it sure isn't what anybody purchasing an album called *The Best of Bill Haley* would want. *—Stephen Thomas Erlewine*

Rock the Joint! / Apr. 5, 1995 / Schoolkids ✦✦✦✦✦
A 22-track collection that collects sides from 1951-1953. Those who haven't heard this material before will be astonished to discover bona fide rock & roll dating from three to four years earlier than the era (1954-1955) more commonly associated with the music's birth. Haley's sound is similar to the country-boogie of the late '40s, retaining the steel guitar prominent in much of the era's country music, but it's clearly more driving and forward-looking. The songs owe a lot to jump R&B but are transformed into the basic model of rock & roll with slapping bass, ricky-tick drums, and extended electric guitar riffing. Listen to his version of Jackie Brenston's "Rocket 88" (which has itself been pegged as one of the first rock & roll records) and you'll be astounded to note the basics of rockabilly already in place—in 1951. The low buzzing, distorted guitar on "Green Tree Boogie" (also from 1951) is also a revelation, as is the guitar solo on 1952's "Rock the Joint," which is almost identical to the much more famous one on "Rock Around the Clock." The later sides introduce a honking sax, which would become such a prominent feature in 1950s rock & roll. Includes "Crazy Man Crazy," the first rock & roll song to make the Top 20. *—Richie Unterberger*

American Legends, No. 20: Bill Haley & The Comets / Apr. 1996 / LaserLight ✦✦
Leaving Decca Records, where he had recorded his hits, at the start of the 1960s, Bill Haley & the Comets landed a deal with then-fledgling Warner Bros. Records, for which they naturally re-recorded their hits. (The 1960 release was called *Bill Haley & His Comets*, Warner Bros. 1378.) There they are again, 36 years later, on a budget label and of course without any indication on the cover that these are not the original versions. In 27 minutes, the group revives "Rock Around the Clock," "Crazy Man, Crazy" and such contemporaneous hits as "Blue Suede Shoes" and "Blueberry Hill." If you aren't expecting the hit versions and pay no more than the budget price, this album is a minor curiosity; otherwise, it's a rip-off. *—William Ruhlmann*

● **20th Century Masters—The Millennium Collection: The Best of Bill Haley & His Comets** / Apr. 20, 1999 / MCA ✦✦✦✦✦
Like any record company worth their salt, MCA knows a good gimmick when they see it, and when the millennium came around ... well, the *20th Century Masters—The Millennium Collection* wasn't too far behind. Supposedly, the millennium is a momentous occasion, but it's hard to feel that way when it's used as another excuse to turn out a budget-line series. But apart from the presumptuous title, *20th Century Masters—The Millennium Collection* turns out to be a very good budget-line series. True, it's impossible for any of these brief collections to be definitive, but they're nevertheless solid samplers that don't feature a bad song in the bunch. For example, take Bill Haley's *20th Century* volume—it's an irresistible 12-song summary of his Decca/MCA years. There may be a couple of noteworthy songs missing, but many of his best-known songs for the label are here, including "Rock Around the Clock," "Shake, Rattle & Roll," "Thirteen Women," "Dim, Dim the Lights," "The Saints Rock n' Roll," "Burn that Candle," and "See You Later, Alligator." Serious fans will want something more extensive, but this is an excellent introduction for neophytes and a great sampler for casual fans, considering its length and price. That doesn't erase the ridiculousness of the series' title, but the silliness is excusable when the music and the collections are good. *—Stephen Thomas Erlewine*

The Warner Brothers Years & More / Jun. 23, 1999 / Bear Family ✦✦✦✦
The rating of this six-CD set is no joke—yes, Bill Haley was supposed to be an irrelevant artist during the 1960s, but he did, in fact, generate well over 100 good and far-better-than-decent sides that are contained in this set. No, there's nothing remotely as earth-shattering or important as his best work for Decca from 1954-1955, and even most hardcore fans of that material may find the cost of this set difficult to justify; but take it from someone who shelled out for this box, it's worth a LOT more than you'd ever guess without hearing it—Haley and his band still knew how to work a song, as demonstrated several dozen times on this set. The title is actually a bit misleading, since the sides that Haley recorded for Warner Bros. Records amount to less than a third of the contents of this box. Disc one is given over to the principal contents of Haley's two Warner albums and their accompanying singles, which include his versions of a brace of rock & roll oldies (among them recuttings of "Rock Around the Clock" and "Shake, Rattle and Roll," as well as hits identified with Jerry Lee Lewis, et al.) and some excellent country standards. Disc two wraps up the Warner Bros. sides (apart from a series of outtakes that appear on disc six) in surprisingly strong form, including a good version of "Let the Good Times Roll, Creole," and unearths a pair of mysterious recordings—"Jack in the Box" and "Pistol Packin' Mama"—by Haley and his band with an unidentified baritone singer; it also offers four songs that he recorded for Gone Records in the early '60s, and an album's worth of tracks (including a hot version of "Yakety Sax") that Haley and company recorded for the Guest Star label in 1962. None of this is bad stuff—it's often a good deal better than, say, the songs that Elvis Presley was doing in his movies of the era, and it shows that Haley was still a solid, viable performer and musician a good decade after his breakthrough, and six years beyond the point where most pop historians have usually written him off. Franny Beecher was with him until the Roulette sides were done—and Johnny Kay was a good substitute on the Guest Star sides—and Rudy Pompilli was there all the way, honking away in generally fine style. Disc three is largely devoted to Haley's sides for the Newtown and Nicetown labels from 1963, and his dance recordings for the Apt Records label in 1965, and his abortive liaison with United Artists Records in 1968; some of the Newtown/Nicetown numbers are embellished with the sound of keyboards and backing vocals, but the core of Haley's music is there, and he's in much finer form even on those tracks than he was on many of the late Decca sides; only the novelty tunes like "Tongue-Tied Tony" and "Tenor Man" fall flat to varying degrees, but his rippling version of "Flip, Flop & Fly" is more than adequate compensation for such lapses. Finally, disc four brings us up to 1969 and Haley's participation in Richard Nader's Rock 'N' Roll Revival shows, and the concerts—best known for their partial release on various Buddah and Kama Sutra albums, but included here in their entirety—that he played at New York's *Bitter End*. Discs five and six, together in a narrow double-pack, are comprised of outtakes, demos, the live sides recorded for Gone Records at the Roundtable, and various tracks of indeterminate date and origin. The box comes with Bear Family's usual thoroughly annotated booklet and complete session information, and it's certain to delight and amaze even serious Bill Haley fans, as well as anyone else who ever wondered about the later work of this lost hero of rock & roll. *—Bruce Eder*

On the Air / Jun. 12, 2001 / Hydra ✦✦✦
The more one hears of Bill Haley & His Comets as they sounded in the 1960s—yes, the 1960s, the decade in which they supposedly became irrelevant—the more impressed one

gets, and this German CD doesn't break that spell. Derived from a pair of mid-1962 studio sessions for the Armed Forces Radio Network, while the group was on tour in Germany, the material on this CD captures the Comets as a still very tight, exciting working rock & roll band, still capable of generating lots of energy in their performances; additionally, the interview segments with Haley in between the songs present the bandleader at the top of his game as a spokesman for rock & roll history as well as the band, even giving Hank Ballard (the forgotten man in the "twist" craze of the era) a big nod in his talk about some of the music. Surprisingly, Haley handles the lead vocals on a few numbers here, "Rock Around the Clock," "Shake Rattle and Roll," "The Saints Rock and Roll," and "See You Later, Alligator," with lead guitarist Johnny Kay, bassist Al Rappa, and steel guitarist Billy Williamson doing the rest of the singing—the band also does a large number of instrumentals, which are excellent showcases for saxman Rudy Pompilli as well as for Kay's playing. The sound is generally good, with only minor distortion and fluctuation in a few short sections (the former just because of overload on the volume), and the performances are mostly all worthwhile, especially on the extended numbers such as the five-minute version of "Honky Tonk." The second broadcast will probably be less appealing, featuring as it does mostly lesser songs (albeit mostly in good performances), such as "The Saints Rock and Roll," "JA-DA," and "Malaguena," but this was all part of the repertory of the band at the time, done live and unedited as they might have performed it at the Star Club. The annotation by Chris Gardner is extraordinarily detailed and very entertaining as well, and this CD is overall the perfect companion to either of the Bear Family Records boxes devoted to Haley's music. *—Bruce Eder*

Connie Hall

b. Jun. 24, 1929, Walden, KY

Vocals / Traditional Country, Nashville Sound/Countrypolitan

Singer/songwriter Connie Hall had a brief country music career during the 1960s, punctuated by her hits "It's Not Wrong" and "Fool Me Once." She was born in Kentucky but raised in Cincinnati, and began performing there while in her teens. After high-school she worked at the Jimmie Skinner Music Center in Ohio and then became a regular singer on radio WZIP in nearby Covington, KY. In 1954, Skinner hired her to sing on his radio show at WNOP Newport, KY. She appeared on his show and others for several years and even worked as a weather girl on an area television station.

Hall's recording debut was a 1957 duet with Skinner, "We've Got Things in Common." She released her first solo effort in 1958, "I'm the Girl in the USA," and had her first hit the following year with "The Bottle or Me," which peaked near the Top 20. She moved to Decca in 1960 where producer Harry Silverstein helped her make it to the Top 25 with "Poison in Your Hand" and the Top 20 with its B-side "It's Not Wrong," a response to Warner Mack's 1958 hit "Is It Wrong (For Loving You)." She remained with Decca for three years and produced seven more respectable hits including "Sleep, Baby, Sleep" and "Fool Me Once." She also appeared on the *Grand Ole Opry, Louisiana Hayride,* and *Midwestern Hayride. —Sandra Brennan*

● **Connie Hall** / 1962 / Decca ✦✦✦✦

Country Songs / 1965 / Vocalion ✦✦✦

Country Style / 1965 / Vocalion ✦✦✦

Tom T. Hall

b. May 25, 1936, Olive Hill, KY

Songwriter, Vocals, Guitar / Progressive Country, Country-Pop, Singer/Songwriter, Country-Folk

Tom T. Hall is known as a storyteller, a songwriter with a keen eye for detail and a knack for narrative. Many musicians have covered his songs—most notably Jeannie C. Riley's 1968 hit "Harper Valley P.T.A."—and he also has racked up a number of solo hits, including seven number one singles. Hall is the son of a bricklaying minister, who gave his child a guitar at the age of eight. He had already begun to write poetry, so it was a natural progression for him to begin writing songs. Hall began learning music and performing techniques from a local musician called Clayton Delaney. At the age of 11, his mother died. Four years later, his father was shot in a hunting accident, which prevented him from working. In order to support himself and his father, Hall quit school and took a job in a local garment factory. While he was working in the factory, he formed his first band, the Kentucky Travelers. The group played bluegrass and gigged at local schools as well as a radio station in Morehead, KY. The station was sponsored by the Polar Bear Flour Company; Hall wrote a jingle for the company. After the Kentucky Travelers broke up, Hall became a DJ at the radio station.

In 1957, Hall enlisted in the Army and was stationed in Germany. While in Germany, he performed at local NCO clubs on the Armed Forces Radio Network, where he sang mostly original material, which usually had a comic bent to it. After four years of service, he was discharged in 1961. Once he returned to the States, he enrolled in Roanoke College as a journalism student; he supported himself by DJ-ing at a radio station in Salem, VA. One day a Nashville songwriter was visiting the Salem radio station and he heard Hall's songs. Impressed, the songwriter sent the songs to a publisher named Jimmy Key, who ran New Key Publishing. Key signed Hall as a songwriter, bringing the songs to a variety of recording artists. The first singer to have a hit with one of Hall's songs was Jimmy Newman, who brought "DJ for a Day" to number one on the country charts in 1963. In early 1964, Dave Dudley took "Mad" to the Top Ten. The back-to-back success convinced Hall to move to Nashville, where he was going to continue his career as a professional songwriter.

After Johnnie Wright had a number-one hit with Hall's "Hello Vietnam," the music industry was pressuring Tom to become a performer. He decided to take the plunge in 1967, signing a contract with Mercury Records. His first single, "I Washed My Face in the Morning Dew," was released in the summer of 1967 and became a minor hit. Hall followed the single with two other singles in 1968 that failed to crack the Top 40. Then, in the late summer of 1968, Jeannie C. Riley had a major hit with Hall's "Harper Valley P.T.A.," which spent three weeks at the top of the charts and was voted the Single of the Year by the Country Music Association. Its success brought attention to Hall's own recording career, which was evident from the performance of "Ballad of Forty Dollars." The song became his first Top Ten hit, climbing all the way to number four. Throughout 1969, he had a string of hit singles, culminated by the release of the number one single "A Week in a Country Jail" at the end of the year. The following year was just as successful, as "Shoeshine Man" and "Salute to a Switchblade" both hit the Top Ten. In 1971, he had his second number one single and his biggest hit, "The Year That Clayton Delaney Died," which was based on his childhood hero.

For most of the early '70s, Hall was a consistent hitmaker as well as a popular concert attraction. Between 1971 and 1976, he had five number-one hits besides "The Year That Clayton Delaney Died": "Old Dogs, Children and Watermelon Wine," "I Love," "Country Is," "I Care," and "Faster Horses (The Cowboy and the Poet)." Hall was appearing on television shows with regularity during this time, particularly *Hee Haw.* He also wrote a book on songwriting, which led to his authorship of a pair of books in the late '70s and early '80s—the semiautobiography *The Storyteller's Nashville* (1979) and the novel *The Laughing Man of Woodmont* (1982). Although he continued to have the occasional Top Ten hit in the late '70s—most notably the number four "You Man Loves You, Honey" (1977)—Hall didn't deliver hit singles as consistently as he did the first half of the decade. That pattern continued in the early '80s, when he began having trouble cracking the Top 40; only 1984's "P.S. I Love You," a cover of a 1934 Rudy Vallée hit, made it into the Top Ten. After 1986, Hall retired from recording, although artists continued to record his songs. In 1996, he delivered *Songs From Sopchoppy,* his first album in ten years. *—Stephen Thomas Erlewine*

☆ **Ballad of Forty Dollars** / 1969 / Mercury ✦✦✦✦✦

Ballad of Forty Dollars and *Homecoming,* two of Tom T. Hall's excellent late-'60s albums, are combined on this single compact disc. Although many of the best songs were featured on *Greatest Hits* and *Storyteller, Poet, Philosopher,* these albums work well as individual records and they're well worth acquiring for any Hall fan. *—Thom Owens*

I Witness Life / 1970 / Mercury ✦✦✦✦✦

Homecoming / 1970 / Mercury ✦✦✦✦✦

☆ **In Search of a Song** / 1971 / Mercury ✦✦✦✦✦

Hall gathered his material while driving solo through rural America, and his songs are literal and compassionate—but not romantic or sentimental. Instead, he fills his heartland stories with extraordinary realism and humanity. *—Michael McCall*

100 Children / 1971 / Mercury ✦✦✦✦

We All Got Together And . . . / 1972 / Mercury ✦✦✦

More great songs from Hall including "Pamela Brown" which was later covered by Leo Kottke and the political satire of "Monkey That Became President"; a song which is still as potent today. Not to be missed. *—Jim Worbois*

Greatest Hits, Vol. 1 / 1972 / Mercury ✦✦✦✦✦

Greatest Hits contains the bulk of Tom T. Hall's biggest hits from the late '60s and early '70s, including all his Top Ten hits from that era—"Ballad of Forty Dollars," "Homecoming," "A Week in a Country Jail," "Shoeshine Man," "Salute to a Switchblade," "The Year That Clayton Delaney Died," and "Me and Jesus"—but the record only hints at the his talent as a songwriter. Many of his best songs are on *Greatest Hits* and the collection does avoid his tendency for cuteness (with only a couple of exceptions), making *Greatest Hits* a good introduction, even though it does bypass plenty of fine songs. *—Thom Owens*

Tom T. Hall . . . The Storyteller / 1972 / Mercury ✦✦✦✦

It seemed like Hall could do no wrong in the early '70s, and this album adds more fuel to that idea. Another fine album of Hall originals (plus one by Billy Joe Shaver); including one of Hall's finest in "Old Dogs, Children and Watermelon Wine." *—Jim Worbois*

The Rhymer and Other Five and Dimers / 1973 / Mercury ✦✦✦✦✦

More great songs from the man called "The Storyteller"; including one from Billy Joe Shaver. This record picked up a little negative publicity when the folks in Spokane took exception with "Spokane Motel Blues." Still, no one else will find anything to complain about. *—Jim Worbois*

For the People in the Last Hard Town / 1973 / Mercury ✦✦✦✦

Songs of Fox Hollow (For Children of All Ages) / 1974 / Mercury ✦✦✦

Country Is / 1974 / Mercury ✦✦✦

I Wrote a Song About It / 1975 / Mercury ✦✦✦✦

Tom T. Hall was impressively consistent in the 1970s, and one of his noteworthy albums was *I Wrote a Song About It,* which contained the major hit "Deal" and the amusing "I Like Beer." Some of the best songs on this LP weren't major hits, and Hall reminds listeners how superb a storyteller he can be on everything from "It Rained in Every Town Except Paducah" to the poignant "The Trees in Philadelphia," a rare example of a country artist singing affectionately about a large Northeastern city. Indeed, Philly is the last place you'd expect to hear about in a country song, but Hall sings this ballad with so much soul that you're ready to make a beeline for the Liberty Bell. The album isn't without a few novelty items—most notably, the abovementioned "I Like Beer." But while they're fun and enjoyable enough, it is songs like "The Trees in Philadelphia" and the philosophical "Deal" that do the most to illustrate just how captivating Hall can be. *—Alex Henderson*

Greatest Hits, Vol. 2 / 1975 / Mercury ✦✦✦✦

Where *Greatest Hits* had the bulk of Tom T. Hall's greatest story songs, *Greatest Hits, Vol. 2* concentrates on his silly, cutesy songs, like "Sneaky Snake," "I Like Beer," "I Love," and "Old Dogs, Children and Watermelon Wine," among seven others. For fans of his detailed narratives, these songs can be quite grating, but for listeners that want all of these hits in one package, *Greatest Hits, Vol. 2* functions quite nicely. *—Thom Owens*

The Magnificent Music Machine / 1976 / Mercury ♦♦♦

There's a down-home country tone to Tom T. Hall's *The Magnificent Music Machine* that both new listeners and longtime fans will find relaxing. Hall has a knack for slice-of-life story songs, from telling of the cold-hearted beauty who "left me to die, like a "Fox on the Run'" to the mellower, more wryly humorous plaint of "Momma's Got the Catfish Blues." In between are tales of horse racing, with "Molly and Tenbrooks," hunting ("Fastest Rabbit Dog in Carter County Today"), and the album rounds out with a nostalgic look at meeting "In the sweet bye and bye/In that 'Bluegrass Festival in the Sky.'" Hall has a likable voice, and his tunes get listeners humming along and joining in on the choruses. —*Murrday Fisher*

Faster Horses / 1976 / Mercury ♦♦♦

About Love / 1977 / Mercury ♦♦♦

Places I've Done Time / 1978 / RCA ♦♦♦♦

New Train—Same Rider / 1978 / RCA ♦♦♦

Greatest Hits, Vol. 3 / 1978 / Mercury ♦♦♦

Beginning with 1976's "Faster Horses" and running through 1977's "Your Man Love You, Honey" and "It's All in the Game," *Greatest Hits, Vol. 3* collects the remainder of Tom T. Hall's '70s hit singles for Mercury Records. It does feature his biggest hit singles from the mid-'70s, as well as some less interesting, lesser-known songs, but the material on *Greatest Hits, Vol. 3* isn't quite as strong as his two previous hit collections. The album does pick up some highlights from a number of weaker albums, but casual fans will be better served by the first two *Greatest Hits* collections or, better yet, the box set *Storyteller, Poet Philosopher*. —*Thom Owens*

Ol T's in Town / 1979 / Koch ♦♦♦♦♦

Back in 1979, during the height of drugstore, er, *Urban Cowboy* mania, there were some artists who were beginning to be forgotten by the public due to the media's obsession with the glamour of the moment. It's a shame, because a number of country artists—such as George Jones, Merle Haggard, David Allan Coe, Mickey Gilley, Tammy Wynette, Gail Davies, and the man whose name is on this album—were making some of the best records of their careers. *Ol T's in Town* is a hard country album recorded during a time when country music was beginning to forget where it came from. Pedal steel, honky tonk pianos, fiddles, banjos, and acoustic guitars saturate the upfront production of Roy Dea (he died shortly after finishing the recording). In addition, some of Hall's most memorable songs are here, including "Jesus on the Radio (Daddy on the Phone)," "The Old Side of Town," "I Left You Some Kisses on the Door," and "You Show Me Your Heart (I'll Show You Mine)." Hall is a storyteller, and in a mix this clean and simple the power of his pastoral images comes across with immediacy and majesty. As an album, this acts like a collection of songs laid out in a grid. The opener, "The Last Country Song," is the first in a series of songs that reflect on the innocence of earlier times ("The Old Side of Town," "Old Habits Die Hard") and as warnings against a future of rampant opportunism ("Greed Kills More People Than Whiskey"). Once the societal concerns are out of the way the topic turns to love—newly discovered, mature ("The Different Feeling"), broken, and resolved ("I Left You Some Kisses on the Door"). The entire album is a journey through the tradition of country music as well as through the emotional terrain of a songwriter who is at a crossroads when the music he loves is changing, and is also observing the lives of the people he has spent his career writing about as they change. *Ol T's in Town* is brilliant; its transfer to CD is sonically flawless and it is an essential building block in Hall's collection. —*Thom Jurek*

Everything From Jesus to Jack Daniels / 1983 / Mercury ♦♦♦

Natural Dreams / 1984 / Mercury ♦♦♦

Song in a Seashell / 1985 / Mercury ♦♦♦

The Essential Tom T. Hall: Story Songs / 1988 / Mercury ♦♦♦♦♦

Tom T.'s songs are stories filled with interesting characters. And, some of his most interesting characters are gathered on this record which celebrates the first 20 years of Hall's career as a performer. (Hall was a writer first with his most famous pre-performer song being "Harper Valley PTA.") Whether you're looking for a hits package (which this isn't, strictly speaking) or just want to learn more about Hall, this is a fine place to start. —*Jim Worbois*

★ **Ballad of Forty Dollars/Homecoming** / 1992 / Bear Family ♦♦♦♦♦

Here are two albums from Tom T. Hall's late-'60s period, both of them stellar examples of his worth as a storyteller and a songwriter. A journeyman songwriter, Hall viewed his work as a job, but one he showed a passion for learning and living. The two albums featured here showcase Hall at one of the creative peaks of his life. There are a total of 26 tracks with Hall and his band, the Storytellers, including classics such as "Shame on the Rain," "That's How I Got to Memphis" (which registers as one of the saddest brokenhearted love songs in country music history), "Forbidden Flowers," "The World the Way I Want It," "Kentucky in the Morning," "Margie's at the Lincoln Park Inn," and many others. The beauty of Hall's work during this period, and indeed for the most of the rest of his career, is that his writing comes from the point of empathy. The grain in his voice on these recordings is that of a friend or a neighbor who witnesses without judgment. Even in the first person there is no instance where the protagonist is saying, "Why me God?" In the desperation and sadness as well as in the joy or bewilderment, there is a quiet or raucous acceptance of life as it is. There is a generosity in this approach extended to the listener, which allows for our place in the narrative, not as an extension of our experience or his, but as a sharing of experience. Bear Family's choices in these two albums, recorded in 1968, is a phenomenal portrait in miniature of one of the greatest storytellers and songwriters of the 20th century. This is essential Tom T. Hall for the collector, and a tremendous introduction for the novice. —*Thom Jurek*

I Witness Life/100 Children / 1992 / Bear Family ♦♦♦♦♦

I Witness Life and *100 Children*, two of Tom T. Hall's excellent late '60s albums, are combined on this single compact disc. Although many of the best songs were featured on *Greatest Hits* and *Storyteller, Poet, Philosopher*, these albums work well as individual records and they're well worth acquiring for any Hall fan. —*Thom Owens*

Greatest Hits, Vols. 1 & 2 / 1993 / Mercury ♦♦♦♦♦

Greatest Hits, Vols. 1 & 2 combines Tom T. Hall's first two greatest hits albums on one CD. Although it is a good bargain, the two albums don't necessarily sit well together—the earlier story songs are considerably more heartfelt and substantial than the pseudo-novelties that comprise the latter songs. Nevertheless, the two-fer CD works as the best single-disc retrospective of Tom T. Hall's career, although it still misses a couple of key tracks. —*Stephen Thomas Erlewine*

☆ **Storyteller, Poet, Philosopher** / Nov. 14, 1995 / Mercury ♦♦♦♦♦

The double-disc box set *Storyteller, Poet, Philosopher* concentrates on Tom T. Hall's talents as a narrative songwriter, eschewing some of his better-known novelties for lesser-known, but better-written, serious songs. That doesn't mean the box is devoid of hits—all of the important ones are here. What that does mean is that *Storyteller, Poet, Philosopher* is the first Tom T. Hall compilation to accurately convey the scope of his talents, as well as his achievements. —*Thom Owens*

Songs from Sopchoppy / 1996 / Mercury ♦♦

Tom T. Hall's two-disc box set—the outstanding *Storyteller, Poet, Philosopher*—revived interest in the one-of-a-kind performer. So Mercury Records, the label that Hall worked for from 1967 to 1986, agreed to release *Songs From Sopchoppy*, his first album of original tunes in ten years (not counting a children's project). Unfortunately, the collection is not up to Hall's usual standards. Part of the problem comes from production. Tom Collins once guided hits for Ronnie Milsap and Barbara Mandrell, but he hasn't been active in leading record production since the mid-'80s. That's where his sound seems stuck, as he saddles Hall with a decidedly old-fashioned, stilted sound. Hall's observations are still witty, but rarely as incisive as on such classics as "Homecoming" and "Ballad of Forty Dollars." Still, the best song on the album, a ballad titled "Shoes and Dress That Alice Wore," is a devastating and artful piece of work. It suggests Hall still has it, if someone is willing to push him to dig a little deeper. —*Michael McCall*

Home Grown / Sep. 16, 1997 / Mercury ♦♦♦

Tom T. Hall returned to recording in 1996 with *Songs from Sopchoppy*, his first collection of new, original material in ten years. While it had its moments, the album wasn't a return to form, and its sequel, *Homegrown*, wasn't either. However, it is closer to classic Hall than its predecessor. The production on *Homegrown* is simpler than on *Sopchoppy*, helping to bring his songs to the forefront. Unfortunately, only a handful of songs are up to Hall's standards, but that's enough to make *Homegrown* worthwhile for dedicated fans. —*Thom Owens*

20th Century Masters—The Millennium Collection: The Best of Tom T. Hall / Feb. 29, 2000 / MCA ♦♦♦♦

Part of Universal's massive *20th Century Masters—The Millennium Collection*, this 12-song budget set draws on a dozen of Hall's best-known tunes. Highlights include "Old Dogs, Children, and Watermelon Wine," "Ballad of Forty Dollars," and "The Year That Clayton Delaney Died." A perfect, bare-bones introduction to this artist. —*Cub Koda*

★ **Ultimate Collection** / Jun. 12, 2001 / Hip-O ♦♦♦♦

Since Tom T. Hall's recording career extends all the way from 1969 to the end of the century, becoming familiar with his music can often feel like a daunting task. Thankfully, the folks at Hip-O have made things much easier for newcomers who don't want to splurge and get the double-disc *Storyteller, Poet, Philosopher*, even if that is the preferred place to begin. Hip-O's *Ultimate Collection* summarizes Hall's career with much efficiency, cramming a total of 24 songs onto one disc—some of the best songs Hall ever recorded. Granted, with a canon as deep as Hall's there's going to be bickering among seasoned fans about the inclusions, but newcomers need not worry about these sort of debates—everything here is top-notch, and that's all that really matters in the end. Obviously though, this is just the tip of the iceberg when it comes to Hall's work. That's undoubtedly why it's nice to have a simple, straightforward best-of such as this to give newcomers a succinct overview of his recording career so they know where to head next. But for those who are really curious about Hall, there's no denying that the aforementioned *Storyteller, Poet, Philosopher* stands as the more comprehensive and preferred best-of; prospective buyers just need to consider that it's also a larger investment on their part relative to *Ultimate Collection*. —*Jason Birchmeier*

George Hamilton IV

b. Jul. 19, 1937, Winston-Salem, NC

Vocals, Guitar / Traditional Country, Country-Pop, Nashville Sound/Countrypolitan, Country-Folk

Proclaimed the International Ambassador of Country Music thanks to his world tours in the '70s, George Hamilton IV began his career in the late '50s as a teen-oriented pop star. After his first hit, "A Rose and a Baby Ruth," hit number six on the pop charts in 1956, he toured with Buddy Holly and the Everly Brothers. However, his later pop efforts stalled on the charts, and in 1959, Hamilton joined the *Grand Ole Opry*. Top ten country singles like "Before This Day Ends," "Three Steps to the Phone (Millions of Miles)" and "If You Don't Know I Ain't Gonna Tell You" paved the way for 1963's "Abilene," which topped the country charts for four weeks and hit 15 on the pop charts. The following year, Hamilton charted three singles and returned to the Top Ten with "Fort Worth, Dallas or Houston." Folk music inspired Hamilton's late-'60s hits, including the Gordon Lightfoot-penned "Steel Rail Blues" and Joni Mitchell's "Urge For Going." Except for 1970's number-three hit "She's a Little Bit Country," chart success eluded him during the '70s, so George

Hamilton IV took country music around the world. Besides more than ten tours of Great Britain and several BBC-TV productions, Hamilton became the first country artist to perform behind the Iron Curtain; he also toured Africa, the Orient, New Zealand, Australia, and even the Middle East. For the rest of his career, Hamilton concentrated on gospel recordings. His son, George Hamilton V, toured with his father's backup band and charted a single in 1988. *—John Bush*

Abilene / 1963 / Collectables ♦♦♦♦

Collectables' reissue of George Hamilton IV's *Abilene* contains the original album, plus three bonus tracks which include the hits "Why Don't They Understand" and "A Rose and a Baby Ruth." The hits augment an album that, as its subtitle suggest, leans more toward folk songs. Of course, these songs aren't given folk arrangements—they are folk songs and standards, like "The Roving Gambler" and "You Are My Sunshine," given appealingly pop arrangements. There are a few dull spots on the record, but on the whole it's quite entertaining, and it's made even better with the bonus tracks. *—Stephen Thomas Erlewine*

Down Home in the Country / 1970 / RCA ♦♦

Down Home in the Country is supposedly George Hamilton IV's bow to traditional country music after years of making teen idol pop and light country-folk, but in reality, the album is no different from his '60s recordings. In a few cases it is exactly what he was doing in the '60s: "The Little Grave" is a re-recording of a song he originally cut in 1963, while "If You Don't Know I Ain't Gonna Tell You" and "I've Got a Secret" are his third recordings of those songs! The Kris Kristofferson staples "Me & Bobby McGee" and "Sunday Morning Coming Down" are far from traditional, and "Everything Is Beautiful" (performed here as a duet with Skeeter Davis) was a number-one pop hit for Ray Stevens. In short, the traditional country billing is complete bunk—as is the promise of anything new. That isn't to say the album is worthless; Hamilton's performances are good even if his repertoire is uninteresting, but *Down Home in the Country* is one of his least substantial efforts. *—Greg Adams*

The ABC Collection: George Hamilton IV / 1977 / ABC ♦♦♦♦♦

1954–65 / 1995 / Bear Family ♦♦♦♦♦

1954-65 is a six-disc box set containing all of George Hamilton IV's most popular recordings, including all of his records for ABC/Paramount and the bulk of his RCA recordings. Hamilton's pop hits often obscured his talents as a country singer, but this set demonstrates that he was a talented and versatile singer. Nevertheless, it's the kind of set that is designed for hardcore fans—there may be several gems buried in this weighty box set, but its sheer bulk makes *1954-65* intimidating to anyone else. *—Thom Owens*

● **Country Boy: The Best of George Hamilton IV** / Dec. 2, 1996 / BMG International ♦♦♦♦

Butch Hancock

b. Jul. 12, 1945, Lubbock, TX

Guitar, Harmonica, Vocals / Progressive Country, Singer/Songwriter, Country-Folk, Alternative Country, Americana, Contemporary Singer/Songwriter

As a member of the groundbreaking Flatlanders, singer/songwriter Butch Hancock helped kick-start the progressive country movement of the '70s. As a solo artist, Hancock recorded a series of country-folk albums for his own independent Rainlight label, which showcased his literate wordplay, quirky humor, and dry, Dylan-esque vocal delivery. Going the independent route certainly cost Hancock some name recognition and wider exposure, but he did earn a devoted cult following, especially in his native Texas. Hancock was born in the West Texas town of Lubbock in 1945 and grew up on a farm, writing his first songs while driving his father's tractor. In high-school, he started playing music with friends Jimmie Dale Gilmore and Joe Ely, fellow long-haired intellectuals who shared a distaste for commercial country. Hancock entered architectural school after graduation, but eventually left to return to his family's farm in Lubbock.

He reconnected with Gilmore and Ely, and in 1970 the three formed a band called the Flatlanders. In 1972, they traveled to Nashville for a recording session with Plantation Records, a low-budget offshoot of the past-its-prime Sun label. When their first single flopped, their lone album, *Jimmie Dale & the Flatlanders*, was barely released in extremely limited quantities in 1973, and the group members gradually went their separate ways. However, when Ely became an acclaimed solo artist in the late '70s, he drew heavily from Gilmore and Hancock's songwriting catalogs, bringing Hancock classics like "West Texas Waltz," "If I Were a Bluebird" (both covered by Emmylou Harris), "She Never Spoke Spanish to Me" (covered by the Texas Tornados), and "Boxcars" to a wider audience.

Ely's recordings helped spark interest in Hancock, but Hancock returned to music on his own terms, moving to the progressive country hotbed of Austin and starting up his own Rainlight label. In 1978, he issued his first album, *West Texas Waltzes & Dust-Blown Tractor Tunes*, a spare, simple collection that spotlighted his impressive lyrical abilities. The double album *The Wind's Dominion* followed a year later, and experimented with a broader musical palette and fuller arrangements. Released in 1980, *Diamond Hill* featured a full backing band, and 1981's *Firewater* was an informal live set; both continued to build his cult reputation on the Texas roots music scene.

Hancock subsequently took a break from recording for several years, pursuing his interests in photography and video, and returned in 1985 with *Yella Rose With Marce Lacouture*; *Split & Slide* followed in 1986. During another break from recording, Jimmie Dale Gilmore decided to return to his solo career, and thanks to the Flatlanders' burgeoning legend, his versions of several Hancock compositions once again renewed interest in the songwriter. In 1989, the bluegrass-oriented Sugar Hill label issued *Own & Own*, a compilation of highlights from Hancock's early albums. Meanwhile, Hancock and Gilmore toured Australia together, which resulted in the live duo album *Two Roads*; Hancock also issued *Cause of the Cactus* on his own label in 1991. Another compilation for Sugar Hill came in 1993, this one called *Own the Way Over Here*, and the following year, Hancock contributed songs to *Chippy*, a musical theater piece about a Texas prostitute co-written by Ely.

In 1995 his first-ever non-compilation studio project for an outside label was released, the acclaimed Sugar Hill set *Eats Away the Night*, which was hailed as one of his most fully realized recordings. In the years that followed, Hancock re-released many of his old albums on CD, and also issued the new Rainlight set *You Coulda Walked Around the World* in 1999. He toured with the reunited Flatlanders in 2000, after which he moved from Austin to the small desert town of Terlingua; there he worked as a white-water rafting guide and returned to architecture, designing, and building his own home. In 2002, the Flatlanders issued the well-received reunion album *Now Again*. *—Steve Huey*

West Texas Waltzes & Dust-Blown Tractor Tunes / 1978 / Rainlight ♦♦♦♦♦

While Sugar Hill released two fine collections of Butch Hancock's recordings in 1989 and 1993, they only scratched the surface of a rich mother lode of Americana music. Recorded in 1978, *West Texas Waltzes* represents the debut of a talented wordsmith whose folk tunes seem to sprout naturally from Western farmland. Stripped-down arrangements, featuring no more than an acoustic guitar and harmonica, underline the bare land and harsh winds of these songs. On "Dry Land Farm," Hancock evokes Woody Guthrie and early Dylan as he plumbs the depths of the history of the American farmer. "Where the West Winds... Have Blow'd" follows, developing the twin themes of a person's relationship to the land and responsibility to it. The West Texas land is hard and unforgiving as "Dirt Road Song" notes, but the rewards, as in "They Say It's a Good Land," balance out the equation. Hancock also doesn't mind subtly passing on a bit of Guthrie-esque politics in "I Grew to Be a Stranger," or writing a love song to his native state, "Texas Air." While these songs sound "serious," Hancock's rough-hewn vocals and clever, down to earth lyrics deliver pieces like "West Texas Waltz" with a joyous gusto. He may have a point to make, but he's going to have fun making it. Indeed, everything works together to create an understated, though powerful, vision of American life, leaving the listener with a taste of dust in his or her mouth. Since Hancock's debut was released on his own Rainlight Records in a musical genre (folk or country-folk) outside the mainstream, it never had the impact of an album like *The Freewheelin' Bob Dylan*. Nonetheless, *West Texas Waltzes* must have seemed like the freshest of breezes to the handful of people who heard it back in 1978. Even today, none of the album's power is diminished. This is simply Americana music at its finest. *—Ronnie D. Lankford Jr.*

The Wind's Dominion / 1979 / Rainlight ♦♦♦

Somewhere within *The Wind's Dominion*, a masterpiece is waiting to get out. At least eight lovely songs, including "Fightin' for My Life," "Row of Dominoes," and "Personal Rendition of the Blues," clock in around 35 minutes, or about the same length as Neil Young's *Harvest*. But Butch Hancock sinks his sophomore effort by loading it down with 30 more minutes of weak tunes and a mixed bag of arrangements. Cuts like "Once Followed By the Wind" and "Long Road to Asia Minor" would have sounded fine as outtakes on a box set, while other oddities like the a cappella "Sea's Deadog Catch" should have been left in the vault. All pale beside the real stuff, and since the good tunes weren't front-loaded, it gives the impression that no one involved could separate the chaff from the wheat. Several of these tunes, like the title cut, "Gift Horse of Mercy," and "Smokin' in the Rain," would show up later on a couple of Sugar Hill collections, and they're as good as anything on his debut, *West Texas Waltzes & Dust-Blown Tractor Tunes*. Besides differences in production, *The Wind's Dominion* also lacks the social-political dimension of his first album. Hancock's left-field point of view, sense of wordplay, and rough and ready vocals, however, remain intact. Despite lapses and misfires, *The Wind's Dominion* qualifies as a valuable album that captures the genius and growing pains of a vital artist. *—Ronnie D. Lankford Jr.*

Diamond Hill / 1980 / Rainlight ♦♦♦♦

After recording the spare masterwork *West Texas Waltzes & Dust-Blown Tractor Tunes* in 1978 and the eclectic double-LP *The Wind's Dominion* in 1979, Butch Hancock opted for a full-band outing on *Diamond Hill* in 1980. Several of these songs—"Diamond Hill," "Neon Wind," "Ghost of Give and Take Avenue," and "Corona del Mar"—were issued on Sugar Hill collections in the '80 and '90s, but the album (available on CD in 1998) is well worth hearing in its entirety. It is much more uniform than *The Wind's Dominion*, and the instrumental muscle adds a new dimension to Hancock's word-heavy songs. One might describe the mixture of pedal steel, acoustic guitar, piano, and occasional saxophone as country-folk. Even with a band, however, Hancock, with his croaky vocals and rich wordplay, is always front and center. The Tex-Mex-flavored "Corona del Mar" begins with the lovely lines, "Golden sunlight... please save us from our dreams/They're not all that bad... but they're sure not what they seem." To anyone familiar with Hancock, no one else could've written the line; to everyone else, the curious phrasing is immediately distinctive. Hancock has too often been compared to Bob Dylan, but the association makes sense if one states that Hancock, as original and idiosyncratic as any singer/songwriter, is one of the rare musical visionaries worth mentioning in the same sentence with Dylan. *Diamond Hill* is a satisfying effort from one of the best songwriters to ever come out of Texas. *—Ronnie D. Lankford Jr.*

1981: A Spare Odyssey / 1981 / Rainlight ♦♦

Firewater / 1981 / Rainlight ♦♦♦♦♦

Butch Hancock's discography is somewhat difficult to piece together. Many of his albums originally appeared on the small Rainlight label, and while a number of these albums have been reissued on CD, some have not. *Firewater* is Hancock's fourth album, a thrown-together live set recorded at *the Alamo Lounge* in Austin in 1980 (and released the following year). Although recorded live, only "The Wind's Dominion" had shown up on his earlier solo albums. "If You Were a Bluebird" would become a Hancock standard, but the standout tune here is the title track. The unpolished band chugs along on all cylinders for "Firewater" while Hancock sings, "You got drunk last nite/You swear you saw the devil/Don't you know firewater seeks its own level?" There's a good version of A.P. Carter's "No Hidin' Place," and Jimmie Dale Gilmore sings a verse or two on "I Keep Wishing for You" and "If You Were a Bluebird." There are other good songs on *Firewater*—"Like the Light at Dawn" and "One More Road"—and they're filled with Hancock's usual clever wordplay and off-the-cuff delivery. The problem, however, is that it all sounds like it was recorded in a barn and just for the fun of it. For those accustomed to Hancock's loose performing style, though, the album will be worth picking up if for no other reason than the title track. —*Ronnie Lankford Jr.*

Yella Rose with Marce Lacouture / 1985 / Rainlight ✦✦✦
This album has a rather big band with occasional horns, congas, accordion, and Marce Lacouture songs on the title cut. A good one. —*Richard Meyer*

Split & Slide / 1986 / Rainlight ✦✦✦

● **Own & Own** / 1989 / Sugar Hill ✦✦✦✦✦
Critics are fond of saying that an artist like Butch Hancock deserves more attention. Hancock, however, never seemed to worry too much about who was listening. At least he didn't until the late '80s, when he allowed Sugar Hill to reissue some of his older material, originally only available on his own small Texas record label. While *Own & Own* didn't make Hancock a country-folk star, it did give a number of people a chance to find out just how good this eccentric songwriter from Lubbock really was. Drawn from his debut in 1978, "Dry Land Farm" and "West Texas Waltz" show that his Dylan-esque vocals and love of wordplay were born in full from the very start. The spare accompaniment, just acoustic guitar and harmonica, seems to reflect the dry, dusty land he sings about. While the stripped-down production would eventually give way to the roots rock of "Firewater" and the country duets with Marce Lacoutre on "Yellow Rose" and "Like a Kiss on the Mouth," Hancock's basic approach remained the same. The only material that really doesn't work here are the last four cuts, recorded in 1989, the same year as the album's release. The lyrics seem forced and the crunchier guitar raises the noise level, meaning that the two main reasons listeners enjoy Hancock, his clever words and spare country-folk sound, are mysteriously missing. Overall, though, *Own & Own* offers a good place to sample the peculiar songs of one of the most peculiar songwriters ever to wonder the dusty Texas plains. —*Ronnie D. Lankford Jr.*

Live in Australia / 1990 / Virgin ✦✦✦
An energetic live album of duets by Hancock and Gilmore, it was recorded in Sydney in 1990. The Flatlander "hit" "Dallas" is here and other ragged but right cuts from these musical pals. —*Richard Meyer*

Cause of the Cactus / 1991 / Rainlight ✦✦✦✦

Two Roads / Jul. 3, 1992 / Caroline ✦✦✦
Gilmore and Hancock take turns singing and accompanying each other on this live album recorded during an Australian tour. —*Kurt Wolff*

Own the Way Over Here / 1993 / Sugar Hill ✦✦✦
Are all the presidents really named after the streets in Amarillo? The answer is yes, but only in the strange lyrical world of Butch Hancock's songs. While often compared, vocally and lyrically, to Bob Dylan, the comparison fails to do justice to Hancock's idiosyncratic approach. *Own the Way Over Here* collects songs from earlier albums like *Yella Rose With Marce Lacoutre* and *Diamond Hill*, released on his own Rainlight Records. "Talkin' About That Panama Canal" sounds a bit dated, as do most protest songs, but it remains entertaining if for no other reason than Hancock's inability to remember all the presidents' names. The epic, ten-minute "Only Born" contains enough wordplay for six songs, and while one might guess that cute phrases would grow tired after seven or eight versus, Hancock's smart enough to avoid clichés. Two of the strongest cuts, "Smokin' in the Rain" and "Gift Horse of Mercy," come from his sophomore effort, *The Wind's Dominion*. *Own the Way Over Here* works as a good thumbnail sketch of Hancock: One may have an inkling of his talents after listening to the album, but less than an in-depth portrait. If the album leads listeners to seek the original Rainlight albums, however, it has done its job. —*Ronnie D. Lankford Jr.*

Eats Away the Night / 1995 / Sugar Hill ✦✦✦✦✦
After about 20 years, Butch Hancock has released his first produced studio album for a national label not compiled from his previously released Rainlight Records LPs. In many ways, Hancock set his style down with his very first self-produced album, *West Texas Waltz*. All the elements from that period remain—the Dylan-esque vocal sound, his love of wordplay, and a deep feeling for the stories that make up an individual's life. The warm sound of this album makes it easier for newcomers to get past his dry voice, and the inclusion of his hit "If You Were a Bluebird" will help a new audience locate him properly in the contemporary Texas songwriting scene. The band is tight and steps back enough to let Hancock's stories and personality shine through. —*Richard Meyer*

No Two Alike / 1996 / Rainlight ✦✦✦✦
This 14-tape series (available by subscription only) is a document of six nights at the Cactus Cafe, where Butch performed with a host of great guests and never repeated a single one of his songs. —*Richard Meyer*

You Coulda Walked Around the World / Jan. 1, 2000 / Rainlight ✦✦✦
Equal parts philosopher and joker, Butch Hancock qualifies as a modern-day renaissance man. Sure, he's a fine musician when the mood strikes him, but he's also an accomplished photographer and architect. On 1997's *You Coulda Walked Around the World*, Hancock returns to a "one man with a guitar and harmonica" mode that harks back to his 1978 debut, *West Texas Waltzes*. While these stripped-down efforts have been referred to as "lo-fi," it's pretty obvious that Rainlight is using better recording equipment than it did 19 years ago. A few of the rougher edges have also been polished out of Hancock's idiosyncratic style on *You Coulda Walked Around the World*. This doesn't mean that his basic stylistic blueprint—rustic vocals and unusual wordplay—aren't evident on songs like "Roll Around" and "Long Sunsets." This mellow set, however, lacks the bite of albums like 1995's *Eats Away the Night*. One is left with the feeling that pieces like "Black Irish Rose"

and "All Curled Up" would blossom with a fuller arrangements and a producer like Gurf Morlix at the helm. The lyrics on songs like "Chase" and "Hidin' in the Hills" are also a bit tired and would benefit greatly from a small dose of Hancock's trademark humor. Despite these flaws, fans will want to pick up a copy of *You Coulda Walked Around the World* for lovely gems like "One Good Time." Even at half-throttle, Hancock is more interesting than most of his songwriting peers. —*Ronnie D. Lankford Jr.*

Wayne Hancock

Vocals, Guitar (Acoustic) / Alternative Country, Neo-Traditionalist Country, Americana, Rockabilly Revival
Alternative country favorite Wayne Hancock is that rare breed of traditionalist, one who imbues his retro obsessions with such high energy and passion that his songs never feel like museum pieces he's trying desperately to preserve. Hancock is most often compared to Hank Williams, and he can indeed be a hardcore honky tonker, but there's more to him than that: he also displays a genuine affinity for stomping rockabilly, Western swing, blues, and old-time country à la Jimmie Rodgers. Plus, he also throws in the occasional pop standard in the manner of Willie Nelson's classic *Stardust* album. Hancock's devotion to classic country sounds, coupled with his strong aversion to the Nashville hit-making machine, earned him an ardent following among alternative country fans (from both the country and rock sides of the movement), as well as a fair amount of critical acclaim.

Wayne "the Train" Hancock was born May 1, 1965, and began writing songs around age 12. His family moved around a lot during his childhood, and often sang to entertain themselves. Hancock started playing juke joints around Texas as a teenager, and at age 18 won a prestigious talent competition, the Wrangler Country Showdown; however, he was unable to reap the benefits, having just enlisted in the Marines. After six years in the military, Hancock returned to Texas and began playing around the state wherever he could, working odd jobs on the side to help make ends meet. Eventually tiring of his itinerant existence, Hancock moved to West Dallas in 1993, and shortly thereafter settled in the music mecca of Austin. In 1994, he got a part in the musical theater production *Chippy*, where he performed alongside progressive country legends Joe Ely, Butch Hancock (no relation), Robert Earl Keen, and Terry Allen. He also made his recorded debut on the soundtrack album *Songs From Chippy*

Thanks to that bit of exposure, Hancock was able to score a deal with the small Texas indie label Deja Disc. His debut album, *Thunderstorms and Neon Signs*, was produced by steel guitar legend Lloyd Maines and released in 1995. Critics fawned over the album, particularly the Hank Williams-ish title track, and despite being on a tiny label with limited distribution, it sold over 20,000 copies, mostly through word of mouth. Its success attracted the attention of the somewhat larger indie Ark 21, which signed Hancock for his second album, *That's What Daddy Wants*. Issued in 1997, the record found Hancock employing elaborate, horn-driven arrangements and delving more deeply into rockabilly and Western swing, which earned some comparisons to the Brian Setzer Orchestra. Reviews were again highly positive, and Ark 21 accordingly reissued Hancock's debut. His third album, *Wild, Free & Reckless*, had more traditional country instrumentation, full of fiddles and steel guitars, and accordingly was more reminiscent of pre-rock & roll country boogie. Hancock subsequently switched to the alt-country hub Bloodshot Records, debuting in 2001 with *A-Town Blues*, which continued the more stripped-down approach of his most recent music. Hancock dug even deeper into his honky-tonk roots with his next album, 2003's *Swing Time*, recorded live during a two-night stand at the Continental Club in Austin, Texas. —*Steve Huey*

Thunderstorms and Neon Signs / Oct. 1995 / Deja Disc ✦✦✦✦
There are moments on Wayne Hancock's debut album, 1995's *Thunderstorms and Neon Signs*, where you could swear that the risen ghost of Hank Williams had somehow found its way into this sawed-off drifter from Texas; but beyond the unavoidable vocal similarity between Hancock and Williams, what the two really have in common is a heartfelt love of the honky tonk tradition and a real gift for making the style sound fresh and vital. While the spare, mostly acoustic arrangements on *Thunderstorms and Neon Signs* are clearly modeled on classic country sounds of the '40s and '50s (with a dash of Western swing thrown in, mostly audible in the occasional appearance of horns), Hancock never sounds like he's aiming for a "retro" sound; this is just what he does, he couldn't sound different if he tried, and there's just enough texture in his rough edges and fiery enthusiasm to convince anyone this isn't a pose, but the real thing. Even better, Hancock can write in the classic style with a breezy confidence and a keen eye for the details. If "Juke Joint Jumping" and "She's My Baby" aren't exactly startlingly original, they show Hancock can find fresh inspiration in traditional country frameworks; while the roadside poetry of the title cut really is something special; and "Double A Daddy" may be one of the only great honky tonk tunes about staying on the wagon. Producer Lloyd Maines and a handful of superb pickers give these songs just the right support, but it's Hancock who's the star of this show, and *Thunderstorms and Neon Signs* shows he's got the guts, sass, and talent to bring honky tonk music back to America's dancehalls, where it belongs. —*Mark Deming*

● **That's What Daddy Wants** / Aug. 26, 1997 / Ark 21 ✦✦✦✦
Hancock approaches classic country themes with a modern flair. Hank Williams couldn't have gotten away with singing about finding his lover with another on "those damp, slick, sticky satin sheets." And Hancock does branch out a bit, utilizing a drummer as well as the occasional horn or accordion. But his most radical departure, a cover of the Clash's "Brand New Cadillac," is a surf music screamer that advances his sound to state of the art circa 1963. You can almost picture Jethro and Granny out twistin' by the cement pond. This music is something of an anachronism, and that is perhaps that greatest criticism one could levy against it. Hancock swings and moans with the best, but don't expect his '90s themes to modernize this sound. Retro is perfectly fine when it's done as well as this. —*Brian Briscoe*

Wild, Free & Reckless / Jul. 27, 1999 / Ark 21 ✦✦✦
Wayne Hancock's third album, *Wild, Free and Restless*, is another richly eclectic melting pot of vintage American sounds with a distinctly rural orientation. Yet, in spite of the fact

that Hancock is an unabashed revivalist, his music never comes off as academic or as mere preservationism; these songs breathe with a lively energy, and the juxtapositions of styles seem natural and unselfconscious. The spirits of Hank Williams, Jimmie Rodgers, and Bob Wills hang the heaviest over Hancock's music, but there's also blues, big-band jazz, and some rockabilly insanity; plus, Hancock covers both Ernest Tubb ("Kansas City Blues") and Carl Perkins ("Blue Suede Shoes") this time out. Another fine effort from a singular stylist. *—Steve Huey*

A-Town Blues / Sep. 4, 2001 / Bloodshot ✦✦✦✦
There are never any big stylistic surprises with Hancock—the man knows what works for him musically and never veers outside of his circle of comfort. In the case of Wayne "the Train" Hancock, this means that he is still pounding out the same retro country/honky tonk/Western swing vibe that he has toyed with since his excellent 1995 debut, *Thunderstorms and Neon Signs*. Hancock's fourth album, *A-Town Blues*, features more anachronistically pleasing old-time music augmented by warbled Southwestern vocals. On his first release for the insurgent country label Bloodshot Records, the wayward troubadour touches on familiar genre subject matter as well. Tales of road weariness ("Route 23"), warnings about booze and breaking the law ("Miller, Jack, and Mad Dog"), and, of course, heartbreak ("Sands of Time") are all recurring themes. Surprisingly, a production hand by longtime collaborator Lloyd Maines (Wilco, Richard Buckner) doesn't really add much to Hancock's naturally sparse sound, though. If anything, it's Maines' appropriately placed steel guitar licks that actually do more for the album. All in all, *A-Town Blues* is yet another excellent release from a homely, all-American artist. *—Bret Booth*

The Handsome Family

f. Chicago, IL
Group / Neo-Traditional Folk, Alternative Country, Indie Rock
Husband and wife duo the Handsome Family has been labeled both alt-country and traditionalist, but truthfully their often-dark music lies in a unique space somewhere in between, blending the sounds of traditional country and bluegrass (and, especially, murder ballads) into a more modern scenery. Vocalist and composer Brett Sparks hails from Texas where he studied music and briefly worked around the oil rigs. By the mid-'90s, he resided in Chicago with his wife Rennie Sparks, a fiction writer originally from Long Island. Brett persuaded Rennie to write lyrics for him, leading to the unusual and striking form of the Handsome Family's songs— evocative scenes and brief tales (of both the daydream and ghost story varieties) in lieu of the standard verse-chorus-verse structure. The Handsome Family's debut album, entitled *Odessa*, was released in January 1995 on the independent label Carrot Top. This first home recording (all of the Handsome Family's albums are recorded in their living room) had slight punk shadings not heard on their subsequent albums. *Odessa* unfortunately made few waves except for some radio stations' ban on the second song, "Arlene," which is about a woman who gets bludgeoned to death. The follow-up came in May of the following year, and the Handsome Family hit the road in support of their new release, *Milk and Scissors*, first touring the U.S. with Wilco, then heading on to Europe for shows in Austria, Germany, and Switzerland. With *Milk and Scissors*, the duo had traded in their previous rock edges for more traditional country sounds. The resulting album won praise from the critics, got named in the Top Ten of 1996 by alt-country/Americana magazine *No Depression* and was featured on John Peel's BBC show.

This was not, however, an easy period for the Handsome Family. Brett suffered an emotional breakdown during this time, which resulted in his hospitalization and diagnosis as manic-depressive. *Through the Trees* (Carrot Top, January 1998), the Handsome Family's third album, was written and recorded in the aftermath of these troubles. The raw, emotional quality of lyrics that deal with the darkness of everyday tragedy is delivered in Brett's deadpan baritone, often met by more traditional country sounds. With this recording, the Handsome Family came into their own sound and received widespread attention as a result. *Through the Trees* was named the best local release and in the Top Ten of 1998 by major Chicago papers, but the attention went far beyond the local press; the album received praise from major magazines, both on-line and in-print. *Through the Trees* was featured on NPR and even named the "Best New Country Album of the Year" by England's *Uncut* magazine, despite the album's overall untraditional sound.

This was the Handsome Family's breakthrough album, which continued to increase in popularity over the next several years, allowing Brett and Rennie Sparks to quit their day jobs and focus on music full time. Following the album's release, the duo began touring extensively, performing regularly in Europe and touring the U.S. twice—once with the Mekons. On the wave of this success, two years later came the somewhat lighter and more natural sounds of *In the Air* (Carrot Top, 2000), with guest appearances by Jeff Tweedy of Wilco and violinist Andrew Bird, formerly of the Squirrel Nut Zippers. The Handsome Family supported the release of their fourth album with a month-long European tour followed by a tour along the West Coast of the U.S. A document of their sound at this time can be found on their 2002 release, *Live at Schuba's Tavern*, which was recorded at a December 2000 show in Chicago. *—Joslyn Layne*

Odessa / Jan. 9, 1995 / Carrot Top ✦✦✦
The Handsome Family's first album certainly stands apart from their later work; at this point, the group still had a live drummer, they were playing more rock-oriented material (the noisy guitars on "Here's Hopin'" and "One Way Up" would have sounded rather out of place on *Through the Trees*), and there's a bit more upfront humor than in their later work. The key phrase, however, is "a bit"; the creepy but amusing Freudianisms of "Pony," the drunkard's hymn of "Water Into Wine," and the morning-after lament of "She Awoke With a Jerk" are witty enough, but there's a dark undertow that wavers between cynicism and hopelessness which allows these songs to sit side by side with the album's takes of murder ("Arlene"), urban alienation ("Moving Furniture Around"), and corrupted faith ("Everything That Rises Must Converge"). Brett Sparks' plain but resonant Midwestern twang gives the songs on *Odessa* the ring of common truth, and he and Rennie Sparks had already established themselves as writers to be reckoned with, conjuring a lyrical voice that sounds homey and terribly alienated at the same time. Listening to *Odessa* today, it's obvious the Handsome Family had a way to travel before they would create their strongest work, but it's obvious they already had the talent and the ideas that would make them one of the most interesting and intelligent bands to emerge from Chicago's alt-country scene. *—Mark Deming*

Milk and Scissors / 1996 / Carrot Top ✦✦✦
On their second album, the Handsome Family began their retreat away from the scrappy, electric guitar-based sound of their debut, *Odessa*, and started to ease into the lovely but unnerving mix of Appalachian textures and 20th century despair that would become their calling card on *Milk and Scissors*. While "Winnebago Skeletons" and "The Dutch Boy" still feature amped-up guitars in all their noisy glory, most of the cuts reflect a more subdued approach, with acoustic guitars and subtle steel work dominating the proceedings. Despite embracing a less-abrasive style, Brett Sparks and his spouse and musical partner, Rennie Sparks, sure didn't sound any happier than they did on their debut; *Milk and Scissors* features a bit less in the way of dark humor and more simple darkness, reveling in bad judgment, cruel fate, heartbreak, and simple disappointment in all its shapes and sizes. Of course, the Handsome Family's gift is in making something beautiful and compelling out of such things, and there are a handful of great songs here, especially the darkly fanciful "Amelia Earhart vs. the Dancing Bear" and the oddly catchy "Drunk By Noon," but for the most part *Milk and Scissors* captures them in mid-stylistic shift, and they would be a lot more compelling when they arrived on the other side. *—Mark Deming*

Invisible Hands / 1997 / Carrot Top ✦✦✦✦
A limited edition, vinyl only EP by the Chicago-via-Albuquerque alt-country duo the Handsome Family, *Invisible Hands* has more of a full-band feel than some of the pair's better-known later albums. A full rhythm section appears on half the tunes, giving the opening "Tin Foil" a more rock-oriented sound, almost akin to Uncle Tupelo's work. Even stripped-down songs like "Grandmother Waits for You" feature nice sonic touches like piano and fiddle behind Brett Sparks' vocals and guitar. ("Bury Me Here," for example, has a deep, foreboding twang guitar solo that sounds like it came from one of Lee Hazlewood's late-'60s albums.) Wife and musical partner Rennie Sparks takes a back-seat role here, taking no lead vocals of her own and adding her signature ghostly harmonies only to an extended, funereal version of the traditional ballad "Barbara Allen," whose doomy folk-rock sound recalls *Liege & Lief*-era Fairport Convention. *Invisible Hands* doesn't have the *Wisconsin Death Trip*-style sense of Victorian creepiness that colors some of the Handsome Family's albums, but the lack of stylistic pretensions might make it an easier listen for some. *—Stewart Mason*

● **Through the Trees** / Jan. 26, 1998 / Carrot Top ✦✦✦✦✦
Through the Trees was the Handsome Family's breakthrough album, garnering enough attention and sales that they were finally able to quit their day jobs and focus on music full-time. The group subsequently toured the U.S. and Europe, while critics on both sides of the Atlantic went nuts for the Sparks' clever, brooding songs. With *Through the Trees*, the transitional phase heard on *Milk and Scissors* was complete and the duo emerged with a more defined style, delivery, and songcraft which became their trademark sound. Brett sings with a deeper resonance and phrases Rennie's mini-stories more skillfully, while the occasional distorted guitar and harder-rocking tunes have been trimmed away, leaving a more consistent, stripped-down country feel. This album includes Rennie's vocal debut (albeit in a self-conscious, exaggerated nasal twang) on "Down in the Ground"; "Cathedrals," a song originally heard on their limited-edition vinyl EP *Invisible Hands* (Carrot Top, 1997); and enduring crowd favorites "The Woman Downstairs" and "Weightless Again." It also includes guest Jeff Tweedy of Wilco. While the albums that followed were excellent, *Through the Trees* remains the Handsome Family's definitive album, and is a wonderful encapsulation of the myths and heartbroken tales that populate the dark, romantic world of Brett and Rennie Sparks. *—Joslyn Layne*

In the Air / Feb. 15, 2000 / Carrot Top ✦✦✦✦
If their last album, *Through the Trees*, came to us from the darkness at the bottom of a well (or a liquor bottle), *In the Air* is the sound of the Handsome Family after they made it out of the depths and up onto the grass—and are now adjusting to a less desperate life. Not to say that it's sunny. Lyricist Rennie Sparks still presents us with dark and bloody tragedies, as well as whimsical fairytales about lonely, but hopeful figures. The difference between *In the Air* and the Handsome Family's last album seems to be the presence of a calm (as opposed to disturbed restraint) and a certain warmth pervading this album. Brett Sparks' vocal delivery comes across as more relaxed and natural and in lieu of the occasional, creepy vocal effects used on the last album. The colorful, sad, and disturbed scenes are often delivered with a country flavor and a folk instrumentation, and include songs that are the rightful offspring of Appalachian murder ballads, such as "My Beautiful Bride" and "Up Falling Rock Hill," and Southern hymns ("Never Grow Old"). The Handsome Family's songs are imbued with a tender romanticism and love of the fantastic—and of a world that, for all it's real twists and sadness, still holds moments of childlike wonder and fairy-tale possibilities. *In the Air* was recorded, as were their three previous albums, in the Handsome Family living room, this time with live percussion (provided by Brett) instead of a drum machine. Also heard are guest musicians Darrell Sparks, who sings backup and plays guitar on two songs, and violinist Andrew Bird (formerly of the Squirrel Nut Zippers, leader of his own roots music-based band) who contributes to "Poor, Poor Lenore," "Up Falling Rock Hill," and "When That Helicopter Comes," a hellfire and brimstone, foot-stomping number with a sparse, bluegrass delivery: "It's gonna rain champagne/and the hills are gonna dance... The sky will swim in lightning fire and the trees will shake and scream." *—Joslyn Layne*

Twilight / Oct. 2, 2001 / Carrot Top ✦✦✦✦

In the world of the Handsome Family, it would appear that the glass is half full. The only problem is that the glass is either upside down or shattered on the floor. Riddled with dark and morbid tales of suburbia, murder, and the demise of carrying pigeons, the baker's dozen offerings seem animal-oriented, but still teem with an eerie old-time country & western sense of foreboding. Although the first track, "The Snow White Diner," seems uplifting with its "Layla"-like intro, the album waltzes along with keyboards and basic bare-bones accompaniment. Particularly pretty is "All the TVs in Town" and the spacy background of "Gravity." There is also a sense of this being a dysfunctional Christmas album, exemplified by "Birds You Cannot See." The husband and wife team of Rennie Sparks on keyboards and singer Brett Sparks lead the listener down a lovely yet dark trail few would dare tread twice. —*Jason MacNeil*

Live at Schuba's Tavern / Jul. 9, 2002 / Digital Club Network ✦✦✦

This live recording documents a December 2000 show in Chicago during which the Handsome Family entertain, performing a good mix of material, drawing songs from all of their albums to date. The sound is decent and fans will definitely enjoy the teasing banter—nine of the 25 tracks—between Brett and Rennie Sparks and the random personal details that get revealed (the magic balls story is hilarious). Of the 14 songs, half are from *Through the Trees*, including the chokingly sad "So Much Wine," "Down in the Ground," the only song in the band's repertoire in which Rennie sings lead (albeit in an affected, old-lady-on-the-porch, nasally tone), the darkly incisive "Weightless Again," and another fan favorite, "The Woman Downstairs," which closes the show. Throughout the set are also heard a few songs each from *In the Air* and *Milk and Scissors* ("Winnebago Skeletons" falls apart, but "Amelia Earhart Vs. the Dancing Bear" and "Drunk By Noon" go well), two from *Odessa* ("Arlene" and "Moving Furniture Around"), and one that would end up on *Twilight* ("I Know You Are There," which Brett effectively delivers with a crooner's tremolo). While not the place for newcomers to start, *Live at Schuba's Tavern* is a good listen. —*Joslyn Layne*

The Happy Goodman Family

Group / Southern Gospel, Country Gospel, Traditional Gospel

For nearly four decades, the Happy Goodman Family brightened the world with their gospel songs. They were founded in Alabama in the 1940s by Howard and Gussie Goodman. Over the years, they expanded and changed membership until finally becoming a quartet composed of Ruth, Sam, Rusty and Bob Goodman. They were later joined by Vestal Goodman and the only non-Goodman, tenor Johnny Cook. The family was most successful during the 1960s and '70s; in 1968, their album *The Happy Gospel of the Happy Goodmans* won a Grammy for Best Gospel Album. The following year, Vestal received a Dove Award for Female Vocalist of the Year. The Happy Goodmans were some of the first members of the TV show *The Gospel Singing Jubilee*, which has won numerous Dove Awards. —*Sandra Brennan*

● **Greatest Hits** / 1985 / Canaan ✦✦✦✦

Always / Jan. 28, 1997 / Chordant ✦✦✦

Always collects both new material and re-recorded gospel favorites from the Goodman family. —*Jason Ankeny*

Set Your Sails / Jun. 20, 2000 / Pamplin Music ✦✦✦

Toe-tapping, fast-moving set of Southern gospel selections from a family trio perhaps best-known for their frequent appearances on Bill Gaither's gospel performance series. Includes a few ballads thrown in for good measure and some very nice, ear-pleasing, tight harmonies, despite the obvious aging of the elder Goodmans. Pretty nice selection, actually, though a bit more suited to daily listening rather than the quiet reverence of a Sabbath observance. The song "Faithful Man" might be one exception, with its quietly moving lyrics and soft country ballad music about an aging "faithful man" nearing the end of his mortal life. Very moving. The title song is also worth a thorough listen with its equally moving lyrics: "set your sails and head for home/you'll find shelter from the storm/there's no need for you to roam/set your sails and head for home." —*Dacia A. Blodgett-Williams*

Southern Gospel Treasury / Jan. 16, 2001 / Sony ✦✦✦

Harden Trio

f. England, AR, **db.** 1968

Group / Country-Pop, Nashville Sound/Countrypolitan

Sibling act the Harden Trio was basically a one-hit wonder, but they spent many years at the *Grand Ole Opry*. Robbie, Arleen, and Bobby Harden were all born in England, AR, an area of the Ozarks noted for its rich musical heritage. They teamed as teens and performed locally, first gaining professional notice when they joined *Barnyard Frolics* in Little Rock. They became popular and joined the *Ozark Mountain Jubilee* in Springfield, MO, and *Louisiana Hayride*. Their success led them to Nashville, where they appeared on WSM's *Opry Almanac*.

In 1965, they made their recording debut with "Poor Boy," which did nothing on the charts. Their second single, "Tippy Toeing," was their biggest; it hit number three on the country charts, crossed over to the pop Top 50, and earned the group a spot on the *Opry*. In 1967, Arleen and Robbie left the group to go solo. Bobby tried to keep the band going with Karen Wheeler and Shirley Michaels, but the trio broke up in 1968, and Bobby went solo as well. Arleen, who changed her name to Arlene, did have some success as a singer, making the charts 16 times over the six years she spent with Columbia. In 1968, she and Bobby had success with a duet, "Who Loves You." In 1974, she changed her name back and scored one minor hit, her version of Helen Reddy's "Leave Me Alone (Little Ruby Red Dress)." Meanwhile, Bobby found his calling as a successful songwriter. —*Sandra Brennan*

Tippy Toeing / 1966 / Columbia ✦✦✦✦

Sing Me Back Home / 1968 / Columbia ✦✦✦

Nashville Sensation / 1969 / Starday ✦✦✦

Great Country Hits / 1970 / Harmony ✦✦✦

● **Tippy Toeing/Sing Me Back Home** / Jun. 4, 2002 / Collectables ✦✦✦✦

Collectables' two-fer of *Tippy Toeing/Sing Me Back Home* captures the Harden Trio at the peak of their popularity, gathering such charming originals as "Tippy Toeing," "Poor Boy," "Sing Me Back Home," "Don't Remind Me," and "My Friend Mr. Echo" and covers like "Skip a Rope." As it collects virtually all of the output of the trio's original lineup (Bobby, Robbie, and Arleen Harden), *Tippy Toeing/Sing Me Back Home* is a convenient compilation worthwhile for anyone interested in mid-'60s country-pop that's slightly off the beaten path. —*Heather Phares*

Linda Hargrove

b. Feb. 3, 1949, Jacksonville, FL

Guitar, Songwriter, Vocals / Country-Rock, Country-Pop, Urban Cowboy

Linda Hargrove was a singer, songwriter, and multi-instrumentalist who forever seemed to be in the wrong place at the wrong time. In the mid-'70s, she was one of the first Nashville artists to blend country sounds with a modern pop/rock sheen; by the time that such a hybrid came to dominate the charts a decade later, however, Hargrove was largely out of the music industry. Born in Tallahassee, FL, on February 3, 1951, Hargrove began playing piano and guitar while still a preteen. Throughout her formative years, she was largely unresponsive to country music, preferring instead pop and R&B, and by the tail end of the 1960s was performing in a local blue-eyed soul band. It was not until the release of Bob Dylan's *Nashville Skyline* album that she became fascinated by the possibilities that country music offered; when another Florida group, After All, decided to record seven of Hargrove's songs, she followed the band to Nashville in 1970. A year later, Sandy Posey recorded Hargrove's "Saw Someone Else Before Me," which brought her to the attention of producers Billy Sherrill and Pete Drake, who helped the fledgling performer find work as a session guitarist and songwriter.

In 1973, Leon Russell recorded a pair of Hargrove tunes for his country album *Hank Wilson Is Back*. In the same year, Drake introduced her to ex-Monkee Michael Nesmith; together with James Miner, Hargrove and Nesmith co-wrote the song "Winonah," which the latter recorded for his *Pretty Much Your Standard Ranch Stash* album. Nesmith also signed Hargrove to his short-lived experimental C&W label Countryside; she recorded an LP for the label, but it never saw the light of day after Countryside was dropped by its parent company, Elektra/Asylum. Elektra did, however, release her 1973 album *Music Is Your Mistress*, as well as its follow-up, the next year's *Blue Jean Country Queen*.

In 1975, Hargrove moved to Capitol Records, for whom she released her only Top 40 hit, "Love Was (Once Around the Dance Floor)," from the LP *Love, You're the Teacher*. In the same year, Johnny Rodriguez took her composition "Just Get Up and Close the Door" to the top of the charts. She released two more country albums, 1976's *Just Like You* and 1977's *Impressions*, but found little commercial success. Shortly thereafter, she began to focus exclusively on inspirational music, and under her married name of Linda Bartholomew released the Christian album *A New Song* in 1981. She was largely out of music for the next several years until issuing another inspirational record, *Greater Works*, in 1987. Following its release, she again left the industry due to health problems; after recovering from leukemia, in the mid-'90s she began making tentative steps towards resuming her career as a country performer. —*Jason Ankeny*

Music Is Your Mistress / 1973 / Elektra ✦✦✦

Hargrove is an excellent songwriter; which is borne out by the fact that several of these songs have been covered other places. She's also a fine performer. But, something in the production keeps this from being the killer record it could have been. In some places it sounds thin and in others the mix works against the voice. Still, the songs make this record worth having. —*Jim Worbois*

Blue Jean Country Queen / 1974 / Elektra ✦✦✦

● **Love, You're the Teacher** / 1975 / Capitol ✦✦✦✦

More good stuff from Hargrove including her original version of the Johnny Rodriguez hit "Just Get Up and Close the Door." Everything is in place (songs, performance, production) making this, easily, one of her best. —*Jim Worbois*

Just Like You / 1976 / Capitol ✦✦✦

Good songs. Some of the best players and singers around. Mike Nesmith is a writing partner on one song. Why didn't this catch on in a big way? That's one of life's great mysteries. This is a good album. —*Jim Worbois*

Impressions / 1977 / Capitol ✦✦✦

Keith Harling

b. Greenwood, SC

Vocals, Guitar, Saxophone, Drums / Contemporary Country, New Traditionalist

New traditionalist country singer Keith Harling was born in Greenwood, SC, and raised in Chattanooga, TN. Influenced by Lefty Frizzell, Conway Twitty, and Keith Whitley, he built himself a drum set at the age of ten and taught himself to play by mimicking the musicians he watched on television; throughout high-school and college, Harling also played bass, saxophone, and trumpet in a variety of local rock bands. After a period in Florida, he relocated to Nashville but found the music industry impenetrable, and after six months returned to Chattanooga. There Harling spent the next seven years honing his writing and performing skills in area clubs. Finally, in 1996, he signed to MCA's publishing division as a songwriter, and after playing a showcase, he landed a recording contract just six weeks later. His debut LP, *Write It in Stone*, followed in 1998; *Bring It On* appeared a year later. —*Jason Ankeny*

● **Write It in Stone** / May 19, 1998 / MCA ✦✦✦✦

Keith Harling's debut album *Write It in Stone* is an engaging, neo-traditional honky tonk record that suggests Harling is as talented a songwriter as he is a vocalist. He has a nice, laid-back delivery and a rich timbre; similarly, his songwriting is effortless and natural.

He wrote six of the songs on his debut, and the best of them match the professional tunes he sings on the remainder of the album. There are a few weak moments, but overall, *Write It in Stone* is a first-class debut. *—Thom Owens*

Bring It On / Nov. 23, 1999 / Warner Bros. ✦✦

As difficult a time as Keith Harling had getting to Nashville, once he got there things got even harder for him. You'd think that a New Traditional singer/songwriter who put three singles from his debut album, *Write It in Stone*, in the country charts, including two, "Papa Bear" and "Write It in Stone," that he wrote himself, would be take his career to the next step with a well set-up second album. Instead, in the bloodletting that accompanied MCA's acquisition of PolyGram, he was dropped from the MCA roster; apparently you had to have gone gold your first time out to make the cut. Happily, he was scooped up immediately by Giant Records, but not so happily the label doesn't seem to trust him to make his own record—while he wrote two-thirds of his first album, he wrote nothing on his second *Bring It On*. No doubt relieved to even have a record contract, he has done his best on the collection of 11 sturdy country songs that the label found for him, but the chance for something individual has been lost. The music is standard-issue country-pop with occasional (but not too frequent) honky tonk elements; the lyrics are the usual sort of catch-phrase clichés—"Bring It On," "As If," "It Goes Something Like This"—wedded to the usual romantic sentiments. The title song was rising on the country charts before the album's release, and there are other songs that sound like possible winners on country radio in its currently pop-compromised state. The promise Harling showed on his first album, however, has been deferred for now. *—William Ruhlmann*

Joni Harms

b. Nov. 5, 1959, Canby, OR

Vocals / Contemporary Country, Country-Pop

Joni Harms grew up on a ranch in Oregon where she combined an interest in singing with the life of a cowgirl. She won a talent contest sponsored by the Future Farmers of America while in high-school and soon began taking trips to Nashville in search of a recording contract. She signed to record executive Jimmy Bowen's Universal label, a co-venture with MCA Records, and reached the country Top 40 in April 1989 with "I Need a Wife." "The Only Thing Bluer Than His Eyes," the follow-up single, reached the country charts in June. Bowen took Harms with him when he moved to Capitol Records in 1990 and there released her debut album, *Hometown Girl*, which did not chart. During the 1990s, Harms maintained her musical career while marrying, raising two children, and continuing to live and work on her family ranch in Oregon. She followed *Hometown Girl* with *Whatever It Takes* and the all-original holiday album *Christmas in the Country*.

By 1998 she was signed to Warner Bros. Records, which released *Cowgirl Dreams*. She made a children's album, *Are We There Yet?*, accompanied by a coloring book, and also wrote and published a children's book, *Stan and Bert*. A second children's book, *The Little Grey Donkey*, appeared in the fall of 2001, as did a new country album, *After All*, released on her Real West Productions label through the independent record company Paras Recordings. *—William Ruhlmann*

Hometown Girl / Jul. 30, 1990 / Capitol ✦✦✦

Cowgirl Dreams / Nov. 17, 1998 / Warner Bros. ✦✦✦

● **After All** / Oct. 30, 2001 / Paras Recording ✦✦✦

This is Joni Harms' eighth album (counting a children's record and a Christmas record), only two of those discs having appeared on major labels, so she is by now an artist with a confirmed style. She calls that style "western music," and it consists of songs that recall the Western swing of Bob Wills, forays into Tex-Mex, and lots of references to cowboys. It's also happy music—Harms' lyrical persona is romantically content, married to a cowboy, raising children, confident in her life and her faith. One song after another proclaims her devotion and satisfaction. Her warm, buoyant voice occasionally suggests Patsy Cline (especially in "Every Cowgirl's Dream"), but she has no interest in the wild side of life that Cline sometimes embraced. This is not a cowgirl who's going to go crazy or fall to pieces; she's going to dance a "West Texas Waltz" and then have some "Cowboy Coffee." One may protest that this is all a bit too wholesome; Harms' West doesn't seem to have a single gunrack or honky tonk in it. She remakes her own "I Want to Sing for You" as the album's closer, and though it's a believably straightforward statement of purpose, its declaration that "I want to make you blue" (which follows "I want to make you happy") is not fulfilled on this album. Maybe it's unfair to expect an artist to concoct a life that isn't true to her experience just for the sake of variety, but Harms' worldview is so well-scrubbed it doesn't seem entirely true to its subject. They say the Old West you see in the movies never really existed. The New West certainly does, but there must be more to it than what you hear in these songs. *—William Ruhlmann*

Bill Harrell

b. Sep. 14, 1934, Marion, VA

Guitar, Vocals / Traditional Bluegrass

A player who favored a subtle, traditional approach to his music, singer and multi-instrumentalist Bill Harrell remained one of bluegrass' most popular figures for several decades. Born in Marion, VA, on September 14, 1934, Harrell's passion for music began during his childhood, when he started playing guitar and taking piano lessons. While attending college in Maryland, he first became enamored of bluegrass, and began playing mandolin in a trio. Tenures in other Washington, D.C.-area groups, including the Rocky Mountain Boys, followed as he played with musicians like Eddie Adcock, Donny Bryant, Smiley Hobbs, Smitty Irvin, Carl Nelson, and Roy Self. While serving in the armed forces, Harrell was injured in an auto accident, and spent close to a year recovering in a military hospital. Upon his release, he returned to Washington and cut his first recordings.

In 1960, he formed the Virginians with Irvin on banjo, Buck Ryan on fiddle, and Stoney Edwards on bass. The group released the album *The Wonderful World of Bluegrass Music* in 1963 and followed it two years later with *Ballads and Bluegrass*. In addition to hosting a weekly television program from Harrisonburg, VA, the group played dates up and down the East Coast and guested frequently on Jimmy Dean's network series. Irvin left the band in 1965, and was replaced by Don Stover. Harrell soon departed to join Don Reno & the Tennessee Cut-Ups, remaining with Reno for over a decade; their partnership coincided with a resurgence in the public's interest in bluegrass as a result of a growing festival circuit. Soon after Harrell joined the group, his Virginians bandmate Buck Ryan signed on as well, and in 1966 Reno and Harrell released the LP *The Most Requested Songs*.

Around the time of 1969's *I'm Using My Bible for a Roadmap*, Reno's former partner Red Smiley returned from retirement, and began performing with the group on-stage and in the studio. After several more records with Reno, Harrell and bassist Ed Ferris amicably left the group to reform the Virginians with Harrell's old friend Carl Nelson on fiddle and newcomer Darrell Sanders on banjo. The band released the record *Bluegrass and Ballads* in 1978, followed by the back-to-back *Bluegrass Gospel, Pure and Simple* and *I Can Hear Virginia Calling Me* in 1980. Despite a revolving-door lineup, Harrell continued to steer the Virginians well into the 1990s, issuing records like 1983's *Walking in the Early Morning Dew*, 1986's *Blue Virginia Blue*, and 1990's *After Sunrise*. *—Jason Ankeny*

● **Classic Bluegrass** / 1991 / Rebel ✦✦✦✦

Kelly Harrell

b. Sep. 13, 1889, Drapers Valley, VA, **d.** Jul. 9, 1942, Virginia

Vocals / Traditional Country

Kelly Harrell was a near-legendary country balladeer during the 1920s, when he cut more than a dozen songs for Victor and OKeh. He was also a gifted songwriter whose music was covered by other artists, including Jimmie Rodgers and Ernest Stoneman, in his own lifetime. Harrell was born in the Virginia highlands in the western part of the state, and from his early teens worked in various textile mills. He enjoyed singing, though he didn't play an instrument, and was inspired to try recording in his belief that he was at least as good a singer as a man he met locally named Henry Whitter, who had made records.

In early 1925, when Harrell was already 35 years old, he went to New York and recorded four sides for Victor Records, among them "New River Train" and "The Roving Gambler." He recorded for OKeh later that year, including a version of "The Wreck of the Old 97," backed by "Blue Eyed Ella." Those sides elicited enough interest that Victor was interested in recording Harrell further in 1926. Those sides were his first using the electrical recording system, which was a considerable advance on the acoustic recordings he'd previously made. In 1927, Victor cut Harrell in another half-dozen songs backed by his own band (as Kelly Harrell & the Virginia String Band), with which he was performing locally.

Harrell recorded another handful of recordings for Victor in 1929, after which his recording career came to a halt, owing to his inability to play an instrument—Harrell always required backing by other musicians, and the Great Depression had so damaged the recording business that Victor was unwilling to pay the cost of hiring backup musicians in 1930 and beyond. Harrell performed locally and worked the textile mills until 1942, when a heart attack took his life. His complete recorded music was reissued by Bear Family on a triple-LP set in the 1970s, and he is also represented by an LP on the County label. *—Bruce Eder*

● **Complete Recorded Works, Vol. 1 (1925–1926)** / May 2, 1998 / Document ✦✦✦

Complete Recorded Works, Vol. 2 (1926–1929) / May 2, 1998 / Document ✦✦✦

Emmylou Harris

b. Apr. 2, 1947, Birmingham, AL

Guitar, Vocals, Leader / Traditional Country, Progressive Country, Country-Rock, Folk-Rock, Alternative Country, Contemporary Country

Though other performers sold more records and earned greater fame, few left as profound an impact on contemporary music as Emmylou Harris. Blessed with a crystalline voice, a remarkable gift for phrasing, and a restless creative spirit, she traveled a singular artistic path, proudly carrying the torch of "Cosmic American music" passed down by her mentor, Gram Parsons. With the exception of only Neil Young—not surprisingly an occasional collaborator—no other mainstream star established a similarly large body of work as consistently iconoclastic, eclectic, or daring; even more than three decades into her career, Harris' latter-day music remained as heartfelt, visionary, and vital as her earliest recordings.

Harris was born on April 2, 1947, to a military family stationed in Birmingham, AL. After spending much of her childhood in North Carolina, she moved to Woodbridge, VA, while in her teens, and graduated high-school there as class valedictorian. After winning a dramatic scholarship at the University of North Carolina, she began to seriously study music, learning to play songs by Bob Dylan and Joan Baez. Soon, Harris was performing in a duo with fellow U.N.C. student Mike Williams, eventually quitting school to move to New York, only to find the city's folk music community dying out in the wake of the psychedelic era.

Still, Harris remained in New York, traveling the Greenwich Village club circuit before becoming a regular at *Gerdes Folk City*, where she struck up friendships with fellow folkies Jerry Jeff Walker, David Bromberg, and Paul Siebel. After marrying songwriter Tom Slocum in 1969, she recorded her debut LP, 1970's *Gliding Bird*. Shortly after the record's release, however, Harris' label declared bankruptcy, and while pregnant with her first child, her marriage began to fall apart. After moving to Nashville, she and Slocum divorced, leaving Harris to raise daughter Hallie on her own. After several months of struggle and poverty, she moved back in with her parents, who had since bought a farm outside of Washington, D.C. There she returned to performing, starting a trio with local musicians Gerry Mule and Tom Guidera. One evening in 1971, while playing at an area club called Clyde's, the trio performed to a crowd which included members of the country-rock pioneers the Flying Burrito Brothers. In the wake of the departure of Gram Parsons, the band's founder, the Burritos were then led by ex-Byrd Chris Hillman, who was so impressed by Harris' talents that he considered inviting her to join the group. Instead, Hillman himself quit to join Stephen Stills' Manassas, but he recommended her to Parsons, who wanted a female vocalist to flesh out the sound of his solo work, a trail-blazing fusion of country and rock & roll he dubbed "Cosmic American music." Their connection was instant, and soon Harris was learning about country music and singing harmony on Parsons' solo debut, 1972's *GP*. A tour with Parsons' backup unit the Fallen Angels followed, and in 1973 they returned to the studio to cut his landmark LP, *Grievous Angel*.

On September 19, just weeks after the album sessions ended, Parsons' fondness for drugs and alcohol finally caught up to him, and he was found dead in a hotel room outside of the Joshua Tree National Monument in California. At the time, Harris was back in Washington, collecting her daughter for a planned move to the West Coast. Instead, she remained in D.C., reuniting with Tom Guidera to form the Angel Band. The group signed to Reprise and relocated to Los Angeles to begin work on Harris' solo major-label debut, 1975's acclaimed *Pieces of the Sky*, an impeccable collection made up largely of diverse covers ranging in origin from Merle Haggard to the Beatles. Produced by Brian Ahern, who would go on to helm Harris' next ten records—as well as becoming her second husband—*Pieces of the Sky*'s second single, a rendition of the Louvin Brothers' "If I Could Only Win Your Love," became her first Top Five hit. "Light of the Stable," a Christmas single complete with backing vocals from Dolly Parton, Linda Ronstadt, and Neil Young, soon followed; Harris then repaid the favor by singing on Ronstadt's "The Sweetest Gift" and Young's "Star of Bethlehem."

For her third LP, 1975's *Elite Hotel*, Harris established a new backing unit, the Hot Band, which featured legendary Elvis Presley sidemen James Burton and Glen D. Hardin as well as a young songwriter named Rodney Crowell on backup vocals and rhythm guitar. The resulting album proved to be a smash, with covers of Buck Owens' "Together Again" and the Patsy Cline perennial "Sweet Dreams" both topping the charts. Before beginning sessions for her fourth effort, 1977's *Luxury Liner*, Harris guested on Bob Dylan's *Desire* and appeared in Martin Scorsese's documentary of the Band's legendary final performance, *The Last Waltz*. *Quarter Moon in a Ten Cent Town* followed in 1978, led by the single "Two More Bottles of Wine," her third number one. The record was Crowell's last with the Hot Band; one of the tracks, "Green Rolling Hills," included backing from Ricky Skaggs, soon to become Crowell's replacement as Harris' vocal partner.

Blue Kentucky Girl (1979) was her most country-oriented work to date, an indication of what was to come a year later with *Roses in the Snow*, a full-fledged excursion into acoustic bluegrass. In the summer of 1980, a duet with Roy Orbison, "That Lovin' You Feelin' Again," hit the Top Ten; a yuletide LP, *Light of the Stable: The Christmas Album*, followed at the end of year, at a time during which Harris had quit touring to focus on raising her second daughter, Meghann. *Evangeline*, a patchwork of songs left off of previous albums, appeared in 1981. Shortly after, Skaggs left the Hot Band to embark on a solo career; his replacement was Barry Tashian, a singer/songwriter best known for fronting the 1960s rock band the Remains. In 1982, drummer John Ware, the final holdover from the first Hot Band lineup, left the group; at the same time, Harris' marriage to Ahern was also beginning to disintegrate. After 1981's *Cimarron*, Harris and the Hot Band cut a live album, *Last Date*, named in honor of the album's chart-topping single "(Lost His Love) On Our Last Date," a vocal version of the Floyd Cramer instrumental. Quickly, they returned to the studio to record *White Shoes*, Harris' final LP with Ahern at the helm. Her most far-ranging affair yet, it included covers of Donna Summer's "On the Radio," Johnny Ace's "Pledging My Love," and Sandy Denny's "Old-Fashioned Waltz."

After leaving Ahern, she and her children moved back to Nashville. There, Harris joined forces with singer/songwriter Paul Kennerley, on whose 1980 concept album *The Legend of Jesse James* she had sung backup. Together, they began formulating a record called *The Ballad of Sally Rose*, employing the pseudonym Harris often used on the road to veil what was otherwise a clearly autobiographical portrait of her own life. Though a commercial failure, the 1985 record proved pivotal in Harris' continued evolution as an artist and a risk taker; it also marked another chapter in her personal life when she and Kennerley wed shortly after concluding their tour. *Angel Band*, a subtle, acoustic collection of traditional country spirituals, followed, although the record was not issued until 1987, after the release of its immediate follow-up, *Thirteen*.

Harris, Dolly Parton, and Linda Ronstadt had first toyed with the idea of recording an album together as far back as 1977, only to watch the project falter in light of touring commitments and other red tape. Finally, in 1987, they issued *Trio*, a collection which proved to be Harris' best-selling album to date, generating the hits "To Know Him Is to Love Him" (a cover of the Phil Spector classic), "Telling Me Lies," and "Those Memories of You." The record's success spurred the 1990 release of *Duets*, a compilation of her earlier hits in conjunction with George Jones, Willie Nelson, Gram Parsons, and others. Fronting a new band, the Nash Ramblers, in 1992 she issued *At the Ryman*, a live set recorded at Nashville's legendary Ryman Auditorium, the former home of the *Grand Ole Opry*. At the time of the record's release, Harris was also serving a term as President of the Country Music Foundation. In 1993, she ended her long association with Warner Bros./Reprise to move to Asylum Records, where she released *Cowgirl's Prayer* shortly after her separation from Paul Kennerley.

Two years later, at a stage in her career at which most performers retreat to the safety of rehashing their greatest hits again and again, Harris issued *Wrecking Ball*, perhaps her most adventuresome record to date. Produced by Daniel Lanois, the New Orleans-based artist best known for his atmospheric work with U2, Peter Gabriel, and Bob Dylan, *Wrecking Ball* was a hypnotic, staggeringly beautiful work comprised of songs ranging from the Neil Young-penned title track (which featured its writer on backing vocals) to Jimi Hendrix's "May This Be Love" and the talented newcomer Gillian Welch's "Orphan Girl." A three-disc retrospective of her years with Warner Bros., *Portraits*, appeared in 1996, and in 1998 Harris resurfaced with *Spyboy*. Following the release of *Trio II* later that year, she and Ronstadt again reunited, this time minus Parton, for 1999's *Western Wall: Tucson Sessions*. Harris returned the following year with *Red Dirt Girl*, her first album of original material in five years, which featured appearances from Bruce Springsteen, Patty Scialfa, Jill Cunniff, and Patty Griffin. *—Jason Ankeny*

Gliding Bird / 1968 / Emus ✦✦
Harris typically omits *Gliding Bird* from her discography; her first record, it was issued on the folk label Jubilee, which filed for bankruptcy within weeks of the LP's release. Cut before her tenure with Gram Parsons, it's a straightforward folk effort, owing more to Joni Mitchell than anything else; although most of the songs were composed by Tom Slocum, Harris' first husband, there are also a number of ill-suited covers, including Hank Williams' "I Saw the Light" and the Burt Bacharach/Hal David composition "I'll Never Fall in Love Again." *—Jason Ankeny*

★ **Pieces of the Sky** / 1975 / Reprise ✦✦✦✦✦
Harris' major-label solo debut quickly establishes the pattern that the vast majority of her subsequent work would follow: *Pieces of the Sky* is bravely eclectic, impeccably performed, and achingly beautiful. Amidst a collection of songs which ranks among her most well-chosen—ranging from the catalogs of the Beatles ("For No One") to Boudleaux & Felice Bryant ("Sleepless Nights") and the Louvin Brothers (the hit "If I Could Only Win Your Love")—the record's centerpiece is one of Harris' rare original compositions, "Boulder to Birmingham," her stirring tribute to fallen mentor Gram Parsons. *—Jason Ankeny*

Elite Hotel / 1975 / Reprise ✦✦✦✦✦
While much of Harris' career has been spent carrying on the legacy of Gram Parsons, *Elite Hotel* ranks among her most overt tributes to his genius, thanks to its covers of the Flying Burrito Brothers' "Sin City" and "Wheels," along with "Ooh Las Vegas" from the *Grievous Angel* album. In addition to the usual eclectic mix of covers—which includes the Beatles' "Here, There and Everywhere" and Hank Williams' "Jambalaya" this time out—*Elite Hotel* offers renditions of the country perennials "Together Again" and "Sweet Dreams," which were, respectively, Harris' first two number-one chart hits. *—Jason Ankeny*

Luxury Liner / 1977 / Reprise ✦✦✦✦✦
Luxury Liner ranks as Harris' best-selling solo record to date, and it's one of her most engaging efforts as well; her Hot Band is in peak form, and the songs are even more far afield than usual, including Chuck Berry's "(You Never Can Tell) C'est La Vie" and Townes Van Zandt's painterly tale of aging outlaws, "Pancho & Lefty." *—Jason Ankeny*

☆ **Profile (The Best of Emmylou Harris)** / 1978 / Reprise ✦✦✦✦✦
Profile (The Best of Emmylou Harris) collects 12 of Harris' biggest hits from the mid-'70s, including the number-one hits "Together Again," "Sweet Dreams," "Two More Bottles of Wine," and the Top Ten hits "One of These Days," "If I Could Only Win Your Love," "You Never Can Tell," "Making Believe," and "To Daddy." *—Stephen Thomas Erlewine*

A Quarter Moon in a Ten Cent Town / 1978 / Reprise ✦✦✦✦
Quarter Moon in a Ten Cent Town is a transitional effort which bridges the curveballs of Harris' earliest solo work with the more traditional country albums which comprise the bulk of the second phase of her career. For the first time, she covers no Gram Parsons tunes or pop music chestnuts, relying instead on newly exited Hot Band member Rodney Crowell for two songs ("Leaving Louisiana in the Broad Daylight" and "I Ain't Living Long like This") and Dolly Parton for another (the devastating "To Daddy"); the highlight is a gorgeous cover of Jesse Winchester's "Defying Gravity." *—Jason Ankeny*

Blue Kentucky Girl / 1979 / Reprise ✦✦✦
In response to criticism that her records weren't "country" enough, Harris recorded *Blue Kentucky Girl*, one of her most traditional outings. Relying on a more acoustic sound, the album largely forsakes contemporary pop songs in favor of standard country fare, including the Louvin Brothers' "Everytime You Leave" and Leon Payne's "They'll Never Take His Love from Me." The cover of Dallas Frazier's "Beneath Still Waters" earned Harris her fourth number-one single. *—Jason Ankeny*

Christmas Album (Light in the Stable) / Jul. 1979 / Reprise ✦✦✦✦
Taking her cue from the title track, a Christmas single first issued in 1975 (complete with backing vocals by Neil Young, Dolly Parton, and Linda Ronstadt), Harris compiled this collection of holiday music, originally issued in 1980. Along with "Angel Eyes (Angel Eyes)," a Rodney Crowell song composed specifically for the project, the album includes traditional fare like "O Little Town of Bethlehem," "Little Drummer Boy" and "Silent Night," rendered in much the same acoustic style as her previous studio effort *Roses in the Snow*. *—Jason Ankeny*

Roses in the Snow / 1980 / Reprise ✦✦✦✦✦
Combining acoustic bluegrass with traditional Appalachian melodies (and tossing one contemporary tune, Paul Simon's "The Boxer," into the mix), *Roses in the Snow* ranks among Harris' riskiest—and most satisfying—gambits. *—Jason Ankeny*

Evangeline / 1981 / Reprise ✦✦✦
Long considered a substandard effort due to its oddly brief running time (it's just barely half an hour long) and scattershot feel (like its sister album, *Cimarron*, also released in 1981, it primarily consists of outtakes from earlier albums), *Evangeline* is not as bad as its detractors claim. It's true that the album has more than a couple of clunkers; the synthesizers and California rock guitars of Rodney Crowell's "I Don't Have to Crawl" and "Ashes By Now" do neither singer nor songs any favors, the version of John Fogerty's "Bad Moon Rising" adds nothing new to the song, and James Taylor's "Millworker" simply isn't very good. On the other hand, two recordings from the then-unreleased *Trio* sessions with Dolly Parton and Linda Ronstadt, a perky "Mr. Sandman" that was a minor pop hit and a reworking of Robbie Robertson's haunting "Evangeline" featuring some outstanding harmonies from Parton, are outstanding, as are "Spanish Johnny," a Springsteen-ish ballad sung with Waylon Jennings, and a dazzling version of the standard "How High the Moon" that uses the same pre-rock arrangement style as "Mr. Sandman." So, *Evangeline* is certainly uneven, but it's not at all worthless. *—Stewart Mason*

Cimarron / 1981 / Reprise ✦✦✦
That *Cimarron*, Emmylou Harris' ninth regular album, was assembled largely from recording sessions held for her previous couple of records is no necessary reflection on

its quality. In fact, *Cimarron* was a typical effort for Harris, presenting her usual mix of country favorites, songs borrowed from the pop/rock arena, and singer/songwriter discoveries. Most prominent among the last category was Townes Van Zandt's "If I Needed You," released as a single three months ahead of the LP. From the pop mainstream, Harris borrowed Poco's "Rose of Cimarron" and Bruce Springsteen's "The Price You Pay." The recent T. G. Sheppard country number-one hit "The Last Cheater's Waltz" and "Tennessee Waltz," best remembered for Patti Page's pop hit, were given respectful readings. And there was a lovely arrangement of the traditional ballad "Spanish Is a Loving Tongue." But the most memorable songs on the album were its two other country Top Tens, Karen Brooks and Hank DeVito's "Tennessee Rose" and Paul Kennerley's "Born to Run." On the whole, the album maintained the high standard Harris had set with her previous releases, and it deserved its 1982 Grammy nomination for Best Country Vocal Performance, Female. Though it matched the success of recent Harris LPs on the country charts, hitting the Top Ten and remaining listed for more than nine months, it did not enjoy as great a pop crossover sale and became Harris' first regular album since her 1975 breakthrough not to go gold. This was more indicative of the overall decline in country's crossover success than of any deficiency of the album itself; nevertheless, Harris' commercial success had crested. *—William Ruhlmann*

Last Date / 1982 / Reprise ♦♦♦

Unlike most recording artists, whose profit-taking live albums simply repeat their best-known material, Emmylou Harris approached her first concert album *Last Date* as her next regular release, including only songs she had not previously recorded. This meant that *Last Date* was another in Harris' series of tasteful song selections mixing covers of traditional country fare with country-styled interpretations of pop songs. One exception to the usual bill of fare was that there were no newly written songs. In their place, Harris harked back to her legendary association with country-pop singer/songwriter Gram Parsons, using former Parsons associate Barry Tashian in his place on four Parsons-related numbers. Beyond her commitment to Parsons, Harris seemed determined to present a catholic interpretation of country music, embracing the Nashville sound and acknowledging the Bakersfield sound, looking to traditional country, trying out rockabilly, and reviving the Everly Brothers' country-pop sound. The choices underscored Harris' position as a student of country music earnestly reproducing all of its forms, rather than an adherent of any particular contemporary school, and this was reinforced by her usual sprinkling of pop material. Though *Last Date* was in many ways a typical Harris disc, the added excitement of playing the material live with the Hot Band gave the album extra kick. Like its predecessor *Cimarron*, *Last Date* reached the country Top Ten and the Top 100 of the pop charts, but did not sell well enough to go gold. It represented the end of Harris' reign as a consistently successful commercial entity; thereafter, she would struggle to sell records in significant numbers. *—William Ruhlmann*

White Shoes / 1983 / Reprise ♦♦♦

Harris' final album with longtime producer (and husband) Brian Ahern is among her most surprising and diverse, perhaps the closest she's ever come to a straight-ahead rock LP. Among the unusual cover choices: Johnny Ace's "Pledging My Love" and Donna Summer's "On the Radio." *—Jason Ankeny*

Profile II: The Best of Emmylou Harris / 1984 / Reprise ♦♦♦♦♦

Harris' second hits collection is highlighted by a pair of chart-toppers, "Beneath Still Waters" and "(Lost His Love) On Our Last Date." It also includes the Top Five smashes "Born to Run," "I'm Movin' On" and "Save the Last Dance for Me." *—Jason Ankeny*

The Ballad of Sally Rose / 1985 / Reprise ♦♦♦

This is one of the most intriguing albums of Emmylou Harris' career, and that is saying a lot. It marked the first album where she wrote or co-wrote all the songs, and the strength of the songwriting makes one wonder why she had never attempted it before. One can tell that this album is truly a labor of love, as it is a semi-autobiographical concept album that she also co-produced. It tells the story of a girl from a small town who gets taken under the wing of singer that takes her (and her angelic voice) out on the road. (The story mirrors her relationship with Gram Parsons, although it is a fictional account of the life of another woman.) As a concept album, it only partly holds together; one must read the liner notes to get a true feeling for the story. However, Emmylou Harris sounds particularly inspired, and the songs themselves are strong both musically and lyrically. As expected, she truly shines on the slower ballads such as "Diamond in My Crown" and the closer "Sweet Chariot." While not essential for casual fans, it is an interesting album worth tracking down for Emmylou Harris fans (the album is not easily available in the U.S.). *—Vik Iyengar*

Thirteen / 1986 / Reprise ♦♦

Thirteen takes its title from the number of solo efforts Harris had recorded to date; her numbering didn't take into account hits collections or her true debut, *Gliding Bird*, an album she later disowned. For that matter, *Thirteen* is no great shakes either—with the exception of a lovely cover of Bruce Springsteen's "My Father's House," both the material and the performances are lackluster. *—Jason Ankeny*

Angel Band / 1987 / Reprise ♦♦♦♦

Angel Band is yet another fascinating left turn, an acoustic record comprised of country-gospel songs like "We Shall Rise," " "If I Be Lifted Up" and "Someday My Ship Will Sail," " performed with great subtlety and nuance. *—Jason Ankeny*

Bluebird / 1988 / Reprise ♦♦♦

Like most of Emmylou Harris' albums, *Bluebird* is an expertly performed album, featuring some truly startling and affecting *tour de forces* by Harris. However, the material—while featuring a handful of truly great songs, like John Hiatt's "Icy Blue Heart" and her original "A River for Him"—is too uneven to rank among her finest efforts. *—Thom Owens*

Brand New Dance / 1990 / Reprise ♦♦♦

In 1990, Emmylou Harris' run of superb mid-'70s albums was over, and she hadn't yet assembled the Nash Ramblers, the acoustic band that gave her music a heady kick-start prior to her first striking collaboration with Daniel Lanois, *Wrecking Ball*. As a result, *Brand New Dance* captures Harris at the end of one cycle and just before the start of another, and the material and production suggest Harris was ready for some changes. Emmylou Harris probably couldn't make a truly bad album if she tried, and as always, she's in lovely voice on *Brand New Dance*, but she doesn't always sound especially engaged with the material, most of which falls into the "good-but-not great" category (notable exceptions—a strong cover of Bruce Springsteen's "Tougher Than the Rest" and the title cut). In addition, producer Allen Reynolds puts a shade too much pop-friendly gloss on the arrangements and mix for several of these tunes, and despite the presence of a truly impressive team of accompanists, this album never quite catches fire as in Harris' best work. *Brand New Dance* is a strong and professional piece of work, but Harris' next few albums would remind fans she was capable of a lot more than that. *—Mark Deming*

Duets / Jul. 24, 1990 / Reprise ♦♦♦

On the heels of *Trio*, Harris' smash studio collaboration with Dolly Parton and Linda Ronstadt, comes the compilation *Duets*, which collects previously released performances recorded in conjunction with Neil Young, Willie Nelson, and others. Obviously intended to cash in on the success of *Trio*, the record is by no means an essential addition to the Harris ouevre: virtually everything included is readily available on other albums, and the selections are erratic at best—by and large, Harris' finest material is her solo work, although the power of "Love Hurts," recorded during her all-too-brief period with Gram Parsons, remains undeniable. *—Jason Ankeny*

At the Ryman / 1992 / Reprise ♦♦♦♦

This is the album debut of the Nashville Ramblers, her acoustic backing band featuring Sam Bush and Roy Huskey Jr. recorded over three nights in the former home of the *Grand Ole Opry*. Harris' choice of songs strikes a balance between hillbilly classics and folk-influenced rock, with Bill Monroe receiving heaviest tribute but sharing space with Tex Owens, Bruce Springsteen, and John Fogerty. *—Brian Mansfield*

Cowgirl's Prayer / 1993 / Elektra ♦♦♦♦

Cowgirl's Prayer, recorded in 1993, was the last album Emmylou Harris recorded before beginning a long association with producer and songwriter Daniel Lanois, creating her band Spyboy, and recording her exit from Elektra with *Wrecking Ball*. In other words, it was the last "traditional" Emmylou Harris record. Produced by Allen Reynolds and Richard Bennett, it features 11 stellar cuts by songwriters such as Lucinda Williams ("Crescent City"), Leonard Cohen ("Ballad of a Runaway Horse"), David Olney ("Jerusalem Tomorrow"), Kieran Kane ("The Light"), Eddy Arnold (the classic "You Don't Know Me"), and, in a welcome change, Harris herself ("Prayer in Open D"). This is also filled with Nashville session aces as well as Kane; backing vocalists who include Trisha Yearwood, Alison Krauss, and Ashley Cleveland; and famed bassist Edgar Meyer. The Arnold track, Harris' own composition, and her reading of Williams' "Crescent City" are standouts to be sure, in that Harris allows her voice to move deeper into the lyric than the arrangements would normally allow. But it is on Olney's "Jerusalem Tomorrow" that the weight of the album rests, with Al Perkins' whining pedal steel and Sam Levine's clarinet winding their way through the mix. The story involves a charlatan who heals the sick and makes a mute speak, a false prophet who feels his game is being eclipsed by a strange, wandering Galilean who doesn't charge for his works of wonder. When the false prophet encounters Jesus, he decides to go along with his game as long as his way is paid, and prepares to go into Jerusalem the next day. Given that it is spoken and not sung, Harris dislocates her way of conveying emotion in a song; that she becomes convincing as a male figure is another shapeshift, and finally that there is no overly moral tone in her delivery, but strictly one of empathy, opens up not only the song, but Harris and the rest of the album to an entirely different set of critical criteria. *Cowgirl's Prayer* is one of Harris' most emotionally honest and musically satisfying recordings that matches the intensity, diversity, and musical ambition of her earliest works. *—Thom Jurek*

Songs of the West / 1994 / Warner Western ♦♦

Following Harris' departure from Warner Bros., the label saw fit to compile *Songs of the West*, a collection of previously released performances linked thematically by their connection, however tenuous, to Western music, life and mythology. Stripped of their original album context, the individual tracks fail to happily co-exist; the record's lone selling point is that a pair of cuts—one culled from her autobiographical song cycle *The Ballad of Sally Rose*, the other a cover of Poco's "Rose of Cimarron"—make their domestic CD bow herein. *—Jason Ankeny*

Wrecking Ball / Sep. 26, 1995 / Elektra ♦♦♦♦♦

Wrecking Ball is a leftfield masterpiece, the most wide-ranging, innovative, and daring record in a career built on such notions. Rich in atmosphere and haunting in its dark complexity, much of the due credit belongs to producer Daniel Lanois; best known for his work with pop superstars like U2 and Peter Gabriel, on *Wrecking Ball* Lanois taps into the very essence of what makes Harris tick—the gossamer vocals, the flawless phrasing—while also opening up innumerable new avenues for her talents to explore. The songs shimmer and swirl, given life through Lanois' trademark ringing guitar textures and the almost primal drumming of U2's Larry Mullen Jr. The fixed point remains Harris' voice, which leaps into each and every one of these diverse compositions—culled from the pens of Neil Young, Bob Dylan, Jimi Hendrix, Steve Earle, and others—with utter fearlessness, as if this were the album she'd been waiting her entire life to make. Maybe it is. *—Jason Ankeny*

Portraits / Oct. 8, 1996 / Warner Archives ♦♦♦♦♦
Portraits is a three-disc, 61-track box set covering Emmylou Harris' entire career for Reprise and Warner Records, which spans from 1974 to 1992. Not only does the box select highlights from classic albums like *Luxury Liner, Roses in the Snow,* and *Blue Kentucky Girl*, but it also features her early duets with Gram Parsons and selections from the *Trio* album she recorded with Dolly Parton and Linda Ronstadt. *Portraits* doesn't dwell too long on unreleased material—there are only five unearthed tracks on the entire set—preferring to sketch out a full overview of her career. While there might be a few favorite tracks missing, the box nevertheless fulfills its goals quite nicely—anyone looking for a comprehensive compilation of Emmylou's career will not be disappointed. *—Thom Owens*

Spyboy / Aug. 11, 1998 / Eminent ♦♦♦♦
This live project, which includes the talents of the always great Buddy Miller, is an interesting reflection of an American icon. Eclectic, it is reflective of Emmylou Harris' excursions into areas of music beyond the country and rock spheres she has already conquered. But it is the country arena that best showcases her ever-flowering ability with a song. "I Ain't Living Long Like This" and "Love Hurts" stand out boldly. "Tulsa Queen," a co-write with Rodney Crowell, is an amazing display of her vocal prowess, as is the a cappella "Calling My Children Home." "Boulder to Birmingham" is equally effective in its power and intensity, while Jesse Winchester's "My Songbird" seems to be custom-made for Harris. She delivers in triplicate on the traditional "Green Pastures." Still, even after all these years, there is a transcendent emotional depth and connection when Harris performs "Wheels," a song written by Chris Hillman and Harris' early mentor, Gram Parsons. Her relationship with Parsons is well documented, but it is best evidenced by her performances of the work he left behind, as this performance of "Wheels" proves. An original, she continues to conjure up interesting and diverse vocals, while giving her talented bandmembers the go-ahead to show off their skills as well. This live project is awe-inspiring, much like Emmylou Harris herself. *—Jana Pendragon*

Singin' with Emmylou, Vol. 1 / 2000 / Reprise ♦♦♦
Singin' With Emmylou, Vol. 1 collects Emmylou Harris' collaborations with friends like Glen Campbell, Rosanne Cash, and George Jones. Harris joins Willie Nelson on "Angel Eyes," Vince Gill on "Oh Carolina," Dan Fogelberg on "Only the Heart May Know," and Waylon Jennings on "Spanish Johnny." A worthwhile compilation of supporting performances from one of country's most gifted female vocalists. *—Heather Phares*

Red Dirt Girl / Sep. 12, 2000 / Elektra ♦♦♦♦
On her 29th album, Emmylou Harris continues the evolution from innocent folkie to present day renaissance woman. Alternately sparse and lush, *Red Dirt Girl* can be seen as a companion piece to 1995's *Wrecking Ball* with the production credits going to Malcom Burn (who previously worked with Harris engineering and mixing *Wrecking Ball*). Here, drum loops and middle eastern melodies nestle in comfortably next to warm guitar work and Harris' gently wavering voice. Her extensive guest work on dozens and dozens of recent releases (showing up on albums by everyone from Guy Clark to Midnight Oil) pays off with great help from Bruce Springsteen, Patti Scialfa, Buddy and Julie Miller, Guy Clark, Kate McGarrigle, and even alternative rock upstarts Dave Matthews and Luscious Jackson's Jill Cunniff. The diverse production only adds to Harris' earthy songwriting, adding interest to what could otherwise be lulls during the more subdued songs, and really showcases the understated lyrics that the singer has slowly become recognized for. The teary dirge "Bang the Drum Slowly" written for her father (who died in 1993) wrings with emotion and ethereal atmosphere, while "J'ai Fait Tout" (co-written with Cunniff) is an upbeat and jangly pop song, complete with hip-shakin' tambourine. While this is a big departure from her rootsy '70s releases like *Blue Kentucky Girl* and *Roses in the Snow,* it still burns with an honest intensity and clear voice that Harris is known for 20 years later. *—Zac Johnson*

● **Anthology: The Warner/Reprise Years** / May 1, 2001 / Rhino ♦♦♦♦♦
Rhino's double-disc *Anthology* concentrates on Emmylou Harris' Reprise recordings, which is a blessing. Once she left Reprise, she started to delve into "experimental," "atmospheric" recordings a bit too heavily, certainly more than her prior recordings would justify, and it almost obscured her purest talents—that of a singer that carried on the tradition of, say, Patsy Cline, becoming the greatest country singer of her generation. Since her generation was the rock generation, her path crossed multiple times with singers that weren't strictly country, most notably at the beginning of her career, when she sung backing and harmony vocals for the incomparable Gram Parsons. This gave her exposure, and she capitalized upon it by turning in recordings that simultaneously appealed to rock and country artists, finding herself as a tremendous interpretive singer, somebody that perfectly balanced the divide between classic and contemporary. Rhino's double-disc *Anthology* perfectly captures that balance and if it has any faults, it's that it illustrates her career a little too well, finding that her classicist approach was as modern as it was reverent. So, there are moments here that seem a little too studied to be true, but that's an accurate representation of her career, illustrating how she walked the tightrope between genuine country and a scholarly interpretation of it. This will appeal to both factions, as it captures both sides of her personality equally well. That means it might not be the perfect choice to convert doubters, yet it still winds up representing Harris' career remarkably well, perhaps being the one disc for casual fans. *—Stephen Thomas Erlewine*

Singin' With Emmylou, Vol. 2 / Apr. 8, 2003 / Raven ♦♦♦♦
The second volume of *Singin' With Emmylou*, a collection of duets and backing vocal appearances by Emmylou Harris, is no barrel scraper. If anything it is even more eclectic than the first. If *Vol. 1* offered names and historical country music and pop figures, *Vol. 2* offers the other side of Harris' contributions—some to lesser-known artists, some to artists well outside of the country music confines, and some appearances with grand legends. The set opens with a duet of Harris with Johnny Cash. The song "As Long as I Live" is a Roy Acuff classic. Coming from Cash's 1988 collaborative album "Water From the Well," it is easily the strongest track on it. Along the way there are some soundtrack appearances such as her duet with Patty Griffin on Beth Nielsen Chapman's "Way Beyond the Blue," from the film *Where the Heart Is*. It is one of Harris' most stirring performances in the last 20 years having a foil that is every bit her vocal equal. There are some killer performances of Harris singing with Bill Monroe, the late Nicolette Larson, Lucinda Williams, Tammy Wynette, and Tanya Tucker as well. On the work of lesser known but wildly talented artists such as Barry and Holly Tashian, the Kendalls, Matraca Berg, German country legend Tom Astor, guitarist Albert Lee, Jim & Jesse, Bobbie Cryner, Mike Auldridge, the Woodys, and Billy Joe Shaver, Harris is a forcer who pushes at the margins in the heart of a song, coaxing phenomenal performances—in most cases from those she is supporting. In Lee's case, nothing could help the song; it sucks eggs and he can't sing to save his life. The duet with Mary Black on Eleanor McEvoy's "Only a Woman's Heart" from 1995 is burning in its honesty. This is a soul-on-fire collaboration despite the balladic nature of the song. Its understatement adds so much weight to the melody and tempo that these women seem to carry the weight of the world inside them. Coming as it does in the middle of the album, it's almost difficult to go on, but there are more jewels, in the mix, but only one of them shines this blue, black, and brilliant, and that's the aforementioned "Beyond the Blue," which seems to be the answer to this one. Look for more volumes in this excellent series because there's plenty more where this came from. *—Thom Jurek*

Freddie Hart

b. Dec. 21, 1933, Lochapoka, AL
Songwriter, Guitar, Vocals / Traditional Country, Country-Pop, Honky Tonk
Singer/songwriter Freddie Hart had a long, fascinating odyssey on his way to becoming a popular country hitmaker in the early '70s. Hart was born in Lochapoka, AL, in 1933, one of 15 children born to a sharecropper. When he was five years old, his grandfather fashioned him a makeshift guitar out of a cigar box and wire from a Model T. He ran away from home at age seven, and was sent to a Civilian Conservation Corps camp at 12. When Hart was 16, he enlisted in the Marines by lying about his age, and served in Iwo Jima and Okinawa; during his off hours, he performed country music in officers' clubs. After his discharge, he worked odd jobs in various locations, and wound up moving to Nashville in 1949 to be a roadie for Hank Williams. He cut a single later that year, the George Morgan-penned "Every Little Thing Rolled into One," and worked on his songwriting, with hints from Williams.

He moved to Phoenix in 1950 to work at a cotton mill, but wound up meeting Lefty Frizzell there; he offered Frizzell one of his songs, but instead was signed up as Frizzell's tourmate. He recorded for Capitol without commercial success, and left Frizzell's show in 1953 to move to Los Angeles. There he made regular appearances on *Town Hall Party*, and also earned his black belt in karate, which enabled him to become an instructor at the Los Angeles Police Academy. Hart also continued to write songs, and in 1955 Carl Smith took his co-composition "Loose Talk" to the top of the country charts. With success to his name, Hart finally landed another record deal with Columbia in 1959, and had minor hits with "The Wall" and "Chain Gang," recording in a style that was mostly honky tonk tinged with rock & roll.

He made his *Grand Ole Opry* debut in 1961, but didn't chart again until 1965, when "Hank Williams' Guitar" narrowly missed the country Top 20. He released several albums on Kapp during the late '60s, and returned to Capitol in 1970, landing a moderate hit with "The Whole World Holding Hands." By this point, Hart had refashioned himself as more of a country-pop singer with a slightly risqué (at least, for the genre and the time) take on romance. The move paid huge dividends when his 1971 single "Easy Living" came out of nowhere to top the country charts (it also crossed over to the pop Top 20). The album of the same name also hit number-one country, and Hart followed it with three more number-one singles in 1972—"Bless Your Heart," "Got the All Overs for You (All Over Me)," and "My Hang-Up Is You." "Super Kind of Woman" and "Trip to Heaven," both from 1973, also hit number one, and "If You Can't Feel It (It Ain't There)" reached the Top Five.

Hart landed three additional Top Five hits with 1974's "The Want-To's" and 1975's "My Woman's Man" and "The First Time." But suddenly, the hits dried up, and after a last album in 1977, Hart and Capitol parted ways. He recorded for a succession of smaller labels during the '80s, and charted several more singles over 1980-1982, with the Top 20 "Sure Thing" being the biggest. Released in 1987, "Best Love I Never Had" was his last commercially oriented appearance; he subsequently performed often in Branson, MO. He issued a gospel album, *I Will Never Die*, in 1996, and another one called *Sermon on the Mountain* appeared in 2002. *—Steve Huey*

Spirited Freddie Hart / 1962 / Columbia ♦♦♦
Folks who are only familiar with Hart's string of hits from the '70s may be surprised by this record. A little honky tonk, a little early-'60s rock, and a ballad or two. Overall, quite a nice record. *—Jim Worbois*

● **Freddie Hart's Greatest Hits** / 1969 / Kapp ♦♦♦♦♦

The World of Freddy Hart / 1972 / Columbia ♦♦♦
While it appears that this record was released to cash in on Hart's 1970s success, it's still a fine collection of his work on Columbia (and includes both of his hits on that label). If you only know Hart's work from the '70s, this record may be a surprise. Still, there are some fine performances here that should not be missed. *—Jim Worbois*

Super Kind of Woman / 1973 / Capitol ♦♦♦♦
Super Kind of Woman was released in the midst of Freddie Hart's commercial renaissance in the '70s, when he was cranking out hits like crazy, and the album reflects the high standards he set for himself. Most of the songs were written or co-written by Hart,

and two tracks ("Super Kind of Woman" and "Trip to Heaven") went to number one. Hart's frequent use of words like "sexy" and phrases like "you turn me on" were a mild manifestation of a fad for risqué or sexually expressive country music, but his songs were typically expressions of love—often marital love—rather than pure physical desire. Perhaps this mix of conservative messages couched in relatively hip terminology helped sell Hart's solid country music to the genre's amorphous audience of the '70s. Whatever the case, Hart showed one way that country music could be updated without losing its identity during a time when the music was moving increasingly toward the pop mainstream. *—Greg Adams*

The Best of Freddie Hart / 1975 / MCA ♦♦♦♦
MCA's *The Best of Freddie Hart* doesn't really contain that many big hits. Instead, it has a selection of Hart's relatively unknown material for Kapp Records that was recorded in the late '60s. The minor hit "Hank Williams' Guitar" is featured, as are fine songs like "The Whole World's Holding Hands," "Battle of the Sexes," "The Fool's Part" and "The Weaker Sex," but on the whole, this set is only necessary for the curious. *—Stephen Thomas Erlewine*

That Look in Her Eyes / 1976 / Capitol ♦♦
Freddie Hart released albums at a rate of two per year throughout most of the '70s, which almost certainly accounted for his increasing reliance on outside songwriters. Although the liner notes to *That Look in Her Eyes* praise Hart's songwriting ability, he wrote or co-wrote only two songs. One of the two is "Why Lovers Turn to Strangers," Hart's final Top Ten hit, which shows that his ability was intact, if under-represented on the album. The title track just missed the Top Ten, but after this album Hart's hits began to taper off in size and frequency. The album contains several love songs of the sort for which Hart was known, but also Merle Haggard's "Can I Still Come Home" and the rueful "Paper Sack Full of Memories." *That Look in Her Eyes* is a middling album from the tail end of Hart's commercial peak, notable mainly for its pair of hits. *—Greg Adams*

● **Best of Freddie Hart** / Apr. 10, 1998 / Cema Special Markets ♦♦♦♦
The Best of Freddie Hart is part of EMI-Capitol Special Markets' excellent *Ten Best Series*, a budget-line series that features an artist's ten biggest hits in their original recorded versions. This disc contains ten of Hart's biggest hits for Capitol Records—including the number one singles "Easy Loving," "My Hang Up Is You," "Bless Your Heart," "Got the All Overs for You (All Over Me)," "Super Kind of Woman" and "Trip to Heaven" albeit not in chronological order. Nevertheless, the very fact that all these hits are on one disc at such an affordable price makes *The Best of Freddie Hart* a terrific choice for budget-minded casual fans. *—Stephen Thomas Erlewine*

John Hartford

b. Dec. 30, 1937, New York, NY, **d.** Jun. 4, 2001, Nashville, TN
Banjo, Fiddle, Guitar, Songwriter, Vocals / Neo-Traditional Folk, Progressive Country, Country-Rock, Old-Timey, Traditional Country
John Hartford remains best known for the country-pop standard "Gentle on My Mind," a major hit for Glen Campbell and subsequently covered by vocalists ranging from Frank Sinatra to Aretha Franklin. The song remains among the most often recorded in the history of popular music, its copyright netting Hartford well over a hundred thousand dollars annually for many years. But there was more to Hartford than that curious mix of highly literary folk music and MOR romantic nostalgia, told from the perspective of a homeless man remembering days of perfect love. Hartford was a multi-talented old-time musician, a riverboat captain, a satirical songwriter, a one-man showman of exceptional talents, and one of the founders of both progressive country music and old-time string music revivalism.

John Harford (the added "t" was the brainchild of Chet Atkins) was born in New York City to a medical resident and his painter wife but grew up in St. Louis near the Mississippi River he would always love. His first job, on a riverboat, came at age ten. As a boy he liked the traditional country music he heard on the *Grand Ole Opry* radio broadcast from Nashville, and by age 13 he was an accomplished fiddler and five-string banjo player whose main influences were Stringbean and Earl Scruggs. Soon he added guitar and mandolin to his repertoire. He founded his first bluegrass band in high-school and dropped out of Washington University after a year to pursue his music. Performing and working as a DJ and sometimes as a commercial graphic artist in Missouri and Illinois, Hartford made a few singles for small local labels in the early '60s. In 1965 he moved with his wife and son Jamie to Nashville, taking a DJ job at radio station WSIX. It didn't take him long to meet the other architects of the city's songwriting renaissance—Kris Kristofferson, Mickey Newbury, and the Glaser Brothers, who owned a state-of-the-art recording studio and began promoting Hartford and his songs around Music Row.

Signed to RCA in 1966, Hartford went into the studio to record his debut album, *John Hartford Looks at Life*, which was produced by Atkins. "He is himself and will not be told how to write or sing, because he has only his own world," wrote Johnny Cash in the liner notes. Hartford's second album, *Earthwords & Music*, featured "Gentle on My Mind" (a modest hit) along with songs that pointed forward to his independent-minded career as a solo performer: "The Good Old Electric Washing Machine Circa 1943" featured a charming mouth-music imitation of that appliance. In 1968 Hartford moved to Los Angeles, appearing regularly on CBS's *Smothers Brothers Comedy Hour* and later on *the Glen Campbell Goodtime Hour*. He also played on the Byrds' 1968 album *Sweetheart of the Rodeo* and Doug Dillard's *The Banjo Album*. By the end of the decade, Hartford also earned his riverboat pilot's license. Financially secure thanks to "Gentle on My Mind," he decided to spend the rest of his life pursuing an artistic vision rooted in country music traditions.

In 1971, Hartford returned to Nashville and founded a bluegrass band featuring guitarist Norman Blake, dobro player Tut Taylor, and master fiddler Vassar Clements. The all-acoustic *Aereo-Plain* album recorded for Warner Bros. that year (and its successor *Morning Bugle*) featured a free bluegrass feel often cited as seminal both by progressive bluegrass musicians and by adherents of the modern jam band movement. Hartford made guest appearances on albums by James Taylor, Seals & Crofts, and Hoyt Axton, and he cut the bluegrass *Tennessee Jubilee* album in 1975 with the assistance of Benny Martin and Lester Flatt.

In the mid-'70s Hartford worked out a solo act in which he appeared in a trademark bowler hat and black vest. He began to record unaccompanied, releasing the unclassifiable *Mark Twang* in 1976 and winning a Grammy award for Best Ethnic or Traditional Recording. That album was the first of a series of mostly solo albums Hartford recorded for the Chicago-based Flying Fish label, featuring a mix of traditional material with Hartford's own trenchant originals. Though Hartford had diverged sharply from the sphere of commercial country music, he continued to live in Nashville and to appear as a session man on such albums as the Dillards' *Permanent Wave* and Shel Silverstein's *The Great Conch Train Robbery*. He also became involved with Opryland, where he helped launch an old-fashioned steamboat ride.

By the late '80s Hartford was battling non-Hodgkin's lymphoma, but he continued to record and perform until he lost the use of his hands shortly before his death in 2001. He performed and recorded with his son Jamie, re-recorded and reissued his earlier work on his own Small Dog Barking label, and kept busy with a host of side projects such as narration for the Ken Burns public-television series *the Civil War*. His later albums, several of them recorded for Rounder, were highly individualistic gems: 1998's *Speed of the Old Long Bow* was a tribute to a little-known fiddler named Ed Haley on which Hartford not only performed Haley's music but also added lyrics that traced his life and career. As word of Hartford's illness spread, his well-wishers included a long parade of musicians he had worked with and influenced profoundly. *—James Manheim*

Earthwords & Music / 1967 / RCA ♦♦♦
Aside from the obvious bonus of containing Hartford's own version of his classic "Gentle on My Mind," this record also contains other gems such as "Washing Machine" on which he imitates the difference in the sounds made by both the old and new machines (using only his voice) and his "rap" about the many uses of baking soda. Also contains some fine straight songs. Good stuff. *—Jim Worbois*

Gentle on My Mind & Other Originals / 1967 / RCA ♦♦♦♦♦
Poetic. Blissful. Wonderfully arranged. Lavishly recorded. This collection of original melodies written and recorded by widely recognized singer/songwriter John Hartford is vivid and beautiful. Each tune throws in hints of creative brilliance and sincerely artistic poetic expression, much to the likings of Bob Dylan and Willie Nelson. Charming songs such as "A Simple Thing as Love" and his radio-friendly single, "Gentle on My Mind," stir the kettle of emotion, where more serious subjects are covered in the deep retrospect song "California Earthquake" and the chilling "Mouth to Mouth Resuscitation." "Mouth to Mouth" is an upbeat, vibrant tune stressing the need for a nation's rebirth, as Hartford chants, "good for the country, good for the nation." Surely it finds itself as song born for a good old time mingling among friends. The album's most deeply gripping tune is the lyrically poetic gem "I Would Not Be There," a passionate six-verse tune detailing the characteristic lives of a man visiting a Baker-street bookstore to check out a book of steamboats and cotton, he who is inspired by a fifth grade replacement schoolmistress, a man at the barracks, and Sam, hung over from drinking. The record's overall lyrical content is mystic and sharp in quality and respectfully strong in arrangement. Perfect for a morning cup of coffee and a kind of pick-me-up for a cloudy day. You can tag along with John Hartford, who never fails the listener of seeking and finding an enjoyable time. Like a day at the annual state fair, *Gentle on My Mind* is folk-rock music at its best during the '60s. Music that can bring together friends in times of laughter and nights of tears, this record can warm the soul, never leaving its power of nostalgia. Though the arrangements are strong, Hartford's lyrical content is not quite as cohesive and powerful as many of Dylan's or Nelson's records. Still, to give merit were it's due, his material ranks somewhat close to that pedestal of more widely loved singer/songwriters of the time. *—Shawn M. Haney*

Housing Project / 1968 / RCA ♦♦♦

The Love Album / 1968 / RCA ♦♦♦
This has too many instances where good songs get buried behind unnecessary strings and things. There is some good material here so the record shouldn't be over looked... just what was added to the tracks. *—Jim Worbois*

John Hartford / 1969 / MCA ♦♦♦♦
RCA probably thought they were just signing the guy who wrote "Gentle on My Mind" when they signed John Hartford back in 1966, but his own albums just kept getting stranger and stranger during the late '60s, culminating in this bizarre piece of orchestrated country-tinged art rock from 1969, which sounds kind of like Nashville's take on Van Dyke Parks' *Song Cycle*. Opening with the descriptively titled "Dusty Miller Hornpipe and Fugue in A Major for Strings, Brass and 5-String Banjo," the album eases into a cockeyed blend of middle-of-the-road orchestrations and Hartford's quirky sense of humor. There are a few almost normal-sounding tunes, but even the most commercial song has the unwieldy title "I've Heard That Tearstained Monologue You Do There By the Door Before You Go" and rueful lyrics to match. After that interlude, the album touches on creepy character studies like "The Collector" and "Mr. Jackson's Got Nothing to Do," interlarded with short instrumental pieces that are as odd and artsy as anything Parks was doing at the same time, including an ironic deconstruction of "Gentle on My Mind" under the title "A Short Sentimental Interlude." The combination of Hartford's remarkable voice, his eccentric but accessible sense of whimsy, and Al Capps' utterly straight strings and brass arrangements is quite fascinating. Fans of the comparatively twee and normal Neon Philharmonic should check out this similar (but much better) album, as should anyone who adores Glen Campbell's Jim Webb collaborations. *—Stewart Mason*

Iron Mountain Depot / 1970 / RCA ✦✦✦
Someone at RCA must have decided Hartford would benefit from more production so strings and background singers have been added this time out. The songs are still good but the added production values keep this from being the record it could have been. *—Jim Worbois*

Aereo-Plain / 1971 / Rounder ✦✦✦✦✦
Shortly after being released in 1971, *Aereo-Plain* achieved cult status. Hartford enlisted such Nashville notables as guitarist Norman Blake, dobro player Tut Taylor, violinist Vassar Clements, and bassist Randy Scruggs to help out in the studio. The cult following of *Aereo-Plain* though, has less to do with the music than with Hartford's quirky songs and even quirkier approach. "Boogie" is a mind-boggling song that includes grunts, foot stomping, and panting. Hartford seems to have no problem progressing from the old-time religion of "Turn Your Radio On" to the irreverence of "Back in the Goodle Days." This later song conjures up images of a future meeting between old friends at the city dump ("Oh you'll pass a joint/and I'll pass the wine") to relive their glory days. Hardly Bruce Springsteen. One of the attractions to this material is that Hartford seems to be in his element, just doing what comes natural to him. He also has quite a sentimental streak that never spills over to the sappy. "First Girl I Loved" is an unabashedly gentle song about trying to find your first love in every subsequent love. Romantic fiddle and mandolin greatly add to the melancholy mood. "Tear Down the Grand Ole Opry" is another love song, memorializing the Ryman Auditorium that would be abandoned in 1974. While Hartford would go on to make other great albums, *Aereo-Plain* signaled the full blooming of his eccentric talent. This is an essential album for any fan, revealing both his genius and the glory days of early '70s progressive bluegrass. [Rounder released a terrific album of outtakes from these sessions entitled *Steam Powered Aereo-Takes* in 2002.] *—Ronnie Lankford Jr.*

Morning Bugle / 1972 / Rounder ✦✦✦✦✦
One of Hartford's finest records. Done mostly live in the studio with virtually no overdubs, this is a fine collection of song covering a variety of subjects. Two of the most poignant are "Howard Hughes Blues" and "Nobody Eats at Linebaugh's," which addresses country music's abandonment of the Ryman and downtown Nashville in favor of "the park." *—Jim Worbois*

Down on the River / 1972 / Flying Fish ✦✦✦
John Hartford's *Down on the River* is an old-timey tribute to the Mississippi River and its steamboats, casinos and saloons, filled with campy salutes to a forgotten lifestyles, as well as surprisingly affectionate paens to a lost era. Hartford's approach may be too kitschy for some—after all, there are several songs driven by calliope—yet its a thoroughly entertaining album for listeners that share his obsessions, or at least his fondness for fine, old-timey banjo. *—Thom Owens*

Nobody Knows What You Do / 1976 / Flying Fish ✦✦
John Hartford was once something of a renegade within traditional music circles. This fact may be less obvious today because there is so little to offend on *Good Old Boys* and *Live From Mountain Stage*. But way back in the '70s, traditional musicians just didn't sing about drugs ("Granny Wontcha Smoke Some Marijuana") or women's breasts ("The Golden Globe Award"). Most still don't. The highly eccentric *Nobody Knows What You Do* was recorded around the same time as the equally unusual and better-known *Mark Twain*. Like *Mark Twain*, Hartford's approach on *Nobody Knows What You Do* is just about as far out as Hartford ever ventured. A couple of songs work beautifully. "In Tall Buildings" and "Joseph's Dream" are shot through with romanticism and a touch of the sentimental, making them the most intriguing pieces on this album. "The False Hearted Tenor Waltz" finds Hartford adding contorted vocals to an otherwise lovely melody, while "Somewhere My Love—We'll Meet Again Sweet Heart" offers a hillbilly version of the *Doctor Zhivago* theme. Really. The album's arrangements, however, veer closer to the country-rock of the New Riders of the Purple Sage than the one-man show of *Mark Twain*. The three instrumentals, including "John McLaughlin," a tribute to the jazz guitarist, sound a little like outtakes of Bob Dylan's "Nashville Skyline Rag." *Nobody Knows What You Do* shouldn't be the first choice for a new Hartford devotee. It may not even appeal to fans of his more recent work. But for those who can't get enough of those heady days of the early- to mid-'70s when an artist could still go into the studio and make an album like this, *Nobody Knows What You Do* will speak to the inner hippie-hillbilly. *—Ronnie D. Lankford Jr.*

Mark Twang / 1976 / Flying Fish ✦✦✦✦✦
From the early to mid-'70s, John Hartford let his eccentric genius run wild, creating the cult favorite *Aereo-Plain* and the lovely, straightforward *Morning Bugle*. *Mark Twang*, released in 1976, proved to be the pinnacle of Hartford's artistic run. Unlike the previous albums though, it was stripped down to only Hartford recording live in the studio. The album's themes circle around the Mississippi river, steamboats, and river men. The songs, as usual, run from sentimental to strange, from the romantic to the weird. "Let Him Go on Mama" is a tribute to a river man with the wonderful refrain, "you say he's old fashioned/well that ain't no big deal." "Skippin' in the Mississippi Dew" pays joyful foot stomping, fiddle sawing homage to the mighty river with a barrage of old-fashioned imagery. Hartford's unconventional side rears its head on "Don't Leave Your Records in the Sun," a song complete with imitations of skips and other odd noises a record might make after becoming warped. "Tryin' to Do Something to Get Your Attention" is a fun, if downright peculiar song, that will, for better or worse, get the listener's attention. Perhaps the most bizarre contribution, though, is "Tater Tate and Allen Mundy," a homage in which Hartford attempts to string together every important name that ever graced a bluegrass stage. This song, and album, may seem at odds with the artist's image as a progressive bluegrass musician, but he never drew lines between the old and new—he just followed his muse. *Mark Twang* may not be the first stopping place for the new Hartford fan, but for those already familiar with his unique talent, it's a must have. *—Ronnie Lankford Jr.*

Tennessee Jubilee / 1976 / Flying Fish ✦✦✦

Headin' Down Into the Mystery Below / 1978 / Flying Fish ✦✦✦✦✦
Besides being a million-selling songwriter and one of the most delightfully idiosyncratic performers in traditional-style folk music, John Hartford is also a licensed steamboat captain with a love for the Mississippi River that rivals Mark Twain's. *Headin' Down Into the Mystery Below* from 1978 is Hartford's purest expression of his love for steamboats and river rides, with 11 original songs on the subject. Hartford's songs are so pure that it sounds like he made them up at the wheel of the boat, which may well be true; in the case of the hilarious "See the Julia Belle Swain," he actually sings the travel brochure for the boat on which he apprenticed for his license, occasionally answered by the five-person chorus who are the only other musicians on the album. Accompanying himself on banjo, guitar, and violin, as well as providing rhythm by dancing on a close-miked sheet of three-quarter-inch plywood, Hartford sings in his friendly tenor tales of boats and trips in such homely, vivid images that it's easy for listeners to imagine themselves on the top decks of the Mississippi Queen even if the closest they've ever come to a steamboat is the old Reprise Records logo. The tunes range from playful ditties like "Mama Plays the Calliope" (which Hartford pronounces "CALLY-ope," to rhyme with "Brother throws the rope"), the bucolic tale of a family-run steamboat, to the title track, the haunting tale of a wreck that's followed by the poignant "Beatty's Navy," a simple field recording of the whistle of a steamboat that's salvaging another from the bottom of the Tennessee River. John Hartford has arguably made better records than *Headin' Down Into the Mystery Below*, but none have been so personal and loving. *—Stewart Mason*

Me Oh My, How the Time Does Fly: A John Hartford Anthology / 1982 / Flying Fish ✦✦✦✦✦
While a number of fine albums—*Aereo-Plain*, *Morning Bugle*, and *Mark Twang*—would serve as a good introduction to John Hartford, *Me Oh My, How the Time Does Fly* offers the best overall collection. The reason? It has the most music, 65 minutes, and offers samples from most of Hartford's albums between 1976 and 1984. "Skippin' in the Mississippi Dew," "The Julia Belle Swain," and "Let Him Go on, Mama" represent *Mark Twang*, an album some consider Hartford's finest, while "Good Old Electric Washing Machine" and "I Would Not Be Here" are drawn from *Catalogue*, an album that revisits his out-of-print RCA recordings. There are also a number of pieces from *All in the Name of Love* and *Slumberin' on the Cumberland*. Three of the most intriguing tracks, "Natchez Whistle," "Miss Ferris," and "On Christmas Eve," come from the also unavailable *Headin' Down Into the Mystery Below*. With no more than a banjo and a few background singers, Hartford spins out the delightful "Miss Ferris" for seven minutes. The downside of this collection is that only two songs show up from Hartford's earlier Rounder albums, and one of them is an inferior, re-recorded version of "Boogie." The other is a fine, though somewhat mellow, version of "Nobody Eats at Linebaugh's Anymore" with the New Grass Revival serving as backup band. One also fears that the song choices, as excellent as they are, purposely downplay Hartford's more eccentric attributes. He had taken a step back toward traditionalism on *Gum Tree Canoe*, which had been released a few years before this collection. Nonetheless, *Me Oh My, How the Time Does Fly* will do a fine job introducing the unfamiliar to Mr. John Hartford. Indeed, even the avid fan will probably want to add this excellent group of tunes to their Hartford collection. *—Ronnie D. Lankford Jr.*

Catalogue / 1985 / Flying Fish ✦✦✦

Gum Tree Canoe / 1987 / Flying Fish ✦✦✦✦✦
Hartford's most even Flying Fish album, with equal measures of songwriting whimsy and expert musicianship, *Gum Tree Canoe* includes a number of tunes that would remain concert staples for the length of his career. From the relaxed stroll of the album's title track to a rendition of Doc Watson's "Your Long Journey" to an original breakneck bluegrass instrumental, "Jug Harris," there's not a clinker to be heard. Hartford's banjo playing is exceptional, as is the accompaniment provided by a host of fine country, bluegrass, and newgrass pickers, Roy Huskey Jr., Sam Bush, and Jerry Douglas among them. Riverboat tales, an R&B staple, and the Rolling Stones couldn't sound more at home together than they do on this fine album from one of roots music's genuine originals. [Flying Fish's remastered CD, issued in 2001, includes two previously unreleased tunes and a short written tribute by Hartford String Band banjo player Bob Carlin.] *—Brian Beatty*

Hartford & Hartford / 1991 / Flying Fish ✦✦✦
Hartford's son Jamie is a fine mandolin player, and he joins his father for this album. *—Charles S. Wolfe*

Cadillac Rag / 1991 / Small Dog A-Barkin' ✦✦✦
As a musician, John Hartford vacillates between writing modern folksinger/songwriter and being an academic revivalist, researching and recording traditional country and folk songs in their original arrangements. *Cadillac Rag* is one of his academic albums—a selection of ten traditional tunes, played simply and directly by Hartford (banjo), fiddler Ted Masden, Buddy Spicher, and John Yudkin. Occasionally the sleek professional production and studied performances make these traditional songs sound lifeless, which prevents *Cadillac Rag* from being a truly engaging listen. However, it is an interesting one, particularly if you're interested in studying traditional country from an academic standpoint. *—Thom Owens*

The Walls We Bounce Off Of / 1994 / Small Dog ✦✦✦✦
This batch of casual solo performances highlights Hartford's humorous sensibilities on tunes that sound made-up on the spot, including "The All Collision All Explosion Song" and "Hooter Thunkit," though they would sometimes appear in his concert set lists. Over the course of 13 numbers, he sings and plays banjo, fiddle, guitar, and his shoes. He also

reads a piece of skeptical fan mail and answers a ringing telephone that interrupts some banjo tuning before the start of a song. Whatever this relaxed album lacks in comparison to the studio polish of his early RCA recordings or the reverence for older traditions that characterized his Rounder releases, there's no refuting that Hartford's love of music and joy for life permeate these seriously silly songs. *—Brian Beatty*

Live at College Station Pennsylvania / Apr. 25, 1995 / Rounder ♦♦♦

It's John Hartford's casual charm—not his substantial instrumental, vocal, and writing talents, which he makes sound tossed-off, too—that puts this album's 17 solo performances over, even when his impromptu clogging throws off his playing. Expected favorites like "Gum Tree Canoe" and "Gentle on My Mind" sound as fresh as pleasant surprises like "I Would Not Be Here" and "The Girl I Left Behind Me." His banjo rendition of the R&B staple "Piece of My Heart" inspires many in the audience to clap and singalong. Whether plucking his banjo, sawing away on his fiddle, or strumming his guitar, Hartford sounds happily at home throughout this entertaining set. All that's missing is a tall tale or three and a good view of his beloved Big Muddy. *—Brian Beatty*

Wild Hog in the Red Brush / 1996 / Rounder ♦♦♦♦

John Hartford would just grin crookedly at you if you brought up the subject of virtuosity in his presence. Half the charm of his music is his loopy sense of humor—he often counts a tune in by grunting rhythmically or by singing the title, and his fiddling is always just a hair away from wobbling off the side of the road. But his knowledge of the traditional repertoire is encyclopedic, and he can fiddle in more idioms than most can recognize. On this outing he's joined by banjoist Bob Carlin, guitarist Ronnie McCoury, mandolinist Mike Compton, and bassist Jerry McCoury for a sprawling tour of obscure tunes, a number of which Hartford learned from old recordings by Ohio fiddler Ed Haley. Each track is annotated and pedigreed (sample: "French and Solly Carpenter who were friends of Ed Haley's played this according to Wilson Douglas"). The whole thing's a hoot and a joy, and is recommended strongly. *—Rick Anderson*

The Bullies Have All Gone to Rest / 1998 / Whippoorwill ♦♦♦

This album of fiddle and banjo duets was recorded over two days in the spring of 1997, as John Hartford battled life-threatening cancer. The album's selection of traditional tunes from fiddler Jim Wood's native middle Tennessee gives both players plenty of room to show off their instrumental skills. This modest album is one of several tributes to older musical traditions that Hartford recorded late in his career. Solid if not the best, it remains worth searching out for the opportunity to hear the legend playing his banjo again. *—Brian Beatty*

Speed of the Old Long Bow: A Tribute to Ed Haley / May 5, 1998 / Rounder ♦♦♦♦

Good Old Boys / Sep. 14, 1999 / Rounder ♦♦♦

Good Old Boys is something of a return to form for John Hartford. As with *Retrograss*, an album he recorded with David Grisman and Mike Seeger, Hartford eschews fiddle tunes to concentrate on a number of good songs. The album kicks off with the melancholy title track, which exalts the virtues of reliable old friends, before delving into tributes to a number of Hartford's bluegrass heroes. "On the Radio" recalls the first time he heard Earl Scruggs' banjo coming in loud and clear, and it's one of the catchiest tunes on the album. The life of Bill Monroe is remembered in "The Cross-Eyed Child," a ten-minute pastiche that combines music and monolog. All of these songs are pleasant, if a bit mellow. The only difficulty rests in their length. Four of the first five songs last over five minutes, while "The Cross-Eyed Child" extends for over ten. This latter piece also becomes tiresome, as Hartford mutters on and on with the musicians plucking away behind him. The second half of the album works better. There's a nifty piece titled "Billy the Kid" and an old song, "Keep on Truckin'," that dates back almost 30 years. *Good Old Boys* doesn't stack up to Hartford's classic '70s albums, but it's a fun album that will please longtime fans. *—Ronnie D. Lankford Jr.*

Live From Mountain Stage / Mar. 7, 2000 / Blue Plate ♦♦♦♦

John Hartford traveled a long road from hippie counterculture figure in the early '70s to standard bearer of tradition in the '90s. Recorded between '94 and '96, *Live From Mountain Stage* represents the finishing touches of his transition into a guardian of traditional music. Indeed, this is only the second *Mountain Stage* release that concentrates on one artist (the first featured Bill Monroe). With fairly simple arrangements, Hartford offers affecting versions of trademark songs like "I Wish We Had Our Time Again" and "Lorena" to an appreciative audience. There are spry renditions of "Bring Your Clothes Back Home and Try Me One More Time" and "Gum Tree Canoe," and a upbeat take on "Gentle on My Mind." It may surprise casual fans, only familiar with the last song, how many good songs Hartford wrote. While he had a penchant for odd points of view, he also had a touching, melancholy streak that gave warmth to his songs. he's in good voice and seems to flourish in a live setting. Sure, it might have been nice to have Hartford lay down a good old rude classic like "Boogie" or "Holding," but his *Aereo-Plain* days were long behind him. Instead, the listener is left with a handful of lovely gems, chosen across the span of his career, that attest to his ability to craft great songs. *Live From Mountain Stage*, then, succeeds on several levels. It's a good live show and a retrospective, suitable for longtime fans and those with a budding interest in the master. *—Ronnie D. Lankford Jr.*

Hamilton Ironworks / Sep. 11, 2001 / Rounder ♦♦♦

Hamilton Ironworks, the last studio recording made by fiddler John Hartford before his untimely death in 2001, is a collection of old-time fiddle pieces in the tradition of Gene Goforth, Ed Haley, and many others. Hartford interprets nearly two dozen traditional melodies. There are few concessions given to modernity, and, while bringing his own distinct voice to the tunes, Hartford is clearly aware of the historical stream he occupies, coming off as both a devoted scholar and respectful practitioner. Where the liner notes feature rough recollections of where Hartford learned each tune and how the melodies might have evolved, the most convincing element is his storytelling on the disc itself. During most of the numbers, his warm and slightly gruff voice comes chortling out of the speakers, perpetually sounding as if it is going to deliver some dry punchline to a joke. The stories told are almost sung, capturing brief moments of spontaneous melodic memory, much like his solos on songs like "Wooliver's Money Musk," "Quail Is a Pretty Bird," "Green Corn," "Comin' Down From Denver on a Trip to Galway Here and There," "Devil's Hornpipe," and many others. Miraculously, Hartford's storytelling is never hokey or overtly self-conscious. Where the half-spoken interludes might seem an interruption on another artist's record, they seem perfectly in place here—like a natural part of the song if one didn't know any better or listen any closer. As usual, he is backed by the Hartford Stringband, including Bob Carlin, Mike Compton, Larry Perkins, and Chris Sharp. *—Jesse Jarnow*

● **RCA Country Legends** / Sep. 25, 2001 / Buddha ♦♦♦♦♦

The clean-cut John Hartford, who dons the cover of *RCA Country Legends*, offers quite a contrast to the scruffy photo of the singer on *Aereo-Plain* just a few years later. One might be lulled into believing that this young man attended Republican rallies and offered no threat to the establishment. But the selections, chosen from several RCA albums recorded between 1966 and 1968, belie the image. While far from the counterculture figure of his *Aereo-Plain* days, songs like "Untangle Your Mind" and "The Girl With the Long Brown Hair" show him on his way. Hartford's idiosyncratic humor shows up on "Big Blue Balloon" and "Whose That," while his ability to write catchy melodies surfaces on "Corn Cob Blues" and, of course, "Gentle on My Mind." Certain traits, like Hartford's low-guttural delivery of lyrics, make cameos here, but clearly RCA and producer Chet Atkins kept certain eccentricities in check. There are also odd touches, like the trumpets on "I'm Still Here," but overall the production and arrangements are better than one might expect from a major studio with an oddity like Hartford. *RCA Country Legends* provides a good snapshot of this long-out-of-print material. Thankfully, Rich Kienzle and Dave Samuelson's liner notes remind everyone of Hartford's central role in the birth of newgrass. Sure, he eventually became part of the establishment, but in the late '60s and early '70s he threatened it. *RCA Country Legends* offers an excellent portrait of Hartford's early work and will be eagerly snatched up by fans. *—Ronnie D. Lankford Jr.*

The Love Album/Housing Project / 2002 / Camden Deluxe ♦♦♦♦

John Hartford's death in 2001 has brought a number of issues and reissues, but none have been more important than Camdem Deluxe's release of his six early RCA albums along with the never-before-released *Radio John*. These albums offer a sidelong view of Hartford in the mid- to late '60s, prior to his *Aereo-Plain* days. *The Love Album/Housing Project* captures Hartford on his third and forth release, both recorded in 1968. *The Love Album* finds him using slightly bigger arrangements, gaining confidence, and more or less coming into his own. "The Six O'Clock Train and a Girl With Green Eyes" bounces along like the happy '60s pop song it is, while the smart and catchy "Why Do You Do Me Like You Do?" manages to be funny without being overly obvious. "I Would Not Be Here" is the type of song Dylan might've written if he'd come from Nashville and didn't take himself quite so seriously, while "Landscape Grown Cold" and "This Eve of Parting" find Hartford feigning country sincerity. *Housing Project* may be Hartford's best RCA album. Great pieces like "I'm Still Here," "The Girl With the Long Brown Hair," and "Big Blue Balloon" fit snuggly between bizarre word-speak poems like "Housing Project" and psychedelic fluff like "Crystallia Daydream." The arrangements are more innovative than his earlier RCA material, but don't go overboard, as would his follow-up, *John Hartford*. The production, nonetheless, will seem a bit much to those accustomed to his more traditional recordings. Nonetheless, *The Love Album/Housing Project* find Hartford taking his place beside Kris Kristofferson and other Nashville songwriters and easily holding his own. *—Ronnie D. Lankford Jr.*

John Hartford/Iron Mountain Depot/Radio John / 2002 / Camden Deluxe ♦♦♦

Both *John Hartford* and *Iron Mountain Depot*, the fifth and sixth RCA albums, will probably surprise fans weaned on his more traditionally minded work from the '80s and '90s. While Hartford remains a fine songwriter here, the overblown production gives the impression that he's cutting a joint effort with Herb Alpert & the Tijuana Brass. Strings and horns smooth out the rustic banjo on pieces with bizarre names like "Dusty Miller Hornpipe and Fugue in A Major for Strings, Brass and 5-String Banjo." "Mr. Jackson's Got Nothing to Do" is vaguely reminiscent of a mid-'60s Dylan putdown song, while "The Poor Old Prurient Interest Blues" offers a bit of wacky nonsense about nudity. Perhaps Hartford was growing bored with the music business, but he still managed to churn out nice pieces like "The Wart" and "Like Unto a Mockingbird." Oh yeah—and make sure to stick around for an instrumental version of "Hey Jude" at the end of *Iron Mountain Depot*. *Radio John* is an entirely different story. Hartford decided to get back to the basics, or at least closer to them, and cut an album with no overdubs. The arrangements—mostly guitar, bass, guitar, and percussion—work pretty well, though the drums seem too loud. *Radio John* provides the missing link in Hartford's career, complete with early versions of "In Tall Buildings" and "Skippin' in the Mississippi Dew." There's also folk-rap ("Self Made Man"), rock & roll-tinged vocals ("Bed on My Mind"), and straight-up bluegrass ("Orange Blossom Special"). *Radio John* alone makes this CD set worth having. *—Ronnie D. Lankford Jr.*

Looks at Life/Earthwords and Music / 2002 / Camden Deluxe ♦♦♦

John Hartford's eccentric outlook and unabashed romanticism are already full-blown on *Looks at Life* and *Earthwords and Music*, both released in 1967. Both "I Shoulda Wore My Birthday Suit" and "(Good Old Electric) Washing Machine (Circa. 1943)" come straight out of left field, while "The Tall Tall Grass" and "Daytime of Life" capture the wistfulness of a summer Sunday. A couple of pieces, "Front Porch" and "Love Song in 2/4 Time," even manage the difficult feat of being both melancholy and comical at the same time. Hartford also shows a penchant for experimenting on pieces like "I Reckon" and "Earthwords": both sound like beat poetry strained through a Nashville sensibility. Counterculture morality dates "Untangle Your Mind" and "When the Sky Began to Fall," but the songs are nonetheless fun. These albums also hold a couple of early classics. "Corn Cob Blues" and "Gentle on My Mind" offer hints at what Hartford would sound like in his prime. While the arrangements are fairly simple on both albums, keeping Hartford's vocals and banjo front and center, fans of his later, more traditional material will probably find them overproduced. Overall, though, both albums provide a fine introduction to Hartford's early work and will be much appreciated by hardcore fans. *—Ronnie D. Lankford Jr.*

Steam Powered Aereo-Takes / Jan. 22, 2002 / Rounder ♦♦♦

With its feet in the most traditional of American folk music and its head peeking through a cloud of psychedelic hippie smoke, John Hartford's 1971 LP, *Aereo-Plain*, was groundbreaking in its ability to sound earnestly faithful to the music it was rooted in, while still twisting words and poking fun in a way that was definitely hip for the time. The informal jam session feel of the recordings created some 80-odd reels of tape that couldn't all fit onto the LP, so in early 2002 Rounder Records' impeccable Select division released *Steam Powered Aereo-Takes*, featuring nearly an hour of song sketches, outtakes, demos, impromptu jams, and goofing-off suites. All the members of the assembled team—including Hartford on guitar, banjo, and vocals, Norman Blake on guitar and mandolin, Tut Taylor on dobro, mandolin, and mandola, Vassar Clements on fiddle and mandocello, and Randy Scruggs on electric bass—were at the top of their musical game in the early '70s, and the recordings show it beautifully. If the sessions that were used on *Aereo-Plain* became the *Revolver* of the progressive bluegrass movement, this disc is more like the White Album or maybe *Let It Be*. The song ideas are there, but they feel looser and more free, with each of the performers playing with ideas and song structures, fiddling with things when they don't work, and milking them when they click. *—Zac Johnson*

● **Natural to Be Gone 1967–1970** / Jul. 2, 2002 / Raven ♦♦♦♦♦

Australia's Raven Records has accomplished the impossible: they have distilled the finest moments from John Hartford's first seven RCA recordings down into 28 songs and issued them with pristine sound on a single CD. What seems impossible is that there aren't any tracks on these albums that are remotely substandard. The fact that these seven albums were done in a four-year period is astonishing. Using only two producers during that time, Felton Jarvis and Rick Jarrard Hartford built a white heat body of work that was as eclectic as it was innovative and high quality. Hartford was the Mark Twain of songwriting and not only because he was from Missouri. His sense of irony, travel, history, humor and commitment to excellence were nearly without peer. Only Mickey Newbury and Kris Kristofferson—who arrived in Music City about the same time Hartford did—were his peers. Most know Hartford as the author of Glen Campbell's smash: "Gentle on My Mind," but that song is only the beginning of the story. "Untangle Your Mind," "Windows," "Go Fall Asleep Now," "Like Unto a Mockingbird," and so many others bring an enormous perspective to the songwriting being done at the time: historical concerns, a zen detachment to the subject matter, which offers a compassionate view of every situation and profound empathy with his protagonists without artifice or sentiment, and the way to construct a line where metaphor and metonymic device become interchangeable. Hartford also used his encyclopedic musical knowledge in his songs, wrapping his lyrics in old folk songs, bluegrass, hillbilly, Celtic influences, vanguard tonal architectures, and good old country and blues hooks. What's even more amazing, that like the best work of Bob Dylan and John Stewart, Hartford's work is timeless, it shows no age either in sits innovative production techniques, nor its composition or lyrical content. This is essential for any fan of singer/songwriters, or for the history of country music as it began flirting with other forms. This is the real Americana music. *—Thom Jurek*

Dale Hawkins

b. Aug. 30, 1938, Goldmine, LA

Vocals, Guitar / Rock & Roll, Rockabilly

Louisiana guitarist Dale Hawkins' 1957 hit "Suzy Q," with its crackling bluesy guitar and insistent cowbell, was one of the most exciting early rockabilly singles. Recording for Chess (as one of its few white artists) between 1956 and 1961, Hawkins never quite duplicated its success, either commercially or artistically, but came close enough on a number of occasions to warrant respect as one of the better rockabilly singers. His drawling delivery, sense of humor, affinity for blues, and sharp guitar work (which was actually provided by such ace players as Roy Buchanan, Scotty Moore, and James Burton) are heard to good effect on his 1958 album and a number of non-hit singles. Hawkins went on to become a producer of some note in the 1960s, working with the Five Americans and Bruce Channel. *—Richie Unterberger*

Susie Q / 1958 / Checker ♦♦♦♦♦

This is a way-above-average '50s rock & roll album, including both sides of Dale's first four singles. Highlights are "Suzie Q," its killer B-side ("Don't Treat Me This Way"), and the goofy "See You Soon Baboon" and "Mrs. Merguitory's Daughter." *—Richie Unterberger*

My Babe / 1987 / Argo ♦♦♦

This features rare singles and other interesting material that Hawkins cut, mostly for Chess, between 1958 and 1962. Includes his sole Top 40 hit besides "Suzie Q" ("La-Do-Dada") and some fine rockabilly interpretations of blues hits. *—Richie Unterberger*

● **Oh Suzy Q** / Oct. 24, 1995 / Chess ♦♦♦♦♦

Here are 18 tracks from Hawkins' Chess prime, all but one from the late '50s. It includes "Susie Q" and some obscure rockabilly cuts that are nearly as good, such as "Don't Treat Me This Way," "Liza Jane," and "Ain't That Lovin' You Babe." James Burton, Roy Buchanan, and Scotty Moore are the most prominent of the excellent guitarists to be heard on these sides. One could quibble over the absence of "Mrs. Merguitory's Daughter," "Yea-Yea (Class Cutter)," and the post-Chess single "Stay at Home Lulu," but this is definitely the best Hawkins compilation ever assembled. *—Richie Unterberger*

Daredevil / May 13, 1997 / Norton ♦♦♦♦

These 12 tracks, compiled from Hawkins' own personal stash of well-worn acetates, brings together the rarest of the rare of this Louisiana rockabilly songwriter/producer. The centerpiece of this 12-track collection is the first-time appearance of the original 1956 demo version of Dale's big hit, "Susie Q." Recorded by country songwriter Merle Kilgore—then a disc jockey at KENT in Shreveport—the original demo is looser and faster than the better-known hit version, moved along with two raw guitar solos from a 16-year-old James Burton (this now becoming his debut recording) and a surprise solo from saxman Sheldon Bazelle. The sound is raw and over-amped, the feel of a band taking a bandstand jam and trying to shape it into something that would fit onto one side of a phonograph record. The flip side of this scratchy 78 acetate is perhaps an even bigger surprise, Hawkins and band playing an impromptu slow blues entitled "If You Please Me" with Burton spraying licks all over the place, Dale mumbling a hastily assembled vocal, and no clear-cut ending. Equally fine is a version of Tarheel Slim's "Number Nine Train" featuring explosive guitar work from Carl Adams and the rare appearance of a slappin' upright bass (played by Bossier Strip regular Shorty Tony) on a Dale Hawkins record. This collection also features Hawkins in a supporting role picking guitar behind local boy vocalist Donnie Ray White and Nashville buddy Roger Miller, while his original band moonlights behind Maylon Humphries on "Weep No More," another cowbell rocker, this time in a minor key. Another noteworthy inclusion is "Superman," featuring Margaret Lewis on backup vocal, Roy Buchanan on guitar, and D. J. Fontana on drums. The title track, a wild instrumental with Adams driving the band on an agitated riff, later became the blueprint for "Lovin' Bug." Later cuts from the early '60s flesh things out (the gospel-styled "Everglades," "On Account of You," "Hey Pretty Baby," "Mumbly Peg"), but these half-dozen tracks—and especially the "Susie Q" demo—are the main reasons to grab this one and add it to the MCA-Chess best-of compilation. *—Cub Koda*

Rock & Roll Tornado / Oct. 27, 1998 / Ace ♦♦♦♦♦

At first glance, this 30-track compilation of Dale Hawkins' late-'50s and early-'60s Checker sides might seem like a preferable collection to MCA's briefer (18-song) best-of. Actually, however, this only repeats 11 of those 18 tracks, with the emphasis on some cuts that haven't been on CD before, as well as no less than eight previously unreleased songs. It's hard to figure if this was meant as a best-of compilation or just a disc that mixes some of his biggest and best singles with obscure items; the omissions of "Ain't That Lovin' You Baby" (which is on the MCA collection) alone prevents this from being definitive. It does include a couple of songs that should be on any Dale Hawkins collection, "Yea-Yea (Class Cutter)" and "Mrs. Merguitory's Daughter," that do *not* appear on the MCA anthology. As for the more obscure material that's only on *Rock & Roll Tornado*, it's largely respectable, but not so essential that you would compare it to "Susie Q," "La-Do-Dada," or others considered among Hawkins' best performances. Sometimes it's heavily derivative—"Boy Meets Girl" sounds like it's trying very hard to imitate Jerry Lee Lewis, and "Someday, One Day" is quite Buddy Holly-like—and some of the unreleased cuts, like the cover of "Caldonia" and the country-soul ballad "Convicted," show him trying styles removed from rockabilly. In all, a good compilation that Hawkins fans should get even if they have the one on MCA. But if you just want one, it's a pretty tough call, each disc containing worthy selections not on the other, though each has his most essential recordings (i.e., "Susie Q," "Liza Jane," "La-Do-Dada"). *—Richie Unterberger*

Wildcat Tamer / Apr. 13, 1999 / Lightyear ♦♦♦♦

Hawkins' first record in over 30 years shows that he had plenty of gas left in the tank as the new century approached. From the opening title track (complete with chaotic false start) to the closing recut of "Susie Q" (done more in a Creedence style than Hawkins' original), it's very obvious that Hawkins is absolutely delighted to be making records again. His bluesy style is put to great use on funky remakes of Leadbelly's "Goodnight Irene" and "Going' Down the Road (Feelin' Bad)" while his country side comes up for air on the whimsical summer hit in the making, "Summertime Down South," which features Vassar Clements on fiddle. Some great rockin' that recalls his Chess salad years without Xeroxing it. *—Cub Koda*

Hawkshaw Hawkins (Harold Franklin Hawkins)

b. Dec. 22, 1921, Huntington, WV, **d.** Mar. 5, 1963, Camden, TN

Vocals, Guitar / Traditional Country, Honky Tonk

Hawkshaw Hawkins is a country singer, guitarist, songwriter, and entertainer. A large man (six-feet six-inch) with a deep singing voice, Hawkins was an immensely popular performer in country music for many years without the benefit of big record success. He started on radio, becoming a regular on WWVA's *Wheeling Jamboree* by 1946 and making his first records for the King label around that time. By 1953 he signed with RCA Victor and became a regular member of the *Grand Ole Opry* by 1955. Described as "the man with 11-and-a-half yards of personality," Hawkins was a warm and engaging performer both on-stage and on records, able to pull off a wide variety of material from maudlin weepers to uptempo novelties. His label-jumping from Columbia by the late '50s and back to King by the early '60s moved his material closer to commercial mainstream country, but his time in the spotlight ran out when he perished in the same plane crash as Cowboy Copas and Patsy Cline.

Hawkins (born Harold Franklin Hawkins, December 22, 1921; died March 5, 1963) was born and raised in Huntington, WV. His first foray into performing came at the age of 15, when he won a talent contest at a local radio station, WSAZ. Following his win, he began working at the station, eventually moving to WCHS in Charleston by the end of the '30s; at WCHS, he frequently sang with Clarence "Sherlock" Jack. During 1941, he traveled the United States with a revue. The following year, he joined the military, where he was stationed in the Philippines; in Manila, he sang on the local Army radio. Following his discharge from the Army, Hawkins signed with King Records, releasing the minor hit—and the song that would eventually become his signature tune—"The Sunny Side of the Mountain." In addition to recording for King, he was a regular on WWVA's *Wheeling Jamboree* between 1946 and 1954. In 1948, he had his first hit single with "Pan American," which climbed into the country Top Ten. Over the next three years, he had four other Top Ten singles—"Dog House Boogie" (1948), "I Love You a Thousand Ways" (1951), "I'm Waiting Just for You" (1951), and "Slow Poke" (1951). In 1953, he left King and signed with RCA, but he had no hits for the label. In 1955, Hawkins became a member of the *Grand Ole Opry*.

Hawkins joined Columbia's roster in 1959, releasing the number 15 single "Soldier's Joy" later that year. The following year, he married fellow country singer Jean Shepard, and they made their home on a farm outside of Nashville, where he bred horses. Hawkins re-signed to King in 1963, releasing "Lonesome 7-7203" as a comeback single early that spring. Though it became a number-one hit, Hawkins didn't live to see it reach the top of the charts—he tragically died in the same airplane crash that killed Cline and Copas on March 5, 1963. Shepard was pregnant with their child at the time of the crash; the child was a son, and he was named after his father. Hawkins' recorded legacy was treated haphazardly in the three decades after his death, but in 1991, Bear Family released a comprehensive, multi-disc overview of his RCA and Columbia Records called *Hawk*. —*Cub Koda*

Hawk / 1953-1961 / Bear Family ✦✦✦✦✦
This collection, featuring 63 songs, isn't a cross-section of Hawkins' history, because it's limited to his RCA and Columbia recordings, thus leaving out his pre-1953 and post-1961 hits for King Records. It is, however, a dazzling array of some of the best honky tonk-based country music this side of Hank Williams. The first thing one notices is what a stunning voice Hawkins had, and also his range as a performer—he could do a lovesick ballad and make it seem like the words came right from his heart, but was equally engaging doing playful novelty numbers. Disc one covers his first two years at RCA, one perfect track after another, great singing backed by crisp, tight playing and note-perfect arrangements across a dazzling range of material. It runs the gamut from the sentimental to some of the brightest dance-type tunes and novelty numbers of their period, and even some not-half-bad efforts at hooking into the new rock craze. Disc two opens with maybe the prettiest, most haunting song that Hawkins ever recorded, the previously unissued "I've Had It Before," a moody country blues driven by Hawkins' own acoustic guitar. His re-recording of "Sunny Side of the Mountain," Hawkins' signature tune beginning in the late '40s, is also here. Disc three is given over to Hawkins' stay at Columbia Records, which marked a major change in his repertory. The sound isn't as crisp, but the material is the real curiosity; Hawkins' arrival coincided with Marty Robbins' huge success with Western songs, and Johnny Horton's mega-hit "The Battle of New Orleans," so Columbia had him do half-dozen folk-based and historical songs and Western numbers. It took a year for Hawkins to return to his old sound, which closes out this set. —*Bruce Eder*

Hawkshaw Hawkins, Vol. 1 / 1958 / King ✦✦✦✦
King Records originally assembled this album in 1958, five years after Hawkins left the label, but long before his return in 1962. Surprisingly, while it contains "Slow Poke" and "Sunny Side of the Mountain," it doesn't have his other big hits from his first period with the label, including "I Love You a Thousand Ways" and "Dog House Boogie." It does offer a cross-section of his honky tonk and traditional country material; Hawkins could be ultra-sentimental, but he could also boogie with the best of them, and this disc fills in some holes left by the Bear Family box. There are, as usual for King, no notes or session information and no information on the year of release of any of the songs. The audio quality on the 1988 remastering leaves something to be desired—the sonics on some of it are a bit compressed, but there may not be much that can be done about this, as some of the stuff goes back to the mid-'40s, and the producers have at least had the courage to pump the volume up high, so the guitars are nice and loud (check "Rattlesnakin' Daddy"). —*Bruce Eder*

Hawkshaw Hawkins / 1959 / La Brea ✦✦✦✦
Hawkshaw Hawkins' smooth and deep country voice first flowered during his 1946-1953 stay at the King label. With behemoths RCA and Columbia still in the future, Hawkins delivered some his biggest hits for the blues-centric, Cincinnati independent. This fine LP spotlights a few of them, including his signature tune, "Sunny Side of the Mountain," and "Slow Poke." Far from being the only highlights, though, these smashes are augmented by some of the best early honky tonk on wax. Reflecting the influence of Jimmie Rodgers and Ernest Tubb, Hawkins ranges freely from weepers ("If I Ever Get Rich Mom") to hillbilly boogie ("Rattlesnakin' Daddy") to country swing ("Somebody Lied"). A vintage set tailored made for the honky tonk faithful. —*Stephen Cook*

● **I'm a Rattlesnakin' Daddy: The King Anthology, 1946–1963** / Feb. 8, 2000 / WestSide ✦✦✦✦✦
Subtitled "The King Anthology 1946-1963," this brings together his earliest recordings as well as two versions of his final single. Kicking off with a previously unissued undubbed version of his biggest hit, "Lonesome 7-7203," the set goes back to the dawn of Hawkins' career with sides like "I Ain't Goin' Honky Tonkin' Anymore," "I've Got the Blues," "Sunny Side of the Mountain," and "You Nearly Lose Your Mind," all distinguished by sparse string backing and bluesy vocals. It isn't until 1949's "Pan American" that normal country instruments (fiddles, steel guitar) start showing up in Hawk's music, as he covers everything from Hank Williams to current R&B hits like Ruth Brown's "Teardrops From My Eyes" and John Greer's "Got You on My Mind." Hawkins further blurs the line between country and blues with proto-rockabilly tracks like "Doghouse Boogie," "Back to the Dog House," and "Rattlesnakin' Daddy." Hawkshaw left King in 1953, and the rest of his career is chronicled on an exhaustive Bear Family box set entitled *Hawk*, but these

are some of his very best and earliest sides and are absolutely essential to getting the big picture on this highly underrated artist. —*Cub Koda*

Ronnie Hawkins

b. Jan. 10, 1935, Huntsville, AR
Vocals, Guitar / Rock & Roll, Rockabilly
Ronnie Hawkins is a rockabilly singer who formed his original backing band, the Hawks, while attending the University of Arkansas. After auditioning unsuccessfully for Sun in 1957, he started working regularly in Canada the following year, eventually taking up permanent residence there. After one release on the Canadian Quality label, he signed with Roulette in New York in 1959, having hits with "Forty Days" and "Mary Lou." The live fervor of Hawkins (known as Mr. Dynamo) and the Hawks' show continued in Canada after all the original members except Levon Helm headed back to the U.S. Hawkins quickly hired Canadian players Robbie Robertson, Garth Hudson, Rick Danko, and Richard Manuel as the new Hawks. They stayed with him until 1963, but later became Bob Dylan's backing group and went on to a career of their own as the Band. Hawkins has remained a legend in Canada, recording unrepentant rockabilly sides and gigging constantly. He's still the original Mr. Dynamo, capable of shaking the walls down any old time he feels like it. —*Cub Koda*

The Folk Ballads of Ronnie Hawkins / 1960 / Roulette ✦✦✦✦
Originally issued on Roulette, this album was a kind of cash-in on the folk boom spawned the year before by Johnny Horton with his recording of "The Battle of New Orleans." The folk material here, includes a wailing version of "Motherless Child" and a subdued version of "The Cherry Song" (as "I Gave My Love a Cherry"), and works like "John Henry" and "Poor Wayfaring Stranger" (done very moodily) in Hawkins' arrangements, and there's also stuff like Gershwin's "Summertime" and "Brave Man" from a Paramount movie *Red Garters*. Hawkins' aggressively moody vocals make all of it appealing. The backing chorus that appears on most of the songs is a bit off-putting, but overall, this is a fairly appealing record of its kind, with Hawkins in fine musical form and generally on target in his interpretive decisions. (British import) —*Bruce Eder*

Sings the Songs of Hank Williams / 1962 / Grand Prix ✦✦✦✦
Hawkins' tribute to Hank Williams is OK, if somewhat unexciting, more conscientious than inspired. His voice is good enough, but the songs aren't done in that interesting a fashion, and the inclusion of an obtrusive female chorus mars the proceedings somewhat—today, or even in the 1980s, this record would have been done leaner and harder. All of the expected numbers are here among the dozen, including "Your Cheatin' Heart," "Hey Good Lookin'," "Cold Cold Heart," "Jambalaya," and "I'm So Lonesome I Could Cry." (British import) —*Bruce Eder*

● **The Best of Ronnie Hawkins & His Band** / Jun. 1990 / Rhino ✦✦✦✦✦
In the late '50s and early '60s, Ronnie Hawkins was one of the few rock & rollers committed to performing and recording unapologetic rockabilly while others were returning to their country roots or going the teen-idol route. This 18-song compilation focuses mostly on his initial burst of activity for Roulette in 1959 and 1960, with a few later odds and ends thrown in. While he deserves respect for keeping the torch of rock & roll's roots burning during some of its leaner years, he didn't match the greatness of rockabilly's kingpins. His voice and performance were energetic but not brilliant; his material was a bit pedestrian. The best of these tunes are "Mary Lou" (his sole Top 30 hit), "Forty Days" (an update of Chuck Berry's "Thirty Days"), and "One of These Days" (later covered by the Searchers). What he's really known for, of course, is giving a bunch of mostly Canadian kids their start as his backing band, the Hawks. A later edition of the Hawks eventually toured with Bob Dylan and evolved into the Band. Only two of these songs, though, feature that lineup, the 1963 single "Bo Diddley"/"Who Do You Love." On "Who Do You Love" especially, Robbie Robertson lets rip with a roaring solo that's a good few years ahead of its time in its manic distorted intensity. It's by far the most exciting track on this compilation of a respectable but minor performer from rock's early days. —*Richie Unterberger*

The Roulette Years / 1995 / Sequel ✦✦✦✦✦
This 57-track double-CD set seems like a no-brainer—get almost all of Ronnie Hawkins' rock & roll recordings in one place. The packaging here is good, thoughtful, and legitimate, but could also be a little misleading to those who are buying this expecting to hear a lot of early work by the musicians who later became the Band—Levon Helm was aboard on drums from the Hawks' first official recordings, but the remainder didn't begin arriving on the scene until almost two years later; they're only on hand more than one or two at a time for less than half of what's here. Additionally, taken on its own terms, this is about as solid a rock & roll collection by a single white artist from this period as you're going to find—in 1959-1960, as Elvis Presley, et al. were generally softening their sounds, Ronnie Hawkins was staying a true rock & roller. The alternate takes and demos featured here are about as worthwhile as any of Hawkins' hits, and the quality of everything about this set makes it practically scream to be purchased—the detailed notes, the complete sessionography, the bright, clean yet raunchy sound on the masters. A straight, enjoyable (and probably revelatory to some) rock & roll document, Sequel deserves an award for this release—only Bear Family does it better, and this is a lot cheaper than one of their double CDs. —*Bruce Eder*

Rock & Roll Resurrection/The Giant of Rock & Roll / Apr. 1996 / One Way ✦✦✦
This two-fer combines a pair of Hawkins LPs dating back to the early 1970s; while the singer is largely past his prime, there are enough solid performances here to make the collection worthwhile for fans. —*Jason Ankeny*

Ronnie Hawkins/Folk Ballads of Ronnie Hawkins / May 18, 1999 / Collectables ✦✦✦✦
In 1999, Collectables released *Ronnie Hawkins/Folk Ballads of Ronnie Hawkins*, which contained two complete albums—*Ronnie Hawkins* (1959, originally released on Roulette)

and *Folk Ballads of Ronnie Hawkins* (1960, originally released on Roulette)—by Ronnie Hawkins on one compact disc. *—Jason Birchmeier*

Mr. Dynamo/Sings the Songs of Hank Williams / Jun. 8, 1999 / Collectables ♦♦♦♦
In 1999, Collectables released *Mr. Dynamo/Sings the Songs of Hank Williams*, which contained two complete albums—*Mr. Dynamo* (1960, originally released on Roulette) and *Sings the Songs of Hank Williams* (1962, originally released on Roulette)—by Ronnie Hawkins on one compact disc. *—Jason Birchmeier*

Wade Hayes

b. Apr. 20, 1969

Guitar, Vocals / Traditional Country, Contemporary Country, Honky Tonk, Neo-Traditionalist Country

Raised in Bethel Acres, OK, Wade Hayes grew up around country music. His father Don was a professional musician who played bars and honky tonks across Oklahoma. Through the influence of his father, he began playing music as a child. Initially, he played mandolin for a while, but he switched to guitar at the age of 11. Inspired by honky tonk, outlaw country, and bluegrass, Hayes developed a distinctive style at an early age. When Wade was a pre-teen, his father signed a contract with a Nashville-based independent record label and moved the family to the Music City. Within a year, the label had folded, leaving the Hayes family broke. They struggled back to Oklahoma, where Wade began playing guitar and singing backup in his father's band, Country Heritage. Following his graduation from high-school, Wade went to three different colleges, but he decided to drop out of school to pursue music after seeing Ricky Skaggs on the 1991 Country Music Awards show.

He moved to Nashville and beginning playing on demo tapes, all the while working on his own original material. Shortly after he settled down in Nashville, Hayes began writing songs with Chick Rains, who arranged an audition for the vocalist with record producer Don Cook (the Mavericks, Brooks & Dunn). Cook was impressed and began working with the singer, eventually getting him in contact with executives at Columbia Records. *Old Enough to Know Better*, Hayes' debut album, was released in 1995. The record was an immediate hit, with its title track becoming a number-one single. The Academy of Country Music nominated him for Top New Male Vocalist of the Year for 1995. Hayes' second album, *On a Good Night*, was released in the summer of 1996. Although it wasn't as big a hit as his debut, it still sold respectably. Hayes' third album, *When the Wrong One Loves You Right*, was released in early 1998 and *Highways and Heartaches* followed two years later. *—Stephen Thomas Erlewine*

● **Old Enough to Know Better** / 1995 / Columbia ♦♦♦♦
Brought up on music recorded by legendary artists like Merle Haggard, Waylon Jennings, Willie Nelson, and George Jones, it's little wonder Wade Hayes has such a feel for their style of country music. On this 1995 debut album, *Old Enough to Know Better*, Hayes offers up some impressive honky tonk numbers, three of which he helped pen: "I'm Still Dancin' With You," "It's Gonna Take a Miracle," and the title track and number-one hit "Old Enough to Know Better." Three other songs from the recording also hit the charts in the Top Ten. One listen and music fans will understand why this album landed so many hits and went gold for the young singer. Don Cook, who has worked with award-winning artists like Brooks & Dunn and the Mavericks, served as producer on this debut, though he didn't do so with a heavy hand and left young Hayes in control of his music. Cook did write or co-write some of the tunes for the album, such as "Don't Make Me Come to Tulsa," "Kentucky Bluebird," "What I Meant to Say," and "Steady As She Goes." Wade Hayes is a talented singer and songwriter. Combined with Don Cook at the controls, the music on this album is the kind country fans will enjoy listening to over and over. *—Charlotte Dillon*

On a Good Night / Jun. 25, 1996 / Columbia ♦♦♦
Wade Hayes' eagerly awaited second album, *On A Good Night*, doesn't have the front-to-back consistency of his debut album, but there are enough first-rate songs—particularly the first single "On a Good Night"—to make it a successful album. *—Thom Owens*

When the Wrong One Loves You Right / Jan. 27, 1998 / Columbia ♦♦♦
Despite a handful of weak moments, *When the Wrong One Loves You Right* finds Wade Hayes maintaining the high standards of his first two records. Hayes' voice is deep and resonant with emotion, helping to distinguish even the weaker cuts, but it's songs like "The Day She Left Tulsa (In a Chevy)," where the melody, lyric and delivery blend perfectly, that illustrate Hayes' true potential. *—Thom Owens*

Highways and Heartaches / Sep. 12, 2000 / Monument ♦♦♦
After scoring four Top Ten country hits off his debut album *Old Enough to Know Better* in 1995-1996, Wade Hayes enjoyed more moderate success with his second and third discs, 1996's *On a Good Night* and 1998's *When the Wrong One Loves You Right*, each of which spawned a sole Top Ten hit and some also-rans. Atypically, his new label Monument (like his old one, Columbia, within the Sony corporation) seems not to have chosen an advance single from his fourth album, but there are several singles possibilities among the record's ten tracks. Possessed of a flexible baritone that can ride roughly over the uptempo numbers and croon smoothly through the ballads, Hayes is equally effective in either mode. The songwriting doesn't rise above Nashville formula style, but among the more fast-paced tunes, leadoff track "Up North (Down South, Back East, out West)" and "That's What Honky Tonks Are For" sound like possible radio fodder, while among the slow ones, "She Used to Say That to Me" and "You Were, You Are, You'll Always Be" stand out. The closer, "I'm Lonesome Too," is a midtempo song on which Hayes breaks into an attractive falsetto on the chorus. *Highways and Heartaches* doesn't sound like the album to turn around Wade Hayes' slowly declining career, but with Monument's promotional muscle behind it may help him maintain his current status. *—William Ruhlmann*

Aubrey Haynie

b. 1974

Fiddle / Progressive Bluegrass, Traditional Bluegrass, Contemporary Country

Born in 1974, Aubrey Haynie has wasted no time in establishing himself as one of the most talented fiddle and mandolin players in contemporary country music. Haynie has been one of the most sought after session players in Nashville, having appeared on releases by George Jones, Porter Wagoner, Trisha Yearwood, and Bryan White among others, and with tours in the bands of Aaron Tippin and Clint Black padding his resumé, as well. Comfortable in a variety of traditional musical genres, from bluegrass and country to more swing and jazz-oriented styles, Haynie has drawn comparisons to swing and bluegrass fiddler Chubby Wise, who served as something of a mentor to Haynie in his youth, and accolades from Ricky Skaggs, who contributed vocals on Haynie's debut. *Doin' My Time* (1997)—an excellent mix of traditionals, covers, and original instrumentals mixed with the occasional vocal track—was well-received in the bluegrass community and netted Haynie a nomination from the International Bluegrass Music Association for Instrumental Album of the Year. The similarly impressive *A Man Must Carry On* followed in the spring of 2000 and only added to Haynie's growing reputation. *—Matt Fink*

● **Doin' My Time** / Sep. 16, 1997 / Sugar Hill ♦♦♦♦
Aubrey Haynie's debut, recorded at the ripe old age of 23, is a *tour de force* in bluegrass, country, and Western swing instrumentals. Taking the title track from Haynie's version of the Flatt & Scruggs classic, *Doin' My Time* never disappoints, as the young artist effortlessly tosses off amazing renditions of traditionals like "Cherokee Shuffle," "Dark Hollow," and "Turkey in the Straw." The jazzy "Cracker Jack" and the Texas swing of "Foolin' Around" are also exceptional. Just as impressive are Haynie's own entries into the genre, with the solemn "Leavin' Rosine," featuring Béla Fleck and Jerry Douglas, "Montgomery Bell," and the gorgeous "Austin's Dream," on which Haynie adds tenor guitar to his fiddle. Given time, these could be the songs that the next generation of bluegrass musicians will be learning, and Haynie's, being young enough, will still be around to teach them firsthand. *—Matt Fink*

A Man Must Carry On / Mar. 21, 2000 / Sugar Hill ♦♦♦♦
Once again joined by members of the bluegrass elite, the ridiculously talented Aubrey Haynie's second Sugar Hill release *A Man Must Carry On* is an exceptional extension of Haynie as an artist, as he composed 11 of the 16 tracks here, with most sounding so familiar that it's hard to think they were written by someone born in 1974. From the gently mournful "Sam's Creek Blues" to the Spanish elements of "Thonotosassa," this is the sound of an artist truly coming into his own. More traditional elements, like the straightforward bluegrass of "Homesick & Lonesome" and the more contemporary country of "Can I Get an Amen" go along perfectly with toe-tapping instrumental workouts like "Buffalo Gals" and "Yeehaw Junction" to make a well-rounded set. *—Matt Fink*

The Bluegrass Fiddle Album / Mar. 11, 2003 / Sugar Hill ♦♦♦♦
The best thing about Aubrey Haynie's fiddling is that he's so smooth and fluid. *The Bluegrass Fiddle Album* is not likely to draw any new fans to the genre, but bluegrass regulars will appreciate how deftly the hugely talented Haynie works through originals, traditionals, and covers of artists like Kenny Baker and Arthur Smith. On his third and most old-school-styled album, Haynie's tone is always dead on, whether he's paying homage to Florida legends like Chubby Wise and Vassar Clements on the slow and gentle "McHattie's Waltz" or burning the barn down with the freewheeling traditional "Bill Cheatham." With legends Tony Rice and Sam Bush in his band, Haynie can't really go wrong. *The Bluegrass Fiddle Album* is an excellent, straight-up bluegrass record played in a traditional style that will impress those wary of bluegrass fusion and crossover, and though it won't break out like a Nickel Creek album, the beauty of Haynie's playing is sure to bring a grin to your face. *—Charles Spano*

Lee Hazlewood (Barton Lee Hazlewood)

b. Jul. 9, 1929, Mannford, OK

Producer, Vocals, Songwriter / Country-Rock, Country-Pop, Pop, Baroque Pop, Obscuro

Country and pop iconoclast Lee Hazlewood has been one of the music world's most irascible geniuses during a long, fruitful career. An Oklahoma Dust Bowl refugee who grew up to become a dedicated Europhile; a production heavyweight who authored success stories for Duane Eddy and Nancy Sinatra but also a recording eccentric who refused to acknowledge mainstream tastes; a songwriter capable of crippling fatalism ("My Autumn's Done Come") and playful country corn ("Dolly Parton's Guitar"), and songs that use elements of both ("Dark in My Heart"); it's all part of the highly contradictory legend of Hazlewood. Hazlewood was born Barton Lee Hazlewood in 1929 in Mannford, OK. (A 1968 recording even took his birthplace as its title.) His father, an oil man, moved the family around continually during the 1930s and '40s while looking for work, with stops in Arkansas, Kansas, and Louisiana before landing on the Gulf Coast in Port Neches, TX. Hazlewood enrolled at Southern Methodist planning to study medicine but was conscripted soon after; he married his high-school sweetheart, Naomi Shackleford, then spent several years overseas, spinning records in Japan for Armed Services Radio but also on active duty in Korea.

Returning from the war, the Hazlewoods moved to California and then Coolidge, AZ, where Lee used a short stint in broadcasting school to land a job with a local radio station. His play lists eventually gravitated toward rock & roll, and following a move to Phoenix several years later, he began producing tracks for his own label, Viv, in 1955. One year later, he wrote a song called "The Fool" and hired local country singer Sanford Clark to record it. Hazlewood's innovative recording techniques—heavily echoed, in similar fashion to Sam Phillips' work at Sun—turned the single into an unlikely Midwestern regional favorite and a national hit after it was reissued by Dot—it eventually peaked inside the Top Ten. Clark failed to repeat its success, however, and a Dot production deal for Hazlewood also fizzled, even after he moved back to California. He then hooked up with entrepreneur Lester Sill, who'd previously been partners with Leiber & Stoller and was still managing the Coasters. Hazlewood cut some tracks back in Phoenix, including a few bizarre guitar-effects records by local sensation Duane Eddy. An unlikely signee to Jamie Records (co-owned by Dick Clark), Eddy hit the big time with "Rebel Rouser" and went on to notch 15 singles in the Top 40. (Hazlewood's influence extended to an associate of Sill's named Phil Spector: he visited the studio in Phoenix to study Hazlewood's taping techniques, and his first productions appeared on the Trey label owned by Hazlewood and Sill.)

With success came a series of complications, however, beginning with Eddy's decision to produce himself after an argument concerning royalties. Then, Sill began focusing his patronage on Spector in the wake of his increasing production acumen during the early '60s. While the duo formed their own Philles label, Hazlewood was having little success with his productions, which included another brief stint with Eddy, longtime friend Al Casey (who a moderate hit with "Surfin' Hootenanny"), and his own folk-pop group, the Shacklefords. In 1963, Hazlewood booked some time at Western Studios (site of a few Brian Wilson/Beach Boys classics) and recorded the tracks for his first solo LP, *Trouble Is a Lonesome Town*. A concept record centered on the eccentric residents of a small Western burg, it introduced Hazlewood's distinctive performing talents; a keen observer of human behavior with a talent for storytelling, he dryly told despairing tales of hard-bitten small-town characters and prefaced each song with a few knowing words about its subject. It wasn't a formula for pop success, but Mercury A&R man Jack Tracy believed in the record and released it with little interference.

After a yearlong break from recording of any kind, he returned to the studio in 1965, when asked by Jimmy Bowen from Reprise to produce Dino, Desi & Billy—a trio of Hollywood teens with royal blood (the first two were the sons of Dean Martin and Desi Arnaz). Hazlewood recorded a pair of Top 40 hits, "I'm a Fool" and "Our Time's Coming," and one of his compositions, "Houston," was recorded for a hit by Martin himself. Reprise showed their gratitude by allowing him to record his second LP, *The N.S.V.I.P.'s* ("The Not-So-Very-Important People"), during 1965. Also, Hazlewood was duly apportioned the career of Nancy Sinatra, another blue-blooded child who'd been at Reprise for four years without earning a hit. By the end of 1965, she'd reached the pop charts with "So Long Babe," and one year later became an international superstar thanks to the cultural milestone "These Boots Are Made for Walkin'." Hazlewood's other production chart-topper was "Somethin' Stupid," featuring a duet with Nancy and father Frank.

After another record for Reprise (*Friday's Child*), his publisher found him a contract with MGM, and he released two LPs in two years: 1966's *The Very Special World of Lee Hazlewood* and 1967's *Lee Hazlewood-ism: Its Cause and Cure*. (A planned third record, 1968's *Something Special*, wasn't actually heard until decades later.) These two comprised the best work of his (solo) career, a collection of desert-dry ballads of the dust boasting a healthy dose of Western fatalism and wanderlust and given impeccable productions that ranged from cowboy minimalism to overblown brassy pop. They were also a place to flesh out material he'd later produce for Sinatra, like "Sand" and "Summer Wine." When the latter, a Nancy & Lee duet tacked onto the B-side of a 1966 Sinatra single, became a hit one year later, it sparked a full-fledged duet album. *Nancy & Lee* sold a million copies during 1968 and earned its place as one of the most influential records associated with either Sinatra or Hazlewood; "Some Velvet Morning," a haunting hymn to the twilight, became an alternative classic thanks to airings, not as much by contemporaries (Vanilla Fudge, Gabor Szabo) as by second- and third-generation inheritors (Lydia Lunch, Thin White Rope, Slowdive, Primal Scream).

Also in 1968, Hazlewood the solo artist returned (briefly) to Reprise to issue *Love and Other Crimes*, another vaguely conceptual record featuring some solid material (though little to compare to his MGM work). He also formed his own imprint, LHI (Lee Hazlewood Industries), which most famously signed the International Submarine Band featuring Gram Parsons but later refused to release Parsons' contract so his work with the Byrds could appear on the country-rock classic *Sweetheart of the Rodeo*. His own LHI debut was 1969's *The Cowboy & the Lady*, recorded with another female foil, Ann-Margret. Increasingly, though, Hazlewood appeared restless in Southern California, recording a few sessions for country stars (including Eddy Arnold and Waylon Jennings) but gradually spending more time in Europe—especially Sweden. During 1970, he recorded *Cowboy in Sweden*, the first of several collaborations with Swedish director Torbjörn Axelman. (Hazlewood even earned a Golden Rose at the Montreux Festival in 1973.) The same year, *Requiem for an Almost Lady* etched onto wax his breakup with Suzi Jane Hokum, who had dueted on several of his MGM singles. More and more, his records weren't even being released in America, though he continued to do solid work—1973's *Poet, Fool or Bum* was one of the best of his career.

After his recording career began drifting during the late '70s, Hazlewood retired briefly resurfaced in 1995, touring America with Sinatra after her comeback album, *One More Time*. He also contributed two vocal tracks to the Casey album *Sidewinder*, recorded in Phoenix and released in 1995 by the German label Bear Family. Since his peak in the late '60s, however, Hazlewood had been revered by figures in the alternative scene ranging from Nick Cave to Tindersticks to Lambchop. In 1999, Smells Like Records (founded by Steve Shelley of Sonic Youth) began reissuing several of Hazlewood's classic LPs and also released his first new album in 20 years, *Farmisht, Flatulence, Origami, ARF!!! and Me*.... —*John Bush*

Trouble Is a Lonesome Town / 1963 / Smells Like ✦✦✦

Trouble Is a Lonesome Town was Lee Hazlewood's first proper solo album, following his prosperous late-'50s partnership with Duane Eddy and prior to his mentoring and making of '60s boot-walker Nancy Sinatra. Hazlewood considered it a "writer's album" from which other artists could cull songs, but *Trouble* is a perfectly legitimate effort in its own right and characteristically wonderful Hazlewood. The songs are succinct, country-drenched cowboy ballads given a certain undeniable authority by Hazlewood's warm, bottomless baritone, which booms out of the music like a voice amplified from the heavens. The album runs through jail songs ("Six Feet of Chain"), railroad songs ("The Railroad"), traveling songs ("Long Black Train"), and cold-hearted love songs ("Look at That Woman") peppered with outlaws, itinerants, dead-end women, card players, and beat-down heroes, too. Between the songs, Hazlewood shows his storyteller's gift by

offering up bits of narration, and the album itself is a storyteller's record. *Trouble* is like a cross between a novel full of idiosyncratic character studies (à la Faulkner) and a John Wayne Western, with Hazlewood—looking a lot like a dharma bum on the album cover, sitting on the railroad tracks with his guitar and a dangling cigarette—spinning out intricate yarns about all manner of interesting souls with names like Orville Dobkins and Emory Zickfoose Brown, all residents of the hard-scrabbled fictitious town Trouble ("nothing with a railroad running through it"), which is loosely based on his birthplace. The music is as somber and loping as such subject matter demands, mostly consisting of strummed acoustic guitars and woeful harmonica wails that weep the blues. But it is in the purposefully humorous, sympathetic, and colorful storytelling that the distinct, dead-on Americana heart of *Trouble* lays. —*Stanton Swihart*

The N.S.V.I.P.'s / 1965 / Hazlewood ✦✦✦

Kooky, funny, but surprisingly insightful songs and stories about small-town weirdos—a companion album to *Trouble*. A quirky anomaly, this album is easily one of the seven wonders of the pop music world. —*Kurt Wolff*

Friday's Child: Lee Hazlewood / 1966 / Reprise ✦✦✦✦

The Very Special World of Lee Hazlewood / 1966 / MGM ✦✦✦✦✦

Although Lee Hazlewood had recorded as a solo performer prior to his brief stint with MGM, his first two MGM albums present his best '60s recordings as a solo vocalist. Issued in 1966, *The Very Special World of Lee Hazlewood* is the first of these. Hazlewood's limitations as a singer kept him, and this album, from being marketable as anything approaching a commercial proposition at the time (unless he was dueting with Nancy Sinatra). Yet with the passage of several decades, this one-of-a-kind blend of country, pop, lounge, nonchalant sub-Johnny Cash vocals, and off-kilter lyrics was recognized as worthy on its own terms and appreciated by a sizable cult audience. And as this album demonstrates, he really wasn't without his more conventionally pleasing pop attributes either, even if it would take other artists to put them onto the hit parade. It does include his own versions of songs far more famous as the versions he produced for Nancy Sinatra: "These Boots Are Made for Walkin'" (done here in a far less effective, self-mocking satirical fashion), "Summer Wine" (done as a duet with Suzi Jane Hokum, though it's his slightly later subsequent duet of the song with Sinatra that's remembered), and "So Long Babe." There's also a bossa nova treatment of the hit he wrote and produced for Dino, Desi & Billy, "Not the Lovin' Kind." But there are a couple of delectable sad pop ballads with gorgeous strings and weepy backup choral vocals ("Your Sweet Love" and "For One Moment"); one of his greatest dark meditations, "My Autumn's Done Come"; and zippier, frivolous fun pop tunes ("I Move Around" and "When a Fool Loves a Fool"). Not everything here's on this level; there are occasional songs that verge on slipping from the humorous to dumb novelties. But it's a worthwhile record, and not solely on kitsch terms. [The music's also now much easier to find than it used to be, all of the tracks having been included on the 2002 Big Beat CD reissue *These Boots Are Made for Walkin': The Complete MGM Recordings*.] —*Richie Unterberger*

Lee Hazlewood-ism: Its Cause and Cure / 1967 / MGM ✦✦✦✦✦

This is the fifth solo attempt by the producer, singer/songwriter, and self-proclaimed Bohemian with "a scotch-scarred heart," who would rather see people remembering his ill-fallen ballpoint "from a rare sort of liver ailment" instead of his songwriting—thus he states in the liner notes to this album. In terms of concept, *Lee Hazlewood-ism: Its Cause and Cure* has much in common with its immediate predecessor, *The Very Special World of Lee Hazlewood*. Both albums include the familiar, Western movie classic-styled orchestration by arranger Billy Strange, who would create a masterpiece with the followup, the duet album *Nancy & Lee*. Combined with Hazlewood's own contradictory performance—the ambiguous content of his half-sung/half-spoken tales is delivered without a hint of irony—the result proves mysterious, funny, and sincere at the same time. Hazlewood's performance is helped a great deal by his unearthly deep voice which, upon hearing, will make friends, family, and stereo equipment alike beg for mercy. In this instance, Hazlewood gets nostalgic about former Parisian mistresses and tries to outdo both Sinatra Sr. (the tender "I Am a Part") and daughter Nancy ("In Our Time," this time delivered by an outraged Hazlewood himself). However, most of the time he seems completely at ease with the development of an unsuccessful solo career ("Home (He's Home)"), and "The Old Man and His Guitar" nearly has Hazlewood sounding like he's been retired for ages. If you don't get the picture by now, there are the album's intriguing highlights—the haunting epics "José" and "The Nights"—to convince you. The former tells the tale of a homeless Mexican boy who's destined to become a glorious bullfighter, while the latter offers a closer look at the ways of life of an Indian tribe—from the perspective of a white female who happens to live with one of them. Essential Hazlewood, if not for the phantom choirs that appear from the background with every chorus to enhance the dramatic effect, then at least for the eccentric lyrics ("The ways of a red man are lonely/And his woman can expect little more/Than a day filled with hard work and sorrow/So she learns to live for: the nights, the nights"). [The entire album was reissued as part of the 2002 Big Beat CD reissue *These Boots Are Made for Walkin': The Complete MGM Recordings*.] —*Quint Kik*

Love and Other Crimes / 1968 / Reprise ✦✦✦✦✦

If you're looking for evidence of Lee Hazlewood the weirdo, this album will not disappoint. As pure music it's another story. Hazlewood usually sounds like Johnny Cash gone pop, after gargling with razor blades; sometimes he sounds like a drunk taking over the cocktail piano, with soused accompaniment by such estimable session greats as guitarist James Burton and drummer Hal Blaine. Check out "She's Funny That Way," which suddenly fades into a silly excerpt of Ray Charles' "Drown in My Own Tears"; there's also "Pour Man'" (sic), a jaunty ballad sung by a convicted murderer on his last night of life. "Forget Marie" is reasonably solid country-pop in the style of the material he fashioned for Nancy Sinatra, but overall this has the ambience of a tax write-off or a vanity project, knocked off with a bit of extra studio time. —*Richie Unterberger*

Nancy & Lee / 1968 / Reprise ♦♦♦♦♦
Lee's first duet album with Nancy Sinatra is a classic of '60s pop. He plays the leering, deep-throated, trail-worn cowboy to her bright-eyed girl-child, and the match on songs like "Summer Wine," "Sand," "Jackson," and "Some Velvet Morning" is a smart, sexy, lip-smacking bowl of mind candy. —*Kurt Wolff*

Something Special / 1968 / MGM ♦♦♦
The *Something Special* album has a strange history, even by the standards of Lee Hazlewood's incredibly strange solo career. Recorded (with the exception of one number) in 1967, it was scheduled for released by MGM and even given a catalog number and a cover, but was canceled. However, it did come out in Germany 20 years later, and the entirety of the album is included on the 2002 Big Beat release *These Boots Are Made for Walkin': The Complete MGM Recordings*. Hazlewood fans eager to investigate an album that's never been easy to hear (at least prior to that Big Beat reissue) may be disappointed to find it a spare, almost nonchalant collection that sounds like the work of a sozzled if unpredictably eccentric lounge combo. It's almost totally lacking the gorgeous, eccentric arrangements and memorably quirky pop songs of his productions for Nancy Sinatra (and for that matter his two prior MGM LPs from 1966-1967, *The Very Special World of Lee Hazlewood* and *Lee Hazlewood-ism: Its Cause and Cure*). One song, "Shades," does recall those first two albums, for the very good reason that it was recorded in 1966 during sessions for *Lee Hazlewood-ism: Its Cause and Cure*, though it wasn't as good as most of the songs that ended up on that LP. Otherwise *Something Special* sounds like an outlet for humorous, slightly off-the-wall, and quite uncommercial Hazlewood ditties blending jazz, country, folksy philosophy, and a bit of folk and blues. Occasional dumb sub-Louis Armstrong scatting in the background (by Billy Strange) adds to the air of a project that doesn't seem intended to have been taken that seriously. —*Richie Unterberger*

The Cowboy & the Lady / 1969 / Smells Like ♦♦
Many listeners are surprised that this combination doesn't click, and as it turns out the best thing about this record is the photography, as the pair strips down to longjohns in what appears to be the frontier city set in Tucson, AZ. After all, brassy Ann-Margret does have things in common with the Hazlewood breadwinner Nancy Sinatra, and that includes a good voice as well as a hard body. The instrumental arrangements reveal that Hazlewood was already brave, bold, and audacious, sometimes changing the texture totally for what winds up to be a fade-out tag; other times dropping so many instruments in one's lap it will seem like a music store has moved in upstairs and caused the floor to collapse. The one missing ingredient is subtlety—this is what good old Nancy Sinatra brought to each and every one of the classic recording collaborations with Hazlewood. She never pushed too hard, and it wasn't just a matter of sounding sultry, either. Even in the diabolical "Boots Are Made for Walkin'" she really just sounds like someone's slightly bitchy girlfriend, whereas judging by the performance of "Sweet Thing" that comes near the close of this collection, one shudders to think of how Ann-Margret might have interpreted the personality behind the tromping boots. She is just over the top much too often, an approach that of course works well for her when an audience is also watching her dance or she is part of a farce such as the hit play *Best Little Whorehouse in Texas*. What can be said for her is that she sometimes accomplishes the not-simple task of stepping into a country & western arrangement when she is not at all a country singer. This does not mean her "Only Mama That'll Walk the Line" will make anyone forget the Waylon Jennings original, but it does mean that the moments when her voice is swathed with the harmonica of Charlie McCoy and Mr. Unidentified on pedal steel are pleasant indeed. Which is more than can be said for some of the atrocious bombast that also came out of this session, material that probably only saw the light of day because some bean counter at the record label wanted something to show for having hired an entire symphony orchestra and big band for the session. —*Eugene Chadbourne*

Forty / 1969 / LHI ♦♦♦
Another dearth of Hazlewood originals in lieu of mediocre showtunes ("It Was a Very Good Year," "September Song"); nonetheless the hardcore downer "The Bed" and his dark, turgid, but almost saucy take on Randy Newman's "Let's Burn Down the Cornfield" are stellar. —*Kurt Wolff*

Cowboy in Sweden / 1970 / Smells Like ♦♦♦♦
At the turn of the '60s, Lee Hazlewood decided to leave America for Sweden. He had already spent time in the country, appearing as an actor in two television productions, so his decision wasn't completely out of the blue—especially since he had become close with the Swedish artist/filmmaker Torbjörn Axelman. The year that he arrived in Sweden, he starred in Axelman's television production *Cowboy in Sweden* and cut an album of the same name. Judging by the album alone, the film must have been exceedingly surreal, since the record exists in its own space and time. At its core, it's a collection of country and cowboy tunes, much like the work he did with Nancy Sinatra, but the production is cinematic and psychedelic, creating a druggy, discombobulated sound like no other. This is mind-altering music—the combination of country song structures, Hazlewood's deep baritone, the sweet voices of Nina Lizell and Suzi Jane Hokum, rolling acoustic guitars, ominous strings, harpsichords and flutes, eerie pianos, and endless echo is stranger than outright avant-garde music, since the familiar is undone by unexpected arrangements. Though the songs are all well-written, *Cowboy in Sweden* is ultimately about the sound and mood it evokes—and it's quite singular in that regard. —*Stephen Thomas Erlewine*

Did You Ever / 1971 / RCA ♦♦♦♦
Not as charmingly succinct a package as the pair's debut, their reunion album "Again" has a more "adult" feel. Nonetheless it contains some excellent work that alternates between the serious ("Down from Dover," a Dolly Parton song, where Lee's voice dips deeper than

any man has gone before) and the silly ("Did You Ever"). "Got It Together" is a cute and personable conversation-style song. —*Kurt Wolff*

Requiem for an Almost Lady / 1971 / Smells Like ♦♦♦
Requiem for an Almost Lady is the rarest of Lee Hazlewood's albums because it was released in 1971 exclusively in Sweden (where Hazlewood also completed his cult classic *Cowboy in Sweden* album) and the U.K. The album is one of the most beautifully agonizing breakup records to ever hit wax, culled from a composite of Hazlewood's relationships gone wrong. Spoken word introductions precede each of the ten brief songs and reveal Hazlewood's poetic soul, while the songs themselves are full of longing and witty, clever cynicism coupled with a sad-eyed idealism that paints the music as even more visceral and grievous. Hazlewood spares none of his past loves. *Requiem* is often cutting, even harsh, as is evident with songs such as "I'd Rather Be Your Enemy" and "I'm Glad I Never…" (as in never owned a gun), but there is an underlying feeling of tenderness, as if Hazlewood is only talking tough to hide his own deep hurt. The album creates an impossibly cavernous warmth, with only acoustic guitar and electric bass backing provided by Jerry Cole, Donnie Owens, and Joe Cannon. Although there are hints of Hazlewood's cowboy sound on "L.A. Lady" and "Must Have Been Something I Loved," *Requiem* actually steers much closer to folky psychedelic pop territory, particularly the sound of California at the end of the '60s. The subject matter is sophisticated and somatic, but the tone of the music veers much more toward the mystical, existential, and hippie-ish. Hazlewood is meditative without seeming overly fragile. His perspective is world-weary, but it doesn't stop him from tossing in a campy sense of humor to leaven his obvious passionate disappointment, and it makes the album that much more lyrical, intelligent, and emotionally poignant. —*Stanton Swihart*

13 / 1972 / Smells Like ♦♦♦
One of the rarest of Lee Hazlewood's original LPs, *13* is a surprisingly swinging album completely indicative of the year of its recording, 1972. But though it's undeniably a period piece, in many ways it's dated in all the right ways. The opener, "You Look Like a Lady," is a gem, complete with soaring horn section, a roving bassline, and scads of wah-wah guitar. Oddly, over-production never hurt Hazlewood's gravelly, off-key delivery, and though the arrangements here aren't always sympathetic to the songwriting ("Tulsa Sunday" is particularly jarring), they're usually entertaining. "She Comes Running," a song originally recorded for 1968's *Love and Other Crimes*, makes another appearance, though with a much more commercial production. The lyrics are vintage Hazlewood, and "Ten or 11 Towns Ago" is a highlight: "Met a girl in Baltimore/Nothing less and nothing more/She was rich and I was poor/So I let her take me on a small vacation" and "One week in San Francisco, existing on Nabisco/Cookies and bad dreams/Sad scenes and dodging paranoia." Not all of the songs are up to Hazlewood's level; "Toocie and the River" and "Rosacoke Street" are both, relatively speaking, duds. But Hazlewood fans will love to hear these songs, especially since none have been collected on the quasi-legal compilations available at the nation's better record stores. [Out of print for decades, *13* returned in early 2000 thanks to a reissue campaign by Smells Like Records.] —*John Bush*

Poet, Fool or Bum / 1973 / Capitol ♦♦♦♦♦
The title track mixes black humor, clever rhymes, and cowboy existentialism; "The Performer" is a stark and somewhat autobiographical picture of a singer who's sick of the game; and the epic "Nancy and Me" is some sort of fantasy-ramble that likely never happened, but stands among the best songs Lee ever wrote. Includes a drawling version of Tom Waits' "Those Were Days of Roses (Martha)." —*Kurt Wolff*

A House Safe for Tigers / 1975 / CBS ♦♦♦
Regarded as one of his more obscure albums, this is the soundtrack to one of the many television movies Hazlewood made as a recluse in early-'70s Sweden. Directed by his friend Torbjörn Axelman, *A House Safe for Tigers* is accompanied by some of his strongest material. Filmed in documentary style, the movie finds Hazlewood and Axelman embarking on a nostalgic trip through their childhood days and contemplating the meaning of life. True, most viewers with a general education might be hard-pressed figuring out any meaning whatsoever, since considerable parts of *A House Safe for Tigers* are spoken in Swedish and sometimes even recited in Latin. Hazlewood makes up for this by offering some marvelous anecdotes, completely in line with his songwriting skills. The story about the bum who one day visited his parents' house and helped a youthful Hazlewood to get rid of his stutter is especially insightful. The movie derives its title from Swedish folklore, wherein everyday life is kept safe from "tigers" (problems, misfortune) by the peculiar practice of throwing flowers around the house. Cultish pretensions left alone, the accompanying soundtrack to *A House Safe for Tigers* could be viewed as the mirror image of 1973's sublime *Poet, Fool or Bum*. While the latter partly dealt with Hazlewood's hectic experiences touring the Las Vegas circuit in the early '70s, the former focuses on enjoying his laid-back, newly found life in Sweden. There's a beautiful ode to Gotland, the island Hazlewood fell in love with during the shooting of the television movie *Cowboy in Sweden*. Its breathtaking orchestral arrangements and never-ending fade-out lends "Souls Island" an epic quality. Axelman's words to a second version even add further fuel to the myth of the "cowboy in Sweden." Next to it there's a mixture of old songs (curiously, a version of the Shacklefords' "Our Little Boy Blue" is included here) and a couple of new ones of which the bravado of "Lars Gunnar and Me" and the moving title song are worth mentioning. The music and images of Hazlewood singing to Axelman's family, running the Gotland marathon, and convincing Swedish children to take sides against Nixon turn both movie and album into a celebration of the enduring friendship between artist and director. —*Quint Kik*

20th Century Lee / 1976 / RCA ♦♦♦
Being responsible for an endless line of albums and international hits for both Duane Eddy in the '50s and Nancy Sinatra thereafter, surprisingly Hazlewood still had time left

to maintain a solo career. Since America had enough of him, the artist migrated to Sweden to fulfill his potential as an actor and screenplay writer. From the moment he made his first movie for television in 1970 (*Cowboy in Sweden*), Hazlewood seemed to experience more artistic freedom than ever before. Not only did he make several more of them, but he also equalled his album output. To the ten between 1963 and 1969, Hazlewood added 11 more albums until 1977. Some of them were truly exceptional (*Poet, Fool or Bum* from 1973), while others remain highly obscure. Although it appeared Hazlewood's creative well didn't run dry immediately, the outcome of his late-'70s, Swedish/German-only releases largely proved an inconsistent affair. For some reason, Hazlewood didn't feel like keeping up anymore with the high standard of '60s albums like *Lee Hazlewood-ism: Its Cause and Cure* or *Love and Other Crimes*. Over-production and the artist's growing tendency to record his favorites instead of writing new material make 1976's *20th Century Lee* a little disappointing at first. However, the specific Hazlewood touch is not lost on all selections here. "That's How I Got to Memphis" and "The Ballad of Lucy Jordan" are well-chosen tearjerkers with a nice, soothing background choir. Elsewhere, "My Girl Bill" offers the kind of tongue-in-cheek phrasing similar to Hazlewood's own lyrics. The only original here is the reappearing "The Fool," one of Hazlewood's biggest commercial successes of the '50s for Sanford Clark. Including this particular song seems either a self-reflecting gesture or a sorry excuse for partly trying to sing in Spanish ("An Old Lullaby") and even in Swedish: a version of Evert Taube's "Brevet Från Lillan proves as much hilarious as uncanny a closing piece on the album. If by chance you think you've heard it all, nothing can prepare you for the ambiguous highlights of *20th Century Lee*, as Hazlewood takes both "Indian Summer" and "Whole Lotta Shakin' Goin' On" to a high and unforeseen level. While the former wouldn't be out of place in a '70s soft-porn pic, the latter—with its interrupting pan flute solos—is on the verge of a porno itself. "Come on over baby/We've got chicken in the barn" sounds outright scary if sung with a voice as deep as Hazlewood's. Both the Swedes and the Germans seemed to have had high commercial expectations of it, because a 12-inch with special disco mixes was issued separately. —*Quint Kik*

Movin' On / 1977 / Polydor ♦♦

Released in the same year as his swan song, *Back on the Street Again*, hearing this initially feels like as a bit of a letdown. Newly composed Hazlewood originals do not appear and overall the album comes close to a not-so-greatest-hits collection. The only two songs by his own hand are taken from the impressive concept album *Requiem for an Almost Lady*. Alas, out of their context and bereft of their superbly funny spoken-word introductions ("And you wake up one morning and you say: I feel good, I don't miss her, I can live without her/And you soon learn: that time will come, but it wasn't that day"), they make less sense. Furthermore, including four songs from 1969's career peak, *Forty*, while leaving out "The Bed" and "Bye Baby" makes you wonder whether Hazlewood had any influence on this at all. Does this turn *Movin' On* into a disappointing experience for long-time fans as well? Thankfully not, for there's still the other half of the album with songs selected by the man himself. You'll find it amazing how well the hilarious "Kung Fu You" matches his own repertoire. In fact, Hazlewood does it so well, you actually picture him getting in position before being hit black and blue with his own black belt. Like the previous *20th Century Lee*, part of *Movin' On* suffers from over-production. Though some of the studio musicians are, in fact, the guys who would make ABBA famous in years to come, they opt for a kind of cheesiness that surpasses even Hazlewood in his own territory. Only incidentally do they hit the right mark, with "The Rising Star" and "It's for My Dad" being done in a tasteful manner and carefully suited to the sort of mourning Vegas act Hazlewood turned himself into on 1973's *Poet, Fool or Bum*. In a helpful mood, he performs both without a hint of irony. A nice Peterbilt truck on the album cover might serve to support a careful recommendation. —*Quint Kik*

Back on the Street Again / 1977 / EMI ♦♦♦

"My friends have seen you 'round old Stockholm town/they say you're wearin' it well"—any country performer who dares to come up with a lyric as awkward as this, must either be slightly mental or desperately looking for a new fan base. Some truth probably lies in both, since back in 1970 Lee Hazlewood decided to start a new life in Sweden. There, he became friends with director Torbjörn Axelman, who was responsible for a series of music videos accompanying 1970s *Cowboy in Sweden*. From that moment on Hazlewood appeared in several more Swedish cult movies. A television special, *The N.S.V.I.P.s*, even earned him a Golden Rose at 1973's Montreux Festival. Parallel to his acting career, Hazlewood remained active in the record industry, way until 1977. He managed to release nearly a dozen more solo-albums in less than eight years. Sadly though, apart from 1971's *Did You Ever*, aka *Nancy and Lee Again*, not one of these gained even the slightest commercial impact. A stronger argument for his retreat into obscurity after *Back on the Street Again* is hard to imagine. As was the case with most of the albums from Hazlewood's Swedish period, *Back on the Street Again* was released sparsely. Only Sweden, Germany, the Netherlands, and South Africa were lucky enough to be bothered with yet another Hazlewood record. Compared to the relatively weak *20th Century Lee* and *Movin' On*, Hazlewood's final album consisted of more original material, as a mere seven out of 11 compositions were from his own hand. They were put together with the help of several German session musicians and Dutch steel guitarist Frans Doolaard. It turned out to be pretty much country flavored, but thanks to Hazlewood's songwriting it seldom becomes average. His black humor is ever present in a tale like "Dolly and Hawkeye," as is his over estimation in the epic monster "Rider on a White Horse," which confronts the listener with some of the most outrageous productions ever. Worthwhile additions to the Hazlewood canon are "Your Thunder and Your Lighting" (strangely similar of Leonard Cohen's "First We Take Manhattan") and finally an uptempo love song with trademark Hazlewood lyrics: "You bragged about me to other folks when you knew I wouldn't go far/you, you made me happier/than Dolly Parton's guitar." Add to this five different

drawings of the artists on the album cover and you're left with an altogether mystifying goodbye note. —*Quint Kik*

Fairy Tales and Fantasies / 1989 / Rhino ♦♦♦♦♦

This CD compilation includes the entire *Nancy & Lee* album and four songs from their follow-up: "Did You Ever," "Down From Dover," "Paris Summer," and "Arkansas Coal (Suite)." —*Kurt Wolff*

● **The Many Sides of Lee** / 1991 / Request ♦♦♦♦♦

This is a 25-song import compilation of rare Hazlewood tracks, most or all dating from the 1960s, including solo numbers and collaborations with Suzi Jane Hokum, the Shacklefords, and Mark Robinson. The most country-ish cuts are like a debauched Johnny Cash; the bullfighter narrative "Jose" is Hazlewood at his most compellingly cheesy and melodramatic; and there are shades of his Duane Eddy roots in the more rock-oriented cuts, like the grungy "Della" and the rockabilly tinged "Pretty Jane." There are also solo renditions of several songs that he produced for Nancy Sinatra, although Sinatra's versions are uniformly better. You could justifiably call this the work of an idiot savant, or (at its worst) just a plain idiot, but it is, like much of Hazlewood's stuff, intriguing in its blend of banal '60s pop-country and eccentric production, lyrics, and vocals. It would have been nice to have even a shred of documentation as far as dates and sources, and there's no question that his collaborations with Nancy Sinatra offer a much better context for his work as a songwriter and producer. But this is the best available distillation of the man's erratic and large solo output into one place, if you can find it. —*Richie Unterberger*

Farmisht, Flatulence, Origami, ARF!!! and Me… / Apr. 27, 1999 / Smells Like ♦♦♦

Some may be disappointed that Lee Hazlewood's first album in over 25 years is a collection of standards, but given time, *Farmisht, Flatulence, Origami, ARF!!! and me…* will work its considerable charms. Essentially an outgrowth of Al Casey's Sidewinder project, which featured Hazlewood's vocals on a pair of tracks, *Farmisht* is a laid-back, jazzy affair, with Hazlewood contributing surprisingly supple and inventive readings of such standards as "Honeysuckle Rose," "It Had to Be You," "She's Funny That Way," "Don't Get Around Much Anymore," and "Am I Blue." The album is as much Casey's as it is Hazlewood's, since his small group strikes a wonderful balance of jazz, pop, and country; it's loose but never sloppy, sophisticated but never pretentious. Thanks to Casey's fleet leadership and Hazlewood's rich vocals—which weathered far better than anyone could have predicted—*Farmisht* is one of the few standards albums that actually works, since it is faithful to the songs while creating an identity of its own. It's a modest achievement, but it's not a bad way to return to recording at all. —*Stephen Thomas Erlewine*

Lounge Legends / Jan. 8, 2002 / Polygram International ♦♦♦♦

Although he has become something of legendary figure in lounge music circles, Lee Hazlewood's body of work is sparsely represented in the compact disc format. However, things are changing as hip labels pick up on the enduring popularity of Hazlewood's unique brand of lounge pop. An important gap in the Hazlewood canon has been filled by the release of *Lounge Legends*, a selection of tracks from three albums that he recorded for MGM Records in the late '60s. The 20 tracks presented on this disc present a one of a kind combination of folk-rock, country, and pure pop, all dished up in a slick style that befits its 1960s Los Angeles studio origins. Standout tracks include "For One Moment," a spooky ballad that backs up the singer's quietly heartbroken vocal delivery with a shivery string section, and "Home," a hymn to the individualist mindset wrapped up in a tasty country-pop melody. Elsewhere, Hazlewood's sly yet oddball sense of humor makes itself felt with "Dark in My Heart," a tongue-in-cheek chronicle of woe set to a jaunty country melody, and "In Our Time," a bemused chronicle of society's advances set to a jangle-rock melody worthy of the Byrds. Fans of Hazlewood's work with Nancy Sinatra will be amused by "Summerwine," a duet with Suzi Jane Hokum that serves as a prototype for the Hazlewood/Sinatra duet style, and Hazlewood's version of "These Boots Are Made for Walking," which he slyly transforms into a commentary on how Sinatra's version was a song that nobody believed until it became a success. However, the album's finest track is "My Autumn's Done Come," a haunting ballad about coming to the end of life that offsets its bitter lyrics with a warm, mellow string arrangement. All in all, *Lounge Legends* is a fine collection of songs that provides an able testament to Lee Hazlewood's gift for eccentric yet catchy pop music. —*Donald A. Guarisco*

These Boots Are Made for Walkin': The Complete MGM Recordings / Nov. 15, 2002 / Ace ♦♦♦♦♦

This double CD is just what it says: all three of the albums Lee Hazlewood recorded for MGM in 1965-1967, with the addition of three instrumentals attributed to Lee Hazlewood's Woodchucks (two of which came out on a 1966 single, the third of which, "Batman," was previously unissued). His first two MGM LPs, *The Very Special World of Lee Hazlewood* (released in 1966) and the far more imaginatively titled *Lee Hazlewood-ism: Its Cause and Cure* (1967), together comprise the 22 songs presented on the first disc. In tandem, these two LPs arguably represented the peak of Hazlewood's mighty long and checkered career as a solo artist, containing some of his finest compositions; sympathetic production and arrangements combining pop, easy listening orchestration, rock, country, cowboy music, and folk; and a unique fusion of droll humor with pop hooks, storytelling, and even some genuine romantic sentiment. There are some silly throwaways, to be sure, but there are also some real standouts, like his 1966 duets with Suzi Jane Hokum on "Sand" and "Summer Wine" (which predate the far more famous duets of those tunes he recorded with Nancy Sinatra); the bullfighting epic "Jose"; the Native American narrative "The Nights"; his own comic version of "These Boots Are Made for Walkin'"; the almost morbidly fascinating moping ballad "My Autumn's Done Come"; and neglected gems of brooding, sumptuously orchestrated melodramatic pop like "Your Sweet Love," "For One Moment," and "I Am a Part." It's a little strange, and perhaps distracting to those who own the original LPs, that these 22 songs don't follow the sequence from the original vinyl (and switch back and forth between those albums), but everything's here. Most of the second disc is devoted to *Something Special*, recorded (save for one song) in 1967 but not released for two decades (and then only in Germany). Sadly, this is far less worthwhile than his prior two MGM LPs, sounding like an eccentric lounge country-jazz-pop singer, with (except for "Shades") none of the full orchestrated arrangements that had distinguished his prior MGM output, the material boasting far fewer pop hooks (if just as much oddball lyrics). The set finishes with the three Lee Hazlewood's Woodchucks instrumentals, which though rare are throwaways, combining generic pop/rock with cheesy mariachi flourishes. In truth, almost all of the memorable songs on here can be found on the single-disc *Lounge Legends* compilation, which has almost everything from *The Very Special World of Lee Hazlewood* and *Lee Hazlewood-ism: Its Cause and Cure*, though the peppy, catchy "When a Fool Loves a Fool" (from *The Very Special World of Lee Hazlewood*) somehow escaped inclusion on *Lounge Legends*. But for those willing to spend a little more money and time, this two-disc anthology covers all the bases of Hazlewood's MGM era, augmented by detailed liner notes and an MGM sessionography. —*Richie Unterberger*

Roy Head

b. Jan. 9, 1943, Three Rivers, TX
Vocals / Rock & Roll, Traditional Country, Blue-Eyed Soul, Pop-Soul
Actually a country and rock vocalist rather than an R&B star, Roy Head nevertheless cut one of the great pieces of uptempo soul in the mid-'60s. "Treat Her Right" on Back Beat made it to number two on the R&B charts and number-two pop, and the fact that Head was white was soft-pedaled in R&B circles while the song made its way up the charts. That performance alone was enough to qualify Head as one of the finest blue-eyed soul singers of the 1960s. But in fact, Roy was one of the most versatile stylists of the era, capable of hard R&B/rock tunes (even cutting material with a pre-fame Johnny Winter on backup guitar); mournful, soul-tinged country; and straight R&B and blues covers. Head was also an excellent entertainer, and his live shows of the period even included some fancy footwork clearly under the influence of James Brown.

The Texan singer is remembered as a one-shot artist, but he actually cut many records (some under the auspices of noted producer Huey Meaux) throughout the 1960s on a confusing variety of labels. A few of these were tiny hits in the wake of "Treat Her Right," with only a couple ("Just a Little Bit" and "Apple of My Eye") sneaking into the Top 40. Quite a few of his records were dynamic, sleek hybrids (in varying degrees) of soul, rock, and country, all featuring Head's cocky, confident vocals. In a sense, though, he was damned by his versatility, not fitting comfortably into any niche or marketing plan; the tiny labels he recorded for lacked national promotional muscle in any case. In the 1970s, after several years without success in the rock or R&B fields, Head returned to country, and landed quite a few chart hits in the arena between 1974 and 1985. —*Ron Wynn & Richie Unterberger*

Treat Me Right / 1965 / Bear Family ✦✦✦✦✦
Read the title carefully; it's not "Treat Her Right," the title of Head's 1965 megasmash, but *Treat Me Right*, an entirely different song. Yes indeed, this is an exploitation release of material Head cut for a different label than the one that issued "Treat Her Right," repackaged after the hit to capitalize on its unexpected success. The final punchline is that, as exploitative as this LP is, it's quite good. The ten songs—mostly revved-up R&B, with a bit of country-soul thrown in—are solid evidence of Head's stature as one of the finest white soul singers of the '60s. The small combo R&B arrangements are spare and tight, investing even overdone standards like "Money" with excitement. Long out of print, it still shows up in the used bins from time to time and is worth picking up. —*Richie Unterberger*

Dismal Prisoner / 1972 / T.M.T. ✦✦✦
While ignored commercially, this was a very respectable piece of swamp-pop that showed Head capable of convincingly updating his white R&B sound into the early '70s. Produced by Steve Cropper, it falls somewhere between the vibe of Van Morrison's early-'70s albums and Tony Joe White; indeed, Head covers Morrison's "You Got the Power" and White's "Dismal Prisoner 0613" (on which White himself guests on guitar). Whether getting into horn rock, quasi-funk, or white soul, Head's vocals are consistently fine and assured, complemented by suitably rootsy Southern rock/R&B arrangements. —*Richie Unterberger*

Slip Away: His Best Recordings / Aug. 5, 1993 / Collectables ✦✦✦
Not only are these *not* his best recordings by a long shot—this package also matches the shoddiest standards of the Collectables label, a company often (justly) criticized for a variety of inadequacies. The documentation on these 14 tracks is totally nonexistent—not a clue as to when they were first released or recorded. A good many came out in the mid-'60s (though "Treat Her Right" and most of the other best Back Beat singles are absent); others have a heavier soul/blues feel that sounds as though they might date from a few years later, or even much later. What's more, a few tracks that appear (in better fidelity) on the Varese Sarabande compilation are presented here with different track titles, although you might mistakenly think at a glance that it doesn't duplicate anything from that anthology. There *are* a few very good cuts here that aren't on *The Best of Roy Head*, such as the talking soul rap "Slip Away," the deep soul ballad "The Feeling Is Gone," and the zany psychedelic/jazz-flavored "Easy Loving Girl" (written by Johnny Winter, who plays fuzz guitar on the song). Just be warned that this is a carelessly assembled package, much inferior to the "Varese Sarabande" compilation, if you only want one disc. —*Richie Unterberger*

● **Treat Her Right: The Best of Roy Head** / Aug. 29, 1995 / Varese ✦✦✦✦✦
A long overdue anthology of Head's best sides, mostly recorded for the Back Beat label in the mid-'60s. Besides "Treat Her Right," it has all five of his other singles that dented the charts at the time. These aren't necessarily the highlights of these 18 tracks; "Pain" is

country-soul moan at its best (although it's a thinly veiled rewrite of Lonnie Mack's "Why"), "To Make a Big Man Cry" is his best foray into country-pop from the period, and "You're (Almost) Tuff" is one of his toughest rockers, with a sound that almost verges on Texas garage. This collection is the most solid evidence of Head's superb talents, which were never rewarded with the consistent material or national recognition he deserved. —*Richie Unterberger*

White Texas Soul Shouter / Feb. 23, 1999 / Edsel ✦✦✦✦
Country Crooner / Apr. 20, 1999 / Edsel ✦✦✦✦✦

Texas Soul and Country Man: The Crazy Cajun Recordings / Jul. 27, 1999 / Edsel ✦✦✦✦
It's good to see that music lovers worldwide are finally recognizing Roy Head. The Texas wailer got busy on soul radio in the '60s with the ladies' favorite "Treat Her Right," included here. Head wriggled more than Presley and could out-sing Conway Twitty without the flashy, theatrical props of showmen like Wayne Cochran. This is pure, uncompromising, gutbucket soul with many standouts including "I Can't Stand It," Johnny Ace's "Pledging My Love," "Don't Want to Make It Too Funky," and "Get Out of My Life Woman," a cuttin' rendition of Lee Dorsey's classic. This 15-song import showcases Head at his down-to-earth best and includes some country cuts, but there's no big style change between Head's soul songs and his country songs; he meshes both genres well. —*Andrew Hamilton*

Head On! / Oct. 9, 2001 / Music Club ✦✦✦
The 15 recordings on *Head On!* were made during a commercial drought following Roy Head's mid-'60s hit streak, but preceding his successful resurrection as a country artist in the early '70s. Although there are a couple of country songs (one of which is a remake of his hit "Treat Her Right"), the rest of the performances fuse James Brown with Mitch Ryder to create high-energy white soul music verging on funk. Head's appropriation of James Brown's vocal affectations is more contrived than exciting, although it is hard to deny that Head had a flair for this kind of music. The formula is most effective on "The Same People" and "Mama Mama," where Head's rock and soul approach foreshadows the music Elvis Presley would make in the '70s (and was just beginning to make at American Studios). Despite its lack of hits, *Head On!* fills a hole in Head's discography for collectors and provides a view of a transitional time in his career. —*Greg Adams*

Health & Happiness Show

Group / Alternative Country-Rock, Alternative Country
James Mastro, a music veteran who played with a post-Television Richard Lloyd as a teenager, and St. Vincent DeNunzio (former Feelies and Richard Hell drummer) first began jamming in their kitchen in the early '90s. After adding bassist Tony Shanahan, guitarist Kerryn Tolhurst, and fiddlers Todd Reynolds and Eileen Ivers, the power country sextet signed with Bar/None and released their 1993 debut, *Tonic. Instant Living* followed two years later, and in 1999 the Health & Happiness Show returned with *Sad & Sexy.* —*John Bush*

● **Tonic** / 1993 / Bar/None ✦✦✦✦✦
The idea of a country-leaning folk-rock album from a band fronted by the former guitarist for the Bongos probably sounded like some sort of a bad joke in 1993, but it didn't take long for the Health & Happiness Show to outshine most folks' memories of James Mastro's past resumé, and one listen to *Tonic* will show why. While Mastro didn't have an especially high profile as a songwriter on his earlier recording projects, he certainly made up for lost time here, with ten songs that are warm, honest, and speak from the heart without sounding saccharine or clichéd, all of them buoyed by melodies that manage to sound graceful and catchy at once. And Mastro put together a great little band to play these tunes, including one-time Feelies percussionist St. Vincent DeNunzio, future Patti Smith bassist Tony Shanahan, and ace multi-instrumentalist Kerryn Tolhurst; the Health & Happiness Show make their arrangements sound full and satisfying without becoming overbearing, and they can ease from folk to country to Celtic accents without missing a step. (Their Celtic side gets a real boost by the presence of Eileen Ivers, who plays alongside HAHS fiddler Todd Reynolds on three cuts.) Despite the downtown credibility of several of the members, the Health & Happiness Show played roots music like they were born to it, and *Tonic* offers conclusive proof even a New Yorker can play a convincing two-step if they put their mind to it. —*Mark Deming*

Instant Living / 1995 / Bar/None ✦✦✦✦
Instant Living jettisons the Celtic influences of their first record and replaces it with a more road-tested, country-influenced rock. The stompin' "Tossed Like a Stone" and the Burritos-like "Anytime" show a band that can ring as clear as a bell, while the "Lo-Fi Intro" which leads into "To Be Free" will have you singing and grinning for days on end. Roots-pop to the max. —*James Chrispell*

Sad & Sexy / 1999 / Cropduster ✦✦✦
Continuing their exploration of the smooth twang groove, this trio offer up more sturdy tunes in a roots & rock style. But while the songs aren't bad, there's nothing that really jumps off the album. Instead, the band seems to just be passing time with tunes like "Waiting for the Light" and "Some Stay Broke." The curious die-hard fan will, however, find their theme song as a hidden first track. —*Tim Sheridan*

Jimmy Heap

b. Mar. 3, 1922, Taylor, TX, d. Dec. 4, 1977
Vocals, Guitar, Leader / Western Swing, Honky Tonk
Western swing bandleader Jimmy Heap led the Melody Masters for over three decades and contributed one country classic to the genre, "The Wild Side of Life," covered by Hank Thompson, Burl Ives & Grady Martin, Freddy Fender, and most recently, Waylon Jennings & Jessi Colter. Heap's "Release Me" also provided Esther Phillips and Engelbert Humperdinck with their first Top Ten popular hits, in 1962 and 1967 respectively.

James Arthur Heap was born on March 3, 1922, in Taylor, TX. He formed the Melody Masters just after his service in World War II, with sidemen Arlie Carter, Louis Renson, Bill Glendining, and Horace Barnett. A continuing spot on local radio gave the Melody Masters a bit of renown around central Texas, and Imperial Records signed the band in 1949. Some time before the initial recordings, Heap—who played only lead guitar—hired Houston "Perk" Williams (born 1926) to provide vocals along with his fiddling duties. Though Williams had never sung before, his good performance on their debut release "Today, Tonight, and Tomorrow" guaranteed him the spot ever after. Another song, "Haunted Hungry Heart," was covered by Slim Whitman, but it was "The Wild Side of Life" that provided Jimmy Heap & the Melody Masters with their big break. Hank Thompson & the Brazos Valley Boys took it to number one in March 1952, and the single spent 15 weeks there.

But even before Thompson had borrowed the biggest hit of his career, the country star had advised Capitol Records to sign Heap. Over five years the Melody Masters recorded 32 sides for Capitol, including their big hit "Release Me," which charted in the Top Five in January 1954. No other Capitol singles charted, and Heap left the label in the mid-'50s to form Fame Records. The Melody Masters recorded for Fame throughout the 1950s and '60s, and even integrated rock & roll inspirations. Heap disbanded the group in July 1977 but drowned in a boating accident before the year was over. *—John Bush*

● **Release Me** / 1992 / Bear Family ✦✦✦✦✦

A great 30-track, single-disc compilation of Heap's earliest and best sides. Includes the title track, "Let's Do It Just Once," "It Takes a Heap of Lovin'," and "Ethyl in My Gas Tank (No Gal in My Arms)." This is great Western swing-style material in transition. *—Cub Koda*

Bill Hearne

Guitar, Vocals / Country-Folk

The husband-and-wife duo Bill & Bonnie Hearne first emerged in the late '60s as proponents of the Austin, TX, country-folk scene; over the following decades, they remained early and enthusiastic supporters of area performers, including Lyle Lovett, Nanci Griffith, and Tish Hinojosa. While many of their protégés subsequently went on to great commercial success, the Hearnes languished in relative obscurity and ultimately moved to Santa Fe, NM; still, they remained a popular draw on the folk festival circuit, and their regular gigs at area hotel bars consistently sold out. After a series of shoestring-budget self-releases, the Hearnes secured the financial backing of friend Barney Crutchfield, and with producer Jim Rooney they recorded their 1997 Warner Western debut, *Diamonds in the Rough*, a celebration of the couple's 25th anniversary, featuring guest appearances from Lovett, Griffith, Hinojosa, and Jerry Jeff Walker. Mid-2000 saw the release of *Watching Life Through a Windshield*. *—Jason Ankeny*

Diamonds in the Rough / Apr. 8, 1997 / Warner Bros. ✦✦✦

Bill & Bonnie Hearne's Warner Western label debut is a low-key affair spotlighting the couple's sweetly ragged harmonies. As *Diamonds in the Rough* proves, the Hearnes have great taste in music and friends—not only does the record feature material from the likes of Lyle Lovett and Nanci Griffith, but both lend vocal contributions as well. *—Jason Ankeny*

● **Watching Life Through a Windshield** / Aug. 1, 2000 / Back Porch ✦✦✦✦

New Mexico's Bill & Bonnie Hearne have been at the top of their game for several decades, rising in the early '70s in the healthy country-folk scene in Austin, TX, and influencing many future singer/songwriter heroes (Nanci Griffith among them). If you need any evidence of their prowess, look no further than the star power that crops up on this album. Chris Hillman (on "You Ain't Goung Nowhere," a track he first recorded with the Byrds for the seminal *Sweetheart of the Rodeo*) and Emmylou Harris (who harmonizes on a rendition of Guy Clark's "L.A. Freeway"). More important, however, are the principals, Bill & Bonnie. Bill's deep, rich voice and flatpicking are the focus here, leading us through remarkable takes on songs by songwriting luminaries with last names like Clark and Hancock. While it would be nice to hear more of Bonnie's lead vocals on this effort, this remains top-notch, heart-piercing Americana. *—Erik Hage*

Hearts & Flowers

f. 1965

Group / Country-Rock, Folk-Rock

Hearts & Flowers were one of the most eclectic groups on the Southern California folk-rock scene in the '60s, skewing more to the folk side of the equation and often adding flourishes of psychedelia and, most importantly, bluegrass and country music. The group was founded by guitarist Larry Murray, a Georgia native who had come to California in the late '50s and played with a bluegrass group called the Scottsville Squirrel Barkers. At various points, the Barkers' membership included Chris Hillman and Bernie Leadon, and they recorded a rare album for Crown in 1962 before breaking up. Murray went on to play in several other bands, including another one with Hillman called the Green Grass Group, before forming Hearts & Flowers with vocalist/guitarist Dave Dawson and vocalist Rick Cunha, who had worked together as a folk duo in Hawaii. The trio played the Los Angeles club scene, sometimes by themselves, sometimes with a rhythm section, and eventually landed a deal with Capitol.

Their debut album, *Now Is the Time for Hearts and Flowers*, was released in 1967 and echoed work by the Byrds, the Stone Poneys, and the Dillards. Its eclectic originals and wide-ranging taste in covers meant that it didn't sell very well, however, and at Capitol's urging, the group underwent an overhaul, adding Terry Paul and Dan Woody to flesh out their live sound, though both left before the group completed its second album. So too did Cunha, who was replaced on guitar by Leadon. The group's sophomore effort, *Of Horses, Kids and Forgotten Women*, was released in 1968 and featured more elements of pop and psychedelia than their debut, in spite of the fact that the band had taken to playing folk-rock arrangements of country tunes almost exclusively at their live shows. *Of Horses* didn't sell either, and the group disbanded not long afterward. Murray and Cunha both went on to release solo country-rock albums. *—Steve Huey*

Now Is the Time for Hearts and Flowers / 1967 / Capitol ✦✦✦✦✦

This debut album is an overlooked precursor to country-rock, echoing the late-'60s Byrds, Stone Poneys, Gene Clark, and most especially, as Brian Hogg points out in his lengthy liner notes, the Dillards. Earnest vocals and conscientious harmonies on this subdued, acoustic, and countrified take on folk-rock, with mild Eastern/psychedelic dabs of autoharp. The songs mix original tunes with covers of Donovan, Tim Hardin, Hoyt Axton, Kaleidoscope, and Carole King. There's little to criticize, but it lacks the innovative spark that characterizes the best folk-rock of the time. *—Richie Unterberger*

Of Horses, Kids and Forgotten Women / 1968 / Capitol ✦✦✦✦✦

Future Flying Burrito Brother/Eagle Bernie Leadon replaced Rick Cunha for the group's second and final album, which is actually a considerably more L.A. pop-flavored production than their debut. Country-seasoned folk-rock remains at the core of the group's sound, but producer Nik Venet provides occasional tasteful, psychedelic-tinged orchestral arrangements. The material—about half original—is fairly strong, especially their covers of Arlo Guthrie's "Highway in the Wind" and Jesse Lee Kincaid's "She Sang Hymns Out of Tune" (also covered by Harry Nilsson on his first album). The unquestioned highlight is Larry Murray's "Ode to a Tin Angel"; by far the group's most psychedelic slice of folk-rock, with its swimming strings, tripped-out lyrics, and sweet harmonies, it's also their most atypical track. A slicker, but better, album than their first effort. *—Richie Unterberger*

● **Now Is the Time for Hearts and Flowers/Of Horses, Kids and Forgotten Women** / Oct. 1995 / Edsel ✦✦✦✦✦

Edsel does '60s collectors a favor by combining both of Hearts & Flowers' hard-to-find LPs onto one compact disc, which puts the group's entire repertoire in one place. *—Richie Unterberger*

The Complete Hearts and Flowers / Jan. 7, 2003 / Collectors' Choice Music ✦✦✦✦✦

In 1967 and 1968, Hearts & Flowers stood at the intersection between folk, country, and rock. The band recorded two albums, *Now Is the Time for Hearts and Flowers* in 1967 and *Of Horses, Kids and Forgotten Women* in 1968, and then disappeared. *The Complete Hearts and Flowers* collects both of these albums and enough extras (13 songs) for another album. In 2003, over 30 years after these albums were recorded, it will surprise many listeners—who've never heard of the group—how well Hearts & Flowers' eclectic blend of California folk/country/rock has held up. Like the Dillards and the Byrds, one quickly notices the band's high-flown harmony and mixture of acoustic and electric instruments. While cuts like "Save Some Time" and Donovan's "Try for the Sun" show their folk revival roots, "Rain, Rain" takes a psychedelic turn and "The View From Ward 3" adds a touch of country. The straight production of the early material expands to tasteful string arrangements on the second album. This leads to a dreamy take on "Second-Hand Sundown Queen" and trippy pop fare like "She Sang Hymns out of Tune." The extra material comes from several scattered sessions, and by and large delves more deeply into country-rock. These bonus tracks hold up well to the officially released material, sounding a lot like a lost album. *The Complete Hearts and Flowers* offers a pleasing musical time capsule to the fertile L.A. scene in the late '60s. *—Ronnie D. Lankford Jr.*

Bobby Helms

b. Aug. 15, 1933, Bloomington, IN, **d.** Jun. 19, 1997

Vocals, Guitar / Rock & Roll, Traditional Country, Country-Pop, Nashville Sound/ Countrypolitan

Though his name is unfamiliar to most, Bobby Helms rules the airwaves every year around December 25th. His single "Jingle Bell Rock" first became a hit in 1957, and it reappeared on the charts four of the following five years to become an all-time Christmas classic. Before he was pigeonholed, though, Helms had a successful country career with two number-one hits to his credit. Born on August 15, 1933, in Bloomington, IN, Helms first performed on his father Fred's Monroe County Jamboree, singing while brother Freddie played guitar. The Helms Brothers, as they were billed, became a regional attraction. Bobby later cut a single called "Tennessee Rock and Roll," but then returned to Bloomington to appear on the *Hayloft Frolic* television show. While on the program, he was encouraged to go to Nashville to sing background vocals on an Ernest Tubb session. Tubb recommended him to Decca Records, and the label signed him in 1956. His debut single, "Fraulein," initially flopped in January 1957 but then hit number one on the country chart in April. (The song also hit the pop Top 40 in July of 1957.) In October, Helms released another number one, "My Special Angel," which stayed four weeks at the top and crossed over to number-seven pop.

Helms' next recording was "Jingle Bell Rock"; though Decca released it only two days before Christmas 1957, the single still peaked at number six on the pop chart. Two 1958 singles—"Just a Little Lonesome" and "Jacqueline"—hit the country Top Ten but flopped elsewhere, though a reissue of "Jingle Bell Rock" made the pop Top 40. The country single "Lonely River Rhine" hit the Top 20 in 1960, but subsequent new material from Helms had little success. (Decca reissued his Christmas hit each year from 1960 to 1962 with diminishing returns.) Helms toured throughout the '60s and recorded two albums for Kapp in 1966, *I'm the Man* and *Sorry My Name Isn't Fred*—a nod either to brother Freddie or father Fred. Two years later, he released *All New Just for You* on the Little Darlin' label. Several singles placed modestly on the country charts during 1967-1968, including "He Thought He'd Die Laughing" and "So Long." The 1970 Certron single "Mary Goes 'Round" was his last hit, but Helms recorded *Pop-A-Billy* for MCA as late as 1983. *—John Bush*

To My Special Angel / 1957 / Decca ✦✦✦✦

The Best of Bobby Helms / 1963 / Columbia ✦✦✦✦

Bobby Helms Sings Fraulein / 1967 / Harmony ✦✦✦

All New Just for You / 1968 / Little Darlin' ✦✦✦

Pop-A-Billy / 1983 / MCA ♦♦♦

● **Fraulein: The Classic Years** / 1994 / Bear Family ♦♦♦♦♦
Fraulein: The Classic Years is a double-disc collection that contains all of Bobby Helms' Decca recordings, including "Fraulein," "My Special Angel," "Jingle Bell Rock," "Just A Little Lonesome," "Jacqueline," "New River Train" and "Lonely River Rhine." In addition to the well-known songs, *Fraulein* also includes several unreleased songs, alternate takes and failed attempts at crossover hits. While the packaging and sound is superb, the set is simply too extensive for anyone but dedicated fans. Casual fans will find cuts like "Captain Santa Claus" and "I Guess I'll Miss the Prom" extraneous, and they'd be right—it's the kind of material that only appeals to hardcore collectors, and *Fraulein* is designed for them. —*Stephen Thomas Erlewine*

Mike Henderson

b. Jul. 7, 1951, Yazoo City, MS
Guitar, Songwriter, Vocals, Slide Guitar / Blues-Rock, Contemporary Country
Guitarist, singer and songwriter Mike Henderson carved a niche for himself as a session guitarist over the years in the Nashville studio scene before he began recording under his own name with his own blues band, the Bluebloods. He began playing mandolin and moved from Missouri to Nashville. Trained as a mandolin player and flat-top guitarist, he soon found work in the Nashville studio scene as a slide guitarist. Henderson's albums on the Dead Reckoning label include *Edge of Night* (1996), *First Blood* (1996) and *Oakland Blues* (1998). Henderson uses a stellar lineup of supporting musicians on *First Blood*—Reese Wynans, Glenn Worf, and John Gardner—making it one of the best (and unfortunately most overlooked) releases of 1996. Collectively, these musicians have recorded and performed with John Hiatt, Emmylou Harris, Kevin Welch, Stevie Ray Vaughan, Mark Knopfler, Lonnie Mack, Aaron Neville, Larry Carlton, Johnny Cash, Al Kooper, Tracy Nelson, Rory Block, Sonny Burgess and Delbert McClinton.

The band got some radio attention on its second release for their song, "Pay Bo Diddley," a song that addressed the inequities in U.S. record royalty laws. Not surprisingly, *First Blood* was recorded in the studio in Nashville over two days, with almost all the songs being recorded on the first take with no overdubs. The band lends their own spin to classic blues material like Sonny Boy Williamson's "So Sad to Be Lonesome," J. B. Hutto's "Hip Shakin'" and Hound Dog Taylor's "Give Me Back My Wig." —*Richard Skelly*

Country Music Made Me Do It / Mar. 15, 1994 / RCA ♦♦♦♦
This is pure roadhouse honky tonk, stoked with bent notes, twisted humor, and a couple of tough, bittersweet ballads. —*Michael McCall*

Edge of Night / 1996 / Dead Reckoning ♦♦♦
Long one of Nashville's best-kept secrets, Mike Henderson's solo debut is all over the roots music map, flirting with Delta blues to honky-tonk to gospel; opening with "I Wouldn't Lay My Guitar Down," which sports a riff ripped from the pages of the Chuck Berry songbook, *Edge of Night* is a showcase for Henderson's blistering guitar work and soulful voice, and what the record lacks in innovation it makes up for in immediacy. —*Jason Ankeny*

First Blood / 1996 / Dead Reckoning ♦♦♦♦
First Blood harks back to the glory days of the '60s blues-rock boom—Mike Henderson and the Bluebloods' gritty sound is far from original, but years on the Nashville bar band circuit have honed their skills to a razor-sharp point, and the record is refreshingly raw and direct, distinguished by rock-solid musicianship. —*Jason Ankeny*

● **Thicker Than Water** / Jan. 12, 1999 / Dead Reckoning ♦♦♦♦
Nashville homeboy Mike Henderson belies his roadhouse roots with this crystalline studio blues record, singing, weirdly, as much like Ben Folds as he does like Stevie Ray Vaughan. This is a jubilant no-nonsense toe-tapping album, staffed by Henderson's ever-present entourage of excellent musicians, including keyboardist John Jarvis and Dead Reckoning label co-captain Glenn Worf on bass. A longtime mandolin and flat-pick guitar player, Henderson gets Jarvis into the Jerry Lee Lewis spirit with a demon-calling "Keep What You've Got" and the house-rockin' "Scared of that Child." As he does on his previous and under-aired album, *First Blood*, Henderson honors his idols Sonny Boy Williamson and Howlin' Wolf on the conga-thick "Mister Downchild" and classic down-home "My Country Sugar Mama." In addition to fine guitar covers, Henderson contributes a particularly clear vocal style with plenty of simultaneous character from both the blues and true-blue country music, which he began to cultivate in his early road days with the Snakes. It's a fine, versatile record for a good mood. —*Becky Byrkit*

Terri Hendrix

b. San Antonio, TX
Composer, Vocals, Guitar / Singer/Songwriter, Contemporary Folk, Alternative Country, Contemporary Country
Singer/songwriter Terri Hendrix was born and raised in San Antonio, TX. She left home to attend Hardin-Simmons University in Abelene on vocal scholarship before transferring to Southwest Texas State University in San Marcos, where she continues to reside. While there she came under the influence of a local philanthropist, Marion Williamson, who owned a property in Hye, TX, called Wilory Farm. In exchange for working on the farm, Hendrix received voice and guitar lessons from Williamson and developed a friendship with her that lasted until Williamson's death from cancer in 1997. To honor her, Hendrix changed the name of her record label from Tycoon Cowgirl Records to Wilory Records and issued an album entitled *Wilory Farm* in 1998. Her previous album, *Two Dollar Shoes* had received critical acclaim by that time, making her a local hit. Hendrix's versatile, folky style—which hangs elements of blues, pop, and traditional music on a country framework—was also featured on a 1999 live recording and 2000's *Wilory Farm* and *Places in Between*. —*Stacia Proefrock*

Terri Hendrix Live / Jul. 6, 1999 / Tycoon Cowgirl ♦♦♦

Wilory Farm / Mar. 11, 2000 / Orchard ♦♦

Places in Between / May 23, 2000 / Wilory ♦♦♦

● **The Ring** / 2002 / Wilory ♦♦♦
While the dusty Texas landscape hardly seems like fertile soil, it nonetheless produces more singer/songwriters per acre than any state besides Massachusetts. The difficulty is to stand out in the crowd. Terri Hendrix makes her latest effort to stand out on *The Ring*, a 40-minute foray into love, relationships, and intergalactic space travel. A bouncy acoustic arrangement gets things off to a good start on "Goodbye Charlie Brown," a song that expresses hope in the face of the millennium and all the fears that came with it. This tune, along with "Spinning Off" and "Truth Is Strange," features Hendrix's attractive and confident vocals against a rich musical backdrop. While these songs work well, the material also calls to mind a number of other singer/songwriters. On a track like "From Another Planet," however, with a barrage of words and a jazzy structure, and "Nightwolves," with its half-sung, half-spoken lyric, she offers something completely different. In fact, on "From Another Planet" Hendrix comes into her own, presenting an exciting, in-your-face vocal with a fun lyric. Even on the somewhat-predictable country romp "I Found the Lions," Hendrix uses a word rap in the middle of song to transform the piece into something original. Even when she doesn't throw in a little something extra, good taste dominates the arrangements and production, creating a good-sounding album. With its tuneful songs and distinctive elements, *The Ring* should make Hendrix conspicuous among her Texas peers. —*Ronnie D. Lankford Jr.*

Don Henry

Guitar / Contemporary Country, Singer/Songwriter
Don Henry came to prominence when Kathy Mattea's version of "Where've You Been" (co-written with Mattea's husband Jon Vezner) won every award in sight in 1990 and 1991. Henry grew up in suburban San Jose, CA, and moved to Nashville in 1979, where he spent four years copying tapes for publisher Tree International (now Sony/Tree) and then became a staff songwriter there. He wrote tunes for Mattea, John Conlee, T. G. Sheppard, and Conway Twitty and won Tree's Writer of the Year award in 1990 before recording his first album. —*Brian Mansfield*

Wild in the Backyard / 1991 / Epic ♦♦♦♦♦
Henry's debut album can only be classified country because of its high moral sense (which it actually gets from folk) and from the styles of the session players. With its malls and Mercedes, *Wild in the Backyard* isn't country—it's suburban. Henry's a singer/songwriter capable of drama and humor within the same song. But his real strength is his ability to create honest humanity, a trait equally present in "Harley," about a boy named after a chopper, and "Half a Heart," a touching tale of unfulfilled promise. —*Brian Mansfield*

Ty Herndon

b. Butler, AL
Vocals / Contemporary Country, New Traditionalist
Like many new country singers of the mid-'90s, Ty Herndon fused neo-traditionalist country with a slick, rock-oriented sense of style and production. Like many of his contemporaries, his blend of genres proved commercially successful, as his first album became one of the biggest hits of 1995. Herndon was a little wilder, at least off the stage, than many of his peers, but his records had a down-to-earth sense of sentimentality that initially gave him a broad fan base. Born and raised in Butler, AL, Herndon became involved in music as he was growing up. He sang gospel music and learned how to play piano. After he graduated from high-school, he moved to Nashville. Initially, he had difficult time gaining a foothold in the music industry, spending ten years without making any real headway. Herndon left the Music City and headed to Texas, where he began slogging it out in local honky tonks, developing a dedicated following of fans. In 1993, he won the Texas Entertainer of the Year. Later that year, he signed to Epic Records.

Herndon's first single, "What Mattered Most," hit number one in the spring of 1995. An album of the same name was released in April and became a Top Ten country hit. The second single, "I Want My Goodbye Back," became a number-seven hit. Seemingly, the world was in his hands, but his first year of stardom was a difficult one, as he was arrested for drug possession on June 13, 1995, in Fort Worth, TX. Nevertheless, the arrest didn't halt his career. The third single, "Heart Half Empty," was a hit, and Herndon's second album, *Living in a Moment*, debuted at number six upon its summer 1996 release. *Big Hopes* followed two years later, and in 1999 Herndon resurfaced with *Steam*. —*Stephen Thomas Erlewine*

What Mattered Most / Apr. 18, 1995 / Epic ♦♦♦♦

Living in a Moment / Aug. 13, 1996 / Epic ♦♦♦
Although he is in fine voice throughout the album, Ty Herndon's *Living in a Moment* is bogged down by mediocre material that fails to given him a proper showcase for his talents. Herndon doesn't write his own material, which might not necessarily be a bad thing—after all, hundreds of country singers don't write their own songs—but he doesn't have the best ear for selecting songs. When he does have a strong song—like the title track or "Don't Tell Mama"—he sounds terrific, but otherwise Herndon simply sounds adequate. Furthermore, on the undistinguished numbers, the production sounds generic and canned, which also hurts the record. Although Herndon still shows promise, it's hard to avoid that *Living in a Moment* sounds like a sophomore slump. —*Thom Owens*

Big Hopes / May 26, 1998 / Epic ♦♦♦
Like its predecessor *Living in a Moment*, Ty Herndon's third album *Big Hopes* comes as close to MOR rock and pop as it does to country. Beneath the glossy production, the music has subtle country roots, but often Herndon is closer to Don Henley than Haggard. That may upset some purists, but by this point in his career, anyone interested in Herndon should know he isn't pure country. Those fans should be pleased by some of the cuts on this disc—"A Man Holdin' On (To a Woman Lettin' Go)" is a good ballad, and "The Only

Way I Know" is better, and "Hands of a Working Man" are about as gritty as Herndon gets—but they may be dismayed that the filler once again slightly outweighs the good stuff. —*Thom Owens*

Steam / Nov. 2, 1999 / Epic ✦✦✦
A bit of a departure from his previous work, *Steam* is an appealing collection of songs from a man who wanted to make "feel-good music." And feel good we do with suggestive lyrics like, "Tonight when we get together, we're gonna make some steam" from the album's title song or "My heart stops when you touch me" from the uptempo "A Love Like That." With a new production team in tow, Herndon has played a bigger part in selecting the album's songs, which have a spiritual undertone, and it's clear he sings from the heart, as he always has. He includes a fan favorite from his live show, the sexy remake of Joe Cocker's "You Can Leave Your Hat On." This fourth album is a step in the right direction for an artist whose career boasts two gold albums and three number-one singles. —*Maria Konicki Dinoia*

● **This Is Ty Herndon: Greatest Hits** / Mar. 26, 2002 / Sony ✦✦✦✦
Although Epic's 2002 compilation *This Is Ty Herndon: Greatest Hits* is a little short at 13 tracks, it does contain most of the contemporary country crooner's biggest hits, from his debut hit "What Mattered Most" through "Steam." The album isn't sequenced chronologically, which may be a problem for some listeners, but the end result has Herndon at his best, making it a nice summary and introduction. —*Stephen Thomas Erlewine*

Caroline Herring

Vocals, Composer / Contemporary Bluegrass, New Acoustic, Contemporary Singer/Songwriter, Bluegrass

Singer/songwriter Caroline Herring grew up in Mississippi, but made a name for herself in Austin, TX, where she began lighting up the music scene. Her debut album, *Twilight*, released toward the end of 2001, earned her Best New Artist honors in the *Austin American-Statesman*. In a town stocked with rookie musical talent, she also took home the same title at the *Austin Chronicle*-sponsored Austin Music Awards (held during the annual South by Southwest festival).

Herring attended Ole Miss and, upon graduation, hooked up with the Oxford, MS, bluegrass outfit the Sincere Ramblers, in which she sang and played guitar and mandolin. During the '90s, the Ramblers hosted the local *Thackeray Mountain Radio Show*, which was broadcast from a used bookstore. Through her involvement with these ventures, Herring was able to meet and play with such Americana notables as Gillian Welch, Peter Rowan, the Bottle Rockets, and Blue Mountain. Herring moved to Austin to pursue a doctorate in American Studies in 1999. A year full of frequent performances with Billy & Bryn Bright (who had played with Rowan in the Texas Trio) led to a deal with Houston's Blue Corn Records, which released *Twilight*. Rowan and veteran player Lloyd Maines appear on the album. —*Erik Hage*

Twilight / Oct. 30, 2001 / Blue Corn Music ✦✦✦✦
There's a moment on the third track of *Twilight* when the listener realizes he or she's listening to something special. "Devil Made a Mess," in fact, has just about everything that the average country hit doesn't: It's tuneful, has a well-crafted lyric, and the singer never overdoes the vocals. Caroline Herring is joined by several great musicians, including steel player Lloyd Maines, fiddler Eamon McLoughlin, and, on several cuts, newgrass luminary Peter Rowan. Whether singing country or folk, Herring seems determined to offer discerning versions of her self-penned material. Her penetrating vocals, deep and rich, deliver the emotional goods on "Standing in the Water" and "Delta Highway." The arrangements and production go a long way toward showing this material in the best light. No more than a guitar and voice are needed to deliver the simple "Whippoorwill," while a fiddle and pedal steel embellish the rolling "Learning to Drive." Call it country-folk. Also call it pretty darn impressive, because *Twilight* is Herring's debut. The album winds up with a cover of "Wreck on the Highway," a particularly gruesome religious song, with whisky, blood, and glass all over the highway, that perfectly captures the spirit of older country music. This is simple, honest music that is occasionally referred to as "authentic," meaning, sadly, that the local country station will probably not play it. Luckily, one can just go out and buy a copy. *Twilight* will please fans of classic country and it shouldn't be missed. —*Ronnie D. Lankford Jr.*

John Hiatt

b. 1952, Indianapolis, IN

Guitar, Piano, Vocals, Slide Guitar / Country-Rock, Singer/Songwriter, Americana, Heartland Rock, College Rock, Roots Rock, New Wave

John Hiatt's sales have never quite matched his reputation. Hiatt's songs were covered successfully by everyone from Bonnie Raitt, Ronnie Milsap, and Dr. Feelgood to Iggy Pop, Three Dog Night, and the Neville Brothers, yet it took him 13 years to reach the charts himself. Of course, it nearly took him that long to find his own style. Hiatt began his solo career in 1974, and over the next decade he ran through a number of different styles from rock & roll to new wave pop before he finally settled on a rootsy fusion of rock & roll, country, blues, and folk with his 1987 album *Bring the Family*. Though the album didn't set the charts on fire, it became his first album to reach the charts, and several of the songs on the record became hits for other artists, including Raitt and Milsap. Following its success, Hiatt became a reliable hit songwriter for other artists, and he developed a strong cult following that continued to gain strength into the mid-'90s.

While he was growing up in his hometown of Indianapolis, IN, John Hiatt played in a number of garage bands. Initially, he was inspired by the Rolling Stones and Bob Dylan, and the music of those two artists would echo strongly throughout his work. Out of all the bar bands he played with in the late '60s, a group called the White Ducks was the one that received the most attention. Following his high-school graduation, he moved to Nashville at the age of 18, where he landed a job as a songwriter for Tree Publishing. For the next several years, he wrote and performed at local clubs and hotels. Within a few years, his

songs were being recorded by several different artists, including Conway Twitty, Tracy Nelson, and Three Dog Night, who took Hiatt's "Sure as I'm Sittin' Here" to number 16 in the summer of 1974. Eventually, his manager secured him an audition at Epic Records, and the label signed him in 1974, releasing his debut album, *Hangin' Around the Observatory*, later that year. Despite their critical acclaim, neither *Hangin' Around the Observatory* nor its 1975 follow-up *Overcoats* sold many copies, and he was dropped by the label. By the end of the year, Tree Publishing had let him go as well.

Following his failure in Nashville, Hiatt moved out to California. By the summer of 1978 he had settled in Los Angeles, where began playing in clubs, opening for folk musicians including Leo Kottke. With Kottke's assistance, Hiatt hired a new manager, Denny Bruce, who helped him secure a record contract with MCA Records. *Slug Line*, his first record for MCA, was released in the summer of 1979. Where his first two records were straight-ahead rock & roll and folk-rock, *Slug Line* was in the new wave vein of angry English singer/songwriters like Elvis Costello, Graham Parker, and Joe Jackson, as if Hiatt was vying for the role of the American angry young man. The new approach earned some strong reviews, yet it failed to generate any sales. *Two Bit Monsters*, his second MCA album, faced the same situation. Although it was well-received critically upon its 1980 release, it made no impression on the charts, and the label dropped him.

Apart from working on *Two Bit Monsters*, Hiatt spent most of 1980 as a member of Ry Cooder's backing band, playing rhythm guitar on the *Borderline* album and touring with the guitarist. Hiatt stayed with Cooder throughout 1981, signing a new contract with Geffen Records by the end of the year. Produced by Tony Visconti (David Bowie, T. Rex), his Geffen debut *All of a Sudden* was released in 1982, followed by the Nick Lowe/Scott Matthews & Ron Nagel-produced *Riding With the King* in 1983. As with his previous records for Epic and MCA, neither of his first two Geffen releases sold well. By this time, Hiatt's personal life was beginning to spin out of control as he was sinking deep into alcoholism. Around the time he completed 1985's *Warming Up to the Ice Age*, his second wife committed suicide. Following the release of *Warming Up to the Ice Age*, Hiatt was dropped by Geffen. By the end of 1985, he had entered a rehabilitation program. During 1986, he remarried and signed a new deal with A&M Records.

For his A&M debut, Hiatt assembled a small band comprised of his former associates Ry Cooder (guitar), Nick Lowe (bass), and Jim Keltner (drums). Recorded over the course of a handful of days, the resulting album, *Bring the Family*, had a direct, stripped-down rootsy sound that differed greatly from his earlier albums. Upon its summer 1987 release, *Bring the Family* received the best reviews of his career and, for once, the reviews began to pay off, as the album turned into a cult hit, peaking at 107 on the U.S. charts; it was his first charting album. Hiatt attempted to record a follow-up with Cooder, Lowe, and Keltner, but the musicians failed to agree on the financial terms for the sessions. Undaunted, he recorded an album with John Doe, David Lindley, and Dave Mattacks, but he scrapped the completed project, deciding that the result was too forced. Hiatt's final attempt at recording the follow-up to *Bring the Family* was orchestrated by veteran producer Glyn Johns, who had him record with his touring band, the Goners. Despite all of the behind-the-scenes troubles behind its recording, the follow-up album, *Slow Turning*, actually appeared rather quickly, appearing in the summer of 1988.

Slow Turning, like *Bring the Family* before it, received nearly unanimous positive reviews and it was fairly well-received commercially, spending 31 weeks on the U.S. charts and peaking at 98. Within the next year, Hiatt successfully toured throughout America and Europe, strengthening his fan base along the way. Inspired by the success of Hiatt's two A&M albums, Geffen released the compilation *Y'all Caught? The Ones That Got Away 1979-1985* in 1989. That same year, other artists began digging through Hiatt's catalog of songs, most notably Bonnie Raitt, who covered "Thing Called Love" for her multi-platinum comeback album, *Nick of Time*.

In 1990, Hiatt returned with *Stolen Moments*, which was nearly as successful as *Slow Turning*, both critically and commercially. "Bring Back Your Love to Me," an album track from *Stolen Moments* that was also recorded by Earl Thomas Conley, won BMI's 1991 Country Music Award. By the time "Bring Back Your Love to Me" won that award, it had become a standard practice for artists to cover Hiatt's songs, as artists as diverse as Bob Dylan, Ronnie Milsap, Suzy Bogguss, and Iggy Pop all covered his songs in the early '90s. In 1993, Rhino Records released *Love Gets Strange: The Songs of John Hiatt*, which collected many of the cover versions that were recorded during the '80s and '90s. During 1991, the group that recorded *Bring the Family*—Hiatt, Cooder, Lowe, and Keltner—re-formed as a band called Little Village, releasing their eponymous debut in early 1992. Based on the success of *Bring the Family* and Hiatt's A&M albums, expectations for Little Village were quite high; yet the record and its supporting tour were considered a major disappointment. Later, the individual members would agree that the band was a failure, mainly due to conflicting egos.

Hiatt decided to back away from the superstar nature of Little Village for his next album, 1993's *Perfectly Good Guitar*. Recorded in just two weeks with a backing band comprised of members of alternative rock bands School of Fish and Wire Train, the album was looser than any record since *Bring the Family*, but it didn't quite have the staying power of its two predecessors, spending only 11 weeks on the charts and peaking at number 47. The following year, he released his first live album, *Hiatt Comes Alive at Budokan?* Hiatt left A&M Records after the release of the record, signing with Capitol Records the following year. *Walk On*, Hiatt's first Capitol album, was recorded during his supporting tour for *Perfectly Good Guitar* and featured guest appearances by the Jayhawks and Bonnie Raitt. *Walk On* entered the charts at 48, but slipped off the charts in nine weeks, indicating that his audience had settled into a dedicated cult following. Fittingly, after 1997's *Little Head* quickly came and went in the marketplace, Hiatt parted ways with Capitol, and his next album, 2000's *Crossing Muddy Waters* was released on the established independent imprint Vanguard Records. After a second album with Vanguard, *The Tiki Bar Is Open*, Hiatt aligned himself with another independent label, New West, for the release of his 2003 set *Beneath This Gruff Exterior*. —*Stephen Thomas Erlewine*

Hangin' Around the Observatory / 1974 / Epic ✦✦✦
John Hiatt mixed pop, folk, rock, R&B, country, and gospel on his debut album, immediately becoming an uncategorizable (and thus uncommercial) entity. Although this album

was cut in Nashville, it owes more to Van Morrison than it does to Conway Twitty, and like the Belfast bluesman, Indianian Hiatt came to his influences somewhat secondhand, however sincerely he evoked them. What he really was, of course, was a singer/songwriter, albeit not in a style easily recognizable in 1974. The title indicates his position: Hiatt's songs show him an acute observer. But the performances require him to dig in, and although he does so with alacrity, the result is too diffuse. Nevertheless, Hiatt earned critical kudos for this album, and Three Dog Night (who knew good songwriting when they heard it) covered "Sure As I'm Sittin' Here," getting a Top 40 single out of it. *—William Ruhlmann*

Overcoats / 1975 / Epic ✦✦
John Hiatt is better at imitating Howlin' Wolf than he is James Taylor, and that he tries both here as well as Bob Dylan and Ben E. King is some indication of his ambition, if not his accomplishment. Conversely, be began to become more himself on his second album, at least on such songs as "I'm Tired of Your Stuff" and "I Killed an Ant With My Guitar," if not on the more lugubrious numbers, such as "Distance" or on the ones that sounded like publishing demos for a more popular singer, such as "Down Home." *—William Ruhlmann*

Slug Line / 1979 / Universal Special Products ✦✦✦
Conventional wisdom at the time was that MCA Records had signed John Hiatt (who had languished without a record contract for four years) with the idea that he would be their Elvis Costello—a singer/songwriter in the fashionable punk/new wave style. Certainly, Hiatt has stripped down and roughed up from his Epic records here, fronting a straight-ahead guitar rock band (that was capable, of course, of playing the obligatory reggae number), eschewing the stylistic diversity he reveled in before, and throwing out snappy, aphoristic lyrics in a highly processed voice. None of this quite turns him into Elvis Costello, although the mean streak he reveals would serve him well later. *—William Ruhlmann*

Two Bit Monsters / 1980 / MCA ✦✦✦
At the time of its release, *Two Bit Monsters* was perceived by critics who had caught up with John Hiatt on *Slug Line* as a less impressive follow-up to that record. In retrospect, it may be the better of the two albums, boasting an even more simplified musical approach and such notable songs (and future Rosanne Cash covers) as "Pink Bedroom" and "It Hasn't Happened Yet." Hiatt here was starting to emerge from the "new Elvis Costello" tag that had been affixed to him with *Slug Line*, but his reviewers, however well-meaning, seemed determined to keep him in that category. (In any case, record buyers were paying little attention—*Slug Line* was Hiatt's fourth straight album to miss the charts, and MCA dropped him as Epic had before.) *—William Ruhlmann*

All of a Sudden / 1982 / Geffen ✦✦✦
Hiatt's fifth album and his first for Geffen, his third record label, was given a somewhat inappropriate big-gloss production (all shimmering keyboards and filtered vocals) by Tony Visconti, known for his work with David Bowie. What counts with Hiatt, though, is the songs, and this album contains "I Look for Love," as knowing a dissection of the dating scene as anyone has yet attempted. *—William Ruhlmann*

Riding With the King / 1983 / Geffen ✦✦✦✦✦
John Hiatt's talents as a singer and songwriter have never been a matter of question, but for the longest time neither Hiatt nor his various record labels seemed to know what to do with him. Epic Records thought he was some sort of a folky, while MCA figured, since his songs were often cranky and angular, he could be sold as a skinny-tie new wave guy. Neither idea made much of a dent in the marketplace, and by the time Hiatt cut his second album for Geffen, *Riding With the King*, someone had come to the reasonable conclusion that Hiatt was a roots rocker at heart—but what *kind* of roots rocker? Side one of *Riding With the King* was produced by Ron Nagel and Scott Matthews of the Durocs, with Hiatt singing and playing guitar and Matthews handling everything else; the results have a thick, glossy retro-pop sound with a vague '50s undercurrent, complete with twinkly keyboards and honking saxophones. Side two was cut with Nick Lowe at the controls, featuring a band assembled from Lowe's touring unit (which at one time included Hiatt); these tunes are leaner and blusier, but also a bit more laid-back. While the two halves of the album have decidedly different sonic personalities, the consistent strength of Hiatt's witty, sweet-and-sour songwriting holds the album together, balancing punchy rockers like "Say It With Flowers" and "Falling Up" against soulful contemplations of the ups and downs of love, such as "She Loves the Jerk" and "You May Already Be a Winner." And while Hiatt's voice doesn't boast much range, he knows how to make the most of what he's got, and his vocals here sound a lot more subtle and incisive than the albums that preceded it. *Riding With the King* may be a bit mixed-up, but it was certainly a step in the right direction for Hiatt. *—Mark Deming*

Warming Up to the Ice Age / Jan. 1985 / Geffen ✦✦✦
Hiatt turned to veteran country producer Norbert Putnam here, but the result still rocked hard, with the occasional soul touch (notably those obnoxious thumb-struck basslines that are so prevalent in '80s music). Highlights here are "The Usual," later covered by Bob Dylan, and "She Said the Same Things to Me." There is also an odd duet with Elvis Costello on the old Spinners hit "Living a Little, Laughing a Little" (try and tell them apart). Critics' darling or not, when this album went into the tank, Geffen became the third label to drop Hiatt. *—William Ruhlmann*

● **Bring the Family** / May 1987 / A&M ✦✦✦✦✦
In 1987, John Hiatt, clean and sober and looking for an American record deal, was asked by an A&R man at a British label to name his dream band. After a little thought, Hiatt replied that if he had his druthers, he'd cut a record with Ry Cooder on guitar, Nick Lowe on bass, and Jim Keltner on drums. To Hiatt's surprise, he discovered all three were willing to work on his next album; Hiatt and his dream band went into an L.A. studio and knocked off *Bring the Family* in a mere four days, and the result was the best album of Hiatt's career. The musicians certainly make a difference here, generating a lean, smoky groove that's soulful and satisfying (Ry Cooder's guitar work is especially impressive, leaving no doubt of his singular gifts without ever overstepping its boundaries), but the real triumph here is Hiatt's songwriting. *Bring the Family* was recorded after a period of great personal turmoil for him, and for the most part the archly witty phrasemaker of his earlier albums was replaced by an wiser and more cautious writer who had a great deal to say about where life and love can take you. Hiatt had never written anything as nakedly confessional as "Tip of My Tongue" or "Learning How to Love You" before, and even straight-ahead R&B-style rockers like "Memphis in the Meantime" and "Thing Called Love" possessed a weight and resonance he never managed before. But *Bring the Family* isn't an album about tragedy, it's about responsibility and belatedly growing up, and it's appropriate that it was a band of seasoned veterans with their own stories to tell about life who helped Hiatt bring it across; it's a rich and satisfying slice of grown-up rock & roll. *—Mark Deming*

Slow Turning / 1988 / A&M ✦✦✦✦✦
After the success of *Bring the Family*, John Hiatt originally intended to reunite that album's all-star backing band (Ry Cooder, Nick Lowe, and Jim Keltner) for a follow-up. Hiatt's "dream band" proved to be unavailable, and he ended up cutting *Slow Turning* with his road band, the Goners, but the finished product proves he remembered well the lessons learned from *Bring the Family*. *Slow Turning* is a lighter and wittier affair than *Bring the Family*; the outlaw rocker "Tennessee Plates" and its more subdued companion piece, "Trudy and Dave," are more rambunctious than anything on the previous album, and the tempos are sharper this time out, with a bit less blues and a touch more twang in the melodies. But *Slow Turning* is also an album of hard-won lessons about life and love, placing a subtle but pronounced emphasis on the nuts and bolts of family life with the mingled joys and annoyances of parenthood dominating both "Georgia Rae" and the title cut, and the newfound maturity that made *Bring the Family* so special is still very much in evidence. And while the Goners aren't quite up to the standards of the quartet that recorded *Bring the Family* (and who, pray tell, is?), they're still a stronger and more empathetic band than Hiatt usually had in the studio, with Sonny Landreth's guitar work a standout. Following the best album of your career is no easy task for most performers, but with *Slow Turning* John Hiatt made it clear that the excellence of *Bring the Family* was no fluke. *—Mark Deming*

Y' all Caught? The Ones That Got Away 1979–1985 / Sep. 1989 / Geffen ✦✦✦
Bypassing 1974's *Hanging Around the Observatory* and 1975's *Overcoats*, *Y'all Caught?* is still an enjoyable collection of John Hiatt's early-'80s material, taking some of the best tracks from albums such as *Slug Line*, *Two Bit Monsters*, and *Warming up to the Ice Age*. Hiatt's blues-based guitar playing and down-home songwriting wonderfully rises to the surface throughout these 13 songs, spotlighting his material before he took on a more commercial rock & roll sound. The rustic simplicity of songs such as "Love Like Blood" and "Pink Bedroom," the latter covered by Rosanne Cash, is helped along by Hiatt's countrified vocal yammering and the looseness of his guitar strumming. 1979's *Slug Line* is represented by the title track, as well as "Radio Girl" and the solemn-sounding "Washable Ink," eventually covered by the Neville Brothers. Slightly more poetic and intricate than Hiatt's usual work, these tracks signify a change in his style, with catchier hooks and a slant toward a more modern rock feel. *Riding With the King* spawned both the title track and "Love Like Blood," both with the help of musician/producer Nick Lowe. "Riding With the King" was redone superbly almost 17 years later by the tandem of B. B. King and Eric Clapton on their collaborated album. Hiatt's more radio-friendly persona begins to take shape on tunes like "She Said the Same Things to Me" and "The Crush" from *Warming Up to the Ice Age*, as his guitar playing and lyrical makeup tends to grow flashier, busier, and less laid-back than the material that made up most of his career to that point. In 1987, Hiatt released *Bring the Family*, one of his best albums, which was where he united blues and rock to perfection, thus starting the second part of his career with a string of successful albums. As far as compilations go, *Y'all Caught* is a friendly romp through Hiatt's early days and is good to have in the collection. *—Mike DeGagne*

Stolen Moments / Jun. 1990 / A&M ✦✦✦
John Hiatt's highest-charting album yet is a step down from the dizzy heights of *Bring the Family* and *Slow Turning*, as he abandons his more acid commentaries and turns in a self-deprecating set full of promises of reformation and celebrations of marriage and family life. But the observations remain acute, and Hiatt's singing (so much camouflaged in his early days) is becoming his secret weapon. *—William Ruhlmann*

Perfectly Good Guitar / Sep. 7, 1993 / A&M ✦✦✦
For all of his ability to rock out, John Hiatt's records usually have more of a soul and/or country feel to them, which makes 1993's *Perfectly Good Guitar* something of an anomaly: This is the most consistently rock & roll-oriented album of Hiatt's career. Produced by Matt Wallace (Replacements, Faith No More), who gives a Neil Young-style guitar crunch to most of the songs, *Perfectly Good Guitar* was a record almost tailor-made for the then-nascent AAA (adult album alternative) demographic. Unfortunately, Hiatt seems to borrow not only Young's guitar sound, but also his sloppy, inconsistent songwriting for this album. The title track is one of Hiatt's all-time best, using smashed guitars as a perfectly realized metaphor for abusive relationships and setting the impressive lyrics to the catchiest chorus of his entire career. But while the tender "Buffalo River Home" and "Blue Telescope" are equally fine, much of the rest of the record sounds hurried and unfocused. "The Wreck of the Barbie Ferrari" sadly fails to live up to its title, and the closing "Loving a Hurricane" takes the Neil Young comparisons right to the edge of outright plagiarism.

John Hiatt has released far worse albums than *Perfectly Good Guitar*, but given how terrific about a third of the songs are, this album's one of his more frustrating efforts. *—Stewart Mason*

Hiatt Comes Alive at Budokan? / Nov. 22, 1994 / A&M ✦✦✦
John Hiatt's first live album was recorded during a 1994 winter-spring tour of the U.S. (the title is a joke) and finds the singer/songwriter backed by the Guilty Dogs, a guitar-bass-drums trio. He doesn't need any more ammunition than that, not when he's got a set of 15 songs drawn from his last four critically acclaimed albums, including "Thing Called Love" and "Tennessee Plates." Hiatt gives his songs a rougher treatment than some of those who have covered them, his throaty voice giving even love songs like "Angel Eyes" an unsentimental force. In the absence of an A&M best-of, *Hiatt Comes Alive at Budokan?* makes a good sampler of his work, 1987-1993. *—William Ruhlmann*

Walk On / Oct. 24, 1995 / Capitol ✦✦✦
Walk On is a classic "road" album in the sense that its songs largely seem written to or about people who are not present, either because the singer is away from them, he is singing about the past, or they are dead. John Hiatt exploits the resulting feelings of longing, anger, and mourning inherent in that premise, sometimes, as in "I Can't Wait," singing about wanting to be back home, sometimes, as in the odd love song "Ethylene," wishing for a departed lover, sometimes, as in "Dust Down a Country Road," reflecting as in a dream on the past. He employs rustic nature imagery, but frequently for ominous effects rather than gentle ones, and he is supported by spare, guitar-dominated backup that is alternately soothing and disturbing. Hiatt's label debut for Capitol (though they didn't do much to promote it), *Walk On* is not among Hiatt's more consistent or more accessible works, but he remains a highly imaginative and craftsmanlike writer who can startle you. The raucous "Shredding the Document" is among the half-dozen best songs of the year, if not the decade. *—William Ruhlmann*

Living a Little, Laughing a Little / Jun. 4, 1996 / Raven ✦✦✦✦
Living a Little, Laughing a Little does a good job as an early-career summary, drawing material from each of his albums released from 1974 to 1985—*Hangin' Around the Observatory, Overcoats, Slug Line, Two Bit Monster, All of a Sudden, Riding With the King*, and *Warming Up to the Ice Ages*. For those who are only familiar with his critically acclaimed work from the late '80s on, this provides a introduction to the formative years and a fascinating look at an man finding his voice—from an average '70s-style singer/songwriter to a rocker à la Elvis Costello to the first hints of his better known, later rootsy incarnation. A 1985 interview and a track Hiatt contributed to the *Cruisin'* soundtrack have been added as bonus to those who already have the albums. *—Chris Woodstra*

Little Head / Jul. 1, 1997 / Capitol ✦✦
By attempting to loosen up on *Little Head*, John Hiatt only accentuates his songwriting slump. Hiatt tentatively backs away from pure Americana, trying to make the rhythms looser and the lyrics funnier. It's supposed to be a lighthearted record, but the humor is so labored and the music so forced that it largely falls flat. But the real problem is Hiatt's shockingly listless songwriting. Although he's recycled past ideas on *Perfectly Good Guitar* and *Walk On*, his craftsmanship made those two efforts at least marginally entertaining. On *Little Head*, his skill has abandoned him—there's no spark to the music, no bite to the lyrics, no hooks in the melodies. "Pirate Radio" comes close to rocking, and "Graduated" is an affecting ballad, yet they pale next to the finest moments not only on *Bring the Family* and *Slow Turning*, but also *Walk On*. Which means it's arguably his weakest album to date. *—Stephen Thomas Erlewine*

The Best of John Hiatt / Aug. 25, 1998 / Capitol ✦✦✦✦
John Hiatt finally achieved some sort of fame in 1987, when his comeback album *Bring the Family* sparked a career renaissance. For the next decade, his albums sold well and his songs were continually covered by other artists, all of which earned him acclaim as one of the finest songwriters of his era. Despite its title, *The Best of John Hiatt 1973-1998* is a chronicle of those successful ten years. Only two songs—"Riding With the King" and "Take Off Your Uniform"—date from before 1987, which means that the collection effectively sidesteps Hiatt's years of searching for a style; it chooses to ride with him once he settled on roots rock. Of course, that's where he did the bulk of his best work, and *The Best Of* does offer a good overview of his prime period. Since much of his best work was recorded for labels other than Capitol, the label releasing *The Best Of*, Hiatt entered the studio to record two new songs ("Love in Flames," "Don't Know Much About Love") and cut his first version of "Angel Eyes," the song he gave to Jeff Healey, who turned it into a hit in 1989. He also re-recorded "Have a Little Faith in Me" and "Drive South," two of his best songs from the late '80s. Although these new versions are OK, they don't compare with the originals and only hammer home the fact that this is merely an acceptable compilation, instead of the perfect one that it could have been. Nevertheless, it's a good sampler for the curious, and the hardcore fan will not be disappointed with the new material, even if they're frustrated that they have to purchase a whole new album to acquire it. *—Stephen Thomas Erlewine*

● **Greatest Hits: The A&M Years '87–'94** / Oct. 27, 1998 / A&M ✦✦✦✦✦
Two months after Capitol's *The Best of John Hiatt 1973-1998* hit the stores, A&M released *Greatest Hits: The A&M Years '87-'94*. It's hard to surmise what weird licensing agreements led to this release pattern, since the similarities will cause confusion even among dedicated fans, but there are notable differences between the two discs. Since Hiatt's albums for A&M in the late '80s were his creative peak, it's not surprising that *Greatest Hits*, which concentrates his A&M work, is a more consistent album than *The Best of John Hiatt*, which balances classic A&M cuts with two re-recorded songs, highlights from his two Capitol albums, and two new songs. Aside from the inexplicable omission of "Slow Turning" and one of his best rockers, *Greatest Hits* contains all the A&M songs that are on *The Best of John Hiatt* ("Thing Called Love," "Memphis in the Meantime," "Child of the Wild Blue Yonder," "Drive South," "Buffalo River Home," "Feels Like Rain," "Perfectly Good Guitar," "Tennessee Plates"), plus the original versions of "Drive South" and "Have a Little Faith in Me" (only available in butchered remakes on the Capitol disc), a live take of "Angel Eyes," and several fine numbers, such as "Thank You Girl," "Real Fine Love," "Paper Thin," "Lipstick Sunset," and "Through Your Hands." There are some excellent songs from *Bring the Family* and *Slow Turning* missing, but *Greatest Hits* remains the compilation to get for casual fans. *—Stephen Thomas Erlewine*

Rollin' into Memphis: Songs of John Hiatt / Aug. 22, 2000 / Telarc ✦✦✦
The variety of artists who have covered John Hiatt's songs is truly staggering. From Iggy Pop to Emmylou Harris, Hiatt's unpretentious Midwestern tunes filled with clever wordplay, nifty singalong melodies, and heartfelt stories seem to resonate with an astonishingly eclectic set of musicians. But the folk, country, and blues crowd like Buddy Guy, Rosanne Cash, and especially Bonnie Raitt have been the most commercially successful Hiatt interpreters, hence an entire album devoted to these genres is a logical, and even obvious, concept. This is not the first anthology of Hiatt covers; Rhino's 1993 *Love Gets Strange* got there first, but that was only a compilation of previously recorded tracks. *Rollin' Into Memphis*, with its title seemingly derived from "Memphis in the Meantime," oddly a song that does NOT appear here, is a well-meaning and generally successful attempt to mine the blues and folk roots of his music and breathe new life into these tunes with imaginative rearrangements from an intriguing assortment of players. The album benefits greatly from utilizing the same backing band on all tracks. Although the singers run the gamut from folk (Odetta, Patty Larkin, Chris Smither) to blues (Raful Neal, Colin Linden) and even to zydeco and Cajun (C. J. Chenier, Terrance Simien), the core group featuring guitarist G.E. Smith and keyboardist Anthony Geraci keeps the music in the same sweaty, swamp rock groove. Highlights are many with Irma Thomas blazing her way through a soulful "Old Habits Are Hard to Break," Kenny Neal's slow-boiling "Love Like Blood," one of Hiatt's best and least-known compositions, and Kris Wiley with James Cotton taking "Wrote It Down" to New Orleans with a subtly scorching harp-driven version that doesn't let up powered by Smith's revved-up guitar, stuttering and lurching though the song. Even the less successful tracks like Tab Benoit's "Feels Like Rain" where the second line beat doesn't mesh with the song's lyrics, Patty Larkin's unspectacular "Have a Little Faith in Me"—one of the only Hiatt pieces that has worn out its welcome—and Cliff Eberhardt's straight-ahead reading of "Back of My Mind" aren't failures. They're just not as compelling or interesting as the rest of the covers here. Hopefully this will be the beginning of a series of likeminded interpretations of John Hiatt songs. The concept is sensible, and Hiatt's catalog, filled with dozens of unheralded tunes, is ripe for the picking. *—Hal Horowitz*

Crossing Muddy Waters / Sep. 26, 2000 / Vanguard ✦✦✦
John Hiatt's 16th effort is a marked departure from his work of the previous 25 years, and a vast improvement over 1997's disappointing *Little Head*. Hiatt retrenched and recorded his first drummer-less, predominantly acoustic record for Vanguard. It's a sympathetic match and a smart move, since the company has a long, rich history working in the unplugged medium before it became trendy. The result is the most natural and relaxed John Hiatt album in years, and a welcome addition to his extensive catalog. With just a duo of acoustic multi-instrumentalists, Davey Faragher and David Immergluck (both longtime associates), Hiatt pulls out some of the most earnest, down-to-earth songs of his career. He sings like a man rejuvenated, totally at ease with his surroundings, and plays with the laid-back, homespun honesty that has infused his best work. Although some comical lyrical touches remain, the majority of the album is a sober reflection on lost love ("What Do We Do Now," the title track) and the resulting psychological scars. Hiatt's voice has never sounded better; its coarse edges sometimes straining for high notes works perfectly with this craggy, unpolished music. The mandolin is the most distinctive instrument here, and its brittle, trebly, crisp tone gives the disc an underlying tension, especially on the ballads that comprise the majority of the album. Heart-rending, sincere, stripped down yet multi-faceted, John Hiatt has taken a step forward by taking a small step back. Although not quite in a class with career highlights like *Bring the Family* or *Slow Turning*, *Crossing Muddy Waters* is a subtle treat and an album whose watercolor brush strokes paint a vibrant picture of stirring delicacy. *—Hal Horowitz*

Anthology / Aug. 7, 2001 / Hip-O ✦✦✦✦✦
As of its 2001 release, there are at least three other single-disc compilations of John Hiatt's prolific career available, but none truly does justice to his immense body of work. Until now. This intelligently collected, sequenced, and annotated double pack delivers 40 tracks covering 15 of Hiatt's albums from his inauspicious yet refreshingly naive debut (1974's *Hangin' Around the Observatory*) to 2000's all-acoustic *Crossing Muddy Waters*, a return of sorts to his rural roots. Fans may quibble with the song selection, lack of previously unreleased material, and the inclusion of only one rarity ("Spyboy," his Jack Nitzsche-produced contribution to the obscure *Cruising* soundtrack), but this is as close to a perfect summation of Hiatt's career through 2001 as one could hope for without expanding to the box set he probably deserves. Hip-O thoughtfully licenses tracks from Sony, Capitol, Reprise (for Little Village's "Don't Think About Her..."), and Vanguard, in addition to including hefty chunks of his defining A&M years as well as the more spotty yet essential MCA and Geffen work. The overall effect is staggering in its stylistic diversity and sheer volume of ruggedly melodic singer/songwriter tunes. Whether it's his vaguely new wave rockers like "Doll Hospital," country weepers such as "The Way We Make a Broken Heart," the twangy pop of "Memphis in the Meantime," heartfelt, emotionally tugging ballads like "Lipstick Sunset" and "Feels Like Rain," or the Stones-esque crunch of "Paper Thin," there are precious few clinkers here. Each disc maxes out at 78 minutes, the 16-page book is filled with an informative essay, quotes from the artist, and rare pictures (but surprisingly lacks specific track personnel, a major omission considering Hiatt has worked with a stellar assortment of talented musicians), and the 24-bit remastered sound

is crisp, lean, and clean. As of its 2001 release date, the modestly titled *Anthology* is the definitive portrait of one of America's most talented, respected, and eclectic songwriters. *—Hal Horowitz*

The Tiki Bar Is Open / Sep. 11, 2001 / Vanguard ✦✦✦✦
On a creative roll after 2000's acoustic *Crossing Muddy Waters*, John Hiatt returns rejuvenated as well as electric. Old backing band the Goners have returned for his 17th—and best—album in the 13 years that have passed since the same outfit accompanied him on 1988's classic *Slow Turning*. Unlike its intentionally cheesy tongue-in-cheek title, *Tiki Bar* is a keenly constructed collection of heartfelt, bluesy tunes that rock—and often rock hard—with tremendous soul. Subtle use of drum loops and the occasional overdub enhances, but doesn't update, Hiatt's roots approach. Like the Band, whose "The Weight" he evokes on "Hangin' Round Here," these songs seemingly spring from a bottomless well of melodies and hooks, all energized by his raw, throaty vocals. The famed Goners guitarist, Louisiana's Sonny Landreth, positively burns throughout, especially on slide, and the group consistently coalesces like Crazy Horse on a hot night. They follow their eclectic leader through waltzy ballads, folksy love songs, midtempo burners, and even an unusual album closing ten-minute psychedelic romp, "Farther Stars," that takes the Beatles' "Tomorrow Never Knows" to the Middle Eastern swamps. Far from winding down in his fifties, John Hiatt is releasing the most inspired work of his life. Fans will be thrilled that he has found his muse, and newcomers who start here will be elated to know there is more where this came from. Not quite as magical as his high-water mark, *Bring the Family*, this is still a superbly crafted disc whose songs quickly sink in and stay lodged in your brain. Come in and have a taste; the tiki bar is open. *—Hal Horowitz*

Beneath This Gruff Exterior / May 6, 2003 / New West ✦✦✦✦
While *Beneath This Gruff Exterior* is credited to John Hiatt & the Goners, a more appropriate designation might be "John Hiatt and Sonny Landreth"—hotshot guitarist Landreth, who has held down a longtime on-and-off tenure in Hiatt's road band, spreads his licks over every nook and cranny of this album, so much so that his guitar spends about as much time in the spotlight as Mr. Hiatt himself. With the guitars turned up and Hiatt willing to push the growl of his voice to the limit, *Beneath This Gruff Exterior* finds Hiatt in stripped-down and rockin' form, much more so than on the albums which immediately preceded it. The production (by Don Smith with Hiatt and the band) is simple and straightforward, sounding loose and live, with Hiatt willing to let a few minor vocal glitches slip into the final mix. In short, this is a John Hiatt rock & roll album, which means his more serious songs are put on hold and stuff like "How Bad's the Coffee" and "Almost Fed Up With the Blues" find their way onto disc. But as has long been the case, Hiatt's lighter stuff still packs more emotional heft than most songwriters you could mention (especially on "Missing Pieces" and "The Most Unoriginal Sin"), and if his voice sounds as if it's starting to fray a tiny bit, he can still belt it out pretty convincingly for a guy who's been making records since 1974. The vast majority of Hiatt's albums fall into one of two categories—brilliant and real good. *Beneath This Gruff Exterior* falls into the latter file, which means it isn't a revelation like *Two Bit Monsters* or *Bring the Family*, but it's got good songs sang by a great songwriter, and played by a rockin' little band with a real fine guitarist up front, and if that's not what you're looking for, you're probably not much on Hiatt anyway. *—Mark Deming*

Sara Hickman

b. Mar. 1, 1963, Jacksonville, NC
Guitar, Vocals / Folk-Pop, Singer/Songwriter, Country-Folk, Alternative Country, Contemporary Folk
Sara Hickman was born on March 1, 1963, in Jacksonville, NC, but was raised in Houston, TX. She launched her professional career at age 14 at a Houston Oilers party with just her guitar and voice. Through the remainder of her teenage years, Hickman performed at bank openings, weddings, and even psychiatric units. Following her graduation from the High School for Performing Arts in Houston, she went on to receive a bachelor of arts degree in painting from the University of North Texas. Hickman released her debut, *Equal Scary People*, in 1989, originally on the independent label Four Dots. Due to overwhelming positive response to the record, Hickman was signed to Elektra in 1989, and they reissued the album. In 1990, Hickman released her follow-up disc on Elektra, *Shortstop*, which yielded the adult contemporary hit "I Couldn't Help Myself." In 1994, after touring with Dan Fogelberg and Nanci Griffith, a third disc was delivered to Elektra called *Necessary Angels*. Unfortunately, Elektra refused to issue it. A dedicated group of Hickman fans raised the money so she could buy the tapes back from Elektra. She did, and it was eventually released on the indie label Discovery.

By 1997, Hickman had released three discs on Shanachie Records: *Misfits*, a collection of odds and ends, the Adrian Belew-produced *Two Kinds of Laughter* in 1998, and *Spiritual Appliances* in 2000. Hickman has also released numerous limited-edition discs and cassettes on her own Sleeveless label, including *This Christmas Wish*, *Faithful Heart*, an official bootleg (*Ready to Pop*), and her children's albums *Newborn* (1999) and the award-winning *Toddler* (2001). Another important aspect of Hickman's work is her concerts dedicated to numerous charities, addressing issues such as (but not limited to) abused and neglected children, breast cancer research, AIDS, women's issues, illiteracy, and the homeless. *—Al Campbell*

Equal Scary People / 1989 / Discoveries ✦✦✦
Her clever debut, it revealed her unusual slant on life—and the fact that she has more musical smarts than most Texas singer/songwriters. *—Michael McCall*

● **Shortstop** / 1990 / Elektra ✦✦✦✦✦
She's clearly enjoying herself, and so will the listener, though the cuteness sometimes becomes a crutch. *—Michael McCall*

Sara Hickman / 1993 / Asylum ✦✦✦

Necessary Angels / 1994 / Discovery ✦✦✦✦✦
An album worth fighting to get out, it's her boldest, most mature, and most musically sophisticated offering to date. *—Michael McCall*

Misfits / Mar. 18, 1997 / Shanachie ✦✦✦
Misfits is a collection of rarities and oddities that Sara Hickman has released over the years, including her concert staple "Dumptruck," and covers of "I Think I Love You" and "Zippity Doo-Da," and a recording she made when she just seven years old, as well as collaborations with Jackopierce, Brave Combo, and Freddie Jones. While this album is primarily of interest of hardcore fans, there are a number of wonderful gems here that should entertain even casual listeners. *—Thom Owens*

Two Kinds of Laughter / Mar. 17, 1998 / Shanachie ✦✦✦✦
Hickman creates an inviting tension in her songs, pitting unusual lyric lines against catchy melodies. That's why choosing Adrian Belew as her producer and co-conspirator on this disc is a stroke of genius. His off-kilter pop sensibility complements Hickman perfectly. The terrific touches, such as the toy soldier fanfare that opens "I Wear the Crown," add to the easy joy of the music rather than overpowering it. The fact that Hickman is a top-shelf singer and songwriter helps, too. *—Tim Sheridan*

Spiritual Appliances / Feb. 22, 2000 / Shanachie ✦✦✦
Sara Hickman's 2000 album *Spiritual Appliances* is her first turn as producer, and the resulting album is another solid addition to her catalog. Hickman's fans will enjoy observing the positive evolution of this lesser-known songwriter. *Spiritual Appliances* also offers as good a beginning point for new listeners as any of her albums. She has been compared to the likes of Shawn Colvin, but this album lacks a song as radio friendly as "Sunny Came Home" from *A Few Small Repairs*. That being said, standout tracks include the moody ballad "Moment of Grace"; the typically intricate and whimsical pop songs "Standing Ground" and "Life"; and the personal "Woman Waiting to Happen." A good find, but not the album to catapult Hickman into the mainstream. *—JT Griffith*

Dan Hicks

b. Dec. 9, 1941
Guitar, Vocals / Western Swing Revival, Rock & Roll, Progressive Country, Country-Rock
Throughout his decades-long career, Dan Hicks stood as one of contemporary music's true eccentrics. While steeped in folk, his acoustic sound knew few musical boundaries, drawing on country, call-and-response vocals, jazz phrasing, and no small amount of humor to create a distinctive, albeit sporadic, body of work which earned him a devoted cult following. Hicks was born December 9, 1941, to a military family then living in Arkansas, and grew up in California, where he was a drummer in a number of high-school bands. He attended college in San Francisco, where he switched to guitar and began playing folk music. He returned to the drums, however, when he joined the Charlatans, one of the Bay City's first psychedelic bands. Although the Charlatans were short-lived—they issued only one single during their existence—they proved influential throughout the San Francisco musical community and were one of the first acts to play the legendary *Family Dog*.

Hicks had formed the acoustic group Dan Hicks & His Hot Licks in 1968 as an opener for the Charlatans, but soon the new band became his primary project. After adding a pair of female backing vocalists—"the Lickettes"—the group issued its debut LP, *Original Recordings*, in 1969. After a pair of 1971 records, *Where's the Money?* and *Striking It Rich*, they issued 1973's *Last Train to Hicksville*, which proved to be the Hot Licks' most successful album yet. At the peak of the group's popularity, however, Hicks dissolved the band and did not resurface until 1978, releasing the solo LP *It Happened One Bite*, the soundtrack to an uncompleted feature by animator Ralph Bakshi. He then phased in and out of the music industry for more than a decade and did not issue another major recording until 1994's *Shootin' Straight*, a live recording cut with a new band, the Acoustic Warriors. In 2000, over two decades after the group's dissolution, Hicks re-formed the Hot Licks and issued *Beatin' the Heat*. *Alive and Lickin'* arrived a year later. *—Jason Ankeny*

Original Recordings / 1969 / Epic ✦✦✦
Sometimes this sextet spreads their sound so thin that they sound like the world's largest populated duo, and not every aspect of what made for an exotic, intriguing, or just plain freaky band in the late '60s still holds one's undivided attention years down the line. Nonetheless, leader Dan Hicks, later to dub himself an "acoustic music warrior," made a good case for himself on this, his debut recording as a bandleader and one that certainly helped put this band on the map, although at the time part of their popularity had to do with the wispy appearance of vocalists Sherry Snow and Christina Viola Gancher. Their contributions tend to sound weak upon repeated listening. Sometimes they are just plain out of tune with each other, a trait that one might forgive if their Western swing gambits paid off a little better. Violinist Sid Page plays just great on this record, though, and the efforts of bassist Jaime Leopold are in the right spot. The five-minute "I Scare Myself" is here in all its glory, one of this outfit's definite triumphs. The string players make a huge addition, but inevitably this is Hicks' show, with the leader often taking over half the rhythm section by overdubbing himself on drums. The presence of a dozen original tunes, all witty and stylistically expressive, and a few downright classics, speaks well for Hicks. Still, he doesn't seem to have figured out a good way to use his vocal sidekicks all the time, other than as scenery. *—Eugene Chadbourne*

Where's the Money? / 1971 / MCA ✦✦✦✦✦
Before they could release a second album of their patented good-time hippie acoustic swing, Hicks and his band parted company with Epic records. That their fresh start would be marked by the release of a live set may seem odd at first. But the album does in fact capture a certain intimacy missing from their studio debut. Songs that would remain staples of the Hot Licks repertoire for years to come are found in their most well-known versions here, including the title track, "I Feel Like Singing," "Shorty Falls in Love," and "By

Hook or By Crook." The between-song banter even stands up to repeated listenings. It's not often that can be said about a live recording. *—Brian Beatty*

Striking It Rich / 1972 / MCA ✦✦✦✦
Striking It Rich features 14 more sides of hipster acoustic swing from Hicks and his helpmates, including the fan favorites "I Scare Myself" and "Canned Music." The band's musicianship remains mostly on the mark, but there are elements of the album that go beyond kitsch and the humor here is considerably darker than in the past—perhaps early signs of fading inspiration? The jazz flourishes of "Flight of the Fly" are nice, but not enough to lift this album's darker spirits. "Moody Richard (The Innocent Bystander)" may be among the most well-known numbers on this album, but with its string arrangements and uncharacteristically slick production, it suggests the band wasn't always above playing the commercial game. Maybe the album's title was meant as more than just wishful thinking. *—Brian Beatty*

Last Train to Hicksville / 1973 / MCA ✦✦✦
Sometimes more of the best thing can become too much. If the train hasn't completely left the station, it certainly sounds as if Hicks and his band could have used a vacation before recording this album, or at least a return ticket to more familiar musical environs. Ambling spontaneity has been replaced by the rushed, nervous propulsion of "Lonely Madman" and the sour twang of "Payday Blues." Drums and steel guitar were never what this band needed, as evidenced by the simple, nostalgic cymbal shuffle of "My Old Timey Baby." Spiffed up to look a little too respectable, Hicks and company sound every bit as uncomfortable as a California hippie trapped in a Nebraska country & western bar. *—Brian Beatty*

Hey Good Lookin' / 1975 / Warner Bros. ✦✦✦✦
Hey Good Lookin' is an animated feature film by Ralph Bakshi—of *Fritz the Cat* and *Heavy Traffic* fame. Dan Hicks' involvement with the project began in 1974, shortly after the dissolution of his Hot Licks. Bakshi solicited the singer/songwriter to provide music for the soundtrack. After almost a year in delays, the film—which satirizes biker and gang movies of the '50s—ended up taking nearly eight years to complete. When eventually released in 1982, the film had been re-scored by pop/rock producer John Madara. So, where did the tracks Hicks created for the project end up? His then record company, Warner Bros., decided that since *Hey, Good Lookin'* had yet to be scheduled for release, they would revisit the recordings for a Dan Hicks solo album—which was humorously titled *It Happened One Bite*. As the music was cinematic in nature and origin, Hicks chose the title as a send-up of the 1934 Frank Capra film *It Happened One Night*. The spirit behind the sounds picks up right where the final Hot Licks album, *Last Train to Hicksville*, left off. Ever the master of timing and rhyming, Hicks unveils more than just a few minor classics on this disc. Among the most notable are the opening track, "Cruizin'," which features a bossa nova-influenced shuffle à la "Where's the Money," as well as "Crazy 'Cause He Is," with its agile tempo and lyrics that border on surrealistic. This is Dan Hicks at his *Mad Magazine* Dadaist best. Likewise, "Dizzy Dogs" is a slightly askew electric jug band instrumental that harks directly back to Hicks' days as a founding member of the psychedelic Charlatans. [In 2001, the Rhino Handmade Internet-only audio boutique reissued a *It Happened One Bite: Widescreen Edition*, including bonus material that consisted of two sessions made subsequent to the film recordings. The release is limited to an edition of 4,500.] *—Lindsay Planer*

● **It Happened One Bite** / 1978 / Warner Bros. ✦✦✦✦✦
A cherished rarity among even his most die-hard fans, *It Happened One Bite* finds Dan Hicks and company—not exactly his Hot Licks, but close enough for hipster folk swing—providing the soundtrack for a 1978 animated film set during the gangster '50s. Unfortunately, the cartoon in question, at least with Hicks' exceptional soundtrack for it, was shelved. A reworked version of the film eventually released in 1982 featured none of the tunes Hicks wrote and recorded. Too bad, too, because his 13 songs are all top-notch tomfoolery of the patented Hicks variety. Though a Warner Bros. album made a brief appearance on store shelves back in the days of vinyl records, U.S. consumers looking for it on CD had only the choice of a pricey Japanese import or going without. Enter Rhino Handmade. [The reissue label remedied the dilemma with a widescreen limited-edition CD pressing of 4,500 in late 2001. This disc includes the original album, plus an additional nine tunes (including the standard "It's Only a Paper Moon"). Available only from the Rhino Handmade Internet site.] *—Brian Beatty*

Rich & Happy in Hicksville / 1986 / See for Miles ✦✦✦

Dan Hicks & His Hot Licks / 1991 / Columbia Special Products ✦✦✦✦
This 1991 CD release contains *Original Recordings* (1969), which was Dan Hicks' initial solo effort as well as the debut of his "Hot Licks." Unlike the overamplified electric jug band music that the Charlatans had been creating during Hicks stint as their drummer and occasional vocalist, this new band performed a refreshing blend of jazz swing with country & western. Their understated performance style stood in stark contrast to the burgeoning heavy metal and acid rock that were *en vogue* as the '60s became the '70s. Featured on this album is a seminal version of the "Hot Licks" that were only together briefly. Included are John Weber (guitar) and Terry Wilson (drums) as well as vocalists Tina Viola Gancher and Sherry Snow. Both Sid Page (violin/vocals) and Jaime Leopold (acoustic bass) would remain with Hicks (guitar/vocals/spoken word) as core members of the band. Of the 11 original compositions on this disc, "How Can I Miss You When You Won't Go Away" followed Hicks from the Charlatans, while "Canned Music," "I Scare Myself," and "Shorty Falls in Love" would be slightly reworked for their inclusion on the upcoming long-players *Where's the Money?* and *Striking It Rich*, respectively. Perhaps because of Hicks' background as a drummer, his sense of timing is a key element to his deceptively complex melodies. Likewise, this has a great deal to do with the success of the call-and-response vocals between Hicks and the female background vocalists he would dub "the Lickettes." Within these pastoral melodies and slightly askew lyrics is the somewhat out of sync and acid-tinged "It's Bad Grammar, Baby." In retrospect, the prominently distorted acoustic guitar lead overwhelms the track—which would have otherwise fit nicely within the context of the remainder of the album. This might have had something to do with it being conspicuously left off the 2001 Sony/Legacy reissue *Canned Music: The Most of Dan Hicks & His Hot Licks*. Those who can locate a copy of these *Original Recordings* are urged to do so. For Hicks-ophiles or Dan-ophites, it is a vital entry into his canon. *—Lindsay Planer*

Shootin' Straight / 1994 / Private Music ✦✦✦✦
In an ideal world, Dan Hicks would be headlining huge sports arenas. But in the real world, someone that hard to categorize is a marketing person's nightmare. Is he Western swing, country-rock, folk, or rock & roll? Hicks is a variety of things. But his followers love him just the way he is; those are the people who will savor *Shootin' Straight*, which was recorded live at McCabe's Guitar Shop in Los Angeles in 1994. Backed by his Acoustic Warriors band, the singer/songwriter is totally uncompromising during his inspired set. Hicks is as humorous and eccentric as ever, and his McCabe's appearance is extremely difficult to categorize. The material owes a lot to pre-bebop jazz, but it also owes a lot to country, rock, folk, and blues. From a marketing standpoint, that's extremely frustrating—from the standpoint of Hicks' small but enthusiastic group of followers, that's what makes him special. If you're the sort of eclectic, adventurous listener who holds Django Reinhardt, Bob Wills, Hank Snow, Jerry Lee Lewis, and Pete Seeger in equally high regard, you can't help but admire the adventurous spirit that Hicks brings to McCabe's. Although excellent, *Shootin' Straight* isn't Hicks' most essential release. But it's an album that his confirmed fans will find to be consistently rewarding. *—Alex Henderson*

Moody Richard / 1995 / MCA ✦✦

● **Return to Hicksville: The Best of Dan Hicks & His Hot Licks—The Blue Thumb Years 1971–1973** / Jun. 17, 1997 / Hip-O ✦✦✦✦✦
Just where to place the free-range music of Dan Hicks & His Hot Licks (are they country? jazz? rock? Western swing? comedy?) has always been a nettlesome problem, confounding the public and hyphen-crazy critics alike. For Hicks and his all-acoustic band were certainly all of those genres and then some, a marvelous amalgam of American music with a large dollop of humor thrown in for good measure. Subtitled "The Blue Thumb Years, 1971-1973," this 16-track collection touches on all of the group's major stylistic bases and more, making this a greatest-hits album on a group who never really had a hit. Pulling half- dozen tracks from their debut album, *Where's the Money?* (the title track, "I Feel Like Singing," "Reelin' Down," "Dig a Little Deeper," "News From Up the Street," and "The Buzzard Was Their Friend"), seven tracks from *Striking It Rich* ("Canned Music," "Walkin' One and Only," "The Innocent Bystander," "I Scare Myself" (which later became a hit for techno rocker Thomas Dolby), the wry humor of "Presently in the Past," "You Gotta Believe," Maryann Price's sendup of "I'm an Old Cowhand (From the Rio Grande)"), and three from their swan-song album, *Last Train to Hicksville the Home of Happy Feet* ("My Old Timey Baby," "Sweetheart (Waitress in a Donut Shop)," and "Long Comma Viper"), this hits almost all the high spots with not a lick of filler anywhere to be found. The transfers to disc sound vivid and dimensional, and the liners by compilation producer and music historian Todd Everett are fun, provocative, and spot-on, getting into just what made this group so special. As all three of their albums are available on compact disc, this compilation makes an excellent first-purchase introduction to this band. *—Cub Koda*

Early Muses / Nov. 24, 1998 / Big Beat ✦✦✦✦✦
Unissued until 1998, these tracks were recorded in 1967 and 1968, serving as the missing link between Hicks' days in the Charlatans and his solo career. Thirteen of the 20 songs were recorded by Hicks in October 1967 (when he was still in the Charlatans) as a publishing demo album, produced by Nick Reynolds of the Kingston Trio; it was intended both to shop Hicks compositions to other artists, and to serve as an example of what he could be capable of as a solo artist. The sound on this disc (aside from a snatch of Hicks doing "Home on the Range" in 1953) is very good and clear, usually using accompaniment from other musicians; David LaFlamme, soon to form It's a Beautiful Day, plays violin on the Reynolds-produced numbers. Historical details out of the way, this is a fine disc on its own terms, not as psychedelically inclined as the Charlatans, and not as Western swing-oriented as his work with the Hot Licks. Like the Holy Modal Rounders and Norman Greenbaum (of Dr. West's Medicine Show & Junk Band), Hicks updated old-timey folk music with contemporary attitude and rock/psychedelic influences. He wasn't as weird as the Rounders or Greenbaum, but he had a similar off-kilter sense of humor and affinity for ticklish wordplay; he was also more melodic and accessible than either of those acts. *Early Hicks* has a few songs that went on to become some of the more popular items in his Hot Licks repertoire ("How Can I Miss You When You Won't Go Away?," "The Innocent Bystander," "Canned Music"), but most of the rest, which include some songs totally unavailable elsewhere, is well up to that standard. "Shall I Ask an Elf?" and "I've Got a Capo on My Brain" are good examples of his engaging screwball humor, with its bemused view of life as a gentle cosmic joke. Cuts like "The Gypsy's Secret," "He Don't Care" (with its unusual autoharp), and "The Innocent Bystander" illustrate his deft way with unconventional and attractive minor-key melodies that fork off in unexpected directions. Heartily recommended to those looking for '60s music combining folk, psychedelia, and witty songwriting. *—Richie Unterberger*

Beatin' the Heat / Aug. 29, 2000 / Hollywood ✦✦✦✦✦
He's never stopped playing live, yet Dan Hicks' first album in six years, and his only studio release since 1978's *It Happened One Bite*, has to be considered a comeback of sorts.

Interestingly, little has changed in the musician's idiosyncratic style that effortlessly meshes country, bluegrass, '40s pop, Western swing, folk, and even blues together to produce music completely unique unto itself. The proof of Hicks' low-key genius is that through his decades of making music, few have attempted to mimic his eclectic and often wacky approach. Stylish guest stars Rickie Lee Jones, Tom Waits, Elvis Costello, Bette Midler, and even guitar slinger Brian Setzer drop by to add color, but thankfully they never hog the spotlight from the self-effacing Hicks. Fiddle/mandolin player Sid Page is the only holdover from the original '70s Hot Licks, but not much has shifted in Hicks' rarefied world. His talk/sung/scatted vocals, bone-dry humor, as well as call and response from the Andrews Sisters-styled backing vocalists are in place, and the 15 tracks are among the best, most fully realized he's ever recorded. Intricate yet swinging, Hicks and his band sound loose and relaxed as if this was a jam session in his living room that was accidentally recorded. Song titles like "Don't Stop the Meter Mack," a song about stalking; "I've Got a Capo on My Brain," which is as loony as its name; and a remake of his most covered tune, "I Scare Myself" (with Jones on duet vocals), exhibit Hicks at his witty best, but everything here is classic Hot Licks. Even an occasional sample and subtle drum loops don't detract from the distinctively stylized slant. Even with the high-profile visitors it's unlikely to put him on the charts, but *Beatin' the Heat* is a glorious, superbly crafted return, and arguably the best album in Dan Hicks' slim catalog. It's a perfect introduction for newcomers and a wonderful treat for established fans wondering if Dan Hicks would ever release another album. —*Hal Horowitz*

The Canned Music: The Most of Dan Hicks & His Hot Licks / May 29, 2001 / Epic ✦✦✦
With nine of the 11 songs from Dan Hicks' debut album, 1969's *Original Recordings*, and seven previously unreleased songs recorded for an unissued second album, this has most but not all of the tracks Hicks did for Epic at the outset of his career. The *Original Recordings* material, though perhaps underproduced, remains a charming mix of Western swing, dryly comic lyrics, and pop-jazz female backup harmony vocals. Some of Hicks' best songs were done for that album (although some would be re-recorded slightly later for Blue Thumb), including "Canned Music," "How Can I Miss You," and "I Scare Myself." Fans who've been following Hicks for a while will be most interested in the seven previously unavailable cuts, which are certainly up to official-release standard. They're pretty much in the same vibe as the songs from the debut LP, perhaps a little tighter in arrangements and production, and not quite as off-the-wall word-wise (the stoner ode "He Don't Care" being an exception). Nice stuff, but it's curious that two songs ("It's Bad Grammar Baby" and "Shorty Falls in Love") from *Original Songs* were omitted, as there would have been plenty of space to accommodate them on this CD. —*Richie Unterberger*

Alive & Lickin' / Aug. 7, 2001 / Hollywood ✦✦✦✦
After the constant joy and flood of creativity Dan Hicks expressed in *Beatin' the Heat*, his previous release, it would be difficult to return with a stronger effort. This live set, recorded during the subsequent touring of *Beatin' the Heat*, doesn't quite hit you over the head with great new songs, but rather keeps you entertained with live versions of Hicks favorites like "Where the Money?" and "Shootin' Straight," as well as the gem "My Cello." The disc's greatest strength, though, comes between the songs, when Hicks' wacky personality shines. His song introductions are so entertaining in their own right that sometimes it almost sounds as if the music is a letdown. After the opening track, he sings a short version of "Don't Get Around Much Anymore" with twisted lyrics about missing the toilet and cleaning up with a toothbrush, "Don't Brush My Teeth Much Anymore." Later, before "How Can I Miss You When You Won't Go Away?," he jokes about how he's been performing the song for years. "This marks the four-billionth time I've done this one," he says as the audience erupts in laughter. His jokes aren't limited to between the songs, though. He also inserts silly but cool one-liners in between sung lines. But don't get the impression that the disc's only value comes in Hick's oddball banter. The music, like all his records with the Hot Licks, is played by top-notch instrumentalists, mixing equal parts Django-inspired jazz with jug band and folk traditions. —*Scott Cooper*

It Happened One Bite: Widescreen Edition / Jan. 12, 2002 / Rhino HandMade ✦✦✦✦✦
According to Hicks' eight-page "Memo From the Office of Dan Hicks" liner notes essay, the saga of the album began shortly after he'd disbanded the Hot Licks in 1974. The project commenced as Hicks began collaborating with motion picture animator Ralph Bakshi—of *Fritz the Cat* and *Heavy Traffic* fame—on a project titled *Hey Good Lookin'*. Initial sessions that incorporated a bevy of Los Angeles musicians and jazz heavyweights—including bop piano legend Lou Levy and bassist Lyle Ritz—proved fruitless, however. So a slightly reassembled version of the Hot Licks—including John Girton (guitars/vocals), Maryann Price (vocals), and Sid Page (violin)—was inaugurated for the project, which was eventually delivered to Warner Bros. in April of 1975. Fast-forward almost two years later and…no film, which inevitably means no soundtrack either. Hicks and the record company decided that since *Hey, Good Lookin'* was still not even scheduled for release, they would revisit the tapes, and voilà, *It Happened One Bite* was hatched. Incidentally, seeing as the music was cinematic in nature, Hicks chose the title as a send-up of the 1934 Frank Capra film *It Happened One Night*. The spirit behind the music picks up right where the final Hot Licks album, *Last Train to Hicksville*, left off. Ever the master of timing and rhyming, Hicks unveils more than just a few minor classics on this disc. The "Widescreen Edition" bonus material consists of two sessions made subsequent to the recording, but prior to the release of *It Happened One Bite* in 1978. The first three tracks are monophonic reference mixes of tunes not used, but recorded for *Hey Good Lookin'*—two of which are "slow versions" of pieces that ended up on the album. The final cache of tunes is from an extremely laid-back and self-produced session at the Sausalito, CA, Record Plant on June 11, 1976. It features five standards as well

as "Hummin' to Myself"—an original blues, highlighted by a duet with Maryann Price. There is likewise an additional track that was unable to fit onto this single-disc volume—which is already maxed out at nearly 79 minutes. Information on how to capture this cyber-Easter egg is available in the 20-page liner notes booklet. *It Happened One Bite: Widescreen Edition* is limited to an edition of 4,500 and is available as one of the final releases from the *RW Hand*-era Rhino HandMade audio boutique. It is truly a package fitting his honor and reign as curator of the Rhino HandMade Institute of Petromusicology. —*Lindsay Planer*

Highway 101

f. 1986, Los Angeles, CA
Group / Contemporary Country
One of the most popular country bands of the late '80s, Highway 101 boasted an influential country-rock sound that helped pave the way for the blockbuster superstars of the '90s. The group was fronted by singer/guitarist Paulette Carlson, a Minnesota native, and assembled by manager Chuck Morris in Los Angeles in 1986. Morris pulled together Jack Daniels (guitar), Curtis Stone (bass, guitar, mandolin), and drummer Cactus Moser, all of whom were seasoned session pros; Daniels and Stone had also worked together as the Lizards. Highway 101 signed with Warner Bros. and issued its self-titled debut in 1987. It was an immediate success, as the first two singles—"The Bed You Made for Me" and "Whiskey, if You Were a Woman"—shot into the country Top Five. The next two, "Somewhere Tonight" and "Cry, Cry, Cry," both went to number one, and seemingly overnight, the group members had become stars.

Their 1988 follow-up, *Highway 101, Vol. 2*, spawned another chart-topper in "(Do You Love Me) Just Say Yes," and three more Top Tens in "All the Reasons Why," "Setting Me Up," and "Honky Tonk Heart." Following 1989's *Paint the Town*, which contained one further chart-topper in "Who's Lonely Now," Carlson left the band for a solo career in 1990. She was replaced by Nikki Nelson, who debuted on 1991's *Bing Bang Boom*; however, despite some decent-sized hits, the new version of Highway 101 wasn't quite as commercially successful, and the band soon parted ways with Warner. They signed with Liberty for 1993's *The New Frontier*, but the album flopped, and Daniels subsequently left the group. He and Carlson temporarily returned to the fold for 1996's *Reunited*, released on the smaller Intersound label. Curtis Stone and Cactus Moser later formed a new version of Highway 101 with vocalist Chrislynn Lee and guitarist Charlie White, and recorded *Big Sky* for FreeFalls in 2000. White left in 2002 and was replaced by Justin Weaver. —*Steve Huey*

Highway 101 / 1987 / Warner Bros. ✦✦✦✦
The main thing that this country-rock quartet had going for it was lead singer Paulette Carlson, who approximated the throaty, torn vocal style of Stevie Nicks, but with a Southern accent. The group was heard best on its debut album, which included such characteristic hits as "Whiskey, If You Were a Woman" and "The Bed You Made for Me." —*William Ruhlmann*

Highway 101, Vol. 2 / 1988 / Curb ✦✦✦
Highway 101's second album followed the same rocking country formula that made their debut a success, but its best songs—"Setting Me Up" and "Honky Tonk Heart"—are as good as anything on the first album. —*Thom Owens*

Paint the Town / 1989 / Warner Bros. ✦✦✦
Highway 101 was beginning to show signs of stagnation on *Paint the Town*. Although there were still some good songs on it—particularly the number one single "Who's Lonely Now"—the quality of material wasn't as strong as their first two albums and the group was sounding tired, verging on the formulaic. —*Thom Owens*

● **Greatest Hits (1987–90)** / 1990 / Warner Bros. ✦✦✦✦
Country-rock band Highway 101 got off to a great start in the late '80s with several hits featuring the powerful voice of Paulette Carlson. Unfortunately, just as the band was enjoying its greatest success, Carlson and the band parted ways. By that time they had chalked up several number-one hits, "Somewhere Tonight," "(Do You Love Me) Just Say Yes," "Who's Lonely Now," and "Cry, Cry, Cry," all of which are included on this recommended *Greatest Hits (1987-90)* package. —*Al Campbell*

Bing Bang Boom / 1991 / Warner Bros. ✦✦
Bing Bang Boom is the first album Highway 101 recorded with vocalist Nikki Nelson. Although Nelson has an attractive voice, she couldn't fill Carlson's shoes. Furthermore, the band had trouble coming up with a consistently compelling material, apart from the hit title track, making *Bing Bang Boom* one of the weakest entries in the group's catalog. —*Thom Owens*

The New Frontier / Sep. 13, 1993 / Liberty ✦✦
On *New Frontier*, Highway 101 sounds like they're floundering. Not only did new vocalist Nikki Nelson not fit into the group particularly well, Jack Daniels left the band—as a result, the group sounds like half a band. Although "You Baby You" isn't bad, Highway 101 is clearly lacking inspiration throughout the album. —*Thom Owens*

Reunited / Feb. 27, 1996 / WillowTree ✦✦✦
Reunited was recorded around Highway 101's tenth anniversary. To celebrate, Paulette Carlson joined the band again and the difference is apparent. The band and Carlson need each other—they are more energetic and dynamic together than they are apart. Unfortunately, Highway 101 didn't create an album of all-new material—out of the 12 tracks, four are re-recordings of their biggest hits. These are fine, but they don't have the spark of the originals, nor do they have the charm of the new songs. Though it isn't as good as their first two albums, it is better than either of their Liberty albums. —*Thom Owens*

Big Sky / May 9, 2000 / FreeFalls ✦✦✦

The Highwaymen

f. 1985, Middletown, CT

Group / Traditional Country

Before rock & roll gave listeners the Traveling Wilburys, country music spawned the Highwaymen, a supergroup of mythic proportions that featured living legends Johnny Cash, Willie Nelson, Waylon Jennings, and Kris Kristofferson. The foursome had worked together in various combinations over the years, but teamed up under the Highwaymen umbrella in 1985. Their first single together, "Highwayman," topped the country charts that year and spawned an album of the same name on Columbia. The album also proved mightily popular, hitting number one on the country listings and producing a Top 20 follow-up single in a cover of Guy Clark's "Desperadoes Waiting for a Train." Afterwards, the members returned to their individual careers for a few years, but reconvened in 1990 to record a sequel, *Highwayman 2*. It reached number four on the country album charts and spun off the minor hit "Silver Stallion," but didn't cause quite the same stir overall as its predecessor. Another layoff followed, and when the Highwaymen returned for a third outing in 1995, they inked a new deal with Liberty/Capitol. *The Road Goes on Forever* was produced by Don Was, but proved a distinct commercial disappointment, and the group did not record again prior to Jennings' death in 2002. *—Steve Huey*

● **Highwayman** / 1985 / Columbia ✦✦✦✦

These old friends have appeared together in various combinations, but never as effectively as on the epic title song here, written by Jimmy Webb. And the rest of the record, including Guy Clark's "Desperados Waiting for a Train" and Woody Guthrie's "Deportee," lives up to the leadoff hit. *—William Ruhlmann*

Highwayman 2 / 1990 / Columbia ✦✦✦

Country music's version of the Traveling Wilburys, the Highwaymen's second album clocks in at just under a mere 33 minutes and covers little new territory for the group of country legends. Sadly, of the ten tracks, only six were penned by any of the members. Even the songs included are a little light for this group of country heavyweights, and the album suffers from an overall homogenous and dated 1980s studio sound. The opening track, "Silver Stallion," was the only minor hit from the album, though Cash, Nelson, and Kristofferson make solid contributions to the album. Overall, *Highwayman 2* features a decent set of rather uneventful songs, but only the most dedicated fan will find this album a necessity. *—Matt Fink*

Road Goes on Forever / 1995 / Liberty ✦✦✦

For their third album, *The Road Goes on Forever*, the Highwaymen hired Don Was to produce. Was had previously worked with every member of the group but Johnny Cash, so he was theoretically a natural choice and, on the surface, *The Road Goes on Forever* has all the trappings of being *the* classic Highwaymen album. It has great material, from standards like Dallas Frazier's "True Love Travels on a Gravel Road" to contemporary favorites by Steve Earle ("The Devil's Right Hand") and Billy Joe Shaver ("Live Forever") to new cuts from all four members. It has a crisp sound and a focused production, with fine performances from everyone involved. The problem is, the whole thing sounds too damn serious; Was and the Highwaymen may have all the right cards, but they don't know how to play them. Instead of capturing a kinetic energy or intense introspection, *The Road Goes on Forever* just sounds studious and over-labored, as if the group wanted to produce music that lived up to their mythological legacy, not the music itself. *—Stephen Thomas Erlewine*

Super Hits / Mar. 2, 1999 / Sony ✦✦✦

Willie Nelson, Johnny Cash, Waylon Jennings, and Kris Kristofferson released two albums together on Columbia Records, 1985's chart-topping *Highwayman* and 1990's *Highwayman 2*. (For the sake of convenience, the quartet itself was sometimes referred to as Highwayman or even the Highwaymen, though they were never actually billed as such.) Three songs from those albums reached the country charts, "Highwayman," "Desperados Waiting For a Train," and "Silver Stallion." So, one wishes a better title than *Super Hits* could have been used for this budget-priced ten-track compilation, which draws five tracks from each album. Nevertheless, the combination of the four country superstars remains amazingly comfortable, as they trade off vocals on songs such as Cash's "Big River" and even harmonize. The first album, which used standards, was superior to the second, for which new material was written, but many of the songs on the first album did not feature all four singers, so the balance of tracks from the two albums here is reasonable. *—William Ruhlmann*

Highwoods String Band

f. 1973, **db.** 1978

Group / Old-Timey, Traditional Country

Any time the word "revival" pops up in connection with a given style of music, it often seems to be the case that a certain tension develops between those who take an academic, preservationist approach, with recital-style performances, and those who seek to recapture the original spirit of the music as something that was done for the sheer joy of it. In the case of the resurgence of interest in the old-time string band music of the Appalachians that took place in the '70s, it would be unfair to say that even the most serious and academic of the folklorists and collectors weren't also having a good-time playing the music, but when it came to making sure everyone was having a good-time, there was nothing quite like seeing the Highwoods String Band. As banjo player Mac Benford liked to say, it was, "all about fun—fun for us and fun for our audiences."

Any discussion of the music scene in San Francisco during the late '60s certainly brings to mind images of the Grateful Dead, Jefferson Airplane, Santana, and many others, but a vibrant mix of many varieties of street music was also an integral part of that era in the Bay Area. Among the bands that eked out a living busking on the streets were All-Skate, a band that performed on stilts and that included fiddler Bob Potts; Dr. Humbead's New Tranquility String Band, whose banjo player was New Jersey native Benford; and the Busted Toe Mudthumpers, featuring fiddle and banjo ace Walt Koken, a New York native. When their respective bands dissolved at about the same time, the three of them came together as Fat City, specializing in driving fiddle-and-banjo tunes from the repertoires of such early country recording artists as the Skillet Lickers and the Georgia Yellow Hammers. Having two fiddles in the band was unusual enough, but the ability of Potts and Koken to play differing yet complementary styles made Fat City one of the more distinctive outfits in the Bay Area, and all three of them had wry, wisecracking stage personas that added much to the entertainment quotient.

Their profile outside California began to grow when they appeared at the Smithsonian Folk Life Festival in Washington, D.C., in 1971. When Koken returned to his Ithaca, NY, stomping grounds in 1972, Potts and Benford followed a short time later. The metamorphosis from Fat City to Highwoods String Band took place when they added a driving rhythm section to the band in the persons of guitarist Doug Dorschug and bassist Jenny Cleland. The guitar as rhythm backup had been a part of old-time music for decades, but as John Cohen of the New Lost City Ramblers would later note, Dorschug's playing often contained an element of ragtime that lent even more character to an already potent musical sound. Cleland's pulsing bass, on the other hand, was an almost radical departure from tradition after all. Bass fiddles weren't exactly something every Appalachian family regarded as a necessary part of their household décor. It all added up to a mix of attitude, showmanship, musicianship, and entertainment bang-for-the-buck that appealed strongly to the remnants of the '60s counterculture who had become jaded with rock and heavy metal.

As festivals like the Brandywine Mountain Music Convention began to spring up around the country, the Highwoods String Band became the marquee act for these events (or, they would have been if these events were the type that had marquees) for most of the '70s until road weariness and family responsibilities caused them to disband at the end of that decade. Benford formed the Backwoods Band and cut an album for Rounder Records before that band broke up in 1981. After heading up Mac Benford's Old Time Band for a few years, he formed the Woodshed All-Stars in 1990 and toured with them for most of the '90s. Walt Koken released a couple of solo banjo albums on Rounder in the early '90s before forming Mudthumper Music with Benford and releasing another solo album, *Finger Lakes Ramble*, in 1998. As of 1999, all five members of the Highwoods were still living in the Ithaca region and still playing together occasionally on an informal basis. Their legacy is that, more than any other band of their time, they were responsible for drawing a legion of new, young fans into old-time music by the force of their musicianship and the fact that they were having such a damn good-time at it. Looking back at their '70s heyday, Walt Koken summed it up by saying, "Ironically, the more well-known we became, the less necessary we were to the growing old-time music scene, since one of the messages is to do it yourself—unplug it, and take it home!" *—John Lupton*

Feed Your Babies Onions: Fat City Favorites / Oct. 18, 1994 / Rounder ✦✦✦✦

This great revivalist band's earlier Rounder albums boiled down to a lone CD for a new generation of hungry old-timey fans. The band's free, adventurous spirit reflects its early '70s heyday but sounds as timeless as the tunes they play. Lively performances and unique dual fiddle arrangements make even the most familiar selections—"Fire On the Mountain" and "Way Down the Old Plank Road" among them—sound fresh. An essential re-issue and necessary addition to all old-timey music collections. *—Brian Beatty*

Highwoods String Band: Dance All Night / Rounder ✦✦✦

This was the group's second album for Rounder, cut about midway through the life of an old-time music revival band that was never accused of approaching its musical subjects with the tone of a librarian. The performances on this record have a fervor that is hard to believe and yet really needs to be a part of every successful string band, be it a revival band or the historical originals. A tasty group of traditional tunes is covered, of course revealing the sure signs of the devoted music lover whose nose has been pressed up against fading labels. It was smart to program "Dance All Night" right at the start of side one, as it lets the listener know that this shall not be a laid-back recording. "Money Musk" is hypnotic old-time banjo music with African influences. "Wild Bill Jones" and "Hawks and Eagles" are other highlights with terrific fiddle interaction. *—Eugene Chadbourne*

No. 3 Special / Rounder ✦✦✦

Quite tight as an ensemble by its third album, the Highwoods Stringband raves forth with a collection of traditional material picked up off the likes of Charlie Poole, Gid Tanner, the Carter Family, and so forth. The almost surreal intensity that marked the original recordings by such artists is traded in here for squeaky-clean studio production and youthful enthusiasm. The acoustic instruments sound really fine, and the twin-fiddle attack of Walt Koken and Bob Potts is not to be sneezed at, no matter how much rosin is in the air. There are those listeners who would rather hear the real item then a revival, even if it was done way back in the distant '70s as this was, decades before Joel and Ethan Coen's *Brother, Where Art Thou?* If one just scratched this record up enough, even these purists might be fooled by a performance as raucous as "Pig Ankle Rag," which closes out the first side. *—Eugene Chadbourne*

● **Fire on the Mountain** / Rounder ✦✦✦✦

This is old-time string band music at its best, it was re-created from old 78s of the '20s and '30s. *—Charles S. Wolfe*

Faith Hill

b. Sep. 21, 1967, Jackson, MS

Vocals / Country-Pop, Contemporary Country, Adult Contemporary

One of the biggest female country stars of the '90s, Faith Hill also took advantage of the inroads Shania Twain made into pop territory, becoming an enormous crossover success by decade's end. Of course, Hill's movie star good looks certainly helped her cause, and her much-celebrated marriage to fellow country star Tim McGraw gave her career an extra kick of glamour and mystique. Hill may not have appealed to country purists, but she had the star power of a diva even before her pop success.

Faith Hill was born Audrey Faith Perry on September 21, 1967, in Jackson, MS, and grew up in the nearby small town of Star. She was singing for her family as young as age three and first performed publicly at a 4-H luncheon when she was seven. Hill spent much of her childhood singing wherever the opportunity arose, influenced primarily by Reba McEntire, and at age 17 formed a band that played local rodeos. At 19, she quit college and moved to Nashville to make it as a singer, first finding work selling T-shirts. During this time, she was married briefly to music executive Dan Hill. Eventually she was hired as a secretary at a music publishing firm, where she was discovered by accident while singing to herself one day. Encouraged by company head Gary Morris, Hill became a demo singer for the firm and also performed professionally as a harmony vocalist behind singer/songwriter/producer Gary Burr, who produced Hill's own demo tape. A Warner Bros. executive caught Burr and Hill's act at a Nashville club, and wound up signing Hill to a solo deal.

Hill released her debut album, *Take Me As I Am*, in late 1993, with producer Scott Hendricks (also her boyfriend) at the helm. Success wasn't long in coming; the lead single "Wild One" raced up the country charts en route to a four-week run at number one early the next year, making her the first female country singer in 30 years to top the charts for that long with her debut single. The follow-up, a countrified cover of Janis Joplin's "Piece of My Heart," also hit number one, as did the album's title track, and *Take Me As I Am* wound up selling over two-million copies. Hill was set to build on her success right away, but had to undergo surgery on her vocal cords, which delayed recording of her next album. Nevertheless, the wait wasn't unreasonable, and *It Matters to Me* appeared in the summer of 1995. The title track became her fourth number-one country single, and it was accompanied by a string of Top Ten hits that helped push sales of the album past the three-million mark. Hill was by now a firmly established country hitmaker, and she continued her active touring schedule by teaming up with Tim McGraw in 1996 for the Spontaneous Combustion Tour; it was an apt name, as Hill broke off her engagement to Hendricks to marry McGraw that October. The couple's first child, daughter Gracie, was born in May of 1997, and not long after, their duet "It's Your Love"—recorded for McGraw's *Everywhere* album—was burning up the country charts, hitting number one for six weeks.

Hill returned in the spring of 1998 with *Faith*, which provided the first signs that she was interested in crossing over to pop audiences, even if the still-countrified music often straddled the fence instead of making her ambitions explicit. The single "This Kiss" proved the savvy of her approach; not only did it top the country charts for three weeks, but it also became her first pop hit, climbing to number seven. By the time "This Kiss" had run its course on the charts, Hill had given birth to her second daughter by McGraw, Maggie. If Hill had been a star in the country world, she was now rapidly becoming a superstar, known not just for her music but also her pure celebrity; she also signed an endorsement deal with Cover Girl makeup. Her next two singles, "Just to Hear You Say That You Love Me" (another duet with McGraw) and "Let Me Let Go," hit number-one country, though they didn't duplicate the pop success of "This Kiss." *Faith* became Hill's biggest-selling album yet, moving over five-million copies and reaching the Top Ten on the LP charts; plus, it was now crystal clear that Hill potentially held major crossover appeal. Accordingly, she re-entered the studio immediately after her supporting tour and cut *Breathe*, a full-fledged bid for pop and adult contemporary success. *Breathe* entered the charts at number one upon its release in late 1999, and its title track became Hill's biggest hit yet; it spent six weeks on top of the country charts and was an even bigger hit on the adult contemporary charts. While it only climbed to number-two pop, the single had such staying power that it wound up the biggest hit of the year 2000. The follow-ups were pretty successful in their own right: "The Way You Love Me" and "There You'll Be" both hit the pop Top Ten, with the former topping the country charts and the latter hitting number one AC. Hill also scored a Top Ten country hit with "Let's Make Love," a third duet with McGraw, and the two teamed up for another tour in 2000. *Breathe* was a bona fide blockbuster, selling over seven-million copies, and earned her a slew of award nominations. Hill spent much of 2001 taking a break and spending time with Audrey, her third daughter with McGraw. The next year, Hill returned to the spotlight with her fifth studio recording, *Cry*. *—Steve Huey*

Take Me as I Am / 1994 / Warner Bros. ✦✦✦✦

Whether she's singing songs associated with Janis Joplin ("Piece of My Heart") or Maura O'Connell ("I Would Be Stronger Than That"), Faith Hill sounds every bit like the new-generation Reba McEntire heir her press makes her out to be. Hill sings with with a natural tear in her voice that recalls McEntire without ever mimicking her. Hill sounds like a star on all ten cuts, whether she's fronting minimal acoustic accompaniment on "Just Around the Eyes" or rocking out on "Wild One." *—Brian Mansfield*

It Matters to Me / 1995 / Warner Bros. ✦✦✦✦

On her second album, Faith Hill confirmed that *Take Me as I Am* was no fluke. Like her debut album, *It Matters to Me* is an ambitious, diverse set of contemporary country that proves Hill can tackle virtually every subgenre of country, singing rockers, ballads, socially aware stories, and love songs with an equal amount of grace. The singles "Let's Go to Vegas" and "It Matters to Me" aren't the only stong songs here—the entire album is rich with first-rate songs, as well as superb singing from Hill, one of the most promising female vocalist of the mid-'90s. *—Stephen Thomas Erlewine*

Faith / Apr. 21, 1998 / Warner Bros. ✦✦✦

Faith Hill moves toward mainstream pop on her third album, *Faith*. Without abandoning the polished contemporary country that defined her first two efforts, she's expanded her sonic palette, evidently with the hope of getting an MOR audience—that's the only reasonable explanation behind the Diane Warren and Sheryl Crow songs on the album. Hill gives it her all, and there are some very nice performances here; anyone who doubted her vocal prowess will be impressed with her showcase performance here. Still, it's a little disconcerting to hear the heavy-handed arrangements that dominate the album—she may never have been a country singer in the classic sense, but here she's hanging to the genre by the most tenuous of strings. *—Thom Owens*

● **Breathe** / Nov. 9, 1999 / Warner Bros. ✦✦✦✦✦

Being married to a sexy country superstar and mom to two little baby girls, along with her sultry new image and a huge crossover hit have all changed not only the way Faith Hill sounds, but also the things she sings about. There's no more spousal abuse, heartbreak, or letting go as heard on all three of her previous albums. On *Breathe*, Hill sings of love, making love, kissing, and simply love (In fact, five of the albums 13 tracks have love in the title), and it works for her. Country music fans might be a bit disappointed that there's very little about this album that sounds country, but Faith Hill fans will never feel an ounce of disappointment over this outstanding album. With each release, Hill's voice gets more and more confident and producers Byron Gallimore and Dann Huff (in addition to herself) utilize that confidence by choosing songs that complement her vocal strengths. And of course, what's a Faith Hill album about love without a duet with husband Tim McGraw? Fans won't be able to take a breath from this album—at least not on the first listen. *—Maria Konicki Dinoia*

There You'll Be: The Best of Faith Hill / Nov. 20, 2001 / Wea International ✦✦✦✦✦

Released in 2001, *There You'll Be: The Best of Faith Hill* was a collection designed for international markets, intending to introduce the American superstar to the world. As such, it presents her as a pop star, including remixes of "Breathe" and "The Way You Love Me" (that are nevertheless also present in their original versions), as well as her biggest crossover hits from *Breathe*, *Faith*, and *It Matters to Me*. This doesn't contain all of her hits, but it contains all the big hits, along with the brand new title track and some dubious selections (why is "Over the Rainbow" here?), but on the whole, it's a good summary of her poppiest material, which is often among her best, but be forewarned—this does not contain *all* of her best, and it was released before her full-fledged pop album, *Cry*, and it's entirely likely that it will be replaced by a better, more comprehensive American collection in the future. With that in mind, this does get a recommendation, since it does have the hits, but for those reasons, it's a qualified recommendation. [In some territories, *There You'll Be* was released with a bonus track, a cover of Bruce Springsteen's "If I Should Fall Behind."] *—Stephen Thomas Erlewine*

Cry / Oct. 15, 2002 / Warner Bros. ✦✦✦

Lavishly produced and packaged, *Cry* marks the continued ascent of Faith Hill from the lowlands of down-home authenticity to the heights of pop superstardom. Though plenty of Nashville A-team players back her up, the sound they churn out has almost nothing to do with country music. Riding a tide of massed synthesizer textures, sweeping orchestral strings, thundering drums, rock guitar licks, and melodramatic dynamics, Hill strives for the biggest possible gestures in her performance. The result is the kind of glitzy fireworks normally associated with *Star Search* or *American Idol*, in which the lyric takes a distant backseat to raw exhibitionism and only the most cursory nod is made toward country lyrical convention. (The nod is particularly schizoid in "This Is Me," as Hill proclaims, "I try to love Jesus and myself... yeah, yeah.") Beyond the general issue of taste, this approach raises twofold problems for Hill in particular, in that her established skills as a song interpreter are lost in all this *Sturm und Drang* and her voice, while undeniably powerful at its peak, doesn't have the range that allows most singers in this style, from proto-diva Barbra Streisand to flameout icon Mariah Carey, to at least milk the material at some superficial level. With all this in mind, it may be significant that Tim McGraw, a guest on previous Hill albums, makes no appearance here. Perhaps there's no room for country credibility, or even for a spouse, when one's career trajectory is as hot as Hill's. *—Robert L. Doerschuk*

Goldie Hill

b. Jan. 11, 1933, Karnes County, TX

Vocals / Traditional Country, Honky Tonk

Country singer Goldie Hill, younger sister of Tommy Hill, was born in 1933 in Karnes County, TX. Music played a huge part in the Hill family. The radio was one way to block out the daily backbreaking work of picking cotton. Goldie soaked up the popular country music of the era and developed a talent for singing. Early on, Goldie's older brothers Tommy and Ken left a life of cotton picking determined to make a name for themselves in country music. Within a few years, they were backing up Hank Williams, Johnny Horton, and Webb Pierce. Sister Goldie officially got her start on the *Louisiana Hayride* in 1953 as part of Tommy's band. Billed as "the Golden Hillbilly," she scored a number-one hit in 1953 with her second single, "I Let the Stars Get in My Eyes," originally written by Tommy for Kitty Wells.

Among her other charting tunes were several duets with either Ernest Tubb's son Justin Tubb or Red Sovine, including the big hit "Yankee Go Home." In 1957 she married country singer Carl Smith following his divorce from June Carter. In the late '60s she made a short-lived comeback as Goldie Hill Smith, without much fanfare. Following Carl Smith's retirement from music in the late '70s, he and Goldie lived on their horse farm outside of Franklin, TN, and the two began to show horses professionally during the course of the decade. *—Al Campbell*

● **Goldie Hill** / 1960 / Decca ✦✦✦✦

Tommy Hill

b. Apr. 27, 1929

Fiddle, Guitar, Drums, Vocals / Rockabilly

Tommy Hill never quite made it as a country star, despite a couple of decades of trying and crossing paths with (and even working for) stars and legends like Smiley Burnette, Webb Pierce, Hank Williams, and Johnny Horton. He wrote some very successful songs and produced important hits by others, and also left some hot rockabilly sides behind. Born on a farm near Coy City, TX, on the eve of the Great Depression, Hill was one of four children. He spent a good part of that childhood picking cotton in order to help his family survive. He also listened to the radio and especially enjoyed the music of Jimmie Rodgers, the Delmore Brothers, Cowboy Slim Rinehart, and Wayne Raney. It was while dragging sacks of cotton through the fields that Hill vowed to try for a career as a musician. He learned guitar listening to Ernest Tubb's lead player, Jimmie Short, and was proficient enough as a teenager to get a gig playing on radio with Big Bill Lister in San Antonio—he was good enough, in fact, to blow the competition out of the studio.

With his brother Ken, Hill got gigs working with Red River Dave McEnery, and one day in 1948, musician/actor Smiley Burnette (of Gene Autry and Roy Rogers fame) passed through San Antonio and found himself in need of a guitar player or two. Tommy and Ken were hired for the gig and stayed with Burnette, who brought them to California, which got them into the background scenes in his movies as extras and musicians. The Hollywood work only lasted for 18 months before Hill and his brother returned to Texas to try and really make it in the music business. Sometime in 1949, Hill was playing in a group called the Texas Hillbillies, and he managed to cross paths during the years that followed with Hank Williams and Johnny Horton. A couple of years later, Hill got picked up by Webb Pierce as a fiddle player. They only worked together for about four months, during which time Pierce cut one of Hill's original songs, "Slowly," before Hill decided to form a band of his own. Pierce's manager, Tillman Franks (who also later managed Horton), got Hill a contract with Decca Records in 1952. He formed his own band in Shreveport, LA, with his sister Goldie, who had a hit with Hill's "Let the Stars Get in My Eyes" (retitled "Don't Let the Stars Get in Your Eyes"), which he had originally written for Kitty Wells.

Hill had little success with Decca and was persuaded to join Hickory Records, the recording arm of Acuff-Rose publishers. By that time, rock & roll was rumbling out of the South and the Midwest, and Hill ran across a fellow Texan with a yen to record, steering him to Decca in Nashville—that marked the start of Buddy Holly's commercial recording career. He also saw Ronnie Self in concert and took to heart the kind of music that the kids were listening to. He tried his hand at rockabilly, recording a single session one night that took more than 35 years to see the light of day.

Somehow, however, success eluded Hill. He had no hits during his three years at Hickory Records, and he subsequently hooked up with Starday Records, where he eventually became a producer, handling many of the label's releases until 1968. After a stint with MGM Records, Hill went into partnership with his fellow guitarist, Pete Drake, in the Stop label, which recorded the Jordanaires and Johnny Bush, among others, during its brief existence. Finally, in 1972, Hill formed Gusto Records, and two years later went into partnership with Moe Lytle; the two eventually bought out the King and Starday labels, and Hill was the producer of Starday's biggest hit, "Teddy Bear" by Red Sovine. Hill hasn't been heard from since the early '60s as a recording artist, and none of his country sides are currently in print. In 1993, however, Bear Family Records released his long-lost rockabilly session from that June night in 1958. Despite his talent and his years of playing and writing, Hill never scored a hit; however, as he observed in Colin Escott's notes for *Get Ready Baby*, he had a habit of always giving his best songs away to others. *—Bruce Eder*

Get Ready Baby / 1993 / Bear Family ♦♦♦♦

There's good news and bad news for people thinking of buying *Get Ready Baby*. The bad news is that the ten songs (two of them in two versions each) on this $20 CD run a total of 18 minutes and change, which is outrageous given the price. The good news is that this is really good rockabilly, a little too midtempo at times, but well played and sung by a guy who otherwise spent his whole career doing mainstream country music. In June of 1958, Tommy Hill and some friends got drunk one night and went into the studio to cut these ten tracks, which were promptly forgotten. The sound is occasionally a little more country than pure rockabilly, but the energy and the beat are all there (with D. J. Fontana on drums, how could they not be?), as Hill, Leo Jackson, and Hank Garland rock out on the guitars and Ace Cannon shows surprising restraint on the sax. This is solid Texas rockabilly, in the style of Buddy Holly. *—Bruce Eder*

Chris Hillman

b. Dec. 4, 1944, Los Angeles, CA

Bass, Mandolin, Vocals / Progressive Bluegrass, Country-Rock, Progressive Country

Along with frequent collaborator Gram Parsons, Chris Hillman was the key figure in the development of country-rock, virtually defining the genre through his seminal work with the Byrds and the Flying Burrito Brothers. Hillman was born on December 4, 1944, in Los Angeles, where he grew up listening to Spade Cooley and Cliffie Stone and taught himself to play guitar. In 1961, he and a pair of high-school friends formed the Scottsville Squirrel Barkers, and cut an album; a year later, he joined the Golden Gate Boys, a bluegrass band featuring Vern Gosdin. In honor of their new vocalist's prowess on the mandolin, the group renamed itself the Hillmen; after recording a self-titled LP with producer Jim Dickson, they broke up in 1963.

In 1964, the Beefeaters, an L.A. folk trio comprised of guitarists Jim (later Roger) McGuinn, David Crosby, and Gene Clark, released a single, "Please Let Me Love You"; after its commercial failure, they decided to add a bassist and drummer to their lineup. Their producer, Dickson, suggested Hillman for the bass position; although he had never picked up the instrument before, thanks to his bluegrass background he was able to quickly develop his own unique, melodic performance style. After the addition of drummer Michael Clarke, the quintet renamed itself the Byrds. At their label's insistence, they cut their first record with session men, which meant that Hillman and Clarke sat on the sidelines during production; the resulting single, a jangly cover of Bob Dylan's "Mr. Tambourine Man," was a tremendous hit which marked the birth of the folk-rock form.

During the mid-'60s, the Byrds ranked as one of the most successful and influential American pop groups, issuing a string of massive hits like "Turn! Turn! Turn!," "Eight Miles High," and "So You Want to Be a Rock 'N' Roll Star" along with acclaimed albums like 1967's *Younger Than Yesterday* and 1968's brilliant *The Notorious Byrd Brothers*. Internal strife dogged the band, however, and by late 1967 only Hillman and McGuinn remained from the original roster. At about the same time, Gram Parsons entered the picture, and in December 1967, McGuinn invited him to join the group as a jazz pianist for a planned project embracing the history of American popular music. However, Parsons' mastery of country soon became the sessions' dominant focus, much to Hillman's delight, and the album the Byrds ultimately recorded, 1968's *Sweetheart of the Rodeo*, became the blueprint for all country-rock efforts released in its wake.

A tour followed, and so did disaster; Parsons did not agree with the group's decision to play apartheid-torn South Africa, and subsequently quit the Byrds in July 1968. Three months later, Hillman followed suit, and joined Parsons as a vocalist and guitarist in the re-formed Flying Burrito Brothers along with bassist Chris Ethridge, pedal steel player "Sneaky" Pete Kleinow, and drummer Jon Corneal. Further honing their hybrid sound by combining the energy and instrumentation of rock with the issues and themes of country, the Burritos recorded the landmark *Gilded Palace of Sin*, followed in 1970 by *Burrito Deluxe*. After Parsons left the group in 1971, Hillman stayed on for two less successful records, a self-titled 1971 effort and the following year's *Last of the Red Hot Burritos*. After they disbanded, Hillman joined Stephen Stills' Manassas, where he remained until 1973, when he briefly rejoined the Byrds.

In 1974, Hillman teamed with singer/songwriters John David Souther and Richie Furay to form Souther-Hillman-Furay Band; after recording two LPs with the trio, Hillman issued a pair of solo albums, 1976's *Slippin' Away* and 1977's *Clear Sailin'*. By 1978, he had rejoined Roger McGuinn and Gene Clark to record a 1979 album under the name McGuinn, Clark & Hillman, producing the Top 40 pop hit "Don't You Write Her Off." The album *City* followed a year later, this time as Roger McGuinn and Chris Hillman Featuring Gene Clark. They soon went their separate ways, and in 1982 Hillman issued a straightforward country record, *Morning Sky*. Two years later, he released *Desert Rose*, which contained the minor country hits "Somebody's Back in Town" and "Running the Roadblocks." The album's title proved indicative of things to come, and in 1986 he formed the Desert Rose Band, a country-rock outfit featuring Nashville session aces Herb Pedersen, John Jorgenson, Jay Dee Maness, Steve Duncan, and Bill Bryson.

The Desert Rose Band proved to be Hillman's most commercially successful post-Byrds project; their first LP, an eponymous-titled 1987 outing, generated a pair of Top Ten country hits in "Love Reunited" and "One Step Forward," which peaked at number two. 1988's "He's Back and I'm Blue" topped the country charts, as did "I Still Believe in You," from the album *Running*. Two other singles from the record, "Summer Wind" and a cover of John Hiatt's "She Don't Love Nobody," reached the Top Five. The follow-up, 1989's *Pages of Love*, was also highly successful, with two more Top Ten hits, "Start All Over Again" and "Story of Love." Subsequent releases like 1991's *True Love* and 1993's *Traditional* failed to achieve the same degree of popularity, however, and after one final LP, *Life Goes On*, the group called it quits in 1994.

At the peak of the Desert Rose Band's success, Hillman had also begun appearing infrequently with McGuinn, releasing the Top Ten country duet "You Ain't Going Nowhere" in 1989. Soon, the pair joined Crosby in a reformed Byrds, playing a handful of club dates. In 1990, they appeared at a tribute to the late Roy Orbison, performing "Mr. Tambourine Man" along with the song's composer, Bob Dylan. The same year, the Byrds cut four new songs for inclusion in a career-spanning box set, and in 1991 were inducted into the Rock & Roll Hall of Fame. In 1996, Hillman reunited with Desert Rose alumnus Herb Pedersen for *Bakersfield Bound*. *Like a Hurricane* followed in 1998. *—Jason Ankeny*

The Hillmen / 1971 / ♦♦♦♦♦

Slippin' Away / 1976 / Line ♦♦♦

Having recently departed Souther-Hillman-Furay Band, this album more heavily reflects his association with Manassas than anything he did with SH&F. A nice batch of songs overall but the high point for me is the killer version of the bluegrass standard "Take Me in Your Lifeboat" that closes the album. *—Jim Worbois*

Clear Sailin' / 1977 / Asylum ♦♦

This is not one of those records that transcends the period in which it was made. It could easily be confused with Fools Gold, Firefall, or any one of a number of bands from the late '70s. *—Jim Worbois*

Ever Call Ready / 1978 / A&M ♦♦♦

● **Morning Sky** / 1982 / Sugar Hill ♦♦♦♦♦

A back-to-the-roots album (of sorts), Hillman has given up the bass in favor of the mandolin and acoustic guitar for this mostly acoustic album of other people's tunes. The band is made up of people with whom Hillman has worked over the years and it's obvious they are comfortable together. Listening to this album is almost like eavesdropping on a group of friends making music in their living room. *—Jim Worbois*

Desert Rose / 1984 / Sugar Hill ♦♦♦♦

Chris Hillman was never the songwriter of the caliber of Gene Clark, Gram Parsons, or Stephen Stills, his bandmates back in the heady days of folk-rock and early country-rock, so it's not surprising to see him mine the treasures of traditional Nashville once he broke free as a solo artist. *Desert Rose* is his second album for the Sugar Hill label, and it features largely the same crack backup musicians as on *Morning Sky*, as well as a lineup of breezy country tunes by the likes of Jimmie Rodgers, and Acuff-Rose publishing. Hillman again plays mandolin, and the use of banjo and fiddle on this record further add to a bluegrass feel. The title track, a Hillman original, would later be used as a name for his band, and you can sense Hillman's contentment at leaving his rock baggage behind. This is a pleasant, understated affair, great music to unwind to while sipping cold lemonade on a hot summer day. *—Peter Kurtz*

Sixteen Roses: Greatest Hits / 1995 / Curb ♦♦♦

Bakersfield Bound / May 21, 1996 / Sugar Hill ♦♦♦♦

Between more commercial projects, Chris Hillman has a tendency to revert to more traditional sounds. A couple of years after the demise of the Desert Rose Band, he reconstituted its primary members—himself, Herb Pedersen, and Jay Dee Maness, along with some studio players—for this genre exercise that finds him and Pedersen making like the Wilburn Brothers, the Louvin Brothers, the Everly Brothers, and Buck Owens with Don Rich, among other country vocal teams, and cutting material by and/or associated with Boudleaux & Felice Bryant, Merle Haggard, Hank Williams, and Skeeter Davis. The duo is steeped in this material, and they perform it with authority and conviction. Having refreshed themselves by returning to their roots, it will be interesting to see what they do next. — *William Ruhlmann*

Like a Hurricane / Jun. 16, 1998 / Sugar Hill ✦✦✦
This is a solid album of new and old songs by one of the founding fathers of country-rock. Hillman has a wonderful voice, great pop instincts, and a finely developed talent for splicing together country, bluegrass, and four-chord rock & roll. A highlight is a cover of the Searchers' "When You Walk in the Room"—two minutes of pure jingle-jangle pop perfection. Although "Like a Hurricane" (the title track is a Hillman original, not the Neil Young song) seldom reaches the heights of "Bakersfield Bound," Hillman and Herb Pedersen's outstanding 1996 tribute to hard California country, this former Byrd and Flying Burrito Brother can still teach the young country crowd a thing or two. —*Joel Roberts*

Way Out West / 2002 / Back Porch ✦✦✦
Here's the perfect antidote for country fans who mourn the loss of old-school flavors in lieu of the modern polished pop crossover approach. First the pedigrees for those who know the names but can't place them: Hillman is one of the great innovators of California country-rock, with legendary associations including the Byrds, the Flying Burrito Brothers, Manassas, and other post-Byrds and Burrito lineups featuring former members. Pedersen's crystal-clear tenor has graced the work of artists like Vince Gill, Johnny Rivers, and Linda Ronstadt, along with his bands the Dillards and the Laurel Canyon Ramblers. These two met as members of the Desert Rose Band and, all these years later, still apparently love folk, bluegrass, and old country—styles which make up the bulk of the influences on this easygoing-down project. There are lots of crisp, twangy guitars and a colorful 17-track run featuring familiar themes like love, heartache, and living life the hard way. "Backporch Boy" is an instrumental bluegrass prelude, followed up by traditional honky tonk flavors on the she-done-me-wrong song "There You Go" and "Problems" (the perfect cross of country instrumentation and Everly Brothers harmonies). Other highlights are the lament "Invitation to the Blues" and "Better Man Than That," which sounds like one of those classic, Eagles-flavored early-'70s Southern California classics. There are also gospel elements here and there on pieces like "The Old Cross Roads." Affiliated with Narada and Virgin, Back Porch Records is billed as a roots rock and Americana label, and this disc offers a throwback to various classic styles that are all at once comfortable and challenging. —*Jonathan Widran*

The Hillmen

Group / Progressive Bluegrass
The Hillmen were a bluegrass-styled combo that featured Chris Hillman, Don Parmley, Vern Gosdin, and Rex Gosdin. Based in Southern California, the short-lived group was an early player in that state's burgeoning bluegrass and country movement. The group made a series of recordings between 1963 and 1964; Hillman eventually left to join the Byrds while Parmley went to Bluegrass Cardinals, Vern Gosdin pursued a career as a country crooner, and his brother Rex became a country songwriter. In 1995, Sugar Hill released the definitive Hillmen retrospective. —*Johnny Loftus*

● **The Hillmen** / 1970 / Together ✦✦✦✦
Before there were the Byrds, the Bluegrass Cardinals, and the Desert Rose Band, there were the Hillmen, a young and earnest bluegrass band with a taste for the high and lonesome sound of Bill Monroe and the faux-folk lyrics of Bob Dylan. Like many young musicians who discovered the world of folk music in the mid-'60s, they combined a deep respect for tradition with a forward-looking sense of exploration; in a few years bands like the New Grass Alliance and the Seldom Scene would take a similar approach into more adventuresome territory, but the early work of the Hillmen helped to blaze the trail. This album is a reissue of recordings made in 1963 and 1964, and while other bands were doing the same sort of thing with a bit more panache (the Kentucky Colonels and the Country Gentlemen both come to mind as more exciting contemporaries of the Hillmen), there's no denying the freshness, enthusiasm, and skill in evidence on this recording. Mandolinist Chris Hillman (who would later come to country-rock prominence as a founding member of the Byrds, the Flying Burrito Brothers, and the Desert Rose Band) shows off some impressive chops on instrumentals like "Blue Grass Chopper" and "Wheel Hoss," while future country star Vern Gosdin shows himself to be a fine if not earthshaking bluegrass singer. His bass-playing brother, Rex, stands out as a high tenor and shines on the gospel standard "Goin' Up." Don Parmley picks the banjo in a straightforward Scruggs style that veers into melodic Bill Keith territory from time to time and prefigures his future work with the Bluegrass Cardinals. The band covers "Barbara Allen," a British folk song that Joan Baez had recently made popular in the U.S., and two Dylan tunes; those song choices and a somewhat fuzzy recorded sound combine to make this album something of a period piece, but it's a fun one. Fans of Gosdin and Hillman, especially, will get a solid retro kick out of this disc. —*Rick Anderson*

Tish Hinojosa (Leticia Hinojosa)

b. Dec. 6, 1955, San Antonio, TX
Guitar, Piano, Vocals / Contemporary Folk, Contemporary Singer/Songwriter
Tish Hinojosa has drawn numerous critical accolades for her borderless approach to music, blending Mexican folk and country music with a modern singer/songwriter sensibility and touches of pop. Born Leticia Hinojosa in San Antonio in 1955, Hinojosa's parents were Mexican immigrants, and she soaked up their music as well as the area's country sounds and the socially relevant rock & roll of the '60s. She started playing guitar as a teenager, singing folk and pop songs in local clubs; she also sang commercial jingles for a Spanish-language radio station, and recorded a few Latin pop songs for a local label as well. In 1979, she moved to Taos, NM, and eventually landed a job singing backup with Michael Martin Murphey. In 1983, she relocated to Nashville and tried to make it

as a singer and/or songwriter, but found that she didn't fit the mold of what record companies wanted, despite recording a one-off single for Curb ("I'll Pull You Through"). In 1985, she moved back to Taos, and two years later completed the self-released cassette *Taos to Tennessee*. In 1988, she moved to Austin and hit the city's thriving roots-music scene, where she knew her distinctiveness would find a better reception.

Hinojosa quickly landed a deal with A&M, and in 1989 she issued her official debut album, *Homeland*, which received highly complimentary reviews. Her next effort, *Culture Swing*, was released by the respected roots label Rounder in 1992 to even greater acclaim; thanks to its free-thinking musical cross-pollination, the National Association of Independent Record Distributors named it Folk Album of the Year. Around the same time, Watermelon issued three archival recordings, including a live album, a holiday album, and the first appearance of *Taos to Tennessee* on CD. Thanks to the attention surrounding *Culture Swing*, Hinojosa landed a deal with Warner Bros., debuting for the label with 1994's *Destiny's Gate*. Although her time with Warner signaled a more polished approach (some naysayers said sanitized), she also continued to record more specific projects for Rounder, starting with 1995's *Frontejas*, an overview of Texas/Mexico border music that won massive respect in the Latin music community. *Dreaming From the Labyrinth* followed on Warner in 1996, and that same year she issued a bilingual children's album, *Cada Niño (Every Child)*, on Rounder. Frustrated by Warner's reluctance to put out more of her material, Hinojosa eventually secured her release from the label and returned to Rounder. In the meantime, she continued her activism on behalf of Latino and women's issues, even as her 20-year marriage broke apart. Finally, after a four-year absence from recording, Hinojosa returned in 2000 with *Sign of Truth*. —*Steve Huey*

Homeland / 1989 / A&M ✦✦✦✦✦

Memorabilia Navideña / 1991 / Watermelon ✦✦✦
Memorabilia Navideña is a pleasing Christmas collection that alternates between English and Spanish renditions of old and new seasonal songs. —*Roch Parisien*

Aquella Noche / 1991 / Watermelon ✦✦✦✦
Recorded live and in Spanish, *Aquella Noche* (1991) offers melodious songs surrounded by rich acoustic guitars and Latin percussion. Unlike *Homeland* in 1989 or *Culture Swing* in 1992, *Aquella Noche* finds Tish Hinojosa fully immersing herself in her Spanish/Mexican heritage. This is less a singer/songwriter album than a portrait of an artist plumbing her roots. The effervescent "Samba San Pedro" reminds one of a bossa nova classic, while the quieter "Anos, Meses Y Dias" is delivered with the simplicity of a traditional Spanish folk song. The multifaceted chords and rhythms of "Una Noche Mas" and the title cut create a rich, layered music. Arturo Garza's bongos and congas add a forceful though bare underpinning, while Marvin Denton Dykhuis' guitar delivers delicate touches that skillfully draw attention to the melody and vocals. The final ingredient, of course, is Hinojosa's emotional vocals. She adds depth of feeling to pieces like "La Llorona" and "Azul Cristal" that resonate whether or not one knows Spanish. The idea of recording one night of music live and issuing it may seem a bit old fashioned, but the results are simple and pure. Hinojosa's exploration of Spanish traditions on *Aquella Noche* results in a lovely album of finely textured songs. —*Ronnie D. Lankford Jr.*

● **Culture Swing** / 1992 / Rounder ✦✦✦✦✦
If Joan Baez or Tracy Chapman were influenced by the Mexican-American music of Texas, they might sound something like Tish Hinojosa—a charming singer/acoustic guitarist who sings mostly in English but can be equally convincing in Spanish. Categorizing this expressive vocalist isn't easy. While "By the Rio Grande," "The Window," and "San Antonio Romeo" bring Tex-Mex touches to the Anglo-American folk and singer/songwriter traditions, "Corazon Viajero (Wandering Heart)" and "Chanate, El Vaquero" are Spanish-language gems that would please Mexican traditionalists. "Drifter's Wind" and "Louisiana Road Song" essentially fall into the country category, while "San Antonio Romeo" pays homage to the Western swing sound defined by Bob Wills. Unpredictable as well as moving, Hinojosa showed considerable promise on this enriching CD. —*Alex Henderson*

Taos to Tennessee / 1992 / Watermelon ✦✦✦✦✦
Tish Hinojosa is an established Mexican-American singer with recent releases on A&M and Electra. Her Watermelon debut *Taos To Tennessee* features country material in English. —*Roch Parisien*

Destiny's Gate / 1994 / Warner Bros. ✦✦✦
Hinojosa continues to move into the mainstream with *Destiny's Gate* without losing the magic of *Culture Swing*. With a beautiful voice reminiscent of Joan Baez and Emmylou Harris, she seems to have perfected her unique blend of Mexican folk and country music. "I Want to See You Again" stands out as one of her finest songs. —*Chris Woodstra*

Frontejas / 1995 / Rounder ✦✦✦

Cada Nino (Every Child) / 1996 / Rounder ✦✦

Dreaming From the Labyrinth (Soñar del Laberinto) / May 1996 / Warner Bros. ✦✦✦
Tish Hinojosa's album, *Dreaming From the Labyrinth* (her second for Warner Bros.), is more what comes to mind with the word "traditional." Hinojosa was born in Texas to Mexican immigrant parents, and her multicultural upbringing is a defining characteristic of her acoustic folk music (she sings in both Spanish and English, for example), as is her association with the current folk and country scene in Austin. Hinojosa's music, however, is often so sweet and nice around the edges that it becomes a turnoff. The songs on *Labyrinth* are as pretty as Hinojosa's voice, but there's no dirt under the fingernails, which is exactly what makes the music of Lucinda Williams, for instance (another Austin-based artist), so vibrant and alive. —*Kurt Wolff*

The Best of the Sandia: Watermelon 1991–1992 / Feb. 25, 1997 / Watermelon ✦✦✦
While Tish Hinojosa only recorded briefly for the Watermelon label at the beginning of her career, *Taos to Tennessee*, *Aquella Noche*, and *Memorabilia Navidena* represented a

distinct body of work from a new singer/songwriter. While Hinojosa grew up in Texas, she kept close ties to her Mexican heritage, often choosing to sing in Spanish. This bilingual, bicultural approach also lent her songwriting a unique subject matter. Add to this her lovely, warm voice and pleasant country-folk arrangements, and there's much to admire on her early albums. The cuts from *Taos to Tennessee* represent five of the best pieces from Hinojosa's delightful debut. These songs, including the title track and "Prairie Moon," are as poignant and tuneful as anything she has written. There's also her achingly beautiful vocal on Irving Berlin's "Always," which evokes Patsy Cline. Recorded live and in Spanish, *Aquella Noche* offers melodious songs surrounded by rich acoustic guitars and Latin percussion. The effervescent "Samba San Pedro" reminds one of a bossa nova classic, while the quieter "Anos, Meses y Dias" is delivered with the simplicity of a traditional Spanish folk song. Only three songs represent *Memorabilia Navidena*, an album of holiday music. Four previously unreleased songs also enrich the disc, including a duet, "By the Rio Grande," with Kris Kristofferson. While this album succeeds as a representative collection, one wouldn't want to miss out on her other albums, especially the delightful *Taos for Tennessee. The Best of Sandia* serves as a good introduction to the early work of Tish Hinojosa. *—Ronnie D. Lankford Jr.*

Soñar del Laberinto / May 5, 1997 / Warner Bros. ♦♦♦

Soñar del Laberinto is the Spanish language version of Tish Hinojosa's fine *Dreaming From the Labyrinth* and her lovely, folky songs are just as affecting in Spanish as they are in English. *—Thom Owens*

Sign of Truth / May 23, 2000 / Rounder ♦♦♦

This Texas born and raised songstress has done nothing but grow stronger, both in vision and her ability to express this understanding, by huge strides as the years have passed. She wrote, or co-wrote, all 12 of the songs on this disc. If you aren't familiar with her she sings in both English and Spanish, and her songs express both the duality and the oneness, as well as the peace and love she has found from being raised in both cultures on the border by a strong and loving family. There is something about her songs and manner that have always spoken strongly of a greater truth, and this is most clearly expressed here. Her longtime friend and accompanist Marvin Dykhuis is on all manner of guitars and stringed instruments, as well as an exceedingly solid group of exceptional musicians that echo the intensity of feelings being expressed very ably assist her. There are people such as Chip Dolan on keyboards, David Grissom on guitar, Lloyd Maines on pedal steel, and the wonderful accordion accents of Joel Guzman. This is a disc that speaks of love and growing, the puzzles in life, and somehow taps into the rhythm of the heart. It is a disc that brings comfort with it carried in her voice even when she speaks of love that has vanished. There is a sincerity here that is getting difficult to find. A disc from the heart, that is aptly named. *—Bob Gottlieb*

Taos to Tennessee [Bonus Tracks] / Oct. 16, 2001 / Texas Music Group ♦♦♦♦

A beautiful simplicity graces the early work of Tish Hinojosa. When mixed with a familiarity of Mexican/Texas border life, her country-folk leanings offer a fresh slant on the genre. Her debut, *Taos for Tennessee*, presents the same lovely songwriting and vocals that would characterize her recordings for the next several years. First issued independently in 1987, *Tao for Tennessee* was reissued by Watermelon in 1992 and by Texas Music Group in 2001. With ease and grace she opens with Peter Rowan's mystical classic "Midnight Moonlight," and follows with "Prairie Moon," a gentle Western ode complete with cowboys, whiskey, and a silver moon. A couple of noteworthy items set her songwriting apart. She never forgets, as on the title track, to write a catchy melody, and the musical accompaniment perfectly underlines the spare Western landscape she paints with her lyrics. Hinojosa sings in Spanish on "Amanecer" (Daybreak), a practice she would continue on later albums, and she offers good interpretations of several writers' songs, as with James McMurty's "Crazy Wind and Flashing Yellows." Lyrically, Hinojosa sets forth a number of poignant lines that subtly integrate the desolate land with the lonely souls that inhabit it. On "The Highway Calls" she sings, "Just one more drink to bring back a mem'ry/Or maybe forget where you've been," and captures the ambiguity of the unsettled life. *Taos for Tennessee* succeeds on every level, establishing Hinojosa as a vital artist with a distinctive vision. *—Ronnie D. Lankford Jr.*

The Best of Tish Hinojosa: Live / May 13, 2003 / Rounder ♦♦♦

This best-of is an unconventional one—though its type is becoming increasingly less so as the 21st century immerses itself in nostalgia from Tish Hinojosa. The recordings were done with a reunion band at the Cactus Café in Austin in 2002. There are 17 songs here, 15 of which come from albums she recorded on four different labels and cover the period from 1980-2002. Along with her regular band, which includes the truly gifted Marvin Dykhuis on all things with strings, pianist Danny Levin, Marty Muse on pedal steel, percussionist Arturo Garza, Glenn Kawamoto on bass, and drummer Bob Madden, there is a guest appearance by the incomparable Santiago Jimenez Jr. on accordion. Everything one would except from Hinojosa is here—"Taos to Tennessee," "Aquella Noche," "Bandera del Sol," "I'm Not Through Loving You Yet," "She's a Highway," "Otra Vez," "Donde Voy," "Roses Around My Feet," "Little Faith," and others. The sound is pristine, which is in keeping with Hinojosa's live mix for anyone who has ever seen her—instruments are perfectly balanced and the volume is kept at a minimum. That's accurate, but it seems that Chet Himes and Bill Johnson, who recorded this set, recorded it even warmer than it comes off live. There is something here that is not quite distant but doesn't quite capture the pure pastoral elegance and grace of Hinojosa at her best. The performances are fine, inspired even, but they just don't "sound" that way. It's too tidy even for Hinojosa, a bit too subdued for the joyousness of the occasion. That said, if you were only looking to have her finest—and favorite—material on one disc, this might be the one for you. *—Thom Jurek*

Rex Hobart

b. St. James, MO

Fiddle, Drums, Guitar (Rhythm), Guitar (Steel), Vocals, Bass (Upright) / Indie Rock, Alternative Country-Rock, Americana

Rex Hobart grew up in St. James, MO, but moved to Kansas City to find his fortune. Around 1989, he was playing in a rock & roll combo called Giant's Chair, but it just didn't feel right. What felt great were the honky tonk and country numbers he was writing in his spare time. So Hobart hooked up with Solomon Hofer, Vincent Floyd, and Blackjack Snow, and the Misery Boys were born. Later, J. B. Morris also joined up. *Forever Always Ends*, their debut, was recorded with Lou Whitney and appeared on the Chicago-based insurgent country label Bloodshot in 1999. Hobart and the boys then road-tested their honky tonk and heartbreak with a series of U.S. tours. Arriving back in K.C., T. C. Dobbs was brought in to replace Floyd behind the kit, and the band re-entered the studio with Whitney, this time emerging with *The Spectacular Sadness of Rex Hobart & the Misery Boys*, again for Bloodshot. They returned in 2003 with the acclaimed *Your Favorite Fool*, which featured more of the band's signature honky tonk and a duet with likeminded Chicago torch rocker Kelly Hogan. *—Johnny Loftus*

● **Forever Always Ends** / Jun. 22, 1999 / Bloodshot ♦♦♦

Hobart's classic Nashville style, complete with mellow baritone twang and unbelievable puns (like the soon-to-be-classic "I Walked in While He Was Changing Your Mind"), is given an energy boost by Vincent Floyd's lively drumming and J. B. Morris' meaty electric guitar. Though it may not appeal to Billy Ray Cyrus' country-pop fans, this is a heady country-rock hybrid. *—Tim Sheridan*

The Spectacular Sadness of Rex Hobart & the Misery Boys / 2000 / Bloodshot ♦♦♦

Much like Mike Ireland and Holler or Dale Watson, Rex Hobart and the Misery Boys fit in with the "alternative country" scene only to the extent that they're playing stuff no one looking for country & western airplay is going to bother with these days—this isn't country-rock, this is old-school honky tonk music served straight up, with no chaser. While Hobart's lyrics are sometimes a bit wordy compared to his obvious influences (Merle Haggard, Buck Owens, and the rest of the Bakersfield crowd), and his sense of melody is occasionally a shade dour, his tales of drinkin', cheatin', and getting on the wrong side of trouble are effectively cut from the classic mold (especially "Bridge Burners Union (Local 36)," "Barstow Barstool," and "Forever Always Ends"), and Hobart's strong, resonant voice is just the right instrument for his material. Hobart's band gets high marks as well, especially J. B. Morris on lead guitar and Solomon Hofer on pedal steel, and Lou Whitney's rich, clean production gets this on tape with a minimum of fuss. Not top-shelf honky tonk, but well worth a listen for enthusiasts, and it'll keep you from hearing Shania Twain for 38 minutes. *—Mark Deming*

Your Favorite Fool / Sep. 24, 2002 / Bloodshot ♦♦♦

Rex Hobart's third Bloodshot release in four years, at ten tracks and just over half an hour of music, is a little on the short side. But how much heartbreak, cryin', and twangy reverbed regret can you take in one sitting? Executive produced by Dwight Yoakam axeman and knob twiddler Pete Anderson, who oughta know his way around a good Bakersfield tune by now, *Your Favorite Fool* is top-shelf, low-down tears-in-yer-beer honky tonk, like in the old Faron Young days. Torchy country & western chanteuse Kelly Hogan goes sob for sob with Hobart on the George Jones/Tammy Wynette styled "Golden Ring," just to prove that hurtin' aches as much on both sides of the altar. Hot dawg double-time licks kick into high gear on the Commander Cody-ish "I Don't Feel It Anymore," proving that the Misery Boys can tear it up with the best of them. But it's the sobbin' steel guitar and classic Buck Owens sound that drives the majority of this disc. Even though it's all been heard before, Hobart's expressively deep baritone and no-frills approach go down like good whiskey after a bad night. Titles like "Gotta Get Back to Forgetting You" and "You've Got Some Cheatin' to Do" tell the story without having to hear a note. It's a slice of pure, dusty country the way they used to make it before the big hats and bigger production budgets moved in. You'll be singing Hobart's songs well after the half-hour it takes to spin this short but sweet album. *—Hal Horowitz*

Adolph Hofner

b. Jun. 8, 1916, Moulton, TX, **d.** 2000

Guitar, Leader, Vocals / Western Swing

Bandleader and vocalist Adolph Hofner was a durable musical icon of south Texas who helped shape Western swing, and whose dual career as a swing bandleader and Czech dance musician showed the ways in which Western swing had roots in Central European dance traditions. Hofner was raised on a farm in Lavaca County, TX, and like many other rural Texans his ethnic background was German and Czech. While growing up, Hofner heard polkas, schottisches, and other forms of local dance music. He and his family moved to San Antonio in 1928, where, four years later, Adolph and his steel guitar-playing brother, Emil, began performing in local clubs. Their sound reflected several strands of the Texas musical mosaic. Adolph was a crooner in the Bing Crosby mold, and Emil, like other early Texas swing musicians, at first emulated Hawaiian sounds—the brothers' first instrument was a ukulele they ordered from a catalog.

After the brothers heard the pioneering music of Milton Brown and Bob Wills, they began playing the jazz-inflected country dance music that in retrospect was labeled Western swing. Hofner worked during the day as a mechanic, and at night he performed with various San Antonio bands. He and Emil joined with Oklahoma-born fiddler Jimmie Revard to form Jimmie Revard's Oklahoma Playboys, a major musical attraction in 1930s San Antonio. Hofner also cut some sides as a solo vocalist and performed on vocals with Tom Dickey's Show Boys; his lead vocals on that band's cover of his friend Floyd Tillman's melancholy honky tonk success "It Makes No Difference Now" became a hit in its own right and inspired Hofner to form his own band in 1939. At first the band was known as Adolph Hofner & His Texans, but when they began recording for OKeh and Columbia in the early '40s with the addition of hot fiddler J.R. Chatwell, they were called the San Antonians. Among their best-known tunes were "Maria Elena" and "Alamo Rag."

The band spent the early '40s working in southern California; during World War II, Hofner went by the nicknames "Dub" and "Dolph" to avoid the highly unfavorable associations of his given first name. After the war he began using his own name again, and returned to Texas where he also began recording Czech and German polka music in addition to Western swing. The Czech-language piece known as "The Shiner Song" and "The Prune Waltz" became standards of Texas music. Though Hofner's polka pieces had a distinctive driving backbeat that was clearly swing-influenced, he generally kept the swing and Czech tracks of his musical life separate. In 1949, in honor of new sponsor Pearl Beer, Hofner's band became the Pearl Wranglers for radio, but remained the San Antonians on record. They recorded for the Sarg label for many years and were fixtures of San Antonio music through the 1980s, but Hofner was finally sidelined by ill health and died in the year 2000. He left behind a musical legacy that was richly American in its diversity and a trail of influence that stretched from Willie Nelson down to modern alt-country stalwarts Charlie and Bruce Robison. —*James Manheim*

Dance-O-Rama / 1955 / Decca ✦✦✦

● **South Texas Swing** / 1980 / Arhoolie ✦✦✦✦
Here are 26 tracks and 78 minutes of music by one of the Texas country swing greats, most cuts dating from the late 1930s and early 1940s, although there are a few stragglers from the late 1940s and early 1950s. This could be heartily recommended to Bob Wills and Milton Brown fans, with the proviso that Hofner favored a slightly more pop-oriented sound; the inclusion of some polka-oriented material betrays his Czech ancestry. His vocal sound is supremely relaxed and easygoing; it sounds like the stage would have to catch fire before his voice betrayed any hint of nervousness. Interesting oddities are five tracks sung in Czech; other than their presentation in a foreign language, they sound quite in line with his usual material. —*Richie Unterberger*

Kelly Hogan
b. Atlanta, GA

Composer, Guitar, Vocals / Alternative Country-Rock, Americana, Singer/Songwriter, Country-Rock, Adult Alternative Pop/Rock

Equally comfortable with indie rock, traditional country, and jazz pop, Georgia-based singer/songwriter Kelly Hogan explored all of those directions and more in her career. As the singer/guitarist for the Jody Grind in the early '90s, Hogan made a name for herself and the band with her lovely, versatile voice. The group released two albums—1990's *One Man's Trash Is Another Man's Treasure* and 1992's *Lefty's Deceiver*—before a car accident killed two of their members. After this loss, Hogan joined the arty garage rock revivalists the Rock*A*Teens; appearing on their 1996 self-titled debut EP; that year, she also released her first solo album, *The Whistle Only Dogs Can Hear*, which featured her own material alongside covers of Palace and Vic Chesnutt songs. After the release of the Rock*A*Teens' full-length debut *Cry* in 1997, Hogan left the group and began collaborating with alt-country and indie rock artists like Will Oldham and the Waco Brothers. In 2000 she released her second solo album and Bloodshot Records' debut *Beneath the Country Underdog*, which featured Jon Langford's Pine Valley Cosmonauts as her backing band, guest vocals by Edith Frost, and photography by Neko Case. A year later, she returned with *Because It Feel Good*, another eclectic set featuring performers like Andrew Bird and covers of songs by the Statler Brothers, Smog, Charlie Rich, and Randy Newman. —*Heather Phares*

Whistle Only Dogs Can Hear / Apr. 16, 1996 / Long Play ✦✦✦✦
Jody Grind frontwoman Kelly Hogan re-emerges with an eclectic collection of country-tinged torch songs and down-tempo rockers that highlight her warm, brassy voice. The album's best moments may be the interpretations of Vic Chesnutt and Will Oldham numbers that sound more personal and intimate than the versions recorded by the songs' own writers. Surprises like the shuffling "Dirtclod" and the slinky "The Idea of You" are all the more enjoyable for their unexpectedness. Only the noisy "Feel Good Hit" disappoints. Though she appears to be a less-than-prolific songwriter, penning just two of this album's 15 tracks, Hogan remains a talent to watch. —*Brian Beatty*

Beneath the Country Underdog / Jan. 1, 2000 / Bloodshot ✦✦✦
After former Jody Grind vocalist Kelly Hogan relocated to Chicago, she became a frequent (and welcome) presence on the recordings of a number of acts on the Windy City alt-country scene, popping up with everyone from Will Oldham to the Waco Brothers, and her first album for Bloodshot), *Beneath the Country Underdog*, makes it clear she has more than enough talent and authority to stand proudly beside anyone she's worked with in the past. Backed by the Pine Valley Cosmonauts (the Jon Langford-led group who invited Hogan to add her voice to a memorable take of "Drunkard's Blues" for their Bob Wills tribute album), *Beneath the Country Underdog* leans toward a country-accented approach as one would expect, but there's also more than a little R&B on deck, especially on the sassy "Wild Mountain Berries" and "I Don't Believe in You" (the latter complete with Stax-style horns), and Hogan's musical world view is broad enough to encompass covers of tunes by Johnny Paycheck, the Band, and the Magnetic Fields. And while this is Hogan's show, she displays the good sense to never overplay her hand; while she has a strong, clear voice and a superb sense of phrasing, she also has a welcome sense of restraint, and she knows when to quietly sneak through the nooks and crannies of a song just as surely as she knows when to belt it out hard and heavy. While covers dominate the album, the three tunes Hogan wrote with guitarist Andy Hopkins are fine stuff, and whether she's feeling blue or getting happy, Hogan never makes a wrong step when she steps in front of a mike. Quite simply, Kelly Hogan is among the finest female vocalist to emerge from the alt-country community, and *Beneath the Country Underdog* is a soul-satisfying delight well-worth listeners' attention. —*Mark Deming*

● **Because It Feel Good** / Oct. 9, 2001 / Bloodshot ✦✦✦✦
You certainly can't accuse Kelly Hogan of dishing up "more of the same" on her third solo album, *Because It Feel Good*—while her previous release, *Beneath the Country Underdog*, was a solid and satisfying dose of rootsy C&W and R&B, *Because It Feel Good* aims for something a good bit more expressive, and much harder to pigeonhole. Hogan has once again teamed up with a handful of superb Chicago-area musicians (including guitarist Andy Hopkins, pedal steel virtuoso Jon Rauhouse, and violinist Andrew Bird, taking a breather from his own band Bowl of Fire), but she's also enlisted David Barbe (best known as the former bassist with Sugar) as producer, and with Barbe's help Hogan has gone for a broader and more impressionistic sound for this album. The opening cut, a cover of the Statler Brothers' hit "I'll Go to My Grave Loving You," sets the tone with its echoey, skeletal guitar patterns, stark and boomy percussion, and Hogan's beautiful, ethereal voice soaring above it all, achieving an effect that's at once gorgeous, heart-tugging, and a little ominous. It's a daring approach and a bravura performance, and it works superbly on both levels. While much of *Because It Feel Good* takes a somewhat more traditional approach (particularly the low-key weeper "(You Don't Know) The First Thing About Love" and the soulful "Please Don't Leave Me Lonely"), for the most part the album strays admirably far from the formulaic constraints of typical alt-country, and Hogan proves just how broad and how keen her talent is. While there are only two originals from Hogan and Hopkins, they're both superb, and as she recasts songs by Charlie Rich, Smog, and Randy Newman—often without changing the gender of the main characters and always with taste, intelligence, and a simply gorgeous voice—she makes it clear she's one of the finest and most imaginative interpretive singers of her generation. If you're looking for updated honky tonk, this might not be your cup of tea, but if you want to hear a gifted and imaginative singer make the most of a diverse collection of fine tunes, then Kelly Hogan's *Because It Feel Good* deserves a place in your CD player. —*Mark Deming*

Roscoe Holcomb
b. 1911, Daisy, KY, d. 1981

Banjo, Vocals / Old-Timey, Traditional Folk, Appalachian Folk

One of the most noted Appalachian old-time musicians, banjo player and singer Roscoe Holcomb spent most of his life in the small town of Daisy, KY, and was one of the most authentic exponents of American mountain folk music. Indeed, he never had any professional ambitions but become a recording artist and participant in the folk revival circuit after being recorded for the first time in the late '50s. Holcomb's style is stark, epitomizing the keening, at times pained vocals associated with Appalachian music, with a repertoire stuffed with traditional songs that had passed among generations, as well as some songs that he likely learned from early country records. Folk musician and archivist John Cohen coined the term "high lonesome sound" to describe Holcomb's music, and the phrase has since passed into common usage to describe bluegrass and Appalachian music as a whole. He cut several albums for Folkways and made some concert appearances on the college/festival scene throughout the 1960s and 1970s, giving his last show in 1978. —*Richie Unterberger*

Close to Home / 1975 / Folkways ✦✦✦✦✦
Without attempting to slight any other Appalachian or old-time artist, many critics have decided the solo recordings of Roscoe Holcomb produced in the '60s by John Cohen represent some kind of pinnacle for this genre. Every quality that is important in this music is represented here in the fullest dimension, by a man who sings like a philosopher while keeping a rhythm going on several stringed instruments that would make a metronome envious. And then there's his voice. He seems to reach with some held notes as if attempting to establish a resonance that will allow him to actually enter a listener's skull. Holcomb didn't make that many recordings, so those who appreciate his music will want them all. This contains 11 pieces and it is hard to decide what is his best, his banjo or guitar playing. Some may put the haunting unaccompanied ballad "The Village Churchyard" ahead of it all. A great talent of Holcomb's is his ability to present material bordering on devastating emotionally in a way that is uplifting and rhythmically intoxicating. It makes for memorable music. —*Eugene Chadbourne*

The High Lonesome Sound / Jan. 20, 1998 / Smithsonian Folkways ✦✦✦✦✦
Here are 21 tracks from his Folkways album, including his accomplished, somber renditions of standards such as "House of the Rising Sun," "Moonshiner," "Trouble in Mind," and "Motherless Children." Holcomb is a big favorite among musicians and folklorists—Bob Dylan, for one, is a big fan—yet it must be said that this is probably *too* authentic for most listeners to play for pleasure. It's straight from the bone, with high, at times harsh vocals that make no concession to popular clichés to make things easier on the ear. That's one thing which makes the parallel to Dylan easy to see. The banjo playing is impressive, and the anthology is embellished by lengthy liner notes and recollections by John Cohen. —*Richie Unterberger*

★ **An Untamed Sense of Control** / Mar. 25, 2003 / Smithsonian Folkways ✦✦✦✦✦
As documented by the Smithsonian Folkways reissue *The High Lonesome Sound*, Roscoe Holcomb, like contemporaries Dock Boggs and Bascom Lamar Lunsford, was the real thing, a raw, solitary musician who expressed the inexpressible, a yearning out of time and place, a sense of the wild, the unseen, the unknowable, perhaps even the unspeakable. The title of this second volume of Holcomb's recordings comes from Bob Dylan, who was describing what he heard in Holcomb's music. And he's right, he knew how to get *that* sound, how to seek and find the mercurial ghost inside whatever instrument he was playing, the banjo, a guitar with a jackknife, or from that graveyard, sorrowful voice of his. His was able to channel the wisdom and tragedy of the ages and allow for both possibility and despair, even in his a cappella numbers. His is the sound of Appalachian midnight, somewhere past bluegrass, folk, and country. These recordings were made not in 1959 like the material on the other volume, but later, between 1961-1973, when Holcomb was touring, though in declining health and spirits. And, while some the material is

duplicated on this set, the versions are very different, and, if anything, this material is somehow spookier, deeper in the trenches of both sorrow and resignation. Some of these tunes were recorded in New York City and in concert in Cambridge, MA, and others on Holcomb's front porch in Daisy, KY. The settings hardly matter; this includes his versions of "Little Maggie," "Frankie and Johnny," the knife-guitar take of "Foggy Mountain Top" that is only rivaled by Maybelle Carter's, his 1961 version of Carter Stanley's "Man of Constant Sorrow" (which *is* the definitive version of the song done a cappella), and his read of "I Ain't Got No Sugar Baby Now" (which rivals Dock Boggs' earlier version). The truth in all of these songs is the way the blues, bluegrass, ancient folk traditions, and Holcomb's uncompromising and truly unusual sense of rhythm and phrasing collide and, rather than cancel each other out, bring one another to life. His blues songs, such as "Milk Cow Blues" and "Sitting on Top of This World," are fraught with edges and trail-offs that unsettle the listener, seeking a kind of completion that could only come from a singer who didn't hold the song as a living, breathing presence that haunts him. The bravado in the latter is offset by the irony that Holcomb's life had been an image in direct opposition to what the braggadocio in its lyrics offers. There is no grain in Holcomb's voice and banjo style; his voice *is* the grain, the American Grain in all its rough-hewn glory and grace and desolation. It is majestic in its reediness and singular in its power. This is an essential collection for anyone interested in American traditional music—be it folk, blues, country, or bluegrass—and is a primer for those who seek to discover what it was that all of those musics sought to express. *—Thom Jurek*

The Hollisters

f. 1994

Group / Honky Tonk, Alternative Country, Rockabilly Revival, Americana

The Hollisters played their first date together in June 1995, and by summer 1997 they had been voted the best country act in Houston. Their 1997 CD, *The Land of Rhythm & Pleasure*, became Houston's best-selling local release. Although this success story sounds like a meteoric rise to fame, the four bandmembers took varied paths through other musical outfits before coming together to form the Hollisters. Lead singer Mike Barfield's most obvious vocal influence is Johnny Cash, but he also credits George Jones, Johnny Horton, and Sun Records artists like Carl Perkins and Elvis Presley with helping to shape his sound. Barfield played in various blues bands in the Texas Gulf Coast area before founding the popular Houston country-rock band the Rounders with lead guitarist Eric Danheim. That group broke up when Danheim left to join Austin's Wagoneers and, later, Chapparal. At the same time, bassist Denny Dale was playing with Webb Wilder, and Kevin Fitzpatrick was playing drums in Atlanta. In 1994, they both came to Houston and joined Barfield and Danheim to form the Hollisters. After playing everywhere they could in Houston for two years, the group hit it big with the aforementioned *Houston Press* award and debut album, which they hoped would take them to a larger audience. *Sweet Inspiration* followed in early 2000. *—Brian Wahlert*

● **The Land of Rhythm & Pleasure** / Nov. 4, 1997 / Freedom ✦✦✦✦

The Hollisters keep dancehall audiences satisfied with their rollicking brand of country music, which translates well to a studio recording on this album. Lead singer Mike Barfield and guitarist Eric Danheim co-wrote nine of the 12 songs here, and their best and most distinctive is "Deacon Brown." The first lilting minute of the song sounds like cowboys singing around the campfire as the singer tells how he "stabbed my Romina with a Barlow knife." Then the drums, electric guitar, and even a Spanish classical guitar kick in, and the tempo increases as the singer describes the consequences of his actions. "Pink Adobe Hacienda" has a more overt south-of-the-border feel with classical guitar and accordion. But these songs are the exception. Midtempo songs that keep the couples dancing are the bread and butter of a band like the Hollisters, whose touring has taken them from one hole-in-the-wall nightclub to another. Songs like "Tyler," "Without Love," and "Good for the Blues" fit that bill. Barfield's baritone has often drawn comparisons to Johnny Cash, and nowhere is this comparison more fitting than on "Heart." Barfield never masters the ruddy resonance of Cash, but his singing is still enjoyable. Overall, this is a very good debut album that should take the Hollisters' music to a broader audience. *—Brian Wahlert*

Sweet Inspiration / Feb. 15, 2000 / Hightone ✦✦✦

It's not hard to hear why the Hollisters are considered one of the finest bands in Houston. Energy, energy, and more energy are what these guys thrive on, and one can imagine that seeing them live must be a heck of a good-time. That is, if you appreciate country music stripped of most of its emotional power, imbued with novelty, and cranked up loud. That's the nutshell review of *Sweet Inspiration*, but there are a few additional things worth mentioning. First of all, these guys can really play. Led by guitarist Eric Danheim, the band has developed a tight, punchy sound which is firmly in its element on rowdy rockers like "Fishin' Man" and "Love Rustler." Mike Barfield's Johnny Cash-like lead vocals are well known, and they are all over this album, especially on "Thrill of the Ride" and "Holes in the Road (Dumptruck)." In the end, though, while the record is fun, it can't cover up the fact that the Hollisters are a party band, no matter how polished their attack. *—Jim Smith*

Buddy Holly (Charles Hardin Holley)

b. Sep. 7, 1936, Lubbock, TX, **d.** Feb. 3, 1959, Clear Lake, IA

Guitar, Vocals / Rock & Roll, Rockabilly

Buddy Holly is perhaps the most anomalous legend of '50s rock & roll—he had his share of hits, and he achieved major rock & roll stardom, but his importance transcends any sales figures or even the particulars of any one song (or group of songs) that he wrote or recorded. Holly was unique, his legendary status and his impact on popular music all the more extraordinary for having been achieved in barely 18 months. Among his rivals, Bill Haley was there first and established rock & roll music; Elvis Presley objectified the sexuality implicit in the music, selling hundreds of millions of records in the process, and defined one aspect of the youth and charisma needed for stardom; and Chuck Berry defined the music's roots in blues along with some of the finer points of its sexuality, and its youthful orientation (and, in the process, intermixed all of these elements). Holly's influence was just as far-reaching as these others, if far more subtle and more distinctly musical in nature. In a career lasting from the spring of 1957 until the winter of 1958-1959—less time than Elvis had at the top before the army took him (and less time, in fact, than Elvis spent in the army)—Holly became the single most influential creative force in early rock & roll.

Born in Lubbock, TX, on September 7, 1936, Charles Hardin "Buddy" Holley (he later dropped the "e") was the youngest of four children. A natural musician from a musical family, he was proficient on guitar, banjo, and mandolin by age 15 and was working as part of a duo with his boyhood friend Bob Montgomery, with whom he had also started writing songs. By the mid-'50s, Buddy & Bob, as they billed themselves, were playing what they called "western and bop"; Holly, in particular, was listening to a lot of blues and R&B and finding it compatible with country music. He was among those young Southern men who heard and saw Elvis perform in the days when the latter was signed to Sam Phillips' Sun Records—indeed, Buddy & Bob played as an opening act for Elvis when he played the area around Lubbock in early 1955, and Holly saw the future direction of his life and career.

By mid-1955, Buddy & Bob, who already worked with an upright bass (played by Larry Welborn), had added drummer Jerry Allison to their lineup. They'd also cut some sides that would have qualified as rock & roll, though no label was interested at that particular time. Eventually Montgomery, who leaned toward more of a traditional country sound, left the performing partnership, though they continued to compose songs together. Holly kept pushing his music toward a straight-ahead rock & roll sound, working with Allison, Welborn, and assorted other local musicians, including guitarist Sonny Curtis and bassist Don Guess. It was with the latter two that Holly cut his first official recording session in January of 1956 in Nashville for Decca Records. They found out, however, that there was a lot more to playing and cutting rock & roll than met the eye; the results of this and a follow-up session in July were alternately either a little too tame and a little too far to the country side of the mix or were too raw. Some good music and a pair of near classics, "Midnight Shift" and "Rock Around With Ollie Vee," did come out of those Decca sessions, but nothing issued at the time went anywhere. At the time, it looked as though Holly had missed his shot at stardom.

Fate intervened in the guise of Norman Petty, a musician-turned-producer based in Clovis, NM, who had an ear for the new music and what made it sound good, especially over the radio, to the kids. Petty had a studio where he charged by the song instead of by the hour, and Holly and company had already begun working there in the late spring of 1956. After Decca's rejection, Holly and his band, which now included Niki Sullivan on rhythm guitar, threw themselves into what Petty regarded as the most promising songs they had, until they worked out a tight, tough version of one of the failed originals that Holly had cut in Nashville, entitled "That'll Be the Day." The title and lyrical phrase, lifted from a line that John Wayne was always quoting in the John Ford movie *The Searchers*, had staying power, and the group built on it. They got the song nailed and recorded, and with Petty's help, got it picked up by Murray Deutsch, a publishing associate of Petty's who, in turn, got it to Bob Thiele, an executive at Coral Records, who liked it. Ironically, Coral was a subsidiary of Decca, the same company to which Holly had previously been signed.

Thiele saw the record as potential hit, but there were some major hurdles to overcome before it could actually get released. For starters, according to author Philip Norman in his book *Rave On*, Thiele would get only the most begrudging support from his record company. Decca had lucked out in 1954 when, at Milt Gabler's urging, they'd signed Bill Haley & His Comets and subsequently saw his "Rock Around the Clock" top the charts, but very few of those in charge at Decca had a real feel or appreciation for rock & roll or any sense of where it might be heading, or whether the label could (or should) follow it there. For another, although he had been dropped by Decca Records the previous year, the contract that Holly had signed prohibited him from re-recording anything that he had cut for Decca, regardless of whether it had been released or not, for five years; though Coral Records was a subsidiary of Decca, there was every chance that Decca's Nashville office could hold up the release and might even haul Holly into court. Amid all of these possibilities, good and bad, Welborn, who had played on "That'll Be the Day," was replaced on bass by Joe B. Mauldin.

"That'll Be the Day" was issued in May of 1957 mostly as an indulgence to Thiele, to "humor" him, according to Norman. The record was put out on the Brunswick label, which was oriented more toward jazz and R&B, and credited to the Crickets, a group name picked as a dodge to prevent any of the powers-that-were at Decca—and especially Decca's Nashville office—from having too easy a time figuring out that the singer was the same artist that they'd dropped the year before. Petty also became the group's manager as well as their producer, signing the Crickets—identified as Allison, Sullivan, and Mauldin—to a contract. Holly wasn't listed as a member in the original document, in order to hide his involvement with "That'll Be the Day," but this omission would later become the source of serious legal and financial problems for him.

When the smoke cleared, the song shot to the top spot on the national charts that summer. Of course, Decca knew Holly's identity by then; with Thiele's persuasion and the reality of a serious hit in their midst, the company agreed to release Holly from the five-year restriction on his old contract, leaving him free to sign any recording contract he wanted. In the midst of sorting out the particulars of Holly's legal situation, Thiele discovered that he had someone on his hands who was potentially a good deal more than a one-hit wonder—there were potentially more and different kinds of potential hits to come from him. When all was said and done, Holly found himself with two recording contracts, one with Brunswick as a member of the Crickets and the other with Coral Records as Buddy Holly, which was part of Thiele's strategy to get the most out of Holly's talent. By releasing two separate bodies of work, he could keep the group intact while giving room for its obvious leader and "star" to break out on his own.

There was actually little difference in the two sets of recordings for most of his career, in terms of how they were done or who played on them, except possibly that the harder, straight-ahead rock & roll songs, and the ones with backing vocals, tended to be credited to the Crickets. The confusion surrounding the Buddy Holly/Crickets dual identity was nothing, however, compared to the morass that constituted the songwriting credits on their work.

It's now clear that Petty, acting as their manager and producer, parceled out writing credits at random, gifting Niki Sullivan and Joe B. Mauldin (and himself) the co-authorship of "I'm Gonna Love You Too," while initially leaving Holly's name off of "Peggy Sue." Petty usually added his name to the credit line as well, a common practice in the 1950s for managers and producers who wanted a bigger piece of the action. In fairness, it should be said that Petty did make suggestions, some of them key, in shaping certain of Holly's songs, but he almost certainly didn't contribute to the extent that the shared credits would lead one to believe. Some of the public's confusion over songwriting was heightened by complications ensuing from another of the contracts that Holly had signed in 1956. Petty had his own publishing company, Nor Va Jak Music, and had a contract with Holly to publish all of his new songs; but the prior year, Holly had signed an exclusive contract with another company—eventually a settlement and release from the old contract might be sorted out, but in order to reduce his profile as a songwriter until that happened, and to convince the other publisher that they weren't losing too much in any settlement, he copyrighted many of his new songs under the pseudonym "Charles Hardin."

The dual recording contracts made it possible for Holly to record an extraordinary number of sides in the course of his 18 months of fame. Meanwhile, the group—billed as Buddy Holly & the Crickets—became one of the top attractions of rock & roll's classic years, putting on shows that were as exciting and well played as any in the business. Holly was the frontman, singing lead and playing lead guitar—itself an unusual combination—as well as writing or co-writing many of their songs. But the Crickets were also a totally enveloping performing unit, generating a big and exciting sound (which, apart from some live recordings from their 1958 British tour, is lost to history). Allison was a very inventive drummer and contributed to the songwriting bit more often than his colleagues, and Joe B. Mauldin and Niki Sullivan provided a solid rhythm section.

The fact that the group relied on originals for their singles made them unique and put them years ahead of their time. In 1957-1958, songwriting wasn't considered a skill essential to a career in rock & roll; the music business was still patterned along the lines that it had followed since the '20s, with songwriting a specialized profession organized on the publishing side of the industry, separate from performing and recording. Once in a while, a performer might write a song or, much more rarely, as in the case of a Duke Ellington, count composition among his key talents, but generally this was an activity left to the experts. Any rock & roller with the inclination to write songs would also have to get past the image of Elvis, who stood to become a millionaire at age 22 and never wrote songs (the few "Presley" songwriting credits were the result of business arrangements rather than any creative activity on his part).

Buddy Holly & the Crickets changed that in a serious way by hitting number one with a song that they'd written and then reaching the Top Ten with originals like "Oh, Boy" and "Peggy Sue," and regularly charging up the charts on behalf of their own songwriting. This attribute wasn't appreciated by the public at the time, and wouldn't be noticed widely until the 1970s, but thousands of aspiring musicians, including John Lennon and Paul McCartney, took note of the fact, and some of them decided to try and emulate Holly. Less obvious at the time, Holly and company also broke up the established record industry method of recording, which was to bring the artist into the label's own studio, working on a timetable dictated by corporate policy and union rules. If an artist were extremely successful—à la Sinatra or Elvis, or later on, the Beatles—they got a blank check in the studio and any union rules were smoothed over, but that was a rare privilege, available only to the most elite of musicians. Buddy Holly & the Crickets, by contrast, did their work, beginning with "That'll Be the Day," in Clovis, NM, at Petty's studio. They took their time, they experimented until they got the sound they wanted, and no union told them when to stop or start their work, and they delivered great records; what's more, they were records that didn't sound like anyone else's, anywhere.

The results were particularly telling on the history of rock music. The group worked out a sound that gave shape to the next wave of rock & roll and, especially, to early British rock & roll and the subsequent British Invasion beat, with the lead and rhythm guitars closely interlocked to create a fuller, harder sound. On songs such as "Not Fade Away," "Everyday," "Listen to Me," "Oh Boy!," "Peggy Sue," "Maybe Baby," "Rave On," "Heartbeat," and "It's So Easy," Holly advanced rock & roll's range and sophistication without abandoning its fundamental joy and excitement. Holly and the band weren't afraid to experiment even on their singles, so that "Peggy Sue" made use of the kind of changes in volume and timbre on the guitar that were usually reserved for instrumental records; similarly, "Words of Love" was one of the earliest successful examples of double-tracked vocals in rock & roll, which the Beatles, in particular, would embrace in the ensuing decade.

Buddy Holly & the Crickets were very popular in America, but in England they were even bigger, their impact serious rivaling that of Elvis and, in some ways, even exceeding it. This was due, in part, to the fact that they actually toured England—they spent a month there in 1958, playing a series of shows that were still being written about 30 years later—which was something that Elvis never did. But it also had to do with their sound and Holly's stage persona. The group's heavy use of rhythm guitar slotted right in with the sound of skiffle music, a mix of blues, folk, country, and jazz elements that constituted most of British youth's introduction to playing music and their way into rock & roll. Additionally, although he cut an exciting figure on-stage, Holly looked a lot less likely a rock & roll star than Elvis—tall, lanky, and bespectacled, he looked like an ordinary guy who simply played and sang well, and part of his appeal as a rock & roll star was rooted in how unlikely he looked in that role. He provided inspiration—and a way into the music—for tens of thousands of British teenagers who also couldn't imagine themselves rivals to Elvis or Gene Vincent in the dark and dangerous department.

At least one star British guitarist of the late '50s, Hank Marvin of the Shadows, owed his look (and the fact that he wore his glasses proudly on-stage) to Holly, and his look can be seen being propagated into the 1970s by Elvis Costello. Additionally, although he played

several different kinds of guitar, Holly was specifically responsible for popularizing—some would say elevating to mystical, even magical status—the Fender Stratocaster, especially in England. For a lot of would-be rock & rollers on the Sceptered Isle, Holly's 1958 tour was the first chance they'd had to see or hear the instrument in action, and it quickly became the guitar of choice for anyone aspiring to stardom as an axeman in England. (Indeed, Marvin, inspired by Holly, later had what is reputed to be the first Stratocaster ever brought into England.)

The Crickets were reduced to a trio with the departure of Sullivan in late 1957, following the group's appearance on *the Ed Sullivan Show*, but that was almost the least of the changes that would ensue over the following year. The group consolidated its success with the release of two LPs, *The Chirping Crickets* and *Buddy Holly*, and did two very successful international tours as well as more performing in the U. S. Holly had already developed aspirations and interests that diverged somewhat from those of Allison and Mauldin. The thought apparently had never occurred to either of them of giving up Texas as their home, and they continued to base their lives there, while Holly was increasingly drawn to New York, not just as a place to do business, but also to live. His romance with and marriage to Maria Elena Santiago, a receptionist in Murray Deutsch's office, only made the decision to move to New York easier.

By this time, Holly's music had grown in sophistication and complexity to the point where he had relinquished the lead guitar duties in the studio to session player Tommy Alsup, and he had done a number of recordings in New York utilizing session musicians such as King Curtis. It was during this period that his and the group's sales had slackened somewhat. The singles such as "Heartbeat" didn't sell nearly as well as the 45s of 1957 had rolled out of stores. He might even have advanced farther than a big chunk of the group's audience was prepared to accept in late 1958. "Well … All Right," for example, was years ahead of its time as a song and a recording.

Holly's split with the group—and Petty—in the fall of 1958 left him free to pursue some of those newer sounds, but it also left him short of cash resources. In the course of ending the association, it became clear to Holly and everyone else that Petty had manipulated the numbers and likely taken an enormous slice of the group's income for himself, though there was to prove almost no way of establishing this because he never seemed to finish his "accounting" of the moneys due to anyone, and his books were ultimately found to be in such disarray that when he came up with various low five-figure settlements to those involved, they were glad to get what they got.

With a new wife—who was pregnant—and no settlement coming in from Petty, Holly decided to earn some quick money by signing to play the Winter Dance Party package tour of the Midwest. It was on that tour that Holly, Ritchie Valens, and J. P. "Big Bopper" Richardson were killed in a plane crash, on February 3, 1959. The crash was considered a piece of grim but not terribly significant news at the time. Most news organizations, run by men who'd come of age in the 1930s or 1940s, didn't take rock & roll very seriously, except to the degree that it could be exploited to sell newspapers or build viewing audiences. Holly's clean-cut image and scandal-free life, coupled with the news of his recent marriage, did give the story more poignancy than it otherwise might have had and probably got him treated more respectfully than would have been the case with other music stars of the period.

For teenagers of the period, it was the first public tragedy of its kind. No white rock & roller of any significance had ever died before, forget three of them, and the news was devastating. Radio station disc jockeys were also shaken—for a lot of people involved in rock & roll music on any level, Holly's death may well have been the first time that they woke up the next day wishing and hoping that the previous day's news had all been a dream. The suddenness and the whole accidental nature of the event, coupled with the ages of Holly and Valens—22 and 17, respectively—made it even harder to take. Hank Williams had died at 29, but with his drinking and drug use he had always seemed on the fast track to the grave to almost anyone who knew him and even to a lot of fans; Johnny Ace had died in 1954 backstage at a show, but that was also by his own hand, in a game of Russian roulette. The emotional resonances of this event was totally different in every way possible from those tragedies.

A few careers were actually launched in the wake of the tragedy. Bobby Vee leaped to stardom when he and his band took over Holly's spot on the tour. In America, however, something of a pall fell over rock & roll music—its sound was muted by Holly's death and Elvis' military service, and this darkness didn't fully lift for years. In England, the reaction was much more concentrated and pronounced—Holly's final single, "It Doesn't Matter Anymore," rose to number one on the British charts in the wake of his death, and it seemed as though the new generation of English rock & rollers and their audiences wouldn't let Holly's music or spirit die. Two years after the event, producer Joe Meek and singer Mike Berry combined to make "Tribute to Buddy Holly," a memorial single that sounded like the man himself reborn and still brings smiles and chills to listeners who know it; it is said that Meek never entirely got over Holly's death, and he did kill himself on the anniversary. On the less extreme front, players from Lennon, McCartney, and Keith Richards on down all found themselves influenced by Holly's music, songs, and playing. Groups like the Searchers—taking their name from the same Wayne movie whence the phrase "that'll be the day" had been lifted—sounded a lot like the Crickets and had a handful of his songs in their repertory when they cut their earliest sides, and it wasn't just the hits that they knew, but album cuts as well. Other bands, like a Manchester-spawned outfit fronted by Allan Clarke, Graham Nash, and Tony Hicks began a four-decade career by taking the name the Hollies.

Holly's record label continued to release posthumous albums of his work for years after his death, beginning with *The Buddy Holly Story* in early 1959, and they even repackaged the 1956 Decca sides several times over under various titles (the mid-'70s British LP *The Nashville Sessions* is the best of the vinyl editions). The company also engaged Petty to take various Holly demos and early country-flavored sides done by Buddy & Bob and dub new instruments and backing voices, principally using a band called the Fireballs. Those releases, including the albums *Reminiscing* and *Showcase*, did moderately well in America, but in England they actually charted. New recordings of his music, including the Rolling Stones' bone-shaking rendition of "Not Fade Away"—taking it back to its Bo Diddley-inspired roots—and the Beatles gorgeous rendition of "Words of

Love" helped keep Holly's name alive before a new generation of listeners. In America, it was more of an uphill struggle to spread the word—rock & roll, like most American popular culture, was always regarded as more easily disposable, and as a new generation of teenagers and new musical phenomena came along, the public did gradually forget. By the end of the 1960s, except among older fans (now in their twenties) and hardcore oldies listeners, Holly was a largely forgotten figure in his own country.

The tide began to turn at the very tail-end of the 1960s, with the beginning of the oldies boom. Holly's music figured in it, of course, and as people listened they also heard about the man behind it—even *Rolling Stone* magazine, then the arbiter of taste for the counterculture, went out of its way to remind people of who Holly was. His image constituted a haunting figure, frozen forever in poses from 1957 and 1958, bespectacled, wearing a jacket and smiling; he looked like (and was) a figure from another age. The nature of his death, in an air crash, also set him apart from some of the then-recent deaths of contemporary rock stars such as Brian Jones, Jimi Hendrix, Janis Joplin, and Jim Morrison—they'd all pushed life right to the edge, till it broke, where Holly stood there seemingly eternally innocent, both personally and in terms of the times in which he'd lived.

Then, in 1971, a little-known singer/songwriter named Don McLean, who counted himself a Holly fan, rose to international stardom behind a song called "American Pie," whose narrative structure was hooked around "the day the music died." After disposing of the erroneous notion that he was referring to President Kennedy, McLean made it clear that he meant February 3, 1959, and Holly. Coverage of "American Pie"'s popularity and lyrics as it soared to the top of the charts inevitably led to mentions of Holly, who was suddenly getting more exposure in the national press than he'd ever enjoyed in his lifetime. His music had never disappeared—even the Grateful Dead performed "Not Fade Away" in concert—and now there was a song that seemed to give millions of people a series of personal and musical reference points into which to place the man. Until "American Pie," most Americans equated November 22, 1963, the day of President Kennedy's murder, with the loss of national innocence and an opening of an era of shared grief. McLean pushed the reference point back to February 3, 1959, on a purely personal basis, and an astonishingly large number of listeners accepted it.

In 1975, McCartney's MPL Communications bought Holly's publishing catalog from a near-bankrupt Petty. To some, the sale was Petty's final act of theft—having robbed Holly and his widow blind in settling the account of what was owed him as a performer, he was profiting one last time from his perfidy. The truth is that it was a godsend to Maria Elena Holly and the Holly family in Lubbock; amid the events of the years and decades that followed, MPL was able to sell and exploit those songs in ways that Petty in Clovis, NM, never could have, and earn hundreds of thousands of dollars for them that Petty never would have. And with McCartney—a Holly fan from the age of 15, and probably the most successful fan Holly ever had—as publisher, they were paid every cent they had coming.

Amid the growing interest in Holly's music, the record industry was very slow to respond, at least in America. At the end of the 1960s, there were exactly two Holly LPs available domestically, *The Great Buddy Holly*, consisting of the 1956 Decca sides, which hardly represented his best or most important work, and the even more dispensable *Giant* album, consisting of overdubbed demos and outtakes. British audiences got access to more and better parts of his catalog first, and a collection, *20 Golden Greats*, actually topped the charts over there in 1978, in conjunction with the release of the movie *the Buddy Holly Story*, starring Gary Busey in the title role. It was a romanticized and very simplified account of the man's life and career, and slighted the contributions of the other members of the Crickets—and never even mentioned Petty—but it got some of the essentials right and made Busey into a star and Holly into a household name.

In 1979, Holly became the first rock & roll star to be the subject of a career-spanning box set, ambitiously (and inaccurately) called *The Complete Buddy Holly*. Initially released in England and Germany, it later appeared in America, but it only seemed to whet hardcore fans' appetites for more—two or three Holly bootlegs were circulating in the early '80s, including one that offered a handful of songs from the group's 1958 British tour. In a rare bold move, mostly courtesy of producer Steve Hoffman, MCA Records in 1983 issued *For the First Time Anywhere*, a selection of raw, undubbed masters of original Holly recordings that had previously only been available with extra instruments added on—it was followed by *From the Original Master Tapes*, the first attempt to put together a Holly compilation with upgraded sound quality. Those titles and *The Great Buddy Holly* were the earliest of Holly's official CD releases, though they were soon followed by *Buddy Holly* and *The Chirping Crickets*. In 1986, the BBC aired *The Real Buddy Holly Story*, a documentary produced by McCartney as a counteractive to the Busey movie, which covered all of the areas ignored by the inaccuracies of the movie and responded to them. There have followed stage musicals and plays, upgraded and audiophile reissues of his work, and tribute albums, all continuing to flow out at a steady pace more than 40 years after Holly's death. *—Bruce Eder*

☆ **The "Chirping" Crickets** / 1957 / MCA ✦✦✦✦✦

The debut album by the Crickets and the only one featuring Buddy Holly released during his lifetime, *The "Chirping" Crickets* contains the group's number-one single "That'll Be the Day" and its Top Ten hit "Oh, Boy!" Other Crickets classics include "Not Fade Away," "Maybe Baby," and "I'm Looking for Someone to Love." The rest of the 12 tracks are not up to the standard set by those five, but those five are among the best rock & roll songs of the 1950s or ever, making this one of the most significant album debuts in rock & roll history, ranking with *Elvis Presley* and *Meet the Beatles*. *—William Ruhlmann*

That'll Be the Day / 1958 / Decca ✦✦✦

The tendency of most critics is to dismiss this album, comprised as it is of the songs from Holly's 1956 Nashville sessions, which yielded a somewhat too tentative, country-oriented sound that suited neither him nor the public. In actual fact, at least ten of the 11 songs on this LP (the one exception being the ballad "Girl on My Mind") have aged almost as well as anything that Holly ever recorded. "Rock Around With Ollie Vee," "Blue Days, Black Nights," "Ting-A-Ling," "I'm Changing All Those Changes," "Modern Don Juan," "Love Me," "Don't Come Back Knockin'," and "Midnight Shift" are all decent, solid early rock & roll; he sounds too countrified by about half on much of the record, especially on the early version of "That'll Be the Day," but these were not bad records, even if they weren't going to break his talent out to a mass audience. What's more, at least at the time of his first sessions in January of 1956, few white artists and even fewer producers at major labels had yet figured out what mix of country, R&B, and blues worked on a rock & roll record. Given all of this, this is a better than decent album with one real gem ("Rock Around With Ollie Vee"), and if not for the fact that they mostly feature a completely different lineup of musicians and were also contractually separate from the rest of his eventual output for Coral/Brunswick/Decca, roughly half of the songs here could have been filtered into either of Holly's later official LPs without doing any violence to the newer material. Even the ballad "You Are My One Desire"—though it doesn't really resemble much else that Holly ever did—is given a hauntingly passionate performance. *That'll Be the Day* isn't a revelatory piece of rock & roll history, but it's a more substantial and enjoyable prelude to the main body of Holly's career than it's usually given credit for being, extending his serious legacy backward a full album. [In 1967, Decca Records reissued *That'll Be the Day* as *The Great Buddy Holly*, with a new cover and stripping off the song "Ting-A-Ling." In 1975, British MCA gathered together the 11 songs off of this album and an alternate take of "Rock Around With Ollie Vee" from a different session and released it as *The Nashville Sessions*.] *—Bruce Eder*

Buddy Holly / Feb. 20, 1958 / Brunswick ✦✦✦✦✦

When Buddy Holly & the Crickets broke through nationally in 1957, they were marketed by Decca Records as two different acts whose records were released on two different Decca subsidiaries—Brunswick for Crickets records, Coral for Holly records. But there was no real musical distinction between the two, except perhaps that the "Crickets" sides had more prominent backup vocals. Nevertheless, coming three months after *The "Chirping" Crickets*, this was the debut album credited to Buddy Holly. It featured Holly's Top Ten single "Peggy Sue" plus several songs that have turned out to be standards—"I'm Gonna Love You Too," "Listen To Me," "Everyday," "Words of Love," and "Rave On." The rest of the 12 tracks weren't as distinctive, though Holly's takes on such rock & roll hits as "Ready Teddy" and "You're So Square (Baby, I Don't Care)" provide an interesting contrast with the more familiar versions by Elvis Presley. This was the final new album featuring Holly to be released during his lifetime. Every subsequent album was an archival or posthumous-collection. [(Originally released on LP by Coral Records [as Coral 57210] on February 20, 1958, *Buddy Holly* was reissued on CD by MCA Records in 1988.)] *—William Ruhlmann*

The Buddy Holly Story / 1959 / Coral ✦✦✦✦✦

This 12-track compilation album was rushed out within weeks of Buddy Holly's death. It combines what previously had been credited as Crickets group-titles and Holly solo recordings, containing all eight of Holly and the Crickets' Top 40 hits, 1957-1959: "That'll Be the Day," "Peggy Sue," "Oh, Boy!," "Maybe Baby," "Rave On," "Think It Over," "Early in the Morning," and "It Doesn't Matter Anymore," plus the chart entries "Heartbeat" and "Raining in My Heart" and the classics "Everyday" and "It's So Easy." There was more great Holly, of course, but this was an excellent single-LP compilation. *—William Ruhlmann*

Reminiscing / 1963 / Pair ✦✦✦✦

Even with Buddy Holly four years in the grave, there were "new" albums of his stuff coming out that were running circles around most of the competition, and *Reminiscing* was a prime example, a bluesy, hard-rocking, moody assembly of material gathered from across more than two years of Holly's history, from among some of his last finished tracks and demos going all the way back to 1956 and extending up as late as his home-recorded demos of January 1959. Apart from "Wait 'Til the Sun Shines, Nellie"—which he may well have done as a sentimental favorite—the main focus of the sound (overdubbed by the Fireballs under the guidance of producer Norman Petty) was rockabilly, sometimes of a very advanced kind. This expanded reissue, courtesy of MCA's British division, features not only excellent sound but is augmented with the presence of seven bonus tracks, including some of the 1956/1957 demos ("Bo Diddley," "Brown Eyed Handsome Man," "Slippin' and Slidin'") that formed the basic tracks for parts of the finished album, coupled with a handful of demos and acetates that were found in the early '80s and turned up originally on the *For the First Time Anywhere* album. The annotation by Colin Escott is as good as the sound—and that's very good—and this release continues the pattern of Holly's catalog generally being treated better in England than America. *—Bruce Eder*

Showcase / 1964 / Coral ✦✦✦

The second of the posthumously overdubbed albums, *Showcase* presented a number of rock & roll cover songs performed by Buddy Holly, most of them recorded during his sessions in Nashville in 1956. It was not Holly at his best, though the performances were often spirited. *—William Ruhlmann*

Holly in the Hills / 1965 / Coral ✦✦✦

On its face, *Holly in the Hills* was seemingly one of the more artistically dubious Buddy Holly albums to appear posthumously. Built around Holly's pre-Crickets recordings circa 1955, as part of the duo of Buddy & Bob, the familiar Holly voice is present and easy to appreciate, though he's sharing the spotlight with Bob Montgomery and doing a repertory that's steeped thoroughly in country music, complete with fiddle accompaniment ("Baby It's Love," "I Gambled My Heart"). Holly was beginning to discover rock & roll and work out a sound of his own, as demonstrated by some of the cuts here, but he was still a country artist and doing a lot of ballads in that idiom as well. Apart from "I Wanna Play House With You," "Wishing," and "Down the Line"—and as it happens, those three are killer tracks, worth the price of the album—little here resembles the sound that Holly subsequently became known for. All of it, however, is fine music, occupying a place in Holly's career to what the Everly Brothers' early Columbia sides represent in their history (though it is far more sophisticated than the Everlys' sides). The presence of the Fireballs, a band managed and produced by producer Norman Petty, on several of the tracks, does bring the material up to a modern standard (circa 1965), and it's easy to see why this record sold well, especially in England, where it rode the charts for six weeks and just missed the Top Ten. *Holly in the Hills* does represent a formative and legitimate component of Holly's music, which is perfectly valid, and he does amazingly well in tandem with Montgomery on numbers like "Queen of the Ballroom" and "Soft Place in My Heart"—had rock & roll not come along, it would be easy to see these Buddy & Bob sides having opened a career in country music for the two of them that could easily have carried them into the 1960s before a very different audience from the one Holly actually ended up finding. —*Bruce Eder*

Western & Bop / 1978 / MCA ✦✦

This is an album made up of the "Buddy & Bob" demos of 1954-1955, country music recorded by Buddy Holly and Bob Montgomery before Holly turned to rock & roll and became a star. —*William Ruhlmann*

☆ The Complete Buddy Holly / 1979 / MCA ✦✦✦✦✦

In the wake of the number one British ranking for *20 Golden Greats* in 1978 and the release of the feature film *the Buddy Holly Story*, MCA U.K. assembled this six-LP box set (which finally was released in the U.S. in February 1981). It traces Buddy Holly's career from his country & western duo with Bob Montgomery in 1954-1955 to his 1956 Nashville sessions for Decca Records; the Clovis, NM, recordings with the Crickets and producer Norman Petty that launched his career in 1957; the New York sessions of 1958; the final 1958 demo recordings; the various posthumously overdubbed versions of the demos; and other assorted rarities. In other words, all the material that Decca/MCA previously had spread across seven LPs—*The "Chirping" Crickets, Buddy Holly, That'll Be the Day, Reminiscing, Showcase, Holly in the Hills*, and *Giant*—between 1957 and 1969 (not counting the many compilations) was here, plus more. The box also contained an extensive scrapbook, lots of liner notes, and a detailed discography. It was, thus, the state of the art in box sets just prior to the CD era, and given Holly's importance in the history of rock & roll, an essential album for any serious collector. With the passing of the LP era, it is out of print, and MCA claims to be gathering more unreleased material for some comparable box set, though years go by without its appearing. Meanwhile, if you needed one record album to demonstrate what the most popular music of the second half of the 20th century sounded like, this would be it. —*William Ruhlmann*

The Great Buddy Holly / 1982 / MCA ✦✦✦

In 1967, Decca Records reissued Buddy Holly's *That'll Be the Day* album with new cover art and this new title, minus one song ("Ting-A-Ling"). That album has remained in print to the present day, due in part to the fact that it's always been popular as a low-priced LP or CD—the latter is a result of the ironing out of the contractual and potential legal difficulties that Buddy Holly had engendered by re-recording "That'll Be the Day" (which appears here in its early version); he surrendered any artist royalties to which he would have been entitled from these sides, so MCA owns them completely. Reference books and experienced listeners have always felt compelled to warn neophyte fans away from *The Great Buddy Holly*, not because it's bad (it's not), but because its ten songs were cut at Holly's 1956 Nashville sessions, before he had evolved and created (in the studio, at least) the sound that made him famous. In fact, this is a fun record, if not really representative of Holly's fully developed style, and ought to interest not only his fans, but also anyone who wants to learn a little more about the early days of the rock & roll boom, when even soon-to-be top artists and their producers were still trying to figure out how big a proportion of country to R&B, blues, and pop there ought to be in a rock & roll record. [But better still, one should track down the imported reissue (part of a two-on-one CD) of *That'll Be the Day* from Beat Goes On Records, or the mid-'70s British LP *The Nashville Sessions*, both of which offer the same songs in better sound and with full annotation. —*Bruce Eder*

For the First Time Anywhere / 1983 / MCA ✦✦✦✦✦

When this album was originally released in 1983, it was a major revelation in collector's circles. Here were the original, undubbed versions of eight songs that had appeared on posthumous Holly albums like *Reminiscing, Showcase*, and others with overdubbed backing provided by the Fireballs and producer Norman Petty, along with two rarities to pad things out. And hearing the stripped-down Holly minus the audio cover-ups and beef-ups revealed strong (and sometimes superior) efforts all by themselves without the assistance. With future Cricket Jerry Allison on drums, a set of revolving bass players, and Sonny Curtis handling lead guitar chores on three tracks, Holly blasts through some bona fide Texas rockabilly here. Four of the eight tracks come from Buddy's pen, and these early efforts ("Rock-a-Bye Rock," "Because I Love You," "Changing All Those Changes," and "I'm Gonna Set My Foot Down") are sign pointers toward his later, more commercial style; in this case listeners get stripped-down, elemental pop tunes disguised as rockabilly ravers and country ballads. The collection is bookended with two more tracks, the original studio swipe of "Maybe Baby" and "That's My Desire," a ballad from the 1958 New York session that produced "Rave On." Although the overdubbing done to Holly's music made sense from a commercial standpoint at the time, this collection only whets your appetite to hear more of the real thing. —*Cub Koda*

☆ From the Original Master Tapes / 1985 / MCA ✦✦✦✦✦

MCA got serious about reissuing vintage music from its library in the 1980s, when it put the responsibility in the hands of producer Steve Hoffman, who was willing to spend the time and do the research required to find the right masters and also to propose doing right by them. One of the first results was *For the First Time Anywhere*, which unearthed a lot of previously unheard undubbed Holly demos, and Hoffman followed it up two years

later with *From the Original Master Tapes*, the first Buddy Holly collection that was a revelation for its sound quality. Although it has been outdone in that department since, what with the advancement of digital technology and its uses, and there are compilations that take into account songs of his that became important in others' hands, this remains the best single-disc collection of Buddy Holly's music, featuring 20 of his biggest hits. The songs aren't presented in chronological order, but the disc flows well, running through every one of his hits and all of his best-known songs—"That'll Be the Day," "Peggy Sue," "Oh, Boy!," "Maybe Baby," "Rave On," "Think It Over," "Heartbeat," "It Doesn't Matter Anymore," "Everyday," "Not Fade Away," "Well ... All Right," and many others. A few terrific songs are missing, but *From the Original Master Tapes* remains a first-rate introduction and a nearly definitive summary of the highlights of Holly's brief recording career. —*Bruce Eder & Stephen Thomas Erlewine*

☆ The Buddy Holly Collection / Sep. 28, 1993 / MCA ✦✦✦✦✦

Given the reluctance of MCA to release a CD version of the complete Buddy Holly recordings (due to either legal issues or a skepticism of its commercial worth), the double-disc 1993 set *The Buddy Holly Collection* stands as the most comprehensive and greatest CD-era retrospective of the legendary rock & roller. Though it contains all the big hits, this is not the place to turn if all that you're looking for are "That'll Be the Day," "Not Fade Away," "Everyday," "Oh, Boy!," "Peggy Sue," "Maybe Baby," "Rave On," "Well...All Right" and It Doesn't Matter Anymore"—they're all here, but they don't start unrolling until track 15 on the first disc. No, this collection is for the listener that knows the hits but needs more. Namely, they need the proof that Holly was one of the greatest, most inventive artists in the first wave of rock & roll, which this collection certainly does, through its selection of lesser-known sides that showcase both his wildman rockabilly ways and his sensitive songwriting. If it takes the *Collection* a little while to get going—it kicks off with the dynamite "Down the Line," but then takes a little while before it, and Holly, finds its groove—there are also no bum tracks here, and, taken as a whole, Buddy's gifts as a songwriter and a rocker are staggering. Until the complete box is finally issued on CD, this will have to stand as the most comprehensive Holly collection on CD, and, as such, it's absolutely necessary for anybody that loves American music of the 20th century. —*Stephen Thomas Erlewine*

★ Greatest Hits / Sep. 24, 1996 / MCA ✦✦✦✦

MCA re-mastered 18 of Buddy Holly's best-known songs for 1996's *Greatest Hits* album. While the sound is fine, it isn't markedly better than that on *From the Original Master Tapes*, which also boasted a more complete track selection. Nevertheless, *Greatest Hits* is one of the most thorough single-disc collections ever assembled on Holly and for audiophiles, it may be worth the extra money. For most fans, *From the Original Master Tapes* remains the definitive single-disc set, with the double-disc *The Buddy Holly Collection* or the LP-only *The Complete Buddy Holly* providing better, more comprehensive overviews, which provide more value for your dollar than *Greatest Hits*. —*Stephen Thomas Erlewine*

20th Century Masters—The Millennium Collection: The Best of Buddy Holly / Apr. 20, 1999 / MCA ✦✦✦

Like any record company worth their salt, MCA knows a good gimmick when they see it, and when the millennium came around...well, the *20th Century Masters—The Millennium Collection* wasn't too far behind. Supposedly, the millennium is a momentous occasion, but it's hard to feel that way when it's used as another excuse to turn out a budget-line series. But apart from the presumptuous title, *20th Century Masters—The Millennium Collection* turns out to be a very good budget-line series. True, it's impossible for any of these brief collections to be definitive, but they're nevertheless solid samplers that don't feature a bad song in the bunch. For example, take Buddy Holly's *20th Century* volume—it's an irresistible 12-song summary of his Decca/MCA recordings. There may be a couple of noteworthy songs missing, but many of his best-known songs for the label are here, including "That'll Be the Day," "Words of Love," "Peggy Sue," "Everyday," "Not Fade Away," "Maybe Baby," "Oh Boy!," "It's So Easy," "Rave On," "True Love Ways," "Think It Over," and "It Doesn't Matter Any More." Serious fans will want something more extensive, but this is an excellent introduction for neophytes and a great sampler for casual fans, considering its length and price. That doesn't erase the ridiculousness of the series title, but the silliness is excusable when the music and the collections are good. —*Stephen Thomas Erlewine*

☆ The Chirping Crickets/Buddy Holly / Jan. 30, 2001 / BGO ✦✦✦✦

Oh boy—that's the first reaction to seeing this British import turn up. RCA/BMG got around to remastering Elvis Presley's original albums at the end of the 1990s, but MCA/Universal, which owns Buddy Holly's legacy, has shown no such interest in the late Texas rock & roll legend's music. So, instead, it's fallen to Beat Goes On (BGO), the U.K. outfit. BGO combined the two albums that Buddy Holly saw released in his lifetime and slapped them onto one CD, remastered in 24-bit digital audio. Everyone who thinks they know this stuff should get ready for a shock when they hear what it sounds like on this disc—the listener can practically hear the action on Jerry Allison's drums, and when the guitar break on "Peggy Sue" comes in, it's like the instrument is in your face. And "Rave On" pretty much booms out the way it did on-stage on a good night. What's more, the resolution on the tracks from both albums enhances the little details, such as the quality of the backup singing on "Send Me Some Lovin'." Also, there are excellent notes written from a uniquely British point of view and a thumbnail sketch of the history of each song. The disc is as essential to any collection as Elvis' Sun sides and his first two years at RCA, or the Beatles' first four years of music. —*Bruce Eder*

Reminiscing/Showcase / Feb. 14, 2001 / BGO ✦✦✦

In recent decades, both *Reminiscing* and *Showcase* have enjoyed less than stellar reputations among Buddy Holly fans and '50s rock purists, as both albums were made up of the products of producer Norman Petty's posthumous redubbing of Holly's unfinished demos. Apart from the bizarre inclusion of "Wait Till the Sun Shines, Nellie"—a B-side chosen by Petty for the single of the title track—*Reminiscing* is a very solid album, and was essential to the maintaining of Holly's memory, reaching number three in a six-month run on the U.K. charts in 1963; one can just about lay odds that various members of the Beatles and the Rolling Stones were among the listeners of this album or its successor. *Showcase*, which sold just about as well, is a slightly less consistent record overall, but has some killer rock & roll tracks, including versions of "Rock Around With Ollie Vee," "Shake, Rattle and Roll," and "Blue Suede Shoes," plus the glittering acoustic number "You're the One" (with Waylon Jennings providing the handclaps). Moreover, even as a two-LP on one CD release, it's rather bite-sized at 48 minutes of music—Holly, like more rock & rollers of his day, made his points quickly. Despite their shortcomings as authentic documents of what Holly might have done with the songs, these are fun albums and fit together perfectly, as enjoyable accounts (if not, for obvious reasons, as revealing) of the talent involved as any LPs that Elvis Presley or Chuck Berry ever released. The fall 2000 release also benefits from state-of-the-art sound and superb annotation by John Tobler. —*Bruce Eder*

The Ultimate EP Collection / Dec. 11, 2001 / See for Miles ♦♦♦♦♦

The four-song Seven-inch EP disc, a vinyl format in between full-length albums and singles, was a popular configuration particularly in financially strapped Europe in the late '50s and early '60s, the heyday of Buddy Holly & the Crickets, so many of them were released on the group. Those releases now provide the excuse for this 53-track, two-CD set from British reissue label See for Miles, its material licensed primarily from MCA, though one track, a radio interview with Holly, comes from elsewhere. "Excuse" is the right word to describe the organizing principle, since, although a list in the hardcover CD packaging traces the origins of most of the songs to British or French EPs, the sequencing does not follow the order of release of those original EPs. This is not to say the album would be better sequenced if it did; assembled as afterthoughts, Holly's EPs made for a haphazard release of his singles and album tracks. A more serious concern is that, since Holly's popularity continued unabated in Europe well after his death in 1959, many of the posthumous EPs contained unfinished demo material given overdubs by Holly's producer, Norman Petty. There are 12 such tracks included here, from EPs released through January 1965. (Had the compilers actually included all of the material released on the British EPs, there would have been even more.) Nevertheless, all of Holly's major hits are featured, and the listener can simply dispense with the "EP" conceit and consider the album a two-hour, randomly sequenced collection of Buddy Holly music. For that, it's fine, although, of course, there are plenty of other Holly compilations out there. —*William Ruhlmann*

Singles + / Dec. 25, 2001 / DJ Specialist ♦♦♦

This collection starts deeper and more interesting than its title would lead one to expect, and for 29 of its 45 songs, it's also wonderfully enjoyable. Assembling all of the Buddy Holly singles and B-sides issued in America and Europe between April of 1956 and September of 1964, it covers Holly's music and career the way the ordinary listener heard it, and pretty much the way that Holly concentrated on it; he only completed two LPs in his lifetime, but he released some 16 singles during the last three years of his life, from early 1956 until early 1959, of which a dozen charted. Those 30 songs provide a step-by-step map of his development as an artist; the dozen or so posthumous releases that followed tell how his name was kept alive (principally in England), in interesting but often awkwardly overdubbed versions of the original recordings. This set treats the first ten singles well enough, but then it goes astonishingly wrong by utilizing the stereo masters on the subsequent singles—true, "It Doesn't Matter Anymore" and "Raining in My Heart" were recorded with orchestral accompaniment, but they were intended to be heard on 45s (exclusively mono in those days) and on AM radio (also mono). The stereo mastering adds nothing to the recordings except an overbearing artificiality; it's nice to hear the details of the scoring and the accompaniment, but not in so obtrusive a manner. Worse still, most of the posthumous singles (apart from the hard, stripped-down rock & roll numbers "Midnight Shift" and "Rock Around With Ollie Vee") are given this same treatment, and suffer from the same problems. The pity is that the producers really had something enjoyable in their grasp—listening to "Blue Days, Black Nights" b/w "Love Me," it's eerie to think that Holly was cutting those sides practically at the same time that Elvis Presley was starting to lay down the tracks for his first RCA single and album, and it is hard to say that Holly's results weren't more accessible than Presley's. As the songs advance, one hears the innovations come in, layer after layer, the way that fans picked them up—and then you run into the stereo masters for those later sides, which make you wince. In fairness, the sound is clean and a decent match for the best work that MCA has issued domestically on Holly. Ideally, these two CDs and their 100-plus minutes of music would be part of a four- (or five-) disc Buddy Holly box, but MCA/Universal doesn't seem capable of getting anything like that out in this lifetime, so this double-disc set will have to suffice, flaws and all. —*Bruce Eder*

Holly in the Hills/Giant / Aug. 2002 / BGO ♦♦♦

England's Beat Goes On Records has done listeners a service with this two-on-one release, though some listeners may hesitate to buy this disc based on the relatively low-ranking reputations of the two Buddy Holly albums featured here. The truth is that while neither *Holly in the Hills* nor *Giant* represent Holly's music as he would have wanted it known, or even would necessarily have recognized it, it's all good listening; the first 12 cuts, off *Holly in the Hills*, veer from hard rockabilly to soft country ballads and feature lots of harmony singing shared by Holly and his then-performing partner, Bob Montgomery, and the last ten are mostly heavily redubbed Holly demos and song fragments, the added accompaniment generally approximating his instrumental style to varying degrees and showing him off in renditions of songs associated with Little Richard, Fats Domino, Mickey & Sylvia, and more, and having fun, in particular, with Clarence "Frogman" Henry's "Ain't Got No Home." It's all a lot of fun to hear and enjoyable enough, if not a serious Holly release, and it's never sounded better, nor are any of these tracks likely to show up anywhere else (like in the U.S. catalog) anytime soon, and the annotation by John Tobler is worth a few reads. —*Bruce Eder*

That'll Be the Day/Remember / Oct. 8, 2002 / BGO ♦♦♦♦

This disc is an interesting pairing, combining the contents of two LPs from opposite ends of the efforts to tap into Buddy Holly's catalog. *That'll Be the Day*, released in April of 1958, was Decca Records' first attempt to give a boost to the available Buddy Holly material, assembling 11 of the songs that he'd cut for the label during his four unsuccessful Nashville sessions of 1956 into an LP, issued one month after the *Buddy Holly* album was issued; *Remember*, released in 1971, was the last posthumous compilation of Holly's work assembled by British MCA, gathering together the last of his officially released singles, B-sides, and more. Curiously, it is the first 11 songs here, from *That'll Be the Day*—which is usually dismissed by critics as not sufficiently representative of Holly's real sound—that make this CD an important release, very close to essential listening. Those tracks, though a fair distance from the music that made Holly famous, are good, solid, occasionally inspired rock & roll, with a decided rockabilly and country flavor; they're as instructive about how the producers at the major labels—in this case, Owen Bradley and his assistants at Decca's Nashville studio—and young artists like Holly, without a lot of studio time under his belt, were finding their way around rock & roll recording. Those 11 sides, which never sounded better than they do here, make this CD a must-own release for anyone with more than the most casual interest in Holly's work or in early rock & roll; if the alternate take of "Rock Around With Ollie Vee" were here, the CD would be perfect as a document of its subject and period. The later songs, from *Remember*, are better crafted and more sophisticated, as well as encompassing some of Holly's best songs, including "Learning the Game" and "Peggy Sue Got Married," but those are all available elsewhere, and as the context of their inclusion on *Remembering* was mere happenstance, they're nothing more than handy bonus tracks here—rather more impressive among those later cuts is "Real Wild Child," a frantically paced rockabilly number credited to Ivan and sung by Crickets drummer Jerry Allison, featuring Holly on guitar and backing vocals. The annotation is surprisingly sketchy concerning *That'll Be the Day*, concentrating far more on Holly's life story, and the original notes from *Remember* tell listeners more about that album's contents than do the new notes for the CD. —*Bruce Eder*

David Holt

b. Oct. 15, 1946, Gatesville, TX

Banjo, Vocals / Old-Timey, Traditional Country, Traditional Folk, String Bands

Contemporary banjo player and storyteller David Holt is devoted to keeping old-time music and stories alive. Best-known as the host of TNN's *Fire on the Mountain* and *the American Music Shop*, he also records children's albums. He was born into an established Texas family and began playing the family's traditional instruments, the spoons and bones, at age ten. When he was a teen, the family moved to California where he began playing the drums and gained experience in several rock & roll and jazz bands. His budding interest in traditional music bloomed after hearing an inspiring 78-rpm single by cowboy singer Carl T. Sprague, whom he traveled to Bryan, TX, to see. Sprague taught Holt to play harmonica and encouraged his interest in old songs.

In 1969, Holt and his college buddy, banjo player Steve Keith, visited the southern Appalachians, where they immersed themselves in the local musical traditions; Holt learned the clawhammer banjo style straight from the sources. Soon after receiving his teaching certificate and degrees in biology and art from the University of California, Holt moved to Asheville, NC, to learn more about mountain music. For many years he interviewed and taped traditional musicians and convinced them to play at local festivals. (Much of the research and the recordings have been placed in the Library of Congress.)

Holt began his own recording career on the June Appal label, and decided to become a full-time performer in 1980. With his trademark white fedora, Holt soon became a major figure in traditional music and won the Best Old-Time Banjoist in *Frets* magazine's Readers' Poll three times. He founded his own label, High Windy, and has released many albums. He also developed shows such as *Banjo Reb and the Blue Ghost* to bring the music to wider audiences. He continues to tour and has appeared on *Hee Haw*, *Nashville Now* and the *Grand Ole Opry*, where he has the distinction of being the first performer to play a paper sack on-stage. In addition to hosting TNN shows, Holt has produced the seven-part series *Folkways* for PBS radio. He also hosted and starred in American Public Radio's *Riverwalk: Live from the Landing*, which was broadcast from San Antonio. In 1992, Holt released the Grammy-nominated *Grandfather's Greatest Hits*, featuring Chet Atkins and Duane Eddy. Two years later, he issued an album called *I Got a Bullfrog: Folksongs for the Fun of It*. —*Sandra Brennan*

Reel & Rock / 1986 / High Windy ♦♦♦♦

● **Grandfather's Greatest Hits** / 1991 / High Windy ♦♦♦♦

David Holt was one of the main old-timey revivalists of the '80s and *Grandfather's Greatest Hits* is his finest achievement. With this release, Holt constructed a set list of classic country songs—from "John Henry" and "Fire on the Mountain" to "Wabash Cannonball," "Pretty Polly," and "Wreck of the Old '97"—drafted in a handful of superstar guests (Mark O'Connor, Doc Watson, Duane Eddy, Jerry Douglas, Chet Atkins) and turned a convincing, good-humored performance that revived traditional country without embalming it. It's a wonderful, fun album that establishes Holt as one of the leading traditional revivalists of the latter-half of the 20th century. —*Thom Owens*

Hairyman—Southern Folktales / Feb. 9, 2000 / High Windy ♦♦♦

Spiders in the Hairdo / Mar. 27, 2002 / High Windy ♦♦♦

Doodle Daddle Day: Old Time Sing-Alongs for Everyone / High Windy ♦♦♦♦

Homer & Jethro

f. 1932, **db.** 1971

Group / Traditional Country, Country Comedy

Known as "the thinking man's hillbillies," Homer Haynes & Jethro Burns got a lot of mileage out of an act that shouldn't have lasted or gone as far as it did, at least on the surface of things. Certainly there were other, far more established duos mining similar turf on the country music circuit, with Lonzo & Oscar leading the way. But Homer & Jethro were far more than just two hayseeds doing cornball send-ups of pop tunes. Underneath the cornpone facade were two top-flight musicians with a decidedly perverse sense of humor and a keen sense of satire.

Homer D. Haynes was the older of the two men, born in Knoxville, TN, on July 27, 1918. Jethro was born with the decidedly non-showbiz moniker of Kenneth D. Burns also in Knoxville on March 10, 1923. The duo met in their early teens and started playing music together almost immediately, with Haynes on guitar and Burns alternating between mandolin and banjo. In the mid-'30s they began working on local radio station WNOX as part of a larger group, the String Dusters. One night, the boys heard a radio broadcast of a pop singer doing a broad—and fairly denigrating—takeoff of a hillbilly singer singing a country tune. Using exaggerated vowel and consonant stressing (trademarks of bluegrass singing) and deliberately going off-key as much as possible, the singer's performance irked the duo to no end. They decided right then and there that payback was the only logical solution to this kind of insult. From here on out, they would take current popular songs and send them up as hillbilly renditions, performed in deadpan earnest by Haynes and Burns, who now took the stage name of Jethro. They started working in the act while the rest of the group took a break during the broadcast. The new duo's "intermission" turn proved to be immensely popular and within four years' time, their characters and their timing were fully honed to a razor edge.

By 1938, they had broken off from the String Dusters and moved up to the more prestigious Renfro Valley Barn Dance, later broadcasting on the Chicago-based *Plantation Party*. World War II split the duo up, with Homer serving in Europe and Jethro serving in the Pacific theater. Getting back together after their respective discharges, they started up their radio appearances again, this time working on the Cincinnati-based *Midwestern Hayride*. Their recording careers also began during this time period, signing with King Records out of Cincinnati, issuing several 78s between 1946 and 1948. By the end of the year, country producer legend Steve Sholes had signed them to RCA Victor, where they would spend the rest of their recording careers, cutting records—especially in the '60s—as if nothing could contain them. The duo joined up briefly with Spike Jones & His City Slickers, appearing in the stage show for a while, recording at least one session with him in 1950 ("Pal-Yat-Chee"), and letting Jones' agency handle all their bookings.

It was in the late '40s into the 1950s, basing themselves out of the Windy City, that the duo hit their true stride. Their first big hit was a takeoff on "Baby, It's Cold Outside" with a quite young June Carter contributing on vocals. The success of this single brought them to the attention of powerful radio station WLS, thus securing Homer & Jethro a regular spot on the *National Barn Dance*. Joining in 1949, the duo would stay faithful to the original version of the *Grand Ole Opry*, staying with the show until 1958. The national hookup did wonders for their career, which got an added boost when they started working double duty as regulars on *Don McNeil's Breakfast Club*, one of the top-rated morning-radio chat shows of its time, also based out of Chicago. The 1950s found them scoring big with numerous guest shots on television. The beauty of Homer & Jethro (as opposed to another country novelty act) was that they could work *anywhere* and be understood. They could be on the bill with Roy Rogers or trading cornball put-downs with Jimmy Dean or slickly one-upping Johnny Carson, and they always held their own. As time went on, their act became more deadpan and, if anything, even more polished, as if to distance themselves from everything else that had existed before them in their little corner of the country world. State-fair work was replaced with the glitzier surroundings of Las Vegas and the like. RCA Victor Living Stereo album covers aside, Homer & Jethro never had to dress up in bib overalls and play hicks to get their act over. If anything, the straighter they dressed and the straighter they acted, the funnier they were.

They were still singing with broad accents, but the satires were getting more acerbic with each release, giving rise to their lasting sobriquet as "the thinking man's hillbillies." Their satire of Patti Page's "How Much Is That Doggie in the Window?" (Homer & Jethro'd into "(How Much Is) That Hound Dog in the Window?") became their first crossover hit in 1953. In 1959, the duo won their first—and only—Grammy award for "The Battle of Kookamonga," their hilarious spoof of Johnny Horton's "The Battle of New Orleans," a country crossover record that cut a wide swath on the charts that year.

When Southern country humor became a small phenomenon of the 1960s with the success of television shows like *The Beverly Hillbillies*, *Petticoat Junction*, and *Green Acres*, Homer & Jethro's career went into overdrive. They (and RCA Victor) released an avalanche of records like there was no tomorrow, issuing eight albums of new material between 1966 and 1967 alone. Their studio efforts were produced by Chet Atkins with the cream of Nashville sidemen, and one album, *Playing It Straight*, found them in an all-instrumental setting, showing there were chops aplenty behind the cornball vocals and broad satires. The duo also participated in a wildly successful advertising campaign in the mid-'60s for Kellogg's Corn Flakes, even issuing an album based on the ad's catch phrase, *Ooh, That's Corny!*, to brisk sales. The duo continued until Homer's death in 1971. Jethro went into semiretirement for a few years, being coaxed back into show business by folksinger Steve Goodman, who brought him out on tour, spotlighting him to much recognition as a fine jazz-influenced mandolinist. Homer & Jethro were inducted into the Country Music Hall of Fame in 2001. *—Cub Koda*

Barefoot Ballads / 1957 / RCA Victor ✦✦✦✦

The Worst of Homer & Jethro / 1957 / RCA Victor ✦✦✦✦✦

Their best early parodies include the hilarious "(How Much Is) That Hound Dog in the Window?" and "Jam Bowl Liar," a recasting of Hank Williams' "Jambalaya." *—Michael McCall*

Homer & Jethro at the Country Club / 1960 / RCA Victor ✦✦✦✦

Homer & Jethro were a popular country comedy duo who continued to record together for decades until the death of Homer. This long-out-of-print live LP was taped at the Hillwood Country Club in Nashville, with many country celebrities evidently on hand, including Grandpa Jones, Jim Reeves, Chet Atkins (the album's producer), and Archie Campbell (the latter wrote the liner notes). The hilarious banter between songs is almost as funny as their parodies of popular favorites. In addition to the expected reworkings of country favorites like "Yaller Rose of Texas, You All," "(How Much Is) That Hound Dog in the Window" (which detours into "Blue Danube"), and "Hart Brake Motel" (skewering Elvis Presley's "Heartbreak Hotel"), the duo has a blast with George Shearing's theme song (which is converted into "Lullaby of Bird Dog") and even Duke Ellington's "C-Jam Blues." Although most of the selections feature the duo by themselves, their backup band includes Nashville saxophonist Boots Randolph. Many folks aren't even aware that they were superb musicians as well. No matter how corny the humor, it still produces chuckles decades later. *—Ken Dryden*

Songs My Mother Never Sang / 1961 / RCA Victor ✦✦✦✦✦

In the early to mid-'60s, Homer & Jethro were RCA Victor's top-selling country comedy act and one of their top sellers in the country field, period. Producer Chet Atkins and the sales department took note of both, and thus began the golden age of the Homer & Jethro album, a form that proliferated during the '60s, with the duo sometimes issuing several in one year alone. For this album, producer Atkins threw caution to the wind and left the tape machine running all during the recording date so he could include on this album some of the wild, between-take goings-on that Homer & Jethro sessions were so well known for. Although the song contents are among the duo's best ("She Was Bitten on the Udder By an Adder," "Please Help Me, I'm Falling," "How Come There's No Dog Day?," "In the Shade of the Apple Tree," "The Tattooed Lady," "I Love Your Pizza," "Don't Jump Off the Roof Dad!," a devastating version of "Among My Souvenirs," "Sweet Violets," "Will You Love Me When," and "Come Here Little Wifey!"), the real highlights here are the false starts, comments about the songs, and occasional ribald jokes that make this such a fly-on-the-wall treat. One can only imagine as to what was deemed too raunchy for the final cut on this very fun session. *—Cub Koda*

Homer & Jethro at the Convention / 1962 / RCA Victor ✦✦✦✦✦

Homer & Jethro already had one live album to their credit (*Homer & Jethro at the Country Club*) when they released this little gem in 1962. The brainstorm this time was to make a recording during the annual Country Music Association banquet at *the Hillwood Country Club* in Nashville, then a closed-to-the-public, non-televised event. As Homer & Jethro state in the liner notes, "... this is the kind of challenge we like. This is a super critical audience, all country music big shots, artists, publishers, writers and many disc jockeys. They've heard all the jokes, and laughs are hard to come by. After the usual cocktails and dinner they had speeches, awards, and they took an hour to read the minutes of the last meeting. By now, they're practically asleep, so they finally introduce us. We had a ball, heckling the speakers table; when we spotted someone we knew we fired away, all in fun of course. We played it all by ear; it's impossible to plan a routine in advance for a crowd like this." As for the tunes in between the ad-libbed patter, they're largely country standards like "San Antonio Rose," "Tennessee Waltz," "Wildwood Flower," and "I Fall to Pieces," along with some special material like "Country Music Blues." Perhaps the most "inside" of all of their album output, this one captures them at their improvisational best. *—Cub Koda*

Playing It Straight / 1962 / RCA Victor ✦✦✦✦✦

Humorous Side of Country Music With Homer & Jethro / 1963 / Camden ✦✦✦✦

As far as combining ridiculous comedy with hot mandolin breaks, there really is nowhere else to shop than the Homer & Jethro mart. Although the pair of grinning pickers made fun of many kinds of music, including the Beatles and Ray Charles, on this album the focus (or should we say out of focus) is on country & western, particularly the overwrought type of song story such as Hank Williams' "Kaw-liga," redone here as "Pore Ol'Koo-liger," and everyone's favorite pioneer hero song, presented by these boys as "The Ballad of Davy Crew-Cut." Old Hank Williams really gets more than one finger poked in his eye here, as he was riding high on the hit parade when this album was released and was obviously a good target for parody. In much the manner of Spike Jones, Homer & Jethro combine superior musicianship with jokes that run the range from corny to sophisticated, sometimes in the course of a single line. Another nice touch on this collection are the funny sound effects, sometimes utilizing el cheapo hi-fi effects like echo. A tasty rhythm section keeps the pace with perfect accompaniment, though the players are not rewarded with a credit for their efforts. All in all, this is as funny or funnier than any other effort by these fellows, which is saying that it should be able to make even the ultra-mean witch known as Old Screwface burst into laughter. *—Eugene Chadbourne*

Ooh, That's Corny! / 1963 / RCA Victor ✦✦✦

Zany Songs of the '30's / 1963 / RCA Victor ✦✦✦

Cornfucius Day / 1964 / RCA Victor ✦✦✦✦

In the mid-'60s, the Kellogg's cereal company hired Homer & Jethro to participate in a number of television commercials utilizing a string of moth-eaten jokes as a sales pitch tie-in for their brand of corn flakes. The commercials were successful enough for the duo to issue an album based on the commercials' catch phrase (*Ooh, That's Corny!*) and certainly successful enough to elicit this sequel. This follow-up walks an uneven path, split between reprisals of the earlier album's TV commercial patter ("Doctor Foo Man Choo," "Oh Golly, Cornfucious," and the title track) and Homer & Jethro's usual fare ("Cousin John and Cousin Mabel," "Chow Hound's Lament," "Monsters of the World, Unite!," "Mother Goose Is Chicken," "Doin' My Homework (While I Watch TV)," and "A Slow Boat to China"). Of particular note is their salute to the Beatles, "Gonna Send 'Em Home," which makes a nice bookend comparison to their version of the Fab Four's "I Want to Hold Your Hand." —*Cub Koda*

Fractured Folk Songs / 1964 / RCA Victor ✦✦✦✦

Songs to Tickle Your Funny Bone / 1966 / Camden ✦✦✦✦

Camden was RCA Victor's $1.98 budget label, glutting the bins in grocery and drug stores nationwide in the late '50s and early '60s. Cobbling together long-playing albums from sides kicking around the vaults—usually issued as singles or in RCA's extended-play 45 format—the country market and the artists the label had in its masters catalog made for some budget albums that were every bit as fine as their upscale product on the parent label. This 1966 collection of tracks cut for RCA Victor back in the early to mid-'50s (1959's "Itsy Bitsy Teenie Weenie Yellow Polka Dot Bikini" is about the latest entry on here) nonetheless does right by Homer & Jethro with a nice cross section of the hillbilly song parodies that were the duo's stock-in-trade. Highlights include the waltz-tempoed "Malady of Love," featuring a warped "romantic" recitation from Jethro Burns ("You said your heart belonged to me, but the rest of ya kept goin' out with other guys!"), the now politically incorrect "You Tell Her, I Stutter," "The Nutty Lady of Shady Lane," "Listen to the Goony Bird," "Throw Mama from the Train," a Mitch Miller parody ("Don't Sing Along (On Top of Old Smoky)"), and takeoffs of Carl Smith ("Hay Shmo!") and Elvis ("Houn' Dawg"). Although there are only ten cuts aboard this budget entry (and no chart hits), it's all top-flight material and as good an introduction to the duo as any. —*Cub Koda*

Assault the Rock & Roll Era / 1989 / Bear Family ✦✦✦

The Best of Homer & Jethro / 1992 / RCA ✦✦✦✦✦

Their latter favorites include their version of the Beatles' "I Want to Hold Your Hand" and "The Battle of Kookamonga," based on Johnny Horton's "The Battle of New Orleans." —*Michael McCall*

★ **America's Song Butchers: The Weird World of Homer & Jethro** / Feb. 18, 1997 / Razor & Tie ✦✦✦✦

Country music has a long and rich tradition of cornball jokes calculated to make audiences laugh and groan at the same time, and few if any acts mined this vein with greater results than Homer & Jethro. No one would ever accuse Homer & Jethro of having a subtle or sophisticated sense of humor, but their twangy parodies of various country and pop hits (and equally goofy original novelty numbers) revealed a genuine gift for prodding the funny bone, and it certainly didn't hurt that Kenneth "Jethro" Burns and Henry "Homer" Haynes had the good sense to make themselves the butt of their own joke more often than not. Even more importantly, they were both top-notch instrumentalists, and those who chose to listen past the gags were treated to some superb picking, especially from Burns, who later would show off his chops on a series of fine recordings with David Grisman. While most of Homer & Jethro's many albums for RCA Victor were frustratingly hit-and-miss, *America's Song Butchers: The Weird World of Homer & Jethro* is a superb compilation which pulls together 20 tunes which represent the duo at the top of their form, including their best-known hits (such as "Baby, It's Cold Outside," featuring June Carter, and "The Battle of Kookammonga") and a few choice obscurities (a silly but beautifully played version of "Misty," and a dead-on parody of the Beatles' "I Wanna Hold Your Hand"). Funnier than the entire series run of *Hee Haw*, and featuring nearly as much good music, *America's Song Butchers* is easily the best introduction to the clown princes of Nashville. A word of warning: don't play this around small children, or they'll be subjecting you to their favorite cuts on a regular basis for days on end. —*Mark Deming*

Hoosier Hot Shots

Group / Novelty, Old-Timey, Traditional Country, Country Comedy

In the 1930s, at the height of the Depression, rural Americans desperate for a laugh tuned in their radios to enjoy the cornball musical antics of the Hoosier Hot Shots. Their odd-sounding blend of a slide whistle and clarinet as the two lead instruments, the solid rhythm of the washboard, and their bizarre song lyrics made them the top novelty act of their day and the true precursor to the latter-day success of Spike Jones & His City Slickers. In the passage of some 50 to 60 years since their heyday and in the current climate of digital samplers, it becomes hard to imagine just how weird this four-piece combo sounded to the average listener. As clarinetist bandleader Gabe Ward put it, "People started to laugh as soon as we started playing. We had a funny sound with the whistle and the clarinet. The way Hezzie played it, it was funny." The Hezzie that Ward refers to was one Paul "Hezzie" Trietsch, the washboard-playing, slide whistle-blowing heart of the group. Ward had met him and his older brother Ken in their teenage years. All three had music in their blood and by the late '20s, they were playing together in an outfit called Ezra Buzzington's Rube Band. Buzzington's outfit worked the vaudeville circuit, its main claim to fame being its huge assortment of freak musical instruments. It was here that the trio stared honing their chops, with Ken becoming equally adept on guitar and banjo, Ward's clarinet style veering from swing to sweet to silly, and Hezzie coming into his own playing washboard, slide whistle, and a wild assortment of whistles, bells, and horns.

They stayed with Buzzington until he disbanded the group in 1929, the three vowing to stay in touch, and playing together in various on and off situations. In 1932, the Trietsch Brothers and Ward—their stage moniker at the time—were broadcasting over WOWO in Fort Wayne, IN. Doing a charity broadcast to help Ohio River Valley flood victims, they quickly found and developed their style doing novelty renditions of good-time songs, playing one after another during the course of the radio-thon. They picked up a 15-minute sustaining program on the station for no pay but with the chance to promote their own live appearances over the airwaves. They soon came to even wider prominence via their radio appearances on the *National Barn Dance*, broadcast over powerful station WLS in Chicago. The show was the first of its type to be broadcast and reach a wide audience, predating the subsequent success of Nashville's *Grand Ole Opry* and counting a young Gene Autry, Lulubelle & Scotty, and Red Foley among its many stars.

The show became a radio staple, broadcasting every Saturday night across the country for over 35 years. The trio—under their new name, the Hoosier Hot Shots—were an immediate hit, considering it an honor to be hooked up with the most prestigious show in country music. But the group just as quickly moved over to a regular guest spot on the *Uncle Ezra Pinex Cough Syrup* program, and when Uncle Ezra secured a national spot with NBC, he took the Hot Shots with him, and the group's national success was quickly assured.

They started making records around this time, and the Hot Shots couldn't have asked for a more sympathetic producer on their sessions than Art Satherly. Satherly, a distinguished Englishman, was in charge of Columbia Records' (at that time ARC) country and blues A&R division. As Gabe Ward put it, "What Art Satherly wanted on record was out visualness; he was trying to get that through. And he succeeded with us, because we were about the only people who could make people laugh after only four bars of music!" Satherly, for his part, would strip down to his shirt, put a bath towel around his neck, and go into the studio and dance to illustrate the tempo he wanted the Hot Shots to record at. The formula—with Gabe calling out, "Are you ready, Hezzie?" at the start of each tune—was a wildly successful one, with the band's records fitting comfortably on jukeboxes around the country in the "novelty dance" category. Among their hits were "I Like Bananas (Because They Have No Bones)," "The Coat and Pants Do All the Work," and "From the Indies to the Andies in His Undies," exactly the type of tunes that fitted the group like a glove. "We were tops in the novelty field," Ward would later reminisce, "all because of Art Satherly. He had the nerve to put them on the jukeboxes, even though they weren't always the top tunes. We'd do it for Art Satherly, with a beat for the jukeboxes." What Ward also fails to mention, however, is the group's tireless promotion of those records, making in-store appearances at all the Sears and Roebuck outlets nationwide when their 78s started appearing on the company's budget label, Perfect.

By the late '30s the Hot Shots started making movie appearances, debuting with a turn in *In Old Monterey* in 1939. The success of this and a couple others led the group to give up their sustaining radio spot with Uncle Ezra, relocating to the West Coast after World War II. Signing a movie deal with Columbia Pictures, the Hot Shots would go on to appear in 22 films into the early '50s. With the advent of changing tastes and the rise of television, the boys' star fell into eclipse somewhat, although they found steady work on the Nevada gambling casino circuit. The group soldiered on into the '70s, when Paul "Hezzie" Trietsch's death broke up the original group. Although nowhere near as wild as Spike Jones, nor possessing the "thinking man's hillbillies" personas of Homer & Jethro, it is impossible to think of either of those two acts existing—much less prospering and finding an audience—without the groundbreaking efforts of the Hoosier Hot Shots. —*Cub Koda*

● **Rural Rhythm** / Aug. 18, 1992 / Columbia/Legacy ✦✦✦✦

A 20-track lunatic collection of sides from the hokey side of country music. Titles include "I Like Bananas (Because They Have No Bones)," "Connie's Got Connections In Connecticut, " "From the Indies to the Andies in His Undies, " "The Coat and the Pants Do All the Work, " and "Moving Day in Jungletown." Corny beyond belief, and great fun every step of the way, there's never been anything in country music that remotely sounds like this. —*Cub Koda*

Havin' Fun With the Hoosier Hotshots / Apr. 8, 2003 / Collectors' Choice Music ✦✦✦✦

Johnny Horton

b. Apr. 30, 1925, Los Angeles, CA, d. Nov. 5, 1960, Milano, TX

Vocals / Traditional Country, Rockabilly, Honky Tonk, Nashville Sound/Countrypolitan, Country Boogie

Although he is better-remembered for his historical songs, Johnny Horton was one of the best and most popular honky tonk singers of the late '50s. Horton managed to infuse honky tonk with an urgent rockabilly underpinning. His career may have been cut short by a fatal car crash in 1960, but his music reverberated throughout the next three decades. Horton was born in Los Angeles in 1925, the son of sharecropping parents. During his childhood, his family continually moved between California and Texas, in an attempt to find work. His mother taught him how to play guitar at the age of 11. Horton graduated from high-school in 1944 and attended a Methodist seminary with the intent of joining a ministry. After a short while, he left the seminary and began traveling across the country, eventually moving to Alaska in 1949 to become a fisherman. While he was in Alaska, he began writing songs in earnest.

The following year, Horton moved back to east Texas, where he entered a talent contest hosted by Jim Reeves, who was then an unknown vocalist. He won the contest, which encouraged him to pursue a career as a performer. Horton started out by playing talent contests throughout Texas, which is where he gained the attention of Fabor Robison, a music manager that was notorious for his incompetence and his scams. In early 1951, Robison became Horton's manager and managed to secure him a recording contract with Corman Records. However, shortly after his signing, the label folded. Robison then founded his own label, Abbott Records, with the specific intent of recording Horton. None of these records had any chart success. During 1951, Horton began performing on various Los Angeles TV shows and hosted a radio show in Pasadena, where he performed under the name "the Singing Fisherman." By early 1952, Robison had moved Horton to Mercury Records.

At the end of 1951, Horton relocated from California to Shreveport, LA, where he became a regular on the *Louisiana Hayride*. However, Louisiana was filled with pitfalls—his first wife left him shortly after the move, and Robison severed all ties with Horton when he became Reeves' manager. During 1952, Hank Williams rejoined the cast of the *Hayride* and became a kind of mentor for Horton. After Williams died on New Year's Eve of 1952, Horton became close with his widow, Billie Jean; the couple married in September of 1953. Although he had a regular job on the *Hayride*, Horton's recording career was going nowhere—none of his Mercury records were selling, and rock & roll was beginning to overtake country's share of the market place. Horton's fortunes changed in the latter half of 1955, when he hired Webb Pierce's manager Tillman Franks as his own manager and quit Mercury Records. Franks had Pierce help him secure a contract for Horton with Columbia Records by the end of 1955. The change in record labels breathed life into Horton's career. At his first Columbia session, he cut "Honky Tonk Man," his first single for the label and one that would eventually become a honky tonk classic. By the spring of 1956, the song had reached the country Top Ten and Horton was well on his way to becoming a star.

"Honky Tonk Man" was edgy enough to have Horton grouped in on the more country-oriented side of rockabilly. Wearing a large cowboy hat to hide his receding hairline, he became a popular concert attraction and racked up three more hit singles—"I'm a One-Woman Man" (number seven), "I'm Coming Home" (number 11), "The Woman I Need" (number nine)—in the next year. However, the hits dried up just as quickly as they arrived; for the latter half of 1957 and 1958, he didn't hit the charts at all. Horton responded by cutting some rockabilly, which was beginning to fall out of favor by the time his singles were released.

In the fall of 1958, he bounced back with the Top Ten "All Grown Up," but it wasn't until the ballad "When It's Springtime in Alaska (It's Forty Below)" hit the charts in early 1959 that he achieved a comeback. The song fit neatly into the folk-based story songs that were becoming popular in the late '50s, and it climbed all the way to number one. Its success inspired his next single, "The Battle of New Orleans." Taken from a 1958 Jimmie Driftwood album, the song was a historical saga song like "When It's Springtime in Alaska," but it was also far more humorous. It was also far more successful, topping the country charts for ten weeks and crossing over into the pop charts, where it was number one for six weeks. After the back-to-back number one successes of "When It's Springtime in Alaska" and "The Battle of New Orleans," Horton concentrated solely on folky saga songs. "Johnny Reb" became a Top Ten hit in the fall of 1959, and "Sink the Bismarck" was a Top Ten hit in the spring of 1960, followed by the number-one hit "North to Alaska" in the fall of 1960. Around the time of "North to Alaska"'s November release, Horton claimed that he was getting premonitions of an early death. Sadly, his premonitions came true. On November 4, 1960, he suffered a car crash driving home to Shreveport after a concert in Austin, TX. Horton was still alive after the wreck, but he died on the way to the hospital; the other passengers in his car had severe injuries, but they survived. Although he died early in his career, Horton left behind a recorded legacy that proved to be quite influential. Artists like George Jones and Dwight Yoakam have covered his songs, and echoes of Horton's music can still be heard in honky tonk and country-rock music well into the '90s. *—Stephen Thomas Erlewine*

Honky-Tonk Man / 1957 / Columbia ✦✦✦✦✦

Honky-Tonk Man contains 12 of Johnny Horton's hardest honky tonk material, including "I'm a One-Woman Man," "The Wild One," "I'm Coming Home" and the title track. It's a brief, but excellent, summation of Horton's often-forgotten talent for pure country and rocking honky tonk. *—Stephen Thomas Erlewine*

The Spectacular Johnny Horton / 1960 / Columbia/Legacy ✦✦✦

Horton's brief flurry of country-pop mega-stardom coincided with some of his less interesting music, as this 1960 album proves. Corny Americana became his meal ticket after "The Battle of New Orleans" (which leads off the disc), and more of the same follows on the gold-prospecting tales "Sam Magee" and "When It's Springtime in Alaska." Those songs are country-pop with a banjo for a whiff of (not quite genuine) authenticity. On several of the other tracks, he didn't bother with the banjo, leaving average or below-average country-pop balladry to remain. Yet he hadn't forgotten how to play and sing gutsy rockabilly cum honky tonk, as shown on the album's best cuts. His self-penned "The First Rain Headin' South" is certainly the best of the crop; the cover of "Cherokee Boogie," like Warren Smith's "Ubangi Stomp," flirts with imagery that will strike many as un-PC these days; and "Got the Bull by the Horns" and the cover of Hank Snow's "The Rocket" are respectable uptempo numbers. Half a good album, then, and Horton wouldn't have a chance to resolve his conflicting directions, dying in the same year as the LP's release. [The 2000 CD reissue adds three bonus tracks: the lame 1958 ballad "Counterfeit Love," the mild 1958 rockabilly number "All Grown Up," and a bizarre version of "The Battle of New Orleans" cut especially for the English market, in which the *rebels* flee from the *British* instead of vice versa.] *—Richie Unterberger*

Johnny Horton Makes History / 1960 / S&P ✦✦✦

America's Most Creative Folk Singer / 1960 / Columbia ✦✦✦

Johnny Horton's Greatest Hits / 1961 / Columbia ✦✦✦✦

Even though he also cut a slew of country ballads and honky tonk tunes, Horton's fame rests with these folk saga songs. After spending the majority of the '50s reworking the classic sound of Hank Williams, Lefty Frizzell, and Webb Pierce, Horton scored with country shuffle cuts like "Honky Tonk Man." It wasn't until 1958, though, that he broke nationally with several geographical and historical themes like "When It's Springtime in Alaska" and "Johnny Reb." And while other drum, fife, and banjo production numbers like "The Battle of New Orleans" and "Sink the Bismarck" come off well, albeit in small doses, more overwrought cuts like "Johnny Freedom" and "Jim Bridger" find this particular stylistic well running dry. Too bad Horton didn't stick to more simple and emotive historical material like "Comanche" and "Whispering Pines." Unfortunately, this hits collection favors the gratuitous flag-waving fare and even ups the kitsch factor with syrupy, string-laden weepers like "The Mansion You Stole" and "All for the Love of a Girl." Still, a tidy collection of Horton's biggest numbers, and one that includes several cuts not featured on Columbia's more balanced two-disc retrospective. *—Stephen Cook*

The Voice of Johnny Horton / 1965 / Hilltop ✦✦✦✦

Before making it big on Columbia during the latter half of the 1950s, Johnny Horton spent five years recording for smaller labels like Cormac, Abbott, Dot, and Briar. Horton fashioned himself as a honky tonk singer in the mold of Webb Pierce and Hank Williams (he would marry Williams' widow Billie Jean in 1953) and made a slew of solid rockabilly-flavored tracks throughout the '50s. More in the vein of his first Columbia smash "Honky Tonk Man" than later historically minded hits like "The Battle of New Orleans" and "Johnny Reb," Horton's early sides are full of fiddles, pedal steel guitar, and shuffle beat drumming: music tailor made for tavern jukeboxes. For those curious about Horton's early material but unable to handle Bear Family's mammoth collection of the singer's pre-Columbia material, this fine yet somewhat skimpy highlights package will do the trick. Including minor hits like "Smokey Joe's Barbecue," the collection also takes in down-home humor à la Little Jimmy Dickens ("Old Gobbler" and "Barefoot Boy Blues") and songs like "Banks of the Nile," which would presage Horton's later predilection for geographical subject matter. A fine sampling of Horton's early sides. *—Stephen Cook*

Johnny Horton on the Road / 1969 / Columbia ✦✦

While the title of this album makes it sound quite ordinary, it is really a very unusual production, more strange than good in the end. There is probably no more reviled form of music than so-called "grave-robbing" recordings in which studio musicians overdub new tracks on top of old ones left behind by dearly departed musicians, and this album belongs in that category. Producer George Richey, who likes to take on gimmicky projects from time to time, was behind this idea to combine what were supposedly off the cuff recordings of Horton entertaining live or casually sitting around picking with new studio overdubs including the sanctimonious sounds of the Jordanaires. While some interesting productions have developed from taking dressing-room recordings and adding on to them, this country vocal group might not be the most subtle choice of an overdub if the idea is to create natural sounding country music, and the move to include them is typical of the sort of production decisions made here. It is almost a given that in cases like this, the more eccentric and unusual the grave that is being robbed, the more bland and lacking in personality will be the new material. From the choice of material, it seems like this is an attempt to present Horton as a straightforward country artist rather than the creator of big studio productions evoking gold rushes and historical battles. Some of the better material here consists of songs he recorded elsewhere when he was actually in control of the proceedings—as in still alive. The original recordings that Richey started out with most likely had promise, including a batch of Horton originals as well as an amusing Johnny Cash cover. The album cover contains the following text in a box, "Collector's Item: Recently Discovered Performances," to which "Now Ruined" would be an appropriate and extremely honest addition. *—Eugene Chadbourne*

Rockin' Rollin' Johnny Horton / 1981 / Bear Family ✦✦✦✦✦

Although several of his hits are featured—including "Honky Tonk Man," "The Woman I Need," and "All Grown Up"—most of *Rockin' Rollin' Johnny Horton* is comprised of obscurities, culled from his early career. The album veers between is rockabilly experiments and honky tonk, and the entire CD is highly enjoyable compilation for fans of his harder-edged music, even though a handful of tracks haven't aged particularly well. *—Stephen Thomas Erlewine*

American Originals / 1989 / Columbia ✦✦✦✦✦

American Originals is a brief, ten-track collection that captures Horton's biggest hits. Though it gives a more balanced overview than *Greatest Hits*, it doesn't have the breadth of the double-disc set *Honky Tonk Man: The Essential Johnny Horton 1956-1960*, which is the definitive collection. *—Stephen Thomas Erlewine*

The Early Years / 1991 / Bear Family ✦✦✦✦

The Early Years was the first extensive Johnny Horton collection that Bear Family assembled. Spanning seven LPs, the set includes all of Horton's recordings for the Cormac, Abbott, and Mercury labels, as well as two albums' worth of demos and two albums' worth of overdubbed Abbott recordings issued on the Briar and Dot labels. Though these early recordings aren't quite as accomplished as his later, better-known work for Columbia, there's a lot of exciting of material here—including proto-rockabilly and off-center honky tonk like "On the Banks of the Beautiful Nile," "I'm a Fishin' Man," and "The Train With the Rhumba Beat"—especially for dedicated fans. Of course, the sheer size of the set means that only dedicated fans will ever pick up the box, but it is worth the investment for those fans, since these obscurities are often more interesting than the more polished recordings that followed later in his career. *—Stephen Thomas Erlewine*

1956–1960 / 1991 / Bear Family ✦✦✦✦✦

This Bear Family box documents the last four years of Johnny Horton's life as a recording and performing artist. It is the second box set issue in their extensive—in fact, complete—Johnny Horton oeuvre. The first documented the Cormac, Abbott, and Mercury recordings as well as two albums' worth of demos and overdubs released while he was alive. This four-CD collection contains Horton's complete issued recordings, unreleased demos, and outtakes as well as overdubbed recordings issued between 1964 and 1969 (during the decade after his death) and working demos. Horton's final period at Columbia is what people (most people) remember. These were the years of "Sink the Bismarck," "Battle of New Orleans," "Honky Tonk Man," "Rock Island Line," "Ole Slewfoot," "The Same Ole Tale the Crow Told Me," his devastating recording of "Lost Highway," as well as his final monster singles recorded in August of 1960 (a mere three months before he was killed in an auto accident), "Go North" and "North to Alaska" (for a soundtrack). Unlike his peers during the later years—Johnny Cash, Webb Pierce, Faron Young, and others—Horton exhibited not only an easy amiability but a combination of confidence and vulnerability. It was as if he knew that making music came naturally to him but couldn't understand why anybody would make a big deal out of it. Here are the songs that ran the gamut of rockabilly, hard honky tonk, hillbilly boogie, blues, patriotic songs of the South, cowboy tunes, and even a recording of "Empty Bed Blues," which Bessie Smith had recorded 30 years before. While most Bear Family boxes—because of their elaborate packaging, liner notes that resemble full critical biographies, and import prices—are not for everyone, this set is an exception. Rock & roll fans interested in the early music, hardcore honky tonk fans, and of course Horton nuts will have to have this. The earlier set would have even more limited appeal, but the sheer quality of the music issued here transcends its genre, time, and place and is eternal in postwar musical history. Highly recommended. —*Thom Jurek*

★ **Honky Tonk Man: The Essential Johnny Horton 1956–1960** / 1996 / Columbia/ Legacy ✦✦✦✦✦
This 36-track double-CD set, running just under an hour and a half, effectively chronicles Johnny Horton's Columbia Records career. The first disc, which is in mono, traces Horton's honky tonk work of 1956–1957, starting with "Honky Tonk Man." Though lacking the crossover appeal of his later work at the time, this is the material on which his reputation stands today, with people like Dwight Yoakam resurrecting it. The end of the first disc and the beginning of the second (which is in stereo) present the stylistic fishing expedition of Horton's commercially unsuccessful middle period, as be goes looking for a bit. He finds it, of course, with the martial rhythms and historical theme of "The Battle of New Orleans," a chart-topping novelty that leads to a string of similar productions. By the end, in songs like "The Mansion You Stole," Horton seems headed toward the lush, string-filled Nashville Sound, though he died before it gained dominance. Along the way, all of Horton's Country chart singles and most of his pop chart singles are included, along with two tracks, previously unreleased in the U.S. Of course, the set could have been considerably longer (or, better yet, shaved by a few tracks and fit onto a single disc), but nothing essential is missing. —*William Ruhlmann*

Somebody's Rockin' / 1996 / Bear Family ✦✦✦✦
Supplementing Bear Family's *Rockin' Rollin' Johnny Horton*, the 31-track *Somebody's Rockin'* contains a selection of good, if obscure, rock & roll and honky tonk Horton recorded in the mid-'50s, including "Devlish Lovelight," "Mean Mean Son of a Gun," "Happy Millionaire," "Coal Smoke, Valve Oil and Steel," "Talk Gobbler Talk," "Bawlin' Baby," and "Tennessee Jive." Much of this material is fun, but it's only for hardcore fans, since the primary appeal of the music is its very obscurity; on the whole, it does not rank among his finest works. —*Thom Owens*

16 Biggest Hits / Aug. 10, 1999 / Sony ✦✦✦✦
16 Biggest Hits may be missing some noteworthy songs, but it does provide an excellent summary of Johnny Horton's Columbia recordings between 1956 and 1960. Since it does contain the majority of his best-known songs—"The Battle of New Orleans," "Honky-Tonk Man," "I'm a One Woman Man," "Johnny Reb," "Sink the Bismark," "Whispering Pines," "North to Alaska"—at a mid-line price, it's an excellent introductory collection. —*Stephen Thomas Erlewine*

Hot Rize

f. 1976, **db.** 1992
Group / Bluegrass, Progressive Bluegrass, Traditional Bluegrass
The eclectic Colorado progressive bluegrass band Hot Rize also played traditional bluegrass, jazz, and rock. They came together in 1976 and were named after the secret ingredient of Martha White Self-Rising Flour, the product Flatt & Scruggs had promoted early in their careers. The bandmembers were Tim O'Brien on lead and harmony vocals, mandolin, and fiddle; Pete Wernick on banjo and harmony vocals; and Charles Sawtelle on bass guitar, guitar, harmonies, and lead vocals. Mike Scap departed in 1976 and was replaced by bass player, guitarist, and vocalist Nick Forster, who also became the group's MC. Hot Rize recorded its self titled debut album, a blend of traditional and new material, in 1979. Their second album, *Radio Boogie*, came out in 1981. A year later, their alter ego Red Knuckles & the Trailblazers, a parody of hardcore '50s country music, recorded their own album, *Red Knuckles & the Trailblazers*. In 1984, Hot Rize released a concert album largely comprised of traditional hits and in 1985 released *Traditional Ties.* In 1988 another Red Knuckles album, *Shades of the Past*, followed. Their final album, *Take It Home*, came out in 1990; O'Brien and Wernick went on to successful solo careers, while Forster went on to executive produce the syndicated radio variety show Etown. Sawtelle passed away in March 1999 after a two-year fight with leukemia. —*Johnny Loftus*

Hot Rize / 1979 / Flying Fish ✦✦✦✦✦
Hot Rize's debut album demonstrated that traditional bluegrass bands could bring the music into the modern era without turning totally progressive or losing the music's roots. Over the album's 14 tracks, Hot Rize turns in consistently engaging and exciting performances, particularly from vocalist/fiddler/mandolinist Tim O' Brien and banjoist Pete Wernick. It's a terrific debut. —*Thom Owens*

Radio Boogie / 1981 / Flying Fish ✦✦✦✦

Red Knuckles & Hot Rize: Live / 1982 / Flying Fish ✦✦✦

In Concert / 1984 / Flying Fish ✦✦✦

Traditional Ties / 1985 / Sugar Hill ✦✦✦✦
Traditional Ties is the first album Hot Rize recorded for Sugar Hill, and it is arguably their best effort ever, capturing their skill for both traditional material, originals (Tim O'Brien's "Walk the Way the Wind Blows," which became a Top Ten hit for Kathy Mattea), and progressive bluegrass (Keith Whitley's "You Don't Have to Move the Mountain"). —*Thom Owens*

● **Untold Stories** / 1987 / Sugar Hill ✦✦✦✦✦
The combo of vocalist/fiddler/mandolinist Tim O' Brien and banjo player Pete Wernick was never stronger than on Hot Rize's 1987 release *Untold Stories.* Never as "progressive" as some of their peers (New Grass Revival, the Seldom Scene, Country Gazette), Hot Rize were able to hold on to the trappings of traditional roots music without ever letting it sound stale or too "old-timey." The underrated vocals of O'Brien harmonize beautifully with Wernick and bassist Nick Foster, and the dobro playing of the ubiquitous Jerry Douglas soars over several tracks. The fluid instrumental "Bluegrass Part Three" serves as an early highlight, and Wernick's beloved phase-shifted banjo pops up on the edgy "Shadows of My Room," but the album's stark high point is the delicate closing number "Late in the Day." This simple love song highlights the singer's restraint and guest player

Douglas' clean, soaring dobro. Warm and crisp all at once, *Untold Stories* tells more than the title would suggest. —*Zac Johnson*

Shades of the Past / 1988 / Sugar Hill ✦✦✦
In addition to comic material, the Hot Rize alias Red Knuckles & the Trailblazers run-through honky-tonk favorites like "The Window Up Above" and "Always Late." —*Jason Ankeny*

Take It Home / 1990 / Sugar Hill ✦✦✦✦
Take It Home, Hot Rize's final album, demonstrates that the group continued to improve the longer they stayed together. The group's instrumental interplay is astonishing and their harmonies are quite beautiful—their performances are effortlessly graceful, making it a farewell album to treasure. —*Thom Owens*

So Long of a Journey: Live at the Bouder Theater / Mar. 5, 2002 / Sugar Hill ✦✦✦✦
A live show by Hot Rize was always something to get excited about, especially the part of the show where the traditional bluegrass quartet morphed into their humorous alter egos, Red Knuckles & the Trailblazers. This disc, recorded live in 1996, is also something to get excited about, even though Red and his boys never show up. Instead, Hot Rize stayed in their suits and baked a tasty set of bluegrass biscuits. Tim O'Brien, Nick Forster, Charles Sawtelle, and Pete Wernick are all perfectly competent players, but their songs set them apart from their peers. In addition to great covers such as longtime favorites "High on a Mountain" and "Radio Boogie," the foursome displayed their strength as writers. Wernick's "Just Like You" is one of the set's highlights, with strong vocal harmonies, though Wernick's banjo often sounds as if it's going through some type of effect pedal. Forster's "Shadows in My Room" is another strong performance, particularly from O'Brien's lead vocal. The band performs one tune by guitarist Sawtelle, an instrumental called "The Butcher's Dog," where his picking is more straight-ahead and less idiosyncratic than his soloing on other songs. The band also performs three songs by frontman O'Brien, whose banter between songs shows how casual Hot Rize was, especially in front of their hometown crowd in Boulder, CO. So casual, in fact, that they asked for and honored a request from the audience, a quick run-though of "Foggy Mountain Breakdown." Also so casual that at the end of the show O'Brien remarks, "Oh, you're still here? We just came back to get our stuff." —*Scott Cooper*

David Houston

b. Dec. 9, 1938, Bossier City, LA, **d.** Nov. 30, 1993
Vocals, Guitar / Traditional Country, Country-Pop, Nashville Sound/Countrypolitan, Honky Tonk
Houston apparently came from good stock: his lineage includes Sam Houston and Gen. Robert E. Lee. Born and raised in Bossier City, LA, Houston became a regular on the *Louisiana Hayride* as a teenager. Apparently his soaring tenor voice wasn't totally appreciated; he found trouble getting work in the music business, and ended up as an insurance underwriter. But record producer Billy Sherrill brought Houston into the fold when Epic Records was still a young label (the early '60s), and Houston brought the company its first real hit with "Mountain of Love." In 1966 he broke through to major status with "Almost Persuaded," which netted a pair of Grammy awards and brought pop recognition as well. A member of the *Grand Ole Opry* since 1971, he racked up 28 hit records over a decade, including duets with Tammy Wynette and Barbara Mandrell. —*Tom Roland*

Golden Hymns / 1969 / Epic ✦✦
David Houston often sang in a lower register on his hits, so fans who are not intimately familiar with his catalog may not realize what a gorgeous tenor voice he has. On *Golden Hymns*, his first gospel album, the purity of his voice in its simple setting is very effective and even stirring. This album is much more conventional and traditional than *David*, Houston's modernized sacred album from 1969, and is ultimately less exciting for that reason. But if you prefer old-fashioned gospel music to revisionism laced with secular influences, *Golden Hymns* is the one to pick. —*Greg Adams*

David / 1969 / Epic ✦✦✦✦
It may seem like sacrilege to describe a gospel album as sexy, but David Houston's performances of sacred standards on *David* are intensely sensual and soulful. Produced by the forward-looking Billy Sherrill and backed by the Jordanaires, *David* is a rarity among the sacred albums cranked out in profusion by major country artists in that it takes well-known spirituals and transforms them into something surprisingly new and compelling. He prolongs "Were You There" into five aching minutes of religious ecstasy, and revives "The Milky White Way"—one of Elvis Presley's best gospel numbers—without echoing The King. One glance at the track list and its roster of chestnuts like "Old Time Religion," "Swing Low, Sweet Chariot," and "When the Saints Go Marching In" may convince potential listeners that there is nothing new to be heard here, but the remarkable *David* should not be judged by its cover. —*Greg Adams*

Greatest Hits / 1969 / Epic ✦✦✦✦

David Houston's Greatest Hits, Vol. 2 / 1972 / Epic ✦✦✦✦

American Originals / 1989 / Epic ✦✦✦✦
Columbia's 1989 collection *American Originals* serves up the ten basics of David Houston's '60s peak—including "Almost Persuaded," "My Elusive Dreams," "I Do My Swinging at Home," and "Mountain of Love"—with little frills or fuss. The sequencing is not chronological but given the similar nature of Houston's hits that doesn't really matter and the songs flow nicely anyway. So, it's a good, basic collection, but it went out of print in the early '90s and it has since been supplanted by other Houston collection, including Collectables' *Almost Persuaded: The Very Best of David Houston*, which replicates the entirety of *American Originals* in its first ten tracks. —*Stephen Thomas Erlewine & Tom Roland*

Pure Country / Aug. 25, 1998 / Sony ✦✦✦✦
Sony Music Special Products' *Pure Country* is a budget-line collection—whose low-budget roots surface on the front cover, where "Mountain of Love" is mistakenly called "Fountain of Love"—that contains ten of David Houston's biggest hits for Epic. Eight of the ten songs were on the 1989 collection *American Originals* ("Where Love Used to Live" and "My Woman's Good to Me" did not make the cut; "A Loser's Cathedral" and "You Mean the World to Me" take their place) and all ten show up on both Collectables' *Almost Persuaded: The Very Best of David Houston* and Collector's Choice's *The Best of David Houston*. Those two discs are considerably more comprehensive and not much more expensive, so they're recommended above this, but for those on a budget, or those needing not much more than the bare-bones basics, this suits the bill nicely. *—Stephen Thomas Erlewine*

● **The Best of David Houston** / Oct. 19, 1999 / Collectors' Choice Music ✦✦✦✦✦
Collectors' Choice Music's 1999 collection *The Best of David Houston* is easily the most comprehensive collection of Houston's work yet assembled. Spanning 24 tracks over the course of one disc, this contains all of his country Top Ten hits for Epic, from "Mountain of Love" in 1963 to "Can't You Feel It" in 1974. No other collection comes close to the scope of this set, which is a little bit of a mixed blessing because, frankly, Houston's soaring falsetto can be a bit much to take over the course of 24 tracks, particularly when so many of the songs have the same slow tempo and the same gentle production. There are brilliant moments, of course, when Billy Sherrill's sweeping production and Houston's voice perfectly mesh, and those are the big hits, "Mountain of Love," "Almost Persuaded," "My Elusive Dreams," and "Livin' in a House Full of Love" among them. No matter how alluring they are in small doses, they can seem a little samey—and Houston's voice can seem a little mannered—when taken in one long sitting like this. Then again, the length of this collection does give room to songs that switch up the tempo a little or give Houston a chance to stretch his voice, as he does on "After Closing Time" when he builds on Jerry Lee Lewis' trademark delivery to great effect. So, even if this collection offers nearly too much to digest at once, it does offer more variety than other Houston collections—which, after all, tend to recycle the same handful of songs—and it's also easily the best and most thorough single-disc collection to ever be assembled on David Houston and will likely remain the standard by which all other Houston comps are judged. *—Stephen Thomas Erlewine*

Almost Persuaded: Very Best of David Houston / Nov. 9, 1999 / Collectables ✦✦✦✦✦
Collectables' *Almost Persuaded: The Very Best of David Houston* is a very, very good collection of Houston's biggest and best singles. In fact, it's essentially an expanded version of the 1989 collection *American Originals*, since the first ten songs duplicate that collection, with the remaining six songs collecting other Billy Sherrill-written and -produced hits from the '60s, including "Livin' a House Full of Love," "You Mean the World to Me," "Wonders of the Wine," and "I'm Down to My Last 'I Love You.'" If there's any problem with this collection it's that all 16 tracks are on Collectors Choice 24-track compilation *The Best of David Houston*, released just months before this disc. This is still a very, very good collection and, since it's a little cheaper, some listeners may opt for this and be very, very happy with what they get; but the Collectors Choice collection is a better value and a better, more comprehensive collection. *—Stephen Thomas Erlewine*

Chuck Howard

d. Aug. 15, 1983
Guitar, Composer, Producer / Truck Driving Country, Country Boogie, Traditional Country
The father in the country & western Chuck Howard dynasty, this guitar picker was a musician's musician type, the kind of guy whose licks are played on a thousand records but nobody knows who he is. One of his most famous credits is on the often overlooked country album by Ringo Starr, *Beaucoups of Blues*. In fact, Howard was one of the main reasons this record happened at all. Howard first entered the extremely private world of the Beatles when he traveled to London with frequent playing partner Pete Drake. The latter player went to London at the bequest of George Harrison, who was hard at work on his epic *All Things Must Pass* album and wanted some of Drake's expertise. In the meantime, Howard became good friends with Ringo Starr and was the man who convinced him to spend an extended stay in the U.S. in order to record the country project. The finished record included four of Howard's songs, as well as extensive contributions from songwriter, picker, and peanut farmer Sorrells Pickard.

The Kentucky-born Howard recorded a series of honky tonk singles in the late '50s and early '60s for esoteric regional labels such as Sand, Kim, Flame, and Do-Re-Me. These songs have become popular candidates for anthologies of hardcore country, hot rod country, honky tonk, or rockabilly, with titles including "Crazy, Crazy Baby," "Out of Gas," "Gossip," and a rockabilly cover of "Chattanooga Shoe Shine Boy." Since rockabilly represents the wildest, least disciplined side of the country & western music spectrum, perhaps it was hearing these records being played around the house that influenced young Chuck Howard Jr. to rebel against his father and become a slick Nashville record producer and A&R man, responsible for many string-laden pop hits as well as launching the careers of many photogenically appealing but strictly bland country artists in the '90s. *—Eugene Chadbourne*

Chuck Howard / 1977 / Cream ✦✦✦

Harlan Howard

b. Sep. 8, 1929, Lexington, KY, **d.** Mar. 3, 2002, Nashville, TN
Vocals, Composer / Traditional Country, Honky Tonk, Bakersfield Sound
Country music's preeminent composer, Harlan Howard boasted an unparalleled body of work encompassing well over 4,000 songs; the writer behind such perennials as "I Fall to Pieces," "Life Turned Her That Way," and "Heartaches By the Number," he scored major chart hits during every decade of the postwar era. Born September 8, 1929, in Lexington, KY, Howard and his family moved to Detroit just two years later. A devoted fan of the *Grand Ole Opry* radio show, his idol was the great Ernest Tubb, whose songs Howard attempted to copy down lyric by lyric; a number of words were subsequently lost in the translation, of course, forcing him to invent new lines—sometimes even entire verses—and in the process an aspiring songwriter was born. After graduating high-school, Howard spent the next four years stationed in Fort Benning, GA, serving as a military paratrooper; in his off hours, he learned to play guitar, and each Friday night he and a friend would hitchhike to Nashville, spending the weekends soaking up live country music.

After leaving the service, Howard spent the last half of the 1950s traveling the country, accepting short-term jobs everywhere from Michigan to Arizona; he finally ended up in California, gravitating towards the Bakersfield area. There performers including Buck Owens and Wynn Stewart were developing the famed Bakersfield sound; Howard's fledgling compositional skills were recognized, and soon artists like Tex Ritter and Johnny Bond agreed to publish his songs. Then Stewart recorded Howard's "You Took Her off My Hands," and virtually overnight his work was in hot demand; with his wife, Jan Howard—herself a rising country star—recording his demos, in 1958 his "Pick Me Up on Your Way Down" was cut by Charlie Walker, and a short time later "What Makes a Man Wander" was covered by Jimmy Skinner. In early 1959, Kitty Wells scored with her rendition of "Mommy for a Day"; however, Howard's true breakthrough came later in the year, when his classic "Heartaches by the Number" became a smash for Ray Price. A pop remake by Guy Mitchell was also an enormous success.

In mid-1960, the Howards relocated to Nashville; he soon authored another hit for Price, "I Wish I Could Fall in Love Today," as well as a pair of tracks for Owens, "Excuse Me (I Think I've Got a Heartache)" and "Above and Beyond." Then, in 1961, Howard and Hank Cochran co-wrote arguably his best-loved song, "I Fall to Pieces," a crossover success for the legendary Patsy Cline. After penning the hit "Three Steps to the Phone (Millions of Miles)" for Jim Reeves, he then wrote a follow-up, "He'll Have to Go"; Reeves rejected the track, however, and it was passed on to George Hamilton IV, in whose hands it was a major success. (Reeves instead cut Howard's "The Blizzard," to significant acclaim.) In all, Howard notched 15 chart hits in 1961 alone; among his other notable compositions that year were "Heartbreak U.S.A." (covered by Wells), as well as "Under the Influence of Love" and "Foolin' Around" (two more by Owens). He was writing a minimum of two or three songs daily, with about a dozen of those recorded each week; not surprisingly, he was named *Billboard*'s Songwriter of the Year two years running.

Also in 1961, *Harlan Howard Sings Harlan Howard*, his debut solo LP, was released; he cut several more albums in the years to follow, even scoring a minor hit a decade later with the single "Sunday Morning Christian," but a serious recording career was clearly never his intention. Instead, he remained Nashville's most prolific composer; between 1962 and 1963, his major hits included Johnny Cash's "Busted" (later a pop hit for Ray Charles), Price's rendition of "You Took Her off My Hands," George Jones' "You Comb Her Hair," Roy Drusky's "Second Hand Rose," and Johnny & Jonie Mosby's "Don't Call Me From a Honky Tonk." In 1964, Howard established his own publishing imprint, Wilderness Music, and Jones notched another hit with "Your Heart Turned Left (And I Was on the Right)"; the following year, he and Owens co-authored the latter's chart-topper "I've Got the Tiger by the Tail." In 1966, Howard and Tompall Glaser teamed to write the superlative "Streets of Baltimore" for Bobby Bare, and a year later wife Jan even hit with "Evil on Your Mind."

In 1967, Waylon Jennings issued *Sings Ol' Harlan*, an album comprised solely of Howard songs; that same year, Mel Tillis cut "Life Turned Her That Way," another of his greatest compositions (it was later successfully covered by Ricky Van Shelton). Hank Williams Jr. scored in 1968 with "It's All Over (But the Crying)," but as the decade drew to a close, Howard fell prey to an extreme case of writer's block which threatened to derail him for the duration of the 1970s. Indeed, he scored only a handful of hits in the years to follow, among them a pair of chart-toppers, Melba Montgomery's "No Charge" and Charlie Rich's "She Called Me Baby." By the 1980s, Howard had settled into semiretirement, although he regularly tutored up-and-coming songwriters at Tree Publishing; in 1982, John Conlee dusted off his "Busted" and reached the Top Ten, and two years later a pair of his more recent gems—"I Don't Know a Thing About Love (The Moon Song)," covered by Conway Twitty, and the Judds' rendition of "Why Not Me"—reached number one. Other contemporary artists to hit with Howard's songs include Reba McEntire, Highway 101, and k.d. lang. Howard died on March 3, 2002, in Nashville. *—Jason Ankeny*

● **All Time Favorite Country Songwriter** / 1965 / Koch ✦✦✦
By 1965, Harlan Howard had seen 400 of his songs recorded, with easily a dozen going on to become not only chart-topping hits but country classics as well. Close friend and Monument Records president Fred Foster thought it would be a great idea to bring in Nashville's best pickers and showcase an album of Howard singing his own greatest hits. The result is an album that's fascinating listening; the musicianship is spot-on and Howard has a way of singing his own material that has a reflectiveness missing from the better-known hit versions, fine as they are. The song lineup is astounding alone: "Busted," "Heartaches by the Number," "I Fall to Pieces," "I've Got a Tiger By the Tail," "Too Many Rivers." Any one of these songs would have made the career of a lesser writer; that they came from the pen of one writer alone is even more staggering. Harlan Howard may not be the greatest interpreter of his own material, but this album nonetheless shines for the small, folksy jewel it is. *—Cub Koda*

Country Music Hall of Fame 1997 / Jul. 23, 2002 / King ✦✦
Harlan Howard is one of the greatest songwriters in country history. His career as a writer far overshadowed his career as a recording artist, which was not nearly as successful or sustained. He had an album in 1965 for Monument, as well as some sessions for the small label Nugget in the early '70s. King's 2002 collection *Country Music Hall of Fame 1997* draws from those Nugget recordings, featuring nine originals, including the minor hit "Sunday Morning Christian." Howard had a warm, pleasant voice and these productions are appealingly dated—witness the fuzz guitars on his version of his standard, "The Chokin' Kind"—but this does not capture him at his best and the packaging is so shoddy

that only hardcore fans who cannot find this material any other way should pick this up. *—Stephen Thomas Erlewine*

Jan Howard (Lula Grace Johnson)

b. Mar. 13, 1932, West Plains, MO

Vocals / Country-Pop, Nashville Sound/Countrypolitan

During the '60s, Jan Howard was one of the hottest female vocalists in country music. Born Lula Grace Johnson in West Plains, Missouri, she moved to L.A. in 1953 and became involved with songwriter Harlan Howard, whom she married a month after they first met. Howard helped her break into country music, sending her demos to various companies. As a result she began singing demos for Tex Ritter and Johnny Bond. In 1959, using the pseudonym "Jan Howard," she recorded "Yankee Go Home."

In 1960, the Howards went to Nashville; there, Jan appeared on the "Prince Albert Show" segment of the *Grand Ole Opry.* Later that year, the Howards moved to Nashville permanently, where Jan's successful duet with Wynn Stewart resulted in her first solo single, "The One You Slip Around With," which made the Top 15; her next song, another duet with Stewart, reached the Top 30. In 1962, she charted with "I Wish I Was a Single Girl Again" and issued an eponymous album. Although she didn't do well on the charts, she continued to tour extensively. Two years later her career finally caught fire. Her songs of the period reflected her troubled marriage; in 1965, she reached the Top 30 with "What Makes a Man Wander?" Later that year, Howard joined Bill Anderson's touring and television shows. In 1966, she and Anderson scored two hits with "In Know You're Married (But I Love You Still)" and "Time Out." She then scored a Top Five hit with her solo "Evil on Your Mind. " Her next hit was "Bad Seed," and towards the end of the year, she had her only number-one hit with "For Loving You," a duet with Anderson.

In October 1968, Howard dreamed that her eldest son had been killed in Vietnam, which turned out to be true; shortly thereafter, she released the Top 15 single "My Son." In 1971, Howard became a member of the *Grand Ole Opry*; two years later, her youngest son committed suicide. She joined the *Johnny Cash Show* and in 1977 had three minor hits, including "To Love a Rolling Stone." In 1979, she and Tammy Wynette embarked on a tour of the U.S. and Great Britain. In 1984, Howard released the album *Tainted Love*, followed by *Life of a Country Girl Singer* in 1987. The same year, she published her best-selling autobiography *Sunshine and Shadow.* Howard remarried in 1990 and continued to appear on the *Opry.* *—Sandra Brennan*

Jan Howard / Sep. 28, 1999 / First Generation ♦♦♦♦

Rebecca Lynn Howard

b. Apr. 22, 1979

Vocals / Country-Pop, Contemporary Country, Adult Contemporary

Crossover country-pop singer Rebecca Lynn Howard grew up in Salyersville, KY, and moved to Nashville in 1997, where she began a career as a songwriter. Her compositions were recorded by singers like Patty Loveless, Reba McEntire, Lila McCann, and John Michael Montgomery. When Howard began recording on her own, she drew just as much from adult contemporary pop as she did from country, much in the manner of Shania Twain's crossover bids. After a delay for some retooling, her self-titled debut album was released in the spring of 2000. The album was a minor success, but she didn't make the splash anyone expected and she returned to the studio to retool her approach. Cutting some of the obvious commercial elements of her debut while alternately bringing in newer ones, resulting in 2002's better received *Forgive.* *—Steve Huey*

Rebecca Lynn Howard / May 2, 2000 / MCA ♦♦♦

This is Howard's debut album, and it showcases an artist with a very pleasing voice and a knack for songwriting. This Kentucky native wrote/co-wrote ten of the 12 songs on the CD. Like too many major-label releases from Nashville in the '90s, Howard's album suffers from an obviously formulaic approach to the assemblage of material. Songs like "You're Real," "Melancholy Blue," and "Believe It or Not" aren't country tunes at all, but tiresome adult contemporary ballads, while "Jesus, Daddy and You," a ridiculous lyric, is evidently intended to nail down the Christian Coalition demographic. Songs that actually have a country feel and original, compelling, lyrical content include "Tennessee in My Windshield," "Heartsounds," "Out Here in the Water," and "Was It As Hard to Be Together," the only genuine country ballad on the album. The good news is that Howard wrote the best songs on the CD, and the bad news is that she also wrote most of the insipid material. Howard needs to decide whether she wants to sing country or pop; too many Nashville artists try to do both, to the detriment of country music. *—Philip Van Vleck*

● **Forgive** / Sep. 10, 2002 / MCA ♦♦♦♦

One of Nashville's best-known songwriters shines on album number two. One can easily draw the conclusion that Rebecca Lynn Howard had many musical influences in her life because you can hear all of them throughout this gripping 12-track collection: country, bluegrass-gospel, and Top 40 pop. But it's the album's title track that could give Howard the breakout status she deserves. The chill-inducing "Forgive" is a masterpiece. But it's not alone, with songs like "It Didn't Look Like Alcohol," about a man who is down on his luck, and "It's My Job to Fall," about a tear. Loaded with diversity, freshness, and inspiration, *Forgive* will no doubt earn its place on one of the top spots on the charts. *—Maria Konicki Dinoia*

Ray Wylie Hubbard

b. Nov. 13, 1946, Soper, OK

Songwriter, Vocals / Progressive Country, Singer/Songwriter

A leading figure of the progressive country movement of the 1970s, singer/songwriter Ray Wylie Hubbard remains best known for authoring the perennial anthem "Up Against the Wall, Redneck Mother." Born November 13, 1946 in Soper, OK, Hubbard and his family relocated to Dallas during the mid-'50s; there he learned to play guitar, eventually forming a folk group with fellow aspiring musician Michael Martin Murphey. Befriended by the likes of Jerry Jeff Walker and Ramblin' Jack Elliott, Hubbard later formed a trio named Three Faces West which regularly performed at the Outpost club in Red River, New Mexico, a musical hotbed also trafficked by artists including Steve Fromholz and Bill & Bonnie Hearne. Upon the breakup of Three Faces West Hubbard toured the southwestern coffeehouse circuit as a solo act before forming another group, Texas Fever; they too proved short-lived, and he returned to New Mexico to again take up residence at the Outpost.

While in Red River Hubbard rekindled his friendship with Walker, who in 1973 recorded Hubbard's most famous (if least representative) composition, "Up Against the Wall, Redneck Mother, " on his acclaimed *Viva Terlingua* LP. The success of the album guaranteed Hubbard instant cult status within progressive country circles, and at much the same time he set about organizing a new backing band, dubbed the Cowboy Twinkies. Considered by many the first cowpunk group—their regular set lists included everything from Merle Haggard songs to a show-stopping cover of Led Zeppelin's "Communication Breakdown"—the Cowboy Twinkies' music met with considerable resistance in both country and rock quarters; frustrated, Hubbard funded a demo tape which won the group a contract with Atlantic. However, the label left the band in limbo, and they finally jumped ship to Warner Bros., who shipped them off to Nashville to record their debut LP *Ray Wylie Hubbard and the Cowboy Twinkies.*

Released in 1975, the album suffered from label-imposed over-production and fared poorly; Hubbard did not resurface prior to 1978, when he signed to Willie Nelson's short-lived Lone Star imprint to record *Off the Wall*, which contained his own version of "Redneck Mother." The following year Hubbard acquired a new backing unit in the form of the Lost Gonzo Band, previously Walker's supporting group; comprised of guitarist John Inmon, bassist Bob Livingston and drummer Paul Pearcy, they recorded the live LP *Caught in the Act.* By 1984 Hubbard was backed by the Bugs Henderson Trio, which featured guitarist Henderson, bassist Bobby Chitwood and drummer Ron Thompson; with them he cut another live effort, *Something About the Night.* Hubbard did not record for another eight years, instead building a small but loyal following through constant touring; finally, in 1992 he issued *Lost Train of Thought* on his own Misery Loves Co. label, followed in 1995 by the Dejadisc release *Loco Gringo's Lament. Dangerous Spirits* appeared two years later, and in 1999 Hubbard returned with *Crusades of the Restless Nights. Eternal & Lowdown*, which was issued in summer 2001, captured the haunting poetics of religion, philosophy, and salvation. *—Jason Ankeny*

Ray Wylie Hubbard & The Cowboy Twinkies / 1975 / Warner Bros. ♦♦♦

Off the Wall / 1978 / Lone Star ♦♦♦

Ray Wylie Hubbard established himself as a different and braver kind of country artist with his great song "Redneck Mother." Not only did he make fun of rednecks, he made fun of their mothers as well. He even managed to irritate the normally calm Merle Haggard by appropriating a line from "Okie From Muskogee." Although the latter song had been delivered tongue in cheek to begin with, Hubbard's song can be considered something of an answer to the right-wing sentiments expressed by the narrator of the Haggard ditty. So Hubbard arrived with a splash, but the relative lack of impact he had on the country scene since then might have something to do with his inconsistency. The listener who has enjoyed the redneck song, which needless to say kicks off the first side of this debut Hubbard album, will immediately come face to face with Hubbard's failings as he launches into the pretentious, whining "What a Way to Go." This song represents something of an innovative fusion, although maybe not one anyone is interested in hearing: the combination of country & western and Meatloaf. Next up is some standard white boy Texas blues, kind of like Delbert McClinton with a headache. But it isn't a one-hit album by any means. The Tony Joe White cover boogies along nicely and can be added to the Saturday night "rock out" radio play list. And the edgy lyrics that made Hubbard so interesting in the first place are back on "Freeway Church of Christ." The many and varied instrumentalists that came together for these sessions really shore up the music at times when the lyrics and Hubbard's dull voice don't have much to offer. Steel guitar player Larry White plays incredible licks, some of them on the worst songs. *—Eugene Chadbourne*

Loco Gringo's Lament / 1994 / Dejadisc ♦♦♦♦♦

With *Loco Gringo's Lament*, this Texas troubadour plants himself firmly in the thick of life and love, delivering a deeply introspective and honest album that rivals his best work. Poignant songs chronicling the self-discovery that comes as a result of living hard and surviving are presented with solid instrumental backing that adds to their power and emotional impact. "After the Fall" is a masterpiece of song, a journey of struggle and enlightenment sung over a prominent choppy guitar vamp, while "Wanna Rock and Roll" rocks hard underneath Hubbard's brilliant telling of a dark and murderous tale. "I've Seen That Old Highway" is a spirited observation in Texas country style, and the title track is a song for musicians, outlaws, and people of the road—a mournful saga of the life. *—Jack Leaver*

Lost Train of Thought / 1995 / Dejadisc ♦♦♦♦♦

Hubbard's 1992 release *Lost Train of Thought* has been given a new life via Dejadisc's reissue program. It was the artist's own independent release available only at performances. He is backed up by a ragged but right band who can easily switch musical gears for more sedate tunes. "Sweet Lips Goodbye" is one classic of the mysterious power of woman brand, while "These Eyes" performed with Willie Nelson is, as it happens, a perfect Willie Nelson-style ballad. The energy is directed and clean. Hubbard has produced himself without excess and finds the right balance to keep his style hopping and songwriting sounding cohesive. *—Richard Meyer*

● **Dangerous Spirits** / Aug. 5, 1997 / Philo ♦♦♦♦♦

Sheer determination is what makes this collection of songs a force to be reckoned with. Hubbard's songs mix styles and genres recklessly, using whatever he needs to get the point across. While he doesn't have the greatest voice around, he puts his soul into his singing, leaving a memorable impression. None of these songs are comfortable, simple ditties about love and loss and all that—these are songs about life and pain in a way that country music usually doesn't cozy up to, with some genuinely creepy moments: "The Last Younger Son" tells the tale of the youngest of the Younger brothers as he faces his death, played out as a slow blues reeling with spiritual obsession and cold destiny. An excellent album. *—Steven McDonald*

Crusades of the Restless Nights / Jul. 20, 1999 / Philo ♦♦♦♦♦

"I wanted to be a folk singer," Ray Wylie Hubbard told annotator Geoffrey Himes of his early goal in the liner notes of his second Philo album, *Crusades of the Restless Knights*, and the record bore out the renewal of that ambition. Although the arrangements of Hubbard's tunes usually found several pickers playing stringed instruments (acoustic and electric guitars, steel guitar, bass, mandolin, Dobro), the simple song structures and restrained lyrics gave them the feel of old folk songs. Even when he waxed verbose, on "Conversation With the Devil," Hubbard was employing the talking blues form that dated back to Woody Guthrie and beyond. More typically, he would sing an entire song about a woman getting dressed up for a night on the town ("Red Dress"), each verse describing another article of clothing or makeup. There was a lot deliberately left out of such songs, but the suggestions of meaning were filled in by Hubbard's world-weary persona and rough, south-Texas-accented singing voice. It was music for anyone who liked his peers, especially Jimmie Dale Gilmore and the name-checked Townes Van Zandt, using a similar language and attitude. The strain of '70s-era Texas singer/songwriters turned out to be amazingly rich, and even this late-breaking legend lived up to his reputation after surviving to sobriety. *—William Ruhlmann*

Live at Cibelo Creek / Jan. 1, 2000 / Misery Loves Company ♦♦♦

Eternal & Lowdown / 2001 / Philo ♦♦♦♦

This is Ray Wylie Hubbard's blues album, though it is not blues in the traditional sense of 12-bar and three-chord progressions. However it is blues in feel, which is far more important. There are elements of slow country blues to the soul styling from Memphis. It is the spoken blues of Woodie Guthrie and Bob Dylan, but Ray Wylie has always been of that school of singer/songwriter going back to his early days. The big kicker here is that he has enlisted the stellar assistance of Gurf Morlix as both producer and guitarist. Gurf's guitar and production adds sound as if it is laid down in the desert with a windstorm ragin' and the sandy grit permeating into every smallest crack and opening there is to be found or not. This, combined with the laconic/wry wit of the Ray Wylie-crafted songs provides a combination that seems so natural you wonder why it was never done before. You know that Ray is no longer imbibing as he did at one time and he has seen his path, but can also laugh at where he was. He is constantly taking a good hard look at that fine line between good and evil and is not afraid to approach it. Ray Wylie pens ten of the 11 songs, and he approaches that minute line and even straddles it fearlessly in this collection that further exposes his/your demons. But under all of it there is a beauty that shines through for the life you have. *—Bob Gottlieb*

Growl / Apr. 1, 2003 / Philo ♦♦♦♦♦

Anybody who has followed the development of Ray Wylie Hubbard as an artist over the last dozen years or so has had to be keenly aware that he's been moving through changes in lyric style, melodic invention, and production styles. He's also been on a spiritual odyssey in his music that culminated on the excellent *Eternal & Lowdown*. *Growl* is a record of an awareness gained; it is expressed in the most basic, elemental physical and emotional truths (from humor to doubt to surrender to anger at hypocrisy) in these songs. The truth expressed on *Growl*—the most aptly named of all Hubbard's recordings—is in a dirty-hands, mud-romping, greasy, rock & roll inbred with Delta blues. This is music comprised of exposed innards, cutting honesty, scab-ripping emotion, and pure, badass Texas attitude. Produced by Gurf Morlix—he also minded the store on *Eternal & Lowdown*—the band is basically Hubbard (on lead—a first—and slide guitars), Morlix (on bass and lead guitars), and Rick Richards (drums), with guests including Mary Gauthier, Scrappy Judd, Buddy Miller, and Jon Dee Graham. And it should be noted that Hubbard has become a heck of a guitar player in the last six years. There isn't a weak cut on the set, all of it drenched in the midnight smoke and grit of the blues as it couples with early rock & roll under a blood-red moon. The set opens with "Knives of Spain," which features a killer guitar part by Miller. It's a songwriter's spiritual, full of "ifs" that have already come to pass for Hubbard, which is why he can write from the craggy fissure in the center of the song's truth: "If I had some poet's wings/I would fly to New Orleans/I'd rhyme my trials and misdeeds/So if you cut the words they would bleed/And in the night when I'm all alone/And the sadness goes to the bone/I'd make the words in the refrain/As lethal as the knives of Spain." As he continues, and the band turns up the volume, bringing the tension to the breaking point, it becomes evident that all of this has already come to pass in Hubbard. His haunted voice speaks that this is the other side of the desert of revelation: it's not bliss, not rapture, but a sincere, if bloodied, gratitude and the desire to always tell a truth so mucky and messy it cuts to the bone. One could write an entire essay on this song alone, or stop here, taking it in over and over, deep within oneself, and never get to the bottom of its mystery. But Hubbard's not done; he revisits the past on "No Lie," a paean to giving up the wasted life and becoming immersed in the roots of his inspiration. *Growl* is not only about bad luck, hard-won wisdom, and knowledge, though. "Name Droppin'" is one of the lightest-weight tunes Hubbard's ever written, but its groove is eternal, it's backbone-slipping, humpin'-on-the-box-springs, sweating blues in raw-rock overdrive. Guitars and fiddles undulate against the rhythm section in a sinful, copulating embrace that feels so good it's a miracle it's still legal. "Purgatory Road" is a blues-drenched painting by Thomas Hart Benton. It's rough truth—stark, knife-slashing images without judgment or anything but reportorial calm. Welcome to the hard times; this is where darkness and light don't know how to identify themselves, let alone one another. "Bones" is almost a part two with hoodoo thrown in, and the redemption in the song is in the slide blues itself. This is bottleneck playing honed razor sharp, and can be praised for plenty in its lyric and melody, but the fineness of its blue-black slash groove is enough. "Preacher" is an indictment of hypocrisy, but it's not obvious; it's rooted in the same tradition as Mississippi Fred McDowell's—he didn't need the minister, he encountered his God personally and let the struggle of that truth come out in his playing. "Rock-n-Roll Is a Vicious Game" is a stomping throb that is equal parts roots rock smoker and is the warning side of an earlier Hubbard song, "Loco Gringos Lament," or could have been the story of the L.A. band Sublime or one of 100 other bands. The cosmic, in Hubbard's own trademark way, is revisited on "Stolen Horses," with a wrist-slipping resonator guitar burn leading his musings on reincarnation. The groove takes the body down the slippery spine road to a place where it wishes for another chance at a smoky, shimmering groove like this one and the mind to place where perhaps it considers the subject in a different, more sensual way. The album closes with a country-rocker destined to be (in)famous, "Screw You, We're From Texas," an anthem that tells the fools who don't understand his music to f&%$ off. "It's Up Against the Wall Redneck Mother," without the drunken pathos, is humor disguised as punked-out roots rock (early ZZ Top meets the White Stripes). It works, but I'm glad it's the album's final track and not its first—and that's not a criticism. The highest praise that can be heaped on *Growl* is that perhaps it should have been released on Fat Possum, the now-legendary Delta label that releases the raw-as-steamy blues records of masters such as R.L. Burnside, the late Junior Kimbrough, Paul "Wine" Jones, and the Jelly Roll Kings. It would have fit without a glitch. This is for rollin' in the hay, fighting in the mud, twisting between the sheets, and turning your partner out all over the dancehall floor; and when it's over, you'll be dirty, sweaty, grimy, and grateful to be alive to enjoy the murkier pleasures of the earth, the flesh, and the spirit. *—Thom Jurek*

Marcus Hummon

Vocals / Contemporary Country, Singer/Songwriter, Alternative Country

The son of a career diplomat, singer/songwriter Marcus Hummon spent his formative years traveling the globe; at various times, he lived in areas as far-ranging as Italy, Africa, and the Philippines. After settling in Washington, D.C., as a teen, he began performing with his three sisters in a group named Harmony; following college, in 1984 he moved to Los Angeles to seek a record deal. After months of frustration, he relocated to Nashville in 1986. While quickly finding success on the city's club circuit, a recording contract consistently eluded Hummon and his band, Redwing, for years; his first taste of success came as a songwriter, when Wynonna notched a Top Three hit in 1993 with his "Only Love." The following year, Alabama scored with his "Cheap Seats," and after his songs were also covered by the likes of Hal Ketchum, Patty Loveless, and the Nitty Gritty Dirt Band, Hummon finally debuted with the LP *All in Good Time* in 1995. *—Jason Ankeny*

All in Good Time / Sep. 5, 1995 / Epic ♦♦♦♦

Michael Hurley

b. Dec. 20, 1941, Pennsylvania

Drums, Vocals / Progressive Bluegrass, Progressive Country, Country-Rock

A singer/songwriter in the subversive Greenwich Village folk scene of the late '60s and '70s, with several songs lent to the Holy Modal Rounders, Michael Hurley (aka Doc Snock) maintained an infrequent solo career into the '90s but was more famed for his writing credits. Born on December 20, 1941, in Pennsylvania, he migrated to Greenwich Village by the early '60s and was ready to sign a major record deal when he contracted mononucleosis; after spending several years in the hospital, Hurley returned to music and released a Folkways album in 1964 titled *First Songs*. Though he was inactive through the rest of the '60s, several songs from his first LP were borrowed by both the Holy Modal Rounders and the Youngbloods, who signed Hurley to their Raccoon label in 1970. He delivered two albums for Raccoon, *Armchair Boogie* and *Hi Fi Snock Uptown*, but was inactive again by 1972.

Four years later, Holy Modal Rounders' leader Peter Stampfel recruited Hurley for a 1976 project, *Have Moicy!*. The group's self-titled album was critically praised, landing recommendations for Album of the Year by the *Village Voice* and Top 20 LPs of the '70s by *Rolling Stone*. Hurley's prominent place on the album—guitar, fiddle, several lead vocals—gave notice that he was ready to resume his solo career, and he signed to the folk label Rounder in 1977. Hurley released only two LPs for the label (*Long Journey* and *Snockgrass*), spending most of his time on his farm in Vermont or playing sideman on several albums. He resurfaced occasionally, recording LPs in 1984, 1988, 1995, and 1999. *—John Bush*

First Songs / 1964 / Folk Era ♦♦♦

These are the eccentric singer/songwriter's first professional recordings, done in 1964 for the Folkways label, after his discharge from Bellevue. The lifelong themes of wine and bumming are addressed in "I Like My Wine" and "Just a Bum." Fan favorites "The Werewolf Song" and "Captain Kidd" make their first recorded appearances, too. In fact, these 12 songs suggest that Hurley's "hippie bard" musical vision was fully formed from the start. Future Holy Modal Rounder Robin Remaily joins in on fiddle for one tune; the rest of the time it's just Snock and his acoustic guitar. *Have Moicy!* indeed. CD-R and cassette copies of the album must be purchased directly from the Smithsonian (as in Institution) on a made-to-order basis. Photocopies of the album's original liner notes are included with each order. *—Brian Beatty*

Armchairboogie / 1970 / Warner Bros. ♦♦♦

Hi Fi Snock Uptown / 1972 / Racoon ♦♦♦♦

● **Long Journey** / 1977 / Rounder ♦♦♦♦♦

Yet another overlooked brilliant singer/songwriter, Hurley mined the roots of American music, delivering warm and heartfelt original songs with an earthy twang. This disc is one of his finest, here reissued with "Watchin' the Show," a previously unreleased track.

This is music will delight folk lovers, but more surprisingly should please Eagles fans as well. —*Tim Sheridan*

Snockgrass / 1980 / Rounder ✦✦✦✦✦

A truly delightful singer/songwriter mix-up from the Vermont-based Hurley, a man who has one of those cheerfully lived-in faces. The cover painting tends to get puzzled and startled reactions for its surreal landscape filled with naked folks and instrument-playing wolves, but that's just the package. Hurley's songwriting tends to switch from the serious to the satirical at the drop of a hat (sometimes in the middle of a song), which can result in unexpected laughter—he's a fine man with a witty line. The musical is congenial, no worries there. Hurley is the sort of artist who leaves listeners regretting that he doesn't record more. [The 1997 reissue comes with an additional cut.] —*Steven McDonald*

Watertower / 1988 / Fundamental ✦✦✦

Wolfways / Oct. 1995 / Koch ✦✦✦

Snock reprises highlights of his song catalog in this collection of new recordings, including "The Portland Water," "Werewolf," and "Hog of the Forsaken." Other songs are lifted from the out-of-print import *Watertower* album. If the arrangements are looser than in Hurley's heyday, when he had the Holy Modal Rounders and company to back him, the Doc himself sounds as feisty and bent as ever. His raw fiddle and banjo work are a pleasure to hear. Though nothing's really new here, sightings of this genuine eccentric are rare enough that any collection is welcome. —*Brian Beatty*

Weatherhole / Oct. 12, 1999 / Rounder ✦✦✦

Not as potent as *Long Journey*, *Blue Navigator*, or *Snockgrass*, *Weatherhole* is more on a par with *Watertower*, and the two Racoon Records albums, *Armchair Boogie* and *Hi Fi Snock Uptown*. In other words, Michael Hurley is even more laid-back than usual; though, with Hurley, "laid-back" can be an asset. The main culprit here is mixing Hurley's vocals a layer or two back in the mix. In fact, the dobro, alternately provided by either Kevin Maul or David Mansfield, seems to be hogging the lead vocal mike. The Hurley dynamic requires his lazy, loopy-yet-effective vocals to be squarely up front. It is no accident that the most successful songs on *Weatherhole*—"The Beggars Terms," "Vanessa," "Mr. Man in the Moon," and "Don't Call Me Sam"—feature Hurley's vocals clearly atop the instrumental mix. These four tunes, along with "The Rue of Ruby Whores," "Extra Love," "Wildegeeses," and "Your Old Gearbox," comprise eight worthy additions to the Hurley canon. "Vanessa," to single out one, with its "holy modal," fiddle-and-banjo backing, is essential. The other four originals on *Weatherhole* are so-so Doc Snock fare, as is the take of the traditional "Rider's Lament." Particularly so-so is the overly cute toker anthem, "Nat'l Weed Growers Association." Still, eight out of 13 is not a bad ratio. What's that, math fans? Sixty percent? One is inclined to accept the percentage because no one else is even remotely capable of providing a Hurley fix other than Hurley himself. Hurley's vivid, primitive artwork for the cover and insert booklet of *Weatherhole*, featuring usual suspects Wood Bill, Kornbred, Jocko, and Boone, is among his best. —*Steve Cooper*

Sweetkorn / 2002 / Trikont ✦✦✦

The question of whether Michael Hurley (aka Dock Snock) is a neglected national treasure or a mildly amusing pseudo-folky aberration is one that must be resolved in the ear of the individual listener. The fact that the question meets different answers in just about every quarter probably explains both Hurley's legendary status among American roots musicians (he has played with everyone from the Youngbloods to Son Volt) and the fact that this album was released on a small German label more usually devoted to historical curiosities. On *Sweetkorn*, the aging Hurley evokes the sound of middle-period Tom Waits, though he comes by his junkyard instrumentation and ugly voice more honestly than Waits does. Same with the aggressively lo-fi production quality, which is a longstanding Waits affectation and, one senses, simply a reflection of the way things are for Hurley. Hurley's "Ohio Blues" is spare and beautiful, as is his eerily lovely rendition of the pop classic "Mona Lisa"; he brings nothing particularly new or noteworthy to "Barbara Allen," but "The End of the Road" sounds like a sly undermining of "Mommas Don't Let Your Babies Grow Up to Be Cowboys," while "Negatory Romance" opens with this deathless couplet: "He's wantin' her more than he's wantin' his wife/Now buddy, that's a good way to screw up your life." Bard, sage, screwup, whatever—Michael Hurley's generally worth hearing, and that's certainly the case on this weird but charming album. —*Rick Anderson*

Blueberry Wine: The First Songs of Michael Hurley / Jun. 25, 2002 / Locust ✦✦✦

These are his earliest professional sides, made in 1964 for the Folkways label, reissued on CD with a new title, new cover art, and new notes by Hurley himself. Favorites like "The Werewolf Song" and "Captain Kidd" made their first recorded appearances on this dozen-song set, and sound just as new nearly four decades later. Though *First Songs* (the album's original title) has long been available on CD-R and cassette on a made-to-order basis from Smithsonian/Folkways, whatever commercial distribution the fledgling Locust label can provide should help save Hurley's fans time, trouble, and money. —*Brian Beatty*

Michael Hurley / Rounder ✦✦✦

Ferlin Husky

b. Dec. 3, 1927, Flat River, MO

Guitar, Vocals / Traditional Country, Country-Pop, Country Comedy, Honky Tonk, Bakersfield Sound, Nashville Sound/Countrypolitan

Ferlin Husky had three separate careers. Out of the three, the best-known is his country-pop career, which brought him to the top of the charts in the late '50s, but he was also known as a honky tonk singer called Terry Preston and a country comic named Simon Crum. Of course, Preston and Crum are just footnotes to Husky's very popular career, even though Crum nearly became a household name as well. During the late '50s and

early '60s, he had a string of Top 40 country hits, highlighted by two number-one hits—"Gone" and "Wings of a Dove"—which each spent ten weeks at the top of the charts. Husky wasn't able to sustain that momentum, but both of the songs became country classics.

Born and raised outside on a Missouri farm, Husky became infatuated with music and began to play guitar as a child. During World War II, he enlisted in the Merchant Marines, where he occasionally entertained the troops onboard his ship. Following the war, he became a DJ in Missouri, then in Bakersfield, CA. While he was in California, Husky began using the name Terry Preston, because he believed his given name sounded too rural. He also began singing in honky tonks, using the Preston name. At one of his gigs, Tennessee Ernie Ford's manager Cliffie Stone heard Husky and took him under his wing. Stone helped Husky secure a record contract at Capitol Records in 1953. As soon as he signed with Capitol, he reverted to using Ferlin Husky as his performing name.

Husky's first records were generally ignored. It wasn't until he sang on Jean Shepard's "A Dear John Letter" that he had a hit. "A Dear John Letter" became a number-one hit, but Husky wasn't able to follow it immediately with a solo hit, although the duo had a sequel, "Forgive Me John," later that year. Husky didn't have a solo hit until 1955, when "I Feel Better All Over (More Than Anywhere's Else)" and its flip side, "Little Tom," climbed into the country Top Ten. Around the same time, he developed his comic alter ego, Simon Crum. Husky signed Crum to a separate record contract with Capitol and began releasing records under that name.

Husky racked up a consistent string of hits during the late '50s, reaching his peak in 1957, when "Gone" spent ten weeks at number one; the song crossed over into the pop charts, climbing to number four. That same year, he began an acting career, starting with a spot on the *Kraft TV Theatre* television program and the film *Mr. Rock & Roll*. In 1958, Crum had a number-two hit with "Country Music Is Here to Stay." Though he had several hits in 1959, none of his songs broke the Top Ten. In 1960, he had his biggest hit, the gospel song "Wings of a Dove," which was number one for a total of ten weeks and reached number 12 on the pop charts.

Despite the massive success of "Wings of a Dove," Husky wasn't able to sustain a presence on the country charts during the '60s. He remained a popular concert attraction, but he had no Top Ten hits between "Wings of a Dove" and "Once," which hit number four in 1966. A year after "Once," he had his final Top Ten hit with "Just for You." In the late '60s, Husky managed to incorporate the slicker, heavily produced sounds of contemporary country-pop into his music, which resulted in his brief career revitalization. Husky kept racking up minor hits until 1975. In 1977, he had heart surgery and briefly retired from performing. During the '80s and '90s, he performed regularly on the *Grand Ole Opry*, as well as Christy Lane's Theater in Branson, MO. —*Stephen Thomas Erlewine*

Ferlin Husky & Jean Shepard / 1955 / Capitol ✦✦✦

Songs of Home and Heart / 1956 / Capitol ✦✦✦✦

Boulevard of Broken Dreams / 1957 / Capitol ✦✦✦✦✦

Gone / 1963 / Capitol ✦✦✦✦

Memories of Home / 1963 / Capitol ✦✦

Some of My Favorites / 1963 / Capitol ✦✦

The Heart and Soul of Ferlin Husky / 1963 / Capitol ✦✦✦✦✦

Ferlin Husky Sings the Songs of Music City, U.S.A. / 1966 / Capitol ✦✦✦

Ferlin Husky's singles enjoyed solid if not often spectacular success on the country charts throughout the '60s, but his dynamic personal appearances and film roles maintained a steady audience for his albums. "Money Greases the Wheels," a catchy and humorous song that Husky performed twice in the film *Las Vegas Hillbillys*, is the sole hit on *Ferlin Husky Sings the Songs of Music City, U.S.A.*, and an undeservedly minor one at that. Ballads dominate the remaining tracks, particularly on the first side, giving exercise to Husky's highly emotional style. "Green, Green Grass of Home" and Merle Haggard's "Strangers" are the obligatory covers of hits, while three of the album's dozen songs aren't performed by Husky at all. Two tracks feature brother-sister duo Orlo and Mavis Thompson, and the Ferlin Husky Orchestra provide an instrumental number ("Sack O' Woe"). Except for the hit, the hodgepodge of material (and artists) makes the album tracks seem more than usual like filler. —*Greg Adams*

What Are We Doin' Lonesome / 1982 / CBS ✦✦

What Are We Doin' Lonesome, recorded in 1982—seven years after Ferlin Husky's last chart hit—may be his final nationally distributed studio album. Thankfully the producer made no attempt to place Husky in a schlocky "modern" context; the instrumentation is straight country with plenty of steel guitar and fiddle. The title track was a major hit for Larry Gatlin in 1981, but Husky's vocals sound aged and a little wobbly. The entire album is devoted to covers of big country hits like Willie Nelson's "On the Road Again" and Johnny Paycheck's "Take This Job and Shove It," which may have been a bid for instant appeal but leaves no surprises for the listener. *What Are We Doin' Lonesome* isn't an embarrassing album, but is far from Husky's best work. —*Greg Adams*

Capitol Collectors Series / 1989 / Capitol ✦✦✦✦✦

Although *Capitol Collector's Series* is a fairly comprehensive overview of Ferlin Husky's hit-making peak, it's missing a couple of essential items, most notably hit first hit, "A Dear John Letter." It concentrates on his country-pop hits, picking up the great majority of his hits, including "Wings of A Dove," "Gone," "A Fallen Star," "Just for You," and 16 other songs. —*Stephen Thomas Erlewine*

Greatest Hits / 1990 / Curb ✦✦✦

Although it's brief and cheaply-produced, *Greatest Hits* contains many of the essential Husky tracks, including "A Dear John Letter," and which isn't on *Capitol Collector's Series*, "Gone," and "Wings of a Dove." For the budget-conscious it isn't a bad purchase, although *Capitol Collector's Series* offers a greater selection for an equivalent price. —*Stephen Thomas Erlewine*

With Feelin' / 1991 / Pair ✦✦✦

On *With Feelin'*, Husky tackles some of country's most revered songs, including "I'm So Lonesome I Could Cry," "I Fall to Pieces," and "She Thinks I Still Care." —*Jason Ankeny*

complete simon / 1993 / Laserlight ✦✦

Country Music Is Here to Stay includes a remake of "Wings of a Dove," Husky's biggest hit. —*Jason Ankeny*

● **Vintage** / 1996 / Capitol ✦✦✦✦✦

Vintage contains nearly all of the essential items from Ferlin Husky's peak years at Capitol Records. Featuring almost 20 tracks—including the hits "Wings of a Dove," "A Dear John Letter," "Once," "Stormy Weather" and "Gone," which is included in both in its hit single version and the original version released under the name "Terry Preston"—it's the closest thing to a definitive retrospective yet assembled. —*Thom Owens*

Feelin' Better All Over / Apr. 18, 2000 / Jasmine ✦✦✦✦

Classic transcriptions of Husky working his magic with his regular road band, the Hush Puppies. Husky has always been one of country music's most versatile performers, alternating between his heartfelt singing and his comedy alter ego of Simon Crum. Here he alternates between both personas, singing his heart out on tunes like "If You Be My Baby," "I'm Sittin' on Top of the World," "I Feel Better All Over (More Than Anywhere's Else)," "(I Love You) For Sentimental Reasons," and "Gone" while doing comedy with Red Foley, George Morgan, and a brace of imitations, including a surreal one of Roy Acuff singing "Hound Dog." This is a superlative package, with clean transfers of the original lacquers that go a long way toward enhancing his image as an all-a-round entertainer with talent to spare. —*Cub Koda*

Country Music Is Here to Stay: The Complete Simon Crum a.k.a. Ferlin Husky on Capitol / Sep. 10, 2002 / Collectors' Choice Music ✦✦✦

It's appropriate that *Country Music Is Here to Stay: The Complete Simon Crum a.k.a. Ferlin Husky on Capitol* was released on Collectors' Choice Music, because this is precisely the kind of music that appeals to collectors. Simon Crum was the alter ego of Ferlin Husky, who created him in the mid-'50s as an outlet for his novelty songs, which were always popular in country music, as evidenced by the popularity in the '50s of Homer & Jethro. The thing about country novelties is, no matter how well they're done, they date very quickly and they can often be way too much to take in one setting. Such is the case with the Simon Crum recordings, which cover a lot of different musical territory from rockabilly to white-bread pop, mock jazz, and, of course, straight-ahead country, and also show that Husky was a skillful imitator, capable of doing anybody from Elvis Presley to Ernest Tubb. All of this is interesting in theory and, played in short doses of a track or two, it's pretty amusing, largely because Husky is indeed so skilled. But there is a big, big caveat—to listen to *more* than one or two tracks in a row takes a Herculean effort for anybody who isn't a crazed novelty fanatic (and, if you're not in the mood, even one track can be a bit much). That's where the collectors angle comes in. By the time CCM released this in 2002, anybody who would be purchasing Simon Crum on CD would be interested enough to want it *all*, not just a selection—after all, if you're interested in this stuff enough to hear it once, you want to immerse yourself, even if it can be a bit much at times—which is where this complete collection comes in. There may not be track-by-track notes, but Greg Adams writes a very good overview, and this does serve up 21 tracks, including five previously unreleased songs, including three written by Dallas Frazier. There's no question that this appeals to a limited audience, but that audience will undoubtedly be satisfied by this collection, not in the least because it covers an area so specialized it's a wonder it came out at all on CD, especially at this late date. —*Stephen Thomas Erlewine*

Walter Hyatt

b. 1950, Spartanburg, SC, **d.** May 11, 1996, Florida Everglades

Vocals, Guitar / Progressive Country, Singer/Songwriter, Americana

He was born and raised in Spartanburg, SC, and died in one of the only places on earth that can be considered worse—the 1996 crash of ValuJet flight 592 into the Florida Everglades swamp. This savage dig at the hot little place known as "Sparkletown" is now out of the way, as is the mention of the notorious circumstances that took away Walter Hyatt. Associated with the Texas music scene, Hyatt was a songwriter and guitarist whose music could not be corralled into any one pen. And this was always an aspect of his musical life dating from his early listening as a child, digging into R&B and rock & roll, the latter style transforming into a maelstrom of styles all in itself in the '60s. Scholars on the subject of what makes for a good career tend to agree that Hyatt was just too eclectic to make a mark on the rather dimwitted roots rock audience at large. Hyatt projects had a huge influence on other musicians, though, and on a regional level the wonderful music of Uncle Walt's Band was a favorite of many a college music lover, in the days before Ronald Reagan locked the under-21 crowd out of the honky tonks.

Other members of the group were Champ Hood on guitar and David Ball on bass, and while claimed along with dozens of other famous acts as an Austin phenomenon, Uncle Walt's Band actually formed not only in Spartanburg, but in one of that city's high-schools when the players were more the age of nephews than uncles. Obviously, the local environment that could inspire the outrageously negative comment that began this biography has done little to hamper the creativity of its citizens, even the teenagers. In fact, the real problem Uncle Walt's Band faced was not just getting out of Spartanburg, but finding somewhere that would accept the group's repertoire wholeheartedly. Hyatt and partners bounced back and forth between Nashville and Austin, releasing several albums that, while eventually reissued by Sugar Hill due to public demand, really did not have that great of an impact at the time of their release.

Uncle Walt's Band broke up several times during the '70s but enjoyed a period of prosperity by the end of that decade and into the early '80s. For several years beginning in 1976, Hyatt and Hood also put together the Nashville-based Contenders, featuring Steve Runkle, Tommy Goldsmith, and Jimbeau Walsh. The group did a fair bit of barnstorming and built up a cult following. 1978 was the Uncle Walt Band's heyday in terms of acceptance in Austin. It appeared on *Austin City Limits* in 1980—Hyatt got on the show again as a solo artist a decade later—and the band itself called it quits to pursue solo careers in 1983.

One of the fans of Uncle Walt's Band as a college student was country singer, songwriter, and actor Lyle Lovett, who would later reach out to Hyatt and offer him opening act slots and production expertise. Hyatt was a fine performer but made an even greater impact as a songwriter. Cover versions of songs such as "Get Out of Dodge" have been done by artists such as Jimmie Dale Gilmore and Allison Moorer, turning out to be highlights of the albums they appear on. Following Hyatt's death, many of his musical colleagues paid tribute to him in a series of live concerts across the U.S. as well a CD project. —*Eugene Chadbourne*

● **King Tears** / 1990 / MCA ✦✦✦✦✦

Music Town / 1993 / Sugar Hill ✦✦✦

Frank Ifield

b. Nov. 30, 1937, Coventry, England
Vocals / Traditional Country, Country-Pop

Australian singer/songwriter/yodeler Frank Ifield was one of the more original country artists to come from overseas. He was born in England, and moved to Australia in 1948. His father was an inventor and engineer famed for creating the Ifield pump, a device used in fuel systems for jet aircraft. While still in his teens, he became a regular on *Bonnington's Bunkhouse*, a popular radio program, and dropped out of school to pursue a music career full-time. He appeared on other radio shows as well, finally landing on the traveling *Ted Quigg Show*, where he stayed for many years.

Ifield signed wtth EMI Australia in 1953 and released two successful singles including "There's a Loveknot in My Lariat." Soon he was hosting a weekly television show *Campfire Favourites*. By 1959, Ifield was appearing on all three of the Sydney television channels. Later that year, he went to London, and had his first British hit in 1960 with "Lucky Devil." He remained in England and in 1962 became a star with his yodeling classic "I Remember You." The song stayed at the top of the British charts for over two months, and when released in the States it hit number five on the pop charts. His most successful year was 1963 when he scored two British number-one hits; one of the chart toppers, "I'm Confessin' (That I Love You," a cover of a Rudy Vallée hit, made it to the middle reaches of the U.S. pop charts as well.

He continued having pop chart success through 1964, but after that his career in Britain began to wane. He came to Nashville in 1966 and was made an Honorary Tennessean by the state's governor, Frank Clement. Ifield recorded two albums in Nashville and debuted on the *Grand Ole Opry*, where he was a great success. During 1966-1967, he had several mid-range hits: "Call Her Your Sweetheart," "No One Will Ever Know," and "Tale of Two Cities," recorded for Hickory. He again found popularity in Europe during the '70s, particularly in Belgium, Holland and Luxembourg, and continued to tour and perform at country music festivals and cabarets. —*Sandra Brennan*

I Remember You / 1963 / Vee-Jay ♦♦♦

I'm Confessin' / 1963 / Capitol ♦♦♦♦♦
This album, half made up of standards and half of country music classics, is done as only Frank Ifield could do them. There's nothing about these songs that makes them stand out on this record, background music at best. Best remembered for "I Remember You" in the U.S.; nothing on this record comes close. —*Jim Worbois*

Portrait of Frank Ifield / 1983 / PRT [UK] ♦♦♦♦
● **The Best of Frank Ifield** / 1991 / Curb ♦♦♦♦♦
● **Someone to Give My Love To/Ain't Gonna Take No** / Jun. 10, 1997 / See for Miles ♦♦♦♦♦
This two-fer follows in the tradition of Ifield's previous recordings, offering charming if forgettable country-pop. —*Jason Ankeny*

The EMI Years / Capitol ♦♦♦♦
The EMI Years is a 20-track sampler of English-born Frank Ifield, who became a country superstar in the U.K. and Australia. Ifield had an unusual vocal style which mixed traditional country yodeling with slick pop stylings. These are the original recordings from the mid-'50s to late '60s, including "I Remember You," "The Days of Wine and Roses," "San Antone Rose," and "Stardust." While a few crucial tracks are missing, this remains the most comprehensive title in his catalog. —*Al Campbell*

Jack Ingram

Drums, Vocals / Contemporary Country, New Traditionalist
The Texas-based modern-day honky tonker Jack Ingram first carved out a niche for himself in the bars and roadhouses between Dallas and Houston. By the mid-'90s after extensive touring with his Beat Up Ford Band, he had released two well-received independent albums and had opened for artists like Merle Haggard and Mark Chesnutt. The end of 1996 brought about a deal with Warner, who reissued his first two indie albums, and in 1997 issued his major-label debut, *Livin' or Dyin'*. Moving to Sony's Lucky Dog label in 1999, Ingram released his fifth roots rock album, *Hey You*. Three years later, he hooked up with Lee Ann Womack's producer, Frank Liddell for *Electric*. —*Stephen Thomas Erlewine*

Jack Ingram / Sep. 30, 1995 / Crystal Clear Sound ♦♦♦♦
In the early '90s, country music was getting a well-deserved shot in the arm by an influx of new and exciting talent. One of these struggling new artists went by the name of Jack Ingram and his self-titled release here is something of a find. Recorded for a tiny independent label, *Jack Ingram* shows the first glimpse of the talent which was lurking in the shadows. These 12 cuts range from rather stunning originals to tasty covers. "Beat Up Ford," which Ingram would name his backing group, is fine indeed; and his covers of Willie Nelson's "Pick Up the Tempo" and Robert Earl Keen's "Road Goes on Forever" are

stunning examples of simplicity using, only voice, guitar, and mandolin for a wonderful effect. Elsewhere, the backings are kept on the money and enhance each tune nicely. *Jack Ingram* is a fine country/folk testament by an emerging artist. —*James Chrispell*

● **Live at Adair's** / Nov. 21, 1995 / Warner Bros. ♦♦♦♦♦
Jack Ingram's independent debut album *Live at Adair's* captures the roadhouse energy of the traditionalist honky tonker. Running through a selection of his original material, Ingram is energetic and convincing, making modern country sound more alive, gritty and vibrant than it usually does. Largely, that's due to his stellar backing band, who drive the songs home for all their worth, but don't discount Ingram's talent for leading the band, as well as his knack for writing tight, memorable weepers and honky tonk ravers. Those are the things that make *Live at Adair's* such an invigorating, promising debut. —*Thom Owens*

Lonesome Question / Dec. 1995 / Crystal Clear Sound ♦♦♦

Livin' or Dyin' / Mar. 25, 1997 / Rising Tide ♦♦♦♦
Country-rock chock full of blue-collar charm, *Livin' or Dyin'* is Jack Ingram's take on life after years of being in the road. While he covers Guy Clark's "Rite Ballou" and Jimmie Dale Gilmore's "Dallas," he makes them both sound like originals. Full of rockabilly guitar licks, Ingram songwriting shows that he has done his lessons and is now ready to graduate. "Imitation of Love" even comes across as an honest-to-goodness pop tune. *Livin' or Dyin'* is a great statement from one of country-rock's finest rising stars. —*James Chrispell*

Hey You / Sep. 21, 1999 / Sony ♦♦♦♦
Bouncing back from his first, abortive major-label experience with the shuttered Rising Tide imprint, Jack Ingram lands on another custom label, Sony's Lucky Dog, for his fifth album overall, *Hey You*. And he just keeps doing what he does, which is producing a lightened version of the kind of Texas singer/songwriter honky-tonk music typical of Joe Ely and Steve Earle. Ingram's primary subject is the difficulty of communication between lovers, a topic he pursues in songs like "Talk About," "How Many Days," and "Work This Out." But his better songs are more specific, and often seem to derive their opening lines. "Biloxi," in which a son criticizes his father for abandoning the family, begins, "Where in hell did you go, " while "Mustang Burn," in which the singer addresses a man whose automobile he may or may not have torched, starts with, "I don't give a damn that your car's on fire." They tell stories that grab you right away, and they're good enough that you wish Ingram's songs were all that good and wonder why they're not. —*William Ruhlmann*

Electric / Jun. 4, 2002 / Lucky Dog ♦♦♦
You know Jack Ingram has to be an "alt-country" performer. For one thing, his songs rock, and for another thing, he's witty enough to have a song lyric like "Everybody loves you/Jesus told you so/Everybody's lying/Hell, even Jesus knows." Ingram's songs mix a subtle background of country and folk with a hefty dose of roots rock, and the result is reminiscent of early Rolling Stones or Bob Dylan without the fancy wordcraft. In fact, Ingram's lyrics are simple but often humorous, as on "We're All in This Together," and the above-quoted "Everybody." While many of the songs on this album are fast-moving and danceable, the last three songs are performed acoustically. While they may not live up to the title *Electric*, they demonstrate Ingram's ability to do "old-style" country—but with a modern twist. Despite the occasional touch of slide guitar, this is country for city folk, music that fits in well with the Adult Album Alternative radio format. —*Lynne Bronstein*

The International Submarine Band

f. 1966, db. 1968
Group / Country-Rock
The International Submarine Band is best remembered as country-rock pioneer Gram Parsons' first band, which isn't surprising since the group received almost no publicity when they were active in the late '60s. Though the band never quite realized their potential, their sole album, 1968's *Safe at Home*, suggests the path Parsons would later follow. Parsons formed the International Submarine band with guitarist John Nuese, bassist Ian Dunlop, and drummer Mickey Gauvin while he was studying theology at Harvard in the mid-'60s. Parsons dropped out of college in 1966 and had the band move its operations to New York, where they began developing their synthesis of country and rock. By the end of the year, they had recorded two singles for Goldstar which were ignored. The group also recorded an album, which went unreleased; the tapes were later lost.

Early in 1967, the band moved out to Los Angeles on the advice of former child actor Brandon DeWilde, who told the band he could get them into the movies. The International Submarine Band did indeed appear in a movie—Roger Corman's *The Trip*, which starred Peter Fonda. However, the group's music was erased, with the psychedelic blues of the Electric Flag overdubbed on the ISB's performance. Still, the band benefited from its performance in *The Trip*, since it increased their profile in the L.A. underground; Fonda even recorded Parsons' original song "November Nights." However, relations between the bandmembers were beginning to fray, and Dunlop and Gauvin left the group in the spring of 1967. A few months later, Parsons' childhood friend Jon Corneal joined as a drummer, and they hired a temporary bassist in order to audition for Lee Hazlewood's LHI Records. On the basis of the audition, the group landed a contract. LHI's in-house producer, Suzi Jane Hokum, was hired as the group's producer and Chris Ethridge was hired as the group's bassist. By the end of 1967, the International Submarine Band had completed their debut album, *Safe at Home*.

Although the group's fortunes were beginning to improve, Parsons left the band in February of 1968 to join the Byrds. However, he hadn't told LHI that he intended to leave the Submarine Band before he became a Byrd, and he had to sell his rights to the ISB name to Hazlewood in order to avoid a lawsuit; Hazlewood was also able to prevent Parsons' vocals from appearing on his first album with the Byrds, 1968's *Sweetheart of the Rodeo*. Following Parsons' departure, the International Submarine Band attempted to replace the vocalist, but they couldn't find any possible candidates. By the time the ISB's debut album, *Safe at Home*, was released in the spring of 1968, the group had broken up. — *Stephen Thomas Erlewine*

● **Safe at Home** / 1968 / Shiloh ✦✦✦✦✦
Safe at Home, Gram Parsons first full-length album (and the only LP he would record with the International Submarine Band), today sounds like a dry run for the country-rock he would later perfect with the Byrds and the Flying Burrito Brothers; it's also major changeup from the psychedelically shaded pop/rock of the ISB's impossible to find debut singles. In many ways, the album sounds more purely "country" than Parsons' best-known work; the Burritos' crucially important R&B edge had yet to make its presence felt in Gram's music, and on these sessions the rock influence is often more felt than heard (probably due in part to the presence of Nashville session veterans who pitched in on piano and pedal steel). But Parsons considerable gifts as a songwriter were already evident on tunes like "Blue Eyes" and "Luxury Liner," and while there's a touch less grace in Gram's vocals than on his best work, his passion, understated wit, and deep love for country music are always in the forefront. And while Gram is the star of this show, his bandmates—John Nuese and Bob Buchanan on guitars, Jon Corneal on drums, and future Burrito Chris Ethridge on bass—are solid, soulful, and firmly in-the-pocket throughout. If *Safe at Home* sounds like a rough draft for Gram Parsons' later triumphs, it's also a fine record on its own terms, and leaves little doubt that the International Submarine Band's leader had something special right from the start. — *Mark Deming*

James Intveld

Bass, Vocals / Neo-Traditionalist Country, Americana, Alternative Country-Rock
James Intveld was a native of Los Angeles who started his career at an early age listening and singing along to his parents' recordings of Hank Williams Sr., Dean Martin, Lefty Frizzell, and Elvis. During the cow punk movement of the '80s, Intveld was working the same clubs as Dwight Yoakam and Rosie Flores, playing his own brand of rockabilly, and so impressed *Town South of Bakersfield* producers Pete Anderson and Dusty Wakeman that he was included on the second volume of the compilation series. Initially, Intveld worked with his younger brother Ricky and friend Pat Woodward in a band known as the Rockin' Shadows. The group dissolved when Ricky and Woodward left to work with Rick Nelson's Stone Canyon Band; both later died in the same airplane accident that took the life of Nelson, a tragedy that cut deeply into Intveld's heart and soul.

On his own, he worked as a singer/songwriter and concentrated on acting. Continuously cast in movies, TV, and videos, he was the singing voice of Johnny Depp's character in the John Waters film *Cry Baby* and served as a prominent player and character in videos by such artists as Kathy Mattea. Still, his music remained the centerpiece of his creative life. As a writer, Intveld wrote the Rosie Flores hit "Cryin' Over You" as well as all the material on his own 1996 effort *James Intveld*. Named the best studio recording project and the best country or roots CD of 1996 by *California's Music Connection* magazine, Intveld successfully produced, arranged, sang, and played all the parts on this magnificent release, dedicated to his brother and best friend, Ricky.

Continuing to write and perform on a continual basis, Intveld also remained in demand for his skills as a player; as adept at the slap bass, slide, steel, and drums as on guitar, he sat in with the Blasters periodically and often held down percussion duties for bluesman Lester Butler. A regular player around L.A., Intveld was also involved on recording projects with Kathy Robertson and the tribute CD *Turning the World Blue*, honoring Gene Vincent. The solo *Somewhere Down the Road* followed in mid-2000. — *Jana Pendragon*

● **James Intveld** / 1996 / Bear Family ✦✦✦✦✦
This self-titled release is by far and away the closest to perfection any studio project has achieved in a very longtime. With every aspect of the production, performance, and choice of material handled by the artist himself, there is a continuity and purity about it that is missing in even the top-selling discs that chart and receive platinum recognition. Vocally, no one can come close to Intveld's irreproachable style. His ability to evoke emotion from a song, even those he did not write, is dumbfounding; his version of Don Gibson's "Blue Blue Day" is evidence of this. As a writer, Intveld is stunning in his clarity and storytelling ability; listen carefully to the earthy tale of "Kermit Vale." While he does not consider himself a country writer per se, he is quite capable of concocting a mean shuffle and accentuating it with the optimal amount of twang, as exhibited on "Your Lovin'" and "Barely Hangin' On." His own rendition of his classic hit, "Cryin' Over You," made famous by Rosie Flores, also demonstrates Intveld's obvious understanding of traditional country music. A noteworthy balladeer, James Intveld takes this art form to the highest level. His own "You Say Goodnight, I'll Say Goodbye" is not only emotionally evocative, but also intelligent. The entire affair is dedicated to his late brother, Ricky Intveld, which makes this, his first Bear Family CD, all the more meaningful for James and his many fans the world over. As they say, nobody does it better than James Intveld; in a perfect world where music and musicians are rewarded for talent, ability, and original creativity, the enticing Mr. Intveld would be constantly sitting at number one on all the music charts and this CD would be double or triple platinum at least. — *Jana Pendragon*

James Intveld / Sep. 23, 1997 / 404 Music Group ✦✦✦
Writing, producing, and playing all instruments is a daunting task for anyone, but young James Intveld handles the responsibilities like an accomplished veteran, while projecting a good deal of charm and personality into each song. He's transparently influenced by Elvis Presley, but a number of songs are updated somewhat by an atmospheric ambience similar to that of Chris Isaak, although without the sleek production of an Isaak album. "Kermit Vale" is the surprise, a black, almost Irish folk song, which reveals that Intveld's heart is clearly not restricted to revival rock & roll. — *Jim Smith*

Somewhere Down the Road / Jun. 6, 2000 / Molenaart ✦✦✦

Alan Jackson

b. Oct. 17, 1958, Newnan, GA

Vocals, Guitar / Contemporary Country, New Traditionalist, Neo-Traditionalist Country
After Garth Brooks, Alan Jackson was the most popular male country singer of the '90s. An heir to the new traditionalist movement of the '80s, Jackson's approach was rooted in classic honky tonk yet remained comfortably within the contemporary mainstream. Jackson's hallmark was consistency—he wrote many of his own hits, and his way with a hook was part of the reason he never really hit a commercial dry spell, even into the new millennium. He also projected a modest, wholesome, down-to-earth image that made him one of the best-liked stars of his era even apart from his music. The total package resulted in an astounding 20 number-one singles and 20 more Top Ten hits, all in the first 12 years of his career.

Jackson was born in the small town of Newnan, GA, on October 17, 1958. He grew up singing gospel music, both in church and at home with his family, and as a teenager performed locally as part of a country duo. He left school to work and married his high-school sweetheart, Denise, who worked as an airline stewardess. During the early '80s, Jackson held down a series of odd jobs—car salesman, construction worker, forklift operator at K-Mart—while playing the local club circuit with his band, Dixie Steel, and working on his songwriting. He caught his big break when Denise found country-pop star Glen Campbell waiting for a flight and gave him a copy of her husband's demo tape; Campbell in turn gave her contact information for his music publishing company, and the Jacksons picked up and moved to Nashville shortly thereafter. Campbell's company suggested that Alan take a year and hone his songwriting even further, and so he worked more odd jobs—including the mail room at the Nashville Network, plus some session singing—before finally signing on as a staff writer. By night, he performed in Nashville clubs and recorded an updated demo with songwriter/producer Keith Stegall. In 1989, Jackson became the first artist signed to Arista's new country division.

Jackson's debut album, *Here in the Real World*, was issued in 1990 and became a platinum-selling hit on the strength of four Top Fives: the title cut, "Chasin' That Neon Rainbow," "Wanted," and the first of many chart-toppers, "I'd Love You All Over Again." He shot to full-fledged superstardom with the follow-up, 1991's *Don't Rock the Jukebox*, whose title track was an inescapable number-one smash that year. The record produced three more number ones ("Someday," "Dallas," "Love's Got a Hold on You") and also contained one of Jackson's signature songs, the Top Five "Midnight in Montgomery," which told the story of a visit to Hank Williams' grave. Also in 1991, Jackson co-wrote several songs with Randy Travis for Travis' *High Lonesome* album. With 1992's *A Lot About Livin' (and a Little 'Bout Love)*, Jackson took his place as not only one of the most popular stars of his time, but also one of the best. The number-one smash "Chattahoochee" became another signature tune, and Jackson also topped the charts with "She's Got the Rhythm (And I Got the Blues)," while scoring three more Top Five hits from the album—which became his first to top the country LP charts.

In late 1993, Jackson released the stopgap holiday album *Honky Tonk Christmas*, which actually avoided standards in favor of lesser-known material. He returned in 1994 with *Who I Am*, his second straight number-one country album, which gave him a staggering four number-one singles: a cover of Eddie Cochran's "Summertime Blues," the music-biz satire "Gone Country" (a dig at executives hopping on the commercial country bandwagon), "Livin' on Love," and "I Don't Even Know Your Name." In only his fifth year on the scene, Jackson was able to issue *The Greatest Hits Collection* in 1995 and scored hits with three newly minted songs: a cover of George Jones' "Tall Tall Trees," "I'll Try" (both number one), and "Home." It took *The Greatest Hits Collection* only a year to sell over three-million copies. And, of course, Jackson was far from done. 1996's *Everything I Love* became his fourth straight release to top the country album charts, and it gave him five Top Ten hits, including the number ones "Little Bitty" (a Tom T. Hall cover) and "There Goes." The 1998 follow-up, *High Mileage*, also hit number one and became Jackson's highest-charting album on the pop side, reaching number four; it contained four more Top Tens, including the chart-topping "Right on the Money."

Jackson paid tribute to his favorite country singers of the past on the easygoing 1999 covers album *Under the Influence*, which featured material by Jones, Merle Haggard, Charley Pride, Jimmy Buffett, Hank Williams Jr., Don Williams (the chart-topping "It Must Be Love"), and Jim Ed Brown (the Top Ten "Pop a Top"), among others. Although *Under the Influence* just missed hitting number one, 2000's *When Somebody Loves You* returned Jackson to the top of the album charts and gave him another number one in "Where I Come From." That year, he also teamed up with George Strait for the duet "Murder on Music Row," a strident defense of traditional country in the face of a new wave of crossover stars. An enormous hit, "Where Were You (When the World Stopped Turning)," a poignant attempt to make sense of the aftermath of September 11; rush-released in 2001 after an awards-show premiere, song rocketed to the top of the country charts and also became his first single to crack the pop Top 30. It was followed by the full-length *Drive* in 2002, which spawned another number one in "Drive (For Daddy Gene)," a tribute to Jackson's late father. The album was Jackson's seventh to top the country charts, and it also became his first to top the pop charts. —*Steve Huey*

Here in the Real World / 1990 / Arista ✦✦✦✦
In 1989, country music honky tonk revivalist Alan Jackson scored his first number one hit with "I'd Love You All Over Again"—not bad for being only his fifth single. Interestingly enough, it was a ballad, but a hard country ballad nonetheless. The songs sits somewhere in the no man's land between George Jones and Randy Travis, and floats uneasily seeking an edge. The title track is another hard country ballad, and with its sweet lonesome fiddle it was a more logical choice, but what the hell. The bottom line is that while *Here in the Real World* may not be Jackson's strongest record, it still stands head and shoulders over most of the competition, and that includes Curtain Shirt Brooks, that is, Garth. Producers Keith Stegall and Scott Hendricks understood that Jackson's country sensibilities are a boon, not a bane, in terms of putting his particular brand of new traditionalism onto the charts. Other winners are the honky tonkers such as "Blue Blooded Woman," "Chasin' That Neon Rainbow," and "She Don't Get the Blues," which feels as much like Merle Haggard doing Bob Wills as it does new country. This is a solid effort and established the fact that Jackson was just beginning to come into his own. —*Thom Jurek*

Don't Rock the Jukebox / 1991 / Arista ✦✦✦✦✦
If there was one record that established Alan Jackson as a bona fide star, *Don't Rock the Jukebox* was it. The set featured no less than two number-one singles in the title track and "Love's Got a Hold on You," and three more entered the Top Ten. This is Jackson at what he does best, being a modern honky tonk singer not quite as tough as Dwight Yoakam, but with more sex appeal and easier on the ears for those who like their "hard country" smoothed a bit. That's more Keith Stegall's fault than Jackson's, as there is no doubt by his having written all but one song here that he's the real thing. The truth of the matter is that Jackson's mettle comes in the ballads, like the criminally overlooked "That's All I Need to Know," or in the story-songs like "Dallas." "Midnight in Montgomery" is a stellar song about encountering the ghost of Hank Williams; its Spanish guitar overtones in the intro made it perfect for the radio, but its innovative video far overshadowed the song as a single. But hits aside, *Don't Rock the Jukebox* is solid as a new traditionalist record, meaning that it's a country record with ever-present pedal steel for every synth or glossy fiddle. Jackson's voice is in the groove, down there with Jones and Haggard, tougher than Travis, leaner than Strait, and almost as hillbilly as Yoakam. This is a great record that stands the test of time. —*Thom Jurek*

☆ **A Lot About Livin' (And a Little 'Bout Love)** / 1992 / Arista ✦✦✦✦✦
Three years after his first number-one single, Alan Jackson took his brand of new honky tonk country and pushed it all the way into the mainstream, making it possible for another batch of acts to follow him. Sticking with producer Keith Stegall, Jackson wrote over half the tracks on the set, including a pair of singles, "She's Got the Rhythm (And I Got the Blues)" and "Tonight I Climbed the Wall," as well as "Chattahoochee." The uptempo numbers with the jukebox kick are what works best with Jackson's restless country-soul voice—check "I Don't Need the Booze (To Get a Buzz On)." The smoking Western swing of "Up to My Ears in Tears" walks a line between Bob Wills and Buck Owens, and could have been covered by Dwight Yoakam. But the set's winner is its closer, the Geddins/Douglas classic "Mercury Blues." Taking the tune back to its country roots and claiming it for the Fender Telecaster's particular brand of pinch and tang, Jackson sings the hell out of it. At this point in his career, Jackson established himself as one of the most consistent talents country had to offer. —*Thom Jurek*

Honky Tonk Christmas / Oct. 12, 1993 / Arista ✦✦✦✦
One of the best country Christmas albums, this smart blend of old and new songs doesn't have a traditional carol in the bunch. He starts off strong with the rocking "Honky Tonk Christmas" and then sings a gorgeous duet with Alison Krauss. He adds his voice to a previously taped track by the late Keith Whitley on "There's a New Kid in Town" and does a credible job with Merle Haggard's "If We Make It Through December." Save for a silly duet with the cartoon Chipmunks, this is a fabulous album. —*Brian Mansfield*

Who I Am / 1994 / Arista ✦✦✦✦
By 1994, Alan Jackson may not have scored as many hit singles, but he definitely began to set himself apart from the onslaught of young country hat bands. First, there are 13 tracks on this set—three more than usually appear on country records because labels don't want to pay for more than that. Second, Jackson showed he had cojones by opening his album with Eddie Cochran's rockabilly classic "Summertime Blues," a song as associated with the Who as it is with Cochran. But Jackson shows the 'billy side of the equation while delivering both humor and soul in his reading. "Living on Love," an original, is a midtempo honky tonker with killer fiddle, telecasters chopping up the middle, and lyrics that make its sentimental subject matter palatable. "Gone Country," by Bob McDill, is an anti-new country anthem accusing a whole lot of folks of coming into the game for the cash. Jackson is the real hillbilly article, so he can sing that song—and so is the writer,

but it's most effective when looking at some of Alan's peers. But it's on Harley Allen's "Who I Am," a midtempo two-step barroom love song where the pedal steels whine and the fiddles cascade with their high lonesome song in the bridge, that Jackson's at his best. He sings with a sincerity that turns sarcasm on its head. The same is true on Rodney Crowell's "Song for the Life." In a version that rivals Crowell's own, Jackson's balladry in three-four time is heartbreakingly beautiful. And then there's Jackson's own songs like "Job Description," which comes right from the Merle Haggard side of the Bakersfield side of honky tonk, and the same goes for "Let's Get Back to You and Me," which is every bit as tough as Dwight Yoakam with a guitar solo to match. This is where Buck Owens and Ernest Tubb meet Johnny Burnette and George Jones. What a way to end a record. This is solid from top to bottom and one of Jackson's strongest outings. —*Thom Jurek*

★ **The Greatest Hits Collection** / Nov. 21, 1995 / Arista ✦✦✦✦✦
As the title indicates, all of Alan Jackson's greatest hits—including the number-one singles "Chattahoochee," "She's Got the Rhythm (And I Got the Blues)," "I'd Love You All Over Again," and "Don't Rock the Jukebox"—are collected on this single disc, making it the perfect introduction to the singer. —*Stephen Thomas Erlewine*

Everything I Love / Oct. 29, 1996 / Arista ✦✦✦✦
Everything I Love is further proof that Alan Jackson is one of the finest country singers of the '90s. Jackson continues to mine traditional country and honky tonk for source material, yet he isn't afraid to update the sound with electronic instruments. That fearless experimentation is kept in check by his ability to keep his music simple and straightforward—there is no question that Jackson deals only in pure honky tonk. Of course, his musical experimentation wouldn't be quite so effective if he didn't have a fine set of songs to back him up, and on *Everything I Love*, he has some of his finest ever, including "Little Bitty," "A House With No Curtains" and "Must've Had a Ball." —*Thom Owens*

High Mileage / Sep. 1, 1998 / Arista ✦✦✦✦
Upon first listen, *High Mileage* seems to have Alan Jackson visiting familiar territory. Jackson's well-earned stardom owes much to his warm vocal delivery, wrapped around gently rolling tunes about the simple things in life. *High Mileage* is no different, but this time the songs reflect some of the personal turmoil the singer was going through at the time. The Jackson-penned tunes "Gone Crazy," "Little Man," "Hurtin' Comes Easy" and "A Woman's Love" make it clear as to the type of soul-searching he was going through. Add to that the daring, spoken-word "I'll Go on Loving You" and the swinging "Right on the Money," and Jackson rewards the listener in the most disarming way. That personal touch, along with his winning traditional country stylings, make *High Mileage* one of his most emotional—and best—releases. —*Inigo C. Figuracion*

Super Hits / Mar. 23, 1999 / Arista ✦✦✦
For most fans, it's inconceivable to have an Alan Jackson hits collection without "Chattahoochee" or "Don't Rock the Jukebox," neither of which are on the budget-line compilation *Super Hits*. And that, naturally, is a problem for the casual fan, the kind who would buy a budget-line disc expecting that their favorites would be present. That's not the case with *Super Hits*, which shares only four songs with the exhaustive 20-track *Greatest Hits Collection*. Those four songs—"Chasin' That Neon Rainbow," "Who Says You Can't Have It All," "She's Got the Rhythm (And I Got the Blues)," "I Don't Even Know Your Name"—are among Jackson's best and the remaining six songs (all album tracks, except "Must Have Had a Ball," a hit from the post-*Greatest Hits* album *Everything I Love*) are good as well, but this collection simply doesn't deliver the hits it promises. Taken on its own terms, as a random sampling of nine songs from Alan Jackson's catalog, it's entertaining and possibly even a bargain for listeners on a tight budget, but most fans are much better-served by the definitive *Greatest Hits Collection*. —*Stephen Thomas Erlewine*

Under the Influence / Oct. 12, 1999 / Arista ✦✦✦✦✦
Anyone who doubts Alan Jackson's roots as a honky tonk singer should turn to *Under the Influences*, his heartfelt salute to his favorite country singers. According to his self-penned liner notes, Jackson has "always wanted to do this album," and that's evident from the songs he chose to cover. There are several hits here, but they're the kind that aren't regularly covered—"Pop a Top," "Kiss an Angel Good Mornin'," "Revenooer Man," "She Just Started Liking Cheatin' Songs," and "Once You've Had the Best." That, along with Jackson's loving reverence, makes this a step above the average covers album. Much of the material dates from the late '70s and early '80s, which makes sense, since he's a fourth-generation honky tonker raised on second and third-generation honky tonk. When he dips into Merle Haggard's catalog, he chose 1979's "My Own Kind of Hat." He picks songs written in the late '70s by Bob McDill. He also pays tribute to Hank Williams—but Junior, not Senior. This all gives Jackson and *Under the Influence* true character. He's not going out of his way to pick historically correct songs, he's just choosing ones he likes. The album is all the better for it—it's relaxed, warm, and entertaining, as he casually shows off his talents with some of his favorite songs. He rarely makes an effort to reinterpret the songs or contemporize the material, although the arrangements can occasionally be a little too clean. It also has to be said that the closer "Margaritaville," performed as a duet with Jimmy Buffett, sticks out like a sore thumb, but these two complaints wind up being nitpicking, since mainstream country didn't produce a better honky tonk album in 1999 than *Under the Influence*. —*Stephen Thomas Erlewine*

When Somebody Loves You / Nov. 7, 2000 / Arista ✦✦✦✦
Before talking about what a fine country album *When Somebody Loves You* is, there's a disclaimer: If you're a woman, or somebody who wants a great deal of change or evolution in an artist's music, this set won't do much for you. Here are 13 songs about love and being a blue-collar guy who doesn't mind being a redneck, digs the old hillbilly sounds, and hates sushi. Alan Jackson's been at these anthems for an entire career. He's also had the same producer for the whole run. But there has been some change. The truth of the matter is, as close to the line as Jackson has kept his brand of country, it's actually become

more so. There are less and less canned sounds on every record, whether it's on a killer love song like the title track with its Spanish guitar overtones that are reminiscent of Marty Robbins or the slamming honky tonk of "The Thrill Is Back" with the rawest sounding fiddle on a country record in a decade. And on the dumbly titled "WWW.Memory," Jackson gets down into a place where the sad lyric fits the tinkling of the upright piano (it's probably synthesized but doesn't feel like it). "Where I Come From" is another redneck anthem, but it rocks a little harder with a ZZ Top-styled guitar. The point is simple: If you like guitars, banjos, pedal steels, and songs about simple things—"I Still Love You" is one of those songs and one of the best Jackson's ever recorded—then *When Somebody Loves You* is your kind of record. This is trad honky tonk country in a country-pop age. Jackson gets a vote not only for holding on to the tradition but because he is able to articulate its heart in a heartless age. As long as Jackson, Montgomery Gentry, and George Strait are hanging in there on the male side of things, country music won't disappear into the ether of pop music schlock. —*Thom Jurek*

Drive / Jan. 15, 2002 / Arista ✦✦✦✦
The odd thing about *Drive* is that its centerpiece and its emotional fulcrum is a song that was likely one of the last recorded for the record. That song, of course, is "Where Were You (When the World Stopped Turning)," Alan Jackson's attempt to capture the hurt, pain, confusion, and overwhelming sadness caused by the terrorist attacks on the World Trade Center and Pentagon on September 11, 2001. The song works because Jackson keeps his sights simple as he conveys the bewilderment and sadness of the average American in the days after the attack, sketching the little things that people did to just get through the hours or how time just stopped cold. Given the enormity of the subject—it's simply not something that can be summarized in song—it's a surprisingly effective and moving tune, something that signals that Jackson is indeed in the forefront of the country singers of his time because it plays to his strengths: it's within the tradition of classic country and delivered simply, but with the vernacular and production of the modern day. And that's why even if it was a last-minute addition to the record, it fits so well into a typically strong collection of material from Jackson—musically, it fits perfectly among these heartache ballads and midtempo honky tonkers, but it also gives it significant emotional weight. It, in effect, acts as the anchor for the rest of the album, lending songs that are very good genre pieces—whether it's outside material like the excellent, poppy "A Little Bluer Than That" or original material—extra weight. The great thing is that *Drive* doesn't really need it, since it's filled with top-notch songs, including the great George Strait duet "Designated Drinker" and "Drive," a tribute to his dad that's nearly as affecting in its own way as "Where Were You." This is not a total shock, since Jackson's track record is one of the strongest in '90s country, but nevertheless a record this solidly crafted and emotionally resonant is a welcome event all the same. —*Stephen Thomas Erlewine*

Aunt Molly Jackson (Mary Magdalene Garland)

b. 1880, Clay County, KY, **d.** Sep. 1, 1960
Vocals / Old-Timey
Aunt Molly Jackson is one of the most overlooked, yet influential, figures in American folk music. Not only was she a contemporary of Woody Guthrie and Leadbelly, she was also a major influence on Pete Seeger. Unfortunately her recorded output consists of one single, recorded in the early '30s. Born Mary Magdalene Garland in 1880 in the coal mining country of Kentucky, she married in her early teens and became a certified midwife by the time she was 18. Since Jackson was so young when she delivered her first baby, instead of following the custom of the times by calling midwives "Grandma," she insisted being called "Aunt Molly" instead.

Jackson was the wife of a miner in the Kentucky coal fields. When the miners decided to strike for better pay and working conditions, she wrote her first song about the experience. In the midst of the strike, a group of writers led by Theodore Dreiser and John Dos Passos came to Kentucky on a fact-finding tour. Among the interviewed miners and family members, Jackson sang her song, "Hungry Ragged Blues." The impressed committee convinced her to go to New York City and use her singing to raise funds for the strikers, which she did. After the strike was settled, Jackson stayed on in New York City and continued as an activist and singer, where she became known among the folk and radical communities. Her earliest compositions to impress listeners in the radical movement were "Miner's Hungry Ragged Blues" and "Poor Miner's Farewell." By 1960 Jackson was impoverished but nevertheless was working on an LP of original material when she died suddenly. During the 1970s, some of those songs were released on a Rounder anthology. —*Al Campbell*

The Songs & Stories of Aunt Molly Jackson / 1961 / Smithsonian Folkways ✦✦✦✦
● **Library of Congress Recordings** / 1972 / Rounder ✦✦✦✦
Tough stuff, this. Folk music archivist Alan Lomax recorded many a cappella performances by this outspoken political singer, who came out of the Kentucky mines bearing a pretty big grudge. In fact, she was exiled from the state because of her political activities. This album focuses on her political songs, and she doesn't mince words. "Hungry Disgusted Blues" is typical of her titles. She isn't a folk artist who uses the troubles of the common people to trigger a sentimental reaction in her audience. Rather, her music is a means to an end, the end being rabble rousing and eventually revolution. Playing this record loud enough might indeed incite a riot in some neighborhoods. A big bonus is the enclosed booklet which includes an intense biography as well as complete song lyrics. —*Eugene Chadbourne*

Carl Jackson

b. Sep. 18, 1953, Louisville, MS
Guitar (Acoustic), Banjo, Vocals / Traditional Bluegrass
Carl Jackson, an accomplished bluegrass instrumentalist and songwriter, was born September 18, 1953, in Louisville, MS. While playing in his father's bluegrass band at the

age of 14, he was approached by Jim & Jesse to join their backing group, the Virginia Boys. He accepted and spent most of his teenage years playing banjo for Jim & Jesse and other groups at the *Grand Ole Opry*. Jackson's talents earned him a contract with the independent Prize label, where he recorded the album *Bluegrass Festival* in the late '60s. In 1971, Jackson left to play with the Sullivan Family, but after less than a year, he moved to Ohio to form the Country Store with Keith Whitley and Jimmy Gaudreau. A short time later, he jumped at the chance to join Glen Campbell's backing band. He spent 12 years with Campbell, but during that time he also recorded the albums *Banjo Player* and *Old Friend* for Capitol. In 1981, Jackson signed with Sugar Hill and released his tribute to Earl Scruggs, *Banjo Man*. The following year brought *Songs of the South*, and in 1983 he joined with old friends Jim & Jesse for *Banjo Hits*.

After signing with Columbia in 1984, Carl Jackson left Glen Campbell and began to hit the charts. His Lefty Frizzell cover "She's Gone, Gone, Gone" reached number 44 in 1984, though three later singles never matched its relative success. (Jackson did write the hit "(Love Always) Letter to Home," which peaked in the Top 15 for Campbell in May 1984.) During the late '80s, his rich harmony vocals brightened recordings by Emmylou Harris, Ricky Skaggs, Vince Gill, Garth Brooks, Roger Miller, and many other acts. In the '90s, Carl Jackson began to be rewarded for his years of work. He earned the International Bluegrass Association's Song of the Year award in 1990 for "Little Mountain Church Home," recorded by Ricky Skaggs and the Nitty Gritty Dirt Band on *Will the Circle Be Unbroken, Vol. 2*, and won a Best Bluegrass Album Grammy the following year with John Starling & the Nash Ramblers for *Spring Training*. —*John Bush*

Banjo Player / 1973 / Capitol ✦✦✦✦

Banjo Hits / 1983 / Sugar Hill ✦✦✦✦

Spring Training / 1987 / Sugar Hill ✦✦✦

Banjo Man: A Tribute to Earl Scruggs / Oct. 17, 1990 / Sugar Hill ✦✦✦

● **Songs of the South** / 2001 / Sugar Hill ✦✦✦✦
Guitar picker, singer, and banjo player extraordinaire Carl Jackson recorded two lovely albums in 1980 and 1982, *Banjo Man* and *Songs of the South*, respectively. Now Sugar Hill has decided to offer a collection that gathers the best cuts from both albums in one place. An impressive guest list weighs in on *Songs of the South*, including Emmylou Harris, Jesse McReynolds, Marty Stuart, Keith Whitley, Jerry Douglas, and Vassar Clements. Lively instrumentals like "Earl's Breakdown," "Grey Eagle," and "John Henry," featuring dobro, fiddle, and banjo, play a central role on the album. The flashy guitar licks on "Lay Down My Old Guitar" would turn Tony Rice's head, while the banjo picking on "Ground Speed" would make Earl Scruggs proud. "On My Mind" and "You Are My Flower" feature old-time country vocals, with Jackson's clear tenor supported by some lovely harmony. "The Lonesome River" is embroidered with bluesy fiddle and dobro, and brought to fullness by a forlorn vocal. Complaints? Only that this disc is a short 38 minutes. Surely a 70-minute disc would hold most of both albums. This means that anyone who listens to this compilation and loves it will have to purchase two more albums to get the other 32 minutes of music. Still, only good things can be said about the tracks chosen for this disc. *Sounds of the South* is a good place to tune in to the wonderful sounds of Carl Jackson's singing and playing. —*Ronnie Lankford Jr.*

Shot Jackson (Harold B. Jackson)
b. Sep. 4, 1920, Wilmington, NC, d. Jan. 24, 1991

Dobro, Guitar (Steel), Session Musician / Traditional Country, Instrumental Country
One of the premier steel guitar and Dobro players of the postwar generation, Shot Jackson was a solo and session artist who also gained fame as a designer and manufacturer of musical instruments. Born Harold B. Jackson on September 4, 1920, in Wilmington, NC, he earned the nickname Buckshot—later abbreviated to simply Shot—while still a child. His interest in music also began at an early age, and he became a devoted fan of the *Grand Ole Opry*, in particular of Roy Acuff's Smoky Mountain Boys and their dobro player, Bashful Brother Oswald. In 1941, Jackson joined the house band on a local country radio station, and in 1944, he moved to Nashville to sign on with the *Opry* as a sideman for Cousin Wilbur Westbrooks.

After a year in the Navy, Jackson began playing electric steel guitar with the Bailes Brothers and continued performing with the group throughout their tenure on the Shreveport, LA, station KWKH's *Louisiana Hayride* program. After the Bailes Brothers left the show, Jackson remained at KWKH, where he performed and recorded with the likes of Webb Pierce, Jimmie Osborne, and Red Sovine. In 1951, he joined Johnnie & Jack's Tennessee Mountain Boys, and over the next half-dozen years, he played dobro on virtually all of the group's live dates and studio sessions. He also played on many of Kitty Wells' first hits, in addition to recording a few solo sides.

In 1957, Jackson fulfilled a personal dream by becoming the electric steel player for Acuff's Smoky Mountain Boys and remained with the group for five years. During his affiliation with Acuff, Jackson and Buddy Emmons designed an electric pedal steel guitar; to market it, they founded their own company, Sho-Bud. Gradually, the company's success began to absorb more and more of Jackson's time, and he left the Smoky Mountain Boys, although he did remain an active musician, particularly as a steel player for Melba Montgomery, who had also left Acuff to go solo some time before. In addition to working with Montgomery (on both her solo work and her duets with George Jones), he recorded with many other artists and even cut his own solo LP, *Singing Strings of Steel Guitar and Dobro*, in 1962.

Jackson rejoined Acuff full-time in 1964, but his tenure abruptly ended in July of 1965 when he, Acuff, and singer June Stearns were all sidelined by a near-fatal car crash. After a long recovery period, he began performing with his wife Donna Darlene, a former vocalist on the *Jamboree* program; in 1965, he also issued the solo record *Bluegrass Dobro*. His latest creation, a seven-string resonator guitar called the Sho-Bro, hit the market not long after, and again, Jackson distanced himself from music to focus on business. Still, he continued to play on occasion, rejoining the Bailes Brothers for a number of reunion concerts and recordings. He also hooked up with the Roy Clark Family Band

for a pair of albums and appearances on the TV program *Hee Haw*. In 1980, Baldwin-Gretsch purchased Sho-Bud, and three years later, Jackson sold his instrument repair business as well. Soon after retirement, he suffered a stroke which left him unable to speak and play music. In 1986, he was inducted into the Steel Guitar Hall of Fame; shortly after suffering another stroke several years later, Jackson died on January 24, 1991. —*Jason Ankeny*

● **Singing Strings of Steel Guitar and Dobro** / 1962 / Starday ✦✦✦✦

Bluegrass Dobro / 1965 / Cumberland ✦✦✦

Stonewall Jackson
b. Nov. 6, 1932, Tabor City, NC

Vocals, Guitar / Honky Tonk, Nashville Sound/Countrypolitan, Traditional Country
Stonewall Jackson was one of the most popular country stars of the early '60s, scoring a string of Top Ten country hits and becoming a fixture at the *Grand Ole Opry* with a pleading voice that seemed to reflect his hard, often abusive upbringing on a south Georgia dirt farm. He was named after the Confederate general Thomas "Stonewall" Jackson, to whom he was related according to family legend. When he was ten he traded his bike for a guitar and began making up songs. Some of his later hits, such as "Don't Be Angry," were written very early in his creative life. Jackson began singing professionally in the mid-'50s, moving to Nashville in 1956. Within a few days of his arrival he delivered an unsolicited demonstration recording to the offices of the Acuff-Rose publishing house, and executive Wesley Rose heard his recorded singing and set up an audition for Jackson at the *Grand Ole Opry*.

He became the first entertainer to join the *Opry* without a recording contract, performing first on the Opry's *Friday Night Frolics* before his official debut. Backed by Ernest Tubb's Texas Troubadours, he proved so popular that the audience demanded four encores. Eventually Jackson hit the road with Tubb, who became a mentor to the young singer and songwriter. By early 1957, Jackson had signed a recording contract with Columbia Records and cut his first record, "Don't Be Angry." Jackson followed up with a cover of George Jones' "Life to Go," which peaked at number two in early 1959. The upbeat "Waterloo," with its mixture of novelty and melancholy, did even better, spending five weeks at the top of the country charts, hitting number four on the pop charts, and garnering Jackson some national television exposure.

Through the early '60s Jackson was a consistent hitmaker with such country standards as "Why I'm Walkin'" (number six, 1960), "A Wound Time Can't Erase" (number three, 1962), and "I Washed My Hands in Muddy Water" (number eight, 1965). Jackson's second number-one hit, "BJ the DJ," arrived in early 1964. During the second half of the '60s, he reached Top 40 less often, scoring only one Top Ten hit: 1967's "Stamp Out Loneliness." His Columbia albums of this period contained ornate wordplay from the pens of well-established Nashville writers like Vic McAlpin; songs such as "Ship in a Bottle" and "Nevermore Quote the Raven" applied literary virtuosity to traditional country themes. By 1970, however, Jackson wasn't even hitting the Top 40. He bounced back briefly in 1971 with a cover of Lobo's "Me and You and a Dog Named Boo." In 1973, he had his last hit with "Herman Schwartz," which reached number 41. After that, Jackson continued to appear regularly on the *Opry* and to record occasionally, releasing albums like the inspirational *Make Me Like a Child Again*. He also re-recorded versions of his old hits, and he privately published his autobiography, *From the Bottom Up*, in 1991. —*Sandra Brennan & James Manheim*

The Dynamic Stonewall Jackson / 1959 / Columbia ✦✦✦✦✦

American Originals / 1989 / Columbia ✦✦✦✦
Like many other installments in Columbia's late-'80s series *American Originals*, the Stonewall Jackson volume contains several of his biggest hits—in this case, "A Wound Time Can't Erase," "Smoke Along the Track," "Waterloo," "Life to Go," and "Blues Plus Booze (Means I Lose)"—but it overlooks many others. These omissions are major: the number one comeback hit "BJ the DJ," "Why I'm Walkin'," "One Look at Heaven," and most importantly, the first recorded version of the classic "I Washed My Hands in Muddy Water." So, it's an ineffective overview but a modestly enjoyable sampler, which would have seemed better if there were better Jackson collections on the market—and there weren't until Collectors Choice's 2002 release, *The Best of Stonewall Jackson*. By the time that was released, this *American Originals* disc was long out of print, and since the 2002 collection is so good, there's no reason to seek this collection out anymore. —*Stephen Thomas Erlewine*

Waterloo / 1993 / Laserlight ✦
Waterloo offers inferior remakes of some of Jackson's hits, including the title cut. —*Jason Ankeny*

Classic Country / Sep. 1, 1998 / Simitar ✦✦✦✦✦
This 14-track CD improves upon previous collections by offering more songs, recording dates, chart information, brief liner notes (including a testimonial from Marty Stuart), and Jackson's 1963 number one hit "BJ the DJ." Every one of Jackson's 11 Top Ten country hits are included, the remaining three cuts having made the Top 20. All but one track from the *American Originals* collection is duplicated here, making *Classic Country* the definitive Stonewall Jackson anthology. —*Greg Adams*

● **Best of Stonewall Jackson** / 2002 / Collectors' Choice Music ✦✦✦✦✦
Stonewall Jackson is a neglected figure in country music. Perhaps it was his name, which gave the impression that he was a singer with a corny stage name, when it was in fact his birth name, given to him by a father who believed he was a descendent of General Stonewall Jackson and died three weeks before his son's birth. Perhaps it's because his breakthrough single, 1959's "Waterloo," a record that superficially seemed to be a historical number like "Battle of New Orleans" but was actually a clever folk-country tune co-written by Marijohn Wilkin and John D. Loudermilk. Perhaps it was because that even when he had a bit of a revival when Dwight Yoakam covered "Smoke Along the Track" in the '80s, there was no accompanying CD reissue of Stonewall's best work to help

restore his reputation. These kind of contradictions camouflaged his excellent traditionalist country that nimbly touched on folky storytelling, barroom ballads, railroad songs, jailhouse tunes, novelties, and honky tonk, encapsulating everything that was pure mainstream country during the '60s. He wasn't as hardcore as his honky tonk contemporaries, which may be one of the reasons he was overlooked, but as Collectors Choice's splendid 2002 compilation *The Best of Stonewall Jackson* illustrates, he had a sturdy, enjoyable body of work that holds its own among the best country of the '60s. Yes, sometimes it gets a little silly, whether it's in production flourishes or in songs like the anti-protest "The Minute Men (Are Turning in Their Graves)," but these are the exceptions, not the rule; Jackson could even give Lobo's fluffy "Me and You and a Dog Named Boo" a country kick in 1971, even if he reportedly wasn't too happy with the song itself, according to Colin Escott's typically excellent liner notes. Over the course of 24 tracks—including all of his major, Top 40 country hits, along with his last charting hit, "Torn From the Pages of Life"—*The Best of Stonewall Jackson* makes the case for his talents, and it's convincing. He was a straight-ahead singer, armed with good songs and a simple, direct delivery that never wavered. It lead to a decade-long streak of hits that may not have been as fondly remembered outside of the '60s as they should have been, but this long-overdue comprehensive retrospective gives them another chance and any fan of unadorned mainstream country will find this very satisfying. *—Stephen Thomas Erlewine*

Tommy Jackson

b. Mar. 31, 1926, Birmingham, AL, **d.** Dec. 9, 1979

Fiddle, Session Musician / Traditional Country, Western Swing, Square Dance

If there was a Jimi Hendrix of country fiddlers, it was Tommy Jackson. And if square dance music had its Eric Clapton, then it was Tommy Jackson. Would-be stars on the country fiddle snapped up his records as fast as he could release them during the late '50s and early '60s. This makes it a special tragedy that Jackson isn't very well remembered today, except by his fellow musicians. In his time, from the end of the 1940s until the beginning of the 1960s, he was the first important session fiddle player in Nashville, and the best and busiest violinist in country music, working on records by Hank Williams, Bill Monroe, and George Jones, among numerous others. One of the sad ironies of his career was that his influence led to Jackson's own forced retirement—so many younger players followed in his footsteps that he found precious little work during the final decade of his life and died in relative obscurity.

Thomas Lee Jackson was born in Birmingham, AL, but his family moved to Nashville before he was a year old, and he grew up there listening all of the best country music that local radio and the *Grand Ole Opry* had to offer. Among his favorite groups growing up were George Wilkerson and the Fruit Jar Drinkers and Arthur Smith's Dixieliners. His father was a barber, not a musician, but he encouraged the boy—by age seven, Tommy was playing fiddle tunes at local bars for nickels and dimes, and at 12 he was going on tour with John Wright and Kitty Wells. He formed a group called the Tennessee Mountaineers and became a regular guest on Nashville's WSIX. By 17, he was playing on the *Opry* with Curly Williams and His Georgia Peach Pickers. A year later, however, his budding musical career was interrupted when Jackson joined the U.S. Army Air Force—he spent 1944 and 1945 as a tail gunner in a B-29 flying missions in the Pacific, earning four Bronze Stars and an Air Medal.

When Jackson returned to civilian life, he re-entered the music world immediately, touring with various stars of the *Opry*. He didn't like life on the road, however, and in 1947 he hooked up with producer Milton Estes, who had a radio show on WSM in Nashville. Jackson became a member of Red Foley's band, the Cumberland Valley Boys, and was regularly featured on his broadcasts. His fiddle playing was in demand, and with the other members of the Cumberland Valley Boys, he began working recording sessions. Jackson played on Hank Williams' "I Saw the Light" in 1947, providing the distinctive fiddle introduction, and later appeared on such records as "Lovesick Blues." He also played sessions with Red Foley ("Satisfied Mind" was one of the resulting singles). The session work only increased after the group moved to Cincinnati, OH, becoming regular participants on recordings at King Records. Jackson played on records by Grandpa Jones, Cowboy Copas, and Hawkshaw Hawkins, among others. In the early '50s, he made his first records for Mercury, which sold well, and in 1953 he signed to Dot Records.

Over the next ten years, Jackson cut 11 albums and 30 singles, hooking into the burgeoning square dance boom. The recordings all sold well and were swept up eagerly by aspiring fiddle players, for whom Jackson rapidly became a major inspiration. In 1954, he left Foley and began playing sessions with Ray Price and Faron Young, and Jackson virtually invented the standard modern fiddle accompaniment.

During the 1960s, Jackson was one of the busiest fiddle players in country music, appearing on hundreds of recordings apart from his own solo sides. The end of the square dance boom saw a slackening off of his own records' sales and production, but he continued to be one of the Nashville session musicians most heavily in demand.

Jackson became a victim of his own success during the 1970s, as the growing number of session fiddlers—their career inspired by him—made it difficult to find work. He'd stopped playing by the middle of the decade, and he was virtually forgotten at the time of his death in 1979, outside of the Nashville music community and the ranks of *Opry* musicians, among whom he'd once been a star. Jackson is remembered today primarily by country music scholars. The acquisition of Dot Records by MCA Records has opened the way for reissues of his solo material on compact disc. *—Bruce Eder*

Greatest Bluegrass Hits / 1962 / Dot ✦✦✦✦✦

● **Good Old Fiddle Music** / 1995 / MCA ✦✦✦✦✦

If this low-priced CD ran about eight more minutes, it might merit the top rating. As it is, it's an indispensable part of any country collection, serious or not, and one of the prettiest, jumpingest records you ever heard, so infectious to listen to that it's a good thing it is a CD, because an LP of it would get worn out real quick. *Good Old Fiddle Music* is also the only compact disc release there is of Tommy Jackson as of the early 2000s, and that's a shame. This is all square-dance material, all-instrumental, bright, upbeat, exquisitely textured fiddle-driven music with lots of detectable banjo, electric guitar, etc., recorded in excellent sound—a pity the band isn't credited and there are no notes. *—Bruce Eder*

Wanda Jackson

b. Oct. 20, 1937, Maud, OK

Vocals / Traditional Country, Rockabilly, Country Gospel

Wanda Jackson was only halfway through high-school when, in 1954, country singer Hank Thompson heard her on an Oklahoma City radio show and asked her to record with his band, the Brazos Valley Boys. By the end of the decade, Jackson had become one of America's first major female country and rockabilly singers. Jackson was born in Oklahoma, but her father Tom—himself a country singer who quit because of the Depression—moved the family to California in 1941. He bought Wanda her first guitar two years later, gave her lessons, and encouraged her to play piano as well. In addition, he took her to see such acts as Tex Williams, Spade Cooley, and Bob Wills, which left a lasting impression on her young mind. Tom moved the family back to Oklahoma City when his daughter was 12 years old. In 1952, she won a local talent contest and was given a 15-minute daily show on KLPR. The program, soon upped to 30 minutes, lasted throughout Jackson's high-school years. It's here that Thompson heard her sing. Jackson recorded several songs with the Brazos Valley Boys, including "You Can't Have My Love," a duet with Thompson's bandleader, Billy Gray. The song, on the Decca label, became a national hit, and Jackson's career was off and running. She had wanted to sign with Capitol, Thompson's label, but was turned down, so she signed with Decca instead.

Jackson insisted on finishing high-school before hitting the road. When she did, her father came with her. Her mother made and helped design Wanda's stage outfits. "I was the first one to put some glamour in the country music—fringe dresses, high heels, long earrings," Jackson said of these outfits. When Jackson first toured in 1955 and 1956, she was placed on a bill with none other than Elvis Presley. The two hit it off almost immediately. Jackson said it was Presley, along with her father, who encouraged her to sing rockabilly. In 1956, Jackson finally signed with Capitol, a relationship that lasted until the early '70s. Her recording career bounced back and forth between country and rockabilly; she did this by often putting one song in each style on either side of a single. Jackson cut the rockabilly hit "Fujiyama Mama" in 1958, which became a major success in Japan. Her version of "Let's Have a Party," which Elvis had cut earlier, was a U.S. Top 40 pop hit for her in 1960, after which she began calling her band the Party Timers. A year later, she was back in the country Top Ten with "Right or Wrong" and "In the Middle of a Heartache." In 1965, she topped the German charts with "Santa Domingo," sung in German. In 1966, she hit the U.S. Top 20 with "The Box It Came In" and "Tears Will Be the Chaser for Your Wine." Jackson's popularity continued through the end of the decade.

Jackson toured regularly, was twice nominated for a Grammy, and was a big attraction in Las Vegas from the mid-'50s into the '70s. She married IBM programmer Wendell Goodman in 1961, and instead of quitting the business—as many women singers had done at the time—Goodman gave up his job in order to manage his wife's career. He also packaged Jackson's syndicated TV show, *Music Village*. In 1971, Jackson and her husband became Christians, which she says saved their marriage. She released one gospel album on Capitol in 1972, *Praise the Lord*, before shifting to the Myrrh label for three more gospel albums. In 1977, she switched again, this time to Word Records, and released another two.

In the early '80s, Jackson was invited to Europe to play rockabilly and country festivals and to record. She's since been back numerous times. More recently, American country artists Pam Tillis, Jann Browne, and Rosie Flores have acknowledged Jackson as a major influence. In 1995, Flores released a rockabilly album, *Rockabilly Filly*, and invited Jackson, her longtime idol, to sing two duets on it with her. Jackson embarked on a major U.S. tour with Flores later that year. It was her first secular tour in this country since the '70s, not to mention her first time back in a nightclub atmosphere. *—Kurt Wolff*

There's a Party Goin' On / 1959 / Capitol ✦✦✦✦

While this doesn't have most of Wanda's best rockabilly sides (check the compilation *Rockin' With Wanda* for those), it's a pretty solid and energetic set. About half of it is taken up with retreads of the "Let's Have a Party" theme and covers of early rock hits like "Tweedlee Dee" and "Kansas City" which are, admittedly, well done. "Fallin'" and especially, "Hard Headed Woman" are really fine cuts that rank among her best rock & roll performances. The real surprise of this album is the lightning-speed rockabilly riffing by Roy Clark; his playing on "Hard Headed Woman" is downright savage, almost enough to redeem all those horrible *Hee-Haw* programs. *—Richie Unterberger*

Early Wanda Jackson / 1986 / Bear Family ✦✦✦

Jackson's earliest material, recorded in 1954 and 1955 (including a couple of duets with Billy Gray), is pure honky tonk and hillbilly country, with no rockabilly whatsoever. It's the rootsiest country she ever recorded, with arrangements that put the fiddles to the fore, and songs that rate as some of her most plaintive. It does not, however, necessarily qualify as some of her most interesting productions: the material isn't as exceptional, and the vocal delivery kind of stilted. Also, rock-oriented fans of Jackson's slightly later work may well find this disappointing and too corny for their tastes. There's not much in the way of uptempo tunes, and nothing in the way of genuine rock & roll. *—Richie Unterberger*

Rockin' in the Country: The Best of Wanda Jackson / Jun. 1990 / Rhino ✦✦✦✦✦

Perhaps the greatest of the rockabilly women, Wanda Jackson later turned to pure country. Rhino's *Rockin' in the Country: The Best of Wanda Jackson* presents the best of both eras here on this 18-track collection. *—Jeff Tamarkin*

Right or Wrong / 1993 / Bear Family ✦✦✦✦

This four-CD set is like a photo album of Wanda Jackson growing up, from innocent adolescent to rockabilly star and the dominant female country singer of the early 1960s. Her complete recordings from the first Decca session in March 1954 until her Capitol session of November 2, 1962, constitute the part of her career that rock & roll and rockabilly fans most care about. Disc one covers those early years, the 15 songs she cut for Decca Records through 1955, when she was still treading a fine line in country music, seemingly trying to be the next Kitty Wells at least part of the time. The singing is glorious and the playing solid, although Jackson, working in this idiom, was like a racing thoroughbred being asked to canter around a track. Then comes "Baby Loves Him," a Jackson original that redefined her for the next few years as a rockabilly star. Disc two features Jackson treading that fine line between straight country and rock & roll, interspersed with slower, more traditional numbers. As late as 1961, Disc three reveals, Jackson was still courting the rock & roll audience, although the main thrust of her career was moving back toward pure country, with forays into pop and country-pop. The country material on Disc four had a serious edge to it by now, and the rock & roll was almost superfluous. By late 1962 and early 1963, however, her sides show the kind of opulent overproduction, complete with choruses and string sections, that would help give country-pop a bad name; her voice is as good as ever, but the material is a stretch after the hot rockin' sides. The booklet is more thorough than most from Bear Family. *—Bruce Eder*

Hits & Rarities / 1996 / Music Collection ✦✦✦
Since *Hits & Rarities* is a single-disc compilation that contains both well-known numbers like "Right and Wrong" and "Let's Have a Party," as well as several obscurities, the result is an entertaining collection, but one that's unsuited for both neophytes, who won't appreciate the rarities, and serious fans, who will find the inclusion of the familiar cuts extraneous. *—Thom Owens*

Vintage Collections Series / Jan. 23, 1996 / Capitol ✦✦✦✦✦
This 20-track anthology of Jackson's early work is roughly equal to Rhino's *Rockin' in the Country* in value. *Rockin' in the Country* offers a considerably wider range, chronologically speaking. *Vintage Collections*, on the other hand, focuses on 1956-1961 recordings, affording greater depth for what is acknowledged as her most fertile period. Although it's issued on Capitol Nashville, it mixes rockabilly and straight country, including her biggest hits in each style ("Let's Have a Party," "Fujiyama Mama," "Right or Wrong") and some worthy obscurities. Those with an appetite for both rock & roll and country will find this the best compilation of her work; those who want just the rock & roll should look for the harder-to-find *Rockin' With Wanda* instead. *—Richie Unterberger*

Tears Will Be the Chaser for Your Wine / Nov. 5, 1997 / Bear Family ✦✦✦✦

● **Queen of Rockabilly** / Oct. 17, 2000 / Ace ✦✦✦✦✦
Ace's *Queen of Rockabilly* is the best overview of Wanda Jackson's raw, early rockabilly recordings yet assembled. Spanning 30 tracks and boasting fine liner notes and great sound, this is a terrific collection of exciting rockabilly. This is the best way to hear one the greatest rockabilly gals of the '50s. *—Stephen Thomas Erlewine*

Wanda Jackson [Bonus Tracks] / Sep. 17, 2002 / Capitol ✦✦✦✦✦
Like many other young recording artists of the late '50s, especially those on major labels, Wanda Jackson was encouraged to straddle musical genres as a hedge against changing trends. She was an accomplished rockabilly singer, but Capitol Records must have worried how long rockabilly was going to stay popular, so the singer cut tracks in several other styles, most frequently country. Her rockabilly fans may have been surprised to hear her first full-length album, *Wanda Jackson*, which leaned more toward country and also showed off her affinity for straight pop. True, she did cover "Long Tall Sally" and "Money, Honey," and she did a particularly raucous version of "Let's Have a Party" (which surprisingly took off for the pop Top 40 two years after the album's release). But more typical of the sound of the album overall were her versions of Kitty Wells' "Making Believe" and Don Everly's "Here We Are Again," traditional country material, and she even tried her hand at Patti Page's 1954 hit "Let Me Go, Lover!," a pop ballad. Add it all up, and you had one versatile singer, able to sing convincingly anything that was thrown at her. The variety made sense at the time, even if subsequent fans may wish Jackson had rocked out a bit more. [The 2002 CD reissue adds six tracks to the original 12, all of them drawn from singles Jackson released between 1956 and 1958. Like the material on the original album, the bonus tracks tend more toward the country side of Jackson's persona. Particularly notable is an early, country version of "Silver Threads and Golden Needles," which went on to become a hit for the Springfields (and to launch the career of Dusty Springfield) six years after Jackson first released it.] *—William Ruhlmann*

☆ **Rockin' With Wanda [Bonus Tracks]** / Sep. 17, 2002 / Capitol ✦✦✦✦✦
When Capitol Records assembled Wanda Jackson's self-titled debut album in 1958, the label was trying to suggest her versatility as a singer who could handle vocal pop and country as well as the rockabilly with which she was most associated. As the title of her next Capitol album, 1960's *Rockin' With Wanda*, suggested, there was less of an attempt at variety (although there were still a couple of examples of her taste in country, and "Don'a Wan'a" had a Latin flavor). The 12-track LP was actually a compilation collecting singles sides dating back to her 1956 Capitol debut 45, "I Gotta Know," the most recent being "You're the One for Me," which had been released a year earlier. (Although all of the tracks had been released previously on singles, none had appeared on an LP before.) This was the raucous Wanda Jackson, barely contained on rave-ups like "Fujiyama Mama" and "Hot Dog! That Made Him Mad," a performer worthy of being called the distaff Elvis Presley. Focusing attention on her talents as a rocker, the album should have broken Jackson in the rock realm, and it might have but for the late-breaking success of "Let's Have a Party," another uptempo number that was not on the album. Clearly, too, 1960 was a little late for crowning a rockabilly queen, and by the following year Jackson was recording more frequently in a country vein. Nevertheless, *Rockin' With Wanda* stands as her finest achievement, at least as far as boppers are concerned. [There was a British CD reissue that added four tracks and re-sequenced the album, but more impressive is the 2002 U.S. reissue, which adds another six songs (most of them more country than rock) drawn from the same batch of singles that produced the original 12.] *—William Ruhlmann*

Wanda Rocks / Nov. 19, 2002 / Bear Family ✦✦✦✦✦

Sonny James (James Loden)

b. May 1, 1929, Hackleburg, AL
Vocals, Guitar / Nashville Sound/Countrypolitan, Country-Pop, Pop
Sonny James, the Southern Gentleman, used the popular Nashville sound of the '60s to countrify pop hits of the past into a form accessible to many, broadening country music's appeal across the nation. James even moved over to the pop charts for a time in the late '50s but found the secret of his success by the time he returned to country. During the late '60s, he scored an incredible five-year run of number-one singles which locked up the top spot for a combined 45 weeks during the late '60s.

Born James Loden on May 1, 1929, he began performing with his show-business family at the age of three and played with his four sisters as the Loden Family while in his teens. The group appeared around the South and on radio shows like the *Louisiana Hayride* and *Saturday Night Shindig*. After spending time overseas during the Korean War, Loden took Sonny James as his stage name—after his teenage nickname—and joined the local bar circuit. He met and played with Chet Atkins, who later got him a tryout with Capitol Records. The label liked what it heard and offered James a contract.

His first single, "That's Me Without You," hit the country Top Ten in early 1953, but it was three years before "For Rent (One Empty Heart)" became his second big hit. James, who played guitar on virtually all of his records, followed up with two 1956 Top Ten near-misses "Twenty Feet of Muddy Water" and "The Cat Came Back." His next single became his biggest hit: "Young Love" spent nine weeks at number one during 1956-1957 and crossed over to top the pop charts also. Beginning in 1957, James began to focus his attention on the popular charts. "First Date, First Kiss, First Love" made the Top 25, but no follow-up placed as high. Several of his failures had still managed to go Top Ten on the country charts, so James returned to country with a vengeance in 1964. "You're the Only World I Know" hit number-one country late that year and spent four weeks atop the chart.

That began one of the greatest tears country music has ever known: 21 of his next 25 singles hit number one (and the other four near-misses hit either two or three). James completely dominated the chart from 1964 to 1972, though only several singles crossed over for modest placements on the popular charts. That fact is somewhat surprising, since three-quarters of James' number ones had previously been pop hits, including "Take Good Care of Her" for Adam Wade, "I'll Never Find Another You" and "A World of Our Own" for the Seekers, "Born to Be With You" for the Chordettes, and Roy Orbison's "Only the Lonely." Backed by his Southern Gentlemen band, James toured the country and overseas, appeared on *the Ed Sullivan Show, Hee Haw*, and *the Bob Hope Show*, and made several movies, including *Las Vegas Hillbillies* (1966), *Second Fiddle to a Steel Guitar* (1967), and *Nashville Rebel* (1967). *Billboard* named him the Number One Artist of 1969.

Even after James' number-one streak ended in January 1972, he continued to place high on the charts. The number two "Only Love Can Break a Heart" (a pop hit for Gene Pitney ten years earlier) was followed by the number ones "That's Why I Love You Like I Do" and—after moving to Columbia in mid-1972—"When the Snow Is on the Roses." James' next chart-topping single, "Is It Wrong (For Loving You)," was released in March 1974, and it began his last major run. He followed with four consecutive Top Ten hits, "A Mi Esposa con Amor (To My Wife With Love)," "A Little Bit South of Saskatoon," "Little Band of Gold," and "What in the World's Come Over You." By the early '70s, James had moved into producing and music publishing also; he oversaw three of Marie Osmond's albums and still managed occasional Top Tens himself. He picked up the prestigious award of Country Music's Male Artist of the Decade from *Record World* in 1977 and moved to the Monument label in 1979, then to Dimension two years later. He retired in 1983, and now raises cattle in Alabama. *—John Bush*

Sonny / 1957 / Capitol ✦✦✦

The Southern Gentleman / 1957 / Capitol ✦✦✦✦✦

Honey / 1958 / Capitol ✦✦

Young Love / 1962 / Dot ✦✦✦✦✦
Young Love includes hits like the title track and "Here Comes Honey Again." *—Jason Ankeny*

The Minute You're Gone / 1964 / Capitol ✦✦✦✦
Sonny James wrote a lot of mediocre material to fill out his late-'60s and early-'70s albums, so it is not very surprising that *The Minute You're Gone*—to which he contributed no original songs—is actually one of his better albums. The probable reason for his non-participation in the songwriting department is that *The Minute You're Gone* was his first Capitol album after returning to the label in 1963, and he would not gain artistic control until he had proven himself commercially. The title track was a Top Ten country hit that crossed over to the pop chart, and "Going Through the Motions (Of Living)" made the country Top 20, but the album tracks are where things really get interesting. "Bad Times a Comin'" has as hard a country sound as James ever adopted in the '60s, and the bilingual "Shina-No-Yuro" could have been a left-field hit like "Sukiyaki." "Tommy Brown" is a long-winded tale involving a laughably maudlin tragedy, and "Gold and Silver" is a charming love song that George Jones also cut around the same time. It may be that only ardent James-watchers will perceive the difference between *The Minute You're Gone* and its successors, but to quote a Johnny Horton song: Hooray for that little difference. *—Greg Adams*

Behind the Tear / 1965 / Capitol ✦✦✦

You're the Only World I Know / 1965 / Capitol ✦✦✦

I'll Keep Holding On (Just to Your Love) / 1965 / Capitol ✦✦✦

Heaven Says Hello / 1968 / Capitol ✦✦✦
"Heaven Says Hello" was another in a long line of number-one hits for Sonny James, with many more to come. The 1968 album that shares its name is an engaging collection of country standards ("Crazy Arms," "She Thinks I Still Care") and songs co-written by James with various partners. All of the songs feature James' acoustic guitar flatpicking and his distinctive fusion of country and pop. "Misery and Agony" is a decent "Wolverton Mountain"-style story song with banjo, and "The Blues Can't Keep a Good Man Down"

adds a spot of blues to the hybridized mix. The best of the album tracks is "Love is a Happy Song," a catchy finger-snapper that recalls James' hit "True Love's a Blessing." *Heaven Says Hello* was recorded during James' commercial peak and contains a fair percentage of original songs, making it a substantial if not spectacular album. *—Greg Adams*

Here Comes Honey Again / 1971 / Capitol ✦✦✦

Here Comes Honey Again is less reliant on cover songs than many of Sonny James' later albums, and in fact he had a hand in writing half of the material. The title track was James' second-to-last number-one hit before leaving Capitol for Columbia, where his incredible streak of number ones would be broken by the flurry of mediocre singles issued by Capitol in competition with his new Columbia sides. Besides "Here Comes Honey Again," the notable originals on this album are "Still Water Runs Deep," with its bass vocal hook, and "Louisiana Bayou," which recycles Cajun clichés into a peppy inducer of déjà vu. The pop oldies that James refurbishes are "Clinging Vine," a mid-'60s hit for Bobby Vinton, and the oft-covered "Pledging My Love." In retrospect, "Here Comes Honey Again" isn't the most memorable of James' number-one hits, but the album that shares its name has a few highlights. *—Greg Adams*

If She Just Helps Me Get Over You / 1973 / Columbia ✦✦✦

If She Just Helps Me Get Over You takes its name from the melancholy song that became a Top 20 country hit for Sonny James in 1973. The album also contains the Top Five hit "I Love You More and More Everyday," which is arguably the inferior of the two songs despite being the bigger hit. James co-wrote half of the album with his frequent collaborator Carol Smith, including the downcast "When Tomorrow's Dark Hours Come" and the plane-wreck tragedy of "Sweet Echoes of Ann." James' familiar trick of modernizing the oldies seems formulaic if you're not enamored with his style, but fans will enjoy his updates of Lefty Frizzell's "Mom and Dad's Waltz" and the Porter Wagoner hit "Satisfied Mind." James was consistent to the point of stasis in the late '60s and early '70s, but his albums offered reliable if unsurprising entertainment. *—Greg Adams*

The Guitars of Sonny James / 1975 / Columbia ✦✦✦

"Eres Tu (Touch the Wind)," originally a hit for the Spanish vocal group Mocedades in 1974, was reinterpreted as an easy listening guitar instrumental by Sonny James for his most unusual single release of the '70s. The record's only connection with country music was James' name on the label, but it became a minor country hit nonetheless, and James produced a full-length instrumental album around it, *The Guitars of Sonny James.* James, whose abilities as an acoustic guitar soloist are very competent, if not often flashy, composed "Kickapoo" and "Theme From Venice." "Apache" is a new recording of the Jorgen Ingmann tune with which James had a minor hit in 1961, and "Paper Roses" is a version of the 1973 hit James produced for Marie Osmond. *The Guitars of Sonny James* is more similar to 101 Strings than Chet Atkins' most schmaltzy efforts, but the subdued blend of James' acoustic guitar with strings and an occasional vocal chorus is hypnotically alluring and tailor-made for quiet moments of relaxation. *—Greg Adams*

This Is the Love / 1978 / Columbia ✦✦

This Is the Love is dedicated to Sonny James' longtime songwriting partner, Carol Smith, who wrote or co-wrote half of the selections. That is an unusually high proportion of original material for a Sonny James album in the '70s, when his successful formula of updating oldies in a glossy country-pop style dominated his output. "No Sand in a Sand Dune" and the straight rocker "It'll Still Be Worth It All" are decent originals, but the recycling of "All Burned out Inside" from James' 1976 album *When Something Is Wrong With My Baby* suggests a deficiency of ideas or effort. The title track and "Caribbean" are the album's two hits, the latter of which is a nice cover of Mitchell Torok's hit from the '50s and the album's highlight. *—Greg Adams*

Love Letters in the Sand / 197 / Pickwick ✦✦

Love Letters in the Sand contains assorted album tracks and B-sides recorded by Sonny James for Capitol Records in the late '60s. His remake of The Seekers' "I'll Never Find Another You" is the only hit, and is here with its B-side, "Goodbye, Maggie, Goodbye," and covers of popular '60s songs like the title track and Skeeter Davis' "End of the World." James' sound became so formulaic from the mid-'60s onward that anyone familiar with his style will know what this album sounds like before it even plays. The tracks were specially selected to create a mellow mood, and *Love Letters in the Sand* may be James' most relaxing record, for what that's worth. *—Greg Adams*

American Originals / 1989 / Columbia ✦✦✦

American Originals is a cross-section of Sonny James' later hits from Columbia, beginning with the 1974 number one "Is It Wrong (For Loving You)" and running through a selection of '70s hits. James was still popular during this period, even if he was showing signs of age. Although it is brief, *American Originals* provides a good summation of his later career. *—Stephen Thomas Erlewine*

Capitol Collectors Series / 1990 / Capitol ✦✦✦✦✦

Capitol Collector's Series has 20 of Sonny James' chart-topping hits for Capitol Records, ranging from 1956's breakthrough "Young Love" to 1972's "When the Snow Is on the Roses." Although it's missing a handful of number-one hits, it remains a thorough, entertaining, and definitive compilation. *—Stephen Thomas Erlewine*

Greatest Hits / 1992 / Columbia ✦✦✦

While by no means comprehensive, *Greatest Hits* is among the best collections of James' chart smashes; it includes the number-one hits "Young Love," "You're the Only World I Know," "Behind the Tear" and "Take Good Care of Her." *—Jason Ankeny*

Sunny Side Up / Dec. 1, 1995 / Sony Special Products ✦✦✦

Sunny Side Up is the album Sonny James recorded for Monument Records in 1979. It produced two hits that year, the biggest of which (a cover of Joe Tex's "Hold What You've Got") barely cracked the country Top 40. The album wasn't especially successful from a commercial standpoint, which makes it a curious choice for reissue on CD. Buyers shouldn't have any complaints, though; *Sunny Side Up* is a strong offering from start to finish, and the cover songs (Ken Copeland's "Pledge of Love," the Box Tops' "The Letter," etc.) are much better than mere filler thanks to creative arrangements. The songs with Mexican themes at the beginning of the album make James sound a bit like Jimmy Buffett, and his voice is much different from what it had been during his late-'60s peak, but *Sunny Side Up* will be a pleasant surprise for adventurous fans. *—Greg Adams*

● **Young Love: The Classic Hits** / Aug. 19, 1997 / Razor & Tie ✦✦✦✦✦

Young Love: The Classic Hits is a definitive 21-track collection that contains all of Sonny James' big hits from the late '50s and '60s—"Young Love," "First Date, First Kiss, First Love," "Uh-Huh-Mm," "Born to Be With You," "Only the Lonely," "Running Bear," "You're the Only World I Know," "I'll Never Find Another You," "Empty Arms," "Bright Lights, Big City"—plus a number of lesser-known singles and album tracks that are as good as the hits. *—Stephen Thomas Erlewine*

Young Love: The Complete Recordings: 1952–62 / May 21, 2002 / Bear Family ✦✦✦✦

The Complete Columbia & Monument Hits / Jul. 14, 2002 / Collectors' Choice Music ✦✦✦✦

By the time that this single-disc compilation picks up the Sonny James (guitar/vocals) story, he had already entered his third decade as a country music artist. His streak of 20 consecutive chart-topping hits in the early to mid-'60s is the stuff of legend. This 22-track title gathers all of James' charting hits extracted from the 11 long-players issued in the '70s for the Columbia and Monument labels. Interestingly, during this seemingly prolific period, James considered his primary focus to be producing and music publishing. Early in his career, the vocalist adopted the persona of Nashville's "Southern Gentleman." His easy, non-threatening demeanor as well as warm and inviting inflection made him a great crossover artist into the pop realm as well. The set opens with the number-one single "When the Snow Is on the Roses," which began another string of hits. Among the higher-profile inclusions are the romantic epic "A Mi Esposa con Amor (To My Wife With Love)," "What in the World's Come Over You," "A Little Bit South of Saskatoon," and "Little Band of Gold." James also found success covering a wide spectrum of genres. These range from his tongue-in-cheek interpretation of the Piedmont blues "He's in the Jailhouse Now"—which sounds as if it may have been mocked up to imitate a live performance featuring the "Tennessee State Prison Band"—to the '60s Stax sound of "When Something Is Wrong With My Baby" and even Gene Autry's signature "Back in the Saddle Again." For the most part, the primary directive of the rather generic backing musicians is to, quite frankly, stay out of the way of the vocalist—which they indeed accomplish. Notably, the latter hits—such as the Top 20 "Caribbean"—retain much of the charm and cozy familiarity of his earlier work. Perhaps it is this stability that has allowed James such a lengthy and prolific career. Enthusiasts will undoubtedly herald Collectors' Choice Music for finally corralling these sides together. *—Lindsay Planer*

20 All-Time Greatest Hits / Aug. 20, 2002 / TeeVee ✦✦✦

20 All-Time Greatest Hits contains several essential items from Sonny James' country/pop crossover years at Capitol Records, including the 1957 hit "Young Love." Several of these tracks from the '60s—including "A World of Our Own," "Take Good Care of Her," and "I'll Never Find Another You"—had previously been hits on the pop charts for other artists, before James' interpretations brought them to the country charts. While this is a decent greatest-hits package, fans of Sonny James would be served better by the single-disc *Young Love: The Classic Hits*, which includes a few early hits missed here. *—Al Campbell*

Jason & the Scorchers

f. 1981

Group / Roots Rock, Cowpunk, College Rock, Heartland Rock

A country/hard rock band formed by Illinois native Jason Ringenberg in 1981, Jason & the Scorchers came careening onto the indie rock scene seemingly out of nowhere (truth was, it was Nashville) with a debut EP whose most killer track (among a slew of killer tracks) was a fire-breathing cover of Bob Dylan's "Absolutely Sweet Marie." This amalgam of speedy hard rock fused with Ringenberg's decidedly country twang, along with the band's ability to deftly negotiate between Rolling Stones-style stomps and quieter, more melodic acoustic country music, led to Jason & the Scorchers becoming a critically lauded and fairly popular '80s band. Capitalizing quickly on the notoriety brought by their debut EP, the Scorchers kicked out two fine LPs (*Lost & Found* and *Still Standing*) that sounded perfect for radio, but not so slick as to sound manufactured. With Ringenberg's yowling voice pushed way up front, the band's sonic power came from the synchronous playing of Nashville rock veterans Warner Hodges (guitar), Jeff Johnson (bass), and Perry Baggs (drums). Sharing similar musical backgrounds that valued the music of Hank Williams and Johnny Cash as much as the Stones or Beatles, these guys could crank out mega-amped hard rock one minute and sound like the Flying Burrito Brothers the next, all of it done with great skill and excitement.

Despite their obvious talent, by the release of 1986's *Still Standing*, it seemed as though the band wasn't going anywhere. They had achieved a modicum of success but weren't able to break through to mass acclaim, partly because they came along just before the explosion of country radio in the late '80s/early '90s. Hence, rock radio was reluctant to play them because they sounded too country, and country radio thought they were too rock; it's an old story that usually spells doom for the band in question. After a three-year break that saw Johnson's departure, the Scorchers released a desultory third album (*Thunder and Fire*) that sounded like a desperate attempt at hard rock credibility. They broke up soon after. Ringenberg went on to record country-oriented solo work, reformed the original Scorchers in 1994, and released a modest reunion record (*A Blazing Grace*) that sounded like the Scorchers of old. Two years later, the reunited Scorchers released *Clear Impetuous Morning*; *Midnight Roads* followed in 1998. *Rock on Germany* appeared three years later. *—John Dougan*

Restless Country Soul EP / 1982 / Praxis ♦♦♦♦
Restless Country Soul is a real treat for longtime fans of Jason & the Scorchers. It led off the group's history in January 1982, one week after the Scorchers' live debut, in a jerry-rigged home studio with Jason Ringenberg singing in a hallway while the band set up in the living room. The five songs off that EP are followed here by five tracks cut at Sun Studios in Memphis, apparent outtakes from the *Fervor* album that have never before seen the light of day. The original *Restless* sides hold their own, but the Sun outtakes are a match for them. The group sounds tighter as they rip through a medley of "I'd Rather Die Young/Candy Kisses," do a completely straight "Pray for Me Momma (I'm a Gypsy Now)," and finish with maybe the best, raunchiest-sounding cover of a Carl Perkins song ever released, "Gone Gone Gone." And there's an uncredited bonus track to boot. As solid musically as any of their official albums. *—Bruce Eder*

Fervor EP / 1983 / EMI America ♦♦♦♦♦
Their debut EP has "Absolutely Sweet Marie" (which you'll play over and over and over), as well as some wonderful country-rock like "Hot Nights in Georgia." Ringenberg's twangy voice is a hoot to listen to, and Warner Hodges plays some great guitar. A wonderful, if too brief, record and a harbinger of some great rock & roll to come. R.E.M.'s Michael Stipe contributes a song ("Both Sides of the Line") and some backup vocals. *—John Dougan*

Lost & Found / 1985 / EMI America ♦♦♦♦♦
Of the Scorchers' three full-length LPs, this is by far the best. There is so much pent-up energy and excitement on this record, it sounds as if it will fly off your turntable (assuming you still have a turntable) at any moment. With Hodges (as usual) driving this machine, Ringenberg's wild-eyed country-punk persona is here in full fury, and the good-times never let up. This should have been the album that made them stars, but it did solidify their audience and place them in larger concert venues, where they tore it up. *—John Dougan*

Still Standing / 1986 / Mammoth ♦♦♦
Produced by veteran hard rock producer Tom Werman, *Still Standing* is a fine record, but also shows subtle signs of the band in decline: the hard-rock is stiffer, Hodges' guitar is smoother and more akin to the anonymous hard-rock/heavy-metal guitar sound that defined AOR radio in the '80s. That notwithstanding, there are still songs like "Golden Ball and Chain," which sounds like an outtake from *Exile on Main Street* and, continuing with the Rolling Stones motif, a ripsnortin' cover of "19th Nervous Breakdown." A teensy bit disappointing in comparison to *Lost and Found*, but by no means a bad record or one to ignore. If you've liked the Scorchers up to this point, you'll want *Still Standing*. *—John Dougan*

Thunder & Fire / Dec. 1989 / A&M ♦♦♦
With the release of *Thunder & Fire*, Jason & the Scorchers should have been set for the top. Unfortunately, that didn't happen. They broke up instead. But the record they left behind does have its moments. Hard-hitting rockers like "Now That You're Mine" and "6 Feet Underground" fit snugly alongside "Close Up the Road," a country-tinged weeper and "Bible & a Gun" which recalls the best things about the roots rock movement of the late '80s. *—James Chrispell*

● **Essential, Vol. 1 (Are You Ready for the Country?)** / Oct. 20, 1992 / EMI America ♦♦♦♦♦
Essential, Vol. 1 (Are You Ready for the Country?) compiles Jason & the Scorchers' first EP, *Fervor*, and their debut LP *Lost & Found*, adding four bonus tracks for good measure. It's an excellent way to acquire their best records, yet it was replaced four years later by the nearly identical *Both Sides of the Line*, which featured the EP and LP without the bonus tracks. *—Stephen Thomas Erlewine*

A Blazing Grace / Feb. 7, 1995 / Mammoth ♦♦♦
Jason & the Scorchers came "blazing" back with this rockin' barrelhouse of a release. Containing surefire rockers in "Where Bridges Never Burn" and "Cry By Night Operator," the Scorchers never sounded better. But also check out their hard-drivin' covers of both John Denver's "Take Me Home, Country Roads" and George Jones' "Why Baby Why." They're great! Coming back with just the original four members, Jason & the Scorchers prove that there is life after punk, or were they roots rock, or maybe cowpunk, or.... Ah, you get the picture. *A Blazing Grace* is superb! *—James Chrispell*

Both Sides of the Line / Sep. 1996 / EMI ♦♦♦♦♦
This is a CD reissue combining the *Fervor* EP and *Lost & Found* album onto one disc, and thus offers the best way to collect their early material. *—Richie Unterberger*

Clear Impetuous Morning / Oct. 1996 / Mammoth ♦♦♦
Here comes yet another steam-rolling country-rock release from Jason & the Scorchers. Pushin' the pedal to the metal, *Clear Impetuous Morning* sounds a lot like a band that has just found an open stretch of highway and is jammin' in high gear. Just about everything here rocks out in fine form including a cover of the Byrds' "Drug Store Truck Drivin' Man." Emmylou Harris even drops by to guest on "Everything Has a Cost" to great effect. You won't be disappointed if you choose to get a hold of this disc. *—James Chrispell*

Midnight Roads & Stages Seen / May 5, 1998 / Mammoth ♦♦♦♦♦
This seminal country-punk outfit proves they haven't lost any power in their punch with this double-live effort. There are even a few unreleased studio tracks tacked on the tail of the second disc. Check out the searing cover of Dylan's "Absolutely Sweet Marie." It just goes to show what many have said for years: there's nothing like a Jason and the Scorchers show. *—Tim Sheridan*

Rock on Germany / Mar. 27, 2001 / Courageous Chicken ♦♦♦♦
This "official" CD issue of a bootleg LP is many things: first, it's a portrait of this band at the height of their power. In June of 1985, Jason & the Scorchers had proven to be the first totally country/totally hard rock band in the world. They owed as much to the Sex Pistols and the Clash as they did Hank Williams and Buck Owens. (And don't give me a hard time about the Byrds or Lynyrd Skynyrd either—the Byrds weren't a hard rock band and Skynyrd only referenced country music, they used more of the blues in their mix.) Second thing is: They were one of the wildest live bands in America at the time, during a period where there wasn't exactly a lot of exciting live music. In fact, it can be argued there weren't any rock bands at all at the time except in the underground. Third, it was this unheralded unit that was the true wave rider for alt-country. Forget the Old 97s or the Bottlerockets. The Scorchers didn't need corny humor because they had all the pieces. With Jason's killer songwriting and stage presence, Warren Hodges' otherworldly guitar playing (he is the definition of a "guitar-slinger"), and an energy level most hardcore bands couldn't match—not for an hour and a half anyway—this is the sound of this band's moment. And that was all they had, a shift in the hourglass before it got turned right side up again. This set is an eye-opener. Musically, the rockabilly and hard country styles of Williams and his contemporaries are wedded to punk rock's energy and hard rock's sophisticated musicality and comes off as raw as a scrape. What makes this disc so revelatory—by the way, it was mastered from an LP; you can hear the pops but it adds to the set's rock & roll ethos—is that this gig was played in front of a sparse audience, referenced a few times by Jason throughout. But you'd never know it by the performance. It was as if they were playing for the audience at the U.S. Festival (remember them?). They rip through their own gems like "Shop It Around," "Broken Whiskey Glass," "Hot Nights in Georgia," "Last Time Around," "White Lies," and "Pray for Me Momma—I'm a Gypsy Now," defining them as live songs as opposed to their recordings, which are also smokin'. However, what defines the Scorchers as a great band is the original manner in which they cover the songs of other people: from Leon Payne's "Lost Highway" and Williams' "You Win Again" and "Honky Tonk Blues" to John Fogerty's "Travelin' Band," Neil Young's "Are You Ready for the Country," and a version of Dylan's "Absolutely Sweet Marie" that would make Dylan proud—or jealous. These songs they put their indelible stamp on, reclaiming them for their own generation, making sure they went on, wider, deeper than before, as valid for any rock & roll generation as they were for the pop and country generations that preceded them. The sound isn't perfect here, but more than adequate; after a track or two, the music is so damn hot, it isn't even an issue. As a document, this is a field recording worth preserving, as a rock & roll record it's worth listening to over and over again. *—Thom Jurek*

Still Standing [Bonus Tracks] / 2002 / Capitol ♦♦♦
While Jason & the Scorchers' first two national releases—the *Fervor* EP and the long-playing follow-up, *Lost & Found*—earned reams of good reviews and blazed a trail for the cowpunk and alt-country movements that followed in their wake, they earned far more fame than record sales. Their second LP, 1986's *Still Standing*, seems to have been an attempt to give Jason & the Scorchers a bit of polish in hopes of attracting a wider audience. Produced by Tom Werman (who had previously worked with Molly Hatchet, Ted Nugent, and Cheap Trick), *Still Standing* has a slicker tone than the group's previous work, especially Warner Hodges' guitar (and Hodges seems all too eager to give his solos a veneer of arena-level bombast), while occasionally veering toward Georgia Satellites-style raunch—not a bad idea but one that doesn't suit Jason Ringenberg's voice all that well. More to the point, the songwriting on *Still Standing* isn't quite up to the level of *Lost & Found*, but while *Still Standing* sounds like an attempt by Jason & the Scorchers to meet the mainstream half way, there's enough of their strength and fiery passion to make the album worthwhile, and "Crashin' Down," "Shotgun Blues," and the delicate ballad "Ocean of Doubt" show that even this band's weaker albums had moments to savor. [The 2002 reissue of *Still Standing* features three bonus tracks, including "Greetings From Nashville," a wild and woolly attack on Music City, and a pedal-to-the-metal cover of "Route 66," both of which add value to the package.] *—Mark Deming*

Wildfires and Misfires: Two Decades of Outtakes and Rarities / Jan. 29, 2002 / Yep Rock ♦♦♦♦
Subtitled *Two Decades of Outtakes and Rarities*, this generous 19-track, 72-minute disc assembles odds and sods from cowpunk's hardest-rocking gang. Although they may be called leftovers, these tunes slice as hard and sharp as what was originally released on their studio albums from 1983-1998 (OK, so it's not quite 20 years), and in some cases better. From an unplugged radio performance of Jimmie Rodgers' "Last Blue Yodel" to a very plugged-in version of Johnny Burnette's "Tear It Up" with guest guitarist Link Wray tearin' it up at the Roskilde Festival in 1985 that must be heard to be believed, Jason Ringenberg and the band obviously find their niche on-stage. That's not to say that the studio outtakes aren't worthwhile too, but these C&W and Stones-loving Southerners let loose in concert like few others. Between Jason Ringenberg's nasal twang and Warner Hodges' limber guitar, their sound seesaws between the heartfelt hillbilly of "The Slow Train Never Ends"—a duet with Hodges' mom—and their fire-spittin' cover of Dylan's "Absolutely Sweet Marie." That song, which got them signed, leads off the album in a 1983 demo that pounds with raw power. From a flaming version of Tony Joe White's "Polk Salad Annie," the only track here sung by Hodges, to the Drivin' N' Cryin' Southern metal swagger of "Too Much Too Young" and the tough ballad "Window Town" (one of their best tracks, previously only available as a B-side to a British EP), this is prime stuff that's not just meant for existing fans who own all the band's material. With their music confusingly scattered over three, now four labels, it's time for a comprehensive collection of Jason & the Scorchers' best work. Until listeners get one, this ragtag anthology will work just fine. *—Hal Horowitz*

Jerry Jaye (Gerald Hatley)

b. Oct. 19, 1937, Manila, AR
Vocals / Traditional Country, Honky Tonk, Memphis Soul
Best remembered for his 1976 country radio hit "Honky Tonk Women Love Redneck Men," singer/guitarist Jerry Jaye was born Gerald Hatley in Manila, AR, on October 19, 1937;

after a handful of independent recordings, he surfaced on Hi Records in 1967 with the rockabilly influenced *My Girl Josephine*, reaching the Top 30 with the title track (a cover of the Fats Domino hit) before spending nearly a decade out of the spotlight. Resurfacing on Columbia in 1975, Jaye notched a minor hit with a cover of the Tommy Edwards chart-topper "It's All in the Game," returning to Hi the following year with *Honky Tonk Women Love Redneck Men* before again receding from view. *—Jason Ankeny*

● **My Girl Josephine** / Mar. 7, 2000 / Edsel ✦✦✦✦

Hello Josephine / Edsel ✦✦✦✦
Jerry Jaye was one of those inexplicable one-hit wonders, scoring in 1967 with his pre-Creedence-like cover of the title track. This brings together the original single version, the stereo re-cut, the two follow-up singles, and the original 12-track album in its entirety. With Roland Janes producing, these sides have "Memphis" written all over them. *—Cub Koda*

The Jayhawks

f. 1985, Minneapolis, MN
Group / Alternative Country-Rock, Americana
Led by the gifted songwriting, impeccable playing, and honeyed harmonies of vocalists/guitarists Mark Olson and Gary Louris, the Jayhawks' shimmering blend of country, folk and bar-band rock made them one of the most widely acclaimed artists to emerge from the alternative country scene. The group sprung up in 1985 out of the fertile Minneapolis, MN, musical community, where Olson had been playing standup bass in a rockabilly band called Stagger Lee until his desire to write and perform his own country-folk material prompted him to begin a solo career. He enlisted Marc Perlman, the guitarist for a local band called the Neglecters, whom Olson then convinced to take up the bass; after the addition of drummer Norm Rogers, the group first played in front of a crowd of less than a dozen people. One of those patrons, however, was Gary Louris, a veteran of the local bands Safety Last and Schnauzer; after the show, he and Olson began talking, and by the end of the evening Louris, a guitarist famed locally for his innovative, pedal steel-like sound, had become a member of the group, eventually named the Jayhawks.

Drawing on influences like Gram Parsons, the Louvin Brothers, Tim Hardin, and *Nashville Skyline*-era Bob Dylan, the Jayhawks quickly became a local favorite, honing their sound in Twin Cities clubs before releasing their eponymous debut in 1986. Issued in a pressing of just a few thousand copies, the album was well-received by those who heard it; a major recording deal did not follow, however, so the band continued to polish their craft live, with more and more of their songs bearing writing credits belonging to both Olson and Louris. In October 1988, after a line-up change which saw the departure of Rogers (who joined the Cows) followed by the addition of drummer Thad Spencer, Louris was nearly killed in an auto accident, and the Jayhawks went on hiatus. At much the same time, however, executives at the Minneapolis independent label Twin/Tone decided to issue the demos the group had been stockpiling over the past few years, and after some overdubbing and remixing, *Blue Earth* appeared in 1989. Richer in sound and more complex in its themes and concerns, the record's release brought the group considerable attention, and also brought Louris back into the fold. After another drummer switch (Spencer for Ken Callahan), the band hit the road for a national tour.

The Jayhawks were signed to major label (Def) American Records after producer George Drakoulias heard *The Blue Earth* playing in the background during a phone call to Twin/Tone's offices. With Drakoulias in the producer's seat, the band recorded their breakthrough album *Hollywood Town Hall* in 1992; a mainstay of critics' annual "best-of" lists, the album generated the alternative radio hits "Waiting for the Sun," "Take Me With You (When You Go)," and "Settled Down Like Rain." After a tour which saw the permanent addition of Minneapolis pianist Karen Grotberg, the individual bandmembers guested on albums from Counting Crows, Soul Asylum, Maria McKee, Joe Henry and others. Before recording the fourth Jayhawks album, Callahan departed, and was replaced by session drummer Don Heffington. The resulting record, 1995's *Tomorrow the Green Grass*, is a beautiful collection of songs led off by the elegiac single "Blue," the recipient of significant airplay. A tour followed, but after some months on the road, Olson announced he was quitting the band. In 1997, the Jayhawks—now consisting of Louris, Perlman, Grotberg and drummer Tim O'Reagan—released the album *Sound of Lies*. Grotberg left the band in early 2000, and was replaced by ex-Dag keyboardist Jen Gunderman for the band's sixth album *Smile*. A move to a new label (Lost Highway) in 2002 brought about more changes in the band's ever evolving lineup, leaving Louris, Perlman and O'Reagan (assisted by newcomer Stephen McCarthy on guitar) to craft 2003's rootsier *Rainy Day Music*. *—Jason Ankeny*

The Jayhawks / 1986 / Bunkhouse ✦✦✦
Though lacking the almost telepathic interplay later developed by frontmen Mark Olson and Gary Louris, the Jayhawks' self-titled debut—issued in a tiny pressing of just a few thousand copies—is a fair indication of the remarkable things still to come from the band. Complete with song titles which could have been cribbed from old Replacements records—"Six Pack on the Dashboard," "The Liquor Store Came First," "I'm Not in Prison," and so forth—the record owes a clear debt to the group's Minneapolis stomping grounds, but evidence of the Jayhawks' own distinct identity can be found in the fluid guitar work as well as in Olson and Louris' harmonies, which even this early in the game are graceful and rich. *—Jason Ankeny*

Blue Earth / 1989 / Twin/Tone ✦✦✦
The songs which make up *Blue Earth* originated as demos, and save for some minor studio tinkering, are presented here in their original embryonic state. As a consequence, the record lacks punch; spare and economical, the songs are simply too primitive to come to life in this setting. Nonetheless, the growth of the band's songwriting skills over their debut is substantial; while many of the themes—drifting, drinking, and lost love—remain the same, they're handled with greater insight and clarity than before, with a keen eye for detail and nuance. *—Jason Ankeny*

● **Hollywood Town Hall** / Sep. 15, 1992 / American ✦✦✦✦✦
It was one of the more unlikely major label releases of 1992—nothing to do with grunge, certainly not a last holdout from '80s mainstream sludge. On the flip side, it wasn't really the incipient alternative country/No Depression sound either, for all that there was a clear influence from the likes of Gram Parsons and fellow travelers throughout the grooves. This wasn't a sepia-toned collection of murder ballads or the similarly minded efforts that were almost overreactions to Nashville's triumphalism throughout the '90s. At base, *Hollywood Town Hall* found a finely balanced point—accessible enough for should-have-been success (sclerotic classic rock station programmers were fools to ignore this while still playing the Eagles into the ground) but bowing to no trends. Its lack of variety tells against a bit—while there are certainly stronger moments than others, most of the songs do have a tendency to blend into each other—but the core strengths of the group come through. George Drakoulias fleshed out the sound just enough, with the side help of performers like Benmont Tench and Nicky Hopkins adding fine extra touches without swamping the identity of the group. Piano and organ may be prevalent, but it's really Olson and Louris' great harmonies that are the core of things, giving songs like "Crowded in the Wings" and "Settled Down Like Rain" a high-and-lonesome sparkle. Callahan's a good drummer, if not particularly noteworthy, but he keeps the pace steady without dominating the tracks, Drakoulias keeping him back in the mix a bit. Olson's eventual departure isn't really explained by this disc—he might have been tired of the attempt to aim for commercial success, but this sounds more like something made for the group's own satisfaction that connects beyond it as well. *—Ned Raggett*

Tomorrow the Green Grass / Feb. 14, 1995 / American ✦✦✦✦
The Jayhawks' final record with singer/songwriter Mark Olson, *Tomorrow the Green Grass* is also the group's finest. While the band's earlier efforts perfected a more traditional brand of country-rock, their fourth record is marvelously eclectic, both musically and emotionally; never before had they rocked as hard as on "Real Light," dug as painfully deep as on "Two Hearts," or hit quite the same peaks of exuberance as on "Miss Williams' Guitar," a tribute to Olson's new wife, neo-folkie Victoria Williams. The addition of keyboardist Karen Grotberg brings rich new layers to the Jayhawks' sound, as does the inclusion of a string section on cuts like "Blue" and "I'd Run Away," a soaring pop song that's quite possibly the best thing the group ever recorded. A fitting legacy, indeed. *—Jason Ankeny*

Sound of Lies / Apr. 22, 1997 / American ✦✦✦
Following Mark Olson's amicable departure, the remaining Jayhawks reconvened under the direction of Gary Louris to record *Sound of Lies*, the band's most ambitious album to date. Like Wilco's *Being There*, *Sound of Lies* uses country-rock as a foundation and wanders off into a variety of different sonic territories, including surf-rock and Beatles-esque pop, bringing the music closer to the sound of adult-alternative pop/rock. Although the surface of the album is pleasant and melodic, Louris has written a uniformly harrowing set of songs, inspired both by the dissolution of his partnership with Olson and a recent divorce. The lyrics have a naked, emotional honesty which would have been more affecting if the music echoed its sentiment, yet the record still has a subtle grace and power, proving that the Jayhawks remain a distinctive band without Olson. *—Thom Owens*

Smile / May 9, 2000 / American ✦✦✦
With *Smile*, the Jayhawks drop yet another sizable chunk of their alt-country sound by the roadside, adding in its place healthy doses of power pop and modern electronic music. Almost half of *Smile*'s songs feature looped percussion, overdubbed drum tracks, or flat-out, funky backbeats. Little blips of sound skitter underneath the mostly acoustic guitars on the wistful "What Led Me to This Town" and make "Queen of the World" a worthy candidate for a dance remix (if the Jayhawks were ever to consider such a thing). Their second record since the departure of founder and leader Mark Olson, *Smile* is meant as a direct reaction to the pessimism of *Sound of Lies*, their underappreciated, moody offering from 1997. Ironically, with the charismatic Gary Louris now fronting the group alone, they sound more like a band than ever before. Despite the modern touches, though, the fact remains that *Smile* retains just enough of a distinctly Americana feeling. On the warm and twangy "Better Days," one of Louris' best songs in years, he sings with genuine regret and heartache the way he treated a long ago lover, and on "Break in the Clouds" he celebrates the comforts of domestic contentment, complete with pedal steel and soaring harmonies that recall the band's landmark work *Hollywood Town Hall* from 1992. The general shift in direction may alienate a few long-term fans, but much like friends Wilco achieved with their adventurous *Summerteeth*, *Smile*'s modern touches may bring even more people into the band's orbit. What never changes on the Jayhawks' albums, it seems, are the blissful melodies and well-constructed tunes, and that may just be enough for even the toughest critics. *—John Duffy*

Rainy Day Music / Apr. 8, 2003 / American/Lost Highway ✦✦✦
The Jayhawks' seventh album backs away from their "super-pop" releases like *Smile* and the underrated *Sound of Lies* and looks back to their earlier, rootsier sound. The band has whittled itself down again following the departures of keyboardist Jen Gunderman and longtime guitarist Kraig Johnson, leaving behind core songwriter and vocalist Gary Louris, founding member Marc Perlman on bass, and longtime drummer Tim O'Reagan assisted by newcomer Stephen McCarthy on guitar. Produced by Ethan Johns (and overseen by Rick Rubin), *Rainy Day Music* goes back even further than the band's first albums, channeling the ghosts of the Byrds, Crosby, Stills & Nash, and Buffalo Springfield, and interpreting their '60s folk jangle and lazy, sunny harmonies through the Jayhawks' own sweetly awkward formula. "Madman," in particular, gives the listener a sense of *déjà vu*, sounding like a long lost CSNY demo, and the chiming Rickenbacker 12-string

guitar of the leadoff track, "Stumbling Through the Dark," could've been lifted right from the master tapes of "Mr. Tambourine Man." The first six tracks are all vintage Louris gems—trembling and honest, with warm melodies and hooks for days. Unfortunately, the album stumbles in the second half with the inclusion of two O'Reagan compositions (which try too hard to evoke John Lennon's world-weary mumble and Bob Dylan's nasal whine), and an unsuccessful stab at heartland gospel on "Come to the River." Although the summertime love song "Angelyne" and the waltzing "Will I See You in Heaven" provide bright spots near the end, the album never *fully* recovers. This is a real shame, since the whole affair starts so strong, and it seems as though if side B could've been trimmed by about four songs (and 15 minutes), *Rainy Day Music* would stand alongside their strongest albums. Still, fans who complained that their last two albums were "too poppy" or "not rootsy enough" should be pleased with this direction, and it's certainly an album that gets better with each listen, so it may yet prove to be worth its weight in acoustic gold. *—Zac Johnson*

Paul Jefferson

Songwriter, Vocals / Contemporary Country, Singer/Songwriter

Combining elements of country, bluegrass, and folk music, singer/songwriter Paul Jefferson writes songs that concentrate on positive examinations of love, whether it be romantic or spiritual. Jefferson's first taste of success was as a songwriter, co-writing Aaron Tippin's chart-topper "That's as Close as I'll Get to Loving You." Hailing from the hills and ranches of Woodside, CA, in the Santa Cruz Mountains above Palo Alto, he began listening to country music as a child. While attending college for engineering, Jefferson—who is also a pilot—developed a large regional following playing in a country band, eventually striking out on his own and marketing a tape of his original songs. After signing a publishing deal in L.A., the company took him to Nashville where he linked up with the newly formed Almo Sounds record label, started by music veterans Herb Alpert and Jerry Moss. The company released Jefferson's debut in 1996, and the album's first single, "Check Please," was a Top 40 hit. *—Jack Leaver*

Paul Jefferson / Jul. 15, 1996 / Almo Sounds ♦♦♦

Before the release of his eponymous debut album, Paul Jefferson had spent some time in Nashville writing songs professionally. In fact, he cowrote Aaron Tippin's number one hit "That's as Close as I'll Get to Loving You," which gives an idea of what kind of music Jefferson plays on his debut. Jefferson sounds like a mainstream new country singer, with polished production and anthemic choruses. However, the actual songs boast more lyrical detail and narrative thrust than the standard Nashville song. That's what makes *Paul Jefferson* an intriguing, promising debut. *—Thom Owens*

Snuffy Jenkins

b. Oct. 27, 1908, Harris, NC, **d.** Apr. 30, 1990

Banjo / Traditional Bluegrass, Old-Timey

Bluegrass banjo pioneer DeWitt "Snuffy" Jenkins was born in Harris, NC, on October 27, 1908; the youngest of ten children, all of whom excelled in music, he began playing the fiddle as a child but was too small to use the bow and as a result picked the instrument like a mandolin. He later turned to guitar and by 1927 was playing in a trio with banjo players Smith Hammett and Rex Brooks; Jenkins copied their three-finger style, and in the years to follow the banjo became his primary instrument, honing his skills playing square dances throughout the western North Carolina region. At this time he began mentoring the young Earl Scruggs; while Jenkins' technique bridged the gap between jagged, old-timey picking and the more fluid contemporary style, Scruggs soon surpassed his teacher, forging a thoroughly modernized sound distinguished by its subtlety and grace.

Jenkins relocated to Columbia, SC, in the spring of 1937, soon joining a string band which performed on local radio station WIS; despite the inevitable lineup changes, the group—later dubbed the Hired Hands—remained active for over half a century. Joining in 1939 was Jenkins' longtime foil, fiddler Homer "Pappy" Sherrill, a onetime member of the Blue Sky Boys; eight years later the Hired Hands welcomed lead guitarist Julian "Greasy" Medlin and bassist Ira Dimmery, followed in 1955 by the arrival of second guitarist Bill Rey. This five-piece lineup cut the first Hired Hands recordings in 1962, released by Folklyric in 1970 and subsequently reissued on Arhoolie as *Pioneer of the Bluegrass Banjo*. In 1971, Jenkins and Sherrill also recorded an LP for Rounder and in 1989 also cut material for Old Homestead; Jenkins died on April 30, 1990. *—Jason Ankeny*

● **33 Years of Pickin' & Pluckin'** / 1971 / Rounder ♦♦♦♦

For a modern recording of old-time music that is hardly played in the copycat manner, one can't do much better than this. It is a relaxed recording of a group of musical veterans getting together to have fun playing, without much regard to genre boundaries or folklorist dogma. Some of the music is kind of an acoustic version of Western swing, some of it is right-on old-time, and the tracks featuring Snuffy Jenkins on washboard suggest both jug band music and the madcap percussion lunacy of Spike Jones. Studio sound really makes one feel as if this entire gang was sitting in one's living room, which would probably be lots of fun. Pappy Sherrill provides many highlights with his superior fiddling. Perhaps the ultimate delight for most listeners will be discovering the hilarious vocal style of Greasy Medlin, a veteran of vaudeville from the days of the medicine tents. *—Eugene Chadbourne*

Pioneer of the Bluegrass Banjo / Aug. 18, 1998 / Arhoolie ♦♦♦

Although credited to Snuffy Jenkins, this is actually an 18-song set by the full Hired Hands band, several of whom also take vocals, recorded at WIS in Columbia, SC, in October 1962. It's straightforward bluegrass with some versatility to the approach, going into instrumentals, old-timey tunes, comic numbers, and a couple tracks ("Step It Up and Go" and "Born in Hard Luck," both sung by "Greasy" Medlin) with a bluesy skiffle flavor. *—Richie Unterberger*

Waylon Jennings

b. Jun. 15, 1937, Littlefield, TX, **d.** Feb. 13, 2002, Chandler, AZ

Guitar, Vocals / Traditional Country, Progressive Country, Country-Folk, Outlaw Country

If any one performer personified the outlaw country movement of the '70s, it was Waylon Jennings. Though he had been a professional musician since the late '50s, it wasn't until the '70s that Waylon, with his imposing baritone and stripped-down, updated honky tonk, became a superstar. Jennings rejected the conventions of Nashville, refusing to record with the industry's legions of studio musicians and insisting that his music never resemble the string-laden, pop-inflected sounds that were coming out of Nashville in the '60s and '70s. Many artists, including Willie Nelson and Kris Kristofferson, followed Waylon's anti-Nashville stance and eventually the whole "outlaw" movement—so-named because of the artists' ragged, maverick image and their independence from Nashville—became one of the most significant country forces of the '70s, helping the genre adhere to its hardcore honky tonk roots. Jennings didn't write many songs, but his music—which combined the grittiest aspects of honky tonk with a rock & roll rhythm and attitude, making the music spare, direct, and edgy—defined hardcore country, and it influenced countless musicians, including members of the new traditionalist and alternative country subgenres of the '80s.

Jennings was born and raised in Littlefield, TX, where he learned how to play guitar by the time he was eight. When he was 12 years old, he was a DJ for a local radio station and, shortly afterward, formed his first band. Two years later he left school and spent the next few years picking cotton, eventually moving to Lubbock, TX, in 1954. Once he was in Lubbock, he got a job at the radio station KLLL, where he befriended Buddy Holly during one of the station's shows. Holly became Waylon's mentor, teaching him guitar licks, collaborating on songs, and producing Jennings' first single, "Jole Blon," which was released on Brunswick in 1958. Later that year, Waylon became the temporary bass player for Holly's band the Crickets, playing with the rock & roller on his final tour. Jennings was also scheduled to fly on the plane ride that ended in Holly's tragic death in early 1959, but he gave up his seat at the last minute to the Big Bopper, who was suffering from a cold.

Following Holly's death, Jennings returned to Lubbock, where he spent two years mourning the loss of his friend and working as a DJ. In late 1960, he moved to Phoenix, AZ, where he founded a rockabilly band called the Waylors. Jennings & the Waylors began to earn a local following through their performances at the local club JD's, eventually signing to the independent label Trend in 1961. None of the group's singles made any impact, and Jennings began working for Audio Recorders as a record producer. In 1963, Waylon moved to Los Angeles, where he landed a contract with Herb Alpert's A&M Records. By this point, Waylon's music was pure country, and Alpert wanted to move him toward the pop market; Jennings didn't cave in to the demands and his sole single, "Sing the Girl a Song, Bill," and album for A&M flopped.

Following the A&M debacle, Jennings landed a contract with RCA with help from Chet Atkins and Bobby Bare, and he moved to Nashville in 1965. After arriving in Nashville, he moved in with Johnny Cash, and the two musicians began a long-lasting friendship, which eventually resulted in a collaboration in the form of the Highwaymen in the '80s. Waylon released his first single for RCA, "That's the Chance I'll Have to Take," late in the summer of 1965, and it became a minor hit. With his second single, "Stop the World (And Let Me Off)," he had his first Top 40 country hit, and it began a string of moderate hits that eventually developed into several Top Ten singles—"Walk on out of My Mind," "I Got You," "Only Daddy That'll Walk the Line," "Yours Love"—in 1968. At this point, he was working with Nashville session men and developing a sound that was halfway between honky tonk and folk. As the next decade began, he started to move his music toward hardcore country.

In 1970, Jennings recorded several songs by a struggling but promising songwriter called Kris Kristofferson, which led to a pair of ambitious albums—*Singer of Sad Songs* and *Ladies Love Outlaws*—the following year. On these two records, he developed the roots of outlaw country, creating a harder, tougher muscular sound with a selection of songs by writers like Alex Harvey and Hoyt Axton. During the following year, Waylon began collaborating with Willie Nelson, recording and writing several songs with the songwriter. Just as importantly, he also renegotiated his contract with RCA in 1972, demanding that he assume the production and artistic control of his records. *Honky Tonk Heroes*, released in 1973, was the first album released under this new contract. Comprised almost entirely of songs by the then-unknown songwriter Billy Joe Shaver and recorded with Jennings' road band, the album was an edgy, bass-driven, and surly variation on stripped-down honky tonk. Jennings and his new sound slowly began to gain more fans, and in 1974 he had his first number one, "This Time," followed by yet another number-one single, "I'm a Ramblin' Man," and the number two "Rainy Day Woman."

Waylon's success continued throughout 1975, as *Dreaming My Dreams*—featuring one of his signature songs, the number one "Are You Sure Hank Done It This Way"—reached number 49 on the pop charts; he was also voted the Country Music Association's Male Vocalist of the Year. Jennings truly crossed over into the mainstream in 1976, when *Wanted! The Outlaws*—a various-artists compilation of previously released material that concentrated on Waylon but also featured songs from his wife Jessi Colter, Willie Nelson, and Tompall Glaser—peaked at number one on the pop charts. Following the success of *Wanted!*, Waylon became a superstar, as well known to the mainstream pop audience as he was to the country audience. For the next six years, Jennings' albums consistently charted in the pop Top 50 and went gold. During this time, he recorded a number of duets with Nelson, including the multi-platinum *Waylon & Willie* (1978), which featured the number one single "Mammas Don't Let Your Babies Grow Up to Be Cowboys." Over the course of the late '70s and early '80s, Jennings scored ten number-one hits, including "Luckenbach, Texas (Back to the Basics of Love)" (which hit number 25 on the pop charts and spent six weeks at the top of the country charts), "The Wurlitzer Prize (I Don't Want to Get Over You)," "I've Always Been Crazy," "Amanda," "Theme from 'The Dukes of Hazzard' (Good Ol' Boys)," and three duets with Nelson.

By the mid-'80s, the momentum of Waylon's career began to slow somewhat, due to his drug abuse and the decline of the entire outlaw country movement. Jennings kicked his substance habits cold turkey in the mid-'80s and formed the supergroup the Highwaymen with Willie Nelson, Kris Kristofferson, and Johnny Cash in 1985; over the next decade, the band released three albums, yet none of them were more successful than their debut, which spawned the number-one single, "Highwayman." Also in 1985, Jennings parted ways with RCA, signing with MCA Records the following year. At first, he had several hit singles for the label, including the number one "Rose in Paradise," but by the end of the '80s, he was no longer able to crack the Top 40. In 1990, Waylon switched labels again, signing with Epic. "Wrong," his first single for the label, reached the Top Ten in 1990, and "The Eagle" reached the Top 40 the following year, but after that minor hit, none of his singles were charting.

Despite his decreased sales—which were largely due to the shifting tastes in country music—Waylon remained a superstar throughout the '90s and was able to draw large crowds whenever he performed a concert, while many of his records continued to receive positive reviews. In 1996, he signed to Justice Records, where he released the acclaimed *Right for the Time. Closing in on the Fire* followed in 1998. His work was slowed by his health in the years following that album, as complications from diabetes made it difficult for him to walk. His foot was amputated in December 2001 because of his illness, and he died on February 13, 2002, at his home in Arizona. *—Stephen Thomas Erlewine*

Waylon at JD's / 1964 / Bat ✦✦✦✦

Don't Think Twice / 1965 / A&M ✦✦✦✦

The country & western and folk music paths come together here as if they were two mountain trails meeting at a truly wonderful vista. This is years before Jennings introduced thudding double bass drums, heavy electric guitars, the thick scraggly beard, and the dark leather cowboy hat. Here he just looks like a well dressed dude who might break your nose in a bar. In the world of used record store buyers who ask for "no beards" on their Waylon, Merle, or Willie, this here is the jackpot. Jennings comes across as an undersung interpreter of Bob Dylan; this is a "Don't Think Twice" one can really take seriously, while the "I Don't Believe You," with its soulful dobro picking and swishing Jerry Lee Lewis-style piano, is one of the best covers ever of a songwriter whose work has been recorded extensively. There's more. Jennings pulls off a fine rendition of "House of the Rising Sun" and is arrogant enough to call his arrangement "The Real Rising Sun." A trio of terrific country tunes are there for the old fans, and things only falter with some banal cover versions on side two. Herb Alpert co-produced, and one wonders if he is blowing the trumpet on the version of Ian Tyson's "Four Strong Winds." Talk about whipped cream and other delights. *—Eugene Chadbourne*

Folk Country / 1966 / Razor & Tie ✦✦✦✦

Folk Country is chapter number one in the Waylon Jennings/Chet Atkins partnership that ended up as a series of pitched battles. *Folk Country* is Waylon's true debut album for the RCA label, and while it is very much embryonic in terms of its revelation of the mature Jennings sound, its roots are clearly audible and the material, while safe, is more than satisfying. The single "Stop the World (And Let Me Off)" is indicative of the kind of countrypolitan fare Atkins was developing at the label. And while this is only 1963, the listener can hear Jennings stretching the song to its limits—at least the limits imposed by a mainstream country single. Also included is a true folk/country song, the traditional "Man of Constant Sorrow," on which the song's hillbilly roots are given a distinctly modern folk sound treatment. Also, "Cindy of New Orleans," one of Jennings' first attempts at writing story-songs, is a curio that works very well as a narrative with a fine and memorable melody, dressed in trappings of silk around a tale of grit. Jennings was still leaning heavily on the songs of Harlan Howard, who has no less than four tunes present here, including the classics "Another Bridge to Burn" and "What's Left of Me," which open and close the set. Jennings treats the country songs as modern folk songs while keeping to the middle of the road, and the folk songs, if indeed there are any aside from the aforementioned traditional number, are treated in a striking progressive country fashion without allowing the entirety of the songs or their intents to slip away into the ether. While it's true this is "straighter" than any Jennings date on the label, its songs have aged amazingly well. *—Thom Jurek*

Leavin' Town / 1966 / RCA ✦✦✦

Love of the Common People / 1967 / Buddah ✦✦✦✦

Love of the Common People is where Waylon Jennings began to come into his own, delivering country, folk, pop, and rock in a distinct blend. To a certain extent, he's still searching here, overpowering on Beatles covers but effective on the title track. There's a certain tendency for country albums of this era to be uneven, and if that's the case on *Love of the Common People*, it isn't because of bad material, but because Jennings is searching the entire time, testing things out, finding that some things work and others don't. It may not be a perfect album, but there are enough remarkable moments to make it nearly essential. *—Stephen Thomas Erlewine*

Sings Ol' Harlan / 1967 / RCA ✦✦✦✦✦

Hangin' On / 1968 / RCA ✦✦✦✦

Sticking to totally musical criteria, the best tracks on this collection are so good that dismissing the gunky ones is easy. There are other criteria for rating a Waylon Jennings album but, however one looks at it, *Hangin' On* is one of this country artist's very special productions. Some might see distinction in the fact that the brief liner notes are written by none other than the wonderful singer Skeeter Davis. Others may treasure this particular album because it really looks like ol' Waylon is lighting up a joint on the front cover. Then, there is the ultimate criterion for judging the value of an album not only by Jennings, but by some of his associates such as Kris Kristofferson, Merle Haggard, and Willie Nelson, at least in the eyes of a used record store buyer from North Carolina: "If they's wearin' beards, I don't want it. If they's shaven, then ah'm interested." While many publications use some sort of star system for rating records, it appears a system based on lack of beards is really the key with some types of country music. In this case, the clean-shaven Jennings was still a few years from the rumbling of heavily rock-influenced music that he would create in the '70s, but had already been pushing at country music's perceived boundaries since the middle of the decade. Considering that his groups featuring two drummers would eventually play as loud as the Rolling Stones, the fact that an acoustic dobro can practically drown out the whole band here is a pretty good indication of how relatively soft, even pretty, the music on this album is. But closer listening reveals that the dobro is being turned up really loud for certain effects, just one of many intricate touches that make certain cuts on this record absolute marvels of country music. The premier track is "I Fall in Love So Easy," which weaves together three completely different sections—and these sections are varied in tempo, in how they are mixed, and in the feeling with which they are played. Subtle use is made of brass, sometimes in written passages in combination with harmonica. There was a lot of work put into this, producing the kind of good feeling one gets from a fine chamber group when it is really playing well. There are also a couple of tracks that clunk, one of which might be the Roy Orbison cover, no matter how well it is sung. This type of submissive personality is not the best character for Jennings to act out in a song. He does much better with the threatening slob who sings "Woman, Don't You Ever Laugh at Me" or, even better, the depressed psycho who destroyed himself over unrequited love for "Julie." A check of the songwriting credits reveals, to no surprise, that it is Jennings who wrote the latter ballad. It is one of his best originals. Those who find the John Hartford song "Gentle on My Mind" heavy trodding will need to soak their feet after listening to this album; if a cover version of the song isn't bad enough, a few minutes later a cheap imitation with similar minor chords burps up. Jennings' backup band, the Waylors, actually plays on a few tracks here, a hard-fought compromise with RCA producer Chet Atkins, who wanted his own session crew to provide backup. There are no further musical credits, and no information about who thought up the wonderful parts of this album. Call it a brilliant collaboration of Jennings and Atkins at the dawn of a new era in country music. *—Eugene Chadbourne*

Jewels / 1968 / RCA ✦✦✦

Country-Folk / 1969 / RCA ✦✦✦✦

Just to Satisfy You / 1969 / RCA ✦✦✦✦

The title track on this album is the strongest track here. Co-written by Jennings and country music funny-man/songwriter Don Bowman, it's been covered several times (including by Glen Campbell), but never done better than Jennings. He sounds good, but overall, not one of his best. *—Jim Worbois*

Singer of Sad Songs / 1970 / RCA ✦✦✦✦

In late 1969, Waylon Jennings was wrapping up his tenure with producer Danny Davis and threw in his lot with Lee Hazlewood. *Singer of Sad Songs* features a title cut produced by the former, with the rest of the album done by the latter. It was, up to that time, Waylon's most compelling album, and stands the test of time based not only on Hazlewood's sympathetic ear and visionary sense of keeping Jennings at the dead center of his mix, but also in the selection of material, which proved to be pivotal for this stage of Jennings' career and the universe that would begin to take place in earnest in early 1972. Here with a host of musicians that includes Reggie Young, Sonny Curtis, Ronnie Dyson, and Randy Meisner is a cycle of songs that over three decades later still sounds electrifying for its poignancy, musical dynamics, and group interplay. From the title track to a rollicking cover of George Jones' "Ragged But Right," an open and moving reading of Tim Hardin's "If I Were a Carpenter," Utah Phillips' "Rock, Salt and Nails," and an early recording of Billy Joe Shaver's "Honky Tonk Heroes," Jennings and Hazlewood up the rock & roll ante in Jennings' sound. Up to three and four guitars play on each track, with Hazlewood stripping everything back while adding the layers of phase and reverb that would become signifiers of Jennings' trademark. The performances here are suave but not smooth, moving but far from melodramatic. In fact, they are archetypal—if not overly rowdy—readings of the renegade freedom songs that literally spawned the outlaw generation's reliance on anthems of alienated individuals at odds with everything and everyone, yet still seeking purpose and a way home from the edge of a drifting way of life. *Singer of Sad Songs* is a myth, one of the hardest of Jennings' records to find, despite its great historical and musical—not to mention pleasurable—significance. *—Thom Jurek*

☆ **The Taker/Tulsa** / 1970 / RCA ✦✦✦✦✦

Despite its excellence in composition, production and sequencing, The Taker/Tulsa stands the rest of time as the first recording by Waylon Jennings to show what it was he had been crucifying Nash Vegas producers over. The end of his long production relationship with Chet Atkins—as Atkins was moved upstairs—his hostile, barely a year tenure with Atkins pick Danny Davis, a successful run with Lee Hazlewood that the establishment on music Row disowned because it wasn't homegrown, and the final straw with Atkins protégé Ronny Light, ultimately led to Waylon hiring a new lawyer and manager and producing himself. Taker/Tulsa is chock full of Kris Kristofferson's songs. Mickey Newbury brought Kristofferson to Jennings' attention a couple of years earlier, but this time out, Jennings decided to theme his recording and showcase Kris' songs. The result—despite the fact that the record was culled from work over two years with Davis and Light—is the first real salvo in the outlaw movement (not *Ladies Love Outlaws*, which was full of demo sessions and unfinished tracks). Kris' tunes, from "Loving Her Was Easier," "Sunday Morning Comin' Down," "Casey's Last Ride," and others, brought Jennings closer than ever to the flame, to the dream of producing his own records with his own band. The Kristofferson tunes stand out, but so does "Tulsa," by Wayne Carson Thompson and Jennings' own "You'll Look For Me." The albums dovetails together like one session and offers a view of what Waylon could issue when he got his way. This is one of Jennings' true classics and with *Lonesome, On'ry and Mean* still a year away, it was the first unruly outing by a man who, along with his friends, was about to change everything. *—Thom Jurek*

Ned Kelly / 1970 / United Artists ✦✦✦✦✦

Waylon / 1970 / RCA ✦✦✦✦
The self-titled album signifies the real beginning of Waylon Jennings' discontent with his career. He is making efforts in the studio here to stretch its boundaries and include material very foreign to Nashville. First off the album opens with Chuck Berry's "Brown-Eyed Handsome Man," a rollicking jump; off the country and T-Bone Walker Texas blues flasgship. Jennings' own version may not be as rollicking as Berry's, but it swings hard and moves inside a groove that twists and turns on its own axis. One can also feel the conflict between producer Danny Davis trying to tamer his singer and Jennings trying to spilt the seam of the track. In addition to beginning the album with so much tension, Jennings even gives more traditional number, such as Sammi Smith's "Yellow Haired Woman," a spacier sound, where the "Nashville Sound," becomes something akin to a bunch of studio guys in Nash Vegas trying to emulate Brian Wilson. Ray Buzzea's "I May Never Pass This Way Again," has honky tonk ballad written all over it, but those marching, shuffling guitars add a new spin. But it's with Mickey Newbury's "33rd of August" that the pokiness of Waylon's mission becomes apparent. In the slow dirge complete with gorgeous layers and textures of strings, aberrant percussion and backing vocals that whisper rather than chorus, Jennings offers another dimension to not only this sad story, but the direction of his musical muse, somewhere in the groove but outside the confines of the studio. *Waylon* is an overlooked gem in the transition period of Jennings career. *—Thom Jurek*

Cedartown, Georgia / 1971 / RCA ✦✦✦
Cedartown, Georgia is another off Waylon Jennings' late '60s recordings that offers a unique view of his restlessness. Made with producer Danny Davis, Jennings taut sense of propriety here is very much in evidence with the simplest and most basic of songs—namely Miriam Eddy's (Jessi Colter's) "It's All Over Now," among them. The window dressing added by Davis waters its impact and makes Jennings' job as a singer more difficult—he knew in advance what would happen to it. Others, such as "Big D," and "Tonight in Baltimore," suffer the same fate though there is nothing particularly wrong with the performances, there does seem to be too much going on. But the tables are turned on "Bridge Over Troubled Water," on which Colter joins Waylon and Davis' Chet Atkins (hell, almost Billy Sherrill) laden string fest to provide something almost blessed out amid the tumultuous arrangements. The conviction on both voices is nothing less than shattering. But aside from this and "It's All Over Now," Cedartown Georgia feels just like what it is, a decent collection of songs and inspired performances marred byproduction nonsense. Take a quick listen to the album and it becomes very easy to see why Davis worked with Jennings for even one year. *—Thom Jurek*

Good-Hearted Woman / 1972 / RCA ✦✦✦✦
Produced by Ronny Light, this is the second of the three albums Waylon Jennings released for RCA in 1972. The other two, *Ladies Love Outlaws* and *Lonesome, On'ry and Mean* were bookends of Waylon's pre- and post-outlaw career. The former was a collection of unfinished songs and demos the singer disowned despite the fact that it contains very solid and viable material, the latter was the crack in Nashville's pavement in which rock & roll took equal stage without country and Jennings wasn't going to go back. The title track written by cowboy savant Steve Young, sums up Jennings' career up to that point and it was time to get rid of the baggage of the past. *Good-Hearted Woman* reveals the singer in full glide from one side of the spectrum to the other. (The first single, Tony Joe White's "Willie and Laura Mae Jones" and the title track, the first stellar` and enduring collaboration by Jennings and Willie Nelson, showcase Jennings' adaptability, but going deeper there is the unique read of Kris Kristofferson's "To Beat the Devil," and Harlan Howard's "One of My Bad Habits." Also is the amazing "Do No Good Woman," with Reggie Young's smoking guitar solo that made the soundboard jump into the red, and Willie's "It Should Be Easier." Shirl Milete's "Unsatisfied" with Ralph Mooney's pedal steel whining in the background is one of the most poignant performances of the period for Waylon as a singer, topped only by his reading of Chip Taylor's "Sweet Dram Woman." In sum, *Good-Hearted Woman* is pretty sensational outing for Jennings; he's feeling his power here, and as the door opened just one more crack, the listener can hear how it never closed again. *—Thom Jurek*

Ladies Love Outlaws / 1972 / RCA ✦✦✦
Even though Waylon Jennings virtually disowned this album as a hoodwink job by RCA brass and that some of these tracks were unfinished and others mere demos, *Ladies Love Outlaws* nonetheless has come very fine moments including Jennings' version of "Delta Dawn," a finely emotionally wrought read of Hoyt Axton's "Never Been to Spin" (that Jennings claimed was never intended for release) and Mickey Newbury's "Frisco Depot"—one of the few tracks the singer considered complete. In addition there's Ralph Mooney's (who plays pedal steel in this band) classic honky tonk anthem "Crazy Arms," and one of the reclusive Lee Clayton's best songs in the title track. We also get a solid, moving duet version of "Under Your Spell Again," with Jessi Colter. These performances offer Jennings in a deeply expressive terrain as a vocalist. He wrings emotion from songs rather than merely projecting them into a microphone, and his band, which includes Norb Putnam, and Kenny Buttery as well as guitarist Dave Kirby and Hargus Robbins, turns the volume up a point or two and lends a slippery greasy hand to the entire proceeding. *Ladies Love Outlaws* is not a perfect Waylon album but it's worth owning for the fact that while Jennings may have disliked the finished result, he proves to be no judge of his own work. In essence, this is the outlaw primer, and the beginning of the opening of the field. *—Thom Jurek*

☆ **Lonesome, On'ry and Mean** / 1973 / RCA ✦✦✦✦✦
Lonesome, On'ry and Mean is the quintessential Waylon outlaw record. The first unfettered by the bonds of RCA, Waylon produced the set with his own band and the results are nothing less than electrifying. While Steve Young, the terminal country and folk music outsider may have penned the cut, it is Waylon's delivery as an anthem that bears in it all of the years of frustration at not being able to make the music he wanted to that is heard in the grain of its lyrics. Fury is a better word. Young's own version is devastating, but this one is transcendent. (And why is it that Travis Tritt was picked to sing this at Waylon's memorial instead of Young who was also present? Talk about misguided justice.) But the boundaries between rock & roll and country come down once again on this album in Kris Kristofferson's "Me and Bobby McGee," as folk and post psychedelia meets Texas in Mickey Newbury's "'Frisco Mabel Joy," and the broken, road-weary pop honky tonk balladry of Danny O'Keefe's "Good Time Charlie's Got the Blues." Add to this Johnny Cash's "Gone To Denver" and Willie Nelson's "Pretend I Never Happened," and you have an outsider's dream. That the rest of the recording is just as consistent, just as seamless in both its execution, production and delivery, makes *Lonesome, On'ry and Mean*," the first seriously pitched battle in the 1970s country music wars. And this one went to Jennings and his fans hands down. *—Thom Jurek*

★ **Honky Tonk Heroes** / 1973 / Buddah ✦✦✦✦✦
When Waylon Jennings hooked up with songwriter Billy Joe Shaver, he found the perfect author for his obsessions, his fascinations, and his very image. Waylon had always been looking, perhaps unintentionally, for a common ground between country and rock, and Shaver's songs—sketching an outlaw stance with near defiance and borrowing rock attitude to create the hardest country tunes imaginable—were perfect. On his previous album, Waylon had sung that "ladies love outlaws," but now he found the music that would soon be called outlaw country, a defiant, ballsy blend of mythmaking and truth-telling. Shaver never had a better voice for his songs, and Jennings never had better songs for his style. *Honky Tonk Heroes* arrived at a crucial moment, a time when true honky tonk was fading, so only a dose of rock & roll could save it. And, no matter how much rock attitude is here, this is pure country in its stance and attitude—yet *Honky Tonk Heroes*' very defiance makes it a perfect discovery album for listeners who never thought they would like country music. And the songs! Shaver earned his stripes here, with songs that were emotional, funny, and clever, utterly bringing the mythic outlaw ethic to life. "Black Rose," "You Asked Me To," and "Honky Tonk Heroes" remain among the greatest things Waylon ever cut, and every other song here matches them. Few country albums have ever been this consistent, and few records, from any genre, have been as consistently compelling. A wonderful album—one that's hard to tire of. *—Stephen Thomas Erlewine*

Nashville Rebel / 1973 / RCA ✦✦✦
Recorded and issued in 1966, *Nashville Rebel* is the soundtrack to a budget film of the same name by Jay Sheridan—who also wrote most of the songs on side two. While the title of the album may be prophetic in terms of the radical changes in Waylon Jennings' career around 1971, the music found here is anything but. While Jennings brought seven of the 12 songs to these sessions, and starred in the film, the soundtrack feels and sounds dated and overwrought—mostly from a production point of view. However, it's also true that some of the material here is less than stellar. Noteworthy tracks include "Nashville Rebel" and "Green River" by Harlan Howard, as well as an interesting if flawed cover of the Beatles' "Norwegian Wood." This is Jennings trying to punch a hole in the sky, but he falls short by trying too hard. The songs here do nothing to advance the narrative of the film and, while interesting, don't really stand on their own. Sheridan's cuts, which close the album, are nothing short of embarrassing. *—Thom Jurek*

☆ **This Time** / 1974 / Buddah ✦✦✦✦✦
This Time appeared just as outlaw hit its stride, thanks in large part to the excellent *Honky Tonk Heroes*. If this record isn't its equal, it's still pretty wonderful all the same. Part of the record's flaw is its heavy reliance on Willie Nelson—actually, not just on Willie, but on *Phases and Stages*, which is the source of no less than four of this record's six songs. Granted, these are great songs, and Waylon's versions are hard to fault, but they nevertheless give the record a slightly recycled feeling. Fortunately, these songs are surrounded by excellent material, such as the number-one single "This Time." Overall, *This Time* is fairly muted and deliberate, surprising for an album coming on the heels of the defiant *Honky Tonk Heroes*. Even the songs that swagger, like Billy Joe Shaver's "Slow Rollin' Low," are laid-back, and the whole thing is fairly reflective (appropriate, if it uses a divorce album as its template). It's not that the monochromatic makes it a lesser affair than its predecessor, yet the whole thing does feel a bit reserved and not quite as overpowering as a sequel to *Honky Tonk Heroes* should be. Still, it's a first-rate record—perhaps not a classic, but a subdued, understated album unlike anything in his catalog. [The 1999 Buddha reissue contained five bonus tracks featuring Waylon supported by the Crickets, running through (mostly) highlights from Buddy Holly's catalog. Though incongruous with *This Time*, these are highly entertaining cuts, packing more immediacy than the album itself.] *—Stephen Thomas Erlewine*

The Ramblin' Man / 1974 / Buddah ✦✦✦✦✦
If you look at the cover of *The Ramblin' Man*, you would think that Waylon Jennings had been a ramblin' man, riding the top of the charts, for years, maybe decades. He looks worn out, whether it's on the close-up on the cover, or the back-cover shot of him drunkenly playing solitaire. In truth, it would be another album before he hit the top of the country charts and before outlaw country became hip. Still, this is the record where it all came home. If he had created a sketch of outlaw on *Honky Tonk Heroes*, he perfected the marketable version of it here, making it a little slicker, a little more commercial, and a whole lot more unstoppable. If the songs aren't the equal of *Honky Tonk Heroes* or even *This Time*, *The Ramblin' Man* has a wilder sound and a greater diversity of songs that make it seem more unruly than its immediate predecessor and more blatantly outlaw. This contains, after all, his first flat-out rock cover, with a good take on the Allman Brothers' "Midnight Rider," plus songs that play into the image of what an outlaw country singer is. There are moments of reflection, yet even those feed into the outlaw picture. Too bad many of the album tracks wind up being agreeable filler instead of knockouts.

There aren't any bad cuts, and the entire thing holds together quite well, but it doesn't add up to a moment of transcendence the way *Honky Tonk Heroes* or its successor would. Still, with "I'm a Ramblin' Man," "Rainy Day Woman," and the heartbreaking "Amanda" on its side, plus highlights like "Oklahoma Sunshine," this is a first-rate Waylon record. [The 1999 Buddha reissue contains three bonus tracks.] —*Stephen Thomas Erlewine*

☆ **Dreaming My Dreams** / 1975 / DCC ✦✦✦✦✦

Dreaming My Dreams was Waylon Jennings' first number-one record, and deservedly so. He had created outlaw country with *Honky Tonk Heroes*, and then delivered two further albums that subtly developed its themes, even if they weren't quite as consistent. *Dreaming My Dreams* maintains the consistency, increasing the country quotient while subtly making it more sentimental than before. This is an unabashedly romantic album, not just in its love songs, but in its tributes to Waylon's heroes. "Are You Sure Hank Done It This Way" opens and "Bob Wills Is Still the King" closes the album—making Jennings an heir apparent to their legacies. Between those two extremes, Waylon appropriates Jimmie Rodgers ("Waymore's Blues"), covers Roger Miller ("I've Been a Long Time Leaving (But I'll Be a Long Time Gone)"), ups the outlaw ante ("Let's All Help the Cowboys (Sing the Blues)"), and writes and records as many sentimental tunes as possible without seeming like a sissy. At times, the emotional undertow may seem a bit much, yet the whole thing adds up as Waylon's best album since *Honky Tonk Heroes*, and one of the few of his prime outlaw period to deliver from beginning to end. —*Stephen Thomas Erlewine*

Are You Ready for the Country / 1976 / RCA ✦✦✦✦

If the heavy-hitters of outlaw country were acting like rock stars during their mid-'70s peak, then perhaps it was inevitable that the outlaws would start singing rock songs—which is precisely what Waylon Jennings did on 1976's *Are You Ready for the Country*. Although the title is taken from Neil Young's song—which provides an absolutely storming opener for this ten-song record—there is a bit of a jibe to its sentiment as well, since Waylon not only sings Young, but also the Marshall Tucker Band and Dr. Hook, along with reviving Jimmy Webb's "MacArthur Park." That selection of material indicates not just the increasing rock-isms of Waylon and the outlaws, it also indicates that Jennings' focus was beginning to blur slightly as he lost the sense of purpose that propelled his records of the first half the '70s, from *The Taker/Tulsa* to *Dreaming My Dreams*. Here, the music hasn't really changed, but the flow is no longer seamless and the shifting tones can be a little jarring. Also, Jennings' songwriting starts to slip a little bit here; none of his originals are bad, and "I'll Go Back to Her" is quite good, but they're all decidedly second tier. All things considered, though, most of the individual moments hold up quite well, with "Are You Ready for the Country" and a wonderful, surging take on Marshall Tucker's "Can't You See" ranking among Waylon's best music of the era. There are other very good moments, such as the cracking "Jack a Diamonds," and the entire record is entertaining, but more for a collection of moments than a cohesive whole. That's the first time since the late '60s that one of Jennings' albums felt like less than the sum of its parts, and if it didn't necessarily mark the end of the era, it did mark the point when he started to ease back from his startling peak of creativity. —*Stephen Thomas Erlewine*

☆ **Waylon Live** / 1976 / Buddah ✦✦✦✦✦

As one of the great live albums, *Waylon Live* is nearly flawless, a snapshot of Waylon Jennings at the height of his powers and, not so coincidentally, at the peak of the outlaw movement. At this time, he was popular and powerful, creating a mythos out of his performances and songs, delivering first-rate material both on record and in concert. This is where it all came together, since a set list limited Waylon to his best songs, whether his own hits or carefully selected covers. This is especially true of 1999's Buddha reissue that included nine bonus tracks (all put into the middle of the record), restoring *Waylon Live* to the double-LP running time it was designed to have. With the restoration of this section—containing such perennials as "Lovin' Her Was Easier (Than Anything I'll Ever Do Again)," "Lonesome, On'ry and Mean," "The Taker," "Look Into My Teardrops," and "Never Been to Spain"—the record really becomes a definitive statement on outlaw country and how it bent the rules, borrowing from country and rock and twisting them into something thoroughly distinctive. On top of it all, Waylon and his band give a bracing, terrific performance, investing these songs with more passion than they had previously seen on record. It winds up as one of the great country records and one of the great live albums, capturing a movement at its peak and transcending it. —*Stephen Thomas Erlewine*

Ol' Waylon / 1977 / DCC ✦✦✦✦✦

Ol' Waylon was released when Waylon Jennings had become a superstar. Outlaw was still popular, perhaps at its peak, but it was no longer the movement that it had been just a few short years before. As if offering proof, Waylon cut his most formulaic album since the early '60s, a record that satisfied the demands of outlaw without ever stretching them. Since this was recorded at a near-peak of not only his popularity but his power, there are some great moments on *Ol' Waylon*, particularly on the lead single "Luckenbach, Texas (Back to the Basics of Love)," a wonderful reminiscence of times back, "If You See Me Getting Smaller," and "I Think I'm Gonna Kill Myself." The rest of the record is a little formulaic and reliant on covers, sometimes enjoyably (including a version of Little Richard's "Lucille"), sometimes not as much ("Sweet Caroline" was never suited for Waylon's style). Overall, *Ol' Waylon* is pretty enjoyable, but it winds up feeling a little hollow, as if Jennings was trying to give the audience what it wanted. There are enough good moments to make it worthwhile, not just to the dedicated but for some casual fans enamored of the outlaw years, but it's still an album that gets by more on its style than substance. —*Stephen Thomas Erlewine*

I've Always Been Crazy / 1978 / RCA ✦✦✦✦

By 1978 Waylon Jennings had been through the ringer with his position as one of the most visible "outlaw" country stars: He'd been busted for drugs and was addicted to both cocaine and alcohol and was tired of the hype surrounding Nashville's co-opting what he, Willie Nelson, and a handful of others started in the name of greater artistic control. *I've Always Been Crazy* is his first "political" statement about his feelings. And while it may not be as great an album as *Ol' Waylon* or *Dreaming My Dreams*, it's still a fine one. With a cast of players that includes the great Tony Joe White, Ralph Mooney, Carter Robertson, Reggie Young, and Bee Spears, the band assembled here smokes. In addition to the title track, this set also features the classic "Don't You Think This Outlaw Bit Has Done Got Outta Hand." But even though these two cuts would have been worth the purchase of the album, the rest is nothing to dismiss. There are fine covers of a medley of Buddy Holly hits, a poignant, barely disguised ode to old friend and rambling mate Billy Joe Shaver, the glorious "A Long Time Ago," and the outlaw shuffle "As the 'Billy World Turns." There are also fine, heartfelt covers of Merle Haggard's "Tonight, the Bottle Let Me Down" and Johnny Cash's "I Walk the Line." The set closes with a pair of ballads, which is uncharacteristic of Jennings during this period; there's "Girl I Can Tell (You're Trying to Work It Out)," with its folk song melody and country music bridge. And finally, the four-and-a-half-minute "Whistlers and Jugglers," a broken love song by Shel Silverstein that talks of surrender and loss so poignant and sharp, it numbers among Jennings' finer performances of the late '70s. In all, *I've Always Been Crazy* is a solid recording, still possessing the piss and vinegar of Jennings' best work with a deeper lyrical edge on most tracks. In fact, despite its obvious origins, the Holly medley is the only thing that keeps the album from being as stellar as the aforementioned ones. Nonetheless, this is necessary for any fan of outlaw country in general and Jennings in particular. —*Thom Jurek*

Waylon & Willie / Feb. 4, 1978 / BMG Special Products ✦✦✦

In 1995, RCA released a truncated eight-track version of 1978's *Waylon & Willie* as a budget-line release. Since the original album ran 11 tracks and 32 minutes, this was a slim album made slimmer—a mere 22 minutes, now!—and the track listing was thrown all out of order, resulting in a jumble. It's a listenable jumble, of course (which is appropriate, since the original album is a bit of a listenable jumble), but the mixed-up, shook-up order and missing songs makes this release absolutely infuriating, especially because the full-length original album—as well as the fine 2001 Buddha reissue—were already moderately priced! If you find this particular edition, don't touch it all—this album is not supposed to be this way. It won't take much effort to find the full-length album, and it won't set you back much more, and unlike this rip-off resequencing, you *will* get off on the proper record. —*Stephen Thomas Erlewine*

What Goes Around Comes Around / 1979 / RCA ✦✦✦✦

When *What Goes Around Comes Around* was released in late 1979, Waylon Jennings was riding a hot streak of seven number-one albums in a row. This didn't reach the top spot only because it was shut out by the phenomenal crossover success of Kenny Rogers' *Kenny*, so it sat at number two for 14 weeks—so, even if it didn't really reach the top of the charts, it came close enough to count. The generally accepted conventional wisdom about Jennings' late-'70s/early-'80s records is that they pale in comparison to his early-'70s records, which is true on the surface but does albums like *What Goes Around* a disservice. Yes, the neon-and-laser studded cover of this record is ridiculous, but the music isn't splashy and the album, as a whole, is more cohesive than *I've Always Been Crazy*, even if it isn't as weighty as *Ol' Waylon*. Reading between the lines, it's easy to hear Jennings getting a little weary under the hot spotlight of stardom—there's the storming opener of Rodney Crowell's "I Ain't Living Long Like This," which easily became an anthem for the waning days of outlaw, but there's an underlying sense of sadness that runs through the record, particularly the ballad-heavy second half. That Jennings doesn't contribute many originals—he just co-writes the silly but charming vaudeville of "It's the World's Gone Crazy (Cotillion)" with Shel Silverstein—but that doesn't matter because the choice of songs is strong, displaying that Waylon still hadn't lost his expert ear for songs that suited his styles. True, it isn't a set of stone-cold classics that compares with *Honky Tonk Heroes*, but "I Ain't Living Long Like This" is iconic, "Come With Me" is moving, "Another Man's Fool" is a sly barroom number, and his take on Mickey Newbury's "If You See Her" is beautiful. Since Waylon's first-rate work is so good and so bountiful, it's easy to overlook the relatively modest pleasures of a record like this, but only a fool would dismiss it out of hand, because there's a lot of good music here—more than enough to justify his continued hot streak. —*Stephen Thomas Erlewine*

☆ **Greatest Hits** / 1979 / RCA ✦✦✦✦✦

RCA's nine-track 1979 *Greatest Hits* collection has since been supplemented by more thorough compilations—most notably the double-disc sets *Only Daddy That'll Walk the Line* and *RCA Country Legends*—but as a snapshot of Waylon at his outlaw peak, this serves quite well. And, make no mistake, this concentrates solely on the outlaw years, leaving off anything from the '60s, including such defining songs as "Only Daddy That'll Walk the Line" and "The Taker." Instead of being hurt by such exclusions, this *Greatest Hits* gains strength by its sharp focus on the peak of his outlaw years. Each of these nine songs has a nearly mythological pull, presenting ol' Waylon as the Nashville rebel, honky tonk hero, and ramblin' man who stormed through country music in the '70s with his piledriving hardcore country (yet wasn't afraid to show a macho sensitive side, as he did with "Amanda"). He made plenty of other great songs than what's here, especially during the outlaw era, but every tune here is at the core of his legend, which is why this *Greatest Hits* remains a great listen, even after it's been replaced by more comprehensive collections. —*Stephen Thomas Erlewine*

Music Man / 1980 / RCA ✦✦✦

Released in the summer of 1980, *Music Man* was the last number one album Waylon Jennings had until he switched labels and scored a chart-topper in 1986 with *Will the Wolf Survive*. So, it capped off a remarkable five-year streak of number-one albums (only one of his records in that time didn't reach the top), and while he still had another winner in him with 1982's *Black on Black*, in retrospect it's easy to hear that Waylon was on some unsteady ground around this time. Not that this is a bad record, but it does show signs that he was relying a little too much on polish and that his ear for material is slightly off. There are no outright dogs in the batch, but covers of Kenny Rogers and Jimmy Buffett are a far cry from the Neil Young and Toy Caldwell covers on *Are You Ready for the Country*; even if they are listenable, they suggest Waylon isn't stretching himself, a sentiment that's contradicted by a surprising but effective cover of Steely Dan's "Do It Again." *Music Man* is best when it sticks to harder country, whether it's in the form of a sweet cover of "Waltz Across Texas," a good version of his wife Jessie Colter's "Storms Never Last," Harlan Howard's joyously lewd "Nashville Wimmin," or a propulsive cover of J.J. Cale's "Clyde." Jennings doesn't write many original tunes here—just a J. J. Cale/George Jones tribute which appropriately follows "Clyde" and "Theme From the Dukes of Hazzard (Good Ol' Boys)," which has actually weathered time very well, sounding leaner and looser than much of the rest of the album. It's an album that, once again, doesn't quite add up to the sound of its parts, and in retrospect, those parts do seem to point toward his commercial and artistic collapse a few years away, but even with these flaws, *Music Man* is a pretty entertaining latter-day Waylon album. *—Stephen Thomas Erlewine*

Leather & Lace / Mar. 21, 1981 / RCA ✦✦✦

Waylon Jennings and Jessi Colter made hits together as early as 1970, but it wasn't until 1981 that they recorded an entire album of duets. *Leather & Lace* reprises "I Ain't the One," the B-side from their 1970 hit "Suspicious Minds," and visits a few familiar titles like Chuck Berry's "You Never Can Tell (C'est la Vie)" and Hank Thompson's "Wild Side of Life." The latter became a Top Ten hit for the duo, and the poignant "Storms Never Last" was also a moderate hit. The outlaw movement had run its course by the time *Leather & Lace* was made, so Colter and Jennings were free to make their overdue duet album without having to prop up that particular facade. The result is an enjoyable half-hour of husband-and-wife music, comfortable as an old shoe. *—Greg Adams*

Black on Black / 1982 / RCA ✦✦✦

Black on Black is the weirdest *sounding* Waylon Jennings record ever made. Issued in 1982 after the rather uninspired *Music Man*, the set was produced by Chips Moman, who had worked with Willie Nelson on *Always on My Mind*. On virtually every track, Jennings' voice seems to come out of a tunnel, someplace out of time and space, as if his ghost is singing these songs. The laid-back angle Jennings was trying to show here is perhaps overwrought, with electric pianos covering for electric guitars on "(We Made It as Lovers) We Just Couldn't Make It as Friends," written by Moman and Bobby Emmons. Jennings also circled his wagons on this set, with Nelson appearing in the fold on yet another recording of Waylon's "Just to Satisfy You," which holds up against the best of them with Jessi Colter being omnipresent on backing vocals here and everywhere else on this set. And while keyboards dominate on "Shine," it's one of the best songs Jennings wrote in the 1980s and is deeply influenced by the work of J. J. Cale. The funky, uninspired cover of "Folsom Prison Blues" is just filler, whereas Hank Williams' "Honky Tonk Blues" feels more like one of Jennings' more adventurous experiments. Paul Kennerley's "Gonna Write a Letter" is one of the more convincing and beautiful love songs that Ol' Waylon delivered between 1975 and the end of his life, as was the Bobby Emmons/Chips Moman ballad "May I Borrow Some Sugar From You." With those electric pianos (two) balanced by acoustic guitars, Waylon's vocal is believable despite its distance from everything in the mix. Rodney Crowell's "Song for the Life" could have been written for Jennings. It's a slow waltz centered around gaining wisdom from a life of folly. The acoustic piano and electric guitar fills, showcased by a gorgeous acoustic solo, would have been a stunning end to this record, but it was not to be—even if it is the strongest thing here and leaves Crowell's own version in the dust. Emmons' "Get Naked With Me" is a stupid song in the old, tired outlaw frame. Given its presentation as a singalong country song à la Jerry Jeff Walker, it only serves to showcase Jennings' tired voice and the strange textures Moman added to the rather simple songs on this set. Somebody should've released the outtakes before all the warm fuzzy bull was put on the proceedings; it might have made for a much stronger album. Jennings is as inspired as he can be, but Moman ruined this set with his trademark over-production. *—Thom Jurek*

WWII / 1982 / Buddha ✦✦

The first time Waylon Jennings and Willie Nelson released a duet record, it was at the height of outlaw country—it was 1978, and the two were the biggest stars in country music, not only selling millions of copies, which was unheard of prior to outlaw, but they were critically respected. They dominated the scene, which allowed them to get away with a patchwork record of solo cuts, duets, and old tunes with overdubbed vocals by Nelson. Five years later, they teamed up again for *WWII* (har har), and while this record displayed considerably more care, it also displayed some of the flaws that marked their solo work of the time. In 1983, Waylon and Willie were still riding high on the country charts, but the quality of Jennings' work was beginning to slip and his sales were responding accordingly, as 1982's *Black on Black* reflected. Nelson had his biggest hit ever that year with *Always on My Mind*, but it also was his worst album to date, the first time he sounded like he couldn't be bothered. The sessions that comprise *WWII* date from before those records (most are from December 1981), but they were all produced by the same producer, Chips Moman, whose touch was a little too slick for either Waylon or Willie to do their best work. Fortunately, he lightens up a bit for this record; it's still polished and not gritty at all, but the choice of material is pretty good, particularly the Jimmy Webb ("Mr. Shuck and Jive"), Guy Clark ("The Old Mother's Locket Trick"), and Tom T. Hall ("The Year That Clayton Delaney Died") covers, and Willie's Nashville-bashing original, "Write Your Own Songs." However, the billing, like last time, is a little misleading, since this is essentially a Waylon Jennings record featuring five duets with Willie Nelson (who contributes no solo cuts this time). This winds up being a little more consistent than *Black on Black* (even though it shares "May I Borrow Some Sugar From You"), largely because Willie's presence helps focus the song selection and performance, but even at its best, *WWII* is nowhere near as good as Waylon and Willie are at their best, since they're coasting on reputation through most of this, a fact that's only enhanced by Moman's glossy showcase production. *—Stephen Thomas Erlewine*

Waylon & Company / 1983 / RCA ✦✦

This is a duets album with some guests you would expect (Hank Williams Jr., Jessi Colter, and Willie Nelson) and some surprises (Ernest Tubb, Mel Tillis, and actor James Garner). Fun for what it is. *—Jim Worbois*

Never Could Toe the Mark / 1984 / RCA ✦✦

Will the Wolf Survive / 1985 / MCA ✦✦✦

Moving to MCA after a long stay at RCA brought Jennings a new producer in Jimmy Bowen and a fresh approach, resulting in one of his better albums, typified by his version of the Los Lobos title track and a cover of Steve Earle's tailor-made "The Devil's Right Hand." *—William Ruhlmann*

Greatest Hits, Vol. 2 / 1985 / RCA ✦✦✦✦

Greatest Hits, Vol. 2 contains ten of Waylon Jennings' biggest hits from the late '70s and early '80s, including "America," "I Ain't Living Long Like This," "Come With Me," "Women Do Know How to Carry On," "Don't You Think This Outlaw Bit's Done Got Out of Hand" and "Dukes of Hazzard." *—Stephen Thomas Erlewine*

Waylon: The Best of Waylon Jennings / 1985 / RCA ✦✦✦

Waylon: The Best of Waylon Jennings is an adequate nine-song budget-line compilation of some of his Top Ten hits from the early '80s, including "Lucille," "Drinkin' and Dreamin'," "I May Be Used (But Baby I Ain't Used Up)," and "Breakin' Down." *—Thom Owens*

Hangin' Tough / 1987 / MCA ✦✦

My Rough & Rowdy Days / 1990 / MCA ✦✦✦

The Eagle / Feb. 1990 / Epic ✦✦

The Eagle includes the Top Five hit "Wrong" as well as "Where Corn Don't Grow," "What Bothers Me Most" and the title track. *—Jason Ankeny*

Clean Shirt / Feb. 1991 / Epic ✦✦✦

Two aging outlaws swap reminiscences and argue good-naturedly about who's caused the most trouble. Every once in a while they work themselves up to doing more damage. Small flashes of tossed-off brilliance appear in nearly every song, but sometimes it's hard to tell what's part of the pair's casual charm and what's just laziness: when the clever "Old Age and Treachery" (always overcome youth and skill) falls apart at the end, it's infuriating. Like much of either singer's output, *Clean Shirt* sounds a bit wrinkled at first, but most of the album holds up to repeated listening. *—Brian Mansfield*

★ **Only Daddy That'll Walk the Line: The RCA Years** / 1993 / RCA ✦✦✦✦✦

Prior to 1993's double-disc box set *Only Daddy That'll Walk the Line: The RCA Years*, there was no comprehensive collection of Waylon Jennings' seminal RCA recordings, only three LP collections, each targeting specific eras in his career: 1970's *The Best of Waylon Jennings* covered his '60s material, including his country-folk hits; 1979's *Greatest Hits* zeroed in on his outlaw peak; and its 1985 sequel concentrated on the post-outlaw hangover. All had their attributes, especially the expertly assembled *Greatest Hits*, but none captured the full scope of his music, particularly because much of his great music never hit the charts. *Only Daddy That'll Walk the Line* doesn't limit itself to just the hits and, in fact, pulls many lesser-known singles and, more importantly, album tracks that were key to his reign as the king of outlaw country in the '70s. That's not to say that all of his great songs are here, since there are big tunes that should have been here: "Cedartown, Georgia," "Pretend I Never Happened," "The Wurlitzer Prize (I Don't Want to Get Over You)," and "Mammas Don't Let Your Babies Grow Up to Be Cowboys" chief among them. That said, they're not particularly missed, since this collection manages to present nearly every facet of Waylon's musical personality, balancing the braggadocio and sensitivity in equal measure. Plus, it also has a great *narrative*, taking Waylon from his first Nashville hits, through his country-folk tunes, to the brilliant progressive country of the late '60s/early '70s, though the peak of outlaw, and to the beginnings of its decline. It's one of the great journeys in American music, and no other Waylon Jennings compilation tells the story so well and offers so much great, timeless music as this essential set. *—Stephen Thomas Erlewine*

Right for the Time / May 21, 1996 / Buddha ✦✦✦

Waylon Jennings' later albums have consistently been more interesting than those of most others from his aging generation, and his new album, *Right for the Time*—his first for his new label, Justice Records—is one of his strongest of the '80s and '90s. His voice is rich and beautiful, his arrangements are spare and casual, and his songs explore life, love, and dreams with honesty and wisdom. He waxes nostalgic for small-town life on "Cactus Texas," and mixes bitter sentiments with a snap-crackle wit on "Kissing You Goodbye." Never shy about his feelings, Waylon again comments (as he has on recent albums) on the "new hats" in country music, doing so with good-natured sarcasm on the spoken-word acoustic song "Living Legends Pt. II." *—Kurt Wolff*

The Essential Waylon Jennings / Jun. 18, 1996 / RCA ✦✦✦✦✦

The Essential Waylon Jennings may not contain every hit Jennings every recorded or every fine album track he cut, but—as the title implies—it does have the bare-bone essentials ("Only Daddy That'll Walk the Line," "Are You Sure Hank Done It This Way," and several others), making it the best single-disc retrospective assembled on the ground-breaking country singer. *—Thom Owens*

Cowboys, Sisters, Rascals & Dirt / Mar. 3, 1998 / RCA ✦✦✦✦

Cowboys, Sisters, Rascals & Dirt is Waylon Jennings' family album, a collection of songs written for children. Jennings always has had a keen eye for detail and a warm voice, and those factors assist him on this record. He doesn't talk down to kids—he treats them as equals, and there's a real tenderness to his songs and performances that makes the album a wonderful record for kids. *—Stephen Thomas Erlewine*

Closing in on the Fire / Jun. 16, 1998 / Ark 21 ✦✦✦✦
With so many classic country & western artists making comebacks in the 1990s, it was only natural that Waylon Jennings did so to. But, rather than follow the surfeit of "comebacks," Jennings took his own sweet time, and we are rewarded justly with *Closing in on the Fire*. It's a fabulous album, spotlighting Jennings powerful vocals as well as his direst, to-the-bone songwriting. Most of the record rocks surprisingly hard, especially Tony Joe White's swampy title track. Gust appearances by Sheryl Crow, Mark Knopfler, Mary Stuart, and others are a plus, but this is Waylon's record—one of his finest in the last 20 years—and the man really doesn't need the help. *—Matthew Greenwald*

☆ **The Journey: Destiny's Child** / 1999 / Bear Family ✦✦✦✦✦
The Journey: Destiny's Child is the first of two box sets from Germany's Bear Family Records covering Waylon Jennings' pre-outlaw period. This set collects his complete recordings, from his first Buddy Holly-produced single to his April, 1968, RCA sessions. His rare, privately-released album *Waylon at JD's* is here, in addition to a number of other complete albums such as *Folk-Country, Sings Ol' Harlan*, and *Love of the Common People*. Also included are early demos, radio ads for Coca-Cola and other products, a number of previously unreleased cuts, and his complete A&M recordings from the early '60s. Many of Waylon's individual '60s albums have been reissued domestically, which means that much of the music herein can be had for far less than the high retail price of this box set. For hardcore fans and completists, though, *The Journey: Destiny's Child* is an all-inclusive survey of Waylon's early years, and the accompanying full-color hardback book is chock full of rare photos and fascinating tidbits. *—Greg Adams*

☆ **The Journey: Six Strings Away** / Dec. 14, 1999 / Bear Family ✦✦✦✦✦
Bear Family's second Waylon Jennings box set covers the late '60s and early '70s, tracing Waylon's journey to outlaw country. Often, it's possible to hear him floundering as he tries to find the perfect balance between rock and country, sometimes flailing about admirably, other times feeling a little out of place. Still, this remains essential for any serious Jennings or country music fan. Even when Waylon wasn't quite sure of what he was doing, he made extraordinary music, from the wah-wah inflected cover of "Lonely Weekends" to the undeniable brilliance of his *Honky Tonk Heroes* material. *Six Strings Away* is a travelogue of Waylon finding his voice—and the remarkable thing is, not only does it deliver some of the greatest country music of all time, but it winds up mirroring the evolution of the genre during those years. *—Stephen Thomas Erlewine*

The Restless Kid—Live at JD's / Apr. 25, 2000 / Bear Family ✦✦✦
In the summer of 1964, Waylon Jennings began a residency at JDs, a new two-story club in Scottsdale, AZ. He had been in Arizona playing for some time, gigging and DJ-ing shortly after the death of Buddy Holly, but his time at JDs was pivotal, since it's where he developed his musical voice and began to establish himself as a solo star in his own right. A few short months after he began playing JDs, he went into Audio Recorders in Phoenix and cut two sessions that resulted in an independent album, *JD's Presents Waylon Jennings*, which was available at JDs and in area record stores. This was not a live album, but it did capture the wide-ranging nature of his live performances of the time. He relied heavily on folk and country, adding a little bit of rock, blues, rockabilly, and R&B to the mix. All of this was captured on the album, which is easily one of the most valuable and interesting items in Jennings' catalog. Bear Family reissued the album as part of their splendid, exhaustive six-disc box *The Journey: Destiny's Child*, but a year later, the label issued *The Restless Kid—Live at JD's*. This disc is not *JD's Presents Waylon Jennings*. Instead, it's a compilation that contains six previously unreleased cuts from those sessions (they aren't on the box set, either), then, best of all, a live performance of Waylon Jennings & the Waylors circa 1965. Understandably, the recording is a little rough, demanding close attention from the listener, but it's worthwhile for the dedicated. *Restless Kid* doesn't necessarily provide revelations, since it's well known what Jennings was playing during this period as he etched out his signature "folk-country," but it does add some color and texture to this period, illustrating how comfortable Jennings was with such a broad variety of material. If there are any surprises here, it's that much of the set list is very low key and leans heavily on folk songs, including cowboy songs, making the Waylors sound like disciples of the Kingston Trio. The only time the tempo really picks up is for kicking versions of "Candy Man" and "Memphis, Tennessee," which is further proof that the folk part of the equation was more dominant than the country. And that's what's really interesting about this disc; it fleshes out and brings to life a time in Jennings' career that is often read about, but seldom heard. Of course, that means it's primarily for the dedicated fans and historians, the kind of listener that knows the arc of Waylon's career by heart, but that doesn't make *The Restless Kid—Live at JD's* any less a welcome addition to Jennings' catalog. *—Stephen Thomas Erlewine*

20th Century Masters—The Millennium Collection: The Best of Waylon Jennings / May 9, 2000 / MCA ✦✦✦
Waylon Jennings' installment in the MCA series *20th Century Masters—The Millennium Collection* features 11 tracks from his mid- to late-'80s albums for the label. In other words, not the prime of his career, but the compilation demonstrates that Jennings did produce some quality work during his time with MCA, landing hit singles like "Will the Wolf Survive?," "Working Without a Net," "What'll You Do When I'm Gone," "My Rough and Rowdy Days," and more. While this isn't the most important or satisfying phase of Jennings' career, *The Millennium Collection* does a nice job of summing it up, and it's a worthy addition to the collections of devoted fans. *—Steve Huey*

Never Say Die: Live / Oct. 10, 2000 / Columbia ✦✦✦✦
At age 63, Waylon Jennings may have reached the point that he is commercially marginal, but his long hit-filled career gives him a repertoire that can make for a powerful concert set, and on this album, recorded at the Ryman Auditorium in Nashville in January 2000, he demonstrates that he remains able to turn in a performance to match. This is a special show, with frequent guest-star appearances from Jennings' accolytes—John Anderson ("Waymore's Blues"), Montgomery Gentry ("(I'm A) Ramblin' Man"), Travis Tritt ("I've Always Been Crazy")—as well as his wife, Jessi Colter, who gets a solo spot with her hit "I'm Not Lisa" and duets with Jennings on their hit "Storms Never Last." In addition to the familiar material, Jennings mixes in songs from his little-heard late-'90s albums, such as the title track from his 1998 collection, *Closing in on the Fire*, and covers the pop hits "Drift Away" and "Never Been to Spain." He makes an engaging host, joking with his guests and talking to the audience, but what matters most is that his bass baritone remains sturdy, while his veteran band (which earns a co-billing) still plays his songs with authority. Jennings vows that he is "Goin' Down Rockin'," and if so, that's appropriate, but this album suggests there's still plenty of life in him. *—William Ruhlmann*

★ **RCA Country Legends** / Nov. 6, 2001 / Buddha ✦✦✦✦✦
Buddha's 2001 release, *RCA Country Legends*, theoretically supplants the peerless 1991 collection *Only Daddy That'll Walk the Line*, since it covers roughly the same time period, also spans two discs, and has many of the same songs. There is a big difference, however: this concentrates more on chart hits, which is part of the reason that it extends further into the '80s than the previous collection. That isn't inherently a bad thing, since Jennings had many chart hits and many were terrific; indeed, this contains such seminal items as "Cedartown, Georgia," "Pretend I Never Happened," "You Can Have Her," "Can't You See," "The Wurlitzer Prize (I Don't Want to Get Over You)," and "Mammas Don't Let Your Babies Grow Up to Be Cowboys." Still, there are some great songs missing from that idiosyncratic collection, songs that give Jennings depth as an artist: "Nashville Rebel," "Love of the Common People," "Just to Satisfy You," "Lovin' Her Was Easier (Than Anything I'll Ever Do Again)," "Black Rose," "Lonesome On'ry and Mean," "Honky Tonk Heroes," "Waymore's Blues," "T for Texas," and "It's Not Supposed to Be That Way." These are missed, but so are the songs not on *Only Daddy That'll Walk the Line*. Ideally, there would be a collection that covers all the territory—the hits on *RCA Country Legends* and the album-oriented outlaw on *Only Daddy*—but until that happens, both are effective introductions and essential parts of any country collection (hell, any collection of American music of the 20th century). Until then, choose which direction you'd prefer to follow when seeking an introduction, but be forewarned, it's a lot easier to find *RCA Country Legends* than the out-of-print *Only Daddy That'll Walk the Line*. *—Stephen Thomas Erlewine*

Phase One: The Early Years 1958–1964 / Mar. 5, 2002 / Hip-O ✦✦✦✦
The recordings on Hip-O's 2002 collection *Phase One: The Early Years 1958-1964* have been collected many times before, in a number of different fashions, but with the exception of Bear Family's exhaustive box set *The Journey: Destiny's Child*, they've never been presented as clearly or as logically as they are here. Essentially, this is the first disc of that set, containing both sides of his Buddy Holly-produced 1958 single "When Sin Stops"/"Jole Blon," both sides of his 1961 single for Trend; two songs from a 1963 session (these may have been re-recorded later, but the documentation is unclear); five sides for A&M produced by Herb Alpert in the spring and fall of 1964; and nine tracks recorded in December 1964 for a Phoenix independent label. Given that chronology, it should not come as a surprise that the music here is all over the map—a little bit of rock & roll; a little bit of Cajun; a lot of country; a little crossover pop; a sappy string-laden tribute to Buddy Holly; a cover of "Rave On," with mariachi horns; a heavy dose of folk, including covers of Ian Tyson's "Four Strong Winds" and Dylan's "Don't Think Twice, It's Alright"; and lots of rock & roll and country covers. In other words, it's formative recordings, finding Waylon as he was trying to find his sound—and even if you can hear him stumble, it's a hell of an interesting journey, since it covers so much ground. Sometimes the covers are faithful, usually quite enjoyably ("Love's Gonna Live Here Again," "White Lightnin'," "Big Mamou," "Jole Blon," all fair well), but occasionally to their detriment (Waylon could sing "Crying," but not in an arrangement that copies Roy Orbison's original); sometimes they're quite inventive ("Don't Think Twice" points toward country-rock, "The House of the Rising Sun" is nicely moody). Apart from the Orbison covers, Waylon sounds comfortable in nearly every style and, in retrospect, it's amazing to hear how all these experiments would later blossom on his RCA work—plus, there's the first version of his first great song, a gently rolling take on "Just to Satisfy You." It all adds up to a fascinating listen; that's not just a boon to collectors, it's also quite an entertaining listen. Perhaps you need to be a dedicated listener to purchase these early recordings, but if you're curious, you will be satisfied. *—Stephen Thomas Erlewine*

☆ **Waylon Live: The Expanded Edition** / May 20, 2003 / BMG Heritage ✦✦✦✦✦
Waylon Jennings' 1976 album *Waylon Live* is generally considered as one of the great live albums in country music—and, when pressed, it's easy to make an argument that it's among the finest of the decade—and Buddha's 1999 reissue seemed to be the final word on the record, since it restored the record to its scrapped original double-album running length, taking it from 11 to 20 songs. Just four years later, however, BMG Heritage issued *Waylon Live: The Expanded Edition*, which more than *doubled* its length to 42 songs over two discs. Most concerts don't last that long and it is true that this expanded *Waylon Live* isn't taken from just one gig; it was taken from three concerts in late September 1974, one show at the Western Place in Dallas on the 25th, and two dates at the Opry House in Austin on the 26th and 27th. Simply put, Jennings was on fire these three days, at the peak of his powers as a performer, turning out music that was rebelliously rowdy and sweetly poignant. These shows were also at a crucial time, just as he was reaching the summit of his creativity, and this new expanded track listing has him looking back ten years while living thoroughly in the moment. There's a little bit of everything here: hits and album tracks, covers of classic country and current rock hits, newly written songs

and tunes he's never sung before, songs recorded for RCA in the '60s, and songs yet to be released. It covers a hell of a lot of ground, but there's not a bad choice or performance here, and its freewheeling, all-encompassing scope makes as strong a case for Jennings' deep, far-ranging gifts as the classic studio albums *Honky Tonk Heroes* and *Dreaming My Dreams*. In its own way, it's as good as an introduction to Jennings as either of the double-disc greatest hits collections *Only Daddy That'll Walk the Line* and *RCA Country Legends*; while those contain original hit versions recordings which illustrate how consistent and adventurous he was in the studio, this is similarly eclectic and contains plenty of heart, guts, soul, and fire. These performances are as good as Jennings ever got, which means it's tremendous and one of the rare cases where the album truly deserves such an expanded treatment. Absolutely essential. —*Stephen Thomas Erlewine*

Are You Ready for the Country/What Goes Around Comes Around / Jul. 8, 2003 / BMG UK/Camden Deluxe ✦✦✦✦

Are You Ready for the Country and *What Goes Around Comes Around* aren't necessarily the most logical choice for a two-fer, since they are separated by three years and four albums (counting the *Waylon & Willie* duet album in 1978). Nevertheless, they're two classic albums from Waylon's commercial peak of the late '70s that had yet to appear in any form on CD when BMG UK/Camden Deluxe released this two-fer in the spring of 2003. There's just enough time separating these two records for even casual listeners to notice the difference between the two records. On 1976's *Are You Ready*, Jennings' creative peak is starting to draw to a close, and while it's a little uneven, it's wholly enjoyable, with cuts like "Are You Ready for the Country" and "Can't You See" ranking among his absolute best sides of the decade. In contrast, 1979's *What Goes Around* certainly arrives after his creative peak—he's no longer innovating; he's found his style and settled into it—but it arguably gels better, providing a solid set of polished outlaw material that may only produce one undeniable classic in "I Ain't Living Long Like This," but nevertheless is quite entertaining on a song-by-song basis, with Waylon's choice of covers revealing the adventurous spirit that the streamlined production sometimes glosses over. Perhaps 1977's *Ol' Waylon*—which followed the same spirit of *Are You Ready*, but did it better—would have been a better pair for the 1976 release, and perhaps 1978's *I've Always Been Crazy* would have been a good companion for *What Goes Around*, since it would have showcased the 1979 album better, but it's hard to complain since these albums are long overdue for a CD reissue and it's a treat to have them out, regardless of the form. —*Stephen Thomas Erlewine*

Music Man/Black on Black / Jul. 8, 2003 / BMG UK/Camden Deluxe ✦✦✦

Waylon Jennings' artistic fortunes started to sink in the late '70s, as the heady peak of the outlaw years gave way to the aftermath where the musical and personal excesses started to catch up with him. He was still a star and still making good music (at least on occasion), but things were becoming erratic, as detailed on this two-fer from BMG/Camden Deluxe in the U.K. Neither 1980's *Music Man* nor *Black on Black* are considered among his finest works, but they were both big hits, and they play like hit albums—singles, surrounded by filler, including many covers. But, ever restless, Waylon chose good, interesting covers, where even if he did something familiar, it would be delivered in an odd way, such as his take on "Honky Tonk Blues" on *Black on Black*. But, those would be tempered by a cover of Kenny Rogers' "Sweet Music Man," which kind of gives away the plot—he's still outlaw, but there's a huge sentimental streak sneaking in here that's a little disarming, particularly when it's given a pretty polished production. Production plays a more obvious role on these two records than previous Waylon records—these *sound* produced, drawing attention to their sound, where his best records, even in the '60s, never sounded constructed; they simply exist. Here, on both records, the production is at the forefront, and it's possible to hear Waylon struggle a bit to keep things interesting. But uneven Waylon albums are still filled with great moments—a good cover of J. J. Cale's "Clyde," followed by a J. J. tribute by Jennings; a surprising cover of Steely Dan's "Do It Again"; "We Made It as Lovers (We Just Couldn't Make It as Friends)"; and of course, "Theme From the Dukes of Hazzard (Good Ol' Boys)," a joke at the time but one that has weathered time to stand as possibly his finest single of the early '80s. These are the reasons why this two-fer isn't just welcome for getting these albums in print in the CD age, it's also welcome in any serious Waylon fan's library. —*Stephen Thomas Erlewine*

Jim & Jesse

f. 1945, Virginia

Group / Bluegrass, Traditional Bluegrass, Close Harmony

One of the great bluegrass bands in history, brothers Jim (born 1927) and Jesse (born 1929) McReynolds & their Virginia Boys remained at the top by changing with the times. Starting as a traditional brothers duet, Jim on guitar and Jesse on mandolin showed their versatility by following country's changing tastes, moving to country/folk when necessary to keep a road band going. Whatever style they played (including *Berry Pickin' in the Country*, an album of bluegrass versions of Chuck Berry tunes), they retained a pure country core, due in no small part to Jim's pure, high tenor and Jesse's virtuoso, cross-picking mandolin playing.

Raised in Virginia, Jim & Jesse were born into a musical family. Their grandfather Charles McReynolds was a fiddler who had recorded a single for Victor in 1927 with the Bull Mountain Moonshiners. The brothers learned to play a number of stringed instruments while they were children, occasionally playing local dances and events as teenagers. However, the duo didn't begin playing professionally until they were in their 20s and Jim left the Army—by this point, Jim was playing guitar and Jesse played mandolin. In 1947, they landed a daily 15-minute spot on a local Norton radio station. For the next few years, they played on a variety of Southern radio stations, securing a regular spot on Augusta, GA's WGAC in 1949. After staying at the station for a year, they moved to the Midwest, where they played stations in Iowa and Kansas without gaining much of a following. In 1951, they relocated to Middletown, OH, where they had a regular spot at

WPFB. While they were at the station they cut ten songs with vocalist Larry Roll under the name the Virginian Trio; the records didn't gain much attention.

For the remainder of 1951 and much of 1952, Jim & Jesse played at a variety of radio stations throughout the country. Finally, in 1952, the group secured a major-label deal with Capitol Records. However, their career was interrupted when Jesse was drafted into the Army to serve in the Korean War. After he was discharged in 1954, he rejoined Jim, who was still playing *the Tennessee Barn Dance* in Knoxville, TN. For the rest of the decade, they played radio and television stations across the country—including ones in Alabama, Georgia, and Florida—building up a fan base. During this time, their band, the Virginia Boys, included such musicians as fiddler Vassar Clements and banjoist Bobby Thompson. In 1958, they recorded a handful of sides for Starday Records.

Martha White Mills flour company became Jim & Jesse's sponsors in 1959; the duo was the company's second major sponsorship, following Flatt & Scruggs. In 1961, they debuted at the *Grand Ole Opry*; three years later, they became members of the *Opry*. Jim & Jesse switched record labels in 1962, signing with Epic Records. The change in labels resulted in success for the duo, as "Cotton Mill Man" became their first charting country single in the summer of 1964. For the next few years, they continued in a straight bluegrass direction, scoring the occasional hit. In the late '60s, Jim & Jesse adopted a more country-oriented direction, which resulted in their biggest hit singles, including the number 18 "Diesel on My Tail."

In 1970, Jim & Jesse re-signed to Capitol Records, and the first album they released under their new contract featured electric instruments. However, the duo quickly returned to a traditional bluegrass sound, since a bluegrass revival had gripped the attention of many country fans and college students across the U.S. For the next two decades, the duo was a staple on the bluegrass festival scene, and they recorded for a variety of independent labels, including CMH, Rounder, and their own Old Dominion and Double J labels. In 1982, they had a minor hit single with "North Wind," which was recorded with Charlie Louvin. —*Stephen Thomas Erlewine & David Vinopal*

☆ **Bluegrass Special/Bluegrass Classics** / 1963 / Epic ✦✦✦✦

Bluegrass Special/Bluegrass Classics is a double-LP set containing 24 tracks Jim & Jesse cut for Epic Records. These songs were recorded in the early '60s, during the era when folk and bluegrass were experiencing a revival in popularity. The bluegrass boom happened to coincide with a time that Jim & Jesse were reaching their musical peak, at least according to many observers. These Epic songs—including many of their popular favorites ("Drifting and Dreaming of You," "Stoney Creek") but none of their hits from that era—feature an accomplished, streamlined band that effortlessly plays dazzling instrumental leads. It's a fine introduction to one of the best duos in bluegrass; while missing some hits, it captures Jim & Jesse at their best. —*Thom Owens*

Jim & Jesse Saluting the Louvin Brothers / 1969 / Epic ✦✦✦

Here are the best of the duo's recordings with electric country, rather than bluegrass accompaniment. —*Richard Lieberson*

The Jim & Jesse Story: 24 Greatest Hits / 1980 / CMH ✦✦✦✦

The Jim & Jesse Story: 24 Greatest Hits contains the majority of the duo's biggest hits and most familiar numbers, including "Diesel on My Tail," "Paradise," "Cotton Mill Man," "Better Times A-Coming" and "Are You Missing Me." However, the disc does *not* contain original recordings—it is all re-recordings from the early '90s. Nevertheless, the album does boast a number of excellent performances, since the duo is supported by several of the finest former Virginia Boys, and they themselves sound energetic and surprisingly lively, making *The Jim & Jesse Story* a fine introduction to the duo's sound. —*Thom Owens*

In the Tradition / 1987 / Rounder ✦✦✦

In the Tradition features new Jim & Jesse material as well as re-recorded versions of their hits. —*Jason Ankeny*

Epic Bluegrass Hits / 1988 / Rounder ✦✦✦✦

The material on this album and other tracks from these recording sessions have been packaged and repackaged a few times via Epic and the parent company that paid the bills, Columbia. This vinyl pressing was done via an arrangement between Rounder and the Columbia Special Products Division. Mastering is gorgeous, so is the color photo on the front of our boys in their blue suits, but have the magnifying glass on hand for the essay printed in smaller than phone book typeface on the back cover. The bluegrass influence on country & western music is easy to discern even for a novice listener. This material and the career of Jim & Jesse as a whole provides an interesting example of influences going back the other way, as these were recordings done for a label that was having lots of chart success with country releases. One of the top country producers, Billy Sherrill, was even called in to produce some of these sides. But, although Jim & Jesse would later record almost totally country & western material, the songs here are definitely from the bluegrass crockpot. It just seems as if a chef came by and sprinkled in some country & western pepper from time to time, and it is a great combination. Like many magic music moments, it is a collaborative effort, with banjo player Allen Shelton coming up with an amazingly rhythmic style. One doesn't need a drummer to keep the time with players such as this, whose way of hitting the beat has the impact of a large hammer driving in a nail. Most of these songs are classics of a sort, but the one-two punch of "Cotton Mill Man," a huge hit with tough lyrics, and "She Left Me Standing on the Mountain" is the musical climax of this set. —*Eugene Chadbourne*

Music Among Friends / 1991 / Rounder ✦✦✦✦✦

A celebration of this bluegrass duo's 25 years on the *Grand Ole Opry* includes guest appearances by Bill Monroe, Emmylou Harris, Porter Wagoner, and others. —*Mark A. Humphrey*

★ **Jim & Jesse: 1952–1955** / 1992 / Bear Family ✦✦✦✦✦

Bear Family's *Jim & Jesse: 1952–1955* contains 20 recordings the duo recorded for Capitol in the prime of their career. Among the highlights are "I'll Wash Your Love from My Heart," "Just Wondering Why," "Virginia Waltz," "Look for Me (I'll Be There)," "Purple

Heart," "Air Mail Special," "My Little Honeysuckle Rose," "My Darling's in Heaven," "Memory of You," "I'll Wear the Banner," and "My Garden of Love." The duo's harmonies never sounded better than they did on these Capitol recordings, and their instrumental work is equally impressive. *—Stephen Thomas Erlewine*

Bluegrass & More / Jun. 28, 1994 / Bear Family ♦♦♦♦♦
Bluegrass & More is a comprehensive multi-disc box set that includes all of the material, including alternate takes and unreleased tracks, from Jim & Jesse's prime years for Epic Records in the '60s. There's plenty of fine music on the set, but it is primarily of interest for completists and historians. *—Thom Owens*

Tribute to Bill Monroe / Jan. 7, 1997 / AMI ♦♦♦
On Jim & Jesse's *Tribute to Bill Monroe*, the brothers & their Virginia Boys tackle the canon of their hero and peer. Mega-popular Monroe tunes such as "Orange Blossom Special" crop up here alongside lesser knowns. Most of the tracks take a fairly true-to-the-original approach, and renderings of "Blue Moon of Kentucky" and "Footprints in the Snow" won't surprise any listeners familiar with the Monroe versions (though, admittedly, the McReynolds brothers put more *Opry* polish on the proceedings and possess little of Monroe's dark-holler intensity). A particular highlight here is Jim & Jesse's nimble, speedy romp through "Uncle Pen." *—Erik Hage*

Y'All Come: The Essential Jim & Jesse / Jan. 27, 1998 / Epic/Legacy ♦♦♦♦♦
Y'All Come: The Essential Jim & Jesse is a 20-track collection that culls highlights from the duo's decade at Epic Records in the '60s, featuring such hits and favorites as "Better Times A-Coming," "Ballad of Thunder Road," "Yonder Comes a Freight Train," "She Left Me Standing on the Mountain," "Stay a Little Longer," "Memphis Tennessee" and "Truck Drivin' Man." This isn't the set for traditional bluegrass fans, although there is plenty of that. Instead, the set is divided between bluegrass and the duo's brief flirtation with straight-ahead country, giving a good picture of their time at Epic. Either way, it's a fine set, showcasing some of the best music Jim & Jesse ever recorded, and it's one of the best anthologies of their Epic years yet assembled. *—Stephen Thomas Erlewine*

Songs From the Homeplace / Aug. 11, 1998 / Pinecastle ♦♦♦
On *Songs From the Homeplace*, the veteran bluegrass duo Jim & Jesse cover songs that they learned growing up in Virginia and that have continued to have a special place with them throughout their career. The aging McReynolds brothers are still in fine throat here and offer up strong versions of tunes by the Carter Family, Grandpa Jones, and Cliff Carlisle, among others. The vocals of Emmylou Harris (who is fast becoming the most ubiquitous album guest in the music industry) meld nicely with the brothers on the plaintive "No Letter in the Mail Today." While possessing a less-haunting sound than peers such as Ralph Stanley (and despite a run at commercial country at one point), the McReynolds brothers are original bluegrass masters. And anytime you hear Jim & Jesse's vocal tones merging together and Jesse's distinctive cross-picking on the mandolin, you're staring down bluegrass history. *—Erik Hage*

The Old Dominion Masters / Mar. 9, 1999 / Pinecastle ♦♦♦♦♦
This four-disc set compiles material from nine Jim & Jesse albums originally released on their own record label in the 1970s and 1980s, as well as a few radio show recordings and some previously uncompiled singles. In 1972, tired of the pressure they were feeling from the major labels to modernize their sound with drums and electric guitars, the brothers Jim & Jesse McReynolds formed the Old Dominion label and began producing and releasing their own albums. Among the nine collected here (some, but not all, in their entirety), there are two gospel albums, a collection of patriotic songs released during the U.S. bicentennial, and an album recorded live in Japan. All feature the McReynolds brothers' winning combination of tradition and innovation; the irony of the Jim & Jesse story is that even as they were resisting the more crass modernizations urged on them by record executives, they were developing a sound that was really quite progressive in bluegrass terms. They adopted the electric bass early on, their banjo players were typically well-versed in the melodic Tony Trischka/Bill Keith approach, and, along with traditional bluegrass standards like "Live and Let Live" and "Blue Ridge Mountain Blues," they frequently performed material with more complicated, country-derived structures. Jesse's own "Jesus Is the Key to the Kingdom" is one good example of that tendency, as is a surprising cover version of Chuck Berry's "Back in the U.S.A." This outstanding box set provides an excellent overview of one of bluegrass music's finest ensembles working at the peak of its powers. *—Rick Anderson*

Our Kind of Country / May 8, 2001 / Pinecastle ♦♦♦
Jim & Jesse McReynolds have always had their own take on the bluegrass tradition. Like their contemporaries the Osborne Brothers, they've always pushed the envelope of the mainstream while never completely losing their aura of old-time traditionalism. This album will change all that. Teaming up with the stage band from the *Grand Ole Opry*, the McReynolds brothers deliver a program of classic honky tonk country music, complete with steel guitar and Telecaster accompaniment. (Interestingly, the band uses an upright instead of an electric bass—an ironic twist, given that Jim & Jesse use an electric instrument in their bluegrass ensemble.) The songs are mostly well selected—there are a couple of great tunes from the Buck Owens catalog ("Foolin' Around," "Til These Dreams Come True"), a Mel Tillis chestnut ("Heart Over Mind"), and others from Roger Miller and Don Gibson, not to mention a few McReynolds originals played in that 1950s country-shuffle style. There's only one misstep (the inexcusably smarmy "Lovin' Machine"); for the most part, this is a completely charming album that may leave hardcore bluegrass fans cold but will appeal greatly to fans of pre-'70s country. *—Rick Anderson*

Jim & Jesse Today! / Mar. 19, 2002 / CMH ♦♦♦
Virginia natives Jim & Jesse McReynolds began in the late '40s as serious-minded bluegrass players; however, throughout their career (and despite inevitable returns to bluegrass) they have flirted with mainstream country and even rock & roll. That nomadic attitude is well represented on this collection. They did a cover album of Chuck Berry songs in the late '60s, and one Berry song, "Johnny B. Goode," shows up here. Meanwhile, the McReynolds originals on this effort, while not exactly mainstream, do tend to tread near commercial country waters (particularly the heart-worn ballad "Where Do We Go From Here"). Nevertheless, whether meeting the precise expectations of the bluegrass idiom or not, what distinguishes a Jim & Jesse album is Jesse's syncopated, crosspicking mandolin style and Jim's unwavering tenor harmony. And the brothers are in fine form here. *—Erik Hage*

First Sounds: The Capitol Years / Oct. 22, 2002 / Capitol ♦♦♦♦
Jim & Jesse's signing to Capitol Records in 1952 marked their recording debut as a duo (they had previously cut some gospel material as part of the Virginian Trio), not to mention their first work for a large record company. This album combines the results of their first two recording sessions, on June 13, 1952, and March 16, 1953. (At the second session, Jesse McReynolds was on leave from the army.) Originally, the tracks were released as singles. They have since been gathered on occasional Capitol albums and by the German Bear Family reissue label, but this is the first time they have reappeared domestically in many years. Accompanied by bandmates Hoke Jenkins (banjo) and Curly Seckler (second guitar), plus session bass player Bob Moore and fiddler James Loden, Jim McReynolds on guitar and vocals and Jesse McReynolds on mandolin and vocals perform an excellent bluegrass repertoire that includes "Are You Missing Me," the frenetic "Air Mail Special," and "A Memory of You." They are more polished than many rural performers, but still rough enough to have an authentic sound, and they benefit from the professional recording facilities of Capitol, so that the tracks are fresh and clear, showing little of their age on this CD reissue. These vintage performances are a welcome return to the ranks of Jim & Jesse's in-print recordings, and they compare favorably with the contemporary work of Bill Monroe and Flatt & Scruggs. The McReynolds brothers add new liner notes to the package. *—William Ruhlmann*

'Tis Sweet to Be Remembered / Apr. 15, 2003 / Pinecastle ♦♦♦
Fans of traditional music become so accustomed to the longevity of favorite bands that it's easy to imagine they'll always be around. Jim and Jesse had been performing mostly good-old-fashioned bluegrass since 1947, combining top-notch harmony and Jesse McReynolds' fancy mandolin work. It came as shock to the bluegrass community, then, when Jim McReynolds died of cancer on December 31, 2002. *'Tis Sweet to Remember* serves partly as a memorial and partly as Jim and Jesse's final project. Jesse McReynolds is joined here by Luke McKnight (his grandson), Matthew Allred (Jim's son-in-law), and Charles Whitstein for a dozen songs performed in the classic bluegrass style. Jesse McReynolds delivers fine versions of "As Long as I Live" and "Grin and Bear It," but the real excitement gets started when he's joined by McKnight and Allred for some good harmony on the choruses. The album is solid, but Jim McReynolds' tenor, an essential component of the brother's distinct sound, is missed. To compare, one only has to listen to "Tennessee" and "She's Running Wild," the two songs on which his vocals have been lifted from early recordings. *'Tis Sweet to Be Remembered* is a fine tribute to a great singer and one of bluegrass' most long-lasting bands. *—Ronnie D. Lankford Jr.*

Flaco Jimenez

b. Mar. 11, 1939, San Antonio, TX
Accordion, Vocals / Tex-Mex, Conjunto, Norteño, Tejano
Flaco Jimenez is the best known of the talented Jimenez family of Tex-Mex accordionists. He has always been popular in the border region, and came to the attention of the wider pop-music-buying public with the help of roots-music enthusiast Ry Cooder. Since then Jimenez has toured internationally, made guest appearances on a number of recordings, teamed up with Doug Sahm and Freddy Fender in The Texas Tornados, and continued to record on small labels for the Texas norteño community. *—Myles Boisen*

Flaco Jimenez & His Conjunto / 1978 / Arhoolie ♦♦♦
Flaco, son of Don Santiago Jimenez Sr., is the second generation of accordion players in his family (his son is now an up-and-comer). There was a time when the fringes of the rock world flirted with him. But here he plays the righteous border sound, with some fancier flourishes and more Anglo touches than the men of his father's era. These are classic polkas, rancheras, corridos (including one on Hurricane Beulah and his father's great "Mojado sin Licencia"). *—John Storm Roberts*

El Sonido De San Antonio / 1980 / Arhoolie ♦♦♦

Ay Te Dejo en San Antonio y Mas! / 1986 / Arhoolie ♦♦♦♦♦
Following on from his father Santiago Jimenez' own successful run as a conjunto musician in San Antonio, Flaco Jimenez put together a conjunto of his own in the '50s, eventually becoming one of the most famous figures in Tex-Mex music (also known as Musica Norteña in Mexico). Based on the polkas and waltzes Mexican performers refashioned as rancheras, the Tex-Mex conjunto style features accordion, the 12-string bajo sexto guitar, bass, and drums. Flaco immediately staked his claim in the music with a distinctly imaginative and lively accordion style, finding the ideal backing from equally able Tejano musicians, including his father and his son David. For this excellent 1985 recording, Flaco teams up with noted bandleader and bajo player Toby Torres, bassist Henry "Big Red" Ojeda, and drummer Isaac Garcia. The group works through a variety of song forms, including rancheras, boleros, danzons, and polkas. Along with a fine rendition of the ubiquitous "El Barrilito" ("Beer Barrel Polka"), other highlights include a version of Jimenez Sr.'s "Ay Te Dejo en San Antonio," the sensuous danzon instrumental "Juarez," and the Toby Torres vocal feature "Un Viejo Amor." Throughout, Flaco's playing comes off as both astonishing and very enjoyable, especially on the live recording "Traigo un Recuerdo." With ten extra tracks on the CD, this Flaco Jimenez release makes for substantial and fine listening. *—Stephen Cook*

Arriba El Norte / 1988 / Rounder ✦✦✦✦
Another in a series of Rounder anthologies featuring Flaco Jimenez. These were all done for the DBL label in San Antonio, and are short, predominantly polka and ranchero tunes. They're mostly rousing, celebratory party songs, sung with passion and played exuberantly by Jimenez. Unlike some other performers, Jimenez's approach and appeal are quite insular; he doesn't attempt to do anything flamboyant, unusual or non-traditional, opting to sing and play the material in vintage conjunto style. As a result, while it's often quite delightful, the differences in song structure over the 14 numbers will seem minimal to those who aren't fans of the idiom. *—Ron Wynn*

Flaco's Amigos / 1988 / Arhoolie ✦✦✦
This album was released by Arhoolie from recordings made between 1986 and 1988 of the great conjunto accordion player Flaco Jimenez playing with various friends of his in the music business—primarily Fred Ojeda, Ry Cooder, and Peter Rowan. Truthfully, on most of the tracks, the influence of his "amigos" is hardly noticeable. When Ry Cooder appears on mandolin by the time of "Jennette," the sound begins to change a bit away from the classic Tex-Mex sound to something almost a bit Hawaiian. Later on in the album, other songs with Cooder hold a less Tex-Mex feel, partially due to the instrumentation, but partly as well due to the change in mood or style from the musicians themselves. They're more relaxed on the Cooder sessions. Again though, the bouncing throb of the conjunto bass returns to pull the listener back to a San Antonio parking lot. Overall, it's quite a nice collection of music, though other Jiminez recordings might be somewhat more representative of his sound. *—Adam Greenberg*

Entre Humo Y Botellas / 1989 / Rounder ✦✦✦✦
Flaco Jimenez has been the most popular accordionist to perform, compose and record conjunto music, not only cutting numerous singles and albums for regional labels but also serving as a sideman for well-known rockers like Doug Sahm and Ry Cooder. This anthology was pulled from singles he recorded between 1982 and 1987 and features the major styles preferred by conjunto performers; these include the swaying, arresting polkas, rancheras and boleros, all done in Spanish, with Jimenez's accordion and vocals prominently in the upper register. Despite the absence of thematic or musical variety, this is a good opportunity to hear one of the masters and popularizers of a folk idiom at his best. *—Ron Wynn*

San Antonio Soul / 1991 / Rounder ✦✦✦
Flaco Jimenez has recorded dozens of conjunto songs and albums and done material for both the American and Latino markets. This 14-cut Rounder anthology featured material recorded for the Mexican-American audience, and includes tunes that address such issues as immigration and the lifestyle of the border community. There are three rollicking instrumentals that showcase Jimenez's ability and flashy style on accordion. Other songs include romantic fare and traditional polkas and rancheros. His vocals and instrumental abilities are quite impressive, and provide solid examples of classic ethnic music seldom heard outside its target area. *—Ron Wynn*

Partners / 1992 / Warner Bros. ✦✦✦
A very nice album from Jimenez, who's attracted attention as part of the Texas Tornados recently. He collaborates with an interesting variety of vocalists, as well as Los Lobos, producing an album filled with heart and warm energy, centered on the conjunto style and Jimenez's accordion work. It's good stuff indeed. *—Steven McDonald*

Un Mojado Sin Licencia / 1993 / Arhoolie ✦✦✦✦✦

Flaco's First! / 1995 / Arhoolie ✦✦✦✦✦
Containing material recorded between 1955 and 1956, *Flaco's First!* contains the first recordings that Flaco Jimenez ever made. Throughout this compilation, he is supported by bajo sexto player Henry Zimmerle, and the duo stand out among the rest of the band. *—Thom Owens*

Buena Suerte Senorita / Jun. 1996 / Arista ✦✦✦
Some good traditional accordion-based Tejano music from the king of the genre. The songs here don't stray far from one another and the basic sound for the style, but that tends to help the album as a whole in its coherence. Here, Flaco Jimenez is in his element, pumping out bouncing waltz and polka one after another, along with the basic song formats. It's dance music that's being put out here, and some quite good dance music at that. For someone who isn't acquainted with Tejano accordion music, this album would probably make a decent introduction, as a relatively standard and bland album in comparison to many others. For old fans of the style, this album might prove a bit unadventurous, but worth a listen for the sake of hearing Jimenez on the accordion in any capacity. *—Adam Greenberg*

● **The Best of Flaco Jimenez** / 1999 / Arhoolie ✦✦✦✦✦
Drawn from his Arhoolie recordings (there is also a live recording from the soundtrack of the Chulas Fronteras documentary), this is a satisfactory 16-track compilation with tracks spanning the '50s to the '80s, although, unfortunately, exact dates are not given in the liner notes. The different sources for the material allow for a greater range of sounds than is frequently heard on conjunto records. Although Flaco sings throughout, he also duets with Fred Ojeda, Toby Torres and Henry Zimmerle. Purists may frown on the inclusion of an instrumental, "Poquita Fe," with slide guitar by high-profile guest Ry Cooder, but frankly, for those who don't specialize in conjunto, it makes for a nice change of pace. Another Anglo, Peter Rowan, takes a guest vocal on his composition, "The Free Mexican Airforce." *—Richie Unterberger*

Santiago Jimenez Jr.

b. 1944

Accordion, Vocals / Zydeco, Tex-Mex, Conjunto, Norteño

Born in 1944, Santiago Jimenez Jr. was a singer and accordionist whose father made a significant contribution to the conjunto instrumental style. Conjunto, the accordion-based social music of Mexico and South Texas, was a style rooted in tradition. While his brother Flaco Jimenez mixed its sound with modern influences like jazz and country, Santiago upheld the traditions of his father and concentrated on the basic formula of two-button accordion with guitar and voice accompaniment. He released numerous albums, including a 1960 collaboration between his brother and him, numerous singles on local pressings, and a series of Spanish-language releases for the Rounder and Watermelon labels throughout the late '80s and 1990s. *—Johnny Loftus*

Familia Y Tradicion / 1989 / Rounder ✦✦✦
The songs on Jimenez's 1988 session for Rounder were mostly rigid, but spirited, emphasizing the polka and midtempo beat and sung in Spanish. Jimenez played the two-row button accordion, and his riffs and solos were fluidly expressed and superbly played, while his singing was intense and earnest. Only on "You Are My Sunshine" did Jimenez veer away from strict ethnic traditions to do a fun/throwaway piece. Otherwise, these were topical and/or vintage numbers that celebrated the conjunto sound with vigor and love. *—Ron Wynn*

El Gato Negro / 1990 / Rounder ✦✦✦
Santiago Jimenez Jr.'s trademarks are the two-row button accordion and passionate, fiery singing in the classic conjunto mode. This session featured 14 tracks, with Jimenez doing polkas, rancheros and boleros, but no pop or rock covers. The short numbers (none longer than four and a half minutes) were structured to give Jimenez's vocals and accordion bursts maximum space, while the backing players filled in tightly underneath him. This was contemporary conjunto with an authentic and vintage sensibility, performed by one of the idiom's major stars. *—Ron Wynn*

● **El Mero Mero De San Antonio** / Nov. 1990 / Arhoolie ✦✦✦✦
Son of conjunto great Santiago Jiminez, and brother of conjunto great Flaco Jiminez, Santiago Jiminez Jr. is in his own right an "ambassador for traditional Tex-Mex accordion music." So say the liner notes to this compilation of songs by the San Antonio musician. The works are from his other two Arhoolie albums: *El Mero Mero* and *Santiago Strikes Back*, along with some material recorded in 1988 but unreleased. The tempos and styles range from the Tejano mainstay the ranchero to polkas to mazurkas, boleros, huapangos, and cumbias. Every facet of the Tex-Mex accordion repertoire is represented. Realistically, even fans of conjunto might have heard of Santiago's father and brother before they've heard of him, but if that's the case, they might be missing out to some degree. Fans of the genre would likely enjoy this recording, though those new to the styles might be better suited listening to Flaco on Los Super Seven's debut album for a start. *—Adam Greenberg*

Corazon de Piedra / 1992 / Watermelon ✦✦✦
Santiago Jimenez Jr. has long labored in the obscuring shadow cast by his famous father Don Santiago Sr. and elder brother Flaco. *Corazon de Piedra* doesn't try to compete, but quietly and assuredly offers an intimate, backporch glimpse of one of Austin's masters of old-time traditional Tex-Mex conjunto music. This vintage working class form originated historically from a mingling of German and Czech settlers' waltzes and polkas with Mexican corrido song stories. The perfect disc for fans of Los Lobos who would enjoy exploring those roots somewhat deeper. *—Roch Parisien*

Canciones de Mi Padre / 1994 / Watermelon ✦✦✦✦
A dish that rarely disappoints is a son's expression of gratitude toward his father in the form of a tribute of some sort. When the subject is Tex-Mex music and the legacy of Don Santiago Jimenez, no one is better suited to create a tribute CD than Santiago Jimenez Jr. Of Don Santiago's two accordion-playing sons, he is the one who has dedicated himself toward carrying on directly in his father's musical tradition. This is one of America's great fusion musics, as it effortlessly combines accordion styles that came over on boats full of German immigrants with the songs of other travelers entering Texas from the north of Mexico. Listeners may want to take the challenge to see if the exact same accordion lick is indeed played on every one of the songs; even after many listens there are still the distractions of the rollicking vocals and the glorious sound of the bajo sexto, the light way it keeps the rhythm almost like a drummer playing brushes on the top of a 12-string guitar. Recorded just as well as any of the superior Arhoolie productions of norteño music, this is a love-filled collection of some of the most good-natured music around. *—Eugene Chadbourne*

Musica de Tiempos Pasados, Del Presente, Y Futuro / 1995 / Watermelon ✦✦✦✦
What a beautiful, moving and great sounding album this is. Jimenez (his friends call him Chief, according to the liner notes) plays great accordion and sings the border songs that he has revitalized, learned from his father in the old-time tradition. It is so great to hear the loose interdependent textures of this music. One can really get a sense of small-town celebrations untouched by the pervasive influence of contemporary American pop. The recording is so wonderfully full that the shifting dynamics through these tracks convey the immediacy of the playing even more. Some terrific tracks are "La Nopalera" (a polka) and "Prisaonero en Tus Brazos" (a ranchero). *—Richard Meyer*

Purely Instrumental / Apr. 21, 1998 / Arhoolie ✦✦✦
Instrumental quartet arrangements of polkas, vals, and the occasional danzon and tango, Jimenez handling the accordion and bajo sexto. All competently done, but it's so similar to so many other releases in the genre that it's difficult to imagine even Tejano enthusiasts getting worked up over this. *—Richie Unterberger*

El Corrido de Esequiel Hernandez: Tragedia de Redford / Jun. 22, 1999 / Arhoolie ✦✦✦
Besides a tejano collection of southwestern polkas, rancheras and cumbias led by bajo sexto guitar and Jimenez on accordion, this recording boasts two corridos (narrative ballads). One tells the tale of American student Esequiel Hernandez' demise (he was mistaken for an illegal immigrant by the Marines) and the other is about a migrant worker who enjoys some success in America but longs to return to Mexico. Notes and lyrics to *El Corrido* are in Spanish and English. *—Tom Schulte*

Johnnie & Jack

f. 1938, Nashville, TN, **db.** 1963

Group / Traditional Bluegrass, Traditional Country, Close Harmony

Johnnie & Jack mined the familiar turf of singing brother duos in the late '40s through the late '50s with a few distinct twists. For openers, they weren't blood brothers, just brothers in law. Secondly, they brought a new rhythmic strain to country music, both in their use of Latin beats and the unfettered drive of their combo, the Tennessee Mountain Boys. And of all the singing duos, they were the most inclined to stretch the boundaries of their sound, from bluegrass to sacred to amazing covers of R&B tunes with none of their country-soul diluted in the bargain. But for all their melding of outside influences, few artists—even in the mid-'50s—were as wholesale committed to sounding as "country" as they were. Whatever they played, sang, or wrote, it *always* sounded like Johnnie & Jack.

Johnnie Wright and Jack Anglin started playing together in 1938, forming a loose-knit country string band featuring Johnnie's new wife Muriel Deason, whom he would later rename Kitty Wells. Their sound in the early days was heavily influenced by both the Delmore Brothers and the Monroe Brothers, Charlie and Bill. As Johnnie plainly put it, "We were so green we didn't know you needed to develop your own style. We just out and out copied their sound in the beginning." An important member of the unit was Jack's brother Jim Anglin who contributed a high, lonesome tenor harmony both live and on records and contributed mightily as a songwriter during the duo's 25-year partnership.

Johnnie & Jack's band, now named the Tennessee Hillbillies, were just starting up the country food chain with sustaining radio broadcasts on local stations when World War II temporarily put the project on hold as Jack joined the Army. Reunited after the war, Johnnie & Jack—with Kitty now a permanent fixture of the band—picked up where they left off, adding an emcee/bass player named Smilin' Eddie Hill and a young guitarist named Chet Atkins to the fold. By 1947, they were filling in for Roy Acuff on the *Grand Ole Opry*, under the edict that they change their billing (*Opry* officials were loath to associate with any acts that used the word "hillbilly" in their name) to the Tennessee Mountain Boys and that Kitty sit out the radio performances as the *Opry* was top-heavy with female singers at the time.

At years' end, they had finally made their first records for the R&B-based Apollo Records out of New York City. After the non-success of those early 78s (the company refused to send promotional copies to radio stations to promote sales and airplay) and a quick side project with Ray Atkins and Clyde Moody as the King Sacred Quartette for the King label, the duo started recording for RCA Victor—their longest lasting label affiliation—in 1949. But even with Kitty recording solo and supplying high baritone harmonies on the duo's records, success proved elusive for the next few years. The troupe moved from one radio station to another, logging in time with the *Louisiana Hayride* and stations as far afield as Georgia and North Carolina. All of that changed with the release of their first hit, "Poison Love," in 1951, the tune making the Top Ten on all three *Billboard* country charts at the time. What Johnnie & Jack had done to crack the charts was to take their straight bluegrass harmonies and wed them to a distinct rhumba beat, principally supplied by studio bassist Ernie Newton, playing a maraca and wire brush simultaneously while handling the bass part. In the dark days of country music, where drums were outlawed on the stage of the *Grand Ole Opry* and electric instruments were only grudgingly accepted, this new approach was novel and influential. The combination proved a winner, one that the duo would return to on several recordings, complete with cha cha endings, which would become a Johnnie & Jack trademark.

With Kitty's success assured after the mega-success of "It Wasn't God Who Made Honky Tonk Angels," the duo combined with her to become one of the most in-demand road shows in country music. Within a couple of years, their sound would change again, adding bass singer Culley Holt from the Jordanaires to countrify a batch of R&B recordings, including the Moonglows' "Sincerely," the Four Knights' "(Oh Baby Mine) I Get So Lonely," the Delta Rhythm Boys' "Kiss Crazy Baby," and the Spaniels' "Goodnight, Sweetheart, Goodnight," all hits in the country field for the duo. This helped handle the onslaught of rock & roll better than most country artists of the day while keeping the roots of their sound intact. Johnnie & Jack made the *Billboard* country charts a total of 15 times and probably would have had more entries if the mid-'50s charts weren't limited to only mirroring the Top Ten songs of the day.

But by the late '50s, Johnnie & Jack's records were being mainstreamed into the Nashville Sound, with the Jordanaires, the Anita Kerr Singers, saxophones, and full rhythm sections burying their plaintive vocals beneath layers of reverb and pop sugar coating. Dissatisfied, the duo let their contract run out and signed with Decca Records in 1961. Their new company changed the spelling of their name to "Johnny & Jack," but at last the duo and Kitty were all on the same label again and with labelmates like Patsy Cline, Ernest Tubb, Webb Pierce, Red Foley, and Bill Monroe, they couldn't have been in better company. The contract produced no more hits than the tail end of their tenure with RCA, but with Kitty racking up hit after hit, the troupe had all the road work it could handle. It was coming back from one of these road trips that they were to learn of the plane crash deaths of Patsy Cline, Cline's manager, Randy Hughes, Hawkshaw Hawkins, and Cowboy Copas. On his way to the funeral parlor to attend memorial services for his fellow performers, Jack Anglin's car spun out of control, killing him instantly, thus ending the duo of Johnnie & Jack on an especially sad note. *—Cub Koda*

All the Best of Johnnie and Jack / 1970 / RCA Victor ✦✦✦✦✦

All the Best of Johnnie and Jack is a double LP that contains 24 of Johnnie & Jack's biggest hits for RCA Records, which were all recorded during the '50s and early '60s. The hit singles "(Oh Baby Mine) I Get So Lonely," "Poison Love," "Cryin' Heart Blues," "Three Ways of Knowing," "Goodnight, Sweetheart, Goodnight," and "Stop the World (And Let Me Off)" are all included, as are several other, lesser-known gems, making it an excellent, concise retrospective. It's the perfect introduction to one of the finest, and most underappreciated, groups in all of bluegrass and it is a shame that it isn't available on compact disc. *—Thom Owens*

Johnnie & Jack and the Tennessee Mountain Boys / 1992 / Bear Family ✦✦✦✦✦

Multi-disc box set of everything this country duo ever recorded. From their early bluegrass and gospel sides (some featuring Kitty Wells) to their rhumba beat hits of the '50s, it's all here. With heartfelt singing and playing, great songwriting and much good humor in abundance, all box set retrospectives should be this much fun to listen to. Highly recommended. *—Cub Koda*

At KWKH / 1994 / Bear Family ✦✦✦✦

Here are rare transcriptions from the original headliners of the *Louisiana Hayride* radio show, Johnnie, Jack, and Jack's wife, the illustrious Kitty Wells. Though the trio—with the rest of the Tennessee Mountain Boys—were at KWKH from 1948 through 1951, these transcriptions, buried in secrecy for decades, were probably recorded between early 1949 and early 1950. The set begins with the *Louisiana Hayride* theme, "Raining on the Mountain," as an introduction, and after the introductions are quickly made slips into a burning version of "Orange Blossom Special" followed by "White Dove," a bluegrass funeral song, full of high lonesome passion and Wells' forlorn alto. Wells is up next with a number from one of the later shows (they were either 15 or 30 minutes in length), "The Singing Waterfall," a pretty love song that takes a contralto vocal and jazzes up the arrangement so it borders on being a Western swing tune. Other folks on the Johnnie & Jack show included Paul Warren and his stomping fiddle, burning down the house at every opportunity as Johnnie & Jack tried to keep up and Wells went out for coffee or a doughnut. There are 19 selections here that don't necessarily add up to the rough-hewn majesty of the six-CD box set of Johnnie & Jack's collected studio recordings, and the sound quality is a bit shabby—though it's not Bear Family's fault, since these transcriptions are from acetates. But collectors will find this indispensable material that sheds light on a little-known period of the trio's beginnings, and the beginnings of the *Louisiana Hayride*. *—Thom Jurek*

● **For Old Times Sake** / Apr. 2003 / Bear Family ✦✦✦✦✦

In 2003, Bear Family released *For Old Times Sake*, a great single-disc compilation on Johnnie & Jack, one of the finest brother acts in country music. Most of their best performances are here, including the title track, "Poison Love," and "Goodnight, Sweetheart, Goodnight." *—John Bush*

The Johnson Mountain Boys

f. 1978, Washington, D.C., **db.** 1988

Group / Progressive Bluegrass, Traditional Bluegrass

During the 1980s, the Johnson Mountain Boys were contemporary masters of traditional bluegrass music who remained faithful to the old styles while keeping the songs fresh and original. The band was founded in the suburbs of Washington, D.C., by vocalist/banjoist/guitarist Dudley Connell, banjoist Richie Underwood, mandolinist David McLaughlin, fiddler Eddie Stubbs, and Larry Robbins on bass. The personnel changed over the years, but the group's sound remained consistent. The Johnson Mountain Boys made their recording debut with a single in late 1978; an EP soon followed and helped build a loyal audience in the D.C. area. They became festival favorites after the release of their self-titled debut. Their second album, *Walls of Time*, came out in 1982 and featured Connell, McLaughlin, Stubbs, and vocalist/banjoist/mandolinist Tom Adams. The same lineup recorded four more albums for Rounder during the early '80s. In 1986 Robbins departed and was replaced by Marshall Wilborn; Underwood left soon after, to be officially replaced by the mandolinist Adams. In 1988, the Johnson Mountain Boys announced that they planned to retire after a farewell concert in Lucketts, VA. Two years later, the Boys reunited briefly to play two festivals. But the reunions were so successful that the band basically reconstituted itself. The *Blue Diamond* LP appeared in 1993, followed by a live recording. By 1997's *Working Close*, Underwood had returned to the fold. *—Johnny Loftus*

Working Close / 1983 / Rounder ✦✦✦✦✦

Dudley Connell's chilling, high-lonesome lead vocals were only one of the delights of this militantly traditional, young bluegrass band. Any of their albums are among the best bluegrass of recent decades. *—Mark A. Humphrey*

Live at the Birchmere / 1984 / Rounder ✦✦✦

Let the Whole World Talk / 1987 / Rounder ✦✦✦

One of the finest records the Johnson Mountain Boys ever recorded, *Let the Whole World Talk* is an audaciously accomplished set of modernized bluegrass. The group slips a couple of excellent contemporary folk songs onto the record, but it is mainly notable for the way they make traditional songs into vibrant, vital and undeniably contemporary music. For its instrumentals, harmonies and arrangements, *Let the Whole World Talk* is one of the finest contemporary bluegrass albums of the late '80s. *—Thom Owens*

● **Favorites** / 1987 / Rounder ✦✦✦✦✦

Favorites features a terrific cross-section of highlights from the Johnson Mountain Boys' early-'80s Rounder albums and is the perfect introduction to their traditionalist bluegrass. *—Thom Owens*

Requests / 1988 / Rounder ✦✦✦

At the Old Schoolhouse / 1989 / Rounder ✦✦✦✦

At the Old Schoolhouse was recorded on the Johnson Mountain Boys' intended "farewell tour" of the late '80s. The group later decided to stick together, perhaps because they knew they were giving performances as good as this. Throughout *At the Old Schoolhouse*, the group gives lively, invigorating performances that prove traditional bluegrass isn't boring. It's a terrific live album, and one of the Johnson Mountain Boys' finest moments. *—Thom Owens*

Blue Diamond / 1993 / Rounder ✦✦✦

Blue Diamond is an excellent newgrass album that juxtaposes contemporary folk songs by Bob Dylan with standards by Carter Stanley, and country songs by Buck Owens. It proves that the Johnson Mountain Boys remain one of the best progressive bluegrass combos of the '70s and '80s. —*Thom Owens*

Earl Johnson

b. Aug. 24, 1886, Gwinnett County, GA

Speech/Speaker/Speaking Part, Fiddle, Guitar / Old-Timey, Traditional Country, String Bands

During the 1920s and '30s, the state of Georgia produced some of the wildest records in old-time or "hillbilly" music. Compared with the relatively steady, subtle, and sedate recordings by such groups as Charlie Poole's North Carolina Ramblers, the Georgia string bands, defined by flamboyant fiddlers like Gid Tanner, produced screeching strings and vocals on the brink of a masterful chaos. Of the Georgia fiddlers, Earl Johnson was one of the most chaotic. Born Robert Earl Johnson on August 24, 1886, in Gwinnett County, GA, he learned to play the fiddle from his father and spent his formative years playing with his two brothers, banjo-player Albert and guitarist Ester. Though both Albert and Ester died in 1923, Earl had by then begun playing with other nearby musicians, including the legendary Fiddlin' John Carson, who released the first commercial hillbilly record, also in 1923, thus paving the way for Johnson's own commercial success. Johnson made his recording debut in 1925 for Paramount, performing under the auspices of the Dixie String Band on some sides and backing banjoist Arthur Tanner on others. He also appeared as second fiddler and vocalist on several of Carson's records, with whom he continued to perform and record sporadically throughout his career. Johnson finally began recording under his own name and with his own bands in February of 1927, and over the next four years he produced close to 50 sides for the OKeh label.

Throughout these sessions, Johnson worked variously with his Dixie Entertainers and his Clodhoppers, both groups matching his characteristically wild fiddling with banjo, guitar, and energetic vocals. Emmett Bankston played banjo for both bands, while Lee "Red" Henderson replaced guitarist Byrd Moore on the Clodhopper recordings. Much of Johnson's sound and repertoire was clearly derived from the very popular Columbia recordings of Gid Tanner's Skillet Lickers, whose shrill falsetto backup vocals and frenzied instrumental breaks echoed throughout Johnson's recordings. Despite obvious debts to Tanner and the Skillet Lickers, Johnson's groups succeeded in creating some excellent, and even distinctive records of their own.

The very first side produced by the Dixie Entertainers was their classic version of "Ain't Nobody's Business," a piece which has itself come to be imitated by later performers and whose bizarre lyrics ("She runs a weenie stand, way down in no-man's land") could only have been sung by such an utter absurdist as Johnson. Occasionally, Johnson's fiddle or the accompaniment of the driving band slips beyond the reaches of rhythm, reason, and pitch, but such moments are more indicative of personal style than lack of mastery. Johnson's performances with the Dixie Entertainers and the Clodhoppers, consistently balancing technical expertise with a rowdy enthusiasm, rank him as one of the most significant fiddlers and string bandleaders of the period. He continued to record until 1931, and his legacy has survived into the 21st century through the performances of modern string bands such as the Freight Hoppers. —*Burgin Mathews*

● **Complete Recorded Works, Vol. 1 (1927)** / Dec. 3, 1997 / Document ✦✦✦✦

This set presents the first half of Earl Johnson's complete recordings with his Dixie Entertainers and, on the later tracks, his Clodhoppers. Recorded in 1927, these tracks are wonderful sides by an excellent, absurd entertainer whose wild fiddling and frenzied falsetto vocals reveal a substantial debt to Gid Tanner, the most famous of the crazy Georgia fiddlers. While Johnson borrows freely from Tanner's style and repertoire, descending occasionally into pure imitation, the body of his work reveals him ultimately as a fine, distinctive, and creative performer in his own right, backed by an able—and equally frantic—band. Easily rivaling Tanner's maniacal personality and performance, Johnson fiddles like a lunatic on the outskirts of a burning city, the instrument screeching and squealing its way through the high parts of one tune after another. His takes on such standards as "John Henry," "Boil Them Cabbage Down," and "Shortenin' Bread" keep the old pieces immensely fresh and exciting, as if they were being played for the first time; certainly they have seldom been played with such urgency. The bands also exhibit a skillfully controlled madness on such pieces as their driving "I Get My Whiskey from Rockingham" and the hilarious "Ain't Nobody's Business." For some listeners, Johnson's sound, with its screeches and lack of restraint, may be an acquired taste never quite acquired, and certainly a few of the performances on this set are wholly unspectacular; his eclectic approach, serious talent, and sheer enthusiasm, however, rank him as one of the most engaging and essential figures of early old-time music, and his best work is included here. Despite a few moments of weakness, this collection is an excellent introduction to Earl Johnson and should satisfy the needs of most listeners; for the collector who wants it all, though, Document has also provided a second volume. —*Burgin Mathews*

Complete Recorded Works, Vol. 2 (1927–1931) / Dec. 3, 1997 / Document ✦✦✦

One might excuse offensive titles like "Nigger on the Wood Pile" and "Nigger in the Cotton Patch" as unfortunate signs of the times when these old-timey tracks were recorded. But the annoying cackle of Earle Johnson (a kind of ugly uncle to Bob Wills' "a-hah") makes many of these tracks supremely unlistenable. As string bands go, Johnson's work was not the finest and this collection is proof. —*Tim Sheridan*

Michael Johnson

b. Aug. 8, 1944, Alamosa, CO

Guitar, Vocals / Soft Rock, Adult Contemporary, Singer/Songwriter, Contemporary Country, Progressive Country

Stylistically, singer/songwriter Michael Johnson has been all over the map, ranging from folk to pop and soft rock to country. But no matter what kind of music he recorded, he maintained a mellow, pleasant tone that served as his hallmark. Johnson was born in Alamosa, CO, in 1944 and started playing the guitar as a teenager, studying both rock & roll and jazz. At 21, he traveled to Barcelona and studied classical guitar with Graciano Tarrago for a year, then returned to the U.S. and joined the later version of the folk group the Chad Mitchell Trio (when John Denver was a member). Initially signing to Atco, Johnson released his first album, *There Is a Breeze*, in 1973 and displayed a gentle, folk-influenced sound.

He recorded three more albums for smaller labels in the mid-'70s, gradually transforming into more of a soft rock artist, and signed with EMI in 1978 in that capacity. He scored a number-one hit on the adult contemporary charts that year with "Bluer Than Blue," which almost made the pop Top Ten, and also made the adult contemporary Top Five with 1978's "Almost Like Being in Love" and 1979's "This Night Won't Last Forever." Johnson recorded five albums in all for EMI and in 1985 moved over to RCA, where he adopted a contemporary country style that stayed compatible with his soft, mellow leanings. He was surprisingly successful, scoring a total of five Top Ten country hits from 1986-1989, including the chart-toppers "Give Me Wings" and "The Moon Is Still Over Her Shoulder." After three country albums on RCA, Johnson moved over to Atlantic in 1991, which effectively halted his commercial momentum. He recorded very sporadically in the '90s for smaller labels. —*Steve Huey*

Wings / 1986 / RCA ✦✦✦✦✦

Johnson's first country album didn't stray far from the formula that gave him pop hits. The band on *Wings* is essentially the same as on "Bluer Than Blue," but Johnson leaned toward songs by Nashville writers. And what songs they were. *Wings* yielded two number-one singles, "Give Me Wings" and the ultra-romantic "The Moon Is Still over Her Shoulder." Those are the hits, but the quality songwriting runs as deep as any country album of the time. —*Brian Mansfield*

That's That / 1988 / RCA ✦✦✦

Dobro great Jerry Douglas guests on *That's That*, which features Johnson's chart-topping "The Moon Is Still Over Her Shoulder." —*Jason Ankeny*

The Best of Michael Johnson / 1990 / RCA ✦✦✦✦✦

A pair of number one hits—"Give Me Wings" and "The Moon Is Still Over Her Shoulder"—highlight *The Best of Michael Johnson*. —*Jason Ankeny*

Michael Johnson / 1991 / Atlantic ✦✦

As mellow as he wants to be, Michael Johnson is truly laid-back. The music is somewhere in the middle of country-ish pop and pop-ish country. This album features songs written by Hugh Prestwood, Mike Reid, Randy Sharp, and Don Schlitz, among others. Most albums are sequenced so that the stronger tracks are near the beginning, but, in this case, the last three songs are the best. The highlight of the ten-track album is "Company Man," by Bob McDill and Dan Seals. There's nothing here as memorable as his hits from the '70s, like "Bluer Than Blue"; but this self-titled release is pleasant enough. —*Tim Griggs*

Departure / 1995 / Vanguard ✦✦✦

Michael Johnson has a relaxed, pleasant voice with an ever-so-slight bluesy feel. The mellow songs on *Departure* complement his voice. The four tracks (including the title track) written by Hugh Prestwood plus the W. T. Davidson-penned "She's Real" are the highlights of this fine pop album. There's not a bad song in the bunch. Alison Krauss makes a subtle guest appearance. —*Tim Griggs*

● **The Very Best of Michael Johnson: Bluer Than Blue (1978–1995)** / Mar. 9, 1999 / Razor & Tie ✦✦✦✦✦

During the late '70s, soft rock and country-pop struck up a friendship and soon the lines separating the two genres were blurred beyond recognition. Glen Campbell was at the forefront of the movement, but few epitomize the entire genre like Michael Johnson, a former folkie who moved into soft rock as the '70s drew to a close. He had two big soft rock hits—"Bluer Than Blue" and "This Night Won't Last Forever"—before the decade finished, and as the '80s progressed, he slowly moved from the adult contemporary charts to the country listings without ever really changing his sound, as Razor & Tie's definitive compilation *Bluer Than Blue (1978-1995)* proves. There's really no difference in sound or style on any of these 17 songs; they all sound like variations on the same mellow vibe. Occasionally, the pop, folk, or country elements are emphasized, but Johnson's work retained a remarkably consistent tone over the course of 17 years. That's not to say that it's always interesting—part of the problem with soft rock is that it's hard to say why certain songs work and others don't, since they all share a similar aesthetic. Johnson was rarely adventurous but he could deliver the goods, even though listeners with a passing interest in the songwriter may find the material a little monotonous. That said, *Bluer Than Blue* does an excellent job of rounding up highlights from a career that was consistent in style but not in quality. Pop fans will be roped in by his two earliest hits, plus "Almost Like Being in Love," while country fans will use "Give Me Wings" and "The Moon Is Still Over Her Shoulder" as their entrance. Chances are both camps will find the entire disc satisfying—providing they were fans already, of course, since this music could sound quite dated to listeners unfamiliar with Johnson. —*Stephen Thomas Erlewine*

● **Classic Masters** / Jan. 29, 2002 / Capitol ✦✦✦✦✦

Michael Johnson was a '70s singer/songwriter with a gift for melody and a fondness for mellow arrangements, which meant that his records turned into warm, soothing soft rock instead of folksy musings. He later abandoned this trait, as he turned to contemporary country and then contemporary singer/songwriters, but his prime remains those late-'70s/early-'80s records, where his songwriting had a strong pop bent and a lush, engaging production. These are showcased to their best effect on EMI/Capitol's 2002 collection, *Classic Masters*. It contains highlights from his records for Capitol, including all of his big hits ("Bluer Than Blue," "This Night Won't Last Forever," "You Can Call Me Blue"), plus a bunch of lesser-known singles and album tracks. Razor & Tie's *You Can Call Me Blue* may cover more chronological ground, but Johnson's work past the early '80s can sound a little sterile no matter how well the songs are written, due to the recording. This boils his prime down to 12 songs, making it a great choice for the less-dedicated fans and soft rock aficionados and a perfect introduction for the curious. *—Stephen Thomas Erlewine*

Freedy Johnston

b. 1961, Kinsley, KS

Guitar, Vocals / Singer/Songwriter, Adult Alternative Pop/Rock, Americana

A gifted songwriter whose lyrics paint sometimes witty, often poignant portraits of characters often unaware of how their lives have gone wrong, Freedy Johnston seemingly appeared out of nowhere in the early '90s and quickly established himself as one of the most acclaimed new singer/songwriters of the day. Johnston was born in 1961 in Kinsley, KS, a small town with the odd distinction of being equidistant between New York City and San Francisco. Growing up, Johnston developed a strong interest in music, but living in a city without a music store or a record shop, doing something about it took some effort. When he was 16, Johnston bought his first guitar by mail order, and a year later, a friend drove him 35 miles to the nearest record store so he could buy an album he'd read about: *My Aim Is True* by Elvis Costello.

After high-school, Johnston enrolled at the University of Kansas in Lawrence; while his academic career didn't last very long (less than one year), Johnston wasted no time in immersing himself in the city's new wave scene and became a passionate fan of local legends the Embarrassment. Johnston also began listening to everything from Neil Young to XTC and developed a taste for country music. After several years of working in restaurants and writing songs on a four-track recorder in the evening, Johnston pulled up stakes in 1985 and moved to New York City. After several years of making the rounds, Johnston's work caught the attention of Bar/None Records, a respected independent label based in Hoboken, NJ.

Johnston made his recording debut in 1989 with two tracks on a Bar/None label sampler, *Time for a Change*, and his first album, the scrappy and genially eccentric *The Trouble Tree*, followed in 1990. While the album received largely positive reviews and became a minor hit in Holland, sales were poor in the U.S., and in order to finance recording of his second album, Johnston was forced to sell some farmland which had been with the Johnston family for generations (an decision Johnston set to music in his song "Trying to Tell You I Don't Know"). However, the risk paid off as 1992's *Can You Fly* earned enthusiastic reviews and was named among the year's best albums by *The New York Times*, *Billboard*, *Spin*, and *Musician Magazine*; Robert Christgau in *the Village Voice* went so far as to call it "a perfect album." The album also earned a healthy amount of alternative radio airplay, and *Can You Fly*'s success convinced Elektra Records to sign Johnston. His first set for Elektra, 1994's *This Perfect World*, received similarly positive press and spawned a minor hit single in the song "Bad Reputation." While Johnston's next three albums for Elektra—*Never Home, Blue Days Black Nights*, and *Right Between the Promises*—didn't fare as well in terms of sales, he maintains a loyal fan following and the respect of critics and peers. Johnston has also dabbled in film scoring by writing incidental music for the Farrelly Brothers comedy *Kingpin*, and he performs occasionally with the Know-It-All Boyfriends, an informal cover band featuring Butch Vig and Doug Erikson of Garbage. *—Mark Deming*

The Trouble Tree / 1990 / Bar/None ✦✦✦✦

Johnston's debut, though not without its rough edges, firmly established him as a talent to be reckoned with—even his earliest songs are marked by great maturity and insight. *—Jason Ankeny*

Can You Fly / Apr. 14, 1992 / Bar/None ✦✦✦✦✦

A giant step forward from his likable but ragged debut, Freedy Johnston's *Can You Fly* is a stunningly accomplished and coherent album that recalls the raw lyricism of such quintessentially American writers as Raymond Carver and Richard Hugo. Johnston sold his family's Kansas farm to finance the recording of *Can You Fly*, a fact that's cited in the record's opening line and reflected in several autobiographical songs about the guilty downside of pursuing a dream. Elsewhere, Johnston creates rich character studies of people who are vaguely aware that their lives have gone awry but aren't sure what to do about it. If Johnston's stories are bleak, however, the delicacy of his melodies and simple, clean production ensure that hearing them is downright exhilarating. Standouts include the wistful gambler's lament "The Lucky One," the tender "Mortician's Daughter," and especially the supernatural-tinged title track. Syd Straw contributes vocals on one track, the lovely duet "Down in Love." *—Kristi Coulter*

Unlucky / 1993 / Bar/None ✦✦✦

The six-song EP *Unlucky* features *Can You Fly*'s tale of Las Vegas woe, "The Lucky One," in both its completed and demo forms. In addition to three new Johnston originals, it also contains a terrific cover of Jimmy Webb's "Wichita Lineman." *—Jason Ankeny*

● **This Perfect World** / Jun. 28, 1994 / Elektra ✦✦✦✦

Freedy Johnston's major-label debut is less consistently stunning than its predecessor, 1992's *Can You Fly* but, taken on its own terms, it affirms his position as one of the best songwriters of his generation. Certainly no one paints more evocative portraits of lonely, disappointed people. The majority of these 12 tracks are about men who either know or strongly suspect that they've done something unforgivable, and such is Johnston's mastery as a lyricist that it's even subtly apparent when his narrators are lying to themselves. Johnston frames his bleak narratives with melodic, chiming folk-rock; if anything, the predominantly midtempo songs and radio-ready Butch Vig production are a little too smooth, robbing *This Perfect World* of the edge that made *Can You Fly* so piercing. The most memorable tracks are the sparsest ones, where Johnston's words and appealingly plain voice take center stage. In addition to the melancholy opener, "Bad Reputation," other highlights include "Can't Shake This Town" and the witty "Dolores"—few songwriters could pack so many *Lolita* allusions into three minutes of guitar pop without sounding too clever by half. Best of all is the mournful, eerie title track, which describes the possibly mortal sins of one man's past and the hopelessness of his future with the economy and punch of a good short story. *—Kristi Coulter*

Never Home / Feb. 25, 1997 / Elektra ✦✦✦✦✦

From the propulsive opener "On the Way Out" to the lilting closer "Something's Out There" (about, of all things, a UFO abduction), the sparkling *Never Home* is Johnston's most musically and emotionally expansive outing to date. Finding a sympathetic ear in producer and guitarist Danny Kortchmar, Johnston's songs transcend their dark themes to reveal unexpected and heretofore unseen moments of warmth and sentimentality; even edgy, Randy Newman-like character studies such as "He Wasn't Murdered" and "Gone to See the Fire" offer moments of tenderness which their subjects (suicide and arson, respectively) can't suppress. *—Jason Ankeny*

Blue Days Black Nights / Jul. 20, 1999 / Elektra ✦✦✦✦

The darkest, most understated Freedy Johnston record to date, *Blue Days Black Nights* is also the singer's most intimate effort, largely rejecting the quirky character studies of prior outings in favor of more plainly personal narratives, and revealing new shades of depth and honesty in the process. Co-producers T-Bone Burnett and Roger Moutenot cloak Johnston's songs in dusky atmospherics which underscore the music's spare beauty—far removed from the crackling pop flavor of the preceding *Never Home* or even the shimmering folk of *This Perfect World*, *Blue Days Black Nights* possesses a hushed gravity which insinuates itself only over repeated listens. At times the results are overly ponderous, but a handful of tracks—the opening "Underwater Life" and "Moving on a Holiday" included—rank among Johnston's finest. *—Jason Ankeny*

Right Between the Promises / Aug. 7, 2001 / Elektra ✦✦✦✦

Right Between the Promises comes across as simultaneously the flip side of, and a companion piece to, 1999's *Blue Days Black Nights*. Where that album's songs flowed with an ominous energy barely concealed by the moody, hushed tones of their surface, *Promises* forces those same emotions out into the light—a cathartic, rocked-out release to *Nights*' endless tension. The result? Smart, darkly ambiguous songs that nevertheless seem built for high volume, summertime play on a car stereo. *Promises* continues the slant toward vague, impressionistic character studies, and away from narrative Johnston started on that previous album. In a way, though, it's telling that his sole cover here is an unabashedly straight version of Edison Lighthouse's '70s bubblegum hit "Love Grows (Where My Rosemary Goes)"—and more telling that he does it so well. Even the strangest stuff here has a certain accessibility: The chunky, harmonically fractured blues "Back to My Machine" holds attention despite its overly ambitious, science fiction-themed lyrics. The few tunes that hark back to the subdued quality of *Nights* have a new aura of poppiness, too; the gentle guitar hook in "Arriving on a Train" sounds breezy rather than just forebodingly delicate, and not even the prominent cellos and violins seem mournful. The disc includes the first studio appearance of "Radio for Heartache," previewed on Johnston's 2000 live record *Live at 33 1/3*. *Right Between the Promises* may not be as richly nuanced as his very best work, but it's still a fine example of his idiosyncratic brand of intelligent, radio-friendly folk-rock. *—Kenneth Bays*

Buddy Jones

d. 1950

Vocals / Traditional Country, Honky Tonk

Buddy Jones is one of the most interesting, but sadly overlooked, figures of early honky tonk. A police officer from Shreveport, LA, Jones recorded several singles for Decca Records during the late '30s and early '40s before abandoning his musical career. Jones began singing with Jimmie Davis, a fellow Louisiana politician, in 1935, recording a number of duets for Decca over the course of the next year and a half. Jones went solo in 1937, recording with his brother Buster on steel guitar. After releasing a series of singles, which were nearly all risqué honky tonk, Bob Dunn, a former steel guitarist for Cliff Bruner, replaced Buster in Buddy's band. Jones continued to record for Decca until 1945, when he essentially retired from the music business. Buddy Jones died in 1950. *—Stephen Thomas Erlewine*

● **Louisiana Honky Tonk Man** / 1984 / Texas Rose ✦✦✦✦

Louisiana Honky Tonk Man covers the highlights of Buddy Jones' recordings for Decca Records. Jones was one of the forgotten pioneers of honky tonk, and these recordings—which were made between 1935 and 1941—are among the most risqué honky tonk of the era. There are prototypical honky tonk blues like "Shreveport County Jail Blues" and "Ease My Troubled Mind," but much of Jones' material grew out of the dirty blues, as evidenced by "She's a Hum-Dum Dinger," "Butcher Man Blues," "I'm Going to Get Me a Honky Tonky Baby," and "She's Sellin' What She Used to Give Away." *Louisiana Honky Tonk Man* has 16 of his best cuts, functioning as the finest retrospective—indeed, the *only* retrospective—of his unappreciated career to date. *—Stephen Thomas Erlewine*

David Lynn Jones

b. Jan. 15, 1950, Bexar, AR

Guitar, Vocals / Contemporary Country, New Traditionalist, Progressive Country

David Lynn Jones began performing in clubs around his Arkansas hometown while still a teenager. For a while during the late '60s, he worked as a car salesman, but he quit in 1970 to become the bass player for Freddy Morrison & the Bandana Blues Band and to hone his songwriting skills. Jones tried to sell his songs in Music City, but he wasn't successful; by 1975, he was barely making a living as a session musician in Houston, TX. Matters improved in 1976 when he provided Randy Corner with "Heart Don't Fail Me Now," which became a Top 40 hit. Later, with the help of producer Ritchie Albright, Jones made a demo tape for Mercury Records. He played every instrument but the saxophone on the tape, which eventually made its way to Willie Nelson, who recorded Jones' song "Living in the Promiseland" in 1986. The song went straight to number one on the country charts.

Jones then released his debut album, *Hard Times on Easy Street* (Mercury, 1980). Albright produced the album and also helmed 1989's glossier, pop-oriented follow-up, *Wood, Wind and Stone*. Jones jumped to Liberty for 1992's *Mixed Emotions*, which he recorded in the studio at his home in Bexar, AR. With the Nashville sheen of the first two records removed, Jones could concentrate on his songs and let his personal style show through. He followed the album with *Play by Ear* in 1994. Since 1985, Jones had written songs for the Nashville publishing house Blue Water Music. He stayed with the company until 1998. He continued to work as a producer for other artists at his Alamo Studios in Bexar. *—Johnny Loftus*

Hard Times on Easy Street / 1980 / Mercury ✦✦✦

David Lynn Jones' debut album *Hard Times on Easy Street* showcases a talent that arrived fully formed. Though Jones doesn't push any musical boundaries, his ear for straightforward, rock-inflected rootsy country is impeccable, as is his talent for Dylan-esque lyrics and Springsteen-esque narratives. Jones would later push out into more adventurous musical directions, but the straightforward country and heartland rock on *Hard Times on Easy Street* remains his most rewarding outing. *—Thom Owens*

Wood, Wind and Stone / 1989 / Mercury ✦✦

Jones' label considered employing *Wood, Wind and Stone* as a means of breaking the singer into the pop market; while the plan fell through, the record still feels slick and overproduced, its glossy sheen at odds with Jones' soul-searching lyrics. *—Jason Ankeny*

● **Mixed Emotions** / 1992 / Liberty ✦✦✦✦✦

After two albums for Mercury that left his promise unfulfilled, David Lynn Jones switched labels and recorded an album in his home studio in Bexar, AR. Like a saved man flirting with sin, Jones forsakes Nashville wisdom and takes his cues from renegade American rockers like Leon Russell and Robbie Robertson. In his heart he's still country, but he revs the tempos, cranks the guitars, and lays on the horns as he takes off screaming into the Arkansas Delta. *—Brian Mansfield*

Play by Ear / Apr. 5, 1994 / Liberty ✦✦✦

George Jones

b. Sep. 12, 1931, Saratoga, TX

Guitar, Vocals / Traditional Country, Country-Pop, Honky Tonk, Nashville Sound/ Countrypolitan, Country Gospel

By most accounts, George Jones is the finest vocalist in the recorded history of country music. Initially, he was a hardcore honky tonker in the tradition of Hank Williams, but over the course of his career he developed an affecting, nuanced ballad style. In the course of his career, he never left the top of the country charts, even as he suffered innumerable personal and professional difficulties. Only Eddy Arnold had more Top Ten hits than Jones, and Jones always stayed closer to the roots of hardcore country.

George Jones was born and raised in East Texas, near the city of Beaumont. At an early age, Jones displayed an affection for music. He enjoyed the gospel he heard in church and on the family's Carter Family records, but he truly became fascinated with country music when his family bought a radio when he was seven. When he was nine, his father bought him his first guitar. Soon, his father had Jones playing and singing on the streets of Beaumont, earning spare change. At 16, he ran away to Jasper, TX, where he sang at a local radio station. Jones married Dorothy, his first wife, in 1950 when he was 19 years old. The marriage collapsed within a year and he enlisted in the Marines at the end of 1951. Though the U.S. was at war with Korea, Jones never served overseas—he was stationed at a military camp in California, where he kept singing in bars. After he was discharged, Jones immediately began performing again.

In 1953, Jones was discovered by record producer Pappy Daily, who was also the co-owner of Starday Records, a local Texas label. Impressed with Jones' potential, Daily signed the singer to Starday. "No Money in This Deal," Jones' first single, was released in early 1954, but it received no attention. Starday released three more singles that year, which all were ignored. Jones released "Why, Baby, Why" late in the summer of 1955 and the single became his first hit, peaking at number four. However, its momentum was halted by a cover version by Webb Pierce and Red Sovine that hit number one on the country charts.

George Jones was on the road to success and Pappy Daily secured the singer a spot on the *Louisiana Hayride*, where he co-billed with Elvis Presley. Jones reached the Top Ten with regularity in 1956 with such singles as "What Am I Worth" and "Just One More." That same year, Jones recorded some rockabilly singles under the name Thumper Jones which were unsuccessful, both commercially and artistically. In August, he joined the cast of the *Grand Ole Opry* and his first album appeared by the end of the year. In 1957, Starday Records signed a distribution deal with Mercury Records and George Jones' records began appearing under the Mercury label. Pappy Daily began recording Jones in Nashville and his first single for the new label, "Don't Stop the Music," was another Top Ten hit. Throughout 1958, he was landing near the top of the charts, culminating with "White Lightning," which spent five weeks at number one in the spring of 1959. His next big hit arrived two years later, when the ballad "Tender Years" spent seven weeks at number one. "Tender Years" displayed a smoother production and larger arrangement than his previous hits, and it pointed the way toward Jones' later success as a balladeer.

In early 1962, Jones reached number five with "Aching, Breaking Heart," which would turn out to be his last hit for Mercury Records. Pappy Daily became a staff producer for United Artists Records in 1962 and Jones followed him to the label. His first single for UA, "She Thinks I Still Care," was his third number-one hit. In 1963, Jones began performing and recording with Melba Montgomery. During the early '60s, mainstream country music was getting increasingly slick, but Jones and Montgomery's harmonies were raw and laden with bluegrass influences. Their first duet, "We Must Have Been Out of Our Minds" (spring 1963), was their biggest hit, peaking at number three. The pair continued to record together throughout 1963 and 1964, although they never again had a Top Ten hit; they also reunited in 1966 and 1967, recording a couple of albums and singles for Musicor. Jones had a number of solo hits in 1963 and 1964 as well, peaking with the number three "The Race Is On" in the fall of 1964.

Under the direction of Pappy Daily, George Jones moved to the new record label Musicor in 1965. Jones' first single for Musicor, "Things Have Gone to Pieces," was a Top Ten hit in the spring of 1965. Between 1965 and 1970, he had 17 Top Ten hits for Musicor. While at Musicor, Jones recorded almost 300 songs in five years. During that time, he cut a number of first-rate songs, including country classics like "Love Bug," "Walk Through This World With Me," and "A Good Year for the Roses." He also recorded a fair share of mediocre material and given the sheer amount of songs he sang, that isn't surprising. Although Jones made a couple of records that were genuine tributes or experiments, he also tried to fit into contemporary country styles, such as the Bakersfield sound. Not all of the attempts resulted in hits, but he consistently charted the Top Ten with his singles, if not with his albums. Musicor wound up flooding the market with George Jones records for the rest of the '60s. Jones' albums for Musicor tended to be arranged thematically and only two, his 1965 duet *George Jones & Gene Pitney* and 1969's *I'll Share My World With You*, charted. That meant that while Jones was one of the most popular and acclaimed singers in country music, there was still a surplus of material.

Like his discography, George Jones' personal life was spinning out of control. He was drinking heavily and began missing concerts. His second wife Shirley filed for divorce in 1968, and Jones moved to Nashville, where he met Tammy Wynette, the most popular new female singer in country music. Soon, Jones and Wynette fell in love; they married on February 16, 1969. At the same time Jones married Wynette, tensions that had been building between Jones and his longtime producer Pappy Daily culminated. Jones was unhappy with the sound of his Musicor Records, and he placed most of the blame on Daily. After his marriage, Jones wanted to record with Wynette, but Musicor wouldn't allow him to appear on her label, Epic, and Epic wouldn't let her sing on a Musicor album. Furthermore, Epic wanted to lure Jones away from Musicor. Jones was more than willing to leave, but he had to fulfill his contract before the company would let him go.

While he continued recording material for Musicor, Epic entered contract negotiations with their rivals and halfway through 1971, Jones severed ties with Musicor and Pappy Daily. He signed away all the rights to his Musicor recordings in the process. The label continued to release Jones albums for a couple of years and they also licensed recordings to RCA, who released two singles and a series of budget-priced albums in the early '70s. Jones signed with Epic Records in October of 1971. It was the culmination of a busy year for Jones, one that saw he and Wynette becoming the biggest stars in country music, racking up a number of Top Ten hits as solo artists and selling out concerts across the country as a duo. Jones had successfully remade his image from a short-haired, crazed honky tonker to more relaxed, sensitive balladeer. At the end of the year, he cut his first records for Epic.

George Jones' new record producer was Billy Sherrill, who had been responsible for Tammy Wynette's hit albums. Sherrill was known for his lush, string-laden productions and his precise, aggressive approach in the studio. Under his direction, musicians were there to obey his orders and that included the singers as well. Jones had been accustomed to the relaxed style of Pappy Daily, who was the polar opposite of Sherrill. As a result, the singer and producer were tense at first, but soon the pair developed a fruitful working relationship. With Sherrill, Jones became a full-fledged balladeer, sanding away the rough edges of his hardcore honky tonk roots.

"We Can Make It," his first solo single for Epic, was a celebration of Jones' marriage to Wynette written by Sherrill and Glenn Sutton. The song was a number-two hit early in 1972, kicking off a successful career at Epic. "The Ceremony," Jones and Wynette's second duet, followed "We Can Make It," and also became a Top Ten hit. "Loving You Could Never Be Better," followed its predecessors into the Top Ten at the end of 1972. By now, the couple's marriage was becoming a public soap opera, with their audience following each single as if they were news reports. Even though they were proclaiming their love through their music, the couple had begun to fight frequently. Jones was sinking deep into alcoholism and drug abuse, which escalated as the couple continued to tour together. Though every single he released in 1973 went into the Top Ten, George Jones' personal life was getting increasingly difficult. Tammy Wynette filed for divorce in August 1973. Shortly after she filed the papers, the couple decided to reconcile and her petition was withdrawn. Following her withdrawal, the duo had a number-one single with the appropriately titled "We're Gonna Hold On." In the summer of 1974, Jones had his first number one hit since "Walk Through This World With Me" with "The Grand Tour," a song that drew a deft portrait of a broken marriage. He followed it with another number-one hit, "The Door." Not long after its release, he recorded "These Days (I Barely Get By)," which featured lyrics co-written by Wynette. Two days after he recorded the song, Wynette left Jones; they divorced within a year.

The late '70s were plagued with trouble for George Jones. Between 1975 and the beginning of 1980, he had only two Top Ten solo hits—"These Days (I Barely Get By)" (1975) and "Her Name Is" (1976). Though they divorced, Jones and Wynette continued to record and tour together, and that is where he racked up the hits, beginning with the back-to-back 1976 number ones, "Golden Ring" and "Near You." The decrease in hits accurately reflects the downward spiral in Jones' health in the late '70s, when he became addicted not only to alcohol, but to cocaine as well. Jones became notorious for his drunken, intoxicated rampages, often involving both drugs and shotguns. Jones would disappear for days at a time. He began missing a substantial amount of concerts—in 1979 alone, he missed 54 shows—which earned him the nickname "No-Show Jones."

Jones' career began to pick up in 1978, when he began flirting with rock & roll, covering Chuck Berry's "Maybellene" with Johnny Paycheck and recording a duet with James Taylor called "Bartender's Blues." The success of the singles—both went Top Ten—led to an album of duets, *My Very Special Guests*, in 1979. Though it was poised to be a return to the top of the charts for Jones, he neglected to appear at the scheduled recording sessions and had to overdub his vocals after his partners recorded theirs. That same year, doctors told the singer he had to quit drinking, otherwise his life was in jeopardy. Jones checked into a rehab clinic, but left after a month, uncured. Due to his cocaine addiction, his weight had fallen from 150 pounds to a mere 100. Despite his declining health, Jones managed a comeback in 1980. It began with a Top Ten duet with Tammy Wynette, "Two

Story House," early in the year, but the song that pushed him back to the top of the charts was the dramatic ballad "He Stopped Loving Her Today." The single hit number one in the spring of the year, beginning a new series of Top Ten hits and number-one singles that ran through 1986. The string of hits was so successful, it rivaled the peak of his popularity in the '60s. "He Stopped Loving Her Today" was followed by the Top Ten "I'm Not Ready Yet" and an album, *I Am What I Am*, in the fall of the 1980. *I Am What I Am* became his most successful album, going platinum.

Throughout 1981 and 1983, he had eight Top Ten hits. Although he was having hits again, he hadn't kicked his addictions. Jones was still going on crazed, intoxicated rampages, which culminated with a televised police chase of Jones, who was driving drunk, through the streets of Nashville. Following his arrest, Jones managed to shake his drug and alcohol addictions with the support of his fourth wife, Nancy Sepulvada. Jones and Sepulvada married in March of 1983. Soon after their marriage, he began to detoxicate and by the end of 1983, he had completed his rehabilitation. Jones continued to have Top Ten hits regularly until 1987, when country radio became dominated by newer artists; ironically, the artists that kept him off the charts—singers like Randy Travis, Keith Whitley, and Dwight Yoakam—were heavily influenced by Jones himself. Jones and Sepulvada moved back to Nashville in 1987. In 1988, he recorded his final album with Billy Sherrill, *One Woman Man*. The title song, which was a hit for Johnny Horton in 1956, was Jones' final solo Top Ten hit. *One Woman Man* was his last record for Epic Records.

After its release, he moved to MCA, releasing his first record for the label, *And Along Came Jones*, in the fall of 1991. In between its release and *One Woman Man* arrived a duet with Randy Travis, "A Few Ole Country Boys," that was a Top Ten hit in the fall of 1990. Jones' records for MCA didn't sell nearly as well as his Epic albums, but his albums usually were critically acclaimed. In 1995, he reunited with Tammy Wynette to record *One*. In April of 1996, Jones published his autobiography, *I Lived to Tell It All*. In 1998, he returned with another studio album, *It Don't Get Any Better Than This*. Following the release of *It Don't Get Any Better Than This*, Jones moved from MCA to Elektra/Asylum, who signed him on the provision that he would record hardcore country music. Jones was completing work on his debut for the label when he crashed his car into a bridge in Nashville on March 6, 1999, critically injuring himself. Amazingly, he pulled through the accident, but the investigation proved that Jones had been drinking and driving—a troubling revelation, given his long history with alcoholism. He pled guilty to a lesser charge, DWI, and entered a rehab program. The release of his Elektra/Asylum debut, *Cold Hard Truth*, went on as scheduled, appearing in stores in the summer of 1999. *—Stephen Thomas Erlewine*

The Grand Ole Opry's New Star / 1957 / Starday ✦✦✦

Long Live King George / 1958 / Starday ✦✦✦✦

Hillbilly Hit Parade / 1958 / Starday ✦✦✦

Country Church Time / 1959 / Mercury ✦✦✦

The Crown Prince of Country Music / 1960 / Starday ✦✦✦

George Jones Salutes Hank Williams / 1960 / Mercury ✦✦✦✦
George Jones Salutes Hank Williams was recorded at Mercury Records, toward the beginning of Jones' career. At this stage, George still sounded similar to Hank Williams, but he had begun to incorporate much of Williams' vocal techniques into a distinctive vocal style of his own. If Jones had recorded these songs while still at Starday, they wouldn't be as exciting as they are now—since he had moved beyond mimicking into his own style, he's able to invest Williams' songs with grit and passion, instead of just copying Hank. It's an affectionate, entertaining tribute, featuring some of the greatest songs ("Cold Cold Heart," "Hey Good Lookin'," "Half As Much," "Jambalaya," "Why Don't You Love Me," "Honky Tonkin'," "Settin' the Woods on Fire") in country music. [The 1984 reissue is slightly shorter than the original issue and features liner notes by Elvis Costello]. *—Stephen Thomas Erlewine*

George Jones Sings Bob Wills / 1962 / Razor & Tie ✦✦✦✦
Bob Wills' songbook—which, of course, includes tunes popularized, not written, by Wills—is one of the most resilient in country music, ranking alongside Hank Williams in popularity and its ability to be reinterpreted in continuously fresh fashions. So, it comes as no surprise that George Jones, one of the greatest singers in country, did a bang-up job with his tribute album, the 1962 platter *George Jones Sings Bob Wills*. Where some Wills tributes are faithful to a fault, Jones, as produced by Pappy Daily, plays these songs as hardcore honky tonk, occasionally informed by Western swing, but only as a coloring device. He is singing these songs in his signature pure country style, and the results are pretty terrific, not only because this is the hardest country he cut at United Artists, fueled by a crackerjack band playing at its peak, but because these are tremendous songs that are open to such a sly reinterpretation as given to them by Jones and Daily. Furthermore, in addition to the standards—"Bubbles in My Beer," "Faded Love," "Roly Poly," "Take Back to Tulsa," "Time Changes Everything," and "San Antonio Rose"—he finds a few obscurities in "The Warm Red Wine," "Worried Mind," and "Silver Dew on the Bluegrass Tonight," which help accentuate his own spin on Wills' music. This record is so good, you're inclined to forgive Jones for sitting out the last two songs and letting the bandmembers play since, after all, they, like the Possum or any other musician, sound at their best when playing the music of Bob Wills & His Texas Playboys. And that's why this is a small treasure in George Jones' discography. *—Stephen Thomas Erlewine*

Sings Country and Western Hits / 1962 / Mercury ✦✦✦
While not a George Jones masterwork, this album is the equivalent of going to hear a really great country cover band in which Jones is the lead singer, and the set includes such numbers as "I Walk the Line" by Johnny Cash. The lights are dim in this imaginary country bar, affording the same amount of informational access as a listener has on the liner notes to this album. Thus, even with the benefit of squinting, it is impossible to say who exactly is in the band, although the bandmembers are obviously adept professional pickers. One and all attack the material with enthusiasm, and on a certain level this can be looked at as some kind of country music ideal. This is a recording of songs played pure and simple, from the heart and for a little bit of money, and recorded properly but without a lot of production hoopla. The three Jones originals that come at the end all have the special zest he brings to his material, especially the rollicking "You Gotta Be My Baby." In retrospect, these originals make the balance of the material actually seem like the work of a cover band in comparison. *—Eugene Chadbourne*

Sings the Hits of His Country Cousins / 1962 / Razor & Tie ✦✦✦✦
A compilation of various performances George Jones recorded at United Artists, including album tracks, singles, and new performances, *Sings the Hits of His Country Cousins* is an entertaining hodgepodge of Jones' versions of classic country songs. There's a wide variety of styles on the album, from the Western swing of Bob Wills' "Silver Dew on the Bluegrass Tonight" and the honky tonk of Hank Williams' "I Could Never Be Ashamed of You" and Webb Pierce's "The Same Sweet Girl" to the pop leanings of Hank Cochran's "A Little Bitty Tear," the traditional country of Roy Acuff's "The Precious Jewel," and the country gospel of "Peace in the Valley" and "Wings of a Dove." Despite the fact that the album features songs recorded at different sessions and music that is stylistically opposed, every cut is first-rate, which makes *Sings the Hits of His Country Cousins* one of his most enjoyable, if not one of his most consequential, United Artists albums. *—Stephen Thomas Erlewine*

Homecoming in Heaven / 1962 / Razor & Tie ✦✦
Boasting a more lavish production than his secular albums, *Homecoming in Heaven* is George Jones' second collection of gospel songs. The majority of the songs on the album are newly written, including selections from Willie Nelson, J.P. Richardson (the Big Bopper), and George himself. Pappy Daily has assembled a choir to support Jones, which places the music somewhere between traditional, stripped-down country gospel and polished, Nashville country-pop. George is in good voice throughout, but there are only two genuine classics on the album, "Wings of a Dove" and "Peace in the Valley," which are both available on Liberty's more consistent collection *All-Time Greatest Hits*. *—Stephen Thomas Erlewine*

My Favorites of Hank Williams / 1962 / Razor & Tie ✦✦✦
George Jones' second tribute to Hank Williams in a matter of years, *My Favorites of Hank Williams* was originally released on United Artists in the early '60s. None of the songs on *My Favorites* were featured on George's Hank tribute on Mercury Records, but given Williams' extensive catalog, that isn't surprising. *My Favorites* does differ from the previous Mercury recordings in terms of production—the UA release is slightly smoother, yet it is still firmly in the honky tonk tradition. George doesn't put a new spin on any of these songs—which include "You Win Again," "Your Cheatin' Heart," "I Could Never Be Ashamed of You," "You're Gonna Change (Or I'm Gonna Leave)," "Mansion on the Hill"—but he delivers them with affection and grit, making the record a thoroughly enjoyable listen. *—Stephen Thomas Erlewine*

The New Favorites of George Jones / 1962 / United Artists ✦✦✦
The New Favorites of George Jones is a mixed bag that is highly indicative of the crossroads country music faced in the early '60s. Stylistically, *New Favorites* is all over the place, as it tries to appeal to not only Jones' hardcore honky tonk audience, but also to country-pop fans and those listener that had been seduced by the burgeoning rock & roll audience. So, honky tonk weepers like "She Once Lived Here" and "She Thinks I Still Care" sit next to uptempo country-pop cuts like "What Am I Worth" and "Imitation of Love," and that only scratches the surface of what's here. There's also folk ballads ("Open Pit Mine"), crossover attempts ("Poor Little Rich Boy," "Running Bear"), the requisite novelties ("Best Guitar Picker"), and the ridiculous "White Lightnin'" rewrite, "Root Beer." Even the dated material like the novelties and crossovers are enjoyable, but Jones is at his best when he's singing honky tonk or country-pop. Still, the wide range of material on *New Favorites* does prove that neither artists, producers, or labels knew how to retain the splintering country audience of the '50s. *—Stephen Thomas Erlewine*

I Wish Tonight Would Never End / 1963 / United Artists ✦✦✦

The Novelty Side of George Jones / 1963 / Mercury ✦✦✦

The Ballad Side of George Jones / 1963 / Mercury ✦✦✦✦✦

George Jones Sings Like the Dickens! / 1964 / Razor & Tie ✦✦✦
Given George Jones' love for novelty songs, it isn't surprising that he recorded a tribute album to the king of country novelties, Little Jimmy Dickens. What is surprising is his approach. On *George Jones Sings Like the Dickens!* Jones bypasses all of Dickens' biggest hits, choosing to concentrate on personal favorites, which happen to be songs that Dickens interpreted, not ones that he wrote (only two of the 12 songs were co-written by Dickens). Jones realizes that although Dickens was famous for his novelties, he was a first-rate balladeer and he patterns his own album according to his idol's strengths. Jones gives a fine performance, but it's a bit too laid-back to make a lasting impression. There are a handful of gems (particularly "We Could," "It Scares Me Half to Death," "Making the Rounds," and "I've Just Got to See You Once More") scattered throughout *Sings Like the Dickens!* and the album is never anything less than enjoyable, even though nothing on the record approaches the transcendent. ["It Scares Me Half to Death" and "Take Me as I Am (Or Let Me Go)" also appear on *The Race Is On*.] *—Stephen Thomas Erlewine*

Bluegrass Hootenanny / 1964 / United Artists ✦✦

Country & Western #1 Male Singer / 1964 / Mercury ✦✦✦

I Get Lonely in a Hurry / 1965 / United Artists ✦✦✦

King of Broken Hearts / 1965 / United Artists ✦✦✦

Old Brush Arbors / 1965 / Musicor ♦♦♦
Old Brush Arbors features 12 country gospel songs notable not only for Jones' particularly strong performances but also for being one of the rare times that George himself is credited with writing more than half of the songs himself. *—Chris Woodstra*

Mr. Country & Western Music / 1965 / Musicor ♦♦♦

New Country Hits / 1965 / Musicor ♦♦♦♦
The music on this album is what is really happening, so the inevitable discussion of the cover will be dispensed with first. It is indeed a beautiful yet garish color picture of a country band. The jackets the guys in the band are wearing are stunning. In fact, the members of the Jones Boys get to wear nicer threads than their boss George Jones, if this album cover is any indication. That is probably just one example of what a nice guy Jones is, that is when he isn't 50 sheets to the wind. But back to the cover. Jones has a fantastic haircut, true. But it inevitably loses out to staring at the pair of glasses one of the sidemen is wearing. These are glasses that comedian Mike Myers would kill for, if only to give his satires of the '60s some authenticity. Johnny Paycheck, eventually a country star in his own right, is one of the Jones Boys, easily recognizable on both front and back cover photos. OK, so it is one of the great country & western album covers. The music totally lives up to whatever expectations are created by this artwork. The musicians sound wonderful here, creating a sentimental old-time country sound when necessary in the devastating "I'm Wasting Good Paper" or delivering the type of twangy honky tonk country fans associate with Bakersfield, CA, Buck Owens & His Buckaroos. The band also handles enough harmony vocal to sound like the type of vocal group that sometimes gets dragged into the studios at country & western recording sessions. The influence Jones had on Paycheck is also demonstrated, as some of the more electric and peppier numbers here could easily keep company on any of that artist's early Starday albums. The rhythm section is excellent; check out "Along Came You" or the classic "Feeling Single—Seeing Double" for prime examples of what a good country band should sound like. The latter tune, sparked here by a guitar solo loaded with interstellar reverb, is one of several numbers here by the under-rated Nashville song craftsman Wayne Kemp. Another good Kemp number here is "I'd Rather Switch Than Fight." Of course the premier, number-one attraction is the voice of Jones. The slightly strained, bluegrass-influenced high-end vocals are here, along with overwhelming dips into the baritone end and phrasing that rivals that of jazz singer Billie Holiday's, although she never got to sing a lyric such as this line from Leon Payne's "Things Have Gone to Pieces": "Someone threw a baseball through my window. . . ." *—Eugene Chadbourne*

Trouble in Mind / 1965 / United Artists ♦♦♦♦

Famous Country Duets / 1965 / Musicor ♦♦♦

George Jones & Gene Pitney: For the First Time! Two Great Singers / 1965 / Musicor ♦♦♦

The Race Is On / 1965 / Razor & Tie ♦♦♦
The title track to *The Race Is On* is one of George Jones' biggest hits. With its galloping beat and clever, funny lyrics, the single gives the impression that the rest of the record is a return to Jones' honky tonk roots. Although there are several uptempo numbers, *The Race Is On* is dominated by ballads, like the majority of his UA albums. But *The Race Is On* boasts a stronger, more varied set of songs than most of his '60s albums, ranging from ballads like "They'll Never Take Her Love From Me" and the Western swing of "Time Changes Everything" and the skittering honky tonk of "Don't Let the Stars Get in Your Eyes." There are a couple of weak moments—ironically, one is "She's Mine," which was co-written by George—but the album remains one of his strongest from the mid-'60s. ["It Scares Me Half to Death" and "Take Me as I Am (Or Let Me Go)" also appear on *Sings Like the Dickens!* and "Time Changes Everything" appears on *Sings Bob Wills*.] *—Stephen Thomas Erlewine*

We Found Heaven Right Here on Earth at "4033" / 1966 / Musicor ♦♦♦

I'm a People / 1966 / Musicor ♦♦♦

Love Bug / 1966 / Musicor ♦♦♦♦

It's Country Time Again! / 1966 / Musicor ♦♦♦

Close Together as You and Me / 1966 / Musicor ♦♦♦

Cup of Loneliness / 1967 / Musicor ♦♦♦

Walk Through This World With Me / 1967 / Musicor ♦♦♦

Book of Memories / 1967 / United Artists ♦♦♦

George Jones & Melba Montgomery / 1968 / Deluxe ♦♦♦

Sings the Songs of Dallas Frazier / 1968 / Musicor ♦♦♦♦♦
Since his beginnings at Musicor, George Jones covered countless songs by Dallas Frazier—Frazier's songs would frequently occupy more than half of an album—so an entire album devoted to his songwriting comes as no surprise. And while the big production numbers, complete with backup by the Jordanaires, may put off some country purists, the album serves as a true testament to both the singer and the songwriter. In light of the label's constant recycling and repackaging of material, the most surprising thing about this record is that none of the songs have appeared on any previous album. *—Chris Woodstra*

If My Heart Had Windows / 1968 / Musicor ♦♦♦
After some experimentation (both failed and successful) at Musicor, George returned for a more-or-less straight honky tonk album with *If My Heart Had Windows*. Though the record boasts his typical overblown late-'60s production, it's kept in check for the most part. Two Top Ten hits—the title track and "Say It's Not You"—are included on the record, as well as the classic "Your Angel Steps Out of Heaven" and the quirky album closer "Poor Chinee." *—Chris Woodstra*

Song Book & Picture Album / 1968 / Starday ♦♦♦
What an unusual item. This typical Starday mishmash of items from the recording archive originally came with what was advertised as a 32-page color songbook with words and music as well as pictures and stories about the songs. This may have not been a large edition, and used record store hounds have to face the unfortunate possibility that this treasured booklet might be long gone by the time a copy of this side makes it their way. Deluxe souvenir book aside, this collection of Jones material is goofier than usual, and will definitely appeal to fans of Jones' old buddy Roger Miller for this reason. Two songs that Jones and Miller wrote together are featured. One of them, "Tall Tall Trees," is often picked as one of Jones' best recordings. The song selection also includes a larger percentage of original Jones material than normal for one of his albums and he seems to be under something of a Miller influence, although there is a little bit more of a honky tonky, near rockabilly feel to some of the material. There are Miller-ish, clever turns of phrase but there is also Jones' own "Window Up Above," one of the great country ballad recordings. Inexplicably, two tracks are given over to fairly lame instrumentals. The liner note claims these numbers are "performed . . . in the Western swing dance style that George Jones uses on his personal appearances"—which fortunately for Jones' career was a lie. *—Eugene Chadbourne*

I'll Share My World With You / 1969 / Musicor ♦♦♦

Where Grass Won't Grow / 1969 / Musicor ♦♦
The album title might be a reference of some sort, perhaps to the top of Jones' head when he has applied an excess of greasy kid's stuff to hold his flattop in place, or perhaps to the spot of former lawn where "ol' possum" regularly keeps his beer cooler. But a song about farmers suffering from harsh climactic conditions? The presence of such a dreary subject alone indicates the degree to which this singer was floundering around during his days with the Musicor label. Weeping over an old flame's coffin is one thing, and party boy Jones even had to be forced to go there. It might be playing into the hands of the Nashville establishment to suggest that the ills of this record can be surmised from looking at the cover photograph of the artist, and that actually listening to the music is not at all necessary. The most casual appraisal of both the haircut and the suit chosen for the photograph indicate a personality crisis. Who am I? Where am I going? No longer a honky tonker, OK but a shame, attempting to be not only respectable but nice, perhaps not such a great idea. It is the equivalent of the Columbia album where Johnny Paycheck was cleaned up and posed on the cover in jaunty leisure suit, a *The New York Times* under his arm. Musically, that project is the equivalent of this one, both needlessly bland and the inevitable result of trying to tame the wild stallion. The label's house crew of pickers, uncredited here as is usually the case with this outfit, do a pretty decent job of sounding like a country band, but neither they nor Jones can do much with the material here. The star seems to be receiving songs from only a handful of sources here, none of which do him much justice. Like grass, much better Jones grows in abundance on the discographical hillside. *—Eugene Chadbourne*

Will You Visit Me on Sunday? / 1970 / Musicor ♦♦
When people criticize George's Musicor recordings for over-the-top arrangements and intrusive sappy vocal choruses, they're probably thinking of albums like this one. Released during Jones' last year at Musicor, *Will You Visit Me on Sunday* doesn't sound like a country album. In fact it doesn't even *look* like a country album—the cover shows a seductive model and spells out the title in neo-psychedelic, wavy orange print. While *Will You Visit Me on Sunday* lacked hits and its sound may have represented a new peak in slick production for Jones, the songs on the album (many of which were written by Dallas Frazier) are all top-notch. Jones' voice has never sounded this confident and his overall approach on this album would serve as a blueprint for his '70s work on Epic. *—Chris Woodstra*

The Best of George Jones / 1970 / Musicor ♦♦♦
This fine package features George Jones tracks from his Musicor output. The only complaint about this record is that it's too short. One standout on this record is "Your Angel Steps Out," which Gram Parsons later covered. *—Jim Worbois*

The Great Songs of Leon Payne / 1971 / Musicor ♦♦♦♦♦
One of many songbook albums that George Jones recorded while at Musicor Records, *The Great Songs of Leon Payne* is one of the finest minor gems in the Possum's catalog. Though Payne's reputation as a terrific honky tonk songwriter was well-known among country music fans, he only had a handful of hits, which were often recorded by other artists. Granted, the biggest of those were Hank Williams' versions of "Lost Highway" and "They'll Never Take Her Love From Me" as well as his own "I Love You Because," but the depth of Payne's songwriting is not well-known to many casual country fans. George Jones' tribute album remedies that fact. Apart from "They'll Never Take Her Love From Me" and Jones' hit single "Things Have Gone to Pieces," these songs are all rather obscure and there's not a bad one in the bunch. From ballads like "Blue Side of Lonesome" to uptempo honky tonkers like "Brothers of a Bottle," all of the cuts on *The Great Songs of Leon Payne* are first-rate and Jones brings each of them to life. It's a forgotten album in Jones' catalog—and Leon Payne's reputation has faded somewhat in the decades following his death—but that doesn't change the fact that *The Great Songs of Leon Payne* is one of his best records of the '60s. *—Stephen Thomas Erlewine*

☆ **George Jones with Love** / 1971 / Musicor ♦♦♦♦♦
By 1970, George Jones' stay at Musicor had been marked by a glut of sloppy releases that would continually repackage and repeat material in different thematically based "concept" albums; initially it would seem that *George Jones With Love*, with its lineup of all love-based songs, would fall into this disposable category. One listen, however, shows this to be an exception to the rule. Beginning with the wonderful "A Good Year for the Roses" (one of his all-time greatest performances), Jones tackles affairs of the heart from all directions—from the joy and excitement of newfound love to the warmth of a settled

relationship to the pain and despair of separation and its aftermath. He's clearly focused on each song, pouring the proper emotion and passion into each performance. It still may not be a "concept album" by rock & roll standards, but it does serve as a high point for Jones' Musicor period as well as one of his greatest, most consistent albums. *—Chris Woodstra*

The Best of Sacred Music / 1971 / Musicor ✦✦✦✦✦

We Go Together / Nov. 13, 1971 / Epic ✦✦✦

Jones made his debut for Epic with *We Go Together*, his first duet album with his wife Tammy Wynette. Recorded only three years into their marriage, the album focuses on the joys of their love and has an optimistic eye toward the future—chapter one of the soap opera the two would commit to vinyl over the next several years. The two redo three songs from George's catalog—"Take Me" (a Top Ten hit both times), "Never Grow Cold," and "A Girl I Used to Know" (this time titled "Someone I Used to Know"). *—Chris Woodstra*

☆ **A Picture of Me (Without You)** / 1972 / Epic ✦✦✦✦✦

Perhaps even George Jones doesn't know how many records he's cut over the course of his career and, given the assembly line production methods that were the order of the day in Nashville throughout the '50s, '60s, and '70s, a great Jones album was often a matter of fate rather than careful design—if Ol' Possum got a batch of good songs that week and was working with a producer who wasn't an utter schlockmeister, then maybe Jones would get the great album he deserved. *A Picture of Me (Without You)* was one such album where Jones lucked into something sublime; it was one of his first sets with producer Billy Sherrill, and while Sherrill's fondness for glossy surfaces wouldn't immediately seem compatible with Jones' hard honky tonk soul, he managed to give these sessions a low-key, late-night feel that was a fine match for the bluesy tone of Jones' voice. And the Music Row publishers sent by a stack of really good demos while they were putting together *A Picture of Me (Without You)*; the title cut is one of Jones' best songs on his favorite theme, failed romance (as are "Another Way to Say Goodbye" and "Tomorrow Never Comes"), "Second Handed Flowers" is a fine story-song from Tom T. Hall, "That Singing Friend of Mine" is just gutsy enough to overcome its innate sentimentality, and "She Loves Me (Right Out of My Mind)" communicates the thrill and despair of a love affair with no future. And as a singer, Jones was at the top of his form when he cut this album; if you want to know why Gram Parsons called Jones "the king of broken hearts," one spin of this album will tell you all you need to know. While it's a bit less ambitious than later albums like *The Battle* and *The Grand Tour* in terms of fine songs sung with beauty and feeling, George Jones albums rarely get much better than *A Picture of Me (Without You)*. [In 1998, it was released on CD in tandem with another solid Jones set from the early '70s, *Nothing Ever Hurt Me (Half as Bad as Losing You)*.] *—Mark Deming*

George Jones (We Can Make It) / 1972 / Epic ✦✦✦

Jones' first solo outing for Epic in 1972 is a rough concept album built around George's own optimism and joy about his marriage to Tammy Wynette, even though cracks were already beginning to show in their real-life relationship. Jones' voice sounds mature, settled and smooth—a perfect combination with Billy Sherrill's decidedly non-country, slick production style. *—Chris Woodstra*

Me and the First Lady / 1972 / Epic ✦✦✦

The second chapter in the George and Tammy saga still finds the couple pretty happy, settling into a mostly imaginary domestic life. Not all is well though, as told in "A Lovely Place to Cry" and "The Great Divide," which contemplate fading love and the possibility of divorce. The two continue to hold on, still in love, and even go as far as to recreate their wedding ceremony in the album closer, "The Ceremony," seemingly to reaffirm their vows. *—Chris Woodstra*

We Love to Sing About Jesus / 1972 / Razor & Tie ✦✦

George Jones and Tammy Wynette had both made fine gospel records as solo artists, but when it came time to record their first together, they failed to come up with something memorable. Over-produced, overwrought, and under-written, *We Love to Sing About Jesus* is largely comprised of songs by Earl Montgomery, with the rest of the album devoted to contemporary country gospel by the likes of Dallas Frazier and Tom T. Hall. Billy Sherrill's trademark grandiose productions are made even bigger by the presence of the Jordanaires and the Nashville Edition on backing vocals. Though the production is overbearing, it would have been forgivable if more than a handful of songs—namely, the single "Old Fashioned Singing," the singalong title track, and Hall's "Me and Jesus"—were memorable. Instead, the songs are almost entirely mediocre and forgettable, making the production the only noticeable thing about the album. Though the album is short, the bombastic production gets a little nerve-wracking about halfway through the album, and by the end of the record the music hasn't provided much inspiration. In all, a wasted opportunity. *—Stephen Thomas Erlewine*

☆ **Nothing Ever Hurt Me (Half as Bad as Losing You)** / 1973 / Epic ✦✦✦✦✦

Nothing Ever Hurt Me (Half as Bad as Losing You) was the second album in the George Jones/Billy Sherrill collaboration and built on the strengths of *A Picture of Me (Without You)*. Sherrill backed off a bit on the lushness of the previous album and retrained more of Jones honky tonk persona on the title track (by Bobby Braddock), "You're Looking at a Happy Man," and "Never Having You" (by Tom T. Hall). The uptempo nature of the disc was the last record Jones would make like this until he recorded with Merle Haggard in the 1980s. This is not to say that ballads aren't plentiful here. There's a fine read of "What's Your Mama's Name?" by Peanut Montgomery and Dallas Frazier, that Sherrill had cut with Tanya Tucker a year earlier when she was just 14 and went straight to number one. Also, Jones' readings of "Made For the Blues," and Left Frizzell's "Mom and Dad Waltz," are solid, tender honky tonk ballads that offer the deep raw emotion in the singer's best material. Tammy Wynette and Peanut Montgomery's "You'll Never Gow Old (To Me)," is a love song delivered in the classic Jones manner with Sherrill using a Phil Spector-ish approach to arrangement and layering the piano on top of a wash of strings and a meandering pedal steel. Sherrill and Jones collaborated on "What Many Woman Can't Do," another of the Jones love songs, but done in midtempo honky tonk strut is dynamite in its presentations. Here the steel is in front of everything except Jones vocal. The strings, backing vocals and acoustic guitar are separated out to offer a sense of space in the mix. The final cut, "Wine (You've Used Me Long Enough")", written by Jones and Wynette is a bitter surrender song to a lover—alcohol. It was prophetic in that it was the single biggest factor in ending their marriage. This is a dynamite set that offered a solid look at what Jones and Sherrill were capable of—and delivered—in the coming years. *—Thom Jurek*

We're Gonna Hold On / 1973 / Epic ✦✦

Only the album cover—two separate, non-smiling photos of George and Tammy partially overlapping each other—and a handful of the tracks attempt to directly tell the story of the dissolving marriage on this, the fourth duet album. Far more telling though is the inclusion of rather disjointed crowd pleasers like "Roll in My Sweet Baby's Arms" and the semi-novelty hit "(We're Not) The Jet Set"—by this point, the two had become a part of the touring machine and the album seems to built around a stage show. The songs, outside of the title track (a number-one hit), aren't particularly memorable. *—Chris Woodstra*

Let's Build a World Together / 1973 / Epic ✦✦✦

The chemistry that develops between partners in a male and female country music duo can sometimes be based on fantasy, as was obviously the case with Loretta Lynn and Ernest Tubb, who no country listener even imagined for a moment were romantically involved. Tammy Wynette and George Jones, on the other hand, did have a relationship. As the details of it became public knowledge, often resembling pages torn out of sleazy novels written by Jim Thompson, the inevitable result was that the music the two made started to sound somewhat dull and dreary in comparison. The reasons for this are musical, however, and were there in the tracks all along. For one thing, and it is a mighty big thing at that, the persona of Jones gets toned down for these tracks. Along with that also goes much of the rocking, honky tonk flavor that is part of the best music this artist makes. The closest Jones gets to the type of losers he normally brings to life is the joker in "My Elusive Dreams," who keeps flitting from one disaster to the next, good ol' "Stand By Your Man" Tammy at his side. This is the best track in the set, despite the fact this is an overplayed number from the '60s country songbook. "After the Fire Is Gone" is also a well done tune, the bitterness and cynicism flavored country style, which means plenty of pedal steel. It is too bad there are not more country songs here of the quality of the Louvin Brothers' "When I Stop Dreaming," as much of this material seems like it was hammered out by country songwriting teams too enamored with these giant country stars to relax and come up with something that isn't just romantic tripe. And that isn't said lightly. Just as some country fans will decide to buy an album based on provocative or amusing song titles, a look at the titles here and one will want to put the record back on the shelf. The singers themselves don't do that much better when whipping out the songwriting notebooks, either. The blend of these two beautiful voices is of course a great moment in country history, but this is one of those albums where it is the songs, and not the singers, that have to provide something for the country fan to gnaw on other than distracted thoughts about what the world they built might have really been like. *—Eugene Chadbourne*

☆ **The Grand Tour** / 1974 / Razor & Tie ✦✦✦✦✦

Creatively, 1974 was a hell of a year for George Jones. Two of his finest Epic recordings were issued during that year, *The Grand Tour*, and *Alone Again*. Jones' partnership with producer Billy Sherrill saw some of its finest fruit here. The Grand Tour in particular was a watershed for Jones, boasting the title track as one of the most devastating country singles ever issued that came so close to crossing over it was being played on some adult pop stations along with Sinatra, Bennett, Dionne Warwick, and Herb Alpert. Ironically, one of the co-author's of the tune was none other than Jones' about to be ex-wife Tammy Wynette's future husband George Richey. If ever there were a song that cut too close to home for the singer it was this one and Sherrill worked his most creative magic over it. With a string section that only revealed the size of itself when he wasn't singing and filled in between the guitars, piano and pedal steel during the sung lines. Jones poured his heart into every syllable and its chilling quality after almost 30 years attests to this. But this cut was only the beginning, "'Pass Me By (If You're Only Passing Through)" with the Jordanaires, is one of those haunting midtempo honky tonk love songs that won't let go after the first chorus has been sung. As ballads go, "She'll Love the One She's With," by Hank Cochran and Grady Martin is one of those jealous country waltzes where obsession and love continually cross each other. Shored up by a small string orchestra, and a pedal steel cascading through the vocal lines, it's wrenching and poetic. Johnny Paycheck's classic ballad "Once You've Had the Best," is given poetic and musical justice by Jones and Sherrill; in fact, this version blows away the author's. And in a nod to both Bakersfield and Jones' "Thumper" period, "The Weatherman," is a honky tonk stomper also partially authored by Richey and it sounds as if it were written just for this session; coming in the middle of a host of broken love songs, this is an optimistic, even giddy tune with a Mickey Raphael harmonica solo and a Don Rich sound-alike guitar break in the middle. Ultimately, this is Jones' country, the kind of country music that is pure, yet as sophisticated as Sherrill wanted it to be. Chet Atkins and all of his countrypolitan productions never had anything on Sherrill, and with the greatest singer in the music's history as part of the team combined with a collection of absolutely staggering songs—only *I Am What I Am* rivals it—this is one of the finest country records of the '70s and perhaps in the Top 100 of all time. *—Thom Jurek*

Memories of Us / 1975 / Epic ✦✦✦✦✦

This is the one country fans both looked forward to and were almost too anxious to speak about, and perhaps dreaded: the first George Jones album after his divorce from Tammy

Wynette. The title track, with its personal historical metaphors of abandoned movie theaters, and other geographical locations are metaphorical for a relationship that is not bittersweet, but full of grief. The same is true of denial in "A Goodbye Joke" and "She Should Belong to Me," and "She Once Made a Romeo Cry." Here is denial and regret and astonishment all rolled into one on a record album. Jones, with Billy Sherrill, let down the guard and answered the forbidden questions before fans and/or media asked them. "What I Do Best," is a song which claims the protagonist's finest skill is missing his lover. There is some comic relief in "Have You Seen My Chicken," a cut about guitar picker, and there is laughter in front of Jones' tears on the swinging two-step of "Bring on the Clowns." The final track is the bitterest cut Jones ever recorded. He claims he wrote it at 3 a.m. in the aftermath of the divorce. It comes right from the Hank Williams' tradition of catharsis songs. Jones condemns everyone and everything including himself. As he denies his shortcomings, he fires back simultaneously, with razor-sharp fineness his anger. That fiddle floating in the background offers a portrait of loneliness and rage that is unbridled and self-destructive in the classic honky tonk style. Jones began a run of recordings with *the Grand Tour* in 1974 that would last pretty much through 1980. *Memories of Us* is one of those records that cannot be played all the time, but when in the proper space for a heartbreak record, none will fit the bill better. —*Thom Jurek*

Battle / 1976 / Epic ✦✦✦

The *Battle* from 1976, is one of the most confusing records George Jones ever released. And, like many records of his mid-'70s period with Epic, it's an effort as inspired and emotionally satisfying as anything he has done. While nothing touches the *Grand Tour* musically, the *Battle* is nonetheless a gorgeous record. Released immediately after *Memories of Us*, it's the first post-divorce album the singer and his producer Billy Sherrill made after the Jones/Tammy Wynette divorce was over. The *Battle* is more poignant of the two because while its title suggested a concept album, it is anything but. In fact, it's an exercise in the conflict of emotions from sadness and loss, denial, anger, and grace. And everything here is a love song. There's "The Battle" itself, which tells the story. It begins with a string section and snare drums playing the refrain from the "The Battle Hymn of the Republic," and as a piano enters on top of the snares, Jones is telling the story of his regret for his ruthlessness and for winning the battle, but he loses to himself in the war. The mixed emotions in "I Can't Get Over What Lovin' You Has Done," and "Baby, There's Nothing Like You," are in classic Jones' balladic style before the rambling rounder honky tonk of "The Nighttime (And My Baby)," and "I'll Come back," are two jumping country tunes that reflect the unwillingness to surrender the inevitable. But "Wean Me," sums it all up… "If you can still believe/Take this bottle from my hand and wean me… I've got a feeling with your help/ I still might be a man/Take this bottle from my hand and wean me." Too little, too late and Jones sings it like he wishes it were still possible. "Love Coming Down," offers more self-recrimination and begs for another opportunity; again it's sung from the other side—the past. It's a devastating track, one that sums up not only the marriage with Wynette, but Jones entire life up to that point. Sherrill's use of the pedal steel here, which is constant in the song, adds to the depth and dimension of the lyric. The album closes with "I Still Sing the Old Songs," by David Allan Coe, with a fiddle mournfully playing "Red River Valley" and "Dixie," in the background. The story is one of continuance, forbearance and the willingness to continue, to move through whatever has befallen the protagonist and "rise again." And he's still rising. —*Thom Jurek*

Alone Again / 1976 / Epic ✦✦✦✦

The classic cover—a picture of George alone in a diner, staring forlornly at his milkshake—pretty much sums up the feeling of this *Alone Again*, a low-key, morning-after look at regret and loneliness. As always, Jones sings from the heart and from his own real life experiences dealing with the aftermath of his failed marriage. Despite a generally depressive mood, George pulls off one of his greatest novelty songs, "Her Name Is…," one of only a handful of hits he managed during his mid-'70s slump. —*Chris Woodstra*

Greatest Hits [George Jones & Tammy Wynette] / 1977 / Epic ✦✦✦

Released in 1977, a few years after they divorced but while they were still occasionally touring and recording together, *Greatest Hits* contains the ten biggest hits George Jones and Tammy Wynette had as a duet, including "Golden Ring," "The Ceremony," "We're Gonna Hold On," "Near You," and "(We're Not) The Jet Set." Since this was a ten-track vinyl collection from the late '70s, it's very, very brief—about 27 minutes long—but it does contain every truly noteworthy hit they had as a duo and is enjoyably concise. However, keep in mind that all ten songs are on the 1999 collection *16 Biggest Hits*, which may be a little bit more, but does indeed offer more songs—and that may be enough of a reason to get that collection instead, even if this is a snappier listen. —*Stephen Thomas Erlewine*

Bartender's Blues / 1978 / Razor & Tie ✦✦

Recorded at the height of the rock & roll establishment's infatuation with George Jones in the late '70s, *Bartender's Blues* is one of the most uneven and mis-directed albums in his catalog. Though the production is dated, leaning too close to the soft-rock with its electric pianos, the main flaw with the album is the material. Apart from the excellent weeper "I'll Just Take It Out In Love," the strongest song is the forced title track, which is essentially James Taylor's impression of what life in a honky tonk must be. The remaining songs don't deal in such hackneyed clichés, but they don't have its melodic force, either. That means that the album becomes just a wash of songs, despite Jones' fine performance. —*Stephen Thomas Erlewine*

The Best of George Jones / 1978 / Epic ✦✦✦✦✦

My Very Special Guests / 1979 / Epic ✦✦✦

Jones duets with some expected country contemporaries (Tammy Wynette, Johnny Paycheck), some outlaws (Waylon Jennings, Willie Nelson), and, most interestingly, some up-and-coming and pop-oriented guests (Emmylou Harris, Linda Ronstadt, Elvis Costello), often to beneficial effect for both. —*William Ruhlmann*

☆ **I Am What I Am** / 1980 / Epic/Legacy ✦✦✦✦✦

I Am What I Am announced that George Jones had officially returned to form artistically and, in the process, it became his biggest hit album ever. It's easy to see why—the production is commercial without being slick, the songs are balanced between aching ballads and restrained honky tonk numbers, and Jones gives a nuanced, moving performance. "He Stopped Loving Her Today," "I'm Not Ready Yet," and "If Drinkin' Don't Kill Me (Her Memory Will)" were the hits, but the remaining seven album tracks are exceptionally strong, without a weak track in the bunch. It's mature country, both in the laid-back approach and subject matter, but that doesn't mean it's dull—like the best country music, these are lived-in songs that are simple, direct, and emotionally powerful, even with the smooth production. *I Am What I Am* is the sound of George Jones at his peak and it's the highlight of his later years. Four bonus tracks—"Am I Losing Your Memory or Mine?," "The Ghost of Another Man," "It's All in My Mind," and "I'm a Fool for Loving Her"—give the 20th anniversary version of the album an added richness. —*Stephen Thomas Erlewine*

Together Again / 1980 / Epic ✦✦✦

Recorded just as George Jones was beginning his remarkable early '80s comeback, the George and Tammy reunion album *Together Again* doesn't have the spark of some of their earlier duets, but it has its share of fine moments. Both of the singers sound terrific, particularly on the hit singles "Two Story House" and "A Pair of Old Sneakers." Even when the material isn't up to their talents, the duo sounds recharged, which makes *Together Again* a thoroughly enjoyable, if inconsistent, listen. —*Stephen Thomas Erlewine*

Double Trouble / 1980 / Razor & Tie ✦

At the time *Double Trouble* was recorded, George Jones was enjoying the attention of hip rock & rollers, thanks to a glowing article in *Rolling Stone*. Jones and Billy Sherrill decided to make the most of his new rock audience, as evidenced by the presence of James Taylor on the previous year's *Bartender's Blues*. But their attempts to court the rock audience came to fruition with *Double Trouble*, recorded as a duet album with Johnny Paycheck. Primarily consisting of '50s rock & roll covers—"Maybellene," "Along Came Jones," "Roll Over Beethoven," etc.—the arrangements are flat, lifeless, and over-produced, featuring an overbearing chorus of female supporting vocalists. That's not to say that Jones and Paycheck are mellow. The pair sound as if they were on one of their notorious drinking and drugging binges, making jokes with each other throughout every song (except the closing "You Better Move On") and singing without regard for key. There is a bizarre fascination in hearing them so completely out of their heads, but it is an embarrassing record, particularly since it illustrates that Jones and Sherrill had no idea why a rock audience would be attracted to Jones' music. It's easily the worst album George Jones ever recorded. —*Stephen Thomas Erlewine*

Still the Same Ole Me / 1981 / Epic ✦✦✦

Recorded at the peak of his popularity, this album is sometimes restrained, and sometimes finds Jones at his uncontrollable best. Though predominantly honky tonk ballads, the best cuts (besides the obvious hits) include: "Good Ones and Bad Ones," "Together Alone," and the raucous "You Can't Get the Hell out of Texas." —*Tom Roland*

Encore: George Jones & Tammy Wynette / 1981 / Epic ✦✦✦✦

One album in an entire series of greatest-hits releases for CBS artists, this package documents the very best singles by George Jones and Tammy Wynette, an act that was once country music's top running soap opera. The sad hitch in Wynette's voice, and the greasy slides in the Possum's make for an interesting contrast. They sound just as good after their 1975 breakup ("Golden Ring," "Two Story House") as before ("We're Gonna Hold On," "Near You"). —*Tom Roland*

A Taste of Yesterday's Wine / 1982 / Epic ✦✦

★ **Anniversary: Ten Years of Hits** / 1982 / Epic ✦✦✦✦✦

Released in 1982 to commemorate a decade at Epic Records, *Anniversary* is a double LP (later reissued as a single CD) spanning 22 tracks and containing all of George Jones' big hits from 1972's "A Picture of Me (Without You)" to 1982's "Same Ole Me," all produced by Billy Sherrill. Broken down to the details, it's an impressive, weighty collection and would be essential just for having such exquisitely crafted and sang hits as "We Can Make It," "The Grand Tour," "The Door," "Once You've Had the Best," and "He Stopped Loving Her Today." What makes *Anniversary* transcendent, one of the best country albums of all time, is the context and subtext, how it reads like an autobiography of the most turbulent, heartbreaking decade in Jones' life. When this was released in 1982, he was hitting rock bottom after a decade of substance abuse and erratic behavior, much of it kick-started by his rocky marriage with Tammy Wynette. *Anniversary* doesn't explicitly tackle any of this—although some of the songs were written with these events in mind—but it does something better: It *dramatizes* it, largely due to Sherrill's near-operatic productions and the song sequencing. The first half of the album starts with songs of devotion, and they slowly give way to songs about heartbreak and loss, ending with the remarkable second half of the record where the songs find Jones broken and alone, drinking and pining for his lost love, even from beyond the grave. It's a thrilling journey that doesn't just showcase his ballad style at its finest, it has a devastating emotional impact that eclipses his excellent '70s albums because of the scope of the narrative; each of the proper LPs were snapshots of a time, while this takes a long view of his troubled decade and the results are heartbreaking and unforgettable and, because of the narrative, utterly necessary even if you have all the actual albums. It's unquestionably one of the 25 greatest country albums of all time. —*Stephen Thomas Erlewine*

Shine On / 1983 / Epic ✦✦✦

One continually waits for an edge to develop or some sense of intense commitment to break through the surface of the smooth, professional '80s productions of this country artist, who too often expresses genius in the subtle inflections of various syllables rather than the artistic majesty of a completely brilliant album or song, often on the same day he wraps himself around a signpost. Are listeners to believe the final track, "Ol' George Stopped Drinkin' Today," or the earlier homage to "Tennessee Whiskey"? The pomposity of an artist who commissions ditties about his own personally destructive habits—the former came from one O. B. McClinton—is just part of the entire legendary parcel of George Jones in his senior years, officially considered to have begun in the '80s since nobody was sure how long he might take to drink himself to death. Never the artistic equivalent of the edgy honky tonk performer of the '60s, this Jones is still a miracle worker vocally, shedding a light on the lyrics to "She Hung the Moon" that is every bit as deep as moonlight, sounding every bit like a normal human being when he admits "I'd Rather Have What We Had," and rising to the challenge of freshly performing a stale country chestnut, "Almost Persuaded." *—Eugene Chadbourne*

Ladies' Choice / 1984 / Epic ✦✦

Conceptually linked to *My Special Guests, Ladies Choice* is a collection of duets with country music's biggest female stars of the time including, Janie Fricke, Barbara Mandrell, Lacy J. Dalton, Deborah Allen, and Emmylou Harris. Though the liner notes claim that Jones personally selected his partners for these recordings, more than likely this was a marketing decision to pair the old-school singer with the up-and-coming country ladies of the '80s. The album did have two moderate hits ("Hallelujah, I Love You So" and "Size Seven Round (Made of Gold)") but rarely does this album strike anything above average. *—Chris Woodstra*

First Time Live / 1985 / Epic ✦✦

Who's Gonna Fill Their Shoes? / 1985 / Epic ✦✦✦

An EP culled from this album would be brilliant, and fans of Jones might want to put up with the mediocre cuts here just to enjoy some of the finer moments of the man's '80s recording career. The title track was the kind of mystical, self-serving necrophilia that country music is all about, powerful despite the fact that 20 years later, the same country singers who were fussing about disappearing from the scene are still going strong. The concept that they would leave shoes behind that need to be filled, regardless of whether they can or not, is an approach to ongoing musical history that is not always positive, so country fans might find that the two duets with female singers here bear up better to repeated listening than the hit record under discussion. The marvelous Lynn Anderson is on hand for "If You Can Touch Her at All," and really few can. Here is a truly classy country singer, who never wasted her time recording songs about how none of the younger singers are up to her level. If she did, she would have had to ignore the raunchy Lacy J. Dalton, who teams up with *el maestro possumo* for the lightweight but enjoyable "That's Good—That's Bad." Jones' ability to bond with Dalton is a good thing, and a full album of them together would probably be more fun than the lion's share of the dreary later Epic Jones catalog. Otherwise, like many Jones releases from this period, the material seems fairly insignificant, prompting the question of why he couldn't find better songwriting than this to record. *—Eugene Chadbourne*

Burn the Honky-Tonk Down / 1986 / Rounder ✦✦✦✦✦

20 Greatest Hits / 1987 / Deluxe ✦

Jones' Musicor recordings have been criminally mistreated through the years with a flood of rip-off collections filled with muddy re-recordings. The budget-priced *20 Greatest* isn't a perfect collection but there are a lot worse. The disc consists mainly of re-recordings but at least they seem to come from the same time period as the originals, and the sound isn't too bad. In addition to the Musicor material, his early hit "Why Baby Why" is included in its original form, although the sound is bad. *—Chris Woodstra*

Super Hits / 1987 / Epic ✦✦✦

Epic's 1987 *Super Hits* is a budget-line sampler of George Jones' '70s and '80s work for the label—which means, of course, that the first three songs on the album ("White Lightning," "Why Baby Why," "The Window Up Above") are *not* original recordings, they're remakes. Billy Sherrill-produced remakes, that is, which means they're better and more interesting than your average remakes, but they're not as good as the Starday/Mercury/UA originals (plus, they're recycled from the 1977 collection, *All-Time Greatest Hits, Vol. 1*). The rest of the song selection is a little hit and miss, highlighted by a four-song stretch in the middle of the record that brings you "A Picture of Me (Without You)," "The Grand Tour," "Bartender's Blues," and "He Stopped Loving Her Today." As samplers go, it's not bad, but other collections offer a fuller picture with a better song selection for about the same price, so there's no real reason to get this. *—Stephen Thomas Erlewine*

Don't Stop the Music / 1987 / Ace ✦✦✦✦✦

With scant material between the two, both this Ace compilation of Jones' early material and Mercury's two-disc *Cup of Loneliness* collection should thrill fans in search of the country star's classic honky tonk sides. Cut for the independent Starday label and Mercury, the 22 cuts on *Don't Stop the Music* chart Jones' gradual maturation in the latter half of the '50s and during the first few years of the '60s. Over the course of such gems as the title track and "Accidentally on Purpose," Jones reveals a fine pen, indelible country pipes, and a keen take on the tavern's wayward world of love and booze. Fiddles, pedal steel guitars, and rustic harmonies ring throughout, fueling a set perfect for a dance under all those hazy neon beer signs. *—Stephen Cook*

Live at Dancetown U.S.A. / 1987 / Ace ✦✦✦✦

There have been very few live recordings of George Jones, particularly of his early years, which makes *Live at Dance Town USA* so valuable. Recorded in June of 1965, the compact disc features 26 tracks—including nine songs performed by Jones' supporting vocalist Don Adams—that capture Jones running through his biggest hits, plus a couple of left-field covers like "Bony Moronie" and "Jole Blon." Jones is wired and energetic, breathing fire into the songs; one of the biggest joys of the entire disc is his between-song patter, such as when he tells the audience that he's taking a "liquor mission" halfway through the set. Not only is the music superb—on this date, the Jones Boys featured steel guitarist Buddy Emmons and Cajun fiddler Rufus Thibodeaux—but it illustrates exactly what a honky tonk concert was like in the '60s. For hardcore George Jones fans, it's an essential addition, one that's revelatory and highly entertaining. *—Stephen Thomas Erlewine*

Golden Hits / 1989 / Hollywood ✦✦

Hollywood's shoddy packaging of George Jones are notorious but *Golden Hits* is one of the company's better efforts. The quality of the recordings is fairly good, though a close listen reveals a few instances of vinyl sources, and the re-recordings are not bad ("I'll Follow You On Up to Our Cloud" and "Walk Through This World With Me" seem to be the only originals). *Golden Hits* only features ten tracks but there are much worse Jones budget-line collections on the market. *—Chris Woodstra*

Greatest Hits, Vol. 2 / 1989 / Hollywood ✦✦

Greatest Hits is hardly an accurate term—"You Comb Her Hair" was the biggest hit here—but *Greatest Hits, Vol. 2* is an interesting hodgepodge of nine tracks of indeterminate origin. These are most likely Musicor recordings, and while several sound like originals, there are also re-recordings and cuts that are so sonically muddy, it's hard to tell where they come from. However, for the dedicated George collector patiently awaiting the official reissue of Musicor material, this isn't a bad purchase, as long as you know that you take the very bad with the very good. *—Stephen Thomas Erlewine*

One Woman Man / Feb. 1989 / Epic ✦✦✦

One of Jones' best Epic albums, it succeeds despite two previously released songs being tagged on to fill it out. One of those is "Radio Lover," a bizarre cheating tale. Things get even stranger with "Ya Ba Da Ba Do (So Are You)," in which Jones gets drunk and talks to a Fred Flintstone glass and an Elvis Presley wine decanter (it also sparked legal action by Hanna-Barbera.) Beyond that, it's quality Jones honky-tonk and weepers, including a first-rate remake of "Just out of Reach (Of My Two Empty Arms)." *—Brian Mansfield*

Heartaches & Hangovers / 198 / Rounder ✦✦✦✦✦

Mr. Country Music / 198 / Classic Country ✦

Mr. Country Music offers a basic 18-track collection of Jones' Musicor recordings. While the occasional re-recording creeps onto the disc, the real downfall of this compilation is the muffled sound and tape dropouts throughout the disc. The three non-hits included ("I'm Wasting Good Paper," "Say It's Not You," "My Favorite Lies") are a nice change but that's not enough to recommend the disc to anyone but Musicor-starved fans. *—Chris Woodstra*

The Greatest Country Hits / 1990 / Curb ✦✦

Greatest Country Hits is a budget-line, 11 track CD covering Jones' biggest hits for United Artists, all presented in their original recordings. While this collection does a fair job, subsequent reissues have made this largely unnecessary. It is notable for the inclusion of "You Comb Her Hair," a number-five hit in 1963 that is unavailable on the other UA collections. *—Chris Woodstra*

Friends in High Places / 1991 / Epic ✦✦✦

This album features duets with some of country's biggest stars, including Buck Owens, Emmylou Harris, Vern Gosdin, Randy Travis, Charlie Daniels, Ricky Van Shelton, and others. *—AMG*

And Along Came Jones / 1991 / MCA ✦✦✦

George Jones ended a long association with Epic and producer Billy Sherrill in 1990 when he jumped ship to MCA and Kyle Lehning. His MCA debut wasn't a masterpiece, but it was stronger than almost everything he'd done in the '80s. The abandoned house in "Where the Tall Grass Grows" is yet another symbol for the unchecked memories of Jones' mind, and the Post-it Notes in "You Couldn't Get the Picture" are the kind of trivial detail he loves. The Cajun remake of "You Done Me Wrong" (co-written in 1960 with Ray Price) works, and the only moment of true silliness is "Heckel and Jeckel." *—Brian Mansfield*

★ **The Best of George Jones (1955–1967)** / 1991 / Rhino ✦✦✦✦✦

Rhino's 1991 collection *The Best of George Jones (1955-1967)* covers his recordings for Starday, Mercury, United Artists, and Musicor—in other words, it's the Pappy Daily years, featuring every label Pappy and the Possum recorded for before Jones severed ties with his producer/manager/mentor and moved to Epic and Billy Sherrill's luxurious productions in 1971. This is the foundation of George Jones' career, with his wildest honky tonk and sweetest ballads, and many of his most iconic songs—"Why Baby Why," "White Lightning," "The Window Up Above," "Tender Years," "She Thinks I Still Care," "The Race Is On," "Walk Through This World With Me"—among them. This is when Jones perfected his heart-wrenching ballad style—still the standard all country singers are measured by—and when he sang the purest hardcore honky tonk, dabbled in bluegrass with duet partner Melba Montgomery, dipped his toes into pop crossover with Gene Pitney (on the delirious "I've Got Five Dollars and It's Saturday Night"), and reveled in his love for novelties and silly songs, a taste he never lost in his entire career. Through it's expertly chosen 18 tracks, this *Best of George Jones* touches on all these sounds, as it offers an abundance of country Top Ten hits, along with a couple other songs that might not have climbed as far on the charts but help fill out Jones' musical portrait. Given the size of the collection, it should be no surprise that it doesn't contain all of his hits from these four labels—it skews toward the Starday and Mercury sides, with five selections from UA and four from Musicor—but it is a little surprising that it stops seemingly arbitrarily in 1967, since his first Epic hit arrived in 1972, leaving five years undocumented. Some great songs were recorded during that time—most notably "A Good Year for the Roses"—and while it would have been nice to have them here, it's also true that during those five years he began to shift toward the ballad-heavy style that distinguished his Epic records, so they're more of a piece with that era. The 12 years covered here constitute his first golden period, when he could and did sing anything, and they're presented perfectly here. Combine this disc with Epic's *Anniversary*, and you have the essential George Jones on CD—and two discs that are just slightly better than Epic/Legacy's very fine 1994 double-disc set, *The Spirit of Country*. —*Stephen Thomas Erlewine*

☆ **The Best of George Jones, Vol. 1: Hardcore Honky Tonk** / 1991 / Mercury ✦✦✦✦✦
At the time Mercury released *The Best of George Jones, Vol. 1: Hardcore Honky Tonk* in 1991, it was their most exhaustive trawl through Jones' Starday and Mercury recordings to date. Just three years later, they produced the double-disc set *Cup of Loneliness*, which provided an exhaustive overview of the same era this 20-track single disc covers. The two albums shared a whopping 18 tracks—"Someone Sweet to Love" and "Into My Arms Again" are the only two songs to not make the cut—so it wasn't a surprise that not only was a second volume never released, but that this disc went out of print a few years after the appearance of *Cup of Loneliness*. Since most of this material is readily available on that collection (and the two songs that are not, while good, aren't a great loss to anyone outside of hardcore collectors), it's not a tragedy that this is no longer in print, but it nevertheless is missed, since it's an excellent summary of Jones' early sides, containing both his biggest hits from this time and the purest hardcore country he ever sang. It's a little on the serious side, containing no novelties like "Who Shot Sam," which is unfortunate since silly songs were always a big part of Jones' music, and it doesn't have all the great songs he cut during this period (no "White Lightning" or "No Money in This Deal," for instance, or "I'm Gonna Burn Your Playhouse Down" or "Big Harlan Taylor"), but these are purposeful omissions: This is intended to be a collection of the hardest honky tonk he cut, a record for heartbreak and late nights, and it's superb on that count. Superb enough, actually, to keep around even if you have *Cup of Loneliness*, and good enough to pick up if you find it in a used record store—but probably not worth spending too much time and energy to seek it out. —*Stephen Thomas Erlewine*

Walls Can Fall / 1992 / MCA ✦✦✦
"Wrong's What I Do Best," Jones sings in one song from *Walls Can Fall*, and listening to the album you almost believe he's telling the truth. Jones makes the same albums he's always made; two producers (this time Emory Gordy Jr.) since Billy Sherrill has failed to do more than decrease the number of novelty songs and tune up Jones' sound, which is still defined by low piano melodies and sawing fiddle. Jones continues to play off his legend: Songs like "I Don't Need Your Rockin' Chair," "Drive Me to Drink," and a cover of Merle Haggard's "The Bottle Let Me Down" sound scarier because of George's past. The thing is, wrong isn't what Jones does best. What Jones does best is consequences, which is why "There's the Door" sounds more emotionally devastating than anything else here. —*Brian Mansfield*

Greatest Hits, Vol. 2 / 1992 / Epic ✦✦✦
Some of the most popular duets from this former husband-and-wife team: "The World Needs Melody," "We Go Together," "Two Story House," and more. —*AMG*

High-Tech Redneck / 1993 / MCA ✦✦
George Jones' third MCA album is a ten-track, pure country outing. Despite the digital sound and short running time (less than 32 minutes), it is produced in classic fiddle/steel instrumental glory. Jones sounds steely on the title cut, and such songs as "I've Still Got Some Hurtin' Left to Do" and "Tear Me Out of the Picture" are the type of earnest, unsophisticated heartache songs that define country. He concludes things with a tribute to the departed Conway Twitty, an urgent "Hello Darlin'" that rivals any version Twitty ever issued. —*Ron Wynn*

Bradley Barn Sessions / 1994 / MCA ✦✦✦
The concept behind *The Bradley Barn Sessions* was an intriguing one: Place George Jones in the hands of traditionalist country producer Brian Ahern, record at Owen Bradley's legendary studios, compile a selection of George's greatest hits and have him sing duets with contemporary vocalists (and Tammy Wynette) that have cited him as an influence. In theory, it should have worked but in practice, it's a stilted, nearly lifeless album. The production is too clean and polished, lacking any of the grit of true honky tonk records. Furthermore, songs like "A Good Year for the Roses" suffer from the stringless, stripped-down arrangements. And though all of George's duet partners—including Marty Stuart, Alan Jackson, Vince Gill, Ricky Skaggs, Trisha Yearwood, and Travis Tritt—are respectful, only Keith Richards captures the spirit of a roadside honky tonk. —*Stephen Thomas Erlewine*

☆ **Cup of Loneliness: The Mercury Years** / 1994 / Mercury ✦✦✦✦
George Jones is widely considered the greatest singer in country music—as well as one of the greatest singers in American popular music—and while his style gradually grew richer and more nuanced, he arrived pretty much fully formed, a force of nature, as Mercury's 1994 double-disc set *Cup of Loneliness* proves. Over the course of 48 tracks (51 tracks on the limited-edition initial box set release, packaged in an exceedingly flimsy cardboard book-style box), the best of Jones' earliest work for Starday and Mercury records is unveiled—not everything, but close enough, particularly because the quality of the material is so consistently strong, whether it's on raw, hardcore honky tonk ravers or on the wrenching ballad style that became his signature. Both are on full display on this tremendous set, which finds George at his purest as a country singer. Later, his songs were sweetened a little, through both production and song choice, but here, even novelties like "Who Shot Sam" or the unhinged "Revenooer Man" sound like wild, unruly complements to the barroom ravers like "If I Don't Love You (Grits Ain't Groceries)," "White Lightning," "No Money in This Deal" and "Why Baby Why," not to mention such great tear-in-my-beer ballads as "Just One More," "Colour of the Blues" and "Window Up Above." What's great about this set is that it fills in the little details and forgotten singles left out of such otherwise excellent collections as Rhino's *The Best of . . .* or Mercury's previous *The Best of George Jones: Hardcore Honky Tonk*. By featuring such weird, woolly songs as "Slave Lover" next to pure gospel like "Family Bible," or by airing such country classics as "You're Still on My Mind," "Heartaches By the Number" and "(I'll Be There) If You Ever

Want Me" next to such great lesser-known songs as "Relief Is Just a Swallow Away," "Big Harlan Taylor" and "I'm Gonna Burn Your Playhouse Down," this is the hardest, funniest, best pure country George Jones ever recorded. Though it's worth the search for the 51-track version, the 48-track version packs the same punch, and it's beyond essential, especially for those who only are familiar with the cinematic scope of his Billy Sherrill Epic recordings. This is the sound of the Possum as the great country singer, where his music bristles with energy and invention. He recorded many, many sides as great as these later, but he never did hardcore country better than he did on the music captured on *Cup of Loneliness*. —*Stephen Thomas Erlewine*

All Time Greatest Hits / 1994 / Liberty ✦✦✦
All-Time Greatest Hits is culled from George Jones' United Artists recordings. During these years, he had two of his definitive hits—"She Thinks I Still Care" and "The Race Is On"—but it was largely a transition period for Jones, as this entertaining but scattershot collection shows. Not all of his hits from his UA recordings are included—particularly the number three "A Girl I Used to Know" and the number five "You Comb Her Hair," which are indeed featured on Rhino's *The Best of 1955-1967*—and several of the songs here weren't hits and don't deserve to be included, particularly his version of "Running Bear." Still, the album gives a good sense of his time at the label and contains the great majority of his hits of the early '60s. —*Stephen Thomas Erlewine*

White Lightning / 1994 / Drive Archive ✦
Based on the track listing, it would seem that *White Lightning*, which boasts 14 tracks mainly from now woefully scarce Musicor years, would be an essential collection. Unfortunately, this disc is marred by horrible sound and inferior re-recordings best exemplified by "A Good Year for the Roses," one of the many re-makes/alternate takes that sound like George is singing under water. A handful of the songs are indeed original versions but it's not enough to make up for the low points. —*Chris Woodstra*

★ **The Essential George Jones: The Spirit of Country** / Nov. 1, 1994 / Epic/Legacy ✦✦✦✦✦
If any artist cried out for a cross-licensed, multi-label retrospective, it was George Jones. When Epic/Legacy released the double-disc *The Essential George Jones: The Spirit of Country* in 1994, he had recorded for no less than six labels—in chronological order: Starday, Mercury, United Artists, Musicor, Epic, MCA (since then, he's added two more labels: Elektra and BNA/RCA)—over the course of four decades, a discographical nightmare if there ever was one. *The Spirit of Country* was the first (and, to date, only) to attempt a serious, multi-label overview of George Jones' lengthy career, and while it has a few flaws, it nevertheless is indeed essential as an overview of his prolific work, tracing his hits from 1955's "Why Baby Why" to 1989's wonderful "The King Is Gone (And So Are You)." That means there's nothing from his MCA records here, but that's not a major problem, since his peak ended when he left Epic, and that entire peak is chronicled here. It is not chronicled evenhandedly, though. Starday and Mercury account for the first seven tracks, then UA is rushed through in three cuts, before moving to five Musicor sides (including "A Good Year for the Roses," previously unavailable on CD). This means the '50s and '60s are finished in 15 tracks, with the remaining 29 songs all from his Epic work of the '70s and '80s. This is a bit of an imbalance, and it's hard not to wish that some of the missing songs—whether it's "What Am I Worth" or "Things Have Gone to Pieces"—were here, but, that said, there are no truly essential items missing from his pre-Epic sides. As far as the Epic material is concerned, the 1982 collection *Anniversary* may have arranged the material in a more dramatic fashion, but 14 of that record's 22 songs are here, including all the really big hits, although there are enough great songs absent—"Nothing Ever Hurt Me (Half as Bad as Losing You)," "What My Woman Can't Do," "The Battle," and "Memories of Us"—to still make that collection necessary (much as Rhino's *The Best of George Jones (1955-1967)* still serves a valuable need). But, this set not only has songs unavailable on other collections, it does do its job very well, providing the best available overview of George Jones' career. It might not have everything, but it has all the important sides, and there simply isn't a better way to get acquainted with George Jones than this. —*Stephen Thomas Erlewine*

One / 1995 / MCA ✦✦
More of a trip down memory lane than an album, *One* is the long-awaited reunion album by George Jones and Tammy Wynette, their first in 15 years. It's a pleasant listen, with both George and Tammy in fine voice. The problem is that much of the material is often indifferent—there are a few fine songs, particularly the title track and a lament about modern country radio called "They're Playing Our Song," but many of the songs fail to make an impression either way. The main pleasure of the record is hearing George and Tammy together again, after all these years, but if *One* is judged by their previous efforts, it looks rather thin. —*Stephen Thomas Erlewine*

George Jones & Gene Pitney / 1995 / Bear Family ✦✦✦✦
When George Jones left United Artists to join Musicor in 1965, it was decided to start off with a duet recording session with teen idol (and labelmate) Gene Pitney. The session resulted in two duet albums—*George Jones & Gene Pitney* and *It's Country Time Again*—as well as a solo country album by Pitney, *The Country Side of Gene Pitney*. Bear Family's *George Jones & Gene Pitney* collects the 31 songs recorded during these sessions. For a seemingly unlikely pairing, the two complemented each other well, with Pitney proving himself not only a fan of the genre but also a competent country singer as well. Though only two hits came from the albums ("Love Bug" and the brilliant "Things Have Gone to Pieces"—the latter absent from this collection for some reason), this disc captures some truly inspired moments by both artists. In light of the scarcity of good CD collections of George Jones' Musicor recordings, this disc is essential to anyone who wants a complete picture of Jones' career. —*Chris Woodstra*

Vintage Collections Series / Jan. 23, 1996 / Capitol ✦✦✦✦
Vintage collects nearly all of George Jones and Melba Montgomery's duets for United Artists. These songs, originally released on *What's in Our Hearts* and *Bluegrass*

Hootenanny, illustrate how well-suited the pair was for each other—there may be a couple of weak songs, but there are no weak performances. In fact, *Vintage* makes a good argument that Montgomery was Jones' best duet partner. —*Stephen Thomas Erlewine*

I Lived to Tell It All / Aug. 13, 1996 / MCA ✦✦✦

A companion piece to his best-selling autobiography of the same name, *I Lived to Tell It All* is a surprising return to form by George Jones. Where *The Bradley Barn Sessions* tried to be an authentic release in the vein of a Hightone record and where *High-Tech Redneck* was clueless in its calculation, *I Lived to Tell It All* is an effortless encapsulation of Jones' gifts. There are honky tonk raveups, there are heart-tugging barroom weepers, and, best of all, there are several novelties that rank among the most clever and self-deprecating that Jones has ever recorded. Those that were seeking the pseudo-gritty production of *The Bradley Barn Sessions* may be discouraged by the slicker sound of *I Lived to Tell It All*, but there's no denying that Jones sounds recharged and energetic; he's getting a genuine kick singing these songs, which are all loosely auto-biographical. In terms of content and performance, it's his best record since *I Am What I Am.* —*Stephen Thomas Erlewine*

She Thinks I Still Care: The George Jones Collection (The United Artists Years) / Apr. 22, 1997 / Razor & Tie ✦✦✦✦✦

She Thinks I Still Care: The George Jones Collection (The United Artists Years) is a comprehensive double-disc retrospective of Jones' four years with UA, featuring 40 songs, including 21 country Top 40 hits. His time with United Artists was essentially a transitional period, as he moved from the hardcore honky tonker of his Starday-Mercury years to the country crooner of his Musicor era, which means there are several cuts on the set that fall somewhere between the two extremes. It also means that there is a handful of mediocre cuts on the collection, but some of George's absolute best is here—not only familiar hits like "The Race Is On," "She Thinks I Still Care," "A Girl I Used to Know," "Your Heart Turned Left (And I Was on the Right)," "You Comb Her Hair," and his remarkable bluegrass duets with Melba Montgomery, but also lesser-known gems like "Open Pit Mine," "My Tears Are Overdue," and "Wrong Number." Although his United Artists recordings are on the whole his most uneven work—the Musicor albums may have been inconsistent, but they were usually interesting—he made a number of terrific records for the label, and *She Thinks I Still Care* is easily the best way to hear them. The set is more thorough, representative, and listenable than *All-Time Greatest Hits*, and the original albums contain so much duplication that they're frustrating for anyone but die-hard fans. —*Stephen Thomas Erlewine*

It Don't Get Any Better Than This / Apr. 7, 1998 / MCA ✦✦✦

The title track to *It Don't Get Any Better Than This* has George lamenting contemporary country celebrating classic country with a bunch of pals—Merle, Waylon, Willie, Bobby Bare, "Johnny Counterfeit"—thereby providing the emotional touchstone for the entire album. Discounting the overly clean production, the album makes no concessions to contemporary country—it's a honky tonk record, filled with steel guitars and fiddles. George even revives an old hit, "When Did You Stop Lovin' Me," which fits right into this collection of traditionalist country. It's not a bad record by any means, and George is in surprisingly good voice, hardly sounding like a man approaching his 70th birthday. Still, there's no truly great performances or unusual songs to make it worth putting on after the initial play. —*Stephen Thomas Erlewine*

16 Biggest Hits / Jul. 14, 1998 / Legacy/Epic ✦✦✦✦

16 Biggest Hits covers much of the same ground as the sublime *Anniversary*—not quite as well, but it's still pretty great nonetheless, simply because the source material is very strong indeed. The first nine songs were all on *Anniversary*, and they're the best tracks here. Many of the remaining songs are culled from post-*Anniversary* albums, and while there are some great cuts—"She's My Rock," "I Always Get Lucky With You," "The King Is Gone (So Are You)," "Who's Gonna Fill Their Shoes"—on the whole they don't match the earlier tracks. Nevertheless, this is a small matter, because it does a good job of sampling lesser work and thereby gives a good overview of his entire time with Epic. It may not be definitive the way the second disc of *The Spirit of Country* is or how *Anniversary* chronicles his peak years, but it's a good, affordable sampler all the same. —*Stephen Thomas Erlewine*

☆ Nothing Ever Hurt Me/A Picture of Me (Without You) / Oct. 20, 1998 / Koch ✦✦✦✦✦

On the back cover of Koch's two-fer reissue of *A Picture of Me (Without You)/Nothing Ever Hurt Me (Half as Bad as Losing You)*, George Jones is quoted as saying: "I am so excited about the release of two of my all time favorite albums. I hope you enjoy every song contained on this special release." This is one of the rare times that the Possum's self-evaluation is entirely accurate, since these are two of Jones' very best records, albums that may still follow the pattern of singles-n-filler, but are of higher quality than many of his other albums, regardless of the era they were released. True, if you scan the track listing, only a few titles will pop out—certainly the title tracks, but also "The Man Worth Lovin' You" and definitely "What My Woman Can't Do"—but what makes these records remarkable is that the rest of the albums are comprised of material that is firmly solid. These are not classics, but they're good songs all the same and producer Billy Sherrill gives them a uniform, appealing production that makes them gel into something that's greater than the sum of their parts. And, when paired on this two-fer, they seem all the stronger—they complement each other, with their professional production, fine songwriting, and passionate performances from Jones. So, even if this doesn't have a lot of classics in the traditional sense, it's essential listening for the dedicated George fan all the same. —*Stephen Thomas Erlewine*

The George Jones Collection / Jun. 1, 1999 / MCA ✦✦✦

George Jones moved to MCA Records in 1990, beginning the decade with the promising *And Along Came Jones*. As it turns out, a new label and a new band of collaborators and producers didn't necessarily mean artistic revitalization for Jones. He still could turn out some fine records, but he often fell prey to formula, particularly in how he always seemed to have a song about how he "don't need your rocking chair" or how country radio won't

play veterans like him. Even if those sentiments may be true, they gave all the albums a homogenous feel, which in turn led to less airplay. So, when Jones left MCA for Elektra and it was time for a compilation of MCA material, there weren't many hits for a compilation. Then again, *George Jones Collection* isn't really a hits compilation, it's a portrait of the MCA years, which were scattershot in terms of quality and remarkably consistent in tone. Accordingly, the 11-track compilation is coherent but uneven, containing some great moments ("Walls Can Fall," "Wrong's What I Do Best," "You Couldn't Get the Picture") and a number of mediocrities. This may mean that it's an accurate portrait of this era, but it doesn't mean that it contains all the best moments from his MCA recordings, which will undoubtedly be frustrating for serious fans that want a definitive compilation of Jones' latter-day recordings. —*Stephen Thomas Erlewine*

The Cold Hard Truth / Jun. 22, 1999 / Elektra ✦✦✦✦

Touted as George Jones' return to hardcore country, *Cold Hard Truth*—the Possum's first record for the revitalized Asylum Records—certainly does achieve that goal. Under the guidance of producer Keith Stegall, Jones returns to the sound of his classic Mercury and UA recordings, meaning that there's nothing but honky tonk ballads and ravers throughout. Impressively, Stegall made sure that Jones didn't take the easy way out: there are no covers or superstar duets, just strong new songs. And, unlike almost any of Jones' previous albums, there's not a single novelty or throwaway. In short, it's the album hardcore fans have said they've always wanted Jones to make. Like most realized fantasies, *Cold Hard Truth* doesn't quite live up to the imagination, yet it still delivers enough that it isn't a disappointment. Much of the credit must be given to Stegall; his production may be a bit too clean and echo-laden, but he made a wise move in adhering to simple, traditional instrumentation and guiding Jones toward a great set of songs. George sounds terrific, not necessarily better than on his latter-day MCA records, but the strength of the material makes it seem so. For all of its virtues, there's a curious distance on *Cold Hard Truth*, possibly because it's too careful in both its song selection, and there's no grit in the production. Silly songs and rushed performances always gave Jones' albums character, and it's hard not to miss that reckless spirit on *Cold Hard Truth*, no matter how good the music is. But ultimately, such complaints amount to nitpicking. There's little question that *Cold Hard Truth* boasts the finest set of songs Jones has had in nearly two decades, and he delivers the performances they deserve. It's refreshing to finally hear a Jones album that holds up from beginning to end. —*Stephen Thomas Erlewine*

Memories of Us/Battle / Jul. 20, 1999 / Koch ✦✦✦✦

So paired because they appear to be reminiscences and elegies to George Jones' legendary failed marriage to Tammy Wynette, this two-fer of *The Battle* and *Memories of Us* reveals that the records aren't all that thematic, no matter what the *Rolling Stone Record Guide* may claim. If anything, these two records are more formulaic than the two records comprising the two-fer of *A Picture of Me (Without You)/Nothing Ever Hurt Me (Half as Bad as Losing You)*, which isn't necessarily a bad thing—it just is. Even if these two records don't just have their share of filler, they have more than their share of novelties, which Jones always loved, and that gives the records the impression of being slightly off-kilter. Even if those tunes are pretty good. Even if these two albums don't gel the way the records on Koch's other 1998 two-fer do, each record has not only its share of hits, it has its share of underappreciated songs, resulting in a two-fer that may not be as essential as its counterpart, but is still quite good. —*Stephen Thomas Erlewine*

16 Biggest Hits / Aug. 10, 1999 / Epic/Legacy ✦✦✦✦

16 Biggest Hits provides an excellent summary of George Jones and Tammy Wynette's duets for Epic between 1971 and 1980. All of their best-known songs—"The Ceremony," "We're Gonna Hold On," "Golden Ring," "The Jet Set (We're Not)," "Rollin My Sweet Baby's Arms"—are here at a mid-line price, making an excellent choice for beginners and casual fans. —*Stephen Thomas Erlewine*

Live With the Possum / Nov. 9, 1999 / Elektra ✦✦

Arriving a mere five months after George Jones' much-hyped Asylum debut, *Cold Hard Truth*—a record that was touted as his return to hardcore country—*Live With the Possum*, his second Asylum outing, seemed on the surface to be a live equivalent of its studio predecessor, but it's not. It's a rushed, cheaply packaged release that simply replicates the 1994 video *Live in Tennessee*. Jones gives a good journeyman performance, balancing classic hits with a couple of latter-day numbers ("She Loved a Lot in Her Time," "The One I Loved Back Then (The Corvette Song)"). It's not an exceptional performance, though, and its sudden, unannounced CD release is a little puzzling—especially since the album sounds as if it was directly transferred from a laser disc. It seems as if Alan Jackson's intro to "No Show Jones" was taped from a TV, while other parts of the mix sound a bit off. The only thing that appears to be changed is the crowd noise, which seem to be enhanced (the end result is that it sounds like everyone in the audience is on the verge of hysteria, as if they were teenage girls watching the Backstreet Boys). The audio transfer is disarming, as is the very appearance of the disc—there's no mention anywhere on the disc that this is indeed *Live in Tennessee*, the cover looks as if it was assembled a half-hour before it went to the printer, and there are no liner notes. This wouldn't be so bad if it was a budget-line release from a fly-by-night operation, but this is Jones' second album for Asylum and it's not unreasonable to expect more, given that his association with the label was supposed to be a dignified affair. If you can ignore all of the disc's shortcomings and just concentrate on the performance, *Live With the Possum* is reasonably entertaining, but it's not an essential release—just something for the hardcore fans, who probably have the video already. —*Stephen Thomas Erlewine*

20th Century Masters—The Millennium Collection: The Best of George Jones / May 9, 2000 / MCA ✦✦✦✦

20th Century Masters—The Millennium Collection: The Best of George Jones draws upon Jones' legendary honky tonk recordings for Mercury during the mid- to late '50s and early

'60s. It's ground that's covered much more thoroughly on the double-disc set *Cup of Loneliness*, and Rhino's *The Best of George Jones 1955-1967* is a more satisfying single-disc overview of the period. However, this 12-track compilation is not without its virtues—it does gather some of the biggest hits and very best cuts that Jones recorded for Mercury, and it's a reasonable, mid-priced sampler perfect for those who don't want to spring for the double-disc. —*Steve Huey*

The Rock Stone Cold Country 2001 / Sep. 11, 2001 / BNA ♦♦♦

One album with Asylum was enough for "the Possum," and even if *The Cold Hard Truth's* mastermind Keith Stegall has been retained for a couple of cuts on *The Rock: Stone Cold Country 2001* (possibly the most awkward title of any George Jones record), it's clear that the pure hardcore country of that album has been abandoned for a refined, commercialized version of that sound. That's not entirely a bad thing, since this is hardly as compromised an album as *High-Tech Redneck* and, by and large, the material is good. But, apart from the last-minute addition of the Garth Brooks duet "Beer Run," few of the songs really stand out—they all occupy a pleasant midlevel that sounds good while playing but doesn't really register in memory. That still doesn't hurt the record, since it's unencumbered by unnecessary superstar duets and is appealingly lean, but it is the kind of record for the dedicated believers who like to hear Jones performing cleanly as a professional. Not really something to celebrate like *The Cold Hard Truth*, but it results in a solid latter-day effort, much like *I Lived to Tell It All*. —*Stephen Thomas Erlewine*

Love Songs / Jan. 14, 2003 / Epic ♦♦♦

One of the more bittersweet entries in the *Love Songs* series, this collection of George Jones' ballads features some of his essential songs, including "Loving You Could Never Be Better," "Once You've Had the Best," "We Can Make It," and "He Stopped Loving Her Today," as well as many other solid tracks from the early '70s and early '80s, the two peaks of Jones' collaboration with producer Billy Sherrill. Sherrill's penchant for lush strings and backing vocals gives songs like "A Picture of Me Without You," "You've Still Got a Place in My Heart," and "I'll Take You to My World" an added richness and depth, though some of the '80s productions, such as "(What Love Can Do) The Second Time Around," aren't quite as warm-sounding as the material from the '70s. "She Hung the Moon," "You Oughta Be Here With Me," and "I Always Get Lucky With You" are some of the other highlights from *Love Songs*. While it doesn't include enough of Jones' definitive songs to make it compare favorably to a straightforward greatest-hits collection, and a duet or two with Tammy Wynette would've been nice, *Love Songs* is a likable collection of some of Jones' mellow musings on the ups and downs of love. —*Heather Phares*

Hank, Bob & Me: Songs of Hank Williams Sr. and Bob Wills / Mar. 11, 2003 / Fuel 2000 ♦♦♦

In 1962 George Jones cranked out a lot of albums. Fuel 2000 has taken two of these (*My Favorites of Hank Williams* and *George Jones Sings Bob Wills*), chopped a few tracks off each, and combined them into one disc. The 14 tracks on *Hank, Bob & Me* have seven songs from each of the records. Why they didn't just go ahead and make it a two-fer is a bit of a mystery. They also decided to mix the tracks together; it would have made more sense, both from a historical and sonic standpoint, to keep them separate. Still, if you are a die-hard fan of George Jones who doesn't already own the two records, you will want to pick up this disc. Hearing him wrap his dulcet tones around the great songs of Hank Williams, like "Your Cheatin' Heart" and "Mansion on the Hill," is a treat. He is pretty faithful to the source material, and while the band could be a little more exciting, the seven Williams songs are a success. The seven Wills tracks are a bit less so, as Jones doesn't really swing. The band turns the Western swing of the Texas Playboys into a smoky honky tonk sound, but Jones sounds a little stiff on dance numbers like "Take Me Back to Tulsa." And if anyone can figure out why they included the instrumental "Steel Guitar Rag" instead of something Jones sings on, please send in the answer. It is really a shame when good music is packaged poorly. Unless you are one of the diehards mentioned above, you should probably look elsewhere for quality George Jones reissues. —*Tim Sendra*

The Gospel Collection / Apr. 1, 2003 / BNA ♦♦♦♦

In 2003, could there be anything more desirable in country music than George Jones reunited with "retired" producer Billy Sherrill? Hardly. Some will complain that the pair should have worked on an album of countrypolitan or love or drinking songs instead of a two-CD, 24-track collection of gospel tunes, but that's just cryin' in their beer. After all, this is a George Jones record, and there isn't a thing the man sings that doesn't have the weathered sound of whiskey, women, and toil in the honky tonks. Jones was supposedly inspired to make this recording during his long recovery from a serious car wreck and a subsequent case of pneumonia. Musically, the material is choice, striking, moving, and full of emotion. Jones is incapable of singing gospel music without emotion. The set is split along traditionals such as "Amazing Graze," "Just a Closer Walk With Thee," "Swing Low, Sweet Chariot," "Peace in the Valley," "The Old Rugged Cross," and about eight others, and classic country gospel tunes like Stuart Hamblen's "It Is No Secret," Cleavant Derricks' "Just a Little Talk With Jesus," the Vaughan/Rowe staple "If I Could Hear My Mother Pray Again," and the Jimmie Davis/Jack Campbell stalwart "I Know a Man Who Can." What matters ultimately is the performance, though, since Jones has released other gospel collections on various labels. Sherrill's silky soundscapes add a lot to Jones' voice, which is no longer the instrument it once was. There is no doubt he is still a great singer, but his ability to throw his voice around and hit the higher notes in his baritone register is all but gone. With his more limited stylistic vernacular, however, Jones digs deep and gets the tunes across, making them swing and sway with emotion and honky tonk swagger. The edges one can hear now are far from crags and they do add a certain hard-won wisdom and change to his sound, but one can't help but miss the smooth delivery of his earlier years. Nonetheless, these songs ring truer than any collection of gospel music

Jones has ever released, thanks to Sherrill being able to get the finest performance possible out of him. If you had to pick one Jones gospel record, it should be this one, hands down. —*Thom Jurek*

Grandpa Jones (Louis Marshall Jones)

b. Oct. 20, 1913, Niagra, KY, d. Feb. 19, 1998
Vocals, Banjo, Guitar / Old-Timey, Traditional Country, Country Comedy

Louis Marshall "Grandpa" Jones was one person who aged right into his makeup. Like his real appearance, however, his actual background and role in country music were deceptive and more complex than they seem. Beginning in the 1920s, he began attracting attention with his boisterous performing style, old-time banjo performing, and powerful singing, and by the 1940s, with hits like "Rattler" and "Mountain Dew," he began receiving national attention. He joined the *Grand Ole Opry* in 1946 and remained there throughout his career; in the 1960s, with hits like "T for Texas," he continued making a place for himself on the country charts, and as a regular on *Hee Haw* since its inception in 1969, he became a television celebrity. But Jones' influence went much further than that chain of successes would indicate—he was almost single-handedly responsible for keeping the banjo alive as a country music instrument during the 1930s and 1940s, and in addition to his own work and songs, he was an important associate and collaborator of Merle Travis.

Jones was born in Niagra, KY, and grew up not in the mountains or the countryside, as one would think from his music, but in industrial Ohio and Kentucky, living in factory towns. His father was a fiddle player, and his mother was a ballad singer. He listened to a lot of radio growing up, especially the *National Barn Dance* out of Chicago, and his strongest influences included old-time country music and gospel songs as well as the music of Jimmie Rodgers, which led him to begin yodeling. He'd made it onto the radio himself by 1929 at the age of 18 as the Young Singer of Old Songs. Later on he moved to Chicago, teamed with Bashful Harmonica Joe, and appeared on the *Lum and Abner* show. During the mid-'30s, he started working with Bradley Kincaid, the man who gave Jones the "Grandpa" name, a result of his grouchy moods during their early-morning radio broadcasts—Jones thought the name worked and adopted makeup to match. Coupled with his skills as a comedian and raconteur, the image was a natural. It was with Kincaid that Jones' career moved to Boston, where their brand of country music proved extremely popular among rural New Englanders.

As a solo act later in the 1930s, Jones had radio shows on numerous stations from West Virginia and Connecticut to Cincinnati, where he sang folk ballads and more old-time country ballads as well as gospel songs. He also learned to play the banjo and made it an integral part of his act at a time when the instrument had all but vanished from country music; it was the combination of Jones' old-time repertory and humor that helped to keep the banjo alive as a viable, popular country instrument. Jones later hooked up with Alton & Rabon Delmore and Merle Travis, and played with them throughout World War II as Brown's Ferry Four. He and Travis also became the first artists to record for the newly founded King label, under the name of the Shepherd Brothers. Jones' own earliest solo records were also done for King during this period, among them "It's Raining Here This Morning," "Eight More Miles to Louisville," "Rattler," and "Mountain Dew."

Those singles brought Grandpa Jones to national attention, and he was poised for the next step in his career, a move to Nashville. Before that, however, he married Ramona Riggins, who became not only his wife but his accompanist on fiddle and mandolin. In 1946, he began playing on the *Grand Ole Opry* and touring with acts such as Lonzo & Oscar and Cowboy Copas. He didn't stay in Nashville too long at first, moving to Lorton, VA, and a radio show in Arlington, and later on the *Old Dominion Barn Dance* in Richmond. Finally, he returned to Nashville as a regular member of the *Opry*. Jones recorded with King Records from 1945 until 1952, when he moved to RCA Victor, where he remained for four years, recording both traditional-sounding country and topical songs ("I'm No Communist").

In 1956, he began a six-year stint on Decca Records, recording a total of 16 songs including the talking-blues country hit "The All-American Boy" in 1959. Jones moved to Fred Foster's Monument Records in 1962 and had a Top Five country hit the following year with "T for Texas." His career during the 1960s continued uninterrupted, and in 1969 he joined the cast of the new country music/comedy showcase *Hee Haw*, which gave him unprecedented national exposure for the next two decades. By 1978, he'd been elected to the Country Music Hall of Fame and, by that time, was taking on the real-life role of elder statesman within the community. He continued recording into the 1980s, although his music is somewhat under-represented today on compact disc, apart from the Monument and Decca sides. In 1984, Jones published his autobiography, *Everybody's Grandpa*. He died February 19, 1998. —*Bruce Eder*

16 Sacred Gospel Songs / 1963 / King ♦♦♦♦♦

Before Grandpa Jones (real name Louis Marshall Jones) became a worldwide personality through his association with the long-running TV show *Hee Haw*, gospel music was a significant part of both his live and studio presentation since the '30s. On *16 Sacred Gospel Songs*, Jones is joined on several cuts by the Brown's Ferry Four, covering many of those songs that remained forever in his repertoire: "Praise God! He Loves Everybody," "You Must Be Born Again," and "Can't You Hear Him Calling." Jones also covers "Dark as a Dungeon," a song written by his one-time Depression-era collaborator, Merle Travis. —*Al Campbell*

Live / 1969 / Monument ♦♦♦

Grandpa Jones Live captures a concert Jones performed in Cincinnati in 1969. Though the album doesn't feature any of his best-known songs, it nevertheless gives a good idea of what Grandpa's shows were like during the latter-half of his career—filled with traditional tunes, warmth and good-times. In fact, the record is largely useful as an example of the friendly exchange between old-time country performers and their audiences, since musically *Live* is only entertaining, not revelatory. —*Stephen Thomas Erlewine*

Grandpa Jones-Live / 1969 / Monument ♦♦♦♦♦

Grandpa Jones had been signed to Fred Foster's Monument label for seven years when producer Ray Pennington recorded this concert at the Black Stallion in Cincinnati, OH, on December 29, 1969. The result is a priceless document of Jones' stage act—ironically, Jones himself regards this as the least favorite of his Monument records because he doesn't feel he was prepared or that his voice sounds very good. None of that is very obvious, for the performance is excellent and his singing seems just fine. Surprisingly, he covers none of his Monument hits such as "T for Texas" or "Mountain Dew," choosing instead new material. The songs range from the rollicking "Dooley" and "Rocky Top" to eloquent gospel such as "The Air, the Sunshine, and the Rain" (a great showcase for Jones' wife Ramona's fiddle playing, as is "I Don't Love Nobody") to traditional folk tunes like a banjo-driven version of "John Henry" and "My Bonnie Lies Over the Ocean" played on cowbells. The band includes Joe Edwards on guitar, and Ramona sings harmony. The tunes are spiced by Jones' vaudeville patter, including his ribald retelling of the story of the three bears as "The Three Old Maids." Nothing on this recording is less than first-rate, including the sound, which captures the mix of instruments and voices with wonderful fidelity. *—Bruce Eder*

The Grandpa Jones Story / 1976 / CMH ♦♦♦♦
The *Hee Haw* banjo comic in a pleasant folksy setting with Ramona. *—Mark A. Humphrey*

16 Greatest Hits / 1978 / Hollywood ♦♦♦♦
The best of Grandpa Jones' King Records sides from the late '40s, including the original hit versions of "Mountain Dew" and "Old Rattler." Among the old-time gems here are Jones' version of the comedy country song "I'm My Own Grandpa" and "Jonah and the Whale." A lot of the material on this generously programmed collection also includes a fair amount of comedy, including "15 Cents Is All I Got," as well as novelty tunes like the rollicking regional anthem "Are You From Dixie?" Among the surprises is the folk-based material, including "Eight More Miles to Louisville" and "Grandpa Boogie," where he slips into a really cool '40s dance groove. The sound is generally OK, though a little bright where it might use more depth, and a few tracks like "East Bound Freight Train" sound as though they're drawn from not quite first-generation sources. There are no notes, alas. *—Bruce Eder*

Family Album / 1979 / CMH ♦♦♦

• **Country Music Hall of Fame Series** / 1992 / MCA ♦♦♦♦♦
The banjo player's entire recorded output for Decca Records between 1956 and 1959, this includes a live performance and previously unreleased tracks. Jones sings about dogs and trains, rerecords some previous hits for King Records, and parodies Johnny Cash's "Don't Take Your Guns to Town." *—Brian Mansfield*

Good Ole Mountain Dew / Dec. 1, 1995 / Sony Special Products ♦♦♦♦
This ten-song, 22-minute budget-priced release includes the hits "T for Texas" and "Mountain Dew" (a 1960s re-recording) as well as such familiar fare as the classic dog songs "Old Rattler" and "Old Blue," the rip-roaring banjo workout "Are You From Dixie," and relatively reflective songs such as the idyllic Tennessee paean "Nashville on My Mind." The most interesting number here is Jones' own, topical "King of the Cannon County Hills," sort of his answer to "Okie From Muskogee," with digs at hippies ("let the hippie have his LSD and pills") and college students amid his description of rural southern life. Anyone who's heard "T for Texas" as done by the Everly Brothers or anyone else since Jimmie Rodgers hasn't really heard the song until they've heard Grandpa Jones' version here, which has the richness of a page out of a William Faulkner novel and about the best playing the song has ever gotten (and some great yodeling too). The sound is crisp if unexceptional, with nice stereo separation, and there are no notes, but until a proper Monument collection is released domestically this seven-dollar job will have to suffice. *—Bruce Eder*

Pickin' and a Grinnin' / Dec. 1, 1995 / Sony Special Products ♦♦♦♦
This is essentially a cut-down version of Grandpa Jones' 1963 album *Yodeling Hits*, basically a Jimmie Rodgers tribute, containing ten songs. It's a fine and valuable recording, despite slight overlap with the other current studio release. *—Bruce Eder*

Everybody's Grandpa / 1996 / Bear Family ♦♦♦♦♦
Five CDs, covering the years 1960 through 1973, more than 120 songs, including all of the hits, A-sides, B-sides, album tracks, and rarities from Grandpa Jones' stay on Monument Records. The sound is excellent, the selection of tracks includes remakes of Jones' classics as well as his new material from the biggest boom years of his career, and the booklet and annotation are the finest ever done on him. The pity is that his King, RCA, and Decca sides haven't been gathered together in the same manner—but that's for another box. *—Bruce Eder*

• **28 Greatest Hits** / May 19, 1998 / King ♦♦♦♦♦
Until a box set of his King recordings appears, *28 Greatest Hits* is the best available anthology of Grandpa Jones' classic early years. Sounding like Uncle Dave Macon with an electric guitar, Grandpa Jones' King sides mixed old-timey novelties with hot Travis-picking (Merle Travis and Grandpa Jones were bandmates in the Brown's Ferry Four gospel quartet), and created an anachronistic style that kept pace with the times in its own way. Not every track is electrified, but Jones' unique update of mountain music is heard most clearly on tracks such as "Five-String Banjo Boogie" and the popular "Eight More Miles to Louisville." While most of the songs are novelties, Jones plays it straight occasionally, as on "Tragic Romance" and the couple of sacred songs. Essential music from everybody's favorite Grandpa. *—Greg Adams*

Stan Jones

b. 1915, Arizona
Bass, Guitar / Traditional Country, Cowboy, Soundtracks
The name Stan Jones doesn't pop up in too many country music reference books, but most fans of cowboy songs and Western movie soundtrack music, not to mention the music of Gene Autry, the Sons of the Pioneers, Vaughn Monroe, and Johnny Cash, know his name, as the author of "(Ghost) Riders in the Sky." Stanley Davis Jones was born in Arizona in 1915 and became a forest ranger. He had an interest in music, could sing a little and play a guitar, and occasionally wrote songs in his spare time. In the fall of 1948, he was assigned as a technical advisor on a Columbia Pictures movie called *The Walking Hills*, starring Randolph Scott and Ella Raines and directed by John Sturges, when the crew was doing their location shooting in Death Valley. During a slow point in the work, Jones pulled out his guitar and started singing some of those songs and was told by Scott and the rest of the crew that the songs might go nicely in Western movies and that he should try and sell them to the Hollywood studios.

Jones followed their advice and tried to publish some of his songs (including "(Ghost) Riders in the Sky," which owed its melody to "When Johnny Comes Marching Home"), only to have them turned down by the music companies that he approached—one even said that "Riders" was too dirgeful and funereal. He recorded that song and a few others on his own, and composer Eden Ahbez (best known for the hit "Nature Boy") heard "(Ghost) Riders in the Sky" and brought it to Burl Ives, who cut it for Columbia Records. It was later picked up by Bing Crosby, Gene Autry, and Vaughn Monroe, as well as dozens of others, and Jones had a new career and major Hollywood representation.

By 1950, Jones was writing songs for major motion pictures, including Ford's *Rio Grande*, starring John Wayne and Maureen O'Hara—Ford learned of Jones' songs when actors Harry Carey Jr. and Ben Johnson brought him and his music to the director in person, during shooting—where they were sang by the Sons of the Pioneers, and he was being looked at by Walt Disney Studios, where he signed on as a composer and recording artist. He wrote and recorded individual songs and began releasing albums in 1961 with *Ghost Riders in the Sky*, followed by *Creakin' Leather* a year later and the concept album *This Was the West*. Jones' other credits include the beautiful theme music to the Warner Bros. television series *Cheyenne*, written in collaboration with Hollywood veteran William Lava—indeed, some viewers say the title theme was the best part of the program—and the title theme from the landmark John Ford Western *The Searchers*. "(Ghost) Riders in the Sky" remains one of the most popular and often-covered post-World War II country & western songs, constantly re-recorded and old recordings constantly revived. *—Bruce Eder*

Ghost Riders in the Sky / 1961 / Buena Vista ♦♦♦♦

Creakin' Leather / 1962 / Buena Vista ♦♦♦

• **This Was the West** / 196 / Disney ♦♦♦♦♦

Esteban Steve Jordan

Accordion / Norteño
When Esteban Jordan showed up at the gates of the 19th Annual Tejano Conjuto Festival in San Antonio, TX, and asked to play, it was such a typical move on his part that one might wonder why his appearance was mentioned in all the headline coverage of the event. It seems that even devoted fans had lost track of this legendary performer, nicknamed "El Parche" for the patch he wears over one eye. He had dropped out of the San Antonio music scene in 1991, and there was a great deal of wild speculation about what happened to him. It turns out he had been in Phoenix, AZ, during the '90s, and he told interviewers at the San Antonio festival that he had been extremely active there, having turned out nine new records during his stay. He "just showed up at the gate," festival organizers told reporters, and was quickly rushed to the stage where he jammed with fellow Tex-Mex star Flaco Jimenez, one again revealing the imaginative playing style that has often earned him a reputation as the Jimi Hendrix of the accordion.

But for Jordan to just appear after nearly a decade of mystery is really not that surprising, as he has always been considered something of a mystery man, one of those characters about whom there are legends simply involving how one might manage to get in touch with him. "You have to call a certain pool hall in such and such a border town..." would be one such myth, while another soothsayer might insist only the captain of a certain charter fishing boat on the Gulf Coast would know how to reach El Parche. These are some of the details that are known about Jordan. He was in his early sixties when he arrived at the San Antonio festival unannounced, and has been playing professionally since the age of seven. He was born somewhere in the Rio Grande Valley but actually grew up in California. His first official recording sessions were in 1963, featuring a group fronted by him and his wife, singer Virginia Martinez. He had actually been featured on a 78 rpm recording made in San Jose, CA, in the late '50s, part of a prize for best young conjunto performer. In the '60s, Jordan made many recordings on small Texas labels, some of which were regional hits. Eventually he began evolving the unique style that led to the comparison with Hendrix.

Unlike many artists in his genre, he has kept pace with technological developments, using devices such as phase shifters, fuzz boxes, and synthesizers, and was one of the few conjunto musicians to weave bits of styles such as fusion jazz and rock into his music. He also recorded country & western numbers. Throughout these diverse recordings he has always performed brilliantly on his instruments, the comparison with Hendrix being an apt one not just because he is "freaky," but because his sound is strong and vivid, literally jumping out of the grooves. Some of the titles he has recorded present a revealing portrait of his musical directions. There is "Polka Psicodelica," a cover of "You Keep Me Hangin' On" that certainly outdoes Vanilla Fudge, and "La Polka Loca." Throughout the '70s, Jordan recorded such material for a variety of Texas labels including Falcon, Fama, and Freddie. Members of his family frequently were heard backing him up, including his son Steve Jr. and daughter Bonnie. He recorded one album for his own El Parche label, entitled *Canto El Pueblo*, in which he played all the instruments himself.

During the '80s a small-scale accordion craze broke out in North America on the heels of the "My Toot Toot." New wave bands such as Brave Combo talked up the music of Jordan and the popularity of a few artists such as Joe King Carrasco helped focus attention on Tex-Mex music. This led to some recording opportunities with the nationally distributed Arhoolie label, which also licensed and re-released many of the Jordan recordings that had been done for smaller labels. In 1986, Jordan was able to cut an album for RCA entitled *Turn Me Loose*, which was nominated for a Grammy. Jordan lost out, however, to his old friend Flaco Jimeniz in this category. His bid for mainstream presence continued in 1986 when he was asked to do the soundtrack for the Cheech Marin film *Born in East L.A.* Nonetheless, as the new millennium began Jordan had left Texas, not a lot of information was available as to what he was doing and whatever recordings he was supposedly producing in Arizona have not been widely distributed even within the conjunto or Tex-Mex market. He is even a mystery man in cyberspace with the once-active website stevejordan.com also coming up missing in action. Fans of this wildflower of Tex-Mex music will just have to be content waiting for him to pop up again. —*Eugene Chadbourne*

La Bamba / 196? / ARV International ✦✦✦✦✦
Judging from the cover artwork and the sound (not to mention the cover of the Beatles' "Run for Your Life"), this is probably from the mid-'60s. It's a really cool mix of conjunto and R&B/rock approaches, not so much a "mix" actually as an alternation. One minute Jordan is grinding out a straight, peppy conjunto instrumental, the next he's belting some prime white soul with little or no hint of Tex-Mex whatsoever. The straight R&B/rock stuff demonstrates convincingly that Jordan could have been one of the all-time greatest non-African-American soul singers, sounding much like L.A.'s Thee Midniters did on their best straight soul material. Singing in both English and Spanish, Jordan is erratic only in terms of style, not quality, delivering a hepped-up version of "La Bamba" that must be heard to be believed. This is the rock & roll skeleton in Jordan's closet, but a very good one, deserving of reissue, especially as it's real hard to locate an original. —*Richie Unterberger*

Corrido de Johnny El Pachuco / 1971 / Arhoolie ✦✦✦✦✦
Lovers of vinyl should be familiar with the concept that certain releases simply can't be appreciated to the full extent in any other format, and this often a case of combined efforts in the artwork department as well as music. Here is a really perfect example, because although this material was eventually combined with other material by this madman of Tex-Mex, there is really nothing like owning the album with its priceless band standing around the tour bus photograph. Collectors will most likely have to settle for the Arhoolie reissue, but the real treasure would be finding the first pressing from the RyN label out of McAllen, TX. Listeners who are unfamiliar with Jordan, but might have heard his music described, should head toward this album, where his concept of working all manner of outside stylistic influences into Tex-Mex songs is given free rein. One would have to head to the Spike Jones band or perhaps the John Zorn *Naked City* project to hear such tight, well-arranged, and rehearsed arrangements involving strange tempo changes, musical jokes, and goofy fills. It is really fantastic music, with the title track one of those pieces of music one simply couldn't possibly improve upon. Plus, the lyrics have a good moral! What else could one ask for? If the answer is country & western, Jordan takes care of that order expertly with the last two tracks. [Note: for some reason, the Arhoolie release has a different album title printed on the label.] —*Eugene Chadbourne*

● Many Sounds of Steve Jordan / 1985 / Arhoolie ✦✦✦✦✦
This is a flamboyant artist operating in a style of music that is already pretty rowdy to begin with. The legend of Jordan being the Jimi Hendrix of the accordion might strike listeners as hype, but in reality is accurate more from a musical point of view than the obvious similarity in freaky appearances that both artists share. (Jordan has a wild mop of black hair and wears an eye patch, for which he was given the nickname "El Parche".) But a typical recording finds him coming across as powerfully as the Hendrix guitar style: right out front of his backing bands, his tone of the industrial strength variety, strong and cutting. This set intelligently combines his earliest recordings with music from about eight years later, during which time he developed from an excellent but fairly typical player to an iconoclastic wild man, throwing in all manner of stylistic asides including fusion jazz drum fills, satirical breakdowns à la Spike Jones, and even country & western. Just as Hendrix mastered a variety of effects devices, Jordan plugs his accordion into phase shifters and fuzz boxes and figures out how to get a totally personal sound, enhancing the traditional tone of the instrument in ways that always draw the listener in. All the music on this set is extremely enjoyable but of course it is the later music that is most innovative. He seems to be forging a trail that few would follow, however, as only a few eclectic artists such as Doug Sahm have even approached this level of musical pioneering, and even proponents of the school of avant-garde accordion playing have yet to get anywhere near Jordan's sound or inventiveness on his instrument. The incredible tale of a small time gangster named Jhonny is told in "El Corrido de Jhonny El Pachuco," definitely one of Jordan's masterpieces. —*Eugene Chadbourne*

Return of El Parche / 1986 / Rounder ✦✦✦✦✦
Steve Jordan's facility with uptempo or ballad material, polkas, waltzes, traditional Mexican and reworked American rock, pop and country helped established his base, as did a number of regional singles and albums. The 12 tunes on this anthology were recorded between 1976 and 1984 for the Freddie and Joe labels in Corpus Christi and San Antonio, including salsa/Afro-Latin jazz cuts, blues and country-tinged numbers. Jordan's vocals were soulful and exuberant, while his accordion playing was fast, dashing and enticing. Jordan also utilized an Echoplex and phase-shifter, getting some intriguing sounds. The songs were mostly short, catchy and diversified, expertly showing Jordan's total range and stylistic adaptability. —*Ron Wynn*

El Hurracane / 1987 / Rounder ✦✦✦✦
Steve Jordan's second Rounder anthology in 1989 included polkas, drinking songs and a couple of more ambitious numbers that blended Afro-Latin and Caribbean rhythmic influences. Once more, his accordion playing was impressive, especially on "Que Tanto Es Tantito" and "Ran-Kan-Kan." Jordan did some tunes in English and showed his skill with poignant ballads on "Goodbye Love," as well as the comedic/novelty fare "Kranke" and "They Say I'm a Drunkard." It was overall a lighter, less traditional date than its predecessor, but no less musically rigorous. —*Ron Wynn*

Las Coronelas / Arhoolie ✦✦✦✦

The Jordanaires

f. 1948, Springfield, MO
Group / Country-Pop, Pop, Nashville Sound/Countrypolitan
For over 40 years, the Jordanaires remained one of the premier backup vocal groups in country music, working with such greats as Jim Reeves, Patsy Cline, George Jones, and, of course, Elvis Presley. The quartet began in Springfield, MO, during the late '40s, featuring original members Bob Hubbard, Bill Matthews, Monty Matthews and Culley Holt who sang barbershop and spirituals. They debuted on the *Grand Ole Opry* in 1949. The group changed members during the early '50s, with Gordon Stoker and Hoyt Hawkins replacing Hubbard (who was drafted) and Bill Matthews (who became seriously ill). In 1953, Monty Matthews left the group for personal reasons, and was replaced by Neal Matthews.

By 1954, the Jordanaires were singing behind artists such as Elton Britt, Red Foley, and Jimmy Wakely. That year they appeared on Eddy Arnold's television show, but didn't get their big break until Elvis Presley, a longtime fan, invited the group to back him after receiving a major recording contract from RCA Victor. When Elvis became a star, he honored his promise to keep them as his backup singers, and they worked with him until 1970, appearing in many of his films and on his gospel recordings. In 1954, Culley Holt became ill and was replaced by Hugh Jarrett; he left in 1958 and was replaced by Ray Walker.

When not backing Elvis, the Jordanaires were busy making their own mark in country music. Neal Matthews was a talented arranger and was responsible for Jim Reeves' massive hit "Four Walls" (1957). In 1959, the Jordanaires began working with Patsy Cline, and also devised the Nashville number system of chords that is still widely used in recording studios and performances. The quartet also recorded their own gospel and country albums. It was the Jordanaires who provided the main impetus for the formation of the American Federation of Television/Radio Artists-Screen Actors' Guild in Nashville. They also established Nashville's commercial jingle market, which helped singers like Janie Fricke and Judy Rodman get their start. —*Sandra Brennan*

Big Country Hits / 1966 / Columbia ✦✦✦
This is not what one would necessarily look for from this group, but with some worthwhile moments for those who appreciate their sound. —*Bruce Eder*

● Monster Makers / 1969 / Stop ✦✦✦✦
The grotesque cover, intended as a joke, hides some superb music making. The hauntingly beautiful rendition of the country-gospel number "Skip-A-Rope" is possibly their best record ever. —*Bruce Eder*

Sing Gospel / 1992 / K-Tel ✦✦✦
After all these years, The Jordanaires are still in good form, and their gospel album is a fine collection, offering ten pleasant readings of mostly traditional material. It's only slightly hampered by rather sterile production and the occasional intrusive synthesizer. —*Stephen Thomas Erlewine*

Will the Circle Be Unbroken / 1992 / CEMA ✦✦✦

Sing the King / Aug. 18, 1998 / Music Club ✦✦✦
The prospect of the Jordanaires doing a tribute album of Elvis' songs was not so much a matter of "if" they were going to do one as much as "when." This reissue, originally cut for the Janus label, proves it was worth the wait, however long, and one well worth getting out there again. As in-demand as they have always been, they've sung these tunes countless times, either on the original recordings, in the movies, or behind somebody else doing a well-intentioned tribute. Although the lead vocals are no rhythmic match for the King, the harmonies are rich and impeccable and the arrangements are sparse and well-played. As these types of albums go, this one seems to be firing on most of its cylinders, right down to the stoic recitation on "Are You Lonesome Tonight?" Like the old saying goes, they ought to know how these songs go by now. —*Cub Koda*

Greatest Gospel Hits / Mar. 19, 2002 / Curb ✦✦✦
For traditionalists who can't handle the modern approach to gospel taken by new pioneers like Kirk Franklin, this type of project is the perfect antidote. It's hard-to-beat classic hymns, simply arranged and so easy to hum along to. The legendary quartet is still going strong after half a century, perfecting their spiritual barbershop harmonies on a collection of such classics as "Amazing Grace" and "How Great Thou Art." Adding to the traditional hymnal are versions of Willie Nelson's "Uncloudy Day" and Kris Kristofferson's tearjerking "Why Me Lord?" Perhaps in response to September 11, 2001, the group includes a close-to-the-vest version of Lee Greenwood's "God Bless the U.S.A.," featuring a break in the middle for "America the Beautiful." —*Jonathan Widran*

John Jorgenson

b. Jul. 6, 1956, Madison, WI
Guitar, Mandolin, Multi Instruments / Progressive Bluegrass, Country-Rock, Bluegrass, Instrumental Country
Southern California native John Jorgenson, a three-time winner of the Academy of Country Music award for Guitarist of the Year, was destined to be a part of the music business from an early age. Classically trained as a child, his father conducted for Benny Goodman. John, who idolized Goodman, played with his hero while his father was leading the way. Later, he went on to work for eight years as a member of the jazz and bluegrass group at Disneyland. While employed at the "happiest place on earth," John contributed his skills on a number of instruments, including mandolin, saxophone, guitar, and clarinet. At another point in his career he was the featured bassoonist for the L.A. Camerata. Still, it was Jorgenson's expertise as a guitarist that brought him fame and respect as he recorded with the groundbreaking Byrds as well as Rose Maddox, Roy Orbison, Bob Dylan, John Prine, Bonnie Raitt, Dan Fogelberg, and even Michael Nesmith.

In 1986 Jorgenson joined forces with some of the biggest guns on the West Coast in order to form a truly traditional country-rock outfit called the Desert Rose Band. With former Byrd Chris Hillman singing lead and assistance from Herb Pedersen, Bill Bryson,

Steve Duncan, and steel player Jay Dee Maness, the Desert Rose Band came out of the gate full force. Jorgenson's power-driven 12-string was one of the reasons. Their first single was a remake of the classic Johnnie & Jack hit "Ashes of Love" from their self-titled debut album. With the release of their second project in 1988, *Running*, they were named the Academy of Country Music's Touring Band of the Year. This honor was repeated in 1989 and 1990. Also, in 1989 and 1990 they were nominated for the Country Music Association's Best Vocal Group award.

In spite of the number-one hits, the classic covers they brought back to life, and all the Top Ten singles, the Desert Rose Band began to crumble by 1992. Jorgenson left to pursue other interests, including his guitar work with the Hellecasters, a band that came together after a one-time-only gig in 1991. Comprised of Jorgenson and fellow Telecaster disciples Will Ray and Jerry Donahue, the Hellecasters were made up of three lead players and no vocalist. *The Return of the Hellecasters*, their debut recording, was voted both Album of the Year and Country Album of the Year in 1993 by the *Guitar Player* magazine Reader's Poll. A second Hellecasters project in 1995, *Escape From Hollywood*, continued to refine and redefine guitar techniques. Jorgenson recorded and toured with Elton John during 1995, and one year later recorded a bluegrass project with the legendary Rose Maddox at Mad Dog Studios. Released in 1996, *The Moon Is Rising* was also produced by Jorgenson. *Emotional Savant* followed in 1999. —*Jana Pendragon*

After You've Gone / 1988 / Curb ◆◆◆◆
This release is a blend of the Django Reinhardt-Stephane Grappelli quintet of the Hot Club of France and David Grisman's Dawg music, the latter being no surprise since Grisman adds his distinctive mandolin to the CD. Jorgenson is a talented guitarist known for his tenure with Chris Hillman's short-lived Desert Rose Band, but he's also right at home with swing era gems like "You're Nobody's Sweetheart Now" and Reinhardt's "Mabel," and his own compositions "Red Shoelaces" and "Mirror in Blue" fit in beautifully. Violinist Daryl Anger, a veteran of Grisman's group and the Turtle Island String Quartet, is also no stranger to classic swing and performs well. Jorgenson's chops on clarinet may be news to some folks but he proves up to the task on a superb take of "I'm Crazy 'Bout My Baby." —*Ken Dryden*

Scott Joss
b. Long Beach, CA
Fiddle, Mandolin / Western Swing, Bakersfield Sound, Neo-Traditionalist Country, Americana
Scott Joss was often praised as the "heir to the Bakersfield throne" because of his early association with Tiny Moore and Merle Haggard and his later affiliation with Buck Owens and Dwight Yoakam. Born in Long Beach and raised in Redding, Joss was a native Californian whose roots ran deep. He learned to play fiddle from Jana Jae, the one-time wife and fiddle player for Buck Owens & His Buckaroos. Befriended by one of Bob Wills' surviving Playboys, Tiny Moore, Joss was encouraged to develop his talent on a professional level after winning numerous California State Fiddle Championships. In 1980, at the age of 18, he got the call from Haggard. His first show as one of the Strangers was at Carnegie Hall. Still a little green, Joss returned to Redding to continue working on his performance skills before joining up with Merle and the band on the road. While with the Strangers, Joss spent time with Bakersfield guitarman Roy Nichols, who saw great promise in the young fiddle player.

Leaving the road and Merle was a hard decision, but Joss wanted to begin work on a band of his own. After moving to Sacramento, he hooked up with Dennis Barney, another California player from the early days. Barney, who became mentor and friend to the fledgling frontman, showed Joss the ropes and became a member of his band. After playing around California for a while, Joss was spotted by Pete Anderson, who produced, arranged, led the band, and played guitar for Dwight Yoakam. Bringing Joss into the fold in 1988 allowed Anderson to keep an eye on him and his career growth. Commuting between Sacramento and Los Angeles became a way of life for Yoakam's fiddle player and harmony vocalist. On the road and in the studio, Joss had a full-time job as a member of the Babylonian Cowboys. Still, whenever he was in Sacramento he would pull together Barney, brother-in-law Don Weeks, and some other players and work on his solo venture. Eight years after signing on with Yoakam, Anderson and respected L.A. producer/engineer/bassman Dusty Wakeman (Rosie Flores, Dwight Yoakam, the Lonesome Strangers, Reach Around) took Joss into the all new Mad Dog Studios to start work on his first solo project.

Souvenirs was released in 1996 and hit Gavin's Americana chart with all the force of a fast moving train, landing at number seven. Top cuts included two Jim Lauderdale songs, "Stay Out of My Arms," a traditional shuffle, and the anthemic "Doin' Time in Bakersfield." Also included was one Joss original, "I Never Got Anywhere With You," which proved that Scott Joss was indeed a worthy successor to Buck, Merle, and all the rest who created the Bakersfield sound. —*Jana Pendragon*

● **Souvenirs** / 1996 / Little Dog ◆◆◆◆◆
The debut album by Scott Joss, an award-winning fiddle player whose musical resumé includes playing behind Dwight Yoakam and legends Merle Haggard and Buck Owens, is an impressive nod to the classic California country sound that also offers up a contemporary feel. Possessing a richly deep and well-oiled voice, Joss especially shines on the traditional-sounding cuts—particularly two cool Jim Lauderdale-penned tunes, "Doin' Time in Bakersfield" and "Stay Out of My Arms." And although most of the 11 cuts come from such notable writers as Kostas, Kevin Welch, and Tom Russell, among others, Joss proves himself more than a capable songwriter with the standout ballad "I Never Got Anywhere With You." His fiddle playing is good, but the spotlight here is on Joss the singer. The rest of the musical muscle—featuring mainly producer Pete Anderson's signature lead guitar and others from Yoakam's band—is inspired and memorable throughout. —*Jack Leaver*

A New Reason to Care / Jul. 4, 2000 / Little Dog ◆◆◆
Scott Joss may be primarily known as a sideman for such artists as Merle Haggard and Dwight Yoakam, but when he's not backing the greats, he's releasing solo albums full of

strong traditional country. He also proves that he was paying attention all those years. On "Even if You Have to Lie," for example, he does a stirring turn on the kind of emotional balladry for which Haggard is known. And like his old boss, Joss is able to get downright sweet and sorrowful without stumbling into overly saccharine territory. "You're the Reason," meanwhile, rolls and stops with rockabilly flair while the title track enters pensive acoustic territory with a rumination on road life. *A New Reason to Care* proves that Scott Joss is a genuinely great country singer, with pipes that fall smack dab between Haggard's bruised baritone and Jimmie Dale Gilmore's goofy, rangy charm. It's clear that this noted sideman is deserving of his own spotlight. There's fine production work here by Pete Anderson. —*Erik Hage*

Benny Joy
Vocals, Guitar, Composer / Rockabilly
Benny Joy was not a talent on the order of top rockabilly stars, but he had more going for him than a lot of the obscure singers in the style that have been rediscovered and championed by collectors. The Tampa guitarist and vocalist cut a few rare singles in the late '50s that didn't get anywhere, although he was represented for a time by Platters manager Buck Ram and did some recording in Nashville with session musicians like saxophonist Boots Randolph, guitarist Hank Garland, and drummer Buddy Harman. Although rockabilly was calming down by the late '50s, Joy seemed in no mood to settle down himself, and on numerous sides he sounds like he's about to shout-sing himself hoarse. Joy wrote most of his material, and although he was derivative of such bigger cats as Elvis Presley, Buddy Holly, Jerry Lee Lewis, and others, on his better tracks he projected a straight-to-the-heart-of-the-matter exuberance along the lines of (although, again, not as good as) Eddie Cochran and Gene Vincent.

Joy was also one of the relatively few minor rock artists to tour Europe in the late '50s—he did so twice, in fact. After parting with Ram, Joy recorded for Decca without success and in the 1960s became a country songwriter, supplying some material for Stonewall Jackson. Like many obscure rockabilly acts, Joy enjoyed renewed appreciation in England after British collectors discovered his work, particularly for his 1958 single "Crash the Party." —*Richie Unterberger*

● **Crash the Rockabilly Party** / Dec. 15, 1998 / Ace ◆◆◆◆◆
Joy only released three singles in the late 1950s (all here), but a bunch of previously unissued material (some without a full band) from the era was scoured up for various reissues in the late '70s and early '80s. With the addition of half a dozen more unissued cuts and three instrumental sides by guitarist Big John Taylor (who played with Joy), *Crash the Rockabilly Party* has 28 cuts from Joy's early years—quite a job, given how little Joy managed to get on the market in the 1950s. Certainly the cuts are rather similar-sounding, and Joy could have really done with a higher grade of material if he had wanted to make the big time. At his best, his all-out enthusiasm conquers the generic tunes, as on "Miss Bobby Sox," "Little Red Book," and "Spin the Bottle." At other times, it's apparent he's trying to follow someone's lead; "Ittie Bittie Everything" is sung as if under instructions to imitate Buddy Holly, for instance, while "Kiss Me" emulates Elvis Presley's ballad style, and "Bundle of Love" sounds like a son of Elvis' "I Got Stung." —*Richie Unterberger*

Cledus T. Judd
Vocals, Producer / Contemporary Country, Country Comedy, Novelty
Country music's answer to Weird Al Yankovic, Cledus T. Judd had a similar approach to song parody, recording backing tracks that were as similar as possible to the original versions. Like Yankovic, he also recorded some original material, but parodies of recent country hits were his bread and butter; also like Yankovic, a Judd parody came to be regarded as a badge of honor by many of the artists he reworked. Judd made his bow in 1995 with the Razor & Tie album *Cledus T. Judd (No Relation)*, a billing that made clear his lack of connection to Wynonna and Naomi. His breakthrough set was the follow-up, 1996's *I Stoled This Record*, which established his long-running preoccupation with Shania Twain—not only did he transform her "If You're Not in It for Love (I'm Outta Here)" into "I'm Not in Here for Love (Just Yer Beer)," he also recorded the original "If Shania Was Mine" and had her guest (along with Joe Diffie) on "(She's Got a Butt) Bigger Than the Beatles." *Did I Shave My Back for This?*, the title cut a parody of Deana Carter, followed in 1998, also featuring redone material from Brooks & Dunn and Tracy Lawrence, among others. 1999's *Juddmental* saw him branching out into pop with a Ricky Martin parody as well as a Garth Brooks/Chris Gaines send-up and another ode to Twain, "Shania I'm Broke."

Judd's albums weren't blockbusters, but they sold consistently enough to earn him a major-label contract with Sony's revived Monument imprint. His 2000 major-label debut, *Just Another Day in Parodies*, skewered material by the Dixie Chicks, Brad Paisley, Kenny Chesney, Toby Keith, and even Kid Rock. The follow-up, 2002's *Cledus Envy*, offered parodies of Faith Hill and Billy Gilman as well as *O Brother, Where Art Thou?*'s "Man of Constant Sorrow." Later that year, Judd issued his first holiday album, *Cledus Navidad*. He returned in 2003 with the mini-album *Six Pack of Judd*. —*Steve Huey*

Cledus T. Judd (No Relation) / 1995 / Razor & Tie ◆◆◆
The parenthetical comment in the title gives you an indication of what you're in for if you listen to Cledus T. Judd's debut album. Cledus' jokes are rarely more clever than his observation that he is "no relation" to the famous singing duo of Naomi and Wynonna Judd—however, that simple-minded humor is part of his appeal. The fact of the matter is, if you don't like corny country humor, you will not find *Cledus T. Judd (No Relation)* amusing. But if you do find Jeff Foxworthy and *Hee Haw* funny, *(No Relation)* is a laugh riot—though he doesn't have a distinctive routine like Foxworthy, Judd is more consistently funny and his music, on its own terms, is pretty enjoyable. —*Leo Stanley*

● **I Stoled This Record** / May 21, 1996 / Razor & Tie ◆◆◆◆
Cledus T. Judd's debut album indicated that he was a first-rate country comic for the '90s, but his second effort, *I Stoled This Record*, is where his talents truly blossom. Judd's

humor is simple and direct—witness how he lusts after superstar country vocalist Shania Twain on "If Shania Was Mine" or the Charlie Daniels parody "Cledus Went Down to Florida" or the obvious Elmo & Patsy sendup "Grandpa Got Runned Over By a John Deere." It doesn't take a comic genius to come up with these endearingly sophomoric and corny jokes, but it does take some guts to actually follow them through, and that's what makes *I Stoled This Record* surprisingly engaging and fun. Besides, the music is better than you would imagine (Joe Diffie and Shania herself guest on "(She's Got A Butt) Bigger Than the Beatles"). *—Thom Owens*

Did I Shave My Back for This? / Mar. 24, 1998 / Razor & Tie ✦✦✦✦
The title of *Did I Shave My Back for This?*—a clever send-up of Deana Carter's *Did I Shave My Legs for This?*—indicates that the album will be another funny collection of song parodies and humorous originals. Cledus T. Judd, it must be said, does not disappoint. Like a redneck Weird Al Yankovic, Judd is an engaging, charismatic performer who possesses a wry wit and a way with words—witness how he twists Brooks & Dunn's "Mama Don't Get Dressed Up for Nothing'" into "Cledus Don't Stop Eatin' for Nothin'." Judd's ear picks up on rhythms and meters inherent in each song, resulting in unexpected, delightful parodies. And country humor rarely comes any smarter than "First Redneck on the Internet" or "Hankenstein." But don't let Judd's brains or goofiness stand in the way of your enjoyment of *Did I Shave My Back for This?*—if you've ever laughed at Ray Stevens, Grandpa Jones, or Weird Al Yankovic, this will surely tickle your funny bone. And if you're wondering if this is just too much frivolity for you, consider that the great Buck Owens lends his musical support, which means that there's substance to the album as well. *—Chuck Donkers*

Juddmental / Oct. 26, 1999 / Razor & Tie ✦✦✦✦
Cledus T. Judd might be the most surprising success story in '90s country music. After all, who would have guessed that country music wanted a Weird Al Yankovic of their very own? Then again, country has a new comedy *cause celebre* each decade or so, and it was inevitable that a cornpone Weird Al would surface at some point. Of course, song parodies have been a staple of country comedy for years, but Judd's sensibility was straight out of Yankovic—copying the original arrangement and recording to a T, only with wacky lyrics. And, like Weird Al, Cledus' stuff doesn't work if you're not familiar with the originals or if you just don't buy into the whole schick. If you're down with Judd, however, you'll find that his catalog is every bit as consistent as Yankovic's—he hits the mark with each of his parodies, and his original songs are strong, too. *Juddmental*, his fourth album, is fundamentally no different than his first three efforts, and it is no better and no worse. That's not laziness—that's consistency. If some of the jokes fall a little flat ("Coronary Life" is disgusting, not funny, and the Ricky Martin sendup "Livin' Like John Travolta" is misguided), there are plenty more that do work (particularly "Shania I'm Broke"—strange how Shania brings out the best in Cledus). And it's hard not to smile when Judd twists Garth Brooks' alter-ego Chris Gaines into Waite Gaines. So, if you've never liked Cledus before, this ain't gonna change your mind. But if you have, you'll find *Juddmental* to your liking. *—Stephen Thomas Erlewine*

Just Another Day in Parodies / Nov. 14, 2000 / Sony ✦✦✦
Cledus T. Judd celebrates his ascension to major-label status on his fifth album by taking on his new labelmates, the Dixie Chicks, on two songs, "Goodbye Squirrel," which rewrites "Goodbye Earl" into a hunting story, and "Wife Naggin'," a self-explanatory takeoff on "Sin Wagon." Brad Paisley's "Me Neither" gets transformed into the double entendre "More Beaver," which is nominally about a desire for more reruns of *Leave It to Beaver*, with help from Paisley himself on several instruments, and John Anderson sings the choruses of the original song "Momma's Boy," essentially a standup routine set to music. But the cleverest parodies are "My Cellmate Thinks I'm Sexy" (think Kenny Chesney's "She Thinks My Tractor's Sexy"), which discusses the legal difficulties of some country stars, and the deconstruction of Toby Keith's massive hit "How Do You Like Me Now," reimagined as "How Do You Milk a Cow." Judd branched out into pop music last time by making fun of Ricky Martin; this time he ventures into rock by turning Kid Rock's "Cowboy" into "Plowboy." But he's on firmer ground with his country satires, which are full of asides about Tim McGraw, Faith Hill, and Billy Gilman that country fans will appreciate. As usual, the more familiar you are with the country music scene, the funnier you will find this stuff, but a lot of it works on its own terms. *—William Ruhlmann*

Cledus Envy / Apr. 30, 2002 / Monument ✦✦✦✦
Either Cledus T. Judd is getting better at writing his musical parodies of country hits or country music itself is getting sillier and more deserving of satire, but this is the funniest of his six albums. The standout tracks are "Breath," a rewrite of Faith Hill's overly sensitive hit "Breathe" that changes the subject to halitosis ("I can feel you breathe" becomes "I can smell your breath"), and "My Voice," a skewering of Billy Gilman's sanctimonious "One Voice" that shows what will happen when the pint-sized singer's voice inevitably starts to change. It isn't only Judd's comic lyrics that make these tracks work, but also the playing that makes fun of the original arrangements, such as the piano on "My Voice" that indulges in all kinds of foolish embellishments and the hip-hop effects on "Man of Constant Borrow" which add to the takeoff on the traditional "Man of Constant Sorrow" from *O Brother, Where Are Thou?* Judd doesn't always rewrite other people's hits—"Let's Burn One" is an original tune about music downloading, while "If George Strait Starts Dancin'" is another new song about over-production on country awards shows—but the parodies provide the best moments. The album is so good it even survives a big downturn in quality on the last three tracks, "Just Another Day in Parodies" (the title of his last album), in which Judd laments the difficulty in getting people to let him write parodies of their songs; "Leave You Laughin'," a sentimental and serious statement of purpose; and the jingoistic "Don't Mess With America." These tracks are worthless, but the first nine are keepers, and that's a good percentage on a comedy album. [Initial copies are packaged with a bonus DVD containing a video of "Breath."] *—William Ruhlmann*

Cledus Navidad / Oct. 15, 2002 / Sony ✦✦✦
On their Christmas albums, most performers draw upon the existing body of holiday music for their selections, re-creating old favorites in their own style. Country music comedian Cledus T. Judd is no exception on his seasonal album, *Cledus Navidad.* Acknowledging the humor of Christmases past, he covers Spike Jones' "All I Want for Christmas Is My Two Front Teeth" (adapting it into a weak rap parody called "All I Want for Christmas Is Two Gold Front Teef"), Ray Stevens' "Santa Claus Is Watchin' You," and Elmo & Patsy's "Grandma Got Run Over By a Reindeer" (done in an outlaw country-rock arrangement). But while remakes are often the highlights of more serious artists' Christmas albums, far superior to the new attempts to join the pantheon, these songs are the least of Judd's collection. The best tracks are the new ones, starting with "Cledus' Christmas Ball," which has sharp remarks for some current country stars, the wittiest being the swipe at Garth Brooks, poking fun at the star's repeated withdrawals from the music business. ("Garth retired early again, but he'll be back next year.") The other standout is a parody of Johnny Cash's "Ring of Fire," "Tree's on Fire," sung in an impersonation of the Man in Black himself. Of course, the humor gets gross ("Don't Serve Beans") and politically incorrect ("Stephon the Alternative Lifestyle Reindeer") on occasion, but that's to be expected from a country comedian. Judd may not be quite up to his predecessors in seasonal humor, but he's trying and frequently succeeding. There are a lot of laughs here. *—William Ruhlmann*

Six Pack of Judd / Apr. 29, 2003 / Monument ✦✦✦
Cledus T. Judd has opted to release half an album this time out, only six songs running less than 23 minutes. His avowed reasons for such a disc are that it allows his fans to spend less than ten dollars for the CD (of course, they also get less), and, perhaps more significantly, he is able to be more current in his parodies of popular country songs. Or, as he puts it in a press release, "I wanted to get these out while the songs I'm rippin' off are still popular." Like his pop counterpart, Weird Al Yankovic, Judd has become an institution much encouraged by the people whose songs he sends up. Maybe that's because most of his parodies are harmless, such as his take on Toby Keith's "Who's Your Daddy?," "Where's Your Mommy?," which effortlessly becomes a song about a father left at home with an infant and quickly descends into poop jokes. The best satires are the ones that have a little bite. "My Crowd," which takes off from Montgomery Gentry's "My Town," actually has better lyrics than the original, and though it nominally comments on Judd's own redneck audience, it's actually speaking, accurately, about the one Montgomery Gentry deliberately cultivates. Technically, "I Was Country When Country Wasn't Pop" is not current, since it is inspired by Barbara Mandrell's 1981 hit "I Was Country When Country Wasn't Cool." But it actually comments on contemporary pop crossover attempts in a witty manner, much assisted by an uncredited vocal duet from George Jones. The other numbers might not be so clever, but Judd's batting average is still pretty good on this mini-album. *—William Ruhlmann*

Wynonna Judd (Christina Ciminella)

b. May 30, 1964, Ashland, KY
Vocals, Guitar / Contemporary Country, Neo-Traditionalist Country
As one-half of the Judds, Wynonna Judd became one of the most popular and respected female country stars of her time. On her own since the early '90s, Judd demonstrated an eclecticism that increasingly confounded hardcore country fans and radio programmers but also helped her retain a core of admiring followers. Her solo records might stick with Judds-style country-pop or delve into roots rock, blues, gospel, adult contemporary pop, folk, or Southern R&B. Judd was born Christina Ciminella in Ashland, KY, on May 30, 1964. Her mother, Naomi (then known by her birth name, Diana), was still in high-school at the time, and her biological father abandoned the family almost immediately; Naomi married another man, Michael Ciminella, to create a traditional family unit. In 1968, they moved to Los Angeles, but the marriage disintegrated in 1972. Wynonna spent parts of the next few years living on welfare and returned to Kentucky with her mother in 1976. They lived in a mountain home with no phone or television, and listening to country music on the radio was a major source of entertainment. Wynonna learned to play guitar after receiving one as a gift and was soon singing close harmony with her mother. By the time she was a teenager, her vocal talents were apparent, and in 1979, the family moved to Nashville to try their luck in the music business.

Naomi and Wynonna landed a contract with RCA in 1983, and over the remainder of the '80s, they became the biggest-selling duo in country music history (a title that would later be taken over by Brooks & Dunn). Wynonna wasn't always as career-minded as her mother, who effectively ran the group, and was growing ever more rebellious when, in 1990, Naomi was diagnosed with hepatitis C; she retired from performing after a farewell tour in 1991. Wynonna was at first unsure whether she wanted to carry on without her mother but quickly decided to embark on a solo career, signing with MCA. Her first album on her own, *Wynonna*, was released in 1992 and was an instant smash, selling over three-million copies; it also topped the country charts, reached the Top Five on the pop side, and earned many positive reviews as well. Her first three solo singles—"She Is His Only Need," "I Saw the Light," and "No One Else on Earth"—all went to number one on the country charts, and "My Strongest Weakness" also made the Top Five.

Judd's 1993 follow-up, *Tell Me Why*, was another platinum-selling, number-one country/Top Five pop album; it gave her five more Top Ten hits in the title track, "Only Love," "Girls With Guitars," "Rock Bottom," and "Is It Over Yet." However, Judd's career hit a snag when it was revealed that, like her mother before her, she had become pregnant out of wedlock. The tabloids had a field day, and more conservative country fans attacked her as being an immoral role model. Judd eventually married her son's father, Nashville businessman Arch Kelly, in 1996, and that year finally released her third album, *Revelations.* It was a more introspective affair that gave her a number-one single in "To

Be Loved By You" and eventually went platinum despite not producing any further Top Ten hits. For the follow-up, 1997's *The Other Side*, Judd refashioned her sound into a bluesy, rock-driven roots-music blend that often recalled Bonnie Raitt. It reached the country Top Five yet failed to sell a million copies for the first time in Judd's solo career, prompting her to split with MCA and move to Mercury.

By this point, Judd had also had a second child, but her marriage fell apart in 1998; instead of releasing another solo album right away, Judd reunited with her mother for a New Year's Eve concert to ring in the year 2000. They embarked on a full-fledged tour together in 2000, and four new Judds songs were released on an exclusive bonus disc with Wynonna's Mercury debut, *New Day Dawning*. Her most eclectic effort to date (and her first as a co-producer), the album featured covers of Joni Mitchell and the Fabulous Thunderbirds, and while it didn't spawn any major hit singles, it again climbed into the Top Five on the country album charts. —*Steve Huey*

Wynonna / 1992 / Curb/MCA ✦✦✦
Daughter Judd stakes out her own territory. It's probably safe to say that she had more in her than most people guessed. From the tender "She Is His Only Need" to the Southern rock & soul of "No One Else on Earth," Wynonna sings With a smoldering sensuality that pulsed beneath the surface of the duo's best records—even "Live With Jesus" sounds sexy. After a few more albums like this, folks may not even remember The Judds. It also includes "I Saw the Light" and "My Strongest Weakness." —*Brian Mansfield*

Tell Me Why / May 11, 1993 / Curb/MCA ✦✦✦✦✦
Wynonna's second album, *Tell Me Why*, is a more confident and diverse collection than her debut. Drawing from sources as varied as gospel, folk, and blues-rock, Wynonna doesn't necessarily deliver a pure country album, but her blend of roots genres does qualify as a cleverly constructed contemporary country record. The selection of material is first-rate, but what makes *Tell Me Why* her best solo effort is how she ties all of the songs together with her assured—and surprisingly subtle—vocals. —*Thom Owens*

Revelations / 1996 / Curb/MCA ✦✦✦✦
Wynonna had no problem with the spotlight; or, as the tabloids regularly revealed, with opening up her private life for all to poke through and ponder. For all of her cultivating of celebrity, her albums continued to turn down the lights and focus on the softer glow of emotional verities her albums. *Revelations* is another worthy solo effort by the younger member of the Judds, the mother-daughter duo through which she first found massive fame. Often somber, and just as often right on the money, she casts a blue tint to several reflective songs that examine spirituality (without sermons) and the quiet discoveries that come with mature relationships. Ballads like "Don't Look Back," "Love By Grace," and "My Angel Is Here"—all album highlights—prove how sympathetic her rich, expressive voice can be when applied to a well-written, sensitive lyric. As in the past, she's equally convincing on uptempo, R&B-infused strutters, such as Delbert McClinton's "Somebody to Love You" or the gospel rave-up "Dance! Shout!" It's a mystery as to why she would include her version of "Free Bird," which previously was released as part of a Lynyrd Skynyrd tribute album. (Maybe someone should tell her that those people who yelled it out during encores were kidding.) Otherwise, *Revelations* is just that; a revealing next step by a country music star who understands the power of subtlety in an age that tends to prefer overstatement. —*Michael McCall*

● **Collection** / Apr. 8, 1997 / MCA ✦✦✦✦✦
Collection contains all of the highlights and big hits from Wynonna's three albums (*Wynonna*, *Tell Me Why*, *Revelations*), including "Tell Me Why," "Rock Bottom," "Girls With Guitars," and the number-one singles "She Is His Only Need," "I Saw the Light," and "No One Else on Earth." —*Thom Owens*

The Other Side / Oct. 21, 1997 / MCA ✦✦✦
The title says it all—*The Other Side* finds Wynonna exploring new territory, repositioning herself as a rootsy blues-rocker in the vein of Bonnie Raitt. While Wynonna has a strong voice, she doesn't have the presence to pull off this sound convincingly. Furthermore, the material just isn't strong. A few songs have catchy hooks, but most of the songs are bland and undistinguished, and when combined with Wynonna's unremarkable delivery, the results are a true disappointment. —*Stephen Thomas Erlewine*

New Day Dawning / Feb. 1, 2000 / MCA ✦✦✦✦
Southern gospel and soul, rockers, and ballads all grace Wynonna Judd's fifth release as a solo artist and her first as co-producer. One of the most recognizable voices in country music, the depth and range of her voice can be heard from the first track, the rhythmic "Going Nowhere," to the last, the soulful "I Can't Wait to Meet You." Fans will be delighted to hear Judd put her rock-influenced country-pop spin on Joni Mitchell's "Help Me." And of course, what's a good Wynonna album without her signature growl? As a bonus for Judd fans, *New Day Dawning* includes a special second CD, *Big Bang Boogie*, available in limited quantities with four new tracks from Wynonna and Naomi. The Judds reunion CD, however brief, is an exciting extra to the already electrifying *New Day....* —*Maria Konicki Dinoia*

The Judds
f. 1979, Nashville, TN, **db.** 1991
Group / Contemporary Country
Up until the rise of Brooks & Dunn in the '90s, the Judds were the most commercially successful duo in country music history. Mother Naomi and daughter Wynonna enjoyed an astounding run of 14 number-one singles from 1984 to 1989, ranking them as one of the most popular country acts of the '80s. Their music combined elements of traditional country harmony singing, bluegrass, and Appalachian folk with pop, rock, and polished contemporary production. Moreover, Wynonna's powerful, bluesy, often sexy lead vocals established her as one of the finest female country singers of her era. But even more important than their widely accessible sound—or their considerable visual appeal—was

their sympathetic understanding of working-class and small-town women, earned through a long, hard struggle of their own. Though their off-stage relationship was often more contentious than it appeared, it took a life-threatening illness to bring the Judds to a halt—Naomi retired from performing when she was diagnosed with hepatitis C but beat the disease to watch Wynonna enjoy an acclaimed solo career.

The Judds' story began in Ashland, KY, where Naomi was born Diana Ellen Judd on January 11, 1946. An honor roll student, she often played piano in the Baptist church her family attended but shocked the town by getting pregnant at age 17 by a man who abandoned her immediately. Hoping to save face, she married new sweetheart Michael Ciminella but missed her high-school graduation, giving birth to Wynonna (born Christina Ciminella, May 30, 1964); to make matters worse, her brother died of cancer not long after, and her parents divorced. In 1968, the family moved to Los Angeles, and new daughter Ashley (later, of course, a successful movie star) was born not long after. Unfortunately, the marriage broke apart in 1972, and the family often survived on welfare while Diana bounced between jobs (waitressing, modeling, serving as secretary for the pop-soul group the 5th Dimension) and endured an abusive rebound relationship.

In 1976, she moved the family back to Kentucky, where they lived in a mountain home with no phone or TV. Music helped pass the time, and Wynonna began playing the guitar and harmonizing with her mother, who was in the meantime studying to become a nurse. She renamed herself Naomi and brought the family back to the West Coast to finish her nursing degree. Wynonna's singing talent was by then readily apparent, and in 1979, the Judds moved to Nashville in hopes of making it in the music business.

Naomi and Wynonna made tapes of themselves on a cheap cassette recorder and sometimes sang on Ralph Emery's local morning show. They caught their first big break through Naomi's nursing job: one of her patients happened to be the daughter of record producer Brent Maher, and that contact eventually led to an audition for RCA executives in early 1983. The Judds were signed on the spot and issued their debut single, "Had a Dream (For the Heart)," late in the year. It reached the country Top 20, and it was accompanied by a quickly assembled mini-album, *The Judds*. Their second single, "Mama He's Crazy," was a breakout hit that went all the way to number one and later won a Grammy for Best Country Vocal by a Duo or Group. Their first true full-length, *Why Not Me*, was released in 1984 and took its place as a classic of modern country, establishing the Judds as spokeswomen for a new generation of female country music fans. The Grammy-winning title track, "Girls Night Out," and "Love Is Alive" all went on to top the country charts, as did the album, which also sold over a million copies.

The Judds were now full-fledged stars, and they spent the rest of the '80s cranking out hit after hit. 1985's exuberant *Rockin' With the Rhythm* spawned four number-one singles in "Have Mercy," "Grandpa (Tell Me 'Bout the Good Old Days" (another Grammy winner), "Rockin' With the Rhythm in the Rain," and "Cry Myself to Sleep." *Heartland* (1987) was widely viewed as more uneven than its predecessors but kept their hit streak going strong with the chart-toppers "I Know Where I'm Going," "Maybe Your Baby's Got the Blues," and "Turn It Loose." The ten-track *Greatest Hits* was released in 1988 and featured two new songs: "Give a Little Love," which went to number two and won another Grammy, and "Change of Heart," which hit number one. *River of Time* (1989) became the first Judds album not to top the country charts since their debut mini-album but continued their streak of consecutive million-sellers all the same. "Young Love (Strong Love)" and "Let Me Tell You About Love" both hit number one and would prove to be the last Judds songs to do so.

By this point in the Judds' career, mother and daughter were clearly distinct personalities. Naomi was the extroverted stage presence, the sometime songwriter, the ambitious businesswoman who steered the group's career and pushed her daughter to keep realizing her talent. Wynonna—despite her quiet, reserved demeanor—was a prodigiously talented vocal stylist who grew surer of herself with every passing release and rebelled more and more forcefully against her mother's direction. By the time *Love Can Build a Bridge* was released in 1990, there was already speculation that Wynonna was ready to mount a solo career. Not long after the album was released, Naomi announced that she had been diagnosed with hepatitis C, a chronic and life-threatening illness that she had likely contracted from a needle during her days as a nurse. The constant touring had already begun to take its toll on her health, and she elected to retire from performing and recording, following one last farewell tour in 1991.

Love Can Build a Bridge produced several hits, including the Top Fivers "Born to Be Blue" and the title track, and the tour was unsurprisingly a blockbuster success.Wynonna released her solo debut in 1992 and followed it with several more successful albums over the course of the '90s. Naomi, meanwhile, sought alternative medical treatment for the disease that was expected to take her life in several years. She published her autobiography, *Love Can Build a Bridge*, in 1993; the book was later turned into a TV-movie. By 1999, Naomi's hepatitis had somehow gone into remission, and she and Wynonna reunited for a gala New Year's Eve concert to ring in the new millennium; it was later released as *The Judds Reunion Live*. A full-fledged reunion tour followed in 2000, and four newly recorded Judds songs were issued exclusively on a bonus disc included with Wynonna's solo album *New Day Dawning*. Following the tour, Wynonna resumed her solo career, while Naomi made her primary living as a motivational speaker. —*Steve Huey*

The Judds / 1983 / RCA ✦✦✦✦✦
Though it lacked a strong set of songs, the Judds' eponymous debut album established that the vocals of Wynonna and Naomi played off of each other beautifully, and songs like the hit "Had a Dream (For the Heart)" provide the foundation for their later hit singles. The best moments on *The Judds* have been compiled on their numerous hits compilation, yet it remains a pleasant listen for most dedicated fans. —*Thom Owens*

☆ **Why Not Me** / 1984 / RCA ✦✦✦✦✦
Despite the promise of their self-titled debut album, Naomi and Wynonna Judd struck pay dirt by issuing the bona fide classic *Why Not Me*, their sophomore outing from 1984. It was produced by Brent Maher and recorded with a small group of session players who were chosen as carefully as the songs were. From the opening track, the title cut, written by greats Harlan Howard, Sonny Throckmorton, and Maher, it is obvious what a showcase

this is for Wynonna Judd's stylized singing. Her big throaty voice rings clear and wide, pulling up every ounce of emotion from the song's root; her phrasing is perfect, and Naomi's harmonies are golden; they soar, float, and lilt in contrast, complement, and counterpoint to her daughter's lead. The elder Judd is also a fine songwriter in that track two, "Mr. Pain," is one of the finest songs on the set, full of beauty and vulnerability but ever present with hope. But it's not until track three, "Drops of Water," that the album breaks wide open. Here Wynonna proves she can sing from the rockabilly side of country as well. From her gritty lead vocal to her sweet swing-style harmony with Naomi and killer dobro runs from Sonny Garrish, the tune is irresistible. "My Baby's Gone" is another such moment, a tough, lean, bluesy shuffle graced with Andrews Sisters-styled harmonies and country guitar picking from Don Potter that turns this into a stomper. The ballads work too, however, on "Sleeping Heart" or the blues-rooted "By Bye Baby Blues," which is penned by the Howard/Throckmorton/Maher team and is country music from the Patsy Cline fake book. The elements of jazz and early-'60s countrypolitan are impossible not to remember. But that's what makes the Judds so special—they can sing it all. All they need is the material, and when they get it—and they do here in spades—they are virtually untouchable. With Wynonna's voice being one of the best in the history of the music, and Naomi's harmonizing being literally the most unconventional, they are wall-to-wall original as an act. With the two closers, "Endless Sleep," a solid rocker in the "Heartbreak Hotel" tradition, and the plaintive "Mama He's Crazy," the duo accomplish the impossible: becoming a longstanding duo who consistently rode the top of the charts until Naomi left for health reasons and who remained a bona fide country music act. Of all their recordings, *Why Not Me* is their best-known, best-selling, and deservedly so. It's perfect. —*Thom Jurek*

Rockin' with the Rhythm / 1985 / RCA ✦✦✦
On the third album, "Have Mercy" and the title track (among others) kick with a funky glee that makes this the most plainly joyous Judds album. —*Mark A. Humphrey*

Heartland / 1987 / RCA ✦✦✦
Opening as it does with "Don't Be Cruel," the listener might be led to believe that *Heartland* was a distinct follow-up to *Rockin' With the Rhythm*. But it's a misleading track. While "Don't Be Cruel" gives you a fresh, new interpretation of the classic so closely associated with Elvis that it feels like an Everly *Sisters* reinvention rather than a redo, it's also different from virtually everything else on the album. Far from the nominal gritty funkiness of its predecessor, *Heartland* walks a thin line between roots rock and mainstream country. Mostly with producer Brent Maher and the same band that had been playing with them from the beginning, this set feels a tad uneven. Perhaps it's because the great songs here such as the aforementioned "Turn It Loose," "Cow Cow Boogie," and "I Know Where I'm Going" outshine the ballads not just in terms of energy, but in vocal experimentation. Only "The Sweetest Gift" with Emmylou Harris adding another voice to an already rich harmonic tapestry equals the bluesier, swinging country-rock tunes. That doesn't make this a bad or substandard record in any way, just one that creates a tension within itself that remains unresolved. —*Thom Jurek*

★ **The Greatest Hits** / 1988 / RCA ✦✦✦✦✦
These singles document the rise of Naomi and Wynonna Judd, a mother-daughter team who seemed, at times, to be singing for every bank teller, teacher, and struggling single mama in every small town in America. Songs like "Why Not Me," "Mama He's Crazy," and "Girl's Night Out" were more than country hits; they're like validation for every woman brave enough to believe in innocence even when she knows better. —*Dan Cooper*

River of Time / 1989 / RCA ✦✦✦✦
Six years after their debut, the Judds were still cranking out the hits, albeit with a funkier, grittier sound that brought electric pianos and Hammond B-3s into the mix. Using the same basic team that had made their career the monstrously successful thing it was, talent like guitarists like Carl Perkins, Mark Knopfler, and Roy Huskey Jr. augment *River of*

Time. That said, it seems like the funkier and less traditionally "country" the Judds became, the wider their appeal. Album to album, their singles still seemed to resonate with country audiences the most. *River of Time* boasted two number-one singles, the plaintive country of "Young Love" and the rockabilly shuffle of Perkins' "Let Me Tell You About Love" with Perkins kicking it on guitar. Naomi Judd is also featured here as a prominent songwriter with her partner, John Jarvis, on the title track, "Cadillac Red," and the closer, "Guardian Angel." There is a stunning cover of Boudleaux Bryant's "Sleepless Nights" that equals the Gram Parsons/Emmylou Harris version. And Knopfler's "Water of Love" was stretching it for the Judds, but in its sultry outlaw country feel and the author's guitar snaking around Wynonna's voice, nocturnal and mysterious, it's the most seductive tune on the set. The strutting country boogie of "Cadillac Red" and the shuffling swinging honky tonk of "Do I Dare" are infectious. "Guardian Angel," which Naomi wrote with Jarvis and Don Schlitz, bears the latter's unmistakable imprint. Having written "The Gambler" for Kenny Rogers, Naomi's story is made elegant by a heartbreakingly beautiful melody and refrain. *River of Time* is another ace in the Judds' hands. —*Thom Jurek*

Love Can Build a Bridge / Sep. 11, 1990 / RCA ✦✦✦✦
The last Judds album may not be their strongest but nonetheless featured some killer tracks and is by no means unsuccessful when taken as a whole. There is plenty of merit here. With an opening track like "Born to Be Blue" that begins as an old swinging blues tune à la the 1930s and moves into a hot fusion of country and R&B, the album is off to a good start. There are a handful of Naomi Judd co-writes that feature everything from roots and progressive country to strutting, punchy rock & roll to heartbreaking ballads. The remake of Lawrence Hammond's "John Deere Tractor" may not have be the best move to make, but then, it's not bad either. "Calling in the Wind" sounds like Bruce Springsteen's "Born in the USA" at the beginning, but Wynonna dispels any of that quickly in the verse. "Rompin' Stompin' Bad News Blues" is a ferocious blues-rocker with acoustic guitars roiling under the voice of Wynonna, who sings as loud as she growls, and guest star Bonnie Raitt's greasy electric slide doesn't hurt either. Ultimately, *Love Can Build a Bridge* is a fine sendoff for one of the most successful and revolutionary bands in country history. There is much pleasure here, and it is all in the way two voices weave, Wynonna's command of her instrument, and Brent Maher's production that accents all the strengths and leaves just enough weakness in the mix to make the band human. —*Thom Jurek*

The Judds Collection 1983–1990 / 1992 / RCA ✦✦✦✦
The three-disc box set *The Judds Collection 1983-1990* is an example of a wasted opportunity. Instead of providing a thorough, exhaustive overview of the duo's immensely popular career, the set simply combines their first two *Greatest Hits* albums with a disc of demos, which are only of interest to hardcore fans, who will already have all of the music on the first two discs. That leaves the set as being useful to no one—casual fans are better served by the individual collections, while dedicated fans are being ripped off by being forced to purchase two discs they already have if they want to get the rarities, which aren't that revelatory in the first place. —*Thom Owens*

Collector's Series / Feb. 1993 / RCA ✦✦✦

The Essential Judds / Oct. 1995 / RCA ✦✦✦✦✦
The Essential Judds contains a great majority of the duo's biggest hits, as well as a wisely chosen selection of rarities, making it a definitive compilation. —*Stephen Thomas Erlewine*

Greatest Hits, Vol. 2 / Nov. 19, 1996 / RCA ✦✦✦✦✦
While songs like "Young Love" and "Love Can Build a Bridge" continue to emphasize the Judds' warm and fuzzy middle-American sensibilities, several other hits—"Let Me Tell You About Love," for instance—showcase the side of Wynonna that admires Bonnie Raitt. —*Dan Cooper*

#1 Hits / Apr. 11, 2000 / Curb ✦✦✦

Kalin Twins

f. Feb. 16, 1934, Port Jervis, NY
Group / Rock & Roll, Close Harmony

Herbert and Harold Kalin, twin brother harmony singers, sang like a pop-focused version of the Everly Brothers, and they charted a few catchy records in 1958, including one Top Five hit. They represent one of the better acts to find a compromise between rock & roll and pop music, even if they weren't the Everlys by a long shot. Although Herbert and Harold were born in the same period as Elvis Presley, they came from more of a middle-class background, and from much further north as well. Not surprisingly, their musical preferences lay more with the pop music that preceded Elvis (so, to some degree, did Presley's own taste), and their music was closer in spirit to that tamer third wave of rock & roll, exemplified by Bobby Darin, Paul Anka, and Dion DiMucci.

The Kalins grew up in Port Jervis, NY, and pursued music as a career while in their teens. Their listening ran toward Tony Bennett, Johnny Ray, and Nat King Cole—they weren't *allowed* to listen to R&B, although they did get to hear records by LaVern Baker, Ruth Brown, and other R&B stars of the period, even if these weren't central to their taste or experience. Their aspirations to a recording career were delayed until Hal's stint in the Army was over, and the two moved to Washington, D.C., in 1957. This led them to a hookup with songwriter Clint Ballard, who helped them land a contract with Decca Records. The Kalins' first recording session took place in December of 1957, by which time the rock & roll boom was in full swing—the record company wanted them to compete for the teen market and insisted that they try something close in spirit and beat to the newer sounds. Their first session yielded a trio of songs that went nowhere, but they struck gold three months later with "When," a catchy romantic pop/rocker with a good beat (originally intended as a B-side) that rose to number five in the United States and number one in England.

They appeared on *The Milt Grant Show*, Washington's answer to *American Bandstand*, and became nationally known, appearing on the typical package tours of the period. "Forget Me Not," a hastily scheduled and recorded follow-up done while they were on the road promoting the big hit, was notably less successful. Their next single, the ethereal and catchy "It's Only the Beginning," however, could have been close in spirit to the Everly Brothers, but for the inclusion of the chorus behind the brothers. During this period, they also recorded a pair of their own songs, "Clickety Clack" and "Oh! My Goodness." By the middle of 1959, they were working in Nashville with Owen Bradley and doing songs by, among others, Felice & Boudleaux Bryant, who had previously supplied the Everlys with material. The Bryants' "Sweet Sugar Lips"—the Kalins' final chart entry, at number 97—was as close to the Everlys' sound as the Kalins ever got, soft country-based rock complete with Hank Garland on guitar and Floyd Cramer at the piano. Meanwhile, out on the road, the Kalins also performed in England, opening for Cliff Richard.

Back home, the Kalin Twins kept recording until 1962, even hooking up with their one-time mentor, Clint Ballard. Among the highlights of the later part of their recording career were the duo's cover of "Zing, Went the Strings of My Heart," which recalled "When," and their soaring cover of "Picture of You," a hit in England for Brit-rocker Joe Brown (Paul McCartney has also been known to sing it, though not formally in concert). They also left behind a body of unreleased material from Nashville, featuring Garland and Cramer, that was fairly solid pop/rock. As the 1960s dawned, the Kalins moved away from teen-oriented numbers, preferring to perform more mature material. Curiously, although their influence in the United States was minimal, it is probable that their number one hit in England with "When" was an influence on the fortunes and perhaps even the sound of the Brook Brothers, an English brother act (signed to Pye Records) with a nearly identical sound. The Kalins ceased recording after 1962, but three decades later, they were still performing as a pop-nostalgia act before audiences in their 50s. —*Bruce Eder*

● **When** / 1984 / Bear Family ◆◆◆◆◆

For once, Bear Family Records has compromised on a retrospective—the Kalin Twins left behind 38 songs, but only 30 of them are here, obviously to hold this to a single disc. Some of the stuff not present includes their covers of Gene Pitney's "Loneliness" and Jackie DeShannon's "Trouble," but there's some fascinating material in its place—the unreleased 1960 vintage "Make Love to Me" was a sincere attempt to give the duo a more mature sound, and their never-before-issued version of "Bye Bye Blackbird" has a surprise or two. "When" is the best-known song here, and it's surrounded by some pleasant, lively teen pop ("Bubbles," "Schoolbell Dream"), but the country-rocker "Picture of You" is also very worthwhile. And "It's Only the Beginning" is one of the most unabashedly beautiful and achingly romantic pieces of pop/rock of the period that one is likely ever to hear. Some of this is too sappy for words ("True Love"), but it's still enjoyable overall. The order of the material is a bit haphazard, skipping around between years and sessions, but that can be fixed with some player programming. —*Bruce Eder*

Kieran Kane

b. Oct. 7, 1949, Queens, NY
Guitar, Mandolin / Traditional Folk, Contemporary Country, Country-Folk

Best known as one half of the acclaimed new traditionalist country duo the O'Kanes, singer/songwriter Kieran Kane was born in Queens, NY, on October 7, 1949; by age nine, he was drumming in his older brother's rock band, while in his teens he turned his focus to bluegrass and folk, performing at festivals throughout the Northeast. At 21, Kane relocated to Los Angeles, where he labored as a songwriter and session guitarist; by the late '70s, he'd moved on to Nashville, where he landed a writing contract with Tree Publishing Co. A deal with Elektra followed, but despite notching a pair of Top Ten country singles—"You're the Best" and "It's Who You Love"—he found himself at odds with the label and soon returned to composing.

Teaming with fellow Tree staff writer Jamie O'Hara, he formed the O'Kanes in 1985, issuing three hit albums and scoring a half-dozen Top Ten singles before disbanding four years later. Kane resurfaced with a more austere, folk-influenced sound in 1993 with the solo effort *Find My Way Home*, issued on Atlantic; soon after he formed the Nashville-based indie label Dead Reckoning with fellow singer/songwriters Kevin Welch, Tammy Rogers, and Harry Stinson, issuing the album *Dead Rekoning* in 1995. *Six Months, No Sun* followed in 1998, and *The Blue Chair* was issued in fall 2000. —*Jason Ankeny*

Find My Way Home / 1993 / Atlantic ◆◆◆◆◆

Kane quietly and effectively examines his relationships and decisions in songs that are as acutely accurate as they are minimally drawn. —*Michael McCall*

Dead Rekoning / Oct. 1995 / Dead Reckoning ◆◆◆

Kieran Kane is one of the new outlaw types surfacing in Nashville these days. Only the "outlaw" aspect doesn't apply to the lifestyle as in the old days. Here, it applies to the music, which bypasses the major labels and trends in favor of independently operated labels and a sense of following one's heart in making music. Kane's own "This Dirty Little Town" has a nice, ragged quality to it, and his cover of Hank Williams' "Ramblin Man" comes off high 'n' lonesome. Pleasing, but not exactly laid-back, Kieran Kane's *Dead Reckoning* has a haunting quality that keeps you coming back for more. —*James Chrispell*

Six Months, No Sun / Apr. 7, 1998 / Dead Reckoning ◆◆◆

On *Six Months, No Sun*, Kieran Kane continues along the path that he started down first as one-half of the O'Kanes, and then on his first two solo albums, *Find My Way Home* and *Dead Rekoning*; solid songwriting embellished by almost understated instrumentation, drawing on country, bluegrass, folk, and rock elements in equal portion. The songs on *Six Months, No Sun*, most of them penned by Kane, are in a range of styles. The two inspired covers, though, demonstrate his range: the bluegrass standard, "I Wonder Where You Are Tonight," and the pop standard, "What a Wonderful World," made familiar by Louis Armstrong. Highlights on the album include the title track, which is a solid country song, and "Table Top Dancer," which is a rather bleak vignette of working-class life. Another stand-out is "Hysteria," co-written with Irish singer/songwriter Andy White. There are also skillfully worded songs of love gone wrong, including "I Wonder Where You Are Tonight" and "Foolish as That May Be." Relying primarily on acoustic instrumentation (including the fiddle and mandolin of Tammy Rogers), Kane places the emphasis squarely on the songs themselves. His skill as a songwriter is such that the songs are substantial enough to stand such stark relief. While perhaps not as strong as his earlier solo efforts, Kane has made another solid album with *Six Months, No Sun*. —*Martin Monkman*

11/12/13: Live from Melbourne, Australia / Jun. 20, 2000 / Dead Reckoning ◆◆◆

These are live recordings from Kane's joint appearances with fellow country-folk songwriter (and fellow *Dead Rekoning* artist) Kevin Welch in Melbourne, Australia, on November 12 and November 13 of 1999. For these shows, the pair played unaccompanied, using just a bass and a guitar. Sometimes harmonizing, sometimes letting one or the other sing solo, they ran through 15 songs, mostly original material composed by Kane and Welch separately, although there are covers of John Hiatt's "Train to Birmingham" and Hank Williams' "Ramblin' Man." There's an informal, playing-before-friends feel to the performances, on tunes that are mostly good-natured and easygoing, even if songs like Kane's "Table Top Dancer" get into something a little darker. Low-key country-folk, suited for Sunday morning tea. —*Richie Unterberger*

The Blue Chair / Oct. 24, 2000 / Dead Reckoning ◆◆◆

● **Shadows on the Ground** / Oct. 8, 2002 / Dead Reckoning ◆◆◆◆◆

Kieran Kane, formerly of the not-quite-neo-trad (but utterly compelling) country group the O'Kanes, has released his finest album to date with the primarily acoustic *Shadows on the Ground*. On this effort, Kane pares back his tunes to only their most essential, suggestive elements, and the result can be compared to the most evocative short stories of Ernest Hemingway. This is his simplest effort yet—but there's great artistry at work. *Shadows on the Ground* was recorded in a couple of days in a single room in Nashville, and is dedicated to Kieran's son Lucas, who had been diagnosed with Hodgkin's disease. The hard, simple truths on the album perhaps stem from that situation, with the lyrics often coming off like unadorned little nuggets of Eastern thought (such as the title track's "Truth is always truth, stone is always stone/We all live and die but not alone/We go by different roads/We go by different names/Shadows on the ground all look the same"). The combination of the stark but intelligent lyrics and low-key yet impressive instrumentation and arrangements—in fact, two songs feature only one chord—results in an album that, like the best art, doesn't telegraph its message. Rather, it's suggestive enough to draw the listener in for the act of discovery. (On a blunter level, it's also a darn fine listen.) The intelligence and artistry at work on this album are remarkable, and here in the new millennium, it baffles the mind that a talent like Kieran Kane and the O'Kanes once hurtled up the mainstream country music charts. *—Erik Hage*

Buell Kazee

b. Aug. 29, 1900, Burton Fork, KY, **d.** Aug. 1976

Banjo, Vocals / Traditional Bluegrass, Traditional Folk, Field Recordings

Buell Kazee was a minister who played banjo and sang the ancient songs of his beloved Kentucky mountains during the 1920s. Considered one of the very best folksingers in U.S. history, he was a master of the high, "lonesome" singing style of the Appalachian balladeer. Kazee was born in the foothill town of Burton Fork, KY, and learned most of his songs from his family. He began picking banjo at age five and often played during local gatherings. He prepared for the clergy even as a teen and after high-school began studying English, Greek, and Latin at Georgetown College, KY. It was there that he began to understand the significance of his family and friends' traditional songs. Kazee formally studied singing and music in order to transcribe the old songs and make them more contemporary. Following his graduation in 1925, he gave a "folk music" concert at the University of Kentucky. He wore a tie and tails while playing the banjo and piano, sang in his specially trained "formal" voice, and gave lectures about the history of the songs. The show was a great success, so he repeated it several times over the following years.

In 1927, he was asked to record the songs for Brunswick in New York, and he was signed to the label on the condition that he sing using his high, tight "mountain" voice and forego his formal vocal training. Over the next two years, he recorded over 50 songs backed by New York musicians. Many were religious, but others ranged from traditional to popular ballads, including "Lady Gay," "The Sporting Bachelors," and "The Orphan Girl." His biggest hit was a version of "On Top of Old Smoky" called "Little Mohee," which sold over 15,000 copies. In the early '30s, the recently married Kazee lost interest in pursuing a music career and stopped touring to become the minister of a church in Morehead, KY. For the next 22 years, he only sang publicly at revival meetings. Much later, he began using folk themes to compose formal music, such as a cantata-based on the old Sacred Harp piece "The White Pilgrim." During the folk revival of the early '60s, he made a comeback and was one of the first to appear at the Newport festivals. In addition to preaching and singing, Kazee also wrote three religious books and a book on banjo playing. He died in 1976. *—Sandra Brennan*

● **Buell Kazee Sings and Plays** / 1958 / Smithsonian Folkways ♦♦♦♦

Originally recorded in 1958 for the Folkways label, *Sings and Plays* is now available on CD and cassette on a made-to-order basis, ordered directly from the Smithsonian label website. These 18 sides include as much oral history as they do fine banjo frailing. Kazee's expert clawhammer playing is the reason this collection remains essential for fans of the archaic performance style. His stories and impromptu banjo lessons are likewise worthwhile. Kazee's brittle singing voice, on the other hand, may require some getting used to for unprepared listeners. But the old familiar tales of "John Hardy" and "Darling Corey" sound like today's breaking news as this Kentucky minister performs them. This is an exceptional collection that chronicles an age of American musical tradition (and spirit) long since lost to history and third-generation imitations. Photocopies of the album's original notes and lyric sheet are included with each order. *—Brian Beatty*

Buell Kazee / 1978 / June Appal ♦♦♦♦

A banjo-playing and singing minister who actually had some hit records in the '20s, Buell Kazee was tracked down during the folk revival of the '60s, resulting in a Folkways album that was recorded casually and released without the artist's knowledge or permission as well as this posthumous set, which apparently came much closer to the new recording Kazee was intent on putting out during his twilight years. Rounder was putting out much of this type of material in the '70s, but word is that this slightly prissy Boston-based label could never really come to terms with the equally picky Kazee. The project eventually saw the light of day on the smaller June Appal label. The artist was basically in good form during his later years. The banjo work is not particularly of the hotshot variety, but this is not what he was known for even during his younger days. Fans of banjo playing will be most interested in the medley in which he blends together three different traditional pieces with relaxed grace. This album is more about the deep emotions he puts across through his vocals, which some listeners may find a bit formal sounding for country music, while others may have no use for the gospel material that concludes the set. All in all, fans of Kazee's earlier work will surely be interested in this, as it both holds up in comparison and reveals a somewhat deeper feeling from the artist than was evident when he was just a whippersnapper. *—Eugene Chadbourne*

Robert Earl Keen Jr.

b. Houston, TX

Guitar, Vocals / Progressive Country, Singer/Songwriter, Country-Folk, Alternative Country, Contemporary Folk, Americana

Among the large contingent of talented songwriters who emerged in Texas in the 1980s and 1990s, Robert Earl Keen Jr. struck an unusual balance between sensitive story-portraits ("Corpus Christi Bay") and raucous barroom fun ("That Buckin' Song"). These two song types in Keen's output were unified by a mordant sense of humor that strongly influenced the early practitioners of what would become known as alternative country music. Keen, the son of an oil executive father and an attorney mother, was a native of Houston. His parents enjoyed both folk and country music, and his own style would land, like that of his close contemporary Nanci Griffith, between those genres. Keen wrote poetry while he was in high-school, but it wasn't until he went to journalism school at musically fertile Texas A&M that he learned to play the guitar. He and Lyle Lovett became friends and co-wrote a song, "This Old Porch," which both later recorded.

Keen made a splash in Austin with his debut album, *No Kinda Dancer*, self-financed in 1984 to the tune of 4,500 dollars. He moved to Nashville during the heady experimentalism of the 1980s that saw Lovett and k.d. lang hit the country Top Ten, but he soon returned to Austin. Texas landscapes and residents provided Keen with creative inspiration, as his second album, *West Textures*, made clear; that album yielded one of Keen's signature numbers, an ambitious crime-spree song called "The Road Goes on Forever." Now recording for Sugar Hill, Keen recorded a live album shortly after *West Textures* but waited several years to release a studio follow-up, 1993's *A Bigger Piece of Sky*. After that album (which contained "Corpus Christi Bay") came *Gringo Honeymoon* (1994), which merged Keen's story songs with the emerging sounds of alt-country: guitars were laid down by the influential Austin musician Gurf Morlix, who later produced albums for both Keen and Lucinda Williams, and a young Gillian Welch provided harmony vocals.

Once again, after taking his career to a new stage, Keen recorded a live album (*No. 2 Live Dinner*, 1996) and took time to accumulate new material. The 1997 album *Picnic*, his first for the Arista Texas label, again moved in the direction of alternative country, featuring Keen in a duet with the Cowboy Junkies' Margo Timmins, while 1998's *Walking Distance* featured sparer textures. Whatever production style surrounded his songs, Keen's musical personality seemed consistent, and his live shows, widely known thanks to a touring schedule that often approached 200 dates a year in the 1990s, grew organically in depth and control. In the early 2000s Keen signed with the Lost Highway label and released the album *Gravitational Forces* (2001). He also devoted time to his influential annual concert series and talent festival, *Texas Uprising*, which took place at several venues around Texas and the Far West. *—James Manheim*

● **No Kinda Dancer** / 1984 / Sugar Hill ♦♦♦♦♦

The Live Album / 1988 / Sugar Hill ♦♦♦♦♦

West Textures / 1989 / Sugar Hill ♦♦♦

Some singers write songs and some songwriters sing. Robert Earl Keen Jr. falls into the latter category. Unlike his pal Lyle Lovett, who has an extraordinary talent for both crafts, Keen's main strength is his writing. (He studied journalism, after all.) Sure, he can sing just fine, well enough to build a solo career, in fact, but his songs often shine a little brighter when performed by more versatile vocalists. Nevertheless, *West Textures* marks Keen's third outing and is a fine collection of tunes, most of which are original compositions. Like Nanci Griffith and Steve Earle, Keen's style lies somewhere between alternative country and contemporary folk. Filled with acoustic guitar, dobro, fiddle, mandolin, accordion, and upright bass, *West Textures* is a pretty consistent set with a handful of standout tracks. "The Road Goes on Forever" and "Don't Turn Out the Light" jump right out on the first listen thanks to their peppy, catchy melodies. With further attention, "Leavin' Tennessee," "Maria," and "Love's a Word I Never Throw Around" should get the kudos due them, as well. A songwriter's songwriter, Keen gets an A for effort. *—Kelly McCartney*

A Bigger Piece of Sky / 1993 / Sugar Hill ♦♦♦

This album contains the radio hit "Tangled up in Blue," sound-alike song "Jesse with the Long Hair," as well as more of Keen's rough and tumble story-songs. *—Richard Meyer*

Gringo Honeymoon / 1994 / Sugar Hill ♦♦♦

Framed by smooth production and tasteful instrumentation, Robert Earl Keen Jr. hands over ten more tunes on this 1994 release. *Gringo Honeymoon* is more lively and immediately likeable than previous efforts and is comprised of all Keen originals, save Steve Earle's "Tom Ames' Prayer." Keen transports the listener to Texas with his stories and the overall tone of the record. But it's not big-hair Dallas that calls, it are the back roads and small towns that form the landscape. From the toe-tapping shuffle of "Think It Over One Time" to the sweeping grandeur of "Lonely Feeling" to the eye-winking swing of "Barbeque," Keen paints the scenes one by one. With the sly humor of "Merry Christmas From the Family," he sketches, in great detail, a dysfunctional family that many may recognize. (Not unsurprisingly, Jill Sobule covered this spirited number for a holiday sampler disc.) Gillian Welch adds her lovely voice to "Lynnville Train" and "The Raven and the Coyote." Both are tales of aching hearts that do well with her gentle harmonies. Overall, *Gringo Honeymoon* is pretty closely in step with Lyle Lovett and Nanci Griffith. If you like either of them, give this one a try. *—Kelly McCartney*

Merry Christmas from the Family / Nov. 21, 1995 / Sugar Hill ♦♦♦

After Keen's mordant yuletide song "Merry Christmas From the Family" was tapped by the country-themed syndicated radio program *the John Boy & Billy Big Show* for heavy airplay during the 1994 holiday season, the singer decided to re-cut the song live for release the following year. The single was packaged with its original source album *Gringo Honeymoon* for release during 1995. *—Jason Ankeny*

No. 2 Live Dinner / Mar. 19, 1996 / Sugar Hill ♦♦♦

Robert Earl Keen Jr. is a Texan who did not take the express lane to the radio airwaves. Instead, he spent more than a decade seasoning his talent while entertaining folks in the—yep, you guessed it—friendly honky tonks of Texas, where music fans tend to like individualists with plenty of personality. *No. 2 Live Dinner* finished off a consistently powerful string of albums recorded for Sugar Hill Records. Taped in front of rowdy, beer-swilling crowds in two Texas towns, Keen bears his good-natured raspiness into songs of desperation, danger, and raucous humor. A contemporary of Steve Earle, Lyle Lovett, and Nanci Griffith, Keen's work has been as consistent and occasionally as strong as that of his friends. It's taken him longer to gain a national profile, but it's coming at a deserving time. For those unfamiliar with him, this live album will convey how well he's loved in his home state. Listen closely, and the songs will explain why, too. *—Michael McCall*

Picnic / Apr. 29, 1997 / Arista ♦♦♦♦
Picnic finds Robert Earle Keen Jr. at the top of his form, telling detailed stories with remarkably simple and expressive rustic accompaniment. The record boasts a somewhat cleaner sound than before, since it's targeted at the alt-country audience who have embraced the artists Keen has influenced. Even with such slight sonic compromises, the essence of his music has not been diluted, and his emotionally direct country-folk is as affecting as ever. Of particular note is "Over the Waterfall," a lovely duet with Margo Timmins from Cowboy Junkies. *—Stephen Thomas Erlewine*

Walking Distance / Oct. 27, 1998 / Arista ♦♦♦♦
Sometimes a disc comes along without any expectations and hits one right out of the ballpark. Such is the case with Robert Earl Keen Jr.'s *Walking Distance.* Although much less of an alt-country affair than his earlier work, *Walking Distance* comes across warm and friendly. Keen's humor crops up on "That Bucking Song," which he says is all about riding a horse, while "Down That Dusty Trail" is full of childhood memories. "Feelin' Good Again" shows that for all the bad times, it is the good-times that make us feel, and then some. Perhaps that's the message that Keen is trying to convey this time out, and if it is, then sit back and feel good about feeling good. We get the next installment of Keen's twisted take on an original Christmas song in "Happy Holidays, Y'All." Once you hear it, you won't be able to help yourself from singing along to a tale that nearly everyone who's spent the holidays with the family can identify with. No matter what, Keen's *Walking Distance* is just around the next bend from wherever you might be. *—James Chrispell*

Gravitational Forces / Aug. 7, 2001 / Lost Highway ♦♦♦♦♦
If anyone needs to be convinced that Robert Earl Keen Jr. is the reigning champion of Texas twangers, *Gravitational Forces* makes one forceful knock-out blow. The disc paints a multitude of vivid pictures backed by memorable melodies and superb instrumental backing. Keen delivers his goods early and often, starting with the singalong chorus to Joe Dolce's "My Home Ain't in the Hall of Fame." It's not perfectly clear what exactly he's singing about in the chorus—something about his home and his songs on Top 40 radio—but with a hook so infectious, you'll mumble along anyway. Of course, none of these tracks are destined for Top 40 radio, but they're surely bound for glory in the realm of Americana. The colorful duo in Terry Allen's "High Plains Jamboree" typify Keen's penchant for vivid caricatures. Few of us—hopefully—can relate to a honky tonk woman with gold teeth and a family man who spends a night at the motel lounge with her while his wife's at home. But Keen's portrait of these two slightly unwholesome but otherwise common folk brings them home like a crazy uncle, a bit on the edge but loveable just the same. After all, these two are just looking for a good-time. And that's precisely what Keen delivers throughout this stellar release. *—Scott Cooper*

Bill Keith

b. Dec. 20, 1939, Boston, MA
Banjo, Guitar (Steel) / Progressive Bluegrass, Instrumental Country
Bill Keith had great impact on modern banjo playing, particularly in the direction of "newgrass." He even had a picking style informally named after him. Born in Boston, MA, Keith began taking banjo lessons at a young age, and also learned to play piano and ukulele. During adolescence, he played in a few Dixieland bands, but by the late '50s, became interested in folk music after listening to such inspirational artists as Pete Seeger and Earl Scruggs. Using instruction books, the Amherst college student began learning their two different styles. Eventually, Keith began developing his own unique style, which became known as the melodic, chromatic or "Keith" picking style. This distinct technique was borne of his desire to play fiddle melodies on his instruments.

In 1958, he teamed up with fellow Amherst student Jim Rooney and began playing at local coffeehouses and on campus. Eventually they hooked up with promoter Manny Greenhill; with his assistance they founded the Connecticut Folklore Society, which sponsored a series of traveling campus concerts throughout New England. Following graduation and a brief stint in the U.S. Air Force Reserve, Keith began learning to make banjos with Tom Morgan. Later he, Rooney, mandolin player Frank Wakefield, and guitarist Red Allen formed the Kentuckians.

In 1963, Earl Scruggs contacted Keith to lay out the tablature for the instructional book *Earl Scruggs and the 5-String Banjo.* Later that year, Keith and his former Amherst classmate Dan Bump developed a new kind of tuning peg that was adopted by Scruggs who provided a name for the resulting company in 1964. In the mid-'60s, Keith joined Bill Monroe's Blue Grass Boys, where he was listed as Brad Keith. He left the band after only eight months to do more session work and by the year's end had joined Jim Kweskin's Jug Band where he would stay for four years. After that he played with the Blue Velvet Band. He abandoned the banjo for a while in 1968 to become a pedal steel guitarist.

In 1970, Keith moved to Woodstock, New York, and spent a year with Jonathan Edwards. He then went on to work with Judy Collins. He and longtime cohort Rooney also toured together in both the U.S. and in Europe during the '70s and '80s, with Keith developing a particularly large following in France. When back home in Woodstock, Keith began playing banjo for the Woodstock Mountain Review. In 1977, he worked briefly as a columnist for *Frets* magazine. Later, in 1989, Keith, Rooney, Eric Weissberg and Kenny Koseck re-formed their old group, calling it the New Blue Velvet Band. *—Sandra Brennan*

Livin' on the Mountain / 1963 / Prestige Folklore ♦♦♦♦

● **Something Auld, Something Newgrass, Something Borrowed, Something Bluegrass** / 1976 / Rounder ♦♦♦♦

Banjoistics / 1984 / Rounder ♦♦♦

Beating Around the Bush / 1992 / Green Linnet ♦♦♦

Fiddle Tunes for Banjo / 2000 / Rounder ♦♦♦

Toby Keith (Toby Keith Covel)

b. Jul. 8, 1961, Clinton, OK
Vocals / Contemporary Country, New Traditionalist
Toby Keith spent the '90s as a solid, workmanlike country star who met with considerable chart success yet never quite broke free of the neo-traditionalist pack to become a household name like Garth Brooks or Alan Jackson. That all changed in 2002 when he recorded "Courtesy of the Red, White and Blue (The Angry American)," a super-patriotic response to September 11 that became one of country's most highly charged political statements since Merle Haggard's "Okie From Muskogee." The media furor ensured that even people with no knowledge of country music still knew him as "the guy with the 'boot in the ass' song," and helped make Keith a genuine phenomenon. Yet he'd been recording for nearly a decade prior and already had several chart-topping country singles to his credit.

Keith was born Toby Keith Covel in Clinton, OK, in 1961 and grew up mostly on a farm in Moore, near the outskirts of Oklahoma City. He took up guitar at age eight, inspired by the country musicians who played at the supper club his grandmother ran. He listened to his father's Bob Wills records and fell in love with Haggard's music. He worked as a rodeo hand while in high-school, and after graduation, he found work in the nearby oil fields. In the meantime, he formed the Easy Money Band and played Alabama-style country-rock in area honky tonks. After about three years, the oil industry hit a major downturn, and Keith turned to playing semipro football for a USFL farm team, even trying out (unsuccessfully) for the short-lived league's Oklahoma City franchise. Following two years as a football player, Keith decided to focus on music and adopted a much more rigorous touring schedule. He cut a few records for local indie labels, and his demo tape eventually found its way to onetime Alabama producer Harold Shedd, who helped Keith land a deal with Mercury.

Keith's self-titled debut album was released in 1993 and made him an out-of-the-box success with its chart-topping single "Should've Been a Cowboy." Three more songs from the record—"Wish I Didn't Know Now," "A Little Less Talk and a Lot More Action," and "He Ain't Worth Missing"—made the Top Five, and the album sold over two million copies. "Who's That Man," the lead single from his second album, *Boomtown*, was released in late 1994 and became his second number one; *Boomtown* hit stores in early 1995 and went gold on the strength of further Top Ten hits "Upstairs Downtown" and "You Ain't Much Fun." Keith followed it later that year with the holiday record *Christmas to Christmas* and returned with the proper album *Blue Moon* in 1996. Its first two singles, "A Woman's Touch" and "Does That Blue Moon Ever Shine on You," went Top Ten, and the third, "Me Too," gave Keith his third number one, also helping the album go platinum.

Dream Walkin' (1997) marked his first collaboration with prolific producer James Stroud, with whom he would work regularly from then on. "We Were in Love" and the title track were both Top Five hits, as was "I'm So Happy I Can't Stop Crying," a duet with Sting. However, Keith longed for an even bigger breakthrough, and he was growing dissatisfied with Mercury's promotional efforts. In 1999, he left the label and followed Stroud over to the Nashville division of DreamWorks. Keith's label debut, *How Do You Like Me Now?!*, appeared in late 1999 and started to bring him the wider recognition he felt poised for. The title cut went to number one on the country charts and brought him his first Top 40 pop hit; its follow-up, "Country Comes to Town," went Top Five, and "You Shouldn't Kiss Me Like This" also hit number one. Overall, the album had a rough, brash attitude that helped give Keith a stronger identity as a performer. It was also the first to bring him those long-desired major industry awards, when in 2001 the Academy of Country Music named him Male Vocalist of the Year and named *How Do You Like Me Now?!* its Album of the Year.

In the meantime, Keith became more visible in the mainstream media, making cameos on *Touched By an Angel* and in a *Dukes of Hazzard* TV reunion movie as well as co-starring in a series of telephone commercials. Later in 2001, his follow-up album, *Pull My Chain*, became his first to top the country charts and also his first Top Ten pop album. It spun off three number-one singles: "I'm Just Talkin' About Tonight," "I Wanna Talk About Me," and "My List." Keith was already a burgeoning superstar when he recorded "Courtesy of the Red, White and Blue (The Angry American)" in the summer of 2002. A raging response to the September 11 terrorist attacks, the song struck a fierce chord with aggressively patriotic listeners, while others condemned it as knee-jerk jingoism. The whole controversy came to a head when *ABC News* anchor Peter Jennings objected to Keith's scheduled performance on a network Fourth of July schedule. Keith was axed from the guest list, and the ensuing media flap proved to be a publicity coup. Meanwhile, the song went to number one on the country charts and crossed over into the pop Top 25. All of this set the stage for *Unleashed*, which sold like hotcakes upon its release later in 2002, debuting at number one on both the country and pop charts. "Who's Your Daddy?" was a number-one country hit, and the Willie Nelson duet "Beer for My Horses" also made the country Top Ten. *—Steve Huey*

Toby Keith / 1993 / Mercury ♦♦♦
Keith's hit "Should've Been a Cowboy" is the featured cut on this self-titled debut. *—Jason Ankeny*

Boomtown / 1995 / Mercury ♦♦♦

Christmas to Christmas / Oct. 17, 1995 / Polygram ♦♦♦
All the songs on *Christmas to Christmas* are new compositions, several by Keith himself. They range from playful ("Blame It on the Mistletoe") and thoughtful ("Jesus Gets Jealous of Santa Claus") to devastatingly sad ("Santa I'm Right Here"). The playing is casual, back-porch rootsy. It is first and foremost a collection of good songs, well-performed, that just happen to be about Christmas. *—Roch Parisien*

Blue Moon / Apr. 1996 / A&M ♦♦♦

Dream Walkin' / Jun. 24, 1997 / Mercury ♦♦♦♦
Although Toby Keith doesn't depart from his trademark new traditionalist formula on *Dream Walkin'*, he comes close to perfecting it. Keith sings with more force than ever before, and he has a stronger selection of songs—songs that showcase his musical strengths. A few weak spots hamper the record's momentum, yet *Dream Walkin'* remains an exciting record from a talented honky tonker. *—Thom Owens*

Greatest Hits, Vol. 1 / Oct. 20, 1998 / Mercury ♦♦♦♦
Five years isn't really a longtime to generate 12 monster-size hits for a greatest-hits album, but that's exactly what Toby Keith did. From his first album in 1993 to the release of his first greatest-hits package in 1998, Keith has culled some of his best singles from the charts to create a 14-track ode. He includes only two newbies—the deliciously suggestive "Getcha Some" and the achingly troubled "If a Man Answers." Those are the first two tracks on the album, so you can get them out of the way quickly if you want to and move on to the music that makes Keith so good, starting with his very first single that went straight to number one, "Should've Been a Cowboy." And you'll kick your heels all the way through "A Little Less Talk and a Lot More Action," "You Ain't Much Fun," "Who's That Man," and "He Ain't Worth Missing." It might be hard to recall at first that Keith had so many hit singles in the Top Ten, but with one listen, it'll be hard to forget. *—Maria Konicki Dinoia*

How Do You Like Me Now?! / Nov. 2, 1999 / DreamWorks ♦♦♦♦
While still staying true to his cowboy roots, Toby Keith delivers an excitingly fresh and original sixth album. Keith's got the vocal prowess to conquer any musical style, but finds a home in country. Having penned nine songs on this rarefied 12-track collection about everything from in-your-face confidence to dying with your boots on, Keith exhibits a propensity for the prolific. Mainstream and chart success have never eluded him with songs like "Should've Been a Cowboy" and "Getcha Some," and this time around it won't be any different. There are a bevy of attention-getting harmonies, gentle hymns, and oddball little ditties. *How Do You Like Me Now?!* is a forum that displays the natural evolution of Toby Keith from likable, talented artist to musical giant. *—Maria Konicki Dinoia*

Pull My Chain / Aug. 10, 2001 / DreamWorks ♦♦♦♦
After a career that spans nine years, Keith finally got his accolades and walked away in 2000 with ACM's Top Male Vocalist and Album of the Year for *How Do You Like Me Now?!* So *Pull My Chain* has some tough footsteps to follow in. But his eighth album and second release for DreamWorks is exemplary. From the album's first release and first track, "I'm Just Talkin' About Tonight," to the 12th, what you get is the natural evolution of Toby Keith at his finest. A top-notch songwriter and one of the most recognizable voices in country music, Keith fits right into the niche that is his and his alone. That makes *Pull My Chain* formidable, strong, and certainly worth adding to your Keith collection. *—Maria Konicki Dinoia*

Unleashed / Aug. 6, 2002 / DreamWorks ♦♦♦♦
Toby Keith was edging in on superstardom prior to the release of *Unleashed*—he appeared on a national long-distance telephone commercial, after all—but this was the record that made him a household name, thanks to the opening track "Courtesy of the Red, White and Blue (The Angry American)" and the media-created controversy surrounding its release. The rabble-rousing, obstinate flip side to Alan Jackson's "Where Were You When the World Stopped Turning"—essentially, a 9/11 song for those who thought Jackson's heartbroken confusion was for pansies, but weren't redneck enough to embrace Charlie Daniels' "That Ain't No Rag, It's a Flag" or "The Last Fallen Hero"—"Courtesy of the Red, White and Blue" is, as its subtitle suggests, filled with anger, telling the terrorists (whose "suckerpunch came flying in from somewhere in the back," a rhyme so tantalizingly close to "somewhere in Iraq," you will yourself to hear it every time it plays) that they'll "get a boot in their ass, it's the American way." Keith was scheduled to sing this on an ABC special on the fourth of July (not too coincidentally mentioned in the song), when apparently Peter Jennings objected to the tone of the song and asked the network to rescind the singer's invitation, which then lead to reams of print and countless TV appearances that effectively sold *Unleashed* before it hit the stores. As it turns out, "Courtesy" is a bit misleading of a lead single, as is the title, since most of this album is hardly tough macho posturing. Sure, there's some of it—such as the absurdly anthemic "Beer for My Horses," a duet with Willie Nelson where the two of them hunt down modern day gangsters like cowboys, then drink to their accomplishments—but most of this album is tuneful singer/songwriterism, particularly on the second side, where this album really takes off with a series of rolling, melodic, acoustic-based songs that truly demonstrate that Keith can be a sturdy, memorable songwriter. True, he does descend into cloying cuteness on occasion ("Huckleberry"), but the stretch of songs from "It Works for Me" through "That's Not How It Is" that ends the record is among his finest, and they're balanced by a couple of good moments from the first side (the silly fun of "Good to Go to Mexico," "Losing My Touch") and, of course, "Courtesy of the Red, White and Blue." That song may mischaracterize what's on *Unleashed*, but those who are brought in by that slice of flag-waving jingoism should be pleased by the sweeter fare here since, ultimately, it proves to be more substantive. *—Stephen Thomas Erlewine*

● **20th Century Masters: Millennium Collection—The Best of Toby Keith** / Apr. 15, 2003 / Universal ♦♦♦♦♦
Toby Keith didn't become a crossover superstar until 2002, when his post-9/11 anthem "Courtesy of the Red, White and Blue" made him a household name, but by then, he had been a country star for nearly a decade, constantly reaching the upper heights of the country charts while on Mercury. That's the era covered on 2003's *20th Century Masters: The Millennium Collection*: the years between his 1993 self-titled debut and his 1997 farewell to Mercury, *Dream Walkin'*. This does its job perfectly, containing all of his big hits from this era, including "Should've Been a Cowboy," "A Little Less Talk and a Little More Action," and "Me Too." In fact, even though this disc has two less tracks, this mid-priced collection is better than 1998's *Greatest Hits, Vol. 1* since it has no filler, all the biggest and best hits, and is presented in chronological order—all factors that make this a near-ideal summary of Keith's Mercury recordings as well as a fine introduction to the man himself. *—Stephen Thomas Erlewine*

The Kendalls

f. 1969, St. Louis, MO
Group / Country-Pop, Traditional Country
One of the rare father-daughter duos in country music history, the Kendalls were also the most successful, racking up a series of hits during the late '70s and early '80s. Daughter Jeannie sang lead on most of the group's material, while father Royce typically double-tracked his harmony vocals behind her and shunned the spotlight on most occasions. Though their production was certainly radio-friendly, they were more grounded in country tradition than many of their contemporaries, working elements of bluegrass, honky tonk, and country gospel into their music. Royce was born in St. Louis, and along with his brother Floyce, he formed a group called the Austin Brothers during the late '50s. Jeannie was also born in St. Louis, and her father taught her to sing as a child. Royce moved the family to Los Angeles as he pursued a career with the Austin Brothers, but after a couple of years, he returned to St. Louis and set up his own barber shop. He and Jeannie teamed up as a family act when she was 15 and started selling their demo tape via mail order. They found a patron in producer Pete Drake, who signed them to the small Stop Records and helmed their very first chart single, a 1970 cover of "Leaving on a Jet Plane" that just missed the country Top 50.

The Kendalls subsequently moved to Nashville in pursuit of greater success, but although they recorded a bit more, their breakthrough was several years in coming. It wasn't until 1977 that they signed to Ovation and released the smash hit "Heaven's Just a Sin Away," which went all the way to number one on the country charts and won a Grammy for Best Country Vocal by a Duo or Group. The Kendalls visited the country Top Ten regularly up into the mid-'80s, establishing a penchant for cheating songs; their biggest hits of the late '70s included "It Don't Feel Like Sinnin' to Me," "Pittsburgh Stealers," the number one "Sweet Desire," and "I Had a Lovely Time." In 1981, they switched from Ovation to Mercury and scored more hits with songs like "You'd Make an Angel Wanna Cheat," "Teach Me to Cheat," and a third number one, "Thank God for the Radio."

Changing tastes in country music meant that their last Top 40 hit came in 1985, and although the Kendalls continued to record for several different labels into the late '80s, their hitmaking run was over. They continued to tour, however, and for a time took up residency in Branson, MO. In 1997, they signed with Rounder Records and began work on a new, bluegrass-flavored album, but Royce died of a stroke on May 22, 1998, just prior to a show in La Crosse, WI. Several tracks had been completed, and Jeannie eventually returned to the project, completing it as her solo debut; *Jeannie Kendall* was finally released in early 2003. *—Steve Huey*

Meet the Kendalls / 1970 / Stop ♦♦♦

Two Divided by Love / 1972 / Dot ♦♦♦
The Kendalls began their career turning pop songs into minor country hits. After making their chart debut with "Leaving on a Jet Plane" for the Stop label, they moved to Dot Records, where they recorded one LP, *Two Divided by Love*. The album produced two hits: the title track, a Grass Roots song that provides a showcase for the Kendalls' tight harmonies while negotiating some unusual chord changes for country music, and Bread's "Everything I Own," which is practically a solo turn by Jeannie Kendall. The song "Two Divided by Love" is one of the Kendalls' finest performances—far better (and more enduring in their stage act) than its modest chart placement suggests. Nothing else on the album is as immediately gripping, but it is a consistent effort with a pair of notable Jeannie Kendall originals and a good cover of Dickey Lee's "Never Ending Song of Love." *Two Divided by Love* was reissued by Pickwick in 1979. *—Greg Adams*

1978 Grammy Award Winner: Best Country Duo / 1978 / Gusto ♦♦

Movin' Train / 1983 / Mercury ♦♦♦

Two Heart Harmony / 1985 / Mercury ♦♦♦

Fire at First Sight / 1986 / MCA/Curb ♦♦♦♦

20 Greatest Hits / 1986 / Deluxe ♦♦
20 Greatest Hits contains all of the Kendalls' biggest hits from the '70s, including "Heaven's Just a Sin Away," "It Don't Feel Like Sinnin' to Me," "Sweet Desire," "I Had a Lovely Time," and "Put It Off Your Tomorrow." *—Stephen Thomas Erlewine*

Break the Routine / 1987 / Step One ♦♦♦♦
Break the Routine offers the minor chart hits "Dancin' With Myself Tonight," "Routine," "Still Pickin' Up After You," and "The Rhythm of Romance." *—Jason Ankeny*

The Best of the Kendalls / Apr. 5, 1994 / Curb ♦♦♦♦♦
Best of the Kendalls is a ten-track budget-priced collection that features some of their biggest hits, including "Heaven's Just a Sin Away," "Sweet Desire," "Thank God for the Radio," "Little Doll," and "If I Get That Close." Although this isn't a bad budget-priced disc, there are better collections available, offering more songs and better sound for not much more money. *—Stephen Thomas Erlewine*

● **The 16 Greatest Hits** / Oct. 5, 1999 / Varese ♦♦♦♦♦
All of the Kendalls number-one country hits can be found on this excellent cross-licensed compilation that draws from the duo's Ovation and Mercury singles. Covering the years 1977 through 1984, *16 Greatest Hits* is packed with chart hits and great music. Jeannie Kendall's voice is very similar to Dolly Parton's, and her father Royce Kendall, despite being a capable vocalist, usually provides harmony vocals rather than taking lead. Cheatin' songs comprise the bulk of this material, but the lack of variety in subject matter is offset by strong performances and material. In terms of quality, the Kendalls' dedication to honky tonk themes and prominent hooks sets them above many other hit-makers of the era; *16 Greatest Hits* is the best-sounding and best-annotated collection of their music. *—Greg Adams*

12 Hits: Five Star Collection / Sep. 10, 2002 / Varese ♦♦♦♦
12 Hits: Five Star Collection is an overview of duets the father and daughter team of Jeannie and Royce Kendall recorded together during the late '70s and early '80s. Their

number-one hits "Heaven's Just a Sin Away" and "Sweet Desire" are coupled with favorites like "It Don't Feel Like Sinnin' to Me," "Pittsburgh Stealers," and "I Had a Lovely Time." While this collection is missing "Thank God for the Radio," the digitally remastered sound makes this a package worth picking up. *—Al Campbell*

Love Is a Long Hard Road / Apr. 1, 2003 / Varese ✦✦✦✦✦
Recorded in the late '80s, *Love Is a Long Hard Road* is the first true showcase for Jeannie Kendall's solo talents. The Kendalls' first country chart hits came as early as the 1970s, and crossed over finally in 1978 with "Sweet Desire." But it wasn't until almost a decade later that Royce Kendall, Jeannie's father, began to step more firmly into the harmony role, though still appearing solo on the occasional bridge. Produced by Buddy Killen, this set accents the truly remarkable strengths of the Kendalls as a unique and gifted country duo. And the word "country" is the operative one here. There is nothing remotely urban about the Kendalls. Just one listen to the title track—with its cascading fiddles, phased steel guitars, and ringing Telecasters—is evidence there. But there's no attempt to make Jeannie's voice anything other than it is: a high lonesome honky tonk voice that has a beautiful range and drips emotion. The duo's reading of Boudleaux Bryant's "Bye Bye Love" (which worked so well for the Everly Brothers) is a delight here, full of dark irony, heartache, and winsome charm. Kevin Welch's "I'd Rather Dance With You" is a far cry from his later Americana version, and Harlan Howard's "Heartaches By the Number," made immortal by Ray Price, is treated as the swinging honky tonk number it is. Jeannie's voice is somewhere between Loretta Lynn's and Patsy Cline's; it's smooth, full, reedy, and almost grainy at the same time. Royce takes a beautiful tenor harmony here, punching the syllables at the end of his lines. The band swings hard in full barroom flush. This is followed by Lee Ross' "Curtain in the Window," given a very empathetic treatment before the whole album just cracks open with Buck Owens' lonely weeper, "Crying Time." The beautiful piano work and orchestration carry the duet vocal over the arrangement and into the emotion of the melody. There are a couple of bonus tracks here, such as "Temporarily Out of Order," a single from 1989, and the disc closes with Bob McDill's "Just Like Real People," an anthem that testifies that no matter how hard the road of love is, it's worth walking and stumbling upon. This is as worthy a reissue as exists in the country world, and a stellar example that true-to-the-roots country music still existed during the time period. *—Thom Jurek*

Kennedy Rose

Group / Country-Rock, Contemporary Country
Roots-pop duo Kennedy Rose teamed Nashville-based singers/songwriters Mary Ann Kennedy and Pam Rose, who first joined forces in 1981 in the group Calamity Jane. Already sought-after session vocalists, the twosome also earned renown for their songwriting skills before returning to performing as Kennedy Rose; signing to the IRS label, they issued *Hai Ku* in 1989, followed five years later by *Walk the Line*. Neither record made much commercial impact, but Kennedy and Rose nevertheless emerged as one of contemporary country's most successful writing teams, authoring a series of hits including Martina McBride's "Safe in the Arms of Love," Restless Heart's "I'll Still Be Loving You," Patty Loveless' "You Will," and Lee Greenwood's "Ring on Her Finger, Time on Her Hands" and "Dixie Road." *—Jason Ankeny*

● **Hai Ku** / 1989 / IRS ✦✦✦✦✦
Kennedy and Rose's decision to turn to performing resulted in this debut, which reprises familiar songs of theirs, such as "Love Like This" and "The Only Chain." The production is deep and echoey, with sharply recorded acoustic instruments, and the swinging is as forceful as the writing. *—William Ruhlmann*

Walk the Line / Feb. 8, 1994 / IRS ✦✦✦
Working with co-producer Ray Kennedy, an unrelated country singer with a few offbeat hits, Kennedy Rose created a tighter, leaner sound for *Walk the Line*. The duo's spacious music resonates with possibilities, and guest appearances by Emmylou Harris and David Lanz suggest that Kennedy Rose is in the process of creating a New Age alternative to country. *—Brian Mansfield*

Jerry Kennedy

Guitar, Producer / Rock & Roll, Singer/Songwriter, Progressive Country, Country-Folk, Outlaw Country, Nashville Sound/Countrypolitan, Country-Pop, Traditional Country
Jerry Kennedy worked for over 30 years as a guitarist, producer, and A&R man for Mercury Records, attaining success in all three endeavors. Born in Shreveport, LA, Kennedy became a teen idol in his local school after he was offered a singing contract at age 11. Although he never became a vocal star, throughout his teens he lent background vocals to several Mercury acts. After doing session work around Shreveport and East Texas, Kennedy was persuaded to move to Nashville by Mercury Records' Shelby Singleton. His arrival in 1961 coincided with country music's boom period of the '60s, and he was soon called upon to not only scout talent for Mercury, but to play and produce sessions as well. Kennedy produced on all, and played on most, of Jerry Lee Lewis' country records, as well as playing guitar for Elvis, Ringo Starr, and Kris Kristofferson. He also became vice president of Mercury Records' Nashville division in 1968 when his mentor Shelby Singleton left. Kennedy himself left Mercury in 1984 and created his own company, producing the Statler Brothers and others. *—Steve Kurutz*

Ray Kennedy

b. May 13, 1954, Buffalo, NY
Guitar, Piano, Keyboards, Vocals, Producer, Bass, Drums / Progressive Country, Neo-Traditionalist Country
In the country music business, multi-talented Ray Kennedy did it all. He was the master of several instruments, wrote and arranged songs, and was a producer and a recording engineer. He was born in New York to Ray Kennedy Sr., the National Vice President for Sears and the man behind the Discover credit card. His father's work kept young Kennedy and his family on the move. As a teen, his parents refused to get him a guitar, so Kennedy built his own. He briefly attended college where he majored in business, but at that time he found himself drawn to music and dropped out to play in midwestern clubs. He spent some time in Oregon and in 1980 moved to Nashville where he built his own studio and learned engineering when he began recording his own demos.

He got his start as an engineer and was responsible for producing most of Tree Publishing's pop demos during that time. Pop singer Stevie Nicks recorded one of his songs, "Battle of the Dragon," and Kennedy became a staff writer at Tree where his tunes were occasionally recorded by John Anderson, Charley Pride, David Allan Coe and others. Because his songs weren't selling well enough to suit him, Kennedy decided to become a recording artist and cover them himself. In 1990, he signed to Atlantic Records and debuted with *What a Way to Go*. Kennedy not only produced the album in his own studio, he also played all of the instruments but the Dobro, steel guitar, and Weissenborn. He also penned or co-penned all of the songs on it. Kennedy made his single debut with the album's title track, which peaked on the Top Ten with the album making it to the Top 60. He released two more singles from the album, but they only became minor hits. In 1991, he produced and engineered an album for songwriter Don Henry, *Wild in the Backyard*. In 1992, Kennedy teamed up with producer/songwriter Monty Powell and made *Guitar Man*. *—Sandra Brennan*

● **What a Way to Go** / 1973 / Atlantic ✦✦✦✦
Recorded entirely in his home studio, Kennedy's debut LP includes the title track, his first Top Ten hit. *—Jason Ankeny*

Ray Kennedy / 1980 / Columbia ✦✦
First off, there is no way anyone would mistake this for a country album. Secondly, Kennedy's claim to fame is that he co-wrote "Sail on Sailor" with Brian Wilson for the Beach Boys' *Holland* album. Aside from an excuse to hear Kennedy's version of that song, there really isn't a lot of reason to get this album. *—Jim Worbois*

Guitar Man / 1992 / Atlantic ✦✦✦
Entertaining rockabilly laden country from Ray Kennedy in this too-brief (32 minutes) outing, ranging from fairly standard country love songs to a rollicking anti-drinking number. Some witty lines mixed in with some fresh, spirited and clean guitar-pickin' makes for a better than average time here. *—Steven McDonald*

The Kentucky Colonels

f. 1963, Los Angeles, CA, **db.** 1965
Group / Bluegrass, Progressive Bluegrass, Traditional Bluegrass
Progressive bluegrass band the Kentucky Colonels had a short but legendary career during the folk revival of the late '50s and early '60s. The band was formed in Los Angeles in the early '50s by brothers Roland, Eric, and Clarence White, and their sister Joann. When Joann dropped out, the three brothers began billing themselves as the Three Little Country Boys and appeared on local television after winning first prize in a talent contest. In 1958, Arkansas native Billy Ray Latham became their banjo player and dobro player Le Roy Mack joined the band the next year. Latham's arrival allowed Roland White to switch to mandolin, his instrument of choice.

As the Country Boys, the group recorded their first single, "I'm Head Over Heels in Love with You." They began appearing on *Town Hall Party* and *Hometown Jamboree* and recording on Gene Autry's label. Bassist and banjoist Roger Bush joined the band in 1961 after Eric dropped out to marry. Three Little Country Boys then recorded *Songs, Themes & Laughs From the Andy Griffith Show* for Capitol. Before the year was out, Roland was drafted and left the band for two years, leaving them without a mandolinist. The group cut its first album on Briar, which disliked the band's moniker and suggested a series of names, the best of which was the Kentucky Colonels. In 1963, fiddler Bobby Sloane joined the Colonels and Roland returned as well. By this time, the Colonels had begun to gather a following through their U.S. tours, and appeared at both the UCLA and Newport Folk Festivals in 1964. The band recorded several albums and appeared in the movie *The Farmer's Other Daughter*. They really took off musically when fiddler Scotty Stoneman replaced Sloane, but broke up shortly thereafter in 1965, with each member going their separate ways. *—Sandra Brennan*

New Sound of Bluegrass / 1963 / Briar ✦✦✦✦

☆ **Appalachian Swing!** / 1964 / World Pacific ✦✦✦✦✦
Appalachian Swing! is one of the most influential albums in the whole of bluegrass music, primarily because of the stunning playing of Clarence White. With his vibrant, innovative flatpicking, White helped pioneer a new style in bluegrass; namely, he redefined the acoustic guitar as a solo instrument instead of confining it to just background status. The sound was revolutionary upon its release in 1964 and the music still sounds alive, even timeless, because of the strength of White's vision and talent. He was one of the greatest musicians in bluegrass history and the fact that *Appalachian Swing!* still sounds fresh makes his tragic death all the more painful. *—Thom Owens*

★ **Long Journey Home** / 1964 / Vanguard ✦✦✦✦✦
These great recordings from a 1964 live performance at the Newport Folk Festival feature Clarence White and many others, including duets with Doc Watson. *—Richard Lieberson & Mark A. Humphrey*

Kentucky Colonels / 1973 / Shiloh ✦✦✦✦✦
This is an expanded version of the group's debut album, *Appalachian Swing*, originally issued in England in this form after Clarence White's death in 1973 and reissued over there in 1997 by the Beat Goes On label. The original 12-song album (which was also available here as a ten-song LP at one point late in the 1970s) is here, newly remastered, along with two additional tracks, "John Henry" b/w "Flat Fork," that came out as a single at around the same time. Highlights on the original album include "I Am a Pilgrim," a song that the Byrds were later to cover during the beginning of their country phase; maybe the prettiest version of the bluegrass standard "Billy in the Low Ground" that you're ever going to hear; White's arrangement of the popular song "Listen to the

Mockingbird"; and traditional numbers like "Wild Bill Jones" (great mandolin showcase), "Lee Highway" (ditto the fiddle), their beautifully sung version of Gordon Lightfoot's "That's What You Get for Lovin' Me," and "Sally Goodin." In addition to the extra song, there are extensive notes giving a detailed biography on Clarence White and a history of the Kentucky Colonels and this recording, all of which make this a choice addition to any collection. *—Bruce Eder*

Livin' in the Past / 1975 / Briar ✦✦✦✦

The Kentucky Colonels only played together for a short period of time, but the legacy of Roland White, and even more so of guitarist Clarence White, has kept the band's name alive. But the White brothers are only two of the many reasons to appreciate this band. For starters, there is the instrumental dexterity of fiddler Scotty Stoneman, banjoist Billy Ray Latham, and bassist Roger Bush. One should also mention that the group is a vocal powerhouse. There are 25 tracks on *Livin' in the Past,* taken from a number of performances during the early- to mid-'60s, and clocking in at over 73 minutes. The material ranges from the four-part gospel singing of "Get on Your Knees and Pray" to wonderful instrumentals like "Julius Finkbine's Rag." On this latter piece, Clarence White transforms "Beaumont Rag" into a guitar standard, filled with phenomenal flatpicking. On "I Am a Pilgrim," his guitar playing—as the saying goes—will knock your hat in the creek. Roland White shows that he's no slouch with some speedy mandolin picking on "Barefoot Nellie," while Stoneman's fiddle shines on "If You're Ever Gonna Love Me." The Whites turn in a great brother duet on "Dark Hollow," and add Bush for a nice trio on "Ocean of Diamonds." This album provides a nice snapshot of the Kentucky Colonels at the height of their powers, and provides a fuller picture of the band's talents than *Appalachian Swing!* because of the inclusion of vocals. For bluegrass fans who enjoy traditional singing and progressive playing, *Livin' in the Past* should prove more than satisfactory. *—Ronnie Lankford Jr.*

The Kentucky Colonels 1965–1967 / 1979 / Rounder ✦✦✦✦

This group was together for a relatively short time during the second half the '60s. Many styles of music were going through revolutions of one sort or another during this period, and bluegrass was no exception. Unique to perhaps this group was the idea of doing modern things to bluegrass not by writing new material with diverse influences as many other groups were doing, but by taking traditional tunes, some of the done-to-death variety, and making all new whoopee with them. This concept has worked to great impact in many styles of music. Certainly bluegrass guitar playing was never the same after Clarence White decided to give it more of a lead element and make it jump out of the ensemble more by using some tricky syncopation. But it certainly isn't going to be one man alone that gets the credit for the success of this group. The fiddler Scotty Stoneman is, in a word, unbelievable, pushing the envelope in his solos and playing with an energy level more normal in free jazz than in the safe little bluegrass world. Then there's the double threat of Billy Ray Latham on banjo and Roland White on mandolin. This album release collects recordings from the group's releases on various independent labels, as well as some never-released sessions. A triumphant meeting of the old and new in a form of music that certainly regards traditions as important. *—Eugene Chadbourne*

The White Brothers Live in Sweden / 1979 / Rounder ✦✦✦

On Stage / 1984 / Rounder ✦✦✦

Kentucky Headhunters

f. 1986, Edmonton, KY

Group / Southern Rock, Contemporary Country

The Kentucky Headhunters created a hybrid of honky tonk, blues, and Southern rock that appealed to fans of both rock and country music. While they were only officially together for a few albums, the band nevertheless left a long shadow. The origins of the Kentucky Headhunters lie in 1968, when Fred and Richard Young began playing together with their cousins Greg Martin and Anthony Kenney at the Youngs' grandmother's home. Mark Orr also later joined them. The first incarnation of the band was called the Itchy Brothers, and the group played together informally for over a decade. After about 13 years, the band-members began launching separate careers: Richard Young went off to write songs for Acuff-Rose, while Fred Young began touring with country beauty Sylvia. Martin became a member of Ronnie McDowell's band, while Kenney dropped out of music.

In 1985, Martin decided to reassemble the Itchy Brothers. When Kenney declined to rejoin the group, Martin remembered Doug Phelps, who he had met while on tour with McDowell. Phelps joined the new project, which was named the Kentucky Headhunters. Besides Martin and Phelps, the band also included the Young brothers and Doug's brother Ricky Lee Phelps. The Headhunters started playing twice monthly on the *Chitlin' Show,* a radio program on WLOC Munfordville, KY. From these 90-minute performances, the Headhunters built up a following. They sent an eight-song demo to Mercury, and soon after, the label signed the group. The original demo tape was remixed and became the basis of the band's first album, 1989's *Pickin' on Nashville,* which upon its release received overwhelmingly positive reviews and quickly became a hit. "Dumas Walker" reached number 15 in the spring of 1990, followed by the group's biggest hit, the number six "Oh, Lonesome Me."

In 1991, the Headhunters released their second effort, *Electric Barnyard.* The album received mixed reviews, couldn't muster a single, and sold weakly. In summer 1992, the Phelps brothers left the group to form Brothers Phelps, a more traditional country group. The remaining Headhunters brought ex-Itchy Brothers Anthony Kenney and Mark Orr to the group, and the rehashed lineup released *Rave On!* in 1993. The album marked a progression towards bluesy Southern rock, which came to fruition with *That'll Work* later that same year. In 1996, Doug returned on lead vocals, and a year later the band issued *Stompin' Grounds. Songs From the Grass String Ranch* followed in 2000, and *Soul* appeared in spring 2003. *—Johnny Loftus*

Pickin' on Nashville / 1989 / Mercury ✦✦✦✦✦

As their album title suggests, The Headhunters aren't entirely comfortable with the country tag, which is appropriate when you hear their guitar-heavy, rambunctious music. The vocals have that twang, but these good old boys are often closer to Lynyrd Skynyrd than they are to Merle Haggard, and all the better for it. *—William Ruhlmann*

Electric Barnyard / 1991 / Mercury ✦✦✦

The Kentucky HeadHunters aren't a remarkable country mutation, just a top-notch Southern rock band with a sense of humor. "The Ballad of Davy Crockett" is the kind of clever novelty that won't work twice; "Big Mexican Dinner" is a novelty that doesn't even work the first time. Once again, the country and bluegrass covers—"Only Daddy That'll Walk the Line," "With Body and Soul"—are the highlights, and most of the originals (the Beatles-esque shuffle "Always Makin' Love" aside) are offbeat, adequate filler. *—Brian Mansfield*

Rave On! / 1993 / Mercury ✦✦

It's hard to tell if it was the new guys or just the direction the band was headed, but most of the novelty wore off the Kentucky Headhunters by the group's third album. New lead singer Mark Orr replaced Richard Phelps' backwoods country voice with a Southern rock wail; Anthony Kenney (cousin to drummer Fred Young and guitarist Richard Young) took Doug Phelps' place on bass. The original songs aren't as idiosyncratic as the ones on *Pickin' on Nashville* or *Electric Barnyard,* and the Headhunters continue to cover Bill Monroe, this time with "Blue Moon of Kentucky." Covers of Carl Perkins ("Dixiefried") and the Lovin' Spoonful ("My Gal") are less obvious. The Headhunters started as a hard rock country band, a novel idea; here, they've devolved into a redneck boogie group. *—Brian Mansfield*

● **The Best of the Kentucky Headhunters: Still Pickin'** / 1994 / Mercury ✦✦✦✦✦

The Best of the Kentucky Headhunters is a first-rate compilation of the highlights from the group's first three albums. Although their debut remains a worthwhile purchase, this collection salvages the good songs from the band's two uneven follow-ups to their exciting breakthrough first album. *—Thom Owens*

Stompin' Grounds / Apr. 29, 1997 / BNA ✦✦✦

Following several Southern-rock detours, the Kentucky Headhunters returned to their country-rock roots on *Stompin' Grounds.* For the record, the brothers Young reunited with the brothers Phelps, which does reinvigorate the Headhunters sound. Still, the extra muscle and skill doesn't necessarily make *Stompin' Grounds* a return to form. Certainly, it's a stronger record than *Rave On!* or *That'll Work,* but they show a lack of imagination—after all, the first single is a cover of "Singin' the Blues"—which makes the record somewhat stultifying. It's nice to hear them play, to be sure, but their whole style sounds considerably less energetic and exciting than it did years before. *—Thom Owens*

Songs From the Grass String Ranch / Jun. 13, 2000 / Audium Entertainment ✦✦✦

Songs From the Grass String Ranch is the fifth release by the Kentucky Headhunters, and while it is enjoyable, there's nothing out of the ordinary here. The band continues to play their crowd-pleasing mixture of Southern countryrock & roll blues boogie, which you either love them for or don't. In this case it would be unfortunate to miss out on the fun. *—Al Campbell*

Anita Kerr

b. Oct. 31, 1927, Memphis, TN

Piano, Vocals, Producer / Nashville Sound/Countrypolitan

Anita Kerr was the vocal embodiment of the "Nashville Sound" which dominated country music throughout the mid-'50s and '60s. Along with the Jordanaires, her group, the Anita Kerr Singers, were the seminal backing vocal unit of the era, and it is estimated that at their early-'60s peak, they graced fully one-quarter of all of the records coming out of Nashville's studios. Kerr was born Anita Jean Grilli on Halloween 1927 in Memphis, TN; her mother hosted a local radio program there, and by the age of four, Anita herself was taking piano lessons. In her early teens, she formed her own girl group, the Grilli Sisters, which soon became a fixture on her mother's radio show. At age 14, she was hired as the station's staff pianist. In 1948, Kerr left Memphis and began playing piano on the club circuit. The following year, she formed the Anita Kerr Singers, which also featured alto Dottie Dillard, tenor Gil Wright, and baritone Louis Nunley. After gaining some fame on regional radio, NBC hired the Singers for the program Sunday Down South, with Kerr brought aboard as chorus director.

In 1951, the group signed to Decca Records and began their career as a studio backing unit. Five years later, the Singers made their first appearance on the New York-based *Arthur Godfrey Talent Scouts* television program and quickly became featured players, splitting their time between the broadcast and their session work. In the mid-'50s, Kerr joined forces with Chet Atkins, then the head of RCA Records' country division and the creator of the pop-centric "Nashville Sound," which employed vocal choruses as a means of smoothing over country music's rougher edges. The Anita Kerr Singers appeared on literally hundreds of the era's most prominent recordings, including releases from Jim Reeves, Roy Orbison, Floyd Cramer, Dottie West, Hank Snow, Eddy Arnold, and Lorne Greene; even pop singers like Perry Como and Brook Benton enlisted Kerr's talents. She also produced Skeeter Davis' *End of the World* album, making Kerr one of the very first women to oversee a Nashville recording.

After touring Europe in 1964, she moved to California the next year to focus her energies on freelance production and songwriting, even as two of the Singers' LPs, *We Dig Mancini* and *Southland Favorites,* were winning Grammy awards (in the Vocal Group and Gospel categories, respectively). In the later years of the decade, Kerr teamed with poet Rod McKuen for a series of mood-music records, titled *The Sea, The Earth,* and *The Sky,* for which the Singers were renamed the San Sebastian Strings & Singers. At the same time, the group were featured weekly on the *Smothers Brothers'* sketch comedy program. By the 1970s, Kerr produced a number of easy listening records before moving to her second husband Alex Grob's native Switzerland to compose music for films.

Eventually, she returned to Tennessee and focused almost all of her talent within the Christian music industry. In 1988, she switched genres yet again and embraced New Age culture with *In the Soul* on the Gaia label. —*Jason Ankeny*

Velvet Voices and Bold Brass / 1969 / Dot ✦✦✦

● **Anita Kerr Singers Reflect on the Hits of Burt Bacharach & Hal David** / 1969 / Dot ✦✦✦✦

The Simon & Garfunkel Songbook / 1971 / Bainbridge ✦✦

Anita Kerr & the French Connection / 1977 / RCA ✦✦

In the Soul / 1988 / Gaia ✦✦

In the Soul bears little resemblance to Kerr's work during the Nashville Sound era; performed almost entirely on synthesizers, the album alternates between spare electronic accompaniment and lush symphonic passages, while maintaining its focus on Kerr's readings of Walt Whitman poetry and new age doctrine. —*Jason Ankeny*

Music Is Her Name / 1992 / Columbia ✦✦✦

Reflect on the Hits Of Burt Bacharach & Hal David/Velvet Voices and Bold Brass / 1999 / Collectors' Choice Music ✦✦✦

It's unclear what segment of the listening population this Collector's Choice Music reissue is targeted to, but it does include the complete contents of two LPs by the Anita Kerr Singers, *Reflect . . .* and *Velvet Voices and Golden Brass*. The focus of the first, on songs written by the team of Burt Bacharach & Hal David, makes for a pleasant (though innocuous) listen. The choir tackles a baker's dozen of the most well-known Bacharach standards, including "Do You Know the Way to San Jose?," "Walk on By," "I Say a Little Prayer," and "The Look of Love." As expected, there are few surprises. The *Velvet Voices and Golden Brass* album presents rock (and a few Broadway) standards of the day given the inimitable Anita Kerr treatment. There are one or two surprises (Donovan's "Lalena," Billie Holiday's "God Bless the Child") that might pique the interest of a few listeners, but the world hardly needed more versions of "The Windmills of Your Mind," "My Way," and "Ob-La-Di, Ob-La-Da." The two-fer makes for an hour of vaguely pleasant, nostalgic wallpaper—but not much else. —*John Bush*

David Kersh

b. Dec. 9, 1979, Humble, TX
Vocals / Contemporary Country, Neo-Traditionalist Country
Born and raised in Humble, TX, contemporary country singer David Kersh spent his early 20s working the local Texas dancehall circuit, eventually landing a major-label record contract. Kersh's debut album, *Goodnight Sweetheart*, was released in the fall of 1996, followed in 1998 by *If I Never Stop Loving You*. —*Stephen Thomas Erlewine*

● **Goodnight Sweetheart** / Oct. 1, 1996 / Curb ✦✦✦

David Kersh's debut album *Goodnight Sweetheart* is a pleasant set of contemporary country that emphasizes slick uptempo, line-dancing country-rock and polished ballads. Kersh has a winning voice and personality, yet he lacks strong material. For every strong number, there's one that doesn't quite catch hold. Despite this, *Goodnight Sweetheart* is a promising debut, simply because it introduces a vocal talent as engaging as Kersh. —*Thom Owens*

If I Never Stop Loving You / Feb. 17, 1998 / Curb ✦✦✦

This album is pretty much an also-ran, settling on competence in spite of numerous up-and-coming talents looking to steal guys like David Kersh's thunder. Kersh works up a bit of steam on a few cuts, most notably "I Breathe In, I Breathe Out" and "Hello Walls," but the vast majority of *If I Never Stop Loving You* is well-covered ground at a time when country needs new voices. Some feel that incorporating rock influences is the key to freshness, but it would be hard to make such a case based on Kersh's version of the Eric Clapton classic "Wonderful Tonight," in which he stumbles blindly through the entire song without finding the right emotional vibe. The brighter moments on this album shouldn't take up too much space on a greatest-hits album, but what is achieved is maintained with consistency. —*Jeremy Ulrey*

Doug Kershaw

b. Jan. 24, 1936, Tiel Ridge, LA
Fiddle, Guitar, Vocals / Traditional Cajun, Traditional Country
1969 was a pivotal year in the musical career of Doug Kershaw (born Douglas James Kershaw). An appearance on the premier broadcast of *The Johnny Cash Show*, on June 7th, brought him to the attention of his largest audience and led to a contract with Warner Bros./ Seven Arts. Two months later, Kershaw's autobiographical tune, "Louisiana Man," became the first song broadcast back to Earth from the Moon by the astronauts of Apollo 12. Kershaw capped the year with a much-publicized, week-long, engagement at the Fillmore East in New York as opening act for Eric Clapton's Derek & the Dominos. While it seemed, to many rock and pop fans, that Kershaw had appeared out of nowhere, he had already sold more than 18-million copies of the records he had done in the early '60s with his brother, Rusty. "Louisiana Man" had been a Top Ten country hit in 1961 and its follow-up, "Diggy Diggy Lo," had done almost as well. The son of an alligator hunter, Kershaw was the seventh born to a family that eventually included five boys and four girls. Raised in a home where Cajun French was spoken, he didn't learn English until the age of eight. By that time, he had mastered the fiddle, which he played from the age of five, and was on his way to teaching himself to play an amazing 28 instruments. His first gig was at a local bar, *the Bucket of Blood*, where he was accompanied by his mother on guitar. After teaching his brother, Rusty (born Russell; February 2, 1938), to play guitar, he formed a band, the Continental Playboys, with Rusty and older brother, Peewee, in 1948.

Although they intially sang in French, J. D. Miller, owner of the Feature record label, persuaded them to incorporate songs in English into their repertoire. With the departure of Peewee from the group, in the early '50s, Doug and Rusty continued to perform as a duo. The brothers quickly built a solid reputation for their high-energy performances of

Cajun two-steps and country ballads. In 1955, they recorded their first single, "So Lovely, Baby." Released on the Hickory label, the tune became a Top Five country hit in August 1955. Shortly afterward, they were invited to become cast members of the *Louisiana Hayride*, a popular radio show broadcast from Shreveport, LA. In 1957, they recorded a Top 40 country hit, "Love Me to Pieces."

They became members of the *Grand Ole Opry* the following year. Despite the demands of his music career, Doug Kershaw enrolled in McNeese State University and earned an undergraduate degree in mathematics. At the peak of their early career, in 1958, Doug and Rusty decided to simultaneously enlist in the U.S. Army. They devoted their attention to the military until their dismissal three years later. Picking up where they left off, in February 1961, the two brothers recorded "Louisiana Man," a song Doug had written while in the Army. The song was eventually covered by more than 800 artists. By the time that their debut album, *Rusty and Doug*, was released in July 1964, however, the Kershaw brothers had elected to go their separate ways.

It took another three years before Kershaw signed a songwriters' contract with BMI. Despite the success of his solo career, Kershaw continued to be plagued by depression and sorrow. His father had committed suicide when he was only seven. Until 1984, Kershaw battled drug and alcohol abuse and he became known for erratic behavior. Although he continued to perform and record, his albums of the 1970s failed to duplicate the commercial success of "Louisiana Man" and "Diggy Diggy Lo." In 1981, Kershaw rebounded with his biggest selling hit, "Hello Woman," which reached the country music Top 40. In 1988, he recorded a duet, "Cajun Baby," with Hank Williams Jr. that became a Top 50 country hit. Marrying his wife, Pam, at the Astro Dome on June 21, 1975, Kershaw began raising his own family that included five sons—Douglas, Victor, Zachary, Tyler, and Elijah—and two grandsons. His son, Tyler, plays drums in his band. Kershaw released a French-language album, *Two Step Fever*, in 1999. Michael Doucet of Beausoleil is featured on the duet "Fievre De Deux Etapes." *Hot Diggity Doug* was released in mid-2000 and *Still Cajun After All These Years* followed in early 2001. —*Craig Harris*

The Cajun Way / 1969 / Warner Bros. ✦✦✦✦

Spanish Moss / 1970 / Warner Bros. ✦✦✦✦

Louisiana Man / 1971 / Warner Bros. ✦✦✦

Doug Kershaw / 1971 / Warner Bros. ✦✦✦✦

Swamp Grass / 1972 / Warner Bros. ✦✦✦

Devils Elbow / 1972 / Warner Bros. ✦✦✦

Douglas James Kershaw / 1973 / Warner Bros. ✦✦✦

Mama Kershaw's Boy / 1974 / Warner Bros. ✦✦✦✦

Alive & Pickin' / 1975 / Warner Bros. ✦✦✦✦

Ragin' Cajun / 1976 / Warner Bros. ✦✦✦

Flip, Flop & Fly / 1977 / Warner Bros. ✦✦

Cajun Country Rockers / 1979 / Bear Family ✦✦✦✦✦

More Cajun Country Rock / 1984 / Bear Family ✦✦✦✦

● **The Best of Doug Kershaw** / Aug. 8, 1989 / Warner Bros. ✦✦✦✦

Fiddle player extraordinaire Doug Kershaw is featured on ten Cajun-drenched country and rockabilly tunes recorded in the '70s for Warner Bros. Some of these songs were initially recorded by Kershaw and his brother, Rusty, in the early '60s and became regional hits in Louisiana before Kershaw went on to mainstream success as "the Ragin' Cajun" in the '70s. Among the ten tracks are "Diggy Diggy Lo," "Louisiana Man," "Mamou Two-Step," "Hippy Ti Yo," and versions of Hank Williams' Cajun classic "Jambalaya (On the Bayou)" and "I'm Walking" by Fats Domino. It's highly recommended. —*Al Campbell*

The Best of Doug & Rusty Kershaw / 1991 / Curb ✦✦✦✦✦

The Best of Doug & Rusty Kershaw collects 12 of the Kershaw brothers' recordings for Hickory Records in the late '50s, including the hit singles "Louisiana Man" and "Diggy, Diggy Lo." During this time, the group sounded like a cross between a Cajun string band and the Everly Brothers, which resulted in one of the most unique sounds of the late '50s. They might not have had many hits and some of their material now sounds dated, but Doug and Rusty's musical interplay still sounds fresh. *The Best of* isn't a perfect collection—it's missing the hits "So Lovely, Baby," "Love Me to Pieces," and "Hey Sherrif"—but what is here is very good, making it an adequate retrospective. —*Thom Owens*

Crazy Cajun Recordings / Feb. 18, 1999 / Edsel ✦✦✦

Diggy Diggy Lo / Mar. 16, 1999 / Ronn ✦✦✦✦

This 1999 album finds Kershaw at the top of his well seasoned game, playing and singing with both conviction and abandon. Kicking off with "Diggy Diggy Lo," Kershaw's fiddle has real bite and a downright nasty tone while his vocals are full of exuberance. Duets with Hank Williams Jr. on "Cajun Baby" (a tune started by Hank Sr. and finished years later by his son) and Fats Domino on "My Toot Toot" are highlights, but every track on this album is an inspired performance, Kershaw pouring his blood and guts into each track on here. If you're looking for great Cajun fiddle music, you've hit paydirt with this one. —*Cub Koda*

Oh Boy Classics Presents: Rusty & Doug Kershaw / Jul. 9, 2002 / Oh Boy ✦✦✦

Fiddle player extraordinaire Doug Kershaw is featured with his brother Rusty on these Cajun-drenched country and rockabilly songs recorded in the early '60s for the Hickory label. Before Doug went on to mainstream success as the Ragin' Cajun in the '70s, he and brother Rusty recorded numerous regional records, some of which gained national attention. Among the 11 tracks included here are "Diggy Diggy Lo," "Cajun Joe (Bully of the Bayou)," and the country standard "Louisiana Man," which has been covered through the years by a host of artists such as Jerry Lee Lewis, Rick Nelson, the Flying Burrito Brothers, Dave Edmunds, and Charley Pride. It's highly recommended. —*Al Campbell*

Easy / Sep. 10, 2002 / Spin Art ✦✦✦

That Rockin' Cajun Country / Bear Family ✦✦✦✦

Rusty Kershaw

b. Feb. 2, 1938, Tiel Ridge, LA, **d.** Oct. 23, 2001, New Orleans, LA

Guitar, Vocals / Traditional Country, Traditional Cajun

As a soloist, Rusty (Russell) Kershaw has yet to match the success that he had in the early '60s when he shared a duo with older brother, Doug Kershaw. His albums, however, have been well-conceived samplings of Cajun two-steps and country ballads, and have featured accompaniment by top-notch musicians. While *Cajun in Blues Country*, released in 1970, featured Charlie Daniels on fiddle, *Now & Then*, released in 1992, was a *tour de force* featuring Art Neville of the Neville Brothers on piano and Ben Keith on dobro, flute, piano, pedal steel, and background vocals. Introduced to Cajun and country music by his multi-instrumentalist brother, Kershaw was only ten when he began performing with Doug and Peewee in the Continental Playboys. The enthusiastic response that the group received helped to sooth the pain he had felt since their father, an alligator hunter, committed suicide five years before. Following the departure of Peewee in the early '50s, Rusty and Doug continued to play together as a duo. Their debut single, "So Lovely, Baby," became a Top Five country hit in August 1955.

Soon afterward, the two brothers were invited to become cast members of the *Louisiana Hayride*, a popular country music radio show broadcast from Shreveport. In 1957, they became members of the *Grand Ole Opry*. Simultaneously enlisting in the U.S. Army, in 1958, the Kershaws devoted their attention to the military for the next three years. Discharged in 1961, the brothers soon recorded their greatest hit, "Louisiana Man," an autobiographical tune written by Doug. Their follow-up single, "Diggy Diggy Lo," was nearly as successful. Although they released their debut album, *Rusty and Doug*, in July 1964, Rusty and Doug had already gone their separate ways. While Doug went on to become an internationally known superstar, Rusty maintained a low-key presence, occasionally popping up on albums by the likes of Neil Young (*On the Beach*) and several of his brother Doug's albums. He performed shows regularly up until his death of a sudden heart attack on October 23, 2001. *—Craig Harris*

● **Cajun in Blues Country** / 1970 / Cotillion ♦♦♦♦♦

Rusty's best Cajun LP as a leader includes both solid vocals and first-rate playing. *—Ron Wynn*

Now & Then / 1992 / Domino ♦♦♦

In the early '90s, producer Rob Fraboni was the man behind Domino Records, a label distributed by Relativity Entertainment Distribution. Domino released *Zoom*, the self-produced album by Ten Years After guitarist Alvin Lee, along with two discs produced by Fraboni, one by blues artist John Mooney, and the other being this excellent effort by Rusty Kershaw. For fans of Neil Young's *Harvest*, this is even more laid-back, but it shows Young's roots, and he actually shows up on six of the 13 tracks. "I Like to Live on the Bayou" has Ben Keith on dobro and pedal steel, and Young playing a melancholy harmonica. This material was recorded and mixed in New Orleans, and it can't be beat for authenticity. *Now & Then* is a record from another time and place, and if you aren't accustomed to the sound, it really needs to be played a couple of times to detox you from what you may be used to listening to; the 12 Kershaw originals and one arrangement of a traditional tune, "Stop Kicking My Dog Around," have an amazing effect when given a proper ear. Fraboni's production is perfect, allowing the music to get absorbed by the analog recording tape. Art Neville's piano on "Musician's Woman" and "I Don't Like the Feeling" is a nice addition to the Subdudes, the band recording with Kershaw on this disc (Steve Armadee on tambourine, Johnny Ray Allen on bass, Tommy Malone providing acoustic guitar, and John Magnie on keyboards). "This Is Rock & Roll" is not rock & roll—it's some blend of folk and Cajun music—but it works, and the instrumentation weaves a nice tapestry here, a little more uptempo than most of the record. "I Don't Like the Feeling" brings things right back down; Kershaw's vocals are almost unintelligible, and the performance feels like B.J. Thomas' 45 rpm version of "I'm So Lonesome I Could Cry" played at 33 rpm. There is amazing precision in these grooves; Kershaw is able to slow things down with more intensity than Vanilla Fudge in its heyday. Fans of modern rock might find this musical morass monotonous, but that would be a pity. "Married Man," with contributions from Young and Keith, is like some sort of Cajun funk. It's music with a well-deserved cult following, and is a treat for connoisseurs of the genre. *—Joe Viglione*

★ **Greatest Hits** / May 21, 2002 / Varese ♦♦♦♦♦

This is a long-overdue, wonderful compilation, containing the bulk of the Hickory singles Rusty and Doug Kershaw released on Hickory Records—either as a duo, or as solo acts—during the late '50s, '60s, and right on into the '70s (thanks to the single "(Our Own) Jole Blon.") They're kind of easy to overlook in some ways: often pigeonholed as Cajun—and they were from Louisiana, they did play Cajun songs—they blew any preconception of what that genre could do, rooting themselves in hardcore country as much as Cajun, while dabbling in rockabilly, wild backwoods weirdness, a little bit of Nashville sweetness (a wonderful cover of Don Gibson's "Sweet Sweet Girl to Me," turning Hank's "Why Don't You Love Me" into a skipping Everly-esque side), and everything in between. This is genuine American music, blending it all together in wild, invigorating, unexpected ways, and while some of the material could be argued as rock-pandering, lightweight teen tunes, there's a grittiness in the production and an inventiveness in the music that keeps all 20 tracks crackling and alive. *—Stephen Thomas Erlewine*

Sammy Kershaw

b. Feb. 24, 1958, Kaplan, LA

Vocals / Contemporary Country, New Traditionalist, Neo-Traditionalist Country

Sammy Kershaw rode in on the new traditionalist wave in the early '90s, finding success with a penchant for ballads and a blend of updated honky tonk (especially the vocal stylings of George Jones), Southern rock, and a hint of Cajun flavor. But as his career progressed, Kershaw moved farther and farther into crossover-minded country-pop, which actually eroded his early following. He was born in 1958 in Kaplan, LA, in the heart of Cajun country; in fact, his third cousin was legendary Cajun fiddler Doug Kershaw. He got his first electric guitar at age 11 from his grandfather, but sadly, his father passed away not long after, forcing Kershaw to get professional as quickly as he could. He debuted at age 12 with local bandleader J. B. Perry and often worked for Perry as both a musician and roadie during his teenage years, touring the Southern club and honky tonk circuit.

In 1980, Kershaw moved to Oklahoma with his wife and worked a day job while singing in local bands. However, his marriage fell apart two years later, and he returned to Louisiana, where he went through a succession of day jobs, remarried in 1985, and joined a touring club band called Blackwater in the mid-'80s. Unfortunately, the honky tonk lifestyle took its toll on Kershaw, who developed major problems with drugs and alcohol. In order to save his marriage, he quit everything cold turkey in 1988—including the music business, taking a full-time job at Wal-Mart as a supervisor of store remodeling. However, his songwriter friend Barry Jackson convinced him to submit a demo tape to Mercury Records in 1990, and after a showcase performance, Kershaw finally landed the record deal he'd spent so long pursuing.

Kershaw's debut album, *Don't Go Near the Water*, was released in 1991 and spawned the breakout hit single "Cadillac Style," which reached number three on the country charts the following year. The title cut and "Yard Sale" both charted in the Top 20, and "Anywhere but Here" became his second Top Ten hit in 1993, helping the album go platinum. Later that year, Kershaw issued his second album, *Haunted Heart*, which many critics and fans still regard as his finest. The lead single, "She Don't Know She's Beautiful," became Kershaw's first number-one hit, and its three follow-ups—the title track, "Queen of My Double Wide Trailer," and "I Can't Reach Her Anymore"—all went Top Ten; plus, the album became his second straight million-seller. Building on that commercial success, Kershaw began his shift away from hard honky tonk and toward more radio-friendly contemporary country with his next effort, 1994's *Feelin' Good Train*. He scored two number-two hits with the anthem "National Working Woman's Holiday" and a cover of the Amazing Rhythm Aces' country-rock hit "Third Rate Romance"; plus, the album featured a duet with his longtime idol George Jones on "Never Bit a Bullet Like This." At the end of the year, Kershaw released a holiday album, *Christmas Time's a Comin'*.

Kershaw returned in 1996 with *Politics, Religion and Her*, which found his sales beginning to slip a bit. Even so, he managed two Top Ten hits off the album: "Meant to Be" and the novelty song "Vidalia." *Labor of Love* (1997) was a ballad-heavy affair that returned Kershaw to the Top Ten of the country album charts; its "Love of My Life" became Kershaw's last big hit to date, peaking at number two. Even so, Kershaw's albums were growing increasingly uneven and pushing him farther into adult contemporary territory. That was especially true on 1999's *Maybe Not Tonight*, which found him covering '70s soft rocker Leo Sayer's "More Than I Can Say"; he also duetted on the Top 20 title track with Lorrie Morgan, who became his third wife in 2001. That year, they teamed up for the duet album *I Finally Found Someone*. Neither it nor Kershaw's last solo album produced any big-time hits, and he wound up parting ways with Mercury in the aftermath. He went on to sign with Koch subsidiary Audium, a newly established home for many country veterans of the '80s and '90s. His first album for the label, *I Want My Money Back*, was released in 2003. *—Steve Huey*

Don't Go Near the Water / 1991 / Mercury ♦♦♦

"Cadillac Style," Kershaw's first single, started him off strong. This album, which made his Jones influence explicit with a cover of "What Am I Worth," also produced the hits "Don't Go Near the Water," "Yard Sale" and "Anywhere but Here." *—Brian Mansfield*

Haunted Heart / 1993 / Mercury ♦♦♦♦♦

The more you know about Sammy Kershaw, the more there is to like about his albums. Though Kershaw doesn't write his songs, he makes some of the most autobiographical albums to come from Music Row. If you know that Kershaw quit performing for a year and a half when it threatened his marriage, "Still Lovin' You" assumes greater significance. Even a song as strange as "Queen of My Double Wide Trailer" makes more sense when you learn that Kershaw still owns a trailer in Louisiana, "in case things don't work out." Sure, he still sounded a lot like George Jones with a south Louisiana accent. But *Haunted Heart* showed that Kershaw was coming into his own as a vocalist. Just as important, he was choosing songs that set him apart from the pack. If some of those were as offbeat as "Double Wide" and "Neon Leon," well, that's just part of what made him distinctive. *—Brian Mansfield*

Feelin' Good Train / 1994 / Mercury ♦♦♦

"National Working Woman's Holiday" was a perfect example of Kershaw's strengths and weaknesses: few people, if any, had sung about the psychological toll the economic reality of the two-income family took on Southern men whose mothers had probably stayed at home to raise them. Unfortunately, Kershaw addresses it with a song whose chorus sounds like it belongs on a T-shirt. He still sounds too much like Jones to be a great singer (just try to tell the two apart on the duet "Never Bit a Bullet Like This"—just try), but he gets in a couple of strong ballads with "If You Every Come This Way Again" and "Southbound." It also contains a cover of the Amazing Rhythm Aces' 1975 hit "Third Rate Romance." *—Brian Mansfield*

● **The Hits: Chapter 1** / Sep. 12, 1995 / Mercury Nashville ♦♦♦♦♦

Sammy Kershaw had only been recording for four years when he released *The Hits: Chapter 1*, but its appearance didn't seem premature. During that time, he had racked up a considerable number of Top Ten country hits, including the number ones "National Working Woman's Holiday" and "She Don't Know She's Beautiful." Both of those songs are included, as well as eight others that prove why he was one of the most popular country singers in the early '90s. *—Stephen Thomas Erlewine*

Politics, Religion and Her / 1996 / Mercury ♦♦

Sammy Kershaw knows the sights and smells of true honky tonks, but he keeps moving further away from the soulful slur and fun-loving style that made him sound so promising a few years ago. After too many novelty songs and mis-directed pop-country moves, Kershaw tries to focus himself and get serious on *Politics, Religion and Her*. Unfortunately, his material fails him. A couple of powerful, soul-baring ballads only serve to show how superficial the rest of the song choices are. And his stiff version of Chuck Berry's

"Memphis, Tennessee" would get the vote for worst cover of the year, except it gets topped by his pale take on Sammy Johns' ludicrous '70s hit, "Chevy Van." —*Michael McCall*

Labor of Love / Nov. 4, 1997 / Mercury ✦✦✦

Labor of Love finds Sammy Kershaw moving further away from the neo-honky tonk that made his first records such a delight. Sure, there are a couple of honky tonkers on the record, but they are fairly tame and don't overshadow the love songs, exemplified by the power ballad "Love of My Life." While these ballads are impeccably crafted, they aren't distinguishable from those of his peers and they aren't as passionate as his earlier, more ragged ballads. Still, Kershaw's voice gives the material—which vacillates from strong to utterly bland—some style, and that's what will make *Labor of Love* appealing to some fans. However, early fans—the ones who loved *Don't Go Near the Water* and *Haunted Heart*—may find Kershaw's increasing professionalism a little distressing. —*Thom Owens*

Maybe Not Tonight / Apr. 13, 1999 / Mercury ✦✦✦

This record is pure Nashville by the numbers. Not a displeasing affair, but certainly not inspired either. Covering all bases, there is a romantic duet with Lorrie Morgan (the title track), the requisite honky tonk rocker ("Louisiana Hot Sauce"), a re-vamped cover of the old Leo Sayer hit, "More Than I Can Say," and plenty of heartbreak songs thrown in for the sensitive crowd. Present throughout *Maybe Not Tonight* are catchy melodies and tasteful playing, but in Nashville, where many of the best studio musicians and writers reside, those elements are a given and the difference between a good album and a great one is a wide bridge to cross. —*Steve Kurutz*

Coverin' the Hits / Jun. 20, 2000 / Mercury ✦✦✦

The title pretty much explains it all on Sammy Kershaw's *Coverin' the Hits*. This is not a collection of his hit singles, it's a compilation of covers Kershaw cut throughout the '90s, including songs from his own albums and selections from tribute albums. That it all sounds like it came from the same session says as much about Kershaw's consistency as it does for his taste. Consider this: the closest he comes to straight country here is "Third Rate Romance," the 1975 classic from country-rockers Amazing Rhythm Aces. It's either that or Chuck Berry's "Memphis, Tennessee," which many a country singer, including Buck Owens, has tackled over the years. No, this reveals that Kershaw is as much a fan of '70s soft rock as he is of country, which is to his benefit. He never treats this material with contempt, he has fun with it, and delivers sincere, effective versions of "More Than I Can Say," "Chevy Van," "Fire and Rain," "Angie," "I Got a Name," and "Little Bit More," plus a respectable version of Lynyrd Skynyrd's rocking "I Know a Little." That might not make *Coverin' the Hits* a major item per se in Kershaw's catalog, but it sure is a lot of fun. —*Stephen Thomas Erlewine*

The Hits: Chapter 2 / May 15, 2001 / Mercury ✦✦✦✦

I Want My Money Back / Mar. 25, 2003 / Audium/Koch ✦✦✦✦

After about a decade, Sammy Kershaw parted ways with Mercury Nashville after his 1999 album *Maybe Not Tonight*, resurfacing four years later on Audium/Koch with *I Want My Money Back*. A switch to an independent at this stage of the game pretty much takes Kershaw out of the running for the charts, but he thanks God in the liner notes "for giving me another chance to do what I love to do so much," so chances are, his eyes aren't on the charts anyway. Kershaw also calls it the best album he's done to date, and he very well might be right, because *I Want My Money Back* boasts a strong set of songs and performances that make it one of his most satisfying efforts. Part of the reason that this works is the fact that he isn't concerned about hits—there are no Leo Sayer covers, in other words—and with producer Richard Landis, he has picked a fine set of songs that highlight Kershaw's country roots. Not that this is an unadulterated honky tonk record; there are plenty of songs that are rock-influenced, neo-traditionalist country, which is now firmly part of contemporary country's tradition. But the difference is, there's not a song that feels pop, not a song with a false performance, not a moment that doesn't feel like Kershaw has made the comeback that he's needed for a longtime now. It's easily his best since 1993's *Haunted Heart*. —*Stephen Thomas Erlewine*

20th Century Masters—The Millennium Collection: The Best of Sammy Kershaw / Mar. 25, 2003 / Universal ✦✦✦

Sammy Kershaw's *20th Century Masters—The Millennium Collection* essentially gathers the highlights of his two Mercury greatest-hits collections, *The Hits: Chapter 1* and *The Hits: Chapter 2*, presenting a decent mix of early singles, like "Don't Go Near the Water," "She Don't Know She's Beautiful," and "Haunted Heart," and more recent hits like "Love of My Life" and "Vidalia." Kershaw is such a consistent artist that his past and current work flows together seamlessly, especially because the same good-natured, rollicking charm flows through "National Working Woman's Holiday" and "Vidalia," and his sentimental streak is just as evident on "I Can't Reach Her Anymore" as it is on "Love of My Life." For what it's worth, *20th Century Masters—The Millennium Collection* draws more from the first part of Kershaw's career, so fans who already own *The Hits: Chapter 1* would be better off getting *Chapter 2* than this collection, but for anyone looking for a sampling of Kershaw's work, this album certainly does the job. —*Heather Phares*

Clark Kessinger

b. Jul. 27, 1896, Kanawha County, WV, d. Jun. 4, 1975

Fiddle / Progressive Bluegrass, Traditional Bluegrass, Instrumental Country

One of the greatest of old-time fiddlers, Kessinger and his nephew, Luches, were billed as the Kessinger Brothers and recorded for the Brunswick company in the late '20s, producing records that greatly influenced other fiddle players around the South. When Kessinger was "rediscovered" during the folk revival of 1960, he appeared on the *Opry*, giving two encores because of audience demand. He entered many of the better-known fiddle contests, winning first place and the title as World's Champion Fiddler at the 47th Annual Union Grove, when he was in his mid-'80s. —*David Vinopal*

● **Clark Kessinger: Fiddler** / 1966 / Smithsonian Folkways ✦✦✦✦✦

These tunes are played with incredible drive. [Like all Folkways albums, it's now available on tape from Smithsonian/Folkways.] —*Charles S. Wolfe*

Clark Kessinger (Old-Time Music w/ Fiddle & Guitar) / 1984 / Rounder ✦✦✦✦✦

A West Virginian who began recording in 1928, Kessinger was rediscovered in the '60s and made several "comeback" albums, of which this is one of the best. —*Charles S. Wolfe*

Live at Union Grove / 1984 / Smithsonian Folkways ✦✦✦✦

Hal Ketchum

b. Apr. 9, 1953, Greenwich, NY

Drums, Vocals / Contemporary Country, Neo-Traditionalist Country

Singer/songwriter/drummer Hal Ketchum was raised in the Adirondack Mountains in upstate New York. He began drumming at age 15 and soon joined an R&B trio. At age 17, Ketchum moved to Florida and then to Texas, where he quickly got involved playing at a local dance hall where he began to hone his songwriting skills. He went to Nashville in 1986 to write songs, and three years later released his debut album, *Threadbare Alibis*; soon after, Ketchum signed with Forerunner Music, which eventually led to a record contract with Curb. He released his first Curb album, *Past the Point of Rescue*, in 1991. "Small Town Saturday Night," the first single, reached number two and the second single, "I Know where Love Lies," reached number 13.

In 1992, he scored two more hits and released his third album, *Sure Love*, which produced three Top 20 hits, including the number two "Hearts Are Gonna Roll." The following year, Ketchum joined the *Grand Ole Opry*. In 1994, he released his fourth album, *Every Little Word*, which, while not quite as successful as its predecessors, still produced two Top 40 hits. In 1995, he released *The Hits*, a collection of vintage 1977 sessions titled *Hal Yes* was due in 1998 but postponed until the following year, when it was finally released as *Awaiting Redemption*. —*Sandra Brennan*

Threadbare Alibis / 1988 / Watermelon ✦✦✦

Recorded as Hal Michael Ketchum in Austin before he moved to Nashville, it's folkier and less musically focused than his country recordings. But the thoughtfulness that informs his best work is in place, as is the willingness to take chances with his songwriting. —*Michael McCall*

Past the Point of Rescue / 1991 / Curb ✦✦✦✦✦

Hal Ketchum writes simple, sometimes moving songs about relationships and/or life's dilemmas, and communicates them in an attractive, unadorned vocal package. But although many of these numbers espouse country themes, Ketchum's delivery, as well as the arrangements and sensibility, lean toward easy-listening pop and light folk. Certainly every country artist isn't a honky tonking, tough-talking, drinker whining about lost love, but Ketchum comes perilously close on "Past the Point of Rescue" or his cover of the Vogues' "Five O'Clock World" to the super-smooth "Nashville Sound" of days past. —*Ron Wynn*

Sure Love / 1992 / Curb ✦✦✦

Ketchum was surprised by the success of his major-label debut, and he followed up with a slicker, peppier album. The melodies are stout, and he's at his best on the working-class tributes "Mama Knows the Highway" and "Daddy's Oldsmobile." —*Michael McCall*

Every Little Word / 1994 / Curb ✦✦✦✦✦

Ketchum reconciles the thoughtfulness of his folkie heart with the verve of modern country, tapping into the directness and earthiness that ties them together. His most country album, it's his most consistent. —*Michael McCall*

● **The Hits** / Mar. 26, 1996 / Curb ✦✦✦✦✦

Although it doesn't collect every worthwhile cut Ketchum recorded, *The Hits* has the great majority of his big hits, making it a good introduction to the vocalist. —*Stephen Thomas Erlewine*

I Saw the Light / May 19, 1998 / Curb ✦✦✦

Hal Ketchum wasn't quite sure what he wanted to achieve with *I Saw the Light*. He returned to Austin to cut a number of songs that are edgier and folkier than many of the songs that made him into a star. However, he didn't want to abandon that smooth sound that gave him hits, so there are quite a few slick songs that were cut together. Each of the sessions have isolated moments where everything works, but put together the Austin and Nashville tracks don't add up to an enjoyable record. It's not only that the two production extremes don't mesh, it's that the material is drastically uneven. There are enough good moments to make the record worth a listen for hardcore fans, but searching for them may be difficult for some less dedicated listeners. —*Thom Owens*

Awaiting Redemption / May 18, 1999 / Curb ✦✦✦

Lucky Man / May 8, 2001 / Curb ✦✦✦

The King of Love / Mar. 25, 2003 / Curb ✦✦✦

One has to ask why in the name of heaven Hal Ketchum allowed "Everytime I Look in Your Eyes" to be the opening track on his first album in two years. Perhaps it was a concession to Curb, or he had a momentary lapse of reason. Whatever the reason, it's one of the most unlistenable, sugary sweet, slicker than schlock excuses for a song to be heard in close to a decade. It's the only track here Ketchum didn't write or co-write, and it wasn't picked as the first single (thank God), so what the hell? Luckily, the 14 other songs here are substantially better. Ketchum produced this album (all but that cursed track) and did a fine job. It's a lot more polished than his Austin material, but the songs themselves are inspired, the arrangements are spare enough to let the subtle emotion in his voice come through the grain in the music, and the performances themselves are solid. Standout tracks include "As Long as You Love Me," a duet with the inimitably brilliant Jonell Mosser, and the title track, with its Bo Diddley shuffle done on acoustic guitars with a snarling electric in the background before it explodes into a pure roots rock extravaganza. The old R&B roots of Ketchum's New York past come through in "On Her

Own Time," a stunning vocal performance. The B-sharp in the background shimmering above the guitars is a particularly nice touch. The passion in Ketchum's voice, with Mosser in the background, cracks the track wide open and what spills out is a truth that both singer and listener can believe in. The evidence here suggests—as it does on his other recordings—that Ketchum couldn't write a bad song if he tried. His work is fine; there are no extra words cluttering up his stories, no overblown phrases and rambling ellipses. The bluesy shuffle in "Takin' My Time" and the near funky "The Way She Loves Me" are nice twists that might have been better served if he employed Austin's Archangels to back him instead of his own band, but they're still fine cuts. Guy Clark makes an appropriate appearance on "The Carpenter's Way"; given his own penchant for tools and woodworking, it's a waltz full of dobro and fiddles and bouzouki. The hippest track here, "Evangeline," a co-write with Charlie Daniels, has echoes of Bob Dylan's "It's Alright Ma (I'm Only Bleeding)," but digs deeper into the blues with backing vocals by Tim O'Brien. The fretless bassline and bodhran in "Skies Over Dublin" make a simple country song into a gorgeous pop tune, with its shape-shifting lines and atmospherics. It's as if Daniel Lanois were producing Celine Dion. In sum, Ketchum has given listeners a fine example of where he's at as a songwriter and proves himself as a producer, as this is a solid work—other than the one offending moment (why didn't he place it last?). *The King of Love* is a fine outing, full of passion, verve, soul, and honesty. *—Thom Jurek*

Jerry Kilgore

Vocals, Guitar / Contemporary Country, Neo-Traditionalist Country

Jerry Kilgore grew up in Tillamook, OR, and developed an interest in country music by listening to his family's Merle Haggard and Buck Owens records. He took up the guitar as a teenager but didn't form his first band until the age of 20, when he began playing in a honky tonk one in Portland. After a couple of years, he moved to Mesa, AZ, and played in a club there five nights a week for three years, then moved to North Carolina and fronted a honky tonk band for two more years before deciding to try his luck in Nashville. His breakthrough came when "Love Lessons," a song he had co-written, peaked in the country Top Ten for Tracy Byrd in December 1995. John Michael Montgomery took his song "Cover You in Kisses" into the country Top Ten in 1998. In January 1999, he became the first male artist signed to the newly formed Nashville division of Virgin Records. His debut single, "Love Trip," came out in the summer of 1999 and made the country charts, followed in September by a debut album of the same name. *—William Ruhlmann*

Love Trip / Sep. 21, 1999 / Virgin ✦✦✦

Jerry Kilgore's debut album has been so carefully calibrated to current commercial notions of Nashville success that its real strengths are nearly obscured. Though his biography emphasizes his love of Merle Haggard and Buck Owens and his years of playing honky-tonks, Kilgore's record is dominated by bland love ballads, many of which he wrote or co-wrote himself. Two of the singer's co-compositions dwell on the potential difficulties of being distracted by love—he risks a car accident in "It's Dangerous With You on My Mind" and almost loses his job in "If a Man Ain't Thinking 'Bout His Woman," all because he's daydreaming about his significant other! But the songs aren't distinctive enough, and Kilgore isn't a distinctive enough singer, to make such notions work, even when they're not so silly. Then, seven songs in, he finally shows a little honky-tonk feel in "All Hell's Breakin' Loose," and the Buck Owens influence starts to make sense. And at the end, with Steve Seskin and Allen Shamblin's story song "Cactus in a Coffee Can," he finally gets his hands on a song that's about something, and he makes the most of it. This is the kind of song that could really do something for him, if he and his handlers weren't so interested in pursuing the young adult female demographic the rest of the album is so squarely aimed at. (As an aside, one can't help wondering why country songwriters keep mentioning crack in their songs, given that it's thought of as such an urban drug. Is there something we don't know about the rural South, or is it just that the word "crack" is so easy to rhyme?) *—William Ruhlmann*

Merle Kilgore

b. 1934, Chickasha, OK

Vocals / Cowboy, Country-Rock, Honky Tonk

Merle Kilgore has had a multi-tiered career in country music as a singer, songwriter, and DJ, and more recently, as the manager of Hank Williams Jr. Born in Chickasha, OK (full name Wyatt Merle Kilgore), and raised in Shreveport, LA, he learned to play guitar at a young age and was working as a disc jockey and musician in his mid-teens. His outgoing personality and musical ability served Kilgore well, and he worked at several stations around the state before joining the *Louisiana Hayride* as the principal accompanying guitarist. He made the jump to television in 1952 on the *Ouachita Valley Jamboree* on KFAZ-TV in West Monroe, LA, then debuted on the *Grand Ole Opry*, and appeared on the *Big D Jamboree* in Dallas, all in a two-year span from 1952 to 1954, during which period he also completed college. Kilgore was signed to Imperial Records in 1953, and wrote the song "More and More," which was recorded by Web Pierce, Guy Lombardo, and Johnny Duncan, among others, with Pierce's making the number one country single for ten weeks.

His own recordings didn't do much, either on Imperial or D Records, but in 1959 Johnny Horton got a Top Ten hit with "Johnny Reb," another Kilgore song. It was only when he signed with Starday Records that Kilgore began generating hit recordings of his own, beginning with "Dear Mama" early in 1960. "Love Has Made You Beautiful" and "Gettin' Old Before Your Time" was a double-sided hit, the A-side making the Top Ten. Kilgore joined the *Grand Ole Opry* in the early '60s, even as other artists—including Frankie Miller—continued to generate their own hits with his songs, such as "Baby Rocked Her Dolly." He also appeared regularly on the *Big 10 Jamboree* and the *Riley Springs Jamboree*, out of Arkansas and Texas, respectively. "Wolverton Mountain," authored by Kilgore and his fellow Louisianan Claude King, became one of the biggest hits of Kilgore's songwriting career in King's hands, holding the number-one country spot for nine weeks in the early '60s, riding that chart for six months and becoming a Top Ten pop hit as well. In 1962, he also co-wrote "Ring of Fire" with June Carter, which became a major country and pop hit for Johnny Cash. Kilgore even followed Cash's path into the august surroundings of Carnegie Hall in New York for a concert and became a major draw in Las Vegas, while his albums, including *There's Gold in Them Thar Hills* and *Merle Kilgore*, kept selling for Starday.

By the mid-'60s, he'd jumped to Mercury Records and also into motion pictures, as a singer, doing the title song for the Steve McQueen revenge Western *Nevada Smith*, and also as an actor in the same movie. He joined Columbia Records in 1967 and did some more onscreen acting in Hewnry Hathaway's *Five Card Stud* (1967), starring Dean Martin and Robert Mitchum. He jumped labels again in 1969 and then in 1973, ending up back on Starday at that time. He continued to record into the 1980s and was assisted by Hank Williams Jr. on the album *Mr. Garfield*. He subsequently began managing Williams. Despite his activities in management, Kilgore still performed in his 60s and remained a familiar figure in country music thanks to his songwriting, which kept his name before the listening public even as he moved into other capacities. In 1995, Bear Family released a CD called *Teenager's Holiday*, made up of Kilgore's classic recordings. And Kilgore's music continues to be covered anew—in 1998, Van Morrison recorded a version of "More and More" as a duet with Bob Dylan. *—Bruce Eder*

● **Teenager's Holiday** / 1995 / Bear Family ✦✦✦

Teenager's Holiday collects none of Merle Kilgore's hits, concentrating instead on his earliest country, rockabilly, and pop recordings for the Imperial and Mercury labels from 1954-1962. Kilgore's original recording of "More and More" (later a hit for Webb Pierce) is here, as well as an attempt to cash in on the commercial folk craze ("Tom Dooley Jr."), and a session with Fats Domino's bandleader and producer Dave Bartholomew. In the early '60s, Kilgore went back to making country music, albeit with pop flourishes, and that comprises roughly half of this set. Kilgore was a talented songwriter and an important figure in country music, and his early recordings are interesting from a historical perspective, but *Teenager's Holiday* chronicles the uneven results of an artist casting about, following trends, and changing styles in pursuit of a hit. *—Greg Adams*

Claude King

b. Feb. 5, 1923, Shreveport, LA

Vocals / Country-Pop, Nashville Sound/Countrypolitan, Traditional Country

Singer/songwriter and actor Claude King is best remembered for his one big hit, "Wolverton Mountain," the tale of one Clifton Clowers who is "mighty handy with a gun and a knife" and keeps his daughter sequestered in their mountain home away from potential suitors. Focusing exclusively on that song results in an incomplete picture of King's career, however; he emerged from the milieu that also produced Johnny Horton, and after "Wolverton Mountain" he scored another 27 chart singles. The Shreveport, LA, native was a natural athlete as a child. When he was 12, he learned how to play guitar. After attending college on a baseball scholarship, he spent the late '40s and early '50s working as a construction engineer and performing music in local clubs and on TV and radio. Early on, he met up with Tillman Franks, who became Horton's manager and also a top talent official with the *Louisiana Hayride* program on Shreveport radio station KWKH.

King recorded his first single for the President label in 1947. He followed up with the hilarious honky tonker "51 Beers" (Gotham, 1949) and with other singles, including four recorded for Specialty in 1952, but despite some *Hayride* appearances lined up by Franks, he remained just under the national radar. In 1961, King signed to Columbia and released his first single, "Big River, Big Man." The song became a Top Ten country hit as well as a minor pop hit. The follow-up, "The Comancheros," also made it to the Top Ten. Around this time King teamed up with Merle Kilgore to write "Wolverton Mountain," a song that neatly blended a classic fairy-tale quality with Horton's storytelling style—and capped off the whole with lush Nashville sound background vocals that accented the song's theme of youthful ardor. "Wolverton Mountain" spent nine weeks at the top of the country charts and peaked at number six on the pop charts.

Two more hits—the Top Ten "The Burning of Atlanta" and the number 11 "I've Got the World by the Tail"—followed, and King and his band, the Nashville Knights, became hot tickets. Through 1964, he continued his string of successes with singles like "Hey Lucille!," "Sam Hill," and "Building a Bridge," but his hits became more sporadic in the latter half of the '60s. King left Columbia in 1971 and began recording with little success on independent labels. "Cotton Dan," which barely nicked the bottom of the charts, became his last hit in 1977. During his career, King also appeared in two feature films, *Swamp Girl* and *Year of the Wahoo*. He also appeared in the 1982 television miniseries *The Blue and the Gray*. *—Sandra Brennan & James Manheim*

Meet Claude King / 1962 / Columbia ✦✦✦

Meet Claude King was Claude King's debut long-player, even though he had been recording for a variety of labels since 1947. As a new Columbia artist he had already made three big hits, all of which are included on this album. The biggest was the enormously successful story-song "Wolverton Mountain." "The Comancheros" was recorded for, but not used in, the film of the same name, and "Big River, Big Man" was the third in King's trio of early Top Ten hits. King was a good songwriter, but had a hand in writing only a couple of songs on this album. Many of the other selections are oldies that smack of filler, like Jimmie Rodgers' "Pistol Packin' Papa" and Karl & Harty's "I'm Here to Get My Baby Out of Jail," although the latter receives an appealingly wistful treatment from King. The hits are the bright spots on *Meet Claude King*, and all of them can be heard on subsequent greatest-hits anthologies. *—Greg Adams*

Tiger Woman / 1965 / Columbia ✦✦✦

I Remember Johnny Horton / 1969 / Columbia ✦✦✦✦

Claude King and Johnny Horton were close friends in real life, and when Horton died King was groomed by Columbia Records to be his replacement. King had his own sound, but the two artists covered enough similar ground that King was right at home with Horton's songs. The title track is a heartfelt recitation on which King recalls Horton and their friendship, and the remainder of the album is drawn from Horton's hits (excepting a few personal favorites, like the early Horton composition "First Train Headin' South" and "She Knows Why," which Horton and King co-wrote). The historical folk song craze was itself history in 1968 when *I Remember Johnny Horton* was recorded, but the album's sincerity and celebration of a sadly missed friend is affecting in any era. —*Greg Adams*

Friend Lover Woman Wife / 1970 / Columbia ✦✦✦

Chip 'n' Dale's Place / 1971 / Columbia ✦✦✦

American Originals / 1990 / Columbia ✦✦✦✦✦
Though he had been recording for since the late '40s, Claude King didn't rise to national attention until the early '60s, when Columbia Records positioned the vocalist as the heir to the departed Johnny Horton's legacy of story-songs. *American Originals* contains all of King's country-pop hits, including "Wolverton Mountain," "Big River, Big Man," "The Comancheros," "The Burning of Atlanta," and "All for the Love of a Girl," among many others, making it the perfect retrospective of his hit-making heyday. —*Thom Owens*

More Than Climbing That Mountain / 1994 / Bear Family ✦✦✦✦✦
Wolverton Mountain is a five-disc box set containing all of Claude King's recordings for Columbia Records, from 1961's "Big River, Big Man" to 1972's "He Ain't Country." In addition to all of the released masters and hit singles, the box also features a number of unreleased songs, rarities, alternate takes and King's early recordings for Gotham Records. Certainly, a box set of this size is only of interest to historians and hardcore fans—there is simply too much marginal material for casual fans—but for those devoted listeners, *Wolverton Mountain* is the definitive retrospective. —*Thom Owens*

● **16 Original Classics** / Aug. 24, 1999 / Collectables ✦✦✦✦
Claude King is remembered for the story song "Wolverton Mountain," which topped the country charts for nine weeks in 1962 and crossed over to the pop Top Ten, but his recording career spanned three decades and 30 country hits. Columbia saw King as a replacement for his friend, the late Johnny Horton, so his early hits like "Big River, Big Man" and "The Comancheros" are similar in production and tone to Horton's historical recordings. "The Burning of Atlanta," the hit most blatantly in the Horton style, caused some controversy by declaring during a time of civil rights agitation that "the South's gonna rise again." King enjoyed only two other Top Ten hits, "Tiger Woman" and "All for the Love of a Girl," but he was a consistent artist with an appealing and subtly distinct style that could just as easily accommodate the country-pop bubblegum of "Catch a Little Raindrop." Columbia's own Claude King anthology, *American Originals*, has been deleted, and *16 Original Classics*, with four additional hits, is its superior replacement. —*Greg Adams*

Pee Wee King (Julius Frank Anthony Kuczynski)

b. Feb. 18, 1914, Milwaukee, WI, **d.** Mar. 7, 2000, Louisville, KY
Leader, Violin, Accordion / Old-Timey, Traditional Country, Cowboy, Western Swing
A flamboyant and influential figure during his heyday, Pee Wee King remains somewhat underappreciated as a performer, though his fame as a songwriter is assured thanks to the smash hit "Tennessee Waltz." King helped modernize the sound and style of country music; he introduced electric instruments, drums, and horns to the notoriously conservative *Grand Ole Opry*, and dressed his band in sharply tailored, Western-style Nudie suits that looked anything but backwoods. Despite his affinity for Western swing and cowboy songs, King actually came from Polish extraction, which helped account for his eclectic approach to country music. He was born Julius Frank Anthony Kuczynski on February 18, 1914, in Milwaukee, and grew up in the northern Wisconsin town of Abrams (or possibly vice versa, according to some sources). His father headed a polka band, and young Frank (as he was called) eventually joined up, learning both fiddle and accordion but concentrating on the latter instrument. He made his professional radio debut at age 14, and eventually started leading his own band, adopting the name Frank King (in tribute to polka bandleader Wayne King) and playing a mixture of polkas and cowboy songs. Starting in 1933, his band played regularly on the Milwaukee radio show The Badger State Barn Dance, where they were discovered by an up-and-coming Gene Autry. Autry hired them as his backup band, and nicknamed King "Pee Wee" for his five-foot six-inch height. In 1934, Autry and King became regulars on Louisville radio, but Autry soon departed for Hollywood.

King elected to stay behind in Louisville, and played with the Log Cabin Boys in 1935; the following year, he formed his own band, the Golden West Cowboys, which initially featured fiddler Abner Sims, guitarist Curly Rhodes, and singer Texas Daisy. In 1937, fiddler Redd Stewart joined the lineup, and would later become King's songwriting partner. Just as importantly, the group was invited to join the *Grand Ole Opry*. They were an unorthodox selection that made traditionalists uncomfortable: not just for their wardrobe, but also for their flashy, professional showmanship and for the polka and waltz rhythms that drove some of their songs. They remained regulars over the next ten years, during which time King also hosted his own radio show in Knoxville; they also evolved into more of a Western swing band. King first used an amplified electric guitar on-stage at the *Opry* in 1940, and introduced drums to the *Opry* stage in 1947. During that run, several prominent vocalists passed through the ranks of the Golden West Cowboys, including Eddy Arnold, Cowboy Copas, Milton Estes, Tommy Sosebee, and Becky Barfield. The Golden West Cowboys recorded and toured as Minnie Pearl's backing band over 1941-1942, and worked with Ernest Tubb as well. Additionally, King appeared in several Westerns playing himself as a bandleader; the first was 1938's *Gold Mine in the Sky*, starring his old friend Gene Autry.

A new era for the band started in 1947. King left the *Grand Ole Opry* to return to Louisville and host his own TV show, which ran for the next ten years and was picked up nationally by ABC in the final two seasons. King also signed a recording contract with RCA, and Redd Stewart took over the lead vocal chores. Inspired by Bill Monroe's hit "Kentucky Waltz," King and Stewart penned lyrics to an instrumental tune they'd been playing; recorded in December 1947, "Tennessee Waltz" became a number three hit for King the following year. Pop singer Patti Page cut her own version in 1950 and it was an

enormous hit, topping the pop charts and selling several million copies; it ranked as one of the biggest country crossovers ever. King followed it in 1951 with "Slow Poke," a novelty tune that topped both the country and pop charts, spending over three months at number one. Other hit King compositions included "Silver and Gold" (1952), "Changing Partners" (1954), "Bonaparte's Retreat," "You Belong to Me," "Walk By the River," "Busybody," and "Bimbo," among others. King also returned to the movies, appearing in a couple of Charles Starrett Westerns during the early '50s.

King's run of commercial success tailed off after 1954; his TV show went off the air in 1957, and he continued to record for RCA until 1959. From then until 1963, he reunited with Minnie Pearl and led the Golden West Cowboys as her supporting band. In 1965, Tennessee adopted "Tennessee Waltz" as its official state song. King broke up the Golden West Cowboys in 1969 and went to work for the Country Music Foundation, at one point serving as its director. He was elected to the Country Music Hall of Fame in 1974, later serving on its board of directors, and also made it into the Nashville Songwriters Hall of Fame. King passed away in Louisville on March 7, 2000, after suffering a heart attack. —*Steve Huey*

The Best of Pee Wee King & Redd Stewart / 1975 / Starday ✦✦✦✦

Rompin', Stompin', Singin', Swingin' / 1983 / Bear Family ✦✦✦✦✦

Hog Wild Too! / 1990 / Zu Zazz ✦✦✦

● **Pee Wee King and His Golden West Cowboys** / 1995 / Bear Family ✦✦✦✦✦

● **Pee Wee King's Country Hoedown** / Jan. 1, 1999 / Bloodshot Revival/Soundies ✦✦✦✦
Until a domestic anthology of Pee Wee King's classic RCA recordings appears, listeners who would like to sample King's innovative and supremely entertaining music can choose between either Bear Family's expensive multi-disc complete recordings box set or this affordably priced two-CD collection of radio transcriptions recorded circa 1952. Certainly owners of the box set would want to augment their collection with these previously unreleased performances, which include versions of hits such as "Slow Poke" and "Silver and Gold" as well as an incredible variety of novelties, love songs, and Western numbers that incorporate elements of swing, jazz, honky tonk, pop, and polka while seldom neatly fitting into any one of those categories. Redd Stewart is the featured vocalist on these 51 cuts, and liner notes were provided by noted country music historian Bill C. Malone. —*Greg Adams*

Country Music Hall of Fame 1974 / Nov. 9, 1999 / King ✦
If you're expecting King's original RCA recordings, guess again. These are later—although nicely done—recuts, albeit a bit heavy in the reverb department. Hits like "Slow Poke" and "Tennessee Waltz" are lovingly replicated, right down to Redd Stewart's honeyed vocals. But spend a little more time and dig up the originals, you're better off. —*Cub Koda*

Sid King (Sid Erwin)

f. 1952, Denton, TX, **db.** 1958
Group / Western Swing, Rockabilly, Country Boogie
One of the first white rock & rollers to record for a major label (Columbia), Sid King (born Sid Erwin) was also one of the first young Southern musicians to go from Western swing to rockabilly in the mid-'50s. Erwin grew up in the Dallas-Fort Worth area. He sang and played guitar at school, and while still in his mid-teens he began appearing on local radio with a friend, Melvin Robinson. The duo eventually took over the program, and Erwin and Robinson (who also played steel guitar and sax) formed a band, bringing in Erwin's brother Billy Joe on lead guitar, Ken Massey on bass, and David White on drums.

The group, by then known as the Western Melody Makers, stuck to playing country and Western swing in their gigs and radio appearances, but they were listening to lots of records by black artists. They were signed to Starday Records in 1954 and recorded a handful of songs, but these yielded no hits. They subsequently got a contract with Columbia Records and rechristened themselves the Five Strings. Erwin, in turn, changed his name to Sid King, all for the sake of a rhyming moniker, Sid King & the Five Strings. The Columbia sessions show just how far afield from country the group's listening had gotten. Their harmonies, the high-compression beat of their playing, and their choice of songs, coupled with Jim Beck's hard, up-front mixing of the rhythm section, made them, for a time, one of the hotter rockabilly acts outside of Memphis. They weren't as wild as the Sparkletones, but within Columbia Records' stable of artists, their music (along with that of the Collins Kids) constituted a tiny corner of rockabilly validity. Hearing their stuff today, they could have been fair rivals to Bill Haley & His Comets or Carl Perkins, with a sound midway between the two.

Sid King & the Five Strings were featured on the *Louisiana Hayride* alongside Elvis Presley and Johnny Horton and inherited "Ooby Dooby" from Roy Orbison (competing head to head with the latter's Sun version), but they never had the success of those whose paths they crossed. Their success was still confined to Texas, and by 1957 their Columbia contract had ended. The group's sound had also softened by that time, and their music no longer had the same edge, so by 1958 the band had called it quits.

King saw recording activity on his own in the early '60s on the Dot label through his acquaintance with Pat Boone, a fellow native of Denton whom he'd met years earlier, but by 1965 he was out of the music business. He resumed performing part-time in the 1980s, drawn back to the stage by a new generation of Europeans eager to hear authentic American rockabilly. He never quite jumped into rock head over heels, nor did he ever break through to a national audience. The only vintage King available on CD domestically is an interesting, but not wholly representative, set of radio broadcasts from the mid-'50s that are closer to hillbilly than rockabilly. His Columbia recordings have been reissued in Germany on Bear Family's *Gonna Shake This Shack Tonight*. —*Richie Unterberger & Bruce Eder*

● **Gonna Shake This Shack Tonight** / 1991 / Bear Family ✦✦✦✦✦
Sid King & the Five Strings were one of the weirdest and most enjoyable of the pre-rock & roll hillbilly country bands. Not only did King & the Five Strings play country boogie and nervy honky tonk, they tore their way through R&B and blues, performing all their songs with a wild, backwoods humor. *Gonna Shake This Shack Tonight* contains all

29 songs the group recorded between 1953 and 1959. Primarily, this is music for collectors—though there is a lot of really weird, wonderful proto-rock & roll here, you have to have a taste for the obscure to truly appreciate it. For those that have a taste for the obscure, the music on *Gonna Shake This Shack Tonight* is a true treasure. *—Thom Owens*

Rockin' on the Radio / Mar. 19, 1996 / Schoolkids ♦♦♦

This has 16 tracks broadcast live on Texas radio stations in 1954 and 1955. With muffled (though listenable) fidelity, this is more of a historical document than a sampling of King at his best; it also finds him and his group much more grounded in hot Western swing (complete with steel guitar) than rock & roll. As an archival glimpse of the first stirrings of hillbilly turning into rockabilly, though, it's not bad. The group runs through the country boogies and ballads with zesty, unpolished flair, and edge close to rockabilly with their covers of "That's All Right," "Maybellene," and "Flip, Flop & Fly." *—Richie Unterberger*

Kinleys

f. Philadelphia, PA

Group / Country-Pop, Western Swing, Contemporary Country

Twin sisters from Philadelphia with impeccable harmonies and an energetic sense of country swing, Heather and Jennifer Kinley, born November 5, 1970, were influenced by the harmonies of other familial country pairings like the Everly Brothers and the Judds. At the age of 19, the twins moved to Nashville and worked on their songwriting and performing, with Heather on guitar and Jennifer on piano. They spent more than five years toiling in Music City's underground before finally finding a winning song, "Just Between You and Me." Co-written with Russ & Debbie Zavitson, it brought the major labels calling, and the Kinleys signed with Epic.

After working with producers Tony Haselden and Peter Greene (as well as Russ Zavitson), the Kinleys released their debut album, *Just Between You and Me*, in September 1997. Their debut single, "Please," hit the country Top Ten and even crossed over to the pop charts, then the song that had started it all for them, "Just Between You and Me," made the country Top 20. The album settled in for a run of almost a year on the country charts, eventually going gold. Meanwhile, album tracks "Dance in the Boat" and "You Make It Seem So Easy" made minor appearances in the country charts. As a result, the sisters were named Best New Duo by the Academy of Country Music and garnered nominations from the Grammys, the Country Music Association, and the American Music Awards.

In the fall of 1998, they were represented by "Somebody's Out There Watching" on the million-selling television soundtrack album *Touched By an Angel*. Released as a single, the song made the country Top 20 and crossed over to the pop charts. In August 1999, the Kinleys returned to the country charts briefly with the one-off single "My Heart Is Still Beating," but they spent a longtime crafting their second album, working with Russ Zavitson and Tony Haselden again for half of it, but turning to Radney Foster for help in completing it. The album was heralded by an advance single, "She Ain't the Girl for You," which broke into the country charts in April 2000. *The Kinleys II* finally appeared in July. *—John Bush*

Just Between You and Me / Sep. 23, 1997 / Sony ♦♦♦

The Kinleys' debut album *Just Between You and Me* is an engaging set of country-pop illustrating that twin sisters Heather and Jennifer are quite gifted vocally. It's a joy to hear them sing these sweet country-pop tunes, even if the songs don't always equal their performances. With a more consistent set of material, the debut could have been even more impressive, but the raw talent the duo displays makes the record a top-notch first effort. *—Thom Owens*

● **The Kinleys II** / Jul. 18, 2000 / Sony ♦♦♦♦

In 1998, the Kinleys were back in the country Top 20 with "Somebody's Out There Watching," from the *Touched By an Angel* television soundtrack. In the summer of 1999, they put out the single "My Heart Is Still Beating," which was intended to be the curtain raiser on their second album. But it fizzled, dropping off the charts after two weeks. Epic decided to go back to the drawing board, bringing in new producer Radney Foster to replace Tony Haselden and Russ Zavitson, who had shepherded the Kinleys for their entire career. The result, a full year later, is *The Kinleys II*, which is really two half-albums, its first six songs handled by Foster and the next six by Haselden and Zavitson, with "Somebody's Out There Watching" following as the conclusion. Like his own modestly successful solo albums, Foster's half consists of craftsmanlike country-pop with blues tendencies. The tempos are restrained, the material well put together but dull, and the sisters are given a lot of solo singing. Foster seems to conceive of the Kinleys as potential successors to the Judds, but with both singers playing the earthy Wynonna role. Yet anyone who leaves the album playing until the seventh track (the first Haselden/Zavitson track) is in for a surprise—suddenly, the record comes into focus as a lively, driving country disc. Maybe it's just that Epic cherry-picked from a scrapped earlier version of this album, but its second half is a vast improvement over its first. The Haselden/Zavitson numbers are honky tonk harmony performances in which the Kinleys sound much more involved than they do with Foster; it's clear that the Kinleys' first producers have a much better sense of their real strengths than the hired gun brought in to save the release. You can't help wondering what would have happened if the whole album were as good as the second half—since a successful country album now has the same sales potential as a pop release, the second effort for an act that had good but not great sales the first time around is crucial to its success. *—William Ruhlmann*

Bill Kirchen

b. Jan. 29, 1948, Ann Arbor, MI

Guitar, Vocals / Country-Rock, Alternative Country, Americana

Bill Kirchen is best known for his work in the '70s with the rebel band Commander Cody & His Lost Planet Airmen. Leading the way, this gang of rock & roll honky tonkers cut a wide path through country and rock, creating an intersection where both could meet and meld together their many guises effortlessly. Bill Kirchen was a dominating force behind the success of the Airmen. Meeting up with George Frayne, later known as Commander Cody, in his hometown of Ann Arbor, MI, set the wheels of Kirchen's musical career into motion.

Born and raised in Ann Arbor, the future guitar god first learned to play the trombone. While in high-school he meet folksinger David Siglin and proceeded to place himself in the middle of the local folk scene. This was a training ground for Kirchen's prospective endeavors. He learned to play banjo and guitar. His fascination with folk eventually segued into an interest in the blues and string bands. While still in college, Kirchen started his own band, an outfit best described as "psycho folk-rock." It was around this same time that Detroit-based Frayne and future airman John Tichy decided to put a country band together. Having gone to the University of Michigan, Ann Arbor, Kirchen, Frayne, and some of the other Airmen knew each other, thus Commander Cody & His Lost Planet Airmen were born.

By 1969 Kirchen knew something had to be done or the band would idle away in obscurity. Aware of the music coming out of San Francisco, he convinced the rest of the band to move to the West Coast, where they took off and became legendary outlaws, lauded by Waylon Jennings and Willie Nelson as well as the Allman Brothers and the Grateful Dead. Kirchen's power as a vocalist, player, performer, and songwriter began to solidify. Known for his vocal treatment and hot guitar licks on "Mama Hated Diesels" and the ever popular "Down to Seeds and Stems Again Blues" from two of their preeminent releases, *Hot Licks, Cold Steel & Truckers' Favorites* and *Lost in the Ozone*, respectively. As a performer Kirchen came into his own while on stage in Austin for the live recording of the critically acclaimed *Live From Deep in the Heart of Texas*, recorded in November of 1973 at *the Armadillo World Headquarters*. Kirchen's work during this phase in the all-too-short career of Commander Cody & His Lost Planet Airmen is still remembered with awe. The 1976 breakup of the band lead Kirchen to form the Moonlighters, a swing orchestra. British star Nick Lowe, who'd become interested in Kirchen's work while he was still with the Airmen, sought him out. The two formed a bond that remained intact years later. As the producer of the first Moonlighters album, Lowe found a soul mate in the talented American. Kirchen toured internationally with his friend and even joined him in the studio. While in England, Kirchen's style was a hot property as is evidenced by his participation on recording projects for Elvis Costello, rockabilly king Gene Vincent, and Link Wray.

By 1986 Kirchen had moved to the Washington, D.C., area, establishing himself as a leader on the music scene. Prior to his signing on with Black Top Records in 1994, Kirchen recorded *Tombstone Every Mile*. This high-powered project was initially released on Costello's label, Demon Records, in England. Available in the U.S. on Black Top, this was just the beginning of Kirchen's personal recording renaissance. *Have Love, Will Travel* was released in 1996. Critically acclaimed, it is an eclectic disc that displays the various aspects of Kirchen's artistry and talent. Praised as one of the pioneers who marked territory for a new radio format, Americana, this still-wild guitar slinger is also noted as a forefather of the twangcore movement that encompasses everyone from the king of California, Dave Alvin, to rockabilly bands and roots rock outfits like Big Sandy & His Fly-Rite Boys and Wilco. It is also believed that fellow madman Junior Brown was given a career boost thanks to Kirchen's dominating spirit, which has served to stand as a point of light for rebels of every stripe and color over these many years. In 1999, Kirchen followed with *Raise a Ruckus*.

Kirchen has been instrumental in keeping the work of many musical pioneers as more than just a memory. Using his 1950s Telecaster and his chameleon-like voice, he has told the tale of Bakersfield's top bard, Red Simpson, and maverick songwriter Blackie Farrell. Ernest Tubb's former man of pedal steel, Buddy Charleton, whose infallible twang and moan can be heard throughout *Have Love, Will Travel*, is a featured player in Kirchen's world. Always ahead of his time, Kirchen remains a man of distinction who looks at music not as something to be categorized, but as an art form that has no boundaries. *—Jana Pendragon*

Tombstone Every Mile / Jul. 5, 1994 / Edsel ♦♦♦♦

This first Black Top release by honky tonker Bill Kirchen is an Americana roots-music vault of valuables. With plenty of traditional C&W riffs underscored by the brilliant pedal steel of one-time Ernest Tubb steel player Buddy Charleton and the powerful piano of Mitch Collins, this project is more than mere buried treasure that contemporary radio overlooked. Kirchen, a living legend of sorts, takes a very broad stance and combines the best elements of C&W, hillbilly, blues, rockabilly, and honky tonk music to come up with cuts like "Bottle Baby Boogie," a rip-it-up rockabilly tune that shows off Kirchen's guitar master skills, and "All Tore Up," another rocker. The Farrell-Preston song "Fool on a Stool" is given an outstanding retooling with plenty of steel that is true to the tenants of C&W music. Covering Johnny Horton's hit "One Woman Man" is a brave move that comes off convincingly and sounding as honest as the original. Teaming up with bassman Jeff Sari and wife Louise Kirchen, this triple threat not only displays Bill Kirchen's songwriting skills, but a spectacular piece of music in "Secrets of Love." Also noteworthy is "Think It Over," a Donley-Meaux tune that is haunting in the hands of a master. With a nod to friend Nick Lowe, Kirchen adds the beautiful harmony vocals of Louise to his own multi-faceted vocal style on Lowe's "Without Love," to come up with a moment that leaves time standing still. A mighty accomplishment in musical terms. This disc is only an indication of what the future holds for one of the few solid survivors of the country-rock phenomenon of the 1970s. With all his talent on display here, it is easy to understand why Kirchen has survived, even in the face of the '90s pop-bubblegum-country cookie-cutter mentality. *—Jana Pendragon*

● **Have Love, Will Travel** / Mar. 19, 1996 / Black Top ♦♦♦♦♦

If all Commander Cody ever aspired to was sounding like a real good Dave Dudley 45, then ex-Lost Planet Airman Bill Kirchen has achieved his dream with this album. The kickoff track, "Womb to the Tomb," would have fit in atmospherically just about anywhere on those early albums, and his rendition here of the Sharps/Rivingtons with Duane Eddy title track seems absolutely tailor-made for Kirchen's twanging roadhouse style. It's like a night in a real good honky tonk with a great little combo up there. There's a lot of great music on this 14-track outing, with the lion's share of it emanating from Kirchen and his tighter-than-Jack Benny rhythm section of Johnny Castle on bass and Jack O'Dell on drums. No big names doing meaningless guest appearances, just some friends adding some horns, some keys, and a little steel guitar. Records seldom come this simple and unaffected, but Kirchen pulls it off with style and grace. *—Cub Koda*

Hot Rod Lincoln Live! / Sep. 16, 1997 / Hightone ♦♦♦♦
Since his early days as a member of Commander Cody & His Lost Planet Airmen, Bill Kirchen has distinguished himself as a showman of the highest order. This, his first live solo recording, captures the vivacious presence of the man who is without a doubt one of the true fathers of the country-rock movement. His significance to country-rock and American roots music was obvious early on; after 30-plus years in the business, his influence can be found in the work of Nick Lowe, Elvis Costello, and every outfit that tried to marry country & western music to rock & roll after the 1976 demise of the Airmen. *Hot Rod Lincoln Live!*, recorded in February of 1997 at the Globe Theater in Berlin, MD, gives credence to the undeniable power and spirit of Bill Kirchen. As a performer, vocalist, guitar virtuoso, and bandleader, Kirchen shines. This live disc contains a fine collection of tunes that include old favorites like "Too Much Fun," "Looking at the World Through a Windshield," and "Hot Rod Lincoln." Newer standouts include "All the Secrets of Love," "Swing Fever," and "Tell Me the Reason." While he is effective on all 12 cuts, his treatment of "Cold Country Blues" allows him to join hands emotionally with the ghosts of Jimmie Rodgers and Hank Williams. His rock & roll edge is underscored by some hillbilly spice on "Sometimes I Think." There are a myriad of magical moments throughout the performance, but the breadth of Kirchen's talent is given wing as he reprises "Hot Rod Lincoln." This time, "Hot Rod Lincoln" is a vehicle Kirchen drives with his expertise as he eases into and out of the signature styles of such greats as Roy Nichols (Merle Haggard), Don Rich (Buck Owens), B. B. King, Link Wray, Muddy Waters, Chuck Berry, Duane Eddy, and Flatt & Scruggs, to name just a few. Always in good humor, Bill Kirchen is one of music's most versatile and glorious treasures. In the studio and live on-stage, Kirchen stands tall. *—Jana Pendragon*

Raise a Ruckus / 1999 / Hightone ♦♦♦♦
As guitarist/singer/songwriter for Commander Cody & His Lost Planet Airmen during the '70s, Bill Kirchen turned out many a classic riff, the most famous of which was "Hot Rod Lincoln," the old Tex Ritter song, updated and rocked up by Kirchen's guitar. With *Raise a Ruckus*, Kirchen brings his rockabilly guitar to center stage with a 14-song collection that is sure to please his fans the world over. The title track has a real Bob Dylan feel to it, with original lyrics by Kirchen that rival any of those penned by the great Zimmerman, and tunes like "Girlfriend" and "Fly on Your Jacket" evoke happy memories of the "Lost in the Ozone" kind. "Man in the Bottom of the Well" slows things down a bit with more of Kirchen's well thought-out lyrics and tasty guitar work, while "Little Bitty Record" bops along with a genuine rockabilly heart. "Big Hat, No Cattle" is a Texas swing ditty that would surely make the late Bob Wills smile and say, "Aw, play it boys!" Kirchen pulls out his trombone for "Dreamworld," a country romp with some Tex-Mex undertones. Johnny Castle on bass and Jack O'Dell on drums are the perfect complement for Kirchen, as evident on "She's a Yum-Yum" and the R&B-influenced "My Heart Has a Mind of Its Own." "Living Dangerously" rocks, and "True Love's the Treasure" is a very nice country duet featuring Bill and his wife, Louise; "Interstate" closes the set with a sound very reminiscent of Commander Cody's old treasures. *Raise a Ruckus* is a fun album for anyone who has followed Kirchen's career, but it is equally enjoyable for those who have missed out on hearing this rockabilly guitar man's work. *—Michael B. Smith*

Big Hat / Apr. 20, 1999 / Hightone ♦♦♦

Tied to the Wheel / Aug. 21, 2001 / Hightone ♦♦♦♦
Though he's plowed roughly the same furrow for more than 20 years, Bill Kirchen's brand of dieselbilly/high-octane country has yet to grow stale. Here, with the same rhythm section from 1999's *Raise a Ruckus*, he offers another set of choice covers and a handful of originals. Red Simpson's forlorn ballad "Roll Truck Roll" and Blackie Farrell's "One More Hour of Blues" are vintage Bakersfield country and, oddly enough, fit perfectly well with a straight reading of Dylan's "Just Like Tom Thumb's Blues" and the lightning-fast newgrass of "How Mountain Girls Can Love" (with drummer Jack O'Dell on lead). The previously unheard Commander Cody era "Truck Stop at the End of the World" is Kirchen at his best—smokin' Telecaster licks and clever lyrics with a sense of humor. The instrumental "Poultry in Motion" is a showcase for his version of chicken-pickin', the plucky playing style with roots in his hometown of Washington, D.C. *—John Duffy*

Sneaky Pete Kleinow

b. Aug. 20, 1934, South Bend, IN
Pedal Steel / Traditional Country, Country-Rock
One of the unsung heroes of the country-rock movement, steel guitarist and songwriter Sneaky Pete Kleinow was born August 20, 1934, in South Bend, IN. Influenced by the music of Jerry Byrd, he took up the steel guitar at the age of 17 and, after graduating high-school, spent over a decade as a road maintenance worker for the Michigan State Highway Department. In 1963, Kleinow relocated to Los Angeles, where he became a regular performer on the city's club circuit; he also found work composing jingles and even wrote the theme music for the children's series *Gumby*. In addition, he began working in Hollywood developing special effects for films. In 1965, Kleinow played on his first record, backing the Ventures on their "Blue Star." While performing in an area club, he met Gram Parsons and Chris Hillman, who approached Kleinow about joining the band they were organizing apart from their current venture, the folk-rock pioneers the Byrds. Kleinow agreed, and after a brief tenure as a Byrds sideman he joined Parsons and Hillman in the Flying Burrito Brothers; the band's 1969 debut, *The Gilded Palace of Sin*, established the very blueprint for the country-rock genre.

Kleinow remained with the Burritos through April 1971, appearing on the 1970 LP *Burrito Deluxe* and its eponymously titled follow-up. At the same time, he became a sought-after session musician who played on records by Joe Cocker, Delaney & Bonnie, and Little Feat. After departing the Burritos, he focused all of his energies on session work, appearing with John Lennon, Frank Zappa, Stevie Wonder, Jackson Browne, Linda Ronstadt, and the Steve Miller Band. In 1974, Kleinow briefly joined the band Cold Steel; the following year, he signed on with a reformed Flying Burrito Brothers for the album *Flying Again*. After two more Burritos LPs—1976's *Airborne* and 1978's *Live in Tokyo*—Kleinow cut his first solo record, *Sneaky Pete*, in 1978. Following one final Burritos album, 1981's *Hearts on the Line*, he gradually withdrew from the music industry to focus on creating special effects; the films he worked on included *The Empire Strikes Back*, *The Right Stuff*, *Gremlins*, and both *Terminator* features. Nevertheless, he occasionally returned to music, performing with diverse artists like Leonard Cohen, Medicine, and the Golden Palominos. In 1994, he released the solo effort *The Legend and the Legacy* and led a new Burritos lineup on a tour of Europe. *—Jason Ankeny*

Cold Steel / 1974 / Ariola ♦♦
Sneaky Pete Kleinow was a founding member of the Flying Burrito Brothers and much in demand as a session player by the time the pedal steel guitarist recorded this solo LP for the Dutch Ariola label during 1973. Although Kleinow is better known as an instrumentalist, he starts the record with an original song wisely rejected while he was with the Burritos, the rather insipidly titled "Wings That Make Birds Fly," which has even worse lyrics. The rest of this country-rock album is also uneven, with rather mediocre compositions by the group's members, which include drummer and lead singer Greg Attaway, pianist David Lovelace, guitarist Richard Bowden, and bassist Michael A. Bowden. Fiddler Gib Guilbeau is a guest on three tracks and sings his "Sweet Suzanna" as well. Not a particularly memorable release by any means, *Cold Steel* will appeal mainly to obsessive fans of Sneaky Pete Kleinow who must have everything he's recorded. *—Ken Dryden*

Sneaky Pete / 1979 / Shiloh ♦♦♦♦♦
By the end of the '70s a certain kind of re-energized approach to country and bluegrass music was a clearly audible phenomenon, and some of the musicians associated with this movement were also well integrated into the American rock scene. Although done on an obscure independent label and under the leadership of a great pedal steel player who is mostly known as a sideman, this album puts some of these important players together in a studio with results that are fine enough to warrant consideration as some kind of epistle rather than just a stray, largely side project. A problem with albums spotlighting pedal steel players is sometimes a loss of emotional content resulting from downplaying lyrical song content at the expense of instrumental virtuosity. In this case, this approach actually works to the overall benefit of the album, since the heartfelt songwriting efforts of Sneaky Pete Kleinow as well as his participants, such as fiddler and vocalist Gib Guilbeau, sometimes don't stand the test of time as well as the solidly traditional showpiece instrumentals such as the opener, "Cannonball Rag." While a popular group from this era, such as Flying Burrito Brothers or the Byrds, would have buried this type of track in the midst of a side, here it starts things off with an effect that will make a listener want to spin around the room. There is marble-solid drumming from Gene Parsons, Mickey McGee, and others, with Jamie Faunt and Skip Battin covering all the bass action as if chicken-frying a steak. Fans of Sneaky Pete Kleinow's pedal steel playing should emerge with a full gut; he takes plenty of breaks through the program, even taking the precautions to identify himself as the guitar soloist on one of the album's highlights, "Sleepy Lagoon," so completely does he succeed in masquerading his instrument's sound in an alien form. In light of such impeccable and inspiring playing, captured to an extent often only hinted at on his sideman appearances, it would be silly to think too many listeners would remember much about the vocal performances on this record. Yet while no major life experience would be lost if the needle was lifted before hearing Sneaky Pete croon the original number "California and You," the vocals of Connie Williams on several tracks are very nice, especially "Trains in the Station." Another highlight is the instrumental cover of the country hit "Love of the Common People," with intricate interplay between the pedal steel and pianist Charlie Harwood. *—Eugene Chadbourne*

● **Legend & The Legacy** / 1994 / Shiloh ♦♦♦♦

Meet Sneaky Pete / Dec. 4, 2001 / Shiloh/Beautown ♦♦♦

Cheri Knight

Bass, Vocals / Alternative Country-Rock, Americana
Cheri Knight made her initial foray into music as the bassist for the alternative bluegrass unit the Blood Oranges. After the band's breakup, she moved from Massachusetts to New York, where she met up with musicians Eric Ambel and Will Rigby, who aided her in recording her 1996 solo debut, *The Knitter*. The acclaimed *Northeast Kingdom* followed in early 1998. *—Jason Ankeny*

The Knitter / Mar. 19, 1996 / East Side Digital ♦♦♦♦
Mandolinist Jimmy Ryan may have been the driving force behind the Blood Oranges, but bassist Cheri Knight's strong, earthy voice and beautifully melancholic songs marked many of that band's finest moments. On "The Knitter," she takes a confident and much-deserved step into the foreground (she even plays guitar this time around). The songs are an organic mix of strong-willed power chords, country-driven rhythms, and rural acoustic ballads, and the lyrics ring with vivid images of loneliness, anger, emotional confusion, and moments of undeniable love. Cheri Knight is the real deal, and *The Knitter* is a solid and promising debut. *—Kurt Wolff*

● **The Northeast Kingdom** / Jan. 20, 1998 / E Squared ♦♦♦♦♦
Although Knight is sometimes classified as something of a maverick modern country artist, her sound is too eclectic to be categorized as country. It's better thought of, perhaps, as extremely ambitious, smart mainstream pop with a lot of indie rock and country elements. If this is the direction country or Nashville might go in (it was produced in Nashville and features Steve Earle on guitar throughout), one can only applaud heartily. On this album, she's developed into a really fine singer/songwriter whose compositions and throaty vocal delivery project a wise weariness. The sound is quite varied by either country or rock standards, from the near-Celtic drone of "Dar Glasgow" and the Byrdsy jangle of "Rose in the Vine" to the Appalachian pluck of "The Hatfield Side" and "Crawling" (one of a couple tunes with Emmylou Harris on backup vocals). Both "Crawling" and "Northeast Kingdom" are particular standouts, compelling songs of troubled relationships with fresh lyrical twists, and with enough hooks to grab rock and pop ears; "White Lies," on the other hand, is an upbeat number that has the makings of a modern honky tonk classic. *—Richie Unterberger*

Chris Knight

b. Slaughters, KY

Composer, Vocals, Keyboards, Guitar (Acoustic) / Country-Rock, Contemporary Country, Singer/Songwriter, Outlaw Country, Alternative Country, Americana

Chris Knight is a singer/songwriter from the tiny mining town of Slaughters, KY, whose self-titled debut album invited comparisons to Steve Earle and John Prine. Knight started on his musical journey at just three years old when he requested a plastic guitar for Christmas. At 15, he became more serious when he began teaching himself dozens of John Prine songs on his older brother's guitar. After earning an agriculture degree from Western Kentucky University, Knight went to work in land reclamation, but in 1986 he heard Earle on the radio and decided to try his hand at writing songs.

After six years of perfecting his story songs about the downtrodden of small-town America, Knight came to Nashville and won a coveted spot on a songwriters' night at the Bluebird Cafe. Performing songs like "Framed," which would eventually wind up on his debut album, he caught the ear of Frank Liddell, who signed him to a publishing deal with Bluewater Music. Knight went back home and kept writing, and when Decca Records hired Liddell for an A&R position, Knight got a record deal. When Decca released his self-titled debut in 1997, Knight still lived in a house trailer on 90 acres in Slaughters. *—Brian Wahlert*

● **Chris Knight** / Feb. 10, 1998 / MCA ♦♦♦♦
With Chris Knight's debut album, released on MCA Nashville's sister label Decca, critics of the new country sound of the late '90s began to hold out hope that Nashville could return to the genuineness that it had been so lacking for years. That hope was rooted partly in Knight's singing, full of country-rock phrasing clearly modeled after Knight's hero, Steve Earle, but even more so in Knight's songwriting. His flair for describing the lower-middle class in Middle America, their difficulties making a living, and run-ins with the law, evokes Earle and even early Bruce Springsteen. For example, "Love and a .45," co-written with Fred Eaglesmith, describes how two lonely people on opposite sides of the law, a cop and a prostitute, find each other. One of Knight's most literate songs, "The River's Own," details the singer's father's (and ultimately, his own) union with the river that runs by the family farm. And on the album's most poignant song, Knight tells the story of "William," a boy who "grew up hard and mean," beaten by his father, only to inflict some of the same pain on his family as an adult and die in a drugstore robbery. The only problem with this album is the instrumental arrangements. Some of Nashville's top studio musicians perform, and therein lies the rub. While technically proficient, the playing never matches up to the raw energy of Knight's songs. Thus, recording for a major label was a double-edged sword. On the one hand, it gave Knight a chance to be a major force in starting a new trend in country music, but on the other, the music might have been more effective had it been recorded live for a small independent record label. *—Brian Wahlert*

A Pretty Good Guy / 2001 / Dualtone ♦♦♦♦
Ah, the return of true redneck rock. Chris Knight, who received more than a few kudos for his self-titled MCA debut, is back with a dirtier and more satisfying effort now that he's been allowed to record exactly what he wants. A victim of the MCA (and every other major label) "let's-throw-it-at-the-wall-and-see-if-it-sticks" theory of ripping off artists and insuring profits no matter who gets hurt, Knight proves he's better off without them. For those who haven't heard Knight, he's got the same rowdy, earthy, Saturday night sensibility that Jerry Jeff Walker blessed us with in the 1970s, the raucous rock & roll smarts of the Faces, the poetry of John Mellencamp all graced with the swampy blues mark of Tony Joe White. It's a damn shame the cat won't be played on the evil empire's radio stations, but given the networking of the alt-country enthusiasts and the occasionally visionary American programmers, he might get a nod. If Knight was allowed to make a video and his records—especially this one—were to get played on the air, he'd make someone beside himself a cool million or so. The cat's got it all in spades: a vision that rides as far as the border of his own town, a wistful romance for the everyday, and a pissed-off streak that honors every American male with dirty hands and scuffed shoes. The set opens with the gambler's lament "Becky's Bible," with guitars charging through the center of the mix, so loud that Knight has to emphasize everything to be heard, which is good because his words are not to be ignored. Dan Baird's production (the Georgia Satellites guy) is tight, raw, and immediate. He equalizes everything at around ten and a half. Any man who starts a song with the words "empty beer bottles rattle on my pistol on the seat of my Chevy pickup truck," you know he means business. He isn't shooting anybody, but he's scared, rock & roll scared, trying to leave a trace, trying to find a placer just to live inside his own shoes. "Oil Patch Town," is an elegiac anthem to the crazy innocence of high-school glory days that weren't so glorious. Knight's brutal; he doesn't paint anything romantically or make it darker than it has to be. He understands the power of both country and rock & roll to carry the message as long as the message is pure, simple, and direct. He doesn't get in the way, and therefore is a hell of a storyteller. One listen to the chilling "Down the River" is enough to make the weak-kneed—or those who deplore violence—go elsewhere for their listening pleasure, but Knight makes his stories, no matter how brutal, white-knuckle rides through the dark side of the imagination. He does so without judgement, reporting the facts as he dreams them just as they are. Baird's electric guitars and Rusty Young's lap steel bring drama and pathos to the stark lyric and drive the tale over the edge into rock tragedy. The way Baird and Knight use fiddles and banjos in tracks like "North Dakota" brings back the feeling of the Band's gothic Americana with Garth Hudson serving as multi-instrumentalist. The dirty-water Dylan-inspired blues-rock of "Highway Junkie" is a stomper. With its open E slide guitar slinging and wrangling greasy posturing, it feels like the Faces' "Loose" and Dylan's "Highway 61" brawling at the local truck stop. In all, Knight has made a far better record this time out—and his first one was pretty damn good. The songs feel more like him and less like Nash Vegas and they have a looser, more heterogeneous feel as the big guy gets to stretch his blues heart and flex his rock muscle in what is at heart, the body of a country singer and songwriter. *—Thom Jurek*

The Knitters

f. 1985

Group / Roots Rock, Alternative Country-Rock

The Knitters was a one-off country side project of the famed Los Angeles punk band X featuring the group's vocalist Exene Cervenka, singer/bassist John Doe, and drummer D. J. Bonebrake as well as the Blasters' guitarist Dave Alvin. (Ironically, when original X guitar player Billy Zoom left the band in 1986, it was Alvin who replaced him, albeit briefly.) The Knitters' lone LP, 1985's *Poor Little Critter on the Road*, was a collection of originals, covers, and acoustic revampings of earlier X material, redone in a variety of country-based styles running from swing to traditional. *—Jason Ankeny*

Poor Little Critter on the Road / 1985 / Warner Bros. ♦♦♦
Before MTV created *Unplugged*, X released a shrewd blend of country, traditional and original songs, as the Knitters, minus Billy Zoom plus Jonny Ray Bartel and Dave Alvin. No longer struggling to incorporate their love of roots musics into their own hard rock sound, X gave over to the acoustic project with songs like "Someone Like You" and "Cryin' But My Tears Are Far Away." John Doe's version of Merle Haggard's "Silver Wings" may be the definitive version, and the previously recorded "The New World" and "Love Shack" sound wonderful in this spare context—think Carter Family. *—Denise Sullivan*

Fred Knoblock

b. Jackson, MS

Guitar, Vocals / Country-Pop, Adult Contemporary, Soft Rock

Country-pop singer Fred Knoblock's smooth, soft, adult contemporary friendly style landed him a few hits at the beginning of the '80s. Born in Jackson, MS, Knoblock spent six years in the '70s as part of the rock band Let's Eat; he later signed to Scotti Brothers as a solo country act. Knoblock's debut album, *Why Not Me*, was released in 1980, producing a Top 20 pop hit in the title track. Knoblock's duet with actress Susan Anton, "Killin' Time," also charted in the pop Top 30, but climbed all the way into the Top Ten on the country charts. Its success prompted a debut album from Anton, to which Knoblock contributed several vocals. A cover of Chuck Berry's "Memphis" became another country hit for Knoblock, and he scored his last success on the country charts with 1982's "I Had It All." Knoblock subsequently formed a trio with Thom Schuyler and Paul Overstreet dubbed SKO (later SKB when Overstreet was replaced by Craig Bickhardt). *—Steve Huey*

● **Why Not Me** / 1980 / Scotti Bros. ♦♦♦♦

Live at the Bluebird Cafe / Sep. 12, 2000 / American Originals ♦♦♦

Buddy Knox

b. Jul. 20, 1933, Happy, TX, **d.** Feb. 14, 1999, Bremerton, WA

Guitar, Vocals / Rock & Roll, Rockabilly

The brand of Texas rockabilly that Buddy Knox cooked up around 1957 wasn't quite as raw as that of his Memphis cohorts at Sun, but it was just as commercially potent. Knox sported a light, almost gentle vocal style, and his band, the Rhythm Orchids, obliged with upbeat backing that suited him well. Formed at West Texas State University, the Rhythm Orchids also included Jimmy Bowen on upright bass, and it was Bowen's equally lighthearted vocal on "I'm Stickin' With You" that originally graced the flip side of Knox's first smash, "Party Doll." Roulette Records astutely picked up the master from the tiny Triple-D logo, separated the sides, and the fledgling label enjoyed two giant hits for the price of one.

"Party Doll" soared to the very top of the pops, and Knox encored with the equally tuneful "Rock Your Little Baby to Sleep" and "Hula Love," which he performed in the 1957 rock flick *Jamboree*. Knox waxed the fine rockabilly based "Swingin' Daddy," "Devil Woman," and a cover of Ruth Brown's "Somebody Touched Me" for Roulette before moving to Liberty and hitting with a pop-flavored rendition of the Clovers' song "Lovey Dovey" in 1960. Over the ensuing decades the Texas rocker remained a popular act on the oldies front. He passed away on February 14, 1999, a victim of lung cancer. *—Bill Dahl*

Liberty Takes / 1986 / Charly ♦♦♦

● **The Best of Buddy Knox** / Jun. 1990 / Rhino ♦♦♦♦
Rhino's *The Best of Buddy Knox* is a definitive 18-track compilation featuring all of the hits the light rockabilly cat ever had, including "Party Doll," "Rock Your Little Baby to Sleep," "Hula Love," "Swingin' Daddy," "Somebody Touched Me," "Teasable, Pleasable You," "That's Why I Cry," "I Think I'm Gonna Kill Myself," "Lovey Dovey," and "Ling-Ting-Tong." *—Stephen Thomas Erlewine*

The Complete Roulette Recordings / May 7, 1996 / Sequel ♦♦♦
Knox only has one-half of this double CD; the second disc is devoted to tracks by his friend and contemporary, Jimmy Bowen. The approach isn't as odd as it seems: When

Knox and Bowen began their recording careers, they were both part of the Rhythm Orchids, and a similar lineup of Orchids backs each solo singer on their respective recordings. Most listeners will be much better off with Rhino's briefer, more selective Knox best-of. Completists, however, will find all 30 of Knox's 1956-1960 Roulette tracks on disc one of this two-pack. Including five previously unreleased songs, it's pleasant Tex-Mex rockabilly, tamer than Buddy Holly, but far gutsier than the Jimmy Bowen solo cuts that take up all of disc two. —*Richie Unterberger*

● **Buddy Knox/Buddy Knox & Jimmy Bowen** / Jun. 22, 1999 / Collectables ✦✦✦✦
In 1999, Collectables released *Buddy Knox/Buddy Knox & Jimmy Bowen*, which contained two complete albums—*Buddy Knox* (1957, originally released on Roulette) and *Buddy Knox & Jimmy Bowen* (1958, originally released on Roulette)—by Buddy Knox on one compact disc. —*Jason Birchmeier*

Fred Koller

b. Chicago, IL
Guitar, Songwriter, Vocals / Progressive Country, Contemporary Country, Singer/ Songwriter, Contemporary Folk
Songwriter Fred Koller was born in Chicago, IL. He moved to Nashville and went on to write numerous hit songs for artists like Kathy Mattea, Nanci Griffith, the Sons of the Pioneers, and the Jeff Healy Band. He also taught the art of writing music in classrooms and at seminars, as well as through his book, *How to Pitch and Promote Your Songs*. In addition to his songwriting work, Koller released numerous solo albums, including *Night of the Living Fred* and *Songs From the Night Before*. In 2001, the Gadfly imprint released *No Song Left to Sell*, which featured songs Koller had co-written with his pal Shel Silverstein. —*Johnny Loftus & Chip Renner*

Night of the Living Fred / 1989 / Alcazar ✦✦✦
Accentuating his broad humor and biting irony—instead of lingering in the shadows, here his wit hogs the spotlight. —*Michael McCall*

● **Songs from the Night Before** / 1989 / Alcazar ✦✦✦✦✦
His first solo album, it portrays the eclectic character of Koller's colorful insights and his balance of troubling observations, hard-eyed irony and sentimental yearnings. "Life as We Knew It" recalls a friendlier, slower America, while "This Hell We Created" and "Showbizness" wonderfully spoofs modern relationships and entertainment. —*Michael McCall*

Where the Fast Lane Ends / 1990 / Alcazar ✦✦✦✦✦
Koller's versions of his songs "Goin' Gone" and "Lone Star State of Mind" are here, but he has a deep, bluesy voice that puts a very different spin on these familiar tunes. —*William Ruhlmann*

Alison Krauss

b. Jul. 23, 1971, Champaign, IL
Fiddle, Vocals / Bluegrass, Progressive Bluegrass, Traditional Bluegrass, Contemporary Country, Neo-Traditionalist Country, Contemporary Bluegrass
Alison Krauss helped bring bluegrass to a new audience in the '90s. Blending bluegrass with folk, Krauss was instantly acclaimed from the start of her career, but it wasn't until her platinum-selling 1995 compilation, *Now That I've Found You*, that she became a mainstream star. Between her 1987 debut *Too Late to Cry* and *Now That I've Found You*, she matured from a child prodigy to a versatile, ambitious, and diverse musician and, in the process, made some of the freshest bluegrass of the late '80s and early '90s.

When she was five years old, Krauss began playing the violin, taking classical lessons. She soon tired of the regiments of classical playing and began performing country and bluegrass licks. At the age of eight, she began entering talent contests in and around her native Champaign, IL. Two years later, she had her own band. In 1983, when she was 12 years old, she won the Illinois State Fiddle Championship and the Society for the Preservation of Bluegrass in America named her the Most Promising Fiddler in the Midwest. In 1985, Krauss made her recording debut on an album, playing on a record made by her brother Viktor, Jim Hoiles, and Bruce Weiss. The album was called *Different Strokes* and appeared on the independent Fiddle Tunes label. Later that year, she signed to Rounder Records. She was 14 years old at the time.

Too Late to Cry, Krauss' debut album, appeared in 1987 to very positive reviews. The album was recorded with Krauss' backup band, the Union Station, which featured guitarist Jeff White, banjoist Alison Brown, and bassist Viktor Krauss; the following year, the group won the Society for the Preservation of Bluegrass in America's National Band Championship contest. In 1989, Krauss and Union Station released *Two Highways*, which was nominated for the Grammy Award for Best Bluegrass Recording. Although the album didn't win the award, her next album, 1990's *I've Got That Old Feeling*, did. The success of *I've Got That Old Feeling* was unprecedented for bluegrass acts in the '80s and it laid the groundwork for Krauss' breakthrough in the '90s. By this time, the Union Station's lineup had more or less settled; it now featured mandolinist Adam Steffey, banjoist/guitarist Ron Block, bassist Barry Bales, and guitarist Tim Stafford; Stafford later left the group and was replaced by Dan Tyminski.

In 1992, Alison Krauss & Union Station released *Every Time You Say Goodbye*, which featured a typically eclectic array of material: everything from "Orange Blossom Special" to the Beatles' "I Will" and Shawn Colvin's "I Don't Know Why" were covered. The album appeared in the country charts and Krauss' videos were shown on Country Music Television. *I Know Who Holds Tomorrow* was released in 1994 and was even more successful. But it was the 1995 compilation, *Now That I've Found You: A Collection*, that made Krauss a star. The album reached number two on the country charts and—even more remarkably—went into the pop Top Ten and sold over a million copies. Its success confirmed her status as bluegrass' leading light in the '90s. Krauss & Union Station followed the unexpected success of *Now That I've Found You* with *So Long, So Wrong* in the spring 1997. *Forget About It* followed in mid-1999. A year later, Alison Krauss & Union Station joined the likes of John Hartford, Ralph Stanley and others for the multi-million selling soundtrack *O Brother, Where Art Thou?* A North American tour showcasing some

of the album's stellar musicians followed in summer 2002, allowing Krauss and her band's popularity to soar. *New Favorite* appeared in November and went gold within four months. —*Stephen Thomas Erlewine*

Different Strokes / 1985 / Fiddle Tunes ✦✦✦
Different Strokes is the first album to feature an appearance by Alison Krauss. Released on the very small independent record label Fiddle Tunes when Krauss was only 14, the record is a collection of bluegrass and traditional folk material performed by Alison, her brother Viktor, Bruce Weiss, and Jim Hoiles. —*Thom Owens*

Too Late to Cry / 1987 / Rounder ✦✦✦
Alison Krauss may have recorded *Too Late to Cry* when she was only 14 years old, but her sound was already well-developed and astonishingly accomplished. Throughout the album, she demonstrates a mastery of bluegrass, singing and playing with a distinctive grace. It's an impressive debut, but it would pale in comparison to the albums that followed. —*Thom Owens*

Two Highways / 1989 / Rounder ✦✦✦✦
Two Highways is the first album Alison Krauss recorded with her excellent backing band, Union Station, and appropriately, it demonstrates that she could lead a band through a number of bluegrass standards, as well as several more contemporary numbers. Of course, her instrumental solo continue to be the most impressive thing about her music on *Two Highways*, but her duets with guitarists Jeff White demonstrate that her vocals are beginning to come into their own. —*Thom Owens*

I've Got That Old Feeling / 1990 / Rounder ✦✦✦✦✦
There's a sweet voice, fine fiddling, and a tight plaintive band on this breakthrough bluegrass/country/pop album that produced the first music video for bluegrass. —*Mark A. Humphrey*

Every Time You Say Goodbye / 1992 / Rounder ✦✦✦
Alison Krauss was born to sing bluegrass. Her voice just wouldn't work in a riot grrrl or hip-hop setting. Not even close. The fiddle wouldn't quite fit either. Lucky thing she found her calling. On *Every Time You Say Goodbye*, Krauss is once again teamed with the stellar craftsmen of Union Station, and she sounds as comfortable as a porch swing and lemonade on a warm summer evening. Although Krauss gets the majority of the accolades, this is truly a group effort as the various musicians share the credit as writers and producers. Ron Block, Tim Stafford, Barry Bales, and Adam Steffey also take their turns stepping up to the mike, offering harmony and lead vocals where fitting. The songs range from traditional country fare to unexpected covers like Shawn Colvin's "I Don't Know Why." Their arrangement might seem oddly peppy to those who know the Colvin version. But to those who don't, it works just fine. Other highlights include the title track, "Who Can Blame You," "Last Love Letter," and the Karla Bonoff composition "Lose Again." And you just have to love a record that includes "Cluck Old Hen," which happens to be a fine showcase for Krauss' outstanding fiddle work. She has done a lot to make bluegrass a viable, contemporary genre of music. *Every Time You Say Goodbye* does much to further that cause. —*Kelly McCartney*

I Know Who Holds Tomorrow / 1994 / Rounder ✦✦✦
I Know Who Holds Tomorrow isn't as consistently engaging as *Every Time You Say Goodbye*, but that's only a relative term—from any other artists, this would be a masterpiece. From Krauss, it's another reliably wonderful collection of jaw-dropping fiddling and breathtaking singing. —*Thom Owens*

★ **Now That I've Found You: A Collection** / Feb. 7, 1995 / Rounder ✦✦✦✦✦
Alison Krauss had been recording a decade before she gained stardom, but she became a star in a big way. *Now That I've Found You: A Collection*, a retrospective of her ten-year recording career for Rounder, became the surprise hit of 1995, rocketing to number two on the country charts and into the Top 15 on the *pop* charts, which is remarkable for a musician who had never captured the attention of a mass audience. It may have been a surprising success, but it also was deserved. Krauss was arguably the leading bluegrass musician of the late '80s and early '90s, pushing the music into new directions without losing sight of its roots. *Now That I've Found You* does a splendid job of chronicling her career, hitting all of the highlights and making a new listener eager to seek out her albums. —*Stephen Thomas Erlewine*

So Long, So Wrong / 1997 / Rounder ✦✦✦✦
After mainstream success happened for Alison Krauss & Union Station, one would have rightly expected a commercial sweetening of their sound, resulting in diminishing (or even abandoning) the simple but very unique thing that brought them into the public eye—and eventual public acclaim—in the first place. But the group's first new recording in the wake of the surprise success of *Now That I've Found You: A Collection* finds Alison Krauss & Union Station happily keeping their eclectic focus firmly on the prize stretched before them with no silly attempts to court the hat-hunk-of-the-month or the boot-scoot-boogie crowd. Despite the media's singling out of Krauss as country's new bluegrass solo diva, Union Station (with Krauss as simply a featured member of it) remains very much a group, and that's the real refreshing news here. It is that collective spirit that remains the re-occurring theme and the resounding musical point being made here, and it is the solid anchor that roots this album into place from beginning to end. Krauss' expert evocative way with a ballad is on full display here, with "Deeper Than Crying" and "It Doesn't Matter" featuring her on violas, adding a new voice to Union Station's sound. But the lead vocals are passed around among Krauss, mandolinist Adam Steffey, guitarist Dan Tymiski, and banjoist Ron Block, while Krauss' fiddle work in a backup capacity is an integral part of the sound as well. All in all, this is a totally un-gimmicky album that flies in the face of what usually happens when mainstream success comes calling. And, as a result of that commitment to quality and musical focus, one that makes you want to play it again when it's all over. —*Cub Koda*

Forget About It / Aug. 3, 1999 / Rounder ✦✦✦
Krauss gets introspective and personal on her seventh album, one of her solo outings that shoves Union Station in the background while conventional country steps up to the spotlight. But Krauss is a little too sharp for Nashville standard, so *Forget About It* sounds more like an adult pop album with occasional notes of country grace. Unfortunately, the material here isn't very inspired (despite a dip into the Todd Rundgren songbook and the fine title tune), and Krauss herself has a hard time elevating it. Still, her fragile, angelic voice is capable of working wonders, which it often does with even the weakest of songs. *—Michael Gallucci*

New Favorite / Aug. 14, 2001 / Rounder ✦✦✦
Following the success of the startlingly popular traditional old-timey soundtrack for the film *O Brother, Where Art Thou?*, contemporary bluegrass pioneers Alison Krauss & Union Station moved in the opposite direction for their 2001 release, *New Favorite*. While Krauss and Union Station guitarist/vocalist Dan Tyminski got deeply in touch with their dust bowl Americana roots for their work on the film, their follow-up studio album is certainly the slickest, most progressive work they've recorded to date. *New Favorite* seems almost neatly divided into two albums: one following the same path as Alison Krauss' 1999 contemporary country solo album, *Forget About It*, and the other helmed by Tyminski, bringing a progressive slant to Union Station's traditional bluegrass feel. The whole album is well crafted (with the exception of Tyminski's laborious, drawn-out "The Boy Who Wouldn't Hoe Corn") but will certainly not sit right with certain elements of the band's core audience, who has come to know them as the strongest traditionally based bluegrass act still recording. The whole album feels a little too slick and reverbed out; the brilliant dobro work of Jerry Douglas seems mired in echoes, and at times Krauss' vocals seem to be coming out of some deep studio well. The musicianship, however, is beyond top-notch. The players (specifically banjo player Ron Block and guitarist Tyminski) are among the best in the genre, and the harmonies between the two vocalists are stunning and chill inducing. Their call-and-response vocals on "Daylight" serve as the highlight of the album, traced delicately by Douglas' dobro and chilling to the end. Unfortunately, the collective spirit that was so evident on their 1997 release *So Long So Wrong* seems to be dissolving, and the award-winning fiddle playing that brought Krauss to the nation's attention seems to be becoming almost a background instrument (if it shows up at all). While there are intriguing moments in the album, it lacks the spark that *So Long So Wrong* had in spades, and even their few moments on the *O Brother* soundtrack seemed to breathe more life into the band than *New Favorite* does. *—Zac Johnson*

Live / Nov. 5, 2002 / Rounder ✦✦✦
Given Alison Krauss' tremendous popularity and her status as the first female bluegrass singer to cross over into genuine pop marketability, and given the fact that her guitarist, Dan Tyminski, is the voice behind "Man of Constant Sorrow" (or at least the version that served as an *idée fixe* in the blockbuster movie *O Brother, Where Art Thou?*), a live album was inevitable. That it should be a two-disc set can simply be chalked up to good luck. Unless you're a bluegrass purist, that is, looking for music that preserves the traditional Appalachian sounds of Ralph Stanley and Bill Monroe. Listeners of that mindset will be bitterly disappointed by the presence of modern singer/songwriter fare ("Lucky One," "Let Me Touch You for a While"), by the drums on "Oh, Atlanta," and, most of all, by those dreadful call-and-response vocals on the chorus of "Man of Constant Sorrow" (which, you can hear them sniff, Tyminski takes at about twice the appropriate speed). All of this would explain why bluegrass purists are no fun to be around and, one suspects, don't have very much fun in private either. The simple fact is that every time Krauss opens her mouth to sing, angels stop what they're doing and take notes. There may be no musical pleasure quite as pure and sweet as listening to Krauss sing "Baby, Now That I've Found You" or "When You Say Nothing at All." And when she starts in on the impossibly beautiful gospel tune "Down to the River to Pray," the effect is almost disturbingly moving. Which brings listeners to the problem with this album, which is the amount of time it spends on stuff other than Alison Krauss singing great songs. The instrumental bits, the Jerry Douglas showcases, and Tyminski's requisite rendition of "Man of Constant Sorrow" are all fine, but they end up feeling like filler. Still, this album can be solidly recommended to modern bluegrass fans in general and to Krauss' many fans in particular. *—Rick Anderson*

Kris Kristofferson

b. Jun. 22, 1936, Brownsville, TX
Guitar, Songwriter, Vocals / Progressive Country, Singer/Songwriter, Outlaw Country, Traditional Country

After a lengthy period of struggle, Kris Kristofferson achieved remarkable success as a country songwriter at the start of the 1970s. His songs "Me and Bobby McGee," "Help Me Make It Through the Night," "Sunday Mornin' Comin' Down," and "For the Good Times," all chart-topping hits, helped redefine country songwriting, making it more personal and serious, much in the way that Bob Dylan's songs had transformed pop music songwriting in the mid-'60s. By 1987, it was estimated that Kristofferson's compositions had been recorded by more than 450 artists. His renown as a songwriter enabled him to launch a moderately successful career as a musical performer and that, in turn, brought him to the attention of Hollywood, leading to a lengthy career as a film actor.

The eldest of three children of an Air Force major general who retired from the military to head up air operations for the Saudi Arabian company Aramco, Kristofferson spent most of his childhood in Brownsville, TX, though his family moved around, finally settling in San Mateo, CA, by his junior high-school years. He graduated from San Mateo High School in 1954 and entered Pomona College in Claremont, CA. There he studied creative writing and he won first prize and three other placements in a collegiate short-story contest sponsored by *Atlantic Monthly* magazine. He graduated Phi Beta Kappa in 1958, having secured a prestigious Rhodes scholarship to continue his studies at Oxford University in England. While at Oxford, he wrote and performed his own songs, which brought him to the attention of manager Larry Parnes (who handled Tommy Steele and other British pop stars). Signing with Parnes, he made recordings for Top Rank Records produced by Tony Hatch (apparently never released) and performed under the name Kris Carson, but he was not successful.

After earning a master's degree in English literature from Oxford in 1960, Kristofferson intended to continue his studies there. But during a Christmas break back home in California, he resumed his relationship with an old girlfriend, Fran Beir, and they married. Instead of returning to Oxford, he joined the Army. Like his father, he became a pilot, learning to fly helicopters. He was assigned to West Germany and went there with his wife and their daughter. During the early '60s, while rising to the rank of captain, he eventually returned to writing and performing, organizing a soldiers' band to play at service clubs. Hearing his songs, a friend suggested sending them to a relative of his, the Nashville songwriter Marijohn Wilkin. Kristofferson did so and he received encouragement from Wilkin, who had become a music publisher by founding Bighorn Music. In 1965, Kristofferson was re-assigned to the West Point military academy, where he was to become an English instructor. He spent a two-week leave in June 1965 in Nashville, where he looked up Wilkin and decided to try to become a country songwriter instead. He resigned his commission and moved his family to Nashville, signing to Bighorn, which gave him a small weekly stipend that he augmented with a variety of jobs including janitorial work, bartending, and flying helicopters to and from offshore oil rigs in the Gulf of Mexico. He and his wife had a son who was born with a defective esophagus, resulting in thousands of dollars in medical bills. Eventually, the couple divorced.

Kristofferson scored his first success as a songwriter with "Viet Nam Blues," which was recorded by Dave Dudley and peaked in the country Top 20 in April 1966. As a recording artist, Kristofferson was signed to Epic Records and released a lone single, "Golden Idol"/"Killing Time" in 1967, but it missed the charts. (He later re-recorded both songs for his *Surreal Thing* album.) Roy Drusky recorded Kristofferson's "Jody and the Kid" and took it into the country Top 40 in the summer of 1968 and Billy Walker & the Tennessee Walkers' version of his "From the Bottle to the Bottom" peaked in the Top 20 of the country charts in April 1969. But by that spring, those three chart placings and his failed single were all Kristofferson had to show for almost four years of effort in Nashville. He had moved to Fred Foster's Columbine Music and begun to collaborate occasionally with Foster and he got a break when Roger Miller decided to record one of their songs, "Me and Bobby McGee," a ballad about hoboing that recalled earlier Miller hits like "King of the Road," but with more of a hippie slant. Miller ended up recording not only "Me and Bobby McGee," but also two other Kristofferson compositions, "Best of All Possible Worlds" and "Darby's Castle," for his August 1969 album, *Roger Miller*. "Me and Bobby McGee" was released as a single in advance of the album and it peaked in the country Top 20. Meanwhile, Kristofferson had begun to gain recognition as a performer, thanks to Johnny Cash, who introduced him at the Newport Folk Festival that summer and featured him on his network television show.

In September 1969, Kristofferson earned another important cover when Ray Stevens released a version of his reflection on a hangover, "Sunday Mornin' Comin' Down," as a single. It entered both the pop and country charts. The following month, Faron Young released "Your Time's Comin'," co-written by Kristofferson and Shel Silverstein. It gave the songwriter his biggest hit so far when it peaked in the country Top Five in December 1969. Jerry Lee Lewis' recording of Kristofferson and Silverstein's "Once More With Feeling" did even better, just missing the top of the country charts in March 1970.

In addition to Columbine Music, Fred Foster also ran Monument Records, an independent label, and he signed Kristofferson to it as a recording artist. Kristofferson went into the studio and cut his own versions of some of the songs others had already done—"Me and Bobby McGee," "Best of All Possible Worlds," "Darby's Castle," "Sunday Mornin' Comin' Down"—as well as some new songs, notably "Help Me Make It Through the Night" and "For the Good Times," both romantic ballads with a decidedly erotic tone. His debut album, titled *Kristofferson*, was released in April 1970 and he promoted it with his first major concert tour, debuting at the Troubadour in Los Angeles on June 23, appearing at the giant Isle of Wight Festival on July 26, and playing the Bitter End in New York in August. But even at a time when standards for singers had fallen noticeably, the album was criticized for Kristofferson's rough vocals; it sold poorly and quickly went out of print. The demand for his songs, however, only increased. The same month that *Kristofferson* was released, Ray Price reached the country charts with "For the Good Times," though it had been intended as the B-side of the single. It hit number one in September and crossed over to the pop charts, where it reached the Top 20; as a result, "For the Good Times" was named Song of the Year for 1970 by the Academy of Country Music. In August, Waylon Jennings reached the country charts with Kristofferson and Silverstein's "The Taker," which peaked in the Top Five in October and crossed over to the pop charts. By then, Johnny Cash had entered the country charts with his version of "Sunday Morning Coming Down" (as he called it, restoring the dropped "g"s). It hit number one in October and crossed over to the pop charts and the same month it won the Country Music Association's Song of the Year Award for 1970, putting Kristofferson in the unusual position of winning the same award from country's two rival organizations for the same year with different songs.

But the string of hits was far from over. In December, Sammi Smith entered the country charts with "Help Me Make It Through the Night," giving the song a surprising twist by having the woman ask the man to sleep with her instead of the other way around. The single crossed over to the pop charts, eventually reaching the Top Ten and going gold and it gave Kristofferson his third country chart-topper in February 1971. Meanwhile, Bobby Bare's recording of Kristofferson's "Come Sundown" also had reached the country charts in December and it peaked in the Top Ten in February 1971. Up to this point, Kristofferson had been getting most of his recognition in country music, but that changed in January 1971 when Janis Joplin's posthumous album *Pearl* was released. Joplin had covered "Me and Bobby McGee" and it was released as a single, shooting up the pop charts to number one in March. That same month, Ray Price followed "For the Good Times" with another Kristofferson song, "I Won't Mention It Again," which crossed over to the pop charts and in May gave the songwriter his fourth country number-one hit within eight months. Meanwhile, Joe Simon got into the pop charts with his version of "Help Me Make It

Through the Night" in April, Bobby Bare charted country in May with Kristofferson's "Please Don't Tell Me How the Story Ends," which peaked in the Top Ten in July and Peggy Little reached the country charts with his "I've Got to Have You."

Despite all this sudden success as a songwriter, Kristofferson had not yet achieved any great notice as a performer. Monument had been purchased by CBS Records and turned into a subsidiary of the Columbia label, giving its artists the benefit of major-label distribution and promotion. Kristofferson released his second album, *The Silver Tongued Devil and I*, in July 1971. Again, it combined the songwriter's own versions of songs that had scored for others—"Jody and the Kid," "The Taker"—with important new work, notably the ballad "Loving Her Was Easier (Than Anything I'll Ever Do Again)," which Roger Miller quickly covered for a Top 40 country hit. The album finally broke Kristofferson as a recording artist, rising into the Top Five of the country charts and the Top 20 of the pop charts and going gold, with the songwriter's own version of "Loving Her Was Easier (Than Anything I'll Ever Do Again)" becoming a Top 40 pop and top five Easy Listening hit. In August, Monument re-released Kristofferson's first album, renaming it *Me and Bobby McGee.* This time, the LP reached the country Top Ten and the pop Top 100 and went gold. Meanwhile, Ray Price released his third consecutive single of a Kristofferson song, "I'd Rather Be Sorry," and it just missed topping the country charts in October while crossing over to the pop charts. Patti Page also made the country charts with her version of the song. Jerry Lee Lewis put "Me and Bobby McGee" into the charts for a third time in November; it was given some country airplay as the B-side of his number-one country single "Would You Take Another Chance on Me," while pop radio flipped the disc over and made it a Top 40 pop hit. The same month, O. C. Smith got into the pop charts with his version of "Help Me Make It Through the Night."

Kristofferson himself, meanwhile, had traveled to Peru at the behest of director Dennis Hopper and he made his film debut in a bit part in *The Last Movie*, released in September, to which he also contributed songs. The same month, part of his performance from the Isle of Wight Festival was in the charts on the triple-record set *First Great Rock Festivals of the Seventies: Isle of Wight/Atlanta Pop Festival.* (In 1997, the film and CD *Message to Love: the Isle of Wight* also featured his appearance.) He had a more substantial film role in *Cisco Pike*, released early in 1972, also getting to sing several more of his songs. In February, he released his third album, *Border Lord.* It was his first collection to consist of all-new material and proved to be a slight commercial disappointment, reaching only the Top 100 of the pop charts and the Top Ten of the country charts, its single "Josie" becoming a pop and country chart entry but not a big hit. In March, however, three of his songs, "For the Good Times," "Help Me Make It Through the Night," and "Me and Bobby McGee," were among the five nominees for the 1971 Grammy Award for Best Country Song, while "Help Me Make It Through the Night" and "Me and Bobby McGee" were also up for the Song of the Year Grammy. Competing against himself, he managed to win his first Grammy for Best Country Song for "Help Me Make It Through the Night." The same month, Gladys Knight and the Pips brought the song back into the pop Top 40 and also made the R&B Top 20 with their rendition. In April, Kristofferson was in the charts with another live recording, appearing on the various artists collection *Big Sur Festival/One Hand Clapping.* In June, Sammi Smith made the country charts with her version of "I've Got to Have You," which peaked in the Top 20 in September and also crossed over to the pop charts.

Having taken only seven months between his second and third albums, Kristofferson waited only nine more months before delivering his fourth album, *Jesus Was a Capricorn*, in November 1972. Initially, the LP did not do as well as *Border Lord*, itself a step down from *The Silver Tongued Devil and I*, as the title song barely made the pop singles charts and a second single, "Jesse Younger," missed the charts entirely. But in March 1973, Monument released a third single, the slow, pious "Why Me," which topped the country charts in July and went gold, also crossing over to the pop Top 20. With that, sales of *Jesus Was a Capricorn* rebounded and the album hit number one in the country charts a year after it was released. (Meanwhile, Brenda Lee had covered "Nobody Wins" from the album for a Top Five country hit and a pop chart entry.)

Kristofferson, meanwhile, had returned to acting, getting more substantial film roles and working with important directors. In 1973, he appeared in Paul Mazursky's *Blume in Love*, also contributing a couple of songs, and in Sam Peckinpah's *Pat Garrett and Billy the Kid*, co-starring as Billy the Kid in the latter. His notices tended to be better than those for the films themselves and indicated that he had a future in films.

On August 19, 1973, Kristofferson married singer Rita Coolidge (who soon bore him a second daughter) and the following month the couple released a duo album, *Full Moon.* It was a big hit, topping the country charts, reaching the Top 40 of the pop charts, and going gold. Its first single, Kristofferson's composition "A Song I'd Like to Sing" was a Top 20 easy listening hit, a Top 40 pop hit, and a country chart entry. "Loving Arms," a second single, made the easy listening Top 40 and also reached the pop and country charts. The couple's version of "From the Bottle to the Bottom" won the 1973 Grammy Award for Best Country Vocal Performance by a Duo or Group. (Due to the peculiarities of the Grammy eligibility rules, "Loving Arms" was nominated in the same category the following year.) Kristofferson also earned 1973 Grammy nominations for Best Country Song and Best Country Vocal Performance, Male, for "Why Me."

In April 1974, "One Day at a Time," written by Kristofferson and Marijohn Wilkin, reached the country charts in a recording by Marilyn Sellars that went on to peak in the Top 20. Later in the year, it reached the pop Top 40. Kristofferson's fifth album, *Spooky Lady's Sideshow,* was released in May. Compared to earlier releases, it was a commercial disappointment, reaching the Top Ten of the country charts but only the Top 100 of the pop charts, with no charting single. From this point on, Kristofferson's albums would be only modest sellers at best. But he remained a potent country songwriter. In July, Ronnie Milsap entered the country charts with a revival of "Please Don't Tell Me How the Story Ends"; by September it had topped the country charts and crossed over to the pop charts. Kristofferson continued to pursue his film career, taking a small part in Sam Peckinpah's *Bring Me the Head of Alfredo Garcia*, released in the summer and a co-starring role in Martin Scorsese's *Alice Doesn't Live Here Anymore*, which appeared in December. Also that month, Kristofferson and Coolidge released their second duo album, *Breakaway.* Though less successful than their first one, it reached the Top 100 of the pop charts and the Top Five of the country charts. The single "Rain" made the country and Easy Listening charts. "Lover Please" also got into the Easy Listening charts and it went on to win the duo a second Grammy for Best Country Vocal Performance by a Duo or Group.

Kristofferson took a break from moviemaking to concentrate on his musical career and his sixth album, *Who's to Bless… and Who's to Blame*, released in November 1975. But the extra effort did not translate into increased sales. The LP reached the country Top 40, but it missed the Top 100 of the pop charts. Johnny Duncan's recording of the Kristofferson song "Stranger" from the album became a country hit, however, reaching the Top Five. Kristofferson returned to the movies and in the spring of 1976 was seen in *Vigilante Force* and *The Sailor Who Fell From Grace With the Sea*, also contributing a song to the latter. His seventh album, *Surreal Thing*, followed his sixth by only eight months. It was another commercial disappointment, reaching the country Top Ten while barely registering in the pop charts. But in December 1976, he enjoyed both a hit movie and a hit record with the release of *A Star Is Born*, in which he co-starred with Barbra Streisand. Critics howled, but the film was a box office smash, second only to *Rocky* among motion pictures released in 1976 as the top grossing hit, while the soundtrack album, which featured several contributions from Kristofferson (among them the pop chart entry "Watch Closely Now"), topped the pop charts and sold several million copies. Of course, Streisand had more to do with all that than Kristofferson did, but he was awarded a Golden Globe for Best Actor.

Monument Records seized upon the occasion of his increased profile to release a compilation, *Songs of Kristofferson*, in April 1977. It did considerably better than his recent releases of new material, making the country Top Ten and the pop Top 100 and earning a gold record. Making only one film in 1977, *Semi-Tough*, released in the fall, he worked on his eighth album for more than a year and a half, not releasing *Easter Island* until March 1978. It marked a slight commercial uptick, charting higher in the pop and country charts than his previous effort, but did not restore his commercial fortunes as a recording artist. Returning to the movies, Kristofferson starred in *Convoy*, a film extrapolation of the 1976 song hit by C. W. McCall, which opened in the summer. In January 1979, he and Rita Coolidge released their third duo album, *Natural Act*, which was another modest seller. Kristofferson's personal life and professional career were both at low points in the late '70s and early '80s. His ninth album, *Shake Hands With the Devil*, was released in September 1979 and did not sell well enough to reach the charts, though the single "Prove It to You One More Time Again" was a country singles chart entry. His next film, *Freedom Road*, was not given a theatrical release in the U.S., instead being broadcast on television in October. And on December 2, he and Rita Coolidge were divorced. At the same time, however, his song catalog continued to prosper. Lena Martell's cover of "One Day at a Time" hit number one in the U.K. in October, then in the U.S. Cristy Lane revived the song, taking it to number one in the country charts in June 1980.

Willie Nelson Sings Kris Kristofferson was released in October 1979 and made the country Top Five, as did Nelson's single release of "Help Me Make It Through the Night." Kristofferson toured with Nelson during the winter of 1979-1980. During this period, he also was working on what should have been his greatest cinematic triumph yet, though it turned into a debacle. This was *Heaven's Gate*, director Michael Cimino's follow-up to his Academy Award-winning film *The Deer Hunter.* The lengthy, expensive film debuted to negative reviews in November 1980 and was such a financial catastrophe that it bankrupted the movie studio that made it. Kristofferson had already been contracted to make another film, *Rollover*, released in 1981, but his association with *Heaven's Gate* may have scared off casting directors, since he didn't appear in another film until 1984. Meanwhile, he released his tenth album, *To the Bone*, in January 1981, and it became his second straight LP to miss the pop charts, though it made the country charts briefly, as did the single "Nobody Loves Anybody Anymore." But the old songs continued to sell; in July, Tompall & the Glaser Brothers just missed topping the country charts with their revival of "Lovin' Her Was Easier (Than Anything I'll Ever Do Again)."

Except for a non-charting single, "Here Comes That Rainbow Again"/"The Bandits of Beverly Hills," Kristofferson was not heard from for the rest of 1981 or most of 1982, resurfacing in November 1982 with the release of the double-album *The Winning Hand*, a group effort credited to "Kris [Kristofferson], Willie [Nelson], Dolly [Parton], & Brenda [Lee]." The album reached the country Top Five, though it failed to cross the 100 mark on the pop charts. On February 19, 1983, Kristofferson married for the third time, wedding attorney Lisa Meyers, with whom he eventually had five more children, for a total of eight. He returned to filmmaking in January 1984 with the television broadcast of *The Lost Honor of Kathryn Beck*, and made it back into movie theaters later that year with *Flashpoint*, a mystery, and *Songwriter.* In the latter, he co-starred with Willie Nelson in a story about the Nashville music industry. He wrote a number of songs for the film, resulting in his first Academy Award nomination for original song score. Columbia Records released *Music from Songwriter*, a duo album by Nelson and Kristofferson on which the two sang separately and shared a couple of duets. The album reached the pop charts and the Top 20 of the country charts, and one of the duets, Kristofferson's "How Do You Feel About Foolin' Around," made the country singles charts.

Kristofferson and Nelson expanded their partnership into a supergroup quartet with the addition of Johnny Cash and Waylon Jennings to create the album *Highwayman*, released in April 1985. The title track, a song about reincarnation written by Jimmy Webb, with each group member taking a verse, topped the country charts in August and the LP was also a number-one country hit, going gold. A second single, Guy Clark's "Desperados Waiting for a Train," made the country Top 20. The recordings were billed to the four participants by name, but the group came to be known informally as "the Highwaymen," though a settlement had to be made with the 1960s folk group the Highwaymen for the name to be used legally.

In December 1985, Kristofferson starred in Alan Rudolph's film *Trouble in Mind*, also contributing the theme song, "El Gavilan" ("The Hawk," after the name of his character), sung by Marianne Faithfull. He put the song on *Repossessed*, his first solo album in six years, which was released on Mercury Records in February 1987. Reflecting his left-wing views particularly on American military involvement in Central America, *Repossessed* spent six months in the country charts and "They Killed Him," a tribute to Christ, Gandhi, and Martin Luther King Jr., placed in the country singles charts. Simultaneous with the release of the LP, Kristofferson appeared in *Amerika*, a controversial weeklong television mini-series that fantasized a U.S. under Communist domination. It was one of many TV movie projects the actor had done in the mid-'80s, a time when his feature film work remained sparse.

Highwayman 2 appeared in February 1990, preceded by a single, "Silver Stallion," that made the country Top 40. The album reached the country Top Five and it earned a Grammy nomination for Best Country Vocal Collaboration. Kristofferson followed *Repossessed* with a second Mercury album, *Third World Warrior*, in March 1990. Another work of agitprop, it failed to reach the charts. In 1991, Columbia/Legacy released the compilation *Singer/Songwriter*, a double-CD set containing both Kristofferson's versions of his best-known songs and the best-known covers of them by people like Janis Joplin and Ray Price. The archival label followed in 1992 with the previously unreleased concert set *Live at the Philharmonic*, recorded in 1972. Kristofferson worked steadily in TV movies and independent features during the late '80s and early '90s; he wrote the score for the 1993 film *Cheatin' Hearts*, in which he also appeared. The Highwaymen's third album, *The Road Goes on Forever*, appeared in April 1995 and made the country charts. As a solo artist, Kristofferson had teamed with producer Don Was to record a new album, *A Moment of Forever*, for Was' Karambolage imprint in 1993, but an initial distribution deal fell through and the album was not released until August 1995, when it appeared on the Texan independent label Justice Records. Four years later, Kristofferson released *The Austin Sessions*, an album of remakes of his most popular songs. (In the mid-'90s, One Way Records reissued many of Kristofferson's Monument albums on CD.)

Kristofferson's appearance in director John Sayles' film *Lone Star* (1996) marked a turning point in his film career. Taking a supporting role as a corrupt sheriff, the 60-year-old actor displayed a flair for character parts and villains that vastly increased his offers from Hollywood in the late '90s and led to his appearances in such major-studio action features as *Fire Down Below*, *Blade*, and *Payback*. He also earned admiring critical notices as a James Jones-like novelist in *A Soldier's Daughter Never Cries* and in another Sayles film, *Limbo*. By the turn of the century, complaining that he hadn't had time to tour as a singer in years, Kristofferson was looking forward to additional film work. —*William Ruhlmann*

☆ **Kristofferson** / 1970 / Monument/Legacy ✦✦✦✦✦
Kris Kristofferson was approaching his mid-'30s and had been kicking around Nashville for several years when he belatedly became an overnight success in 1969-1970. The impetus was "Me and Bobby McGee," which he co-wrote with Fred Foster, who ran Monument Records. Roger Miller cut the song, and his recording peaked in the country Top 20 in August 1969. By that time, Kristofferson had performed at the Newport Folk Festival at the behest of Johnny Cash, and Foster decided to sign him to Monument as a recording artist. Before this debut album was released in 1970, Ray Stevens had scored a pop and country chart entry with Kristofferson's "Sunday Mornin' Comin' Down."

On the evidence of his first collection of songs, Kristofferson was ahead of his country music peers in realizing that, despite Nashville's conservative political tilt, there was a natural affinity between the country archetype of a hard-drinking, romantically independent loner and the rock & roll archetype of a drug-taking, romantically free hippie. (Of course, lots of rock musicians, especially in Los Angeles, had already noticed this similarity, and formed bands like Poco and the Flying Burrito Brothers to exploit it.) He opened the album with what sounded like an answer to the criticisms of the Rolling Stones in the wake of Altamont. "Blame It on the Stones" contrasted various conservative stereotypes, starting with "Mr. Marvin Middle Class," with the supposedly evil rock group, its chorus a parody of "Bringing in the Sheaves." Needless to say, that was not a typical way to open a country album in 1970 (or any other time), but Kristofferson quickly followed with the somewhat more reverent "To Beat the Devil," which he dedicated in a spoken introduction to Johnny Cash and June Carter, and in which he established a persona he would maintain through much of the album, the character of a poor songwriter struggling against despair. "Me and Bobby McGee," a classic on-the-road song, was next, with Kristofferson, despite the country grammar, displaying his background as an English teacher in its chorus, "Freedom's just another word for nothin' left to lose/Nothin' ain't worth nothin', but it's free." Then came "The Best of All Possible Worlds," which used a reference to Voltaire to reflect wryly on the viewpoint of a drunken vagrant. (You could see what attracted Roger Miller to Kristofferson in a song like this, which clearly was influenced by Miller's "King of the Road," though Kristofferson's treatment of the subject was grittier.) Of course, the ultimate example of the subject was the album-closing "Sunday Mornin' Comin' Down," which was basically a first-person description of a hangover. The romantic side of the hard-living drifter character was glimpsed in the album's two tenderest statements, "Help Me Make It Through the Night" and "For the Good Times," both of which were pleas by the narrator to sleep with the object of his affection.

A sleeve note suggested that Kristofferson had been reluctant to record, but while he didn't have much range as a singer, he brought a conviction to his vocals and a complete understanding of the nuances of the lyrics. The songs were so personal that they seemed to demand a personal interpretation. Nashville, as it turned out, didn't have much use for countercultural songs like "Blame It on the Stones" and "The Law Is for Protection of the People" (which had some choice words for the police), but the country music community could recognize a good love song with an erotic edge that was on the cusp of the era's changing mores, and Ray Price quickly cut "For the Good Times," which topped the country charts. Then, Johnny Cash covered "Sunday Morning Coming Down" for a number-one country hit, leading to its winning the Country Music Association's Song of the Year award for 1970, and Sammi Smith gave a twist to "Help Me Make It Through the Night" by recording it as a woman's song for yet another country number one. The finishing touch to Kristofferson's sudden renown was Janis Joplin's cover of "Me and Bobby McGee," released shortly after her death, which topped the pop charts.

When it was released in 1970, *Kristofferson* did not reach the charts. By the following year, however, its creator was on his way to becoming a major star, and after his second

album, *The Silver Tongued Devil and I*, broke into the pop charts in July 1971. Monument re-titled the first album *Me and Bobby McGee* and reissued it. This time around, it made the pop and country charts and went gold. [On February 6, 2001, Monument/Legacy reissued *Kristofferson* as part of its American Milestones series. Featuring 24-bit remastering, the CD added four previously unreleased tracks from the same sessions that produced the album, among them an early version of "Come Sundown," later recorded for a Top Ten country hit by Bobby Bare and re-cut by Kristofferson himself for his *Shake Hands With the Devil* album in 1979.] —*William Ruhlmann*

★ **The Silver Tongued Devil and I** / Jul. 1971 / Monument ✦✦✦✦✦
By the time Monument came to release Kristofferson's second album, *The Silver Tongued Devil and I*, in July 1971, he was the author of four songs that had topped the country or pop charts for others. Kristofferson himself had not yet reached the charts with a recording of his own, but his spectacular success as a songwriter made *The Silver Tongued Devil and I* a much-anticipated record. One consequence of this was that Monument was willing to spend more money; three of the album's songs boasted strings and another a horn section. But the key, of course, was still the songwriting, and though there were several excellent songs, the album could not live up to its predecessor, which was the culmination of years of writing. Typically for a second album, Kristofferson reached back into his catalog, presenting his own treatments of "Jody and the Kid" and "The Taker," which had been hits for Roy Drusky and Waylon Jennings, respectively. In his newly written material, Kristofferson continued to examine the lives of society's outcasts, but the anti-establishment tone of some of *Kristofferson* was gone along with much of the wry humor, and in their place were touches of morbidity and sentimentality. Kristofferson retained his gift for intimate love songs, and the album's most memorable selections turned out to be "Loving Her Was Easier (Than Anything I'll Ever Do Again)" (which became a semi-standard) and "When I Loved Her." And even if his observations seemed less acute, his talent for wordplay often rescued the songs from banality. On its way to becoming a gold record, *The Silver Tongued Devil and I* reached the pop Top 20, Kristofferson's career high on that chart, and the country Top Five; thus, Kristofferson made the transition from being a successful songwriter to a successful recording artist. —*William Ruhlmann*

Me and Bobby McGee / Aug. 1971 / Monument ✦✦✦✦✦
In the late '60s and early '70s, Kris Kristofferson's adult, reality-based songs were the most shocking thing to hit Nashville in a longtime, and what's more, they were hits. This album contains his own versions of some of the best, including the title song, "Help Me Make It Through the Night," and "Sunday Mornin' Comin' Down." —*William Ruhlmann*

Border Lord / Feb. 1972 / One Way ✦✦✦
Border Lord was a crucial album for Kris Kristofferson. After five years of scuffling in Nashville, he had broken through in 1970-1971 largely because of a series of song hits recorded by others, though his first two albums, *Kristofferson* (aka *Me and Bobby McGee*) and *The Silver Tongued Devil and I* had enjoyed healthy sales, the latter even spawning a Top 40 pop hit in "Loving Her Was Easier (Than Anything I'll Ever Do Again)." But he needed to consolidate that success and even increase it, especially as a recording artist. Yet, as is so often the case, he was afforded precious little time to craft his next work. *Border Lord*, which, like its predecessors, was an album of all-original compositions, was in record stores only seven months after *The Silver Tongued Devil and I*, and it was his third such collection in 20 months. He continued to draw upon the dwindling store of songs in his trunk, using the 1967 copyright "Burden of Freedom," as well as "Somebody Nobody Knows," published in 1968, while two others, "Smokey Put the Sweat on Me" and "When She's Wrong," were published by his first publisher, Buckhorn Music, suggesting that they may have been written well before their 1972 copyright dates. New or old, the songs on *Border Lord* often seemed like retreads of already familiar Kristofferson themes. His interest on lowlife characters, especially fallen women, was so pervasive it practically turned the disc into a concept album. Of the ten songs, six—"Josie," "Stagger Mountain Tragedy," "Somebody Nobody Knows," "Little Girl Lost," "Smokey Put the Sweat on Me," and "When She's Wrong"—treated the subject of women in debased conditions, several specifically described as prostitutes. And Kristofferson tended to reuse his allusions and imagery, especially references to the Devil (already the subject of earlier songs such as "To Beat the Devil" and "The Silver-Tongued Devil and I"), who appeared in no less than five songs. The songwriter was almost, but not quite, as interested in the Lord, who was name-checked here and there, and with whose Son Kristofferson identified in the philosophical "Burden of Freedom" ("Lord, help me forgive them, they don't understand"). Among the religious and roadhouse references, the only really new subject was life on the road, which was treated in such new songs as "Border Lord" and "Gettin' By, High and Strange," an indication that this always confessional songwriter was writing about his current life as a touring musician. Though it consisted of material that was noticeably inferior by Kristofferson's standards, the album was full of poetic lines effectively performed by a road-honed singer and a touring band heavily augmented by Nashville pros; even second-rate Kristofferson was pretty good in 1972. Still, Monument Records had difficulty finding an obvious candidate for a hit single, finally settling on "Josie," which must have seemed to have some of the same qualities as "Me and Bobby McGee," but which only struggled into the lower reaches of the pop charts. With that, *Border Lord* proved a commercial disappointment, slowing the momentum of a career that had been accelerating over the past three years. No doubt Kristofferson and Monument would have been better advised to have waited until he had a collection of songs to match his early hits; instead, he quickly began work on yet another album, *Jesus Was a Capricorn*, which was out before the end of the year. —*William Ruhlmann*

Jesus Was a Capricorn / Nov. 1972 / Monument ✦✦✦
Kris Kristofferson is pictured smiling in sunglasses on the cover of *Jesus Was a Capricorn*, accompanied by his girlfriend and soon-to-be-wife Rita Coolidge. The album followed his

previous LP, *Border Lord*, by only nine months and was his fourth album to be released within two-and-a-half years, which meant that a man who had struggled for half a decade to get anybody to listen to his songs was now writing and recording them as fast as he could. Not surprisingly, he was having trouble filling the pipeline; he borrowed the melody of John Prine's "Grandpa Was a Carpenter" for the title song and even recorded a cover song for the first time, performing a duet with Larry Gatlin on Gatlin's "Help Me." There was nothing here that matched his best songs, but the overall quality of the material was quite good, as Kristofferson went back over familiar ground, singing about religion, romance, and roughhousing with equal fervor. Especially impressive were the two duets with Coolidge, "It Sure Was (Love)" and "Give It Time to Be Tender," which looked forward to their duo albums. Commercially, *Jesus Was a Capricorn* can be seen either as a case of record company ineptitude or perseverance, or both. *Border Lord* had marked a falloff in sales from Kristofferson's first two albums, and initially *Jesus Was a Capricorn* looked like it was going to do even worse, as Monument Records couldn't seem to figure out what the right single was. The label started by releasing a single version of the title track, in which Kristofferson described Christ as a sandals-wearing hippie, and, despite the subject matter, pop radio gave it enough play to get it into the bottom of the charts for a few weeks. But the LP quickly peaked in the charts and started to fade, not helped by the second single, the medium-tempo rocker "Jesse Younger," which made no impression. (Meanwhile, Brenda Lee had no trouble locating the album's best song; she covered "Nobody Wins" and established herself in country music by taking it into the country Top Five.) Finally, four months after the album's release, Monument issued a third single, the slow-paced statement of faith that closed the LP, "Why Me." (Actually, a disc jockey had started playing the song, which Monument hadn't even wanted on the album. Though sometimes described as a spoof, "Why Me" sincerely reflects a religious experience, according to Kristofferson.) It quickly entered the country and pop charts, hitting number one in country in July 1973, and peaking in the pop Top 20 after a slow climb in November. That turned around the fortunes of *Jesus Was a Capricorn*, which marched back up the charts and reached number one on the country charts a full year after it had been released. Both album and single went gold, giving Kristofferson his greatest success as a recording artist. *—William Ruhlmann*

Full Moon / Sep. 1973 / A&M ✦✦✦✦

Kris Kristofferson was at his commercial peak as a recording artist at the time that *Full Moon*, his first duo album with Rita Coolidge, was released in September 1973. His single "Why Me" had topped the country charts two months earlier, and his album *Jesus Was a Capricorn* was about to do the same thing. And, only weeks before *Full Moon*'s release, the couple had gotten married. All of that made for a terrific send-off for the record, which benefited the careers of both participants. Not surprisingly, it was an album of love songs. Despite Kristofferson's greater celebrity, the LP was made with Coolidge's strengths in mind. David Anderle, its producer, was her producer, and it was released on her record label, A&M. The songs were set in her key, with Kristofferson crooning along in an unusually high register. The tempos were mostly slow, emphasizing the dreamy quality of Coolidge's voice. And the songs were mostly covers, though there were two joint compositions by the couple, one old Kristofferson song ("From the Bottle to the Bottom," a Top 20 country hit for Billy Walker in 1969), and one new Kristofferson tune, the Caribbean-flavored "A Song I'd Like to Sing," which was released as the first single and became a Top 40 pop hit while also reaching the country and easy listening charts. With that, the album became a number-one country hit. "From the Bottle to the Bottom" won the 1973 Grammy Award for Best Country Vocal Performance by a Duo or Group. The album's second single, a cover of Tom Jans' "Loving Arms," also made the pop, country, and easy listening charts, and because it was released in the 1974 eligibility period for the Grammy Awards, it earned the couple a second nomination in the same category the following year. *—William Ruhlmann*

Spooky Lady's Sideshow / May 1974 / One Way ✦✦✦

Kris Kristofferson has complained that no album he released after 1972's *Jesus Was a Capricorn* was given any promotion, and 1974's *Spooky Lady's Sideshow* is the first record that falls into that category. If his statement is true, it is understandable why Monument Records would have refrained from a major campaign on behalf of the album. Record companies tend to reserve their greatest promotional effort for developing artists who show commercial promise, expecting established artists to fend for themselves. And at the time of the release of *Spooky Lady's Sideshow*, the company probably considered Kristofferson an established artist; after all, two of his last three albums had gone gold, and he had hit number one in the country singles charts the year before with the gold-selling "Why Me" while at the same time topping the country albums charts twice, with *Jesus Was a Capricorn* and his duo album with Rita Coolidge, *Full Moon*. Also, in the interim between his last album and this one, he had become a movie star with his appearances in *Blume in Love* and *Pat Garrett and Billy the Kid*. But all that success masked a relatively fragile status as a recording artist. Kristofferson was actually more successful as a songwriter than as a singer; his third album, *Border Lord*, had been a commercial disappointment, and so had *Jesus Was a Capricorn* until "Why Me" belatedly became a fluke hit. He didn't really have as firm a fan base as the statistics indicated, and the movie stardom was a double-edged sword, suggesting that his commitment to music-making was compromised. But a second reason for Monument not to commit its resources to promoting *Spooky Lady's Sideshow* must have come from listening to the record itself. On paper, Kristofferson may have seemed to be at the top of his game, not only because of his record sales and box office appeal, but also because of his apparently successful marriage to Coolidge. And yet *Spooky Lady's Sideshow* was practically a concept album about dissipation and decline. Over and over, Kristofferson sang of characters and of himself (or, at any rate in the persona of a first-person narrator) going downhill while consuming liquor and drugs. From the back of the album cover, which was festooned with fictional negative reviews, to song titles like "Star-Spangled Bummer (Whores Die Hard)" and "Stairway to the Bottom," the album was a portrait of excess and deterioration. Monument was unable to locate a "Me and Bobby McGee" or even a "Why Me" to release as a single and settled for "I May Smoke Too Much," a Dixieland-style tribute to hedonism, which made no impact. With that, the album faded from its peak in the lower reaches of the pop Top 100, Kristofferson's lowest and briefest charting LP so far. It's hard to blame anyone but the artist himself for this. While he had been rushed in making his third and fourth albums, the belated success of "Why Me" afforded him a year-and-a-half to come up with the material for *Spooky Lady's Sideshow*. Its songs featured his usual wordplay and repeated many of his usual interests—freedom, the Devil, Jesus Christ. Leaving longtime producer Fred Foster and Nashville behind, Kristofferson worked with David Anderle and a team of Los Angeles session pros, but his country-rock sound remained much the same. The problem was that his songs were so saturated in controlled substances and so determinedly focused on self-destruction that they became a self-fulfilling prophecy. You might say that *Spooky Lady's Sideshow* is Kris Kristofferson's version of Neil Young's *Tonight's the Night* (which was recorded around the same time though released later). But Kristofferson lacked Young's humorous perspective on his wasted condition, and instead of reinvigorating his career, the album was a misstep from which he never recovered as a recording artist. *—William Ruhlmann*

Breakaway / Dec. 1974 / Monument ✦✦✦

The success of Kris Kristofferson and Rita Coolidge's first duo album, *Full Moon*, which topped the country charts, went gold, and won a Grammy Award for Best Country Vocal Performance by a Duo or Group for the track "From the Bottle to the Bottom," whetted appetites for its follow-up, *Breakaway*. But just as Kristofferson's solo album *Spooky Lady's Sideshow*, released earlier in 1974, had been a commercial disappointment following the popularity of its predecessor, *Jesus Was a Capricorn*, so *Breakaway* failed to match the impression *Full Moon* had made. That may have been in part because Monument Records, which released the album (*Full Moon* had been on Coolidge's label, A&M), was treating Kristofferson as an established artist who didn't need a lot of promotion, and in part because *Breakaway* was the seventh new Kristofferson album released within four-and-a-half years, too much product for the market to absorb. In any case, the album was a worthy successor to *Full Moon*. The Kristofferson/Coolidge albums were very different from each artist's solo albums, though somewhat closer to Coolidge's because they consisted largely of cover songs and the keys were set to her voice, with Kristofferson singing at the upper edge of his narrow range. This forced him to work harder and sing more, which made him a better vocalist than he usually was on his own albums. He tended to take brief vacations from songwriting for their sessions of love songs, but this album was sparked by two of his old songs, neither of which he had previously recorded, though they had been hits for others. "I'd Rather Be Sorry" was a country hit for Ray Price in 1971 and "I've Got to Have You" for Sammi Smith in 1972. (There is also an effective version of the latter on Carly Simon's second album, 1971's *Anticipation*.) The husband-and-wife team handled these songs well, making you wish they would tackle an entire album of Kristofferson love songs. But the tracks that garnered the most attention were their revival of the old Clyde McPhatter hit "Lover Please" (written by Kristofferson sideman Billy Swan), which reached the easy listening charts as a single and won the duo a second Grammy, and their version of Larry Gatlin's "Rain," a country and easy listening chart entry. Those semi-hits were enough to get the album into the country top five and the Top 100 of the pop charts, but like Kristofferson's solo recording career, his teaming with his wife had passed its commercial peak. *—William Ruhlmann*

Who's to Bless and Who's to Blame / Nov. 1975 / One Way ✦✦✦

Having suffered a commercial disappointment with his fifth album, *Spooky Lady's Sideshow*, Kris Kristofferson re-affirmed his movie stardom in *Alice Doesn't Live Here Anymore* and made a second album with Rita Coolidge, *Breakaway*, then spent some time coming up with material for his next recording, *Who's to Bless and Who's to Blame*, which appeared 18 months after its predecessor. The album was far more accessible, containing several catchy songs with commercial possibilities. Lyrically, Kristofferson was largely concerned with moral compromise and the difficulty of distinguishing right from wrong, the conundrum contained in the album title. In the leadoff track, "The Year 2000 Minus 25," he took on politics and recent news events from a sarcastic viewpoint, finally concluding, "It don't hurt so bad when you're high." Songs like "Easy, Come On" and "Stranger" extended the discussion to emotional politics, and the title song took a philosophical tone, contrasting clichés to reveal the murkiness of morality. Even minor songs like "Rocket to Stardom" and "Don't Cuss the Fiddle," humorous looks at celebrity life, introduced unresolved contradictions. The album-closing "Silver (The Hunger)," at eight minutes-plus Kristofferson's longest song, dealt with moral compromise in its allegorical story of a mysterious man's encounter with a woman, even if the songwriter seemed more interested in his alliterative wordplay than in the song's meaning. Monument Records, perhaps hoping to hit the pop and country markets with its different sides, released a single of "The Year 2000 Minus 25"/"If It's All the Same to You," but radio didn't bite, and the album marked another slide in Kristofferson's sales. Four months later, Johnny Duncan covered "Stranger" and took it into the country Top Five. *—William Ruhlmann*

Surreal Thing / Jul. 1976 / One Way ✦✦✦

The fall-off in the quality of Kris Kristofferson's albums after his initial success is sometimes ascribed to his moonlighting as a film actor, dividing his time and attention between two careers. A better reason is probably a country music-style recording contract that called for him to turn in an album a year consisting of his own all-new compositions, a pace that did not allow him enough time to write songs of the caliber of the standards he produced in the late 1960s and early '70s. *Surreal Thing* (1976), his seventh album since 1970 (not counting two duet LPs with his wife, Rita Coolidge), is a good case in point. It was released only eight months after its predecessor, 1975's *Who's to Bless and Who's* to Blame, and while Kristofferson had come up with a few good songs in the interim, he simply didn't have ten new keepers. As a result, he reached back nine years and re-cut both sides of the long-lost single he had made for Epic Records in 1967, "The Golden Idol" and "Killing Time," songs written in a more verbose style than his current one. "The Golden Idol" sounded heavily influenced by Bob Dylan's mid-'60s poetic approach, while "Killing Time" was a put-down of unimaginative average people. Its tone of criticism was picked up in two new songs, both of which lashed out at Kristofferson's detractors. "Eddie the Eunuch" was his portrait of a rock & roll critic who attacked his subjects "'cause he wasn't Jackson Browne," and "If You Don't Like Hank Williams" was a roll call of the artist's favorite rock and country artists that criticized people who lacked his broad taste (and who, by implication, wanted to categorize him as either rock or country). When he wasn't venting his spleen, the songwriter brought in a couple of good country ballads, "It's Never Gonna Be the Same Again" and "Bad Love Story," though his more philosophical efforts, such as "I Got a Life of My Own," for which he adopted a Gospel sound complete with a choral backing, were ponderous and seemed underwritten. Not helping the spotty quality of the songwriting were arrangements and performances that sometimes seemed like run-throughs and, particularly, Kristofferson's rough vocals, which were often inept. *Surreal Thing* sounded like an album made by a man who was rushed, both as a songwriter and as a performer. Though it rose into the country Top Ten, it barely made the pop charts, and with the single "It's Never Gonna Be the Same Again" a flop, it quickly disappeared. — *William Ruhlmann*

Songs of Kristofferson / Apr. 1977 / Monument ✦✦✦✦
In the spring of 1977, Kris Kristofferson was at the apex of his film career, having recently co-starred in the box-office hit *A Star Is Born* and won a Golden Globe Award for it. At the same time, his recording career was on the wane; his two most recent solo albums, *Who's to Bless...and Who's to Blame* (1975) and *Surreal Thing* (1976) had failed to break into the Top 100 of the pop LP charts. Monument Records seized on his movie celebrity to release his first compilation, which emphasized his early success as a songwriter over his actual recordings. In 1970-1971, he had scored four number one hits as a writer—"Help Me Make It Through the Night," "For the Good Times," and "Sunday Mornin' Comin' Down" on the country charts, and "Me and Bobby McGee" on the pop charts. All four songs had appeared on his debut album, *Kristofferson* (aka *Me and Bobby McGee*), and they were featured on the first side of *Songs of Kristofferson* along with the title track of his second album, *The Silver Tongued Devil and I* (1971), and his first Top 40 pop hit as a performer, "Loving Her Was Easier (Than Anything I'll Ever Do Again)," also from his second album. The second side of the LP plucked another song, "The Pilgrim: Chapter 33," from the second album, along with two tracks each from *Who's to Bless...and Who's to Blame* and *Surreal Thing*, plus "Why Me," Kristofferson's 1973 country chart-topper and Top 20 pop hit. The compilers left out such minor chart entries as "Josie" and "Jesus Was a Capricorn," giving undue weight to the later, less successful work, which keeps *Songs of Kristofferson* from being a true best-of. But it does contain the highlights of his early recordings, which remained his best-known material over time, and fans responded favorably to having the material on one album, as the LP went gold within two years of release. — *William Ruhlmann*

Easter Island / Mar. 1978 / One Way ✦✦✦
The portents seemed good for Kris Kristofferson's eighth album. Though his sixth and seventh LPs had missed the pop Top 100, his profile had increased due to his involvement in the film *A Star Is Born*, with its million-selling soundtrack featuring his pop singles chart entry "Watch Closely Now." And his first compilation, *Songs of Kristofferson*, had been a good seller. All of that allowed him more than a year and a half to craft *Easter Island*. He responded with an effort that combined ponderous, highly poetic compositions with several commercial-sounding love songs that might have been expected to ensure the set's popular success. "Risky Bizness" opened the album with the image of a boxer who had some of the characteristics of Jesus Christ, an image picked up again toward the end of the album on "The Fighter." The title track considered those mysterious stone heads on Easter Island, while "The Sabre and the Rose" and "Spooky Lady's Revenge" treated romantic encounters in heightened language. "Living Legend," which closed the album, sounded like it could have been written for *Pat Garrett and Billy the Kid*, the 1973 film that Kristofferson co-starred in and Bob Dylan scored. Any one of the four conventional love songs—"How Do You Feel (About Foolin' Around)," "Forever in Your Love," "The Bigger the Fool (The Harder the Fall)," and "Lay Me Down (And Love the World Away)"—all of them co-written with Mike Utley and Stephen Bruton, sounded like it might be a country hit. Monument chose "Forever in Your Love," but it didn't catch on. (Six years later, Kristofferson and Willie Nelson's remake of "How Do You Feel" was a country chart entry.) As a result, while the album marked a slight improvement over Kristofferson's recent sales, it was another commercial disappointment. — *William Ruhlmann*

Shake Hands With the Devil / 1979 / One Way ✦✦
By the time of *Shake Hands With the Devil*, the ninth album of Kris Kristofferson's ten-album contract with Monument Records, he must have considered his recording career an afterthought to his more prominent career in the movies. That's what's suggested by this album, to which he's given little thought. It consists mainly of old material: The title song is a previously unheard 1970 copyright; "Come Sundown" and "Once More With Feeling" are also 1970 songs, both of them country hits, one for Bobby Bare, the other for Jerry Lee Lewis; Atwood Allen and Kim Fowley's "Michoacan" was featured in Kristofferson's 1971 film *Cisco Pike*; Tom Ghent's "Whiskey, Whiskey," a 1970 country hit for Nat Stuckey, was in Kristofferson's concerts as far back as 1972; "Killer Barracuda" is a 1975 copyright; and Kristofferson wrote "Seadream" for his 1976 film *The Sailor Who Fell From Grace With the Sea*. Of the remaining three songs, "Lucky in Love" and "Fallen Angel" are co-compositions with Mike Utley and Stephen Bruton ("Fallen Angel" is also co-credited to Kristofferson's soon-to-be-ex-wife Rita Coolidge). So, the only new

composition solely by Kristofferson is the regretful ballad "Prove It to You One More Time Again." The result is a patchy collection with no really unified feeling. "Prove It to You One More Time" and "Lucky in Love" both have a slight Caribbean feel, while "Michoacan" is in Tex-Mex style, and "Once More With Feeling" employs a horn section for a Dixieland effect. Kristofferson sounds unusually relaxed, though his wheezy vocals, augmented by Utley, Bruton, Coolidge, and Billy Swan, are no better than usual. *Shake Hands With the Devil* became Kristofferson's first album not to reach the charts at all, though surprisingly "Prove It to You One More Time Again" got into the lower reaches of the country singles charts. — *William Ruhlmann*

Natural Act / Jan. 1979 / Karrussel ✦✦✦
Kris Kristofferson and Rita Coolidge inaugurated their musical partnership in 1973 (also the year of their marriage) with *Full Moon*, which topped the country charts, and they quickly followed with 1974's *Breakaway*, another album with healthy sales. By the time of their third and final duo LP, *Natural Act*, a little more than four years later, much had changed. At the time of their earlier efforts, Kristofferson was the dominant force in the partnership, coming off his gold records of the early '70s, his movie stardom, and his songwriting renown, while Coolidge was a developing artist who benefited from the exposure the albums brought her. By the start of 1979, the positions were reversed. Coolidge's 1977 album *Anytime...Anywhere* had generated two gold singles and gone platinum, and its follow-up, 1978's *Love Me Again*, had gone gold. Kristofferson's albums, on the other hand, struggled to get into the Top 100 bestsellers of the pop chart. Still, *Natural Act*, like its predecessors, came off as a busman's holiday for Kristofferson and his band with Coolidge along for the ride. The song list was dominated by contributions from Kristofferson cronies like Billy Swan and Donnie Fritts, and he himself brought in three songs, as usual two of them old items from his catalog. "Loving You [sic] Was Easier (Than Anything I'll Ever Do Again)" was an old hit of his that he used to dedicate to Coolidge; now they performed it together perfunctorily. "Please Don't Tell Me How the Story Ends," which had been a hit for Ray Price, and the previously unrecorded "Love Don't Live Here Anymore" seemed to hint at the couple's dissatisfaction with each other; they were divorced within a year of the album's release. Much of the material seemed inappropriate for this vocal team, especially a reading of the Bobby Fuller Four hit "I Fought the Law," and unlike the first two albums, Kristofferson didn't seem to be making much of an effort as a vocalist, while Coolidge just seemed listless. *Natural Act* sounded like a contractual obligation record from a musical act that had lost the chemistry that fueled it early on, just as the marriage apparently had. It was the duo's last album together. — *William Ruhlmann*

To the Bone / 1981 / One Way ✦✦✦
The period between the September 1979 release of Kris Kristofferson's ninth album, *Shake Hands With the Devil*, and the January 1981 release of his tenth, *To the Bone*, was an eventful one in his life. In December 1979, he and Rita Coolidge divorced, and he spent much of the period working on *Heaven's Gate*, an epic film that opened to disastrous reviews in November 1980, devastating his movie career. Since *Shake Hands With the Devil* had also been a commercial failure, and *To the Bone* was the last album on his contract with Monument Records, his singing career didn't seem to be in any better shape. Not surprisingly, he used the record to vent his feelings about his personal life. Many of the songs were addressed directly to a former romantic partner, and they detailed a relationship that had exhausted itself, leaving behind it considerable emotional pain and domestic complications, in particular a small child whose concerns were discussed in "Daddy's Song." Kristofferson quoted verses from the 1952 Hank Thompson hit "The Wild Side of Life" in two songs and filled his own lyrics with references to aging, though he found space for his favorite references—freedom and the Devil—as well. The result was a painful recording to listen to, but a worthwhile one as well, comparable to Marvin Gaye's 1979 album *Here, My Dear*. And Kristofferson's pain was not without its commercial aspect. Though Monument, itself nearly moribund, had little ability or incentive to promote the album, a single, "Nobody Loves Anybody Anymore," made the country charts, and the LP charted for several weeks, too. But that was it, and the singer/songwriter/movie star entered a career eclipse, not appearing in a feature film for three years and not releasing another solo album for six. — *William Ruhlmann*

The Winning Hand / Nov. 1982 / Monument ✦✦✦
In 1982, Willie Nelson, at a commercial peak, was recording prolifically, releasing albums not only under his own name alone, but also in duos with other artists. Still, this record was more expansive than most, a double-LP featuring Nelson, Dolly Parton, Brenda Lee, and Kris Kristofferson in solo performances and in duets. The genesis of the unusual project may have been Nelson and Parton's debt of gratitude to Monument Records and its founder, Fred Foster. The label had fallen on hard times lately, and *The Winning Hand* seems to have been an attempt to reactivate it. Kristofferson had recorded for Monument since 1970 (and his two solo selections on the album, "Here Comes That Rainbow Again" and "The Bandits of Beverly Hills," had been released as a single the year before). Lee had no association with Monument, but must have welcomed the opportunity to record with currently bigger stars like Nelson. The result is a typically mixed collection of re-made oldies and new songs. Going with the two big stars, Monument released Parton and Nelson's rendition of Parton's "Everything's Beautiful" and was rewarded with a Top Ten country hit. Lee and Nelson's "You're Gonna Love Yourself (In the Morning)" was also a country chart entry. Other highlights include Kristofferson's "Here Comes That Rainbow Again" (a musicalization of a passage in *The Grapes of Wrath*), Kristofferson and Lee's remake of his 1978 song "The Bigger the Fool, the Harder the Fall," Nelson and Kristofferson's remake of Nelson's 1967 song "To Make a Long Story Short, She's Gone," and Nelson's "King of a Lonely Castle." (When *The Winning Hand* was released originally as a double-LP running only an hour, it was something of a ripoff for the money; since reissued as a single budget-priced CD, it's now a bargain.) — *William Ruhlmann*

Repossessed / 1986 / Mercury ✦✦
After Kris Kristofferson's ninth and tenth solo albums, *Shake Hands With the Devil* (1979) and *To the Bone* (1980), missed the charts, he did not make another album on his own for more than six years, in the meantime contributing to three albums recorded with others: *Kris, Willie, Dolly & Brenda… The Winning Hand* (1982) (with Willie Nelson, Dolly Parton, and Brenda Lee); the soundtrack *Music From Songwriter* (1984) (with Nelson), which contained four Kristofferson solo tracks; and *Highwayman* (with Nelson, Johnny Cash, and Waylon Jennings). The last was a major success, topping the country charts, and probably interested Mercury Records in giving Kristofferson a new contract as a solo artist. The result was his 11th solo album, *Repossessed*, its title containing a telling double meaning. Kristofferson billed his backup group, the Borderlords, on the cover, a reasonable decision since they included such notable figures as Donnie Fritts and Billy Swan, who occasionally stepped in to sing a verse of a song here and there in place of the leader. Also, the tracks had a true country-rock band feel, and Kristofferson sometimes introduced the songs or called out solos as if they were playing a set in a club. The tracks thus had a kinetic feel, and that was all to the good since the songs themselves were not very impressive. 1986-1987 was a period of political unrest, as left-wing activists feared another Vietnam in El Salvador, and Kristofferson explored that concern in "What About Me," while such songs as "Shipwrecked in the Eighties," "They Killed Him," and "Anthem '84" reflected on various aspects of politics and war. But there were no real insights to be found in the songwriter's sketchy and abstract descriptions, either in these songs or the more philosophical statements such as "The Heart" (chorus: "The heart is all that matters in the end") and "Love Is the Way." In a lull in his film career, Kristofferson promoted *Repossessed* with extensive touring and managed to keep it in the country album charts six months, with "They Killed Him" (which Bob Dylan had thought enough of to cover) getting into the lower reaches of the singles charts. But it was not one of his better records. *—William Ruhlmann*

Third World Warrior / Mar. 6, 1990 / Mercury ✦✦
A danger in writing topical material is that it may be overtaken by the news before you can get it out, but no collection of topical songs has been quite as unfortunate in that regard as Kris Kristofferson's *Third World Warrior*. As his recording career declined from the late '70s on, Kristofferson became increasingly interested in writing and singing about left-wing political concerns, especially with regard to Central America, and *Third World Warrior* was the logical extreme of this tendency, consisting entirely of agitprop pronouncements. "If you don't like it mister I don't care," Kristofferson sang in the opening song, "The Eagle and the Bear." That song closed with the lines, "And I'll say until the day we free Mandela/All the world will be in chains," while the album's final song, "Sandinista," declared support for the Nicaraguan rebels of that name. *Third World Warrior* was released on March 6, 1990. But on February 12, Mandela had been released, and on February 26, Sandinista leader Daniel Ortega had conceded defeat in the Nicaraguan election. Thus, *Third World Warrior* was largely irrelevant the day it arrived in record stores. Probably it was also hobbled by the release a week earlier of *Highwayman 2*, the second album by the quartet of Willie Nelson, Johnny Cash, Waylon Jennings, and Kristofferson that had considerably more commercial clout. But leaving aside issues of timing, *Third World Warrior*, however committed its statements, was simplistic and heavy-handed, a perfect example of politics overwhelming art. *—William Ruhlmann*

Singer/Songwriter / 1991 / Monument ✦✦✦✦✦
Kris Kristofferson is known for a half-dozen compositions that became pop or country hits in the early '70s, most of them for other artists: "Me and Bobby McGee," "Help Me Make It Through the Night," "Sunday Mornin' Comin' Down," "For the Good Times," "Loving Her Was Easier (Than Anything I'll Ever Do Again)," and "Why Me." But in the country market, he had many other hits as a songwriter over a period of more than 20 years. The two-CD compilation, an unusually ambitious undertaking for Sony Music's Special Products division (why didn't Legacy, the company's top-of-the-line reissue division do it?), devotes one disc to Kristofferson's own versions of some of his hits, with the second disc given over to the hit versions recorded by others, some of them licensed from other labels. There are a couple of his songs that he himself had hits with ("Josie," "Why Me"), and only his versions are included, and there are a couple of the many songs he had hits with but never recorded himself ("Vietnam Blues," "Please Don't Tell Me How the Story Ends"). There are also two cover versions each of "Me and Bobby McGee" (by Roger Miller and Janis Joplin) and "Help Me Make It Through the Night" (Sammi Smith and Willie Nelson). The result is revelatory. His rough voice an acquired taste and his arrangements given to loose country-rock, Kristofferson makes his songs sound like personal statements. Then you hear the slick country versions of the same songs, and they sound like good commercial Nashville product. Sammi Smith's "Help Me Make It Through the Night," sung from a woman's viewpoint, has a completely different feel from Kristofferson's. "If You Don't Like Hank Williams" sounds like it was written for Hank Williams Jr.'s typically belligerent reading, though Kristofferson's own is, if anything, more raucous. The early "Vietnam Blues," the artist's first-ever cut back in 1966 by Dave Dudley, demonstrates the pro-war, anti-demonstrator attitude of the just-discharged former army captain, a vastly different political viewpoint from the one he would espouse two decades later. *Singer/Songwriter* is not perfect—a thorough collection would have dredged up his 1967 Epic Records single "The Golden Idol" and included more of his lost masterpieces and big country hits, notably the great love song "I've Got to Have You" and the major country hits "Your Time's Comin'," "I Won't Mention It Again," and "One Day at a Time." But this is the first compilation to give listeners a sense of the scope of Kristofferson's achievement as a songwriter, beyond the handful of songs for which he is best known. (Though the annotations do not say so, the Kristofferson performance of "From the Bottle to the Bottom" appears to be previously unreleased.) *—William Ruhlmann*

Live at the Philharmonic / 1992 / Sony Music Special Products ✦✦✦✦
Having gone above and beyond the usual effort for the sort of discount-priced, secondary-market compilations that are the typical province of its division with the elaborate Kris Kristofferson double-CD *Singer/Songwriter* in the fall of 1991, Sony Music Special Products followed it in the spring of 1992 with another special Kristofferson title, *Live at the Philharmonic*. The album of previously unreleased recordings was drawn from a concert performed at Philharmonic Hall in New York City on December 2, 1972. It was an unusual show, packed with guest stars and including three cover songs that never appeared on Kristofferson's studio albums. The singer/songwriter, who was near the peak of his musical popularity and not yet a movie star, had just released his fourth album, *Jesus Was a Capricorn*, and after opening the show with John Prine's "Late John Garfield Blues," he quickly played five songs from the LP, interrupted only by one of his hits, "Loving Her Was Easier (Than Anything I'll Ever Do Again)," and a new song, "Late Again (Gettin' Over You)," that he would not put on record until 1974's *Spooky Lady's Sideshow*. The unfamiliarity of most of the early material made for a slow start to the concert, but there then followed half a dozen songs from earlier albums that were greeted with cheers of recognition, among them "For the Good Times" (which was tossed off perfunctorily) and "Sunday Mornin' Comin' Down"; also included was a version of Merle Haggard's right-wing anthem "Okie From Muskogee" with altered lyrics (after which Kristofferson spoke admiringly of Haggard, though not of the song). Next up, the star of the show introduced a guest star, Willie Nelson, who would have been largely unknown to a New York audience in 1972, but who was greeted generously, performing a four-song mini-set including two of his better-known compositions, "Funny How Time Slips Away" and "Night Life." Taking back the spotlight, Kristofferson soon brought on the woman he called his "better half," Rita Coolidge (though the couple would not marry for another eight months) and then another unknown country musician on the verge of stardom, Larry Gatlin. The encore song was Tom Ghent's "Whiskey, Whiskey," a 1970 country chart entry for Nat Stuckey that wouldn't turn up on a Kristofferson studio album until 1979's *Shake Hands With the Devil*. It's notable that "Help Me Make It Through the Night" was not performed, and neither was "Why Me." Kristofferson had just released the latter, which would become his biggest hit as a recording artist, on *Jesus Was a Capricorn*, but it was still months away from being issued as a single. If those omissions keep this album from being a definitive live document of Kristofferson's career, it is nevertheless a special performance that occurred at a key moment in that career. *—William Ruhlmann*

Singer/Song Writer: 36 All-Time Greatest Hits! / 1993 / Sony Special Products ✦✦✦
Not to be confused with the 1991 two-CD set *Singer/Songwriter* released by Sony Music Special Products, which combines Kris Kristofferson's own performances of his best-known songs with cover versions, the 1993 three-CD set *Singer/Song Writer: 36 All-Time Greatest Hits!*, released by Sony Music Special Products through GSC Music is a compilation drawn from Kristofferson's tenure at Monument Records in the 1970s consisting entirely of his own recordings. A bare-bones, no-frills album (no liner notes, not even any songwriting credits, strangely enough), the package, which sells for about $30 in mail-order catalogs, selects tracks from nine of the 11 albums Kristofferson released on Monument. The choices weighted heavily toward his first (1970s *Kristofferson*, aka *Me and Bobby McGee*, 11 of 12 songs), second (1971's *The Silver Tongued Devil and I*, seven of ten songs), and fourth (1972's *Jesus Was a Capricorn*, six of ten songs) LPs, which were his three regular albums that were certified gold. Conversely, nothing at all has been chosen from 1974's *Spooky Lady's Sideshow* or 1981's *To the Bone*. In chart terms, Kristofferson did not actually score 36 hits, but he did have quite a few, especially as a country songwriter, and his versions of many of them are included, notably "Come Sundown," "For the Good Times," "Help Me Make It Through the Night," "I'd Rather Be Sorry," "Jesus Was a Capricorn," "Jody and the Kid," "Loving Her Was Easier," "Me and Bobby McGee," "Nobody Wins," "Once More With Feeling," "Stranger," "Sunday Mornin' Comin' Down," "The Taker," and "Why Me." But there are also some omissions: "Josie," a pop chart entry, and "Prove It to You One More Time Again" and "Nobody Loves Anybody Anymore," both of which reached the country charts, all in versions by Kristofferson himself, and "I've Got to Have You," which Sammi Smith covered for a country hit and which Kristofferson recorded on *Breakaway*, his one duet album with Rita Coolidge to be released by Monument. The set has been divided up roughly thematically, with the first 12-song disc subtitled "Silver Tongued Devil" and featuring philosophical and otherwise discursive songs, the second called "Me and Bobby McGee" and containing story songs, and the third, dubbed "Easy," featuring love songs. That doesn't explain what the devotional "Why Me" is doing on the second disc or the sardonic talking blues "The Best of All Possible Worlds" on the third, but maybe they weren't a thematic fit anywhere. *Singer/ Song Writer: 36 All-Time Greatest Hits!* runs over two hours, but it could have fit onto two CDs rather than three, and it seems a little pricey for what you get. Still, it presents a big chunk of Kristofferson's recordings, including his best-known songs, in one album. *—William Ruhlmann*

A Moment of Forever / 1995 / Buddha ✦✦✦
After salvaging several recording careers, producer Don Was formed his own imprint, Karambolage, to continue such efforts in the early '90s, and among other artists worked with Kris Kristofferson, dormant as a solo singer/songwriter since the commercial failure of his two politically oriented Mercury albums *Repossessed* and *Third World Warrior* in the late '80s. But *A Moment of Forever*, the comeback album Was produced for Kristofferson, was shelved when Karambolage lost its distribution deal, and the album wasn't released until the summer of 1995 by the independent Justice label. That means it's a far more ambitious undertaking than you might expect, packed with Los Angeles studio heavyweights like drummer Jim Keltner, guitarist Waddy Wachtel, and Heartbreakers organist Benmont Tench, as well as studio wiz Was on bass and behind the glass. In his late 50s, Kristofferson has retreated slightly from the agitprop, but fighting is still a recurring motif in his songs, along with an old favorite subject, freedom.

(Picking up on this, designer Cynthia S. Kinney even sticks the dictionary definition of freedom into a collage on one of the CD booklet pages.) But the songwriter often comes off as a sage elder rather than an active combatant, and the album is as concerned with emotions as it is with politics. Two old songs, "Casey's Last Ride" and "Good Love (Shouldn't Feel So Bad)," and two later ones, "Shipwrecked in the Eighties" and "Under the Gun," join the new compositions, and the old ones have a lyricism and clarity that makes you wish Kristofferson's mature writing wasn't so rhetorical. *A Moment of Forever* doesn't seem like the place to start in listening to Kristofferson, but those who have been following his work thus far will find it a good representation of his philosophical concerns, expressed in strong musical performances. *— William Ruhlmann*

Super Hits / Mar. 2, 1999 / Sony ✦✦✦✦
As advertised, this album contains many of Kris Kristofferson's "super hits," though it's worth noting that, with the exception of the gold, chart-topping "Why Me," none of them were super hits for Kristofferson: "Me and Bobby McGee" was a country hit for Roger Miller, then a pop hit for Janis Joplin; "Sunday Mornin' Comin' Down" was a country hit for Ray Stevens and for Johnny Cash; "For the Good Times" topped the country charts for Ray Price; Sammi Smith did the same with "Help Me Make It Through the Night"; and both Roger Miller and Tompall & the Glaser Brothers had country hits with "Lovin' Her Was Easier (Than Anything I'll Ever Do Again)." The versions here are Kristofferson's, with "Me and Bobby McGee," "The Pilgrim: Chapter 33," and "Casey's Last Ride" (the last two among the several songs that weren't actually hits, but are among the songwriter's best material) in live renditions. Given its budget price, this ten-track compilation may be the best place for a neophyte to get a sense of the songwriting prowess of a man no doubt better known as a movie actor (in part because all of these songs date from the late '60s and early '70s). *— William Ruhlmann*

The Austin Sessions / Aug. 24, 1999 / Atlantic ✦✦✦
For the follow-up to *Moment of Forever*, his first set of new original songs in years, Kris Kristofferson decided to record a set of stripped-down new versions of his classic songs. This project, released on Atlantic Records and entitled *The Austin Sessions*, was a star-studded affair, featuring harmony vocals from Jackson Browne, Steve Earle, Matraca Berg, Vince Gill, Marc Cohn, Alison Krauss, Catie Curtis, and Mark Knopfler. In one sense, it's easy to question why Kristofferson needed to record these songs again, since much of his catalog seems to consist of reinterpretations of these songs, but taken on its own terms, it's a good listen. In a way, Kristofferson's voice—which never had too much range, even at its peak—sounds better now that its older; the ragged edges and wear give it more character, which lend character to the songs. Ultimately, *The Austin Sessions* isn't a major addition to his catalog, but there's enough warmth and personality to these recordings to make it worth a listen for longtime fans. *— Stephen Thomas Erlewine*

All Time Greatest Hits / Sep. 25, 2001 / Varese ✦✦✦✦
With so many Kris Kristofferson collections featuring basically the same material already available, it's questionable why the compilers felt it was necessary to repackage these songs again into this 2001 disc. What's especially frustrating is as of this release, there still was not a comprehensive multi-label Kristofferson compilation. While the bulk of his best-known material was recorded for Monument in the '70s, he's had a smattering of hits for other labels in the decades since. Even tracks from Monument's belatedly released live album, recorded at a New York City concert in 1972, aren't included here, making this an adequate but extremely disappointing compilation of well-worn Kristofferson classics. That said, for those unaware of the charms of the country singer/songwriter's early recordings, this is a sufficient introduction, as these 18 tracks include almost everything of significance Kristofferson recorded during the '70s. His gritty talk-singing on classics like "Why Me?" and "Sunday Mornin' Comin' Down" recalls Waylon Jennings and perfectly meshes with his tales of down and outers, life on the skids, and characters with little left to lose. The bulk of his best songs during these years are ballads, which infuse this album with a rather bleak, samey atmosphere, especially when they are programmed next to each other. Only the barroom romp of the Shel Silverstein collaboration "How Do You Feel About Foolin' Around?," one of this set's least engaging tunes, lightens the mood. Although *Billboard* chart position information is welcome, the lack of any musician credits is troublesome, making this a less satisfying anthology than it should be. But for those who just want the basics of Kris Kristofferson's claim to fame, you needn't look any further. *— Hal Horowitz*

Sleepy LaBeef (Thomas Paulsley La Beff)

b. Jul. 11, 1935, Smackover, AR

Guitar, Vocals / Traditional Country, Rockabilly

Sleepy LaBeef became the ultimate rockabilly survivor, his live performances retaining the same raw power as he approached his eighth decade that they had in the years when he was among the music's pioneers. He was born Thomas Paulsley LaBeff in Smackover, AR. The 6-feet 7-inch singer has heavily lidded eyes which make him appear half-asleep, hence his nickname. He was raised on a melon farm and grew up hearing both country and blues music. LaBeef moved to Houston at age 18, working at several odd jobs before beginning to sing gospel music on local radio shows. Soon he was working with a band of his own at local bars, and he appeared on the *Houston Jamboree* and *Louisiana Hayride* radio programs. The new rockabilly style fit his blazing voice perfectly, and in the late '50s he recorded about a dozen sides in that style for various labels. His first single, "I'm Through," was released in 1957 on Starday. Sometimes he was billed as Tommy LaBeff or Sleepy LaBeff.

LaBeef moved to Nashville in 1964 and soon was signed to Columbia. In the 1960s he recorded mostly country music. His sixth single for the label, "Every Day," provided LaBeef with his chart debut in 1968, and after moving to Shelby Singleton's Plantation label in 1969, he hit the Top 20 with his version of "Blackland Farmer," Frankie Miller's heartfelt ode to the soil. The late '60s also saw the towering baritone's film debut in the bizarre Southern drive-in horror musical *The Exotic Ones*; LaBeef played a swamp monster. LaBeef moved to Sun Records in the mid-'70s after Singleton acquired that original institution of rockabilly, and there he reconnected with his rockabilly roots. Singles such as "Thunder Road," "There Ain't Much After Taxes," and "Boogie Woogie Country Girl" saw little chart action but helped form the beginnings of the LaBeef legend as his indefatigable touring exposed audiences to his wildman energy. LaBeef remains more popular in Europe than in the U.S. and appeared at England's Wembley Festival twice. Among his U.S. fans was soul-music historian Peter Guralnick, who saw LaBeef perform in Massachusetts in 1977 and praised his performances in a widely read article.

That plus the general revival of rockabilly around 1980 at the hands of such groups as the Stray Cats paved the way for the emergence of Sleepy LaBeef, rockabilly revivalist. He signed to Rounder in 1981 and released *It Ain't What You Eat (It's the Way How You Chew It)* in the U.S. and in Europe. The live album *Nothin' but the Truth* gave CD buyers a taste of the booming vocals and slashing guitar that had made LaBeef a prime club attraction. LaBeef returned to regular recording in the mid-'90s, releasing several more albums on Rounder: *Strange Things Happening* (1994) and *I'll Never Lay My Guitar Down* (1996) contained a variety of country and blues tunes and revealed the depth of LaBeef's musical experiences. Four years later, he issued *Tomorrow Never Comes*, which featured guest vocals from Maria Muldaur. Compilations of the numerous unissued tracks from earlier in LaBeef's career began to surface in the early 2000s, and by that time Sleepy was nothing less than a rockabilly legend. —*James Manheim*

● **Nothin' but the Truth** / 1985 / Rounder ✦✦✦✦✦
There aren't many legitimate characters left in popular music; the rotund Sleepy LaBeef isn't a media concoction or collection of outrageous clichés exploiting a carefully built image. He's a simple, hard-rocking vocalist with a manic performance style and musical approach that seamlessly blends rockabilly, classic rock and roll, gospel and country boogie into a non-stop, attacking mode. This 12-track live set from 1985 includes LaBeef renditions of "Milk Cow Blues," "Ring of Fire," "Tore Up Over You," "My Toot Toot" and a rousing concluding medley that includes "Jambalaya" and "Folsom Prison Blues." It's no-frills, unsophisticated, joyous roots music without reverence or pomp. —*Ron Wynn*

Strange Things Happening / Mar. 30, 1994 / Rounder ✦✦✦
Sleepy LaBeef is a bawdy, exuberant performer whose musical skills are slightly above average, but whose heart and energy are kingsize. He rips through Western swing, rockabilly, R&B, and rock on this 14-track set, doing originals and vintage pieces with equal ferocity. LaBeef doesn't coast through any song; he sings "Standing in the Need of Prayer" and "Strange Things Happening" with the same aggressiveness as "Sittin' on Top of the World" and "Stagger Lee." His slashing guitar riffs and authoritative vocals setting the pace, Sleepy LaBeef makes music for those who feel the spirit, no matter what the song. —*Ron Wynn*

Human Jukebox / Oct. 25, 1995 / Sun ✦✦✦
This is a nice budget collection of some of the sides Sleepy cut for Shelby Singleton's reactivated Sun label in the late 1960s and early '70s. Although there isn't nearly enough of Sleepy's own electric guitar in the mix and the Nashville session players backing him sound a bit stiff at times, these sides come as close as any to capturing a small chunk of Sleepy's prodigious song list. That Rolodex of songs covers everything from rockers like "Tore Up" and "Boogie Woogie Country Girl" to R&B ballads like "Raining in My Heart" and "There's Something on Your Mind" to straight-ahead country tracks like "Faded

Love" and "Blackland Farmer," the closest Sleepy has ever come to having a hit. It's an eclectic set, just like the man performing it. —*Cub Koda*

Larger Than Life / 1996 / Bear Family ✦✦✦✦✦
All of Sleepy LaBeef's most important records—from his early singles for Starday to his latter-day sides for Sun—are included on the mammoth, six-disc box set *Larger Than Life*. LaBeef recorded for a number of different labels during his career, and during that time, he explored a variety of roots music, from rockabilly and country to blues and soul. Spanning three full decades, *Larger Than Life* contains 158 tracks, including all of his recordings for Starday, Dixie, Columbia, and Sun. The box begins in the '50s and ends in the '70s, hitting all of LaBeef's best moments in the interim. A set of this size is designed for hardcore fans, and they are the ones who will treasure it—for less-dedicated listeners, the music may become rather monotonous, since the sheer length of the box is overwhelming. However, *Larger Than Life* is a treasure for devoted followers, since it collects many rare items—LaBeef's records have never been very easy to track down—adding an excellent booklet and many demos and outtakes in the measure. For those fans, it's a necessary addition to their collection. —*Thom Owens*

I'll Never Lay My Guitar Down / Jun. 1996 / Rounder ✦✦✦✦
Original rockabilly basso profundo Sleepy LaBeef returned with *I'll Never Lay My Guitar Down* and the great news was that it's even better than the last album he had put out on the Rounder imprint, the truly involved *Strange Things Happening*. Like the last one, this biscuit is produced by Jake Guralnick (who guests on lap steel and guitar) and features Duke Levine on guitar, Paul Bryan on bass, Dave Keyes on piano, and the right-in-the-pocket Lisa Pankratz on drums. For his part, LaBeef tears through 11 country, rockabilly, rock & roll, and bluesy favorites, giving each of them the flattening stamp of his whole personality. When LaBeef's into it, he's just the best, and this time it's evident by his screams and yelps that the pilot light was lit full blast. If your idea of rockabilly is some guy with a pompadour hiccuping himself into an early grave, do yourself a favor and pick up *I'll Never Lay My Guitar Down*. LaBeef may have been 60 years old, but he knew how to rock; after all, he was there when they invented it. —*Cub Koda*

Flying Saucers Rock 'n' Roll: The Very Best of Sleepy Labeef / Feb. 2, 1999 / Collectables ✦✦✦✦
Sleepy LaBeef did not record for Sun Records in the '50s, but his reputation as a rockabilly artist might mislead a few buyers into thinking *Flying Saucers Rock 'n' Roll* is a collection of '50s rockabilly recordings. In reality, this 24-track anthology spans LaBeef's 1970-1979 tenure with Plantation and the reactivated Sun Records. The disc includes LaBeef's lone hit from this period, a cover of Frankie Miller's "Blackland Farmer" that inched onto the country charts in 1971. LaBeef's deep-voiced country efforts sound a bit like Dave Dudley, although, ironically, the resemblance is less pronounced on LaBeef's trucking song, "Asphalt Cowboy." The rockabilly cuts, taken from albums like *1977 Rockabilly* and *Down Home Rockabilly*, don't attempt an "authentic" sound, but are nonetheless fun and rockin' performances that are thankfully untouched by dated production flourishes. All of these tracks are duplicated on Bear Family's six-disc box set *Larger Than Life*. —*Greg Adams*

The Bull's Night Out/Western Gold / Oct. 12, 1999 / Collectables ✦✦✦✦
In 1999, Collectables released *The Bull's Night Out/Western Gold*, which contained two complete albums—*The Bull's Night Out* and *Western Gold* (both originally released on Sun)—by Sleepy LaBeef on one compact disc. —*Jason Birchmeier*

Tomorrow Never Comes / Aug. 22, 2000 / M.C. ✦✦✦✦
On his first studio album in four years, the big man with the big baritone voice and a seemingly limitless knowledge of classic rock & roll, blues, country, gospel, and honky tonk, pumps out another 14 tracks of joyful genre crossing roots music. Not a songwriter, LaBeef reinterprets classics like Chuck Berry's "Too Much Monkey Business," Big Joe Turner's "Honey Hush," and Tony Joe White's "Polk Salad Annie" as if he wrote the tunes himself, filtering them though his own eclectic influences. There aren't many artists who sound as comfortable blowing through the surf instrumental "Wipeout," then immediately nuzzling up to Maria Muldaur as a duet partner on the following track with a bluesy cover of Slim Harpo's "Raining in My Heart," but LaBeef makes it seem simple and natural. At 65, he's refined his unique approach, which he's been honing for the past 40 years, but that doesn't mean there aren't surprises here. Even when the singer tackles hoary fare like "Will the Circle Be Unbroken," it seems fresh and inspired. Obscure covers from Hank Williams ("The Blues Come Around,") and Ernest Tubb (the title track) show LaBeef's depth of knowledge from his sources, and place him as one of the most talented and under-recognized interpreters of traditional C&W…and blues…and rock & roll. Sleepy LaBeef may not do it all, but he does a lot and, most importantly, on *Tomorrow Never Comes* he makes it look easy. —*Hal Horowitz*

Rockabilly Blues / Jan. 23, 2001 / Bullseye Blues ✦✦✦
Although it's comprised entirely of previously unissued studio material predominantly recorded in 1980 and 1981 that didn't make the first cut on his Rounder albums, there's nothing second-rate about this compilation. The big man with the droopy eyes from Sun records sounds equally inspired on upbeat bluesy rearrangements of tracks rescued from the vault, such as Jimmy Reed's "Bright Lights, Big City," the roof-raising Little Richard cover "Long Tall Sally," and the album closing "Rip It Up." Sure, these chestnuts have been recorded thousands of times, but LaBeef tears into them with enthusiasm and passion, adding fresh nuances and a creative approach. Even Hank Williams' "Fool About You," where Buddy Spicher's fiddle injects a backwoods feel, is augmented by LaBeef's meaty twang guitar and gutsy vocals. His rearranged "Mannish Boy" maintains the classic song's energy but runs it through a swampy rhythm, transforming it into a chugging locomotive. Like Sun's stable of artists, in particular one Elvis Presley, LaBeef sees little difference between rockabilly, country, and blues. It's in the way he incorporates and combines those genres through that deep baritone and skittering guitar that makes him unique. Not just for fans, *Rockabilly Blues* is as good an introduction to Sleepy LaBeef's charms as any of his other albums. A bit more rockin' and bluesy than most of his stuff, only the album's abbreviated 37-minute length is disappointing about this rollicking, infectious disc. Roots rock & roll at its finest. *—Hal Horowitz*

Jimmy LaFave

b. 1955
Guitar, Vocals / Singer/Songwriter, Alternative Country, Americana
Austin-based singer/songwriter and guitarist Jimmy LaFave brings a passionate rock & roll energy to his original folk songs, whether he's playing solo or with a band. LaFave grew up in Wills Point, east of Dallas, but at 17, his family moved to Stillwater, OK. When he was in his teens, his mother purchased his first guitar for him with green stamps. While Stillwater was not exactly bustling with musical activity, it wasn't a ghost town either, and it was close enough to Tulsa that LaFave found all the opportunities he was seeking as a young singer/songwriter. The musical heritage of the area certainly was rich enough: folksinger Woody Guthrie, jazz trumpeter Chet Baker and jazz fiddler Claude "Fiddler" Williams, plus songwriter J.J. Cale and Leon Russell's Shelter Studios. But to find a wider audience, and more importantly, a record deal, LaFave thought it would be worthwhile to move to Austin. He found both after moving to Austin in 1985, and he's been based there ever since.

LaFave found a home in Chicago House, an Austin coffeehouse, and he spent the next eight years hosting open mikes there, honing his presentation skills as a solo artist. Through the latter half of the 1980s, he also worked with his band, Night Tribe, at other Austin clubs. With backing from Mark Shumate, a computer entrepreneur, LaFave was finally able to record his debut for Bohemia Beat Records, a company Shumate founded in 1992. LaFave has released three albums for Bohemia Beat: *Austin Skyline* (1992), his debut, a live recording titled as a play on Bob Dylan's *Nashville Skyline* album; *Highway Trance* (1994), a studio album that showcases his considerable skills as a guitar picker, singer and songwriter; and 1995's *Buffalo Return to the Plains*, which contains just one cover, prime inspiration Bob Dylan's "Sweetheart Like You." LaFave counts among his other influences Jackson Browne, Chuck Berry and Jerry Lee Lewis. LaFave's grass-roots approach should give him a better foundation on which to build a successful career. The way he blends country, blues, folk and early rock & roll, his work ethic and low-key rapport with fans are all factors that work in his favor. *Trail* was issued in 1999; *Texoma* followed in early 2001. *—Richard Skelly*

● **Austin Skyline** / 1992 / Bohemia Beat ✦✦✦✦✦

Highway Trance / 1994 / Bohemia Beat ✦✦✦✦
His plaintive voice embraces his lyrics with the feelings of his heart. His singing and song writing (he wrote all the songs except "Early Summer Rain") evoke the wide open sky of Texas, with the great spaces between people as evident as the stars in the wide-open sky. His tight band keeps the sound moving behind him. He deftly varies the rhythms and song styles so that the album never lets you fall into that "Highway Trance" which he sings of. His lyrics are sharp on the variety of subjects he addresses. Maybe a notch below *Austin Skyline*, but its a small step down, and a big step forward. *—Bob Gottlieb*

Buffalo Return to the Plains / 1995 / Bohemia Beat ✦✦✦✦
This is the third of singer/songwriter Jimmy LaFave's albums, and each one reveals new dimensions. The songs are socially conscious and idealistic without being the least bit melancholy. His voice has that rasp that comes from living near the edge, and is one of his best assets. He can take a ballad and make you feel its pain and sadness; listen to "I'm Thinking of You" and "Never Be Mine." Then listen to the tenderness, joy, and love in "Going Home," the gentleness and caring now in his voice reinforcing the lyrics. Then there are the times he just puts his foot down and rocks out in the Western rhythm that so effectively drives the work of contemporaries like Joe Ely, plus the one who started the West Texas sound, Buddy Holly; take a listen to "That I Can't Control." LaFave's band is only getting tighter and tighter, staying with him at all times, but never hidden behind him; he allows them to step out and show their chops in ways that effectively highlight the songs. *—Bob Gottlieb*

Road Novel / 1997 / Bohemia Beat ✦✦✦✦✦
The raspy warm voice wrapping around his—he wrote or co-wrote 13 of the 15—well-written songs, with real solid playing has become a trademark of this artist, in fact if it weren't so that would be the surprise. It is not necessarily more of what we come to expect from him, but you better understand that as a compliment. This is by far his best songwriting effort, and with the progress he has shown from album to album one can't wait for the next batch of songs. His ballads tear into your heart and mind with their tone nuance, yet they are not soppy, but real life that most can feel because we have worn those boots also. Take a journey into the moods and thoughts of "Into Your Life." Remember that day when you had the same experience, and all the emotions that went with that day. Go right into the infectious "Ramblin Sky" and see if you know "why my feet are tappin'," look down at yours and see what they are doing. Listen to the wondering that goes on during "Long Ago With Miles Between," can you say that those same thoughts haven't run-through your mind, in one form or another? It's not only his songs that he puts it all into, but he also does some fantastic work on Bob Dylan's songs. His musical tone reflects the thoughts and mood tone almost perfectly, so that each builds on the other. *—Bob Gottlieb*

Trail / Feb. 9, 1999 / Bohemia Beat ✦✦✦✦✦
Containing 31 previously unreleased tracks, this two-CD set highlights the past two decades of LaFave's growth both as a songwriter and as a prime interpreter of Dylan material. Here he tackles no less than a dozen of Dylan's classics, ranging from the opening "Positively 4th Street" to "Just Like Tom Thumb's Blues" to the quiet stillness of "If Not for You." Equally as satisfying are LaFave's own originals, with "Red Dirt Roads at Night," "Burden to Bear," "How It Must Remain," "Ellie's Song," "Loved You Like Rainbows" and "The Open Road" all being particularly compelling statements. The sound, taken from live performances and radio broadcasts from Texas and around the world, is rough and right, giving this an official bootleg kind of feel that fits the music nicely. *—Cub Koda*

Texoma / Mar. 13, 2001 / Bohemia Beat ✦✦✦
Jimmy LaFave built his reputation as an interrupter of Dylan songs and as an up-and-coming singer-songwriter from the Austin music scene. On his sixth album, *Texoma*, he is joined by a talented band and some excellent background singers (the Burns Sisters). The material features a number of covers and originals, and ranges from the quiet "Never Is There a Moment" to the slow rocking blues of "Bad Bad Girl." "Woody Guthrie" is a folk-tribute to an idol, with a soulful vocal and some nice dobro by Larry Wilson. There is a fresh take on John Phillips' classic, "San Francisco," and an upbeat "This Glorious Day," a song full of hope and joy. "Elvis Loved His Mama" may remind the listener more of Jerry Lee Lewis than the King, but either way the song works as a quirky, funny homage to the roots of rock & roll. Glancing at other titles like "Rock and Roll Music to the World" and "On the Road to Rock and Roll," one might gather that while LaFave is a clever songwriter, he also enjoys a little straightforward Memphis rock & roll. This roots approach is also given its due when it comes to LaFave's considerable guitar skills. "Emotionally Yours" is the obligatory Dylan song, and it's nice that LaFave chose a less recognized—and less cliché—song from the master. *Texoma* is fine release, filled with good songs, fitting arrangements, and country-soul. LaFave's fans and followers of the Texas country-folk scene should enjoy this one. *—Ronnie Lankford Jr.*

Lambchop

f. 1993, Nashville, TN
Group / Indie Rock, Alternative Country-Rock, Chamber Pop
Touted as "Nashville's most f*cked-up country band" by their label Merge Records, Lambchop was arguably the most consistently brilliant and unique American group to emerge during the 1990s. Their unclassifiable hybrid of country, soul, jazz, and avant-garde noise seemed at one time or another to drink from every conceivable tributary of contemporary music, its baroque beauty all held together by the surreal lyrical wit and droll vocal presence of frontman Kurt Wagner. Although Lambchop's ever-rotating roster would later expand to over a dozen members, the group formed in 1986 as a simple three-piece teaming Wagner, guitarist Jim Watkins, and bassist Marc Trovillion, former high-school classmates already ten years removed from the educational system. Originally dubbed Posterchild, the trio made its earliest recordings in Trovillion's bedroom, self-releasing a series of cassettes with titles like *I'm Fucking Your Daughter*. In time, the lineup began to grow and the band regularly performed live in and around the Nashville area, often at the area record shop, Lucy's (not coincidentally owned by Wagner's wife, Mary).

In 1992, Posterchild—now consisting of Wagner, Trovillion, guitarist Bill Killibrew, clarinetist Jonathan Marx, multi-instrumentalist C. Scott Chase, drummer Steve Goodhue, and percussionist Allen Lowery—released *An Open Fresca + A Moist Towlette*, a split single with friends Crop Circle Hoax. The 7-inch brought the group to the attention of entertainment lawyer George Regis, who issued cease-and-desist orders on behalf of his clients, the noise pop band Poster Children. After rejecting the names REN, Pinnacles of Cream, and Turd Goes Back, the band settled on Lambchop, added vocalist/saxophonist Deanna Varagona, steel guitarist Paul Niehaus, and organist John Delworth, and signed to Merge to release the 1993 single "Nine." Their debut LP *I Hope You're Sitting Down* (aka *Jack's Tulips*) followed a year later. In many ways, this album would be the most conventional Lambchop record. Its Nashville origins and torch-and-twang ambience would saddle the band with the increasingly erroneous alt-country tag, although Wagner's Lou Reed-like vocals and bizarre narrative conceits—in particular the fan-favorite "Soaky in the Pooper," a vivid recounting of a bad LSD trip—immediately signaled their obvious distance from the likes of Uncle Tupelo or the Jayhawks.

The lovely *How I Quit Smoking* appeared in 1996 (although on the subsequent "Cigaretiquette" single, Wagner would proudly announce, "I'm smoking again"). Recorded live the previous Independence Day, the *Hank* EP followed later in 1996. Marking the debut of drummer Paul Burch, the disc represented the apotheosis of Lambchop's Billy Sherrill-inspired phase, its lush production evoking the Nashville sound so popular three decades earlier, but now completely passé among Music City's chart superstars. *Thriller* (1997) proved a major turning point; highlighted by the Muscle Shoals soul of "Your Fucking Sunny Day" and including no fewer than three songs penned by East River Pipe's F. M. Cornog, this sprawling, difficult album introduced the uncompromising eclecticism that would dominate Lambchop's work from here on out. The follow-up, 1998's *What Another Man Spills*, upped the ante further; for remarkably soulful covers of Curtis Mayfield's "Love Song (Give Me Your Love)" and Frederick Knight's "I've Been Lonely for So Long," Wagner's baritone drawl even gave way to a Prince-like falsetto. That same year, the group also backed Vic Chesnutt on his album *The Salesman and Bernadette*.

Lambchop's fifth full-length, *Nixon*, appeared in the spring of 2000. Supposedly a concept album exploring the presidency of the infamous Tricky Dick, Wagner even included a bibliography in the liner notes—a direct connection to the Watergate scandal remains unidentified. Though still criminally unknown at home, Lambchop enjoyed a much more substantial following overseas, and on May 13, 2000, they appeared at the London Royal Festival Hall; the gig was recorded and made available at U.K. appearances that fall as *The Queens Royal Trimma* limited-edition EP. (A 2001 European tour yielded the *Treasure Chest of the Enemy* EP.) In addition to Lambchop, several members of the group pursued side projects. Burch led his own band, the WPA Ballclub, Varagona released a fine 2000 solo record, *Tangled Messages*, and Mark Nevers led CYOD. Wagner even teamed with Josh Rouse for the 1999 EP *Chester*. The 2001 collection *Tools in the Dryer* assembled many of Lambchop's scattered singles, compilation tracks, and remixes. *—Jason Ankeny*

I Hope You're Sitting Down [aka Jack's Tulips] / Sep. 1994 / Merge ✦✦✦
A mix of post-modernism and straight (not roots) country music. The spooky organ fills, saxes, clarinets, and cello make this sound at times like the Art Ensemble of Chicago-as-country-band. Kurt Wagner's morose, resigned lyrics and dry, almost spoken delivery can get hard to take over the course of the hour-plus disc. "Soaker in the Pooper," a song about suicide in the bathroom, gave Wagner almost instant notoriety, and many of the other songs deal with similarly downbeat matters, although usually not as directly. *—Richie Unterberger*

Hank / 1996 / Merge ✦✦✦✦
In hindsight, the seven-track *Hank* EP would seem to herald the conclusion of Lambchop's "straight" country period—assuming, of course, that songs with titles like "Poor Bastard" and "I Sucked My Boss' Dick" could ever be considered pure country in the first place. The impossibly lush production which buoys tracks like "I'm a Stranger Here" and the gorgeous "Blame It on the Brunettes" screams Billy Sherrill, however, and the melancholia which permeates the disc is the stuff of which endless nights in smoky honky tonks are made; ultimately, in their own singularly bizarre way, Lambchop has made what might just fly in under the radar as a classic country record, provided no one listens too closely. Of course, with the subsequent *Thriller*, they produced the most dissonant and difficult album of their career, kissing fame and fortune goodbye forever. Nashville's loss, not ours. *—Jason Ankeny*

● **How I Quit Smoking** / Jan. 30, 1996 / Merge ✦✦✦✦✦
Bona fide string arrangements give Lambchop's second album a much more "authentic" Nashville country feel than the first—meaning, ironically, that it sometimes sounds as gloppy, sentimental, and superficial as "real" Nashville country records. The arrangements are more inventive as well, mixing conventional country instruments like steel and acoustic guitars with saxes, clarinet, cornet, banjo, tin whistle, and more, along with the same kind of off-center organ featured on the first album. Wagner continues to mine the same offbeat lyrical territory, though unlike other audio *vérité* talents like (say) Lou Reed, he doesn't bring much passion to his inner monologues. *—Richie Unterberger*

Thriller / Sep. 23, 1997 / Merge ✦✦✦✦
Following in the tradition of the brilliant "Cigaretiquette" single, which immediately preceded it, *Thriller* moves Lambchop sharply away from their signature alt-countrypolitan sound, pushing instead toward a punchier, noisier aesthetic; borrowing its title from the best-selling album of all time and devoting no less than three of its eight tracks to East River Pipe covers, it's a strange, difficult record likely to baffle even the group's most devoted fans. Opening with the surreal doo wop of "My Face Your Ass" and then sliding into the oddly funky "Your Fucking Sunny Day," which comes complete with a Muscle Shoals-styled horn section, the record defies expectations at every turn; almost completely abandoning the string-laden, Nashville sound-influenced approach of earlier efforts, *Thriller* is dark and dissonant, with an edgy, menacing lyrical slant to match. Not everything here works, but the album's sheer audacity alone makes it well worth a listen, again confirming Lambchop's status among the most consistently weird and fascinating bands around. *—Jason Ankeny*

What Another Man Spills / Sep. 8, 1998 / Merge ✦✦✦✦✦
It's a safe bet to expect the unexpected in regards to any new Lambchop effort, but the cryptically titled (and beautifully packaged) *What Another Man Spills* is the band's most consistently surprising and deliriously eclectic outing to date, with new twists around every corner. While it's their loveliest record since *How I Quit Smoking*, that album's countrypolitan gauze is largely a thing of the past, replaced here by a dreamy, jazz-like patina which proves a remarkably versatile backdrop not only for Kurt Wagner's originals but for a vast range of covers, from Dump's "It's Not Alright" to Curtis Mayfield's "Give Me Your Love (Love Song)." The latter is easily the most jaw-dropping track on *What Another Man Spills*, with the group easily slipping into the song's soulful groove without a hint of irony, not even in Wagner's amazingly Prince-like falsetto; a later cover of the Frederick Knight smash "I've Been Lonely for So Long," while less surprising, is no less engaging, further solidifying Lambchop's growing debt to the Stax/Volt sound. Where the album's jumble of styles and offbeat covers might seem self-indulgent coming from any other band, Lambchop somehow makes it all work with their wit, style, and intelligence intact—even five records in, they never cease to amaze. *—Jason Ankeny*

Nixon / 2000 / Merge ✦✦✦
As time went on, Lambchop got a little more musically accomplished, and Kurt Wagner more inclined to write songs that were a little less of a stream-of-consciousness jumble, and a little less random. This will still strike most as a mighty odd record, though. Ostensibly much of this record was inspired by former president Richard Nixon (there is even a suggested reading list of Nixon-related books on the sleeve). But there are no direct references to him, and even any indirect ones are so oblique that you'd never make the connection if the record had a different title (or contained no reading list). Wagner's songs are less of a laundry list of bringdown imagery and a tad more direct than in the past, but still suggestive of, well, the kind of voices and snatches of conversation a schizophrenic might hear and utter. The music? Yes, another incongruous clash of lush orchestrated countrypolitan music and alternative singer-songwriter rock, but the Philadelphia/'70s soul influences are pretty upfront on some tracks. Wagner even adopts a thin, breaking soul falsetto on "What Else Could It Be?" that sounds as much like a satire as an homage. There are some inventive, hard-to-identify, eerie reverberant effects on several tracks, adding a sense of atmosphere even if they're not particularly complementary to the songs or melodies. All of this contributes to the sensation of hearing a radio stuck between a 1990s alternative college station and a 1970s oldies one, without the static. There's still the sense that it's an in-joke outsiders will have a hard time puzzling through, even if it's more approachable than some of Lambchop's previous outings. *—Richie Unterberger*

Tools in the Dryer: A Rarities Compilation / Sep. 18, 2001 / Merge ✦✦✦✦
The Nashville-based Lambchop "is and has been" almost two-dozen different members with a discography that boasts something like 23 cassettes, singles, EPs, and full-lengths, as well as numerous one-off appearances on compilations, best-of collections, and the like. It's fairly safe to say, then, that *Tools in the Dryer*—unlike most odds-and-ends collections—isn't entirely uncalled for. In fact, for fans of the prolific band, a collection of 16 "A-sides, B-sides, live tracks, and remixes" is downright appreciated. Spanning 1987 to 2000 and compiled by member Jonathan Marx, the excellent *Tools in the Dryer* is a consistently enjoyable—though anything but comprehensive—collection that includes everything from the Vic Chesnutt-penned "Miss Prissy" to disorienting dance remixes and demos recorded before the band even officially formed. Newcomers to the quirky, countrified world of Lambchop should start with *Nixon* or *How I Quit Smoking*, but die-hard fans should dive right into this trip through the band's memory lane of musical miscellany. *—Jimmy Draper*

Is a Woman / Feb. 19, 2002 / Merge ✦✦✦✦
Many of the attributes that numerous alternative listeners have found endearing or annoying about Lambchop remain on this, the band's sixth album. There's the fragmented, sometimes mundane subject matter of Kurt Wagner's lyrics, his dry sing-speak voice, and an overall air of resignation that blurs the line between contentment and containment. *Is a Woman* has to rank as one of the group's better efforts, though, primarily since the coyness that could lead to aggravating pretensions has been muted, almost to the point of absence. It's also fair to say that, at this point, Lambchop was no longer an alt-country act. Perhaps there's still a touch of countrypolitan to the subdued songs and languorous tempos. But the effect is rather more like that of an arty lounge singer, with the deft piano, rich vibes, and occasional science fiction-like guitar effects. Wagner sounds something like an alternate-universe Randy Newman, not nearly as concise or direct in his imagery, but possessed of similar weary, reflective Americana. By focusing less on quotidian (i.e., boring) experiences of the proletariat and more on less-tangible allusions to death, troubled romance, and loneliness, Wagner's music is simply more approachable and meaningful, if still hard to puzzle out in its specific intent. Too, the sound is much more consistent from cut to cut than it has been on past Lambchop albums, with enough inventive tinges of soul and jazz to leaven the super-somber after-hours ethos. This is still way too idiosyncratic for mass digestion, but it's a definite positive artistic progression. *—Richie Unterberger*

Cristy Lane (Eleanor Johnston)

b. Jan. 8, 1940, Peoria, IL
Vocals / Country-Pop, CCM, Inspirational
Cristy Lane is best remembered for her 1979 single "One Day at a Time," a gospel song that blended Protestant fervor with the language of self-help in a seamless, heartfelt whole. She is also noteworthy as one of the builders of the Branson, MO, live-entertainment phenomenon. Lane was born Eleanor Johnston to a family of 12 in Peoria, IL. Married before she was 20, she had three children by 1964. Her husband, Lee Stoller, a salesman, encouraged her to sing professionally, but she was painfully shy. After some tentative attempts, she landed several nightclub appearances and then a guest slot on Chicago's WLS *Barn Dance* radio program in 1968. She took her stage name from that of a Peoria DJ, Chris Lane.

Several early attempts to break into country music in Nashville came to nothing, and Lane struggled with the pressures of the performing career her husband was urging upon her. She attempted to commit suicide twice in the late '60s, once after a difficult 1969 tour of Vietnam, organized by Stoller during which Lane performed 120 shows and was involved in a helicopter crash that left her stranded in the midst of a battle. Lane and Stoller returned to Peoria and opened a pair of nightclubs that featured Lane as the marquee attraction. In 1972, the Stoller family moved to a Nashville suburb and continued its attempts to get Lane's career off the ground. The reaction from established label executives ranged from indifference to sexual come-ons for Lane, and finally Stoller formed his own label, LS, in the mid-'70s. He was tireless in promoting Lane's career, and his efforts were rewarded when the label's debut single, "Tryin' to Forget About You," and its follow-up, "Sweet Deceiver," made the charts in 1977.

That year she also made it to the Top Ten and the Top 20 with "Let Me Down Easy" and "Shake Me, I Rattle," respectively. Lane scored three more hits the following year and in 1979 was named New Vocalist of the Year by the Academy of Country Music. During the awards ceremony Lane sang "I Just Can't Stay Married to You," which later became a Top Five hit. In late 1979, Lane was signed to United Artists Records and had three more hits. But the label balked at releasing the song Lane and Stoller had planned for their next single, "One Day at a Time." That song was a several-years-old entry from Kris Kristofferson's catalog of compositions; co-written with Nashville veteran Marijohn Wilkin, it was of a piece with other religious songs (such as "Why Me, Lord?") the hard-living Kristofferson had written in soberer moments. Shortly before Lane's version appeared, the song had topped British charts in a version by vocalist Lena Martell. For country radio in 1980, it was an unorthodox song, but Lane and Stoller correctly estimated its powerful impact. After it hit number one on the country charts, Lane released "Sweet Sexy Eyes," her final Top Ten hit.

Her career hit the skids temporarily when Stoller was imprisoned on racketeering charges in 1982, but the couple bounced back after Stoller observed the spectacular success yodeler-crooner Slim Whitman had experienced after beginning direct television marketing of his music. By 1986 Lane and Stoller had put together a strong pair of linked materials: a *One Day at a Time* album and a Lane autobiography of the same name. Marketed through television advertising and later on the World Wide Web, these items sold well for years and kept Lane's name before a demographic just waiting to be tapped: that of country fans in late middle age. As Branson began to emerge as a major entertainment destination in the late '80s and early '90s, Lane and Stoller jumped on the bandwagon. Their Cristy Lane Theatre became a major Branson attraction, hosting not only Lane's own performances but also early appearances by Branson stars-to-be such as Yakov Smirnoff (in 1992). Lane sold her Branson theater in the mid-'90s but remained active as a performer. She has recorded several albums of gospel and sentimental standards for marketing through her website and elsewhere. Plans were laid in the early 2000s for a film depicting Lane's life story. *—James Manheim*

One Day at a Time / 1978 / Cema Special Markets ♦♦♦♦♦

Love Lies / 1979 / LS ♦♦♦♦

Before "One Day at a Time" and "Footprints in the Sand" propelled Cristy Lane toward a career in contemporary Christian music, she made a moderately successful string of cheating and divorce songs for the country audience. Her bright, chipper sound and country-pop style on the 1978 album *Love Lies* is a little more toward the country side than Barbara Mandrell's "Crackers," and her voice has a sweet girl-next-door quality that lends character to the otherwise sterile production. "Sweet Deceiver" was a minor hit, but the album's standout is "Somebody's Baby," a song written by Lane's husband and manager, Lee Stoller, that should have been issued as a single. The Top Five divorce song "I Just Can't Stay Married to You" was Lane's biggest hit after "One Day at a Time" but was omitted from her first greatest-hits album in an apparent attempt to sanitize her image for her large Christian following. Fans of Lane's early country recordings will agree that *Love Lies* ranks among her best efforts. *—Greg Adams*

● **Footprints in the Sand** / 1983 / Liberty ♦♦♦♦♦

Because of the strong selection of songs and consistent performances, this compilation is the one to get out of the several Lane discs available from Arrival. *—Stephen Thomas Erlewine*

Amazing Grace, Vol. 2 / 1986 / Arrival/K-Tel ♦♦♦

This is a solid, if unspectacular, set of popular gospel tunes that are nicely performed by Lane, even if she is occasionally dominated by an intrusive synthesizer. *—Stephen Thomas Erlewine*

All in His Hands / 1989 / Heartwarming ♦♦♦

20 Greatest Hits / 1991 / TeeVee ♦♦♦♦

My Best to You / 1992 / Arrival/K-Tel ♦♦♦

Here is a good compilation of some of Lane's most popular gospel material, which is somewhat undermined by the number of tracks duplicated from *Footprints in the Sand*. *—Stephen Thomas Erlewine*

k.d. lang

b. Nov. 2, 1961, Consort, Alberta, Canada

Vocals / Adult Alternative Pop/Rock, Alternative Country, Neo-Traditionalist Country

When k.d. lang released her first major-label album in 1987, she caused considerable controversy within the traditional world of country music. With her vaguely campy approach, androgynous appearance, and edgy, rock-inflected music, very few observers knew what to make of her or her music, although no one questioned her considerable vocal talents. That confusion never quite dissipated over the course of her career, even when she abandoned country music for torchy adult contemporary pop in 1992 with her fourth album, *Ingenue*.

Born in Alberta, Canada, lang was first drawn toward music while she was in college. In particular, she was attracted to the music of Patsy Cline. She became acquainted with Cline's music while she was preparing to star in a collegiate theatrical production based on the vocalist's life. Soon, lang immersed herself within Cline's life and music and decided that she would pursue a career as a professional singer. With the help of guitarist/co-songwriter Ben Mink, she formed a band, named the Reclines in tribute to Patsy Cline, in 1983, and they recorded a debut album, *Friday Dance Promenade*, which received some positive notices in independent papers. A follow-up album, *A Truly Western Experience*, was released in 1984 and received even better reviews and led to national attention. In 1985, lang was named the Most Promising Female Vocalist by the Juno Awards.

All of the Canadian attention led to the interest of a number of American record labels. Sire signed lang in early 1986, and she recorded her first record for the label later that year. The result, *Angel With a Lariat*, was produced by Dave Edmunds and appeared in the fall of 1986. The mix of '50s-styled ballads, kitschy rockabilly, and honky tonk numbers on *Angel With a Lariat* received good reviews, especially from rock critics. The album had heavy support from college radio as well as cutting-edge country stations. Though it was a mainstream hit in Canada and an underground smash in the U.S., Nashville resisted lang, especially her tongue-in-cheek concert appearances. As she was recording her second Nashville album in 1987, lang duetted with Roy Orbison on his old hit "Crying," which was recorded for the film *Hiding Out*. The single was released at the end of the year and was hit, marking her first appearance on the country charts.

Shadowland, her second Sire album, made her debt to Patsy Cline explicit. Recorded with Cline's producer, Owen Bradley, the album lacked the campy humor of *Angel With a Lariat*, which helped it succeed in traditional country circles—"I'm Down to My Last Cigarette," the first single from the record, was her first to break the country Top 40. *Shadowland* became a sizable word-of-mouth hit, both in modern country and alternative music circles, which led to it going gold. The following year lang released the harder-edged *Absolute Torch and Twang*, which increased her mainstream American country audience, in addition to being a college radio and Canadian hit. lang won a Grammy—Best Country Vocal Performance, Female—for the album in 1989, and "Full Moon of Love" became a Top 25 hit in the summer of 1989. The attention made lang a minor celebrity, which meant that when she launched a protest against meat eating in 1990, it became a media sensation.

Before the release of her fourth album, lang declared that she was a lesbian in an interview in *The Advocate*, which could have been a risky proposition, since Nashville's industry was notorious for not accepting people that fell outside of the margins of the mainstream. However, the new album was not a country album. *Ingenue* was a set of adult contemporary pop that owed very little to country. Its first single, "Constant Craving," became a Top 40 American hit and won the Grammy Award for Best Pop Vocal Performance, Female, leading the album to platinum status in America, Britain, and Australia; it went double platinum in Canada.

Ingenue won lang a new audience, but she didn't immediately produce a follow-up to the album. Instead, her next recorded work was the largely instrumental soundtrack for Gus Van Zant's film adaptation of Tom Robbins' *Even Cowgirls Get the Blues* in 1993; the soundtrack was actually released several months before the before the film. It wasn't until 1995 that lang delivered *All You Can Eat*, her full-fledged follow-up to *Ingenue*. *All You Can Eat* continued the pop direction of its predecessor, showing no traces of country. The album didn't enjoy the mass commercial acceptance of *Ingenue*, but it was a moderate success, proving that she had a dedicated cult following. Subsequent efforts include 1997's *Drag* and 2000's *Invincible Summer*. *—Stephen Thomas Erlewine*

Friday Dance Promenade / 1983 / Bumstead ♦♦

A Truly Western Experience / 1984 / Bumstead ♦♦♦

k.d. lang's first independent album is an uneven but exciting revamp of '50s country. She alternates between rocking honky tonk numbers and Patsy Cline-influenced weepers, sometimes assuming an ironic distance. It may be flawed, but *A Truly Western Experience* has an almost punky kick and illustrates why lang would soon be considered as the freshest female vocalist in country music in the late '80s. *—Stephen Thomas Erlewine*

Angel With a Lariat / 1987 / Sire ♦♦♦

k.d. lang's first major-label album (and debut American release) was a bit of a switch from the polished retro-country of her best known work; with Dave Edmunds in the producer's chair, *Angel With a Lariat* often sounds more like rockabilly or roots rock than classic C&W, with a big, snappy drum sound, plenty of guitars mixed upfront, and lots of slapback of lang's vocals (a production decision lang mentioned with little enthusiasm several years after the album came out). "Turn Me Around" and "High Time for a Detour" rock significantly harder than most of lang's body of work, and "Watch Your Step Polka," "Diet of Strange Places," and "Tune Into My Wave" find lang and her band (who are in fine form throughout) indulging her sly sense of humor, which tended to get lost in the shuffle on later albums such as *Ingenue*. While the production and arrangements tend not to focus on the subtleties of lang's voice (with the exception of the weepy closer, "Three Cigarettes in an Ashtray"), she's one heck of a belter on this set, with a set of pipes as big as all outdoors. And the cover of the old Lynn Anderson chestnut "Rose Garden" actually tops the original. Fast, fresh, and funny, *Angel With a Lariat* may not be k.d. lang's best album, but it's probably the best one to put on at a party—it's got a good beat, and you can dance to it. *—Mark Deming*

☆ **Shadowland** / 1988 / Sire ♦♦♦♦♦

k.d. lang is not an ordinary country singer: Born in Canada, she has neither the pedigree nor the charisma of the average female country star. By 1988, she had only released one original album, and it was commercially unsuccessful. Despite the long odds against her, she had not escaped the notice of Owen Bradley, a veteran Nashville producer who had worked with the likes of Loretta Lynn, Brenda Lee, and Patsy Cline. In fact, lang brought Bradley out of retirement with *Shadowland*, and it's easy to understand why he was eager to work with her. lang's wonderful voice is showcased throughout the album, as she sings cover tunes that remain true to the originals while receiving her indelible vocal stamp. The versatility of her voice allows her to tackle heartache ballads ("Lock, Stock and Teardrops") and playful tunes ("Don't Let the Stars Get in Your Eyes") with equal effectiveness. This album also reveals lang's connection to the past and her genuine affection for Owen Bradley—their friendship and collaboration clearly paved the way for her breakthrough album *Ingenue*, released a few years later. Although this is an album of country standards, the production and arrangements (which include strings) indicate her shift toward a more polished pop sound. An excellent introduction to her early music. *—Vik Iyengar*

★ **Absolute Torch and Twang** / 1989 / Sire ♦♦♦♦♦

Absolute Torch and Twang was the last bona fide country album of k.d. lang's career (as of this writing), and while external circumstances may have forced her hand in exploring other musical avenues, this set suggests she may have already been headed that way. *Absolute Torch and Twang* is the definitive statement of lang's country period; by this time, she'd moved past the slightly kitschy Patsy Cline homages of her earliest work and developed a strong musical personality of her own, using her rich and supple voice to approach material both witty and heartfelt. Lang's collaboration with producer and songwriter Ben Mink was reaching its peak as well, with the performances and arrangements hitting a superb grace note between polish and passion. Lang's songwriting had matured, most notably on "Nowhere to Stand," a powerful number about child abuse, and she'd developed a knack for writing about misfits, both defiant and otherwise; as a Canadian Lesbian vegetarian performance artist trying to work within mainstream country music, you have to know her heart was with the heroines of "Big Boned Gal" and "Wallflower Waltz." And while lang had embraced vintage countrypolitan sounds on *Shadowland*, *Absolute Torch and Twang* found her bridging a gap between Cline-style balladry and polished lounge styles on "Trail of Broken Hearts" and "Pullin' Back the Reins," and finding a comfortable home in the middle ground. While some fans were disappointed when lang retreated from country music on her next album, *Ingenue*, it's hard to imagine her (or anyone else) topping an album quite as strong as *Absolute Torch and Twang.* —*Mark Deming*

Ingenue / 1992 / Sire ✦✦✦✦

Canada's angel with a lariat has chucked the spurs for *Ingenue* in favor of a classic, Tin Pan Alley pop approach. lang's turnaround is a great success. *Ingenue* is an achingly beautiful work, all melancholy longing and heartbreak that strikes a perfect balance between the pain and pleasure of love. To stake out her own individual territory somewhere between Patsy Cline and Billie Holiday without relying on pop standards is a feat in itself. The ten original compositions allow full reign to lang's spectacularly expressive voice. One misses the sense of humor and playful spirit that has infused lang's music in the past, but that can wait until next time 'round when she's recovered from whatever major personal crisis served as inspiration for *Ingenue*. For now, listen and weep. —*Roch Parisien*

All You Can Eat / Oct. 10, 1995 / Sire ✦✦✦✦

k.d. lang followed through on the promise of her adult contemporary changeover *Ingenue* with *All You Can Eat*. A more experimental and realized record than its predecessor, there are more daring production touches on *All You Can Eat*—it's clear that she has been listening to contemporary pop, not just torch songs. It isn't immediately accessible—the production is low-key, the melodies are gentle and subtle (although her cutesy, tongue-in-cheek song titles suggest otherwise), and lang gives a nuanced, sophisticated performance. Though it lacks a standout song like the aching "Constant Craving," *All You Can Eat* has a more consistent set of songs and, given time, is a more rewarding listen. —*Stephen Thomas Erlewine*

Drag / Jun. 10, 1997 / Warner Bros. ✦✦✦

Returning, however tentatively, to the torch stylings that made *Ingenue* her most successful album, k.d. lang crafted an odd commercial comeback with *Drag*. A collection of covers that are somehow related to smoking, *Drag* is by far more ambitious than the average cover record. She recasts Steve Miller's "The Joker" and the Hollies' "The Air That I Breathe" as slow, bluesy cabaret numbers, while traditional '50s pop like "Don't Smoke in Bed" and "Smoke Rings" act as seductive counterpoints. lang's rich voice and the measured arrangements make *Drag* a ringer for *Ingenue* in places, but the tone is considerably lighter and more humorous, which certainly makes it an enjoyable listen. Nevertheless, the very presence of a tongue-in-cheek, all-covers tribute to smoking is a little disheartening in the wake of the wonderful, if severely underappreciated, *All You Can Eat*, which found lang pushing herself forward. *Drag*, in comparison, can't help but sound like a retreat. —*Stephen Thomas Erlewine*

Invincible Summer / Jun. 20, 2000 / Warner Bros. ✦✦✦

The k.d. lang who played tribute to Patsy Cline in her band the Reclines seems a millennium away from the smooth, pop-infused chanteuse on this album. Glowing with happiness and lovey bliss, this lush album is dripping with the kind of bright, slick production that hasn't seen much light since the Brill Building's heyday. Swelling strings, electronic bubbles and warbles, and the occasional mandolin combine to create a sound that manages to evoke a warm feeling of nostalgia without sounding retro. Topping it all off is lang's smooth-as-maple-syrup voice, which shows even greater range than before, occasionally issuing the bell-like tones more often heard from fellow Canadians Jane Siberry and Sarah McLachlan. If there is a fault to this album, it is that it is too smooth; while the listener is surfing these waves of happiness and cushiony pop, an occasional desire for edges and bones surfaces. While "The Consequences of Falling," "Love's Great Ocean," and "Simple" are all fine songs, this recording also lacks the kind of hooky, knockout singles that have been featured on her best albums. —*Stacia Proefrock*

Live By Request / Aug. 14, 2001 / Warner Bros. ✦✦✦

Live By Request is a series of occasional television specials broadcast on the A&E cable network, conceived by Tony Bennett's son and manager Danny Bennett. It works well for musical artists with loyal followings and established catalogs who may no longer be at the forefront of the record industry but are anxious to promote new albums. Viewers and fellow celebrities call in carefully screened requests that allow the performers to revisit their old favorites and mix in some new ones. k.d. Lang was a good choice for such a show, and here she becomes the first artist to use the *Live By Request* rubric for a corresponding album. Lang usually makes concept albums with distinctive themes that can be quite different from each other stylistically and, of course, she moved toward an adult contemporary pop sound after beginning her career as a country singer, so her discography sometimes seems to be all over the map. By mixing songs from her different albums here, she is able to demonstrate the similarities in them, suggesting that the apparent diversity in her music is not as extreme as it might have seemed. Also, never having released a compilation, she compresses her catalog into an excellent introduction here. All that's missing is another important aspect of the *Live By Request* shows—the spontaneous personal interaction they tend to provide between artist and audience. Lang just goes from one song to another on the disc, never saying anything more elaborate than "Thank you so much" in between. No requests from fans are heard, no comments by the singer. In that sense, the album is just a straightforward (and somewhat cut and dried) live album, with none of the special flavor of the TV show. —*William Ruhlmann*

Roy Lanham

b. Jan. 16, 1923, Corbin, KY

Guitar / Rock & Roll, Traditional Country, Cowboy, Country-Pop, Rockabilly, Instrumental Country

Although known primarily as guitarist for the Sons of the Pioneers from 1961 through 1986, Roy Lanham also led the Whippoorwills for many years and performed as a solo

artist, recording albums of country-jazz guitar instrumentals under his own name in the late '50s and early '60s. Despite his relative obscurity, Lanham is often esteemed on the level of such well-known guitar greats as Chet Atkins and Merle Travis. Lanham was born in Corbin, KY, on January 16, 1923, and picked up the guitar at an early age. Beginning as a teenager he found radio work as a rhythm guitarist in a number of instrumental combos, one of which was eventually hired by pop vocalist Gene Austin and renamed the Whippoorwills. In this group Lanham functioned as lead guitarist, performing in a jazzy style influenced by Charlie Christian and Django Reinhardt but distinguished by his development of a four-part harmony chord technique he would alternate with single-string figures.

In 1943 Lanham joined Cincinnati's WLW, a 50,000-watt station that allowed him the opportunity to work with King Records, for which he soon performed regularly as a session guitarist, appearing on recordings by Hank Penny and the Delmore Brothers, among others. After participating in one Chet Atkins session in 1946 for the Bullet label, Lanham moved to Dayton and re-formed the Whippoorwills. For the next few years the combo toured, recorded transcriptions for Smiley Burnette's radio show in Hollywood and collaborated with Merle Travis on six sides for Capitol in the early '50s. It was during his tenure with Smiley Burnette's show that Lanham first met the Sons of the Pioneers, who invited the Whippoorwills to fill in for them on their radio show while the Sons were on tour. Lanham found additional session work recording separately with Johnny and Dorsey Burnette as well as Johnny Horton, Jim Reeves, Bonnie Guitar, the Browns, and the Fleetwoods, in addition to recording singles under his own name and with the Whippoorwills. The success of the Fleetwoods singles on which he appeared led to his recording of a solo LP in 1959 and the sole Whippoorwills album, *Sizzling Strings*, later that year. —*Greg Adams*

● **Sizzling Strings/The Fabulous Guitar** / 1996 / Bear Family ✦✦✦✦

Sizzling Strings is a 1959 instrumental album from Lanham's group, the Whippoorwills, and *The Fabulous Guitar* is his 1961 solo album. This two-fer collects both albums on one CD, and the sonic and stylistic differences between the two are slight. Both are heavily oriented toward instrumental versions of pop hits and jazz tunes with mellow guitar leads that emphasize melody over virtuosic display. In fact, compositions by such cowhands as Stan Kenton, Artie Shaw, and Benny Goodman far outnumber country songs. Only "Air Mail Special" and the Delmore Brothers' "Sand Mountain Boogie" work up a fret-happy steam, and the remainder provides pleasant, if not jaw-dropping evidence of Lanham's guitar mastery. Listeners looking for guitar wizardry may not immediately appreciate Lanham's subtlety, but fans of instrumental music bordering on easy listening may enjoy these jazzy, laid-back takes on such chestnuts as "Tea for Two" and "In the Mood." —*Greg Adams*

The Hard Life Blues: Standard Transcriptions / Oct. 24, 2000 / Soundies ✦✦✦✦

Before becoming a successful session guitarist and longtime member of the Sons of the Pioneers, Roy Lanham led his own variety act, the Whippoorwills. A top-notch instrumental and vocal combo, the Whipps covered everything from Western swing to pop and jazz, as well as virtuoso instrumentals that showcased Lanham's unique guitar stylings. *Hard Life Blues* collects 31 recordings for the Standard Transcription Service from 1950 and, because the group made few commercial recordings, is a rare document of their vocal sound. Occasionally compared to the Modernaires, the Whippoorwills managed to create a distinct musical personality despite their rampant diversity. No other release better demonstrates the range of Lanham's talents as guitarist, songwriter, and arranger. —*Greg Adams*

Nicolette Larson

b. Jul. 17, 1952, Helena, MT, d. Dec. 16, 1997

Guitar, Percussion, Vocals / Country-Rock, Country-Pop, Soft Rock, Urban Cowboy

After working as a backup vocalist for several country-rock acts and serving as a member of Commander Cody's Lost Planet Airmen for several years during the mid-'70s, vocalist Nicolette Larson launched a solo career in the late '70s. Initially, Larson followed the sound of laid-back Californian country-rock, which resulted in a Top Ten pop hit in 1979 with "Lotta Love." In the years following the success of "Lotta Love," Larson continued to mine the soft rock California sound, eventually leaving it behind for country music in the mid-'80s. During the course of the '80s, she racked up a number of country hits before moving into semi-retirement.

Born in Montana, Nicolette Larson and her family eventually settled in Kansas City. Following her high-school graduation, she moved out to San Francisco, where she began working on the Golden Gate Country/Bluegrass Festival. While she was working the festival, she met a number of musicians, who were all impressed by her voice and encouraged her to pursue a professional musical career. Larson followed their advice, joining David Nichtern & the Nocturnes, playing clubs around the Bay Area. Eventually, she came to the attention of Commander Cody & the Lost Planet Airmen, who invited her to sing on their 1975 album, *Tales From the Ozone*. Following its release, Larson toured with the band, and over the next three years, she sang on two of the group's albums—*Rock 'n' Roll Again* and *Flying Dreams*—in addition to touring with the band.

Around the same time as she began singing with Commander Cody, Larson moved to Los Angeles, where she began singing as a studio musician. Over the next four years, she appeared on numerous albums by country and rock musicians, including records by Neil Young, Linda Ronstadt, Hoyt Axton, Guy Clark, Jesse Winchester, Emmylou Harris, Jesse Colin Young, John Stewart, the Doobie Brothers, Rodney Crowell, and Graham Nash. In 1978, she signed a record contract with Warner Bros., releasing her first single, a cover of Young's "Lotta Love," at the end of the year. "Lotta Love" became a huge hit, reaching number eight on the pop charts, helping to send her debut album, *Nicolette*, into gold status. Though *Nicolette* and "Lotta Love" were hits right out of the box, she wasn't able to replicate her success, as "Rhumba Girl" stalled at number 47, which also happened to be the peak chart position of her second album, *In the Nick of Time*. The album did spawn a hit with the Top 40 "Let Me Go, Love," a duet with Michael McDonald, but her third album, *Radioland* (1980), was largely ignored.

Following one other attempt at pop success with 1982's *All Dressed Up & No Place to Go* and the single "I Only Want to Be With You," Larson retreated from the mainstream and starred in the country musical *Pump Boys and Dinettes*. Larson received positive reviews for her performance, which led to a record contract with MCA in 1983. On the basis of her performance, the Academy of Country Music named her the Best New Female Vocalist in 1984, even though she had yet to have any country hits. Larson finally released a country album in 1985 with *... Say When*, but the record didn't live up to its hype. Though it was critically acclaimed, the album was far from a commercial success, with only one single, "Only Love Will Make It Right," reaching the Top 50, yet the record was strong enough for *Cash Box* to name Larson the Best New Female Vocalist of the year.

Larson finally broke into the country charts in 1986 when "That's How You Know When Love's Right," a duet with Steve Wariner, climbed into the Top Ten and stayed in the charts for five months. "That's How You Know When Love's Right" was drawn from *Rose of My Heart*, which performed respectably. However, Larson didn't choose to follow the album up with another country record. In 1987, she recorded an album, *Shadows of Love*, in Italy, and in the next year, she began pursuing an acting career. In 1988, she appeared on *Family Reunion*, a black gospel television show and the Arnold Schwarzenegger/Danny DeVito comedy *Twins*, as well as the television series *Throb*. During the early '90s, she began touring with singers Valerie Carter and Lauren Wood, and the trio went on a USO tour. In 1994, she released a children's album titled *Sleep Baby Sleep*. Larson died on December 16, 1997. *—Stephen Thomas Erlewine*

Nicolette / 1978 / Warner Bros. ✦✦✦✦

Nicolette Larson first came to public attention when she backed up Neil Young on his *American Stars 'n Bars* disc. She went on to duet with him on his much anticipated *Comes a Time* album, which was the genesis for *Nicolette*. Using an even wider-ranging style than friends Linda Ronstadt or Emmylou Harris, Larson hit it big right out of the starting gate with Young's "Lotta Love," a super Top Ten smash. From there, she broadens her approach to include a soulful "You Send Me," the Louvin Bros' "Angels Rejoiced," Motown's "Baby, Don't Do It," and a hard-rockin' "Can't Get Away From You." No matter which genre she aspired to, she seemed to have the chops to do a fine job. *Nicolette* was a surprise for many when it first came out and is still a pleasure to listen to today. After this, her first effort, the sky was the limit for Larson. *—James Chrispell*

In the Nick of Time / 1979 / Warner Bros. ✦✦✦

In the Nick of Time was much more highly polished than Nicolette Larson's first effort. Here, Nicolette Larson is backed up by a crack team of L.A. studio musicians, and the results are sort of mixed. True, she doesn't suffer from the dreaded sophomore jinx that plagues so many first hit artists, but *In the Nick of Time* doesn't have that wow-charm that Larson did. Her styles have broadened even more here to include '40s dance tunes alongside Motown surefire hits and '50s rockin'. While nothing here grabs the listener's attention, there is plenty of fine listening in store. Larson even co-wrote the title cut and was helped out by such stellar friends as Karla Bonoff and Michael McDonald, who duets with her on his own "Let Me Go, Love," which comes off as an almost too slick cut for the listener to grab hold of. Culled from the late '70s Hollywood slick machine, *In the Nick of Time* could use a little dirt to help make it all sound just a bit more real. *—James Chrispell*

Live at the Roxy / 1979 / Warner Bros. ✦✦

Radioland / 1980 / Warner Bros. ✦✦✦

Larson's third Warner Bros. album, reissued on CD in Germany but not in the U.S., is a bold, melodic collection of midtempo country-inspired pop-rock. Her voice isn't always strong or rich enough to sustain interest in which she's singing, but the diversity of sounds, including one great Allen Toussaint number ("Tears, Tears and More Tears") holds the interest. The remastering is adequate but not especially impressive. *—Bruce Eder*

All Dressed Up & No Place to Go / 1982 / Warner Bros. ✦✦✦

Nicolette Larson's final album for Warner Bros., *All Dressed Up & No Place to Go*, got her a fair amount of airplay and TV exposure, thanks to her hit version of "I Only Want to Be With You"—a fairly daring move, considering that the Bay City Rollers had also charted with it as a single not too many years before. Larson's version is sparked by some pleasing guitar ornamentation by Andrew Gold and some achingly beautiful backing vocal flourishes on the fade, and only the '80s drumming sound dates it today. She attempted to make the jump from country singer to pop diva here, especially on "Just Say I Love You" and "I'll Fly Away (Without You)," and somehow it didn't take. The album isn't as strong as it might've been, and part of the problem involves the production, which mixes '80s-style electric drumming with country-pop sounds. Another, albeit minor weakness, involves Larson's own songwriting on "I Want You So Bad," which comes off as filler next to numbers like Lowell George's "Two Trains"—a true highlight of this record. [Reissued on CD as a European import in the late '90s.] *—Bruce Eder*

... Say When / 1985 / MCA ✦✦

Rose of My Heart / 1986 / MCA ✦✦

Sleep, Baby, Sleep / 1994 / Sony ✦✦✦✦

● **The Very Best of Nicolette Larson** / Aug. 17, 1999 / Rhino ✦✦✦✦

Nicolette Larson was a staple of California pop and soft rock in the '70s, not only as a solo artist, but as a backing vocalist for artists as diverse as Commander Cody & His Lost Planet Airmen, the Nitty Gritty Dirt Band, Van Halen, and Neil Young. As a matter of fact, Young gave Larson her breakthrough hit, "Lotta Love." The song turned out to be the peak of her popularity, climbing into the Top Ten in early 1979. She never had that kind of widespread popularity again, even if she had a few smaller pop hits to her credit, along with some success on the country charts. The charts may have changed, but the music really didn't—she always walked the line separating country-pop and Californian soft rock. Throughout it all, her sweet voice was continually engaging, even when she worked with material that wasn't always convincing. That much is evident from Rhino's definitive retrospective, *The Very Best of Nicolette Larson*. Spanning her entire solo career, from her 1978 debut to her 1994 children's album, the 16-song collection contains all the major highlights, but its momentum sort of sags toward the end of the disc, as her material grew weaker and her productions became too clean. Nevertheless, this is an accurate portrait of her career. If *The Very Best Of* isn't quite as cohesive as her first few albums, so be it—it charts the ups and downs of her career quite well, and in doing so, it offers a definitive, warts-and-all summary. *—Stephen Thomas Erlewine*

Jim Lauderdale

b. Apr. 11, 1957, Statesville, NC

Songwriter, Vocals / Singer-Songwriter, Neo-Traditionalist Country, Americana, Traditional Country, Honky Tonk

Singer-songwriter Jim Lauderdale helped lay out the blueprint for the Americana movement of the '90s, earning high critical marks for an eclectic series of albums that spanned hard country, slick pop, rootsy rock & roll, blues, folk, R&B, and bluegrass. He never sold that many records on his own, but his compositions were recorded—often with considerable success—by a number of contemporary country stars, including George Strait, Patty Loveless, Vince Gill, Mark Chesnutt, Kathy Mattea, and George Jones, among others. Lauderdale was born in Statesville, NC, in 1957 and grew up loving country music; however, he was also drawn to the theater and later moved to New York, where he landed roles in two national touring productions. He subsequently settled in Los Angeles, where he began playing the now-legendary alt-country hot spot the Palomino Club. With Dwight Yoakam producer Pete Anderson behind the boards, he recorded a track for the seminal compilation *A Town South of Bakersfield*, which helped him—briefly—land a record deal with CBS. He completed an album in 1989, but the label declined to release it; it finally appeared over ten years later on an overseas label as *Point of No Return*.

Undaunted, Lauderdale signed with the Bluewater music publishing firm in Nashville, where his compositions found immediate success in the contemporary country world. Additionally, he sang backup on records by Yoakam, Lucinda Williams, and Rosie Flores and toured with everyone from Freedy Johnston, Nick Lowe, and Hootie & the Blowfish to Johnny Cash and Merle Haggard. He earned another shot with Reprise and issued his debut album, *Planet of Love*, in 1991, with production from Rodney Crowell and John Leventhal. The album was greeted with strong reviews by many critics, who hailed Lauderdale as a major new talent. Still, it would be three years before he would release another record; he returned in 1994, now on Atlantic, and issued two acclaimed albums over the next two years in *Pretty Close to the Truth* and *Every Second Counts*.

In 1996, he moved over to roots label Rounder's Upstart subsidiary for *Persimmons*, yet another critical success. Hopping to BNA, Lauderdale released *Whisper* in 1998, then returned to the majors on RCA, issuing the somewhat slicker-sounding, more commercial *Onward Through It All* in 1999. That same year, Lauderdale also took a detour into traditional bluegrass, recording the collaborative album *I Feel Like Singing Today* with the legendary Ralph Stanley for Rebel. Lauderdale finally found a more permanent home on Dualtone and debuted with 2000's *The Other Sessions*, a return to hardcore country. Two projects arrived in 2002: another album with Stanley, called *Lost in the Lonesome Pines*, and a country record called *The Hummingbirds*. *—Steve Huey*

Planet of Love / 1991 / Reprise ✦✦✦✦✦

Jim Lauderdale's *Planet of Love* is one of the most auspicious debuts a singer-songwriter could release. While Lauderdale had been on the scene for quite a while hanging on the West Coast—where his actual first album was recorded by Columbia and never released—he spent most of his time (and still does) writing songs for other acts. *Planet of Love* is one of the first records of the new country. It has modern adult contemporary sensibilities built into its production by the once and future husbands of Rosanne Cash, Rodney Crowell, and John Leventhal, solid country singing from Lauderdale—who was raised in North Carolina—and country songs that are so mercurial they seem to defy the genre. In many ways, *Planet of Love* is the '90s version (post-cocaine) of outlaw country. It may not fit any one place stylistically, but Crowell and Leventhal had long been pushing at country radio's boundaries, and *Planet of Love* is truly the first Americana and adult alternative record to land. Reprise had no idea how to market it, and though it sold acceptably and was reviewed very favorably, it was a blip on the screen. That doesn't mean it's not a classic. Lauderdale's songwriting, especially when paired with Leventhal, is flawless: there's enough rock, enough country, enough striking pop hooks, and killer bridges to make any music fan swoon. (It also doesn't hurt that Lauderdale is an amazing vocalist who has sung with the cream of country's crop.) The hard rural edge in Lauderdale's voice is inescapable, but it was in Elvis' too. The ten songs here are interchangeable in terms of excellence but the slick, rockabilly-tinged "Heaven's Flame," and "Maybe" with its Traveling Wilburys' shuffle, are mind blowers to open a record with. Likewise, the honky tonkin' "I Wasn't Fooling Around" has all the marks of being inspired by Faron Young, though it's thoroughly postmodern; but in Lauderdale's voice it could be sung by either George Jones or Bono! The track "Bless Her Heart" proves that he can sing a ballad as well. This is heartbreaking without sentimentality. The emotion in it is one of honesty, confessional shame and spine-breaking regret. (The chorus of backing vocalists that includes Shawn Colvin is also noteworthy.) Emmylou Harris made her first, though certainly not last appearance on a Lauderdale record doing a stunning (what else?) harmony vocal on "The King of Broken Hearts," echoing both Merle Haggard and Gram Parsons. The last two cuts are the bluesy rocker "What You Don't Know" with a Howlin' Wolf moan at the end of each line in the refrain, and the Everly Brothers-inspired "My Last Request," with a chilling harmony vocal by Crowell. If any record from the 1990s deserves to be reissued, it's this one. It's a masterpiece top to bottom and broke open the floodgates for the Americana format in that decade, while kicking off an eclectic but consistently interesting recording career. *—Thom Jurek*

● **Pretty Close to the Truth** / 1994 / Atlantic ✦✦✦✦✦

Jim Lauderdale did his share of label hopping in the 1990s, recording for Reprise and RCA, as well as Upstart/Rounder. Released in 1994, *Pretty Close to the Truth* was the first of two albums he provided for Atlantic. Some might wonder why an artist who was talented enough to write songs for the likes of Patty Loveless and George Strait did so much label hopping, and it came down to the fact that—from a commercial standpoint—he had too much integrity for his own good. Sure, Lauderdale could have taken the easy way out and tried to become just another radio-oriented Garth Brooks clone, but if he had done that, *Pretty Close to the Truth* would not have been half as interesting and heartfelt as it is. This CD isn't easy to categorize; is it Americana, roots rock, alternative country-rock? However you describe it, *Pretty Close to the Truth* is a diverse, unpredictable effort that draws on influences ranging from Merle Haggard to the Rolling Stones to classic soul. While the title song has a strong Stones influence and "This Is the Big Time" would not be out of place on a Dwight Yoakam album, the soul-minded "Why Do I Love You?" isn't unlike something Al Green would have recorded in the early '70s—take away the steel guitar and add a Memphis-style horn section, and you can easily imagine Green recording "Why Do I Love You?" for one of his Hi albums. In a perfect world, this album would have been a favorite at country radio. But, in 1994, Lauderdale was determined to do things his own way, and while that free-spirited attitude can frighten marketing people and radio programmers, it makes for a lot of first-class listening on *Pretty Close to the Truth*. *—Alex Henderson*

Every Second Counts / Sep. 5, 1995 / Atlantic ✦✦✦

Jim Lauderdale has had success by writing songs others have had hits with. Jim Lauderdale has been favorably compared to the late Gram Parsons. Jim Lauderdale sounds an awful lot like a tame Rodney Crowell. Jim Lauderdale is playing it safe when he releases albums such as *Every Second Counts*. Jim Lauderdale should be more famous than he is. Either all, some, or none of the above are true. If you want to find out which statement is which, seek out a copy of *Every Second Counts* and find out for yourself. It's as simple as that. You will not be disappointed. *—James Chrispell*

Persimmons / Sep. 3, 1996 / Upstart ✦✦✦✦

Persimmons continues Jim Lauderdale's string of excellent albums. Though it isn't any different than his previous solo albums—it still is a down-to-earth fusion of roots music from soul to blues, all tied together by a basic country songwriting template—what impresses is Lauderdale's consistency and imaginative songwriting. Though he uses the same ingredients every time out of the gates, he puts enough of an original spin on his rockers and ballads, giving them slight melodic or lyrical twists which make *Persimmons* more rewarding with each listen. *—Thom Owens*

Whisper / Feb. 10, 1998 / BNA ✦✦✦✦

Whisper, Jim Lauderdale's major-label debut, continues to expand on the singer/songwriter's slightly modernized version of the classic, traditional country sound. In addition to his own compositions, Lauderdale gets songwriting help from Harlan Howard, Melba Montgomery, and Frank Dycus. *—Steve Huey*

Onward Through It All / Aug. 10, 1999 / RCA ✦✦✦

It may be a little streamlined and polished, especially when compared to his previous releases, but *Onward Through It All* is another reminder of why Jim Lauderdale is considered one of the finest songwriters in Nashville. Even his lesser material is classy, well-crafted and sturdy, which may be why it's a little disappointing that much of this album is designed for radio play. Then again, he deserves some success on his own terms—and that's why it's hard to be angered by the creeping slickness, since not only should he be heard by a wider audience, it doesn't distract from the fine craft behind the music. *—Stephen Thomas Erlewine*

I Feel Like Singing Today / Aug. 31, 1999 / Rebel ✦✦✦

North Carolina native Jim Lauderdale is well-known in Nashville as a proficient songwriter and an excellent performer in his own right. This album finds Lauderdale taking a shot a bluegrass music. He even wrote or co-authored nine of the 15 tunes on the CD, including two of them with former Grateful Dead songwriter Robert Hunter. He also had the good sense to throw in with Ralph Stanley & the Clinch Mountain Boys, one of the premier bluegrass/mountain music bands in the world. This is a unique project for Lauderdale. The fact that he succeeds so thoroughly is due not only to his eminent songwriting chops but also because he has obviously learned his bluegrass lessons very well over the years. Given that anyone who can sing will sound like a veteran bluegrasser if they're singing with Ralph Stanley, it's still remarkable how convincingly Lauderdale has slipped into this genre. *—Philip Van Vleck*

The Other Sessions / 2000 / Dualtone ✦✦✦✦

When Jim Lauderdale issued his 1991 masterpiece *Planet of Love*, the critics were falling all over themselves proclaiming him the king of progressive country who was ushering in the era of Americana. He wrote songs for everyone from Kathy Mattea to the glorious Patty Loveless to the two Georges: Jones and Strait. Ten years later, Lauderdale's made almost as many records of all kinds of music, from rootsy rock to slick, funked-up country to a bluegrass album with Ralph Stanley. All of them had their moments, and most of them were good, but until now he's never issued a record as pure and solid as *The Other Sessions*. It's a 12-pack of hardcore, honky tonk country songs written in the tradition of Merle Haggard, Hank Thompson, Bobby Bare, and Del Reeves. And it should, since 11 of the 12 tunes were co-written with country stalwarts like Reeves, Harlan Howard, Melba Montgomery, Kostas, and Clay Blaker. But it doesn't end with the songs. The musicians on this set read like a who's who of contemporary music—country and otherwise. There's Billy Bremner from Rockpile, pedal steel god Bucky Baxter, Stan Lynch from Tom Petty & the Heartbreakers, Reese Winans, Tammy Rodgers, Roy Huskey Jr., Pat Buchanan—and that's not even half of the musicians involved. The quality lies in Lauderdale's delivery as both a singer and a visionary. He takes hard country songs, plays them the hard country way, and makes them sound as contemporary as the latest Nelly record. There isn't a fusion or crossover bone in the guy's body, but he can make any rock & roll fan fall head over heels for these tracks. The best stuff here—the truck rock anthem "Diesel, Diesel, Diesel," the wine-swilling "Honky Tonk Haze," and the deep, down-in-the-flesh love song "Just to Get to You," co-written with Montgomery—will be covered by others but never with as much raw gumption and swagger. This is the country record Elvis Presley could never have made though he wanted to, and it's the rock record Haggard's been trying make since the '80s. None of the alt-country, "americorna" kids can touch this because it's not about riffs and postures, it's about craft and vision. *The Other Sessions* is one of the finest hard country records to be issued since the 1960s. Period. It's also the new watermark by which Lauderdale has to judge himself. Forget Americana—this is country music. *—Thom Jurek*

Point of No Return: The Unreleased 1989 Album / Apr. 10, 2001 / WestSide ✦✦✦

Lost in the Lonesome Pines / May 7, 2002 / Dualtone ✦✦✦✦

Songwriter and vocalist Jim Lauderdale's second pairing with bluegrass legend Ralph Stanley retains much of the vitality of 1999's *I Feel Like Singing Today*, and if anything, the duo seems to have become more comfortable working together on *Lost in the Lonesome Pines*. One can only imagine the jitters Lauderdale must have felt working in the studio with one of American music's true treasures, so the hints of apprehension revealed in the cracks of the earlier album have been brushed away, and the two sound like old pals sitting on a sunlit porch trading songs and licks. The gruff sentimentality in Lauderdale's lead vocals provide the perfect canvas for Ralph Stanley's high lonesome tenor to color, echoing the close harmonies of the Stanley Brothers from 50 years earlier. In many ways, this album is reminiscent of the spectacular collaboration between Steve Earle and Del McCoury on *The Mountain*; both albums paired a respected maverick singer-songwriter with a legendary bluegrass figure, and the results on both are not quite bluegrass and not quite contemporary folk, but both feel just about right. *—Zac Johnson*

The Hummingbirds / May 7, 2002 / Dualtone ✦✦✦✦

A consummate Nashville songwriter, Jim Lauderdale has penned hits for folks like George Strait and Patty Loveless over the years, but he has long been underappreciated as a solo artist. One of Lauderdale's songwriting strengths is to craft seemingly simple tunes set around smart but not excessively clever lyrics, and several songs here serve as excellent case studies. On "Morning," he uses the start of the day as a metaphor to gently suggest the possibilities life holds that often slip by "as the afternoon pulls you away." The twangy, jazz-flavored "It's a Trap" utilizes the games cats and mice play to discuss human relationships. The title track, one of the disc's crowning glories, uses hummingbird imagery in a story of love renewed. Lauderdale's voice, while perhaps not slick enough for music row, is full of character and warmth. He can give a suitably rough edge to rocking honky tonk numbers like "There and Back Again" and "Rollin' the Dice," while also projecting a poignancy in the bittersweet ballads "I'm Happiest When I'm Moving" and "I Know Better Now." The disc's bluegrass-flavored closing cut, "New Cascade," creates a natural segue to his Ralph Stanley collaboration, *Lost in the Lonesome Pines*, an album released simultaneously with *The Hummingbirds*. The song also highlights Lauderdale's hillbilly roots and demonstrates how he effortlessly synthesizes them into a more country-pop sound. It wouldn't be surprising if more than a tune or two off this stellar effort were recorded by other artists (Kelly Willis has already covered "I Know Better Now"), but Lauderdale deserves to have his splendid original renditions recognized and enjoyed for their own impressive merits. *—Michael Berick*

Wait 'Til Spring / 2003 / Skycrunch ✦✦✦

It's difficult to pigeonhole musicians like John Lauderdale. He's been called "country," but that seems more of a convenient label than an accurate description of his talent. Lauderdale, after all, recorded an album with Ralph Stanley in 2000, and joined with Donna the Buffalo in 2003 for *Wait 'Til Spring*. Country singers, after all, don't make a habit of associating with jam bands (imagine Merle Haggard recording with the Grateful Dead). The combination, however, works remarkably well here. Lauderdale obviously wanted a sonic twist to his homegrown songs, and Donna the Buffalo obliges. The six-piece band, in fact, has a bewildering arsenal of instruments, ranging from fiddle, accordion, electric guitars, and an organ, and also helps out on background vocals. Lauderdale delivers a lovely, soulful vocal on "Ginger Peach," while Jim Miller and Jeb Puryear's guitar work lovingly underlines the melody. The upbeat, reggae flavored "Sapphire" seems custom-made for serious dancing, and "This World Is Getting Mean" cuts a bit deeper than the average country song. Interestingly, Donna the Buffalo's work here, sandwiched between Lauderdale's three and four minutes songs, seems more focused than usual. Both artists take a leap of faith on *Wait 'Til Spring* and come up with a finely executed album that should please fans on both sides of the aisle. *—Ronnie D. Lankford Jr.*

Tracy Lawrence

b. Jan. 27, 1968, Atlanta, TX

Vocals / Contemporary Country, New Traditionalist

Part of the commercial rise of rock-tinged honky tonk in the early '90s, Tracy Lawrence was one of the decade's most reliable country hitmakers. Born in Atlanta, TX, in 1968, he grew up mostly in Foreman, AR, where he soaked up traditional and outlaw country as well as Southern rock. He started performing in public when he was 15 and was a regular presence on the local honky tonk circuit by 17. After college, he moved to Nashville in 1990 and worked day jobs while winning numerous talent shows. That led to a live radio performance and, in 1991, a showcase gig that netted him a deal with Atlantic. In May 1991, just prior to the scheduled release of Lawrence's debut album, he was walking a girlfriend back to her hotel room when the two were mugged by several gun-wielding attackers. Lawrence fought back to allow his companion time to escape and was shot four times; two bullets only grazed him, but one had to be surgically removed from his knee, and the other remained deeply embedded in his pelvis. Fortunately, he progressed rapidly through physical therapy, and the album, *Sticks and Stones*, was released later in the year when Lawrence could return to promotional duties. Its lead single, the title track, went all the way to number one on the country charts, helped out by all the publicity.

More hits followed in the Top Tens "Runnin' Behind," "Today's Lonely Fool," and "Somebody Paints the Wall," and Lawrence was on his way to stardom. He arrived there with *Alibis*, the platinum-selling 1993 follow-up that produced an astounding four chart-topping singles: the title track, "Can't Break It to My Heart," "My Second Home," and "If the Good Die Young." In 1994, Lawrence contributed the Top Ten hit "Renegades, Rebels and Rogues" to the soundtrack of the movie version of *Maverick* and also released his third album, *I See It Now*. "Texas Tornado" became his sixth number-one hit, and three more singles—the title track, "As Any Fool Can See," and "If the World Had a Front Porch"—all went to number two. Somewhat lost in all the success was Lawrence's arrest that same year on a weapons charge, but it didn't slow his career momentum at all. He tossed off the *Live and Unplugged* set in 1995, which compiled acoustic tracks and concert performances with his backing band, Little Elvis. In 1996, he returned with the proper follow-up album *Time Marches On*. The title track was a huge hit, topping the country charts, and "If You Love Me," "Stars Over Texas," and "Is That a Tear" all went Top Five.

His hit streak continued with 1997's *The Coast Is Clear*, which contained two more Top Five singles in the title track and "Better Man, Better Off." However, all was not well behind the scenes. In January 1998, Lawrence was convicted on charges stemming from an incident in which his wife accused him of hitting and threatening her; the couple soon divorced. Lawrence laid low for a while, putting his life back together, and returned in 2000 with the uneven but highly personal *Lessons Learned*. The title track was a Top Five smash, but it was the only major hit from the record, and Lawrence soon parted ways with Atlantic. He subsequently signed with Warner Bros. and debuted for them in 2001 with an album titled simply *Tracy Lawrence*. Despite some good reviews, it failed to halt his downward commercial momentum. —*Steve Huey*

Sticks and Stones / 1991 / Atlantic ✦✦✦

Lawrence's first two chart-toppers, "Sticks and Stones" and "Today's Lonely Fool," are included on this debut outing. —*Jason Ankeny*

Alibis / 1993 / Atlantic ✦✦✦✦

While not as consistent as his debut *Sticks and Stones*, Lawrence's strong baritone is still well-served on *Alibis*. —*Jason Ankeny*

I See It Now / Sep. 20, 1994 / Atlantic ✦✦✦✦

Live and Unplugged / Sep. 19, 1995 / Atlantic ✦✦

Time Marches On / Jan. 23, 1996 / Atlantic ✦✦✦

Tracy Lawrence's *Time Marches On*, the singer's fourth album, is another crowd-pleasing set of contemporary country. Like his previous albums, the song selection is a hit-or-miss affair, with about half of the songs failing to make much of an impression. The remainder, however, proves why Lawrence is one of the most popular singers in Nashville. —*Stephen Thomas Erlewine*

The Coast is Clear / Mar. 18, 1997 / Atlantic ✦✦✦✦

The Coast is Clear again demonstrates that Tracy Lawrence was one of the finest new honky tonkers of the '90s. Lawrence can wring tremendous emotion out of a song, adding nuances that give each line heart-tugging resonance. Unfortunately, his material is not the equal of his skills. Although there are bright spots, such as "Livin' in Black and White," about half of the record is saddled with pedestrian material performed without style. Try as he may, Lawrence cannot bring material of this level to life. Still, *The Coast Is Clear* remains a winning record, since Lawrence sings well no matter what the material, and when he is given a good song, the results are first-rate. —*Thom Owens*

● **The Best of Tracy Lawrence** / Sep. 1, 1998 / Atlantic ✦✦✦✦

Lessons Learned / Feb. 1, 2000 / Atlantic ✦✦✦

Given the three years separating it from its predecessor, it's a little disappointing that *Lessons Learned* isn't a little livelier, or at least a little different from his previous records. It's not. It's not bad, however. Lawrence sticks with the polished, modern-day honky tonk that made him a star, toning down the rough edges and adding gloss to the surface. That means the record heavily favors ballads, and even the peppier material is midtempo. The most exciting it gets is "Up All Night," a credible, mild-spirited rocker, graced by a moment of genius when the music stops and Lawrence sings "I Been Up, I Been Up, I Been Up" in mesmerizing cadence. In other words, it's a well-crafted, adult album. How that plays is a matter of taste. Strictly speaking, this isn't really a straight-up country record, but it's hardly the country-pop of Shania Twain either. It falls between the two extremes, borrowing the form of hardcore country, but the sound and attitude of country-pop. This isn't out of character for Lawrence, but it's a little surprising just how measured *Lessons Learned* is. It's certainly pleasant, yet it tends to fade into the background. It doesn't help that the material is, by and large, not particularly distinguished. A few tunes jump out, and there's nothing bad here, but there's nothing particularly noteworthy. It's the kind of record only a veteran could produce: accomplished, professional, and modestly—yet only mildly—entertaining. —*Stephen Thomas Erlewine*

Tracy Lawrence / Oct. 23, 2001 / Warner Bros. ✦✦✦✦

There's a reason why Tracy Lawrence is on his ninth studio release, and a listen to the honky-tonk good album opener "Crawlin' Again" off his self-titled release reminds listeners why. Here, Lawrence's simple and lighthearted approach to addressing heartache is a refreshing and sorely needed touch in contemporary music—country and otherwise. Look at these lyrics: "It takes a mama 20 years to make a boy a man/and another woman 20 seconds to have him crawlin' again." "Lawrence" wrote two sentences to describe what musicians fill four-minutes worth of song to express. Then there's the twangy and laid-back title track, where Lawrence, with no trickery or Shakespearean prose, expresses one of people's most fundamental desires: to live well, fully and simply. "Sit down in the porch

swing/sip a little ice tea/play with the kids in the yard/it's time to get lazy/had enough crazy/life ain't gotta be so hard." You can't top that. Lawrence's ability to plainly and vividly portray life's moments is sheer artistry. This is best evidenced on "What a Memory," an ode to a mother-son relationship that could make a steer cry. Musically speaking, this set is noticeably more scaled down—simple guitar lines, 4/4 rhythms, and vocals—compared to Lawrence's past efforts. His minimalist musical style is in winning tandem with his delightfully direct and honest approach to songwriting. Together, you couldn't ask for more abundant fare. *Tracy Lawrence* is simply a great, *real* piece of work. It restores faith in jaded audiences who believe music has degenerated into one huge bucket of cookie-cutter swill. Less is so much more sometimes, and if artists can pull this off successfully, as Lawrence does here, God bless them. —*Liana Jonas*

Doyle Lawson

b. Apr. 20, 1944, Kingsport, TN
Mandolin, Vocals / Traditional Bluegrass, Country Gospel
One of the top mandolin players in bluegrass music since the early days of his career in the 1960s, Doyle Lawson incorporated traditional gospel quartet singing into his music after forming his own band, Quicksilver, and honed his unique bluegrass-gospel sound to a remarkable intensity. Lawson was born in unincorporated Ford Town, TN, near Kingsport. Several members of his family sang in local gospel quartets, but the Lawsons also listened to the *Grand Ole Opry* on the radio during the years when Bill Monroe was creating the music that took the name of bluegrass. Monroe inspired young Lawson to take up music and to learn the mandolin. He borrowed his first one at age 11 from a member of his father's gospel quartet and eventually taught himself the five-string banjo and guitar as well. In 1963, Lawson began playing banjo with Jimmy Martin & the Sunny Mountain Boys. He moved to Kentucky and played with various groups before joining J. D. Crowe & the Kentucky Mountain Boys in 1966, first on guitar and then on mandolin. Lawson made his recording debut with Red Allen on the album *Bluegrass Holiday* and temporarily returned to Martin's band in 1969 but otherwise stayed with Crowe until 1971 and recorded two albums with him.

In 1971, Lawson joined the Country Gentlemen and toured Japan with them the following year. He remained with the Country Gentlemen for eight years, recording ten albums with the band. Lawson also recorded an album of mandolin instrumentals, *Tennessee Dream*, in 1977; the album also featured Crowe, Jerry Douglas, and Kenny Baker. In 1979, he put Quicksilver together, including banjo player Terry Baucom, guitarist Jimmy Haley, and electric bass player Lou Reid. In 1980, Quicksilver released its eponymous debut album and followed it up with *Rock My Soul*.

In 1981, *Quicksilver Rides Again*, featuring Douglas, Mike Auldridge, and Sam Bush, came out. The group also released a gospel album, *Heavenly Treasures*, which sold better than the group's initial secular LPs, and Lawson himself proclaimed in 1985 that he had rededicated his life to Jesus Christ. Lawson's next album, *Once and for Always*, appeared that year and featured both bluegrass and gospel tunes. In 1986, Lawson recorded the all-gospel *Beyond the Shadows* with new players Scott Vestal on banjo, Curtis Vestal on electric bass, and Russell Moore on guitar, and the following year brought the first of several a cappella gospel albums, *Heaven's Joy Awaits*. Lawson & Quicksilver gained a reputation for razor-sharp gospel harmonies that incorporated virtuosic vocal moves drawn from the African-American gospel tradition as well as from white quartet singing (some of it already rooted in black styles). Lawson recruited new members into Quicksilver but maintained consistency in the group's style.

Continuing to record mostly gospel music, Lawson explored styles and presentation modes of the past in such albums as *Gospel Radio Gems* (1998), which was recorded with only a single microphone. Several of the 1980s Doyle Lawson & Quicksilver LPs were re-released in pairs on CD in the late '90s by the group's longtime label, Sugar Hill. Lawson resurfaced with the new gospel albums *Just Over in Heaven* and *Gospel Parade* in the early 2000s, and in 2002 Lawson released the masterly *Hard Game of Love*, his first secular disc in some years. He bounced back from coronary problems later that year and continued to perform. Married and the father of three children, Lawson is the long-time host of his own Doyle Lawson & Quicksilver bluegrass festival in Denton, NC. —*James Manheim*

Tennessee Dream / 1977 / County ✦✦✦

Doyle Lawson & Quicksilver / 1980 / Sugar Hill ✦✦✦✦✦

Quicksilver Rides Again / 1981 / Sugar Hill ✦✦✦✦✦

Heavenly Treasures / 1981 / Sugar Hill ✦✦✦

This is one of the earliest all-gospel recordings by Doyle Lawson with Quicksilver, the band he formed after leaving the Country Gentlemen in the late '70s. You can hear hints of his future direction all over this album: ornate a cappella quartet arrangements alternating with driving bluegrass settings, the willingness to cross stylistic boundaries (note the pedal steel on "Too Much to Gain to Lose"), an obvious admiration for African-American gospel traditions ("Jezebel"). All of these elements would be further refined in future projects, and the fact is that as powerful as this album is, there are flaws that would gradually be eliminated as Quicksilver's personnel shifted and coalesced over the following 20 years. The lead voice on "Too Much to Gain to Lose" is a bit off, for example—not something Lawson would stand for just a few years later. All in all, this is a worthy gospel album, but not quite up to Lawson's highest standards. —*Rick Anderson*

Rock My Soul / 1981 / Sugar Hill ✦✦✦✦

Rock My Soul is the first gospel album that Doyle Lawson recorded and it's a wonderful record of simple, graceful beauty. The key to the success of *Rock My Soul* is that Lawson has opened up bluegrass-gospel by incorporating elements of country and Southern gospel, which made it accessible to a wider audience. —*Thom Owens*

Once and for Always / 1985 / Sugar Hill ✦✦

The News Is Out / 1987 / Sugar Hill ✦✦✦

I'll Wander Back Someday / 1988 / Sugar Hill ✦✦✦
Relying primarily on traditional songs and standards, *I'll Wander Back Someday* is another excellent effort from Doyle Lawson and Quicksilver, highlighting the group's innovative vocal arrangements and acumen for driving, straight-edged instrumental support. *—Thom Owens*

Heaven's Joy Awaits / 1988 / Sugar Hill ✦✦

Hymn Time in the Country / 1988 / Sugar Hill ✦✦✦
Doyle Lawson & Quicksilver's *Hymn Time in the Country* is an excellent contemporary bluegrass-gospel album. Though there's a couple of weak tracks—it would have been nice to hear "John the Revelator" with a full instrumental accompaniment, the album has enough terrific harmonies and spirit to satisfy both traditional bluegrass fans and contemporary Christian fans. *—Rodney Batdorf*

I Heard the Angels Singing / 1989 / Sugar Hill ✦✦✦
Lawson returns to gospel on *I Heard the Angels Singing*, which features his rendition of Carl Jackson's "The Little Mountain Church House." *—Jason Ankeny*

My Heart Is Yours / 1990 / Sugar Hill ✦✦✦✦✦

The Gospel Collection 1 / 1990 / Sugar Hill ✦✦✦✦✦
Gospel Collection, Vol. 1 contains 13 tracks that Doyle Lawson & Quicksilver released on their earliest albums, as well as two previously unreleased songs, all of which that demonstrate that Lawson's talent for modernizing bluegrass-gospel was unparalleled in his era. *—Thom Owens*

Pressing on Regardless / 1992 / Brentwood ✦✦✦
Pressing on Regardless is one of Lawson and Quicksilver's occasional secular recordings, released in tandem with the gospel record *Treasures Money Can't Buy*. *—Jason Ankeny*

Treasures Money Can't Buy / 1992 / Brentwood ✦✦✦
The all-gospel *Treasures Money Can't Buy* features "Just a Little Talk With Jesus" and "Buckle of the Bible Belt." *—Jason Ankeny*

Never Walk Away / 1995 / Sugar Hill ✦✦✦✦✦
This album is crystal clear from the first notes of the Buck Owens tune "Rosie Jones" to the end of "Ancient History." It is a tight ensemble album where the instrumental playing is all the more impressive for being excellent but not showy. Strong songs include "Jealous," "In the Gravel Yard" and "Your Crazy Heart." There's nothing groundbreaking here, just a solid rootsy bluegrass band album, and that's not bad. *—Richard Meyer*

Doyle Lawson with Bobby Hicks & Jerry Douglas / Nov. 17, 1995 / Koch ✦✦✦✦

There's a Light Guiding Me / Feb. 20, 1996 / Sugar Hill ✦✦✦✦
Doyle Lawson & Quicksilver are among bluegrass music's most heavenly harmonizers, as they prove once again on the timeless music featured in *There's a Light Guiding Me*. Largely a cappella and completely focused on spirituals, these songs will fill the soul with warmth. No matter what one believes, this music—just like that of spiritual singers from Tibet, Hungary, Pakistan, or Cambodia—strikes a resonant chord deep within. *—Michael McCall*

Kept & Protected / May 20, 1997 / Sugar Hill ✦✦✦✦✦
Doyle Lawson's band Quicksilver has long been known as a launching pad for young bluegrass musicians—you could almost call the group a farm team if it wasn't so consistently of major-league quality. The lineup on this all-gospel album features singers and multi-instrumentalists Dale Perry and Barry Scott, both of whom would remain with Quicksilver for longer than most and would, with guitarist and singer Jamie Dailey, form the nucleus of what may be Lawson's finest band. *Kept & Protected* finds the group sticking mainly to straight-ahead bluegrass-gospel, performing such standards as "I Have Found the Way" and "The Glory Land Way," but also expanding into gospel styles that draw explicitly on other traditions. "My Lord Is Writing All the Time" is a funky a cappella quartet piece that harks back to the African-American gospel groups that Lawson heard throughout his childhood, while "You Are My Hiding Place," with its solfege introduction, refers to the shape note hymn singing tradition even as it employs a fruitier, more modern chord progression. This is a rich and varied program that stands easily with the best of Lawson's work. *—Rick Anderson*

Gospel Radio Gems / Jun. 16, 1998 / Sugar Hill ✦✦✦✦

Original Band / Feb. 16, 1999 / Sugar Hill ✦✦✦✦
What has always set Doyle Lawson's groups apart from other progressive bluegrass outfits is their equal focus on both vocal and instrumental virtuosity. Where colleagues like the Country Gentlemen, the Seldom Scene, and the New Grass Revival tended to emphasize unusual repertoire and instrumental pyrotechnics, Lawson's band, even with its kaleidoscopically shifting membership, has always maintained a consistent dual focus on fiery playing and tight, rich, gospel-flavored harmonies. *The Original Band* compiles the first two albums (*Doyle Lawson & Quicksilver* and *Quicksilver Rides Again*) that Lawson made with his own group after leaving the Country Gentlemen in 1979, and it will probably stand as the definitive document of his early work as a bandleader. There are blistering versions of Bill Monroe's "On and On" and the traditional "Shady Grove," the forward-looking "A Touch of Pennsylvania," and several absolutely stunning gospel numbers, including the standard "He Put a Rainbow in the Clouds for Me" and "Calm the Storm." If you had to limit your bluegrass collection to only 20 discs, this would have to be one of them. *—Rick Anderson*

Once and for Always/News Is Out / Feb. 16, 1999 / Sugar Hill ✦✦✦✦
This disc was released simultaneously with *The Original Band*, and, like its counterpart, it combines the contents of two Quicksilver albums from the early '80s. If this one is the less-consistently satisfying of the two compilations, it's probably due in part to the stress of a constantly changing lineup—bassist and singer Lou Reid had left by the time *Once and for Always* was recorded, and by the following album the entire band was different with the exception of Lawson. There was a slight but noticeable drop in vocal quality during this period; while the ensemble singing is still uncannily tight, no member of the band emerges as an outstanding lead singer. Nor is the song quality as consistent. There are still great moments, such as the a cappella gospel number "A Lover of the Lord" and the very high and lonesome "I've Heard These Words Before." But "The Grass That I'm Playing Is Really Blue" is a complete clunker and there are just a few too many others like it. This one's worth owning, but if you have to choose between it and *The Original Band*, the latter's your best bet. *—Rick Anderson*

● **Winding Through Life** / Jul. 27, 1999 / Sugar Hill ✦✦✦✦✦
It almost doesn't seem fair—not only is Doyle Lawson's band arguably the finest in traditional bluegrass, but he seems to be determined to lead the best gospel group as well. Several things set his ensemble apart from the pack. It's not just the consistently high quality of his singers (though that alone would be enough to put Quicksilver in the top rank of gospel groups)—it's also the group's surprising stylistic variety. On *Winding Through Life*, they move easily from upbeat bluegrass tunes like "The Lord Will Answer Thee" and "Gladness, Peace and Love" to a more modern country sound on "Just Let Me Fly" and "River of Tears." But most impressive of all is "If Jesus Is There," which sounds like it draws equally on barbershop and shape-note influences, and "Do Right and Come Smiling Thru," which comes squarely from the African-American gospel harmony tradition. "Closer I Must Be" sounds like a Louvin Brothers tune (although it isn't). Everything is delivered with an effortless blend that somehow manages to reconcile the conflicting qualities of creamy smoothness and mountain astringency. Excellent. *—Rick Anderson*

Just Over in Heaven / Jun. 20, 2000 / Sugar Hill ✦✦✦✦
Doyle Lawson & Quicksilver, without doubt the finest bluegrass-gospel group performing today, seems unable to make a bad album, and Lawson's current lineup may be the best one he's ever had. *Just Over in Heaven* combines band arrangements with a cappella numbers, but even when the instruments are playing the vocal arrangements are at the center of the group's sound; where most bluegrass bands use standard parallel harmonies in their gospel arrangements, Lawson's approach is far more complex and is rooted equally in shape, note, and African-American gospel traditions. On tracks like "I Am Glad" and "We Need the Light" the parts move in intricate counterpoint, like cogs in a perfectly designed watch; the sound borders on that of a barbershop quartet. In fact, that effect is a little bit cloying on one or two tracks (notably "Listen to the Bells"), but, for the most part, this album succeeds spectacularly and is highly recommended. *—Rick Anderson*

Gospel Parade / Oct. 9, 2001 / Sugar Hill ✦✦✦
A new gospel album from Doyle Lawson & Quicksilver isn't much of a surprise—Lawson's groups have been recording gospel and secular albums in about a two-to-one ratio since the 1980s. But this is the first that departs so completely from the traditional bluegrass format. Although the album opens and closes with standard-issue bluegrass arrangements (guitar, banjo, mandolin, high mountain harmonies, etc.) just about everything in between comes from a very different tradition. "Gloryland Boogie" finds the group testifying in rich four-part harmony, accompanied by rollicking piano; "I Heard Zion Moan" harks back explicitly to the great black gospel quartets of the 1950s; "He Knows How Much You Can Bear" brings back the piano-and-quartet arrangement. Those who love bluegrass-gospel music mainly for its bluegrass component will be disappointed by this album, but those whose taste for the gospel tradition ranges a bit more widely will find much to love here. *—Rick Anderson*

The Hard Game of Love / May 7, 2002 / Sugar Hill ✦✦✦✦
Doyle Lawson's gospel albums have been gradually moving away from the bluegrass mainstream and toward the gospel mainstream; the last one even featured that least bluegrassy of all instruments, the piano. But traditional bluegrass fans who were starting to get nervous will be greatly reassured by this release, which is not only a solid return to straight-ahead bluegrass, but an all-secular program to boot. (On the other hand, if you were looking forward hopefully to a Hammond organ and swaying church choirs, you'll be disappointed.) While Lawson's bands are notoriously changeable, this lineup has been surprisingly stable, and that consistency is reflected in their almost superhuman vocal tightness. But the incredible harmonic blend they've cultivated through years of gospel singing may not be quite as much of an asset in such astringent lyrical contexts as "Nightingale" and the bemusedly heartbroken "Standing Room Only" as it is on more lighthearted fare like "Poor Boy Working Blues." Overall, though, there's really very little to complain about here: the picking is virtuosic without being overbearing, the songs are traditional-sounding but not actually traditional (and therefore not over-represented on other bluegrass releases), and the singing is a pure pleasure, even when it flirts with slickness. And those who prefer the straight gospel stuff have plenty of other Doyle Lawson releases to fall back on. *—Rick Anderson*

Shannon Lawson

b. 1974, Taylorsville, KY

Composer, Vocals, Guitar / Contemporary Country, Progressive Country, Singer/Songwriter, Country-Rock

Blending country and bluegrass with healthy side portions of blues and rock & roll, singer-songwriter Shannon Lawson was born in Taylorsville, KY, in 1974. Lawson's family was full of amateur musicians who had frequent picking sessions at home, and he first began trying his hand at his uncle's guitar at age four; three years later, he got a nylon-string acoustic of his own. In high-school, Lawson formed a rock band, but along with a slew of hard rock covers, he threw in twangier numbers by John Anderson or the Eagles to the setlists. After graduating from high-school, Lawson relocated to Louisville to attend college and in his freshman year, he scored a gig with a local blues act (all of whom were

African-American, except for Lawson), first playing lead guitar and then adding lead vocals to his resumé.

After a couple years, Lawson left the band and began playing Louisville's coffeehouses as a solo acoustic act; before long, he hooked up with a bluegrass band called the Galoots and they soon developed a passionate local following for their high-energy mixture of acoustic country and blues. The Galoots released two successful self-distributed albums, and the group obtained a manager, Mandy Snider, who developed a particular interest in Lawson; the two fell in love and eventually married. While in the Galoots, Lawson began writing songs for the group, and his tunes won him a deal with a Nashville publishing house, though his move to Music City also forced Lawson to leave the band. After hearing Lawson sing on one of his publishing demos, an A&R man from MCA Records' Nashville office became curious and after a showcase solo gig in Nashville, Lawson scored a major-label deal in 2001. His debut solo album, *Chase the Sun*, was released in the spring of the following year. —*Mark Deming*

Chase the Sun / Jun. 4, 2002 / MCA ✦✦✦
Imagine if some mad scientist working for the Nashville office of a major record label created a cross between Marty Stuart and Mark McGrath, and you start to get an idea of what to expect from Shannon Lawson. Lawson shares Stuart's fondness for both traditional country flavors and uptempo rock & roll, and like McGrath he's a high-attitude bad-boy type with the kind of photogenically unruly hair that's all the rage with marketing departments. Trouble is, judging from Lawson's debut album, *Chase the Sun*, Lawson falls short of Marty Stuart's chops and good taste; while his guitar and mandolin work are pretty good, his rock influences are strictly by-the-numbers, especially on the high-bombast "Who's Your Daddy" (which the overly polished production from Mark Wright only emphasizes), and his honky tonk and bluegrass gestures are neither strong nor original enough to make more than a surface impact (and no matter what Lawson thinks, his acoustic version of Marvin Gaye's "Let's Get It On" is a fun idea, but it sure ain't bluegrass). And while Lawson's pipes are at least as good as Mark McGrath's, he lacks Mr. Sugar Ray's sly humor and easy (if hardly earth-shaking) grasp of musical eclecticism (which, given Lawson's attempted genre-hopping, would help a lot). And as a songwriter, Shannon Lawson suggests he has potential on several tunes here, but never enough to overcome his habit of wandering into clichés. *Chase the Sun* proves that Shannon Lawson has talent, but also suggests he got his record deal because he's easy to market rather than being better than his competition; maybe if this is a hit, listeners will get to hear a stronger and leaner presentation of his style in the future. —*Mark Deming*

Ledford String Band

Group / Old-Timey, String Bands
The Ledford String Band was led by master fiddler Steve Ledford, who first found success as one of the most popular players of the 1930s. Ledford was born and raised in Bakersville, NC, and won his first fiddling contest at age nine. He and his family began performing as a string band at local one-room school houses in the Roan Mountain region. Eventually, they became known as the Carolina Ramblers Stringband and moved to New York in 1931, where they began playing on area radio. In 1932, they recorded 20 songs for the American Record Company, eight of which were released on labels such as Perfect, and Romeo. Ledford later returned to his home to marry and farm. A few years later, he teamed with Wade Mainer; while with Mainer's band, Ledford recorded his signature fiddle tune "Little Maggie." Through the early '40s, Ledford appeared regularly on a Roanoke radio station with Jay Hall and his brother Roy. He returned to farming in 1942; a few more years passed and Ledford formed a new incarnation of the Carolina Ramblers with his little brother Wayne and their relative James Gardner. They eventually called themselves the Ledford String Band, and in 1971 cut an album for Rounder. They also released a couple singles on the Roan Mountain label. —*Sandra Brennan*

Ledford String Band / 1972 / Rounder ✦✦✦✦

Chris LeDoux

b. Oct. 2, 1948, Biloxi, MS
Guitar, Vocals / Cowboy, Contemporary Country, Neo-Traditionalist Country, Urban Cowboy
Prior to becoming a successful independent country artist, Chris LeDoux was a rodeo champion known for his bareback-riding skill and made his name in music by writing countless songs about the rodeo life. LeDoux was born in Biloxi, MS, in 1948 and moved around often as a child since his father was in the Air Force. He first tried his hand at rodeo riding in Denison, TX, at age 13 and was soon winning junior competitions. His family moved to Cheyenne, WY, while he was in high-school, and he continued to ride; after graduating, he won the Wyoming State Rodeo Championship, which earned him a rodeo scholarship to Caspar College. He also studied the sport at Sheridan and Eastern New Mexico and won the Intercollegiate National Bareback Riding Championship. He turned pro in 1970 and eked out a living on the national rodeo circuit, winning just enough prize money to keep himself going.

At the same time, LeDoux began writing songs about the rodeo lifestyle, since no other country performer had yet filled the niche (the way trucker songs became a specialized country subgenre). His first composition was "Bareback Jack," and he soon recorded an album's worth of songs in a friend's basement in 1972. He and his father set up a recording company, American Cowboy Songs, and LeDoux began selling his tapes at rodeo events out of the back of his pickup truck. As this side business became more lucrative, LeDoux started traveling to Nashville for quickie recording sessions rather than relying on local musicians.

LeDoux's hard work on the rodeo circuit paid off when he won the 1976 world bare-back riding championship at the National Rodeo Finals in Oklahoma City. He remained active until 1980, when small nagging injuries and a desire to be with his family led him to retire. He settled on a ranch in Kaycee, WY, but kept up his songwriting and recording and developed an increasingly large following as well as a reputation for exciting concerts. By 1982, he'd sold over 250,000 copies of his self-released albums, of which he

completed 22 by the end of the '80s. LeDoux had long refused to sign a record deal, valuing his independence more, but when rising superstar Garth Brooks name-checked him on the 1989 hit "Much Too Young (To Feel This Damn Old)," the attention was too much to resist. LeDoux signed with Capitol subsidiary Liberty and released his national debut, *Western Underground*, in 1991. The 1992 follow-up, *Whatcha Gonna Do With a Cowboy*, featured a duet with Brooks on the title track. The single became LeDoux's first (and only) Top Ten country hit, and the album also entered the Top Ten and went gold.

Though he hasn't had another single that big, LeDoux recorded steadily for Liberty through the '90s, and all of his albums—1993's *Under This Old Hat*, 1994's *Haywire*, 1996's *Stampede*, 1997's *Live*, and 1998's *One Road Man*—made the country Top 40, selling well to LeDoux's extensive fan base. 2000's *Cowboy* found LeDoux re-recording his earliest compositions, and he subsequently battled a liver illness that threatened his life and required a transplant. He recovered fully and returned to music with the more personal album *After the Storm* in 2002. —*Steve Huey*

Songs of Rodeo Life / Oct. 28, 1971 / Liberty ✦✦✦

Rodeo Songs "Old & New" / 1973 / Liberty ✦✦✦✦✦
With his second album *Rodeo Songs "Old & New,"* Chris LeDoux found his style. Namely, he found his voice as a contemporary cowboy, telling tales of horses and the rodeo with charming, down-home melodies. Balancing traditional songs with new material, LeDoux has created a fine work that fulfills the promise of his debut. —*Thom Owens*

Rodeo & Living Free / 1974 / Liberty ✦✦✦
Rodeo & Living Free, first issued in 1974, contains the bronc-riding tributes "Bucking Maching" and "Fourth of July Rodeos." —*Jason Ankeny*

Songs of Rodeo & Country / 1974 / Liberty ✦✦✦✦✦

Life as a Rodeo Man / 1975 / Liberty ✦✦✦

Songbook of American / 1976 / Liberty ✦✦

Sing Me a Song Mr. Rodeo Man / 1977 / Liberty ✦✦
Tributes to "Billy the Kid" and a "Bad Brahma Bull" flesh out the 1977 release *Sing Me a Song Mr. Rodeo Man*. —*Jason Ankeny*

Cowboys Ain't Easy to Love / 1978 / Liberty ✦✦

Paint Me Back Home / 1979 / Liberty ✦✦

Old Cowboy Heroes / 1980 / Liberty ✦✦✦
The 1981 LP *Old Cowboy Heroes* includes the character studies "Little Joe the Wrangler" and "Old Jake." —*Jason Ankeny*

Sounds of the Western Country / 1980 / Liberty ✦✦✦

Western Tunesmith / 1980 / Liberty ✦✦✦
Western Tunesmith features LeDoux's rendition of "My Heroes Have Always Been Cowboys" and the hit "Ten Seconds in the Saddle." —*Jason Ankeny*

He Rides the Wild Horses / 1981 / Liberty ✦✦✦

Used to Want to Be a Cowboy / 1982 / Liberty ✦✦✦
Used to Want to Be a Cowboy includes the minor hit "This Cowboy Hat." —*Jason Ankeny*

Old Cowboy Classics / 1983 / Liberty ✦✦✦
Old Cowboy Classics, which first appeared in 1983, collects LeDoux favorites like "Old Paint," "Ballad of Will Rogers," and "Tennessee Stud." —*Jason Ankeny*

Thirty Dollar Cowboy / 1983 / Liberty ✦✦
Thirty Dollar Cowboy offers "It Ain't the Years, It's the Miles" and "They Couldn't Understand My Cowboy Songs." —*Jason Ankeny*

Melodies & Memories / 1984 / Liberty ✦✦✦✦

Wild & Wooly / 1986 / Liberty ✦✦
"Little Long-Haired Outlaw" and "Foggy Mountain Breakdown" are two of the highlights of 1986's *Wild & Wooly*. —*Jason Ankeny*

Radio & Rodeo Hits / 1990 / Liberty ✦✦✦

Western Underground / Jul. 22, 1991 / Liberty ✦✦✦
After nearly 20 years and as many self-produced albums, LeDoux found himself attracting attention as the rodeo singer mentioned in Garth Brooks' first hit, "Much Too Young (To Feel This Damn Old)." Brooks' company soon offered the cowboy his first major-label contract. Here, his producers try to turn him into a conventional Nashville hat act. —*Michael McCall*

Chris LeDoux & the Saddle Boogie Band / Sep. 2, 1991 / Liberty ✦✦✦✦
Chris LeDoux was born in Mississippi, but his music and lyrics both have plenty of Texas heart—maybe brought on by the fact that by the time he hit his teens he was already living in Texas, and soon began the normal cowboy path of taking part in rodeos and spending his summers doing ranch work. The recording *Chris LeDoux & the Saddle Boogie Band* has been called a great cowboy-style album, like most of LeDoux's work. Country fans will find both ballads and upbeat numbers on this offering. Songs such as "Cowboys Like a Little Rock and Roll," "Night Rider's Lament," and "Hooked on an 8 Second Ride" showcase his skill at tapping into the celebrated world of the everyday cowboy that he knows so well and shares even better. All you need to do is tug off your cowboy boots, tip back your hat, get comfortable, and have a nice long listen. —*Charlotte Dillon*

Gold Buckle Dreams / Sep. 2, 1991 / Liberty ✦✦✦
Released shortly after Chris LeDoux returned to recording following an extended rodeo absence, *Gold Buckle Dreams* collects highlights from his '70s and '80s recordings. It's not a comprehensive collection, but among the 12 songs are several of his finest—including "So You Want to Be a Cowboy," "A Cowboy's Got to Ride," "Born to Follow Rodeo," "Bareback Jack," "National Finals Rodeo" and "Photo Finish"—which makes *Gold Buckle Dreams* worth its price for casual fans. —*Thom Owens*

Whatcha Gonna Do with a Cowboy / Jul. 20, 1992 / Capitol ♦♦♦♦♦
Brooks helps out his new friend again by joining him for a duet on the title cut, and LeDoux flashes more of his own personality and gritty charm. *—Michael McCall*

Under This Old Hat / Jul. 5, 1993 / Capitol ♦♦♦
LeDoux learns to rock, taking to the punched-up sound like he's been riding the horse all his life. Included is his wild 'n' woolly version of Joe Ely's "For Your Love." *—Michael McCall*

Haywire / 1994 / Capitol ♦♦♦♦
By the time guitarist and singer Chris LeDoux completed this album, *Haywire*, he had already seen the release of more than two-dozen others—impressive enough—but he doesn't show any sign of slowing in his career. The songs on *Haywire* are mostly what is common LeDoux cowboy country-style, done the way he does it best. Since he is a real cowboy—he spent time riding in the rodeo and became a champion bareback rider—maybe he just has a better feel for the subject matter than many singers, and it comes through in his voice. LeDoux's skills really shine on this offering, with numbers like "Hairtrigger Colts," "Dallas Days and Fort Worth Nights," "Tougher Than the Rest," and the 1991 Billy Dean hit "Billy the Kid." This album isn't as long as a best-of collection, carrying only ten tracks, but they are all strong songs, and that makes *Haywire* a good addition to your country shelf. As a bounce, the album comes with a booklet that holds a few pictures. *—Charlotte Dillon*

American Cowboy / 1994 / Liberty ♦♦♦♦♦
If you are a Chris LeDoux fan, or just a fan of good ol' country music, this is a must-have box set for your collection. This noteworthy offering contains three compact discs; that's three full-length compact discs with more than two and half hours' worth of music on them—54 tracks altogether. *American Cowboy* carries a number of LeDoux's most popular songs, including "Amarillo by Morning," "Look at You Girl," "Cadillac Ranch," "Whatcha Gonna Do With a Cowboy?," "Workin' Man's Dollar," and "Riding for a Fall." *American Cowboy* covers a lot of LeDoux's long career, pulling together recordings he did in the '70s, '80s, and '90s. Many of the tunes on these albums are Western or cowboy-style numbers, the kind of storytelling songs about that simple way of life that LeDoux is known for. Inside the box set are a number of photos of the artists, as well as a booklet about his life. *—Charlotte Dillon*

The Best of Chris LeDoux / Mar. 8, 1994 / Liberty ♦♦♦♦
Here are 12 tracks from the genuine rodeo cowboy and former bareback bronc-riding champion of country music. *The Best Of* collects the strongest tracks from *Western Underground, Whatcha Gonna Do With a Cowboy*, and *Under This Old Hat*, serving up an almost perfect blend of earthy honesty and commercial tunefulness. *—Roch Parisien*

Rodeo Rock and Roll Collection / Aug. 15, 1995 / Liberty ♦♦
An entertaining live compilation, featuring many of Chris LeDoux's biggest hits, including "Cadillac Ranch," "Call of the Wild," and a version of "Copenhagen," recorded with Toby Keith. *—Stephen Thomas Erlewine*

Stampede / Mar. 19, 1996 / Capitol ♦♦♦
On this 1996 offering, *Stampede*, Chris LeDoux leaves a little of his traditional cowboy/country style behind to try something more contemporary sounding, but you'll still find the familiar resonance of the fiddle and steel guitar present. The title track, "Calico Moon," and "Take Me to the Rodeo" all offer some of the Western country feel fans are used to from LeDoux, but other numbers have a definite sprinkling of pop and rock flavor added to the mix. LeDoux brought some impressive help into the studio for this Capitol Nashville recording, including fiddler Larry Franklin and guitarist John Jorgensen. The result is well worth a listen, so don't let the new stylings keep you from giving this album a try. *—Charlotte Dillon*

Live / Jun. 17, 1997 / Capitol ♦♦♦♦♦
Chris LeDoux's *Live* captures the modern-day cowboy at his best, leading a devoted audience through his rowdy contemporary country. LeDoux is more energetic and exciting in concert than he is in the studio, which means the record is tougher than many of his other albums, and that makes *Live* a standout in his catalog. *—Stephen Thomas Erlewine*

One Road Man / Jul. 14, 1998 / Capitol ♦♦♦♦
While it has been said before, Chris LeDoux is a *real* singing cowboy. And while he has tended to get bogged down in the pop/rock country factory business in the more recent past, he has a solid background of independence and rodeo buckles that few artists can claim. He is seemingly fueled by the kind of fire and combustible energy that only a man who has sustained eight seconds on the back of a wild beast can muster up. With a little help from pals Willie Nelson, Charlie Daniels, and rock & roll cowboy Jon Bon Jovi, LeDoux hits his mark and rides out of the chute with panache. The title cut is sweet as is his version of "Old Paint." "One Ride in Vegas" and Bon Jovi's "Bang a Drum" highlight LeDoux's faster spirit. Wilder still is "The Fever," "Sometimes You Just Gotta Ride," and the Tex-Mex sizzle of "The Borderline." Pulling out all the stops, LeDoux does a tremendous version of the Johnny Horton tune "Old Slew Foot" that is immensely satisfying. Always a showman, LeDoux is champion outside the rodeo area as well as within. *—Jana Pendragon*

● **20 Greatest Hits** / Jun. 8, 1999 / Capitol ♦♦♦♦♦
20 Greatest Hits may not cover Chris LeDoux' entire career, but it does provide a definitive summary of his recordings for Liberty in the '90s. Over the course of the album, all of his big hits, plus a selection of fine album tracks and rarities, are hauled out. It may run a little long for some listeners, but it's nevertheless the ideal LeDoux record for casual fans, since it captures the best from the peak of his popularity. *—Stephen Thomas Erlewine*

Cowboy / Aug. 1, 2000 / Capitol ♦♦♦♦
After recording 22 albums and developing a cult following of rodeo and pure-country enthusiasts, Chris LeDoux re-recorded 11 of his early songs on this compilation to bring new listeners up to speed and to throw a thank you to the fans who have supported him. So many contemporary country singers try to come across like salt of the earth but end up sounding like the country & western version of Michael Bolton. LeDoux, on the other hand, is a former rodeo cowboy, and that experience shows in his choice of material and his emotive voice. He sings about raising crops, for crying out loud. How bold is that in the 21st century's plasticized country scene? That integrity is probably what's kept him from becoming a megastar but also what has gained him fiercely loyal fans. Literate, poetic, moving, and with a killer sense of humor, LeDoux has a wisdom in his voice that enables him to be the consummate storyteller he is. Additionally, it's nice that the songs on this album aren't all love songs; he sings about family, marriage, bar brawls, and, of course, riding the rodeo. He takes you on a journey in each, from the devastating kick in the pants of "Silence on the Line" to a tender, wistful ode to the Cowboy State, "Song of Wyoming." *Cowboy* is a solid collection that spotlights the strengths of one of the most underrated male country artists of the time. *—Bryan Buss*

After the Storm / Apr. 9, 2002 / Capitol ♦♦♦

Capitol Collection: 1990–2000 / Jun. 4, 2002 / Capitol ♦♦♦♦
Capitol Collection: 1990-2000 gathers all six of Chris Ledoux's albums for Capitol—*Haywire, One Road Man, Stampede, Under This Old Hat, Western Underground*, and *Whatcha Gonna Do With a Cowboy*—into a box set. Along with the hits these albums spawned, such as *Under This Old Hat*'s "Cadillac Ranch" and the title track from *Whatcha Gonna Do With a Cowboy*, the set also features a bonus track on each disc. At nearly 70 tracks long, this set certainly isn't for casual fans (who would be better served by LeDoux's *20 Greatest Hits*), but *Capitol Collection* is worthwhile for die-hard fans of his contemporary and neo-traditionalist country work. *—Heather Phares*

Albert Lee

b. Dec. 21, 1943, Leominster, England
Guitar, Vocals, Session Musician / Country-Rock, Neo-Traditionalist Country, Rockabilly Revival
British guitarist Albert Lee made a name for himself as a consummate country and rockabilly stylist, picking out virtuosic licks both on his solo records and as a top-notch sideman. Lee was born in Leominster, England, in 1943 and first made a splash with the blues-tinged country-rock outfit Head, Hands & Feet, which recorded several albums in the early '70s. Lee subsequently formed his own band for a time before joining Emmylou Harris' backing group in the late '70s. He spent several years in the early '80s as a member of Eric Clapton's band and departed to become the musical director for the Everly Brothers' mid-'80s reunion. In the meantime, Lee released his first solo album, *Hiding*, on A&M in 1979 and followed it with a more rock-oriented, self-titled effort for Polydor in 1982. Most critics agreed that Lee reached the high point of his solo career on a pair of albums for MCA, 1987's *Speechless* and 1988's *Gagged but Not Bound*.

In the meantime, Lee continued to play on numerous country and rock sessions through the '90s and also performed with a backing band dubbed Hogan's Heroes, which featured steel guitarist Gerry Hogan, keyboardist Mike Bell, bassist Brian Hodgson, and drummer Pete Baron. They released the live album *In Full Flight* in 1994. Lee joined ex-Rolling Stones bassist Bill Wyman's Rhythm Kings project in the late '90s and issued another album with Hogan's Heroes, *Tear It Up*, in 2002. *—Steve Huey*

Hiding / 1979 / A&M ♦♦♦

Albert Lee / 1982 / Polydor ♦♦♦

Country Guitar Man / Nov. 1986 / Magnum ♦♦♦♦

Speechless / Feb. 1987 / MCA ♦♦♦♦♦
One of the guitar world's best-kept secrets, the former Everly Brothers and Emmylou Harris sideman explores his roots in this instrumental jewel. Albert Lee co-produced this album. Included is a very clean sound, very good cover of "Arkansas Traveler" featuring Lee on guitar, mandolin and piano; Jim Cox, Greg Humphrey, Sterling Biff Ball, and Chad Wackerman. *—Jeff Tamarkin & Chip Renner*

● **Gagged but Not Bound** / Mar. 1988 / MCA ♦♦♦♦♦
The master musician plays unworldly guitar on this acoustic/electric country-, rock-, and traditional-oriented masterpiece. Exquisitely recorded. *—Jeff Tamarkin*

Black Claw & Country Fever / Oct. 1991 / Line ♦♦♦♦
This collection of late-'60s material is raw yet engaging; the musicianship is stunning. *—Jeff Tamarkin*

Brenda Lee (Brenda Mae Tarpley)

b. Dec. 11, 1944, Lithonia, GA
Vocals / Rock & Roll, Country-Pop, Rockabilly, Pop, Nashville Sound/Countrypolitan
One of the biggest pop stars of the early '60s, Brenda Lee hasn't attracted as much critical respect as she deserves. She is sometimes inaccurately characterized as one of the few female teen idols. More crucially, the credit for achieving success with pop-country crossovers usually goes to Patsy Cline, although Lee's efforts in this era were arguably of equal importance. While she made few recordings of note after the mid-'60s, the best of her first decade is fine indeed, encompassing not just the pop ballads that were her biggest hits, but straight country and some surprisingly fierce rockabilly.

Lee was a child prodigy, appearing on national television by the age of ten, and making her first recordings for Decca the following year (1956). Her first few Decca singles, in fact, make a pretty fair bid for the best preteen rock & roll performances this side of Michael Jackson. "BIGELOW 6-200," "Dynamite," and "Little Jonah" are all exceptionally powerful rockabilly performances, with robust vocals and white-hot backing from the cream of Nashville's session musicians (including Owen Bradley, Grady Martin, Hank Garland, and Floyd Cramer). Lee would not have her first big hits until 1960, when she tempered the rockabilly with teen idol pop on "Sweet Nothin's," which went to the Top Five.

The comparison between Lee and Cline is to be expected, given that both singers were produced by Owen Bradley in the early '60s. Naturally, many of the same session musicians and backup vocalists were employed. Brenda, however, had a bigger in with the pop audience, not just because she was still a teenager, but because her material was more pop than Cline's, and not as country. Between 1960 and 1962, she had a stunning series of huge hits: "I'm Sorry," "I Want to Be Wanted," "Emotions," "You Can Depend on Me," "Dum Dum," "Fool #1," "Break It to Me Gently," and "All Alone Am I" all made the Top Ten. Their crossover appeal is no mystery. While these were ballads, they were delivered with enough lovesick yearning to appeal to adolescents, and enough maturity for the adults. The first-class melodic songwriting and professional orchestral production guaranteed that they would not be ghettoized in the country market.

Lee's last Top Ten pop hit was in 1963, with "Losing You." While she still had hits through the mid-'60s, these became smaller and less frequent with the rise of the British Invasion (although she remained very popular overseas). The best of her later hits, "Is It True?," was a surprisingly hard-rocking performance, recorded in 1964 in London with Jimmy Page on guitar. 1966's "Coming on Strong," however, would prove to be her last Top 20 entry. In the early '70s, Lee reunited with Owen Bradley and, like so many early white rock & roll stars, returned to country music. For a time she was fairly successful in this field, making the country Top Ten half-dozen times in 1973-1974. Although she remained active as a recording and touring artist, for the last couple of decades she's been little more than a living legend, directing her intermittent artistic efforts to the country audience. *—Richie Unterberger*

Brenda Lee / 1960 / Decca ♦♦♦♦

Miss Dynamite / 1961 / Brunswick ♦♦♦♦♦

By Request / 1964 / Decca ♦♦
By Request, a Top 100 album for Brenda Lee in 1964, is heavy on ubiquitous easy listening ballads like "Days of Wine and Roses," "Tammy," and "Blue Velvet," but don't pass it over just yet. It also contains four of Lee's hits from 1963: "My Whole World Is Falling Down," "I Wonder," "The Grass Is Greener," and "As Usual," all of which charted in the Top 25. *By Request* offers a useful roundup of hit singles for vinyl addicts, but no surprises for completists. [They are also reissued on the two-disc set *Anthology, Vols. 1 & 2 (1956-1980)*, which leaves half a dozen overly familiar adult contemporary songs for your consideration.] *—Greg Adams*

Let Me Sing / 1964 / Decca ♦♦♦
Even ardent consumers of Brenda Lee's prolific album output can be forgiven for feeling as though her '60s albums all began to sound the same. That impression only deepened as the decade wore on, but in 1963 Lee's bottomless fund of pop ballads could still seem fresh. *Let Me Sing* begins predictably enough with a Cole Porter song ("Night and Day") but also includes "Break It to Me Gently"—one of Lee's greatest '60s hits—and "Losing You." Bobby Darin's "You're the Reason I'm Living" is the kind of cover material preferable to the traditional pop songs that tended to dominate Lee's ballad albums, but *Let Me Sing* manages to sound vital where very similar albums failed later in her career. Not surprisingly, *Let Me Sing* was also Lee's second-to-last Top 40 album. *—Greg Adams*

Songs Everybody Knows / 1964 / Decca ♦♦♦

Coming on Strong / 1966 / Decca ♦♦♦
"Coming on Strong" was Brenda Lee's last major pop hit, very nearly reaching the Top Ten in 1966. The album of the same name is an underwhelming collection of adult contemporary material with a heavy emphasis on ballads, which became the standard formula for her LPs in the late '60s. Buck Owens' "Crying Time" and Don Gibson's "Sweet Dreams" are presented as torchy pop ballads that highlight Lee's impeccable and wonderfully expressive vocals, although one might wish for a more varied approach. The most unusual selection is a rendition of Stevie Wonder's hit "Uptight (Everything's Alright,)" which Brenda Lee comfortably negotiates. That isn't too surprising considering her obvious R&B influences and vocal similarity to Little Esther Phillips. "Coming on Strong" is an excellent single that shows that Brenda Lee could still hit with quality material, but the remainder of the album is too middle-of-the-road in its execution to be fully satisfying. *—Greg Adams*

Johnny One Time / 1969 / Decca ♦♦♦
"Johnny One Time" was Brenda Lee's first country hit in over a decade and the beginning of her commercial "second wind" on the country charts that reached gale force in the mid-'70s. Mike Berniker's production makes the song sound little different from the other straight pop ballads Lee recorded during this period, but "Johnny One Time" had been a minor hit for Willie Nelson a few months earlier, so that made it country enough to cross over. The album of the same name is no different from Lee's typical late-'60s output and in no way foreshadows her coming revival as a country artist. The cover art portrays Lee as a sophisticated pop vocalist, an image that is supported by the material, particularly the several songs with European roots. The Jacques Brel and Rod McKuen composition "If You Go Away" is in a similar cosmopolitan vein, but the cover of the Box Tops' "The Letter" is a bit of a surprise. Brenda Lee is a sadly underrated vocalist who could have gone in any direction she chose; on *Johnny One Time* she dabbles in various styles, but the prevailing mood is one of adult pop. *—Greg Adams*

New Sunrise / 1974 / MCA ♦♦♦
New Sunrise is an apt title for this album, made in 1973 when Brenda Lee received a makeover as a country-oriented MCA recording artist. The big hits began anew, and Lee spent much of the next three years in the country Top Ten. Two songs from *New Sunrise* were successful singles: "Sunday Sunrise" nearly made the Top Five, and Shel Silverstein's "Wrong Ideas" performed equally well. Lee is an excellent ballad singer, but after years of churning out serious, often continental, adult pop, it was a breath of fresh air to hear her perform lively material with down-home accompaniment. That said, much of *New Sunrise* is no different from her late-period Decca recordings, particularly the pop covers like Stevie Wonder's "You Are the Sunshine of My Life." The handful of country songs are a welcome departure; the rest is typical late '60s style Brenda Lee. *—Greg Adams*

The Brenda Lee Story (Her Greatest Hits) / 1974 / MCA ♦♦♦♦
This 22-song, two-LP set included the bulk of her biggest hits, although it misses somes some significant singles (like "Is It True?"). The two-volume *Anthology* CD, with nearly twice as much material, is a much better investment. *—Richie Unterberger*

Even Better / 1980 / MCA ♦♦♦
Brenda Lee may have seemed like an old timer when *Even Better* was released in 1980, but she was 36 years old—only a few years older than Barbara Mandrell and Dolly Parton. The album contains two of Lee's last major hits, the biggest of which is the Top Ten "Tell Me What It's Like." "The Cowgirl and the Dandy," also a Top Ten hit, explores love across class boundaries in what is practically a rewrite of the Tommy Cash hit "The Cowboy and the Lady." Rafe Van Hoy is a major player on the album, contributing several songs and lead guitar, while his wife, country star Deborah Allen, co-wrote "Goodbye Love" with Jim Stafford. The roster of well-known songwriters on *Even Better* certainly contributed to its success, as did Lee's willingness to tackle adult material despite her perpetual little girl image, as on the mildly lascivious "Do You Wanna Spend the Night." Ultimately *Even Better* was designed for the contemporary country audience of 1980 rather than the oldies nostalgia crowd, so there is no guarantee that fans of her early music will take a liking to this slick, modern country music. *—Greg Adams*

Kris, Willie, Dolly and Brenda . . . The Winning Hand / 1983 / Monument ♦♦♦
Recorded for Monument in 1983 thanks to the leniency of the artists' respective labels, *Brenda, Dolly, Kris & Willie* brought together Brenda Lee, Dolly Parton, Kris Kristofferson and Willie Nelson for a double album of duets featuring every possible combination of the four, as well as a handful of solo numbers. Certainly a delight for fans of the individual performers, this album is nonetheless too redolent of a various-artists anthology to truly succeed as a piece. Much of the music is highly enjoyable, however, particularly the Dolly and Kris novelty, "Ping Pong," and Brenda and Dolly's duet on What Do You Think About Lovin'." As a bizarre bonus, Johnny Cash provided the half-poetry, half-prose liner notes. *—Greg Adams*

★ **Anthology, Vols. 1 & 2 (1956–1980)** / 1991 / MCA ♦♦♦♦♦
A 40-song, two-CD collection, this proves Lee was the best white female rock singer of the pre-Beatles '60s. By the time she turned 18, Lee had hit the pop Top Ten 11 times. All of those cuts are here, from the innocently salacious "Sweet Nothin's" to the string-laden "I'm Sorry" and her remake of Earl "Fatha" Hines' "You Can Depend on Me." Her best country singles, "Johnny One Time" and "Big Four Poster Bed," are also included. The compilers wisely passed over some minor hits in favor of obscure sides like the odd rockabilly "Let's Jump the Broomstick," a cover of Edith Piaf's "If You Love Me (Really Love Me)," and "Is It True?" a midding hit from 1964, which features guitarist Jimmy Page (who is 11 months older than Lee). *Anthology* thoroughly traces Lee's development as a vocalist, from early-childish exuberance to mature, graceful phrasing. *—Brian Mansfield*

EP Collection / 1995 / See for Miles ♦♦♦
Most of the tracks on Brenda Lee's *EP Collection* are duplicated on Bear Family's four-disc box set, *Little Miss Dynamite*, but there are a handful of rare '60s recordings for collectors. One of the notable cuts that makes its CD debut here is Lee's cover of Ernest Tubb's "Thanks a Lot" from her album *Top Teen Hits*. The mix of '50s and '60s recordings shows her evolution from rock & roll to adult pop, beginning with "Rock the Bop" and building toward "If You Love Me (Really Love Me)" and "Georgia on My Mind" before returning to her early rock-oriented sides toward the end of the collection. There may not be enough unique material here to justify its purchase for owners of the box set, but *EP Collection* offers an interesting assortment of (mostly) obscurities for anyone who owns only a greatest-hits package or two. *—Greg Adams*

Little Miss Dynamite / 1997 / Bear Family ♦♦♦♦♦
Here are five hours of pure gold on four CDs, covering the 127 songs that Brenda Lee recorded during the years 1956 through 1962, with the added allure of an 84-page *hardcover* book. What's more, there's hardly a second-rate song or performance here, and Lee's singing style evolved so far that there are surprises throughout. Her early rockabilly sides are among the best in the field, and disc one covers her evolution from country-rockin' teen rockabilly queen to an astonishingly precocious pop star with rock roots. Even Lee's early sides, whether hot rockabilly or slow ballads, are all intense experiences—there's just something eerily compelling about 12-year-old Brenda Lee delivering "Your Cheatin' Heart" and sounding like she means all of the yearning and torment behind it. By 1957, her voice and her style had evolved more toward mainstream pop, virtually paralleling Elvis Presley's musical moves of the same era, but, like Elvis, Lee occasionally burst out with hard-rocking sides as late as 1959. Disc two shows off Lee's mid-teen years, when she was doing pop standards that shouldn't have worked with anyone less than 30, but making them pay off—her hot, raspy voice made even her pop stuff work better than Elvis' and outclassed the work of any other female singer who made that same jump to mainstream music. Disc three may be the best of the four here, her rock sides alternating with equally compelling pop performances. Much of disc four is on the softer side, but even here she comes up with exciting pop/rock songs. By this time, she was nearing 18 years old, and already had a catalog of recordings behind her that would have been the envy of any veteran. As usual with Bear Family, the book is as fascinating as the music. *—Bruce Eder*

In the Mood for Love: Classic Ballads / Aug. 11, 1998 / Hip-O ♦♦♦
She can sing rockers and turn around and sing Hank Williams songs as well as anyone. But nobody can put across a ballad the way Brenda Lee can, and this 18-track collection proves it in a most musical way. Drawn from 11 different albums and recorded between

1961 and 1971, this collection forgoes the usual hits and formulaic choices and instead concentrates on Brenda's interpretations of standards and cover versions of then-current hits by the likes of Dusty Springfield and others. Perhaps it's Owen Bradley's uniformly excellent production that helps to band it all together around Brenda's pipes, but everything on here works together as a whole concept, solid as a brick. Great songs, great singing, and production that still sounds crisp some 35-40 years after it was cut. A noteworthy addition to anyone's Brenda Lee collection, covering material not found on her box set anthologies. *—Cub Koda*

20th Century Masters—The Millennium Collection: The Best of Brenda Lee / Aug. 10, 1999 / MCA ♦♦♦

Like any record company worth their salt, MCA knows a good gimmick when they see it, and when the millennium came around, *20th Century Masters—The Millennium Collection* wasn't too far behind. Supposedly, the millennium is a momentous occasion, but it's hard to feel that way when it's used as another excuse to turn out a budget-line series. But apart from the presumptuous title, *20th Century Masters—The Millennium Collection* turns out to be a very good budget-line series. True, it's impossible for any of these ten-track collections to be definitive, but they're nevertheless solid samplers that don't feature a bad song in the bunch. For example, take Brenda Lee's *20th Century* volume. Yes, there are some great songs missing, but what's here is terrific, including "I'm Sorry," "Sweet Nothin's," "I Want to Be Wanted," "That's All You Gotta Do," "Emotions," "Break It to Me Gently," "Dum Dum," "Everybody Loves Me but You," and "All Alone Am I." Serious fans will want something more extensive and neophytes would be best-served by better-chosen collections, but this disc is quite entertaining, considering its length and price. That doesn't erase the ridiculousness of the series' title, but the silliness is excusable when the music and the collections are good. *—Stephen Thomas Erlewine*

Rockin' Around the Christmas Tree / Oct. 5, 1999 / MCA ♦♦♦

Brenda Lee's *Rockin' Around the Christmas Tree* includes the festive title track and a mix of classic holiday tunes, including "Winter Wonderland," "Silver Bells," "White Christmas," and "Santa Claus Is Coming to Town." Unique Christmas and winter tunes like "Christy Christmas," "A Marshmallow World," "Strawberry Snow," and "I'm Gonna Lasso Santa Claus" round out this happy holiday collection. *—Heather Phares*

I'm Sorry / Aug. 28, 2001 / Polygram International ♦♦♦♦

"Little Miss Dynamite" stormed the late-'50s and early-'60s charts with several spot-on classics, and in the process showed a deft vocal touch with pop, country, rockabilly, and rock & roll material. Especially displaying an affinity for both Wanda Jackson's snarled delivery and Dottie West's earnest tone, Lee electrified even the most banal of songs. This is made clear on Polygram's Lee roundup, *I'm Sorry*, as the singer transcends cloying sides like "Speak Pretty to Me" and "Rockin' Around the Christmas Tree" with unerring rhythmic verve and in-the-pocket phrasing. Featuring 20 cuts in all, the collection includes a slew of other highlights like the title track, "Dum Dum," and "Sweet Nothin's." A perfect way to get to know the fabulous Miss Lee. *—Stephen Cook*

Dickey Lee (Dickey Lipscomb)

b. Sep. 21, 1936, Memphis, TN

Songwriter, Vocals / Country-Pop, Rockabilly

Country songwriter Dickey Lee began his career recording for the Sun label. He was born Dickey Lipscomb on September 21, 1936, in Memphis and began playing in a band while in high-school. The group won several talent shows, earning them a spot on a local radio station. DJ Dewey Phillips convinced Sun Records to sign Dickey Lee, so the singer recorded two singles in 1957, "Good Lovin'" and "Fool, Fool, Fool." Neither did especially well, so he moved to Texas and continued to play. Dickey Lee finally hit the big time in early 1962 when George Jones took his song "She Thinks I Still Care" to the top of the country charts, where it stayed for six weeks. The record became one of Jones' biggest hits and also hit number one when Anne Murray recorded it in 1974.

On the wings of Jones, Lee's "Patches" hit number six on the pop charts in August 1962; "I Saw Linda Yesterday" entered the same year and ended up at number 14 early in 1963. Lee recorded one other pop hit, 1965's "Laurie (Strange Things Happen)," but then focused strictly on production and songwriting during the late '60s. Persuaded to return to Nashville in 1969, he signed to RCA and in 1971 recorded a modest hit called "The Mahogany Pulpit." Dickey Lee's next single, "Never Ending Song of Love," crashed the country Top Ten in late 1971 and eventually reached number eight. He continued to record over the course of the '70s, usually peaking in the Top 30s and 40s except for two massive hits—"Rocky," which topped the charts in 1975, and its number three follow-up, "9,999,999 Tears."

Lee stayed with RCA until 1978 and re-emerged on Mercury a year later. His two highlights during the Mercury years were Top 30 singles from 1980, "Workin' My Way to Your Heart" and "Lost in Love." The latter, a duet with Kathy Burdick, became a pop hit for Air Supply the same year. After his contract expired, Lee continued to write songs and perform on occasional package shows. *—John Bush*

● **Tale of Patches** / 1962 / Smash ♦♦♦♦♦

Laurie and the Girl From Peyton Place / 1965 / TCF Hall ♦♦♦

Peyton Place / 1965 / TCF Hall ♦♦♦

Never Ending Song of Love / 1972 / RCA ♦♦♦

Ashes of Love / 1976 / RCA ♦♦

Angels, Roses & Rain / 1977 / RCA Victor ♦♦♦

Dickey Lee wasn't the only teen idol who turned to country music—there was also Johnny Tillotson, Paul Evans, and Pat Boone, to name only a few. Lee made the country charts nearly 30 times in the '70s and '80s, occasionally dealing in death-obsessed material that hearkened back to the "teen tragedy" roots of his early hits like "Patches." Two of Lee's four Top Ten country hits are on the album *Angels, Roses & Rain*: the title track (a reprise of the dead wife theme that gave Lee a number one with "Rocky" in 1975) and the brilliant Razzy Bailey-penned crossover hit "9,999,999 Tears." "Makin' Love Don't Always Make Love Grow," about sex in exotic places and family values, was a minor chart hit as well. Lee sings with a Southern accent that he didn't have on his early pop records, but his sound is light and pop-flavored, recalling John Denver's country-leaning efforts. *—Greg Adams*

Everybody Loves a Winner / 1981 / Mercury ♦♦♦

Johnny Lee

b. Jul. 3, 1946, Texas City, TX

Vocals, Guitar / Country-Pop, Adult Contemporary, Urban Cowboy, Contemporary Country

Like many his age, Johnny Lee grew up on the music of Chuck Berry, Elvis Presley, and Jerry Lee Lewis. Raised on a dairy farm in Alta Loma, TX, he formed his first band, Johnny Lee & the Road Runners, during high-school. He tricked his way into playing on-stage with Mickey Gilley at a Houston club called the Nesadel, and that shot brought him a long-term run at Gilley's clubs. When *Urban Cowboy* was shot at Gilley's, record executive Irving Azoff offered Lee an opportunity to sing in the picture, and he ended up with a song that more than 20 artists had previously rejected. In his hands, that song—"Lookin' for Love"—became a million-seller and the musical centerpiece of the movie. Stardom occurred practically overnight for Lee, but it was a mixed bag. He and Gilley toured steadily; Lee got a substantial string of hits for about three years and ended up marrying *Dallas* starlet Charlene Tilton. But when the marriage soured, he found his name constantly in the tabloids, and he was forced to record a large amount of same-sounding material. Nevertheless, Lee had an important role in a huge era for country music, and his easygoing vocal style still makes him very listenable.

Following the demise of his high-school band, the Road Runners, Lee enlisted in the Navy, serving in Southeast Asia (including Vietnam) during the mid-'60s. After his discharge, he floated between California and Texas before settling near Houston. Lee convinced Gilley into letting him join his band as a backup singer and trumpeter in 1968, telling the pianist that they had previously met in Galveston, when in fact they hadn't. For the next ten years, Lee worked closely with Gilley, becoming an integral party of the pianist's Pasadena club, Gilley's. When Gilley was on tour, Lee acted as the headliner at the club. Lee decided to go solo in 1973, but his records for the independent label Astro were unsuccessful, so he returned to the club within a year.

By the end of 1975, he signed a contract with ABC/Dot and his first single for the label, "Sometimes," became a minor hit. The following year, he moved to GRT, where he released several minor hits in the next two years, highlighted by the number 15 placing of "Country Party" in 1977; the song was a reworking of Rick Nelson's hit "Garden Party." In 1979, he appeared in a made-for-television film, *The Girls in the Office*, which paved the way for his appearance in the 1980 film, *Urban Cowboy*. Starring John Travolta, *Urban Cowboy* glamorized the sound and style of modern honky tonks like Gilley's, and the movie and its soundtrack became huge hits. Lee contributed "Lookin' for Love" to the soundtrack, and the single became a gigantic crossover success, spending three weeks at the top of the country charts in the summer of 1980 while peaking at number five on the pop charts. Lee became a star thanks to *Urban Cowboy*, and his records for his new label, Full Moon, began appearing in the country Top Ten with regularity. "One in a Million" became another number-one hit late in 1980, followed by "Pickin' Up Strangers" early the next year.

In the wake of the success of "Lookin' for Love" and *Urban Cowboy*, Lee officially left Gilley's band in 1981, forming not only his own group, the Western Union Band, but also his own rival nightclub, Johnny Lee's, which was located just down the road from Gilley's. Throughout 1981 and 1982, Lee's star burned bright, as the Academy of Country Music named him the Best New Artist of 1980, and he had Top Ten hits like "Prisoner of Hope" (1981), the number one "Bet Your Heart on Me" (1981), and "Be There for Me Baby" (1982). In 1982, he married actress Charlene Tilton, one of the stars of the nighttime soap opera *Dallas*. Lee's success continued in 1983 and 1984 with Top Ten singles like "Sounds Like Love" (1983), "Hey Bartender" (1983), and the number-one singles "The Yellow Rose" (1984) and "You Could've Heard a Heart Break" (1984).

Lee's career cooled down as quickly as it heated up. Though he had one Top Ten single, "Rollin' Lonely," in 1985, by the beginning of 1986 he had trouble reaching the Top 40. Warner, who inherited his Full Moon contract in 1984, dropped him from their roster in 1986, and his marriage to Tilton collapsed in 1987. Over the next two years, he struggled to find a contract, as he came to the realization his management took most of his earnings from his hitmaking days. During this time, he released a single and three EPs on his own Lee record label as well as an independent record on JMS. In 1989, he signed to Curb Records, but none of his records for the label were hits. By the end of the decade, he published his autobiography, *Lookin' for Love*. During the '90s, Lee continued to tour across the country, playing clubs and honky tonks. He lacked a record contract, and he had long been estranged from his mentor, Gilley, due to his management problems and his rival club, but he continued to draw sizable crowds at his concerts. *—Tom Roland*

For Lovers Only / 1977 / JMS ♦♦♦♦

Lookin' for Love / 1980 / Asylum ♦♦♦♦

It's easy to see why Nashville tastemakers like Ralph Emery were unimpressed with Johnny Lee on first listen—his relaxed style doesn't exactly ooze personality. But the MOR country-pop of "Lookin' for Love" is so appealing that one suspects it could have been a hit even without the publicity from *Urban Cowboy*. The 1980 album containing that hit, *Lookin' for Love*, also includes the wistful chart-topping follow-up, "One in a Million," and the Top Three "Pickin' Up Strangers." Most of the album tracks sound quite a bit like the hits but with varying degrees of memorability (Lee's own "Anni" is the best of the bunch), but the two slick rockers, "Down and Dirty" and "Too Damned Old," are awful. The presence of three of Lee's biggest hits will attract listeners to *Lookin' for Love*, but there are at least a couple of comparable album cuts that will sustain interest beyond the hits. *—Greg Adams*

Bet Your Heart on Me / 1981 / Full Moon ✦✦✦

Hey Bartender / 1983 / Full Moon ✦✦

● **Greatest Hits** / 1983 / Full Moon ✦✦✦✦✦
Lots of midtempo love songs are here, much in the vein of "Lookin' for Love." Too bad Lee couldn't break out of that mold a little sooner—"Sounds like Love" and "Hey Bartender" show some real teeth. —*Tom Roland*

Johnny Lee / 1984 / Audio Fidelity ✦✦

Johnny Lee & Willie Nelson / 1984 / Astan ✦✦✦

'Til the Bars Burn Down / 1984 / Full Moon ✦✦✦

New Directions / 1989 / Curb ✦✦
The songs which comprise *New Directions* fail to live up to the standard enjoyed by Johnny Lee at his early-'80s peak. —*Jason Ankeny*

The Best of Johnny Lee / 1990 / Curb ✦✦✦
The Best of Johnny Lee is a ten-track budget-priced collection that features some of his biggest hits, including "Lookin' for Love," "Cherokee Fiddle," "You Can't Fly Like an Eagle," "I Can Be a Heartbreaker Too," "Maybe I Won't Love Anymore" and "Treat Her Like a Lady." Although this isn't a bad budget-priced disc, there are far better Lee collections available, offering more songs and better sound for not much more money. —*Stephen Thomas Erlewine*

Robin Lee (Robin Irwin)
b. Nov. 7, 1953, Nashville, TN
Vocals / Contemporary Country, Urban Cowboy
Singer-songwriter Robin Lee was born and raised in Nashville. She began her career in music while attending high-school, performing at school dances and talent shows. She later made demo recordings for local publishing companies. In 1982, Lee debuted on the charts with the minor hit "Turning Back the Covers"; "Heart for a Heart" came the following year. In 1984, four songs became low-level hits, including "Angel in Your Arms," "Paint the Town Blue" and "Safe in the Arms of Love" both hit the Top 50 the next year. In 1988 she had three Top 50 hits, including "This Old Flame." Lee did not appear on the charts again until 1990 with the title cut of *Black Velvet*, which made the Top 15 and became her biggest hit to date. The album hit the Top 25, and two other cuts from it reached the Top 70. She had one hit in 1991, "Nothin' But You." After her own recording career slowed, Lee signed as a songwriter for Big Tractor Music, the service owned by Virgin Records Nashville. She married songwriter Trey Bruce and saw her songs recorded by such country music luminaries as LeAnn Rimes and Jo Dee Messina. —*Johnny Loftus*

This Old Flame / 1984 / Atlantic ✦✦

● **Heart on a Chain** / 1990 / Atlantic ✦✦✦✦
A significant improvement over Lee's debut, *Heart on a Chain* focuses on more straight-ahead country material, performed by a crack session band. —*Jason Ankeny*

The Best of Robin Lee / Sep. 19, 2000 / Atlantic ✦✦✦
Country singer Robin Lee only released a few albums in the '80s and early '90s that are now out of print. This ten-song best-of collection finds some of her top Atlantic hits easily accessible once again. Along with "Back to Bein' Blue," "Nothin' But You," and her biggest hit "Black Velvet," a previously unreleased track "When Love Comes Callin'" is also included. —*Al Campbell*

The Lewis Family
f. 1951
Group / Country Gospel, Traditional Bluegrass
With a distinctive sound marked by the blazing (and often hilariously comic) banjo theatrics of Little Roy Lewis, a big bass drum, and robust harmonies from a contingent of identically dressed Lewis daughters, the Lewis Family has remained an institution of Georgia music and of the bluegrass festival scene for several decades. The "First Family of Bluegrass Gospel" got its start, in a way, when Roy Lewis Sr., known as "Pop," used a ladder to spirit 15-year-old Pauline Holloway ("Mom" Lewis, who died in 2002) away from her house and to an elopement in McCormick, SC, in 1925. In the late '40s they joined with four of their eight children to form a family singing group, taking the name the Lewis Family for a gospel performance at a Woodmen of the World meeting in 1951. That year they made their first recordings on the small Sullivan label, and by 1957 they were recording for Starday. The family was influenced by the gospel quartet harmonies of the Chuckwagon Gang and by the big-beat gospel of Martha Carson, but their sound and shows were distinctive from the start. In 1954 the Lewis Family began appearing on a weekly television show in Augusta, GA, near their hometown of Lincolnton; it ran until 1992. The family's live performances likewise had a durable consistency; through about 60 album releases on Starday, Canaan, Riverson, and Daywind, their sound remained largely unchanged. They began touring full time in the early '60s.

By the end of the 20th century the Lewis Family played roughly 200 shows a year, appearing at annual Southern gospel events such as the Albert E. Brumley Memorial Singing in Springdale, AR, as well as at bluegrass festivals far and wide. Their shows, marked by cornball humor and stage razzle-dazzle along with a gospel message, offer a unique window on the musical past in their traveling family-group setup. Although the group operates in a sphere separate from the bluegrass mainstream, Little Roy Lewis is recognized as one of the top masters of the five-string banjo in bluegrass. For sheer speed on the fretboard he is unmatched. Daughters Miggie, Polly, and Janis Lewis joined the group gradually in the 1960s and 1970s as several brothers dropped out to pursue business careers, and their harmony singing anchors many of the family's songs; a third generation of Lewis musicians have found their way into the family band. Many Lewis Family members are talented multi-instrumentalists, and the group plays several upbeat numbers, including "The Good Time Get Together," that are structured so as to allow multiple virtuoso solos on various instruments, sometimes including such novelties as an

autoharp. Their repertoire, particularly heavy on the works of bluegrass songwriter Randall Hylton, also contains numerous traditional pieces and unique songs from a network of local Georgia musicians little heard elsewhere. The Lewis Family hosts an annual festival of its own, the Lewis Family Homecoming & Bluegrass Festival, in Lincolnton. They were inducted into the Georgia Music Hall of Fame in 1992 and have won several Dove awards. —*James Manheim*

● **16 Greatest Hits** / 1977 / Hollywood ✦✦✦✦
16 Greatest Hits is an adequate overview of the Lewis Family's biggest hits, featuring such songs as "Time Is Moving On," "Go Tell It on the Mountain," "Will the Circle Be Unbroken," "The Old Rugged Cross," "The Purple Rose" and "Climbing Jacob's Ladder." —*Stephen Thomas Erlewine*

Jerry Lee Lewis
b. Sep. 29, 1935, Ferriday, LA
Piano, Vocals / Rock & Roll, Traditional Country, Rockabilly, Honky Tonk
Is there an early rock & roller who has a crazier reputation than the Killer, Jerry Lee Lewis? His exploits as a piano-thumping egocentric wild man with an unquenchable thirst for living have become the fodder for numerous biographies, film documentaries, and a full-length Hollywood movie. Certainly few other artists came to the party with more ego and talent than he and lived to tell the tale. And certainly even fewer could successfully channel that energy into their music and prosper doing it as well as Jerry Lee. When he broke on the national scene in 1957 with his classic "Whole Lotta Shakin' Goin' On," he was every parents' worst nightmare perfectly realized: a long, blonde-haired Southerner who played the piano and sang with uncontrolled fury and abandon, while simultaneously reveling in his own sexuality. He was rock & roll's first great wild man and also rock & roll's first great eclectic.

Ignoring all manner of musical boundaries is something that has not only allowed his music to have wide variety, but to survive the fads and fashions as well. Whether singing a melancholy country ballad, a low-down blues, or a blazing rocker, Lewis' wholesale commitment to the moment brings forth performances that are totally grounded in his personality and all singularly of one piece. Like the recordings of Hank Williams, Louis Armstrong, and few others, Jerry Lee's early recorded work is one of the most amazing collections of American music in existence.

He was born to Elmo and Mamie Lewis on September 29, 1935. Though the family was dirt poor, there was enough money to be had to purchase a third-hand upright piano for the family's country shack in Ferriday, LA. Sharing piano lessons with his two cousins, Mickey Gilley and Jimmy Lee Swaggart, a ten-year old Jerry Lee Lewis showed remarkable aptitude toward the instrument. A visit from piano-playing older cousin Carl McVoy unlocked the secrets to the boogie-woogie styles he was hearing on the radio and across the tracks at *Haney's Big House*, owned by his uncle, Lee Calhoun, and catering to blacks exclusively. Lewis mixed that up with gospel and country and started coming up with his own style. He even mixed genres in the way he syncopated his rhythms on the piano; his left hand generally played a rock-solid boogie pattern while his right played the high keys with much flamboyant filigree and showiness, equal parts gospel fervor and Liberace showmanship. By the time he was 14, by all family accounts, he was as good as he was ever going to get. Lewis was already ready for prime time.

But his mother Mamie had other plans for the young family prodigy. Not wanting to squander Jerry Lee's gifts on the sordid world of show business, she enrolled him in a bible college in Waxahatchie, TX, secure in the knowledge that her son would now be exclusively singing his songs to the Lord. But legend has it that the Killer tore into a boogie-woogie rendition of "My God Is Real" at a church assembly that sent him packing the same night. The split personality of Lewis, torn between the sacred and the profane (rock & roll music), is something that has eaten away at him most of his adult life, causing untold aberrant personality changes over the years with no clear-cut answers to the problem. What is certain is that by the time a 21-year-old Jerry Lee showed up in Memphis on the doorstep of the Sun studios, he *had* been thrown out of bible college; been a complete failure as a sewing-machine salesman; been turned down by most Nashville-based record companies *and the Louisiana Hayride*; been married twice; in jail once; and burned with the passion that *he* truly was the next big thing.

Sam Phillips was on vacation when he arrived, but his assistant Jack Clement put Roland Janes on guitar and J. M. Van Eaton on drums behind Lewis, whose fluid left hand made a bass player superfluous. This little unit would become the core of Lewis' recording band for almost the entire seven years he recorded at Sun. The first single, a hopped-up rendition of Ralph Mooney's "Crazy Arms," sold in respectable enough quantities that Phillips kept bringing Lewis back in for more sessions, astounded by his prodigious memory for old songs and his penchant for rocking them up. A few days after his first single was released, Jerry Lee was in the Sun studios earning some Christmas money, playing backup piano on a Carl Perkins session that yielded the classics "Matchbox" and "Your True Love." At the tail end of the recording, Elvis Presley showed up, Clement turned on the tape machine, and the impromptu *Million Dollar Quartet* jam session ensued, with Perkins, Presley, and Lewis all having the time of their lives.

With the release of his first single, the road beckoned and it was here that Lewis' lasting stage persona was developed. Discouraged because he couldn't dance around the stage strumming a guitar like Carl Perkins, he stood up in mid-song, kicked back the piano stool and, as Perkins has so saliently pointed out, "a new Jerry Lee Lewis was born." This new-found stage confidence was not lost on Sam Phillips. While he loved the music of Carl Perkins and Johnny Cash, he saw neither artist as a true contender to Elvis' throne; with Lewis he thought he had a real shot. For the first time in his very parsimonious life, Sam Phillips threw every dime of promotional capital he had into Lewis' next single, and the gamble paid off a million times over. "Whole Lotta Shakin' Goin' On" went to number one on the country and the R&B charts, and was only held out of the top spot on the pop charts by Debbie Reynolds' "Tammy." Suddenly Lewis was the hottest, newest, most exciting rock & roller out there. His television appearances and stage shows were legendary for their manic energy, and his competitive nature to outdo anyone else on the bill led to the story about how he once set his piano on fire at set's end to make it impossible for Chuck Berry to follow his act. Nobody messed with the Killer.

Jerry Lee's follow-up to "Shakin'" was another defining moment for his career, as well as for rock & roll. "Great Balls of Fire" featured only piano and drums, but sounded huge with Phillips' production behind it. It got him into a rock & roll movie (*Jamboree*) and his fame was spreading to such a degree that Johnny Cash and Carl Perkins left Sun to go to Columbia Records. His next single, "Breathless," had a promotional tie-in with Dick Clark's Saturday night *Bandstand* show, making it three hits in a row for the newcomer. But Lewis was sowing the seeds of his own destruction in record time. He sneaked off and married his 13-year-old cousin, Myra Gale Brown, the daughter of his bass-playing uncle, J. W. Brown. With the Killer insisting that she accompany him on a debut tour of England, the British press got wind of the marriage and proceeded to crucify him in the press. The tour was canceled and Lewis arrived back in the U.S. to find his career in absolute disarray. His records were banned nationwide by radio stations and his booking price went from $10,000 a night to $250 in any honky tonk that would still have him. Undeterred, he kept right on doing what he had been doing, head unbowed and determined to make it back to the bigs, Jerry Lee Lewis style. It took him almost a dozen years to pull it off, but finally, with a sympathetic producer and a new record company willing to exact a truce with country disc jockeys, the Killer found a new groove, cutting one hit after another for Smash Records throughout the late '60s into the '70s. Still playing rock & roll on-stage whenever the mood struck him (which was often) while keeping all his releases pure country struck a creative bargain that suited Lewis well into the mid-'70s.

But while his career was soaring again, his personal life was falling apart. The next decade and a half saw several marriages fall apart (starting with his 13-year-long union with Myra), the deaths of his parents and oldest son, battles with the I.R.S., and bouts with alcohol and pills that frequently left him hospitalized. Suddenly the Ferriday Fireball was nearing middle age and the raging fire seemed to be burned out. But the mid-'80s saw another jump start to his career. A movie entitled *Great Balls of Fire!* was about to be made of his life and Lewis was called in to sing the songs for the soundtrack. Showing everyone who was the real Killer, Lewis sounded energetic enough to make you believe it was 1957 all over again with the pilot light of inspiration still burning bright. He also got a boost back to major-label land with a one-song appearance on the soundtrack for *Dick Tracy*.

With box sets and compilations, documentaries, a bio flick, and his induction to the Rock & Roll Hall of Fame all celebrating his legacy, Lewis still continued to record and tour, delivering work that vacillated from tepid to absolutely inspired. While his influence will continue to loom large until there's no one left to play rock & roll piano anymore, the plain truth is that there's only *one* Jerry Lee Lewis and American music will never see another like him. *—Cub Koda*

Jerry Lee Lewis / 1957 / Rhino ♦♦♦♦♦
The Killer's original album for Sun Records makes the compact disc sweepstakes with his big hit, "Whole Lotta Shakin' Going On," appended to the original 12-track lineup. It's a curious mixture, as Sam Phillips pulled songs from all avenues of Jerry Lee's repertoire, everything from handkerchief weepers like "It All Depends," "Fools Like Me," and a staid "Goodnight Irene" to rockers like "Put Me Down," "Matchbox," "Ubangi Stomp," "Don't Be Cruel," and "High School Confidential." But Jerry Lee even rocks up stuff like Hank Williams' "Jambalaya" and "When the Saints Go Marching In," making this one terrific debut, even if a great deal of his best material was inexplicably left off. *—Cub Koda*

Jerry Lee's Greatest / 1961 / Rhino ♦♦♦♦♦
This was Jerry Lee's second album released on the Sun label and, with the exception of "Great Balls of Fire," it's all late-period Killer sides from his tenure at the label. While tracks like "Let's Talk About Us," "What'd I Say," and "As Long as I Live" have their own charm, this set simply isn't the place to start a Jerry Lee collection; stick with the Rhino single-disc best-of to fill that need. For original album freaks and completists only. *—Cub Koda*

The Golden Hits of Jerry Lee Lewis / 1964 / Mercury ♦♦♦
Though the majority of the classic Jerry Lee Lewis hits were recorded for the Sun label, he did manage to resurrect his career and record some fine songs during his tenure on the Smash label. It was during this period that Lewis finally courted and was embraced by his country roots, and *The Golden Hits of Jerry Lee Lewis* highlights that portion particularly well with the inclusion of "Fools Like Me," "I'll Make It All Up to You," and excellent Hank Williams covers like "You Win Again" and "Your Cheatin' Heart." Not surprisingly, Lewis came off as a true natural in this venture, with his voice emerging as amazingly well-suited to the material—this is one side of his career that shouldn't be, though too often is, overlooked in the recorded Lewis canon. Of course, like many of the original rock & roll greats, Lewis couldn't keep himself from re-recording all his major hits, with the result being slightly more polished, less immediate-sounding versions that are only slightly inferior to the originals. "Great Balls of Fire," "Whole Lotta Shakin' Goin' On," "Breathless" and "High School Confidential" are given an overall bigger, booming sound with backup vocalists and a brass section, but most would probably still give the originals preeminence. Overall, this collection is terribly brief with only ten songs, but still is not a bad place to start for an overview of Lewis' years on Smash records. *—Matt Fink*

Country Songs for City Folks / 1965 / Smash ♦♦♦

The Return of Rock / 1965 / Smash ♦♦♦

Soul My Way / 1967 / Smash ♦♦♦

By Request / 1967 / Smash ♦♦♦

Memphis Beat / 1967 / Smash ♦♦♦

All Country / 1969 / Smash ♦♦♦

☆ **She Still Comes Around (To Love What's Left of Me)** / 1969 / Smash ♦♦♦♦♦
Another Place Another Time kicked off Jerry Lee Lewis' career as a straight-ahead country singer, bringing him his first hit in nearly five years. Renewed success was a longtime in coming, so it made perfect sense to follow it up with a record that pretty much mirrored its predecessor, right down to another fine Merle Haggard cover (this time, "Today I Started Loving You Again"). While it is accurate to call *She Still Comes Around (To Love What's Left of Me)* similar to *Another Place*, it's hardly devoid in inspiration; it was more like Jerry Lee found a good groove and continued to ride it, turning out another terrific hardcore country record. This time, the pain perhaps runs even stronger, with the Killer sounding tormented on the classic title track, remorseful on "Listen, They're Playing My Song" and heartbreaking on "To Make Love Sweeter for You," where his phrasing gives lie to the sentiments he's crooning. He also sounds a little emboldened by his success, not afraid to revisit the Sun side "Let's Talk About Us" and rock "Louisiana Man" pretty hard. Still, this is hardly a rock & roll record—it's a pure country record, made for late nights and smoky bars, and it's nearly as good as *Another Place*, containing the same consistent high quality of songs and performance. Based on this, the Killer had clearly entered a second golden age at the end of the '60s. [Note: the cover of this album, featuring a reflected Jerry Lee in the mirror of a desolate motel room—a tremendous visualization of the title song—is one of the greats.] *—Stephen Thomas Erlewine*

☆ **Another Place Another Time** / 1969 / Smash ♦♦♦♦♦
Jerry Lee Lewis had been at Smash Records for several years, searching for a hit and searching for a direction, prior to releasing *Another Place Another Time* in 1968. While the quality of his music didn't necessarily dip—he was still capable of transcendent moments on a regular basis—he was out of step with the times and lacked focus, simply cutting whatever he or producers laid across his piano. With *Another Place*, he snapped into focus and moved toward country. Not that the Killer had avoided country—his first single for Sun was a version of Ray Price's "Crazy Arms," and he cut many Hank Williams songs and country standards while at Sam Phillips' label—but here, he deliberately sticks to pure, hardcore country throughout the record, refashioning himself as a barroom balladeer and honky tonk raver. This reignited his career, sending him to the top of the charts with this album and its singles "What's Made Milwaukee Famous (Has Made a Loser Out of Me)" and "Another Place Another Time." Even though this brought him success, this was not the sound of Jerry Lee pandering for a mass audience. In 1968, hardcore country was not a stranger to the top of the charts—Merle Haggard and Johnny Cash were charting regularly—but it was not a surefire success, either, especially in a year when Glenn Campbell had *six* different number-one albums. Also, there were no other singers as stubbornly hardcore as the Killer, who not only made everything sound as if it was written for him, he made everything sound like it could only be played in a dark, damp bar late, late in the evening. This is seriously pure country music, and while he tackles some familiar songs, it's not in predictable ways—witness the storming "Walking the Floor Over You" or the heavy backbeat on "Break My Mind," where Jerry Lee takes standards and imparts his own signature. Then, there are the ballads and barroom weepers that form the heart of this record—the two hits, plus "Play Me a Song I Can Cry To," a sadly elegant "Before the Next Teardrop Falls," a high lonesome take on "I'm a Lonesome Fugitive," and a duet with Linda Gail Lewis on "We Live in Two Different Worlds." Song for song, there's not a bad tune here, and each performance is a stunner, making for not just a great second beginning, but for one of the greatest hardcore country albums ever. *—Stephen Thomas Erlewine*

☆ **She Even Woke Me up to Say Goodbye** / 1970 / Smash ♦♦♦♦♦
Jerry Lee Lewis turned to pure country in 1968, releasing two killer albums (no pun intended) in a row with *Another Place Another Time* and *She Still Comes Around (To Love What's Left of Me)*, which brought him the elusive success he so desired, so he and Smash cemented his reputation as a country crooner by releasing several albums in 1969 that were explicitly collections of covers of classic country albums. So, it wasn't until early 1970 that he unveiled a record of primarily new songs with *She Even Woke Me Up to Say Goodbye*. He was riding high on his new hits—so successful that new collections of his Sun singles made it to the country Top Ten—and took that as encouragement to do whatever he damn well pleased on this new record. So, he cut pure rock & roll (a thundering cover of "Brown Eyed Handsome Man"), inserted his name in every other song (in every verse on "Since I Met You Baby," where he manages to find a place to say his full name), laughed and leered, growled and crooned, pounding and gliding down the keyboard in equal measure. These are the fieriest, loosest performances he's given since leaving Sun (not counting, of course, the then-unreleased *Star Club* live recording), which jolts the hardcore country of *Another Place* and *She Still Comes Around* to a different stratosphere. Those were spectacular pure country records by any measure, but this is a spectacular pure *Jerry Lee* country record, where he's the center of every cut, every performance, and the record is tremendously addictive for it. Another stellar Smash platter from the Killer. *—Stephen Thomas Erlewine*

The Killer Rocks On / 1972 / Mercury ♦♦♦♦♦

Would You Take Another Chance on Me / 1972 / Mercury ♦♦♦

Who's Gonna Play This Old Piano / 1972 / Mercury ♦♦♦

Rockin / 1972 / Mercury ♦♦♦

The Session: London '73 / 1973 / Mercury ♦♦♦

I-40 Country / 1973 / Mercury ♦♦♦

Sometimes a Memory Ain't Enough / 1973 / Mercury ♦♦♦

Live at the International / 1973 / Mercury ♦♦♦

Southern Roots / 1974 / Mercury ♦♦♦
Southern Roots is commonly acknowledged as Jerry Lee Lewis' comeback, or at least his last great gasp. And, to a certain extent, that prevailing opinion is correct, since after this 1974 release, the quality of the Killer's releases fluctuate, but this attitude also implies that the Mercury records that preceded it were weak, which they were not (inconsistent,

perhaps, but all worthy). *Southern Roots* got the attention not just because it was deliberately touted as a comeback, but because it had the form, presentation, and attitude of a rock record, not least because there's a fair share of oldies here. Apart from the gospel closer, country has been consciously removed from the menu, a move that feels like the producer's choice, since Lewis' performances aren't all that much different or more impassioned than what came before. Sure, "Meat Man" is gleefully lascivious and sports a carnal growl not heard in years on his records, but it's the exception that proves the rule, since the rest of the record is as on-point as the country records of the early '70s. Jerry Lee doesn't sound relieved to be in this setting; he simply sounds like himself, barreling through a set of songs as he twists them to suit his needs. He's supported by a crack band who may be a little bit too polished to give this the kick that it allegedly has, but it's nevertheless highly enjoyable, particularly when the Killer throws in something unexpected, like slowing down "Hold on I'm Coming" to a sexy crawl or finding more spirit in "Haunted House" than "Blueberry Hill." And the latter points out a bit of a problem with the record—just enough of the song selections are too pat, as if the producers were saying, "Wouldn't it be great if Jerry Lee did 'When a Man Loves a Woman'?" instead of finding something he'd be great at singing. That doesn't make for a bad record, and it is indeed a good listen, but it does mean *Southern Roots* does show its seams, which is one of the reasons why it feels more like a manufactured comeback than an actual comeback. *—Stephen Thomas Erlewine*

Boogie Woogie Country Man / 1975 / Mercury ♦♦♦

Odd Man In / 1975 / Mercury ♦♦♦

I'm a Rocker / 1975 / Mercury ♦♦♦

Jerry Lee Lewis Keeps on Rockin' / 1978 / Mercury ♦♦♦

In Loving Memories / 1978 / Mercury ♦♦♦

Jerry Lee Lewis' sister, Linda Gail Lewis, wisely makes no attempt to portray her wildman brother as a holy-roller in her liner notes to his first gospel album, *In Loving Memories*. Lewis' dynamic and exuberant playing is certainly rooted in his enthusiastic religious upbringing, but the contradictions inherent in a hedonistic, so-called "Killer" cousin of Jimmy Swaggart do not put him first on the list of likely spiritual leaders. These personal conflicts lend a certain tension to Lewis' gospel music, whether or not you believe the humility and servitude he professes. The uptempo songs like "My God's Not Dead" and "I'll Fly Away" are the highlights of the set, as are Jerry and Linda's duet on the country gospel "I Know That Jesus Will Be There" and the falsetto fade-out on "Too Much to Gain to Lose." *—Greg Adams*

☆ **Live at the Star Club, Hamburg** / 1980 / Bear Family ♦♦♦♦♦

Words cannot describe—cannot *contain*—the performance captured on *Live at the Star Club, Hamburg*, an album that contains the very essence of rock & roll. When Jerry Lee performed the concert that became this album in the spring of 1964, his career was at its lowest point. Following his scandalous marriage to his teenage cousin, he was virtually blacklisted in the U.S., and by 1964, it had been six years since he had a real hit single, he was starting his recording career again with a new label and, to make matters worse, America had fallen in love with the Beatles and the bands that followed on the British Invasion, leaving him exiled from the charts. Ironically, he wound up in the Beatles' old haunt of the Star Club in Hamburg, Germany, in the spring of 1964, backed by the Nashville Teens, who had still had yet to have a hit with "Tobacco Road" (which would scale the charts later that year). Lewis and the Nashville Teens had been touring throughout the group's native England for about a month, capped off by a stint at the Star Club, where the band played for two weeks, but were only joined by the Killer for one night, which was what was captured on this incendiary recording. Who knows *why* this was a night where everything exploded for Jerry Lee Lewis. It sounds like all of his rage at not being the accepted king of rock & roll surfaced that night, but that probably wasn't a conscious decision on his part—maybe the stars were aligned right, or perhaps he just was in a particularly nasty mood that night. Or maybe this is the way he sounded on an average night in 1964. In any case, *Live at the Star Club* is *extraordinary*, the purest, hardest rock & roll ever committed to record. It starts with the Killer launching into "Mean Woman Blues" at a tempo *far* faster than the band is prepared for, and he never, ever lets go from that moment forward. He pounds the piano into submission, sings himself hoarse, berates the band ("What'd I Say, Pt. 2" has him yelling at a Nashville Teen to "play that thing right, boy!"), increases the tempo on each song, and joins in with the audience chanting his name. It's a crazed, unhinged performance, with the Nashville Teens running wild to follow his lead, and it's a great testament to the band that they nearly manage to keep up with him. One of the profound pleasures of this record is hearing the band try to run with Jerry Lee, which is exceeded only by the sheer dementia of the Killer's performance; he sounds possessed, hitting the keys so hard it sounds like they'll break, and rocking harder than anybody had before or since. Compared to this, thrash metal sounds tame, the Stooges sound constrained, hardcore punk seems neutered and the Sex Pistols sound like wimps. Rock & roll is about the fire in the performance, and nothings sounds as fiery as this; nothing hits as hard or sounds as loud, either. It is no stretch to call this the greatest live album ever, nor is it a stretch to call it the greatest rock & roll album ever recorded. Even so, words can't describe the music here—it has to be heard to truly be believed. *—Stephen Thomas Erlewine*

Fan Club Choice / 1984 / Mercury ♦♦♦

★ **18 Original Sun Greatest Hits** / 1984 / Rhino ♦♦♦♦♦

This 18-song CD contains Jerry Lee Lewis' best rock & roll sides from the 240 or so tracks that he recorded for Sun Records. If that sounds like the very tiny tip of a very large iceberg—it is. But this 1984 compilation remains 40 of rock & roll's hottest minutes, revealing as much about Jerry Lee Lewis as it's possible to learn from watching the movie *Great Balls of Fire!* The hit singles and best B-sides are assembled around the core of his 1957 Sun album—a great, and instructive, musical decision. Lewis' rocking version of "Jambalaya" and his ivory-based rendition of "Matchbox," "Big Blon' Baby," "Big Legged Woman," and "It'll Be Me," are all prime examples of his fiercely sexual personality, pounding away on those keys and whooping and hollering like a white version of Piano Red. Equally important, "Crazy Arms" held what would prove to be the key to his professional salvation: a distinct way with a country song that didn't blow the song right apart and also didn't lose the rock & roll audience. A big hunk of this stuff is available on the Sun debut album, which should be heard at least once (assuming one can't afford the Bear Family label's *Classic* box with his whole Sun output), but this is the place to start. The mid-'80s digital transfer still sounds good; its quality proves that Rhino always gave good value to its customers. The guitars on "Put Me Down" and "Wild One"—yes, there is guitar on a lot of these sides—are nice and crunchy, even though they're buried under the piano. If there's a flaw here, it's the absence of any liner notes (not that much needs to be said about music like this). *—Bruce Eder*

I'm on Fire / 1985 / Mercury ♦♦♦

Milestones / 1985 / Rhino ♦♦♦♦♦

There are so many Jerry Lee Lewis compilations out, ranging from single-disc Sun retrospectives to mammoth German imports documenting a few years in particular, that it's easy to lose track of what the best ones are. All you need to know about this double LP is that it's a good selection of his most famous material, properly emphasizing the late-'50s classics, with excellent liner notes. It also throws on enough of his most notable post-Sun cuts ("What's Made Milwaukee Famous," "Me and Bobby McGee") to make rock-oriented listeners feel that they have a sense of his post-rockabilly career without boring them to death. Those looking for one Jerry Lee album should get Rhino's *All Killer, No Filler* anthology instead. Those who are satisfied with *Milestones* as supplying all the Jerry Lee they want have no need to replace it. *—Richie Unterberger*

The Complete Palomino Club Recordings / 1989 / Tomato ♦♦♦♦

In the late '80s, Tomato released several CDs focusing on Jerry Lee Lewis' performances at the Palomino in L.A.'s suburban San Fernando Valley. First, Tomato released *Rockin' My Life Away, Rocket 88*, and the country-oriented *Heartbreak*. Then, in 1989, Tomato combined the contents of those three CDs on the double-CD *The Complete Palomino Club Recordings* and added ten bonus tracks. Though *Live at the Star Club* remains the Killer's most essential live album, the performances on this collection (which spans 1979-1985) find him in generally excellent form as both a honky tonker and a rock & roller. If one were asked whether Lewis was more convincing as a country singer or a rocker, it would be an impossible choice to make because the fact is that he's equally convincing in both areas. Rockabilly fans will savor his performances of hits like "Great Balls of Fire" and "Whole Lotta Shakin' Goin' On," but he's no less captivating when he turns his attention to several Hank Williams gems (including "Your Cheatin' Heart," "Cold Cold Heart," "Hey Good Lookin'," and "You Win Again") as well as Dottie West's "Careless Hands," Don Gibson's "I Can't Stop Loving You," and his own country smash "What Made Milwaukee Famous." The ten bonus tracks, meanwhile, range from "You Are My Sunshine" and "High School Confidential" to the country gospel favorite "Will the Circle Be Unbroken," which is an interesting choice for the Killer given his reputation for decadence. Boasting a total of 42 selections, this is a collection that Lewis' devotees will find to be a musical feast. *—Alex Henderson*

Classic / 1989 / Bear Family ♦♦♦♦♦

At eight discs, including numerous alternate takes all presented in sequential order, Bear Family's thorough retrospective of Jerry Lee Lewis' Sun recordings on *Classic* is a monumental, even exhausting experience, even for those serious listeners prepared to immerse themselves in this music. Not that the music itself is taxing; it's among the very finest music of its time, probably of the 20th century. The key is the presentation: When these takes are strung together in the sequence of their recording (which can mean that the master is sandwiched between alternates), it may be possible to hear Lewis' approach develop, but the impact of his Sun recordings—the core mastertakes—becomes diffuse because it's impossible to hear those, as a body of work, without significant tweaking. Of course, this approach does enhance appreciation of Jerry Lee's music (there was serious craft behind it, as well as a staggering amount of raw talent), but it does make it the province of scholars and dedicated fans. Even with these problems—the fact that this does not make for easy listening—it's still an essential part of a comprehensive rock & roll, country, or American music collection, because Jerry Lee's music is that good. As he said, he was one of the master stylists, and years later, that is more evident than ever. *—Stephen Thomas Erlewine*

Rocket '88 / 1989 / Tomato ♦♦♦

In the late '70s and early to mid-'80s, it was clear that Jerry Lee Lewis wasn't interested in radical change. His strong points were still rockabilly and country, and the Killer continued to excel by zeroing in on them. Although not in a class with the outstanding *Live at the Star Club*, the live performances documented on this CD (all recorded at the Palomino in North Hollywood, CA) prove that the Killer was still more than willing to go that extra mile. Lewis' voice had held up impressively well, and he sounds quite confident and assured—perhaps even cocky—on everything from Hank Williams' "Hey, Good Lookin'" and Ray Charles' "What'd I Say" to Chuck Berry's "Johnny B. Goode." And when he rips into hits like "Great Balls of Fire" and "Whole Lotta Shakin' Going On," it's crystal clear that one of the all-time masters of rock & roll is very hard at work. *—Alex Henderson*

Rockin' My Life Away / Oct. 15, 1991 / Tomato ♦♦♦♦

Like his other Tomato CDs, *Heartbreak* and *Rocket '88, Rockin' My Life Away* documents Jerry Lee Lewis' hot-blooded performances at his preferred venue in L.A., the Palomino. Much of the material is the same. Excelling as both a rockabilly dynamo and a honky tonk hero, the Killer sounds as inspired on "Great Balls of Fire," "Whole Lotta Shakin' Goin' On" and "Meat Man" as he does on country classics like "What Made Milwaukee

Famous," "Your Cheatin' Heart" and "I Can't Stop Lovin' You." In fact, Lewis still sounds like he's very much in his prime. For more casual listeners, *Rockin' My Life Away* would be as strong a choice as *Rocket '88*. And for completists, hearing even more versions of these songs will be a treat. *—Alex Henderson*

The Greatest Live Show on Earth / 1991 / Bear Family ✦✦✦✦✦
Combining two live albums originally issued in the '60s, Lewis proves that the onslaught of the British Invasion hadn't lowered his rocking quotient one single bit. Blazing performances. *—Cub Koda*

★ **All Killer, No Filler: The Jerry Lee Lewis Anthology** / May 18, 1993 / Rhino ✦✦✦✦✦
The Sun material stops 12 songs into Rhino's double-disc, 42-track collection, *All Killer, No Filler: The Jerry Lee Lewis Anthology*. Since Jerry Lee's legacy is built on his scintillating sides for Sun—they're among the fiercest rock & roll ever recorded—that could seem to be a problem, but the Killer didn't stop making great music when he left the label. He continued to cut classics for Smash and Mercury well into the '70s, after he toned down the rock & roll and turned up the country. Prior to *All Killer, No Filler*, no other collection attempted to tell this story, but this set does, taking it all the way into the early '80s, when Lewis wrapped up his career as an active recording artist. The scope of this alone is to be admired, particularly because most listeners tend to concentrate on "Crazy Arms," "Whole Lotta Shakin' Going On," "Great Balls of Fire," "Down the Line," "Breathless," and "High School Confidential," overlooking everything else he did, even his string of number-one country singles in the late '60s and early '70s. Those singles are justly celebrated, but this proves that his sides for Smash and Mercury are equally stellar—maybe not as visceral or potent, but surely as musically satisfying. They also offer a clear argument for Jerry Lee's versatility and strength as a stylist, how he can make any song sound as if it were written especially for him. *All Killer, No Filler* accomplishes this by not providing a laundry list of hits—although all the key ones are here—but by wisely choosing among his vast catalog of album tracks, forgotten singles, and even live cuts. Apart from arguably "In the Mood," which demonstrates his instrumental prowess but slows the flow, there's not a wrong move here, and it would be hard to better this as either a concise career summary or introduction. Neophytes who just want a heavy dose of Sun should stick with *18 Original Sun Greatest Hits*, but anybody who truly wants to appreciate the richness of Jerry Lee Lewis' music should start here. *—Stephen Thomas Erlewine*

The Locust Years . . . And the Return to the Promised Land / Nov. 29, 1994 / Bear Family ✦✦✦✦✦
Picking up where the eight-CD set *Classic* left off, the eight-CD box *The Locust Years . . . And the Return to the Promised Land* rivals its predecessor in musical quality. Tracing Jerry Lee Lewis' '60s career at Smash Records, the first two discs find the pianist trying to replicate his rock & roll success; while the performances were good, it was clear he was out of touch with the times. During the third disc, he begins to concentrate on country music. The fourth, fifth, and sixth discs match his Sun recordings for consistently brilliant performances; several of the songs became big hits on the country charts, establishing him as a country star. The seventh disc chronicles an exciting unreleased show, while the eighth disc is an unexceptional interview. For dedicated Jerry Lee Lewis fans, *The Locust Years* is every bit as essential as *Classic*. *—Stephen Thomas Erlewine*

Killer Country / 1995 / Mercury ✦✦✦✦✦
For obvious reasons, *Killer Country* has been a popular title for collections of Jerry Lee Lewis' Smash and Mercury recordings, and the 1995 Mercury collection that bears this name is pretty much a typical collection with this title. Spanning 20 tracks over the course of one disc, this hits many of Jerry Lee's big country hits for the two labels, from the career-reviving 1968 hit "Another Place Another Time" to the defining 1977 hit "Middle Age Crazy." Between those two, there are many other great sides—"She Still Comes Around (To Love What's Left of Me)," "What's Made Milwaukee Famous," "She Even Woke Me Up to Say Goodbye," "Once More With Feeling"—but it misses just as many great songs. "To Make Love Sweeter for You," "Chantilly Lace," "One Has My Name (The Other Has My Heart)," "Invitation to Your Party," "Don't Let Me Cross Over," "Would You Take a Chance on Me," and "Sometimes a Memory Ain't Enough," are nowhere to be found, and while there's nothing *bad* here, these songs are all missed and prevent this from being the definitive single-disc overview it could have been. Still, it's a good sampler, and a good introduction to the classic Smash/Mercury recordings, even if it could have been better. *—Stephen Thomas Erlewine*

Young Blood / May 23, 1995 / Sire ✦✦
Jerry Lee Lewis made a comeback effort in 1995 with *Young Blood*. Although the Killer's performance is impressive—his voice continues to weather well with age and he hasn't lost much of his instrumental prowess—the selection of material is fairly uninspired and predictable. This wouldn't have been a problem if Jerry Lee was allowed to work with a top-notch backing band, elevating the pedestrian material to a new level. Instead, *Young Blood* was made like most albums in the mid-'90s—each song was constructed track-by-track, with the musicians laying down their parts at different times. Consequently, the record is stripped of most of its potential power, leaving behind a well-produced but thoroughly unengaging album. *—Stephen Thomas Erlewine*

Greatest Hits: Finest Performances / Jul. 11, 1995 / Sun ✦✦✦
This would serve as a true greatest-hits package of Lewis' early Sun days, except it's missing "High School Confidential," "What'd I Say," and "Sweet Little Sixteen." "Whole Lot of Shakin' Going On," "Great Balls of Fire," and "Breathless" are here, however, flanked by "Crazy Arms," "End of the Road," "Move on Down the Line," and "Lewis Boogie." The big bonus for Lewis completists is in the production foul-up that puts yet another alternate take of "It'll Be Me" in place of the single or album version. If it wasn't for the couple of tracks of filler, this would be the perfect JLL hits set. *—Cub Koda*

EP Collection, Vol. 2 . . . Plus / Oct. 29, 1996 / See for Miles ✦✦✦

Mercury/Smash Years Recordings: Featuring Live & Studio Recording / Nov. 5, 1996 / Collectables ✦✦✦

The Best of Jerry Lee Lewis / May 26, 1998 / Music Club ✦✦✦✦
A blanket statement here: *any* compilation made up of any of Jerry Lee Lewis' Sun recordings is worth owning, as few artists left behind so consistent a body of work. This 20-tracker has just about all the essentials (it's docked a few points for leaving off "Crazy Arms," "End of the Road," and "It'll Be Me") that get your JLL collection off to a fine start. Off-the-wall bonus tracks like "Pumpin' Piano Rock," "In the Mood," and "Drinkin' Wine Spo-Dee-O-Dee" not included in these usual best-ofs make this set great listening, with enough of his country weepers to break things up quite nicely. If you see this one in the bin, by all means pick it up. *—Cub Koda*

Whole Lotta Shakin' Goin On: The Very Best of Jerry Lee Lewis / Feb. 2, 1999 / Collectables ✦✦✦

Invitation to Your Party: The Very Best of Jerry Lee Lewis / Feb. 2, 1999 / Collectables ✦✦✦

Original Golden Hits, Vol. 1-2 / Oct. 12, 1999 / Collectables ✦✦✦✦

Rockin' Rhythm & Blues/Golden Cream of the Country / Oct. 12, 1999 / Collectables ✦✦✦✦
In 1999, Collectables released *Rockin' Rhythm & Blues/Golden Cream of the Country*, which contained two complete albums—*Rockin' Rhythm & Blues* (1969, originally released on Sun) and *Golden Cream of the Country* (1969, originally released on Sun)—by Jerry Lee Lewis on one compact disc. *—Jason Birchmeier*

Taste of Country/Ole Tyme Country Music / Oct. 12, 1999 / Collectables ✦✦✦✦
In 1999, Collectables released *Taste of Country/Ole Tyme Country Music*, which contained two complete albums—*Taste of Country* and *Ole Tyme Country Music* (both originally released on Sun)—by Jerry Lee Lewis on one compact disc. *—Jason Birchmeier*

Monsters/Roots / Oct. 12, 1999 / Collectables ✦✦✦
In 1999, Collectables released *Monsters/Roots*, which contained two complete albums—*Monsters* and *Roots* (both originally released on Sun)—by Jerry Lee Lewis on one compact disc. *—Jason Birchmeier*

20th Century Masters—The Millennium Collection: The Best of Jerry Lee Lewis / Oct. 19, 1999 / Hip-O ✦✦✦
20th Century Masters: The Millennium Collection collects 12 highlights from Jerry Lee's Smash recordings, which means the first four tracks—"Whole Lotta Shakin' Goin' On," "Great Ball of Fire," "Breathless," and "High School Confidential"—are re-recordings. Good re-recordings, but re-recordings all the same. That doesn't really matter, since the remaining eight songs are all prime hardcore honky tonk from the killer. "Another Time Another Place," "What's Made Milwaukee Famous," "She Even Woke Me Up to Say Goodbye," "Drinkin' Wine Spo-Dee-O-Dee," and "Middle Age Crazy" are all classics, and the remaining three cuts are just a notch below their high quality. So, while *20th Century Masters* may not deliver the classic Sun hits, it does provide a good budget-line introduction to his country work, which is still underappreciated by audiences who just know his rocking classics. *—Stephen Thomas Erlewine*

The Very Best of Jerry Lee Lewis / Feb. 8, 2000 / Collectables ✦✦✦

Live / May 4, 2000 / EMI-Capitol Special Markets ✦✦✦
An unidentified and undated live concert that aurally sounds like a radio broadcast from a late-'70s outing. It's well recorded and Jerry Lee is in decent cruise-control mode, rocking out when he needs to, but certainly not the caliber of *Live at the Star Club* or *Greatest Live Show on Earth*, two of the strongest live albums by *anyone*. The backing band gamely keeps up with the Killer as he simply makes it all up as he goes along, jumping between country weepers and blues ("C.C. Rider," "Who Will the Next Fool Be," "Careless Hands," "You Win Again," "Georgia on My Mind") and rockers like "Mean Woman Blues," "Chantilly Lace," "Great Balls of Fire," "Meat Man," and the inevitable "Whole Lot of Shakin' Going On." No notes at all, but a decent late-model Jerry Lee nonetheless. *—Cub Koda*

By Invitation Only / Jun. 6, 2000 / Ember ✦✦
Here's a two-disc set of live private recordings of Jerry Lee playing some place in Dalton, GA, in December of 1972. The quality is bootleg at best, and while the Killer is rocking on here, the Podunk sound quality ultimately sinks this collection. Save your money and buy *Live at the Star Club* instead if you want the ultimate Jerry Lee live album. *—Cub Koda*

25 All-Time Greatest Sun Recordings / Jun. 6, 2000 / Varese ✦✦✦✦✦
Just one of many of Jerry Lee's Sun best-ofs, this one largely sticks to the original single releases with a few strays like "Drinkin' Wine Spo-Dee-O-Dee" thrown in to fill things out. The transfers are as clean as it gets and although this doesn't replace Rhino's version of essentially the same material, it does offer a few stray tracks ("Love on Broadway," "Waitin' for a Train," "I Can't Seem to Say Goodbye," "One Minute Past Eternity," "Invitation to Your Party") you might want or need if you don't feel like popping for Bear Family's exhaustive eight-disc box set. *—Cub Koda*

Mercury Smashes . . . and Rockin' Sessions / Dec. 13, 2000 / Bear Family ✦✦✦✦✦
The third installment of Bear Family's exhaustive reissue of Jerry Lee Lewis' complete recordings, *Mercury Smashes . . . and Rockin' Sessions*, covers the era that many listeners, even some fans, dismiss—his late-'60s and '70s recordings for Mercury. Conventional wisdom claims that the Killer was pretty much spent as a creative force during this time, since he had already made his near-triumphant comeback as a hard country singer on Mercury in the mid-'60s, and that he coasted on formula, except for the concentrated burst of the *Roots* album. Like most conventional wisdom, this one has a hint of truth,

because his recordings did start to have a bit of formula and he did coast for a bit, but it ignores the fact that this was enjoyable formula and that Lewis remained an expert stylist, kicking out songs that may not have been first-rate, but were often given first-rate performances. This is why this set is enjoyable for the dedicated, even at its length of ten discs, because it's at a fairly consistent quality throughout; it also helps that the alternates are all stowed away on the final few discs, which means it's much easier to hear Lewis' main Mercury recordings and much easier to simply listen to, unlike either the *Classic* or *Locust Years* set. To be sure, this is for the dedicated, but if you're of the opinion that Lewis is one of the musical titans of the 20th century, this will enhance and deepen your love and respect instead of sully it. *—Stephen Thomas Erlewine*

Rockin' the Blues: 25 Great Sun Recordings / 2002 / Varese ✦✦✦✦

These 25 tracks focus on the blues-slanted side of Jerry Lee Lewis' large Sun discography, running from 1957 to 1963. Certainly it's not a recommended first or second choice for people looking for the best of Lewis' Sun output, and Jerry Lee fanatics might well already have all of these on box set reissues of Lewis on Sun. Actually, though, it's not a bad buy for those who want to hear more of Jerry Lee than a greatest-hits set, but whose budget, time, and interest prohibit investment in Bear Family's *Classic* box set. There aren't any really well-known Lewis hits here, though "Whole Lotta Shakin' Going On" is represented by an alternate take, and his cover of "What'd I Say" by a 1960 recording that precedes the one used on the 1961 hit version. There are few Lewis originals on a disc that testifies to his broad repertoire of blues and R&B covers, including such standards as "Drinkin' Wine Spo-Dee-O-Dee," "Matchbox," "Hound Dog," "Mean Woman Blues," "C.C. Rider," "Good Rockin' Tonight," and "Be-Bop-A-Lula" (though some would quibble whether that Gene Vincent hit is "blues"). A dozen of these were never issued on Sun (indeed, eight of them make their first U.S. appearance here), and many of the others didn't first surface until the late '50s and early '60s, so there's little danger of coming across overexposed material. And while it's not the first Jerry Lee Lewis you'll slap in the spinner, it's pretty consistently good stuff, containing some of the more overlooked highlights of his early work. There's the percolating "Mean Woman Blues," for example, and the obscure 1963 single "Teenage Letter," which adds some uncharacteristic elements to the arrangement (an organ and a yakety sax) without diminishing the quality of the result. *—Richie Unterberger*

★ **Another Place Another Time/She Even Woke Me Up to Say Goodbye** / Nov. 5, 2002 / Raven ✦✦✦✦✦

Raven's 2002 two-fer CD reissue of Jerry Lee Lewis' 1968 album *Another Place Another Time* and 1970's *She Even Woke Me Up to Say Goodbye* contains the added bonus of six tracks—over half the album—from 1969's *She Still Comes Around (To Love What's Left of Me)*. By doing this, the disc transcends typical two-fer status (which, frankly, would have been enough, since these two albums are so tremendous, their first CD release is something to celebrate) and becomes the best single-disc collection of Jerry Lee's country material. There have been other discs that tackle the same recordings for Smash (all unfortunately out of print as of this writing), but their scope was a little broader, including many of his '70s hits for Mercury as well as Smash sides unheard here. On the surface, this may seem to be a drawback—more is usually better, after all—but the narrow focus of this two-fer highlights his peak as pure country singer, when he found his voice and ran with it. He made great music after *She Even Woke Me Up to Say Goodbye*, to be sure, and had plenty of hits, but these three albums are classics, bristling with excitement and infused with hardcore honky tonk pathos. It's not just that Jerry Lee sounds great on these songs—he rarely sounded bad, after all—but it's that the songs are perfectly suited for him, and the performances are as bold and robust as he is. Also, all the key country hits—"What's Made Milwaukee Famous (Has Made a Loser Out of Me)," "Another Place Another Time," "She Still Comes Around (To Love What's Left of Me)," "Once More With Feeling," "She Even Woke Me Up to Say Goodbye"—are here, and the depth of quality of this material is richer than on some hit collections. These are not just three of the best Jerry Lee albums, they're three of the best and hardest country music ever waxed, and even if one of the records isn't here in its entirety (the best cuts are, though), this is the best way to currently hear them. It's an absolutely essential collection. *—Stephen Thomas Erlewine*

Johnie Lewis

b. Oct. 8, 1908, Eufaula, AL

Vocals, Guitar / Country Blues

Johnie Lewis was a decent, if unexceptional, singer and guitarist in the Southern rural style, particularly accomplished at playing slide. Though he was born in Alabama and grew into adulthood in Georgia, Lewis spent most of his life in Chicago, moving the city in the 1930s. A painter by profession, Lewis only pursued music as an avocation, but through one of his painting jobs, he came to the notice of a filmmaker doing a documentary about Chicago blues. His appearance in that film lead to recording sessions for Arhoolie in the early '70s. *—Richie Unterberger*

Alabama Slide Guitar / 1970 / Arhoolie ✦✦✦

Here are 18 songs recorded by Lewis in 1970 and 1971. If Lewis were one of the few practitioners of the Southern country slide blues guitar, this would be an important document. But the fact is that because there are so many similar performers in the style who recorded more prolifically and with greater imagination, it's just a solid journeyman entry in the field. Lewis does have an affable storytelling manner to his songwriting, and gets in some nifty laidback slide licks; a couple of the more ambitious tunes were inspired by Dr. Martin Luther King Jr. *—Richie Unterberger*

Laurie Lewis

b. 1950, Berkeley, CA

Fiddle, Violin, Vocals / Neo-Traditional Folk, Progressive Bluegrass, Traditional Bluegrass

Laurie Lewis learned to play the violin as a child in the San Francisco Bay Area. As a teenager in the 1960s, she immersed herself in the city's thriving folk scene and fell in love with the innovative bluegrass of Flatt & Scruggs, the Stanley Brothers, and especially Doc Watson. She won numerous fiddling contests during the 1970s and was in and out of assorted area combos. Together with friend Kathy Kallick, Lewis co-founded the pioneering bluegrass group Good Ol' Persons in 1975 and remained with the popular group until 1979. She then formed the Grant Street String Band before bowing as a solo artist with 1986's *Restless Rambling Heart* (Flying Fish), which mixed old-timey sounds with contemporary bluegrass and folk. *Love Chooses You* followed in 1989.

The 1990 album *Singin' My Troubles Away* was attributed to Laurie Lewis & Grant Street and featured guitarist Scott Nygaard, banjoist Tony Furtado, and mandolin player Tom Rozum. Lewis re-teamed with Kallick for 1991's *Together*, which was also the first of many releases for Rounder. After the release of *True Stories* in 1993, Lewis and her bandmates were in a serious auto accident. She took a few years off but returned with *The Oak and the Laurel*, which featured a series of duets with mandolinist Rozum. (The album was nominated for a Best Traditional Folk Album Grammy in 1996.) *Seeing Things* appeared in 1998 and focused on Lewis' considerable talents as a songwriter and singer. A year later she issued the rollicking *Laurie Lewis & Her Bluegrass Pals*. In the early 2000s Lewis made guest contributions to other artists' albums, devoted some time to her second love, the acoustic bass, and dabbled in producing. *—Johnny Loftus*

● **Restless Rambling Heart** / 1986 / Flying Fish ✦✦✦✦✦

The first solo album from this Bay Area singer and fiddler is sweet but not saccharine, a mix of old-time, bluegrass, and rootsy contemporary folk. *—Mark A. Humphrey*

Love Chooses You / 1989 / Flying Fish ✦✦✦✦

Laurie Lewis' second album is a diverse crowd-pleaser that features some of her very best songs. Lewis exposes a certain naiveté in her self-penned song notes, but perhaps most revealing are her comments on the title track, which are almost absurdly modest. In truth, "Love Chooses You" is a gorgeous song that by all rights should enjoy a long life as a folk classic. In general, this plays like a live concert and covers an astonishing number of styles, with "Old Friend" and "Texas Bluebonnets" being the other high spots. *—Jim Smith*

Singin' My Troubles Away / 1990 / Flying Fish ✦✦✦✦

With *Singin' My Troubles Away*, Laurie Lewis balances her music between folk-tinged country and progressive bluegrass. Though Lewis' fiddle certainly takes the center-stage, she has assembled a first-class backing band—featuring guitarist Scott Nygaard, banjoist Tony Furtado, bassist Tammy Fassaert and mandonlinist Tom Rozum—that keeps the music vibrant and alive. *—Thom Owens*

Together / 1991 / Rounder ✦✦✦

Country's relationship with bluegrass is a lot like the relationships between reggae and ska, soca and calypso, or zydeco and Cajun music—they aren't identical, but they're quite similar and share a common heritage. Country and bluegrass are both descendants of the Irish, British, and Scottish traditions that immigrants brought to the United States from the British Isles in the 19th and 20th centuries; thus, some country artists can fit right in at a bluegrass festival if they're rootsy enough, and many bluegrass-oriented artists include a lot of country in their repertoire. At bluegrass festivals, it isn't uncommon for someone to play Bill Monroe one minute and Ernest Tubb or Hank Williams Sr. the next. Teaming up with longtime ally Kathy Kallick, Laurie Lewis provides a healthy blend of bluegrass and old-time country on *Together*. At times, it is hard to tell where the bluegrass ends and the old-time country begins. But, however one might choose to categorize a particular performance, this is a rewarding album. When Lewis and Kallick recorded *Together* in 1991, they had been working together for 17 years—the singer/musicians first joined forces in 1974. So, not surprisingly, they enjoy a strong rapport whether they're embracing original material like Kallick's "Count Your Blessings" (which borders on country gospel) or putting their spin on the Carter Family's "Little Annie" and the traditional "Going Up on the Mountain." Lewis and Kallick share the lead and background vocals, and both of them play acoustic instruments—Lewis is heard on fiddle, upright bass, and banjo, while Kallick sticks to the guitar. *Together* isn't among Lewis or Kallick's essential releases, but it's a solid and pleasing example of the Northern Californians' bluegrass/country collaborations. *—Alex Henderson*

True Stories / 1993 / Rounder ✦✦✦

Laurie Lewis has enjoyed most of her support from traditional bluegrass and folk audiences, and yet, she's hardly a slave to tradition. A varied release, *True Stories* ranges from the traditional Irish song "Singing Bird" to the country gems "Who Will Watch the Home Place," "Still a Fool" and "Val's Cabin" to folk-pop numbers like "Knocking on Your Door Again" and "Swept Away." The Bay Area native is as excellent a songwriter as she is a vocalist, and it isn't hard to imagine "Val's Cabin" or "You'll Be Leaving Me" being big country hits with slicker production and some of Nashville's promotional muscle. Lewis' audience is a small one, but her music is definitely well worth getting to know. *—Alex Henderson*

The Oak and the Laurel / 1995 / Rounder ✦✦✦

Earth & Sky: Songs of Laurie Lewis / Jul. 8, 1997 / Rounder ✦✦✦

Excerpting Laurie Lewis' trio of albums for Flying Fish, and adding four new cuts, the collection does a good job of tracking her development as a country/bluegrass performer, and her adoption of more open forms that cater to more of a singer-songwriter mode—the concluding "Magic Light," in fact, is quite haunting. A good starting point. *—Steven E. McDonald*

Seeing Things / May 5, 1998 / Rounder ✦✦✦✦

While previous albums have explored Lewis' prodigious fiddle talents and her ability to put a new spin on bluegrass music, *Seeing Things* zeroes in on her glorious voice and her ability to tell a story with it. Eight of the 11 tunes come from her pen; tunes like "The

Refugee," "Kiss Me Before I Die," "Angel on His Shoulder," and "Bane and Balm" all show tremendous growth as a writer, while the opening "Blues Days, Sleepless Nights" bears strong comparison to her best bluegrass work. Tom Russel's "Manzanar" (the story of a World War II Japanese POW), her duet with Cris Williamson on "Let the Bird Go Free" and the traditional "The Blackest Crow" set moods bleak, somber and ethereal. But mostly it comes down to Lewis' voice, an instrument of uncommon beauty, depth and versatility. This is one special album. *—Cub Koda*

Laurie Lewis & Her Bluegrass Pals / May 4, 1999 / Rounder ✦✦✦

Laurie Lewis comes full circle and brings a batch of her friends together for an inspired session of straight-ahead bluegrass. There's an empathy to the playing of Lewis with mandolinist Tom Rozum, banjoist Craig Smith, bassist Todd Phillips, and rhythm guitarist Mary Gibbons that grows on you as the album unfolds with the strong trio singing of Lewis, Gibbons, and Rozum that's equally as seductive. Highlights include "Tall Pines," Jimmy Martin's "Stepping Stones," Jean Ritchie's "Black Waters," "Acony Bell," and Lewis' own "Wind at Play," "Blow, Big Wind," and "Big Eddy." It's an inspired session. *—Cub Koda*

Winter's Grace / Jul. 20, 1999 / Signature ✦✦✦

Margaret Lewis

Vocals / Rock & Roll, Country-Pop, Rockabilly, Swamp Pop

In the late '50s Margaret Lewis recorded some obscure rockabilly and bluesy swamp pop singles for the small Shreveport, LA, label Ram. Her sides attract interest by simple virtue of the fact that there weren't many woman rockabilly or swamp pop singers at all, and there weren't even a whole lot of performers, male or female, concentrating on rockabilly by the beginning of the 1960s. Nonetheless, she had a thin and average voice that seemed willing to, but did not, bring out the gutsiest elements in our earthy material, which sometimes crossed rockabilly with down-home blues, gospel, and country-soul. That wouldn't have been as much of a problem if the material had not been average as well. Sometimes, indeed, it was below average, as was the production. Still, she did get to work with some big names, doing backup vocals with Dale Hawkins in the late '50s (on-stage and in the studio). In addition, Johnny Winter played on a couple of numbers she cut in New Orleans, which were not issued until 1995.

After Ram began to fold in the early '60s, Lewis did some recordings for Capitol in the mid-'60s and worked in Las Vegas clubs. She then joined forces with Ram owner Mira Smith—who had played guitar on some of Lewis' Ram sides and co-written some of them with Lewis—to push themselves as a songwriting team. They penned hits, mostly in the country style, for Margaret Whiting ("I Almost Called Your Name"), David Houston ("Mountain of Love"), Jeanne C. Riley ("Country Girl," "The Girl Most Likely," "The Rib," "The Singer"), Connie Francis ("Wedding Cake"), and Peggy Scott and Jo Jo Benson ("Soul Shake"). A compilation of her Ram sides and unreleased material, most from the Ram era by the sound of it, was released by Ace as *Lonesome Bluebird* in 1995. *—Richie Unterberger*

● **Lonesome Bluebird** / Feb. 7, 1995 / Ace ✦✦✦✦✦

This 27-song anthology combines a dozen songs that came out on Ram between 1959 and 1961 with previously unreleased material. Dates aren't given for the previously unreleased stuff, not even general ones, but from the sound of things they probably also date from the 1960s, although one, "Reconsider Me," has 1980 noted on the track listing. Although a woman singing earthy, occasionally raunchy, rockabilly, and swampy pop/blues/country/gospel sounds intriguing, Lewis is no Bobbie Gentry or Tony Joe White. Her voice is enthusiastic, but average at best, and the material (much of which she wrote or co-wrote) would have benefited from performance by better singers. The production sometimes lets down the songs (which aren't so outstanding anyway), either because of a demo thinness or, in the case of the previously unissued "Raggedy Ann and Player Piano," a ragged arrangement that veers close to Hasil Adkins territory in its erratic sense of time. A reasonable amount of stylistic ground is covered, from sax-driven rock and fairly raw rockabilly (the 1959 single "Shake a Leg") to spare, underproduced numbers with reverb swamp guitar, and country-pop tunes that probably date from well after the 1959-1961 Ram sides ("And There Was No You"). Johnny Winter and his band are on the previously unreleased "Bow Wow Puppy Love" and "Lover's Land," given an early-'60s New Orleans rock production, which is no surprise given that it was done at Cosimo Matissa's studio in New Orleans. One should also note that this version of "Dust My Blues" is one of the less effective treatments of that blues standard. *—Richie Unterberger*

The Light Crust Doughboys

f. 1931

Group / Western Swing

One of the original Western swing bands, the Light Crust Doughboys once featured the combined talents of Western swing's two most renowned figures, Bob Wills and Milton Brown. That lineup was unfortunately short-lived, due in large part to issues with the group's overly controlling manager, W. Lee "Pappy" O'Daniel (who would later become governor of Texas). However, even after all three of those figures were gone, the Light Crust Doughboys soldiered on, becoming one of the most popular prewar Western swing bands in Texas; versions of the group continued to perform, off and on, right up to the turn of the millennium. The group that became the Light Crust Doughboys was formed in 1929 as the Wills Fiddle Band, when Bob Wills joined up with guitarist Herman Arnspiger in Fort Worth, TX. The duo began playing dances and radio shows, and hooked up with singer Milton Brown in 1930. Brown's brother Durwood soon joined the band as a second guitarist, and banjoist Clifford "Sleepy" Johnson arrived not long after. The group landed a regular radio gig in Fort Worth sponsored by the Aladdin Lamp Company, and accordingly changed their name to the Aladdin Laddies.

That didn't last long, however; in 1931, the band landed their own morning show on a rival station, sponsored by Burris Mill, the makers of Light Crust Flour. Pappy O'Daniel managed the company at the time, and he convinced them to adopt Light Crust Doughboys as their new name. Still, O'Daniel disliked the group's music, dismissing it as "hillbilly"; he attempted to cancel the show after just two weeks, but popular demand kept the group on the air (as well as a deal with O'Daniel whereby the bandmembers agreed to work in the flour mill). With their regular radio show and wide-ranging musical repertoire (country, blues, jazz, pop, gospel, and more), the Light Crust Doughboys became one of the most popular and widely exposed bands in Texas. Musicians like singer/yodeler Leon Huff, steel guitarist Leon McAuliffe, and banjoist Johnnie Lee Wills began playing with the group. Realizing he had a good thing on his hands, O'Daniel became the Doughboys' manager and sometime songwriter as well as the show's announcer; he first moved the Doughboys to a new station, and then landed their show on a syndicated radio network that spread their sound across the Southwest. But his refusal to allow the band to play gigs outside the radio show was frustrating to its members, who felt they weren't seeing enough money.

Wills, Johnson, and the Brown brothers recorded a single for Victor in 1932 under the name the Fort Worth Doughboys, which was a precursor to Milton Brown leaving the group several months later. Wills replaced him with Tommy Duncan, but clashed frequently with O'Daniel, and wound up leaving himself in the summer of 1933, taking Duncan with him. Undeterred, O'Daniel reorganized the Doughboys and brought them to Chicago later in the year for a recording session with Vocalion. However, his days with the band were numbered as well; disputes with the Burris Mill Company led to his being fired in 1935. O'Daniel put together a new band called the Hillbilly Boys, and thanks to his radio exposure, he made a successful run for governor of Texas in 1938. Meanwhile, the Light Crust Doughboys' new lineup had solidified by 1937: fiddle players Kenneth Pitts and Clifford Gross (plus Cecil Brower on occasion), banjoist Marvin "Smokey" Montgomery (who would remain with the group right up to his death in 2001), lead guitarist Muryel Campbell, rhythm guitarist Dick Reinhart, pianist John "Knocky" Parker, and bassist Ramon DeArman. This lineup's recordings were among the biggest selling in their hometown, and were quite popular across the region thanks in part to their continued radio exposure, which now reached over 170 stations.

Their success continued right up to World War II, at which point most of the members joined either the Army or the defense industry. The Doughboys' radio show was thus canceled in 1942; Burris Mill attempted to mount a new version of the program in 1946, featuring Jack Perry as the leader of the band (a post Smokey Montgomery took over in 1948). But despite a series of new recordings for King, interest had dissipated, and the radio show was canceled for good in 1950. While Montgomery kept the band going in some form, off and on, during the remainder of his life, the first large-scale revival of the Light Crust Doughboys took place during the '60s, featuring Montgomery (now on guitar as well as banjo), guitarist Billy Hudson, fiddler Johnny Strawn, bassist Artie Glenn, and steel guitarist Paul Blount. During the '90s, when the band began recording again, the lineup featured Montgomery, guitarist Jerry Elliott, bassist Art Greenhaw, fiddlers John Walden and Jim Baker, and pianist Bill Simmons. Montgomery passed away on June 6, 2001, after a bout with leukemia. *—Steve Huey*

The Lightcrust Doughboys / 1959 / Audio Lab ✦✦✦

String Band Swing / 1981 / Longhorn ✦✦✦✦

● **Light Crust Doughboys 1936-39** / 1982 / Texas Rose ✦✦✦✦✦

These 16 sides catch the band long after Wills and Brown left, but still laying down solid, bluesy licks. "Pussy, Pussy, Pussy" is simply not to be believed. *—Dan Cooper*

The Lilly Brothers

f. 1938, Clear Creek, WV, **db.** 1980

Group / Traditional Bluegrass

The Lilly Brothers, Everett and Bea, played old-time/bluegrass music together for over three decades. They may best be remembered in New England, where they were a fixture in the downtown Boston music scene from the early '60s through 1980. Charles Everett Lilly and older sibling Mitchell Burt Lilly, who went by Everett and Bea respectively, were born three years apart in Clear Creek, WV. Everett played the mandolin, banjo and fiddle while Bea played guitar; both brothers sang; early influences included the Delmore Brothers, the Callahan Bros, and the Monroes. The Lillys debuted in 1938 singing old-time country on a West Virginia radio station. They initially billed themselves as the Lonesome Holler Boys. Later they added a banjo and became a bluegrass group. In 1939, they began performing regularly at the newly established WKLS Beckley, where they performed together and with other musicians. After that they spent a few years at various southern stations playing in such groups as the Smiling Mountain Boys and Red Belcher's Kentucky Ridge Runners.

They made their recording debut in 1948 while working with the latter group at WWVA. They remained at the station through 1950, whereupon they returned home after a heated fight with Belcher over money. From there the Lillys split up for a time; Everett became a mandolin player and tenor with Flatt & Scruggs' Foggy Mountain Boys, and remained with them through early 1952 when he left to join his brother, fiddler Tex Logan, and banjo picker Don Stover in Boston. They got their first job playing on WCOP's *Hayloft Jamboree* and from there hit the local club circuit.

The Lilly Brothers recorded fairly frequently during the 1950s. Between 1958 and 1959, Everett spent another year with Flatt & Scruggs while Stover did a bit of touring with other bands. But for that, the Lilly Brothers remained intact through 1970. In addition to playing downtown Boston, they also played the local festival circuit and were instrumental in the development of urban bluegrass. In the early '70, Everett's son was killed in a car crash, causing him and his wife Joann to leave Beantown and return to West Virginia. Bea Lilly came down a while later to help Everett host a local television show, but eventually returned to the city. After 1971, Everett infrequently joined the band to perform at festivals during the summers and occasionally recorded with them. The Lilly Brothers' career was later chronicled in a 1979 documentary *True Facts in a Country Song*. *—Sandra Brennan*

Folk Songs from Southern Mountains / 1961 / Folkways ✦✦✦

This album is split half-and-half between the Lilly Brothers dueting in the traditional bluegrass "brother" style of the Monroe Brothers and the Blue Sky Boys; and a larger band session that brings in the phenomenal Don Stover on banjo, as well as band regular Herb Hooven on fiddle and bass and Mike Seeger contributing occasional bass and detailed liner notes. The material focuses totally on the traditional side of things and might be too somber in general tone for some listeners. Although the Lilly Brothers recorded modern pieces and liked to mix the repertoire up, it must be said that they really sink their teeth into this chance to focus on old time music exclusively. The vocals from brothers Everett and Bea are piercing and as clean as a West Virginia mountain stream might have been before the mines were opened. Instrumentally, things only really jump when Stover steps in and drives ten-penny nails through the front of his banjo head. Recording quality is a trifle mousy sounding; it was supposedly done with an Ampex machine and Electrovoice microphones, so it must have happened in the mastering. —*Eugene Chadbourne*

Bluegrass Breakdown / 1963 / Prestige Folklore ✦✦✦✦

This classic bluegrass "brother" duet is particularly known for popularizing bluegrass music in the New England area, as the group held forth regularly at Boston's Hillbilly Ranch, among other sympathetic venues. It was the '60s, the height of the folk boom, and the Lilly Brothers were soon tapped to do some recording for the ever-expanding Prestige label. That the New England-based Rounder Records would jump on reissuing this material is only appropriate; that the parent company would get around to also re-releasing it a few decades later just adds to the multiple confusion that is known collectively as the Lilly Brothers' discography. Listeners slanted toward a more rural perspective may immediately imagine that this bluegrass is a bit more polished around the edges than many Southern groups, and they would be right. The vocal delivery of brothers Everett and Bea also sounds downright cosmopolitan in comparison with some bluegrass outfits. Some of the slickness comes from the way the original recordings were made. Prestige had a certain sort of sound established for its jazz artists and tended to try to create a similar ambience when establishing its *Folklore* series. The instruments are thus cleanly and deeply recorded. There is a lot of good picking, especially from banjo maestro Don Stover, who worked regularly with the Lilly boys. These sessions consisted of quintet, trio, and duo tracks, and the latter reveal just how strongly the brothers feel the rhythm of this music together. The instrumental tracks allow Stover, Everett Lilly on mandolin, and fiddler Herb Hooven to stretch out impressively. Another interesting aspect of these sessions are the more modern tunes from the pure country camp, but pushed back into a bluegrass and old-time style. Very effective. —*Eugene Chadbourne*

Country Songs / 1964 / Prestige Folklore ✦✦✦✦

These driving, late-'50s performances have breathtaking banjo from Don Stover and hand-in-glove vocal harmonies. It is one of the best bluegrass albums ever. —*Mark A. Humphrey*

★ **Early Recordings** / 1971 / Rebel ✦✦✦✦✦

The pure soul of this country "brother" duo is laid out in all its glory here. With nothing but bass backup from yet a third sibling, Everett Allen Lilly, it is like a heaping buffet consisting of nothing but steaming mashed potatoes, meat, and green beans. This delicious material, ranging from old-time material to a current country hit, originated on the Prestige label. The jazz label was jumping on the resurgence of interest in folk music of the '60s by starting up a Folklore line. The Lilly Brothers were kingpins on the New England folk scene, specializing in an interpretation of Bill Monroe they had tweaked until it practically sparkled. They are captured with the pristine recording quality of a Rudy Van Gelder jazz session. Some of the tracks, such as "I'm Troubled I'm Troubled," are total classics. The Lilly Brothers are as swinging as they are moving. And listeners may not be able to get over just how beautiful sounding an album this is. —*Eugene Chadbourne*

What Will I Leave Behind / 1973 / Country ✦✦✦

In 1973, young, progressive musicians attempted to add folk and rock elements to bluegrass. If the new music didn't offend old timers, Bill C. Malone once noted, their long hair did. In the midst of this revolution, a number of musicians stayed the course and continued to deliver traditional bluegrass for the pure at heart. The Lilly Brothers & Don Stover, in fact, never sounded better than on 1973's *What Will I Leave Behind*, a bluegrass/gospel effort filled with lovely harmony and no nonsense accompaniment. The straightforward arrangements feature guitarist/vocalist Bea Lilly, mandolinist/vocalist Everett Lilly, banjoist/vocalist Don Stover, and bassist Kevin Smith. The quartet hold forth on a dozen old songs including "I Would Not Be Denied," "On the Sunny Side of Life," and "What Would the Profit Be." The beauty of the project is its simplicity, with the quartet adorning but never overwhelming gems like "In a Little Village Churchyard." This allows the emotion and conviction of the lyrics to come forward. Interestingly, both the Lilly Brothers and Stover came from above the Mason-Dixon line—New England and West Virginia respectively—and *What Will I Leave Behind* is the only religious album the Lilly Brothers ever recorded. Listeners will be glad they did. Whether one enjoys gospel bluegrass or old-time songs simply rendered, *What Will I Leave Behind* offers fine introduction to the Lilly Brothers & Don Stover. —*Ronnie D. Lankford Jr.*

Prestige/Folklore Years, Vol. 5: Have a Feast Here Tonight / Jan. 26, 1999 / Prestige ✦✦✦✦✦

In 1999, Fantasy reissued two classic Lilly Brothers albums on *Vol. 5* of its *Prestige/Folklore Years* series: *Bluegrass Breakdown* (recorded in either late 1962 or early 1963) and *Country Songs* (recorded in 1964). Hearing the albums back to back on a single 75-minute CD, the listener is exposed to two very different but equally appealing sides of vocalist/mandolin player Everett Lilly and vocalist/guitarist Bea Lilly. On one hand, they're heard playing some very passionate, hot-blooded bluegrass; the siblings' versions of Bill Monroe's "Bluegrass Breakdown," Charlie Monroe's "Rollin' On," and Earl Scruggs' "Foggy Mountain Breakdown" aren't exactly short on exuberance. Much of the CD, however, finds them focusing on the gentle, old-time, pre-Hank Williams country styles of the

1920s and 1930s. The influence of the Carter Family and Jimmie Rodgers (country's most important pre-Williams stylists) can be heard on Everett's "Beneath the Old Southern Skies" as well as such Carter gems as "Rosewood Casket" and "The Storms Are on the Ocean." The Lilly Brothers' treatment of Lefty Frizzell's "The Long Black Veil" is especially interesting; Frizzell, one of the top electric honky tonkers of the 1950s, didn't record the ballad until 1959, but the Lilly Brothers give it an acoustic 1930s-style makeover. This is a CD that lovers of bluegrass and unplugged, pre-World War II country should make a point of obtaining. —*Alex Henderson*

On the Radio 1952–1953 / 2002 / Rounder ✦✦✦

If the Lilly Brothers had stayed in their native West Virginia and pursued a bluegrass career there, they would have gone down in the history books as a classic brother act on a par with Jim & Jesse McReynolds or the Osborne Brothers (though probably not in the same class as the Stanley Brothers). But by relocating to Boston in the early '50s and building the bulk of their career in New England, they did more than that: they also built a foundation for the New England bluegrass scene that burgeoned in the 1960s and 1970s, providing training and nurturance for such top-flight talents as Joe Val, Dave Dillon, Bill Keith, Peter Rowan, and Herb Applin. That said, this collection of live radio transcriptions is something of a mixed bag. The sound quality is a bit dodgy, as might be expected for the medium and the time period, but unfortunately both the performances and the song choices are rather uneven as well. When the Lilly Brothers haul off and tear down on barnburning renditions of "Why Did You Wander" and the gospel classic "Sinner You Better Get Ready," or on their charming bluegrass arrangement of "When the Saints Go Marching In," the effect is electric. But their instrumental performances—especially their brief intro and outro segments and an awkward take on "Rawhide"—get kind of sloppy, and "Don't Make Me Go to Bed and I'll Be Good" is perhaps the worst of the many maudlin dying-child tearjerkers scattered throughout the bluegrass repertoire. This is a valuable document of an important and impressive ensemble, but it will be of primary interest to hardcore fans. —*Rick Anderson*

Little Big Town

Group / Honky Tonk, Neo-Traditionalist Country, Close Harmony

The country vocal quartet Little Big Town began with Kimberly Roads and Karen Fairchild, both from Georgia, who began singing together in college. Arkansan Jimi Westbrook, a friend of Fairchild's husband, joined them to make a trio and the group was completed in 1998 by Phil Sweet, another native of Arkansas. Little Big Town was devoted to harmony and multiple lead vocals which, along with their unusual lineup, made them a hard sell in Nashville at first. They finally landed a deal at Mercury Records, but it fell through in disagreements about musical direction. In the wake of the success of the Dixie Chicks, they seemed a more likely commercial proposition and they were next taken up by the Dixie Chicks' label, Monument Records, in 2000. Recording sessions lasted longer than usual for a country release, but Monument finally issued their debut single, "Don't Waste My Time," in the winter of 2002. It was on its way up the charts as their first album, *Little Big Town*, followed in May. —*William Ruhlmann*

Little Big Town / May 21, 2002 / Sony ✦✦✦

Little Big Town is a vocal quartet consisting of two men and two women who sing their songs by mixing up lead vocals and harmonies, such that one may start a song only to have another take the second verse, while some other combination sings the choruses. This, of course, is not typical of country music, nor are the song arrangements, which lean heavily to a folk-rock sound with prominent acoustic guitars and rhythm section, but only touches of fiddle and steel guitar; nor, for that matter, are the songs themselves, most of them written by the group members, which tend toward a pop sensibility with their generalized romantic sentiments. In the inevitable game of describing a new act by its antecedents, one must throw out names like Fleetwood Mac rather than any specifically country artists. Actually, Little Big Town does call to mind certain country acts of the past, though not prominent ones. They may remind knowledgeable country fans of such late-'80s performers as Foster & Lloyd and Kennedy Rose, duos that earned critical kudos (especially from non-country critics), but struggled to earn a commercial footing and ultimately found greater success behind the scenes as writers. Championed by Monument Records, the same label that changed the parameters of conventional country success with the Dixie Chicks, Little Big Town may succeed by re-writing the Nashville rule book in a similar way. But probably not. The Dixie Chicks had great songs, a powerful image, and an undeniable connection to hardcore country. Little Big Town does not have great songs, their image is diffuse, and they seem ready to cross over to pop at any minute. At least on their first album, the group is more a concept than a fully formed entity, which will make revolutionizing country music a challenge. —*William Ruhlmann*

Little Texas

f. 1984, **db.** 1997

Group / Contemporary Country

One of the most popular country bands of the early '90s, Little Texas was influenced by modern country outfits like Alabama and Restless Heart, as well as country-rock groups like the Eagles, which was underlined by their rowdy, long-haired image. The band was founded by singer Tim Rushlow and singer/guitarist Dwayne O'Brien, who first performed together in Arlington, TX, in 1984; they renewed their partnership in Nashville in 1987 and fleshed out the band with lead guitarist Porter Howell and bassist Duane Propes. They spent the next couple of years working the club circuit and added drummer Del Gray and singer/keyboardist Brady Seals, whom they met while out on tour; Seals also began to share lead vocals with Rushlow and O'Brien. Finally settling on Little Texas as their name, the group landed a contract with Warner Bros. in 1989 and toured heavily to help build an audience.

Their debut single, "Some Guys Have All the Love," was released in 1991 and quickly hit the Top Ten, and its follow-up, "First Time for Everything," just missed duplicating that feat. Finally, the group's debut album, also titled *First Time for Everything*, was released in 1992. It spawned two further hits in "You and Forever and Me" (their first Top Five single) and "I'd Rather Miss You." Their 1993 follow-up album, *Big Time*, was a smash, selling over 1.5 million copies and spinning off two Top Five country hits in "What Might Have Been" and "God Blessed Texas." The third single, the Seals-sung "My Love," became Little Texas' first number-one hit. *Kick a Little* (1994) was another platinum success, with two Top Five singles in the title track and "Amy's Back in Austin." In 1995, Seals departed for a solo career and was replaced by multi-instrumentalist Jeff Huskins, formerly of Clint Black's band; the same year, the band issued *Greatest Hits*, which featured the newly recorded Top Five single "Life Goes On." Unfortunately, 1997's self-titled album marked a significant downturn in Little Texas' commercial momentum and to date remains their final effort. —*Steve Huey*

First Time for Everything / Mar. 3, 1992 / Warner Bros. ✦✦
First Time for Everything bears the strong influence of mellow '70s pop, especially on hits like "You and Forever and Me." —*Jason Ankeny*

Big Time / 1993 / Warner Bros. ✦✦✦
Little Texas hit chart paydirt with the aptly titled *Big Time*, which features the number one smash "My Love" along with "What Might Have Been" and "God Blessed Texas." —*Jason Ankeny*

Kick a Little / 1994 / Warner Bros. ✦✦✦✦
Super country group Little Texas certainly gives country music a little kick with this 1994 album, *Kick a Little*. There are ten tracks on this recording, and not a dud in the mix. Little Texas seems to be proving good at making big hits. Many of the songs on *Kick a Little* are rowdy and filled with attitude, including the title track, "Kick a Little," "Your Days Are Numbered," and "Red Neck Like Me." There are a couple of kind of sedate numbers here to be had as well, such as "Inside" and "Southern Grace." By the time this album was finished, Little Texas had already landed three number-one hits from their second album and earned Vocal Group of the Year honors at the Academy of Country Music Awards. Members of this group are Dwayne O'Brien, Duane Propes, Tim Rushlow, Del Gray, Porter Howell, and Brady Seals. —*Charlotte Dillon*

• **Greatest Hits** / Oct. 1995 / Warner Bros. ✦✦✦✦✦
Collecting all of Little Texas' best numbers, *Greatest Hits* is the perfect introduction to the country-pop band, as well as being their most consistent and enjoyable album. —*Stephen Thomas Erlewine*

Little Texas / Apr. 22, 1997 / Warner Bros. ✦✦✦✦
It took Little Texas three years to deliver the follow-up to *Kick a Little*, but it was worth the wait. Entitled *Little Texas*, the album demonstrates the band's continued improvement. Not only is the songwriting stronger and more melodic than before, but the performances are tighter and more effective, making the record one of their best. —*Thom Owens*

Super Hits, Vol. 3 / Feb. 8, 2000 / Warner Bros. ✦✦✦

Hank Locklin (Lawrence Hankins Locklin)
b. Feb. 15, 1918, McLellan, FL
Vocals, Guitar / Traditional Country, Honky Tonk, Nashville Sound/Countrypolitan
Hank Locklin (b. Lawrence Hankins Locklin), one of country music's great tenors, was born February 15, 1918, in the small town of McLellan, located in the lumbering district of the Florida Panhandle. The youngest son of four children, he went to a one-room schoolhouse and was musical even as a young child. Locklin was injured at the age of eight in an accident and the long recovery process was the time when he first begin to learn music. Although interested in the guitar early on, it was not until his mid-teens that he really began to master that instrument. Locklin was active in music in high-school (which he never finished), and at 18 won first prize in a talent show. He went on to do spots on the local radio station as he became more and more interested in entertaining.

By the mid-'40s he was playing on the radio and doing in-person performances in Florida and nearby states. For the next ten years or so, Locklin worked many jobs (musical and otherwise), played with a variety of groups, and, through a variety of trials, gradually worked his way up the country music ladder to recognition. (A good account of these years can be found in the Bear Family box set liner notes, written by Otto Kissinger.) Locklin was exempted from military service due to his old leg injury, and during the war he began playing guitar in various bands around Mobile, AL, and also started singing and writing songs. His vocal style was originally influenced by Ernest Tubb, but he later began developing his own approach to singing. Late in World War II, he joined Jimmy Swan's dance band as a guitarist—whose ranks included Hank Williams sitting in occasionally—and he spent much of 1945 and 1946 playing gigs across the Southeast, from Florida to Alabama.

It was Locklin's association with a group called the Four Leaf Clover Boys that led to the formation of his first group. In the wake of their breakup, Locklin formed the Rocky Mountain Boys in 1947. The group's lineup later changed radically, but it was this original outfit—Locklin on vocals and guitar, Clint Holmes on rhythm guitar, "Tiny" Smith on bass, Felton Pruett on steel guitar, and Douglas "Dobber" Johnson playing fiddle—that got Locklin his first break. They were popular on the radio, and were sponsored by wealthy businessman Elmer Laird, who was also a songwriter. Laird proposed starting a record label around Locklin and the group with his songs, but he died in a stabbing incident on the eve of Locklin's first recording session.

They soldiered on, recording for Gold Star and later Royalty without much success, and eventually the band broke up (Holmes and Pruett hooked up with Hank Williams soon after). Locklin ended up based in Houston and signed to Four Star, where he had his first major regional hits with such songs as "The Same Sweet Girl" and "Send Me the Pillow That You Dream On." In those days, Locklin's sound was that of Texas-style dance band, and lacked the smooth, romantic commercial veneer of his later Nashville-based recordings for RCA. In 1953, he finally achieved national recognition with a number-one

country hit, "Let Me Be the One." His success, however, was still sporadic, particularly in the face of an awkward contractual arrangement that had Locklin recording for Decca but belonging to Four Star and largely restricted to recording Four Star-owned songs. This didn't change until 1955.

His career took off when he joined the RCA Victor label in the spring of 1955. Locklin's work with RCA has the added advantage that almost all of it was produced by Chet Atkins, often with Atkins himself on rhythm or lead guitar and with the added trills and fill-ins of Floyd Cramer on piano. The extreme simplicity of his early works makes the combination of his clear voice and these particular sidemen very effective. Everyone knows Locklin's big hits—"Send Me the Pillow That You Dream On" (written by Locklin), "Geisha Girl," and "Please Help Me I'm Falling"—but real fans are in love with his very simple heartfelt tunes like "Who Am I to Cast the First Stone," "A Good Woman's Love," "Seven or Eleven," "I'm Tired of Bummin' Around," "Golden Wristwatch," "Sitting Alone at a Table for Two," and many others. These early songs are characterized by Locklin's crystal-clear tenor, the ultra-simplicity of the songs themselves, and their straight-to-the-heart emotional plea. (Kitty Wells has this same kind of gift.) The result is a group of incredible songs that, first released as singles, later became available on Camden, RCA's budget label. After many years of neglect, many of these songs became available on the Bear Family box set *Hank Locklin, Please Help Me I'm Falling*. Locklin stayed with the RCA label until the mid-1960s.

Locklin helped pioneer the idea of concept albums; his albums *Foreign Love* and *Irish Songs, Country Style* are examples. He also recorded an album tribute to Roy Acuff, *A Tribute to Roy Acuff, King of Country Music*. His Irish songs are pretty near definitive. As time goes by, the vocal chorus begins to creep into the Locklin albums a little more than purists might like, but his crystal-clear tenor never deserts him. Hank Locklin hit the Top Ten charts again in the 1968 with "The Country Hall of Fame." In the 1970s he toured overseas often, was very popular in Ireland and Great Britain, and made at least one tour with Chet Atkins to Japan. After leaving RCA, he went on to record for a number of labels including MGM and Plantation. He since has retired and lives in Brewton, AL, only some 20 miles from his birth place. After a hiatus of over twenty years, Locklin returned to the studio and recorded the surprisingly strong *Generations in Song*, which was released in 2001. —*Michael Erlewine*

Foreign Love / 1958 / RCA Victor ✦✦✦
Hank Locklin's first album grew out of his hits "Fraulein" and "Geisha Girl," which rode the country charts for a big chunk of late 1956 and 1957, the latter also finding its way onto the pop charts. It's a winner almost all the way around—beyond the two hits, there's the surprisingly rocking (country-style, described in the trades at the time as a "rock-ahula") "Blue Grass Skirt," the sentimental "Filipino Baby," and the bouncy yet romantic "Foreign Love." Locklin's twangy tenor is ideally suited to this midtempo material, and he even acquits himself well on the awkwardly fitting "Lili Marlene," included so that the potential German-based G.I. audience for his records would have something to relate to. He gets through "Mademoiselle" well enough, with help from Grady Martin's tasteful guitar embellishments under each verse, and Chet Atkins also participated on guitar for this album, in addition to producing the session. The only weak moment comes on "My Wild Irish Rose," where Locklin seems uncomfortable, and that is more than made up for by his bouncy renditions of "Mexicali Rose" and "Blue Hawaii" and the deeply expressive "Anna Marie." —*Bruce Eder*

Please Help Me I'm Falling / 1960 / RCA Victor ✦✦✦✦✦
Hank Locklin's second album is made up of material cut between December of 1956 and January of 1960, when he was rapidly headed for the top of his game and fully embraced the Nashville sound, giving up the steel guitar and fiddle accompaniment in favor of the smoother sound of the piano, with some drums as well. In contrast to his first LP, *Foreign Love*, which was a concept album built around a specific body of songs, *Please Help Me I'm Falling* offers a cross section of Locklin's styles and sounds drawn from numerous sessions. The album was actually hooked around several hits: the RCA Victor version of "Send Me the Pillow That You Dream On," highlighted by Millie Kirkman's soaring accompaniment, which had charted in the country Top Five in 1957; the amusing 1959 single "Foreign Car"; and the smooth, elegant title track. Interspersed among these singles are the nine other songs in a multitude of styles, including the achingly beautiful and catchy ballad "Seven Days (The Humming Song)," the lean country lament "(I'm So Tired Of) Goin' Home All by Myself," the slow, moody "Blues in Advance," the more lushly produced "Livin' Alone," with its mixed male and female chorus, and the jaunty "Why Don't You Haul Off and Love Me" and "It's a Little More Like Heaven," with their crisp, stripped-down guitar-dominated textures. Even the non-hits are excellent recordings, and at least four of them could compete for places on a genuine best-of Hank Locklin. —*Bruce Eder*

Encores / 1961 / RCA ✦✦✦✦
A Tribute to Roy Acuff, King of Country Music / 1962 / RCA Victor ✦✦✦
Hank Locklin / 1962 / Wrangler ✦✦✦✦✦
Irish Songs, Country Style / 1964 / RCA Victor ✦✦
Sings Hank Williams / 1964 / RCA Victor ✦✦✦✦
My Kind of Country Music / 1965 / RCA Camden ✦✦✦✦
Released on RCA's subsidiary Camden Records, *My Kind of Country* may only contain only one hit ("Wooden Soldier") but the LP demonstrates Hank Locklin's gift for tear-jerking ballads and pure traditional country. —*Thom Owens*

The Girls Get Prettier / 1966 / RCA Victor ✦✦✦
The Best of Hank Locklin / 1966 / RCA Victor ✦✦✦
Classic country tenor Locklin came out of the Texas dance band scene but had his real chart success in Nashville under the helm of Chet Atkins. It was before Atkins and his simple studio approach would become bloated by choruses and string sections, so some

of the most famous performances here—such as the hit "Send Me the Pillow You Dream On"—are marked by the understated presence of Atkins on guitar and the unmistakable midnight tinkle of pianist Floyd Cramer. Some listeners may find the Locklin repertoire a bit on the sentimental side; the point is, he had both the voice and the passion to pull off this kind of material—even "Danny Boy." This is a nice collection; the four Locklin collections advertised on the back cover are even better bets. *—Eugene Chadbourne*

Nashville Women / 1967 / RCA Victor ✦✦✦✦
Although it has a couple of slow spots, *Nashville Women* is a highly enjoyable LP, boasting a number of engaging country-pop songs like "Nashville Women," "After the Hurt Is Gone," "Hasta Luego (See You Later)," "The Best Part of Loving You," "Release Me," and "I Feel a Cry Coming On." *—Thom Owens*

Country Hall of Fame / 1968 / RCA Victor ✦✦✦✦✦
Country Hall of Fame is a terrifically entertaining tribute not to only the institution of the Country Music Hall of Fame (the hit title song is a corny but strong tribute to the foundation), but the performers that grace its halls. Over the course of the LP, Hank Locklin sings standards like "High Noon (Do Not Forsake Me)," "Four Walls," "Walking the Floor Over You," "Lovesick Blues," "Blue Yodel ('T' for Texas)," and "Peace in the Valley," giving them each his patented high, lonesome tenor. It's a very entertaining and even moving record, and it ranks as one of his best albums of the late '60s. *—Thom Owens*

My Love Song for You / 1968 / RCA Victor ✦✦✦✦
My Love Song for You is an excellent collection of country ballads highlighted by "Danny Boy," "Longing to Hold You Again, " "I Came So Close to Living Alone, " and the hit single "Lovin' You (The Way I Do)." *—Thom Owens*

Lookin' Back / 1969 / RCA Victor ✦✦
Though Hank Locklin is in fine voice throughout *Lookin' Back*, the LP is burdened by too many average songs and overblown production that makes the record a frustrating listen. *—Thom Owens*

Hank Locklin & Danny Davis & the Nashville Brass / 1970 / RCA ✦✦✦
Hank Locklin & Danny Davis & the Nashville Brass is an awkward fusion of Locklin's pure country with brass bands. A few of the tracks—namely "Blue Moon of Kentucky," "Laura (What's He Got That I Ain't Got)," "Once a Day," and the hit single "Flying South"—work, but many of the songs, particularly "Please Help Me, I'm Falling," sound overburdened with horns. *—Thom Owens*

Please Help Me I'm Falling [Box Set] / Dec. 1995 / Bear Family ✦✦✦✦✦

Send Me the Pillow You Dream On [Box Set] / 1997 / Bear Family ✦✦✦✦✦
This triple-CD set is fascinating as well as priceless—66 sides cut by Hank Locklin between 1948 and 1954 for Gold Star, Four Star, and Decca. The majority of the tracks here will be new to most listeners, never having been reissued in any form (or in redubbed form) from their original 78 rpm appearances. They present Locklin doing a rougher, harder honky-tonk brand of music, derived from Texas dance-band roots, but different from the Nashville countrypolitan sound with which he achieved lasting fame—compared to his later, softer material, this stuff rocks. The early Gold Star and Royalty sides come from decent masters, with a certain amount of noise (the bass tends to boom) that is unavoidable, but otherwise they're pretty impressive. Of his early Four Star releases, the most unexpected treats are "Knocking at Your Door," Locklin's theme song in his Texas period, and the heavily Hank Williams-influenced "Born to Ramble." The latter is a revelation, showing Locklin to be a talented yodeler, among other surprises. "Send Me the Pillow That You Dream On" is also here in its original version, a lot less slick than the 1957 hit version off of RCA. Even at this point, Locklin's music was weighted toward ballads, although he interjected bright dance numbers. Disc two is still honky tonk-based but slicker, with better players all around. Disc three opens with Locklin's move to Nashville in 1952, under the aegis of Owen Bradley—the sound on those first sessions is smooth, almost elegant compared with the Texas-based stuff, and shows Locklin hitting his stride as a singer and bandleader, predating the full bloom of his Nashville period. The music on this disc flows seamlessly into the RCA period covered by the next Bear Family box, and Locklin's better-known RCA sides. *—Bruce Eder*

● **Please Help Me I'm Falling** / Jan. 5, 1998 / Collectables ✦✦✦✦✦
This is a strange collection, not to be confused with Bear Family's multi-disc set of the same name. It's not a best-of or a greatest-hits collection, despite the presence of some monster sellers—the title track and "Send Me the Pillow You Dream On" are present in their hit versions, along with "Livin' Alone," "It's a Little Bit Like Heaven," and "Geisha Girl." The rest are good songs, but hardly hits, including the spritely "Seven Days" (written by Locklin), which could've been a great song for Buddy Holly to cover; the mournful "Blues in Advance"; the comical "Why Don't You Haul Off and Love Me" and "Foreign Car"; and John D. Loudermilk's angst-filled "When the Band Plays the Blues." The sound is bright and loud, although some of the textures seem harsh, especially the reverb on certain tracks, and the notes are a little haywire, claiming that Locklin wrote "Send Me the Pillow You Dream On" in 1958, when he'd previously recorded it twice for other labels and had already charted with it. *—Bruce Eder*

Generations in Song / 2001 / Coldwater ✦✦✦✦
Hank Locklin was in his eighth decade when he cut this killer album in Nashville with a cast of supporting musicians that included Dolly Parton, Vince Gill, Jimmy Capps, Buddy Harmon, Jeannie Seely, Jeanne Pruett, and others. His voice sounds at least three decades fresher than it has a right to, and the harmonizing and the playing are first-rate, along with the arrangements, which makes this more than an exercise in nostalgia—Locklin and Parton, and steel player Weldon Myrick, positively luxuriate in the notes of "Send Me the Pillow You Dream On," and banjoman Charlie Cushman romps with Locklin through the rollicking "Country Honey" and "Flying South" like it was the first time either was working with either; similarly, Locklin, Gill, and fiddle-player Herbert "Hoot" Hester pull every iota of melody there is to draw out of "Danny Boy." Perhaps the most unexpected track here is "Hey Good Lookin'," which gets a beat similar to Elvis Presley's "Don't Be Cruel." Even better than his handling of the rhythm numbers are the ballads like "Almost Persuaded," where Locklin's range and interpretive skills should be the most taxed—age goes well with Locklin on this repertory, and he's never been surrounded by more sympathetic production, mixing modern country elegance with some of the lean, raw vibrancy of his early honky tonk sides. Rather than a late-career thrust at reclaiming lost glory, *Generations in Song* sounds more like the work of a man in the prime of life, still with something to say as a singer. [Note: Hank Adam Locklin, the singer's son, who also produced the album, takes the lead vocals on four of the 19 numbers here, but no one should feel cheated by his presence; their voices are so alike it's almost scary.] *—Bruce Eder*

★ **RCA Country Legends** / Mar. 4, 2003 / RCA ✦✦✦✦✦
Hank Locklin had a high, plaintive voice and a taste for heartbreaking barroom ballads and pure honky tonk that made him one of the best straight-ahead country singers of the '50s and early '60s. Although he had some big hits—most notable his original "Send Me the Pillow That You Dream On" and "Please Help Me, I'm Falling," along with "Why Baby Why," "Geisha Girl," and "It's a Little More Like Heaven"—he was more of a country singer's country singer, which led to smaller hits as the '60s wore on, as well as a lack of available material even during the CD boom. Bear Family fixed that to a certain extent with two big, comprehensive box sets, and there was a decent Collectables collection in the late '90s, but it wasn't until 2003's *RCA Country Legends* that his greatest hits were available as strong single-disc collection. *RCA Country Legends* spans 16 tracks, running from 1956 to 1968, and unlike some volumes in the series, it concentrates on Locklin's hits—which is appropriate since, as mentioned above, they had yet to make it to disc. So, 14 of these 16 tracks are hits, covering the great majority of his charting singles, and the result is necessary for any serious country collection. The times may have changed considerably in those ten-plus years covered on this collection, but Locklin held firm to his country ideals, and whittled down to the essentials as they are here, they offer proof of why country connoisseurs consider him among the best pure singers in the genre. This long-awaited collection finally offers the average listener a chance to hear why. *—Stephen Thomas Erlewine*

Tex Logan (Benjamin Logan Jr.)

Fiddle / Old-Timey, Bluegrass, Traditional Bluegrass, Progressive Bluegrass

From the kind of activities he is renowned for, most people might get a bit envious of Tex Logan. He is a famous and influential fiddler who hosts annual barbecues in his Madison, NJ, home that attract guests such as Doc Watson, Bill Monroe, and Oscar Brand. Monroe not only attends these events, he also plays music at them, and even did a routine dressed in drag once. Logan has written songs that have been recorded not only by Monroe, but by Emmylou Harris and even Bob Dylan, who normally prefers to write his own songs. Logan is also an electrical engineer who got so far in this field that he is sometimes referred to as a rocket scientist. Which is a bit of exaggeration, but the designation of "rocket scientist and bluegrass fiddler" just sound so perfect.

Born Benjamin Logan Jr., his father was also a violinist, although Logan Jr. quickly realized the vast difference between classical violin training and fiddling once he went from one to the other. He took violin lessons as a child in Texas and from as far back as his adolescent days he was torn between his interest in science and his love of playing the fiddle. Certainly, the latter won out in terms of personal enthusiasm, as he said at one point he would gladly trade 20 years of engineering for one night of fiddling. But in practical career terms, he spent much of his life employed by electrical engineering firms before retiring. He received his bachelor's degree in the subject from Texas Technical College, and went on to be a research assistant at the Massachusetts Institute of Technology. He literally fiddled his way out of this posting, heading for Wheeling, WV, and a stab at full-time musicianship before returning back to the technical world in 1951.

During his Wheeling days, Logan was a member of the Coal River Valley Boys which also featured another half and half player, banjoist Don Stover. (This meant Stover was spending half his time playing bluegrass, and the other half actually working in the coal mines.) The band also featured the well-known Lilly Brothers, as well as Red Belcher on banjo. When Logan returned to M.I.T. in 1951, it was by no means an end to his bluegrass connections. In his second year there, he lined up work for the Lilly Brothers in Boston. Perhaps there was a mental cross-reference between bluegrass and mathematics, considering the rapid pace at which chord changes fly by, especially when the musicians involved try to play the fastest tempos possible, or not possible.

Logan himself would usually mention the speed at which bluegrass was played whenever describing the reasons for liking it in interviews, and the following reaction is typical of comments about Logan from fans of this genre, that is when they aren't drooling over the reputed quality of his barbecue or homemade baked beans: "The most impossibly fast tune I've heard recorded is "Fire on the Mountain" with Tex Logan setting the pace playing with Bill Monroe." This performance is featured on the Smithsonian Folkways collection of live Bill Monroe tracks, entitled *Off the Record, Vol. 1*, while the comment was taken off an Internet chat room site dedicated to, of all things, bluegrass performances at rapid speeds. Monroe was particularly enthusiastic during the early '50s about banjo and fiddle breakdowns at manic tempos, when Logan was in and out of the mandolinist's Blue Grass Boys. Monroe was one of many artists to have recorded and performed Logan's most famous original song, "Christmas Time's A-Comin'," a real favorite with country artists looking for a seasonal song for that inevitable yuletide theme album. There seems to be a new recording of this number for every generation of country music audiences, from bluegrass grandpappy Monroe to '80s country-rock goddess Emmylou Harris to '90s country radio sharpies Diamond Rio. Dylan, on the other hand, preferred Logan's "Diamond Joe," pulled off as a sardonic folk number on his *Good As I've Been to You* album.

In 1956, Logan went to work in the communications theory department of the New Jersey Bell Telephone labs. The bluegrass world never let him rest in peace, however, and he was continually pressed back into service by enterprising pickers from the New Jersey area such as flatpicker and vocalist Peter Rowan, with whom he toured Scotland in the '80s, and versatile mandolinist Barry Mitterhoff, who created a revival group in the '90s devoted to Logan's music that performed at the New York City new music venue *Tonic*. Logan was one of the musicians profiled in *Prairie Nights to Neon Lights: The Story of Country Music in West Texas*, a collection of biographical essays by Joe Carr and Alan Munde. The jam band generation adopted Logan as one of their own through his connection with big daddy Jerry Garcia, with whom he performed and recorded on several versions of Old & in the Way's new-grass projects. *—Eugene Chadbourne*

Bluegrass Get Together / 1964 / Folkways ✦✦✦✦

Jimmie Logsdon

b. Apr. 1, 1922, Panther, KY

Vocals / Traditional Country, Nashville Sound/Countrypolitan

During the 1950s, Jimmie Logsdon was an extremely popular singer and a top country DJ. He was born in Panther, KY, to a Methodist minister, and began performing at age 12 in the church choir with his sister Martha Jean. He later played clarinet in his high-school band, and also learned to play guitar. He was married in 1940, and entered the Air Force and World War II in 1944, where he sang songs he had written to his comrades. Upon his return, Logsdon opened a record and radio shop in LeGrange, KY, and continued to perform professionally. He began his radio career in 1950 on WGN Chicago, and later got his own 15-minute show in Louisville, Kentucky. In 1952, he toured with his friend Hank Williams; following Williams' death, Logsdon honored his friend and mentor with the double-sided single "The Death of Hank Williams/Hank Williams Sings the Blues No More."

Logsdon's career was boosted in 1953 when he became the host of the live *Country & Music Show* on WHAS-TV, which also featured his backup group, the Golden Harvest Boys. Although he released singles and albums through 1962, Logsdon never appeared on the charts. During the '60s, he returned to his career as a DJ and penned songs for such stars as Johnny Horton, Carl Perkins, and even jazz artist Woody Herman. He augmented his income by working in his brother-in-law's swimming pool business, while also making commercials and singing in nightclubs. *—Sandra Brennan*

Howdy Neighbors / 1963 / King ✦✦✦

Doing It Hank's Way / 1980 / Castle ✦✦✦✦

● **I Got a Rocket in My Pocket** / 1993 / Bear Family ✦✦✦✦✦

The complete '50s output of this second-line country artist who also recorded rockabilly under the name Jimmy Lloyd. Includes the title track, one of rockabilly's finest moments, as well as traditional country material like "The Death of Hank Williams" and "That's When I'll Love You the Best." Fans of '50s-style country will love this one. *—Cub Koda*

Lone Justice

f. 1984, **db.** 1986

Group / Roots Rock, College Rock, Heartland Rock

The roots rock band Lone Justice was formed in Los Angeles by guitarist Ryan Hedgecock and singer Maria McKee. The half-sister of Bryan MacLean, a member of the seminal psychedelic outfit Love, McKee's involvement in the L.A. club scene dated back to her infancy; at the age of three, she joined MacLean at a performance at the famed Whisky-a-Go-Go and was befriended by Frank Zappa and members of the Doors. As a teen, she studied musical theater, and briefly performed in duos with MacLean and local blues singer Top Jimmy. McKee and Hedgecock first met while dabbling in the L.A. rockabilly scene, and their mutual affection for country music inspired them to found Lone Justice in 1982. Initially, the group was strictly a cover band, but the additions of veteran bassist Marvin Etzioni and Don Heffington, a former drummer in Emmylou Harris' Hot Band, prompted McKee to begin composing original material inspired by Dust Bowl-era balladry.

Gradually, elements of rock began creeping into the Lone Justice sound as well, and soon the band became a local favorite. At the urging of Linda Ronstadt, they were awarded a contract with Geffen Records; their self-titled debut appeared in 1985, followed by a tour in support of U2. Still, despite good press and media hype, *Lone Justice* failed to sell; slickly produced by the band's manager, Jimmy Iovine, it failed to connect with either country or rock audiences. In the record's wake, Hedgecock, Etzioni, and Heffington all exited the band, leaving McKee to lead Lone Justice alone. After enlisting guitarist Shayne Fontayne, bassist Greg Sutton, drummer Rudy Richman, and keyboardist Bruce Brody, Lone Justice recorded their second LP, *Shelter*. Shortly after the record's release, McKee broke up the band for good and went on to a solo career. Heffington became a successful session drummer, while Etzioni recorded under the guise Marvin the Mandolin Man. After a decade removed from the music industry, Hedgecock returned in 1996 as half of the duo Parlor James. A posthumous Lone Justice retrospective, *This World Is Not My Home*, followed in early 1999. *—Jason Ankeny*

● **Lone Justice** / 1985 / Geffen ✦✦✦✦

Few new bands receive the kind of critical buzz that Lone Justice generated prior to the release of their first album in 1985, and one senses the band (not to mention producer Jimmy Iovine and Geffen Records) wanted to deliver something special to merit the hype. Which was not necessarily a good thing; *Lone Justice* is an album that tries so hard to be great that it sometimes ends up tripping over its own ambitions. The record leaves no doubt that the first edition of Lone Justice was a very good band; on the best cuts, Maria McKee's voice sounds like a force of nature, bassist Marvin Etzioni and bassist Don Heffington are a strong and imaginative rhythm section whether they were playing souped-up country shuffles or fifth-gear rock & roll, and if guitarist Ryan Hedgecock isn't quite a virtuoso, he's solid and inspired when he gets to step to the forefront. But guest keyboardist Benmont Tench and the other high-priced help (including Little Steven, Mike Campbell, and an uncredited Annie Lennox) often overwhelm the group's personality, and while McKee's songs celebrating the heart and soul of rural America are unquestionably sincere, they don't always ring true ("After the Flood" and "Pass It On" sound more like writing exercises than narratives centered around believable characters), and they also seem to inspire Iovine's most bombastic production decisions. Where *Lone Justice* succeeds is on straight-ahead rockers like "East of Eden" and "Working Late," the C&W weeper "Don't Toss Us Away," and the tough "love gone bad" number "Way to Be Wicked," all of which prove that this band really did have the goods. In the wake of the 1990s alt-country movement, in which dozens of bands mined similar musical territory with more satisfying results, *Lone Justice* sounds like an example of too many cooks spoiling the soup; there's enough good stuff to make it worth hearing, but its hard not to wish Lone Justice had gotten the sort of sympathetic but hands-off production that allowed Wilco and the Jayhawks to do their best work. *—Mark Deming*

Shelter / 1986 / Geffen ✦✦✦

Shelter finds Lone Justice abandoning the cowpunk image of their debut in favor of a more polished '80s sound. What they came up with is rather a mishmash of material that only points the way for Maria McKee to don a solo outfit and carry on alone. *Shelter* falls into the trap of a record company dictating how a disc should sound no matter what might happen to the group producing it. There are strong cuts here—most notably, "I Found Love" (a real '80s-sounding product), "Wheels," and "Dixie Storms" (which foretells Maria McKee's future in music) all have something to recommend them. The rest falls into the trap of songs produced to fulfill obligations. Lone Justice was a group not unlike Big Brother & the Holding Company, who had a great female lead singer and focal point along with competent sidemen. Once the record execs ventured to guess that McKee would sell more on her own, they urged her to jettison the band, which she did after *Shelter*. Such is life in the record biz. *—James Chrispell*

This World Is Not My Home / Jan. 12, 1999 / Geffen ✦✦✦

This hot elegy album for the dearly departed Lone Justice is sheer rockabilly road-trip, as well as an illuminating artifact by a smart (albeit frustrated) "crossover" band. Blends of hardcore old-country roots and fast modern originality can be iffy on the charts, but the efforts of post-Emmylou Harris drummer Don Heffington, Little Steven collaborator Ryan Hedgecock on guitar, and bassist Marvin "Mandolin Man" Etzioni are committed. In typical Justice fashion all songs are tagged by the distinct Kate Pierson-meets-Dolly Parton vocals of Maria McKee; in Emmylou-like "East of Eden" we hear great drums behind a rambly hand jive riff and lots of big-hair yelling. Highway rocker "Ways to Be Wicked" is all tambourines and banshee vibrato, and dramatic Maria gets talkative on-stage with the lovestruck "Sweet Sweet Baby." A foot-stompin' good-time record. *—Becky Byrkit*

Lonesome Pine Fiddlers

f. 1938, **db.** 1966

Group / Traditional Bluegrass

The Lonesome Pine Fiddlers were an enduring force in the development of bluegrass music for over three decades. Over the years, the band underwent many personnel changes and played a variety of styles, ranging from old-time string music to bluegrass to country. The group was founded in 1938 by Ray Cline in Baisden, West Virginia. Originally it consisted of Cline and his adolescent cousins. The Lonesome Pine Fiddlers started out playing at WHIS Blufield, and soon after, Gordon Jennings joined them. The Fiddlers temporarily broke up during World War II. After the war they reunited back on WHIS, joined by Charlie Cline, who sang duets with Ray. In 1949, the Cline Brothers were replaced by fiddler Ray Morgan, Bob Osborne and Larry Richardson. By 1950, they had become a full-fledged bluegrass band. Bob and Larry left the following year and were replaced by Jimmy and Paul Williams. More personnel changes ensued and in 1953, the band began playing at WJR in Detroit. There they cut six sides for Victor in Chicago, among them their best-known song, "Dirty Dishes Blues."

The Lonesome Pine Fiddlers then moved to WLSI Pikeville, KY, and stayed there the rest of their career. They recorded eight singles in 1954, including two bluegrass classics, "Windy Mountain" and "No Curb Service." The band had a golden opportunity that year to perform on the Martha White-sponsored program at WSM, but they refused and Flatt & Scruggs took it instead. This refusal limited the band's exposure to the Appalachian area, where they remained popular on radio and television shows while recording and performing full-time through 1964, when they decreased the pace of their schedule. By 1966, the members of the Lonesome Pine Fiddlers had gone their separate ways. In 1988, some of the founding members reunited for a reunion album. Charlie Cline still uses the band's name for his own country music group. *—Sandra Brennan*

14 Mountain Songs Featuring 5-String Banjo / 1961 / Starday ✦✦✦

14 Mountain Songs Featuring 5-String Banjo, a nice, solid recording of mostly midtempo numbers, was among the first full-length albums cut by Lonesome Pine Fiddlers, who, although active performing as far back as 1938, didn't start recording until the mid-'50s. Fiddler Ray Cline is sometimes the soaring voice that brings the group's music to life; at other times it is the comforting, captivating rhythm they bring to material such as the corny "Eatin' Out of Your Hand." Membership changed quite a lot over the years with this group; for this album there are the two sets of brothers Cline and Goins, and it seems to be a pretty good match-up of talents. Despite the prestige of liner notes by bluegrass messiah Bill Monroe, the packaging sets new lows even for the ultra-cheap Starday folks. The front cover is pasted on the back by mistake, the songs titles are printed in a nearly illegible bright yellow typeface, and "High Fidelity" is printed in type five times the size of the group's name. And the album's title must have been designed to attract accountants. *—Eugene Chadbourne*

Early Bluegrass, Vol. 1 / 1979 / Old Homestead ✦✦✦✦✦

Early Bluegrass, Vol. 2 / 1983 / Old Homestead ✦✦✦✦✦

● **Windy Mountain** / 1992 / Bear Family ✦✦✦✦✦

Windy Mountain contains all of the material the Lonesome Pine Fiddlers recorded for Cozy and RCA Records during the early '50s. Though the 26-track collection is exhaustive, it is also exhausting; no matter how good these tracks are as individual songs, the relentless chronological sequencing of the material on this compact disc makes the record more of a history lesson than a casual listen. Nevertheless, *Windy Mountain* functions as the definitive retrospective of one of the finest and most important bluegrass bands of the '50s, and features great performances by Bobby Osborne, Charlie Cline, Paul Williams, and Curly Ray Cline. For bluegrass historians, it's essential. —*Stephen Thomas Erlewine*

The Lonesome River Band

f. 1983
Group / Contemporary Bluegrass
The Lonesome River Band have withstood numerous personnel changes to merge as one of the best respected bands in bluegrass. Although rooted in the traditional sounds of Flatt & Scruggs and Bill Monroe, the Lonesome River Band continue to set standards of their own. The recipients of the SPBGMA award as Vocal Group of 1997, the Lonesome River Band continue to fuse ultra-tight vocal harmonies with virtuosic musicianship and well-conceived arrangements. The original lineup of the Lonesome River Band was assembled by banjo player-turned-lead vocalist and -rhythm guitarist Tim Austin and featured Steve Thomas on mandolin and fiddle, Rick Williams on banjo, and Jerry McMillan on bass. After attracting attention on the local bluegrass circuit in Virginia, the Lonesome River Band released their debut album, *I Guess Heartaches Are in Style This Year*, in 1985 on the regional label Shar-Lynn. Their national debut came with a self-titled album, released by Rebel, the following year.

The Lonesome River Band have been evolving at a steady clip since the early-'90s with the arrival of lead vocalist and bass player Ronnie Bowman and banjo ace Sammy Shelor. North Carolina-born Bowman sang gospel music with a family group from age three until his late teens and is equally effective singing traditional bluegrass tunes as he is voicing songs by contemporary singer-songwriters. Shelor, who inherited his love of the banjo from his grandfathers, began to play the five-stringed instrument at age five. Although he learned his early technique from an old-timey clawhammer banjo player Carp Ayers, Shelor's approach to the instrument has been as much influenced by the playing of Earl Scruggs, J.D. Crowe, Ben Eldridge, Allen Shelton, Pete Wernick, and Béla Fleck. Shaping his performance skills with local bluegrass bands in North Carolina and Virginia, Shelor was a founding member of the Virginia Squires in 1983. He remained with the Squires until 1989 when he was joined the Lonesome River Band.

The reorganized Lonesome River Band hit their stride with their first album together, *Carrying the Tradition*, which debuted at the top slot on the best-selling charts compiled by *Bluegrass Unlimited*. It remained on the charts for five months before being supplanted by the band's next release, *Old Country Town*, which remained at the number-one position for six months. In the aftermath of their success, founding member Tim Austin left the Lonesome River Band to devote more time to working in his home recording studio, Doobie Shea. Although he was replaced by Kenny Smith, of Claire Lynch's Front Porch String Band, Austin continued to work with the Lonesome River Band on their albums. The newest member of the Lonesome River Band, Don Rigsby, who sings tenor vocals and plays mandolin, is a veteran of such bands as J.D. Crowe & the New South, the Bluegrass Cardinal, and previously worked with Vern Gosdin. The first album by the reconstructed lineup, *One Step Forward*, was released in 1996.

Each member of the current Lonesome River Band has recorded memorable solo albums. Bowman, who was named Vocalist of the Year by the International Bluegrass Music Association (IBMA) in 1995, delivered the most successful of the solo albums, *Cold Virginia Night*, which won the IBMA award as Best Album of the Year in 1997. Bowman followed it with a second solo album, *The Man I'm Tryin' to Be* in 1998. Shelor, who was named the IBMA's Banjo Player of the Year in 1995 and 1998, released *Leading Roll* in 1997 with guest appearances by Tony Rice, Sam Bush, Jerry Douglas, and Alan O'Bryant of the Nashville Bluegrass Band. Rigsby's solo debut, *A Vision*, celebrated his religious views and featured a duet with Ralph Stanley. Smith's *Studebaker*, released in 1997, spotlighted his songwriting talents and featured instrumental and vocal support from the other members of the Lonesome River Band. The Lonesome River Band were featured on several tracks of John Fogerty's 1997 album, *Blue Moon Swamp*. Their *Finding the Way* album followed a year later, and in mid-2000 the group returned with *Talkin' to Myself.* —*Craig Harris*

Looking for Yourself / 1989 / Rebel ✦✦✦

Carrying the Tradition / 1991 / Rebel ✦✦✦

● **Old Country Town** / 1994 / Sugar Hill ✦✦✦✦

One Step Forward / Mar. 19, 1996 / Sugar Hill ✦✦✦

Finding the Way / Aug. 18, 1998 / Sugar Hill ✦✦✦✦
Certainly, the Lonesome River Band is one of the most significant proponents of traditional bluegrass music to canoe down any river in a long while. And *Finding the Way* is reflective of their status as a band of integrity and purpose. In every way—musicianship, vocals, harmonies, performance and execution—this is a solid outing. "Love's Come Over Me," an upbeat tune that highlights Sammy Shelor's banjo and the harmony vocals of Don Rigsby and Kenny Smith, recalls the best of the Louvins and the Stanleys. In fact, "Sweet Sally Brown," penned by Wandell M. Smith and Dr. Ralph Stanley, displays the intensity and talent of the Lonesome River Band in full bloom. They could very well stand side by side with Ralph & Carter Stanley. The Tommy Morse tune "Perfume, Powder and Lead" is filled with all the dark mystery that many classic bluegrass tunes are known for. Again, Rigsby and Smith provide the harmony vocals that make this performance so haunting. Jason Carter's fiddle underscores the moaning quality of a song sung high upon a hill into a dark, unknown holler as the protagonist reaches out to eternity. "Baby Come Home," "Another By My Side," "Don't Worry 'Bout Daddy," and "Up on the Shelf" are all high steppin', while "Finding Your Way" is a nod of the head to the softer side of bluegrass music. Ending with the traditional tune "Devil Chased Me Around the Stump" places this project among the finest in the annals of bluegrass history. Produced by Jerry Douglas, *Finding the Way* is a fine introduction to the Lonesome River Band or to the more contemporary forms of bluegrass music. —*Jana Pendragon*

Talkin' to Myself / Jun. 20, 2000 / Sugar Hill ✦✦✦✦
Since their debut in the mid-'80s, the Lonesome River Band has spent time both in the middle of the bluegrass road and along its margins, experimenting with newer, more progressive sounds while periodically returning to their traditional bluegrass roots. *Talkin' to Myself* finds them in the latter mode, running through a program of bluegrass standards ("Are You Afraid to Call Me Darlin'," the Stanley Brothers' classic "Dog Gone Shame") and tradition-minded originals and covers (bassist Ronnie Bowman's "Talkin' to Myself," Bill Castle's "Swing That Hammer"). This lineup may be the strongest vocal ensemble the group has had yet: Mandolinist Don Rigsby is one of the best tenors in bluegrass right now, and Bowman is just as good singing lead. Dan Tyminski's production offers just the right balance of slickness and grit. This is one of those rare bluegrass albums that is likely to appeal equally to fans of the traditional and progressive schools. —*Rick Anderson*

Window of Time / Aug. 27, 2002 / Doobie Shea ✦✦✦✦
Although it's hard to know exactly why one would recommend this uniformly excellent release over most of the others in their catalog, not to mention the majority of the like-minded rank and file of the genre, there is no denying that the Lonesome River Band play to the status quo of the bluegrass elite exceptionally well. As always, their picking and harmonies are found to be in tremendous form, even with the lineup changes that continue to reshuffle the band's lineup. Continuing its return to the foundational tenets of the music, with driving rhythms and themes of home, love, and God provided in abundance, the band clearly ranks among the absolute best in the genre, whether plowing through a high-energy rendition of the Delmore Brothers' "Honey I'm Ramblin' Away" or finding an easygoing, more contemporary feel with the plaintive "Missed It By a Mile." All in all, you're unlikely to hear anything here that isn't exactly what you'd expect from these guys, and for most of their fans, that should be more than enough —*Matt Fink*

Lonesome Strangers

f. 1984, Los Angeles, CA
Group / Alternative Pop/Rock, Roots Rock, Alternative Country-Rock, Alternative Country, Americana
Part of the roots music explosion that took place in Southern California during the '80s, the Lonesome Strangers' harmonies evoked great fraternal duos like the Delmore Brothers and Everly Brothers, even though leaders Randy Weeks and Jeff Rhymes weren't related at all. Weeks, a transplant from Minnesota, and Rhymes, a Colorado native, founded the band in Los Angeles in 1984 (some accounts have it as early as 1982); their initial rhythm section featured bassist Nino Del Pesco and ex-Wall of Voodoo drummer Joe Nanini. Blending their vocal harmonies effortlessly over a blend of vintage country and roots rock, the Lonesome Strangers played around the L.A. club scene and quickly attracted the attention of producer Pete Anderson, who would soon make his name helming Dwight Yoakam's records. Anderson included their "Lonesome Pine" on the 1985 compilation *A Town South of Bakersfield*, which gave crucial early exposure to Yoakam, Rosie Flores, James Intveld, and other Americana-minded artists from the resurgent Los Angeles/Bakersfield scene. Anderson produced their debut album, also called *Lonesome Pine*, which was released on the small Wrestler label to positive reviews. Nanini left the band after the album was completed but before it was released, allowing new drummer Mike McLean to appear with the group on the artwork. The Strangers toured behind Yoakam and Dave Alvin, after which Del Pesco departed to form Snakefarm with Barry McBride; he was replaced by Lorne Rall.

Weeks and Rhymes lent backup vocals to Yoakam's acclaimed *Buenos Noches From a Lonely Room* in 1988, and the Lonesome Strangers moved to a larger label in Hightone. They issued their second album, an eponymous effort, in 1989, once again to highly complimentary reviews. However, when Rhymes relocated to the East Coast in the early '90s, the band went on hiatus. Rhymes' return to Los Angeles several years later quickly brought about a reunion with Weeks, and eventually a new album, 1997's *Land of Opportunity*. It was released on Anderson's Little Dog imprint and co-produced by him and Dusty Wakeman, who filled the empty bass slot (drummer Jim Christie and keyboardist Skip Edwards also played on the album). Jeff Roberts was later hired as the touring bassist, and the drum chair was filled first by ex-Plowboy Kenny Griffin, then Greg Perry. —*Steve Huey*

● **The Lonesome Strangers** / 1989 / Hightone ✦✦✦✦
The self-titled sophomore effort by one of California's most influential bands, the Lonesome Strangers, not only brought them fame, if not fortune, but also helped them build a strong following that continues to support their efforts. Fronted by the brotherly harmonies of Randy Weeks and Jeff Rhymes, the Lonesome Strangers borrowed from such great brother duos as the Stanley Brothers, the Delmores, and the Everlys while bringing a fresh and harder edged perspective to their rock & roll hillbilly style. Their remake of Johnny Horton's "Goodbye Lonesome, Hello Baby Doll" brought the country music industry to attention. Adding a Buddy Holly twist, the very hillbilly "Daddy's Gone Gray" takes things to a whole new level. "We Used to Fuss" recalls the humor that old-time country music and Buck Owens made so pleasing. As for ballads, "Clementine" and "Oh My Train" are bittersweet and executed with genuine feeling. Also good is their crack cover of a Delmore Brothers standard, "Lay Down My Old Guitar," "Don't Back Down," and the almost morose "Another Fool Like Me." Simply put, every cut counts. With production credits going to friend and sometime Lonesome Stranger Wyman Reese and Hightone mogul Bruce Bromberg and the mixing handled by another intimate and major California player, Dusty Wakeman, this second Lonesome Strangers project is ground-breaking. —*Jana Pendragon*

Land of Opportunity / 1997 / Little Dog ✦✦✦✦
From the jaunty opening track, "And It Hurts," to the norteño rendering of the Louvin Brothers' gem "I Don't Believe You've Met My Baby" that closes the set, the Lonesome Strangers demonstrate that they just might be the closest country music will ever get to a reincarnation of the Delmore Brothers. Capturing the same fun and wild abandon of

that early hillbilly boogie, Jeff Rhymes and Randy Weeks could easily be mistaken for one of the great brother duos, melding their nasal voices seamlessly. Just listen to the backwoods treatment and vitality they inject into the winded, but still spooky classic "Tobacco Road." Rhymes and Weeks' style is based in country and roots rock, but they also have a great pop sense, writing songs with a Buddy Holly-esque flair such as "Sharon," which sounds like something Holly might have thrown the Everly Brothers' way. Other highlights include the swampy, tremolo-drenched "Ton of Shame" and the cheerful, dance-inspiring "Ramblin' Around." Guitar ace and Little Dog founder/president Pete Anderson produced this ten-song collection, and his band backs the duo solidly, with musical touches that include some tasty Hammond B-3. —*Jack Leaver*

Lonesome Val

Bass, Vocals / Singer/Songwriter, Country-Folk, Americana
Manhattanite Lonesome Val first came to national and critical attention in 1988, when her country- and folk-tinged tunes got her named *Musician Magazine*'s Best Unsigned Artist of the Year. But Val went through a difficult breakup which left her musical career in shambles until she met Roches member Suzzy Roche. The two started playing together, and Roche helped Val make a demo tape. The Bar/None record label was impressed enough to ask for an entire album from Val, which Roche produced and played guitar on. The result, *NYC*, was released in the summer of 1994. —*Steve Huey*

● **Lonesome Val** / 1990 / Restless ✦✦✦✦
Here is a fun, rockin', slightly country, guitar-driven album with songs and vocals by Lonesome Val. She sets up the mood with the lead-off track "To Be Young." The album features electric guitars by Stuart Lerman, drums by Howie Wyeth, vocals by Greg Trooper and lots of others. —*Richard Meyer*

NYC / 1994 / Bar/None ✦✦✦
Lonesome Val is quite the fetching live performer—she just bubbles over with cuteness. On record, some of that country music cuteness does manage to shine through; however, her material is not quite as infectious on record as it is live. For those who have not seen Val in concert, the performances on *NYC* and her preceding self-titled album will probably be more than satisfactory. Highlights on *NYC* include "New York Town," "He Never Gives Up," and "Spanish Eyes." Lonesome Val's music is fine on record, but it's better live. —*Tim Griggs*

Lonestar

f. 1992, Tennessee
Group / Contemporary Country, Neo-Traditionalist Country
Though their name might lead you to believe that Lonestar was formed in Texas, the quintet actually hails from Tennessee. Originally called Texassee, the band features Richie McDonald (lead vocals, guitar), John Rich (lead vocals, bass), Michael Britt (lead guitar, background vocals), Dean Sams (keyboard, background vocals), and Keech Rainwater (drums). All the members are in fact Texas natives—they just formed in Tennessee in 1992.

In 1993, Lonestar played their first concert at Backstage Pass in Nashville in January of 1993. A booking agent happened to hear the show. Impressed, he added the group to his roster, and the group headed out on the road. Over the next two years, they played nearly 500 shows. In 1994, the group landed a record contract with BNA Records. The following year they released their eponymous debut, which spawned the Top Ten hit "Tequila Talkin'." *Crazy Nights* followed in 1997, and two years later Lonestar returned with *Lonely Grill*, which featured the hit "Amazed." Their seasonal effort *This Christmas Time* followed in fall 2000, and *I'm Already There* appeared the next spring. —*Stephen Thomas Erlewine*

Lonestar / Oct. 10, 1995 / BNA ✦✦✦✦
The Texan group Lonestar's self-titled debut is an accomplished and impassioned hardcore honky tonk, drawing from such influences as Lefty Frizzell, George Jones, and Merle Haggard. —*Stephen Thomas Erlewine*

Crazy Nights / Jun. 17, 1997 / BNA ✦✦✦
For better and for worse, Lonestar's second album *Crazy Nights* finds the band veering toward smooth, Eagles-influenced contemporary country. When the group has a strong song, such as the first single "Come Cryin' to Me" or the Pure Prairie League's "Amie," the band sounds appealingly professional, but when they're churning out generic material, they simply sound slick and bland. The singles won't disappoint any fan of the debut, yet *Crazy Nights* suggests that Lonestar might be only a good singles band, not album artists. —*Thom Owens*

Lonely Grill / Jun. 1, 1999 / BNA ✦✦✦
Lonestar began as a fairly straight-ahead country band, indebted to pure honky tonk. With their second record, they moved themselves toward pop and, ironically, it didn't pay off in great dividends, even if it spawned a Top Ten single. For their third album, *Lonely Grill*, they take a middle ground, moving back toward hardcore country while retaining elements of the pop sheen of *Crazy Nights*. The results aren't always successful, but overall, the album is stronger than its immediate predecessor, largely due to the increased grit. There are still some slow spots and mediocre songs scattered throughout the record, but the strong moments, such as "Amazed" and "I've Gotta Find You," keep the record entertaining and suggest that Lonestar will find a way to fuse their two inclinations into a signature sound. —*Stephen Thomas Erlewine*

This Christmas Time / Sep. 12, 2000 / BNA ✦✦
An unfortunately slick and forgettable collection of holiday tunes, cloyingly done in a soulless pop-country style. Fans of their crossover hit "Amazed" will know what to expect and will probably find it enjoyable, but those who respect the band's honky tonk upbringing will wonder where their earthy soul disappeared to. They sound most natural playing their own material like "Reason for the Season" and the title track, but on the whole, *This Christmas Time* feels as comfortable as coal in your stocking. —*Zac Johnson*

I'm Already There / Jun. 19, 2001 / BNA ✦✦✦
Lonestar has a way with passionate songs that either make hearts soar or eyes well up with tears; think previous number ones "Amazed," "Smile," and "Tell Her" from the triple platinum *Lonely Grill*. That album solidified and shaped their career—and yet, they don't want to be known as a "ballad band." *I'm Already There* has five ballads, including the title track, so it doesn't seem they're working overtime to change their image. But why fix what isn't broken? This four-member band delivers full-on on those moving ballads, due in part to Richie McDonald's big vocal prowess. But they do pretty well on the other seven tracks of up- and midtempo tunes too, including mentionables "Unusually Unusual" and "Every Little Thing She Does." Accomplished songwriters Annie Roboff, Holly Lamar, Lari White, Chuck Cannon, Mark McGuinn, and McDonald himself lend themselves to the pool of talent that makes *I'm Already There* another platinum album in the making. —*Maria Konicki Dinoia*

● **From There to Here: Greatest Hits** / Jun. 3, 2003 / BNA ✦✦✦✦
Greatest Hits is the first collection of Lonestar's greatest hits, released after four albums and one holiday record. Not all of their singles are here—the holiday tunes, of course, are left behind, as are smaller singles— but all the big songs are here, highlighted by "Tequila Talking," "Everything's Changed," "What About Now," "Smile," and the big crossover hit "Amazed." These tunes, along with the nine other songs that comprise this record, illustrate that even though Lonestar proudly takes its name from Texas, the band doesn't belong to that state's legacy of musical mavericks. They're a straightforward bunch, whether they're singing ballads or midtempo country-rockers, and even when there's plenty of twang in the voice and the guitars, the melodies are firmly in the pop-leaning country mainstream. Still, that twang counts for something—at its best, it made Lonestar's music seem rootsier, more real than many of its peers, and while it wasn't always consistent, the band did make some very good singles that may not have been the best of contemporary country in the late '90s, but captured the sound of the time well. They're all here on this fine retrospective. —*Stephen Thomas Erlewine*

The Long Ryders

f. 1981, db. Dec. 15, 1987
Group / Roots Rock, Paisley Underground, Jangle Pop, College Rock
Although they played the same clubs as most of Los Angeles' "paisley underground" bands (i.e., Dream Syndicate, Rain Parade) and even featured Dream Syndicate leader Steve Wynn in an early lineup, the Long Ryders were actually more a roots rock group strongly influenced by Gram Parsons. The group was founded by Kentucky native Sid Griffin, a Parsons devotee who moved to Los Angeles after hearing about that city's punk scene, with guitarist Stephen McCarthy and drummer Greg Sowders. The group's first bassist Barry Shank, along with Griffin, had previously been a member of the L.A. garage revivalists Unclaimed. He was replaced by Des Brewer just before the band went into the studio for the first time.

The Long Ryders' 1983 debut EP, *10-5-60*, was a blend of punk attitude, '60s rock, and traditional country (Griffin played steel guitar, autoharp, and mandolin). Brewer soon left as he was not committed to touring. His replacement, Don McCall, lasted for one tour before he was asked to leave. The band's lineup was stabilized when Indiana native Tom Stevens joined. Their first full-length album, the following year's *Native Sons*, was also arguably their best, and featured guest vocals from former Byrd Gene Clark. Subsequent albums, while still of considerable artistic merit, failed to find an audience despite the band's incessant touring.

Reeling from the defections of Stevens in June of 1987 and McCarthy in September, and unhappy with Island's promotional efforts and seeming disregard for the group, the Long Ryders called it quits on December 15, 1987. McCarthy formed Gutterball and, along with Griffin, contributed to the 1993 Gram Parsons tribute album *Conmemorativo*. Griffin, meanwhile, moved to London and formed the Coal Porters; today he works as a music critic and writer, foreshadowed by his definitive 1985 biography of (who else?) Gram Parsons. —*Steve Huey*

10-5-60 / 1983 / PVC ✦✦✦
It didn't take a genius to figure out that Sid Griffin and his fellow Long Ryders loved the Byrds with all their hearts, but they rarely made their affection quite so obvious as on their debut EP, *10-5-60*. The photos on the front and back cover clearly echo old Byrds promo shots, and the opening cut, "Join My Gang," sounds like some long-lost outtake from *Turn! Turn! Turn!*, while "I Don't Care What's Right, I Don't Care What's Wrong" and "Born to Believe in You" wouldn't have been out of place on *The Notorious Byrd Brothers*. But if *10-5-60* doesn't always speak of a startlingly original vision, the truth is hardly anyone short of the Byrds did this kind of stuff quite so well, and they absorbed the trappings of mid-'60s folk-rock so completely that they sound less like a throwback than some vintage band who somehow passed through a wrinkle in time and ended up in 1983—they walk the walk *and* talk the talk. And Griffin was thankfully still getting the revved-up snottiness of his days with garage mavens the Unclaimed out of his system, because the rave-up title track (written with fellow Unclaimed vet Barry Shank) is one of the hardest rocking cuts the Long Ryders ever released, and it ranks among the most exciting performances to come out of the '80s garage revival. The Long Ryders would gain a lot in the way of depth and ambition by the time they next entered a studio, but *10-5-60* proved they already had the talent, vision, and energy that would make them one of the more memorable American bands of the 1980s. [*10-5-60* later appeared as a bonus on the CD release of the group's first full-length album, *Native Sons*, with an outtake, "The Trip," added to the running order.] —*Mark Deming*

Native Sons / 1984 / Zippo ✦✦✦✦✦
Native Sons was the first full-length album by the Long Ryders and the one that established their eclectic mixture of Byrds/Clash/Flying Burrito Brothers' influences. The band wore those influences on their sleeve, literally, going so far as to recreate the cover of an

unreleased Buffalo Springfield album, *Stampede*, for *Native Sons* and using the producer of the first two Flying Burrito Brothers albums, Henry Lewy. *Native Sons* lovingly captures the band's musical obsessions, while turning in an original sound that became the banner for both the paisley underground and cow punk styles in the mid-'80s. Highlights include several forays into country on "Final Wild Son," the Mel Tillis composition "Sweet Mental Revenge," "Fair Game," and the humorous "Never Got to Meet the Mom," complete with a raging down-home banjo break. "Ivory Tower," featuring the late ex-Byrd Gene Clark on vocals, remains the greatest song the Byrds never wrote and one of the most sincere tributes to that band's sound. The album's final track, "I Had a Dream," reveals the punk sensibility, cranking the jangling Rickenbackers up to ten, closing with cacophonous feedback. On *Native Sons*, the Long Ryders pioneered a musical design that future alternative roots rockers would use as a manual. [*Native Sons* has been reissued on CD with the Long Ryders' initial EP, *10-5-60*.] *—Al Campbell*

The State of Our Union / 1985 / Island ♦♦♦♦

The Long Ryders kicked off their major label debut, *The State of Our Union*, with one of their most anthemic *and* most explicitly political songs, "Looking for Lewis and Clark," and that tune set the tone for the rest of the album—*The State of Our Union* found the Long Ryders reaching for a larger audience at the same time that they were using their music to say a great deal more than they had in the past. Musically, plenty of roadwork had tightened the band's interplay to an even finer point than on *Native Sons* (Sid Griffin and Stephen McCarthy were both in superb voice, and their guitar work meshed perfectly), and Will Birch's production gave the songs a poppier sheen that still allowed the band's roots-conscious sound to shine through. Lyrically, *The State of Our Union* took a long look at Reagan-era America as the gulf between the rich and the poor began to divide the nation, with "You Can't Ride the Boxcars Anymore," "Two Kinds of Love," and "Good Times Tomorrow, Hard Times Today" all exploring issues of economic injustice, and even the less obvious political songs often having a progressive subtext ("WDIA," a tribute to the great Memphis R&B radio station, deals with how the love of music brought together black and white listeners in the 1960s). *10-5-60* and *Native Sons* had already made it clear that the Long Ryders knew how to make great rock & roll, but *The State of Our Union* suggested they had a lot else on their minds, and they were able to air their concerns while playing music that could move the masses... assuming that the masses ever heard them. (Ironically, a large portion of the audience for this very American album was in England, where the Long Ryders had become press favorites, and "Looking for Lewis and Clark" became a hit single.) [A deluxe edition, with bonus tracks, was issued in the mid-'90s by Griffin's label, Prima Records.] *—Mark Deming*

Two Fisted Tales / 1987 / Island ♦♦♦

This, *Two Fisted Tales*, the last album by the Long Ryders, pulls together all the various elements that had distinguished them from the rest of the jangly, '60s revisionist rock bands of the mid-'80s. The Long Ryders' sound was a unique blending of McGuinn-esque guitar figures with well-defined parameters that encompassed Gram Parsons' country-rock sensibilities and the various tenet of traditional roots rock. Highlights include the kickoff track, "Gunslinger Man," a powerful guitar assault that displays the band's ability to rock strong and hard. In contrast, "I Want You Bad," a Terry Adams-penned tune also covered by Dave Edmunds, is a melodic song of long-distance desire. Here the vocal quality is particularly expressive and fitting to the song's message. On the other hand, formative years in the South are reflected on Sid Griffin's "Harriet Tubman's Gonna Carry Me Home." The overall instrumentation—which includes mandolin, autoharp, lap steel, and a guest accordion by David Hidalgo from Los Lobos—reflects their allegiance to traditional Americana music. Unfortunately, *Two Fisted Tales* was to be the Long Ryders' swan song. However, in the '90s there were still those who recalled the pioneering spirit of the Long Ryders. [In the mid-'90s a deluxe edition with four bonus tracks was issued by Griffin's label, Prima Records.] *—Jack Leaver*

Metallic B.O. / 1989 / Long Ryders Fan Club ♦♦♦

The Long Ryders were one of the finest retro/roots bands to emerge from the U.S. in the 1980s. Their recorded legacy on Island and Frontier easily bears this out. When the Ryders disbanded in 1987, they left behind miles (well, at least hundreds of yards) of unreleased tapes. This release, a fan-club-only compilation, illustrates the band's power and diversity, especially on cover tunes like "What Goes On" and "I Shall Be Released." The whole affair has been lovingly and intelligently put together, and is a nice tribute to one of the finest bands of the decade. *—Matthew Greenwald*

BBC Radio 1 Live in Concert / 1995 / Windsong ♦♦♦

● **Anthology** / Jul. 21, 1998 / Polygram Chronicles ♦♦♦♦♦

The Long Ryders were one of the greatest bands to come out of L.A. during the 1980s. The band combined rootsy influences such as Gram Parsons and Buffalo Springfield with an unlikely punk sensibility. They were refreshing, they cared about the songwriting, and they could rock. Coming from the long-lamented paisley underground scene, which included such bands as the Dream Syndicate, the Bangles, and Rain Parade, the Ryders were easily the tightest, and well-deserving of their major-label deal with Island Records, following their brilliant debut for Frontier in 1984. Polygram Chronicles has neatly compiled all the above material, plus the early *10-5-60* EP and loads of rare and unreleased tracks, on the Long Ryders' *Anthology*. It's an excellent collection from one of the most honest and genuinely gifted bands of the period. Tracks such as Ryders founder Sid Griffin's "Final Wild Son" and bassist Tom Stevens' "Years Long Ago" capture the essence of the band, which can almost be compared to a meeting of the Flying Burrito Brothers, Neil Young, and the Sex Pistols. Lead guitarist Stephen McCarthy's material has probably aged the best, with such polished tracks as "I Had a Dream" (one of the band's finest) and "Mason-Dixon Line" leaving you to wonder why listeners haven't heard a solo album from him. Individual praise, however, is not what the Long Ryders were about. They were a great *band*, and should be remembered as such. The Long Ryders' *Anthology* accomplishes just that. *—Matt Greenwald*

The Lost & Found

f. 1973

Group / Progressive Bluegrass

Formed in 1973, the original lineup of the Lost & Found bluegrass band consisted of bass fiddler Allen Mills, banjo player Gene Parker, mandolin player Dempsey Young and guitarist Roger Handy. The band became quite popular playing bluegrass festivals, with Mills' exceptional songwriting contributing much to the group's fame; "Love of the Mountains," recorded by the original lineup, has become a contemporary bluegrass standard. In addition to contemporary songs, the band also recorded more traditional fare, such as "The Man Who Wrote 'Home Sweet Home' Never Was a Married Man." Most of their albums feature similar material, and the band continues to be a strong positive force in contemporary bluegrass music. By the mid-'90s, only Mills and Young had stayed, recruiting guitarist Ray Berrier and banjo player Lynwood Lunsford as replacements. *—Sandra Brennan*

● **The Best of Lost and Found** / 1984 / Rebel ♦♦♦♦♦

Hymn Time / 1988 / Rebel ♦♦♦

New Day / 1989 / Rebel ♦♦♦♦♦

New Day features a new lead vocalist/guitarist in Ronnie Bowman, plus new banjoist Jody King. The addition of the two new members has reinvigorated Lost & Found, giving them a new kick which is evident both on the covers (particularly a tough version of Buck Owens' "Trouble"), but also on their original numbers. *New Day* does indeed represent a new beginning for Lost & Found. *—Thom Owens*

The Lost and Found / 1991 / Rebel ♦♦♦

Classic Bluegrass / 1991 / Rebel ♦♦♦♦

Bluegrass Classics / 1991 / Rebel ♦♦♦♦

January Rain / 1992 / Rebel ♦♦♦

It's About Time / 2002 / Rebel ♦♦♦♦

As Bill C. Malone points out in the liner notes, there's a certain old-fashioned quality to Lost & Found that never seems self-conscious or premeditated. In other words, the group never seems to be purposely trying to counter progressive bluegrass. Instead, *It's About Time* includes the same kind of music that the band might play at a local festival or on the back porch. Guitarist Barry Berrier, bassist Allen Mills, mandolinist Dempsey Young, and banjoist Ronald Smith form a small but nicely matched unit. Indeed, Lost & Found's small size works to the group's advantage, guaranteeing plenty of space for a spare, clean sound. The band also avoids fancy soloing and breakneck pacing. Pieces like "Teardrops in My Eyes" and "The Hurt's All Gone" roll along like a lazy afternoon, while old classics like "Down the Road" and "Wreck of the Old '97" receive respectful treatments. Mills sings most of the lead vocals and, interestingly, often adds a bass vocal to match his lead. Berrier also sings a number of fine leads, including the fun ghost song "Cold, Icy Fingers." While Lost & Found may have had no conscious intention of making a traditional bluegrass album, the results are the same. Fans, traditionalists, and anyone who longs for the simpler things of yesteryear will enjoy *It's About Time*. *—Ronnie D. Lankford Jr.*

John D. Loudermilk

b. Mar. 31, 1934, Durham, NC

Songwriter, Vocals, Trombone, Trumpet, Drums (Bass), Saxophone / Rock & Roll, Traditional Country, Country-Pop, Rockabilly, Nashville Sound/Countrypolitan

Although his music isn't exactly weird, John D. Loudermilk is one of the weirdest figures of early rock & roll. Much more famous as a songwriter than a performer (although he made plenty of records), his material was incredibly erratic. He could range from the most mindless, sappy pop to a hard-bitten, bluesy tune that rang with as much authentic grit as a Mississippi Delta blues classic. That tune was "Tobacco Road," and if he'd written nothing else, Loudermilk would have been worth a footnote in any history of popular music. Loudermilk wrote plenty of other songs, though, in a lengthy career that saw him straddling the fields of rock, pop, and country. Originally striving to be a performer in a very mild pop/rockabilly style, he found his first success as a songwriter, when George Hamilton IV took "A Rose and a Baby Ruth" into the Top Ten in 1956.

Recording as Johnny Dee, Loudermilk made a few singles for the small Colonial label in North Carolina. The best and most successful of these was "Sittin' in the Balcony," which made the Top 40 in 1957. Eddie Cochran's cover, based closely on Loudermilk's version (though performed with more force and style), stole most of Johnny Dee's thunder when it outsold the original by a wide margin, making the Top 20. Johnny Dee changed his name back to John Loudermilk when he signed with Columbia in 1958, and also decided to concentrate on songwriting when he relocated to Nashville, eventually working for Chet Atkins at RCA. Although Loudermilk had a pleasantly passable voice, his early records aren't worth much, often purveying material that was mindlessly lightweight or, worse, idiotically humorous ("Asiatic Flu"). "Tobacco Road" was a different story—a stark, stomping tale of hard-bitten Southern poverty, it had a strong blues flavor that was virtually absent from most of his material. It took a one-shot British Invasion group, the Nashville Teens, to fully realize the song's menace in their magnificent, hard rocking 1964 cover, which made the U.S. Top 20. The song was also covered by Lou Rawls, the Jefferson Airplane, Edgar Winter, and others.

"Tobacco Road" was far from Loudermilk's only success. In the late '50s and early '60s, he supplied material for country stars, teen idols, and pop/rock singers, including "Waterloo" (Stonewall Jackson), "Angela Jones" (Johnny Ferguson), "Ebony Eyes" (the Everly Brothers), "Norman" (Sue Thompson), and "Abilene" (George Hamilton IV). In the mid-'60s, he was briefly in vogue in Britain: the Nashville Teens did both "Tobacco Road" and "Google Eyes" (the latter of which was a hit in the U.K., though a flop stateside), and Marianne Faithfull had a British hit with the moody "This Little Bird."

Loudermilk continued to record on his own, though more as an afterthought than a specialty, reserving most of his focus for writing songs for other performers. Much of his material followed a faint-hearted, goofy pop/novelty thread, which made his somber efforts seem all the more incongruous. His last big songwriting success was another of his serious-minded tunes, "Indian Reservation," which topped the charts for Paul Revere & the Raiders in 1971 (it had previously been a hit for British singer Don Fardon). He withdrew from professional activities to spend most of the '80s and '90s studying ethnomusicology. —*Richie Unterberger*

Language of Love / 1962 / RCA Victor ✦✦

When Frank Zappa parodied doo wop, or when Lee Hazlewood made odd amalgams of country and pop, it's funny because there are indications that these guys were aware that they were deconstructing established idioms. Loudermilk is like Zappa and Hazlewood, except he's not funny, just banal, and it's not clear whether these lightweight country-pop-rock ditties are tongue-in-cheek or simply the work of a hack who can't do any better. The songs are clichés, except that Loudermilk will throw in things to arouse suspicion that he's cranking these out as sort of an in-joke. What to make of a line like "since Dad's been laid off work, Mary's no longer mine," in a song ("Mary's No Longer Mine") bemoaning the narrator's lack of access to his Dad's car to take out Mary, delivered with all the emotion of a demo singer (which Loudermilk was)? Hardly the usual stuff of 1960 country and pop, and hardly likely to be covered by someone to bring in royalties, so what was the point? The high point of the record is "Two Strangers in Love," very much in the style of the Everly Brothers (who covered Loudermilk's "Ebony Eyes" for a hit); one wouldn't be surprised if it turned out it was submitted to the duo for consideration. —*Richie Unterberger*

12 Sides of / 1962 / RCA Victor ✦✦

Although this contains some of Loudermilk's own versions of some of his most famous songs, it's a surprisingly disposable effort. The production is period Nashville pop-lite, Loudermilk's voice is almost devoid of character, and the songs themselves are usually downright dippy in their slightness. Much of this is Loudermilk at his worst—chipper, mindless romantic trifles, or trivial tunes about characters who are, one would guess, supposed to be laughably eccentric, though the results are about as funny as your average prime-time sitcom. Includes versions of "Angela Jones," "Google Eye," and "This Little Bird" (here titled, for some reason, "The Little Bird"), all of which were big hits in the hands of others. Beware, though—the version of "Tobacco Road" here is not the original, basic thumper on Loudermilk's 1960 Columbia single, but a vastly inferior remake with an inappropriately jaunty arrangement. —*Richie Unterberger*

Sings a Bizarre Collection / 1965 / RCA Victor ✦✦✦

Suburban Attitudes in Country Verse / 1967 / RCA Victor ✦✦✦

Country Love Songs Plain and Simply Sung / 1968 / RCA Victor ✦✦✦

The Open Mind of J D Loudermilk / 1969 / RCA Victor ✦✦✦

Elloree, Vol. 1 / 1971 / Warner Bros. ✦✦✦

Although this album is about as inscrutable in tone and intention as the average Loudermilk LP, it's preferable to most, chiefly because the production is so sparse. The acoustic arrangements emphasize Loudermilk's own guitar and occasional harmonica, although Norman Blake adds some mandolin and dobro. As Loudermilk often segues from one song to another without a break, there's an intimate living-room feel to the proceedings, accentuated by occasional indications that Loudermilk is not taking the project entirely seriously (he breaks into bird whistles at one point, for instance). The program is something of a greatest-hits set, with "Tobacco Road," "The Lament of the Cherokee Reservation Indian," "Google Eye," and "Abilene" all present, although these are not all Loudermilk's first versions of these compositions (if any are); it's at least the third time around for "Tobacco Road," in fact. The versions of "Lament of the Cherokee Reservation Indian" and "Tobacco Road" are bluesier and more down-home than you might expect, though he punctures "Cherokee"'s effect with pseudo-Indian war chants and a flip spoken aside in the middle. On lesser-known items like "The Jones'" and "Ma Baker's Little Acre," it's really hard, as always, to figure out where Loudermilk is coming from—if he's trying to offer social protest, social satire, or just make up some silly ditties reflecting the absurdity of contemporary society. —*Richie Unterberger*

Blue Train / 1989 / Bear Family ✦✦✦✦

Blue Train is one of three Bear Family discs that collect the recordings of famed Nashville songwriter John D. Loudermilk. Some of the tracks here were actually minor hits (Loudermilk rarely did anything to promote his recordings as an artist), but Loudermilk's writing and unique interpretations are of primary interest. The songwriter's vocals are pleasant, if not spectacular, and the production is nicely sparse and folky, often featuring Loudermilk's own excellent classical guitar playing. His quirky compositions have always straddled the line between pop and folk, and the tunes here are no exception. Although much of this music will sound lightweight to modern ears, it is certainly the product of an intensely creative mind, unafraid to tackle any topic, no matter how bizarre or seemingly inconsequential. Highlights include "All of This for Sally," a song about a millionaire who willed his fortune to a cocker spaniel, and "The Bully of the Beach," which was inspired by those ubiquitous Charles Atlas muscle building ads. Although many of the tunes are lighthearted, Loudermilk could occasionally get serious, as evidenced by "Darling Jane," where he details a man's loss of his new wife to hurricane floodwaters. Although not really for the casual country or oldies fan, *Blue Train* should appeal to any fan of brilliant songwriting or slightly left of center vintage pop and country music. —*Pemberton Roach*

It's My Time / 1989 / Bear Family ✦✦✦✦✦

● **Sittin' in the Balcony** / Jul. 5, 1995 / Bear Family ✦✦✦✦✦

This is a 23-song collection of his earliest material from 1957-1960. Includes both sides of all five singles he recorded for Colonial (when he was known as Johnny Dee), and early

Columbia singles, as well as three previously unreleased songs from the early Columbia era. "Sittin' in the Balcony" and the original, stark version of "Tobacco Road" are the clear highlights here. Most of the rest is timid rockabilly/pop, with songwriting that's riddled with goody-goody teen clichés; the novelty "Asiatic Flu" and "The Happy Wanderer (Val-De-Ri Val-De-Ra)" are downright unbearable. Still, it's probably Loudermilk's best work, considering that from 1960 on he principally worked as a songwriter, recording his own work only as a sideline. The previously unissued "The Angel of Flight 509" stirs mild interest, as it's a prototype of sorts for "Ebony Eyes," minus the tragic elements. —*Richie Unterberger*

The Louvin Brothers

f. Jul. 4, 1940, Rainesville, AL, db. Aug. 18, 1963

Group / Traditional Bluegrass, Traditional Country, Close Harmony, Bluegrass-Gospel

From the close-harmony brother acts of the '30s evolved Charlie and Ira Louvin, ranking among the top duos in country music history. With Ira's incredibly high, pure tenor and Charlie's emotional and smooth melody tenor, they learned well from the Bolick Brothers (the Blue Sky Boys), the Monroe Brothers, the Delmore Brothers, and other major family duos of the previous generation, preserving the old-time flavor while bringing this genre into the '50s, when country music moved to a newer sound. Whatever type of songs they recorded—gospel, folk, hillbilly, or '50s pop—those songs became the Louvins'. Add to the list the many Louvin compositions (for example, "If I Could Only Win Your Love," Emmylou Harris' first hit), and you have an act that is outstanding in country music history.

Their career took awhile to get going, partly because of interruptions from WWII and the Korean War. In the early '50s, after making a reputation for unexcelled gospel singing, the Louvins broadened their repertoire, recording "The Get Acquainted Waltz" (with Chet Atkins adding another guitar to Charlie's and to Ira's mandolin), a fair hit that showed success was reachable with non-religious music. The electric guitar, with the duo's unique harmony and Ira's exceptional tenor, created a sound that fans asked for in increasing numbers. In 1955, after ten unsuccessful auditions, they finally joined the *Opry*, where they performed to great acclaim until 1963, when they broke up. They had a number of hits, including the much-covered "When I Stop Dreaming" and "Cash on the Barrel Head." Following the duo's breakup, Ira and Charlie both pursued solo careers.

Born and raised in the Appalachian mountains in Alabama, both Charlie (born Charlie Elzer Loudermilk, July 7, 1927) and Ira (born Lonnie Ira Loudermilk, April 21, 1924; died June 20, 1965) were attracted to the close-harmony country brother duets of the Blue Sky Boys, the Delmore Brothers, the Callahan Brothers, and the Monroe Brothers when they reached their adolescence. Previously, they had sung gospel songs in church, and their parents encouraged them to play music, despite the family's poverty. Ira began playing mandolin while Charlie picked up the guitar, and the two began harmonizing. After a while, they began performing at a small, local radio station in Chattanooga, where they frequently played on an early-morning show.

The Brothers' career was interrupted in the early '40s when Charlie joined the Army for a short while. While his brother was in the service, Ira played with Charlie Monroe. Once Charlie returned from the Army, the duo moved to Knoxville, TN, where they received a regular spot on a WROL radio show; they later moved to WNOX. Around this time, they decided to abandon their given name for Louvin, which appeared to be a better stage name. (Their cousin John D. Loudermilk retained the family name.) Following their stint in Knoxville, they moved to Memphis, where they broadcast on WMPS and cut one single for Apollo Records. After their brief stay in Memphis, they returned to Knoxville.

In 1949, the Louvin Brothers recorded a single for Decca Records which failed to make much of an impact. Two years later, they signed with MGM Records and over the next year recorded 12 songs. Shortly after their MGM sessions were finished, Charlie and Ira moved back to Memphis, where they worked as postal clerks while playing concerts and radio shows at night. Eventually, they earned the attention of Acuff-Rose, who signed the duo to a publishing contract. Fred Rose, the owner of the publishing house, helped the duo sign a contract with Capitol Records. The Louvins' debut single for the label, "The Family Who Prays," was a moderate success (it would later become a gospel standard), yet they were unable to capitalize on its success because Charlie was recalled by the Army to serve in the Korean War.

Upon Charlie's discharge from the Army, the Louvins relocated to Birmingham, where they planned to restart their career through appearances on the radio station WOVK. However, a duo called Rebe & Rabe had already carved out a close-harmony niche in the area, using several of the Louvins' own songs. When Charlie and Ira were reaching a point of desperation, Capitol's Ken Nelson was able to convince the *Grand Ole Opry* to hire the duo. Prior to joining the *Opry*, the duo had been marketed as a gospel act, but they began singing secular material as soon as they landed a slot on the show, primarily because a tobacco company sponsoring its broadcast told the *Opry* and the Louvins "you can't sell tobacco with gospel music." While they didn't abandon gospel, the Brothers began writing and performing secular material again, starting with "When I Stop Dreaming." The single became a Top Ten hit upon its release in the fall of 1955 and would eventually become a country standard. It was followed shortly afterward by "I Don't Believe You've Met My Baby," which spent two weeks at number one early in 1956. No less than three of the duo's other singles—"Hoping That You're Hoping," "You're Running Wild," "Cash on the Barrel Head"—reached the Top Ten that year, and they also released the albums *Tragic Songs of Life* and *Nearer My God to Thee*. The Louvins' success in 1956 was particularly impressive when considering that rock & roll was breaking big that year, sapping the sales of many established country artists.

However, the Louvins weren't able to escape being hurt by rock & roll. They had two relatively big hits in 1957 ("Don't Laugh" and "Plenty of Everything but You"), "My Baby's Gone" reached the Top Ten in late 1958, and their classic version of the traditional ballad "Knoxville Girl" was a moderate hit in early 1959, but those four hit singles arrived in the space of three years; they charted four songs in 1956 alone. Soon, the Louvins were receiving pressure from Capitol to update their sound. They tried to cut a couple of rockabilly numbers, but they were quite unsuccessful. Eventually, Ken Nelson suggested that the duo abandon the mandolin in order to appeal to the same audience as the Everly Brothers. The Louvins didn't accept his advice, but the remark did considerable damage to Ira's ego and he began to sink into alcoholism. The Louvin Brothers continued to record during the early '60s, turning out a number of theme albums—including tributes to the Delmore Brothers and Roy Acuff, as well as gospel records like *Satan Is Real*—as well as singles. "I Love You Best of All" and "How's the World Treating You" reached numbers 12 and 26, respectively, in 1961, the first year they had two hit singles since 1957. However, the duo began fighting frequently, and Ira's alcoholism worsened. Following one last hit single, "Must You Throw Dirt in My Face," in the fall of 1962, the duo decided to disband in the summer of 1963.

Charlie and Ira both launched solo careers on Capitol Records shortly after the breakup. Charlie was the more successful of the two, with his debut single, "I Don't Love You Anymore," reaching number four upon its summer release in 1964. For the next decade, he racked up a total of 30 hit singles, though most of the records didn't make the Top 40. Ira's luck wasn't as good as his brother's. Shortly after the Louvins disbanded, he had a raging, alcohol-fueled argument with his third wife, Faye, that resulted in a shooting that nearly killed him. He continued to perform afterward, singing with his fourth wife, Anne Young. The duo were performing a week of concerts in Kansas City in June of 1965 when they were both killed in a car crash in Williamsburg, MO. After his death, his single "Yodel, Sweet Molly" became a moderate hit.

The Louvin Brothers' reputation continued to grow in the decades following their breakup, as their harmonies and hard-driving take on traditional country provided the blueprint for many generations of country and rock musicians. The Everly Brothers were clearly influenced by the duo, while country-rock pioneer Gram Parsons drew heavily from the Louvins' deep catalog of classic songs, recording "The Christian Life" with the Byrds and "Cash on the Barrelhead" as a solo artist. The Louvin Brothers and their music is truly legendary. —*David Vinopal*

Nearer My God to Thee / 1956 / Capitol ✦✦✦✦✦

☆ **Tragic Songs of Life** / 1956 / Rounder ✦✦✦✦✦

The first album by the Louvins has been lovingly transferred to compact disc, with new historical notes as well as a reproduction of the original art work. This disc is more cheerful than its title would suggest, with even the saddest songs sung with such beauty that there is an inherent joy in hearing them. The Louvins had only been recording popular songs (as opposed to gospel) for a year before they cut the majority of the 12 numbers here in May of 1956. There's a lot that will be familiar, including Carl Davis' "Kentucky" (which the Everly Brothers covered on *Roots*) and traditional standards like "Let Her Go, God Bless Her" and "Knoxville Girl," which later became a hit single, intermingled with a few originals. All of the material was drawn from the Louvins' own roots, including the first song they ever sang, "Knoxville Girl." The digital remastering is impeccable, with crisp textures on the guitars and mandolins throughout and barely a trace of hiss or noise. —*Bruce Eder*

The Louvin Brothers / 1957 / JS ✦✦✦✦✦

Ira and Charlie / 1958 / Capitol ✦✦✦

Issued in Capitol in 1958 (and reissued on LP in England), this is a fairly traditional outing, with only one song penned by the Louvins. It's solid enough, but some of their other Capitol work (such as the 1960 LP *My Baby's Gone*) is more imaginative, and places a greater weight on original material. —*Richie Unterberger*

The Family Who Prays / 1958 / Capitol ✦✦✦✦✦

Country Love Ballads / 1959 / Capitol ✦✦✦

A Tribute to the Delmore Brothers / 1960 / Capitol ✦✦✦✦✦

You could listen to music for 50 years and not hear harmonies as sweet or playing as nimble as what's on *A Tribute to the Delmore Brothers*. The album was one top-flight brother harmony duo paying tribute to the first great brother harmony duo in recording history. It sometimes seems like every country duo did tribute records to Alton & Rabon Delmore, and Capitol has at least one other (by Johnny Bond and Merle Travis), but this is the best one, recorded in three days, with Ira Louvin using the late Rabon Delmore's own guitar, former Delmore collaborators Grandpa Jones and Merle Travis standing by, and Chet Atkins on hand. The execution of the record is dazzling, with soaring harmonies and exquisite instrumental textures throughout—stereo was invented just for acts like the Louvins. The song selection is also impeccable (chosen with help from Alton Delmore), including "Brown's Ferry Blues," "Weary Lonesome Blues," "Midnight Special," "When It's Time for the Whippoorwill to Sing," and the hauntingly nostalgic "Put Me on the Trail to Carolina." Also included is "Blues Stay Away From Me," a future part of Bob Dylan's repertory, and a rockin' version of "Freight Train Boogie." It's only a pity that there weren't any leftover tracks from the session to include on the CD. —*Bruce Eder*

My Baby's Gone / 1960 / Capitol ✦✦✦✦✦

The Louvins' Capitol output was extremely consistent, and this 1960 LP (reissued on LP in England by Stetson) is no exception. Working under producer Ken Nelson, the traditional core of their harmonies and guitar remained intact, updated only very slightly with some fuller arrangements and mild pop touches. Most of the material is love laments, with "I Wish It Had Been a Dream" and "She Didn't Even Know I Was Gone" (mournfully heartbreaking even by country standards) being standouts. —*Richie Unterberger*

☆ **Satan Is Real** / 1960 / Capitol ✦✦✦✦✦

Much of *Satan Is Real*'s reputation stems from its cover, a bizarre photo depicting the Louvins—awkwardly posed and in gleaming white suits—standing amid the flames of hellfire, a 12-foot-tall plywood Lucifer looming behind them. The jacket is so notorious, in fact, that it merited inclusion in the second volume of the *Incredibly Strange Music* book series. It's a shame the album has acquired such a high kitsch quotient, because in reality *Satan Is Real* is one of the Louvins' finest and most impassioned recordings. The duo's second all-gospel LP, its songs—most of them originals—explore the brothers' deeply held beliefs without pulling any punches. The title track, in which Ira preaches

that any acknowledgment of a higher power demands a similar nod to the reality of darker forces, sets a haunting tone which carries throughout the course of the set; from "The Christian Life" (later covered by the Byrds on their country-rock landmark *Sweetheart of the Rodeo*) to the stinging "Are You Afraid to Die," these tales of death, sin, and despair resonate with raw power and stark beauty. —*Jason Ankeny*

Weapon of Prayer / 1962 / Capitol ✦✦✦

Keep Your Eyes on Jesus / 1963 / Capitol ✦✦✦

Sing and Play Their Current Hits / 1964 / Capitol ✦✦✦

Sing and Play Their Current Hits isn't exactly a greatest-hits collection, but neither was it recorded as an album. The songs are taken from various sessions recorded between 1960-1962, including the three hits the Louvin Brothers charted in the '60s. "How's the World Treating You" and "Must You Throw Dirt in My Face" were relatively minor entries, while the old-fashioned "I Love You Best of All" nearly reached the Top Ten. Ken Nelson's production alternates between the modern Nashville sound of "I Can't Keep You in Love With Me" and the more traditional approach for which the duo is known. "I Ain't Gonna Work Tomorrow" is handled as a commercial folk number with prominent banjo, an instrument that also features heavily in "Ruby's Song." While by no means a representative anthology, *Sing and Play Their Current Hits* offers a fair look at the Louvin Brothers' early-'60s output. —*Greg Adams*

Thank God for My Christian Home / 1965 / Capitol ✦✦✦

Less and Less and I Don't Love You Anymore / 1965 / Capitol ✦✦✦

Songs That Tell a Story / 1981 / Rounder ✦✦✦✦✦

Arguably the greatest duet and brother act in country history, Ira & Charlie Louvin made remarkably moving, simply performed songs about their faith and lives, with only guitar and mandolin backing, and reflecting the values of country with more sincerity and genuine feeling than hundreds of elaborately produced and packaged albums have since. Rounder issued these numbers on album in the late '70s, and reissued them on CD in 1991. The digital backdrop doesn't drain the authority from their voices; instead, it simply reaffirms the glory and splendor of the Louvins on 15 short, but brilliant gospel numbers. —*Ron Wynn*

Radio Favorites 1951–57 / 1987 / Country Music Foundation ✦✦✦✦✦

Radio Favorites 1951-57 contains a selection of radio performances from the Louvin Brothers, largely drawn from appearances at the *Grand Ole Opry*. Over the course of the compilation, several of the Louvins' best-known songs are featured, including both gospel numbers and secular songs. Though the performances and sound quality aren't quite as strong as the original studio versions, *Radio Favorites* remains of considerable interest for dedicated fans, since the brothers occasionally offer a new, unexpected turn in both their harmonies and instrumentals. —*Thom Owens*

Live at New River Ranch / 1989 / Copper Creek ✦✦✦

Recorded in Maryland in 1956, *Live at New River Ranch* perfectly captures the Louvin Brothers' live show of the late '50s, presenting not only their stunningly affecting music, but also their surprisingly goofy on-stage banter. For dedicated fans, this mix of great music and corny schtick is an invaluable find. —*Thom Owens*

☆ **Close Harmony** / 1992 / Bear Family ✦✦✦✦✦

A gargantuan, eight-disc box set *Close Harmony* is essential for serious country fans and scholars. Collecting everything the Louvin Brothers recorded for Capitol, Apollo, Decca, and MGM, the set may have too much music for casual fans, but those willing to delve deeply into these 219 tracks will learn much not only about the duo, but about the evolution of country music in the '50s—many of the roots of contemporary country and rock & roll are apparent throughout the set. —*Stephen Thomas Erlewine*

★ **When I Stop Dreaming: The Best of the Louvin Brothers** / 1995 / Razor & Tie ✦✦✦✦✦

In the 1950s, a time when Nashville was beginning to sand off the rough edges of country music and move in a more "modern" and pop-influenced direction, the Louvin Brothers were at once a breath of fresh air and a reminder of the music's Appalachian traditions. The close harmonies of Ira & Charlie Louvin reflected the influence of earlier family harmony acts such as the Delmore Brothers, and Bill & Charlie Monroe, but few (if any) duos in country history brought their voices together with such thrilling and heart-tugging clarity as the Louvins. Whether they were singing about the pain of heartbreak or the trials of sin and redemption, their performances spoke of a plain and unaffected sincerity that's uncommonly moving. Despite the group's importance and lasting influence, *When I Stop Dreaming: The Best of the Louvin Brothers* was the first genuinely comprehensive single-disc collection of the duo's most memorable work, and while it focuses strictly on their recordings for Capitol Records without referring to their earlier sides for MGM and Decca, only the most rabid completist is likely to mind. The 24 tracks included capture the Louvin Brothers at the very peak of their abilities, and features not only their biggest charts hits but a handful of superb album cuts; if there was ever a best-of album that lived up to its billing, this is it. Beautifully remastered and featuring a fine biographical essay by Marshall Crenshaw, *When I Stop Dreaming* is the best way to introduce yourself to the Louvin Brothers and their music short of the eight-disc Bear Family anthology *Close Harmony*; and as a sampler, it's far more affordable (and portable). —*Mark Deming*

Charlie Louvin (Charles Elzer Loudermilk)

b. Jul. 7, 1927, Rainesville, AL

Guitar, Vocals / Traditional Country, Close Harmony

As half of the Louvin Brothers, Charlie Louvin (born Charlie Elzer Loudermilk, July 7, 1927) was one of the most influential musicians of the '40s and '50s; the Louvins defined close harmony duet singing for several generations of country fans. After the Louvins disbanded in 1963, Charlie began a solo career, recording for Capitol Records until 1972.

During that time, he had two Top Ten hits—"I Don't Love You Anymore" (number four, 1964) and "See the Big Man Cry" (number seven, 1965)—as well as a series of minor hits. Louvin continued to perform and record for a variety of labels well into the '90s. —*Stephen Thomas Erlewine*

Less and Less & I Don't Love You Anymore / 1964 / Capitol ✦✦✦✦
Charlie Louvin scored more hits as a solo artist than as one-half of the Louvin Brothers, but his solo recordings are not nearly as well remembered. Although his solo sides for Capitol are less essential and were less successful on the charts overall, they are very good and deserve to be reissued. The title of *Less and Less & I Don't Love You Anymore* is an example of that weird '60s convention of naming an album after two of its songs, both of which in this case became hits. "I Don't Love You Anymore" was Louvin's only Top Five solo hit and "Less Is Less" was a minor hit. Another track on the album, the wonderful "See the Big Man Cry," became his only other Top Ten entry. The album tracks include covers of hits like Connie Smith's "Once a Day" and "Just Between the Two of Us," a hit for Merle Haggard and Bonnie Owens. The few originals include two songs Charlie wrote with his brother and one written solely by Ira Louvin. This strong album is notable for containing Louvin's two biggest hits, but a greatest-hits collection is needed. —*Greg Adams*

It Almost Felt Like Love / 1974 / United Artists ✦✦✦✦
On his own, Charlie Louvin of the Louvin Brothers is like the hitchhiker with a "Need a Ride to Nashville" sign. He seems to love straight-ahead country music of the meat and potatoes variety. On this superb session he picks up the equivalent of a comfortable ride all the way to his destination. Producer Kelso Herston has the wisdom to provide a very natural sound on the vocals, which although hardly imitative could sometimes be compared in style to George Jones. And that certainly should be taken as a compliment. Billy Sherrill, who produced many a Jones album, is on hand as engineer, which couldn't have hurt. Choice of material is very good, including a great Bill Anderson song entitled "As Much as I Love You." The overall theme is love, hardly a novel idea for a country record but also hardly problematic when the artist is this sincere and straightforward. Too bad none of the musicians are credited—the pickers add plenty to the arrangements, making excellent use of striking little instrumental touches. —*Eugene Chadbourne*

● **50 Years of Makin' Music** / 1991 / Playback ✦✦✦✦✦

Hoping That You're Hoping / 1992 / Copper Creek ✦✦✦

Longest Train / Sep. 24, 1996 / Watermelon ✦✦✦
Longest Train is an album designed for fans who became interested in Charlie Louvin and the Louvin Brothers through the music of Gram Parsons and the Byrds. The album features latter-day recordings of signature Louvin songs like "The Christian Life" and "In the Pines," all songs that country-rockers and rockers have covered. Consequently, it's not a bad way to learn about the Louvins, but it really isn't as compelling as the original Louvin Brothers recordings, and those do provide a better introduction than *Longest Train*. —*Thom Owens*

Charlie Louvin / Aug. 24, 1999 / First Generation ✦✦

Ira Louvin (Lonnie Ira Loudermilk)
b. Apr. 21, 1924, Rainesville, AL, **d.** Jun. 20, 1965, Jefferson City, MO
Mandolin, Vocals / Traditional Country, Yodeling
One of the top country musicians of the '40s and '50s, Ira Louvin teamed up with his brother Charlie Louvin to form the Louvin Brothers. The duo's hits included "When I Stop Dreaming," "Cash on the Barrelhead," and "If I Could Only Win Your Love," also recorded by Emmylou Harris. The Louvin Brothers were famous for their ability to sing many styles of music. During their musical career, the two recorded gospel, folk, hillbilly, and '50s pop songs. Born in the Appalachian Mountains of Alabama, Ira was born Lonnie Ira Loudermilk. Together with his brother Charlie, Ira began his musical career singing gospel songs in church. Despite the family's poverty, the two were encouraged to pursue their musical interests. Ira began playing the mandolin and his brother played the guitar. The two began playing together and eventually brought their sound to the airwaves on a small Chattanooga morning radio show. They were influenced by such recording artists as the Blue Sky Boys, the Delmore Brothers, the Monroe Brothers, and the Callahan Brothers.

When Charlie entered the Army in the early '40s, Ira played with Charlie Monroe. After the Army stint, the brothers moved their career to Knoxville, TN, where they played the radio circuit; first on WROL, then on WNOX. It was in Knoxville that the two changed their last name of Loudermilk to their stage name of Louvin. In 1951 the Louvin Brothers signed a contract with MGM Records and recorded 12 songs, all of which were only moderate hits. After the contract expired with MGM, the two headed back to Memphis, where they played concerts and radio shows. Capitol Records eventually signed the Louvin Brothers, and they became famous for their gospel standard "The Family Who Prays." Charlie was once again called to the Army to serve in the Korean War, so the group's career again came to a halt. When Charlie returned, the brothers went to Birmingham and sang for the *Grand Ol Opry*. Labeled as a gospel artist, the Louvin Brothers broadened their style to include pop and hillbilly music. Their song "When I Stop Dreaming" became a Top Ten hit as well as "I Don't Believe You've Met My Baby." In 1956 the two released the albums *Tragic Songs of Life* and *Nearer My God to Thee*. The two stayed together until 1963 and produced such favorites as "My Baby's Gone," "Don't Laugh," and "Plenty of Everything but You."

After the breakup, Ira pursued a solo music career, signing with Capitol Records. An alcoholic, Ira was almost killed in an argument with his third wife, Faye. He performed with his fourth wife, Anne Young, until 1965, when he died in a car accident in Williamsburg, MO. Despite the Louvin Brothers' breakup, their influence lived on decades later. Their reputation of versatility and their combination of harmonies influenced rock, gospel, and country musicians, including Gram Parsons, the Byrds, and the Everly Brothers. —*Kim Summers*

The Complete Recordings of Ira Louvin / Jul. 11, 2000 / King ✦✦✦
After the dissolution of the Louvin Brothers in 1963, Ira Louvin went on to record two albums for Capitol Records. The sum of these recordings have been combined on *The Complete Recordings of Ira Louvin*, which showcases the smooth traditional country stylings of the older, less volatile brother. This collection is a fair sample of the country-pop style popular in the late '50s and early '60s through Louvin's familiar voice, with a smattering of old-time religion and Appalachian yodeling. Unfortunately, these last recordings fail to display any of the excellent mandolin picking that Louvin exhibited in the previous decades and really lacks the spark and bittersweet charm of the music performed with brother Charlie. —*Zac Johnson*

Patty Loveless (Patricia Lee Ramey)
b. Jan. 4, 1957, Pikeville, KY
Vocals / Contemporary Country, Neo-Traditionalist Country
One of the most popular female singers of the new traditionalist movement, Patty Loveless rose to stardom thanks to her blend of honky tonk and country-rock, not to mention a plaintive, emotional ballad style. Her late-'80s records for MCA were generally quite popular, earning her comparisons to Patsy Cline, but most critics agreed that she truly came into her own as an artist when she moved to Epic in the early '90s. Loveless was born Patricia Lee Ramey in Pikeville, KY, in 1957, and spent most of her childhood in nearby Elkhorn City, where her father worked in the coal mines. Her immediate family loved music, and two of her distant cousins later found fame as Loretta Lynn and Crystal Gayle. Unfortunately, her father contracted black lung disease, forcing the family to move from their rural home to Louisville for the sake of convenient medical treatment. Patty found escape from the culture shock in music, and her father gave her a guitar when she was 11.

Soon she was singing and writing songs with her older brother Roger, and the two started performing at local country jamborees. At one such show, the Wilburn Brothers caught their act and gave them a standing invitation to Nashville. Roger and a 14-year-old Patty made the trip on a weekend when the Wilburns were out of town, but managed to talk their way into Porter Wagoner's office instead, impressing him with a performance of Patty's original "Sounds of Loneliness." Wagoner took Patty under his wing, inviting her to perform with him and Dolly Parton on the weekends. In 1973, after finishing high-school, she became a featured vocalist with the Wilburn Brothers' band (a post once held by Loretta Lynn), and also signed with their publishing company. She later married the band's drummer, Terry Lovelace, and moved to his hometown near Charlotte, NC, in 1976. There she sang pop, rock, and R&B material with a local cover band for several years, and endured bouts with alcoholism and drug use.

In the early '80s, she returned home, hired her brother Roger as her manager, and altered the spelling of her married name to Loveless. After traveling to Nashville to record demos of country songs, she landed a publishing deal with Acuff-Rose, and moved to Nashville permanently in 1985; she also divorced Lovelace around the same time, and her demo tape impressed MCA exec Tony Brown enough that he offered her a contract later that year. With Roger's producer friend Emory Gordy Jr. at the controls, Loveless released her first chart single, "Lonely Days, Lonely Nights," and her self-titled debut album in 1987. She enjoyed some modest success, but didn't really make a splash until the 1988 follow-up *If My Heart Had Windows*, which gave her two Top Ten hits in the title cut (originally recorded by George Jones) and Steve Earle's "A Little Bit of Love." Late in 1988, she released the follow-up album that made her a star, *Honky Tonk Angel*. "Timber, I'm Falling in Love" became her first number-one hit in 1989, and three more singles—"Blue Side of Town," "Don't Toss Us Away," and "The Lonely Side of Love"—reached the Top Ten before year's end, by which time Loveless had married producer Gordy.

In 1990, the album's fifth single, "Chains," became her second number one. Her next album, *On Down the Line*, came out later that year and brought her two Top Five hits in the title cut and "I'm That Kind of Girl." Following 1991's *Up Against My Heart* and its Top Five hit "Hurt Me Bad (In a Real Good Way)," Loveless made some major changes in her career. She parted ways with her brother as manager, and switched labels to Epic, taking husband Gordy with her as producer; moreover, she was forced to undergo throat surgery to repair her vocal cords before she was able to complete her label debut. *Only What I Feel* was released in early 1993 and earned Loveless the best reviews of her career to date, thanks to a newfound level of confidence. The number-one smash "Blame It on Your Heart" helped the record go platinum, and "How Can I Help You Say Goodbye?" and "You Will" also went Top Ten. *When Fallen Angels Fly* (1994) won equal acclaim, not to mention the CMA's Album of the Year award; it spun off four Top Ten hits in "I Try to Think About Elvis," "Halfway Down," "You Don't Even Know Who I Am," and "Here I Am." *The Trouble With the Truth* (1996) continued Loveless' renaissance with two more number one smashes, "You Can Feel Bad (If It Makes You Feel Better)" and "Lonely Too Long," and the Top Five "She Drew a Broken Heart"; that year, she won the ACM's Female Vocalist of the Year award.

However, 1997's *Long Stretch of Lonesome* abruptly halted her commercial momentum; despite a similar level of consistency, none of its singles made the Top Ten. Perhaps a shift toward slick country-pop played a role in Loveless' sales slump, as 2000's solid *Strong Heart* met with a similar fate. In response, Loveless turned away from hitmaking and embraced the acoustic Kentucky bluegrass of her youth, which was enjoying a renaissance of its own thanks to *O Brother, Where Art Thou?* The result, *Mountain Soul*, was released in 2001 and earned numerous critical plaudits, also selling decently in spite of its lack of concern for commercialism. Loveless kept that acoustic approach for her 2002 holiday album *Bluegrass and White Snow: A Mountain Christmas*, and it also informed her proper follow-up, 2003's *On Your Way Home*. —*Steve Huey*

Patty Loveless / Feb. 1987 / MCA ✦✦

If My Heart Had Windows / 1988 / MCA ✦✦✦✦✦

Honky Tonk Angel / 1988 / MCA ✦✦✦
The song subjects hardly classify Loveless as a honky-tonk angel, at least by Hank Thompson's definition. But this was the album that established Loveless as a major

presence, and it includes two of her biggest singles—"Chains," "Timber I'm Falling in Love"—and two of her best—"Blue Side of Town" and "Don't Toss Us Away," a duet with Rodney Crowell. *—Brian Mansfield*

On Down the Line / May 15, 1990 / Universal Special Products ♦♦♦
Patty Loveless entered the 1990s with *On Down the Line*, an excellent album that contained such major hits as "The Night's Too Long," the gutsy "Blue Memories" and the infectiously rockin' "I'm That Kind of Girl." Despite all the talk about Loveless being part of a neo-traditionalist movement in country, this isn't an album for purists—there's plenty of pop and rock influence here, and a 33-year-old Loveless is undeniably folky on the haunting ballad "Some Morning Soon." Loveless still found herself being compared frequently to Patsy Cline, who was no stranger to pop and rock elements either. Not that Loveless excludes more hardcore country—"I've Got To Stop Loving You (And Start Living Again)" is a honky tonk gem. Unpredictable and consistently inspired, *On Down the Line* remains one of Loveless' finest albums. *—Alex Henderson*

Up Against My Heart / 1991 / MCA ♦♦♦
Loveless gets a little more adventurous with each album, though she never forgets to include surefire hits like "Hurt Me Bad (In a Real Good Way)" and "Jealous Bone." This time she invites comparisons to Patsy Cline with "Can't Stop Myself from Loving You" and implies that God is female by switching the pronouns in Lyle Lovett's "God Will." *—Brian Mansfield*

Only What I Feel / Apr. 20, 1993 / Epic ♦♦♦♦♦
Loveless underwent throat surgery and switched labels before creating this album, and both helped. She sounds stronger and more impassioned than she had in years, and her artistic drive seemed more confident and determined. "Nothin' but the Wheel" ranks with her best ballads. *—Michael McCall*

Greatest Hits / May 11, 1993 / MCA ♦♦♦♦♦
The inevitable hits compilation chronicling Patty Loveless' five years and five albums at MCA is, in the Nashville tradition, not exactly generous: It contains only ten tracks and runs 31 1/2 minutes. In that space, though, you get most of Loveless' big hits between 1988 and 1992, from "If My Heart Had Windows" to "Jealous Bone," and including the chart-toppers "Timber I'm Falling in Love" and "Chains." Oddly, "A Little Bit in Love," which just missed hitting number-one, is not included. The set traces Loveless' rise as part of the neo-traditionalist movement of the 1980s, a movement that had faded, and that Loveless was ready to move beyond, by the time she ended her tenure at MCA. The music included here is fine, bedrock country, but a little faceless for all its authenticity. This is one artist whose second hits collection is likely to be more interesting than her first. *—William Ruhlmann*

When Fallen Angels Fly / 1994 / Epic ♦♦♦♦♦
Patty Loveless expanded on the success of her comeback album, *Only What I Feel*, on its successor, *When Fallen Angels Fly*, which made the country Top Ten, went gold, spawned four Top Ten singles, and was named the Country Music Association's Album of the Year. Songs like the feisty hit "Halfway Down" had a bouncy rockabilly feel, and Loveless rode the rhythms well, while on the ballad "Here I Am," another hit, she sounded like a country Stevie Nicks. And then there was "I Try to Think About Elvis," a comic rocker that was one of the best pieces of material to turn up in Nashville that year, and that Loveless performed with just enough tongue in her cheek. Of course, there were a couple of those hopelessly hokey Gretchen Peters ballads, but even one of those, "You Don't Even Know Who I Am," was a hit. *—William Ruhlmann*

The Trouble With the Truth / Jan. 23, 1996 / Epic ♦♦♦♦
Having broken through at the tail-end of the neo-traditionalist trend in country in the 1980s, Patty Loveless was one of the few established artists to navigate the transition into the post-Garth pop-country trend of the '90s. *The Trouble With the Truth*, her third album after the turn and the follow-up to the CMA Album of the Year *When Fallen Angels Fly*, found her again relying on her steady stable of writers—Gary Nicholson, Jim Lauderdale, Tony Arata, Matraca Berg—for another series of songs that acknowledged the country tradition of twang, yet kept to a sharp beat, and that maintained the female country sensibility of faithful loving, while avoiding victimization. "You Can Feel Bad," the album's first single and a number-one hit, was a breakup song with a twist or two, while the second single, "A Thousand Times a Day," treated love as a 12-step addiction, and "I Miss Who I Was (With You)," caught a sense of regret tempered with acceptance. Some of the writing was a bit abstract, notably the title track, and there didn't seem much reason to cover Richard Thompson's uptempo, Cajun-flavored "Tear-Stained Letter," which Jo-El Sonnier took into the Top Ten in 1988 (except, of course, that it's a great song). But *The Trouble With The Truth* was a consistent collection that consolidated Loveless' prominent place in the country music scene of the mid-'90s. *—William Ruhlmann*

Long Stretch of Lonesome / Sep. 30, 1997 / Epic ♦♦♦♦
Patty Loveless has created one of the most consistent bodies of work within contemporary country, and *Long Stretch of Lonesome* does nothing to erase the notion that she is one of the finest singers of the '90s. Stylistically, there isn't much difference between *Long Stretch of Lonesome* and her other records, but the key to its success is Loveless' unerring knack for picking the right material. Usually, contemporary country albums have a few hit singles surrounded by filler, but with any Loveless album, you can expect consistently excellent material, and this is no exception. *—Thom Owens*

● **Classics** / Mar. 23, 1999 / Epic ♦♦♦♦♦
As expected, Patty Loveless' second hits compilation, covering her first five years on Epic Records, was even better than her earlier *Greatest Hits* on MCA, showing off a more confident singer who rocked out convincingly and was comfortable on weepy ballads, even if the latter tended not to be the best compositions she got to sing. Typical of country hits collections, this one was on the skimpy side, containing only 12 tracks, and typical of nearly all contemporary hits collections, it failed to contain all the hits while tossing in a few new songs. The most serious omission was "Halfway Down." But Loveless' biggest hits of the era, "You Can Feel Bad," "Lonely Too Long," and "Blame It on Your Heart" were included, and there was enough here to justify all those Female Vocalist of the Year awards she won during the half-decade. At the same time, the selection reflected the recent downturn in the singer's fortunes, containing nothing from the commercially disappointing 1997 album *Long Stretch of Lonesome*. As so many hits collections do, this one seemed a summing up that confirmed the artist's past triumphs, while she herself stood at a crossroads. *—William Ruhlmann*

20th Century Masters—The Millennium Collection: The Best of Patty Loveless / Aug. 15, 2000 / MCA Nashville ♦♦♦♦
The Millennium Collection: The Best of Patty Loveless gathers highlights from the singer's body of work, including "If My Heart Had Windows," "A Little Bit of Love," "Blue Side of Town," and "Timber, I'm Falling in Love." Choice album tracks and radio favorites make up the rest of this concise, affordable hits collection from one of the most popular country songbirds from the late '80s. *—Heather Phares*

Strong Heart / Aug. 29, 2000 / Epic ♦♦♦♦♦
"I tell you what, we're in a rut," Patty Loveless sang in "That's the Kind of Mood I'm In," the single released in May 2000 in advance of her tenth album, *Strong Heart*, which followed in August. The song, a plea from one lover to another to shake up a stale romance, also worked as an unintended metaphor for Loveless' career, as the 43-year-old, who had enjoyed widespread success in country music from the late '80s to the mid-'90s, struggled to standup to a newly pop-oriented Nashville. "That's the Kind of Mood I'm In" bowed somewhat to Faith Hill's approach, though (to its credit) it ended up sounding more Cajun than crossover, but by the time *Strong Heart* was released it had only gotten into the lower reaches of the country Top 40, not boding well for the album's commercial prospects. Even so, it turns out to be another well-balanced set of songs from a singer who can give effective performances in a variety of styles and tempos. The most impressive harder-rocking tunes are "You Don't Get No More," which sounds like a ZZ Top song, and the bluesy "The Key of Love," songs you can imagine Loveless singing in a roadhouse on a Saturday night. The chaste ballads "My Heart Will Never Break This Way Again" and "Thirsty" (the latter featuring Travis Tritt on harmony vocals) sound like singles, but the song that cries out to be a country hit is "She Never Stopped Loving Him," one of those big, sentimental, string-filled country ballads that ends in the cemetery. True to form, Loveless and Gordy somewhat underplay it, when this kind of tearjerker should be done all out or not at all. At any rate, *Strong Heart* is a worthy addition to her catalog. *—William Ruhlmann*

Mountain Soul / Jun. 26, 2001 / Sony ♦♦♦♦
A 180-degree departure from contemporary commercial country music, album number six from the always dynamic Loveless is like a breath of fresh air on a steamy summer afternoon. *Mountain Soul* is a rare and brilliant acoustic 14-track album of bluegrass mountain music. Amidst the mandolins, fiddles, and banjos is Loveless' harking alto voice, singing from her soul to the music she grew up with. Just when you thought the days of Lester Flatt, Earl Scruggs, Bill Monroe, and the Stanley Brothers were gone, Loveless brings them back with new life and staggering grace. Rounding out this ubiquitous collection are soft-singing collaborators Travis Tritt, Ricky Skaggs, and Rebecca Lynn Howard. *—Maria Konicki Dinoia*

Bluegrass and White Snow: A Mountain Christmas / Oct. 29, 2002 / Sony ♦♦♦

Lyle Lovett

b. Nov. 1, 1957, Klein, TX
Guitar, Vocals / Singer/Songwriter, Alternative Country
Lyle Lovett was one of the most distinctive and original singer-songwriters to emerge during the '80s. Though he was initially labeled as a country singer, the tag never quite fit him. Lovett had more in common with '70s singer-songwriters like Guy Clark, Jesse Winchester, Randy Newman, and Townes Van Zandt, combining a talent for incisive, witty lyrical detail with an eclectic array of music, ranging from country and folk to big-band swing and traditional pop. Lovett's literate, multi-layered songs stood out among the formulaic Nashville hit singles of the late '80s as well as the new traditionalists who were beginning to take over country music. Drawing from alternative country and rock fans, Lovett quickly built up a cult following which began to spill over into the mainstream with his second album, 1988's *Pontiac*. Following *Pontiac*, his country audience declined, but his reputation as a songwriter and musician continued to grow, and he sustained a dedicated cult following throughout the '90s.

Born in Klein, TX—a small town named after his great-grandfather, a Bavarian weaver called Adam Klein, which later became a Houston suburb—Lovett was raised on his family horse ranch. He didn't begin his musical career until he began writing songs while he attended Texas A&M University in the late '70s, where he studied journalism and German. While he was a student, he performed covers and original songs at local folk festivals and clubs. As a graduate student, he traveled to Germany to study and continued to write and play while he was in Europe. However, he didn't begin to pursue a musical career in earnest until he returned to America in the early '80s. Upon his return to the U.S., Lovett played clubs throughout Texas, eventually landing a spot in the 1983 Mickey Rooney TV-movie *Bill: On His Own*. The following year Nanci Griffith, whom Lyle had interviewed for a school paper while he was in college, recorded his "If I Were the Woman You Wanted" on her *Once in a Very Blue Moon* album. He also sang on the album as well as her 1985 record *Last of the True Believers*. Guy Clark heard a demo tape of Lovett's songs in 1984 and directed it toward Tony Brown of MCA Records. Over the next year, MCA worked out the details of a record contract with Lyle. In the meantime, he made his first recorded appearance on *Fast Folk Magazine, Vol. 2 #8* later in the year.

Lovett signed with MCA/Curb in 1986, releasing his eponymous debut later in the year. *Lyle Lovett* received excellent reviews, and five of its singles—"Farther Down the

Line," the Top Ten "Cowboy Man," "God Will," "Why I Don't Know," and "Give Back My Heart"—reached the country Top 40. Despite his strong showing on the country charts, it was clear from the outset that Lovett's musical tastes didn't rely on country, though the genre provided the foundation of his sound. Instead, he incorporated jazz, folk, and pop into a country framework, pushing the musical boundaries of each genre. *Pontiac*, his second album, revealed exactly how eclectic and literate Lovett was. Greeted with overwhelmingly positive reviews from both country and mainstream publications upon its 1987 release, *Pontiac* expanded his audience in the pop and rock markets. The album charted in the lower reaches of the pop charts and slowly worked its way toward gold status. While his pop audience grew, his country fan base began to shrink—"She's No Lady" and "I Loved You Yesterday" both made the Top 30, but after those two songs, none of his other singles cracked the country Top 40.

It didn't matter that Lovett's country audience was disappearing—*Pontiac* had gained enough new fans in the pop mainstream to guarantee him a strong cult following. To support *Pontiac*, he assembled His Large Band, which was a modified big band complete with guitars, a cellist, a pianist, horns, and a gospel-trained backup singer named Francine Reed. Lovett recorded his third album, *Lyle Lovett and His Large Band*, with his touring band. Like its two predecessors, the album was well-received critically upon its early 1989 release, and it performed well commercially, peaking at number 62 and eventually going gold. Perhaps because of the album's eclectic, jazzy sound, the album produced only one minor country hit in "I Married Her Just Because She Looks Like You," but his straight rendition of Tammy Wynette's "Stand By Your Man" received a great deal of attention in the media.

Following the release of *His Large Band*, Lovett settled out in California, which signaled that he was abandoning country. After settling in Los Angeles, he spent the next two years collaborating and working on his fourth album. In 1990, he produced Walter Hyatt's *King Tears* album; the following year, he sang on Leo Kottke's *Great Big Boy* and donated a cover of "Friend of the Devil" to the Grateful Dead tribute album *Deadicated*. Also in 1991, he made his acting debut in Robert Altman's *The Player*, which was released in the spring of 1992. A few months after *The Player* hit the theaters, Lovett's fourth album, *Joshua Judges Ruth*, was released. Boasting a heavy gospel and R&B influence, *Joshua Judges Ruth* was his most successful album to date, peaking at number 57 and going gold. On the whole, the album was ignored by country radio, but pop audiences embraced the record, and Lovett became a staple on adult alternative radio and VH-1.

Despite the success of *Joshua Judges Ruth*, Lovett became a near-superstar for a completely different reason in 1993—his surprise marriage to actress Julia Roberts. Upon the announcement of their marriage, Lovett became the subject of many gossip segments and tabloid stories, elevating him to a level of fame he had not experienced before. Lyle's first project after his marriage was a role in Altman's 1993 film *Short Cuts*. He didn't release another album until the fall of 1994, when *I Love Everybody* hit the stores. A collection of songs Lovett wrote in the late '70s and early '80s, *I Love Everybody* continued his move away from country, and it was the first record he had released that didn't expand his audience in some way. After it entered the charts at number 26, it disappeared 13 weeks later, failing to go gold.

Lovett and Roberts divorced in the spring of 1995, and Lyle began to retreat from the spotlight somewhat, spending the remainder of the year touring and writing. Lovett reemerged with *The Road to Ensenada*, the first album since *Pontiac* to be dominated by country songs, in the summer of 1996. In addition to performing well on the pop charts, where it entered at a career peak of number 24, *The Road to Ensenada* performed strongly on the country charts, entering at number four. The two-disc covers album *Step Inside This House* followed in 1998, featuring mostly underexposed material penned by some of Lovett's favorite songwriters (many of whom hailed from Texas). In 1999, Lovett issued his first concert record, *Live in Texas*, and his soundtrack to the Altman film *Dr. T. & the Women* followed a year later. *—Stephen Thomas Erlewine*

☆ **Lyle Lovett** / 1986 / Curb ♦♦♦♦♦

While Lyle Lovett's debut album is easily the closest he's ever come to making a straight country disc, right out of the box Lovett made it clear he was an eccentric in the great Texas tradition, and rather than sounding like the new boy in Nashville, he presented himself as the odd but likable distant relative of Guy Clark and Jesse Winchester. While "This Old Porch" and "If I Were the Man You Wanted" proved he could write a sincere and affecting song as well as anyone, they also made clear that he wasn't cutout for Nashville-style radio-ready singles, while the ironic "Cowboy Man" and the wickedly cynical cheating song "God Will" proved Lovett possessed a genius for taking traditional formulas and giving them a hard twist. The jazzy sway of "An Acceptable Level of Ecstasy (The Wedding Song)" offers a witty and engaging preview of the blues-flavored sound Lovett would hone on later album, and in this context the tunefully obsessive "You Can't Resist It" sounds like the great pop hit he never had. While under Tony Brown's production (and with a team of Nashville session vets backing him up) some of the sharper edges of Lovett's musical personality were smoothed down, Lovett's reedy but soulful voice shines through, and a casual listen confirms that Lovett's music was just as strong as his lyrics. Along with Steve Earle's *Guitar Town*, *Lyle Lovett* was one of the most promising and exciting debut albums to come out of Nashville in the 1980s, and like Earle's album, this set a high bar for what would become an exciting and idiosyncratic career, proving first-rank singer-songwriters didn't just come from New York or Los Angeles. *—Mark Deming*

★ **Pontiac** / 1987 / Curb ♦♦♦♦♦

While Lyle Lovett's self-titled debut album made it clear he was one the most gifted and idiosyncratic talents to emerge in country music in the 1980s, his follow-up, 1987's *Pontiac*, took the strengths of his first disc and refined them, and the result was a set whose sound and feel more accurately reflected Lovett's musical personality. While much of *Pontiac* favors the country side of Lovett's musical personality, the bouncy swing of "Give Back My Heart" and the weepy stroll of "Walk Through the Bottomland" have a lighter touch that suits them noticeably better than the stiffer production and arrangements of the first album, while the breezy snap of "L.A. County" serves as a perfect contrast to the tune's violent *dénouement*. The second half of the album gives Lovett a chance to indulge his fondness for jazz and blues flavors on the cynical "She's No Lady," "M-O-N-E-Y," and "She's Hot to Go," and if Lovett would follow this path with great musical success on his next few albums, he was already traveling in the right direction and the songs and the arrangements are aces. And it's all but impossible to imagine anyone being given a big push by a major label in Nashville who could get away with the fanciful whimsy of "If I Had a Boat" and the stark and unsettling character sketch of "Pontiac" on the same album. If *Lyle Lovett* left any doubts at all about this man's gifts as a performer and songwriter, *Pontiac* proved that he had even more tricks up his sleeve than he'd let on first time out, and it's the first of several masterpieces in Lovett's career. *—Mark Deming*

Lyle Lovett and His Large Band / 1989 / Curb ♦♦♦♦♦

While from the outset Lyle Lovett sounded like a hard artist to pigeonhole, his sponsors at Curb Records and MCA Records seemed determined to sell him as a country artist, though the blues and retro-jazz leanings of Lovett's second album, *Pontiac*, suggested that strategy would only be practical for so long. With his third album, 1989's *Lyle Lovett and His Large Band*, Lovett seemingly sidelined any career aspirations as a mainstream country act he or his handlers may have held. The album kicks off with a lively cover of Clifford Brown's "The Blues Walk," and the next five tunes all bear the smoky, late-night vibe of a low-key jazz joint, with top marks going to the hilariously off-kilter "Here I Am," the witty scenario of potential infidelity "What Do You Do/The Glory of Love," and the marvelously sly "Good Intentions." The second half of the album is steeped in twang, but it was hardly more comforting for country radio programmers; "I Married Her Just Because She Looks Like You" is a "sweet on the outside and sick on the inside" tale of romantic obsession, "Nobody Knows Me" bears a punchline that makes "God Will" sound generous, and Lovett's straight-faced cover of "Stand By Your Man" stubbornly refuses to either announce itself as a joke or suggest another interpretation. Wherever you choose to file it, *Lyle Lovett and His Large Band* made it clear that Lovett was only getting better with each album; the songs are uniformly well-crafted, Lovett's vocals are full of subtle nuance, and his band is in brilliant form throughout (with special kudos to Lovett's frequent vocal foil, Francine Reed). If you're going to burn your bridges, you could hardly find a better way to do it than this. *—Mark Deming*

Joshua Judges Ruth / Mar. 31, 1992 / Curb ♦♦♦

While *Lyle Lovett and his Large Band* wasn't a massive chart hit, it was successful enough to establish an audience for Lovett outside the boundaries of the country market, and 1992's *Joshua Judges Ruth* found Lovett seemingly free to follow his muse wherever it cared to go. *Joshua Judges Ruth* only bore the faintest glimmers of Lovett's country leanings (notable exception: "She's Leaving Me Because She Really Wants To"), and more surprisingly it suggested he was also moving away from the broad-shouldered jazz and blues accidents that dominated much of *Pontiac* and *Large Band*. Compared to his previous work, *Joshua Judges Ruth* sounds startlingly spare—producer and engineer George Massenburg brings a clear and keenly detailed sound to these sessions that allows all the details of the low-key arrangements to be heard, and "She's Already Made Up Her Mind," "Baltimore," and "Family Reserve" seem to have been recorded with this in mind. The songs also reflect a shift toward more serious and introspective themes for Lovett; outside of the gospel-influenced "Church" and the easygoing "She Makes Me Feel Good," his trademark humor is conspicuous in its absence, and loss, loneliness, and heartbreak dominate the lyrics. While the craft of *Joshua Judges Ruth* ranks with the finest work of Lovett's career, its spare and sober surfaces aren't especially engaging, and it's the sort of album fans are more likely to admire than embrace with pleasure. *—Mark Deming*

I Love Everybody / Sep. 27, 1994 / Curb ♦♦♦♦

Lyle Lovett's 1992 album, *Joshua Judges Ruth*, was a highly ambitious project for the Texas-born singer-songwriter—perhaps too ambitious, since despite the album's beautiful surfaces, the results simply weren't especially absorbing. Released in 1994, *I Love Everybody* seemed to find Lovett taking a step back—it consists of 18 tunes Lovett had written prior to the recording of his first album—but for the most part it succeeds where *Joshua Judges Ruth* disappoints, largely because the songs offer enough changeups to keep the listener engaged at all times. Also, for a set of tunes that were apparent leftovers, the writing on *I Love Everybody* is startlingly strong, from the saucy "Hello Grandma" and "Record Lady" to the stark and edgy storytelling of "I Think You Know What I Mean" and "The Fat Girl." The album also offers up plenty of Lovett's trademark dour humor and playfully sinister undertones; the title song was originally intended to be "Creeps Like Me," and it's hard to decide if one should laugh or frown in disgust while listening to it. And like *Joshua Judges Ruth*, *I Love Everybody* is dominated by clean, stripped-down arrangements and transparent production, but the players bring a lot more spirit and swing to these sessions (top honors go to bassist John Leftwich and drummer Russ Kunkel, a superb and soulful acoustic rhythm section), and the dynamics bring more drama to the performances rather than weighing them down. *I Love Everybody* is just eccentric enough to be best recommended to folks already familiar with Lovett's work, but anyone attuned to his sensibility will find plenty to enjoy here—and a little to make you a shade uncomfortable. *—Mark Deming*

The Road to Ensenada / Jun. 18, 1996 / Curb ♦♦♦♦♦

Since *Pontiac*, Lyle Lovett has been experimenting with different sounds, whether it was the big band posturing of *Lyle Lovett and His Large Band*, the gospel overtones of *Joshua Judges Ruth*, or the '70s singer-songwriter flourishes of *I Love Everybody*. With *The Road to Ensenada*, he hunkers down and produces his most straightforward album since *Pontiac*. As it happens, it is also his best record since that breakthrough album. Lovett strips the sound of the album down to the bare country essentials, allowing it to drift into Western swing, country-rock, folk, and honky tonk when necessary. He also decides to balance his weightier material ("Private Conversation," "Who Loves You Better," "It Ought to Be Easier," "I Can't Love You Anymore," "Christmas Morning") with fun, light-hearted numbers like "Don't Touch My Hat," "Fiona," and "That's Right (You're Not From Texas)," which are funny without being silly. In fact, *The Road to Ensenada* is the lightest album Lyle Lovett has ever made—the darkness that hung around the fringes of *Pontiac*, *Joshua Judges Ruth*, and *I Love Everybody* has drifted away, leaving his wry sense of humor and a newly found empathetic sentimentality. The combination of straightforward instrumentation and lean, catchy, and incisive songwriting results in one of the best albums of his career—he's just as eclectic and off-handedly brilliant as he has always been, but on *The Road to Ensenada* he's more focused and less flashy about his own talent than he's ever been. *—Stephen Thomas Erlewine*

Step Inside This House / Sep. 22, 1998 / MCA ✦✦✦
Step Inside This House, in a way, is a perfect follow-up to *The Road to Ensenada*, his straightest country album since his debut, taking Lyle Lovett back to the very beginning, as he covers his favorite songwriters. He consciously avoids such obvious influences as Randy Newman and Jesse Winchester, choosing to concentrate almost solely on Texan singer-songwriters, resulting in a minor revelation. Lovett's place in Texas' progressive country tradition has always been evident, and his good taste has never been in question, but this not only confirms his strength as a performer, but also illustrates the origins of his clear, wry narratives. He not only sheds light on songwriters known better for their reputation than their actual recordings (Townes Van Zandt, Guy Clark, Walter Hyatt, Michael Martin Murphey, Robert Earl Keen), yet he carries a torch for obscure names like Eric Taylor, Vince Bell and Craig Calvert, David Rodriquez, and Steve Fromholz, who has no less than four songs on the album. For all the different writers, what's striking about *Step Inside This House* is how all the songs seem to spring from the same worldview. Few covers albums are as unified and Lovett's achievement is particularly noteworthy since none of the songs are standards. *—Stephen Thomas Erlewine*

Live in Texas / Jun. 29, 1999 / MCA ✦✦✦✦
In a way, Lyle Lovett has operated on two different levels since the beginning of his career. For many listeners, including critics, he's an exceptionally talented songwriter, revealing himself as the equal to such inspirations as Randy Newman. However, unlike most singer-songwriters, he's an entertainer, putting on one hell of a show every time he takes the stage. And that may be why *Live in Texas* is such a good album: For the first time, Lovett the entertainer has been captured on record. Not that his previous albums have been dry, but it's a pleasure to hear Lovett play with an audience (they love it, laughing at the punch lines in "Here I Am" and listening dead quiet to "North Dakota") and his songs, delivering vibrant, loose-limbed performances that confirm what a rich catalog he has. Recorded in Austin and San Antonio just prior to the release of his 1998 covers album *Step Inside This House*, *Live in Texas* is nearly a greatest-hits collection, graced with a couple of idiosyncratic choices (including a showcase for vocalist Francine Reed, "Wild Women Don't Get the Blues") that are nice additions to a uniformly excellent set of songs. Since Lovett never breaks from his recorded arrangements, what brings *Live in Texas* to life is the spirit of the performances, which not only rival the original recordings, but at times are more energetic or humorous. That doesn't necessarily make it a better album than any of his studio efforts—like most live albums, it plays better if you already know the material—but it's undeniably hard to resist. *—Stephen Thomas Erlewine*

Dr. T. & the Women / Sep. 26, 2000 / MCA ✦✦
The score to the 2000 Robert Altman film about the chaotic life of a Dallas gynecologist features a largely instrumental score by Lovett. There are just three vocals here, among them a remake of "Ain't It Somethin'," leaving the rest to be occupied by 13 instrumentals. It's ordinary, perhaps a bit above-average incidental soundtrack music, jumping from subdued themes and jazzy lounge sounds to hoe-down jazzy bluegrass and items that sound like barroom odes sans words ("Golf Cart Love"). A very minor, even forgettable entry in the discography of Lovett (who, if you're wondering, does not appear as an actor in the film, although he has acted in other Altman-directed movies). *—Richie Unterberger*

Anthology, Vol. 1: Cowboy Man / Oct. 23, 2001 / MCA ✦✦✦
Check the subhead in the title—yes, this may be an anthology, but this isn't a greatest hits, it's a collection of songs that emphasize Lyle Lovett's country side and, therefore, is pitched directly at the country audience that never had much truck with him after he started singing "Stand By Your Man," playing with His Large Band, and indulging his passion for Randy Newman. In other words, it's not really representative, particularly in how it consciously avoids his status as a leader of the alt-country movement in the first Bush era. *His Large Band*, *Joshua Judges Ruth*, and *I Love Everybody* are entirely avoided (perhaps saved for *Vol. 2*), and even good portions of Lovett's country work are ignored, such as "You're Not From Texas" and the rest of *The Road to Ensenada*, for that matter. That's not really a complaint, but their absence feels more puzzling since two new songs are thrown in for good measure (the really good "The Truck Song," plus "San Antonio Girl"). In any regard, this is a good summary of Lovett's first two albums, containing most of the great songs from those records—"God Will," "This Old Porch," "If I Were the Man You Wanted," "If I Had a Boat," "Walk Through the Bottomland," and "L.A. County" are as good as music got in the '80s, and it's a pleasure to hear them in any context. Even so, it's hard to shake the nagging feeling that the whole story isn't told with this collection, and it's even harder not to notice that Lovett hasn't released a collection of original songs since 1996—and, for the hardcore fans who are suckered in by the two new songs, it'll be hard not to wish that a full-fledged album is around the corner sometime soon. *—Stephen Thomas Erlewine*

Smile / Feb. 25, 2003 / MCA ✦✦✦
Since *The Road to Ensenada* in 1996, Lyle Lovett has released a collection of covers in 1998, a live album in 1999, a predominately instrumental soundtrack in 2000, and now, in 2003, *Smile*, a collection of songs he recorded for movie soundtracks between 1992 and 2002. None of these were on his official albums and none of them are originals (meaning that it's been nearly seven years since he's released a collection of new songs; this may or may not be a sign of writer's block). Most are covers of pop standards, with a couple of R&B and gospel standards thrown in for good measure (the one contemporary tune is "You've Got a Friend in Me," the Randy Newman duet from *Toy Story*). All are given perfectly tasteful, perfectly pleasant Large Band-styled arrangements; they're very faithful to the songs yet are styled to Lovett's idiosyncratic delivery. Overall, it's a nice listen and it's nice for collectors to get these all tunes in one place, but it's not essential and it's hard not to wish that Lovett would just finally do an album of new material already. *—Stephen Thomas Erlewine*

Nick Lowe

b. Mar. 25, 1949, Woodchurch, Suffolk, England
Bass, Songwriter, Vocals, Producer / Rock & Roll, Country-Rock, New Wave, Power Pop, Pop/Rock, Pub Rock, Roots Rock

As the leader of the seminal pub rockers Brinsley Schwarz, a producer, and a solo artist, Nick Lowe held considerable influence over the development of punk rock. With the Brinsleys, Lowe began a back-to-basics movement that flowered into punk rock in the late '70s. As the house producer for Stiff, he recorded many seminal records by the likes of the Damned, Elvis Costello, and the Pretenders. His rough, ragged production style earned him the nickname "Basher" and also established the amateurish, D.I.Y. aesthetics of punk. Despite his massive influence on punk rock, Lowe never really was a punk rocker. Lowe was concerned with bringing back the tradition of three-minute pop singles and hard-driving rock & roll, but he subverted his melodic songcraft with a nasty sense of humor. His early solo singles and albums *Jesus of Cool* and *Labour of Lust* overflowed with hooks, bizarre jokes, and an infectious energy that made them some of the most acclaimed pop records of the new wave era. As new wave began to fade away in the early '80s, Lowe began to explore roots rock, eventually becoming a full-fledged country-rocker in the '90s. While he never had another hit after 1980's "Cruel to Be Kind," his records found a devoted cult audience and often were critically praised.

The son of a British Royal Air Force officer, Lowe spent part of his childhood stationed in the Middle East before his family settled in Kent. As a teenager, he played in a variety of bands, including Three's a Crowd and Sounds 4 Plus 1, with his friend, guitarist Brinsley Schwarz. In 1965, the pair formed the guitar-pop band Kippington Lodge, which landed a contract with Parlophone Records the following year. Over the next four years, the group released five singles, none of which received much attention. In 1969, Kippington Lodge evolved into the country-rock band Brinsley Schwarz, who secured a record contract with United Artists the following year. At the outset of their career, the Brinsleys attempted to gain fame by holding a showcase concert at the Fillmore East, but the publicity stunt backfired, making the band outcasts from the British music scene by the time their first album was released. Over the next five years, the group slowly built a following as the leading exponents of pub rock, a back-to-basics movement of good-time rock & roll that earned a niche in the early '70s.

With their unassuming appearance and unpretentious music, pub rockers set the stage for punk rock in the late '70s, not only by relying on three-chord rock & roll, but also establishing a circuit of pubs to play. Of all the old-guard pub rockers, Lowe was the most significant in the development of punk rock. By the time Brinsley Schwarz broke up in 1975, he had already gained a reputation as an excellent, eccentric songwriter, and he was beginning to produce artists like Graham Parker, Dr. Feelgood, and the Kursaal Flyers. At the time, his songwriting was veering away from the country-rock and bluesy rock that distinguished his Brinsley work, and he was beginning to write inventive pop songs. Lowe wanted to leave United Artists, but the label refused to let him go, so he proceeded to record a series of deliberately unmarketable singles in hopes of getting kicked off the label. The first was "Bay City Rollers We Love You," a tongue-in-cheek tribute to the teen pop sensations credited to the Tartan Horde. Inexplicably, the single became a hit in Japan—the Japanese branch of UA even asked for a full album—and the label kept him as an artist. However, after "Let's Go to the Disco," credited to the Disco Brothers, UA dropped him from the label.

After leaving UA, Lowe became the first artist on Jake Riviera and Dave Robinson's fledgling independent label Stiff Records as well as the label's in-house producer. Recorded for just 65 pounds and released in the summer of 1976, "So It Goes"/"Heart of the City" became the first British proto-punk single of the late '70s, earning glowing reviews if not sales. Lowe began producing records at a rapid rate, helming the Damned's debut album, *Damned Damned Damned*—the first British punk album—and Costello's *My Aim Is True* in 1977; he would produce all of Costello's albums between *My Aim Is True* and 1981's *Trust*. Lowe also produced singles by Wreckless Eric, the Rumour, and Alberto y los Trios Paranoias as well as Graham Parker's early albums. In the summer, he became part of Dave Edmunds' touring band Rockpile, which would become his backing band within a year. He also released the *Bowi* EP (a play on the title of David Bowie's *Low* LP) in 1977, and toured with the Stiff package tour *Live Stiffs* before leaving the label with Costello to join Riviera's new label, Radar Records.

Lowe released his debut album, *Jesus of Cool* (retitled *Pure Pop for Now People* for its American release), in 1978, which featured his first British Top Ten hit, "(I Love the Sound Of) Breaking Glass." The single "American Squirm" was released in the fall of 1978 to little success. After producing the Pretenders' debut single, "Stop Your Sobbing," Lowe recorded his second album, *Labour of Lust*, supported by Rockpile; Edmunds' *Repeat When Necessary* was recorded at the same session. *Labour of Lust* featured Lowe's one big American hit, "Cruel to Be Kind," which was a reworked version of an old Brinsley Schwarz song. Between the recording and touring in 1979, Lowe married Carlene Carter, the step-daughter of Johnny Cash; he would produce her albums *Musical Shapes* (1980) and *Blue Nun* (1981).

Lowe and Edmunds toured with Rockpile to support their respective 1979 albums, and the pair were the subject of the BBC documentary *Born Fighters* later that year. Rockpile's shows became notorious for their wild, frequently drunken performances and the group's spirited selection of originals and obscure covers. In 1980, the band decided to record an album together, but the sessions were plagued by tension between Lowe and Edmunds. *Seconds of Pleasure*, the group's lone album, was released in the fall of 1980 to mixed reviews; it generated one hit single, the Lowe-written "Teacher Teacher." Rockpile split only months after the release of *Seconds of Pleasure*, with the remaining members choosing to support Edmunds on his solo album.

Lowe returned with *Nick the Knife* in February of 1982, supporting the album with a band featuring guitarist Martin Blemont and keyboardist Paul Carrack; the group was first called the Chaps, but their name changed to Noise to Go during the American tour. *Nick the Knife* was a moderate hit, but its follow-up, 1983's *The Abominable Showman*, was a flop. Lowe retaliated by shifting his music toward roots rock on his 1984 album *And His Cowboy Outfit*. Both *Cowboy Outfit* and its 1985 successor, *The Rose of England*, were greeted with positive reviews and improved sales; the former featured his last U.K. hit, "Half a Boy Half a Man," and the latter featured his last U.S. hit, a reworking of his chestnut "I Knew the Bride (When She Used to Rock & Roll)." In 1986, he reunited with Costello to produce *Blood & Chocolate*. The album was one of many records—including efforts by the Fabulous Thunderbirds, John Hiatt, and Paul Carrack—he produced in the '80s.

During much of the mid-'80s, Lowe suffered from alcohol abuse, but with the assistance of his old mates Costello and Riviera, he recovered and gave up looking for a crossover pop hit, concentrating on country-rock and roots rock. *Pinker and Prouder Than Previous* (1988) was the first indication of this shift in style, but the record largely went unnoticed. Produced by Dave Edmunds, *Party of One* (1990) became his first charting album since 1985. Later that year, Lowe divorced Carter. The following year, he formed the supergroup Little Village with John Hiatt, Ry Cooder, and Jim Keltner; all of the musicians played on Hiatt's 1987 breakthrough album, *Bring the Family*. Little Village was fraught with tension, and their eponymous 1992 album and its supporting tour suffered as a result. The group disbanded upon the tour's conclusion. While he was working on material for a new album, Lowe's Brinsley Schwarz composition "(What's So Funny 'Bout) Peace, Love and Understanding," which had previously been a hit for Costello, was covered by Curtis Stigers for the soundtrack to Whitney Houston's film *The Bodyguard*. The album became the biggest-selling soundtrack album in history and, in the process, Lowe unexpectedly became a millionaire from the songwriting royalties.

Lowe made a comeback in 1994 with the straight country album, *The Impossible Bird*. Hailed as his finest effort in years, the album became a hit in the burgeoning Americana movement in the U.S., and he supported the album with his first solo tour in five years; his touring band featured former Commander Cody guitarist Bill Kirchen. In 1998, Lowe returned with *Dig My Mood*. *—Stephen Thomas Erlewine*

★ **Jesus of Cool** / 1978 / Demon ✦✦✦✦✦

☆ **Labour of Lust** / 1979 / Demon ✦✦✦✦✦

Nick the Knife / 1982 / Demon ✦✦✦

The Abominable Showman / 1983 / Demon ✦✦

☆ **16 All Time Lowes** / 1984 / Demon ✦✦✦✦✦

The Rose of England / 1985 / Demon ✦✦✦✦✦
Following through on the roots rock leanings of *Cowboy Outfit*, Nick Lowe delivered the delightful *The Rose of England*. While some of the material is still rather lightweight— "Lucky Dog" and "Bo Bo Skediddle" are defiant and thoroughly entertaining throwaways—much of the record is clever and charming, delivered with laid-back confidence from the Cowboy Outfit. "Darlin' Angel Eyes" and "The Rose of England" are minor classics in the Lowe canon, while his cover of John Hiatt's "She Don't Love Nobody" and the revival of the rockabilly standard "7 Nights to Rock" keep the album moving. Still, it's his stark take on Elvis Costello's lovely "Indoor Fireworks" that gives the album an anchor, and it's a performance so affecting that it makes the neutered reworking of "I Knew the Bride" completely forgivable. *—Stephen Thomas Erlewine*

Pinker and Prouder Than Previous / 1988 / Demon ✦✦✦
Abandoning the Cowboy Outfit but not roots rock, Nick Lowe followed the winning *The Rose of England* with the amiable but muddled *Pinker and Prouder Than Previous*. Working with the same blend of classic pop, rock & roll, and country-rock, Lowe gets thing off to a roaring start with the driving "(You're My) Wildest Dream," but the record quickly bogs down in mediocre material. Many of the songs are certainly not bad, yet they rarely distinguish themselves from each other—only "Lover's Jamboree," John Hiatt's "Love Gets Strange" and Graham Parker's "Black Lincoln Continental" stand out, and they would have been second-string songs on *The Rose of England*. That doesn't necessarily make *Pinker and Prouder Than Previous* a bad record; it's just not particularly memorable. *—Stephen Thomas Erlewine*

• **Basher: The Best of Nick Lowe** / Sep. 1989 / Columbia ✦✦✦✦✦
Containing no less than 25 tracks, *Basher: The Best of Nick Lowe* is an excellent overview of Lowe's solo career, detailing how he evolved from a quirky, innovative new wave pop craftsman to a fine roots rocker. All of Lowe's absolutely essential songs—from "So It Goes" and "Heart of the City" through "Cracking Up," "Born Fighter," and "Cruel to Be Kind" to "American Squirm," "The Rose of England" "Half a Boy and Half a Man" and "Raging Eyes"—are here, and while *Jesus of Cool* and *Labour of Lust* are essential in their own right, *Basher* is a terrific introduction to his body of work. *—Stephen Thomas Erlewine*

Party of One / 1990 / Upstart ✦✦
Nick Lowe settled a long-standing feud with Dave Edmunds with *Party of One*, hiring his former Rockpile mate to produce the album. Edmunds gives Lowe a sharper sound than before, keeping a tight reign on the performances and the songs—for the first time, there are no covers on a Nick Lowe album. Theoretically, that wouldn't be a problem, but Lowe was in a songwriting slump at the time of *Party of One*. "All Men Are Liars," with its weird jab at dance-pop idol Rick Astley, is symptomatic of the record's flaws—ingratiating melodies are undercut by forced humor and bland support. Even the best moments—

"(I Want to Build A) Jumbo Ark," "What's Shakin' on the Hill," "I Don't Know Why You Keep Me On"—are undercut by stiff, colorless performances. For an artist who is defined by his relaxed charm, the stilted *Party of One* comes as an unwelcome surprise. *—Stephen Thomas Erlewine*

The Wilderness Years / 1991 / Demon ✦✦✦✦✦

☆ **The Impossible Bird** / Nov. 29, 1994 / Upstart ✦✦✦✦✦
Nick Lowe's best records have always been full of clever lyrics and undeniable pop craftsmanship; the exception is *The Impossible Bird*. For most of the 1980s, Lowe had been appropriating country and R&B influences, but *The Impossible Bird* is where he fully incorporates those styles into his songwriting. Lowe doesn't abandon his gift for melody; "Soulful Wind" and "12-Step Program (To Quit You Babe)" are as catchy as anything he's ever written. The difference is haunting songs like "The Beast in Me" and "Withered on the Vine," two rich, sad, introspective numbers that Lowe would never have put on previous albums. And that's what makes *The Impossible Bird* his best album since *Labour of Lust*—it's the most focused, mature, personal music of his career, without a single throwaway. *—Stephen Thomas Erlewine*

Dig My Mood / Jan. 26, 1998 / Upstart ✦✦✦✦
The Impossible Bird revitalized Nick Lowe's career, finding him in a rare moment of reflection and focus, resulting in one of the very best records of his career. Its follow-up, *Dig My Mood*, doesn't reach the same peaks, but it matches the same high standard, offering 12 songs with no filler or novelties. The dark, torchy opener, "Faithless Lover," may come as a bit of a surprise, especially since it's followed a song later by "You Inspire Me," another torch number, this time in the vein of k.d. lang. These two songs actually are a good indicator of the tone of *Dig My Mood*, since the country-rock that dominated *The Impossible Bird* actually fades into the background over the course of the album, popping up most directly on the funny Johnny Cash homage "Man That I've Become" and "I Must Be Getting Over You." The rest of the record is a skillful, laid-back hybrid of torchy pop, R&B, and country that is subtle in its execution. Lowe's voice is in the forefront, but it's gentle and unassuming, blending perfectly with the guitars, pianos, and accordions. His songs are quietly ambitious, exploring new territory lyrically and musically, without leaving his signature style. As always, his taste in covers is impeccable, finding Henry McCullough's little-known "Failed Christian" and the wonderful, overlooked Ivory Joe Hunter gem "The Cold Grey Light of Dawn." They are the final, irresistible grace notes to an album that finds Lowe at his best. *—Stephen Thomas Erlewine*

The Doings / Jul. 27, 1999 / Demon ✦✦✦✦
The subtitle of the four-disc box set *The Doings* is *The Solo Years*, and the 86-track compilation never once strays from that edict. Disc one kicks off with Nick Lowe's seminal single "So It Goes," bypassing his early work with Brinsley Schwarz. By the end of that first disc, the compilation is already at *Nick the Knife*, his first album after the disbandment of Rockpile, and none of that group's official recordings are here. As it stands, *The Doings* falls just below the definitive mark, mainly because of those omissions. It's still a worthwhile set, though, playing much like an expanded version of *Basher*. It could be argued that it moves a little too quickly through Lowe's '70s and '80s material, especially since the third disc contains almost all of his '90s albums *Impossible Bird* and *Dig My Mood*. Then again, those two records really are among the best music he's ever made, so they deserve such an elevated position. Still, such decisions help point out what's missing from *The Doings*, and there are some great songs not included, but that's nit-picking. What's here is excellent, tracing a good history of Nick's solo career, perfect for casual fans wanting a comprehensive anthology. But *The Doings* is really for obsessive fans, and they'll be pleased by the rarities. Not only is the original fast version of "Cruel to Be Kind" here, but there's a full disc of live recordings, demos, and home recordings, all of high quality. Not only does *The Doings* do a good job of collecting obscurities, it does an even better job of drawing a portrait of Lowe's solo recordings. Ultimately, that's what makes *The Doings* a success. *—Stephen Thomas Erlewine*

The Convincer / Oct. 11, 2001 / Yep Roc ✦✦✦✦
The Convincer is the last installment in a trilogy begun with *The Impossible Bird* and musically it falls between that record's country-rock and the torch songs of 1997's *Dig My Mood*. No surprises then, but that's fine, because Lowe hasn't delivered three records this consistent in a very longtime, if ever. All three records are warm, intimate affairs, yet they all have a different mood. *Bird* was a quintessential breakup record, *Mood* was the soundtrack to a late-night seduction, while *The Convincer* is a laid-back record that simply feels good. It's a smooth affair, whether Lowe is crooning a cover of Johnny Rivers' "Poor Side of Town" or "Homewrecker," where it's clear that he still loves the title seductress, even if she turned his life upside down. And that's the key to the record—there's a real sense of joy from Lowe, a sense that he knows he's been in a creative renaissance and that he's enjoying every second of it, and that spills over to the record itself. It's a record comprised of little triumphs—the relaxed rockabilly of "Has She Got a Friend?," the telling details of "Lately I've Let Things Slide," and the wry ballad "I'm a Mess." At the end of the record, when he's convincing his sweetheart "Let's Stay in and Make Love," the listener is as smitten as the object of his affection. That may not be earth-shaking, but it's thoroughly charming all the same. *—Stephen Thomas Erlewine*

Lulu Belle (Myrtle Eleanor Cooper)

b. Dec. 24, 1913, Boone, NC, **d.** Feb. 8, 1999
Vocals / Traditional Country
Lulu Belle and husband Scotty were a popular duo during the 1930s credited with helping make country music more popular and accessible to mainstream audiences. Scotty Wiseman also penned songs such as "Remember Me" and "Have I Told You Lately That I Love You" which went on to become country standards. In addition to headlining WLS Chicago's *National Barn Dance* for close to two decades, the duo appeared in seven

motion pictures, including *Shine on Harvest Moon.* Lulu was born Myrtle Eleanor Cooper in Boone, NC, and got her start on the *National Barn Dance* when she was 19. There she worked as a cornball comedian à la Minnie Pearl with Red Foley. Later the station teamed her up with Skyland Scotty Wiseman, another North Carolina native, when Foley's wife began getting jealous of Lulu. It was a good move, as she and Scotty clicked both professionally and personally, and they married in 1934.

Though Lulu Belle and Scotty did record periodically, they were never as popular on wax as they were on the air. The couple left the *Barn Dance* in 1958, at which point Scotty returned to college and obtained a Master's degree. He then became a teacher, a farmer, and a bank director. Lulu Belle was active in community activities and eventually went on to serve two terms in the legislature of North Carolina as the Democratic representative for three counties. They also occasionally recorded during these years, and made three albums for Starday during the '60s and one in 1974 for Old Homestead. Scotty died in 1981 and two years later Lulu Belle remarried an old family friend. In 1986, she recorded a solo album for Homestead. *—Sandra Brennan*

• **The Sweethearts of Country Music** / 1963 / Starday ✦✦✦✦✦

Down Memory Lane With Lulu Belle and Scotty / 1964 / Starday ✦✦✦✦
A straight reissue of a 1964 album, this CD is one of very few examples of Lulu Belle and Scotty's music that has appeared on compact disc. Recorded late in their careers, *Down Memory Lane . . .* may not be the most representative collection, but it is an excellent album that alternates acoustic hillbilly ballads and novelties with more modern-sounding efforts. "Wonderful Lies" flirts with the Nashville sound and rock & roll, while "The Devil's Tramping Ground" is a spooky minor-key cautionary tale. This isn't prime Lulu Belle & Scotty, but it's a fine collection by a duo that deserves a more comprehensive retrospective. *—Greg Adams*

Lulu Belle & Scotty / 1965 / Starday ✦✦✦

Sweethearts Still / 1991 / King ✦✦

Bob Luman

b. Apr. 15, 1937, Nacogdoches, TX, **d.** Dec. 27, 1978, Nashville, TN
Guitar, Vocals / Traditional Country, Rockabilly, Country-Rock
Bob Luman started out as a rockabilly performer, switched to country and then in the late '50s nearly ditched the music industry altogether. Through his teens, Luman was primarily interested in singing country music like his idol Lefty Frizzell, but then he saw Elvis, which inspired him to try his hand at the rockabilly sound. Soon after graduating, Luman won a talent contest, leading to his debut on the *Louisiana Hayride.* He became a regular in the mid-'50s, and had a small role in the 1957 film *Carnival Rock*; still, his singles did nothing on the charts. In 1959, the Pittsburgh Pirates offered Luman a contract; fed up with his lack of success, he announced his intention to accept the offer during a concert one night. However, the Everly Brothers talked him into recording the Boudleaux Bryant song "Let's Think About Living"; sure enough, it was a Top Ten hit on both the country and pop charts. His follow-up, "The Great Snowman," was also a hit, but he was drafted, and spent the next two years in the military.

In 1964, he began recording for Hickory Records, and the following year, he became a member of the *Grand Ole Opry.* Luman eventually signed with Epic Records and had a string of Top 25 hits over the next ten years. He toured extensively and became the first country singer to perform in Puerto Rico; he also remained a regular on the *Opry,* where his lively performances veered close to rock & roll at times. Luman had a major heart attack in 1975, and it took him nearly five months to recover. His final chart appearance came in 1977; the following year he contracted pneumonia and died at the age of 41. *—Sandra Brennan*

• **American Originals** / 1984 / Columbia ✦✦✦✦✦
American Originals offers most of Luman's hits, including "Lonely Women Make Good Lovers," "Still Loving You," "Let's Think About Living" and "Ain't Got Time to Be Unhappy." *—Jason Ankeny*

10 Years: 1968–1977 / Apr. 25, 2000 / Bear Family ✦✦✦✦
Somewhere between Elvis Country and Waylon Jennings resides Bob Luman, a former rock & roll artist who turned to country and enjoyed a healthy string of hits. This five-disc box set compiles everything Luman recorded for Epic and Polydor from 1968 until his death, including 30 Top 100 country hits. Except for a few K-Tel re-recordings, this box set is a complete chronicle of the last years of Luman's career. Luman was very consistent, the box and hardbound book are beautiful, and there are many lost gems on this set, but only the most ardent collector will shell out the high price for this import set. *—Greg Adams*

Loretta / May 16, 2000 / Sundown ✦✦✦
By the time Luman got around to cutting these tracks for Hickory Records, he was straddling the fine line between his old rockabilly style and vying for entry in the world of country music. As such, the tracks move between those two poles, rocking furiously one minute (the title track) and lapsing into maudlin tear-jerker sentiments the next ("It's a Sin," complete with corny recitations). Not his best, nor a good introduction to his work, but not awful, either. *—Cub Koda*

Loretta Lynn

b. Apr. 14, 1934, Butcher Hollow, KY
Vocals, Guitar / Honky Tonk, Nashville Sound/Countrypolitan, Traditional Country
Loretta Lynn is one of the classic country singers. During the '60s and '70s, she ruled the charts, racking up over 70 hits as a solo artist and a duet partner. Lynn helped forge the way for strong, independent women in country music. As her song (and movie and book) says, Loretta Lynn is a coal miner's daughter, born in Butcher Hollow, KY, in 1934. As a child, she sang in church and a variety of local concerts. In January 1948, she married Oliver "Mooney" Lynn. She was 13 years old at the time. Following their marriage, the couple moved to Custer, WA, where they raised four children.

After a decade of motherhood, Lynn began performing her own songs in local clubs, backed by a band led by her brother, Jay Lee Webb. It took her a decade of gigging before she was noticed by a record label. In 1959, she signed a contract with Zero Records, which released her debut single, "I'm a Honky Tonk Girl," in 1960. The honky tonk ballad became a hit thanks to the insistent, independent promotion of Lynn and her husband. The pair would drive from one radio station to the next, getting the DJs to play her single, and sent out thousands of copies to stations. All of the effort paid off—the single reached number 14 on the charts and attracted the attention of the Wilburn Brothers. The Wilburns hired Lynn to tour with them in 1960 and advised her to relocate to Nashville. She followed their advice and moved to the city in late 1960. After she arrived in Nashville, she signed with Decca Records. At Decca, she would work with Owen Bradley, who had produced Patsy Cline.

Lynn released her first Decca single, "Success," in 1962 and it went straight to number six, beginning a string of Top Ten singles that would run-through the rest of the decade and throughout the next. She was a hard honky tonk singer for the first half of the '60s and rarely strayed from the genre. Although she still worked within the confines of honky tonk in the latter half of the decade, her sound became more personal, varied and ambitious, particularly lyrically. Beginning with 1966's number-two hit "You Ain't Woman Enough," Lynn began writing songs that had a feminist viewpoint, which was unheard of in country music. Her lyrical stance became more autobiographical and realistic as time wore on, highlighted by such hits as "Don't Come Home A Drinkin' (With Lovin' on Your Mind)" (1966), "Your Squaw Is on the Warpath" (1968), "Woman of the World (Leave My World Alone)" (1969), and a tune about birth control called "The Pill" (1974).

Between 1966 and 1970, Loretta Lynn racked up 13 Top Ten hits, including four number-one hits—"Don't Come Home A Drinkin'," "Fist City" (1968), "Woman of the World," and the autobiographical "Coal Miner's Daughter." In 1971, she began a professional partnership with Conway Twitty. As a duo, Lynn and Twitty had five consecutive number-one hits between 1971 and 1975—"After the Fire Is Gone" (1971), "Lead Me On" (1971), "Louisiana Woman, Mississippi Man" (1973), "As Soon as I Hang Up the Phone" (1974), and "Feelins'" (1974). The hit-streak kick-started what would become one of the most successful duos of country history. For four consecutive years (1972-1975), Lynn and Twitty were named the Vocal Duo of the Year by the Country Music Association. In addition to their five number-one singles, they had seven other Top Ten hits between 1976 and 1981.

Loretta Lynn published her autobiography, *Coal Miner's Daughter,* in the mid-'70s. In 1980, the book was adapted for the screen, with Sissy Spacek as Lynn. The film was one of the most critically acclaimed and successful films of the year and Spacek would win the Academy Award for her performance. All of the attention surrounding the movie made Loretta Lynn a household name with the American mainstream. Although she continued to be a popular concert attraction throughout the '80s, she wasn't able to continue her domination of the country charts. "I Lie," her last Top Ten single, arrived in early 1982, while her last Top 40 single, "Heart Don't Do This to Me," was in 1985. In light of her declining record sales, Lynn backed away from recording frequently during the late '80s and '90s, concentrating on performing instead. In 1993, she recorded the *Honky Tonk Angels* album with Tammy Wynette and Dolly Parton. *Still Woman Enough* was released in mid-2000. *—Stephen Thomas Erlewine*

Loretta Lynn Sings / 1963 / Decca ✦✦✦

Before I'm Over You / 1964 / Decca ✦✦✦

Hymns / 1965 / King ✦✦✦✦
Loretta Lynn's fourth album—fifth if you count her duet record with Ernest Tubb from earlier in 1965—is a collection of Christian songs but, despite the title, the record is actually about evenly divided between traditional church music and what would eventually come to be called contemporary Christian music. The rollicking opening track, "Everybody Wants to Go to Heaven (But Nobody Wants to Die)," biblical verse or no, sounds more like a classic Sun Records rockabilly single, complete with slapback bass and Scotty Moore-style guitar, than anything one would be likely to hear on a Sunday morning. That song is a Lynn original, as is the closing "Where I Learned How to Pray," a sentimental weeper in the classic style. In between, Lynn essays traditional hymns and newer classics of the style like the Rev. Thomas A. Dorsey's immortal "There'll Be Peace in the Valley for Me," the arrangement of which strongly recalls Elvis' hit version. A relative rarity among Lynn's albums, this disc was reissued by King Records in 1998. *—Stewart Mason*

Songs From My Heart / 1965 / Decca ✦✦✦

Ernest Tubb & Loretta Lynn / 1965 / Decca ✦✦

Blue Kentucky Girl / 1965 / Decca ✦✦✦

I Like 'Em Country / 1966 / Decca ✦✦✦

You Ain't Woman Enough / 1966 / MCA ✦✦✦✦
This is one budget-line release that rewards collectors as well as casual fans. Despite the shoddy packaging, the CD comprises Lynn's entire 1966 album *You Ain't Woman Enough,* including her number-two country hit of the same name. In addition, listeners are treated to a collection of originals and covers of uniformly fine quality, including an excellent version of the Wilburn Brothers' 1965 hit "It's Another World" featuring Lynn's double-tracked harmony vocals. Only two of the 12 songs on this package are duplicated on the *Honky Tonk Girl* box set, making this a necessary—and inexpensive—addition to any fan's collection. *—Greg Adams*

A Country Christmas / 1966 / MCA ✦✦✦
There are those who would like to set every Christmas album ever recorded ablaze over a Yuletide fireplace, but let's hope these cheerless arsonists overlook this already well-roasted chestnut of a record. If anyone has the personality to make a good Christmas record, it would be Loretta Lynn. But there are surprise goodies in her gift bag, as she even manages to come up with three great original numbers based on the holiday, the best of the batch being "To Heck With Ole Santa Claus." Her playful side helps her extract

nice feelings from too-familiar numbers such as "Silver Bells" and "Frosty the Snowman." And she's such a great vocalist she is able to give both Elvis Presley and Bing Crosby a run for the mistletoe as she takes Christmas from shades of blue to white and back again. Some good country session pickers hold things together whenever she stops for a holiday smooch. *—Eugene Chadbourne*

☆ **Don't Come Home A Drinkin'** / 1967 / MCA ✦✦✦✦✦
The title track was one of those defining songs for Lynn, not only one of the best but one of the most likable country and western artists. She bats one home run after another in these vocals, singing her brains out and coming across as totally convincing in each role she takes on. The cynical "I Got Caught" is one of her finer originals, while she also has the knack of picking covers that suit her perfectly, such as "The Shoe Goes on the Other Foot Tonight" by the underrated Buddy Mize. No country fan will mind that she covers a number by her old sidekick, Ernest Tubb. Then there's the pickers who came along for the ride, totally tearing it up. The series of lead guitar/pedal steel interchanges that run-through this album are certainly more attractive than the Nashville freeway system, and definitely contributed more to 20th century civilization. Lynn would later record the song "You're Looking at Country," and that pretty much sums up the view of this mighty lady. This here is stone cold country, and it doesn't get much better. *—Eugene Chadbourne*

Singin' With Feelin' / 1967 / Decca ✦✦✦✦
She was into the double digits with albums on Decca by the time this was released, and although recording them involved a formula and must have settled into a kind of science, what a great scientist Loretta Lynn is. "Vocal with instrumental accompaniment" is the understated totality of the liner notes. Permanent pedal steel partner Hal Rugg, joined at the hip to Lynn, is his brilliant self. He is sometimes driven into near frenzy by his trading partner on electric guitar. Drums are especially crisp and snappy on the numbers that shuffle or swing. Lynn also has her fingers in the pop pie, making "Secret Love," at that time a hit for Doris Day, sound just like it was a Loretta Lynn song. Country music is of course known for tragedy and there is plenty of that here to savor. But the high point of the album is, surprisingly, a cute bit of fluff entitled "It's Such a Pretty World Today." Lynn puts literally oodles of good feeling into the lyrics by Dale Noe, resulting in a song that could probably brighten up the worst of days. *—Eugene Chadbourne*

Who Says God Is Dead! / 1968 / MCA ✦✦✦✦
Considering the amount of conviction Loretta Lynn sings with here, no one has probably ever debated the singer about this album title. And buckets full of retro-kitsch aside, this late-'60s follow-up to Lynn's gospel debut, *Hymns*, nicely packs it in with dreams of the apocalypse, testaments of the heaven-bound, and several classic gospel songs. In addition to romping through "Harp With Golden Strings" and "He's Got the Whole World in His Hands," Lynn really sinks her sanctified teeth into waltz-time ballads like "In the Garden" and "Ten Thousand Angels." Adding to these venerable selections, Lynn contributes a few of her own testimonies on the judgment-day narrative "Standing Room Only" and the title track. And for that ethereal touch, the Jordanaires bless the proceedings with their airily dulcet harmonies. Whether laughing or crying, partying or praying, this album should fit the bill if you need a break from Nashville's slew of cheatin' songs and other tragic tales of co-dependency. *—Stephen Cook*

Fist City / 1968 / Decca ✦✦✦✦✦

Here's Loretta Lynn / 1968 / Columbia ✦✦✦✦
Certain expectations arise when an artist's first recordings are repackaged and resold after they have made it big. Often a listener expects nothing from such a release and is pleasantly surprised. Such a reaction would be expected with this particular set, because, after all, Lynn's first recording sessions for the Vancouver Zero label created the material that, along with a hundred-thousand miles or so of tire tread, got her started along the road to becoming the country legend she is today. But repeated listenings to this material will result in the appraisal going up a few notches. For a debut effort no doubt done under a lot of pressure with not so ideal conditions, this material is pretty impressive. One striking thing about this recording is that all the songs were written by Lynn, not a common thing for a country artist, especially when they are going into the studios for the first time. The songs are really very good, rich with detail and, needless to say, convincing in emotion. Lynn is already coming into her own, but there is more of a Kitty Wells influence. The backup is of a more standard variety, with none of the showboating, breath-stopping pedal steel, and lead guitar interplay that makes her later recording career so exciting. The band does surprise, though, coming up with a near B. B. King sound for the cute "Heartaches Meet Mr. Blues." Session men are uncredited, but, since this was recorded in Los Angeles, the listener can assume for sure that they weren't Nashville cats. *—Eugene Chadbourne*

☆ **Greatest Hits** / 1968 / MCA ✦✦✦✦✦
She had a big hand in raising Nashville's perception of women as capable and competent (although the city still has a way to go). "Don't Come Home A-Drinkin'" and "You Ain't Woman Enough" are particularly representative: sassy, honest, and aggressive. *—Tom Roland*

Your Squaw Is on the Warpath / 1969 / Decca ✦✦✦✦
Boasting one of the classic politically incorrect album covers—which depicts Loretta as a sexy, tomahawk wielding Native American—*Your Squaw is on the Warpath* takes its title from the equally inappropriate track that begins the album. And while it may seem that this album's real value comes from its now kitschy artifact status, the rest of the album stands as a good collection, showcasing Lynn's talents as singer and interpreter of others' songs. *—Chris Woodstra*

Woman of the World/To Make a Man / 1969 / Decca ✦✦✦
A couple of misfire tracks keep this from being among the best of this country singing queen's many fine albums for this label. Normally a pretty reliable songwriter, she comes up with a pretty embarrassing dud in "To Make a Man Feel Like a Man," but it must have been the season for this kind of thing as she also does a cover version of "Stand By Your Man," which is a much better song and also in this case provides the interesting contrast of getting to hear one country song queen doing her interpretation of one of her rival's biggest hits. Elsewhere, Lynn has the taste to do a moving Merle Haggard cover, and her original "Big Sister, Little Sister" is almost uncomfortably tragic, even by country music standards. As for musical backup, the uncredited players are right in the pocket with heartfelt tinkling piano, honky tonk pedal steel, and all other expected stylings. *—Eugene Chadbourne*

Loretta Lynn Writes 'Em and Sings 'Em / 1970 / Decca ✦✦✦✦✦

Wings Upon Your Horns / 1970 / Decca ✦✦✦

I Wanna Be Free / 1971 / Decca ✦✦✦

One's on the Way / 1971 / Decca ✦✦✦

Coal Miner's Daughter / 1971 / MCA ✦✦✦✦✦
Unlike the song, autobiography and film of the same name, the album *Coal Miner's Daughter* isn't a reflection on Loretta Lynn's upbringing. Instead, it's merely a standard, early '70s collection of originals and covers, all performed with gusto by Lynn. *Coal Miner's Daughter* boasts a stronger, more consistent selection of material than most of her other albums from the period, and contains a number of her classics, like the title song and "I'm a Honky Tonk Girl," plus a handful of lesser-known gems. *—Thom Owens*

You're Lookin' at Country / 1971 / Decca ✦✦✦

Alone With You / 1972 / MCA ✦✦✦

God Bless America Again / 1972 / Decca ✦✦

Here I Am Again / 1972 / Decca ✦✦✦
Here I Am Again is practically a concept album for all its songs about men. A few express love and devotion, such as "My Kind of Man," "Be Proud of Your Man," and the Top Three title track written by Shel Silverstein. But Lynn has always been a spitfire where gender relations are concerned, and she balances the sugar with characteristically sassy songs like "There's a Built-In Trouble Maker in Every Man" and "A Woman a Day" ("keeps my man away"). Her personality is conveyed through her interpretive ability rather than her songwriting since she shares a composer credit on only one song. A by-the-numbers rendition of "Delta Dawn" is neither a benefit nor a detraction, but the touching "Where Do Babies Go" could have been a single considering all of Lynn's well-received songs about family and reproduction. *—Greg Adams*

Entertainer of the Year / 1973 / MCA ✦✦✦

Love Is the Foundation / 1973 / MCA ✦✦

The Ernest Tubb/Loretta Lynn Story / 1973 / MCA ✦✦✦✦
Perhaps the greatest of all country male/female duos created three albums worth of material for Decca. When MCA launched its series of two-fer vinyl packages in the '70s, it grabbed a bunch of the Ernest Tubb and Loretta Lynn material and threw together this package. They could have wrapped it in a paper bag; in fact, considering what they did use for artwork they would have been better off. They could have put the material in any order, they could have chosen any material, in fact they could have fit all of it onto the four sides but they chose not to. All these criticisms simply don't matter as the skill and charm of these two shine forth as if they were coming to us directly from their own Mt. Olympus, and not via the packaging and re-packaging enterprises of various record companies. This was something of a father/daughter relationship, although the singers did the love style songs, too. They try out a lot of different approaches on the nearly two-dozen tracks included. It is often a case of the singer not the song, as much of this material only comes to life because it is Tubb and Lynn. None of the songs are really bad; this was certainly the popular duo to try to get a track recorded by, so the songs chosen have to be some of the best of what might have been available at that point in time. The listener can sometimes hear the songwriter's wheels turning, trying to come with something cute and smart, but some of the material is really hilarious. A bit more of Lynn's original material would have been good. Those wishing to sample one and only one song should head straight for "Who's Gonna Take the Garbage Out?" The backup bands don't hurt in the least, and the listener can assume the players are a combination of Texas Troubadour members and Nashville session men, seeing as how MCA couldn't find space to inform us as to their identities somewhere on all this cardboard. *—Eugene Chadbourne*

They Don't Make 'Em Like My Daddy / 1974 / MCA ✦✦✦
A real gem! Loretta Lynn has always been one of country music's great singers, but on this album she transcends the often rigid boundaries of country music and lays down some great honky tonk, rock & roll tunes, as well as several convincing tear-swept ballads. "Trouble in Paradise," for one, is an amazingly melodic and gritty rocker that sounds like the lost song of the Stones' country catalog, a perfect counterpart to "Dead Flowers" or "Torn & Frayed," and "I've Never Been This Far Before" perfectly evokes the anxiety of first love. *—Steve Kurutz*

Greatest Hits, Vol. 2 / 1974 / MCA ✦✦✦✦✦
In the liner notes, Pete Axthelm cites "the range of her personality," and that range is in evidence here: reflective ("Coal Miner's Daughter"), feisty ("Fist City"), humorous ("One's on the Way"), and sentimental ("Love Is the Foundation"). *—Tom Roland*

Back to the Country / 1975 / MCA ✦✦✦
It is a misleading album title from an artist who never left country except to market a fried chicken recipe. For one thing, it would have to be a country project to rope in the gang of session pickers here, the best of the best; names such as Charlie McCoy, Pete Wade, Grady Martin, Johnny Gimble, and the pope of the pedal steel, Hal Rugg. A bit of a tougher edge might have helped the song selection, though. It is as if the opening track,

the notorious "The Pill," was considered so rowdy that they thought they had to tone it down after that. And though the choice of Tom T. Hall's "You Love Everybody But You" is commendable, some of the other material just seems a little light for Lynn. Production by the great Owen Bradley is creamy smooth. *—Eugene Chadbourne*

Home / 1975 / MCA ✦✦✦

Blue-Eyed Kentucky Girl / 1976 / MCA ✦✦✦✦
Blue-Eyed Kentucky Girl assembles ten tracks from Loretta Lynn's 1970s recordings for RCA, perhaps the singer's most creatively fertile period; highlights include "Rated 'X'," "When the Tingle Becomes a Chill" and the perennial "Coal Miner's Daughter." *—Hank Small*

When the Tingle Becomes a Chill / 1976 / MCA ✦
It is gratifying that, at the height of Loretta Lynn's popularity, record buyers rejected the confusing and ridiculous "Red, White and Blue," a self-penned "Kaw-Liga" rip-off about Native American pride (or something). The song barely made the Top 20 at a time when Lynn was one of the hottest stars around. "Red, White and Blue" was probably intended to cash in on the American bicentennial, and the accompanying album, *When the Tingle Becomes a Chill*, bore an advertisement for Lynn's autobiography, published the same year. The whole enterprise could be written off as crass money-making if not for the gorgeous title track, a big hit and by far the best cut on a very poor album. Does anyone really want to hear Loretta Lynn sing "Rhinestone Cowboy?" Embarrassing. *—Greg Adams*

Somebody Somewhere / 1976 / MCA ✦✦

I Remember Patsy / 1977 / MCA ✦✦✦

Out of My Head and Back in My Bed / 1978 / MCA ✦✦✦

Greatest Hits Live / 1978 / K-Tel ✦✦
Lynn shines throughout this live performance from 1978, which features some of her best-known material; the supporting musicians could have been a little better, but they don't hurt the disc in the slightest. *—Stephen Thomas Erlewine*

We've Come a Long Way, Baby / 1979 / MCA ✦✦

Lookin' Good / 1980 / MCA ✦✦✦

Loretta / 1980 / MCA ✦✦✦

I Lie / 1981 / MCA ✦✦

Making Love From Memory / 1982 / Universal Special Products ✦✦✦

Lyin' Cheatin' Woman Chasin' Honky Tonkin' Whiskey Drinkin' / 1983 / MCA ✦✦✦

Just a Woman / 1985 / MCA ✦✦✦

The Very Best of Loretta and Conway / 1988 / MCA ✦✦✦
The Very Best of Loretta Lynn and Conway Twitty contains the duo's 14 biggest hits, including the number-one singles "After the Fire Is Gone," "Lead Me On," "Louisiana Woman, Mississippi Man," "As Soon As I Hang Up the Phone," "Feelins'," and "The Letter" among several other hits. The record is definitive proof that Loretta and Conway were one of the greatest—if not *the* greatest vocal duos in country music history. *—Stephen Thomas Erlewine*

20 Greatest Hits / 1988 / MCA ✦✦✦✦✦

Who Was That Stranger / 1989 / MCA ✦✦✦
Who Was That Stranger is a mildly successful attempt at updating Lynn's sound to fit with the hard-country sound in vogue at the tail end of the 1980s. *—Jason Ankeny*

Peace in the Valley / 1990 / MCA ✦✦

★ **Country Music Hall of Fame Series** / 1991 / MCA ✦✦✦✦✦
Usually including a sage cross-section of the artist's work, the *Country Music Hall of Fame Series* from MCA provides some of the best introductory discs for the country music neophyte. This time, one of country's undisputed queens is given the royal treatment. In fact, it's Loretta Lynn's prime stretch (early '60s to the mid-'70s) that's excavated here. The 16 tracks take in both the hits ("Coal Miner's Daughter," "The Pill," "Success") and the relatively obscure gems ("Wings Upon Your Horns," "Out of My Head and Back in My Bed"), with plenty of Lynn's powerful Kentucky siren songs to enjoy. Yes, that's right, "You're Lookin' at Country." *—Stephen Cook*

☆ **Honky Tonk Girl: Collection** / 1994 / MCA ✦✦✦✦✦
Loretta Lynn's three-disc box set *Honky Tonk Girl* has the requisite rarities, but the real strength of the collection is how it offers all of her essential tracks—from 1960's "I'm a Honky Tonk Girl" to 1988's "Who Was That Stranger"—in one place. Not only are her classic hits like "Fist City" and "Coal Miner's Daughter" are included, but so are most of her hit duets with Conway Twitty, such as "After the Fire Is Gone" and "As Soon As I Hang Up the Phone." A few hits are missing—notably "Louisiana Woman, Mississippi Man"—but *Honky Tonk Girl* remains the one comprehensive and essential Loretta Lynn collection. *—Stephen Thomas Erlewine*

20th Century Masters—The Millennium Collection: The Best of Loretta Lynn / Aug. 10, 1999 / MCA ✦✦✦
Like any record company worth their salt, MCA knows a good gimmick when they see it, and when the millennium came around, the *20th Century Masters—The Millennium Collection* wasn't too far behind. Supposedly, the millennium is a momentous occasion, but it's hard to feel that way when it's used as another excuse to turn out a budget-line series. But apart from the presumptuous title, *20th Century Masters—The Millennium Collection* turns out to be a very good budget-line series. True, it's impossible for any of these ten-track collections to be definitive, but they're nevertheless solid samplers that don't feature a bad song in the bunch. For example, take Loretta Lynn's *20th Century* volume. Yes, there are some great songs missing, but what's here is terrific, including "Coal Miner's Daughter," "You Ain't Woman Enough," "Lead Me On," "Don't Come Home a Drinkin' (With Lovin' on Your Mind)," "Louisiana Woman, Mississippi Man," and "Blue Kentucky Girl." Serious fans will want something more extensive and neophytes would be best-served by better-chosen collections, but this disc is quite entertaining, considering its length and price. That doesn't erase the ridiculousness of the series title, but the silliness is excusable when the music and the collections are good. *—Stephen Thomas Erlewine*

20th Century Masters—The Millennium Collection: The Best of Loretta Lynn, Vol. 2 / Aug. 7, 2001 / MCA ✦✦✦
This 12-track addition to the *20th Century Masters* series contains a few of Loretta Lynn's iconic hits—"Fist City," "As Soon As I Hang Up the Phone," and "The Pill." The rest, however, concentrates on hits that were big at the time, but remain on the second tier of her catalog. That's not to say they're bad, because they're not—they're really good, actually—but they're not necessarily the tunes that casual listeners are looking for. However, if you see several of your favorite songs here, or if you followed the charts at the time these dominated the rungs, this certainly will be a good listen. *—Stephen Thomas Erlewine*

★ **All Time Greatest Hits** / May 23, 2002 / MCA ✦✦✦✦✦
This straightforward hits collection contains all 16 of Loretta Lynn's number-one country hits according to *Billboard*, five of them duets with Conway Twitty, plus three number two hits and three number-three hits, all released originally between 1964 and 1979. The singer also scored one other number-two hit, the Twitty duet "I Still Believe in Waltzes" from 1981, and several other number three hits, as well as numerous other major songs that are not included. Some of them could have fit on a CD that runs less than 57 1/2, but from a record company point of view the issue is less the time than the number of tracks, since song publishers must be paid royalties on each title. That makes 22 tracks (none of which run longer than three minutes and 15 seconds) a packed disc from a profit perspective, even if consumers wonder why the album isn't more complete. As it is, there are enough of Lynn's big records to justify the title and make this a good purchase for anyone seeking a single-disc hits collection. *—William Ruhlmann*

Shelby Lynne (Shelby Lynne Moorer)

b. Oct. 22, 1968, Quantico, VA
Vocals, Fiddle / Contemporary Country, Adult Alternative Pop/Rock, Americana, Singer/Songwriter, Alternative Country-Rock

By the time Shelby Lynne won her Best New Artist Grammy, she'd already completed six albums, and had over a decade of recording experience under her belt. Yet in a way, the award was appropriate, since *I Am Shelby Lynne* was the album that finally found her taking control of her music, following years of casting about in search of an identity. Lynne's work ranged through country, blues, Southern soul, roots rock, Western swing, jazz, and adult contemporary pop; naturally, that eclecticism made her difficult to market, and it also resulted in pressure to record more commercial, radio-friendly material that didn't really suit her. Once Lynne put all the pieces together, she found herself embraced not by the country mainstream, but by rock critics, British audiences, and the alt-country/Americana crowd.

Lynne was born Shelby Lynne Moorer in Quantico, VA, in 1968, and grew up mostly in Jackson, AL. Her father was a local bandleader and her mother a harmony-singing teacher, and as children, she and her younger sister Allison—later a country recording artist in her own right—sometimes joined their parents on-stage to sing along. However, Lynne's father was a violent alcoholic who at one point had her thrown in jail; when Lynne was 17, he shot his wife dead in the family's driveway, then turned the gun on himself while his daughters looked on. Lynne took charge of raising her sister, and married her high-school sweetheart (albeit briefly) prior to their move to Nashville. There, Lynne recorded some demo songs, which landed her an appearance on TNN's *Nashville Now* series. That in turn led to a duet with George Jones, 1988's Top 50 hit "If I Could Bottle This Up," and a record deal with Epic, where Lynne teamed with legendary producer Billy Sherrill for her 1989 debut album *Sunrise*. The follow-up, 1990's *Tough All Over*, took more of a Reba McEntire-esque direction, and 1991's *Soft Talk* found Lynne moving into slick country-pop.

Lynne placed several songs on the country charts during this period, but none managed to break into the Top 20. Critics generally regarded her as a promising talent, and she even won the CMA's Horizon Award (given to the year's top emerging artist) in 1991. However, she was tiring of the lack of control she was afforded over her image and musical direction. She split from Epic and signed with the smaller Morgan Creek label, debuting with 1993's *Temptation*, an exercise in Bob Wills-style Western swing and big band jazz. Unfortunately, the label folded not long after, and she moved on to Magnatone for 1995's *Restless*, which marked a return to contemporary-style country. Afterward, Lynne disappeared from recording for several years. During that time, she moved to Palm Springs, CA, and convinced producer Bill Bottrell—best known for his early work with Sheryl Crow—to work on her next album.

Lynne signed with Island Records and finally returned in 2000 with *I Am Shelby Lynne*. Effectively a roots rock album with Sheryl Crow overtones and strong hints of Lynne's eclecticism, the record was greeted enthusiastically in the U.K., and was released in the U.S. several months later. Positive word of mouth led to effusive critical praise, with many hailing *I Am Shelby Lynne* as a major statement of purpose as confident as its title's declaration. It won her a Grammy for Best New Artist in early 2001, and she began working on a follow-up with producer Glen Ballard, best known for his work with Alanis Morissette. *Love, Shelby* appeared later in 2001, but was received with confusion and disappointment by many reviewers, mainly because of its smoother, less country-infused production. *—Steve Huey*

Sunrise / 1989 / Epic ✦✦✦
Lynne's debut album, released when she was barely out of her teens, contains a duet with George Jones called "If I Could Bottle This Up." *—Brian Mansfield*

Tough All Over / Aug. 1990 / Epic ✦✦✦✦
Before Shelby Lynne reinvented herself at the end of the 1990s and began recording for Mercury, she made a number of fine recordings that were unfortunately lost in the heap

of "new traditionalist" and female superstar recordings that were popping out of Nash Vegas like zits. This 1990 effort, produced by the great Bob Montgomery, is a case in point. Not only does this hold up to her best work, it's at the very least on a par with Kathy Mattea, Trisha Yearwood, Martina McBride, etc. It just isn't a strictly country outing, but it's a truly fine pop-country record. Interestingly, it also has the range of her later records. While there are songs here from the then-current crop of Nash Vegas song churners, like the opener, "I'll Lie Myself to Sleep," there are also cuts like the gorgeous gentle Western swing of "Don't Mind if I Do," by the legendary Skip Ewing. The tune borrows as much from Billie Holiday's "Ain't Nobody's Business" as it does from early Bonnie Raitt and Maria Muldaur. And then there's a burning, hard-rocking cover of Charlie Rich's early hit "Lonely Weekends." It's more Dixie-fried than Rich's version, but it comes across as a thoroughly contemporary country-rock song with ringing guitars à la the Doobie Brothers' *Toulouse Street*, an Elvis-styled delivery, and a piano shuffle in the background that keeps the lyric from sinking under the weight of a cooking band. Wayne Carson's "Dog Day Afternoon" sounds like a latter-day Rich number, or one Tom Waits wrote for Crystal Gayle for the *One From the Heart* soundtrack; it's all jazzy, warm, and sensual. If there were any doubts about Lynne's country pedigree, it vanishes when her radical working of "I Walk the Line" comes through the speakers. Bluesy, shuffling, and the slightest bit funky, her sense of Cash's melody remains untouched. The set ends with another Western swing-influenced nugget, but this one comes from Duke Ellington, "Don't Get Around Much Anymore," before it breaks out into a full-blown Patsy Cline country-jazz tune. She saved the best moment for last here, and it is so original in its swinging elegance that listeners can only wonder if she might have taken the Diana Krall route, in that she not only has the pipes and the chops, but the feel for this material. *Tough All Over* is wonderful from start to finish. —*Thom Jurek*

Soft Talk / 1991 / Epic ♦♦♦

Temptation / Jul. 6, 1993 / Morgan Creek/Mercury ♦♦♦

An album of big-band country swing, it was produced by Brent Maher (the Judds). "Feelin' Kind of Lonely Tonight" had limited success as a single. —*Brian Mansfield*

Restless / Jul. 18, 1995 / Magnatone ♦♦♦

Country singer Shelby Lynne has a powerful and versatile voice that can deliver a touching ballad as well as a fast-paced swing number, all without uttering one single off-key note. On this 1995 album, *Restless*, her undeniable vocal talent shines through best on demanding tunes like "Slow Me Down." Brent Maher, who worked with the Judds until they split, served as Lynne's producer on this recording as well as on the album before this, *Temptation*. Though Lynne's music style ranges from Texas swing to pop/rock, she goes standard contemporary country on *Restless*—almost as to give country one last try after not reaching the success she had hoped for, and deserved, in the genre. Some of the songs on this album that fans shouldn't miss include "Talkin' to Myself Again," "Another Chance at Love," "Wish I Knew," and "I'm Not the One." This recording is a keeper for country lovers, since it might be the last real country album this singer offers the music world for a longtime, seeing as how she has turned her attention toward rock. —*Charlotte Dillon*

Epic Recordings / 2000 / Lucky Dog ♦♦♦

Shelby Lynne's early career on Epic Records frustrated fans of her rich, soulful contralto because, though she placed three albums and nine singles in the country charts between 1988 and 1991, she never scored the big hit needed to propel her to star status. Not all collections are hit oriented, of course, but *Epic Recordings* makes a particular point of second-guessing Epic's singles choices. Of the 16 tracks drawn from the 30 recordings released on her three Epic albums, *Sunrise*, *Tough All Over*, and *Soft Talk*, only one, "I'll Lie Myself to Sleep," was released as a single. That leaves the compilers plenty of room to emphasize

Lynne's diversity, from her Western swing renditions of Duke Ellington's "Don't Get Around Much Anymore" and the Louis Armstrong hit "I'm Confessin'" to a stirring country-rock version of Charlie Rich's "Lonely Weekends" and a fierce performance of Johnny Cash's "I Walk the Line." There are also plenty of lesser album tracks, but it remains odd that the opportunity of an anthology did not inspire Lucky Dog to put Lynne's non-LP chart singles "Under Your Spell Again" and "Don't Cross Your Heart" on disc or to select some of her better-known material. You can't help wondering whether parent label Sony denied Lucky Dog the right to use those songs, preferring to hold them for a Lynne release in its popular *Super Hits* or *16 Biggest Hits* series. It's significant that this album is not billed as a "best-of"; what it really constitutes is "the rest of Shelby Lynne." —*William Ruhlmann*

● I Am Shelby Lynne / Jan. 25, 2000 / Mercury ♦♦♦♦♦

After years of kicking around Nashville to great acclaim but nonexistent sales, Shelby Lynne got fed up with the system and reinvented herself on *I Am Shelby Lynne* as a tough and sexy singer, equal parts Bonnie Raitt and Sheryl Crow. Though this album is undeniably classicist in approach, borrowing from classic R&B, country, soul, and rock & roll, it's cleverly constructed, as producer Bill Bottrell gives it a wonderful, warm production graced by slight contemporary flourishes (such as the rolling rhythms behind "Thought It Would Be Easier") that keep it fresh, not entrenched in history (even though its succinct ten tracks and half-hour running time are welcome holdovers from classic rock). Ultimately, of course, the triumph of the record belongs to Lynne, who finally sounds comfortable in her writing and voice. This music is so warm and welcoming, it's easy to overlook the darker themes running through the songs, particularly because Lynne's greatest strength is that she never oversings, shading her phrasing and drawing listeners in with her easy confidence and sexy rasp. This isn't an album that flaunts its strengths—it's expertly constructed, subtle music that grows in stature with each spin, revealing Lynne as a trad rocker of uncommon skill and charm. It may have taken her years to finally find her groove, but *I Am Shelby Lynne* is so good, the wait seems worthwhile. —*Stephen Thomas Erlewine*

Love, Shelby / Nov. 13, 2001 / Universal ♦♦♦

Following her somewhat belated Best New Artist Grammy award (six albums and 13 years into her musical career), Shelby Lynne's follow-up to the truly heartbreaking and spectacular *I Am Shelby Lynne* finds her reaching out to a more rock-oriented audience with mixed results. After some last minute retooling from the record label, *Love, Shelby* proves Lynne can still write a hook, but much of what makes or breaks the finished results ultimately falls in the hands of her producer. While the critically acclaimed mix of Memphis soul and whispered almost-country on *I am Shelby Lynne* reverberated with an honest longing, thanks in large part to producer Bill Bottrell (Sheryl Crow, Lisa Germano), the follow-up seems slickly over-produced at times and occasionally forced, with some of the blame certainly falling on new producer Glen Ballard (Alanis Morissette, Dave Matthews). While Ballard's clean rock production really worked for Alanis (and almost no one else, truth be told), an artist like Shelby Lynne who oozes a raw sexuality and an almost primal passion for her song subjects, could have benefited from a less contemporary feel in the studio, as was evidenced by Bottrell's earlier collaboration with the artist. That being said, *Love, Shelby* hits its stride about mid-album, starting with the dynamic "I Can't Wait," continuing through "Tarpoleon Napoleon" and the single "Killin' Kind," which all stand side by side with some of her best songs. In all honesty, this would actually be a more successful album if her previous work hadn't been so strong. It seems as though the singer had such artistic success with her "rock-tinged'" record that she thought it would be a good idea to push the envelope further into an almost strictly rock environment. Unfortunately, by stripping almost all of the country elements out of the songs, she stripped out a good deal of the fire along with it. The few songs that embrace her rough, soulful edge are pretty terrific, and (hopefully) smarter choices in the future will bring about another strong album along the same lines as *I Am*... —*Zac Johnson*

Ronnie Mack

b. Apr. 18, 1954, Baltimore, MD

Guitar, Vocals / Rockabilly, Roots Rock, Americana

Ronnie Mack made a name for himself as a savior of sorts on the Los Angeles country and roots music circuit. A native of Baltimore, he was born on April 18, 1954. From an early age he was impressed by the guitar. Both of his grandfathers were musical and influenced him greatly. His paternal grandfather Bill Mack gave the youngster toy instruments upon which he played and began to learn chords. The radio also was an important tool in Mack's development as a musician. This is where he first heard Elvis, the Everly Brothers, Eddie Cochran, and his hero, Ricky Nelson. Almost as a preview of his future loyalty to Nelson, Mack's first performance consisted of "Hello Mary Lou" when he was in second grade. A six-chord song, the budding performer knew only three but still pulled off a somewhat exemplary performance. As a teenager he was surrounded by the psychedelic world that followed the British Invasion of the early '60s. Convinced that this was not the way to go, Mack devoted himself more and more to the ideals of "Blue Suede Shoes." But, he still needed to play and did so with some reservations. While he had to learn the latest Cream or Hendrix single, he also began to write his own rockabilly songs.

After high-school he began to think about moving west to Los Angeles. Nelson's Stone Canyon Band was doing well and the Flying Burrito Brothers, Poco, the New Riders of the Purple Sage, and Commander Cody & His Lost Planet Airmen were all twangin' away, a much closer cousin to the rockabilly he loved so much more than what was happening in Baltimore. Packing up and moving to the West Coast, Mack broke into the diverse L.A. music scene with a fury. The punk rock aspect of the scene was open to anything, even rockabilly. Putting together a band, Ronnie Mack & the Black Slacks, Mack followed the punker circuit, the same one that allowed Dwight Yoakam to play his music. He also played showcases with the Blasters and other roots rock acts and made a bid for his share of the audience with his rockabilly sound. The pay off came around 1979 when roots music took off. For the first time since the 1950s, rockabilly had garnered some respect. Signing with the roots rock label Rollin' Rock, Mack recorded a series of singles; "You Make Me Wanna Rock" and "I Wanna Dance With You" were two of the most memorable, both co-writes with partner Greg Loeb. He later went on to record a country track for volume three of the *Town South of Bakersfield* compilation and worked with Yoakam, Ray Campi, Rosie Flores, Buck Owens, James Intveld, Cliffie Stone, Marty Stuart, the Jordanaires, and D. J. Fontana, to name just a few.

In 1988 Intveld began *the Barn Dance*, a weekly showcase for big names as well as newer artists living and working around Los Angeles. But, with a career that was taking off in several directions at once, Intveld soon found he could not keep up with the demands, so he turned *the Barn Dance* over to Mack. Moving from the small Little Nashville Club to the world-renowned Club Palomino in North Hollywood, Mack's *Barn Dance* continued to promote California roots music until shortly before the Pal closed for good in 1995. Moving to a new venue at the corner of Hollywood and Vine gave new life to Mack, the show, and the entire scene. Located at Jack's Sugar Shack, every Tuesday night was a celebration as well as a meeting place for local musicians and those from out of town seeking some companionship and a cold one. Visitors like Connie Smith, Robert Reynolds, Bruce Springsteen, and Bob Woodruff were not uncommon in the audience or on the stage.

Another aspect of Mack's good standing in the community was his work with and for various charities. As the host of the annual Elvis Birthday Bash, another event that was the brainchild of Intveld, Mack worked alongside local industry insider Art Fine in order to pull off the big show that features a wide variety of acts all doing Elvis songs. Besides Mack, Yoakam, Flores, and Intveld, the Elvis tribute attracted Dave Alvin, Wanda Jackson, Johnny Rivers, Lee Rocker, Big Sandy, and roots rock royalty Barry Holdship and Florida Slim. The money raised from this event always went to a charity for the homeless. While his own success was fleeting, he never faltered from his chosen path. In 1996 the Swedish SunJay label released a 28-cut compilation built around the many singles he recorded for Rollin' Rock, Lonesome Town, and SunJay Records between June of 1981 and ending with a live recording from the Palomino in 1994, including Mack's 1986 cover of the Intveld hit "My Heart Is Achin' for You." *—Jana Pendragon*

● **Ronnie Mack Is Born to Rock** / 1996 / SunJay ✦✦✦✦✦

This is a compilation project that spans the period between 1981 through 1990, an important time for Ronnie Mack professionally. With an emphasis on rockabilly, Mack's largess to that genre has kept rockabilly alive for many fans around the world. Like many American artists who are overlooked at home, Mack is a star in Europe, where his singles are hits that still merit air play. Respected too for his devotion to country and roots music, that devotion is reflected here via Mack's covers of John Hiatt's "Doll Hospital," the Merle Travis tune "Kentucky Means Paradise" and the Bryant & Bryant penned "Brand New Heartache," a duet with Rosie Flores. As a chronicle of a vibrant career that has benefited many, this CD defines Mack's genius. *—Jana Pendragon*

Warner Mack (Warner MacPherson)

b. Apr. 2, 1938, Nashville, TN

Guitar, Vocals / Traditional Country, Nashville Sound/Countrypolitan

Warner Mack was a popular performer for Decca Records during the 1960s. He was born Warner MacPherson, the son of a Presbyterian minister, and raised in Vicksburg, MS, where he taught himself to play guitar as a youth. A talented athlete, he had offers to play both college baseball and football; he was also offered a spot on the St. Louis Cardinals, but Mack really wanted to be a musician. He got his start on the KWKH *Louisiana Hayride* and then appeared on Red Foley's *Ozark Jamboree*, gaining an even greater following. He still kept a day job at a tire company and also worked as an announcer on a Vicksburg radio station.

Mack moved to Nashville in the late '50s; in 1957, he began his profitable association with Decca, becoming "Mack" thanks to an inattentive secretary. He wrote his debut single "Is It Wrong (For Loving You)" and scored a Top Ten hit that remained on the country charts for over nine months and crossed over to become a minor pop hit. He later signed with Kapp Records and produced several albums for them. After performing on the *Grand Ole Opry*, he re-signed to Decca, where "Sittin' in an All Nite Cafe" made it to the Top Five. Unfortunately, he had a serious auto accident in 1964 and spent several months recovering. In 1965, he scored his career hit with "Bridge Washed Out," which topped the charts for months. This was followed by a series of hits that stretched until 1973; among his most popular songs were "Sittin' on a Rock (Crying in a Creek)," "Talkin' to the Wall," and "Leave My Dreams Alone." Mack left Decca in 1973. Four years later he signed to Pageboy Records and had one minor hit, "These Crazy Thoughts (Run Through My Mind)," his final chart entry.*—Sandra Brennan*

● **Golden Country Hits, Vol. 1** / 1961 / London ✦✦✦✦✦

The Country Touch / 1966 / Decca ✦✦✦

Country Touch is from Warner Mack's peak year and contains two of his biggest hits: "Sittin' on a Rock (Cryin' in a Creek)" and "Talking to the Wall." Mack's Decca hits have yet to be anthologized on CD and are scarce on compilations, so his original albums are the place to go to hear this fine country singer. The album tracks are mainly covers of recent hits like Ernest Tubb's "Thanks a Lot," Jimmy Dean's "First Thing Ev'ry Morning (And the Last Thing Ev'ry Night)," and Webb Pierce's "Alla My Love." There are a few interesting originals, too, particularly Liz Anderson's grim heartbreak ballad, "The Way It Feels to Die." Mack's music falls somewhere between the Nashville sound and traditional country, in the neighborhood of Stonewall Jackson and Webb Pierce's '60s recordings. *—Greg Adams*

The Many Country Moods of Warner Mack / 1968 / Decca ✦✦✦

Warner Mack's self-penned "I'm Gonna Move On" was the bit hit from *The Many Country Moods of Warner Mack*, an album of mostly original compositions that points up Mack's prolificacy during his peak years. The title promises a wide variety of styles or emotions, but Mack sticks with his familiar groove throughout. "I'd Give the World (To Be Back Loving You)" just missed the Top Ten, an anomaly for this part of Mack's career, when his singles usually charged into the Top Ten with ease. His revival of Bobby Edwards' "You're the Reason" coincides—perhaps coincidentally—with Johnny Tillotson's minor hit version from 1967, although Webb Pierce recorded it around this time, too. Mack's enormous success and latter-day obscurity call to mind Webb Pierce, who also enjoyed comparable popularity in the '60s but could have ceased to exist as far as the compilers of modern anthologies are concerned. The similarities between Mack's and Pierce's '60s efforts are prodigious enough to recommend each artist to fans of the other. *—Greg Adams*

20 Country Hits / 1993 / Country Routes ✦

Country Routes would have you believe that *20 Country Hits* compiles the Decca hit versions, since original chart dates and positions are given. The liner notes go so far as to state that "this…collection provides a retrospective of two decades of the best country music recordings" of Warner Mack. In reality, the package consists of re-recordings of ten of Mack's hits from the late '50s through the early '70s. Furthermore, the remaining ten songs are recordings of obscure originals and non-hits by other songwriters. In short, this package deliberately misleads consumers. Even as re-recordings go, these versions are poor, suffering from muddy sound and lackluster performances. *—Greg Adams*

Early Years: Southern Rockabilly 1957–1962 / Dec. 15, 1998 / Lost Gold ✦✦✦

Early Years: Southern Rockabilly 1957-1962 is a good budget-line sampling of Warner Mack's early, lesser-known days, including more than ten previously unreleased demos and singles he recorded for Decca and Scarlet. This release also offers the first CD appearance of "Roc-a-Chica," Mack's Top 100 hit in 1958 that was abruptly banned after a DJ thought he heard "the F-word" in the background. "Roc-a-Chica," Mack's take on "Someone Somewhere," and "Now I'm Living" are some of the best of the catchier, upbeat tunes heard here, while "Tell Me Darlin'" stands out among the ballads. *—Joslyn Layne*

Kate MacKenzie

Vocals / Progressive Bluegrass, Contemporary Folk

Kate MacKenzie is probably best known for her regular performances on Garrison Keillor's *Prairie Home Companion* radio broadcasts as a member of the Hopeful Gospel Quartet, which also features Keillor and Robin & Linda Williams. MacKenzie's duties on the program have required her to sing in numerous genres of music, and her listening tastes range from the Elvis Presley and Patsy Cline records she grew up with to Motown, Irish folk, classical, pop, bluegrass, blues, and country. The latter three styles are most prevalent on her solo debut album, *Let Them Talk*, which was released in 1994. She became interested in folk and bluegrass music while at the University of Minnesota and taught herself to play the guitar, but it took awhile to overcome her shyness about singing—until she was 28, in fact. Her first singing gig was with the bluegrass band Stoney Lonesome, and from there, MacKenzie went on to *A Prairie Home Companion* and finally recorded her first album, *Age of Innocence*, 15 years later. *—Steve Huey*

Age of Innocence / Oct. 15, 1996 / Red House ✦✦✦✦

Kate MacKenzie's solo debut album *Age of Innocence* is a shining demonstration of her talents. MacKenzie is able to push bluegrass music into new directions without diluting its purity. The key to the success of *Age of Innocence* is how MacKenzie delivers folk and country as gracefully as bluegrass. There's depth and beauty to this music but most of all there's a gentle, subtle charm which makes it a rewarding musical experience. *—Stephen Thomas Erlewine*

Uncle Dave Macon (David Harrison Macon)

b. Oct. 7, 1870, Smart Station, TN, **d.** Mar. 22, 1952, Readyville, TN

Banjo, Vocals / Old-Timey, Traditional Country, Field Recordings

Uncle Dave Macon, beginning his professional musical career after the age of 50, brought musical and performance traditions of the 19th century South to the radio shows and the recording catalogs of the early country music industry. In 1925, he became one of two charter members of the *Grand Ole Opry*, then called the *WSM Barn Dance*. A consummate showman on the banjo and a one-man repository of countless old songs and comic routines, Macon remained a well-loved icon of country music until and beyond his death in 1952.

Born David Harrison Macon in Smart Station in middle Tennessee's Warren County, he was the son of a Confederate officer who owned a large farm. Macon heard the folk music of the area when he was young, but he was also a product of the urban South: after the family moved to Nashville and began operating a hotel, Macon hobnobbed with traveling vaudeville musicians who performed there. After his father was stabbed near the hotel, Macon left Nashville with the rest of his family. He worked on a farm and later operated a wagon freight line, performing music only at local parties and dances.

Macon's turn toward a musical second career was due partly to the advent of motorized trucks, for his wagon line fell on hard times in the early '20s after a competitor invested in the horseless novelties. In 1923, he struck up a few tunes in a Nashville barbershop with fiddler Sid Harkreader, and an agent from the Loew's theater chain happened to stop in. Soon Macon and Harkreader were touring as far afield as New England, and when George D. Hay began bringing together performers two years later for what would become the *Opry*, Macon was a natural choice. The tour also brought Macon the first of his many recording dates, held in New York for the Vocalion label in 1924. Macon would record prolifically through the 1930s (and occasionally up to 1950) for various labels, accompanied at different times by Harkreader, the brother duo of Sam & Kirk McGee, the Delmore Brothers, the young Roy Acuff, and other string players including a then-unknown Bill Monroe. For secular material, his backing band took the name of the Fruit Jar Drinkers.

Macon's recordings are richly enjoyable in themselves and are priceless historical documents, both for the large variety of banjo styles they preserve and for the window they afford on American song of the late 19th century. Macon performed musical-comic routines such as the "Uncle Dave's Travels" series, topical songs, often of his own composition ("Governor Al Smith"), playful folk songs ("I'll Tickle Nancy"), gospel with his Dixie Sacred Singers, blackface minstrel songs, unique proto-blues pieces that Macon learned from African-American freight workers ("Keep My Skillet Good and Greasy"), and songs of other types. Yet "the Dixie Dewdrop" was loved most of all for his presence as a live musician, captured not only on the weekly *Opry* broadcasts (which were broadcast nationally for a time in the 1930s) but also in the 1940 film *Grand Ole Opry*. Macon delivered what an 1880s southern vaudeville audience would have demanded for its hard-earned dollar: showmanship (he handled the banjo with Harlem Globetrotters-like trick dexterity), humor, political commentary (often of the incorrect variety by modern standards), and unflagging energy.

Macon continued to appear on the *Opry* almost until his death, gradually taking on the status of a great-hearted living link to country music's origins. He became the tenth member of the Country Music Hall of Fame in 1966, and the revival of old time music that flourished as part of the folk movement focused the attention of younger listeners on his music. Yet Macon remains less well understood, and less present in the musical minds of country listeners, than Jimmie Rodgers or the Carter Family, even though he was nearly as well-known in his own day. Perhaps that's because he represents an older layer of American music-making than almost any other performer known to country audiences: modern hearers can easily connect with Rodgers' blues or the Carters' homespun sentiment, but Macon may require greater effort. Such effort, in any case, is well repaid by an acquaintance with his musical legacy. *—James Manheim*

Early Recordings / 1971 / County ✦✦✦✦✦

Yes, this is the real deal, a dozen monumental tracks lifted off the original 78 slabs that comprised the early-recording career of this eccentric and almost endlessly amusing old-time country star. Practically every track is some kind of classic, all of them driven by a banjo sound that has enough energy to plow the back 40 and whip up biscuits when that's done. Sound, of course, is not high-tech, but if the listener can ignore original scratches, which were, of course, placed there on the 78s with love by the original owner, the primitive recording quality doesn't even come close to obscuring all the wonderful things about the music. Banjo playing is, of course, overwhelming, but not enough can be said about his entertaining vocal style. On one great track entitled "Worthy of Estimation" he sounds something like an auctioneer who's been given a snootfull of laughing gas. Half the tracks feature backup from the immortal Fruit Jar Drinkers, whose hotshot picker Sam McGee also joins Uncle Dave for a couple of terrific duets. The Delmore Brothers also have a cameo, showing up for a final gospel number. *—Eugene Chadbourne*

Go Long Mule / 1972 / County ✦✦✦

A wild romp through 18 tracks recorded during Uncle Dave Macon's heyday period of 1926 through 1934, *Go Long Mule* is uniformly strong if not exceptionally complete. These are some of the most vibrant examples of old-timey music likely to be found, with Macon charging through shouters like "I'm Goin' Away in the Morn" and "Sail Away Ladies," even literally stomping out the rhythms of "Way Down the Old Plank Road." Joined by the Fruit Jar Drinkers, the call and response of "Hold the Woodpile Down" and "Carve That Possum" are prime examples of the very best of early string band music. With pleas to abandon automobiles in favor of the horse and buggy, Macon's songs frequently make deceptively poignant statements about Depression-era America. He even slows the pace down for a few well-chosen ballads, occasionally displaying intricate banjo work for which he rarely gets sufficient credit. Overall, there may be better Macon sets on the market, but *Go Long Mule* is, nonetheless, a wildly enjoyable ride. *—Matt Fink*

The Gayest Old Dude in Town / 1973 / Folk Variety ✦✦✦✦

This is a very nice German repackaging of material by old-time music hero Uncle Dave Macon, including a booklet with complete lyrics. The album combines the earliest recordings of Uncle Dave with what are represented to be his last sessions, although there are other releases of his material purporting to be from even 12 years later. Information is hazy in the booklet, and the listener will have to bring in an old-time music detective in order to identify which tracks feature the notorious Fruit Jar Drinkers and so forth. It is instructive, however, to be reminded that Uncle Dave did not begin performing professionally until the age of 48, after already achieving success in two careers, farmer and "haulage contractor." There are a lot of genres and approaches to old-time music, from ultra-serious to ultra-corny, with a separate section for ridiculous loudmouths armed with banjos, of which Uncle Dave has got to be the looniest. But he can also dim the lights and sit back and deliver a straight country tune, or a banjo instrumental that sounds like three other players, on the wrong speed to boot. A highlight of this program is the extended "Uncle Dave's Travels," featuring his bizarre spoken comments as well as singing and picking. *—Eugene Chadbourne*

At Home / 1976 / Bear Family ✦✦✦

Featuring "Banjo Solo," "Rabbit in the Pea Patch," "Mountain Dew," and others, these were his last recordings, made in 1950. *—AMG*

Laugh Your Blues Away / 1979 / Rounder ✦✦✦

When this album was released, none of the material on it had ever been distributed outside the hands of various collectors, some of whom had made the recording themselves off radio broadcasts. Although the wonderful Uncle Dave Macon recorded prolifically at least in the early stages of his career, and much of his catalog has continued to remain in print, the tracks contained herein hardly represent needless repetition, as the performer seems looser than usual in settings outside the recording studio. Sometimes the looseness results in off-the-cuff commercial announcements for his radio sponsors, such as the patter he goes into at the end of "Eleven Cent Cotton" and "Chewing Gum." But even more enjoyable is just how boisterous this already wild performer gets in these settings. Recording quality varies, as the tracks were done over several decades and on all manner of tape recorders. Uncle Dave's powerful banjo has managed to sound more than just acceptable on various vintage recordings done in antiquated studio conditions, but on some of these home recordings the distortion makes it difficult to even tell what instrument is being played. *—Eugene Chadbourne*

Keep My Skillet Good & Greasy / 1979 / Old Homestead ✦✦✦✦

Country Music Hall of Fame Series / 1992 / MCA ✦✦✦✦✦

"Shout if you are happy!" Uncle Dave Macon exclaims during "Tom and Jerry" as Mazy Todd saws away at her fiddle. "Kill yo'self!" That's the kind of enthusiasm Macon brings to these 16 fine examples of string band music, recorded between 1926 and 1934 for the Vocalion, Brunswick, and Champion labels. Macon, who was 55 at the first of these recording sessions, frequently starts the songs with a spoken anecdote (including a plug for his Macon Midway Mule and Wagon Transportation Company). This collection is essentially an expanded version of *Uncle Dave Macon: First Featured Star of the Grand Ole Opry*, a retrospective issued in 1966 after his posthumous election to the Country Music Hall of Fame. *—Brian Mansfield*

★ **Travelin' Down the Road** / 1995 / County/BMG ✦✦✦✦✦

This CD is a reissue containing many of Uncle Dave Macon's best sides. All these tunes were transfers from original 78s recorded in 1935. The sound is still quite clear and enjoyable. There is a good selection of religious and secular tunes, all performed with vitality. You can really hear what draws people to old-timey music after listening to these records. *—Richard Meyer*

The Maddox Brothers & Rose

f. 1933, **db.** 1956

Group / Traditional Country, Bakersfield Sound

The Maddox Brothers (Cliff, Cal, Fred, Don, and "friendly Henry, the working girl's friend") and their sister Rose called themselves "America's Most Colorful Hillbilly Band."

They weren't kidding. It wasn't just a matter of hillbilly couture—though with their matching Turk suits and spangles the family had style in spades. But colorful described their sound, as well. On the air in Modesto, CA, by 1937, the group made their first records, for the 4-Star label, in 1946. From 1951 till 1956, they recorded for Columbia. At that point, the family act broke up, though Rose maintained a successful solo career for many years after. But throughout the 1940s and '50s, the Maddox Brothers & Sister Rose tore down the honky tonks from the Pacific Northwest to the Gulf Coast with slap-bass boogie and an iconoclastic attitude towards the stiffer mores of conventional country. In other words, they rocked the house.

It all started in 1933, when the Maddox family—Charlie and Lula, and five of their seven children—hitchhiked and rode the rails from Boaz, AL, to California, where they worked in the migrant labor camps of the San Joaquin Valley. Fred quickly tired of picking fruit and wrangled a radio spot on KTRB Modesto for his intensely musical family (which featured 11-year-old Rose on decidedly raw lead vocals). In addition to playing on KTRB, the group performed at local barns and festivals, and in 1939, they were named the best band at the California State Fair. Early the following year, they began playing at KFBK in Sacramento, and their show was syndicated throughout the West Coast.

Though the future was bright for the Maddox Brothers & Rose, their career was interrupted by the advent of World War II in the early '40s. Fred, Cal, and Don were all drafted into the military (Cliff was too ill and Henry was too young to serve), leaving the remaining members to play with different bands during the course of the war. Rose sang with Arky Stark and Dave Stogner; she also was turned away from the Texas Playboys. Meanwhile, Cliff headed his own band, the Rhythm Ramblers. Following the war, the Maddox Brothers & Rose re-formed, settling at KGDM in Stockton, CA. Over the next decade, their fan base steadily grew, as their blend of music and comedy played well not only in concert, but on the radio as well. During the '40s and early '50s, they cut a number of records for 4-Star.

In 1951, the Maddoxes switched labels and signed with Columbia Records. Over the next six years, they recorded over 40 singles for the label. During the '50s, the group appeared on both the *Louisiana Hayride* and the *Grand Ole Opry*, often performing with an augmented lineup that featured steel guitarist Bud Duncan and either Roy Nichols, Jimmy Winkle, or Gene Breeden on lead guitar. At the end of their stint with Columbia, Rose began to pursue a solo career, leading toward the band's breakup in the summer of 1956. Rose began a solo career with the assistance of Cal, while the remaining members operated as a new band. Despite the breakup, the Maddox Brothers & Rose recorded a final session for Columbia in the summer of 1957.

Following the disbandment of the Maddox Brothers, Rose had a successful solo career on Capitol Records, while the band comprised of the remaining members quickly fell apart. Fred opened a nightclub, the Fred Maddox Playhouse, which was quite successful during the late '50s and early '60s. Henry went on to accompany Rose on her recordings for Capitol. Over the course of the '70s and '80s, all of the members of the Maddox Brothers—quietly retired from music. *—Dan Cooper*

A Collection of Standard Sacred Songs / 1956 / King ✦✦✦✦

In between their raucous and ribald proto-rockabilly recordings, the Maddox Bros. & Rose made a number of religious recordings, some of which were quite popular with their listeners. Twelve of their sacred recordings for the 4-Star label from the late '40s and early '50s are collected here, including a studio version of "Flowers for the Master's Bouquet," one of two songs they performed on their sole *Grand Ole Opry* appearance. These tracks emphasize the family's group harmonies, and demonstrate the serious side of an ensemble better known for its wild humor. *—Greg Adams*

★ **The America's Most Colorful Hillbilly Band: Their Original Recordings 1946–1951, Vol. 1** / 1961 / Arhoolie ✦✦✦✦✦

The Maddox Brothers & Rose first started recording in 1946 for the tiny 4-Star label, and it was there that they cut their most uninhibited sides, in the years immediately after World War II, freely mixing comedy, raw hillbilly sounds (including elements of what would later evolve into rockabilly), and mainstream country. The sides here move freely from hillbilly to blues to honky tonk to what we would later call rock & roll. Their version of "Move It on Over" is one of the hottest tracks of its era—and all the most amazing since the lead singer is Rose Maddox, and white women performers in those years seldom got to express themselves with the lack of inhibition displayed here. They romp and stomp their way through 27 songs that were so wild and raw, that by the early '50s they made many country music producers cringe at their lack of couth. The CD is worth it just for Rose Maddox's performance on "Milk Cow Blues," a dissolute, cackling, ultimately compelling piece of work that stands next to any other rendition of the song that one cares to name. The group also has savage fun at the expense of sentimental numbers like the ballad "Brown Eyes," and it's hard to listen to too much of this collection without breaking into laughter. The sound is generally excellent and the notes are thorough, although one wishes that there were more information to be found on the history of these actual recordings, which is barely touched upon. *—Bruce Eder*

Go Honky Tonkin' / 1965 / Hilltop ✦✦✦

☆ **1946–1951, Vol. 1** / 1976 / Arhoolie ✦✦✦✦✦

Better than Hank Williams Sr.? Some country fans might light a bonfire in order to burn at the stake anyone voicing such an opinion about a country recording. But many listeners may agree that as great as Hank Sr. was, the versions of his songs done by this wild family band are so energetic and over-the-top that they practically defy description. Every female country singer including the great Patsy Cline picked up on the Rose Maddox growl which makes the words "honky tonk" sound like so much more than slang for a lively roadside bar. Above and beyond Rose's efforts there is the busy instrumental backup including terrific playing from steel guitar innovator Bud Duncan. Sound effects and crazy licks fly through the air thicker than the sounds at a Western swing convention. This is part of a series documenting the group's efforts, and if they are all as fine as this then the whole collection is worth having for sure. Highlights here, besides the Hank covers, include a medium-tempo take on "Blue Eyes Crying in the Rain," previously unreleased; Woody Guthrie's hysterical "Philadelphia Lawyer," complete with gun shots; and the equally manic "Careless Driver." *—Eugene Chadbourne*

Maddox Brothers & Rose On the Air, Vol. 1 / 1983 / Arhoolie ✦✦✦

Rockin' & Rollin' / 1983 / Bear Family ✦✦✦✦✦

The Maddox Brothers & Rose / 1986 / Forum Circle ✦✦✦

The America's Most Colorful Hillbilly Band: Their Original Recordings 1946–1951, Vol. 2 / 1995 / Arhoolie ✦✦✦✦✦

Like *Maddox Brothers & Rose, 1946-1951, Vol. 1*, this has a wealth of material—30 cuts in all—from their early 4-Star era. The quality is on the same level as the first volume, and it's difficult to imagine that anyone who enjoyed the previous installment will be dissatisfied with this collection. The recording quality has the odd effect of making the records seem older than they actually are, but the music is actually as adventurous as any in country in the time, particularly on the fast boogies. Even collectors who kept up with Arhoolie's various vinyl reissues of pre-Columbia Maddox material may want this CD anthology too, as it has eight previously unissued acetates from the same era. *—Richie Unterberger*

On the Air: The 1940's / 1996 / Arhoolie ✦✦✦

These 1940s radio broadcasts have been issued on previous Arhoolie vinyl albums and cassettes, and without those original releases handy as reference, it's difficult to say whether this 32-track compilation gathers every bit of material from these sources that has seen the light of day. Should you still be building your Maddox Brothers collection, however, it's certainly good value, with tracks from 1940, 1945, and 1949, as well as some from a similar vintage whose exact year of broadcast is not known. What matters most is the content, which is good, and sometimes actually of better fidelity than their 4-Star recordings from the same era; Cal Maddox's harmonica in particular seems more prominent here than in their other early work. *—Richie Unterberger*

The Maddox Brothers and Rose / Sep. 23, 1997 / King ✦✦✦

Chronologically positioned between their early acoustic sides and radio broadcasts that grace the various Arhoolie CDs and the later and arguably more polished performances for Columbia in the 1950s, these 12 sides cut for 4-Star and later acquired by King catch the group honing their style to a fine edge. Rose's voice is in full bloom (as indicated by the opener, "Philadelphia Lawyer," and "No One Is Sweeter Than You") and the group's rough and rowdy approach to putting over a tune is well to the fore on uptempo novelty material like "Chocolate Ice Cream Cone," "Whoa Sailor" (also a hit for Hank Thompson), "New Step It Up and Go," "Sally Let Your Bangs Hang Down," and "You've Been Talking in Your Sleep." Not that the group can't be traditional, but even pieces like "Gosh, I Miss You All the Time," "I'm Sending Daffydils," and "I Wish I Was Single Girl Again" sound like they're getting more than they bargained for in the energy department, a trademark of their high-octane style. Highly deserving of a wider hearing on compact disc (hopefully with bonus tracks), this is the missing piece of the Maddox puzzle in absorbing their unique take on the country string band sound and style. *—Cub Koda*

★ **The Most Colorful Hillbilly Band in America** / Mar. 25, 1998 / Bear Family ✦✦✦✦✦

The Maddox Brothers & Rose belong in that upper echelon of performers whose contributions shaped country music for the ages. The difference is that the Maddox Brothers & Rose have not been inducted into the Country Music Hall of Fame, never charted a national hit, and are far from being household names. The artists who credit their influence include Merle Haggard and Dolly Parton, to name only a couple. Their outrageous appearance (they popularized the garish Nudie suits that would later become the uniform of country stars), risqué material, and crazed performances punctuated by brother Cal's maniacal cackle made the group one of the most exciting and innovative acts of its time. They were rockabilly before such a thing existed, and Rose Maddox's brash, assertive style opened up new possibilities for women in country music beyond Patsy Montana's comparatively demure cowgirl image. *The Most Colorful Hillbilly Band in America* collects on four discs the group's complete Columbia recordings, plus early solo recordings by Rose, the Rosie & Rhetta singles, and a few stunning sides by the Maddox Brothers alone. There are many classic performances, from intense readings of sacred songs to hillbilly rock & roll to wild revisionist covers of current hits. The band's loose, energetic playing and surreal sense of humor make for some of the most awe-inspiring music of its era. This is the first legitimate release of this material on CD, and certainly the most complete anthology of the band's studio recordings ever assembled. Damn the charts—if you want to know about '50s country, this box set belongs in your collection. *—Greg Adams*

Live on the Radio: Excerpts from 1953 Radio Broadcasts / Aug. 18, 1998 / Arhoolie ✦✦✦

Recorded from radio broadcasts on KXLA in Pasadena, CA, in 1953 (there are also a couple of tunes from a television program from that year), the fidelity on these isn't so hot. That's understandable; they were recorded by a teenager using early-'50s technology, after all, with no eye for professional release. As was already demonstrated by other radio performance collections of the groups on Arhoolie, the Maddoxes had a large repertoire and enjoyed using their radio time to cover everything from novelties to boogies to spirituals to classics like "Mule Skinner Blues" and "Silent Night, Holy Night." Their exuberance is unfailing, though as the sound is lo-fi and the presentation riddled with corny jokes and short skits from the bandmembers, it's not a suitable introduction to their significant body of music. That observation, and the low rating assigned to the album, should not be taken to mean it's not a worthwhile release for Maddox Brothers fans. The performances are good, there's much historical interest in hearing the band in a live-ish setting, and with 74 minutes of material (including, minus the skits, about 30 songs), it's decent value for the money. *—Richie Unterberger*

Columbia Historic Edition / Columbia ✦✦✦✦✦

Originally released on LP, these are the original Columbia recordings of the Maddox Brothers & Rose from the '50s. The 13 tracks run the gamut between sacred songs, hillbilly, rockabilly, and novelty tunes including "Old Black Choo Choo," "Bringing in the Sheaves," "Ugly and Slouchy," "The Death of Rock & Roll," and "The Hiccough Song." Since Arhoolie and Bear Family have reissued this material on CD, you won't need to spend your time searching used record stores or websites for it. *—Al Campbell*

Rose Maddox (Roselea Brogdon)

b. Aug. 15, 1925, Boaz, AL, d. Apr. 15, 1998

Vocals / Bluegrass, Traditional Bluegrass, Traditional Country, Western Swing, Honky Tonk

Rose Maddox exerted a heavy influence on honky tonk females through her recordings with the Maddox Brothers but later turned to traditional bluegrass forms as well to inspire folk revivalists of the 1960s and '70s. Born Roselea Brogdon on August 15, 1925, she moved from Alabama to Modesto, CA, with her family to make a better living as farm laborers. After several years of hard work and occasional amateur musical appearances, Fred Maddox lobbied KTRB-Modesto to give a time slot to him and his brothers Cliff, Cal, Don, and Henry. The radio station agreed, but on the condition that the Maddoxes include a female singer. Rose was recruited—as an 11 year old—and the group soon appeared in bars as well as on the radio show. They won a contest at the California State Fair in 1939, and began to broadcast at KFBK-Sacramento, which included several stations in nearby states as part of its coverage.

World War II interrupted the career of the Maddox Brothers & Rose, with Cal, Fred, and Don entering the services. The group re-formed in the late '40s and became more popular than ever: They recorded for 4-Star and Columbia, making annual trips east to appear on the *Louisiana Hayride* and the *Grand Ole Opry*. The Maddoxes' popularity was biggest on the West Coast, however; they performed on several radio shows with good music and comic hillbilly routines that appealed to the masses of dispossessed Southerners in California.

The Maddox Brothers last recorded in 1957, and Rose decided to go solo a year later with help from brothers Cal and Henry. She signed to Capitol but didn't have much success until 1961, in which she accounted for five Top 20 hits. Both "Kissing My Pillow" and its B-side "I Want to Live Again" hit the country Top 15 early in the year. "Mental Cruelty" made it to number eight in May, and her duet with Buck Owens called "Loose Talk" hit number four the same month. She ended the year with another Top 15 single, "Conscience, I'm Guilty." Her biggest hit, "Sing a Little Song of Heartache," came the following year, reaching number three in late 1962. More Top 20 singles followed in 1963, including "Lonely Teardrops," "Down to the River," "We're the Talk of the Town," "Somebody Told Somebody," and another duet with Owens, "Sweethearts in Heaven." After hearing suggestions that her voice would be perfect for bluegrass recordings, the resulting *Rose Maddox Sings Bluegrass* (with Bill Monroe, Don Reno, and Red Smiley) became a big hit with folk revivalists of the mid-'60s. Maddox's Capitol contract ended in 1965, and after recording with several smaller labels, she began to concentrate on tours, with brothers Cal and Henry in addition to her son, Donnie. During the '80s, Rose suffered several heart attacks but continued to perform at folk and bluegrass festivals and record for Arhoolie, Varrick, and Takoma. Maddox spent most of the '90s relatively quietly, performing at a few festivals and recording an occasional album, including *The Moon Is Rising* in 1996. Maddox died of kidney failure on April 15, 1998. She was 71 years old. *—John Bush*

● **Rose Maddox Sings Bluegrass** / Nov. 5, 1962 / Capitol ✦✦✦✦✦

Of the many fine (and now rare) LPs she cut for Capitol, this humdinger is the best one to break your neck trying to find. On this bluegrass sung with honky tonk fire, sparks do fly. *—Dan Cooper*

Rose of the West Coast Country / 1980 / Arhoolie ✦✦✦

The One Rose: The Capitol Years / 1993 / Bear Family ✦✦✦✦✦

All 111 tracks—and not a weak one among them—that Rose Maddox cut for Capitol Records between 1959-1965, including seven numbers (one live) with Buck Owens, spread among four CDs and topped off with a 16-page booklet. As usual, the quality is excellent, in addition to the material being exceptionally attractive. Maddox's singing (sometimes joined by her brother, John, or Buck Owens) is powerful throughout, whether she's introducing new numbers like "Custer's Last Stand" or "Lies and Alibis," or covering familiar territory like Hank Williams' "Whoa Sailor" or "Honky Tonkin'," or Woody Guthrie's "Philadelphia Lawyer." Her honky tonk numbers are in a class by themselves, among the boldest material in this vein ever cut by a woman, and hearing it, it's easy to understand why her influence crosses generational lines in country music—she was well ahead of her time. But it's also filled with surprises: her wonderfully robust and raspy rendition of "Honky Tonkin'," which could melt a lumberjack's chain saw, but also features a jewel of a mandolin break that would be a blessing on any bluegrass record; a frantic, rockabilly flavored version of Williams' "Move It on Over" that ought to be part of any serious rock & roll collection; an enticing (and rocking) version of Tommy Collins' "Down Down Down" (never on any album); a stunningly moving version of "Please Help Me I'm Falling," which was later buried by Hank Locklin's version, recorded after but issued just a few weeks ahead of Maddox's; a dozen gospel numbers (most notably "That Glory Bound Train") that are among the most sincere, exuberant, upbeat, and rousing songs of their kind ever assembled in one place; and a killer live rendition of Buck Owens' "Down to the River" cut at an Owens concert in Bakersfield in September 1963. The complete contents of her albums—including *The One Rose*, *Glorybound Train*, and *Rose Maddox Sings Bluegrass*—are here, along with the dozens of tracks that the label never found room on its roster to release. The booklet is also fascinating, explaining how Maddox came to record so much and release so little during her years with Capitol (more than a

third of the contents here have never been heard before), and how she came to be dropped from the label along with other country legends like Hank Thompson. *—Bruce Eder*

$35 and a Dream / 1994 / Arhoolie ✦✦✦

Rose Maddox's first album following seven heart bypasses and three months spent in a coma, after which she had to re-learn to talk, let alone sing, is an excellent and welcome addition to the Maddox family catalog. Rose Maddox's voice had weathered very well, and with an excellent backing band, including most of the Desert Rose Band and the fiddle of Byron Berline, her signature sound remains in top form. A fine testament to her legendary status within the country music community, Merle Haggard and composer David Price contribute songs written especially for the occasion, with Haggard contributing harmony vocals on "Dusty Memories." Johnny Cash even sings her praises in a non-musical dialogue. The final product is a fine combination of bluegrass, Western swing, and Bakersfield country, all presented with a very professional sound. Fine examples of the latter are covers of Buck Owens' "Falling for You" and "We're Gonna Let the Good Times Roll." A beautifully understated rendition of Gram Parsons' "Sin City" and the exemplary musicianship on the traditional "Blue Ridge Mountain Blues" are also highlights. David Price's three songwriting contributions range from the completely appropriate gospel of "Blood Stained Hands" to the somewhat maudlin "Tonight I'm on Stage" and "$35 and a Dream," which charts the history of the Maddox family and puts Rose Maddox in the strange position of singing about her own legacy. All in all, there still isn't a bad track here, and *$35 and a Dream* would be one listeners' last looks at a true country legend. *—Matt Fink*

The Moon Is Rising / 1996 / Country Town Music ✦✦✦✦

The Moon Is Rising was started in 1987 and finally finished at Mad Dog Studios in 1996. Between the time Rose Maddox and John Jorgenson began the bluegrass project and the time they finished it, their lives had taken drastic twists and turns. Still, California country & western legend Maddox is without a doubt one of the consummate performers to come out of the central valley and make a contribution to the Bakersfield sound. Known for her solo work as well as her time as a member of the Modesto-based Maddox Brothers & Sister Rose, her joining with the younger Jorgenson provides an interesting look at how two generations can come together for the sake of the music. Both are outstanding and Rose has a feel for Western bluegrass that has inspired Laurie Lewis and her band, Front Range. Their cover of Buck Owens' "Down to the River" is most entertaining. Another California legend, Bill Bryson, who also adds his skills as a bluegrass bass man and background vocalist to the mix with good results, contributes his song "Love Me or Leave Me Alone," an outstanding composition made better because of the talent involved. Making their presence known on this recording are expert L.A. players Jay Dee Maness on pedal steel and dobro and percussion master and background vocalist Steve Duncan. Overall, Jorgenson's production works nicely with Rose's vast experience. The material is steeped in tradition as are the players, making for a pleasant and uplifting experience. *—Jana Pendragon*

J.E. Mainer

b. Jul. 20, 1898, Weaversville, NC, d. Jun. 12, 1971

Fiddle, Leader, Vocals / Old-Timey, String Bands, Field Recordings

Mainer's Mountaineers, with their leader J.E. Mainer on fiddle, were one of the most popular string bands of the 1930s. They formed an important link between old-time string music and bluegrass, and their musical life exemplified several important aspects of the musical culture of the mountain southeast: the importance of the brother duet, the early link between country music and radio advertising, and the prevalence of turn-of-the-century sentimental song in the repertories of 1930s musicians. Mainer was born in Buncombe County, NC, and was raised in the mountains. His first instrument was the banjo, which he played at local square dances. Mainer's music, like that of other southeastern performers, offered an alternative to working in North Carolina's hellish textile mills; Mainer left home for mill work in his mid-teens, landing first in Knoxville, TN, and then in Concord, NC, where he moved in 1922 and lived for the rest of his life. At one point, having turned his banjo over to his brother Wade temporarily, he sold some agricultural seed on commission and drew his pay in the form of a tin fiddle. After he mastered the showpiece "John Henry," he invested in a better instrument. Soon he and Wade had joined with other local musicians to form a band. Mainer's appetite for performing was whetted when he started winning top prizes at fiddle contests.

By the early '30s, the commercial potential of country music on radio had been amply demonstrated, and Charlotte's Crazy Water Crystals Company (a purveyor of bottled water containing mineral salts of dubious medical value) offered Mainer's Mountaineers a series of promotional appearances and a slot on Charlotte's powerful WBT radio station. The group, now featuring John Love and Zeke Morris on guitars, was re-christened the Crazy Mountaineers and remained on WBT for four years. The fame they attained interested record companies in turn, and the group recorded its first sides for the Bluebird label in Atlanta in 1935.

One of the 14 songs recorded at that session was "Maple on the Hill," a turn-of-the-century sentimental standard originally composed by the African-American Cincinnati janitor-composer Gussie Davis. The song had been introduced to country audiences by both Vernon Dalhart and the Carter Family, but the mournful warmth of J.E.'s fiddle and Wade's banjo made it a country standard. In 1936, Wade and Zeke Morris left to form the Sons of the Mountaineers, while J.E. and his new lineup, consisting of Snuffy Jenkins, George Morris, and Leonard Stokes, spent over a year playing on radio stations in Spartanburg and Columbia. In 1939, with new musicians once again, Mainer recorded once more for Bluebird with Clyde Moody and Jay Hugh Hall. After World War II, Mainer became one of the first artists signed to the independent Cincinnati label King and made recordings with a band featuring his sons Curly and Glenn. New musical trends were in the air by then, however, and Mainer returned home to Concord. For the next 15 years he made mostly local appearances.

The Mountaineers were rediscovered during the folk revival in 1962 by Chris Strachwitz of the California-based Arhoolie label. At that time, Mainer's Mountaineers recorded *The Legendary Family From the Blue Ridge Mountains*, which introduced Mainer's music to a whole new generation. King reissued some of the Mountaineers recordings (such as *Good Ole Mountain Music*) in the early '60s, and over the course of that decade Mainer recorded several more albums and made appearances on the radio and at festivals. He continued to perform until his death in 1971. *—James Manheim*

A Legendary Family From the Blue Ridge Mountains / 1963 / Arhoolie ✦✦✦✦

● **Run Mountain** / Jan. 21, 1997 / Arhoolie ✦✦✦✦
Somewhere near the crossroads of traditional string band music and early bluegrass, you'll find J.E. Mainer's Mountaineers. Though this recording was made in 1963, with Mainer having replaced all his former bandmembers with his own children and a few friends, the collection is still nothing short of superb, with over 70 minutes of high spirited and rambunctious old-timey music. Drawing on lively fiddle tunes, classic spirituals, ballads, and standard string band fare, a very loose and impromptu feeling runs through the 23 cuts, as the band seems to be having more than a little fun on tracks like "If I Lose Let Me Lose" and "Crying Holy." Good harmonies, excellent musicianship and an authentic and sincere presentation make *Run Mountain* a nearly flawless document of traditional string band music. *—Matt Fink*

Wade Mainer

b. Apr. 21, 1907, Weaversville, NC
Banjo, Vocals / Traditional Bluegrass, Traditional Country
Banjoist/singer Wade Mainer was an influential figure whose innovative two-fingered picking technique expanded the traditional clawhammer style and helped pave the way for the three-finger virtuosity of modern bluegrass players like Earl Scruggs. Mainer was born in 1907 and raised on his family's small mountain farm near Weaverville, NC, where he was inspired to try his hand at traditional mountain music by his brother-in-law, fiddler Roscoe Banks. After moving to Concord to work in a cotton mill, he began performing with his brother J.E. Mainer's group the Mountaineers, playing frequent gigs on local radio and appearing on some of their classic recordings. In 1936, he left to form a short-lived duo with bandmate Zeke Morris, and put together his own band the following year. Dubbed the Sons of the Mountaineers, their initial lineup featured guitarists Jay Hugh Hall and Clyde Moody, and fiddler Steve Ledford. Also in 1937, Mainer married singer Julia Brown, who performed under the name Hillbilly Lilly. He and his group recorded for Bluebird through 1941, and are best remembered for 1939's "Sparkling Blue Eyes"; personnel changes brought in other members like Jack and Curly Shelton, Tiny Dodson, Red Rector, and Fred Smith, among others.

World War II curtailed Mainer's musical activities quite a bit, partly because he couldn't afford to use gasoline rations to travel to radio stations. He and a version of the Sons of the Mountaineers did perform at the White House in 1942, and following the war, Mainer reorganized the group. By this time, however, traditional mountain music was becoming passé, and recording opportunities came only sporadically. In 1953, Mainer renewed his commitment to Christianity and retired from the music business; he and Julia moved to Flint, MI, where he worked at an automobile plant. In the meantime, he returned to recording (for King) with his wife in 1961, when Molly O'Day convinced him that the banjo was a perfectly acceptable instrument in gospel music.

He recorded occasionally through the '60s, and after retiring from the auto industry in the early '70s, he entered the studio more often. He issued a series of albums on the Old Homestead label spanning from the late '70s to the early '90s, and also played at several bluegrass and folk festivals, mostly around Michigan. In 1987, he received the Nation Heritage Fellowship from the National Endowment for the Arts. *—Steve Huey*

Soulful Sacred Songs / 1961 / King ✦✦✦✦✦

Sacred Songs of Mother and Home / 1971 / Old Homestead ✦✦✦✦

The Songs of Wade Mainer / 1973 / County ✦✦✦

● **In the Land of Melody** / 1987 / June Appal ✦✦✦✦✦
In the Land of Melody is a latter-day recording (and first compact disc) by Wade Mainer, one of the most prolific and influential country stars of the '30s. When Mainer re-emerged in the '70s, he began performing with his wife Julia and the pair recorded *In the Land of Melody* in the late '80s. The record is divided between standards, originals, instrumentals, and novelties, with none of Wade's obvious hits making an appearance. Instead, the record is a carefully assembled collection that intends to revive the feeling of '30s traditional country, not just Mainer's career. Though the sound is too clean and Wade and Judy occasionally show signs of wear and tear, *In the Land of Melody* is a joyous celebration that hints at the accomplishments Mainer has achieved in his career. *—Thom Owens*

Charlie Major

b. Dec. 31, 1954, Aylmer, Quebec, Canada
Vocals / Contemporary Country, Singer/Songwriter
A major star in his native Canada, Charlie Major had a string of number-one hits and numerous awards, including winning the Juno Award for Country Male Vocalist of the Year three years running, beginning in 1994. Deciding he wanted to be a musician in 1974, Major became a traveling troubadour, and for the next 15 years sharpened his writing and playing skills on the road. At one point he lived in Spain, where he played for tourists and put together a few country bands. Back in Canada, he entered and won a songwriting contest in 1986, part of the prize entitling him to record and release a single. Soon, his songs were being recorded by the likes of Canadian stars Matt Minglewood and Patricia Conroy.

On a visit to Nashville in 1989, he did some recording, and one of the songs, "Backroads," ended up being a number-one hit for Ricky Van Shelton three years later. Then in 1993, Major released his first album, *The Other Side*, in Canada, and it sold double platinum there, yielding six number-one hits and winning numerous awards, including the Canadian Country Music Association 1994 Album of the Year and Single of the Year ("I'm Gonna Drive You Out of My Mind"). He moved to Nashville in 1994 and was briefly signed to Arista Records, before Imprint Records bought his contract and issued his second album and U.S. debut, *Here and Now*, in 1996. *Everything's Alright* appeared a year later, and in early 2000 Major resurfaced with *444*. *—Jack Leaver*

● **The Other Side** / May 8, 1995 / Arista ✦✦✦✦
The Other Side introduced Charlie Major's blue-collar, rock-influenced brand of country, and was a significant hit in Canada, going double platinum (sales of over 200,000). The album spawned six singles that went to number one on the Canadian country charts, including the debut hit "I'm Gonna Drive You Out of My Mind." *The Other Side* is littered with first-rate examples of journeyman country-rock. Major writes and sings about working-class life, songs that have quite a lot in common with some of Bruce Springsteen's blue-collar anthems. "Running in the Red" is about working from paycheck to paycheck, working hard just to get by, while "I'm Somebody" recognizes the lives of ordinary people. However, most of the songs concern love, either people looking for love or trying to escape the pain of love gone wrong. In "Walk Away," Major says goodbye to a lover; on "The Other Side" he's inviting love into his heart, while in "I'll See You in My Dreams" he's pining for a lover who's far away. Producer Steve Fishell gathered a crack band consisting of some Nashville's best players. Led by lead guitarists Albert Lee and Steuart Smith, these musicians are obviously sympathetic to Major's music. Harry Stinson plays an important role, both drumming and singing throughout the album, and Kim Richey is also on hand to provide harmony vocals on "I'm Here" and "I'll See You in My Dreams." *The Other Side* is a fine debut from a gifted writer and singer, and established Charlie Major as a significant talent in the Canadian country music scene. *—Martin Monkman*

Lucky Man / Feb. 26, 1996 / Arista ✦✦✦
Lucky Man, Charlie Major's second album, continues in much the same vein as his first, *The Other Side*. That is to say, it's the same heartland country-rock, essentially a slightly twangier version of John Hiatt or a harder-rocking Rodney Crowell. Major is a journeyman writer and singer, never rising above the pack, and *Lucky Man* demonstrates his talent for making consistently solid music. There are songs about the grind of everyday working life, including the Canadian hit "(I Do It) For the Money," written by Major in 1986 when he was working as a restaurant cook. There are also driving songs, including the opening track "Someday I'm Gonna Ride in a Cadillac," which finds the singer achieving his dream of a Cadillac, but only for the trip to heaven. And there are Major's love songs, which invariably manage to sound heartfelt in spite of the preponderance of clichéd phrases (one case in point: "I Can See Forever in Your Eyes" was a phrase Major used on the song "Walk Away" from *The Other Side*). The album closes with a fine cover of Donovan's "Remember the Alamo," as inspired a selection as you'll find on a country record. Major does the song as a stately ballad, with synthesized strings underpinning some bluesy slide guitar. The production, by Steve Fishell (the Mavericks, Pam Tillis, and Radney Foster), is always sympathetic, bringing out Major's strengths. A strong ensemble of some of Nashville's best players helps, too. Reprising the roles they played on *The Other Side*, guitarists Steuart Smith and Dan Dugmore are on hand to play tasteful guitar solos and fills, and drummer Harry Stinson does double duty on many tracks, adding harmony vocals. *Lucky Man* contains four number-one Canadian singles and sold over 100,000 copies in Canada, garnering platinum certification. *—Martin Monkman*

Here and Now / Oct. 8, 1996 / Imprint ✦✦✦
An award-winning singer/songwriter in his native Canada, Major shines on his sophomore album and first American release. Major's record will appeal to country fans who like the rootsy, rock side of the genre. The vocals, as well as music bear a strong resemblance to Lee Roy Parnell, in the way that it combines blues-based country with infectious upbeat melodies. Strong cuts include the memorable "(I Do It) For the Money," and the slide guitar-driven "I Can See Forever in Your Eyes." Some might remember Major's song "Backroads," which was a number-one hit for Ricky Van Shelton. *—Jack Leaver*

Everything's Alright / 1997 / BMG ✦✦✦
Charlie Major's third album, *Everything's Alright*, doesn't break any new ground—it sticks to the course set by his first couple of recordings. Unfortunately, in doing so, it lacks some of the freshness that characterized those earlier albums. Kicking off with the rocking "I'm Feeling Kind of Lucky Tonight," the 11 songs on the album traverse familiar terrain. These are models of blue-collar, rock-influenced country, drawing equal inspiration from Bruce Springsteen (and his followers) and Rodney Crowell. Major has made a name writing driving songs—this time around it's the optimistic "I Keep on Driving"—but instead of driving as escape, this song deals with driving as a return to his lover's embrace. One of the album's best tracks is Neil Diamond's "Thank the Lord for the Night Time," which is given a rock-solid performance. Like his previous efforts, *Everything's Alright* is characterized by solid playing by lead guitarist Steuart Smith and bass player Glenn Worf. Major is a journeyman writer and singer, producing solid if unexceptional material. All in all, *Everything's Alright* will appeal to Major's fans, but it won't convert those who weren't convinced by his earlier efforts. *—Martin Monkman*

444 / Mar. 21, 2000 / Artemis ✦✦✦
Contemporary country singer Charlie Major had a string of number-one records in his native Canada during the '90s. Then with a U.S. deal and an eye toward breaking into Nashville, Major released *444*. Nevertheless, despite a strong batch of performances and guest appearances by folks like Joy Lynn White and Cowboy Junkie Margo Timmins, Major presents a conundrum for Music City. His tunes have a lot of polish, but not that extra bump of pomp and saccharine needed to succeed in mainstream country. Conversely, he's not quite "alternative" or "insurgent" enough to find any elbow room in the *No Depression* camp (as Patty Loveless, a one-time hit machine, and Kelly Willis, a would-be Young Lion in the early '90s on MCA, have). Major writes strong, cosmopolitan country tunes with lots of heartfelt appeal, however. And highlights such as "Right Here,

Right Now" and "Why Don't We Stay Home Tonight" show why he has had such great success in his homeland (where popular country music has a much more catholic reach). The album also includes a stirring take on Bob Dylan's "Oh, Sister." *—Erik Hage*

Raul Malo

b. Aug. 7, 1965, Miami, FL

Vocals / Lounge, Pop, Latin Pop, Cuban Pop, Progressive Country, Contemporary Country, Neo-Traditionalist Country

Originally making his mark in the county music world and then slipping into the Latin and jazz arenas via rock & roll, Raul Malo has proven to be an ever expanding musical talent. Malo, born in Miami of Cuban parents, started playing bass guitar in high-school and soon found his way into several small bands. In 1987, he made his first recording with the Basics, and one song, "Paperheart," appeared on the promotional album *Unsigned*. While the album wasn't a success, the experience whet Malo's appetite for more. Later in the '80s Malo and a high-school friend, Robert Reynolds (bass), joined together to form their own country band, based on their mutual love for Hank Williams, Johnny Cash, and Patsy Cline. Paul Deakin, with experience in several progressive rock bands, became the drummer, and the group chose the name the Mavericks. This band went on to become one of the outstanding country bands of the '90s.

Under Malo's leadership, the Mavericks released their debut self-titled album in the fall of 1990. The album managed to grab the attention of many big labels and MCA Records signed the band on in May 1991, when they played their first gig in Nashville. David Lee Holt, who previously played with Carlene Carter, Joe Ely, and Rosie Flores, became the lead guitarist for the band, with Malo concentrating on the songwriting and vocals. MCA released *From Hell to Paradise* in 1992 and released five more albums for the band during the '90s. *Hell to Paradise* was critically acclaimed, but not financially a success. However, *What a Crying Shame* brought forth financial fortunes when it was released in 1994, with its title-track reaching the Top 40; the album went platinum by spring 1995.

Holt was replaced with Nick Kane as lead guitarist for the next releases. Many of the bands singles reached the Top 40, with "O What a Thrill" making number 18 in the summer of 1994, and "There Goes My Heart" reaching number 20. *Music for All Occasions*, released in 1995, made gold. The Mavericks eventually won a Grammy and the Country Music Association named it the Top Vocal Group twice. One of the highlights of the band's career was playing at the Royal Albert Hall in London. As Malo began to integrate Latin rhythms into his songwriting during the latter part of the '90s, the albums picked up more Havana influence, leaving the country rhythms in the shadows. The band became an eclectic mix of rockabilly, honky tonk, tejaño, native Cuban, and country. The MCA label continued to release the Maverick's albums and singles throughout the '90s, while two compilations (*20th Century Masters—The Millennium Collection: The Best of the Mavericks* and *O What a Thrill: An Introduction to the Mavericks*) were released in 2001. Although the Mavericks quit playing gigs together in early 2001, they haven't really broken up as a band and Malo still has tight connections with the members.

During the later years of the '90s, Malo began doing parallel solo work, sometimes accompanied by the Dennis Burnside Orchestra. During October 1999, he completed his first solo tour in the U.K., performing many of his new songs. By 2000, he had become a producer with Ethan Allen and K.T. Oslin, and joined the Los Super Seven as a lead vocalist and songwriter, in addition to working with the Latin singer Rick Trevino in his studios. Malo's first solo recording, "Bailare (El Merecumbe)," was self-penned in Spanish, and he also did a solo recording of "Downbound Train" by Bruce Springsteen. When the Country Music Association needed a voice that could handle singing all the different hits of those being inducted into the *Country Music Hall of Fame* in 2001, they called on Raul Malo because of his ability to handle diverse rhythms.

Malo's first album as a single, *Today*, reflects his Cuban background, but doesn't entirely leave out the deep-twang guitar that country music gives. His exuberance flows as he mingles the pop sounds of the '60s with salsa and country. Released by Omtown/Higher Octave Music in October 2001, the album also features Shelby Lynne on vocals and a backup band of 11 that produces the big band sounds of which Malo is becoming fond. Malo sings *Today* in both Spanish and English, reflecting calypso, carnival, jazz, salsa, and country influences playing out the theme of universal love. Malo also covered "Black Is Black," a Latin rock hit, on Los Straitjacket's 2001 album, and sang on Raffi's compilation of country singers for children. Although it may not be realistic to mix everything in music together, it makes sense to Malo and he succeeds in doing it. He sees only a fine line between rock & roll, country, and salsa rhythms. Because he loves all kinds of music and doesn't like classifying tunes into set genres, his music will undoubtedly continue to slip in and out of the various rhythms, crossing cultures, and blurring musical boundaries. *—Eleanor Ditzel*

Today / Oct. 23, 2001 / Omtown/Higher Octave ♦♦♦♦

From the start, it was obvious that the Mavericks were comprised of a more interesting variety of flavors than most C&W hitmakers, and by the time they released *Trampoline* in 1998, the band had evolved from an eclectic country-accented outfit into an adventurous adult pop group willing to dip their toes into practically anything. So it shouldn't surprise anyone that Raul Malo's first solo album doesn't have a single country bone in its body, but not everyone might have expected Malo to walk so boldly in a single direction. Malo began exploring his Cuban musical heritage with a few Latin-flavored numbers on the Mavericks' *Music for All Occasions* and *Trampoline*, and on *Today* he steeps himself in Latin rhythms, from the fiery dance groove of the title track and the sensuous tension of "Every Little Thing" to the jazzy sway of "Ya Tu Veras" (four of the album's 12 cuts are sung in Spanish, and Malo's estimably rich voice communicates beautifully in either tongue). *Today* bears more than a few hallmarks of Malo's earlier work along the way; the sly humor that marked the Mavericks' best work is evident in a playful duet with Shelby Lynne on "It Takes Two to Tango," his Roy Orbison-esque way with a ballad doesn't escape him on "Let's Not Say Goodbye," and Malo's fondness for lounge jazz takes the place of his Latin sounds on the closing track, "Since When." In terms of style and approach, *Today* isn't what most people might expect from Raul Malo, but one listen makes it clear the man has a great voice, sure instincts, and talent to spare—and anyone who has ever listened to his music ought to be well-aware of that. *—Mark Deming*

Barbara Mandrell

b. Dec. 25, 1948, Houston, TX

Vocals, Guitar (Steel) / Country-Pop, Urban Cowboy, Contemporary Country

Thanks to a string of hit singles and a popular television variety series, vocalist Barbara Mandrell was arguably the biggest female star in country music in the late '70s and early '80s. Born the oldest daughter into a musical family in Houston, TX, on Christmas Day, 1948, Mandrell was already reading music and playing accordion by the age of five. Just six years later, she was so adept at playing the steel guitar that her father escorted her to a music trade convention in Chicago, where her talents caught the attention of Chet Atkins and Joe Maphis. Soon after, she was a featured performer in Maphis' Las Vegas nightclub show, followed by television performances and tours with Red Foley, Johnny Cash, and Tex Ritter.

When Mandrell was 14, her family formed its own group, with her father Irby on vocals and guitar, her mother Mary Ellen on bass, and Barbara handling pedal steel and saxophone. The band also included drummer Ken Dudney, whom Mandrell would eventually marry. The Mandrells toured the U.S. and Asia before Barbara made her first recordings in 1963, among them the minor hit "Queen for a Day." After a few more years of touring, Mandrell briefly retired in order to become a housewife, but she soon grew restless and returned to the music business. After signing with Columbia in 1969, she notched her first chart hit, a cover of the Otis Redding classic "I've Been Loving You Too Long." In 1970, Mandrell scored the first of many Top 40 hits with "Playin' Around With Love." In the same year, she began performing with singer David Houston, and their partnership also generated considerable chart success.

In 1975, Mandrell jumped to the ABC/Dot label, and under the guidance of producer Tom Collins reached the Top Five for the first time with the single "Standing Room Only." After a series of successive hits, she earned her first number one with 1978's "Sleeping Single in a Double Bed," which was immediately followed by another chart-topper, "(If Loving You Is Wrong) I Don't Want to Be Right," in early 1979. Later in the year, "Years" also reached number one, as did three more singles—"I Was Country When Country Wasn't Cool," "'Till You're Gone," and "One of a Kind Pair of Fools"—between 1981 and 1983, a period during which Mandrell also received numerous industry awards and accolades.

In 1980, the TV program *Barbara Mandrell and the Mandrell Sisters* premiered on NBC. In addition to hosts Barbara, Louise, and Irlene Mandrell, the show featured musical guests and comedy sketches. Each broadcast also closed with a gospel song, and in 1982 Mandrell released her own inspirational album, *He Set My Life to Music*. As a result of her busy schedule, she began suffering from vocal strain, and on doctor's orders pulled the plug on the television program in 1982. In 1983, she premiered *The Lady Is a Champ*, a Las Vegas stage show, and released two LPs, *In Black & White* and *Spun Gold*.

A collection of duets with Lee Greenwood, *Clean Cut*, followed in 1984. Tragedy struck later in the year, however, when Mandrell and two of her children were involved in a nightmarish head-on car crash that left the other driver dead. Though Mandrell and her kids survived, all three faced a long period of recovery. When she finally returned to performing a year later, the country music landscape had changed dramatically, with the "new traditionalist" movement gaining dominance while the glitzier, more pop-influenced music Mandrell favored began falling out of favor. As the 1980s became the 1990s, she began focusing almost exclusively on live performing, where she remained a significant draw; she also published her autobiography, *Get to the Heart: My Story*. *—Jason Ankeny*

● **The Best of Barbara Mandrell** / 1979 / MCA ♦♦♦♦♦

The Best of Barbara Mandrell collects her biggest hits from the late '70s, including "After the Lovin'," "Married But Not to Each Other," "Tonight," "Woman to Woman," and "Sleeping Single in a Double Bed." *—Stephen Thomas Erlewine*

Greatest Country Hits / 1987 / Curb ♦♦♦

While *Greatest Country Hits* does, as advertised, contain some of Mandrell's most popular recordings, many of these 11 songs were minor hits, and others never reached the charts at all. However, it does offer three of her chart-toppers—"Years," "One of a Kind Pair of Fools," and "I Was Country When Country Wasn't Cool." *—Jason Ankeny*

Super Hits / Aug. 12, 1997 / Columbia ♦♦♦

For those who know Barbara Mandrell only by her pop-oriented recordings of the late '70s and '80s, *Super Hits* may come as a welcome surprise. Compiling ten of her singles recorded for the Columbia label in the early '70s, *Super Hits* features two Top Ten country hits, including "The Midnight Oil" and seven other Top 40 entries. The second Top Ten entry, "Tonight My Baby's Coming Home," is a thoroughly enjoyable trucking song told from the perspective of the trucker's woman. Other selections are more rock-oriented, although even the otherwise straight-ahead rock track "Show Me" incorporates a fiddle breakdown. Billy Sherrill's production on these selections is glossy and firmly rooted in the '70s, and the disc is unfortunately brief, but *Super Hits* offers some of the best recordings Barbara Mandrell ever made. *—Greg Adams*

20th Century Masters—The Millennium Collection: The Best of Barbara Mandrell / Oct. 31, 2000 / MCA ♦♦♦

20th Century Masters—The Millennium Collection: The Best of Barbara Mandrell spans her '70s and '80s hits over the course of 11 tracks, including definitive moments such as "(If Loving You Is Wrong) I Don't Want to Be Right," "I Was Country When Country Wasn't Cool," "Sleeping Single in a Double Bed," and "One of a Kind Pair of Fools." One of the better Mandrell retrospectives currently available, *The Millennium Collection* is a good introduction to her body of work. *—Heather Phares*

The Midnight Oil/Treat Him Right / Nov. 14, 2000 / Collectables ✦✦✦✦
This two-fer from Collectables features a pair of out of print Barbara Mandrell LPs: *Midnight Oil* and *Treat Him Right*, both originally issued on Columbia in the early '70s. Highlights among the 27 tracks include "The Midnight Oil," "Do Right Woman, Do Right Man," and "Treat Him Right," which provide an interesting combination of pop, country, and soul. *—Al Campbell*

● **Ultimate Collection** / Jul. 31, 2001 / Hip-O ✦✦✦✦✦
Like most of the entries in Hip-O's excellent *Ultimate Collection*, Barbara Mandrell's volume of *Ultimate Collection* pretty much fulfills the promise of the title, offering 23 tracks, including nearly all of her biggest hits. A few cuts are indeed missing, but all the iconic numbers are here—"Sleeping Single in a Double Bed," "I Was Country When Country Wasn't Cool," "Happy Birthday Dear Heartache" among them—and the quality of the material is consistently high, making this a great summary of her career. *—Stephen Thomas Erlewine*

Carl Mann

b. Aug. 24, 1942, Huntingdon, TN
Guitar, Piano, Vocals / Rockabilly, Rock & Roll
One of the last discoveries on Sam Phillips' legendary Sun label, piano player Carl Mann was best known for his rockabilly reworking of the Nat King Cole pop standard "Mona Lisa." That million-selling hit positioned him as something of a softer, smoother Jerry Lee Lewis, possessed of a crooner's instincts and a velvety vibrato. Unfortunately, Mann was never able to land another hit on the level of "Mona Lisa," despite waxing a fair amount of high-quality rock & roll. Like many early rock vets, he eventually moved into country music when the rockabilly market dried up, but never successfully established himself in that arena, and gradually drifted out of music.

Carl Mann was born in Huntingdon, TN, on August 24, 1942. He grew up in a strongly rural area, where his family ran a lumber business, and fell in love with country music as a child. He began singing in church at age nine and soon moved on to performing country songs at area talent contests. He learned guitar at age ten, and piano at 13, by which time he'd already become a regular on local radio. He also formed a band with several other young musicians, and soon took an interest in the R&B and rockabilly records that some of his DJ friends played on the radio, especially those of Elvis Presley. In 1957, Mann successfully auditioned for the Jaxon label and cut his debut single, "Gonna Rock and Roll Tonight" b/w "Rockin' Love"; those sides marked his first collaborations with guitarist Eddie Bush, who would become an important member of Mann's band, and assisted him on his rearrangement of "Mona Lisa." Mann cut several more unreleased sides for Jaxon over the next year, and caught a break when Carl Perkins' drummer Bill "Fluke" Holland offered to become his manager. Holland brought Mann to Sun Records in 1959, and Sam Phillips signed him to a three-year deal. Mann cut his take on "Mona Lisa" early that year, and while Phillips wasn't keen on releasing it as a single, Conway Twitty heard the demo tape and quickly cut his own version, which began climbing the charts. Phillips hurriedly issued Mann's, which battled Twitty's all the way up the pop charts. Both hit the Top 30, and while they tended to cancel each other out in terms of placement, Mann's wound up selling over a million copies; and he wasn't even 17 years old.

Despite the newfound stardom and several TV appearances, "Mona Lisa" turned out to be the pinnacle of Mann's commercial success. At first, he tried to repeat the formula by rocking up other vintage pop standards, which failed to return him to the Top 40, and perhaps even obscured the virtues of original tunes like "I'm Coming Home." Mann also wasn't helped by the fact that he'd appeared at the tail end of rockabilly's prime, or that Charlie Rich had taken his place as Sun's rising new star. Mann's first album, *Like Mann*, was released in 1960, but sold disappointingly, and he began to develop a drinking problem that necessitated some time away from music. In 1964, he was drafted into the Army; upon returning to the U.S., he signed with the Monument label, but the single "Down to My Last 'I Forgive You'" failed to return him to prominence. Mann soon left music to return to his family's business, settling down with a wife and finally overcoming his problems with alcohol.

In 1974, Mann attempted a comeback singing straight country material; he issued several singles over the next few years on ABC and Dot, but they didn't fit in with the slick countrypolitan records then dominating the charts. In 1977, Mann got an offer from the Dutch label Rockhouse to record for European audiences; he issued a couple of albums on that label, 1978's half-live/half-studio *Gonna Rock'n'Roll Tonight* and 1981's *In Rockabilly Country*. Mann toured periodically during the '80s, returning to Europe every so often, and finally retired to concentrate on the family logging business. He still resides in Huntingdon, TN. *—Steve Huey*

Mona Lisa / 1994 / Bear Family ✦✦✦✦
Carl Mann managed a one-million-selling single with his rock & roll interpretation of Nat King Cole's "Mona Lisa," and then spent years rocking up familiar oldies in an attempt to duplicate that success. He stayed with the formula for way too long, but the rock & roll recordings he made are enjoyable, mild rockers vaguely reminiscent of Ricky Nelson. Mann switched to country in the mid-'60s, briefly signing with Monument and then ABC in the '70s, but never recaptured his early success. *Mona Lisa* is nearly a complete recordings collection, beginning with Mann's first single on Jaxon, all of his Sun and Phillips recordings, his Monument and ABC sides, and a lot of non-commercial demos from his country phase. Four decent solo sides by his longtime guitarist, Eddie Bush, are included as well. The bottom line is that Mann's country material is fairly pedestrian, and it comprises half of the set. The two discs of rock & roll recordings are very good, but single-disc anthologies would satisfy 99 percent of listeners. Consequently, *Mona Lisa* is even more of an artifact for hardcore fans than many of Bear Family's other box sets. *—Greg Adams*

● **Mona Lisa: The Very Best of Carl Mann** / Feb. 2, 1999 / Collectables ✦✦✦✦✦
Like fellow Sun pianists Charlie Rich and Jerry Lee Lewis, Carl Mann found a way to mix pop, country, and rock & roll into his own unique style. Taking a cue from Rich's penchant for crooning vocals à la Sinatra, Mann gave a rockabilly spin to one of the Chairman's classic sides, "South of the Border," while also revving up the likes of the Nat King Cole hit "Mona Lisa." In fact, this 20-track Collectables roundup of Mann's 1959-1962 material takes its name from the singer's million-selling smash version of that musical ode to DaVinci's diva. Actually recorded for Sam Phillips' Sun subsidiary, Phillips International, the Cole number and a fine mix ranging from more inimitable covers ("Kansas City") to top-notch rockabilly staples ("Ubangi Stomp") make this a must for fans looking to dig a bit deeper into their Sun history. *—Stephen Cook*

Joe Maphis (Otis Wilson Maphis)

b. May 12, 1921, Suffolk, VA, **d.** Jun. 27, 1986
Guitar, Session Musician / Traditional Country, Instrumental Country, Bakersfield Sound, Honky Tonk, Rockabilly
Joe & Rose Maphis were a popular husband-and-wife act in the late '40s and early '50s, singing traditional material backed by the amazing instrumental talent of Joe, who played everything with strings on it, especially the twin-neck guitar. The honky tonk anthem "Dim Lights, Thick Smoke (And Loud, Loud Music)" was their big hit. Until his death in 1986, Joe was a sessions instrumentalist, backing such stars as Rick Nelson, Tex Ritter, and Wanda Jackson. *—David Vinopal*

● **Fire on the Strings** / 1957 / Columbia ✦✦✦✦✦
Once upon a time, hotshot guitar pickers were a valued, though perhaps underrated, part of the country-western scene. Jimmy Bryant accompanied Speedy West on a number of historic sessions in the '50s, and *Hee Haw* alumnus Roy Clark made his first mark on the guitar. Among guitar heroes of the era, none loomed larger than Joe Maphis with his trademark double-neck guitar, complete with his name inscribed on the fret board. Unlike the fingerpicking method favored by Merle Travis and Chet Atkins, Maphis preferred to string notes together in such rapid-fire succession that the title *Fire on the Strings* is more than just hyperbole. From the infectious boogie of "Guitar Rock and Roll" to the electrified bluegrass of the "Katy Warren Breakdown," these instrumentals are spontaneously bursting at the seams. It is curious that many of the arrangements add banjo and fiddle to the electric guitar, creating something akin to progressive bluegrass a few years before the term was in vogue. The title cut is a variation on the fiddle tune "Fire on the Mountain," and transforming fiddle tunes into guitar tunes surely formed part of Maphis inspiration. But his music cannot be pigeonholed as progressive bluegrass, country, or any particular genre. Instead, think of it as expertly played instrumental music brought to life by an energetic electric guitar. There are seven bonus tracks, including the Latin-tinged "The Rockin' Gypsy," that generously lengthen the album. While Maphis never became a household name, his rapid-fire style would influence numerous guitarists. To aspiring guitarist players and lovers of good instrumental work, *Fire on the Strings* shouldn't be missed. *—Ronnie Lankford Jr.*

Flat-Picking Spectacular / 1982 / CMH ✦✦✦✦✦

Flying Fingers / Mar. 25, 1997 / Bear Family ✦✦✦✦✦
Along with Chet Atkins and Merle Travis, Joe Maphis was one of the most widely heard session guitarists from the 1940s until the 1980s, but his solo recordings weren't nearly as popular—which doesn't mean they weren't good. The 24 brisk, crisp instrumental tracks on *Flying Fingers* (running under one hour) were cut mostly for Columbia between 1955 and 1960; the 1955-1957 stuff was recorded between sides by Rose Lee Maphis, and she is present there playing guitar, with Larry Collins (featured on four numbers, on top of which his sister Lorrie is the subject of the title of the Maphis original "Lorrie Ann"), Johnny Bond, and Leon Silby joining the guitar accompaniment on the later sessions. In addition to guitar, Maphis himself plays banjo and autoharp on various tracks. The best showcase to date of Maphis' work, the music features what seem like superhuman feats of dexterity, reminiscent of Jascha Heifetz's 1930s recordings on the violin, only better—every note is hit spot-on, but the playing never loses its warmth or seems mechanical. Listeners may swear that the masters of "Flying Fingers," "Fire on the Strings," and "Floggin' the Banjo" *must* have been sped up, but they weren't. While they may constitute highlights, they're not alone. Other high spots include "Katy Warren Breakdown," by session fiddle player Fiddlin' Kate Warren, and the cover of "Sweet Fern" by A.P. Carter. There's also a lot of variety, especially with the presence of the four Collins sides, which rock pretty hard; "Early American" shows some strong blues elements. *—Bruce Eder*

Rose Lee Maphis (Rose Lee Schetrompf)

b. Dec. 29, 1922, Baltimore, MD
Vocals / Traditional Bluegrass, Traditional Country, Honky Tonk
During the 1950s and 1960s, Joe and Rose Lee Maphis—"Mr. and Mrs. Country Music"—ranked as one of show business' most successful husband-and-wife duos, thanks largely to Joe's distinctive, highly influential brand of guitar picking. While Otis Wilson Maphis was born on May 12, 1921, in Suffolk, VA, Rose Lee Schetrompf was born over a year later on December 29, 1922, in Baltimore, MD. Both became active in music at a young age: after playing guitar in a group with his family's group, the Railsplitters, at local square dances, in 1938 Joe became a full-time musician, and not long after joined Sunshine Sue (Workman)'s backing outfit, the Rangers, in Cincinnati, OH. With the group, he began to perfect his unique approach to playing, which favored hyperkinetic fingerpicked melody lines over more basic chord accompaniment. Rose Lee, meanwhile, began singing on local radio in Hagerstown, VA, at the age of 15 as a member of the girl group the Saddle Sweethearts and soon graduated to appearances in large markets like Baltimore and St. Louis.

After serving in World War II, Joe returned to Virginia, where he briefly joined Sunshine Sue's radio jamboree, *the Old Dominion Barn Dance*, which also featured young singer Rose Lee Schetrompf. However, Maphis soon departed for Chicago; when he came back to Virginia in 1947, he took up the electric guitar and rejoined the radio program.

He and Rose Lee soon began performing together on the air and on the road; however, in 1951 Merle Travis convinced Joe to move to California to work in television, and only after Rose followed a year later did the couple finally wed. In 1953, the duo cut their first sides, among them the self-penned "Dim Lights, Thick Smoke (And Loud, Loud Music)," which has since become a honky tonk standard.

Throughout the decade, "Mr. and Mrs. Country Music" (as they were dubbed) remained staples of the West Coast scene, and even as Rose turned her attentions to raising a family, Joe continued performing both as both a solo instrumentalist and a highly regarded session musician. In 1954, he became one of the very first performers to play a double-necked guitar by adopting the Mos-Rite Special, an instrument he helped design. Through his work on solo records like 1957 *Fire on the Strings* and on sessions for other country stars as well as rockers like Ricky Nelson and vocal groups such as the Four Preps, Maphis earned another nickname, "the King of Strings." In addition to a number of duets with his young protégé Larry Collins (of the Collins Kids), Joe also released a tenor banjo record, *Hi-Fi Holiday for Banjo*, in 1959. Two years later, Rose Lee followed with a self-titled solo collection of country standards.

In 1962, the couple joined with the Blue Ridge Mountain Boys for *Rose Lee & Joe Maphis*, an album of bluegrass duets; later in the year, Joe released another solo effort, *King of the Strings*. Two years later, he and Merle Travis teamed for a record of guitar duets, followed shortly by another collaboration with Rose titled *Mr. and Mrs. Country Music* along with another solo outing, *Hootenanny Star*. In addition to a lucrative side career composing theme music for television programs, Joe released the solo offerings *Golden Gospel* in 1966 and *New Sound of Joe Maphis* a year later. The Maphis family moved to Nashville in 1968, and largely dropped out of music for a few years until Joe and the couple's eldest son, Jody, released the LP *Guitaration Gap* in 1971. Six years later, Joe released the solo *Grass 'n' Jazz* and was joined by Rose in 1978 for *Dim Lights, Thick Smoke*. Two more albums—1979's *Boogie Woogie Flattop Guitar Pickin' Man* and 1980's *Honky Tonk Cowboy*—followed. In 1986, Maphis succumbed to lung cancer; as a result, Rose Lee left performing to work as a costumer at Opryland. *—Jason Ankeny*

Rose Lee Maphis / 1961 / Columbia ✦✦✦✦

Carolyn Mark

b. Sicamous, B.C., Canada

Vocals / Alternative Country

Canadian alt-country singer/songwriter Carolyn Mark was born and raised in Sicamous, British Columbia, growing up on her family's dairy farm. Taught piano by her father, himself an accomplished violinist, in 1991 she surfaced as a member of the Victoria, B.C.-based all-girl rock combo the Vinaigrettes, touring Canada and the western U.S. relentlessly over the next seven years. After the group's 1998 dissolution, Mark formed the Corn Sisters, a duo with fellow insurgent country diva Neko Case—a Seattle live performance later constituted their 2000 debut, *The Other Women*. Mark also mounted a solo career, backed by guitarist Tolan McNeil and drummer Garth Johnson (her real-life housemates, hence their professional moniker the Room-Mates), and after signing to the Mint label, she again hit the road—her 2000 solo debut, *Party Girl*, assembled 11 songs cut across Canada, at least one from each province.

Mark's long-standing fascination with the classic Robert Altman film *Nashville* led to the 2002 release of an all-star tribute to the movie's soundtrack, with contributions from Case, Kelly Hogan, the New Pornographers' Carl Newman, and other stalwarts of the Canadian indie scene; her sophomore solo effort, the excellent *Terrible Hostess*, followed that summer. *—Jason Ankeny*

Party Girl / 2000 / Mint ✦✦✦✦

Carolyn Mark doesn't hold back on the boogie of old-time country music. With her guitar and a notebook full of lyrical heartache, the astounding results of *Party Girl* is a fine documentation on the roots of country. Although Mark doesn't perfectly capture the haunting vocals of Patsy Cline, her honesty of love and other tragedies are perfectly captured on tracks such as "Don't Come Over Baby." As Mark bellows: "Don't come over baby/You're not invited/Love is so much better when it's unrequited/So go to hell, leave me alone/And please don't answer baby/When I call you on the phone." The added lo-fi touch of basement recordings only contributes to the sincerity that gives *Party Girl* its rugged, open appeal. *—Mike DaRonco*

● **A Tribute to Robert Altman's Nashville** / Feb. 5, 2002 / Mint ✦✦✦✦

Finally, a tribute album that works. Featuring an all-star roster of Mint Records artists and friends, including Neko Case, Kelly Hogan, the New Pornographers' Carl Newman, and headliner/organizer Carolyn Mark, this homage to Robert Altman's classic film satire *Nashville* succeeds because the performances transcend the material—they're heartfelt readings of songs that were largely written for maximum irony and corniness. Sure, there's a tongue-in-cheek element at work here as well—the reproduction of speeches and dialogue from the film at times undercuts the effectiveness of the music—but the vocal performances are much stronger than in the actual film, and while some of the songs are still too campy to salvage, the truly solid material (like Hogan's heartbreaking reading of "Dues," Dallas Good's Lee Hazlewood-inspired "Bluebird," and Tolan McNeil's lovely take on Keith Carradine's Oscar-winning hit "I'm Easy") seems far more substantial and authentic on CD than it ever did on celluloid, enhancing the undeniable catchiness of these faux-country classics. An appreciation of Altman's film is certainly recommended, but not necessary. *—Jason Ankeny*

Terrible Hostess / Aug. 6, 2002 / Mint ✦✦✦✦

In the self-penned press release accompanying her superb second album, *Terrible Hostess*, Carolyn Mark self-deprecatingly dubs herself "The Other Girl in the Corn Sisters," and while it's true she's never earned the notice or acclaim justly heaped on duet partner Neko Case, it's time people started paying closer attention. Mark's songs are boozy and brassy, and her voice suggests a tough, salt-of-the-earth Natalie Merchant—moving deftly from the Red Bull-and-vodka bluegrass of the opening "Fuzzy Slippers" to the juke-joint torch balladry of "Inevitable," *Terrible Hostess* is both rooted in traditional country & western and a repudiation thereof, smarter and saucier than anything to come out of Nashville in eons. *—Jason Ankeny*

The Marshall Tucker Band

f. 1971, Spartanburg, SC

Group / Country-Rock, Southern Rock, Boogie Rock

One of the major Southern rock bands of the '70s, the Marshall Tucker Band was formed in Spartanburg, SC, in 1971 by singer Doug Gray, guitarist Toy Caldwell (born 1948, died February 25, 1993), his brother bassist Tommy Caldwell (born 1950, died April 4, 1980), guitarist George McCorkle, drummer Paul Riddle, and reed player Jerry Eubanks. The group's style combined rock, country, and jazz and featured extended instrumental passages on which lead guitarist Toy Caldwell shone. The band was signed to Capricorn Records and released its debut album, *The Marshall Tucker Band*, in March 1973. They gained recognition through a tour with the Allman Brothers Band and found significant success during the course of the '70s, with most of their albums going gold. Their peak came with the million-selling album *Carolina Dreams* and its Top 15 single "Heard It in a Love Song" in 1977.

The band was slowed down by the death of Tommy Caldwell in a car accident in 1980 and faded from the album charts after 1982. Toy Caldwell left for a solo career soon after, and the original lineup disbanded in 1983. Later that same year, Doug Gray and Jerry Eubanks hired some Nashville studio musicians and took the band back out onto the road; a little over a year later, the second wave of the Marshall Tucker Band began, as Gray and Eubanks returned home to Spartanburg, SC, and hired guitarist Rusty Milner, bassist Tim Lawter, drummer Ace Allen, and guitarist Stuart Swanlund.

During the years since the original band dissolved, the group has had country chart hits, toured constantly, made forays into the blues and adult contemporary, and suffered the loss of founding member Toy Caldwell, who died in 1993. Some bandmembers left, some joined, and some stayed right where they were, but through it all, the Marshall Tucker Band endured. The band continued to record steadily, maintained a loyal fan base, and eventually began to receive their due as Southern rock pioneers. The 1998 Marshall Tucker Band consisted of Gray, Milner, Lawter, Swanlund, David Muse (formerly of Firefall, on sax, flute, and keys), and drummer B. B. Borden (formerly of Mother's Finest). The band took several stylistic detours with 1998's all-blues outing *Face Down in the Blues* and the 1999 spiritual album *Gospel*. *—William Ruhlmann & Michael B. Smith*

The Marshall Tucker Band / 1973 / AJK ✦✦✦✦

Taking a page from their Capricorn Records labelmates and Southern rock contemporaries the Allman Brothers, the Marshall Tucker Band issued a self-titled debut blending the long and winding psychedelic and jam band scene with an equally languid and otherwise laid-back country-rock flavor. Into the mix they also added a comparatively sophisticated jazz element—which is particularly prominent throughout their earliest efforts. The incipient septet featured the respective talents of Doug Gray (vocals), Toy Caldwell (guitar/vocals), his brother Tommy Caldwell (bass/vocals), George McCorkle (guitar), Paul Riddle (drums), and Jerry Eubanks (flute/sax/vocals). Their free-spirited brand of Southern rock was a direct contrast to the badass rebel image projected by the Outlaws or Lynyrd Skynyrd. This difference is reflected throughout the 1973 long-player *The Marshall Tucker Band*. The disc commences with one of the MTB's most revered works, the loose and limber traveling proto-jam "Take the Highway." The improvised instrumental section features some inspired interaction between Toy Caldwell and Eubanks. This also creates a unique synergy of musical styles that is most profoundly exhibited on the subsequent cut, "Can't You See." Caldwell's easygoing acoustic fretwork babbles like a brook against Eubanks lonesome airy flute lines. The remainder of the disc expounds on those themes, including the uptempo freewheelin' "Hillbilly Band." Unlike what the title suggests, the track is actually more akin to the Grateful Dead's "Eyes of the World" than anything from the traditional country or bluegrass genres. "Ramblin'" is an R&B rave-up that leans toward a Memphis style with some classy brass augmentations. The effort concludes on the opposite side of the spectrum with the tranquil gospel rocker "My Jesus Told Me So," offering up Caldwell's fluid guitar work with a sound comparable to that of Dickey Betts. "AB's Song" is an acoustic folk number that would not sound out of place being delivered by John Prine or Steve Goodman. This eponymous effort established the MTB's sound and initiated a five-year (1973-1978) and seven-title run with the definitive Southern rock label, Capricorn Records. *—Lindsay Planer*

A New Life / 1974 / AJK ✦✦✦✦

On their second release, The Marshall Tucker Band becomes slightly rootsier and bluesier without sacrificing any of the relaxed charm of their first record. Overall, it is a stronger, more consistent album, highlighted by "Southern Woman," "Blue Ridge Mountain Sky," and "Too Stubborn." *—Stephen Thomas Erlewine*

Where We All Belong / 1974 / AJK ✦✦✦✦✦

Although it runs a little long, *Where We All Belong* captures the sound of the Marshall Tucker Band coming into its own. Half the tracks are new studio recordings, which are more focused than their previous releases; the other half is a harder-edged, jam-oriented live set. Taken together, they show that the band was progressing musically. *—Stephen Thomas Erlewine*

Searchin' for a Rainbow / 1975 / AJK ✦✦✦✦

With *Searchin' for a Rainbow*, the Marshall Tucker Band retreats somewhat from the grittier sounds of *Where We All Belong* without abandoning their country and blues roots. *—Stephen Thomas Erlewine*

Long Hard Ride / 1976 / AJK ✦✦✦

On *Long Hard Ride*, the Marshall Tucker Band's country influences come to the fore, resulting in a strong record that failed to gain many hits. Still, the final product is well worth listening to—it's one of their better releases. Be sure to listen for Charlie Daniels' guest appearance. —*Stephen Thomas Erlewine*

Carolina Dreams / 1977 / AJK ✦✦✦
Carolina Dreams marks a retreat from the more pronounced country leanings of *Long Hard Ride* to the more successful country-tinged pop-rock of "Heard It in a Love Song" and "Fly Like an Eagle." They gathered more hits with this approach, and although the hits hold up well, the rest of the album doesn't live up to their quality. —*Stephen Thomas Erlewine*

Together Forever / 1978 / AJK ✦✦✦
Together Forever boasts a more mainstream rock approach than any of its predecessors, halfway between the country-tinged *Long Hard Ride* and the pop-oriented *Carolina Dreams*. Although the band sounds good, the songs don't match the strength of their performances. —*Stephen Thomas Erlewine*

Greatest Hits / 1978 / AJK ✦✦✦✦✦
Fusing country-rock with bits of loose-structured jazz that popped up here and there, the Marshall Tucker Band found themselves alongside bands like Little Feat and Pure Prairie League in the middle of the mid-'70s Southern rock explosion. While maybe not as prominent as other bands in their field, the addition of saxophone and flute in their music gave them an edge that was a distinguishing attribute to their music. Lead guitarist Toy Caldwell, with brother Tommy on bass, churned out some appealing jamboree-flavored rock as well some charming slow material. Only eight tracks make up this sparse hits collection, and even though it includes their two biggest singles with "Fire on the Mountain" and the beautiful "Heard It in a Love Song," it's not enough to truly represent this band's music. The album kicks off with "Can't You See," made famous by country superstar Waylon Jennings in 1976, as well as FM radio staples "24 Hours at a Time" and "Searchin' for a Rainbow." With over 13 albums under their belt, the spirited mix of traditional country and electrified rock that exists in the Marshall Tucker Band's repertoire is impossible to appreciate within the radius of only eight songs. —*Mike DeGagne*

Running Like the Wind / 1979 / Ramblin ✦✦✦
Running Like the Wind finds the Marshall Tucker Band returning to their ever popular cowboy theme, with Toy Caldwell's strong, melodic title track, and George McCorkle's "Last of the Singing Cowboys." The music is well-produced, with some fine vocal arrangements from singer Doug Gray. Tommy Caldwell sings the only lead vocal of his career in a heartfelt love song to his wife, "Melody Ann." —*Michael B. Smith*

Tenth / 1980 / Ramblin ✦✦✦
Tenth, the last album to feature the late Tommy Caldwell, comes out of the chute rocking, with some of the Marshall Tucker Band's most moving material ever. "Cattle Drive," written by the Caldwell brothers, Toy and Tommy, drives with such intensity that the listener may feel as though they are riding drag on a real cattle drive. George McCorkle contributes another of his Western-themed story songs with "Gospel Singin' Man," and the guitarists pay homage to Jimi Hendrix with an instrumental original. —*Michael B. Smith*

Dedicated / 1981 / Warner Bros. ✦✦✦
Guitarist Toy Caldwell lost two brothers within one year, and this album is dedicated to their memory, culminating with the final track, "Ride in Peace." Former Garfeel Ruff bassist, Franklin Wilkie, steps in as bass guitarist, and the band shines on the moderate Top 40 single "This Time I Believe" and the bluesy "Tell the Blues to Take Off the Night." —*Michael B. Smith*

Tuckerized / 1981 / Warner Bros. ✦✦✦
On this, their 12th outing, the Marshall Tucker Band covers some of their personal favorite songs written by artists as diverse as Randy Newman and Guy Clark. The band also contributes a couple of writings, including George McCorkle's "Sweet Elaine," and Toy Caldwell's "Sea, Dreams and Fairytales." Guest pianist Ronnie Godfrey adds his own flavor to the recording, wrapping beautiful keyboard passages around the soaring vocals of Doug Gray on "Unforgiven" and "Even a Fool Would Let Go." —*Michael B. Smith*

Just Us / 1983 / Warner Bros. ✦✦✦✦✦
The second Marshall Tucker Band album to be recorded at their own studios in Spartanburg, S.C., *Just Us* stands as one of the five best MTB records to date. Newly christened bandmember Ronnie Godfrey brings more than his share to the party, penning some of the best tunes on the album, as well as playing his own unique and heartfelt style of piano. Godfrey's "Time Don't Pass By Here" is an excellent country song, with poetic lyrics, as is his "When Love Begins to Fade." Other outstanding tracks include the bluesy "Testify" and "Wait for You," which delivers a heart and soul rhythm and blues groove. —*Michael B. Smith*

Greetings From South Carolina / 1983 / Warner Bros. ✦✦✦
Greetings From South Carolina was the last album to be recorded by the original (except for the late Tommy Caldwell) lineup of the Marshall Tucker Band, prior to a breakup and a restructuring in 1984. While there are a few good songs on this one, it lacks the energy and creativity that burned so brightly within the band during the 1970s and into the early '80s. Exceptions include the Franklin Wilkie composition, "Closer to Jesus," and the country "I May Be Easy But You Make it Hard." Of the three recordings produced at their Spartanburg, S.C., studios, *Greetings From South Carolina* stands as the weakest. Still, there are always a few rare gems in any Tucker recording. —*Michael B. Smith*

Still Holdin' On / 1988 / Polygram ✦✦
In 1988, the Marshall Tucker Band released their first album following the break-up of the original band. Doug Gray and Jerry Eubanks had decided to continue touring and recording, and recruited some of Nashville's best session players to travel as well as record under the MTB name. Unfortunately, *Still Holdin' On* falls short of the band's previous efforts in many ways, not the least of which is an obvious state of confusion in

regards to musical direction. Although it did yield a pair of country Top 40 charting singles, *Still Holdin' On* stands as one of the Marshall Tucker Band's least interesting recordings. —*Michael B. Smith*

Southern Spirit / 1990 / Capitol ✦✦✦✦✦
Following the moderate success of *Still Holdin' On*, original Marshall Tucker Band members Doug Gray and Jerry Eubanks broke ties with the Nashville studio musicians they had used for a little over a year, and came back home to Spartanburg to hire a fresh new set of musicians who had grown up in the shadow of the Marshall Tucker Band, making the entire band, except for keyboardist Don Cameron, hometown boys. Perhaps familiarity breeds creativity, because *Southern Spirit* is filled with the good old-fashioned Southern energy and down-home sound that the Tuckers cut their teeth on. All 12 songs were written by the band, including the country and adult contemporary charting "Stay in the Country," penned by bassist Tim Lawter. Other outstanding tracks include Rusty Milner's "Destruction," a heavy electric blues offering, and the harmonizing gospel number that closes the set, "Closer Today," written by Gray. A fine set of musicians coupled with some very pleasing songs make *Southern Spirit* a very listenable Marshall Tucker Band record. —*Michael B. Smith*

Still Smokin' / 1992 / Cabin Fever ✦✦✦✦✦
With *Still Smokin'*, the Marshall Tucker Band continues the same pattern they initiated with the 1991 release, *Southern Spirit*. Solid, catchy pop-rock and country-tinged tracks like "Frontline," and "Southern Spirit," help to round out a fine selection of tunes that found the band once again cracking into the country Top 40 with "Driving You Out of My Mind." —*Michael B. Smith*

Walk Outside the Lines / 1993 / Cabin Fever ✦✦✦
The Marshall Tucker Band followed their 1992 release, *Still Smokin'* with another memorable set of songs, including the title track, "Walk Outside the Lines," co-written by Garth Brooks. On this outing, the MTB manages to produce their most country-oriented album to date, and the country Top 40 track, "Down We Go," written by fellow Spartanburg, S.C., resident Sam Spoon, brings it all back home. Other choice cuts include, "Daddy's Eyes," written by bassist Tim Lawter and "Lost in Time," co-written by Doug Gray and Rusty Milner. While *Walk Outside the Lines* may not go down in the books as one of the Marshall Tucker Band's best recordings ever, it still manages to hold its own in the country music field. —*Michael B. Smith*

● **The Best of the Marshall Tucker Band: The Capricorn Years** / 1995 / ERA ✦✦✦✦✦
This fairly self-explanatory double-disc compilation gathers 27 sides from '70s Southern rock staples the Marshall Tucker Band. With a blend of intricate jamming and straight-ahead guitar-driven rock & roll, the MTB were among the predecessors to the success of their Capricorn labelmates—the Allman Brothers Band, Cowboy, and Sea Level. They also incorporated elements of jazz, folk, and country to create a unique and original sound that effortlessly crossed genres, yet never strayed too far away from their decidedly down-home essence. The MTB only scored a handful of hits—such as "Heard It in a Love Song," "Take the Highway," "Can't You See," and "Fire on the Mountain"—which of course are represented here. However, the seven long-players that featured the incipient incarnation(s) of the MTB reveal a synergy among bandmates Doug Gray (vocals), Toy Caldwell (guitar/vocals), his brother Tommy Caldwell (bass/vocals), George McCorkle (guitar), Paul Riddle (drums), and Jerry Eubanks (flute/sax/vocals). Their laid-back ethos hung equally on the band's diversity of styles and skills. Toy Caldwell's prowess as a guitar player stretches beyond that of a standard acoustic and electric picker. Tracks such as "See You Later, I'm Gone" and "Virginia" show off his amazing depth as a steel guitarist as well. The deep and somewhat reverential twang that commences "Fire on the Mountain" harks back to the roots of the MTB's high and lonesome bluegrass origins. Then, mix in Eubanks' light and airy reed work for a truly liberating experience that is also distinctly American. *The Best of the Marshall Tucker Band: The Capricorn Years* (1994) features examples of the combo's loose instrumental jamming on "In My Own Way," "A New Life," and the 13-plus minute live rendering of "24 Hours at a Time." This cut definitely rivaled the Lynyrd Skynyrd epic "Free Bird" or the Allmans' "Whipping Post" for spin time on many FM album rock radio stations, back when they were still spinning LPs. This collection features several "45 versions"—which may best serve the burgeoning or casual enthusiast. However, diehards will want to seek out the full-length renderings of "Can't You See," "This Ol' Cowboy," "Searchin' for a Rainbow," and "Long Hard Ride." The accompanying 26-page booklet is replete with discographical and biographical information as well some black-and-white photos. *The Best of the Marshall Tucker Band: The Capricorn Years* is a good place for all interested parties to begin. —*Lindsay Planer*

Country Tucker / Aug. 1996 / K-Tel ✦✦✦✦
Country Tucker compiles tracks from the Marshall Tucker Band's mid-'70s heyday. As the title implies, all of the songs included on this collection lean toward the group's country roots—many of them, including "Heard It In A Love Song," were minor country hits. In fact, *Country Tucker* works as a greatest hits collection, since it does feature pop hits like "Fire on the Mountain" (presented in its original single version) and "Can't You See" that nevertheless demonstrate strong country leanings. In short, it's a useful introduction and a nearly definitive compilation that should satiate the desires of most casual fans. —*Stephen Thomas Erlewine*

Asa Martin

b. Jun. 28, 1900, Winchester, KY, **d.** Aug. 15, 1979
Guitar, Vocals / Old-Timey, Traditional Country
Old-time Kentucky singer Asa Martin made many records during the '20s and '30s and was closely associated with the famed fiddler Doc Roberts, for whom he played rhythm guitar. In turn, Roberts frequently played mandolin on Martin's recordings; Roberts' son James even sang duets with Martin under the name Martin and Roberts. Martin was born

in Clark County, KY, and grew up listening to the traditional music presented in minstrel shows and vaudeville productions. Inspired to become a performer, he joined a traveling show or two and learned to play guitar. It was during this time that he met Doc Roberts, who had him sit in on a recording session in Richmond, IN. His first solo songs were mostly parodies, such as "The Virginia Bootlegger" and "There's No Place like Home (For a Married Man)."

Martin moved to more traditional ballads after he teamed up with James Roberts in the late 1920s, including "Knoxville Girl," "Lilly Dale," and "Give My Love to Nell." Occasionally, the two also sang contemporary old-time style songs, such as "The Little Box of Pine on the 7:29." They continued to record together until 1934, when Martin became the host of the *Morning Roundup* in Lexington. He returned to recording in 1938, again focusing on comedy songs with the occasional ballad, like the haunting "Harlan Town Tragedy."

Martin quit music after the outbreak of World War II, initially working for a munitions factory in Middletown, Ohio. He retired in 1965 and moved to Kentucky, where he founded the Cumberland Rangers. In 1968, his early contributions were unearthed by music scholars Archie Green and Norm Cohen, who helped arrange a reunion concert between Martin and Roberts. In 1974, Martin and the Cumberland Rangers recorded an old-time music album, *Dr. Ginger Blue*. *—Sandra Brennan*

● **Asa Martin** / Rounder ♦♦♦♦

Dr. Ginger Blue / Rounder ♦♦♦

Benny Martin

b. May 8, 1928, Sparta, TN, **d.** Mar. 15, 2001

Fiddle, Vocals / Progressive Bluegrass, Traditional Bluegrass, Country Gospel

Benny Martin was one of bluegrass music's premier fiddlers and the inventor of the eight-string fiddle. Born to a musical family in Sparta, TN, he made his debut on a local radio station when he was only eight. He played in a local band for a while and when he was 13 went to Nashville to work with Big Jeff & the Radio Playboys at WLAC. He remained with the group for nearly ten years, and also began working as a session man for Dot Records. Martin also recorded a solo album on the Pioneer label; one of his early singles, "Me and My Fiddle," became his signature song.

Frequently, Martin worked as a sideman for such performers as Bill Monroe, Roy Acuff, Kitty Wells and Flatt & Scruggs. He founded his own band in 1954 and also briefly joined the *Grand Ole Opry*. During the mid-'50s he was managed by Col. Tom Parker and opened for Elvis Presley 35 times. This was not a great time to be a country performer, and Martin began doing more session and sidework than solo recording. In 1963 he had his only chart hit, "Rosebuds and You." In the mid-'60s, he briefly teamed with Don Reno and recorded a gospel album. Martin continued working behind others, performing at festivals and recording frequently on various labels through the early '80s, when his health began failing. *—Sandra Brennan*

All Time Great Country & Western Songs / 1962 / Guest Star ♦♦♦

A very deceptively titled record. Fiddle player Benny Martin, whose fun-loving photo graces the cover, performs only on one cut, "Tennessee Rag." He's a fine player, and it is a fun recording with a wonderful bluegrass spirit. The remainder of the record contains recordings by a wide array of country artists from the period, such as Moon Mullican, George Jones, Jim Glaser, and others. It's actually a fine, if somewhat misguided sampler, though. Mullican's "Wabash Cannonball" is one of the finest recordings of the period, and the same can be said of George Jones' classic "It's OK." Also, the Willis Brothers excellent harmony exercise, "Footprints in the Snow," is quite a nice addition. It's a little uneven, but nevertheless, a fun sampler. *—Matthew Greenwald*

The Greatest Hits of Benny Martin / 1973 / Power Pak ♦♦♦

This guy is a pretty hot fiddler, when he wants to be, and even is known as the originator of the eight-string fiddle in bluegrass. The cover of this hits collection is a large color close-up of the man sweating over his fiddle. No information is given about where the shot was taken, in fact there is not much information about anything available on the jacket, save for song titles and composers. But we can be sure the picture was not taken at any of the recording sessions here, because Martin barely breaks a sweat on his instrument. And, unfortunately, there were long stretches of his career where he had to downplay instrumental virtuosity to suit the trends in the marketplace. There are many tracks here that barely feature fiddle at all, and the ones that do are along the lines of the half-hearted "Orange Blossom Special," complete with an el wimpo fade. Martin's vocal talents keep things from being a complete write-off, however. He has a deep, and thick country & western voice similar to artists such as Hank Locklin. This is an album of country played as straight as possible, the pedal steel the only instrument with any kind of electric sound to it. Although some tracks lack a spark, there are several that are absolutely classic, most notably "Falling Star," a career-on-the-skids tune that makes a good companion to John Fogerty's "Lodi." The clever country songwriter Bobby Braddock is represented with "Three Hundred Thousand Unmarried Women in Georgia," but it turns out the title is the best thing about this one. *—Eugene Chadbourne*

● **Fiddle Collection** / 1976 / CMH ♦♦♦♦♦

Tennessee Jubilee w/John Hartford and Lester Flatt / 1993 / Flying Fish ♦♦♦♦

Brad Martin

b. May 3, 1973, Greenfield, OH

Guitar, Vocals / Honky Tonk, Neo-Traditionalist Country, Progressive Country, Contemporary Country

Country singer Brad Martin grew up in the suburbs of Ohio with a healthy dose of Merle Haggard and Conway Twitty. His love for country music encouraged him to start playing guitar as a young kid. By his mid-'20s, he was a songwriter and moved to Nashville to follow his dream. Epic Records snatched him up in the new millennium and Martin made his proper debut with *Wings of a Honky Tonk Angel* in June 2002. *—MacKenzie Wilson*

Wings of a Honky Tonk Angel / Jun. 18, 2002 / Epic ♦♦♦

Brad Martin's debut album has the steeped-in-traditional country title *Wings of a Honky Tonk Angel*, and his press biography is littered with references to Merle Haggard, Johnny Paycheck, Johnny Cash, and George Jones. But the ten-song collection actually mixes up traditional and contemporary styles, making it a good example of the way Nashville is compromising, trying to figure out where country music is going. Hardcore country comes to the fore on such tracks as the title song, a steel guitar-infused ballad that would not be out of place in Hank Williams' repertoire; "The Fifth," a good formula country song ("the fifth" refers both to the Fifth Amendment and a fifth of liquor) and one of only two songs on which Martin does not earn a co-writing credit; and "Damn the Whiskey," an uptempo honky tonk number. On such songs, Martin's tenor often takes on a Haggard- or Jones-like cry. But there are other influences at work on the record. You can hear traces of popsters Don Henley in "Completely" and Kenny Loggins in "That's a Woman," while the Fleetwood Mac-influenced "Run to Me" is the sort of pop/rock many people wouldn't call country at all and "Just Like Love" seems aimed more at the adult contemporary charts than the country ones. Not surprisingly, the album's advance single, "Before I Knew Better," the other song Martin did not co-write, attempts to split the difference. It's a confusing time for country music, and you can't blame record executives and new artists for hedging their bets. But Martin probably would be better off leaning more toward traditional country, which sounds like a better fit, and aiming at the sort of new traditional country audience Brad Paisley has identified. His first album gets it about half-right. *—William Ruhlmann*

Janis Martin

b. Mar. 23, 1940, Sutherlin, VA

Vocals / Rockabilly, Rock & Roll

Janis Martin was a unique figure in the history of rockabilly—there were other women working in that male-dominated field (Lorrie Collins for one), but Martin was the one dubbed "the Female Elvis Presley" by RCA, reportedly with the approval of Colonel Tom Parker. This was probably the kiss of death, evoking images so contradictory that no one could really hold it properly in their mind. The fact that she was signed to RCA probably didn't hurt, but as a hot-rocking female in a field where men's libidinal gyrations weren't approved, she had too many strikes against her for a lasting career. She was good, though, and she left behind the records to prove it.

Martin was born in Sutherlin, VA, in 1940 and had a stage mother on one side and a father and uncle who were amateur musicians on the other, a mix that practically made her predestined for a performing career. She was playing and singing before age five. By six, she'd mastered chords on her junior-sized guitar and was singing in a style influenced by Eddy Arnold and Hank Williams. She became a fixture in local talent contests and won all of them. Martin was playing and singing on the WDVA *Barndance* out of Virginia by age 11. By her mid-teens, she'd appeared alongside the likes of Ernest Tubb, the Carter Family, Sonny James, and Jean Shepard.

Her amazing amount of experience for one so young helped push her into rock & roll. It turned out that Martin had tired of country music by her mid-teens, especially the slow ballads, having been doing them for a decade. Her timing was perfect, for she discovered R&B in the mid-'50s and was soon bringing that material into her own song lists. RCA A&R chief Steve Sholes heard one of her demos and Martin was signed to the label at age 15, only two months after Elvis was signed up. "Drugstore Rock 'n Roll," a Martin original, was her debut record and her biggest hit, selling some 750,000 copies. By the middle of 1956, she was making the rounds of the *Today Show, the Tonight Show*, and other variety programs, as well as appearing on the *Grand Ole Opry*, and was voted Most Promising Female Vocalist in *Billboard*, the record industry's bible.

Some of the "Female Elvis" publicity rebounded fairly early, as fans felt she was hooking herself and her style of singing to him as a means of exploitation. Ironically, for all of the publicity that seemed to link them, and her recording of the single "My Boy Elvis" at the insistence of her management, plus the fact that they used the same session musicians and shared the same country-cum-R&B interests, Martin never saw the Memphis Flash perform until he made it to national television. By that time her own performing style—amazingly similar to his, but developed independently—was established and locked down. Additionally, she only met Elvis twice, both times very briefly, with hardly a word exchanged. The two found themselves converging on a similar point.

For all of her early success, Martin was never able to sustain a rock & roll career, mostly because of her gender and the changing times. Her stage moves and lusty delivery appeared unseemly (or so people said, especially on the country circuit) in a girl, once the initial furor and enthusiasm for rock & roll quieted down. Additionally, the country shows on which she was booked usually put her on bills and in front of audiences that weren't overly enamored of rock & roll to begin with, and Martin found herself caught between conflicting currents. Her record company and management wanted her to keep pushing rockabilly in her stage act, while promoters doing the bookings preferred that she do straight country. Martin might have finessed it all but for a personal situation that came up in 1958. She'd been secretly married since 1956, and her husband was stationed overseas in the army; she went on a European tour and got to see him in 1958. The result was that the 17-year-old rockabilly star became pregnant and was dropped by the label in short order.

Martin tried to keep a music career going and was courted by both King Records and Decca Records before signing with a Belgian-owned label called Palette, for which she cut four sides in 1960. She was on her second marriage by then, and husband number two (whom she later divorced) didn't take well to her career. She withdrew from music except for appearances near her home in Virginia and then in the 1970s, on her own again, formed her own band, the Variations, and toured Europe, where she encountered strikingly enthusiastic audiences, ready to embrace her as though it were still 1958. She continued to figure in some Elvis-related discographies, thanks to "My Boy Elvis" and also as a result of a 1959 South African album called *Janis and Elvis*, a 2,000 dollar collectible that was heavily bootlegged in the late '70s. Martin's RCA records, however, were forgotten and neglected by the company (which, in those days, could hardly reissue an Elvis recording without screwing it up in some way). In the 1980s, Bear Family Records finally gathered together Martin's complete recorded history on one CD, entitled, appropriately enough, *The Female Elvis*, making her ultra-rare sides easily available for the first time in decades. *—Bruce Eder*

The Female Elvis: Complete Recordings 1955–60 / 1987 / Bear Family ♦♦♦♦♦

Here are 30 songs, and not a loser in the bunch. This little lady rocks—hard—and she doesn't start to slow down until 21 songs in. The best is sort of like Elvis' early RCA sides, only better, mixed with some wildness that makes one wonder if Sun Records wouldn't have been a better home for her. As it happens, Martin is a good enough singer that even the slow ballads like "Cry Guitar" and "One More Year to Go" come off well—she had a rich, strong, slightly throaty voice that would have allowed her to make it in country music, or even pop (check out the Duke Ellington-authored "Squeeze Me") as easily as rock & roll, if that was what she wanted. What's more, she could write songs as well, and that was pretty rare for female performers of the time; her originals here compare pretty favorably with standards like "Ooby Dooby." "Blues Keep Calling" is a hot number in any discography. *—Bruce Eder*

Jimmy Martin

b. 1927, Sneedville, TN

Guitar, Vocals / Bluegrass, Traditional Bluegrass, Truck Driving Country

Blessed with a great tenor voice, traditional bluegrass singer and guitarist Jimmy Martin mastered his craft as lead vocalist for Bill Monroe's Blue Grass Boys for much of 1949-1951 and again in 1952-1953. Martin's vocals and his dynamic guitar playing both complemented Monroe perfectly, and in the opinion of many, he was the finest lead singer and guitarist Bill ever had. In 1951, between stints with Monroe's band, Martin joined with the Osborne Brothers, forming the Sunny Mountain Boys. Though this association lasted only until 1955, Martin has used this band name up to the present. In keeping up such high standards over the years, Martin has hired numerous major-league musicians, including banjo players J.D. Crowe, Bill Emerson, Vic Jordan, Alan Munde, and mandolin player Paul Williams, all of whom subsequently made it big in bluegrass. Martin is required listening for anyone with more than a passing interest in bluegrass.

Martin was born and raised in the Cumberland Mountains of East Tennessee. As a teenager, he fell in love with Monroe's music, which inspired him to pursue a career as a singer. He began working at radio stations around Morristown, TN, to gain experience; he also worked as a housepainter to make ends meet. At the age of 22, he auditioned in Nashville for Monroe's band to replace Mac Wiseman, and he successfully passed the audition. For the next four years, Martin stayed with Monroe, recording 46 sides for Decca Records. In 1951, Martin briefly sang with Bob Osborne, which was captured on a series of singles for King Records. At the same time, he was a member of the Monroe side project the Shenandoah Valley Trio, which cut several songs for Columbia.

Martin split from Monroe for good in 1954, joining Bobby and Sonny Osborne's duo as a lead singer. He stayed with the Osbornes for about a year, recording several sessions for RCA-Victor. Jimmy left the brothers the following year, taking the band name Sunny Mountain Boys—which had previously been used by the Osborne Brothers—with him. In the spring of 1956, Martin signed with Decca Records and made his first solo recordings. Through his solo records and performances on the *Grand Ole Opry* and the *Louisiana Hayride*, Martin helped bring bluegrass into the mainstream. This was primarily because he concentrated on bluegrass that focused on the vocals, not the instruments. Within two years, he began charting in the country Top 40, beginning with the number 14 single "Rock Hearts." Throughout the '60s, he had the occasional hit single and became a staple of the bluegrass festival circuit.

Over the years, Martin's Sunny Mountain Boys hosted a wealth of new musical talents, including Doyle Lawson, Bill Emerson, Clarence "Tater" Tate, Paul Williams, Alan Munde, and J.D. Crowe. Although the lineup of the band changed constantly, the quality of the musicians remained high throughout his career. In 1971, Martin sang "I Saw the Light" and "Sunny Side of the Mountain" on the Nitty Gritty Dirt Band's *Will the Circle Be Unbroken*, which helped increase his audience. Martin parted from Decca Records in 1974, signing with Starday/Gusto Records shortly after his departure. He stayed at Gusto for nearly a decade, releasing six albums during his tenure at the label. After Gusto went out of business in the '80s, Martin began his own record label, King of Bluegrass, which reissued his classic Decca recordings. Martin continued to perform concerts and bluegrass festivals into the 2000s. *—Stephen Thomas Erlewine & David Vinopal*

Sunny Side of the Mountain / 1965 / Decca ♦♦♦

Jimmy Martin's 1965 album *Sunny Side of the Mountain* spawned three unsuccessful singles, one of which—"Guitar Picking President"—suggests the frightening possibility of a Jimmy Martin presidency. The album places standards ("In the Pines") alongside originals like the murder ballad "Poor Ellen Smith" and the patriotic "I'd Rather Have America." An instrumental rendition of "John Henry" provides a showcase for Mike Miller's five-string banjo picking, and Vernon Derrick's contributions on the mandolin are also noteworthy. Major label bluegrass was becoming a rarity in the mid-'60s, and Martin was one of few who could still put bluegrass on the country charts. *—Greg Adams*

20 Greatest Hits / 1988 / Deluxe ♦♦

20 Greatest Hits contains re-recorded versions of Martin favorites done in the mid-'70s. *—Jason Ankeny*

Greatest Bluegrass Hits / 1989 / Hollywood ♦♦♦

Here are '70s-era rerecordings of Martin's bluegrass classics are compiled on *Greatest Bluegrass Hits*. *—Jason Ankeny*

☆ **You Don't Know My Mind (1956–1966)** / 1990 / Rounder ♦♦♦♦♦

This is a Monroe band veteran with astonishing high pipes and a penchant for blending bluegrass and honky tonk. *You Don't Know My Mind (1956-1966)* is a 14 track collection that boasts many highlights from his ten-year stint at Decca Records. These are great bands, great songs, and classic sides. *—Mark A. Humphrey*

Jimmy Martin and the Sunny Mountain Boys / 1994 / Bear Family ♦♦♦♦♦

This five-CD set covers Jimmy Martin's complete recorded output from 1954 until 1974, 20 years and 146 tracks cut primarily for Decca-MCA, with a handful for RCA at the very outset. Disc one covers the early days, from his sides with the Osborne Brothers to his formation of a band of his own—once Martin gets people like banjo man J.D. Crowe and fiddler Gordon Terry, the sound tightens up and gets smoother, and Martin's singing grows in power and confidence. Disc two represents Martin and the Sunny Mountain Boys at their peak, at least in the studio—these tracks display a range of singing, emotion, and restrained instrumental virtuosity that are almost overpowering. By that time, Martin had managed to incorporate the best components of Nashville's "countrypolitan" sound into his bluegrass work, and was reaping rewards both musical and financial. Disc three is a direct continuation, with a growing body of fare that country-rock bands would later pick up from Martin and others. Disc four, gets into the mid- to late '60s, when Martin's music achieved an incredibly high level of dexterity. His fourth distinct lineup of Sunny Mountain Boys are as good as any but the originals; different, with a more brittle, dexterous approach. This disc is dominated by the 1966 instrumental album *Big and Country Music*; as it will probably never be issued as a CD, this material alone may justify the purchase of this box. Disc five goes into the mid-'70s, when Martin had a more obviously smooth and commercial sound than his earlier work—the music is more sentimental and a little less impressive technically, but still worth hearing. The sound is all high quality, and the essay by Chris Skinker and the discography are impressive in their own right. *—Bruce Eder*

★ **The King of Bluegrass** / Feb. 27, 2001 / Audium ♦♦♦♦♦

Since this is a bit more extensive than the Rounder compilation *You Don't Know My Mind (1956-1966)*, with four more songs and a greater chronological breadth, it probably assumes the position of first-choice Martin anthology. The 18 songs are all drawn from his 1956-1970 Decca catalog, including his biggest hit, "Rock Hearts." The bluegrass giant explores various nuances of the form in this material, capable of both fairly witty plays on words ("Hit Parade of Love"), odes to the heartland ("Tennessee"), and a George Jones cover ("Milwaukee Here I Come"). The harmonies and arrangements are excellent throughout, with just a touch of country-pop giving much of the material greater crossover accessibility than much bluegrass has. At the same time, Martin's vocals retain an engaging brashness that steers his music clear of over-polish, while his use of snare drums, though it might pass unnoticed by many listeners, was considered radical by bluegrass purists. *—Richie Unterberger*

Mason Dixon

f. Texas

Group / Country-Rock, Urban Cowboy

Mason Dixon was a rock-tinged country band from the '80s that was formed by New York native Frank Gilligan and Texan Rick Henderson, who adopted the band's name in tribute to their mixed Northern/Southern roots. The two met in college during the mid-'70s and started playing around southern Texas together; in 1979, onetime solo act Jerry Dengler, who was originally from Odessa, TX, joined the group to make it a trio. They hired several supporting musicians and attempted to mount a tour, but a shortage of bookings forced them to shed most of the additional lineup. A self-released single, "Armadillo Country," caught the ear of promoter/producer Don Schafer, who signed Mason Dixon to his local Texas Records label. Starting with a 1983 cover of the Police's "Every Breath You Take," they scored a few local hits, which also included "I Never Had a Chance With You" and "Gettin' Over You"; in 1985, they also released an album called *The Spirit of Texas*, in conjunction with the state sesquicentennial.

In 1986, the band moved to another indie, Premier Once, and issued several singles with producer Dan Mitchell. These led to a deal with Capitol, and the band's major-label debut, *Exception to the Rule*, was released in 1988. They had limited success with the singles "Dangerous Road" and "When Karen Comes Around," but Henderson left the group in 1989, to be replaced by Terry "Caz" Casburn. A follow-up album, *Reach for It*, appeared in 1990, but didn't sell particularly well, and the group later disbanded. *—Steve Huey*

● **Exception to the Rule** / 1988 / Capitol ♦♦♦♦

Reach for It / 1990 / Capitol ♦♦♦

Mason Proffit

f. 1969, Chicago, IL, **db.** 1973

Group / Country-Rock, Folk-Rock

Mason Proffit is widely considered by obscure rock aficionados to be one of the best bands who never made it to the big time. Although they are mostly overlooked today, along with the Byrds, Michael Nesmith, and others, they helped to invent country-rock. The band was formed in 1969 by members of the recently disbanded Sounds Unlimited, a tough Chicago garage band with a well-developed melodic sense. John and Terry Talbot were the main movers behind Sounds Unlimited and in Mason Proffit they took the vocal harmonies they had developed in Sounds Unlimited and went in a folk and country direction. They were among the first to combine the energy and instrumentation of rock with the subject matter and twang of country. Perhaps the reason they were not hailed as visionaries at the time is that their first three records came out on small labels and didn't sell many copies. 1969's *Wanted! Mason Proffit* and 1971's *Movin' Toward Happiness* were released by Happy Tiger and 1971's *Last Night I Had the Strangest Dream* was released by Ampex.

The band's fortunes took a positive turn in 1972 when they were signed by Warner Bros. and released *Rockfish Crossing*. They used their Warner Bros. connection to tour with the Grateful Dead but it didn't help them with the record buying public. In 1973 they released one last album, *Bare Back Rider*, and then broke up. In 1974, Warner Bros. released a two-record set of Mason Proffit's Happy Tiger recordings. This has been reissued on CD by One Way and is a great place to start if you want to discover the roots of country-rock. In the years after the breakup of Mason Proffit, the Talbot brothers shifted their attention to Christian music, recording albums for Warner Bros., Sparrow, and other labels. *—Tim Sendra*

Wanted! Mason Proffitt / 1969 / Happy Tiger ✦✦✦✦
"Hear the voice of change," command the Talbot brothers at the opening of their debut album, and the song, "Voice of Change," is both a political statement calling out to President Nixon's "silent majority" and a statement of purpose from the band. Like their peers on the West Coast, the Midwestern Talbots attempt to merge the musical and social concerns of the folk-rock movement with elements of traditional country. But they are a bit more Western-styled than the Flying Burrito Brothers and less of a good-time outfit than Poco. Forging a connection between the hippie ethos and the Old West's outlaw myth, they conjure up a portrait of long-haired cowboys riding across the plain. In "Two Hangmen," the brothers alternate vocals (and stereo speakers) to tell the odd tale of an executioner who comes to doubt his profession and is sentenced to death for it, only to be spared by a second executioner, the two then hung to preserve the status quo. It's a bizarre Western fable, to be sure, but one that illustrates the brothers' sense that they are trying to invent a new society within the terms of the old and may have to pay for it. (*Wanted!*, after all is a title that cuts at least two ways.) The music takes off from folk and country sources into progressive rock ("Sweet Lady Love" is even reminiscent of Creedence Clearwater Revival), the pedal steel guitar and fiddle augmented here and there by strings, while the brothers' tenor harmonies give the group a distinctive vocal sound. Like many debut albums, this one is ambitious, both musically and thematically; Mason Proffit wants to change musical tastes and political beliefs at the same time. Whether or not they succeed, they have crafted a good opening argument. *—William Ruhlmann*

Movin' Toward Happiness / Mar. 1971 / Happy Tiger ✦✦✦
Based in Chicago, Mason Proffit played a style of country-rock that owed less to the more pop-oriented style of L.A. bands like Poco than it did to the newly bluegrass-happy Grateful Dead of *American Beauty* and its emerging offshoot, the New Riders of the Purple Sage. Despite the pedal steel guitar, fiddle, banjo, and dobro, the Talbot brothers, who led the group, were less about a new Nashville than about a fusion of the Old West with hippiedom. They lamented the plight of Native Americans in "Flying Arrow," and while they could pick a mean hoedown on "Old Joe Clark," their version somehow managed to express anti-war sentiments. They recognized the connection between the cowboy myth and the independent spirit of truck drivers, and they managed to mix it all in with a sort of primitive Christianity. In this, they were very much of their time. Mike Cameron's "Good Friend of Mary's" fit into the emerging Jesus cult that identified the Christian savior as a kind of proto-hippie, preaching peace and love while wandering the country in long hair and sandals, and the Talbots sang it with their warm tenor harmony in complete sincerity. Such music wasn't going to make it far out of the early 1970s, but in 1971 it was perfectly appealing, and *Movin' Toward Happiness* managed to make the national charts despite being released on the band's own label, suggesting that they had the potential to appeal beyond a cult. *—William Ruhlmann*

Last Night I Had the Strangest Dream / Oct. 1971 / Ampex ✦✦✦✦✦
Though this album sank without a trace when it was released, time has been kind to *Last Night I Had the Strangest Dream*, and it is now hailed as a work of genius. Justifiably so, since every track is proof of a band with wonderful instincts for melody and how to frame a musical idea. Mason Proffit was an ensemble that played a blend of music that was more country than rock, with occasional folk and blues influences to make things interesting. Though a few of their songs were straightforward love songs and celebrations of country virtues, many were uncommonly sophisticated for 1971. The song "Jewel" is a pure tearjerker, a sad tale of a young black woman who is used and abandoned by a wealthy white man. The tragic story is set to a weeping steel guitar and is sung in a voice that sounds anguished, and it is a marvelously affecting track. The title track and "Eugene Pratt" are noteworthy for their gentle insistence that something is wrong with the society in which we live, and something should be done about it immediately. Other bands were experimenting with country-rock but never achieved this subtlety and grace, and there was a whole genre of protest music which lacked those same two attributes. The fact that both were in the same package, but were ignored at the time that they were released, is just a darn shame. This band's catalog cries out for a re-evaluation and re-release, starting with this album. *—Richard Foss*

Rockfish Crossing / 1972 / One Way ✦✦✦✦
Mason Proffit earned a major-label contract with Warner Bros. Records in 1972 after its second and third albums, *Movin' Toward Happiness* and *Last Night I Had the Strangest Dream*, both made the charts in 1971 despite being released on small independent labels. Warner probably thought it was getting in on the country-rock trend already receiving national exposure via the Flying Burrito Brothers on A&M and Poco on Epic, and it might well have worked out that way. *Rockfish Crossing*, the group's Warner debut, was an accomplished blend of country and rock on which the Talbot brothers, who led the band, sang pure harmonies on folk-rock songs, played convincing country hoedowns, covered country standards like "You Win Again," and even included some timely social consciousness in "Were You There," with its references to My Lai and Wounded Knee. They dressed up in Western gear on the album cover like 19th century desperadoes, Civil War soldiers, and buffalo hunters. It's hard to say why this appealing and apparently trendy package wasn't successful, but *Rockfish Crossing*, unlike its two predecessors, didn't sell well enough to make the charts, much less expanding Mason Proffit's following. The country-rock hybrid was a delicate mixture, one not really perfected until the Eagles did it a little later. (Neither the Flying Burrito Brothers nor Poco actually sold records in significant quantities.) It may be that Mason Proffit, despite earlier indications, simply fell between the stools of being too country for the rock audience and too rock for the country audience. But the group's music was an accomplished blend of the two styles. *—William Ruhlmann*

Bare Back Rider / 1973 / One Way ✦✦✦✦
Mason Proffit's second major-label album and fifth album overall was similar in construction to its predecessor, *Rockfish Crossing*. Once again, the Talbot brothers and their supporting players turned in a combination of effective originals that touched on subjects from romance to politics with some enthusiastically performed country covers, notably a version of "Setting the Woods on Fire" that sounded like a deliberate attempt to impersonate Jerry Lee Lewis and featured a furious kazoo solo. The political element came out in "Black September/Belfast," with its reflections on Northern Ireland and Vietnam. You'd have thought that music this impressive could get a hearing, but Mason Proffit appeared at a time when music fans were more polarized than musicians, not only by music but by politics and culture. Despite the band's evident affection for traditional country music, their left-wing political stance and status as hippie rock musicians meant they could never be accepted in Nashville. And their music was too overtly country for them to score a pop hit. Thus, they were doomed to appeal only on the country-rock-oriented Los Angeles club scene and to some music critics. *Bare Back Rider* did a little better than *Rockfish Crossing* had, even scraping into the charts for a couple of weeks, but that wasn't the level of success a major label expected, and Mason Proffit was forced to hang up its spurs. *—William Ruhlmann*

● **Come & Gone** / 1974 / One Way ✦✦✦✦
After Mason Proffit signed to Warner Bros. Records, the label reissued the band's first two albums, *Wanted* and *Moving Toward Happiness*, as a double-LP set under the title *Come & Gone*. "Hear the voice of change," commanded the Talbot brothers at the opening, and the song, "Voice of Change," was both a political statement calling out to President Nixon's "silent majority" and a statement of purpose from the band. Like their peers on the West Coast, the Midwestern Talbots attempted to merge the musical and social concerns of the folk-rock movement with elements of traditional country. But they were a bit more Western-styled than the Flying Burrito Brothers and less of a good-time outfit than Poco. The music took off from folk and country sources into progressive rock, the pedal steel guitar and fiddle augmented here and there by strings, while the brothers' tenor harmonies gave the group a distinctive vocal sound. Mason Proffit wanted to change musical tastes and political beliefs at the same time. They lamented the plight of Native Americans in "Flying Arrow," and while they could pick a mean hoedown on "Old Joe Clark," their version somehow managed to express anti-war sentiments. They recognized the connection between the cowboy myth and the independent spirit of truck drivers, and they mixed it all in with a sort of primitive Christianity. In this, they were very much of their time. Mike Cameron's "Good Friend of Mary's" fit into the Jesus cult that identified the Christian savior as a proto-hippie, preaching peace and love while wandering the country in long hair and sandals, and the Talbots sang it with their warm tenor harmony in complete sincerity. Such music wasn't going to make it far out of the early 1970s, but in 1973 it remained appealing. *—William Ruhlmann*

Mila Mason

Vocals / Country-Pop, Contemporary Country
Born and raised near Dawson Springs, KY, modern country singer Mila Mason secured a record contract with Atlantic Nashville by the mid-'90s, releasing her debut album, *That's Enough of That*, in the fall of 1996. *The Strong One* followed in 1998. *—Stephen Thomas Erlewine*

That's Enough of That / Sep. 17, 1996 / Atlantic ✦✦✦
Mila Mason's debut album *That's Enough of That* is a competent but undistinguished set of modern country. The album boasts a number of songs written by professional Nashville songwriters, as well as a clean commercial production, and Mason has a fine voice, but nothing on *That's Enough of That* demonstrates much originality or spark. It's simply pleasant background music. *—Thom Owens*

● **The Strong One** / Jan. 20, 1998 / Atlantic ✦✦✦✦
Mila Mason's *Strong One* is a marked improvement from her debut, *That's Enough of That*. Throughout the album, Mason demonstrates more musical personality than she did on her first record, and she has a stronger set of songs. There's still a little too much polish for the album to really qualify as traditional country or honky tonk, but there's enough slick country-pop gems to make it an entertaining listen. *—Thom Owens*

Johnny "Country" Mathis

b. Sep. 28, 1933, Maud, TX
Vocals / Traditional Country, Nashville Sound/Countrypolitan
Not to be confused with pop singer of the same name, Johnny "Country" Mathis was born on September 28, 1933, in Maud, TX. He became a longtime member of the *Louisiana Hayride* from 1951 thru 1960. Johnny "Country" Mathis started out as part of the duo Jimmy & Johnny, with Jimmy Lee Fautheree. While they only released a handful of records, the duo hit the country & western Top Ten in 1954 with "If You Don't Somebody Else Will." It was recorded for the Chicago blues label Chess; it was one of the only country songs the label ever released. By the mid-'50s, Mathis went solo, recording a string of records for Dallas' renowned D Records, (including a rockabilly single, "Bee-Boppin' Daddy," under the name Les Cole & the Echoes), Decca, United Artists, and Little Darlin.' His last chart entry was in 1963 "Please Talk to My Heart" on UA. A fairly prolific songwriter, his work was recorded by Johnny Paycheck, George Jones, and Webb Pierce. At the beginning of the new millennium, Mathis was still active, based in Texas, and devoting his talent to Christian music. *—Al Campbell*

- **Country Johnny Mathis** / 1965 / Hilltop ✦✦✦

The liner notes to Johnny "Country" Mathis' self-titled album state that in 1964 Mathis "renounced country music to become a full-time missionary in the Lord's word." The album is Mathis' first long-player despite his having been a recording artist since the early '50s, and asserts his change of direction on 12 country gospel songs colored with chiming steel guitars. Sacred standards such as "Old Time Religion" and "Precious Memories" accompany lesser-known selections on this sturdy, old-fashioned spiritual offering. Mathis' renunciation of country music was very short-lived, and he returned to recording secular songs for the Little Darlin' label one year later. *—Greg Adams*

Kathy Mattea

b. Jun. 21, 1959, Cross Lane, WV

Guitar, Vocals / Contemporary Country, Country-Folk

Kathy Mattea was one of the most respected female country stars of her era, a commercially successful hitmaker who was able to bring elements of folk, bluegrass, gospel, and singer/songwriter intimacy to her music. Mattea was born in Cross Lane, WV, in 1959, and received classical voice training starting in junior high, but also took up the guitar when she discovered folk music. In 1976, while in college, she joined the bluegrass band Pennsboro, and two years later dropped out of school to move to Nashville. She worked odd jobs and perfected her songwriting, and in 1983 she landed a deal with Mercury on the strength of her demo tape. Her self-titled debut was released in 1984, and the follow-up *From My Heart* appeared the following year; none of the singles from either record managed to breach the Top 20. However, Mattea's third effort, 1986's folky *Walk the Way the Wind Blows*, proved to be her breakthrough both critically and commercially. Her cover of Nanci Griffith's "Love at the Five and Dime" was her first Top Five hit, and the record produced three other Top Tens in the title track, "Train of Memories," and "You're the Power."

Her 1987 follow-up album *Untasted Honey* confirmed Mattea's newfound stardom, featuring two number-one country hits in "Goin' Gone" and "Eighteen Wheels and a Dozen Roses"; "Untold Stories" and "Life as We Knew It" also made the Top Five. 1989's *Willow in the Wind* boasted an even stronger folk influence, and it became her first album to go gold on the strength of the number-one hits "Burnin' Old Memories" and "Come From the Heart," and the number two "She Came From Fort Worth." Additionally, the album's Top Ten hit "Where've You Been," which Mattea co-wrote with her new husband Jon Vezner, won her a Grammy for Best Female Country Vocal. Seeking to keep her music fresh by returning to its roots, Mattea made several trips to Scotland in the early '90s, studying the links between country music and traditional Scottish folk. Her own music kept getting rootsier and more eclectic, as 1991's ambitious *Time Passes By* featured guest spots by Emmylou Harris, folkies the Roches, and Scottish singer/songwriter Dougie MacLean. The album's title track and "A Few Good Things Remain" both hit the Top Ten, but overall the album's singles didn't chart as well as was usual.

She subsequently had throat surgery, but recovered fully to record 1992's *Lonesome Standard Time*, a less ambitious but still eclectic album whose title track was a near-Top Ten hit. Mattea backed off her critically acclaimed recent sound for 1993's more commercial *Walking Away a Winner*, whose title track became yet another Top Five hit; however, the same year, she also issued the gospel-oriented Christmas record *Good News*, which won a Grammy for Best Southern/Country/Bluegrass Gospel Album. After a several-year hiatus, Mattea returned in 1997 with *Love Travels*, which balanced her folk and mainstream country leanings; it sold decently well, but failed to produce any major singles. Mattea subsequently moved to MCA for 2000's ballad-heavy *The Innocent Years*, a heartfelt tribute to her ailing father. Wanting to explore her taste for Celtic folk, Mattea hopped labels to Narada, for whom she debuted in 2002 with the eclectic *Roses*. *—Steve Huey*

Kathy Mattea / 1984 / Mercury ✦✦

From My Heart / 1985 / Mercury ✦✦✦

Walk the Way the Wind Blows / 1986 / Mercury ✦✦✦

Oh yeah, 1986, when Kathy Mattea was still a country singer, she was one of them, the "new traditionalists" at that point in time, before she became such an awesome pop singer. *Walk the Way the Wind Blows* is the rootsiest (in the American sense of the word) album Mattea had recorded up to that time. With a cast of players that included progressive bluegrass upstart Béla Fleck, country legend Don Williams, Wendy Waldman, Buddy Spicher, up and comer Vince Gill, bass king Bob Wray, and a slew of others, Mattea took honky tonk songs, shimmied them up against bluegrass energy and funky horns ("Train of Memories"), and came up with something entirely different. And while it's erratic in places, *Walk the Way the Wind Blows* is a fine outing overall. It's on the funky, rocked-up or old-timey down swing jazzers like "Evenin'" where the disc works the best. Her ballad singing hadn't gotten to the place it did just three years later; on "Reason to Live" it falls a tad flat, and the stirring conviction of her later singing is not yet in place here. The one exception is her cover of Nanci Griffith's "Love at the Five and Dime." Its pacing and restraint—courtesy of expert production by Allen Reynolds and Don Williams' harmony vocal—make the song a mind movie. Mattea's vocal tells the story as if she is looking back on her own life instead of being a reportorial account of fictional characters. The refrain with Williams is chillingly beautiful, as if, now old and gray, they are singing to one another in the moonlight. The stellar dobro and Cajun accordion carry the lyric into the stratosphere on "Back Up Grinnin' Again." Mattea found a formula; restless as she is, changing direction and producers so often, she didn't stick with it long. Nonetheless, *Walk the Way the Wind Blows* is one of her better efforts. *—Thom Jurek*

Untasted Honey / Sep. 28, 1987 / Mercury ✦✦✦

In many ways, Kathy Mattea's *Untasted Honey* is about as close as she's ever come to recording a bluegrass album. Of course, it's not bluegrass; it's more like Nash Vegas grass. The appearance of players and singers like Tim O'Brien, David Schnaufer, Ray Flynn, Ray Flacke, and a host of others suggests Mattea is sticking close to the roots formula. Her reliance on songs by O'Brien, Fred Koller, Don Henry, and Pat Alger also directs the mix in a certain direction. With producer Allen Reynolds and backing vocals by O'Brien, Beth Nielsen Chapman, and John Thompson, this set is consistently fine. All of the songs seem to segue into one another, creating a tapestry, or a series of snapshots placed together in an album. "Untold Stories," a flashy stomp & roller with the influence of Bill Monroe haunting the background, is a hell of an opener—especially with the mandolin and guitar solos. The Nelson Brothers' "Eighteen Wheels and a Dozen Roses" is a song Rodney Crowell wishes he would have written, and as storyteller here, Mattea is so deep inside the story it's difficult to tell if she's recording a story or giving the listener a recounting of something that happened to her. "Late in the Day" is another O'Brien winner, full of rambling pedal steel and entwined acoustic guitars. Other standouts include the title track, with a virtual choir of backing vocalists and the punch of Bob Ray's voice. This is the most '80s neo-trad country track on the set, and it works. The funky country blues of Pat Alger and Mark D. Sanders' "Like a Hurricane" has that high lonesome ring to it, and Mattea's voice—which is so large you can hear it echo within itself—was created to sing a tune like this. In all, this is solid for such a young effort; the selection of tunes, particularly near the end of the record, falls apart, but there's plenty here to engage even the most casual of listeners. *—Thom Jurek*

Willow in the Wind / 1989 / Mercury ✦✦✦✦✦

The year 1989 was awesome for Kathy Mattea. Her brand of country-pop music began to evolve toward folk and Celtic-oriented influences, which were actually encouraged by her label—changes like this in Nash Vegas are few and far between—and what's more, it all translated in terms of chart success and record sales. A strong and indeed the first completely realized project of her career, *Willow in the Wind* boasted three hits, "Burnin' Old Memories," "Where've You Been," and "Come From the Heart." The hard honky tonk/West Texas swing of "Burnin' Old Memories," with its slightly rocked-uptempo, is more than just catchy; it's infectious. "Hills of Alabam'" is one of those gorgeous songs where the weary traveler—with a lonesome harmonica in the background—romanticizes home as contrasted with the harsh questions of the present and the uncertain future. Mattea's phrasing is impeccable in that she becomes an itinerant musician riding endless hours on some forsaken urban freeway in the predawn light. But the true stunner on *Willow in the Wind* is, of course, a love song. Written by Zen bluegrass queen Laurie Lewis, it's the most springlike testament to new love and is free of sentimentality or emotional manipulation, and Mattea's voice is perfect for its utterance. Slippery acoustic guitars, a piano, and a strolling bass anchored by a small drum kit are what frame the verses, with a shimmering pedal steel on the refrains. It's simply orchestrated, with an old-timey feel, and when Mattea takes the last verse she lays all cheesy, false, and clichéd love songs to waste: "Love cuts like a torch to a heart behind steel/And though you may hide it, love knows how you feel/And though you may trespass on the laws of the land/Your heart has to follow when love takes your hand/And it seems we're two people/Within the same circle/It's drawn tighter and tighter/'Till you're all I can see/I'm full and I'm empty and you're pouring through me/Like the warm rain fallin' through the leaves on a tree/Tell me now if I'm wrong are you feeling the same/Are your feet on the ground/Are you callin' my name/Do you lie awake nights/Please say you do/You can't choose who you love/Love chooses you." The record closes two tracks later, but it hardly matters—the case has been made. *—Thom Jurek*

- **A Collection of Hits** / 1990 / Mercury ✦✦✦✦✦

Kathy Mattea has risen to near the top of the Nashville ranks because of a haunting, soulful voice, well-produced recordings that have a simple, folkie directness, and, most especially, an amazing talent for picking the best songs being written for the country market, among them "Eighteen Wheels and a Dozen Roses," "Goin' Gone," and the heartbreaking "Where've You Been." *—William Ruhlmann*

Time Passes By / 1991 / Mercury ✦✦✦✦

On her most ambitious album, Mattea gets impeccably chosen songs (as usual) and strong supporting performances (from Emmylou Harris, Dougie MacLean, and the Roches). She doesn't write her own stuff, so she may not be the romantic dreamer of "Asking Us to Dance," but she sure sounds like it. Songs like "Time Passes By," co-written by husband Jon Vezner, suggest there's more honesty here than image. She can even make the half-baked "From a Distance" convincing. *—Brian Mansfield*

Lonesome Standard Time / 1992 / Mercury ✦✦✦✦✦

Mattea had vocal-cord surgery that threatened to end her career before she made *Lonesome Standard Time*, but you couldn't prove it by listening: her voice hasn't lost a bit of its deep alto warmth. *Lonesome Standard Time* isn't as ambitious as *Time Passes By*, but it's filled with lovely performances from Mattea's favorite sources: bluegrass ("Lonesome Standard Time"), gospel-influenced country ("Standing Knee Deep in a River (Dying of Thirst)") and Nanci Griffith ("Listen to the Radio"). *—Brian Mansfield*

Good News / 1993 / Mercury ✦✦✦✦

Kathy Mattea's album for the Christmas season is unlike any country Christmas record ever released. For starters, she and producer Brent Maher commissioned original songs rather than taking them from the canon, or adapted obscure songs from the ages. Secondly, the band was formed around what served each song to make it feel as organic as possible. Strange instruments appear, such as the marimbas on "New Kid in Town," recorders and a high string guitar and recorders on "Christ Child Lullaby" (courtesy of Dougie MacLean and Jim Horn), and a full choir on the closing title track. This doesn't feel like any Christmas record you've ever heard before, either. It sounds like a well-crafted, gorgeously wrought folk/country/Celtic-flavored Kathy Mattea record. Give a listen to any of the above, or especially the haunted traditional song "Brightest and Best," completely reworked by Mattea and Maher. The guitars caress the open space between themselves and Mattea's voice, as the pipes and recorders float within. Likewise, listen to

"Mary Did You Know," which is one of the most stunningly beautiful Christian folk songs written in decades (by Mark Lowry and Buddy Greene). But then, while songs can be many things, they cannot be given life without a singer, and on *Good News*, in Mattea's instrument, the grains of truth add up to something incalculable: high art. — *Thom Jurek*

Walking Away a Winner / Oct. 1993 / Mercury ✦✦✦✦
Walking Away a Winner is the rocked-up/pop side of Kathy Mattea. With records by Mary-Chapin Carpenter gathering steam as well as those of Beth Nielsen Chapman, Lucinda Williams getting some notice, and Bonnie Raitt riding the very top of the charts over the previous two years, Mattea took a listen and apparently liked what she heard. There are layers and layers of guitars on the album, and nowhere are they borne out more than on the title track that opens the album. With producer Josh Leo and a deck of tough songs, Mattea showed a side her country audience hadn't yet seen, and one that the adult contemporary and emerging AAA formats could embrace. In other words, the album, with its tightly knit group of astonishingly well-written pop songs done in a slight country manner by a crack group of players, was a winning formula. It's a record that stands the test of time. What makes Mattea such a great singer—besides her gift of a voice—is her empathy. She finds herself in every song she records. On tape, there is no separation between her and her characters, whether it's the woman finally walking away from a dead relationship and seeing herself not as beaten but as free in the title track, the rambling woman relentlessly seeking that lost love no matter where the search takes her in the rollicking "Streets of Your Town," or the overworked, underappreciated wife and mother who breaks down in "Maybe She's Human." From "Clown in Your Rodeo," with its ringing electric 12-strings and hard-swinging refrain, through the final track, the haunting jazzy ballad "Who's Gonna Know," conviction and commitment are fully on display, along with an elegance that is both accessible and sophisticated. This is a winner indeed. — *Thom Jurek*

Love Travels / Feb. 4, 1997 / Mercury ✦✦✦
Though the glossy production may put off some of her old country-folk fans, *Love Travels* is a typically tasteful and compelling record from Kathy Mattea. While it is more uneven *Walking Away a Winner*, most of the record is first-rate, finding the perfect middleground between country-folk and mainstream contemporary country. — *Thom Owens*

The Innocent Years / May 16, 2000 / MCA ✦✦✦
A brisk song with tempo and lyrical substance, "Trouble With Angels" is one of only two songs on this 11th studio release from Mattea that isn't a ballad. Written and recorded during a time when she was facing the declining health of her father, much of the music on *The Innocent Years* is about the tender mercies of life: love, family relationships, faith in God, perseverance, commitment, and growing old. Most notably poignant is "That's the Deal," a tribute to her father and the health struggles he's recently faced. The album gets high marks for vocal collaborations with the likes of Suzy Bogguss, Alison Krauss, and pop singer Graham Nash. And the album's bonus track, "BFD," a crowd favorite in her live shows, ends the album on a playful note. — *Maria Konicki Dinoia*

Roses / Jul. 30, 2002 / Narada ✦✦✦
Kathy Mattea has always teetered on the Nashville edge with her music. On *Roses*, her 13th studio album, she pushes the envelope, bringing to the forefront the blending of the Scottish/Irish music found in small doses on her last few albums. "That's All the Lumber You Sent," the first track, screams Celtic, as does the instrumental "Isle of Inishmore." But whatever the musical style, brooding and contemplative lyrics accompany all of the tracks. Mattea's warm alto voice comes across opulently in "The Slender Threads That Bind Us Here" and the Kim Richey remake "I'm Alright." This album isn't the country music of the former Grammy-winner and CMA vocalist of the year, but it wins high marks for creative expression and originality. — *Maria Konicki Dinoia*

Matthews, Wright & King

f. 1991, db. 1994
Group / Country-Rock, Contemporary Country
Matthews, Wright & King were a studio assembly masterminded by Columbia Nashville producer Larry Strickland. At the time (the early '90s) Shenandoah had drowned under a wave of bad publicity, lawsuits, and label woes. It was Columbia's idea to step into the breach left by Shenandoah's departure. To that end, Strickland and the label rounded up vocalist/guitarist Raymond Matthews (who was already contracted with Columbia to do a solo album), bassist/vocalist Woody Wright, and guitarist/vocalist Tony King. *The Power of Love* appeared in December 1991; while the title cut made the Top 50, "Mothers Eyes" and "House Huntin'" weren't nearly as successful. *Dream Seekers* followed in 1993, but was met with even less enthusiasm, and soon after the trio dissolved. Tony King joined Brooks & Dunn's backing band in 1995; Woody Wright founded an inspirational country/gospel trio with Michael Sykes and David Ponder; and Raymond Matthews embarked on a solo career. (Incidentally, Shenandoah reunited on a different label and continued to release music throughout the 1990s.) — *Johnny Loftus*

● **Power of Love** / Dec. 1991 / Columbia ✦✦✦✦
The debut from this country-rock trio contains the hits "Mothers Eyes" and "House Huntin'." — *Jason Ankeny*

Dream Seekers / 1993 / Columbia ✦✦✦

The Mavericks

f. 1990
Group / Contemporary Country, Neo-Traditionalist Country, Americana
Fusing traditional country with traditional rock & roll, the Mavericks became one of the most critically acclaimed and commercially successful groups of the early '90s. Led by singer/songwriter Raul Malo (born August 7, 1965, Miami, FL), the band was formed in Florida in the late '80s. Malo had previously played in several different bands while he

was in high-school, as did bassist Robert Reynolds (born Robert Earl Reynolds, April 30, 1962, Kansas City, MO). The pair met at school and discovered they had similar musical tastes—they both enjoyed the music of Roy Orbison, Patsy Cline, Elvis Presley, Hank Williams, and Johnny Cash—and decided to form a band. Reynolds persuaded his best friend, Paul Deakin (born Paul Wylie Deakin, September 2, 1959, Miami, FL)—who had been a drummer in progressive rock bands before and had done some session work—to join the fledgling country band.

Taking the name the Mavericks, the band began playing rock clubs around the Miami area and built up a solid local following. The group chose to play rock clubs because the country bars only wanted to book bands that played covers and the Mavericks preferred to concentrate on original material. In the fall of 1990, the band released an eponymous independent album. The record worked its way onto play lists across Florida and made its way to Nashville, where it gained the attention of nearly every major record label. In May of 1991, the group went to Nashville to play a showcase gig. Scouts from all of the town's major labels were in attendance, but the band decided to sign with MCA Records. Later that year, the Mavericks set about recording their first major-label album; before the sessions began, they added lead guitarist David Lee Holt, who had previously played with Joe Ely, Rosie Flores, and Carlene Carter. Titled *From Hell to Paradise*, the record primarily consisted of Malo's original songs and was released in 1992. Although it was critically acclaimed, the album wasn't a commercial success; only a cover of Hank Williams' standard "Hey Good Lookin'" made the charts and that peaked at number 74.

The Mavericks' commercial fortunes turned around with their second major-label album, *What a Crying Shame*. Produced by Don Cook (Brooks & Dunn, Mark Collie), the album was more streamlined and focused. It became a hit upon its release early in 1994, with the title track becoming a Top 40 hit. Shortly after the release of *What a Crying Shame*, the group replaced Holt with Nick Kane (born Nicholas James Kane, August 21, 1954, Jerusalem, GA). Throughout 1994, the band racked up Top 40 hit singles. "O What a Thrill" went to number 18 in the summer, with "There Goes My Heart" reaching number 20 in the fall. By the spring of 1995, *What a Crying Shame* had gone platinum. During the first half of 1995, the Mavericks recorded their fourth album, *Music for All Occasions*, which appeared in the fall of the year. Like its predecessor, it was critically acclaimed and a commercial success. By the spring of 1996, the album had gone gold. *Trampoline* followed in 1998. — *Stephen Thomas Erlewine*

Mavericks / 1990 / Hip-O ✦✦✦
The Mavericks' debut album was a pale shadow of the music they'd be putting on plastic a few years later, but it's strong enough to make clear this was a significantly more interesting band than one would expect to hear on the country charts in 1990. Vocalist (and principle songwriter) Raul Malo was still learning how to control his spacious, Orbisonesque tenor, but anyone with ears could tell the man already had a great voice, and if the group would become more adventurous with time, this material sounds tight, enthusiastic, and pretty ambitious for a band aiming toward the mainstream recording market (and cutting the sessions on their own dime). It's significant that four of the best songs from this album would be re-recorded for the Mavericks' major-label debut in 1992, and that by that time guitarist Ben Peeler (whose style is solid but more than a bit rote) would be out of the picture, but *The Mavericks* is hardly an embarrassing place for a band this good to start their recording career; it's a stylish and enthusiastic album from a band who would get much better with time. — *Mark Deming*

From Hell to Paradise / 1992 / MCA ✦✦✦✦
The Mavericks made their major-label debut with their second album, 1992's *From Hell to Paradise*, and while co-producer Steve Fishell added a lot more gloss than the band could summon up on their first independently released disc (not all of which works in their favor), overall this set sounds noticeably stronger and more sure-footed than the Mavericks did their first time at bat. The slicker sound certainly makes the most of Paul Deakin's sharp drumming and Robert Reynolds' rock-solid bass, and vocalist Raul Malo gained plenty of control and confidence this time out, with his clear, flexible tenor shining bright on every track, especially the plaintive "This Broken Heart" and the dramatic title song. Between the Farfisa-flavored pop of "I Got You," the rockabilly-accented locomotive charge of "End of the Line," and the Latin accents of "From Hell to Paradise," the broad stylistic range of the group's best work was beginning to make itself felt, as well as intelligent and challenging lyrical themes which set them apart from the average bunch of Nashville cats (significantly, *From Hell to Paradise* was recorded in that noted country music Mecca of Miami, FL). A few tunes are a bit more formulaic than one might hope for, and while the Hank Williams and Buck Owens covers are fun (and show good taste), they aren't especially enlightening. But there's enough good stuff on *From Hell to Paradise* to confirm the musical promise of the Mavericks' first album, and pave the way for their breakthrough with *What a Crying Shame*. — *Mark Deming*

★ **What a Crying Shame** / 1994 / MCA ✦✦✦✦✦
The Mavericks fully hit their stride with their third album, 1994's *What a Crying Shame*, in which the band's blend of rootsy country and vintage pop sounds finally found the balance they'd been searching for. While producer Don Cook gave the band a significantly glossier sound than that of their first two albums, with a hefty number of guest musicians (and guest songwriters) on board, remarkably enough the Mavericks' personality wasn't subsumed in the process; if anything, the high-priced help seemed to have prodded the boys into playing at the top of their game. Raul Malo's keening tenor gets a superb workout on "I Should Have Been True" and the title cut (the latter of which boasts a guitar hook Roger McGuinn would have been proud to come up with), while "Pretend" and "There Goes My Heart" are honky tonk floor-fillers of the first order. Robert Reynolds and Paul Deakin are a rhythm section who can give these songs the nervy drive of a rock band without betraying the Mavericks' country leanings, and they give the covers of "All That Heaven Will Allow" and "O What a Thrill" a taut foundation most contemporary Nashville acts lack. Truth to tell, *What a Crying Shame* doesn't have a single dud track, and offers encouraging proof that it's still possible to make an engaging and idiosyncratic

country album while signed to the Nashville division of a major label… and the best news is, the band managed to turn that accomplishment into a hat trick over the next few years. *—Mark Deming*

Music for All Occasions / Oct. 1995 / MCA ✦✦✦
With their third album, The Mavericks added slick country-pop to their arsenal of retro-country styles. The result straddles the line between affection and camp, since the band never goes completely overboard by drenching their songs with strings, and Raul Malo retains his aching Orbison-esque voice. However, that doesn't mean their songwriting has slipped, as all 11 originals are first-rate updated honky tonk ravers or countrypolitan numbers. And the closing cover of "Somethin' Stupid," recorded with Trisha Yearwood, is a fun, kitschy delight. *—Stephen Thomas Erlewine*

Trampoline / Mar. 10, 1998 / MCA ✦✦✦✦✦
As their career progresses, the Mavericks are becoming more of a showcase for vocalist/frontman Raul Malo, both for better and for worse. They may be losing their band identity, but that may have been inevitable, considering that Malo is such a gifted, powerful musician. He is the driving force behind all of the group's stylistic fusions, their blend of honky tonk with country-rock, classic rock & roll, pop, and Latin. On *Music for All Occasions*, the stylistic blends sounded a little gimmicky, but the band sounds revitalized on *Trampoline*—even the vaudevillian "Dolores" rings as true as the shuffling, cha-cha "I Should Know." If anything, the album is the least "country" album the Mavericks have ever done, but that's primarily because all of their influences have blended seamlessly together, creating an original, altogether intoxicating sound. Furthermore, they're not simply surface—Malo's songs are clever constructions, ranking among the most imaginative roots songwriting of the '90s. His writing, combined with his band's musical panache, makes *Trampoline* a ride worth taking. *—Thom Owens*

It's Now! It's Live! / May 26, 1998 / MCA International ✦✦✦✦
The guys who make up the country group the Mavericks began their professional music career performing together at rock clubs in Florida. Now you might think that's a long ride from Nashville, but they found their way easy enough. Once they did, they didn't leave everything they learned in those rock clubs behind though, and listeners won't miss the rock & roll flavor that the Mavericks stir into a number of the songs on this 1998 album, *It's Now! It's Live!* As the title foretells, this is a live album. It was made during a couple of shows the group did in Canada. This is great country-rock music done the way the Mavericks do it best, but the album is a little short with only seven tracks. The songs are fan favorites though, like "There Goes My Heart," "Tonight the Bottle Let Me Down," and "I Don't Care if You Love Me Anymore." *—Charlotte Dillon*

The Super Colossal Smash Hits of the 90's: The Best of the Mavericks / Jan. 25, 2000 / Mercury ✦✦✦✦
The Mavericks were one of the most acclaimed country bands of the '90s and, for a brief moment, were among the most popular. With their third album, *What a Crying Shame*, they were at the zenith of their creative powers and were rewarded with great reviews and sales. They maintained a high level of creativity with its two follow-ups, 1995's *Music for All Occasions* and 1998's *Trampoline*, but their audience shrank somewhat, turning into a cult following much like Lyle Lovett's—they were popular, going gold with their new albums, but they didn't have crossover hits. That was a crying shame, because as the 1999 singles collection *Super Colossal Smash Hits of the 90's: The Best of the Mavericks* proves, they kept a high level of quality. That doesn't mean that *Super Colossal* is a perfect collection, however. Like most '90s hits compilations, it's baited with unreleased material. Usually, that means there's just one or two new cuts. This time, there are no less than four new tracks, which means there are only eight hits on the record. The new material—including covers of "Here Comes My Baby" and "Think of Me (When You're Lonely)"—isn't bad, and the Tex-Mex-flavored "Pizziricco" in particular is pretty good, but the fact that a quarter of the album is devoted to new material means that there's a lot of good stuff missing here. Still, it's a good roundup of the best of the best, and a nice reminder to casual fans that haven't paid attention since *What a Crying Shame* that the Mavericks have a lot more to offer. *—Stephen Thomas Erlewine*

O What a Thrill: An Introduction to the Mavericks / May 22, 2001 / MCA ✦✦✦✦
O What a Thrill: An Introduction to the Mavericks conspicuously avoids the phrase "greatest hits" in its title, and for a good reason: This collection appears to consciously avoid most of the group's best-known songs, instead focusing on some of the lesser-known gems in the group's catalog. Featuring material from all the group's first six albums, *O What a Thrill* does an admirable job of capturing the eclectic spirit of the Mavericks, ranging from the honky tonk stomp of "Hey Good Lookin'," the jazzy countrypolitan mood of "Foolish Heart," the country-rock shuffle of "All That Heaven Will Allow," and the pure pop melody of "I Don't Even Know Your Name." On this set, the Mavericks cover a lot of bases and cover their territory admirably well, with Raul Malo's superb vocals at the forefront throughout and his partners Paul Deakin, Robert Reynolds, and Nick Kane offering first-class support. Given the Mavericks' eclectic approach and the distinct personalities of their studio albums, *O What a Thrill* takes on a hefty challenge by attempting to represent the group's multifaceted body of work, but it achieves its goal with admirable success, and its a fine calling card for the group's excellent back catalog. *—Mark Deming*

20th Century Masters—The Millennium Collection: The Best of the Mavericks / Aug. 28, 2001 / MCA ✦✦✦
One of the more current groups to have a *20th Century Masters—The Millennium Collection* the Mavericks' volume in the best-of series isn't quite as comprehensive as their best retrospective, *Best of the Mavericks*. However, this collection does provide an ample amount of their definitive tracks, including "What a Crying Shame," "There Goes My Heart," and "Dance the Night Away." While *Best of the Mavericks* might still be the preferable best-of, *The Millennium Collection: The Best of the Mavericks* does a better-than-average job of collecting their most popular singles. *—Heather Phares*

Buddy Max (Boris Max Pastuch)

b. 1929

Vocals, Guitar / Honky Tonk, Traditional Country, Country Comedy

In a genre full of colorful characters, Buddy Max is certainly not the most famous, but might be the most weird. Collectors of oddball, self-produced recordings have held a long-time devotion to Max's song "The Birthmark Story," which, at nearly eight minutes, is longer than "McArthur Park" and has much better lyrics, namely a blow-by-blow description of a GI having a birthmark removed by a bloodthirsty Korean surgeon. Dwelling on this song would give a false impression of what Max is all about, however. Born Boris Max Pastuch, he is very much a sentimental country artist from the old-school, whose early influences were cowboy singers such as Gene Autry and Johnny Bond. According to his online biography, Max made his first recording in 1949 on Broadway and 42nd Street in New York City, evidence that he has been a do-it-yourself artist from the start, as this could very well be a reference to the booth that used to stand in this location where one could cut an instant record for a quarter.

A few years later, Max was playing with the Kingwood Township Plowboy Band in Hollywood, CA, and he cut a second record in 1955 in Tampa, FL, although perhaps not in a 25-cent recording booth. Eventually, he settled in Florida, where his wife-to-be, Freda, heard him singing on a radio station in Tampa. The great part of Max's career and recorded output centered around his home base of Lecanto, FL, where he bought his own flea market in 1957 and reigned as America's Singing Flea Market Cowboy. He performed at the flea market and printed a series of albums and CDs, some of which contain songs about flea markets and the public who shops at them. He has also performed out of state at events such as the Northwoods Bluegrass and Country Festival in White Cloud, MI; he performed country music on roller skates. Max's son, Johnny Pastuch, was a journalist, musician, and actor and was closely involved with his father, playing bass in his bands. In 1996, Johnny Pastuch was murdered in his sleep at his home in Pike County, AL. A group calling themselves Friends of John Pastuch started a website offering a 250,000 dollar reward for information about this murder. *—Eugene Chadbourne*

• **Many Styles and Sounds** / 1980 / Cowboy Junction ✦✦✦
This particular album by Buddy Max gets the "pick" designation because it includes his most famous song, "The Birthmark Story." In this long narrative, a GI writes home to tell his mother all about how he has had that "dreaded birthmark" removed by a bloodthirsty Korean surgeon. The lyrics will cause most listeners' hair to stand on end, despite the polite waltz background. This song may have spread far and wide—anarchistic rocker Jad Fair even recorded an as yet unreleased cover version—but its author has chosen to stay pretty much put, singing and hawking his self-published records out of a flea market he owns in Lecanto, FL. It would take a total cad to question this artist's sincerity, which he has in spades. The material itself is sometimes squashed by a sentimentality that overwhelms the often plodding accompaniment, yet this pathos is real and not a contrivance of some Nashville songwriting scheme. In fact, one could argue that the work of artists such as Max is really a true representation of what country music is supposed to be all about—the music of ordinary working people. This series of vinyl productions shares a production design that is richly entertaining: a color photo of Max on the front and a series of black-and-white shots on the back accompanied by crudely written text, which makes almost random use of punctuation. The shot of Max performing as the first Biblical man in a local Adam and Eve pageant is worth the price of the LP, especially if one finds it at a flea market. *—Eugene Chadbourne*

The Great Nashville Star Is a Flea Market Cowboy / 1984 / Cowboy Junction ✦✦✦
This is one of flea market owner and country singer Buddy Max' self-produced vinyl outings from the '80s. It is kind of a concept album focusing on the goings-on at his flea market in Lecanto, FL. The first side is all Max performances, while the flip features two more Max numbers and four songs by other performers who work at the flea market. "Dedicated to the Flea Market People," the opening of the liner notes, would have been a more appropriate album title. Describing Max as a "Great Nashville Star" is about as accurate as saying he was the first man to walk on the moon; he has never recorded in Nashville and the type of country music represented here is about as far from the slick, contrived Nashville milieu as a concert by Funkadelic. The performances are all rock-solid in their own way; these are regular people playing music, and although the shortcomings are obvious there is nothing phony about it—and that in itself is a quality not always so easy to come by. The lines of text pasted up around the selections of photos are wonderful, not only describing the day jobs of all these players, but even providing their phone numbers. If only Garth Brooks could make a record like this. *—Eugene Chadbourne*

Mac McAnally

b. Jul. 1, 1959, Red Bay, AL

Guitar, Vocals, Producer / Country-Pop, Singer/Songwriter, Country-Folk

A prolific Nashville singer/songwriter who authored hits for Jimmy Buffett, Alabama, and Steve Wariner, Mac McAnally was born July 15, 1957, in Red Bay, AL. Singing in church throughout childhood, at age eight he began taking piano lessons and within five years was performing professionally; McAnally later took up guitar and at 15 composed his first song, "People Call Me Jesus." After quitting high-school he went to work as a session player at Muscle Shoals' Wishbone Studios; one night, during a break in a Hank Williams Jr. date, McAnally began playing some of his own original material, so impressing producers Terry Woodford and Clayton Ivey that they convinced Williams to record the tune "I Need You Tonight." Signing to Ariola, in 1977 McAnally issued his self-titled debut album, scoring a crossover hit with the single "It's a Crazy World" and touring in support of Randy Newman.

Acclaimed for the richly literary appeal of his songcraft, McAnally returned in 1978 with *No Problem Here*, followed two years later by *Cuttin' Corners*; neither sold as well as his debut, but he remained one of Nashville's most sought-after writers, penning material for Buffett ("It's My Job") and Alabama (the chart-topping "Old Flame"). In the wake of 1983's *Nothin' But the Truth*, McAnally did not release another new LP until *Finish Lines* five years later, in the interim penning hits for Buffett ("When the Coast Is Clear") and Ricky Van Shelton ("Crime of Passion"); with 1990's *Simple Life*, he returned to the charts with "Back Where I Come From," and a year later authored the Wariner smash "It's a Precious Thing." After 1992's *Live and Learn* (which generated the minor hits "The Trouble With Diamonds" and "Junk Cars"), McAnally resurfaced two years later with *Knots*, remaining silent until releasing *Word of Mouth* in mid-1999. *—Jason Ankeny*

Mac McAnally / 1977 / Ariola ✦✦✦✦✦
McAnally's debut revealed uncommon wisdom and spiritual reflection for such a young singer/songwriter. It features the favorite, "It's a Crazy World." *—Michael McCall*

Finish Lines / 1980 / Geffen ✦✦✦

Nothin' But the Truth / 1983 / Geffen ✦✦✦

Simple Life / Feb. 13, 1990 / Warner Bros. ✦✦✦
McAnally has an ability to inject exceptional compassion into mannered, country-pop songs. The album features well-crafted lyrics, fastidious acoustic-pop arrangements and his unremarkable voice. *—Michael McCall*

● **Live and Learn** / 1992 / MCA ✦✦✦✦✦
Writing songs packed with gentle emotions and hard-earned life lessons seems to come easy for McAnally. However, hits don't—at least not when he's singing. *—Michael McCall*

Knots / Sep. 27, 1994 / MCA ✦✦✦

No Problem Here / 1999 / Ariola ✦✦✦

Word of Mouth / Jun. 1, 1999 / DreamWorks ✦✦✦
Mac McAnally's *Word of Mouth* features the singer/songwriter/producer/arranger's multiple talents in effect. Songs like "The Ass & the Hole," "Cold Day in Hell," and "Better Than the Good Old Days" reflect McAnally's dry wit, which has endeared him to Nashville's best and brightest. *—Heather Phares*

Leon McAuliffe (William Leon McAuliffe)

b. Mar. 1, 1917, Houston, TX, **d.** Sep. 20, 1988, Tulsa, OK
Guitar (Steel) / Traditional Country, Western Swing
Steel guitarist Leon McAuliffe made his name as a member of Bob Wills' Texas Playboys, ranking as one of the best of his era on his chosen instrument. Born William Leon McAuliffe in Houston in 1917, he started playing both acoustic and steel guitar at 14, and quickly joined the Waikiki Strummers, a Hawaiian-style group, on the latter instrument in 1931. In 1933, he joined the early Western swing band the Light Crust Doughboys, and found a major influence in Milton Brown's steel guitarist Bob Dunn, who taught him how to electrically amplify his instrument. In 1935, he moved on to the Texas Playboys, who would soon become the premier Western swing band in existence. One of their earliest recordings was "Steel Guitar Rag," an instrumental showcase that McAuliffe had adapted from bluesman Sylvester Weaver's "Guitar Rag." The record helped make McAuliffe a star and a standard-setter on his instrument, and Wills' directive of "Take it away, Leon!" became something of a musical catch phrase. McAuliffe remained with the Texas Playboys until being called to serve in World War II in late 1942, during which time he worked as a flight instructor.

After the war, McAuliffe decided to form his own big band, which he dubbed the Cimarron Boys. The group played regularly on a Tulsa radio station and soon signed a contract with Columbia, and McAuliffe's instrumental showcase "Panhandle Rag" became a Top Ten hit in 1949. Over the course of the '50s, McAuliffe's band mixed down-home Western tunes with smooth big band jazz, which sometimes brought him fairly close to mainstream swing territory. He recorded for a variety of labels during the '60s, including Dot, Capitol, and Starday, but by this time Western swing was a phenomenon of the past, and he performed mostly on a local basis; he later purchased a radio station in Rogers, AR. He played on a reunion recording with Wills in 1973, and led occasional Texas Playboys reunions following Wills' death a short time later. McAuliffe himself passed away in 1988. *—Steve Huey*

● **Columbia Historic Edition** / 1984 / Columbia ✦✦✦✦✦
Leon McAuliffe came to prominence as a member of Bob Wills' Texas Playboys. He had to leave the group to serve in World War II and after he returned from the army, he chose to form his own band. After recording a couple of tracks for Majestic Records, McAuliffe signed to Columbia Records, who were looking for a Western swing star to replace Wills. *Columbia Historic Edition* collects the highlights from McAuliffe's time at Columbia, including the Top Ten hit "Panhandle Rag" and "The Steel Guitar Polka." The compilation is a good testament to McAuliffe's prodigious instrumental skill and features some of his best playing. It may be a little brief, but it nevertheless borders on a definitive overview of his Columbia recordings. *—Thom Owens*

Take It Away the Leon Way! / Aug. 14, 2001 / Jasmine ✦✦✦✦
This compilation contains McAuliffe's finest records of the 1950s. His solo work lacked originality, true, but the Cimarron Boys were an excellent band who played tight and sparkly, with excellent engineering at the sessions. McAuliffe played down-home hillbilly stompers like "Boil 'Em Cabbage Down," but his other specialty was smooth big band jazz, and it can be argued that McAuliffe came closer to that realm of popular music than any other Western swing band. This disc has some of both, and plenty in between. It also happens to be the only available collection of McAuliffe's solo work on compact disc. *—Jim Smith*

McBride & the Ride

f. 1989
Group / Country-Rock, Contemporary Country
In the tradition of Alabama came McBride & the Ride, a country trio noted for their close harmonies and contemporary honky-tonk sounds. The group was the creation of Tony Brown, MCA Nashville's Executive Vice President, who introduced songwriter Terry McBride to session players Ray Herndon and Billy Thomas. The three clicked, and their harmonies blended perfectly. McBride, the son of vocalist Dale McBride, was born and raised in Texas. He played guitar since childhood and had a longtime interest in traditional and Texas music. Following high-school, he auditioned to join his father's band and worked with him for three years before joining Delbert McClinton and touring with John Fogerty. He then moved to Nashville to work on his songwriting.

Herndon and his siblings started out as child stars on the Phoenix-based TV show *Lew King Rangers*, where the three-year-old played accordion, guitar, sang and tap-danced. At age four, Herndon cut the novelty single "Christmas Eve." Later he teamed with Lyle Lovett, singing a duet on his debut album and joining Lovett's Large Band. Like the others, drummer Billy Thomas began playing as a child. He started out in rock & roll and in 1973 moved to L.A. to work with Rick Nelson, Mac Davis, and the Hudson Brothers. Two years later, he was doing session work in Nashville, and worked with numerous stars including Emmylou Harris, Vince Gill, Dan Seals, and Jann Brown. McBride & the Ride debuted in Detroit and soon launched an extensive cross-country tour. Their debut album, 1991's *Burnin' Up the Road*, featured nine songs written or co-written by McBride, and won them a gig as the Judds' opening act. By the end of the year viewers discovered the video of their single "Can I Count on You," which saved the group from losing their contract with MCA as the single soon made the Top 15. Their next single, "Same Old Star," made it to the Top 30. In 1992, the Ride scored their first Top Five hit with the title cut from their album *Sacred Ground*, which also produced two more Top Ten hits.

Their 1993 album *Hurry Sundown* contained four popular singles, including "No More Cryin'," which appeared on the soundtrack of the film *8 Seconds*. In early 1994, Herndon and Thomas left and were replaced by Kenny Vaughn, Randy Frazier and Keith Edwards. The band was then renamed Terry McBride & the Ride and released one album this way before the band officially broke up. In September of 2000, the group reunited for a show, until Ray Herndon suggested they go back to the studio. The band recorded demos and shopped them around, eventually landing on Dualtone and releasing *Amarillo Sky* in the summer of 2002. *—Sandra Brennan*

Burnin' up the Road / 1990 / MCA ✦✦✦
Terry McBride had a hand in writing all but one of the ten cuts on this debut effort, which features the hit "Can I Count on You." *—Jason Ankeny*

● **Sacred Ground** / 1992 / MCA ✦✦✦✦✦
The title cut was the biggest hit from *Sacred Ground*, a more confident and thoughtful record than the band's debut *Burnin' Up the Road*. *—Jason Ankeny*

Hurry Sundown / 1993 / MCA ✦✦✦✦✦
The third record from McBride & the Ride continues to hone the group's close harmony style. *—Jason Ankeny*

Terry McBride & The Ride / Sep. 13, 1994 / MCA ✦✦✦

Amarillo Sky / 2002 / Dualtone ✦✦✦
Nine years after their last outing, the trio reunites and, with help from a passel of Nashville aces, turns in a performance that sounds like they'd never taken a break. All but three of the tracks are original; a spirited cover of "Squeeze Box" proves that Pete Townshend could fit right in on Music Row if he had to. In its details and in the broad picture, *Amarillo Sky* is tight, seamless, a bit impersonal in the commercially acceptable sense, and chopped into radio-friendly bits; only one track tiptoes near five minutes in length. (The album as a whole is concise even by LP-era measure.) It is, in other words, emblematic of contemporary country music, no warts and all. *—Robert L. Doerschuk*

Martina McBride (Martina Mariea Schiff)

b. Jul. 29, 1966, Sharon, KS
Vocals / Contemporary Country, New Traditionalist
Contemporary country singer Martina McBride rose to stardom in the late '90s, starting out with a more traditionalist approach and moving into pop-friendlier territory. She was born Martina Mariea Schiff in Sharon, KS, in 1966, and discovered country music through her father, who led a local band called the Schifters. By her teen years, she was singing and playing keyboards with the Schifters, and after high-school she gigged around Kansas with several different bands. She married soundman John McBride, and in 1990 the couple moved to Nashville, where John worked for artists like Charlie Daniels and Ricky Van Shelton; Martina, meanwhile, worked as a demo singer, and her husband produced her own demo tape, which got her signed to RCA in 1991. Around the same time, John was hired as Garth Brooks' production manager, which helped land Martina an opening slot on tour with Brooks.

Her debut album, *The Time Has Come*, was released in 1992, offering a set of songs indebted to traditional honky tonk and progressive-minded country-folk. The pop-inflected 1993 follow-up *The Way That I Am* was her commercial breakthrough, with the lead single "My Baby Loves Me" zooming up the country charts to the number-two position. The affecting story-song "Independence Day" became something of a signature number, and another single, "Life #9," also reached the Top Ten.

McBride's 1995 follow-up *Wild Angels* gave her a second Top Five hit in "Safe in the Arms of Love," and its title track became her first-ever number-one single in 1996. 1997's *Evolution* became her first Top Ten country album, and the Jim Brickman duet "Valentine" not only went Top Ten, but crossed over to become her first big hit on the adult contemporary charts. *Evolution* went on to spawn two number-two hits ("Happy Girl" and "Whatever You Say") and two number-one hits ("A Broken Wing" and "Wrong Again"), and sold over two-million copies, launching McBride into the top rank of country stardom. She issued a Christmas album in late 1998, and returned with the proper follow-up *Emotion* in 1999. Its lead single, "I Love You," hit number-one country and also crossed over to adult contemporary radio, and the follow-ups "Love's the Only House," "There You Are," and "It's My Time" were all successful as well, with the former two reaching the Top Ten. 2001's *Greatest Hits* compilation was the first McBride album to top the country charts, and sold well enough to make the pop Top Five as well. It contained four new tracks, all of which were eventually released as singles; "Blessed" hit number one, and "When God-Fearin' Women Get the Blues" and "Where Would You Be" both reached the Top Ten. *—Steve Huey*

The Time Has Come / 1992 / RCA ✦✦✦

Rest assured, it's highly unlikely that Martina McBride will ever issue another record that sounds like *The Time Has Come.* With co-producers Paul Worley and Ed Seay (who also worked with her on her breakthrough, *The Way That I Am*), McBride delivers a set of neo-traditionalist country and progressive country-inflected folk songs that showcase her ability to get to the heart of a song and turn it into something communicative and thought provoking. With a host of Nashville superpickers and backing vocalists from Garth Brooks and Carl Jackson to Kathy Chiavola, McBride turns in intense performances of the Emory Gordy/Jim Rushing classic "Cheap Whiskey" for a neo-honky tonk feel, as well as the stompin' nightclub country of the Longacre/Wilson-penned title track and the Lonnie Wilson/Charlotte Wilson/Herbert Wilson weeper "Losing You Feels Good." The album ends with Gretchen Peters' "When You're Old," a meditative love song delivered with the empathy, grace, and elegance that have become McBride's trademark. This is a very solid debut, even if it resembles none of her other work. *—Thom Jurek*

● **The Way That I Am** / 1993 / RCA ✦✦✦✦✦

While Martina McBride's blend of traditional country and progressive folk styles—along with her powerful, remarkable voice—got country audiences to sit up and take notice in 1992, it was *The Way That I Am,* and most notably its Gretchen Peters-penned single "Independence Day," that blew minds. While the song itself—told from the point of view of a surviving daughter of an alcoholic wife-beater and an abused, long-suffering wife and mother—ends in a tragedy of suicide and death, it is nonetheless a redemptive song that makes no moral judgments yet asks real questions about what "independence" actually means. Set on the Fourth of July, it pointedly asks, Does Independence Day mean independence for everyone or does it mean making the choice to free yourself from your bonds, no matter how horrific the consequences? Is it a choice made independent of society, morals, and cultural and religious mores because of the depth of one's convictions? McBride delivers the story with a tough, matter-of-fact, barely concealed rage, and yet that gives way to a transcendence in the refrain so stirring and shatteringly moving it was used in the aftermath of September 11th (even if it was taken out of context in the same way that Bruce Springsteen's "Born in the USA" was). It was an instant classic and remains one two decades later. It's the kind of troubling song you cannot immediately—or perhaps ever—fathom. The listener is carried into the heart of the contradiction of a day of celebration and raw horror inside a tune so seductive and catchy it feels at odds with its lyric, yet comes together on the refrain only to split again into more fragments than can be counted. When McBride declares, "Now I ain't sayin' it's right or it's wrong/Maybe it's the only way/Talk about your revolution/It's independence day," the entire world inside the song comes apart, and you are left wondering who the right, wrong, and guilty are in the refrain, and you have to make out your own point of consideration regarding a "day of reckoning." There are no answers, just facts, questions, and ciphers. The single could have sold the album alone, but the other nine tracks here are quality as well. From the opener, "Heart Trouble," to "She Ain't Seen Nothing Yet," to the closer, "Ashes," the feel on the album, set by the completely modern country-pop sound of the single, is uptempo, glossier, and more streamlined in its focus than her debut, but that's fine because McBride proves herself capable of delivering any kind of song in the end. There isn't a weak track in the bunch, and despite the more modern, less traditional sound, it makes little difference because McBride is a singer's singer: tough, true, and in full control of her gift. *—Thom Jurek*

Wild Angels / Sep. 26, 1995 / RCA ✦✦✦✦

Coming two years after her smash *The Way That I Am* and her mind-bogglingly successful single, "Independence Day," Martina McBride had nothing to prove—except to the folks in accounting at her record company. *Wild Angels* continues her exploration of melding classic country influences and modern pop—long before Shania Twain dreamed it—in the same way (albeit in a radically different time and context) that Patsy Cline did 30 years earlier. Using the same production team of Ed Seay, Paul Worley, and herself—with a literal boatload of engineers—McBride and company assembled a fine collection of songs and performers, including the Band's Levon Helm and Ashley Cleveland on backing vocals, to deliver a powerful set that is her most consistent yet despite not having a single as memorable as "Independence Day" (but you only get those once or twice in a lifetime anyway, right?). Here there are many standout tracks, not the least among them being a rocking & rolling country version of Delbert McClinton's classic "Two More Bottles of Wine" that blows away Emmylou Harris' version and rivals McClinton's. In addition, there are a couple of Matraca Berg cuts, including the modern country title track and the soulful weeper "Cry on the Shoulder of the Road." The Bunch/Stinson-penned "You've Been Driving All the Time" has that irresistible lead-in of acoustic guitars that gives way to compressed ringing electrics that underscore her voice so well and make the track a winner. But there aren't any weak moments here, and McBride proves for the third time that she not only is for real, but that she has the ability a lot of her peers don't to make consistently engaging, moving, and memorable music from album to album. That's an achievement. *—Thom Jurek*

Evolution / Aug. 26, 1997 / RCA ✦✦✦✦

Evolution is an appropriate title; it's clear that Martina McBride has grown—evolved—between *Wild Angels* and this terrific follow-up. That's not to say *Wild Angels* wasn't wonderful in its own right—its blend of rootsy country and contemporary production was clever, and her singing and songs were spot-on—but *Evolution* is different and special in its own way. It is true that it's smoother than its predecessor, especially with polished duets like "Valentine" (with Jim Brickman) and "Still Holding On" (Clint Black). What makes *Evolution* work is the purity and power of McBride's voice—she is one of the few contemporary country singers who can pull off this kind of country-pop. And that's not all she can do, as the rocking "Keeping My Distance" or the gospel-inflected "A Broken Wing" prove. Furthermore, McBride's songs remain staunchly independent and strong-willed, with clear feminist overtones, which helps make *Evolution* a rarity among contemporary country albums—it's catchy and it has a heart. *—Thom Owens*

Emotion / Sep. 14, 1999 / RCA ✦✦✦✦

Emotion is the fifth installment in a series of platinum albums from one of the most underrated voices in country music. After two years since the release of her double platinum *Evolution*, Martina McBride tears into these tracks showcasing the range and power of her incomparable voice. *Evolution* was a big-sounding record with lots of overdubbing and production. *Emotion* scales back musically using a very small band and the result is fresh and authentic, allowing McBride to captivate us with her resounding vocals. Aptly titled, *Emotion*, with lyrics like "anything's better than feelin' the blues" and "love's the only house big enough for all the pain in the world," tugs at the heart strings at times. But it's in "Do What You Do" that McBride lets us know that she's just doing what she does: "If you want to give them something different—something to sink their teeth into—well baby, you just do what you do." *—Maria Konicki Dinoia*

Greatest Hits / Sep. 18, 2001 / RCA ✦✦✦✦

Fans of McBride who have waited a longtime for a greatest-hits album from the always-fresh, always-captivating McBride won't be disappointed. A stellar collection packed with 18 songs: 14 previously recorded smashes and four new, striking originals. Perhaps the greatest voice in contemporary country music, McBride revisits popular favorites from her last four platinum albums—from her 1994 Top Ten breakthrough "My Baby Loves Me" through to the propulsive "Love's the Only House." And in between, McBride's incomparable voice belts out a generous mix of familiar favorites, like "Independence Day," "Wild Angels," "Valentine," "Happy Girl," and "Whatever You Say." McBride's magnetic vocals and unmatched artistry reinforce her musical dominance with new songs, such as "Where Would You Be," "Concrete Angel," and "Blessed." A brilliant career retrospective and a must-have for fans. *—Maria Konicki Dinoia*

Don McCalister Jr.

Leader, Vocals / Progressive Bluegrass, Neo-Traditionalist Country, Western Swing Revival

From the musical hotbed of Austin, TX, sprang Don McCalister Jr., a singer/songwriter with a revolving group of friends and musicians that made up his Cowboy Jazz Revue. Intelligent songwriting and McCalister's smooth tenor, backed by a Western swing and jazz-tinged country sound, drew comparisons to other Texas mainstays, including Ray Benson (Asleep at the Wheel), Lyle Lovett, Hal Ketchum, and the music of Bob Wills & His Texas Playboys. On any given night, the Revue could appear as just a trio, with McCalister and Boomer Norman on guitar and Carl Keesee on bass, or expand to a full orchestra with as many as 14 musicians on-stage. Some of the notable musicians that occasionally played with McCalister included the Grammy award-winning Floyd Domino on piano, Champ Hood on fiddle, Lynn Frazier on pedal steel, Stan Smith on clarinet, and Maryann Price on vocals.

The son of a college professor, McCalister was raised in several places, including California, Arkansas, Tennessee, North Carolina, Maine, Alabama, and New Orleans. As a result, he cites a variety of musical influences, such as Muddy Waters, Flatts & Scruggs, Norman Blake, and Duane Allman. Moving to Austin in 1981, McCalister formed his first band, the short-lived Bluegrass Demons, in 1986 before helping found the Flakey Biscuit Boys, which became a popular central Texas bluegrass band which performed regularly at the renowned Kerrville Folk Festival. After that group dissolved, McCalister independently released a cassette in 1990 entitled *Silver Moon* which moved in a folk music direction and concentrated on his songwriting. Shortly thereafter, he assembled the Cowboy Jazz Revue. McCalister was signed to Dejadisc in 1993 and his debut album, *Brand New Ways*, garnered McCalister rave reviews in and around Austin, plus airplay on regional radio stations. *—Jack Leaver*

● **Brand New Ways** / 1993 / Dejadisc ✦✦✦✦

A solid 12-song debut ensconced in the tradition of Western swing, and flavored with jazz, with a sprinkling of blues for good measure. McCalister's smooth tenor has a light and relaxed feel that's inviting, and is reminiscent of the late Walter Hyatt and also Ray Benson of Asleep at the Wheel. The playing is first-rate, provided by the core of the Cowboy Jazz Revue, with help from stellar Austin musicians that include, Johnny Gimble, Floyd Domino, Maryann Price, and Champ Hood. This record swings, and highlights include the romantic "Silver Moon," co-written by McCalister, which could easily be mistaken for a standard, and a swingin' cover of the Louvin Brothers' classic "Cash on the Barrelhead." *—Jack Leaver*

C.W. McCall (William Fries)

b. Nov. 15, 1928, Audubon, IA

Vocals / Country-Pop, Bakersfield Sound, Urban Cowboy, Truck Driving Country, Novelty, Country Comedy

Essentially a character created by advertising executive William Fries, C. W. McCall was the instrumental figure behind the truck-driving craze that swept America in the mid-'70s. Fries was born November 15, 1928, in Audubon, IA, and while he displayed musical promise as a child, he was more interested in graphic design. While attending the University of Iowa, Fries studied music and played in the school's concert band, but his major was in fine arts, and after graduation he began handling the art chores at an Omaha, NE, television station. After five years there, he was hosting his own program, on which he drew caricatures of celebrities.

Fries signed on as the art director for an Omaha advertising agency in the early '60s, and it was there that he created the character C.W. McCall as a selling tool for an area bakery. A trucker for the fictional Old Home Bread company who spent much of his time in a diner called Old Home Filler-Up an' Keep On a-Truckin' Café, the McCall character was a huge hit with viewers, and the radio campaign won Fries the advertising industry's prestigious Clio Award. In 1974, Fries decided to cut a record under the McCall moniker, and the single, a monologue with country backing titled after the aforementioned cafe, was a Top 20 hit. A follow-up, "Wolf Creek Pass," was even more successful.

In 1975, McCall released the album *Black Bear Road*; the single "Convoy" hit number one on both the pop and country charts, and a national craze was born. The song proved so successful that it influenced the famed filmmaker Sam Peckinpah to direct the 1978 film *Convoy*, starring Kris Kristofferson. By the time of the film's release, however, McCall's career was largely over. He released two more LPs, 1975's *Wolf Creek Pass* and 1977's *Roses for Mama*, which did spawn a major hit in its title track. But shortly after the latter album's release, McCall turned his back on the music industry to focus on the burgeoning environmental movement and moved to the small town of Ouray, CO, of which he was elected mayor in 1982. An attempt at a comeback in 1990 proved unsuccessful. *—Jason Ankeny*

Wolf Creek Pass / 1975 / MGM ✦✦✦
Though this album will never win any awards for depth or transcendence, it shows that C. W. McCall (aka William Fries) did have a way of investing his truck-driving songs with charm and humor. The Johnny Cash soundalike wades through ten selections that deal mostly with life on the highway, including the hits "Wolf Creek Pass" and "Old Home Filler-Up an' Keep On a-Truckin' Café." Humor is the main element in most of the songs, and one can almost see McCall smiling his way through these tunes. ("Eight stools and a promise" is one way that he describes the "Old Home Filler-Up an' Keep On a-Truckin' Café.") In "Sloan," a song about a dog, McCall laments that "he didn't have a license or shots or nuthin'/I thought he was a goner." Female backup singers on several cuts sound like they were rounded up from a local coffee shop, but they add an element of kitsch to the recordings, whether intended or not. One seeming exception to the tongue-in-cheek humor of most of the cuts is the last song, "Glenwood Canyon." Lamenting the loss of natural habitat through development, it is surprisingly affecting and foreshadowed McCall's later political involvement in environmental issues. *—Michael Ofjord*

Black Bear Road / 1975 / MGM ✦✦✦✦

Wilderness / 1976 / Polydor ✦✦✦✦

Around the World With a Rubber Duck / 1977 / Polydor ✦✦✦

Roses for Mama / 1978 / Polydor ✦✦✦✦

● **Greatest Hits** / 1990 / Polydor ✦✦✦✦
No other artist took advantage of the CB craze of the '70s better than C.W. McCall. Chock full of trucker lingo, his songs bordered on the novelty type and would have been classified as just that if it wasn't for the popularity it gained from radio play. While much of McCall's material is either out of print or extremely hard to find, his *Greatest Hits* more than suffices. Although outdated, there is still some humor left to be found in some of his campy tunes. His hillbilly drawl is front and center on "Wolf Creek Pass," while terms like "smoky" and "10-4" are hilariously rekindled on "'Round the World With a Rubber Duck." His claim to fame, the mighty "Convoy," which was loosely based on protests by truck drivers on state-issued border tolls, hit number one on *Billboard*'s Top 40 back in 1975. McCall rarely sang, as his long-tongued songs usually involved him spinning the yarn while a chorus of females with high-pitched voices sang the middle. "Roses for Mama" was a serious attempt for McCall that was in the same vein as Red Sovine's "Teddy Bear," and "Crispy Critters" sounds like a Jeff Foxworthy offering. The music, which is a light spattering of countrified guitar and banjo, helps to guide the *Hee Haw* whimsy of the songs to the height of 18-wheel silliness. Still fun to listen to, but undoubtedly dated, this disc will still conjure up the odd chuckle. *—Mike DeGagne*

Best of C.W. McCall / Apr. 8, 1998 / PSM ✦✦

Darrell McCall

b. Apr. 30, 1940, New Jasper, OH
Vocals / Traditional Country, Honky Tonk
Though his initial singles were pop, Darrell McCall was a hardcore country vocalist to the core, singing tough honky tonk during the majority of his career without caring for trends and fashions. After coming to prominence as a member of the Little Dippers in 1960, McCall broke away from the group the following year, and by 1963 his sound had evolved into pure country. He sang both traditional country and honky tonk during the '60s, but he eventually became devoted to roadhouse country. As a result, his sales suffered somewhat. McCall had a few hits over the course of his career, sliding into the charts every few years, whenever hardcore country crossed over into the mainstream, but for the bulk of his career, he essentially remained a semi-popular artist with a die-hard cult following. Born in and raised in New Jasper, OH, McCall began his musical career by landing a slot as a Saturday morning DJ on a local radio station when he was 15 years old. Around the same time, he was playing local dances and events as a musician. Following his high-school graduation, he joined the Army, where he was stationed in Kentucky. After his tour of duty was completed, he and his childhood friend Johnny Paycheck moved to Nashville in 1958. McCall and Paycheck attempted to record as a duo, but they were unsuccessful. Eventually, McCall became a studio harmony vocalist, singing on records by Faron Young, George Jones, and Ray Price, among others. In a short time, the studio work metamorphosed into road work, as he played bass and sang harmony for several different touring bands, including those of Young, Price, and Hank Williams Jr.

During a recording session in 1959, McCall met Buddy Killen, a famous Nashville producer and publisher. Impressed with Darrell's abilities, Killen asked him to join a group he was assembling called the Little Dippers, which also featured Hurshel Wigintin, Delores Dinning, and Emily Gilmore. McCall agreed, and the Little Dippers had one major pop hit, the Top Ten single "Forever," in 1960. The following year, he signed a solo contract with Capitol. During 1961, he released two pop singles for the label, "My Kind of

Lovin'" and "Call the Zoo," but both failed miserably, and the label dropped him. In light of his unsuccessful forays into the pop marketplace, McCall returned to country in 1962 and signed a contract with Phillips. In January of 1963, "A Stranger Was Here," his first—and, as it would turn out, his biggest—country hit, appeared. Peaking at number 17 on the charts, the single spent eight weeks on the charts and seemed to be a positive beginning to his country career, but he wasn't able to deliver a hit follow-up, even though he sang the theme to the Paul Newman film *Hud* that same year.

McCall decided to abandoned music for a short while in the mid-'60s, launching an acting career in 1965. That year, he appeared in the film *Nashville Rebel*, and the following year, he was in *Road to Nashville* and *What Am I Bid*. During that time, McCall also worked as a cowboy in the Southwest and appeared in several minor rodeos. He didn't return to recording until 1968, when he joined the roster of the independent label Wayside Records. Over the next two years, he had four minor hits for the label—"I'd Love to Live With You Again," "Wall of Pictures," "Hurry Up," "The Arms of My Weakness"—and released one album, 1970's *Meet Darrell McCall*, which was distributed by Mercury. The contract with Wayside expired in 1971, and McCall didn't immediately sign another recording contract. However, Hank Williams Jr. took McCall's "Eleven Roses" (which he co-wrote with Lamar Morris) to number one, which led to Tree International signing him as a professional songwriter.

McCall didn't reactivate his recording career until 1974, when he signed with Atlantic. His debut single for the label, "There's Still a Lot of Love in San Antone," nearly reached the country Top 50 that year. In 1975, he left Atlantic for Columbia, where he had his greatest period of chart success since the early '60s. Although his first single for the label, "Pins and Needles (In My Heart)," didn't do much better than "There's Still a Lot of Love in San Antone," his second single, "Lily Dale," was a duet with Willie Nelson that cracked the country Top 40. McCall's new success was partially due to the popularity of outlaw country, and how he neatly fit into its rough and ready musical style. "Lily Dale" was named Best Duet of 1977 by *Cash Box* magazine, and it was followed by "Dreams of a Dreamer," McCall's first solo Top 40 hit since 1963. Of course, the brief McCall renaissance began to lose its luster in 1978, as outlaw country began to lose its stronghold on the country charts. His singles "Down the Roads of Daddy's Dreams" and "The Weeds Outlived the Roses" failed to make the Top 40, and he was soon dropped by Columbia.

In 1980, he signed with Hillside Records, where he had only one hit single—a duet on "San Antonio Medley" with Curtis Potter. After that reached the lower levels of the country charts in the spring, he switched labels to RCA, where he nearly reached the Top 40 in the fall with "Long Line of Empties." At that time, the tastes of country radio and the genre's audience had shifted completely away from outlaw country and settled on the smooth, rock-influenced textures of urban cowboy. Consequently, McCall's recording career suffered. Over the next four years, he recorded only sporadically, most notably as the uncredited "friend" on Connie Hanson & Friend's minor 1982 hit, "There's Still a Lot of Love in San Antone." Two years later, he had his final charting hit with "Memphis in May," which was released on Indigo Records. In 1986, McCall cut two albums: a record with his old backing group the Tennessee Volunteers called *Reunion* (released on BGM) and *Hot Texas Country*, a duet record with Johnny Bush. Following 1986, McCall essentially retired from recording, though he continued to play the occasional concert and worked constantly for the Muscular Dystrophy Association. McCall spent the remainder of the '80s and most of the '90s at his Texas home with his wife Mona Vary, who used to play in Audrey Williams' band. *—Stephen Thomas Erlewine*

● **The Real McCall** / 1996 / Bear Family ✦✦✦✦✦
Darrell McCall was a hardcore traditional country singer, keeping the flame of pure, gritty honky tonk alive during the country-pop crazes of the '60s and '70s. Though he never had many hits—only his debut single, "A Stranger Was Here," broke the Top 20—he gained a dedicated cult following among fans of traditional country, which translated into a string of moderate hits that ran from the early '60s until 1980. The five-disc box set *The Real McCall* collects all of the recordings he made during that time, including every song he cut for Starday, Wayside, Atlantic, American Heritage, Columbia, and RCA, among others. In addition to the released recordings, *The Real McCall* also features a handful of demos (including some he made for Jimmy Reed), radio transcriptions, and radio commercials—everything a dedicated fan could ever want from McCall. Of course, such an exhaustive approach means that listening to the box is a daunting task for anyone but the most devoted fan, yet it will satisfy all of his hardcore followers with its excellent sound and lavish, detailed packaging. *—Thom Owens*

Lila McCann

b. Dec. 4, 1981, Steilacoom, WA
Vocals / Country-Pop, Contemporary Country
Another teenage female country star to join the ranks of LeAnn Rimes, Lila McCann debuted singing "You Are My Sunshine" with her father's country band at the tender age of four. Influenced by Reba McEntire and the Judds (though she also listened to No Doubt and Boyz II Men), McCann began performing regularly several years after her debut, balancing her education in small-town Washington with shows at local Eagle's Lodges and bars. While just a freshman at Steilacoom High School, she was given a demo of the song "Down Came a Blackbird" by her new manager, Kasey Walker. The song so impressed Elektra Records president and longtime industry insider Seymour Stein that he signed McCann to Elektra/Asylum. After working with producer Mark Spiro (also the writer of "Down Came a Blackbird"), McCann released her debut album, *Lila*, in June 1997. Though the album's maturity was quite remarkable, it failed to break into the Top 40 album charts but did go gold. *Something in the Air* followed in 1999. *Complete* appeared in spring 2001. *—John Bush*

● **Lila** / Jun. 17, 1997 / Elektra ✦✦✦✦
Upon the first glance, it could be easy to dismiss Lila McCann's debut album, *Lila*, as a byproduct of LeAnn Rimes' astounding success—after all, there couldn't be two talented teenage female vocalists arriving within a year of each other. However, upon further investigation, McCann reveals herself as a promising singer in her own right—arguably one

with more potential than Rimes. McCann has a pure, pretty voice that can simply soar, as the hit single "Down Came a Blackbird" proves. At this stage, she hasn't reached artistic maturity, and she frequently has trouble delivering songs with subtlety, yet there's a passion to her singing that makes this point a minor one. Musically, *Lila* may stray a little too close to adult contemporary for some tastes (a Sheena Easton cover—"Almost Over You"—wasn't a great choice), but there's enough spirit and conviction in McCann's performances to make her rank as a contender. —*Stephen Thomas Erlewine*

Something in the Air / Mar. 23, 1999 / Elektra ✦✦✦
The second album from teenage country singer McCann goes through the usual post-Shania motions as elements of glossy pop merge with typically overproduced Nashville standard. McCann is likable enough, and the spunky songs ("With You," "Rhymes With") can be addictive. And the sweet "Kiss Me Now," with Vince Gill on backing vocals, is a tentative step into the adult world with genuine emotion. But the blandness of it all (and McCann's own misfortune of sharing many personal and professional qualities with LeAnn Rimes) makes it a bit difficult to distinguish her from the rest of the '90s hat pack. —*Michael Gallucci*

Super Hits / Jun. 4, 2002 / Warner Bros. ✦✦✦✦
Super Hits gathers ten of the young country star's biggest hits, including early successes like "Down Came a Blackbird" to the more mature sound of "Come a Little Closer." Selections like "I Wanna Fall in Love," "Almost Over You," and "Crush" emphasize her youthful, romantic side, which is also the most genuine-sounding aspect of her work. Though it's not an especially deep retrospective, the budget price and the fact that not many McCann collections exist make *Super Hits* worth the time of casual fans. —*Heather Phares*

The McCarters
f. Sevierville, TN
Group / Contemporary Country, New Traditionalist
Jennifer McCarter (born 1964) and her twin sisters Lisa McCarter and Teresa McCarter (born 1966) were born in Sevierville, a Tennessee town best known as the birthplace of Dolly Parton. The daughters of an amateur banjo-playing father and gospel-singing mother, Jennifer and her sisters were born to perform. However, they reassessed their burgeoning career as a clog-dancing troupe when the endeavor proved to have a glass ceiling. Jennifer picked up her father's Martin guitar and learned to sing, and soon her sisters were adding harmony vocals. After performing on-stage and in the streets of their hometown, the young trio moved to Nashville, where pestering and tenacity led to an audition with Randy Travis' manager, Kyle Lehning. In 1987, the McCarters signed a contract with Warner Bros., who were seeking an act like their successful Forester Sisters.
A year later, their debut LP, *The Gift*, appeared. It included the Top Ten hits "Timeless and True Love" and its title track, and the group promoted the album with a worldwide tour supporting Travis. The girls returned three years later with *Better Be Home Soon*, which heightened the role of lead vocalist Jennifer and diminished the harmonies that had been the hallmark of their success. The album's reception was lukewarm at best, and mustered only minor chart activity. The McCarters were released from Warner Bros., and spent the 1990s focusing on live performances, appearances, and celebrity endorsements. —*Johnny Loftus*

● **The Gift** / Jun. 21, 1988 / Warner Bros. ✦✦✦✦
The Gift is an exceptional debut album from the McCarters, a group of three sisters that hails from Tennessee. Throughout the record, the trio demonstrates their remarkable vocal talents, as their beautiful harmonics grace a set of traditional country tunes. —*Thom Owens*

Better Be Home Soon / 1990 / Warner Bros. ✦✦✦
While the McCarters' debut focused on the trio's harmonies, *Better Be Home Soon* focuses the spotlight almost exclusively on sister Jennifer, pushing twins Lisa and Teresa into the background. —*Jason Ankeny*

Mary McCaslin
b. Dec. 22, 1946, Indianapolis, IN
Banjo, Guitar, Vocals / Singer/Songwriter, Country-Folk, Contemporary Folk
As a singer/songwriter who wrote story-songs combining elements of country, folk, and pop, Mary McCaslin was one of the most appealing contemporary folk performers of the 1970s. As a country-folksinger working totally outside of the Nashville sphere, singing of prairies and Old West images in almost mythic terms, her audience was confined to the folk circuit (though within that boundary, it was very wide). Yet her ability to appeal to rock and pop listeners helped pave the way for country-folk-pop stars like Nanci Griffith and Mary-Chapin Carpenter, although her influence in this area has remained relatively unacknowledged.
Born in Indiana, McCaslin moved to southern California with her family at a young age. Inspired both by country narrators like Marty Robbins and singer/songwriters like Joni Mitchell, she recorded her first album, *Goodnight, Everybody*, for Barnaby in 1969. At this point her repertoire consisted entirely of covers; she didn't begin writing until her 20s, coming up with one of her signature tunes, "Way Out West," on her second try. That composition would be the title track of her first Philo album (1973), recorded after a brief liaison with Capitol (which produced one single). *Way Out West* was the first of three albums that she made for Philo in the 1970s, featuring her finely wrought songs, strong upper-register vocals, and sympathetic, fully arranged accompaniment. Two of the tracks which attracted widest notice were her acoustic interpretations of two Beatles songs ("Things We Said Today" and "Blackbird"), which were not only among the few truly fine folk renditions of Lennon-McCartney tunes, but among the best Beatles covers ever attempted.
Her Philo era is recognized as her artistic peak, although she maintained her presence on the folk scene with albums for Mercury (*Sunny California*, 1979) and Flying Fish (*A Life and a Time*, 1981). She also did a duo album with her husband, guitarist and songwriter Jim Ringer (who also played on McCaslin's albums), in the late '70s. Surprisingly

little was heard from McCaslin in the 1980s. Ringer (from whom she separated in 1989) became very ill, and her family problems put her songwriting on hold; she once estimated that she wrote only three songs between 1981 and 1989. 1994's *Broken Promises* was her first album in 13 years. —*Richie Unterberger*

Goodnight, Everybody / 1969 / Barnaby ✦✦✦
Rarely discussed in overviews of McCaslin's career, this debut album is unfairly overlooked, even if it's a little different from the sound for which Mary is most familiar. Actually, it's not *too* much different from the folkier albums she would record for Philo in the 1970s. The singing is excellent: sensitive without being sappy, rooted in folk-country but flexible enough to interpret contemporary material. McCaslin's passion for doing unexpected rock and folk songs in a folk context is already apparent with her covers of the Beatles' "Help!" and "Blackbird," and the slow reading of the Supremes' "You Keep Me Hangin' On"; in fact she liked "Blackbird" well enough to record it again in her Philo days. The production is a bit slicker and more mainstream than what she would use on her home-spun folk records, but not much fussier, despite the presence of a rhythm section (Jerry Scheff, who played sessions for the Doors, Elvis Presley, and many others, is on bass) and subtle strings. It's still understated, with a dramatic yearning quality. McCaslin did not write any of the material, another key difference between this and her subsequent work. But the songs are pretty strong, whether by well-known writers such as Lennon-McCartney, Hoyt Axton, Barry & Maurice Gibb ("With the Sun in My Eyes"), or unheralded composers like the producer of the album, Larry Murray (who wrote "Jamie," and had been in the early country-rock group Hearts & Flowers). —*Richie Unterberger*

Way Out West / 1974 / Philo ✦✦✦✦✦
This was the album that established McCaslin as a major folk performer. Her interpretive skills are in evidence on covers of "Let It Be" and Randy Newman's "Living Without You," but most of the set was devoted to original material, showing her to be an impressive songwriter (if not quite as impressive a singer). The title track and "San Bernardino Waltz" are standouts, the latter being probably her most famous song. —*Richie Unterberger*

Prairie in the Sky / 1976 / Philo ✦✦✦
Public perception of what a particular musical artist was all about sometimes fades, leaving the poor confused record buyer in the predicament of trying to figure out what sort of music to expect from cover artwork alone. In the case of this album one might think this is some kind of new age cowboy drivel, the cover decorated with airbrushed cowgirls, cacti, horses, and pink flowers. It is all very ugly and could very well hide the respectable and sincere music that lies within. The voice of Mary McCaslin is the kind of female folk or country voice that has gotten harder and harder to find since the '70s passed by. With both country and rock music getting slicker, vocalists tend to almost intentionally avoid this kind of warmth and personality, as if afraid of sounding real. The Western theme of this album is in reality a haphazard umbrella over songs that deal with Western settings or something just vaguely Western. Many of the artist's lyrics have a vague quality, which will appeal to listeners who like to think about lyrics and what they might mean rather than getting whacked over the head with an obvious message. There is also some well-done orchestration involving instruments such as French horn. All in all, quite a good album and one thing is for sure—it doesn't sound what it looks like. —*Eugene Chadbourne*

Old Friends / 1977 / Philo ✦✦✦
McCaslin wrote only one of the ten songs (the title track) on her fourth album. The remainder of the program stressed her abilities as one of folk music's most eclectic interpretive artists, as in addition to folk-country tunes, there were two Lennon-McCartney compositions ("Things We Said Today" and "Blackbird," both among her best-known tracks); the Who's "Pinball Wizard"; the Supremes' "My World Is Empty Without You"; Cole Porter's "Don't Fence Me In"; and the huge 1950s pop hit "The Wayward Wind." At a glance, the breadth of repertoire seems outlandish. But McCaslin's vocals are consistently strong, and she does make all of these work as folk songs (with occasional light rhythm section), without sounding like a dilettante. Perhaps "Pinball Wizard" would have been better, though, with just McCaslin's voice and banjo and without the rhythm section. —*Richie Unterberger*

The Bramble & the Rose / 1978 / Philo ✦✦✦
The only duet album by McCaslin and Ringer (who were married to each other at the time) doesn't click too well, and indeed for McCaslin fans especially might be a disappointment. Their voices and musical persona's—McCaslin's high, sweet and vulnerable, Ringer's earthy and gruff—weren't well-suited for a collaboration. Stated more harshly, McCaslin was a greater talent than Ringer, and the combination of the two does more to lower McCaslin than it does to elevate Ringer. Beyond that, the material and arrangements are ordinary, all coming from outside sources, whether the traditional folk tune "Oh Death" or compositions from country-rockers like Herb Pedersen and Larry Murray. The low point is certainly the cover of "Hit the Road, Jack." Probably McCaslin was trying to do for it what she did for the rock songs "Things We Said Today," "Pinball Wizard," and "Blackbird," but it's leaden, and the dual vocals by McCaslin and Ringer don't possess chemistry. It's not a terrible album, just unmemorable and, probably, unnecessary. —*Richie Unterberger*

● **The Best of Mary McCaslin** / 1990 / Philo ✦✦✦✦
The best of her 1970s material, taken from her first three solo albums. Many strong originals, and two excellent Beatles covers ("Things We Said Today" and "Blackbird") that remain among the best folk interpretations of Lennon/McCartney compositions. —*Richie Unterberger*

The Best of Mary McCaslin: Things We Said Today / 1992 / Philo ✦✦✦✦✦
If Mary McCaslin's name fails to jump out at the listener as a singer/songwriter of note, it has nothing to do with the quality of her music. She made a fine series of LPs for Philo

in the mid-'70s, and *The Best of Mary McCaslin* collects 18 songs from those efforts. Unlike a number of singer/songwriters today, McCaslin never minded offering fresh interpretations of other writers' material. She infuses Lennon and McCartney's "Things We Said Today" and "Blackbird" with folk-country flavorings, and gives Randy Newman's "Living Without You" a twangy down-home quality. She also offers deft versions of familiar fare like "Ghost Riders in the Sky" and "Wayward Wind," and an appealing duet with Jim Ringer on "The Bramble and the Rose." The quality of McCaslin's countrified vocals would be enough to turn these songs into something special, but she's also an artist, putting a piece of herself in each song and filling it with emotional significance. A number of her self-penned songs also appear on this volume, and they easily hold their own with the covers. "Northfield" features a superior vocal, while "Way Out West" gives the listener a taste of her most noted album of the same name. *The Best of Mary McCaslin* doesn't replace the need for albums like *Way Out West* and *Prairie in the Sky*, but it does offer an excellent introduction to a wonderful singer/songwriter from the mid-'70s. —*Ronnie D. Lankford Jr.*

Broken Promises / May 2, 1994 / Philo ✦✦✦

Rain: The Lost Album / Sep. 27, 1999 / Bear Family ✦✦✦
It's not well known that McCaslin was very briefly with Capitol Records in the late '60s, in her early '20s. Only one single, 1967's "Rain"/"This All Happened Once Before," was released, but in 1967-1968 she, in fact, did a few sessions, resulting in almost 20 tracks. All of these tracks, including both sides of the single, were finally unearthed on this 1999 CD. While of undeniable historical interest, these really do show McCaslin to still be a fairly unformed artist, even relative to her very obscure (and good) 1969 debut album, *Goodnight Everybody*, on Barnaby. She's just an average folksinger here, her voice not sounding as assured as it would be subsequently, with a repertoire entirely comprised of cover tunes. That's not necessarily a problem as McCaslin was a gifted interpreter as well as songwriter, but that interpretive gift is not as strongly in evidence as it would be later. In truth this seems to be bear the stamp of producer Nick Venet—who also produced country-folk-rock artists Linda Ronstadt & the Stone Poneys, Hearts & Flowers, Fred Neil, and Karen Dalton in the same era—more than it does the imprint of McCaslin herself. The low-key-to-the-point-of-sedate, lightly electrified arrangements will be extremely familiar to those who know the Stone Poneys and Hearts & Flowers records well. It's a good sound, but McCaslin, at this point, was not as original an artist as those acts, and did not have access to material that was as interesting. She does take in an eclectic assortment of songwriters on this collection, including Michael Nesmith, Hoyt Axton, the Bee Gees, Tom Paxton, Bert Jansch, and Leonard Cohen, as well as three Beatles songs, a harbinger of her oft-tapped love of Lennon-McCartney rearrangements. Yet of the songs that aren't well known, few are that memorable (the sad "Windigo" and "Please Don't Go" are exceptions), and some of the covers not only fail to leave a mark, but actually diminish the songs. Tim Buckley's "Aren't You the One" was handled much better by Buckley, for instance, and she changes George Harrison's Beatles composition "I Need You" so radically that she strips it of most of its recognizable melody, though to no good end. Incidentally, Bernie Leadon, Doug Dillard, and Larry Murray are among the country-rock musicians of note who contributed to the sessions at various points. —*Richie Unterberger*

Charly McClain
b. Mar. 26, 1956, Memphis, TN
Vocals / Country-Pop, Urban Cowboy
Originally named Charlotte, Charly McClain was given her masculine moniker by neighborhood friends in Memphis, and she also used it when she started playing hotel lounges. When Epic Records decided it sounded catchier than Charlotte, it became a permanent professional banner. McClain's father had tuberculosis when she was eight, and, since she was under age for visitation rights at the hospital, she had to communicate with him through a tape recorder. That inspired her interest in recording, and by age 17 she was a regular on the club circuit. Signed to her first recording contract in 1976, McClain's distinct vocal sound provided an edge in recognizability—as did her appearance. She hit country's Top Ten for the first time in 1978 with "That's What You Do to Me," followed up with 1980's "Men," and hit the top spot one year later with "Who's Cheatin' Who."

She stayed in the upper reaches during 1982 with "Dancing Your Memory Away" and "The Very Best Is You," then hit number one again in 1983 with her Mickey Gilley duet "Paradise Tonight." McClain married former soap star Wayne Massey in 1984, and their own duet ("With Just One Look in Your Eyes") reached number five. Her last number one came with 1985's "Radio Heart," but she continued to chart until her last recording came in 1989. —*Tom Roland*

Greatest Hits / 1982 / Epic ✦✦✦✦✦
McClain's Southern heritage is very much in evidence in her vocal style. No other woman sounds as simultaneously tough and feminine as she does; this is simply McClain at her best—"Men," "Sleepin' With the Radio On," "Who's Cheatin' Who," and "The Very Best Is You." —*Tom Roland*

Paradise / 1983 / Epic ✦✦✦
Charly McClain is a pleasant-sounding female vocalist who came to fame by opening for such artists as Mickey Gilley and George Jones. In fact, Gilley even duets with Charly on the track "Paradise Tonight." While it doesn't break any new ground, *Paradise* is a strong collection of easy-listening honky tonk for the discerning country fan. —*James Chrispell*

● **Biggest Hits** / 1985 / Epic ✦✦✦✦✦
Covering the ground since 1982's *Greatest Hits*, *Biggest Hits* does indeed contain Charly McClain's most popular songs. From the number one "Paradise Tonight" to her biggest hit, "Radio Heart," the collection not only is a good representation of her mid-'80s peak, it's an excellent introduction to her music. —*Thom Owens*

Pure Country / Aug. 25, 1998 / Sony ✦✦✦
Pure Country is a decent overview of Charly McClain's hits recorded in the late '70s and early '80s. Several of her Top Ten hits are here, including "Who's Cheatin' Who," "Men," "Sleepin' With the Radio On," and the number-one duet with Mickey Gilley, "Paradise Tonight." While this collection is missing a few crucial songs ("Radio Heart," "With Just One Look in Your Eyes"), the mid-line pricing makes this a package worth picking up. —*Al Campbell*

Anthology / Mar. 16, 1999 / Renaissance ✦✦✦✦
Anthology is a fairly complete, 34-track overview of Charly McClain's country/pop hits recorded in the late '70s and early '80s. All of her Top Ten hits are here, including "Radio Heart," "Who's Cheatin' Who," "Men," "Sleepin' With the Radio On," and her duets with Mickey Gilley, "Paradise Tonight," and husband Wayne Massey, "With Just One Look in Your Eyes." Even though the cost is a bit more for this set than other similar packages, this is the one to own. —*Al Campbell*

Delbert McClinton
b. Nov. 4, 1940, Lubbock, TX
Harmonica, Vocals / Americana, Modern Electric Blues, Blues-Rock, Country-Rock
The venerable Delbert McClinton is a legend among Texas roots music aficionados, not only for his amazing longevity, but for his ability to combine country, blues, soul, and rock & roll as if there were no distinctions between any of them in the best time-honored Texas tradition. A formidable harmonica player long before he recorded as a singer, McClinton's career began in the late '50s, yet it took him nearly two decades to evolve into a bona fide solo artist. A critics' darling and favorite of his peers, McClinton never really became a household name, but his resurgence in the '90s helped him earn more widespread respect from both the public at large and the Grammy committee.

Delbert McClinton was born in Lubbock, TX, on November 4, 1940, and grew up in Fort Worth. Discovering the blues in his teenage years, McClinton quickly became an accomplished harmonica player and found plenty of work on the local club scene, where musicians often made their living by playing completely different styles of music on different nights of the week. His most prominent early gig was with the Straitjackets, the house band at a blues/R&B club; it gave McClinton the opportunity to play harp behind blues legends like Howlin' Wolf, Jimmy Reed, Sonny Boy Williamson II, and Bobby "Blue" Bland. In 1960, McClinton's cover of Williamson's "Wake Up Baby" made him the first white artist to have a record played on the local blues station KNOK. McClinton's harmonica was prominently featured on Fort Worth native Bruce Channel's 1962 number-one smash "Hey! Baby"; brought along for Channel's tour of England, McClinton wound up giving harp lessons to a young John Lennon. Upon returning to the U.S., McClinton founded a group called the Rondells (sometimes listed as the Ron-Dels), which had a minor chart single in 1965 with "If You Really Want Me to, I'll Go." Although the Rondells recorded for several different labels, wider success eluded them and McClinton spent much of the '60s making the rounds of the Texas club and roadhouse circuit, where his reputation kept growing steadily.

In 1972, McClinton moved to Los Angeles, where he teamed up with Fort Worth singer/songwriter Glen Clark as Delbert & Glen. Signed to the small Atlantic affiliate Clean Records, Delbert & Glen recorded two albums in a mostly country-rock vein, 1972's *Delbert & Glen* and 1973's *Subject to Change*. Neither sold well and McClinton returned to Texas in 1974, where he was able to land a solo deal with ABC on the strength of his emerging songwriting talent. His first solo album, *Victim of Life's Circumstances*, was released in 1975; although he was marketed as part of the emerging progressive country movement, McClinton's music was too indebted to blues and R&B to neatly fit that tag. *Genuine Cowhide* (1976) and *Love Rustler* (1977) followed to highly positive reviews, if not much commercial attention, and other artists started to mine McClinton's catalog for material; in 1978, Emmylou Harris took his "Two More Bottles of Wine" all the way to the top of the country charts. A switch to Capricorn produced two albums, 1978's *Second Wind* and 1979's *Keeper of the Flame*; the former featured his original version of "B Movie Boxcar Blues," later a part of the Blues Brothers repertoire. When Capricorn folded, he moved to the Muscle Shoals Sound imprint and his 1980 label debut, *The Jealous Kind*, gave him his first Top 40 single in "Givin' It Up for Your Love," which hit on both the pop and country charts.

Unfortunately, Muscle Shoals Sound folded not long after McClinton's follow-up, 1981's *Plain From the Heart*, and he subsequently took a long hiatus from recording, concentrating instead on live performances. His next prominent appearance was an acclaimed vocal turn on guitarist Roy Buchanan's 1986 album *Dancing on the Edge*; that guest appearance helped land him a deal with Alligator. In 1989, McClinton issued the comeback album *Live From Austin*, which earned him his first Grammy nomination (for Best Contemporary Blues Album). He signed with Curb in 1990, debuting that year with *I'm With You*, and moved to Nashville, where he soon became a much sought-after songwriter (often in tandem with new partner Gary Nicholson) in the contemporary country field. Over the next few years, McClinton placed material with stars like Wynonna, Vince Gill, Lee Roy Parnell, and Martina McBride, among others. His biggest break, though, came when he was tapped for a duet with Bonnie Raitt on 1991's *Luck of the Draw*, the follow-up to her much-lauded comeback *Nick of Time*. The result, "Good Man, Good Woman," brought McClinton his first Grammy for Best Rock Vocal, Duo or Group, which suddenly raised his profile tenfold. He capitalized with 1992's *Never Been Rocked Enough*, which featured not only his duet with Raitt, but also guest appearances from Tom Petty and Melissa Etheridge, and his biggest hit single since 1980, "Every Time I Roll the Dice." Later that year, he hit the country charts with another duet, this time with Tanya Tucker on "Tell Me About It." The song later appeared on McClinton's next album, 1993's simply titled *Delbert McClinton*.

Despite enjoying the greatest commercial success of his career, McClinton's relationship with Curb was beginning to sour. His next two albums were released to comparatively little attention and he finally extricated himself from his contract to sign with Rising Tide, a small label associated with Universal. *One of the Fortunate Few* (1997) was designed to restore McClinton to his early-'90s stature, featuring an array of guest stars, including Vince Gill, Patty Loveless, Lyle Lovett, Pam Tillis, B.B. King, John Prine, and Mavis Staples. It was still definitely McClinton's show, however, and as such it received mostly complimentary reviews; it also sold more than 250,000 copies before Rising Tide went belly-up. McClinton next returned in 2001 on the Austin, TX-based New West imprint with another acclaimed effort, *Nothing Personal.* It proved to be one of the most popular recordings of his career, gaining substantial airplay on Americana radio and ending up one of the year's biggest hits on *Billboard*'s blues chart; it also won him another Grammy for Best Contemporary Blues Album. *—Steve Huey*

Delbert & Glen / 1972 / Clean ✦✦✦

Subject to Change / 1973 / Clean ✦✦✦

Victim of Life's Circumstances / 1975 / ABC ✦✦✦✦

Victim of Life's Circumstances was Delbert McClinton's first solo album and his debut for the ABC label that signed him in 1974 after the dissolution of Delbert & Glen. Even at this early date McClinton, as a solo artist, arrived fully developed. From the outset McClinton's many influences and style masteries are present. The album brought questions at the time—in an era of Bruce Springsteen's *Born to Run* and the Marshall Tucker Band topping the charts (as well as David Bowie's latter-day glam experiments)—like "Who is this guy?" and "What's he trying to do?" On this album McLinton took hard stompin' honky tonk, including the tile track, his first solo recording (and most Texas country version) of "Two More Bottles of Wine," "Object of My Affection," and "Real Good Itch," which rocked harder than anything coming out of Nash Vegas at the time and, other than Montgomery Gentry, rocked harder than any country music coming from there today. In addition, there was the nasty, funky soulful R&B of "Honky Tonkin' (I Guess I Done Me Some)" with a horn section, Fender Rhodes pianos, and Hammond B-3s alongside acoustic and electric guitars, deep in the groove with a Texas drawl, punched in the cut by the horn charts. "Lesson in the Pain of Love," with its swirling horns and on-the-one funk, echoes the Stax/Volt sound and features the most out-of-character soulful backing vocals Janie Fricke ever cut. Reggie and Chip Young (who produced the set) distorted the hell out of their guitars and made everything greasy and edgy. "Solid Gold Plated Fool" borrows the rhythm from the Band's "Up on Cripple Creek" and turns it into a groove number with keyboard and brass popping in the margins and McClinton's voice digging deep for both the humor and pathos in the song. McClinton's harmonica on the final cut, "Troubled Woman," is pure gold. It floats in understated lines in the refrains and in the bridge and delves as deep into the blues as any white boy ever had the nerve to. McClinton comes off as not authentic, but awe inspiring. And top it off, despite a performance that delighted, confounded, and infuriated critics, McClinton wrote every track here. And despite the range, this is as focused a debut as you are likely to run across, not to mention one that will get you off your ass and moving. *—Thom Jurek*

Genuine Cowhide / 1976 / ABC ✦✦✦✦

Issued in 1976, Delbert McClinton's second genre-busting date for ABC proved to be more outrageous, more out of step with the times—as in far ahead—than *Victim of Life's Circumstances.* On his debut for the label, McClinton wrote all of his own material, showcasing his mastery of crossing hard country, rock, soul, R&B, and blues and expressing them all with emotional authenticity, musical expertise, and raw power. On *Genuine Cowhide,* McClinton shifted gears and, with a smaller group of Nashville's finest, cut a set largely made up of covers. But these were not just any covers; they were James Brown's "Please, Please, Please," Memphis Curtis' nugget "Lovely Dovey," Fats Domino's "Blue Monday," Bo Diddley's "Before You Accuse Me," Jesse Stone's "Lipstick, Powder and Paint," and a couple of tunes by Leiber & Stoller such as Leonard Lee's "Let the Good Times Roll," Washington and Robie's "Pledging My Love," and a couple of originals. In 1976, this took balls—trying to get on the charts with a collection of tunes that had been basically regarded as so classic they should never have been touched (Brown's, Domino's, and Memphis Curtis') or were considered so hopelessly out of date no one cared to remember them if they could. To put your own songs on an album of classics was nearly unheard of. Who cares? This album is steeped harder in blues and R&B than it is country. It moves, rattles, rolls, snakes, and funks in dirty, deep, raw emotion and good-time raucousness. The covers of "Please, Please, Please" and "Pledging My Love" are astonishing in their raw-boned honesty and lack of artifice. Stone's doo wop tune has been revamped into a smoking R&B behind the beat groover, and the Leiber & Stoller tunes—"One Kiss Led to Another" and "My Baby Comes to Me"—have been given the Memphis treatment with funky Rhodes pianos and horns driving the tunes. McClinton's "Special Love Song" is as naked as it gets, full-on, down-on-one-knee woman worship. The only complaint is that the production techniques Chip Young used sound a bit dated in the 21st century, but it's hardly a problem for more than a minute or two. The other is that McClinton's lover song should have closed the set instead of "Let the Good Times Roll," to go out on that deep soul note, but that's the quibble of a writer who has never produced an album. *Genuine Cowhide* is as fine a place as any to discover McClinton if you've been living under a rock for the past three decades. *—Thom Jurek*

Love Rustler / 1977 / ABC ✦✦✦✦

Delbert McClinton's final album for ABC, issued in 1977, came on the heels of momentum built up by two albums that gradually warmed him to critics and audiences alike. *Love Rustler* dared to take the fusion of virtually all the music McClinton had come up around working as a musician from the early '60s on. Chip Young and McClinton chose a slate of songs that were contemporary in their arrangement but retained the deep rootsiness of McClinton's established approach. The cast and crew were the same musicians who played on *Genuine Cowhide.* The title track is, for all intent practical purposes, a disco song, but one read through the lessons of hard soul and funk with a huge horn section kicking it over the top of the vocal. "Let Love Come Between Us," which had been a mid-level hit for Bootsy's Rubber Band, is given a more solid soul treatment here. Both these tracks are significant in that they offer a view into what is McClinton's focused record from his early periods. R&B, funk, and soul are the basis for virtually everything here. Even the country tunes, such as Jimmie Rodgers' "In the Jailhouse Now" or the prison chain gang song "No More Cane," are given this treatment. And while that may sound hideous to purists of traditional music, truth is, you'd never get McClinton anyway, so take your musical fascism somewhere else. "Under Suspicion" takes a groove sensibility from Marvin Gaye's "Heard It Through the Grapevine" and turns it into snaky, overdriven groove 'n' roll. There's a read of Tony Joe White's "Hold on to Your Hiney" that's less swampy but way funkier. Horns punching up the fill between the lines and synthesizers kick the edges of the melody as popping bass and razor-wire guitars create the body. McClinton shoves White's humorous lyric over the line into the deeply sexual. It works despite some of the dated-sounding synth washes. Like its predecessor, McClinton wrote minimally for this recording, but it hardly matters; he makes all these songs his own anyway, and nowhere is this more evident than in the closer, "Turn on Your Lovelight," which is a stomping, Ray Charles soul-based arrangement with country edges in the backbeat and funked-up fat-belly bass. It goes on forever and one can feel the horns and McClinton's voice in the spine, right where they belong. Highly recommended. *—Thom Jurek*

Second Wind / 1978 / Mercury ✦✦✦✦

After his ABC deal collapsed, Delbert McClinton signed with Phil Walden's Capricorn Records in 1978. *Second Wind* was his debut for the label and was produced by the legendary Johnny Sandlin (of the Allman Brothers' *Fillmore East* and *Brothers and Sisters* fame), with backing by the entire Muscle Shoals stable—horns and rhythm section, and Sandlin on lead guitar, and Clydie King and Bonnie Bramlett leading a quartet of female backing vocalists. The recipe was right for a burning session of Southern-fried soul, R&B, and funky rock & roll. The material was solid. First there was "'B' Movie" (aka the notorious "'B' Movie Boxcar Blues" from the *Blues Brothers* movie in 1980) from the Delbert & Glen project that derailed a few years earlier. McClinton's own "Take It Easy," "It Ain't Whatcha Eat But the Way That Ya Chew It," "Maybe Someday Baby," and "Lovinest Man" were also on the set; each one a soulful funky groover, with "Take It Easy" being a straight-up Memphis-styled soul tune. The new arrangement of Taj Mahal/Jesse Ed Davis' take on "Corrina" shuffled and simmered the pot with a burgeoning intensity. The Allmans themselves, immediately following "In Memory of Elizabeth Reed" during their live set, could have executed this spooky, jazzed-up read of Willie Dixon's "Spoonful." The horn chart in Chris Kenner and Dave Bartholomew's "Sick and Tired" is so greasy it nearly slides off the platter. Add McClinton's harmonica to the break, and it's groove-a-licious dirty gumbo. In addition, McClinton's rhythmic delivery on Johnny Cash's "Big River" completely reinvents the tune before the set gets carried out with McClinton's Allen Toussaint-inspired "Lovinest Man," on which Barry Beckett's electric piano shines. *Second Wind* is a smoldering slow burn of an album and sounds as fresh in the 21st century as when it was recorded. *—Thom Jurek*

Keeper of the Flame / 1979 / Mercury ✦✦✦✦

Keeper of the Flame was the follow-up to *Second Wind* and was to prove once again to be the last record Delbert McClinton would record for a label that was going out of business; in this case it would be Capricorn. The sound of the album is quite different in that it was cut in Los Angeles rather than in Macon. Also, there are no Muscle Shoals players on the date. McClinton's road band was augmented by bassist Willie Weeks, pianist John Jarvis, and Hammond B-3 king Old Joe Walk; Bob Harwell was the entire horn section, playing all four saxophones with John Hug; and Billy Sanders played guitars (they were with Johnny Sandlin on *Second Wind* as well). Sandlin was still in the producer's chair and seemed to understand intrinsically all of the seeming contradictions in McClinton's sound—he exploited them to the maximum. The album is a laid-back mix of killer soul, white-hot R&B, and country funk; there's little rock & roll on this set, perhaps because Jarvis' style was already so rooted in the barroom barrelhouse style of pianists there was no room for another pursuit. In terms of material there was no shortage of great songs. Randall Bramblett's "Plain Old Makin' Love" is restless country-soul; with its Memphis-styled horn lines grafted onto the refrain, one could hear Otis Redding singing the sh*t out of this tune. As it stands, McClinton makes it his own. In addition there are two Don Covay covers, both "Have Mercy" and "See Saw," as well as a Doc Pomus tune ("A Mess of Blues") and Chuck Berry's "I'm Talking About You." Glen Clark's "I Don't Want to Hear It Anymore" from the old Delbert & Glen days resurfaces here completely reworked and funked up to the max. The album's highlight, however, is the oft covered yet never equaled McClinton tune "Two More Bottles of Wine" with a trio of backing vocalists singing gospel. Rather than the anthem Emmylou Harris made of it; here it is a hymn of resignation and acceptance that, come what may, right now is all you've got to make the most of it. McClinton's harp solo adds to the street-cred nature of the tune. This is a soulful shoulder shrug that could have closed the album but instead precludes "See Saw." No matter. Like its predecessor, there isn't a weak link in this bunch, and despite the fact that the album went nowhere, it endures as a prime example of McClinton's genius as a singer, writer, and performer. *—Thom Jurek*

The Jealous Kind / 1980 / Capitol ✦✦✦✦✦

Vocalist, songwriter, and harmonica ace Delbert McClinton has label-hopped more than just about anybody still recording. He also experienced a number of popular rebirths after fallow periods. There was never any need for a critical reevaluation of McClinton; his work has always been above the standard. This 1980 date on the Muscle Shoals Sound imprint for Capitol was produced by legend Barry Beckett. It showcased what McClinton's strong suits were at the dawn of the decade: hard funky soul and gritty R&B. It charted at number 34. Whether it be on the opening Larry Henley-penned "Shotgun Rider," which was already a hit for flash-in-the-pan country singer Joe Sun, or Van Morrison's "Bright Side of the Road," McClinton transformed them all into driving, smoking, gritty Southern white soul. Backed by the Shoals rhythm section and a host of stellar musicians and backing vocalists, McClinton turns in an absolutely burning performance. Ten tracks of rubber-meets-the-road, rollin', strollin', hip-grindin', rocked-up soul were out of time and space in the 1980 in terms of the pop charts, but that doesn't mean the record was out-dated. It was merely ahead of its time. With songwriters on board like New Orleans legend Bobby Charles, who contributed the title track and "I Can't Quit You," with its killer second-line rhythm. Bonnie Bramlett offers a searing backing vocal on "Givin' It Up for Your Love," and John D. Whyker's "Baby Ruth," which flopped via John Prine's limp version, is turned into an anthem of dirty love here. In addition there is a completely sexed-up version of Al Green's "Take Me to the River"—forget the Talking Heads' anorexic white-boy version, will ya? Add another four variations on the Southern-fried R&B formula with rock overdrive, indulgence, and edginess, and you have one of McClinton's best records of the era. —*Thom Jurek*

Plain from the Heart / 1981 / Capitol ◆◆◆◆
Despite the fact that the previous year's album *The Jealous Kind* charted at number 34, and that Delbert McClinton used a similar approach to *Plain From the Heart*, it topped at a disappointing number 181. Perhaps it's the fact that McClinton had been out on the road working his ass off with a crack band for a year and didn't have as much time to carefully consider the material choices. Where *The Jealous Kind* was a blend of soul and R&B variations that included basic rock & roll and country, *Plain From the Heart* relied heavily on hard R&B standards and material. It's a much funkier album than *The Jealous Kind*, but its drive is caught in third gear the entire time. There's not a weak song here, but neither is there a "Shotgun Rider" or "Givin' It Up for Your Love." Two covers—"In the Midnight Hour" and "Lipstick Traces (On a Cigarette)"—were surprising choices in that they'd been done so often that, while McClinton's versions are meaty enough and shovel out the grit, they add little new to these nuggets. Two Frankie Miller tunes come closer: "Heartbreak Radio," a solid rocker with killer horn work fill around in the vocals from the pocket, and "A Fool in Love," with its jagged guitar lines snaggling around the verses while becoming punchy chorded riffs in the refrains. The best cuts here are McClinton's own contributions, the steamy bluesified "I Wanna Thank You Baby," with stinging Jimmy Johnson guitar lines, and "Sandy Beaches," written with John Jarvis. It's a slow to midtempo soul groover; gorgeous Barry Beckett keyboard work underlines McClinton's best vocal on the set. Chuck Willis' "I Feel So Bad" is wonderfully reinterpreted by McClinton here, turned into a greasy funky groover instead of the desperate moaner it was originally. The set closes with Jerry West's "Rooster Blues," and while it's an acceptable Joe Turner-styled blues shouter, it's a surprising choice for the album, let alone as its closer. But this is quibbling. In all, *Plain From the Heart* is prime McClinton and deserved a hell of a lot better than it got in the marketplace at the time. —*Thom Jurek*

Honky Tonkin' / 1989 / Alligator ◆◆◆

The Best of Delbert McClinton / 1989 / Curb ◆◆◆◆◆
It's only 11 tracks, but *The Best of Delbert McClinton* contains nearly everything you need to know about how the eclectic blues/country/soul performer sounds, even if it doesn't have every good song he recorded. Nevertheless, it has the best moments from his early '70s records, and is a terrific introduction to his work. —*Thom Owens*

Live From Austin / 1989 / Alligator ◆◆◆◆

I'm With You / 1990 / Curb ◆◆◆
I'm With You is another solid release from the road-tested, fan-approved vocalist Delbert McClinton. At the time of this release, McClinton hadn't done a studio effort since 1981's somewhat disappointing *Plain From the Heart*. The gift of *I'm With You* is that McClinton makes it sound like he had been away for ten days rather then almost ten years. "That's the Way I Feel" is an effortless country blues bop with great, punchy Memphis by way of Tower of Power styled horns. Unlike many artists, McClinton wasn't stingy with a good track, and Jimmy Hall shows up on the old-fashioned "Got You on My Mind" and offers great harmony. Although *I'm With You* has McClinton is good voice and spirits, the tracks tend to run together, and the results don't click during the first listen. The album standout, "The Real Thing," has McClinton put through the ringer in a good way by a conquest as he bellows the title and the lyrics with glee. The last track, "My Love Is Burnin'," has McClinton extending the album's horny nature with another great vocal. *I'm With You* was co-produced by McClinton and Muscle Shoals stalwart Barry Beckett. Rather than trying to replicate McClinton's late-'70s sound, *I'm With You* has subtle touches of the newer commercial and polished country of the time mixed with the soul McClinton is known for. Although many fans may think they've heard this all before and better, this has a way of impressing with repeated plays. —*Jason Elias*

Never Been Rocked Enough / 1992 / Curb ◆◆◆
One of those influential "musician's musician" types, vocalist/harp-player Delbert McClinton was able to call on the likes of Bonnie Raitt, Tom Petty, and Melissa Etheridge for support on *Never Been Rocked Enough*. The results cover the whole checkerboard while remaining vintage McClinton: his harp wails on "Everytime I Roll the Dice," "Can I Change My Mind" flirts with Motown soul; "Blues as Blues Can Get" defines the confessional blues ballad; "I Used to Worry" and the title track chug into Band/Little Feat territory. The disc also includes the performer's Grammy winning duet with Bonnie Raitt, "Good Man, Good Woman." —*Roch Parisien*

Delbert McClinton / Jul. 13, 1993 / Curb ◆◆◆◆

Honky Tonk 'n Blues / 1994 / MCA ◆◆◆

Classics, Vol. 1: The Jealous Kind / Apr. 5, 1994 / Curb ◆◆◆◆
Classics, Vol. 1: The Jealous Kind is a ten-track, budget-priced collection that features a good cross-section of highlights from McClinton's Curb and Capitol recordings, including "Shotgun Rider," "I Can't Quit You," "Going Back to Louisiana," "Take Me to the River" and "My Sweet Baby." —*Stephen Thomas Erlewine*

Classics, Vol. 2: Plain From the Heart / 1994 / Curb ◆◆◆◆
Classics, Vol. 2: Plain From the Heart is a ten-track budget-priced collection that features a good cross-section of highlights from McClinton's Curb and Capitol recordings, including "Be Good to Yourself," "A Fool in Love," "I've Got Dreams to Remember," "In the Midnight Hour," "Sandy Beaches," "Lipstick Traces (On a Cigarette)" and "I Feel So Bad." —*Stephen Thomas Erlewine*

Great Songs: Come Together / 1995 / Curb ◆◆

Victim of Life's Circumstances/Genuine Cowhide / Dec. 17, 1996 / Raven ◆◆◆◆◆
Raven is to be congratulated for their Delbert McClinton series. There are three two-fers in the series available covering his years at ABC, Capricorn, and Capitol's Muscle Shoals Sound (MSS) imprint. *Victim of Life's Circumstances* and *Genuine Cowhide* were his first two albums for ABC and basically his first two solo recordings. They show the restless musical vision that McClinton, a Lubbock, TX, native like fellow adventurer Buddy Holly, was possessed by that blurred the lines between hard honky tonk country, Memphis soul, funk, classic New Orleans R&B, Chicago blues, and more. McClinton is unique in that not only does he display here his considerable gift as a singer and musical gadfly, but he's also a stunning harmonica player—who taught John Lennon the licks that ended up on "Love Me Do" and songwriter. The former album is comprised entirely of McClinton's compositions, the latter a set of rock, soul, and R&B covers with two of his own gems tossed in for measure. Both records were cut in Nashville with a set of studio musicians known for their outside playing—Bobby & Buddy Emmons, Reggie & Chip Young (who produced both records), Buddy Spicher, and more. Both of these albums are indispensable for McClinton fans and are the best possible introduction to those who only know his later work. The sound is impeccable, having been completely remastered from original tapes, and the package includes liners by Don McLeese and session photos. In addition to these two outings, Raven includes four bonus tracks from McClinton's third ABC album, *Love Rustler*. Another four are spread over the other two-fers. Price is standard, though these all come from Australia. —*Thom Jurek*

One of the Fortunate Few / Oct. 7, 1997 / Rising Tide ◆◆◆
Like the first track says, Delbert McClinton is like an old weakness, comin' on strong. McClinton's music is a hybrid of rock, country and blues, though that's much too analytical for this roadhouse. Sung and played throughout with sass and a knowing grin, this is music that speaks to everyone. And for once the guest artists add just the right amount, neither dominating nor lessening the proceedings. —*Ross Boissoneau*

Crazy Cajun Recordings / Feb. 18, 1999 / Edsel ◆◆◆

● **The Ultimate Collection** / Jun. 1, 1999 / Hip-O ◆◆◆◆◆
Hip-O's *The Ultimate Collection* comes very close to fulfilling the promise of its title. Over the course of 18 tracks, the compilation traces the evolution of Delbert McClinton's career, concentrating on his recordings for ABC, Capricorn, Capitol and Rising Tide, while hitting almost all of the major highlights. True, there may be a personal favorite or two missing for hardcore fans, but there is no better introduction to this acclaimed Texas musician than this. —*Stephen Thomas Erlewine*

Genuine Rhythm & the Blues / Mar. 28, 2000 / Hip-O ◆◆◆
Far from a comprehensive overview of Delbert McClinton's four decade career, this is an enjoyable yet relatively brief disc focusing entirely on covers of classic R&B material. Compiled from the rugged Texas singer's four early solo albums recorded from 1974 through 1979, it shines a light onto McClinton's varied influences as well as being a consistently enjoyable listen. A cursory scan of the song titles initially indicates there's not much exciting here. Many of these classics such as Bobby "Blue" Bland's "Turn on Your Lovelight," Fats Domino's "Blue Monday," and Don Covay's "Have Mercy" are well known through either their original versions or numerous renditions throughout the years. Upon closer listen though McClinton's approach to them is effortlessly soulful, and some of his arrangements—in particular transforming Willie Dixon's "Spoonful" from a wailing Chicago blues to a swampy soul stirrer—are refreshingly unique. McClinton's sand- and honey-inflected vocals flow easily, and his sharp band including horns, female backing vocals and tight ensemble playing, wrap themselves around the songs with loose precision. The songs of Elvis Presley, Jimmie Rodgers, Chuck Berry, Johnny Ace, Big Joe Turner, the Clovers, and Bo Diddley all become McClinton tunes as he latches onto their varied genres and transforms them into rollicking R&B. The anthology shares only one selection with the excellent *Ultimate Collection*, but even though it's cobbled together from albums recorded over five years, McClinton's cohesive style bonds these tracks into a surprisingly unified whole. Thoughtful and informative liner notes explain the source material, and the lack of individual personnel listings, as well as the album's relative brevity, prove to be minor shortcomings. —*Hal Horowitz*

Nothing Personal / Mar. 6, 2001 / New West ◆◆◆◆
McClinton's first outing for the independent Austin label New West, *Nothing Personal* features more of the Texan harp player's loose blend of rock, blues, and honky tonk. He penned all the cuts here, sometimes in tandem with producer Gary Nicholson and Benmont Tench of Tom Petty & the Heartbreakers fame (Tench also sits in on keyboards for a few cuts). The lyrical concerns take in the usual stories of love and its travails, which McClinton consistently phrases in his own rough-hewn yet sweet way. He also contributes some of his ace harmonica work to several of the tracks. The selections feature McClinton's standard variety, ranging from barroom rockers like "Squeeze Me" and the vintage country side "Birmingham Tonight" to the south-of-the-border ballad "When Rita Leaves." Another fine release from one of Texas' best. —*Stephen Cook*

Jealous Kind/Plain from the Heart / Jun. 5, 2001 / Raven ◆◆◆◆
This two-fer from the Australian Raven label is a part of a series of Delbert McClinton reissues. All of them come with new liner notes, session photos, and bonus tracks. These two albums, from 1980 and 1981, respectively, represent a renaissance for McClinton of sorts.

While he never had a fallow period creatively, *The Jealous Kind* allowed him a renewed commercial viability even if it was short-lived. Both records were issued by the Muscle Shoals Sound imprint of Capitol Records and were produced by Barry Beckett with the Muscle Shoals rhythm section and horns. While the first disc is centered around diversity in its song choices—by everyone from Larry Henley to Bobby Charles to Van Morrison to Al Green to Jerry Williams—and took radical approaches to reinterpreting the material through soul, blues, funk, rock, and country, the latter chose hard-driving Southern-fried funk and R&B and a relatively close-to-the-vest approach in terms of material—most notably covers of "In the Midnight Hour" and Naomi Neville's "Lipstick Traces (On a Cigarette)." The material is strong and inspired, but the best cuts are the two McClinton contributed himself—the acid blues of "I Wanna Thank You Baby" and the soulful midtempo ballad "Sandy Beaches." Nonetheless, it's a tough album full of great performances. In addition to the two albums, three tracks from McClinton's classic *Love Rustler* LP are included—"As Long as I Got You," Tony Joe White's "Hold on to Your Hiney," and a stirring wooly version of Jimmie Rodgers' "In the Jailhouse Now." *—Thom Jurek*

Second Wind/Keeper of the Flame / Jun. 11, 2002 / Raven ✦✦✦✦

This two-fer represents both albums Delbert McClinton cut for Capricorn Records, which was to close its doors for the first time in 1979. Esteemed producer Johnny Sandlin was on board for both recordings and brought unique touches to each. On *Second Wind* he brought the entire Muscle Shoals rhythm and horn sections from Alabama to Macon and enlisted a host of other studio hotshots—including himself on lead guitar. From the salacious "B-Movie" to the a new take on the Taj Mahal/Jesse Ed Davis arrangement of "Corinna," to McClinton's own "Lovinest Man" and a sultry read of Willie Dixon's "Spoonful," the album was pure Dixie-fried grease and gravy. *Keeper of the Flame* was recorded in L.A. with McClinton's road band, bassist Willie Weeks, a trio of backing vocalists, the incredible pianist John Jarvis, and B sharp whiz Old Joe Walk (both of whom drove the album). It's a more laid-back affair, less raw and immediate perhaps, but what it gives up in punch it more than compensates for in material, emotion, and delivery. McClinton's own version of "Two More Bottles of Wine" registers here as far superior to any other as it comes from the bottom of the grain in his voice. Unlike Emmylou Harris' version, this is not a party anthem, but a "sh*t at least I still have this and that's OK" statement of acceptance. In addition are Don Covay's two classics, "See-Saw" and "Have Mercy," as well as Glen Clark's "I Don't Want to Hear It Anymore," Doc Pomus' killer "A Mess of Blues" (that McClinton goes over the top to deliver the full emotion in), and a reinvented version of Chuck Berry's "I'm Talkin' About You." Here are two awesome recordings from the beginning of McClinton's prime for a great price with great sound and notes. *—Thom Jurek*

Room to Breathe / Sep. 24, 2002 / New West ✦✦

McClinton's ebullience is undeniable on *Room to Breathe*, yet a sense of going through the paces permeates the project. Chord progressions are predictable; this is expected, of course, when playing the blues, as McClinton does frequently here, but with the exception of the lovely ballad "Don't Want to Love You," not much compositional substance is evident. Too often, he compensates by leading his band through overly exuberant performances, but on cuts like "Money Honey," this only creates an impression of the artist as a kind of Cowtown Tom Jones. He seems as well to strain for his lyrics; lines like "You love a man that don't love you/You musta got a lot of abuse" reflect both a lenient rhyme scheme and an overly topical vernacular for the idiom. One track, "Lone Star Blues," stands out for its splashy presentation; over a clip-clop beat that might have been more effective if slightly slowed down, an eye-crossing assembly of Americana superstars gathers to sing on each chorus. Outside of *Will the Circle Be Unbroken*, this much talent has rarely been herded into one studio, yet all that makes each guest distinct gets buried into a single harmonized holler. This feeling of being hurried, and of misplaced creative energy, is what *Room to Breathe* leaves behind. *—Robert L. Doerschuk*

The McCormick Brothers

Group / Traditional Bluegrass, Bluegrass-Gospel, Bluegrass

The McCormick Brothers are not as well-known as other country and bluegrass harmonizers who were popular in the 1950s, such as the Stanley Brothers and the Louvin Brothers. But they were a good bluegrass band, though they weren't as long-lived as the most renowned ones working the same turf, and certainly didn't record as often or sell as many records. The seeds for the act were planted when Lloyd McCormick and Kelly McCormick formed a guitar-mandolin duo as youngsters, performing duets on Kentucky and Tennessee radio stations. Their personnel and instrumentation expanded, and younger brother Haskel McCormick joined on banjo in the early '50s. At one point, the lineup was filled out with a couple of cousins, Hayden Clark (on bass) and Billy Clark (on fiddle), before the youngest brother joined on bass and Dewel Bullington on fiddle; Charlie Nixon later joined on dobro.

From the mid-'50s to the early '60s, the McCormick Brothers recorded for Hickory, run by Fred Rose (who co-ran the enormously successful Nashville publisher Acuff-Rose with Roy Acuff). The McCormicks did some rockabilly sides in an attempt to boost their sales, but are known primarily for the fairly straight bluegrass recordings they did on Hickory, alternating between harmony vocals and purely instrumental workouts. Their biggest seller was their first single for the label in 1954, "Red Hen Boogie," penned by Charlie Louvin and Ira Louvin. They also did an album after leaving Hickory for Metromedia. Eighteen sides from their bluegrass Hickory singles were assembled for the 2002 Varese Sarabande compilation *The Very Best of the McCormick Brothers*. *—Richie Unterberger*

● **The Very Best of the McCormick Brothers** / Mar. 19, 2002 / Varese Vintage ✦✦✦✦✦

These 18 songs, taken from singles issued on the Hickory label between the mid-'50s and early '60s, comprise the heart of the McCormick Brothers' discography. It deliberately focuses on their bluegrass recordings, though it might have been nice to include one or two of their rockabilly cuts for those not intimately familiar with those rare and little-known records. What's here is high-quality bluegrass with a mere touch of modernized 1950s country production, heavy on brotherly harmonies. It's not as top drawer as the most famous artists working the style, but it's certainly respectable and nothing that fans of harmonizing bluegrass groups of the mid-20th century, family acts or otherwise, wouldn't take a shine to. The vocal numbers share space with instrumentals showcasing their instrumental virtuosity, particularly the fast banjo-picking of Haskel McCormick. Their debut single and biggest seller, a cover of the Louvin Brothers' "Red Hen Boogie," is here as well, though it's not too typical of their recordings, both in its slight boogie flavor and insertion of novelty hen clucks. *—Richie Unterberger*

The McCoury Brothers

Group / Close Harmony, Traditional Bluegrass

Del and Jerry McCoury pursued individual careers in bluegrass before the Pennsylvania-born siblings teamed up for the 1987 Rounder album, *The McCoury Brothers*. Older brother Del had played banjo before switching to guitar and singing lead with Bill Monroe's Blue Grass Boys in 1963-1964. He subsequently led his Dixie Pals and recorded for both Rounder and Rebel. Jerry sang and played bass with Red Allen and the Kentuckians, as well as with Don Reno and Bill Harrell. The McCoury Brothers' sole album together to date is a wonderful close-harmony exposition of bluegrass, rooted in the "brother duo" tradition. *—Mark A. Humphrey*

The McCoury Brothers / 1995 / Rounder ✦✦✦✦✦

Jerry and Del McCoury fit together like hand-in-glove on these fine performances. *—Mark A. Humphrey*

Del McCoury (Delano Floyd McCoury)

b. Feb. 1, 1939, Bakersville, NC

Guitar, Vocals / Bluegrass, Traditional Bluegrass

Among the most distinguished practitioners of traditional bluegrass, for over three decades Del McCoury's voice was the epitome of the "high lonesome sound." Born Delano Floyd McCoury, he was raised in Bakersville, NC. In 1941, he and his family moved to Glen Rock, PA, where he got his start as a five-string banjo picker with Keith Daniels and the Blue Ridge Ramblers. Later he played with Jack Cooke's Virginia Mountain Boys in Baltimore. McCoury got his first big break in 1963 when Bill Monroe hired the Virginia Mountain Boys to play a few New York gigs. Monroe was impressed by the young banjo player and invited him to join his Blue Grass Boys. Shortly after accepting Monroe's offer, McCoury became the group's lead vocalist and took up rhythm guitar. In early 1964, he recorded one single with Monroe, but a month later returned home to marry.

Following his marriage, he and fiddler Billy Baker spent three months in California playing with the Golden State Boys. Upon his return back east, McCoury began playing and recording with the Shady Valley Boys. McCoury left the group in 1967 and founded the Dixie Pals with Bill Emerson, Wayne Yates and Billy Baker. McCoury and his Dixie Pals, which underwent several membership changes, played together for over 20 years and recorded on such labels as Rounder, Revonah, Leather and Rebel. In 1987, the unit was renamed the Del McCoury Band following the additions of his sons Ronnie on mandolin and Robbie on banjo along with fiddler Tad Marks and bass player Mike Brantley.

The period following the formation of the Del McCoury band proved to be very productive, with several terrific releases for Rounder. The band carefully bridged the gap between the interesting song choices and instrumentation of the best progressive bluegrass groups, while still retaining the high lonesome style of traditional bluegrass. In early 1999, the band reached a whole new group of listeners when they backed singer/songwriter Steve Earle on his successful traditionally themed album *The Mountain*. Around that time, McCoury and sons amicably ended their relationship with Rounder, moving to Ricky Skaggs' Ceili label for their next series of albums. *—Sandra Brennan*

I Wonder Where You Are Tonight / 1968 / Arhoolie ✦✦✦✦

McCoury's first album as a bandleader was recorded in two days in December 1967. Although he didn't have a regular band at the time, he was backed by a solid quartet (though five other musicians appear in all, with Tommy Neal and Dewey Renfro alternating on bass), three of them capable background singers as well. McCoury's vocals had the high, lonesome sound for which bluegrass is esteemed, but put over with more easy-going, engaging friendliness than some slicker, flashier singers and players. The songs were a well-chosen mix of traditional standards and songs by his one-time boss Bill Monroe; the Monroe-Lester Flatt collaboration "Sweetheart You Done Me Wrong"; Johnny Bond; Kitty Wells; Jimmie Rodgers; and, on just one tune (the ballad "Dreams," one of the more pensive heartfelt numbers), McCoury himself. [According to Chris Strachwitz's liner notes, the 2002 CD reissue discards the compression heard on the stereo mix of the original LP and more accurately reflects the music as it was originally recorded.] *—Richie Unterberger*

Del McCoury Sings Bluegrass / 1968 / Arhoolie ✦✦✦

Livin' on the Mountain / 1971 / Rebel ✦✦✦

Recorded in 1971, with a band that doesn't meet McCoury's usual standards, it wasn't released for five years. *—Brian Mansfield*

Collector's Special / 1971 / Grassound ✦✦

High on a Mountain / 1972 / Rounder ✦✦✦✦

A bit less than 40 minutes in length, this set of tunes can be considered as revolutionary as the arrival of Bill Monroe on the country music scene. While nobody is going to give Del McCoury credit for inventing bluegrass, he and his Dixie Pals seem well past the midpoint in developing a new way to interpret the genre on this classic early-'70s recording, reissued on compact disc more than two decades later. McCoury's style on this record can be compared to the Modern Jazz Quartet. Like that long-running and popular group, Del McCoury & the Dixie Pals commonly were described simply by tacking the word "chamber" in the right place, as if it were a Post-it note, making "chamber bluegrass" out of the proceedings just like the MJQ were critically served up as a "chamber jazz" group. It is more than attire that inspired these descriptions, not that clothing isn't considered an important part of a performer's image by some. Indeed, it was enough for the MJQ to walk on-stage in their normal attire of suits and ties to turn off certain jazz listeners. Avant-garde jazz maestro Anthony Braxton has written about this, calling it "the sweaty brow syndrome." The desire to see a player really "gittin' down and sweatin'" as the music heats up on-stage is in complete contrast to the commonly accepted notion of a chamber music ensemble, expected to stay cool and dry. The bluegrass audience is philosophically ruled by something called "the yee-haw factor," which sounds like it could even be a sub-department of the sweaty brow syndrome, or vice versa. This McCoury record "will never be among the records I play constantly," Jack O'Ryan wrote in *Old Time Music* magazine the year this album was originally released. Referring to the term "chamber bluegrass," the writer bemoans what he hears as a lack of "precipitous, exhilarating flangdang." For the record, the MJQ would have considered McCoury and band underdressed on their album cover photo: white shirts, but no ties and jackets. Brows are sweating, true, but it is probably because the group is posing in the middle of a pasture. The huge audience that McCoury built up through dedicated, almost nonstop touring is hardly there to hear a Hindemith quartet, make no mistake. Neophytes in the bluegrass world might even think they had entered an alternate universe when a number such as "Big Rock in the Road" can be compared to chamber music. What is interesting about the notion is not the perversity of judging players by their sweat secretions; such a problem could easily be balanced out by having players pedal an exercise bike while performing. But in both jazz and bluegrass, the subject of chamber music is essentially another example of these genres drawing in outside influences, one of the great sustaining factors in either style. The musical atmosphere that makes some critics think they are breathing the stuffy air of a classical recital hall can better be described as a sense of precise articulation, and a concept of sustaining certain moods, that seems to be a part of the way bluegrass pickers from McCoury's generation on up play their instruments. Logically, these stylistic developments are related to the players' exposure to the big wide world of musical styles. The early generations of players learned music from parents, relatives, and other locals, and heard their first country & western on *Grand Old Opry* broadcasts. By the '70s, Dixie Pal members such as sibling Jerry McCoury on bass and the superb banjoist Bill Runkle had absorbed these essential influences along with everything else from James Brown to Leonard Bernstein, and were just as likely to enjoy a broadcast of Bob Marley as Roy Acuff. The groundbreaking that McCoury did on this album turned out to be the foundation for a new and expanding audience for bluegrass. And since it inevitably led listeners back to Ralph Stanley, it can be assumed that even the old-time music crowd is happy about it by now, yee-haw factor or not. The quintet gets a wonderfully full sound on tracks such as the title number and the lovely "When I Stop Dreaming." Fiddler Billy Sage and Runkle mesh all over the place—"In My Mind to Ramble" is a journey for the listener as well as the narrator, while "I'm Lonely Tonight" is just not going to be the case for the listener to whom bluegrass is the best company of all. —*Eugene Chadbourne*

Del McCoury and the Dixie Pals / 1975 / Revonah ✦✦✦

Live in Japan / 1980 / Copper Creek ✦✦✦
A live concert with excellent performances and strong material, the recording nevertheless leaves something to be desired. —*Brian Mansfield*

Don't Stop the Music / 1988 / Rounder ✦✦✦✦✦
Don't Stop the Music is a typically entertaining and surprisingly bluesy release from the Del McCoury Band, featuring a selection of originals and covers, including a version of the George Jones title track. —*Thom Owens*

★ Classic Bluegrass / 1991 / Rebel ✦✦✦✦✦
It would be impossible to pinpoint the high point of Del McCoury's career in bluegrass for two reasons: one being that he has been so consistently good in everything he's done, and the other being that he seems to incredibly keep getting better and better, making any speculation prone to revision. That being said, this compilation of his recordings for Rebel Records from 1974-1984 showcases one of bluegrass' great voices at one of the many peaks of his career. The album is set up without chronology in mind, but the change from one lineup of the Dixie Pals into another isn't noticeable, and the whole thing flows quite naturally from beginning to end. High harmonies and excellent musicianship have long been McCoury trademarks, and these recordings are especially interesting where they showcase the first appearances of mandolin player Ronnie McCoury, who would eventually go on to become one of the most celebrated pickers in bluegrass. Longtime fans of the Del McCoury Band's work will want to complete their collection with this album, and recent converts to the man would be well-suited to start their collections here. —*Zac Johnson*

Blue Side of Town / May 15, 1992 / Rounder ✦✦✦✦✦
Named for his version of the Patty Loveless hit "The Blue Side of Town," McCoury covers Steve Earle's "If You Need a Fool" and Arthur "Big Boy" Crudup's "That's Alright Mama." When it comes to song choice, he may be the most well-rounded man in bluegrass. —*Brian Mansfield*

☆ Deeper Shade of Blue / 1993 / Rounder ✦✦✦✦✦
A classic from the word go, McCoury's love affair with blues is never more explicit than here, where songs with the titles like "Cheek to Cheek With the Blues," "A Deeper Shade of Blue," and "The Bluest Man in Town" are the order of the day. Never a purist when it comes to songs, McCoury covers Kevin Welch's "True Love Never Dies," Willie Nelson's "Man with the Blues," and the Jerry Lee Lewis hit "What Made Milwaukee Famous." His version of Lefty Frizzell's "If You've Got the Money Honey" is downright piercing. —*Brian Mansfield*

Cold Hard Facts / Sep. 17, 1996 / Rounder ✦✦✦
An exemplary album from the group that roots music figurehead David Grisman has referred to as "my favorite bluegrass band," *The Cold Hard Facts* features everything one

has come to expect from the McCourys: virtuoso (but never unnecessarily flashy) playing, innovative song selection, and the finest tenor lead vocals since Bill Monroe. The band imbues originals and cover tunes by a broad selection of writers (Tom Petty, Robert Cray, Ray Price, and others) with a passion and energy that gives these odd choices the emotional weight of bluegrass standards—a feat that even less traditionally rooted, "progressive" bands can rarely accomplish. Although the elder McCoury always leads the way with his flawless singing, Del's sons have developed into stellar musicians as well. Ronnie McCoury's expert rhythm mandolin playing is the secret ingredient to many songs' driving grooves and brother Rob McCoury's muscular, bluesy, Roland White-like banjo stylings give the music an appealing heft. Bassist Mike Bub also deserves special mention, his classically understated, near-perfect bass work serving as the prototypical low-end glue. Anyone who claims to be a fan of bluegrass really can't go wrong with a Del McCoury Band album and, simply put, *The Cold Heart Facts* finds this stellar ensemble at the top of its game. —*Pemberton Roach*

Del Doc & Mac / Oct. 20, 1998 / Sugar Hill ✦✦✦✦

Family / Feb. 9, 1999 / Ceili Music ✦✦✦✦
Del McCoury has one of those high tenor voices that seems to be enriched, rather than undermined, by age. Although you'd never mistake him for a youngster, he can still let the high notes fly with the confidence of a singer half his age. And in collaboration with his mandolin-playing son Ronnie, he has built a top-notch traditional bluegrass band that manages to keep itself firmly rooted in the verities while still conducting such (largely successful) experiments as collaborating with punk-country icon Steve Earle and recording songs by commercial folkie John Sebastian. The band's latest finds McCoury covering Bill Monroe ("Get Down on Your Knees and Pray") and Jimmy Martin ("She's Left Me Again"), as well as the aforementioned Sebastian (the cute and clever "Nashville Cats"), and delivering a few fine originals as well. Highlights include Ronnie McCoury's vinegary instrumental "Red Eyes on a Mad Dog" and a great version of Verlon Thompson' s "Backslidin' Blues," not to mention the group's spookily beautiful rendition of "Get Down on Your Knees and Pray." —*Rick Anderson*

Del and the Boys / Jul. 10, 2001 / Hollywood ✦✦✦✦
On their second effort for Ricky Skaggs' Ceili label, Del McCoury and his band, the reigning kings of bluegrass (even if Ralph Stanley is the Pope) turn in a another solid, haunting, and even completely astonishing set that features everything from tunes about haunted train rides, biker outlaws who remain focused on their quest unto death, a Richard Thompson tune ("1952 Vincent Black Lightning"), and a blues tune supposedly gleaned from listening to Frank Sinatra, as well as more traditional bluegrass stompers about being high and lonesome, grief, lost love, and hanging out at the barnyard. Right, that sentence was a mouthful, but then, this is an album full of surprises and affirmations of how great Del and his boys are—especially that monster Ronnie McCoury on his mandolin and as a backing tenor singer. When music like this comes down the pipe and a record is structured as well as the band's live set (and just like the live set; other than microphones there are no electric instruments to be heard anywhere), bearing listeners out of their shells in the opening moments, taking them deep into the reality of the stories being offered in glorious four-part harmony with Del soaring above the band with a voice that encompasses all the emotion in the world in its grain, listeners are carried through each pitfall and blessed moment as the music kicks, whispers, slips, and slithers around them until they are moved by this band of minstrels into the heart of all things human and most things American. This is perhaps McCoury's finest outing yet. —*Thom Jurek*

My Dixie Home / Jul. 27, 2001 / Rebel Records ✦✦✦✦
The national music scene took notice of Del McCoury in 1999 when he and his band collaborated with country-punk icon Steve Earle, making the time right for some reissues and compilations. This collection is a good place to start. *My Dixie Home* compiles tracks originally released on various Rebel albums between 1974 and 1984 (along with one previously unreleased effort, the inessential "Call Collect on Christmas"); the plurality of selections comes from the excellent *Sawmill* album, which featured banjo player Paul Silvius (later a member of Joe Val's New England Bluegrass Boys), as well as McCoury's young son, Ronnie, already a fine mandolinist by this point. But the main attraction, of course, is McCoury's voice, a sharp and nasal whine that pierces the soul on hardcore traditional numbers like "My Dixie Home" and "White House Blues." This collection finds McCoury at the top of his form, and when he's at his best there are few bluegrass singers better. —*Rick Anderson*

Charlie McCoy

b. Mar. 28, 1941, Oak Hill, WV
Bass, Guitar, Harmonica / Country-Rock, Country-Pop, Nashville Sound/Countrypolitan
Charlie McCoy was perhaps the definitive Nashville session musician, a multi-talented performer best known for his harmonica playing and whose mastery of the instrument virtually defined its role within the context of modern country music. Though born in West Virginia on March 28, 1941, Charles Ray McCoy was raised in Miami, FL, where he first picked up the harmonica at the age of eight. By his mid-teens, he was playing harmonica and guitar in an area rock & roll band, and a few years later graduated to traveling the Florida rock and country circuits as a backup performer. At one local gig, he met Mel Tillis, who instructed McCoy to move to Nashville, which he did in 1959. After finding little work as a session player, he journeyed back to Florida, where he began studying musical theory and taking vocal lessons in addition to work as an arranger and conductor.

In 1960, McCoy auditioned as a guitarist for singer Johnny Ferguson, only to learn that the opening had been filled. Ferguson was still looking for a new drummer, however, so McCoy bought a kit, learned to play, and won the job. After contacting Tillis, he was introduced to agent Jim Denny, who helped the upstart musician find some work in Nashville. McCoy's first session was Roy Orbison's 1961 "Candy Man," and within months he was one of the most sought-after players on the scene. He also toured extensively as a drummer in Stonewall Jackson's band throughout the early '60s and released a handful of solo singles.

By the mid-'60s, McCoy was a fixture on Elvis Presley's Nashville and Los Angeles sessions, and in 1965, he began working with Bob Dylan, appearing on a string of legendary LPs that included *Highway 61 Revisited*, *Blonde on Blonde*, *John Wesley Harding*, and *Nashville Skyline*. As a result, McCoy became as much in demand among rock and folk artists as he was within the Nashville community and began performing with the likes of Ringo Starr, Al Kooper, Gordon Lightfoot, and John Stewart. At his peak, he was performing on over 400 sessions annually. In 1969, McCoy joined the country-rock band Area Code 615, with whom he recorded a self-titled LP, followed by *A Trip in the Country* in 1970. Also in 1969, he released a solo effort, *The Real McCoy*; while the album garnered little notice at the time of its release and was quickly deleted, in 1971 a Florida DJ began playing the track "I Started Loving Her Again" to massive listener response. A single was soon available, and the song reached the Top 20 in 1972. Even as his solo career began taking off, McCoy remained a constant in Nashville studios, and in the early '70s alone he worked with Paul Simon, Joan Baez, Kris Kristofferson, Leon Russell, and Steve Young.

When the remnants of Area Code 615 reformed as Barefoot Jerry, McCoy signed on and, with the group, issued three albums—1975's *You Can't Get Off With Your Shoes On*, the following year's *Keys to the Country*, and 1977's *Barefootin'*. At the same time, he played on records for Waylon Jennings, Tanya Tucker, and Wanda Jackson and also began a tenure as the musical director for the country comedy program *Hee Haw*, where he remained for many years. In 1978, he played England's Wembley Festival with Lloyd Green, and his popularity across the Atlantic soared. In the 1980s, he toured Europe frequently and began recording extensively there as well. By the early '90s, McCoy had cut back considerably on his studio work, although he continued to play with many prestigious artists. In 1996, he led a number of Nashville studio luminaries like the Jordanaires, Russ Hicks, Hargus "Pig" Robbins, and Bobby Ogdin during the sessions for the cult duo Ween's *12 Golden Country Greats*. *—Jason Ankeny*

The World of Charlie McCoy / 1968 / Monument ✦✦✦

The Real McCoy / 1969 / Monument ✦✦✦

Charlie McCoy / 1972 / Monument ✦✦✦

When it comes time to put together a project of his own, harmonica man Charlie McCoy seems to want to make up for all the empty space in his car trunk, never needed for much but a spare six-pack when he was off to another recording session packing his entire instrumental arsenal in his shirt pocket. Here listeners have nearly an army of various musicians conducting skilled maneuvers in and out of various recording sessions, hoping not to trod on each other's toes as the intricate arrangements unfold. A sure sign of someone trying to pack every possible instrument into his car is the presence of both bongos and vibraphone, and this album has both, along with some of the first use of Moog synthesizer on a country record, courtesy of the clever John Harris. There's no denying that it all sounds pretty good, that is unless the listener's tastes veer far afield from strongly country-pop-flavored instrumental music with the occasional chanting choir popping in. The strongest conceptual factor with this set of songs is that each tune is something of a show-stopper in some way, be it the rousing crowd-pleaser "Me and Bobby McGee" cut when it was in its full glory, the heart-melting (and potentially stomach-churning) "Danny Boy" featuring glorious pedal steel work from Curly Chalker, or a desperate "I Can't Stop Loving You." What philosophy was motivating this artist to create such an over the top, emotionally trying album is intriguing. On some levels, it just seems like someone trying way too hard, resulting in performances that have no choice other than to succumb to the basic inner rottenness of the material. Yet the music also seems to be sailing off into the sky at other times, the fine musicianship of the players more than enough to transform a mere "Rocky Top" or "Woman (Sensuous Woman)" into much more than just a song. Well, maybe not "Woman (Sensuous Woman)." *—Eugene Chadbourne*

Harpin' the Blues / 1975 / Monument ✦✦✦✦

One of McCoy's strongest solo efforts, *Harpin' the Blues* is an homage to his hero, Chicago blues master Little Walter. *—Jason Ankeny*

● **Greatest Hits** / 1982 / Monument ✦✦✦✦

Beam Me Up Charlie / 1989 / Step One ✦✦✦

McCoy recut a pair of old Area Code 615 numbers, "Southern Comfort" and "Katy Hill," for this release recorded in Denmark. He also covers Hank Williams' "Cold, Cold Heart" and fellow session ace Russ Hicks' "Funky Country Music." *—Jason Ankeny*

The Fastest Harp in the South / 1991 / Monument ✦✦✦✦

Out on a Limb / Dec. 1991 / Step One ✦✦✦

For *Out on a Limb*, McCoy enlisted the diverse talents of the well-regarded European touring unit the United, the Jordanaires, and Nashville session kings like Bobby Ogdin, Russ Hicks and Pig Robbins to tackle chestnuts like "You Don't Know Me" and Leon Payne's "You've Still Got a Place in My Heart." *—Jason Ankeny*

Charlie McCoy's 13th / Jan. 1, 1995 / Step One ✦✦✦✦

McCoy focuses on country standards for album number 13, including Hank Williams' "I'm So Lonesome I Could Cry" and Merle Haggard and Buck Owens' "I Started Loving You Again." He also makes an excursion into jazz to take on Count Basie's "One O'Clock Jump." *—Jason Ankeny*

Neal McCoy (Hubert Neal McGaughey Jr.)

b. Jul. 30, 1963, Jacksonville, TX

Vocals / Contemporary Country, Neo-Traditionalist Country

Neal McCoy's brand of neo-traditionalist honky tonk brought him a string of hits in the mid-'90s. McCoy was born Hubert Neal McGaughey Jr. in Jacksonville, TX, in 1963, to a father of Irish descent and a Filipino mother. He grew up listening to all kinds of music—country, swing, rock, disco, R&B—and first sang in local gospel choirs. His voice developed into a rich baritone, and he first put it to professional use in an R&B band; soon, however, he returned to country music, playing bars and clubs all over Texas. In 1981, he won a talent contest that was attended by Janie Fricke, and she helped him land a slot on tour as Charley Pride's opening act. He spent six years in that capacity, and finally left to pursue his own recording career in 1988, when he released his debut single, "That's How Much I Love You," under the name Neal McGoy (the pronunciation of his birth name). Modifying it to the more common McCoy, he released his debut album, *At This Moment*, on Atlantic in 1990. Despite McCoy's growing reputation for exciting, freewheeling live shows, neither it nor the follow-up, 1992's *Where Forever Begins*, sold all that well.

However, McCoy's fortunes took a turn for the better with his third album, 1994's *No Doubt About It*. Both the title track and "Wink" topped the country charts, and "The City Put the Country Back in Me" went Top Five, helping *No Doubt About It* sell over a million copies. Suddenly a breakout star, McCoy returned in 1995 with *You Gotta Love That*, another platinum seller that produced a total of three number-three singles: "For a Change," "They're Playin' Our Song," and the title track. 1996's *Neal McCoy* kept his hit streak going strong, giving him a third straight platinum album and another Top Five single in "Then You Can Say Goodbye." The following year saw the release of a *Greatest Hits* compilation, and McCoy offered a new album later in 1997 called *Be Good At It*. Despite another Top Five smash in "The Shake," album sales dipped below the million mark for the first time since McCoy's breakthrough. 1999's *The Life of the Party*, contrary to its title, was an album of ballads and soft country-pop tunes, and both it and 2000's *24-7-365* found McCoy's sales progressively slipping. Taking some time off to recharge, McCoy returned in early 2003 with *The Luckiest Man in the World*. *—Steve Huey*

At This Moment / 1990 / Atlantic ✦✦✦

This debut's most notable song is its title track, a country version of the Billy Vera prom-night pop hit. *—Brian Mansfield*

Where Forever Begins / 1992 / Atlantic ✦✦✦

It includes the singles "Where Forever Begins," "There Ain't Nothin' I Don't Like About You," and "Now I Pray for Rain." *—Brian Mansfield*

No Doubt About It / 1994 / Atlantic ✦✦✦✦✦

This Barry Beckett-produced disc was the first to capture the rock-influenced sound of McCoy's stage show (which usually included a rap version of *The Beverly Hillbillies* theme). Though McCoy had never had a single chart above number 21, the album gave the singer his first two number-one hits: "No Doubt About It" and "Wink." *—Brian Mansfield*

You Gotta Love That / 1995 / Atlantic ✦✦✦✦

Neal Mccoy / Jun. 1996 / Atlantic ✦✦✦

Neal McCoy's eponymous album is another set of immaculately crafted contemporary country music. From McCoy's polished but heartfelt performance to the slick, seamless selection of songs, there isn't an obvious flaw on the album. Some may complain that McCoy's approach is getting a bit pat and predictable, but the highlights—including the longtime stage favorite "Hillbilly Rap," and which features segments of "Day-O," "The Ballad of Jed Clampett," and "Rapper's Delight"—are well worth the time of any fan. *—Thom Owens*

● **Greatest Hits** / Jun. 10, 1997 / Atlantic ✦✦✦✦✦

Greatest Hits contains all of Neal McCoy's biggest contemporary country hits, including "Wink," "For a Change," "They're Playing Our Song," "You Gotta Love That" and "Then You Can Tell Me Goodbye," plus the new song "The Shake." *—Thom Owens*

Be Good At It / Oct. 28, 1997 / Atlantic ✦✦✦

The first album to follow a *Greatest Hits* collection usually provides an artist the opportunity to break free from his formulas and pursue a new path. It can also mean nothing, the artist just continuing to turn out the kind of music that supplied hits in the first place. That's what Neal McCoy chooses to do with *Be Good At It*, a perfectly fine collection of smoothed-over honky tonk and slick contemporary country ballads. McCoy has considerable charm—he's so engaging that he can effortlessly sell the weaker material here—and that's what makes the unadventurous nature of *Be Good At It* forgivable. Simply put, McCoy may have the potential to achieve more than this kind of contemporary country, but he's very good at this kind of music and it's still entertaining to hear him at the top of his form. *—Thom Owens*

The Life of the Party / Jan. 19, 1999 / Atlantic ✦✦✦

Ironically, *Life of the Party* is one of the slowest albums Neal McCoy has ever recorded—not the bustling collection of honky tonk ravers and country-rockers the title promises. Instead, it's an accomplished collection of midtempo country-pop and tearjerker ballads, all of which McCoy can deliver quite convincingly. After all, by this stage in the game, McCoy is undoubtedly a professional. He knows all the right notes, all the strings to pull, even though ballads aren't necessarily his forte. As a result, *Life of the Party* is listenable, even though it only occasionally matches the heights of his previous work. *—Stephen Thomas Erlewine*

24-7-365 / Aug. 22, 2000 / Warner Bros. ✦✦

McCoy's cheeseball brand of country has always been pretty simple stuff. On this straightforward set of songs he sets himself up in a singles bar, teaches the meaning of life and love to young 'uns, proclaims his everlasting devotion to some lucky lady, and generally sleepwalks through the entire lackluster group. Good intentions aside, there's no muscle to McCoy's work, and *24-7-365* is about as toothless as they come. *—Michael Gallucci*

Super Hits / Sep. 19, 2000 / Atlantic ✦✦✦

Neal McCoy was one of the most successful country artists of the '90s, mixing a commercial formula of contemporary country with honky tonk. This budget collection contains ten of his biggest Atlantic hits, including "You Gotta Love That," "Love Happens Like That," "No Doubt About It," and "Then You Can Tell Me Goodbye." Also included on this set is McCoy's version of the Nat King Cole hit "Straighten Up and Fly Right" originally released on his 1999 disc *Life of the Party*. *—Al Campbell*

Luckiest Man in the World / Jan. 28, 2003 / Warner Bros. ✦✦✦✦
With barely a nod to "Wink" and his other riff-happy hits, McCoy fills this album with quality material and digs into it with some of his finest singing to date. Aside from one novelty number, the goofball romp "Elvis in the Airport," these are straightforward songs, most of them adorned with melodies and chord changes any singer would adore. The title cut, an affirmation of virtues taken for granted, is especially dramatic, with a soaring chorus that can't help but ignite stage lights and pull audiences up to their feet. Eloquent lyrics abound, from a meditation on the familial admixture of love and hate in "All at the Same Time" to a moving examination of love lost in "Never Got to Say"—and "Put Your Best Dress On" qualifies as one of the finest romantic ballads in years. There are less-solemn moments too, but these—the simplistic ditty "Sing" and a boot-scoot throwaway called "Honky-Tonk Mona Lisa"—are the weakest links in an otherwise strong chain of songs. The last title, "I'm Your Biggest Fan," deserves special mention: Recorded live at Nashville's annual *Fan Fair*, it is quite simply the warmest expression on record of an artist's gratitude to his fans. Listen to it and you're guaranteed to feel better about yourself. *—Robert L. Doerschuk*

Mindy McCready (Malinda Gayle McCready)

b. Nov. 30, 1975, Fort Meyers, FL
Vocals / Contemporary Country
Mindy McCready's debut album, *Ten Thousand Angels*, elevated her into Nashville's music spotlight and established her as a promising singer. Born and raised in southern Florida, McCready (born Malinda Gayle McCready) graduated from high-school at the age of 16 with the intention of beginning her musical career early. Following her graduation, she took a part-time job in her mother's ambulance company and began concentrating on performing her music. When she was 18 years old, she moved to Nashville. She had made her mother a promise that she would go to college if she failed to break into the music industry within the space of a year. After a few months in Nashville, she met producer/songwriter Norro Wilson, who directed her demo tapes to producer David Malloy. Impressed with her tapes, Malloy agreed to work with McCready.

For the next year, McCready and Malloy refined the singer's style and crafted a high-class demo tape. Eventually, Malloy took the tape to RLG Records, who signed McCready after seeing her perform a live concert; she completed the deal exactly 51 weeks after she moved to Nashville. McCready released her debut album, *Ten Thousand Angels*, in April of 1996 to positive reviews. Within six months of its release, it had gone gold. *If I Don't Stay the Night* followed in 1997, trailed two years later by *I'm Not So Tough*. *—Stephen Thomas Erlewine*

Ten Thousand Angels / Apr. 1996 / BNA ✦✦✦✦
Mindy McCready's debut *Ten Thousand Angels* is an appealing debut album, despite a handful of flaws. The songwriting on the album is occasionally a little weak, but throughout the record McCready turns in a powerhouse performance that elevates her to the front ranks of young female contemporary country singers. *—Thom Owens*

If I Don't Stay the Night / Nov. 4, 1997 / BNA ✦✦✦✦
If I Don't Stay the Night fulfills the promise of Mindy McCready's debut album *Ten Thousand Angels*, finding the singer developing a stronger voice, both as a singer and a storyteller. Although McCready doesn't write any original songs, she has selected a set of songs—ranging from the title track to a cover of Linda Ronstadt's "Long Long Time"—that establish her as a strong, independent female voice in country music. Furthermore, her voice is growing stronger, turning even the mediocre songs into something special. It's a record that confirms that she is one of the strongest singers in the post-Shania world. *—Thom Owens*

I'm Not So Tough / Aug. 10, 1999 / BNA ✦✦✦
Taking a bit of a cue from Faith Hill and Shania Twain, Mindy McCready shoots for the crossover adult contemporary audience with her third album, *I'm Not So Tough*. She doesn't take things quite as far as either Faith or Shania, retaining a distinct country twang to the music (if not the voice) throughout the album, but it's clear that the album has a smoother, brighter sheen, all the better for pop radio, plus ballads and midtempo pop cuts that are designed for wider plays. This may dismay some longtime fans, but McCready pulls it off because she sings with conviction and she has true charisma. That said, the music itself isn't as appealing as that on her first two albums and the material is a bit more uneven, but it is often entertaining and is ultimately at least a musically successful bid at a crossover adult pop record. *—Stephen Thomas Erlewine*

● **Super Hits** / Jan. 11, 2000 / BNA ✦✦✦✦
Super Hits may be a budget-line compilation—usually a sign of cut-rate product—but it's nevertheless an excellent summation of Mindy McCready's two hit country albums for BNA. It bypasses her third and final record for the label, *I'm Not So Tough*, but that's fine, since that was a pop crossover move that didn't quite work out. That means that *Super Hits* contains nothing but the cream of *Ten Thousand Angels* and *If I Don't Stay the Night*—ten songs, including the hits "Ten Thousand Angels," "Guys Do It All the Time," "A Girl's Gotta Do (What a Girl's Gotta Do)," "Maybe He'll Notice Her Now," "What if I Do," "You"ll Never Know," and "The Other Side of This Kiss," plus a handful of album tracks. It may not be packaged like a first-rate compilation, but that's its only flaw, since *Super Hits* contains everything most McCready fans could want. *—Stephen Thomas Erlewine*

Mindy McCready / Mar. 26, 2002 / Capitol ✦✦✦
With her bellybutton ring and in-your-face songs (e.g., "Guys Do It All the Time"), 20-year-old Mindy McCready seemed like the next big thing in Nashville in 1996-1997, especially after her million-selling debut album, *Ten Thousand Angels*, turned out to feature three Top Ten country singles. But 1997's *If I Don't Stay the Night* was a relative disappointment, and 1999's *I'm Not So Tough* an outright disaster, after which she parted ways with her record company, BNA, and switched to Capitol. The new label showed the flag by distributing the promotional single "Scream" in the fall of 2000 but, when it didn't attract much attention, McCready woodshedded before emerging with the radio track "Maybe, Maybe Not" in early 2002, followed by this self-titled fourth album. Despite its mediocre showing, "Scream," with its emotive vocal and elements of traditional country, is the most impressive track here, and McCready might have been better advised to record more material in a similar vein. Instead, she opted for highly produced country-pop recordings—often reminiscent of Faith Hill—that don't show her voice off to advantage. Typical of them is "Maybe, Maybe Not," which ought to be a rollicking tune with some of the lyrical bite fans are accustomed to hearing from McCready, except that the overly busy arrangement buries the punch line in the chorus when, after rehearsing the possibility of returning to a former lover, she sings, "Maybe not." Elsewhere, on "I Just Want Love," she throws in a hint of Latin pop, an odd touch for a country album. You can't blame her for trying a variety of approaches in attempting a comeback, but the result is schizophrenic and tends to confirm the view of McCready as a calculating careerist in a field that, despite all, still respects tradition more than anything. *—William Ruhlmann*

Mel McDaniel

b. Sep. 6, 1942, Checotah, OK
Vocals, Guitar, Trumpet / Country-Pop, Urban Cowboy
Mel McDaniel decided on a career in music at age 14, after seeing Elvis Presley on television. After establishing himself in the bars and clubs of his hometown of Tulsa, OK, McDaniel briefly landed in Nashville before settling in Anchorage, AK. It was there that he refined his songwriting and performance skills; when McDaniel returned to Nashville in 1976, he promptly signed a record deal with Capitol. He had some early success with the single "Have a Dream on Me," but really began to steamroll thereafter, ending up with a string of country Top Tens that stretched through the 1980s. His biggest hit came in 1993 with "Baby's Got Her Blue Jeans On," a song that was nominated for a Grammy and a CMA. McDaniel continued to perform throughout the '90s and into the 2000s, usually at the *Grand Ole Opry*, of which he became a member on January 11, 1986. *—Johnny Loftus*

● **Greatest Hits** / 1987 / Capitol ✦✦✦✦✦
He is gravelly voiced and has a limited range, but McDaniel gets the most out of his talents by concentrating on songs with the proper "groove." "Louisiana Saturday Night" and "Baby's Got Her Blue Jeans On" are staples; "Stand Up" and "Big Ole Brew" are pretty damn good. *—Tom Roland*

Skeets McDonald (Enos William McDonald)

b. Oct. 1, 1915, Greenway, AR, **d.** Mar. 31, 1968
Vocals / Traditional Country, Honky Tonk
Best known for his self-penned chart-topper "Don't Let the Stars Get in Your Eyes," Skeets McDonald was a honky tonk singer and songwriter whose work helped serve to bridge the gap between country and rock & roll. The youngest of seven children, Enos William McDonald was born on October 1, 1915, in Greenway, AR, and earned his nickname after an incident involving a swarm of mosquitoes. He became interested in music at a young age and, according to McDonald family legend, even traded his hound dog for a guitar and six dollars. When his older brother moved to Michigan several years later, McDonald followed and joined his first band, the Lonesome Cowboys, in Detroit in 1935. He continued to perform on local radio stations until he was drafted to serve in World War II in 1943.

After returning from battle, McDonald began performing on a Detroit-area television program and in 1950 cut his first records with fiddler Johnnie White & His Rough Riders. In 1951, McDonald and his family moved to Los Angeles, where he was signed to perform on Cliffie Stone's TV program *Hometown Jamboree*. Soon after, he joined Capitol Records and in 1952 released "Don't Let the Stars Get in Your Eyes," by far his biggest hit. McDonald remained with the label until 1959, the year he released the LP *The Country's Best*, and while he scored few chart successes, his music's evolution from honky tonk to straightforward rockabilly proved to be influential with other musicians.

In 1959, McDonald signed with Columbia, which mandated that he return to country music. In the early '60s, he notched a handful of hits, including "Call Me Mr. Brown," which reached the Top Ten in 1963. A year later, he issued the album *Call Me Skeets!* As the decade wore on, he began branching out from the West Coast music scene, recording in Nashville and appearing on the *Grand Ole Opry*. Despite the country industry's shift towards slicker, more pop-oriented productions, McDonald remained a purist throughout his career; he died on March 31, 1968, after suffering a massive heart attack. *—Jason Ankeny*

Goin' Steady With the Blues / 1958 / Capitol ✦✦

The Country's Best / 1959 / Capitol ✦✦✦✦

Call Me Skeets! / 1964 / Columbia ✦✦✦

Skeets / 1966 / Sears ✦✦✦✦

● **Skeets McDonald's Tattooed Lady** / 1969 / Fortune ✦✦✦✦✦
McDonald checks in here with the risqué title track and "Birthday Cake Boogie," while the rest of the album features equally naughty fare by the York Brothers, Tommy Odim, Johnny Buckett, Roy Hall, and Rufus Shoffner. Great fun all. *—Cub Koda*

● **Don't Let the Stars Get in Your Eyes** / Nov. 25, 1998 / Bear Family ✦✦✦✦✦

Ronnie McDowell

b. Mar. 26, 1950, Fountain Head, TN
Vocals, Guitar / Country-Pop, Urban Cowboy
Best known for his visual and vocal resemblance to Elvis Presley, Ronnie McDowell enjoyed a series of Top Ten hits on the country charts during the first half of the '80s.

McDowell was born in 1950 and raised in the small town of Portland, TN, and started singing publicly while serving the Navy in the Philippines. He hit big in 1977 with "The King Is Gone," a tribute to Presley written immediately after the singer's death; released on the Scorpion label, the song climbed into the Top 20 of both the pop and country charts. McDowell capitalized on the exposure to land another hit, the Top Five country single "I Love You, I Love You, I Love You," in 1978. The following year, he was tapped to sing the vocals for an Elvis TV-movie starring Kurt Russell. Afraid he was becoming pigeonholed, McDowell teamed up with producer Buddy Killen at Epic Records in hopes of broadening his style. The plan worked, as McDowell became a consistent country hitmaker.

He scored a number one hit in 1981 with "Older Women," which kicked off a string of 11 consecutive Top Ten hits on Epic; of those, "Wandering Eyes," "Watchin' Girls Go By," "You Made a Wanted Man of Me," and "In a New York Minute" all made the Top Five, and 1983's "You're Gonna Ruin My Bad Reputation" went to number one. McDowell jumped labels to Curb in 1986, but despite getting some attention via duets with Conway Twitty (a remake of "It's Only Make Believe") and Jerry Lee Lewis ("You're Never Too Old to Rock 'n' Roll"), his commercial momentum ground to a halt. He served as the singing voice of Elvis for a few more TV productions, and also sang some national commercial jingles, while continuing to record for Curb through the early '90s. Toward the end of the decade, he started performing R&B and beach music with Bill Pinkney's Original Drifters, and they teamed up to release an album in 2002. —*Steve Huey*

A Tribute to the King / 1979 / Scorpion ♦♦
This album came about after an August 1992 concert commemorating the 15th anniversary of the death of Elvis Presley. McDowell, who in addition to being a country star had emulated Elvis for television soundtracks, asked Scotty Moore, D.J. Fontana, and the Jordanaires—all of whom had played on Presley's early recordings—if they wanted to do a recording project. *A Tribute to the King* was the result. Perhaps if popular music was a math equation, this would be the formula for the best possible emulation of Presley in the singer's absence: the most competent Elvis sound-alike, teamed with the surviving musicians most important to supporting Presley on record. But life's not that simple, is it? Although McDowell does sound more like Elvis than just about any lounge imitator, there isn't any reason to buy this collection of Presley covers (with a couple of Elvis tribute songs thrown in) when the immeasurably superior originals are still available, and always will be as long as people are buying records. These are faithful, watered-down covers of many of the hits from Elvis' early career, from "Heartbreak Hotel" and "Love Me Tender" to the best of his early-'60s tracks, like "His Latest Flame (Marie's the Name)" and "(You're The) Devil in Disguise." McDowell only covers songs from Presley's first decade, feeling (and he has a strong argument) that this was Elvis' good period. The backing is agreeably competent, the arrangements sometimes straight-ahead and sometimes disagreeably slicked-up with contemporary production. The two non-Elvis-identified songs are a remake of McDowell's 1977 tribute hit, "The King Is Gone," and another Presley-inspired tribute, "Tupelo's Too Far." —*Richie Unterberger*

Greatest Hits / 1982 / Epic ♦♦♦

Country Boy's Heart / 1983 / Epic ♦♦♦

Personally / 1983 / Epic ♦♦♦

In a New York Minute / 1985 / Epic ♦♦♦

● **Older Women and Other Greatest Hits** / 1987 / Epic ♦♦♦♦♦
McDowell fell into this "clone" thing for a couple of years where he remade his own hits; and all three soundalikes ("Older Women," "Wandering Eyes," "Watchin' Girls Go By") are curiously placed back-to-back. His later material is the most emotive, especially "I Dream of Women like You," "In a New York Minute," and "Love Talks," recorded with Exile. —*Tom Roland*

American Music / 1989 / Curb ♦♦♦♦
On *American Music*, McDowell is backed by musicians Doug Phelps and Greg Martin, who went on to form the Kentucky Headhunters. —*Jason Ankeny*

The Best of Ronnie McDowell / 1990 / Curb ♦♦♦♦
Along with "The King Is Gone," the song which forever established McDowell's remarkable vocal similarities to Elvis Presley, this hits collection includes "I Love You, I Love You, I Love You," "All Tied Up" and "It's Only Make Believe." It does not, however, feature either of his chart-topping hits, "Older Women" and "You're Gonna Ruin My Bad Reputation." —*Jason Ankeny*

Your Precious Love / 1991 / Curb ♦♦♦
On *Your Precious Love*, McDowell covers a number of soul classics, including "Lover's Question" and, of course, "For Your Precious Love." —*Jason Ankeny*

Unchained Melody / 1991 / Curb ♦♦♦
Duets with Jerry Lee Lewis, Wayne Newton, Jack Scott, and Bobby Vinton highlight *Unchained Melody*. —*Jason Ankeny*

Country Dances / Oct. 5, 1993 / Curb ♦♦

Great Gospel Songs / 1996 / Curb ♦♦
Although he had numerous country hits of his own in the '80s, singer Ronnie McDowell has never been able to shake his initial guise as an Elvis impersonator, the man who wrote "The King Is Gone" and provided the vocals for the 1979 TV movie *Elvis*. With that in mind, guess who this collection of *Great Gospel Songs* sounds like? Nothing original here, just versions of "Just a Closer Walk With Thee," "The Old Rugged Cross," and "Peace in the Valley" as if Elvis were singing them. Pass on this disc and instead check out *The Best of Ronnie McDowell* on Curb. —*Al Campbell*

Ronnie McDowell with Bill Pinkney's Original Drifters / Sep. 17, 2002 / Curb ♦♦♦
Any project that finds a playful version of *The Little Mermaid*'s "Kiss the Girl" appropriate is obviously something conceived in a tropical wonderland. Veteran country singer

Ronnie McDowell takes a break from the honky tonkin' and teams up with the legendary doo wop-era group the Drifters to create a fun, reggae-influenced trip down to the islands (that takes a few detours through the history of rock & roll). Classics include "Honey Love" and a moody rendering of "For Your Precious Love," while McDowell's own sense of novelty songwriting leads to the inspired "I Wanna Shag With You" and "Boardwalk Girl." The closing number, "Shama Lama Ding Dong," blends the best of the two worlds together. —*Jonathan Widran*

Country / Sep. 17, 2002 / Curb ♦♦♦
Singer Ronnie McDowell launched his career with a novelty hit about Elvis' death and has spent much of his career doing King-related things, so it's easy to overlook his fine contributions to country music over the past two decades. This lively new project shows that with the right material he can still be in fine form with the help of his band, the Rhythm Kings. "Gimme Some More" is spirited honky tonk pop fun, while "Amazing Grace" isn't the hymn but a colorful lament for a girl who loved the song. Unlike most popular country singers who rely solely on the material of others, McDowell writes a good half of these songs, including the clever "Treat Me Like a Dog," the poignant "Linda, You're Losing a Good Thing," and the lust-filled punchy rocker "Is It Hot in Here." It's doubtful that this will knock guys from the new generation off the charts, but it's good to see there's still a fire burning in the members of the old guard. —*Jonathan Widran*

Reba McEntire
b. Mar. 28, 1955, Chockie, OK
Vocals, Guitar / Contemporary Country, Neo-Traditionalist Country
Reba McEntire was one of the most successful new country vocalists to emerge in the early '80s. The only problem was, she began her recording career in the mid-'70s. It may have taken her several years to reach the top of the country charts, but once she got there she stayed there—McEntire was the single most successful female country vocalist of the '80s and '90s, scoring a consistent stream of Top Ten singles and a grand total of 18 number-one singles. McEntire is the daughter of Clark McEntire, a professional rodeo rider. As a child, Reba was a rodeo rider, as were her sisters Alice and Susie and her brother Pake. While their father taught them how to ride, their mother, Jackie, taught them music. As young adults, the four siblings formed a vocal group that landed a local hit in 1971 with "The Ballad of John McEntire," a song dedicated to their grandfather.

The McEntire children intended to become a professional singing group, but those plans were thrown for a loop when Reba sang the national anthem at the National Rodeo Finals in Oklahoma City in 1974. Red Steagall had heard her sing the anthem and immediately suggested that she go to Nashville and record a demo. McEntire was initially hesitant to pursue a solo career, but the family eventually decided it was better for her to take the chance while it was there. With some help from Steagall, McEntire signed with Mercury Records in 1975, releasing her first record that same year. Initially, she was a traditional hard country singer at a time when the radio wasn't receptive to that sound—her first singles didn't come close to cracking the Top 40. Around the time of the release of her first album, she married Charlie Battles, a professional steer wrestler and bulldogger, and completed her teaching degree, in case her musical career floundered.

In 1978, McEntire began to make some headway on the charts, as the double A-sided "Three Sheets in the Wind"/"I'd Really Love to See You Tonight" reached number 20. However, she didn't have any significant hits until the summer of 1980, when "(You Lift Me) Up to Heaven" made it to number eight. By this time, she had begun to cut more ballad-oriented material and the slight shift in musical direction paid off. McEntire stayed with Mercury Records for three more years. In that time, her audience dramatically expanded—at the end of 1982, she had her first number one single, "Can't Even Get the Blues."

McEntire switched labels in 1984, abandoning Mercury for MCA Records. At MCA, she established herself as one of the decade's most popular artists, selling over 20-million albums and winning four Female Vocalist of the Year awards from the Country Music Association. Between 1985 and 1992, she had 24 straight Top Ten hits, including 14 number-one singles. McEntire began toying with rock and pop influences, both in her music and in her image.

McEntire divorced Charlie Battles in 1987. Two years after the divorce, she married Narvel Blackstock, her road manager and steel guitarist; the pair assumed complete control of all aspects of her career, from recording to merchandising and marketing. In the '90s, McEntire stayed as popular as she was in the previous decade, as both her albums and her singles consistently charted in the Top Ten, frequently at number one. McEntire also begun an acting career in the early '90s, appearing in TV movies and feature films, most notably the cult horror film *Tremors*. She released *If You See Him* in 1998, returning a year later with a second seasonal collection, *The Secret of Giving*, as well as *So Good Together*. —*Stephen Thomas Erlewine*

Reba McEntire / 1977 / Mercury ♦♦♦♦♦
The average listener of Reba McEntire's first album will most likely have one of two minds about it. On the one hand, fans of McEntire's later recordings might reject this album on the grounds that it is more tradition-oriented and less contemporary-sounding than the material for which she is best known, while traditionalists might embrace it as the one Reba McEntire album to own. Whatever the listener's bias, this album has more to do with the early-'70s sounds of Tanya Tucker and Tammy Wynette than the contemporaneous pop-country hits of, say, Barbara Mandrell. Although such individual tracks as "Glad I Waited Just for You" and McEntire's version of "Right Time of the Night" hardly constitute hard country, her recording of Roger Miller's "Invitation to the Blues" is probably as close as she comes. Ironically, it is the very listeners who would likely dismiss any Reba McEntire album out of hand that might find this the most surprising and enjoyable, whereas only the most accepting fans of her later recordings will react so positively. This is a strong album that rewards exploration. —*Greg Adams*

Out of a Dream / 1979 / Excelsior ♦♦♦♦
Reba McEntire is one of the great ladies of country music who needs not be introduced. Her albums have won her numerous awards, and sold millions of copies. This one, *Out*

of a Dream, was originally released way back in 1979, as only her second full-length recording. It was brought back to life on compact disc almost two decades later. Even with the passing of so much time, this offering can still please country music lovers with songs like "Runaway Heart," "Last Night, Ev'ry Night," "It's Gotta Be Love," "Sweet Dreams," and "That Makes Two of Us," a duet sung with Jacky Ward. The second track on the album was the first sampling the music world got of McEntire's songwriting talents. It might not have been a chart-topper, but its lyrics seem to come from the heart. A great album for longtime Reba McEntire fans, as well as the new ones. —*Charlotte Dillon*

Feel the Fire / 1980 / Mercury ✦✦✦✦

Heart to Heart / 1981 / Mercury ✦✦

Unlimited / 1982 / Mercury ✦✦✦

Just a Little Love / 1984 / MCA ✦✦✦

The Best of Reba McEntire / 1985 / Mercury ✦✦✦✦✦
The Best of Reba McEntire contains ten of her biggest hits from the early '80s, which were all recorded for Mercury Records. These hit singles—including "(You Lift Me) Up to Heaven," "Today All Over Again," "I'm Not That Lonely Yet," "Can't Even Get the Blues," "You're the First Time I've Thought About Leaving," and "Why Do We Want (What We Know We Can't Have)"—represent the first songs where McEntire truly found a voice of her own. Occasionally, Jerry Buckler's productions are a little too sanitary, but McEntire overcomes any overly commercial flourishes with her gritty, gutsy vocals, and the best of these songs are as good as her finest moments for MCA. —*Thom Owens*

My Kind of Country / 1986 / MCA ✦✦✦✦✦
McEntire's celebration of the back-to-basics movement in country has many country shuffles. These are her purest country performances and most straightforward production. —*Mark A. Humphrey*

Whoever's in New England / 1986 / MCA ✦✦✦✦✦
This is the album that elevated McEntire from pretty good country singer to megastar. A number of the melodies have pop sensibilities, but the production is decidedly country. —*Tom Roland*

What Am I Gonna Do About You / 1986 / MCA ✦✦✦✦✦
The chart-topping title cut highlights *What Am I Gonna Do About You*, which also features the number-one hit "One Promise Too Late." —*Jason Ankeny*

The Last One to Know / 1987 / MCA ✦✦✦
Recorded as McEntire went through the process of divorce from first husband Charlie Battles, it's understandably heavy on songs about breakups and the uncertainty of the future, "The Stairs"—about domestic violence—is particularly moving. Despite her personal pain, she still holds out hope in "Love Will Find Its Way to You." —*Tom Roland*

★ **Greatest Hits** / 1987 / MCA ✦✦✦✦✦
Reba McEntire's first collection of hits on MCA Records draws entirely from the beginning of her string of Top Ten hits in the mid-'80s. *Greatest Hits* cover her singles from 1984, 1985, and 1986 and features nearly every Top Ten hit she had, including the number-one hits "How Blue," "Somebody Should Leave," "Whoever's in New England," "Little Rock," "What Am I Gonna Do About You," and "One Promise Too Late." —*Stephen Thomas Erlewine*

Reba / Apr. 18, 1988 / MCA ✦✦✦
This contains the hits "I Know How He Feels," "Sunday Kind of Love," and others. —*AMG*

Sweet Sixteen / 1989 / MCA ✦✦✦
It features "Somebody Up There Likes Me," "Cathy's Clown," and "Walk On," among other hits. —*AMG*

Reba Live / 1989 / MCA ✦✦✦
Live is a predictable but enjoyable live set featuring 19 of Reba McEntire's biggest hits and best-known songs, plus a selection of covers ("Mama Tried," "San Antonio Rose," "Night Life," "Sweet Dreams," "Respect"). For fans, it's a fun but ultimately unnecessary set, since it offers no revelations and very little kinetic energy. —*Thom Owens*

Rumor Has It / 1990 / MCA ✦✦✦
It features "Fallin' Out of Love," "You Lie," "Climb that Mountain High," and other hits. —*AMG*

☆ **For My Broken Heart** / 1991 / MCA ✦✦✦✦✦
Only the quietly moving "If I Had Only Known" might be considered a tribute to the members of McEntire's band who died in a 1990 plane crash, but the tragedy creeps into McEntire's voice and her song selection. Throughout the album, McEntire dwells on regrets, unvoiced feelings, and missed chances. The best songs aren't the hits "For My Broken Heart" and "Is There Life Out There" but a group of evocative story-songs which unfold slowly, leaving loose threads and developing complex emotional undercurrents. *For My Broken Heart* may be the strongest album of McEntire's career; it's certainly her most heartbreaking. —*Brian Mansfield*

It's Your Call / 1992 / MCA ✦✦✦
McEntire possesses one of the most undeniably emotional voices in country music—one well-phrased word in her Oklahoma accent can start hearts breaking. The overwhelming number of ballads on *It's Your Call* take maximum advantage of that talent, especially on "Straight From You" and "The Heart Won't Lie," a duet with labelmate Vince Gill. While *It's Your Call* may have the same intensity of emotion as the double-platinum *For My Broken Heart*, it lacks similar depth—taken as a whole, these songs make McEntire sound like a victim, a role she no longer plays well. The ballads leave few places for McEntire's strength of character, and the bluesy "Take It Back" and "Go Down Easy" only serve as breaks in the despair. McEntire showed her best on *For My Broken Heart*; while

she's not holding back here, only casual or partial listeners will be moved as much. —*Brian Mansfield*

☆ **Greatest Hits, Vol. 2** / Oct. 1993 / MCA ✦✦✦✦
Greatest Hits, Vol. 2 collects Reba McEntire's biggest hits of the late '80s, including the number-one singles "You Lie," "For My Broken Heart," and her biggest hit, "Is There Life Out There," and seven other songs. —*Stephen Thomas Erlewine*

Oklahoma Girl / 1994 / Mercury ✦✦✦✦
Country singing star Reba McEntire was born and raised in Oklahoma, so *Oklahoma Girl* seemed a fitting title when producers began putting this album together, picking songs that covered a lot of McEntire's early career. This album is a must-have for any McEntire fan, and for almost any country fan at all. *Oklahoma Girl* is a solid two-disc offering. Each disc carries 20 tracks, a total of 40 songs in one buy. The first disc holds numbers such as "A Cowboy Like You," "Right Time of the Night," "The Blues Don't Care Who's Got 'Em," and "Tears on My Pillow." Some of the songs on disc two that fans probably remember the best include "I'm Not That Lonely Yet," "Can't Even Get the Blues No More," "You're the First Time I've Thought About Leaving," and "Pins and Needles." Unless you have all of McEntire's early works, you'll probably find a number of tunes on this set that you are missing—including a few previously unreleased tracks. This is a great way to get a good country collection started with one purchase. —*Charlotte Dillon*

Read My Mind / Apr. 26, 1994 / MCA ✦✦✦✦
This 1994 album, *Read My Mind*, is another wonderful offering of songs performed by the gifted country singer Reba McEntire. Half of the tunes on this album became hits. Many carry a deep emotional impact, with themes that move from a wife confronting a cheating husband in "I Won't Stand in Line" to lost love in "And Still" to a young woman dealing with AIDS while her friends and family face her nearing death in "She Thinks His Name Was John." There are also a couple of good everyday love ballads on this offering, and the fun and fast-paced song "Why Haven't I Heard From You." Mixed in with the expected country styling on this album you'll find a little soul, a little swing, and some pop, too. This is one of the few albums music lovers will find out there where almost every song is a good one, and worth repeated listening. —*Charlotte Dillon*

Starting Over / Oct. 3, 1995 / MCA ✦✦✦
Starting Over isn't quite a rebirth for Reba McEntire; rather, it's a tribute to her formative influences. Consisting of nothing but covers of a selection of her favorite songs from the '50s, '60s, and '70s, the album is an engaging listen. Some of the tracks demonstrate her roots, while others are nothing more than entertainment. McEntire doesn't re-imagine these songs, but she delivers strong, confident performances that make them sound fresh. —*Stephen Thomas Erlewine*

What If It's You / Nov. 5, 1996 / MCA ✦✦✦
What If It's You doesn't offer any new tricks from Reba McEntire, but it is nevertheless an excellent reminder of her deep talents as a vocalist. The album is slightly uneven, but at its best—such as on the single "The Fear of Being Alone," "She's Calling it Love" and "I'd Rather Ride Around With You"—it is as good as anything McEntire has ever done. —*Thom Owens*

If You See Him / Jun. 2, 1998 / MCA ✦✦✦
To stir interest in her record as well as Brooks & Dunn's, Reba McEntire recorded a duet with the duo called "If You See Him/If You See Her," and both artists named their respective new albums after the song. It was a way to draw attention for both parties, since they were no longer new guns—they were veterans in danger of losing ground to younger musicians. Brooks & Dunn happened to deliver an enjoyable, albeit workmanlike, album, which only puts in perspective the opportunity McEntire missed with *If You See Him*. She remains a powerful, charismatic vocalist, but she's stripped away many of her country roots on this record, deciding to craft a country-pop album that plays as an adult contemporary record. Her pop material isn't bad in small doses, but it simply doesn't have the same personality or variety as her country material. And that's the problem with *If You See Him*—McEntire has enough presence to make you aware of what she's capable of achieving, and then she doesn't deliver. —*Thom Owens*

Behind the Scene / 1999 / Rebound ✦✦✦
Behind the Scene was her last album for Mercury, featuring strong songs like "Love Isn't Love ('Til You Give It Away)," "Nickel Dreams" and her own "Reasons." —*Keith Farley*

So Good Together / Nov. 23, 1999 / MCA ✦✦✦✦
It hasn't been hard to notice that Reba McEntire's usually reliable stream of number-one hits has slowed lately. But *So Good Together* re-examines McEntire's artistry and puts fans back in touch with the Reba we know and love. No one sings emotion better than McEntire, and the relaxed warmth of her voice produces one of the finest vocal performances she's bestowed on listeners since before *Starting Over*. *So Good Together*'s first release, the introspective "What Do You Say," has been making its way up the charts in glowing Reba style. —*Maria Konicki Dinoia*

Greatest Hits, Vol. 3: I'm a Survivor / Oct. 23, 2001 / MCA ✦✦✦✦
The grand dame of country music delivers a potent greatest-hits album—her third—and her 27th album overall. She had 31 huge hits from which to choose that hadn't previously appeared on her first two greatest-hits albums. Longtime producer Tony Brown and manager/husband Narvel Blackstock chose 12 of those 31 goodies and mixed in three newbies worthy of praise, including the old Kenny Rogers tune "Sweet Music Man," produced by Alison "Make It Sound Pure" Krauss. Among the old 1990s favorites are "And Still," "She Thinks His Name Was John," "Fear of Being Alone," and "Why Haven't I Heard From You." Time and again the reigning diva of Music City just keeps hitting them out of the park—about as effortlessly as Barry Bonds at PacBell Stadium. —*Maria Konicki Dinoia*

John McEuen

b. Dec. 19, 1945, Garden Grove, CA

Banjo, Guitar, Mandolin, Vocals, Violin / Progressive Bluegrass, Progressive Country

Best known for his long tenure as a key member of the venerable Nitty Gritty Dirt Band, John "the String Wizard" McEuen was one of the most influential figures in contemporary American country, bluegrass and even pop music. Credited with introducing both the banjo and the mandolin to pop, he was a master string player who developed a devoted fan base on the festival circuit.

Born and raised in Garden Grove, CA, McEuen began learning to play the banjo when he was 18. At that time he was attending college and earning extra money by working at nearby Disneyland; comedian Steve Martin was a co-worker, and McEuen taught him how to play banjo. (Much later Martin and the NGDB would frequently appear together in concert.) McEuen decided to become a professional musician in 1964 after seeing the Dillards perform live; inspired by their energy and musicianship, he began to study the banjo in earnest. In 1965 he hooked up with Michael Martin Murphey for a year and subsequently performed on all five of Murphy's albums. In 1966, he was visiting a guitar shop in Long Beach when he met the Illegitimate Jug Band, who had just lost member Jackson Browne and were deciding to regroup. McEuen joined and the group became the Nitty Gritty Dirt Band. He remained with them for over two decades, singing and playing banjo, mandolin, fiddle and other stringed instruments through the watershed period that produced such classic albums as *Uncle Charlie and His Dog Teddy* (1970) and the landmark compilation *Will the Circle Be Unbroken* (1972). McEuen was also there during the band's subsequent dry spells, as they struggled to reshape their style before again finding success in the mid-'80s. For reasons that remain unclear, McEuen abruptly left the Dirt Band in 1987.

During his years with the group, McEuen had played solos at every show and occasionally appeared as a solo act. He also made guest appearances on other albums and did session work for such artists as Bill Wyman, Marshall Tucker, and Hoyt Axton. McEuen also composed music for film and television soundtracks, including the scores for *Paint Your Wagon* (1969) and *Samuel Beckett Is Coming Soon* (1993). In 1989, he briefly rejoined the Dirt Band to perform on their *Will the Circle Be Unbroken II* album. The following year he directed a concert video and produced an album for the Dillards. In 1991, he released the album *String Wizards*, an all-star venture featuring such illustrious artists as Earl Scruggs, Vassar Clements, and Byron Berline. A follow-up, *String Wizards II*, appeared in 1993, at about the same time McEuen founded his own label—named, appropriately enough, String Wizard. *Acoustic Traveller* was released in 1996, followed three years later by *Round Trip: Live in L.A.* He and former Nitty Gritty Dirt Band member, Jimmy Ibbotson came together in March 1999 to record *Stories and Songs*. The traditional rock-bluegrass sound is combined with behind-the-scene anecdotes and commentary. *Stories and Songs* was released in May 1999. *—Sandra Brennan*

John McEuen / Apr. 1985 / Warner Bros. ✦✦✦✦

String Wizards / 1991 / Vanguard ✦✦✦

Considering the bluegrass superstars who drop in, maybe the expectations are unfairly raised. But with players that include Josh Graves, Vassar Clements, Earl Scruggs, Sam Bush, Byron Berline, and Jerry Douglas, it's hard to not anticipate more than what is delivered here. The high points such as "Return to Dismal Swamp" are high indeed, but too much is too laid-back. Perhaps the players were too respectful of each other. "Miner's Night Out" is a delightful little surprise that would sound more at home in the English North Country than in the Appalachians. Much as Doc Watson and Merle Watson did for "Take Me Out to the Ballgame," this album gives "Stars and Stripes Forever" a new life as a bluegrass anthem. *—Mark Allan*

String Wizards 2 / Sep. 1993 / Vanguard ✦✦✦

● **Acoustic Traveller** / 1996 / Vanguard ✦✦✦✦✦

John McEuen plays a variety of stringed instruments, including mandolin, guitar, banjo, dulcimer, lap steel guitar, and even a Japanese koto on this accomplished album of folk-, country-, bluegrass-, and Western-flavored traditional-sounding original instrumentals, with one vocal track, "I Am a Pilgrim." There are many familiar sounds from McEuen's long career, including "Mr. Bojangles (suite)." *—William Ruhlmann*

String Wizard's Picks / Apr. 29, 1997 / Vanguard ✦✦✦✦

Round Trip: Live in L.A. / Nov. 30, 1999 / Cedar Glen ✦✦✦✦

This delightful live recording finds John McEuen (former leader of the Nitty Gritty Dirt Band) on-stage in his hometown, obviously completely at ease and spinning out a long program of tunes both standard ("I Am a Pilgrim," "Sheik of Araby") and original ("Good Old Boys Texas," "Night Flight"). The focus is on instrumentals, with McEuen taking the lead on guitar and banjo, but he also sings a few (including the inevitable "Mr. Bojangles") in his agreeably undistinguished voice. Surprises include a very attractive banjo arrangement of an old Muzio Clementi piano etude and a boot-stomping version of "Kiss" that probably makes the diminutive purple artist formerly known as Prince go into convulsions whenever (if ever) he hears it—young Jonathan McEuen approximating a soul falsetto is not something you'd want to hear without a good night's rest and a fully functioning sense of humor. Best of all are the Merle Travis songs and stories; McEuen's renditions of "Cannonball Rag" and "I Am a Pilgrim" are warm and wonderful. It's highly recommended. *—Rick Anderson*

Sam McGee

b. May 1, 1894, Franklin, TN, **d.** Aug. 21, 1975, Franklin, TN

Guitar / Old-Timey, Traditional Country

Flat-top guitar picker Sam McGee and his fiddling brother Kirk were among the earliest fraternal duets in country music, and were also extraordinary sidemen for such legendary performers as Uncle Dave Macon and Fiddling Arthur Smith. The McGee brothers were born just south of Nashville in Williamson County, TN, and were influenced by their old-time fiddle-playing father and other members of their family. Sam got his professional start playing at a square dance in the early 1900s. He began as a banjo player, as guitars were very rare in Tennessee during that era, but became intrigued with the instrument and the blues songs sung by black railroad laborers congregating outside his father's store. Meanwhile, Kirk followed his father and learned to play the fiddle while also practicing his singing. He enjoyed more traditional, sentimental songs, while Sam was drawn to comic material. Kirk also found the blues interesting and learned songs from the records of such performers as Papa Charlie Jackson and Kokomo Arnold.

In 1925, Sam began a longtime affiliation with Uncle Dave Macon, who would become his mentor and occasional rival. It was with Macon that Sam made his recording debut on guitar instrumentals like "Buck Dancer's Choice" and "Knoxville Blues." Two years later, Kirk also joined Macon's band, the Fruit Jar Drinkers, and recorded with them in New York. Around this time, the brothers also began recording their own songs; in 1928, Kirk and his cousin Blythe Poteet cut a few singles for Gennett, including the popular "Kicking Mule," and also performed on the *Grand Ole Opry* with Macon. In 1931, the brothers began working with fiddler Arthur Smith as the Dixieliners, becoming one of the most popular string bands during the 1930s. Although they played during most of Smith's live performances, the McGees never recorded with him.

The brothers abandoned country music during the 1940s for a time. Later, Kirk began his decade-long intermittent association with Bill Monroe. By 1955, the McGees were in danger of losing their tenure at the *Opry* and were told to resume touring. The following year, they staged a comeback, entertaining a new generation of folk music lovers. The brothers reunited with Smith in 1957 and recorded two albums for Folkways, also playing Northern folk festivals. The McGees began to specialize in old-time music during the 1960s. They recorded together and separately on a variety of independent labels before forming their own record company, MBA, in the early 1970s. They played their final engagement at the old Ryman Auditorium, the original home of the *Opry*, in 1974; by that time they were the senior members of the show and were honored by being the first act to play at the new *Opry* house. One year later, Sam was killed in a farming accident. Kirk kept on playing alone and with the Fruit Jar Drinkers. *—Sandra Brennan*

Opry Old Timers / 1962 / Starday ✦✦✦

The Starday label puts together two groups that revolve around "brother" duets for an album that is certainly enjoyable, if a bit confusing in presentation. The song credits would make it seem that this is a sort of split disc, in which the tracks alternate between Sam and Kirk McGee and the Crook Brothers, and, to the extent of who is handling the leadership of a particular tune, that would be true. However, there is an overlap of the musicians in the different groups; for example, the Crook Brothers are on-stage with the McGees, and Sam McGee is picking guitar with the Crook Brothers, and so forth. Best thing is probably to just sit and back and enjoy this program, which is sort of an anniversary card for 35 years of active service with *the Grand Old Opry*, which started out in 1925 as the WSM *Barn Dance*. Listeners may want to quibble about whether they want to hear some of these numbers for the umpteenth time, yet the musicians crank out some of these too-familiar songs as if they were proving their worth, so no complaint there. Fiddler Gerry Rivers, who also worked with Hank Williams, is on hand for all the tracks, and gets pushy in the instrumental exchanges with both bands. *—Eugene Chadbourne*

● **Grand Dad of the Country Guitar Pickers** / 1963 / Arhoolie ✦✦✦✦✦

Recorded over the course of 1969 and 1970, *Grand Dad of the Country Guitar Pickers* showcases the considerable talents of Sam McGee through exercises in gorgeous, finger-picked parlor songs, blues guitar playing, banjo tunes, waltzes, and spirituals. Though the majority of the tracks highlight McGee's idiosyncratic instrumental skills, renditions of the nostalgic "When the Wagon Was New" and the durable and oft-repeated theme in "Penitentiary Blues," both with his colorful word-slurring singing, are standouts themselves. Traditional instrumentals like the fiddle tune "Black Mountain Rag" and the spiritual "Wayfaring Stranger" are also major highlights. With a repertoire stretching back to the early days of the 20th century, McGee was able to incorporate elements of the many forms he'd come across in his 75 years and craft a truly vibrant work, all done with a very warm and expressive style. Though more like Doc Watson than Uncle Dave Macon, with whom he performed extensively, McGee was a truly unique talent. *Grand Dad of the Country Guitar Pickers* is a fine introduction. *—Matt Fink*

Country Guitar / 1997 / Arhoolie ✦✦✦✦✦

McGee's country guitar picking is bright and impressive. The compact tunes contain a chugging rhythm from guitar and bass over which he flourishes bursts of notes on banjo, guitar, and banjo-guitar. This mostly instrumental disc is interspersed with songs on which Sam McGee provides the vocals. He was a pioneer among hot country guitar pickers, being the first to record, broadcast, and perform road shows. Blues and urbane styles ("Franklin's Blues," "Railroad Blues") are included with the strident examples of hyper-country guitar. Mike Seeger, who made these recordings in 1969 and 1970, provides the liner notes. The booklet of this excellent, early country guitar album also contains an interview with Sam and track-by-track notes. *—Tom Schulte*

1926–1934 / Oct. 12, 1999 / Document ✦✦✦

Although he enjoyed a career as country music's first hot guitarist, Sam McGee's name is all but unknown to modern fans. Even his long partnership with Uncle Dave Macon produced very little that survives in the CD era, and as a solo performer he is even more obscure. It's unfortunate, then, that country guitar obsessives should be led compulsively to these early solo recordings, which to say the least are underwhelming. Why? Well, quite simply, McGee couldn't sing, and on most of his early records, he does. There are some transcendent moments during the instrumental "Buck Dancer's Choice" and "Knoxville Blues," but for the most part, McGee's cracked, stick-thin tenor is difficult to listen to, even by these antiquated standards. But since the truly obsessed will probably explore these recordings anyway, it's fair to say that there are other good songs here, most notably a version of the Delmore Brothers' "Brown's Ferry Blues," "Salt Lake City Blues," and McGee's signature song, "Railroad Blues," heard in its earliest incarnation. The curious, however, are advised to initially seek out Arhoolie's *Grand Dad of the Country Guitar Pickers* because of its mostly instrumental program and sound quality, as *1926-1934* is probably going to be enjoyed primarily under the auspices of historical interest. —*Jim Smith*

Tim McGraw (Samuel Timothy McGraw)

b. May 1, 1967, Delhi, LA

Vocals / Country-Pop, Contemporary Country, Neo-Traditionalist Country, Adult Contemporary

When Tim McGraw debuted in the early '90s, few would have predicted that he would eventually take over Garth Brooks' position as the most popular male singer in country music. Yet that's exactly what he did, thanks to a string of multi-platinum albums, a high-profile marriage to fellow superstar Faith Hill, and Brooks' own inevitable decline. His sound epitomized the strain of commercial country that dominated his era: updated honky tonk and Southern-fried country-rock on the uptempo tunes, well-polished, adult contemporary-tinged pop on the ballads. Helped out early in his career by several jokey novelty items, McGraw simply wound up cranking out hookier hits on a more consistent basis than any of his peers. By the late '90s, he was not only a superstar among country fans, but a mainstream celebrity with a large female following.

Samuel Timothy McGraw was born in Delhi, LA, on May 1, 1967. Though he didn't know it until years later, his father was baseball player Tug McGraw, a star relief pitcher for the Philadelphia Phillies and New York Mets who'd had a brief affair with McGraw's mother. He was raised mostly in the small town of Start, LA, near Monroe, and grew up listening to a variety of music: country, pop, rock, and R&B. He attended Northeast Louisiana University on a baseball scholarship, studying sports medicine, and it was only then that he started playing guitar to accompany his singing. He played the local club circuit and dropped out of school in 1989, heading to Nashville on the same day his hero Keith Whitley passed away. He sang in Nashville clubs for a couple of years and landed a deal with Curb in 1992.

His debut single, the minor hit "Welcome to the Club," was released later that year, and his self-titled debut album appeared in 1993 but failed to even make the charts. McGraw's fortunes changed with the lead single from his 1994 sophomore effort, *Not a Moment Too Soon*. "Indian Outlaw" was embraced as a light-hearted, old-fashioned novelty song by fans but was heavily criticized for what some regarded as patronizing caricatures of Native Americans. Despite some radio stations' refusal to air the song, it reached the country Top Ten and even crossed over to the pop Top 20. All the publicity helped send McGraw's next single, the ballad "Don't Take the Girl," all the way to the top of the country charts; it too made the pop Top 20. The album kept spinning off hits: "Down on the Farm" hit number two, the title track went to number one in 1995, and the novelty tune "Refried Dreams" also reached the Top Five. *Not a Moment Too Soon* was a genuine blockbuster hit, eventually selling over five-million copies and topping both the country and pop album charts; it was also the best-selling country album of the year.

McGraw's follow-up, 1995's *All I Want*, immediately consolidated his stardom with the number-one smash "I Like It, I Love It." The album topped the country charts, reached the pop Top Five, and sold over two-million copies. Once again, it functioned as a hit factory thanks to the number two "Can't Be Really Gone," the number one "She Never Lets It Go to Her Heart," and the Top Five "All I Want Is a Life" and "Maybe We Should Just Sleep on It." Over 1996, McGraw supported the album with an extensive tour, accompanied by opening act Faith Hill. In October, after the tour was over, McGraw and Hill married, in a union of country star power that drew plenty of attention from mainstream media. It doubtlessly helped McGraw's next album, 1997's *Everywhere*, become another crossover smash; it topped the country charts, fell one spot short of doing the same on the pop side, and sold four-million copies. The lead single was a McGraw-Hill duet called "It's Your Love," which not only hit number-one country, but made the pop Top Ten. Three more singles from the album—"Everywhere," "Where the Green Grass Grows," and "Just to See You Smile"—hit number one, and two others—"One of These Days" and "For a Little While"—reached number two. Meanwhile, "Just to Hear You Say That You Love Me," another husband-and-wife duet from Hill's 1998 album *Faith*, climbed into the Top Five.

With the multi-platinum success of *Everywhere*, McGraw was poised to take over Brooks' throne as the king of contemporary country, a transition that only accelerated when Brooks confounded his fans with the *Chris Gaines* project. McGraw, meanwhile, just kept topping the charts. His next album, 1999's triple-platinum *A Place in the Sun*, hit number-one country and pop, and four of its singles also hit number-one: "Please Remember Me" (which featured Patty Loveless), "Something Like That," "My Best Friend," and "My Next Thirty Years." McGraw's first *Greatest Hits* compilation, came out in 2000 and was predictably a best-selling smash, as was and another Top Ten duet from Hill's *Breathe* album, "Let's Make Love." The song later won McGraw his first Grammy, for Best Country Vocal Collaboration. Also in 2000, McGraw had a brush with the law when he and tourmate Kenny Chesney got involved in a scuffle with police officers, after Chesney attempted to ride one of the officers' horses; McGraw was later cleared of assault charges and spent the rest of 2000 on a second tour with Hill. *Set This Circus Down* (number-one country, number two pop), from 2001, kept McGraw's hit streak going into the new millennium, giving him four more number-ones—"Grown Men Don't Cry," "Angry All the Time," "The Cowboy in Me," and "Unbroken"—just like that. In 2002, his duet with protégée Jo Dee Messina, "Bring on the Rain," also went to number one. For the follow-up album, McGraw defied country convention by entering the studio not with session musicians, but with his road band, the Dancehall Doctors, a unit that had been together since 1996 (with some members around even before that). *Tim McGraw* was released in late 2002 and produced Top Ten hits in "Red Rag Top" and "She's My Kind of Rain"; it also featured a startlingly faithful cover of Elton John's "Tiny Dancer." —*Steve Huey*

Tim McGraw / 1993 / Curb ✦✦✦

Three songs—"Welcome to the Club," "Memory Lane," and "Two Steppin' Mind"—appeared on the bottom half of the *Billboard* singles chart, which suggested McGraw had

some talent but wasn't anything special. During a year that introduced Clay Walker and Doug Supernaw, hardly anybody noticed this young hat act. —*Brian Mansfield*

Not a Moment Too Soon / Mar. 22, 1994 / Curb ✦✦✦✦

"Indian Outlaw," with its controversy and its resemblance to the Raiders' "Indian Reservation," made McGraw a star, and the ballad "Don't Take the Girl" reinforced the image. *Not a Moment Too Soon* contained better hooks than its predecessor, but it also belabored the obvious with songs like "It Don't Get Any Countrier Than This" and "Give It to Me Strait." —*Brian Mansfield*

All I Want / Sep. 19, 1995 / Curb ✦✦✦

Tim McGraw's albums always suffer from uneven material, but *All I Want* is a surprisingly consistent record that consolidates his strengths while expanding him into new territory. He hasn't abandoned the honky tonk and jokey country-rock that made his famous, but he's made it harder and more believable. Similarly, his ballads are heartfelt, delivered with convincing sincerity. In other words, he has grown musically and developed into a thoroughly entertaining vocalist. And that growth is what makes *All I Want* his best record. It is still fairly uneven, with several weak songs, but McGraw now knows how to disguise the flaws in the material with his singing. —*Stephen Thomas Erlewine*

Everywhere / Jun. 3, 1997 / Curb ✦✦✦

Everywhere, Tim McGraw's fourth album, finds the vocalist following the same formula of slick ballads and measured rockers that made his second record *Not a Moment Too Soon* a blockbuster success. That's not necessarily a bad thing, since he remains an appealing singer when he has the right material, such as on the single "It's Your Love." When he has a lesser tune, however, the results are bland and uneventful. Those songs don't prevent *Everywhere* from being a pleasant listen, and it should satisfy his legions of fans, but it does suggest that he should break free from these constraints on his next record. —*Stephen Thomas Erlewine*

A Place in the Sun / May 4, 1999 / Curb ✦✦✦

Everywhere may have continued Tim McGraw's streak of hit albums, but it also suggested that he was falling into a bit of a rut. That doesn't seem to have bothered McGraw, since *Everywhere*'s sequel, *A Place in the Sun*, is much like its predecessor in its balance of polished ballads, country-pop and uptempo ravers, which are supposed to sound like honky tonk but are closer to country-rock. Since he's a professional and works with professionals, *A Place in the Sun* sounds good and has a number of highlights, from ballads like "My Best Friend" and the Patty Loveless duet "Please Remember Me" to harder numbers like "Something Like That," "My Next Thirty Years" and "She'll Have You Back." The problem is, there's nothing new here—not only is the music in the same vein as his previous efforts, it has nearly the same ratio of hits to misses. Since the moments that do work are very good, and since it is a stronger overall record than its predecessor, it will be worthwhile for fans, but it doesn't help erase the impression that McGraw won't deliver a truly satisfying album until a greatest-hits compilation comes along. —*Stephen Thomas Erlewine*

● **Greatest Hits** / Nov. 21, 2000 / Curb ✦✦✦✦✦

Greatest Hits lives up to its title, offering the bulk of Tim McGraw's big hits over the course of its 15 tracks. Thankfully, there are no new recordings to bait hardcore fans—just "Let's Make Love," the duet with Faith Hill that originally appeared on her *Breathe* album. Consequently, this is one of the rare modern-day incidences of a *Greatest Hits* that really offers all the hits, and nothing but, which not only makes it a boon to fans, but also makes it the most consistent record in McGraw's catalog. —*Stephen Thomas Erlewine*

Set This Circus Down / Apr. 24, 2001 / Curb ✦✦✦✦

Tim McGraw's first studio album on Curb Records after his multi-platinum *A Place in the Sun* delivers a more polished and diverse collection of 14 quality tunes with producers Byron Gallimore and James Stroud. From the energetic honky tonk sound of "Forget About Us," to the upbeat tempo of "Telluride," to the Latin-laced "Let Me Love You," McGraw masterfully flows from one sound style to the next. Yet McGraw's familiar country-pop sound remains evident throughout, especially on the title track, "Set This Circus Down," about a fast-paced couple yearning to kick back and relax by the countryside. Sung with such confidence, one might believe it's a self-imposed goal set by McGraw. Just as convincing are the heartfelt ballads of "The Cowboy in Me" and "You Get Used to Somebody," along with riveting guitar solos and synthesizing techniques heard on "Angel Boy." McGraw's wife, Faith Hill, contributes subtle harmonic vocals on the emotionally compelling "Angry All the Time," written by Bruce Robison. It portrays a relationship gone sour, which McGraw claims is a far cry from his own marital bliss, but was added to digress from his usual proverbial love songs. Although the sentimental "Grown Men Don't Cry," written by Steve Seskin and Tom Douglas, was the first official release from the album, McGraw's uplifting performance of "Things Change" at the Country Music Awards mysteriously found its way onto Napster first. Subsequently, "Things Change" hit the country radio airwaves, where it received rave success. McGraw's aggressive approach with this album is also a success; *Set This Circus Down* is one of his finest efforts and one you won't want to miss. —*Deborah Wong*

Tim McGraw / Nov. 26, 2002 / Curb ✦✦✦✦

Tim "Outlaw" McGraw has been one of the most consistent of the late-'90s country superstars. Never content to reply on his reputation, he continually pushed at the pillars of the hall that created him, namely Nash Vegas. McGraw's particular gift as an interpreter of other songwriters' works is almost singular among his generation of singers. Not relying solely on production, McGraw uses numerous voices to get to the heart of a song. On this album, McGraw convinced his label and co-producers, Byron Gallimore and Darran Smith, to use his road band, the Dancehall Doctors, to make a more organic and immediate sounding record. It worked. From the stunning opener, "Comfort Me," by Craig Wiseman and Don Poythress, an ancient military sounding snare drum and a bleeding guitar note usher in a tune that is the only non-cloying patriotic song that was recorded after September 11, 2001. It's a hymn equal parts country and Celtic that is an homage to all of those who entered this country by going past the Statue of Liberty and entered the American experience. When he reaches the end, "I am the tired, I am your poor in spirit/yearnin' to breathe, breathe free . . . ," the listener is caught up in the "us" of the song; it's inclusive, and captures in McGraw's prayer for comfort, for deliverance not from something else but to the space that freedom is—defined both individually and collectively—is unique among the country songs that came up after the disaster struck. Interestingly enough, it sets the tone for a record full of romantic archetypes, not only the icon of Lady Liberty, but family ("Home"); the reliving of experience unconsciously ("Red Ragtop"); escape and recreation of oneself ("That's Why God Made Mexico"); the idealization of love as a force in and of itself ("Watch the Wind Blow By", a killer soul-oriented track by Anders Osborne, and McGraw sings the hell out of it); dislocation and the realization that home isn't such a bad place to be ("Sing Me Home"); and others. McGraw closes the record with Elton John's and Bernie Taupin's "Tiny Dancer," and for a verse or so, you'd swear it was the same song. It's frightening how close to the original it is. Why would anyone try to recreate a song so close to its original version; simple, because they love it. And McGraw's version is gorgeous, soulful, and deep like the rest of *And the Dance Hall Kings.* *—Thom Jurek*

McGuinn, Clark & Hillman

f. 1977, California

Group / Country-Rock, Folk-Rock

McGuinn, Clark & Hillman (later McGuinn-Hillman) came about in 1979, after three former members of the original Byrds—Roger McGuinn, Gene Clark, and Chris Hillman—decided to do a joint tour of Europe, each fronting his own band. The tour itself didn't go off as planned, but the experience of singing together on-stage for the first time in more than ten years worked so well that McGuinn and Clark ended up touring the U.S. together as a duo, with Hillman and even David Crosby occasionally showing up at their performances (this was how the unofficial "Byrds" reunion concert at the Boarding House in San Francisco came about, later released from a radio tape as *Doin' Alright for Old People*). Capitol Records became interested in recording the duo, and a contract was signed with McGuinn and Clark, with Hillman coming aboard soon after.

The resulting album, *McGuinn, Clark & Hillman*, was a bit stiff at times, and in its best moments was closer in spirit to the Eagles than the Byrds, which wasn't so bad—the Eagles being indirect offshoots of the Byrds, by way of the Flying Burrito Brothers. A tour followed, and things were going well until Clark's health began deteriorating, forcing his exit from the tour. This also created a rift between the ex-bandmates that was never fully healed, and may have been responsible for Clark's not having been asked to participate in the "reunion" tracks recorded for the Byrds box set in the early '90s. A second album, *City*, released in 1980, included a pair of Clark songs but was otherwise a McGuinn-Hillman album ("featuring Gene Clark"). It was successful enough to justify a third release, *McGuinn/Hillman*, but that record proved a group-breaker—the producers, Jerry Wexler and Barry Beckett, were renowned R&B specialists who evidently just didn't embrace the Byrds' sound or its modern permutations, and neither musician was comfortable with the results. There were a few good songs, mostly written by McGuinn or Hillman, but none of the outside material was really suitable.

Hillman returned to bluegrass, where he'd started his career, and later won several country music awards and cut a string of successful albums with the Desert Rose Band, while McGuinn resumed his solo career, playing the occasional concert and eventually cutting a fairly successful album, *Back From Rio.* Clark toured nationally with a band called the Firebyrds and cut one album (with another left unfinished) for Allegiance Records in the early '80s, and subsequently recorded with Carla Olsen, but he never really resumed a full-time career. He died in 1991, just a few months after taking the stage with McGuinn, Hillman, and Crosby at the Rock & Roll Hall of Fame induction ceremony honoring the Byrds. *—Bruce Eder*

● **McGuinn, Clark & Hillman** / 1979 / Capitol ♦♦♦♦

Although Roger McGuinn, Gene Clark, and Chris Hillman were founding members of the Byrds, when they reunited as a trio at the end of the 1970s they seemed determined to create a sound that did not remind listeners of the earlier group. Though their music was still mainstream pop/rock with folk antecedents, it sounded like contemporary 1970s studio rock, even to the point of including a song with a disco arrangement, "Release Me Girl." More important, the trio's vocal blend, heavily augmented by the voices of John Sambataro and Rhodes, Chalmers & Rhodes, did not remind listeners of the Byrds. The major reason for this was the back seat that McGuinn, the virtual leader of the Byrds, took in the new group. He had only two compositions, to Hillman's three and Clark's four, on the record, and they were his only lead vocals. Otherwise, his reedy tenor faded into the background, with Clark and Hillman singing lead most of the time. But if the group didn't sound like the Byrds, they often did sound like the Eagles, the group that had inherited the Byrds' mantle in the 1970s. Hillman's "Sad Boy," for example, could have passed for a Glenn Frey-led Eagles song. Ironically, and perhaps deliberately, given record company machinations, the single released from the album was McGuinn's "Don't You Write Her Off," which rose into the Top 40, taking the album with it. But what probably helped the group and the album most was that in 1979 more than two years had passed since the last Eagles album, leaving fans hungry for a soundalike. If the trio had an appealing sound, however, they lacked substance. The songwriting was pleasant but slight, songs of romance that were nowhere near the quality of the Eagles' or Crosby, Stills & Nash's material. [The 2001 reissue adds three demos: "Surrender to Me," "Little Girl," and "I Love Her."] *—William Ruhlmann*

City / 1980 / One Way ♦♦♦♦

The second McGuinn, Clark & Hillman album turned into a McGuinn-Hillman album "featuring Gene Clark" when the latter dropped out of the tour ahead of it and then only contributed to two songs to this record, one of which was ironically called "Won't Let You Down." Apart from Clark's two songs, none of this really sounds much like the Byrds, although the stuff is pleasant late-'70s Byrds-influenced rock, sort of folky at its best moment and driven by McGuinn's mournful lead vocals and the soaring harmonies. "One More Chance" was the most Byrds-like of the non-Gene Clark numbers, and "City" was a good song, but, ironically, the two Gene Clark numbers were the best on the record, as good as anything he ever wrote after leaving the Byrds—and this CD is the only way to get them (they didn't make it onto Edsel's anthology). *—Bruce Eder*

McGuinn/Hillman (Mean Streets) / Mar. 1981 / Capitol ♦♦

Return Flight / 1992 / Edsel ♦♦♦♦

A sort of best-of McGuinn, Clark & Hillman and McGuinn-Hillman, drawn from all three Capitol albums, its 14 songs distilling most of their best and liveliest (and most Byrds-like) moments. The highlights include McGuinn's "Eight Miles High"-inspired 12-string playing on "City," plus the soaring "Givin' Herself Away," the haunting "Angel," and the Beach Boys-like "Skate Date." The only flaw is the absence of the two Gene Clark numbers off of *City*, which were good songs, regardless of Clark's state of mind. The notes are very detailed, but the lack of music credits is a slight drawback. *—Bruce Eder*

3 Byrds Land in London / Jun. 30, 1998 / Strange Fruit ♦♦♦

In 1977, Roger McGuinn, Chris Hillman, and Gene Clark all had new albums to promote, and all three were trying to set up promotional tours in Europe; some clever promoter got the bright idea of booking them on a package tour of the U.K., and faster than you could say "Byrds reunion," the three former bandmates found themselves sharing a bill for the first time in years, leading to a short-lived reunion for the three singer/songwriters. *3 Byrds Land in London* comes from BBC recordings of the tour's two-night stand at London's Hammersmith Odeon in the spring of 1977. The woefully underappreciated Gene Clark gets the short end of the stick as usual, performing only four tunes on this set (two of which he never recorded elsewhere), but he's in great voice and his band (including Thomas Jefferson Kaye) is in strong, rollicking form, especially on the good and greasy "Hula Bula Man." Chris Hillman delivers a typically strong and polished performance on his eight songs, ranging from solid country to sharp R&B, and if Hillman isn't a terribly charismatic frontman, he was a hell of a good bandleader, judging from this recorded evidence. Roger McGuinn and his band (called Thunderbyrd, just in case you had forgotten a key part of his resumé) get the longest set (nine songs) and play a solid selection of vintage Byrds material, highlights from McGuinn's solo career (including the rare and blazing "Shoot 'Em" and a slightly odd cover of Tom Petty's "American Girl"; at least McGuinn was sharp enough to spot the influence); guitarist Rick Vito serves up more than his share of fiery leads. Finally, the three former Byrds join forces for the encore, performing "So You Want to Be a Rock 'n' Roll Star," "Mr. Tambourine Man," and "Eight Miles High," and if the legendary harmonies aren't quite spot on, they're close enough to bring a smile to any fan who's listening. All in all, *3 Byrds Land in London* is a solid and well-recorded souvenir for fans of the three artists; while it captured all of them in the midst of a career lull, they also sound happy to be playing before a packed house again, and their enthusiasm shows. *—Mark Deming*

McGuinn, Clark & Hillman [Bonus Tracks] / Jul. 10, 2001 / One Way ♦♦♦♦

Roger McGuinn (James Joseph McGuinn)

b. Jul. 13, 1942, Chicago, IL

Banjo, Guitar, Vocals / Rock & Roll, Country-Rock, Folk-Rock

As the frontman of the Byrds, Roger McGuinn and his trademark 12-string Rickenbacker guitar pioneered folk-rock and, by extension, country-rock, influencing everyone from contemporaries like the Beatles to accolytes like Tom Petty and R.E.M. in the process. James Joseph McGuinn was born on July 13, 1942, in Chicago, where by his teenage years he was already something of a folk music prodigy. After touring with the Limelighters, in 1960 he signed on as an accompanist with the Chad Mitchell Trio, appearing on the LPs *Mighty Day on Campus* and *At the Bitter End*; frustrated with his limited role in the group, he soon joined Bobby Darin's group when the singer moved from pop to folk. After appearing on sessions for Hoyt Axton, Judy Collins, and Tom & Jerry (soon to be known as Simon & Garfunkel), McGuinn began playing solo dates around the Los Angeles area, where he soon formed the Jet Set with area musicians David Crosby and Gene Clark. After a failed single under the name the Beefeaters, the group recruited bassist Chris Hillman and drummer Michael Clarke, changed their name to the Byrds, and set about crystallizing McGuinn's vision of merging the poetic folk music of Bob Dylan with the miraculous pop sounds heard via the British Invasion. McGuinn was the only member of the Byrds to play on their landmark debut single "Mr. Tambourine Man," but his jangly guitar work quickly became the very definition of the burgeoning folk-rock form; still, despite the Byrds' immediate success, both commercially and critically, the group was plagued by internal strife, and following the release of their 1968 country-rock breakthrough *Sweetheart of the Rodeo*, McGuinn was the only founding member still in the band.

Under the direction of McGuinn—who had changed his first name to Roger after a flirtation with the Subud religion—the Byrds soldiered on, delving further and further into country and roots music before finally dissolving in February 1973. That same year, McGuinn issued his self-titled solo debut, an ambitious, eclectic affair which explored not only folk and country but surf and even space rock. 1974's *Peace on You* and 1975's *Roger McGuinn & His Band* preceded a stint with Bob Dylan's *Rolling Thunder Revue*, which helped revitalize his standing within the musical community. 1976's *Cardiff Rose* was regarded as his best solo effort to date, but the next year's *Thunderbyrd*, which featured a cover of Tom Petty's "American Girl," failed to connect with audiences.

In late 1977, McGuinn reunited with Byrds mates Chris Hillman and Gene Clark; the resulting LP, 1979's *McGuinn, Clark & Hillman*, notched a Top 40 pop hit with the McGuinn-penned "Don't You Write Her Off." Midway through recording the follow-up, 1980's *City*, Clark departed, and the album was released under the name "Roger McGuinn and Chris Hillman Featuring Gene Clark." Following another effort, 1981's

McGuinn/Hillman, they went their separate ways. After undergoing another religious conversion, this time becoming a born-again Christian, McGuinn spent the remainder of the 1980s without a recording contract and performing solo dates.

The appearance of a faux Byrds led by Michael Clarke prompted McGuinn to reform the group with Hillman and David Crosby in 1989, resulting in a series of club performances, an appearance at a Roy Orbison tribute, and a handful of new recordings for inclusion on a box set retrospective. In 1991—the same year the Byrds were inducted into the Rock & Roll Hall of Fame—McGuinn issued his first new solo recordings in over a decade, the all-star *Back from Rio*, which was met with great public and critical acclaim. *Live From Mars*, a retrospective of songs and stories, appeared in 1996. —*Jason Ankeny*

Roger McGuinn / 1973 / Columbia ✦✦✦
Coming after the Byrds' reunion record, *Roger McGuinn* is an extension of those sessions, with the Byrds showing up on the cut "My New Woman." The rest of the disc is full of McGuinn's typical country-rock-folk-space music. Highlights include "Lost My Drivin' Wheel," "I'm So Restless," which includes Bob Dylan on harmonica, and the traditional "The Water Is Wide," which wouldn't have sounded out of place on the Byrds' *Sweetheart of the Rodeo*. It's a fine, focused effort. —*James Chrispell*

Peace on You / 1974 / Columbia ✦✦
The solo career of this great rock artist took awhile to gather some steam; his 1976 album, *Cardiff Rose*, showed that with at least some consistent production and a tight backing ensemble, he could put across a powerful musical vision without having to rely totally on re-creating the sound of the Byrds. For this 1974 album his focus is as wandering as a glaucoma patient who has just gone through a two-hour field test. Many different influences come into his musical world, like strange cooks passing through a kitchen and dropping odd things into the stew. There is heavy collaborating with songwriter Jacques Levy, who like McGuinn was part of Bob Dylan's chaotic music world during this period. While Levy has fans who feel he brought great riches to the kingdoms of artists such as McGuinn, the offerings from the McGuinn and Levy songwriting team on this album, such as "Together" and "The Lady," are packed with corny images and shallow sentiments—in other words, not exactly what one is used to hearing from McGuinn in his practically angelic role as a lead vocal spokesman for the Byrds. A bit of Turtles sauce goes in courtesy of vocal contributions from Howard Kaylan and Mark Volman—it doesn't add much, but at least doesn't detract, which is more than can be said for the song contributions of session pro Al Kooper or the wimpy Dan Fogelberg. The title of the former artist's tune is a gift to critics and the public alike: "Please Not One More Time." Another pair of nothing songs comes from one Donnie Dacus, while the album's title number, courtesy country singer Charlie Rich and hyped to the hilt via the album's artwork, is also pretty much a disappointment, a one-idea song that badly muddles the all-important opening track parade. —*Eugene Chadbourne*

Roger McGuinn & His Band / 1975 / Columbia ✦✦✦
Rather a mismatch of material awaits the listener on *Roger McGuinn & Band*, what with the inclusion of such Byrds-related tunes as "Born to Rock and Roll" and "Lover of the Bayou." Along with those, Dylan's "Knockin' on Heaven's Door" and other cuts written by members of his new band, you'll find a rather mediocre album. For McGuinn completists only. —*James Chrispell*

Cardiff Rose / 1976 / Columbia ✦✦✦✦✦
Coming after Bob Dylan's Rolling Thunder Revue, *Cardiff Rose* is full of the collective spirit which shone through in that tour. McGuinn uses his fellow travelers to great advantage by turning in his most concise and well-recorded album to date. It's rock & roll to the foreground with help from Mick Ronson & the Rolling Thunder touring band "Guam" helping out. Everything here works, from the opening "Take Me Away," written about the tour, through the quiet of "Friend" and Joni Mitchell's "Dreamland," this is where McGuinn got everything and everyone to work together. His best yet. —*James Chrispell*

Thunderbyrd / 1977 / Columbia ✦✦✦
Following his high-water mark of *Cardiff Rose*, McGuinn's *Thunderbyrd* is a bit of a letdown. With most of the tracks being covers ranging from Dylan to Peter Frampton to George Jones to Tom Petty's "American Girl," the songs all have a sort of weariness to them which detracts from what should have been a great effort. His last solo disc for a long, longtime. —*James Chrispell*

Back from Rio / 1990 / Arista ✦✦✦✦✦
After spending the better part of the 1980s as a solo acoustic troubadour, Byrds cofounder Roger McGuinn landed a contract for a solo album with Arista Records at the turn of the 1990s. Featuring Tom Petty, Mike Campbell, and ex-Byrds David Crosby and Chris Hillman, the resultant album had a strangely modern feel, although it was primarily driven by McGuinn's trademark Rickenbacker 12-string. Songwriting had never been McGuinn's strong suit, and on this album he wisely chose some excellent material by Jules Shear and Tom Petty, who provided the album's unexpected hit, "King of the Hill." —*Matthew Greenwald*

● **Born to Rock & Roll** / Mar. 1992 / Columbia ✦✦✦✦✦
Nitty Gritty Dirt Band–Roger Mcguinn Live / 1994 / Javelin ✦✦✦✦
Someday someone may put out a full live Roger McGuinn album with 16 or 20 songs from across his repertory and history, but in the meantime, these four songs ("Turn Turn Turn," "Mr. Spaceman," "Mr. Tambourine Man," "Tiffany Queen") recorded at Little Darlin's Rock N' Roll Palace in Kissimmee, FL, will have to do. They're very well recorded, with McGuinn in excellent voice, backed by an uncredited band—the latter-day Byrds didn't do them much different, though Clarence White's presence is missed (as it always will be). An announcer intro sort of blows the opening of "Mr. Tambourine Man," but otherwise this is a decent concert vignette. —*Bruce Eder*

Live from Mars / Nov. 19, 1996 / Hollywood ✦✦✦
Taking his cue from Ray Davies' "Storyteller" tour to support his autobiography *X-Ray*, Roger McGuinn constructed his live performances of the mid-'90s as a series of greatest hits, new songs, neglected gems and witty, affectionate anecdotes of his life in the music industry. *Live from Mars* replicates one of these concerts, featuring classics like "Mr. Tambourine Man," "Turn, Turn, Turn," and "So You Want to Be a Rock N' Roll Star" intercut with humorous stories and two new songs, "May the Road Rise to Meet You" and "Fireworks." For fans, *Live from Mars* is a small treasure, since it is one of McGuinn's friendliest and most relaxed recordings. —*Stephen Thomas Erlewine*

McGuinn's Folk Den Vol. 1 / 2000 / mp3.com ✦✦✦
McGuinn's Folk Den Vol. 1 is the first of four short, discount-priced albums of traditional folk songs that Roger McGuinn offered for sale on www.mp3.com/mcguinn. The varied song selection touches on gospel, country, Irish, and whaling songs. McGuinn's familiar light, vibrato-laden tenor is a good vehicle for the material, which he clearly knows well. Though several acoustic instruments are sometimes overdubbed along with double-tracked or harmony vocals, these are not sophisticated recordings; in fact, "John Henry" has a primitive sound that makes one suspect it was recorded quite a few years back. But the sound quality matches the folk material, and this is clearly a case of an artist re-investigating his roots affectionately. —*William Ruhlmann*

McGuinn's Folk Den, Vol. 2 / 2000 / mp3.com ✦✦✦✦
McGuinn's Folk Den, Vol. 2 is the second of four short, discount-priced recordings of traditional folk songs that Roger McGuinn distributed through www.mp3.com/mcguinn. These recordings sound a bit more polished than those on *Vol. 1*, with McGuinn overdubbing several guitar tracks and creating harmony parts that sometimes echo his work with the Byrds, particularly on the leadoff track, "John Riley," which appeared on the Byrds' third album, *Fifth Dimension*, back in 1966. Songs like "900 Miles," "Old Paint," and "Buffalo Skinners" were favorites during the folk boom of the early '60s that McGuinn emerged from, and one can listen to this album as a primer of the music that influenced the singer when he went on to help create folk-rock. —*William Ruhlmann*

McGuinn's Folk Den Vol. 3 / 2000 / mp3.com ✦✦✦
McGuinn's Folk Den Vol. 3 is the third of four short, low-priced collections of traditional folk songs recorded by Roger McGuinn and available at www.mp3.com/mcguinn. McGuinn mixes cowboy songs, whaling songs, and Celtic songs in this collection, including both familiar titles ("I'm Alabama Bound," "The Greenland Whale") and more obscure ones. He overdubs extra guitar parts and harmony vocals such that he is often performing duets with himself. The tracks range from those with good sound quality to a few with rudimentary sound, as if the album had been compiled from different sources, some better than others. —*William Ruhlmann*

McGuinn's Folk Den, Vol. 4 / 2000 / mp3. com ✦✦✦✦
McGuinn's Folk Den, Vol. 4 is the fourth in a series of low-priced recordings of traditional folk music Roger McGuinn made available online at www.mp3.com/mcguinn, and it is the best one so far. Sound quality has occasionally been iffy in the series of short CDs, but that is not a problem here, and, at 35 minutes, this is the longest of the discs. McGuinn overdubs his vocals and several different instruments, especially acoustic guitar and banjo, and he even breaks out his 12-string electric Rickenbacker on a couple of tracks, notably "If I Had Wings," which gives the music a Byrds-like feel. He has also expanded his concept of traditional folk music to include standards such as "Star Spangled Banner" and "Auld Lang Syne." Anyone who enjoyed the sound of McGuinn's reedy tenor over his 12-string guitar in the Byrds subsequently will like the *McGuinn's Folk Den* series, and, though this is the fourth one, it does not find him running out of songs to cover—quite the opposite. If you want to buy one of these albums to see whether you will like them all, start here. —*William Ruhlmann*

Treasures From the Folk Den / Aug. 28, 2001 / Appleseed ✦✦✦
In late 1995, as part of his official website, Roger McGuinn launched a feature called The Folk Den, in which each month he recorded a traditional folk song in his home studio and posted the results on his web page along with brief essays on the histories of the songs and how he came to learn them. McGuinn used this ongoing experiment as the inspiration for his album, *Treasures From the Folk Den*, which was recorded in a series of informal sessions (mostly in people's homes, none in a traditional recording studio) using McGuinn's Apple G4 computer as a mobile recording setup. Unlike the online "Folk Den" recordings, which feature McGuinn solo (occasionally overdubbing himself for accompaniment), for these performances he enlisted a number of friends as accompanists and duet partners, including Joan Baez, Judy Collins, Pete Seeger, Odetta, Eliza Carthy, and Tommy Makem. The results are a shade more polished than McGuinn's Folk Den sessions (several of which have been released on disc by mp3.com) and McGuinn is in fine voice, as are his guests (though neither McGuinn nor Odetta and Jean Ritchie have quite enough grit to do justice to "John the Revelator"). *Treasures From the Folk Den*, however, is flawed somewhat by the material; while nearly all of these songs are foundation blocks of the folk repertoire, as a consequence they've been recorded dozens of times by a number of major artists (including several who appear on this disc), and while these recordings are strong, they aren't that much different than the others that are already available. *Treasures From the Folk Den* would make a good introduction for someone just dipping their toes into the basic folk repertoire, and it's always a pleasure to hear these artists in strong and committed form, but there isn't much here that longtime folk enthusiasts haven't heard before; it's enjoyable, but hardly essential. —*Mark Deming*

Live From Electric Lady Land: 7/18/91 / 2002 / Fusion ✦✦
Roger McGuinn recorded rather sporadically during the 1990s, so this live bootleg would seem like it would have appeal to his fans. Unfortunately, this is not the case, as several

mitigating factors work against this sloppily produced CD. A number of the songs are incorrectly identified, most notably McGuinn's "Tiffany Queen" (first recorded for the Byrds' final LP, *Farther Along*), which is listed as "The Party"; Elvis Costello's "You Bowed Down" is titled "You Bow Down" and Bob Dylan's well-known "Mr. Tambourine Man" is called "Mr. Tambourin." What is even more inexcusable is that this 1991 live broadcast from Electric Ladyland Studio has been truncated with all of McGuinn's comments to his audience excised, the music has been resequenced, and there is a fade-up on nearly every number, along with abrupt endings. The band isn't identified at all, though presumably many of the musicians appeared with McGuinn on his *Back From Rio* CD (a studio session also released in 1991 featuring many of the songs present). The performances are fine, though several of the newer songs (particularly "Car Phone") fail to compare with McGuinn's writing from the 1960s and 1970s. Anyone interested in the music found on this CD is advised to look for the far-superior McGuinn bootleg *Back to New York*, which has far-superior sound and correctly identifies all of the songs and their composers, and has all of McGuinn's talk between numbers intact. —*Ken Dryden*

Back to New York / 2002 / Oh Boy ✦✦✦
Following his series of solo albums for Columbia, Roger McGuinn recorded infrequently during the 1990s, so this live bootleg, taped during a 1991 concert broadcast from Electric Ladyland, will have some appeal to his fans. Although the supporting cast of musicians is not identified, it was a Tampa Bay based band called the Headlights, led by Steve Connelly. McGuinn revisits some older material with success, including "Tiffany Queen" (first recorded for the Byrds' final LP, *Farther Along*), Bob Dylan's well-known "Mr. Tambourine Man," and Pete Seeger's famous recasting of Biblical verse ("Turn! Turn! Turn!"), though the finale of "Eight Miles High" lacks the drama of versions he recorded as leader of the Byrds. Most of the set leans toward newer material, including collaborations with his wife ("Someone to Love," "The Trees Are All Gone," and "Car Phone") and Tom Petty ("King of the Hill"), though none of this material (especially "Car Phone") compares to McGuinn's writing from the 1960s and 1970s. The excellent recording quality and good playing make this CD stand far above typical bootlegs, especially the alternate version of this concert put out as *Live from Electric Ladyland*, which has lousy sound, mislabels songs, and chops up the performance. —*Ken Dryden*

Maria McKee

b. Aug. 17, 1964, Los Angeles, CA

Guitar, Vocals / Alternative Country-Rock, Roots Rock, College Rock, Alternative Pop/Rock, Americana

After making her name as the gritty, soulful lead singer of roots rockers Lone Justice, Maria McKee embarked on an often-rewarding solo career. A native of Los Angeles, McKee was born in 1964; her half-brother was Bryan MacLean, the guitarist and sometime singer of the groundbreaking psychedelic band Love. After studying musical theater as a teenager, McKee started performing on the L.A. club scene in a duo with MacLean and also teamed up with local blues singer Top Jimmy (who inspired the Van Halen song of the same name). A roots-music scene sprang up in L.A. during the early '80s, and McKee—a country music fan—met likeminded guitarist Ryan Hedgecock; the two co-founded Lone Justice in 1982, and with McKee often composing material, the group became a local favorite. They signed with Geffen on the recommendation of Linda Ronstadt, but in spite of highly positive media attention, their two albums—1985's *Lone Justice* and 1986's *Shelter*—failed to sell well, hampered by slick production and a sense of not-quite-fulfilled potential. McKee went solo after the latter record and released her self titled debut in 1989, with Mitchell Froom producing.

McKee scored a critical breakthrough with her second album, 1993's *You Gotta Sin to Get Saved*, which was helmed by Black Crowes/Jayhawks producer George Drakoulias. Its rootsy, countrified rock and McKee's ever more powerful vocals led many reviewers to call it her most fully realized work to date. She went on to contribute the song "If Love Is a Red Dress (Hang Me in Rags)" to the hit soundtrack of *Pulp Fiction*, and in 1996 she released a third solo album, the much artier *Life Is Sweet*, on which she played all the guitar parts. McKee subsequently took a hiatus from recording, during which time she extricated herself from her deal with Geffen in search of greater creative control. She finally returned in 2003 with another ambitious outing, *High Dive*. —*Steve Huey*

Maria McKee / Jun. 1989 / Geffen ✦✦✦
Three years after Lone Justice's last album, Maria McKee released her self-titled debut, which showed that her skills as a songwriter had grown considerably since her first band. Not only were her songs better, but McKee's singing had improved; while it was still a little thin, her voice had grown grittier and more soulful, which made her songs all the more convincing. Unfortunately, most of McKee's musical growth was obscured by Mitchell Froom's mushy overproduction. —*Stephen Thomas Erlewine*

You Gotta Sin to Get Saved / Jun. 22, 1993 / Geffen ✦✦✦✦✦
A few years after an underappreciated solo album, former Lone Justice leader Maria McKee returns with *You Gotta Sin to Get Saved*, her best album yet. With Black Crowes and Jayhawks producer George Drakoulias at the helm, *You Gotta Sin to Get Saved* evokes the country-rock vibe of the early '70s (much like the aforementioned groups) without sounding like a studied replica. McKee sings a dynamic mix of originals and covers with genuine conviction, making *You Gotta Sin to Get Saved* an album that demands repeated plays. —*Stephen Thomas Erlewine*

Life Is Sweet / Mar. 26, 1996 / Geffen ✦✦✦
For most of her career, Maria McKee has never deviated from country-rock, but *Life Is Sweet* is a bold departure from her trademark sound, taking her into new sonic territories. Although the loud, distorted guitars are the first noticeable change, it soon becomes apparent that the thing that makes the album sound so different is its latent progressive rock influences. Throughout the album, McKee weaves complex, layered arrangements

that interweave strings, guitars, and keyboards. Appropriately, her melodies are more convoluted than ever before, yet they never become too obtuse. Lyrically, she has become more cryptic and angry, but that is all part of the plan—*Life Is Sweet* is McKee's bid to be taken seriously as an artist. For some reason, that means she has constructed a hybrid of the prog rock arrangements that dominate the first half of the album and the confessional songwriting that is prominent on the second. Fortunately, the results sound better than they read, primarily because beneath all of the bombastic arrangements, McKee has retained her keen sense of songcraft. Still, with its art rock tendencies and naked ambition, *Life Is Sweet* may not appeal to fans who have become attached to McKee's country-rock. For those willing to accept her pretensions, it is a frustrating but rewarding album. —*Stephen Thomas Erlewine*

● **Ultimate Collection** / Aug. 22, 2000 / Hip-O ✦✦✦✦✦
Ultimate Collection collects Maria McKee's definitive moments with Lone Justice and as a solo artist. Her sensual yet down-to-earth vocals and gritty songwriting stand out on Lone Justice tracks like "Don't Toss Us Away," "Shelter," and "Ways to Be Wicked"; her growth as both a singer and a writer is reflected on solo songs such as "Absolutely Barking Stars," "Breathe," and "What Else You Wanna Know." The collection also includes some interesting bonuses, including Lone Justice's live version of "Sweet Jane," an acoustic demo of "Show Me Heaven," and "If Love Is a Red Dress," which originally appeared on the *Pulp Fiction* soundtrack. At 17 tracks long, it comes pretty close to being an ultimate collection of McKee's body of work. —*Heather Phares*

High Dive / Apr. 2003 / Viewfinder ✦✦✦✦✦
Seven years between albums is a longtime. But in her quest for artistic freedom and total control over her own material, Maria McKee took the time to get out from under the Geffen imprint, write a host of new songs, and create a new band. And as is her wont, her effort on *High Dive* is something as different from her earlier recordings as they were from one another. In 1996, when *Life Is Sweet* was released, McKee had left behind the country-rock that had established her for a raucous and woolly aggressive rock sound where she played all the guitars—in overdrive. That record was full of grief, rage, and the desire to shed her skin. It was a misunderstood work of high, inimitable art. *High Dive* is by turns a gorgeous rock record and a Baroque pop masterpiece. Strings, horns, and a full-on rock band grace its 14 tracks—including an absolutely stunning redo of *Life Is Sweet's* title track. McKee has always possessed two gifts as a lyricist: her ability to make all images completely vivid and her naked compassion and empathy. All of the songs here are loaded with both. Her melodies are positively irresistible and infectious, and her lyrical tomes are full of everything from the longing for freedom—"To the Open Paces," to codependence, "Be My Joy," to a near Buddhist sense of loving kindness, "Life Is Sweet," to all notions of love and loss. All of these have come to be expected from McKee, who is one of the most underrated lyricists pop music has ever produced. But on *High Dive*, it's the sound of the record that is also stunning. Along with Jim Akin, McKee employed a virtual string orchestra and a group of chamber horns and arranged them for a sound that is as timeless as it is current. There are echoes of Scott Walker's first four albums ("We Pair Off"), the Kinks' preservation (the title track), Love's more baroque psychedelic textures ("Love Doesn't Love"), Brian Wilson's tenderness ("After Life"), and Jimmy Webb's musical and poetic excesses—yes, that's good—("Non Religious Building"), and countless other influences. But these groundings in the popular vernacular are merely signposts. This sound is McKee's alone, and ultimately, despite the range of emotions she addresses and conveys, this is an album about amorous love, full of its dizzying heights and its turbulent spirals into the abyss of loss. Its particular gift is how, no matter how dark or even horrifying the lyrics are, the music is upbeat, full of a life-affirming transcendence that makes it the ultimate statement from love's battlefield, where scars and wounds are the gateways to a deeper understanding of what it means to be human; they add depth and dimension in such grandeur, no matter how tortured, that you're still willing to risk everything to find its promise. McKee is never morbid, just unflinching, and *High Dive* is a leap from the cliff of who she was and was perceived to be into being what she is: an artist of considerable vision, passion, and both musical and literary acumen. That these songs, in all of their sophistication and layered surfaces, can communicate so immediately and accessibly is an achievement; that they do so without looking away from the bottomless cavern of the heart's labyrinthine journey is an artistic achievement and one of the last slices of rock & roll poetry at its most honest and direct. McKee's *High Dive* is simply an awe-inspiring album and easily her finest recorded moment. —*Thom Jurek*

Tommy McLain

Vocals / Zydeco, Rockabilly, Swamp Pop, Swamp Blues
With his gutsy blend of rockabilly and Cajun music, Tommy McLain helped to lay the foundation of Louisiana's swamp pop tradition. The writer of more than 150 songs, McLain is best known as the writer of Freddy Fender's hit, "If You Don't Love Me Alone (Leave Me Alone)," and the performer of a swamp pop version of "Sweet Dreams" that sold more than three-million copies in 1966. In addition to being twice inducted into the Louisiana Hall of Fame, McLain was inducted into the Rock & Roll Hall of Fame in Sweden. McLain has had a career-long involvement with country singer Clint West. In the late '50s, they were both members of Red Smiley's Vel-Tones and moved together to the Boogie Kings in the mid-'60s. In 1965, McLain and West recorded a duet single, "Try to Find Another Man."

A native of the small central Louisiana city of Jonesville, McLain began playing guitar at the age of five. He soon added piano, keyboards, drums, bass, fiddle, and bagpipe. A former DJ at KREH in Oakdale, LA, McLain toured with Dick Clark's Caravan of Stars and Where the Action Is in the 1960s. He also appeared in the film *The Drowning Man* starring Paul Newman. McLain continues to perform with his group, Tommy McLain and the Mule Train Band. —*Craig Harris*

- **The Cajun Rod Stewart: Crazy Cajun Recordings** / Jul. 27, 1999 / Edsel ✦✦✦✦
McClain, believe it or not, had the only version of "Sweet Dreams" to ever make the pop charts. This companion volume to Edsel's other McClain compilation features his entire faux live album from 1979, four sizzling duets with Freddy Fender on some old rock & roll classics, and some odds and ends that were left off the other package due to time constraints. Still active today and still a massive draw in his home state, this package makes a nice introduction to McClain and his brand of Cajun soul music. *—Cub Koda*

Clayton McMichen

b. Jan. 26, 1900, Allatoona, GA, **d.** Jan. 4, 1970
Vocals, Fiddle / Old-Timey, Traditional Folk
Clayton McMichen fused his interests in country, folk, jazz, swing, and pop music into one of the most recognizable fiddle styles. His playing with Jimmie Rodgers and Gid Tanner & His Skillet Lickers in the 1920s helped to lay the foundation for country music. From the time that he arrived in Atlanta to work as an automobile mechanic in 1921 until shortly before his death from emphysema nearly five decades later, he continued to allow his fiddling to evolve. McMichen's band, the Georgia Wildcats, was one of the most eclectic groups of the 1930s. Formed as a string band, they switched to Dixieland jazz in the mid '40s. From 1945 until 1955, the group was featured daily on the Louisville radio station, WAVE. McMichen & the Georgia Wildcats also appeared on their own television show in the early '50s.

A native of Allatoona, GA, McMichen learned to play fiddle as a youngster. By his early '20s, he had mastered the instrument. After moving to Atlanta, he won the first of numerous fiddle championships. A close friend of the "singing brakeman" Jimmie Rodgers, McMichen and Rodgers toured and recorded together throughout the 1920s. Among the songs that they co-wrote was the classic "Peach Pickin' Time in Georgia." McMichen recorded his first songs as a bandleader, a series of jazz tunes played by fiddle, clarinet, and guitar in 1925. The following year, McMichen accepted an invitation to join an all-star country band organized by Columbia talent scout, Frank Walker. The group, which McMichen named the Skillet Lickers, went on to become one of country music's early successes. During the five years that they were together, the band, which also featured fiddler Gid Tanner, guitarist Riley Puckett, and banjo player Fate Norris, recorded more than 100 tunes.

McMichen's first solo hit came with a fiddle tune arrangement of a pop standard, "Sweet Bunch of Roses." Released in 1927, the song sold more than 100,000 copies. Although he tried his hand at sentimental ballads, recording under the pseudonym Bob Nichols, only one recording, "My Carolina Home," became a hit. Forming the Georgia Wildcats after the breakup of the Skillet Lickers in 1931, McMichen was unable to match his early success. To supplement his income as a musician, he promoted fiddle contests and, in 1936, operated a medicine show. He continued to compete, as well. In 1932, he won the first of 18 national fiddle championships. Despite remaining active as a musician, McMichen had no interest in recording his new repertoire. In 1955, he retired from music. Although he was sought out during the folk revival of the 1960s, he was frustrated by the folklorists' reverence for the Skillet Lickers.

While he maintained a low profile for the rest of his life, he agreed to perform at the Bean Blossom festival in 1964 and 1966 and the Newport Folk Festival in 1964. McMichen continued to dazzle audiences with his virtuosic fiddling. At the age of 68, he placed first in the senior division of the Kentucky State Championship. Merle Travis and Mac Wiseman celebrated McMichen's legacy with an album, *The Clayton McMichen Story*, released by CMH Productions in 1988. *—Craig Harris*

The Traditional Years / 1970 / Davis Unlimited ✦✦✦✦✦
From the moment the needle drops on the vinyl, the listener is in the presence of musical greatness. Fiddler Clayton McMichen takes off on a fast version of "McMichen's Reel," backed by the nimble guitar work of Riley Puckett. This album collects 15 such brilliant performances, including solo examples of old time contest-style fiddling, a "Fire on the Mountain" that verges on bluegrass, the Western swing feel of "Yum Yum Blues," McMichen crooning a Hawaiian-style vocal on "Honolulu Moon," and the out and out sentimentality of "Sweet Bunch of Daisies." One half expects W.C. Fields to come stumbling into the room half drunk during the latter number. So all in all, the hero, McMichen, is all over the place, as was his style, pushing the envelope in every setting with both his energy and superior musicianship. Other great players seemed to have flocked around him like moths to a flame, and tastes of various collaborations are provided as this anthology skips around. Fellow fiddler Bert Layne and even a squeaky clarinetist show up on "Sweet Bunch of Daisies"; hotshot picker Slim Bryant helps jazz up the "Wild Cat Rag"; and the entire Skillet Lickers show up for other tracks. McMichen's Melody Men harmonize deliciously for "My Carolina Home." The small Tennessee label behind this reissue likes to use rows and rows of tiny typeface, which produces eyestrain but not the identities of every musician involved in this material. *—Eugene Chadbourne*

Shannon McNally

b. Hempstead, NY
Vocals / Adult Alternative Pop/Rock, Alternative Country-Rock, Singer/Songwriter
Shannon McNally was born in Hempstead, on Long Island. While studying anthropology in college, McNally began singing and playing guitar in clubs, and after graduating honed her skills on the streets of Paris as a busker. The willowy, graceful McNally secured a deal with Capitol in 1997. While the label was interested in marketing her as a second-wave Alanis Morissette, McNally herself was intent on making an acoustic record. Eventually, she won the execs over and entered the studio with a talented bunch of studio pros that included Jim Keltner, Benmont Tench, and Greg Leisz. The result was *Jukebox Sparrows*, a soulful, countrified affair that mixed the well-crafted professionalism of Sheryl Crow with more disparate '70s influences like the Band and Little Feat.

Despite the album's promise, it was shelved indefinitely amidst power struggles at Capitol. In the interim, McNally opened for Stevie Nicks and Ryan Adams, and was part of the *1999 Girl's Room* tour with Tara MacLean, Kendall Payne, and Amy Correia. She also modeled for Urban Decay cosmetics. In 2000, McNally issued the holdover EP *Bolder Than Paradise*. When Capitol finally issued *Jukebox Sparrows* in January 2002, it did so into a market that had already embraced such roots-flavored material as Ryan Adams and the *O Brother, Where Art Thou* phenomenon. McNally embarked on an extensive press tour, and spent the summer of that year supporting John Mellencamp. In late 2002, she released the *Ran on Pure Lightning* EP. A casual, easygoing recording, the project was a collaboration with songwriter Neal Casal. *—Johnny Loftus*

- **Jukebox Sparrows** / Jan. 8, 2002 / Capitol ✦✦✦✦
In a post-Sheryl Crow/Shelby Lynne world, Shannon McNally has a real shot of stardom, since there have already been artists who have opened the doors for her classy, urbane, slyly roots singer/songwriterism. That's not to say that McNally is totally indebted to those artists, even if her debut, *Jukebox Sparrows*, recalls both, along with touches of everyone from Lucinda Williams to Stevie Nicks. It's that she's departing from the same point—post-alternative singer/songwriter pop, with a heritage in classic rock and a fondness for classic country, but with enough hipness to know when to keep things calm and measured and when to haul out the obligatory trip-hop drum loop. So *Jukebox Sparrows* is very much an album of its time, at least as far as its musical approach and production is concerned, but what suggests that Shannon McNally is more than a transitory pleasure is the very quality of her material and voice. She has a rich, textured voice that may not quite be distinctive on its own merits, but is pleasing within her tradition, and the songs are tuneful, passionate, and well-written (well, as long as she keeps her ambitions in check—the Tom Waits-meets-Garbage closing title track gives this fine album a sour aftertaste). This is very much a debut—at times it's hard to not wish it would soar a little higher or shake off the formula of its genre—but it's a very enjoyable, promising debut from an artist who could turn into something special. *—Stephen Thomas Erlewine*

Larry McNeely

b. Jan. 3, 1948, Lafayette, IN
Banjo, Guitar, Harmonica, Vocals / Traditional Bluegrass
A talented session musician, Larry McNeely is known best for his work with Roy Acuff and Glen Campbell. A native of Lafayette, IN, he was born into a musical family, but didn't begin learning to play piano until he was 13. He then added guitar and banjo, and got his professional start at the age of 17 when he joined the Pinnacle Mountain Boys. In 1965, after moving to Nashville to work for the Sho-Bud Guitar Company (formed by Shot Jackson and Buddy Emmons), he met Acuff and joined his Smoky Mountain Boys. He remained with them through decade's end and then moved to California, where he joined Glen Campbell's band after John Hartford left. He recorded his first solo album, *Glen Campbell Presents Larry McNeely*, in 1971. He remained with Campbell through 1974, then left the touring circuit to work as a session man.

McNeely played on numerous albums (including work by the Carpenters and Roger Miller) as well as movie soundtracks, commercials, and in 1977, he recorded two albums for different labels. He went back to Nashville in 1984 to try the bluegrass scene, but soon returned to work with Acuff, with whom he played until Acuff's death in 1992. After that McNeely began working with Russ & Becky Jeffers and Smoky Mountain Sunshine. *—Sandra Brennan*

- **Rhapsody for Banjo** / 1979 / Flying Fish ✦✦✦
That this guy is one of the flashiest and technically adept banjo pickers around would be a fact many bluegrass fans would be happy to wager a set of fingerpicks or two over. Many tracks on this album are simply killer, and the presence of mandolinist Jethro Burns will definitely be of interest to listeners who would like to hear more of his fine, serious picking outside the wacky confines of the famous Homer and Jethro unit. The originals by McNeely, highlighting fast-moving developments with a particularly aggressive sense of time, would predict the later work of artists such as Béla Fleck, and younger fans of this latter artist should definitely check out the playing of artists such as McNeely who have received a whole lot less hype in their lifetime. However it is something of a shame that McNeely also chose to play guitar in a hot jazz or swing style, his work vastly in the debt of jazz picker supreme Django Reinhardt, to whom he dedicates a tune. When it comes to these tracks the music is just much less original and exciting, unless the listener is a bluegrass fanatic who has never heard any other styles of music before, in which case it might be difficult to predict what the reaction might be. Nashville session king Roy Husky is solid on bass, no doubt smoking a cigar the whole time. *—Eugene Chadbourne*

The McPeak Brothers

f. 1963, Wytheville, VA
Group / Progressive Bluegrass, Traditional Bluegrass
The McPeak Brothers were a popular bluegrass trio from Wytheville, VA, comprised of banjo/guitar player Dewey, bassist/guitarist Larry and guitarist/lead vocalist Mike. Their older brother Udell broke into music first when he joined the Lonesome Pine Fiddlers during the 1950s. In 1963, he, Dewey and Larry formed the first version of the McPeak Brothers. Soon after, Udell left to play with Red Smiley's band and was replaced by Mike. Following the addition of fiddler Ernest Atkins and mandolin player Gus Ingo, the group began appearing weekly on a local radio show in 1969. The McPeaks made their recording debut in 1970 and cut their first album (*Virginia, Where It All Began*) two years later. They released a second effort, *Bluegrass at Its Peak*, in 1973. Atkins' friendship with Mel Tillis helped the McPeaks get onto Tillis' syndicated TV show, which led to a contract with RCA Victor and an album in 1974.

They soon left the label and recorded three more albums on independent labels. Several McPeak Brothers tunes—"Somebody Socked It to Mine," "Simon Crutchfield's Grave," and "Bobbi,"—became quite popular with progressive bluegrass players. The group slowed down considerably during the mid-'80s and only played local engagements. They did cut a new album in 1992, though, and later put together an anthology containing the best of their independently released songs. *—Sandra Brennan*

- **Classic Bluegrass** / 1992 / Rebel ✦✦✦✦✦

Bottom Line / Apr. 14, 1998 / Copper Creek ✦✦✦✦

Larry, Mike, and Dewey McPeak have been around as a group for almost 25 years but have made relatively few albums during that period. Their eighth is a winning program of originals by Larry and cover versions of material by such legendary country and bluegrass artists as Bill Monroe, Marty Robbins, and Jimmie Davis. Though the McPeaks' voices are starting to roughen with age, their trio harmonies are still sweet and tight, and they work particularly nicely on a version of the Delmore Brothers' "Gonna Lay Down My Old Guitar" and Larry McPeak's aching "Why You're Leaving Me This Time." Dewey McPeak's banjo playing is another of this group's prime attractions—though he avoids ostentatious displays of virtuosity, his blend of straight-ahead Scruggs-style playing, melodic licks, and single-string Reno-esque passages makes him a pleasure to listen to, especially on "I Can't Get Over You" and "Don't Count the Rainy Days." Other highlights on this album include fine versions of the creepy (and rarely recorded) murder ballad "Poor Ellen Smith" and of Bill Monroe's "Used to Be." —*Rick Anderson*

Randy Meisner

b. Mar. 8, 1946, Scottsbluff, NE

Bass, Vocals / Country-Rock, Adult Contemporary, Soft Rock

Meisner is probably best known as the bassist of the Eagles. His career began in the early '60s with obscure bands such as the Dynamics and the Poor. He became a founding member of the country-rock band Poco, but disagreements led him to leave for Rick Nelson's Stone Canyon Band. In 1971, he joined the Linda Ronstadt backing band which eventually became the Eagles, leaving in 1977 to pursue a solo career. He had several Top 40 singles before taking some time off. Meisner joined a reunited Poco in 1989, but friction resurfaced, and he joined a group called Black Tie, which then had a country hit with Buddy Holly's "Learning the Game." —*Steve Huey*

Randy Meisner / 1978 / Asylum ✦✦

- **One More Song** / 1980 / Epic ✦✦✦

One More Song highlights Meisner's knack for writing honest, heartfelt love songs with a countrified rock candor that reveals his rustic, down-home roots. With help from songwriter Eric Kaz, two of the album's tracks found their way onto *Billboard*'s Top 40. "Deep Inside My Heart," with backing from Kim Carnes made it to number 22, while "Hearts on Fire" reached the number 19 spot three months later. Both of these singles bask in the sweetness of laid-back AOR, but Meisner's velvety voice and homespun innocence carried them above the insipidness of average radio schlock. The rest of the songs hold up just as solidly, especially the title track with both Don Henley and Glenn Frey contributing to the background vocals, not to mention Craig Hull's lonely steel guitar playing. Closing out with Richie Furay's rollicking "Anyway Bye Bye," *One More Song* ends up being a pleasurable set of modest songs from a musician who was glad to be home. —*Mike DeGagne*

Randy Meisner / 1982 / Epic ✦✦✦

After finishing a tour of Northern Europe with the Eagles in September of 1977, Randy Meisner retreated back to his home state of Nebraska to record his self-titled solo debut album. —*Mike DeGagne*

Meisner, Swan & Rich / Sep. 11, 2001 / Varese ✦✦✦

This frustratingly brief ten-track album is a lovely re-creation of the '70s West Coast country-pop sound as best practiced by the Eagles (of which Randy Meisner was a founding member), CSN, Poco (another Meisner group), and various lesser-known offshoots like the Souther-Hillman-Furay Band and Firefall. It's a little on the slick side, but these songs are all top-notch, well-crafted, and splendidly sung by three titular country-rock vets whose beautiful voices melt collectively. Charlie Rich Jr., who like his dad plays piano, is responsible for the majority of the songwriting, co-writing a few tunes with Billy Swan. Sadly Meisner, who wrote some of the Eagles' best ballads, only pens one track, the reflective "My How Things Have Changed." There are a few upbeat rockers, like "Who's Gonna Love You Baby?," but the majority of the disc stays focused on peaceful, easy-feeling-styled, broken-hearted slow songs that go down smooth and sad. Meisner in particular is in fine form, singing in his teary tenor on weepers like "(It's Like I) Never Had a Broken Heart," a track that sounds like a great lost Eagles B-side. Swan adds some swamp on "Honey (Sweet Sweet Honey)," but Rich Jr.'s earnest tunes dominate this collection. Actually it's the harmonies that rivet your attention, as these three voices effortlessly coalesce and sound like they've been singing together for years. Even though it leans toward easy listening, it's a far cry from the soulless, sterile country clogging up the radio waves in 2001. This is a highly recommended debut, geared to those pining for the days when the singer/songwriter L.A. sound ruled the charts. Maybe next time they can write a few more songs and push past an anemic but enjoyable half hour of music. —*Hal Horowitz*

Dallas / Feb. 25, 2002 / Rev-Ola ✦✦✦

About five years after he'd left the Eagles, Randy Meisner recorded this live set in Dallas on December 2, 1982, before a none-too-big or (at times, at least) enthusiastic-sounding crowd. To his credit, at this point he wasn't resting on his work with the Eagles, filling up most of the set with songs from his trio of albums from the late '70s and early '80s, though he did include the Eagles' "Try and Love Again" and "Take It to the Limit." Still, it's bland if slickly executed singer/songwriter rock, touched with traces of country, folk, and pop, but less so than the work of the Eagles. Like many live albums, it's one for fans only, whether of the Eagles and/or (less likely) Meisner's solo work. The packaging is disappointing in that it has few details of the show, though it does at least list the musicians and print the lyrics. There are, incidentally, two versions of "Take It to the Limit," one of them identified as an "alternate mix." —*Richie Unterberger*

Ken Mellons

b. Jul. 10, 1965, Kingsport, TN

Vocals / Contemporary Country

A resident of Nashville since the age of three, Ken Mellons found a Music City contract with Epic in 1994, after several appearances on the *Grand Ole Opry* spread the word about his talents. Born in Kingsport, TN, on July 10, 1965, Mellons soon moved with his family to Nashville, where he grew up on the standard honky tonk heroes: Merle Haggard, George Jones, and Lefty Frizzell. He played guitar and sang at school talent shows, and moved on to the clubs after high-school graduation. Impressed by one performance, the general manager of the *Grand Ole Opry* invited Mellons to make a guest appearance. He was invited back several times—in fact, his *Opry* residence lasted from 1989 to 1992. While most kids his age were studying in college, Mellons was honing his craft alongside future country stars like Chely Wright and Lonestar's Dean Sams.

After slugging it out on the *Opry*'s "Country Music USA" show, Mellons caught the attention of impresarios Hal Durham and Bud Wendall, who bumped him up to a Friday night spot at the *Opry*. Producer Jerry Cupit took notice, and a deal with Epic was proffered in 1993. Mellons' self-titled debut album was released one year later; the single "Jukebox Junkie" was a hit and continued to receive airplay for the rest of the decade. Mellons followed up his debut's success in 1995 with *Where Forever Begins*. He was married that same year and also moved from EMI to Curb, where he issued the confusingly titled *Best of Ken Mellons* in 2001. The record was actually made up of all new material, but for a "dance remix" of "Jukebox Junkie." In early 2003, Mellons issued the successful single "Mr. DJ," in anticipation of his next album for Curb. —*Johnny Loftus*

- **Ken Mellons** / 1994 / Epic ✦✦✦✦

Where Forever Begins / 1995 / Sony ✦✦✦

On his second album, Ken Mellons constructs a balanced mix of tearjerking ballads, honky tonk rockers, and plaintive, straightforward traditional country. Mellons performs the songs convincingly, but he is occasionally hurt by a lack of quality songwriting, as evidenced by the single "Rub-A-Dubbin." Although he might not be powerful enough of a vocalist to pull off lightweight material, he can deliver good songs forcefully, which is what makes the majority of *Where Forever Begins* an entertaining listen. —*Stephen Thomas Erlewine*

Best of Ken Mellons / Apr. 3, 2001 / Curb ✦✦✦

Country singer and songwriter Ken Mellons had only completed two full-length albums when he went to work on this best-of recording. Those first two albums were done under the Epic Records label, before he switched over to Curb. There are only ten tracks on *Best of Ken Mellons*, including "Farmer's Daughter," "Was It As Good for You," "Ladies Night," and a kind of dance mix of his popular "Jukebox Junkie" number from his debut album. Mellons co-wrote all of the songs on this album except the last track, "Cool As You." This album shouldn't really be titled as a best-of offering, since these are not hits from other recordings; they are actually all new numbers except the reworked "Jukebox Junkie," so don't pass this one up thinking you have these songs if you have his first two albums. If you are a Ken Mellons fan, you'll find this album sticks with his traditional and honky tonk country sound—a sound that many country artists are giving up to cross over that pop line. —*Charlotte Dillon*

Tift Merritt

b. 1975, Houston, TX

Vocals, Guitar, Composer / Contemporary Singer/Songwriter, Alternative Country, Contemporary Country

Singer/songwriter Tift Merritt seemingly appeared out of nowhere in the spring of 2002 with her acclaimed debut album *Bramble Rose*, but as is often the case, this triple-threat artist—a gifted singer, superb songwriter, and skillful guitarist—actually has plenty of experience under her belt. Born in Houston, TX, in 1975, Merritt's family moved to North Carolina when she was young and she's lived there ever since. Merritt first developed an interest in music when she was a child and learned to sing harmonies with her father, who had dabbled in folk music in his younger days; in her early teens, she picked up a guitar and her dad taught her her first four chords. While Merritt was drawn to the rebellious spirit of punk and indie rock, she felt a greater emotional connection with more acoustic-oriented artists, particularly Joni Mitchell (Merritt once told a reporter, "I went through a Joni Mitchell phase—and all girls go through a Joni Mitchell phase; if any girl tells you she never did, don't believe her."). Hearing Emmylou Harris' album *Quarter Moon in a Ten Cent Town* opened Merritt's ears to roots music and she soon began to immerse herself in North Carolina's active alt-country scene. Merritt began appearing on a semi-regular basis with the band the Two Dollar Pistols, singing duets with lead singer John Howie and playing rhythm guitar; she eventually appeared on a seven-song EP of classic country covers the group released in the fall of 1999. Looking for a vehicle for her own songwriting, in 1998 Merritt formed a band called the Carbines with drummer Zeke Hutchins, guitarist Greg Reading, and bassist Jay Brown; the band soon became a fixture on the North Carolina club scene and they released a well-received seven-inch single.

Between the Carbines and the Two Dollar Pistols, Merritt was becoming a popular figure in the North Carolina roots-music community and in early 2000, Merritt and the Carbines seemed poised to sign a contract with Sugar Hill Records. The deal fell through at the last minute, but when Merritt won the Chris Austin Songwriting Contest at the annual 2000 Merlefest Music Festival, it sparked a new round of interest in her work. Fellow North Carolina native Ryan Adams brought Merritt to the attention of his manager, Frank Callari, and he began shopping a record deal for her; when he was hired as an A&R executive for the Universal-distributed roots music label Lost Highway, Merritt became one of his first signings. (While Merritt was signed as a solo act, she's continued to use the Carbines as her backing band, both for live shows and for the recording of *Bramble Rose*). Her debut album was released to enthusiastic reviews in June 2002. —*Mark Deming*

- **Bramble Rose** / Jun. 4, 2002 / Universal ✦✦✦✦✦

In his short story *Billy the Kid*, Steve Earle spun the tale of a fresh-faced kid who arrived in Nashville with a handful of brilliant songs, cut a stone classic album, scored a record deal most musicians would give their eye teeth to get, and married the girl of his dreams, all in a few weeks before cruel fate caught up with him. While one can only hope the powers that be have a more generous final act planned for Tift Merritt, listening to her first album, *Bramble Rose*, is a reminder that such things could possibly happen in the real world. If *Bramble Rose* is a bit short of perfect, it leaves no doubt that Merritt is already a talent of the first order. As a singer, she has a simply gorgeous vocal instrument (imagine the passion of Lucinda Williams and the real-world twang of Iris Dement fused with the silky beauty of Emmylou Harris), and her songs are nearly as impressive as her vocals. At 27, Merritt's lyrical perspective speaks of the often-unfortunate twists and turns of fate, but without bitterness or spite, and she can jump from the wistful sway of "Virginia, No One Can Warn You" to the R&B-influenced bite of "Neighborhood" and back to the classic weeper style of the title cut without missing a step or ever sounding less than committed or convincing. Merritt also has the good fortune of having a superb backing band who support her songs with grace and impeccable taste, and producer Ethan Johns gets this music on tape with a sound that's at once intimate and comfortably wide open. It's difficult to imagine that an artist whose previous recording experience amounted to one self-released 45 and a split EP could turn in an album so strong and well-crafted, but it's even harder to imagine that listeners are likely to hear many debut albums nearly as good as *Bramble Rose* in the final six months of 2002, and by all rights this should be the first offering in a long and successful career for Tift Merritt. *—Mark Deming*

Jo Dee Messina

b. Aug. 25, 1970, Framingham, MA

Vocals, Vocals (Background) / Contemporary Country, Neo-Traditionalist Country

Part of country music's late-'90s crop of female crossover stars, Jo Dee Messina's appeal nonetheless remained more with country fans than pop audiences. Messina was born August 25, 1970, in Framingham, MA, and grew up in nearby Holliston. She sang in musical plays starting at age eight but discovered country music at age 12 and got hooked on the likes of the Judds, Reba McEntire, and Dolly Parton. She soon started performing live, and by 16 she was playing local clubs with a rhythm section made up of her brother and sister. At age 19, she moved to Nashville in search of greater exposure and sang regularly for prize money in local talent competitions. One win led to a regular gig on the radio show *Live at Libby's*, which in turn caught the interest of producer Byron Gallimore, who helped her assemble a demo tape. Gallimore was also working with the young Tim McGraw around the same time, and Messina befriended him. Backstage at one of his concerts, Messina met an executive from his label, Curb, and jokingly suggested that they needed a redhead. Producer James Stroud, who had just heard Messina's demo, stepped up to vouch for her, and she soon wound up on Curb, with Gallimore and McGraw serving as her producers.

Messina's self-titled debut album was released in 1996 and gave her two Top Ten hits in "Heads Carolina, Tails California" (number two) and "You're Not in Kansas Anymore." The album sold well, setting the stage for Messina's star-making sophomore effort, *I'm Alright*. Released in 1998, it made Messina the first female country artist to score three multiple-week number-one hits from the same album: "Bye Bye," "I'm Alright," and "Stand Beside Her." She nearly had a fourth, but "Lesson in Leavin'" stalled at number-two. Honored by both the CMA and ACM in 1999, Messina staked out even pop-friendlier territory on her third album, 2000's *Burn*. It became her first number-one album, and the lead single, "That's the Way," her fourth number-one single. Two more Top Tens followed in "Burn" and "Downtime," and a fourth single, the Tim McGraw duet "Bring on the Rain," also topped the charts, helping *Burn* sell over a million copies. Messina followed it with the holiday album *A Joyful Noise* in late 2002, and just months later, with only three albums to her credit, Curb released a *Greatest Hits* compilation. *—Steve Huey*

Jo Dee Messina / Mar. 26, 1996 / Curb ✦✦✦✦

Country singer Jo Dee Messina has been voted top new female vocalist by the Academy of County Music, and walked away with the Country Music Association's Horizon Award. Before then she made her full-length debut into the music world with this 1996 self-titled album. Producers Byron Gallimore and well-known singer Tim McGraw oversaw the recording. The resulting album was an impressive outing for Messina. On this recording, music lovers can enjoy country ballads like "He'd Never Seen Julie Cry," "On a Wing and a Prayer," and "Every Little Girl's Dream," as well as upbeat, energetic pop-flavored numbers such as "Do You Wanna Make Something of It" and "Heads Carolina, Tails California." The latter is an early favorite of many Messina fans. After such a great first effort, it wasn't surprising that her next album, *I'm Alright*, released two years later, went double platinum. *—Charlotte Dillon*

I'm Alright / Mar. 17, 1998 / Curb ✦✦✦

Released two years after her breakthrough debut, Jo Dee Messina's second album, *I'm Alright*, essentially follows the same polished country-pop formula as her first. Messina again worked with producers Byron Gallimore and Tim McGraw, who supply arrangements that are just a little too clean. Nevertheless, many of the songs are solid contemporary country tunes, even if they lean a little close to adult contemporary pop, and her delivery is assured and convincing. Like many country albums, *I'm Alright* essentially features a handful of very, very good singles, surrounded by filler that's either pleasant or forgettable, but the best moments on the record ("Bye, Bye," "I'm Alright," "Silver Thunderbird") prove that Messina's debut was no flash in the pan. *—Thom Owens*

Burn / Aug. 1, 2000 / Curb ✦✦✦✦

Messina's third release with Curb, *Burn* is a riveting collection of 11 songs guaranteed to make even the faintest of heart feel energized. Byron Gallimore and Tim McGraw throw their hats into the ring again as co-producers putting out an album that speaks volumes to Messina fans. "Downtime," the album's lead track, is an upbeat song about needing a little space in order to mend a broken heart; "Burn," the title track and one of the album's slower songs, is about being what you want to be in life; the soulful "Bring on the Rain" is the culmination of the McGraw/Messina friendship with McGraw singing background vocals about those days in life when you're feeling like everything's going wrong; and perhaps part autobiographical is "Dare to Dream," a snappy song with lyrics like "Live, love, seize the day, and dare to dream." Having taken two years to make this album was worth it; the third time's a charm. *—Maria Konicki Dinoia*

A Joyful Noise / Oct. 29, 2002 / WEA ✦✦✦

● **Greatest Hits** / May 20, 2003 / Curb ✦✦✦✦

A greatest-hits album appearing after just three studio albums and following a Christmas album by months can only mean one thing—an artist is reaching the end of her contract, and she's riding it out. So appears to be the case with Jo Dee Messina, whose *Greatest Hits* was released in May of 2003, seven years after her first album. During those seven years, she amassed quite a number of hits, including five chart-toppers. All of them are here on this generous 15-track collection, along with four new tracks, highlighted by the opening track and lead single "Was That My Life." Only two of her charting singles for Curb are missing—the first, "Do You Wanna Make Something of It," and the last, "Dare to Dream"—which makes this an excellent summary and introduction to an artist who may not have blazed trails, but delivered consistently enjoyable mainstream and fairly traditional country, as this fine collection proves. *—Stephen Thomas Erlewine*

Ramsay Midwood

b. Arlington, VA

Composer, Vocals, Guitar / Americana, Blues-Rock, Singer/Songwriter, Folk-Rock, Country-Rock

It isn't likely that anyone is going to accuse Ramsay Midwood of being glossy or ultra-slick anytime soon. Earthy, gritty, rugged, and soulful, Midwood is an Austin, TX-based singer/songwriter whose folk-rock, Americana, and roots rock owe a major debt to the blues—in fact, his songs are soaked in blues feeling. Midwood brings a variety of influences to the table. Woody Guthrie, Pete Seeger, Levon Helm, and Ramblin' Jack Elliott have obviously had a major impact on his work; so have Bob Dylan and Tom Waits (especially Waits' early recordings). There are traces of Bruce Springsteen in some of Midwood's writing, and there are times when he brings to mind the darker, moodier side of bluesmen John Lee Hooker and Lightnin' Hopkins.

Midwood isn't from Austin originally; he was born and raised in Arlington, VA, a suburb of Washington, D.C. Both of his parents were interested in the arts. His father was a tuba player, and his mother (who volunteered at the Smithsonian Institute) did a lot to encourage his interest in roots music, especially folk, bluegrass, and the blues (both acoustic country blues and electric urban blues). After reaching adulthood, Midwood moved to Chicago and got into acting. In the Windy City, he hooked up with the famous Steppenwolf Theater Company and played two roles in a production of *The Grapes of Wrath*: Al Joad and Floyd Knowles. Financially, Chicago was a struggle for Midwood, and when he had a chance to make some money by appearing in a beer commercial (which was being filmed in Los Angeles), he decided to visit the West Coast. The fact that he was dating a woman who was planning to move to L.A. permanently also affected his decision, and after he got there, he realized that he liked the weather and ended up staying.

In L.A., Midwood performed his songs in small coffeehouses, and one of the people who admired his singing and writing urged him to submit a demo to a small German indie label called Glitterhouse Records. Midwood ended up recording his debut album, *Shoot Out at the OK Chinese Restaurant*, for Glitterhouse, which released it in Germany in 2000. The album received its share of favorable reviews in various European countries and earned Midwood a small but enthusiastic following on that continent. After a fire destroyed Midwood's L.A. apartment in February 2002, he decided to move to Austin, TX. In November 2002, *Shoot Out at the OK Chinese Restaurant* was released in the U.S. by Vanguard. *—Alex Henderson*

Shoot Out at the OK Chinese Restaurant / 2002 / Vanguard ✦✦✦✦

Originally released in 2000 on the German Glitterhouse label, *Shoot Out at the OK Chinese Restaurant* draws deep from two American wells. Traditional music nourishes these performances, but so does that part of American culture that produces idiosyncratic, somewhat twisted individualists. In a laconic drawl that recalls both Woody Guthrie and Levon Helm, Midwood projects an ageless, enigmatic quality; like Leon Redbone, he might be a prematurely rustic twentysomething, a crotchety yet poetic septuagenarian, or anything in between. Vivid images fill his lyrics and drift over shambling tracks marked by banjo plucks, beat-up old pianos, and other garage-sale relics. His songs offer romantic insights based on distant experience ("Feed My Monkey,"), bits of aphoristic wisdom fashioned as koans from a Dust Bowl Buddha ("Grass'll Grow"), reflections on redneck bravado ("Monster Truck,") and stream-of-consciousness ramblings that seem more wise than coherent ("Alligator's Lament.") Perhaps his most compelling lyric, "Spinnin' on a Rock," documents the murderous fantasy of a laid-off dockworker in couplets more reminiscent of a playground game. In one song, Midwood advises listeners to hear him out with the wry line, "Take a tip from a real smart feller." That's a suggestion worth listening to, given the broken-down brilliance of this debut. *—Robert L. Doerschuk*

Bill Miller

b. Jan. 23, 1955

Flute, Guitar, Piano, Vocals / Contemporary Singer/Songwriter, Contemporary Folk, Americana

The strength of the Native American people and the hardships of their lives are captured through the folk-like balladry of Nashville-based singer/songwriter Bill Miller. Miller's best-known tune, "Tumbleweed," co-written with Peter Rowan and included on Rowan's 1990 album *Dust Bowl Children*, reflects on a memorable Native American character; *Trail of Freedom*, however, focuses on alcoholism among Native Americans.

The son of Mohican-German parents, Miller was born on the Stockbridge-Munsee Reservation in northern Wisconsin. Music played an essential role in tribal life, and Miller, whose Mohican name is Fush-Ya Heay Aka (meaning "bird song"), learned to sing traditional songs at an early age. The sounds of nature including the howling of coyotes and the hooting of owls were also influential. Contemporary popular music, however, had a powerful effect on Miller's musical evolution. An enthusiastic fan of the Byrds, the Rolling Stones, and the Beatles, Miller often traveled into town to buy records.

At the age of 12, Miller acquired his first guitar. His first gig came when he sat in with a cousin's polka band. Although he played in a teenaged rock & roll/Top 40 band for two years, he tired of pop music. Trading his electric guitar for an acoustic, Miller began to play folk music and bluegrass. A musical turning point came when Miller attended a Pete Seeger concert shortly after leaving the reservation to study art at the University of Wisconsin at LaCrosse (he later attended the Lake School of Art and Design in Milwaukee). The experience inspired Miller, who moved to Nashville in 1984, to pursue a career as a singer/songwriter.

Miller's biggest break came when Tori Amos asked him to be her opening act on her *Under the Pink* tour of the United States. The tour, which sold out venues across the country, was extended to over 200 shows. Although he mostly accompanies his baritone vocals on acoustic guitar, Miller has mastered the Native American flute. His 1991 album *Loon, Mountain and Moon* was a showcase of traditional Native American flute songs. —*Craig Harris*

The Red Road / Aug. 3, 1993 / Reprise ✦✦✦

Raven in the Snow / Oct. 1995 / Reprise ✦✦✦✦✦
Native American artist Bill Miller released his second album, *Raven in the Snow*, in 1995. Any preconceived notion that this might be new age or traditional music is put to rest immediately with the opening track, "River of Time." The song is a harmonica-driven, midtempo rocker that compares favorably with the music of artists like Peter Himmelman. The song contains a heavy spiritual vibe that runs through the entire record, from the powerful lyric of "Listen to Me" to the fire-and-brimstone tone of "The Final Word." The proceedings, however, never fail to be highly melodic. There are several instrumentals that take a more traditional Native American bent; these don't really add to the record, but they don't detract from it either. —*Tom Demalon*

● **Ghostdance** / May 18, 1999 / Vanguard ✦✦✦✦✦
Combine Native American touches with a healthy appreciation of storytellers like Bruce Springsteen, Neil Young, and Leonard Cohen and you have Bill Miller, a distinctive singer/songwriter who shows how compelling he can be on *Ghostdance*. This superb CD is essentially folk-rock, but it's folk-rock with Native American elements. Not only has Native American culture influenced him musically, but his reflective lyrics are also greatly influenced by the history and culture of Native Americans. Like Springsteen, Miller realizes that great singer/songwriters often draw on their own backgrounds and experiences. The Boss' frame of reference is working-class New Jersey—he sings so convincingly about blue-collar life that you know he has been there—whereas Miller's is the Native American experience. And his insights as a Mohican help to enrich "There Is You," "Every Mountain I Climb," and other pearls on *Ghostdance*. But you don't have to have a Native American background to be moved by this album any more than you have to be from New Jersey to savor Springsteen's *Born to Run*. The Boss might be writing about people in Asbury Park, NJ, but listeners in Melbourne, Australia, or Dublin, Ireland, can easily relate to his stories; and similarly, *Ghostdance* offers insights that people from a variety of backgrounds will appreciate. —*Alex Henderson*

Loon, Mountain and Moon / Jul. 25, 2000 / Vanguard ✦✦✦

Reservation Road Live / Jul. 25, 2000 / Vanguard ✦✦✦

The Art of Survival / Jul. 25, 2000 / Vanguard ✦✦✦

Spirit Rain / Jul. 9, 2002 / Paras Recording ✦✦✦✦
Bill Miller never seems to be in a hurry. He doesn't mind opening an album with a two-minute instrumental piece called "Approaching Thunder," making sure he sets the mood right. He proceeds with the confidence of an artist who knows he has the goods, and who plans to deliver them when the time is right. "Approaching Thunder" segues into the country-folk of "You Are the Rain," a gentle wash of acoustic guitars, flutes, and organ backed by percussive brushes. While Miller's lyrical quality may suggest a singer/songwriter's disposition, his utterances cut a broader swath than the average wordsmith. "Rain Down Your Love" poetically captures one person's search for God, while "Never Too Far" offers a lyrical rendering of a person's connection to nature and perhaps to a higher being that permeates all things. Miller never feels the need to spell out his message, but paints it in impressionistic images of red skies and empty prairies. *Spirit Rain* adapts non-folk material easily, as with the inclusion of "Face the Blues," a bit of 12-bar Texas blues with an electric guitar reminiscent of the Vaughan Brothers. A lovely piece titled "Love Sustained" even evokes Dylan without sounding derivative. All of this works and works well on *Spirit Rain* because Miller steps into the moment and keeps the faith throughout. Anyone who appreciates uncompromised folksingers who actually have something to say will want to pick up a copy. —*Ronnie D. Lankford Jr.*

Buddy Miller

Guitar, Vocals / Neo-Traditionalist Country, Americana, Country-Folk, Country-Rock
Soulful Americana songwriter, singer, and producer Buddy Miller began his career in the early '60s as an upright bassist is high-school bluegrass combos. Later, he traveled the backroads of America as an acoustic guitarist, eventually landing in New York City, where his Buddy Miller Band included a young Shawn Colvin on vocals and guitar. He also forged an enduring relationship with country-rock iconoclast Jim Lauderdale. Miller eventually landed in Nashville, where he did session guitar and vocal work on albums by Lauderdale, Victoria Williams, and Heather Myles, among others. He self-produced his criminally overlooked solo debut, *Your Love and Other Lies* (Hightone, 1995), and followed it with 1997's equally superb *Poison Love*.

By this point Miller was the lead guitarist in Emmylou Harris' band, and Harris returned the favor with backing vocals throughout *Poison Love*. 1999's *Cruel Moon*

continued Miller's string of home-recorded masterpieces; this time around, Steve Earle dropped by for the sessions. A big part of all Miller's recordings was the songwriting and harmonies of his wife, Julie Miller. Their 2001 duet album *Buddy & Julie Miller* brought her contributions to the front of the mix and delivered them with gritty, soulful country arrangements enhanced by the interplay of his scowl and her lilt. His fifth album for Hightone, *Midnight and Lonesome* was released in 2002. It again featured contributions from Julie, Harris, and Lauderdale and mixed honky tonk with heartfelt balladry and the occasional soul cover. In addition to his stellar solo career, Miller held down his gig in Harris' backing band, played guitar with Earle, produced albums by his wife Julie, Jimmie Dale Gilmore, and the Vigilantes of Love, and wrote songs for the Dixie Chicks, Lee Ann Womack, Lauderdale, and Hank Williams III. —*Johnny Loftus*

● **Your Love and Other Lies** / 1995 / Hightone ✦✦✦✦
A talented guitarist/singer/songwriter and producer, Buddy Miller merges a love for classic country, with a rock & roll sense of urgency and do-it-yourself ethic. Witness the fact that a good share of this record was recorded in Miller's living room. The results, however, are memorable—not low-budget. Miller enlists some great vocal support from longtime duo partner Jim Lauderdale, Lucinda Williams, Emmylou Harris, and Dan Penn. His wife, Julie Miller, also provides moving harmonies, particularly on a stunning cover of the Louvin Brothers' classic "You're Running Wild," as well as sharing writing credits with her husband on a good share of the songs. She solely authored two of the album's strongest tracks, the haunting "Don't Listen to the Wind" and the tender ballad "Through the Eyes of a Broken Heart." And although it's been largely overlooked, Miller arguably turns in the finest version of Tom T. Hall's lonesome "That's How I Got to Memphis" since the original. —*Jack Leaver*

Poison Love / Aug. 19, 1997 / Hightone ✦✦✦✦
Poison Love picks up where Buddy Miller's debut, *Your Love and Other Lies*, ended, offering a set of exhilarating traditional country laced with blues and soul. Half of the album was recorded with Emmylou Harris' backing band (Miller is its lead guitarist), including Emmylou on backing vocals, but those aren't the only tracks that kick. The entire album, from his sturdy originals to smart covers, demonstrate that he has superb taste and a flair for down-home, gritty performances. And although Miller is a terrific guitarist, he knows enough to keep his solos concise, serving the purpose of the song; that, in the end, is what makes *Poison Love* so good—it's an album of great songs, delivered without pretension and with a whole lot of heart. —*Thom Owens*

Cruel Moon / Oct. 19, 1999 / Hightone ✦✦✦✦
Here's a homemade album that totally hits the spot. Buddy Miller cut this twangy little masterpiece at his home studio, enlisting the aid of friends who dropped by to help out on various tracks. The end result, which normally would make a nice-but-disjointed demo tape, ends up being the freshest new country album to hit the boards in a while. Miller plays tasty lead guitar fills that fit like a glove with his vocals, no matter what the material. He has a world-weary, whiskey-soaked voice, full of crazed hillbilly nuances that are on open display, even on left-field entries like Gene Pitney's "I'm Gonna Be Strong," turned into a modern country radio-ready tearjerker. Along the way, Emmylou Harris, Joy Lynn White, and Steve Earle make guest appearances. But it isn't the guests that make *Cruel Moon* so special; it's Miller's commitment to the material at hand, whether it's an old favorite or something he and his wife, Julie Miller, wrote together; like the lilting title track or "In Memory of My Heart," which sounds like it was recorded in an old-time radio station. There's so much personality coming off of this disc, it takes you awhile to realize that Miller's no young chicken, with a receding hairline that'll surely keep him out of whatever new hat-hunk meat-factory sweepstakes is currently dominating country music. Bypass such fashion front-running and make a beeline straight for this disc; it's as real, honest, and forward looking a country album as you're likely to encounter in these image-encrusted times. —*Cub Koda*

Buddy & Julie Miller / Sep. 18, 2001 / Hightone ✦✦✦
Earthy husband and wife singer/songwriters Buddy & Julie Miller offer more rootsy, countrified folk music on their self-titled 2001 release, this time with a full, more rock-influenced sound. While the two have made involved appearances on each others' albums, *Buddy & Julie Miller* marks their first release as a true duo. The leadoff track, "Keep Your Distance," is a full and lush stomper, humming with rich Hammond organ and rattling tambourine, while the breathy trembler "You Make My Heart Beat Too Fast" is a bluesy throwback to late-'70s era Rolling Stones, with heavy electric guitar and throbbing drums. Fans of the Millers' traditional folk love songs needn't worry; the achingly bittersweet "Forever Has Come to an End" is on par with the honest American folk on their previous releases, and the dark murder ballad "Rock Salt and Nails" is as gripping and chilling as Gillian Welch's gritty recordings. The harmonies of Julie's sweet, girlish singsong and Buddy's gruff, dark voice still remain their strongest trademark, with their honest songwriting following closely behind. Buddy & Julie Miller continue to grow and experiment with their sound, and while this may ruffle the feathers of folk purists, Americana fans will certainly embrace this new direction wholeheartedly. —*Zac Johnson*

Midnight and Lonesome / 2002 / Hightone ✦✦✦✦
Buddy Miller's fourth solo release (fifth if you count 2001's collaboration with wife Julie Miller) slots comfortably into the established formula around which he's structured all of his albums. Lots of honky tonk infused into heartfelt ballads (Jesse Winchester's "A Showman's Life"), upbeat rockers (the Everly Brothers' "The Price of Love"), rural hillbilly ("Wild Card"), and a stray soul cover (Percy Mayfield's "Please Send Me Someone to Love"). Emmylou Harris, whose band he plays in, adds backing vocals. Wife Julie does as well, and also contributes four songs in addition to co-writing three others. Old pals like songwriter Jim Lauderdale, Tammy Rogers on fiddle, and Al Perkins handling steel guitar also make appearances. But even though he's following his own blueprint, Miller never just goes through the motions, making this one of his most consistent and enjoyable

works. The couple successfully shifts gears by delving into traditional Cajun on "Oh Fait Pitié d'Amour" and acoustic jazz/blues with standup bass on the Mayfield cover. The tracks range from playful on a silly but jaunty "Little Bitty Kiss" to serious on the somber and stark closing "Quecreek," a song written and recorded a few hours after the rescue of workers at the titular mine. Miller teams up with Vigilantes of Love frontman Bill Mallonee for "Water When the Well Is Dry," a crackling country-rocker and one of the most powerful and catchy tunes he has recorded. Established fans will be thrilled by this rugged and rootsy addition to his catalog. Those who haven't experienced Buddy Miller's grits-and-honey voice, inventive guitar playing, and gutsy no-frills country approach can start their collections here. *—Hal Horowitz*

Emmett Miller

b. Feb. 2, 1900, Macon, GA, **d.** Mar. 29, 1962, Macon, GA
Vocals / Old-Timey, Minstrel

Although his vocal delivery was influential on several major country singers, Emmett Miller was basically a vaudeville singer, with far stronger aural links to Al Jolson than Merle Haggard. A white man performing in blackface, Miller was an exponent of the minstrel school of performance, touring widely with minstrel shows for several decades. The most influential aspect of his recordings were his yodeling trill, and there can be no doubt that it heavily influenced country singers such as Jimmie Rodgers, Lefty Frizzell, and Hank Williams (who learned "Lovesick Blues" from a Miller record). Bob Wills asked his early lead singer to copy Miller's style, and a bit of Miller's easygoing ragtime sensibility can be heard in Leon Redbone.

But Miller, to quote Donald Sutherland's description of John Milton in *Animal House*, does not speak well to our generation. That's not just because the vaudeville arrangements of his 1920s recordings will strike most modern-day listeners as quaint. It's also because the blackface minstrel tradition—which was just part of the scene in Miller's heyday—strikes as somewhat distasteful in the post-segregation era in its perpetuation of some disagreeable black stereotypes. Miller began recording for OKeh in the mid-'20s and made his most important singles for the label at the end of the decade with accompaniment by the Georgia Crackers, which included both Tommy & Jimmy Dorsey. The minstrel tradition faded drastically in popularity after 1930, although Miller did record for Bluebird in 1936 and continued to perform in minstrel shows to dwindling crowds through the early '50s. *—Richie Unterberger*

● **Minstrel Man from Georgia** / Feb. 6, 1996 / Columbia/Legacy ♦♦♦♦
God knows what this is doing in Legacy's *Roots N' Blues* series; it's a long way from Blind Willie McTell and Bukka White to this. Anyway, this has 20 of his OKeh sides from the late '20s, including a "Lovesick Blues" that served as the model for Hank Williams' hit with the same song in 1949. The Georgia Crackers accompany Miller on every cut, with a cast including Tommy & Jimmy Dorsey (present on every track), Jack Teagarden, and Gene Krupa. More of historical interest and musical significance than anything else, with a thorough sleeve note from country music authority Charles Wolfe. *—Richie Unterberger*

Frankie Miller

b. Dec. 17, 1931, Victoria, TX
Guitar, Vocals / Traditional Country

Frankie Miller recorded several dozen sides for Starday during the late '50s and '60s, including two country hits in 1959. Born in Victoria, TX, on December 17, 1931, Miller earned a football scholarship to a local junior college, at which time he formed the Drifting Texans and began broadcasting on the area station KNAL. He also worked in Houston, where he gained a contract with the 4-Star subsidiary, Guilt Edge. Though he recorded several numbers in 1951, Miller soon left to serve in the Korean War. He returned two years later with a Bronze Star, and signed to Columbia in 1954. None of the dozen sides he recorded in the subsequent year placed on the charts, though. Miller appeared around Texas (including on Fort Worth's Cowtown Hoedown) during the late '50s and recorded occasional one-off singles for local labels.

Don Pierce, owner of the Starday label, had been of the few who appreciated Miller's Guilt Edge recordings, so he signed the young singer in 1959. Miller rewarded the label-owner's confidence that same year when "Blackland Farmer" hit the country Top Five and became one of Starday's most popular recordings. "Family Man" reached number seven in October 1959, and Miller was tapped as *Cashbox*'s Most Promising Country Artist for 1960. He joined the *Louisiana Hayride* and appeared on the *Grand Ole Opry* several times. Unfortunately, Miller had already reached the pinnacle of his success—he hit the charts only three more times. "Baby Rocked Her Dolly" entered the Top 15 in 1960 and "A Little South of Memphis" hit number 34 in 1964, while a re-release of "Black Land Farmer" hit number 16 in 1961. Miller recorded for United Artists in 1965 but retired from music to work at a Chrysler dealership in Arlington, TX. The German label Bear Family re-released three of his albums during the '80s. *—John Bush*

Rockin' Rollin' Frankie Miller / 1983 / Bear Family ♦♦♦♦♦

Hey! Where You Going? / 1984 / Bear Family ♦♦♦♦♦

● **Sugar Coated Baby** / 1996 / Bear Family ♦♦♦♦♦
Taking the album *Hey! Where You Going?* one step further, *Sugar Coated Baby* contains his complete 1954-1956 Columbia sides, including many of his hits. This single-disc, 30-track collection is absolutely essential for Miller Fans. *—Thom Owens*

Jody Miller (Myrna Joy Miller)

b. Nov. 29, 1941, Phoenix, AZ
Vocals / Traditional Country, Country-Folk

Although she became famous for "Queen of the House," her response to Roger Miller's "King of the Road," Jody Miller pioneered a fusion of folk, country, and pop that set the stage for the folky country-pop of the '70s. Raised in Oklahoma, she was born Myrna Joy Miller, and, inspired by the music of Joan Baez, learned to play guitar at the age of 14. Soon after, Miller joined a folk trio and began performing at a local coffeehouse. Lou Gottlieb, a member of folk group the Limelighters, heard her sing and was impressed enough to offer to help her get a recording contract, provided she move to Los Angeles. Miller initially declined as she had recently married, but eventually she and her husband went to California to test the waters. A friend of the family arranged an audition with Capitol Records, which signed Miller while suggesting that she change her name from Myrna to the folkier "Jody."

In 1963, Miller recorded her debut album *Wednesday's Child Is Full of Woe*, which did fairly well and led to appearances on Tom Paxton's folk music television show. In 1964, she had a minor pop hit with "He Walks Like a Man" but her breakthrough arrived in 1965, when "Queen of the House" reached number five on the country charts and number 12 on the pop charts. Despite her success on the country charts, Miller continued to have more hits as a pop act; "Silver Threads and Golden Needles," her follow-up to "Queen of the House," was a minor hit in the summer of 1965, as was the protest song "Home of the Brave." During the latter half of the '60s, she released a handful of albums and singles, none of which gained much attention.

At the end of the '60s, Miller left the West Coast and returned to her Oklahoma ranch to spend more time with her family. After a few years of semi-retirement, she began recording with Billy Sherrill in Nashville in late 1970; the result, *Look at Mine*, was released in 1971 and featured a mixture of country-pop songs a few traditional tunes. The album produced her first string country hits, as "He's So Fine" and "Baby I'm Yours" reached the Top Ten, and several other songs from the record reached the Top 40. Throughout 1972 and 1973, Miller hit the Top Ten with regularity. However, her comeback ended as quickly as it began—as of 1974, she no longer was able to crack the Top 40, although she did have a string of minor hits. She managed to bounce back into the Top 40 in 1977 with "Darling, You Can Always Come Back Home," but by and large, her career had stalled. In 1979, her contract with Epic expired and she chose to retire to her ranch with her family.

Miller returned in 1987 with the independently released *My Country*, which consisted entirely of patriotic songs; it caught the attention of President-elect George Bush, who invited her to perform at his 1988 inaugural ball. Afterward, Miller's now-grown daughter Robin encouraged her to return to country music and the two formed a duo. In 1990, they tried to secure a record contract in Nashville, but were unsuccessful. *—Sandra Brennan*

Wednesday's Child Is Full of Woe / 1963 / Capitol ♦♦♦♦

The Story Of . . . / Marginal ♦♦♦♦
Most likely an illegitimate release, this 29-song compilation mostly concentrates on Jody Miller's 1960s recordings for Capitol, though it does have her early-'70s Epic country hit cover of Barbara Lewis' "Baby I'm Yours." In that respect it's considerably different from the authorized 2000 *Anthology* collection, which has a lot of post-'60s Epic material and duplicates only four songs from *The Story Of*.... Miller is most often categorized as a country singer, but in the 1960s she was actually pretty eclectic, roving among and combining country, folk, pop, and girl group-like pop/rock. That means there isn't much stylistic consistency here, though there are some good songs. Those include her two big hits, the "King of the Road" "answer" record "Queen of the House" and the 1965 Barry Mann-Cynthia Weil girl group-style protest song against the expulsion of a boy from school for long hair, "Home of the Brave." What makes this most interesting to the small group of listeners curious enough to spring for a Jody Miller collection in the first place, however, are the many obscure oddities. There's the cover of the Crystals' "He Hit Me (And It Felt Like a Kiss)," one of the most unfeminist-friendly rock songs of all time; a very pop arrangement of Bob Dylan's "All I Really Want to Do"; a late-'60s Nashville country-pop version of Joni Mitchell's "Urge for Going," complete with brief spoken recitation; "Sea of Heartbreak," which puts Bo Diddley, blues harmonica, and country-folk-pop into the same blender; and "The Fever," which recalls Jackie DeShannon's rowdiest early- to mid-'60s sides, though DeShannon would have done the song with more vocal power. As is the case with all CDs on the Marginal label, the packaging is maddeningly inadequate. The graphics are decent and the sound quality good considering that it's an unauthorized anthology, but there are no liner notes aside from songwriting credits and a reprint of the text from the back cover of a 1965 LP, and the title is given as "Home of the Brave" on the front sleeve and "The Story Of..." on the spine. Its value lies in assembling some fairly good, unclassifiable '60s pop music, albeit by a singer without much vocal character, that official labels have little interest in reissuing. *—Richie Unterberger*

Queen of the House / 1965 / Capitol ♦♦♦♦♦

Home of the Brave / 1965 / Capitol ♦♦♦

The Great Hits of Buck Owens / 1966 / Capitol ♦♦♦

The Nashville Sound of Jody Miller / 1969 / Capitol ♦♦♦

The Best of Jody Miller / 1973 / Capitol ♦♦♦♦

Will You Love Me Tomorrow / 1976 / Epic ♦♦♦

Here's Jody / 1977 / Epic ♦♦♦

● **Anthology** / Mar. 14, 2000 / Renaissance ♦♦♦♦♦
Jody Miller, Jan Howard, and Jeannie Seely were a few of the women who pioneered pop-oriented country music in the '60s, and their sound has since come to dominate the field. Miller's clear, professional-sounding voice has more in common with Vikki Carr than Loretta Lynn, and it lacks any of the rural or working-class character that typified earlier country singers. Miller's first hit was "Queen of the House," an answer to Roger Miller's "King of the Road," followed by the pop hit "Home of the Brave," a patriotic defense of non-conformity. *Anthology* includes those two songs and most of Miller's other early hits for Capitol and later hits for Epic, including a surprising 1972 duet with Johnny Paycheck, and "There's a Party Goin' On," her biggest country hit. Miller followed Sonny James' lead throughout the '70s by making country-pop updates of pop and R&B oldies, particularly girl group hits in Miller's case, but was usually even less identifiably country than James.

The strong performance of Miller's crossover hits on the adult contemporary chart attests to broad appeal of her MOR pop style. *—Greg Adams*

Ned Miller

b. Apr. 12, 1925, Raines, UT

Songwriter, Vocals / Traditional Country, Nashville Sound/Countrypolitan

While Ned Miller was best known for his international 1962 hit "From a Jack to a King," during the 1960s he had 11 chart hits and made it to the pop charts three times. Miller was born in Raines, UT, and started writing songs and singing at local parties and on the radio when he was only 16. After his discharge from the Marines, Miller worked at several jobs before moving to California in 1956 to become a full-time songwriter. The following year, singer Gale Storm scored a Top Five hit with his song "Dark Moon"; Bonnie Guitar also had a hit with the composition, and both continued to record Miller's songs.

He began his own recording career in 1957 for the Fabor label, issuing "From a Jack to a King" as his debut single. Later that year, he released "Roll O Rollin' Stone," again without much notice. In 1962, following a short detour to Capitol Records, Miller persuaded the Fabor label to re-release his prior version of "From a Jack to a King"; this time, the single soared to the Top Three on the country charts, the Top Ten on the pop charts, and even made it to number two on the British pop charts. The following year, Miller scored two Top 30 hits, "One Among the Many" and "Another Fool Like Me." In 1965, he had another Top Ten hit, "Do What You Do Do Well," which later provided success for Ernest Tubb; Miller's version also crossed over to the Top 60 on the pop charts.

Later that year, he returned to Capitol. Songs he wrote or co-wrote with his wife Susan also found chart success for other artists, among them Gale Storm's "Love by the Juke Box Light," Faron Young's "Safely in Love Again," Porter Wagoner's "Your Kind of People" and Hank Snow's "The Man Behind the Gun." Miller faded into obscurity after the 1960s, but decades later Ricky Van Shelton recorded "From a Jack to a King" and had a number-one hit. *—Sandra Brennan*

From a Jack to a King / 1963 / Fabor ✦✦✦

Ned Miller recorded "From a Jack to a King" in 1957, but the resulting single was unsuccessful. Years later, label head Fabor Robison reissued the same recording and it became one of the biggest crossover hits of 1963. That song and one other from 1957 ("Lights in the Street") were added to ten new cuts to fill out Miller's sole Fabor LP, *From a Jack to a King*. The album has a surprising number of Western songs like "The Man Behind the Gun" and "Stagecoach," some of which were written by Miller. Miller later acknowledged that the album was slapped together and suffers from uneven material, but another flaw is the album's production, which yielded a distant, hollow sound. In 1981, Plantation recycled the album cover of *From a Jack to a King* for a new ten-song album that omitted four tracks and added the hits "Do What You Do, Do Well" and "Invisible Tears." *—Greg Adams*

Ned Miller Sings the Songs of Ned Miller / 1965 / Capitol ✦✦✦✦

The Best of Ned Miller / 1966 / Capitol ✦✦✦✦✦

Teardrop Lane / 1967 / Capitol ✦✦✦

In the Name of Love / 1968 / Capitol ✦✦✦

Ned Miller's Back / 1970 / Republic ✦✦

From a Jack to a King / 1981 / Plantation ✦✦✦

This budget CD version of Miller's original 1963 Fabor album features the title track, the biggest hit of his career, as well as the minor hit "One Among the Many," in addition to an original composition "Do What You Do, Do Well," which was later a hit for Ernest Tubb. In fact, seven of these ten selections were written or co-written by Miller. The sound quality is fair and the packaging mediocre, and all of these recordings are included in better fidelity on Bear Family's expanded CD of the same name. *—Greg Adams*

● **From a Jack to a King [Anthology]** / 1991 / Bear Family ✦✦✦✦✦

From a Jack to a King is a 31-track anthology that collects everything Ned Miller recorded for Fabor Records (some of which was released through Dot) plus a handful of recordings from a brief stint with Capitol. Miller's complete commercial output through 1964 is accounted for, with the exception of a lone single on Jackpot. His career hit, the crossover smash "From a Jack to a King," is here, as well as "Do What You Do, Do Well," "Invisible Tears," and "Dark Moon," which was a hit for both Bonnie Guitar and Gale Storm. Miller's album tracks and B-sides were very uneven, and a number of the Fabor Robison-produced tracks have a peculiar sound, as though the music is emanating from a speaker in another room. The hits are the clear highlights on this package, and there are otherwise too few quality tracks to recommend this disc to anyone but serious collectors. *—Greg Adams*

Polk Miller

d. Oct. 1913

Vocals / Old-Timey, Country Gospel

One of the oldest "old-time" performers on record is Polk Miller, who fought as an artilleryman in the American Civil War on the Confederate side and, according to his son, is said to have furled the confederate flag at Appomattox. Settling in Richmond, VA, in 1868, Miller opened a drugstore and specialized in pet remedies. He marketed them under the name of his own prized pet dog, Sergeant, and as Sergeant's Pet Care Products the company Polk Miller founded continues to sell many of these same remedies today.

Miller's professional involvement in music began late in life; although he learned the banjo before the Civil War, he laid it aside during the postwar years, citing that his choice of instrument "was beneath the notice of the cultivated." However, in 1892, he had a change of heart and began to tour with his banjo, singing old Southern and African-American songs. Miller was an immediate hit, and garnered endorsements from celebrities such as Mark Twain and Joel Chandler Harris.

Around 1900, Polk Miller added four black male singers to his show, whom he called the Old South Quartette. The line-up of this group was constantly changing and, according to Miller, recruited from Richmond's street corners and bars. One member who proved more lasting than others was the bass voice, James L. Stamper. Stamper helped Miller arrange some of the Old South Quartette's material and ultimately became known as a popular songwriter in his own right. While the group was a huge success in Northern cities, the group's appearances in the South were less common and sometimes held in black churches, appropriate as they were heavily reliant on gospel material. Although the Old South Quartette performed songs and skits that were drawn from minstrelsy, Miller did not wear blackface and the Quartette dressed in ordinary work clothes.

In November 1909, Polk Miller & the Old South Quartette made seven cylinders for Edison, including versions of "The Bonnie Blue Flag," "The Old Time Religion," and "Jerusalem Mournin'." These were well received in rural markets, where cylinders were still king in 1910, but did especially well in the West—a Kansas City phonograph dealer suggested to Edison that a thousand such records should be made! But the seven titles would remain the only recordings made by Polk Miller. In 1912, Miller parted company with the Old South Quartette, and Miller himself died not long after, in October 1913. In a newspaper interview made shortly before his death, he declared that he was forced to take leave of the group as racial attitudes towards them had made touring impossible, saying "in some places I had to call upon the police to guard my men." Nonetheless, the cylinder recordings made by Polk Miller and his Old South Quartette are of crucial historical importance, documenting the shared musical heritage between white and black Southern songsters in a style that jumps right out of the 19th century. *—Uncle Dave Lewis*

Roger Miller

b. Jan. 2, 1936, Fort Worth, TX, **d.** Oct. 25, 1992

Guitar, Songwriter, Vocals / Traditional Country, Country-Pop, Honky Tonk, Nashville Sound/Countrypolitan, Country Comedy

Roger Miller is best known for his humorous novelty songs, which overshadow his considerable songwriting talents as well as his hardcore honky tonk roots. After writing hits for a number of artists in the '50s, Miller racked up a number of hits during the '60s which became not only country classics, but popular classics as well. Miller was born in Fort Worth, TX, but raised in the small town of Erick, OK, by his aunt and uncle, following the death of his father and his mother's debilitating sickness. Initially, he was attracted to music by hearing country over the radio as well as by his brother-in-law, Sheb Wooley. By the time he was ten, he earned enough money picking cotton to buy himself a guitar. At the age of 11, Wooley gave him a fiddle and encouraged him to pursue a performing career. Miller completed the eighth grade and left school to become a ranch hand and rodeo rider. Throughout his adolescence, he played music in addition to working the ranch. Soon, he was able to play not only guitar and fiddle, but also piano, banjo, and drums.

He enlisted in the Army during the Korean war and was stationed in South Carolina, where he met the brother of Jethro Burns who arranged an audition at RCA Nashville for him. Early in 1957, Miller left the army and auditioned for Chet Atkins at RCA. The session was unsuccessful, and he spent a year as a bellhop at a Nashville hotel. While in Nashville, Miller met George Jones and Pappy Dailey, who introduced him to Don Pierce, an executive at Mercury Records. Pierce signed Miller and had him cut three songs. His first single, "Poor Little John," disappeared without a trace. Following the failure of his first single, Miller continued to work at the hotel and tour with other musicians—he played fiddle with Minnie Pearl for a short time, then he became the drummer for Faron Young. After a few months, he was signed as a songwriter for Tree Music Publishing and stopped performing as a supporting musician. Instead of playing music, he became a fireman in Amarillo, TX. The abandonment of performing was short-lived, however—within a few months, he became the drummer for Ray Price's Cherokee Cowboys.

In 1958, Price recorded Miller's "Invitation to the Blues," and it went to number three. It was soon followed by three other successful versions of his songs—Young's "That's the Way I Feel" and Ernest Tubb's "Half a Mind" both went Top Ten, while Jim Reeves had a number one hit with "Billy Bayou." That same year, Jones recorded "Tall Tall Trees" and "Nothing Can Stop My Love," which he had written with Miller; neither of the songs were hits. The following year, Reeves had a hit with another one of Miller's songs, "Home." Since his songwriting career was flourishing, Miller decided it was again time to try to become a performing artist as well. He recorded a few tracks for Decca which weren't successful, and then he signed to RCA Records. "You Don't Want My Love," one of his first singles for the label, reached number 14 in early 1961, followed by the Top Ten "When Two Worlds Collide" later that summer.

Miller wasn't able to immediately follow the songs with another hit single. Two years later, "Lock, Stock and Teardrops" scraped the charts, and he left the record label. Around that time, Miller moved to Hollywood began appearing regularly on *the Jimmy Dean Show* and *the Merv Griffin Show*, two of the most popular television programs in the country. His guest spots showcased his new style—instead of concentrating on hardcore country, he had developed a willfully goofy persona, singing silly novelty songs. He signed a record contract with Smash Records and released his first single for the label, "Dang Me," in the summer of 1964. It was an immediate smash, vaulting to number one and spending six weeks at the top of the charts; it also crossed over into the pop charts, peaking at number seven. "Chug-A-Lug" followed a few months after it, reaching number three on the country charts and nine on the pop charts. At the end of the year, "Do-Wacka-Do" was released, becoming a number-15 hit.

Miller began 1965 with his best-known song, "King of the Road." The single spent five weeks at the top of the country charts and became his biggest pop hit, peaking at number four. Its accompanying album, *The Return of Roger Miller*, was another crossover success, also peaking at number four on the pop album charts and going gold. Miller was at his peak in 1965. Every song he released that year—"Engine Engine #9," "One Dyin' and a Buryin'," "Kansas City Star," "England Swings"—reached the country Top Ten, and at the end of the year, his *Golden Hits* album went Top Ten; it would eventually go gold. In the summer of 1965, he released *The Third Time Around*, a record that leaned toward his honky tonk roots; it peaked at number 13.

After the watershed year of 1965, Miller's career dipped slightly. Although other artists were still having hits with his songs—Eddy Arnold took "The Last Word in Lonesome Is

Me" to number two—Miller had trouble breaking the Top 40 following the number five hit "Husbands and Wives" in early 1966. He continued to record throughout the late '60s, but fewer and fewer of the songs were becoming hits. Occasionally, he would record the songs of emerging songwriters, whether it was Bobby Russell's "Little Green Apples" (number six, 1968) or Kris Kristofferson's "Me and Bobby McGee" (number 12, 1969). Toward the end of the decade and beginning of the '70s, he began to concentrate on honky tonk, although he still made his trademark novelties. During the '70s, he recorded sporadically, preferring to concentrate on his hotel chain, appropriately called King of the Road. "Tomorrow Night in Baltimore," released in the spring of 1971, was his biggest hit of the decade, climbing to number 11. Early in the decade, he wrote songs for Walt Disney's animated adaptation of *Robin Hood*—he also provided a voice for the rooster in the film—as well as the movie *Waterhole Three*. In 1973, he left Smash/Mercury for Columbia Records. He spent four years at Columbia and only his debut single for the label, "Open Up Your Heart," was a hit, peaking at number 14.

Miller didn't record much during the '80s—his biggest hit was "Old Friends," recorded with Willie Nelson and Ray Price. In the mid-'80s, he wrote the music for *Big River*, a Broadway adaptation of Mark Twain's works. Both the play and Miller's music were critically acclaimed and enormously popular. *Big River* won seven Tony Awards and two of those went to Miller, for Best Musical and Outstanding Score. *Big River* would be the last major work of Miller's career. In 1991, he was diagnosed with throat cancer and died a year later. After his death, his legacy remained strong, as each new generation of country singers found songs in his catalog to cover and reinterpret. —*Stephen Thomas Erlewine*

Dang Me! (Roger and Out) / 1964 / Smash ✦✦✦✦

This was the first album released from a whole gob of tracks cut over a marathon two-day recording session. The title song was so totally bizarre and out of step with all the British Invasion material of the day that it was something of a shock how much of a hit it became. Roger Miller's talent was so unique, and the results so different than anything anyone else was doing in country or pop, that it was as if he had carved out his own dominion to rule with nary a challenge, although there were attempts to imitate him from time to time. With all this richness of talent, Smash records herein doles out portions of Miller as if serving up the vegetable sides in a French restaurant. Perhaps the label was scared that too much of Miller at once would send the audience scrambling for their old Hank Williams records. This entire album could easily fit on one side of a slab of vinyl. A quick glance at the songs and their timings might lead one to believe that this is a punk album, since half are under two minutes. Two classics from the Miller canon are here, "Chug-A-Lug" and "Dang Me," and among the lesser-known numbers is the catchy "Got Two Again," a children's song disguised as a Roger Miller song. Make no mistake about it, the playing is top-notch, the concept original, and the delivery as sparkling as a slab of crystal from Miller's Arkansas homeland, but the brevity of it all is a bit like trying to get there from Nashville on half a tank of gas. —*Eugene Chadbourne*

Roger Miller Featuring Dang Me! / 1964 / Smash ✦✦✦✦✦

Roger Miller Featuring Dang Me! is Smash Records' third configuration of Miller's debut album, originally released in 1964 as *Roger and Out* and soon thereafter as *Dang Me!/Chug-A-Lug* to advertise the hit singles. Miller unveiled his unique scat-singing novelty persona on these 11 cuts, and enjoyed two of the biggest hits of his career. The album is packed with songs that were widely covered, from the oft-quoted "The Moon Is High" ("and so am I") to "If You Want Me To," which could have been the blueprint for one of Jeff Foxworthy's standup comedy routines. Some lesser-known but highly entertaining songs are tucked in between, like "Squares Make the World Go Round" and "Got 2 Again." Here is the birth of one of the most beloved and original sounds in American country music. —*Greg Adams*

☆ **The Third Time Around** / 1965 / Smash ✦✦✦✦✦

Third time the charm, this is one of the classic Roger Miller records on Smash. At least half of the dozen titles here are among his most famous, and every song is written by him. Many were recorded in a marathon two-day session featuring just Miller and his guitar plus a few lead guitarists, piano, drums, and bass. What a range of themes and characters are presented, from the little "Swiss Maid" to "Big Harlan Taylor" and the sad sack who sobs "The Last Word in Lonesome is Me" Miller gets so much out of so little, evidence "Kansas City Star," a rockabilly-flavored classic starring a bragging kiddie show host. The Jerry Kennedy arrangements and picking from session pros who were uncredited at the time are really superb. Every track seems as if extra effort was made to make it sound fresh and different. Miller is indeed fortunate that such an individualistic style as he had was allowed plenty of breathing room, ample proof that a recording company can be successful when it is wise enough to allow an artist to present new music on its own terms, without compromise or interference. —*Eugene Chadbourne*

☆ **The Return of Roger Miller** / 1965 / Smash ✦✦✦✦✦

Allowed to hit with full power on his second album for Smash, Roger Miller presents an album made up completely of his own compositions, quite an achievement in country music circles. The songs reach way beyond the genre into stylistic realms that are difficult to pinpoint, although certain facts are beyond question. They are classic American songs which hold up alongside the best of any generation. They are also songs that appeal to children of all ages, partly due to a whimsical nature that borders on anarchy. His portrait of the "King of the Road" is packed with detail and nuance like a Vincent van Gogh painting, while other songs skip along as if they are about absolutely nothing, tongue firmly in cheek when eventually revealing the message. Like many country releases of this era, this is hardly a bargain in playing time, but Miller gets it all in, balancing the humorous and serious songs, stretching out just a touch on the more swinging numbers and packing something of six verses of gibberish into well less than two minutes of "You Can't Roller Skate in a Buffalo Herd." All praises to Miller the songwriter, but let's not forget the terrific sidemen and arrangements that make each of these

recordings so special. It would have been nice if they had credited the guys at the time! One of the most unique things about this material, much of it recorded over a two-day marathon session, is that the sound almost always focuses around the leader's guitar style, which was eccentric to say the least. Scat singing was certainly not the norm in country, let alone combined with instrumental leads in the Slam Stewart tradition. Mainstay instruments of country music, such as fiddle or pedal steel, don't make much of an appearance, instead the sound is built up around doubling of acoustic and electric guitars, with a piano-heavy rhythm section holding everything in place. Small but telling touches make the tracks happen big time, the best example of which would be the finger snapping on "King of the Road," credited over the years to everyone from Miller's sidekick guitarist Thumbs Carlisle to the Lone Ranger. —*Eugene Chadbourne*

The One and Only / 1965 / Camden ✦✦✦

Clocking in at 22 minutes from the RCA vault, this album presents some of the songs that were country chart items before Roger Miller really hit the jackpot with his Smash recordings. "Burma Shave" must have been some kind of vision, taking listeners into the realm of fantasy and silliness that would become Miller's private territory a few years later. It is a crazy, almost soul music arrangement, as all over the place as are many of the tracks here, as if Miller's songwriting hadn't quite gotten as far out as some of the musical situations he wanted to get into. He redid "It Happened Just That Way," but this earlier version is lovely. For a shortie "cash-in" collection, this holds up rather well. —*Eugene Chadbourne*

Wild-Child / 1965 / Starday ✦✦✦

No one can blame Starday for attempting to cash in on Roger Miller's chart success in the mid-'60s, and it might be understandable though questionable to leave any dates off the album cover so that nobody would be able to guess how far removed these sessions are from the type of productions and songs that made Miller a star. They even subtitle it "The Madcap Sensation of Country Music" so that the buyer thinks it will be a typically crazy Miller album, even though he only wrote four out of the dozen songs included. The choice of covers by country stalwarts such as Buck Owens, Mel Tillis, and Harlan Howard is respectable and a lot more exciting than the type of material Miller would cover later in his career, but there really isn't anything that madcap about it, especially by this artist's standards. A more appropriate title would have been "Some Pleasant Early Sessions by Roger Miller Featuring Relaxed Picking by Uncredited Nashville Sidemen," but that surely wouldn't have sold as many copies. —*Eugene Chadbourne*

★ **Golden Hits** / 1965 / Smash ✦✦✦✦✦

Years before Waylon Jennings and Willie Nelson grew their hair long, Miller took country to the counterculture with these hipster twists on the Nashville sound. No tunesmith in Music City had ever tossed off songs like "Dang Me," "King of the Road," "Chug-a-Lug," and "Engine Engine #9." No one has since. —*Dan Cooper*

Words and Music / 1966 / Smash ✦✦✦✦

Perhaps Roger Miller's weirdest song ever kicks off this album from the batch he recorded for Smash in the mid-'60s. It is "My Uncle Used to Love Me But She Died," and it is an attack of pure dementia just two seconds shy of two minutes. But it is the next song, "Husbands and Wives," that really sets the tone for this album, saying so much with so few words while coming up with very clever ways to offset one's expectations of where the same old country phrases and chord changes are going to go. The laziness that would plague later Miller recordings is perhaps visible through the haze here, and it would be hard to argue the necessity of the cover version of "Heartbreak Hotel"; it certainly takes the wind out of the proceedings. He recovers fast, though, building the album to a strong climax purely through emotion and sentimentality, the cornpone humor in reserve but not needed. Liner notes are an endorsement by the great Johnny Mercer. —*Eugene Chadbourne*

Walkin' in the Sunshine / 1967 / Smash ✦✦✦

After a triumvirate of near-perfect albums came this harbinger of the decline of a particularly imaginative and original country artist. Upon listening to the first side, one wonders if this is the same Roger Miller whose string of zany hits had made listening to the hit parade so much fun. We get three of his most inconsequential and unformed songs ever recorded, and sandwiched between are covers of "Ruby, Don't Take Your Love to Town" and "Green Green Grass of Home" that should never have been hatched. Miller positively sleepwalks his way through these performances. Things definitely look up upon a flip of the side, though. We get three high quality Miller songs, and, although close inspection reveals these also to be a bit imitative of his past glories, they are still full of the detail and spiky twists this artist is known for. "Pardon My Coffin" is really a fantastic song, despite the "Sixteen Tons" lick in there. And how about this bit of poetry tossed in at the end of "I'd Come Back to Me": "If egg was foo, if I was you, you'd be too young for me." Miller's cover of "Hey Good Lookin'" by Hank Williams makes one wonder why he didn't approach more of his cover versions like this. He takes total liberty with the lyrics and structure of the song, turning it inside out very casually, as if what he was doing was the original version. Not all the material on the second side is that good, but the high points would certainly have become more well-known parts of the Miller canon if they had not been surrounded by such drek on their original release. The session backup sounds great when they stick to a small jazz-flavored country combo. The strings are the last thing Miller needs, weighing him down worse than if arranger Jerry Kennedy himself had climbed onto the artist's back and demanded a shoulder ride. A key part of Miller's sound all along, Kennedy should have known better. —*Eugene Chadbourne*

A Tender Look at Love / 1968 / Smash ✦✦

In a perfect world this record would never have happened, but it did, and at the height of Roger Miller's popularity, too. Was there a suspicion he wasn't a complete enough artist in his own right and had to project a leading man side as well, by sticking to a program of mushy romantic ballads? Of course the concept would have been brilliant if Miller had been knocking the wind out of this material à la Spike Jones or Homer and Jethro. Nay, these are serious runs at a list whose contents need not be itemized once it is revealed that the noxious "Honey" is amongst the titles. The real shame is that Miller wrote a lot of beautiful romantic songs of his own which could have been utilized for this album to much better effect. Pretty nice version of "Dear Heart," though bear in mind this is a Miller fanatic panning for gold dust in a muddy stream. *—Eugene Chadbourne*

Roger Miller / 1969 / Smash ✦✦✦

Roger Miller turns out to be a very good set that features Miller's hit rendition of Kris Kristofferson's "Me and Bobby McGee." The tracks that follow are far from being filler, from the beautiful folk-pop of "Darby's Castle" to the slightly Beatlesque "Meanwhile Back in Abeline." Lighter tracks like "Colonel Maggie" and "Boeing Boeing 707" are nice additions, as is the poignant "Where Have All the Average People Gone." Overall, the album might not feature as many hits as other Miller albums, but the material is first-rate, nonetheless. *—Matt Fink*

Roger Miller / 1969 / Camden ✦✦✦

Smash records was really the NASA of the Roger Miller launch, but any label with tapes of the guy was re-releasing them in the '60s. The stuff from the RCA vault is definitely more vintage Miller than earlier recordings circulating; he would even do reworkings and re-recordings of some these numbers later. The most famous song here is "Sorry, Willie," as it has evolved into a launch pad of its own for various artists trying to summon the spirit of Willie Nelson. When it was originally recorded in 1960, neither Miller nor Nelson were household names, both struggling with their careers and the forces attempting to shape them into more conventional Nashville talent. Each of these tracks has an edge to it, and sometimes Miller packs himself into a box he doesn't exactly fit into. Not essential Miller, but certainly lots of fun. *—Eugene Chadbourne*

Roger Miller 1970 / 1970 / Smash ✦✦

So, where was Roger Miller by 1970? Possibly in worse shape than Boris Karloff was when he filmed the dreadful *Frankenstein 1970*. Miller contributes three originals that have the sound of scraps from the back of the songwriting pad. Otherwise, he goes for setting himself up as a kind of Ernest Tubb figure, benevolently turning his recording session over to the songs of then new, upcoming songwriters Bobby Russell, Kris Kristofferson, Don Linde, and Mickey Newbury. The story is that this is one of the first recordings of "Me and Bobby McGee," with Kristofferson poking his head into the studio every now and then clutching a freshly written verse. On paper this might all seem jake, as Miller's voice is good and he has a way of bringing sincerity to just about any lyric. Not everything written during this sensitive, maudlin, and sincere era in Nashville history holds up to the test of time, however. Even when it is interesting, as it surely is to hear Miller doing a Newbury tune, it still has nowhere near the impact of the artist doing his own songs. An overwhelming sense of drag haunts this recording, some of the tracks hanging in for as much time as the Miller of the mid-'60s would have spent on three completely different songs. "Me and Bobby McGee" goes on for four minutes, and, to paraphrase Muddy Waters, that's four minutes too long. *—Eugene Chadbourne*

A Trip in the Country / 1970 / Mercury ✦✦

Roger Miller revisits some of his earliest songs on *A Trip in the Country*, many of which were hits for artists such as Faron Young ("That's the Way I Feel"), Ernest Tubb ("Half a Mind"), and Ray Price ("Invitation to the Blues"). A couple of these songs were hits for Miller, too, in the early '60s, which makes *A Trip in the Country* seem less like an interesting concept and more like a dubious re-recording project. Miller's early songs were very different from the ones he wrote after "Dang Me," and exhibit little of the humor and surrealism for which he became known. The album's brush with commercial success came when "Don't We All Have the Right" saw a little chart action when recycled as the B-side of Miller's minor 1970 hit "South." *—Greg Adams*

Dear Folks, Sorry I Haven't Written Lately / 1973 / Columbia ✦✦

☆ **The Best of Roger Miller, Vol. 1: Country Tunesmith** / 1991 / Mercury ✦✦✦✦✦

Downplaying his humorous muse in favor of showing off his skill as a straight-ahead country writer, these 21 tracks (including some strongly Ray Price-influenced fare from 1957) were either written or co-written by Miller. It's well worth the money to hear his own versions of such standards as "Invitation to the Blues," "Half a Mind," and "Don't We All Have the Right." *—Dan Cooper*

☆ **The Best of Roger Miller, Vol. 2: King of the Road** / Aug. 4, 1992 / Mercury ✦✦✦✦✦

Where *The Best of Roger Miller, Vol. 1: Country Tunesmith* concentrated on Miller's lesser-known honky tonk numbers and hits he wrote for other artists, *Best of Roger Miller, Vol. 2: King of the Road* is strictly Miller's biggest hits. From the novelties of "Dang Me," "Chug-A-Lug," "Do Wacka Do," and "Kansas City Star" to the relatively straightforward "King of the Road" and "Engine Engine #9," all of Miller's big hits from the mid-'60s are included, as are selected lesser hits from the late '60s like "Little Green Apples" and "Me and Bobby McGee." Combined, *Country Tunesmith* and *King of the Road* offer a definitive overview of Roger Miller's career that even eclipses the subsequently released box set, *King of the Road*. *—Stephen Thomas Erlewine*

King of the Road / Jun. 27, 1994 / Bear Family ✦✦✦✦✦

★ **King of the Road [Box Set]** / 1995 / Mercury ✦✦✦✦✦

The subtitle of Mercury Nashville's three-disc box set *King of the Road* is "The Genius of Roger Miller," a sentiment that listeners only familiar with his deliberately silly smashes would dispute, but as this three-disc, 70-track set plays out, it becomes clear that this is hardly hyperbole. If genius is a unique voice, either in writing or delivery, Miller certainly qualifies. If genius is an artist who displays a depth and variety of material, Miller fills the bill. If genius is creating a body of work unlike no other, Miller certainly fits the bill. Miller's genius lay in his command of small details, unassumingly witty wordplay, and seemingly effortless songcraft. Apart from "King of the Road," which developed an iconic status separate from his career, his hits were so funny, so *easy*, that it seemed his music was too light to withstand such an exhaustive retrospective, but that's hardly the case. Miller's hits were often wonderful, often the pinnacle of his talents, but look closer and it becomes clear that they happened to be the songs that were the singles; he often wrote songs that could have been as big as his hits, but weren't released as singles, or were tucked away on records to be discovered by diligent fans. It's a testament to his talent that not all of these are featured on this otherwise comprehensive box set; the 1991 *Country Tunesmith* collection alone contains many great songs that could have made the cut. They are missed, as are Miller's brilliant songs from Walt Disney's 1973 animated adaptation *Robin Hood* ("Not in Nottingham" is as lovely as anything he's done), but that doesn't mean that *King of the Road* doesn't work as a retrospective—it just means that, like other great artists, he has more than enough great music to fit onto three CDs. The three CDs are filled with wonderful music—songs that prove Miller is one of the great country songwriters, capable of songs wrenching in either their humor or pain, and one of the most distinctive voices in the genre. Needless to say, it's essential to any serious country collection. *—Stephen Thomas Erlewine*

Super Hits / Mar. 19, 1996 / Epic ✦✦

Consumer advisory: Although this album does contain a small-print statement on the back reading, "This compact disc was previously released as 'Roger Miller King of the Road,'" it does not explain that that album contained '70s re-recordings of Roger Miller's '60s hits. Here then are ten selections running 22 minutes and 19 seconds, among them such popular songs as "Dang Me," "King of the Road," "Chug-A-Lug," and "England Swings," redone. The originals were on Smash, a division of Mercury that in turn is owned by PolyGram. *—William Ruhlmann*

Hits / May 5, 1997 / Mercury ✦✦✦

Hits is a budget-line collection of ten of Roger Miller's biggest hits, including "King of the Road," "Chug-A-Lug" and "Do Wacka Do." While several hits are missing and the double-volume *The Best of Roger Miller* and the box set *King of the Road* are better, more comprehensive collections, *Hits* is a nice sampler for casual fans. *—Thom Owens*

20th Century Masters—The Millennium Collection: The Best of Roger Miller / Sep. 14, 1999 / MCA ✦✦✦✦

Roger Miller's output for the Smash Mercury label was at its peak in 1964-1965. Even though he would never achieve that level of success again, he did occasionally make the charts until his time with the label expired in 1973. It's unfortunate that lesser hits like "Walkin in the Sunshine," "Little Green Apples," and "Me and Bobbie McGee" weren't included on this compilation along with obvious choices like "King of the Road" and "Dang Me." To really grasp Miller's creativity beyond 1964 and 1965, it's advisable to skip the *20th Century Masters- The Millennium Collection* and pick up the three-CD box set *King of the Road*. *—Al Campbell*

Country Music Hall of Fame 1995 / Nov. 9, 1999 / King ✦✦

A budget collection of Miller's early Smash recordings. This ten-track set features the biggies "King of the Road," "Dang Me," "Chug-A-Lug," "England Swings," and "Engine #9." Not a definitive package, and the transfers sound a bit muffled, but overall a good budget buy. *—Cub Koda*

Roger Miller Classics / May 21, 2002 / Varese ✦✦✦

The bulk of Varese Sarabande's 2002 collection *Roger Miller Classics* is devoted to re-recordings Miller cut in the mid-'80s with producer Buddy Killen. That means that all the hits here—"Dang Me," "Chug-a-Lug," "Do Wacka Do," "King of the Road," "Kansas City Star," etc.—are latter-day recordings; the only original hits here are three early-'70s minor hits for Columbia: "Open Up Your Heart," "I Believe in the Sunshine," "Our Love." This, of course, means this is hardly the first choice for anybody who wants only one Roger Miller disc, or a collection of Miller at his best. That said, these are pretty lively, entertaining re-recordings—they may not be originals, but they'll still bring a smile to your face. So, instead of being a collection for beginners, this is better seen as a collection for the diehards who want to hear Miller sing the old songs in a different way, one more time. *—Stephen Thomas Erlewine*

★ **All Time Greatest Hits** / Apr. 22, 2003 / Mercury ✦✦✦✦✦

There have been many collections of Roger Miller's hitmaking peak on Mercury over the years, but few have been as comprehensive or as good as Mercury/Chronicle's 2003 CD, *All Time Greatest Hits*. Spanning 20 tracks over the course of one CD, this contains all the big songs: "Dang Me," "Chug-A-Lug," "Do Wacka Do," "In the Summertime (You Don't Want My Love)," "King of the Road," "You Can't Roller Skate in a Buffalo Herd," "Kansas City Star," "England Swings," and "Husbands and Wives," among others. All but one track from the seminal 1965 collection *Golden Hits* is here ("Atta Boy Girl" is the missing culprit—a good song but not enough to tip the scales in favor of the 38-year-old collection), and it spans further than that record, collecting hits from 1967-1970 and ending with the 1986 hit "River in the Rain." While that final song isn't quite of the standard of what preceded it, it provides a nice closer to a set of songs that unequivocally proves Miller's genius. That might seem like a weighty word for a singer/songwriter whose specialty was lightweight funny songs, but the thing is, those songs have a certain mad ingenious sensibility that nobody else could replicate, and he could dig deeper—witness "I've Been a Long Time Leavin' (But I'll Be a Long Time Gone)"—when he wanted to. That side might not be mined as deeply as it could have been here, but that's what previous comps like the *King of the Road* box is for. This is a hits collection, a summary overview and introduction to his genius, and it succeeds brilliantly on that level. It's absolutely essential. *—Stephen Thomas Erlewine*

Ronnie Milsap

b. Jan. 16, 1944, Robbinsville, NC

Piano, Vocals / Country-Pop, Urban Cowboy, Contemporary Country

Ronnie Milsap was one of the major figures of country music in the 1970s, developing a hybrid of country and pop which brought him a large audience. Milsap was born in Robbinsville, NC, and was raised by his father and grandparents following his parents' divorce. He was born blind from congenital glaucoma, and when he was five began attending the Governor Moorhead School for the Blind. When he was seven, his instructors noticed his extraordinary musical talents and he began to study classical music formally. A single year after he began learning the violin, Milsap was declared a virtuoso; he also mastered piano, guitar and a variety of other stringed instruments, as well as various woodwinds. Eventually, he became interested in rock & roll music and while still in school formed his first rock band, the Apparitions. He briefly attended college in Atlanta where he studied pre-law; though he was awarded a comprehensive scholarship, Milsap decided to become a full-time musician instead. His first professional gig was as a member of J.J. Cale's band in the early '60s.

In 1965, Milsap started his own band and four years later, after having an R&B hit with "Never Had It So Good," moved to Memphis to become a session musician. There he frequently worked for Chips Moman and can be heard playing keyboards on Elvis' "Kentucky Rain" and singing harmony on "Don't Cry Daddy." When not doing session work, Milsap and his backing group were the house band at TJ's Club. In 1970, he had a pop hit with "Loving You Is a Natural Thing." Following its success, in 1971 he released his eponymous debut. Two years later, Milsap moved to Nashville in hopes of jump-starting his flagging career, and became a client of Charley Pride's manager Jack D. Johnson. Within a year, he signed to RCA Victor, where he would remain for the bulk of his career. "I Hate You," his first single for RCA, reached the country Top Ten in the summer of 1973. The following year, he had three number-one hits in a row—"Pure Love," "Please Don't Tell Me How the Story Ends," and "(I'd Be) A Legend in My Time," a cover of Don Gibson's classic.

Milsap had a handful of Top Ten hits in 1975 and but in late 1976, he became a genuine star, with a string of six number-one hits in a row. In turn, that string of hits begat a remarkable run where Milsap didn't leave the Top Ten for 15 straight years. During that time, he had a number of pop crossover hits, beginning with 1977's "It Was Almost like a Song." Between 1980 and 1982, Milsap had ten more consecutive number-one hits including the crossover smashes "Smoky Mountain Rain," "No Gettin' Over Me" and "Any Day Now." Milsap had yet another string of uninterrupted number-one hits between 1985 and 1987, racking up eight consecutive chart toppers. He had his last number-one hit in 1989, when "A Woman in Love" spent two weeks on the top of the charts. In total, he had 35 number-one singles. In the early '90s, Milsap's commercial appeal began to decline—after 1992, he wasn't able to break into the country Top Ten. Nevertheless, he continued to record. In 1992, he left RCA and signed to Liberty, where he recorded *True Believer*, which failed to yield any major hits. Despite his decline in popularity, Milsap continued to record and perform successfully into the 2000's. *—Sandra Brennan*

Pure Love / 1974 / RCA ✦✦✦✦✦

Ronnie Milsap had been paying dues as a session musician before cutting a record in 1971 for Warner Bros. that promptly made little impact. Three years later, he moved from Memphis to Nashville, signed with RCA, and released *Pure Love*. It was kind of like his second debut, a record that found Milsap carving out his own musical identity—one that brought him to the top of the country charts. Taking cues from Elvis Presley and Charlie Rich (Milsap's cover of "Behind Closed Doors" is a revelation for anyone unfamiliar with his earlier work, since the Rich influence seeming shockingly present throughout Milsap's work), Milsap had a warm, friendly croon and an easy delivery to his music, which made it easy to overlook the hints of soul, gospel, and pop in his music. That's because his mellow country-pop was so relaxed, it simply seemed to exist without any effort. His music only got easier over the years, but on *Pure Love*, it still had a solid country foundation; while it never had *grit*, it did have weight and it felt like country music. He also had one of his strongest sets of songs, highlighted by the singles "Pure Love" and "Please Don't Tell Me How the Story Ends," but running deeper than that, thanks to songs like "My Love Is Deep, My Love Is Wide" and "Blue Ridge Mountains Turnin' Green." Milsap may have been sweeter and more romantic than even other country-pop crooners of the '70s, but it made from some good easy listening, and it was rarely better than it was on *Pure Love*. *—Stephen Thomas Erlewine*

Where My Heart Is / 1974 / RCA ✦✦✦✦

A Legend in My Time / 1975 / RCA ✦✦✦

On *A Legend in My Time*, his third album for RCA Victor, Ronnie Milsap followed through on the sound of its predecessor, *Pure Love*, but he switched up the tempo a little. Where *Pure Love* was unabashedly romantic, there was a bit more variety here—not just in terms of speed, since there were some sprightly numbers here, but also within the ballads, which now showed some signs of heartbreak. While he was changing his tune slightly, when he stayed in his sweet territory he got a little sticky, as on his take on Olivia Newton-John's "I Honestly Love You," but it is nowhere near as slick as his later soft crossover material. He also got a little silly on "Country Cookin'," a Nashville spin on "Memphis Soul Stew," but, overall, this excelled both in strength and variety of material, highlighted by the singles "Too Late to Worry, Too Blue to Cry" and "(I'd Be) A Legend in My Time," but also the good barroom weeper "The Busiest Memory in Time," "She Came Here for the Change," and his original "I'm Still Not Over You." It was a very good mainstream country-pop record—good enough to win the CMA's Album of the Year for 1975—and remains one of the highlights in Milsap's extensive catalog. *—Stephen Thomas Erlewine*

Night Things / 1975 / RCA ✦✦✦✦✦

Night Things is an appropriate title for Ronnie Milsap's fourth LP for RCA, since this ten-track collection from 1975 carries the distinct mood of a late-night album. But where most late-night country albums are built for solitary listening, this is a romantic record, where even songs about separation and being no good at goodbyes are better for slow dances than for crying in your beer. On that level, *Night Things* would seem to offer further proof that Milsap simply plays nothing but slick, commercial pop, but the opposite is true. While there are a couple of bright, catchy items here, including the bouncy title track, along with a few sweeping strings, this is his purest country album yet, since most of the songs are given relatively spare production (there is only one truly corny moment, thanks to the backing vocals and canned synths on the classic "I'll Be There (If You Ever Want Me)") and Milsap's singing is impassioned and convincing. Plus, there's a consistency in the songs: "(After Sweet Memories) Play Born to Lose Again" and "Who'll Turn Out the Lights (In Your World Tonight)" constitute a terrific one-two opener, and the rest of the album follows through on its promise, thanks to songs like "Just in Case," "Remember to Remind Me (I'm Leaving)," and a fine version of Conway Twitty's "(Lying Here With) Linda on My Mind." All this pushes *Night Things* to the forefront of Milsap's catalog. *—Stephen Thomas Erlewine*

☆ **20/20 Vision** / 1976 / RCA ✦✦✦✦✦

Oh yeah, Ronnie Milsap circa 1976. A contemporary of Mickey Gilley's in spirit and Conway Twitty's in pure emotion and dedication to the early rock sounds of the late '50s, Milsap was a monster when he was this on. *20/20 Vision* is one of the—if not the—finest records he ever cut. It perfectly balances his strengths, a honky tonk singer's repertoire, a rock & roll vocalist with a taste for doo wop and countrypolitan, and a delivery that was seamless due to possessing a gorgeous, silky baritone voice. With longtime producer Tom Collins and a band that included Pig Robbins, Chip & Reggie Young, Charlie McCoy, Larrie Londin, Kenny Malone, the Jordanaires, Nashville Edition, and of course himself on piano, they couldn't miss with this collection of songs by Kent Robinson, Cindy Walker, Kent Schweers, and Geoffrey Morgan, who wrote the title track. True to tradition, however, there's also a completely rocked-up version of the classic "Lovesick Blues" that's more suited to Jerry Lee Lewis and Hank Williams. In addition, Milsap does a devastating cover of Leon Payne's "You've Still Got a Place in My Heart." Side one, with the title cut, Walker's awesome tearjerker "Not That I Care," and "Lovesick Blues," is already worth the price of admission, but side two is a killer. It opens with a pair of Schweers tracks that are devastating in their heart-rending emotion: "Looking Out My Window Through the Pain" tells the story of a man who watches his wife go out to cheat with an old flame, over and over again as he watches. The track is countered with a honky tonk love song called "What Goes on When the Sun Goes Down." Along with a deep read of the Payne jewel is Wayne Kemp's slippery honky tonk nightmare, "I Got Home Just in Time to Say Goodbye," with Pig Robbins' signature upright plunking along in pure beer-garden style next to Lloyd Green's sweeping pedal steel. The set closes with Robinson's "I'm a Stand By My Woman Man," a bluesy answer to Tammy Wynette's "Stand By Your Man" (it quotes a few notes of the tune in the refrain), and as on virtually every Milsap album, love wins in the end and all is redeemed, right out of the barroom and into the barroom where everything is resolved. This is country music at its best. *—Thom Jurek*

It Was Almost like a Song / 1977 / RCA ✦✦✦

This album features such Milsap favorites as "Here in Love," "What a Difference You've Made in My Life," and "Long-Distance Memory." *—AMG*

Live / 1977 / RCA ✦✦✦

Only One Love in My Live / 1978 / RCA ✦✦

Images / 1979 / RCA ✦✦

Milsap Magic / 1980 / RCA ✦✦

There's No Gettin' Over Me / 1980 / RCA ✦✦✦✦

By 1981, Ronnie Milsap had become a superstar and was still riding the crest of the wave that began in the early '70s. But Milsap had taken his version of country music as close as he could get to the pop charts without quite crossing over. In many ways his sound is indicative of the times and the artists making hit records at the same time (Eddie Rabbitt, Ronnie McDowell, Johnny Lee, etc.), but Milsap possessed something that none of the aforementioned did: a direct link to the rock and doo wop sounds of the late '50s and early '60s. His urban country is evidenced in the title track, which was a Top Ten single, has a sweet alto saxophone solo in it, and has a chorus that reflects James Taylor's late-'70s attempts at crooning early rock. And there are Milsap's ballads, such as "It's All I Can Do," "Two Hearts Don't Always Make a Pair," and "Too Big for Words." There's the other single, "I Wouldn't Have Missed It for the World," which is urban cowboy country music in its purest essence and was rewarded with the number-one spot for a few weeks in late 1981. The sweeping backing vocals, a harp, a barely present pedal steel added for atmosphere, and enough acoustic guitars to supply an army of big-feathered hat-wearing drugstore cowpokes. It's also an awesome pop song. The chorus alone is so infectious it could be heard being hummed and whistled on street corners and its words being sung in barrooms and dancehalls throughout the rest of 1981. It also, finally, crossed over. *There's No Gettin' Over Me* is a perfect example of what Milsap was about in his middle period. There's humility in his confidence and a genuine empathy in his croon. Yeah, it's slick, and even schlocky in places ("Jesus Is Your Ticket to Heaven"), but it's also terrific. *—Thom Jurek*

Greatest Hits / 1980 / RCA ✦✦✦✦✦

This is a solid, albeit random assessment of Milsap's first seven years in country music. Mainstream country is featured, with "Pure Love" and "(I'm A) Stand By My Woman Man," but Milsap really shines on the elaborate and challenging arrangements of "(I'd Be) A Legend in My Time," "It Was Almost like a Song," and "Let's Take the Long Way Around the World." One previously unreleased track is here: "Smoky Mountain Rain." *—Tom Roland*

Inside / 1982 / Buddha ✦✦✦✦✦

Inside is arguably the strongest album Ronnie Milsap released at the peak of his slick contemporary country hit-making streak. The key to the album is that its consistency is married to a thoroughly appealing production equal parts Nashville and Californian soft rock. Make no mistake, this is glossy, slick music, but that's its charm—the surface is seductively slick, giving Milsap's warm baritone a sympathetic musical bed. Though he does dip outside of adult contemporary-oriented country-pop on "I Love New Orleans Music," this truly soars when its feet are planted firmly in the mainstream and he has melodic tales of heartbreak, whether it's on the hits "Any Day Now" and "He Got You" or album tracks like "Hate the Lies—Love the Liar" or "It's Just a Room." These are corny and slick, but they work thanks to their production and Milsap's performances. He had a number of number one singles and albums, but few were better than *Inside*. —*Stephen Thomas Erlewine*

Keyed Up / 1983 / RCA ✦✦✦

The eclectic *Keyed Up* features a pair of number one singles, "Show Her" and "Don't You Know How Much I Love You," as well as the Top Five hit "Stranger in My House." —*Jason Ankeny*

One More Try for Love / 1984 / RCA ✦✦✦

In his effort to expand the boundaries of country, Milsap pushes the edge harder here than in any other album. The electronically altered vocals in the tracks "She Loves My Car" and "Suburbia" have a winning effect—tasteful, not overdone. —*Tom Roland*

Greatest Hits, Vol. 2 / 1985 / RCA ✦✦✦✦✦

Juxtaposed to the first *Greatest Hits* package, this one nicely displays the evolution of a motivated risk-taker. Milsap redefines the outer limits of the commercial country format with his soul- and/or rock-inflected singles "(There's) No Gettin' Over Me," "Lost in the Fifties Tonight," and (most dramatically) "Stranger in My House." —*Tom Roland*

Heart & Soul / 1987 / RCA ✦✦✦

One of Milsap's more diverse efforts, *Heart and Soul* includes the chart-topping "Snap Your Fingers," "Make No Mistake, She's Mine" (a duet with Kenny Rogers), and "Where Do the Nights Go." —*Jason Ankeny*

Back to the Grindstone / 1991 / RCA ✦✦✦

Back to the Grindstone was an excellent return to form from Ronnie Milsap and, not coincidentally, it was his last great record, as well as his last hit album. Throughout *Back to the Grindstone*, Milsap displays his talent for eclectic, soul-inflected R&B, tearing through a gritty duet with Patti LaBelle on "Love Certified," covering "Since I Don't Have You" with heart, and then slipping into hard country with "Turn That Radio On." Not one of the ten songs on the record is weak, and Milsap responds with a gutsy, powerful performance, easily making *Back to the Grindstone* one of his best albums. —*Thom Owens*

Greatest Hits, Vol. 3 / 1991 / RCA ✦✦✦

Greatest Hits, Vol. 3 collects the bulk of Ronnie Milsap's late-'80s hits, including "Happy, Happy Birthday Baby," "How Do I Turn You On?," "Snap Your Fingers," "Where Do the Nights Go," "Button Off My Shirt," "A Woman in Love," and "Stranger Things Have Happened." Although it bypasses some of his hits ("In Love," "Houston Solution," "Are You Lovin' Me Like I'm Lovin' You") at the expense of lesser-known material ("L.A. to the Moon"), the collection remains a good sampling of Milsap's final round of Top Ten hits. —*Thom Owens*

True Believer / Jun. 7, 1993 / Liberty ✦✦✦

If only the whole album had the energy of the John Hiatt title track (not to mention the wit of the Hoss Allen intro), Milsap's Liberty debut would have been a record to reckon with. —*Dan Cooper*

The Essential Ronnie Milsap / 1995 / RCA ✦✦✦✦✦

RCA's 20-track, single-disc 1995 collection *The Essential Ronnie Milsap* doesn't live up to the billing of its title, largely because it bypasses a huge portion of his career—namely, the '70s. This doesn't dent the number of hits on the collection, since Milsap was one of country's most successful hitmakers of all time, charting toward the top until well into the '90s, but it doesn't necessarily provide the most accurate reading of his career, because many of his best songs—along with his purest country—are simply not here, including "Pure Love," "Please Don't Tell Me How the Story Ends," "Daydreams About Night Things," and "Smoky Mountain Rain," among others. To find those, turn to either the double-disc *40 #1 Hits* or to the 2001 release *RCA Country Legends*. This disc concentrates on the poppier material and crossover hits, many of which are excellent, ranking among his best work: It's hard to deny that "He Got You," "Stranger in My House," and "Any Day Now" are not among the best smooth country-pop of the early '80s (or among the best soft rock, for that matter). *Essential* continues in that vein, pursuing it into the '90s as the productions got clearer and cleaner, but the hits only got a little smaller. For listeners that prefer that era, this is a terrific, even necessary, purchase. For those who want to follow the '70s-oriented *RCA Country Legends*, this is a good next purchase, although they may just be better off getting the double-disc set for a full-fledged, comprehensive overview. —*Stephen Thomas Erlewine*

Sings His Best Hits for Capitol Records / Sep. 17, 1996 / Capitol ✦✦

As the title suggests, Ronnie Milsap's *Sings His Best Hits for Capitol Records* consists of re-recorded versions of ten of his biggest hits—including "Lost in the Fifties Tonight," "Snap Your Fingers," "(I'm A) Stand By Your Woman Man" and "(There's) No Gettin' Over Me"—which were all originally recorded for RCA Records. Though these new versions aren't particularly bad, they are neither as good or familiar as the originals, making it collection to avoid, especially if you're looking for a strong hits collection. —*Thom Owens*

Crazy Cajun Recordings / Feb. 18, 1999 / Edsel ✦✦✦

★ **40 #1 Hits** / Jun. 6, 2000 / Virgin ✦✦✦✦✦

Those of you who pay attention to record labels are liable to assume that this two-disc compilation consists of re-recordings of Ronnie Milsap's hits. After all, he spent his hit-making years on RCA Victor, which is owned by BMG, while Virgin Records, which released this set, is owned by EMI, a competing major label. While the majors occasionally license a track or two to their rivals, they never loan out the bulk of an album, and Milsap, like many music veterans, has re-recorded his material before. Surprisingly, however, *40 #1 Hits* is an exception to these suppositions; it does contain Milsap's original RCA Victor recordings, digitally remastered. Meanwhile, those of you who are fans of statistics and who consult only the charts in the best-known music trade magazine (or who have perused the *AMG*'s biography of Milsap) may suppose that the artist hasn't had 40 country chart-toppers, only 35. But there is more than one music trade magazine and more than one country singles chart, and a record that stopped short of the summit on one may have made it on another. For the sake of interest, the number-one songs according to other charts found here are "Too Late to Worry, Too Blue to Cry," "Just in Case," "Back on My Mind," "Stranger Things Have Happened," and "Since I Don't Have You," all of which made the Top Ten in that well-known magazine's rankings. Finally, those of you who are good at addition will note that there are actually 43 tracks on *40 #1 Hits*. "Stranger in My House," which is one of those extra recordings, didn't get to number one by anybody's estimation, but it did hit the country Top Five and the pop Top 40, and it won the Best New Country Song Grammy Award for 1983. The other two are newly recorded songs, "Livin' on Love" and "Time, Love and Money," both of which rock a little harder than Milsap usually does. All told, Ronnie Milsap's *40 #1 Hits* is a compilation that exceeds expectations and stands as the definitive collection of the most popular work by one of the most successful country artists of the 1970s and '80s. —*William Ruhlmann*

● **RCA Country Legends** / Jun. 19, 2001 / Buddha ✦✦✦✦✦

Ronnie Milsap had a staggering number of hits, staying near the top of the country charts for 20 years between 1973 and 1992. It's too much material to fit on a single disc, which is why the double-disc *40 #1 Hits* exists, and for those who want a comprehensive collection, they should turn there. Single-disc collections are still useful as overviews and introductions to his lengthy career, largely because they're easier to absorb, but his volume of BMG Heritage's *RCA Country Legends* isn't necessarily a straight hits collection, even if every one of these 16 tracks was a charting hit. There are many very big hits missing, including "(I'm A) Stand By My Woman Man," "Stranger in My House," and "Smoky Mountain Rain," along with the giant pop crossover tunes "He Got You" and "Any Day Now." The absence of the latter suggests that this, like other installments in the *RCA Country Legends* series, intends to offer a country-centric view of the featured artist—an admirable intent, but one that doesn't quite work in the case of Milsap, who always cheerful spun his work toward pop. Plus, the song selection contains such slickly produced pop-bait as "Lost in the Fifties Tonight (In the Still of the Night)" and "Happy, Happy Birthday Baby," two numbers that feel far more pandering than "He Got You" and "Any Day Now," which really should have been on here instead. Apart from those two cuts, the rest of this disc actually has an expert song selection, even finding gems from the late '80s in "Don't You Ever Get Tired (Of Hurting Me)" and "A Woman in Love" but really gaining its strength by concentrating on his terrific '70s and early-'80s sides like "Pure Love," "(All Together Now) Let's Fall Apart," "Daydreams About Night Things," and "Please Don't Tell Me How the Story Ends." All of those tunes did not appear on the 20-track 1995 collection *The Essential Ronnie Milsap*, which focused on '80s material, thereby playing up his pop side. This, in comparison, gives a better indication of his country roots (even with the couple of MOR selections toward the end of the collection) than any compilation outside of *40 #1 Hits*, and in that sense, it winds up fulfilling its intention of being a country-oriented Milsap overview, and it's very entertaining and a very good introduction for those listeners who don't want a full two discs. —*Stephen Thomas Erlewine*

Waddie Mitchell (Bruce Douglas Mitchell)

b. 1950, Elko, NV

Vocals / Cowboy

Waddie Mitchell was a real cowboy who became a world-renowned cowboy storyteller and poet, enchanting contemporary audiences with tales of life in the rugged West. He was born Bruce Douglas Mitchell on the enormous Horseshoe Ranch, located over 30 miles south of Elko, NV. Young Bruce, nicknamed "Waddie" (a synonym for "cowboy") by his father, spent most of his time with real cowboys and at night listened to their stories and memorized their poems. He dropped out of school at age 16 to become a full-time wrangler and chuck wagon driver. He was drafted into the Army and was stationed at Fort Carson, CO, on a 24,000-acre ranch where he broke and trained horses for the U.S. Cavalry. While working as the foreman of a ranch, Mitchell appeared in an early-'80s PBS documentary about the last real cowboys in America, *The Vanishing Breed*. The documentary featured some of Mitchell's own poetry, and Johnny Carson invited him to visit *the Tonight Show*. Mitchell didn't even know who Carson was, but he was a big hit on the show after reciting Wallace McCray's famous poem *Reincarnation*, and later returned several times. He also appeared on several other programs, including Larry King's radio show and a *National Geographic* special.

In 1984, he and pal Hal Cannon organized the first Elko Cowboy Poetry Gathering. Two thousand people attended the first year and by 1994, the attendance soared to nearly 14,000. Later in 1984, Mitchell recorded his first album of poetry at Cannon's house in Idaho. His second album sold over 10,000 copies. In 1992, Mitchell was one of the first artists to record on Warner Bros.' newly established Warner Western label with *Lone Driftin' Rider*. He and colleague Don Edwards embarked upon an extensive promotional tour of festivals, concert halls, schools and universities to sell the album and to educate audiences about their nearly extinct way of life. Mitchell released his second Warner album, *Buckaroo Poet*, in 1994. He next appeared as a guest host on the cable-TV channel VH1's *Country Country* show. He also won numerous honors for his poetry and storytelling, and was inducted into the Cowboy Poets and Singers' Hall of Fame. —*Sandra Brennan*

● **Lone Driftin' Rider** / Jan. 1992 / Warner Bros. ✦✦✦✦
Waddie Mitchell revives the tradition of story-telling cowboy songs with the intimate, entertaining "Lone Driftin' Rider," which is equally divided between standards and poetic originals. —*Thom Owens*

Buckaroo Poet / Aug. 3, 1993 / Warner Bros. ✦✦✦✦

Bard & The Balladeer: Live From Cowtown / Nov. 1, 1994 / Warner Bros. ✦✦✦

Live w/ Norman Blake, Don Edwards & Rich O'Brien / Mar. 17, 1998 / Shanachie ✦✦✦✦

That No Quit Attitude / Oct. 8, 2002 / Shanachie ✦✦✦
Most Americans assume that the only place where one could find a real cowboy is on TV. While the breed is certainly scarcer in the 21st century, Waddie Mitchell is walking, talking proof that honest to God cowboys still exist. He's also intent on preserving Western traditions. *That No Quit Attitude*, however, doesn't romanticize the Western plains with close harmony and songs of the coyote's lonesome call. Instead, Mitchell recites original poetry, cataloging the life he's lived growing up and working on ranches in the West. When he talks about horses, as he does in "Who But the Horse," he doesn't just give an idealized picture of the happy cowboy riding along with his tried and true companion. Instead, his poem offers a lengthy rumination on the life of a horse. There's plenty of humor on *That No Quit Attitude*. "Don" recalls a contemporary story of a man in the supermarket who—as some people are wont to do—unloads his opinions on unsuspecting bystanders. It's fascinating how Mitchell is able to juxtapose old and new values while still keeping his distance from the material. There are life lessons ("Harsh Words"), biscuit recipes ("Bisquits and Gravy"), and, surprisingly, reflections on suicide ("Through the Pain"). Waddie Mitchell's poetry runs as deep as the Colorado River and as wide as the Grand Canyon, and *That No Quit Attitude* provides an in-depth portrait of a fading way of life. —*Ronnie D. Lankford Jr.*

Moby Grape

f. Sep. 1966, San Francisco, CA

Group / Country-Rock, Psychedelic, Folk-Rock

One of the best '60s San Francisco bands, Moby Grape were also one of the most versatile. Although they are most often identified with the psychedelic scene, their specialty was combining all sorts of roots music—folk, blues, country, and classic rock & roll—with some Summer of Love vibes and multi-layered, triple-guitar arrangements. All of those elements only truly coalesced, however, for their 1967 debut LP. Although subsequent albums had more good moments than many listeners are aware of, a combination of personal problems and bad management effectively killed off the group by the end of the 1960s.

Many San Francisco bands of the era were assembled by recent immigrants to the area, but Moby Grape had even more tenuous roots in the region than most when they formed. Matthew Katz, who managed the Jefferson Airplane in their early days, helped put together Moby Grape around Skip Spence. Spence, a legendarily colorful Canadian native whose first instrument was the guitar, had played drums in the Airplane's first lineup at the instigation of Marty Balin. Spence left the Airplane after their first album, and reverted to his natural guitarist and songwriting role for the Grape (the Airplane had already recorded some of his compositions). Guitarist Jerry Miller and drummer Don Stevenson were recruited from the Northwest bar band the Frantics; guitarist Peter Lewis had played in southern California surf bands like the Cornells; and bassist Bob Mosley had also played with outfits from southern California.

The group's relative unfamiliarity with each other may have sown seeds for their future problems, but they jelled surprisingly quickly, with all five members contributing more or less equally to the songwriting on their self-titled debut (1967). *Moby Grape* remains their signature statement, though the folk-rock and country-rock worked better than the boogies; "Omaha," "Sittin' by the Window," "Changes," and "Lazy Me" are some of their best songs. Columbia Records, though, damaged the band's credibility with overhype, releasing no less than five singles from the LP simultaneously. Worse, three members of the group were caught consorting with underage girls. Though charges were eventually dropped, the legal hassles, combined with an increasingly strained relationship with manager Katz, sapped the band's drive.

Moby Grape's follow-up, the double-LP *Wow*, was one of the most disappointing records of the '60s, in light of the high expectations fostered by the debut. The studio half of the package had much more erratic songwriting than the first recording, and the group members didn't blend their instrumental and vocal skills nearly as well. The "bonus" disc was almost a total waste, consisting of bad jams. Spence departed while the album was being recorded in New York in 1968, as a result of a famous incident in which he entered the studio with a fire axe, apparently intending to use it on Stevenson. Committed to New York's Bellevue Hospital, he did re-emerge to record a wonderful acid folk solo album at the end of 1968, but that would be his only notable post-Grape project; he struggled with mental illness until he died in 1998.

Another unexpected blow was dealt when Mosley, despite his membership in a band that emerged from the Haight-Ashbury psychedelic scene, joined the Marine Corps at the beginning of 1969. The band did struggle on and release a couple more albums during that year, and the best tracks from these (particularly the earlier one, *Moby Grape '69*) proved they could still deliver the goods, though usually in a more subdued, countrified fashion than their earliest material. The group broke up at the end of the '60s, although they would periodically reunite for nearly unheard albums over the next two decades, in lineups featuring varying original members. Their problems were exacerbated by Matthew Katz, who owns the Moby Grape name, and has sometimes

prevented the original members from using the name when they worked together. —*Richie Unterberger*

★ **Moby Grape** / Jun. 1967 / San Francisco Sound ✦✦✦✦✦
Moby Grape's career was a long, sad series of minor disasters, in which nearly anything that could have gone wrong did (poor handling by their record company, a variety of legal problems, a truly regrettable deal with their manager, creative and personal differences among the bandmembers, and the tragic breakdown of guitarist and songwriter Skip Spence), but their self-titled debut album was their one moment of unqualified triumph. *Moby Grape* is one of the finest (perhaps *the* finest) album to come out of the San Francisco psychedelic scene, brimming with great songs and fresh ideas while blessedly avoiding the pitfalls that pock marked the work of their contemporaries—no long, unfocused jams, no self-indulgent philosophy, and no attempts to sonically recreate the sound of an acid trip. Instead, Moby Grape built their sound around the brilliantly interwoven guitar work of Jerry Miller, Peter Lewis, and Skip Spence, and the clear, bright harmonies of all five members (drummer Don Stevenson and bassist Bob Mosely sang just as well as they held down the backbeat). As songwriters, the group blended straight-ahead rock & roll, smart pop, blues, country, and folk accents into a flavorful brew that was all their own, with a clever melodic sense that reflected the lysergic energy surrounding them without drowning in it. And producer David Rubinson got it all on tape in a manner which captured the band's infectious energy and soaring melodies with uncluttered clarity, while subtly exploring the possibilities of the stereo mixing process. "Omaha," "Fall on You," "Hey Grandma," and "8:05" sound like obvious hits (and might have been if Columbia hadn't released them as singles all at once), but the truth is there isn't a dud track to be found here, and time has been extremely kind to this record. *Moby Grape* is as refreshing today as it was upon first release, and if fate prevented the group from making a follow-up that was as consistently strong, for one brief shining moment Moby Grape proved to the world they were one of America's great bands. While history remembers the Grateful Dead and Jefferson Airplane as being more important, the truth is neither group ever made an album quite this good. —*Mark Deming*

Grape Jam / 1968 / Columbia ✦✦
Recorded during downtime from the *Wow* sessions, *Grape Jam* was originally issued with the aforementioned album as a bonus record. It's a shame that a few cuts weren't incorporated into *Wow*—it would have made one hell of a great album. Some of *Grape Jam* is a bit ponderous, especially "Marmalade" with Mike Bloomfield playing piano. However, there are some excellent cuts, such as Bob Mosley's slow and soulful blues number "Never," which was later taken (*stolen*) by Led Zeppelin for a track on their third album. "Black Current Jam" with guest pianist Al Kooper is overloaded with a wonderful, graceful funk that illustrates what a fine *band* the Grape really were. The record concludes with a "poem" by one Michael Hayworth; loaded with sound effects and backward tapes, it comes off sounding not unlike "Revolution # 9." —*Matthew Greenwald*

Wow / 1968 / Columbia ✦✦
Moby Grape's self-titled 1967 debut album was a tight, seamless record that wedded folk, psychedelic rock, blues, and R&B into a cohesive whole. It's no wonder they were considered the next big thing, and much has been written about the managerial and marketing screw-ups which prevented that from happening. But this, their second album, was considered a failure. Granted, parts of this record are almost unlistenable (literally), but there is still a certain magic prevalent on several cuts. "Murder in My Heart for the Judge" is without a doubt one of the finest hard rock/blues performances ever committed to vinyl in San Francisco during the period. While Peter Lewis and Jerry Millers' guitars wail, bass player Bob Mosley gives a vocal performance worthy of Otis Redding. Also on the album is the amazing "He," featuring guitar work from Lewis very reminiscent of Bryan MacLean's on *Forever Changes*. On the less listenable side, there is the Skip Spence cut "Just Like Gene Autry," which—when the original vinyl version was released—had to be played at 78 rpm. Spence does score with a gender-bending version of "Leader of the Pack" titled "Motorcycle Irene." The entire album is somewhat confusing and a little misdirected, but the finer moments are among the Grape's greatest. —*Matthew Greenwald*

Wow/Grape Jam / 1968 / San Francisco Sound ✦✦✦
Could Moby Grape live up to the hype following the release of their first album? The answer was "No." That fact alone nearly broke up the band. They went back into the studio and recorded a flawed but essential gem which they titled *Wow*. Great R&B and blues workouts co-existed alongside hallucinogenic raveups and introspective ballads. Production gimmicks did mar such near-classic cuts such as "The Place and the Time" and "Bitter Wind," but on the whole, this album is well worth the time. *Grape Jam* is just that, a jam between Moby Grape members and famous friends such as Mike Bloomfield and Al Kooper essentially making things up as they went along. For historical purposes only. —*James Chrispell*

Truly Fine Citizen / 1969 / Columbia ✦✦
Recorded in just three days down in Nashville, *Truly Fine Citizen* was little more than a contractual obligation with the Grape pared down to a trio. Augmented by session men, it does have its moments. "Right Before My Eyes" has a relaxed country feel to it and the title track rocks out like the old days, if only briefly. The end of Moby Grape came about just as the "country-rock" sound was about to become the Next Big Thing. —*James Chrispell*

Moby Grape '69 / Jan. 30, 1969 / Columbia ✦✦✦
After the unfortunate departure of Skip Spence, Moby Grape continued as a four-piece band. They still had the power, songwriting, and talent, but Spence's exit was something that robbed the band of an indefinable magic. Nevertheless, '69 is a good and very real album. Sounding like it was cut from a variety of sessions at different times, this album

isn't exactly what you would call cohesive, but it is still excellent, in places. Bob Mosley shines on the rocker "Hoochie" and the gorgeous pop/folk ballad "It's a Beautiful Day Today," which is underscored by some brilliant fingerpicking guitar from Peter Lewis. Lewis also has some excellent country-oriented songs here, notably "I Am Not Willing" and "If You Can't Learn From My Mistakes," the latter of which still graces his solo performances. The record concludes with "Seeing." Recorded (partially) before his exit, it remains one of Spence's finest songs, easily one of Moby Grape's most glorious (and disturbing) achievements, and a good reason to get this record as well. *—Matthew Greenwald*

20 Granite Creek / 1971 / Reprise ✦✦✦✦✦

The story of Moby Grape has been told and re-told countless times, with its tales of excess, mismanagement, and record company screwups. By the end of the '60s the Grape was all but finished—or so everyone thought. After an aborted attempt at a Peter Lewis solo album, producer David Rubinson was able to help engineer this re-formation of all five original members, along with extra member Gordon Stevens on various stringed instruments. Written and recorded at the Grape's communal house in the Santa Cruz mountains, the results of the experiment rendered *20 Granite Creek*, an album that is rightfully the successor to the first album (1967's *Moby Grape*). One of the most shining examples is Peter Lewis' funky and fast "Goin' Down to Texas," which clearly illustrates the power Moby Grape had in this, one of the original three-guitar lineups. Skip Spence, who was one of the more interesting writers in the band, contributes one song, the delicate and gorgeous oriental-sounding "Chinese Song." The whole record is quite similar in feel to the Doors' *L.A. Woman*, another truly great, homemade comeback album. Of course, it didn't sell anything. A true crime in a never-ending saga. *—Matthew Greenwald*

Moby Grape '84 / 1984 / San Francisco Sound ✦✦✦

● **Vintage: The Very Best of Moby Grape** / May 11, 1993 / Columbia/Legacy ✦✦✦✦✦

It's hard to imagine a better-produced package of Moby Grape's work than this two-disc, 48-track condensation of their best late-'60s recordings. The first disc of this set centers around their entire 1967 self-titled debut LP (included in its entirety), which mixed blues, country, and folk influences with hard-charging psychedelic rock & roll. The result was one of the Summer of Love's more enduring works. The second disc boils their wildly inconsistent 1968-1969 material down to a fairly strong and coherent selection. While it doesn't match the peak of the group's initial burst, it features some strong folk and country-rock originals that wear much better in the absence of the bloated jams and half-baked hard rock that could make their albums a chore to sit through. Each disc includes interesting demos, outtakes, and live performances that round out the legacy of this prodigiously talented but ill-fated band, which was overcome by internal strife and label/management difficulties after their promising debut. *—Richie Unterberger*

Hugh Moffatt

b. Nov. 10, 1948, Fort Worth, TX

Guitar, Vocals / Progressive Country, Singer/Songwriter, Country-Folk

Country-folksinger/songwriter Hugh Moffatt penned several big hits for other country artists during the '70s and '80s before making his own critically acclaimed solo records. Moffatt was born in Fort Worth, TX, in 1948 and played classical piano and jazz trumpet during his teen years. While studying English at Rice University, he started listening to blues music, learned guitar, and went on to join a pop band called Rollin' Wood. He briefly moved to Austin, then set out for Washington, D.C., in 1973, but a detour to Nashville wound up becoming permanent, as he decided to try his hand at professional songwriting. Influenced by the literary-minded Kris Kristofferson, Moffatt found a mentor in Ed Penney, and in 1974 his composition "Just in Case" became a major hit for Ronnie Milsap. Moffatt landed a solo deal with Mercury in 1977, but after two flop singles, he was let go and returned to songwriting.

Moffatt's songs were recorded by a number of country stars during the '80s, including Dolly Parton ("Old Flames (Can't Hold a Candle to You)"), Johnny Rodriguez ("How Could I Love Her So Much"), Lacy J. Dalton ("Wild Turkey"), and Alabama ("Words at Twenty Paces"), among others. In the meantime, Moffatt formed a band called Ratz, recording a five-song EP in 1984 titled *Puttin' on the Ratz*. He cut some solo sessions in 1986 and the following year signed to Rounder subsidiary Philo, which released his solo debut, *Loving You*. It earned generally positive reviews, as did the 1989 follow-up, *Troubadour*.

For his next album, Moffatt teamed up with his sister, country singer Katy Moffatt; *Dance Me Outside* was released in 1992. The following year, Moffatt teamed with Memphis-based composer Michael Ching to co-author the one-act opera *King of the Clouds*. 1995 brought *The Wognum Sessions*, an album released on the Dutch label Strictly Country and credited to the Hugh Moffatt Trio. Follow-ups included 1996's *The Life of a Minor Poet*, on the independent Watermelon, and the concert album *Live and Alone*, on Brambus. He and Ching composed a second opera, *Out in the Rain*, which premiered in 1998. After some time away from recording, Moffatt finally returned with 2003's *Ghosts of the Music*, also on Brambus. *—Steve Huey*

Loving You / 1987 / Philo ✦✦✦✦✦

● **Troubadour** / 1989 / Philo ✦✦✦✦✦

Dance Me Outside / 1992 / Philo ✦✦✦

The Wognum Sessions / Apr. 25, 1995 / Strictly Country ✦✦✦

The Life of a Minor Poet / 1996 / Watermelon ✦✦✦

Katy Moffatt

b. Nov. 19, 1950, Fort Worth, TX

Guitar, Vocals / Progressive Country, Contemporary Country, Country-Folk, Americana

Katy Moffatt has never broken through to the country mainstream, but she has earned a substantial cult following among roots-music fans and plenty of critical respect for her blend of country, folk, rock, pop, and blues. The younger sister of singer/songwriter Hugh Moffatt, she was born in Fort Worth, TX, in 1950 and first performed in local coffeehouses. She attended St. John's College in Santa Fe, NM, and while there, she appeared in the 1971 film *Billy Jack*. She subsequently dropped out of school and moved to Corpus Christi, TX, where she worked at a television station and sang with a local blues band. Unfortunately, the station was destroyed by a hurricane, and she moved first to Austin and then to Colorado, where she found a regular gig singing on a Denver radio station in 1973. That helped her land a deal with Columbia in 1975, and she issued two country-rock albums for the label: 1976's *Katy* and 1978's *Kissin' in the California Sun*, the latter of which featured members of the Allman Brothers. Neither broke her commercially, and she made ends meet as a backup singer, working with the likes of Willie Nelson, Jimmy Buffett, Poco, John Prine, Tanya Tucker, and Lynn Anderson, among others.

In 1983, Moffatt signed with the independent Permian label and recorded several acclaimed singles for them; although she didn't release an album or score a major chart hit, she still managed to land a nomination as the Academy of Country Music's Female Vocalist of the Year in 1985. Permian later folded, and she moved on to a new deal with Rounder subsidiary Philo, issuing her label debut, *Walkin' on the Moon*, in 1989. The 1990 follow-up, *Child Bride*, was a more electrified, rock-oriented effort, and both started to earn Moffatt some attention in the roots-music community. She recorded an album of duets with brother Hugh, *Dance Me Outside*, and saw the live set *Indoor Fireworks* released on the overseas Red Moon label. Her next proper solo effort, *The Evangeline Hotel* (originally released under the title *The Greatest Show on Earth*), was hailed by many critics as her best ever and an instant classic. It proved to be her last release for Philo, however; a pair of albums on Watermelon, 1994's *Hearts Gone Wild* and 1996's *Midnight Radio*, failed to maintain her critical momentum. 1998's *Angel Town*, issued on HMG, received good reviews, however, and she followed it with the straight-ahead country album *Loose Diamond* on Hightone in 1999. Her next project, 2001's *Cowboy Girl*, was a collection of traditional (and traditional-style) western songs, issued on Shanachie. *—Steve Huey*

Katy / 1976 / Columbia ✦✦✦✦

Kissin' in the California Sun / 1978 / Columbia ✦✦✦

Walkin' on the Moon / 1989 / Philo ✦✦✦✦

By the time Katy Moffatt had recorded this debut acoustic record for Rounder's Philo label with guitarist Andrew Hardin in 1989, she had issued two albums of trailblazing country-rock on Columbia, a handful of singles for Permian, and backup vocal gigs for everyone from Jimmy Buffett to Tanya Tucker. Away from the production slickness of Billy Sherrill, Moffatt strips down her sound; she asserts herself as a songwriter. The tracks "Carnival Man," "Fire in Your Eyes," and "I'm Sorry Darlin'" prove beyond a shadow of a doubt that Moffatt is more than just a pretty voice. Her writing cuts to the bone; the songs come from the heart of emotion more than just clever ideas. In addition, the songs she wrote with Tom Russell, which include the titles "If Anything Comes to Mind" and "I'll Take the Blame," transcend country altogether and become storyteller's songs that would work in any genre. Given Hardin's aesthetically beautiful guitar playing and Moffatt's restraint, the essence of these songs just bubbles up and out of the grooves. But the true evidence of Moffatt's mastery of a lyric and her ability to convey the grain of truth in its construction is on "Mr. Banker," by members of Lynyrd Skynyrd. Their harsh guitar-driven blues becomes a country plea with the Delta blues framing the entire proceeding and accented by Hardin's tasty runs. For all those who came to the game late with Moffatt, *Walkin' on the Moon*, which boasts one of the most tender title tracks in country music's long history, is a way of diving headlong into the mystery that is Katy Moffatt. *—Thom Jurek*

Child Bride / 1990 / Philo ✦✦✦✦✦

On the follow-up to 1989's *Walkin' on the Moon*, Katy Moffatt decided to crank up the volume a bit and let her hair down. *Child Bride* is anything but a delicate recording. It's closer to rockabilly and the woolly side of country than any singer/songwriter outing. Some of the musicians who appear here are Carlo Nuccio from the Continental Drifters, former Lone Justice guitar ace Marvin Etzioni (who wrote the title track and another one), guitarist Duane Jarvis, Dave Alvin, the late Donald Lindley, Pat McLaughlin, Greg Leisz, and Los Lobos' Steve Berlin, among others. This is a singer's effort; uncharacteristically, Moffatt didn't pen a track here, but in her readings of these songs, they become hers. From the rolling country-rockabilly of the title track to her deep Memphis soul meets Nashville contemporary country reading of John Hiatt's "We Ran" to a loose-wristed rocking reading of Arthur Alexander's "You Better Move On," Moffatt digs deep into her cowboy angel alto and delivers with raucous passion and a gritty verve that's closer to Wanda Jackson than it is Tammy Wynette—and that's only on side one. The second half opens with another Etzioni rocker, entitled "False Alarm," that pulls out the stops before Moffatt turns to a slower—though not slow—articulation of the Doc Pomus classic "Lonely Avenue." Pat McLaughlin's "You Done Me Wrong" is given classic rockabilly treatment, but it leans a lot heavier on honky tonk country than it does on rock. The set closes with the Wesley Rose classic "Settin' the Woods on Fire," so closely associated with Hank Williams. It's a duet with Dave Alvin and the feel is steaming honky tonk with a beautiful pair of guitars courtesy of Alvin and Richard Stekol. Juke Logan's harmonica break gives the track a serious blues edge before Leisz returns on Weissenborn slide guitar to anchor it back in the out-of-control Saturday midnight honky tonk country bus. *Child Bride* is easily the hardest-rocking record Katy Moffatt ever issued; it's also the closest to country music's heart. *—Thom Jurek*

Indoor Fireworks / 1992 / Red Moon ✦✦✦

This release is closer in style to *Childe Bride* than other recent Moffatt albums. She takes on ballads and rockers such as Dave Alvin's "Rich Man's Town" and "Words at Twenty Paces." Recorded in Switzerland in 1991 with a country band live, this CD has a loose country-rock sound. As always, Katy Moffatt's captivating voice pulls it all together. *—Richard Meyer*

★ **The Evangeline Hotel** / 1993 / Philo ♦♦♦♦♦
This album has since been released with a different cover and title—*Evangeline Hotel*. Be assured, it is the same album and a great one it is too. Many of the tracks were co-written with Tom Russell who produced the CD. Andy Hardin plays great parts as usual and it's all held together by some of the most open and honest-sounding vocals among contemporary songwriters. —*Richard Meyer*

Hearts Gone Wild / 1994 / Watermelon ♦♦
Hearts Gone Wild is Katy Moffat's seventh album. This one most closely resembles *Walkin' on the Moon* in that the arrangements are primarily acoustic and the songs are mostly personal and romantic. Many of the songs were co-written with Tom Russell, but the emphasis is not on stories as much as on her previous CD *The Greatest Show on Earth*. Her voice, as always, is a wonder, heartbreaking and reassuring. —*Richard Meyer*

Midnight Radio / 1996 / Watermelon ♦♦♦

Angel Town / Aug. 25, 1998 / HMG ♦♦♦♦♦
Katy Moffatt is all perfection and substance, an endearing figure in the music business whose talent is just as admirable. Sturdy and enduring, Moffatt's beauty belies the great strength of character with which she operates. Both in the studio and on-stage, Moffatt is a power to be reckoned with. Subtle and soft, she reaches out to her audience and takes them by the heart. As both an interpreter of the work of other songwriters as well as a marvelous voice for her own compositions, Moffatt sparkles. This time around she covers Chris Smither's gigantic blues hit "Love Me Like a Man" with aplomb and grace, while retaining all the baser animal instincts Smither so delicately wove into his song. Just as good is Cole Porter's "Miss Otis Regrets," an out-of-time tidbit that comes to life in an different time and place. Steve Goodman's "I Just Keep Falling in Love" is brilliant. As for herself, Moffatt presents several wonderful tunes which she wrote with longtime friend Tom Russell. "Jigsaw Love Affair," "The Game," and "Mother of Pearl" are reflective of the high caliber of talent both Moffatt and Russell possess. Magnificent is the only word one can use to describe this steely yet gossamer-like project. Moffatt never sounded better. —*Jana Pendragon*

Loose Diamond / Oct. 5, 1999 / Hightone ♦♦♦
Katy Moffatt has assembled some daunting Americana talent for her straight-shooting country album *Loose Diamond*, including producer Dave Alvin (the Blasters) and the pedal steel player at the top of everyone's wish list, Greg Leisz. Members of Alvin's group, the Guilty Men, and Dwight Yoakam's band also spur things along. The result is a trad country album with a lot of scope and breadth (and a wonderfully full sound). The crown jewel in the arrangement, however, is Moffatt's voice, which hunkers down into these tracks with heart-rending ease. The Rosie Flores/Moffatt original "Wheels" is a folk-inflected country beauty in the Townes Van Zandt vein, while a turn through Leiber & Stoller's "Fools Fall in Love" finds Moffatt successfully skirting the pop perimeters of country without falling in. Moffatt even tackles an old Blasters tune, "Goodbye Baby So Long," and in her hands it becomes a slowed-down, heart-piercing country-rocker. She also throws open the doors of honky tonk (and shows a set of fierce pipes) on Hank Williams Jr.'s "Stoned at the Jukebox." Moffatt is in fine form throughout and shows impressive range and diversity within the classic country idiom. —*Erik Hage*

Cowboy Girl / Sep. 11, 2001 / Shanachie ♦♦♦♦
While mainstream country continues to ignore its roots, a number of "alternative" acts purposely seek them out. Katy Moffatt's new album is a superior example. She decided to record a number of Western songs on *Cowboy Girl*, both traditional and contemporary, classics and little known gems. "Black Diamond" starts things quietly, with sparse accompaniment and a restrained, affecting vocal. She's joined by guitarists David Wilkie and Rich O'Brien, and bassist Mary Stribling, providing a simple, tasteful backdrop for songs like "Midnight the Unconquered Outlaw" and "Ol' Bill Miner (The Gentleman Bandit)." For the most part this is a calm, low-key effort that matches the dusty, bare plains of the West. An exceptional version of John Phillips' "Me and My Uncle" gives the song a new life, freeing it from some 500 Grateful Dead performances. Wilkie joins Moffatt for a lovely duet on "Magdalena and the Jack of Spades," a minor-key effort that more than lives up to its evocative title. *Cowboy Girl* will grow on listeners as it gently introduces western geography through its 15 songs. It's also nice that she chose to include modern material, showcasing writers like Joe Ely and Tom Russell. The only false note rings on the over-familiar "John Hardy," with Moffatt's boisterous vocal overpowering the lyrics and the band. It is perhaps ironic that artists who sing within the tradition are labeled alternative, because *Cowboy Girl* is the real thing. Cowboys and cowgirls alike will enjoy this one. —*Ronnie D. Lankford Jr.*

Katy/Kissin' in the California Sun / Oct. 22, 2002 / WestSide ♦♦♦♦♦
In 2002, WestSide released *Katy/Kissin' in the California Sun*, which contained two albums—*Katy* (1976, originally released on Columbia) and *Kissin' in the California Sun* (1978, also originally on Columbia)—by Katy Moffatt on one compact disc. —*Gregory McIntosh*

The Monroe Brothers

f. 1932, **db.** 1938
Group / Traditional Bluegrass, Old-Timey, Traditional Country, Country-Folk, Close Harmony
The Monroe Brothers began as a trio of Birch, Charlie, & Bill Monroe on fiddle, guitar and mandolin, respectively, performing square dance songs as well as traditional and gospel numbers. In 1932, Bill and Charlie began touring professionally with the WLS touring company as dancers, appearing with the Hoosier Hot Shots and Red Foley among others, and in 1934 secured the sponsorship of the Texas Crystals Company, a manufacturer of laxatives. The association provided the Monroes with a steady stream of radio work for over a year until competing laxative maker Crazy Water Crystals took over sponsorship of the duo while they continued working on many of the same stations. The radio appearances made the Monroe Brothers a popular live act, which prompted the interest of RCA to recording the two.

In mid-February the Monroe Brothers made their first recordings for RCA's Bluebird imprint, and went on to wax 60 sides in the following two years. Their music at this point was firmly within the brother duo tradition and exhibited only hints of the style Bill Monroe would later pioneer as the Father of Bluegrass. They were set apart from other harmony duos by Bill's piercing harmonies and mandolin leads, as well as the energy and often fast tempos of their performances. The very use of the mandolin as a lead instrument would revolutionize its application in country music, as would Bill's unique fiddle-influenced style. It would be silly to label them the "rock & roll of the '30s," but certainly there was an excitement and an edge to their music that put them on the frontier of hillbilly innovation in their day. In early 1938, Bill and Charlie parted ways due to personality conflicts and business disagreements, and each formed his own band shortly thereafter. Charlie formed a group called the Kentucky Pardners, and by 1941 (after a short stint with a band called the Kentuckians and an abortive attempt at recreating the Monroe Brothers sound with partner Cleo Davis) Bill Monroe was recording again for RCA with a band he named the Blue Grass Boys. In this new group, Monroe built upon his earlier innovations and developed the distinctive and enduring style that came to be known as bluegrass. —*Greg Adams*

★ **The Legendary Monroe Brothers** / 1997 / BMG Japan ♦♦♦♦♦
Available only as a pricey Japanese import, this three-CD collection contains the Monroe Brothers' complete 1936-1938 recordings. The historical importance of this package cannot be overstated, providing, as it does, a link between the brother-duo sound and the birth of bluegrass. Although the seeds of bluegrass can be heard among these 86 recordings, and some of the material would later surface as standards of bluegrass repertory, the music of the Monroe Brothers is unique in its own right. Bill Monroe's high harmonies and aggressive mandolin leads were revolutionary at the time, and the influence of the brothers' choice of material and presentation would resonate throughout country music for decades to come. Some of the recordings on this set have been mastered from off-center or damaged 78s, but most of the material is quite listenable. Despite the high import price, *The Legendary Monroe Brothers* is essential for serious fans of Bill Monroe or anyone with a deep interest in the history of country music. —*Greg Adams*

Monroe Brothers, Vol. 1: What Would You Give in Exchange for Your Soul / May 16, 2000 / Rounder ♦♦♦♦♦
This is the first of a four-volume set covering the entirety of the 60 sides the duo recorded for RCA/Bluebird. It would have been nice if dates, even estimated ones, were included with the tracks in the liner notes, but it can be gathered that the 15 cuts represent the first chronological fourth of the Monroe Brothers' RCA/Bluebird material. Again it's not certain from Charles Wolfe's liners (which are, it should be added, in the main excellent), but most or all of them date from 1936. There was no run up the ramp to a level of musical accomplishment when the brothers started recording. Right from the start, they were tight instrumentalists and harmonizing vocalists. The guitar (Charlie Monroe) and mandolin (Bill Monroe) blended in a way that foreshadowed, indeed virtually was, bluegrass on the rapid "My Long Journey Home" and "Nine Pound Hammer Is Too Heavy," the latter getting heavy exposure in 2000 via its inclusion on *Harry Smith's Anthology of American Folk Music, Vol. 4*. Much of the material on this disc was gospel in origin; they were also able interpreters of both traditional folk songs and contemporary compositions (some of which were their own). Although this was mastered from old 78s, the sound is pretty good, certainly about as good as it's going to get via the remastering process. —*Richie Unterberger*

The Monroe Brothers, Vol. 2: Just a Song of Old Kentucky / Jun. 12, 2001 / Rounder ♦♦♦♦
Although the Monroe Brothers initially made their name singing gospel, *Vol. 2* of Rounder's series features mostly secular material. All 15 sides (including a few on *Vol. 1*) were recorded during two "quick and dirty" sessions in June and October 1936, most of them in a single take. Still, the playing is tight and the material generally excellent, highlighted by "Where Is My Sailor Boy?" (also known as "What Does the Deep Sea Say?") and Monroe's first recording of "Roll in My Sweet Baby's Arms." "Will the Circle Be Unbroken," heard here in its original 1912 incarnation, might prove to be a revelatory listen for anyone familiar only with A.P. Carter's adaptation. —*Jim Smith*

Bill Monroe

b. Sep. 13, 1911, Rosine, KY, **d.** Sep. 9, 1996, Springfield, TN
Mandolin, Vocals, Fiddle, Guitar, Leader / Bluegrass, Traditional Bluegrass, Bluegrass-Gospel
Bill Monroe is the father of bluegrass. He invented the style, invented the name, and for the great majority of the 20th century, embodied the art form. Beginning with his Blue Grass Boys in the '40s, Monroe defined a hard-edged style of country that emphasized instrumental virtuosity, close vocal harmonies, and a fast, driving tempo. The musical genre took its name from the Blue Grass Boys, and Monroe's music forever has defined the sound of classical bluegrass—a five-piece acoustic string band, playing precisely and rapidly, switching solos and singing in a plaintive, high lonesome voice. Not only did he invent the very sound of the music, Monroe was the mentor for several generations of musicians. Over the years, Monroe's band hosted all of the major bluegrass artists of the '50s and '60s, including Flatt & Scruggs, Reno & Smiley, Vassar Clements, Carter Stanley, and Mac Wiseman. Though the lineup of the Blue Grass Boys changed over the years, Monroe always remained devoted to bluegrass in its purest form.

Monroe was born into a musical family. His father had been known around their hometown of Rosine, KY, as a step-dancer, while his mother played a variety of instruments and sang. His uncle, Pendelton Vanderver, was a locally renowned fiddler. Both of his older brothers, Harry and Birch, played fiddle, while his brother Charlie and sister Bertha played guitar. Bill himself became involved with music as a child, learning the mandolin at the age of ten. Following the death of his parents while he was a pre-adolescent, Monroe went to live with his Uncle Pen. Soon, he was playing in his uncle's band at local dances, playing guitar instead of mandolin. During this time, Monroe met a local blues guitarist called Arnold Shultz, who became a major influence on the budding musician. When Monroe turned 18, he moved to East Chicago, IN, where his brothers Birch and Charlie were working at an oil refinery. Monroe also got a job at the Sinclair oil refinery and began playing with his brothers in a country string band at night. Within a few years, they performed on the *Barn Dance* on WLS Chicago, which led to the brothers' appearance in a square dance revue called the WLS Jamboree in 1932. The Monroes continued to perform at night, but Birch left the band in 1934. Ironically, it was just before the group landed a sponsorship of the Texas Crystals Company, which made laxatives. Charlie and Bill decided to continue performing as the Monroe Brothers.

The Monroe Brothers began playing in other states, including radio shows in Nebraska, Iowa, and both North and South Carolina. Such exposure led to record label interest, but the Monroe Brothers were initially reluctant to sign a recording contract. After some persuasion, they inked a deal with RCA-Victor's Bluebird division and recorded their first session in February of 1936. One of the songs from the sessions, "What Would You Give in Exchange," became a minor hit and the duo recorded another 60 tracks for Bluebird over the next two years.

In the beginning of 1938, Bill and Charlie parted ways, with Charlie forming the Kentucky Pardners. Bill assembled his own band with the intention of creating a new form of country that melded old-time string bands with blues and challenged the instrumental abilities of the musicians. Initially, he moved to Little Rock, where he formed the Kentuckians, but that band was short-lived. He then relocated to Atlanta, where he formed the Blue Grass Boys and began appearing on the Crossroad Rollies radio program. Monroe debuted on the *Grand Ole Opry* in October of 1939, singing "New Muleskinner Blues." It was a performance that made Monroe's career as well as established the new genre of bluegrass. In the early '40s, Monroe & the Blue Grass Boys spent some time developing their style, often sounding similar to other contemporary string bands. The most notable element of the band's sound was Monroe's high, piercing tenor voice and his driving mandolin. The Blue Grass Boys toured with the *Grand Ole Opry's* road shows and appeared weekly on the radio. Between 1940 and 1941, he cut a number of songs for RCA-Victor, but wartime restrictions prevented him from recording for several years. The classic lineup of the Blue Grass Boys fell into place in 1944, when guitarist/vocalist Lester Flatt and banjoist Earl Scruggs joined a lineup that already included Monroe, fiddler Chubby Wise, and bassist Howard Watts. This is the group that supported Monroe when he returned to the studio in 1945, recording a number of songs for Columbia. Early in 1946, he had his first charting hit with "Kentucky Waltz," which climbed to number three; it was followed by the number five hit "Footprints in the Snow."

Throughout 1946, the Blue Grass Boys were one of the most popular acts in country music, scoring hits and touring to large crowds across America. At each town they played, the band would perform underneath a large circus tent they set up themselves; the tent would also host a variety of other attractions, including Monroe's baseball team, which would play local teams before the concert began. During the late '40s, the Blue Grass Boys remained a popular act, landing five additional Top 20 singles. Numerous other acts began imitating Monroe's sound, most notably the Stanley Brothers. Flatt & Scruggs left the Blue Grass Boys in 1948 to form their own band. Their departure ushered in an era of stagnation for Monroe. After Flatt & Scruggs parted ways from his band, he left Columbia Records in 1949 because they had signed the Stanley Brothers, who he felt were simply imitating his style. The following year, he signed with Decca Records, who tried to persuade Monroe to attempt some mainstream-oriented productions. He went as far as cutting a few songs with an electric guitar, but he soon returned to his pure bluegrass sound. At these sessions, he did meet Jimmy Martin, who became his supporting vocalist in the early '50s.

Throughout the '50s—indeed, throughout the rest of his career—Monroe toured relentlessly, performing hundreds of shows a year. In 1951, Monroe opened a country music park at Bean Blossom, IN; over the years, the venue featured performances from a number of bluegrass acts. Monroe suffered a serious car accident in January of 1953, which sidelined his career for several months. The following year, Elvis Presley performed Monroe's "Blue Moon of Kentucky" at his one and only *Grand Ole Opry* appearance, radically reworking the arrangement; Presley apologized for his adaptation, but Monroe would later perform the same arrangement at his concerts.

Monroe released his first album, *Knee Deep in Bluegrass*, in 1958, the same year he appeared on the country singles chart with "Scotland"; the number 27 single was his first hit in over a decade. However, by the late '50s his stardom was eclipsed by Flatt & Scruggs. Monroe was not helped by his legendary stubbornness. Numerous musicians passed through his band because of his temperament and his quest for detail, he rarely granted press interviews and would rarely perform on television; he even canceled a concert at Carnegie Hall because he believed the promoter, Alan Lomax, was a communist. In the '60s, Monroe received a great career boost from the folk music revival, which made him popular with a new generation of listeners. Thanks to his new manager, ex-Greenbriar Boys member Ralph Rinzler, Monroe played bluegrass festivals across the U.S., frequently on college campuses.

In 1967, he founded his own bluegrass festival, the Bill Monroe Bean Blossom Festival, at his country music park, which continued to run into the '90s. In 1970, he was inducted into the Country Music Hall of Fame; the following year, the Nashville Songwriters Association International Hall of Fame. Throughout the '70s, he toured constantly. In 1981, Monroe was diagnosed with cancer and underwent treatment for the disease successfully. After his recovery, he resumed his busy touring schedule, which he kept into the '90s. In 1991, he had surgery for a double coronary bypass, but he quickly recovered and continued performing and hosting weekly at the *Grand Ole Opry*. In 1993, the Grammys gave Monroe a Lifetime Achievement Award. After suffering a stroke in early 1996, Monroe died on September 9, 1996, four days short of his 85th birthday. *—Stephen Thomas Erlewine*

Live Duet Recordings 1963–1980 / 1963-1980 / Smithsonian Folkways ✦✦✦✦✦
Any time two greats who admire each other and are musically compatible team together, the results are usually mutually beneficial. That was true for Bill Monroe and Doc Watson, whose spirited union on this 17-song disc is a sampler of American musical styles. They ripped through bluegrass, folk, blues, spirituals, mountain tunes, work songs, reels and breakdowns. Monroe's mandolin and Watson's guitar playing were masterful, wondrous and performed without any trace of self-indulgence. Their vocals were also delivered with ease, fluidity and conviction, the product of two performers completely at ease with themselves and only interested in spotlighting the material. *—Ron Wynn*

Bean Blossom / 1973 / MCA ✦✦✦✦✦
There is very little in the world quite like a good, live bluegrass album, and this is as good as it gets. The album was recorded in 1973 at the seventh annual Bill Monroe Bluegrass Festival in Bean Blossom, IN, and features, alongside Monroe, most of the greats of early bluegrass, still kicking in the 1970s-Jim & Jesse, Jimmy Martin, James Monroe, Lester Flatt & the Nashville Grass, and 12 of the period's greatest fiddlers. The only notably absent figures of the classic bluegrass canon are the Stanley Brothers and Earl Scruggs; Carter Stanley died in 1966, and Scruggs, who had recently broken from Flatt to pursue more "modern" sounds in bluegrass music, was still getting the silent treatment from Monroe for leaving his Blue Grass Boys in the first place. Curly Ray Cline, Clarence "Tater" Tate, Tex Logan, Kenny Baker, and the other eight fiddlers play simultaneously on three instrumental standards, "Soldier's Joy," "Grey Eagle," and "Down Yonder," backing Monroe on the album's final track, a lively and unforgettable "Swing Low, Sweet Chariot." The music is played, for the most part, at a tightly reined turbo speed and, along with the steady claps and yells and sure-enough screams of an enormously rowdy audience, makes for about the most exciting 75 minutes of music imaginable. *Bean Blossom* captures the true, original spirit of the music created by Monroe as much or more than any other album, and provides a sturdy backbone to any bluegrass collection. *—Burgin Mathews*

Bill Monroe & Friends / 1984 / MCA ✦✦✦
Bill Monroe & Friends features the "Father of Bluegrass" on ten duets with such stalwarts of old-time music as Barbara Mandrell and the Gatlin Brothers. It's an all-acoustic affair that stays fairly true to Monroe's vision (with the exception of Johnny Cash's contribution, "I Still Miss Someone," which is straight country). It is fun to hear ultra-commercial artists like Mandrell and the Gatlins in this setting, but other guests, including Ricky Skaggs, Emmylou Harris, and John Hartford, didn't have to make as much of a stretch. Each track begins with a spoken intro in which Monroe thanks the artist(s) for appearing, followed by humble declarations of respect by the guest(s). *Bill Monroe & Friends* hangs together better than many such all-star packages, since most of the guests conform to Monroe's style instead of asserting their own in an ersatz bluegrass context, so in that sense it is very successful. Ultimately, the album is a satisfying tribute that is much better than one might think from looking at the track list. *—Greg Adams*

Bill Monroe at His Best / 1989 / Highland ✦✦
The title of *Bill Monroe at His Best* is a bit of a misnomer. Although this is fine Monroe—and he never was particularly bad—it isn't the best way to hear him, since the audio quality is terrible and the presentation is shoddy. There are good performances of "Muleskinner Blues," "Blue Moon of Kentucky," "Uncle Pen," "I Saw the Light" and "Bluegrass Breakdown," among many others, but there are better performances and collections on the market. *—Stephen Thomas Erlewine*

Columbia Historic Edition / 1989 / Columbia ✦✦✦✦✦
Columbia Historic Edition has a nice selection of ten songs that Bill Monroe cut for Columbia in the early '40s, including "Kentucky Waltz," "Blue Yodel No. 4 (California Blues)," "Bluegrass Special." Several hits are missing and there are several compilations released in the '90s that cover the same ground more thoroughly, but this record remains an enjoyable listen. *—Thom Owens*

Live at the Opry: Celebrating 50 Years on the Grand Ole Opry / 1989 / MCA ✦✦✦
Recorded live in 1989, Monroe has by this time turned over a majority of lead vocal turns to guitarist Tom Ewing. But the music proves how vibrant and aggressive Monroe's mandolin skills remain. It also features one fantastic cut from a 1948 *Opry* date. *—Michael McCall*

☆ **Bluegrass 1950–1958** / 1990 / Bear Family ✦✦✦✦✦
In 1950, Bill Monroe had been on his own with the Blue Grass Boys for over 11 years and had been a *Grand Ol Opry* member for over ten. More importantly, he had had a successful run with Columbia records and had left it, as his music had continued to develop for what he perceived to a brighter, more lucrative future with Decca in 1950. As usual, Monroe's instinct was correct. The 103 selections compiled here are from Monroe's most fertile, creative period, many of the songs recorded during this era became his signature tracks, such as "Uncle Pen," "Raw Hide," "Get Down on Your Knees and Pray," "Little Georgia Rose," "On and On," "Roanoke," "The Little Girl and the Dreadful Snake," "Kentucky Waltz," and many others. It was while at Decca that he introduced and recorded his original and trademark mandolin tuning—where instead of four pairs of strings tuned to the same pitches as a violin, he tuned several pairs of strings to two different notes that added the otherworldly timbres to his "high lonesome" sound. In addition to Monroe's recording with the Blue Grass Boys, there are a number of sessions here that put Monroe in the solo spotlight with some of Nashville's hottest session cats, in an attempt by Decca to put Monroe's music in a more modern and mainstream country setting. What is most noteworthy about the period of recordings here, however—besides the tracks themselves—are the musicians that played with Monroe during those very fertile and adventurous years. Guitarists included none other than Jimmy Martin from 1950-1954, then Carter Stanley briefly before Eddie Mayfield signed on, as did Jackie Phelps for a time, and Doug Kershaw. Bassists Ernie Newton and Bessie Lee Mauldin joined the

band for the first time on these recordings, as did Buddy Killen briefly, and then Culley Holt. Fiddle players were plentiful and stunning during the '50s. Monroe certainly had the pick of the crop in Vassar Clements, Charley Cline, Bobby Hicks, and others. And banjo pickers, while hard to come by still in that three-finger style, were as fine as they came in Rudy Lyle, Don Stover, and Joe Stuart. There is the association here with legendary producer Owen Bradley as a sideman toward the end of the '50s, and the influence of Monroe on the music of the time, where his main competition, Flatt & Scruggs, grudgingly (briefly) adopted Monroe's Nashville style to further their own careers, and the spin-offs by Jimmy Martin and others began successful recording careers as well. The story the recordings themselves tell is one of ambition, vision, and restlessness. The songs come in strange batches: There are the numerous co-writes with Hank Williams, sometimes credited, other times willfully—but for no known reason—obscured in their authorship. But Monroe's own writing was red-hot as well. His own compositions easily overshadow anything he covered during these years. Monroe was hunting ever deeper and wider for the elusive element that was the very grain of his style of music. He fought hard to keep it contemporary while not giving up anything in return. While it is not explained in the liner notes, his two Decca sessions with Nashville studio cats were perhaps a compromise Monroe himself made to keep the music of the Blue Grass Boys pure. These sessions, five and seven, included many fine songs, including "Sailor's Plea," "Highway of Sorrow," "My Carolina Sunshine Girl," "Peach Picking Time in Georgia," and others, but only three of them were ever issued before the compilation of this box, the rest, as fine as they were, left in the bins and the liner notes in the book, as fine as they are does not explain why the choices were made at the time to leave them on the shelf. In all, this is a stunning collection of Monroe's music at the beginning of his modern era, his first fully mature recordings that would prove so timeless and influential are here, not on the Columbia recordings. The sound here is also, for the most part, pristine, and never less than very good, with great balancing and equalization. As is customary with Bear Family, the book is chock-full of information and complete session notes making it an indispensable package, and, along with its companion set, from 1959-1969, the only recordings by Monroe anybody would ever need to really take in his contribution. *—Thom Jurek*

Cryin' Holy Unto the Lord / 1991 / MCA ♦♦♦

An all-gospel album propped up with some stellar guests, it includes Ricky Skaggs, Ralph Stanley, the Osborne Brothers, Jim & Jesse McReynolds, and Mac Wiseman. *—Michael McCall*

★ **Country Music Hall of Fame** / 1991 / MCA ♦♦♦♦♦

Bill Monroe made his most famous and popular—and arguably his best—recordings after he signed to Decca Records in 1950. For the next 40 years, he cut a number of classics, and 16 of his finest tracks are collected on *Country Music Hall of Fame*. The original versions of many of Monroe's best-known songs, including "New Mule Skinner Blues" and "Uncle Pen," are included, as well as his popular remake of his standard "Blue Moon of Kentucky." Of course, with a career as long and varied as Monroe's, it's hard to boil it down to just 16 tracks and, inevitably, some of the latter-day cuts won't please some dedicated fans. Nevertheless, it's hard to beat *Country Music Hall of Fame* as a single-disc introduction to one of the greatest musicians in country music history. *—Stephen Thomas Erlewine*

Mule Skinner Blues / 1991 / Roadracer ♦♦♦

Mule Skinner Blues contains the first recordings that Bill Monroe made with the Blue Grass Boys in 1940 and 1941 for RCA. On these recordings of the earliest and loosest bluegrass band, Monroe is wearing his blues, old-time, and even swing influences on his sleeve. *—Mark A. Humphrey*

Bluegrass 1959–1969 / 1991 / Bear Family ♦♦♦♦♦

For starters, the only reason this four-CD box didn't garner a perfect score was that the band Monroe led in the early '50s is a tough one to beat—especially since it contained Jimmy Martin. Musically, the songs Bill Monroe recorded during this very difficult period for bluegrass music—rock & roll was killing off country, as well as a host of pop music, and had all but finished off Western swing—were every bit as compelling as the earlier ones and moved into the gorgeous, grainy space that offered a pure view of his commitment to the music. As the liner notes attest, the early '60s were very difficult for the Blue Grass Boys on the concert circuit. They often traveled days at a time to make one gig, and musicians got paid for the time they actually worked rather than a steady salary. Recordings, too, were fewer and farther between, but each of them seemed to count for so much more. These were the years that Monroe hooked up with Owen Bradley—who produced the majority of these sessions (Harry Silverstein did the rest), the man who would finally put Monroe back on the charts chasing his arch rivals Flatt & Scruggs—who had embraced the folk revival movement in its entirety and were in turn embraced by it; they never lacked for a place to play and charted no less than 13 times in the same period. This is also the time Monroe met and befriended Ralph Rinzler from New York, who ran a group called "The Friends of Old Time music." Rinzler became involved with booking Monroe and his recording session with Bradley. The first real fruit of the association came with "Gotta Travel On," which charted number 15 with *Billboard*, and was followed up with "Come Go With Me" a full year before Marty Robbins recorded it. It also landed in the Top 50. This box tells that story, and tracks the confounding path of the complete sessions of those years as much of that the music found here never made it onto domestic LPs or CDs. For starters, there are songs such as "Dark as the Night, Blue as the Day," which ranks among one of Monroe's finest vocal performances. Of the 111 performances found here, among many alternate takes, unissued tracks, and domestically unissued sides, there are none left wanting. There is no substandard Bill Monroe material during these leaner years at all. As a plus, many of the music's most well-known performers today began with Monroe at this time, and many of the newgrass revival types were short- or long-term members of the Blue Grass Boys and appear here, including Vassar Clements, Peter Rowan, Buddy Spicher, Roland White, Vic Jordan, Richard Greene, Jackie Phelps, Joe Stuart, and many others. While influenced deeply by Monroe, they were also able, in small ways, sometimes intangibly, to influence his evolving sound. But it is the sound that matters here. While Flatt & Scruggs and others were embracing new trends in pop, folk, and country music, Monroe refused to integrate his music; though the '60s were tumultuous times, Monroe stayed close to the heart of his original bluegrass and old-time music and put it in anybody's face that would book him. As a result, many of the sides here are timeless, and with the possible exception of recording technology and studio sound, they could have been recorded at the time of the Carter Family. There is something that enters Monroe's voice about 1965, which is a permanent moan toward the past. In all these four CDs represent the second part of a long story that the folks at Bear Family are hell bent on telling, or letting it be told through the music. Their packaging as always is superb, and the liner notes by Charles Wolfe and Neil Rosenberg are flawlessly researched and written, as are the session notes taken from the master tapes themselves and the session notes by Bradley or Silverman. Truly inspiring is what this is. *—Thom Jurek*

★ **The Essential Bill Monroe (1945–1949)** / 1992 / Columbia/Legacy ♦♦♦♦♦

On the surface, *The Essential Bill Monroe (1945-1949)* seems like the perfect compilation, containing 40 tracks of Monroe and the Blue Grass Boys' Columbia recordings. However, the set wasn't executed with care—no less than 16 of these songs are represented with alternate takes, not the original versions. Though these alternates are interesting, they don't have a place in a set like this, which purports to be an extensive *introduction*, not an exhaustive compilation of Monroe's complete recordings; the alternates would have been more acceptable if they were placed in conjunction with the master takes. Still, *The Essential Bill Monroe* is a necessary set for bluegrass historians, since it does contain the bulk of his groundbreaking '40s recordings, including versions of "Blue Moon of Kentucky," "Kentucky Waltz," and "Rocky Road Blues." It's just not quite as good as it could have been. [The 16 master takes that were not included on this box were later issued by Columbia as the single-disc *16 Gems* collection.] *—Stephen Thomas Erlewine*

Blue Moon of Kentucky / 1993 / MCA ♦♦♦

Though terribly brief, at less than 30 minutes in length, this compilation is a consistently enjoyable listen from start to finish. None of the ten tracks are particularly rare, but all are classic Monroe, from the standard "Blue Moon of Kentucky" and "Kentucky Waltz" to the driving "Toy Heart" and "Molly and Tenbrooks (The Race Horse Song)." That said, this set is a decent companion piece to the more complete collections on the market, as the majority of the material here isn't generally featured on the better-known compilations. *—Matt Fink*

Live Recordings 1956–1959 / 1993 / Smithsonian Folkways ♦♦♦

The 27 numbers presented here offer Monroe in more intimate settings, including workshops, jam sessions and live performances where he's casually swapping yarns, offering anecdotes, and displaying the blistering, yet folksy and down-home style that's made him a musical legend. His group included a number of marvelous players and future stars, such as Del McCoury, Peter Rowan, Bill Keith, and Tex Logan. Monroe was also playing with brothers Charlie and Birch. This is 75 minutes of breakdowns, folk tunes, railroad and work songs, such classics as "Blue Grass Stomp" and "Blue Moon of Kentucky" and many others performed in a loose, next-door neighbor atmosphere. *—Ron Wynn*

☆ **The Music of Bill Monroe** / 1994 / MCA ♦♦♦♦♦

A four-disc set covering his entire career from 1936 to 1994, this is a meticulously remastered and researched four hours and 20 minutes of music and features important recordings from seven decades of recordings for RCA, Columbia, Decca and MCA. It's an exceptional box set, put together with great care and knowledge, and it's essential for any fan of bluegrass or traditional country music. *—Michael McCall*

Bluegrass 1970–1979 / 1995 / Bear Family ♦♦♦♦♦

Bluegrass (1970-1979) is a four-disc box set containing all of Monroe's '70s recordings for Decca, including several unreleased cuts and a live album featuring Jim & Jesse, James Monroe, Jimmy Martin, Lester Flatt, and Carl Jackson. By the time he made these recordings, Monroe was no longer making any innovations with his music. Instead, he just demonstrated his skill and artistry—the music on *Bluegrass (1970-1979)* is for aficionados, the kind of listener that can discern subtle differences between supporting bands and solos. Overall, the material on the box isn't as strong as the previous two box sets, but any Monroe completist will not be disappointed by the set. *—Stephen Thomas Erlewine*

☆ **16 Gems** / 1996 / Columbia/Legacy ♦♦♦♦♦

Sony's decision to use 16 alternate takes for the double-CD *Essential* collection was disagreeable to some completists. That omission is rectified by *16 Gems*, which makes all 16 of the official versions of those tunes available on CD, and creates a useful adjunct to the *Essential* set for collectors. On its own merits, it's hardly dismissable, with an appeal not limited to Monroe obsessives. Spanning 1945-1949, it includes such notable cuts as "Kentucky Waltz" and "Blue Grass Special." *—Richie Unterberger*

The Essential Bill Monroe & Monroe Brothers / Apr. 29, 1997 / RCA ♦♦♦♦♦

The Essential Bill Monroe & the Monroe Brothers chronicles Monroe's very first recordings from the late '60s. Selecting 24 highlights, including nine selections from the Monroe Brothers, from the 60-plus tracks he recorded for Bluebird, *The Essential* is the best single-disc overview of the beginning of Monroe's career and the roots of bluegrass, featuring such classics as "Mule Skinner Blues," "In the Pines" and "Crying Holy Unto My Lord." These are neither the best nor the best-known versions, yet they are historically invaluable, demonstrating the birthing pangs of bluegrass. —*Stephen Thomas Erlewine*

The Early Years / Jul. 14, 1998 / Vanguard ♦♦♦♦

Featuring an excellent cross-section of tracks from the definitive 1945-1949 period, *The Early Years* charts Bill Monroe's evolving sound through Western swing-influenced pieces, waltzes, blues, spirituals, ballads, and instrumentals. Though there are definitely far more comprehensive collections on the market, and the tracks here aren't particularly rare, *The Early Tapes* does a good job of representing Monroe's early recordings, the inclusion of Flatt & Scruggs, and the period following their departure. The material included is first-rate, with "Blue Moon of Kentucky," "Toy Heart," and the sharp "Blue Grass Breakdown" among the 14 tracks included. Good liner notes also make this an excellent introductory collection. —*Matt Fink*

☆ **The Father of Bluegrass: Early Years 1940–1947** / Jul. 20, 1999 / ASV ♦♦♦♦♦

Containing Monroe's first hit, "Mule Skinner Blues," as well as classic performances like "Blue Moon of Kentucky" and "Footprints in the Snow," *Father of Bluegrass* is an outstanding sampler that follows the the Blue Grass Boys through their first three lineups. It is especially valuable for its inclusion of 12 of Monroe's 1940-1941 recordings for RCA-Victor, which, while they may not be his most famous work, are nonetheless exhilarating sides that set the stage for the Maddox Brothers and just about every other slap-bass boogie outfit in the country. There's also ten tracks' worth of material from the Flatt & Scruggs-era band, rounding out a collection that says everything you need to know about this period in Monroe's development. —*Jim Smith*

20th Century Masters—The Millennium Collection: The Best of Bill Monroe / Oct. 5, 1999 / MCA ♦♦♦

MCA's *20th Century Masters: The Millennium Collection* is a good, basic collection of many of the best-known recordings of Bill Monroe's best-known songs, including "Blue Moon of Kentucky," "In the Pines," "New Mule Skinner Blues," "Uncle Pen," "I'm Sitting on Top of the World," "I Saw the Light," and "My Sweet Blue-Eyed Darlin'." These may not be his most historically important recordings, and undeniably there are some classic songs missing, but this should satisfy casual listeners on a tight budget. —*Stephen Thomas Erlewine*

Live, Vol. 1 / May 15, 2001 / Rural Rhythm ♦♦♦♦

This is relatively late-period live Monroe (recorded six years before his death), but don't think there are any signs of age in the performance. This double-CD set, from Monroe's Bean Blossom Festival in Indiana, captures him at 79, still completely vital, with fleet fingers and that trademark high, lonesome voice, leading the umpteenth incarnation of the Blue Grass Boys. As always, they're up to the mark, even if they're not the big names of yesteryear. But Tom Ewing, Blake Williams, Tater Tate, and Billy Rose do a fine job and establish their own presence among the shadows of the greats. However wonderful they might be, though, they really have only one function, and that's to back up Monroe, who's the undoubted star. There's a good mix of sings and instrumentals and of the sacred and the secular, and it's interesting to note just how many truly familiar pieces there are in his repertoire, like "Uncle Pen," one of his real signature tunes; "Muleskinner Blues"; and the famous "Rawhide." Inevitably, Monroe ends with "Roll in My Sweet Baby's Arms" to close out another excellent set. But excellence was always his benchmark, and the fact that he demanded a lot of both himself and the people around him is apparent here. Everything is spot-on, the musicians can turn on a dime, and the master can still play a mandolin like no other. —*Chris Nickson*

Blue Moon of Kentucky 1936-1949 / 2002 / Bear Family ♦♦♦♦♦

RCA Country Legends / Jun. 11, 2002 / RCA ♦♦♦♦

Bill Monroe is one of the most influential and important American musicians to ever pick up an instrument. He is undoubtedly the father of bluegrass and at least an uncle of country. This set captures Monroe near the beginning of his long and storied career and does a nice job showing the roots of bluegrass. The 16 tracks include many classic songs like "Orange Blossom Special," "Mule Skinner Blues (Blue Yodel No. 6)," and "In the Pines" and encompass Monroe's entire 1940-1941 tenure at RCA. This set is a not an essential purchase; a collection of Monroe's Columbia years would fit that bill. However, it is a good set for those who wish to dig a little deeper. —*Tim Sendra*

★ **The Very Best of Bill Monroe and His Blue Grass Boys** / Aug. 27, 2002 / MCA ♦♦♦♦♦

Bill Monroe's recorded legacy resides in the vaults of three major labels. His RCA Victor recordings are controlled by BMG, his Columbia sides are in the possession of Sony, and his Decca/MCA tracks are claimed by Universal. Monroe signed to Decca in November 1949 at the age of 38 and remained with it and its successor, MCA, until his death in 1996. His catalog with the label is vast, but uneven. In its strategy of putting into the marketplace compilations at different price points, MCA issued a four-disc box set, *The Music of Bill Monroe*, in 1994 and a discount-priced collection, *20th Century Masters—The Millennium Collection: The Best of Bill Monroe*, in 1999. *The Very Best of Bill Monroe and His Blue Grass Boys* supersedes the label's now out-of-print 1991 album *Country Music Hall of Fame* as a single-disc, full-priced examination of his Decca/MCA years. It chooses 22 tracks at a running time of less than an hour, ranging from Monroe's first recording session for Decca in 1950 to a 1981 MCA session. Since Monroe didn't really score hits in this period (his two country chart entries, "Scotland" and "Gotta Travel On," are included), the compiler must make many subjective choices to augment certain obvious favorites such as "Uncle Pen," and Mary Katherine Aldin has leaned toward familiar songs from the pens of such well-known figures as Hank Williams ("I Saw the Light") and Jimmie Rodgers ("New Mule Skinner Blues"). She has also included four re-recordings of songs that were successful for Monroe on Columbia in the 1940s. And she has avoided chronological sequencing in favor of a mixed approach. The result is more a sampler than a real best-of, only emphasizing the necessity for the Monroe fan to obtain collections from each of the labels for which Monroe recorded. —*William Ruhlmann*

Anthology / Apr. 22, 2003 / MCA Nashville/Decca ♦♦♦♦♦

So much has been said about the founding father of bluegrass music, that it would be nice if there was an all-encompassing collection of Bill Monroe's music to accompany the legend. Although the nearly-correctly titled *Anthology* comes close, there is still a wealth of Columbia and RCA-Victor recordings missing from this Decca-centric collection which runs chronologically from 1950 to 1969 (with one final track from 1981). Unfortunately this means that the classic lineup of Lester Flatt and Earl Scruggs, with fiddler Chubby Wise and bassist Howard Watts is not represented. Still, bluegrass luminaries Vassar Clements, Jimmy Martin, Kenny Baker, Del McCoury, Peter Rowan, and many others all drifted in and out of the Blue Grass Boys during these 20-some years and make appearances on classic tracks like "Sally Goodin," "Uncle Pen," "Blue Moon of Kentucky" and "New Mule Skinner Blues". All told, this may be the perfect collection of Monroe's work for Decca but it falls only slightly short of being The Bill Monroe Anthology. —*Zac Johnson*

Charlie Monroe

b. Jun. 4, 1903, Rosine, KY, **d.** Sep. 27, 1975

Guitar, Vocals / Traditional Bluegrass, Old-Timey, Honky Tonk

The older brother of Bill Monroe, Charlie joined his younger brother in laying the foundation for bluegrass music. Although they only recorded together for two years, the ripples caused by Charlie & Bill Monroe's collaboration continue to be felt. Raised on a family farm in rural Kentucky, Charlie grew up in a musical home. After learning to sing hymns as children, via the traditional "sacred note" technique, each member of the Monroe family chose a musical instrument. Charlie and his sister Bertha chose guitar, while Birch opted for fiddle and Bill for the mandolin.

Although Charlie joined with Birch and Bill to form a band in the mid-'20s, and made his radio debut in 1927, he left with Birch to seek employment in the Midwest after the death of their parents. After temporarily stopping in Detroit, Charlie and Birch went on to work in the oil refineries of Hammond, Whiting, and East Chicago, IN. In 1929, they were joined by Bill, who found a job at a Sinclair refinery.

The three reunited Monroe brothers resumed their musical collaboration, performing at small clubs, dances, and house parties. While performing at a dance in 1932, the Monroes were overheard by Tom Owens, whose band had a feature slot on the radio show WSM *Barn Dance*. Impressed by their performance, Owens invited the Monroe brothers to join his group as dancers. The Monroes continued to dance with Owens' troupe for two years. The Monroes got their chance to be musicians again when they were hired to play on WAE in Hammond, IN, and WJKS in Gary, IN. Before long, Charlie and Bill were dreaming of playing music full-time. Their dreams became reality when Texas Crystals, a patent medicine company, offered to sponsor a radio show showcasing their music. When Birch turned down Charlie's invitation to join him on the show, the Monroe Brothers became a duo featuring Charlie & Bill. The duo was so successful that they soon moved to a larger radio station. The show was eventually expanded into a daily event broadcast by WBT in Charlotte, NC.

Although sponsorship of Charlie and Bill Monroe's show was dropped by Texas Crystals in 1936, it was quickly picked up by the Crazy Water Crystal Company. In addition to performing daily on the show, the Monroe Brothers performed on the weekly Saturday night show, *Crazy Barn Dance*. They also appeared on WFPC in Greenville, SC, and WPTF in Raleigh, NC. Charlie and Bill Monroe made their recording debut in February 1936, cutting several tracks in a Charlotte, NC, studio that were released on RCA's Bluebird label. A mixture of gospel and secular tunes, the tunes set the standard for bluegrass with their high harmony vocals, bass guitar runs, and hard-driving mandolin arrangements.

Their partnership, however, was increasingly strained as Bill became frustrated by Charlie's determination to sing lead on every tune. In 1938, the brothers went their separate ways, with Bill forming the Kentuckians, who later became the Blue Grass Boys, and Charlie forming the Kentucky Pardners. Among the many musicians who played with Charlie's band were guitarist and vocalist Lester Flatt and mandolin players Red Rector, Curly Seckler, and Ira Louvin. The Kentucky Pardners, who played a mixture of bluegrass and honky tonk-style country music, became one of the most successful tent shows and played continuously throughout the South and Midwest in the 1940s.

Charlie, who signed a solo contract with RCA Victor in 1946 and moved to Decca in 1950, wrote a large number of tunes, including "It's Only a Phonograph Record," "Who's Calling You Sweetheart Tonight," and "Rubber Neck Blues." Tired of non-stop touring, Monroe retired from music in 1957. Although he intended to remain on his farm, he left Kentucky to work for a lift company in Indiana after his wife was diagnosed with cancer. He remained within the company until his wife's death. Monroe remarried in 1969 and moved to Tennessee, and later to Reidville, NC. Monroe remained inactive until he was persuaded by Jimmy Martin to perform at the Gettysburg Bluegrass Festival in 1972. The response to their performance was so overwhelming that Monroe, often with Martin, continued to perform at similar festivals until 1974, when he was diagnosed with cancer. Monroe died on his farm in Reidville on September 27, 1975, and was buried in the Monroe family plot on Jerusalem Ridge in Rosine, KY. —*Craig Harris*

● **Vintage Radio 1944** / 1994 / Rebel ♦♦♦♦

Patsy Montana (Ruby Blevins)

b. Oct. 30, 1914, Hot Springs, AR, **d.** May 3, 1996

Vocals / Traditional Country, Cowboy, Yodeling

Patsy Montana was the first woman in country music to have a million-selling single—1935's "I Want to Be a Cowboy's Sweetheart"—and was a mainstay on *the National Barn Dance* on Chicago radio station WLS for many years. She might also have been country music's first female session musician. In the '30s and '40s she was the sweetheart of many a movie cowpoke, appearing in numerous western films, and her success encouraged the traditionally male-oriented country music business to welcome and respect the scores of female performers that followed her.

Patsy Montana was born Ruby Blevins in Hot Springs, AR, the 11th child and first daughter of a farmer, and she attended schools in President Bill Clinton's hometown of Hope. She was influenced early on by the music of Jimmie Rodgers, and as a child she learned to yodel and play organ, guitar, and violin. Dropping out of the University of Western Louisiana, she moved to California around 1930 with her older brother and his wife. Montana won a talent contest there and began appearing on a local radio station as "Rubye Blevins, the Yodeling Cowgirl from San Antone" (she thought the added "e" brought sophistication to her image). Appearing on station KMIC with western-music star Stuart Hamblen, she joined with two other female singers to form a group called the Montana Cowgirls. The presence of champion yodeler Monty Montana on the show inspired her to take Montana as her own last name, and Hamblen suggested the first name of Patsy because one of the other singers in the group was named Ruthie—the names Ruby and Ruthie sounded too similar on the radio.

In 1932 she returned to Arkansas for a visit and performed briefly on Shreveport, LA, radio station KWKH. Those performances caught the attention of Shreveport recording star, Jimmie Davis, who would go on to record "You Are My Sunshine" but at the time was in the midst of a series of often risqué blue-yodel recordings for the Victor label. Montana backed Davis on several recordings and then was given the chance to make a few of her own; her debut record, released in 1933, included "When the Flowers of Montana Are Blooming."

In 1933, Montana headed for Chicago to see the Century of Progress World's Fair and to audition at WLS. She got acquainted with a string band called the Kentucky Ramblers and signed on as the group's vocalist as it changed its name to the Prairie Ramblers to fit the increasingly cowboy-oriented programming at WLS. Soon she was a regular on *the National Barn Dance*, the variety show that at the time was the *Grand Ole Opry*'s biggest competitor and helped launch the careers of various western film stars. Despite her experience with the raunchy Davis, Montana had to leave the room when the Prairie Ramblers recorded some off-color numbers of their own under the name the Sweet Violet Boys. But she was at the microphone in 1935 to record the peppy polka-rhythm "I Want to Be a Cowboy's Sweetheart," which married the new dance energy of country music to a perfect set of Hollywood cowboy (or cowgirl) images. Recorded in New York on the ARC label, it became her signature song, but it was not her only hit; others included "Rodeo Sweetheart," "Montana Plains," and "I Want to Be a Cowboy's Dream." In 1939, she made her full-length feature film debut with Gene Autry in *Colorado Sunset*.

Montana moved to the Decca label in 1941, releasing a dozen singles during the war years. After a stint on the ABC radio network as leader of a program called *Wake Up and Smile* in 1946 and 1947, she returned to Arkansas to live on a farm with her husband, Paul Rose, and their two children, appearing on the radio daily in Hot Springs and many Saturdays on the *Louisiana Hayride*. Later she and her husband moved back to California. Over the years, Montana remained active in the music industry, appearing on many country music shows and continuing to record. In 1964, she cut a live album at the Matador Room in Safford, AZ; among her backing musicians was a young guitarist named Waylon Jennings. In the '80s and '90s, she recorded albums (several of them gospel) for a number of independent labels before her death on May 3, 1996. *—Sandra Brennan and James Manheim*

The New Sound of Patsy Montana / 1964 / Sims ♦♦♦

Columbia Historic Edition / 1984 / Columbia ♦♦♦♦

The Cowboy's Sweetheart / 1988 / Flying Fish ♦♦♦♦
These are late recordings by the Western radio star. The title track, from 1935, was the first million-selling female country vocal performance. *—Mark A. Humphrey*

★ **The Best of Patsy Montana** / Jul. 10, 2001 / Collectors' Choice Music ♦♦♦♦♦
Here is a reissue of great historical importance: the only CD anthology of the classic recordings of Patsy Montana, the first female country artist to enjoy a million-seller ("I Want to Be a Cowboy's Sweetheart") and the preeminent woman in early hillbilly music after the Carter Family gals. *The Best of Patsy Montana* has 24 of her seminal Vocalion and Conqueror recordings spanning the years 1935-1940, concluding with "I Want to Be a Cowboy's Dreamgirl," a barely rewritten reprise of her big hit. "The She Buckaroo" displays a proto-feminist outlook that balances the cowboy worship of "I Want to Be a Cowboy's Sweetheart," but most of the remaining material consists of straight Western fare. Although a glimpse at the record charts may suggest that Montana was merely a one-hit wonder, *The Best of Patsy Montana* belongs in the collection of any serious enthusiast of early C&W music. *—Greg Adams*

Montgomery Gentry

f. Lexington, KY
Group / Contemporary Country, New Traditionalist
Country duo Montgomery Gentry evoke the sound and spirit of Southern rockers like Lynyrd Skynyrd, the Marshall Tucker Band, and Charlie Daniels, painting themselves as rowdy redneck rebels who still hold small-town values. Eddie Montgomery and Troy Gentry first met in Early Tymz, a Lexington, KY, band led by Montgomery's brother, future country star John Michael Montgomery. Both Eddie and Troy had been performing on the local club scene since their teenage years, the former as a drummer in his father's band. After Early Tymz broke up, a new group called Young Country formed from its ashes, with John Michael billed out front. He eventually went solo, of course, and Montgomery Gentry first formed not long after, initially calling themselves Deuce.

After playing around Lexington for a time, Montgomery Gentry landed a deal with Columbia thanks to a showcase performance. Their debut album, *Tattoos & Scars*, was released in 1999 and made the country Top Ten on the strength of the Top 20 singles "Hillbilly Shoes" and "Daddy Won't Sell the Farm," plus the Top Five smash "Lonely and Gone" and the Charlie Daniels collaboration "All Night Long." They were named the CMA's Duo of the Year in 2000, breaking a run of eight consecutive years by Brooks & Dunn. The follow-up album, *Carrying On*, came out in 2001 and also made the country Top Ten and produced the number-two smash "She Couldn't Change Me." A third album, *My Town*, was completed quickly and released in 2002, bringing the duo their third Top Five hit in the title track. *—Steve Huey*

● **Tattoos & Scars** / Apr. 6, 1999 / Columbia ♦♦♦♦
With all of the comparisons to Southern rock legends Lynyrd Skynyrd, Marshall Tucker, Charlie Daniels, the Outlaws, and so forth, this solid, hardcore rockin' honky tonk duo and their amazing band is an entity unto themselves. Eddie Montgomery (brother of John Michael) and Troy Gentry are equal parts country music that comes from Merle Haggard, George Jones, Wynn Stewart, Dwight Yoakam, and even Hank Williams. At the same time, they play a scorching brand of rock & roll that has everything to do with the aforementioned heroes of the 1970s and the Allmans too because the blues are at the root of everything they do. This is an auspicious debut album, one that not only shows promise, but delivers the goods in the form of great songs written by a host of Nash Vegas' and Texas' finest—if unknown new breed—and absolutely tremendous performances. Check the hard rocking opener, "Hillbilly Shoes," with its flatpicking guitar intro supplanted by overdriven fiddles and screaming dual lead guitars. And "Trying to Survive" with its guitar, pedal steel, and piano fills is reminiscent of the feel, not sound, of Tucker's "Can't You See." It's easy to embrace Tim McGraw and a host of others who use rock & roll as way of framing their country music, but Montgomery Gentry don't use rock; they are a rock band who make country music, real country music. Check the gorgeous chorus on "Lonely and Gone" that is commenced with a heavy metal guitar intro only to become a gorgeous midtempo ballad. Other tracks, like "Self-Made Man," are pure modern honky tonk. Vocally, the harmonies between this pair are a perfect balance of beer and fine whiskey. Montgomery's rough hewn baritone and Gentry's almost unreal range and trademark phrasing make something highly original in the face of so much cookie-cutter Nash Vegas big-hatted crap. The funky blues on "Daddy Won't Sell the Farm" with those fiddles and pedal steels wrapping around a greasy keyboard line lead into a rebel Southern son's admiration for a man and a way of life that is quickly disappearing. The drums propel the tune forward, and the guitars fill what little space there is with rollin' and tumblin' blues. The Bakersfield honky tonk of "I've Loved a Lot More Than I've Hurt" is as traditional as it gets, and Jones or Yoakam could have cut it. The title track is a great morality tale, and "Trouble Is" is a Gentry showcase with his singing tenor in the hillbilly groove that is equal parts blues, tonkin' stride, and arena rock. Montgomery Gentry should be nothing less than amazing in a few years if they keep this up, because this is solid, ass-kickin' country-rock. This is one of the best pop records of the year. Period. *—Thom Jurek*

Carrying On / May 1, 2001 / Sony ♦♦♦
On their second album, Eddie Montgomery and Troy Gentry continue to resurrect the sound and persona of Southern rock and outlaw country performers like Charlie Daniels and the Marshall Tucker Band. They may not have been much involved in the songwriting for this album, managing one co-writing credit each along with Kenny Beard on "Lucky to Be Here" and spreading the rest of the writing among no less than 23 other names, but that large staff knew to craft a collection of songs full of boastful Southern pride and not a little belligerence. For the most part, the sentiments never go too far, restricting themselves to playful bluster, though on one occasion the duo takes on an issue it might have been better advised to leave alone. That's when, in "Carrying On," they sing, "It ain't nobody's business what kind of flag I fly 'cause that's my right." Getting into the Confederate flag controversy may well attract attention to them, but not necessarily the kind they want. Southern clannishness is one thing, but the Klan is another. That's the exception, however, since Montgomery Gentry usually is careful only to put on the airs of rebelliousness without actually being offensive. Similarly, the music never turns into real barroom stomp or bluesy country-rock, skirting the edge of a hard sound but never boiling over. That's why the correct comparisons are to softer acts like Charlie Daniels and Marshall Tucker rather than real rowdies like Hank Williams Jr. and Lynyrd Skynyrd. Next time around, the duo ought to try varying the message a little bit; all these songs about what he-men they are make it sound like they're trying to hard to be macho, especially when the music doesn't entirely back up the boasts. *—William Ruhlmann*

My Town / Aug. 27, 2002 / Sony ♦♦♦
The core of Montgomery Gentry's musical appeal lies in the duo's vocal contrast, alternating lead singing between the gruff low tenor of Eddie Montgomery and the sweeter high tenor of Troy Gentry. The core of their cultural appeal lies in another dichotomy, between the hell-raising and church-going aspects of stereotypical Southern rural life. "My Town," the leadoff track, title song, and advance single from their third album, concerns itself with the latter, depicting a small community in which you have to get up early on Sunday morning to be able to find a seat in church. But by the fifth track, the singers are having trouble keeping to the straight and narrow, deciding that they'll be "Bad for Good," and that song is a good candidate for a single, too. To a country fan, of course, there isn't that much of a conflict between the duo's rowdy Saturday night and reverent Sunday morning postures. In fact, they're two sides of the same coin. Similarly, to Montgomery Gentry, as to many fans, contemporary country music isn't just acoustic instruments and cheating songs, it's also the legacy of 1970s Southern rock. The session musicians number Allman Brothers Band alumni Chuck Leavell and Johnny Neel, and the album, which rocks harder as it goes along, concludes with a cover of "Good Clean Fun" from the Allmans' 1990 album, *Seven Turns*. Just as their image, with Montgomery decked out in a black jacket with tails and a big, flat-brimmed hat and Gentry in excessively casual wear, is calculated, so their musical approach is tempered. But the contradictions are the same ones their listeners live with every day. You may want to jump on the bar and yell "Hell Yeah," but "Montgomery Gentry supports responsible drinking," as a sleeve note discloses. And be early for church. *—William Ruhlmann*

John Michael Montgomery

b. Jan. 20, 1965, Danville, KY

Vocals / New Traditionalist, Contemporary Country

Part of the '90s wave of honky tonk hitmakers that brought country to new commercial heights, John Michael Montgomery made his name primarily as a romantic balladeer. Yet despite his sometime adult contemporary leanings, his vocal style remained solidly grounded in country tradition. Montgomery was born in 1965 in Danville, KY, near Lexington and learned guitar from his father, a local musician. He first performed in public at age five with his father's band, which also featured his mother on drums. By 15, he was performing regularly on the local scene and at 17 became the lead singer of a group with his father and brother after his parents divorced. Following high-school, he played around the local honky tonk circuit and was discovered at a favorite venue in Lexington, which led to a contract with Atlantic in 1991.

Montgomery issued his debut album in 1992, titling it after the lead single, "Life's a Dance." The song rocketed into the Top Five, and its follow-up, "I Love the Way You Love Me," went all the way to number one, helping the album climb into the country Top Five. That set the stage for 1994's *Kickin' It Up*, a bona fide, multi-platinum blockbuster that topped both the country and pop charts and made Montgomery a star. Three number-one country hits—"I Swear," "Be My Baby Tonight," and "If You've Got Love"—sprang from the album as well as another Top Five hit, "Rope the Moon." A self-titled 1995 follow-up also topped the country charts and kept Montgomery's hit streak alive with the number-one smashes "Sold (The Grundy County Auction Incident)" and "I Can Love You Like That," plus more Top Fivers in "No Man's Land," "Cowboy Love," and "Long as I Live." Late in 1995, Montgomery was forced to take time off for surgery to repair his vocal cords.

Montgomery recovered in time to put out *What I Do the Best* in 1996. "Friends" and "How Was I to Know" both hit number two, and "I Miss You a Little" was also a Top Ten hit. A *Greatest Hits* compilation was released in 1997, and Montgomery returned in 1998 with *Leave a Mark*, which found him continuing to move into more polished territory. "Cover You in Kisses" and "Hold on to Me" were the Top Five hits this time out. Things got even smoother on the very adult contemporary-styled *Home to You*, which appeared in 1999 and whose title cut reached number two on the country charts. Still, Montgomery's crossover-friendly approach was beginning to affect his sales in the country marketplace. *Brand New Me* (2000) featured a higher percentage of uptempo tracks, and it peaked at number two on the country charts; plus, his duet with Alison Krauss, "The Little Girl," gave him another number-one hit. His next album, 2002's *Pictures*, was an attempt to move into more mature, adult territory. —*Steve Huey*

Life's a Dance / 1992 / Atlantic ◆◆◆

Montgomery's baritone lends itself well to the romantic songs, ensuring his success in the heartthrob-heavy country field of the early '90s. That he also does some competent Oklahoma swing counts in his favor. —*Brian Mansfield*

Kickin' It Up / Jan. 25, 1994 / Atlantic ◆◆◆◆◆

As the title suggests, Montgomery kicks up the tempos and reveals a stronger country-rock bent. He still leans heavily on contemporary ballads ("I Swear," "Rope the Moon"), but proves just as capable on the brawnier songs. It became a number one album on the pop charts shortly after its release. —*Michael McCall*

John Michael Montgomery / Mar. 28, 1995 / Atlantic ◆◆◆◆◆

It doesn't really matter that *John Michael Montgomery* replicates the formula of its hit predecessor, *Kickin' it Up*. Even though it has the same country-pop ballads, slick country-rock and honky tonk numbers that made *Kickin' It Up* a monster commercial success, the record doesn't sound dull or repetitive. Most of the album's success is due to the clean, commercial production, which makes even the weak material entertaining. —*Stephen Thomas Erlewine*

What I Do the Best / Sep. 24, 1996 / Atlantic ◆◆◆

John Michael Montgomery's fourth album, *What I Do the Best*, doesn't tamper with his hitmaking blueprint at all. Essentially, it follows the same pattern as its three predecessors, relying equally on heart-tugging ballads and clean, uptempo neo-honky tonk and country-rock. Occasionally, the material is below par and Montgomery's delivery doesn't quite save the weaker songs, yet the best moments of *What I Do the Best* are among his best, blending well-written songs with crisp production and assured singing. —*Stephen Thomas Erlewine*

● **Greatest Hits** / Oct. 14, 1997 / Atlantic ◆◆◆◆◆

After only four albums and five years of recording, it may be a little soon for John Michael Montgomery to release a *Greatest Hits* album, yet this collection does everything it should do—it features all of Montgomery's biggest hits and best-known songs in one place, providing an excellent summary of the first part of his career, as well as an ideal introduction for listeners unacquainted with his brand of contemporary country. —*Thom Owens*

Leave a Mark / May 5, 1998 / Atlantic ◆◆◆◆

John Michael Montgomery didn't take the release of his career summary *Greatest Hits* as an opportunity to change direction and explore new musical territory. Instead, he continues with the slick contemporary country that made his reputation. Often, Montgomery's ballads are indistinguishable from MOR pop, and his uptempo numbers a similarly clean and well-produced. When the material is subpar, this can all sound homogenous, and there are times on *Leave a Mark* where everything blends together. Still, Montgomery is a professional vocalist, and he delivers a handful of surefire hits, like "Love Working on You," which makes the album worthwhile for longterm fans, even if they suggest he'll have to work harder to ensure career longevity. —*Thom Owens*

Home to You / May 25, 1999 / Atlantic ◆◆◆

John Michael Montgomery settled into a groove early into his career, choosing to never push things too far. He had an easygoing style and a mellow baritone that sounded equally good on country-rockers and love ballads. To the dismay of hardcore country purists, Montgomery chose to keep things easy—his rockers never pushed too hard and

his ballads were clean and calm. This inclination to keep things smooth only increased as his career progressed, and his sixth album, *Home to You*, is his smoothest yet. Nearly every song on the album is a love ballad, and all of them sound better-suited for adult contemporary radio than contemporary country radio (in the case of "Nothing Catches Jesus By Surprise," it could fit right into a CCM station's play list). Not that this is necessarily a bad thing, since Montgomery's strength has always been ballads, but the album winds up sounding very homogenous and bland after a while. It's hardly an unpleasant listen, yet few songs distinguish themselves from their peers. Those that do will undoubtedly sound fine on the inevitable second greatest-hits collection, but in this context they're part of the sonic fabric on an album that is essentially romantic country mood music. —*Stephen Thomas Erlewine*

Brand New Me / Sep. 19, 2000 / Atlantic ◆◆◆

Montgomery's eighth album *Brand New Me* will no doubt meet with the same kind of success many of his storytelling songs like "Hello L-O-V-E" and "Home to You" have before. But songs that tell a story and tug at the heartstrings are what he's about. And there isn't much that differs on this album from anything you've heard from Montgomery before. Produced by Buddy Cannon, Norrow Wilson, and Montgomery himself, fans will surely enjoy "Bus to Birmingham," a touching ballad about a man who has to let the love of his life go; "Even Then," another moving ballad about a man who can't love his partner enough; and, for fans looking for the upbeat Montgomery that gave you previous hits like Sold!" and "Cowboy Love," there's the likable "Brand New Me" and the catchy ditty "That's What I Like About You." —*Maria Konicki Dinoia*

Love Songs / Feb. 5, 2002 / Warner Bros. ◆◆◆

This romantically themed greatest-hits collection features most of John Michael Montgomery's best-known love songs, including "I Swear," "I Love the Way You Love Me," and "I Can Love You Like That." Sweet, idealistic songs like "Holding an Amazing Love," "Oh How She Shines," and "High School Heart" play to Montgomery's strengths as a vocalist; likewise, his distinctive, consistent style gives the collection a nice flow, despite the fact that it covers nearly a decade's worth of music. Though it doesn't paint as representative a picture of his work as his regular *Greatest Hits* compilation does, *Love Songs* does highlight one of the best facets of his music. —*Heather Phares*

Pictures / Oct. 8, 2002 / Warner Bros. ◆◆◆

Perhaps it's a sign that time is creeping along, but after ten years of success, John Michael Montgomery dilutes some of his lovable rascal persona with a more mature perspective on *Pictures*. The titles hint at his broadening focus: "Love and Alcohol," with its good-time beat and shouts of "Hey, bartender," admits right up front that the women get better looking with each new round. But on the title track, Montgomery offers grandkids yet to come and wedding pictures that are far from yellowed as measures of a life well spent, and on "I Wanna Be There" he similarly anticipates a future of idyllic fatherhood with his young daughter. He presents all of this with his reassuring baritone croon, backed by an idiomatically correct assembly of Nashville studio all-stars. If there's any distressing detail here, it's the formulaic writing. Each song, whether sentimental or mischievous in its intent, projects a one-dimensional image of a life concerned with nothing weightier than drinkin', dancin', drivin', or looking back on those wild days, or forward to a time when other things matter more. Attempts to push past these limits seem a little awkward; nobody who talks like the folks in these songs would say, as Montgomery does in "It Goes Like This," that some little hottie over there has a "thunderstorm of love" inside of her. On the other hand, these concerns are real to lots of people, and if they need a singer to articulate them in song, then *Pictures* serves that purpose. —*Robert L. Doerschuk*

Kevin Montgomery

Vocals / Contemporary Country

Nashville, New York, and Los Angeles all figure prominently into the musical landscapes that singer/songwriter Kevin Montgomery paints with his high lonesome voice and heartfelt lyrics. As the child of Buddy Holly's musical partner and Elvis Presley's backup singer, Montgomery had little choice in the matter of his musicality. With that bloodline, the nature angle is covered pretty well. As for the nurture side, growing up in Nashville set the rootsy Americana sound as the basis of Montgomery's work, while busking in subways adds New York's sly, street-smart sensibilities to the mix. The wide-open, sun-filled skies of Los Angeles top it all off with an optimism and melodicism reminiscent of Jackson Browne.

Montgomery made a strong debut in 1993 with *Fear Nothing* on A&M Records. It showcased a young talent with obvious potential, earned him slots fronting for labelmate Sheryl Crow and David Crosby, and garnered limited airplay on Triple-A radio. With that foundation, Montgomery bounced around for several years before departing A&M. He got himself onto a number of compilation discs, including the Buddy Holly tribute *Not Fade Away* where he duets with Mary-Chapin Carpenter. Montgomery also took some time to collaborate with folks like Lee Ann Womack, Cindy Alexander, Rodney Crowell, and Anna Wilson. Both Martina McBride and Juice Newton sought out Montgomery's tunes to cover. In 2000, *Another Long Story* came to light in the U.K. and Europe. A great collection of Montgomery's strongest work yet, it caught Paul McCartney's ear and got Montgomery invited to perform at the former Beatles' annual Buddy Holly birthday event in London. His popularity overseas has been further proven by the numerous television performances and sold-out concerts enjoyed on every visit. To capture the feel of his acoustic European shows, Montgomery recorded *Kevin Montgomery Live* at Nashville's legendary Bluebird Café in 2001. Also released in 2001 was the EP *Paint* which features a duet with Trisha Yearwood on the aptly titled "Tennessee Girl." That track was chosen by the BBC as their lead-in to the CMA Awards. —*Kelly McCartney*

Fear Nothing / Oct. 5, 1993 / A&M ◆◆◆

As far as first steps go, Kevin Montgomery's *Fear Nothing* is on fairly solid footing. He's a little bit country, owing not in small part to the fact that his father wrote songs for Buddy Holly. And he's a little bit rock & roll, perhaps credited to his mother's role as Elvis

Presley's backup singer. The opening track, "Red-Blooded American Boy," quite appropriately sums up Montgomery, title and all. It's a pretty song, thoughtful and melodic, not a whole lot of edge—signals that this is a nice guy, doing what he can, writing what he knows. You can tell he's just getting started, finding his way through the craft. He's young but smart enough to be leaning on some awfully talented crutches. No doubt A&M Records had no clue how to market Montgomery. If he had leaned a little more toward one side or the other, they would have had a shot, though it's not a very likely bet they would've taken it. Had it been a few years later when Montgomery was on a major label, he would have had an opening slot on a Faith Hill, Kelly Willis, or even a Chris Isaak tour. *—Kelly McCartney*

Melba Montgomery

b. Oct. 14, 1938, Iron City, TN

Vocals / Bluegrass, Traditional Bluegrass, Traditional Country

While a successful singer in her own right, Melba Montgomery is perhaps best remembered in tandem with her string of duet recordings with the likes of George Jones, Charlie Louvin, and Gene Pitney. Born October 14, 1938, in Iron City, TN, and raised in Florence, AL, Montgomery gained her first exposure to music through her father, a fiddler and guitarist who taught vocal lessons at the town's Methodist church. At the age of ten, she was given her own guitar, and a decade later, she and her brother won an amateur talent contest held at Nashville radio station WSM's Studio C, which then housed the *Grand Ole Opry.* Montgomery's performance so impressed contest judge Roy Acuff that he asked the young singer to replace his departing lead vocalist June Webb; she accepted and toured with Acuff for the next four years.

After going solo in 1962, Montgomery released a self-titled LP and then teamed for a series of duets with Jones. Their first joint effort, a rendition of Montgomery's self-penned "We Must Have Been Out of Our Minds," reached the Top Three in 1963, and the follow-up, "What's in Our Heart"/"Let's Invite Them Over," was a two-sided Top 20 hit. Between 1963 and 1967, the Jones-Montgomery team generated a total of five Top 40 hits and two LPs (1966's *Close Together* and 1967's *Let's Get Together*), and while Montgomery maintained a successful solo career during the same period, she remained best known as a duet singer and so recorded an album of collaborations with Pitney titled *Being Together* in 1966.

After a few minor solo hits in the late '60s, in 1970 Montgomery found new partners in Louvin and producer Pete Drake. The duo's first hit, "Something to Brag About," was also their biggest, and after a string of singles and a 1971 album—also titled *Something to Brag About*—she and Louvin parted ways, although Montgomery did continue on with Drake. In 1974, he produced her lone number-one hit, a rendition of Harlan Howard's "No Charge," culled from the LP *No Charge.* While she continued to record throughout the decade, subsequent albums like *Don't Let the Good Times Fool You* and *Aching Breaking Heart* found little commercial success, and by the 1980s Montgomery focused largely on touring and appearing at festivals. In 1988, she even published a cookbook of family recipes. *—Jason Ankeny*

Down Home / 1964 / United Artists ✦✦✦

America's Number One Country and Western Girl Singer / 1964 / United Artists ✦✦✦

Blue Grass Hootenanny / 1964 / United Artists ✦✦✦

I Can't Get Used to Being Lonely / 1965 / United Artists ✦✦✦

The Hallelujah Road / 1966 / Musicor ✦✦✦

Being Together / 1966 / Musicor ✦✦✦✦

Country Girl / 1966 / Musicor ✦✦✦

Melba Toast / 1967 / Musicor ✦✦✦✦

Don't Keep Me Lonely Too Long / 1967 / Musicor ✦✦✦

I'm Just Living / 1967 / Musicor ✦✦✦

The Mood I'm In / 1967 / Unart ✦✦✦

● **Something to Brag About** / 1971 / Capitol ✦✦✦✦

Do You Know Where Your Man Is / 1992 / Playback ✦✦

Do You Know Where Your Man Is mixes remakes of songs Montgomery recorded in her heyday alongside other classic songs. The production is tasteful, but the album sounds a bit sterile and too bright. The standout track is "We Must Be Crazy," performed as a duet with Charlie Louvin (who sounds his age), although Montgomery's performances are good throughout. She sounds great and the material is fine, but *Do You Know Where Your Man Is* isn't up to the standards of the music she made in her prime. *—Greg Adams*

Golden Moments / Jan. 30, 2001 / Classic World ✦✦✦

The golden voice of Melba Montgomery delivered homegrown country for a strong 30-year period between the '50s and the '80s. *Golden Moments* is a collection that tries to sample from virtually every aspect of her career, from the zydeco-influenced "Crawdad Song" to the country-fried weeper "He Thinks I Still Care." With all the variety found here, the album feels very disjointed, as many of these songs have been picked from vastly different moments in her career. Her wonderful singing voice is really what stands out here, unfortunately the songs that were chosen do not complement her range and several excellent songs have been left off. Fans of Montgomery may enjoy this album, but the casual listener may want to try a different album if they want to give her a chance. *—Bradley Torreano*

Clyde Moody

b. Sep. 19, 1915, Cherokee, NC, **d.** Apr. 7, 1989

Guitar, Vocals / Traditional Bluegrass

Best remembered as one of Bill Monroe's original Blue Grass Boys, singer/songwriter/string player Clyde Moody also played in almost every other subgenre of country music during his over fifty-year career, and even performed as a solo artist. During the '40s, he was known as the "Hillbilly Waltz King" after his song "Shenandoah Waltz" became a certified gold hit.

Moody was born and raised in Cherokee, NC, and was very influenced by the traditional mountain music he heard there. During the mid-'30s, he and Jay Hugh, the brother of Roy Hall, teamed up to appear as the Happy-Go-Lucky Boys on the radio in Spartanburg, SC. They then joined Wade Mainer, and with fiddler Steve Ledford they became the Sons of the Mountaineers. Moody joined Monroe in 1940 and performed with the Blue Grass Boys at WSM and at the *Grand Ole Opry.* About this time, Monroe and his Boys were becoming a bluegrass band, and the changes can clearly be heard in Moody's mandolin playing on the classic "Six White Horses." A year later, Moody spent a few months in Burlington, NC playing radio duets with Lester Flatt. He later returned to the Blue Grass Boys and remained with them until again attempting a solo career in 1945.

He joined the *Opry* as a featured artist for a few weeks and then recorded for Columbia. He had his biggest hit, the sentimental "Shenandoah Waltz," in 1947, and followed it up with a series of similar tunes such as "Cherokee Waltz" and "I Waltz Alone." He had a few more hits through the end of the decade and then moved to Washington, D.C., to work for Connie B. Gay. In 1952, Moody signed with Decca, but only had a few singles up through the mid-'50s, when his health began to fail. He left music to become a mobile home salesman, but returned in 1962 with a solo album. He then tried a modern country album. During the folk revival, he played at bluegrass festivals and moved back to Nashville in 1972, where he performed both bluegrass and country music until his death in 1989. *—Sandra Brennan*

● **The Best of Clyde Moody** / 1964 / King ✦✦✦✦✦

Ralph Mooney

b. Sep. 16, 1928, Duncan, OK

Guitar (Steel) / Traditional Country, Bakersfield Sound

Along with Speedy West, Buddy Emmons, and Pete Drake, Ralph Mooney is one of the true steel guitar innovators in country music. He was born in Duncan, OK, and first became interested in the instrument after hearing another steel pioneer, Leon McAuliffe. As a teenager in the '40s, Mooney moved to California, where he gradually developed his style by exhaustive playing with numerous bands, in both live and studio situations. In the '50s and '60s, Mooney was hired as a staff musician for Capitol Records, where he played on the early recordings of Buck Owens and is heard prominently on several Merle Haggard hits, including "Swinging Doors," "The Bottle Let Me Down," and "(All My Friends Are Gonna Be) Strangers."

Throughout the years, Mooney left his mark on recordings by Wynn Stewart (that's his steel on "It's Such a Pretty World Today"), Warren Smith, Rose Maddox, Skeets McDonald, Bobby Austin, Bonnie Owens, Wanda Jackson, Donna Fargo, and Jessi Colter. His longest running stint was with Waylon Jennings, whom Mooney joined in 1970 and stayed with until he retired in the early '90s. While Mooney is known mainly for his steel playing, he also dabbled in songwriting. His biggest hit was "Crazy Arms," which he co-wrote with Chuck Seals in the mid-'50s. Even though Mooney spent most of his life playing on the recordings of others, he did release an instrumental album on Capitol Records in 1968 called *Corn Pickin' and Slick Slidin'* with guitarist James Burton. *—Al Campbell*

● **Corn Pickin' and Slick Slidin'** / 1968 / Capitol ✦✦✦✦

This reissue of a 1968 instrumental album features steel guitar hero Ralph Mooney. *—Dan Cooper*

Charlie Moore

b. Feb. 13, 1935, Piedmont, SC

Vocals / Traditional Bluegrass, Country Gospel, Bluegrass-Gospel

Known as one of classic bluegrass music's most soulful vocalists, Charlie Moore also contributed the undying "Legend of the Rebel Soldier" to the genre's stock of songs known to all. Raised in Piedmont, SC, Moore learned guitar when he was young and heard mountain music on radio stations from Charlotte and Greenville. Landing a radio slot in Asheville, NC, in 1956 and starring in a short-lived television show in Spartanburg, SC, the following year, Moore cultivated a vocal style that perfectly blended the forceful nasal sound of Bill Monroe and other pioneers with a smoother, quieter voice production influenced by contemporary country developments. Moore put together the first version of his Dixie Partners band in 1957 and made his recording debut for Starday the following year. In 1960 Moore and Bill Napier (formerly a member of the Stanley Brothers' band) teamed up to form the duo of Moore and Napier, signing with King Records and recording nine albums during the '60s. Among the 108 songs Moore and Napier released on King were several that would become bluegrass standards: "Truck Driver's Queen," for example, was covered by both Jimmy Martin and the Willis Brothers. After splitting with Napier in 1969, Moore staged a comeback in the early '70s with a new edition of the Dixie Partners. The band cut one album for the Country Jubilee label and recorded for other independent labels during the next two years.

During this time, Moore became a member of the popular *Wheeling Jamboree* radio show and made frequent appearances on the festival circuit and in clubs. After 1973, Moore recorded mostly for Michigan's Old Homestead label. One of his most widely heard songs was "The Legend of the Rebel Soldier," a ballad of a Confederate fighter, dying "in a dreary Yankee prison," who asks, "Oh, parson, tell me quickly, will my soul pass through the southland?" The song was later included in the *Smithsonian Collection of Classic Country Music.* During the '70s, Moore endured several personal tragedies, and his drinking habits led to liver difficulties and poor health. Although he attempted to keep performing and touring, Moore finally died in 1979 after falling into a coma. *—Sandra Brennan and James Manheim*

● **The Best of Charlie Moore & Bill Napier** / 1975 / Starday ✦✦✦✦

Truckin' Favorites / Jan. 1, 1996 / King ✦✦

Truckin' Favorites is a skimpy eight-track budget-priced collection that contains versions of songs like "Long White Line," "Bluegrass Truck Driver," "Lonesome Truck Driver" and "Truck Driver's Romance" that are most likely re-recordings or alternate takes. Stick to the more comprehensive, expensive collections—they offer a better value. *—Stephen Thomas Erlewine*

Merrill Moore

b. Sep. 26, 1923, Algona, IA, **d.** Jun. 14, 2000, San Diego, CA
Piano, Vocals / R&B, Boogie-Woogie, Traditional Country

Pianist Merrill Moore's unique style fused Western swing, boogie-woogie, and early R&B in a melting pot that many critics felt was a distinct influence on rockabilly, especially Jerry Lee Lewis. Born in Algona, IA, in 1923, Moore began playing the piano at age seven and by 12 was performing on a Des Moines radio station. After high-school, he played in a band on the Midwestern ballroom circuit, taking a break to serve in the Navy during World War II. Afterwards, he married his high-school sweetheart and moved to San Diego, where he started playing the club circuit. He got a regular gig with local club king-pin Jimmy Kennedy and put together the Saddle, Rock & Rhythm Boys as his backing band in 1950.

Kennedy helped get Moore a record deal with Capitol in 1952, and that year he released his first single, "Big Bug Boogie." 1953's "House of Blue Lights" became a national hit, but Kennedy refused to allow the band to tour or promote the record: He'd signed them to a seven-year deal to play six nights a week and had only gotten them the record contract to increase their local drawing power. Moore continued to record occasional boogies and novelty tunes for Capitol, issuing an extremely rare self-titled EP in 1955. That same year, he walked out on his contract with Kennedy and moved to Los Angeles.

Moore performed regularly on Cliffie Stone's music program *Hometown Jamboree* and also worked as a session pianist, appearing on records by the likes of Tommy Sands ("Teenage Crush"), Johnny Cash, Faron Young, Hank Thompson, Sonny James, and Kay Starr, among others. He recorded only one more session for Capitol, a selection of instrumentals that wasn't released until 1990 by Bear Family. Moore returned to San Diego in 1962, taking up residency in a hotel lounge. He worked clubs and similar venues for the next couple of decades, sometimes venturing into Nevada and Arizona. A car accident in 1986 put him on hiatus for a few years, but Moore spent most of the '90s playing regularly at Mr. A's in San Diego, leaving in 1998. He lost a battle with cancer on June 14, 2000. *—Steve Huey*

● **Boogie My Blues Away** / 1958 / Bear Family ✦✦✦✦✦

Scotty Moore

b. Dec. 27, 1931, Gadsden, TN
Guitar / Rockabilly, Rock & Roll

Scotty Moore is one of the great pioneers of rock guitar. As the guitarist on Elvis Presley's Sun Recordings, he may have done more than anyone else to establish the basic vocabulary of rockabilly guitar licks, as heard on classic singles like "That's All Right," "Good Rockin' Tonight," "Baby Let's Play House," and "Mystery Train." Moore took the stinging licks common to both country music and blues, and not only combined elements of country & western and R&B, but added a rich tone through heavier amplification. His concise, sharp phrasing, and knack for knowing both what to play and when not to overplay were perfect accents to Presley's vocals. Although his Sun riffs may be his most famous, Moore in fact continued to play on Presley records until the late '60s and laid down some of his best accompaniments to the star on RCA discs. Unsurprisingly, the best of these were in Elvis' early RCA years in the 1950s, when Moore added more wattage and recklessness to his riffs to come out with classic solos on "Hound Dog," "Jailhouse Rock," and "Too Much," among others.

As extensive as Moore's resumé with Presley is and as well-known as his solos are, he actually contributed more to Presley's career than is often realized. He was crucial to Presley's early live shows and did much to help advance Elvis' career in business capacities. He also did quite a bit of production and recording work, for several decades, in which Presley was not involved. He also had a brief career as an instrumental solo artist, although the mid-'60s album released under his name, *The Guitar That Changed the World*, was not the ideal showcase for his skills.

After a lengthy stint in the Navy, Moore settled in Memphis in the early '50s, playing honky tonk music when not working at a dry cleaners. His band, Doug Poindexter & the Starlite Wranglers, recorded a routine country single for Sun Records in the spring of 1954. Although the record did nothing, and the band would soon break up, Moore gained a valuable musical partner in their bassist, Bill Black. When Sun Records, and its owner/producer, Sam Phillips, were mulling over trying a recording with young hopeful Elvis Presley, and in general looking for a new musical direction, Moore, Black, and Presley started to play together, groping for some common musical ground. Very shortly after Moore met and played with Presley for the first time, they were in Sun on July 5, 1954. This was the session that resulted in "That's All Right," the first great rockabilly record and possibly the first great rock & roll record made by white musicians. All three musicians made stellar contributions to the track by shedding their inhibitions, mixing country and blues, and going into new territory, Moore's soloing imbued with a masterful fluidity and crisp reverb.

In 1954 and 1955, Moore and Black were nearly equal partners with Presley; indeed, on Sun releases they were billed as Elvis Presley, Scotty, and Bill. What's more, Moore became Presley's first manager in a July 1954 contract that identified Moore as the bandleader. The trio played together live and with increasing success on the Southern circuit, and inevitably, as Presley started to attract wide attention and come into his own as a frontman, more powerful interests edged Moore out of his business role in the band. First Bob Neal, and then Colonel Tom Parker, took over Presley's management. By the summer of 1955, Moore and Black became salaried employees of the act rather than the partners. Drummer D.J. Fontana was added to the band shortly afterwards, and the musicians continued to record, and play live with, Elvis when the singer began recording with RCA in 1956.

While additional musicians on RCA sessions would sometimes make Moore's role less prominent than it had been at Sun, Scotty still added a great deal to Elvis' earliest and best RCA discs. There was the chilling, fiercely echoing solo on "Heartbreak Hotel," the almost avant-garde mad runs up and down the scales on the solos of "Hound Dog" and "Too Much," the brief but blasting one on "Jailhouse Rock," and the bubbly one on "My Baby Left Me," which was as pure and sparkling as anything Moore had played at Sun. Still, Moore and Black became less close to Elvis both personally and professionally.

Some biographers have speculated that Parker viewed anyone who had a close personal and artistic relationship with Elvis as a threat to his own power over the singer and that the manager tried to drive a wedge between Elvis and the other musicians, or even force Moore and Black out of the picture. For the soundtrack of *Love Me Tender*, Scotty and Bill were not allowed to record with Presley. (They did help on other soundtracks from the period, as well as appearing in some Presley movies.)

Frustrated with their limited salaried incomes as Presley became a superstar and earned more and more, Moore and Black gave Presley letters of resignation in September 1957. Although this was patched up after about a month, tension remained, and in any case Moore and Black were out of work again early in 1958, when Presley was drafted. Moore began working at Fernwood Records in production and got a big national hit with Thomas Wayne's "Tragedy" in 1959. When Elvis returned from the Army in 1960, Moore resumed playing sessions for him, although Black was not involved any longer, having started a successful solo career as the leader of the instrumental Bill Black Combo. There wasn't a lot of income from either Fernwood or Elvis, though, so Moore began working for Phillips as a production manager in 1960, continuing to work with Elvis occasionally. In 1964, perhaps influenced by the success of former bandmate Black, Moore released an entire album of instrumentals for Epic in 1964, consisting of versions of songs recorded by Elvis in the 1950s, on which (with one exception) Scotty had played. Although Moore played well on the LP, it was rather pointless given the superiority of the Elvis versions and sold few copies. In March of 1964, Moore was fired by Phillips, and the guitarist moved to Nashville to work at Music City Records as an engineer, as well as doing some producing. His ongoing work with Presley as a session guitarist finally came to an end in the late '60s, although he did appear on-stage with Elvis on the singer's heralded 1968 television comeback special.

Moore continued to work as an engineer, occasionally crossing paths in this capacity with unexpected clients such as Ringo Starr, Tracy Nelson, Mother Earth, and the Holy Modal Rounders. He got back into playing guitar again, after a layoff of about 25 years, on recordings and live shows with Carl Perkins in the early '90s. In 1997, he did a tribute album to Elvis Presley with D.J. Fontana, *All the King's Men*, which included appearances by Keith Richards, Levon Helm, Jeff Beck, and Ronnie Wood. The presence of such heavyweights was a testament to the influence of Moore on other guitarists, not just rockabilly ones, but also rockers of a later generation, such as Richards. The Rolling Stones guitarist, indeed, is quite vocal and enthusiastic in his praise of Moore, even saying that it was hearing "Heartbreak Hotel" that made him want to devote his life to playing guitar. Moore's life story, both with and without Elvis, is recounted in the autobiography *That's Alright, Elvis*, co-written with James Dickerson. *—Richie Unterberger*

The Guitar That Changed the World / 1964 / Epic ✦✦✦

Scotty Moore's guitar, as represented on Elvis Presley's Sun sides in 1954 and 1955, did help in a big way to change the world. But 1964 was definitely not the year in which for Moore or Epic Records to try and remind anyone that fact, even with Elvis alumni D.J. Fontana (drums), Bob Moore (bass), Boots Randolph (sax), Jerry Kennedy (guitar), Buddy Harman (drums), Bill Pursell (piano), and the Jordanaires aboard. *The Guitar That Changed the World* passed largely without notice that year, becoming a curiously mistimed attempt at a career move. Apart from its sense of timing, the album's problems included having more of a Nashville than a Memphis sound, being a little too midtempo and relaxed, and having too much sax and country piano. Without Elvis' presence, there wasn't going to be an overabundance of sexuality, nothing like the excitement of the originals, in these re-recordings of "That's All Right," "Hound Dog," "Money Honey," "Heartbreak Hotel," "Milk Cow Blues," "Mystery Train," and so on, but the country sound here is a little too pale, and a little too close in spirit to Chet Atkins. Rather than trying to pick up where he'd left off at Sun in 1955, or even recreating the pseudo-Sun sound of Elvis' early RCA singles, Moore aimed for more of a mature, virtuoso performance—he plays beautifully and dexterously, but not with much excitement or any attempt to elicit excitement from the listener; he and the rest concentrate more on precision, and the resulting album is strong there and weak in most other departments. It's beautifully, carefully played but nothing like spontaneous, cutting-edge rock & roll. Guitar buffs and Elvis completists will want the CD, but others should hear it, if only to get a glimpse of what Elvis' sidemen (and collaborators, in Moore's case) could do on their own. [The compact disc is very clean, with a brighter sound than the original LP or the 1980s European vinyl reissue, and the stereo separation does wonders in delineating the playing.] *—Bruce Eder*

● **All the King's Men** / Aug. 12, 1997 / Sweetfish ✦✦✦

Forty years after making history as Elvis Presley's sidemen, guitarist Scotty Moore and drummer D.J. Fontana reunited to record *All the King's Men*. The album is a tribute to Elvis but not in the traditional sense. Most tributes devote themselves to covering shop-worn classics by familiar artists, but this one tries to nail down the spirit of Elvis. With a number of guest artists in tow, Moore and Fontana run-through a number of new songs—Rick Nielsen's "Bad Little Girl," Joe Ely's "I'm Gonna Strangle You Shorty," the BoDeans' "Locked in the State of Illinois," and the Mavericks' "I Told You So"—revamping them to sound like lost rock & roll classics. It's not always a successful effort, but most of *All the King's Men* is roots rock at its best and least pretentious. It's hard to resist Keith Richards and Levon Helm's duet on "Deuce and a Quarter," or Jeff Beck and Ronnie Wood playing on "Unsung Heroes," and Moore and Fontana play superbly throughout. For die-hard rockabilly cats, *All the King's Men* will sound like a tribute fit for a king. *—Thom Owens*

Tiny Moore (Billie Moore)

b. May 12, 1920, Hamilton County, TX, **d.** Dec. 15, 1987, Jackpot, NV
Mandolin / Progressive Bluegrass, Traditional Bluegrass, Traditional Country, Western Swing, Bluegrass, Instrumental Country

Best known for his work in Bob Wills' Texas Playboys, Tiny Moore earned a reputation as one of the greatest mandolin players of all time. He was born Billie Moore in

Hamilton County, TX, in 1920 and learned to play not only the mandolin, but also fiddle, banjo, and drums. Earning his nickname due to his large frame, his first professional job in music was with the Port Arthur Jubileers. He joined Wills' band in 1946, playing on classic sides like "Three Guitar Rag" and "Bubbles in My Beer." Tired of touring, he spent some time running Bob's Wills Point Ballroom in Sacramento, where he also played in brother Billy Jack Wills' early-'50s band and from 1956-1962 hosted a local children's TV show.

Also during the '50s, Moore developed an electric five-string mandolin that helped bring the instrument into country's amplified age as well as proved its viability in jazz combos. Moore later spent 13 years in Merle Haggard's backing band, the Strangers, and recorded two jazzy albums of his own for Kaleidoscope Records: *Back to Back* (an album of collaborations with fellow mandolin virtuoso Jethro Burns) and *Tiny Moore Music*. On December 15, 1987, he suffered a fatal heart attack while performing in Jackpot, NV. —*Steve Huey*

Tiny Moore Music / 1972 / Kaleidoscope ✦✦✦✦✦

● *Back to Back* / 1979 / Kaleidoscope ✦✦✦✦✦

Allison Moorer

b. Frankville, AL

Vocals / Contemporary Country, Neo-Traditionalist Country, Americana, Progressive Country

Allison Moorer was born into a musical family and raised in the small southern Alabama town of Frankville; when Moorer's father shot her mother and then turned the gun on himself, older sister Shelby Lynne—soon to become a country singer herself—took charge of raising Allison. After attending the University of South Alabama, Moorer moved to Nashville, hoping to get her start as a studio backing vocalist. She struck up a songwriting partnership with musician and future husband Butch Primm, and soon signed a publishing deal. Performances of Walter Hyatt's "Tell Me Baby" at benefit shows for the late singer's family landed Moorer a contract with MCA Nashville. Moorer's big break came when "A Soft Place to Fall," a track she had co-written with Gwil Owen, was tapped for inclusion on the soundtrack of *The Horse Whisperer*, it garnered rave reviews, as well as an appearance in the film itself for Moorer, and set the stage for the singer's 1998 debut album, *Alabama Song*.

She returned with another solo effort in 2000 with *The Hardest Part*. Two years later, Moorer had a new deal with Universal South and released a third album, *Miss Fortune* later that summer. *Show*, which was recorded in January 2003 at Nashville's 12th & Porter, was slated for a June release. Her sister, Shelby Lynne and country-rock boy Kid Rock joined Moorer for this first time live recording. —*Steve Huey*

Alabama Song / Sep. 22, 1998 / MCA ✦✦✦

Allison Moorer's debut album delicately balances and divides '90s country aesthetics into two parts: one wants to stick pretty close to classic Nashville structure and songwriting, while the other is acutely aware of the rising pop saturation of the music. Fortunately, she sticks near the former throughout most of this glowing, but somewhat derivative, album—at times, almost too near. Moorer is so intent on keeping herself and *Alabama Song* grounded that they occasionally have trouble lifting off. But her commitment and integrity eventually win (Moorer co-wrote ten of *Alabama Song*'s 11 tracks), giving the album the trad-country boost it needed. Best is "A Soft Place to Fall" (which was originally featured on the soundtrack to *The Horse Whisperer*), a bittersweet tale of love's securities and insecurities that shows off both Moorer's husky, vibrant voice and her sharp way around a tune. —*Michael Gallucci*

The Hardest Part / 2000 / Island ✦✦✦✦

The year 2000 proved to be a momentous year for this Alabama native. Obviously influenced by the soulful, mature departure from contemporary country music taken by her sister Shelby Lynne on *her* 2000 release *I Am Shelby Lynne*, Alison Moorer has similarly grown since her 1998 album *Alabama Song*. While her debut CD flirted with the fine line between traditional country and the slick Nashville sound, *The Hardest Part* dives headfirst into a Southern soul-tinged countrypolitan sound, complete with string and horn sections. The Beatles-esque, mellotron-infused "Send Down an Angel" sounds almost like "Strawberry Fields Forever" with less LSD and more whiskey, while "Is It Worth It" feels like Dusty Springfield is back in Memphis again. The dark final track (unlisted in the liner notes) is a somber murder ballad, a heart-wrenchingly honest reaction to the death of her parents. Her brash, husky vocals hold the album together through heartache and pedal steel, and the fact that she co-wrote and co-produced the album proves that she's more than just a pretty voice. While it took six albums for her sister to realize her dissatisfaction with the limits of the pop country sound, Allison Moorer has made great strides in just two. —*Zac Johnson*

● **Miss Fortune** / Aug. 6, 2002 / Universal South ✦✦✦✦

Rather than open her Universal South debut with a boot-stompin' rave, Moorer sounds an autumnal tone—not just on the opening track, but on the first three. Though several uptempo tunes do follow, this muted quality pervades *Miss Fortune*. Clearly the point is that Moorer intends to move past her identification with traditional country into a more personalized and varied realm in which she exercises full creative control. Make no mistake: This is a country album, but it's closer to what the music might have become rather than to where it has sunk in its current doldrums. A honey-toned and expressive singer, Moorer does seem more at home with slower, thoughtful material; on faster numbers, like "Ruby Jewel Was Here" and "Hey Jezebel," her phrasing is more affected—in fact, the grooves are transparently derivative, reflecting the Band and the Stones, respectively. On the other hand, when she slinks into a Kurt Weill pose on the closing track, "Dying Breed," she feels totally at home with the idiom and its interpretive implications. Despite the ambiguity of the title, *Miss Fortune* suggests an intriguing turn for Moorer, not to mention

affirmation that there are still opportunities to experiment outside the boardrooms of Music Row. —*Robert L. Doerschuk*

Show / Jun. 24, 2003 / Universal South ✦✦✦✦

On *Show*, singer/songwriter Allison Moorer follows up her stellar *Miss Fortune* album with a live collection recorded at Music City's famed 12th & Porter. Playing songs drawn from her three previous studio outings, she also includes a tough and trashy version of Neil Young's barroom classic "Don't Cry No Tears." In addition to performing her material with uncompromising honesty and brutal emotional intensity, Moorer gets the most from her backing band and a couple of guests. For those who own the studio records and wonder, the versions of well-known songs here—such as "Alabama Song," "Easy Place to Fall," "Send Me Down an Angel," "Is Heaven Good Enough for You," or "Day You Said Goodbye"—along with virtually every other cut here, are wrought with a raw immediacy that's impossible to capture in a recording studio. The balance of ringing acoustic guitars, whinnying pedal steels, and crunching electric guitars juxtaposed with Hammond B-3s and honky tonk pianos is stirring. And Moorer's voice, unedited and in its natural state, offers further proof of her originality and rough-hewn grace. In this landscape, her songs stand out individually as mini-epics of burning love, unrequited passion, and an affair's aftermath in the ashes. Whether it's the slow groove of "Steal the Sun," the burning country-rock of "Going Down" (with sister Shelby Lynne on backing vocals), the funky strut of "Bully Jones" (a duet with up-and-coming country crooner Bob Richie (aka Kid Rock)), or the undulating gypsy-ballad-music-meets-Brecht-ian-substance-abuse-tragedy in "Dying Breed," the effect is the same: badass country music delivered with an edgy testiness and musical professionalism. In sum, this is how live records should be made. —*Thom Jurek*

Chad Morgan

b. Queensland, Australia

Vocals, Guitar / Novelty, Country Comedy

There are those listeners who feel that country & western music would be better off if there were less people imitating Hank Williams and more people imitating Roger Miller. Failure to add the name Chad Morgan to the Miller side of the tally is an excusable mistake, because despite a half of a century of service to the art of zany country music, Morgan remains pretty much unknown outside of his native Australia. Chadwick Morgan hails from a spot in Queensland known as Scrubby Creek. Just as Paul McCartney would return to the "Penny Lane" of his childhood for lyrical inspiration, Morgan would later score one of his biggest hits with his song "Sheik of Scrubby Creek." A few seconds of this record is all one needs to get a full bearing of what Chad Morgan is all about. The groove is basic country with a bit of a folk feeling. The voice begins sounding absurd; by the chorus, Morgan is yodeling, cooing, squeaking, and sometimes sounding like a raccoon with operatic ambitions. The lyrics, if they can be made out, snatch at whatever words might be needed to describe whatever strange goings-on he has in mind. Like Miller, he is not afraid to head for black comedy in order to make a point: Morgan's "In the Cemetery" is every bit as brilliant as Miller's "Pardon My Coffin." And also like the best of Miller, Morgan is able to use very commonplace incidents as well as the absurd. In "You Just Can't Win," the sensitive hubby gets up in the middle of the night to feed the baby, then gets chewed out by his wife for moving the blanket.

But one look at a picture of Chad Morgan tells the true tale. Roger Miller was just using weird as a stylistic device, but Morgan really is weird. No press release or Morgan website exists that does not almost immediately mention his trademark buck teeth. The teeth, which seem to extend a good inch past his lower lip, are definitely real—something that brought him a good deal of negative attention back in the Scrubby Creek days. Music was, perhaps, a way of getting some positive feedback for the lad, who entered the *Australia Amateur Hour* contest and wound up getting to record a song for the Regal Zonophone label in 1952. This label was one of the main companies documenting the Australian country music scene, which has always been healthy, if not as exportable as the country's film industry. Morgan won the contest with his "Sheik of Scrubby Creek," inspiring a move from Brisbane up to the more populous and exciting Sydney.

For a few years, he worked with other big names on the Australian country & western scene, such as Kevin King, Slim Dusty, and Reg Lindsay. Package tours were popular in Australia at this time, as they were on the American country scene. A particularly successful venture for Morgan was participating in the *1958 Star Western Show*. These were up-and-down years for Morgan, as he was in conflict about whether to be a straight country performer or continue playing up his goofy side. At one point, he considered having his teeth straightened (he even made a dental appointment). Fate intervened in the form of his car breaking down on the way to the dentist, and after that he decided to keep the buck teeth. His career seems to have two main sections. There is a gap of three years after the contest recording before he was able to get into the studio again. After that and running until 1970, he was able to release about a dozen different album titles, each with many of his original songs.

In the '70s, he got off the road and apparently cleaned up his health and personal habits, which he summed up once thusly: "I've been wild and I've seen a lot without remembering a great deal the morning after." In 1977, an appearance with Slim Dusty at the Sydney Opera House led to a revival of his career. Much of Morgan's later activity is focused around an Australian country & western theme park called Tamworth, located in Brisbane. There is a wax figure of him in the Tamworth gallery of stars, and Morgan performs at events such an annual festival and the Gympie Muster. He is considered the supreme Australian country & western artist, and is sometimes credited with creating a style known as White Outback.

In the manner of certain country artists, such as Minnie Pearl and Stringbean, Morgan is expected to be as wacky as he can be on-stage. Acknowledgement of Morgan's work outside Australia has been limited. It seems there might at least have been a possibility for international success following in the trail of Rolf Harris, an Australian folksinger who scored a huge hit with the song "Tie Me Kangeroo Down Sport," with lyrics about as down under as one can get. The public's interest in this type of material seems to have been limited, though, because Harris wasn't able to repeat his success, and there was no more room on the charts for any other weird Australian singers. As Morgan developed his status as a senior statesman of Australian country, critical appraisal of his work began to notch up a few levels. As is the case with many performers, his skill at comedy had prevented some listeners from also noticing his musical skills. He was described as "the only original artist in Australia" by singer Tex Morton.

There has been at least one attempt to produce a compilation of international artists performing Morgan's songs. And in 1998 there was an announcement of a film planned on the life of Morgan, supposedly to star actor Steve Buscemi. But as the titles of Morgan albums—such as *Double Decker Blowflies* and *Sheilas, Dills, and Drongos*—make it clear, Morgan is pretty much interested in communicating only with his fellow Australians. *—Eugene Chadbourne*

Chad Charms the Birds / 1984 / EMI Australia ✦✦✦
Albums by this loony Australian country legend are hard to come by, so there might be a certain delight in finding any of the dozen some album titles Chad Morgan has waxed. And there is an urge to give any and all Morgan products five stars because he is such a loveable nut, with the weirdest looking teeth in country & western music, performers from Arkansas excluded. This album comes a bit later in Morgan's career, when he was beginning to look on himself as a survivor and a legend. In fact, he even wrote a song about himself for the session entitled "The Legend," but must have gotten bashful because he credited it to a scrambled version of his own name, Dach Nagrom. So he hasn't exactly calmed down here, but he is in a good-sounding studio with a professional backup unit that gives him a pretty straight-ahead country sound. The overwhelming Australian flavor of the material might overwhelm some country fans, but this sense of place and background is a strong part of any country & western music. Witness to what extent American country performers will go to make their material sound authentically "Southern," for example. No listener will doubt for a moment that Morgan is Australian. Unlike George Jones who might sing about smashing up his car, it is a kangaroo that Morgan hits when driving on a bender. And so forth, with the pile upon pile of Australian slang, gibberish, and jargon combining with the sameness of the music to create an overwhelming feeling of ennui—not the normal state when listening to a Chad Morgan album, if that experience could ever be described as normal. Strangely enough it is the serious "A Lover's Plea" that stands out, with bassist Glen Mooney adding a superb line. Morgan overdoes the affectation of ending many tracks with rambling narrative that slowly fades out. The material is just not crazy enough to support this kind of stuff. *—Eugene Chadbourne*

George Morgan

b. Jun. 28, 1924, Waverly, TN, **d.** Jul. 7, 1975
Vocals, Guitar / Nashville Sound/Countrypolitan, Traditional Country, Country-Pop
The Candy Kid—as George Morgan was known after his first hit "Candy Kisses" spent three weeks at the top of the country chart—was a grand country crooner in the tradition of Eddy Arnold, whom he replaced on the *Grand Old Opry* in 1948. Born in Waverly, TN, on June 28, 1924, Morgan and his family moved to Ohio not long after. He grew up listening to the *Opry* and formed his first band in the mid-'40s. Occasional spots on local radio did little for Morgan's career, but after he wrote "Candy Kisses," WWVA-Wheeling (WV) hired him for the *Wheelin Jamboree*. The *Grand Old Opry* called soon after, and Columbia Records contracted Morgan in 1948.

"Candy Kisses" was finally released early the following year and it hit number one in April; though it proved George Morgan's only chart-topper, he placed six of his next seven singles in the Country Top Ten. "Please Don't Let Me Love You," the B-side of "Candy Kisses," reached the Top Five soon after, and another double-sided hit, "Rainbow in My Heart"/"All I Need Is Some More Lovin'" continued the success. Three Top Ten singles (plus the near-miss "All I Need") in the span of a month was simply astonishing for a debut artist, and Morgan proved he was no fluke by closing out 1949 with three more Top Five hits: "Room Full of Roses," "Cry-Baby Heart," and "I Love Everything About You." It was almost inevitable that Morgan's chart success would taper somewhat, though the three-year gap between hits from late 1949 to 1952 was surprising. "Almost" reached number two in April 1952, however, and Morgan's performances on the *Grand Old Opry* sustained his reputation.

He left the show in 1956 to host a TV program in Nashville, but returned to the *Opry* three years later. He christened his return in 1959 with "I'm in Love Again," which hit number three. Early the following year, "You're the Only Good Thing (That's Happened to Me)" hit number four, but it was Morgan's last Top 20 entry. From 1965 to 1975, George Morgan remained with the *Opry* and recorded frequently, hitting the nether reaches of the Country charts consistently. Morgan witnessed his daughter Lorrie's debut on the *Opry*, but didn't live to see her musical success in the late '80s: he passed away in July 1975 after a heart attack. His posthumous father-daughter duet, "I'm Completely Satisfied With You," hit the charts in 1979. *—John Bush*

Morgan, by George / 1957 / Columbia ✦✦✦✦

Golden Memories / 1961 / Columbia ✦✦✦

Red Roses for a Blue Lady / 1965 / Columbia ✦✦✦✦✦

American Originals / 1977 / Columbia ✦✦✦✦
All of his famous hits, including "Candy Kisses" and "Room Full of Roses," are featured, although not necessarily in their original form. Contrary to the album title, a few of these songs are 1959 remakes of earlier hits. *—Michael McCall*

● **Room Full of Roses: The Best of George Morgan** / 1996 / Razor & Tie ✦✦✦✦✦
Room Full of Roses contains a generous selection of George Morgan's hits from the late '40s and '50s, including "Candy Kisses," "Please Don't Let Me Love You," "Almost," "I'm in Love Again" and the title track. Every cut is presented in its original hit versions, making the compilation the definitive single-disc retrospective of his hit-making peak at Columbia Records. *—Stephen Thomas Erlewine*

Candy Kisses / 1996 / Bear Family ✦✦✦✦
Candy Kisses contains George Morgan's complete recordings for Columbia between 1949 and 1966. Spanning eight discs and 200 songs, all of Morgan's major hits—"Candy Kisses," "Almost," "I'm in Love Again," "Room Full of Roses," "Please Don't Let Me Love You" and "You're the Only Good Thing (That's Happened to Me)"—are included on this extensive compilation, which is designed for hardcore fans. The consistency of Morgan's material is somewhat uneven, which makes the set a little tedious for any listener that isn't a fanatic or a historian, yet the box—with its excellent biography, sound and sessionography—is worthwhile for anyone willing to invest the time and money. *—Stephen Thomas Erlewine*

Country Music Hall of Fame 1998 / Nov. 9, 1999 / King ✦✦
Part of King's *Country Hall of Fame* series, this brings together ten tracks from this hall of famer. Unfortunately, these are *not* the originals, but late-period recuts—which is obvious from their stereo mixes and Music City, U.S.A., backings. Although the booklet is nonexistent, there's a nice, short bio on Morgan on the tray card, and the versions of hits like "Room Full of Roses" and "Candy Kisses" still work, despite the modern backing. *—Cub Koda*

Candy Kisses Are Best of All / Apr. 18, 2000 / Jasmine ✦✦✦
Those who find country crooner George Morgan's classic Columbia recordings a bit on the bland side might take a liking to this collection of 1950s radio transcriptions. Morgan tackles a wide variety of material, including gospel, uptempo honky tonk, covers of others' hits, and the obligatory sentimental slow songs. "Up and Down My Heart Strings" is weirdly interrupted by Ferlin Husky's comedic persona, Simon Crum, and backing group Don Davis and the Candy Kids turn in an instrumental performance of "Panhandle Rag." Two different versions of Morgan's career hit "Candy Kisses" are included. Roy Drusky was often called the "Perry Como of Country Music," but George Morgan may have better deserved the nickname. *—Greg Adams*

Lorrie Morgan (Loretta Lynn Morgan)

b. 1960, Nashville, TN
Vocals / Contemporary Country, Neo-Traditionalist Country
Although she spent most of her life singing, Lorrie Morgan didn't become a star until the early '90s, when she scored a string of Top Ten country hits. Born Loretta Lynn Morgan, she was the daughter of *Grand Ole Opry* star George Morgan and made her professional debut at age 13 on the *Opry*, where her rendition of "Paper Roses" received a standing ovation. When her father died in 1975, she took over his band and began leading the group through various club gigs. Within a few years, she disbanded the group, and in 1977, she went on to play with the Little Roy Wiggins band. She then became a receptionist and demo singer at Acuff-Rose, where she also wrote songs. In 1978 she had one minor hit single; the following year another minor hit with "I'm Completely Satisfied," an electronically dubbed duet with her late father.

She began touring Nashville nightclubs and opened for a number of acts, including Jack Greene, Billy Thunderkloud, and Jeannie Seely. She also toured as a duet partner with George Jones and spent two years as part of the Opryland USA bluegrass show and as a guest singer on TNN's *Nashville Now*. In 1984, Morgan scored a minor hit with "Don't Go Changing." That year she became the youngest singer ever to join the *Grand Ole Opry*. She married Keith Whitley in 1986 and two years later had a Top 20 hit, "Trainwreck of Emotion." Morgan's popularity was blossoming and she had just scored a major hit with "Dear Me" when Whitley died suddenly in 1989. Though devastated, Morgan continued to work, and that year her album *Leave the Light On* went gold. In 1990 she had her first number-one single, "Five Minutes," along with several other Top Ten hits. *Something in Red*, her second album, was released in 1991; it went platinum and spawned the number-one single "What Part of No."

Morgan's third album, *Watch Me*, was released in 1992; *Merry Christmas From London* (1993) and *War Paint* (1994) followed before she issued her *Greatest Hits* in 1995. She released her fifth studio album, *Greater Need*, in 1996; *Secret Love* followed two years later. In 1999, Morgan returned with *My Heart*; the hits collection *Side By Side* appeared the following spring. *I Finally Found Someone*, featuring a duet with Sammy Kershaw, was released in spring 2001. *—Sandra Brennan*

Leave the Light On / 1989 / RCA ✦✦✦✦✦
Lorrie Morgan's debut album for RCA Records, *Leave the Light On*, is a skilled and assured blend of traditional country, honky tonk, country-rock and modern pop sensibilities that pointed the direction toward the sound, style and musical eclecticism of '90s contemporary country. Boasting a clean production and uncluttered arrangements, the record shifts between straightforward country-rockers and ballads, to soul-inflected numbers, all of which help showcase Morgan's exceptional voice. *—Thom Owens*

Something in Red / 1991 / RCA ✦✦✦
Morgan backs off the sad songs for her second album—a wise move. (She went through the first part of her life known as George Morgan's daughter; she wouldn't want to spend the rest of it as Keith Whitley's widow.) Instead she concentrates on laid-back country and ballads like the title track, which is about the dress colors during different stages of a woman's life. Dolly Parton duets on "Best Woman Wins." *—Brian Mansfield*

Watch Me / Oct. 1992 / RCA ✦✦✦✦✦
Morgan's second and third albums each improved on the last. *Watch Me* contains more good songs than the first two combined, including "I Guess You Had to Be There" and "From Our House to Yours" but not "What Part of No" or the remake of Bonnie Tyler's 1978 hit "It's a Heartache." *—Brian Mansfield*

Trainwreck of Emotion / 1993 / BNA ✦✦✦

War Paint / May 10, 1994 / BMG Special Products ✦✦✦
War Paint falls somewhere between the excellent *Watch Me* and the drastically uneven *Trainwreck of Emotion*, *War Paint* finds Lorrie Morgan making a tentative comeback

after *Trainwreck*. Morgan still sings beautifully, but her clean contemporary country arrangements are as predictable as her material. The three hit singles—"My Night to Howl," "War Paint," "If You Came Back From Heaven"—hold up really well, but the rest of the album is a little too familiar for comfort. —*Thom Owens*

● **Greatest Hits** / Oct. 1995 / BNA ✦✦✦✦✦
Lorrie Morgan's *Greatest Hits* highlights 11 tracks from the contemporary country vocalist's late-'80s and early-'90s recordings for RCA. Among the number-one singles are "What Part of No," "Five Minutes," "Something in Red," and "Dear Me." Also featured is the posthumous duet recorded with Morgan's late husband, Keith Whitley, "Til a Tear Becomes a Rose," released following his death in 1989 from alcohol poisoning. —*Al Campbell*

Greater Need / Jun. 1996 / BNA ✦✦✦
On *Greater Need*, Lorrie Morgan perfectly balanced slick contemporary country with rootsy honky tonk. Although the album is peppered with filler, like most country records, Morgan's performance is consistently stunning, and the best moments rank among her very finest work. —*Thom Owens*

Super Hits / Mar. 24, 1998 / BNA ✦✦✦
Super Hits contains ten hits from the peak of Lorrie Morgan's career, including "Good as I Was to You," "Go Away," "Half Enough," "What Part of No," "Five Minutes," "He Talks to Me," "Out of Your Shoes" and "By My Side," her duet with Jon Randall. Ultimately, this collection isn't as good as her *Greatest Hits* compilation, but it's still a good bargain for the budget-conscious. —*Thom Owens*

The Essential Lorrie Morgan / Jun. 2, 1998 / BNA ✦✦✦✦
Although it falls short of being a definitive collection, *The Essential Lorrie Morgan* contains a handful of her greatest hits—including "Dear Me," "Back in Your Arms Again" and "I Didn't Know My Own Strength"—plus a number of great album tracks and rarities that give a good idea of her artistic range. As a result, it's a nice sampler and not a bad introduction, but it isn't ideal for listeners just looking for a concise hits collection. —*Thom Owens*

Secret Love / Sep. 29, 1998 / BNA ✦✦✦✦
This 1998 Lorrie Morgan offering, *Secret Love*, is dedicated to her late father. The songs you'll find on this album aren't the normal country fare fans might expect from Morgan. That doesn't mean it's not worth a listen, or maybe a number of them. As always, her voice and emotional delivery are up to the test, even for old ballads and standards. It helps that she had the backing of some top instrumental artists, along with the Nashville String Machine. *Secret Love* was a career risk for Lorrie Morgan. It meant moving out of the comfort zone that country fans held her in and taking a step away from all of the success she had in one genre to try a new one. It seems she gambled and won. This album is filled with classic romantic numbers, many from the '50s and earlier, including such songs as "Fly Me to the Moon," "Good Morning Heartache," "Once Upon a Time," "I've Got the World on a String," and "My Foolish Heart." *Secret Love* makes a great accompaniment to candlelight and dinner for two. —*Charlotte Dillon*

My Heart / Apr. 13, 1999 / BNA ✦✦✦
My Heart, a 1999 album recorded by Lorrie Morgan, earned a Grammy award nomination, but not as much attention as expected. It would have probably done a lot better with more backing from Morgan's label at the time and the release of a few more singles from its track list. Though not well celebrated, it is still a good album filled with all new material. Morgan had some special help on this offering, including the vocal talents of gifted singer Jo Dee Messina on the tune "The Things That We Do." There is also a duet, "Maybe Not Tonight," with popular country singer Sammy Kershaw. This album is filled mostly with ballads, such as "I Did," "Where Does That Leave Me," "Strong Enough to Cry," and "Between Midnight and Tomorrow." There are a few songs added in to pick up the pace and invite a little toe-tapping, like the title track and "The Only Thing That Looks Good on Me Is You." —*Charlotte Dillon*

To Get to You: Greatest Hits Collection / Feb. 22, 2000 / BNA ✦✦✦✦
To Get to You: The Greatest Hits Collection weighs in at a generous 17 tracks, but it falls short of being definitive. In fact, it's not necessarily even a hits collection, although it contains a fair share of big singles, including "We Both Walk," "Half Enough," "Good as I Was to You," "Go Away," and "He Talks to Me." Instead, it's a bit haphazard, containing the aforementioned hits, some smaller hits, previously released material that never charted, unreleased recordings (including a fine reading of Tammy Wynette's "Another Lonely Song"), and new recordings (including a live version of Sarah McLachlan's "Angel"). That means *To Get to You* is hardly a greatest-hits collection, but it nevertheless is a fine, fairly representative sampler, showcasing Morgan's terrific voice and ability to tackle everything from straight country to smooth ballads. It should satisfy casual fans, even if it may not have everything they're looking for, and the rarities make it worthwhile for longtime followers. —*Stephen Thomas Erlewine*

I Finally Found Someone / Apr. 17, 2001 / RCA ✦✦✦
Real life lovers singing duets together in country music is nothing new, but this 12-track collection does offer something fresh—a wide-ranging group of songs from traditional country to a bit of mellow rock to tender ballads. Lorrie Morgan's voice is raspy and pleasant and Sammy Kershaw's is distinctively country, and when they come together for their six duets, they sound smooth and melodious. The more notable duets are uptempo songs and not the standard romantic fare—"He Drinks Tequila" describes what a trailer park queen and her hard-working husband do on weekends, and "3 Seconds" is how long you have to explain your wrongdoing in a relationship—are playful and fun. Both artists have three solos each, including a song Morgan wrote in just five minutes when she was only 18, the insightful "I Must Be Gettin' Older," and a song with a rock edge that Kershaw wrote in 15 minutes, titled "Sugar." *I Finally Found Someone* is a half-decent album, especially for a first-time full-length pairing. —*Maria Konicki Dinoia*

The Color of Roses / Mar. 12, 2002 / Image ✦✦✦✦
Lorrie Morgan says that she has always wanted to do a live album, but it wasn't until 2001 until the opportunity "arose," no pun intended. *The Color of Roses*, released in March 2002, encapsulates Morgan's remarkable career while celebrating her ability to move live audiences with her music. Most of the singer's hits are bundled in the package, including an emotional performance of "Something in Red," the uplifting "I Didn't Know My Own Strength," and the sassy "Watch Me." One hit that would have perfectly rounded the collection, "Heart Over Mind," is conspicuously absent, however. Still, the album offers enough nostalgia to satisfy longtime Lorrie Morgan fans, yet opens the door to build new bridges with songs such as the title cut and a classy version of "My Favorite Things." No one can deny that Lorrie Morgan is one of the foundations of modern country music. It is one thing to be top-notch recording artist, but quite another to be able to connect with an audience. Morgan can do both. It's high time people stop the chatter about Morgan's personal life and put an ear to the music. —*Rick Cohoon*

RCA Country Legends / Apr. 9, 2002 / RCA ✦✦✦✦✦
Lorrie Morgan's *Country Legends* is a good 16-track collection that contains most of Morgan's hits—all of those that most listeners want—along with a handful of album tracks, all taken from her recordings for Arista. It's a good, solid collection, the best yet assembled on Morgan, and is an expert introduction. —*Stephen Thomas Erlewine*

Oh Boy Classics Presents: Lorrie Morgan / Jul. 9, 2002 / Oh Boy ✦✦✦
This is Lorrie Morgan of the late '70s, before her marriage to Keith Whitley and her chart-topping singles for RCA in the early '90s. These ten tracks, originally recorded for Hickory Records, are good, but not essential for anyone but the most ardent fan. They are somewhat flat when compared to her RCA output. Basically, this is second-tier Nashville pop crossover material that includes a decent version of the easy listening standard "Love Letters," "Two People in Love," and an early example of Morgan's songwriting on "Making Love for the First Time." —*Al Campbell*

Morris Brothers

Group / Traditional Country
The Morris Brothers were a popular fraternal duo during the late '30s best known for their song "Let Me Be Your Salty Dog," which later became the bluegrass standard "Salty Dog Blues." Zeke & Wiley Morris were born three years apart in Old Fort, NC. Their eldest brother, George, was the first to get into music, working with J.E. Mainer and his brother Wade. Mainer's fiddler, John Love, tried to convince George to join the band, but Love instead ended up with 17-year-old Zeke, who remained with the Mainers for three years and participated in the band's first recording session for Bluebird in 1935. Wade Mainer and Zeke soon left to form their own group, adding fiddler Homer Sherrill. They continued recording for Bluebird and also worked at a Raleigh radio station. After Mainer left, Morris, Sherrill, and the rest of the group stayed together to appear on a Danville station. By 1938, Wiley Morris had joined them, and Wiley, Zeke, & Homer recorded several singles for Bluebird, changing their name to the Morris Brothers a few months later for a nine-song session that included the first version of "Salty Dog Blues." The Brothers continued appearing on local radio stations, occasionally joined by George.

During their career, the Morris Brothers usually worked as a duo and didn't always have a backing band; sometimes they even led separate groups. The two split up in Knoxville in the early '40s; Wiley joined the Dixie Pardners, while Zeke joined a band at Johnson City radio. The Morris Brothers recorded together for the last time in 1945 for RCA Victor. Among the songs was a new version of their signature tune, plus "Tragic Romance" and "Somebody Loves You Darling." They went into semi-retirement, eventually moving to Black Mountain, NC, and opening an auto body shop. They did perform infrequently through the '60s and '70s at various festivals and in 1972 recorded an album featuring the fiddle playing of Homer Sherrill. They also joined Earl Scruggs and appeared on a PBS-TV special on which they recorded yet another version of "Salty Dog Blues." In 1985, the Morris Brothers appeared at a Charlotte radio old-timers reunion for their final performance. Five years later, Wiley died; Zeke remained at his body shop and expressed no further interest in performing. —*Sandra Brennan*

Wiley Zeke & Homer / 1973 / Rounder ✦✦✦

Gary Morris

b. Dec. 7, 1948, Fort Worth, TX
Vocals / Progressive Country, Country-Folk
The romantic ballads of Texas-born Gary Morris were staples of country radio in the 1980s—none more than "The Wind Beneath My Wings," which was covered by Bette Midler later in the decade and became a song heard at weddings perhaps more often than any other. From the start, Morris had a powerful voice well suited to the musical theater stage, and after his string of country hits came to an end he enjoyed a successful theatrical career. Morris was born in Fort Worth, TX. Although his own style would become thoroughly contemporary, he was descended from a long line of traditional country and gospel musicians on both sides, and in the third grade he and his twin sister won a talent contest with a rendition of "This Old House." Morris played four sports in high-school and won an athletic scholarship to Cisco Junior College near Abilene, intending to go on to Texas Tech. But music intervened as Morris and two college friends spent a summer working in Colorado, which would become the singer's permanent home.

The trio asked a Colorado Springs bartender if they could get up on the bandstand and perform a few songs, and the audience's response (and tips) convinced Morris to put his college plans on hold and to pursue a performing career. He made a living singing in Denver clubs in the early '70s, also composing advertising jingles for local corporations such as Frontier Airlines. In 1976, Morris signed on with Jimmy Carter's presidential campaign and sang at several fundraisers. That got him invited to perform at the White House after Carter won the election, and Nashville producer Norro Wilson happened to be in the audience as well. When Morris later presented Wilson with a demo tape, the producer remembered him well and signed him to the Warner Bros. label.

Morris notched a few hits with uptempo country-rock pieces, but it was his decisive turn toward ballad material on the 1983 *Why Lady Why* album that put him at the top of the charts. That album spawned several Top Ten hits, including the title track, "The Love She Found in Me," and "The Wind Beneath My Wings," which steadily grew in popularity. In 1984 and 1985 Morris won a host of awards and made guest appearances on several daytime and evening television series. That made it clear to entertainment-industry insiders that although Morris had never studied either singing or acting formally, he was that rare animal: a natural performer and a vocal powerhouse. He was offered the role of Jean Valjean in the Broadway production of *Les Misérables* in 1987, becoming the first American to play the part in that European musical.

Morris didn't give up on country music at first; he recorded 12 country albums in all, including the innovative, mostly acoustic *Plain Brown Wrapper*, and he notched 16 Top Ten singles. But his role in *Les Misérables* evolved into a part in the show's touring production and then in its symphonically accompanied recording. These activities took time, and Morris' country career suffered. His live-theater activities, on the other hand, flourished; he appeared with another former progressive country singer, Linda Ronstadt, in the Broadway adaptation of Puccini's opera *La Bohème*, and he spent much of the 1990s working on other pop projects such as a PBS special concert performance in the Tretyakov Gallery in Moscow, Russia. Morris returned to country music as a performer in Branson, MO, and as a producer in the late '90s. He has shepherded the career of his son, Matthew, and has often performed private concerts for corporate clients. Morris resides at his own fly-fishing lodge in the Colorado Rockies. —*James Manheim*

Morris, Gary / 1982 / Warner Bros. ✦✦✦

Why Lady Why / 1983 / Warner Bros. ✦✦✦
Morris' second recording contains his first significant hits, including "Velvet Chains," "The Love She Found in Me," "The Wind Beneath My Wings" and the title cut, all of which reached the Top Ten. —*Jason Ankeny*

Faded Blue / 1984 / Warner Bros. ✦✦✦

Anything Goes / 1985 / Warner Bros. ✦✦

Plain Brown Wrapper / 1986 / Warner Bros. ✦✦
Plain Brown Wrapper features "Leave Me Lonely," Morris' fourth number-one hit, as well as the title cut, which reached the Top Ten. —*Jason Ankeny*

Second Hand Heart / 1986 / Warner Bros. ✦✦✦

What If We Fell in Love / 1987 / Warner Bros. ✦✦✦

● **Hits** / 1987 / Warner Bros. ✦✦✦✦✦
Morris may have the best "pipes" in country music, but he works so hard at showcasing them that most of his studio albums are bogged down by ballads. This collection includes the best of those ballads ("The Love She Found in Me," "100% Chance of Rain"), plus his best overall material ("I'll Never Stop Loving You," "Baby Bye Bye," "Velvet Chains"), which he seemingly undervalues. For those who appreciate such things, it also includes a sampling of his Broadway work, with a song from *La Bohème*. —*Tom Roland*

Stones / 1989 / Liberty ✦✦

These Days / 1990 / Liberty ✦✦✦

Greatest Hits, Vol. 2 / 1990 / Warner Bros. ✦✦✦✦✦
Greatest Hits, Vol. 2 contains most of Gary Morris' biggest hits from the mid-'80s that didn't make his first compilation, including "Why Lady Why," "Between Two Fires," "Second Hand Heart," and the duet with Lynn Anderson, "You're Welcome to Tonight." —*Thom Owens*

Full Moon, Empty Heart / 1991 / Liberty ✦✦✦
Gary Morris may have the best voice in country music. However, he's really not a country singer; in fact, his voice is more suited for the Broadway stage. Accordingly, he was the original (and maybe best) Jean Valjean in the musical version of *Les Misérables*. Morris has even ventured into opera. While his voice is magnificent, most of the material on *Full Moon, Empty Heart* is only pleasant, at best. "The Man Upstairs" is a nice ballad, but none of the songs match up to his superb voice, which seems restrained on this release. —*Tim Griggs*

Lynn Morris

Guitar, Vocals / Progressive Bluegrass, Traditional Bluegrass
Sometimes a woman has to push the door open and force people to take notice so she can prove herself as capable in a chosen profession as any man. Three decades ago the world of bluegrass bands, especially bandleaders, was firmly dominated by the male gender. There are a few women who opened the path for others to follow, and Lynn Morris was, and still is, one of those talented, determined trailblazers. Singer, bandleader, and musician, Morris grew up in the little rural town of Lamesa, TX. She wasn't into bluegrass at first, but she loved music, and early on became a guitar player. In college she found bluegrass music—or maybe it found her. Soon the guitar was sold, and the money was put to good use, the purchase of a banjo. Morris finished college, graduating with an art degree, then turned her full attention to a professionally music career. Her first steady gigs came as a member of the bluegrass band City Limits. Later she joined other groups, like Whetstone Run. It was amazingly hard for her to find spots in many bands, since most were all-male, and wanted to stay that way.

Morris began to break new ground for women bluegrass artists, in 1974, when she walked away as the winner in the National Banjo Championship that year. She was the first female to ever win. She was also the International Bluegrass Music Association's first female member on the board of directors, a position she retained for six years. In 1988, Morris took fate into her hands, and put together her own bluegrass band, the Lynn Morris Band. One of the first members was a gifted bassist, her husband, Marshall Wilborn. Additional members are mandolin player Jesse Brock and banjo player and fiddler Ron Stewart. Other artists have served as part of the group, too, like David McLaughlin with his guitar and mandolin, banjo player Tom Adams, and fiddler Stuart Duncan. In 1990

Morris released a debut album, titled *The Lynn Morris Band*. It was recorded under the Rounder Records label, and received rave reviews from bluegrass music critics.

During the '90s a number of other astounding albums followed, like *The Bramble and the Rose*, the chart-topping *Mama's Hand*, and *You'll Never Be the Sun*. Some of the enjoyable tracks bluegrass fans can sample on these albums are "No One Has to Tell Me," "Freight Train Blues," "Valley of Peace," "Kisses Don't Lie," "You'll Get No More of Me," "Heartstrings," and "Blue Skies and Teardrops." Over the years Morris has toured across the U.S. and overseas. She has appeared at festivals, clubs, in U.S.O. shows for service men, the *Grand Ole Opry*, and even at Leavenworth Federal Penitentiary. Her music and skills have earned her many top awards, including IBMA Female Vocalist of the Year, IBMA Song of the Year, SPBGMA Traditional Female Vocalist of the Year, and other honors, some more than once. In 2001, with something like 30 hard-earned years in the business, Lynn Morris and her music are still going strong. —*Charlotte Dillon*

● **The Lynn Morris Band** / 1990 / Rounder ✦✦✦✦✦

The Bramble and the Rose / 1992 / Rounder ✦✦✦

Mama's Hand / Oct. 1995 / Rounder ✦✦✦
Lynn Morris, one of the pioneer women banjo performers to break into bluegrass, returns with *Mama's Hand*, her 1995 release. Morris and her band, which includes her husband, expert bassist Marshall Wilborn, put the blues in bluegrass with "It Rains Everywhere I Go," "Freight Train Blues," "Tell Me How to Mend a Broken Heart," and more. Morris has an upbeat side as well, though, with such fast-paced pickin' as the humorously titled "Dancing in the Hog Trough." It's definitely recommended for traditional-style bluegrass fans. —*Murrday Fisher*

You'll Never Be the Sun / May 11, 1999 / Rounder ✦✦✦✦
Lynn Morris and her bassist/significant other Marshall Wilborn have made beautiful understated music for three albums, but this fourth for Rounder finds new blood spurring the duo onto even greater heights. Banjoist and fiddler Ron Stewart and mandolinist Jesse Brock bring a new sheen to this Texas couple's music, shining brightly on "Wrong Road Again," "The Likes of You," and the instrumental "Twister," which features a guest appearance from former bandmate David McLaughlin. It's a solid collection of performances with a heart as pure as they come. —*Cub Koda*

Shape of a Tear / Mar. 11, 2003 / Rounder ✦✦✦

Muleskinner

f. 1973
Group / Traditional Bluegrass, Contemporary Bluegrass, Progressive Bluegrass, Bluegrass
Muleskinner was perhaps the one and only bluegrass supergroup. Composed of David Grisman (mandolin, vocals), Clarence White (guitar), Peter Rowan (guitar, vocals), Richard Greene (fiddle), and Bill Keith (banjo), the group formed as a favor to a California public television station looking for someone to perform on a show with Bill Monroe's Blue Grass Boys. The choice of musicians was perfect for all had began their careers with bluegrass bands (Rowan, Greene, and Keith with Bill Monroe's band; Clarence White with the Kentucky Colonels; and Grisman with the New York Ramblers) and all had gone on to find success and respect in the industry (White with the Byrds; Grisman and Rowan with Earth Opera). Their appearance on the show was so successful that the band was offered a one album deal with Warner Bros. The subsequent soundtrack to the TV special, an instant hit among bluegrass fans for its mastery of the idiom, has been re-issued several times throughout the '80s and '90s. With the exception of White, who died tragically in an auto accident, the members have reunited from time to time for one-off performances. —*Steve Kurutz*

● **Muleskinner** / 1973 / Warner Bros. ✦✦✦✦✦
How smart are the major labels, such as Warner Bros.? In the early '70s, the company had the rights to this totally historic recording by one of the finest lineups in the history of bluegrass, at least from the perspective of the young, progressive (read: hippie) players of the time. Five years later, the Warners Bros. geniuses had let the *Muleskinner* album go out of print and the dinky bluegrass label Ridge Runner got the rights to reissue it. The resulting printing and layout job, despite a touching tribute to the late great bandmember and bluegrass giant Clarence White, was ironically tacky enough to pass for one of the self-produced sides made up for on-stage sales in the '50s by the cutting-edge early-bluegrass bands who had been so influential. At any rate, the interplay between fiddler Richard Greene and banjoist Bill Keith unlocks harmonic doors inside the old bluegrass mansion, with White and the masterful Peter Rowan providing a wall of rhythm guitar whose strength makes a mockery of the word "acoustic." Fans of the Jerry Garcia bluegrass explorations will want to find this set, as it goes in many of the same musical areas, but with an intensity of invention far beyond the efforts of the grateful bluegrasser. This album also represented one of the first uses of a drum set on a bluegrass album. —*Eugene Chadbourne*

A Potpourri of Bluegrass Jam / 1994 / Sierra ✦✦✦✦
Sierra/Hollywood's *A Potpourri of Bluegrass Jam* is a retitled reissue of Muleskinner's debut album, *Muleskinner*. The bluegrass supergroup—featuring Clarence White, Peter Rowan, David Grisman, Richard Greene and Bill Keith—were one of the first bluegrass bands to push at the limits of the genre, adding elements of contemporary folk, pop, rock and blues to the traditional sound. Years after its initial release, the debut remains a vital, vibrant effort, thanks to the amazing, sympathetic interplay between the musicians. There's an electric spark to this acoustic music that still shocks decades after it was recorded, and their ideas sound just as fresh. Along with *Old & In the Way*, Muleskinner's debut is a landmark in progressive bluegrass. —*Stephen Thomas Erlewine*

Muleskinner Live—Original Television Soundtrack / Feb. 24, 1998 / Sierra/Hollywood ✦✦✦✦
For progressive bluegrass aficionados, *Muleskinner Live—Original Television Soundtrack* is something of a watershed event. Originally broadcast on public television in the

late '70s, the documentary captured the bluegrass supergroup at the peak of their powers in from of a live studio audience in Hollywood. Muleskinner's lineup was a knockout, boasting the talents of Clarence White, David Grisman, Peter Rowan, Bill Keith and Richard Green, so it should come as little surprise that this live record is a powerhouse, illustrating everything that was right about progressive bluegrass. All nine songs that were originally aired on the TV program are here, along with four songs that were edited for broadcast. These tapes were often believed to be lost, so the presence of Sierra's meticulous, loving reissue is quite a boon indeed. *—Thom Owens*

Moon Mullican (Aubrey Mullican)

b. Mar. 29, 1909, Corrigan, Polk County, TX, **d.** Jan. 1, 1967, Beaumont, TX

Piano, Vocals / Western Swing, Honky Tonk, Traditional Country, Instrumental Country

By rights, Moon Mullican should be a legend twice over, in country music and rock & roll. He merged them both—as well as blues, pop, and honky tonk—into a seamless whole at the drop of a hat and the ripple of a keyboard, and also managed to play a seminal role in the history of Western swing, all in a recording career that lasted less than 30 years. Instead, for decades he was one of those "lost" musical figures from the '40s and early '50s, whose career paved the way for rock & roll, who was born just a little too early and was a little too old to take advantage of what he'd started.

Aubrey "Moon" Mullican was born in 1909 in Corrigan, TX, a little more than an hour's drive north of Houston, to a family that owned an 87-acre farm that was worked (at least partly) by sharecroppers. It was one of them, a black blues guitarist named Joe Jones, who introduced Mullican to the blues before he was in his teens. Mullican's instrument of choice, however, was the keyboard: first the family organ, which had been bought so that his sisters could practice playing hymns, and later the piano. By the time he was 14, he was able to make 40 dollars—a good deal more than a day's wages in 1923—for two hours of piano playing at a local café. Music was not only something he loved, but it offered a lot more remuneration than farming (or even overseeing land worked by tenant farmers) seemed to; it was also something that his father, a three-time-a-week churchgoer who regarded blues as the devil's music and the places where people listened to it as the devil's playground, despised. Thus at 16, Mullican left home for the big city of Houston. He made his living playing music and earned the nickname "Moon," which stuck for the rest of his life. During the mid-'30s, he joined the Western swing band the Blue Ridge Playboys, and moved from there to playing in Cliff Bruner's Texas Wanderers, as well as recording with the Sunshine Boys and Jimmie Davis.

Mullican's talents at the ivories were long established by the end of the '30s—he played the piano like it was a part of him—but he moved to the lead singer's spot in 1939 when Bruner recorded the pioneering country trucker song, "Truck Driver's Blues." He turned out to be every bit as good a singer as he was a pianist, with a stunningly expressive voice even if it didn't have an overly great range. This recording and the advent of the '40s heralded the busiest phase of Mullican's career, as he juggled a long-term association with Bruner, a stint in the backing band for Jimmie Davis during the latter's successful campaign for governor of Louisiana, and recording dozens of sides for Decca, RCA Victor, and Columbia Records. It was with King Records, however, beginning in 1946, that he came into his own as a recording artist, cutting a decade's worth of superb music, including a uniquely stylized version of "New Jole Blon" that was a hit in 1947, and the ballad "Sweeter Than the Flowers" in 1948. However, it was in the realm of hillbilly boogie that Mullican had his greatest influence, his versions of "Shoot the Moon" and "Don't Ever Take My Picture Down" pre-figuring rock & roll (especially Jerry Lee Lewis' brand of it) in tone and beat, if not youthful subject matter. In particular, the sides that Mullican cut with producer Henry Glover at King crossed over easily into R&B, though he was equally comfortable with pop standards, honky tonk, and traditional country. By the end of the '40s, he was a member of the *Grand Ole Opry* and found a national audience from its radio broadcasts, which helped propel the sales of his biggest hit, "Cherokee Boogie," in 1951.

Mullican was a star in the world of country music, and may have had more influence there than the sales of his records would lead one to believe. For decades, it was an open secret that he'd co-written "Jambalaya (On the Bayou)" with his fellow *Grand Ole Opry* member Hank Williams, collecting a 50 percent share of the royalties on the sly because of his contractual relationship to King Records. By the mid-'50s, he was trying to get out of King Records, however, and onto one of the major labels. It didn't happen for Mullican until the end of the '50s, a point where his star had fallen considerably. Rock & roll had taken a lot of the edge off the sales of country records, effectively stealing the youngest, most active, and most pliable portion of country's audience. Mullican's record sales, ironically, had fallen even as the stars of such stylistic emulators and successors as Jerry Lee Lewis rose. If Bill Haley, who didn't have half of Mullican's singing ability, seemed over the hill as soon as his balding, pudgy post-30-ish image became well-known, then Mullican, with his cowboy hat, Western twang in his singing, and 50-ish appearance was definitely not what the kids were buying.

By the end of the '50s, he'd been released from King but couldn't get another recording deal very easily, as his sales had declined through the middle of the decade. A move to Coral Records led to a toned-down country approach, which managed to intersect with rock & roll, blues, and pop music, but success still eluded him, even when he recut his King Records hits. Mullican entered the '60s as an overlooked figure, apart from country listeners with long memories and those people lucky enough to catch his performances in Texas and around the Southern and border states. A 1962 heart attack on-stage sidelined him into the following year, but he was back performing and recording in 1963, this time locally for the Hall-Way label of Beaumont, TX, where he made his home. He never gave up performing or his love of pleasing an audience. Finally, on New Year's Eve of 1966-1967, he suffered another heart attack, and died early in the morning on January 1, 1967. Two years later, Kapp Records released *The Moon Mullican Showcase* LP, which included those last sides of his done in Beaumont more than half-a-decade earlier. In the decades since, Mullican's name has gradually become known to a generation of listeners attuned to the roots of rock & roll and pre-Nashville country music, and labels like Ace and Bear Family have issued compilations of his King, Coral, and Hall-Way sides on CD. *—Bruce Eder*

I'll Sail My Ship Alone / 1958 / Sterling ✦✦✦✦✦

One of the first issues in Proper's "Pairs" series, this budget two-disc set is the most comprehensive overview of Moon Mullican's music available, spanning his career from his days with the Blue Ridge Playboys in the mid-'30s to his solo recordings of the early '50s. Its 50 tracks don't contain all of his best recordings (no Mullican collection does), but his most important songs—"I'll Sail My Ship Alone," "New Jole Blon," and "Cherokee Boogie"—are here, along with many other greats. The booklet contains one of the better essays on Mullican's life and career, as well as detailed session notes. *—Jim Smith*

Moon Mullican Sings His All-Time Greatest Hits / 1958 / King ✦✦✦✦✦

Originally released in 1958, *Sings His All-Time Greatest Hits* is Moon Mullican's first album and, essentially, it *is* a greatest-hits collection, featuring 12 of his hit singles from the late '40s and '50s. Drawn entirely from his King Recordings, this collection contains the bulk of his signature songs—including "I'll Sail My Ship Alone," "Cherokee Boogie," "Mona Lisa," "You Don't Have to Be a Baby to Cry," "Pipeliner's Blues," and "I Was Sorta Wondering"—which means it's a fine introduction and retrospective. [There is one slight problem: The compact disc reissue is a little cheaply packaged and contains slightly poor sound, but the music is good enough to make those flaws forgivable.] *—Stephen Thomas Erlewine*

Seven Years to Rock: The King Years, 1946–56 / 1981 / Western ✦✦✦✦✦

Not a hits compilation, it's still a good sampling of Moon in his boogie phase. His take on Tiny Bradshaw's "Well, Oh Well" is required listening for anyone who thinks Elvis invented the hillbilly/R&B cover. *—Dan Cooper*

Moon's Rock / 1992 / Bear Family ✦✦✦✦

This draws from Mullican's later years, after his career had gone into commercial decline. *—Dan Cooper*

★ **Moonshine Jamboree** / 1993 / Ace ✦✦✦✦✦

The "king of the hillbilly piano players" shows up at his best on these 24 tracks, cut during his prime years, 1946 through 1954, when he was associated principally with King Records. It's easy to hear the roots of Jerry Lee Lewis' (as well as elements of Carl Perkins') sound in early cuts like "Cherokee Boogie," on which Moon Mullican and his band find room for a rippling, pounding performance on piano as well as a short, hot guitar solo around a jaunty, funny honky tonk core, and most of the rest of what's here is as good as that. Indeed, 90 percent of this collection would have passed as rock & roll a few years later, with "Rocket to the Moon" so suggestive as to have had the potential to be banned—the latter also features one of the rare sax solos heard on this collection, which mostly features hot piano and guitar. There is some purer country here as well, including "I'll Sail My Ship Alone," Mullican's one serious hit, a ballad of lost love made special primarily by his flashy piano solo and its catchy chorus; the jaunty "Downstream," a lament about a life misspent; and a country waltz version of Leadbelly's "Goodnight Irene." There also a fair amount of country blues, including "I Done It" and "Moonshine Blues," both showcases for the artist's piano. The sound is excellent and the programming generous, and if there is one flaw, it's the lack of information about the recordings or the sessions in the notes, but that doesn't detract from the music at all. *—Bruce Eder*

Showboy Special: The Early King Sides / May 16, 2000 / WestSide ✦✦✦✦✦

This gathers the first 18 sides cut by Moon & His Showboys at their first session for King Records in 1946, plus another five from his first sessions of 1947. The Showboys were a wild Western wing band that played equal parts blues and jazz, mixed in with polka, weepers, and other Texas dancehall fare. They rocked hard on sides like "Shoot the Moon," "Don't Ever Take My Picture Down," "Showboy Special," and "Let Me Rock You Baby," while getting effectively sentimental on tunes like "I Didn't Think You'd Ever Really Go," "When a Soldier Knocks and Finds Nobody Home," and "There's a Chill on the Hill Tonight." Classic Texas honky tonk music from the late '40s, and an essential part of Moon's catalog. *—Cub Koda*

The EP Collection / Jul. 12, 2000 / See for Miles ✦✦✦✦✦

Spanning most of Mullican's career with King Records (1946-1956) and featuring crucial hits that weren't included on Ace's *Moonshine Jamboree* compilation, this is a nice volume two of sorts for people looking for more of the pianist's prime work. Surprisingly, even though it covers nearly identical years, there are only a few overlaps from *Moonshine Jamboree*, and among *The EP Collection*'s treasures is the early classic "New Jole Blon," the wonderfully raucous boogie "Showboy Special," and Mullican's own version of "Jambalaya," the Hank Williams hit that is generally acknowledged to have been co-written by the pianist. It also boasts "Country Boogie," a 1951 recording which, if the drummer at the session had maintained a backbeat instead of merely flirting with one, would have certainly passed as one of the first genuine rock & roll instrumentals ever recorded. *—Jim Smith*

Moon's Tunes / Jun. 26, 2002 / WestSide ✦✦✦

WestSide's second volume of Mullican's King recordings covers the years 1947-1950, featuring more traditional country and Western swing fare. Some of Mullican's big hits are here, including "Sweeter Than the Flowers" and "I'll Sail My Ship Alone," as well as choice lesser tracks like "I Was Sorta' Wonderin'," the bluesy "Trouble, Trouble," and "A Million Regrets." The emphasis throughout is on Mullican's easy vocal style, and while these years weren't the most exciting period of his career, there is some fine, relaxed stuff to be found. *—Jim Smith*

Alan Munde

b. Norman, OK

Banjo, Vocals / Traditional Bluegrass, Progressive Bluegrass, Instrumental Country

Alan Munde was an Oklahoman banjoist who first emerged in 1969 as a player with bluegrass guitarist Jimmy Martin's band. Munde remained with Martin until 1971, when he left to join Country Gazette with Roger Bush (bass), Kenny Wertz (guitar), and Byron

Berline (fiddle). The combo released *Traitor in Our Midst* in 1972 through United Artists. Munde would remain the constant in Country Gazette over the next 20 or so years, even as its membership fluctuated around him. But he also found time to release solo albums and collaborate with likeminded modern bluegrass musicians like Sam Bush and Joe Carr, with whom he released 1996's *Windy Days and Dusty Skies*. Munde also released a series of how-to and transcription books through AcuTab that detailed his banjo style. *—Johnny Loftus*

Festival Favorites Revisited / 1993 / Rounder ✦✦✦✦

Alan Munde is one of those phenomenally talented banjo players who very quietly go around making other, more flamboyant characters look like mere showoffs. He can do that because he's possessed of both incredible chops and transcendent taste (a rare combination in banjoists). As he shows here, he can take bluegrass chestnuts like "Cripple Creek" and "Clinch Mountain Backstep" and reveal new depths of melodic content in them while simultaneously bringing out the best in his supporting musicians. In this case, those musicians include some of the best—the tracks on this album were culled from several LPs and feature performances by mandolinists Roland White and Sam Bush and dobroist Jerry Douglas, just to name a few. But unassuming as he may be, it's Munde's picking that takes center stage here; he plays with both the rock-hard intensity of Earl Scruggs and the melodic inventiveness of Tony Trischka (again, how many banjo players can do either of those things, let alone both?). Check out in particular his rendition of "Earl's Breakdown," a Scruggs classic. It's highly recommended. *—Rick Anderson*

• **Blue Ridge Express** / 1994 / Rounder ✦✦✦✦

Blue Ridge Express is a wonderful compilation, consisting of the best cuts from bluegrass banjo player Alan Munde's three '70s solo albums on the Ridge Runner label. Recorded a few years after his stint as a touring member of country-rockers the Flying Burrito Brothers, the performances here are uniformly high energy. As a founding member of the pioneering bluegrass super group Country Gazette, Munde is credited as one of the first players to successfully combine the rhythmic drive of old school "Scruggs-style" banjo picking with the newer, fiddle-based melodic style propagated by younger folk-influenced players like Bill Keith. The resulting innovative style is displayed to great effect on *Blue Ridge Express*. Munde's playing is often pianistic in its stunning clarity, and his notes have a bright, yet full and round, timbre unmatched by just about any other banjoist. The choice of material here is wide-ranging, and Munde performs each tune with equal conviction, from the simple, oft-covered traditional-sounding melody of folkie Steve Gillette's "Darcy Farrow" to the straight-ahead jazz of Munde's original composition "Munde's Child." The recordings here are somewhat of a revelation in that their stylistic diversity—offering subtle hints of "new grass" to come—and Munde's purity of tone make him seem like a direct influence to later smooth players like guitarist David Grier. *—Pemberton Roach*

Welcome to West Texas / Apr. 7, 1998 / Flying Fish ✦✦✦

The dexterity of these "pickin' professors" from South Plains College in Levelland, Texas cannot be denied. Unfortunately, the music itself sounds academic: nothing formally wrong, but it lacks vitality. You almost want to shout at the speakers to get these guys to loosen up on their breakdowns. *—Tim Sheridan*

Michael Martin Murphey

b. Mar. 13, 1945, Dallas, TX

Guitar, Harmonica, Piano, Vocals / Cowboy, Progressive Country, Country-Rock, Singer/Songwriter, Neo-Traditionalist Country

In many ways, Michael Martin Murphey has the career that Michael Nesmith of the Monkees—with whom Murphey performed early in both of their careers—might've had if he'd never been picked for the NBC series. A guitarist/songwriter, Murphey led the country-rock group the Lewis & Clarke Expedition in the mid- to late '60s and had some pop success, and even got one song, "What Am I Doing Hangin' 'Round?," recorded by the Monkees (with Nesmith singing lead, natch). His songs were cut by the likes of Flatt & Scruggs, Kenny Rogers, Roger Miller, and Bobbie Gentry, and he eventually began recording for A&M Records, and later for Epic Records, where he enjoyed a huge pop hit in the 1970s with "Wildfire." For a time he was known as the Cosmic Cowboy after one of his early songs. Murphey moved to Liberty Records in the early '80s and later jumped to Warner Bros., where his interest in cowboy and Native American subjects led to the foundation of the Warner Western imprint, a subsidiary label devoted to cowboy music and poetry.

Murphey was born in Dallas, TX, and quickly took to playing the ukulele. He had a special love for cowboy stories and songs and also read avidly as a boy—especially the work of Mark Twain and William Faulkner—and was writing poetry before he was in his teens. He began performing as an amateur while in junior high-school and within a few years was playing the clubs around Dallas in the early '60s, combining country, folk, and rock music. Somehow, despite the inherently conservative nature of all of those audiences, Murphey made it work, and he formed a band with a decent following in the area around Dallas. He studied poetry and writing at the University of California, and soon after arriving in the Golden State he was signed up as a songwriter with Sparrow Music. By 1964, he was a popular figure in the folk clubs around Los Angeles and had formed up with three likeminded musicians, Nesmith, John London, and John Raines, under the name the Trinity River Boys, who recorded one never-to-be-released album before disbanding. In 1967, Murphey formed the Lewis & Clarke Expedition with Owen Castleman (aka Boomer Clarke). This group recorded one self-titled album for the Colgems label—not coincidentally, the label for which the Monkees, of whom Nesmith was a member, recorded—and got a moderate hit out of the single "I Feel Good (I Feel Bad)." It was around this time that the Monkees recorded Murphey's "What Am I Doing Hangin' 'Round?"

Murphey left Los Angeles in 1968 to take up residence in the San Gabriel Mountains, where his songwriting blossomed anew. He was signed to Screen Gems (the publishing arm of Columbia Pictures, which also owned Colgems) as a songwriter, and with the exposure that he received from this association, both songs recorded by Flatt & Scruggs and Bobbie Gentry. It was Kenny Rogers who gave Murphey his best showcase as a songwriter, however, by cutting an entire album, *The Ballad of Calico*, comprised of songs Murphey had written about a Mojave Desert ghost town.

Back in Texas, in the Austin area, during the early '70s, he resumed his singer/songwriter career and fell in with Jerry Jeff Walker, Willie Nelson, and B.W. Stevenson. He also put together a new band that specialized in country-rock and folk-rock. In 1971, he was signed to his first solo recording contract on A&M Records, and his first album, *Geronimo's Cadillac* (1972), yielded a modest hit in the title song, which was covered by several other artists, including Hoyt Axton, and also taken up as an anthem by Native American civil rights activists. A second album, *Cosmic Cowboy Souvenir*, was well received critically and also a modest hit in the Austin area.

In 1974, Murphey moved to Epic Records, a division of Columbia, and recorded the first of six albums, *Michael Murphey*, that same year. It was his second album, *Blue Sky—Night Thunder*, recorded in 1975, however, that marked Murphey's commercial breakthrough. He had first heard the story about a ghost horse rescuing people on the desert when he was a boy, from his grandfather, and Murphey dreamed of something similar one night as an adult and set it down to music and words in half an hour that same evening. The resulting song, "Wildfire," got to number three on the pop charts in 1975 and became Murphey's first gold record. Another song off of the same album, "Carolina in the Pines," also made the Top 30. He saw more success with *Swans Against the Sun*—which included his first country chart hit, "A Mansion on the Hill" and "Flowing Free Forever," both in 1976. "Cherokee Fiddle" off of that album was a modestly successful single for Murphey, but six years later Johnny Lee brought it into the Top Ten and into the movie *Urban Cowboy*. Up until 1981, he'd been known as Michael Murphey, but that year he began making a series of film acting appearances, starting with Gus Trikonis' *Take This Job and Shove It*, and began using his middle name in films and on albums, as a way of distinguishing himself from the actor Michael Murphy (*Manhattan*).

In 1982, Murphey signed a recording contract with Liberty Records, which yielded two original albums, *Michael Martin Murphey* and *The Heart Never Lies*, as well as a best-of—made up of superb re-recordings of his A&M and Epic hits as well as his original Liberty hits "Still Taking Chances," "Love Affairs," "Don't Count the Rainy Days," "Will It Be Love," and "Radio Land," the latter a sort of country-flavored equivalent to "American Pie." By that time he'd been voted Best New Male Vocalist of the year 1983 by the American Country Music Association. Additionally, his re-recording of "Carolina in the Pines" rose to the country Top Ten in 1985, outperforming the original Epic version.

In 1985, Murphey moved to Warner Bros. records, making his debut on the label with *Tonight We Ride*. A year later he got to the country Top Five with "A Face in the Crowd," recorded with Holly Dunn, and then reached the number one spot with "A Long Line of Love." Murphey's singles chart success slackened off after 1989 with "Never Givin' Up on Love," which had been used in the Clint Eastwood film *Pink Cadillac* that same year. It was after this that Murphey returned to one of the first loves of his life, cowboy music. In 1990, he cut an album, *Cowboy Songs*, made up of traditional and well-known popular songs from the genre, including "The Yellow Rose of Texas" and "Tumbling Tumbleweeds." That record uncovered a niche waiting to be filled, selling several times more than any of Murphey's other Warner Bros. releases. That success, in turn, led the label to establish its Warner Western imprint, which, in addition to Murphey (who also produces a lot of the work), has also recorded the harmony group the Sons of the San Joachin, veteran singing cowboy Herb Jeffries, and poet Waddie Mitchell.

Murphey has since recorded two subsequent albums of Western songs. *Cowboy Songs III* (1993) features a duet with the late Marty Robbins, no doubt inspired by the success of Natalie Cole's "Unforgettable" duet with her own father—using a voice track recorded by Robbins in 1960—on the song "Big Iron." In 1996, Murphey released a live album on which he is backed by a full orchestra. He has also organized a series of annual celebrations of the American West, called West Fest, which he stages in various western states. *Cowboy Songs 4* appeared in 1998 and several collections followed. In summer 2002, his storytelling continued on *Cowboy Classics: Playing Favorites II*. *—Bruce Eder*

Geronimo's Cadillac / 1972 / A&M ✦✦✦✦✦

After all of Michael Martin Murphey's material is taken into consideration, *Geronimo's Cadillac* comes out on top as one of his finest albums, even though his "cosmic cowboy" persona was yet to be developed. The title track was Murphey's first Top 40 hit, later covered by Cher and Hoyt Axton, while the Monkees eventually sang their own version of "What Am I Doing Hangin' 'Round?" But the most relevant aspect of *Geronimo's Cadillac* is the fact that it merges Murphey's slight left of center country sound with a little bit of gospel in a few places, giving his material greater depth and a genuine "reflective" quality that was often absent from commonplace country music. Tracks like "Backslider's Wine," "Calico Silver," and "Boy From the Country" all contain a unique musical complexion inspired by Murphey's voice and by the simplicity of the harmonica and mandolin. Later albums expose more of Murphey's penchant for being pensive and openly contemplative but, as a debut, *Geronimo's Cadillac*, with its three parts country to one part AM rock, is an enjoyable album as well as a worthy indication as to what kind of artist Michael Martin Murphey would soon become. *—Mike DeGagne*

Cosmic Cowboy Souvenir / 1973 / A&M ✦✦✦

Revealing Michael Martin Murphey's philosophical tendencies as well as his preference to drift into deep, thoughtful songs, *Cosmic Cowboy Souvenir* addresses the type of artist that Murphey truly is. The material on *Cosmic Cowboy Souvenir* is borderline romantic, but the album doesn't get too convoluted, too intricate, or too commercial sounding, and it manages to keep its simplicity and rustic charm intact. Tracks like "Cosmic Cowboy, Pt. 1," "Alleys of Austin," and the beautiful "South Canadian River Song" blend a certain amount of guilelessness with Murphey's own brand of urban poignancy, laying claim to Murphey's trademark as a "non-traditional" country music artist. The songs emerge as wholesome and wonderfully unceremonious, cashing in on Murphey's unconfined image and using it to give his material its wandering, nomadic quality in both the lyrics and the wide variety of string work. Even cuts like "Prometheus Busted" and "Drunken Lady of the Morning" keep the album's unbounded feel from sounding conventional or overindulgent without much effort. Although it spawned no hits, *Cosmic Cowboy Souvenir* is the album that quietly proclaimed Murphey as a progressive country artist, even though the material that was to follow would extend this style to even greater lengths. *—Mike DeGagne*

Michael Murphey / 1973 / Epic ✦✦✦
Despite titles that still promote the Texas movement, this record was done in Nashville with Nashville Cats. Songs like "Nobody's Gonna Tell Me How . . ." and "You Can Only Say So Much" seem to indicate this has worn thin for Murphey. Still, there is some good stuff on here. *—Jim Worbois*

● **Blue Sky—Night Thunder** / 1975 / Epic ✦✦✦✦✦
Blue Sky—Night Thunder is one of the great albums completed by cowboy singer Michael Martin Murphey in the '70s, when he was simply known as Michael Murphey and his career was just beginning. He wrote or co-wrote every song on this recording. Fans will find many of their old favorites on this gold album, including his big hit "Carolina in the Pines" and maybe his most popular song of all time, "Wildfire." This album originally appeared on the market in 1975, but was re-released on compact disc in 1990. Murphey first drew plenty of public attention as a songwriter, and earned a name for himself writing songs for country singer Kenny Rogers. Murphey was soon rubbing elbows with artists like John Denver and Willie Nelson. Listeners will spot the influences of many singers on *Blue Sky—Night Thunder*, but that doesn't cover the sound and talent of the main man behind each song, Michael Martin Murphey. *—Charlotte Dillon*

Flowing Free Forever / 1976 / Epic ✦✦✦
Flowing Free Forever lent "Cherokee Fiddle" to the movie *Urban Cowboy*, but the rest of Michael Martin Murphey's efforts are just as pleasing. Not only does the album establish Murphey's love of wide open spaces and his desire to let his soul roam freely, but there's also a great deal of saxophone, steel guitar, banjo, fiddle, and mandolin to accompany his modern cowboy poetry. Although the album wasn't as commercially successful as a few of his earlier releases, Murphey's visions and persona remain intact, from the slight down-home feel of "See How All the Horses Come Dancing" to songs with a little more depth like "Wandering Minstrel" and "North Wind and a New Moon." *Swans Against the Sun* was released in the same year as *Flowing Free Forever* and it may have stolen a little bit of *Flowing*'s thunder, but for Michael Martin Murphey fans, this album should be included in their collections. *—Mike DeGagne*

Swans Against the Sun / 1976 / Epic ✦✦✦
With guests that include Willie Nelson, John Denver, and Charlie Daniels, 1976's *Swans Against the Sun* is a little different in some respects when compared to rest of Michael Martin Murphey's material. It's not that the music is contrary or eccentric itself, it's the fact that there's a little more juice and fire added to the tracks than usual when compared to the rest of Murphey's albums. But this slight change of pace is definitely for the better, and many of the tracks sound refreshing and novel. Murphey travels in and out of the country music norm, and he even lets John Denver sing a version of Hank Williams' "Mansion on the Hill," which is truly one of the album's highlights. Easily the best cut on *Swans*, "Renegade" broke into the Top 40 on the pop side, reaching number 39 and netting Murphey his fourth Top 40 pop hit. As far as the rest of the tracks, most of them hold up as catchy hybrids of country and country-rock, like "Seasons Change," "Wild West Show," and the affecting "Dancing in the Meadow." *Swans Against the Sun* was a brave release for Murphey in a sense, since many figured it would have to live up to 1975's *Blue Sky—Night Thunder*, which yielded hits in both "Wildfire" and "Carolina in the Pines," yet aside from the "Renegade" single, its makeup, character, and overall presence sound substantially less commercial. *—Mike DeGagne*

Peaks, Valleys, Honky Tonks & Alleys / 1979 / Epic ✦✦✦
This live album heavily showcases Murphey's early work with some interesting twists. His "Cosmic Cowboy" turns into a breakdown, while his song "Another Cheap Western" is coupled with The Olympics' 1958 hit, "Wester Movies." Although it's not a particularly memorable album, it's still kind of fun. *—Jim Worbois*

The Best of Michael Martin Murphey / 1982 / EMI America ✦✦✦✦✦
The 12 songs that make up Capitol's *The Best of Michael Martin Murphey* compilation are a perfect initiation for those who want a taste of Murphey's biggest hits on both sides of the charts. The tracks are divvied up appropriately, with his earlier "cosmic cowboy" era represented by hits like "Carolina in the Pines," "Geronimo's Cadillac," "Cherokee Fiddle" (from *Urban Cowboy*), and "Wildfire," his most renowned single. Five other tracks make up some of Murphey's biggest country singles of the early '80s, with "Don't Count the Rainy Days," "What She Wants," and "Still Taking Chances" all making the Top Ten on the country charts. "What's Forever For" gave Murphey his first number one single on the country side, while it went all the way to number 19 on the pop charts at the same time. Both "Disenchanted" and "Radio Land" could have been replaced with more familiar singles, but even so, this set is an inexpensive and satisfying route for exploring both sides of Michael Martin Murphey's material. *—Mike DeGagne*

The Heart Never Lies / 1983 / Liberty ✦✦

Tonight We Ride / 1986 / Warner Bros. ✦✦✦

Americana / 1987 / Warner Bros. ✦✦

River of Time / 1988 / Warner Bros. ✦✦✦✦✦
Murphey's best includes "From the Word Go," "I'm Gonna Miss You Girl," "Talking to the Wrong Man," and "What Am I Doin' Hanging Around," a song Murphey originally wrote for the Monkees. *—Kenneth M. Cassidy*

Land of Enchantment / 1989 / Warner Bros. ✦✦✦

Cowboy Songs / 1990 / Warner Bros. ✦✦✦✦✦
The first of three albums of cowboy material by Michael Martin Murphey, and one of the better modern collections. Murphey approaches his material with both reverence and humor, which makes this disc less serious than many more grimly authentic efforts. For repertory he draws on the songs of Bob Nolan ("Tumbling Tumbleweeds"), Dale Evans ("Happy Trails"), and Ian Tyson ("Cowboy Pride"); traditional songs that were recorded by the likes of Tex Ritter ("I Ride an Old Paint," "Jack o' Diamonds"), Carl T. Sprague ("When the Work's All Done This Fall"), and Powder River Jack & Kitty Lee ("Tying Knots in the Devil's Tail"); a few of a more general nature, such as the gorgeous "Wild Ripplin' Waters"; and a handful of originals, of which the best is "What Am I Doing Here," which acknowledges the spiritual side of cowboy songs. Murphey doesn't imitate any of the singers associated with earlier versions of these songs in terms of delivery or arrangements, but he does try for a rough-hewn authenticity in his singing, laced with a certain amount of humor, which makes it all the more effective. The backing vocals are provided by Sons of the San Joaquin, and by Tammy Wynette, Red Steagall, Suzy Bogguss, Jim Bob Tinsley, Paulette Carson, Cactus Moser, and others. It was this record that led to the founding of the Warner Western label. *—Bruce Eder*

The Best of Country / 1990 / Curb ✦✦
Best of Country is a ten-track budget-priced collection that features some of Michael Martin Murphey's biggest hits from the early '80s, including "What's Forever For," "Still Taking Chances" and "Love Affairs." Although this isn't a bad budget-priced disc, there are better collections available, offering more songs and better sound for not much more money. *—Stephen Thomas Erlewine*

Cowboy Christmas / May 1991 / Warner Bros. ✦✦
A "Western cowboy" holiday album might seem like a contradiction in terms, but Michael Martin Murphey, in his typical tradition, is able to pull off the unexpected with *Cowboy Christmas*. Like his other records, Murphey balances traditional songs with originals that manage to capture not just the style, but the very feel of classic cowboy songs and it has a down-home warmth and honesty that is lacking from most Christmas albums, including most country Christmas albums. *—Thom Owens*

Cowboy Songs 3 / Oct. 12, 1993 / Warner Western ✦✦✦
Murphey's third album of songs devoted to cowboy folklore and true tales of the West (the second was a Christmas album of Western songs) focuses on real-life outlaws, from Jesse James to Billy the Kid to Belle Starr, and related topics, such as "Birmingham Jail" and "Prisoner's Song." All are performed with a scholar's eye and a fan's heart. *—Michael McCall*

Sagebrush Symphony / Sep. 12, 1995 / Warner Bros. ✦✦
Recorded live with the San Antonio Symphony Orchestra, *Sagebrush Symphony* contains a selection of Michael Martin Murphy's most popular songs, as well as several cowboy standards. Although the combination of orchestra and cowboy songs initially seems forced, it works quite well, particularly because Murphy turns in an impassioned performance. In addition, the presence of guest artists Sons of the San Joaquin, Ric Orozco, Herb Jeffries, and Robert Mirabal adds to the musical diversity and richness of the album. *—Stephen Thomas Erlewine*

● **Wildfire 1972–1984** / Oct. 13, 1998 / Raven ✦✦✦✦✦
This collection of Michael Murphey's work is from his earliest period, when he was hanging out with Jerry Jeff Walker's Lost Gonzo Band and issuing some of the most forward-thinking, philosophical, cosmic cowboy music of the outlaw era. And Michael Murphey was no outlaw. The tracks from his first three albums—*Geronimo's Cadillac*, *Cosmic Cowboy Souvenir*, and *Blue Sky—Night Thunder*, where the mega-smash "Wildfire" originally came from—are the most satisfying. The cuts from these albums—such as the title track from *Geronimo*, "Natchez Trace," "Alleys of Austin," "Cosmic Cowboy," "Boy From the Country," and "What Am I Doin' Hangin' Around?"—reflect an artist who is looking to widen his path, searching restlessly through the country, rock, and blues music he loves for a sound that embodies them all but stays true to the spirit of the West. It's as if Murphey were looking to *become* a cosmic cowboy rather than already seeing himself as the embodiment of the ghosts of mythical Western figures he did later. The music from the early records is wild and untamed, full of experimentation and raw fire. Even "Wildfire" and "Carolina in the Pines" embody the seeker's vision, although it's more closely defined by an uncynical wonder and the willingness to let some of the recording studio in on the journey. And no one can ever argue—unless they're out of their damned minds—that "Wildfire" isn't an amazing pop single. It gave Dan Fogelberg a career for a decade or so. "Carolina in the Pines" is one of the most successful fusions of bluegrass, country, and American schlock pop ever accomplished—and the song is stunningly beautiful. In essence, as this collection of Raven's proves, Murphey didn't completely lose his country heritage until after 1984. While the albums that embodied these songs may not have kept to the standard that these songs do, there was at least one track on each that stood out and is worthy of repeated listening by anyone interested in country music, such as the Murphey/Willie Nelson duet on the stomping "Rhythm of the Road." "Dancing in the Meadow," "Cherokee Fiddle," "Texas Morning," a stunning live version of "Backslider's Wine," and "Take It as It Comes," with its whining pedal steel and slowed-down 4/4 tempo, embody the folky spirit of country with all of its contradiction—though Murphey is on the politically correct side of things. It is only on the pop tracks—such as the synthed-out "Renegade," the Steely Dan jazz-funk of "Nothing Is Your Own," the other mega-smash, "What's Forever For," the Eagles/America-like crossover of "Still Takin' Chances," and the insipid "Don't Count the Rainy Days" that was written for the charts—that fall really short in terms of the cosmic cowboy vision. Murphey got caught up in what people said about him rather than his music. The Jackson-Eagles production blends well with Murphey's gorgeous tenor voice, but the song gets lost, too. As far as compilations go, this one is as

good as it gets and should be readily available despite being an import. Despite its shortcomings, there is more than enough good material to satisfy the curious and begin to satiate those who mourn the loss of that restless cowboy who was looking not for compromise, but the soul of the West. —*Thom Jurek*

Acoustic Christmas Carols / Aug. 4, 1999 / Valley ♦♦♦
Michael Martin Murphey's second Christmas album, subtitled *Cowboy Christmas II*, is, as its title declares, a record of carols played on acoustic instruments. The titles all come from the nineteenth century or earlier, among them such favorites as "Silent Night" and "Joy to the World," and Murphey's arrangements usually feature his own fingerpicked guitar, frequently accompanied by John McEuen on banjo or mandolin, or Paul Sadler on hammer dulcimer, over which he sings solemnly in his slightly wheezy tenor. Things get a bit livelier when Murphey's sons Ryan and Brennan trade blues guitar licks on "Go Tell It on the Mountain" and when daughter Laura duets on "Silent Night." But this is a spare and reverent Christmas album, appropriate for a rustic celebration in a Western church. —*William Ruhlmann*

Playing Favorites / Aug. 21, 2001 / Paras Recording ♦♦♦♦♦
Listening to the songs on this disc is the musical equivalent of inviting a handful of old and dear friends over to dinner. They're a bit older and wiser since they were last seen, and the details of the stories they share have changed slightly with age, but their warmth and familiarity win listeners over instantly. More than simply an exciting greatest-hits project from one of contemporary music's most beloved and enduring artists, the collection features completely new recordings of 11 country, cowboy, and pop crossover classics that perfectly capture the romance and adventurous Western spirit of the singer/songwriter's 30-year recording career, including his best loved hits: "Wildfire," "Carolina in the Pines," and "What's Forever For." Murphey also includes a new, previously unrecorded track, the heartfelt ballad "Dancing Horses," which was written with his oldest son, Ryan Murphey, and has been part of the singer's live repertoire for several years. Murphey's liner notes begin with the on-target comparison that "songs are like children, they grow, evolve, change with time," and the concept behind the project was to document the way his best-loved tunes have gone through this process—using many new musicians and modern recording technology which was not available when the original recordings were done. *Playing Favorites* opens with "Carolina in the Pines" (from 1975's *Blue Sky, Night Thunder*), which was a Top 30 pop hit and the follow-up to "Wildfire." Murphey adds more vocal muscle to this version, but still marvels that the original "was a hit despite having a banjo solo on the radio during the dawning of the disco era." "Adobe Walls" is a more recent song (from 1995's live recording, *Sagebrush Symphony*), inspired by the Hispanic culture of the southern Colorado/northern New Mexico region which is now his home. This is a more stripped down version of the song, which was originally done with an orchestra. Singer Johnny Lee's version of "Cherokee Fiddle" is better known than Murphey's original (from *Flying Free Forever*, 1976) because John Travolta heard Lee sing it at *Gilley's* and wanted it on the soundtrack to the film *Urban Cowboy*. This version features mandolin and is closer to Lee's Cajun fiddle arrangement than Murphey's original two-step. "Cowboy Logic" (from 1990's *Cowboy Songs, Vol. 1*) epitomizes Murphey's lifelong love for cowboy music. This version was developed on-stage, with Murphey doing the old man's voice in a spoken, low tone and with different guitar licks throughout. "I'm Gonna Miss You, Girl" (from 1989's *Land of Enchantment*) features fewer backing vocals than the original and a more stripped-down arrangement. "From the Word Go" (from 1988's *River of Time*) closely approximates the original, while "Geronimo's Cadillac" (from his 1972 debut of the same name) is a beloved song among Native Americans; it spearheaded Murphey's involvement with the American Indian movement, and led to his becoming a member of the Sioux tribe. —*Jonathan Widran*

● **Ultimate Collection** / Oct. 2, 2001 / Hip-O ♦♦♦♦♦
Michael Martin Murphey presents great challenges to anyone trying to construct a one-disc compilation of his work. For one thing, he has recorded for several record companies, all of which have catalogs now controlled by different major labels: A&M (Universal) 1972-1973; Epic (Sony), 1973-1981; Liberty (EMI), 1982-1983; and Warner Bros. (Warner) (1986-1997). (He has recorded independently since 1998.) For another, he has had at least three different careers, one in the 1970s as a pop singer/songwriter, another in the 1980s as a country singer, and a third as a Western artist. The least likely label to assemble a compilation would seem to be Universal, which possesses only two of his albums. But Hip-O, Universal's reissue arm, is nothing if not ambitious, and so we have this *Ultimate Collection*. You've got to admit that they've made an effort. No less than 12 of the 79-minute disc's 21 tracks have been licensed from other labels, including the major pop hit "Wildfire" and the number-one country hits "What's Forever For?" and "A Long Line of Love." They've even dug up "I Feel Good (I Feel Bad)," the 1967 chart single by Murphey's early group, the Lewis & Clark Expedition. That said, the disc will not entirely satisfy any of Murphey's constituencies. Necessarily, there is a focus on his early solo work, with seven tracks drawn from A&M's *Geronimo's Cadillac*, while the rest of his career is presented very selectively. Only five tracks cover the Epic years, Murphey's peak as a singer/songwriter, and his period as a mouthpiece for Nashville songwriters is represented by only his biggest country hits. But as of the appearance of this set, neither Epic nor Warner Bros. had bothered to issue a Murphey best-of, which makes this miscast but well-intended effort by far the best Murphey collection ever released. —*William Ruhlmann*

Cowboy Classics: Playing Favorites II / May 14, 2002 / Paras Recording ♦♦♦
In 1990, after 25 years of performing folk and country-rock and a brief fling on the pop charts, Michael Martin Murphey returned to his cowboy pedigree. While such a move might be considered a commercial one designed to capture the "roots" audience following the *O Brother, Where Art Thou?* craze, at the time he was only helping to revive a niche that seemed to be going the way of the longhorn. Furthermore, Murphey's attraction to the cowboy's way of life had less to do with a romantic whim than an attempt to preserve his own heritage. In 2002, Murphey continued to mine Texas tradition with *Cowboy Classics: Playing Favorites II*. Anyone with even a passing knowledge of Western music will recognize classics like "I Ride an Old Paint," "Red River Valley," and "Yellow Rose of Texas." There's a stately six-minute version of "Streets of Laredo," adorned with fiddle and piano, and a fine two-stepping take on "Whoopie Ti-Ti-Yo." Like a number of old-time musicians, Murphey includes a short note concerning each of the song's origins. He has no intention, however, of reproducing the music as it might have sounded around the campfire. Full acoustic arrangements of guitars, fiddle, accordion, and bass tastefully adorn Murphey's relaxed vocals. For anyone drawn to music flavored by the open Western landscape, *Cowboy Classics: Playing Favorites II* more than satisfies the inner cowpoke. —*Ronnie D. Lankford Jr.*

David Lee Murphy

Vocals / Contemporary Country, New Traditionalist
David Lee Murphy's polished blend of neo-traditional country and mainstream rock flourishes made the vocalist a star in the mid-'90s. Murphy moved to Nashville with hopes of become a star in 1983. For ten years he struggled in the Music City, honing his craft but never catching the attention of the music industry. By the early '90s, he had gained a reputation in Nashville and in 1992 signed with MCA Records. Murphy's first recording was a contribution to the soundtrack of the Luke Perry rodeo movie *Eight Seconds*.

Out With a Bang, his first album, was released in early 1995. "Party Crowd" became the most-played song on country radio in 1995, and the record's second single, "Dust on the Bottle," spent two weeks at number one. *Out With a Bang* would go platinum become the best-selling debut album by a male country single for the entire year of 1995. The Academy of Country Music nominated him for Top New Male Vocalist at the end of the year. Released in the summer of 1996, his second album, *Gettin' Out the Good Stuff*, wasn't quite as successful, although the single "The Road You Leave Behind" reached number 14. —*Stephen Thomas Erlewine*

Out With a Bang / 1995 / MCA ♦♦♦♦
Out With a Bang should have had one extra word added to the front of its title—"Starting." This debut solo recording did start things out with a bang for country singer/songwriter and guitarist David Lee Murphy. This first full-length offering was finished a year after he signed with MCA. The album carries ten tracks, including major hits like "Party Crowd" and "Dust on the Bottle," both of which went on to become signature songs for Murphy. You'll also find his first hit, "Just Once," from the movie *8 Seconds*, on this one. Many of his songs are simple country-rocking fun that will find your toes tapping and your lips following the words. Since he wrote or co-wrote every number on this album, the lyrics give fans a peek into the world that survives inside Murphy's mind; a little taste of what he thinks of life and what he has found that he feels is worth sharing. —*Charlotte Dillon*

● **Gettin' out the Good Stuff** / May 21, 1996 / MCA ♦♦♦♦
A number of David Lee Murphy's songs can make listeners have visions of a jukebox spinning tunes in a crowded room filled with the scents of beer and cigarette smoke, like his 1995 hit "Party Crowd." At the core though, his albums offer a good sample of county-pop stylings without forgetting to add in the fiddle and the steel guitar. There are ten tracks on *Gettin' out the Good Stuff*, Murphy's second full-length recording. He co-wrote three of the songs on this album, but penned the remainders on his own, including "Genuine Rednecks," "I've Been a Rebel (And It Don't Pay)," "She's Really Something to See," and "Every Time I Get Around You," as well as the title track. Murphy's Southern drawl and strong, real-life lyrics make this album a keeper for country fans. —*Charlotte Dillon*

We Can't All Be Angels / Sep. 23, 1997 / MCA ♦♦♦

Jimmy Murphy

b. Oct. 11, 1925, Birmingham, AL, **d.** Jun. 1, 1981
Guitar, Vocals / Rock & Roll, Traditional Bluegrass, Rockabilly
Jimmy Murphy is one of the more enigmatic figures to come out of the country/rockabilly scene of the early to mid-'50s. A virtuoso guitar player and a gifted and inspired songwriter, he had a knack for composing and performing quirky, clever songs that hooked into unusual thematic angles—his first song, "Electricity," equated rural electrification with religious salvation, while the closest he ever got to a real hit, "Sixteen Tons Rock n' Roll," was a satire of the 1956 Tennessee Ernie Ford hit of the Merle Travis song. His music was also strangely archaic in both its form and content, elements that may have doomed his chance for a successful recording career.

Murphy's music drew from a multitude of influences, most notably the blues. His father was an admirer of numerous bluesmen, including Blind Boy Fuller and Leadbelly. He joined his father in the bricklaying trade and always split his time between construction and music. By the mid-'40s, Murphy was an occasional guest on the *Happy Hal Burns Show* on Birmingham's WBRC. He moved to Knoxville, TN, sometime in late 1949 and auditioned successfully for a spot on future *Hee Haw* cast member Archie Campbell's Dinner Bell Show on WROL. He later moved over to WNOX. Campbell was responsible for introducing Murphy to guitarist Chet Atkins, who arranged for Murphy to record a demo tape. This resulted in a publishing contract and also led to a formal recording session for RCA Victor in January of 1951, with Murphy backed only by Anita Carter's bass. The resulting single, "Electricity," was received enthusiastically by all those present, but it died on the vine, as did its B-side, a cautionary tale about a teenage girl gone astray called "Mother Where Is Your Daughter Tonight." Both songs were stylistic and thematic throwbacks practically to the 1930s and displayed the eclectic nature of Murphy's music. None of his other RCA sides sold, including "Big Mama Blues" and "Ramblin' Heart"—both of which featured more prominent backup with electric instruments—and the label dropped him after a year.

Murphy was still a regular on radio in Knoxville and switched from WROL to WNOX in the mid-'50s. In late 1955, he took another shot at a recording career when he was signed by producer Don Law to Columbia Records. He still hadn't come up with the right song, despite the presence of some fairly lively rockabilly-style songs ("Sweet Sweet Lips"), which may have been intended as much as satires of the sound, and none of the material from his first Columbia session in November of 1955 managed to chart. Part of the problem of his music's appeal may have been its spare, almost minimalist sound—in an era of increasing amplification and ever more prominent rhythm instruments, he was an anachronism. For all of his occasional references to contemporary hit songs and pop culture fixations, Murphy's music also had a strangely antiquated feel, as though it would have fit in better in 1940 or 1945, rather than 1955.

He tried to solve problem this at his second session in May of 1956, where he cut a number called "Sixteen Tons Rock n' Roll," a piece that seemed to everyone like the song he'd been looking for. It failed to hit, however, and none of the other material from that session did any better. Murphy was dropped by Columbia in 1956, but he kept playing around Knoxville between bricklaying jobs, and in 1962 he recorded again for the Cincinnati-based Ark label, turning in what was probably his best individual song, "I Long to Hear Hank Sing the Blues." He also recorded for the Midnite label in Grand Rapids, MI, and for King/Starday as well as the Loyal and Rimrock labels, but none of this took. Murphy receded to the memories of listeners in Knoxville and rockabilly collectors and probably would have stayed there if not for a series of events in the mid-'70s.

The reissue of "Electricity" as part of a Library of Congress folk collection in the 1970s got the song more exposure than it ever had back in 1951 and drew one listener in particular, Richard Spottswood, to try and track Murphy down. In 1978, Murphy recorded a new album called *Electricity* with the Sugar Hill label, which had already been making some noise by helping to revive the bluegrass careers of people like veteran rocker Chris Hillman. The record, which had a pre-stardom Ricky Skaggs aboard, was an artistic and commercial success, and another record and a tour were in the works when Murphy died in 1981. Murphy was a true original, almost a stylistic mutant, incorporating blues and country influences from across three decades and casting them in a strangely topical yet anachronistic form. He never found the formula for major commercial success, yet his music lingered over the decades in the minds of many rockabilly enthusiasts (his records were highly prized and highly priced during the 1960s and 1970s). In 1989, Bear Family Records finally responded to the demand for his music by issuing a CD that combined Murphy's complete RCA and Columbia recordings on one CD, *Sixteen Tons of Rock & Roll*. *—Bruce Eder*

● **Sixteen Tons of Rock & Roll** / 1989 / Bear Family ✦✦✦✦

The complete recordings of Jimmy Murphy for RCA and Columbia Records, strangely enough assembled far out of sequence, although one can sequence the songs properly on one's player. The sound is raw and usually pretty bluesy, with Murphy's lively acoustic guitar playing sparking all of it. The subjects and sentiments are a strange mix of contemporary pop culture and what were already dated notions of religion and morality (after all, the Rural Electrification Act had pretty well removed the wonder, if not the novelty, of electricity from a lot of the South, or at least the white population of the South, during the 1930s), making this an extraordinary and unique body of work. The sound, as usual, is excellent, and the sessionography and notes are very thorough. *—Bruce Eder*

Electricity / 1999 / Sugar Hill ✦✦✦

The late Jimmy Murphy always defied categorization. His influences ranged from Jimmie Rodgers and rockabilly to honky tonk and bluegrass. Fact is, Murphy was quite comfortable performing any of these styles and more. With the reissue of *Electricity*, some of Murphy's best performances are highlighted, including a pair of live tracks, "John the Baptist" and "Holy Ghost Millionaire," recorded at the National Folk Festival in 1977. Murphy delivers a thoughtful country number, "Mother Where Is Your Daughter Tonight," one minute, and blues the next, with "Shanty Boat Blues" and "Big Mama Blues." "I Get a Longing to Hear Hank Sing the Blues" is an apt tribute to fellow Alabama singer/songwriter Hank Williams. There are also several gospel tunes, including "The Morning Light Is Breaking" and "He's Always the Same." Murphy, who died in 1981, possessed a dazzling guitar technique and a tried and true, hard country voice. The critics could never decide whether he was bluegrass or straight country, but the fact is, he was both and neither. He was a hardcore country artist grounded in the blues, with an obvious love for bluegrass and gospel music. Nowadays, Murphy would be lumped into the same category with Dwight Yoakam and Steve Earle, but during the '50s and '60s, no one knew exactly what to make of him. Now, years after his death, Murphy has found his niche. Maybe the critics can rest easy now and just enjoy this fine music. *—Michael B. Smith*

● **Southern Roots: The Legendary Starday-Rem Sessions** / May 12, 1999 / Ace ✦✦✦✦

Only nine of the 21 songs on this collection of 1960s recordings were previously released, showing up on obscure independent singles and albums between 1964 and 1969. The precise dates of recordings are not known, although the liner notes speculate that some could date from the early 1960s. Regardless of the exact vintage, the album offers interesting, sparse country that sounds tangled between its roots in the 1920s and 1930s and the modern postwar sound. Murphy was an excellent 12-string guitarist, and his busy picking and strumming creates the effect of hearing more than one instrumentalist. On many of the cuts it sounds as if a bass is pulsing away in the background. The liner notes don't mention any such accompaniment, however, so perhaps it's a one-man show, with the exception of a few harmony vocals by his wife Florine (who takes lead on "I Feel Jesus (My My My)"). Murphy sticks largely to sacred material on this compilation, with a few witty, more contemporary tunes, such as "Hub Cap" ("Just 'cause your head looks like a hubcap, it's no sign that you're a big wheel") and "Tears in the Eyes of a Potato." The minimal country-rockabilly feel and stark singing sound a bit like early Johnny Cash recordings, though the similarities don't go that far—Murphy's vocals have a higher and wider range, and his repertoire has much stronger roots in Appalachian country-folk styles. The only concessions to more contemporary trends are the 1965 single "Half a Loaf of Bread," which has some rockabilly guitar, and its B-side "Take This Message to Mother," a bathetic son-mother battlefield letter, and the only track to feature piano. *—Richie Unterberger*

Anne Murray (Morna Anne Murray)

b. Jun. 20, 1945, Springhill, Nova Scotia, Canada

Vocals, Ukulele / Country-Pop, Soft Rock, Adult Contemporary

Nova Scotia-born Anne Murray built her musical influences from the pop sounds that her parents listened to (Rosemary Clooney, Perry Como) and the Top 40 sounds that AM New York radio stations piped into Canada (Buddy Holly, Elvis Presley, Brenda Lee). Originally she intended to work as a physical-education instructor, but she continued to pursue an interest in music. After she was turned down for a spot on a national TV show called *Singalong Jubilee*, she received a call from the show's producer two years later. He offered her a chance to make records, and when she agreed, she found herself with a million-selling crossover single in 1970, "Snowbird." Murray was frequently at odds with the trappings of success—she even performed barefoot in Las Vegas—and when she got married in 1975, she seemingly dropped out of the business. With her family established, she started working in 1978 with a new producer, Jim Ed Norman, who returned her to prominence with "Walk Right Back" and the million-selling follow-up, "You Needed Me." Throughout the late '70s and early '80s, Murray successfully walked the line between country and pop with a rich alto voice and a knack for romantic material.

As a child in Nova Scotia, music was always one of Murray's hobbies. While she was enrolled at the University of New Brunswick studying physical education, she auditioned for a spot on the Halifax-based weekly CBC television series, *Singalong Jubilee*, but she wasn't hired because they already had an alto singer. Following the rejection, Murray graduated from college and began teaching physical education at the high-school level. Two years after the initial *Singalong Jubilee* audition, the show's producer, Bill Langstroth, called her with the information that a new television show, *Let's Go*, needed an altoist. After some persuasion, Murray agreed to join the program, although she did not give up her teaching job. For the next four years, she sang on *Let's Go*, eventually striking up a professional relationship with the program's musical director, Brian Ahern.

Murray began her career as a recording artist in 1968. Early that year, she was still teaching when she received a call from Ahern, asking her to record for the independent label Arc. Accepting the offer, Murray recorded and released her debut album, *What About Me*, that year. The record was well-received and popular for an independent album, thereby earning the attention of Capitol Records, whose Canadian division signed her to a long-term contract in 1969. The following year, her debut single for the label, "Songbird," became an international hit, reaching the Top Ten on both the country and pop charts in America, while reaching the British Top 40. Following the success of "Songbird," Murray moved to Los Angeles, where she began to regularly appear on Glen Campbell's syndicated television show. However, she didn't like the Californian lifestyle, and she quickly returned to Canada.

Over the course of 1971, it looked like "Snowbird" would be Murray's only big hit, since none of her follow-up singles gained much attention; only "A Stranger in My Place" cracked the Top 40. A cover of Gordon Lightfoot's "Cotton Jenny" in early 1972 returned her to the higher regions of the country Top 40, peaking at number 11, while its follow-up, "Danny's Song," became a Top Ten hit on both the pop and country charts in early 1973. Following two minor country hits, she returned to the Top Ten early in 1974 with "Love Song." The single was followed by two Top Ten country hits—the number one "He Thinks I Still Care" and "Son of a Rotten Gambler." Following those two success, Murray spent a number of years struggling to crack either the pop or country Top 40; during this time, she concentrated on raising a family (she married Bill Langstroth and had a son) more than her musical career.

Murray entered her period of greatest commercial success in 1978, as a cover of "Walk Right Back" climbed to number four on the country charts, followed shortly afterward by "You Need Me," her biggest hit since "Songbird"; the single reached number four on the country charts and topped the pop charts, going gold by the end of the year. For the next eight years, she had a virtually uninterrupted string of Top Ten country hits, highlighted by nine number-one hits: "I Just Fall in Love Again" (1979), "Shadows in the Moonlight" (1979), "Broken Hearted Me" (1979), "Could I Have This Dance" (1980), "Blessed Are the Believers" (1981), "A Little Good News" (1983), "Just Another Woman in Love" (1984), "Nobody Loves Me Like You Do" (1984), and "Now and Forever (You and Me)" (1986). Murray prospered during the era of *Urban Cowboy*, since her music drew as much from pop and easy listening as it did from country.

Murray's sales began to decline in the latter half of the '80s, primarily due to the shifting tastes of the country audience, who was beginning to seek out harder-edged, new traditionalist performers. Nevertheless, she maintained a dedicated following during the late '80s and '90s through her occasional recordings ("Feed This Fire" became a surprise Top Ten hit in the summer of 1990) and her concerts. *—Tom Roland*

What About Me / 1968 / Pickwick ✦✦✦

What About Me is Anne Murray's first album, originally released in 1968 on Canada's tiny Arc label. After Murray signed with Capitol in 1969 and began making hits, Pickwick reissued her Arc recordings for the American market. The folk arrangements bring the acoustic guitar to the foreground, and Murray's confident vocals show that she was already fully developed as a singer. "There Goes My Everything" ventures into folk-rock territory, but most of the music, which includes songs by Tom Paxton and Joni Mitchell, is in the tradition of the Canadian folk scene associated with Gordon Lightfoot and Ian & Sylvia. Murray looks even younger in the cover photos than she would have been when this album was made, but her mature performances make her debut nearly as appealing as her better-known major-label recordings. *—Greg Adams*

Anne Murray's Christmas / 1970 / Liberty ✦✦✦

Anne Murray/Glen Campbell / 1971 / Capitol ✦✦✦

A delightful half hour with Anne Murray and Glen Campbell, the two singers looking like lovers on the front cover, casually dressed, Murray's smiling profile face to face with the man nine years her senior. The music inside, produced and arranged by Brian Ahern and Al DeLory, is perfect light country-pop. There are no hits here, though that is surprising, both "Canadian Sunset" and "Bring Back the Love" should have been contenders. At times Campbell's voice overpowers Murray, but it doesn't detract from the album. The familiarity of these personalities on a well-crafted set of songs works for their audience as well as those who enjoy middle-of-the-road music which can fade into the background. "United We Stand" is a nice duet between the two, but it is missing the production punch that made Brotherhood of Man's version so special the year before. Though there are strings on the interesting version of Randy Newman's "Love Story (You & Me)," for the most part the album is produced very low-key, letting Anne and Glen do their thing without heavy sounds barging in. Murray does a nice job opening up Hoyt Axton's almost gospel-ish "Ease Your Pain," Campbell making it country-pop when he gets his chance at the microphone. Glen had two hits with duets with Bobbie Gentry and in 1976 broke the Top 30 with a medley, "Don't Pull Your Love"/"Then You Can Tell Me Goodbye." Here he takes his first hit, Jimmy Webb's "By the Time I Get to Phoenix," and is offset by Anne Murray crooning Bacharach/David's "I Say a Little Prayer." He's leaving, and she's praying he won't. Everything here has a special charm, "Let Me Be the One" as pleasant as the opening track, "You're Easy to Love," and the nice country finish that is Dallas Frazier's "My Ecstasy" just as satisfying. It's a good job from both singers, and worthy of an encore. —*Joe Viglione*

● **Greatest Hits** / 1980 / Liberty ✦✦✦✦✦

It covers Murray's first decade in the international limelight, beginning with "Snowbird" and concluding with "Could I Have This Dance?," a track from the 1980 movie *Urban Cowboy.* It ranges from the folky "Danny's Song" to her cover of The Beatles' "You Won't See Me," but the middle-of-the-road approach is quite obvious. —*Tom Roland*

Greatest Hits, Vol. 2 / 1989 / Liberty ✦✦✦✦

With her country base firmly established, Murray grew restless in the early and mid-'80s, very much desirous of conquering the pop market. It never quite happened, though she made a nice stab at it in her duet with Dave Loggins, "Nobody Loves Me like You Do." She may not be country in the classic sense, but good music is good music and it's hard not to like "Time Don't Run Out on Me" or "Now and Forever (You and Me)." —*Tom Roland*

15 of the Best / Apr. 27, 1992 / Liberty ✦✦✦✦✦

15 of the Best contains the majority of Anne Murray's best-known songs, including "Snowbird," "Danny's Song," "I Just Fall in Love Again," "Broken Hearted Me," "Shadows in the Moonlight," and "You Need Me," making it an excellent introduction to her smooth country-pop style. —*Thom Owens*

Croonin' / 1993 / ERG ✦✦✦

Murray drops any pretense of singing pure country and steps into a Patti Page/Peggy Lee guise instead. The whole set consists of her taking on chestnuts like "The Wayward Wind," "Secret Love," and "Cry Me a River." —*Dan Cooper*

Now & Forever / 1994 / Capitol ✦✦✦✦✦

This three-disc box contains an excellent booklet and 64 freshly remastered tracks, with a generous helping of alternate mixes, live recordings, and previously unreleased material, including several early, pre-fame nuggets. —*Roch Parisien*

● **The Best . . . So Far** / 1994 / Capitol ✦✦✦✦✦

A serviceable 20-song distillation of the biggest hits from the box set. However, here's the kicker: the single disc includes "Over You," a new-old track from the vaults (released as a single) which is not included in the box set. So if you want to have it all . . . —*Roch Parisien*

Anne Murray / Aug. 7, 1996 / Capitol ✦✦✦

Anne Murray is the vocalist's 30th album and, unlike some of the ones that immediately preceded it, this record is carefully assembled and produced. Murray always straddled the line between country-pop and adult contemporary pop and, with this album, she abandons country for smooth, easy listening pop, designed for adults. For the most part, the results are successful. Producer Ed Cherney has crafted some meticulous arrangements that are easy on the ears and the duet with Aaron Neville on "That's What My Love Is For" is a nice touch. Of course, that means the music is never ear-grabbing, but as pleasant background music *Anne Murray* works. —*Rodney Batdorf*

An Intimate Evening With Anne Murray . . . Live / Mar. 10, 1998 / Capitol ✦✦✦

Anne Murray returned to her Canadian hometown in 1997, performing in Nova Scotia for the first time in 29 years. *An Intimate Evening With Anne Murray . . . Live* captures that performance, and the results are surprisingly strong. After all these years, Murray remains in strong voice, and she delivers 13 songs, including such favorites as "Danny's Song," "Save the Last Dance for Me" and "You Needed Me." Jann Arden joins her for "Insensitive" and "Snowbird," while Bryan Adams duets on "What Would It Take," and both duets are quite engaging. While the album relies a little too heavily on recent material, condensing a number of favorites to a "Croonin' Medley," it remains a welcome reminder of Murray's way with a song. —*Stephen Thomas Erlewine*

This Way Is My Way/Honey Wheat & Laughter / Oct. 20, 1998 / EMI ✦✦✦

This two-fer from EMI Music Canada features a pair of out-of-print Anne Murray LPs: *This Way Is My Way* and *Honey Wheat & Laughter,* both originally issued on Capitol in 1969 and 1970. Highlights among the 22 tracks include Murray's first hit in the U.S., "Snowbird," and a pair of Gene MacLellan tunes, "Hard as I Try" and "Bidin' My Time," which provide a perfect combination of country and soft rock. —*Al Campbell*

Straight, Clean & Simple/Talk It Over in the Morning / Oct. 20, 1998 / EMI ✦✦✦

This two-fer from EMI Music Canada features a pair of out-of-print Anne Murray LPs: *Straight, Clean & Simple* and *Talk It Over in the Morning,* both originally issued on Capitol in 1971. Several of these 20 album tracks are top quality and with the right kind of promotion could have made a much bigger dent in the country charts at the time, especially "Child of Mine," "Talk It Over in the Morning," "A Stranger in My Place," and the Gordon Lightfoot-penned "Cotton Jenny." —*Al Campbell*

Love Song/Highly Prized Possession / Apr. 20, 1999 / EMI ✦✦✦

In 1999, EMI released *A Love Song/Highly Prized Possession,* which contained two complete albums—*A Love Song* (1974, originally released on Capitol) and *Highly Prized Possession* (1974, originally released on Capitol)—by Anne Murray on one compact disc. —*Jason Birchmeier*

Let's Keep It That Way/New Kind of Feeling / Apr. 20, 1999 / EMI ✦✦✦

This two-fer from EMI Music Canada features a pair of out-of-print Anne Murray LPs: *Let's Keep It That Way* and *New Kind of Feeling,* both originally issued on Capitol in 1978 and 1979. These albums highlight Murray's forays onto the pop charts with a cover of the Everly Brothers' "Walk Right Back," "You Needed Me," "I Just Fell in Love Again," and her MOR breakthrough "Shadows in the Moonlight." —*Al Campbell*

Anne Murray and Glenn Campbell/Danny's Song / Aug. 28, 2001 / Capitol ✦✦✦

This two-fer from EMI Music Canada features a pair of out-of-print Anne Murray LPs: *Anne Murray & Glen Campbell* and *Danny's Song,* originally issued in 1971 and 1973, respectively. Surprisingly, there were no hits from the duet album even though both artists were hot at the time. Highlights of the 20 tracks include "Bring Back the Love," "What About Me," "Danny's Song," and the country standard "He Thinks I Still Care." —*Al Campbell*

I'll Always Love You/Somebody's Waiting / Aug. 28, 2001 / Capitol ✦✦✦

This two-fer from EMI Music Canada features a pair of out-of-print Anne Murray LPs: *I'll Always Love You* and *Somebody's Waiting,* both originally issued on Capitol in 1978 and 1980. These albums highlight Murray's adult contemporary hit "What's Forever For" and two cover versions of '60s pop tunes, "Daydream Believer" and "I'm Happy Just to Dance With You." —*Al Campbell*

Heather Myles

b. Riverside, CA

Vocals / Honky Tonk, Neo-Traditionalist Country, Americana

An artist who combines the Bakersfield honky tonk tradition with a very here-and-now intelligence and sass, Heather Myles has developed a reputation as one of the finest traditional-style country singers to emerge in the 1990s and her songwriting is just as strong as her voice. Heather Myles was born and raised in Riverside, CA, where her parents, Jim and Vera Myles, raised her on a ranch. Myles grew up with an enthusiasm for horses, as well as the traditional California country sounds her parents loved. When she was a child, Myles picked up a ukulele belonging to her father and tried to learn how to play it; in time, she graduated to a guitar and in the 1980s, she began performing live with a group called the Lonesome Myle Band. Myles in time developed a strong reputation among the West Coast roots music community and in 1992, she released her first album, *Just Like Old Times,* recorded under her own name for the blues and country-oriented Hightone label.

Her second album, *Untamed,* was released in 1995 and a live album, *Sweet Little Dangerous: Live at the Bottom Line,* followed from the British Demon label in 1996. In 1998, Myles moved to Rounder Records; her first album for the label, *Highways and Honky Tonks,* featured a guest appearance by one of her musical heroes, Merle Haggard, on the tune "No One Is Gonna Love You Better." Another Bakersfield boy, Dwight Yoakam, stopped by to sing a tune on Myles' fifth album, 2002's *Sweet Talk & Good Lies.* —*Mark Deming*

Just Like Old Times / 1992 / Hightone ✦✦✦✦

Untamed / 1995 / Hightone ✦✦✦

It's hard not to root for Myles. She is a singer/songwriter rooted in honky-tonk music who is going the indie route and eschewing Nashville, and those breeds are too rare. Nonetheless, the recipe hasn't yet delivered on all of its promising ingredients. She actually sounds best when she is at her most imitative of vintage '50s sounds: "When You Walked Out on Me" is a rougher-voiced Patsy Cline, "Cadillac Cowboy" is very much in the rockabilly-pop mold of early Brenda Lee. The more contemporary-sounding efforts are blander, and she is occasionally prone to vocal swoops that sound a little hokey. As modern California country goes, it's not bad—it's certainly not overly slick—but it lacks the edge or personality that would establish her as a major contender. —*Richie Unterberger*

Sweet Little Dangerous: Live at Bottom Line / Mar. 19, 1996 / Diablo ✦✦✦✦

● **Highways and Honky Tonks** / Jun. 9, 1998 / Rounder ✦✦✦✦✦

Myles is not a groundbreaker in her mining of Bakersfield and honky-tonk styles, but as classicists go she's pretty good. This is an improvement over her previous studio album (*Untamed*), due mostly to the better material (most of it self-penned); her vocals sound more confident and assertive as well. "You're Gonna Love Me One Day," with its Buddy Holly-ish vocal lines, would have obvious hit potential if country radio would throw its corporate consultants out the window; "Broken Heart for Sale," with its sad steel guitar, is a ballad throwback to the best aspects of the early-'60s Nashville sound. As a lyricist, Myles trots out standard honky-tonk phrases, but overall the execution and sincerity here are at a pretty high level. —*Richie Unterberger*

Sweet Talk & Good Lies / Jun. 2002 / Rounder ✦✦✦✦

While there are more than a few hardy souls still recording honest-to-goodness country music in the Nash-Vegas era, not many of them are women, so it's a good thing that Heather Myles is around and making records, and her fifth album, *Sweet Talk & Good Lies,* finds her in typically strong form. Myles' voice is a superb honky tonk instrument, tough but evocative and capable of registering a wealth of emotions, and she and her band have mastered the nuts and bolts of the classic Bakersfield sound without sounding like they've gotten trapped in some sort of retro time warp ("Never Had a Broken Heart" even sounds like it could be a hit if country & western radio was willing to play actual country & western music). If *Sweet Talk & Good Lies* isn't quite as good as 1998's *Highways and Honky Tonks*, it's still a great showcase for Myles' gifts as a vocalist and songwriter. While Myles sounds like someone you would not want to mess with on "Sweet Little Dangerous," "Homewrecker Blues," and the title cut, she can let down her guard on "One Man Woman Again" without losing her backbone, and on her cover of "By the Time I Get to Phoenix," she manages to find something new in that old chestnut. (Friend and fellow honky tonk enthusiast Dwight Yoakam even pops up to duet on the norteño-flavored "Little Chapel.") She's a great singer, a fine songwriter, knows how to make a solid record, and looks real good in a pair of torn jeans—if Nashville can't figure out what to do with Heather Myles, they deserve everything she gives 'em in "Nashville's Gone Hollywood," while fans who love real country music will want to add this to their personal play list ASAP. —*Mark Deming*

The Nashville Bluegrass Band

f. 1984, Nashville, TN
Group / Progressive Bluegrass, Traditional Bluegrass

The conventional bluegrass categories of traditional and progressive are of little help in describing the music of the Nashville Bluegrass Band. Made up of top Nashville musicians who have devoted themselves to cultivating a unique group sound rather than displaying their individual talents, the band performs classic bluegrass numbers and contemporary songs from the likes of Gillian Welch and Kate Campbell with equal ease. They have been especially noted for their close harmony singing and, almost alone among bluegrass bands, for their investigation of the African-American roots of many modern harmony styles.

The four original members of the Nashville Bluegrass Band—banjoist Alan O'Bryant, guitarist and vocalist Pat Enright, mandolinist Mike Compton, and bassist Mark Hembree—came together as a backing band for a 1984 tour featuring country veterans Vernon Oxford and Minnie Pearl. All were veterans of the Nashville scene and had been involved with top bluegrass bands in the 1970s; Enright was a member of the progressive supergroup the Dreadful Snakes. The Nashville Bluegrass Band was signed to the Rounder label, and their debut, *My Native Home*, was released in 1985. Produced by Béla Fleck, the album announced its innovative leanings with its very first track, an a cappella version of Sister Rosetta Tharpe's "Up Above My Head." *My Native Home* became one of several releases on which the band turned to black gospel, specifically to the virtuoso harmony sounds of the decades on either side of World War II. The all-gospel 1987 album *To Be His Child* included several pieces of African-American origin, and in 1991 the Nashville Bluegrass Band released an entire album, *Home of the Blues*, that featured the Fairfield Four as guest vocalists. Such a project was unheard-of in the virtually all-white world of bluegrass, but it made the Nashville Bluegrass Band into a major touring attraction well beyond the usual festival circuit. Sometimes sharing the stage with the Fairfield Four, they appeared in major U.S. folk venues and became the first bluegrass band to perform in the People's Republic of China. They performed in nearly 20 countries on five continents.

The band experienced several changes in membership: Hembree was replaced by Gene Libbea and Compton by Roland White, and fiddle stalwart Stuart Duncan appeared on every album beginning with 1987's *Idletime*. Still, they maintained a consistent sound and experienced strong success over a series of albums in the late '80s and much of the 1990s. They moved to the Sugar Hill label with 1988's *New Moon Rising* (which featured Peter Rowan and Maura O'Connell), and worked mostly with Jerry Douglas as producer in the '90s. After the Grammy-nominated 1998 album *American Beauty*, the group seemed ready to wind up a stellar career as Libbea and White departed for other projects. But the Nashville Bluegrass Band got a second wind after Enright became one of the voices of the Soggy Bottom Boys, the fictional old-time singing trio led onscreen by George Clooney in the unlikely hit film *O Brother, Where Art Thou?* (the others were Dan Tyminski and Harley Allen). Compton and Duncan also appeared on the film's soundtrack, and Compton began performing as part of the *Down from the Mountain* band that backed the variety of bluegrass headliners that appeared as part of a successful concert tour and documentary of that name. From these events emerged a reconstituted Nashville Bluegrass Band, now with bassist Dennis Crouch (a student of the group's original bassist, Mark Hembree) and Compton on mandolin once again. The group undertook major tours in 2002 and 2003. —*James Manheim*

My Native Home / 1985 / Rounder ✦✦✦✦

The Nashville Bluegrass Band / 1987 / Rounder ✦✦✦✦✦
The Nashville Bluegrass Band selects highlights from the group's first two albums for Rounder Records. Though the band's music would improve with time, this is a terrific overview of the group's origins. —*Thom Owens*

Idletime / 1987 / Rounder ✦✦✦

To Be His Child / 1987 / Rounder ✦✦✦✦✦
To Be His Child is an affecting sampling of the Nashville Bluegrass Band's gospel material, featuring both their string work and several tracks that feature an a cappella quartet. —*Thom Owens*

New Moon Rising / 1988 / Sugar Hill ✦✦✦

The Boys Are Back in Town / 1990 / Sugar Hill ✦✦✦✦

Home of the Blues / 1991 / Sugar Hill ✦✦✦
Home of the Blues is one of the Nashville Bluegrass Band's finest albums, boasting a handful of excellent originals like "Blue Train," and interpretations of standards like "Old Daingerfield," and, as a bonus, a live cut with the black gospel group the Fairfield Four. —*Thom Owens*

★ **Waitin' for the Hard Times to Go** / 1993 / Sugar Hill ✦✦✦✦✦
Waitin' for the Hard Time to Go is an excellent collection from a stellar bluegrass band. Instead of choosing to follow either a traditional or progressive direction, the Nashville

Bluegrass Band decide to alternate between the two approaches, which makes it a considerably richer and eclectic record than most contemporary bluegrass albums. *Waitin' for the Hard Times to Go* won the 1993 Grammy Award for Best Bluegrass Album. —*Thom Owens*

Still Unplugged / Oct. 1995 / Sugar Hill ✦✦

Unleashed / Oct. 1995 / Sugar Hill ✦✦✦
The new CD from the all-star Nashville Bluegrass Band is a jaunty, highly musical collection of contemporary tunes with a few trads. thrown in for good measure. The bluegrass and light gospel singing is very agreeable, unforced and as always with this band, it seems completely natural. Too often this style of country singing is adopted but not lived in. Not the case here. This is a very strong album. Instrumentalists trade licks back and forth with casual authority. Some of the highlights are "I Got a Date," "Tear My Stillhouse Down" and "The Doorstep of Trouble." —*Richard Meyer*

American Beauty / Jul. 21, 1998 / Sugar Hill ✦✦✦✦
Always a delight, this band is one of the best in any genre. Pure and true to the music, they pull off such classics as the Flatt & Scruggs song "The Johnson Boys" and Ralph Stanley's "Holiday Pickin'" with finesse. They do a wonderful cover of Bob Dylan's "Livin' the Blues" and make the Gillian Welch-David Rawlings tune "Red Clay Halo" feel almost ancient. "All Alone," penned by Candice Randolph, is outstanding, with Alan O'Bryant's banjo calling out to the faithful. —*Jana Pendragon*

Nashville West

f. California
Group / Outlaw Country

The genesis of the legendary, short-lived country-rock group Nashville West came in the mid-'60s when multi-instrumentalist Gene Parsons (no relation to Gram) and fiddler Gib Gilbeau, who had been together in a band called the Castaways years earlier, were brought in to do a Gosdin Brothers session. The Byrds' Chris Hillman, who was producing, also brought in guitarist Clarence White, formerly of the Kentucky Colonels, to play on the session. White, Parsons, and Guilbeau would go on to form a core unit that played behind country acts as the house band for Bakersfield International Productions. The three also wrote and performed together in various incarnations before forming Nashville West. Around this time, Parsons came up with the mechanism that would give White his trademark sound. The Stringbender allowed him to play licks on his Fender Telecaster that sounded like steel guitar.

In 1967, White, Parsons, and Guilbeau brought in bassist Wayne Moore, who had been in the Castaways with Parsons and Guilbeau, and they became an official group. The quartet adopted their moniker from a California club at which they had a residency, the Nashville West. Country-rock notables such as Gram Parsons and future Flying Burrito Brother Sneaky Pete Kleinow would sit in with the group. However, Nashville West came to an end in 1968 when Gram Parsons abruptly left the Byrds and the group asked White to replace him. (White had already guested on three Byrds albums, including his important role on the seminal *Sweetheart of the Rodeo*.) At White's instigation, Gene Parsons was also brought into the Byrds to replace drummer Kevin Kelley. Hillman, who had pushed to bring in White, quit soon after to form the Flying Burrito Brothers with Gram Parsons. Reportedly, White and Gene Parsons were asked to join the Burritos, but stayed on with Roger McGuinn in the Byrds. On 1969's *Dr. Byrds & Mr. Hyde* album, the Byrds recorded White's signature instrumental, "Nashville West," named after the group in which the song was born.

In July 1973, Clarence White was struck and killed by a drunk driver while loading equipment into a car after a gig with the re-formed Kentucky Colonels (which included his brothers) in Palmdale, CA. Guilbeau went on to work with Linda Ronstadt, play in the group Swampwater, and team-up with Sneaky Pete Kleinow in Cold Steel. In 1974, Guilbeau and Gene Parsons joined a latter-day version of the Flying Burrito Brothers. In 1978, ten years after Nashville West's demise, Sierra Records issued the group's only album, a self-titled LP recorded during a gig. The album, which was recorded on a two-track that Gene Parsons had hooked up to the sound system and microphones at the club, represents an important missing link in country-rock history. In 1997, the album was reissued on CD with several bonus tracks. —*Erik Hage*

● **Nashville West** / 1976 / Sierra ✦✦✦✦
There are a few records that can be considered birthplaces of what has become known as "country-rock." Two Gene Clark albums, *Echoes* and *Fantastic Expedition*, come to mind, as well as the Byrds' *Sweetheart of the Rodeo* and the International Submarine Band's debut. Add to that list—and put it high up there—*Nashville West*, a self-titled debut by a group that consisted of Gib Guilbeau, Wayne Moss, and two future Byrds, Gene Parsons and the great Clarence White, and it's White's awesome guitar work that puts this album in a legendary context. Aside from the revolutionary playing by White, the group has a forceful yet laid-back groove that, if you like it on the first cut, "Nashville West,"

will have you digging the whole record. Parsons' drumming has a slightly soulful edge, which predates the Flying Burrito Brothers' experiments by several years. One of the best cuts on the album is a cover of "Ode to Billy Joe," which has White and Parsons laying into a groove that is indescribably delicious. Ignoring the historical value of this CD, the whole record is a hell of a lot of fun. Vocally, not really what you'd call a masterpiece, but it doesn't matter—*Nashville West* is a record that should be owned by any fan of the Byrds, the Flying Burrito Brothers, Dillard & Clark, and country music as a genre. It's brilliant. *—Matthew Greenwald*

The Legendary Nashville West Album / 2003 / Rev-Ola ✦✦✦
This CD reissue of the only album of Nashville West material, originally titled *Nashville West*, is preferable to the LP version of *Nashville West* as it adds four extra tracks (which had also been available on a previous CD reissue of the record on the Sierra label). It also has detailed historical liner notes, though the Nashville West story is so confusing and labyrinthine (the band was not called Nashville West while it was active, for instance) that it's not easy to follow no matter how well it's written. The music, while of considerable historical interest for anyone interested in the roots of country-rock, isn't as revolutionary or exciting as some might expect. This live material wasn't recorded with the intention of release, for one thing, so although the fidelity is OK, it's not nearly as pristine or polished as those of most official releases, even by late-'60s standards. The impression is one of a congenial Californian country bar band rather than one of innovators, though Clarence White's guitar work sparkles, and the band sprinkles in far more electric rock influences than most country acts were using at the time. Too, the mix and material were selected to spotlight the instrumental rather than the vocal facets of the band, giving a somewhat unbalanced picture of what the group sounded like. It's certainly pleasant stuff, and occasionally the songs are outstanding, particularly "Love of the Common People" and the tremolo-soaked cover of "By the Time I Get to Phoenix." *—Richie Unterberger*

Rick Nelson

b. May 8, 1940, Teaneck, NJ, **d.** Dec. 31, 1985, DeKalb, TX
Guitar, Vocals / Rock & Roll, Country-Rock, Rockabilly, Teen Idol
Rick Nelson was one of the very biggest of the '50s teen idols, so it took awhile for him to attain the same level of critical respectability as other early rock greats. Yet now the consensus is that he made some of the finest pop/rock recordings of his era. Sure, he had more promotional push than any other rock musician of the '50s; no, he wasn't the greatest singer; and yes, Elvis, Gene Vincent, Carl Perkins, and others rocked harder. But Nelson was extraordinarily consistent during the first five years of his recording career, crafting pleasant pop-rockabilly hybrids with ace session players and projecting an archetype of the sensitive, reticent young adult with his accomplished vocals. He also played a somewhat underestimated role in rock & roll's absorption into mainstream America—how bad could rock be if it was featured on one of America's favorite family situation comedies on a weekly basis?

Nelson entered professional entertainment before his tenth birthday, when he appeared with father Ozzie (once a jazz musician), mother Harriet, and brother David on a radio comedy series based around the family. By the early '50s, the series was on television, and Ricky grew into a teenager in public. He was just the right age to have his life turned around by rock & roll in 1956 and started his recording career almost accidentally the following year. The story's sometimes been told that he had no professional singing ambitions until he recorded his debut single to impress a girlfriend. The single, a cover of Fats Domino's "I'm Walkin'" that went to number four, was helped immensely (as all of his early singles would be) by plugs on the *Ozzie & Harriet* TV show.

So far the script was adhering to the Pat Boone teen idol prototype—a whitewash of an R&B hit stealing the thunder from the pop audience, sung by a young, good-looking fella with barely any musical experience to speak of. What happened next was easy to predict commercially but surprisingly satisfying musically as well. Nelson was a fairly hip kid who preferred the rockabilly of Carl Perkins and Elvis Presley to the fodder dished out for teen idols, and over the next five years he would offer his own brand of rockabilly music, albeit one with some smooth Hollywood production touches and occasional pure pop ballads. Nelson recruited one of the greatest early rock guitarists, James Burton, to supply authentic licks (another great guitarist, Joe Maphis, played on some early sides). Some of his best and toughest songs ("Believe What You Say," "It's Late") were written by Johnny and/or Dorsey Burnette, who had previously been in one of the best rockabilly combos, the Johnny Burnette Rock & Roll Trio. Ricky could rock pretty hard when he wanted to, as on "Be-Bop Baby" and "Stood Up," though in a polished fashion that wasn't quite as wild and threatening as rockabilly's Southern originators.

Nelson really hit his stride, though, with midtempo numbers and ballads that provided a more secure niche for his calm vocals and narrow range. From 1957 to 1962, he was about the highest-selling singer in the U.S. except for Elvis, making the Top 40 about 30 times. "Poor Little Fool" and "Lonesome Town" (1958) were early indications of his ballad style; in the early '60s, "Travelin' Man," "Young World," "Teen Age Idol," and other hits pointed to a more countrified, mature style as he honed in on his 21st birthday (by which time he would shorten his billing from "Ricky" to "Rick"). He could still play rockabilly from time to time, the most memorable example being "Hello, Mary Lou" (co-written by Gene Pitney), with its electrifying James Burton solos.

Nelson was lured away from the Imperial label by a mammoth 20-year contract with Decca in 1963 (which would be terminated prematurely in the mid-'70s), and for a year or so the hits continued, at a less frenetic pace. Early-1964's "For You," however, would be his last big smash of the '60s. The fault wasn't all the Beatles and changing music trends—on both singles and albums, much of the material was either substandard pop or dusty Tin Pan Alley standards, although isolated tracks still generated some sparks. He wasn't exactly starving, as he continued to appear on *Ozzie and Harriet*. But by the mid-'60s even that institution was declining in popularity, leading to its cancellation in 1966.

Nelson had a strong country feel to much of his material from the beginning, and by the late '60s it was becoming dominant. He covered straight country material by the likes of Willie Nelson and Doug Kershaw and formed one of the earliest country-rock groups, the Stone Canyon Band, with musicians who had played (or would play) with Poco, Buck Owens, Little Feat, and Roger McGuinn. A cover of Bob Dylan's "She Belongs to Me" made the Top 40 in 1970, but his country-rock outings attracted more critical acclaim than commercial success, until 1972's "Garden Party." A rare self-composed number, based around the frosty reception granted his contemporary material at a rock & roll oldies show, it became his last Top Ten hit.

Nelson would continue to record off and on for the next dozen years and toured constantly, yet he was unable to capitalize on his assets. A big part of the problem was that although Nelson wanted to play contemporary music, he didn't write much of his own material, which was a basic precept of self-respecting rock acts after the advent of the Beatles. Nor did he tap into good outside compositions, and there's little of interest on the albums he recorded over the last decade or so of his life. He died (along with his fiancée) in a private plane crash on December 31, 1985, on his way to a New Year's Eve gig in Dallas, at the age of 45. *—Richie Unterberger*

Ricky / Oct. 1957 / United Artists ✦✦✦
After releasing his first two singles, "A Teenager's Romance"/"I'm Walkin'" and "You're My One and Only Love," on Verve Records, Ricky Nelson switched to Imperial Records in the fall of 1957 for his third single, "Be-Bop Baby"/"Have I Told You Lately That I Love You?," and his debut album, *Ricky*. The result was even greater success: the single's A-side reached the top five and its B-side the Top 40, making for a gold record, and the LP topped the charts. Heard at length for the first time on the 12-track album, the 17-year-old continued to display the combination of natural pop instincts and genuine rock & roll feel that set him apart from the burgeoning pack of Elvis Presley imitators. He was derivative, to be sure, a TV star from a celebrity family who attended Hollywood High School and whose life had been scripted for public consumption since he was eight years old, making him a far cry from the Hillbilly Cat. But he also sang rhythmically in his smooth voice, negotiating the rock & roll beat with far greater ease than Pat Boone. Two songs were borrowed from Carl Perkins and one from Jerry Lee Lewis, and Nelson covered Jimmie Rodgers' recent hit "Honeycomb." All of his covers were more relaxed, less frantic than the originals, but the band, pushed way back in the mix, kept up a steady guitar combo sound. There were also several updates from what could have been the Ozzie Nelson catalog: "Have I Told You Lately That I Love You" (1945), "Am I Blue?" (1929), and "I'm Confessin'" (1930), plus a version of the recent Cole Porter hit "True Love." In Nelson's hands, these songs sounded more like Elvis Presley than Bing Crosby, though the older generation was never quite forgotten, and that was the idea. *—William Ruhlmann*

Ricky Nelson / Jul. 1958 / Imperial ✦✦✦✦
Elvis Presley's first LP was called *Elvis Presley*, and his second *Elvis*. In stark contrast, Ricky Nelson's first LP was called *Ricky*, and his second Ricky Nelson. Nelson remained a slavish imitator of the Sun Records rockabilly style on his sophomore long-player, but he had improved enormously in the endeavor. The production was closer to the Sun Studio sound, with the same kind of vocal echo, and in James Burton, Nelson had found the real article, a classic rock & roll guitarist with a style that was both distinctive and perfectly attuned to the essentials of the sound. But the improvement over the first album was also attributable to Nelson himself, who had become a far more involved singer. He may have been turning out carbon copies of Presley ("There's Good Rockin' Tonight") and Roy Orbison ("Down the Line") from Sun, as well as old favorite Fats Domino ("I'm in Love Again"), whose "I'm Walkin'" had launched his career, and even Little Walter ("My Babe"), but he executed these approximations with the fervor of a true believer. And he was beginning to write his own material ("Don't Leave Me This Way") and introduce the writing of his band (Burton and bass player James Kirkland's "There Goes My Baby"). As usual, there was a complement of tricked-out pop covers from the past—the 1940 copyright "Someday (You'll Want Me to Want You)," the 1944 song "I'll Walk Alone," the recent movie hit "Unchained Melody"—songs that Nelson also managed to be comfortable singing. And there was his latest (and biggest) hit, "Poor Little Fool." *Ricky Nelson* thus marks a distinct advance over *Ricky*, even if was not embraced as enthusiastically as its predecessor, peaking only in the Top Ten and remaining in the charts only a couple of months. *—William Ruhlmann*

Songs by Ricky / 1959 / Imperial ✦✦✦✦
By the summer of 1959, a little more than two years into his performing career, 19-year-old Ricky Nelson had put together a regular band consisting of guitarist James Burton, pianist Gene Garf, bass player James Kirkland, and drummer Richie Frost (with the Jordanaires brought in for background vocals on recordings), and he had what amounted to house songwriters. Brothers Johnny & Dorsey Burnette, separately and together, had written his hits "Waitin' in School," "Believe What You Say," and "It's Late," all uptempo rockabilly-tinged numbers, while Baker Knight contributed the lighter hits "Lonesome Town," "I Got a Feeling," and "Never Be Anyone Else But You." These composers had just written Nelson's latest double-sided Top Ten single, "Just a Little Too Much" (by Johnny Burnette)/"Sweeter Than You" (by Knight), and it served as the anchor for his fourth album, *Songs by Ricky*. For the LP, the Burnettes also brought in "You're So Fine," "Don't Leave Me," "A Long Vacation," and "I've Been Thinkin'," while Knight's additional tracks were "You'll Never Know What You're Missin'" and "One Minute to One." The result was a consistent record by a writing and performing team at the peak of its powers, everyone contributing to an overall sound that was a rhythmic, smooth development on the kind of raw rockabilly invented in Memphis by the original artists at Sun Records. Nelson & co.'s take on the style never worked up quite as much of a sweat, but they clearly had their hearts in the right place, and Nelson had turned into a supple vocalist with a sure sense of the material. Occasionally, the songs leaned a bit too much to teen sentiments, but that was in keeping with the trend of the times, which was leading away from rock to softer sounds. *—William Ruhlmann*

Ricky Sings Again / Jan. 1959 / Imperial ♦♦♦
By the time of his third album, most of which was recorded when he was 18 years old, Ricky Nelson had lots of performing under his belt, and the roadwork showed in his much more confident vocals. Also, as a major recording artist, he was having material written for him instead of having to fill up his LPs with covers of other people's hits. In those songs and in the covers he still did, he hewed to the rockabilly sound developed by Elvis Presley and others in and around Memphis, TN. In particular, he had become a follower of Dorsey Burnette, who co-wrote his 1958 hit "Believe What You Say" with his brother Johnny and took sole writing credit on the album's first two tracks, "It's Late" (soon to be a Top Ten hit) and "One of These Mornings." Such songs were tailored for Nelson, but they were very much in the style of what was currently popular; "It's Late," for example, in sound and subject matter, bore similarities to the Everly Brothers' 1957 hit "Wake Up Little Susie." Thus, even on his own songs, Nelson still sounded like a carbon copy of his betters, and when he tackled a classic like "Trying to Get to You," an Elvis Presley Sun sessions song, or Hank Williams' "I Can't Help It," his inadequacies were accentuated. In a sense, Nelson was a victim of his own success; he was still a promising, developing artist in terms of his abilities and experience, but he was also the second most successful pop singles artist of 1958, right behind Presley, which raised the bar of expectations. *Ricky Sings Again* found him branching out toward country music and anticipating the rise of teen pop, but it did not live up to his star status. *—William Ruhlmann*

Ricky Sings Spirituals / Feb. 1960 / Imperial ♦♦♦
Ricky Nelson followed the lead of other pop stars of his day, particularly Elvis Presley, by recording this four-song, 45-rpm EP of religious material. The only oddity about it was that the songs were all originals. The term "spiritual" is usually thought to mean traditional material, but the songs on *Ricky Sings Spirituals* were written by his in-house songwriter, Baker Knight ("Glory Train," "I Bowed My Head in Shame"); his pianist, Ray Johnson ("March With the Band of the Lord"); and his father, Ozzie Nelson ("If You Believe It"). Nevertheless, the songs were in the style of old-time gospel music, in arrangements that emphasized a driving rhythm, Johnson's piano, and a female chorus. Nelson sang the songs with assurance, but not with the feeling that Presley put into his gospel recordings. As with Nelson's rock & roll performances, his gospel recordings were sincere imitations of music he seemed to like. *—William Ruhlmann*

More Songs By Ricky / Jul. 1960 / Imperial ♦♦♦
Eight of Ricky Nelson's first nine singles hit the Top Ten (sometimes even the B-sides made the Top Ten) and seven went gold. The string was broken in the fall of 1959, and though "I Wanna Be Loved," his tenth single, and "Young Emotions," his 11th, went Top 20, changes were clearly in order. The rockabilly Nelson loved and had imitated was out of fashion, replaced by softer pop music, some of it in a neo-big band style. On *More Songs By Ricky*, his first album in 11 months, Nelson shifted gears. One change was probably inevitable: Johnny and Dorsey Burnette, upon whom Nelson had relied for material, had launched their own solo careers and were less available to him, providing only one title, Dorsey's characteristic "Hey Pretty Baby." Nelson's other songwriting standby, Baker Knight, had three songs on the LP, but he too was adapting to the new style. His "Ain't Nothin' But Love," like another of the album's songs, "Here I Go Again," sounded a lot like the horn-filled productions of Lloyd Price, who had replaced Nelson as the country's second biggest pop singles artist in 1959. Horns, in fact, abounded on the record, particularly a saxophone that took several fat solos. Without the Burnettes, Nelson turned back to the music of his bandleader father Ozzie, cutting covers of songs from the 1920s ("Baby Won't You Please Come Home," "I'd Climb the Highest Mountain"), the 1930s ("When Your Lover Has Gone"), and the 1940s ("Time After Time," "Again") in arrangements that incorporated not only horns, but also strings and chirpy female backup vocals. It was all a big change from Nelson's previous recordings, and it did not restore his commercial fortunes. *—William Ruhlmann*

Rick Is 21 / May 1961 / Imperial ♦♦♦♦
When his record sales began to sag in 1959, Ricky Nelson turned away from the rockabilly sound of his early recordings to a more middle-of-the-road style on his fifth album, 1960s *More Songs by Ricky.* But that didn't help, and in early 1961, the artist returned to a modified rock sound, bringing in new writers like Jerry Fuller and Gene Pitney, and coming up with a streamlined pop/rock approach. The result was a comeback when the single "Travelin' Man"/"Hello Mary Lou" took off, the A-side hitting number one and the B-side the Top Ten, for the singer's eighth gold record. He had already recorded all of *Rick Is 21* before that happened, though, and the album fulfills the promise of the single. There are a couple of the compromised covers of oldies that filled *More Songs By Ricky*—"Do You Know What It Means to Miss New Orleans" and "Stars Fell on Alabama"—no doubt suggested by his father Ozzie, but the rest of the album is guitar rock arrangements of songs written by old hand Dorsey Burnette ("My One Desire") and new recruits Fuller, Pitney, Johnny Rivers, and Dave Burgess. Fuller is the real hero, contributing the excellent rocker "Break My Chain" (complete with a terrific James Burton guitar solo) in addition to "Travelin' Man," but the overall quality of the material is high, and Nelson's band plays it well. The singer himself sounds far more comfortable than he did on his last album, finally having acquired his own sound after years spent copying either Elvis Presley or his father's big band. As its title suggests, *Rick Is 21* is Rick—not Ricky—Nelson's first mature statement as a recording artist. And 21 is a good age for a teen idol to be making his first comeback. *—William Ruhlmann*

Album Seven By Rick / Mar. 1962 / Imperial ♦♦♦
Rick Nelson achieved his first comeback in the spring of 1961 with the double-sided hit "Travelin' Man"/"Hello Mary Lou," and he made it last into 1962 by tapping "Travelin' Man" songwriter Jerry Fuller for the further hits "A Wonder Like You" and "Young World." Nelson did not hold recording sessions for LPs per se, but rather assembled his albums from a series of sessions. In a sense, this meant that a disc like *Album Seven by Rick* tended to consist of tracks that hadn't already been chosen as singles, presumably because they were deemed weaker than the ones that were picked. Be that as it may, the album is a good set of songs mostly written for Nelson by his old guard of songwriters—Sharon Sheeley ("Thank You Darling," with Jackie DeShannon), Dorsey Burnette ("Excuse Me Baby," "Mad Mad World"), and Baker Knight ("Stop Sneakin' 'Round")—and the new boys Fuller ("Congratulations," "Poor Loser," "Baby You Don't Know," "History of Love," the last two with Dave Burgess) and Gene Pitney ("Today's Teardrops," with Aaron Schroeder). The writers have a good sense of Nelson's taste in rock & roll, even if on occasion they sound like they're trying to clone earlier triumphs ("Today's Teardrops" particularly sounds like an attempt to rewrite "Hello Mary Lou"). For once, even the covers are striking: "Summertime" is given a rock & roll arrangement that would have surprised George Gershwin, and the choice of the 1958 country hit "I Can't Stop Loving You" was inspired, even if Ray Charles was to present his overhauled version to the world within months. *Album Seven by Rick* was a disappointing seller, probably because it didn't contain any hits, not even "Young World," just then ascending the singles charts. But it is a worthy follow-up to *Rick Is 21*. *—William Ruhlmann*

For Your Sweet Love / 1963 / Decca ♦♦♦
Nelson's first album for Decca set the pattern for the mid-'60s LPs he would record for the label: professional, respectable, and somewhat tame, although there would always be some bright spots worth a listen (usually in the form of James Burton solos). The material often recalls, but does not match, his earlier '60s ballads such as "Travelin' Man." "Gypsy Woman" is an uncommonly tough number for the period, and "I Will Follow You" is a decent cover of the Little Peggy March hit "I Will Follow Him." Some of the better numbers show up on the best-of anthologies covering Nelson's Decca period, and most listeners are best off limiting themselves to those. *For Your Sweet Love* was combined with his subsequent 1963 album *For You* on a single-disc CD compilation on Ace Records. *—Richie Unterberger*

Best Sellers By Rick Nelson / 1963 / Imperial ♦♦♦
By 1963 standards, Rick Nelson's first hits compilation is a rather curious affair, bypassing chart blockbusters like "I'm Walkin'," "Travelin' Man," and "Hello, Betty Lou" altogether in favor of lesser-known entries like "That's All" and "I'm in Love Again" (neither of which cracked the *Billboard* Top 40, making the *Best Sellers* claim more than a little spurious). By contemporary standards, however, the album affords a wonderful opportunity to experience hits like "Waitin' in School" and "Stood Up" that have been marginalized (if not altogether disregarded) by myopic oldies radio play lists—particularly revelatory is 1958's "Believe What You Say," a chugging rocker in the mold of vintage Buddy Holly. *—Jason Ankeny*

Rick Nelson Sings "For You" / Dec. 1963 / MCA ♦♦♦
"Fools Rush In," with its classic James Burton guitar work, overshadowed everything else on Nelson's second Decca album, which contained another big hit in the title track. The singer moved into some more country-oriented material on cuts like "A Legend In My Time," but as a whole the atmosphere was too sedate and the material was unexceptional, sometimes sounding like inferior derivations of his early-'60s hits for Imperial. [*For You* was combined with his previous 1963 album *For Your Sweet Love* on a single-disc CD compilation on Ace Records.] *—Richie Unterberger*

The Very Thought of You / 1964 / Decca ♦♦
Passable, mostly medium-tempo pop/rock that did little to either embarrass the singer or raise the listener's temperature. The title track was a Top 40 hit, and his last, it turned out, for six years. There are obscure songs by Mann-Weil ("I Don't Wanna Love You") and Charlie Rich ("Just a Little Bit Sweet"), but it all sounds like pleasant throwaway filler, the best cut being his cover of the great lost Drifters-like tune "I Wonder" (a small hit in 1961 for the Pentagons). [A 1997 CD reissue on Ace combines this and another 1964 LP, *Don't Breathe a Word*, onto one disc.] *—Richie Unterberger*

Ricky Sings for You / Jan. 1964 / Imperial ♦♦♦

Spotlight on Rick / 1965 / Decca ♦♦
Nelson's mid-'60s albums would have seemed like far more respectable efforts had they been able to escape comparison with a fast-changing rock scene. As it was, the innovations of the British Invasion, Beach Boys, Phil Spector, and much more made his records, as professional and pleasant as they were, seem hopelessly outdated. Nelson continued to tread water on this album, which had some average contributions by above-average writers like Baker Knight and Jerry Fuller. An energetic stab at Chuck Berry's "I'm Talking About You," and a nice tune from the pen of ex-Cricket Sonny Curtis ("Don't Breathe a Word"), were mild highlights. [A 1997 CD reissue on Ace combines this and another 1964 LP, *The Very Thought of You*, onto one disc.] *—Richie Unterberger*

Best Always / 1965 / Decca ♦♦♦
Not a bad mid-'60s effort from Nelson, although there's little to distinguish it from the other easygoing pop/rock albums he made during the period, except for the slightly higher quality of the material. "Mean Old World," and both more forceful and moodier than anything else he cut in 1964-1965, is by far the best song, but there are some OK numbers from the pens of Johnny Burnette & Jerry Fuller; Jimmy Seals & Dash Crofts also contribute to a couple of tunes, "Only the Young" (written by Seals & Charles Eugene) boasting a quite good pop melody. Rick stretches his vocal range on the cover of the Skyliners' "Since I Don't Have You," and gives a taste of his upcoming move into country with a version of "You Don't Know Me." [A CD reissue on Ace combines this and another 1965 LP, *Love and Kisses*, onto one disc.] *—Richie Unterberger*

Love and Kisses / 1966 / Decca ✦✦
Even by the modest standards of Nelson's early Decca albums, *Love and Kisses* is a tepid, stagnant collection. Some of the cuts sound vaguely updated with harder-edged guitars than unusual, and there's a hint of his future country direction with the cover of Roger Miller's "I Catch Myself Crying." But had the album never appeared, it wouldn't have added to or subtracted a whit from the total sum of his legacy. Three of the numbers were featured in Nelson's forgotten *Love and Kisses* film, including the embarrassing single "Come Out Dancin'." [A CD reissue on Ace combines this and another 1965 LP, *Best Always*, onto one disc.] *—Richie Unterberger*

Bright Lights & Country Music / 1966 / Decca ✦✦✦
Although Nelson's move into straight country music didn't result in notable commercial gains, it made sense given that his last few rock albums hadn't done much, and that most rockabilly performers had long since gone into the country market. Nelson had recorded some country material throughout his career, and this album didn't really require a radical rethink. He still used his regular band, but augmented them with Glen Campbell and future Byrd Clarence White, and regular guitarist James Burton played dobro. It wasn't country-rock, but straight country without any Nashville gloss in the production, emphasizing covers of songs by Willie Nelson, Merle Travis, Bill Anderson, and Doug Kershaw. Nelson sounded more engaged with the material than he had in years, and the album was a decent effort, but as it relied so heavily on songs that had already been made famous by others, it wasn't going to make him stand out as an innovator. Nelson acquitted himself well with his one original, "You Just Can't Quit," and Campbell contributed "Here I Am," yet the best cut was the fastest, "Night Train to Memphis." [The album has been combined with 1967's *Country Fever* onto a single-disc CD reissue on Kent.] *—Richie Unterberger*

Country Fever / 1967 / Decca ✦✦✦
Country Fever continued the country direction of Nelson's previous album, *Bright Lights & Country Music*, and the approach of each record was similarly weighted toward interpretations of country classics. Hank Williams, Jimmie Rodgers, and Acuff-Rose all get covered here, and his sensitive reading of Willie Nelson's "Funny How Time Slips Away" is a standout. There's no denying, though, that the best cut is the one that gets closest to rockabilly (a cover of "Mystery Train"). Nelson's two original compositions weren't much, but on the other hand there was an obscure Bob Dylan tune that the composer had not released ("Walkin' Down the Line"), and "Things You Gave Me," with its steady beat and harmonies, sounded more like a foreshadowing of late-'60s California country-rock than anything else Nelson had recorded up to this point. [The album has been combined with 1966's *Bright Lights & Country Music* onto a single-disc CD reissue on Kent.] *—Richie Unterberger*

Another Side of Rick / 1967 / Decca ✦✦
By 1967 Nelson's records were no longer selling, and out of step with contemporary trends. So why not, someone must have reasoned, try to put Nelson *in* step with contemporary trends? It was about as good a strategy as any, considering his tried-and-true rockaballad format wasn't working. But giving him fruity psychedelic baroque production was not the answer, indeed yielding rather embarrassing results. Nelson showed good taste by covering three Tim Hardin songs, but producer John Boylan's five songs (one co-written with Rick) not only weren't that good, but weren't a good match for the vocalist. Nelson wasn't totally blameless, penning one of the album's crummiest songs, the overdone pop-psychedelic "Marshmallow Skies," twith James Burton. At one point during the cover of "Georgia on My Mind," the musicians suddenly slip into double-time, as if they can't wait to get the obviously doomed-to-failure album over with. [The LP has been reissued, together with 1968's *Perspective*, on an Ace CD that combines both albums onto one disc.] *—Richie Unterberger*

Perspective / 1968 / Decca ✦✦
Although released in August 1968, this album had actually been recorded 16 months before it came out, an indication that Decca wasn't of a great mind to keep Nelson in the forefront of the market in the late '60s. Like his previous *Another Side of Rick*, this had him making ill-advised efforts to modernize his sound with a more orchestrated production, whose nature sometimes often verged on the rococo. Nelson did have good taste in selecting material, covering songs by Paul Simon, Richie Havens, Harry Nilsson, and Randy Newman, all of whom (except Simon) were little known by most of the public in 1967; indeed, Nelson covers five Newman songs in a row to end the album, creating the effect of an aborted *Nelson Sings Newman* concept record. Producer John Boylan added most of the remaining tunes, including the odd "Hello to the Wind (Bonjour Le Vent)" (co-written with Nelson), which with its Burt Bacharach-type piano-based melody and brief interlude of spoken female French narration might find a comfortable home on some lounge music reissue. [The LP has been reissued, together with 1967's *Another Side of Rick*, on an Ace CD that combines both albums onto one disc.] *—Richie Unterberger*

Rick Nelson in Concert / 1970 / Decca ✦✦✦

Rudy the Fifth / 1971 / MCA ✦✦✦

Ricky Nelson / 1971 / United Artists ✦✦✦✦
If vinyl's your preference, this two-album, 26-track compilation is a fine overview of his prime, although it misses some minor hits. Otherwise, it makes much more sense to pick up EMI's two lengthy CD retrospectives of the same era. *—Richie Unterberger*

Garden Party / 1972 / Decca ✦✦✦✦✦

Playing to Win / 1981 / Capitol ✦✦✦✦
Playing to Win was an album of beginnings and endings for Rick Nelson. It was his first LP in more than three years, marking the start of his fifth label affiliation, this one with Capitol Records, and, though it was released just short of five years before his death, it was his last album of new, original material to be released during his lifetime, followed only by 1985's *All My Best*, a collection of re-recordings of his hits marketed on television. In his bid for yet another commercial comeback, Nelson updated his rock & roll sound to take into consideration the heartland rock of artists like Bruce Springsteen, Bob Seger, and Tom Petty, as well as punk/new wave. As always, he had great taste, which allowed him to pick great material: John Fogerty's forgotten 1975 song "Almost Saturday Night"; "Back to Schooldays" from Graham Parker's 1976 debut album *Howlin' Wind*; John Hiatt's "It Hasn't Happened Yet," which would become a country hit for Rosanne Cash in 1983; and Ry Cooder's lilting "Do the Best You Can." He also contributed two of his own compositions, both of which seemed to have bitter personal meanings: "The Loser Babe Is You," a romantic kiss-off perhaps directed at his soon-to-be-ex-wife, and "Call It What You Want," likely addressed to his last label, Epic Records. He never intended the result to be his final statement, but it will serve. [The 2001 CD reissue adds six tracks, including the 1982 one-off single "No Fair Falling in Love"/"Give 'Em My Number"; three tracks that first appeared on the *Legacy* box set, among them a convincing version of Buddy Holly's "Rave On" and the previously unreleased John Hiatt song "Radio Girl." That makes three Hiatt songs on the disc, and Nelson should have done even more of them.] *—William Ruhlmann*

The Best of Rick Nelson / 1987 / EMI America ✦✦
Best of Rick Nelson is a 12-track budget-priced collection that features some of his biggest hits, including "Poor Little Fool," "Travelin' Man," "Hello Mary Lou," "Garden Party," "Lonesome Town," "Never Be Anyone Else But You," and "Teenage Idol," as well as some lesser-known songs like "Don't Leave Me This Way" and "Young World." Although this isn't a bad budget-priced disc, there are far better collections available, offering more songs and better sound for not much more money. *—Stephen Thomas Erlewine*

Live 1983–1985 / 1989 / Rhino ✦✦

★ **Legendary Masters** / 1990 / EMI America ✦✦✦✦✦
Legendary Masters compiles all of the hits Ricky Nelson released for Imperial Records in the late '50s, including "Be-Bop Baby," "Stood Up," "Lonesome Town," "It's Late," "Poor Little Fool," "Sweeter Than You," "Just a Little Too Much," "Never Be Anyone Else but You," and "Believe What You Say." A few essential items are missing—such as the Verve sides "A Teenager's Romance" and "I'm Walkin' "—and it would have been nice if the disc had extended into the early '60s, so songs like "Travelin' Man" and "Mary Lou" could have been included, but *Legendary Masters* remains a vital collection from one of the most undervalued early rock & rollers. *—Stephen Thomas Erlewine*

Best of 1963–1975 / 1990 / MCA ✦✦✦
No longer Rockin' Ricky, but Responsible Rick, his Decca output was wildly inconsistent. The early efforts like "Fools Rush In" and "String Along" still feature guitarist James Burton prominently. *—Bill Dahl*

The Best of Rick Nelson, Vol. 2 / Mar. 18, 1991 / Capitol ✦✦✦✦✦
Focusing primarily on Rick's early-'60s material for Imperial, this 27-cut disc is not quite as rocking as *Vol. 1*, but still offers plenty of worthy moments. It includes all of his massive, midtempo teen idol ballad hits of the era: "Young World," "A Wonder Like You," "Teenage Idol," "It's Up to You," and the number-one hit "Travelin' Man." Teen ballads they might have been, but James Burton's masterful guitar licks and Nelson's assured, committed delivery placed them leagues above other teen-idol hits of the period. Of more interest to serious fans are the inclusion of several minor hit singles and covers of R&B tunes. And of course, there's the first-class rockabilly hit "Hello Mary Lou" (penned by Gene Pitney), perhaps his best recording of the decade. His surprisingly raucous cover of "Summertime" features, amazingly, the same bassline used as a hook on the Blues Magoos' psych-pop-garage hit "We Ain't Got Anything Yet" years later. The pleasures of this CD are modest but consistent. *—Richie Unterberger*

Stay Young: The Epic Recordings / Aug. 31, 1993 / Epic ✦✦✦✦✦
There's not a lot on this CD that even longtime Rick Nelson fans are likely to recognize—not a lot of good seemed to come out of Rick Nelson's two-year stay at Epic Records, based on the released evidence at the time, and certainly there were no hits, just an uneven first album (*Intakes*) and an entire second LP (titled Back To Vienna) produced by Al Kooper that was never issued, plus a four-song EP that contained badly remixed versions of three songs that he'd cut in Memphis. This 18-song CD contains all of the material that audiences should have had a chance to hear from his Epic recordings, the way they were intended to be heard. It's better than anything that anyone ever heard at the time, and were some of the best sides Nelson ever records, running the gamut from engaging country-pop to heavily produced art-rock and raw rockabilly. Reissue producer Bob Irwin distilled down the best of the songs off of *Intakes* and the best four songs from the Al Kooper-produced sessions, and the original, undubbed Memphis sides from the third album. The highlights, in addition to ornate pop/rock renditions of "Mama You've Been on My Mind" and "Carl of the Jungle" from the Kooper sessions, include the raw, stripped down "That's Alright Mama," "Almost Saturday Night," and "Rave On" from Memphis, Nelson's great lost single, his touchingly introspective rendition of "Dream Lover" from the fall of 1978, and his achingly beautiful country ballad "Send Me Somebody To Love," one of the prettiest records he ever made. Most of this CD was entirely new material at the time of its release and it has held up startlingly well over the decades, as strong as any other collection of his work that one can buy, despite the absence of any hits. *—Bruce Eder*

Ricky Nelson & Stone Canyon Band / Apr. 25, 1995 / Edsel ✦✦✦✦✦

Rockin' With Ricky / 1996 / Ace ✦✦✦✦✦
Originally released as an LP in 1984, the CD version of this collection of Nelson's hardest-rocking early material doubles in length to include a whopping 32 tracks (on one disc) from the late '50s and early '60s. This has most of his uptempo smashes, à la "Be-Bop Baby," "Waitin' in School," and "Believe What You Say," with a host of LP tracks, many of

them covers of songs made famous by Elvis, Carl Perkins, Roy Orbison, and the like. The two volumes of greatest hits on EMI are more well-rounded and, on the whole, better retrospectives of his classic era. This is pretty good proof that he could rock respectably, though, with some good cuts that are hard to find on reissues, like "You're So Fine" and "Poor Loser." *—Richie Unterberger*

The Best of the Later Years (1963–1975) / 1997 / Ace ♦♦♦
On the surface, this would appear to have the advantage over its American counterpart (MCA's *Best of 1963-1975* compilation). It's got far more material, for one thing: 26 songs, which is 11 more than the domestic retrospective. There are a couple of significant omissions of tracks that appear on the U.S. set, though, most notably the moody Billy Vera-penned "Mean Old World." Its absence from this anthology is inexcusable, as it was his best mid-'60s recording. Judgment calls aside, this does have the hits Nelson managed to squeeze in on Decca before the rise of the Beatles ("For You" and the great "Fools Rush In"), along with some rocking obscurities like "I Got a Woman" and "Gypsy Woman"; the ballads "The Very Thought of You," "I Wonder," and "There's Nothing I Can Say" are also quite good. After 1964 he slid into early country-rock, which veered from decent to dispensable. "Garden Party" is here, of course, but the additional late-'60s and early-'70s cuts not present on MCA's disc really don't add much. *—Richie Unterberger*

For Your Sweet Love/Sings for You / 1997 / Ace ♦♦♦
This combines Nelson's first two Decca albums (each originally released in 1963) into one CD. Although "Gypsy Woman," "I Got a Woman," and "Fools Rush In" standup to the best of his early-'60s hits, the rest of the material is too average, and the execution too low-energy, to merit attention from anyone except fervid Nelson fans. It's nonetheless among the best stuff that Nelson would record for the label. Some of the best tracks are also on the anthologies covering the singer's Decca's work, which are recommended alternatives for those not seeking a complete Nelson discography. *—Richie Unterberger*

The Very Thought of You/Spotlight on Rick / Dec. 9, 1997 / Ace ♦♦♦
Two 1964 albums are combined onto one CD on this reissue, which adds historical liner notes. Nelson's mid-'60s albums would have seemed like far more respectable efforts had they been able to escape comparison with a fast-changing rock scene. As it was, the innovations of the British Invasion, Beach Boys, Phil Spector, and much more made his records, as professional and pleasant as they were, seem hopelessly outdated. *The Very Thought of You* was passable, mostly medium-tempo pop/rock that did little to either embarrass the singer or raise the listener's temperature. The title track was a Top 40 hit, and his last, it turned out, for six years. There are obscure songs by Mann-Weil ("I Don't Wanna Love You") and Charlie Rich ("Just a Little Bit Sweet"), but it all sounds like pleasant throwaway filler, the best cut being his cover of the great lost Drifters-like tune "I Wonder" (a small hit in 1961 for the Pentagons). Nelson continued to tread water on *Spotlight on Rick*, which had some average contributions by above-average writers like Baker Knight and Jerry Fuller. An energetic stab at Chuck Berry's "I'm Talking About You" and a nice tune from the pen of ex-Cricket Sonny Curtis ("Don't Breathe a Word"), were mild highlights. *—Richie Unterberger*

Best Always/Love and Kisses / Mar. 10, 1998 / Ace ♦♦♦
A two-fer CD reissue combining two 1965 LPs onto one disc. *Best Always* isn't bad, although there's little to distinguish it from the other easygoing pop/rock albums he made during the period, except for the slightly higher quality of the material. "Mean Old World," both more forceful and moodier than anything else he cut in 1964-1965, is by far the best song, but there are some OK numbers from the pens of Johnny Burnette & Jerry Fuller; Jimmy Seals & Dash Crofts also contribute to a couple of tunes, "Only the Young" (written by Seals and Charles Eugene) boasting a quite good pop melody. Rick stretches his vocal range on the cover of the Skyliners' "Since I Don't Have You" and gives a taste of his upcoming move into country with a version of "You Don't Know Me." Even by the modest standards of Nelson's early Decca albums, *Love and Kisses* is a tepid, stagnant collection. Some of the cuts sound vaguely updated with harder-edged guitars than unusual, and there's a hint of his future country direction with the cover of Roger Miller's "I Catch Myself Crying." But had the album never appeared, it wouldn't have added to or subtracted a whit from the total sum of his legacy. Three of the numbers were featured in Nelson's forgotten *Love and Kisses* film, including the embarrassing single "Come Out Dancin'." *—Richie Unterberger*

Bright Lights & Country Music/Country Fever / Jun. 23, 1998 / Ace ♦♦♦
This is a reissue of the two albums—1966's *Bright Lights & Country Music*, and 1967's *Country Fever*—on which Nelson plunged for the first time into country music whole hog. On *Bright Lights* he still used his regular band, but augmented them with Glen Campbell and future Byrd Clarence White, and regular guitarist James Burton played dobro. It wasn't country-rock, but straight country without any Nashville gloss in the production, emphasizing covers of songs by Willie Nelson, Merle Travis, Bill Anderson, and Doug Kershaw. Nelson sounded more engaged with the material than he had in years and the album was a decent effort, but as it relied so heavily on songs that had already been made famous by others, it wasn't going to make him stand out as an innovator. Nelson acquitted himself well with his one original, "You Just Can't Quit," and Campbell contributed "Here I Am," yet the best cut was the fastest: "Night Train to Memphis." *Country Fever* was similarly weighted toward interpretations of country classics. Hank Williams, Jimmie Rodgers, and Acuff-Rose all get covered, and his sensitive reading of Willie Nelson's "Funny How Time Slips Away" was a standout. There's no denying, though, that the best cut is the one that gets closest to rockabilly (a cover of "Mystery Train"). Nelson's two original compositions weren't much, but on the other hand there was an obscure Bob Dylan tune that the composer had not released ("Walkin' Down the Line"), and "Things You Gave Me," with its steady beat and harmonies, sounded more like a foreshadowing of late-'60s California country-rock than anything else Nelson had recorded up to this point. *—Richie Unterberger*

Another Side of Rick/Perspective / Sep. 29, 1998 / Ace ♦♦♦
A reissue that combines 1967's *Another Side of Rick* and 1968's *Perspective* onto one CD. By 1967, Nelson's records were no longer selling, and were out of step with contemporary trends. So, why not, someone must have reasoned, try to put Nelson in step with contemporary trends on *Another Side of Rick*? It was about as good a strategy as any, considering that his tried-and-true rockaballad format wasn't working. But giving him fruity psychedelic baroque production was not the answer, indeed yielding rather embarrassing results. Nelson showed good taste by covering three Tim Hardin songs, but producer John Boylan's five songs not only weren't that good, but weren't a good match for the vocalist. Nelson wasn't totally blameless, penning one of the album's crummiest songs, the overdone pop psychedelic "Marshmallow Skies," with James Burton. At one point during the cover of "Georgia on My Mind," the musicians suddenly slip into double-time, as if they can't wait to get the album over with. Although released in August 1968, *Perspective* had actually been recorded 16 months earlier, an indication that Decca wasn't exactly eager to keep Nelson in the forefront of the market in the late '60s. Like *Another Side of Rick*, this found him making ill-advised efforts to modernize his sound with a more orchestrated production that often verged on the rococo. Nelson did have good taste in selecting material, covering songs by Paul Simon, Richie Havens, and Harry Nilsson, plus five by Randy Newman to end the album. Producer John Boylan added most of the remaining tunes, including the odd "Hello to the Wind (Bonjour Le Vent)" (co-written with Nelson), which, with its Burt Bacharach-type piano-based melody and brief interlude of spoken female French narration, might find a comfortable home on some lounge music reissue. *—Richie Unterberger*

Rick Sings Nelson/Rudy the Fifth / Feb. 10, 1999 / BGO ♦♦♦
In 1999, BGO released *Rick Sings Nelson/Rudy the Fifth*, which contained two complete albums—*Rick Sings Nelson* (1970, originally released on Decca) and *Rudy the Fifth* (1971, originally released on Decca)—by Rick Nelson on one compact disc. *—Jason Birchmeier*

25 Greatest Hits / Mar. 2, 1999 / EMI ♦♦♦♦

A&E Biography / Jun. 8, 1999 / Capitol ♦♦♦♦
Released to coincide with the cable television documentary of the same name, *A&E Biography* provides a concise summary of Ricky Nelson's career from "I'm Walking" to "Garden Party." It isn't quite definitive, since such gems as "Waitin' in School" and "Stood Up" are missing, but it does have the lion's share of Nelson's greatest hits, including "Be-Bop Baby," "Believe What You Say," "Poor Little Fool," "Lonesome Town," "Travelin' Man" and "Hello Mary Lou," along with the previously mentioned pair of bookends. For the collectors, there a previously unreleased "Cindy (Get Along Cindy)," which also features Dean Martin and Walter Brennan, but this is primarily for the casual fan and neophyte, and they'll be quite pleased with it. *—Stephen Thomas Erlewine*

A Night to Remember / Oct. 8, 1999 / Varese ♦♦♦

Legacy / Nov. 21, 2000 / Capitol ♦♦♦♦♦
As a four-CD set spanning Rick Nelson's entire career, this will likely stand as the most thorough overview of the singer's music ever issued. This doesn't mean, though, that it's the best anthology of his work, unless you subscribe to the viewpoint that his post-mid '60s records were about as good as his pre-mid-'60s ones, since a full two discs (or half) of this package is devoted to that post-mid-'60s output. Basically, it illustrates his trajectory in phases: disc one, as a good-to-great pop-rockabilly singer; disc two, as a still-good but not quite as vital teen idol in the late '50s and early '60s; disc three, as a fair but not great country-rocker; and disc four, as a has-been playing out the string with uninspired adult contemporary and revival tracks during his final years. The album is an impressive feat of cross-licensing, though, starting with three songs from his first singles (for Verve, and never easy to find on reissues), drawing a lot from his creative peak at Imperial, and then from his spottier efforts for Decca and other labels. All of his Top 40 hits are here, along with a dozen or so previously unreleased tracks, none too remarkable, as well as the 45-single versions of a few early hits. The song selection is very good, but not infallible: The absence of the moody "Mean Old World," which was about the best thing he did in the mid-'60s, is inexplicable. If you are a big fan and do like Nelson's country-rock phase, this is a reasonable investment, but if you don't, you should stick to those collections that focus on his 1957-1965 recordings. *—Richie Unterberger*

Album Seven by Rick/It's Up to You / Jan. 30, 2001 / BGO ♦♦♦

Ricky/Ricky Nelson / Jun. 19, 2001 / Capitol ♦♦♦♦
Ricky Nelson's first two albums and assorted singles, recorded when he was 17 years old, are triumphs of taste over experience. As chronicled in James Ritz's liner notes, Nelson turned to music more or less on a dare, and while he could carry a tune, he had little personality as a singer when he started, relying for his popularity more on his familiarity as a television star and his good looks. The sound of the day was Elvis Presley-styled rockabilly and the even wilder sounds of Jerry Lee Lewis and black R&B performers, but unlike such pale imitators as Pat Boone, Nelson didn't have to be talked into awkwardly appropriating such material; clearly, he really liked it. Especially on the earliest cuts here, he was barely competent, completely draining "Whole Lotta Shakin' Goin' On" of its sexual threat, for example. But he learned fast; by the time of recording the material for his second album, *Ricky Nelson* (tracks 16-27), he had vastly improved, and his band, led by guitarist James Burton, was first-class, so that, for example, "There's Good Rockin' Tonight" sounded like it could have been made at Sun Studio in Memphis instead of Master Recorders in Los Angeles. Of course, all that meant was that he was still an imitator, albeit a good one, but everyone starts out imitating, and his choices of what to copy, along with his enthusiasm, marked him as a promising new artist. The onrush of pop celebrity tended to obscure this at the time *Ricky* made him the youngest recording artist ever to

have a number-one LP—but more than four decades later it's much easier to appreciate Nelson's early efforts as a teen rocker. —*William Ruhlmann*

Ricky Sings Again/Songs by Ricky / Jun. 19, 2001 / Capitol ✦✦✦✦

The second of four discs containing Rick Nelson's complete recordings for Imperial Records, *Ricky Sings Again/Songs by Ricky* combines the singer's third and fourth albums, both released initially in 1959, with alternate takes and a few other stray tracks. By this point in his career, Nelson, who turned 19 that year, had begun to distinguish himself from the rockabilly legends he admired, at least to the extent of retaining his own songwriters to pen original (if derivative) material, notably brothers Dorsey & Johnny Burnette, who handled the more rocking tunes, and Baker Knight, who wrote ballads and some light rhythm numbers; between them, they contributed 15 of the 27 different songs heard here. It's easy to tell what they were listening to—"It's Late" is reminiscent of the Everly Brothers' "Wake Up Little Susie," "You'll Never Know What You're Missing" is a rewrite of Elvis Presley's "Treat Me Nice," and "A Long Vacation" apes Buddy Holly's "Not Fade Away." The similarity to Presley's records is accentuated by the use of the Jordanaires, who also sang backup for him, but Nelson's band is distinctive, particularly lead guitarist James Burton, and the singer himself had grown in confidence since his early recordings. As such, this is the peak of Nelson's early career, a time when he was scoring hit after hit with his singles (six of the songs on the disc made the Top Ten) and even assaulted the LP charts (according to *Cash Box*, *Ricky Sings Again* hit number one and *Songs by Ricky* made the Top Ten, though *Billboard*'s rankings were much lower). Also featured are Hank Williams and Johnny Cash covers that anticipate Nelson's turn toward country music, as well as the bizarre reading of Billie Holiday's suicide ballad "Gloomy Sunday" that first turned up on the *Legacy* box set. —*William Ruhlmann*

Album Seven by Rick/Rick Sings Spirituals / Jun. 19, 2001 / Capitol ✦✦✦✦

The fourth and final disc reissuing the complete recordings of Ricky Nelson on Imperial Records (1957-1962) contains his final newly recorded album for the label, *Album Seven by Rick*, four non-LP singles originally released in 1961 and 1962, and, to round things out, a long out of print four-song gospel EP, *Ricky Sings Spirituals*. The bulk of the material comes from the point in Nelson's career when he had re-established himself with "Travelin' Man" after the fade-out of his early teen idol success. Not surprisingly, he turned again to "Travelin' Man" songwriter Jerry Fuller, who provides a full third of the tracks on this disc, among them the hits "A Wonder Like You," "Young World," and "It's Up to You." Other frequently heard songwriters are Dave Burgess (five cuts, three of them with Fuller), Baker Knight (four cuts), and Dorsey Burnette (two cuts). Having such writers shape material for him was a boon to Nelson, and if nothing here quite rises to the level of his biggest hits, there is much good early-'60s pop/rock. The covers of "Summertime" and "I Can't Stop Loving You" are effective, and Nelson and his band turn in believable renditions of some original gospel songs. There's even "Teenage Idol," which comments on his early career and became yet another hit. The recordings he was making in the early '60s suggested Nelson had made the transition from the earnest, derivative music he performed at the start of his career to a stream of high-quality material that would seem to assure him a place near the top of the pop heap, which is probably why at this point Decca made him an unprecedented offer and spirited him away from Imperial. Who could have known that his hitmaking days were just about over? —*William Ruhlmann*

More Songs by Ricky/Rick Is 21 / Jun. 19, 2001 / Capitol ✦✦✦✦

The third in a series of four CD reissues containing the complete Imperial Records recordings of Rick Nelson combines his fifth and sixth albums with his five singles from the same period, November 1959 to May 1961. The story told here is one of musical exploration, as Nelson's early success as a teen heartthrob who liked to play Sun Records-style rockabilly faded and he began casting around for other approaches to maintain his popularity. After the relatively disappointing performance of a pair of singles, "I Wanna Be Loved" and "Young Emotions," ballads that peaked only in the Top 20, he made *More Songs by Ricky*, an album that found him attempting to update decades-old standards like "Time After Time" and come up with brass-heavy production numbers in emulation of then-popular Lloyd Price. As annotator James Ritz writes, the best way to appreciate the results is to "take everything he had already done musically and throw it out the window," but even if you do, you are still left with an artist who sounds comfortable only when he gets back to rocking, notably on the Dorsey Burnette composition "Hey Pretty Baby." Amazingly, however, he pulled out of this tailspin, artistically and commercially, with his sixth album, *Rick Is 21*, on which he developed a new pop/rock sound that contained echoes of his rockabilly past but also made its peace with early-'60s pop, especially on the double-sided hit "Travelin' Man"/"Hello Mary Lou," and also on other custom-written songs by Dave Burgess, Jerry Fuller, Gene Pitney, and Johnny Rivers. As a result, the collection might be subtitled "The Fall and Rise of Rick Nelson," and if the going gets rough early on, the tale has a happy ending. [*More Songs by Ricky* is presented for the first time in true stereo here.] —*William Ruhlmann*

The American Dream: The Complete Imperial and Verve 1957–1962 / Nov. 6, 2001 / Bear Family ✦✦✦✦✦

This is one of the more difficult Bear Family sets to take on simply because it is such an intimidating package. Never mind that Nelson is an American myth, having eked his way into that terrain by dying in a plane crash while still in his 40s, and despite being managed by Colonel Tom Parker, he still looked fantastic despite the unsubstantiated rumors of drugs, alcoholism, and twisted sex that poured forth from the tabloids after his passing. But that Ricky (or Rick as he was known then) Nelson doesn't even appear inside this box set. The material documented here begins near the end of the rockabilly era in 1957 and ends before the Beatles came stateside. The 180 tracks contained on this set represent five years in the recording life of Ricky Nelson, who before he even began his recording career was a television star with his real-life family, the Nelsons, parented by Ozzie and Harriet. In fact, Ricky Nelson starred in a number of motion pictures during the era when these recordings were made—most notably *Rio Bravo* with John Wayne and Dean Martin and *The Wackiest Ship in the Army*—and remained on the TV program until 1966, four years after these sessions leave off in 1962. Ricky Nelson was indeed America's most popular and respectable teen idol. For starters there's the hardbound book that's 180 pages long with rare photographs galore, including some risqué shots of a "party" at Nelson's house; some shots with Eddie Cochran's widow, Sharon Sheeley; shots from the TV show; wedding day photos; record covers from seven different countries; all of the original singles and LP sleeves; press clippings; and magazine and fan club shots, as well as stills from the movies and even a full four-color reproduction of the Ricky Nelson comic book. A large chunk of the book is dedicated to an exhaustive essay by Todd Everett that fills in not only biographical details, but cultural ones as well, and quotes many of the major figures in Nelson's life at the time at length, including, but not exclusively, Gene Pitney, Johnny Rivers, Johnny Cash, and Larry and most notably Lorrie Collins of the Collins Kids, whom Nelson was romantically linked to early in his career. In addition to Everett's essay there are copious production notes on remasters and mono and stereo mixes as well as how most of the recordings were constructed in the studio. This adds up to an insanely beautiful package and we've yet to comment on the music. Of the 180 tracks included here, part of disc five and all of disc six have previously unreleased alternate takes, unheard masters, and unreleased tracks—impressive by even Bear Family standards. Disc one begins with Nelson's first Verve single, his cover of Fats Domino's "I'm Walkin'" (that featured Domino's drummer, Earl Palmer, on the session all the way from New Orleans), backed with "My One and Only Love," a syrupy teen anthem that rocketed to the top of the charts. The rest, in a sense, was history, though it didn't run out all over the margins of press and radio like a river. After leaving Verve Nelson went to Imperial, and it is from here and Challenge that the rest of the recordings on this set come—in complete chronological order, which means track duplication in sequence. For whatever reason, since there are usually only two or three takes, it's not as irritating as it is, say, on the complete Verve Bird sessions when there are sometimes 13 versions of the same tune all in a row. All of the hits are here, such as "Hello Mary Lou," "Travelin' Man," and the stuff you'd expect to find on the Imperial masters LPs and CD, but those tracks only tell a small part of an amazing musical odyssey. This set proves beyond the shadow of a doubt that Nelson was not gifted with a golden voice, but it was a good one, and he interpreted material well. One such cover is his 1962 version of the Gershwins' "Summertime." This is a version that rivals Janis Joplin's for its raw, steamy emotion and one that equates with the Clash's version of "Brand New Cadillac" in its rock & roll firepower. (And James Burton's guitar playing on this track is not even to be believed—only heard and whistled at.) The material Nelson got—whether it was from Domino, Leiber & Stoller, Carl Perkins, Don Gibson, Jerry Fuller, J.D. Loudermilk, Scotty Wiseman, Johnny & Dorsey Burnette, Johnny Cash, Baker Knight, and dozens of others—was mostly top shelf. Nelson and producer Jimmy Haskell's choice of standards by Sammy Kahn, the Gershwins, Hank Williams, and many more were not idle or random selections. Everything was picked first for musical value and then with the notion of selling it. But there's so much more: the gospel EP of *Glory Train* plus three Nelson recorded after Elvis' "Pace in the Valley"—his truly moving version of "The Stars Fell on Alabama," his wicked early "Be-Bop Baby," and a throat-clenching rendition of "Have I Told You Lately (That I Love You)"—and the list goes on and on, including one of the spookiest covers of "Gloomy Sunday" ever. Of the unreleased material, it's fascinating to hear Nelson's awesome band with guitarist James Burton (where do you think Gram, Emmylou Harris, and Merle Haggard first heard him?), bassist James Kirkland (and later Joe Osborn), and drummer Richie Frost, who put together the backing tracks before adding a vocal. Or to hear jazz musicians like pianist Jimmy Rowles and bassist Leroy Vinnegar, or country guitar ace Joe Maphis, or the fabulous vocal groups the Jordannaires and the Four Preps sit in. These folks all appear on final issued masters as well, but the process involved is an intimate experience collectors and hardcore fans will be delighted to hear. Listening to this set through is exhausting, draining, and obsessively thought-provoking. It asks questions that cannot yet be articulated let alone answered as to not only how this kid did it—and Elvis being in the army for a couple of those years cannot be the simple explanation—but why he did this, put himself through this much sweat and blood and agony in five years with another whole life or two to live. But ultimately, *The American Dream* is a remarkable rock & roll experience. So massive is the contribution enclosed in this 12-by-12-inch box, that it will without doubt be poured over and analyzed by fans, historians, musicologists, and trivia nuts for decades to come. Well done Bear Family. —*Thom Jurek*

The Greatest Hits: Revisited / Nov. 20, 2001 / Varese ✦✦✦

The Greatest Hits: Revisited features many of Rick Nelson's best-known songs. It's not a definitive collection; however, what is featured on this best-of is of high quality. Featured performances include "Hello Mary Lou," "Travelin' Man," "I Got a Feeling," and "I'm Walkin'," in addition to ten other songs. —*Jason Birchmeier*

★ **Greatest Hits** / Feb. 12, 2002 / Capitol ✦✦✦✦✦

There's nothing more frustrating than an excellent retrospective that nevertheless has a serious shortcoming. Such is the case in Capitol's near-definitive 2002 Rick Nelson compilation, *Greatest Hits*, which has so many hits and so many great songs, it's easy to believe upon a glance that they're all here. But they're not. Most egregiously, "Waiting in School," the flip side of "Stood Up" (which made it perhaps the greatest rock & roll single ever, as no less of an authority than Cub Koda stated), is not here, but such classic sides as "If You Can't Rock Me," "My Bucket's Got a Hole in It," and "String Along," among others, aren't here, along with good cuts from his recordings with the Stone Canyon Band. Of course, since this is a Capitol release called *Greatest Hits*, it's little surprise that it doesn't cover the Stone Canyon Band, but the absence of "Waiting in School" is enough to keep this from bliss. Even so, it's essential because it contains the great majority of Nelson's great songs, and because he really was one of the best of the first generation of rockers. Perhaps not a trailblazer nor a genius on the level of either Chuck Berry or the Everlys, but one of the greatest pure singers of his time, fronting a crackerjack band and singing his peerless material with a conviction overshadowed only by Elvis. And, unlike Elvis, he was one of the legions of teens that wished he *was* Elvis, giving his music a distinctive edge, even if he was backed by unflappable pros. And that's something he didn't lose in his career—he was always a superior interpreter with impeccable taste, which is evident by the two Stone Canyon Band cuts that close this collection (including his comeback classic, "Garden Party"). Much of what Rick Nelson cut is enjoyable, a lot of it is worth hearing, but *Greatest Hits* comes as close as any single disc could to capturing his greatest—even if it's missing one of his greatest songs. *—Stephen Thomas Erlewine*

Garden Party/Windfall / Mar. 13, 2002 / BGO ♦♦♦♦

In 2002, BGO released *Garden Party/Windfall*, which contained two albums—*Garden Party* (1972, originally released on Decca) and *Windfall* (1974, originally on MCA)—by Rick Nelson on one compact disc. *—Tim Sendra*

20th Century Masters—The Millennium Collection: The Best of Rick Nelson / Mar. 4, 2003 / MCA ♦♦♦

20th Century Masters: The Best of Rick Nelson covers the artist's years at Verve and Decca between 1957 and 1972. Beginning with the squeaky clean rockabilly of 1957's "I'm Walkin'" to the laid-back singer/songwriter sound of 1972's hit single "Garden Party," the collection covers a lot a ground and stylistic changes in a brief time. Twelve tracks are really not enough to do justice to 15 years worth of Nelson's career. The first six songs chart his move from rockabilly wildcat to pop dreamboat. After the romp through "I'm Walkin'," tunes like 1963's "String Along" and 1963's "For You" are lightweight mediocrities, and 1964's "The Very Thought of You" is practically a novelty number that shows Nelson to be very near to complete artistic oblivion. Luckily Nelson's achingly pure voice keeps the songs from getting too soppy, and by 1966 things start to look up as Nelson turned to country music for inspiration. His *Country Fever* record was an early salvo in the country-rock explosion, and that album's "Mystery Train" is a blast; James Burton tears it up on guitar and Nelson sounds positively joyous to be free from the bounds of saccharine pop. It would have been nice to have another song or two from this exciting era, but the compilation jumps ahead to 1969 and Nelson's mellow take on Dylan's "She Belongs to Me." He was firmly in the country-tinged singer/songwriter camp at this point and pulls it off very well, both vocally and compositionally. His original song from 1970, "Easy to Be Free," is a beautiful song with lovely vocal harmonies and an uplifting message. The disc includes live versions of Nelson's old hits "Hello Mary Lou, Goodbye Heart" and "Believe What You Say" that show how he was successfully dealing with his past by incorporating it into his new style. Still, it might have been nice to include more original songs from this fertile period in Nelson's career. His "Garden Party" from 1972 shows just what a talented and assured songwriter he had become. Nelson's work for Verve and Decca is worth more than a just a quick glance. A better collection is Ace's *The Best of the Later Years (1963-1975)*, which takes more time and even shows Nelson dipping his toe into psychedelia. Of course, if all you want is the two-dollar tour, this disc does the trick: The sound is flawless, the liner notes are decent, there is a wonderful picture of Nelson at the mic gracing the booklet, and there is some great music by the truly underrated Rick Nelson. *—Tim Sendra*

Willie Nelson

b. Apr. 30, 1933, Fort Worth, TX

Guitar, Songwriter, Vocals, Bass / Traditional Country, Progressive Country, Country-Pop, Nashville Sound/Countrypolitan, Outlaw Country

As a songwriter and a performer, Willie Nelson played a vital role in post-rock & roll country music. Although he didn't become a star until the mid-'70s, Nelson spent the '60s writing songs that became hits for stars like Ray Price ("Night Life"), Patsy Cline ("Crazy"), Faron Young ("Hello Walls"), and Billy Walker ("Funny How Time Slips Away") as well as releasing a series of records on Liberty and RCA that earned him a small, but devoted, cult following. During the early '70s, Willie aligned himself with Waylon Jennings and the burgeoning outlaw country movement which made him into a star in 1975. Following the crossover success of that year's *The Red Headed Stranger* and "Blue Eyes Crying in the Rain," Nelson was a genuine star, as recognizable in pop circles as he was to the country audience; in addition to recording, he also launched an acting career in the early '80s. Even when he was a star, Willie never played it safe musically. Instead, he borrowed from a wide variety of styles, including traditional pop, Western swing, jazz, traditional country, cowboy songs, honky tonk, rock & roll, folk, and the blues, creating a distinctive, elastic hybrid. Nelson remained at the top of the country charts until the mid-'80s, when his lifestyle—which had always been close to the outlaw clichés his music flirted with—began to spiral out of control, culminating in an infamous battle with the IRS in the late '80s. During the '90s, Nelson's sales never reached the heights that he experienced a decade earlier, but he remained a vital icon in country music, having greatly influenced the new country, new traditionalist, and alternative country movements of the '80s and '90s as well as leaving behind a legacy of classic songs and recordings.

Nelson began performing music as a child growing up in Abbott, TX. After his father died and his mother ran away, Nelson and his sister Bobbie were raised by their grandparents, who encouraged both children to play instruments. Willie picked up the guitar, and by the time he was seven, he was already writing songs. Bobbie learned to play piano, eventually meeting—and later marrying—fiddler Bud Fletcher, who invited both of the siblings to join his band. Nelson had already played with Raychecks' Polka Band, but with Fletcher, he acted as the group's frontman. Willie stayed with Fletcher throughout high-school. Upon his graduation, he joined the Air Force but had to leave shortly afterward, when he became plagued by back problems. Following his disenrollment from the service, he began looking for full-time work. After he worked several part-time jobs, he landed a job as a country DJ at Fort Worth's KCNC in 1954. Nelson continued to sing in honky tonks as he worked as a DJ, deciding to make a stab at recording career by 1956. That year, he headed to Vancouver, WA, where he recorded Leon Payne's "Lumberjack." At that time, Payne was a DJ and he plugged "Lumberjack" on the air, which eventually resulted in sales of 3,000—a respectable figure for an independent single, but not enough to gain much attention. For the next few years, Willie continued to DJ and sing in clubs. During this time, he sold "Family Bible" to a guitar instructor for 50 dollars, and when the song became a hit for Claude Gray in 1960, Nelson decided to move to Nashville the following year to try his luck. Though his nasal voice and jazzy, off-center phrasing didn't win him many friends—several demos were made and then rejected by various labels—his songwriting ability didn't go unnoticed, and soon Hank Cochran helped Willie land a publishing contract at Pamper Music. Ray Price, who co-owned Pamper Music, recorded Nelson's "Night Life" and invited him to join his touring band, the Cherokee Cowboys, as a bassist.

Arriving at the beginning of 1961, Price's invitation began a watershed year for Nelson. Not only did he play with Price—eventually taking members of the Cherokee Cowboys to form his own touring band—but his songs also provided major hits for several other artists. Faron Young took "Hello Walls" to number one for nine weeks, Billy Walker made "Funny How Time Slips Away" into a Top 40 country smash, and Patsy Cline made "Crazy" into a Top Ten pop crossover hit. Earlier in the year, he signed a contract with Liberty Records and began releasing a series of singles that were usually drenched in strings. "Willingly," a duet with his then-wife Shirley Collie, became a Top Ten hit for Nelson early in 1962, and it was followed by another Top Ten single, "Touch Me," later that year. Both singles made it seem like Nelson was primed to become a star, but his career stalled just as quickly as it had taken off, and he was soon charting in the lower regions of the Top 40. Liberty closed its country division in 1964, the same year Roy Orbison had a hit with "Pretty Paper."

When the Monument recordings failed to become hits, Nelson moved to RCA Records in 1965, the same year he became a member of the *Grand Ole Opry.* Over the next seven years, Willie had a steady stream of minor hits, highlighted by the number-13 hit "Bring Me Sunshine" in 1969. Toward the end of his stint with RCA, he had grown frustrated with the label, who had continually tried to shoehorn him into the heavily produced Nashville sound. By 1972, he wasn't even able to reach the country Top 40. Discouraged by his lack of success, Nelson decided to retire from country music, moving back to Austin, TX, after a brief and disastrous sojourn into pig farming. Once he arrived in Austin, Nelson realized that many young rock fans were listening to country music along with the traditional honky tonk audience. Spotting an opportunity, Willie began performing again, scrapping his pop-oriented Nashville sound and image for a rock- and folk-influenced redneck outlaw image. Soon, he earned a contract with Atlantic Records.

Shotgun Willie (1973), Nelson's first album for Atlantic, was evidence of the shift of his musical style, and although it initially didn't sell well, it earned good reviews and cultivated a dedicated cult following. By the fall of 1973, his version of Bob Wills' "Stay All Night (Stay a Little Longer)" had cracked the country Top 40. The following year, he delivered the concept album *Phases and Stages*, which increased his following even more with the hit singles "Bloody Mary Morning" and "After the Fire Is Gone." But the real commercial breakthrough didn't arrive until 1975, when he severed ties with Atlantic and signed to Columbia Records, who gave him complete creative control of his records. Willie's first album for Columbia, *The Red Headed Stranger*, was a spare concept album about a preacher, featuring only his guitar and his sister's piano. The label was reluctant to release with such stark arrangements, but they relented and it became a huge hit, thanks to Nelson's understated cover of Roy Acuff's "Blue Eyes Crying in the Rain."

Following the breakthrough success of *The Red Headed Stranger* as well as Waylon Jennings' simultaneous success, outlaw country—so named because it worked outside of the confines of the Nashville industry—became a sensation, and RCA compiled the various-artists album *Wanted: The Outlaws!*, using material Nelson, Jennings, Tompall Glaser, and Jessi Colter had previously recorded for the label. The compilation boasted a number-one single in the form of the newly recorded Jennings & Nelson duet "Good Hearted Woman," which was also named the Country Music Association's single of the year. For the next five years, Nelson consistently charted on both the country and pop charts, with "Remember Me," "If You've Got the Money I've Got the Time," and "Uncloudy Day" becoming Top Ten country singles in 1976; "I Love You a Thousand Ways" and the Mary Kay Place duet "Something to Brag About" were Top Ten country singles the following year.

Nelson enjoyed his most successful year to date in 1978, as he charted with two very dissimilar albums. *Waylon and Willie*, his first duet album with Jennings, was a major success early in the year, spawning the signature song "Mammas Don't Let Your Babies Grow Up to Be Cowboys." Later in the year, he released *Stardust*, a string-augmented collection of pop standards produced by Booker T. Jones. Most observers believed that the unconventional album would derail Nelson's career, but it unexpectedly became one of the most successful records in his catalog, spending almost ten years in the country charts and eventually selling over four-million copies. After the success of *Stardust*, Willie branched out into film, appearing in the Robert Redford movie *The Electric Horseman* in 1979 and starring in *Honeysuckle Rose* the following year. The latter spawned the hit "On the Road Again," which became another one of Nelson's signature songs.

Willie continued to have hits throughout the early '80s, when he had a major crossover success in 1982 with a cover of Elvis Presley's hit "Always on My Mind." The single spent two weeks at number one and crossed over to number five on the pop charts, sending the album of the same name to number two on the pop charts as well as quadruple-platinum status. Over the next two years, he had hit duet albums with Merle Haggard (1983's *Poncho & Lefty*) and Jennings (1982's *WWII* and 1983's *Take It to the Limit*), while "To All the Girls I've Loved Before," a duet with Latin pop star Julio Iglesias, became another major crossover success in 1984, peaking at number five on the pop charts and number one on the singles chart.

Following a string of number-one singles in early 1985, including "Highwayman," the first single from the Highwaymen, a supergroup he formed with Jennings, Johnny Cash, and Kris Kristofferson, Nelson's popularity gradually began to erode. A new generation of artists had captured the attention of the country audience, which began to drastically cut into his own audience. For the remainder of the decade, he recorded less frequently and remained on the road; he also continued to do charity work, most notably *Farm Aid*, an annual concert that he founded in 1985 designed to provide aid to ailing farmers. While he career was declining, an old demon began to creep up on Willie—the IRS. In November of 1990, he was given a bill for 16.7 million dollars in back taxes. During the following year, almost all of his assets—including several houses, studios, farms, and various properties—were taken away, and to help pay his bill, he released the double-album *The IRS Tapes: Who'll Buy My Memories?* Originally released as two separate albums, the records were marketed through television commercials, and all the profits were directed to the IRS. By 1993—the year he turned 60—his debts had been paid off, and he relaunched his recording career with *Across the Borderline*, an ambitious album produced by Don Was and featuring cameos by Bob Dylan, Bonnie Raitt, Paul Simon, Sinead O'Connor, David Crosby, and Kris Kristofferson. The record received strong reviews and became his first solo album to appear in the pop charts since 1985.

After the release of *Across the Borderline*, Nelson continued to work steadily, releasing at least one album a year and touring constantly. In 1993, he was inducted into the Country Music Hall of Fame, but by that time, he had already become a living legend for all country music fans across the world. Signing to Island for 1996's *Spirit*, he resurfaced two years later with the critically acclaimed *Teatro*, produced by Daniel Lanois. Nelson followed up that success with the instrumental-oriented *Night and Day* a year later; *Me and the Drummer* and *Milk Cow Blues* followed in 2000. *The Rainbow Connection*, which featured an eclectic selection of old-time country favorites, appeared in spring 2001. *—Stephen Thomas Erlewine*

And Then I Wrote / 1962 / Liberty ♦♦♦♦

Here's Willie Nelson / 1963 / Liberty ♦♦♦

Country Willie: His Own Songs / 1965 / Buddah ♦♦♦♦♦
The back of this record says, "Willie writes the songs... You make them into hits" and proceeds to talk about some of the artists who have had hits from the pen of Willie Nelson. While some of these tunes showed up in their original versions on the United Artist album *Best of Willie Nelson*, this is still worth tracking down. *—Jim Worbois*

Country Favorites, Willie Nelson Style / 1966 / Buddah ♦♦♦♦
It may be hard to believe but Willie Nelson wasn't always a national icon. In the mid-'60s, he regularly hit the charts but from behind the scenes as a busy and acclaimed songwriter. His own recordings were less successful until, in 1966, *Country Favorites Willie Nelson Style* became his first album to enter *Billboard*'s country album charts, staying there 17 weeks and eventually reaching number nine. Perhaps because the album is a collection of familiar songs, Nelson's idiosyncratic vocals went over better—or maybe his time had just come—but in any case, it's certainly a small treasure. Supporting Nelson was Ernest Tubb's wonderful band the Texas Troubadours who went uncredited because they were under contract to a different record label. The Troubadours' experience and sympathetic ears made a reliable backing for Nelson as they tackled such material as "San Antonio Rose," "My Window Faces the South," "Heartaches By the Number," and "Columbus Stockade Blues." There's nothing cynical or calculated to their light swing and openhearted feeling, despite such a potentially unpromising album concept. Nelson had already learned how to handle his unconventional voice effectively, giving these songs the honest freshness and sharp sense of rhythm that would characterize his later work. Like many rebels, Nelson has always shown a deep respect for tradition; here he shares his affection with everyone. *—Lang Thompson*

Live Country Music Concert / 1966 / RCA ♦♦♦
This is an interesting album chronicling an early show by Nelson. From time to time, the audience will shout song titles, and he actually talks between songs. While many people don't like live albums, this is actually more fun than some of his later live records. *—Jim Worbois*

Make Way for Willie Nelson / 1967 / RCA ♦♦♦

The Party's Over and Other Great Willie Nelson Songs / 1967 / RCA ♦♦♦♦♦
The title track sums up this album perfectly. This is one of those records that sounds incredible at 2 o'clock in the morning when one is feeling reflective after a busy night. Included are 12 Willie Nelson originals and 12 strong performances. *—Jim Worbois*

Texas in My Soul / 1968 / RCA ♦♦♦♦
Five years before heading to Texas was the popular thing to do, Willie celebrated his home state in song. Despite the fact that there's not a Nelson original on this record (though there are three by fellow Texan, Ernest Tubb), there's not a weak track here. *—Jim Worbois*

Good Times / 1968 / RCA ♦♦♦
This is kind of an odd record. One side is very sparse instrumentally, while the other side has three different people providing arrangements. The songs are OK (maybe subpar for Nelson), with one of the most interesting being his cover of Mickey Newbury's "Sweet Memories." *—Jim Worbois*

My Own Peculiar Way / 1969 / RCA ♦♦♦
When Nelson gets into a song, he has a way of playing with the sounds and rhythm of words to get everything possible from a song. Nearly every song on this record is like that, whether it's one he penned or a cover like John Hartford's "Natural to Be Gone." The only song on this record that doesn't work is "That's All." But, don't let that stop you. *—Jim Worbois*

Both Sides Now / 1970 / RCA ♦♦
The title track aside, this is a pretty good album. While there aren't as many originals on this record as some of his albums released around this time, he manages to get something new out of several of his covers. Listening to "Everybody's Talkin'," you don't find youself longing for Nilsson's version. Similarly, after Jerry Lee ripped up "One Has My Name," Nelson still makes it sound fresh. *—Jim Worbois*

Laying My Burdens Down / 1970 / RCA ♦♦♦
This is what can best be described as a pleasant album. There are some nice things on here, but too many are buried under the Nashville Sound and don't seem to be able to stand on their own. It's not great, but you could do worse. *—Jim Worbois*

Columbus Stockade Blues / 1970 / RCA ♦♦
For this record, RCA raided their vaults for vintage tracks of Nelson doing favorites made hits by other artists. Included are songs by his former boss, Ray Price ("Don't You Ever Get Tired...," "Heartaches by the Number"), George Jones ("Season of My Heart"), Bob Wills ("San Antonio Rose"), and Leon Payne. It's not a bad album. *—Jim Worbois*

Willie Nelson & Family / 1971 / RCA ♦♦♦
Over the years, Nelson has shown that he sometimes looks at relationships differently than the average songwriter (such as "Crazy"), with a little more thought and from new perspectives. After all, not everyone's life is moon, June, and honeymoon. Two of the finest examples of the Willie way are on this album: "I'm A Memory" and, especially, "What Can You Do to Me Now?" By his standards, this isn't good enough to be called a classic album, but it would still blow many other artists out of the water. *—Jim Worbois*

☆ **Yesterday's Wine** / 1971 / Justice ♦♦♦♦♦
By the time Willie Nelson released *Shotgun Willie* in 1973, he had already established himself as a Nashville songwriter of the first order, having penned timeless material like "Crazy" and "Nite Life" for other artists. It was *Shotgun Willie*, however, that established Nelson as a quality album artist as well. *Phases and Stages* (1974) and *Red Headed Stranger* (1975) followed, exploring their chosen themes over the course of records that played like unified song suites. Though these albums are often held as the finest examples of Nelson's album craft, *Yesterday's Wine*, their 1971 predecessor had long been neglected. Reissued in 1997 by Justice Records, it finally took its rightful place amongst the singer's best-loved body of work. A series of meditations on God, love, and aging, these songs are fragmented reflections on the life of Nelson's "imperfect man" as he approaches death. Though the story isn't as tightly constructed as that of *Red Headed Stranger*, this fact lends *Yesterday's Wine* a feeling of malleability that adds to its power. At the album's heart are "Summer of Roses," "December Day," and the title track—songs that detail a sense of longing and loss with the changing seasons mirroring the narrator's own life. Throughout, the outlaw subtext Nelson would become associated with a few years later is replaced by an underlying religious faith. While there may not be any songs here of the same caliber as "Whiskey River" (*Shotgun Willie*) or "Blue Eyes Crying in the Rain" (*Red Headed Stranger*), many of the numbers stand on their own, outside the album context. "Family Bible," "Me and Paul," and the title track are all particularly fine examples of Nelson's songcraft. As a whole, *Yesterday's Wine* provides further insight into the development of his art during this prolific period. *—Nathan Bush*

The Willie Way / 1972 / RCA ♦♦♦
Classic Willie Nelson songwriting fills this album (except for two covers) with performances as only he knows how. "You Left Me a Long, Long Time Ago" is worth the price of this record alone. Also, Willie's version of "Undo the Right" is easily as good as Johnny Bush's 1968 hit. *—Jim Worbois*

The Words Don't Fit the Picture / 1972 / RCA ♦♦♦
Another fine album of Willie originals, it's not quite as strong as some of his other albums released about this time, but still good. *—Jim Worbois*

☆ **Shotgun Willie** / 1973 / Atlantic ♦♦♦♦♦
Transferring his allegiance to Atlantic (where he would record two remarkable albums that would get him kicked off the label), for his debut Willie Nelson offered his finest record to date—possibly his finest album ever. *Shotgun Willie* encapsulates Willie's worldview and music, finding him at a peak as a composer, interpreter, and performer. This is laid-back, deceptively complex music, equal parts country, rock attitude, jazz musicianship, and troubadour storytelling. Nelson blurs the lines between his own tunes and covers to the point that "Whiskey River," this record's best-known song, seems thoroughly original, yet it was written by Johnny Bush and Paul Stroud. This, along with two songs apiece by Leon Russell and Bob Wills, provides context for his originals, with *Shotgun Willie* becoming a musical autobiography, offering not only insights into his musicality (witness how he slows down "Stay All Night [Stay a Little Longer]" to a slow shuffle) but, seemingly, into himself (most notably on the title track and the wonderful, funny travelogue "Devil in a Sleepin' Bag"). Nelson wasn't just at a peak of performing here—he also wrote some of his greatest songs, highlighted not just by the previously mentioned tunes but also by the lovely slow waltz "Slow Down Old World" and "Sad Songs and Waltzes." All of it adds up to possibly the finest record in a career filled with hits and highlights. *—Stephen Thomas Erlewine*

The Best of Willie Nelson / 1973 / EMI America ♦♦♦
Willie Nelson didn't spend much time at Liberty Records, but he did record some of his best early material for the label, including his takes on "Funny How Time Slips Away," "Hello Walls," "Crazy," and "Mr. Record Man." The 1973 collection *The Best of Willie Nelson* offers those four along with nine other well-chosen songs, resulting in a nice summary of the first major phase of Willie's career. Other collections of the Liberty material have been more comprehensive, but this remains the best, most concise overview of those early recordings. *—Stephen Thomas Erlewine*

☆ **Phases and Stages** / 1974 / Atlantic ♦♦♦♦♦
If *Shotgun Willie* played a bit like a concept album, *Phases and Stages* was a full-blown one, tracing the dissolution of a marriage and devoting one side to the wife's perspective,

the second to the husband's. If anything, Willie overplays his hand a bit, insisting on grafting the "Phases and Stages Theme" between crucial songs to the point of genuine irritation. But, pretend that never happened, erase it from your mind, and *Phases and Stages* is easily the equal of its remarkable predecessor, a wonderful set of music that resonates deeply, as deeply as the words. Make no mistake—the deceptively relaxed arrangements, including the occasional strings, not only highlight Nelson's clever eclecticism, but they also heighten the emotional impact of the album. And this is a hell of an emotional record, where even each side's celebratory honky tonk numbers (the medley "Sister's Coming Home/Down at the Corner Beer Joint" and "Pick Up the Tempo," respectively) are muted by sadness. Then, there are the centerpieces: "Walkin'," where the woman decides it's time to move on; "Pretend I Never Happened," perhaps the coldest ending to a relationship ever written; "Bloody Mary Morning," a bleary-eyed morning-after tale that became a standard; "It's Not Supposed to Be That Way," a nearly unbearably melancholy account of a love gone wrong; and "Heaven and Hell," a waltz summary of the relationship. Any two of these would have formed a strong core for an album but, placed together in a narrative context, their impact is even more considerable. As a result, this is not just one of Willie Nelson's best records, but one of the great concept albums overall. *—Stephen Thomas Erlewine*

☆ **Red Headed Stranger** / 1975 / Columbia/Legacy ♦♦♦♦♦

Red Headed Stranger perhaps is the strangest blockbuster country produced, a concept album about a preacher on the run after murdering his departed wife and her new lover, told entirely with brief song-poems and utterly minimal backing. It's defiantly anti-commercial and it demands intense concentration—all reasons why nobody thought it would be a hit, a story related in Chet Flippo's liner notes to the 2000 reissue. It was a phenomenal blockbuster, though, selling millions of copies, establishing Nelson as a superstar recording artist in its own right. For all its success, it still remains a prickly, difficult album, though, making the interspersed concept of *Phases and Stages* sound shiny in comparison. It's difficult because it's old-fashioned, sounding like a tale told around a cowboy campfire. Now, this all reads well on paper, and there's much to admire in Nelson's intimate gamble, but it's really elusive, as the themes get a little muddled and the tunes themselves are a bit bare. It's undoubtedly distinctive—and it sounds more distinctive with each passing year—but it's strictly an intellectual triumph and, after a pair of albums that were musically and intellectually sound, it's a bit of a let-down, no matter how successful it was. *—Stephen Thomas Erlewine*

The Sound in Your Mind / 1976 / Columbia ♦♦♦

Red Headed Stranger propelled Willie Nelson to stardom, finally giving him a smash hit, yet its spare arrangements and hushed intimacy were a bit of an anomaly, both in his prior work and the albums that followed on Columbia. His second LP for the label, 1976's *The Sound in Your Mind*, opened up the sound of *Stranger*, retaining some of the low-key vibe, but fleshing out music and even picking up the tempo on occasion. In addition to that, he started delving deep into standards, not just from country artists, but the American popular songbook, pointing the way toward *Stardust* a few years down the road. So, in many ways, *The Sound in Your Mind* sets the template for the next few years of albums by Willie. Even if it set a sound in motion, the album wasn't one of his strongest. He would often better it—and did so immediately, with the tremendous *The Troublemaker*—and sometimes he did worse, but *The Sound in Your Mind* has a little bit of everything that would come on Columbia, both for better and worse. It's a little uneven and unfocused, not because it's so split between covers and originals, but because it meanders, sometimes drifting into overly familiar territory which elicits somewhat lazy performances ("Amazing Grace," for instance), but songs equally familiar—"That Lucky Old Sun (Just Rolls Around Heaven All Day)," or a medley of his standards: "Funny How Time Slips Away," "Crazy," and "Night Life"—are given subtle, inspired arrangements. The true highlights are the original "The Healing Hands of Time," revived from his RCA years and given possibly the definitive treatment here, and especially a vigorous version of Lefty Frizzell's "If You've Got the Money I've Got the Time," so good that it led to a stellar tribute record just a year later. The rest of the album is good but rather standard-issue Willie—worth hearing and very enjoyable, but not enough to compel regular listens. *—Stephen Thomas Erlewine*

The Troublemaker / 1976 / Columbia ♦♦♦♦♦

Released in late 1976, at the height of Willie-mania, *The Troublemaker* is Willie Nelson's first all-gospel album, but country gospel in his hands doesn't sound like traditional country gospel—it's a Willie album, through and through, performed with the freewheeling Family as support. Consequently, it's every bit as wonderfully idiosyncratic as any of his other mid-'70s work and, in some ways, even more so, because inspirational songs and religious material are usually not given arrangements as imaginative and free-spirited as this. Although the album can be divided pretty evenly between ballads and rollicking uptempo numbers, there is the inherent jazz-like unpredictability in the performances of Nelson and his band that makes even familiar numbers like "Will the Circle Be Unbroken" sound spontaneous. Then again, the choice of material also helps, because that song is the most familiar here; while many of the other numbers are also country gospel standards, they're not recorded nearly as often as "Circle" and these song choices also give *The Troublemaker* a unique, fresh feel. Another interesting thing about the album is that the music, not the message, is at the forefront, which is why it doesn't sound separate from his other mid-'70s peaks. Although it is overshadowed by them both, the sublime subtlety of the performances on *The Troublemaker* make it sound of a piece with *The Red Headed Stranger* and *Stardust*. It may not be nearly as popular as either, but musically, it's just as satisfying and one of the quiet highlights in Willie's vast catalog. *—Stephen Thomas Erlewine*

To Lefty From Willie / 1977 / Columbia ♦♦♦♦♦

To Lefty From Willie is an affectionate and thoroughly enjoyable salute to Lefty Frizzell, featuring stellar versions of a number of Lefty's best-known songs—including "Always Late (With Your Kisses)," "She's Gone, Gone, Gone," "I Never Go Around Mirrors" and "That's the Way Love Goes"—plus revealing takes on a number of obscurities from the influential vocalist's catalog. Nelson is respectful without being overly reverential, giving his own spin to each song without abandoning their honky tonk roots. *—Stephen Thomas Erlewine*

☆ **Stardust** / 1978 / Columbia/Legacy ♦♦♦♦♦

At the height of outlaw country, Willie Nelson pulled off perhaps the riskiest move of the entire bunch. He set aside originals, country, and folk and recorded *Stardust*, a collection of pop standards produced by Booker T Jones. Well, it's not entirely accurate to say that he put away country and folk, since these are highly idiosyncratic interpretations of "Georgia on My Mind," "All of Me," "Moonlight in Vermont," and "Don't Get Around Much Anymore," blending pop, country, jazz, and folk in equal measures. It's not that Willie makes these songs his own, it's that he reimagines these songs in a way that nobody else could, and with his trusty touring band, he makes these versions indelible. It may be strange to think that this album, containing no originals from one of America's greatest songwriters, is what made him a star, and it continues to be one of his most beloved records, but it's appropriate, actually. *Stardust* showcases Nelson's skills as a musician and his entire aesthetic—where there is nothing separating classic American musical forms, it can all be played together—perhaps better than any other album, which is why it was a sensation upon its release and grows stronger with each passing year. *—Stephen Thomas Erlewine*

Willie and Family Live / 1978 / Columbia ♦♦♦♦♦

This exceptionally long two-record set seems to prove two things: the Family can jam (sometimes to the extent that you ask yourself what the point is), and Nelson seems to be bored with some of his own material. Instead of singing, he talks his way through the songs. If you need this to fill out the collection, that's one thing. If you want to hear him do these songs, look for the studio albums. *—Jim Worbois*

Sings Kris Kristofferson / 1979 / Columbia ♦♦♦♦

A return to country-rock after the smash success of *Stardust* the year before, this is one of Willie Nelson's best albums. Admittedly, it doesn't withstand comparisons to *Shotgun Willie* or any of his earlier triumphs, but it holds up as one of his most enjoyable second-stringers. "Me and Bobby McGee" is given an exciting, thunderous performance and "Why Me" is terrific, but perhaps more memorable are Nelson's renditions of lesser-known Kristofferson treasures, such as the loping "The Pilgrim, Chapter 33" and the beautiful "Please Don't Tell Me How the Story Ends." As he demonstrated from the beginning, Nelson had one of the best interpretive gifts of any singer, and this album only strengthened that reputation. *—Jim Smith*

One for the Road / 1979 / Columbia ♦♦♦♦

One for the Road, Willie Nelson's duet record with fellow American music maverick Leon Russell, followed months after his freewheeling, jam-heavy double album *Willie and Family Live*. This record (once a double LP, now a single CD) wasn't recorded live and the songs run a little shorter, but it shares the same sort of loose spirit and easy-rolling eclecticism as the two, essentially backed by the Family, run-through a mess of country and pop standards. The latter makes up for the second half and its appropriately a little more subdued feel, but it's earthier than *Stardust* and it makes a good companion for the irresistible first half, which is often cheerfully rowdy (particularly on the dynamite opening triptych of "Detour," "I Saw the Light," and "Heartbreak Hotel") and convincingly bluesy on the ballads and midtempo groovers like the excellent "Trouble in Mind." Both Nelson and Russell are known as sharp interpreters of other people's material, and teamed together, they might not reinvent these songs (though they come close on "Heartbreak Hotel"), but they infuse a lot of sound and spirit into these songs. It's a little bit too laid-back and easy to qualify as a no-holds-barred classic (particularly on the second half), but that mellow charm is precisely why it's a small, priceless gem for any serious fan of either singer. *—Stephen Thomas Erlewine*

Pretty Paper / 1979 / Sony Music Special Products ♦♦♦♦

Artists almost always release Christmas albums when they have a comfortable level of sales, and when Willie Nelson was at a popular peak during the late '70s, he chose to exploit his popularity by releasing *Pretty Paper*. Fortunately, the album was hardly a toss-off—it was one of the finest country holiday records ever released. It's not just because the title track became a classic, or that his choice of material is terrific (all familiar tunes, but all great)—it's because Nelson is a great interpreter, capable of making standards like "White Christmas" and "Silent Night" fresh and unpredictable. Few other artists are willing to put their personal stamp on these standards, and that alone is enough to make *Pretty Paper* a holiday record to cherish. *—Stephen Thomas Erlewine*

San Antonio Rose / 1980 / Columbia ♦♦♦♦

One of the first in a series of duet albums with country legends that Willie Nelson undertook during a period of seemingly uncontrolled output at Columbia, this remains one of the best. Ray Price may be regarded as something of a laid-back smoothie by listeners whose ears are stuffed with wax, but the reality is that Price is one of country's most expressive vocalists as well as a man interested in kicking country tempos as well as ballads. In fact, a certain type of swing boogie beat favored in Texas is known by musicians as "the Ray Price shuffle." Nelson and Price have a relationship typical of this bearded, bandana-wearing outlaw's collaborations with many country stars of Price's era. When Nelson was struggling to survive in Nashville, he penned or co-wrote some hits for Price, including the wonderful "Night Life," which has become something of a standard not only in country music but in jazz and blues as well. The crossover between these music forms is bound to come up in the discussion of this album. It is performances such as these that interested the jazz great Miles Davis in Nelson, and it is easy to see why when one hears the relaxed phrasing and inventive approach to many of these songs. Of course it is the swinging numbers such as the album's title track that really take off, but even "Release Me" sounds fresh here. That's quite an accomplishment considering that this song was so played to death at one point that jukebox customers began to wish that the song's title had been "Don't Release Me" and that someone at the record label had followed instructions accordingly. "This Cold War With You," a haunting Floyd Tillman tune, gets a superior reading and, on the version of "Funny How Time Slips Away," there is singing that rivals in inspiration any such performance released, although the duet version Nelson recorded with Faron Young for this series comes darn close. Comparing the vocalists as they trade verses is one of the best aspects of this Nelson duet series and, in this case, the styles of the singers are perfectly matched. *—Eugene Chadbourne*

Honeysuckle Rose / 1980 / Columbia ✦✦✦✦

Somewhere Over the Rainbow / 1981 / Columbia ✦✦✦

Somewhere Over the Rainbow is a collection of more '40s pop standards, as arranged by Willie Nelson. While it isn't quite a continuation of what he did on *Stardust* and *Always on My Mind*, the record is a safe resting spot and something all the grandmas can enjoy. *—James Chrispell*

★ **Greatest Hits (& Some That Will Be)** / 1981 / Columbia ✦✦✦✦✦

Greatest Hits (& Some That Will Be) was released in the fall of 1981, summarizing a remarkable seven-year stretch of extraordinary success that began when the iconoclastic *Red Headed Stranger*, Willie Nelson's first album for Columbia, became a smash hit not long after its 1975 release. From that point on, Nelson became an American popular music icon and a fixture at the top of the country charts, something that was all the more remarkable because he rarely played it safe: he sang pop standards, jammed like the Grateful Dead, recorded tributes to heroes like Lefty Frizzell, and did duet albums with both mentor Ray Price and fellow maverick Leon Russell. It was a far-ranging, unpredictable body of work, with each individual album retaining its own distinctive character, and *Greatest Hits* manages to pull off the nifty trick of making sense of these records in two records (now one CD) and 20 songs. Sequenced like a set list, not according to strict chronological order, the collection manages to hit all the major singles, but does so judiciously, making sure each of the records and musical moods get equal pay. So, there is no overdose of *Stardust* material, and even album tracks like a moving version of "Look What Thoughts Will Do" get a hearing. Consequently, this *Greatest Hits* is far more than a mere recitation of familiar items. It is something much better—a rounded, full-bodied portrait of Willie in all of his idiosyncratic spleandor, which is about as much as could be asked from a hits collection. And that's why it's worth having, not just as an introduction, but just as a splendid listen on its own terms. *—Stephen Thomas Erlewine*

Always on My Mind / 1982 / Columbia ✦✦

Whether intentionally or not, the first album after a greatest-hits collection always raises the curtain on a new era, and in Willie Nelson's case, the difference between the era recapped on 1981's *Greatest Hits (& Some That Will Be)* and the one started with 1982's *Always on My Mind* is startling. Throughout the late '70s, Nelson's freewheeling, organically eclectic music was not just the biggest thing in country, it was also some of its best, most adventurous music. Sometimes, it could fall a little flat, particularly when he kept replicating *Stardust*, but that was part of the charm of Nelson's unpredictability. With *Always on My Mind*, he teams with producer Chips Moman and embarks on a period of pernicious predictability, giving himself completely over to Moman, who moves him toward rock covers and adult contemporary pop with this record. At the time, it was a huge, huge hit—his biggest ever, actually, spending 22 weeks at the top of the country charts, selling over four-million copies, launching a platinum single with the title track (which reached number five on the pop charts), and winning the CMA's Album of the Year award. Listening to it now, all that success seems undeserved, since the album not only plays as the country-pop record Willie avoided making all these years, but by consisting primarily of familiar rock covers, it also plays as pandering to the mass audience he's achieved. This is uniformly *pleasant*, but it's also rather straight-jacketed, hemmed in by Moman's sterile, synth-heavy productions. With "Always on My Mind" and, to a lesser extent, "Let It Be Me," it works because his production style suits the songs and Nelson sings well, but "Do Right Woman, Do Right Man," "A Whiter Shade of Pale" (complete with vocals from Waylon Jennings), and "Bridge Over Troubled Water" are all flat readings, never showing the spark in either delivery or arrangement that marks Nelson as one of popular music's great interpretive singers. Here, he sounds as he's sleepwalking and turning out product for the first time in his career (at least the early Liberty recordings were a hungry attempt at hits). It may have been a hit, but years later, it clearly sounds like one of his worst records. *—Stephen Thomas Erlewine*

Poncho & Lefty / 1982 / Columbia ✦✦✦

Nelson teamed up with Merle Haggard for this album and, for my money, theirs is the definitive version of "Pancho & Lefty." At first they might seem to be an odd couple, but they do sound good together. Not all the tracks are as strong as "Pancho & Lefty" but it's still a nice album. *—Jim Worbois*

W W II / 1982 / RCA ✦✦✦

Tougher Than Leather / 1983 / Columbia ✦✦✦

After *years* of singing standards, putting out duet albums, starring in movies, appearing in soundtracks, and taking other detours, Willie Nelson *finally* returned with an album of (almost) all-new material with 1983's *Tougher Than Leather*, his first collection of original songs since 1975's *Red Headed Stranger*. Like that record, *Tougher Than Leather* is a concept record, but unlike *Stranger*, it's nearly impossible to figure out what the record is about. In all likelihood, it's about a gunfighter, who may or may not be a metaphor for Willie himself, in his last days, and there are four songs with "rose" in the title, two parts of "Somewhere in Texas," and a version of "Beer Barrel Polka" thrown in for good measure. Musically, it's right in the vein of *Red Headed Stranger*—a little more robust, since it was cut with his touring band, which also leads to a greater variety of sounds, something that doesn't necessarily jibe with the intended intimacy of the songs, even if it's wholly welcome after the stilted Chips Moman productions. The problem with *Tougher Than Leather* is that the album simply doesn't hold together thematically, which wouldn't be a major problem if the songs were consistently good, but they're often too minimal to catch hold, with only the revived "Summer of Roses" (originally on *Yesterday's Wine*), "Little Old Fashioned Karma," and the elegiac "Nobody Slides, My Friend" standing out among the pack, and they're modest in their success as well. Consequently, *Tougher Than Leather* winds up being more admirable for what it tries to do than what it accomplishes. *—Stephen Thomas Erlewine*

Without a Song / 1983 / Columbia ✦✦

The title track, a cover of the 1930 Paul Whiteman hit, was the lone chart entry from *Without a Song*. *—Jason Ankeny*

Take It to the Limit / 1983 / Columbia ✦

Billed as "with Waylon Jennings," *Take It to the Limit* is not a return of the Outlaws from just a few years back. In fact, it sounds like these two hombres are just plain tired and saddle-sore from all the high riding days of the past. Most of the tunes are covers of previous hits by other artists and have little in association with what Willie (or Waylon) are about except for their take on George Jones' "Why Baby Why." By this time, fans were beginning to say the same thing. *—James Chrispell*

Angel Eyes / 1984 / Columbia ✦✦

Angel Eyes boasts only eight songs and is billed as "featuring the guitar of Jackie King." By this time, Willie seemed to be releasing an album every three months or so, and this record certainly sounds like he was spreading himself too thin. *—James Chrispell*

City of New Orleans / 1984 / Columbia ✦✦

The Steve Goodman-penned title cut of *City of New Orleans* was Nelson's umpteenth number-one hit; other highlights include his renditions of "Please Come to Boston" and "Wind Beneath My Wings." *—Jason Ankeny*

Music From "Songwriter" / Oct. 1984 / Columbia ✦✦✦✦

Willie Nelson was making so many records in the mid-'80s that it was easy for one to get lost in the shuffle, and that's what happened to this album. Tri-Star, the company that distributed Nelson's film *Songwriter*, gave it very little promotion, even though it was a good movie that contained one of the singer/actor's finest screen performances. He played Doc Jenkins, a country singer/songwriter who signs an onerous record deal and then finds a way out of it by enlisting the help of his friend Blackie Buck, played by Kris Kristofferson. Music filled the movie, much of it written and performed by the principals, and rather than release a soundtrack album, Columbia Records issued *Music From "Songwriter,"* an album billed to Nelson and Kristofferson. Each side of the LP began with a duet by the two performers, with the rest of side one given over to Nelson tracks and the rest of side two to Kristofferson tracks. The opening duet, "How Do You Feel About Foolin' Around," became a country singles chart entry, but the best material was Nelson's, including the title song and the caustic "Write Your Own Songs," addressed to "Mr. Music Executive" and "Mr. Purified Country," and sung in the character of Doc Jenkins, though it no doubt expressed the feelings of Nelson as well. Kristofferson hadn't made a solo album in four years, and his four solo tracks found him concerned with topical issues having to do with illegal immigration ("Crossing the Border") and war ("Under the Gun"). Such songs had little to do with the movie, but a lot to do with the singer/songwriter's own current concerns, and he delivered them with fervor over a rocking band. The album made the pop and country charts, and *Songwriter* earned an Academy Award nomination for best original song score, losing to *Purple Rain*. *—William Ruhlmann*

Me and Paul / 1985 / DCC ✦✦✦✦

A separate building such as a quonset hut would have to be built to accomodate all the releases this lovable country artist pumped out during the '80s. Some of his records from this period are disposable, but this was definitely one of the better ones. It seems that focusing on his longstanding relationship with bandmembers, especially drummer Paul English, was an effective emotional touchstone for the entire set of songs, some of which are remakes of Nelson songs from his early Nashville period. "Me and Paul" was a song he wrote for English in the early '70s, and it is a classic bit of songwriting, detailing some hilarious exploits on the road as well as being one of the few songs in existence that is about a drummer. The album kicks off excitingly with "I Been to Georgia on a Fast Train," and there really aren't any noticeably weak moments. The band is superb and, by the standards of a normal country artist, the record would be considered a masterpiece. Nelson's discography is so vast, however, that competition for such an honor is a bit tough. Or as Nelson himself would put it, tougher than leather. *—Eugene Chadbourne*

Half Nelson / 1985 / Columbia ✦✦✦

This is an appropriate collection, since Nelson has recorded more duets with more fellow performers than any other country singer in history. This runs the gamut, from traditional country singers Merle Haggard and George Jones, to soulman Ray Charles, to Latin-lover Julio Iglesias, and the rock band Santana. It even has a duet with the late Hank Williams, arranged through modern studio recording technology. *—Tom Roland*

Funny How Time Slips Away / 1985 / CEMA ✦✦✦✦

Country music fans of course have lots of things to be thankful to Willie Nelson for. One area that is often overlooked when the praises begin rolling out are some of his recording projects from the '80s. At that point, Nelson had achieved massive commercial success with a project his record label had apparently fought him tooth and nail against releasing. This was the album of standards entitled *Stardust*, and after it had sold more than a million copies, the honchos at Columbia basically decided to let Nelson do whatever he wanted, within reason. With the intensity of a thirsty bricklayer diving into a six-pack after a hard day, Nelson went right to work putting out duet projects with some of his favorite traditional country singers, most whom had been having trouble getting albums out at all as the country audience shifted to disco. The charming photography reveals Nelson in a jean jacket while Young has on a tux. Judging musicians from their clothing has never been useful, however, and this is no exception. The two really have a lot in common, above and beyond the fact that Nelson wrote Young's biggest hits, many of which are reprised here. Both men come from the hard-edged Texas country scene, so the tracks tend to have a honky tonk quality. And both performers have skirted the line of acceptability in country by doing songs that are considered too "depressing." This album includes more than one side's worth of numbers written for Young by Nelson as well as performances of songs that are heavily associated with Young, such as the kicking "Live Fast, Love Hard, Die Young." In terms of material here, there is nothing really suprising—but the performances are outstanding, featuring such superb pickers as pedal steel guitarist Buddy Emmons and fiddler Johnny Gimble. Considering the restrictive atmosphere in Nashville studios when some of these songs were done the first time around, a case could even be made that these tracks are improvements over the originals, considering the clear recording quality and the more relaxed interplay of the musicians. A main attraction is hearing these great singers trade verses, an experience that could convince skeptical listeners of the relation between country and jazz. Some of the duo projects with Nelson fell flat, such as the ill-fated one with Roger Miller. But this baby is a winner all the way. *—Eugene Chadbourne*

The Promiseland / 1986 / Columbia ✦✦

Partners / Sep. 1986 / Columbia ✦✦✦

Island in the Sea / 1987 / Columbia ✦✦

What a Wonderful World / Mar. 1988 / Columbia ✦✦✦

Nelson makes one of his occasional dips into the Great American Songbook for *What a Wonderful World*, which features his renditions of "Moon River," "Twilight Time," and "Spanish Eyes," another successful duet with Julio Iglesias. *—Jason Ankeny*

Horse Called Music / 1989 / Columbia ✦✦✦

★ **Nite Life: Greatest Hits and Rare Tracks, 1959–1971** / 1989 / Rhino ✦✦✦✦✦

Nite Life: Greatest Hits and Rare Tracks collects material Willie Nelson wrote and recorded while he was trying to launch a career as a professional songwriter during the '60s. At this time, he also made two albums and several singles for Liberty, and many recordings for RCA. These songs, including some rarities, are compiled for this flawless single-disc collection. *Nite Life* runs through all of the songs other performers had hits with and made standards, including the title tracks, "Crazy," "Funny How Time Slips Away," and "Hello, Walls." Not only does it have the songs that established Nelson's reputation, the disc shows that even early in his career, he was creating an eclectic, far-reaching music that never stayed within the boundaries of traditional country. *—Stephen Thomas Erlewine*

All-Time Hits, Vol. 1 / 1989 / RCA ✦✦✦✦

All-Time Greatest Hits, Vol. 1 covers Nelson's mid- to late-'60s tenure on RCA; among the selections are "The Party's Over," "Blackjack County Chain," "San Antonio" and "Funny How Time Slips Away." *—Jason Ankeny*

Born for Trouble / 1990 / Columbia ✦✦

IRS Tapes: Who'll Buy My Memories? / 1992 / Columbia ✦✦✦✦

Commonly known as *The IRS Tapes* because it was made to help pay for Willie Nelson's IRS debts, *Who'll Buy My Memories* is a double disc, 25-track collection of demos, outtakes and stripped-down recordings that feature only Nelson and his guitar. Over the course of the set, Nelson plays a handful of unusual tracks, several new tunes, and a few of his most familiar songs. The result is one of Nelson's most direct and affecting albums, featuring several of his finest vocal performances. *—Thom Owens*

Across the Borderline / 1993 / Columbia ✦✦✦✦

If ever there were doubts about the breadth and depth of Willie Nelson's ambitions and talents, *Across the Borderline* should put them to rest. Nelson surveys roughly two decades of popular music, tackling songs by writers as varied as Paul Simon, Bob Dylan, Willie Dixon, and Lyle Lovett. That Nelson covers such a variety shouldn't really come as such a surprise: the songs on *Across the Borderline* simply consolidate the range of material he's covered previously, from the Bing Crosby-inspired pop standards albums *Stardust* to the folk-rock of "City of New Orleans." Nelson, along with producer Don Was, assembled a stellar cast of musicians for the album. Paul Simon, Bonnie Raitt, and Mose Allison all guest, and a rock band is Nelson's backup unit for most of the tracks. Of course, country music is at the center of Nelson's vast repertoire, and the two Lyle Lovett compositions he chose to cover for *Across the Borderline* are wonderfully done, with the accompaniment of Nelson's regular backing band. There are also Nelson's own songs, both new ("Valentine") and old (the rather gloomy "She's Not for You"), as well as a writing and singing collaboration with Bob Dylan ("Heartland"). For all the strengths of the other 13 tracks, the most stunning song on the album is Peter Gabriel's "Don't Give Up." The parts originally sung by Kate Bush on Gabriel's *So* album are sung here by Sinead O'Connor, a brilliant piece of casting. Nelson and O'Connor's rendition is quietly triumphant and every bit as powerful as Gabriel & Bush's original. The result of the apparently scattershot song selection and numerous musicians is an album that possesses a quiet majesty, further establishing Willie Nelson as one of the most important writers and interpreters of the last half of the 20th century. *—Martin Monkman*

Healing Hands of Time / 1994 / Capitol ✦✦✦

Since 1978's *Stardust*, Willie Nelson recorded a number of standards collections. *Healing Hands of Time* is the most ambitious, in that it's the furthest from what might be expected of Nelson, but at the same time it's the closest to the "album of standards" formula employed by other artists. Unfortunately, it's also perhaps the least successful of Nelson's standards collections. The songs on the album are bathed in a lush wash of strings and low-key rhythmic instrumentation (arranged by David Campbell) that recalls the arrangements Nelson Riddle wrote for Frank Sinatra, Ella Fitzgerald, and Linda Ronstadt. But rather than singing just pop standards, Nelson opts to include five country standards of his own composition, including "Crazy" and "Night Life." A sixth Nelson composition, "There Are Worse Things Than Being Alone," with an arrangement by Jimmy Webb, appears to be a new song. There are also four pop standards, including Jerome Kern and Oscar Hammerstein's "All the Things You Are." While it's interesting to hear Nelson tackle this genre, there are some significant shortcomings. Nelson's guitar—his other voice—is notable in its absence. While there's no faulting the playing of Reggie Young or Billy Joe Walker Jr., it's just not the same. Also, string-heavy standards albums are frequently dismissed as lacking swing, and this record is no exception. In fact, with Nelson's behind-the-beat phrasing, the songs sound even more stilted than they would in the hands of a less idiosyncratic singer. Nelson's ambition is admirable, but in execution, *Healing Hands of Time* is only partially successful. *—Martin Monkman*

The Early Years / Feb. 15, 1994 / Scotti Bros. ✦✦✦

Those who enjoyed Willie Nelson at his most unadorned on the *IRS Tapes* might also enjoy hearing the bare-bones arrangements of *The Early Years*. These 14 tracks were recorded by Nelson as songwriter demos in the early '60s, just before he signed with Liberty. At this point, Nelson was considered more of a songwriter than a performer. Accordingly, there is a sparse feel to most of these performances, which sometimes feature nothing more than his voice or guitar. Not that there's anything especially wrong with that. Willie re-recorded several of these tunes for Liberty and RCA, and one could argue that the arrangements were sometimes less sympathetic than the minimal backing on these tapes. While the demo ambience could be said to add warmth and character, one should also be aware that these aren't the most polished performances; perfunctory arrangements, flat production, and the occasional bum vocal phrase are also found. But fans of Nashville country without the syrup should find something to like here. It includes an early version of "I Hope So," a country hit for Nelson in 1969, and "Undo The Right," which would be a Top Ten country hit for Johnny Bush in 1968. *—Richie Unterberger*

Moonlight Becomes You / Feb. 15, 1994 / Justice ✦✦✦

It's an indication of how out of whack the country boom has gotten at major labels when a proven giant like Willie Nelson must cut tremendous records for tiny independents. There are wonderful originals and sympathetic, engaging covers, Nelson approaches his *Stardust* peak vocally, and a great cast plays these songs with consummate skill and ease, blending country, Western swing, jazz and pop elements. Those with rigid definitions of country may wonder how a CD with "Sentimental Journey" and the title track fits into the genre; anyone with open ears knows the answer. *—Ron Wynn*

☆ **The Early Years: The Complete Liberty Recordings Plus More** / May 3, 1994 / Liberty ✦✦✦✦✦

Not only a fine compilation, it was a gutsy move. Nelson's 1962-1964 sessions for Liberty Records, the first label to sign him as an artist, have never been held in high regard by his fans. On many cuts, the strings were poured on so thick even Eddy Arnold would have protested. But if one dispenses with prejudice and gives this two-CD box set an open-minded listen, there's a wealth of fine work to appreciate among the 61 singles, album cuts, and alternate takes. And no matter the production—lush or spare—his songwriting is a continual joy. Besides the familiar (including a riveting, pre-Liberty version of "Night Life" that opens the set) are any number of near-forgotten songs that would have been another writer's best work. Excellent liner notes are provided by Joseph F. Laredo, who deserves credit for not pretending the strings aren't there. *—Dan Cooper*

A Classic & Unreleased Collection / 1995 / Rhino ✦✦✦✦

Originally released via the Home Shopping Network and later issued through Rhino, *A Classic & Unreleased Collection* is a three-disc box set that, given its origins, could seem like a quick cash-in but it's really an unexpected delight, necessary for any serious fan of Willie Nelson at his prime. It would have been easy for this to be a collection of released album tracks or half-baked outtakes, but this is a veritable treasure trove, containing no "classic" recordings in the classic sense (in other words, there are no hits), but instead a wealth of valuable rarities spanning from 1957 to the mid-'80s. Some of this borders on the legendary, as in the case of the Pamper Music demo recordings, while others are albums so lost they've not even been rumored, but the overall quality of the music is remarkably high. The first disc contains the most historic material, containing his first single for D Records ("No Place for Me"/"Lumberjack") and 11 songwriting demos he cut for Pamper, only a handful of which appeared on Sugar Hill's 2003 collection *Crazy: The Demo Sessions*. While the D single is a little slight, it is appealing and Nelson's style is apparent even at this formative stage, and the Pamper recordings are rich and textured, highlighted by early versions of "Healing Hands of Time," "A Moment Isn't Very Long," and "Slow Down Old World." Then, the collection moves into 11 unreleased cuts from his short stint at Atlantic in the early '70s. He released two of his best albums, *Shotgun Willie* and *Phases and Stages*, at Atlantic, and while these songs don't have the cohesive themes of those records, the music is at a similar high quality, highlighted by an alternate take of "Bloody Mary Morning" and a great duet with Tracy Nelson on "After the Fire Is Gone." The middle of the second disc is devoted to the complete unreleased album *Live at the Texas Opry House*, which captured a 1974 gig. Up to that point, Willie hadn't had a live album, and while this is hardly as epic as the subsequent *Willie and Family Live*, it offers a different take, capturing Willie and his band as a Texas roadhouse band, kicking out storming versions of "Stay All Night (Stay a Little Longer)," "Whiskey River," and "Truck Drivin' Man," while slowing down for some slow-dance numbers; it's a hell of a performance and reason enough to get the collection. From there, the box moves into the '80s, starting with the unreleased *Sugar Moon* album, yet another collection of standards, like so many of his post-*Stardust* albums, but this has the benefit of a really swinging, relaxed vibe with interesting songs and arrangements that actually let Nelson and his band breathe and play; it's better than most of the post-*Stardust* sound-alike records. Then, there are four songs from the scrapped guitar-and-voice album *Willie Alone*, before ending up with *Willie Sings Hank Williams*, a fine record that doesn't deliver any surprises, either in song selection or delivery, but still is a nice listen, one that' s more modest and enjoyable than many of his released '80s efforts on Columbia. Simply put, everything here is very good indeed—maybe not seminal, but always enjoyable and often fascinating. Any serious Willie Nelson collection needs to have this. *—Stephen Thomas Erlewine*

Revolutions of Time: The Journey 1975–1993 / 1995 / Columbia/Legacy ✦✦✦✦✦
Compiling material from Willie Nelson's later career, the box set *Revolutions of Time: The Journey 1975-1993* provides a thorough overview of the singer's most popular recordings, as well as some of his most obscure. Divided into three thematic discs—*Pilgrimage*, *Sojourns*, and *Exodus*—the box contains most of his hits from the era, including selections from *The Red Headed Stranger* and *Stardust*. These songs are on *Pilgrimage*. *Sojourns* concentrates on his duets, while *Exodus* is filled with songs from the late '80s and early '90s. It doesn't round up all of his best songs of the era—there are still several gems hidden away on the original albums—but it does provide an effective and thoroughly entertaining portrait of Nelson's later career. *Revolutions of Time* could be all that the casual fan needs to hear from Nelson's later career, and every country fan should be familiar with much of these songs. *—Stephen Thomas Erlewine*

The Essential Willie Nelson / Aug. 1, 1995 / RCA ✦✦✦✦✦
The 20 songs on this set were recorded between 1965 and 1971, long before his commercial breakthrough with "Blue Eyes Crying in the Rain." All of the songs were produced by Chet Atkins or his able assistant, Felton Jarvis. As explained in the album notes, the producers were trying to marry Nelson's folksy blues style with commercial country-style arrangements, a union which produced no major country hits. Still, these were some of Nelson's best-known songs which had been popularized by other artists. Spare Nelson standards such as "Healing Hands of Time," "Hello Walls," "Funny How Time Slips Away," "Night Life" and "The Party's Over" are all here. *—Bill Carpenter*

Super Hits, Vol. 2 / Sep. 5, 1995 / Epic ✦✦✦
Epic's 1995 collection *Super Hits, Vol. 2* does contain a few very big hits for Willie Nelson—namely, "Mamas Don't Let Your Babies Grow Up to Be Cowboys," "Stardust," and "Let It Be Me." However, the remaining seven selections seem somewhat arbitrary, resulting in a sampler that is sporadically enjoyable but not representative even of Willie's '80s material for Columbia. *—Stephen Thomas Erlewine*

Just One Love / Jan. 1996 / Transatlantic ✦✦✦
Willie Nelson's *Just One Love* is, for the most part, a collection of country standards. There are hard songs by the likes of Hank Williams (a wonderful "Cold Cold Heart"), Floyd Tillman (represented by both "Each Night at Nine" and the timeless "This Cold Cold War With You"), and Fred Rose ("It's a Sin"). There's also the old-timey "Alabam" and "Bonaparte's Retreat." The arrangements are straight country, with most of Nelson's regular band on hand. Standout soloists include Bobbie Nelson on piano and Buddy Emmons on steel guitar, and, of course, Willie Nelson's own nylon-string guitar. While most of the album is given over to old country tunes, two tracks were written by Texas songwriter Kimmie Rhodes. Both are performed as duets with Rhodes, and are arguably the best performances on the record. The title track is a tender love song, while "I Just Drove By" is an exercise in nostalgia. The album closes with Grandpa Jones' rollicking "Eight More Miles to Louisville," featuring the ragged vocals and banjo of Jones himself. This is one duet where Nelson's laid-back delivery seems entirely wrong; Jones is just too hyperkinetic. It's no masterpiece, but *Just One Love* is a solid country record. Unfortunately, Nelson's prolific nature ensures that solid albums like this get overlooked in the big picture, but for his fans and for those of good country music in general, it is well worth investigating. *—Martin Monkman*

Spirit / Jun. 1996 / Island ✦✦✦✦✦
Of all the records Willie Nelson made in the 1990s and since that time, none is more misunderstood or ignored than *Spirit*. Coming as it did so quietly and unobtrusively in 1996, a year and a half before the celebrated *Teatro*, *Spirit* is Willie Nelson's most focused album of that decade. Self-produced and featuring the sparest of instrumental settings—Willie & Jody Payne play guitars, Bobbie Nelson plays piano, and Johnny Gimble plays fiddle on certain tracks—Nelson weaves a tapestry, a song cycle about brokenness, loneliness, heartbreak, spiritual destitution, and emerging on the other side. The set begins with the instrumental "Matador," which seems to usher in the atmospheric texture for this album. "She's Gone" tells its heartbreak story with as much lilt and pastoral grace as is possible without being sentimental. Willie's guitar soloing is gorgeous; he's deep in the groove of the washes of Bobbie's chords. Hearing a steel-string guitar play rhythm and a nylon-string guitar play lead is an interesting twist as well. But Nelson digs the notion of "She's Gone" deeper into the listener's consciousness with "Your Memory Won't Die in My Grave": "Been feelin' kinda free/But I'd rather feel your arms around me/Because you're takin' away/Everything I ever wanted.... /It's a memory today, it'll be a memory tomorrow/I hope you're happy someday/"Your memory won't die in my grave...." And when Nelson moves to the full acceptance issue as he does on "I'm Not Trying to Forget You," the music is slightly off-kilter in the intro, as if the singer cannot come to grips with the song. Payne plays just behind Willie, stretching time, making it slip and shimmer all the way into "Too Sick to Pray," the most devastating country waltz to be recorded since Johnny Paycheck's Little Darlin' albums. On "I'm Waiting Forever" and "We Don't Run," the sun begins to rise out of the heart's bleak night and comes to the dawn of a new day in the life of love and spiritual connection. This is Nelson writing conceptually as he did early on with *Phases and Stages* and *Red Headed Stranger*, but he is at his understated best here, moving deeply into the skeleton of the song itself and what it chooses to reveal through the singer. And while *Spirit* is quiet, it's a tough, big record that makes you confront the roar of silence in your own heart. *—Thom Jurek*

Nashville Was the Roughest / Jun. 10, 1998 / Bear Family ✦✦✦✦✦
Willie Nelson's '60s recordings for RCA have long been the subject of critical disdain due to the supposed ill fit between Nelson's idiosyncratic style and the conventions of the Nashville sound era. In fact, Nelson's RCA material is largely of high quality, his modest hits from this period were often excellent, and his uniqueness comes through no matter how syrupy the orchestration (which isn't always the case—the production on many of these tracks is quite spare). This deluxe eight-CD box set compiles everything Nelson recorded during his eight years with RCA, including a complete live set, unreleased recordings, rough takes of songs that would later surface on his A&M albums, and his few early-'60s recordings for Monument. Nelson covers Western swing, pop country, ballads, and versions of classic country songs in minimalist fashion with his jazzy phrasing fully developed. In fact, those who have been frightened away from these recordings by critics may be surprised by how little they differ from his '70s sound. Fans will delight over the LP-sized hardback book that accompanies this set and the opportunity to review a neglected episode in the Willie Nelson saga. *—Greg Adams*

16 Biggest Hits / Jul. 14, 1998 / Legacy/Columbia ✦✦✦✦
Not all of Willie Nelson's hits are on *16 Biggest Hits*—after all, it only features recordings he made for Columbia and skips over any hit duet he's had—but it never was intended to be a definitive compilation. Instead, it's a worthy summation of his biggest hits of the late '70s and '80s, from 1975's "Blue Eyes Crying in the Rain" to 1989's "Nothing I Can Do About It Now." In between those two songs, plenty of classics—"If You've Got the Money, I've Got the Time," "Georgia on My Mind," "My Heroes Have Always Been Cowboys," "Always on My Mind," "City of New Orleans"—are hauled out, making for an excellent listen that's ideal for novices and casual fans. Of course, Nelson's catalog is so rich it's impossible to pare it down to 16 songs, but this is certainly a terrific sampler on its own terms. *—Stephen Thomas Erlewine*

Teatro / Sep. 1, 1998 / Island ✦✦✦✦
For whatever reason, Willie Nelson's *Teatro*—like Emmylou Harris' *Wrecking Ball*—seems to exist in a vacuum, completely set apart from his other recordings. It's untrue in either case, but especially in Nelson's. A scant year or so before *Teatro* was released—and its recording sessions filmed in an old movie theater in Mexico—Nelson issued his most brilliant album of the 1990s, *Spirit*. Island's publicists had no idea what to do with *Spirit*'s subtle, unsentimental, moody, and sparsely arranged and performed songs, but the roots of *Teatro* lie firmly planted there on its opening instrumental, "Matador." As for *Teatro* itself, Harris is present on 11 of the 14 tracks. In addition, Daniel Lanois, the same mercurial talent who spearheaded *Wrecking Ball*, produced this set. The mood is set in an arid space where a forlorn mariachi band meets the Harmonica Man (courtesy of Mickey Raphael) on Ennio Morricone's score for *Once Upon a Time in the West*. Lyrically, Nelson is as ambitious as he was on *Spirit*, and rhythmically he's more so, but that doesn't necessarily serve him as well. *Teatro* is a fine record with its sadness and bitterness in "I Never Cared for You" and the Spanish two-step of "Darkness on the Face of the Earth." But Lanois is one busy guitar picker here, and it stands at odds with Nelson's more spare yet lyrical style. But it's a good tension. It works better on "My Own Peculiar Way," with the percussion floating and evening out the guitars. The touch of Afro-Cuban rhythm in "These Lonely Nights" is sharp in contrast to Nelson's relatively staid and conventional country melody. Here is where Lanois works his magic; he staggers an organ, an electric piano, an accordion, his own electric guitar, a trap kit, and hand percussion all around the beat without anyone playing dead on it. Nelson's voice is the only constant, and it draws the listener right to it. Nelson's cover of Lanois' "The Maker," with Lanois layering thick slaps of sweet, melodic distorted guitar over its intro, is amazing. Harris and Nelson work so well together—throughout the album but on this track especially—it's almost a shock they aren't always together. Lyrically, Nelson strides out ahead of all his late-'80s and early-'90s material, continuing the great strides he made with *Spirit*. Clearly, the slump is over here, and the poetry he spins is accessible, profound, and moving. *Teatro* is a special album, but it's part two of a story that began with *Spirit*, and both recordings should be heard in tandem with one another for the full effect. Striking, beautiful, and affecting, *Teatro* is a sonic film that displays its moving images in the minds and hearts of its listeners. *—Thom Jurek*

The Very Best of Willie Nelson / Mar. 2, 1999 / Columbia ✦✦✦✦
Spanning two discs and 30 songs, *The Very Best of Willie Nelson* isn't as sublime as *Greatest Hits (& Some that Will Be)*, which came close to capturing the essence of Nelson's Columbia recordings in 20 tracks. *The Very Best* covers more ground and, technically, it has more charting hits, but it isn't as far-reaching and diverse as *Greatest Hits*, which gave equal ground to country, Western swing, folk and pop. This collection tends toward obvious choices, emphasizing covers of pop songs instead of his more obscure choices or original material. Consequentially, it isn't the most representative collection possible, but it will satisfy many casual fans that want Nelson's late-'70s and '80s hits and songs that sound like them. *—Stephen Thomas Erlewine*

A&E Biography / Jun. 8, 1999 / Capitol ✦✦✦
Released to coincide with the cable television documentary of the same name, *A&E Biography* provides a quick, entertaining summary of Willie Nelson's career, beginning with his Liberty recordings and touching briefly on every major development of his career, from the Outlaws to the Highwaymen. Since Nelson's career is filled with terrific music—not only hits, but concept albums and terrific songs tucked away on the second

side of a record—it shouldn't come as a surprise that this collection is hardly definitive and at times even a bit scattershot. Nevertheless, there's not a bad cut among these 14 songs, which balance the familiar ("Hello Walls," "Crazy," "Funny How Time Slips Away," "My Heroes Have Always Been Cowboys," "Blue Eyes Crying in the Rain") with a healthy selection of album tracks, forgotten favorites, and live tracks, including the Waylon Jennings duet "Good Hearted Woman." There's not really anything here that would entice collectors and there may be a bit too much unfamiliar material for some casual fans, but it's still a thoroughly enjoyable listen that would nicely serve anyone whose curiosity was sparked by this episode of *Biography*. *—Stephen Thomas Erlewine*

Night and Day / Jul. 13, 1999 / Free Falls Entertainment ✦✦✦✦

It might come as a surprise to learn that *Night and Day* is a jazz-minded instrumental album, but it shouldn't. Willie Nelson had been bringing jazz elements to his country-pop foundation since the late '50s, so recording an instrumental album that spotlights his guitar playing and illustrates his appreciation of jazz was a logical move. *Night and Day* isn't a hard bop blowing date; fusing pre-swing jazz with country and pop, Nelson draws on such influences as Django Reinhardt and Stephane Grappelli and favors lyricism that is melodic, straightforward, and uncomplicated. When he tackles well-known standards like "All the Things You Are," "Night and Day," Fats Waller's "Honeysuckle Rose," and Reinhardt's "Nuages," Nelson the guitar-playing instrumentalist isn't much different from Nelson the singer: He still brings a great deal of charm, vulnerability, and charisma to the studio. One of Nelson's strongest assets on this CD is fiddler/mandolinist Johnny Gimble, who fits in perfectly. Released when Nelson was 66, *Night and Day* is an album that was long overdue. *—Alex Henderson*

Me and the Drummer / Jun. 6, 2000 / Lockdown ✦✦✦✦✦

One of country music's true superstars is back with one of his best collections of tunes ever, coupled with an impressive interactive scrapbook, all on one CD. Originally available only on the internet, the CD's interactive features include interviews with everyone from Johnny Cash and Waylon Jennings to George W. Bush. But it is the music here that takes center stage. The songs on *Me and the Drummer* are a flashback to a simpler time, reminiscent of the Western-flavored tunes featured on his *Red Headed Stranger* and *Tougher Than Leather* releases. The lyrics are compelling, Nelson's vocals are as smooth as ever before, and the music provided by the Offenders is Texas cool. They operate on the "less-is-more" principle, and it is the perfect complement for Nelson's distinct vocal style. "Rainy Day Blues" is a shuffling, country blues with a lot of Nelson's trademark acoustic lead picking, and "I'd Rather You Didn't Love Me" is pure Nelson at his best. From the swing of "I Guess I've Come to Live Here in Your Eyes" to the waltz of "Me and the Drummer," this is Willie Nelson at his honky tonkin' best. *—Michael Smith*

In the Jailhouse Now/Brand on My Heart / Sep. 12, 2000 / DCC ✦✦✦

Milk Cow Blues / Sep. 19, 2000 / Island ✦✦✦

Willie Nelson's idiosyncratic vocal style has always been heavily influenced by the blues, just as much as it has been by country, pop, and folk, but he'd never recorded a straight blues album until 2000's *Milk Cow Blues*. Any longtime Nelson fan will undoubtedly be quietly thrilled with the idea of a straight blues album, and the very first notes make it seem like the record will deliver on its promise. Then Francine Reed starts singing. Yes, *Milk Cow Blues* is designed as a star-studded duets album, which is apparently the only way major labels think a new album from a veteran superstar will attract press attention and fan curiosity. Sometimes, the concept works, at least commercially, as proved by the stunning success of Santana's *Supernatural*. Here, the idea just guts the album of any power it may have had, since Nelson immediately finds an appealingly unusual groove in each song, and you want to hear him follow it through to the end. The duets always seem like an intrusion to his musical vision, especially since everybody except Dr. John oversells these songs, singing like a cliché instead of finding their own sound. It's all the more frustrating because Nelson really does find his voice on each song here, a fact that's apparent on the three songs he has to himself. These are great recordings and they can't help but put the rest of the album into sharp relief, since even though they have the same great performances from Nelson and his stellar band, they feel cluttered with guests. Ultimately, those cameos, which are intended to broaden the audience, wind up short-circuiting a record that could have been a modest highlight of Nelson's latter-day catalog. As it stands now, *Milk Cow Blues* is largely a wasted opportunity. *—Stephen Thomas Erlewine*

Love Songs / Sep. 26, 2000 / Sony ✦✦✦

Willie Nelson achieved broad-based popularity in the late '70s and '80s by singing pop standards on a series of albums starting with 1978's *Stardust*. This discount-priced, ten-song compilation mixes romantic ballads largely drawn from those albums and includes well-known songs from a range of periods, dating back to the 1940s ("I Can't Begin to Tell You," "To Each His Own," "Some Enchanted Evening") and continuing up to the inclusion of those twin monuments to pompous insincerity, "Always on My Mind" and "Wind Beneath My Wings." As such, the material is more uneven than might have been hoped, but every song is given the same measured, half-spoken, oddly timed Nelson vocal performance. Any one of the full-length albums in which these recordings originated—*Without a Song*, *What a Wonderful World*, etc.—is recommended over this sampler. But at a modest price, it is at least a mood-setter. *—William Ruhlmann*

Rainbow Connection / Jun. 12, 2001 / Island ✦✦✦

The Great Divide / Jan. 15, 2002 / Universal ✦✦

Like most star-studded superstar comeback albums of the late '80s, '90s, and 2000s, Willie Nelson's *The Great Divide* isn't meant for longtime fans of the artists, or even the artists themselves; it's meant for listeners who always liked the idea or persona of the featured artist, but never liked the artist's music. That's certainly the case with *The Great Divide*, which finds Willie Nelson inexplicably recast as an adult alternative artist, singing songs written by Rob Thomas—who, not coincidentally, led Carlos Santana to the biggest hit of his career in 1999—and other professional tunesmiths, all corralled by producer Matter Serietic. Since professionals are involved—including Nelson himself, who gives an admirable vocal performance throughout—this is an accomplished, classy album, but it sure as hell isn't a Willie Nelson album. The closest it comes is on the title track, the only song co-written by Nelson himself, and the Bernie Taupin-co-written numbers, including a pretty good deliberate ballad called "Let Stand in Open Country" featuring Kid Rock. The rest is radio-ready adult pop, produced fairly well but not inherently interesting, no matter how professional it is. And that's the problem with the record; sure, it may get those who like Nelson the star, but if it alienates those who love his music, including his legions of quiet masterpieces from *The Troublemaker* to *The Rainbow Connection*, then what's the point? *—Stephen Thomas Erlewine*

RCA Country Legends / Sep. 10, 2002 / RCA ✦✦✦✦✦

Absolutely the Best, Vol. 1 / Oct. 22, 2002 / Varese ✦✦✦

Stars & Guitars / Nov. 5, 2002 / Universal ✦✦

Superstar guest albums are the bane of the veteran artist. Designed to introduce a new audience to a legend via duets with a variety of stars, they never do justice to the artist, their music, or even the guests who leap at the opportunity to record with an idol. So, you wind up with albums by John Lee Hooker and Santana that don't sound like albums by Hooker and Santana—just an ad-hoc collection of marketing moves, good intentions, and bad ideas. Willie Nelson, a singer who always sounds unique, even fell prey to this curse on 2002's flop *The Great Divide*, which was promoted by a star-studded concert later released that year as *Willie Nelson & Friends: Stars & Guitars*. This live show has one advantage over the studio set: it *sounds* like Willie Nelson music. Ironically, it has even more guests that distract from the man himself, sounding like an open-mike night where anybody with a record contract who happened to be in town could climb on-stage with the legend. Perhaps everybody here loves Willie, and some are surely even influenced by him, but there's no rhyme or reason to who is featured here, and while some fit well—Patty Griffin, Ray Price, Emmylou Harris, Sheryl Crow, Vince Gill among them—many are downright bewildering or irritating. Ryan Adams twice reveals himself as a posturing blowhard, Norah Jones sounds sweet but out of place, Rob Thomas & Matchbox Twenty might be getting better all the time but share no affinity with Willie's music, and on and on. Perhaps the best illustration of why this doesn't work is Toby Keith's Waylon Jennings impersonation on "Good Hearted Woman," where he copies the classic Waylon & Willie phrasing down to the toss-off cry of "Willie" when handing off the verse. It's studied and kind of affectionate, but there is none of the chemistry between most of the guests and Willie—the kind he had with Waylon, or countless others that he's performed duets with over the years. Even worse, most of the artists are so confined to their own style, they can't roll with Nelson's idiosyncrasies, which are always engaging. Listen to the last two songs, "On the Road Again" and "Move It On Over," performed by just Willie and the band. They've done these songs countless times over the years, but they sound fresher, livelier than anything else here, and it's hard not to think that a real tribute would be a live show cut at any other night in 2002 than this well-intentioned star-soaked dud. *—Stephen Thomas Erlewine*

Crazy: The Demo Sessions / Feb. 11, 2003 / Sugar Hill ✦✦✦✦✦

Prior to become a recording artist, Willie Nelson cut a number of demos for Pamper Music, a publishing company co-owned by Ray Price and Hal Smith. Though he had some success once he started pursuing his recording career in earnest in the '60s, he continued to cut publishing demos, partially because he was better known as a writer than a performer. Some of these demos have come out on assorted reissues over the years, but Sugar Hill's 2003 collection *Crazy: The Demo Sessions* is the first comprehensive collection of this work, and it's a very welcome addition to Nelson's often unwieldy discography. Nelson's earliest recordings for Liberty (and to a lesser extent, his recordings for RCA in the '60s) have been roundly criticized for awkward, string-laden country-pop arrangements—a criticism that may have been overstated, but is certainly valid—and this serves as a counterpoint to those polished recordings, since these publishing demos are spare and unadorned, all recorded in one take. The first eight songs are Nelson alone with a guitar and occasionally a harmony vocalist, and these songs sound like precursors to *Red Headed Stranger* in their intimate directness. The remaining seven feature Nelson backed by a band, which follows his lead and turns in loose, warm performances that follow his trademark idiosyncratic delivery. (There are also three other unlisted songs added as an unlisted bonus on the 16th track, recorded with band.) Many of these songs were made into hits by artists other than Nelson: Of course, there is Patsy Cline's "Crazy," which was cut after hearing this demo, but several other songs were brought to the charts by such Nelson patrons as Ray Price and Faron Young. Many of these songs remained in Nelson's repertoire over the years, highlighted by "Crazy," the great honky tonk raver "I Gotta Get Drunk," "Three Days," and "The Local Memory," but several of these also showed up on his 1998 album *Teatro*. Nevertheless, many titles won't be especially familiar to anyone outside of hardcore Nelson followers—and one title, "I'm Still Here," was not known to exist prior to this release—and it's a testament to his body of work that they seem like minor works compared to his other songs; by any other standard, they're major works. Certainly, the quality of the songs is excellent—it's easy to see why other singers would want to cut the songs after hearing them here—but it's not just the quality of the songs that makes this a revelation, since Nelson's stature as a songwriter is secure. What is revelatory about *Crazy: The Demo Sessions* is how it illustrates that Nelson had a handle on his distinctive, idiosyncratic vocal and performing style very early in his career—much earlier than his records suggested. But what makes this such a wonderful, even essential release, is that these performances are as good and affecting as anything Nelson ever cut, and are endlessly listenable not for historical reasons, but for pure musical enjoyment. *—Stephen Thomas Erlewine*

★ **The Essential Willie Nelson** / Apr. 1, 2003 / Columbia ♦♦♦♦♦

Willie Nelson recorded for many labels during the course of his lengthy career, but his greatest commercial success arrived during his time on Columbia during the late '70s and early '80s, which is one of the reasons that the career-spanning double-disc collection *The Essential Willie Nelson* appeared on Columbia/Legacy in 2003. The other reason, of course, is that during the first part of the 2000s, Legacy had been turning out cross-licensed, multi-label compilations of artists who hopped around from label to label or had unwieldy careers. Willie is a perfect example of this, as he had five significant stays at labels (in chronological order: Liberty, RCA, Atlantic, Columbia, Island), surrounded by a bunch of detours to independent labels, or duets never featured on his official records, all of which makes the task of assembling a concise, definitive collection a difficult one. With its 41 tracks, spanning nearly 40 years of recording, *The Essential Willie Nelson* gets about as close as a set could to providing the basics. That doesn't mean that it's perfect, of course. It naturally relies heavily on the Columbia recordings, since it was both his popular peak and the label that released this collection, with 25 of the tracks dating from this era. To a certain extent, this shortchanges the brilliant Atlantic records *Shotgun Willie* and *Phases and Stages*, as well as his fascinatingly erratic RCA recordings (found in their entirety on the Bear Family box *Nashville Was the Roughest*), but it's also true that the entire first disc, which runs from "Night Life" and "Hello Walls" through "Me and Paul" and "Bloody Mary Morning," all the way to *Stardust*, has a great momentum and summarizes this transition very well. The second disc picks up this thread well for the first 12 songs or so, covering *Honeysuckle Rose* and "Always on My Mind," along with some duets ("Pancho & Lefty" with Merle Haggard, "To All the Girls I've Loved Before" with Julio Iglesias) before it loses steam as it approaches the mid-'80s—not so coincidentally, precisely the time that Willie's career was briefly derailed in a dispute with the IRS. From here on out, the compilation relies too heavily on idiosyncratic selections (partially because he stopped having hits, making selection a matter of picking fan favorites) and duets, including the rarities "Slow Dancing" and "One Time Too Many," where Willie is backed by U2 and Aerosmith, respectively, giving the very end of this collection an inappropriately sour aftertaste. These are minor problems, since the overall collection is as generous as Willie Nelson's music itself and it will likely satisfy the needs of most listeners wanting only one disc in their collection. *—Stephen Thomas Erlewine*

It's Been Rough and Rocky Travelin' / Jun. 2003 / Bear Family ♦♦♦♦

To Lefty From Willie [Expanded] / Jun. 24, 2003 / Columbia/Legacy ♦♦♦♦♦

The remastered and expanded edition of *To Lefty From Willie*, truly one of Willie Nelson's classic recordings, is worth the cash for a number of reasons: The first is that it features as its lone bonus track an absolutely killer rendition of "If You've Got the Money I've Got the Time" from a different recording session. It's live in the studio and blows away the version of *Willie and Family Live*. Another is that the sound brings a warmth to this set that was missing from the shrill transfer of the set when it first appeared on CD. Finally, and most importantly, this remaster presents yet another opportunity for fans and those who may be discovering Nelson for the first time to become acquainted with two of the most kindred spirits in the history of country music. Nelson and Lefty Frizzell were made for each other. Frizzell composed songs that were meant to be *sung*. Their meanings came out in the grain of the singer's voice, and this was certainly true on his own recordings. Nelson, who arguably has the most recognizable male voice in the history of the music with the possible exception of George Jones, turns Frizzell's words into emotions before sending them out into a microphone. These narratives, broken love songs, memories, and ruminations on the blessings and hardships of life are living entities in Nelson's interpretations. "Mom and Dad's Waltz" has no false sentimentality. "I Love You a Thousand Ways" is a declaration without boasting. "Always Late With Your Kisses" is sung with a kind of stunned resignation and heartbroken longing that is taking place in the present in the protagonist's very being. "I Never Go Around Mirrors" is one of the most soothing honky tonk songs ever recorded—especially when the subject matter is so wrenching. Nelson takes the edge off, but as a result the song becomes even sadder. The acceptance in "That's the Way Love Goes" is one where the reward for patience is still one that can be squandered with a false move and one in which that false move can never be known. The way Nelson turns the chorus in on itself and makes it a statement of undying love irregardless of the circumstances or whatever comes next underlines the uniqueness of Frizzell's lyric. The album proper ended with Nelson performing a song by Jimmy Buffett and Jerry Jeff Walker. The reason is not clear, but it feels like Frizzell might have written it, and Nelson delivers it in the same phrasing he uses for all of the Frizzell tunes. *To Lefty From Willie* is known as the great lost Nelson record, and though it did get to number two, it remains one of his least well-known outings but is certainly one of the best. *—Thom Jurek*

Willie and Family Live [Expanded] / Jun. 24, 2003 / Columbia/Legacy ♦♦♦♦♦

Recorded live at Harrah's in Lake Tahoe at the height of Willie madness in 1978, the double-CD remaster of *Willie and Family Live* makes an already long set even longer by the addition of two bonus tracks. Fortunately, those cuts added to the end of disc two are from the same show and include a soul-bearing alternate version of Rodney Corwell's "Til I Gain Control Again" and a tender and moving read of the Hoagy Carmichael classic "Georgia on My Mind." As for the rest, the newly warmed-up sound makes all the difference in the world. While the LP version was fantastic, this set's previous CD incarnation was shrill and lacked bottom. That's all remedied here, and what made that evening so exciting for the folks at Harrah's is plenty evident here: Nelson's band of family (sister Bobbie on piano) and friends—including guest appearances by Johnny Paycheck and Emmylou Harris—kicks ass. The material is classic Nelson, from his own songs such as "Good Hearted Woman" and "I Can Get Off on You," written with Waylon Jennings, to "Crazy" and "Funny How Time Slips Away," as well as a long suite from *Red Headed Stranger*. These of course are on disc one. Disc two is where the gig really heats up and the band stretches out and loosens up, playing largely segueing tunes ranging from Nelson standards and nuggets such as "Bloody Mary Morning" and "Hello Walls," a beautiful combination of "Will the Circle Be Unbroken" and "Amazing Grace," before inviting Paycheck up for "Take This Job and Shove It!" But Nelson goes right back to gospel on "Uncloudy Day" before he moves secular again. In a long suite that starts with "Only Daddy That'll Walk the Line" and continues through Leon Russell's "A Song for You," the original of "Georgia on My Mind," "I Gotta Get Drunk," and back to the show opener, "Whiskey River," Nelson returns back to "Only Daddy That'll Walk the Line" one more time before the bonus versions kick in. In all, it's a solid, rollicking ride with one of the best bands in the business at the time and one of Nelson's more inspired performances. *—Thom Jurek*

Honeysuckle Rose [Expanded Edition] / Jun. 24, 2003 / Columbia/ Legacy ♦♦♦♦

The soundtrack to *Honeysuckle Rose* is an anomaly in the genre. It is really a collection of songs by Willie Nelson & His Family band as well as a host of friends like Jody Payne, Johnny Gimble, Amy Irving, Hank Cochran, Jeannie Seely, Kenneth Threadgill, Dyan Cannon, and Emmylou Harris, all of it set in a concert-like atmosphere and performed live in front of an audience. Now it's true that Nelson is the hero of the movie, but the movie hardly matters when it comes to the soundtrack because it stands so well as a document on its own. Cochran's performances are as inspiring as anything he ever did in his life. Nelson's readings of his own tunes like "Bloody Mary Morning," "On the Road Again," "Pick Up the Tempo," "Heaven or Hell," and others are solid, inspired, and rollicking. His versions of tunes written by Kris Kristofferson ("Loving Her Was Easier Than Anything I'll Ever Do Again"), Rodney Crowell ("Angel Eyes"), and Lee Clayton ("If You Could Touch Her at All") blow away the studio versions. And the duets with Cannon, Harris, and Irving are moving and direct. The sound is much improved on this remastered version with a real bass presence and far less crowd noise during the performances. In addition they restore Irving's reading of Nelson's "If You Want Me to Love You I Will," which was omitted from the original CD release, and add a pair of bonus tracks, making it a superb value. *—Thom Jurek*

San Antonio Rose [Expanded Edition] / Jun. 24, 2003 / Columbia Legacy ♦♦♦♦

Usually projects like this one are a shambles. In 1980 Willie Nelson was a superstar and Ray Price was packing concert halls but not selling records. In 1961 Nelson was Price's bass player and in the band that recorded Price's smash *San Antonio Rose* album. This date is a kind of reprise of Price as king of the honky tonk singers—something he willfully abandoned in the mid-'60s. Recorded in the same studio they'd used 19 years earlier, Nelson & His Family band augmented their sound with Johnny Gimble playing that lonesome fiddle that had become a Price trademark in the same way it was Bob Wills'. In addition, Buddy Emmons, who was also a former Price employee, played steel, and Blondie Calderon, who was Price's bandleader, plays piano and vibraharp here. The program is pure Price, though many of these tunes were present in Nelson's live shows of the era and some remain so. Beginning with the title track and slipping into Price's gorgeous "I'll Be There (If You Ever Want Me)," and of course into "I Fall to Pieces," Hank Cochran, and Harlan Howard, with Price's smooth baritone and Nelson's thin reedy tenor, it's a match made in heaven. Price proves here that he could still be a honky tonk singer when he wanted to be. Other country classics on the set include Floyd Tillman's "This Cold War With You" and Nelson's "Funny How Time Slips Away" (which Price had cut a number of times pre- and post-pop). "Crazy Arms," which is Price's trademark song, is begun by Nelson, but Price's presence on the first chorus takes the spotlight, and in the verse, it's no secret why it's his vocal signature on the tune. As if that weren't enough, they follow it with "Release Me," another Price classic from yesteryear and still a gauge for how well any country singer performs. There's also Fred Rose's "Deep Water," Bob Wills' "Faded Love," and a few unreleased bonus tracks from the session, including Rex Griffin's "Just Call Me Lonesome" and Jesse Ashlock's "My Life's Been a Pleasure." The sound, as it is on the rest of the releases in this series—*To Lefty From Willie*, *Willie and Family Live*, and *Honeysuckle Rose*—is pristine, full of warmth and depth. *—Thom Jurek*

Run That By Me One More Time / Jul. 1, 2003 / Lost Highway ♦♦♦♦

Thirteen years after their first duet recording, the venerable San Antonio Rose, Willie Nelson and Ray Price reconvene for a second outing of Texas honky tonk and Western swing tunes. Recorded and engineered by Joe Gracey at the World Headquarters studios in Luck, TX, *'Run That By Me One More Time* was produced by Nelson and Price. It features 11 really glorious selections that run the gamut from classic Fred Rose number such as "Deep Water" which opens the album, and "Home In San Antone," as well as sentimental reading of Floyd Tillman's "This Cold War With You," and co-writes like the amazing "I've Just Destroyed The World I'm Living In," by the dynamic duo themselves. While Price wrote the beautiful and moving "Soft Rain," that appears here, it is pair of Nelson cuts that are the finest things on the record, "I'm So Ashamed," and "I'm Still Not Over You." Both of them have appeared on recent Nelson outings available only on the internet, but with Price's voice added to the mix, they have a deeper resonance. With the exception of Rose's "Home in San Antone," that appears in the dead center of the recording, the album is comprised of nothing but broken love songs offering a counterweight to the good-time feel of the disc. Speaking of feel, the sound of this album is quite remarkable. It's been awhile since Willie's guitar playing has been given this kind of showcasing or has sounded so rich and full, and the Texas fiddle band setup is recorded as such without a boatload of embellishment. Price's voice, considerably more ragged but even more right lends texture, warmth and a kind of West Texas edge to the sound of the band here as does David Zettner's pedal steel. Of all the recent Willie Nelson recordings out there from

2000 to the present, this is easily the best of them. It's consistent, full of warmth, good-natured looseness and absolutely killer songs. —*Thom Jurek*

Mark Nesler

Vocals, Guitar, Banjo / Contemporary Country, Neo-Traditionalist Country, Singer/Songwriter

Country performer and songwriter Mark Nesler grew up in Texas, where he began playing guitar at an early age. Influenced by his father's bluegrass records, he also picked up a little bit of banjo. After playing in pickup bands during high-school in the Beaumont area, Nesler graduated to a band that toured in support of the Wrangler Star Search. After the tour finished, Nesler formed the 2 Pistols. But despite the band's incessant touring, labels weren't interested.

Nesler's real break came in 1994, when Nashville big wig Jerry Crutchfield signed him to a songwriting deal with MCA Publishing. But then up-and-coming country musician (and fellow Texan) Tracy Byrd asked Nesler to join his touring band as well as write some songs. Nesler accepted and found himself back on the road. But he continued to write songs, and in 1998 Tim McGraw took his "Just to See You Smile" all the way to number one. *I'm Just That Way*, Nesler's own solo debut, appeared in June 1998. That same year, he also married contemporary country artist Jennifer Hanson. Nesler continued to write for Trace Adkins and other Nashville artists. In 2002, Daryl Worley performed his "I Miss My Friend." —*Johnny Loftus*

I'm Just That Way / Jun. 23, 1998 / Elektra ◆◆◆

Although it has a few rough spots, Mark Nesler's debut album *I'm Just That Way* is a promising first effort from the Texan singer/songwriter. Prior to releasing his debut, he had been known as a professional songwriter—he wrote Tim McGraw's number-one hit "Just to See You Smile"—and his craft is evident throughout the album. At times, the craft overwhelms any individual identity Nesler might have, but the moments where it all comes together—the songwriting, the clean production, the appealing, laid-back delivery—it becomes clear that Nesler could reach great heights, given the proper collaborators and artistic environment. —*Thom Owens*

Michael Nesmith

b. Dec. 30, 1942, Houston, TX

Guitar, Vocals / Country-Rock, Singer/Songwriter, Folk-Rock

The comparatively level-headed member of '60s teen sensation the Monkees, Michael Nesmith was the most proficient instrumentalist in the group and wrote their best in-house songs, rootsy pop numbers like "Papa Gene's Blues," "You Told Me," "You Just May Be the One," and "Tapioca Tundra." In fact, he had written many songs before even joining the group, and one of his compositions, "Different Drum," was a hit for Linda Ronstadt and the Stone Poneys in 1968. After he left the Monkees one year later, it wasn't a surprise that he became the only one of his bandmates to sustain a solo career; in fact, his dozen (or so) '70s LPs were among the most groundbreaking country-rock recordings of the era.

Throughout the 1970s and into the '80s, Nesmith continued to record sporadically, though his communications company Pacific Arts began taking up more of his time by the early '80s. Pacific Arts proved to be an important pioneer in the development of music video, the concept he had furthered in the rough-and-tumble pace of the Monkees' TV show. Nesmith, born in 1943 in Houston, listened to the blues and played saxophone while growing up. After spending two years in the Air Force, however, Nesmith became fascinated with folk music and learned to play the guitar. He played around the area, but then moved to Memphis to play backup on recordings for Stax-Volt. Nesmith was in Los Angeles by the mid-'60s, and formed the folk-rock duo Mike & John with John London. He also recorded several singles as a solo act before auditioning to join the Monkees in 1965.

Almost immediately—and even before their show premiered on TV—the Monkees became one of the biggest pop groups of the late '60s. By the end of 1966, the band had notched two number one singles ("Last Train to Clarksville," "I'm a Believer") with the first two Monkees LPs spending more than 30 weeks at number one during 1966-1967. The TV show was a big hit as well, but the group's fabricated origins and subservience to songwriting teams and session musicians betrayed them in the eyes of the rock & roll intelligentsia. While the rock community became smarter every day about the machinations of the music industry, Nesmith led the fight to have the Monkees play instruments on and write songs for their own albums. The band's record label Colgems acquiesced, and on 1967's *Headquarters* the Monkees played their own instruments, wrote eight of the 14 selections, and produced the album (with a little help from their friend Chip Douglas). *Headquarters* reached number one (though with no obvious hits) and the Monkees appeared ready to finally enter the rock elite, artistically as well as commercially. Critics and older listeners weren't impressed with the transformation, however, and the album ended up as something of an artistic peak instead of the beginning of a gradual ascent. Nesmith soothed his wounds in 1968 by recording his first solo album, *Wichita Train Whistle Sings*, which featured new arrangements of his best-known Monkees songs. He continued with the Monkees for one more year, but then left the band in 1969. Nesmith's first act independent of the Monkees was the formation of the First National Band, with old friend John London on bass, John Ware on drums, and one of country music's best steel guitarists, O.J. "Red" Rhodes.

The First National Band signed to RCA Victor and released two albums in 1970, *Magnetic South* and *Loose Salute*. The single "Joanne" hit the pop Top 25, and "Silver Moon" also charted later in the year. Nesmith added several members for 1971's *Nevada Fighter*, and credited it to the Second National Band. The title track skirted the bottom of the charts for several weeks, but Nesmith proved his pop savvy yet again by providing the Nitty Gritty Dirt Band with their hit, "Some of Shelly's Blues." The following year, the National Band released *Tantamount to Treason*. Nesmith dropped the group credit later that year, recording *And the Hits Just Keep on Comin'* as a solo artist—though Red Rhodes continued to play with him. Nesmith's 1973 album *Pretty Much Your Standard Ranch Stash* was his last for RCA Victor, as he formed the music/communications label Pacific Arts in 1974. The following year he released *The Prison* and co-wrote Olivia Newton-John's hit "Let It Shine." Nesmith re-entered the charts with 1977's *From a Radio Engine to the Photon Wing*; the single "Rio" was a hit in the U.K., and a filmed version of the song helped develop the concept of music video.

In 1977, Nesmith furthered his efforts in the field of music video by creating a TV chart show called *Popclips*. When Warner bought the idea from him several years later, the company then developed it into MTV. A stop-gap live album (*Live at the Palais*) appeared in 1978, while *Infinite Rider on the Big Dogma*, Nesmith's last solo album for 13 years, was released the following year. During the '80s, Pacific Arts became the most important video publishing company in America, and Nesmith moved into film and TV production as well, winning the first video Grammy award in 1981 for *Elephant Parts*. He returned to the music business in 1989, appearing with the Monkees once on-stage during their reunion tour. Nesmith also released a compilation of rare solo tracks called *The Newer Stuff* for England's Awareness Records. Rhino Records followed two years later with the best of his early-'70s material, *The Older Stuff*. In 1992, Nesmith released his first album of new material in 13 years, *Tropical Campfires*. Four years later, he reunited with the Monkees again to record *Justus*, the first Monkees album since 1968 to feature all four original members. —*John Bush*

Wichita Train Whistle Sings / 1968 / Dot ◆◆◆

It took over three decades before Michael Nesmith would consent to any subsequent pressings of the instrumental *Wichita Train Whistle Sings* album. However, overwhelming requests—as well as the reality that savvy enthusiasts had already began creating their own inferior CD-R versions—convinced Nesmith to quietly reissue the title under the auspices of his own Videoranch (www.videoranch.com). The legend of this sonic oddity fits in well with the other peculiarities inherent in the Monkees' collective saga. In order to legally circumvent what would have been by all accounts a crippling income tax assessment, Nesmith cleverly financed this one-off scheme. In keeping with his goals, a 52-piece ensemble of studio all-stars was hired for a two-day session on November 18 and 19, 1967, at RCA Studios in Hollywood. Likewise, Nez had the whole affair catered by Chasen's Restaurant. When Dot Records issued the album in August of the following year, it received very little attention except from the inevitably confused Monkees fans. Their reaction was easily understandable as the songs—most of which were Nesmith's solid contributions on the first four Monkees long-players—had been given a decidedly orchestral overhaul. Immediately evident is the big-band style in which these sides were physically documented—incorporating an open microphone placement which is used when recording larger orchestration. The resulting effect lends a natural-sounding warmth that closely miked and/or amplified techniques often lack. The music itself reflects Nesmith's left-of-center attitude and often unpredictable sense of humor. For instance, the full-bodied and otherwise bombastic arrangement of "Nine Times Blue" is speared right through the middle with a Doug Dillard banjo solo. He throttles up the tempo as the full orchestra breaks into a double-time mambo for the second half of the song. Other reinventions include the once psychedelic "Tapioca Tundra" into a free-wheeling escapade replete with a soaring string section that remains amazingly agile throughout. The *Wichita Train Whistle Sings* project also allowed Nesmith the opportunity to record a few songs that he would revisit during his solo career, such as the pseudonym-esque "Carlisle Wheeling." The strict, if not somewhat lumbering, 4/4 time signature performed here is the antithesis of the easy country-rock sound most synonymous with the tune. He would eventually issue it under the name "Conversations" on his second solo album, *Loose Salute*. Also worthy of note is "Don't Cry Now," as it is the only track on the album to have never been issued by either the Monkees or Nesmith. *Wichita Train Whistle Sings* is much more of a timepiece or cultural artifact than an album designed to express artistic achievement or in any way reestablish Nesmith's post-Monkees direction. Fans of his quirky and offbeat sense of humor as well as his delicious melodies will find much to enjoy. —*Lindsay Planer*

Magnetic South / Jul. 1970 / Pacific Arts ◆◆◆◆◆

Anyone who'd been listening closely to the songs Michael Nesmith wrote while a member of the Monkees (or heard his hard to find 1968 solo debut for Dot) already knew that Nesmith had a soft spot for country music. But when Nesmith left the pre-Fab Four to form the First National Band, he dove head first into the twangy stuff, and if he wasn't the first guy to merge country and rock (Gram Parsons easily beat him to the punch on that), he was certainly doing it well before country-rock became the next big thing, and *Magnetic South* made it clear he had his own distinct way of bringing the two genres together. Nesmith put together a top-flight band who sound at once relaxed and thoroughly committed, whether easing through a laid-back number like "Joanne" or kicking up some dust on "Mama Nantucket"; O.J. "Red" Rhodes' pedal steel work is superb throughout, while bassist John London and drummer John Ware offer strong, unobtrusive support (the great Earl P. Hall also sits in on piano). And though the phrase "cosmic cowboy" wasn't coined for Nesmith, it could have been; here, he indulges himself in a consciously poetic and philosophical lyrical style that's a good bit more abstract than one would expect from a former Monkee, though Nesmith's dry sense of humor is always lurking around the corner, ready to rescue him when he slips too deep into pretension. Mixing a country sound with a rocker's instincts and blending airy thoughts on the nature of life and love with iconography of life in the West that brought together the old and the new, Michael Nesmith reveled in contradictions on *Magnetic South*, making them sound as comfortable as well-worn cowboy boots and as fun as a Saturday night barn dance. It's a minor masterpiece of country-rock, and while the Eagles may have sold more records, Nesmith yodels a hell of a lot better than any of them. —*Mark Deming*

Loose Salute / Nov. 1970 / Pacific Arts ◆◆◆◆

After reinventing himself as an engagingly spacey cowboy on the splendid *Magnetic South*, Michael Nesmith took a slightly more eclectic approach on his second album with the First National Band, *Loose Salute*. While country flavors still dominate the album (and O.J. "Red" Rhodes' pedal steel work was even stronger this time out), the uptempo numbers swing a bit harder (especially the rollicking "Dedicated Friend"), there's a funky R&B undertow to "Bye, Bye, Bye," the rhythm guitars on "Silver Moon" suggest Nesmith had heard a bit of reggae, and "Tengo Amore" brings a Latin influence into the mix. But Nesmith's love of old-school country still rings clear on every cut (especially the steel-dominated remake of the Monkees' "Listen to the Band"), and after letting the world know about his deeper side on *Magnetic South*, *Loose Salute* found Nesmith writing about more direct and organic themes (love, faith, ditching work, leaving the Monkees). Nesmith also took over as producer, and he gets a tougher and tighter sound from the band than Felton Jarvis managed on *Magnetic South*. *Loose Salute* doesn't cohere quite as well as *Magnetic South*, but the material is strong, the band sounds great, and Michael Nesmith offered even more surprises than he had in his first turn at bat; it's one of the strongest records in his catalog as a solo artist. —*Mark Deming*

Nevada Fighter / 1971 / Pacific Arts ♦♦♦

Nevada Fighter kicks off with the witty and loose-limbed "The Grand Ennui," and for a moment it sounds like the album will pick up where Michael Nesmith's previous album with the First National Band, *Loose Salute*, left off. But before long, the album shifts gears, and it becomes obvious that Nesmith had something different in mind this time. Except for the rollicking side-closer, "Nevada Fighter," most of the material on side one suggests the more introspective moments of *Magnetic South* but without the same balance of charm and dry humor that made that album so appealing (though "Propinquity (I've Just Begun to Care)" is a fine love song that's a good bit more approachable than its title would lead you to expect). Side two is turned over to material by other songwriters, and while this shifts the album's lyrical tone rather dramatically, Nesmith reveals himself to be a fine interpretive vocalist, and "Texas Morning" and "The Rainmaker" are splendid songs that would merit anyone's attention. The First National Band were also augmented by a number of session musicians on *Nevada Fighter* (including James Burton and Ronn Tutt from Elvis Presley's band), and the arrangements have a decidedly different flavor than on Nesmith's previous two albums, especially in the second half (though Red Rhodes' pedal steel is predictably splendid throughout). *Nevada Fighter* is a fine album, but it's also the weakest of the three Nesmith would cut with the First National Band, and it's not hard to imagine that Nesmith was starting to look for new pastures while he was recording this set. —*Mark Deming*

Tantamount to Treason / 1972 / Pacific Arts ♦♦♦♦

This is Michael Nesmith's first LP backed by the Second National Band, which like its predecessor, is a loose aggregate of studio musicians. This "next generation" was only featured on this disc and heralds the return of former First National Bandmates O.J. "Red" Rhodes (pedal steel) and Michael Cohen (keyboards). The most notable variation between the two units lies in the ethereal style which Nesmith delivers his earthy Southwestern-flavored lyrics and melodies. From right out of the starting gate, Papa Nez unleashes the atypically heavy "Mama Rocker"—which would not have sounded out of place on an early MC5 record. Even compared to his edgier material like "Mama Nantucket," this track is on the verge of early-'70s electric heavy metal. Nez also dips into the avant-garde juxtaposition of jarring sound effects on the introduction to the idiosyncratic tongue-in-cheek narrative "Highway 99 With Melange." These anomalies aside, however, the rest of the album consists of a decidedly more pastoral pastiche of songs. "In the Afternoon" is particularly appealing, and features a blend of folkie-tinged psychedelia with Nesmith's trademark winsome lyrics. Similarly, the other originals—such as the tranquilly trippy "Lazy Lady" or the straight ballad "You Are My One"—reveal the artist's depth as an equally engaging singer and songwriter. This disc is likewise notable for including the Richard Stekol-penned "Wax Minute"—which became both a treasured favorite for artist and enthusiast alike—resulting in its revival during Nesmith's brief return to the concert stage in the early '90s. [In 2001, the U.K.-based Camden label paired the long-players *Nevada Fighter* and *Tantamount to Treason* in their series of two-fer releases. Included on this title are three previously unissued tracks from the early '70s—the original instrumental "Cantata & Fugue in C&W," as well as a cover version of "Rose City Chimes" and the anti-tobacco anthem "Smoke! Smoke! Smoke! (That Cigarette)."] —*Lindsay Planer*

And the Hits Just Keep on Comin' / 1972 / Pacific Arts ♦♦♦♦♦

In 1972, Michael Nesmith had released four albums for RCA Records that didn't sell especially well, and he had parted ways with his band, with only pedal steel guitarist O.J. "Red" Rhodes interested in working on Nesmith's next project. RCA gave Nesmith a limited window of time to make his next album for them, so it was necessity rather than design that led Nesmith to cut *And the Hits Just Keep on Comin'* with just himself on acoustic guitar and Rhodes on pedal steel. But the results were truly inspired; Nesmith and Rhodes use the album's spare instrumentation to their advantage, with the performances both empathetic and intimate, and Rhodes' masterful steel gives these songs a graceful resonance few full bands could muster. And while the ten songs find Nesmith in one of his more introspective phases, here he manages to keep one foot planted firmly in the real world while the other traipses the cosmos (even the trippiest song here, "The Candidate," manages a certain tongue-in-cheek wit that keeps it on *terra firma*, and "Keep On" offers neo-hippie philosophy rooted in good ol' Texas horse sense). He also offers up a superb folk-styled remake of "Different Drum" that has a bluesy lope missing from Linda Ronstadt's better-known version. *And the Hits Just Keep on Comin'* is modest in approach but very satisfying in execution, practically defining the phrase "happy accident." —*Mark Deming*

Pretty Much Your Standard Ranch Stash / 1973 / Pacific Arts ♦♦♦♦♦

After hitting a groove with *And the Hits Just Keep on Comin'*, which Michael Nesmith recorded with just pedal steel guitarist O.J. "Red" Rhodes for accompaniment, Nesmith beefed his sound up again with a full band on *Pretty Much Your Standard Ranch Stash*. But the previous album seems to have reminded Nesmith about the virtues of restraint, and while he had a six-piece band at his disposal this time out, the arrangements are tight and efficient, offering the warmth and immediacy of his *First National Band* sessions (and sometimes even beating them for subtle, understated swing). Red Rhodes, as always, is the star soloist here, but the rest of the band also shines, in particular the guitars of Jay Lacy and Dr. Robert Warford and the solid drumming of Danny Lane. Nesmith wrote one of his best and purest country songs for this set, "Winonah," and offered up a solid remake of the Monkees obscurity "Some of Shelly's Blues," while dipping into bluegrass for the lovely acoustic medley "Back Porch and a Fruit Jar Full of Iced Tea." *Pretty Much Your Standard Ranch Stash* was Michael Nesmith's final album for RCA Records, and if it didn't fare especially well in the marketplace, from a musical standpoint he certainly left the House That Nipper Built on a high note—it was hardly your standard '70s country-rock album. —*Mark Deming*

The Prison / 1974 / Pacific Arts ♦♦♦

The Prison (1974) is a brilliant multimedia concept marrying the personal and inner visual experience of Michael Nesmith's novella with the aural medium of an equally original soundtrack. Earliest pressings came housed in a 12-inch-by-12-inch box set. The short story was presented in an LP-sized booklet with the music featured on the respective A and B sides of a single long-player. As opposed to much of his previous recordings, Nesmith's approach is decidedly more ethereal as the songs drift and dance one into the other with purpose and subjective intent. While Nez's prose as well as the songs' overall lyrical content are not inextricably linked, they aptly balance the respective chapters that correspond to each of the LP sides. The music is a definite departure from the straight-ahead country-rock leanings that Nesmith had exhibited with his First and Second National Bands. Even the copious contributions of David Kempton's ARP synthesizer and the metronome-esque Roland drum machine can't dismantle what are some of his most heartfelt and affectively enchanting melodies to date. "Hear Me Calling?" and "Dance Between the Raindrops" capture much of the Southwestern and Tex-Mex motifs that would continue to evolve on *From a Radio Engine to the Photon Wing* (1977) right through to his *Tropical Campfires* (1994) long-player. The sage advice and thematic moral of *The Prison* deal directly as well as metaphorically with achievement and existing through experience rather than fear. "Elusive Ragings" is pure existential Nez, with a decidedly more personal slant toward relationships and the otherwise inner turmoil of humanity. These concepts also directed *The Garden* (1994), which was a continuation of this story, although neither are mutually exclusive or necessary to the other. [Notably, the 1990 CD reissue has much improved sound quality and the technological advancement allows for a seamless experience. The short story and the music are independently compelling when experienced individually. However, when practiced as complementary media, *The Prison* is nothing short of a quiet revolutionary occurrence.] —*Lindsay Planer*

From a Radio Engine to the Photon Wing / 1977 / Pacific Arts ♦♦♦

This cryptically titled disc seamlessly takes Michael Nesmith from his firmly established southwestern Americana roots and into a much more pop-oriented setting, without compromising his signature laid-back delivery. The disc was cut in Nashville at the height of the disco era. As such, there are a few slightly rhythm-heavy tracks—including the album's signature piece and leadoff track "Rio" and "Love's First Kiss." However, rather than emphasizing a mindless and otherwise repetitive tempo, Nesmith tastefully incorporates the beats into his otherwise country-flavored rockers. As always, the lyrical content is impeccable and at the very least intriguing. The same is true of the sole cover tune—"Navajo Trail"—incorporating the lolloping country & western bassline with his trademark minor chord changes. The lyrical desolation is compounded by some ethereal sound effects that act as a sonic link from song to song—as if the listener is physically drifting from composition to composition. This technique was most likely a remnant from his previous effort, *The Prison*, which was a musical novella featuring text and tunes by Nez. The lovelorn ballad "Wisdom Has Its Way" is practically two decades ahead of its time, as the style is uncanny in the lyrical and musical likeness that would redefine Nesmith on his *Tropical Campfires* (1993) album. The tune is well-crafted and expansive enough musically that it could very well be interpreted as a slow acoustic ballad in addition to a fuller band version—as heard here. The two rockers on the album, the bluesy "We Are Awake" and the honky tonkin' "The Other Room," are somewhat disparate in musical approach, yet they are distinctly Nesmith, with clever metaphysical and witty double entendre-filled lyrics. These tracks pave the way for the decidedly upbeat and edgier *Infinite Rider on the Big Dogma*. This studio follow-up sheds the disco rhythms and features Nesmith with a full-blown rock band. —*Lindsay Planer*

Live at Palais / 1978 / Pacific Arts ♦♦♦♦

Live at Palais is one of the rare concert recordings released by Michael Nesmith. In the early '90s, when the rest of his back catalog was being issued on CD, Nesmith refused to allow the disc to be included in overhaul—citing dissatisfaction with the performance. Due to the demand of enthusiasts worldwide, consent was granted to not only reissue the disc, but also to complement the package with nearly a half-hour of additional music. The material covered here is primarily derived from the half-dozen albums Nesmith did on RCA Records in the early '70s—the singular exception being "Capsule" from the cryptically titled *Infinite Rider on the Big Dogma* long-player. A majority of the tracks are refugees from one of Nesmith's most fertile creative periods in the late '60s, just prior to leaving the Monkees. "Calico Girlfriend," "Propinquity," "Some of Shelly's Blues," "Crippled Lion," and "Listen to the Band" are all tunes Nesmith recorded as both a Monkee and solo artist. On *Live at Palais*, Nesmith's folk-tinged originals are replaced by electric and decidedly more emotive renderings. While much of the folksy spirit remains, songs such as "Calico Girlfriend" and "Some of Shelly's Blues" have matured—featuring the essence of the southwest Americana that Nesmith's music so aptly depicts. The bonus material is as strong as—if not arguably more potent than—the *Palais* performance. From a 1981 show at *the Armadillo World Headquarters* in Austin, TX, comes another, albeit heavier, version of "Grand Ennui" as well as the only live version of the previously mentioned "Capsule." The other pair of bonus tracks is from a concert sponsored by Gretsch Guitars in 1995. Incidentally, Nesmith owned one of only three electric 12-string Gretsch guitars manufactured in the mid- to late '60s. His affinity is obvious and translates into some outstanding music ranging from the tender "Crippled Lion" to the raucous "Listen to the Band." *Live at Palais* is only available through Nesmith's online mail order www.videoranch.com site. *—Lindsay Planer*

Infinite Rider on the Big Dogma / 1979 / Pacific Arts ✦✦✦✦

As the '70s drew to a close, Michael Nesmith's music had still retained all of the intellect, intrinsic charm, and dry wit that had defined his tenure as a Monkee, as well as his country-rock-flavored solo material from earlier in the decade. The cryptically titled *Infinite Rider on the Big Dogma* was "Papa Nez"'s ninth post-Monkees solo studio effort in as many years. The Southwestern motif that practically defined Nesmith's First and Second National Band(s) remained throughout his late-'70s releases, although now the distinct pedal steel guitars had been morphed into the more traditional rock & roll electric ones. The ten tracks cover a lot of ground, from the '50s sock-hop ballad "Magic" to a more modern approach to love songs on "Carioca"—featuring one of Nesmith's finest unions of lyric to melody. These contrast well with the full-fledged heavy-rockers "Factions" and "Horserace," or the slightly Caribbean feel of the uptempo "Flying." Not only does this variety of styles aptly demonstrate Nesmith's maturity as a composer, it is also a more accurate reflection of the versatility in his work. Concurrent to this album, Nesmith was also investing his time and money into a new venture that took the best part of the Monkees project—the marriage of music to a visual image—a step further with the creation of his own Pacific Arts Video company. It was here that Nesmith planted the seeds of what would become MTV—as well as producing the first Grammy-winning musical home video—*Elephant Parts*. The feature-length title contains videos for several tunes on this album—including "Crusin'," "Magic," and "Flying." *—Lindsay Planer*

The Newer Stuff / 1989 / Rhino ✦✦✦

This compilation of later solo material is often glossy and overreaching but still quite impressive. *—Jeff Tamarkin*

The Older Stuff: Best of Michael Nesmith (1970–1973) / 1991 / Rhino ✦✦✦✦✦

This 18-track compilation was a follow-up to the similarly titled *Newer Stuff*, highlighting Michael Nesmith's post-1974 sides as well as featuring some previously unissued material. *Older Stuff* (1991) includes a healthy sampling of tracks from the half-dozen long-players Nesmith issued prior to 1974 as the respective leader of both the First and the Second National Band and then later as a solo artist. As these cuts demonstrate, he consistently turned out some of the best music in the country-rock subgenre that he was helping to pioneer. The tune stack is well represented by the National Band LPs *Magnetic South* (1970), *Loose Salute* (1970), and *Nevada Fighter* (1971), plus, to a much lesser extent, *Tantamount to Treason* (1972) and *And the Hits Just Keep on Comin'* (1972) as well as its follow-up, *Pretty Much Your Standard Ranch Stash* (1973). Nesmith's penchant for penning quirky country & western-flavored pop songs can be directly traced back to his more prominent Monkees contributions. During this period he was also woodshedding material for his future endeavors—although cuts such as "Some of Shelly's Blues," "Cripple Lion," and "Listen to the Band" were all worked up during his waning days as a teen pop idol. Ultimately, autonomy as a solo artist allowed him to further develop a singular voice rooted in folk and country, while remaining ever unique. Stylistically, his range became more eclectic—encompassing both driving rockers such as "Roll With the Flow" and the lilting relationship ballad "Continuing." This release not only visits those extremes, it also hits upon many of the more subtle facets from Nesmith's prolific early-'70s recordings. The obvious inclusions of "Joanne" and "Different Drum" sit well alongside his reworking of Derek & the Dominos' "I Looked Away" or the pair of sides made famous by the Sons of the Pioneers—"Tumbling Tumbleweeds" and "Prairie Lullaby." While some may wish to seek out the six albums from which these cuts were extracted, this is a worthwhile primer for the curious and potential enthusiast. *—Lindsay Planer*

Tropical Campfires / Oct. 27, 1992 / Pacific Arts ✦✦✦✦

Along with Lindsay Buckingham's *Out of the Cradle*, this album may be one of the finest and most underrated albums of the 1990s. Nesmith and his crack band run-through 12 of the most delicious slices of Americana to be put on record in ages. The mood of the album is a cross between Bahamian, tropical, country, and other forms, all forging a unique synthesis of pop that might be very hard to match. Nesmith's songs and vocals are wholly original and personal, and tunes such as "I Am Not That" and "Laugh Kills Lonesome" bear the indefinable Nesmith stamp of humor with a compact and irresistible force. In addition to the excellent originals, Nesmith and his band cover two classic Cole Porter songs with excellent results, and both ("In the Still of the Night" and "Begin the Beguine") fit the menu perfectly. Absolutely delectable. *—Matthew Greenwald*

● **Complete** / Sep. 28, 1993 / Pacific Arts ✦✦✦✦✦

This two-CD set brings together the three albums Michael Nesmith recorded with his group the First National Band in 1971 and 1972, *Magnetic South*, *Loose Salute*, and *Nevada Fighter*. In his liner notes to this set, Nesmith says that he always intended the three First National Band albums to be a trilogy, and while the individual albums do have subtle but distinct personalities of their own, they also play well as a set, with the laid-back *Magnetic South* easing comfortably into the slightly more rock-oriented *Loose Salute* and *Nevada Fighter*'s addition of session men and a handful of covers leading the group into the sunset. Nesmith's notes also declare his status as "one of the pioneers of Country Rock" to be "nonsense," and while anyone whose listened to these albums might think Nez protests too much on this point, it's certainly true that his fusion of country's sound and rock & roll's soul was decidedly his own and bore little resemblance to that of anyone else working in the same direction. (He also was fortunate to have one of the best pedal steel players alive, O.J. "Red" Rhodes, in his band, and his playing alone would make these discs worth your time.) The First National Band albums were among the finest music of Michael Nesmith's solo career, and anyone interested in his body of work (or in country-rock and its best and most intelligent) would do well to pick up *Complete*. *—Mark Deming*

The Garden / 1994 / Rio Royal ✦✦✦✦

The Garden (1994) is Michael Nesmith's companion release to *The Prison* (1974). Both works are a departure from his more traditional releases, as the music is specifically designed to aurally complement an equally engaging written novella/short story—included in the extended liner notes booklet. The idea is for consumers to commence reading Nesmith's prose while simultaneously listening to the recording. The concept may at first seem unusual, although the results are nothing short of profound. No special speed-reading skills are required. Rather, the most useful thing that a potential enthusiast can bring to the multimedia project is an open mind, sense of adventure, and respect for the infinite possibilities inherent within such an subtly demanding correlation. As Nesmith is quick to point out in his preface, *The Garden* is not a sequel in the strictest sense of the term—meaning that there isn't a true continuation of the narrative which began in *The Prison*. Instead, they are correlated thematically and stylistically as both are presented in a linear and consecutive approach. Each of *The Garden*'s seven chapters are also visually enhanced, if not somewhat inspired by a series of Claude Monet paintings. There is a much more subtle connection between the prose and these unqualified masterworks, yet he is able to relate them in a contextual sense. The music retains Nesmith's inimitable and signature sound, yet compared to his most concurrent effort, *Tropical Campfires* (1992), *The Garden* is exceedingly ethereal and more often than not instrumental. There are vocals that feature not only the artist, but also his children Jason—who is likewise the central character in the short story—Christian, and Jessica. The backing band also includes Christian Nesmith as well as most of the musicians the senior Nez had collaborated with on the aforementioned *Tropical Campfires*, most notably Desert Rose Band string man John Jorgenson (guitar/sax/bassoon/mandolin/oboe/bandurila/mandocello), Joe Chemay (bass), and John Hobbs (keyboards), as well as studio maven Sid Page (violin). *—Lindsay Planer*

Listen to the Band / 1997 / Camden ✦✦✦✦✦

This is a particularly fine single-disc compilation, offering 22 tracks of Nesmith's countrified work with his First National Band after he departed the Monkees. What stands out is his real gift as a songwriter (particularly on tunes like "Joanne," "Harmony Constant," and "Some of Shelly's Blues") as well as a hitmaker (as with his original version of "Different Drum" that was such a hit for Linda Ronstadt). The sound also owes a great debt to the fine pedal steel work of O. J. "Red" Rhodes. *—Tim Sheridan*

16 Original Classics / Sep. 28, 1999 / Collectables ✦✦✦

16 Original Classics is actually the 1970 Mike Nesmith album *Magnetic South* with five extra bonus tracks tacked on. This was one of the highlights from any of the post-Monkee recording careers, confirming Nesmith as a pioneer of the country-rock genre with an incredible vocal range, proven talent as a songwriter, and the ability to arrange a group of top-notch country pickers. The First National Band featured longtime Nesmith cohorts pedal steel guitarist "Red" Rhodes, bassist John London, and drummer John Ware. The moderate success of the single "Joanne" (included on this package) made Nesmith the first ex-Monkee to put a solo record on the charts. *—Al Campbell*

Magnetic South/Loose Salute / Apr. 4, 2000 / BMG International ✦✦✦✦

This European two-fer CD contains Michael "Papa Nez" Nesmith's first two post-Monkees recordings—*Magnetic South* and *Loose Salute*—as a member of the First National Band. Although the heavily orchestrated *Wichita Train Whistle Sings* (1968) is credited to Nesmith as a solo artist, it was technically released while he was still a Monkee. As a bonus for collectors, this single-disc anthology also includes the instrumental track "1st National Dance." As enthusiasts of post-*Headquarters* Monkees will assuredly attest, Nesmith's country & western-flavored material is not only the highlight of those albums, but arguably the only worthwhile tracks on them. During his tenuous final days as a pop idol, Nesmith took full advantage of the unique situation by recording his compositions outside of the Monkees pre-manufactured confines—using his own musicians. Several of those tracks are revisited on these recordings. Among them, "Calico Girlfriend," "Nine Times Blue," "Little Red Rider," "Crippled Lion," "Hollywood," and "Conversations" were recorded and available for potential inclusion on the last three Monkees long-players that Nesmith had any involvement in—*The Birds, the Bees & the Monkees*, *Instant Replay*, and *The Monkees Present*. The First National Band featured O. J. "Red" Rhodes (pedal steel guitar), Glen D. Hardin (keyboards), John London (bass), and John Ware (drums). Along with Nesmith (guitar/vocals), they provided a tight yet sublimely down-home platform for Papa Nez to weave his unique brand of country-rock—which was in its infancy at the time. Other West Coast artists such as the Eagles, the post-David Crosby Byrds, and the Flying Burrito Brothers were creating similar sounds and providing an alternative to the recently unleashed aural attack of heavy metal. Although the prolific nature of Nesmith's writing during the late '60s and early '70s is evidenced on both *Magnetic South* and *Loose Salute*, he reworks two Hank Cochran/Harlan Howard standards, "I Fall to Pieces" and "Beyond the Blue Horizon," with sensitivity and to tremendous effect. These are among the highlights of both recordings as well as this era of Nesmith's career. *—Lindsay Planer*

And the Hits Just Keep on Comin'/Pretty Much Your Standard Ranch Stash / Nov. 7, 2000 / BMG International ✦✦✦✦✦

After leaving the Monkees, Michael Nesmith recorded a handful of superb country-rock albums for RCA Records in the early '70s, and this two-fer CD reissues his two final albums for the label—which were also two of his best. *And the Hits Just Keep on Comin'* was recorded in 1972 by Nesmith with just a single accompanist, pedal steel guitarist "Red" Rhodes, after Nesmith suffered a falling out with the rest of his band. Nesmith turned this challenge into a triumph; the album boasts an uncommon warmth and intimacy, and the interplay between Nesmith's vocals and Rhodes' steel is a wonder to behold. Nesmith was back to working with a band on *Pretty Much Your Standard Ranch Stash*, but he did so without robbing the album of the empathy and subtlety that made *Hits* so special; highlights include the lovely "Winonah" (about as close to a straight country ballad as Nesmith would ever get) and a fine bluegrass medley, "Back Porch and a Fruit Jar Full of Iced Tea." Michael Nesmith often had a hard time shaking off the image he picked up in the Monkees, and his solo career suffered as a result, but if his albums for RCA didn't sell very well, it was never because of their quality; this disc finds Nesmith in superb form on two different albums, and if you're at all curious about his solo career in the 1970s, it's a fine place to start exploring. *—Mark Deming*

Nevada Fighter/Tantamount to Treason / Apr. 3, 2001 / BMG International ✦✦✦✦✦
This U.K. import is the second in a series of three separate two-fer releases gathering Michael Nesmith's first six albums with additional materials—such as the three previously issued bonus tracks included on this package. While each album contains a substantially different backing band, they are both continuations of the intricate country & western-influenced songs that Nesmith was both writing and covering in the early '70s. The 1971 release *Nevada Fighter* was the third and final from the First National Band, containing a bevy of both highly melodic originals—much in the same vein as *Magnetic South* and *Loose Salute*. As a songwriter, it is hard to beat the collection of tunes Nesmith corralled for these albums. "Propinquity (I've Just Begun to Care)" ranks among the compositions that Papa Nez had been woodsheding during his final days as a Monkee—a version of which can be heard on the odds-and-sods *Missing Links, Vol. 3* collection. The song's intrinsic beauty didn't escape the ears of Nesmith's influences, as Earl Scruggs included a cover on his disc *I Saw the Light* (1972). His contemporaries also took note of Papa Nez's prowess. The Nitty Gritty Dirt Band rendered a sublime version of not only "Propinquity," but also "Some of Shelly's Blues" on their *Uncle Charlie & His Dog Teddy* release (1970). Speaking of cover material, both titles include a few defining versions of country & western standards "Tumbling Tumbleweeds" (Sons of the Pioneers), "Rainmaker" (Harry Nilsson), and a sentimental "I Looked Away" (Derek & the Dominos). The trio of bonus material is of particular note, as very little seems to exist from these sessions. The two covers are "Rose City Chimes"—which was originally done by Hank Thompson as well as Jim & Jesse—and Merle Travis' anti-tobacco anthem "Smoke! Smoke! Smoke! (That Cigarette)." The one original, "Cantata & Fugue in C&W," is an upbeat boot-stomper of an instrumental that dates circa Tantamount to Treason. This extended-play disc is the ideal way for prospective enthusiasts to collect these recordings. *—Lindsay Planer*

Best Of: Original Hits / Apr. 23, 2002 / Paradiso ✦✦✦

Silver Moon / Jul. 16, 2002 / Audiophile Classics ✦✦✦✦✦
Although the cover art might suggest that this compiles, features, or in some way includes material from Michael Nesmith's four-year (1966-1970) tenure as a Monkee, this isn't the case at all. Additionally confusing matters is that the same 25 tracks on this collection are replicated—right down to the exact running order—on the unimaginatively titled *Best Of: Original Hits*. Regardless, the contents of both have been culled from Nesmith's first half-dozen post-Monkees long-players. The tune stack is well represented by the First National Band LPs *Magnetic South* (1970), *Loose Salute* (1970), and *Nevada Fighter* (1971)—plus, to a much lesser extent, *Tantamount to Treason* (1972), *And the Hits Just Keep on Comin'* (1972), as well as *Pretty Much Your Standard Ranch Stash* (1973). Nesmith's penchant for penning quirky country & western-flavored pop songs can be directly traced back to his Monkees material, such as "St. Matthew," "Good Clean Fun," and "Magnolia Simms." During this period he was also woodshedding material for future endeavors. Although never issued, he recorded a significant backlog of original compositions while still a Monkee. Of the tracks included on this collection, "Cripple Lion," "Some of Shelly's Blues," "Calico Girlfriend," "Nine Times Blue," "Hollywood," "Little Red Rider," and "Conversations," originally titled "Carlisle Wheeling" are among the titles first recorded by Nez prior to gaining artistic independence from his decidedly manufactured image. Ultimately, autonomy as a solo artist allowed him to further develop a singular voice rooted in folk and country, yet remaining ever unique. Stylistically, his range became more eclectic—encompassing both driving rockers, such as "Mama Nantucket," and lilting, heartsick ballads, such as "Joanne." This compilation not only visits those extremes, it also hits upon many of the more subtle facets from Nesmith's prolific early-'70s recordings. *—Lindsay Planer*

New Coon Creek Girls

f. 1979
Group / Traditional Bluegrass, Traditional Folk
Formed by John Lair in 1979, the New Coon Creek Girls carried on the bluegrass tradition established by Lair's original Coon Creek Girls in the 1930s. Just as he had with the first group, Lair promoted the New Coon Creek Girls through his radio show and concert hall, the *Renfro Valley Barn Dance*. Guitarist and banjoist Vicki Simmons was one of the first performers to sign on to the group. Besides her musical talent, Simmons also had a connection to the original Coon Creek Girl, Lilly Mae Ledford, who had taught her the clawhammer banjo style. While the NCCG lineup would fluctuate over the years, Simmons was always a constant.

The band remained on Lair's show until 1983, at which point they struck out on their own. Throughout the 1980s and '90s, the Girls were a popular attraction on the bluegrass and folk festival circuit. By 1991, the lineup included Simmons, banjoist Ramona Church Taylor, vocalist and guitarist Dale Ann Bradley, and Pam Perry on vocals and mandolin. This lineup released 1994's *The L&N Don't Stop Here Anymore* as well as *Ain't Love a Good thing* a year later. The mandolin of Deanie Richardson replaced Perry's for 1996's *Everything You Do*, but Perry and Richardson both appeared on *Our Point of View* two years later. By this point, Bradley and Simmons were playing in another combo, simply called Coon Creek. Teenage fiddling sensation Kati Penn also contributed to latter-day NCCG recordings. *—Johnny Loftus*

Pictures / 1988 / Turquoise ✦✦✦

Playing Our Respect / 1989 / Turquoise ✦✦✦

● **So I'll Ride** / 1991 / Turquoise ✦✦✦✦✦

L&N Don't Stop Here Anymore / 1994 / Pinecastle ✦✦✦

Ain't Love a Good Thing / 1995 / Pinecastle ✦✦✦

Everything You Do / 1996 / Pinecastle ✦✦✦✦

Our Point of View / 1998 / Pinecastle ✦✦✦✦✦
The New Coon Creek Girls is a bundle of bluegrass talent. Foremost, we have the dulcet vocals of Dale Ann Bradley—she makes "Danny Boy" sound fresh as she expresses it here. The instrumentalists step out and tear it up with lightning exchanges like the fiddle-mandolin-banjo frenzy of "On Fire." Other standards they give new life to are Jimmie Rodgers' "Muleskinner Blues" and "Sassafras." The combined chops in this band simply cannot be overlooked. After nearing 20 years of performance, three-way harmonies and stunning melodies mark *Our Point of View* as a stellar bluegrass album of skill and tradition. *—Thomas Schulte*

New Grass Revival

f. 1972, **db.** 1990
Group / Progressive Bluegrass
New Grass Revival, formed in 1972 by four former members of the Bluegrass Alliance, flourished in a decade when numerous groups took traditional bluegrass and changed it to varying degrees. The group was successful enough to have the group's name become a generic label: "newgrass." The band's image, with long hair and occasionally electrified instruments, as well as its musical material contrasted greatly with standard (traditional) bluegrass like that played by Bill Monroe, Ralph Stanley, the Lilly Brothers, and Lester Flatt's band. In terms of longevity, popularity, and exposure, the Revival, with its hip reputation, was perhaps the most successful in competition against II Generation, Seldom Scene, the Country Gentlemen, and others.

The origins of New Grass Revival lay in the Bluegrass Alliance, which Sam Bush (vocals, fiddle, guitar, mandolin) and Courtney Johnson (banjo, vocals) joined in 1970. At the time, the Alliance also featured bassist Ebo Walker and fiddler Lonnie Peerce. Within a year after Bush's and Johnson's arrival, Curtis Burch (dobro, guitar, vocals) joined the band. In 1972, Peerce left the band, and the remaining members decided to continue under a new name—New Grass Revival. The band released their eponymous debut, *Arrival of the New Grass Revival*, later that year on Starday Records.

After the release of their debut, Walker parted ways with the band, and the group replaced him with Butch Robbins, who was only with the band for a short time. He was replaced by John Cowan, an Evansville, IN, native. This lineup was stable throughout the '70s, recording a number of albums for Flying Fish Records. As their name suggested, New Grass Revival never played traditional bluegrass—all of the members brought elements of rock & roll, jazz, and blues to the group's sound. Consequently, certain portions of the bluegrass community scorned them, but they also gained a devoted following of listeners who believed they were moving the genre in a new, fresh direction.

In 1981, Johnson and Burch left the band, claiming they were tired of touring. Bush and Cowan continued the group, replacing them with banjoist Béla Fleck and mandolinist/guitarist Pat Flynn. New Grass Revival moved to Sugar Hill Records in 1984 and released their first album featuring the new lineup, *On the Boulevard*. Two years later, the band signed with EMI Records and released an eponymous album, which proved to be their breakthrough into the mainstream. Two of the singles from the album—"What You Do to Me" and "Ain't That Peculiar"—were minor hits on the country charts, and Fleck's showcase "Seven By Seven" was nominated for a Grammy for Best Country Instrumental. *Hold to a Dream*, released in 1987, was just as successful as its predecessor, featuring the hits "Unconditional Love" and "Can't Stop Now," which both nearly made the Top 40. In 1989, New Grass Revival released their third major-label album, *Friday Night in America*, which was yet another commercial success. "Callin' Baton Rouge" became their first Top 40 single, followed by the number-58 hit "You Plant Your Fields." Even though the band was more popular than ever, Bush decided to pull the plug on the group after the release of *Friday Night in America*. Bush became a session musician, and Fleck went onto a very successful and respected solo career. *—Stephen Thomas Erlewine & David Vinopal*

The Arrival of the New Grass Revival / 1972 / Starday ✦✦✦✦
Even conservative traditions like bluegrass have their rebels, and the New Grass Revival, with their long hair and rock & roll repertoire, certainly qualified as such. *The Arrival of the New Grass Revival* may sound like just another bluegrass album today, but in 1973 it created quite a stir. The first incarnation of the band rose from the ashes of the Bluegrass Alliance, and included mandolinist/fiddler Sam Bush, bassist Ebo Walker, banjoist Courtney Johnson, and guitarist/dobroist Curtis Burch. While a track like Bill Monroe's "Body and Soul" was anchored to tradition, the Revival specialized in progressive material like Leon Russell's "Prince of Peace" and Jerry Lee Lewis' "Great Balls of Fire." Like a rock band, the New Grass Revival also enjoyed stretching out a piece like "Lonesome Fiddle Blues" to seven minutes, allowing everyone plenty of room to solo. As Jon Hartley Fox points out in the liner notes, two of the strongest pieces, "I Wish I Said (I Love You One More Time)" and "Whisper My Name" were written by the band. Besides strong material, the band plays with so much raw energy that *The Arrival of the New Grass Revival* almost sounds live. Perhaps the intensity of the band's approach, bluegrass with a rock & roll attitude, frightened the old guard at the time. Today, it just sounds like great acoustic music. *—Ronnie D. Lankford Jr.*

Fly Through the Country / 1975 / Flying Fish ♦♦♦♦♦

When the Storm Is Over / 1977 / Flying Fish ♦♦♦

Too Late to Turn Back Now / 1977 / Flying Fish ♦♦♦

With a reputation as a crack live unit, it's perhaps surprising that the New Grass Revival only released two official concert albums (and on one of those they shared the bill with Leon Russell). Recorded at progressive bluegrass stronghold Telluride, CO, *Too Late to Turn Back Now* followed two fine mid-'70s studio efforts, *Fly Through the Country* and *When the Storm Is Over.* The set kicks off with an energetic take on "Lonesome and a Long Way From Home," a song that shows off the group's splendid harmony. There's a long instrumental intro to the album's highlight, "With Care From Someone," an eight-minute extravaganza of wild vocals and lively solos. John Cowan offers his characteristic rock & roll take on "Watermelon Man" before tackling *Fly Through the Country*'s ten-minute title track. While versions of both tunes are vigorous enough, the first is a bit rough around the edges while the second is way, way too long. Perhaps concertgoers "got into it," but at home, Sam Bush's slide mandolin sounds like an out-of-tune dobro. The seventh and final cut, "Red Man Blues," gives the band a chance to kick out the jams on an extended instrumental. Bush offers some strong, progressive fiddle work, and sounds as though he's ready to do a duet with Jean-Luc Ponty, while Curtis Burch turns in a bit of fancy flatpicking. Alas, though the results are pretty good, *Too Late to Turn Back Now* is over in a short time. Fans of the New Grass Revival's '70s lineup, however, will definitely want to add this live recording to their collections. *—Ronnie D. Lankford Jr.*

Barren County / 1979 / Flying Fish ♦♦♦♦

By 1979, the New Grass Revival's name defined the progressive branch of the bluegrass tree. Furthermore, they had developed into a crack unit, with a good reputation as live performers and polished studio players. Both mandolinist Sam Bush and bassist John Cowan covered the lead vocals, while guitarist/dobroist Curtis Burch and banjoist Courtney Johnson filled out the band's sound. The band's eclectic song choices, acoustic/electric arrangements, and professionalism are all on display on its fifth album, *Barren County.* Things really start clicking on the third number, "How About You," with Cowan singing a fine rock & roll lead and Bush adding electric guitar. Bush follows with "Crazy in the Night," one of the band's many odes to romance, before Cowan delves into Steven F. Brines and Bush's "Don't Look Back." Brines, in fact, co-wrote four of the nine songs on the album, qualifying him as a silent fifth member of the group. "Souvenir Bottles" stands as perhaps the strongest piece on the album, featuring an energetic joint lead vocal by Bush and Cowan. As good as *Barren County* is, however, the album's airtight sound has stripped away the rougher edges associated with traditional bluegrass. This approach seems to render the material soulless at times, as though little has been left to chance. Nonetheless, one never doubts the ability of the players or the quality of the material, and fans will consider this a fine effort by the pre-Béla Fleck/Pat Flynn version of the band. *—Ronnie D. Lankford Jr.*

Commonwealth / 1981 / Flying Fish ♦♦♦♦

The New Grass Revival had proven just about everything an innovative band could prove by 1981. Not only had their name come to define the progressive branch of the bluegrass tree, they continued to adhere to high standards. On *Commonwealth*, the band stretches its arrangements and production to the very edge with the addition of drummer Kenny Malone and pianist Leon Russell. A jubilant "Reach" inserts a joyous mood into the music from the very start, while John Hartford's "Steam Powered Aereo Plane" receives a rousing rendition. Bassist John Cowan brings his soulful vocals to the lovely "One Day I'll Walk" with a little help from Sharon White, before mandolinist Sam Bush and Cowan cut loose on a fine duet, "Nothing Wasted, Nothing Gained." The inclusion of a traditional piece like "Wicked Path of Sin," deep into the album, seems more like an afterthought than a deliberate nod to tradition. Nonetheless, aficionados of newgrass instrumentals will want to stick around for an eight-minute take on Bush's "Sapporo." The only downside, in retrospect, is that *Commonwealth* would be banjoist Courtney Johnson and guitarist Curtis Burch's last album with the group. *Commonwealth*, then, represented the culmination of a seven-year partnership and brought to a close the era the band had prospered in. Anyone who ever wondered what all the fuss was about will not regret picking up a copy of *Commonwealth. —Ronnie D. Lankford Jr.*

On the Boulevard / 1984 / Sugar Hill ♦♦♦♦

Live / 1984 / Sugar Hill ♦♦

Live captures a boisterous, lively performance from the New Grass Revival, as they tear through their best material. The new additions to the band—banjoist Béla Fleck and guitarist Pat Flynn—have energized the band, and vocalist John Cowan helps spur the band on to truly remarkable performances. *—Thom Owens*

New Grass Revival / 1986 / EMI America ♦♦♦♦♦

Brightly directed by legendary Nashville producer Garth Fundis (his fourth with the band), the simply titled *New Grass Revival* is another in their strong line of progressive bluegrass recordings. The instrumental prowess of Béla Fleck and Sam Bush take center stage on many songs, including Fleck's signature banjo piece "Seven By Seven." The Grammy-nominated composition (named for its unusual, jazzy time signature) is certainly a highlight, as is the mandolin and banjo conversation on "Someone Like Me." A little less successful is their misguided cover of Marvin Gaye's "Ain't That Peculiar," but the high points outweigh the low, making this one of their more successful releases. *—Zac Johnson*

Hold to a Dream / 1987 / Capitol ♦♦♦

The band who originated the term "newgrass" continued their progressive bluegrass stylings on *Hold to a Dream.* As their work grew, the band explored new textures and instrumentation, including the use of fretless bass on Béla Fleck's jazz-inspired "Metric Lips" and the sea shanty roll of Pat Flynn's "I'll Take Tomorrow." Lead singer John Cowan is expressive but still relatively restrained (compared to some of his other recordings), and the interplay between Fleck's banjo and Sam Bush's fiddle or mandolin really sparks. While this album drifts closer to their contemporary country side than their bluegrass roots, it certainly makes for an entertaining listen. *—Zac Johnson*

Friday Night in America / 1989 / Southern Music ♦♦♦

On what would turn out to be New Grass Revival's final album, *Friday Night in America*, the band advanced their sound beyond their own previous pioneering. Their genre-busting brand of rocked-out progressive bluegrass is at its most rockin'—almost bordering on hair metal with banjos. John Cowan's emotive vocals soar above the delicate picking of Béla Fleck's banjo and the occasional electronic drums or fretless bass. From this point, it is easy to see how effortlessly Fleck slipped into the prog jazz-grass of his Flecktones, particularly on the epic jam "Big Foot." Similarly, this jazzy noodling may be precisely why Sam Bush left the group for the earthier tones of Emmylou Harris' Nash Ramblers. Aside from the "historical document" element of the album, there are some fine moments, particularly the hits "Callin' Baton Rouge" and "You Plant Your Fields." While songs like "Angel Eyes" sound almost like the members of Mr. Big couldn't find their guitars so they picked up mandolins and fiddles, fans of contemporary country and tight instrumentation will want to pick this up. *—Zac Johnson*

● **New Grass Anthology** / Aug. 27, 1990 / Liberty ♦♦♦♦♦

Culling tracks from the first three New Grass Revival discs cut for Capitol Records, *Anthology* has all the highlights, including "Callin' Baton Rouge," later made world famous by one Garth Brooks. It also includes one unreleased cut, "Reach" which adds to *Anthology*'s charm. It's a good compilation. *—James Chrispell*

Fly Through the Country/When the Storm Is Over / 1991 / Flying Fish ♦♦♦♦

Fly Through the Country/When the Storm Is Over is a two-for-one deal, representing New Grass Revival releases from 1976 and 1977 respectively. Mandolin player Sam Bush, bassist John Cowan, guitarist Curtis Burch, and banjoist Courtney Johnson form the core of the band on these 20 selections. This material separates itself from traditional bluegrass by its easy air and romantic sensibility. One has a difficult time imagining Ralph Stanley or any traditional act choosing to sing Townes Van Zandt's "White Freightliner Blues." The disc kicks off with a nice version of John Hartford's "Skippin' in the Mississippi Dew," before letting Cowan take the lead vocal on the lovely, "Good Woman's Love." His vocals, unlike traditional bluegrass, are soulful, as though he grew up listening to rock & roll. Sam Bush also offers nice lead vocals on songs like "Glory" and "When She Made Laughter Easy." The song choice in general has more in common with '70s figures like Jackson Browne than any standard bluegrass repertoire. This gives the album a contemporary feel. The overall musicianship is also superb. Burch is the paragon of good taste whether playing guitar or dobro, while Bush, known for his mandolin chops, is equally apt at fiddle, and on one song, Jackson Browne's "These Days," he even breaks out an electric guitar! A wider variety of instruments has been thrown into the musical stew on *When the Storm Is Over*, including electric piano and drums. These electric moments, while clearly not traditional, never overpower the music. Both of these albums offer a great starting place to discover the earlier version of the New Grass Revival (as opposed to the later version, which included Béla Fleck and the glories of early progressive bluegrass). *—Ronnie Lankford Jr.*

The Best of New Grass Revival / Mar. 8, 1994 / Liberty ♦♦♦♦

The Best of New Grass Revival is a first-rate, 18-track collection of the band's output from the late '80s, when the lineup included innovative banjo player Béla Fleck. Among the highlights are "Unconditional Love," "Can't Stop Now," "Callin' Baton Rouge," "You Plant Your Fields," and they even cover the Beatles' "I'm Down." This is a nearly perfect way to get acquainted with these progressive bluegrass innovators. *—Al Campbell*

Today's Bluegrass / Aug. 15, 1994 / Hollywood ♦♦♦

The New Lost City Ramblers

f. 1958, **db.** 1975

Group / Neo-Traditional Folk, Old-Timey, Traditional Folk, String Bands, Folk Revival

During the folk boom of the late '50s and early '60s, the NLCR introduced the authentic string band sound of the 1920s and '30s, in the process educating a generation that had never heard this uniquely American sound of old-time music. While maintaining music with a social conscience, they added guts and reality to the folk movement, performing with humor and obvious reverence for the music. Mike Seeger, John Cohen, and Tom Paley in 1958 modeled their band after groups like the Skillet Lickers, the Fruit Jar Drinkers, and the Aristocratic Pigs, choosing a name in keeping with the past. When Tracy Schwarz replaced Paley in 1962, The Ramblers added solo songs from the Appalachian folk repertoire, religious and secular, educating a large segment of the American population about traditional music.

Folkways recorded the NLCR on five albums in the early 60s, making the Ramblers famous and leading to TV appearances, successful tours, and appearances at the Newport Folk Festival. A songbook with 125 of their songs came out in 1964 and sold well. The NLCR served at least three important purposes: They brought real folk music to a huge audience, they entertained us well with their highly entertaining acts, and they led us to rediscover the original music on which they had based their band. Tracy Schwarz went on the road with his wife and then his son, gradually leaning toward Cajun squeezebox music; Mike Seeger toured with his wife, Alice, and did many solo spots; and John Cohen continued playing in another string band, while making award-winning documentaries about the old music. *—David Vinopal*

The New Lost City Ramblers, Vol. 1 / 1958 / Smithsonian Folkways ♦♦♦

The performances of this group certainly improved with age, with the eventual replacement of one of the members not upsetting the status quo. That is not to say there is anything at all wrong with this album, the very first of the group's efforts and one of the miraculous times Folkways released a project the same year it was recorded. Perhaps this demonstrated great enthusiasm for the concept. For a young group to record new versions of traditional folk and old-timey music classics from the early 20th century turned out to be something along the line of marching orders for the entire folk revival of the '60s, as well as the basic operating principle for groups such as the Rolling Stones and the Beatles when they started digging into Delta blues and rockabilly. An important aspect of the Ramblers' music, and something that has continued to make their records highly enjoyable over the years, was the type of material they would find. Demonstrating the widest range of material was always a priority, nobody caring whether a tune was "hip" or not. The presence of a number such as "It's a Shame to Whip Your Wife on Sunday" shows that the politically correct police were also not supervising this project. Many of the songs are also tied in with social concerns, a theme that each of these players would return to again and again in their own work. While someone involved felt it was important to put someone else's picture on the front—and anyone who looked like a hillbilly old-timer would do—the members of the group even at this early juncture were seeking to put a personal imprint on the material. One of the highlights is the very first track on the album, a simple but riveting instrumental entitled "Forked Deer." Another is Seeger's solo version of "East Virginia Blues" which gives Bob Dylan a run, although perhaps not for his money. Some of the multi-tracking done by Seeger is also quite interesting. The enclosed booklet includes lyrics, complete documentation of the chosen selections with information about the original artists, and several statements of purpose from the group members. *—Eugene Chadbourne*

The New Lost City Ramblers, Vol. 2 / 1959 / Smithsonian Folkways ♦♦♦

It was the end of the '50s and the New Lost City Ramblers were warmed up and ready for the intense revival of folk music that was begining to break out around the world. It is true that the three members of this old-time revival band might not have exactly looked the part for what was about to happen in the '60s. At least somebody at Folkways thought so, since the original black-and-white photograph of bandmembers Mike Seeger, Tom Paley, and John Cohen wearing neat suits and ties was eventually replaced by a color shot with a much hipper, contemporary feel. Certainly nobody would have thought the music the group played was contemporary, although it has proven to be eternally hip. The material on this collection largely comes through the early 20th century, and all the original artists such as Gid Tanner and Charlie Poole are identified as well as strongly recommended for further listening, both by this reviewer and the Ramblers themselves, who never failed to give credit where credit was due. Highlights here include some tasty slide guitar, Seeger's solo vocal and fiddle take on "Texas Rangers," a fine autoharp and banjo duet on "When First Unto This Country," and both the whimsical "Hawkins Rag" and the driving "George Collins." The latter two tracks are fine examples of the trio really locking into instrumental sounds. The range of material is less wide and the playing much less assured than on later recordings, however, and some numbers such as "Tom Dooley" may have become overfamiliar to a point bordering nausea. *—Eugene Chadbourne*

Old-Timey Songs for Children / 1959 / Smithsonian Folkways ♦♦♦

The original lineup of this group, with Tom Paley delivering some his most heartfelt and also funnest vocals, came up with this ten-inch vinyl collection of so-called children's songs. The small album cover done in the typical Folkways card-stock and glue method will certainly appeal to collectors of nifty album packages, and fans of old-timey music won't have any problem sitting through these songs. The instrumental talents of these players have been well-established, and although this was early in the development of the band, there is some traditional playing that is technically pristine in a cozy, comfortable manner. What might not be automatic is any appeal of this music for children, except of course toddlers, who are so young that they practically like any record their mom and dad puts on, including the solo saxophone of Anthony Braxton. Of course these were children's songs when they were first handed down, and there was a time when a set of parents could comfortably predict that a wee lass or lassie would love to rock out to the sounds of "Cotton Eyed Joe" or giggle at the irony of "Soldier, Soldier, Will You Marry Me?" Forty years after this set was released, however, the mass media had succeeded in making pop music attractive to younger and younger age groups, not completely wiping out the need for so-called children's music, but making it a much tougher sell. When rap music is part of the daily diet of young children, their taste for the lyrics of, say, "Old Bell Cow" might be severely compromised. Now, old-timey music does contain lyrics and tell stories that makes rap music pale by comparison, but these aren't the types of tunes the New Lost City Ramblers picked out for their kiddie set in the late '50s. The song "Knoxville Girl," for example, contains worse sex and violence than an hour's worth of programming on a rap station, so try that if one is trying to sell kids on old-timey and meeting with resistance. Or just skip directly to the last track here, "Johnny Get Your Gun," which at least has some shooting and an explosion in it. *—Eugene Chadbourne*

The New Lost City Ramblers, Vol. 3 / 1961 / Smithsonian Folkways ♦♦♦

Although the collected recording legacy of this group more than establishes its ability to rise above the status of mere revivalists or archivists, some collections of New Lost City Ramblers material come off worse than others. Most fans of the group would agree that substituting Tracy Schwarz for Tom Paley brought in a harder instrumental edge and lightened the folky vibe considerably. Paley is still present on this early-'60s effort, however, but he shouldn't take the blame completely for any apparent dullness in the material and the delivery. The group was obviously in some sort of combat with its own aims and how it was being perceived, a fact made clear by the incredible contradiction between the opening of bandmember John Cohen's liner notes, in which he says "we are getting to sound more like the New Lost City Ramblers than anything else," and the photograph chosen for the front cover, a picture not of the Ramblers but of a group of four hillbilly musicians carrying on. If the idea is to establish one's own identity, why put a picture of a different group on an album? Design and imagery might have been the province of the record label, but in either case it indicates a desire to fool consumers into thinking this is the genuine article, and not a trio of college-educated middle-class men. As usual for the Ramblers, all the tunes chosen are credited with the original performers and recording information, so that anyone with a real prejudice against the revival scene can sniff out the original goods. There are fine moments here, such as "Fly Around My Pretty Little Miss" and "Baltimore Fire," but the tracks tend to lack the spirit of the group's later performances, while some of the efforts are just not convincing, such as Paley's dobro playing on "Weaveroom Blues." Other numbers such as "Rollin' in My Sweet Baby's Arms" have become such warhorses since this album was originally released that the Ramblers' versions just seem inconsequential. *—Eugene Chadbourne*

The New Lost City Ramblers, Vol. 4 / 1961 / Smithsonian Folkways ♦♦♦

American Moonshine & Prohibition / 1962 / Smithsonian Folkways ♦♦♦♦

The New Lost City Ramblers, Vol. 5 / 1963 / Smithsonian Folkways ♦♦♦

String Band Instrumentals / 1964 / Smithsonian Folkways ♦♦♦

Songs of the New Lost City Ramblers / 1965 / Smithsonian Folkways ♦♦♦

Rural Delivery No. 1 / 1965 / Smithsonian Folkways ♦♦♦

Remembrance of Things to Come / 1966 / Folkways ♦♦♦

This was the one album by the New Lost City Ramblers to be bartered into an arrangement between Verve and Folkways in the mid-'60s, when one of the U.S.' reoccurring folk music revivals was in full swing. This meant that, at least for a time, entertainment conglomerate MGM was actually pressing the records of this group. How members such as Mike Seeger felt about having their platters touched by the same machinery that was pressing records by Herman's Hermits may not be known, but the big label made absolutely no changes to the production, that's for sure. Other than using a different cover photo, the two albums are completely identical, even to the point of having catalog numbers that are within a few digits of each other. The collection of pieces is mixed in quality due to the incredible range these three musicians go for. It is difficult enough to create the magic of an old-time performance in a ragtime or Appalachian mode without turning around and trying to sound authentic on a Cajun number. Some of the vocalizing the group does together comes across as flat and even bored-sounding, as if they felt a step removed from what was going on or didn't want to lose their composure through excessive involvement. On the other hand, the players have their instrumental chops down cold and have wonderful ways of combining different instruments within the band. The opening "Soldier's Joy" makes great use of harmonica, played adeptly by Seeger, while manic instrumental numbers such as "Black Bottom Strut" or "New Lost Hometown Blues" are done with great flair, Tracy Schwarz breaking out the spoons for the former and providing a historically early example of thrash guitar on the latter. There are also tracks with great dual fiddling and superior banjo playing in several styles, both solo and in duo. Songs that are highlights from the pure fun perspective include "Cat's Got the Measles and the Dog's Got the Whooping Cough" and "Rock About My Saro Jane." *—Eugene Chadbourne*

The New Lost City Ramblers With Cousin Emmy / 1968 / Folkways ♦♦♦

Putting this distinctive old-time music together with the New Lost City Ramblers was a great idea. It could even satisfy picky folk music fans that might find the vocal talents of the Ramblers a bit lacking in authenticity. (Those that want to further discuss whether one has to be a coal miner to sing this type of material properly can meet at 8 p.m. at the coffee house.) Listeners who object entirely to this revival group of the '60s and '70s can also approach this album as a safe object, as Tracy Schwarz, Mike Seeger, and John Cohen tend to fade so far into the background that the results sound more like a solo album at times. Of course it is good that nobody got in the way of Cousin Emmy, who comes on strong with her musical talent. She has a vocal style that is like Loretta Lynn and Ethel Merman rolled into one, the exact opposite of the archivist nature of a Mike Seeger vocal. On banjo it is more a matter of respect that may have led the fellows to leave their instruments in the cases. Cousin Emmy is a terrific banjo player, but so are all three of them. The decision for Seeger to play only mandolin, with Cohen on guitar and Schwarz and guest George Winston handling the bass duties, may have keep distractions to a minimum, but in the process removed one of the better features of the New Lost City Ramblers, the colorful textures of changing instruments. In terms of highlights, there is one hands-down masterpiece: "Graveyard" is simply one of the most beautiful Appalachian ballads ever recorded. *—Eugene Chadbourne*

On the Great Divide / 1973 / Smithsonian Folkways ♦♦♦♦

Well into their career as a trio, the faithful three of Mike Seeger, Tracy Schwarz, and John Cohen came up with one of the best New Lost City Ramblers albums. The choice of material is particularly fun, that adjective being chosen to stress an important, and sometimes neglected, element of this genre. From the opening combination of dulcimer, fiddle, and banjo, the sound of the group is rich, the high overtones of the stringed instruments shimmering like sun over the water. Unfortunately, this track is treated to a fadeout, while an actual ending would have only increased the beauty of "John Brown's Dream." The banjo picking by Schwarz is sensational on "Love of Polly and Jack Monroe," a song originally done by George Davis. Oh yes, of course all the proper references are here, so folk music fanatics of all ages can continue conducting the proper research. This group always includes a few solos on each album and here these are particularly memorable, possibly a reflection of the various members' growing strengths as players. Cohen takes on "Walking Boss," the bassline from his banjo sounding positively intimidating. On "A Night at the Country Opera," Schwarz does a slightly strained but well-intentioned tribute to the vaudeville spoofing of good old Fiddler Joe. Seeger takes on a Roscoe Holcomb tune as a one-man duo, playing fiddle and harmonica simultaneously. Performances such as this tend to be highlights of his solo sets; they also fit nicely into a band program such as this. —*Eugene Chadbourne*

20 Years of Concert Performances / 1978 / Flying Fish ✦✦✦
Culled from a wide variety of sources, including radio broadcasts, *20 Years of Concert Performances* by the New Lost City Ramblers is a treasure trove of music. Using Library of Congress archives of folk music and other sources too numerous to mention here, the New Lost City Ramblers have, in this release, allowed listeners to discover for the first time, or else reintroduced them to, songs long forgotten and nearly lost for all time. Traditional tunes such as "Turkey in the Straw," "Sally Goodin," and "On Some Foggy Mountain Top" are put alongside such nearly forgotten gems as "Country Blues," originally by Dock Boggs, Tom Ashley's "Dark Holler Blues," and the Carter Family's "Worried Man Blues," all to great effect. All of the 34 cuts here are a must for musicologists everywhere, and for the casual listener these same tracks provide a history lesson as to where so many of our contemporary artists have either learned their trades or discovered classics to rearrange. A truly inspirational disc. —*James Chrispell*

Songs from the Depression / 1981 / Smithsonian Folkways ✦✦✦✦
The third album by this group definitely gets an "A" for effort, as simply gathering up so many worthwhile songs about the American depression was worth doing, no matter how listeners might feel about individual tracks. The choice of material doubles up on numbers by Blind Alfred Reed and Bill Dixon, includes fascinating historical material by Fiddling John Carson and Slim Smith, and wisely includes the genre of instrumental music, which sometimes makes the most succinct comment of all, such as the tough fiddle solo "Boys, My Money's All Gone." Many of the medium-tempo numbers are played with the finesse of a fine classical chamber quartet, the fiddle and banjo playing sharp and radiant. The Tom Paley-era Ramblers have a bit more of a college campus-type folky sound, but in some cases this suits these types of songs, making this one of the better early albums by this band. Mike Seeger is busy on an assortment of instruments, livening up one track with harmonica, another with mandolin. As usual, his fiddle and banjo playing is top-notch. There is also nice use made of Hawaiian and steel guitars. While some albums by this group seem like the ensemble is taking on a bit too much territory, here the clear focus of the subject matter creates a more relaxed atmosphere, despite the despair of the lyrics. But OK, it is not a record to put on when one wants to serenade away a bad mood. The original booklet includes lyrics and much interesting information about the original artists and the depression era in general. —*Eugene Chadbourne*

20th Anniversary Concert: Live at Carnegie Hall / 1987 / Flying Fish ✦✦✦
This is a nicely spirited celebration of a band that was longer-lived than many of its old-time role models. —*Mark A. Humphrey*

● **The Early Years (1958–1962)** / 1991 / Smithsonian Folkways ✦✦✦✦✦
Moses Asch had a unique method of recording artists back in the '40s and '50s. Someone like Woody Guthrie, for instance, would just drop by Folkways when he had an idea and record. Asch might pay him five dollars for the session, and in this way he accumulated a vault full of material. Perhaps this explains the incredible fact that the New Lost City Ramblers recorded 12 albums between 1958-1962. *The Early Years (1958-1962)* collects 26 songs, over 70 minutes of music, from these dozen discs, creating an excellent document of the band's years with Tom Paley. Paley, John Cohen, and Mike Seeger formed the New Lost City Ramblers in 1958 with the idea of playing old-time music recorded between the late '20s and 1940. While it has often been stated that the trio intended to copy—phrase for phrase, lick for lick—the old 78s, Jon Pankake points out in the liner notes that this wasn't the case. Instead, the New Lost City Ramblers wanted to insert the same vim and vigor into "The Battleship of Maine" and "Fly Around My Pretty Little Miss" as the original players. What stands out now, some 40 years after these recordings, is the band's versatility. Whether cutting loose on an instrumental like "Colored Aristocracy" or singing tight harmony on "Brown's Ferry Blues," the three comrades form a tight unit. While the arrangements never outgrow the number of persons in the band, each player's ability to play multiple instruments lends diversity to the material. *The Early Years (1958-1962)* offers a very good introduction to an innovative and influential band. —*Ronnie D. Lankford Jr.*

New Lost City Ramblers Vol. 2, 1963–1973, Outstanding in Their Field / 1993 / Smithsonian Folkways ✦✦✦✦
This 72-minute companion piece to *The Early Years (1958-1962)* is drawn from the seven Folkways albums that the New Lost City Ramblers recorded between 1963 and 1973, following the entry of Tracy Schwarz and the departure of Tom Paley, and it's every bit as essential as the first volume. Continuing their emphasis on careful replication of many difficult regional and popular folk forms, one is continually amazed by the versatility of Schwarz, John Cohen, and Mike Seeger, as they bounce from lively fiddle tunes, to instrumental waltzes, from more traditional bluegrass songs to Cajun influences. No doubt, this was a productive period for the NLCR, as many of the 27 tracks should be required listening for fans of traditional string band music. Excellent liner notes and commentary by Jon Pankake also make this a quality collection. —*Matt Fink*

☆ **There Ain't No Way Out** / May 20, 1997 / Smithsonian Folkways ✦✦✦✦✦
More than 20 years after the New Lost City Ramblers' last studio recordings, Mike Seeger, John Cohen, and Tracy Schwarz got back together for *There Ain't No Way Out*, a 26-track celebration of old-timey music, including bluegrass, yodel blues, spirituals, Cajun, and what is usually referred to generically as "folk" music. They haven't lost much of their edge, even if—by their own admission—there are younger, sharper players out there in the wake of the path they opened. Highlights include a sweetly sung "God's Gonna Ease My Troublin' Mind," A.P. Carter's "Anchored in Love Divine," the Dixon Brothers' "Weave Room Blues" (which has a Jimmie Rodgers sound to it), "Cumberland Gap," "Shady Grove," "Skip to My Lou," and "Crapshooters Hop." They still harmonize

beautifully, their instruments sing even sweeter, and the advantages of modern recording aren't lost on this sharp body of music. The notes, featuring contributions by all three players, are exceptionally detailed and informative about their history, as well as that of the songs. —*Bruce Eder*

40 Years of Concert Performances / Jun. 12, 2001 / Rounder ✦✦✦✦✦
Unlike many bands, the history of the New Lost City Ramblers is fairly easy to trace. John Cohen and Mike Seeger joined with Tom Paley between 1958 and 1962, reviving string band music from the '20s and '30s. In 1962, Tracy Schwarz' replaced a departing Paley, adding new material to the band's repertoire. *40 Years of Concert Recordings* proves as straightforward, offering nearly 50 live songs from "Soldier's Joy" in 1958, capturing the band's first performance, to the "Tennessee Blues" recorded in 1999. These live performances, quality wise, vary little from the group's studio work. The difference, however, lies in the Ramblers' sense of humor and interaction with audiences. Whether offering an earnest introduction or just having a little fun, the group leaves the impression of a bunch of nice guys having a good-time doing what they love. Their repertoire is broad and diverse: the anti-war "The Battleship of Maine" makes way for the hoary "Poor Ellen Smith" which moves aside for the joyful "Too Tight Rag." A version of "Sourwood Mountain" finds the Ramblers jamming with the Stanley Brothers, while Seeger offers a superb take on "Little Maggie." With such variety, the band takes on the persona of a walking folk song encyclopedia. The Ramblers also proved amenable to changing times. A particularly odd and enjoyable "Wildwood Weed" turns tradition on its head, crossing the Carter Family with the counter-culture to sing the praises of the weed cannabis. Though many of these recordings have been available before, 16 are new to this collection. This two-CD set provides a detailed portrait of one of the premiere revival bands, searching for new directions over the years, while remaining firmly planted in yesteryear. *40 Years of Concert Recordings* will please longtime fans and work as a grand introduction to those unfamiliar. —*Ronnie D. Lankford Jr.*

The New Riders of the Purple Sage

f. 1969, San Francisco, CA, **db.** 1982
Group / Country-Rock

For most of the early '70s, the New Riders of the Purple Sage™ (yes, the name is trademark-protected) were the successful offshoots of the Grateful Dead. Although they never remotely approached the success or longevity of the Dead, they attracted a considerable audience through their association with Jerry Garcia, Phil Lesh, and Mickey Hart, whose fans couldn't be satisfied with only the Dead's releases—the New Riders never reached much beyond that audience, but the Deadheads loved them as substitutes (along with Garcia's periodic solo projects) for the real article. Their initial sound was a kind of country-acid rock, somewhat twangier than the Dead's usual work and without the Dead's successful forays into experimental jams, but they later acquitted themselves as straight country-rockers.

Essentially, the New Riders of the Purple Sage (their name derives from an old country outfit, Foy Willing and the Riders of the Purple Sage, who in turn took the name from an old Western novel) were initially formed as a vehicle for Garcia, Lesh, and Hart to indulge their tastes for country music beyond the albums *Workingman's Dead* and *American Beauty*. Their original lineup at early performances consisted of Garcia on pedal steel, Lesh on bass, John Dawson (born 1945) on rhythm guitars and vocals, sometime Dead contributor-member David Nelson on lead guitars, mandolin, and vocals, and Mickey Hart on drums. The New Riders quickly evolved into more of a free-standing unit, with Dave Torbert succeeding Lesh, and ex-Jefferson Airplane member Spencer Dryden on the drums, succeeding Hart. They also developed an identity of their own through Dawson's songwriting, which had an appealing command of melody and beat.

The group was a little shaky as a country-rock outfit, without the strengths of soulfulness or strong in-house songwriting of, say, Poco or the Burrito Brothers, but their association with Garcia and the Dead (Lesh co-produced one album) gave them a significant leg up in terms of publicity and finding an audience. High-school and college kids who'd scarcely heard of Gram Parsons or Jim Messina but owned more than one Dead album, were likely in those days to own, or have a friend who owned, at least one New Riders album. That translated into many thousands of sales of the self-titled first album, which proved an apt and pleasing companion to *Workingman's Dead* and *American Beauty* with its mix of country and psychedelic sounds. By the second album, Buddy Cage had come in on pedal steel, replacing Garcia, and their sound had firmed up, helped by the fact that Dawson and Torbert were good songwriters.

Powerglide, their second album, proved that they had what it took to stand separate from the Dead, even though Garcia and Bill Kreutzmann played on a handful of cuts. The group continued to attract a following through the early and mid-'70s, mixing country-rock and folk sounds (Buffy Sainte-Marie was a guest vocalist on the 1974 hit album *The Adventures of Panama Red*) and attracting the mellower component of recreational drug users. By the end of the decade, following a label change from Columbia to MCA, it seemed as though they were running out of steam and originality, however, and the growth in popularity of punk, disco, and power pop made them seem like an anachronism, along with most other country-rock outfits of the era. Ex-Byrd Skip Battin joined in 1975, replacing Torbert; Dryden gave up playing in 1978 to assume management of the band, and by 1981, Nelson was gone.

The New Riders essentially disbanded in 1982, although the name was later picked up by a new lineup built around Gary Vogenson (guitar) and Rusty Gautier (bass). Nelson subsequently played with the Jerry Garcia Acoustic Band and assumed the de facto role of group archivist, supervising the release of unissued tapes by the band through the Relix label. —*Bruce Eder*

● **New Riders of the Purple Sage** / 1971 / Columbia ✦✦✦✦✦
Anyone who enjoyed the Grateful Dead's *Workingman's Dead* or *American Beauty* and wanted more, then or now, should get the New Riders of the Purple Sage's eponymous release and follow it with the Riders' next two albums. With Jerry Garcia and Mickey Hart

in tow, and Jefferson Airplane's Spencer Dryden playing what drums Hart didn't, plus Commander Cody at the piano, *New Riders of the Purple Sage* is some of the most spaced-out country-rock of the period. Even ignoring the big names working with John Dawson, David Nelson, and Dave Torbert, however, this is a good record, crossing swords with the Byrds, the Burrito Brothers, and even Crosby, Stills, Nash & Young and holding its own. Maybe a few of the cuts (especially "Henry") are predictable at times, but mostly, *New Riders of the Purple Sage* was full of surprises then (the amazingly sweet, brittle guitars, in particular) and has tunes that have held up well: "Portland Woman," "Whatcha Gonna Do," "I Don't Know You," and "Louisiana Lady," not to mention the eight leisurely paced minutes of acid-country found in "Dirty Business." There are no added notes, but they'd hardly be vital—the album is an open book. *—Bruce Eder*

Powerglide / 1972 / Columbia ✦✦✦✦

The group's second album is pretty much definitive, especially in its remastered version from Columbia's Legacy division (issued in 1996), which has really crisp, loud sound. Joe Maphis' "Dim Lights, Thick Smoke (And Loud, Loud Music)" is a great opener, a honky tonk-style number featuring David Nelson's lead vocals and Nicky Hopkins' piano sharing the spotlight with Nelson's and John Dawson's axes. The guitars on Dawson's "Rainbow" are nearly pretty enough to be a Flying Burrito Brothers or Poco number. Most of what follows is as good or better, especially Dave Torbert's "California Day" and "Contract," and Dawson's "Sweet Lovin' One." The one letdown is their cover of "Hello Mary Lou," a flat, dullish rendition that could be any bad country-rock bar band, and which isn't going to make anyone forget the numerous versions before and since—they do somewhat better with Johnny Otis' "Willie and the Hand Jive." *Powerglide* is a fun record and offers one virtue that the Dead, in particular, sometimes forgot—they know how to end a song. Jerry Garcia is present on banjo ("Sweet Lovin' One," "Duncan and Brady") and piano ("Lochinvar")—Bill Kreutzmann and Nicky Hopkins also turn up—but the best lead guitar work here comes courtesy of David Nelson and Buddy Cage, who plays the pedal steel. *—Bruce Eder*

The Adventures of Panama Red / 1973 / Columbia ✦✦✦

One has to wonder if 1973 was the year of drug references in songs... never mind. In any case, *The Adventures of Panama Red* established the New Riders of the Purple Sage as something more than a Jerry Garcia side project—which they never were. John Dawson, Spencer Dryden, David Nelson, and Dave Torbert along with pedal steel ace Buddy Cage—replacing Garcia—and producer and multi-instrumentalist Norbert Putnam crafted a smoking, hard country-rock and bluegrass hippie record. Also along for the ride were guest vocalists Donna Jean Godchaux from the Grateful Dead and no less than Buffy Sainte-Marie and the Memphis Horns. Trad country it ain't, and dated it is; but nonetheless, *Panama Red* has considerable charm as a relic from the era. Nelson, Torbert, and Dawson were decent songwriters and enthusiastic performers, and Columbia knew a good thing when they saw one and got behind the album—which was a minor hit. The title track and "Lonesome L.A. Cowboy," with Cage's whinnying steel, carry a lot of the band's weight and separate them from virtually every other West Coast outfit trying the same thing. The Flying Burrito Brothers were more country and Commander Cody's Lost Planet Airmen swung harder, but one thing the New Riders were more of than anyone was stoned, and these songs with titles like "Important Exportin' Man" and "Kick in the Head" and lyrics like "I've been smokin' dope, snortin' coke/tryin' to write a song/ forgettin' everything I know until the next line comes along" only underline this. The freakiest thing is that the record segues together so beautifully and the songs are so tight with nothing extra between, it feels like it's a lot longer than the mere 29 minutes it is. The listener feels satisfied that after 12 songs it's all been said done in a delightful way. This endures despite its obvious lyrical stupidity. Musically it can do a lot to teach modern-day alt-country cookie cutters something about knowing the rules before trying to break them. *—Thom Jurek*

Brujo / 1974 / Columbia ✦✦✦

Home, Home on the Road / 1974 / Columbia ✦✦

Oh, What a Mighty Time / 1975 / Columbia ✦✦

By the time of this, their sixth album, The New Riders of the Purple Sage had deteriorated to the point of recording novelty songs like "I Heard You've Been Layin' My Old Lady" and aging standards like "La Bamba." They managed to talk old friend Jerry Garcia into sitting in on a few songs, but that was no indication that they were back at the level of their first album. Rather, *Oh, What a Mighty Time* sounded like the work of a competent Marin County bar band, which is pretty much what The New Riders were by this time. The album, their worst seller so far, was their last for Columbia Records. *—William Ruhlmann*

Before Time Began / 1976 / Relix ✦✦

Before Time Began is an album of archival material assembled for Relix Records by New Rider Dave Nelson. It contains: two songs recorded by New Rider John Dawson on July 31, 1968; The New Riders' (Nelson, Dawson, Jerry Garcia, Phil Lesh, and Mickey Hart) four-song demo tape of November 1969; and an entire LP side of experimental tapes made by Nelson, recording tracks backwards. The first side will be of interest to New Riders fans who are interested in hearing the elements that went into making the group's 1971 debut album. The second side may interest members of Nelson's family. *—William Ruhlmann*

New Riders / 1976 / One Way ✦✦

The Best of the New Riders of the Purple Sage / 1976 / Columbia ✦✦✦✦

This ten-song collection, clocking in at an anemic 30 minutes, is probably as much New Riders as the casual listener might need, and all they're likely to hear. Some of the highlights of their five years at Columbia are here, but some great tracks are also missing. On the plus side, the live version of "Hello Mary Lou" is somewhat more interesting than the studio rendition, but they still don't do this song justice. And "Glendale Train," "Louisiana Lady," "Panama Red," and "You Angel You" are great fun, if a little obvious. *—Bruce Eder*

Who Are Those Guys? / 1977 / One Way ✦

Marin County Line / 1978 / One Way ✦✦

Vintage NRPS / 1988 / Relix ✦✦

Vintage collects unreleased material from the New Riders' prime, when the band's lineup included guitarists David Nelson and John Dawson and featured the Grateful Dead's Jerry Garcia on steel guitar. While the opening cuts represent some fairly strong country music, as the album progresses the playing begins to grow increasingly lifeless and mediocre; for the most part, the music on *Vintage* went unreleased for a reason. *—Jason Ankeny*

Live (1982) / 1995 / Avenue/Rhino ✦✦✦✦

When this archival concert tape from September 21 and November 20, 1982, was recorded, David Nelson and Buddy Cage were no longer in the lineup, having been succeeded by Rusty Gauthier and Val Fuentes (ex-It's a Beautiful Day drummer). The band is featured doing a mix of classic material ("Henry," "Panama Red") and newer stuff ("Crazy Little Girl"), as well as standards by other artists ("You Can't Judge a Book," "Dead Flowers"). John Dawson and Allen Kemp handle two of the guitars and the vocals, joined by Gauthier (who also plays lap steel), with Billy Wolf on lead guitar. The playing is louder and more forceful than anything on their classic records, but the songs retain their charm and have a lot more energy here. The sound quality is excellent, in vivid stereo and exceptionally crisp clarity, although some of the melodic beauty of the songs is lost amid the electric instrument textures that dominate. *—Bruce Eder*

Take a Red / Jan. 1, 1995 / MCA ✦✦

Between 1976 and 1978, The New Riders of the Purple Sage made three albums for MCA Records, *New Riders, Who Are These Guys?,* and *Marin County Line. Take a Red* is an eight-track compilation album culled from those releases and issued by the discount-priced MCA Special Products division. The late '70s edition of the band was a tighter, more country-oriented unit than the bunch of hippies who made the Columbia Records albums in the early '70s, but also much less fun. The early New Riders were funny and fey, even if you sometimes wondered whether they'd make it to the chorus. There's no such suspense here, but also nothing to distinguish the new New Riders from other country bands. *—William Ruhlmann*

Wasted Tasters / Aug. 21, 1998 / Raven ✦✦✦✦✦

This Australian single-disc compilation corrals two-dozen tracks from the New Riders of the Purple Sage (NRPS) during their prolific four-year run with Columbia Records (1971-1975). *Wasted Tasters* (1998) draws upon the long-players *New Riders of the Purple Sage* (1971), *Powerglide* (1972), *Gypsy Cowboy* (1972), *The Adventures of Panama Red* (1973), the live *Home, Home on the Road* (1974), *Brujo* (1974), and *Oh, What a Mighty Time* (1975). Initially, NRPS were primarily considered a country-flavored Grateful Dead spin-off band. Jerry Garcia (guitar/pedal steel guitar/vocals), Phil Lesh (bass), Mickey Hart (percussion), Bill Kreutzmann (drums), and, occasionally on-stage, Bob Weir (guitar/vocals) floated in and out of incipient versions of the band, which was more permanently manned by John Dawson (guitar/vocals), former Jefferson Airplane member Spencer Dryden (drums), Dave Nelson (guitar/mandolin/vocals), Dave Torbert (bass/guitar/ vocals), and at times Commander Cody (piano). While the personnel seemingly changed from album to album, the New Riders' strong blend of boot-kickin' country & western-tinged originals remained one of the band's most consistently cohesive forces—as evidenced throughout *Wasted Tasters.* Their earliest efforts—such as the smugglin' saga "Henry" or the high and lonesome bluegrass vibe of "Glendale Train"—set a lofty compositional standard from within the band's ranks. This is especially true of Dawson—who penned a majority of the material on the first few NRPS albums—and later Torbert, whose seminal contributions are highlighted by "Contract" and "She's No Angel." Their choice and execution of cover tunes featured on this collection include a rousing reading of "I Don't Need No Doctor" and an affective "Dim Lights, Thick Smoke (And Loud, Loud Music)." They were also able to sustain that momentum on future reworkings of the Stones' "Dead Flowers" and Gene Pitney's "Hello Mary Lou." Sadly, the later incarnations of the New Riders were not able to maintain a stable lineup. As such their efforts suffered from seeming indecision as well as lackluster performances. However, *Wasted Tasters* is a definitive single-disc compilation of early highlights. *—Lindsay Planer*

Gypsy Cowboy/The Adventure of Panama Red / Mar. 9, 2002 / BGO ✦✦✦✦✦

In 2002, BGO released *Gypsy Cowboy/The Adventures of Panama Red*, which contained two albums—*Gypsy Cowboy* (1972, originally released on Columbia) and *The Adventures of Panama Red* (1973, also originally on Columbia)—by the New Riders of the Purple Sage on one compact disc. *—Tim Sendra*

Mickey Newbury

b. May 19, 1940, Houston, TX, **d.** Sep. 28, 2002, Vida, OR

Guitar, Songwriter, Vocals / Progressive Country, Singer/Songwriter, Outlaw Country

Along with fellow songwriters such as Kris Kristofferson, Willie Nelson, and Tom T. Hall, Mickey Newbury helped revolutionize country music in the 1960s and '70s by bringing new, broader musical influences as well as a frank, emotional depth to the music—while at the same time never losing respect for tradition. Newbury infused his country music with haunting beauty and spiritual melancholy, creating an impressive collection of introspective, emotionally complex songs that are more spiritual cousins of the work of Leonard Cohen than that of Roy Acuff. (Newbury, in fact, calls himself a folksinger, and has never toured with a band, prefering the ambience of a quiet coffeehouse.) The fact that many of his songs became hits for singers from Don Gibson to Elvis Presley was proof that the industry and the public were hungry for a change. Like many of his generation, however—such as his friend Townes Van Zandt—Newbury was better known as a songwriter than as a singer. Newbury recorded 15 albums over a nearly 30-year period—right up to 1996's *Lulled by the Moonlight*, a limited-edition release sold by mail order—but his soft, beautiful tenor voice rarely reached the charts.

Newbury spent his teens in Houston absorbing a wide range of music, learning to play guitar, and writing poetry, which he began reading in local coffeehouses. Folk music was on the rise at the time, and he soon turned to writing songs. He sang in a vocal group called the Embers during this time (they were briefly on Mercury), and played and hung out in Houston's black R&B and blues clubs, where he was nicknamed "The Little White Wolf" by Clarence "Gatemouth" Brown. Newbury joined the Air Force and was stationed in England. After his discharge, he turned back to music. In 1963, a friend of his landed him a writing job with Acuff-Rose, and Newbury moved to Nashville. During the next several years, he became friends with such singers as Roy Orbison, Roger Miller, Kris Kristofferson, and Townes Van Zandt. He was also instrumental in getting both Kristofferson and Van Zandt, among others, noticed in Nashville.

In 1966 Don Gibson had a Top Ten hit with Newbury's "Funny Familiar Forgotten Feelings," and Newbury's writing career was off and running. A long string of hit songs followed, recorded by such artists as Kenny Rogers and the First Edition ("Just Dropped In"), Eddy Arnold ("Here Comes the Rain, Baby"), and Andy Williams ("Sweet Memories"). Newbury's first album of his own was *Harlequin Melodies* for RCA in 1968, recorded in RCA's big Nashville studio (it's an album he later detested). He quickly got out of his RCA contract and instead turned to a small four-track studio run by engineer Wayne Moss in a converted garage (becoming, before the word "outlaw" ever became fashionable, one of the first Nashville artists to work outside the studio system). It was here that he recorded some of his best solo albums, starting with *It Looks Like Rain* for Mercury; this contained initial versions of two of his most enduring songs, "San Francisco Mabel Joy" (which he's recorded several times more) and "33rd of August."

But Mercury didn't support the album, and so Newbury switched to Elektra in 1970. With this label, he released a string of superb albums, including *Frisco Mabel Joy*, *Heaven Help the Child*, and the acoustic *Live at Montezuma Hall*; the latter was paired with a rerelease of *Looks Like Rain*. These contained such songs as "Cortelia Clark" (about a blind street singer), the almost painfully lonely "Frisco Depot," and "Heaven Help the Child," a sweeping mini-epic of a song that makes references to Fitzgerald and Paris in the 1920s. In 1972 Newbury had a Top 30 hit with "American Trilogy," a suite-like arrangement of "Dixie," "Battle Hymn of the Republic," and "All My Trials." The song later became a major hit for Elvis Presley and a standard in his repertoire.

Newbury recorded three albums for ABC/Hickory in the late '70s, and was inducted into the Nashville Songwriter's Hall of Fame in 1980, but he was more and more becoming something of a recluse. He had given up concert touring some years before, and also had moved to Oregon. In the 1980s, he only released two albums. In 1994 he resurfaced with *Nights When I Am Sane*, an acoustic album recorded live with guitarist Jack Williams. Since he was out of the spotlight for more than a decade, though, he wasn't well-known in contemporary country circles. People familiar with his work, however, recognized Newbury as one of country music's most inspired and moving artists. After fighting respiratory illness for several years, Newbury passed away in the fall of 2002 at age 62. *—Kurt Wolff*

Harlequin Melodies / 1968 / RCA Victor ✦✦✦

To paraphrase Marc Antony, the listener may not be able to decide whether to praise Mickey Newbury or bury him. This record hits one with the full Newbury experience, because, debut album or not, he comes across as a fully developed artist. His originality and talent is wonderfully evident in a series of songs that, whether brilliant or dreadful, always reveal an incredible amount of care being taken. Newbury never settled into any kind of standard arrangements or simple combo sound in his career, preferring to perform solo on acoustic guitar. But he and his producers went wild in the recording studio, baking in multiple layers that are likely to include any and all possible instruments, combined in a manner both audacitious and typical of the anything-goes '60s. Newbury came out of the country & western scene, and no matter how far away he went the heritage was always evident in his vocal phrasing as well as his subject matter, frequently tragic, as is the C&W norm. There was also a Roy Orbison side to Newbury. His control of falsetto and penchant for heavy sentimentality and great dramatic moments will only appeal to listeners who enjoy Orbison. But he is gifted at many other types of material, and in the memorable "Just Dropped In" he created an absolute classic, undoubtedly the most perfect fusion of country and western and freaky psychedelic music ever recorded. The original Newbury version is really weird, even compared to the more well-known cover version by Kenny Rogers & the First Edition. Rogers' band had a hit with this song when the band was still considered a rock outfit, years before the leader emerged in his true colors as a country artist, all of which is very appropriate to the Newbury story. The sadness of the songs is deep, at times hard to take. "Here Comes the Rain, Baby" is a gorgeous bit of tragedy. Some of the tunes are just too much, though, such as the obnoxious, pretentious "Weeping Annaleah." Sitars, orchestras, backup singers, gospel piano licks, and the kitchen sink all share equal space in the arrangements. Liner notes by Larry King. *—Eugene Chadbourne*

Sings His Own / 1968 / RCA ✦✦✦

After the issue of 1968's *Harlequin Melodies*, an album Mickey Newbury disowned as not being at all what he was looking to get across—despite some success with "Just Dropped In," which would later prove to be Kenny Rogers' first hit —Newbury went his way, writing for others and recording. In 1969 Newbury turned in *It Looks Like Rain* to Elektra, whose label boss hated it. He bought the album back and sold it to Mercury. *It Looks Like Rain* should be considered Newbury's first proper release. *Sings His Own*, like its RCA predecessor, *Harlequin Melodies*, is nothing more than a collection of songwriting demos overbaked by Elvis Presley producer Felton Jarvis. Some of the tracks duplicated those on harlequin and others were added, most notably those recorded by others artists. As a collection of Newbury's songs, it's interesting in an historical manner. As a way of hearing Newbury's unique and beautiful singing voice, it's worthwhile, but as a testament to Newbury's vision, it doesn't fit the bill at all. Unless you are a Newbury completist, this is one to leaving languishing in the bins. It doesn't mean the material isn't good—it's excellent—but it's only half Newbury's and half RCA's idea of what he *should have* sounded like. Like its predecessor, it was the second chapter in a book full of music biz misunderstandings. *—Thom Jurek*

It Looks Like Rain / 1969 / Mountain Retreat ✦✦✦✦✦

In sonic terms, *Looks Like Rain* sounds as far from the studio slickness of the "countrypolitan" machine rock & roll was from Lawrence Welk. In fact, Newbury's sound held more in common with that of Tim Buckley's or Simon & Garfunkel's. But even here, comparisons fail miserably. Aided by co-producers Bob Beckham and guitarist Jerry Kennedy, Newbury created an album haunting, so elegant, full of melancholy and mystery, it sounds out of time, out of space. It is a sound that seemingly comes from inside the mind of the listener than from the speakers on the stereo. When the sound of thunder and rain appears at the beginning of "She Even Woke Me Up to Say Goodbye," we are hardly surprised. Newbury's stories are movies; all the settings are in place before the story begins. He can move back and forth in time while changing images to suit the evolving narrative. "San Francisco Mable Joy," is a long tale of dispossession, dislocation, failure, and death, but so poetically beautiful, it can't help but be heard then echoed, deep in the heart of the listener. The thunderstorm is in full flood now, running through each track, from speaker to speaker in one long line, sheets of rain pouring down around the place the singer emotes from. Suddenly a gunshot cuts just loudly enough to jar us from the reverie. At six minutes and 43 seconds, there is plenty of room for the song's drama to create a tension so mournful it becomes nearly unbearable. And even though we know what's coming as the story winds down, the song's ending is totally devastating. *Looks Like Rain* is so fine, so mysterious in its pace, dimension, quark strangeness and charm, it defies any attempt at strict categorization or criticism; a rare work of genius. *—Thom Jurek*

'Frisco Mabel Joy / 1971 / Mountain Retreat ✦✦✦✦✦

Newbury jumped from Mercury to Elektra and in 1970 recorded the second of his amazing trilogy that concluded with *Heaven Help The Child*. Produced by Dennis Linde, a songwriter, and recorded at the same converted garage studio (Cinderella Sound) *Looks Like Rain* had been, *'Frisco Mabel Joy* adapts its title from a song on the previous album. Once again, texture, atmosphere ands above all mood and mystery were the central tenets of what would become Newbury's trademark sound. The album opens with Newbury's arrangement of what he called "The American Trilogy," a suite containing three songs that have their origin in the Civil War. If this sounds familiar, it is: Elvis Presley made a much more bombastic version of this the centerpiece of his Vegas shows. Newbury's version, full of soft strings, guitars, Charlie McCoy's haunting harmonica bleeding into a muted brass section, is full of drama and pathos. *Looks Like Rain* moves into an entire series of songs that talk of dislocation, emptiness and endless searching through regret, remorse, and ultimately acceptance and resignation. And Newbury's vocal abilities are just astonishing. He has a different voice for literally every song. It is tempting to write about every single song here, but it would be fruitless. Newbury's tunes are so slippery and mercurial. They shift shape and disappear into a puff of smoke the minute you think you have them pinned down. And if the stories and arrangements aren't enough to confound the listener, the melodies, all of which have their roots in country music, are so much more deceptive, they turn in on themselves and extend each measure with complex phrasing and mode changes. *—Thom Jurek*

● **Heaven Help the Child** / 1973 / Mountain Retreat ✦✦✦✦✦

After issuing two solid critical successes that went nowhere commercially, Newbury was more determined than ever to get his idea of what music was across to a the American public. He was also hell bent on changing Nashville's stolid, conservative way of recording, producing, marketing and selling music. He failed on both counts but left another stunner of an album along the way. *Heaven Help The Child* opens with the title track, a wondrously arranged, and gorgeously sung, three-generational American Odyssey that offered, with all of its tragedy the clearly visible line of hope on the horizon. Also included here are three definitive interpretations of songs from his very first album, *Harlequin Melodies*: "Sunshine" "Sweet Memories," and "Good Morning Dear." These songs haven't been re-recorded so much as reinvented from the ground up. Newbury changes pace with an awesome dobro-drenched, country-rock sing along, "Why You Been Gone So Long." "Cortelia Clark" a tale of a young man and an older, blind black musician coming to the train yards in Georgia, is one of Newbury's great achievements as a songwriter. Acoustic guitars and strings woo each other through Newbury's glorious tenor and offers a coming of age tale that is both morally instructive and imagistic ally evocative; only Newbury could tell a story that echoed both the blues of the 20s and 30s and the folk songs of the 40s and 50s. The album closes with the Bob Beckam-produced reinvention of "San Francisco Mabel Joy" and it's a punch-in-the-guts way to end an album. With *Heaven Help The Child*, Newbury, for the third time in as many recording sessions, came up with a record that defied categorization or gentrification. And for the third time in a row, he had done the impossible, created a masterpiece, a work of perfection. *—Thom Jurek*

Live at Montezuma Hall / 1973 / Mountain Retreat ✦✦✦✦

This is Newbury's first live set and it's revelatory to hear him in front of an audience with nothing but an acoustic guitar. It's obvious that Newbury has his audience from the opening of "How I love Them Old Songs" and by the time he tells the heartbreaking story of "Cortelia Clark," they are falling apart and Newbury is soaring with the inspiration he's taking from the songs and the audience entranced in front of him. The second part of the album begins with a long, rambling story that ends in "Bugger Red Blues," is a kind of ruse to break the tension. Newbury is a master showman here (the set was not edited in any way), carrying his audience through "How Many Times (Must The Piper Be Paid For

His Song)," and a raggedly beautiful rendition of "American Trilogy." It sounds like the place is coming apart at the seams! But it's in the encores that Newbury reveals just who he is as an artist. Newbury does a soulful cover of Percy Mayfield's "Please Send Me Someone To Love." It's as if Ray Charles and Charlie Rich met each other in New Orleans barroom and sang together. And while that may be the scenario, the delivery is all Newbury's. He breaks the song-and himself-down and builds it back up again before taking the set out with his own "She Even Woke Me Up to Say Goodbye." Man, there must not have been a dry eye in the place because I can't get through it straight after hearing it over a hundred times! Newbury has recorded numerous live records since Montezuma Hall, but none have come even close to matching its power and intensity. In fact, there are few live records by anybody that can hold a candle to this classic. *—Thom Jurek*

I Came to Hear the Music / 1974 / Mountain Retreat ✦✦✦✦

Produced by Chip Young, *I Came to Hear the Music* is Newbury's most diverse recording from his early period. Along with the bittersweet love songs that defy categorization, there are bona fide country waltzes like "You Only Live Once in a While," rock & roll songs such as "Dizzy Lizzy," and "1 X I Ain't 2," and some blues and gospel. The rain and thunderstorms are back, and there are appearances by the Jordanaires and Bobby Emmons. The lushly orchestrated "countrypolitan" sound of "Yesterday's Gone" and the folk-country "If You See Her" mark two ends of the acoustic spectrum for Newbury. The last half of the album features the most diversity; it begins and ends with the aforementioned rock tracks, and Newbury, with his killer guitar pickers and piano player, could rock with anybody. Traffic sounds open "Organized Noise," which could have been a vintage Neil Diamond track, with its African percussion and off-meter rhyme. It's full of drama, of bitter reverie, of remorse, and as the orchestra swells behind the singer and the cut begins to open itself up, it just abruptly ends... a squandered idea, an emotion best left unexplored. There is also the ballad "Love Look (At Us Now)," which was covered by no less than five different artists, none of them coming close to Newbury's bone honest, tell-it-like-it-is delivery. The song is full of shame and bewilderment, unable to resolve the emotions contained within it (with the strings swelling repeatedly to underscore this) or stand against them. An amazing tome that lasts less than three minutes! Alas, this album sold only as well as its predecessors, but it pointed its creator in new directions, or at least revealed the many simultaneous directions he'd been capable traveling all along. *—Thom Jurek*

Lovers / 1975 / Elektra ✦✦✦

Given the sadness, melancholy, and even grief expressed on his earlier recordings, Newbury's familiarity with the shadow side of the soul is well-known, but none of his recordings cuts such a deep furrow into pain, pessimism, heartbreak, and futile longing as *Lovers*. Newbury plays more styles than one can shake a stick at on *Lovers*. It's as if he's trying, through hard country, blues, gospel, R&B, lounge jazz, folk balladry, and even rock, to plead, beg, borrow, and scheme his way (apparently unsuccessfully) from under the bleak cloud that surrounds him. Hell, you gotta give the guy credit for even trying. The album opens with yet another Newbury trilogy, the epic "Apples Dipped in Candy," coming out stomping in a country-rock manner reminiscent of Waylon Jennings. With a narrative so tense and full of pain, Newbury literally barely makes it through the title cut; the crack and pauses are all left in. The string arrangement assures there won't be a dry eye in the house. This track, and in fact the entire album, are on a par with Frank Sinatra's '50s classic, "In the Wee Small Hours of the Morning." Then comes "Sail Away," a brief respite, where the singer of these songs summons his courage for one more attempt at optimism. It's a beautiful country ballad, but it's short-lived, as "When Do We Stop Starting Over" bares its mournful honky tonk heart. The only other glimmer of hope that comes from these sides happens on the gospel tune "Lead On." As solid as *Lovers* is, it still failed to ignite on the chart level. It was greeted with indifference by radio and, hence, Elektra—which had believed and invested in Newbury's creative vision and proven credibility as a songwriter—let him go. *—Thom Jurek*

Rusty Tracks / 1977 / ABC/Hickory ✦✦✦✦

Newbury hooks up with Bobby Bare as a producer and puts out *Rusty Tracks*, a record full of pedal steel guitars, fiddles, cut time rhythms, and lyrical darkness, for his first album for ABC/Hickory. This concentration on one music and its classic themes and rougher-edged production proved to be as great as anything he had done since his early records. "Makes Me Wonder if I Ever Said Goodbye" answers in true loner fashion his early '70s classic "She Never Even Woke Me Up to Say Goodbye," and the whispering gospel prayer "Bless Us All" takes the darkness Newbury held so firmly in his grasp and opens it up for all of us to be a part of; it expresses our own longing and wish for fulfillment. But it's the close of the album that knocks the listener out of her chair. Mirroring his own "American Trilogy" of half a decade before, Newbury strings together—once more without seams—four pieces of classic Americana with breathtakingly gorgeous arrangements: "Shenandoah," "That Lucky Old Sun," "Danny Boy," and "In the Pines." On this set, the orchestra appears and Newbury's singing is as good as anybody's ever was. He doesn't merely sing these songs—he *is* them, a part and parcel of the fabric of the notes themselves and what they represent. Just when Americans were trying to forget who they were by embracing European disco and punk rock as well as dumbed-down versions of both country and jazz, Newbury reveals—much to his own commercial detriment—who and what we are as a nation. There is no more stunning finish to a Newbury record—maybe anybody's record. *—Thom Jurek*

His Eye Is on the Sparrow / 1978 / Hickory ✦✦✦✦

His Eye Is on the Sparrow is one of Newbury's prettiest records. It's intimate in a way that none of his others are; it's a lonely but not world-weary set. The songs are fraught with a more fragile and tender beauty, and are underscored by his production team's subtle nuances and textures. The album shows a return to the sound effects (particularly the rainstorm) of his earliest sides. "Westphalia Texas Waltz" is a country waltz showcasing a beautiful chamber string section set against Charlie McCoy's harmonica and the endless sound of rain falling. Newbury's version of the title track—arranged here by film score producer Alan Moore—is an American classic in the public domain. It's a gospel song that isn't gospel, a sacred song that is secular enough to include the sounds of gulls (and, one supposes, sparrows). "The Dragon and the Mouse"'s deep metaphorical narrative is missed because of the deceptive simplicity of the arrangement, instrumentation. Another pleasant weirdness is the brief "St. Cecelia," with its church bell and stacked choirs courtesy once again of the Nashphilharmonic. It's a country hymn to everything that has passed away except for the burden of inspiration to do what's right. The disc closes with a reprise (of sorts) of its opener. But "Juble Lee's Revival Shout" is no gospel song; it's a small, bleak testament to the most intimate kind of loneliness—the kind found in the mirror at the end of the day. It's a chilling way to end a record than began so tenderly, so simply, if not optimistically. But that's Newbury. The most horrible truths are the ones that are gorgeously told to us by sages and well-meaning hucksters, and he's both. It is a truly awesome and off-putting finish. *—Thom Jurek*

It Looks Like Rain/Live at Montezuma Hall / 1979 / Elektra ✦✦✦✦✦

Mickey Newbury is in fine form on *It Looks Like Rain/Live at Montezuma Hall*, a release which could be called his "greatest hits," even though most of these songs are better-known by other artists. *Live at Montezuma Hall* is just Newbury and his guitar before an appreciative audience. The record boasts such Newbury staples as "San Francisco Mabel Joy" and "Heaven Help the Child," but the song that truly stands out is his version of "An American Trilogy." *It Looks Like Rain* is a studio effort backed by some of Nashville's finest pickers and includes such excellent tracks as "She Even Woke Me Up to Say Goodbye," "T" Total Tommy, and a studio version of "San Francisco Mabel Joy." The only thing which may mar your enjoyment of this record is the "Rain & Train Sound Effects" courtesy of the Mystic Moods Orchestra. They must have been used as an idea to set a certain mood for the enjoyment of these tunes, but the songs themselves set the mood perfectly. Nevertheless, the album is a good look at Mickey Newbury and it's worth seeking out. *—James Chrispell*

The Sailor / 1979 / Hickory ✦✦✦✦✦

Who would have thought that Mickey Newbury would issue a 100 percent, crackling fresh country-pop record in 1979? Produced by Ronnie Gant with (massive) string arrangements by Alan Moore at Cowboy Jack Clement's studio, *The Sail* reveals that Newbury knew what it took all the time, but by the time he let his muse follow him down the commercial country rabbit hole, it was too late. The first track, "Blue Sky Shinin'," is a country love song arranged and exquisitely performed as if written for Patsy Cline. Next, "Let's Have a Party" is perhaps Newbury's anthem, not because of its title, but because it's one of the most beautiful confessional songs he's ever written. The production by Gant is straightforward and Newbury's voice is clearly in the foreground. The sound effects are replaced with layers of instrumentation and backing vocals. Newbury's relaxed delivery offers the listener a way to see just *how* sincere these songs are. While there are no weak cuts, the aforementioned stand out. So does "Let It Go," done in 2/4 time, beginning as a country song and ending by transforming itself inside out into a gospel shouter. *The Sailor*, once again, refused to sell, perhaps because it was too late, perhaps because it was too early—Merle Haggard and George Jones made records that sounded exactly like this only three years later and scored big. As great as this record is, and as good as Newbury knew it was, it was the same old story. Nashville's radio machine wasn't having it, and therefore the public never got the chance to make up its mind. In fact, the way Newbury's entire career was handled by Nashville is evidence enough to raze the entire town and start over. *—Thom Jurek*

After All These Years / 1981 / Mercury ✦✦✦✦

After All These Years is completely different in content and production from its predecessor *The Sailor*. While "The Sailor" is a classic seafaring tragedy worthy of a film, "Song of Sorrow" and "Let's Say Goodbye One More Time" are both broken love songs, one in the aftermath of an affair and one at the moment of its breaking point. What they have to do with each other is only in Newbury's mind, but it works. Somehow from the vastness of the sea expressed in the suite's first song to the individual sitting alone in a room at night staring at a clock, we find the spectrum of human regret and grief. These songs—most of them country songs although there is a strangely wonderful country-rock ballad called "Truly Blue"—reveal for the first time Newbury's sense that he may have wasted his career. Truth be told, he may have been difficult to work with, but Nashville—that great eater of talent—never gave him a chance, considering him a songwriter rather than a recording artist. Evidence is on the waltz "That Was the Way It Was Then," a nostalgic lament for the 1950s. Never issued as a single, this track was later a hit for no less than three other artists and recorded by perhaps a dozen, yet none of them came close to the emotional depth of Newbury's version. Other standouts include "I Still Love You (After All These Years)," an astonishingly sincere non-corny homage to Newbury's parents. There is also the Dave Loggins-styled vocal on "Over the Mountain," co-written with Joe Henry, who was just beginning his career when this record was made, and wanted to be a country songwriter! *—Thom Jurek*

In a New Age / 1988 / Airborne ✦✦

Newbury is accompanied only by his own guitar playing, violinist "Arizona St. Marie" Rhines, and bassist Edgar Meyer. The versions of "Cortelia Clark," "Frisco Depot," "Poison Red Berries," "San Francisco Mabel Joy" and other Newbury regulars are sweeter and less emotionally piercing than his Elektra recordings. *—Kurt Wolff*

Sweet Memories / 1988 / MCA ✦✦✦

This collection of Newbury material pretty much accents his more sentimental side, with none of his more off the wall psychedelic country material. In this vein he still comes across as a country singer who did not stick to routine chord changes or arrangements, and even avoided much trace of the honky tonk or traditional country sounds he praises so righteously in his classic "How I Love Them Old Songs." The funny brass band fade-in after the listener thinks the song has already ended is a goofy touch in the manner of the Beatles "All You Need Is Love," "She Even Woke Me Up to Say Goodbye," and "The Future's Not What It Used to Be" are examples of Newbury's tragic, kick me when I'm down humor. The album includes at least one re-recording of a song he had recorded much earlier in his career; "Good Morning Dear" comes in at almost twice the length of the original version, dragging itself all the way to the finish line. Some of the other tracks are over the top in the kitsch department, with Newbury giving Roy Orbison some serious competition in falsetto crooning. One may wind up wanting to dump a pitcher of cold water over Newbury's head at the end of a number such as "I'll Remember the Good." Despite the low points, this album will give listeners plenty of reason to check out the collected recordings of this very special songwriter and performer. *—Eugene Chadbourne*

The Best of Mickey Newbury / 1991 / Curb ✦✦

Curb's *The Best of Mickey Newbury* has a misleading title. Not only are many of his best-known songs not included, neither are his best-known versions. Instead, it has a handful of his famous songs—including "She Even Woke Me Up to Say Goodbye" and "An American Trilogy"—in slick, overly-polished versions that only give a hint of his talents. *— Thom Owens*

Nights When I Am Sane / 1994 / Winter Harvest ✦✦✦✦

Released by the tiny Nashville label Winter Harvest, *Nights When I Am Sane* was Newbury's first album in six years and his first live album since *Live at Montezuma Hall* 20 years earlier. Those decades may have deepened Newbury the singer's voice a bit, but it only made him a more powerful performer. As one would expect, *Nights When I Am Sane* is comprised of a batch of Newbury's most well-known songs, but the power these performances hold make them the definitive versions. With one guitar or at most one accompanist, Newbury has always been able to convey what most others would need an entire band to try to get to. Songs like "Just Dropped In (To See What Condition My Condition Was In)" (bet you didn't know he wrote that, did ya?) come across with so much feeling, pathos, and depth that it's possible to see clear into the darkness in the soul of the man when he wrote it. When Newbury gets to his famous refrain on "Nights When I Am Sane," he's telling a hidden truth, one so obscured by legend and the grime of time and music-business bullsh*t that it almost slips though in its gentleness. "We would sweat and moan/Until the need in us was gone/In one another's arms all through the night," begins "What Will I Do Now," the track that ends this set. A song of a lover left to bear his grief in the darkness now that she's gone, Newbury's falsetto conveys the grief with so much empathy, it's hard to believe this isn't some man crying on his best friend's shoulder. Only Newbury would have the naked, unpretentious honesty to end a concert with a song like this, and only he could get away with it. *— Thom Jurek*

Live in England / 1998 / Roadhouse ✦✦✦

After releasing 12 albums in 13 years (1968-1981), Mickey Newbury dropped out of full-time recording to rest on his considerable song royalties. MCA Records released a best-of (*Sweet Memories*) in 1985, and he re-recorded some of his songs for Airborne (*In a New Age*) in 1988, but he did not really begin to re-emerge until the mid-'90s. This live album chronicles his 21-date tour of England in 1993, his first extensive bout of stage work in nearly two decades. (He helpfully explains in a stage remark that over the past 19 years, his concertizing has been restricted to a tour of Australia in 1984, a tour of Poland in 1988, and a few charity shows in the U.S. Actually, his live work in America has been more extensive than that, but not much.) It is curious, then, that when the disc was released belatedly in 1998, it was his third live recording and his second in four years. Newbury released *Live at Montezuma Hall* in 1973 and returned to recording with the concert album *Nights When I Am Sane* in 1994. On the latter, he employed a second guitarist, but all three records are spare efforts that focus on the singer and his guitar, and feature many of the same songs. "Cortelia Clark," "Easy Street," and "American Trilogy," heard here, are getting their second live releases, and "San Francisco Mabel Joy" is on all three albums. On his studio albums, Newbury's dirge-like performances are augmented with often elaborate arrangements, which relieves the gloom and the relentless tempo somewhat. In concert, his work can be forbidding unless you are already a fan, and especially for those who picked up *Nights When I Am Sane* four years earlier, *Live in England* is not an essential purchase. *— William Ruhlmann*

The Mickey Newbury Collection / 1998 / Mountain Retreat ✦✦✦✦✦

The Mickey Newbury Collection is an eight-CD box set containing ten albums originally released between 1969 and 1981. (The first six discs contain one album each, while the last two each combine two albums.) They are: *It Looks Like Rain* (1969), '*Frisco Mabel Joy* (1971), *Heaven Help the Child* (1973), *Live at Montezuma Hall* (1973), *I Came to Hear the Music* (1974), *Lovers* (1975), *Rusty Tracks* (1977), *His Eye Is on the Sparrow* (1978), *The Sailor* (1979), and *After All These Years* (1981). While this is not a complete set of Newbury's recordings, it constitutes the bulk of his work as a recording artist, tracing the most productive periods of one of popular music's most impressive, if least known, singer/songwriters. *The Mickey Newbury Collection* uses transfers from vinyl records, the master tapes having long-since disappeared. (The resulting sound quality is good, though the occasional click can be heard in quiet passages.) At his best, Mickey Newbury is an original, compelling singer/songwriter who ranks with the best to come out of Nashville; at his worst, he is a highly competent writer of generic country songs. He may have been too well compensated for the latter to feel challenged sufficiently to be the former with any consistency, but one hears many examples of his great and only good work in this lengthy collection. *— William Ruhlmann*

● **It Might as Well Be the Moon** / 1999 / Mountain Retreat ✦✦✦✦

In one of the odder moments in an odd performing career, Mickey Newbury was nudged out of retirement in 1988 by a virtual bootleg. He had last made an album in 1981, and had long since moved to Oregon to live on his song royalties. But Airborne Records acquired some of his early demos, overdubbed some trendy "new age" synthesizer parts, and prepared to release the results under the title *In a New Age*. (Apparently, a few copies did escape in Canada.) Newbury managed to stop the release by agreeing to cut new recordings of the same material for Airborne (the record sleeves already having been printed). He went into a studio accompanied only by violinist Marie Rhines and, in one day, recorded the nine selections, which included some of his better known songs such as "San Francisco Mabel Joy" and "An American Trilogy." Then, since he suddenly had a new album out, he did some concerts with Rhines. This two-CD set on Newbury's own label, from 11 years later, reissues the *In a New Age* recordings on one disc and one of the concerts, recorded at the Great American Music Hall in San Francisco, on the other. The spare *In a New Age* material has had bass, percussion, and sound effects newly added to it. You might suppose that since this collection consists of an album of re-recordings and what is Newbury's third live album to be released within five years (following 1994's *Nights When I Am Sane* and 1998's *Live in England*, drawn from 1993 shows), it would not be an essential album. In fact, it is nearly definitive, presenting a good sampling of Newbury's oeuvre on one disc (a sampling otherwise unavailable, since there is no good Newbury best-of) and the finest of his live recordings yet. Newbury had written and recorded too many great songs for a nine-song set (actually eight, since leadoff track "All My Trials" is also included in "An American Trilogy" at the end) to be anything like a thorough compilation. But many of his great ones are here, notably "'Frisco Depot," "Poison Red Berries" (aka "I Don't Think Much About Her Anymore"), and "Willow Tree" (aka "Wish I Was"). They should give the listener a good idea of Newbury's range and depth. The live disc, meanwhile, is a delight in which Newbury, clearly much more comfortable than on his other live releases, banters with the audience, explains many of his songs, and performs some other great ones not included on the first disc, among them such hits as "She Even Woke Me Up to Say Goodbye" and "Sweet Memories." There are several previously unheard songs ("Lie to Me Darlin'," "That's the Way It Goes," "Ain't No Blues Today")— one hesitates to go out on a limb and call them new, since Newbury has a bottomless songwriting trunk—and they are worthy additions to his catalog. And he alters lyrics to old favorites. The result is a collection that sums up Newbury's career effectively and should serve as an excellent introduction to anyone wanting to find out about this neglected songwriter. *—William Ruhlmann*

Lulled By the Moonlight / Feb. 29, 2000 / Mountain Retreat ✦✦✦✦

In 1994, Mickey Newbury gave his patient fans hope by releasing the live album *Nights When I Am Sane*, his first recording of any kind in six years and his first to contain any new material in 13 years. Two years later, he answered their prayers with *Lulled By the Moonlight*, his first new studio album consisting primarily of new material since 1981's *After All These Years*. Put out on his own record label, it was a typically eccentric effort. Always fond of recycling his own work, Newbury borrowed the track "Blue Sky Shining" from his 1979 album *The Sailor* as well as musical interludes from LPs dating back to 1969's *Looks Like Rain*; re-recorded "The Future Is Not What It Used to Be," which had first appeared on his 1971 album '*Frisco Mabel Joy*, and included studio recordings of three of the four new songs that had appeared on *Nights When I Am Sane*. He also turned over one entire track on the album to Toni Jolene Clay, who co-wrote (with J. Weatherly), sang, played piano on, and produced "Silver Moon" with no apparent input from him. All those digressions, however, still left room on a 73-minute CD for 11 new (or at least previously unrecorded) Newbury compositions. The songwriter dedicated the album to Stephen Foster, with whom he must identify. Foster was the first man to become well-known as a songwriter, and he came up with material that has been absorbed into American popular music. Newbury, who has always shown a fondness for 19th century song styles, began this comeback collection with "Three Bells for Stephen," asking, "Do you remember me, dear hearts and gentle people?" His new songs were full of backward glances over a long life and were tinged with regret, which was a typical stance for him. But he could also be surprising. "Captured in Blue" was a doo wop love song on which his voice was reminiscent of fellow East Texan Don Henley, for example, while "Just Another Lovely Day" was a light, jazzy number, and "Freight Train Howlin'" a rocker. More characteristic were songs, like "Shades of '63" and "Time Was," that reflected philosophically on the past. *Lulled By the Moonlight* was not a masterpiece, which necessarily made it a disappointment given the high standard of the artist's best work, but it demonstrated that he continued to ply his craft a decade and a half after he had given up on a full-time performing career, and that was encouraging. *— William Ruhlmann*

Stories From the Silver Moon Cafe / Oct. 10, 2000 / Mountain Retreat ✦✦✦✦

Stories From the Silver Moon Cafe was a characteristic effort in many respects. As on all Mickey Newbury albums, the spaces between tracks were filled with atmospheric sound effects such as chirping crickets, barking dogs, a passing car, trains, and plenty of rain and thunder. As on all Mickey Newbury albums, the selection of songs mixed new compositions and re-recordings of old songs. And as on all Mickey Newbury albums, there were some classic country songs. "Don't it sound like something you have heard before?" Newbury asked in "Oh Mama," and he easily could have been referring to his own work. Even the imagery was repeated: Two songs employed the phrase "one thin dime," and freight trains were mentioned in three. It had always been a talent of Newbury's to write country songs that sounded like they had been around forever, and such works as "Ain't No Blues Today" (which probably dated back to at least the 1970s) and "Ain't No Sunshine" (not the Bill Withers hit) certainly did. So did "Why You Been Gone So Long," but that was no wonder, since it had been a country hit in 1969. As ever, Newbury was a master at expressing emotional pain brought on by dislocation or romantic discord, but he also expanded into a more general sense of dread. However drawn he was to darkness, though, he concluded with the formal statement of faith and family, "A Father's Prayer," underlying a basic paradox in his lifelong stance as an artist, that this poet of the depressed and dissolute had long since settled into a stable family life himself and, at 60, was now looking serenely toward his golden years. —*William Ruhlmann*

A Long Road Home / Jan. 22, 2002 / Mountain Retreat ✦✦✦✦✦
Fate can be a funny thing. Into his fourth decade as a singer/songwriter and battling emphysema (he's hooked up to an oxygen tank around the clock), Mickey Newbury has made his *pièce de résistance*. Newbury rose amidst friends and colleagues such as Willie Nelson, Kris Kristofferson, and the late, great Townes Van Zandt as a formidable Texas songwriter in the late '60s and early '70s. He wrote memorable hits for other artists while recording his own, less-recognized albums. *A Long Road Home* finds the embattled singer/songwriter deeply reflecting upon the journey, and it's a touching and strong song cycle. There are memories of when he was a teen with vinegar in his veins tearing down endless highways toward something or another (and more importantly away from something or another), in the form of "In '59." There are also multiple tales of romantic regret, such as "I Don't Love You," with its parsimonious lyrics, and "Where Are You Darlin' Tonight." There's also the stirring and disconcerting "So Sad," which ranks among Newbury's best compositions. He also revisits past victories with an updated take on "Here Comes the Rain, Baby," which was originally recorded for 1968's *Harlequinn Melodies*. Newbury may be embattled physically, but the creative fires burn fiercer than ever. This is a remarkable album. —*Erik Hage*

Winter Winds / May 8, 2002 / Mountain Retreat ✦✦✦

Harlequin Melodies: The Complete RCA Recordings Plus / 2003 / Raven ✦✦✦✦
It is ironic that the CD release of Mickey Newbury's debut album and initial RCA recordings are the very ones he despised and disowned, yet have better sound than those reissued on his own label. (The reason for this is that the master no longer existed for many of his later records and they were remastered from pristine LPs.) Nonetheless, despite Newbury's own discontent, this album holds up amazingly well. It is easy to hear how Felton Jarvis' production may not have exactly been to his liking in that it was not quite as subtle as his own, and these textures are a bit thinner and less impressionistic, but that can easily be forgiven—especially considering what else was going on in Nashville in 1968 (there are no reverb or echo chamber effects on his vocals). The CD combines *Harlequin Melodies* from 1968 with *Sings His Own* from 1972. Here are several Newbury firsts, whose re-recorded and reinvented versions on later albums—"Sunshine," "Sweet Memories," and "Good Morning Dear" from *Heaven Help the Child*—became definitive takes. There is also the original version of his infamous "Just Dropped In (To See What Condition My Condition Was In)." Also included is a stripped-down, honky tonk version of "How I Love Them Old Songs" and the rocker "Dizzy Lizzy." Most significant is the first version of Newbury's signature medley, "An American Trilogy." There are two tracks here, "Mister Can't You See" and "Weeping Annaleah," co-written with a very young Townes Van Zandt. For a deeper analysis of the music and production techniques here, reference the review of the original LP by Eugene Chadbourne at the top the Newbury listing of recordings. For fans, this is a must-have; for those who have only heard the legend, you can shell out a mere 15 dollars to what it would sound like if a Bob Dylan-literate Nick Drake was from Texas and produced by *Pet Sounds*-era Brian Wilson. Newbury arrived in Nash Vegas in full possession of his nearly limitless power as both a singer and songwriter. This CD attests to that in spades. —*Thom Jurek*

Jimmy C. Newman

b. Aug. 27, 1927, High Point, LA
Vocals / Traditional Cajun, Traditional Country
The "C" stands for Cajun, and though much of Jimmy C. Newman's early country material has little swamp stylings, he developed a fusion on several 1960s albums that established him as a forerunner in Cajun-country music. Newman was born on August 27, 1927, in High Point, LA; as a child, he listened more to Gene Autry than the Cajun music of the area but still included several Cajun songs in his repertoire with Chuck Guillory's Rhythm Boys, which he joined while still a teenager. Newman recorded several unsuccessful sides in the late '40s for J.D. Miller's Feature label, but Miller later convinced Nashville legend Fred Rose to give the budding singer a shot. After recording four songs in 1953, Newman signed to Dot Records and scored a hit the following year when "Cry, Cry, Darling" reached number four in the country charts.

Newman's chart success prompted the *Louisiana Hayride* to hire him as a regular performer. His next four hits all made Top Ten, including 1955's "Daydreamin'," "Blue Darlin'," and "God Was So Good." Newman moved up to the *Grand Ole Opry* in 1956 and released "A Fallen Star" the following year. The single, his biggest hit, spent two weeks at number two and also entered the pop Top 25. The singer was unhappy with his Dot contract, though, and moved to MGM in 1958. By November of that year, Newman charted another Top Ten hit, "You're Makin' a Fool Out of Me"; he closed out the decade with three Top 30 singles and the Top Ten "Grin and Bear It" in July 1959. Newman began the '60s with success also, bringing "A Lovely Work of Art" to number six and "Wanting You to Be With Me" to number 11. Not content with his popularity at MGM, he switched labels again, signing with Decca in 1961.

Now that he was an established artist, Newman began to integrate Cajun influences in such Top 25 singles as "Alligator Man" and "Bayou Talk." His 1963 album *Folk Songs of the Bayou Country* was a milestone in the popularization of Cajun music and included great work by accordionist Shorty LeBlanc and Newman regular Rufus Thibodeaux on fiddle. He hit the country Top Ten at the end of the year with "D.J. for a Day," and his recordings soon moved back to the Nashville sound, with occasional Cajun influences. (One notable exception is 1967's *Louisiana Saturday Night*.)

Newman reached the Top Ten twice within six months in 1965-1966 with "Artificial Rose" and "Back Pocket Money," but they proved to be his final hits. The following three

years saw occasional placements in the Top 30, and his last chart entry was 1970's "I'm Holding Your Memory (But He's Holding You)." Following his commercial decline, Newman moved back to Cajun music, recording Cajun albums for the La Louisianne, Swallow, and Rounder labels. His performances continue to excite many in Europe as well as America, and his *Grand Ole Opry* slot also kept him busy. —*John Bush*

Louisiana Saturday Night / 1967 / Charly ✦✦✦
Louisiana Saturday Night is divided between new songs and re-recorded versions of Newman's '50s and '60s hits. The re-recordings are far from an embarrassment—if anything, they help give the album some weight. The old songs mesh with a handful of excellent new tracks, resulting in a thoroughly engaging and entertaining record. —*Thom Owens*

● **Bop A Hula** / 1990 / Bear Family ✦✦✦✦
Here are 47 songs cut by Jimmy C. Newman for Dot Records between late 1953 and February of 1958, showcasing the singer in his early prime—Newman's recordings go back to 1946, but these were the ones where he hit his stride. The sound is a mix of Cajun and country, with the strong influence of Ernest Tubb, whom Newman grew up idolizing along with Gene Autry—Tubb's lead guitarist Billy Byrd even played on Newman's first sessions (alongside Chet Atkins), although Jimmy's real sound can be heard on the songs from his second and third sessions, which prominently feature Cajun fiddler Rufus Thibodeaux. Newman's earliest Dot sessions, directed by Fred Rose (who was then looking for a successor to the recently deceased Hank Williams), show him working in a hillbilly vein, on songs like "You Didn't Have To" and "Cry, Cry Darling"—the early sessions also show Newman with a marked lisp from a badly fitted gold tooth, which was later corrected. Surprisingly, a lot of the better material here, such as "Do You Feel Like I Feel About You," was not released until a decade later, when Dot started putting out albums on Newman and dipped into their vaults. Disc two includes Newman's attempts to crack the rock & roll and pop markets, with numbers like "Bop a Hula," "Step Aside Shallow Water," and "Carry On," which work to varying degrees (the last is considered a classic by rockabilly fans) but were more aberrations than a genuine new direction for him. When asked to do an Elvis-like piece like "I Can't Go on This Way" (complete with the Jordanaires, who also appear on the same session's cover of Jim Reeves' "Need Me"), however, he gave a good account, and rock & roll history buffs will find at least a half-dozen tracks worth hearing on this disc. —*Bruce Eder*

The Alligator Man / 1991 / Rounder ✦✦✦✦
Jimmy C. Newman has artfully integrated a country sensibility into his Cajun roots and crafted a style with a foot in both camps. This session emphasized the Cajun side, although it still contained numbers that were thoroughly country, from arrangements to Newman's earnest vocals. But he displayed his Cajun side quite forcefully, whether paying tribute to such greats as Johnnie Allen and D. L. Menard with crackling versions of their songs or doing his own arrangements of traditional Cajun music backed by a quality band. —*Ron Wynn*

More Cajun Music / Feb. 28, 1995 / Universal Special Products ✦✦✦

The Cajun Country Music of a Louisiana Man / Feb. 27, 2001 / Edsel ✦✦✦✦

Juice Newton (Judy Kay Newton)

b. Feb. 18, 1952, Lakehurst, NJ
Guitar, Vocals / Country-Pop, Adult Contemporary, Urban Cowboy
Juice Newton (born Judy Kay Newton, February 18, 1952, Lakehurst, NJ) was part of the first wave of country singers raised on rock, folk-rock, and singer/songwriters, which is evident from her hit singles. "Angel of the Morning" and "Queen of Hearts," her two crossover hits, have country-pop arrangements, but their roots are in '60s pop and new wave roots rock, respectively. That's why she managed pop crossover hits in the early '80s and also why she was able to sustain country success throughout the decade. Although Newton was born in New Jersey, she was raised in Virginia. As she entered high-school, her mother gave her a guitar, prompting her infatuation with folk music. After graduating from high-school, she attended Foothill College in Los Altos Hills, CA, where she continued to play folk in coffeehouses. During this time, she met Otha Young, a fellow guitarist and songwriter. The two formed a folk-rock band called Dixie Peach and began playing bars around northern California.

Dixie Peach only lasted a year, but they did gain a local following while they were active. After the band broke up, Newton & Young formed Juice Newton & Silver Spur, which had more country leanings than Dixie Peach. They were also more successful. Their fan base was large enough to convince the band to go to Los Angeles and try to land a record contract. In 1975, Juice Newton & Silver Spur signed to RCA Records and released an eponymous debut which spawned the minor hit single "Love Is a Word" in early 1976. Later that year, the group released *After the Dust Settles*, which didn't attract much attention, and RCA dropped them after its release. The band signed with Capitol Records, releasing *Come to Me* in 1978. Like its predecessor, the album was more or less ignored, causing the Silver Spur to disband.

Though Silver Spur had broken up, Newton & Young continued to work together. Newton still had a contract with Capitol, and the pair immediately began working on her solo debut. The result, *Juice*, was released in early 1981 and quickly became a crossover hit. The first single from the record, "Angel of the Morning," reached number four on the pop charts, and it peaked at 22 on the country charts. "Queen of Hearts" was a bigger hit, reaching number two on the pop charts and number 14 on the country charts. "The Sweetest Thing (I've Ever Known)," the third single taken from *Juice*, was her biggest country hit, peaking at number one; on the pop charts, it hit number seven. *Juice* would eventually go platinum.

Newton's follow-up album to *Juice*, *Quiet Lies*, was released in the spring of 1982. It was also a hit, spawning the pop Top Ten "Love's Been a Little Bit Hard on Me" and the number-two country hit "Break It to Me Gently." The album won a Grammy for Best Country Vocal Performance, Female; it also went gold by the end of the year. *Dirty Looks*, her third solo album, was released in 1983. The record marked the first time Newton failed to crack either the pop or country Top 40. In 1984, she switched labels, signing with RCA. Newton's first album for the label, *Can't Wait All Night*, was a transitional album, seeing her move away from pop and begin to concentrate on country. *Old Flame*, released in 1985, was her country breakthrough, spawning the hits "You Make Me Want to Make You Mine," "Hurt," and the duet with Eddie Rabbitt "Both to Each Other (Friends & Lovers)," which all went to number one; the album had three additional Top Ten hits—"Old Flame," "Cheap Love," and "What Can I Do With My Heart."

Old Flame happened to be Newton's only major country hit. Its follow-up, 1987's *Emotion*, only yielded one Top Ten hit, "Tell Me True." In 1989, she released *Ain't Gonna Cry*, which featured the single "When Love Comes Around the Bend," which barely scraped the Top 40. *Ain't Gonna Cry* turned out be Newton's last album for several years. She abandoned country and began performing showy mainstream pop, which she performed in nightclubs. Throughout the '90s, she continued to perform live concerts without recording any new material for years. Finally, she reunited with producer Richard Landis in 1997, recording *The Trouble With Angels*, a collection of re-recorded hits and new songs that was released in the spring of 1998. *—Stephen Thomas Erlewine*

Juice Newton & Silver Spur / 1975 / RCA ♦♦♦

While on many of the albums Silver Spur act more as a backup band than a real group, this record works more as a group effort. Juice still handles most of the vocals, but Silver Spur check in with "Roll on, Trucker" which sounds very much like mid-period Pure Prairie League. *—Jim Worbois*

After the Dust Settles / 1976 / RCA ♦♦♦

Come to Me / 1978 / Capitol ♦♦♦♦

Otha Young's writing style has always seemed to suit Newton's vocal style the best, and that continues to be the case with this record. Of the two tracks written by her labelmate, Bob Seger, "Fire Down Below" works the best, though Newton's soaring voice doesn't quite equal Seger's growl. *—Jim Worbois*

Well Kept Secret / 1978 / Capitol ♦♦♦

The title of this album seems to apply to her career as much as anything. She was still a couple years away from any substantial success. Newton seems to be without direction on this record and, as such, is trying some harder-edged material. While she doesn't do a bad job, there are so many others who do it better. *—Jim Worbois*

Take Heart / 1979 / Capitol ♦♦

This is not the place to start if you are just getting into Newton's music. It features less original music than many of her albums, and the covers she chooses to do don't really stand out. It's an average album at best. *—Jim Worbois*

Juice / 1981 / DCC ♦♦♦♦♦

Juice was Juice Newton's breakthrough album, sending her into not only into the country Top Ten, but also to the top of the pop charts. The key to her success was how her country-pop not only drew from country roots, but also '60s AM pop, folk-rock, and roots rock. For instance, the country production on "Angel of the Morning" can't disguise its soft rock roots. Similarly, "Queen of Hearts" simply replicates Dave Edmunds' version from *Repeat When Necessary*, down to the vocal inflections and guitar breaks. But Newton's version is slicker, which appealed both to country and pop radio. Throughout *Juice*, Newton straddles the line between country and pop, playing to both sides of the market. As it happened, she appealed to both. As an album, *Juice* has its weak moments, but she sings well throughout the record, and when she has the right material—as on the hit singles—the results are highly entertaining. *—Stephen Thomas Erlewine*

Quiet Lies / 1982 / Capitol ♦♦♦♦♦

This album assured Newton three country hits (the first three tracks) as she found her way back to the country-rock sound she seems to do best. Her choice of covers works better this time as well. Her Brenda Lee netted her a hit, and her Gene Pitney cover wasn't bad either. *—Jim Worbois*

Dirty Looks / 1983 / Capitol ♦♦♦♦

Can't Wait All Night / 1984 / RCA ♦♦

A largely uninteresting album, Newton seems to have lost not only her direction but her drive. *—Jim Worbois*

● **Greatest Hits (And More)** / 1984 / Liberty ♦♦♦♦♦

One of a series of single-artist CD anthologies on Liberty sharing this title, this collection compiles 15 of Juice Newton's hits and album tracks. Her best-known songs such as "Queen of Hearts" and "Love's Been a Little Bit Hard on Me" are included, as well as interesting items such as a cover version of the Zombies' "Tell Her No." The hits are the highlights here; although the fusion of new wave, power pop, and country may sound dated, the hooks are timeless. *Greatest Hits (and More)* makes for enjoyable listening, and provides an excellent and concise overview of Newton's early-'80s output. *—Greg Adams*

Ain't Gonna Cry / 1985 / RCA ♦♦♦

Old Flame / 1986 / RCA ♦♦♦♦♦

Out of all of Juice Newton's albums, *Old Flame* has the strongest country roots and influences. Newton is still equally informed by rock and pop—after all, she doesn't sing hardcore honky tonk on the album, she sings somewhat roots country-pop . However, *Old Flame* proves that she can perform this material with conviction. Most of the production on the record is too slick and indicative of its time, but the singles—as well as Newton's singing—remain effective. *—Thom Owens*

Emotion / 1987 / RCA ♦♦♦

Greatest Country Hits / 1990 / Curb ♦♦♦

Greatest Country Hits is a ten-track budget-priced collection that features some of Juice Newton's biggest hits, including "Sweetest Thing (I've Ever Known)," "Break It to Me Gently," "Queen of Hearts," "Angel of the Morning," "Sunshine," "Stranger at My Door" and "It's a Heartache." Although this isn't a bad budget-priced disc, there are better collections available, offering more songs, more hits and better sound for not much more money. *—Stephen Thomas Erlewine*

Greatest Hits / 1991 / CEMA ♦♦♦

This ten-song assortment that is part of Capitol's *10 Best* series includes six of Juice Newton's Top 40 pop singles, leaving out her lowest charting hit in "Tell Her No," a Zombies hit from 1965. Her three-part recipe of folk, country, and rock comprises her better material, found here with the number two *Billboard* single "Queen of Hearts," recorded two years earlier by Dave Edmunds, and the subtle "Angel of the Morning," which shows off Newton's melodious voice. One of her most vibrant tunes, led by the friendly jangle of acoustic guitar, is included here as well with 1982's "Love's Been a Little Bit Hard on Me." The sweetness of "Break It to Me Gently" was both a pop and country hit thanks to its accommodating radio-friendly formula, and "It's a Heartache," a charted single for Bonnie Tyler in 1978, is sung in a much more delicate fashion by Newton. While this brief dose of Juice Newton's most popular efforts may suffice for some, there is still plenty of material that can be found on more thorough collections. Her country material, such as "You Make Me Want to Make You Mine," "I'm So Hurt," "Old Flame," and "Both to Each Other," to name just a few, all reached number one positions on the country & western charts during the mid-'80s and are absent from this short set. For a meager, inexpensive collection of Newton's pop hits, this disc will do the trick, but like most hits compilations, it's short and suffers from subpar sound. *—Mike DeGagne*

The Trouble With Angels / Apr. 28, 1998 / Platinum/A&M ♦♦♦

Juice Newton spent most of the '90s as a concert act, staying out of the studio for years. As the decade drew to a close, she reunited with producer Richard Landis, the man who helmed the boards for her biggest hits, to record *The Trouble With Angels*. Unfortunately, the album wasn't a full-fledged comeback—seven of the ten tracks were re-recordings of hits like "Angel of the Morning" and "Queen of Hearts," with only three songs being new to her repertoire. Presumably, this course was taken with the idea that it would remind audiences of why Newton was a star, but the lack of new material is nevertheless quite disappointing for longtime fans. That said, she's in fine voice on the record, and the album is hardly bad. It's just that it would have been nice if Newton had decided to make her comeback with an album that felt brand new, not like a retread. *—Stephen Thomas Erlewine*

● **Anthology** / Oct. 13, 1998 / Renaissance ♦♦♦♦♦

The budget-priced *Anthology* is the most comprehensive overview of Juice Newton's career to date, a well-assembled 19-track retrospective which includes all of the singer's biggest country-pop hits from 1976 (her first chart entry "Love Is a Word," recorded with Silver Spur) to 1989 ("When Love Comes Around the Bend," her final Top 40 single). In addition to Newton's four Nashville number ones—"The Sweetest Thing (I've Ever Known)," "You Make Me Want to Make You Mine," "Hurt" and the Eddie Rabbitt duet "Both to Each Other (Friends and Lovers)"—the disc also includes the pop smashes "Angel of the Morning" and "Queen of Hearts." *—Hank Small*

American Girl / Oct. 12, 1999 / Renaissance ♦♦♦♦

Maybe best known for her hit songs "Queen of Hearts" and "Angel of the Morning," Juice Newton has done plenty of other tunes over the years worth recalling. Her music has won her a long list of platinum and gold albums, top hits, and awards. In the '70s, when there was for the most part a pretty defined line between country and rock, Newton marched over that line with success, mixing the best of both and winning fans from each side long before singers like Chely Wright, Faith Hill, Shania Twain, or the Dixie Chicks showed up on the scene with their own crossover hits. On this album, *American Girl*, Juice Newton steps out with some new material for the first time in a number of years. She wrote "Nightime Without You," but many of the additional songs were recorded by other artists first, like Tom Petty's "Keeping Me Alive," Nanci Griffith's "Listen to the Radio," and Queen's "Crazy Little Thing Called Love." Newton's husky voice puts an original touch to each tune, sure to please both new and old fans. An album worth having. *—Charlotte Dillon*

Olivia Newton-John

b. Sep. 26, 1948, Cambridge, England

Vocals / Country-Pop, Adult Contemporary, Soft Rock

Olivia Newton-John skillfully made the transition from popular country-pop singer to popular mainstream soft rock singer, becoming one of the most successful vocalists of the '70s in the process. The transition itself wasn't much of a stretch—her early-'70s hits "I Honestly Love You" and "Have You Never Been Mellow" were country only in the loosest sense—yet the extent of her success in both fields was remarkable. As a country singer, her first five charting singles all went Top Ten in the U.S.; as a pop singer, she had no less than 15 Top Ten hits, including five number one singles, highlighted by "Physical," which spent ten weeks at number one in 1981-1982. Newton-John's sweet voice suited both country-pop and soft rock perfectly, which is what kept her at the top of the charts until the mid-'80s. After 1984, she was no longer able to reach the Top 40, partially because of shifting musical tastes and partially because she was unable to successfully record sexy dance-pop, no matter how hard she tried. Nevertheless, her '70s and '80s hits remained soft rock and adult contemporary staples into the '90s, when she was no longer recording frequently.

Although she was born in Cambridge, England, Newton-John was raised in Melbourne, Australia, where her father was the headmaster of Ormond College (her grandfather Max Born won the Nobel Prize for physics). She tentatively entered show business at the age of 12, when she won a local Haley Mills-lookalike contest. A few years later, she formed an all-female vocal group called the Sol Four with three school friends. Once the Sol Four disbanded, Newton-John entered a television talent contest, winning the grand prize of a trip to London, England. Once in London, she formed a duo with Pat Carroll, another Australian-based vocalist, and tried to work her way into the music industry. Though her partnership with Carrol was short-lived—Pat was sent back to Australia once her visa expired—Olivia was making inroads in the business. Following Carrol's departure, Newton-John recorded and released her first single, a version of Jackie DeShannon's "Till You Say You'll Be Mine." Shortly afterward, she became a member of Toomorrow, a bubblegum group assembled by Don Kirshner in hopes of creating a British version of the Monkees.

Toomorrow appeared in a science fiction movie of the same name and had one minor British hit single, "I Could Never Live Without Your Love," in early 1970 before the group quietly disbanded. Following the failure of Toomorrow, Newton-John became part of Cliff Richard's touring show, appearing both as an opening act at his concerts and on his British television series, *It's Cliff!* The exposure as a singer and comedienne on the show helped Olivia's career immeasurably, and her first single for Uni Records, a version of Bob Dylan's "If Not for You," became a Top Ten hit in the U.K. in the spring of 1971; in America, it was surprisingly successful, spending three weeks at the top of the adult contemporary charts and peaking at number 25 on the pop charts. For the next two years, Newton-John's success was primarily contained in Britain, where she had a string of lesser hits with covers of George Harrison's "What Is Life" and John Denver's "Take Me Home Country Roads." In America, her career was stalled—her follow-up single, "Banks of the Ohio," barely scraped the lower reaches of the Top 100. On the other hand, she didn't release a full-length album in the U.S. until 1973, when *Let Me Be There* appeared. The title track from the record became a huge hit, going gold in early 1974 and peaking in the Top Ten country and pop charts. "Let Me Be There" was so successful it won the Grammy award for Best Country Vocal Performance, Female, much to the consternation of many members of Nashville's music industry.

"Let Me Be There" was followed by four other Top Ten hits—"If You Love Me (Let Me Know)" (number-two country, number-five pop, 1974), "I Honestly Love You" (number-six country, number-one pop, 1974), "Have You Never Been Mellow" (number-three country, number-one pop, 1975), and "Please Mr. Please" (number-five country, number-three pop, 1975). Newton-John moved to Los Angeles late in 1974, and early the following year, she won the Female Vocalist of the Year award from the Country Music Association. As a protest, several members of the CMA quit the organization. Ironically, Newton-John was already planning to move away from country. During 1976 and 1977, she had a number of minor hits with soft rock songs. Though none of these were big pop successes, they began to establish her as a pop singer, not a country-pop singer.

Newton-John's transformation into a mildly sexy pop singer was complete in 1978, when she starred in the movie version of the popular Broadway musical *Grease*. Also starring John Travolta, *Grease* was an international hit and spawned three huge hit singles—"Hopelessly Devoted to You," "Summer Nights," and "You're the One That I Want"; the latter two were duets between Newton-John and Travolta. "You're The One That I Want," in particular, was a massive success, reaching number one in both America and Britain; in the U.K., it spent a staggering nine weeks at number one. During 1979, Newton-John released the *Totally Hot* album, which boasted a mixture of soft rock and light disco. The record was another hit, with the first single, "A Little More Love," peaking at number three on the U.S. pop charts and going gold. Early in 1980, Newton-John starred in the roller-disco fantasy film *Xanadu*. While the movie was an unqualified bomb, the soundtrack was a huge hit. "Magic" spent four weeks at the top of the U.S. pop charts, while the ELO duet "Xanadu" reached number eight and her duet with Cliff Richard, "Suddenly," peaked at number 20.

With her next album, *Physical*, Newton-John continued to rework her image, reinventing herself as a sexy aerobics fanatic. The first single from the record, the suggestive "Physical," was a huge hit, spending ten weeks at number one during the fall and winter of 1981-1982. *Physical* spawned another Top Ten hit—"Make a Move on Me"—and became her most successful record. Following the album's success, she was awarded with an Order of the British Empire. In 1983, Newton-John again starred with Travolta, this time in the comedy *Two of a Kind*. The movie was a bomb, but a song she recorded for the soundtrack, "Twist of Fate," became a Top Ten hit in early 1984.

By the end of 1984, Newton-John had married actor Matt Lattanzi. The following year, she released the *Physical* clone *Soul Kiss*, which produced only one minor hit with its title track. In 1986, she had a daughter named Chloe and opened a clothing store chain called Koala Blue. Newton-John attempted to launch a comeback in 1988 with *The Rumour*, but the album was ignored. She signed with Geffen the following year, releasing the children's album *Warm and Tender*. During the late '80s and '90s, she devoted herself to her family and business as well as several environmental activist organizations. In 1992, Koala Blue folded and Newton-John was diagnosed with breast cancer. Over the next year, she successfully underwent treatment for the disease. In 1994, she returned to recording with the independently released and self-produced album *Gaia*. *Back With a Heart*, a return to Nashville, followed in 1998. *One Woman's Live Journey* was issued two years later. *—Stephen Thomas Erlewine*

Olivia Newton John / 1971 / Pye ✦✦✦

If Not for You / 1971 / UNI ✦✦✦✦

Olivia Newton-John's *If Not for You* covers Gordon Lightfoot, the Band, Leslie Duncan, David Gates, Kris Kristofferson, Tom Rush, and others. Though "If" is a pedestrian cover of Bread's song which hit this same year, it would be a mistake to think these are all mere "covers." The production and arrangements by Bruce Welch and John Farrar are innovative and worthwhile. The only song they contribute is a moving version of "Banks of the Ohio"; the interpretation of Richard Manuel's "In a Station" is respectful and intuitive. *Music From Big Pink* was only three years old when this recording was pressed, and it is one of the few albums to survive the hype and get better with age. Olivia Newton-John dipping into the *Big Pink* songbook was a stroke of genius. Labelmate Elton John released Leslie Duncan's "Love Song" on his *Here and There* live album, but that version doesn't have the sensitivity of this spiritual reading. Both Kris Kristofferson tunes, "Me and Bobby McGee" and "Help Me Make It Through the Night," have arrangements that bring new life to what had become tired bar band favorites in the early '70s. "Where Are You Going to My Love?" was covered by the Brotherhood of Man and the Osmonds, but finds its niche here, as does the superb version of Duncan's "Lullaby." Tom Rush's "No Regrets" and Gordon Lightfoot's "If You Could Read My Mind" are well done, but it is Olivia Newton-John's cover of Bob Dylan by way of George Harrison's *All Things Must Pass* which garnered her a number one adult contemporary and Top 25 hit record. "If Not for You" brought Olivia the attention she deserved. The musicianship by Lou Reed/David Bowie session man Herbie Flowers along with Dave Richmond, John Farrar, and the ever present Brian Bennett is top-notch. After all her own hit records, hearing this superstar sing so many familiar tunes, and performing them so well, is utterly charming. *—Joe Viglione*

Let Me Be There / Dec. 1973 / MCA ✦✦✦✦

Two years after the single "If Not for You" hit the Top 25 on the Uni label, the MCA imprint re-released most of the *If Not for You* album, along with Newton-John's second U.S. hit, "Let Me Be There," and titled the disc after the new smash. With seductive blue ink shadowing her beautiful face and the word Olivia splashed atop the cover, the company created a collector's item with the original LP, a respect from the aficionados that couldn't have been predicted in the '70s, and well-deserved credibility for the popular artist. The first single hit number one on the middle-of-the-road charts, and that market, along with her country base, enabled Newton-John to rack up 26 additional hits, concluding with 1985's "Soul Kiss," the last one almost mirroring her initial success, going Top 20. This collection is a little awkward for the fans who purchased the original hit album, and it gets more confusing: Pye released a 1971 disc, entitled *Olivia Newton-John*, with most of these tracks, while EMI pressed two different titles in 1974, *Crystal Lady* and *First Impressions*, also containing much of this music. Along with the excellent title track, "Let Me Be There," MCA added a cover of John Denver's "Take Me Home Country Roads," a nice rendition of the Merilee Rush classic, Chip Taylor's "Angel of the Morning," and a convenient country tune, "Just a Little Too Much." Tunes missing on *Let Me Be There* which appeared on the original *If Not for You* release are the weak version of David Gate's "If," the Band's "In a Station," a second Lesley Duncan tune, "Lullaby," Tom Rush's "No Regrets," "If I Gotta Leave," and "Where Are You Going to My Love." It's early Newton-John, a bit naïve and far from the sophistication of her *Warm and Tender* release on Geffen, but it works, especially because it contains her first two hit records. *—Joe Viglione*

If You Love Me, Let Me Know / May 1974 / MCA ✦✦✦✦✦

In May and August of 1974, Olivia Newton-John broke through in a big way with this album, the number-five title track written by John Rostil, and the number-one smash "I Love You, I Honestly Love You" by Jeff Barry and Peter Allen quickly established Olivia as a superstar to be reckoned with. The album is beautifully produced by John Farrar with his friend Bruce Welch of Marvin, Welch & Farrar fame helping out with the production on two of the tracks, Gerry Rafferty's "Mary Skeffington" and Olivia Newton-John's sole composition, the acoustic "Changes." The singer is a very good songwriter, and why she didn't put more songs together, or cover some of the wonderful material her mentor was releasing elsewhere, is something to speculate. "Home Ain't Home Anymore" is the one co-write of Farrar's on this collection. Their version of Brian Wilson's "God Only Knows" is short and intriguing, and it is interesting to hear Farrar create a light environment for what was such a big production number for "The Beach Boys." "You Ain't Got the Right" is smart country-pop, with Newton-John in excellent voice and showing a remarkable consistency. Barbara Keith's "Free the People" is, in the hands of Delaney & Bonnie, a wonderfully deep gospel experience. Countrified and given a snappy treatment here, it remains a good song, but doesn't have the balance that Bonnie Bramlett breathed into her version. It's the hits here, though, which are outstanding, and the bright pop is better suited to the title track than to Barbara Keith's masterpiece. "If You Love Me Let Me Know" is a great question for lovers who aren't quite sure, and a marvelous bridge from country music to pop. It might not have the intensity of Tammy Wynette's "Stand By Your Man," but it climbed higher up the charts and, along with Kenny Rogers work, helped Nashville find a wider audience. Topping it off by literally owning adult contemporary on the same album with the ballad "I Love You, I Honestly Love You" is pretty amazing when one looks back at how effectively Farrar and Newton-John set out to conquer the charts, and succeeded. *If You Love Me Let Me Know* works on many levels, and is a strong chapter in Olivia's catalog. *—Joe Viglione*

Have You Never Been Mellow / Feb. 1975 / MCA ✦✦✦✦

The hit single "Have You Never Been Mellow" carried Olivia Newton-John right back to number one, six months after "I Honestly Love You" brought the singer to that coveted position for the first time. The title track is a masterpiece of songwriting by her producer, John Farrar, an exquisitely pleasant melody with a sunny and peaceful theme. Having covered John Denver's "Take Me Home Country Roads" on the *Let Me Be There* album in 1973, Newton-John goes back to the Denver catalog twice on this project, including her beautiful rendition of one of his lesser-known gems, "Follow Me," with Farrar's lush country-pop instrumental backing. "The Air That I Breathe" was a hit for the Hollies when Newton-John was filling the airwaves with "I Honestly Love You"; she does a nice interpretation of the Albert Hammond/Mike Hazlewood song here, along with an intriguing look at Rick Nelson's "Lifestream." The album also includes a soulful reading of Graeme Hall's "And in the Morning" and a John Farrar/Hank Marvin composition, "It's So Easy," a fun melody that is not the Buddy Holly title of the same name. Years after it was recorded, *Have You Never Been Mellow* continued to stand as an entertaining and full album by a woman who would record hits for another 11 years. The title track opens the album and it closes with former producer Bruce Welch's co-write of "Please Mr. Please," a pretty pop tune that went Top Three. From beginning to end *Have You Never Been Mellow* is Olivia Newton-John showing why she could hold her own on the charts with as powerful a star as Elton John. Recorded at EMI Studios, London, it has impeccable sound and a special vibe. —*Joe Viglione*

Clearly Love / Sep. 1975 / MCA ✦✦✦
Nine beautiful photos accompany the lyrics—Olivia with horses, Olivia in the hay, Olivia with a doggy; following up the phenomenal success of *Have You Never Been Mellow* was pretty elementary—Newton-John ruled the Top 40, adult contemporary, and country charts at this point in time. From the end of 1975 to early 1976, *Clearly Love* generated a Top 20 and two Top 30 hits: "Something Better to Do" and "Let It Shine" b/w "He Ain't Heavy…He's My Brother," respectively. They both topped the adult contemporary charts while the flip of "Let It Shine," a rare female-vocalist cover of "He Ain't Heavy…He's My Brother," also garnered radio and sales action. The choices for cover songs on this album are strange indeed: an unnecessary "Summertime Blues" which adds nothing to Eddie Cochran's song of hot-weather angst and the interesting remake of the Hollies' hit "He Ain't Heavy," with its big country-ballad ending to what started as a lilting love song. The gems here are what sound like Olivia Newton-John bread-and-butter staples—"Slow Down Jackson," which is as bubbly and beautiful as "Have You Never Been Mellow"; "Crying, Laughing, Loving, Lying"; the stunning title track "Clearly Love"; along with, of course, the hits. "Let It Shine" has lots of country twang—John Farrar's impeccable production was pretty much automatic after all their previous success. "Something Better to Do" might not be among her biggest hits, but the class and style the Newton-John/Farrar team brought to the table—a prime example being this title—was very well-crafted pop and set the stage for the movie soundtracks down the road, which would bring her back to chart dominance. The transition from the Linda Ronstadt soft rock of "Summertime Blues" to the harmonica-laden "Just a Lot of Folk (The Marshmallow Song)" had Newton-John covering all the bases. Very pleasant, inoffensive, and able to put the listener in a good mood, *Clearly Love* is a nice addition to Newton-John's collection. —*Joe Viglione*

Come on Over / Mar. 1976 / MCA ✦✦✦
Olivia Newton-John's *Come on Over* is country tunes, folk ballads, and more. Her own arrangement and adaptation of the traditional "Greensleeves" is exquisite, haunting, and shows Newton-John is more than just a pretty face. Her hit catalog was already nine songs deep, and "Come on Over" was the tenth of close to 30 visits to the Top 40 in a 14-year period. Fred Rose's "Blue Eyes Crying in the Rain" and a cover of Dolly Parton's classic "Jolene" open and shut side one with the country side of things while the Diane Berglund/Jim Phillips composition "Pony Ride" is more of a piano ballad, nicely bridging the Western music with the song which would go to the top of the adult contemporary charts, the brilliant title track written by Barry Gibb and Robin Gibb of the Bee Gees. "Come on Over" came right on the heels of one of the Bee Gees' most brilliant compositions, "Fanny (Be Tender With My Love)," charting just three months prior to "Come on Over." What this record becomes is a textbook on the separation between what is good and what is great. The album is quality stuff through and through, but even a good reading of a Beatles classic like "The Long and Winding Road" pales next to the majesty of John Farrar's simple production and Olivia's direct and heart-wrenching vocal on the title track. It is so moving that every other performance becomes a supporting act to the main attraction. It is also the only song that charted on the Top 40 from this consistent and entertaining project. "It'll Be Me" is the next best thing to "Come on Over," a Hank Marvin/John Farrar composition showing Newton-John's relationship to Cliff Richard's Shadows, drummer Brian Bennett providing the backbeat. Cliff Richard had his biggest U.S. success up to this point in time with "Devil Woman" as this record was charting simultaneously. It would be four years until Olivia and Cliff's duet "Suddenly," from the *Xanadu* soundtrack, made its splash. "Don't Throw It All Away" and "Who Are You Now?" are beautiful middle of the road performances here, and Farrar's production is really understated and sadly underrated. His grasp of the pop format is major league and worthy of note. Farrar's "Small Talk and Pride" and Harlan Collins' "Wrap Me in Your Arms" are elegant and perfect in their construction. Olivia Newton-John was a superstar before Mariah Carey and Celine Dion, and as beautiful as those pop divas can sing, it is John Farrar's understanding of his artist which makes these albums by Olivia so heartfelt and magical. "Come on Over" is a tremendous song on a very good album. More than just the Bee Gees meets the Shadows featuring Olivia Newton-John, *Come on Over* is a true pop classic. —*Joe Viglione*

Don't Stop Believin' / Oct. 1976 / MCA ✦✦
The 1976 edition of Olivia Newton-John continues the positive vibe that *Have You Never Been Mellow* initiated, and though the title track hit number one on the adult contemporary charts, it, surprisingly, failed to go higher than Top 30 pop. A shame because exactly five years later a different song with the exact same title and sentiment went Top Ten for Journey; the comparison is appropriate because *Don't Stop Believin'* is one of the slickest of Newton-John's country-pop releases. Despite the extra gloss producer John Farrar put on this, it still retains some of the warmth of earlier Newton-John projects while making that inevitable pitch to the '70s record buying public. "New Born Babe" contains elegant musicianship, while Bruce Welch's "Hey Mr. Dreammaker" is bouncy country—the antithesis of Gary Wright's "Dream Weaver," which was released, not so coincidentally, the same year. That Gary Wright, Olivia Newton-John, and Journey influenced each other's works, even if just thematically, says something about that period in music, but the real oddity here is Chris Christian showing up co-writing "Compassionate Man" with producer Farrar. The highly touted Christian pop singer was supposed to cross over as big as Christopher Cross, but made hardly a dent in the pop consciousness of the time. Like his career, the contribution here is not going to overwhelm anyone, though it's not bad either. The Don Black/Hank Marvin/John Farrar composition "Sam" works much better, and hit the Top 20, as well as gaining number-one adult contemporary status, in early 1977. Despite the silly rhyme à la Elton's John's plane & Spain in "Daniel," "Sam" (you know where I am) boasts a gorgeous conclusion with soaring music that drove it

higher on the pop charts. That Olivia didn't cover more Marvin, Welch & Farrar is a mystery, though 60 percent of *Don't Stop Believin'* is comprised of a song written by one or more of that trio, a unique incident and worthy of note. That she and Cliff Richard only had one duet that was a hit, four years after this release, is a pity. So many individuals involved in her music came from Cliff Richard & the Shadows, which created an opportunity for this album to be more than it is. As the new wave was breaking, this highly commercial artist would have been viewed as more hip, broadening her appeal, had she embraced her Cliff Richard & the Shadows heritage. Nonetheless, the title track, like the song "Come on Over," which preceded it by five months, is one of her best moments, and as "Come on Over" should have had a lengthier stay at the top of the charts, the same goes for "Don't Stop Believin'." Both "Magic" and the song "Physical" accomplished what these songs should have—sustained dominance of the pop charts. They came from albums that were even more slickly produced than this. *Don't Stop Believin'* is almost the mid-point in her chart reign, the 11th and 12th out of 28 Top 40 hits, and it is a transition period, as the soundtrack phase of her career kicked in after this. —*Joe Viglione*

Making a Good Thing Better / 1977 / MCA ✦✦
Newton-John has actually made a good thing blander on her 1977 release, in which she milks her tender innocence and soft vocals until all that is left is a drought-driven yearning for substance. She would later learn the rules of rock on *Grease* and *Physical*, but here she makes you suffer through an array of drippy ballads and folk music. "Don't Cry for Me Argentina" has been turned from soaring death-bed proclamation to bone-thin ballad. It is rare that a musical artist of Newton-John's stature would turn out an album that is completely bad, and indeed there are still some songs that make a showcase for her. Johnny Cash admirers will probably cringe at her version of "Ring of Fire," but it is great fun. "I Think I'll Say Goodbye" is upbeat country-pop in tradition of her hit "If You Love Me Let Me Know." Newton-John, whose voice is overtly feminine, works best with songs that are raw and untamed. It does not mean she should keep away from ballads, but on this selection of monotonously low-key ballads, she would at least benefit from less whimpering. —*Peter Fawthrop*

Totally Hot / Nov. 1978 / MCA ✦✦✦✦

Physical / Oct. 1981 / MCA ✦✦✦✦✦

Soul Kiss / Oct. 1985 / MCA ✦✦✦

The Rumour / 1988 / MCA ✦✦

Warm and Tender / 1989 / David Geffen Co. ✦✦✦

● **Magic: The Best of Olivia Newton-John** / Sep. 11, 2001 / UTV ✦✦✦✦✦
UTV Records' *Magic: The Very Best of Olivia Newton-John* is the best compilation ever assembled on Newton-John's career, largely because it does cover her entire career, hitting every major point from her early-'70s soft country-pop hits, like "I Honestly Love You," through her star-making turn in *Grease*, selections from *Xanadu*, up to the *Physical* era and its fallout. That takes a total of 20 tracks, plus the bonus track of "The Grease Megamix," and that gives a listener nearly everything they need from Olivia. When the biggest complaint is that the collection sequences "You're the One That I Want" before "Summer Nights," it means that this is certainly a collection that can be called definitive. —*Stephen Thomas Erlewine*

20th Century Masters—The Millennium Collection: The Best of Olivia Newton-John / Feb. 5, 2002 / Hip-O ✦✦✦
Olivia Newton-John scored 15 Top Ten pop hits between 1973 and 1983; ten of them are included on this 12-track midline-priced best-of, along with a couple of Top 20 hits from the same period. Personal taste (perhaps Newton-John's own, since she served as executive producer) may have governed the choice of selections, but the Newton-John fan nevertheless is likely to be disappointed by the absence of four gold or platinum singles, among them the *Grease* duets with John Travolta, "You're the One That I Want" and "Summer Nights." The singer's development from a country-pop singer on songs like "Let Me Be There" to a dance diva on "Physical" is traced in nearly chronological order through her hits over a decade, so the album does provide a *précis* of her recording career. But fans are likely to want to plump for a more complete hits collection than this one. —*William Ruhlmann*

Joe Nichols

b. Rogers, AR
Vocals, Guitar / Neo-Traditionalist Country, Contemporary Country, Americana
Joe Nichols took the roundabout way to country success, scoring his first major hit six years after landing his initial record deal. A native of Rogers, AR, Nichols grew up watching his father play bass in a local country band. He himself played in a rock band during his teenage years but soon came back to country and after high-school took a night job as a DJ while supporting himself as a mechanic by day. He met producer Randy Edwards at the latter job, and under Edwards' guidance, he performed regularly and worked on his songwriting. He landed a record deal with Intersound and released his self-titled debut in 1996, naturally with Edwards producing. The single "Six of One, Half a Dozen (Of the Other)" was a minor hit, but the album didn't sell particularly well. It did manage to earn Nichols a shot with Warner Bros., but a series of label mergers left him out in the cold, and he worked a series of day jobs around Nashville while looking for a new deal.

In 2000, he struck up a songwriting partnership with session guitarist Brent Rowan, and two years later he signed with Universal. His label debut, *Man With a Memory*, was released in 2002, and its lead single, the ballad "The Impossible," went to number three on the country charts, also crossing over to the pop Top 30. In the wake of its success, his first album was reissued under the title *Six of One, Half Dozen of the Other*. Another single from *Man With a Memory*, "Brokenheartsville," became Nichols' first number-one country hit in early 2003, which helped send the album into the country Top Ten. —*Steve Huey*

● **Joe Nichols** / 1996 / Intersound ◆◆◆

Man With a Memory / Jul. 23, 2002 / Universal ◆◆◆

From the looks of him —long, unkempt hair and wrinkled jeans jacket over a black T-shirt—on the cover of his major-label debut, *Man With a Memory*, you might expect that Joe Nichols aspires to be the next Kris Kristofferson-style Nashville rebel. Appearances can be deceiving, however. Nichols may look like a slacker, but if his music were accurately represented in his coiffure and wardrobe, he'd have razor-cut, blown-dry locks tucked under a cowboy hat. Vocally, he sounds like Alan Jackson trying to make like George Jones, and he sings formula Nashville country songs played by the usual suspects among Music City's session players. The album's lead single, typically released months ahead of the album and slowly climbing the charts when it appeared, is "The Impossible," an unfortunate piece of confused country philosophy about how supposedly impossible things happen. In the first verse, the narrator's apparently invincible father turns out to be able to feel pain after all; in the second a paralyzed friend learns to walk. The unfortunate part is that the chorus inescapably evokes September 11 ("Sometimes the things you think would never happen/Happen just like that"), which is in very bad taste, especially when the song comes to its real point, as the narrator concludes that maybe his girlfriend will come back. Most of the other songs range from barroom weepers ("She Only Smokes When She Drinks" is a virtual rewrite of the John Anderson hit "Straight Tequila Night") to bland expressions of romantic devotion. Tom T. Hall's "Life Don't Have to Mean Nothing at All" is a welcome respite from the mediocrity, but it's only one song. Nichols may make it to country stardom, especially if he cleans up his appearance, but his first major-label effort doesn't make that an appealing prospect. — *William Ruhlmann*

Nickel Creek

f. 1989, San Diego, CA

Group / Contemporary Bluegrass, Contemporary Country, Singer/Songwriter, Bluegrass

Distinguished by their youth and eclectic taste, Nickel Creek became a word-of-mouth sensation on the progressive bluegrass scene and soon found their appeal spreading beyond the genre's core audience. Guitarist Sean Watkins, fiddler Sara Watkins (his younger sister), and mandolin/banjo/bouzouki player Chris Thile first started performing together in 1989, when all three were preteens and taking music lessons in their native San Diego. They met while watching the local band Bluegrass Etc., which put on weekly performances in a pizza parlor. A bluegrass promoter liked the idea of such a young band, and thus Nickel Creek was formed, with Thile's father Scott joining them on bass. Nickel Creek were regulars on the festival circuit through most of the '90s, and during that time, Thile recorded two solo albums, 1994's *Leading Off . . .* and 1997's *Stealing Second*.

In 1998, with help from Alison Krauss, Nickel Creek landed a record deal with the roots-music label Sugar Hill. Krauss produced their self-titled debut album, which was released in 2000; with the kids apparently all right, Scott subsequently retired from the band. Though it was decidedly a bluegrass record, *Nickel Creek* boasted elements of classical, jazz, and rock & roll both classic and alternative; naturally, the influence of progressive bluegrass figures like Krauss, Edgar Meyer, and Béla Fleck was also apparent. Perhaps aided by the success of *O Brother, Where Art Thou?*, which brought traditional roots music to a whole new collegiate audience, *Nickel Creek* became a slow-building hit; by early 2002, it had gone gold, climbed into the country Top 20, and earned a Grammy nomination for Best Bluegrass Album. Meanwhile, Sean released his solo debut, *Let It Fall*, in 2001, and Thile followed suit with *Not All Who Wander Are Lost*. Nickel Creek released their sophomore set, *This Side*, in 2002; it debuted in the Top 20 of the pop charts and went all the way to number two on the country listings. Even more eclectic than its predecessor, the Krauss-produced album turned indie rock fans' heads with a cover of Pavement's "Spit on a Stranger." *This Side* won a Grammy for Best Contemporary Folk Album in early 2003, after which Sean issued his second solo album, *26 Miles*. — *Steve Huey*

● **Nickel Creek** / Mar. 21, 2000 / Sugar Hill ◆◆◆◆◆

Few artists will offer the story of a lighthouse, sung in the first person, but Nickel Creek has a flair for the unusual. "The Lighthouse's Tale," is but one of a dozen good reasons to enjoy this self-titled release. Produced by Alison Krauss, it features an eclectic collection of material, original and borrowed. Highlights include the instrumentals "Ode to a Butterfly," "Robin and Marian," and "Pastures New." Perhaps most striking, though, are the evocative vocals, particularly on "Out of the Woods" and the band's cover of "When You Come Back Down" written by Tim O'Brien and Danny O'Keefe. Nickel Creek, the group and album, are altogether exhilarating. — *Bill Ashford*

This Side / Aug. 13, 2002 / Sugar Hill ◆◆◆◆◆

This Side, Nickel Creek's sophomore release, finds bandmembers Chris Thile, Sara Watkins, and Sean Watkins out of their teens and into their 20s after playing together for 12 years. The southern California band's self-titled debut received wide critical acclaim for welding jazz, rock, and classical music to a bluegrass base. But *This Side* solidifies Nickel Creek's position as the single most original and inventive bluegrass band to emerge in the early '00s. Hardcore bluegrass fans wary of experimentation or even progressive bluegrass may scoff at this claim. But, when it comes down to it, the gorgeous, open production by Alison Krauss gives Nickel Creek's guitars, mandolins, and fiddles the space to dance through sparkling and genuine arrangements. Covers of everything from Pavement's rollicking *Terror Twilight* highlight, "Spit on a Stranger," to Carrie Newcomer's scathing folk "Should've Known Better" to the traditional "House Carpenter" are given elegant and unique twists. Plus, Thile and the Watkins siblings' originals, like the sleepy, subtle "Speak" and the darker "Beauty and the Mess," easily outdo the likes of folk-rockers Dave Matthews and Hootie & the Blowfish, while forging a new style to rejuvenate a genre that has always been a bit of a dark horse. It's decidedly more pop than post-rock-gone-folk outfits like Papa M, David Grubbs, Palace, and Miighty Flashlight,

and lacks the rock & roll flash of Ryan Adams. But Nickel Creek's music is endlessly rewarding nonetheless, and accessible to just about everyone. — *Charles Spano*

The Nitty Gritty Dirt Band

f. 1965, Long Beach, CA

Group / Progressive Bluegrass, Progressive Country, Country-Rock

Founded in California during 1965, the Nitty Gritty Dirt Band has lasted longer than virtually any other country-based rock group of their era. Younger contemporaries of the Byrds, they played an almost equally important role in the transformation from folk-rock into country-rock, and were an influence on such bands as the Eagles and Alabama. The Nitty Gritty Dirt Band's beginnings lay with the New Coast Two, a folk duo consisting of Jeff Hanna (guitar, vocals) and Bruce Kunkel (guitar, washtub bass), formed while both were in high-school in the early '60s. By the time the duo were college students, they were having informal jams at a Santa Monica, CA, guitar shop called McCabe's. It was there that they met Ralph Barr (guitar, washtub bass), Les Thompson (vocals, mandolin, bass, guitar, banjo, percussion), Jimmie Fadden (harmonica, vocals, drums, percussion), and Jackson Browne (guitar, vocals).

This lineup became the Nitty Gritty Dirt Band in late 1965, and began playing jug band music at local clubs. At that time, southern California was undergoing a musical renaissance, courtesy of the folk-rock movement, and the Nitty Gritty Dirt Band fit in with these other folkies-turned-rockers. Browne left after a few months to pursue a solo career, and was replaced by John McEuen (banjo, fiddle, mandolin, steel guitar, vocals), the younger brother of the group's new manager, Bill McEuen. With Bill McEuen's guidance, the group landed a recording contract with Liberty Records and released their debut album, *The Nitty Gritty Dirt Band*, in April of 1967. Their first single, "Buy for Me the Rain," became a modest hit and got the band some television appearances.

A second album, *Ricochet*, released seven months later, was a critical success but a commercial failure. The group now found itself at an impasse over the issue of whether to go electric. During the dispute, Kunkel, who wanted to add an electric guitar to their sound, exited the lineup. He was replaced by Chris Darrow (guitar, fiddle). Ironically, by mid-1968 the group had gone electric, and also added drums to their sound. Their first electric album, *Rare Junk*, released in June of 1968, was also a commercial failure. The band was barely working, a far cry from their success of a year earlier. The band persevered, however, and released *Alive!* in May of 1969. The album was another commercial disaster, and the Nitty Gritty Dirt Band closed up shop soon after.

The members scattered for several months, but six months later the group was back for another try; the new lineup included McEuen, Hanna, Fadden, Thompson, and Jim Ibbotson (guitars, accordion, drums, percussion, piano, vocals). They returned to their record company with a demand for control over their recordings and the record company agreed. Bill McEuen became the group's producer as well as its manager. The first result of this new era in the Nitty Gritty Dirt Band's history was *Uncle Charlie & His Dog Teddy*, issued in 1970. Rooted tightly in their jug band sound, the album had a country feel but no trace of the vaudeville and novelty numbers that had appeared on their earlier records. The album yielded what is the group's best-known single, their cover of Jerry Jeff Walker's "Mr. Bojangles," and suddenly, the band had a following bigger than anything they'd known during their brief bout of success in 1967. Their next album, *All the Good Times*, released in early 1972, had an even more countrified feel.

By 1972, several rock bands, most notably the Byrds and the Beau Brummels, had gone to Nashville seeking credibility from the country music community there, only to be received poorly by that community and to have their resulting work ignored by the press and public. At the suggestion of manager Bill McEuen, however, the Nitty Gritty Dirt Band went to Nashville in 1972 and recorded a selection of traditional country numbers with the likes of Roy Acuff, Earl Scruggs, Mother Maybelle Carter, and other members of country and bluegrass music's veteran elite. Some of the veteran Nashville stars were skeptical and suspicious at first of the bandmembers and their amplified instruments, but the ice was broken when they saw how respectful the band was toward them and their work, and their music, as well as how serious they were about their own music. The resulting triple album, *Will the Circle Be Unbroken*, released in January of 1973, became a million-seller and elicited positive reviews from both the rock and country music press. The band had, by now, eclipsed the competition as a "crossover" act, reaching country and bluegrass audiences even as their rock listeners acquired a new appreciation for musicians such as Acuff and Carter. The Nitty Gritty Dirt Band succeeded with *Will the Circle Be Unbroken* because they were willing to meet country and bluegrass music on the terms of those two branches of traditional music, rather than as rock musicians.

During the year and a half that followed the success of *Will the Circle Be Unbroken*, Les Thompson left the group, reducing the Dirt Band to a quartet. Their next album, *Stars & Stripes Forever*, issued in the summer of 1974, was a peculiar live album, mixing concert performances and dialogue. Following one more original album, *Dream* (1975), the group received its first retrospective treatment, a triple-LP compilation entitled *Dirt, Silver & Gold*, issued late in 1976. Jim Ibbotson left the lineup at around this time, and was replaced initially by session player Bob Carpenter. The remaining trio of Jeff Hanna, John McEuen, and Jimmie Fadden shortened the band's official name to the Dirt Band. In this incarnation, the group became a much more mainstream, pop/rock outfit with a smoother sound, with Jeff Hanna guiding them as producer. Their records were far less eccentric, although they continued to be popular. The band's next albums were decidedly more laid-back than previous records, and didn't attract nearly as much attention. *American Dream*, released in 1980, did relatively well, as did *Make a Little Magic* (1981). By 1982, however, they were back to their country roots, renamed the Nitty Gritty Dirt Band, and Jim Ibbotson was playing with them again. *Let's Go*, released in the middle of 1983, heralded their return to country music, as a largely acoustic band. In 1984, after 17 years with Liberty/UA/Capitol, they switched labels to Warner Bros., and that same year made some headlines as the first American rock band to tour the Soviet Union. Their Warner albums sold well, but by the end of the 1980s the group was moving between labels.

In 1989, both as a reflection of the changing times, and as though to make sure that everyone got the point that the band was once again mining its country roots, they made

Will the Circle Be Unbroken, Vol. 2 for MCA/Universal Records, reuniting with surviving country and bluegrass veterans from the original album and adding a whole roster of new players, including Johnny Cash, Chris Hillman, and Ricky Skaggs. This album won the Grammy for Best Country Vocal Performance (duo or group) and the Country Music Association's Album of the Year Award in 1989. By this time, the Dirt Band was working in their field alongside any number of country/bluegrass crossover artists whose career paths were made easier by that first record, including John Hiatt, Mary-Chapin Carpenter, and Rosanne Cash. Their next several albums saw them never veering very far from their country/bluegrass roots. The group continued to record a new album every year or so, including a concert album, *Live Two Five*, celebrating their 25th anniversary as a band, and the self-explanatory *Acoustic*. In 1999, they returned with *Bang Bang Bang*. *—Bruce Eder*

The Nitty Gritty Dirt Band / 1967 / Liberty ✦✦✦

A strong debut album by one of the most offbeat folk/country-rock bands of the 1960s, the Nitty Gritty Dirt Band. Apart from the one unabashed classic, "Buy for Me the Rain," which was a modest hit and the group's biggest claim to musical fame for the next three years, the album also contained the delightful banjo-dominated John McEuen/Bill McEuen instrumental "Dismal Swamp" (which was anything but dismal), the Jackson Browne ballad "Holding," the rousing "You're Gonna Get It in the End," and Bruce Kunkel's haunting, ethereal "Song to Jutta" (as fine a song as anything the Byrds were doing at the time, and better played). In those days, the band wasn't too far removed from the sound of the early Grateful Dead or the Charlatans, but as this album reveals, drugs played less of a role in their music-making than humor, and some of the material was a little too comedic—Rev. Gary Davis' "Candy Man," for example, comes off more upbeat than blues covers were supposed to be in those days, and may have *seemed* a little too much like a minstrel show interpretation (though one suspects Davis would have loved it), in a time when white versions of such songs were supposed to be either heavily electrified or reverent to the point of being somber. *—Bruce Eder*

Ricochet / 1967 / BGO ✦✦✦✦

The Nitty Gritty Dirt Band's second album is a masterpiece. From the opening bars of Jackson Browne's "Shadow Dream Song," the high spirits overflow the grooves (or ones and zeros, on the CD) of the record. The singing and playing are more confident, and some of the songs—including the bluesy "Ooh Po Pe Do Girl" and the hook-laden "I'll Search The Sky" by Jeff Hanna, and Copeland & Noonan's (the "Buy for Me the Rain" team) "Tide of Love"—are as solid as anything coming out of California. Even the kazoo-dominated "Coney Island Washboard" and "Happy Fat Annie" and the nostalgic '20s-styled Jackson Browne-written "It's Raining Here in Long Beach" fit well into the mix, reflecting the full range of the band's influences. As to why this record never caught on, it could be the timing—released late in 1967, in the wake of *Sergeant Pepper* (which had its own musichall influences, albeit of the English variety, and covered with lots of psychedelic overdubbing) and the Summer of Love, it just wasn't what college kids starting their search for the Lost Chord were looking for. Maybe a kazoo or two less would've helped, and a real drug song or two wouldn't have hurt, but these guys would play a jug band number ahead of a drug anthem anytime. Their cover of Brewer & Shipley's "Truly Right" is pretty spacy in its production, though, but "The Teddy Bear's Picnic"—an adaptation of an old children's song—was probably beyond the pale of most listeners. Beyond NGDB completists, anyone looking for a companion to *Notorious Byrd Bros.* or the Monkees' *Aquarius, Capricorn Pisces & Jones Ltd.*, or a precursor to Crazy Horse's *At Crooked Lake*, need look no further. (British import) *—Bruce Eder*

Rare Junk / 1968 / Liberty ✦✦✦✦

This, the group's third album release, was actually an odds-and-sods type compilation of leftover tracks and singles that formed a respectable ten-song, 30-minute plus LP. As a sign of just how strong the band was, it still represented a step forward from their second album, and is one of the great unknown albums of 1968. *—Bruce Eder*

Pure Dirt / 1968 / BGO ✦✦✦✦

The group's first compilation album, made up of six songs from the first album and eight from *Ricochet*, assembled and released by Liberty Records in England (where neither of the original albums had appeared). A fair representation of the original Nitty Gritty Dirt Band, though serious fans would be more advised to pick up the complete albums. "Buy For Me the Rain" is here, along with some of the more rousing cuts off of the first LP. (British import) *—Bruce Eder*

Alive! / 1969 / Liberty ✦✦✦✦

How many live albums—forget decent ones—were left behind by bands in 1967/1968? This is one, and it's better than decent, and almost a gift from heaven, capturing an early incarnation of the group (circa 1967) on a good night at the L.A. *Troubadour*. Someone has earned a place in musical heaven for seeing to recording the show. *—Bruce Eder*

Uncle Charlie & His Dog Teddy / 1970 / Liberty ✦✦✦✦

The first album issued by the Nitty Gritty Dirt Band after they had temporarily disbanded in 1969, this greatly expanded their pop audience, due primarily to the Top Ten hit cover of Jerry Jeff Walker's "Mr. Bojangles" (which actually wasn't a hit until early 1971). The group moved into a more accessible rock-oriented fusion of country, bluegrass, pop, and rock & roll, relying primarily on smartly chosen covers of tunes by the likes of Walker, Mike Nesmith, Randy Newman, and Kenny Loggins. Few bands had incorporated instruments more commonly associated with country and bluegrass, particularly mandolin and banjo, as comfortably into a rock setting prior to this release, and their well-crafted harmonies help put the songs over for those not-steeped-in backwoods sounds. It was an extremely diverse program for a country-rock album, too, moving from rustic instrumentals and snippets of tapes of elderly musicians performing rural Americana to the Buddy Holly cover "Rave On." The group were actually at their best, though, when doing softer, melodic pop tunes. "Mr. Bojangles" was a deserved huge success in that regard, but Nesmith's "Some of Shelley's Blues" and Loggins' "House at Pooh Corner" were almost as catchy and appealing. *—Richie Unterberger*

★ **Will the Circle Be Unbroken** / 1972 / EMI America ✦✦✦✦✦

With all due respect to the Byrds and the Flying Burrito Brothers, it took the Nitty Gritty Dirt Band with this album to come up with a merger of rock and country music that worked for both sides and everyone involved. The opening number, "The Grand Ole Opry Song," set the tone for the album, showing that this band—for all of their origins in rock and popular music—was willing to meet country music on its terms, rather than as a vehicle for embellishment as rock music. The result, without a false or strained note anywhere among its 37 songs, was an all-star country project that worked (and transcended its country and rock origins), with the Nitty Gritty Dirt Band serving as catalyst and intersecting point for all of the talent involved, all of who gave superbly of themselves. Not only did this album result in new exposure to a new and wider audience for the likes of Mother Maybelle Carter, Roy Acuff, Earl Scruggs, Merle Travis, and others, but this was the first real country album that a lot of rock listeners under the age of 30 ever heard. Thus, it opened up pathways and dialogue in all directions, across several generations and cultural barriers; the dialogue between Doc Watson and Merle Travis alone was almost worth the price of admission. This was also one of rock's very few multi-disc sets to be fully justified in its length and content; at a time when unnecessary double LPs were all the rage, the Nitty Gritty Dirt Band and company gave a triple album that, if anything, left audiences asking for more. [The 2002 CD adds four bonus tracks, though only "Foggy Mountain Breakdown" is a proper song; two of the others consist of warmups and studio chat, while "Remember Me" (featuring Doc Watson) is just a fragment.] *—Bruce Eder*

Stars & Stripes Forever / 1974 / Capitol ✦✦✦✦✦

In many ways, the mixed collection of live and studio recordings on *Stars & Stripes Forever* accomplished for the Nitty Gritty Dirt Band and rock music what *Sweetheart of the Rodeo* failed to do for or with the Byrds, showing the rock band plunging deeply into country music. Two years in the making, it incorporated new studio cuts and live tracks recorded at five concerts over a two-year period, as well as interview material with guest fiddle player Vassar Clements. The mix works better than just about any genuine country (as opposed to country-rock) effort ever done by a rock band, mostly because the band was so careful in their recording and editing, and they gave themselves time to get this stuff just the way they wanted it. Beyond the excellent concert renditions of "Mr. Bojangles" or "The Battle of New Orleans" (which became a single in the wake of this album), and covers of Hank Williams songs and numerous traditional tunes, listeners found they'd walked in on something very deep and profound, tapping into a special creative process. Whatever the reason, this album gave the public more than its money's worth and was a success, charting higher than any other record the group ever released. It still packs lots of power. *—Bruce Eder*

Dream / 1975 / United Artists ✦✦✦

The Nitty Gritty Dirt Band's first pure studio recording since *Will the Circle Be Unbroken*, *Dream* is another very different earful sort of psychedelic country/bluegrass. The band is joined by Linda Ronstadt, Leon Russell, and actor Gary Busey (as "Teddy Jack Eddy," and on drums). The sound is more varied than on previous albums, with a harder electric country feel on "Bayou Jubilee," which segues directly into the bluegrass instrumental "Sally Was a Goodun." Ronstadt does a great job singing "Hey Good Lookin'," but mostly it's the Dirt Band singing, including a superb rendition of "(All I Have to Do Is) Dream." The group had previously released a fun live rendition of Jimmie Driftwood's "The Battle of New Orleans," and they cover it here in a somewhat funkier studio version. John McEuen also offers a taste of some of the sounds he'd later explore more fully on his solo releases with "Classical Banjo I/Malaguena/Classical Banjo II." They offer a non-country instrumental, "Sleeping on the Beach," which could have come from a '50s mood instrumental album—of course, they follow it up with William McEuen's carnival music-inspired "Santa Monica Pier," which segues into the gorgeous lost single "Ripplin' Waters," by Jim Ibbotson, one of two hits that should have been off this album (the other is Ken Edwards' "Mother of Love"). The disc ends with William McEuen's wind harp instrumental and a music-box piece called "Symphonion Montage." *—Bruce Eder*

Dirt, Silver & Gold / 1976 / One Way ✦✦✦✦✦

The 37 songs here were originally on three LPs (now two CDs), and this remains the biggest anthology ever done on the NGDB. As is usual with such collections, the group's early history is represented by only five songs, one of which is (of course) "Buy for Me the Rain." A lot of the rest will be familiar to people who came in after *Uncle Charlie & His Dog Teddy*, but in lieu of owning all of those subsequent albums (though why anyone would want to pass up owning *Will the Circle Be Unbroken* is beyond this writer's ability to understand), this is a handy assembly of songs, covering their output up through 1976 and the album *Dream*. *The Best of the Nitty Gritty Dirt Band* from EMI has fewer songs, but it does have notes, which this was (and is still) sorely lacking, despite the presence of a list showing some of the different lineups of the NGDB. *—Bruce Eder*

Dirt Band / 1978 / United Artists ✦✦✦

Shortly after compiling the retrospective *Dirt, Silver & Gold*, the Nitty Gritty Dirt Band was shrunk to a trio of Jeff Hanna, John McEuen, and Jimmie Fadden, who seized the opportunity to draft in new members and take a stab at the commercial country-rock of their Californian brethren. Sensing that this was the start of a new era, they also decided to lop off "Nitty Gritty" from their name, which was appropriate, since as 1978's *The Dirt Band* illustrated, they were no longer nitty nor gritty. They were a smooth, slick outfit with an eye on the charts. Occasionally, they hauled out banjos for an instrumental jam, but this was a mellow soft rock record, and as such, it was excoriated by their fans who cherished the group's freewheeling roots music, something that already seems a distant memory due to polish of this music. And, it's true—anybody looking for something like

Will the Circle Be Unbroken will be heartbroken. That said, *The Dirt Band* is really good within its chosen milieu, stumbling only when it tries to hearken back to the group's nitty, gritty roots. The production is sleek and stylish, perfectly suiting midtempo songs like "In for the Night," "For a Little While," and "Whoa Babe" as well as softer ballads like "Wild Nights," "Escaping Reality," and the lovely "You Can't Stop Loving Me Now." These are all attributes that will not matter to those appalled that the band took this detour in the late '70s, but to those who like Californian soft rock, this, and its successor *American Dream*, are overlooked minor gems. —*Stephen Thomas Erlewine*

American Dream / 1979 / United Artists ✦✦✦
Any Nitty Gritty Dirt Band fan who thought the smooth soft rock of 1978's *The Dirt Band* was a fluke was proven wrong by the following year's *American Dream*, which took the template of its predecessor and improved it with a streamlined production and some very strong material. Chief among these, of course, was the title song, a winningly polished take on Rodney Crowell's clever "American Dream" that became a hit, climbing all the way to 13 on the pop charts and thereby establishing the band in the public's eyes as the soft rock act they'd become. It's a brilliant single, one of the best Californian soft rock songs of its era, and *American Dream* the album delivers at least on the level of sound—sonically, it's a sleek and appealing collection of midtempo pop songs, ballads, and lazy jams. It's the latter that hurt the momentum of the album; although the instrumental "Jas'moon" works better than "White Russian" on *The Dirt Band*, there are some really silly good-time numbers—"New Orleans," "Happy Feet"—that deflate the mellow vibe of the record (as does the reggae-fied cover of "Wolverton Mountain" that closes the LP on a sour note). Though these are stumbles, they don't hurt the record, since the rest of *American Dream* glides by on its smooth surfaces—all electric pianos, slick guitars, saxophones, and glistening polish—and songs as light but appealing as "In Her Eyes," "Take Me Back," "Dance the Night Away," "Do You Feel the Way That I Do," and "What's on Your Mind." This won't win over the fans lost on *The Dirt Band*—it would be some time before they returned to the progressive country that made their reputation—but this is another small late-'70s soft rock gem. —*Stephen Thomas Erlewine*

Make a Little Magic / 1980 / United Artists ✦✦

Jealousy / 1981 / Liberty ✦✦

Plain Dirt Fashion / 1984 / Warner Bros. ✦✦
While this is a nice-sounding album, there is really nothing here to distinguish it from Poco, the Eagles, or any of the other country-rock bands making records throughout the late '70s and early '80s. —*Jim Worbois*

Twenty Years of Dirt: The Best of the Nitty Gritty Dirt Band / 1986 / Warner Bros. ✦✦✦✦✦
Representing the band's most lucrative years, *Twenty Years of Dirt* is a collection of hits from the Nitty Gritty Dirt Band's late-'70s to mid-'80s era, with tracks from 1979's *American Dream*, 1984's *Plain Dirt Fashion*, and 1985's *Partners, Brothers, and Friends*, among others. Songs like Jerry Jeff Walker's "Mr. Bojangles," which gave them their only Top Ten hit, and the soothing vocal stylings of the Jimmy Buffet-like "American Dream" showcase the group's country-rock finesse. While "American Dream" has Linda Ronstadt helping out on vocals, "Make a Little Magic" utilized Nicolette Larson's sweet-sounding voice. "High Horse" is dominated with an old country sound, led by jangly guitar strumming and quick singing, and "Dance Little Jean" pulls firmly at the heartstrings, making it a country radio mainstay. With such a lengthy career and numerous personnel changes since their formation in 1966, *Twenty Years of Dirt* in no way sums up the lifespan of the band, but it does do a good job at bunching their best commercial years onto one album. —*Mike DeGagne*

Workin' Band / Aug. 9, 1988 / Warner Bros. ✦✦✦
Much of the magic of the Nitty Gritty Dirt Band returned on *Workin' Band*. Switching labels and signing to Warner Bros., the group put a lot of effort into this disc and it shows. Perhaps the assistence of former Eagle Bernie Leadon helped gel their ideas, but by now, they had embraced country music with arms open wide, and the result was a fine effort from a veteran band. —*James Chrispell*

Will the Circle Be Unbroken, Vol. 2 / 1989 / Universal ✦✦✦
This easily won the Country Music Association's Album of the Year Award, thanks to a stellar cast that includes John Denver, Johnny Cash, the Carter Family, Bruce Hornsby, Ricky Skaggs, Chris Hillman, Roger McGuinn, Rosanne Cash, Steve Wariner, Roy Acuff, Chet Atkins…you get the message. Tracks were all recorded in one "take," with no over-dubs, making the outstanding musicianship particularly noteworthy. Atheists beware: there's a lot of gospel. —*Tom Roland*

More Great Dirt (Best, Vol. 2) / 1989 / Warner Bros. ✦✦✦✦✦
Tight harmonies and infectious arrangements are the staple of this compilation. "I've Been Lookin'," "Fishin' in the Dark," and "Baby's Got a Hold on Me" are the musical equivalent of a good book—you can't put 'em down. —*Tom Roland*

The Rest of the Dream / Jun. 26, 1991 / MCA ✦✦✦
This features "Wishing Well," "Hillbilly Hollywood," "Waitin' on a Dark-Eyed Gal," "From Small Things (Big Things One Day Come)," and other hits. —*AMG*

Live Two Five / Jul. 8, 1991 / Liberty ✦✦✦
Recorded during three shows at the Red Deer Fine Arts Center in Alberta, Canada, in 1991, *Live Two Five* contains a healthy portion of the band's significant hit output. Consisting mostly of faithful, slightly extended versions of their classic laid-back country-rock classics, only a meandering 11-minute "Ripplin' Waters" and a completely unnecessary harmonica instrumental on "Harpo" are significant low points. Of course, many of the songs eventually descend into bandmembers pandering for applause and crowd

singalongs, so this is aimed at the more avid fan. Still, there is more than enough to keep the casual fan interested. —*Matt Fink*

Acoustic / May 31, 1994 / Liberty ✦✦✦✦
A couple of years after the Nitty Gritty Dirt Band's string of country hits ended, the band returned to its roots to record this appropriately titled collection of original material. Most of the songs are very good, and the sound is refreshingly unadorned with any concessions to the soundalike country mainstream. Because the NDGB was among the many fine artists swept aside by the faceless hat acts and young country babes birthed by the Garth era, *Acoustic* never found a sizable audience. However, this blend of acoustic guitars, mandolin, dobro, harmonica, accordion, washboard and beautiful vocal harmonies delivers a bevy of country/folk delights. —*Jim Newsom*

Alive/Rare Junk / 1995 / BGO ✦✦✦✦✦
Two superb albums on one CD equal one must-own CD. The studio sides on *Rare Junk* include covers of the jazz standard "Willie the Weeper" (with its familiar "Hi de hi dee ho" chorus), "Collegiana" (done jug band style), "Cornbread and 'Lasses," Tim Hardin's "Reason to Believe," and Jackson Browne's "These Days" in one of its better (and surprisingly upbeat) versions. Some of this stuff is so self-conscious in its humor—"Sadie Green the Vamp of New Orleans" and "Dr. Heckle and Mr. Jibe" come to mind—that it's hard to believe that it was recorded with much confidence of success, but it works musically, capturing the vaudeville side of the band's orientation better than anything on their first two LPs. *Alive*, recorded at the L.A. Troubadour circa 1967, is one of the great live albums of its decade, capturing the early group in top form, clowning around in a loosely structured show that has them covering "Buy for Me the Rain" (which was already a hit), as well as B. B. King's "Rock Me Baby," the Reverend Gary Davis' "Candy Man" (in a version superior to the first album's studio cover), and Earl Scruggs' "Foggy Mountain Breakdown." It is a great set, the guitars, mandolins, and banjos glitter in the clarity of the recording; and it is an honest, fully representative show, complete with wrong notes, false starts, jokes that usually (but don't always) work, and the ten tracks are a vital addition to any folk-rock, country-rock, or even a partly serious NGDB fan's collection. —*Bruce Eder*

Bang Bang Bang / Apr. 21, 1999 / DreamWorks ✦✦✦
While it pales in comparison with their classic early '70s releases, *Bang Bang Bang* is far from being a lesser latter-day effort from the Nitty Gritty Dirt Band. The group are seasoned professionals, capable of making even second-rate material sound fine, which is fortunate since there's a little bit too much filler on the record. Nevertheless, it's a pleasure to hear the group play, and there are moments where they nearly recapture the magic of yesteryear, which may make the album worthwhile for dedicated fans. —*Thom Owens*

Dirt Band/An American Dream / Aug. 25, 1999 / BGO ✦✦✦
In 1999, BGO reissued the Nitty Gritty Dirt Band's 1978 and 1979 albums, *The Dirt Band* and *American Dream*, as a CD two-fer. These were the first two (of three) albums they recorded as the Dirt Band, which is what they renamed themselves when they were diminished to the trio of Jeff Hanna, John McEuen, and Jimmie Fadden, who rebuilt them as a Californian soft rock outfit. That's the key to these two albums—those who are too attached to the sound of *Will the Circle Be Unbroken* will find this too slick, but those who prefer Californian soft rock will be glad these two underappreciated records have finally made their way to CD. Neither record is perfect—the instrumentals don't quite work, for instance, and the boogie numbers on *American Dream* aren't great—but they're both very appealing, thanks to the highly polished, stylized production and a good set of songs highlighted by their hit version of Rodney Crowell's "An American Dream." The rest of these two records delivers on the promise of that single, so if you enjoyed the hit, this is certainly worth seeking out. —*Stephen Thomas Erlewine*

Will the Circle Be Unbroken, Vol. 3 / Oct. 1, 2002 / Capitol ✦✦✦✦
Like a comet that periodically returns and lights up the sky, the *Will the Circle Be Unbroken* series manages to be predictable and illuminating at the same time. Once again, the Nitty Gritty Dirt Band draws an assembly of deities and wannabes around the campfire. Some of these are familiar, though veterans from the first volume have grown scarce: Doc Watson plays "I Am a Pilgrim" as a tribute to the late Merle Travis, who cut the same tune on the 1972 Circle session. Jimmy Martin returns too, his galloping, almost-reckless delivery undimmed by the years. From the 1989 sequel comes Johnny Cash, whose "Tears in the Holston River" eulogizes Maybelle Carter, his mother-in-law and the soul of the first Circle. New faces take the place of those who have departed: Willie Nelson is a logical addition, though his duet partner, Tom Petty, sounds uncomfortable and awkward on "Goodnight, Irene." Emmylou Harris assumes her place in this pantheon, her voice breaking hearts even in harmony with Matraca Berg on "Oh, Cumberland." No performance stands out more than that of Taj Mahal, whose presence has a demographic significance and whose rollicking rendition of "Fishin' Blues" nearly steals the show. But Mahal also contributes to the album's only serious blemish: On the inevitable title cut, he and the other soloists play with a solemnity that deletes the song's communal energies. A congregational enthusiasm distinguished its performance on the first album; here, the singers—particularly Alison Krauss—pass it along, verse by verse, as if it were priceless china. This music is about soul, not trepidation, so it's to everyone's credit that such moments are scarce here. Let's hope that they don't dress it up with string samples or breakbeats once *Will the Circle Be Unbroken, Vol. 4* rolls around. —*Robert L. Doerschuk*

Terry Noland

Photography / Rock & Roll, Rockabilly
Of the assorted Texas rockabillies who plied their wares in Norman Petty's Clovis, NM, studio, the least heralded is Terry Noland. Much of this has to do with Noland jumping

ship early in the ball game from Petty's direction to head to New York City with teen stardom waiting in the wings. He cut sides there with *Tonight Show* musical director Milton DeLugg swinging the baton and little else, jumping from the back-to-back West Texas rockabilly sound of "Ten Little Women" and the title cut to lightweight pop fluff like "Puppy Love," "Teenage Teardrops," and "Let Me Be Your Hero." That Noland (real name Terry Noland Church) adapted well to this watered-down approach—even writing the majority of pop confections—has certainly diminished his rockabilly credentials in the eyes of most hardcore collectors. This is regrettable, simply because Noland laid down some incredible sides during his quest for the diamond ring and the solid gold Cadillac.

As is the case with many before and after him, his best stuff is also his earliest. But after jumping ship from Petty's Clovis rockabilly operation, his sound and style became increasingly watered down. After a few more singles and an album that went nowhere, Noland hung up his guitar. Returning back to Texas, he started dabbling in real estate, eventually moving to Oklahoma and becoming the largest and most successful land developer in that state. —*Cub Koda*

● **Hypnotized** / 1990 / Bear Family ✦✦✦✦✦
This single-disc compilation collects 28 tracks in all—including alternate takes—and is split almost evenly between his energetic rockabilly efforts and his later overproduced sides with strings and backing from the likes of the syrupy Anita Kerr Singers. The title track—heard here in both the master and a breathless, faster alternate take from the session that produced its flip, "Ten Little Women"—is West Texas rockabilly at its most energetic and rockin', yet imbued with a musicality that separates it from the rest of the pack. Using many of his fellow Lubbock teen band players in support and recruiting the Picks on backup vocals, the handful of sides Noland cut in Clovis have that unmistakable Crickets sound without either aping Buddy Holly or his all pervasive style. "Come Marry Me" from a 1957 session integrates the Picks into a seamless mix while still retaining the classic rockabilly style. The closest thing Noland had to a hit was another Clovis session that yielded "Patty Baby," with backing from a combo called the Big Beats featuring a young Trini Lopez on lead guitar. Also on board are two early tracks with Noland's first band, the Teenbeats, which featured Holly band alumni Joe B. Mauldin and Larry Welbourn. Their renditions of "Hound Dog" and Noland's "That Ain't Right" are taken from extremely worn acetates but are well worth the effort, as they further illuminate the rocking side of Noland's scant discography. —*Cub Koda*

Norma Jean (Norma Jean Beasler)

b. Jan. 30, 1938, Wellston, OK
Vocals / Traditional Country, Honky Tonk
"Pretty Miss Norma Jean" may be best-remembered as Porter Wagoner's stage partner before he was paired with Dolly Parton, but she was also well known for an often hard-edged group of songs that spoke of poverty, hard work, and the instability of romantic relationships. Although she didn't have the songwriting creativity of Loretta Lynn or Dolly Parton, she was comparable to those stars in her general outlook. Norma Jean Beasler was no stranger to poverty herself, born into a hard-working farm family near Wellston, OK. As a child, she wanted to be a country star like Kitty Wells, whom she tried to emulate. She made her professional debut singing "If Teardrops Were Pennies" at age 12 on the radio in Oklahoma City. In high-school, she toured with a few Western swing bands, including those of Billy Gray and Merle Lindsay.

Her big break came in 1958 when she became a cast member of the Springfield, MO-based ABC-TV show *Ozark Jubilee*, where Red Foley suggested shortening her name to "Norma Jean." She recorded briefly for Columbia and then moved to Nashville in 1960, becoming a backup vocalist for Porter Wagoner's touring and television shows. She had met Wagoner on the *Jubilee*, and her new level of exposure led to a contract with RCA Victor. She had her first chart single, "Let's Go All the Way," in 1964; the song made the Top 15 and was followed by the Top 25 hit "I'm a Walkin' Advertisement (For the Blues)." That year she had her first Top Ten single, "Go Cat Go," which stayed on the country charts for four months and became a minor pop hit as well. Her chart success continued through the mid-'60s with songs such as "I Wouldn't Buy a Used Car From Him" and the innovative love-triangle trio "The Game of Triangles" (1965), which also featured Bobby Bare and Liz Anderson.

On television, Norma Jean presented a wholesome image at odds with her hurtin' and cheatin' songs, yet in her personal life both those themes were relevant. Around the mid-'60s, she became romantically involved with her mentor Wagoner, who was separated from his wife at the time. The affair led her to leave Wagoner's organization, but she

continued to appear on the *Grand Ole Opry* (between 1965 and 1969) and recorded more singles for RCA. In 1967 she had two Top 30 hits, "Don't Let That Doorknob Hit You" and "Heaven Help the Working Girl," an early feminist song. In the late '60s, Norma Jean returned to Oklahoma after marrying Jody Taylor; she had her last chart hit in 1971 with "The Kind of Needin' I Need." The 1972 album *I Guess That Comes From Being Poor* echoed Parton's *In the Good Old Days (When Times Were Bad)* and bore comparison with that masterwork. In later years Norma Jean struggled with alcoholism and announced a new commitment to Christianity. She continued to tour and to record occasionally on independent labels, and in 1982, she and Claude Gray teamed for a minor hit with a remake of "Let's Go All the Way." —*Sandra Brennan & James Manheim*

Let's Go All the Way / 1964 / RCA Victor ✦✦✦✦✦

Pretty Miss Norma Jean / 1965 / RCA Victor ✦✦✦

Please Don't Hurt Me / 1966 / RCA Victor ✦✦✦✦

Norma Jean Sings a Tribute to Kitty Wells / 1966 / RCA Victor ✦✦✦

● **Norma Jean Sings Porter Wagoner** / 1967 / RCA Victor ✦✦✦✦✦

Jackson Ain't a Very Big Town / 1967 / RCA Victor ✦✦✦

Heaven's Just a Prayer Away / 1968 / RCA Victor ✦✦✦

● **Best of Norma Jean** / Feb. 8, 2000 / Collectors' Choice Music ✦✦✦✦✦
The Best of Norma Jean consists of Norma Jean's 21 Top 100 country hits in chronological order, including her biggest hit, "The Game of Triangles," on which she is joined by Bobby Bare and Liz Anderson. "Go Cat Go" and "I Wouldn't Buy a Used Car From Him" were Norma Jean's only other Top Ten entries, and are among the best cuts on this anthology. Despite her association with Porter Wagoner, he doesn't appear anywhere on these recordings, which span the years 1964-1971. With a new breed of female country singers on the rise—ones who looked like models and sang with hardly a trace of rurality in their voices—the days were numbered for the hard(er) country sound of Norma Jean. —*Greg Adams*

The Notting Hillbillies

f. 1990
Group / Country-Rock, Americana
After the mega-platinum success of Dire Straits' 1984 *Brothers in Arms* LP, the group's frontman, guitarist extraordinaire Mark Knopfler, opted to temporarily shift gears by forming the Notting Hillbillies, a one-off country side project. Among the band's first recruits was Steve Phillips, a fellow guitar player whom Knopfler had first met in Yorkshire in 1968 when both men interviewed a local country and blues musician (also named, curiously enough, Steve Phillips). Soon, the two aspiring journalists formed the two-man Duolian String Pickers and continued performing together until Knopfler entered college in 1970; after graduating three years later, he moved to London to start Dire Straits.

Phillips, in the meantime, formed a rockabilly outfit, the Steve Phillips Juke Band. In 1976, he met Brendan Croker, a onetime member of the Juke Band, and the pair began performing as Nev & Norris. By 1980, Phillips had left the music scene to focus on an art career, leaving Croker to form Five O'Clock Shadow. In 1986, Knopfler came calling, and in May of that year the Notting Hillbillies played their first gig at a tiny Leeds club with a lineup featuring Knopfler, Phillips, and Croker as well as drummer Ed Bicknell (moonlighting from his day job as Dire Straits' manager), guitarist Guy Fletcher, pedal steel guitarist Paul Franklin, and Croker's fellow Five O'Clock Shadow Marcus Cliff on bass. A tour followed, although the group's lone album, *Missing...Presumed Having a Good Time*, did not appear until 1990, at which point the members of the Notting Hillbillies had already returned to their main projects. —*Jason Ankeny*

Missing . . . Presumed Having a Good Time / 1990 / Warner Bros. ✦✦✦✦
On hiatus from Dire Straits, guitarist Mark Knopfler joined with Brendan Croker, Steve Phillips, and Guy Fletcher for 1990's *Missing . . . Presumed Having a Good Time*. The result is a low-key, joyous run-through of mostly traditional, blues-based songs with a handful of originals. Despite the high-profile presence of Knopfler, the Notting Hillbillies succeed in sounding like a band with Knopfler often taking a backseat to his bandmates, although he does sing lead on the lovely "Your Own Sweet Way." The styles range from the gorgeous harmonies of "Railroad Worksong" with some mournful guitar from Knopfler, to the '50s-style rock ballad "Bewildered," to the breezy, tropical-flavored "One Way Gal." *Missing: Presumed Having a Good Time* is a delightful record that doesn't overstay its welcome. —*Tom Demalon*

The Oak Ridge Boys

f. 1961, Oak Ridge, TN
Group / Country-Pop, Country Gospel

One of the longest-running groups in country music, the Oak Ridge Boys began as a gospel quartet before gradually modernizing their style and moving into secular country-pop. Yet even at the height of their popularity in the late '70s and early '80s—when they were big enough to cross over to the pop charts—their sound always remained deeply rooted in country gospel harmony. Their existence dates all the way back to World War II, circa 1942-1943, when a Knoxville, TN, group began performing gospel songs in nearby Oak Ridge, the home of an atomic bomb research facility. The group's members also performed in a larger aggregation called Wally Fowler & the Georgia Clodhoppers, which recorded for Capitol. However, lead singer Fowler decided to focus on gospel music in 1945. Dubbed the Oak Ridge Quartet, the group first appeared at the *Grand Ole Opry* that year and made their first recordings in 1947 with a lineup of Fowler, Lon "Deacon" Freeman, Curly Kinsey, and Johnny New.

Numerous personnel shifts ensued over the next few years, particularly in 1949, when the entire group split from Fowler; at that point, he hired a completely different group, the Bob Weber-led Calvary Quartet, to assume the Oak Ridge name. With a core of Fowler and Weber, plus a revolving-door cast of supporting vocalists, the group became one of the top draws on the Southern gospel circuit, continuing up to the end of 1956. At that point, Fowler disbanded the quartet and sold the name to group member Smitty Gatlin, who organized a new lineup in early 1957. In 1961, Gatlin changed their name to the Oak Ridge Boys, made them a full-time professional act, and started to modernize their sound on record with fuller arrangements and elements of country and folk. Future mainstay William Lee Golden joined as the group's baritone vocalist in 1964, and when Gatlin retired to become a full-time minister two years later, the group, acting on Golden's recommendation, hired ex-Southernairs singer Duane Allen as his replacement on lead vocals.

With bass singer Noel Fox and tenor singer Willie Wynn, the Oak Ridge Boys continued to broaden their appeal by adapting their sound to the times, adding a drummer to their backing band and incorporating bits of pop and even rock into their country gospel style. As a result, they grew into one of the most popular gospel acts of the late '60s, despite purist criticism over their secular influences and increasingly long-haired image. They even won their first Grammy in 1970 for "Talk About the Good Times." Fox and Wynn were replaced by Richard Sterban (ex-Keystone Quartet) and Philadelphia native Joe Bonsall in 1972 and 1973, respectively, and this lineup would remain intact for the next decade and a half. In 1973, they recorded a single with Johnny Cash & the Carter Family called "Praise the Lord and Pass the Soup," which brought them their first appearance on the country charts. In 1975, they opened a series of tour dates for Roy Clark, whose manager was highly impressed and encouraged them to try their hands at secular country. The Oak Ridge Boys signed with Columbia later that year but found the initial transition a rough one: They split their time between country and gospel, and without a strong identity their sales dropped. The resulting financial problems nearly forced them to disband, and a discouraged Columbia gave up on them after the 1976 single "Family Reunion" barely charted, even though labelmate Paul Simon had tapped them to sing backup on his hit "Slip Slidin' Away." Fortunately, they got another chance with MCA and scored a breakout Top Five hit in 1977 with "Y'all Come Back Saloon," the title song from their label debut. The follow-up, "You're the One," reached number two, and their next album, 1978's *Room Service*, gave them their first number-one hit in "I'll Be True to You" as well as two more Top Five hits in "Cryin' Again" and "Come On In."

Thus established as country hitmakers, the Oak Ridge Boys embarked on a run of chart success that would last through the '80s. Golden stopped cutting his hair and beard altogether, giving the group a hugely recognizable visual signature as well. They hit number one again in 1980 with "Trying to Love Two Women," but it was the following year that would make them a genuine phenomenon. Their recording of "Elvira," an obscure, doo wop-style novelty song from the '60s, became a major, Grammy-winning crossover smash. Not only did it hit number one on the country charts, but its infectious "oom-pop-a-mow-mow" bass vocal hook boosted it into the Top Five on the pop charts. Its accompanying album, *Fancy Free*, became their first to top the country charts, not to mention their biggest seller ever. The title cut of their chart-topping 1982 follow-up, *Bobbie Sue*, also went number-one country and nearly made the pop Top Ten as well. *American Made*'s title track also topped the charts in 1983, as did its follow-up, "Love Song." In early 1984 *Deliver* became their third number-one country album, and they landed two more number-one singles that year with "Everyday" and "I Guess It Never Hurts to Hurt Sometimes." "Little Things," "Make My Life With You," and "Touch a Hand, Make a Friend," were all number ones from 1985. The Oak Ridge Boys' sales began to slow a bit in the latter half of the '80s, but they still produced big hits with regularity. They hit number one in 1987 ("It Takes a Little Rain," "This Crazy Love"), 1988 ("Gonna Take a Lot of River"), and 1990 ("No Matter How High"), giving them a total of 16 career country chart-toppers (and 29 Top Ten hits). However, by that point, the group's longtime lineup had split—Golden, whose mountain-man appearance was increasingly supported by his rugged lifestyle, was given the boot in 1987 in an attempt to remake the group's image.

He was replaced by longtime backing-band guitarist Steve Sanders and sued his former bandmates, eventually settling out of court.

In 1991, the Oak Ridge Boys parted ways with MCA and signed with RCA, but after just two albums, it was apparent that their commercial prime had passed, and the relationship ended. The group returned to traditional-style country gospel on occasion during the '90s and continued to tour. Meanwhile, Sanders' marital problems worsened, causing him to leave the group in late 1995; Golden and the other members resolved their differences, and he returned at their New Year's Eve show that year; they still performed often, notably in Branson, MO. Sadly, Sanders shot and killed himself in 1998. Fox, who moved on to run the group's publishing arm and later became a high-ranking music executive, passed away in April 2003. —*Steve Huey*

Y'all Come Back Saloon / 1977 / MCA ✦✦✦✦✦
"You're the One" and the title cut are the featured selections on *Y'All Come Back Saloon.* —*Jason Ankeny*

Room Service / 1978 / MCA ✦✦✦✦
Room Service finds the Oak Ridge Boys in 1978 continuing to establish themselves as a secular act, following a risky decision to expand their repertoire from strictly gospel into country-pop. Among the 11 tracks are three hits: "Come on In," "Tryin' Again," and their first number one on the country charts, "I'll Be True to You." —*Al Campbell*

The Best of the Oak Ridge Boys / 1978 / CBS ✦✦✦✦✦
The Best of the Oak Ridge Boys collects the group's early, gospel-styled recordings. —*Jason Ankeny*

Together / 1980 / MCA ✦✦✦
Together, released in early 1980, found the Oak Ridge Boys on their way to becoming a successful country crossover act. The Oaks had already chalked up enough hits to release their *Greatest Hits, Vol. 1* the same year, including two tracks from this album, "Trying to Love Two Women" and "Heart of Mine." A third track, "Beautiful You," also made the country charts. —*Al Campbell*

Greatest Hits, Vol. 1 / 1980 / MCA ✦✦✦
Greatest Hits, Vol. 1 highlights ten of the Oak Ridge Boys' early MCA hits. This is the Oaks' earliest blend of country and pop after leaving the gospel circuit exclusively. These tracks remain some of the finest: "Leaving Louisiana in the Broad Daylight," "Come on In," "Sail Away," "Y'all Come Back Saloon," and their first number-one single in 1978, "I'll Be True to You." —*Al Campbell*

Fancy Free / 1981 / MCA ✦✦✦✦✦
By the release of *Fancy Free* in 1981, the Oak Ridge Boys were on a roll. They not only had another number-one hit on the country charts with "Elvira," but the single gained so much airplay that it crossed over onto the pop charts as well, becoming a signature song for the band, and the biggest hit of their career. The remainder of the album included similarly enjoyable material including another hit "I'm Settin' Fancy Free," and the obligatory gospel tune "I Would Crawl All the Way (To the River)." —*Al Campbell*

● Greatest Hits, Vol. 2 / 1984 / MCA ✦✦✦✦✦
This covers the Oaks at their peak, with repetitive, singalong choruses predominating in "American Made," "Love Song," and "Everyday." The delicate "I Guess It Never Hurts to Hurt Sometimes" is a nice change of pace, but why did MCA hold out "Bobbie Sue" until *Greatest Hits 3*? —*Tom Roland*

Monongahela / 1987 / MCA ✦✦✦✦✦
Though *Heartbeat* was recorded after the dismissal of William Lee Golden, this is the first album in which replacement Steve Sanders was involved from beginning to end in the recording process. Harmonies are understandably more soulful—and more in tune—and the project is generally more uplifting. It includes "Gonna Take a Lot of River." —*Tom Roland*

Sensational Oak Ridge Boys / 1987 / Starday ✦✦✦✦✦
This is a solid collection of their early gospel recordings. It's interesting to compare to their secular success. —*Cub Koda*

American Dreams / 1989 / MCA ✦✦✦
It features such hits as "An American Family," "Cajun Girl," "Bed of Roses," and others. —*AMG*

Greatest Hits, Vol. 3 / 1989 / MCA ✦✦✦✦✦
This contains "Gonna Take a Lot of River," "Take Pride in America," "This Crazy Love," and other hits from the mid- and late '80s. —*AMG*

The Long Haul / 1992 / RCA ✦✦✦
While the title proved wholly inappropriate—this LP was the group's last with longtime label MCA—*The Long Haul* is one of the Oaks' more consistent efforts, and contains the minor hit "Fall." —*Jason Ankeny*

The Back to Back: Oak Ridge Boys/J.D. Sumner & the Stamps / 1992 / Arrival ♦♦♦
If you don't remember when the Oaks were a gospel group or have never heard the Stamps except in their role as background singers for Elvis, here is a disc that will introduce you to each group as they perform the type of the music they were first known for. Among the five tracks by the Oaks are "Less of Me," "At Last," and "I Wouldn't Take Nothing for My Journey," while the Stamps do "My Savior Knows," "The Old Rugged Cross," and "Amazing Grace." *—Jim Worbois*

The Collection / Apr. 21, 1992 / MCA ♦♦♦
Featured are "Fancy Free," "Trying to Love Two Women," "Thank God for Kids," "American Made," and other hits. *—AMG*

The Very Best of the Country Gospel Years / May 23, 2000 / Goldenlane ♦♦♦
Before gaining their many Top Ten country hits in the late '70s and early '80s, the Oak Ridge Boys had a gospel background, which they maintained throughout their career. *The Very Best of the Country Gospel Years* is a compilation of gospel material recorded in the early '60s. These 20 tracks from the Golden Lane label are at a budget price and recommended for fans of Southern traditional gospel harmonies. *—Al Campbell*

● **20th Century Masters—The Millennium Collection: The Best of the Oak Ridge Boys** / Aug. 15, 2000 / MCA Nashville ♦♦♦♦♦
The Millennium Collection: The Very Best of the Oak Ridge Boys gathers highlights from the country-pop group's body of work, including number one hits like "Elvira," "Leavin' Louisiana in the Broad Daylight," "American Made," and "It Takes a Little Rain (To Make Love Grow)." Choice album tracks and radio favorites make up the rest of this concise, affordable hits collection from one of the most popular country acts of the '70s and '80s. *—Heather Phares*

Mollie O'Brien

Vocals / Traditional Bluegrass, Progressive Country
The older sister of Hot Rize member Tim, bluegrass performer Mollie O'Brien grew up in Wheeling, WV, where during high-school she and her brother teamed as a folk duo. After studying voice in college, O'Brien moved to New York City, where she worked as a buyer for the garment industry. In 1980, inspired by Tim's success in Hot Rize, she joined him in Colorado, where she became a fixture on the R&B and jazz club circuits. In 1984, the O'Brien siblings reunited for a Mother's Day concert, and four years later, they recorded a duets album, *Take Me Back.* Concurrently, O'Brien continued her solo career, issuing her debut LP, *I Never Move too Soon*, in 1987. She also joined with the group the Mother Folkers for 1989's *Live at the Arvada Center.* In the decade that followed, O'Brien continued to divide her time between solo and duo work, releasing her *Everynight in the Week* in 1990 and rejoining Tim two years later for *Remember Me.* Another duet collection, *Away Out on the Mountain*, appeared in 1994, and in 1996, O'Brien issued the solo effort *Tell It True. Big Red Sun Blues* followed two years later, and *Things I Gave Away* was issued in 2000. *—Jason Ankeny*

I Never Move Too Soon / 1987 / Resounding ♦♦♦

● **Tell It True** / Mar. 19, 1996 / Sugar Hill ♦♦♦♦
This wonderful album is peppered with excellent material, interpreted with style and grace. Some of Mollie's best work is on her duet albums with Tim, but this album is a great place to discover this lady, who is actually confident enough to cover the '80s classic "Sign Your Name" by Terence Trent D'Arby. Also features a great old Tin Pan Alley song, "Having the Time of My Life." *—William Ashford*

Big Red Sun Blues / Aug. 18, 1998 / Sugar Hill ♦♦♦♦♦
Mollie O'Brien has a great voice and knows how to use it. It is perfectly feasible to believe she can sing anything. This time out, O'Brien hits the ground running with Memphis Minnie's blues tune "In My Girlish Days." It is an amazing look back from a female perspective that climbs to new heights under Mollie's capable vocals. Just as enticing are "Denver to Dallas" and John Hiatt's "Love Like Blood." "Eleezah" is intoxicating with John Magnie's accordion, and Chuck Berry's "Brown Eyed Handsome Man" is presented in a smooth, easy style. The title track, penned by Lucinda Williams, displays all of Mollie O'Brien's ability nicely. With a wide variety of tunes from traditional to Willie Dixon to Steve Goodman and Randy Newman, O'Brien creates a patchwork quilt of American roots music all sewn together with the strong threads that are her undeniable talent. *—Jana Pendragon*

Things I Gave Away / Aug. 29, 2000 / Sugar Hill ♦♦♦♦
O'Brien's brand of the country blues weaves in strands of Cajun and bluegrass with a distinct pop influence. Equally eclectic is her choice of tunes by the likes of Lennon & McCartney, Abbey Lincoln, and Percy Mayfield. But as diverse as the elements may seem, it makes for a satisfying whole. At the center of it all is O'Brien's sweet, clear alto voice. *—Tim Sheridan*

Tim O'Brien

b. Mar. 16, 1954
Bouzouki, Fiddle, Guitar, Mandolin, Vocals, Mandocello / Neo-Traditional Folk, Singer/Songwriter, Country-Folk, Contemporary Folk
Tim O'Brien is one of the spearheads of contemporary bluegrass. As co-founder and lead vocalist of Hot Rize and Red Knuckles & the Trailblazers, O'Brien served as a bridge between the traditional sounds of the hill country and the modern styles of bluegrass in the 1980s. Since the band's breakup, O'Brien has continued to expand the music's borders as a soloist, a duo partner with his sister Mollie, and with his band, the O'Boys. O'Brien's songs have additionally been recorded by Kathy Mattea, the Seldom Scene, New Grass Revival, and the Johnson Mountain Boys.

O'Brien's earliest memories of music are the Benny Goodman and Glenn Miller records favored by his parents and the Lawrence Welk recordings played by a Polish housekeeper. A turning point came when O'Brien began listening to a weekly country music radio show, *the Saturday Night Jamboree.* Discovering that the show was broadcast from a local theater, O'Brien became a frequent audience member and saw performances by Jerry Lee Lewis, Buck Owens, Merle Haggard, and Roger Miller. Acquiring his first guitar at the age of 12, O'Brien took to the instrument almost immediately. Although he played with numerous high-school rock bands, O'Brien was steered toward country music and bluegrass by Roger Bland, a banjo-playing patient of a girlfriend's psychiatrist father. A former member of Lester Flatt's band, Bland taught O'Brien to play in the three-finger style of Earl Scruggs.

O'Brien had earlier discovered that his father had played mandolin banjo in college. Although his father no longer played the instrument, O'Brien bought new strings and learned a few rudimentary techniques. While attending Colby College in Maine, O'Brien began to play mandolin. Leaving the college after a year, O'Brien headed to Wyoming and then to Colorado. Before long, O'Brien hooked up temporarily with a jug band, Ophelia's String Band. Meeting future Hot Rize bandmates Pete Wernick and Charles Sawtelle, O'Brien formed a bluegrass band, the Drifting Ramblers. Nick Forster, a guitar repairman at the Denver Folklore Center, soon joined the group. The band, however, soon drifted apart with O'Brien and Wernick going on to record solo albums. Assembling a new group to help promote the solo recordings, O'Brien, Wernick, Sawtelle, and Forster launched Hot Rize. The band remained together for 12 years. Although their initial sound was very traditional, Hot Rize continued to evolve in a more progressive direction. A popular highlight of Hot Rize's performances came when the four musicians left the stage, changed their clothes, and re-emerged as the Western honky tonk group Red Knuckles & the Trailblazers. The gag continued to grow with the offshoot band recording several albums on their own.

While performing at the Summerlights Festival in Nashville, O'Brien met country music songstress Kathy Mattea. When Mattea subsequently had hits with her covers of his songs "Untold Stories" and "Walk the Way the Wind Blows," O'Brien announced that he was leaving Hot Rize to seek his fortune as a songwriter. Although O'Brien signed as a solo performer with RCA, the contract was doomed, and the label turned down O'Brien's first album attempt and dropped him from their roster. O'Brien went on to sign with bluegrass label Sugar Hill.

The O'Boys were formed to help promote O'Brien's solo album, *Odd Man In*, in 1991. Although Forster was an original member, he left the group to host the National Public Radio show *etown* and was replaced by Scott Nygaard. Mark Schatz continued to play bass for the group. O'Brien joined with his sister, Mollie, to record an album of old-timey country songs, *Take Me Back*, in 1988. Although they had sung together in church and school choirs, they had spent most of their later teens apart. Since being reunited, they've collaborated on several albums. O'Brien and Hot Rize temporarily resumed their partnership in 1996. They continued to occasionally get together since. *—Craig Harris*

Hard Year Blues / 1984 / Flying Fish ♦♦♦

Take Me Back / 1988 / Sugar Hill ♦♦♦♦♦

Odd Man In / 1991 / Sugar Hill ♦♦♦♦
This album rocks the borders of country, folk and pop. The songs are smart and ironic. There is great playing throughout. "Lonely at the Bottom" is a really good track. *—Richard Meyer*

Remember Me / 1992 / Sugar Hill ♦♦♦
When brother and sister Tim and Mollie do a project together, it is an interesting amalgam of their individual styles and interests—he primarily in acoustic bluegrass and country, she nestled into blues and jazz. This album includes such a variety of material; the gospel writing of Reverend Gary Davis, a contempory ballad by Judy Roderick & William Ashford, and Mollie's scat offering of a blues by Eddie "Cleanhead" Vinson. Although the album as a whole is a little unfocused, it is still a joy to hear these two work together. Extra pleasant for the inclusion of guest players John Magnie, Steve Amedee and Tommy Malone of the Subdudes. *—William Ashford*

Oh Boy! O'Boy! / 1993 / Sugar Hill ♦♦♦
More gospel pop than *Odd Man In*, this record with his band the O'Boys lets us hear O'Brien run down Dylan's "When I Paint My Masterpiece," the bluegrass spiritual "Church Steeple" and the ancient "The Farmer's Cursed Wife." *—Richard Meyer*

● **Away Out on the Mountain** / 1994 / Sugar Hill ♦♦♦♦♦
If you ever wished you could hear brand new music with the conviction and flawless vocal vork of the classic Everly Brothers recordings this album by brother and sister Mollie and Tim O'Brien is for you. The cuts are mostly contemporary gospel-bluegrass sounding tunes with an A.P. Carter and Leadbelly song tossed in. There is not a misplaced note. *—Richard Meyer*

Rock in My Shoe / 1995 / Sugar Hill ♦♦♦
True fans of Tim O'Brien find all of his albums to be excellent, some simply more so than others. This one falls somewhere in the middle. There's the expected eclectic choice of material, and at least a few killer tunes. In this case, "Brother Wind," "One Girl Cried," and the continuing saga of "Daddy's on the Roof Again" fill the bill. A nice album, featuring the usual suspects. *—William Ashford*

Red on Blonde / 1996 / Sugar Hill ♦♦♦♦♦
In case you had forgotten, this album will remind how pertinent and beautiful the songs of Bob Dylan are. The trouble with Tim O'Brien is that he makes it seem so easy; the challenge of reinterpreting classics may escape many. The repertoire covers decades and styles in one giant stroke. The playing is, as usual, impeccable. The inclusion of "Lay Down Your Weary Tune" is excellent; if only he hadn't been in such a hurry on "Forever Young." *—William Ashford*

When No One's Around / 1997 / Sugar Hill ♦♦♦♦♦
This is one of Tim O'Brien's most engaging projects. Known as a writer, he chooses here to co-write with others, including sister Mollie O'Brien, Hal Ketchum, and the elusive Danny O'Keefe. The songs range from celebratory ("Out on the Rolling Sea") to sardonic

("How Come I Ain't Dead") to reflective ("First Days of Fall"). In spite of his attempts to the contrary, O'Brien is still his own best writer, with kudos especially to "Think About Last Night" and "First Days of Fall." The feel of this music is more mainstream country than some of his other albums. The players are quite good, with high praise for drummer John Gardner for his accents and exclamation marks. — *William Ashford*

The Crossing / May 4, 1999 / Alula ✦✦✦✦

It might be a cliché to say that to understand where you are and where you're going, you must know where you've been, but it's a very accurate cliché—especially when it comes to music. If you're going to have a thorough understanding of the history of country, bluegrass, and Anglo-American folk, it's important to have some knowledge of the music that paved the way for those forms—namely, the music that immigrants from the British Isles brought with them to the U.S. On *The Crossing*, singer/instrumentalist Tim O'Brien does a fine job reminding listeners how great a role Celtic music played in the development of Anglo-American styles. As a vocalist, O'Brien shows how Irish and Scottish ballad traditions have influenced American folk and country, and as an instrumentalist, O'Brien (who plays fiddle, mandolin, guitar, and other instruments) shows how the jigs and reels of Ireland and Scotland paved the way for Appalachian bluegrass. A fine storyteller, he describes the experiences of Irish immigrants to the U.S. on gems like "The Crossing" and "Lost Little Children"—and on the humorous, Bob Dylan-influenced "Talkin' Cavan," O'Brien (himself an Irish-American from West Virginia) recalls traveling to Ireland in 1998 to visit the land of his ancestors. This CD is not to be missed. — *Alex Henderson*

Real Time / Apr. 18, 2000 / Howdy Skies ✦✦✦✦

Music has occasionally been born of a couple of friends playing both new and familiar songs in a relaxed setting. Words that are often used to describe the music they make are "natural" or "unaffected." Examples would include John Hartford's *Morning Bugle*, Hartford, David Grisman, and Mike Seeger's *Retrograss*, and Tim O'Brien and Darrell Scott's *Real Time*. The songs on *Real Time* were recorded in Scott's living room over the period of a week. Both musicians play multiple instruments including banjo, mandolin, guitar, and bouzouki; they also exchange lead vocals and sing some very fine harmony. Both the song choice and songwriting add to this project. Hank Williams' "Weary Blues from Waiting" receives an acoustic revision, with both singers sharing lead vocals and providing affecting harmony. O'Brien sings a charged version of "Little Sadie" driven by Scott's aggressive guitar playing. Part of the beauty of this album is how fresh and vital these traditional songs become with these simple and straightforward arrangements. *Real Time* also contains a handful of refined originals, including O'Brien's "Walk Beside Me" and "I'm Not Gonna Forget You." Scott has written the impressive "There Ain't No Easy Way," complete with the same soulful singing found on his last release, *Family Tree*. There are even moments when Scott's vocal style reminds one of the soulful delivery of Little Feat's Lowell George. *Real Time* brings together two artists who love to make music and who give the impression that making good music is as simple as hanging out with friends. While this may not be how all good music is made, it has produced a gem of an album in the hands of Scott and O'Brien. Fans of both artists, and fans of good traditional and folk music, should enjoy this one. — *Ronnie Lankford Jr.*

Two Journeys / Oct. 9, 2001 / Howdy Skies ✦✦✦✦✦

Itinerant American folk musician Tim O'Brien has been on a tear since 1996's *Red on Blonde*, bluegrass interpretations of Bob Dylan songs (and don't laugh, it stands as one of the very finest Dylan tributes ever recorded). Since that time he has issued collaborations with Dirk Powell and John Hermann (*Songs From the Mountain*—inspired by the novel *Cold Mountain*) and Darrell Scott (*Real Time*), as well as issuing the original inspiration for this recording, *The Crossing* in 1999, which offered a rootsy musician's ear-view of how Irish music informed the folk traditions of the American South and found a home in a mutated yet no less soulful form. *Two Journeys* is *The Crossing*'s mirror image. This album shows O'Brien—and a company of the British Isles and American South's finest musicians—looking toward the coastlines of Ireland to express those traditions as they prepared to leave the homeland for the "new world." Digging deep into his own bag of folk songs, traditional ballads, and a few slick bluegrass moves, O'Brien has managed to tell a story, mostly with his own songs, of the cultural miscegenation that took place in the vast Irish exodus during and after the potato famine. From the opening track, "Turning Around," we hear the song of a captain in the middle of the Atlantic, looking back on the homeland with a sense of loss, regret, and heartbreak, and toward the new with a shred of hope, fear, and trepidation. This leads into the glorious swagger of "Mick Ryan's Lament" by Robert Lee Dunlap. The tune extrapolates "Garryowen," George Custer's marching song that was likely his final one at Little Big Horn. And then we're off, deep into the middle ground of a sea rife for the picking with fiddle tunes, jigs, reels, bluegrass, folk-blues and Celtic soul. With help from the aforementioned Yankees, and Paddy Keenan on uilleann pipes, traditional percussionist Kevin Burke, keyboard work from Triona No Drohmnaill, and the vocal support of Karan Casey and Maura O'Connell, O'Brien doesn't merely create facsimiles of Irish songs, but showcases the log, knotty rope between traditions, being not part one or the other but fully both. The most moving track on the disc, and also its most spooky, is "Demon Lover," a duet between O'Brien and Casey. It's a ballad so old it nearly dates antiquity, the rendering here, which doesn't even resemble modern versions, is chock full of pathos, lust, and regret. This may very well be his finest outing. — *Thom Jurek*

Maura O'Connell

b. County Clare, Ireland

Vocals / Progressive Bluegrass, Singer/Songwriter, Contemporary Folk

Maura O'Connell embodies many paradoxes: lead singer for De Dannon, she was not a traditional Celtic singer; resident of Nashville, she is not American; collaborator with New

Grass Revival, she is not a bluegrass performer. Nevertheless, O'Connell has made a name for herself on two continents as a superb singer.

O'Connell was born and raised in County Clare, Ireland, where she began singing at an early age. Involvement in the folk club scene led to an invitation from celtic traditionalists, De Dannon, to join their ranks. Her involvement with De Dannon resulted in the recording of *Star Spangled Mollie*, a clear indication of interest in trans-Atlantic culture. O'Connell then began to collabrate with members of New Grass Revival, and in particular with Béla Fleck who produced several of her tracks. Together with Fleck and others, she recorded *Just in Time* and made the decision to settle in Nashville, TN. Since then, she has released *Helpless Heart*, *Blue is the Colour of Hope*, and *A Real Life Story*, each album registering a move toward a pop synthesis. *Stories* followed in 1995, with *Wandering Home* appearing two years later. — *Leon Jackson*

Just in Time / 1988 / Philo ✦✦✦

This album, produced by Béla Fleck with string arrangements by Edgar Meyer, is one of O'Connell's cleanest and most uncluttered releases. Her voice sounds beautifully free; while some of her recordings sound forced, this one is relaxed and natural. This album demonstrates why she is often compared with Mary Black. The album's band is an all-star affair with Jerry Douglas, Béla Fleck, Mark O'Conner and Nanci Griffith contributing, among others. Maura O'Connell can be given credit here for picking up Paul McCartney's "I Will" seven years before Alison Krauss. — *Richard Meyer*

● Helpless Heart / 1989 / Warner Bros. ✦✦✦✦✦

Irish interpretive singer O'Connell has suffered from the inability of her record company to figure out whether she's a folkie, a country singer, or a pop artist. Meanwhile, she keeps singing her heart out, cherrypicking the work of such writers as Paul Brady, Nanci Griffith, Linda Thompson, and others. If you already own the albums those writers have made, maybe she's redundant. However, great songs still benefit greatly from being performed by great singers, and if you're looking for a sympathetic sampler of the best of today's songwriters, here it is. — *William Ruhlmann*

A Real Life Story / 1991 / Warner Bros. ✦✦✦

Blue Is the Colour of Hope / 1992 / Warner Bros. ✦✦✦

This charmingly eclectic album may be O'Connell's best. Working with producer Jerry Douglas, O'Connell finds sympathetic accompaniment on all these songs, whether its the piano and arco bass on the gently painful "So Soft Your Goodbye," the small-combo swing on "Love to Learn," or the full-band acoustic pop on "Still Hurts Sometimes." Though O'Connell records songs by Nashville stalwarts like Pat McLaughlin and Tom Kimmel, her ear for a wider range of material makes *Blue Is the Color of Hope* such a joy. "Bad News at the Best of Times," by rockers Paul Carrack and John Wesley Harding, is a real find, and O'Connell's cover of Mary-Chapin Carpenter's "It Don't Bring You" is simply gorgeous. — *Brian Mansfield*

Stories / Oct. 1995 / Hannibal ✦✦✦✦

Stories is Maura O'Connell's tribute to great singer/songwriters, and as such it features songs by a number of the usual suspects, including John Gorka ("Blue Chalk") and Shawn Colvin ("Shotgun Down the Avalanche"), as well as a gently lovely rendition of Lennon & McCartney's "If I Fell." The jazzy, stripped-down guitar and bass accompaniment on "The Town Can't Get Over You" provides a nice counterpoint to the lushness that characterizes most of the album, but the high point is probably Mary-Chapin Carpenter's gorgeous (if slightly trite) "Wall Around Your Heart." Any songwriter would be grateful to have a singer like O'Connell interpret his or her music—she combines an Ella Fitzgerald-ish respect for the composer's work with an equally impressive ability to make that work her own, and her voice is a thing of exquisite, honeyed beauty. This disc is highly recommended. — *Rick Anderson*

Wandering Home / Jun. 10, 1997 / Hannibal ✦✦✦✦

Wandering Home is an apt title for Maura O'Connell's first all-Irish album since leaving the Old Sod. The players are a who's who of modern Celtic music—among them guitarist Arty McGlynn, fiddler Ciaran Tourish (of Altan), and bouzouki player Donal Lunny—and the tunes are mostly traditional, if not always rendered in a strictly traditional style. For instance, there are shades of Roy Orbison in the more operatic moments of "I Hear You Calling Me," and her bluesy adaptation of an old folk tune such as "Irish Blues" has more than a hint of Billie Holiday to it. Needless to say, these are not the strongest tracks on the album. The transcendent moments come on the more hardcore trad numbers—her heartbreaking rendition of "Teddy O'Neil," her revelatory take on the old chestnut "Down by the Sally Gardens"—and on the startlingly out-of-place "Down Where the Drunkards Roll," which is one of the grimmest songs Richard Thompson ever wrote, but which O'Connell manages to imbue with a warmth and humanity miles removed from the jaded resignation of Linda Thompson's original version. Jerry Douglas is a brilliant producer and knows just how to showcase O'Connell's stunning voice. — *Rick Anderson*

Walls & Windows / Nov. 13, 2001 / Sugar Hill ✦✦✦✦

A number of fascinating opposites characterize Maura O'Connell's approach to music. Born and raised in Ireland, she currently lives in Nashville. She's recorded Celtic and country albums, but also worked with newgrass pioneers Jerry Douglas and Béla Fleck. Her rich, powerful voice, however, travels with her wherever she goes. *Walls & Windows* is her first recording in several years and her debut on the Sugar Hill label. This time she's backed by a full band with players like Darrell Scott and Dave Francis providing soulful, layered sound. This approach works well for O'Connell's potent vocals, providing lots of cushion on upbeat pieces like "Every River" and "Walls." Her song choice, as with previous projects, serves her well. She has chosen several pieces by Patty Griffin, including a passionate version of "I Wonder" with a backing vocal by the writer. There are two tracks, "To the Homeland" and "A Far Cry," by relative newcomer Malcolm Holcombe, and a lovely version of Van Morrison's "Crazy Love." "Blessing"'s emotional tug reminds one of Tony Price in a late-night bluesy mode, while a mellow version of John Prine's "Sleepy Eyed Boy" offers the perfect note to close the album on. It's refreshing that a singer purposely chooses to interpret and expose goods songs as opposed to writing new ones. Producer Ray Kennedy finds the right balance between singer and material, delivering a recording infused with rhythm and depth. *Walls & Windows* will be warmly welcomed by O'Connell's fans and anyone who enjoys soulful music. —*Ronnie D. Lankford Jr.*

Mark O'Connor

b. Aug. 5, 1961, Seattle, WA
Fiddle, Mandolin, Violin, Session Musician / Progressive Bluegrass, Classical Crossover, Progressive Country, Instrumental Country

Born and raised in Seattle, O'Connor was always a bit out of sync with his teenage peers. Understandably so, since he was winning fiddle contests and had mapped out a sketchy career path. O'Connor moved to Nashville in 1983, already a former sideman for jazz violinist Stephane Grappelli, a job that allowed him to play the stage at Carnegie Hall. At the time O'Connor arrived in Music City (the post-*Urban Cowboy* era), fiddle was hardly in vogue, and it took a couple of years for him to make his mark. Finally, in 1985 the Nitty Gritty Dirt Band used him in their single "High Horse"; thanks to that work, O'Connor's phone number became a popular one with country record producers. Over the next five years he played on 450 albums, including such stellar projects as *Trio* by Dolly Parton, Linda Ronstadt, and Emmylou Harris; *Always & Forever* by Randy Travis; *Killin' Time* by Clint Black; and *Loving Proof* by Ricky Van Shelton. Despite his success, O'Connor gave up session work to concentrate on his own solo career, increasingly rooted in the classical realm thanks to collaborators including Yo-Yo Ma, Wynton Marsalis, and Edgar Meyer. —*Tom Roland*

National Junior Fiddle Champion / 1975 / Rounder ◆◆◆

Pickin' in the Wind / 1976 / Rounder ◆◆◆

Markology / 1978 / Rounder ◆◆◆◆

On the Rampage / 1980 / Rounder ◆◆◆

Soppin' the Gravy / 1981 / Rounder ◆◆◆◆

False Dawn / 1982 / Rounder ◆◆◆

Meanings Of... / 1986 / Warner Bros. ◆◆◆

Elysian Forest / 1988 / Warner Bros. ◆◆◆

Stone From Which the Arch Was Made / 1988 / Warner Bros. ◆◆◆

On the Mark / 1989 / Warner Bros. ◆◆◆
Top touring and session violinist O'Connor (formerly of the Dixie Dregs) is indeed right on the mark with this lovely, melodic collection that can be summed up in three words— sweet, sweeter, and sweetest. The virtuoso seems to be aiming for a pop/country crossover, with running times all under five minutes and a guest vocal by James Taylor, but who can argue when the music is this darn enjoyable? John Jarvis' piano and keyboards prove most effective on the harmonies of "March of the Pharoahs" and the romance of "Miniatures," and Michael Brecker gets to blow his heart out on daring pieces like "Get Set, Go" and the Old West movie chase music of "We're Surrounded." O'Connor's playing is smooth, lush yet urgent throughout, and above all, there's an air of excitement that would continue on through a series of eclectic dates in the '90s. —*Jonathan Widran*

Championship Years / 1990 / Country Music Foundation ◆◆◆◆◆
O'Connor at his earliest and most traditional, these recordings were made during his National Fiddling Championships competitions and were made between 1975 and 1984. —*Brian Mansfield*

● **Retrospective** / 1990 / Rounder ◆◆◆◆◆
Retrospective contains 18 of Mark O'Connor's progressive and traditional bluegrass tunes from his first six albums on Rounder. O'Connor is one of the finest fiddle players of his era, and this collection contains the absolute best of his output during that period. The track selection features equal parts traditional material "Dusty Miller," "Dreamer's Waltz," and "Wild Fiddler's Rag" mixed with O'Connor originals, "Floating Bridge of Dreams," "Pickin' in the Wind" and (the longest piece on the disc at 6:28) "Beserkeley." —*Al Campbell*

The New Nashville Cats / 1991 / Warner Bros. ◆◆◆◆◆
With an incredible lineup of Nashville's very best musicians, this package covers a wide range of musical territory, from bluegrass to the blues, with plenty of stellar pickin'. Ironically, this mostly instrumental album won a vocal Grammy when Vince Gill, Ricky Skaggs, and Steve Wariner teamed with O'Connor on "Restless." —*Tom Roland*

Heroes / 1993 / Warner Bros. ◆◆◆◆◆
O'Connor performs with his favorite fiddlers from a variety of styles, including Jean-Luc Ponty, Johnny Gimble, Vassar Clements, Pinchas Zukerman, and L. Shankar, among others. The set features "The Devil Comes Back to Georgia," a sequel to Charlie Daniels 1979 hit "The Devil Went Down to Georgia." —*Brian Mansfield*

The Fiddle Concerto / 1995 / Warner Bros. ◆◆◆

Liberty / Oct. 28, 1997 / Sony ◆◆◆◆

Midnight on the Water / Apr. 28, 1998 / Sony ◆◆◆◆
Midnight on the Water may be Mark O'Connor's best classical album yet. The album is comprised entirely of his solo recitals, which have earned him great acclaim, not only from fans but from critics. *Midnight on the Water* fulfills all of the high expectations fans and critics may have had, as its filled with lush, sympathetic and unexpected readings of classical and folk pieces alike. Anyone who has pigeonholed O'Connor as just another fiddler will have their perceptions come crashing down after hearing this record. —*Thom Owens*

Hot Swing! / Jun. 26, 2001 / Omac ◆◆◆◆◆
Violinist Mark O'Connor joined forces with bassist Jon Burr and guitarist Frank Vignola for this sensational concert in tribute to Stephane Grappelli, the grand old man of jazz violin until his death just shy of 90 in 1997. O'Connor was captivated at an early age by the Frenchman's playing and played along side him on several occasions, while Burr was Grappelli's regular bassist during the final decade of his career. O'Connor salutes his mentor without emulating his style directly; in fact, only three of the songs are associated with Grappelli: the lovely ballad "Nuages," composed by Grappelli's partner, Django Reinhardt; a wild reworking of "Minor Swing" (a Grappelli-Reinhardt collaboration); and an easygoing stroll through Duke Ellington's "Satin Doll," a song which Grappelli played often on-stage. But it is O'Connor's swinging originals that command the most attention. "Swingin' on the 'Ville" is a lively opener that features blistering solos by all three men, while the complex swinger "Sweet Suzanne" seems to be inspired by the chord changes to a mix of different standards (including "(Back Home Again In) Indiana" and "Limehouse Blues"), and "In the Cluster Blues" is a subtle but soulful blues. Burr's emotional ballad "Lament" is another memorable highlight. The finale is O'Connor's amusing "Pickles on the Elbow." The playing by all three musicians is at a consistently high level throughout the concert. This should be considered an essential CD for swing fans. —*Ken Dryden*

American Seasons / Sep. 25, 2001 / Sony ◆◆◆◆◆
The virtuoso violinist is a roots rock U.S. fiddle champ and one-time king of Nashville's blue chip session players who has spent recent years exploring the riches of classical music. This amazing session is broken up into two main sections, a four movement thrust through the seasons and then a 13 track segment entitled "Strings and Threads Suite" which draws both poignantly and happily from the intense spirit of his Irish heritage. Both are performed with the Metamorphosen Chamber Orchestra, conducted by Scott Yoo. The seasonal sequence is an explicit nod to Vivaldi, wedding to the Shakespearean notion of the seven stages of man. There's also an interesting pull towards grounding the section in very American sounds like the acoustic steel string guitar. "Spring" opens optimistically with a growing rhythmic energy, while "Summer" goes from lazy and laid-back to suddenly dance-driven with speedy fiddle stroking. "Fall" dawns with a sense of wistful melancholy, then "Winter" zips in with a rush of energy, a musical snowstorm that ebbs and flows in fits and starts; there's even a jig in the snow. The second suite keeps the jig vibe alive with "Fair Dancer Reel," then goes from jigs to waltzes to a darker shade of the blues. The impulse with both is to bring folk, jazz, and blues into the classical environment, not contrasting them but mixing them in a completely unique and logical way. The project closes with a seven minute orchestral mood piece called "Appalachia Waltz," which comes across as a meditation after a hectic day spent exploring seasons of both nature and the heart. It's close to a modern masterpiece. —*Jonathan Widran*

In Full Swing / Jan. 14, 2003 / Odyssey ◆◆◆◆
Mark O'Connor's second CD with his Hot Swing Trio is more than just a salute to the late, legendary jazz violinist Stephane Grappelli; it firmly establishes as him as a bona fide jazz violin virtuoso, thanks to being distributed by a major label this time around. The capable guitarist Frank Vignola plays gypsy swing à la Django Reinhardt without sounding like a clone; bassist Jon Burr, who spent a decade as a member of Grappelli's rhythm section in his last years, provides a perfect match for his two bandmates. Each member of the trio contributed originals to the session. O'Connor's "In Full Swing" is absolutely breathtaking, while it is fun imagining how Grappelli and Reinhardt might have interpreted his enticing "Stephane and Django." Burr's pulsating "Three for All" and Vignola's lyrical "A Beautiful Friendship" are also worthwhile songs. The remaining selections all come from the repertoire of either Grappelli or the Grappelli-Reinhardt partnership, with occasional guest appearances by Wynton Marsalis and singer Jane Monheit. There are plenty of fireworks in the trio's wild ride through "Limehouse Blues" (which, of course, isn't a blues at all). The high-flying duo introduction to "Tiger Rag" by O'Connor and Marsalis is a meeting of two masters. Monheit's interpretations of "Misty" and "As Time Goes By" are merely average, and she doesn't loosen up enough to appreciate the fun within Fats Waller's "Honeysuckle Rose," though Marsalis makes up for her shortcomings. In any case, Mark O'Connor's Hot Swing Trio provide first-rate swing all by themselves, so adding guests isn't really necessary. —*Ken Dryden*

Molly O'Day (Lois LaVerne Williamson)

b. Jul. 9, 1923, Pike County, KY, **d.** Dec. 5, 1987
Guitar, Vocals / Traditional Country, Honky Tonk

A pioneering vocalist whose soulful, gut-wrenching performances helped redefine the role of the female country solo artist, Molly O'Day's career was relatively brief, but her lasting influence has proven massive. Born Lois LaVerne Williamson on July 9, 1923, to a coal mining family living in a remote Appalachian community in eastern Kentucky, she spent her childhood enamored of cowgirl singers like Patsy Montana, Lulu Belle Wiseman, Texas Ruby Owens, and Lily May Ledford and eventually began singing and playing guitar in a string band with her brothers Cecil ("Skeets") on fiddle and Joe ("Duke") on banjo. In 1939, Skeets began playing on a radio station in Charleston, WV, and his sister soon followed, adopting the stage name "Mountain Fern." A year later, now under the name "Dixie Lee Williamson," she joined guitarist Lynn Davis' band the Forty Niners, and in 1941, she and Davis married.

Over the next five years, the Forty Niners extensively toured the South, building a substantial fan base along the way. By the time the group settled in for an extended stay in Louisville, KY, in 1946, the name "Molly O'Day" was firmly entrenched. While Davis and O'Day's duets were popular with audiences, it was her deeply felt solo performances of inspirational songs which had the biggest impact and which led writer/publisher Fred Rose to sign the singer to Columbia Records. There, O'Day performed a number of songs written by a young Hank Williams, whom she had already known from their days on the radio circuit; in fact, it was Williams who taught O'Day her best-loved song, "Tramp on the Street," one of eight tunes she cut during her first studio session in late 1946. Backed by Davis, her brother Skeets, bassist Mac Wiseman, and George "Speedy" Krise on the dobro, the recordings gave a further boost to O'Day's surging popularity, but already she was having trouble coping with her success.

O'Day and Davis spent much of 1947 out of music, but in December of that year she returned to the studio, where she recorded her crowd-pleaser "Matthew Twenty-Four." She and Davis spent much of the next several years on the road, where she began performing religious material almost exclusively; in mid-1949, she cut another session, recording songs like "Teardrops Falling in the Snow," "Poor Ellen Smith," and Williams' "On the Evening Train." In the latter half of the year, O'Day suffered a nervous breakdown and was hospitalized; although she did record again in 1950 and 1951, she largely turned her back on show business afterward, instead focusing on performing in churches. In 1954, Davis became an ordained minister, and in the decades following, the couple preached throughout the coal mining communities of West Virginia. O'Day did record for a few small gospel labels in the 1960s, and in 1973 she and Davis began hosting a daily gospel program on a West Virginia radio station. She died of cancer December 5, 1987. *—Jason Ankeny*

★ **Molly O'Day and the Cumberland Mountain Folks** / 1992 / Bear Family ✦✦✦✦✦

Molly O'Day and the Cumberland Mountain Folks is a double-disc, 36-track collection that compiles all of the recordings O'Day made for Columbia Records between 1946 and 1951. Though her music presages the upcoming honky tonk era, O'Day was more closely tied to the mountain music that dominated country music in the first half of the 20th century. As such, her music can be a little difficult for contemporary ears—her thick nasal twang is something that modern listeners will have to accomodate. For country historians, however, *Molly O'Day and the Cumberland Mountain Folks* is worthwhile. Not only did she bridge the gap between string bands and honky tonk with her old-timey banjo playing and twang, but she was one of the first country artists to record a Hank Williams song. As such, this double-disc set is worth investigation for serious musicologists. *—Stephen Thomas Erlewine*

James O'Gwynn

b. Jan. 26, 1928, Winchester, MS

Vocals / Traditional Country, Nashville Sound/Countrypolitan

"The Smilin' Irishman of Country Music," James O'Gwynn was briefly popular between the late '50s and the early '60s. He was born a Mississippi farmboy and raised near Hattiesburg, the son of a mechanic and a talented musician. He learned the guitar as a child from his mother, and his earliest influences were Jimmie Rodgers and Hank Williams. He dropped out of grade school to help out at his father's business and later served as a U.S. Marine for four years. During his tour of duty, he decided to become a country singer. He made his debut appearance during a campaign rally for a gubernatorial candidate while on leave. The candidate suggested O'Gwynn contact Houston DJ Hal Harris, who in turn introduced the young soldier to Biff Collie, the producer and host of *Houston Jamboree*. O'Gwynn joined the show in 1954, as did George Jones. Eventually he hooked up with renowned producer Pappy Dailey and in 1956 recorded "Losing Game." O'Gwynn joined the *Louisiana Hayride* and released two more singles the following year.

In 1958, he signed with Dailey's D label, where he finally found chart success with such songs as the Top Ten "Talk to Me Lonesome Heart" and "Blue Memories," which peaked in the Top 30. In 1959, O'Gwynn released two more hit singles, and, with the help of Jim Reeves, debuted on the *Grand Ole Opry*. He moved to Nashville in 1961 and appeared on the *Opry* for the next two years. During this time, he scored two more minor hits, including "My Name is Mud," his last chart appearance. During the 1960s, O'Gwynn worked with different major and independent labels, but to no avail; by the end of the decade, he had moved to Arkansas and gone into semi-retirement. In 1971, O'Gwynn tried a comeback, with no success. *—Sandra Brennan*

● **The Best of James O'Gwynn** / 1962 / Mercury ✦✦✦✦✦

Heartaches and Memories / 1964 / Mercury Wing ✦✦✦✦

Jamie O'Hara

b. Aug. 8, 1950, Toledo, OH

Songwriter, Vocals / Contemporary Country, Neo-Traditionalist Country

Singer/songwriter Jamie O'Hara was born August 8, 1950, in Toledo, OH. Originally a college football star, a knee injury forced him to look for career opportunities outside of the NFL. He picked up a guitar and eventually began to sing and play his songs at shows throughout the Midwest. Other performers took notice, and O'Hara began to establish himself as a songwriter. In 1975, he signed a publishing contract with Nashville's Tree Records. In 1985, O'Hara and another Tree songwriter named Kieran Kane collaborated on the song "Bluegrass Blues," which the Judds would eventually record. That meeting led the duo to begin writing and performing together as the O'Kanes. They secured a deal with Columbia and went on to release three acclaimed country albums between 1987 and 1990. After the O'Kanes broke up, O'Hara returned to his duties as a songwriter. But he also found time to release his solo debut. *Rise Above It* appeared on RCA in 1994; O'Hara wrote the entire album himself. While the album was a success, its follow-up didn't appear until 2001, when O'Hara released the richly textured *Beautiful Obsession*. *—Johnny Loftus*

Rise Above It / Apr. 1994 / RCA ✦✦✦✦

O'Hara wrote all ten songs himself, a rare and commendable thing in Nashville. The songs are primal and direct, with a slight but chugging rhythm and bluesy underpinning lending a swagger to his lean, seductive lyricism. "Cold, Hard Truth" is a great hard-country ballad about a man coming face-to-face with his deceitful ways. *—Michael McCall*

● **Beautiful Obsession** / Sep. 25, 2001 / Valley ✦✦✦✦

The thick, layered sound of *Beautiful Obsession* matches the dark intensity of its themes. Expansive steel and guitar work along with a B-3 organ stir these proceedings into a rich country stew, while Jamie O'Hara's soulful vocals add the final ingredient. "Come Swim the Rivers With Me" invites both a lover and the listener to come along on a spiritual journey immersed in darkness. The title cut confesses overwhelming desire set against a relaxed rhythm, seductively pulling in the object of the singer's obsession. The journey continues through surrender and fear, examining the need for total emersion followed by a feeling of entrapment. Several of the songs at the heart of the album—"That ain't the Way I Heard It," "Lovin' You Against My Will," and "See if I Care"—were written several years before the album was recorded, suggesting that O'Hara has lived with these themes for some time. Kenny Greenburg's guitar work adds tasteful flourishes on a number of cuts, while Vicki Hampton's background vocals add a little something extra to the choruses. O'Hara cut several classic albums as a member of the O'Kanes in the mid-'80s, and some time elapsed between this and his last solo album. He's still got the touch, though. *Beautiful Obsession* represents a rare album where sound, vision, and execution weld the material into a thematic whole. In other words, this is good stuff that will resonate deeper with each listen. *—Ronnie D. Lankford Jr.*

The O'Kanes

f. 1986, **db.** 1990

Group / Country-Rock, Contemporary Country, New Traditionalist, Neo-Traditionalist Country

During their relatively brief time together, Kieran Kane and Jamie O'Hara, otherwise known as the O'Kanes, produced three albums of absolutely superb country music. The self-titled, first, and arguably strongest effort contains everything that is best about the O'Kanes' sound. It is rich in country music's finest traditions, yet it is by no means a nostalgia album. It is sparse in instrumentation, yet richly textured. Most of all, the album contains direct, honest music whose emotional intensity stays with the listener long after the sound waves have stopped vibrating. The O'Kanes' vocals recall the best of country harmony. Some critics liken them to the Louvin Brothers. Others, because of the more driving sound of their backing, compare them to the Everlys. The instrumental sound ranges from bluegrass (prominent mandolin) to the tense drive of Sun rockabilly (their hit "Oh Darlin'" is evidence of this). The addition of an accordion adds both Tex-Mex and unmistakably bluesy feels to the proceedings. This is truly hybrid music.

Out of the core members of the O'Kanes, Kane was always the more musically inclined of the two. At the age of nine, he began playing drums in his older brother's rock & roll band. By the time he was in his teens, he was also playing bluegrass and folk, performing at festivals across the Northeast. Eventually, his reputation had grown large enough that he was opening for rock & roll groups like Country Joe & the Fish and the Steve Miller Band. When he was 21, he moved to Los Angeles, where he worked as a session guitarist and a professional songwriter. Eight years later, he relocated to Nashville, where he also worked as a session musician and songwriter. Within two years, he had landed a contract with Elektra, and over the next three years, he had a string of minor hits for both Elektra and later Warner. For his part, O'Hara didn't begin playing guitar when he was 22 years old, following a knee injury that prevented him from pursuing a career as a professional football player. After writing several original songs, he began to play clubs across the Midwest, while working odd jobs. In 1975, he arrived in Nashville, landing a publishing contract with Tree Publishing. By the early '80s, artists had begun to cover his songs, with Ronnie McDowell taking "Wandering Eyes" and "Older Women" to the Top Ten in 1981.

Kane and O'Hara began collaborating in 1985, when the two songwriters worked on "Bluegrass Blues" for Tree. Southern Pacific and the Judds would both later record the song. Throughout 1985, the pair wrote songs and recorded demos together, deciding to become a performing duo in 1986. Columbia signed the duo, and their eponymous debut consisted entirely of their demo tapes. "Oh Darlin'," the first single from the record, became a hit, climbing into the Top Ten; the album also reached the country Top Ten as well. In 1987, the group had three Top Ten hits—including the number one "Can't Stop My Heart From Loving You," "Daddies Need to Grow Up Too," and "Just Loving You"—all taken from *The O'Kanes*. The following year, they released their second album, *Tired of the Runnin'*, which produced an additional two Top Ten singles in "One True Love" and "Blue Love." However, the third single from the record, "Rocky Road," didn't even make the Top 40.

Following the recording of their third album, Kane and O'Hara parted ways in 1989; the third record, *Imagine That*, was released posthumously to little attention in 1990. Following the group's breakup, both members continued to work as professional songwriters. In 1993, Kane released his eponymous solo debut on Atlantic Records; O'Hara released his first solo album, *Rise Above It*, the following year on RCA. *—Hank Davis*

The O'Kanes / 1987 / Columbia ✦✦✦

Introspective lyrics and occasional guitar/mandolin jams make an interesting concept from Music City before the "hat" proliferation of 1990. *—Mark A. Humphrey*

● **Tired of the Runnin'** / 1988 / Columbia ✦✦✦✦✦

A strong title song, austerely folkish, represented this short-lived duo at its best. *—Mark A. Humphrey*

Imagine That / 1990 / Columbia ✦✦✦

In the late '80s, the O'Kanes offered a commercially viable update on a venerated country music tradition, the brother duo. Although the two members were not brothers, their close harmonies recalled the Everly Brothers, and their largely acoustic sound tied them to the music of the past despite their undeniable modernity and originality. After two excellent albums the O'Kanes released *Imagine That*, the most straightforward country album of their three, and the only one to fail to provide a Top 40 C&W hit. *Imagine That* doesn't differ radically from the two previous O'Kanes albums, but the material is weaker and the hypnotic quality that made the others so engaging is lacking here. *—Greg Adams*

The Only Years / 2000 / Lucky Dog ✦✦✦

Between 1986 and 1988, the O'Kanes, along with such peers as the Desert Rose Band, led the bluegrass division of the new traditionalist movement in country music, scoring a series of six consecutive Top Ten hits. But the duo of Kieran Kane and Jamie O'Hara split up by the end of the decade, leaving three strong albums as their legacy. Columbia Records, their label, never issued a compilation, but in 2000, parent company Sony's Lucky Dog imprint did, and it's a curious album. Only three of the band's seven chart entries are included, with the number one hit "Can't Stop My Heart From Loving You" not among them. In place of the hits are some low-key album tracks that show off Kane and O'Hara's talent for the high and lonesome sound of bluegrass but will be less familiar to fans. One can only assume that Lucky Dog, issuing this compilation in its discount-priced "Pick of the Litter" series, was not allowed to do a real best-of, Sony perhaps intending to issue an O'Kanes title in its *Super Hits* or *16 Biggest Hits* series. (A Shelby Lynne compilation, *Epic Recordings*, released simultaneously by Lucky Dog, is similarly devoid of singles.) If so, those interested in the O'Kanes might want to wait, since this set does not contain their best-remembered material. *—William Ruhlmann*

Old & In the Way

f. 1973, California

Group / Bluegrass, Traditional Bluegrass

Old & In the Way was a one-shot bluegrass band whose legacy lasted far longer than the band. Led by Grateful Dead member Jerry Garcia (banjo, vocals), the band also featured David Grisman (mandolin, vocals), Vassar Clements (fiddle), Peter Rowan (guitar, vocals), and John Kahn (bass). Garcia formed the band in 1973 as a way to revisit his bluegrass roots and demonstrate his affection for the music. To round out the lineup, he recruited Clements and Kahn as well as Grisman and Rowan, who were both West Coast session musicians who had previously played together in the band Muleskinner. Taking their name from a Grisman composition, Old & In the Way played a handful of gigs, most of them at the Boarding House in San Francisco in October. An album, also called *Old & In the Way*, was culled from these shows but not released until 1975 on the Grateful Dead's own record label, Round. The record combined standards and Rowan originals, which later became standards.

Although the album was the only one the lineup released during the 1970s, the members continued to play together in various permutations over the next two decades, and the record continued to sell steadily. The group reunited after Garcia's death in 1995, releasing a second album (actually composed of 1973 recordings), *That High Lonesome Sound*, in early 1996. A third album of 1973 vintage appeared at the end of 1997. *—Stephen Thomas Erlewine*

● **Old & In the Way** / Oct. 1973 / Grateful Dead ✦✦✦✦✦

The first release from Jerry Garcia's short-lived backcountry bluegrass act was this 1973 recording that also highlighted the amazing skills of mandolin player David Grisman. The quintet actually released only this record, recorded at a series of performances in 1973, but the sound caught on with Grateful Dead fans and the record actually built up the group's legacy long after they disbanded. The songs themselves, mostly penned by guitarist Peter Rowan and Grisman as well as a handful of traditional numbers and even a revamped version of the Rolling Stones' classic "Wild Horses," are delivered with the sincere reverence of true bluegrass fanatics. Soaring multi-part harmonies; fiddle, guitar, banjo, bass, and mandolin lines that seamlessly intertwine with a good-time feel; and exceptionally solid musicianship round out the ten-track effort. Fans of the Grateful Dead's jolly throwback tunes should already have this in their collection, but even those put off by the member's psychedelic resumés will find that Old & In the Way is nothing of the sort. This is the sound of purists re-creating the music they grew up with and it's both enjoyable and inspiring to listen to. Like *American Beauty* and *Workingman's Dead*, this record showcases Garcia going back to his roots, and it shows that he and his buddies have more than the chops required to live up to their legend. *—Peter J. D'Angelo*

That High Lonesome Sound / Feb. 20, 1996 / Acoustic Disc ✦✦✦✦✦

Old & In the Way came out with their second album 21 years after the first one, an amazing development for a group that existed for only nine months and about 30 gigs in 1973. *That High Lonesome Sound*, like its predecessor, *Old & In the Way*, was drawn from the group's stand at the Boarding House in San Francisco in October 1973. And like that release, it combined traditional bluegrass material, in this case standards like "Orange Blossom Special" and "Uncle Pen," with interpolations from the world of rock & roll ("The Great Pretender") and new originals that touched on contemporary issues (Peter Rowan's "Lonesome L.A. Cowboy," a comment on the southern California country-rock scene of the time). *Old & In The Way* was a great crossover album, largely because the band-members had enjoyed careers in rock, especially banjo player and singer Jerry Garcia, moonlighting from his day job in the Grateful Dead. What was less-well-known was that the group had real roots in the music, as Neil V. Rosenberg pointed out in the second album's liner notes. Four of the five members had experience in bluegrass, and two had been members of Bill Monroe's Blue Grass Boys. Old & In the Way was a hybrid, but it was far more bluegrass than rock. *—William Ruhlmann*

Breakdown: Live Recordings 1973 / Nov. 18, 1997 / Acoustic Disc ✦✦✦✦✦

Breakdown: Live Recordings 1973 collects 18 unreleased tracks from the group's legendary 1973 concerts, including two Jerry Garcia banjo songs that aren't available on any other disc and six alternate takes of songs like "Panama Red," "Pig in a Pen," "Wild Horses" and "Midnight Moonlight." In short, it's quite similar to their second record *That High Lonesome Sound*, a compilation of leftovers from the original *Old & In the Way* album that was released the year before *Breakdown*, but when music is as joyous as this, there's no reason to complain. Old & In the Way were one of the greatest progressive bluegrass bands of the early '70s, and each subsequent release proves that they were a special band. Even if you are intimately familiar with its two predecessors, it's unlikely you'll be disappointed with *Breakdown*. *—Thom Owens*

The Old Dogs

Group / Traditional Country, Honky Tonk

A supergroup comprised of country music legends Waylon Jennings, Mel Tillis, Bobby Bare, and Jerry Reed, the Old Dogs were formed after Bare complained to author Shel Silverstein that there were no good songs about growing old. Silverstein proceeded to pen an album's worth of material on the subject, with the end result forming the basis for the Old Dogs' 1998 Atlantic Records debut. *—Jason Ankeny*

Old Dogs / Dec. 1, 1998 / Atlantic ✦✦✦✦✦

Old Dogs, indeed: At the time of this album's release, the combined ages of its principals—Waylon Jennings, Mel Tillis, Bobby Bare, and Jerry Reed—exceeded 250 years, and to these sixtysomethings really should have been added the disc's true auteur, Shel Silverstein, who wrote all the songs. Beginning with the title track, Silverstein's theme, naturally enough, was aging, and being Silverstein, his take on it was expressed in pointed, usually humorous novelty songs with titles like "I Don't Do It No More," "Cut the Mustard," and "Still Gonna Die." The singers took turns singing lead on successive songs, with one or more sometimes joining in for asides or choruses. The album was recorded live in the studio before a raucously enthusiastic audience that sang along, and producer Bare gave it a heavily echoed, trebly sound. The songs could be touching, especially "Me and Jimmie Rodgers," which mixed false reminiscences about real people and movie stars, and the album-closing "Time." But more often Silverstein affected a gallows humor, for example, on "I Never Expected," in which he complained about having lived so long, and "Still Gonna Die," a list song that described the ultimately futile things you can do for your health. Of course, Silverstein was right; he died five months after the album's release. But that only made it a final monument to his unique, irrepressible worldview. *—William Ruhlmann*

Old 97's

f. 1993, Dallas, TX

Group / Alternative Country-Rock, Americana, Indie Pop

One of the most popular bands in the alternative country movement's rock & roll wing, Old 97's hailed from Dallas and drew their inspiration from classic country, bar-band rock, the raw sound of early punk, and—especially on their later records—the tight songcraft of power pop. The band was formed in 1993 by singer/guitarist Rhett Miller and bassist Murry Hammond; Miller had previously played around the Dallas area as a folksinger and a British-style pop devotee and actually earned a creative writing scholarship to Sarah Lawrence College but dropped out to return to Texas and concentrate on music. When he teamed up with Hammond, his original material was allowing the influence of Texas country to seep in. The two soon added lead guitarist Ken Bethea and recorded their initial demo tape at Austin's famed Cedar Creek studio. Drummer Philip Peeples also came onboard, and in 1994, Old 97's issued their debut album, *Hitchhike to Rhome*, on the indie label Big Iron. It received positive reviews and began to build the group's alt-country fan base, which they consolidated on the follow-up, *Wreck Your Life*.

Issued on alt-country stalwart Bloodshot Records in 1995, *Wreck Your Life* fleshed out the group's sound and presented them as a sharp, eclectic country-rock outfit.The positive attention given to the band's two indie albums led to a major-label deal with Elektra, for whom Old 97's debuted in 1997 with *Too Far to Care*. Critics hailed the album as the best balance yet between the group's Texas traditionalism and pop leanings and placed the band among the leaders of the alt-country movement. Their next release, 1999's *Fight Songs*, actually began to move away from their country influences, offering a more polished, pop-friendly set of songs. By this time, Miller had moved to Los Angeles and shed the thick '50s-style glasses that had become a major part of his image; he and Hammond were also performing in an informal side project dubbed the Ranchero Brothers. *Satellite Rides* (2001) had an even stronger power pop flavor and once again received highly positive reviews. Miller subsequently took a temporary leave from Old 97's to record his solo power pop debut, *The Instigator*, which was released in late 2002. *—Steve Huey*

Hitchhike to Rhome / 1994 / Big Iron ✦✦✦

Many bands blend country and rock, but few brew this concoction as well as the Old 97's on *Hitchhike to Rhome*. Energetic frontman Rhett Miller commands attention as a charismatic vocalist and clever songwriter on tracks such as "St. Ignatius" and "If My Heart Was a Car." On the album's highlight "Stoned," he even manages to successfully infuse the adjectives "dope" and "fly" into a country song. Bass player Murry Hammond supplies smooth harmonies throughout the album, in addition to lead vocals on the excellent Merle Haggard cover "Mama Tried." Musically, the Old 97's are capable of shifting comfortably between bluegrassy honky tonk ("Doreen") and the occasional serene ballad ("Dancing With Tears.") Ken Bethea's guitar leads the band throughout their rowdy ride while Philip Peeples' steady drumming manages to somehow hold everything together. Other standouts include "Drowning in the Days," "Hands Off," and "504." Further demonstrating their country roots, there is even a secret hidden version of Webb Pierce's "Tupelo County Jail" after the last listed track. Though their debut sounds more sparse and simplified than their subsequent releases, *Hitchhike to Rhome* showcases the spark of a truly original band with endless potential. *—Michael Frey*

Wreck Your Life / Oct. 3, 1995 / Bloodshot ✦✦✦

While Old 97's second album, 1995's *Wreck Your Life*, continues the forlorn West Texas twang-a-billy that they pioneered with their debut, the sharp songwriting of vocalist Rhett Miller steps out to the forefront this time around. He weeps through the lovesick romp "Doreen" and chunks through longtime favorite "Big Brown Eyes" with a newfound poetic touch to the age-old traumas of love ("I'm callin' time and temperature just for some company," "You made a big impression for a girl of your size"). At the same time, it's hard to believe the barroom ballad "W-I-F-E" wasn't written by George Jones back in the late '50s. Supporting Miller's keening vocals is bassist and yodeler Murry Hammond, whose musical accents are understated, but without them many a song would fall flat. Well-chosen covers, including the Tex-Mex standard "You Belong to My Heart" and a stomp through "My Sweet Blue-Eyed Darlin'" that would do Bill Monroe proud round out the album, although a few songs near the end seem to lose steam. Nevertheless, *Wreck Your Life* contains some killer tracks and the band exudes an honest energy that would only improve on future releases. —*Zac Johnson*

● **Too Far to Care** / Jun. 17, 1997 / Elektra ✦✦✦✦✦
Serving as the ideal apex between the Old 97's Texas twang and smart pop fascinations, *Too Far to Care* is instantly catchy and endearing; heartbreaking desert soul and punk-fueled swagger all at the same time. Chief songwriter Rhett Miller turns a phrase like a doorknob and opens doors to dusty barrooms and tattered bedrooms, both containing the same boozy characters in various states of emotional undress. The initial blast of "Timebomb" carries through the first three songs, relenting finally in the breathy croon of "Salome," accented warmly by bassist Murry Hammond's light harmonies and guitarist Ken Bethea's airy tremolo-heavy guitar. Other highlights include the high-speed chase of "Melt Show," the reckless surge of "House That Used to Be," and their confident re-recording of "Big Brown Eyes" (originally appearing on their 1995 album *Wreck Your Life*). Throughout the album, Miller's swooning howl aches with too many miles on the road and too many lonely nights, familiar topics to be sure but he still manages to tackle them like he invented heartache. The curse of Old 97's may be that country fans consider it too rock & roll, and rock fans can't get past the twang, but for those who dip both feet into these streams, it really doesn't get any better than this band and this album. —*Zac Johnson*

Fight Songs / Apr. 27, 1999 / Elektra ✦✦✦
Texas troubadours Old 97's moved farther away from their traditional C&W sound on their 1999 release, *Fight Songs*, instead incorporating warmly distorted guitars and crunchy rhythms into their brash pop songs. Thankfully for fans of the band, the terrific songwriting is still there, but the sound is a little more polished than the twang-a-billy bombast of their previous album, *Too Far to Care*. The heavy grit of the lead track, "Jagged," is augmented by Rhett Miller and Murray Hammond's bright vocals, whereas the rhumba stylings of "What We Talk About" slinks along like two strangers locked in a tango. Songs seem more thoroughly constructed this time around, relying less on pure bravado and more on structure. That works well for the most part, but there's something lacking that was unrelenting and instantly likable in their previous release. That being said, *Fight Songs* is still a bright and worthwhile album with as many strong songs as any of their releases. —*Zac Johnson*

Early Tracks / May 23, 2000 / Bloodshot ✦✦✦
A collection of out-of-print seven-inch singles and previously unreleased tracks, *Early Tracks* exhibits the Old 97s' uncanny ability to play witty, memorable, country-rock that chugs along at a freight train's pace. Despite the fact that this EP has been pieced together from spare parts, the material is surprisingly strong. With its unrelenting twang and Rhett Miller's nimble wordplay, "Ray Charles" would have fit perfectly into place on *Wreck Your Life*, while "Cryin' Drunk," a swaggering track that is stylistically similar to "Just Like California," would find *Too Far to Care* to be a better fit. Bassist Murry Hammond makes strong contributions, handling lead vocals on "Sound of Running," "Harold's Super Service," and a cover of Johnny Cash's "Let the Train Blow the Whistle." Also present are the dynamic "Por Favor," a swaying, breezy version of "W.I.F.E.," and the devilish "Eyes For You." *Early Tracks* is sure to please fans pleading for a return to the days before the pop sheen of *Fight Songs*, as well as those who just can't get enough of this truly arresting and irresistible quartet. —*Michael Frey*

Satellite Rides / Mar. 20, 2001 / Elektra ✦✦✦✦
Moving even further away from their alt-country roots, the Old 97's fifth effort is a consistently engaging and unpretentious strummy power pop nugget. Bits of the effortless hook-driven approach of Marshall Crenshaw and Nick Lowe mesh with winning melodies that stick in your skull after the first spin. Hints of Brit Invasion Beatles/Badfinger-styled harmonies also infiltrate these songs, bringing a crisp vocal attack to play, especially in bassist Murray Hammond's subtle backing work. Guitarist/singer/songwriter Rhett Miller has honed his composing and arrangement skills to a fine edge, cramming these compact cuts (nothing runs over four minutes, most clock in around three) with smart lyrics and sharp, unaffected playing. There's still a little twang remaining from the old days in the driving double-time "Am I Too Late," and even a solo acoustic guitar ballad in "Question," but the band seems most comfortable pounding out crafty, infectious instant singles like "Rollerskate Skinny." Miller's voice is perfect for these songs, mixing just the right amount of pride, innocence, and youthful exuberance into the predominantly upbeat lyrics. But just as importantly, there's a presence and immediacy to *Satellite Rides*, partially due to the expert touch of mixer Tchad Blake, that makes it jump out of the speakers like the locomotive that provides the band with its name. Deftly incorporating their Texas roots with yodeling and a snappy punch makes "Up the Devil's Pay" one of the disc's most successful tracks, but there really isn't a lackluster performance here. The six-song live bonus EP that came free with early pressings proves how skillful the quartet is in concert, and that their biting, cohesive style is no studio-concocted fluke. The Old 97's sound is organic and natural, and on *Satellite Rides* they find the perfect balance between their roots in rugged country and pure chiming pop. —*Hal Horowitz*

Will Oldham

b. Louisville, KY
Guitar, Vocals / Singer/Songwriter, Lo-Fi, Indie Rock, Alternative Country
For most of the '90s, Will Oldham was the mastermind of Palace Music, a shambling, country-tinged indie rock group that recorded under a variety of names. The only constant in Palace was Oldham, and he would often record as a solo artist under the Palace name. That fact made his decision to retire the Palace name in 1997 somewhat baffling,

since for all intents and purposes, he was the band. Nevertheless, *Joya*, Oldham's first album as a solo artist, was slightly different than Palace, boasting a slightly darker and somber tone. Like all the Palace records, *Joya* was released on Drag City to positive critical notices and a moderately successful cult following. Although the subsequent *I See a Darkness* was attributed to Bonnie "Prince" Billy, Oldham continued using his given name for releases, including *Ode Music* and *Guarapero: Lost Blues 2*. The second Bonnie "Prince" Billy album, *Ease Down the Road*, arrived in early 2001, featuring collaborators David Pajo, Catherine Irwin, Mike Fellows, and Harmony Korine. *Master and Everyone* appeared two years later. —*Stephen Thomas Erlewine*

● **Joya** / Oct. 21, 1997 / Drag City ✦✦✦✦
Retiring the Palace moniker for no reason other than a whim, Will Oldham doesn't necessarily explore new territory on his first official solo album, *Joya*. Oldham sticks to the simple, slow acoustic country-folk songs that dominated the latter-day Palace albums, and like before, the songs teeter between apparent sincerity and inscrutible irony. The hushed dynamics of the music and his whispered vocals suggest that Oldham means what he's saying, but his appropriation of American folk imagery and impenetrable wordplay suggest otherwise. As always, there are a few songs that have a quiet power (including "Antagonism" and a collaboration with the Silver Jews' Dave Berman), but the overall effect of *Joya* is a familiar one—it's a promising, ultimately unfulfilling record that doesn't quite prove whether Oldham is a songwriter of pretense or genuine talent. —*Stephen Thomas Erlewine*

Western Music / Mar. 24, 1998 / Acuarela Ovni ✦✦✦
Keeping up to date with Will Oldham's complete output can be an arduous task—he has always exploited the shorter formats of the seven-inch and EP, producing a healthy amount of material in between his full-length releases. However, seeking out the seven-inch and EP formats can be rewarding, as the material often matches—and occasionally surpasses—the quality of his albums. The genesis of *Western Music* (released by the combined forces of two obscure labels for *The Affliction Series*) is typical, coming from a variety of sessions. Two tracks are solo Oldham, while Mick Turner and Jim White of the Dirty Three and former Gastr del Sol member David Grubbs play anonymous roles elsewhere. On nearly every song, Oldham approaches the level of his best work although, ultimately, each has its shortcomings. "Always Bathing in the Evening" relishes in its simple language. "Wade in/Wade in," he sings, as voices in the distance chime in with "Blowing/Jump in/Waiting/Jump in." While there is little lyrical matter to speak of, it sounds fantastic. *Western Music*'s most complete song is "Jump in Jump In, Come in Come In," though even this, with its plodding tempo, feels more like a rehearsal on disc. Inspiration only seems to strike with the final verse. Only on "Three Photographs" (an oddity in a career full of them) does Oldham manage to throw us yet another curve. It's an intriguing, fragmentary story told through pictures. Over the most rudimentary, lo-fi guitar strum, Oldham's voice is sped up slightly, producing a humorous, Paul Simon effect. *Western Music* came during a particularly prolific time for Oldham, though *Joya*, his full-length album from the period, is more consistent. —*Nathan Bush*

Get on Jolly / 2000 / Palace ✦✦✦
Credited to Marquis de Tren and Bonny Billy, *Get on Jolly* is performed by Will Oldham along with Dirty Three member and Tren Brother Mick Turner. With words adapted from *Gitanjali* by Rabindranath Tagore (1861-1941), a Nobel Prize-winning poet from India, Oldham sings in a somber, yet expressive mode, giving an air of sacredness to the effort. Turner's low-key accompaniment, meanwhile, provides a loose, meandering minor-key backdrop. Though a pleasant enough listen, *Get on Jolly* is by no means an essential release for either artist; only ardent fans will find it worth their while. —*Jason Nickey*

Guarapero: Lost Blues 2 / Feb. 22, 2000 / Drag City ✦✦✦
Guarapero/Lost Blues 2 gathers seven years' worth of rarities from Will Oldham, including an unusual reading of D.H. Lawrence's poem *The Risen Lord*, with a clunky, cheesy drum machine in the background, as well as a radical reworking of Lynyrd Skynyrd's "Every Mother's Son." Several of these songs come from BBC sessions, but the sound quality on tracks like "Gezundheit" and "Let the Wires Ring" suggests they were recorded on wax cylinder and transmitted by a crystal set, which, of course, only amplifies the songs' sparse, timeless feel. "The Spider's Dude Is Often There" and "For the Mekons Et Al" are among the most exuberant Palace songs on *Guarapero*, while Oldham tracks like "No More Rides" and "Sugarcane Juice Drinker" trace his development as a performer and songwriter. Due to the time span it covers, it's natural that *Guarapero/Lost Blues 2* is a bit disjointed; nevertheless, it fills in the gaps for Oldham completists and is an entertaining, if scattered, look at some of his musical sketches over the years. —*Heather Phares*

Carla Olson

Guitar, Vocals / Country-Rock, Roots Rock, Americana
Along with Kathy Valentine (a future member of the Go-Go's), Carla Olson formed the Textones in the early '80s for a few singles on IRS. (Most of these tracks appear on *Through the Canyon* (Rhino) and *Back in Time* (Demon U.K.).) The band's major-label debut, *Midnight Mission* (A&M), included help from Don Henley, Ry Cooder, Barry Goldberg, and Gene Clark. *Cedar Creek*, the band's second album, appeared in 1987 on Enigma Records. Olson then worked on many projects, including ones by John Fogerty, Henley, and Eric Johnson and a duet album with Clark. In 1988, she recorded a self-titled solo album (for Amigo Musik) in Sweden, backed by Wilmer X. After another duet project, this time with former Rolling Stones guitarist Mick Taylor, Olson's second solo LP (*Within an Ace*) was released in 1993 on Watermelon Records; *Reap the Whirlwind* followed the next year. That album signaled a period of relative quiet from the guitarist, as she disappeared into private life while her best-of collection hit the shelves. It wasn't until 2001 that she returned, boasting *The Ring of Truth*, an album featuring Taylor and a handful of roots rock tunes that showcased her weathered vocals and comfortable sound. —*John Bush*

Midnight Mission / 1984 / Varese ✦✦✦✦✦
Midnight Mission is an excellent, low-key collection of roots rock distinguished by terrific support from the likes of Gene Clark and Ry Cooder, as well as Olson's remarkable vocals. *—Thom Owens*

So Rebellious a Lover / 1987 / Razor & Tie ✦✦✦✦

Carla Olson / 1988 / Still Sane ✦✦✦

Live / 1991 / Demon ✦✦✦✦✦
Recorded at the Roxy Theatre in Hollywood, CA, in March of 1990, *Live* is an entertaining if ultimately non-essential addition to the catalogs of both artists; the clear highlight is a fiery rendition of the Rolling Stones' *Sticky Fingers* track "Sway," a song Taylor clearly relishes performing as much as Olson does. (*Live* is the European title of the material released in America as *Too Hot for Snakes*). *—Jason Ankeny*

Within an Ace / 1993 / Watermelon ✦✦✦

Reap the Whirlwind / 1994 / Watermelon ✦✦✦

Wave of the Hand: The Best of Carla Olson / Oct. 17, 1995 / Watermelon ✦✦✦✦✦
It continues to amaze me that people keep snapping up Bonnie Raitt's recent snoozeramas while Carla Olson continues to go relatively unnoticed. A "female Tom Petty" is the easy comparison, but Olson is definitely her own roots rockin' woman. *Wave of the Hand* gathers choice material from her former band the Textones, the excellent *So Rebellious a Lover* collaboration with ex-Byrds Gene Clark, several solo albums, and three newly recorded tracks. Guests and sidemen who know a good thing when they hear it include Mick Taylor, Ry Cooder, Ian McLagan, Percy Sledge, and Don Henley. *—Roch Parisien*

• **Honest as Daylight: The Best of Carla Olson (1981–2000)** / 2001 / Houston Party ✦✦✦✦✦
Austin-to-L.A. transplants the Textones were one of the few post-new wave "roots rock" bands of the mid-'80s to deserve the appellation. (Unfortunately, they're mostly remembered, if at all, only as the band Kathy Valentine left to join the Go-Go's.) Unlike the terribly overrated Lone Justice or the beer salesmen in the Long Ryders or the Del Fuegos, Carla Olson and company came off like a punkier version of the Gram Parsons-era Byrds, with a poppy edge on unexpected covers like the Searchers' "Silver" and Neil Sedaka's "Keep a Walkin'." Although Olson ditched the Textones name fairly early in her career, her smoky voice (think Lucinda Williams with Janis Joplin's accent) and proto-alt-country mentality remain constant through this well-chosen, reverse-chronology collection. Pay particular attention to the pair of remixed tracks from 1993's *Within an Ace*, which sound worlds better now. This album far surpasses the earlier Carla Olson best-of, 1995's *Wave of the Hand*. *—Stewart Mason*

The Ring of Truth / Jul. 2, 2001 / Evangeline ✦✦✦
Carla Olson was one of the best roots rockers to emerge from L.A.'s new wave scene in the '80s, and with the possible exception of the Long Ryders, no one slipped into the groove of folk-rock and country-rock with as much élan and commitment as Olson (she may well have been the best collaborator Gene Clark had outside of the Byrds). *The Ring of Truth* was Olson's first studio album in six years, and it finds her in excellent form; Olson's voice, tough but clear and full-bodied, sounds great, and the set kicks off with three especially fine originals from Olson: the tough-rocking "Loserville" and "Never Fade Away" and the moody "The Low Way." Olson also has a pretty impressive band on board, including former Electric Flag keyboardist Barry Goldberg; bassist Gregg Sutton, who's worked with Dave Alvin and Lone Justice; and John Sebastian, who adds a harmonica solo to a rollicking cover of Bob Dylan's "Won't You Please Crawl Out Your Window." However, one of the album's best-known guest stars also turns out to be its most crippling flaw; former Rolling Stones guitarist Mick Taylor, who's recorded with Olson in the past, contributes to a number of songs on *The Ring of Truth*, and while it's probably very difficult to tell a man who played on *Sticky Fingers* and *Exile on Main Street* that he needs to cut back on his soloing, the truth is his pointlessly extended workouts sink several tracks here, especially the nine-and-a-half-minute "Great Black Hole" and a cover of the Stones' "Winter" that meanders on for a torturous 12 minutes. Carla Olson is a great talent, and with a little editing *The Ring of Truth* would be a great album, but a little less instrumental showboating and more concise arrangements would do many of these songs a world of good. *—Mark Deming*

Jamie O'Neal (Jamie Murphy)

b. Australia
Vocals, Vocals (Background) / Contemporary Country
Jamie O'Neal first struck Music City gold as a sought-after songwriter; it was only later that her own singing career blossomed. O'Neal was born Jamie Murphy in Australia to professional musician parents who eventually moved to Las Vegas and a casino gig via Hawaii. Eventually, Jamie and her sister Samantha began to perform with their parents. This led to a vagabond childhood spent traveling across America in an RV, performing at state fairs, conventions, and as an opening act for touring country stars. The family then moved to Nashville, where it recorded three self-released albums. But the divorce of O'Neal's mom and dad broke up the band, and she moved to Los Angeles with her father. Regular high-school wasn't for her however, and soon O'Neal had dropped out in order to try and make in Music City all on her own. She found some work as a demo performer for a Nashville song factory but soon left America altogether to visit her mother in Australia. There she began performing in clubs and on street corners and landed a gig as a backup singer for pop tart Kylie Minogue. But O'Neal was still writing her own songs and still thought that Nashville might be her ticket. A demo tape sent by her mother to old contacts in Nashville generated interest, and in 1996 O'Neal was offered a songwriting contract under producer Harold Shedd.

This exposure led to a sweeter songwriter/artist-development deal with EMI Music. While O'Neal sang backup for established country acts like Clay Davidson and Ronnie Milsap, her songs were covered by the likes of LeAnn Rimes and Chely Wright. But despite this success, O'Neal still felt stifled, as she still wasn't performing her own material. That changed in 1998, when an audition with Mercury Nashville's Keith Stegall led to a recording contract with the label. Her country-pop debut, *Shiver*, was released in early 2000; it was nominated for three Grammy awards. A self-titled effort followed almost immediately; O'Neal returned in 2003 with a new album and single. *—Johnny Loftus*

• **Jamie O'Neal** / 2000 / Mercury ✦✦✦✦
Country singer and songwriter and Sydney, Australia, native Jamie O'Neal first drew major public attention in the music world with her hit single "There Is No Arizona." It's one of the strongest tunes on this album—a song about being left behind with nothing more than a broken heart and shattered promises. O'Neal has the perfect sultry voice for this kind of contemporary country music. She also has the ability to transfer the emotions of the lyrics into each note she sings. Before recording her own music, O'Neal spent time as a backup singer and even penned songs for many well-known country artists, such as Chely Wright, LeAnn Rimes, Mindy McCready, Tammy Cochran, and many others. O'Neal co-wrote most of the tunes on this album, including "She Hasn't Heard It Yet," "When I Think About Angels," "Sanctuary," "Shiver," and "You Rescued Me." One of the songs, "I'm Not Gonna Do Anything Without You," was performed as an enjoyable duet with Mark Wills. O'Neal's husband, Rodney Good, sang harmony on some of the tunes, while her little sister, Samantha Murphy, did backup vocals. *—Charlotte Dillon*

Shiver / Oct. 31, 2000 / Mercury ✦✦✦
Solid songwriting and powerful vocals course throughout Jamie O'Neal's debut album, *Shiver*. Though billed as a country recording artist, O'Neal's voice lends itself more to pop; therefore, the album comes across as a country-pop blend, with mandolins and the occasional fiddle giving it a country identity. The best cuts on the album are "When I Think About Angels" and "There Is No Arizona," both of which Mercury Records had the musical foresight to release as singles. This was probably a smart move to introduce the world to Jamie O'Neal, as almost all the remaining songs, with the exception of "Sanctuary" and "Frantic," will probably not be running through the listener's head all day at work. The mixing and engineering elements are all here and work in the album's favor, but the whole package, while not at all bad, lacks the polish of the pros. That said, *Shiver* would still be a fine CD to pop in while going down the road or for a quiet evening at home. As her career progresses, O'Neal's music will most surely get better and better. *—Rick Cohoon*

Roy Orbison

b. Apr. 23, 1936, Vernon, TX, **d.** Dec. 6, 1988, Madison, TN
Guitar, Vocals / Rock & Roll, Rockabilly, Pop, Pop/Rock
Although he shared the same rockabilly roots as Carl Perkins, Johnny Cash, and Elvis Presley, Roy Orbison went on to pioneer an entirely different brand of country/pop-based rock & roll in the early '60s. What he lacked in charisma and photogenic looks, Orbison made up for in spades with his quavering operatic voice and melodramatic narratives of unrequited love and yearning. In the process, he established rock & roll archetypes of the underdog and the hopelessly romantic loser. These were not only amplified by peers such as Del Shannon and Gene Pitney, but also influenced future generations of roots rockers such as Bruce Springsteen and Chris Isaak, as well as modern country stars the Mavericks.

Orbison made his first widely distributed recordings for Sun Records in 1956. Roy was a capable rockabilly singer, and had a small national hit with his first Sun single, "Ooby Dooby." But even then, he was far more comfortable as a ballad singer than as a hepped-up rockabilly jive cat. Other Sun singles met with no success, and by the late '50s he was concentrating primarily on building a career as a songwriter, his biggest early success being "Claudette" (recorded by the Everly Brothers). After a brief, unsuccessful stint with RCA, Orbison finally found his voice with Monument Records, scoring a number-two hit in 1960 with "Only the Lonely." This established the Roy Orbison persona for good: a brooding rockaballad of failed love with a sweet, haunting melody, enhanced by his Caruso-like vocal trills at the song's emotional climax. These and his subsequent Monument hits also boasted innovative, quasi-symphonic production, with Roy's voice and guitar backed by surging strings, ominous drum rolls, and heavenly choirs of backup vocalists.

Between 1960 and 1965, Orbison would have 15 Top 40 hits for Monument, including such nail-biting mini-dramas as "Running Scared," "Crying," "In Dreams," and "It's Over." Not just a singer of tear-jerking ballads, he was also capable of effecting a tough, bluesy swagger on "Dream Baby," "Candy Man," and "Mean Woman Blues." In fact, his biggest and best hit was also his hardest-rocking: "Oh, Pretty Woman" soared to number one in late 1964, at the peak of the British Invasion. It seemed at that time that Roy was well-equipped to survive the British onslaught of the mid-'60s. He had even toured with the Beatles in Britain in 1963, and John Lennon has admitted to trying to emulate Orbison when writing the Beatles' first British chart-topper, "Please Please Me." But Orbison's fortunes declined rapidly after he left Monument for MGM in 1965. It would be easy to say that the major label couldn't replicate the unique production values of the classic Monument singles, but that's only part of the story. Roy, after all, was still writing most of his material, and his early MGM records were produced in a style that closely approximated the Monument era. The harder truth to face was that his songs were starting to sound like lesser variations of themselves, and that contemporary trends in rock and soul were making him sound outdated.

Orbison, like many early rock greats, could always depend on large overseas audiences to pay the bills. The two decades between the mid-'60s and mid-'80s were undeniably tough ones for him, though, both personally and professionally. A late-'60s stab at acting failed miserably. In 1966, his wife died in a motorcycle accident; a couple of years later, his house burned down, two of his sons perishing in the flames. Periodic comeback attempts with desultory albums in the 1970s came to naught. Orbison's return to the public eye came about through unexpected circumstances. In the mid-'80s, David Lynch's

Blue Velvet film prominently featured "In Dreams" on its soundtrack. That led to the singer making an entire album of re-recordings of hits, with T-Bone Burnett acting as producer. The record was no substitute for the originals, but it did help restore him to prominence within the industry. Shortly afterward, he joined George Harrison, Bob Dylan, Tom Petty, and Jeff Lynne in the Traveling Wilburys. Their successful album set the stage for Orbison's best album in over 20 years, *Mystery Girl*, which emulated the sound of his classic '60s work without sounding hackneyed. By the time it reached the charts in early 1989, however, Orbison was dead, claimed by a heart attack in December 1988. —*Richie Unterberger*

Crying / 1962 / Columbia ✦✦✦
Roy Orbison's second album was above-average considering the slight standards of the time, but was a fairly slight effort nonetheless. In its favor, the album features nearly all original material by Orbison and some of the writers who frequently tailored songs for him, such as Boudleaux & Felice Bryant and Joe Melson. The trademark early Orbison production flourishes, with swooping strings and full vocal choruses, are also present. What's missing is truly first-rate songwriting. With the exception of "Love Hurts," the title track, and the epic hit "Running Scared," most of the cuts lean toward the Big O's more sentimental side, and are pleasantly forgettable. Of the obscure cuts here, the best are the uptempo "Nite Life" and "Let's Make a Memory," with its bouncing string arrangement, but neither could be classified among his best early work. —*Richie Unterberger*

There Is Only One / 1965 / MGM ✦✦
Orbison explains in the liner notes that MGM will allow him "a new climate of freedom" as an artist, but the results of his first album for the label were unimpressive. He forsakes much of the rock & roll foundation of his classic early-'60s hits for Nashville country & western on most of the LP, complete with barroom piano. The material (mostly written by Orbison with various collaborators) doesn't approach the magnificence of his best work, and his version of his composition "Claudette" isn't nearly as good as the Everly Brothers' hit rendition from 1958. The highlight is the strange, almost rambling minor hit single, "Ride Away." —*Richie Unterberger*

The Fastest Guitar Alive / 1968 / Columbia ✦✦
Orbison's one bid for film stardom, *The Fastest Guitar Alive*, was an unqualified flop. The soundtrack fares slightly better, but only slightly. With ten songs clocking in at a mere 27 minutes, most of the tunes—which Roy composed with longtime collaborator Bill Dees—borrow from the cheesiest elements of cowboy music, with quasi-Mexican guitar riffs, silly Indian chants, and uneasy spaghetti-Western pathos. For all its ill-conceived failure, it includes what may be his best obscure tune, the little-anthologized "Whirlwind." With its galloping rhythm, emotive operatic vocals, swirling strings, and ghostly backing vocals, it recalls the best uptempo ballads that he recorded during his early-'60s heyday at the Monument label. In 1968, of course, few listeners were interested. —*Richie Unterberger*

All-Time Greatest Hits of Roy Orbison, Vol. 2 / 1972 / Monument ✦✦✦
All-Time Greatest Hits, Vol. 2 is a ten-track collection that contains several classics not on the first volume, including "Running Scared," "Love Hurts," "I'm Hurtin'," "Mean Woman Blues," "Pretty Paper," "Blue Bayou," and "Oh Pretty Woman." It's an excellent compilation, but it's now somewhat redundant, since both volumes have been combined on a single CD that surpasses either individual volume. —*Stephen Thomas Erlewine*

The All-Time Greatest Hits of Roy Orbison, Vols. 1 & 2 / 1976 / Monument ✦✦✦✦
Although it missing his early Sun hit "Ooby Dooby," and the 20-track *All-Time Greatest Hits of Roy Orbison* contains every one of his big hits for Monument Records, including "Up Town," "Only the Lonely," "Blue Angel," "I'm Hurtin'," "Running Scared," "Crying," "Dream Baby," "Leah," "Working' for the Man," "Candy Man," "In Dreams," "Falling," "Mean Woman Blues," "Blue Bayou," "Pretty Paper," "It's Over," and "Oh, Pretty Woman." In other words, it is nearly as complete as Rhino's 18-track *For the Lonely*. The main difference between the two collections is the fact that the Rhino disc contains some Sun material, which makes it the preferable retrospective. Nevertheless, *All-Time Greatest Hits* remains a first-rate collection, especially if you're just looking for hits. —*Stephen Thomas Erlewine*

All-Time Greatest Hits of Roy Orbison, Vol. 1 / 1978 / Monument ✦✦✦✦✦
For reasons difficult to fathom, when Monument Records released their fine two-LP Roy Orbison anthology, *The All-Time Greatest Hits of Roy Orbison*, on compact disc, they opted to issue the entire 20-song set on one disc, but also made available two ten-song discs that split the track listing in half. The full-length set obviously offers better value for the money, but either disc offers up a handful of Orbison's timeless hits, and it's hard to argue with the quality of an album that includes "Only the Lonely," "Crying," "In Dreams," and "It's Over." Someone looking for a definitive Roy Orbison package should look elsewhere, but if you're looking for a budget-priced Orbison disc to throw in the car or the boombox, this serves up ten of his spine-tingling hits in fine fidelity; melodramatic heartbreak never sounded this beautiful, either before or since. —*Mark Deming*

All-Time Greatest Hits of Roy Orbison, Vols. 1 & 2 / 1982 / Columbia ✦✦✦

In Dreams: Greatest Hits / 1987 / Virgin ✦✦
In Dreams: Greatest Hits is one of many shoddy Roy Orbison repackagings flooding the market; while it contains a generous 19 tracks of Orbison's best material, none of the songs are present in their original versions, but rather in re-recordings that fail to match the power of the originals. —*Steve Huey*

RCA Sessions / 1987 / Bear Family ✦✦✦
Only Bear Family would issue a CD like this. The pairing of Roy Orbison with Sonny James isn't because the two performed together—and the consumer is nowhere led to believe this is so—but because the sessions featured here showcased both artists in transition and between hits. For Orbison it was this initial period at RCA doing sessions in 1958 and 1959 for Chet Atkins where the record company was trying to make the best use of

Orbison's original voice. The first session doesn't feature any original material, but instead the putrid Billy Sherrill ballad "Sweet and Innocent," J.D. Loudermilk's syrupy "I'll Never Tell," and Boudleaux Bryant's equally drippy "Seems to Me." Have no fear, though, there are four other Orbison tracks, from the silly, yet totally rocking "The Bug," to his teen midtempo rocker "Jolie," "Paper Boy," and "Happy Little Bluebird." It's true none of these are the strongest Orbison tracks, but they nonetheless showcase him beginning to work that voice to dark effect and feature the Jordonaires on backing vocals. As for the James material, all of it is taken from his RCA sides, recorded between 1961 and 1962. There are 12 little-documented sides that are sown in the pipe of James' ballad style that was a signature with that tenor voice of his. His guitar playing added a special kind of rock & roll darkness to the proceedings. These sides, including "Magnetism," "Legend of the Brown Mountain Light," "Hey Little Ducky," and "No Lana," feature James' ringing Telecaster against standard teen rock arrangements and production for the time. It's obvious Atkins and company had no idea the Beatles were coming. The songs are, like the Orbison tracks, interesting, but not compelling and are strictly for the collectors. —*Thom Jurek*

★ **For the Lonely: 18 Greatest Hits** / 1988 / Rhino ✦✦✦✦✦
Appearing as it did just a few months before Roy Orbison's death, this single CD best-of was incredibly fortuitous for Rhino Records. It was the first compilation to include both Orbison's early successes on Sun Records along with his early-'60s hits for Monument Records and, thus, was as definitive as most casual fans needed it to be. The sound is impeccable, as is the choice of material (which was not difficult to assemble). One gets only a somewhat sketchy overview of Orbison's developing talent, ignoring the years between his Sun and Monument recordings, but that's usually the purpose of a greatest-hits collection anyway. For those who want more, *The Legendary Roy Orbison* gives a better overall account, but as a four-CD set is a lot more expensive; *All-Time Greatest Hits* gives a somewhat fuller account of the Monument years (and all of his Monument albums were available individually as well); and the out-of-print MGM best-of covers the music from the years following his departure from Monument. (The best of the latter doesn't sound that different from the Monument material—Orbison's post-Monument songs just never caught the public's ear or managed to become hit records.) But *For the Lonely* is the best account of the music that everyone already recognizes and knows. —*Bruce Eder*

The Legendary Roy Orbison / 1988 / Columbia ✦✦✦✦✦
Tracing Roy Orbison's career from its beginnings at Sun through his big hits at Monument to his largely forgotten late-'60s recordings for MGM, the four-disc set is an exhaustive, definitive history of Orbison's peak years. Yes, his late-'80s comeback is missing (this was released a year before *Mystery Girl*, after all), but this is still as exhaustive as most serious listeners will likely need, since it contains nearly every crucial track, plus such rarities as non-LP soundtrack contributions (including the title song to the Orbison-starrer *Fastest Guitar Alive*). It does lose momentum toward the end, since Orbison's material starts to dip in quality, but there still are some hidden gems to be discovered. Hardcore fans will probably be better off with Bear Family's exhaustive *Orbison*, which has all the Sun and Monument recordings, and wait for the inevitable MGM sequel. Those that want a comprehensive, but not complete, overview will be more than satisfied with this set. —*Stephen Thomas Erlewine*

Our Love Song / 1989 / Monument ✦✦
Skimpily assembled package of a dozen obscurities, most from the early- and mid-'60s Monument era. "(I Get So) Sentimental" and "Born on the Wind" count as some of his better unknown tunes from that time, but on the whole it's a poor and haphazard collection. —*Richie Unterberger*

Best-Loved Standards / 1989 / Monument ✦✦✦
Best-Loved Standards is a 12-track collection that concentrates on Roy Orbison's interpretations of classic pop, country and R&B songs instead of his hits. There are no hits here at all, in fact, just very good versions of "I Can't Stop Loving You," "Distant Drums," "Great Pretender," "Let the Good Times Roll," "Bye Bye Love," "I'd Be a Legend in My Time," "All I Have to Do is Dream," "Cry" and "What'd I Say." It's certainly not a hits collection, but curious fans who know the hits and want to dig a little deeper may find this of interest. —*Stephen Thomas Erlewine*

The Classic Roy Orbison (1965–1968) / 1989 / Rhino ✦✦✦
The hits dried up when Orbison left the Monument label for MGM in 1965. The 14 recordings here, taken from singles and LP tracks, feature arrangements and production not far removed from his classic Monument era. The singing is wonderful, but stacked up against his classic hits, a lot is missing. Lacking the ace songwriting of his best work, there's lots of midtempo, melodramatic rock balladry here, but somehow nothing nearly as gripping as his best compositions. —*Richie Unterberger*

Sun Years / 1989 / Rhino ✦✦✦✦
Here is a 20-track compilation of Orbison's Sun sides, including both sides of all four of his official Sun 45s, and a dozen tracks he recorded for the label that remained unissued at the time. Orbison at this point was a decent but somewhat also-ran rockabilly singer, and not nearly as suited for the style as fellow Sun artists Elvis Presley, Jerry Lee Lewis, and Carl Perkins. He also had yet to find his songwriting or singing voice with balladeering pop/rock material, so this collection may disappoint those who expect something along the lines of Roy's famous Monument hits. It's not at all bad, though, with standout cuts such as "Ooby Dooby," "Rock House," and "Devil Doll"; it's just not Orbison at either his best or his most comfortable. —*Richie Unterberger*

Mystery Girl / 1989 / Virgin ✦✦✦✦
Although it had been years since his last recording, Roy Orbison was inducted into the Rock & Roll Hall of Fame in 1987. Perhaps as a result of the newfound interest in his music, he was invited to record with the supergroup the Traveling Wilburys. Roy Orbison

had a renewed sense of purpose, and also began recording material for a new solo album. Collaborating with Jeff Lynne and Tom Petty, Orbison recreates the feel of his old recordings while sounding modern. His voice sounds as strong as ever, and he is still able to hit the high notes that convey a sad, lonely ache. The highlight of the album is "She's a Mystery to Me," a haunting ballad penned by U2's Bono and the Edge that perfectly plays to all of Orbison's strengths as a singer. Released in the months after his death, *Mystery Girl* was the highest-charting album of his career and spawned the hit "You Got It"—it is a shame that Orbison was not around to experience his success. This comeback album represents Roy Orbison at his best. — *Vik Iyengar*

The Sun Years 1956–58 / Apr. 1989 / Bear Family ✦✦✦✦✦

Roy Orbison wasn't among the great rockabilly cats, as his voice was a little too rich and his performances a little too mannered to truly rock with abandon. Nevertheless, he did cut a pair of terrific rockabilly singles for Sun with "Ooby Dooby" and "Domino." He never quite reached those heights again while on Sun, as Bear Family's single-disc collection *The Sun Years 1956-58* illustrates. Containing every track he recorded for the label, including alternate takes and undubbed mixes, the collection suffers from too much similar-sounding material. Apart from the previously mentioned singles, Orbison only made a handful of songs that really rocked, and they tend to lose their impact when mixed in among the mediocre songs and minutely different alternate takes. For hardcore Orbison and rockabilly collectors, the very comprehensiveness of *The Sun Years 1956-58* makes the disc necessary, but most fans—especially those enamored with his grandiose, theatrical ballads—will find that this collection is overkill. — *Stephen Thomas Erlewine*

Rock Legends / 1990 / RCA ✦✦✦

A compilation of rare and early works by Roy Orbison and Little Richard that makes odd bedfellows of two extremely dissimilar performers, borne out of the necessity of cleaning out old vault material to capitalize on the CD reissue explosion. The first eight tracks belong to Little Richard, who won a recording contract with RCA after winning a talent contest in Atlanta. These sides, cut in 1951 and 1952, show barely a hint of his later wildness, owing far more to the jump blues R&B of Roy Brown and others. Orbison's seven songs were cut in the late '50s, between his rockabilly days at Sun and his ascent to stardom on Monument. You can hear tentative explorations of the soaring romanticism that he'd find his niche with in 1960, but the material is basic, weak, typical late-'50s teen fodder, courtesy of Roy himself and noted songwriters John Loudermilk, Boudleaux Bryant, and Felice Bryant. The yearning "Seems To Me" (written by Boudleaux, who would write many fine hits for Orbison and the Everly Brothers) is the only track which begins to even approximate his future glory. This cheese & chalk compilation is only recommended to those wishing to glean historical insight into these giants' beginnings, though it may well be that the Little Richard fanatic isn't necessarily a Roy Orbison devotee (and vice versa). — *Richie Unterberger*

Singles Collection / Oct. 1990 / Polygram ✦✦✦

Overlooked at the time of its issue, as it was almost simultaneously released with Rhino's *The Classic Roy Orbison (1965-1968)*, this offers a more comprehensive look at his post-Monument recordings. That doesn't mean that it's better. Most of the 1965-1968 cuts on this album are also on the Rhino one, though "She" and "Heartache," which are only on *Singles Collection*, are a couple of his better late-'60s songs. The post-1968 tracks that take up the rest of the anthology are a waste, an embarrassment at worst, as Orbison failed to either successfully incorporate contemporary influences or offer quality variations on his tested formula. Stick with the cheaper, more succinct, and easier to find *The Classic Roy Orbison* for an overview of this era. — *Richie Unterberger*

The Best of His Rare Solo Classics / 1991 / Curb ✦✦✦

The Best of His Rare Solo Classics is a bit of a misleading title for this ten-track budget-priced collection. There isn't much that's rare on this collection; everything has been released before. However, these songs didn't become hits—the first side is filled with Monument recordings, the second with rockabilly Sun sessions like "Ooby Dooby," "Rock House" and "Devil Doll." The result has some good moments, but it's too uneven to be a worthwhile purchase for even a semi-serious Orbison fan. — *Stephen Thomas Erlewine*

King of Hearts / Oct. 20, 1992 / Virgin ✦✦✦

The posthumously released *King of Hearts* collects a handful of Orbison's final vocal tracks along with a few demos and non-LP singles, including the Jeff Lynne-produced "Heartbreak Radio." The highlight, however, is an amazing duet of "Crying" recorded with k.d. lang. — *Jason Ankeny*

Sings Lonely and Blue/Crying / 1993 / Monument ✦✦✦✦

Two of legendary singer Roy Orbison's LPs are collected here on this CD two-fer. Released in 1993 by Monument. — *Chris True*

In Dreams/Orbisongs / 1993 / Monument ✦✦✦✦

In 1993, Monument released *In Dreams/Orbisongs*, which contained two albums—*In Dreams* (originally released 1963) and *Orbisongs* (originally released1966)—on one compact disc. — *Chris True*

Super Hits / Sep. 5, 1995 / Epic ✦✦✦

Roy Orbison's *Super Hits* contains a sampling of his greatest hits, yet it is so skimpy that it isn't a bargain for serious fans, even at its budget-line price. — *Thom Owens*

The Very Best of Roy Orbison / 1996 / Virgin ✦✦✦

Yes, the song selection for *The Very Best of Roy Orbison* is excellent, containing all of his hits. However, all of the material on the record consists of re-recordings Orbison made during the mid-'80s, and while he's in fine voice, these versions simply aren't as special or magical as the originals. — *Stephen Thomas Erlewine*

★ 16 Biggest Hits / Feb. 2, 1999 / Monument/Legacy ✦✦✦✦✦

Roy Orbison scored 20 consecutive Top 40 hits between 1960 and 1965, all but the last of them on the Monument Records label. This compilation presents 16 of the first 17 of those hits (missing is the 1963 Christmas song "Pretty Paper"), from the 1960 gold-seller "Only the Lonely" to the 1964 chart-topper "Oh, Pretty Woman," with Orbison's seven other Top Ten hits of the era in between. Technically, a few of Orbison's singles of 1965 and 1966 did a little better in the charts than a few of the ones here, and, of course, he scored a final, posthumous Top Ten hit with "You Got It" on Virgin Records in 1989. But this collection presents the music from the hottest part of his career in chronological order, with standards like "Crying" sharing space with lesser, but still worthy songs like "I'm Hurtin'." Aficionados know Orbison's Sun works, and his later recordings earned him a new audience, but the Monument hit singles of the early '60s are what he is best remembered for, and they're all here. — *William Ruhlmann*

Ooby Dooby: The Very Best of Roy Orbison / Feb. 2, 1999 / Collectables ✦✦✦

Roy Orbison: Authorized Bootleg Collection / Oct. 26, 1999 / Orbison ✦✦✦

Orbison's widow, Barbara, organized the release of these four live concert recordings taken from various points in Orbison's career. The set list doesn't vary much from show to show; an artist like Orbison would be hidebound to sing his hits, and the audience certainly lets him know which ones they want to hear throughout this four-disc collection. Regarding sound quality, these are soundboard tapes cleaned up as much as possible; don't expect them to sound awful and they won't, but don't expect them to sound like a record either, because they fall quite short. However, you don't come to a Roy Orbison concert, tap your foot, and say, "Nice mix on the bass player." No, you come to hear Orbison, and here's one time when a vocal-heavy board tape has the spotlight falling on the right set of shoulders. If you're going to subject yourself to listening to four hours of one person singing louder then the entire band track put together, it might as well be somebody great like Roy Orbison. He never falters once in these shows, presiding over all of them with a laid-back, good-natured stage personality that perfectly fits the music. For completists and hardcore fans only, perhaps, but here's one of rock & roll's greatest singers tearing it up in four hit-packed concerts; it doesn't get much better than that, sound quality be damned. — *Cub Koda*

Orbison / May 8, 2001 / Bear Family ✦✦✦✦✦

Trying to describe the voice of Roy Orbison is like trying to describe the night sky—it's evocative and full of hues, shades, colors, and feelings, but it's impossible to accurately reflect their shape or meaning, so I won't try. What is possible, however, is to discuss this gigantic wonder of a box set. The German label Bear Family has issued a seven-CD Roy Orbison retrospective from 1955 to 1965; it collects virtually every known Orbison recording from what has been tagged his "golden decade." And when the folks at Bear Family say "every known recording," they mean it. The first treasure trove is the material recorded by the Teen Kings in Odessa, TX, which was the first version of "Ooby Dooby," backed with "Tryin' to Get to You." There is also the Sun version, of course, with the backing side of "Go! Go! Go!" and, of all things, the issue of "Tryin' to Get to You" released by Orbison's former label boss at Je-Wel, Weldon Rogers (only it was Orbison's own take he was trying to pass off as his own!). There are oodles of unissued alternates takes, unreleased demos—including Orbison's original versions of songs written for Buddy Holly ("An Empty Cup") and the Evely Brothers ("Claudette" as well as "Love Hurts"). There is an entire CD dedicated to the complete recordings of the material recorded by the Teen Kings—a first for any Orbison collection. In addition, the latter third of the last disc offers all of Orbison's Coca Cola commercials as a cap off (no pun intended) to the golden decade.

Reissue producers Howard Cockburn, Richard Weize, and John Beecher (for the Teen Kings material) looked under every rock and found tracks believed lost or erased from the period—including the Wink Westerners material (most likely the Teen Kings under another name)—and have assembled the most complete Roy Orbison collection of the period ever. This one is definitive. In addition is an authoritative—and most likely definitive—musico-biographical essay by Colin Escott bound in hardcover (the cover for book and set are deep blue, of course), with over 100 photographs of Orbison posed, candid, in session, and reproductions of various artifacts from his career, including the jackets to his singles and albums and even his high-school drawings.

This set completely leaves the travesty that is the Columbia box released in 1988 in the dust. Not only was it ugly, its sound was turgid even for the period. This Orbison box has pristine sound in most cases, and where it doesn't, it is certainly far superior to any other collection on the market—foreign or domestic, featuring these tunes—and far better than any of the semi-legal pirates.

Containing 151 tracks painstakingly sequenced to give an authoritative picture of one of the rock and pop era's most complex and profoundly influential figures, the Bear Family set tells Orbison's story in bits and pieces, like patches on a quilt, not in chronological order necessarily—the Teen Kings material, for instance, does not appear in full until disc three—but more in terms of his development as a singer and writer of songs. The material he wrote with Joe Melson, which included "Only the Lonely," "Blue Angel," and "Running Scared," is featured to stand alone for its particular contribution to the Orbison legacy. While it's true that earlier Orbison/Melson collaborations are featured separately from this material on the set, it is because they were either A: recorded earlier as demos rather than as singles, or B: they aesthetically fit together better with other material from a particular year—whether the material was with the Wink Westerners, the Teen Kings, or with Melson.

There are certainly arguments against this approach of not issuing material strictly chronologically, though most of it is, but in this writer's opinion, it beats to hell all of the arguments that to have every version of "Ooby Dooby" all stacked on top of one another was the best way to portray either a given session or Orbison's development as some labels have done; that is asinine and a complete burden for the listener (anyone remember the Verve Charlie Parker box with 17 takes of "Ornithology" all in a row?). Orbison, as both singer and songwriter, was a storyteller, a massive one, and what better way to document his legacy than to present it as an unfolding story with twists and turns in the plot along the way. In fact, the argument could be made for looking at creating archival sets in this manner if the artist warrants it. What the producers of the Bear Family set have done is instead issue tracks together from a particular year, where few takes were done. For instance, on the first disc there are two versions each of "Ooby Dooby" by the Teen Kings and the Sun A-side "Tryin' to Get to You"—same thing on the B-sides—and "Claudette" the demo version given to the Everlys and the single Orbison recorded himself. None of the tunes stacked on top of one another. The reason is simple: The Sun and Teen Kings sessions were identical material recorded the same year and were similar in approach but not in sound.

As for the Teen Kings material, it is revelatory in how much a solid rockabilly band they were, and they would try anything once, including "Brown-Eyed Handsome Man" and "Bo Diddley"! By the time the set reaches the "modern" period of Orbison's sound, when his voice had developed from a thin reedy frail lilt to a full-blown operatic force of nature on discs four, five, and six (where many of the more familiar Orbison tunes will be found, including the Melson material, "Crying," "The Great Pretender," "Dream Baby," "In Dreams," a second, very different version of "Blue Bayou," "Oh, Pretty Woman," "Pretty Paper," "Darkness," and others), the sound quality of the material is just stunning. It's never been heard like this before, probably not even on the original masters. All of the drama and dynamic in Orbison's music comes through as if the moon were opening the clouds and shining through. In the lesser-known songs, "Party Heart," "The Crowd," "Leah," "Sleepy Hollow," "Yes," the Orbison version of "Love Hurts," and others, the full story emerges and we see the singer who believed in his voice but not himself emerge as a believer in both things. Orbison wanted big music for his voice, the bigger the mix the more he was able to push his limit, and this is true to a song across the entire collection. Finally, on the last disc, Bear Family's producers opted to place either alternate or re-recorded and released versions of tunes such as "Gigolette," "Born on the Wind," "It's Over" (usually for the overseas market), and many more, with numerous alternate takes of "Double Date" (four), "Paper Boy" (five), and "With the Bug" (five). These are all minor tunes in the Orbison canon, but they do reveal his working process if not his best work. Finally, the awesome Coca Cola adverts—which will have you laughing your ass off—tell the rest of Bear Family's version of the story.

The only argument with this set is that the MGM material through 1968 wasn't included because there are still so many pieces of Orbison's expansive vision from that time that remain in the vault—for instance, there are reportedly three completely different versions of "Southbound Jericho Parkway." The only CD that ever collected that material was a shoddy, cash-in attempt based on the resurgence of Orbison's fame after David Lynch used his music in *Blue Velvet*. It's easy to see Bear Family's point in that from 1955 to 1965, Roy Orbison couldn't miss charting, even if it was near the bottom of the rack. After 1965, with the dawn of the Beatles' *Revolver*, music would change forever, and for a time, at least, Roy Orbison would be a forgotten man. Thankfully, as Colin Escott states in his wonderful notes, "that while many of his peers were trying to stage comebacks, Roy died in the middle of one." The box tells the story of the glory years, the years that created the man, the myth, and the legend. Bravo, Bear Family, you've done it again. *—Thom Jurek*

The Complete Sun Sessions / Jun. 26, 2001 / Varese ✦✦✦✦✦
Roy Orbison's Sun period has often been documented, but was never really given its proper critical due until the 21st century with its 20/20 hindsight. The Bear Family label issued a complete Orbison collection from his earliest Teen Kings recordings—all of them—to 1965, and other compilations have documented some of the material Orbison recorded for Sun between 1956 and 1958. This set on Varese Sarabande documents—with excellent sound quality—Orbison's oeuvre with Sam Phillips and Sun Studios, from the Teen Kings' redo of the Je-Wel classic "Ooby Dooby," with an amazing Orbison guitar solo, to his version of Conway Twitty's "Rock House" to less well-known tracks such as "Domino," "Mean Little Mama," "The Cause of It All," "I Was a Fool," and a handful of alternate takes of tracks like "Claudette," "The Clown," "Chicken Hearted," "Problem Child," and "This Kind of Love." There are 31 tracks in all. The revelatory thing about the Sun material is just how hard and consistently Orbison *rocked*! His guitar playing is amazing, his voice had not yet taken on the glissandi quality it would at Monument, and his producers at Sun, Phillips and Cowboy Jack Clement, among others, worked that West Texas vibe, that hillbilly vibe deep into the Orbison sound. This is essential for rockabilly fans in general and those who understand that there was far more to Orbison than "Pretty Woman." *—Thom Jurek*

Oh Pretty Woman / Apr. 16, 2002 / Collectables ✦✦
Oh Pretty Woman collects ten Roy Orbison tracks recorded for Monument Records in the early '60s. While this budget compilation includes "Oh Pretty Woman," "Only the Lonely," and "Blue Bayou," it's really unnecessary since many superior Orbison hits packages are available in the same price range containing more tracks. This is essentially a reissue of a mid-'90s cheapo compilation *Shades of Roy Orbison* with the same track listing. Recommended to budget-minded casual fans only. *—Al Campbell*

Monumental Hits / Aug. 27, 2002 / Collectables ✦✦✦✦
Collectables Records' Roy Orbison compilation *Monumental Hits*, issued at a discount price, compares favorably with other single-disc Orbison hits collections. As the title suggests, these are original Monument Records recordings licensed from Monument's corporate parent, Sony Music. Orbison recorded for the label between 1960 and 1965, and scored all his early major hits there. All of those Top 20 singles are included—"Only the Lonely (Know How I Feel)," "Blue Angel," "Running Scared," "Crying," "Dream Baby (How Long Must I Dream)," "In Dreams," "Mean Woman Blues," "Pretty Paper," "It's Over," and "Oh, Pretty Woman"—along with most of Orbison's Top 40 hits of the period. A few of those lesser hits are missing ("Falling," "Goodnight," and "(Say) You're My Girl"), and, oddly, the album concludes with eight B-sides of the hit singles, including the B-sides of the missing A-side hits. None of them are great lost songs. ("Love Hurts," a B-side, heard earlier in the collection, is, however.) As a hits collection, the album would have been better if it had been sequenced chronologically, if it had included such non-Monument Orbison favorites as "Ooby Dooby" and "You Got It," and if there were fewer obscurities. But the sound is good, all the big Monument hits are here, and the price is right. *—William Ruhlmann*

50 All Time Greatest Hits / Oct. 8, 2002 / Collectables ✦✦✦✦✦
Perhaps Collectables Records should not get their hopes up on receiving "Truth in Advertising" awards for this two-disc Roy Orbison collection; a handy double set which compiled Orbison's classic Monument sides along with highlights from his releases for Sun, MGM, and Virgin would be a more than welcome addition to his catalog, but despite the title that's not what *50 All Time Greatest Hits* has on board. This set features a whopping 47 tunes from Orbison's Monument years, with his three best known Sun sides ("Ooby Dooby," "Rock House," and "Go! Go! Go!") closing out disc two. All of Roy's classic '60s hits can be found on disc one, while a healthy selection of covers and lesser-knowns dominate the second half; it's all splendid material, even if the sequencing seems just a bit clunky in spots, and the mastering is more than adequate (though some of this material has sounded cleaner on previous CD releases). In short, as an overview of Orbison's most creatively and commercially fruitful period, this compilation does a fine job, but as a full career retrospective, it falls considerably short of the mark, and the sudden emergence of "Rockabilly Roy" at the very end is both odd and disorienting. (The liner notes and cover art aren't much to write home about, either.) In short, the definitive Roy Orbison hits package still remains to be assembled, though if you're looking to replace or upgrade your old copy of Monument's *The All-Time Greatest Hits of Roy Orbison*, this will give you just what you've been looking for. *—Mark Deming*

Orion (Jimmy Ellis)

b. 1945, Orrville, AL
Vocals / Rock & Roll, Traditional Country, Country-Pop, Rockabilly
The music industry is filled with many strange tales of artists whose lives took unexpected turns on the winding road to success, but the saga of singer Jimmy Ellis is perhaps one of the weirdest of them all. He was professionally known as Orion, and his double-edged claim to fame was that his natural speaking and singing voice sounded almost exactly like that of Elvis Presley. Ellis hailed from Orrville, AL, and began his recording career in 1964. In 1972, he worked for Sun Records (Presley's label) with producer Shelby Singleton in Nashville. His first two singles were covers of two of the King's former hits, "That's All Right" and "Blue Moon of Kentucky."

The strange part of the tale began in January, 1979 when author Gail Brewer-Giorgio received a bizarre early morning phone call. Two years before she had begun a novel about a musical superstar, Orion, who faked his own death to find much-needed peace and privacy, based on the circumstances surrounding Elvis' death. The mysterious phone call came from a stranger with a Presley-like voice, claiming to be Orion. A year prior, Jimmy Ellis' voice had been overdubbed with Jerry Lee Lewis on an old single from the Sun archives, "Save the Last Dance for Me;" on it, Ellis was billed only as "Friend." The single made the Top 20 and caused quite a stir as listeners tried to guess the mysterious "Friend's" identity. An album featuring the duet came out and the controversy really heated up when *Good Morning America* had the Friend's voice "scientifically scanned and analyzed" and concluded that it could be no one but Presley. Giorgio's book had just come out, so Singleton decided to cash in on its popularity and transform Jimmy Ellis into the mysterious "Orion" who had phoned the author earlier that year. Ellis' hair and long sideburns were dyed black, and he dressed in a loud, bejeweled polyester jumpsuits, with a mask to protect him from crazed fans.

"Orion" recorded a single, "Ebony Eyes," for Sun in 1979, which became part of his debut album, *Reborn*. The album cover itself generated controversy because it depicted a phantom singer rising from a coffin, and was later withdrawn. He released two more albums in 1980; the third, *Trio Plus*, featured Orion's voice overdubbed on old cuts with Lewis, Carl Perkins, and Charlie Rich. The albums were quite popular, and Orion had three Top 70 hits, including "Am I That Easy to Forget." He had four minor hits the following year, including the contemporary rockabilly song "Crazy Little Thing Called Love," originally recorded by the rock group Queen. Ellis continued recording and performing through 1983 as Orion, and scored only one more minor hit before trying to break his Sun contract to become a recognized performer in his own right.

While performing at the Eastern States Exposition, Ellis took off the mask and swore to never wear it again. Unfortunately, despite the fact that most of the songs he recorded were not covers of Elvis songs, he could not escape the uncanny similarities between their natural voices. At one point he even released the single "I'm Trying Not to Sound Like Elvis." During his time with Sun, Ellis/Orion cut over 11 albums and toured with the Oak Ridge Boys, Jerry Lee Lewis, and other stars like Dionne Warwick. As Jim Ellis, he released an album in 1987 and continued to tour North America; interestingly, he resumed wearing his mask. *—Sandra Brennan*

Who Was That Masked Man? / Jun. 23, 1999 / Bear Family ✦✦✦✦✦
Let's call a spade a spade. Orion is an Elvis impersonator. No more, no less. That he's a good Elvis impersonator is important, since if he wasn't, Sun probably wouldn't have tried to promote his recordings as if they were genuine Elvis material, even going to the extremes of overdubbing Orion's voices on recordings by such Sun stalwarts as Jerry Lee Lewis and Carl Perkins. This doesn't make him any better, but it sure makes him fascinating, particularly because he is gifted at mimicry and these are pretty good evocations of Elvis at his peak. Bear Family's four-disc box *Who Was That Masked Man?* contains all of his '70s masterworks, including original recordings and fake duets, and it's a singularly fascinating listen. Really, it's pretty good music, but for God's sake, the blatant

charlatanism behind this can grate even those with an inclination for kitsch. Taken on surface value, it's enjoyable, but dig a little deeper and it becomes a little silly and a little creepy and completely fascinating. That's not necessarily justification for a four-disc set, but if you're inclined to purchase this on the basis of what Orion is, you won't be disappointed, no matter how uneven the music is. *—Stephen Thomas Erlewine*

Rockabilly/Sunrise / Oct. 12, 1999 / Collectables ✦✦✦✦

In 1999, Collectables released *Rockabilly/Sunrise*, which contained two complete albums—*Rockabilly* (1980, originally released on Sun) and *Sunrise* (1979, originally released on Sun)—by Orion on one compact disc. *—Jason Birchmeier*

● **The Man Who Would Be King: The Best of Orion** / Apr. 2, 2002 / Fuel 2000 ✦✦✦✦

Osborne Brothers

f. 1956, Hyden, KY

Group / Bluegrass, Progressive Bluegrass, Traditional Bluegrass, Close Harmony

The Osborne Brothers were one of the most popular and innovative bluegrass groups of the postwar era, taking the music into new directions and gaining a large audience. Among their most notable achievements are their pioneering, inventive use of amplification, twin harmony banjos, steel guitars, and drums—they were the first bluegrass group to expand the genre's sonic palette in such a fashion. Bobby and Sonny Osborne were born in Hyden, KY, but raised in Dayton, OH. As children, their father instilled a love for traditional music. Bobby picked up the electric guitar as a teenager, playing in various local bands. A few years after his brother began playing the guitar, Sonny picked up the banjo. In 1949, Bobby formed a duo with banjoist Larry Richardson. The pair was hired by a West Virginian radio station and stayed in the state for a while, eventually hooking up with the Lonesome Pine Fiddlers. During their stay with the Fiddlers, they helped change the group's sound to bluegrass and made four singles for Cozy Records. Bobby Osborne left the band in the summer of 1951, forming a band with Jimmy Martin that fell apart shortly after its inception. After making a one-shot single, "New Freedom Bell," with his siblings Louise and Sonny, he joined the Stanley Brothers for a short while before being drafted into the Army.

Sonny spent some time with Bill Monroe's Blue Grass Boys in the early '50s, appearing on several sides on Decca Records. He also cut some covers of popular Monroe and Flatt & Scruggs songs for the budget label Gateway. After Bobby returned from the Army, he and Sonny formed a band. Initially, they supported Jimmy Martin on his RCA session while they had their own spot on a Knoxville radio station. In 1956, they joined the *Wheeling Jamboree*; they would stay with the radio program for four years. In March of that year, Red Allen joined the brothers—four months after his arrival, they recorded their first session for MGM Records. For the next year, they toured and recorded, steadily gaining a large audience. In the spring of 1958, "Once More" became a number-13 hit on the country charts. Its success helped push the band into the mainstream.

Shortly after the success of "Once More," Allen left the band, and the Osbornes filled his vacancy with a string of musicians and vocalists, including Johnny Dacus and Benny Birchfield. The duo stayed with the *Wheeling Jamboree* and MGM Records into the early '60s. The Osbornes became the first bluegrass act to play a college campus in 1960, when they played Antioch College in Yellow Springs, OH. That appearance ushered in a new era for bluegrass, creating a new, younger audience for the music. The Osbornes left MGM in 1963, signing with Decca Records. On their mid-'60s records for Decca, the duo began experimenting more with their music, adding piano, steel guitar, and electric instruments to their music. Their adventurousness made them more accessible to a mass audience, as their string of late-'60s and early-'70s hit singles proves. Although their experimentation angered many bluegrass traditionalists, the Osbornes were the only bluegrass group to consistently have country hits during this time, even if all their singles were only minor hits.

In 1975, the Osbornes left Decca but continued to play the *Grand Ole Opry* and bluegrass festivals across America. Later in the '70s, the duo returned to a more traditional sound. Throughout the '80s and '90s they stuck to this sound, playing concerts and festivals frequently and recording albums for CMH, RCA, Sugar Hill, and Pinecastle. Forty years after their formation, the Osborne Brothers remained an active act in the late-'90s and into the '00s. *—Stephen Thomas Erlewine*

Country Pickin' and Hillside Singin / 1959 / MGM ✦✦✦

☆ **The Osborne Brothers** / 1971 / Rounder ✦✦✦✦✦

Great vocal harmonies and tightly woven banjo-mandolin conversations come together on this, the best early material from 1959-1963. *—Mark A. Humphrey*

Early Recordings of Sonny Osborne, Vol. 1–3 / 1973 / Gateway ✦✦✦

The Best of the Osborne Brothers / 1975 / Sugar Hill ✦✦✦✦

The Osborne Brothers' early- to mid-'60s output for Decca is included on this compilation from Sugar Hill. These are the original recordings that blended the Osbornes' smooth harmonies and bluegrass instrumentation with the burgeoning countrypolitan production of the time. Among the 18 tracks are "Roll Muddy River," "Rocky Top," "Tennessee Hound Dog," and "You Win Again." *The Best of the Osborne Brothers* is highly recommended if you're just getting familiar with their mid-period material. *—Al Campbell*

From Rocky Top to Muddy Bottom / 1977 / CMH ✦✦✦

This album contains such cuts as "We Could," "Love Hurts," "Rocky Top," and more. *—AMG*

The Bluegrass Collection / 1978 / CMH ✦✦✦✦✦

Recorded in 1978, *Bluegrass Collection* is the Osborne Brothers' tribute to the fathers of bluegrass—Bill Monroe, Flatt & Scruggs, and the Stanley Brothers. The duo throws in nice, but unremarkable, remakes of their older hits as well, making the album a pleasant exercise in nostalgia. *—Thom Owens*

★ **The Essential Bluegrass Album** / 1979 / CMH ✦✦✦✦✦

The Essential Bluegrass Album features 24 of the finest songs Mac Wiseman and the Osborne Brothers recorded together in the '60s and '70s. Instead of adhering to the rigid traditionalism of Bill Monroe, the Osbornes and Wiseman open the music up, bringing in a drummer and elements of Western swing, Tex-Mex and traditional country. It's an excellent collection, epitomizing the best of progressive bluegrass in the '60s and '70s. *—Thom Owens*

The Osborne Brothers & Red Allen / 1980 / Rounder ✦✦✦✦

This label's *Special Series* was devoted to licensing material that had gone out of print. Anyone familiar with the Rounder story will know that it was the cheesy boogie rock of George Thorogood that paid the bills at the label, but the golden space on the warehouse shelves was devoted to releases such as this, restoring availability to a classic heritage of music. Response to this release and others in the series among fans was overwhelmingly positive, suggesting wandering souls being attracted to a beacon of light. The surrounding darkness would symbolize the state of the country & western music scene by the early '80s, particularly in Nashville where these tracks were cut at the "old" Victor studios. Sadly enough, musicians seeking to release a recording such as this, produced in this manner, have gone through decades of determined opposition from record companies and radio stations, despite what the fans seem to want. If a country artist had gone to Rounder itself with a project such as this in the '80s, they would have most likely been turned down flat. Or if by chance a deal was struck, a simple production such as this would never have been allowed. This is the real thing, just guys sitting in a room playing music. The use of the recording studio itself was a prime element in developing the essence of what would come to be known as country & western music. The heart and soul might have come from the hills, but the swoop of the pedal steel was strictly urban technology, the producer and mixer conspiring to deliver the finished goods with the panache of a big-budget special effect from Hollywood. While it is not difficult to tell typical country & western from typical bluegrass, here one finds a melding of forces as well as some innovative steps being taken. It means the listener is literally standing on the edge of a cliff, observing musicians making bold leaps into the great unknown. The claim is made that one of these recordings represents the first time the dobro and the drums were used in the recording studio together. The use of drums in the context of bluegrass was itself an innovation pushed by the Osborne Brothers. The type of material here could, and would, wind up being silly putty in the hands of Nashville producers obsessed with making it sweet enough for the radio. But what listeners have here is untouched, and it is gorgeous. "Lost Highway" was a country hit recorded by many, including papa Hank Williams. It has never sounded better than it does here, which is saying a lot. The vocal blend of Red Allen and the Osbornes is wonderful, putting to shame the background singers cluttering so many country records. Other tracks benefit from this ensemble's ability to effectively switch off lead vocals. Repertoire that is more fitting of a bluegrass outfit includes the Irish ballad "Down in the Willow Garden," a delightful track. Fans of the dobro should put a check next to this album: The solos by Shot Jackson and Jimmy Crawford are worth the price of admission. The original release came with an insert featuring an excellent essay on the Osborne/Allen collaboration. One glaring lack is enough information about songwriting credits. Although a great deal of the material is traditional, some of the tunes don't seem like they would be, such as "She's No Angel," a hit for Kitty Wells. *—Eugene Chadbourne*

Bobby & His Mandolin / 1981 / CMH ✦✦✦

Singing Shouting Praises / 1988 / Sugar Hill ✦✦✦

Hillbilly Fever / 1991 / CMH ✦✦✦

Recorded in 1991, *Hillbilly Fever* might not live up to the standards of the Osborne Brothers' earliest and best recordings, but it's a fun listen that shows the duo still has life in them, nearly 40 years after their formation. *—Thom Owens*

Once More, Vols. 1 & 2 / 1991 / Sugar Hill ✦✦✦✦✦

Once More, Vols. 1 & 2 combines two original vinyl albums, which originated from the same sessions, onto one compact disc. The *Once More* albums were recorded in the mid-'80s for Sugar Hill. At these sessions, the Osborne Brothers tackled a large chunk of their earlier repertoire, including songs that were originally recorded for Decca and MGM. These versions are harder and purer than the originals, which frequently featured electric instruments, and—unlike many re-recordings—these cuts don't sound labored or tired. If anything, *Once More, Vols. 1 & 2* contains music that is even more alive and vital than the originals and, since it contains a diverse selection of material, it functions as an excellent primer on one of the finest bluegrass bands ever. However, if you're looking for hits, go elsewhere—*Once More, Vols. 1 & 2* concentrates on pure bluegrass, so the Osbornes have excised their hits in favor for high, lonesome obscurities. *—Thom Owens*

Our Favorite Hymns / 1995 / MCA ✦✦✦

MCA Special Products' *Our Favorite Hymns* rounds up ten inspirational highlights from the Osborne Brothers' recordings for Decca in the '60s. Although these recordings aren't among the Osbornes' very best, they're still enjoyable and effective, particularly for casual fans who aren't looking for anything more than a sampler of the duo's religious material. Among the featured songs are "How Great Thou Art," "I Pray My Way Out of Trouble," "Light at the River," "Rock of Ages," "What a Friend We Have in Jesus," "Will You Meet Me Over Yonder" and "Medals for Mothers." *—Stephen Thomas Erlewine*

1956–1968 / 1995 / Bear Family ✦✦✦✦✦

1956-1968 is a multi-disc box set that contains everything the Osborne Brothers recorded between those years. During that time they recorded for two major labels, MGM and Decca Records. All the songs the duo released on those two labels, plus alternate takes and unreleased tracks, are included on the box. With all of that material, the set is simply too large for anyone but historians and completists to enjoy. Nevertheless, there's lots of wonderful music on the collection and anyone with the patience (and the funds) to invest in the box will not be disappointed. *—Thom Owens*

1968–1974 / 1995 / Bear Family ✦✦✦✦✦

Picking up where Bear Family's previous box set left off, the four-disc set *1968-1974* contains all of the recordings the Osborne Brothers made for Decca Records during the late '60s and early '70s. Though the Osbornes were past their creative peak, they were experiencing a commercial revival during this era. Much of this music ranks among the duo's most enjoyable music, and any serious Osborne Brothers fan will need to invest in this excellent set. *—Thom Owens*

Greatest Bluegrass Hits / 1996 / CMH ✦✦✦

Greatest Hits, Vol. 1 is an excellent cross-section of the Osborne Brothers' finest material for MGM Records, including the hits "Poison Love," "Rocky Top" and "Pain in My Heart," making it an excellent introudciton to one of the finest bluegrass bands of the late '50s. *—Thom Owens*

Country Bluegrass / Nov. 5, 1996 / Universal Special Products ✦✦✦

MCA Special Products' *Country Bluegrass* rounds up ten highlights from the Osborne Brothers' recordings for Decca in the '60s. Although these recordings don't find the Osbornes at their most traditional, they're nevertheless quite enjoyable, particularly for casual fans who aren't looking for anything more than a sampler. Among the featured songs are "Roll Muddy River," "Blue Heartache," "Don't Let Smokey Mountain Smoke Get in Your Eyes," "Lizzie Lou" and "My Old Kentucky Home (Turpentine and Dandelion Wine)." *—Stephen Thomas Erlewine*

Dayton to Knoxville: 1949–1952 / Jan. 1, 2000 / Pinecastle ✦✦✦

Before they plugged their mandolin and banjo into guitar amps, before they hired a drummer and basically served as godfathers of the progressive bluegrass movement that took off the in '60s, Bobby & Sonny Osborne led a straight-ahead bluegrass band that had more in common with Flatt & Scruggs than with stylistic descendants like the New Grass Revival (or even the Country Gentlemen). The second disc in this four-volume series documents the group's early years, when their repertoire leaned heavily towards Louvin Brothers songs and crowd-pleasing patriotic novelty tunes. On this program, the latter are represented by "Alabama" and the rather maudlin "Wrap My Body in Old Glory When I Go," neither of which is a bad song, but both of which are just a bit over the top lyrically. The Louvin material includes excellent versions of "Seven Year Blues" and "I'm Gonna Love You One More Time." But the best tracks on this disc are the last two, both of them featuring the young Jimmy Martin on lead vocals and guitar. These two selections, "Can't You Hear Jerusalem Mourn" and "Across the Sea Blues," are demo recordings salvaged from beat-up acetate transfers, and the sound quality is abysmal. But the performances are spectacular—Martin's voice is at its piercing best, and the blend he achieves with Bobby Osborne is hair-raising. Most of this album will be of primary interest to bluegrass historians, but those last two tracks will be worth the price of the album to any bluegrass lover. *—Rick Anderson*

The Essential Osborne Brothers Collection / Sep. 11, 2001 / CMH ✦✦✦✦✦

The MGM Days of the Osborne Brothers / Polydor ✦✦✦✦✦

The MGM Days of the Osborne Brothers is an extensive, three-disc set that covers 60 tracks the group cut for MGM Records between 1956 and 1963. Over the course of this set, it's possible to hear the group develop from Bill Monroe imitators to distinctive, progressive musicians in their own right; their introduction of electric instruments, varied tempos and complex vocal harmonies still sounds stunning when placed in this chronological context. Despite the wealth of fine music included on *The MGM Days of the Osborne Brothers*, it is an album that is designed only for historians, musicologists and dedicated fans—there is simply too much material for casual fans to digest. *—Thom Owens*

K.T. Oslin (Kay Toinette Oslin)

b. May 15, 1942, Crossett, AR

Vocals / Contemporary Country, Country-Pop

For a short time in the late '80s, K.T. Oslin was one of the most popular female country singers around. Her worldly, distinctly modern persona was quite unlike any of her peers, and she matched it with utterly contemporary country-pop production, complete with synthesizers. Born Kay Toinette Oslin on May 15, 1942, in Crossett, AR, she soon moved to Mobile, AL, and at age five settled in Houston after the death of her father. Oslin's mother had been an aspiring country singer before being forced to support her family, and she passed along her love of music to her daughter. Oslin studied drama at junior college and during the '60s performed in a folk trio with singer/songwriter Guy Clark and producer David Jones. She later went to Los Angeles to work on an album with Frank Davis, but the sessions were never completed, and she returned to Houston and worked in musical theater. A part in the national touring company of *Hello, Dolly!* led to a trip to Manhattan and a spot in the chorus of the Broadway version. She remained in New York for a time, appearing in shows, singing demos and commercial jingles, and working on her songwriting.

In 1978, she sang harmony on a Guy Clark album and in 1981 released two singles on Elektra as Kay T. Oslin. Neither "Clean Up Your Own Tables" nor "Younger Men (Are Startin' to Catch My Eye)" did well at country radio, which simply wasn't ready for such a feisty, feminist-minded woman—who was pushing 40 at that. However, Oslin's original compositions were becoming popular with other artists; her songs were recorded by Gail Davis, Dottie West, and Judy Rodman, among others. She appeared on a live radio broadcast alongside more established musicians in 1984, and two years later she staged her own showcase performance in Nashville. Alabama producer Harold Shedd was in attendance and helped her land a deal with RCA. Oslin debuted in 1987 with *80's Ladies*, whose anthemic title track made the country Top Ten and won her a Grammy for Best Female Country Vocal. The follow-up singles, "Do Ya" and "I'll Always Come Back," both hit number one and so did the album, which went on to sell over a million copies. The follow-up, 1988's *This Woman*, was another chart-topping platinum smash, paced by the

number-one, double-Grammy-winning hit "Hold Me," and the Top Five singles "This Woman" and "Hey Bobby."

Her third album, 1990's *Love in a Small Town*, was something of a concept record about, well, exactly what the title said. "Come Next Monday" became her fourth number-one hit, but Oslin abruptly slowed down afterward, partly because menopause was sapping some of the stamina she needed for touring. Oslin took several years off from music, in the meantime issuing the compilation *Greatest Hits: Songs From an Aging Sex Bomb* in 1993. She tried her hand at acting, appearing in the films *This Thing Called Love* and *Murder So Sweet*. Contemplating a singing comeback in 1995, Oslin experienced chest pains while mowing her lawn and was soon in the hospital for a quadruple bypass. Fortunately, she made a full recovery and signed with the smaller BNA label for a covers album, *My Roots Are Showing*, that drew selections from across the spectrum of 20th century popular music. After another recording hiatus, she teamed up with co-producer Raul Malo of the Mavericks for 2001's *Live Close By, Visit Often*, which inched into the country Top 40. *—Steve Huey*

80's Ladies / 1987 / RCA ✦✦✦

With her breakthrough album *80's Ladies*, K.T. Oslin established a new voice in country music—that of an upscale, middle-aged divorcee, trying to cope with the turmoils with life. The subject matter basically remained the same, but it was given a new viewpoint—Oslin sounded like no other singer, in terms of viewpoint, in the late '80s. *80's Ladies* suffered from a few weak tracks, but on the whole, it was an exciting, fresh change. *—Rodney Batdorf*

This Woman / 1988 / RCA ✦✦✦

K.T. Oslin was at the height of her popularity when she recorded *This Woman*, which went platinum thanks to such major country hits as "This Woman," "Didn't Expect It to Go Down This Way," and "Hold Me." Definitely a late bloomer, the lady with the white gloves reached her commercial peak in her mid-'40s and was 45 when this album soared to the top of the country charts. Oslin is far from a honky tonker, and *This Woman* was hardly recorded with country purists in mind. The title song could have been done by Fleetwood Mac, while "Hold Me" and "Jealous" wouldn't sound out of place on an Eagles album. Make no mistake: "She Don't Talk Like Us No More," "Hey Bobby," and "Round the Clock Lovin'" have as much to do with pop and rock as they do with country. But for all its slickness, *This Woman* is a generally appealing release that successfully balances commercial and artistic considerations. *—Alex Henderson*

Love in a Small Town / 1990 / RCA ✦✦✦✦

Oslin built this loosely defined concept album from ten years of song, including the first one she wrote. Oslin sings of the guises romance wears in the small-town South: Nelda Jean Prudie waxes nostalgic about weekend dances of her Texas youth; a young girl enthuses about a pick-up-driving Romeo named Cornell Crawford; and people searching for perfect partner wind up lonely. *Love in a Small Town* also contains a low-key version of the 1946 standard "You Call Everybody Darling" and a cover of Mickey & Sylvia's "Love Is Strange." Oslin's coyness isn't always flattering, and the arrangements sometimes border on a new countrypolitan, but those moments are rare. On most of *Small Town*, Oslin displays her best assets: her worldly sensibility and complex maturity. *—Brian Mansfield*

● **Greatest Hits: Songs From an Aging Sex Bomb** / Apr. 27, 1993 / RCA ✦✦✦

You'll find K.T. Oslin in the country section, but don't be fooled. This music is to country as Kenny G is to jazz—a slicker, poppier variation on a familiar formula. And Kenny G's example to the contrary notwithstanding, there's nothing necessarily wrong with that. Oslin's reedy alto doesn't have much of that mountain twang to it (her singing owes much more to Phoebe Snow than to Loretta Lynn, whether she knows it or not) and you're not going to hear any tearjerking steel guitar on this collection. But you will certainly hear lots of snappy pop music with good melodies and slick production. Country radio listeners will recognize staples like "Hold Me" and "80's Ladies," but if no one told you that "You Can't Do That" was a country song, you'd never guess. And who cares? This is great pop music, no matter what bin you find it in. *—Rick Anderson*

My Roots Are Showing / Oct. 1, 1996 / BNA ✦✦✦

After quadruple bypass surgery in 1995 and a lengthy recording hiatus, the '80s lady came back in 1996 with updated yesteryear's music, an album of dance songs. Rockers and waltzes too. K.T. Oslin has always shown a degree of quality in her song selection, but she may have topped her own exacting standards here. Every song is a gem and no one track is exactly alike. The only issue is that this was marketed as a country album when the Nashville element isn't terribly conspicuous. Webb Pierce's "Pathway of Teardrops" is like a yearning mellow calypso, "Hold Whatcha Got" rocks so hard it could have shot straight from the Jerry Lee Lewis songbook, and Irving Berlin's "I'll See You in C-U-B-A" could fit snug into Maurice Chevalier's act. The closest Oslin comes to Nashville here is Jimmie Rodgers' "Miss the Mississippi and You," where Oslin gets in a little light yodeling, the hard-driving "Silver Tongue and Goldplated Lies," "My Baby Came Back," and "Down in the Valley," which she translated into blues. But, Oslin's greatest strength is her soulful ballad renderings, and she didn't fail to deliver them on Richard Thompson's "A Heart Needs a Home," the Delmore Brothers' "Sand Mountain Blues," and Wilma Burgess' classic "Tear Time." *—Bill Carpenter*

Super Hits / Jun. 3, 1997 / RCA ✦✦✦

Super Hits is a fine budget-price collection of K.T. Oslin's biggest hits from the late '80s and early '90s, featuring such singles as "80's Ladies," "Do Ya," "I'll Always Come Back," "Hold Me," and "Didn't Expect It to Go Down This Way." *—Thom Owens*

Live Close By, Visit Often / Mar. 6, 2001 / BNA ✦✦

Describing the collection of songs on Oslin's first album in five years as diverse is an understatement. It's always nice to hear from Oslin, but this comeback is bittersweet. Too eclectic to call country, too divergent to call pop, the 12 songs on *Live Close By, Visit Often* are an undefinable mix of various musical styles. Perhaps it was the influence of the

Mavericks' frontman, Raul Malo, who served as co-producer. Either way, music doesn't have to be definable or categorized to make it good—or even interesting—and Oslin's unmediated vocals are always a pleasure to listen to, no matter what she's singing about. *—Maria Konicki Dinoia*

RCA Country Legends / Sep. 10, 2002 / RCA ♦♦♦♦
When K.T. Oslin came along in the mid-'80s, she was a true original. She broke the mold of young, cute singers doing cookie-cutter songs and injected some much-needed spunk and maturity to pop country. This collection rounds up tracks from her tenure at RCA in the '80s and her stay at BNA in the '90s. The 16 tracks include ten Top 40 hits, including the number ones "Do Ya'," "I'll Always Come Back," "Hold Me," and "Come Next Monday." This collection is recommended to anyone who loves women who sing real country music, like Patsy Cline or Loretta Lynn or k.d. lang. Be sure to add K.T. Oslin to that list. *—Tim Sendra*

Marie Osmond

b. Oct. 13, 1959, Ogden, UT
Vocals / Pop, Soft Rock, Country-Pop
As part of a family act that came to be virtually synonymous with wholesome entertainment, Marie Osmond enjoyed a lengthy career switching between several different areas of show business. Born Olive Marie Osmond in Ogden, UT, in 1959, she was raised in a strict Mormon family along with her eight brothers. She made her first TV appearance at the age of three, when her oldest brothers performed on *the Andy Williams Show* as the Osmonds. After spending the '60s as variety-show fixtures, the Osmonds shot to pop stardom in 1970, and before long the group's management encouraged Marie to try her hand at recording as well. She made several concert appearances with her brothers (though she was never officially a member of the Osmonds), and in 1973 she cut her first single, the country tune "Paper Roses." The song was a gold-selling smash, going to number one on the country charts (the first time a female artist's debut single had ever done so) and into the Top Five on the pop charts. Her accompanying album of the same name also topped the country charts, and Osmond followed it with two more albums for MGM and several more singles, none of which matched its success.

In 1976, she and brother Donny began hosting their own weekly variety show, *Donny & Marie*, which ran until 1979. In the meantime, she also began to pursue acting; she famously turned down the lead role in *Grease* because she didn't approve of the script's moral content but found limited success in a series of TV-movies and later did voice-over work for several children's cartoons. In the mid-'80s, she returned to country music and signed with Curb, scoring a number-one hit right out of the box with the Dan Seals duet "Meet Me in Montana." Her solo follow-up, "There's No Stopping Your Heart," also topped the country charts, and she landed two more big hits in 1986 with the Top Five solo track "Read My Lips" and the number one Paul Davis duet "You're Still New to Me." None of her subsequent singles breached the country Top Ten, though 1987's "I Only Wanted You" came close, and she charted for the final time in 1990 with "Like a Hurricane." Osmond spent much of the '90s in touring musicals and returned to television in 1998 as co-host of the daytime talk show *Donny & Marie*, which ran for two seasons. *—Steve Huey*

25 Hits Special Collection / Nov. 7, 1995 / Curb ♦♦♦
A good budget-priced compilation of Marie Osmond's biggest hits, *25 Hits Special Collection* spans from 1973's "Paper Roses" to 1990's "Like a Hurricane." It's a thorough overview of her solo career, hitting all of her best-known songs, including her hit duets with Dan Seals and Paul Davis ("Meet Me in Montana" and "You're Still New to Me," respectively). It's not just for the budget-minded—it's a complete retrospective that offers an excellent encapsulation of Osmond's solo career. *—Thom Owens*

Paul Overstreet

b. Newton, MS
Songwriter, Vocals / Country-Pop, Country Gospel, Contemporary Country
Paul Overstreet was one of the most successful songwriters in contemporary country music, penning hits for artists like George Jones, Randy Travis, Tanya Tucker, and Marie Osmond, as well as scoring hits on his own. He wrote his first songs as a boy in Newton, MO. In 1973, he graduated from high-school and headed for Nashville, where he played in country bands at night and worked blue-collar jobs during the day. Despite his efforts, Overstreet couldn't break into the industry. Eventually, his songs were being recorded by other, more established artists. In 1982, his "Same Ole Me" was recorded by George Jones, who took the song to number five. That same year, Overstreet had his first charting single, when "Beautiful Baby" climbed to number 76. Three years later, the Forrester Sisters took his "I Fell in Love Again Last Night"—which he co-wrote with Thom Schuyler—to number one. Later in 1985, Randy Travis had hits with two Overstreet compositions—"On the Other Hand" (which was co-written with Don Schlitz) and "Diggin' Up Bones," the singer's first number-one hit.

Tanya Tucker, Marie Osmond and Paul Davis also had success with Overstreet songs that year. Overstreet became a full-fledged recording artist in 1986 when he teamed up with Schuyler and Fred Knobloch to form SKO, which scored a number-one hit with "Baby's Got a New Baby." In 1987, Overstreet scored one of his biggest songwriting hits when he provided Randy Travis with "Forever and Ever, Amen." As his string of hits for other artists continued, Overstreet released his 1989 debut album, *Sowin' Love*, which made it to the Top 40 and produced a few hits. His second album, *Heroes*, came out in 1991 and stayed on the charts for nearly a year. When his third album, 1992's *Love is Strong*, was a commercial disappointment, Overstreet shifted his focus to writing more religious material and began recording with Susie Luchsinger, the sister of Reba McEntire. *Time* was released in February 1996. *Living By the Book* followed five years later. *—Sandra Brennan*

Sowin' Love / 1989 / RCA ♦♦♦♦♦
In addition to the popular title cut, *Sowin Love* offers the hits "Seein' My Father in Me," "All the Fun," "Love Helps Those" and "Richest Man on Earth." *—Jason Ankeny*

Heroes / 1991 / RCA ♦♦♦
Heroes is highlighted by Overstreet's first solo number-one hit, "Daddy's Come Around;" both the title track and "Ball and Chain" also reached the Top Five. *—Jason Ankeny*

Love Is Strong / 1992 / RCA ♦♦♦
Love Is Strong represents Overstreet at his most eclectic, exploring pop ("Me and My Baby"), country-rock ("Take Another Run") and swing ("Still Out There Swinging"). *—Jason Ankeny*

• **The Best of Paul Overstreet** / Feb. 1994 / RCA ♦♦♦♦♦
The ultimate new traditionalist factory songwriter, Overstreet's best work is the series of hits he wrote (usually with Don Shlitz) for Randy Travis in the 1980s. On his own, as evidenced by this collection, he's a bit too obsessed with convincing everybody that he's a good Christian man who just can't wait to get home to his wife. There's more to life—and music—than family values, no matter how you define them. *—Dan Cooper*

Tommy Overstreet

b. Sep. 10, 1937, Oklahoma City, OK
Vocals / Country-Pop, Nashville Sound/Countrypolitan
Tommy Overstreet was a countrypolitan-styled singer who achieved his greatest success in the early '70s, although he probably gained his most significant exposure as a frequent guest on the program *Hee Haw*. He was born on September 10, 1937, in Oklahoma City, and an early interest in music was encouraged by his cousin Gene Austin, a singer who had garnered some fame in the 1920 with records like "My Blue Heaven" and "Ramona." In his teens, he began performing pop music on radio stations in the Houston, TX, area and appeared in a musical titled *Hit the Road*. While studying broadcasting at the University of Texas, he began playing in local clubs under the name Tommy Dean From Abilene and toured frequently with Austin.

After a stint in the Army, Overstreet moved to Los Angeles in the early '60s to begin a songwriting career, contributing material to pop crooner Pat Boone. He also signed a recording deal, although none of his studio work from the period was ever issued. After returning to Texas, he began appearing on the TV program *the Slim Willet Show* and formed his own group to play club dates. In 1967, he moved to Nashville, where he became the regional professional manager of Dot Records in addition to signing with the label as a recording artist. His debut single, 1969's "Rocking a Memory (That Won't Go to Sleep)," was a minor hit, and his next record, "If You're Looking for a Fool," did even better. In 1971, he scored his first smash with "Gwen (Congratulations)," the title track from his debut LP, followed by "I Don't Know You (Anymore)."

In 1972, Overstreet scored his biggest hit, "Ann (Don't Go Runnin')," which reached number two on the charts. A series of Top Ten hits followed, among them the same year's "Heaven Is My Woman's Love," 1974's "(Jeannie Marie) You Were a Lady," and 1975's "That's When My Woman Begins." Although he continued to chart throughout the 1970s, he failed to reach the same heights he did in the first half of the decade. Overstreet's hit-making days were largely over by the 1980s, but he remained a popular concert draw and continued touring with his group the Nashville Express. *—Jason Ankeny*

Gwen, Congratulations / 1971 / MCA ♦♦♦

Greatest Hits / 1989 / Highland ♦♦♦♦
This album features such hits as "Send Me No Roses" and "Heaven Is My Woman's Love," among others. *—AMG*

• **The Very Best of Tommy Overstreet** / Sep. 22, 1998 / Varese ♦♦♦♦
Tommy Overstreet is not especially well-remembered—as of this writing, none of his original recordings for ABC and Dot were in print—but during the '70s, he had a steady string of hits for Dot and ABC, including 11 country Top Ten singles. All of those songs are here, along with five other smaller hits, on Varese's comprehensive 1998 summary, *The Very Best of Tommy Overstreet*. Overstreet's baritone, as well as his selection of material, was reminiscent of Don Williams. Occasionally, he sounded strained where Williams let the words roll easy, but he had a similar laid-back Western warmth and walked a similar musical path; where a traditional country sound was given pop overtones in the song selection and the lush production, heavy on layers of vocals and guitars. Although he had no classics, he did have a good ear for songs, often relying on tunes written by his producer Ricci Mareno, often with the assistance of either Jerry W. Gillespie and Charlie Black. They were good genre numbers—as Overstreet puts it in Laurence Zwisohn's liner notes, songs about "the heartaches, the heartbreaks, the success, the failure, the booze, the blues"—and they're delivered in a commercial, straightforward manner and sung with conviction by Overstreet. It's generic music, but in the best possible sense; it's good mainstream '70s country, not gutsy enough for outlaw, but too country to be called countrypolitan, and it's all the better for it. *—Stephen Thomas Erlewine*

Bonnie Owens (Bonnie Campbell)

b. Oct. 1, 1932, Blanchard, OK
Vocals / Traditional Country, Bakersfield Sound
Apart from her solo career, singer Bonnie Owens is well known for the work she did with her former husbands, Buck Owens and Merle Haggard. Born Bonnie Campbell on October 1, 1932, in Blanchard, OK to a pair of sharecroppers and one of eight children, she first met Buck in the mid-'40s when he had a local daily 15-minute radio show. Once Buck discovered that Bonnie could sing, he helped her get a job with him on another radio show in 1947. The following January, Buck and Bonnie married, but the union would be short lived. By 1951, after giving birth to two sons, the marriage was over. Since neither could afford a divorce, they stayed legally married, but separated, for several years. Bonnie and the two boys left for Bakersfield, where she worked as a cocktail waitress. It was during this period that Bonnie met Fuzzy Owen and guitarist Roy Nichols, who would be instrumental in the career of Haggard.

By the late '50s Bonnie was recording on the Mar-Vel label with Fuzzy and his band, the Sun Valley Playboys. She cut a well-received duet album with Fuzzy, her sometime boyfriend, on Tally Records, which would later be re-released on Capitol Records as "Just Between the Two of Us." In 1961, Bonnie saw Haggard singing for the first time at a Lefty Frizzell concert. At the time, Haggard was just a few months out of San Quentin prison for breaking and entering. By 1964 Fuzzy was managing Haggard and suggested that Bonnie and Haggard re-record "Just Between the Two of Us." Taking Fuzzy's advice paid off; the song hit the top of the country charts but not for long. It was replaced by "(My Friends Are Gonna Be) Strangers," Haggard's breakthrough single.

In 1965 Haggard signed with Capitol Records, married Bonnie, and signed the Strangers (including Bonnie) with a booking agency owned in part by Buck. Bonnie's marriage to Haggard lasted until 1978, but the two had already separated in 1975. Eventually Bonnie resumed touring with the Strangers in the late '70s and remarried for the final time to Fred McMillenher. She continued to tour regularly with Haggard and the Strangers. While Bonnie released half a dozen albums and numerous singles on Capitol Records in the mid- to late '60s, she remained satisfied singing backup as a member of the Strangers. *—Al Campbell*

Don't Take Advantage of Me / 1965 / Capitol ✦✦✦✦

All of Me Belongs to You / 1967 / Capitol ✦✦✦

Somewhere Between / 1968 / Capitol ✦✦✦

Lead Me On / 1969 / Capitol ✦✦✦

Hi-Fi To Cry By / 1969 / Capitol ✦✦✦

Mother's Favorite Hymns / 1970 / Capitol ✦✦

● **The Best of Bonnie Owens** / 1999 / Capitol ✦✦✦✦

Buck Owens (Alvis Edgar Owens Jr.)

b. Aug. 12, 1929, Sherman, TX

Guitar, Songwriter, Vocals, Trumpet, Leader, Saxophone / Traditional Country, Honky Tonk, Bakersfield Sound

Buck Owens, along with Merle Haggard, was the leader of the Bakersfield sound, an twangy, electricified, rock-influenced interpretation of hardcore honky tonk that emerged in the '60s. Owens was the first bona fide country star to emerge from Bakersfield, scoring a total of 15 consecutive number-one hits in the mid-'60s. In the process, he provided an edgy alternative to the string-laden country-pop that was being produced during the '60s. Later in his career, his musical impact was forgotten by some as he became a television personality through the country comedy show *Hee Haw.* Nevertheless, several generations of musicians—from Gram Parsons in the late '60s to Dwight Yoakam in the '80s—were influenced by his music, which wound up being one of the blueprints for modern country music.

Owens was born in Texas, but his family moved to Mesa, AZ, when he was a child, seeking work during the Great Depression. Owens developed a fervent interest in music as a young child, learning to play guitar in his early teens. He dropped out of high-school in ninth grade, working on the farm to help his family but also spending a significant amount of time learning how to play the guitar. By his late teens, he had an occasional spot on a local radio station, KTYL Mesa, and was playing gigs in honky tonks and clubs around Phoenix with his friend Theryl Ray Britten. When he was 19 years old, he married Bonnie Campbell, who was also a country singer. By 1950, the couple had two sons. Buck and Bonnie Owens decided to leave Arizona in 1951, moving to Bakersfield, CA. In Bakersfield, he became a regular performer in a number of clubs, particularly the Blackboard, where he was the lead singer and played rhythm guitar for Bill Woods & the Orange Blossom Playboys. Soon, he formed his own band, the Schoolhouse Playboys, which also played the Blackboard. Buck's exposure in Bakersfield led to some session work for Capitol Records, beginning with Tommy Collins' 1954 hit "You Better Not Do That." During all of this, Buck and Bonnie grew apart and divorced in 1953; they remained friends and shared custody of their children.

Between 1954 and 1958, Owens played guitar on a number of Capitol country records produced by Ken Nelson, including some by Faron Young, Tommy Sands, and Wanda Jackson. Occasionally, he was a session musician at the local Bakersfield studio Lu-Tal, run by Lewis Talley. Owens made his first solo recordings at Talley's studio in 1956, cutting ten songs for an independent label called Pep. The singles—which included the often-covered "Down on the Corner of Love" and "Sweethearts in Heaven" as well as two rockabilly sides released under the name Corky Jones—were unsuccessful, yet they attracted the attention of many country music business insiders. Around this time, Owens met Harlan Howard, a struggling country singer/songwriter. The pair became friends and collaboraters, with Buck writing the music and Harlan writing the lyrics. Owens and Howard formed Blue Book Music that year in order to publish their songs.

Owens continued to play regularly in Bakersfield clubs. At these concerts, he attracted the attention of Johnny Bond and Joe Maphis, who were performers on *Town Hall Party* and signed to Columbia Records. Impressed with Owens' music, the pair sent a demo to their record label, who immediately became interested in signing Buck. Several people at Capitol were trying to persuade Ken Nelson, the label's country A&R head, to sign Owens as a recording artist, but he wasn't convinced that Buck was a capable lead singer or songwriter. It wasn't until a Capitol recording artist, the Farmer Boys, picked Owens' songs to record instead of Nelson's that the A&R head decided to sign the guitarist in February 1957.

Initially, Owens' singles for Capitol Records were ignored. They were country-pop numbers, complete with a choral group singing backing vocals. Such a big production didn't fit comfortably with his unvarnished honky tonk roots and both singles sank without a trace when they were released in 1957. Hurting financially from the lack of sales, Owens moved to a suburb of Tacoma, WA, to work at a radio station, KAYE, in January 1958. In addition to DJ-ing and selling ads for the station, he played clubs around the area. By the summer, Owens was convinced that his recording career was over, but Ken Nelson refused to let him out of his contract. In the fall of 1958, Owens had another session for Capitol Records, but this time he was allowed to use a steel guitar and a fiddle. One of the songs from the session, "Second Fiddle," was released as a single and became a surprise hit, climbing to number 24 on the country charts. Even though he had his first taste of success, Owens remained skeptical about his future as a recording artist, so he remained in Tacoma, hosting his own live show on KTNT. On the show, he featured a new local singer named Loretta Lynn. More importantly for Owens, he met Don Rich (born Donald Eugene Ulrich) at this radio show. Rich would become Owens' partner in the next decade and would have an immense influence over his music.

"Under Your Spell Again," the fall 1959 follow-up to "Second Fiddle," broke the doors open for Owens. Climbing to number four, the single began a streak of Top Ten singles that ran more of less uninterrupted into the '70s. After "Under Your Spell Again" became a success, Owens moved back to Bakersfield. That winter, Rich also moved to Bakersfield, joining Owens' band as a fiddler and guitarist. Early in 1960, Owens took over Howard's share of Blue Book Music, leaving him in total control of the publishing of all of his songs. "Above and Beyond" became a number three hit in the spring.

Owens had his next hit, "Excuse Me (I Think I've Got a Heartache)," in the fall of 1960. It was followed in January 1961 with *Buck Owens,* his first album, as well as the single "Foolin' Around," which spent eight weeks at number two. That spring he had a hit single, "Mental Cruelty"/"Loose Talk," recorded with Rose Maddox. Owens and Rich began touring the country together, playing with pickup bands in each honky tonk they visited. Soon, the pair stopped playing acoustic guitars and began playing Fender Telecasters, electric guitars with a bright, punchy twang. Rich would eventually become the lead guitarist. This change was evident in Owens' two Top Ten hits in 1962, "Kickin' Our Hearts Around" and "You're for Me." Instead of being the shuffling honky tonk numbers that had been Owens' signature, the songs were bright, driving tracks in 2/4 that showed a hint of rock & roll influence. By the beginning of 1963, Owens had begun to assemble his own band, featuring a drummer, bassist, and a pedal steel guitarist. One of the first bassists for the band was Merle Haggard, who named the group the Buckaroos.

Owens' first number-one single, "Act Naturally," arrived in the spring of 1963. "Act Naturally" elevated Buck from a successful singer into stardom, starting a streak of 15 consecutive number-one singles. Its follow-up single, "Love's Gonna Live Here," became his biggest hit, spending 16 weeks at number one. "My Heart Skips a Beat," released in the spring of 1964, was nearly as successful, spending seven weeks at the top of the charts. It was replaced at the top by its B-side, "Together Again"; later that year, "I Don't Care (Just as Long as You Love Me)" spent six weeks at number one.

In 1965, his number-one hits included "I've Got a Tiger by the Tail," "Before You Go," "Only You (Can Break My Heart)," and the instrumental showcase "Buckaroo." That spring, Owens took out an advertisement in the Nashville-based publication *Music City News* claiming: "I shall make no record that is not a country record." He then released his ninth album, *I've Got a Tiger by the Tail,* which featured a version of Chuck Berry's "Memphis." Owens explained that "Memphis" was a rockabilly song, a genre he believed to be part of country music. Also in 1965, he demonstrated his knack for business by forming Buck Owens Enterprises (which was managed by his sister Dorothy) and the booking agency OMAC Artists Corporation. Blue Book Music was also becoming quite successful, with the songs of both Owens and Haggard earning the company significant amounts of money. The following year, Owens began purchasing radio stations; by the end of the decade, he owned four stations.

Owens' success had spearheaded the national acceptance of the Bakersfield sound. Haggard, Wynn Stewart, and Tommy Collins were all grouped under this heading in addition to Owens. The Bakersfield artists updated honky tonk, standing in direct contrast to the smooth country-pop of Nashville. Consequently, Owens was one of the biggest stars in popular music in the mid-'60s. He was playing hundreds of shows a year, selling thousands of records, and selling out concerts across the country. He continued to build his streak of number-one hits with "Waitin' in Your Welfare Line," "Think of Me," and "Open Up Your Heart" in 1966. That year, Owens launched his first television series with *Buck Owens' Ranch.* The program was a half-hour music show that ran throughout the year and was syndicated to 100 markets at the peak of its popularity. Owens' string of number one hits continued throughout 1967, as "Where Does the Good Times Go," "Sam's Place," and "Your Tender Loving Care" all hit the top of the charts. His streak ended at the end of the year, when "It Takes People Like You (To Make People Like Me)" peaked at number two.

Owens began to branch out musically in 1968, adding more textures, tempos, and stylistic flourishes to his music. Though he only had one number-one hit that year with "How Long Will My Baby Be Gone," all of his singles from 1968—"How Long Will My Baby Be Gone," "Sweet Rosie Jones," "Let the World Keep On a Turnin'," "I've Got You on My Mind Again"—charted in the Top Ten, and all but one reached the Top Five. The following year, Owens opened a state-of-the-art, 16-track recording studio in downtown Bakersfield appropriately called Buck Owens Studios. Capitol allowed him to record himself and several other artists—including Susan Raye, Tony Booth, and Buddy Alan—at the studio; the label would merely press and package the records.

While Owens had a dedicated country following, he also had picked up a number of pop and rock fans as well. Not only did the Beatles cover "Act Naturally" on their 1965 *Help!* album, but in the fall of 1968, Owens headlined and sold out two concerts at the legendary rock & roll venue Fillmore West. Owens continued to experiment musically, as evidenced by the two 1969 number-one singles, "Who's Gonna Mow Your Grass" and "Tall Dark Stranger." In the summer of 1969, Owens' second television show, *Hee Haw,* premiered. *Hee Haw* was the concept of two Canadian TV producers, who envisioned it as a down-home, country version of the popular *Laugh-In.* Owens was hired as its host, and he brought on singer/guitarist Roy Clark as a co-host. Owens only had to tape the show twice a year—once in June and once in October—and his segments were spread throughout the season's shows. Initially, the show was just a summer replacement for *the Smothers Brothers Comedy Hour,* but its summer run was so successful that CBS scheduled it for the fall. As *Hee Haw* became more popular, so did Owens. In the span of just over a year—December 1969 to February 1971—Capitol released no less than nine Owens albums, including reissues and three new studio records. During that time, he continued to chart in the Top Ten with regularity, as "The Kansas City Song" peaked at number two in the summer of 1970 and "I Wouldn't Live in New York City (If They Gave Me the Whole Dang Town)" reached the Top Ten at the end of the year.

At the beginning of 1971, Owens signed what would turn out to be his last contract with Capitol. He would record for the label for another four years and after his contract expired, he would gain ownership of all of his Capitol recordings, from 1957 to 1975; Capitol could continue to manufacture Owens records until 1980, when the masters would all return to Buck. Throughout 1971, he continued to have Top Ten hits, including a version of Simon & Garfunkel's "Bridge Over Troubled Water," "Ruby (Are You Mad)," and "Rollin' in My Sweet Baby's Arms." In 1971, CBS cancelled *Hee Haw*, and the show moved into syndication, where it became even more popular. By 1973, it had been so successful that it forced *Buck Owens' Ranch* off the air, simply because Owens' first program couldn't compete with the high ratings of his second show. In the spring of 1972, he had his final number-one single as a solo artist, the ballad "Made in Japan." However, his career began to slide after that. It took him over a year to reach the Top Ten again with "Big Game Hunter" at the end of 1973. Two other Top Ten hits followed in the spring and summer of 1974, though both songs—a rewrite of Dr. Hook's "On the Cover of the Rolling Stone" called "On the Cover of the Music City News" and "(It's A) Monsters' Holiday"—were novelty numbers.

In July of 1974, Rich, Owens' longtime partner and guitarist, died in a motorcycle crash, which sent Buck into a deep depression. Though he had one more Top Ten hit that fall with "Great Expectations," he had trouble breaking the Top 40 in the years following Rich's death. Owens' contract with Capitol expired in 1975, and he moved to Warner Bros., where he began recording in Nashville. Appropriately, his music began to sound more like country-pop than the hard-edged Bakersfield sound he had become famous for, but that's because he relinquished creative control of his records to the producers. Owens' record sales had significantly declined, but *Hee Haw* remained popular. Ironically, its success had an unwanted side effect—for many listeners in the general audience, Owens became the cornball country comedian he was in the show, not the hardcore honky tonker he was at heart. That perception remained throughout the end of the '70s and even a hit duet with Emmylou Harris, "Play Together Again Again," in 1979 couldn't erase it. In 1980, Owens decided he didn't want to continue with the grind of constant performing and recording. He ended his contract with Warner and drastically cut back his performances. Even though he was semi-retired, he continued to tape *Hee Haw* until 1986.

Owens was out of public view for the early and mid-'80s, which is when a new generation of country singers was developing. Like Buck in the '60s, they stood in opposition to the pop-inflected country of Nashville, building their sound on the Bakersfield country of Owens and Haggard. One of the leading performers of the new traditionalists, Dwight Yoakam, persuaded Owens to join him on a re-recording of Buck's 1972 song "Streets of Bakersfield." After they performed it on a CBS television special, the duo recorded the song, releasing it in the summer of 1988. "Streets of Bakersfield" became a major hit, reaching number one; it was the first time since 1972 that Owens had a number-one hit. Its success spurred him back into the recording studio, where he made a new album called *Hot Dog!* It was a moderate success and it re-energized Owens. He assembled a new version of the Buckaroos and continued to perform and record, including a duet of "Act Naturally" with Ringo Starr. Owens didn't record or perform frequently in the '90s, but his classic Capitol recordings began to appear on compact disc; they hadn't been in print since 1980, when he gained control of the tapes from Capitol. Furthermore, Owens' influence continued to reverberate throughout country music as well as some quarters of rock & roll. *—Stephen Thomas Erlewine*

Buck Owens / Jan. 30, 1961 / Capitol ♦♦♦♦
This is a reissue of Buck's debut album, originally issued on Capitol in 1961. Featuring Owens' early development of the Bakersfield sound (the classic Buckaroos lineup had yet to be assembled and Don Rich is only listed as the fiddle player on "Excuse Me (I Think I've Got a Heartache)"), this opening salvo sports his early hits "Above and Beyond," "Under Your Spell Again" and "Second Fiddle." This 14-track reissue also sports two extra bonus tracks in addition to the original album, "High as the Mountain" (a 1961 single) and the first recorded version of "Nobody's Fool But Yours," originally issued on a Capitol country compilation. Transfers are astonishingly crisp and clear, showing producer Ken Nelson's touch to good advantage. The sound that became the legend starts right here. *—Cub Koda*

☆ **Buck Owens Sings Harlan Howard** / Aug. 28, 1961 / Sundazed ♦♦♦♦♦
Harlan Howard wrote many of Buck Owens' biggest hits and best songs, including "I've Got a Tiger By the Tail," "Above and Beyond," "Excuse Me (I Think I've Got a Heartache)," and "Under the Influence of Love," so it's only natural that Buck recorded an entire album of Howard's material. And it's also not surprising that it's a stunner, too. Owens sang Howard better than nearly anybody and *Buck Owens Sings Harlan Howard* is full of wonderful songs and performances. Only "Foolin' Around" is regularly featured on Buck's hit compilations, which means there's a wealth of lesser-known gems—including "Heartaches By the Number," "Pick Me Up on Your Way Down," "Keys in the Mailbox" and "Let's Agree to Disagree"—that form the core of this record, one of Owens' most enjoyable LPs of the '60s. *—Stephen Thomas Erlewine*

You're for Me / Oct. 1, 1962 / Sundazed ♦♦♦♦

On the Bandstand / Apr. 29, 1963 / Sundazed ♦♦♦
One of Buck's rootsier '60s Capitol albums, including only one hit ("Kickin' Our Hearts"), and giving plenty of instrumental and vocal space to the rest of the band. It's not as heavy on original material as some of his other Capitol LPs, including numbers by Wanda Jackson, Willie Nelson, Leadbelly, and John D. Loudermilk, as well as an arrangment of "Orange Blossom Special." The CD reissue adds two cuts from a 1963 Top 20 duet single he recorded with Rose Maddox. *—Richie Unterberger*

Buck Owens Sings Tommy Collins / Nov. 11, 1963 / Sundazed ♦♦♦♦♦
Tommy Collins' legacy was greater than his success on the charts, which, despite a few Top Ten singles in the mid-'50s, was never sustained. However, he was a king in California, and he exerted considerable influence on Bakersfield country and its two figureheads, Merle Haggard and Buck Owens, who frequently cited his importance and recorded his songs. Owens, in fact, was a guitarist in Collins' band, which gave him one of his first big breaks, and he decided to return the favor by recording an album of 12 Collins songs in 1963. Like any tribute by an artist who knows his subject intimately, the song selection is highly individualized, but in the case of a cult act like Collins, this works to his favor, since it captures all sides of his character. Owens doesn't rely only on the silly songs that brought Collins some success, but he does cut "It Tickles," a goofy, annoying song about a moustache. But Owens knows what makes Collins an unheralded great: how he could be silly but also have plaintive weepers like "High on a Hilltop" and rocking juke-joint ravers like "If You Ain't Lovin' (You Ain't Livin')," popularized by Faron Young. Owens plays up these two sides, slightly favoring the uptempo side, which comes as little surprise to those familiar with the high-octane, high-twang country of his early Capitol records. Owens didn't have hits with this record, but it did go to number one, and it does stand as one of his most consistently satisfying long-players, thanks to the pen of Tommy Collins and the wonderful performances of Buck Owens & His Buckaroos. *—Stephen Thomas Erlewine*

Country Hit Maker #1 / 1964 / Starday ♦♦♦

☆ **Together Again/My Heart Skips a Beat** / 1964 / Sundazed ♦♦♦♦♦
Named after his double-sided number-one hit single of early 1964, *Together Again/My Heart Skips a Beat* is one of Buck Owens' strongest albums of the '60s, as well as one of his few records to stick firmly in the honky tonk camp. Despite the rolling drums of "My Heart Skips a Beat," the jumpy "Truck Drivin' Man," the jokey "Ain't It Amazin' Gracie," and a Bakersfield overhaul of "Save the Last Dance for Me," the majority of the album is straight-ahead honky tonk. Whether it's Owens' excellent weepers "I Don't Hear You" and "Getting Used to Losing You," or terrific versions of classics like "Close Up the Honky Tonks" and "A-11," the record is filled with superb, pure honky tonk. Sundazed's CD reissue adds the singles "Love's Gonna Live Here" and "Act Naturally," which don't follow in the honky tonk theme of the album, but since both are classics, it's not worth complaining. *—Stephen Thomas Erlewine*

The Best of Buck Owens, Vol. 1 / Jun. 1, 1964 / Capitol ♦♦♦

I Don't Care / Nov. 2, 1964 / Sundazed ♦♦♦
Buck Owens' career was in high enough gear by this point for *I Don't Care* to be his third album for the year. The reason was simple: the hit status of the title track, which held the number-one position on the country charts for six weeks. Like his previous albums, this one features solo performances from Owens (this batch featuring "Don't Let Her Know," "You're Welcome Anytime," "Playboy," "This Ol' Heart," and a duet with Rose Maddox, "Loose Talk") mixed with solo turns by the rest of the band. In addition to Don Rich's takes on Roger Miller's "Dang Me" and "Louisiana Man," this also features two vocals from bassist Doyle Holly ("Abilene" and a version of "Understand Your Man" that's positively growly), "Bud's Bounce," a showcase for steel guitar man Tom Brumley, and a surprise guitar solo from Owens on "Buck's Polka." [The two bonus tracks feature instrumental versions of "Don't Let Her Know" and the title track, both under the direction of Rich from the 1966 *Buck Owens' Songbook* album.] *—Cub Koda*

☆ **I've Got a Tiger By the Tail** / Mar. 1, 1965 / Sundazed ♦♦♦♦♦
Buck Owens had his share of country hits prior to the release of *I've Got a Tiger By the Tail* and the hit single that spawned it. But "I've Got a Tiger by the Tail" was Owens' national breakthrough, featuring everything right about his Bakersfield honky tonk sound sweated down to a 2:12 single that proved to be a irresistible piece of crossover magic to non-country fans without diluting his basic sound one iota. This 14-track CD reissue brings together the original Capitol tracks from that album (which also included the hit "Cryin' Time," later to be a crossover hit of its own when recorded by Ray Charles), along with two bonus tracks. These are live versions recorded in Bakersfield at the Civic Auditorium in October 1963 of "This Ol' Heart" and "Act Naturally," taken from the Capitol anthology album *Country Music Hootenanny*. The sound of Don Rich is all over this album, with his signature biting Telecaster guitar style, plus his vocalizing on "Wham Bam" (which features Owens on lead guitar) and a feature with Buck on a duet of Chuck Berry's "Memphis." Bass player Doyle Holly handles the vocal chores on "Streets of Laredo," while Don Rich's fiddle work is highlighted on the instrumental "A Maiden's Prayer." But ultimately it's Owens' show with tracks like "Trouble and Me," "We're Gonna Let the Good Times Roll," "If You Fall Out of Love With Me," "The Band Keeps Playin' On," and the ballad "Let the Sad Times Roll On" being classic examples of Owens' Bakersfield honky tonk sound at the height of its freight-train rumbling powers. *—Cub Koda*

Before You Go / Jul. 26, 1965 / Sundazed ♦♦♦
When it comes to Owens' mid-'60s Capitol LPs, there really isn't much to choose between. If you like his Bakersfield sound, you'll like all of them; if you're trying to zero in on just one or two collections, you'd be better off with greatest-hits surveys, because the individual albums sound rather interchangeable to the non-enthusiast. This has the usual competent original material and accomplished guitar picking, paced by the number-one title track, with occasional instrumentals thrown in for a change of pace. The CD reissue adds a couple of instrumental bonus cuts from his 1966 album, *The Buck Owens Songbook*. *—Richie Unterberger*

The Instrumental Hits of Buck Owens & His Buckaroos / Jul. 26, 1965 / Sundazed ♦♦♦
When originally issued in July of 1965, no one either noticed or cared that in reality *The Instrumental Hits* was actually a compilation of tracks already available on early Buck Owens & His Buckaroos albums (except for the band's signature song "Buckaroo," which is unique to this package). Regardless of the ratio of new to recycled material, this collection amply highlights the remarkable talents of Owens & His Buckaroos. Note: This title should not be confused with *The Buck Owens Songbook*, another all-instrumental album comparable to a karaoke (read: sans lead vocals) "greatest hits" package. The retrospective nature of this disc allows listeners to experience the evolution of the potent instrumentalists who accompanied Owens circa 1961-1966. Although it would take several years before a stable touring and recording lineup would be forged, the strong influence

and collaborative efforts of Don Rich were there right from the beginning. Whether it's with a fiddle under his chin on songs such as "Bile 'Em Cabbage Down" and "Faded Love" or duelling guitars on "Buckaroo," Rich is undoubtedly the soul of the band, if Owens is the heart. Owens—who is most notable as a lead vocalist—is highlighted on this release as one heck of an underrated instrumentalist. The restless grace in his picking thrusts "Country Polka," "Raz-Ma-Taz Polka," and "Buck's Polka" into orbit via the trademark full-toned electric C&W feel that would ultimately create the Bakersfield sound. [The Sundazed Music CD reissue contains two additional bonus tracks: "Act Naturally" and "Tiger By the Tail," Buck Owens & His Buckaroos' biggest crossover hits. These are taken from the previously mentioned *The Buck Owens Songbook* collection of music and are minus one thing—the vocals. This compilation should not be missed.] *—Lindsay Planer*

Christmas With Buck Owens / Oct. 4, 1965 / Sundazed ✦✦✦✦✦
This 1999 reissue of Owens' 1967 Christmas album is a straight-up affair; with no hidden bonus tracks, just the straight 12 tracks from two 1965 sessions (odd they waited two years to put this stuff out), this is prime Buck Owens & His Buckaroos in the holiday mode. Featured here are "Santa Looked a Lot Like Daddy," "Santa's Gonna Come in a Stagecoach," and enough Yule-time weepers to make you realize that the holidays have a mighty dark side, too. *—Cub Koda*

Roll Out the Red Carpet / Feb. 7, 1966 / Sundazed ✦✦✦
While *Roll Out the Red Carpet* continued the tradition of solid long-players for Buck Owens & His Buckaroos, it ironically was their first album not to have a single in the charts. The stability of the lineup as well as a few Buckaroo instrumentals and vocal duets—featuring lead Buckaroo and longtime Owens collaborator Don Rich—contribute to the power of this oft-overlooked effort. The increasingly subtle yet significant impact of rock & roll can be heard throughout *Roll Out the Red Carpet.* The cross-referencing of the British Invasion with the equally guitar-heavy Bakersfield sound is more than evident. Beatles classics such as "What Goes On," as well as the vocal arrangements to "And Your Bird Can Sing," have audible roots in compositions such as Rich's "I'm Layin' It on the Line" or "There Never Was a Fool." The unique vocal blend that Owens and Rich share could have easily been the prototype for the Lennon & Starr duet on the former Fab Four favorite. The Buckaroos' instrumentals are particularly potent this go-round as well. On "Cajun Fiddle," Owens marries the light electric guitar sound of Bakersfield with a swampy bayou fiddle from Rich. The same airy groove would be incorporated into performance favorites such as "Fishin' on the Mississippi." "Tom Cattin'," the other instrumental on *Roll Out the Red Carpet*, is a more traditional hoedown featuring an ethereal sounding pedal steel guitar rhythm track—presumably overdubbed by Buckaroo steel string man Tom Brumley. [Instrumental versions of "Only You (Can Break My Heart)" and "My Heart Skips a Beat" are added as bonus tracks on the Sundazed Records CD reissues. Both tracks were originally issued on the karaoke-style *Buck Owens' Songbook* long-player.] *—Lindsay Planer*

Dust on Mother's Bible / May 2, 1966 / Capitol ✦✦✦

☆ **The Carnegie Hall Concert** / Jul. 25, 1966 / Sundazed ✦✦✦✦✦
Buck Owens & the Buckaroos' 1966 concert at Carnegie Hall was a landmark not only for the band, but for country music: It signaled that country had firmly integrated itself not only into America's popular music mainstream, but also urban centers like New York. Owens & His Buckaroos had to deliver a stellar performance, and they did—the group sounded like dynamite, tearing through a selection of their classic hits with vigor. Several decades removed from the performance itself, what really comes through is how musical and gifted the Buckaroos were, particularly Don Rich. For dedicated fans, it's a necessary addition to their collection. *—Stephen Thomas Erlewine*

Open Up Your Heart / Dec. 27, 1966 / Sundazed ✦✦✦
Open Up Your Heart arrived in 1966, in the midst of Buck Owens' remarkable streak of success—success that would propel him to the stage of Carnegie Hall in March of that year. This album followed a few months later, and while it is still firmly within his trademark Bakersfield sound, there are slight moves away from his twangy, purer material and toward material that was just a little sillier and a little poppier. Not that anybody could accuse Buck Owens & His Buckaroos of abandoning country music, or even making an overture toward the kind of country-pop coming out of Nashville, but the presentation of the music is a little streamlined and not quite as down-home as it used to be. To begin with, Owens handles all of the lead and harmony vocals on the album, with no instrumentals for Don Rich, even. Then, the songs are getting a little sillier, whether it's the characters who populate the chorus on "Sam's Place" or the corny jokes on "Waitin' in Your Welfare Line." Finally, the production is a little more open and bright, sounding like something coming out of an AM radio instead of a dark honky tonk. These are all subtle changes, and they don't change the fundamental sound of Owens' music, even if they change the feel. As such, *Open Up Your Heart* doesn't resonate quite as strongly as earlier efforts from Owens, nor does it warrant as many repeat plays, but it is still crafted and played well enough to make it a satisfying listen. *—Stephen Thomas Erlewine*

America's Most Wanted Band / 1967 / Capitol ✦✦✦

In Japan! / 1967 / Sundazed ✦✦✦✦✦
Long one of the finer efforts in the Buck Owens album catalog and also one of the finest live country records of all time, *In Japan!* shines in its compact disc reissue. Originally released by Capitol in 1967, this finds Buck Owens & His Buckaroos in the prime of their chart-topping existence and playing like a well-oiled machine, firing exquisitely on all cylinders. The opening and closing remarks and between-song translating banter to the audience from MC Tetsuo Otsuka make for wonderful ambience throughout, and Owens' good-natured master-of-ceremonies turns work hand in glove with him. Musically, the Buckaroos, led by Don Rich, are at the top of their game, and the live versions here of "Open Up Your Heart," "Roll Out the Red Carpet," and "Where Does the Good Times Go" sometimes eclipse their better-known hit studio versions. Although his *Live at Carnegie Hall* album is considered by most fans as definitive, here's another one that shouldn't be dismissed for a second. *—Cub Koda*

Buck Owens & His Buckaroos in Japan! / May 1, 1967 / Capitol ✦✦✦✦✦
There is something palpably avant-garde in the frenetic energy of Owens' unmistakably American (read: Bakersfield) sound set against the cultural backdrop of Tokyo. However, Buck Owens & His Buckaroos prove the adage that the currency of music defies borders and is indeed the universal language. On *Buck Owens & His Buckaroos in Japan!* the band rises to the occasion, performing perennial favorites and previewing tracks from its upcoming album, *It Takes People Like You to Make People Like Me.* The Buckaroos—under the direction of Don Rich—recreate a very Western concert experience. A prime example occurs during Owens' spoken-word prelude, signifying the importance of the Mississippi River in American geography as depicted in "Fishin' on the Mississippi." The band then launches into the song with the bold verve of true Yankee pride. Buck Owens & His Buckaroos frequently display their seemingly double-jointed sense of rhythm. From right out of the gate, their opening number "Adios, Farewell, Goodbye, Good Luck, So Long" features a blazing guitar solo from Rich supported by the taut flexibility of an intuitive musical organization. The audience's affection for tracks such as the ultimately catchy "Open Up Your Heart" propels the quintet's performance level to exceed, at times, the familiar studio version. The instrumentals are also top-shelf and performed with the added edge a live audience often provides. Such is the case with Owens' Eastern-flavored "Tokyo Polka," the Rich masterwork "Fiddle Polka," and Willie Cantu's brief "Drums So Low" percussion solo. History has only reinforced the status of *Buck Owens & His Buckaroos in Japan!* as a key component not only in the canon of Buck Owens & His Buckaroos, but additionally as part of any comprehensive overview of the state of popular C&W music in the mid-'60s. *—Lindsay Planer*

Your Tender Loving Care / Aug. 7, 1967 / Capitol ✦✦✦
The consistent quality of Buck Owen's '60s albums is impressive considering the half-heartedness that typified many albums of the period. *Your Tender Loving Care* is a CD reissue of a 1967 album that was assembled from recordings made at various sessions from 1965-1966. Despite the impression that it is a collection of leftovers, the singularity of Owens' stylistic vision prevents the album from seeming like a hodgepodge. No surprises await the faithful, but this is solid material. The disc includes two bonus tracks, single versions of the title song and "Sam's Place" (both of which were number-one hits). The album tracks are nearly all Buck Owens originals, a few of which were co-written with Red Simpson or Don Rich. *—Greg Adams*

A Night on the Town / 1968 / Capitol ✦✦✦

The Buck Owens' Buckaroos Strike Again! / 1968 / Capitol ✦✦✦

Meanwhile Back at the Ranch / 1968 / Capitol ✦✦✦

It Takes People Like You to Make People Like Me / Jan. 2, 1968 / Sundazed ✦✦✦
This reissue of Buck's original 1968 Capitol album finds himself and the original Buckaroos Don Rich in fine form. By this time, Owens had found his groove, crafting one fine single after another, making each new album almost seem like a greatest hits collection, even if every song wasn't actually a chart number. Highlights include "The Way That I Love You," "You Left Her Lonely Too Long," the title track and "Where Does the Good Times Go," both also offered as mono single release bonus tracks. *—Cub Koda*

The Best of Buck Owens, Vol. 2 / Apr. 1, 1968 / Capitol ✦✦✦✦✦

Christmas Shopping / Oct. 7, 1968 / Sundazed ✦✦✦
Owens' second Christmas album emanates from five session held between February and June of 1968. At this stage of the game, the Buckaroos were a well-oiled studio machine and even the tinkly keyboard stylings of Earle "Poole" Ball doesn't detract from the twang quotient, although this is arguably a more slickly produced album than its predecessor. The usual batch of uptempo, optimistic opuses paired off with holiday weepers ("All I Want for Christmas Is My Daddy" is spot on target) makes this a country Christmas album with a nice, original touch to it. *—Cub Koda*

I've Got You on My Mind Again / Dec. 30, 1968 / Capitol ✦✦✦

Close-Up / 1969 / Capitol ✦✦✦✦

Anywhere U.S.A. / 1969 / Capitol ✦✦✦

Roll Your Own With Buck Owens' Buckaroos / 1969 / Capitol ✦✦✦

Buck Owens in London / Jun. 2, 1969 / Capitol ✦✦✦✦
In 1969, at the height of anti-war fever in America and elsewhere around the world, Buck Owens & His Buckaroos went to the London Palladium as if there was nothing a little Bakersfield country music couldn't cure. And the London audience loved it; they ate it up like chocolate. The audience frenzy—actual, not added—of the first medley of "Act Naturally" and "Together Again" is unnerving. The cornball humor is everywhere and this sophisticated London audience falls for this terrible sh*t—but the music rocks in true Buck fashion. Check out the bad-ass Ventures-meets-Bakersfield boogie of "A Happening in London Town." Buck and crew whip through "Sweet Rosie Jones," Merle Haggard's "Sing Me Back Home," and "Sam's Place" before the side ends. Side two has two medleys, one of Buck's hits, "Love's Gonna Live Here," "Cryin' Time," "I've Got a Tiger By the Tail," and "Open up Your Heart." It's raw and wild and louder than sh*t. There's a short medley of Louisiana Cajun tunes before Buck goes from the sacred ("Dust on Mother's Bible") to the wonderfully profane ("Johnny B. Goode") to close the show. Buck playing Chuck Berry—now there's some deep paradox that proves that music is the universal language, and the significance of it was not lost on the London audience. *—Thom Jurek*

Tall Dark Stranger / Sep. 29, 1969 / Capitol ✦✦

The Guitar Player / Oct. 7, 1969 / Capitol ✦✦✦

The Kansas City Song / 1970 / Capitol ✦✦✦

Buck Owens / 1970 / Capitol ✦✦✦

The Great White Horse / 1970 / Capitol ✦✦✦

Rompin' & Stompin / 1970 / Capitol ✦✦✦

Boot Hill / 1970 / Capitol ✦✦✦

Your Mother's Prayer / Mar. 2, 1970 / Capitol ✦✦✦

Big in Vegas / Dec. 29, 1970 / Capitol ✦✦✦

Bridge Over Troubled Water / 1971 / Capitol ✦✦

Buck Owens' Ruby & Other Bluegrass Specials / 1971 / Capitol ✦✦✦

I Wouldn't Live in New York City / Nov. 2, 1971 / Capitol ✦✦✦

Too Old to Cut the Mustard? / 1972 / Capitol ✦✦

Live at the White House / 1972 / Capitol ✦✦✦

Buck Owens Live at the Nugget / 1972 / Capitol ✦✦✦

In the Palm of Your Hand / 1973 / Capitol ✦✦✦✦
Though a few of the ten tracks on *In the Palm of Your Hand* appeared on previous albums and have been included on subsequent releases, the majority of them appear here for the first and only time in Buck Owens' recorded catalog. Songs such as the classic Bakersfield sound of "Arms Full of Empty" and the excellent ballad "Something's Wrong" are too strong to be overlooked to the extent that they have been. "There Goes My Love" is one of the most insanely catchy songs to ever appear on an Owens album, as well. His last number one hit as a solo artist, "Made in Japan," is also included, making this one of his more overlooked albums. Sadly, the entire album squeaks in at just under 26 minutes, though there are definitely more than enough reasons to check it out. *—Matt Fink*

Ain't It Amazing Gracie / 1973 / Capitol ✦✦✦✦

Arms Full of Empty / 1973 / Capitol ✦✦✦
Considering the era and the album's billing as an "unforgettable collection of love songs," one might suppose that Buck Owens' 1973 LP, *Arms Full of Empty*, is a pop-oriented collection of schmaltzy ballads. Fortunately, that's not the case. Owens sticks to his trademark style and every song on the album was written solely by Owens, with the exception of "Colors I'm Gonna Paint the Town," which was co-authored by his son, Buddy Alan. The love songs are not predominately slow and the distinctive guitar leads are intact. This was one of the last albums to feature Owens' guitarist and partner, Don Rich, who died in 1974. The title track was only a minor hit, and Owens doesn't rigidly adhere to the "love" theme ("Songwriter's Lament" is about the glut of pickers and songwriters in Nashville), but *Arms Full of Empty* is typical of his quality approach to album-making. *—Greg Adams*

Good Old Days / 1973 / Capitol ✦✦✦

It's a Monster's Holiday / 1974 / Capitol ✦✦

41st Street Lonely Hearts Club / 1975 / Capitol ✦✦

Buck 'Em / 1976 / Warner Bros. ✦✦

Hot Dog! / Nov. 16, 1988 / Capitol ✦✦✦
When Buck Owens' career stalled in the mid-'70s, he began concentrating on his many business ventures and investments. He seemed to be waiting for the Bakersfield sound that he helped develop to come back into style. It did in 1988 in the guise of Dwight Yoakam, who recorded "Streets of Bakersfield" as a duet with Owens, briefly re-establishing him with a number one single. That same year he released *Hot Dog!*, his first album since 1976. While the snappy title track received light country airplay, it disappeared quickly. This isn't one of Owens' best albums by a long shot, but it is a fun session, with Buck covering a few rock & roll classics from the '50s ("Summertime Blues" and "Memphis Tennessee"), plus a reworking of his 1959 hit "Under Your Spell Again." *—Al Campbell*

Act Naturally / Oct. 4, 1989 / Capitol ✦✦✦
On *Act Naturally*, Buck Owens runs through his back catalog, re-making several of his classic hits and a handful of obscurities, as well as recording three unremarkable new songs. Though Buck is in fine voice and his backing band can replicate the twangy Bakersfield sound, the record's production is a little too thick, sterile and unaffecting to make the album consistently enjoyable. *—Thom Owens*

All-Time Greatest Hits, Vol. 1 / Aug. 13, 1990 / Curb ✦✦✦✦✦
Curb's *All-Time Greatest Hits* was released two years before Buck Owens allowed Rhino Records to release his catalog in the form of a box set and two compilations. Consequently, the compilation isn't much more than a place-holder—12 songs that contain a few of his biggest hits ("Act Naturally," "Streets of Bakersfield," "I've Got a Tiger By the Tail") plus several lesser-known singles ("Think of Me," "Big in Vegas"). It's an adequate collection, but it doesn't have the comprehensiveness, nor the listenability, of any of the Rhino collections, which are all better introductions and retrospectives. *—Stephen Thomas Erlewine*

☆ **The Buck Owens Collection (1959–1990)** / 1992 / Rhino ✦✦✦✦✦
Spanning three discs, *The Buck Owens Collection* is the most comprehensive compilation ever assembled on one of the founders of the Bakersfield sound. Although his earliest recordings aren't included, all of his greatest Capitol hits are present, as is his 1988 duet on "Streets of Bakersfield" with Dwight Yoakam and its follow-up single, "Hot Dog." The box is a necessary purchase, simply because it presents all of Buck's biggest hits in one place. There might not be many rarities on *The Buck Owens Collection*, but with an artist as consistent as Buck, all you need is the good stuff and that is all on this essential set. *—Stephen Thomas Erlewine*

All-Time Greatest Hits, Vol. 2 / 1992 / Curb ✦✦✦
This compilation features 11 Capitol recordings by Buck Owens from 1963 through 1971. The twangy honky tonk hits include "Love's Gonna Live Here," "Open Up Your Heart," and "Your Tender Loving Care." There's also a fun cover of Chuck Berry's "Johnny B. Goode." A third volume of hits from one of the originators of the Bakersfield sound is also available on Curb. *—Al Campbell*

★ **The Very Best of Buck Owens, Vol. 1** / 1994 / Rhino ✦✦✦✦✦
The Very Best of Buck Owens, Vol. 1 contains a great deal of Buck's most essential songs, including "Under Your Spell Again," "Act Naturally," "I've Got a Tiger By the Tail," and "Waitin' in Your Welfare Line." The set runs from 1959 to 1971, picking up a good cross-section of his biggest hits along the way. The compilation is a perfect introduction and what songs it doesn't cover are readily available on *The Very Best of Buck Owens, Vol. 2*. *—Stephen Thomas Erlewine*

☆ **The Very Best of Buck Owens, Vol. 2** / 1994 / Rhino ✦✦✦✦✦
The Very Best of Buck Owens, Vol. 2 contains all the essential Owens songs the first volume didn't cover, including "Above and Beyond," "Love's Gonna Live Here," "My Heart Skips a Beat," "Cryin' Time," "Buckaroo," and "Big in Vegas." Like its predecessor, the collection spans from 1959 to 1971, and features an excellent cross-section of his biggest hits along the way. Not only is it a perfect supplement to *The Very Best of Buck Owens, Vol. 1*, the compilation works as a good introduction, even though the first collection is a better choice for a new fan. *—Stephen Thomas Erlewine*

Young Buck: The Complete Pre-Capitol Recordings / Feb. 27, 2001 / Audium ✦✦✦✦
Although the exact dates of the original recording and release dates of some of this material is unclear, it's known for sure that all predate his signing to Capitol in 1957. Eight of them appeared as 1955-1956 singles on the small Pep label; the others were originally issued, in unauthorized fashion, on the Chesterfield and La Brea labels (except for the previously unreleased demo "Blue Love"). While the fidelity and production is not as slick as Owens would be accustomed to on Capitol, and the arrangements less heavy on the more electric elements of Owens' subsequent '50s and '60s work, it's still unmistakably Owens, and pretty good. These are virtually all original compositions, and comprise a quality mixture of rhythmic earthy honky tonkers and slower weepers, Owens already a strong and versatile singer. One of those Pep singles, incidentally, is the rockabilly single he cut as Corky Jones, "Hot Dog"/"Rhythm and Booze," and shows that he was quite competent in that style, although he didn't follow it as a career path. The most oddball item is the most ill-fitting: The "Blue Love" demo, an ordinary midtempo Western swing number, includes not just steel guitar but also trumpet in the arrangement. *—Richie Unterberger*

Tex Owens (Doye Hensley Owens)

b. Jun. 15, 1892, Kileen, TX, **d.** Sep. 9, 1962
Songwriter, Vocals / Traditional Country, Cowboy

Best remembered today as the author of the Eddy Arnold hit "Cattle Call," Tex Owens was a fixture on local radio in Kansas City and the CBS network during the 1930s and early '40s, and he was one of the first artists signed to Decca Records back in the '30s. He was the youngest of 13 children in a sharecropper family whose musical interests began with his generation—his brother Chuck was a singer and songwriter, and his sister Texas Ruby was a performer with the *Grand Ole Opry*. Despite their musical activities, however, it took Owens until he was nearly 40 to decide on a career in music.

Doye (some sources spell it Doie) Hensley Owens was born in Kileen, TX, but the family moved to Cushing, OK, while he was still a boy. The name "Tex" logically seemed to stick after the move to Oklahoma. Beginning when he was 15 years old, he worked lots of jobs, especially on ranches in the surrounding area, and even spent a stint as a chuck wagon cook. He did gravitate a little toward singing—he could play guitar well enough to accompany himself, and as a lanky six-feet three-inch vocalist, he looked natural enough as the center of attention. He made his first foray into music at a traveling tent show as a blackface singer, doubling as a hired hand, and spent up to a year with one such tent show. The life didn't appeal to him enough to stay with music, however, and by his late teens Owens was back working more conventional and reliable jobs. He was just young enough, having been born in 1892, to avoid being drafted into military service during World War I.

Owens worked oil fields in Texas, and then jobs in Missouri and Kansas, and after marrying Maude Neal, he settled for a time in Drexel, MO. He worked as a farm hand and mechanic, and later even served as a lawman in Bridgeport, OK, before the family—which now included two daughters, Laura Lee and Dolpha Jane—moved west to Colorado. It was the combination of acute appendicitis and a freak blizzard in Lamar, CO, that brought Owens back to music. While recovering from an appendectomy, Owens saw a group of school children (five of whom had frozen to death before being rescued) who had been stranded in a blizzard brought into the hospital, and he entertained them with some songs.

This proved to be the most appreciative audience to which Owens had ever played, and their reaction pulled him back into music for the first time in years. After the family moved back to Kansas, Owens began singing with his two daughters, including performances at medicine shows. Finally, in the very early '30s, Owens got his first indoor gig, singing to audiences between features at a local movie theater. This led him to a radio audition at KMBC in Kansas City, MO, and his being hired full-time as a singer and general on-air performer.

He was billed as "The Original Texas Ranger" and performed regularly with two groups, the Texas Rangers and, later, the Prairie Pioneers. They were popular enough locally and regionally that the record industry beckoned—Gene Autry, another young Texan with roots in Oklahoma, was burning up the airwaves and selling millions of records, and every record company was looking for another Autry. In the summer of 1934, Owens was signed along with the Texas Rangers to the newly founded Decca label. (Curiously, Decca had also signed another "Tex," by the last name of Ritter, around the same time). They recorded a comedy single, "The Dude Ranch Party, Pts. 1 & 2," on August 27, 1934, on which Owens sang a bit of "The Cattle Call" amid a series of songs that included "Git Along Little Dogies" and "Prance Along," plus comedy material. The Texas Rangers included Bob

Crawford as leader, with the two Massey brothers, Curt (who later wrote much of the background music for the television series *The Beverly Hillbillies*) on fiddle and Allen on fiddle and banjo, respectively, Gomer Cool on fiddle, and Hugh Studebaker on guitar, with George Washington White doing comic relief, often in blackface.

It was Owens' full recording of "Cattle Call," made solo the following day, that ultimately proved more important, introducing a song he'd written and copyrighted in Kansas City that year. According to his wife, he'd written it ahead of a show during a snowstorm when they were stuck at the hotel where the radio station was headquartered, borrowing the melody from "The St. Paul Waltz." The song, one of four he recorded in Chicago that day, wasn't a success at the time, and Owens' relationship with Decca ended after that session. He next recorded ten songs for RCA in September of 1936, none of which—including another version of "Cattle Call"—were issued and all of which are lost today.

Most of Owens' career was spent not in the recording studio, but rather on the radio, performing with either the Texas Rangers or the Prairie Pioneers; he also made personal appearances and, on rare occasions, performed in movies. He began seriously writing songs in the early '30s, more than a dozen of which were published by the radio station in a songbook in 1934. It is also rumored that Owens' KMBC show was telecast in experimental broadcasts by the engineering departments of Kansas State, Purdue, and Iowa State University in 1932. He was a star as a singer and storyteller on KMBC's *Brush Creek Follies*, which included in its cast comedy acts like Uncle Ezra and Aunt Faye, the hillbilly yodelers Bud and Spike, and the Fiddling Minstrels. He was popular enough that in 1939 the governor of Texas declared Owens & the Texas Rangers honorary Texas Rangers. Owens' show on KMBC lasted for more than 11 years, a period during which he was also picked up by the CBS radio network and carried nationally. At the end of his time at KMBC, Owens moved to Cincinnati and a new gig at WLW, where he sang and also hosted a country variety show called *the Boone Country Jamboree*. In 1943, Owens moved once again, this time to Hollywood, and began making appearances in movies and short films. He frequently appeared in a trio with his two daughters, and Laura Lee (1920-1989) later began a career of her own, leading a musical group called Laura Lee & Her Ranger Buddies. In 1943, she became the first female singer hired by Bob Wills for his band, the Texas Playboys. Owens himself continued his work on radio and in movies, but his footage had to be removed from the biggest film in which he ever appeared. He was cast in a supporting part in Howard Hawks' epic Western *Red River*, starring John Wayne and Montgomery Clift, when his horse fell on him during the shooting of one scene and broke his back.

Owens spent a year recovering and never fully got over the injuries. He returned to performing with a new backing group, the Prairie Pirates, and cut a pair of sessions with them in 1953 and 1954. The four songs from these sessions were released on the Wrightman label but failed to excite any major public interest, despite the presence of such gorgeous songs as Alice Canterbury's "Give Me the Plains at Night" as well as the Tex and Chuck Owens-authored instrumental "Porcupine Serenade." During this period, "Cattle Call" twice became a hit, but not for Owens. In 1944, Eddy Arnold cut a hugely successful single of the song, which became his signature tune; in 1955 Arnold had a chart-topping country hit with it again in an orchestrated version. Owens wrote more than 100 songs, but "Cattle Call" was far and away the biggest success he ever had. Unfortunately, he never achieved a fraction of the success as a recording artist that Arnold did during those decades, and by the time Arnold's second version was topping the charts, the author was past 60 and partly forgotten; most listeners assumed Arnold had written it.

By the end of the 1950s, Owens was retired from Hollywood. Now past 60, he'd seen his oldest daughter, Laura Lee, embark on a successful career as the first female vocalist ever hired by Wills. He and his wife moved to Baden, TX, in 1960, and it was there that Owens died of a heart attack in 1962 at the age of 70. His sister Ruby, a star of the *Grand Ole Opry*, died the following year in a fire. Nine years later, in 1971, Owens was posthumously inducted into the Nashville Songwriters' Hall of Fame in recognition of his work as a composer. *—Bruce Eder*

● **Cattle Call** / 1995 / Bear Family ✦✦✦✦
Sadly, the majority of Tex Owens' official commercial recordings, done for RCA-Victor in 1936, are missing. Still, this CD runs to 22 tracks, encompassing the four songs he cut as a solo artist for Decca in August of 1934, his Texas Rangers collaboration "Dude Ranch Pts. 1 & 2," and the four 1953-1954 sides for Wrightman. The rest are previously unissued demos of unknown origin or date, licensed from Owens' widow and comprising songs that only show up on lists of Tex's compositions, not his recordings. The sound is generally good, with only moderate noise on the worst of the masters. Owens' demos are nearly as engaging as his formal recordings, and surprisingly include some backing musicians, as well as Owens' requisite guitar. Highlights, in addition to the title track and the pair of songs with the Texas Rangers, include "Daddy's Old Rocking Chair," "Cowboy Call," and "Don't Hide Your Tears My Darling." *—Bruce Eder*

Vernon Oxford

b. Jun. 8, 1941, Rogers, AR
Vocals / Traditional Country, Honky Tonk
Vernon Oxford was a hard honky tonk singer with unlucky timing, coming up during an era when traditional country simply wasn't counting for much on the charts. However, he was able to find a different route to success, touring the U.K. extensively to capitalize on his surprising popularity there. Oxford was born in Rogers, AR, in 1941 and grew up mostly in Wichita, KS. He discovered country music through his father, an old-time-style fiddler, and learned to play both fiddle and guitar as a youth. His first professional gig came in 1960 at a Utah club, and he spent the next several years playing clubs and dances around Kansas. In 1964, he moved to Nashville to try his luck in the business but found the going rough because of his more old-fashioned style. Fortunately, he also found an ally in the legendary songwriter Harlan Howard, who helped him get a contract with RCA Victor in 1965 and supplied some of his material.

Oxford released seven singles over the next two years as well as an album, *Woman, Let Me Sing You a Song*. While traditional country fans applauded his work, he never managed to hit the charts, and RCA dropped him. He recorded briefly for the smaller Stop label but caught a break when British audiences discovered him as a fine traditional-style artist who'd slipped through the cracks of American popular taste. RCA issued a retrospective of his work in Britain in 1974, re-signed Oxford, and sent him on a tour. Oxford scored his first chart single in America with "Shadows of My Mind" and had his biggest hit with "Redneck (The Redneck National Anthem)"; a few more singles charted in America, and Oxford also scored some British hits with the likes of "I've Got to Get Peter Off Your Mind" and "Field of Flowers." He toured actively through 1977, then took a few years off and re-emerged in 1981 as a born-again Christian dedicated to gospel music. He continued to record and tour Britain. *—Steve Huey*

Keeper of the Flame / 1995 / Bear Family ✦✦✦✦✦
Keeper of the Flame is a five-disc box set containing all of Vernon Oxford's recordings for RCA Records, including all of his minor hit singles from the mid-'70s and a wealth of album tracks and rarities. Though Oxford was a talented hard country singer, his talent was limited, which means that a set of this size is of interest only to hardcore fans. Casual listeners will find the sheer bulk of the set rather tedious, even though there are a number of forgotten treasures buried in the comprehensive box. *—Thom Owens*

● **Let Me Sing You a Song** / Oct. 17, 2000 / WestSide ✦✦✦✦
Let Me Sing You a Song collects Vernon Oxford's RCA Victor recordings from the '60s. Oxford's traditional country approach never really caught on in the U.S., but he became a star in the U.K. due to the copious amount of touring he did there. Several of these tracks were written by songwriter and friend Harlan Howard. It was Howard who brought Oxford to RCA and continuously gave him songs, hoping for a hit. This 28-song compilation includes such Howard-penned numbers as "Woman, Let Me Sing You a Song," "Goin' Home" (two versions), "Nashville Women," "The Old Folks Home," and "That's the Way I Talk." This sampler of Vernon Oxford will satisfy the curious, but aficionados should plunge into the massive five-CD set *Keeper of the Flame* on Bear Family. *—Al Campbell*

Ozark Mountain Daredevils

f. 1971, Springfield, MO
Group / Country-Rock, Southern Rock
The Ozark Mountain Daredevils were among the most popular of mid-'70s country-rock outfits, slotting in chronologically between the Eagles and Firefall, although they were never remotely as successful as either. As exponents of '70s country-rock, the group rode a wave of success for five years on A&M Records and survived in some form into the 1990s, with a following just large enough to justify occasional record releases.

The sextet was formed in Missouri during the early '70s, consisting of guitarists John Dillon and Steve Cash, blues harpist/singer/guitarist Randle Chowning, drummer/guitarist/singer Larry Lee, keyboard player Buddy Brayfield, and bassist-vocalist Michael Granda, and was signed to A&M Records in 1973. Their first album, recorded under the supervision of producer Glyn Johns, was a critical success and yielded a Top 30 hit in "If You Want to Get to Heaven." A year later, they had the biggest hit in their history, "Jackie Blue," a mellow piece of country-rock that got to number three on the charts and still gets played occasionally as a '70s oldie. They had an ethereal edge to their sound and songs that made them especially appealing to college-age listeners during the middle of the decade—sort of Steely Dan with a country twang. Their self-titled debut album set the tone for the group's next four releases, although by 1978's *Don't Look Down*, the sound was somewhat closer to country-pop than country-rock. Collegiate girls and their boyfriends could relate to them, and a sense of humor didn't hurt (their third LP, *The Car Over the Lake Album* had cover art featuring—you guessed it—a car over a lake).

Lee, Dillon (who later played with fellow Daredevil Steve Cash on the Waylon Jennings/Jessi Colter *White Mansions* concept album), and Chowning authored most of the songs that anyone knows ("Jackie Blue," "Following the Way I Feel," "Fly Away Home"). The group enjoyed success primarily on FM radio from 1973 until 1978—they switched labels to CBS in 1980, losing Lee and Chowning by the end of the decade but picking up Buddy Emmons on steel guitar and Rune Walle on mandolin. The group ceased recording activity in the 1980s, but reformed and began making records again in the mid-'90s. *—Bruce Eder*

The Ozark Mountain Daredevils / 1973 / A&M ✦✦✦✦✦
The group's first album is also their most successful rock effort, an ebullient country-rock collection that sounds a lot like the Flying Burrito Brothers of around the same period, with richer production and more of a sense of humor than the Burritos had, and highlighted by some excellent songs ("Country Girl," "Road to Glory," "If You Wanna Get to Heaven"). Randle Chowning's "Country Girl," in particular, is amazing as a harmonica-driven near-twin of the Eagles' "Take It Easy" that you sort of wish ran for ten minutes instead of just three. Steve Cash's jew's harp/harmonica showcase "Chicken Train" brings the band back to its roots. *—Bruce Eder*

It'll Shine When It Shines / 1974 / A&M ✦✦✦✦
A successful second album, containing one hit ("Jackie Blue") and sound solid country-rock ("You Made It Right"), even better harmonies than the first album, and even a few Robert Johnson lyrical references ("Walkin' Down the Road"), not to mention some superb hybrid blues/country guitar. This is probably the album that one should own among all of their individual records, but it has yet to be reissued on CD. *—Bruce Eder*

The Car Over the Lake Album / 1975 / A&M ✦✦✦✦
The Ozark Mountain Daredevils' third album for A&M continues their good-natured Southern chooglin' with hints of a newfound mid-'70s AM pop vibe. Although it was recorded in Nashville, *The Car Over the Lake Album* has a distinctly Californian vibe on several tracks, particularly those written and sung by drummer Larry Lee, whose contributions could ride along "Ventura Highway" with any of America's recordings. Despite this warm Beach Boys influence, the album is still a Southern rocker, evident on "Keep on Churning," "Leatherwood," and the slightly goofy "Gypsy Forest." The hard-rockin' push of "If You Want to Get to Heaven" is nowhere to be found on this album,

but the laid-back porch-sittin' hum of "From Time to Time" and the spectacular "If I Only Knew" acts as an acceptable substitute. —*Zac Johnson*

Men From Earth / 1976 / A&M ✦✦✦
The group's last fully successful record, mixing soft, romantic sounds ("You Know Like I Know") dressed up in restrained, tasteful orchestrations with harder country sounds ("Homemade Wine"). "Fly Away Home" is probably the best rock number here, and also has room for some very pretty noodling on the mandolin. —*Bruce Eder*

It's Alive / 1978 / A&M ✦✦✦✦✦
Ozark Mountain Daredevils left A&M Records in 1978, and in lieu of the obligatory best-of compilation, which would follow a little later, the label put out this double LP. By this time the lineup was an eight-piece, with lots of guitars and a full-time keyboardist (Ruell Chappell) and mandolin player (Jerry Mills). The sound is smooth and close, and very polished (they never really rock out on numbers like "River to the Sun"), this album generating from the same era (and label) that yielded *Frampton Comes Alive*. One suspects there was a certain sweetening of the harmonies, especially on songs like "You Know Like I Know" and "Fly Away Home," while other songs, like "Following the Way That I Feel" and "Horse Trader," sound pretty raw and honest. The big hits are all here, with a fast-paced, crunchy-textured "Jackie Blue" and "If You Wanna Get to Heaven" saved for side four, but the best number here is an acoustic version of "A Satisfied Mind" cut live in a men's shower backstage at an arena in Springfield, MO. The 1997-released *Archive Alive* concert from early in their history is rougher and more viscerally exciting, but this double LP captures what concert work was like in the late '70s and captures a big chunk of the group's repertory. —*Bruce Eder*

Don't Look Down / 1978 / A&M ✦✦✦
The Ozark Mountain Daredevils, while not being the most successful country-rock outfit, had released five fine albums prior to *Don't Look Down*. Their sound had changed little over the years, which suited most fans who frankly wanted more of the same. This release, the bands last on A&M Records, is somewhat more polished than earlier recordings, however, and the style is rather more country-pop than many would have liked. Fine musicianship is present as usual, but the move to a lighter rock style has forced guitar solos to take a backseat throughout. *Don't Look Down* is consistent enough, and is undoubtedly an enjoyable album. Similarity is its key problem, however, and nothing truly original is present. —*Ben Davies*

The Best of Ozark Mountain Daredevils / 1983 / A&M ✦✦✦✦
One of two CDs of classic material by the Daredevils, 12 songs drawn from their first five A&M albums, showing the different sides of the group to very good advantage, from the hard-rocking "If You Wanna Get to Heaven" to the soaring, upbeat, mandolin- and electric-guitar-driven "Homemade Wine." Some of the material seems soft today, and it's hard to imagine that this sound was ever considered viable, but a lot of it is very pretty and eminently listenable. The starting point for anyone interested, and with a little luck this and the first album will be joined at least by reissues of *It'll Shine When It Shines* and *Men from Earth*. —*Bruce Eder*

13 / 1997 / New Era ✦✦✦
The Ozark Mountain Daredevils' return to recording after 17 years of solo projects and festival appearances finds the Daredevils' voices sounding a little older and a little gruffer. However, if Neil Young and Johnny Cash have taught the world anything, it's that a singer/songwriter can improve with age as long as what he's saying is still worth listening to. Unfortunately, it seems as though these guys were torn between making either a smooth Nashville country album or a laid-back Jimmy Buffett-style good-time album. The chunky "Bar Hoppin'" is a loose handful of fun, as is the leadoff track, "Dream-O," but the slick "I'm Still Dreamin'" and the radio-friendly "Everywhere She Goes" are a little too clean in contrast. Still, it's a well-produced album with a grab-bag of solid songs, particularly "If It's True," the sole contribution by original Daredevil Larry Lee (whose voice hasn't slackened a bit since the mid-'70s). As is evidenced by *13*, the band is older, a little less reckless, and a little more cautious, but the people who bought the Ozark Mountain Daredevils' records in their heyday have aged too, and maybe this is just the sound they're looking for. —*Zac Johnson*

● **Time Warp: The Very Best of Ozark Mountain Daredevils** / Dec. 5, 2000 / A&M ✦✦✦✦
Although it omits three songs from the far less comprehensive (and deleted) 1983 12-track *Best Of*, and doesn't include any live or post-A&M music, this 2000 release stands as the final word on the Ozark Mountain Daredevils' career. Cherry-picking 21 tunes from their five studio album stint circa 1974-1978—with the lion's share coming from their first three albums and only three selections from the final two—this is pretty much all you'll need from the under-recognized band that worked in the '70s country-rock shadows of Poco and Firefall, but weren't as dependable or pop savvy as either. In fact, their biggest hit, the Hall & Oates, blue-eyed soul-styled "Jackie Blue," was so atypical of the band's characteristically down-home approach that it ultimately may have been more damaging to their career than if they had clicked with a song more representative of their crisp, rural country-pop/rock. As enjoyable and pleasantly organic as they were, the group lacked a distinctive vocalist, direction, and most importantly great songs. This collection focuses on their less commercially rocking, more rootsy side, and as such it's a consistently listenable, predominantly chronological compilation that is all any but the most die-hard fan will ever need. An extensive essay (including quotes from bandmembers) and rare photos in the disc's 16-page booklet sweeten the pot and make this as definitive an overview from a talented also-ran outfit as necessary. Like its closing title track, the Ozark Mountain Daredevils lived in a stylistic time warp, comfortable within its own limitations and unwilling—but not unable—to break free of them. —*Hal Horowitz*

The Best of the Ozark Mountain Daredevils: 20th Century Masters—The Millennium Collection / Sep. 24, 2002 / A&M ✦✦✦✦
The Best of the Ozark Mountain Daredevils: 20th Century Masters—The Millennium Collection collects a dozen easygoing country-rock hits from the band, including "If You Want to Get to Heaven," "Jackie Blue," and "Homemade Wine." Strong album tracks such as "Country Girl," "Spaceship Onion," "Road to Glory," and "Following the Way That I Feel" give the collection some added depth, even if it isn't as comprehensive as *Time Warp: The Very Best of Ozark Mountain Daredevils*. Nevertheless, it's a solid, if somewhat too concise, overview of this somewhat overlooked band's output. —*Heather Phares*

Patti Page (Clara Ann Fowler)

b. Nov. 8, 1927, Muskogee, OK

Vocals / Country-Pop, Vocal Pop, Nashville Sound/Countrypolitan, Traditional Pop
The best-selling female singer during the 1950s, Patti Page in many ways defined the decade of earnest, novelty-ridden adult pop with throwaway hits like "The Doggie in the Window" and "I Went to Your Wedding." By singing a wide range of popular material and her own share of novelty fluff, she proved easily susceptible to the fall of classic adult pop but remained a chart force into the mid-'60s.

Born Clara Ann Fowler in Muskogee, OK, she began singing professionally at a radio station in Tulsa and took weekend gigs on the side. (After being billed as Patti Page for a program sponsored by Page Milk, she decided to take the name even after leaving.) Page toured the country with a band led by Jimmy Joy and ended up in Chicago by 1947, where she sang in a small-group outing by Benny Goodman and gained a recording contract with Mercury. Her first hit, "Confess," came that same year and made her the first pop artist to overdub harmony vocals onto her own lead. After a few more successes, Page gained her first million-seller in 1950 for "With My Eyes Wide Open I'm Dreaming," which cashed in on the novelty effect of overdubbing (the added touch came with listing it as "the Patti Page Quartet"). Also in 1950, "All My Love" became her first number-one hit and spent several weeks at the top. That same year produced the biggest hit of her career, "The Tennessee Waltz." Notched at number one for months, it eventually became one of the best-selling singles of all time and prompted no less than six Top 40 covers during the following year.

During 1952-1953, Patti Page scored two more huge hits with "I Went to Your Wedding" and "The Doggie in the Window," both of which spent more than two months at number one. She gained her own television program, *the Patti Page Show*, in 1955 and moved into full-lengths with *In the Land of Hi Fi* and *Manhattan Tower*. Page also proved more resilient to the rise of rock & roll than most of her contemporaries, hitting big in 1956 with "Allegheny Moon" and "Old Cape Cod" the next year. Indeed, she kept reaching the charts (if only in moderate placings) throughout the '60s, paced by the Top Ten theme to the film *Hush, Hush, Sweet Charlotte* in 1965. Though she stopped recording for the most part in 1968, she continued performing into the '90s. —*John Bush*

Country & Western Golden Hits / 1961 / Mercury ✦✦✦✦

Patti Page was perfectly comfortable with country music and could even yodel, although she doesn't do it on *Country & Western Golden Hits*. This 1961 album offers some of the crossover country music you would expect a pop vocalist to tackle, like "Dark Moon," but Page also does "You All Come," which is as country as it gets. "Mom and Dad's Waltz" was a minor hit on the pop and country charts for Page, and the album's track list is full of classics like "I Walk the Line," "Walking the Floor Over You," and "Crazy Arms." This isn't your typical attempt to turn country material into lushly orchestrated mood music—*Country & Western Golden Hits* is a bona fide country-pop album, and a good one at that. —*Greg Adams*

Patti Page Sings America's Favorite Hymns / 1966 / CBS ✦✦✦✦

Originally issued in 1966, *Patti Page Sings America's Favorite Hymns* contains 11 of the best-known sacred standars in American history, including "The Old Rugged Cross," "Nearer, My God to Thee," "Rock of Ages," "Amazing Grace," and "Bringing in the Sheaves." —*John Bush*

★ The Patti Page Collection: The Mercury Years, Vol. 1 / Jan. 1991 / Mercury ✦✦✦✦✦

When Mercury Records finally got around to compiling a Patti Page's hits for the CD era (the ten-track LP *Golden Hits* had been in print since 1960), the label opted to create two separate volumes, one containing the singer's early hits, the other her later ones. While fans might have preferred a single-disc greatest hits album containing all of her biggest singles, the two-volume approach allowed Mercury to bring back into print many of Page's lesser hits of the 1950s. The first volume, a 20-track collection, includes most of the 26 chart entries she achieved between 1948 and 1952. All 13 Top Ten hits from the period are included, among them the chart-toppers "All My Love," "The Tennessee Waltz," "Mockin' Bird Hill," and "I Went to Your Wedding." Below the Top Ten, however, compiler Ron Furmanek has made judgment calls so that, for example, "So in Love," which made the Top 20, is not here, while "Evertrue Evermore" is, which only made the Top 30. This is a solid collection which contains some excellent material that, despite its popularity, rarely gets onto compilations, such as Page's recording of "I Don't Care If the Sun Don't Shine," later cut by Elvis Presley. But fans wanting any of her hits from after 1952, starting with "The Doggie in the Window," will have to invest in the second volume as well. —*William Ruhlmann*

The Patti Page Collection: The Mercury Years, Vol. 2 / Feb. 1991 / Mercury ✦✦✦✦✦

A Golden Celebration / Jun. 3, 1997 / Polygram ✦✦✦✦✦

A Golden Celebration is a comprehensive, four-disc box set that contains all of Patti Page's biggest hits and best-known songs for Mercury Records, from "The Tennessee

Waltz" in 1951 to "Most People Get Married" in 1962. Along the way, nearly all of her hits are featured, as are a handful of rarities. Although the set may be too extensive for the casual fan, any listener wanting a definitive overview of her '50s and '60s heyday should acquire *A Golden Celebration*. —*Thom Owens*

Hush, Hush, Sweet Charlotte/Gentle on My Mind / Aug. 24, 1999 / Collectables ✦✦✦

In 1999, Collectables released *Hush, Hush, Sweet Charlotte/Gentle on My Mind*, which contained two complete albums—*Hush, Hush, Sweet Charlotte* (1965, originally released on Columbia) and *Gentle on My Mind* (1968, originally released on Columbia)—by Patti Page on one compact disc. —*Jason Birchmeier*

20th Century Masters—The Millennium Collection: The Best of Patti Page / Mar. 4, 2003 / Mercury ✦✦✦✦

Brad Paisley

b. Oct. 28, 1972, Glen Dale, WV

Guitar, Vocals / Contemporary Country, Neo-Traditionalist Country, Western Swing Revival
Contemporary country singer/songwriter Brad Paisley was born October 28, 1972, in Glen Dale, WV; given his first guitar at age eight, he delivered his first public performance at church two years later. With his 50-something guitar teacher Clarence "Hank" Goddard and two of the older man's seasoned musician buddies, the teenaged Paisley formed his first band, the C-Notes, and at age 12 began writing his own material. After performing in front of the local Rotary Club, he was invited to appear on Wheeling station WWVA's famed Saturday night broadcast Jamboree USA. Paisley's debut was so well-received that he was invited to join the program full-time, and in the years to follow he opened for the likes of the Judds, Roy Clark, and Little Jimmy Dickens. He later attended Nashville's Belmont University, serving an internship with ASCAP; the contacts Paisley made there helped him land a songwriting deal with EMI, and he also appeared on countless demos.

Signing to Arista, he issued his debut solo album, *Who Needs Pictures*, in 1999. The record produced two chart-topping singles in "He Didn't Have to Be," an ode to loving stepfathers, and "We Danced" and also earned generally positive reviews for its diversity of country styles. In the meantime, Paisley recorded a duet with Chely Wright, "Hard to Be a Husband, Hard to Be a Wife," for the *Backstage at the Grand Ole Opry* compilation; the two later collaborated on several songs for Wright's *Never Love You Enough* album. The sequel to Paisley's debut, *Part II*, was released in 2001 and promptly returned him to the Top Five with "Two People Fell in Love." "I'm Gonna Miss Her (The Fishin' Song)" gave Paisley his third chart-topper, and "Wrapped Around" fell one spot short of becoming his fourth. "I Wish You'd Stay" became the fourth Top Ten hit from the record in early 2003. —*Steve Huey*

● Who Needs Pictures / May 18, 1999 / Arista ✦✦✦✦

It's easy to glance at Brad Paisley and assume that he's another in a long line of contemporary country artists that get by on their good looks instead of their talent, but his debut album *Who Needs Pictures* suggests otherwise. Paisley follows the pattern set by such neo-traditionalists as George Strait, Randy Travis, and Alan Jackson, yet he adds a bit of a pop sheen—never as much as John Michael Montgomery, but similar to Tim McGraw. Although it boasts a shiny, clean production, *Who Needs Pictures* keeps itself firmly within country territory, even if it doesn't feel like its roots dig that deep. Similarly, Paisley's voice is a little thin, lacking the resonance of a Travis, but it is appealing, as are his songs, all of which he co-wrote with a host of collaborators (most notably Chris DuBois and Kelley Lovelace). His material may be a little cutesy, but it's catchy, particularly on the faster numbers. Those tunes are surprisingly diverse, ranging from the Western swing-styled "It Never Woulda Worked Out Anyway" and the breezy "I've Been Better" to the skittering Bakersfield instrumental "The Nervous Breakdown," the rocking contemporary country opener "Long Sermon," and the winning honky tonk of "Sleepin' on the Foldout." And even if his ballads tend to drag, "He Didn't Have to Be" is strikingly autobiographical and heartfelt, showcasing his potential in that area, as well. So, even if *Who Needs Pictures* is a little uneven, it hits considerably more than it misses, and those hits suggest Brad Paisley is an artist worth following. —*Stephen Thomas Erlewine*

Part II / May 29, 2001 / Arista ✦✦✦

Brad Paisley was catapulted to stardom with his debut album, *Who Needs Pictures*, and became a household name with songs like "He Didn't Have to Be" and "We Danced." It's almost hard to imagine that this sophomore album could have the same fate, but *Part II* certainly does live up to its predecessor. The strength of Paisley's songs seems to be in the stories they tell. This 13-track collection, ten of which Paisley wrote or co-wrote, is like an ode to tradition. "Two Feet of Topsoil," the first track, sets a tone of banjos, fiddles, and steel guitars. The title track features the lovely Chely Wright on harmony, and other notables include the bluesy-sounding "You Have That Effect on Me" and "Too Country" featuring welcome vocals from old-timers Buck Owens, George Jones, and Bill Anderson. —*Maria Konicki Dinoia*

Palace

f. 1992

Group / Singer/Songwriter, Indie Rock, Alternative Country-Rock, Alternative Country
Will Oldham, the brains and brawn behind releases as Palace Brothers, Palace Songs, Palace Music, and just plain Palace, is loosely grouped with the '90s anti-folk movement that also includes Bill Callahan of Smog, a labelmate of Oldham's on Chicago's Drag City Records. Often mistaken for an old man due to his cracking vocals, sparse guitar pickings, and biblical dialect, Oldham has recorded since 1992 with a variety of sidemen— basically, any friends or acquaintances that can play an instrument.

Raised in Louisville, KY, Oldham first became involved in acting; he starred in John Sayles' 1987 mining film *Matewan*, playing—with considerable ease—an elderly miner who relates the action over a series of flashbacks. Two years later, he moved to TV for *Everybody's Baby: The Rescue of Jessica McClure* and returned to the cinema in 1991 for *Thousand Pieces of Gold*, another mining film. At the same time, Oldham was also involved in the fertile indie rock scene in Louisville, picking up his first musical credit with Slint, for the photograph on the cover of the band's 1991 album, *Spiderland*.

Oldham the musical artist debuted in 1992 with the single "Ohio River Boat Song" on Drag City Records. Though he's credited as Palace Songs on the single, Oldham's debut album the following year was filed under Palace Brothers—in part to denote the work of Todd Brashear. *There Is No-One What Will Take Care of You* introduced several of Oldham's continuing themes: drunkenness, sin in general, and the varied results of each. Recording regularly during 1993-1994, Oldham released several singles and an EP (*An Arrow Through the Bitch*) before his second album—self-titled but also listed as *Days in the Wake*—was issued by Drag City in 1994. Again, Oldham followed with a string of limited-release singles and one EP, but mixed things up for late-1995's *Viva Last Blues* (as Palace Music); Oldham recruited a band, with guitarist Bryan Rich, organist Liam Hayes, and bassist Jason Loewenstein (from Sebadoh). The following year's *Arise, Therefore* found Oldham back in a largely solitary setting. —*John Bush*

There Is No-One What Will Take Care of You / Jun. 14, 1993 / Drag City ◆◆◆

Will Oldham's first album under the Palace rubric, *There Is No-One What Will Take Care of You*, seemed to emerge from under a cloud of mystery on its first release in 1993. The first edition had no credits save a list of names under the heading "Impossible Without," leading to all manner of speculation in the indie community about who was responsible; the album sounded as if some ancient songsters who had somehow escaped Harry Smith's attention years before had recorded a session in their living room, which somehow found its way to the offices of Drag City. On *There Is No-One What Will Take Care of You*, Oldham sounds like a lost-lost cousin of the Louvin Brothers who, after ending up on skid row, is equally convinced that Satan is real, since he smells his foul breath every waking moment of his life. Oldham's stark, intimate tales of sin, lust, alcohol, and hopelessness are fascinating, horribly compelling stuff, and while it would be easy for this material to sound ironic or condescending, it isn't—Oldham makes his characters' shame, confusion, and desperate search for grace real and genuinely moving. *There Is No-One What Will Take Care of You* may not be the best Palace album, but it is the work where Will Oldham's obsession with sin and redemption shines forth with the most painful and absorbing clarity. —*Mark Deming*

Days in the Wake / Aug. 29, 1994 / Drag City ◆◆◆◆

The second album from Palace Brothers would seem to barely qualify on either count— at a shade over 27 minutes, *Days in the Wake* seems a bit skimpy in the era of the 80-minute CD, and only one song, "Come a Little Dog," clearly features any musicians besides Will Oldham and his rickety acoustic guitar. But the stark simplicity and *audio vérité* ambience of *Days in the Wake* builds on the already dramatic emotional power of *There Is No-One What Will Take Care of You*, and if Will Oldham's obsession with sin and retribution is less forcefully stated in these songs, that's not to say it isn't clearly present on most of these songs, especially the cautionary tale "You Will Miss Me When I Burn," the mournful but fiercely proud "No More Workhorse Blues," and "Pushkin," which begins with the declaration "God is the answer/God lies within," without making it sound like a concept in which Oldham can take much comfort. Oldham's lyrics would become increasingly cryptic from this point on, but while the literal meaning of songs like "Wither Thou Goest" and "I Am a Cinematographer" is elusive, the emotional power of these performances is as eloquent as anyone could hope for. *Days in the Wake* is the simplest work in the Palace canon, and among the very best. [*Days in the Wake* was originally released simply as *Palace Brothers.*] —*Mark Deming*

Viva Last Blues / Aug. 21, 1995 / Drag City ◆◆◆◆◆

This incarnation of Palace, one of its more impressive, sees frontman Will Oldham turning out some of the strongest bleak country-rock in his career and taking the music in a few intriguing and even upbeat directions. With a great supporting cast that includes, among others, Sebadoh's Jason Loewenstein on drums and Oldham's brother Ned on bass, the group busts out laid-back twangy tunes that can really rock when the opportunity comes up. Most notably, tracks like "Work Hard/Play Hard" and the opening "More Brother Rides" are brimming with energy that may not overwhelm, but certainly provides a hefty backbone. Alternately, slower brooding tracks like the longing "New Partner" see the band proving their chops in a more refined setting. Oldham's cracking backcountry voice may be a bit of an acquired taste, but it's worth the time, as his inflections are capable of powerful feelings and certain honesty. The Palace team has put out many a record, but as far as accessible and slightly upbeat musical ruminations go, *Viva Last Blues* certainly sees the players near the top of their game. Things are a little thicker and dirtier than on the more laid-back acoustic records this prolific artist has put out, but

the rock approach adds worlds to the delivery and creates a powerful palette for the equally important lyrics. Oldham is a truly underrated American talent, and this is among his best work, so take the time to find it. —*Peter J. D'Angelo*

Arise, Therefore / Apr. 1996 / Drag City ◆◆◆◆

Once again, Will Oldham emerges out of the murky, Midwestern haze with another helping of lovely, low-key musings on his fourth full-length album, *Arise, Therefore*, this time recorded under the name Palace Music (previously Palace Brothers, Palace Songs, or just plain Palace). Much quieter than *Viva Last Blues* and less-Appalachian in its folk spirit than Palace's earlier music, the songs on *Arise, Therefore* shift and moan with breathy cracks and shivers; Oldham's meandering, poet-speak vocals; and guitar accompanied by his brother, Ned's bass, David Grubbs' piano, and (surprise!) a Maya Tone drum machine. The lyrics (included for the first time) are beautiful in their stark, pale honesty as often as they are indecipherable. "I watch things painted on public walls/Now but I see other things as well/Behind but right f*ck in front of my spirit is how the real road's laid out in a line," he sings on "Kid of Harith." Don't ask for an interpretation: It will come with time, or it won't. —*Kurt Wolff*

● **Lost Blues & Other Songs** / Mar. 24, 1997 / Drag City ◆◆◆◆◆

Despite the overall excellence of albums like *There Is No-One What Will Take Care of You* and *Viva Last Blues*, Will Oldham tended to save his best Palace offerings for the group's singles; *Lost Blues & Other Songs* is a career-capping collection of those seven-inch releases which serves as a superb overview of the Palace project's mercurial history. Although a few stray tracks (like the German-only "Gezundheit," a cover of Lynyrd Skynyrd's "Every Mother's Son," and the live *Lounge Ax* single) are MIA, the set includes all of the truly crucial Palace singles from the first (1993's "Ohio River Boat Song") to the last (1997's "Little Blue Eyes"), along with unreleased material like "Valentine's Day," "Lost Blues," and a more ragged rendition of the debut album's classic, "Riding." The highlights are many, but the true standouts are the anthemic cover of the Mekons' "Horses" and both sides of the "West Palm Beach"/"Gulf Shores" single, a luminously pastoral effort reminiscent of Red House Painters. A stunning recapitulation of a truly unique musical vision, *Lost Blues & Other Songs* is an essential record from an essential band. —*Jason Ankeny*

Billy Parker

b. Jul. 19, 1939, Okemah, OK

Vocals / Traditional Country, Honky Tonk
While Billy Parker was a mainstay on country radio, his claim to fame was as an influential disc jockey, not as a performer; ironically, for all of the Top 40 hits he spun over the course of his decades on the air, not one of them was his own. Born July 19, 1939, in Okemah, OK, he began playing guitar as a child and by the age of 14 had made his professional debut on the Tulsa radio program *Big Red Jamboree*. A few years later, he began performing in clubs and in 1959 landed his first DJ work.

By 1963, Parker was the regular daytime disc jockey on Wichita, KS' KFDI and also hosted a Tulsa television program. In the same year, he cut his first single, "The Line Between Love and Hate," and was named "Mr. DJ U.S.A." in a nationwide poll, which helped land him at Nashville's WSM. After releasing another record, "I'm Drinking All the Time," in 1966, Parker began playing with Ernest Tubb's Troubadors in 1968 and stayed with the group for three years, when he joined Tulsa's KVOO.

In 1975, Parker was named Disc Jockey of the Year by the Academy of Country & Western Music; he won the award again in 1977, 1978, and 1984. In 1976, he scored his first chart hit with "It's Bad When You're Caught (With the Goods)," from the album *Average Man*. A series of singles followed, including a tribute to Ernest Tubb titled "Thanks E.T. Thanks a Lot"; while most charted, none came in higher than number 50. In 1982, he scored his biggest success with the title track from the LP *(Who's Gonna Sing) The Last Country Song*, an album of collaborations with the likes of Darrell McCall and Vassar Clements. After a record of duets, 1983's *Something Old, Something New*, he retreated from performing to focus on his work as KVOO's program director but returned in 1988 with the album *Always Country*. In 1990, he released a gospel record, *I'll Speak Out for You, Jesus*; two years later, he was inducted into the Country Music Disc Jockey Hall of Fame. At about the same time, he was appointed KVOO's executive director. —*Jason Ankeny*

Billy Parker & Friends / 1990 / Bear Family ◆◆◆

Some of Parker's friends (Webb Pierce, Jack Greene, and Ernest Tubb) join Parker on this re-release of material originally recorded during the '80s for the Soundwaves label. An informative booklet accompanies this release. —*AMG*

Lee Roy Parnell

b. Dec. 21, 1956, Abilene, TX

Guitar, Vocals, Slide Guitar / Contemporary Country, New Traditionalist, Western Swing Revival
Part of a long line of Texas roots-music eclectics, Lee Roy Parnell's music was a blend of hardcore honky tonk, barroom rock & roll, blues, boogie, Western swing, blue-eyed soul, and occasional gospel. Unlike many other hard-to-pigeonhole artists, Parnell actually enjoyed a run of success on the country charts in the early '90s. He was born in Abilene, TX, on December 21, 1956, and grew up on his parents' ranch; his father had toured with a teenage Bob Wills in traveling medicine shows, and his first public performance came on Wills' radio show at age six. As a teenager, he played drums in a local band and soon picked up guitar as well, eventually concentrating on slide playing. He joined Kinky Friedman's Texas Jewboys in his late teens and moved to Austin in 1974 to join the city's budding music scene.

Parnell spent over a decade playing clubs in Austin, Houston, and Dallas/Fort Worth, honing his style and songwriting; he also married and held down a day job in radio. He moved to Nashville in 1987 and quickly landed a publishing contract and a regular spot at the famed Bluebird Café. He signed to Arista's Nashville division in 1989 and the next year released his self-titled debut album, a collection of horn-driven country-soul. It received good reviews but didn't break him commercially; that would happen with 1992's *Love Without Mercy*, which mostly dispensed with the horns and emphasized Parnell's slide guitar. "What Kind of Fool Do You Think I Am" and "Tender Moment" both went to number two on the country charts, and the title track also made the Top Ten. 1993's *On the Road* produced two more Top Tens in its title track and "I'm Holding My Own," and his duet with Ronnie Dunn (of Brooks & Dunn) on Hank Williams' "Take These Chains From My Heart" made the Top 20. 1995's *We All Get Lucky Sometimes* found Parnell tailoring his sound to country radio a bit more and featured duets with Trisha Yearwood, Mary-Chapin Carpenter, and Tex-Mex accordionist Flaco Jimenez. It also spawned two Top Five hits in "A Little Bit of You" and "Heart's Desire." However, 1997's commercially disappointing *Every Night's a Saturday Night* proved to be Parnell's last new album for Arista, which issued the compilation *Hits and Highways Ahead* in 1999 to coincide with his departure. Parnell next wound up on the rootsy Vanguard label, debuting for them with 2001's *Tell the Truth*. *—Steve Huey*

Lee Roy Parnell / 1990 / Arista ♦♦♦♦
Hard-rocking country-soul, complete with horn section, this album was produced by Barry Beckett, whose experiences at Muscle Shoals mean he knows how to make this kind of record. *—Brian Mansfield*

Love Without Mercy / 1992 / Arista ♦♦♦♦
For his second album, Parnell dropped the horns and gave his slide guitar a bigger role. He was still a Texas rocker disguised by a pedal steel, but the album produced three Top Ten hits—"Love Without Mercy," "What Kind of Fool Do You Think I Am," and "Tender Moment." *—Brian Mansfield*

On the Road / Oct. 26, 1993 / Arista ♦♦♦
More roots rocking road music, though not as perfectly realized as *Love Without Mercy*. The title track and "I'm Holding My Own" were hits, and Parnell sang with Brooks & Dunn's Ronnie Dunn on the Hank Williams standard "Take These Chains From My Heart." *—Brian Mansfield*

We All Get Lucky Sometimes / 1995 / Career ♦♦♦
On *We All Get Lucky Sometimes*, Lee Roy Parnell tempers his mixture of country, R&B, blues, and rock & roll somewhat with a subdued production, designed to attract the attention of country radio. Even when his music is slightly tamed, Parnell turns in a fine effort, filled with enough true grit to satisfy his fans. *—Stephen Thomas Erlewine*

Every Night's a Saturday Night / Jun. 17, 1997 / Arista ♦♦♦♦

● **Hits And Highways Ahead** / Aug. 24, 1999 / Arista ♦♦♦♦
Hits and Highways Ahead compiles the majority of Lee Roy Parnell's hits from his first five albums, adding two new songs ("She Won't Be Lonely Long," "Long Way to Fall") plus "John the Revelator," taken fro, the various-artists album *Peace in the Valley: A Country Music Journey Through Gospel*. It isn't quite definitive—not only are there a handful of hits missing, there are also some good album tracks absent, and nothing is taken from his fine debut—but it's nevertheless a strong, entertaining hits collection, blessed with two strong new entries and such highlights as "Tender Moments," "Love Without Mercy," "On the Road," "I'm Holding My Own," and "What Kind of Fool Do You Think I Am." For casual fans and the curious, this is the ideal choice. *—Stephen Thomas Erlewine*

Tell the Truth / Jun. 12, 2001 / Vanguard ♦♦♦
Parnell's music is a very Texan mix of multiple popular music forms: bar-band rock, honky tonk country, boogie, blues, soul, and gospel. It's no surprise to find some similar-minded vets with high profiles, like Delbert McClinton, Bonnie Bramlett, and (as song-writing contributor) Dan Penn, among the supporting cast of this record. He's similar, yes, but not as outstanding—as a songwriter, stylist, or singer—as any of those figures are at their best. It's serviceable earthy Texas music that's suitable for bars and clubs at both party time on the stompers and closing time on the slow tunes, but kind of middle of the pack as far as it goes. When he trots out the high-energy blues-rock riffs, it wanders closest to clichéd ground. For that reason, the blue-eyed soul ballads, like "Breaking Down Slow" (one of the ones that Penn co-wrote and Bramlett sings on), are better, but there are better blue-eyed soul singers around, like Bramlett, to invite the comparison that it lays right on the table for you. *—Richie Unterberger*

Gene Parsons (Eugene Victor Parsons)

b. Sep. 4, 1944, Los Angeles, CA
Guitar, Drums, Vocals, Bass / Country-Rock, Folk-Rock
Best known as the drummer during the Byrds' groundbreaking country-rock period, Gene Parsons later cut a few solo records that underlined his position as a country-rock pioneer. Parsons was born in Los Angeles on September 4, 1944, and grew up mostly in the Mojave Desert. He played bass and drums in the Castaways starting in 1963, and he and bandmate Gib Gilbeau subsequently teamed up as Cajun Gib & Gene, recording for several small labels. In 1968, they signed on with Nashville West, which featured inventive guitarist Clarence White, and played on the group's self-titled debut. Later that year, both Parsons and White joined the Byrds, debuting on *Dr. Byrds & Mr. Hyde*. Parsons stuck around until 1972, with high points including the albums *The Ballad of Easy Rider* and *Untitled*, and then left for a solo career. His debut album, *Kindling*, was released in 1973 on Warner Bros. and featured appearances by White, Ralph Stanley, and Vassar Clements, among others. The same year, Parsons reunited with Gilbeau and backed Arlo Guthrie and Elliott Murphy in the studio.

In 1974, Parsons took a break from his solo career to join another groundbreaking country-rock group, the Flying Burrito Brothers; he appeared on 1975's *Flying Again* and 1976's *Airborne* before a wrist injury forced him to take several years off of music. In 1980, he joined the Sierra label as both an artist and A&R executive and issued the album *Melodies* in 1979; he subsequently performed with the Gene Parsons Trio, which also included bassist Peter Oliba and drummer Richie Rosenbaum. In 1985, he formed a performing partnership with singer/guitarist Meridian Green, the daughter of folksinger Bob Gibson. The two married in 1986 and formed an official band dubbed Parsons Green in 1991. Their Sierra debut, *Birds of a Feather*, was released in 1992. A couple of live albums were released on Parsons' own StringBender label in 2001. *—Steve Huey*

● **Kindling** / 1973 / Warner Bros. ♦♦♦♦
A torrid love affair between popular music and its old-timey Appalachian music roots occurred in the early '70s, more than a quarter of a century before the much-publicized success of the *O Brother, Where Art Thou?* soundtrack. Some of the '70s' examples of pop roots music homages were definitely worth forgetting, such as the overrated and sanctimonious *Will the Circle Be Unbroken* triple-album project by the Nitty Gritty Dirt Band. And too often, a sort of snot-nosed influence from pop music would erase out the more interesting, smudgy aspects of old-timey music. *Kindling* is also a project that some listeners may find too smooth around the edges, the vocal harmonies treated to a kind of dry, too-hip studio reverb and the instruments themselves occasionally sounding more like a greeting card than a reading from the good book of bluegrass. But the best parts of this Gene Parsons album have that clear taste of a mountain stream, at least one of the ones that some company hasn't dumped waste in. It involves many pickers who were crusading heroes of this period, including Clarence White, who, like Parsons, overlapped into the roster of Byrds sidemen, as well as the always-creative fiddler Vassar Clements, who was simply everywhere in the '70s. Ralph Stanley is also on hand to take part in sections of this cross-generational musical communication, just as he would be ready and willing decades later for the aforementioned soundtrack's success. Some of the most interesting aspects of a program that is packed with nice touches include Parsons' skill at overdubbing, innovative if not strictly down-home use of Bill Payne on synthesizer, and the nice use made of Red Callender's tuba on "Long Way Back"; Parsons must have decided he needed someone to play tuba, but handles all the other instruments himself, including drums, bass, and pedal steel. "Banjo Dog" is a wonderful track, while "Sonic Bummer" has to be heard to be believed, the drumming of Andy Newmark contributing to the combined weirdness of a track that has to be one of the strangest mutant offspring of psychedelic rock and country music. *—Eugene Chadbourne*

Melodies / 1979 / Sierra ♦♦♦
Something of a "comeback" album (after a several-year mid-'70s recording hiatus), Gene Parsons' *Melodies* is a quality record through and through, though it occasionally suffers from lifeless vocal performances and overly slick production. Parsons is at his best when he sticks to more traditionally oriented country and bluegrass material and instrumentals. Although he is best known as the drummer in the early-'70s Clarence White-era Byrds, Parsons is an excellent guitarist, bassist, and banjo player, and his considerable skills are on display throughout the record. Strangely, the problems only arise when Parsons tries his hand at the smooth, California country-rock that his old band pioneered. Simply put, Parsons, though his voice is pleasant and his singing technically competent, is not in the same league, vocally, as great stylists like Roger McGuinn, Gram Parsons, or Don Henley. As a result, a few of the songs on the record sound like outtakes from a bad Firefall session, rather than the work of one of country-rock's founding fathers. In fact, some tracks (particularly "No Fire Here Tonight" and the Clarence White tribute "Melodies From a Bird in Flyght") anticipate the sound of the first wave of slick '80s Nashville country-pop (groups like Alabama, Shenandoah, and Exile). Despite this, however, the album has many high points, the best of which is Parsons' absolutely gorgeous interpretation of the Gram Parsons classic "Hot Burrito #1." *—Pemberton Roach*

Birds of a Feather / 1987 / Sierra ♦♦♦♦

Kindling Collection / 1995 / Sierra ♦♦♦

Gram Parsons (Cecil Ingram Connor)

b. Nov. 5, 1946, Winter Haven, FL, **d.** Sep. 19, 1973, Joshua Tree, CA
Guitar, Vocals / Country-Rock
Gram Parsons is the father of country-rock. With the International Submarine Band, the Byrds, and the Flying Burrito Brothers, Parsons pioneered the concept of a rock band playing country music, and as a solo artist he moved even further into country music, blending the two genres to the point that they became indistinguishable from each other. While he was alive, Parsons was a cult figure that never sold many records, but influenced countless fellow musicians, from the Rollings Stones to the Byrds. In the years since his death, his stature has only grown, as numerous rock and country artists build on his small, but enormously influential, body of work.

Gram Parsons was born Cecil Ingram Connor on November 5, 1946. Parsons was the grandson of John Snivley, who owned about one-third of all the citrus fields in Florida. Snivley's daughter married Coon Dog Connor. As a child, Parsons learned how to play the piano at the age of nine, the same year he saw Elvis Presley perform at his school; following that performance, Parsons decided to become a musician. When he was 12, Parsons' father committed suicide. After Connor's death, Parsons and his mother moved in with her parents in Winter Haven, FL; a year after the move, his mother married Robert Parsons, who adopted Gram and the child legally changed his name to Gram Parsons. At the age of 14, Parsons began playing in the local rock & roll band the Pacers, which evolved into the Legends. During its time together, the Legends featured Jim Stafford and Kent Lavoie, who would later come to fame under the name Lobo. In 1963, Parsons formed a folk group called the Shilos who performed throughout Florida and cut several demos. In 1965, Parsons graduated from high-school; on the same day he graduated, his mother died of alcohol poisoning.

Following his graduation, Gram Parsons enrolled at Harvard, where he studied theology. Parsons only spent one semester at Harvard and, while he was there, he spent more time playing music than attending classes. During this time he formed the International Submarine Band with guitarist John Nuese, bassist Ian Dunlop and drummer Mickey Gauvin. After he dropped out of college, he moved to New York with the International

Submarine Band in 1966. The group spent a year in New York, developing a heavily country-influenced rock & roll sound and cutting two unsuccessful singles for Columbia. The band relocated to Los Angeles in 1967, where they secured a record contract with Lee Hazlewood's LHI record label. The group's debut album, *Safe at Home*, was released in early 1968, but by the time it appeared in the stores, the group had already disbanded.

Around the time the International Submarine Band dissolved, Parsons met Chris Hillman, the bassist for the Byrds. At that time, the Byrds were rebuilding their lineup and Hillman recommended to the band's leader, Roger McGuinn, that Parsons join the band. By the spring of 1968, Parsons had become a member of the Byrds and he was largely responsible for the group's shift towards country music with their album *Sweetheart of the Rodeo*. Originally, the album was going to feature Parsons' lead vocals, but he was still contractually obligated to LHI, so his voice had to be stripped from the record.

Gram Parsons only spent a few months with the Byrds, leaving the band in the fall of 1968 because he refused to accompany them on a tour of South Africa, allegedly because he opposed apartheid. Chris Hillman left the band shortly after him and the duo formed the Flying Burrito Brothers in late 1968. Parsons and Hillman enlisted pedal steel guitarist "Sneaky" Pete Kleinow and bassist Chris Ethridge to complete the band's lineup and recorded their debut album with a series of session drummers. *The Gilded Palace of Sin*, the Flying Burrito Brothers' debut album, was released in 1969. Although the album only sold a few thousand copies, the group gathered a dedicated cult following, which was mainly composed of musicians, including the Rolling Stones. In fact, by the time the album was released, Parsons had begun hanging around the Rolling Stones frequently and became close friends with Keith Richards. Prior to his time with the Stones, Parsons had experimented with drugs and alcohol, but in 1969 he dove deep into substance abuse, which he supported with his huge trust fund.

Parsons recorded a second album with the Flying Burrito Brothers, but by the time the record—titled *Burrito Deluxe*—appeared in the spring of 1970, he had left the band. Shortly after leaving the group, he recorded a handful of songs with producer Terry Melcher, but he never completed the album. Following these sessions, Parsons entered a holding pattern were he acted the role of being a rock star instead of actually playing music. He spent much of his time either hanging out with the Stones or ingesting large amounts of drugs and alcohol; frequently, he did a combination of the two. In 1971, he toured with the Rolling Stones in England, attended the recording of the band's *Exile on Main Street*, and it appeared that he would sign with the band's record label. Instead, he headed back to Los Angeles late in 1971, spending the rest of the year and the first half of 1972 writing material for an impending solo album. In 1972, he met Emmylou Harris through Chris Hillman and Parsons asked her to join his backing band; she accepted. By the summer of 1972, he was prepared to enter the studio to record his first solo album. Parsons had assembled a band—which included Harris, guitarist James Burton, bassist Rik Grech, Barry Tashian, Glen D. Hardin, and Ronnie Tutt—and had asked Merle Haggard to produce the album. After meeting Parsons, Haggard turned the offer down, and Parsons chose Haggard's engineer, Hugh Davis, as the album's producer. The resulting album, *G.P.*, was released early in 1973 to good reviews but poor sales.

Following the release of *G.P.*, Parsons embarked on a small tour with his backing band, the Fallen Angels. After the tour was completed, they entered the studio to record his second album, *Grievous Angel*. The album was completed toward the end of the summer. A few weeks after the sessions, Parsons went on a vacation near the Joshua Tree National Monument in California. He spent most of his time there consuming drugs and alcohol. On September 19, 1973, he overdosed on morphine and tequila, and was rushed to the Yucca Valley Hospital; he was pronounced dead on arrival. According to the funeral plans, his body was to be flown back to New Orleans for a burial. However, Parsons' road manager stole the body after the funeral and carried it back out to the Joshua Tree desert, where he cremated the body. Phil Kaufman revealed that the cremation had been Parsons' wish. Kaufman could not be convicted for stealing the body, but he was arrested for stealing and burning the coffin. In the two decades following Gram Parsons' death, his legacy continued to grow, as both country and rock musicians built on the music he left behind. Everyone from Emmylou Harris to Elvis Costello has covered his songs and his influence could still be heard well into the next millennium. *—Stephen Thomas Erlewine*

☆ **G.P.** / 1973 / Reprise ♦♦♦♦♦

Given Gram Parsons' habit of taking control of the bands he played with (and his disinclination towards staying with them for very long), it was inevitable that he would eventually strike out on his own, and his first solo album, 1973's *G.P.*, is probably the best realized expression of his musical personality. Working with a crack band of L.A. and Nashville's finest (including James Burton on guitar, Ronnie Tutt on drums, Byron Berline on fiddle, and Glen D. Hardin on piano), he drew from them a sound that merged breezy confidence with deeply felt Southern soul, and he in turn pulled off some of his most subtle and finely detailed vocal performances; "She" and "A Song for You," in particular, are masterful examples of passion finding balance with understatement. Parsons also discovered that rare artist with whom he can be said to have genuinely collaborated (rather than played beside), Emmylou Harris; Gram and Harris' spot-on harmonies and exchanged verses on "We'll Sweep out the Ashes in the Morning" and "That's All It Took" are achingly beautiful and instantly established her as one country music's most gifted vocalists. On *G.P.*, Parsons' ambitious vision encompassed hard-country weepers, wistful ballads, uptempo dance tunes, and even horn-driven rhythm and blues. He managed to make them all work, both as individual tunes and as a unified whole. If it falls just short of being his greatest work (an honor that goes to The Flying Burrito Bothers' *The Gilded Palace of Sin*) thanks to a couple songs that are a bit too oblique for their own good ("The New Soft Shoe" may be beautiful, but who knows just what it's supposed to be about), this album remains one that is hauntingly and has only gotten better with the passing years. *—Mark Deming*

☆ **Grievous Angel** / 1974 / Reprise ♦♦♦♦♦

Gram Parsons fondness for drugs and high living are said to have been catching up with him while he was recording *Grievous Angel*, and sadly he wouldn't live long enough to see it reach record stores, dying from a drug overdose in the fall of 1973. This album is a less ambitious and unified set than his solo debut, but that's to say that *G.P.* was a great album while *Grievous Angel* was instead a very, very good one. Much of the same band that played on his solo debut were brought back for this set, and they perform with the same effortless grace and authority (especially guitarist James Burton and fiddler Byron Berline). If Parsons was slowing down a bit as a songwriter, he still had plenty of gems on hand from more productive days, such as "Brass Buttons" and "Hickory Wind (which wasn't *really* recorded live in Northern Quebec; that's just Gram and the band ripping it up live in the studio, with a handful of friends whooping it up to create honky-tonk atmosphere). He also proved to be a shrewd judge of other folks material as always; Tom T. Hall's "I Can't Dance" is a strong barroom rocker, and everyone seems to be having a great time on The Louvin Brothers' "Cash on the Barrelhead." As a vocal duo, Parsons and Emmylou Harris only improved on this set, turning in a version of "Love Hurts" so quietly impassioned and delicately beautiful that it's enough to make you forget Roy Orbison ever recorded it. And while he didn't plan on it, Parsons could hardly have picked a better closing gesture than "In My Hour of Darkness." *Grievous Angel* may not have been the finest work of his career, but one would be hard pressed to name an artist who made an album this strong only a few weeks before their death—or at any time of their life, for that matter. *—Mark Deming*

Sleepless Nights / Apr. 1976 / A&M ♦♦♦

A&M Records seemed to have exhausted its stock of Flying Burrito Brothers outtakes on *Close Up the Honky-Tonks* in 1974, but the continuing posthumous regard for Gram Parsons caused the company to unearth another seven tracks, six covers of country classics like "Tonight the Bottle Let Me Down" and "Green, Green Grass of Home," plus a version of the Rolling Stones' "Honky Tonk Women," all originally intended for what annotator Bud Scoppa called "a pure, honest country album" that the Burritos apparently never finished. To this half-of-an-album, A&M added two tracks from *Close Up the Honky-Tonks* and three Parsons solo outtakes (with Emmylou Harris on backup vocals) licensed from Reprise Records. The result, credited to "Gram Parsons/The Flying Burrito Brothers," is a tribute to Parsons' heartbreaking tenor, especially because the tracks are little more than underproduced demos. It's not on par with *The Gilded Palace of Sin*, *Burrito Deluxe*, or *G.P.*, but should be of interest to fans. *—William Ruhlmann*

Gram Parsons & the Shilos: The Early Years, Vol. 1 / 1979 / Sierra ♦♦♦♦

This wonderful album contains the complete recorded legacy of the Shilos, nine songs cut as a demo tape at Bob Jones University in March of 1965, and one home recording of Gram Parsons improvising a potential theme song for a park at Cypress Gardens, Florida. The harmonizing on the group numbers is gorgeous, a rival to the best work of the Kingston Trio or the Journeymen, and the playing is spirited and of virtuoso quality. Opening up with a very bracing, energetic cover of Dick Weissman's "I May Be Right," the album carries you through myriad sounds and genres, including a beautiful Parsons original called "Zah's Blues" that sounds like a descendant of the Kingston Trio's "Scotch and Soda," and the sweetly passionate "Mary Don't You Weep." The group was equally fine doing covers of Pete Seeger songs (there's a very animated rendition of "The Bells of Rhymney" here) and gospel-themed material. And then there's "Surfinanny," the Parsons theme park theme song—he never cut another song as sweetly innocent or beguiling in the eight years he had left to live. Any of the tracks here were worthy of release, and "On My Journey Home" and "They Still Go Down" should have been especially attractive as potential singles at the time. Anyone who loves the Kingston Trio or similar groups will have to own this record, and it's worth tracking down, especially with the killer photo book/biography that came with it as an insert. *—Bruce Eder*

Gram Parsons & the Fallen Angels / 1981 / Sierra ♦♦♦♦♦

This is a good live document of Parsons' last tour, it was recorded at radio station WLIR in New York. *—Kenneth M. Cassidy*

★ **G.P./Grievous Angel** / 1990 / Reprise ♦♦♦♦♦

In the year before his death in the fall of 1973, Gram Parsons recorded two superb solo albums, and Warner Bros. has conveniently reissued them in their entirety on a single compact disc. Since many of the same musicians played on both *G.P.* (released in January of 1973) and *Grievous Angel* (which appeared in stores almost exactly a year later), the two albums flow together quite well as a single set. And while no bonus tracks were added, the booklet features well-written essays on Parsons from John M. Delgatto and Marley Brant, the complete liner notes from both albums, and lyrics for all the songs on the disc (which weren't included in the original vinyl issues). While the material and performances on *G.P.* are a shade stronger than on *Grievous Angel*, both albums have more than their share of pearly moments, and this disc is a treat from start to finish; James Burton's guitar leads are chicken-pickin' at its smartest and most tasteful, Al Perkins' pedal steel is the definitive sound of country & western heartache, fiddler Byron Berline effortlessly reveals how he became one of Nashville's leading session musicians, and Parsons' duets with the young Emmylou Harris are nothing less than sublime. And would anyone who loves either country or rock really want to be without a CD that includes songs like "A Song for You," "The New Soft Shoe," "Big Mouth Blues," "$1,000 Wedding," or "In My Hour of Darkness"? While the definitive Gram Parsons collection has yet to be compiled, *G.P./Grievous Angel* gives you everything you really need from his solo career, and these 20 performances are among the most influential and satisfying music the genre of country-rock would ever produce. *—Mark Deming*

Warm Evenings, Pale Mornings, Bottled Blues / 1992 / Raven ♦♦♦♦♦

Although all of Parsons' albums are essential, this import-only collection provides an excellent sampling of his entire career, including his stints with the Shilos, the International

Submarine Band, the Byrds (complete with Parsons' vocals restored), the Flying Burrito Brothers, and the solo years. *—Chris Woodstra*

Cosmic American Music / Jul. 18, 1995 / Sundown ✦✦

Cosmic American is a collection of demos made in various homes and hotel rooms in 1972. In an informal, sing-a-long environment, Parsons works through embryonic versions of songs and old favorites with friends Emmylou Harris, Barry Tashian, and Rik Grech (among others)—several songs never making to the studio. Though the quality of the recordings can be off-putting to the casual fan, those who count themselves among GP's ever-growing cult will find this intimate look a compulsive listen. *—Chris Woodstra*

Live 1973 / Mar. 4, 1997 / Rhino ✦✦✦✦

Gram Parsons may have been one of rock's first great trust-fund hippies, but he couldn't match the kind of paycheck Elvis Presley was able to offer for a Vegas gig. So when he hit the road in 1973 to promote his superb solo debut *G.P.*, James Burton, Ronnie Tutt, and most of the band that anchored that album were otherwise engaged. He instead threw together a rough-and-ready crew of roadhouse pickers he dubbed "The Fallen Angels" (Emmylou Harris, thankfully, was available to make the trip), and they began making their way through America's rock clubs and honky-tonks. *Live 1973* was recorded live for radio broadcast in the midst of that tour, and if you imagine it sounds a good bit rougher and leaner than *G.P.* (which includes six of the 12 cuts featured here), you'd be right. On "We'll Sweep Out the Ashes" and "Cry One More Time," the Fallen Angels aren't quite up to the task of recreating the studio arrangements, but they're surprisingly strong on the quieter numbers, especially "The New Soft Shoe" and "Love Hurts" (the latter of which earned a Grammy nomination), and when they pick up the tempo for some end-of-the-set covers (including Merle Haggard's "California Cottonfields" and Dave Dudley's "Six Days on the Road"), guitarist Jock Bartley and pedal steel player Neil Flanz sound like the core of a great bar band. Gram Parsons and Harris' duets are rougher around the edges on-stage than on vinyl, but they sound as emotionally keen as ever, and Parsons and drummer N.D. Smart II made a pretty good comedy team. *Live 1973* isn't an essential release like *G.P.* or *The Gilded Palace of Sin*, but anyone already familiar with Parsons' body of work will love it. *—Mark Deming*

Another Side of This Life: The Lost Recordings of Gram Parsons, 1965–1966 / Dec. 19, 2000 / Sundazed ✦✦

The 18 previously unreleased, solo acoustic performances on this collection were recorded between March 1965 and December 1966. These show Parsons not as a country singer, rock singer, or even folk-rock singer, but very much as a mid-'60s folkie, in the mold of so many artists to be heard in the Greenwich Village scene. There's no straight country music in his repertoire, comprised largely of covers of songs by then-contemporary writers such as Buffy Sainte-Marie ("Codine"), Tim Hardin, Tom Paxton, and Fred Neil, along with high-caliber compositions that would be popularized by rock groups (Billy Wheeler's "High Flyin' Bird" and Hamilton Camp's "Pride of Man"). There are also five Parsons originals, a few not available elsewhere, and others recorded at other points either by himself ("Brass Buttons" and "Zah's Blues") or different performers ("November Nights," placed on an obscure single by Peter Fonda). A bit of R&B pokes out in his covers of "Searchin'" and "Candy Man." This disc is definitely of historical interest, if only to demonstrate that Parsons' roots were certainly not country-soaked, but largely indebted to '60s folk as well. As music, it's very average (though certainly not bad) mid-'60s folk, of the kind you might hear by numerous coffeehouse support acts. He sings best on the jazzy "Zah's Blues," where he seems to reach further into himself than he does on most of the other material here. *—Richie Unterberger*

★ **Sacred Hearts and Fallen Angels: The Gram Parsons Anthology** / May 1, 2001 / Rhino ✦✦✦✦✦

Gram Parsons' legend is so great that it's easy for the neophyte to be skeptical about his music, wondering if it really is deserving of such effusive praise. Simply put, it is, and if you question the veracity of that statement, turn to Rhino's peerless double-disc set, *Sacred Hearts and Fallen Angels: The Gram Parsons Anthology*. This is the first truly comprehensive overview of Parsons' work, running from the International Submarine Band, through the Byrds, to the Flying Burrito Brothers and his two solo albums, scattering appropriate rarities or non-LP tracks along the way. This is no small feat, since it depends on extensive cross-licensing between record labels, plus concentration from the compilers, who won't allow personal biases to get in the way of telling the story. Miraculously, this happens, and the result is a lean, yet thorough, utterly addictive set that summarizes the brilliance of Gram Parsons, capturing his magnificent songwriting abilities and how he made country sound like rock & roll, while giving rock a sense of country's history. It's possible to complain about the handful of omissions—"Break My Mind" is one of the greatest recordings he did with the Byrds, the version of "Do You Know How It Feels" is better with the Burritos, the barroom anthems of his solo records ("Cry One More Time," "Big Mouth Blues," "I Can't Dance," "Cash on the Barrellhead") gave the weepers context—but this still hits every major point. After all, counting the early version of "Do You Know," only two songs are missing from *The Gilded Palace of Sin* and only four songs are missing from the two-fer of *G.P./Grievous Angel*, *plus* this has the best of the ISB, Byrds, and songs that didn't make the solo album. So, even if there may be a personal favorite or two missing, *nothing* major is missing, which means this is a perfect, irresistible summation of Parsons' career, containing every great moment from all of his bands. His genius has never seemed purer than it does here, since it conveys the true scope of his talents and his career. If you are a fan of Parsons, this isn't necessary, even if it is an excellent listen (there's only one unreleased track, the ISB's "Knee Deep in the Blues"). If you haven't fallen in love with him, skip every other disc—this is what you need. Once you hear it, there's no way that you won't become a life-long fan. *—Stephen Thomas Erlewine*

Dolly Parton

b. Jan. 19, 1946, Locust Ridge, TN

Songwriter, Vocals, Banjo, Guitar / Traditional Country, Progressive Country, Country-Pop, Country-Folk, Honky Tonk, Urban Cowboy, Contemporary Country

It's difficult to find a country performer who has moved from country roots to international fame more successfully than Dolly Parton. Her autobiographical single "Coat of Many Colors" shows the poverty of growing up one of 12 children on a run-down farm in Locust Ridge, TN. At 12 years old she was appearing on Knoxville television; at 13 she was recording on a small label and appearing on the *Grand Ole Opry*. Her 1967 hit "Dumb Blonde" (which she's not) caught Porter Wagoner's ear, and he hired Parton to appear on his television show, where their duet numbers became famous. By the time her "Joshua" reached number one in 1970, Parton's fame had overshadowed the boss', and she had struck out on her own, though still recording duets with him. During the mid-'70s, she established herself as a country superstar, crossing over into the pop mainstream in the early '80s, when she smoothed out the rough edges in her music and began singing pop as well as country. In the early '80s, she also began appearing in movies, most notably the hit *9 to 5*. Though her savvy marketing, image manipulation—her big, dumb blond stage persona is an *act*—extracurricular forays into film, and her flirtations with country-pop have occasionally overshadowed her music, at her core Parton is a country gal and a tremendously gifted singer/songwriter. Among her classics are "Coat of Many Colors," "Jolene," "Kentucky Gambler," "I Will Always Love You," "But You Known I Love You," and "Tennessee Homesick Blues," and they give a hint to why her contribution to bringing country music to a wide audience, not only in America but throughout the world, cannot be underestimated.

The fourth of 12 children, Parton was born and raised in Locust Ridge, TN, just next to the Smoky Mountains National Forest. Parton's family struggled to survive throughout her childhood, and often she was ridiculed for her poverty, yet often music soothed their worries. Though her farming father did not play, her half-Cherokee mother played guitar and her grandfather Reverend Jake Owens was a fiddler and songwriter (his "Singing His Praise" was recorded by Kitty Wells). When she was seven, her uncle Bill Owens gave her a guitar, and within three years she became a regular on WIVK Knoxville's *the Cas Walker Farm and Home Hour*. Over the next two years, her career steadily increased, and in 1959 she made her debut on the *Grand Ole Opry*; the following year, she recorded her first single, "Puppy Love," for Goldband.

When she was 14 years old, Parton signed to Mercury Records, but her 1962 debut for the label, "It's Sure Gonna Hurt," was a bomb and the label immediately dropped her. Over the next five years, she shopped for a new contract and did indeed record a number of songs, which were later reissued through budget-line records. She continued to attend high-school, playing snare drum in the marching band. After she graduated, she moved to Nashville where she stayed with Bill Owens. Both songwriters pitched songs across Nashville to no success, and Parton began singing on demos. Early in 1965, both Parton and Owens finally found work when Fred Foster signed them to his publishing house, Combine Music; Foster subsequently signed her to Monument Records. Parton's first records for Monument were marketed to pop audiences, and her second record, "Happy, Happy Birthday Baby," nearly made the charts. In 1966, Bill Phillips took two of Parton's and Owens' songs—"Put It Off Until Tomorrow" and "The Company You Keep"—to the Top Ten, setting the stage for Parton's breakthrough single, "Dumb Blonde." Released early in 1967, the record climbed to number 24, followed shortly afterward by the number 17 "Something Fishy."

The two hit Monument singles attracted the attention of country star Porter Wagoner, who was looking to hire a new female singer for his syndicated television show. Parton accepted the offer and began appearing on the show on September 5, 1967. Initially, Wagoner's audience was reluctant to warm to Parton and chanted for Norma Jean, the singer she replaced, but with Wagoner's assistance, she was accepted. Wagoner convinced his label, RCA, to also sign Parton. Since female performers were not particularly popular in the late '60s, the label decided to protect their investment by releasing her first single as a duet with Wagoner. The duo's first single, "The Last Thing on My Mind," reached the country Top Ten early in 1968, launching a six-year streak of virtually uninterrupted Top Ten singles. Parton's first solo single, "Just Because I'm a Woman," was released in the summer of 1968 and was a moderate hit, reaching number 17. For the remainder of the decade, none of her solo efforts—even "In the Good Old Days (When Times Were Bad)," which would later become a standard—were as successful as her duets. The duo was named Vocal Group of the Year in 1968 by the Country Music Association, but Parton's solo records were continually ignored. Wagoner and Parton were both frustrated by her lack of solo success, because he had a significant financial stake in her future—as of 1969, he was her co-producer and owned nearly half of the publishing company Owepar.

By 1970, both Parton and Wagoner had grown frustrated by her lack of solo success, and Porter had her sing Jimmie Rodgers' "Mule Skinner Blues (Blue Yodel No. 8)," a gimmick that worked. The record shot to number three on the charts, followed closely by her first number one single, "Joshua." For the next two years, she had a number of solo hits—including her signature song "Coat of Many Colors" (number four, 1971)—in addition to her duets. Though she had successful singles, none of them were blockbusters until "Jolene" reached number one in early 1974. Parton stopped traveling with Wagoner after its release, yet she continued to appear on television and sing duets with him until 1976.

Once she left Wagoner, Parton's records became more eclectic and diverse, ranging from the ballad "I Will Always Love You" (number one, 1974) and the racy "The Bargain Store" (number one, 1975) to the crossover pop of "Here You Come Again" (number one, 1977) and the disco experiments of "Baby I'm Burning" (number 25 pop, 1978). From 1974 to 1980, she consistently charted in the country Top Ten, with no less than eight singles reaching number one. Parton had her own syndicated television show, *Dolly*, in 1976 and by the next year had gained the right to produce her own albums, which immediately resulted in diverse efforts like 1977's *New Harvest, First Gathering*. In addition to her own hits during the late '70s, many artists, from Rose Maddox and Kitty Wells to Olivia Newton-John, Emmylou Harris, and Linda Ronstadt, covered her songs, and her siblings Randy and Stella received recording contracts of their own.

Though she was quite popular, Parton became a genuine superstar in 1977, when the Barry Mann/Cynthia Weil song "Here You Come Again" became a huge crossover hit, reaching number three on the pop charts, spending five weeks at the top of the country charts, and going gold. Its accompanying album went platinum and the follow-up, *Heartbreaker*, went gold. Soon, she was on the cover of country and mainstream publications alike. With the new financial windfall, a lawsuit against Wagoner—who had received a significant portion of her royalties—ensued. By the time it was settled, she regained her copyrights while Wagoner was given a nominal fee and the studio the duo shared. In the wake of the lawsuit, a delayed duet album, *Making Plans*, appeared in 1980; its title track hit number two on the country charts.

Parton's commercial success continued to grow during 1980, as she had three number-one hits in a row: the Donna Summer-written "Starting Over Again," "Old Flames Can't Hold a Candle to You," and "9 to 5." The latter was the theme song to Parton's acting debut, *9 to 5*. Also starring Jane Fonda and Lily Tomlin, the movie became a huge success, establishing Parton as a movie star. The song became her first number-one pop single, as well. *9 to 5* gave Parton's career momentum that lasted throughout the early '80s. She began appearing in more films, including the Burt Reynolds musical *The Best Little Whorehouse in Texas* (1982) and the Sylvester Stallone comedy *Rhinestone* (1984). Parton's singles continued to appear consistently in the country Top Ten: Between 1981 and 1985, she had 12 Top Ten hits and half of those were number-one singles. Parton continued to make inroads on the pop charts as well with a re-recorded version of "I Will Always Love You" from *The Best Little Whorehouse in Texas* scraping the Top 50 and her Kenny Rogers duet "Islands in the Stream" (which was written by the Bee Gees and produced by Barry Gibb) spending two weeks at number one.

However, by 1985 many old-time fans had felt that Parton was spending too much time courting the mainstream. Most of her albums were dominated by the adult contemporary pop of songs like "Islands in the Stream," and it had been years since she had sung straightforward country. She also continued to explore new business and entertainment ventures such as her Dollywood theme park, which opened in 1985. Despite these misgivings, she had continued to chart well until 1986, when none of her singles reached the Top Ten. RCA Records didn't renew her contract after it expired that year, and she signed with Columbia in 1987. Before she released her Columbia debut, Parton joined forces with Linda Ronstadt and Emmylou Harris to record the rootsy *Trio* album. *Trio* became a huge hit, earning both critical and popular acclaim, selling over a million copies, and peaking at number six on the pop charts; it also spawned three Top Ten country singles: "To Know Him Is to Love Him," "Telling Me Lies," and "Those Memories of You." Following the success of the album, she had a weekly variety television show, *Dolly*, on ABC that lasted only one season. *Trio* also provided a perfect launching pad for her first Columbia album, 1989's *White Limozeen*, which produced two number one hits in "Why'd You Come in Here Lookin' Like That" and "Yellow Roses."

Though it looked like Parton's career had been revived, it was actually just a brief revival before contemporary country came along in the early '90s and pushed all veteran artists out of the charts. Parton had a number-one duet with Ricky Van Shelton, "Rockin' Years," in 1991, but after that single, she slowly crept out of the Top Ten and later the Top 40. Parton was one of the most outspoken critics of radio's treatment of older stars. While her sales had declined, she didn't disappear. Despite her lack of sales, Parton remained an iconic figure in country music, appearing in films (the 1991 TV-movie *Wild Texas Wind*, 1992's *Straight Talk*), selling out concerts, and releasing a series of acclaimed albums—including 1993's *Honky Tonk Angels*, a collaboration with Tammy Wynette and Loretta Lynn—that all sold respectably. Furthermore, "I Will Always Love You" was covered in 1992 by Whitney Houston, who took it to number one on the pop charts; the single spent 14 weeks at number one, becoming the biggest pop hit of the rock & roll era (it was unseated four years later by Mariah Carey and Boyz II Men's "One Sweet Day"). In 1994, she published her autobiography *My Life and Other Unfinished Business*. *Treasures*, her 1996 album, was a praised collection of unusual covers, ranging from Merle Haggard to Neil Young. *Hungry Again* followed in 1998, and early the following year she reunited with Ronstadt and Harris for a second *Trio* collection in addition to releasing the solo *The Grass Is Blue*. A solo effort, *Little Sparrow*, was issued in early 2001. —*David Vinopal*

Hello, I'm Dolly / 1967 / Monument ◆◆◆◆◆

The charismatic Parton came on strong with these early session for Monument. At least half the songs are among her classics, while the rest of the material is hardly weak. The pedal steel playing is fantastic, and it would be worth the research to find out who the session men were, as they have gone uncredited on the original release, as well as subsequent repackagings. (In one two-fer release combining this album with *As Long As I Love*, the label squandered the inner gatefold on self-advertising rather than provide any information about these wonderful sessions.) The personality that Parton brought to her material is here in full force. "Dumb Blonde" and "Something Fishy" are the wisecracking, smart cookie side of Parton, while "The Company You Keep"and "I've Lived My Life" show how adept she is at cramming country songs full of moralizing while providing the listener with plenty of enjoyment. —*Eugene Chadbourne*

Just Because I'm a Woman / 1968 / RCA ◆◆◆◆◆

It's a measure of how impressed producer Bob Ferguson must have been with Parton that he (and possibly Porter Wagoner in the background) made no attempt to crowd her with strings or choruses on her first RCA album. In fact, it's almost frightening to hear how fully realized her talent was in 1968. —*Dan Cooper*

The Fairest of Them All / 1969 / RCA ◆◆◆

In the Good Old Days (When Times Were Bad) / 1969 / RCA ◆◆◆

My Blue Ridge Mountain Boy / 1969 / RCA ◆◆◆

Just the Two of Us / 1969 / RCA ◆◆◆

As Long as I Love / 1970 / Monument ◆◆◆◆

Parton's years for the Monument label were good ones, resulting in terrific straightforward country numbers, many of them written by her. The uncredited pickers, in particular the pedal steel, keep things really cooking. The arrangement on the opening number

"Why, Why, Why" makes the listener's head spin with both the precision of the pedal steel riffs and the clever shuffling of chords from the standard 1-4-5 progression. Even a skeptic will be able to follow Parton into her private realm of despair, always delivered in a beautiful voice promising hope. This might be one of the most enduring country artists and superstars early in her career, but she already has it all together. It is superb country and western, which, combined with the highly-praised old-time traditions she would return to later in her career, establishes Parton as a visionary artist in traditional American music. —*Eugene Chadbourne*

A Real Live Dolly / 1970 / RCA ◆◆◆◆◆

Once More / Oct. 10, 1970 / RCA ◆◆◆

Golden Streets of Glory / 1971 / RCA ◆◆◆

Joshua / 1971 / RCA ◆◆◆

Two of a Kind / 1971 / RCA ◆◆◆◆

☆ **Coat of Many Colors** / Oct. 1971 / Buddha ◆◆◆◆◆

Dolly Parton had a number of hits in the late '60s as Porter Wagoner's duet partner, yet solo success eluded her until her 1971 album, *Coat of Many Colors*. The title track was a Top Ten single, and it effectively became her signature song, largely because it was a sweetly autobiographical tune about her childhood. That song, along with its two hit predecessors "Traveling Man" and "My Blue Tears," were evidence that Parton was a strong songwriter, but the full album reveals the true depth of her talents. She wrote seven of the ten songs (Wagoner wrote the other three), none of which are filler. There isn't really a theme behind *Coat of Many Colors*, even if its title track suggests otherwise. Instead, it's a remarkably consistent album, in terms of songwriting and performances, but also remarkably diverse, revealing that Dolly can handle ballads, country-rockers, tearjerkers, and country-pop with equal aplomb. And while it is very short, clocking in at under a half hour, there isn't a wasted moment on the album. It's a lean, trim album that impresses because of succinctness—with its ten songs, it announced Parton as a major talent in her own right, not merely a duet partner. —*Stephen Thomas Erlewine*

My Favorite Songwriter, Porter Wagoner / 1972 / RCA ◆◆◆◆◆

Touch Your Woman / 1972 / RCA ◆◆◆◆

Bubbling Over / 1972 / RCA ◆◆◆

The Right Combination/Burning the Midnight Oil / 1972 / RCA ◆◆◆◆◆

Together Always / 1972 / RCA ◆◆◆

We Found It / 1973 / RCA ◆◆◆◆

Mine / 1973 / RCA ◆◆◆◆◆

This is an early-'70s effort that shows the great country songstress to be literally bursting with a spirit of independence, proud of her unique approach to the genre. Listeners who think she didn't really revel in the Appalachian sound until abandoning the commercial country world in the late '90s will find this to be an innovative blend of the country session band sound with mountain ballad-style chord changes, including some dark-sounding minor and modal action. She wrote practically every song on this record, and she co-wrote the exception, a fantastic number entitled "When Possession Gets Too Strong" that should be added to the country & western canon of possible counterattacks to "Stand By Your Man." The material is all strong enough to make this seem like an actual original album effort, but something is rotten in the state of Denmark, or should we say Tennessee. The liner notes hint at this being a repackaging or collection, although it doesn't exactly explain for where or from what. The painting on the front cover is, in a word, horrifying. This also has to be one of the shortest albums ever released. There are people who would be upset if these tracks represented the contents of one side of an album, let alone both sides of the vinyl slab. Perhaps the song "I'm Doing This for Your Sake" was written for the mastering engineer, who had to leave early for a golf date. Besides all that, vintage Parton. —*Eugene Chadbourne*

☆ **Jolene** / 1974 / Buddha ◆◆◆◆◆

Jolene was Dolly Parton's first solo outing after officially leaving Porter Wagoner's show, so naturally many wondered if she could succeed without her old partner's influence. However, any such questions were quickly dispelled when the album spawned two number-one hits, the title track and "I Will Always Love You." Emotional yet not maudlin, the latter song is a bittersweet nod to Wagoner, and is far superior to Whitney Houston's more famous—and over the top—interpretation from the soundtrack to *The Bodyguard*. Dolly's pure and resonant voice is the main attraction, whether on ballads like "Early Morning Breeze" or more upbeat numbers like "Highlight of My Life." The whole album sounds professional, but is still deeply rooted in tradition. This homespun approach would be sorely lacking once Dolly embarked on her more pop-oriented phase just three short years later. Luckily, this release came out before this slick and glitzy period, so it remains perhaps the only time in Dolly's career when artistic integrity successfully mixed with commercial success. *Jolene*, while short by today's standards, is the album that gave Dolly confidence and made her a star, and it should be regarded as one of her best moments. —*Brian Downing*

My Tennessee Mountain Home / 1975 / RCA ◆◆◆

My Tennessee Mountain Home is one of the rootsiest records of Dolly Parton's career. With its affectionate homages and salutes to her childhood in Tennessee, the record is a direct and moving slice of mountain music that isn't dressed up in cosmopolitan production. Parton wrote every song on the record, creating a loose, musical autobiography with its 11 songs. Though the sound of the record isn't particularly rowdy, it is heartfelt and rootsy and Parton's songs—"Old Black Kettle," "The Letter," "The Good Old Days When Times Were Bad," and "The Better Part of Life"—are among her best, most affecting songs, much like *My Tennessee Mountain Home* itself. —*Stephen Thomas Erlewine*

Bargain Store / 1975 / RCA ✦✦✦✦✦

Love Is Like a Butterfly / 1975 / RCA ✦✦✦

Dolly-The Seeker, We Used To / 1975 / RCA ✦✦✦

The Best of Dolly Parton / 1975 / RCA ✦✦✦✦✦

She projects an admirable child-like sense of hope and positivism, which is matched to some degree by her thin, girlish vocal quality. It translates well in her pre-Hollywood, unencumbered productions, notably "Coat of Many Colors," "Love Is like a Butterfly," and "The Bargain Store." —*Tom Roland*

Say Forever You'll Be Mine / 1976 / RCA ✦✦✦

All I Can Do / 1976 / RCA ✦✦✦✦

Here's a generous portion of Parton's original songs, topped off with a pair of Merle Haggard and Emmylou Harris covers. The blend of country and pop here has perhaps never been matched: songs such as "All I Can Do" and the marvelous "Lucky Lady" bounce like an over-inflated beachball. She was breaking free from the influence of her boss Porter Wagoner here, but hadn't quite gotten all the way loose. He still nabs kind of half a producer's credit (he's only identified as Porter, no Wagoner) and may have had something to do with, or at least surely enjoyed, the liner notes and their smarmy references to "spending the night" with Dolly. It is truly her music, and not her looks, that have made her a reputation as a favorite songwriter among session pickers. These tracks bring out the best in the players and the arrangements allow lots of room for neat fills. The appropriately named Tom Pick was on hand to record the proceedings. —*Eugene Chadbourne*

Here You Come Again / 1977 / RCA ✦✦✦

It might be the short length of this album that inevitably makes it feel like it just didn't quite all come together, yet there are plenty of high points, such as the catchy title tune, the grooving "It's All Wrong, But It's All Right," "Two Doors Down," and the typically Parton-esque charm of "Cowgirl and the Dandy." Some problems originate with the studio backup, which just isn't country enough. Sure, there's some pedal steel here and there, but an effort is obviously being made to steer her away from the hardcore country sound to whatever might have been perceived as being popular in the late '70s. This is still a few years before disco was to temporarily monopolize her aesthetic. The musicians here represent a smooth Los Angeles sound, with pickers such as David Lindley aboard. There are even synthesizer contributions from Ian Underwood, but from what he does one would hardly know that he had been a member of the avant-garde rock outfit the Mothers of Invention. —*Eugene Chadbourne*

New Harvest, First Gathering / 1977 / RCA ✦✦✦

Heartbreaker / 1978 / RCA ✦✦✦✦

Dolly Parton found increasing success in the late '70s, and *Heartbreaker* showcases her increasing confidence beautifully. In 1978 Parton was the winner of the Country Music Association's Entertainer of the Year award, probably due in part to *Heartbreaker*'s rise to number one on the country charts and its two number-one singles ("I Really Got the Feeling" and the title track). While the clean country-pop is a step away from her much rootsier previous albums, it is the natural progression toward her *9 to 5 and Odd Jobs* pop crossover success in the years to come. Unfortunately with this BMG Special Products release, the liner notes are nonexistent (Parton's duet partner, Richard Dennison, on "We're Through Forever ('Til Tomorrow") goes completely uncredited) and the disco remixes of "Baby I'm Burning" and "I Wanna Fall in Love" (which were two of the year's biggest club hits) would've been terrific bonus cuts, but they are nowhere to be found. Still, it's great to have *Heartbreaker* back in print, no matter the shortcomings of the packaging. —*Zac Johnson*

Great Balls of Fire / 1979 / RCA ✦✦

Critics had gone along with Parton's ascension into pop and film stardom until this album was released. It was the sense at the time that she had gone a little too far with choice of rock covers, throwing in a version of the Beatles' "Help" along with the title song, which, despite Parton's chutzpah, is more like a pathetic heat spark flicking off of the head of a match than a great ball of fire. As the years passed, Parton would provide a payoff with her cover version of the disco hit "Shine," but that triumph still doesn't make this flop sound better in retrospect. The originals are the best tracks on the record, but they even seem like she consciously is trying for the pop hits she wasn't getting in this period. A few years later, the Bee Gees would come up hit tunes for her and country smoothie Kenny Rogers. An army of session men plink and plunk away, but they're not the Nashville cats. Fans of the hot picking on Parton records will have to make do with a few runs from David Grisman on mandolin and Herb Pedersen on banjo. —*Eugene Chadbourne*

Making Plans / 1980 / RCA ✦✦✦

Dolly Dolly Dolly / 1980 / RCA ✦✦

9 to 5 and Odd Jobs / 1980 / Buddah ✦✦✦✦✦

Dolly Parton has never been an albums artist, and RCA has always been adept at shoving poorly organized products onto the market (look how they've treated Elvis Presley). Hence, though she is an important country figure, most of Parton's albums are hard to recommend. This one contains the title hit, plus a few other Parton originals and a version of Woody Guthrie's "Deportee" among its eight tracks. But that's enough to put it a notch above most of Parton's RCA catalog. —*William Ruhlmann*

Heartbreak Express / 1982 / RCA ✦✦✦

Greatest Hits / 1982 / RCA ✦✦✦✦✦

This is a good sampling of Parton's work in the first few years that she deliberately chased a crossover career in Hollywood. The country-pop stuff might offend purists, but it still

gets the toe tappin'. "Hard Candy Christmas" and her updated version of "I Will Always Love You" (both from *The Best Little Whorehouse in Texas*) show her growth as an interpreter. —*Tom Roland*

Burlap & Satin / 1983 / RCA ✦✦✦

The Great Pretender / 1984 / RCA ✦✦

The Great Pretender includes Parton's hit remake of the Drifters' "Save the Last Dance for Me," along with a rendition of Petula Clark's "Downtown." —*Jason Ankeny*

Rhinestone [Original Soundtrack] / 1984 / RCA ✦

Real Love / 1985 / RCA ✦✦✦

A lot of critics would push this one aside, perhaps with good reason since she turned over much of the creative control on the project to David Malloy. But Malloy set out to highlight the bright, bubbly facet of her personality, and he succeeded. —*Tom Roland*

Collector's Series / 1985 / RCA ✦✦✦

This is a well-programmed selection of Parton's RCA hits, among them "Jolene," "Coat of Many Colors," and "Me and Little Andy." —*William Ruhlmann*

The Best There Is / 1987 / RCA ✦✦✦

The Best There Is is a solid, if too-brief overview of Dolly Parton's hits from the 1970s and early '80s; it includes many of her signature songs, among them the autobiographical "Coat of Many Colors," and the country chart-toppers "Jolene" and "I Will Always Love You," and the pop crossovers "Here You Come Again" and "9 to 5." —*Jason Ankeny*

Rainbow / 1988 / CBS ✦✦✦

The World of Dolly Parton, Vol. 1 / 1988 / Monument ✦✦✦✦✦

This captures young Parton on Monument Records circa 1967, just before she hooked up with Porter. —*Dan Cooper*

The World of Dolly Parton, Vol. 2 / 1988 / Monument ✦✦✦✦✦

World of Dolly Parton, Vol. 2 contains the remaining 12 songs from Parton's days at Monument Records, including "Daddy Won't Be Home Anymore," "This Boy Has Been Hurt," and "I'm Not Worth the Tears." Though they didn't storm the charts like her RCA material, Parton's Monument recordings are among her rootsiest and hardest country recordings, and should be heard by any of her fans. —*Thom Owens*

White Limozeen / 1989 / Columbia ✦✦✦✦✦

Parton moved to Columbia in the late '80s and started paying more attention to her recordings, the best of which is this album. It's produced by Ricky Skaggs, who brought in such fast-picking cronies as Béla Fleck and Jerry Douglas and used more of Parton's own songs than usual. The result is an unusual consistency and a musical revitalization for the singer. —*William Ruhlmann*

Eagle When She Flies / 1991 / Columbia ✦✦✦

She confirms that she's fully returned to the country fold, and is rewarded with her first million-selling album that wasn't a greatest-hits package. The title song is a powerful female anthem. —*Michael McCall*

Slow Dancing With the Moon / 1993 / Columbia ✦✦✦

Slow Dancing With the Moon features a who's who of country music circa 1993; guests including Tanya Tucker, Vince Gill, Mary-Chapin Carpenter, Chet Atkins, Kathy Mattea and Billy Ray Cyrus are just a handful of the singers and players joining Parton on this outing. Ironically, it's the simpler, sparer songs that work best here; stripped of all the gloss and star power that sinks the guest-dominated tracks, they allow Parton's emotional vocals to really shine through. —*Jason Ankeny*

★ **The RCA Years 1967–1986** / May 25, 1993 / RCA ✦✦✦✦✦

The long-overdue box set turns out to be a cursory two-CD set that cheats on her better early years in favor of latter-day hits. Still, it's the best retrospective available, and it emphasizes her stature as a truly significant songwriter, which is easy to forget in the shadow of her Daisy Mae in Hollywood image. —*Michael McCall*

Honky Tonk Angels / Nov. 2, 1993 / Columbia ✦✦✦

Legend is a hefty title to carry, especially if you're still kicking. The standards are high, the expectations immense. Dolly Parton, Loretta Lynn, and Tammy Wynette are, nevertheless, legends of country music with decades of albums and awards to prove it. And they are very much still kicking on *Honky Tonk Angels*—just in case anyone needs a little reminder. You can even hear how much fun they had singing together, setting aside any historic competition and letting their love of country music shine through, each gracefully moving between lead and harmony vocals. As for the song selection, it covers a wide swath of country history from tunes made famous by early pioneers like Ferlin Husky, the Davis Sisters, and Hank Locklin to their own more contemporary compositions. If that weren't enough credibility, Kitty Wells lends her amazing voice to the opening anthem "It Wasn't God Who Made Honky Tonk Angels." Pure goodness. In another twist, Patsy Cline sings on "Lovesick Blues" with Parton, Lynn, and Wynette backing her. The closing track sums up the humorous reverence that permeates much of country music. "I Dreamed of a Hillbilly Heaven" was a hit for Tex Ritter in 1961 and is a surprising choice that seems a bit out of place, but somehow works well enough. For fans of traditional country or great singers, this is a fun listen because it nicely captures three of the best voices around. —*Kelly McCartney*

Something Special / 1995 / Columbia ✦✦✦

Something Special is something of a mixed bag from Dolly Parton, featuring a selection of new songs and re-recorded old material. While the newer songs are fine, they pale in comparison with classics like "Jolene" and "I Will Always Love You," recorded as a duet with Vince Gill. If the new songs had been included on an album that only featured new material, they would have formed a strong record but they take a back seat to Parton's older songs, which are more inspired and better-written. Nevertheless, the album provides several fine moments, even it doesn't rank among her best works. *—Stephen Thomas Erlewine*

The Essential Dolly Parton, Vol. 1: I Will Always Love You / Mar. 28, 1995 / RCA ✦✦✦✦✦

This set kicked off RCA's long-overdue "essential" reissue series with a package by country's best-known ambassador, Dolly Parton. The volume one imprint on the album implies that there will be another Parton set, which is good news, considering that this set is geared toward her late-'70s and thereafter pop recordings. Parton fans must demand a respectful set featuring Parton's very early hits, when she was hungry to establish herself—songs like "Mule Skinner Blues," "Try Being Lonely," "Joshua," "She Never Met a Man (She Didn't Like)," "Coat of Many Colors," "Touch Your Woman," "Dumb Blonde," "The Bargin Store," or "Just Because I'm a Woman." And how about throwing in a couple of Porter Wagoner duets like "If Teardrops Were Pennies" or "Please Don't Stop Loving Me" for good measure? That those tracks aren't included here shouldn't inhibit anyone from picking this set up. There's not a rotten apple in this bunch. There's the 1982 version of her 1974 country smash "I Will Always Love You," which was used in the film *The Best Little Whorehouse in Texas*; the equally familiar "Islands in the Stream" duet with Kenny Rogers; and the title song from the 1980 film *9 to 5*. The rest of the material is divided between what RCA hoped to cross over to the pop charts and what they planned to program to Parton's base country audience. Of the former there is the spirited "Think About Love" and the all-out MOR ballads "Starting Over Again" and "You're the Only One." As for the latter, there are the fun, snappy "Do I Ever Cross Your Mind," "Sweet Summer Lovin'," and "Heartbreak Express," among others. *—Bill Carpenter*

Treasures / Sep. 24, 1996 / RCA ✦✦✦

If the listener senses déjà vu, it's only the idea they've heard before. Parton tried an album of covers called *The Great Pretender* in 1983 or so; those pop arrangements of "Downtown" and "Save the Last Dance for Me" did very well on the country charts, but flopped on the pop charts. For this go-round, Parton has compiled mostly country chestnuts. Parton's voice is sweet, often sinewy. These arrangements are clean and for the most part faithful to the original arrangements. None other than die-hard Parton fans will find real excitement in Charlie Rich's "Behind Closed Doors," Merle Haggard's "Today I Started Loving You Again," Freddy Fender's "Before the Next Teardrop Falls" (although there's a nice Spanish sequence with David Hidalgo sharing vocals), and Ray Price's "For the Good Times." Otherwise, Parton does a swell job of jazzing up one of Mac Davis' least-memorable hits, "Something's Burning." She gives it an anxious, almost rock flavor which brings the song to life. With viola accompaniment and harmony vocals from Alison Krauss, Parton's take on Neil Young's "After the Gold Rush" foretells the Rapture in beautiful poetry. A true surprise, Parton transformed Katrina & the Waves' new wave hit "Walking on Sunshine" into a country swing tune, complete with fiddle solo. Two of the least-familiar songs are also two of the best. "Don't Let Me Cross Over," a woman's angst over the temptation to steal another woman's man, and "Satin Sheets," about a woman who's grown tired of her wealthy husband's lack of affection, are delicious, pure country ballads. Perhaps the album's centerpiece is Cat Stevens' joyous "Peace Train." Backed by South Africa's Ladysmith Black Mambazo, Parton never sounded more exhilarated than when she and the ensemble sang the "ooh-wah-ee-ah-ooh-ah" line. As always, there was fine frilly cover art on Parton, which might find Mambazo singing "ooh-la-la." *—Bill Carpenter*

☆ **The Essential Dolly Parton, Vol. 2** / Apr. 29, 1997 / RCA ✦✦✦✦✦

The Essential Dolly Parton, Vol. 2 doesn't cover the late-'60s and early-'70s pure country hits that were also ignored by its predecessor, choosing to concentrate on her '70s crossover hits. Although that still leaves a large portion of her best work unanthologized, *Vol. 2* is still a very good compilation. It's true that including the original version of "I Will Always Love You"—which was presented in a re-recorded take from 1982 on *Vol. 1*—is a bit redundant, but the remainder of the disc is filled with hits, from her faithful cover of Jimmie Rodgers' "Mule Skinner Blues" to the soft-rock of "Here You Come Again." Such diversity doesn't make for a coherent collection, but it does illustrate exactly why Dolly had such a large fan base. *—Stephen Thomas Erlewine*

Hungry Again / Aug. 25, 1998 / MCA ✦✦✦✦✦

Dolly Parton has long held her place in country music with a style of class and dignity. A tangible physical presence, her songwriting and singing sometimes tend to be pushed into the shadows. But, even after all these years, Parton is still hip-deep in the game and a player of the highest caliber. This release, her first for the resurrected Decca label, is a powerful trip into the foundation of Parton's music. From gospel to honky tonk to mountain music, she paints exquisite landscapes of intense color and emotion. A pioneer, she asks, "Why don't more women sing honky tonk songs" in "Honky Tonk Songs," a worthy question considering all the glib pop tunes the majority of women in modern country try to pass off as country music. But Parton, who can top the pops with the best of 'em, still remains firmly grounded in tradition, as evidenced by "The Camel's Heart," a tune with the wild emotional strength of her legendary hit "Jolene." Always the center of fun and delight, Parton gives her listeners a fast banjo ride on the uptempo "Time and Tears." "Paradise Road" explores poverty and the transcendence of such a state while providing inspiration and hope. As beautiful as anything she has ever written is "Blue Valley Songbird," an autobiography of sorts. And she ends things with a gospel singalong that flies high. Throughout, Parton is joined by the equally talented and traditional Rhonda Vincent on backing vocals, adding a nice layering to the vocal tracks. *Hungry Again* is a timely, heartwarming project that displays all of the many aspects and facets of Parton's talent. She is endearing and respected, and she can still roll right over most anyone who gets in her way with a single note. *—Jana Pendragon*

The Grass Is Blue / Oct. 26, 1999 / Sugar Hill ✦✦✦✦✦

It was inevitable, especially considering her recent albums, that Dolly Parton would eventually go all the way back to the mountains with a bluegrass project. A child of the southern Appalachians, Parton would have absorbed this music straight through her skin during her formative years. And, indeed, her performance on this CD is impeccable, as is her choice of material. Producer Steve Buckingham has taken care to bring together a group of accomplished bluegrassers to accompany Parton. Alison Krauss, Stuart Duncan, Dan Tyminski, Jerry Douglas, Rhonda Vincent, and Bryan Sutton are major contributors, as is Patty Loveless. Parton wrote two songs for the CD—the title tune and "Endless Stream of Tears"—and she also reworked two of her previously recorded numbers, "Will He Be Waiting for Me" and "Steady As the Rain" as bluegrass pieces. She convinced her producer that Billy Joel's "Travelin' Prayer" and Blackfoot's hard-rocking "Train, Train" could work as bluegrass songs and, sure enough, they do. She also reached into the traditional folk repertoire and crafted a beautiful, haunting version of "Silver Dagger." Parton shows a terrific knack for this genre and, as always, her approach is a bit eccentric, but that's one of her gifts as a musician. She's always followed her own muse; this time it has led her to a singular interpretation of bluegrass that is one of the important bluegrass releases of 1999. *—Philip Van Vleck*

Legendary Dolly Parton / May 23, 2000 / BMG International ✦✦✦✦✦

Once again the Australians put the Nashvilleans to shame when it comes to packaging the finest tracks of a country music artist for reissue. This three-CD collection of Dolly Parton's hits, near misses, and cornerstone tracks is a finer compilation than any that has been released in the U.S.—and the price is right, too; a triple for about the price of a single disc. Here are the classics such as "Coat of Many Colors," "Jolene," "The Good Old Days (When Times Were Bad)," "One of Those Days," "Old Flames," "The Last Thing on My Mind," with Porter Wagoner, and literally dozens more. But, as if the country classics weren't enough, the compilers sought to present a well rounded portrait of Parton by offering many of her pop hits, such Carl Smith's "Higher and Higher" (whose definitive version was done by Jackie Wilson) and her duets with Kenny Rogers ("Real Love" and "Islands in the Stream"), as well as her attempts at rock & roll ("Great Balls of Fire") and swinging for the popular standards fences ("Downtown," "We'll Sing in the Sunshine," "We Had It All," etc.). There are also glimpses of her return to the deep roots music of her early years with covers of "Mule Skinner Blues" and her own "Joshua." Parton's own formidable songs are well represented among this collection's 50 tracks, and there are many surprises included, such as "Baby I'm Burnin'" and "Traveling Man." The only off points are a lack of documentation of when songs were released, what albums they're from, and whether or not they charted, but this is for those of us who don't feel complete without such things. For those illuminated souls who are merely seeking a definitive Dolly Parton collection because her voice is what moves them, this is the one to get. *—Thom Jurek*

Little Sparrow / Jan. 23, 2001 / Sugar Hill ✦✦✦✦

Swooping down from the Appalachian Mountains, *Little Sparrow* is a nice companion piece to 1999's *The Grass Is Blue* and a return to the bluegrass roots that Dolly Parton loves so dearly. Half originals, half covers, *Little Sparrow* cuts a wide swath as it meanders through pop, country, rock, and gospel songs all done up in Parton's "blue mountain music" style. A number of the original compositions, such as "Down From Dover" and "My Blue Tears," were written many years ago but deserved another chance. Others sprang from the well of good titles, and were written to fit into the old-timey musical landscape. "Mountain Angel," "Bluer Pastures," and the title track fall into that category. With her pristine, pitch-perfect voice right out front and backed by the best bluegrass players around, Parton makes you want to pull up a rocking chair and strum right along. However, being drawn to the kindness of the lyrics (and her husband's love of pop standards and hard rock) caused Parton to select a couple of awfully unlikely tunes to grass up. Collective Soul's "Shine" and Cole Porter's "I Get a Kick Out of You" seem ever so out of place, despite the banjos and mandolins. Somehow their melodic lines just don't lend themselves well to this genre, not that she didn't try real hard. Sore thumbs, they are, sticking right on out. Parton does manage to make "Seven Bridges Road" flow smoothly though, doing it up with a female trio of harmony rather than the customary male take on it. In the grand tradition of mountain music, the themes are drawn from love, death, and faith. Being the bold gal that she is, Parton tosses once forbidden lyrics about kissing on the mouth, pregnancy, and the like into "Marry Me" and "Down From Dover." And to fulfill the thematic prophesy, she draws inspiration from her childhood Sunday mornings for the gentle rendition of "In the Sweet By and By." All in all, *Little Sparrow* is about as down-home and old-timey as you are going get in this day and age, and Parton's voice is a classic. *—Kelly McCartney*

Jolene/My Tennessee Mountain Home / Apr. 3, 2001 / BMG International ✦✦✦✦

Two of the things Dolly Parton has utilized as an artistic muse throughout her solo recording career are her rural Appalachian upbringing and her brave split from her mentor, Porter Wagoner. This BMG two-fer of *Jolene* and *My Tennessee Mountain Home* showcases each of these life events almost autobiographically. Beginning with the powerfully pleading hit "Jolene," the first half of this release finds Parton exploring her freedom and independence from Wagoner's influence. In fact, fans have spent years trying to decipher exactly which songs ("Highlight of My Life"? "When Someone Wants to Leave"?) were about her relationship with the country star. One song undoubtedly recounts their split, and if it is possible to block out all of the eye-rolling and baggage unfortunately associated with the "other" version, "I Will Always Love You" should stand on its own as one of the most starkly honest and heartwrenchingly beautiful love songs of the 20th century. While the first half of the two-fer celebrates Parton's first strong steps to country superstardom, *My Tennessee Mountain Home* is a gentle stroll back to the earthy roots of her poor rural upbringing. Beginning with the slightly hokey reading of her first letter home from "Naish-Ville," each song is filled with homesick memories of family, church, and "the good old days when times were bad." Where *Jolene* utilized any number of advanced studio techniques to enhance Parton's countrypolitan love songs, the banjos, dobros, and fiddles on the second half illustrate the songs and accent her voice just as well. Although either of these albums stand strongly on their own, together they paint a much more complete picture of who Dolly Parton was, and who she would become. *—Zac Johnson*

★ **Mission Chapel Memories 1971–1975** / Oct. 9, 2001 / Raven ✦✦✦✦✦

Dolly Parton is such an American icon that it is easy to forget how she achieved her fame and success. Years of magazine covers, movies, crossover hits, and Dollywood have tended to obscure the small-town girl who first came to light as a duet partner with Porter Wagoner and then quickly established herself as a major talent in her own right with a series of quiet adventurous records for RCA that blended country, folk, bluegrass, and pop. Raven's brilliant collection *Mission Chapel Memories 1971-1975* concentrates on that period, taking a bold decision to sidestep a predictable recycling of hits in favor of drawing a full portrait of Dolly's considerable musical achievements during the early '70s. There are hits here, of course, including "Coat of Many Colors," "Jolene," and "The Bargain Store," but they're here because they support the collection's musical thesis that during this short span of time Parton grew considerably. And the disc proves that thesis to be absolutely true. With the exception of Bill Owens' "Love Is Only as Strong (As Your Weakest Moment)," everything here was written either by Parton or Wagoner, and they are as low-key as her later hits were splashy. While they are straightforward and often low-key, they're not simple; the words are evocative, as is the music, which grows from unadorned singer/songwriter-styled tunes to complex, multi-layered music, filled with little details yet retaining that pure, unadorned sound and feel. Parton was making this music while she was having hits, but this is every bit as adventurous and unpredictable as the folk-influenced progressive country at the time, and it still retains a highly individual, compelling sound years later. Yes, this an idiosyncratic compilation without many hits, but it's arguably more essential than the stacks of hits collections she's had over the years because it cuts to the heart of her music and explains exactly why she's important. Consider this as a compliment to one of those hits collections or, better yet, go here first and gain a new appreciation for the depth of her music and work backward toward the familiar items. *—Stephen Thomas Erlewine*

Joshua/Coat of Many Colors / Oct. 9, 2001 / BMG International ✦✦✦✦

In 2001, BMG International released *Joshua/Coat of Many Colors* on one compact disc, which combined a pair of Dolly Parton albums originally released in 1971 by RCA—*Joshua* and *Coat of Many Colors*. *—John Bush*

RCA Country Legends / Feb. 19, 2002 / RCA ✦✦✦✦

Dolly Parton's volume in the *RCA Country Legends* series attempts to survey territory previously covered by two volumes of *The Essential Dolly Parton* series, still the best retrospective of her period as a Nashville and (later) American icon. This collection has only 16 tracks, but still stretches all the way from her earthy late-'60s material to the heavily pop-slanted hits of the early '80s. Fans of her early recordings will enjoy hearing a pair of early album tracks (1967's "False Eyelashes" and 1969's "Evening Shade"), but will surely wonder why the volume bypassed not only all of her charting singles from the '60s, but one of her signature songs, "Coat of Many Colors." Those who know her best for pop performances will find a handful of hits, but not nearly enough to love. At best, *RCA Country Legends* does function as a competent hits collection; it includes plenty of country number ones ("Joshua," "The Bargain Store," "Jolene") as well as most of her pop crossovers of the late '70s and early '80s ("I Will Always Love You," "9 to 5," "Here You Come Again"). *—John Bush*

Halos & Horns / Jul. 9, 2002 / Sugar Hill ✦✦✦

More angelic than devilish, *Halos & Horns*, the third in a series of back-to-the-roots styled acoustic albums the legendary country singer recorded for Sugar Hill label, again boasts superior musicianship and a loose but not necessarily low-key style. A mix of new songs, re-recorded obscurities Parton felt deserved another chance ("What a Heartache" got lost on the soundtrack to *Rhinestone*, "Shattered Image" is a little-known gem from 1976's *All I Can Do* album, and an unrecorded oldie "John Daniel" goes back nearly 35 years), and high-profile covers of Bread's "If" and Zeppelin's "Stairway to Heaven" find the singer/songwriter is in excellent voice and exuberant spirits. Some of the new compositions, such as the ballad "If Only" (written for a movie about Mae West that Parton was making when recording this album, but deemed too sad for the soundtrack) and the stirring "Raven Dove," with a full gospel backing, are nearly the equal of the singer's best work. The jaunty tempo but sorrowful lyrics of "Dagger Through the Heart" is classic bluegrass complete with banjo and fiddle and an example of Parton at her finest. Not everything works; "These Old Bones," a winding story-song marred by Parton taking the voice of an old woman on the chorus, is sappy if well intentioned, and her version of "If" remains a bit smarmy, even torn down to its acoustic roots. But her take on an album-closing "Stairway to Heaven" (given the thumbs up from no lesser experts than Jimmy Page and Robert Plant, who had to approve Parton's slightly altered lyrics) smartly and successfully refashions the song's dense themes into a contemporary gospel ode which retains the mystery of the original even as it is rearranged for this project's folk/bluegrass direction. Stirring, unpretentious yet powerful, *Halos & Horns* effectively continues Parton's glorifying of her mountain roots. She subsequently launched her first tour in a decade after this disc's 2002 release. *—Hal Horowitz*

★ **Ultimate Dolly Parton** / Jun. 3, 2003 / RCA ✦✦✦✦✦

Dolly Parton has had countless collections, including many billed as either "definitive" or "ultimate," which is the billing given BMG Heritage's 2003 release. Running 20 tracks over the course of a single disc, this *Ultimate Dolly Parton* keeps its focus on the big hits, including a large stretch of hits from the late '70s and early '80s, including "Here You Come Again," "It's All Wrong, But It's All Right," "Heartbreaker," "9 to 5," and "Islands in the Stream." In addition to this, there are a couple of latter-day tracks, her Trio recording of "To Know Him Is to Love Him" and early hits "Joshua," "Coat of Many Colors," "I Will Always Love You," and "Jolene." So, in short, it's her most familiar material on one disc, something that has certainly been done before in her catalog, but it's done particularly well here. As a roundup of her hits, it works very well and it's also a good introduction, although listeners who are interested in her purer country and more ambitious music are advised to pick up Raven's superb *Mission Chapel Memories: 1971-1975* instead. *—Stephen Thomas Erlewine*

Stella Parton

b. May 4, 1949, Sevier County, KY

Guitar, Autoharp, Vocals / Country-Pop

Stella Parton was the younger sister of Dolly Parton and had a few hits of her own during the latter half of the '70s. She was born in Sevier County, KY, in 1949 and first sang on a local Knoxville TV show with Dolly at age seven. Her radio debut came two years later, and she and two other Parton sisters soon formed a group to sing both gospel music and commercial jingles around eastern Tennessee. Parton started working on her own songwriting in high-school but married and got pregnant with her first child prior to graduation. After some time away from music, she started her own record label, Country Soul, in 1975 and released an album called *I Want to Hold You in My Dreams Tonight*. Its title track was a substantial national hit, climbing into the country Top Ten, and she landed a major-label deal with Elektra in 1976. Her 1977 duet with Carmol Taylor, "Neon Woman," was somewhat successful, and she scored three Top 20 hits over 1977-1978 with "The Danger of a Stranger," "Four Little Letters," and "Standard Lie Number One."

She recorded a total of three albums for Elektra through 1979, then departed to record sporadically for smaller labels during the '80s. She scored minor chart singles in 1982 and 1989 but spent most of the decade working as an actress in Broadway musicals like *The Best Little Whorehouse in Texas* and *Seven Brides for Seven Brothers*; she also wrote and choreographed shows at her sister's Dollywood theme park and in the early '90s published a Southern cookbook. *—Steve Huey*

Country Sweet / 1978 / Elektra ✦✦✦

Stella Parton will always be known as the younger sister of Dolly Parton, but she has songwriting talent and a voice that is similar to, but distinct from, her more famous sibling. *Country Sweet*, one of a few albums she released on Elektra in the mid-'70s, contains two of her biggest hits: "Standard Lie Number One" and the slick Shel Silverstein co-composition "The Danger of a Stranger," which verges on country-disco. Parton's own songs are more down to earth, with the best of the bunch being the haunting "The More the Change." A handful of good songs by name songwriters and a cover of the old Burl Ives classic "A Little Bitty Tear" round out an appealing album that is, in places, even better than the hit singles it generated. *—Greg Adams*

The Best of Stella Parton / 1979 / Elektra ✦✦✦

The budget-priced *Best of Stella Parton* is a decent retrospective encompassing her early country hits from the '70s recorded for Elektra, including "Four Little Letters," "Neon Woman," and her first hit, "I Wanna Hold You in My Dreams." If you're looking for a collection containing Stella Parton's post-Elektra hits, check out *Anthology* on Renaissance. *—Al Campbell*

● **Anthology** / Oct. 13, 1998 / Renaissance ✦✦✦✦

The budget-priced *Anthology* is a solid retrospective encompassing Stella Parton's country hits from 1975 to 1989. Its two dozen tracks include most of the singer's biggest smashes (including "I Want to Hold You in My Arms Tonight," "The Danger of a Stranger," "Standard Lie Number One" and "Stormy Weather") as well as selected album cuts; only the omission of chart entries like the Top 20 hit "Four Little Letters," "It's Not Funny Anymore" and "I'll Miss You" keeps it from being a definitive overview. *—Hank Small*

Johnny Paycheck (Donald Lytle)

b. May 31, 1938, Greenfield, OH, **d.** Feb. 18, 2003, Nashville, TN

Vocals, Bass, Guitar, Guitar (Steel) / Traditional Country, Outlaw Country, Honky Tonk

The first time that many people ever heard of Johnny Paycheck was in 1977, when his "Take This Job and Shove It" inspired one-man wildcat strikes all over America. The next time was in 1985, when he was arrested for shooting a man at a bar in Hillsboro, OH. That Paycheck is remembered for a fairly amusical novelty song and a violent crime (for which he spent two years in prison) is a shame, for it just so happens that he is one of the mightiest honky tonkers of his time. Born and raised in Greenfield, OH, Paycheck was performing in talent contests by the age of nine and riding the rails as a drifter by the time he turned 15. After a Navy stint landed him in the brig for two years, he arrived in Nashville, where he performed in the bands of Porter Wagoner, Faron Young, Ray Price, and George Jones. He recorded several singles under the name Donny Young, then, in 1965, cut his first sides as Johnny Paycheck for the Hilltop label.

A year later, he and gadfly producer Aubrey Mayhew started the Little Darlin' label, for which Paycheck recorded his greatest work. Marked by Lloyd Green's knockout steel guitar and Paycheck's broad, resonant vocals (not to mention his rounder's sense of humor) his Little Darlin' records of the 1960s have since become cult favorites. After splitting with Mayhew (and after running his life into the gutter), Paycheck made a celebrated comeback on Epic in the 1970s. "Take This Job and Shove It" was the most famous result, though ballads like "She's All I Got" and "Someone to Give My Love To" are far more indicative of his stylistic range.

Born Donald Lytle, Paycheck began playing guitar when he was six, and within three years, he was performing talent contests across the state. When he was 15, he ran away from home, hitchhiking, and hoboing his away across the country, singing in honky tonks and clubs along the way. By his late teens, he had joined the Navy, but while he was serving, he assaulted a superior officer and was convicted of court martial. As a result, he spent two years in the brig. Upon his release, he moved to Nashville, where made the acquaintance of Buddy Killen at Decca Records, who offered him a contract. At Decca,

Paycheck released two rockabilly singles on the label under the name Donny Young; neither were hits. Shortly afterward, he moved to Mercury, where he released two country singles, which were also failures. By that time, he had begun supporting other musicians, playing bass and occasionally steel guitar with Porter Wagoner, Faron Young, and Ray Price. He frequently moved between employers because of his short-fused temper. Paycheck finally found his match in George Jones. He stayed with Jones for four years, fronting the Jones Boys between 1962 and 1966, and singing backup on George's hits "I'm a People," "The Race Is On," and "Love Bug."

Toward the end of his stint with Jones, Donald Lytle refashioned himself as Johnny Paycheck, taking his name from a Chicago heavyweight boxer. Late in 1965, he relaunched his solo career with the assistance of producer Aubrey Mayhew, who produced a pair of singles—"A-11" and "Heartbreak Tennessee"—for Hilltop Records. Though it only charted at number 26, "A-11" caused a sensation within the country community, earning several Grammy nominations as well as reviews that compared Paycheck to his mentor, Jones. In 1966, he and Mayhew formed Little Darlin' Records, primarily designing the label to promote Paycheck, but also recording Jeannie C. Riley, Bobby Helms, and Lloyd Green. That summer, "The Lovin' Machine" became Paycheck's first Top Ten hit. Also that year, he wrote Tammy Wynette's first hit, "Apartment #9," with Bobby Austin and Fuzzy Owen; Paycheck also wrote Ray Price's number-three hit "Touch My Heart."

All of Paycheck's recordings for Little Darlin' Records rank among his grittiest, hardest country, but they weren't necessarily big hits. Between 1967 and 1969, Paycheck had eight more hit singles, with each record progressively charting at a lower position than its predecessor—"Motel Time Again" reached number 13 in early 1967, while "If I'm Gonna Sink" climbed to number 73 in late 1968. Though "Wherever You Are" showed signs of a comeback in the summer of 1969, peaking at number 31, the label went bankrupt shortly after its release, partially due to Paycheck's declining commercial performance, partially due to his heavy drinking and erratic behavior. Over the course of the next year, he moved to California and sunk deeply into substance abuse. Meanwhile, Billy Sherrill at Epic Records had been searching for Paycheck with the hopes of producing his records. The label finally tracked him down in 1971 and offered him a contract, provided that he cleaned himself up. Paycheck accepted the offer and, with Sherrill's assistance, kicked his addictions.

Like many of Sherrill's records of the early '70s, his Paycheck recordings were heavily produced and often layered with strings. Though this was a shift from the hardcore country that Paycheck made on Little Darlin', the new approach was a hit—his debut single for the label, "She's All I Got," became a number-two hit upon its fall 1971 release. It was quickly followed by another Top Ten hit, "Someone to Give My Love To," and Paycheck was finally becoming a star. During the next four years, he had 12 additional hit singles—including 1973's Top Ten singles "Something About You I Love" and "Mr. Lovemaker," and 1974's "For a Minute There"—with the more accessible, pop-oriented songs Sherrill crafted for him, but Paycheck's wild ways hadn't changed all that much. In 1972, he was convicted of check forgery and, in 1976, was saddled with a paternity suit, tax problems, and bankruptcy. Accordingly, he shifted his musical style in the mid-'70s to put him in step with the renegade outlaw country movement.

Paycheck's first outlaw album, 1976's *11 Months and 29 Days* (which happened to be the length of his suspended sentence for passing a bad check), featured a photo of him in a jail cell on the cover, signalling his change of direction. Initially, his outlaw records weren't hits, but early in 1977 he returned to the Top Ten with a pair of Top Ten singles, "Slide Off of Your Satin Sheets" and "I'm the Only Hell (Mama Ever Raised)." Later that year, he released his cover of David Allan Coe's "Take This Job and Shove It," which became his biggest hit, spending two weeks at number one; its B-side, "Colorado Kool-Aid," also charted at number 50. Soon, Paycheck's records were becoming near-parodies of his lifestyle, as the title "Me and the I.R.S." and "D.O.A. (Drunk on Arrival)" indicated. Nevertheless, he stayed at the top of the charts, with "Friend, Lover, Wife" and "Mabellene" both reaching number seven in late 1978 and early 1979.

Shortly after the twin success of those singles, his career began to crumble due to his excessive, violent behavior. In 1979, his former manager Glenn Ferguson began a prolonged and difficult legal battle. In 1981, a flight attendant for Frontier Airlines sued him for slander after he began a fight on a plane. The following year, he was arrested for alleged rape. The charges were later reduced and he was fined, but by that point, Epic had had enough and dropped him from the label. Paycheck moved over to AMI, where he had a number of small hit singles between 1984 and 1985. Later in 1985, he had a barroom brawl with a stranger in Hillsboro, OH, that ended with Paycheck shooting and injuring his opponent. The singer was arrested for aggravated assault and spent the next four years appealing the sentence while he recorded for Mercury Records. None of his singles for the label reached the Top 40, and he was dropped from the label in 1987. He spent 1988 at Desperado Records before signing with Damascus the following year, after his conversion to Christianity.

In 1989, Paycheck's appeals had expired and he was sentenced to the Chillicothe Correctional Institute. He spent two years at the prison, even performing a concert with Merle Haggard at the jail during his stint, before being released on parole in January 1991. Following his release, Paycheck kept a low profile, playing shows in Branson, MO, and recording for the small label Playback Records. After battling diabetes and emphysema for a number of years, Paycheck passed away in February 2003. He was 64. *—Dan Cooper*

☆ **The Lovin' Machine** / 1966 / Little Darlin' ✦✦✦✦✦

Upon glancing at the awesome cartoon cover of Johnny Paycheck's classic *The Lovin' Machine* album, one thing becomes immediately apparent—that you know the music in the grooves will be as amazing as the cover. Another oddity makes itself apparent when you flip it over: There are 14 tracks instead of the standard ten that usually appear on country albums. Finally, there is one more, a single performance credit: Lloyd Green on pedal steel. Musically, this is the hardest of honky tonk records. First there's the loopy title track, where it becomes difficult to tell whether Paycheck is talking about a woman or his ride that he picks up women in. Next comes "Miller's Cave," a murder ballad of the most desperate kind, with a character who is unrepentant and yet gains his punishment by becoming lost in the same cave where he buries the bodies of his lover and her backdoor man. In typical Paycheck psychobilly fashion, this is followed with a cheating torch song. Side one's most chilling song, however, is Paycheck's definitive outlaw mayhem ballad, the Mayhew-Lytle song that is as infamous as it is great, "(Pardon Me) I've Got Someone to Kill." Green's steel colors the end of each line with an atmospheric tension that grows with every syllable. It's the story of a cuckolded man whose revenge will not be complete until he kills everyone, including himself. "This gun will buy back the pride they took from me/And also end this life of mine that's worthless now." In addition, there's a killer read of Merle Haggard's "Swinging Doors," done in swinging honky tonk style. As if "I've Got Someone to Kill" wasn't enough, there's an avenging rocking honky tonker in "The Johnsons of Turkey Ridge," which celebrates the mass murder of a family. But the classics don't end there; Paycheck's stellar read of "Between Love and Hate," with it's sonorous cello underneath the mix, is moving and strange. The set ends with "I Know I Never Will," with Green playing counterpoint to Paycheck's devoted romantic lyric, although he still sounds menacing. In all this is a crazy golden-era honky tonk record, one that allows for no compromise, no Nashville input (a good portion of it was recorded in New York), and no allowance for resolving any of the contradictions in Paycheck's voice and delivery. It's a true masterpiece. *—Thom Jurek*

Johnny Paycheck at Carnegie Hall / 1966 / Little Darlin' ✦✦✦✦✦

Despite the title and the photo of Paycheck in black-tie garb, his debut album is actually a Nashville studio product. But what a hopped-up product it is, making most mid-'60s honky tonk sound like Jim Nabors with steel guitar. *—Dan Cooper*

Jukebox Charlie / 1967 / Little Darlin' ✦✦✦✦✦

Country Soul / 1967 / Little Darlin' ✦✦✦

Here's Paycheck in an album of country cover versions, pretty much all big hit songs from the mid-'60s. Some of them are of the done-to-death variety, others forever tainted by Tom Jones and there's even "Danny Boy." The liner notes are not completely out of whack when they promise that Paycheck can bring a certain type of soul to a song that no one else can, and anyone who doubts that Paycheck possesses a highly polished vocal style and superior singing abilities just needs to check out the way he navigates his way through these titles. Nonetheless, he tries to play it too straight here and while it certainly would have been fun to hear his outlaw outfits of the '70s tackle this material, nothing quite like that happened and the song choices are largely pedestrian. Two Paycheck originals—"Apartment Number 9" and "Touch My Heart"—are head and shoulders above everything else. A curiosity of the original album sleeve is, in small print, Paycheck endorsing Baldwin guitars and amplifiers. *—Eugene Chadbourne*

Greatest Hits / 1968 / Little Darlin' ✦✦✦

The eager to please Little Darlin' outfit put together this collection of Johnny Paycheck recordings from 1965-1968; eight out of these 14 songs were later included in the Country Music Foundation's *The Real Mr. Heartache* compact disc retrospective from 1996. It would be nice to say that the best songs from these years were assembled for this album but, as is the norm with this company, there isn't much rhyme or reason to the choice of tracks or the sequencing. Nonetheless, it is hard to find much fault with the material or performances included, and much has been written about the high quality of playing from a group of session regulars that includes fiddler Buddy Spicher and pedal steel whiz Lloyd Green, the latter providing big old buckets of fat, distorted lead runs. In point of fact, an experimental distortion unit was invented for some of these sides by the engineer, Glenn Snoddy. Fans of country & western at its most miserable probably can't do better than Paycheck from this period, with one song beginning "Lately life with you has been unbearable." And of course there should be mention of "The Cave," a rare country & western song about a nuclear holocaust and one of the finest protest songs ever recorded. And here it is on an album with "Ballad of the Green Berets." Truly something for everybody. *—Eugene Chadbourne*

Wherever You Are / 1969 / Little Darlin' ✦✦✦✦

Again / 1970 / Certron ✦✦✦

Post-Little Darlin', but still Mayhew-produced, he keeps right on kicking. Included is "Living the Life of a Dog," a hilarious romp that probably had multiple meanings for Paycheck. *—Dan Cooper*

☆ **She's All I Got** / 1971 / Koch ✦✦✦✦✦

Moving over to Epic in 1971, Johnny Paycheck soon aligned with the label's top producer, Billy Sherrill. Given Paycheck's reputation for rowdy honky tonk and Sherrill's proclivity for opulent productions, the pairing did seem a little odd, but at that point, Johnny hadn't had a Top Ten single in five years and needed a jolt to send him back to the charts. So, he tempered his wild ways and made a Billy Sherrill record in *She's All I Got*, complete with the strings and heavy emphasis on romantic material. Paycheck had not been strongly associated with love songs prior to *She's All I Got*—and once his wild-eyed outlaw days began, he was hardly seen as an ambassador of love—but his slower sides for Little Darlin' proved that he had a strong honky tonk ballad style, similar to his protégé/peer George Jones, and Sherrill exploited that side of him throughout this lovely record. What makes the album work is that the singer and producer found a common ground by muting both the gritty hardcore country of Paycheck and Sherrill's lush, layered arrangements. Strings have been left behind, but there are plenty of choirs and weeping steel guitars, and even when the production is a little thick for a Paycheck song, or the tempos a little too sprightly, it works because the material is first-rate, because Sherrill's production is deft and sensitive, and, of course, because Johnny Paycheck is a superb singer, easily adapting his style to this setting. With its romantic bent, it may be somewhat of an anomaly within his catalog, yet it no doubt stands as one of his consistently greatest albums (all the while setting the template for the great Sherrill-produced George Jones albums of the '70s). *—Stephen Thomas Erlewine*

Someone to Give My Love To / 1972 / Epic ✦✦✦✦

Somebody Loves Me / 1972 / Epic ✦✦✦

Song & Dance Man / 1974 / Epic ✦✦✦

11 Months and 29 Days / 1976 / Epic ✦✦✦

Slide Off of Your Satin Sheets / 1977 / Epic ✦✦✦✦

Take This Job & Shove It / 1978 / Epic ✦✦✦✦

Greatest Hits, Vol. 2 / 1978 / Epic ✦✦✦✦✦

The volume two separates more than just a pair of greatest-hits collections. In this case, it was the second coming of Johnny Paycheck as a chart hitmaker with David Allan Coe's "Take This Job and Shove It" and a major-label contract after years of country hits on the indie Little Darlin' label. This is pretty much the whole arc of his career with Epic and even at that the label had to come up with some padding in order to fill up even a shortie album. The half-dozen hits that are here strut their stuff right proudly and the cover version of "Rhythm Guitar" with its great line "Nobody wants to play rhythm and guitar behind Jesus" is enjoyable. Paycheck shouldn't have bothered trying to cover a Paul Simon song, though. *—Eugene Chadbourne*

The Outlaw / 1978 / Little Darlin' ✦✦✦

No surprise that the Little Darlin' folks would have wanted to cash in on Johnny Paycheck's Top Ten status during 1978, so they slapped out this item, barely half the length of a normal LP and sporting a photo of Paycheck about ten years older, and ten times more the outlaw, than he was when he recorded the tracks herein, which are plucked from his 1966-1968 recording period. But what is here is fantastic country music from the honky tonk tradition yet strangely influenced by '60s rock as well as Cajun and blues. What gives it all that special edge is that Paycheck is willing to go just a bit further in his stories and portraits than other country artists. The supreme example of this could be the infamous "I've Got Someone to Kill," one of three tracks here chosen in 1996 for the Country Music Foundation's *The Real Mr. Heartache* Paycheck retrospective. Just as good is "The Johnsons of Turkey Ridge," mistakenly written in the possessive in the credits, an ironic mistake since the song has to do with feudin' and fightin' over land ownership up in the hills and has to be in the running for the honor of country song with the highest body count. "The Ballad of Frisco Bay" is a unique and marvelous prison escape ballad, while "California Dreams" is wonderfully '60s influenced, telling the tale of a galoot on the roam while the pickers come up with various sitar and fuzz box style riffs. Plus, there are also the "Bayou Bum," "The Loser," and the morose character quick to admit "I'm a Coward." *—Eugene Chadbourne*

Bars, Booze & Blondes / 1979 / Little Darlin' ✦✦✦✦

This slice-of-life LP comes from Johnny Paycheck's late-'60s heyday, when the future boss-hater was still championing rough-hewn honky tonk during the rise of Billy Sherrill's slick Nashville sound (Paycheck would soon switch ranks and cash in with several Sherrill-produced hits of his own during the '70s). Cut for the Paycheck-focused Little Darlin' label, *Bars, Booze & Blondes* finds the pre-rehab singer telling it straight from the tavern heart, wryly musing about his alchy predicament ("The Pint of No Return," "I Drop More Than I Drink"), barroom denizens ("We're the Kind of People"), and cheatin' songs ("The Meanest Jukebox in Town"). He even finds time for some therapy on "Problem Solvin' Doctor," which features a barroom shrink in office between nine p.m. and two a.m. and offering a nice line in jug prescriptions. Nicely peppered with shades of George Jones and Ray Price (both former employers), Paycheck's account of life in the shadows of Oly and Hamms neon makes for a welcome complement to Country Music Foundation's excellent *The Real Mr. Heartache* roundup of many of the singer's other Little Darlin' highlights. *—Stephen Cook*

Armed and Crazy / 1979 / Epic ✦✦✦

Everybody's Got a Family, Meet Mine / 1980 / Epic ✦✦

On the cover we see a gang of sleazy individuals, the members of Johnny Paycheck's band and road crew. The song titles promise us a peek into a depraved honky tonk lifestyle, but they don't really tell a good story the way the best country songs do, and in the end it seems this is the album where the Paycheck outlaw image, although still greasy and grungy, starts to seem like an imitation of itself. The "family" was his finest working band, and the efforts of instrumentalists such as the striking harmonica player P.T. Gazell insure that everything has a nice kick to it. But Paycheck is capable of much more substance than this, and some of the moves just backfire. After success in the past grabbing chestnuts out of the oldtime music bag, this album's "Rollin' in My Sweet Baby's Arms" just comes across as corny. Right in the middle of it all lies an absolute masterpiece, though, the brooding and frightening "Billy Bardo," a tale of a narc that is told with the sing-songy repetition of something like "Froggie Went a Courtin'," making the violent surprise ending that much more potent. Despite the high visible profile of the working band in the artwork, the tracks actually feature a larger than usual quotient of session sidemen, which doesn't seemed to have helped matters. *—Eugene Chadbourne*

New York Town / 1980 / Epic ✦✦✦✦✦

Country & western music is not a genre known for superior live albums, but here is one of the best and a feather in the cap to producer Billy Sherrill, commonly known for his slick studio productions. Here it is Paycheck's best working band on the other end of the microphones, cranking out a pretty typical set down at New York's Lone Star Café. In 1980, there were not many country artists working regularly in the Big Apple; it was mostly those who could offer outlaw credential that were offered a stage. On the strength of this and his Top Ten hit "Take This Job and Shove It," Epic brought Paycheck into New York City to record live, publicizing the outlaw image while simultaneously attempting to tone him down slightly for the cosmopolitan New Yorkers. The success of this advertising campaign was diminished slightly by a Paycheck interview in *the Village Voice* in which he described his condition during parts of his career thusly: "I coulda puked and opened a liquor store." He is shown looking jaunty on the cover, and the album's opening track and title song is a puffy bit of fluff, Paycheck mouthing highly original lines such as "They call it the Big Apple . . ." in his ever so smooth baritone. From then on, things kick off beautifully with a manic-tempo, almost punk rock version of the old-time sawhorse "Ragged but Right." Editing is subtle as the group moves from one tune right into the next. The turn between "Ragged but Right" and "'She Thinks I Still Care" would most certainly cause a wreck if done on the highway. This band is absolutely as tight as a band can get, and features two outstanding soloists: P.T. Gazell on harmonica and Jim Murphy on pedal steel. Most of the songs have been previously recorded by Paycheck, but the new ballad "In Memory of a Memory" is something of a showstopper, the type of tragic material this artist does to the hilt. "Take This Job and Shove It" gets a pretty perfunctory run-through at the end, yet some of the other performances earn the rare distinction of sounding even better than the original studio versions. *—Eugene Chadbourne*

Encore / 1981 / Epic ✦✦

☆ **Mr. Hag Told My Story** / 1981 / Epic ✦✦✦✦✦

Tribute albums are part of country music's bread and butter, with artists routinely paying tribute to their favorite vocalists and songwriters through records filled with covers. Since it's such a routine event, it's easy to take them for granted, particularly when they often cover familiar ground, recycling the same hits over and over again, which is why a tribute record as sublime and subtle as Johnny Paycheck's *Mr. Hag Told My Story* can sometime slip through the cracks. Which is unfortunate, since this is a sterling example of what a tribute album can be. Released in 1981 as his final album for Epic—and thereby inadvertently capping off Paycheck's prime—*Mr. Hag Told My Story* finds Johnny digging through the Merle Haggard songbook, assembling ten perfect barroom ballads and then, in a great coup, recording them with the Strangers themselves, including three duets with Merle. Instead of picking predictable songs, Paycheck avoids the really big hits, choosing a bunch of lesser-known gems Haggard has penned. There are some big hits here—"Turnin' Off a Memory" and "You Don't Have Very Far to Go" as well as the Tommy Collins-written "Carolyn," which is given a great duet—but the emphasis is on personal favorites of Johnny and Merle. Paycheck states exactly that in the liner notes, but the performances are where he offers proof, because he and the Strangers give these a wonderful, lived-in feel, rich with emotion and graceful interplay between the band. Since there aren't many big hits here, it may have been overlooked at the time, barely scraping the country Top 40, but this perfectly executed tribute ranks not just as one of Paycheck's finest, but as one of the great late-night honky tonk records in country. *—Stephen Thomas Erlewine*

Biggest Hits / 1983 / Epic ✦✦✦✦✦

Biggest Hits was released in 1983, just after Johnny Paycheck's streak of big hits on Epic was ending. It was the perfect opportunity to summarize his extended commercial peak, but the compilers chose not to strictly follow chart positions. Many big tunes—Top Ten hits, even—are missing, but the ten songs here hold together because they're nearly all great barroom anthems, whether it's a weeper like "She's All I Got," "Fifteen Beers," the saloon saga "Colorado Cool-Aid," or David Allan Coe's rowdy "Take This Job and Shove It." Subsequent collections covered more ground, with 2002's *The Soul & the Edge* taking the crown for its comprehensiveness, but as a lean slab of Paycheck's best outlaw music, this can't be beat. *—Stephen Thomas Erlewine*

Live In Branson, MO, USA / 1993 / Laserlight ✦✦

Outlaw country artist Paycheck, who increasingly tried to settle down in his later years, cut this promising live set when he was on the verge of starting his own theatre in the resort town of Branson, MO, a mecca for performers who are tired of the road and want the audience to come to them for a change. From the look of things, this is the sort of country & western set that is released too infrequently—a live set recorded direct to two-track without any studio gloss. And particularly in the case of Paycheck, it has none of the homogenized production that has plagued recordings from his post-prison comeback years, as if an unsuccessful attempt was being made to drain all the personality out of the music for fear of offending anyone. Unfortunately, this CD is hampered byproduction problems that are more serious than the lack of punctuation in the abbreviation for Missouri on the front cover. The live recording balance is tilted unfavorably toward the drummer, which is a total drag, as this is an uninteresting drummer, able to keep a beat and pull off some fancy double time stuff, but lacking even the simplest notion of how to create a drum sound that makes the other players and the song sound good. Picking from guitar and steel guitar is pretty good, but it is never loud enough to have the impact it ought to. Remember, Paycheck is a fellow who made a name for himself not only with rowdy lyrics and attitude, but by featuring over-the-top, heavily distorted pedal steel licks on his early Starday albums. The program here is an intelligent mix of his famous hits and tasteful choices such as Hank Cochran's wonderful "A-11" and Paycheck himself is in superior vocal form. He connects with the material each time out, and the song he wrote before serving his prison sentence, "Old Violin," is really moving. His comments between songs are enjoyable and add character to the proceedings, especially the intro to "Colorado Kool-Aid," wherein he recounts how he realized it was possible to score a hit song based on any subject, so why not "one about some old boy who gets his ear cut off?" Production also gets in the way here, as these spoken asides are mixed so low the listener would have to adjust the volume each time in order to understand what Paycheck is talking about, then turn it back down again when the band starts up. Quieter parts of songs—and the band definitely has a knack for dynamics—annoyingly also almost vanish in the mastering. Lead guitarist Jeff Lytle is possibly a relation of the star, whose real name is Donald Lytle. *—Eugene Chadbourne*

★ **The Real Mr. Heartache: The Little Darlin' Years** / 1996 / Country Music Foundation ✦✦✦✦✦

For the casual country fan who only knows Johnny Paycheck from his late-'70s outlaw period ("Take This Job and Shove It," a hit song so huge that its title was made into a major film), these 24 sides from the mid-'60s will come as a major revelation. Paycheck has always come by his outlaw image honestly and he had been knocking around Nashville since 1958, cutting rockabilly country singles under the name Donny Young when he came to the attention of producer/record executive Aubrey Mayhew in 1962. Forming a partnership, they produced a spate of hard country singles for Hilltop before starting up their own label, Little Darlin'. Figuring the easiest way to get noticed was to be as wild as possible, they uncorked a rash of singles (and a couple of albums) that pushed the darkest side of honky tonk lyrics to their limits while simultaneously widening the limits of 45-rpm reproduction with stinging, high-end mixes perfect for AM country radio stations and truck-stop jukeboxes alike. These weren't merely honky tonk records bucking the tide of the '60s Nashville sound; this was country music with a wild-hair, unrepentant redneck attitude to it. This dissolute persona is reflected in many of the titles alone, from "If I'm Gonna Sink (I Might as Well Go to the Bottom)," to "He's in a Hurry (To Get Home to My Wife)," to the absolutely scary "(Pardon Me) I've Got Someone to Kill," the mood getting blacker and blacker with each keening wail of Lloyd Green's steel guitar. Paycheck may have had bigger (much bigger) hits than the 24 tracks collected here, but he never made any greater music than this. *—Cub Koda*

The Best of Johnny Paycheck / Jul. 15, 1996 / Curb ✦✦✦✦
The Best of Johnny Paycheck, Vol. 1 is a budget-line collection that draws from material written during his heyday in the '70s. With such hits as "Take This Job and Shove It," "She's All I Got," "Mr. Lovemaker," and "Slide Off of Your Satin Sheets," this disc functions as a good introduction to Paycheck's sound for the budget-minded. *—Thom Owens*

Super Hits / Aug. 12, 1997 / Sony ✦✦✦

16 Biggest Hits / Aug. 10, 1999 / Sony ✦✦✦✦
16 Biggest Hits may be missing some noteworthy songs, but it does provide an excellent summary of Johnny Paycheck's Columbia recordings between 1971 and 1978. Since it does contain the majority of his best-known songs—"She's All I Got," "Someone to Give My Love To," "Slide Off of Your Satin Sheets," "I'm the Only Hell (Mama Ever Raised)," "Drinkin' and Drivin'," "Me and the I.R.S.," "The Outlaw's Prayer," "Take this Job and Shove It"—at a mid-line price, it's an excellent introductory collection. *—Stephen Thomas Erlewine*

★ **The Soul & the Edge: The Best of Johnny Paycheck** / Mar. 2002 / Epic/Legacy ✦✦✦✦✦
Most listeners know Johnny Paycheck from "Take This Job and Shove It"—a song so popular and so iconic that it overshadows everything else Paycheck did, not just for pop fans but for country listeners. Couple that with a reputation for being a roughneck hellion and you have somebody who is known as a persona, not as a musician. And that's a real shame, as Epic/Legacy's *The Soul & the Edge: The Best of Johnny Paycheck* proves. As the first comprehensive CD collection of Paycheck's hit-making peak years of the '70s and '80s—his early years are documented on the stellar *The Real Mr. Heartache* collection—this collection is a revelation, offering definitive proof that he was one of the very greatest hardcore country singers. He could do it all: blue-collar rage ("Take This Job and Shove It," "Me and the I.R.S."), barroom weepers ("Slide Off of Your Satin Sheets," "I Did the Right Thing") and barroom ravers ("Fifteen Beers"), lush country-pop (the Billy Sherrill-produced "She's All I Got") and gritty country-soul (a George Jones duet on "You Better Move On"), tough-guy laments ("I'm the Only Hell (My Mama Ever Raised)") and tough-guy bravado ("Ragged Old Truck," "The Outlaw's Prayer"). Plus, there's a wicked, bizarre sense of humor, evidenced clearly on the neo-talking blues "Colorado Cool-Aid," illustrating that he didn't tame his wildness even at his popular peak. Then there's that voice—a resonant baritone with impeccable phrasing that some claim was an inspiration for George Jones' style (and listening to this and *Mr. Heartache* makes those claims quite credible). It all adds up to a collection that not only captures Paycheck at his peak, but also lays claim as one of the great country albums of its era, if not all time. It's the kind of collection an artist the stature of Johnny Paycheck deserves. *—Stephen Thomas Erlewine*

Tribute to George Jones / Jun. 18, 2002 / K-Tel ✦✦✦
The great unspoken truth behind this cheap, budget-line *Tribute to George Jones* is that the Possum's style owed a great deal to Johnny Paycheck. It's been argued (very convincingly, by the way) that George borrowed many of his signature phrases from Johnny, but there was no ill will there, since the two palled around for years, even recording a charmingly wretched, coked-out duet album at the end of the '70s. This release doesn't illustrate the care even of that release. It was sneaked into the market in 2002 without any fanfare, and it's impossible to tell when the album was recorded since there are no notes whatsoever. Given the clean, clean production and the edges on Paycheck's voice, it's likely that these are recent recordings. So, it's probably not of interest to anybody who isn't among the hardcore (unless you happen to pick this up at a truckstop on a road trip), but they will be pleasantly surprised by how nice this album is. Sure, Paycheck's voice *is* a little rough, stained with whiskey and tobacco, but it's still sweet and hits all the notes, and each of these ten songs (all predictable choices, outside of "Take Me" and "She's Mine") is given an unadorned hardcore country arrangement that isn't even sullied by the occasional synthesizer. No, it's not going to be the first Johnny Paycheck album you'd choose to play, nor is it as good as *Mr. Hag Told My Story in a Song*, but once it starts spinning, it sucks you in and proves itself to be an engaging, convincing listen. And that's a wondrous, welcome surprise. *—Stephen Thomas Erlewine*

Leon Payne

b. Jun. 15, 1917, Alba, TX, **d.** Sep. 11, 1969, San Antonio, TX
Songwriter, Vocals / Traditional Country, Honky Tonk, Nashville Sound/Countrypolitan
A popular singer and multi-instrumentalist of the postwar era, Leon Payne achieved his lasting fame as a songwriter whose most successful works—among them "Lost Highway" and "I Love You Because"—remain among the country music canon's most enduring compositions. Payne was born blind on June 15, 1917, in Alba, TX, and until the age of 18 he attended the Texas School for the Blind in Austin. There, he was encouraged by teachers to begin learning music as a method of supporting himself and became adept on guitar, piano, organ, drums, and trombone. In the mid-'30s he began performing with a number of area groups and began playing on radio in 1935.

Payne joined Bob Wills' Texas Playboys in 1938, and he remained affiliated with the group to some degree for the majority of his career. At about the same time, he began writing the first of the several thousand songs he would compose over the course his lifetime. In 1939, he cut his first solo recordings, including "You Don't Love Me but I'll Always Care" and "Down Where the Violets Grow," which evidenced his smooth, subtle vocal technique. After spending the large part of the next decade drifting through Texas performing under the moniker "The Texas Blind Hitchhiker," he hooked up with Jack Rhodes & the Rhythm Boys in 1948. He also played frequently with Wills.

In 1949, Payne formed his own band, the Lone Star Buddies, which guested on programs like the *Grand Ole Opry*, the *Louisiana Hayride*, and the *Big D Jamboree*. Two of his songs also reached the charts in cover versions: George Morgan scored a big hit with "Cry-Baby Heart," and more significantly, Hank Williams cut "Lost Highway," one of his most popular efforts. Payne's own recording of his "I Love You Because," penned for his wife Myrtle, became his biggest hit in 1950; in the same year, both Ernest Tubb and Clyde Moody cut their own versions of the song. Williams also had another hit with Payne's "They'll Never Take Her Love From Me." As the decade wore on, his songs grew even more popular among his contemporaries; among the most successful were Hank Snow's 1953 "For Now and Always" as well as a pair of hits for Carl Smith, 1954's "More Than Anything Else in the World" and 1956's "Doorstep to Heaven."

Payne continued to record through 1964; in 1963, he issued two LPs, *Leon Payne: A Living Legend of Country Music* and *Americana*, and at one point even cut a rockabilly single, "That Ain't It," under the alias Rock Rogers. Still, he never repeated the success of "I Love You Because," which was later resurrected by Johnny Cash in 1960 and as a huge 1963 pop hit for Al Martino. A year later, it was also covered by Jim Reeves, who earned posthumous success with Payne's "Blue Side of Lonesome" in 1966 and "I Heard a Heart Break Last Night" in 1968. Also charting with renditions of "I Love You Because" were Smith in 1969, Don Gibson in 1978, and Roger Whittaker in 1983; most importantly, it was one of the songs recorded by Elvis Presley during his legendary Sun Records sessions of 1954. In 1965, Payne suffered a heart attack which forced him to curtail his touring; that same year, his "Things Have Gone to Pieces" was a hit for George Jones. In 1967, Gibson covered "Lost Highway," and Johnny Darrell was successful with "They'll Never Take Her Love From Me." On September 11, 1969, Payne died following another heart attack. *—Jason Ankeny*

★ **I Love You Because** / Jun. 7, 2001 / Bear Family ✦✦✦✦✦
Leon Payne is a legendary figure in country music, but it's for his songs more than his recordings. He wrote hundreds of songs during the '40s, '50s, and '60s, including such perennial classics as "Lost Highway," "I Love You Because," "They'll Never Take Her Love Away From Me," "Blue Side of Lonesome," "You've Still Got a Place in My Heart," and "Things Have Gone to Pieces," but he never had the same rate of success as a recording artist, never following through on his initial success with "I Love You Because." This lack of success kept his recordings out of print for years, until Bear Family finally released the 30-track compilation *I Love You Because* in 1999. It's not just that this is the first serious reissue effort on this major artist—it's the first reissue *period*, and after listening to it, it's stunning that his recordings haven't gotten more attention before, since this is about as honky tonk as traditional country got in the early '50s. Unlike many Bear Family sets, this is not a complete recorded works set: It concentrates on Payne's recordings for Capitol between 1949 and 1952, when he was at his peak as a performer and when his records were selling at least regionally. Although this collection does include previously unreleased sides, it doesn't contain some of his major early work, including no version of "Lost Highway"; that song was recorded for the Nashville independent Bullet, and it, along with other tracks he cut for the label, is available on the superb Bear Family box set *A Shot in the Dark: Tennessee Jive*, which chronicles music made for Nashville indies and is unconditionally recommended. Payne also continued recording until the '60s, but it's actually better that this set is narrowly focused on the Capitol recordings, because it's not only all of a piece, but the shorter length will mean more country fans will be able to afford the time and money to explore this great music. Payne wrote all but two of the songs on this collection, and they cover a wide range of material, from weepy ballads and honky tonk ravers to novelties, romantic tunes, religious songs, and dance numbers, both slow and fast. Payne had a crackerjack band and a versatile voice that could be sweet or catch in his throat when the song called for it. While this music sounds familiar on the surface, it stands among the best country of the early '50s—even if it wasn't widely heard, Payne's Capitol work is consistently satisfying and musically rich, living up to his reputation as a songwriter. It's a shame it took so long for a collection like *I Love You Because* to be released, but it's hard not to be grateful that it finally came out, just like it's hard not to wish that the rest of his recordings will eventually be reissued. *—Stephen Thomas Erlewine*

Minnie Pearl (Sarah Ophelia Colley)

b. Oct. 25, 1912, Centerville, TN, **d.** 1996
Vocals / Traditional Country, Country Comedy
Minnie Pearl, a member of the *Grand Ole Opry* cast from 1940 until her death in 1996, was country music's preeminent comedian and one of the most widely recognized comic performers American culture has ever produced. With her straw hat and its dangling $1.98 price tag, her representation of herself as a man-chasing spinster in the small town of Grinder's Switch, TN, and her great-hearted holler of "How-DEE! I'm just so proud to be here" as she took to the *Opry* stage, Pearl became an icon of rural America even as she lovingly satirized its ways.

Cousin Minnie Pearl grew up among people quite different from the Uncle Nabob, Brother, and boyfriend Hezzie who populated her comic routines. Born Sarah Ophelia Colley, she was the daughter of a prosperous lumberman in Centerville, TN, and she attended tony Ward-Belmont College in Nashville as a theater major. As a young woman she favored classical music, not country. In college she focused especially on her dance classes, which would serve her well as she developed her top-notch stage presence, and after college she taught dance for several years. Then she took a job as a dramatic coach with a touring theater company based in Atlanta. As the group barnstormed through the Depression-era south, she would try to promote the group's shows by making brief appearances at local Lions' clubs and the like. She hit on a routine in which she delivered an impression of a small-town girl, Minnie Pearl, and then began to amplify the impression with traits she observed in people she met along the way. By 1939, the Minnie Pearl character was well developed, but Colley had to return to Centerville that year to help care for her ill mother.

In 1940 Colley appeared at a banking convention in Centerville at which some of the executives of the *Opry's* host station, WSM, happened to be in attendance. One suggested that she audition for the *Opry*, and despite the misgivings of *Opry* managers that she might be seen as ridiculing country people, she was accepted for a late-night slot. Several hundred cards and letters addressed to Minnie Pearl arrived at the station over the following weeks, and her place in the cast was assured. "I don't think people think of her so much as a show business act as a friend," Colley would later observe. During World War II, Pearl toured with the Camel Caravan, and she married Nashville pilot Henry Cannon in 1947. She authored a cookbook and became a prominent figure in Nashville social circles under the name of Sarah Cannon. But her greatest fame came from her *Opry* performances, some of which were broadcast nationally when the show hit prime time in the 1940s. In the late '40s and early '50s, Pearl often worked as part of a duo with comedian Rod Brasfield, and by 1957 she was famous enough to be featured on NBC television's *This Is Your Life* program.

Pearl went on to make many more television appearances in the '60s and '70s, eventually joining the cast of the hillbilly-themed variety show *Hee Haw*. That show made varied use of her comedic talents, featuring her in such segments as "Driving Miss Minnie" in addition to her usual Grinder's Switch settings. She was inducted into the Country Music Hall of Fame in 1975. Pearl was still a television fixture in the 1980s, when she appeared on TNN's *Nashville Now*. She also toured the country for much of her career and made a number of recordings. One of them, the recitation "Giddyup Go Answer," a rejoinder to Red Sovine's sentimental trucker number, became a Top Ten hit. Performing into the 1990s, Pearl suffered a stroke in 1991 and died five years later. *—James Manheim*

Howdee / 1963 / Starday ♦♦♦♦

America's Beloved Minnie Pearl / 1965 / Starday ♦♦♦

The Country Music Story / 1966 / Starday ♦♦♦

Howdy / 1967 / Sunset ♦♦♦

Lookin' for a Feller / 1970 / Nashville ♦♦

Queen of the Grand Ole Opry / Jul. 18, 1994 / Legacy/Columbia ♦♦

Queen of the Grand Ole Opry focuses solely on the standup comedy of Minnie Pearl, eschewing her occasional forays into music. The shoddy packaging provides no dates for the performances or other information, and in fact the six tracks are simply named "Track One" through "Track Six." Such deficiencies aside, this is a passable document of Minnie Pearl's schtick, which didn't change substantially over time, and which occasionally borrowed from other sources (Uncle Dave Macon, for one). Her humor was straightforward, repetitive and corny with occassional (very) mild double entendres, and might test the patience even of fervent Jerry Clower fans. Whatever prejudice or fondness one may have regarding Minnie's brand of country comedy, her significance in the history of the *Grand Ole Opry* is indisputable, and here is a record of her act for those who care to investigate. *—Greg Adams*

● **The Best of Minnie Pearl** / 1996 / Nashville ♦♦♦♦♦

Starday Years / Mar. 24, 1998 / Starday ♦♦

A good demonstration of the many facets of Minnie Pearl would be welcome, but this isn't it. First, the program length of each of the three CDs in this set is approximately thirty minutes, which means that two CDs could have easily sufficed. Second, the studio musical numbers are spliced onto the end of live comedy performances without indexing, which means that listeners must manually scan through the comedy bits if they want to hear only the songs. Finally, no recording dates or session information is given, and the "color photographs" and "liner notes" advertised on the cover amount to two color photos the size of postage stamps (the rest are black and white) and a paragraph of text. Although *The Starday Years* provides a fair sampling of Minnie Pearl's comedy and music, this set promises more than it delivers. *—Greg Adams*

Herb Pedersen

b. Apr. 27, 1944, Berkeley, CA

Banjo, Guitar, Vocals / Progressive Bluegrass, Traditional Bluegrass

A longtime staple of the bluegrass scene, singer and multi-instrumentalist Herb Pedersen was born April 27, 1944, in Berkeley, CA. The child of a policeman, he was introduced to country music at numerous Bay Area folk festivals, finding kindred spirits in fellow aspiring musicians like Jerry Garcia (who went on to form the Grateful Dead) and David Nelson (later of the New Riders of the Purple Sage). In his mid-teens, Pedersen formed his first bluegrass band, the Pine Valley Boys. In 1961, Pedersen began working in Nashville, performing on *Carl Tipton's Bluegrass TV Show*. After a 1963 stint with David Grisman's Smokey Grass Boys, he joined the veteran bluegrass performers Vern and Ray as a singer and five-string banjo player. His work with the duo brought him to the attention of Earl Scruggs, who in 1967 tapped Pedersen to fill in for him during his recovery from a hip operation. A year later, he replaced Doug Dillard in the Dillards for 1968's *Wheatstraw Suite* and 1970's *Copperfields*.

After leaving the Dillards, Pedersen remained in Los Angeles, where he became a highly regarded session player, working with the likes of Gram Parsons, Emmylou Harris, Linda Ronstadt, Kris Kristofferson, and John Prine. After spending the first half of the decade in the studio, in 1975 Pedersen joined Jackson Browne's tour, and the following year released his first solo LP, *Southwest*. After 1977's *Sandman*, he joined John Denver's band from 1977 to 1980 and continued his extensive session and production work well into the next decade before cutting a third solo effort, *Lonesome Feeling*, in 1984. He also ventured into scoring television programs, composing the music for series including *The Rockford Files*, *Kojak*, *The Dukes of Hazzard*, and *The A-Team*.

Throughout the years, Pedersen had occasionally reunited with his old friend Chris Hillman, who had made his mark as a member of the Byrds and the Flying Burrito Brothers. In 1986, the two musicians again joined forces to form the Desert Rose Band, a highly successful country-rock act which scored a series of major hits. After the group disbanded in 1993, a year later Pedersen founded the bluegrass outfit the Laurel Canyon Ramblers, which released the LP *Rambler's Blues* in 1995. The group's second effort, *Blue Rambler 2*, followed in 1996, as did *Bakersfield Bound*, another reunion between Pederson and Hillman. *—Jason Ankeny*

● **Southwest** / 1976 / Epic ♦♦♦♦

This is a solid album featuring David Lindley, Mike Post, Larry Carlton, Josh Graves, Al Perkins, Jim Gordon, and some fine backing vocals by Linda Ronstadt and Emmylou Harris. (Out of print.) *—Chip Renner*

Sandman / 1977 / Epic ♦♦♦

This has the same backups as on the *Southwest* album, with the additions of Lowell George and Dolly Parton. This album is out of print, but worth the search. *—Chip Renner*

Lonesome Feeling / 1984 / Sugar Hill ♦♦♦♦

It's a very fine blend of bluegrass and country. Sugar Hill lets Pederson shine. *—Chip Renner*

Hank Penny (Herbert Clayton Penny)

b. Aug. 18, 1918, Birmingham, AL, **d.** Apr. 17, 1992, California

Leader, Vocals / Traditional Country, Western Swing

While he never achieved the kind of success enjoyed by fellow bandleaders like Bob Wills or Spade Cooley, during the late '40s and early '50s Hank Penny ranked as one of the foremost practitioners of the Western swing sound. Born Herbert Clayton Penny on August 18, 1918, in Birmingham, AL, his father was a disabled coal miner who inspired young Hank with his skills as a guitarist, poet, and magician before his death in 1928. By the age of 15, Penny was performing professionally on local radio; in 1936, he moved to New Orleans, where he first fell under the sway of Western swing pioneers like Wills and Milton Brown. A friendship with steel virtuoso Noel Boggs only served to further his enthusiasm for the swing form.

After a few years with New Orleans' WWL as a solo performer, Penny returned to Birmingham, where he formed the group the Radio Cowboys, which featured guitarist Julian Akins, steel guitarist Sammy Forsmark, tenor banjo player Louis Dumont, bassist Carl Stewart, and vocalist, guitarist, and fiddler Sheldon Bennett. In 1938, the group (minus Akins) first entered the studio under the guidance of legendary producer Art Satherly to record numbers like "When I Take My Sugar to Tea" and Penny's own "Flamin' Mamie." After the Radio Cowboys joined the cast of the Atlanta-based program Crossroad Follies, Forsmark left the group, to be replaced by Noel Boggs; at the same time, they also welcomed a new fiddle player by the name of Boudleaux Bryant.

After turning down offers to take over vocal chores for both Pee Wee King's Golden West Cowboys and the Light Crust Doughboys, Penny moved the group to Nashville in 1939, where they again recorded with Satherley. Shortly after, Boggs left the group to join Jimmy Wakely and was replaced by Eddie Duncan. After recording songs like "Tobacco State Swing" and "Peach Tree Shuffle" in Chicago in mid-1940, the band was forced to dissolve after most of its members were drafted. Penny remained in Chicago working as a disc jockey before assembling a new group for a 1941 session in North Carolina, which generated the songs "Why Did I Cry" and "Lonesome Train Blues."

After signing on with the Cincinnati station WLW's programs *Boone County Jamboree* and the *Midwestern Hayride*, Penny formed a new band called the Plantation Boys, which included Radio Cowboy Carl Stewart on fiddle along with guitarist/bassist Louis Innis, fiddler Zed Tennis, and lead guitarist Roy Langham. In addition to work with the Delmore Brothers, Merle Travis, Bradley Kincaid, and Grandpa Jones, they also backed WLW's pop singer Doris Day. After the departure of Langham, in 1944 the band toured with the USO before Penny traveled to California at the urging of Travis. There, he became enamored with the music of Spade Cooley and met Cooley's onetime manager Foreman Phillips, who offered Penny work as a bandleader. After a brief return to Cincinnati which led to a brief recording date, Penny returned to California to assemble another band which included Boggs; however, when Phillips began ordering Penny how to play, the bandleader balked and the group promptly disbanded.

Soon, he was fronting an all-girl band at a Los Angeles club but was quickly approached by Bobbie Bennett, Cooley's then-manager, to lead one of several groups formed to play at the bookings Cooley and his orchestra were themselves too busy to fulfill. While Tex Ritter led one band and Travis led another, Penny fronted the Painted Post Rangers, which scored a pair of significant chart hits with "Steel Guitar Stomp" and "Get Yourself a Redhead." When the Painted Post Club went bankrupt, he moved to lead the large house band at the Riverside Rancho. In 1946, he joined Slim Duncan's ABC network show *Roundup Time* as a comedian. After moving first back to Cincinnati and then to Arlington, VA, he returned to California and took a disc jockey position. He also formed yet another new band, the Penny Serenaders, which included guitarist Speedy West as well as accordion player Bud Sievert, fiddler Billy Hill, and bassist Hank Caldwell. Together with club owner Amand Gautier, Penny also opened his own dancehall, which featured Bob Wills on its opening night.

In June 1948, Penny joined Cooley's massively popular television program, where he performed as a comedian best known for his backwoods character "That Plain Ol'

Country Boy." A year later, he entered the studio to record a number of songs, among them "Hillbilly Bebop," the first known bop effort cut by a country act, and the 1950 hit "Bloodshot Eyes." After he and Gautier opened another club, the legendary Palomino, he reformed the Penny Serenaders, which included singer Mary Morgan, later known as Jaye P. Morgan. The group issued "Remington Ride" and "Wham Bam! Thank You, Ma'am" before calling it quits and then reforming again, this time with guitarist Billy Strange and steel guitar whiz Joaquin Murphy. In 1952, Penny left Cooley to join Dude Martin's program; after first stealing Martin's wife, singer Sue Thompson, he began hosting his own series, *the Hank Penny Show*, which was canceled after only seven weeks.

By 1954, Penny had moved to Las Vegas, where he began a seven-year run as a performer at the Golden Nugget Casino, fronting a band which included the likes of Roy Clark. He also continued to record, even cutting a jazz record in 1961. After divorcing Thompson, he also recorded a comedy album before moving to Carson City, NV, in 1970 to begin performing with his protégé, Thom Bresh, the son of Merle Travis. After leaving his band to Bresh, Penny moved to Nashville, where he was in the running for a slot hosting *Hee Haw* but lost out, ironically enough, to Clark. After a tenure on radio in Wichita, KS, he and fifth wife Shari returned to California in the mid-'70s, and for the most part he retired. Penny died of a heart attack on April 17, 1992. *—Jason Ankeny*

Hank Penny Sings / 1959 / Audio Lab ♦♦♦♦

Tobacco State Swing / 1981 / Rambler ♦♦♦♦

On this LP, Hank Penny's early career as a Western swing bandleader with his Alabama-based Radio Cowboys is explored. The 14 selections (which include four instrumentals) feature Penny along with such players as fiddlers Sheldon Bennett and Boudleaux Bryant, banjoist Louis Dumont and steel guitarists Noel Boggs and Eddie Duncan. An enjoyable and often hard-driving set. *—Scott Yanow*

Rompin', Stompin' / 1983 / Bear Family ♦♦♦♦♦

Hollywood Western Swing 1944–1947 / May 11, 1999 / Krazy Kat ♦♦♦♦

This gathers the cream of Hank Penny's early King sides, beginning with the 1944 "Plantation Boy" session featuring Roy Lanham, though it also highlights sessions with Merle Travis, Noel Boggs, and Red Foley. This is good material, highlighted by the hits "Steel Guitar Stomp" and "Get Yourself a Red Head." In addition, there is an excellent alternate take of "Hope You're Satisfied." *—Jim Smith*

● **Crazy Rhythm: The Standard Transcriptions** / Jul. 18, 2000 / Bloodshot ♦♦♦♦

Until someone puts together a good anthology of his classic RCA sides, excellent sound quality and tight performances make this the best available Hank Penny collection. These 30 radio transcriptions from 1951 (his complete output for Standard) range from novelties and covers of popular songs to swingin' instrumentals and remakes of his RCA hits. A young Jaye P. Morgan (then known as Mary Morgan) was in Penny's band and she appears on "I'm Waiting Just for You" and "I Like the Wide Open Spaces." Highlights include "Flamin' Mamie," "Peroxide Blonde," and the boogie "Big Footed Sam." *—Greg Adams*

The Penny Opus #1 / Oct. 31, 2000 / Jasmine ♦♦♦

The Penny Opus #1 is completely overshadowed by Bloodshot Revival's collection of Hank Penny's complete Standard transcriptions, *Crazy Rhythm: The Standard Transcriptions*, which has all 22 of these tracks plus eight others. That alone makes *The Penny Opus #1*—with its inferior packaging, notes, and sound quality—thoroughly redundant, although it at least costs a few dollars less. Penny's duet with a young Jaye P. Morgan on the Arthur Godfrey hit "I Like the Wide Open Spaces" and his cover of the Bill Davis Trio's "Catch 'Em Young, Treat 'Em Rough, and Tell 'Em Nothing" were omitted, both of which are well worth hearing. As for the performances that do appear, Penny leads his hot Western swing band through a program of novelties in the vein of Tex Williams. Penny could match Williams' talking blues style, but usually sang. A couple of instrumentals, including the intriguingly titled "Progressive Country Music for a Hollywood Flapper," showcase the talented supporting players. These transcriptions were made in 1951, but Penny didn't re-record his King hits from a couple of years earlier; those can be found on the WestSide anthology *Hillbilly Bebop*. *—Greg Adams*

● **Hillbilly Bebop** / Jun. 26, 2002 / WestSide ♦♦♦♦

Perfect Stranger

f. 1986, Carthage, TX

Group / Contemporary Country, Neo-Traditionalist Country

Perfect Stranger formed in Carthage, TX, in 1986. Led by bassist Shayne Morrison and guitarist Richard Raines, the band also included vocalist Steve Murray and drummer Andy Ginn. The band's formative years were spent fighting for fans at dive bars, honky tonks, and rodeos across Texas. But by 1992, the band had established themselves enough to enter a Nashville recording studio. Their debut LP, *You Have the Right to Remain Silent*, was released in 1995, and soon its Vince Gill-penned single, "Ridin' the Rodeo," was the number-one independent country song in America. The album's title track became Perfect Stranger's second single. It hit the airwaves in the spring of 1995 and garnered widespread airplay both on radio and CMT. The exposure didn't go unnoticed by the major labels, and soon Nashville powerhouse Curb came calling. The label signed Stranger within a week and immediately picked up distribution rights for *Right* from the indie Pacific.

Curb re-released the album with additional tracks, and it spent an additional 26 weeks on the country charts. In 1998, Marty Arbter replaced original drummer Ginn, and the band continued to tour as they readied their follow-up release. *The Hits* appeared in summer 2001; it included another version of the band's biggest hit, "You Have the Right to Remain Silent." In 2002, the band readied for another album and continued to tour the honky tonks and rodeos where they first found their fans. *—Johnny Loftus*

● **You Have the Right to Remain Silent** / Jun. 13, 1995 / Curb ♦♦♦

The Hits / Jun. 26, 2001 / Curb ♦♦♦

Carl Perkins

b. Apr. 9, 1932, Tiptonville, TN, **d.** Jan. 19, 1998

Guitar, Vocals, Guitar (Electric) / Rock & Roll, Traditional Country, Rockabilly

While some ill-informed revisionist writers of rock history would like to dismiss Carl Perkins as a rockabilly artist who became a one-hit wonder at the dawn of rock & roll's early years, a deeper look at his music and career reveals much more. A quick look at his songwriting portfolio shows that he composed "Daddy Sang Bass" for Johnny Cash, "I Was So Wrong" for Patsy Cline, and "Let Me Tell You About Love" for the Judds, big hits and classics all. His influence as the quintessential rockabilly artist has played a big part in the development of every generation of rockers to come down the pike since, from the Beatles' George Harrison to the Stray Cats' Brian Setzer to a myriad of others in the country field as well. His guitar style is the other twin peak—along with that of Elvis' lead man Scotty Moore—of rockabilly's instrumental center, so pervasive that modern-day players automatically gravitate toward it when called upon to deliver the style, not even realizing that they're playing Perkins licks, sometimes note for note. As a singer, his interpretation of country ballads is every bit as fine as his better-known rockers. And within the framework of the best of his music is a strong sense of family and roots, all of which trace straight back to his humble beginnings.

He was born to sharecroppers Buck and Louise Perkins (misspelled on his birth certificate as "Perkings") and was soon out in the fields picking cotton and living in a shack with his parents, older brother Jay, and his younger brother Clayton. Working alongside blacks in the field every day, it's not at all surprising that when Carl was gifted with a secondhand guitar, he went to a local sharecropper for lessons, learning firsthand the boogie rhythm that he would later build a career on. By his teens, Carl was playing electric guitar and had recruited his brothers Jay on rhythm guitar and Clayton on string bass to become his first band. The Perkins Brothers Band, featuring both Carl and Jay on lead vocals, quickly established itself as the hottest band in the get-hot-or-go-home cutthroat Jackson, TN, honky tonk circuit. It was here that Carl started composing his first songs with an eye toward the future. Watching the dancefloor at all times for a reaction, Perkins kept reshaping these loosely structured songs until he had a completed composition, which would then be finally put to paper. Perkins was already sending demos to New York record companies, who kept rejecting him, sometimes explaining that this strange new hybrid of country with a black rhythm fit no current commercial trend. But once Perkins heard Elvis on the radio, he not only knew what to call it, but knew that there was a record company person who finally understood it and was also willing to gamble in promoting it. That man was Sam Phillips and the record company was Sun Records, and that's exactly where Perkins headed in 1954 to get an audition.

It was here at his first Sun audition that the structure of the Perkins Brothers Band changed forever. Phillips didn't show the least bit of interest in Jay's Ernest Tubb-styled vocals but flipped over Carl's singing and guitar playing. A scant four months later, he had issued the first Carl Perkins record, "Movie Magg"/"Turn Around," both sides written by the artist. By his second session, he had added W.S. Holland—a friend of Clayton's—to the band playing drums, a relatively new innovation to country music at the time. Phillips was still channeling Perkins in a strictly hillbilly vein, feeling that two artists doing the same type of music (in this case, Elvis and rockabilly) would cancel each other out. But after selling Elvis' contract to RCA Victor in December, Perkins was encouraged to finally let his rocking soul come up for air at his next Sun session. And rock he did with a double whammy blast that proved to be his ticket to the bigs. The chance overhearing of a conversation at a dance one night between two teenagers coupled with a song idea suggestion from labelmate Johnny Cash inspired Perkins to approach Phillips with a new song he had written called "Blue Suede Shoes." After cutting two sides that Phillips planned on releasing as a single by the Perkins Brothers Band, Perkins laid down three takes each of "Blue Suede Shoes" and another rocker, "Honey Don't." A month later, Phillips decides to shelve the two country sides and go with the rockers as Perkins' next single. Three months later, "Blue Suede Shoes," a tune that borrowed stylistically from pop, country, and R&B music, sat at the top of all charts, the first record to accomplish such a feat while becoming Sun's first million-seller in the bargain.

Ready to cash in on a national basis, Carl and the boys headed up to New York for the first time to appear on *the Perry Como Show*. While en route their car rammed the back of a poultry truck, putting Carl and his brother Jay in the hospital with a cracked skull and broken neck, respectively. While in traction, Perkins saw Presley performing his song on *the Dorsey Brother Stage Show*, his moment of fame and recognition snatched away from him. Perkins shrugged his shoulders and went back to the road and the Sun studios, trying to pick up where he left off. The follow-ups to "Shoes" were, in many ways, superior to his initial hit, but each succeeding Sun single held diminishing sales, and it wasn't until the British Invasion and the subsequent rockabilly revival of the early '70s that the general public got to truly savor classics like "Boppin' the Blues," "Matchbox," "Everybody's Trying to Be My Baby," "Your True Love," "Dixie Fried," "Put Your Cat Clothes On," and "All Mama's Children."

While labelmates Cash and Jerry Lee Lewis (who played piano on "Matchbox") were scoring hit after hit, Perkins was becoming disillusioned with his fate, fueled by his increasing dependence on alcohol and the death of his brother Jay to cancer. He kept plugging along, and when Cash left Sun to go to Columbia in 1958, Perkins followed him over. The royalty rate was better, and Perkins had no shortage of great songs to record, but Columbia's Nashville watch-the-clock production methods killed any of the spontaneity that was the charm of the Sun records. By the early '60s, after being dropped by Columbia and moving over to Decca with little success, Perkins was back playing the honky tonks and contemplating getting out of the business altogether. A call from a booking agent in 1964 offering a tour of England changed all of that. Temporarily swearing off the bottle, Perkins was greeted in Britain as a conquering hero, playing to sold-out audiences and being particularly lauded by a young beat group on the top of the charts named the Beatles. George Harrison had cut his musical teeth on Perkins' Sun recordings (as had most British guitarists) and the Fab Four ended up recording more tunes by him than any other artist except themselves. The British tour not only rejuvenated his outlook, but suddenly made him realize that he had gone—through no maneuvering of his own—from has-been to legend in a country he had never played in before. Upon his return to the U.S., he hooked up with old friend and former labelmate Cash and was a regular fixture of his road show for the next ten years, bringing his battle with alcohol to an end. The '80s dawned with Perkins going on his own with a new band consisting of his sons backing him. His election to the Rock & Roll Hall of Fame in the mid-'80s was no less than his due. After a long battle with throat cancer, Perkins died in early 1998, his place in the history books assured. *—Cub Koda*

On Top / 1969 / Columbia ✦✦✦✦

Carl Perkins' first attempt at an album of new material in a decade is surprisingly successful, and one of the better records to come out of the early days of the rock & roll revival. Cut during the summer of 1969, it sort of follows the lead of Elvis Presley's 1968 comeback special, presenting Perkins doing blues ("Baby, What You Want Me to Do"), rock & roll ("C.C. Rider," "Brown Eyed Handsome Man"), and a few originals such as "Soul Beat" which, if they weren't distinguished, also do no harm to his reputation. There were a few touches that the album might've done well without, like the organ that occasionally crops up on some of the arrangements, and a runaway performance on the wah-wah pedal during one song, but the bulk of this was some of the better LP work up to this point in the career of an artist who was otherwise not especially known for his strong LPs. Among the real highlights is the obscurity "Superfool," written by a friend of Perkins; "Champagne Illinois," a collaboration between Perkins and Bob Dylan that grew out of the sessions for the latter's *Nashville Skyline*; Ronnie Self's "A Lion in the Jungle"; Perkins' powerful and touching "Power of My Soul"; and Buddy Holly's "I'm Gonna Set My Foot Down." [*On Top* was subsequently deleted and, with a new cover and the deletion of a couple of songs, reissued on the budget Harmony Records line under the title *Brown Eyed Handsome Man*.] *—Bruce Eder*

Greatest Hits / 1969 / Columbia ✦✦✦

Contrary to what its title would lead one to expect, Columbia Records' Carl Perkins *Greatest Hits* album wasn't a compilation but, rather, a new LP, comprised of freshly recorded versions of most of his best-known Sun songs (for some reason, "Everybody Trying to Be My Baby" didn't make the cut), as well as his more recent composition "Daddy Sang Bass," which had become a number-one country hit for Johnny Cash, and a Perkins' version of Cash's "Folsom Prison Blues" (Perkins had been touring with Cash for the two years prior to his getting a Columbia contract of his own in 1968). And all of that was augmented by the presence of the artist's own recent success "Restless," which had reached number 20 on the country singles chart. The content makes it a pretty fair representation of where Perkins was, as of early 1969, and is not a bad place to start in enjoying his work from this part of his career. The versions of "Blue Suede Shoes," "Match Box," "Honey Don't," "Boppin' the Blues," etc., included here aren't bad, though they're not remotely as edgy or exciting as the Sun originals. Perkins does a good enough job singing, but the playing—though crisp, and spirited where his own guitar was concerned—lacks the spontaneity that one would hope to find. The Nashville session men involved evidently had little special resonance to the songs, simply starting and stopping on cue; and the presence of a backup chorus, albeit a restrained one that only shows itself over certain parts of songs, was an unnecessary embellishment, but the results were still eminently listenable. At the time these sides were recorded, there was no LP collection of Perkins' Sun hits (though that soon changed); helped, no doubt, by the presence of "Restless," Columbia's *Greatest Hits* album made the Top 40 on the country LP charts, a modest placement but also a milestone in Perkins' career. *—Bruce Eder*

Boppin' the Blues / 1970 / Columbia ✦✦

An ambitious and well-intentioned, but ultimately unsatisfying, experiment by Columbia Records, putting Perkins together with NRBQ. Despite some intersections of interest, neither meshes with the other, although they try hard—basically, it's a difference in philosophy; Perkins says and plays as little as he needs to in putting over his songs, like the rockabilly equivalent of Count Basie at the piano, and the NRBQ stretches out, overly complicating and embellishing most of what they touch here. The results aren't horrendous, and some critics liked what they heard, but this record wasn't what Perkins' fans, country or rock, were paying to hear him do, and amounts to a curious digression from his real music and sound. *—Bruce Eder*

Man Behind Johnny Cash / 1972 / Columbia ✦✦✦

Ol' Blue Suede's Back / 1978 / Jet ✦✦✦

Up Through the Years, 1954–1957 / 1986 / Bear Family ✦✦✦✦✦

An import collection of Perkins' groundbreaking Sun singles, *Up Through the Years* offers eight more tracks than Rhino's *Original Sun Greatest Hits*; both discs are definitive collections. *—Stephen Thomas Erlewine*

★ **Original Sun Greatest Hits** / 1986 / Rhino ✦✦✦✦✦

While Carl Perkins recorded many fine records and enjoyed a long and successful career after he left Sun Records, there's no arguing that the sides cut during his tenure with Sam Phillips are his best-known and most influential work; it's all but impossible to imagine the rockabilly revolution of the 1950s happening without hits like "Blue Suede Shoes" and "Boppin' the Blues," and literally thousands of rock guitarists from George Harrison to Lou Reed first had their heads turned around by his trademark licks. *Original Sun Greatest Hits* compiles 16 of Perkins' best and best-known recordings for Sun, and you could hardly ask for a better introduction to the man's music. From the hillbilly blues of "Sure to Fall" to uptempo rockers like "Matchbox," "All Mama's Children," and "Honey Don't" and lesser-known gems like the down-home delinquency of "Dixie Fried" and the well-oiled sartorial splendor of "Put Your Cat Clothes On," every song is a winner, and Perkins' ringing guitar lines, warm and playful vocals, and loose but emphatic interplay with his band are a joy to hear. If you're only going to own one Carl Perkins album, *Original Sun Greatest Hits* is certainly the one to get. *—Mark Deming*

Honky Tonk Gal / Apr. 1989 / Rounder ✦✦✦✦

While at Sun Records in the mid-'50s, Carl Perkins made his name with "Blue Suede Shoes." Partly due to some bad timing, though, Perkins was unable to achieve the same level of fame his Sun contemporaries Elvis Presley and Jerry Lee Lewis would. But historically speaking, Perkins is just as responsible as those two for the country and blues mix that makes up rock & roll. The proof is heard on this rarities collection, which spotlights his hillbilly roots, Hank Williams-inspired sound, and blues-tinged delivery. A perfect complement to the many hits packages available, *Honky Tonk Gal* includes solid alternate versions of "Turn Around," "Let the Jukebox Keep on Playing," and "Dixie Fried," as well as stunning covers like "You Can't Make Love to Somebody," "Caldonia," and the title track. A fine record for dedicated fans of classic rock & roll, country, and rockabilly. *—Stephen Cook*

The Classic / Feb. 1990 / Bear Family ✦✦✦✦✦

This is a Bear Family release that even casual listeners can sort of agree with. The five CDs contain close to 150 tracks, most notably Perkins' complete Sun Records output in close, glittering sound, plus all of his Columbia sides from 1958 through 1962, and his oft-overlooked early-'60s recordings for both American and English Decca. The Sun material is the best part of this box, and while it has been available as a triple CD from Charly, the latter is now out of print and had nothing like the crisp, clean sound you get here. The Sun outtakes may make the casual listener hesitate, but it's in the multiple takes that rock & roll as you know it was born, and all of the stuff is different enough between the takes to make hearing it worthwhile even for the non-scholar, to show that classics like that don't just "happen." Moreover, these differences aren't the little arrangement polishes and little tempo changes that one finds in most outtakes, but represent the evolution of a style—musically, they're at least as interesting as any of Elvis' Sun session outtakes. Beyond the rock & roll history, however, the reality is also that anyone buying it should have as much love of good honky tonk-style country music as they do for rock & roll. The Columbia sides are available separately, but they just aren't as interesting. The Decca stuff, which is unique to this set, represents Perkins' serious attempts at a comeback in the face of his huge concert success in England in the wake of the Beatles' recording of his music. The booklet is good, though not quite as comprehensive as one would have liked. *—Bruce Eder*

Jive After Five: The Best of Carl Perkins (1958–1978) / Sep. 1990 / Rhino ✦✦✦✦

A nice single-disc set that examines the best of Perkins' recordings after his tenure at Sun Records. The earlier Columbia sides continue the rockabilly mold that launched him, although tracks like "Pink Pedal Pushers" and "Jive After Five" are literally swimming in tape echo and reverb, unlike the sparseness of the Sun sides. The later tracks on Decca, Mercury, and others find him moving from rockabilly into a more mature country style, closing with a solo instrumental, "Just Coastin,'" which shows his deep playing debt to both Chet Atkins and Merle Travis. It's a nice and important companion to the Sun sides. *—Cub Koda*

Restless: The Columbia Recordings / May 12, 1992 / Columbia ✦✦✦✦✦

A strong collection of Perkins' singles for Columbia, concentrating on the late '50s and early '60s; some of his finest songs, including "Pink Pedal Pushers" and "Jive After Five," are included here. *—Stephen Thomas Erlewine*

Country Boy's Dream: The Dollie Masters / Jun. 1994 / Bear Family ✦✦✦

Upon signing to Dollie records in 1966, Carl Perkins decided to concentrate on country music. The result was two minor country hits, "Country Boy's Dream" and "Shine, Shine, Shine," that marked the first time he was on the charts since the late '50s. Though the Dollie recordings weren't blockbusters, they were solid, straight-ahead country and paved the way for Perkins' major label deal with Columbia, as well as a slot in Johnny Cash's band. *Country Boy's Dream: The Dollie Masters* contains all of Perkins' recordings for Dollie, including a handful of unreleased and rare tracks. Fans of Perkins' harder-edged, rocking sound won't find much to like on the compilation, yet it demonstrates that he was equally adept at country. Nevertheless, even fans of Carl's country records will find *Country Boy's Dream* a little tedious, since many of the songs on the album are simply unremarkable. *—Stephen Thomas Erlewine*

Go Cat Go / Oct. 15, 1996 / Dinosaur ✦✦✦

This album is a curious mixture; it isn't really a Carl Perkins album per se as it is an all-star tribute album with some of the big name guests actually getting to interface with their hero. Both John Lennon and Jimi Hendrix appear via the grave and the tape vaults, contributing their own versions of "Blue Suede Shoes" to the proceedings. And Carl works in tandem with live guests Tom Petty, Johnny Cash, Bono, Ringo Starr, George Harrison, Paul McCartney, John Fogerty, and Paul Simon in right fine fashion. But the bottom line is that the real star of the show is Perkins himself, just playing and singing in a most masterful and rockin' way. If stars of this magnitude are tipping their hat, Carl shows on this waxing that their idolatry is well placed. *—Cub Koda*

Silver Eagle Cross Country Presents Live: Carl Perkins / Feb. 11, 1997 / Silver Eagle ✦✦✦✦✦

Recorded live at New York's Lone Star Cafe on June 25, 1983, this show—originally broadcast nationwide—captures Carl Perkins in excellent form before a highly enthusiastic audience. Perkins was still going strong in the early '80s. He was always more complex a performer than any one of his songs would have indicated, and the repertory here shows why, juxtaposing an ebullient "Got My Mojo Working" between "Matchbox" and "Gone, Gone, Gone." "Blue Suede Shoes," "Dixie Fried," and "Honey Don't" are also here, along with "High Heel Sneakers" and Perkins' cover of Arthur Crudup's "That's Alright." The sound is excellent, and the only drawbacks are that the band is never identified, and that the disc runs a mere 44 minutes—one wishes he could've worked in a few more numbers. *—Bruce Eder*

Turn Around / Apr. 7, 1998 / Culture Press ✦✦✦
The 16 songs here consist of demos that Carl Perkins recorded during early 1964, just before he went on tour in England with Chuck Berry, the Animals, and the Nashville Teens, augmented with some slightly later tracks from the following year. In any case, they show Perkins more animated and spirited than he'd been in several years on record, and a number of these songs, including "Help Me Find My Baby," later found their way to the public in finished versions as part of his brief stay with Decca and Brunswick Records. "Big Taxes" has an edgy sound that mixes rockabilly with a guitar style that's definitely early-'60s Brit-beat in nature, while "A Man Without a Home" has a more traditional country sound in just about every nuance, and "Big Bad Blues" has Perkins trying for a sound not too far removed from Chess Records' output of the period—the latter song ought to be dragged down by the female chorus backing him, but his vocal performance and the punky playing just can't be derailed, and the girls add an element of camp that works. And somewhere in the midst of this, a live cut ("Turn Around") has found its way onto this CD. The sound on some of the songs is a bit uneven, as several appear to have come from something other than original master tapes, but it's generally decent, if a bit bass-heavy and slightly ragged. —*Bruce Eder*

Blue Suede Shoes: The Very Best of Carl Perkins / Feb. 2, 1999 / Collectables ✦✦✦

Blue Suede Shoes/Original Golden Hits / Oct. 12, 1999 / Collectables ✦✦✦✦
In 1999, Collectables released *Blue Suede Shoes/Original Golden Hits*, which contained two complete albums—*Blue Suede Shoes* (1970, originally released on Sun) and *Original Golden Hits* (1970, originally released on Sun)—by Carl Perkins on one compact disc. —*Jason Birchmeier*

The Complete Sun Singles / Jun. 6, 2000 / Varese ✦✦✦✦✦
As part of their Sun series, this brings together all 18 of Perkins' original singles for the Flip and Sun labels. In addition to the 16 sides, there's also the inclusion of "Tennessee" and "Sure to Fall," the single by the Perkins Brothers band that features both Carl and Jay. Although there's much duplication with Rhino's *All-Time Greatest Sun Recordings* collection here, there are still enough new wrinkles aboard this one to make a nice stand-alone set. —*Cub Koda*

Back on Top / Jul. 12, 2000 / Bear Family ✦✦✦✦
Back on Top, Bear Family's four-disc retrospective of Carl Perkins' late-'60s and early-'70s work, collects everything he recorded during his second tenure with Columbia, his tribute to Elvis ("E.P. Express"), and his complete recordings with NRBQ. Over the course of 99 tracks, the set also covers his two-year stint with Mercury, the complete *My Kind of Country* sessions, and a full disc's worth of previously unreleased demos. As with all of Bear Family's releases, *Back on Top* also features impressive supplemental material, including liner notes by Grammy winner Colin Escott, a complete discography, and previously unpublished photos. A Perkins completist's dream come true, *Back on Top* paints an expansive portrait of his comeback years. —*Heather Phares*

Jet Propelled: The 1978 Comeback / Oct. 8, 2002 / Sanctuary ✦✦

Gretchen Peters
b. Westchester County, NY
Piano, Vocals, Vocals (Background), Guitar (Acoustic), Dobro / Contemporary Country, Singer/Songwriter, Country-Folk
Known as a writer of intelligent and introspective songs in the country/folk/pop vein, Gretchen Peters achieved notoriety through country stars covering her material. Among the artists to have hits with her songs were Trisha Yearwood, Pam Tillis, George Strait, Martina McBride, and Patty Loveless. Peters was born in Westchester County, NY, and lived there until her parents divorced when she was eight, at which point she moved with her mother to Boulder, CO, where as a teenager she wrote songs and performed in the town's thriving live music scene. She moved to Nashville in 1988 and signed several writing deals before moving to Sony Tree in 1992. Having written a string of critically acclaimed hits, Peters received her first Grammy nomination for Song of the Year in 1995 for "Independence Day" (recorded by McBride), her powerful anthem about a women who fights back against an abusive husband.
In the Country Music Awards that year, the song took home the same award, as well as a CMA Video of the Year in 1994. She was nominated again for a Song of the Year Grammy in 1996 with the Loveless chart-topper "You Don't Even Know Who I Am." Peters' scope wasn't limited to the country music arena, as she demonstrated by co-writing "Rock Steady" with rock artist Bryan Adams—a song that appeared on Bonnie Raitt's *Road Tested*. Peters released her debut album, *The Secret of Life*, on Imprint Records in 1996. Her self-titled sophomore effort was issued five years later. —*Jack Leaver*

The Secret of Life / 1996 / Imprint ✦✦✦
Although this record is stylistically more folk and pop than country, Peters' songs are similar to Mary-Chapin Carpenter's work in that they contain thoughtful and intelligent lyrics that are at times highly introspective. Ten of the eleven tracks on the album were written or co-written by Peters and she turns in a credible cover of Steve Earle's "I Ain't Ever Satisfied," and with Earle and Harris providing harmony vocals. Other guests include Raul Malo singing background on the beautiful "Border Town," and James House on "A Room With a View," a song written from the perspective of a cab driver. Another highlight is the opening track "Waiting for the Light to Turn Green," co-written with Suzy Bogguss. Overall an impressive first outing for this talented singer/songwriter, whose songs have been hits for Trisha Yearwood, George Strait, Patty Loveless and Martina McBride. —*Jack Leaver*

● **Gretchen Peters** / Feb. 13, 2001 / Valley ✦✦✦
On her second album, the Nashville-based singer/songwriter spins straightforward narrative tales that name-drop Kerouac and Picasso, among others, and journeys across America in a used car, taking notes along the way. It's all amiable enough, if not exactly

original. At her worst, Peters sounds like she wants to be Sheryl Crow. When she hits the open road and finds herself, though, it's smart, personal stuff, worthy of its subjects. —*Michael Gallucci*

Pierce Pettis
Guitar, Vocals, Songwriter / Country-Folk, Contemporary Folk, Contemporary Singer/Songwriter
You know you've got a shot when Joan Baez covers one of your songs. That's what sparked the career of Alabama singer/songwriter Pierce Pettis in 1979 when Baez chose to include "Song at the End of the Movie" on her *Honest Lullaby*. From there, Pettis was involved with the Fast Folk movement in New York in the '80s alongside artists such as Shawn Colvin and Suzanne Vega. He continued to write songs and eventually embarked on his solo career in 1987 with the independent release of *Moments*, an album which some still consider his finest. Following that, Pettis made his way onto High Street Records, issuing four releases between 1991 and 1996. *Tinseltown, While the Serpent Lies Sleeping, Chase the Buffalo*, and *Making Light of It* all garnered much critical praise, but failed to find a widespread audience. What Pettis did find were fans in other artists who began adding his original tunes to their own repertoires. Dar Williams snagged "Family" for her *Mortal City* disc, while Garth Brooks tapped "You Move Me" for his hit *Sevens*.
Maintaining his status as a songwriter has always been a focus for Pettis, from his time at Muscle Shoals Sound Studios to his work as a staff writer for PolyGram Publishing in Nashville. Making his name as an artist is another matter, and one that Pettis continues to pursue. In 1998, he aimed himself in a slightly different direction, he signed on with Compass Records and released *Everything Matters*. A fine collection of poignant character sketches, *Everything Matters* has a more refined, mature sound than previous efforts, perhaps due to the production of Grammy winner Gordon Kennedy who is best known for his work on Eric Clapton's "Change the World." —*Kelly McCartney*

Moments / 1987 / Small World ✦✦✦✦✦
Containing the title cut, "Grandmother's Song," and "St. Paul's Song," this is his first album, and still his best. —*Richard Meyer*

Tinseltown / 1991 / High Street ✦✦✦

● **While the Serpent Lies Sleeping** / Jan. 15, 1992 / Windham Hill ✦✦✦✦✦
While the Serpent Lies Sleeping. The keen observations in Pettis' songwriting gain force from the caught-in-the-throat emotionalism of his singing. As befits this record label, the instrumental settings are somewhat busy in a new-age way. But where the drum and keyboard programming leave off, a strong contemporary folk album remains, especially on "Legacy," in which Pettis confronts the conflicts of his Southern heritage. —*William Ruhlmann*

Chase the Buffalo / 1993 / High Street ✦✦✦
On Pierce Pettis' fourth album, *Chase the Buffalo*, he shows a great deal of growth as a writer and studio performer. Pettis' other releases have had some high points, but on this CD, Pettis' politics and Southern gothic folk style are integrated better. His writing is more consistent and stands up to his mature and controlled vocals. The production by David Miner is also more focused on Pierce's style than before. This is an album worth tracking down. —*Richard Meyer*

Making Light of It / Oct. 8, 1996 / High Street ✦✦✦✦
Produced by David Miner, *Making Light* has a somewhat more polished surface than Pierce Pettis' previous albums, yet that doesn't diminish the quiet power of his songs. —*Thom Owens*

Everything Matters / Jun. 16, 1998 / Compass ✦✦✦✦✦
Pierce Pettis is an engaging vocalist and an excellent guitarist, but he's primarily one of the preeminent songwriters of our time. Any disc of his is an event, and this one is no exception. His fifth album and second for Compass, *Everything Matters* is a series of self-portraits capturing the passion, longing, faith, release, compassion and humanity that is Pierce Pettis. He wraps his baritone voice lovingly around clever phrases and rich, everyday language which results in a fine disc by an artist of exceptional ability. —*Sigmund Finman*

State of Grace / Jul. 10, 2001 / Compass ✦✦✦✦
A primitive painting of a simple village bathed in yellow and pale green, inscribed with the promise of peace forever, graces the cover of Pierce Pettis' *State of Grace* album. Of course, Howard Finster's apocalyptic cover art alone couldn't make an album successful, but it sure helps to make a good first impression. With his third Compass release, Pettis returns with some tight accompaniment, a couple of good covers, and the well-written songs that his fans have come to expect. Things push off with a nice version of Mark Heard's "Rise From the Ruins," a catchy tune with the catchy lyric, "There ain't nobody asks to be born/There ain't nobody wishes to die," setting the mood for this spiritual journey. The title cut draws a parallel between a state of grace and life in the South, celebrating the land, the agriculture, and the people. Pettis' reverent delivery transforms the song into a prayer of thanks to his homeland and the richness of its culture. The journey continues, first in the general sense of returning to one's home after a long absence, and then to specific locations like Atlanta, GA, and Orlando, FL. In "Georgia Moon," memories are tinged with the melancholy of what has been lost, though "We Will Meet Again" holds out hope for transcendence in the next world. All of these moods—memories, lost love, and faith—mingle together on *State of Grace*, creating a portrait of an artist perceptively exploring his roots. Listeners should also stick around for a lively take on Bob Dylan's "Down in the Flood" near the end of the album. This is a solid effort, made by a singer who understands how to shape his vision into an artistic whole as well as please old fans. —*Ronnie D. Lankford Jr.*

The Picketts

f. Seattle, WA

Group / Contemporary Country, Alternative Country-Rock, Americana, Indie Pop

The Picketts were Seattle's only "grange rock" combo. Led by vocalist Christy McWilson, the band also included drummer "Blackie" Sleep, McWilson's guitarist-husband Scott McCaughey, and rhythm guitarist Jim Sangster. McWilson and McCaughey had met at San Francisco State. They moved to Seattle in 1980, where McWilson started a '60s retro/new wave band called the Dynette Set, and McCaughey fell in with the ragged pop combo Young Fresh Fellows. Raised in northern California, McWilson had grown up on the Bakersfield sound and the cosmic country of Gram Parsons and Emmylou Harris. But Seattle was pretty much devoid of that sound, and what little did exist didn't have the greatest reputation. Nevertheless, after McWilson noticed Sleep's distinctive standup drumming style during a gig his rockabilly band played opening for the Dynette Set, she asked him about collaborating, and the earliest form of the Picketts was born.

Originally known as the Power Moves, the band eventually lost their grittier edge and became the Picketts. McWilson also took over most of the lead vocal duties around this time. The Picketts' first appearance on wax was a seven-inch for the Seattle indie PopLlama that featured a country-fried version of the Clash's "Should I Stay or Should I Go." It wasn't such an odd choice. Rather than play straight-ahead country, the Picketts were more inclined to mix '50s rockabilly or pop in with more traditional influences like Wanda Jackson or Merle Haggard. *Paper Doll*, their debut full-length, was released in 1992 through PopLlama. Extensive touring followed, and eventually the Picketts landed a showcase at the influential Austin music festival South by Southwest. That exposure led to a deal with Rounder, who released *The Wicked Picketts* in 1995. A more polished version of their sound, the album nonetheless featured the Picketts' engaging mixture of rock and pop elements with traditional country songwriting. *Euphonium* followed on Rounder in 1996, at which point the band went on an extended hiatus while McCaughey focused on touring as a guitarist with R.E.M. or leading his revolving-door side project, the Minus 5. McWilson went on to release two solo albums, both of which featured a stellar supporting cast, including Dave Alvin, Peter Buck, Syd Straw, and Rhet Miller. *—Johnny Loftus*

Paper Doll / 1992 / PopLlama ♦♦♦

The Picketts are a country-rock group that is heavily in debt to classic '50s honky tonk and '60s Bakersfield country, as well as punk, rockabilly and rock & roll. *Paper Doll* is an energetic, rollicking record, full of stomping rockers and terrific ballads. The Picketts might just be a revival band, but when it is performed as well as *Paper Doll* is, a lack of originality is excusable. *—Thom Owens*

● **The Wicked Picketts** / 1995 / Rounder ♦♦♦♦♦

The Picketts draw equally from country and rock & roll, including punk rock, which makes their stripped-down, Bakersfield-influenced honky tonk quite exciting. Their second album, *The Wicked Picketts*, has a bit more studio gloss than *Paper Doll*, but it remains a tough, enjoyable listen. *—Stephen Thomas Erlewine*

Euphonium / 1996 / Rounder ♦♦♦

Jo Carol Pierce

b. Jul. 20, 1944, Texas

Songwriter, Vocals / Progressive Country, Singer/Songwriter, Country-Folk, Alternative Country

An unconventional singer/songwriter from the musical wellspring of Lubbock, TX—home to the likes of Buddy Holly, Joe Ely, Jimmie Dale Gilmore, and Butch Hancock—Jo Carol Pierce was as much a monologuist and performance artist as she was a musician. Her songs, a blend of country and postmodern folk sung in a shaky, conversational style, were steeped more in theater than in any traditional musical idiom; nonetheless, her work proved so popular with other performers that a tribute LP was ultimately recorded in her honor.

Pierce was born on July 20, 1944, near the old Route 66 in Wellington, TX. After her father was killed in Korea, she and her mother moved to Lubbock, where she attended school with the likes of Ely and Hancock. In 1963, she married her high-school sweetheart, Gilmore; after having a child, Elyse, the couple divorced in 1967. Pierce moved to the state's capital of Austin in the early '70s, where she found employment as a social worker. After hours, she also began writing a novel and composing the occasional song. By the next decade, she had become a playwright and screenwriter, authoring such works as *Falling*, *Papergirls*, *New World Tango* (a musical scored by Ely), *Bad Girls Upset by the Truth*, and *In the West*, a drama performed at the Kennedy Center in 1991.

Pierce did not begin to take songwriting seriously until the middle of the 1980s, when Ely and fellow Lubbock alum David Halley started encouraging her to become a performer. After enlisting backing vocalist Robert Jacks and accordionist Mike Maddux, she quickly became a popular fixture on the Austin club circuit. Friends and fans Michael Hall (formerly of the Wild Seeds) and Troy Campbell (of the Loose Diamonds, named after a Pierce song) began organizing the 1993 album *Across the Great Divide: Songs of Jo Carol Pierce*, a tribute LP compiling renditions of Pierce songs performed by musicians like Ely, Gilmore, Terry Allen, Darden Smith, and Kathy McCarty and Gretchen Phillips. A group tour in support of the record followed, and in 1996, at the age of 51, Pierce finally made her own recording debut with *Bad Girls Upset By the Truth*, a semi-autobiographical performance piece drawn from her earlier absurdist musical comedy. *—Jason Ankeny*

● **Bad Girls Upset By the Truth** / Jan. 23, 1996 / Monkey Hill ♦♦♦♦

Pierce's debut, while for all practical purposes a country record, is virtually unprecedented stuff: based on the singer's autobiographical absurdist satire of the same name, *Bad Girls Upset By the Truth* is essentially a performance piece, grounded more in theater than in music. A comic tale masking bitter themes including mental illness and victimization, the narrative kicks off with the central character's (also named Jo Carol) suicide and culminates with the birth of the baby girl Jesus inside a supermarket. Stuffed in between are meditations on sex, monogamy, and spirituality, sung in Pierce's conversational style and set against country, folk, rock, and even Cajun backdrops. *—Jason Ankeny*

Webb Pierce

b. Aug. 8, 1926, West Monroe, LA, **d.** Feb. 24, 1991, Nashville, TN

Vocals, Guitar, Leader / Traditional Country, Honky Tonk

Webb Pierce was one of the most popular honky tonk vocalists of the '50s, racking up more number-one hits than similar artists like Hank Williams, Eddy Arnold, Lefty Frizzell, and Ernest Tubb. For most of the general public, Pierce—with his lavish, flamboyant Nudie suits—became the most recognizable face of country music, as well as all of its excesses; after all, he boasted about his pair of convertibles lined with silver dollars and his guitar-shaped swimming pool. For all of his success, Pierce never amassed the reputation of his contemporaries, even though he continued to chart regularly well into the '70s. Webb's weakness for gaudy ornaments of his wealth, as well as his reluctance to break away from hardcore honky tonk, meant that he had neither supporters in the industry, nor the ability to sustain the ever-changing tastes of a popular audience. Nevertheless, he remains one of the cornerstone figures of honky tonk, both for his success and his artistic achievements.

As a child in West Monroe, LA, Pierce became infatuated with Gene Autry films and his mother's hillbilly records, particularly those of Jimmie Rodgers and various Western swing and Cajun groups. He began to play guitar before he was a teenager. At the age of 15, he was hired as a singer by Monroe's KMLB. During World War II, Pierce enlisted in the Army. While he was in the service, he married Betty Jane Lewis; their wedding was in June of 1942. After he was discharged, Webb and his wife moved back to Monroe, but by 1944 he moved to Shreveport. Getting a job at Sears Roebuck, Pierce began singing on radio stations, nightclubs, and dances with Betty Jane. At first, they were featured on an early morning radio show on KTBS, while they would perform in the evening at clubs. It took them five years before they were noticed by the industry. In 1949, the California-based 4 Star Records signed the duo under separate recording contracts. Webb signed under his own name, while his wife was signed for duets with her husband under the name Betty Jane & Her Boyfriends. However, success didn't come to the duo—it only came for Webb; in the summer of 1950, the couple divorced.

In late 1949, Pierce accepted a spot on the *Louisiana Hayride*, a radio program on KWKH that was instrumental in launching the careers of many country artists. Webb began to assemble a band of local Shreveport musicians, which included recruiting pianist Floyd Cramer, guitarist/vocalist Faron Young, bassist Tillman Franks, and vocalists Teddy & Doyle Wilburn. The Wilburns and Franks all wrote songs, which provided the basis for Webb's initial set list. Pierce also founded a record label called Pacemaker and Ark-La-Tex Music, a publishing company, with Horace Logan, the director of the *Louisiana Hayride*. On Pacemaker, Pierce made several records between 1950 and 1951. They weren't designed to be big sellers—they were created with the intent of attracting radio play around Louisiana. In 1951, he was able to get out of his 4-Star contract and Decca Records signed him immediately. Webb's second single, "Wondering," became his breakthrough hit, climbing to number one early in 1952. After the single became a hit, Pierce left Louisiana for Nashville, where he met and married his second wife, Audrey Grisham. In June of 1952, he had his second number-one single with "That Heart Belongs to Me." The following September, the *Grand Ole Opry* needed to fill the vacancy left by the firing of Hank Williams, so they invited Pierce to join the cast. After Williams' death, Pierce became the most popular singer in country music. For the next four years, every single he released hit the Top Ten, with a total of ten reaching number one, including "There Stands the Glass" (1953), "Slowly" (1954), "More and More" (1954), and "In the Jailhouse Now" (1955).

Pierce and *Opry* manager Jim Denny formed Cedarwood Music, a music publishing company, in 1953; later, the pair would invest in radio stations together. Their business ventures were not looked upon kindly by the *Opry* superiors, and they began pressuring the duo to cease any outside interests. At the same time, Pierce was growing tired of being confined to the *Grand Ole Opry*—he thought he wasn't being treated with the respect a star of his stature deserved, and he wanted to be able to partake in the lucrative financial rewards that came with touring. Pierce left the *Opry* in 1955 and began appearing on *Ozark Jubilee*, a television program on the ABC network. He left *Ozark Jubilee* in 1956 and returned to the *Opry* but left for good the following year.

Pierce continued to have hits until the end of the '50s, but he did take a significant dip in popularity after rock & roll's arrival in the late '50s. Nevertheless, Pierce stayed on the charts, primarily because he kept in close touch with DJs across the country, which meant that he was able to keep his streak of 34 consecutive Top Ten hits running into 1957. For a while, Pierce tried to keep up with rock & roll, covering the Everly Brothers and recording pseudo-rockabilly numbers. Once those proved unsuccessful, he stuck with honky tonk and continued to rack up Top Ten hits right through 1964.

By 1965, the country-pop leanings of the Nashville Sound had pushed honky tonk from the top of the country charts. Pierce remained a star, but he simply didn't have many big hits in the latter half of the '60s—the most notable was "Fool Fool Fool" in 1967. Since his music had faded from the spotlight, he became known for his excessive lifestyle. Instead of indulging in intoxicants, Webb indulged in material items. Pierce had Nudie Cohen, a Hollywood tailor famous for his custom-made flamboyant clothing, line two Pontiac convertibles with silver dollars. He built a guitar-shaped swimming pool at his Nashville home. The swimming pool became a popular tourist attraction—nearly 3,000 people visited it each week—causing his neighbors, led by Ray Stevens, to file a legal suit against Pierce in order to prevent visitors from coming into their neighborhood.

Throughout the '70s, Pierce continued to record, but most of his income came from his highly lucrative financial investments. Pierce left Decca Records in 1975, making a handful of records for Plantation Records that didn't experience much chart success. His last hit came in 1982, when his duet on "In the Jailhouse Now" with Willie Nelson scraped the bottom of the country charts. Despite all of his success, Pierce was never inducted into the Country Music Hall of Fame during his lifetime; it's likely that the members never forgave him for his rejection of the *Grand Ole Opry* and the Nashville industry. Pierce died of pancreatic cancer on February 24, 1991. Just months before his death, he didn't receive enough votes to be inducted into the Hall of Fame. Nevertheless, his career stands as one of the most successful in the history of country music. *—Stephen Thomas Erlewine*

That Wondering Boy / 1956 / Decca ✦✦✦✦✦
That Wondering Boy is an original ten-inch album released on Decca Records in the mid-'50s. Though all of this material has been reissued in various forms, this original track sequence is dynamite, featuring Pierce classics like "There Stands the Glass," "Back Street Affair" and "Slowly," and is one of his best albums of the '50s. *—Stephen Thomas Erlewine*

Bound for the Kingdom / 1959 / Decca ✦✦✦
Bound for the Kingdom is Webb Pierce's gospel album from 1959. Nearly every country artist of note made at least one religious album, and Pierce is no exception. He had taken a stab at gospel material when he cut four sacred songs in 1954, but only one of the four was released at the time. Here he lets loose with a full dozen, including some uncommon selections that add to the album's appeal. Accompanied by the Anita Kerr Singers and an orchestra directed by Owen Bradley, Pierce's unmistakable voice takes center stage as always. He tackles three Albert E. Brumley hymns, and the leadoff track is a snappy rendition of "He's Got the Whole World in His Hands." The liner notes promise that this album will bring the listener peace of mind, but this isn't the kind of material at which Pierce excelled, and in reality it's more of a curiosity than a spiritual masterpiece. *—Greg Adams*

The One and Only Webb Pierce / 1959 / King ✦
In 1950, before signing with Decca and beginning his five-year stretch of chart domination, Webb Pierce recorded 13 sides for King. Most of these songs were never re-recorded by Pierce, so the appearance of 12 of them on CD would normally make for an interesting—if not essential—purchase. Unfortunately, the tracks are utterly ruined by the addition of incongruous acoustic guitar and vocal chorus overdubs that sound as though they were recorded in a different decade (as they probably were). Even die-hard fans will have difficulty enduring this one. The unadulterated King recordings were once available on LP, and we can only hope that they will someday arrive in the digital age. *—Greg Adams*

Webb! / 1959 / Decca ✦✦✦✦
After an incredible run of country hits through most of the '50s and early '60s, honky tonker Webb Pierce began to slowly lose favor with the buying public. Nonetheless, he continued to record with respectable success for the next 20 years, having already ensured his legendary status with those classic early sides. Better known in ways for his taste in one-of-a-kind swimming pools and convertibles, Pierce was still in his musical prime when this 1959 collection of classic honky tonk songs was taped. And while there are no smashes like "In the Jailhouse Now" and "There Stands the Glass," *Webb!* still delivers with renditions of the Ray Price hit "My Shoes Keep Walking Back to You," George Jones' "Life to Go," and the self-penned "Sittin' Alone." Pierce's nasally, high-toned voice is equally well-situated on his and Mel Tillis' rock & roll-tinged "Tupelo County Jail" and the Charlie Walker chart-topper "Pick Me Up on Your Way Down." Topped off with Owen Bradley's clean musical backing, *Webb!* is a rare gem from the days before Pierce and his honky tonk kind were squeezed out by crossover country's arrival on the scene. *—Stephen Cook*

Walking the Streets / 1960 / Decca ✦✦
By the time this country legend died in 1991, fans had no doubt gotten used to the older version of the man, walking tall as a veteran honky tonker and croaking out "Heebie Jeebie Blues" with a ten-gallon hat astride his head. This album comes from an era when hit country records were sounding smoother and smoother, and the label had designs on turning Pierce into a male version of Patsy Cline. She was "Wallking After Midnight," so he's "Walking the Streets." It might have been nice to run into her, but all the listener meets is this fairly dull song. There is some pedal steel, but the edges are smoothed off everything, and frequent use is made out of background singers and choirs even when they destroy the intimacy as surely as if they had burst into your own home. Pierce was involved in the writing of a good chunk of this material, so it can be assumed it was done to his taste. Between the label pressure and his own insecurity about what she should sound like as a country singer, this isn't an example of The artist at his best, coming to life only briefly on the almost rocking "All Night Long" before lapsing back into another Cline rip-off. She's "Down Mexico Way," he's "Down Panama Way." Get it? *—Eugene Chadbourne*

Webb With a Beat! / 1960 / Decca ✦✦✦✦

Fallen Angel / 1961 / Decca ✦✦✦✦
When Webb Pierce made *Fallen Angel*, he had already settled into the formula that would last him throughout the decade: crisp and precise country-pop songs given a hint of rock & roll flavor with prominent drums and electric bass. His trailblazing was behind him, although his blending of pop-oriented instrumental backing with hard country vocals put him in a unique class with the likes of Ernest Ashworth and, occasionally, Rose Maddox. The product was more successful than Pierce receives credit for—two songs on *Fallen Angel* crossed over to the pop Top 100, and Pierce would wind up ranked seventh in *Billboard*'s accounting of the top country artists of the '60s. The title track and "(Doin' The) Lovers Leap" were the two hits on this brief album, and the cookie-cutter songs yield no surprises but ensure a baseline level of quality that fans of Pierce and country music of the era will appreciate. *—Greg Adams*

Cross Country / 1962 / Decca ✦✦✦✦✦

Hideaway Heart / 1962 / Decca ✦✦✦

I've Got a New Heartache / 1963 / Decca ✦✦✦

Bow Thy Head / 1963 / Decca ✦✦✦

Sands of Gold / 1964 / Decca ✦✦✦✦✦
Webb Pierce's '60s albums are all cut from the same cloth—some are better than others, but if you like one you'll probably like them all. *Sands of Gold* yielded three Top 20 country hits: the dreamy, tropical-flavored "Sands of Gold," the perfectly wistful "Those Wonderful Years," and "If the Back Door Could Talk," which, despite its modern production flourishes, sounds like a song Pierce would have recorded in the '50s. Although many critics act as though Pierce fell off the earth after 1959, he was still a very visible and commercially relevant country artist at this point, and the title track even bubbled under the pop Top 100. The album tracks are mostly covers of other recent country and pop favorites, such as the number one hits "Don't Let Me Cross Over" and "Roses Are Red (Violets Are Blue)," but Pierce has such a unique voice it's fun to hear him walk through these performances. [*Sands of Gold* is one of Pierce's best albums of the '60s, and was remixed and reissued on CD with the album *Sweet Memories* in 1993.] *—Greg Adams*

Country Music Time / 1965 / Decca ✦✦✦

Sweet Memories / 1966 / Decca ✦✦✦
Sweet Memories is a typical '60s album for Webb Pierce, containing a few originals aimed at the singles market and too many covers of recent country hits. Pierce himself scored no hits this time around, but turned in competent versions of "Wolverton Mountain," "Love's Gonna Live Here Again," and "Welcome to My World." "The Champ" is a tedious recitation with narration by Jackie Fargo, and the title track is a slow shuffle with a weak hook. Pierce had a real gift for picking chart-bound material, but he struck out this time around. [*Sweet Memories* was remixed and reissued on CD with the album *Sands of Gold* in 1993.] *—Greg Adams*

Webb's Choice / 1966 / Decca ✦✦✦
Every album Webb Pierce made was "Webb's choice" in the sense that he had a reputation for picking great material and was permitted to exercise that talent, unlike many artists who were presented with songs or allowed to choose from a short list (or stack of demos). The fact that *Webb's Choice* calls attention to Pierce's involvement in the selection of material shows that it was unusual, but the album fails as a test of his predictive abilities since the single, "You Ain't No Better Than Me," missed the Top 40. Nevertheless, that song is a good if typical example of Pierce's '60s single A-sides, and there actually are a few surprises lurking in the track list. "Danny Boy" is an uncharacteristic song for Pierce, as is the traditional folk tune "Cotton Fields." Pierce was never associated with Western swing, and yet two songs from that field, "San Antonio Rose" and "Time Changes Everything," are assimilated into Pierce's snappy country style. Most of the songs come from Pierce's usual gang: Wayne P. Walker, Max Powell, and Merle Kilgore (but nothing by Mel Tillis this time around). The questionable theme notwithstanding, *Webb's Choice* is a fine album on which Pierce stretches just a little bit. *—Greg Adams*

Where'd Ya Stay Last Night? / 1967 / Decca ✦✦✦

Fool, Fool, Fool / 1968 / Decca ✦✦✦

Webb Pierce Sings This Thing / 1969 / Decca ✦✦✦✦
This Thing is exemplary of the consistent quality and sound that Webb Pierce maintained throughout the '60s—it could be played side by side with one of his records from 1960, and there would be no discernible difference. The title track was his final Top 20 hit, and "If I Had Last Night to Live Over" also made the country Top 40. Half of the songs are credited or co-credited to Pierce's wife, Audrey Grisham (including "This Thing"), and other songs are from the pens of Pierce's longtime confederates Wayne P. Walker and Mel Tillis. Pierce covers Bobby Edwards' hit "You're the Reason," although his arrangement is more similar to Johnny Tillotson's version than the original, and "Lo-Lenna" is a watered-down Cajun number. The album would have benefited from a couple more uptempo songs, but *This Thing* is a solid album that is sure to please Pierce's fans. *—Greg Adams*

Saturday Night / 1969 / Decca ✦✦✦

Merry-Go-Round World / 1970 / Decca ✦✦✦

Love Ain't Never Gonna Be No Better / 1970 / Decca ✦✦✦
The title track from *Love Ain't Never Gonna Be No Better* was Webb Pierce's second-to-last Top 40 hit in 1969-1970, although it is standard (but pleasant) fare that doesn't stand out for that distinction. Pierce's sound had remained practically static for a decade, so he had no chance of weathering the profound changes that country music had already begun to experience in the late '60s and early '70s, but his fans could take comfort in the reliability of his albums. That said, *Love Ain't Never Gonna Be No Better* has some real highlights, including a wonderful, haunting version of "Faded Love" and a clap-happy inspirational song, "Everyday Will Be Sunday After While." "Send My Love to Me" is based on the melody of "Silver Bells," which Pierce recorded many years earlier. There was a time when ol' Webb Pierce was more adventurous than he came to be during his late period, but he seldom made a bad record. *—Greg Adams*

Webb Pierce Road Show / 1971 / Decca ✦✦✦

I'm Gonna Be a Swinger / 1972 / Decca ✦✦✦

In the Jailhouse Now / 1982 / Columbia ✦✦✦✦✦
Willie Nelson had to try pretty hard to follow-up his brilliant duet album with Ray Price, and certainly came up with a winning, and quite different, combination by teaming up with Webb Pierce. Unless the idea of a fellow in a tall cowboy hat is repulsive, the photography on this album is worth the purchase price alone. Pierce looks the part, talks the talk, and walks the walk of a no-nonsense country singer, and one who—in the manner of Hank Thompson—seems obsessed with drinking songs. But these are songs that touch on the misery of alcoholism as well as barroom revelry. "There Stands the Glass," the opening track on this album, is one of the best country songs about booze ever written, and if that judgment was made by actually listening to every single one of them it would keep somebody busy a longtime, and probably lead them to get drunk more than

once in the process. The listener will want to hear a few more tracks when this album ends, not only because the playing time is a bit ungenerous but because the performances are so much fun. "In the Jailhouse Now" simply rocks and rolls, Pierce's unmannered delivery meshing perfectly with Nelson's jazzy vocal style. At first listen, the pairing of these vocalists might seem a bit awkward, as Pierce is kind of a belter who hits the rhythm right on the head, unlike Nelson, who phrases behind the beat in the manner of jazz master Lester Young. Emotion is where the two really come together; they mean every word they say, and they put the lyrics across with the sentimental and meaningful spirit that is the essence of all great country & western. Pierce is not an artist who Nelson had much of a relationship with as a songwriter, so this record is not dominated by Nelson songs, focusing more on classics from the Pierce repertoire. Fine picking all around from a whole studio full of great musicians hardly hurts either. The players are a mixture of Nelson sidemen, top-rank Nashville session men, and pianists Leon Russell and Richard Manuel, both legendary rock players. *—Eugene Chadbourne*

☆ **The Wondering Boy (1951–1958)** / 1990 / Bear Family ✦✦✦✦✦
For the devout, Germany's Bear Family offers a four-CD boxed set of Pierce's primal honky tonk, a total of 113 songs by one of the seminal post-war country artists, including duets with Kitty Wells, Red Sovine, and the Wilburn Brothers. This is the best sound quality and presentation available of this influential music. *—Mark A. Humphrey*

Sands of Gold/Sweet Memories / 1993 / Mobile Fidelity ✦✦✦✦✦
Oo-oooh, what a little remastering can do. Two Nashville Sound LPs from the downside of Pierce's career feature Webb singing more of other people's hits than his own. But reissued Mofi-style, Pierce and the echo chamber sound great. *—Dan Cooper*

★ **King of the Honky-Tonk: From the Original Decca Masters** / 1994 / Country Music Foundation ✦✦✦✦✦
No one ever accused Pierce of being a singer's singer; neverthless, his classic country oeuvre is totally individualistic, which is really more important. Any fan of '50s fiddle-and-steel honky tonk will want this collection, which features such Pierce immortals as "There Stands the Glass," "Slowly," a rollicking 1954 remake of Jimmie Rodgers' "In the Jailhouse Now," and the to-the-point "Honky Tonk Song." The latter is one of several cuts from the pen of a young Mel Tillis. *—Dan Cooper*

The Unavailable Sides (1950–1951) / Sep. 13, 1994 / Krazy Kat ✦✦✦
Between his first recordings for the Four Star label and his long tenure with Decca Records, Webb Pierce formed the Pacemaker label and Ark-La-Tex Publishing in partnership with Horace Logan, the emcee of the *Louisiana Hayride.* The story of Pierce's recordings for Pacemaker are tangled and confused, and it seems that he was recording under a pseudonym for Pacemaker while still under contract to Four Star. *The Unavailable Sides 1950-1951* attempts to make some sense of this early period of Pierce's career by presenting 21 Pacemaker sides and two rare Four Star recordings credited to his then-wife Betty Jane Lewis, but featuring Pierce on duet vocals. A few tracks are instrumentals or have other vocalists, but the players are interesting: Tillman Franks, Shot Jackson, and Buddy Attaway, to name a few. There are several early recordings of songs Pierce later remade for Decca, including "In the Jailhouse Now," "California Blues," and "Drifting Texas Sand." Pierce would later re-record "Hayride Boogie" with new lyrics as "Teenage Boogie," but most of the songs are exclusive to this collection. The liner notes are full of interesting facts and make a noble effort to solve various mysteries surrounding Pierce and these sessions. The recordings are more raw and primitive than his early Decca cuts, but *The Unavailable Sides 1950-1951* is an important document of rare, formative recordings by the most spectacular country hitmaker of the '50s. *—Greg Adams*

Greatest Hits: Finest Performances / May 2, 1995 / Sun ✦✦
Despite what the packaging may lead you to believe, *Greatest Hits: Finest Performances,* like the Intersound collection *In the Jailhouse Now,* consists of '70s re-recordings of Pierce's '50s and '60s hits, and there is some overlap between the two discs. Pierce is in fine voice throughout, and the instrumentation is tasteful and mostly true to the originals, the only update being the occasional inclusion of a drum kit. Fans may find these recordings interesting, if redundant, and newcomers should hold out for the original recordings. For those who are desperate to hear Pierce's unique voice for a budget price, though, *Greatest Hits: Finest Performance* is adequate and enjoyable. *—Greg Adams*

The Wondering Boy (The King of 50's Country) / Jul. 11, 2000 / Edsel ✦✦✦✦✦

20th Century Masters—The Millennium Collection: The Best of Webb Pierce / Jan. 30, 2001 / MCA ✦✦✦✦
There aren't many Webb Pierce compilations on the market, but *20th Century Masters—The Millennium Collection* isn't necessarily a solution to the problem. Of its 12 tracks, 11 are already featured on the more thorough *King of the Honky-Tonk: From the Original Decca Masters* (the exception is the number one hit "Love, Love, Love," which for some reason was left off the previous compilation). If you'd rather pay a little less money for a Webb Pierce best-of, *The Millennium Collection* certainly isn't bad—all of the songs featured were huge hits. But most listeners will prefer to acquire the more extensive compilation. *—Steve Huey*

Honky-Tonk Hero / Apr. 22, 2003 / Fuel 2000 ✦✦
The back cover of Fuel 2000's *Honky-Tonk Hero* trumpets the chart position of each of the 15 songs on the collection: "Back Street Affair" (number-one country); "In the Jailhouse Now" (number-one country); "Wondering" (number-one country). Too bad that the chart position, in all but two cases, refers to versions not heard on this collection. Webb Pierce did have a remarkable string of chart-topping country hits, but those were cut for Decca. The versions here are remakes Pierce cut in the mid-'70s for Plantation Records, a fact buried until the very end of Bill Dahl's typically fine liner notes (in fact, the liners are better than this deserves). These remakes aren't bad, necessarily—they're professional, well-recorded, and Pierce is in good voice—but they don't hold a candle to the originals, a comparison that can't help but be made because so many of the cuts closely adhere to original arrangements, thereby increasing the feeling that this is a bit of a scam. What is noteworthy are the two exceptions—two largely unheard singles for Plantation that barely scraped the charts in the mid-'70s. Of the two, "The Good Lord Giveth (& Uncle Sam Taketh Away)," is the lost gem, thanks to its post-psychedelic country production, swirling fuzz-tone guitars, and funny lyrics, but the loping Tex-Mex beat of "I've Got Leaving on My Mind" (mildly reminiscent of Doug Sahm) is also nice to hear. These two songs aren't found elsewhere and suggest that Pierce's '70s recordings, while surely tied to the times, would be worth excavating on a real reissue, which this certainly isn't, but it's hard not to wish it was. *—Stephen Thomas Erlewine*

Hayride Boogie, 1950–1951 / Krazy Kat ✦✦✦✦✦
The 16-track album *Hayride Boogie, 1950-1951* contains nearly all of the material Webb Pierce recorded for the local Shreveport, LA, record label, Pacemaker. Though some of this material does capture Pierce at a rough, developmental stage, much of it is downright terrific and it is all fascinating listenings for dedicated fans or country music historians. *—Stephen Thomas Erlewine*

Ray Pillow

b. Jul. 4, 1937, Lynchburg, VA
Vocals / Country-Pop, Nashville Sound/Countrypolitan
Ray Pillow was a singer and songwriter best known as a prominent publisher renowned for his rare gift of matching performers with high-quality songs right for their style. Pillow was born in Lynchburg, VA, and first learned to play the guitar while bedridden as a teen. He graduated from high-school in 1954 and then joined the Navy. Following his discharge, Pillow earned a bachelor's degree in business and made his professional and personal singing debut playing with his uncle's band, the Stardusters. Later, he became their leader and remained with the band for several years. In 1961, Pillow won second place at the regional National Pet Milk talent contest in Nashville. Though he needed to go back to Lynchburg, he accepted an invitation to appear on the *Grand Ole Opry.* He soon returned to Nashville and looked up Joe Taylor, the head of promotion with the Martha White Company, who had promised to help Pillow after hearing him perform. Taylor was true to his word and Pillow signed a personal management contract with the company.

In 1963 he released his first two singles, but didn't really have chart success until 1965, with the Top 50 "Take Your Hands Off My Heart" and his first Top 20 hit, "Thank You Ma'am." In 1966, he had two Top 40 hits and a Top Ten duet with Jean Shepard, "I'll Take the Dog." He later joined the *Opry,* and remained there for over two decades. He continued with a steady stream of hits through 1970, but fell off the charts until 1972 with the minor hits "Since Then" and "She's Doing It to Me Again." Pillow's involvement in the administrative end of the business began the mid-'60s, when he paired up with Taylor in Joe Taylor Artist Management, Shoji Music Publications, and Ming Music, Inc. In the early '80s, Pillow teamed with Larry McFaden and they began Sycamore. In the late '80s, he began working with the A&R team at Capitol Records and later became an independent record consultant. *—Sandra Brennan*

● **Presenting Ray Pillow** / 1965 / Capitol ✦✦✦✦✦

Even When It's Bad, It's Good / 1967 / Capitol ✦✦✦✦

Ray Pillow Sings / 1969 / ABC ✦✦✦

Slippin' Around With Ray Pillow / 1972 / Mega ✦✦✦

One Too Many Memories / 1984 / Allegiance ✦✦

Ray Pillow / Sep. 28, 1999 / First Generation ✦✦✦

Pinkard & Bowden

f. 1983
Group / Traditional Country, Country Comedy
In the tradition of Homer & Jethro came the riotous barnyard humor and song parodies of Sandy Pinkard & Richard Bowden. Unlike their forebears, Pinkard & Bowden's humor was often coarse, and their language was sometimes rough enough to warrant explicit language warnings on their records; in fact, they were the first country comedy artists to have such an advisory posted on their music. Both Pinkard & Bowden were successful singers and songwriters before teaming up. Pinkard began his music career with Ramblin' Jack Elliott in California. He made one unsuccessful bid to get signed in Nashville and entered the professional rodeo in Fort Worth, Texas. He met John Anderson in 1975, who listened to Pinkard's demos and encouraged him to try Nashville again, even purchasing him a round-trip ticket. This time he succeeded, and such artists as Tanya Tucker, Ray Charles, and Brenda Lee recorded his songs; in 1979, Mel Tillis had a number-one hit with Pinkard's "Coca Cola Cowboy." Other singers scoring top hits with his songs included David Frizzell and Shelly West ("You're the Reason God Made Oklahoma"), Anne Murray ("Blessed Are the Believers") and Vern Gosdin ("I Can Tell By the Way You Dance").

Bowden got his start working in the Texas band Shiloh alongside future Eagle Don Henley. After their group disbanded, the two joined Linda Ronstadt's band, which included another future Eagle, Glenn Frey. When Frey and Henley left to form the Eagles, Bowden briefly teamed with former Flying Burrito Brother "Sneaky" Pete Kleinow. He then hit the road and played with different performers, including Roger McGuinn. During the early '80s, he and his band Blue Steel opened for the Eagles.

Pinkard & Bowden were introduced to each other through their mutual friend, record producer Jim Ed Norman. They began writing songs together; although they tried to write seriously, they found that everything they penned was funny, so they took their act onto the national comedy club circuit and built up a following. Their debut album *Writers in Disguise* featured such musical parodies as "Blue Hairs Drivin' in My Lane." The two had their first chart success with "Adventures in Parodies," a montage of clips. Among their other favorites: "Elvis Was a Narc," "She Thinks I Steal Cars," and "Libyans on a Jet Plane." In 1992 they released *Cousins, Cattle, & Other Love Stories,* which featured takeoffs on pop songs like Eric Clapton's "Cocaine" ("Propane"). By the early '90s, Pinkard & Bowden were more involved in performing at comedy clubs than with country music; they also began appearing on rock radio station morning shows to promote their evening gigs. After making the switch, their comedy has became a little bluer and definitely blacker, as seen in their song "Friends in Crawl Spaces," inspired by serial killer/cannibal Jeffrey Dahmer. *—Sandra Brennan*

Writers in Disguise / 1984 / Warner Bros. ♦♦♦

● **Live in Front of a Bunch of Dickheads** / 1990 / Warner Bros. ♦♦♦♦♦
On this concert LP, Pinkard & Bowden offer up crowd-pleasers like "Elvis Was a Narc," "Driving Others to Christ Through Barnyard Innuendo," and "She Dances with Meat." Their families must be very proud. *—Jason Ankeny*

Cousins, Cattle, & Other Love Stories / 1992 / Warner Bros. ♦♦♦
Unlike the homespun country comedy of a bygone era, the music of Pinkard & Bowden is proudly and defiantly raunchy; the opening cut even taunts their label to "Censor Us." (The album does indeed bear a parental advisory sticker, by the way.) Also featured: "Trailer Park Woman" and "Since My Baby Turned Gay." *—Jason Ankeny*

Pinmonkey

Group / Country-Rock, Progressive Bluegrass
The Nashville-based band Pinmonkey likes to refer to their music as progressive country, but that moniker hardly encapsulates the group's range. Pinmonkey boasts a heady blend of country/Americana styles: traditional Southern gospel, Appalachian folk, Carter Family harmonizing, Muscle Shoals pop-soul, and even traces of '70s rock. The band released its debut album, *Speak No Evil*, in early 2002.

Lead singer and Virginia native Michael Reynolds first made his way to Nashville with dreams of a career as a Music City songwriter. After years of struggle and menial jobs, Reynolds started performing small gigs on the writers' night circuit. He found musical allies in brothers Chad and Michael Jeffers (who play dobro/lap steel and bass, respectively) and Rick Schell, a golden-throated, soprano-singing drummer who boasted stints with Steve Earle and Allison Moorer. The group's debut album featured tracks penned by Gillian Welch and Duane Jarvis along with a strong batch of Reynolds originals. The album, as well as the group's rousing live shows, soon caught the attention of RCA Records, which signed Pinmonkey shortly after their self-financed debut came out. *—Erik Hage*

Speak No Evil / Feb. 26, 2002 / Drifter's Church ♦♦♦
Nashville-based Pinmonkey has a smooth, melodic country-rock style that would be received well in the executive offices of Music Row as well as the bars on lower Broadway. The young band's chief strength rests in its vocals. Lead singer Michael Reynolds boasts a clear tenor that is both sturdy and sweet. He moves from being soulful and sorrowful on "Augusta" to commanding and soaring on "The Devil's Front Door." The group also graces its songs with some fine harmonizing, which only enhances Reynolds' strong singing. With its accent on vocals and easygoing sound, Pinmonkey brings to mind such '70s country bands as the Eagles and Poco. The band's sublime rendition of "Love Sometimes" makes such an immediate impact that you'd swear you've heard it on the radio for years. Band originals are in the minority here—only four of the ten tunes—but songs like "Cheap Motel" and "Black Train" demonstrate that singer Reynolds has the songwriting skills to match his singing ability. The group also displays some smarts in its cover choices. Besides selecting tunes from veteran Nashville songwriters such as Gwil Owen (author of "Augusta") and Joy Lynn White and Duane Jarvis (they co-wrote "Love Sometimes"), the bandmembers reveal their affection for backwoods music by covering the Carter Family's "Lonesome Pine Special" and Gillian Welch's "Two Days From Knowing." The disc's main shortcoming is that the music sometimes comes off as a bit too slick and soft-edged. While the songs are catchy and appealing, they too frequently slip past without making an indelible impression. Still, the band displays a number of good qualities and the self-released *Speak No Evil* should serve as a calling card for entry into the major-label arena. *—Michael Berick*

● **Pinmonkey** / Oct. 8, 2002 / BNA ♦♦♦♦
To call an artist "country" is to enter a hall of mirrors. By country, do you mean the Diane Warren-penned pap that has dominated mainstream country radio from the great credibility scare of the '90s (as Steve Earle terms it) through the new millennium? Or do you mean those progressive country/Americana/alt-country artists who ride waves of critical respect and receive their due in *No Depression* magazine? Or do you mean classic country or honky tonk? Or country-rock? So suffice it to say that Pinmonkey is a country band par excellence precisely because it embodies this kind of confusion. The group's sweet-as-mountain-water vocals and tight musicianship could hold a comfortable place in both *No Depression* circles and on country radio. "Every Time It Rains" and "Barbed Wire & Roses" are dosed with enough pop sensibilities to please mainstream Nashville, while the brooding, stirring gospel of "Jar of Clay" and the bruised, drop-dead gorgeous "Augusta" are, frankly, too darn good to survive that milieu. This is a strong country album with pop smarts, and (complicating the picture even more) it isn't too many DNA strands removed from the country-rock of the Flying Burrito Brothers—Pinmonkey's edges are just a whole lot smoother than those of their ancient predecessors. Dolly Parton offers her nod of approval with a guest slot on "Falling Out of Love With Me." The album also features a nearly unrecognizable and joyous take on alternative pop group Sugar Ray's "Fly." *—Erik Hage*

Pirates of the Mississippi

f. 1987
Group / Contemporary Country
A group of five session musicians who formed in 1987 in order to have a little fun, the Pirates of the Mississippi were one of a handful of country bands who emerged in the wake of the Kentucky Headhunters' success in the early '90s. The Pirates of the Mississippi didn't blend genres or joke around like the Kentucky Headhunters, and they weren't smooth country-rock like Alabama. Instead, they were a straightforward country band, with hints of ragged enthusiasm and exceptional instrumental and vocal skills. Though the band wasn't able to capitalize on the success of their one big hit single, 1991's number 15 "Feed Jake," the group continued to record through the mid-'90s.

All five members of the Pirates of the Mississippi—Bill McCorvey (lead vocals, guitar), Rich Alves (guitar), Dean Townson (bass), Jimmy Lowe (drums), and Pat Severs (steel guitar)—were Nashville session musicians during the '80s. In 1987, they began playing together regularly, usually in clubs around Nashville. Eventually, an A&R representative at Capitol Nashville signed the group to a deal. In the summer of 1990, their eponymous debut was released, as was their cover of Hank Williams' "Honky Tonk Blues." The single reached number 30, yet the follow-up, "Rollin' Home," stiffed.

Walk the Plank, the band's second album, appeared in 1991 and proved to be their breakthrough release, thanks to the single "Feed Jake." A sentimental song about the death of a childhood friend, "Feed Jake" and its video became a big hit, leading to the band being named the Top New Vocal Group by the Academy of Country Music. Though they had two other singles from the album—"Speak of the Devil" and "Fighting for You"—nothing else from the record was a hit. *A Street Man Named Desire*, the band's third album, also suffered from poor sales upon its 1992 release, as did their fourth record, 1993's *Dream You*. Following the poor sales of *Dream You*, the compilation *Best of the Pirates of the Mississippi* appeared in 1994, and the band was dropped from Liberty and Capitol Nashville. Later that year, Pat Severs left the group and was replaced by Greg Trostle. In 1995, the Pirates of the Mississippi signed with Giant Records and released *Sure Sign*. *—Stephen Thomas Erlewine*

Pirates of the Mississippi / Jun. 18, 1990 / Capitol ♦♦♦♦♦
The Pirates made their name with their third single, "Feed Jake," which had a video that became country music's version of *Old Yeller*. The rest of the debut is a cross between Alabama country and Southern rock. (The album starts with a speeded-up version of "Honky Tonk Blues," if that's a hint at what's to come.) There are a few twists, though, namely a Guy Clark song ("I Take My Comfort in You") and a surf-country instrumental. *—Brian Mansfield*

Walk the Plank / Sep. 30, 1991 / Capitol ♦♦♦
As country, the Pirates' Allman Brothers cops are more exciting than their stone-country material, although that's certainly competent enough. The white-country-soul "Till I'm Holding You Again"—which tries to rock out when you're not looking—is probably the best of all. *—Brian Mansfield*

A Street Man Named Desire / Sep. 28, 1992 / Liberty ♦♦♦
"Street Man Named Desire" may not be the most clear-cut metaphor given the phrase's origins, but if you're going to make literary allusions, you can do worse than Tennessee Williams. While that's the title tune, the Allman and Doobie Brothers influences in the instrumental "Mystery Ship" tell more about the band—namely, that they're a tamed biker band. The Pirates are good-natured renegades, but they never take the image too far. So "Mississippi Homegrown" is about music, not marijuana (and contains another Williams reference), "The Hard Side of Love" only hints at the Southern boogie the guys might have in them, and "All Your Eyes Can See" is a tender love song for the ladies. Powerful in spots, the album is pedestrian in others. *—Brian Mansfield*

Dream You / Oct. 11, 1993 / Liberty ♦♦♦
Basically a party album, it contains songs like "Save the Wild Life," "Pop from the Top," "The Night They Rocked the Grand Ole Opry," and a full-tilt cover of Hank Thompson's "The Wild Side of Life." *—Brian Mansfield*

● **The Best of the Pirates of the Mississippi** / Mar. 8, 1994 / Liberty ♦♦♦♦♦
Beyond the video for "Feed Jake," The Pirates of the Mississippi never found great success (five Top 40 hits in four years, none making the Top Ten). Even so, they were a pretty decent singles band, as this collection shows, especially when they nail the fast stuff (like "Rollin' Home" and "Speak of the Devil"). *Best Of* also includes dance mixes of two tunes from *Dream You*: "Dream You" and "Pop from the Top." *—Brian Mansfield*

Paradise / 1995 / Giant ♦♦♦

Poco

f. 1968, Los Angeles, CA, **db.** 1984
Group / Country-Rock, Soft Rock, Pop/Rock
One of the first and longest-lasting country-rock groups, Poco had its roots in the dying embers of the Buffalo Springfield: After co-founders Neil Young and Stephen Stills exited in the spring of 1968, only guitarist/singer Richie Furay and bassist Jim Messina remained to complete the group's swan song, *Last Time Around*. The final Springfield track, "Kind Woman," included only Furay and Messina, with a guest appearance on steel guitar by Rusty Young, formerly of Boenzee Cryque. He stuck with Furay and Messina, passing on a scheduled audition for a new group that Gram Parsons was putting together; auditions followed before the fledgling group reached out to Young's ex-Boenzee Cryque bandmate George Grantham on drums and vocals and to bassist/singer Randy Meisner. This lineup rehearsed for four months before making their debut at the L.A. Troubadour in November. A month later, they made their first appearance at the Fillmore West on a bill with the Steve Miller Band and Sly & the Family Stone.

At the time, they were using the name Pogo, but that didn't last; Walt Kelly, the creator of the comic strip Pogo, from which they'd freely admitted borrowing the name, didn't appreciate the group's choice and filed a lawsuit. Not wanting to lose all of the recognition and goodwill they'd built up locally over the previous five months, the result was a change of just one consonant, to Poco. Just one day after signing to Epic in early 1969, Meisner suddenly left the band, apparently over personality clashes; he later joined the Eagles. Recorded as a four-piece, Poco's debut, *Pickin' Up the Pieces*, was released in June of 1969. The group was back to being a quintet in 1970 with the addition of bassist Timothy B. Schmit, whose arrival coincided with the recording of their second album, *Poco*.

It wasn't long after that Messina decided to leave, feeling that Furay had assumed too much control over the group's sound. Before departing, he secured the services of a capable replacement member—Paul Cotton, a onetime member of the Illinois Speed Press—and also played on and produced their subsequent album, *Deliverin'*, which rose to number 26 and yielded the minor hit "C'mon." Their next album, 1971's *From the Inside*, was produced in Memphis by Booker T. & the M.G.'s guitarist Steve Cropper. The same lineup became the first Poco membership to last for more than one studio album; their second, *A Good Feelin' to Know*, was released in 1972, but by this time, even Furay had begun to lose heart over the band's lack of commercial success.

The band made one renewed effort, *Crazy Eyes*, their most accomplished studio album to date; released late in 1973, it became their most successful work. However, just as the LP was released, Furay left the group to hook up with Chris Hillman and John David Souther to form the Souther-Hillman-Furay Band. Still, Poco continued as a quartet; their next album, *Seven*, released in the spring of 1974, failed to replicate the success of *Crazy Eyes*. The group was at a critical point in their history following the release of one more Epic album, *Cantamos*, which appeared in the fall of 1974 and got no higher than number 76. After parting with Epic, Poco signed with ABC Records in 1975; their first album, *Head Over Heels*, issued in mid-1975, surpassed expectations to fall just shy of the Top 40.

After the album *Rose of Cimarron*, the group came close to splitting up in 1976, with new member Al Garth exiting in the middle of the year. Finally, in the spring of 1977, *Indian Summer* was released; four months later, Timothy Schmit exited the lineup to replace Meisner in the Eagles. Grantham followed him out of the band in January of 1978, eventually becoming Ricky Skaggs' drummer. The group re-formed with Charlie Harrison and Steve Chapman joining Young and Cotton; Kim Bullard, a Crosby, Stills & Nash alumnus, came in on keyboards in December of that year, and Poco was once again a quintet. All of these personnel changes seemed to have done the trick, because their next album, *Legend*, released late in 1978, became the best-selling LP in their history, earning a gold record in the course of rising to number 14. The accompanying single, "Crazy Love," reached number 17, far and away their biggest seller to date. It was matched by Cotton's "Heart of the Night," which got to number 20 during the summer of 1979.

However, their subsequent albums—*Under the Gun*, *Blue and Gray*, and *Cowboys & Englishmen*—did progressively poorly; *Ghost Town*, issued late in 1982, peaked at an anemic number 195. Furay rejoined the group briefly in mid-1984 along with Schmit, resulting in the *Inamorata* album, which scarcely made any impact; a five-year hiatus followed before the original quintet re-formed in the spring of 1989. Their comeback single, "Call It Love," hit the Top 20, accompanied by the album *Legacy*, which made it to number 40. Although the 1968 lineup didn't stay together, Poco was restored as a working band, touring periodically with Cotton and Young at its core. In 2002, the band released a new album, *Running Horse*, through their website, www.PocoNut.com. *—Bruce Eder*

Pickin' Up the Pieces / 1969 / Epic/Legacy ✦✦✦✦✦
The group went into the studio with a sudden loss of one member (Randy Meisner), an engineer who didn't quite get what they were trying for, and a lot of pressure for a first album—and came up with this startlingly great record, as accomplished as any of Buffalo Springfield, and also reminiscent of the Beatles and the Byrds. *Pickin' Up the Pieces* is all the more amazing when one considers that Jim Messina and George Grantham were both covering for the departed Meisner in hastily learned capacities on bass and vocals, respectively. The title track is practically an anthem for the virtues of country-rock, with the kind of sweet harmonizing and tight interplay between the guitars that the Byrds, the Burritos, and others had to work awhile to achieve. The mix of good-time songs ("Consequently So Long," "Calico Lady"), fast-paced instrumentals ("Grand Junction"), and overall good feelings makes this a great introduction to the band, as well as a landmark in country-rock only slightly less important (and more enjoyable than) *Sweetheart of the Rodeo*. *—Bruce Eder*

Poco / May 6, 1970 / Epic ✦✦✦✦
The first two-thirds of Poco's second album is 25 minutes of some of their best music. These songs represent the group's blend of country and rock at its finest and brightest, with the happy harmonies of "Hurry Up" and "Keep on Believin'" totally irresistible. Jim Messina's "You Better Think Twice" is a perfectly constructed and arranged song, one that should have been a huge hit but mysteriously never found its place in the Top 40 pantheon. Listening to this recording, though, it's easy to see why unimaginative radio programmers and much of the record-buying public couldn't find a niche for Poco. The knock was "too country for rock, too rock for country," but in fact, they were just ahead of their time, a tough spot to be in the world of popular entertainment. What about the last 15 minutes of this disc? It's a lengthy instrumental called "El Tonto de Nadie, Regressa." A cynic would say it's filler, but given the trend at the time toward side-long cuts, it's probably simply Poco's attempt at hipness. In retrospect, it can be seen as the forerunner to Messina's lengthy jams with Loggins & Messina a few years later; the sound is remarkably similar. While overshadowed by *Pickin' Up the Pieces*, which preceded it, and *Deliverin'*, which followed, *Poco* is well worth owning by anyone interested in the early days of this particular band, and of country-rock in general. The trademark sweet, high harmonies belying the heartbreak expressed in Richie Furay's lyrics, Messina's distinctive lead guitar, and Rusty Young's amazing ability to get an organ sound out of his pedal steel guitar are all here in full blossom. *—Jim Newsom*

Deliverin' / Jan. 13, 1971 / Epic ✦✦✦✦✦
Poco had originally made their name as a live act, and they'd always been at their best and most easygoing on-stage. The result is this live album of all new material, featuring Jim Messina's swan song with the band and some of the tightest playing and best singing in their recorded history. Jewels include "C'mon," "Hear That Music," "Kind Woman," and "You'd Better Think Twice." About as perfect an album as they ever made and, not coincidentally, by far the biggest seller the early group ever had. *—Bruce Eder*

From the Inside / 1971 / Epic ✦✦
Umm, crunchy guitars. *From the Inside* is the group's most unusual record, and one the band didn't like all that much, but a very good one anyway. Produced in Memphis by guitar legend Steve Cropper, *From the Inside* features a leaner, more stripped-down, somewhat bluesier sound. The harmonies are less radiant and the guitars (mostly acoustic) more radiant. The spirits are also a little more low-key than usual, but this is still a wonderful record, if a little offbeat. Grantham's drums and Schmit's bass are nice and up front in the mix, and the guitars have a really close presence. Highlights include "You Are the One," "Hoe Down," "Railroad Days" (maybe their hardest rocker) and "Ol' Forgiver." *—Bruce Eder*

A Good Feelin' to Know / Oct. 25, 1972 / Epic ✦✦✦
A Good Feelin' to Know was Poco's big attempt to broaden their audience—the title track, one of their most popular concert numbers, was the group's push for a hit single, which didn't work. The album as a whole, however, features a louder, harder-rocking sound a step or two removed from the country-rock they'd been known for, even on numbers like "Ride the Country," which has a more brittle sound than the group would have achieved on their earlier records. The guitars are all turned up really loud, and the harmonies are less sweet, overall making for a very heavy sound, surprisingly similar to the Buffalo Springfield (one of their old numbers, "Go and Say Goodbye," is even included, in an arguably better version), making this a curious throwback/advance. This album's relative failure made Furay begin to lose faith in his own group's prospects. *—Bruce Eder*

Crazy Eyes / 1973 / Epic/Legacy ✦✦✦✦✦
The third biggest-selling album in the group's history, *Crazy Eyes* is also the group's most lively and bracing work and contains some of their most soulful music. In short, it's the fruition of everything they'd been working toward for four years. Curiously, it's also one of a handful of examples of their use of outside help, including Chris Hillman on mandolin. The resulting sound is richer than anything found on any other Poco album, and the only tragedy is that the band reportedly cut enough tracks for two whole albums—one longs to hear the material that remained in the can. As it is, there's not a weak song, or even a wasted note anywhere on this album, and most bands would kill for a closing track as perfect as "Let's Dance Tonight." [The sound is excellent on this CD reissue, and only some historical notes would have improved it.] *—Bruce Eder*

Seven / 1974 / Epic/Legacy ✦✦✦
With strong, soaring harmonies, a healthy balance between acoustic country-rock and heavy rock & roll, and some fairly strong songs, *Seven* is a major surprise, given that this is the group's first post-Richie Furay album. George Grantham's drumming is a special highlight (check out his solo on "Drivin' Wheel"), but all of the playing is superb, and with one or two additional strong songs, this would be a highly recommended album, and as it is it is quite good. Unfortunately, not everything here is as strong as "Drivin' Wheel" or "Rocky Mountain Breakdown." *—Bruce Eder*

Cantamos / Dec. 1974 / Epic ✦✦✦
This album marks the emergence of Rusty Young as a composer of merit. Side one rocks out hard and fresh while the second side deals with lost love and broken-hearted romance. Much of the magic of their earlier albums has been recaptured. *—James Chrispell*

Head Over Heels / Jul. 1975 / MCA ✦✦✦✦
Keeping the songs short and to the point, Poco lets loose with a fine batch of material. This time out, they even cover the Becker-Fagen song "Dallas" with great verve. There's less country, but a lot more pop. *—James Chrispell*

The Very Best of Poco / Sep. 1975 / Epic ✦✦✦✦✦
Originally a two-LP set, *The Very Best of Poco* was a decent compilation in its time, assembling the group's best-known songs from singles and album cuts in a straightforward order with no particular surprises. It was reissued with upgraded sound in 1999, and for the very casual fan with a budget to consider the latter is adequate, showing their evolution as a band from the first flourish of their birth, as an offshoot of the Buffalo Springfield, with the same sort of vast potential displayed by the latter group (similarly unrealized by constant membership changes) into one of the premier country-rock outfits of the 1970s. Anyone serious about a deep enjoyment of the group, however, will opt for the more extensive and revelatory *The Forgotten Trail* instead, which contains numerous outtakes and—no pun—forgotten tracks. *—Bruce Eder*

Rose of Cimarron / 1976 / One Way ✦✦✦
Lushly produced pop/rock, *Rose of Cimmaron* hosts an array of sidemen, most notably Al Garth, formerly of Loggin & Messina, and keyboardist Steve Ferguson. The country influence is nearly abandoned except for the Rusty Young tune "Company's Comin'/Slow Poke." There are great tunes with great arrangements throughout. *—James Chrispell*

Live / Apr. 1976 / One Way ✦✦✦
In 1975, Poco left Epic Records after six years and jumped to One Way. Less than a year later, Epic released this 38-minute live album recorded at a series of November 1974 shows. By this time in their history, Richie Furay and Jim Messini were long gone, and steel guitar player Rusty Young and guitarist Paul Cotton were the dominant musical personalities in the group, between them providing all but one of the songs represented here. The group still had a beautiful sound and put on a lively, spirited show, laced with strong lead singing and sweet harmonies—"Ride the Country," which shows the strong influence of Neil Young in both its writing and playing, is a radiant piece of hard country-rock highlighted by Timothy B. Schmit's powerful bass work, Cotton's searing yet smooth lead, and Young's haunting steel sound. In contrast to a lot of live albums of this era, the group stretches out elegantly on the repertory without altering the general shape of the songs, so that this is more than a rehash of the familiar studio versions of the music at hand. "Angel" and "High and Dry" get good performances, and the group finishes with Richie Furay's "A Good Feelin' to Know." The recording is very clean and, typically for concert

albums of this period, pushes the sound of the audience far into the background, with very crisp separation of the instruments between the two stereo channels. [The late-2000 One-Way Records CD reissue is a straight transfer of the LP with no extras, but also carrying a temptingly low retail price, and is the first reappearance of this album in more than 20 years.] *—Bruce Eder*

Indian Summer / 1977 / MCA ✦✦
Although *Indian Summer* wasn't the commercial breakthrough Poco had hoped for (it would come a year later with *Legend*), there's nothing inherently bad here. The band was more compact than ever, evenly sharing songwriting duties, and Rusty Young's confident pedal steel seemed to distinguish Poco from most other country-rock bands. However, this record is also a few notches down from their best, early material. The strongest song is the title track, which has some nice steel guitar and harmony vocals, but this high point is balanced by the closing number, "The Dance," a clumsy suite that's burdened by an over-the-top string and horn arrangement. The only other item of note is a courtesy appearance by Steely Dan's Donald Fagen, who plays Arp synthesizer on a couple songs. File this under the "treading water" category. *—Peter Kurtz*

Legend / Nov. 1978 / MCA ✦✦✦
The departure of Timothy B. Schmit to the Eagles should have signalled the end for Poco. However, they turned in a surprisingly tight set here and got their first Top 40 hit with "Crazy Love." *—James Chrispell*

Under the Gun / 1980 / MCA ✦✦
A deliberate follow-up to *Legend*, *Under the Gun* was a workmanlike but unremarkable effort. *—William Ruhlmann*

Blue and Gray / 1981 / One Way ✦✦

Cowboys & Englishmen / 1982 / One Way ✦
Poco's contractual obligation album to get off MCA Records (which had taken over ABC Records). A throwaway effort at a time when their career needed rejuvenation, not another wound. [Originally released on LP by MCA Records, *Cowboys & Englishmen* was licensed to One Way Records for CD reissue.] *—William Ruhlmann*

Ghost Town / 1982 / Atlantic ✦✦✦
Surprise! Just when they had been written off by even the most loyal fans, Poco rebounds nicely here. Songs "Shoot for the Moon," "When Hearts Collide," and the title track are pleasant reminders of a band that once was. *—James Chrispell*

Backtracks / 1982 / MCA ✦✦✦✦
A nine-song compilation of Poco's tenure at ABC (later MCA) Records, 1975-1982, judiciously chosen. [Later expanded for CD release and retitled *Crazy Loving: The Best Of Poco 1975-1982*.] *—William Ruhlmann*

Inamorata / 1984 / Atlantic ✦✦
Poco was down to the duo of Rusty Young and Paul Cotton by this point, which may be why, having been visited in the studio by former members Richie Furay, Timothy Schmit, and George Grantham, they structured the credits in such a way that you might think the old group had reformed. Not so. Rather, this was a mediocre (and final) effort by an act long past its prime. *—William Ruhlmann*

Legacy / Aug. 1989 / RCA ✦✦✦
The original 1968 lineup of Richie Furay, Jim Messina, Randy Meisner, George Grantham, and Rusty Young, which never got to record (Meisner quit on the eve of their first session), finally goes into the studio, and it's as though 20 years dissolve away. The singing is impeccable, the playing awesome—maybe a little too good—and unlike a lot of reunion projects of this kind, the songs are as good as any the group *ever* recorded, with a couple ("When It All Began," "Call It Love") that would belong on any truly honest best-of collection. The only flaw, if that's what it is, is the decidedly modern sound and production—the group's country-rock sound is nearly compromised by the modern engineering, which gives the drums too much presence and the guitars too much volume. The playing is loud and precise and often beautiful, but also at times mechanical and soulless compared with the group's old recordings; the exceptionally passionate singing more than compensates for this flaw, however. It might have been interesting to see the re-formed group do a couple of the songs off of the first album that they never got to do as a quintet, but the point behind that had long ago been made by the quartet that did record. A must-own alongside the MCA best-of and the original eight Epic albums (or the Epic double-disc *Forgotten Trail* anthology). David Cole was the overall producer, but Richard Marx signed his name as producer to one of the best tracks here, "Nothin' to Hide," which he also co-wrote. *—Bruce Eder*

Crazy Loving: The Best of Poco 1975–1982 / Oct. 1989 / MCA ✦✦✦✦
Known for their country-rock ease and light harmonies, Poco netted two of the finest soft rock tunes of the late '70s in "Crazy Love" and "Heart of the Night," which highlight *Crazy Loving*, one of the more accessible compilations from this California band. After these tracks, the rest of this package takes minor hits from rather lackluster albums such as *Blue and Gray*, *Under the Gun*, and *Cowboys & Englishmen*, gradually losing interest along the way. Although the group's countrified feel wraps itself tightly around songs like "Too Many Nights Too Long," "Indian Summer," and the instrumental "Ashes/Feudin'," Poco's occasional knack for a catchy hook or a sincere lyric fails to rise to the top on most of these cuts. "Midnight Rain" and "Keep on Tryin'" are almost there, but the departure of Richie Furay in 1973 dealt somewhat of a blow to the band's material, and their laid-back sound pales in comparison to what the Eagles were putting out at the same time. This set makes for a better buy than any of the albums that these tracks originate from, but heartier collections contain material from earlier recordings, like *Pickin' Up the Pieces* or *A Good Feeling to Know*, right up to 1989's *Legacy*, the album that gave them their last two Top 40 hits in "Call It Love" and "Nothin' to Hide." *—Mike DeGagne*

The Forgotten Trail (1969–1974) / Oct. 1990 / Epic ✦✦✦✦✦
This excellent two-disc collection captures Poco's finest moments from the days when they were laying down the template for all the country-rock music that was to follow. It's hard to remember, but when the Eagles first hit the scene, they were thought by many to be a Poco-wannabe band. Listen to this set and you'll hear why. *The Forgotten Trail (1969-1974)* culls tracks from Poco's first eight albums, as well as unreleased cuts and singles. From the classic anthem "Pickin' Up the Pieces," which kicks things off, through "You Better Think Twice," "C'mon," "Kind Woman," "From the Inside," "A Good Feelin' to Know," "Crazy Eyes," and on and on, this is wonderful music, ahead of its time in many ways. If Poco had arrived on the scene in the early '90s, they would have been kings of the country charts. Of course, without Poco, country music wouldn't have taken on the rock trappings that it did in the '80s and '90s. As it was, the band was considered too country for the Top 40 rock format of the time, and too rock & roll for country radio. This set is the place to start for an appreciation of the original Poco, when the group was considered to be Richie Furay's band. All the ingredients are here that made their music so delightful: the trademark high-vocal harmonies; Rusty Young's pedal-steel guitar wizardry; Furay's patented juxtapositions of sad lyrics against bouncy, harmony-filled tunes; and their spirit of optimism and good feelings even in the face of hard luck and bad weather. The 36-page booklet does a fine job of telling the story in print, and the 38 songs speak volumes about the band's place and influence. Thanks to this compilation, Poco's trailblazing days need be forgotten no longer. *—Jim Newsom*

● **Ultimate Collection** / Nov. 17, 1998 / Hip-O ✦✦✦✦✦
There has been no lack of Poco compilations, but this is the first one to span the four record labels the band recorded for between 1969 and 1989. Ten of the group's 13 chart singles are included, among them its biggest hits, "Crazy Love," "Call It Love," and "Heart of the Night." Also included are some of its best songs, such as "Pickin' Up the Pieces" and "A Good Feelin' to Know." The country-rock hybrid Poco achieved during its lengthy, commercially under-rewarded recording career is on display in songs written by Richie Furay, Jim Messina, Paul Cotton, Timothy B. Schmit, and Rusty Young. Anyone looking for the missing link between Buffalo Springfield and the Eagles will find it here. *—William Ruhlmann*

The Very Best of Poco / Aug. 31, 1999 / Epic/Legacy ✦✦✦✦
Legacy's 1999 reissue of *The Very Best of Poco* may not contain any songs from the group's reunion, but they're not missed, since this winds up being a generous, 14-track overview of the band at its peak. Yes, there may be a fan favorite or two missing (they may be satiated by the inclusion of a couple of live tracks), but the key songs from Richie Furay and Jim Messina's country-rock outfit are here, making this an excellent representation of the band's best work. *—Stephen Thomas Erlewine*

20th Century Masters—The Millennium Collection: The Best of Poco / Feb. 29, 2000 / MCA ✦✦✦✦
Another excellent entry in MCA's Millennium Collection, this features 11 of the group's best-known tunes. Poco never reached the country-rock commercial heights of the Eagles, but their music was every bit as essential and groundbreaking. Of course, Timothy B. Schmit and Randy Meisner were both members of Poco before becoming Eagles, almost reinforcing the point. Highlights include "Heart of the Night," "Crazy Love," "Under the Gun," "Midnight Rain," and "Making Love." An essential collection for all fans of country-rock. *—Cub Koda*

The Very Best of Poco / Jul. 25, 2002 / BGO ✦✦✦✦

Charlie Poole

b. Mar. 22, 1892, Alamance County, NC, **d.** May 1931, Eden, NC
Banjo, Leader, Vocals / Old-Timey, String Bands
Charlie Poole & the North Carolina Ramblers were one of the most popular string bands of the 1920s. If they didn't have the foot-stomping exuberance of their chief competitors, Georgia's Skillet Lickers, they offered a debonair precision that was equally infectious. Infused with ragtime and pop, their music almost seemed to swing at times (even though the use of that word to describe music was still several years in the future). Poole strongly influenced later banjo players, including those who would become the creators of bluegrass.

Poole was born in Alamance County, NC, and spent much of his adult life working in textile mills. He learned banjo as a youth and also played baseball. (He may have adopted his three-finger playing style, a version of classical banjo technique, due to a baseball accident involving his thumb.) When not working in mills, he would travel from town to town across the country, playing the banjo and taking what work he could get. He ended up settling in Spray, NC, in 1918 and married two years later. He and his brother-in-law, fiddler Posey Rorer, would often play together with other local musicians, and out of these performances grew a distinct group called the North Carolina Ramblers. Poole and Rorer teamed up with guitarist Norm Woodlieff in 1925, and the trio auditioned in New York for Columbia Records. They were accepted and cut four songs; all were successful, including the bluesy "Don't Let Your Deal Go Down." That became a bluegrass and country standard, and Poole and the Ramblers were soon a popular string band.

The band's unusual sound remained consistent through several changes in personnel. As vocalist, Poole sang with a plain, uninflected style that complemented his complex banjo picking. Often, and perhaps intentionally, Poole obscured parts of the lyrics when he sang; record buyers sometimes purchased Ramblers recordings simply so that they could try to parse out what he was saying. The songs they sang were a mixture of minstrel songs, Victorian ballads, and humorous burlesques often delivered with Poole's straight-faced, dry wit. Several more songs' paths to popularity in the country tradition led through Poole's band, including "Sweet Sunny South" and "White House Blues," and his catalog is full of unexpected charmers like "If the River Was Whiskey," which deftly weaves that Irish tale of drunkenness with the then-up-to-the-minute "Hesitation Blues" (also known as "Sittin' on Top of the World"). Through the rest of the 1920s, the Ramblers recorded close to 70 sides for Columbia.

Like many country performers to follow, Poole lived a fast life; he was a hard-drinking man, rowdy and reckless. Poole was significant as one of the first country artists to gain widespread popularity through recordings, and when the Depression slowed record sales dramatically, he was hard hit. Around 1930 his self-confidence began to wane with his popularity, and he began drinking even more heavily. Scheduled to appear in a film in 1931, he unfortunately went on a bender and died of heart failure before he could get to Hollywood. After his death, Rorer (who had left the band in 1929) and guitarist Roy Harvey (who'd replaced Woodlieff around the same time) began leading the North Carolina Ramblers. (The group continued to record and perform for a quite a few years afterward.) Poole's music enjoyed renewed popularity during the folk revival of the '60s, and several reissue LPs followed. His complete recordings were issued on CD by the County label in the 1990s, and Kinney Rorrer wrote and published a biography of the great bandleader and banjo player. *—Sandra Brennan & James Manheim*

Charlie Poole & The North Carolina Ramblers, Vol. 4 / 1976 / County ✦✦✦
This North Carolina old-time music legend and his merry crew of sidemen recorded a great deal of material in the '20s and early '30s, and the County label has reissued just about everything Poole did at one point or another. A listener might expect that, by the time the archivists get around to compiling a fourth volume, it might be something like trying to create a meal out of leftovers found in the back of the refrigerator; although some tracks on this collection might confirm such a suspicion, the Poole group operated on a much higher level then most households do when it comes to storing food. Thus, there are delights galore on this collection, such as the edgy "You Ain't Talkin' to Me" and the lovely "Sunny Tennessee," the latter the artist's first recording ever, and pretty darn good at that. Several instrumentals are also included, some of them showcases for the superb fiddler Lonnie Austin. *—Eugene Chadbourne*

Old Time Songs Recorded from 1925 to 1930 / 1994 / County ✦✦✦
Old-Time Songs contains 16 songs Charlie Poole recorded for Columbia Records between 1925 and 1930. This sampling features nearly every one of his best songs—including the hits "Don't Let Your Deal Go Down Blues" and "Can I Sleep In Your Barn Tonight, Mister"—and provides the definitive retrospective of Poole, as well as a good glimpse into the style and sound of old-timey country music in the first half of the 20th century. *—Thom Owens*

Charlie Poole & the North Carolina Ramblers, Vol. 2: Old Time Songs Recorded From 1926 / Feb. 27, 1996 / County ✦✦✦✦
County Records' second installment of Charlie Poole & the North Carolina Ramblers is another great testament to this seminal band: while most or all of Poole and the Ramblers' best-known songs are included on the earlier volume of *Old Time Songs*, the lesser-known tunes on this disc are every bit as entertaining, if often less familiar. The opening "If the River was Whiskey" (known in other circles as "Hesitation Blues") is one of the smoothest, most subtly infectious recordings of old-timey music available anywhere. True to the Ramblers' style, the playing and vocals are always spotlessly clean and brimming with good humor, the three musicians on each song interacting perfectly. Occasional banter between guitarist Roy Harvey and Poole adds nicely to the atmosphere without delving into gross stereotype or cheap laughs; unlike many of their contemporaries, this band consistently rejected the hillbilly image of the backwoods yokel, creating a music that is instead both sophisticated and inescapably country. Songs on this disc draw from traditional folk sources as well as Tin Pan Alley pop, with each piece rendered in the Ramblers' distinctive style. Sound quality is excellent throughout the compilation, which retains little evidence of the original 78 crackles and hisses; though the first volume of *Old Time Songs* may have the better song selection, its sound quality is sadly less consistent. All in all, this is a sturdy compilation from what is arguably the greatest string band in the annals of old-time recorded music. *—Burgin Mathews*

● **Legend of Charlie Poole, Vol. 3** / Jan. 25, 1999 / County ✦✦✦✦
County continues its excellent survey of works by this popular banjoist and vocalist with this third volume of rural, old-time string band dance tunes, novelties, minstrel songs, and folk ballads. This time-capsule disc of Poole's North Carolina Ramblers features his nimble three-fingered playing and dry-humored tenor singing with fiddle and guitar. Their tunes were well received in their day; their first eight sides sold almost half a million copies by 1927, and their first two alone sold 167,000 in one year. These first-class transfers belie their age and make enjoying the music easy. This is moving stuff. *—Sigmund Finman*

Sandy Posey

b. Jun. 18, 1947, Jasper, AL

Vocals / Country-Pop, Nashville Sound/Countrypolitan, Girl Group

Despite having several moderate hits in both the country and pop charts, Sandy Posey was never fully embraced by either audience and is far from being a household name. Posey was born in Jasper, AL, in 1947. In her teens she relocated to Memphis, where she secured a job as a receptionist in a local studio. Eventually she was given a chance to sing backup during recording sessions which led to work at several other studios in Memphis and Nashville—where her clear voice was perfectly suited for the ultraslick Nashville "countrypolitan" sound of the day. MGM Records signed her at age 18 to a solo deal on the strength of her demo recording of "Born a Woman," and despite her country roots and the country feel of her material, MGM marketed her as a pop singer—in retrospect, a wise decision. "Born a Woman" and "Single Girl" became her first two hits (both reached number 12 in the pop charts in 1966). Since both songs were written by Martha Sharp, it was mistakenly reported during this time that Sandy Posey was a pseudonym assumed by Sharp for recording purposes. Posey had two more pop hits with the Top 40 "What a Woman in Love Won't Do" and the number 12 "I Take It Back." By 1968, Posey's woman-as-a-helpless-victim themes were decidedly out of touch with the times, and the hits stopped coming. She went into semiretirement.

She returned in 1970 for phase two of her career—"the country years." She signed to Columbia Records, where she had another string of hits—this time in the country charts, including the Top 20 Vietnam War-inspired "Bring Him Home Safely to Me," the slightly risqué "Why Don't We Go Somewhere and Love" (a minor hit in 1975), "Happy Birthday Baby," and "Don't" (both Top 40). She moved to Monument Records in 1976 and later to Warner Bros., where she hit again with a series of oldies revivals—the Chordettes' "Born to Be With You" and a medley of "Love, Love, Love" and "Chapel of Love." Her last hit was in 1979 with "Love Is Sometimes Easy." In 1983, she signed to the independent label Audiograph and released her final solo album. She then stayed busy as a session singer and infrequently toured with her husband, Wade Cummings, an Elvis impersonator. *—Chris Woodstra*

Born a Woman / 1966 / MGM ✦✦✦✦
Sandy Posey's debut record starts off with her signature hit song, "Born a Woman" and the rest of the songs, which are mostly laments on lost love and loneliness, set the blueprint she would follow for her pop phase with MGM. The ultra-slick Nashville pop gloss of the arrangements helped secure a pop audience but Posey clearly demonstrated that she had the soul of a country singer. *—Chris Woodstra*

I Take It Back / 1967 / MGM ✦✦✦
Posey's third album features a mix of originals and covers, including songs that had been hits for Miss Toni Fisher ("The Big Hurt"), Tony Orlando ("Halfway to Paradise"), and the Fleetwoods ("Come Softly to Me"). *—Jim Worbois*

Single Girl / 1967 / MGM ✦✦✦
Posey's defiant stance on the cover and the title are slightly deceptive—this isn't a testament to the independence and joy of being a "single girl" but rather another case of Sandy mourning her life without "her man." The title track preaches, "A single girl needs a good hearted man to lean on." Aside from outdated anti-feminist statements, the album's real strengths lie in the haunting, slightly skewed arrangements which cross "countrypolitan" with pure '60s pop best exemplified in the overlooked classic, "Hey Mister." *—Chris Woodstra*

Looking at You / 1968 / MGM ✦✦
While there is really nothing outstanding about this record, it is a pleasant record to listen to and doesn't really get in the way while one is doing something else. One song of some interest is her version of "Shades of Gray," which was issued by the Monkees as a single around this time. *—Jim Worbois*

Why Don't We Go Somewhere and Love / 1972 / Columbia ✦✦✦
Producer Billy Sherrill stripped away the double-tracked vocals and gave her records the same type of feel he applied to the records of Tammy Wynette. This resulted in a modest hit on the title track. The record is also interesting because it includes one track co-written by future game-show host Chuck Woolery and another by future country music star Eddie Rabbitt. *—Jim Worbois*

Tennessee Rose / 1983 / 51 West ✦✦

● **The Best of Sandy Posey** / 1996 / Collectables ✦✦✦✦✦
The Best of Sandy Posey is a 14-track collection covering Posey's first recording period for MGM, including the classic forgotten hits, "Born a Woman," "Single Girl," and "I Take It Back"—oddly, all three peaked at number 12. Posey's mid-'60s songs, almost all depicting a woman helpless without—or alternately, trapped with—"her man," were slightly out-of-touch at the time and are artifacts now, but the slick pop-country arrangements have a timeless charm. Posey would have later success in the country charts in the '70s but unfortunately, those hits are not represented here. Though the album appears to be a straight reissue of the MGM's *The Best of Sandy Posey*, this package actually expands on it by three tracks. *—Chris Woodstra*

● **A Single Girl: The Very Best of the MGM Years** / Dec. 3, 2002 / RPM ✦✦✦✦✦
This replaced Collectables' mid-'90s collection, *The Best of Sandy Posey*, as the best overview of the artist's 1960s material, and hence the best Posey record available. It has 23 tracks where *The Best of Sandy Posey* has only 14, and has extensive liner notes with quotes from Posey herself, whereas the Collectables release had typically (for that label) scant annotation. Actually *The Best of Sandy Posey* does have four songs that don't appear on *A Single Girl*, but the latter album does include the hits that anyone searching for a Posey best-of would demand: "Born a Woman," "Single Girl," "What a Woman in Love Won't Do," and "I Take It Back." Though on the whole the music is rather unadventurous, in its time it struck a peculiar chord: countrypolitan songs that on occasion crossed over to the pop audience (sometimes even in Britain) in a big way, with some echoes of rock, soul (particularly on "What a Woman in Love Won't Do," "One Man Woman," and "Hey Mister"), easy listening pop, and dippy submissive teen idol/girl group vocal flavors that were anachronistic by the time these were made in 1966-1968. There are some big name writers here—Dan Penn-Spooner Oldham, John D. Loudermilk, and Joe South—but their contributions aren't nearly as memorable or biting as the songs for which they're most famous. Even though many of these tracks frankly aren't striking, there are some fair non-hits here, particularly those that go into some (for countrypolitan) unusually brooding pop melodies, like "Shattered" and "Patterns." *—Richie Unterberger*

Johnny Powers (Leon Joseph Pavlik)

b. 1938, East Detroit, MI

Vocals, Producer / Rock & Roll, Rockabilly

Rockabilly artist Johnny Powers' story is one of the more intriguing the genre has to offer. Born John Leon Joseph Pavlik in 1938 in East Detroit, MI, he was the oldest of five children. The family later moved to the small town of Utica, MI, north of Detroit, where he was raised. Pavlik was exposed to music from an early age by members of his father's family, which included several amateur and semi-professional musicians who played weddings and local dances. It was country music, however, that first drew Pavlik into music on a personal level; he discovered Lonnie Baron, a veteran country singer with a show on local radio and would listen and try to play along with a guitar that he'd bought for $2.50 from a neighbor. He later got some helpful instruction from Marvin Maynard, a professional musician who lived in Utica. In 1954, at age 16, Pavlik joined Jimmy Williams & the Drifters, a local country band that played at a local venue called Bill's Barn and got a featured radio spot on a radio station out of Marine City, MI. He also played on one single cut by the band, but it wasn't long before rock & roll attracted Pavlik. It was Jack Scott's single, "Baby She's Gone," that drew him into rock & roll.

Courtesy of Jimmy Williams' brother Russ, Pavlik discovered Elvis Presley when he was still a Memphis-based phenomenon, and his current single was "Milk Cow Blues Boogie," which really interested him, as a country song with a rock & roll beat. Soon he was adding the beat to his own country songs, and in 1957, Johnny Powers, as he was now known, got an audition with Fortune Records in Detroit. He paid $100 for his own session to record a pair of songs, "Honey Let's Go (To a Rock and Roll Show)" b/w "Your Love" on the Hi-Q label. A black DJ named Ernie Durham played his record on WJLB, and Johnny Powers was one of the few white artists who would play the record hops that Durham sponsored. He later put together a band, Johnny Powers & His Rockets, with his friend Marvin Maynard on bass, Clark Locker on the drums, and Stan Getz on guitar. Powers jumped to the Fox label in 1958, getting a pair of regional hits with "Rock Rock" and "Long Blond Hair." The group got steady work cutting demos, some of which have surfaced as bootleg releases in recent years. Among his strongest work from this period were a pair of originals, "Mama Rock" and "Indeed I Do," cut for Leedon. On both, he sounds like the young, wild Elvis Presley that just arrived at RCA, and the group sings uncannily like the Jordanaires on the latter track.

Things began to happen faster for Johnny Powers when his manager, Tommy Moers, got him a contract with Sun Records in 1959, heralded with the release of "With Your Love, With Your Kiss" b/w "Be Mine early that year. A second single followed, but Powers was dropped by Sun in 1960. He later became the first white artist signed to Motown Records, but with the passing of the '60s into the '70s, Power's career found him on the other side of the studio glass, producing hits with Tim Tam & the Turn-Ons' "Wait a Minute" and Jack Kittel's oddball country sickie "Psycho." Still active today, Johnny Powers is proof positive of rock's ability to produce a true survivor who also is a true believer in the strength that lies within the music itself. *—Cub Koda & Bruce Eder*

- **Long Blond Hair** / Nov. 16, 1993 / Norton ✦✦✦✦✦

An excellent 23-track retrospective of Powers' early career. All the landmark Fox (the title cut), Fortune ("Honey Let's Go (To a Rock and Roll Show)") and Sun ("With Your Love, with Your Kiss") singles from the '50s are here, along with a batch of unissued material from the same time frame. Great, true, high powered rockin' that makes up in raw enthusiasm what it may sacrifice in commercial pleasantries. *—Cub Koda*

New Spark (for an Old Flame) / 1994 / Schoolkids ✦✦

Here is modern-day rockabilly from an obscure veteran of the '50s, with few surprises: some covers of familiar oldies, new material that strains to recreate classic rockabilly patterns, some countryish stuff. Actually, there is a surprise: a couple of the "bonus" tracks (covers of old Hank Ballard tunes) have guest appearances by George Clinton. *—Richie Unterberger*

Prairie Oyster

f. 1975, Canada

Group / Western Swing Revival, Contemporary Country, Neo-Traditionalist Country

The Canadian Western swing group Prairie Oyster made a brief splash on the U.S. charts in the early '90s but began playing together in 1975, when they were a trio consisting of lead singer/bassist Russell de Carle, guitarist Keith Glass, and steel guitar player Denis Delorme. Initially, they toured and appeared on television but did not record; they disbanded in 1978, but in 1982 reunited along with new member John P. Allen to do some gigs. They also took on keyboardist/songwriter Joan Besen and finally, in 1986, drummer Bruce Moffett. As the new Prairie Oyster, they recorded their debut *Oyster Tracks*. Eventually some of their demos, recorded by Steve Berlin, made it to RCA executive Joe Galante in Nashville, who signed them after seeing the group perform.

For RCA, Oyster recorded *Different Kind of Fire*, with guest appearances by Berlin; the first single, "Goodbye, So Long, Hello," made it to the Top 70 on the U.S. country charts in 1990. In 1991, they again won numerous kudos for their second album, *Everybody Knows*, and its resulting singles. They did not appeared on the U.S. charts beyond 1991, but continued to work and record in their native Canada through the rest of the '90s. *String of Pearls: A Greatest Hits Collection* was released on both sides of the border in 2000. *—Sandra Brennan*

Different Kind of Fire / Apr. 1990 / RCA ✦✦✦✦

The first U.S. release from this Canadian sextet puts a modern spin on traditional country sounds. *—Jason Ankeny*

- **Everybody Knows** / Sep. 1991 / RCA ✦✦✦✦✦

On *Everybody Knows*, Prairie Oyster shed their other influences to fully embrace honky tonk. *—Jason Ankeny*

Only One Moon / May 29, 1995 / Arista ✦✦✦

Blue Plate Special / Mar. 18, 1997 / Velvel ✦✦✦

String of Pearls: A Greatest Hits Collection / Jun. 20, 2000 / Arista ✦✦✦

In the early '90s, the Canadian Western swing group Prairie Oyster made a brief splash on the U.S. charts and unfortunately disappeared shortly thereafter. *String of Pearls: A Greatest Hits Collection* highlights 14 of their chart-topping country hits, including "Goodbye, So Long, Hello," "Will I Do ('Til the Real Thing Comes Along)," "One Precious Love," and "Man in the Moon." Since the majority of Prairie Oyster's discs are out of print in the U.S., look for this set in the cutout bin. *—Al Campbell*

Elvis Presley

b. Jan. 8, 1935, Tupelo, MS, **d.** Aug. 16, 1977, Memphis, TN

Guitar, Vocals / Rock & Roll, Rockabilly, Pop, Pop/Rock

Elvis Presley may be the single most important figure in American 20th century popular music. Not necessarily the *best*, and certainly not the most consistent. But no one could argue with the fact that he was the musician most responsible for popularizing rock & roll on an international level. Viewed in cold sales figures, his impact was phenomenal. Dozens upon dozens of international smashes from the mid-'50s to the mid-'70s, as well as the steady sales of his catalog and reissues since his death in 1977, may make him the single highest-selling performer in history.

More important from a music lover's perspective, however, are his remarkable artistic achievements. Presley was not the very first white man to sing rhythm & blues; Bill Haley predated him in that regard, and there may have been others as well. Elvis was certainly the first, however, to assertively fuse country and blues music into the style known as rockabilly. While rockabilly arrangements were the foundations of his first (and possibly best) recordings, Presley could not have become a mainstream superstar without a much more varied palette that also incorporated pop, gospel, and even some bits of bluegrass and operatic schmaltz here and there. His 1950s recordings established the basic language of rock & roll; his explosive and sexual stage presence set standards for the music's visual image; his vocals were incredibly powerful and versatile.

Unfortunately, to much of the public, Elvis is more icon than artist. Innumerable bad Hollywood movies, increasingly caricatured records and mannerisms, and a personal life that became steadily more sheltered from real-world concerns (and steadily more bizarre) gave his story a somewhat mythic status. By the time of his death, he'd become more a symbol of gross Americana than of cultural innovation. The continued speculation about his incredible career has sustained interest in his life, and supported a large tourist/entertainment industry, that may last indefinitely, even if the fascination is fueled more by his celebrity than his music.

Born to a poor Mississippi family in the heart of Depression, Elvis had moved to Memphis by his teens, where he absorbed the vibrant melting pot of Southern popular music in the form of blues, country, bluegrass, and gospel. After graduating from highschool, he became a truck driver, rarely if ever singing in public. Some 1953 and 1954 demos, recorded at the emerging Sun label in Memphis primarily for Elvis' own pleasure, helped stir interest on the part of Sun owner Sam Phillips. In mid-1954, Phillips, looking for a white singer with a black feel, teamed Presley with guitarist Scotty Moore and bassist Bill Black. Almost by accident, apparently, the trio hit upon a version of an Arthur "Big Boy" Crudup blues tune, "That's All Right Mama," that became Elvis' first single.

Elvis' five Sun singles pioneered the blend of R&B and C&W that would characterize rockabilly music. For quite a few scholars, they remain not only Elvis' best singles, but the best rock & roll ever recorded. Claiming that Elvis made blues acceptable for the white market is not the whole picture; the singles usually teamed blues covers with country and pop ones, all made into rock & roll (at this point a term that barely existed) with the pulsing beat, slap-back echo, and Elvis' soaring, frenetic vocals. "That's All Right Mama," "Blue Moon of Kentucky," "Good Rockin' Tonight," "Baby Let's Play House," and "Mystery Train" remain core early rock classics.

The singles sold well in the Memphis area immediately, and by 1955 were starting to sell well to country audiences throughout the South. Presley, Moore, and Black hit the road with a stage show that grew ever wilder and more provocative, Elvis' swiveling hips causing enormous controversy. The move to all-out rock was hastened by the addition of drums. The last Sun single, "I Forgot to Remember Forget"/"Mystery Train," hit number one on the national country charts in late 1955. Presley was obviously a performer with superstar potential, attracting the interest of bigger labels and Colonel Tom Parker, who became Elvis' manager. In need of capital to expand the Sun label, Sam Phillips sold Presley's contract to RCA in late 1955 for 35,000 dollars; a bargain, when viewed in hindsight, but an astronomical sum at the time.

This is the point where musical historians start to diverge in opinion. For many, the whole of his subsequent work for RCA—encompassing over 20 years—was a steady letdown, never recapturing the pure, primal energy that was harnessed so effectively on the handful of Sun singles. Elvis, however, was not a purist. What he wanted, more than anything, was to be successful. To do that, his material needed more of a pop feel; in any case, he'd never exactly been one to disparage the mainstream, naming Dean Martin as one of his chief heroes from the get-go. At RCA, his rockabilly was leavened with enough pop flavor to make all of the charts, not just the country ones.

At the beginning, at least, the results were hardly any tamer than the Sun sessions. "Heartbreak Hotel," his first single, rose to number one and, aided by some national television appearances, helped make Elvis an instant superstar. "I Want You, I Need You, I Love You" was a number one follow-up; the double-sided monster "Hound Dog"/"Don't Be Cruel" was one of the biggest-selling singles the industry had ever experienced up to that point. Albums and EPs were also chart-toppers, not just in the U.S., but throughout the world. The 1956 RCA recordings, while a bit more sophisticated in production and a bit less rootsy in orientation than his previous work, were still often magnificent, rating among the best and most influential recordings of early rock & roll.

Elvis' (and Colonel Parker's) aspirations were too big to be limited to records and live appearances. By late 1956, his first Hollywood movie, *Love Me Tender*, had been released; other screen vehicles would follow in the next few years, *Jailhouse Rock* being the best. The hits continued unabated, several of them ("Jailhouse Rock," "All Shook Up," "Too Much") excellent, and often benefiting from the efforts of top early rock songwriter Otis Blackwell, as well as the emerging team of Jerry Leiber-Mike Stoller. The Jordanaires added both pop and gospel elements with their smooth backup vocals.

Yet worrisome signs were creeping in. The Dean Martin influence began rearing his head in smoky, sentimental ballads such as "Loving You"; the vocal swoops became more exaggerated and stereotypical, although the overall quality of his output remained high. And although Moore and Black continued to back Elvis on his early RCA recordings, within a few years the musicians had gone their own ways. Presley's recording and movie careers were interrupted by his induction into the Army in early 1958. There was enough material in the can to flood the charts throughout his two-year absence (during which he largely served in Germany). When he re-entered civilian life in 1960, his popularity, remarkably, was at just as high a level as when he left.

One couldn't, unfortunately, say the same for the quality of his music, which was not just becoming more sedate, but was starting to either repeat itself, or opt for operatic ballads that didn't have a whole lot to do with rock. Elvis' rebellious, wild image had been tamed to a large degree as well, as he and Parker began designing a career built around Hollywood films. Shortly after leaving the Army, in fact, Presley gave up live performing altogether for nearly a decade to concentrate on movie-making. The films, in turn, would serve as vehicles to both promote his records and to generate maximum revenue with minimal effort. For the rest of the '60s, Presley ground out two or three movies a year that, while mostly profitable, had little going for them in the way of story, acting, or social value.

While there were some quality efforts on Presley's early-'60s albums, his discography was soon dominated by forgettable soundtracks, mostly featuring material that was dispensable or downright ridiculous. In time he became largely disinterested in devoting much time to his craft in the studio. The soundtrack LPs themselves were sometimes filled out with outtakes that had been in the can for years (and these, sadly, were often the highlights of the albums). There were some good singles in the early '60s, like "Return to Sender"; once in a while there was even a flash of superb, tough rock, like "Little Sister" or "(Marie's the Name) His Latest Flame." But by 1963 or so there was little to get excited about, although he continued to sell in large quantities.

The era spanning, roughly, 1962-1967 has generated a school of Elvis apologists, eager to wrestle any kernel of quality that emerged from his recordings during this period. They also point out that Presley was assigned poor material, and assert that Colonel Parker was largely responsible for Presley's emasculation. True to a point, but on the other hand it could be claimed, with some validity, that Presley himself was doing little to rouse himself from his artistic stupor, letting Parker destroy his artistic credibility without much apparent protest, and holing up in his large mansion with a retinue of yes-men that protected their benefactor from much day-to-day contact with a fast-changing world.

The Beatles, all big Elvis fans, displaced Presley as the biggest rock act in the world in 1964. What's more, they did so by writing their own material and playing their own instruments; something Elvis had never been capable of, or particularly aspired to. They, and the British and American groups the Beatles influenced, were not shy about expressing their opinions, experimenting musically, and taking the reins of their artistic direction into their own hands. The net effect was to make Elvis Presley, still churning out movies in Hollywood as psychedelia and soul music became the rage, seem irrelevant, even as he managed to squeeze out an obscure Dylan cover ("Tomorrow Is a Long Time") on a 1966 soundtrack album. By 1967 and 1968, there were slight stirrings of an artistic reawakening by Elvis. Singles like "Guitar Man," "Big Boss Man," and "U.S. Male," though hardly classics, were at least genuine rock & roll that sounded better than much of what he'd been turning out for years. A 1968 television special gave Presley the opportunity he needed to reinvent himself as an all-out leather-coated rocker, still capable of magnetizing an audience, and eager to revisit his blues and country roots.

The 1968 album *Elvis in Memphis* was the first LP in nearly a decade in which Presley seemed cognizant of current trends, as he updated his sounds with contemporary compositions and touches of soul to create some reasonably gutsy late-'60s pop/rock. This material, and 1969 hits like "Suspicious Minds" and "In the Ghetto," returned him to the top of the charts. Arguably, it's been overrated by critics, who were so glad to have him singing rock again that they weren't about to carp about the slickness of some of the production, or the mediocrity of some of the songwriting.

But Elvis' voice *did* sound good, and he returned to live performing in 1969, breaking in with weeks of shows in Las Vegas. This was followed by national tours that proved him to still be an excellent live entertainer, even if the exercises often reeked of showbiz extravaganza. (Elvis never did play outside of North America and Hawaii, possibly because Colonel Parker, it was later revealed, was an illegal alien who could have faced serious problems if he traveled abroad.) Hollywood was history, but studio and live albums were generated at a rapid pace, usually selling reasonably well, although Presley never had a Top Ten hit after 1972's "Burning Love."

Presley's 1970s recordings, like most of his '60s work, are the focus of divergent critical opinion. Some declare them to be, when Elvis was on, the equal of anything he did, especially in terms of artistic diversity. It's true that the material was pretty eclectic, running from country to blues to all-out rock to gospel (Presley periodically recorded gospel-only releases, going all the way back to 1957). At the same time, his vocal mannerisms were often stilted, and the material—though not nearly as awful as that '60s soundtrack filler—sometimes substandard. Those who are not serious Elvis fans will usually find this late-period material to hold only a fraction of the interest of his '50s classics.

Elvis' final years have been the subject of a cottage industry of celebrity bios, tell-alls, and gossip screeds from those who knew him well, or (more likely) purported to know him well. Those activities are really beyond the scope of a mini-bio such as this, but it's enough to note that his behavior was becoming increasingly instable. His weight fluctuated wildly; his marriage broke up; he became dependent upon a variety of prescription drugs. Worst of all, he became isolated from the outside world except for professional purposes (he continued to tour until the end), rarely venturing outside of his Graceland mansion in Memphis. Colonel Parker's financial decisions on behalf of his client have also come in for much criticism.

On August 16, 1977, Presley was found dead in Graceland. The cause of death remains a subject of widespread speculation, although it seems likely that drugs played a part. An immediate cult (if cult is the way to describe millions of people) sprang up around his legacy, kept alive by the hundreds of thousands of visitors who make the pilgrimage to Graceland annually. Elvis memorabilia, much of it kitsch, is another industry in his own right. Dozens if not hundreds make a comfortable living by impersonating the King in live performance. And then there are all those Elvis sightings, reported in tabloids on a seemingly weekly basis.

Although Presley had recorded a mammoth quantity of both released and unreleased material for RCA, the label didn't show much interest in repackaging it with the respect

due such a pioneer. Haphazard collections of outtakes and live performances were far rarer than budget reissues and countless repackagings of the big hits. In the CD age, RCA finally began to treat the catalog with some of the reverence it deserved, at long last assembling a box set containing nearly all of the 1950s recordings. Similar, although less exciting, box sets were documenting the 1960s, the 1970s, and his soundtrack recordings. And exploitative reissues of Elvis material continue to appear constantly, often baited with one or two rare outtakes or alternates to entice the completists (of which there are many). In death, as in life, Presley continues to be one of RCA's most consistent earners. Fortunately, with a little discretion, a good Elvis library can be built with little duplication, sticking largely to the most highly recommended selections. —*Richie Unterberger*

★ **Elvis Presley** / Mar. 1956 / RCA ✦✦✦✦✦

Today it all seems so easy—RCA signs up the kid from Memphis, television gets interested at around the same time, and the rest is history. The circumstances surrounding the music on this album were neither simple nor promising, however, nor was there anything in the history of popular music up to that time to hint that Elvis Presley was going to be anything other than "Steve Sholes' folly." That was what rival record-industry executives were already whispering about this latest talent acquisition by the head of RCA's country division (there were even whispers that Sholes had left Sam Phillips at Sun with a performer whom he regarded as potentially bigger than Elvis, in one Carl Perkins). So a lot was unsettled and untried at the first of two groups of sessions that produced the songs on the *Elvis Presley* album—it wasn't even certain that there was any reason for a rock & roll artist to cut an album, because teenagers bought 45s, not LPs, and it was something of an inspiration on Sholes' part that he was thinking of an LP release on Elvis Presley from his first RCA recording session. The January 10, 1956, Nashville session where the first of Elvis' RCA sides were cut yielded one song, "Heartbreak Hotel," that seemed a potential single, but which no one thought would sell, and a few tracks that would be good enough for an album, if there was one. No one involved knew anything for sure about this music—Chet Atkins, the session guitarist who usually ran the RCA country sessions out of Nashville and often led whatever band was involved, mostly strummed along on rhythm guitar or sat on the sidelines, deferring to Elvis' established band of guitarist Scotty Moore (ironically, a huge Atkins fan) and bassist Bill Black. "Heartbreak Hotel" was released 17 days later, and for about a month it did nothing; then it began to move, and then Elvis Presley made his appearances on the Dorsey Brothers' show and Milton Berle's show, and had a number-one pop single. The album Sholes wanted out of Elvis came from two groups of sessions in January and February, augmented by five previously unissued songs from the Sun library. This was as startling a debut record as any ever made, representing every side of Elvis' musical influences except gospel—rockabilly, blues, R&B, country, and pop were all here in an explosive and seductive combination. *Elvis Presley* became the first rock & roll album to reach the number-one spot on the national charts, and RCA's first million dollar-earning pop album. For the 1999 remastering, the sound has been upgraded numerous steps so that one gets a much clearer impression of what Scotty Moore, Elvis, and Atkins are playing (and of the rhythm section of Bill Black and D.J. Fontana), and the bonus tracks show just how far Presley's sound evolved in the space of only two months—in addition to "Heartbreak Hotel" b/w "I Was the One," the extra songs include "Shake, Rattle & Roll" and "Lawdy, Miss Clawdy," rejects from the initial sessions for a projected second album are here, and so is "I Want You, I Need You, I Love You," recorded the month of the original album's release (the single's B-side was "My Baby Left Me," from the album), which shows Presley having developed into a much more dramatic singer, more mature and far more controlled as an artist and technical performer. The notes are a little more sketchy than they need have been, but the quality of everything else—especially the sound—makes this an essential part of any collection. —*Bruce Eder*

☆ **Elvis** / Oct. 1956 / RCA ✦✦✦✦✦

Elvis Presley's second album was really his first to be conceived and cut as an album—his debut long-player, *Elvis Presley*, although a brilliant record, was assembled from busted singles attempts and a quintet of Sun Records outtakes. "Anyway You Want Me (That's How I Will Be)" and the classic "Love Me," display glimpses of sophistication and control as a singer on this album that would increasingly drive his singing in years to come. The rhythm numbers include three Little Richard songs that he performs extremely well, most notably "Long Tall Sally," indicating either a strong preference by Elvis or a dearth of acceptable material brought to the September 1956 sessions by Steve Sholes. The surprises on this album include "Paralyzed," one of the lesser known Otis Blackwell compositions, and Elvis' cover of Arthur "Big Boy" Crudup's "So Glad You're Mine" (cut at Elvis' late-January 1956 RCA sessions, but unused), which would have been among any artist's top output during this period. [The 1999 remastering, in addition to significantly improved sound on the existing tracks, extends the CD by eight songs including "Hound Dog" and "Don't Be Cruel," the two sides of the biggest selling single by anybody in 1956, which were cut at sessions overlapping the conception of this album, "Too Much" and "Playing for Keeps," which came from these sessions, and "Love Me Tender," which was cut at a session overlapping the making of this album.] —*Bruce Eder*

Loving You / Jul. 1957 / RCA ✦✦✦

Purporting to be the soundtrack to Elvis' second film, this album collects songs used in the film on one side with new material on the other. The weakness of a couple of the movie tunes and the fact that the new songs were leftovers from the sessions used to produce Elvis' first gospel EP and latest single add up to his weakest album offering, although any album with "Got a Lot o' Living to Do" is alright. If you think of *Loving You* as simply an Elvis Presley album, rather than a somewhat misleadingly packaged soundtrack, it was actually one of his more coherent and cohesive long-players, assembled from sessions all conducted in the first two months of 1957. By this time, he was doing precious little that was wrong, and his range and control were growing geometrically—thus, amid some powerful rock & roll, including "Mean Woman Blues" (which could almost have passed for one of his Sun tracks), "Teddy Bear," the electric guitar-driven "Got a Lot 'o Livin' to Do," Ivory Joe Hunter's "I Need You So," and a hard, brittle-textured outtake of "I Beg of You," the King does some brilliant ballad singing on "One Night of Sin" and "Is It So Strange," and belts out one of his great blues performances on "When It Rains, It Really Pours"—which boasts a killer Scotty Moore guitar part—and moves into Sons of the Pioneers territory with the hauntingly beautiful Western ballad "Lonesome Cowboy." He doesn't do badly with "Blueberry Hill," either. [The 1997 CD remastering adds eight more songs, only three of them associated with the movie, which becomes sort of incidental to the whole album at that point.] *—Neal Umphred & Bruce Eder*

Elvis' Golden Records / Apr. 1958 / RCA ✦✦✦✦✦

This was rock & roll's first greatest-hits album, and it set the standard for all others to follow. As originally conceived, it was a 14-song collection of most of the King's biggest hits up to that time, released on the eve of his start of military service—a dearth of material being in the offing, it seemed only logical to assemble these hits. Each of the 14 songs had earned a gold-record award for a million sales, a record unequaled at that time by anyone else in rock & roll. The album wasn't intended as a history lesson, so "Hound Dog" and "Loving You" precede "Heartbreak Hotel"—the 1997 remastering also tampers with the concept a bit, adding six bonus tracks. Elvis' singing never sounded richer or more expressive, and one can fully appreciate in vivid detail the delicate nuances of his phrasing on songs like "Too Much." On the downside, the remastering has made the sound so clean on some of the harder songs that some of the raw, "dirty" ambience that characterized this stuff on the radio and the original 45s is lacking. Still, Scotty Moore's groundbreaking lead guitar part on "Hound Dog" and the Jordanaires' backup singing never came through more sharply or cleanly, and the all-important rhythm section is almost up front in the mix. Those who own the first Elvis box from RCA, covering the '50s masters, may hesitate to pick up this or the other parts of this latest remastered series, but the sound has been upgraded one more level, and *Golden Hits* does give a bite-sized glimpse of where Elvis had come from and where he was going (for better or worse) musically on the eve of heading into the Army. *—Bruce Eder*

King Creole / Aug. 1958 / RCA ✦✦✦

King Creole was the last movie that Elvis Presley made before he entered the army in the spring of 1958—it was also his last film in black-and-white, as well as his final effort directed by a serious old-time filmmaker (Michael Curtiz); and, apart from a few isolated, quirky efforts like *Flaming Star, Change of Habit*, and *Charro*, this was the last of his serious movies, in which Presley was trying hard, pushing himself as an actor and, really, all through the score, as a musician. This is reflected in the soundtrack, which is one of the stronger film-related releases of his career. The original 11 songs included a hot title track by Jerry Leiber & Mike Stoller that was a dazzling showcase for Scotty Moore's and Tiny Timbrell's guitars as well as Elvis' intense, exciting lead vocal. Leiber & Stoller's "Trouble" and Claude Demetrius' "Hard Headed Woman" have Moore's and Timbrell's electric guitars competing successfully with a five-man brass and reed section. Even "Dixieland Rock," if not up to the level of those other two numbers, features good playing and a strong performance by Presley, and "Young Dreams" is a decent midtempo number. The slow ballads are where the soundtrack falls flat, "As Long As I Have You" coming up to standard but "Lover Doll" and "Don't Ask Me Why" failing to excite or maintain interest; "Crawfish" can only have been included to bring the album up to the minimum acceptable length for an LP. [The 1997 remastered CD features rather upgraded sound and seven additional numbers that are outtakes from the score; these include two alternate takes of "King Creole" with considerably different guitar and brass parts, and two superior alternate versions of "As Long as I Have You," both in a much more spare arrangement—basically just Elvis and a single piano accompanying him—plus a discarded alternate title track ("Danny"). The undubbed "Lover Doll" is superior to the released version, featuring Presley accompanied by a single acoustic guitar. Even with the bonus cuts, this CD only runs 34 minutes and change.] *—Bruce Eder*

For LP Fans Only / Feb. 1959 / RCA ✦✦✦✦✦

OK, to be fair, *For LP Fans Only* is no more a real Elvis Presley album than, say, *Yesterday and Today* was a real Beatles album—Elvis was nine months through his two-year hitch in the army and RCA needed to get something "new" in the way of an LP out on him, so they threw together a quartet of sides from his Sun Records singles that had never been on album, five of his early RCA sides (which don't sound too different from the Sun stuff stylistically) that had similarly missed being put onto long-player, and one odd song off of the *Love Me Tender* soundtrack EP, and voila—a new Elvis LP. It doesn't sound like much from that description, but in its time *For LP Fans Only* was (along with its follow-up, *A Date With Elvis*) one of the choicest of all Elvis Presley albums. From 1959 until 1976, unless you wanted to try hunting down the original singles, this was the only way that any listeners got to hear the King's Sun Records singles "That's All Right," "Mystery Train," and "My Baby Left Me," and the only album to offer such early RCA sides as "Shake, Rattle & Roll" as well. Maybe it could all have been done better and more coherently, and it would've been nice if the producers had avoided the electronically rechanneled stereo through which the original mono sides were processed, but all RCA was trying to do was get some Elvis Presley material out there—they didn't get interested in the history or the particulars of the music until about 20 years later, and considering their obliviousness, they did astonishingly well. At least the songs were out there—a lot of listeners wore out copies of this album just lending them around to the uninitiated—and taken on its own terms, there weren't five more exciting rock & roll albums than this that you could buy in 1959 (or a lot of years after). It still holds up as one of the best rock & roll albums ever released, and for anyone who wants to remember (or find out) how most listeners discovered Elvis' early stuff during the 1960s and 1970s, this is one place to start, though vinyl connoisseurs will want to get a mono copy, and CD purchasers should get hold of the 2001-release audiophile Japanese version, mastered in 24-bit digital audio. *—Bruce Eder*

A Date With Elvis / Sep. 1959 / RCA ✦✦✦✦✦

Like its companion release (*For LP Fans Only*), *A Date With Elvis* has left varying impressions on different generations of Elvis Presley fans. If you were around in 1959, the first thing you probably noticed was that it was the gatefold jacket, with lots of really cool photos inside and out of Elvis Presley in uniform. Hearing this album—which contained not a word about where or when the music on it was recorded—one would have been struck by just how raw and lively the music was, more exciting, in fact, than the music on his last pre-Army LP release, the *King Creole* soundtrack. As they had with *For LP Fans Only*, RCA had assembled a "new" Elvis Presley album by reaching back to five of the best of his best Sun Records sides, augmented with a few songs left over from the *Love Me Tender* and *Jailhouse Rock* soundtrack EPs. The 1954-1955 recordings of "Milk Cow Blues Boogie," "Good Rockin' Tonight," "Baby Let's Play House," etc., with their lean textures, frantic sound, and Scotty Moore's slashing lead guitar, were a far cry from anything heard on *King Creole*. It was the height of irony that the two "new" Elvis albums of 1959 gave national audiences their first real chance to plunge into the sound of the "old" Elvis of 1954-1955, when he was known as "The Memphis Flash" and "The Hillbilly Cat." A few years later, during the mid- to late-'60s, when some listeners started getting serious about Elvis' music, and others, born too late to have been buying the records in 1956, started discovering his work for the first time, the word got out about *A Date With Elvis* and *For LP Fans Only*—that these were the real article, at least as worthwhile as the first two RCA albums and the easiest way to get the King's early Memphis sides. By the second half of the 1960s, *A Date With Elvis* and its packaging had become irrelevant to 99 percent of rock listeners, but serious fans grabbed up copies—even *Rolling Stone* magazine recommended *A Date With Elvis* and *For LP Fans Only* (especially their mono pressings) in the course of guiding readers through the already confusing maze of his releases. By the late '70s, when the Sun material had been gathered together in a more orderly fashion, *A Date With Elvis* fell out of favor once again, and it has seemed superfluous for most of the time since, in terms of musical scholarship. But listening to it 43 years after its release, one is still hard-put to find too many albums that are more viscerally exciting; what's more, it is a reminder of how those Sun sides were best known for the first two decades after their release, and how they first got out to most of us. It's a keeper in any form, with special regard for mono vinyl pressings or the 2001 Japanese CD reissue, in 24-bit digital audio. *—Bruce Eder*

50,000,000 Elvis Fans Can't Be Wrong: Elvis' Golden Records, Vol. 2 / Dec. 1959 / RCA ✦✦✦✦✦

The release of this album, seen in its proper historical context, is an indicator of just how bright Elvis Presley's star shone in the late '50s. His first hits collection was issued in March 1958, on the eve of his going into the Army; his second was the first "volume two" greatest-hits album ever issued on a rock & roll star, appearing weeks ahead of his leaving the Army in March 1960. Anyone who buys the notion that Elvis was "tamed" during his first years at RCA will find revelation in "A Big Hunk of Love," "I Need Your Love Tonight" and "I Got Stung," some of the greatest pieces of hard rock & roll that the King ever cut—and all were recorded in the midst of Elvis' stay in the Army, in a hastily arranged session in Nashville during June 1958. The 1997 remastering works better on this material than it did on the earlier *Golden Hits*; the more expansive sound doesn't detract a bit from the power of the music, and the quality of Elvis' singing, coupled with his choice of material, was reaching its peak. By this time, his voice was becoming one of the finest instruments in rock & roll, his idolization of Dean Martin and other popular singers paying off with a degree of control and articulation that his rivals could only envy, and it's all laid out here on what are still some pretty hard-rocking sides. The remastered edition not only improves the sound significantly, but adds eight songs to the original ten. The notes are thorough, although they reveal the stretching that the producers were engaged in by citing British releases as the justification for inclusion. But the quality of the music is undeniable. *—Bruce Eder*

Elvis Is Back! / Apr. 1960 / RCA ✦✦✦✦✦

The 1999 remastering of this classic album features the complete contents of the March 20, 1960, RCA Hollywood session plus the dawn-to-dusk April 2 Nashville session that rounded out the album, for a total of 18 songs, including the three singles and their B-sides from those sessions. Although they have common recording origins, two of the three singles, "It's Now or Never" and "Are You Lonesome Tonight," were very quirky by the standards of Elvis songs at the time—the former inspired by Elvis' admiration for Tony Martin's 1949 hit "There's No Tomorrow," while the latter was recorded at the request of Col. Parker as a favor to his wife. They add to the diversity of sounds on this record, which shows a mature Elvis Presley. "Dirty, Dirty Feeling" and "It Feels So Right" showed he could still rock out and challenge authority and propriety, while "Reconsider Baby" and "Like a Baby" offer some of his best blues performances; but "The Thrill of Your Love" (a very gospel-tinged number), "Soldier Boy," "Girl of My Best Friend," and "Girl Next Door Went a' Walking," also displayed the rich, deep vocalizing that would challenge critics' expectations of Elvis Presley playing rhythm guitar throughout. He also comes off better than on any of his other albums since arriving at RCA, as a musician as much as a "star" (he'd always had a lot more to say about running his sessions than the critics who loathed his RCA years indicated). [The sound on the 1999 remastering is extraordinarily close yet natural, giving the listener full value for the presence of Scotty Moore, Hank Garland (who also plays bass on a few tracks), D. J. Fontana, Boots Randolph, and Floyd Cramer.] *—Bruce Eder*

G.I. Blues / Oct. 1960 / RCA ✦✦✦

Elvis Presley's first post-Army movie, *G.I. Blues*, was scored to music that the King had begun recording in April of 1960, immediately after his discharge from the service. He was in excellent voice—even better than he had been before his induction two years before, in terms of his intonation and control—and he still had one of the best bands in the business, including Scotty Moore on lead guitar and D.J. Fontana on drums. What he didn't have here was a first-rate score. There are some OK rock & roll songs present, including "Shoppin' Around," and a pair of good ballads, "Doin' The Best I Can" and "Wooden Heart"—the latter was co-authored by pop bandleader Bert Kaempfert, thus making him one of the few (and perhaps the only) musicians to cross paths creatively with Elvis and the Beatles during this period. There's also one beautiful tune, "Pocketful of Rainbows," that Elvis treats in a subdued, gentle, moody style that recalls his classic Sun Records recordings of "Harbor Lights" and "Blue Moon." And there are a handful of better-than-decent filler numbers, such as "Frankfort Special" and the gentle pop ballads "Big Boots" and "What's She Really Like," but none of those is close to being a truly first-rate composition—most of it is predictable by-the-numbers compositions. Not only would most of the music not be of any interest had anyone other than Elvis recorded it, but it's impossible to imagine any other singer wanting to record any but two of the songs on this album. And "G.I. Blues" and "Didja Ever," in particular, are little more than military-themed novelty tunes, with which Elvis has some fun, but are hardly worth the two slots they take up in the score. And then, right in the middle of this uneven selection, is a fresh, 1960-vintage recording of "Blue Suede Shoes" that shows exactly what Elvis Presley and company were still capable of doing. It's because of tracks like that and the other strong numbers here that *G.I. Blues* can be recommended as Elvis' best full-length post-Army soundtrack release, and the 1997 reissue can be bought with even greater confidence, offering good sound and seven bonus tracks that include some lively alternate takes of five of the better songs. The soundtrack also contains an anomaly from the film—it opens with the main title song from the U.S. version of the film *Tonight Is so Right for Love*, based on the "Barcarolle" from Offenbach's *Tales of Hoffmann*. For the European issue of the movie, however, the opening credits played over "Tonight's All Right for Love," adapted from Johann Strauss. Both tracks date from the same period and the same conception of a popular song that yielded the single "It's Now or Never." There's little in the way of annotation, even on the remastered CD, though some of the factoids listed in the booklet are interesting, such as that *G.I. Blues* was the King's longest-charting album at 111 weeks, including five at number one. *—Bruce Eder*

His Hand in Mine / Dec. 1960 / RCA ✦✦✦✦✦
Presley cut several gospel albums over the course of his career, most of them overblown affairs. This one's easily his best; stripped down arrangements with Elvis passionately involved every note of the way. *—Cub Koda*

Something for Everybody / Jun. 1961 / RCA ✦✦✦
Elvis Presley's third non-soundtrack post-Army album is, in many ways, his most interesting from those years, though nowhere near his best. *Something for Everybody* offers a tamer body of songs than *Elvis Is Back*, but also shows the effect of Presley's maturation—the voice is better than ever, and this is reflected in the arrangements, most of which are closer in spirit to the finely crafted pop symphonies of Roy Orbison than they are to any of Presley's earlier work. His ballad performances are impeccable, displaying a richness of intonation and delicacy of nuance that is downright seductive. Rather less successful are the rockers, including "I'm Coming Home," "Judy," and "Put the Blame on Me," which show a cooling of some of the white heat that Presley used to generate on the rhythm numbers. The one moment where the old Elvis Presley manifests himself is "I Want You With Me," a shouter that's only missing maybe a Gene Vincent-style scream or two from the backing band on the choruses. The 1999 remastered edition of the album is augmented with six extra tracks that turn that version of *Something for Everybody* into a much harder rocking record, with rhythm numbers like "I Feel So Bad," "(Marie's the Name) His Latest Flame," and "Little Sister" that generally are far more successful than those on the original LP. Even at 18 songs, the remastered version only runs 40 minutes, but the skimpy running time is dominated by a brace of beautifully sung ballads and the sound of Elvis as a maturing but still exciting rocker. *—Bruce Eder*

Pot Luck with Elvis / Jun. 1962 / RCA ✦✦✦
One of the great ironies about *Pot Luck With Elvis* is its title, from which one could reasonably infer that it was a collection of leftovers. In fact, *Pot Luck* was Elvis Presley's last collection of new secular material recorded with a specific album release in mind until seven years later, and a lot less of a "pot luck" affair musically than any of the non-hits studio albums that were ever released of Elvis' material. The album is still a bit uneven, continuing the decline begun with *Something for Everybody*. While there are several excellent, continually underrated tracks ("Gonna Get Back Home Somehow," "Night Rider," "(Such An) Easy Question" and, of course, "Suspicion"), the quality of the songs is somewhat uneven, the ballads especially tending toward the lugubrious. The original release, which charted for 18 weeks and reached number four at its peak, never registered as strongly with the public as his soundtracks of the period did, and this relative failure (the *Blue Hawaii* soundtrack having charted for more than a year, with months spent at number one) may have forced Presley and his manager to concentrate on film work from this point on, as a commercial necessity. The sad part of that decision was that *Pot Luck* was a great vehicle for Presley's voice as it was evolving—"She's Not You" brilliantly showcased the softer, more intense singing style that had manifested itself just a few months earlier with "Can't Help Falling in Love." The 1999 remastering benefits from superior sound and a 17-song lineup, reaching back to March 1961 for its songs, including the gorgeous "Fountain of Love" and the haunting, gospel-like "That's Someone You Never Forget," which was co-authored by Presley and is one of his best non-hit songs of this era. *—Bruce Eder & Neal Umphred*

Elvis' Golden Records, Vol. 3 / Sep. 1964 / RCA ✦✦✦✦✦
The original *Elvis' Golden Records, Vol. 3* was, like its predecessors, an unprecedented release—no one in rock & roll up to that point, other than Elvis, had ever earned a second greatest-hits volume, much less a third. This is also the place where the softer, more mature Presley replaces the angry young Elvis represented on the first two volumes. On a sexual level, songs like "Stuck on You," "It's Now or Never," "Fame and Fortune," "I Gotta Know," and "Surrender" offer the fantasy of seduction rather than diverting violation. He might no longer have been a rebel, but as represented on the original dozen songs of this album, he was still making the Top Five and even the top of the charts regularly with work that was legitimately fine early-'60s rock & roll and pop/rock. "His Latest Flame" or "Good Luck Charm" might not have been groundbreaking musical statements of the caliber of "Heartbreak Hotel" or "Blue Suede Shoes," but in Elvis' hands they were worth hearing over and over. The original 12 songs have been augmented by six more, including "Can't Help Falling in Love" (which should have been on this disc to begin with) and the hauntingly beautiful "Girl of My Best Friend," which was a number-two hit in England, plus "Wild in the Country" and "Wooden Heart" (a hit in Europe) from *G.I. Blues*. The producers have stuck with the most tasteful and intriguing numbers from the films, within the time frame of the original release, the annotation is thorough, and the 1997 remastered sound runs circles around all prior editions. *—Bruce Eder*

How Great Thou Art / Mar. 1967 / RCA ✦✦✦✦✦
Between 1966 and 1968, Elvis recorded just enough studio material to fill one complete secular album and *How Great Thou Art*, a far more polite (and slightly surreal) reading of traditional religious material than the previous outing, a half-dozen years earlier. The performances throughout are superb, the sound impeccable; this actually beat *Sgt. Pepper* as the Best Engineered Album of 1967 in the Grammys! This album is also much closer to mainstream gospel and may not be so immediately accessible to the unconverted; don't let that steer you away from an otherwise great record. *—Neal Umphred*

Elvis' Gold Records, Vol. 4 / Feb. 1968 / RCA ✦✦✦✦✦
The fourth volume of *Elvis' Gold Records* was the first of his hits compilations to be issued at a point when Elvis Presley wasn't considered a very important rock & roll star anymore (a few months later he would embark on his network television "comeback"). Indeed, it appeared at a point when it seemed, as Neal Umphred pointed out, "Elvis' gold was drained up and he was reduced to filling up the fourth volume with B-sides." Covering the early '60s through the end of 1967, the original collection had the bad fortune to appear at a point when politics, international affairs and a generational change in the listening public all combined to render Elvis Presley seemingly irrelevant. A great deal of social and musical change had taken place while Elvis withdrew from concerts and television appearances, made his movies, and scarcely attempted the recording of any non-soundtrack albums. So at the time, the album's arrival and even its title might have seemed like a joke to a lot of observers. That having been said, there is some extraordinary music on *Gold Records Vol. 4*, especially in its remastered 18-song version. "Wooden Heart" and "Can't Help Falling in Love" have been moved from *Vol. 4* to *Vol. 3* in reconfiguring the *Elvis' Gold Records* series. The additional songs have been chosen with care and even some inspiration, the remastered sound is most impressive, and the notes are reasonably thorough. Pop-culture mavens may want to note the presence of the indirect Ed Wood connection here—"Rock-A-Hula" was co-written by Dolores Fuller, Wood's companion and collaborator during the period of *Glen or Glenda*. *—Bruce Eder*

Elvis TV Special / Dec. 1968 / RCA ✦✦✦✦✦
After years of making abysmal movies, Presley appeared before a live audience, scared to death. That he more than rose to the challenge is evidenced here, a masterly performance highlighted by the jam-session segment with D.J. Fontana and Scotty Moore, where Presley plays electric guitar and knocks out drop-dead versions of "Baby, What You Want Me to Do" and "Tiger Man." *—Cub Koda*

★ **From Elvis in Memphis** / May 1969 / RCA ✦✦✦✦✦
After a 14-year absence from Memphis, Elvis Presley returned to cut what was certainly his greatest album (or, at least, a tie effort with his RCA debut LP from early 1956). The fact that *From Elvis in Memphis* came out as well as it did is something of a surprise, in retrospect—Presley had a backlog of songs he genuinely liked that he wanted to record and had heard some newer soul material that also attracted him, and none of it resembled the material that he'd been cutting since his last non-soundtrack album, six years earlier. And he'd just come off of the NBC television special which, although a lot of work, had led him to the realization that he could be as exciting and vital a performer in 1969 as he'd been a dozen years before. And for what was practically the last time, the singer cut his manager, Tom Parker, out of the equation, turning himself over to producer Chips Moman. The result was one of the greatest white soul albums (and one of the greatest soul albums) ever cut, with brief but considerable forays into country, pop, and blues as well. Presley sounds rejuvenated artistically throughout the dozen cuts off the original album, and he's supported by the best playing and back-up singing of his entire recording history. The spring 2000 remastered edition matches the sound quality on the two-CD set *Suspicious Minds*, but restores the original album's classic cover and song order, with six bonus tracks cut at the same sessions but only released as singles at the time. This disc proves that he not only came back—he was *better* than he'd ever been as a singer or stylist—and is an essential part of any music collection. *—Bruce Eder*

From Memphis to Vegas/From Vegas to Memphis / Nov. 1969 / RCA ✦✦✦✦✦
One-half of the imponderably titled *From Memphis to Vegas/From Vegas to Memphis* (later issued as a separate album, *Elvis in Person at the International Hotel, Las Vegas, Nevada*), captures Elvis from the summer of 1969, while the exhilaration of conquest was still evident. It's a nice compromise between mere entertainment and the revelatory: The first few songs are old hits to pull you in; the second side opens with a roaring medley of "Mystery Train" and Rufus Thomas' "Tiger Man" and leads to a staggering seven-minute "Suspicious Minds." The studio album, ten tracks from the previous Memphis sessions, are a letdown and, even at the time of release, the two-fer concept seemed ill conceived.

Had the best of the rest of the Memphis material been collected on a single album and titled "Suspicious Minds," it's possible this album could have leapt to number one and outsold the first. *—Neal Umphred*

Elvis in Person at the International Hotel, Las Vegas, Nevada / Apr. 1970 / RCA ✦✦✦✦✦

When Elvis and the Colonel decided it was time to start appearing live again, they assembled a crackerjack band (featuring James Burton) and took on Vegas full-bore. Easily the King's best live album, *In Person at the International Hotel* featured a slew of hits, including "Johnny B. Goode," "My Babe," the "Mystery Train/Tiger Man" medley, and "Suspicious Minds." If the album had a flaw, it was its skimpy running time (36 minutes). We now know, from the unissued tracks from these same performances that were added to the remastered *On Stage (1970)*, that there was more to the repertory of those five days of August 1969 shows than is represented here; but the producers, limited to a single LP, faced a major problem: Should they weigh the tracks more toward his current repertory and recent singles, or toward his classic songs? The classic songs sort of won out, but in the decades since, those then-recent singles have risen in stature. Regardless of what they're playing, the band really rock throughout, and that's not just Burton—who sounds like he's wearing his fingers ragged as he puts a new edge on "Hound Dog," coming up with something different than, yet vaguely similar to, Scotty Moore's approach to the song in concert 14 years earlier—but also the entire guitar contingent of John Wilkinson and Charlie Hodge (not to mention Elvis himself, who strums along here and there) and the muscular rhythm section of bassist Jerry Scheff and drummer Ronnie Tutt. The vocal support by Hodge, Millie Kirkham, the Sweet Inspirations, and the Imperials is soaring and tasteful, never more so than on the album's seven-minute version of "Suspicious Minds" and the soaring finale, "Can't Help Falling in Love." *—Cub Koda & Bruce Eder*

On Stage / Jun. 1970 / RCA ✦✦✦✦

Elvis' second live album, partly cut at the International Hotel in Las Vegas in early 1970, is one of his most unfairly underrated releases. In its original form, it did seem a bit cheap, offering ten songs that weren't necessarily associated with Elvis Presley. By this time, he was adding covers of other artists' contemporary hits to his set, not to capitalize on their success but to keep his hand in contemporary music and show audiences of the era that he was capable of doing more than reprising his own 1950s and early-'60s songs. The critics failed to notice two things, however: Presley had the same first-rate band who had graced the previous tour, led by James Burton on guitar; when he performed Neil Diamond's "Sweet Caroline," Tony Joe White's "Polk Salad Annie," or (most especially) Del Shannon's "Runaway," he did them extremely well. "The Wonder of You" might not have been "That's All Right" or even "Heartbreak Hotel," but it was a towering performance by a singer who, even then, could run circles around virtually anyone in the business this side of Roy Orbison. [The 1999 full-priced reissue not only improves the sound, but adds six songs (for a total of 16), four of them—"In the Ghetto," "Kentucky Rain," "Don't Cry Baby," and "Suspicious Minds"—recent Elvis Presley hits. Although he didn't do any of the songs from his movies or any of the early-'60s hits, he did those four, and that makes this CD essential for any Elvis fan who cares about his comeback or the best work that followed; it also makes this the perfect companion to the 1968 television comeback and the *Suspicious Minds* (aka *Memphis Record*) album.] *—Bruce Eder*

That's the Way It Is / Dec. 1970 / RCA ✦✦✦✦✦

Possibly due to the retro, irony-filled vogue for easy listening giants like Burt Bacharach and—to a lesser extent—roots pop figures like Glen Campbell and Neil Diamond, Elvis Presley's Vegas-era recordings have been given new life after a cruel stretch of put downs by kitsch-wary critics. The praise is not just so much posing, though, since many of Elvis' live albums from this period, in particular, contain a substantial store of quality material—dinner-show horn charts, strings, grandstanding vocals, and all. This 1970 offering from Las Vegas proves to be one of his best (it's actually the soundtrack to Denis Sanders' documentary of Elvis' summer run at the International Hotel). Acting on his affinity for country-pop figures like Campbell and Mac Davis, Elvis especially shines on the slow to midtempo ballads "I Just Can't Help Believin'" and "Just Pretend" (both seamless blends of torch song glitz and contemporary rock elements). And to provide the requisite amount of sweat for those nightly towel giveaways, the King works out extra hard on showstoppers like "Patch It Up" and "You Don't Have to Say You Love Me." Throughout the album, Presley sounds as commanding and powerful as he ever would and gets optimal backing by well oiled, Nashville-to-L.A. session luminaries like guitarist James Burton, bassist Jerry Scheff, and drummer Ronnie Tutt (Aretha Franklin's '60s backup singers, the Sweet Inspirations, deserve special mention as well). Also available as a deluxe three-disc set (including expanded concert highlights and rehearsal takes), *That's the Way It Is* is essential listening for Elvis fans, both die-hard and casual. *—Stephen Cook*

☆ **Elvis Country (I'm 10,000 Years Old)** / Jan. 1971 / RCA ✦✦✦✦✦

Western swing, blues, countrypolitan, traditional country, gospel—if it was music that even brushed the airwaves of a Southern state, Elvis Presley at his best could make it his own, and Elvis was at his peak when he cut *Elvis Country*. Actually, Elvis Presley was positively on a roll at the time. A decade after the end of what were thought to be his prime years, he was singing an ever-widening repertory of songs with more passion and involvement than he'd shown since the end of the 1950s. What's more, his voice had achieved a peak of perfection as an instrument, acquiring a depth and richness, a beauty to go with its power at which even his best work of the early years had only hinted. And it all came together on *Elvis Country*, which has lots of country music on it but also a lot else. His greatest long-player of the 1970s, and one of his three or four best albums ever, *Elvis Country* was a record that he threw himself into with every bit of the passion displayed on the better known, soul-oriented *From Elvis in Memphis*, and it was even more personal; he was cutting songs that he was either very impressed with at the moment or had loved for a lot of years, but they were all songs he cared about, which gives him a commanding and charismatic vocal presence. He doesn't necessarily supplant the originals, but he gives you more than enough reason to listen, again and again, to everything here. Producer Felton Jarvis and a cadre of Nashville sidemen (augmented by James Burton) provided backup as good as Presley ever got. *—Bruce Eder*

Elvis as Recorded at Madison Square Garden / Jun. 1972 / RCA ✦✦✦

This was one of several live recordings by "the King" to appear during the early '70s and was extremely popular, owing to the quality of the performance and the range and number of songs included, as well as the timing of its release—older fans, having been denied Elvis Presley's presence on-stage for more than a decade, responded to his sudden re-emergence with more enthusiasm than they'd shown for any of his non-hits albums in years; and new listeners, too young to have heard him in the 1950s but latching onto Elvis either directly or as part of the oldies boom, started checking out what all of the excitement was about. The show itself, from June 10, 1972, is the more elaborately produced follow-up to his Las Vegas performances of 1969-1970, Elvis backed by an eight-piece band, an orchestra, and at least eight male and female backup singers (including the Sweet Inspirations)—once one gets past the opening fanfare of "Also Sprach Zarathustra," there isn't a lot of difference between this and the best of his Vegas shows, except that Elvis is a lot more confident and self-assured here than he is at the early post-"comeback" concerts. Emboldened by the success of those releases and the fact that he was able to sell out arenas like the Garden, RCA also did something here that they hadn't taken the chance on doing with his previous live albums, loading it up with songs new and old, and also a generous 52 minutes' running time. As with all of his shows of this era, the King interspersed his own established repertory—which embraced everything from "That's All Right" to "Suspicious Minds"—with songs identified with other performers: "Proud Mary," "You Don't Have to Say You Love Me," and "You've Lost That Lovin' Feeling" were all very suitable for him. Presley was in good form for this show and, by all accounts, this series of concerts, and gave beautifully wrought performances of the ballads, as well as highly energetic renditions of the harder rocking numbers. The sound is surprisingly close, betraying little of the cavernous acoustic of Madison Square Garden—there is, conversely, very little audience ambience as well, but that's not terribly important, either; much more to the point is that the accompaniment, from James Burton's guitar on down, is all captured reasonably well, thus making this one of the best of the big-venue Elvis Presley concert documents available: exciting, diverting, and mostly impressive as a performance. [The American CD reissue is decent enough, and a mid-priced bargain, but the 2001 vintage Japanese 24-bit/96k digital remastering has to be heard to be believed.] *—Bruce Eder*

Aloha From Hawaii Via Satellite / Feb. 1973 / RCA ✦✦✦

Aloha From Hawaii Via Satellite is a double-album set that captures Elvis' celebrated live television concert from 1973. Arguably, it also captures the peak of the Presley live extravaganzas of the '70s. Spanning two albums and 30 songs, the record finds Elvis pulling out all the stops, running through a set that favors covers and new material at the expense of classics. That's hardly a complaint, since the whole point of his concerts in the '70s was a sensory onslaught, where a bluesy (albeit over the top) version of "See See Rider" could sit next to a schmaltzy showstopper like "American Trilogy." And the key to the whole thing is that Elvis actually sounds more committed to "American Trilogy" than "See See Rider." That passion and energy are carried over to each song, and that's what makes the entire enterprise so entertaining. It's also why the record was a massive hit upon its release and why so many fans have fond memories of *Aloha from Hawaii* decades after the actual concert. [The single-CD reissue from 1992 trims the number of songs to 24.] *—Stephen Thomas Erlewine*

Elvis Recorded Live on Stage in Memphis / Jul. 1974 / RCA ✦✦✦

This oft-ignored album, recorded in March 1974 at Memphis' *Midsouth Coliseum* (formerly the center of controversy when the proposed title, the Elvis Presley Coliseum, was poo-pooed), is easily the strongest live package of the '70s, the one worth having. Elvis is in exceptional vocal form and, between all the stuff that showed up on every other live album of the period, there is a great "Trying to Get to You" and strong versions of "My Baby Left Me" and "Lawdy, Miss Clawdy," material he otherwise left unnoticed. *—Neal Umphred*

Promised Land / Jan. 1975 / RCA ✦✦✦✦

Promised Land came from the last recording sessions that Elvis Presley ever had in Memphis, the city where his fame and his legend started. The December 1973 Stax Records studio sessions showed him, as he had on *From Elvis in Memphis*, reaching out to publishers other than those he owed for songs, and the repertory embraces material by Chuck Berry, Waylon Jennings, and Larry Gatlin, among others. With the best players on hand and an upbeat mood when these songs were cut, and the singer himself lean and rested after a couple of years of concertizing, the vibes throughout this album were positive and then some. Elvis sounds bold and confident in ways that make this album a diverting, if not profoundly exciting experience. It's not as distinctive or as involved a personal document as *Elvis Country* or the concentrated soul workout of *From Elvis in Memphis*, but it does feature some fine passionate singing throughout (most notably on "It's Midnight," a wrenching performance). [The eight bonus tracks on the spring 2000 remastering (in excellent sound) are drawn from the same sessions but originally appeared on the album *Good Times*.] *—Bruce Eder*

Today / May 1975 / RCA ✦✦✦

Elvis Today is often cited by writers as Elvis' uncertain return to his Sun origins. There really isn't that much difference from the trio that resulted from 1973's Stax sessions, with the lesser tracks being a bit more substantial. The sound is better but the packaging had become, at this point, practically offensive: One color close-up after another, almost all from the *Aloha From Hawaii* special (or that pre-bloated period), back covers with no notes or technical data, just ads for other Presley Product. Still, an album with "Susan When She Tried," "T-R-O-U-B-L-E," and a hilariously appropriate reading of "I Can Help" is worth listening to any time. —*Neal Umphred*

From Elvis Presley Boulevard, Memphis, Tennessee / May 1976 / RCA ✦✦✦
By 1976 Elvis was recording at home in Graceland, cutting what would be the final recordings of his career. Filled with bathos and showing little rock & roll vitality, these remain interesting nonetheless, as it implied his accepting his age somewhat and attempting to combine old-fashioned, melodramatic soul with contemporary country-pop. While the pain and decay are evident—especially in hindsight—Elvis could still sing: "Hurt" is excellent, one of his best and, on "Danny Boy," Elvis reaches with an aching falsetto that closes the song, appropriately. Still, this is hardly the album to begin your collection with. —*Neal Umphred*

Moody Blue / Jul. 1977 / RCA ✦✦✦
The last Elvis Presley album released in the singer's lifetime, *Moody Blue* has a somewhat checkered history, especially among fans. Issued two months before Presley died, the album sold moderately well until Presley died—then it soared up the charts to number three, as his most current album, and it ultimately sold two-million copies. As to the music, the original ten-song album was a mixed bag of live recordings, interspersed with new studio work from the previous fall at *Graceland*. For all of its slapped-together feel, however, *Moody Blue* held up. The title song, authored by Mark James (who'd previously written "Suspicious Minds"), was just about as good a single as Elvis released in the 1970s, topping the country charts earlier in 1977; additionally, he did a superb re-interpretation of the George Jones hit "She Thinks I Still Care." "Little Darlin'" was almost more of a burlesque of the '50s rock & roll standard than a real performance, but it is more than made up for by the presence of the Johnny Ace classic "Pledging My Love," done with depth and sincerity. [At the time, "Let Me Be There" was also on the album, drawn from the 1974 Memphis live album, but it has been removed from the spring 2000 CD remastering, with nine songs from a series of early February 1976 session substituting for it. Some of the 1976 material doesn't hold up as well, but the bonus tracks end this CD on a high note with Presley's rendition of the Tom Jones hit "I'll Never Fall in Love Again." The 24-bit remastering has added a good deal of luster to the 19 songs here, making this the first proper way to hear this material.] —*Bruce Eder*

Elvis' Gold Records, Vol. 5 / 1984 / RCA ✦✦✦✦
Sixteen years after Elvis' *Gold Records, Vol. 4* and seven years after his death came *Vol. 5* in the series, courtesy of Joan Deary, the first RCA executive to take a sensible, intelligent approach to handling the Elvis Presley library. The original ten-song LP has been expanded to a 16-song CD. Later country chart hits like "Moody Blue" work well juxtaposed with numbers like "Suspicious Minds" and "Big Boss Man," and odd B-sides like "For the Heart" (which, as "Had a Dream," became the Judds' first hit in 1984) and Elvis' cover of "You Don't Have to Say You Love Me" don't seem out of place. The only real loser here (mostly thanks to its ponderous chorus) is "Edge of Reality," a song that originally showed up in the movie *Live a Little, Love a Little* as a psychedelic number in a dream sequence in which Elvis dances with a man in a great-dane costume—even stripped of that image, it doesn't work as a song, and comes off even less well since it precedes the superb "Memories" and "If I Can Dream." The decade represented by the 16 songs on *Vol. 5* shows an Elvis Presley every bit as secure as an artist as the rebel represented on *Vols. 1* or *2*, searching for and generally finding a sound and an audience that could go together. —*Bruce Eder*

☆ Reconsider Baby / 1985 / RCA ✦✦✦✦
A 12-song, budget-priced compilation of Elvis' most notable blues sides for the label. A good place to start digging Elvis' commitment to the music—always returning to it right up through the '70s like an old friend, whenever he needed a quick fix of the *real* thing—as he takes on everything from R&B slices like Tommy Tucker's "High Heel Sneakers" to Percy Mayfield's "Stranger in My Own Home Town." Major highlights on this collection are Elvis playing acoustic rhythm guitar and driving the band through a take of the Lowell Fulson title track, blistering versions of two Arthur "Big Boy" Crudup songs, an unreleased Sun recording of Lonnie Johnson's "Tomorrow Night," and the R-rated take of Smiley Lewis' "One Night (of Sin)." —*Cub Koda*

Return of the Rocker / Mar. 1986 / RCA ✦✦✦
A companion to the *Rocker* compilation, *Return of the Rocker* presented harder-edged material recorded by Elvis Presley in the early '60s. Presley was moderating his sound in this period, so even the rockier stuff wasn't as hard as what he had recorded in the 1950s. But songs like "Little Sister," "A Mess of Blues," and "Return to Sender" still maintained his standard for uptempo rock & roll, and this is some of the best material Presley recorded in the decade. —*William Ruhlmann*

★ The Top Ten Hits / 1987 / RCA ✦✦✦✦✦
The Top Ten Hits is exactly what it says it is—every Top Ten hit that Elvis Presley ever had during the course of his career, from "Heartbreak Hotel" in 1956 to "Burning Love" in 1972. Even though this double-disc set covers a lot of ground, there's a huge amount of terrific material that *isn't* included on the compilation. There's none of his Sun recordings, none of his gritty blues, none of his gospel, precious little of his country recordings, and many great singles for RCA aren't included. Still, the 38 songs on *The Top Ten Hits* are absolutely first-rate—there's no arguing with "I Want You, I Need You, I Love You," "Don't Be Cruel," "Hound Dog," "Love Me Tender," "Love Me," "All Shook Up," "Jailhouse Rock," "One Night," "A Fool Such as I," "(Marie's the Name) His Latest Flame," "Can't Help Falling in Love," "Little Sister," "Return to Sender," "Suspicious Minds," and many, many others. It's the perfect way to start an Elvis collection and, for many casual fans, the only set to own. —*Stephen Thomas Erlewine*

Elvis in Nashville / 1988 / RCA ✦✦✦
One of two albums assembled by the Country Music Foundation's Jay Orr (the other is *Elvis Gospel*), *Elvis in Nashville* is, as its title suggests, a sampler of material recorded by Elvis Presley in Nashville. Especially during the 1960s, when he was dividing his time between Tennessee and California, Presley took a different approach to his Hollywood and Nashville sessions, cutting the mediocre soundtracks to his movies in the West and aiming the Music City dates "at producing a hit single, an LP, or a batch of gospel or Christmas songs," as Orr puts it in his liner notes. The material and performances were a cut above the movie work, but the songs were also diverse and, again to quote Orr, "If any conclusion can be drawn from such a limited review (as this album provides), it is that Elvis, with his unique vocal gift and his inherited musical sensibilities, could prevail in any setting given the will to do so." But the same conclusion could be drawn from just about any sampling of his work, and while *Elvis in Nashville* features such classics as "I Got a Woman" and "Guitar Man," there is nothing musically that marks the tracks by their location of recording. At least in this compilation, the Presley Nashville sessions, while not undistinguished, are indistinguishable from those held in other cities. —*William Ruhlmann*

Known Only to Him: Elvis Gospel 1957–1971 / 1989 / RCA ✦✦✦✦✦
The second of two albums assembled by the Country Music Foundation's Jay Orr (the other is *Elvis in Nashville*), *Elvis Gospel 1957-1971: Known Only to Him* was a 14-track compilation culled largely from Presley's inspirational records, the 1957 EP *Peace in the Valley* and the albums *His Hand in Mine* (1960), *How Great Thou Art* (1967), and *He Touched Me* (1972). The music is consistently effective, confirming Presley's affection for gospel. [This album was largely superseded by the two-disc 1994 compilation *Amazing Grace*, which contained most of its selections.] —*William Ruhlmann*

☆ The Million Dollar Quartet / Feb. 1990 / RCA ✦✦✦✦
One of the most important things to remember about this album is it's really just three guys in a room shooting the breeze, goofing around, and stumbling through a few old songs they happen to remember. This wouldn't be the least bit interesting under most circumstances, but the three guys in question happen to be Elvis Presley, Jerry Lee Lewis, and Carl Perkins, which, as you might imagine, makes quite a difference. Perkins was doing a recording session at the Sun Records studio in Memphis on December 4, 1956, with Lewis playing piano on the date, when Elvis, in the midst of his first burst of fame and back in Memphis after a stretch of the road, stopped by to say hello. Elvis, Perkins, and Lewis began casually jamming—mostly on old gospel tunes they remembered from a shared Baptist upbringing—and Sam Phillips had the presence of mind to switch on the tape machine and record the proceedings. (A famous picture taken that day shows Johnny Cash with the group, but if he stuck around to sing a few tunes, he stayed far enough away from the mike to be absent on these recordings.) To call the performances casual taxes understatement, and if you were expecting the ultimate rockabilly moment from these guys, be aware it's about halfway through the session before rock & roll begins to rear its head, and even then it's obvious these guys can play "Farther Along" or "Down by the Riverside" off the top of their heads a lot more easily than "Brown Eyed Handsome Man" or "Too Much Monkey Business." But half the fun of this album is the playful casualness of the performances (and hearing three of rock's great legends in such non-legendary form). And their personalities certainly manifest themselves right off the bat: Elvis is effortlessly authoritative, and at once amused and perplexed by his sudden fame, while Lewis harmonizes like a wild man, determined to show he's the star of the show, and Perkins displays characteristic modesty, content to add churchy harmonies and the occasional signature guitar break. It's also fun to hear Elvis imitate Jackie Wilson imitating him, and Perkins marveling at the genius of Chuck Berry. Like I said, just three guys goofing off—but from these three guys, "goofing off" is really something to hear. —*Mark Deming*

☆ The King of Rock 'n' Roll: The Complete 50's Masters / Jun. 23, 1992 / RCA ✦✦✦✦
Prior to the 1992 release of the five-disc box set *The King of Rock 'n' Roll: The Complete 50's Masters*, RCA's approach to reissuing Elvis Presley on CD—or on LP, for that matter—was rather scatter-shot, seeming to follow the dictates of the market more than the demands of history. There were some excellent releases of archival material and in 1987, on the tenth anniversary of the King's death, there was a stellar series of compilations, but most of what was released was a constant stream of recycled hits, which this box most certainly is not. This set is sharply and expertly assembled, presenting Elvis' peak as a creative and cultural force in staggering detail. Despite the subtitle of this box, this does not contain *everything* Presley recorded in the '50s; there are alternate takes not present on this set, including second takes for Sun that were included on the subsequent collection *Sunrise*, and after this release, more acetates recorded around the same time as his privately recorded "My Happiness" (unveiled here for the first time) were found and released. That said, those alternate takes are the province of collectors, particularly since the best of those are chronicled on the fifth and final disc of this set. That means, anything a real serious fan or listener needs is on this exhaustive set, since it chronicles the rise of the greatest figure of American music in the 20th century. The first disc is largely devoted to the released Sun singles, both the As and Bs, and this remains the rawest, liveliest, nerviest music Presley ever cut, retaining its power over the years; decades later, it still sounds alive and unpredictable—it still is possible to hear rock & roll being created in its very grooves and it's just as thrilling to hear the kinetic energy of this lean combo create an entirely new music; anybody who doubts Elvis as an innovator need only hear this to be proven wrong. Toward the end of the first disc, Elvis leaves Sun for RCA, and the production is a little cleaner and the material a little more streamlined, but that's just a relative judgment. This is still the birth of rock & roll, and when "I Got a Woman" and "Heartbreak Hotel" inaugurate the RCA years, that wild energy is still palpable, even now. As this set illustrates, partially through its sheer scope, that energy

could be dissipated by an inclination to move toward the pop mainstream, which could result in beautiful, heartbreaking ballads, but also the safe pop crooning that debilitated his career in the '60s. Fortunately, at no time in the '50s did he sink into the murk that enveloped him for a period in the '60s. He may have recorded forgettable ballads and trifle (including, ironically, one of his few compositions, the corny "We're Gonna Move"), sometimes succumbing to either his trite side or the demands of the marketplace, but the remarkable thing about this box is how consistently compelling, even thrilling, this music is. The overly familiar hits, and they're all here, are given new life in this context, which has the feeling of history unraveling in front of your ears. That's what makes this box set transcendent—the music and annotation alone would make it necessary for libraries, but this is better because it is thoroughly listenable, while presenting history in a compelling narrative context. Yes, some of these tunes sound like light pop tied to their time, but they make for very few cuts on this 140-track box. Most of this is dynamic, thrilling music that presents Elvis at his very best. Historically, this is surely essential, but what makes the box so great is that it's so entertaining, providing ample proof that Elvis' music is indeed every bit as influential and timeless as the history books state. —*Stephen Thomas Erlewine*

☆ **From Nashville to Memphis: The Essential 60's Masters** / Sep. 28, 1993 / RCA ✦✦✦✦✦
Since *The King of Rock 'n' Roll* was the *complete* '50s masters, it was easy to assume that its five-disc '60s sequel, *From Nashville to Memphis: The Essential 60's Masters*, rounded up all the masters from that decade, which is simply not the case. The producers deliberately avoided the soundtracks to Elvis' movies, which perhaps makes sense, given that they are roundly and rightly disparaged as Presley's low point, which then opened the doors to presenting just what they judged as the best non-soundtrack recordings he made during the '60s. They also disregarded the gospel recordings, saving them for the double-disc 1994 collection *Amazing Grace: His Greatest Gospel Songs*, leaving this as an overview of the best of his pop and rock material of the '60s, all recorded after he got back from the Army. Instead of being a detriment, this is a *brilliant* move, distilling his erratic, wide-ranging '60s recordings to their very best, providing a relatively comprehensive overview of the greatest material Elvis recorded during his most inconsistent decade. Its biggest flaw is that in its zeal to overlook the soundtracks, the box skips over even the hits from the films, so this does not have "Can't Help Falling in Love," "G.I. Blues," "Follow That Dream," "Viva Las Vegas," "Little Less Conversation," and "Return to Sender," as well as other, lesser hits. They are missed, particularly because there is a surfeit of pop-oriented material from the early '60s. That's one area where this box excels: It proves that Presley did turn toward pop in the early '60s. Contrary to conventional wisdom, he did not *abandon* rock & roll, and there are many tough performances from the early years of the decade that stand their own with the '50s RCA sides, but by the middle of the box—which roughly corresponds with the middle of the decade—it becomes clear that Elvis needed to change his approach, and he did with stunning power. That's where the scope of the box comes into play: By disc three, there's been plenty of good, sometimes great, music, but when Elvis gets his swagger back just before the songs that formed *From Elvis in Memphis*, the growing energy is kinetic, and the fourth disc, along with half of the fifth, are intoxicating in how Presley rediscovers his power and starts to not only sing songs worthy of his talents, but have productions and performances that match. This is the greatest music on this set—"Long Black Limousine," "Rubberneckin'," "Wearin' That Loved on Look," "In the Ghetto," "Suspicious Minds," "True Love Travels on a Gravel Road," and "Kentucky Rain" are among the best of this batch—towering over the rest of the music here and holding its own with the Sun material. This is presented in more thorough form elsewhere, but the long view and scope of this set really make his comeback dramatic on *From Nashville to Memphis*. That narrative makes the set essential, as does the judicious selection of his early- and mid-'60s highlights. It's done well—well enough to almost excuse the very, very big hits that are missing, even if it doesn't completely account for their absence. That is a pretty big flaw, but even so, *From Nashville to Memphis* is necessary for any serious pop library, which speaks volumes for the quality of the music within the box. —*Stephen Thomas Erlewine*

Amazing Grace: His Greatest Sacred Songs / Oct. 25, 1994 / RCA ✦✦✦✦
Elvis recorded quite a bit of gospel over the course of his career, and this two-CD, 55-song set has the bulk of it. Most of this is drawn from his three gospel LPs (*His Hand in Mine*, 1960; *How Great Thou Art*, 1967; *He Touched Me*, 1972), as well as a 1957 EP. Presley was undoubtedly heavily influenced by gospel (at times he indicated regret at not having chosen to become a gospel singer), and this material has played pretty well with critics. Elvis sings with skill and reasonable commitment, and the backing musicians include such Elvis/Nashville standbys as Scotty Moore, Hank Garland, Floyd Cramer, Charlie McCoy, Pete Drake, the Jordanaires, and James Burton. At the same time, let's have a reality check here. Rock- and pop-oriented fans are going to find this two-and-a-half hour set tough going, unless they have a taste for spirituals as well. Things get a little more accessible when the tempos brighten, but often it's on the sedate side. For both collectors and listeners, highlights of the collection are five previously unreleased tracks from 1972. Recorded with only Charlie Hodges on piano and J.D. Sumner & the Stamps on backing vocals, they present Presley's gospel at its sparsest and most spontaneous. —*Richie Unterberger*

Command Performances: The Essential 60's Masters II / Jul. 18, 1995 / RCA ✦✦✦
Elvis Presley's 1960s film soundtracks are renowned as the repository of his most frivolous (many would say ridiculous) material. This 62-song, double CD draws from no less than 26 of those screen vehicles to present the "best" of these performances; the idea is to complement the first volume of *Essential 60's Masters*, which focused on his non-soundtrack recordings from the decade, and doesn't include any of the cuts from this collection. The goal of this package may have been to boil away the dross (as big as this is, there's a *lot* of stuff they left off). But if anything, it perhaps inadvertently demonstrates just how lousy most of those recordings were; even this selective, chronologically programmed set feels way too long, and could have probably been cut in length to a single CD without too much loss. That's not to say that what's here is entirely negligible. There are some classic singles ("Return to Sender," "Can't Help Falling in Love"), fair rockers ("What'd I Say," "Little Egypt"), and more than a few cuts that are transcendentally great/awful in their mindless silliness ("Rock-A-Hula Baby," "Viva Las Vegas," "Do the Clam"), songs which are archetypes, for better or worse, of the kitschiest facet of Presley's myth. But much of the rest is just unremarkable, or even bad: stupid novelties ("Poison Ivy League"), drab ballads, and many mediocre rock tunes. This doesn't include such legendarily idiotic tunes as "No Room to Rhumba in a Sports Car," "Yoga Is as Yoga Does," and "Fort Lauderdale Chamber of Commerce"; you can find those on the original soundtracks, or a famous bootleg, the aptly-titled *Elvis' Greatest Shit*. —*Richie Unterberger*

☆ **Walk a Mile in My Shoes: The Essential 70's Masters** / Oct. 10, 1995 / RCA ✦✦✦✦✦
Since *From Nashville to Memphis: The Essential 60's Masters* gave up the ghost of being a complete overview of Elvis Presley's '60s recordings, the compilers of the companion five-disc box set *Walk a Mile in My Shoes: The Essential 70's Masters*—the third and final installment in RCA's justifiably acclaimed Elvis box set reissue series—decided to throw even the illusion of comprehensiveness out the window and just serve up five discs and 120 tracks of highlights. Instead of adhering to a strict chronological sequencing, which the two previous boxes did, this is divided into two discs of singles, two discs of studio highlights, then one disc that attempts to present the ultimate Elvis Presley live show by culling peaks from several gigs throughout of the decade. This is a sharp move, since there is simply too much recorded material from the '70s to be presented either completely or chronologically, and his high points are easier to digest broken down in this fashion. Truth be told, he didn't have too many outright classics during this time—just "Burning Love," "Always on My Mind," "Raised on Rock," "Promised Land," and "Moody Blue," along with 1971's excellent album *Elvis Country (I'm 10,000 Years Old)*—but it was a far more consistent era than the '60s, and it was more adventurous in terms of material and production, never sounding like pandering, which the early '60s could on occasion. This is more evident on the studio highlights than on the singles discs, particularly because those two discs delve into records like *Elvis Country*, but the end result is a set that is far more consistent and entertaining than *From Nashville to Memphis*, even if it doesn't sustain the delirious heights of his late-'60s comeback. If the fifth, final live disc is the kind of thing that you listen to only once or twice, it still crackles with energy, and the two studio highlights discs prove that Presley was still a sensitive, inventive interpreter of strong material, and the productions have a rich, robust diversity that keeps this interesting and enjoyable. To say that the '70s recordings are more consistent than the '60s is true, but it does give the impression that Elvis was as consistently brilliant as he was a decade earlier. That's simply not the case—the best of the '60s recordings overshadows the best cuts here without effort—but this does have a diversity of material and sound (even if it sometimes borders on the splashy excess of Vegas) that not only keeps it interesting, it proves that, when pressed, Elvis was still restless and inventive. Maybe the music here isn't as outright classic as those on the previous box sets, but it captures its era just as well, and provides the final piece of musical narrative while serving up some terrific music. And if the final chapter of the most iconic figure in American popular music is not essential to a library, then you don't truly care for American popular music. —*Stephen Thomas Erlewine*

Elvis 56 / Mar. 5, 1996 / RCA ✦✦✦✦✦
Sure the music on here's great. How could it not be? It has 22 of his hottest tracks from his first year at RCA, including not only the hits "Heartbreak Hotel," "Hound Dog," "Don't Be Cruel," and "Too Much," but such noted early rockers as "My Baby Left Me," "Blue Suede Shoes," "Money Honey," and "So Glad You're Mine." From a collector's viewpoint, though, you have to wonder whether it was really necessary. The only previously unreleased item is a sparser earlier take of "Heartbreak Hotel." Everything else has been widely available (even on CD) for years, and it's a good bet that many of the Elvis fans who buy this already have virtually all of the contents on the *King of Rock 'n' Roll* box set. —*Richie Unterberger*

Great Country Songs / Oct. 15, 1996 / RCA ✦✦✦✦
Great Country Songs compiles 24 of the finest country songs Elvis Presley recorded between 1955 and 1976, from "I Forgot to Remember to Forget" to "Guitar Man." Many familiar performances are available, as are five previously unreleased tracks designed to bait collectors, and the collection does a good job of establishing Elvis' credentials as a country singer, even if it isn't as effective as the blues collection, *Reconsider Baby*. —*Stephen Thomas Erlewine*

Platinum: A Life in Music / Jul. 15, 1997 / RCA ✦✦✦
Released on the eve of the 20th anniversary of Presley's death, *Platinum: A Life in Music* attempts to trace an alternative history of Elvis' career by concentrating on alternate takes and unreleased material. Over the course of four discs, 23 hit singles are interspersed with 77 previously unreleased items. The hits function as touchstones, so the listener has an idea of where Elvis was in his career when he was recording such unreleased gems as a 1966 cover of "Blowin' in the Wind" or the 1959 "Bad Nauheim Medley." Certainly, the sheer amount of unreleased material means that *Platinum: A Life in Music* is targeted at hardcore collectors, but what is surprising is how listenable the set is, even for casual fans. The homemade recordings and demos are occasionally sonically rough, but the rarity of these items make the sound a moot point. Some of the performances aren't particularly remarkable—alternates of "Always on My Mind" and "Heartbreak Hotel" simply sound like the released versions, only not as good—but there's an abundance of gems scattered throughout the set, making it worthwhile for any serious Elvis collector. —*Stephen Thomas Erlewine*

Tiger Man / Sep. 15, 1998 / RCA ✦✦✦
Thirty years after its recording, the complete set from the second of two concerts given by Elvis on June 27, 1968 was released by RCA as *Tiger Man.* Only a handful of tracks had been previously released; three were edited into the first concert, broadcast by NBC (and later released on record by RCA) as the knockout *Elvis TV Special.* The newly compiled material displays Presley even more confident and relaxed than at the earlier show. In fact, he may be a bit *too* relaxed. He flubs a few songs, forgets lyrics (even on "Heartbreak Hotel"), banters excessively with the audience and his band, and appears to treat the entire show as one of his relaxed recording sessions instead of a performance. For most Elvis fans, this is a goldmine, yet another revelation into his career to file alongside *One Hundred Years From Now* and *Sunrise* in RCA's massive reissue campaign. For everyone else, it's simply too disjointed and incoherent to stand on its own worth next to the original *Elvis TV Special* album. *—John Bush*

★ **Sunrise** / Feb. 9, 1999 / RCA ✦✦✦✦✦
Elvis Presley's legendary recordings for Sun Records had been reissued many times before *Sunrise* appeared in early 1999, most notably in the 1987 collection *The Complete Sun Recordings.* Despite its title, *The Complete Sun Recordings* was missing a few odds and ends, plus its sequencing on CD was a little didactic, resulting in a repetitive listen. Those flaws are corrected on the exceptional *Sunrise,* a generous 38-song double-disc set that contains all of Elvis' Sun recordings, including alternate takes and several previously unreleased live performances. The compilers wisely decided to devote the first disc to the original takes, dedicating the second to alternate takes: six live cuts from 1955 and four private demos from 1953 and 1954. This sequencing emphasizes the brilliance of this music. Not only is listening to all 19 masters in a row quite breathtaking, but the second disc winds up as a revelatory experience, since it offers a kind of alternate history by following Elvis' pre-professional recordings from his Sun sessions to early live performances. As such, *Sunrise* is essential for the curious and the collector alike. *—Stephen Thomas Erlewine*

Home Recordings / Mar. 9, 1999 / RCA ✦✦
Here's one for the cult of Elvis Presley: 22 home recordings (15 previously unreleased) of Presley and pals sitting around the piano and belting out favorites. The sound quality is often poor, but, as the notes say, "priority has been given to historic content." The historic content, besides the fact that it's Presley, is the inclusion of many songs Presley did not otherwise record, and the opportunity to hear the King in informal settings singing alone and in harmony with Red West, Charlie Hodge, and others. If you are fascinated by every detail of his life, then you will find this to be a rare and precious glimpse at the private Presley. If you are a more casual fan hoping for raw or unproduced rock & roll, the spirituals and pop ballads that comprise the majority of the tracks will be a disappointment. *—Greg Adams*

☆ **Suspicious Minds** / Apr. 13, 1999 / RCA ✦✦✦✦✦
Elvis Presley's comeback recordings from the late '60s are generally regarded as some of the finest music he ever made, not only because they proved he could still be exciting, but because they're musically diverse and emotionally rich. That was evident on *From Elvis in Memphis,* the first record released from his landmark sessions of 1968 and 1969, and latter-day compilations like *The Memphis Record* made clear how deep those recordings were. Twelve years after *The Memphis Record,* the double-disc set *Suspicious Minds* was released, and it stands as the definitive overview of these sessions. All of the familiar hits are here, of course, but for collectors, what makes this essential is that it not only contains all the master takes, but it provides nine alternate takes of classics such as "True Love Travels on a Gravel Road," "Kentucky Rain," "Suspicious Minds," "In the Ghetto," and "I'm Movin' On." None of these are particularly revelatory, but they are interesting enough to be the icing on the cake on an exceptional collection. Since they're more concise, *The Memphis Record* or *From Elvis in Memphis* remain better bets for some listeners, but any true aficionado or rock historian will need to add *Suspicious Minds* to their collection. *—Stephen Thomas Erlewine*

Tomorrow Is a Long Time / May 18, 1999 / RCA ✦✦✦✦
Many critics and listeners think of Elvis Presley's pre-comeback, mid-'60s recording period as a creative graveyard filled with awful soundtrack songs. While he definitely did record too much soundtrack dreck during this period, Presley also managed to sneak some rock & roll gems out of the studio during the time. Most of this material was previously only available via singles or as bonus tracks on soundtrack albums, but they have finally been given a proper compilation in *Tomorrow Is a Long Time.* Two of the most notable tracks on this album are a pair of Jerry Reed-penned tracks that became hits, "Guitar Man" and "U.S. Male." The former is a fast-paced and witty tale of Southern boy's travails on the way to stardom, and the latter is a talking blues presenting Presley at his most macho as he warns a would-be Romeo to stay away from his girl. *Tomorrow Is a Long Time* a hefty complement of rootsy rock performances, including gritty takes on Chuck Berry's "Too Much Monkey Business" and the R&B classic "High Heel Sneakers." It's truly a joy to hear Presley cut lose on tracks like these. Elsewhere, the album's rock & roll contingent is balanced by some effective ballads: "Love Letters" is a quietly moving, almost hymn-like reading of the Ketty Lester classic, and "Indescribably Blue" features Presley hitting operatic heights of melodrama over a backing that effectively mixes a flamenco guitar melody with ghostly choral backing vocals. The biggest surprise in the ballad department is the title track, a subtle, country-inflected take on the Bob Dylan classic that Dylan once named his personal favorite cover version of his work. Some of the material doesn't hit the same heights as these highlights: "Come What May" and "Fools Fall in Love" come off as slight, insubstantial pop tunes despite tight, energetic production on both. Despite these occasional inconsistent moments, Presley delivers fine, committed vocal performances throughout the album, and there are more than enough worthwhile moments to make it worthwhile for Presley fans. As a result, *Tomorrow Is a Long Time* shapes up as a definitive retrospective of an underappreciated period in the career of one of rock's finest performers. *—Donald A. Guarisco*

Artist of the Century / Jul. 13, 1999 / RCA ✦✦✦✦✦
Elvis Presley doesn't really need more compilations—either single discs or box sets—in his catalog, but RCA's 1999 triple-disc set *Artist of the Century* does wind up filling a need, of sorts. Over the course of 75 tracks, nearly all of Elvis' most popular songs are presented in their original hit versions. Given the number of hits he had, plus the high quality of his recordings in the late '50s and late '60s, there are inevitably big songs missing, but many of his very biggest are here, and the first two discs, in particular, are quite strong (the late-'60s/'70s selections slip somewhat, lacking such necessary items as "Kentucky Rain" and "Moody Blue"). So, this winds up being good one-stop shopping for those who just want one fairly comprehensive Elvis set in their library—although you should be forewarned that "fairly" is the key word in that statement, since this will not contain all the hits or necessary recordings. *—Stephen Thomas Erlewine*

Can't Help Falling in Love: The Hollywood Hits / Sep. 14, 1999 / RCA ✦✦✦
Can't Help Falling in Love: The Hollywood Hits compiles 22 hit singles that were originally featured on soundtracks for films starring Elvis Presley. Where the double-disc set *Command Performances: The Essential 60's Masters II* concentrated on the '60s, specifically the cream of what was not on the five-disc box *From Nashville to Memphis,* this compilation draws from a random selection of movies Elvis made between 1956 and 1972. That's not necessarily a bad thing, even if the sequencing is also at random, since these featured songs are usually either quite good ("Jailhouse Rock," "Loving You," "King Creole," "Return to Sender," "Viva Las Vegas") or are embarrassing guilty pleasures ("Bossa Nova Baby," "Rock-A-Hula Baby," etc.). So, this isn't a definitive collection of movie hits, nor does it have all the movie hits that a casual fan may want. It's simply a reasonably enjoyable Elvis collection, one among many others of the same stripe in his catalog. *—Stephen Thomas Erlewine*

Peace in the Valley: The Complete Gospel Recordings / Sep. 12, 2000 / RCA ✦✦✦
An expanded three-disc collection that attempts to trump a 1994 double-disc set (*Amazing Grace: His Greatest Sacred Songs*) by offering virtually every single Elvis recording of a sacred song, *Peace in the Valley: The Complete Gospel Recordings* accomplishes the mission in its title, but at a hefty price that won't appeal to any but the most obsessive-compulsive fan. Obviously, it includes each track from his three gospel LPs—1960's *His Hand in Mine,* 1967's *How Great Thou Art,* and 1972's *He Touched Me*—plus scattered alternate takes that are previously unreleased. The third disc is padded out with an array of Elvis' sacred recordings that are easily available elsewhere, like the 13 gospel tracks on the raw *Million Dollar Quartet* session recorded at Sun in 1956, the "Gospel Medley" from his 1968 TV Special, and a version of "(There'll Be) Peace in the Valley" originally aired on Ed Sullivan's television show. Though there's no doubt that *Peace in the Valley: The Complete Gospel Recordings* is a complete set, most Elvis fans will gain little from owning it. *—John Bush*

Country Side of Elvis / Nov. 6, 2001 / RCA ✦✦✦
This classy, 51-track reissue featuring Elvis' country-styled tunes through his entire career starts promisingly enough with the early Sun sides from 1954, including his version of Bill Monroe's "Blue Moon of Kentucky." But like the artist himself, it dissipates disappointingly as the years progress. Elvis' almost universal appeal was grounded in how effectively he mixed blues, gospel, and classic vocal pop along with his country & western influences to produce, well, rock & roll, along with his own unique hybrid of styles. Hence his country recordings even as early as 1956's "Old Shep" and 1958's version of Hank Williams' "Your Cheatin' Heart" are often marred by sappy backing singers and a commercial slickness that was a harbinger of his Vegas years. Additionally, much of these selections are only vaguely country-sounding, at least in Elvis' hands. "There's Always Me" from 1961 is a pop ballad that is about as far from Hank Williams as Hank Williams Jr.'s rowdy redneck rock. Far better is Presley's version of Hank Snow's "I'm Movin' On," which starts out with stark accompaniment but adds horns and backing singers as the tune progresses. The best songs here, like the powerful "Kentucky Rain," add drama and pomp to basic country themes of loss, loneliness, and heartache, all emotions that ran rampant in Elvis' own tumultuous life. Colin Escott's liner notes are excellent, but the track documentation—which omits which album the songs originally appeared on, where the live performances are from, and any personnel—is frustratingly sketchy. The graphics and book are adequate, but not up to the standard of other post-early-'90s Elvis collections on RCA. From his first primitive Sun tracks to the last song he commercially recorded, a version of Joe Allison's "He'll Have to Go," Elvis was always at least partially a country singer, and country radio was traditionally his most dedicated outlet. This generous compilation is an indication of how he slotted the Nashville sound into his own larger-than-life palette. Weighed down by its schlocky numbers—and there are a lot of them—*The Country Side of Elvis* is still a fascinating look at one of the many sides of this legendary American artist. Even at his most facile, Elvis sounded inspired when singing this traditionally Southern music, and it's that emotional grip that keeps this collection listenable even through its many rough spots. *—Hal Horowitz*

Today, Tomorrow, & Forever / Jun. 25, 2002 / RCA ✦✦
A surprising perfectionist, Elvis was known to record dozens of takes for many of his records, often loosening up at the beginning of a session by playing around with different readings of the songs he'd decided to record; and while he got the feel of how he wanted his performances to go, the tape rolled. Commemorating the 25th anniversary of his death, RCA's four-disc *Today, Tomorrow, & Forever* presented fans with 100 tracks of previously unreleased Presley, a parade of alternate takes—both very welcome and curiously not so—and scattered live recordings from throughout his career. (Although not a

career record, the version of 1958's "Doncha' Think It's Time" used here was the 48th, and final take.) Among the highlights: seven songs from an incendiary set recorded in Arkansas on May 16, 1956, a 1959 version of "The Fool" recorded with Elvis alone at the piano while serving in Germany, and a few songs each of previously unreleased material from his first two seasons at Las Vegas' *International Hotel*, in 1969 and 1970. It's not clear, however, why the compilers deemed it necessary to include almost two dozen selections from the notoriously weak material used on Presley's '60s soundtracks, including "The Love Machine" (which the liners admit is "a ghastly song") and "My Desert Serenade" (with the added apology/defense, "he had every reason to sound desperately uncomfortable"). RCA certainly deserves credit for refusing to pad this collection with hits or old material unnecessary for collectors, but that's really the only audience left interested by this exhaustive display. *—John Bush*

● **Elvis: 30 #1 Hits** / Sep. 24, 2002 / RCA ✦✦✦✦✦
RCA and the Elvis estate made no bones about their intention on replicating the blockbuster success of the Beatles' *The Beatles 1* with their own single-disc collection of number-one hits—hence, the 2002 release of *Elvis 30 #1 Hits*. The idea of collecting all the number-one hits is simple enough, but there are problems inherent with the concept, not the least of which is that RCA did this once before. Unlike the Beatles, who went through numerous changes in just seven years of recording, Elvis had nearly three times as many years' worth of material and hits to choose from. Also, he hit on a number of different charts—not just pop, but also R&B, country, and adult contemporary. Furthermore, where almost all of the Beatles' number-one hits sampled at least part of their music, there are significant chunks of Elvis' best material—including the visionary sides for Sun—that didn't hit the top of the charts. All of this makes assembling a similar comprehensive sampler of Elvis' biggest hits much more difficult, and it doesn't help that RCA has decided not to have a rigid aesthetic and sample from different charts all over the world, resulting in a collection that feels more of a patchwork than it should, even if the bulk of the material is from the early '60s; at least five songs feel like they should have been replaced with better, and better-known, sides. And, even if much of this material is exceedingly familiar, there also feels like there is a lot missing because, frankly, there is. No Sun singles and very little from his classic 1968 comeback or early-'70s hits like "Moody Blue," not to mention sides that would showcase Elvis "the rocker" better than what's here, which plays closer to Elvis the '60s pop crooner than anything else. And, let's face it, no matter what the packaging is, *Elvis 30 #1 Hits* can't feel that new because of the veritable flood of Elvis collections RCA has issued since the King started having hits. This is a very good compilation, covering many of the basics, but it's hardly close to the only Elvis disc you'll ever need, and it's not even that great of a starting place, since it lacks so much of his best material. (Also, even though this is one of the most carefully considered compilations of Elvis hits, it can't help but feel a little shoddy since there's actually 31 number-one hits here, with the addition of the JXL remix of "A Little Less Conversation" tacked onto the end, no matter how good the single is.) *—Stephen Thomas Erlewine*

Ray Price

b. Jan. 12, 1926, Perryville, TX
Vocals, Guitar, Leader / Traditional Country, Country-Pop, Honky Tonk, Nashville Sound/Countrypolitan

Ray Price has covered—and kicked up—as much musical turf as any country singer of the postwar era. He's been lionized as the man who saved hard country when Nashville went pop, and vilified as the man who went pop when hard country was starting to call its own name with pride. Actually, he was—and still is—no more than a musically ambitious singer, always looking for the next challenge for a voice that could bring down roadhouse walls. Circa 1949, Price cut his first record for Bullet at the Famous Jim Beck in Dallas. In 1951, he was picked up by Columbia, the label for which he would record for more than 20 years.

After knocking around in Lefty Frizzell's camp for six months or so (his first Columbia single was a Frizzell composition) Price befriended Hank Williams. The connection brought him to the *Opry* and profoundly effected his singing style. After Hank died, Price starting stretching out more as a singer and arranger. His experimentation culminated in the 4/4-bass driven "Crazy Arms," the country song of the year for 1956. The intensely rhythmic sound he discovered with "Crazy Arms" would dominate his—and much of country in general's—music for the next six years. To this day, people in Nashville refer to a 4/4 country shuffle as the "Ray Price beat." Heavy on fiddle, steel, and high tenor harmony, his country work from the late '50s is as lively as the rock & roll of the same era. Price tired of that sound, however, and started messing around with strings. His lush 1967 version of "Danny Boy," and his 1970 take on Kris Kristofferson's "For the Good Times," were, in their crossover way, landmark records. But few of his old fans appreciated the fact. In the three decades following "For the Good Times," Price's career was often an awkward balancing act in which twin Texas fiddles are weighed against orchestras.

Born in tiny Perryville, TX, Price spent most of his youth in Dallas. It was there where he learned how to play guitar and sing. Following his high-school graduation, he studied veterinary medicine at North Texas Agricultural College in Abilene before he left school to join the Marines in 1942. Price stayed in the service throughout World War II, returing to Texas in 1946. After leaving the Marines, he initially returned to college, yet he began to perform at local clubs and honky tonks, as well as on the local radio station KRBC, where he was dubbed the Cherokee Cowboy. Three years later, he was invited to join the Dallas-based *The Big D Jamboree*, which convinced him to make music his full-time career. Shortly after joining *The Big D Jamboree*, the show began to be televised by CBS, which helped him release a single, "Your Wedding Corsage"/"Jealous Lies," on the independent Dallas label Bullet.

Price moved to Nashville to pursue a major-label record contract in 1951. After auditioning and failing several times, Ray finally signed to Columbia Records, after A&R representative Troy Martin convinced the label's chief executive Don Law that Decca was prepared to give the singer a contract. Previously, Law was uninterested in Price—he turned him down 20 times and threatened Martin never to mention his name again—but he was unprepared to give a rival company a chance at the vocalist. Just before "Talk to Your Heart" became a number-three hit for Price in the spring of 1952, Ray met his idol, Hank Williams, who immediately became a close friend. Over the next year, Hank performed a number of favors for Price, including giving him "Weary Blues" to record and helping him join the *Grand Ole Opry*. Ray also became the permanent substitute for Hank whenever he was missing or too drunk to perform. Following Williams' death in 1953, Price inherited the Drifting Cowboys.

Following the success of "Don't Let the Stars Get in Your Eyes" in the fall of 1952, Price was quiet for much of 1953. It wasn't until 1954 that he returned to the charts with "I'll Be There (If You Ever Want Me)," a number-two hit which kicked off a successful year for Price that also included the Top Ten singles "Release Me" and "If You Don't, Somebody Else Will." Instead of capitalizing on that success, he disappeared from the charts during 1955, as he spent the year forming the Cherokee Cowboys. Over the course of the past two years, he had realized that performing with the Drifting Cowboys had made him sound too similar to Hank Williams, so he decided to form his own group. Originally, most of the members were lifted from Lefty Frizzell's Western Cherokees, but over the years a number of gifted musicians began their careers in this band, including Roger Miller, Johnny Paycheck, Buddy Emmons, Johnny Bush and Willie Nelson.

Ray returned to the charts in 1956, first with "Run Boy" and then with "Crazy Arms," a driving honky tonk number that immediately became a country classics. The song was one of the first country records to be recorded with a drum kit, which gave it a relentless, pulsating rhythm. Until Price, most country artists were reluctant to use drums and the instrument was even banned from the stage of the *Grand Ole Opry*. The blockbuster status of the single helped change that situation. Spending an astonishing 20 weeks at the top of the country charts, "Crazy Arms" not only crossed over into the lower reaches of the pop charts, but it also established Price as a star. After the success of the single, he remained at or near the top of the charts for the next ten years, racking up 23 Top Ten singles between the 1956 and 1966. During this time, he recorded a remarkable number of country classics, including "I've Got a New Heartache" (number two, 1956), "My Shoes Keep Walking Back to You" (number one, 1957), "Make the World Go Away" (number two, 1963) and "City Lights," which spent 13 weeks at the top of the charts in 1958.

The momentum of Price's career had slowed somewhat by the mid-'60s; though he was still having hits, they weren't as frequent nor as big. His musical inclinations were also shifting, bringing him closer to the crooning styles of traditional pop singers. Ray abandoned the cowboy suits and brought in strings to accompany him, making him one of the first to explore the smooth, orchestrated sounds of late '60s and early '70s country-pop. While it alienated some hardcore honky tonk fans, the change in approach resulted in another round of Top Ten hits. However, it took a little while for the country audience to warm to this new sound—it wasn't until 1970, when his cover of Kris Kristofferson's "For the Good Times" hit number one, that he returned to the top of the charts. Over the next three years, he scored an additional three number-one singles ("I Won't Mention It Again," "She's Got to Be a Saint," "You're the Best Thing That Ever Happened to Me"). By the mid-'70s, the appeal of his string-laden country-pop hits had diminished, and he spent the rest of the decade struggling to get into the charts. In 1974, he left his longtime home of Columbia Records to sign to Myrrh, where he had two Top Ten hits over the next year. By the end of 1975, he had left the label, signing to ABC/Dot. Though he hadn't changed his style, his records became less popular around the same time he signed to ABC/Dot; only 1977's "Mansion on the Hill" gained much attention.

In 1978, he switched labels again, signing with Monument, which proved to be another unsuccessful venture. In 1980, Price reunited with his old bassist Willie Nelson, recording the duet album *San Antonio Rose*, which was a major success, spawning the number-three hit "Faded Love." *San Antonio Rose* reignited Ray's career, and in 1981 he had two Top Ten singles—"It Don't Hurt Me Half as Bad," "Diamonds in the Stars"—for his new label, Dimension. Price left Dimension in 1983, signing with Warner Records. He remained at the label for one year, and by that time, his new spell of popularity had cooled down considerably; now, he was having trouble reaching the Top 40. That situation didn't remedy itself for the remainder of the decade, even though he signed with two new labels: Viva (1983-1984) and Step One (1985-1989). By the late '80s, Ray Price had stopped concentrating on recording and had turned his efforts toward a theater he owned in Branson, MO. For most of the '90s, he sang and performed at his theater in Branson, occasionally stopping to record. Of all of his '90s records, the most notable was the 1992 album *Sometimes a Rose*, which was produced by Norro Wilson. *—Dan Cooper*

Ray Price Sings Heart Songs / 1957 / Columbia ✦✦✦✦✦

Talk to Your Heart / 1958 / Columbia ✦✦✦✦✦

Faith / 1960 / Columbia ✦✦✦

☆ **San Antonio Rose** / 1962 / Koch ✦✦✦✦✦
Fans of Ray Price or Bob Wills won't want to miss the Price's 1961 album, *San Antonio Rose: A Tribute to the Great Bob Wills*. Price, who acknowledged Wills as a primary influence, became the first of many to devote an album to covering the songs of the renowned master of Southwestern dance music. Price recorded the album in a nine-hour period, utilizing many of Nashville's best musicians, including guitarist Grady Martin, fiddler Tommy Jackson, pedal steel specialist Jimmy Day and pianist Pig Robbins (in one of his first Nashville sessions). Also sitting in on acoustic guitar was a new Music City arrival, a little-known songwriter named Willie Nelson, who had just been hired to crank out songs for Price's publishing company. The record finds Price crooning with smooth, easy richness while the band lets it fly. *—Michael McCall*

☆ **Night Life** / 1962 / Koch ✦✦✦✦✦
Depending upon which lens of the historical perspective you view this through, this 12-song collection is the last gasp of true honky tonk, the first stab at mainstreaming it into the Nashville sound of the 1960s, or country music's first concept album. In 1962, Ray Price was at the peak of his form as a honky tonker of major repute. His regular touring band, the Cherokee Cowboys, were the finest of their kind and Price's voice was an

instrument of wonder, full of reflection with every lyrical reading. As a traveling musician, Price knew well of the "night life" depicted in Willie Nelson's title track, a life spent on the road full of hotels, barrooms, one-night stands, heartache, and regrets. This album, full of well-written songs paying homage to that sinful life and its road to nowhere, evokes the sound, feel, and ambience of classic honky tonk music like few others do. As the decade wore on, Price would go on to major superstardom as a mellow balladeer, working with full string sections, reaching audiences that never heard this music or the other honky tonk classics that preceded it. More's the pity, for this album just may be Price's defining moment as an artist. *—Cub Koda*

Love Life / 1964 / Columbia ♦♦♦♦

☆ **Burning Memories** / Dec. 21, 1964 / Columbia ♦♦♦♦♦

Holy Hillbilly Fiddlers, Batman! Ray Price left the honky tonk and hooked up with a string section! At least that's what country fans must have been thinking when they heard Ray Price's *Burning Memories*. Here, the only identifying country marker is the corny cowboy hat he's wearing on the cover. While it's easy to see why Price took so much guff from country die-hards because this is a radical change from his Ernest Tubb-influenced honky tonk persona, it's still a badass country record. Full of Floyd Cramer's and Pig Robbins' pianos, Buddy Emmons' pedal steel and Price's awesome baritone voice in its finest form ever. Begun in 1962, *Burning Memories* was the beginning of the Price transition from hillbilly singer to serious crossover smash. This is the album that boasts the stellar, timeless and unforgettable "Make The World Go Away" by Hank Cochran, and Eddie Miller's mind-blowing "Release Me," two Price signature tunes. In addition, there are amazing reads of Buck Owens' "Together Again," Conway Twitty's "Walk Me to the Door," and Willie Nelson's "Are You Sure," among others—including Harlan Howard's fearsome nugget "You Took Her Off My Hands (Now Take Her Off My Mind)." Truth be told, *Burning Memories* holds no filler, which is astonishing for a country record from that era. Frank Jones production is full of space and slippery genre blurs and allows Price's ambition to soar without abandoning his strengths. [Burning Memories, masterpiece that it is, is only available on CD as part of a two-fer series by Audium. The other record? The amazing follow-up, *Touch My Heart*.] *—Thom Jurek*

Western Strings / 1965 / Columbia ♦♦♦

The Other Woman / 1965 / Koch ♦♦♦♦♦

The Other Woman was Ray Price's follow-up to his classic *Night Life* album and on it he continued to work the seasoned Texas honky tonk he and the Cherokee Cowboys had been perfecting since the mid-'50s—this in the midst of his initial foray into the country-pop style he would eventually embrace. With Cherokee alumni Buddy Emmons on guitar and pedal steel, Tommy Jackson on fiddle, and Buddy Harmon handling the drums, Price works some choice country terrain including a lazy shuffle rendition of the perennial "Born to Lose" and a show-stopping version of Floyd Tillman's "This Cold War With You." He turns in a smoldering version of the classic, blues-tinged "Funny How Time Slips Away," penned by one-time Cherokee Cowboy Willie Nelson. Price's famous shuffle beat style is still intact here, too, on the chart-topping title track, Hank Cochran's codependency nugget "Don't You Ever Get Tired of Hurting Me," and a pair of Fred Carter gems—"Too Much Love is Spoiling You" and "Rose Colored Glasses"—all benefiting from Emmons' stellar pedal steel work. The album is rounded out by a touching version of the Patsy Cline hit "Unloved, Unwanted" and the beautiful waltz "The Last Letter." *The Other Woman* does not quite match the variety or song quality of *Night Life*, but the steady delivery of fine country material as well as the spacious Grady Martin production make for very enjoyable listening. *—Stephen Cook*

Another Bridge to Burn / 1966 / Columbia ♦♦♦

Touch My Heart / Dec. 19, 1966 / Columbia ♦♦♦♦♦

Touch My Heart is the 1966 follow-up to Ray Price's uber-masterpiece *Burning Memories*. Issued two whole years later, this is in many ways a retrenchment for Price, who left the vast layers of strings off this one and, with producer Don Law, concentrated on a more organic approach, but could not give up the ballad style he was forging. While *Touch My Heart* features a more directly connected "country" sound, it is no less a pop album than the ingenious *Burning Memories*. Reemploying songs by Hank Cochran and Willie Nelson, and the Bakersfield sound—instead of Buck Owens, this time Price used Merle Haggard and his classic "Swingin' Doors"—he also relied heavily on former bandmember Johnny Paycheck for the title track and Dallas Frazier's hit "There Goes My Everything." The band was scaled back and the strings aren't quite so sweeping, but there is still plenty of Price's new sound grafted on to his old honky tonk singer's. While the aforementioned make up the album's highlights—especially the four Cochran tunes—other notable moments include Price's cover of Marty Robbins' "The Same Two Lips and Jeannie Seely's "Enough To Lie," for insurance. As suggested on the earlier album, *Burning Memories*, *Touch My Heart* is full of amazing contradictions, wondrous moments of musical whimsy and inspiration while managing to hold together not only as an album, but as an enduring country classic. [*Touch My Heart* is available on CD as part of a two-fer with *Burning Memories* from Audium, distributed by Koch. Necessary.] *—Thom Jurek*

Danny Boy / 1967 / Columbia ♦♦

Take Me as I Am / 1968 / Columbia ♦♦♦

She Wears My Ring / 1968 / Columbia ♦♦♦

Having for most part left behind the shuffle-beat honky tonk style he helped forge, Ray Price found new success as a country-pop singer by the mid-'60s, and although fans of his early hits "Crazy Arms" and "Heartaches By the Number" had difficulty with the change, many listeners accustomed to the pop-heavy Nashville sound or smooth croon of Jack Jones began listening up—Price eventually reaped the benefits by scoring big hits with "Don't Mention It" and Kris Kristofferson's "For the Good Times." Out of the numerous pop albums Price recorded for Columbia, *She Wears My Ring* stands out with very decent material, strong arrangements, and Price's powerful, high lonesome voice. The title track opens with some light country-style guitar and piano as if to hint at the pure country left behind, but soon all thoughts of honky tonkin' are banished as a timpani roll, full-blown strings, and vocal choir all make it clear this is not going to be a barnburning affair; more like the preferred soundtrack for cocktail hour. Thankfully, though, Price's commanding voice and the urbane Ray Ellis arrangements keep the schmaltz in check. The easy listening wave rolls on as Price lays down the oft-recorded "Little Green Apples," the gently swaying "Remembering," and "Welcome to My World," which prefigures the country power ballad style of "For the Good Times." To spice up the laid-back mood a bit, Price includes the jazz-me-blues tinged "Trouble" and the mellow swinging "I'm Gonna Change Everything," even tipping his hat to one of country-pop's early stylists with the Patsy Cline-inspired "I've Been There Before." The standout track of the set, though, is the Jimmy Webb masterpiece "By the Time I Get to Phoenix," rivaling Glen Campbell's definitive version as Ray Ellis' opaque flute/vibe introduction and eerie vocal chorus beautifully frame Price's weather-beaten voice. In contrast to the grandly laid-back mood that dominates the album, Price is able to work up a little steam on the medium-tempo "Set Me Free" and hoe-down spirited "Walking on New Grass." With honky tonk touches, pungent country vocals, and pat lyrics of codependency and tavern life meshed seamlessly in with tasteful string and choir arrangements, *She Wears My Ring* remains the best release from Price's countrypolitan period. *—Stephen Cook*

Sweetheart of the Year / 1969 / Columbia ♦♦♦♦

For the Good Times / 1970 / Columbia ♦♦♦♦♦

I Won't Mention It Again / 1971 / Columbia ♦♦♦

The singer/songwriter movement wrought fundamental changes in the lyrics, chord progressions, and attitudes of country music—changes that were arguably more profound than those of the Nashville sound era. Whereas the Nashville sound was a production style that draped essentially "country" music in pop trappings, the singer/songwriters materially altered the nature of the songs. Kris Kristofferson was one of the leading forces in the world of progressive country in the early '70s, and *I Won't Mention It Again* paired legendary honky-tonker Ray Price with Kristofferson's songs. The result was very successful: The title track spent three weeks at number one and nearly reached the pop Top 40 (thanks to the hipness and rock-orientation of Kristofferson's style), and "I'd Rather Be Sorry" was a respectable crossover hit as well. It is hard to say whether Price sounds uncomfortable or simply unfamiliar in the context of the "new" country music, but his age—which is apparent in his voice—contrasts strangely with Kristofferson's aggressively contemporary lyrics. The strong sales of this material suggests that it was either artistically successful or, perhaps more likely, a palatable midway point between the old and the new during a time of transition. *—Greg Adams*

Welcome to My World / 1971 / Columbia ♦♦♦

The Lonesomest Lonesome / 1972 / Columbia ♦♦♦

She's Got to Be a Saint / 1973 / Columbia ♦♦♦

Like Old Times Again / 1974 / ABC/Myrrh ♦♦♦

Hank 'n' Me / 1976 / ABC ♦♦♦

Say I Do / 1976 / ABC/Dot ♦♦♦

Rainbows and Tears / 1976 / ABC/Dot ♦♦♦

The Best of Ray Price / 1976 / Columbia ♦♦♦♦♦

This compilation presents the highlights of Price's string-laden years. "For the Good Times" is simply one of the most mature singles ever recorded. "She's Got to Be a Saint" has somehow gotten lost over the years. *—Tom Roland*

Reunited / 1977 / ABC/Dot ♦♦♦

After a stellar and rewarding honky tonk run during the '50s and early '60s, Ray Price traded in his band's fiddle for a battery of stringed instruments. The result was much less tavern-worthy than before and all about easy listening bigness on par with Andy Williams or Robert Goulet. Yes, Price embraced the Nashville sound and all its gloss to the extreme. He didn't fail miserably, though, as a respectable group of performances prove, but for earlier fans attuned to Price and his Cherokee Cowboys' prime honky tonk work ("Crazy Arms," "Heartaches by the Number," "Nightlife"), the move was a travesty. Thankfully for those fans, Price returned to his crack Cherokee Cowboys for this fine 1977 reunion LP. Featuring such band standouts as steel guitar player Buddy Emmons and fiddle master Tommy Jackson, Price goes all autumnal and golden on a mix that takes in old favorites ("My Shoes Go Walking Back to You"), a Jessi Colter gem ("Storms Never Last"), and even a bit of Dylan via *Nashville Skyline* ("I'll Be Your Baby Tonight"). His range may be bit compromised thanks to all those smoky supper clubs of his MOR days, but Price still delivers with a wealth of barroom pathos and rough-yet-burnished singing to make this more than just a lukewarm exercise in nostalgia. A must for all those Price purists who waited a longtime for their hero to return home. *—Stephen Cook*

Help Me / 1977 / Columbia ♦♦♦

American Originals / 1989 / Columbia ♦♦♦♦♦

The brief, ten-track collection *American Originals* contains several of Ray Price's biggest hits—including "Crazy Arms," "Under Your Spell Again," "Faded Love," "For the Good Times" and "Funny How Time Slips Away"—dividing the album between his '50s honky tonk hits and his '60s countrypolitan singles. *American Originals* misses many of Price's most famous songs, such as "My Shoes Keep Walking Back to You" and "City Lights," usually at the expense of covers of songs made famous by other vocalists ("Crazy"). And that means, *American Originals* isn't an ideal collection and only of use to budget-minded, casual fans, and those who want a handful of his latter-day singles; *The Essential Ray Price: 1951-1962* is a preferable compilation. —*Stephen Thomas Erlewine*

★ **The Essential Ray Price (1951-1962)** / 1991 / Columbia/Legacy ✦✦✦✦✦

Ray Price may not exert the mythic power of Hank Williams, Bob Wills, or even Lefty Frizzell, but he is unquestionably one of the titans of 20th century country music, one of the musicians who created the foundation of modern country through his skipping shuffles, soulful ballads, and exceptional ear for talent in songwriters and supporting musicians. He was one of the most popular singers of his era, staying on the charts until the early '80s (!), but Columbia/Legacy's 20-track 1991 collection *The Essential Ray Price (1951-1962)* chronicles his peak of creative powers and as a hitmaker. It's possible to hear him evolve from a Hank/Lefty disciple to minting his own style, equal parts hardcore honky tonk and Western swing, supported by a prominent swinging two-step backbeat that was known as the Ray Price Shuffle even after countless other singers used it as the foundation for their own music. It's thrilling to hear this develop over the course of his '50s hits, taking hold around 1955 (about a third into this collection) and reaching full flower on 1956's "Crazy Arms," which arrives halfway through the collection. From this point on, Price's music is propelled by the shuffle, even on the ballads, and it's a body of work as individual and influential as anything else in country music, perhaps best heard on the hits "My Shoes Keep Walking Back to You," Roger Miller's "Invitation to the Blues," Bill Anderson's "City Lights," and Harlan Howard's timeless "Heartaches By the Number." This is the sound of modern honky tonk music—Hank and Lefty were the godfathers, but on the sides Ray Price cut from 1955 onward, he invented the template that neo-traditionalist country singers followed. It remains vital, lively, and essential music, and there's no better place to hear it than Columbia/Legacy's excellent *The Essential Ray Price (1951-1962)*. —*Stephen Thomas Erlewine*

Hits on Monument / 1993 / CBS ✦✦

Ray Price made the Top 40 only three times during his two years on Monument in the late '70s, with "Feet," "There's Always Me," and "That's the Only Way to Say Good Morning," all of which were fairly modest hits. Price's recordings during this period were slick and pop sounding, and his voice exhibited that distinct vibrato that often comes with age. These 11 songs aren't among Price's best, but serious fans will appreciate such a generous view of a relatively brief and minor chapter in his recording career. —*Greg Adams*

☆ **The Honky Tonk Years (1950-1966)** / 1996 / Bear Family ✦✦✦✦✦

The Honky Tonk Years (1950-1966) is an accurate title for this mammoth ten-disc set. Tracing Ray Price's career through his heyday in the '50s and stopping in the late '60s, just as he abandoned honky tonk for country-pop, the set documents one of the finest singers and bandleaders in country music. During this era, Price had a long, impressive string of Top Ten singles—including "Don't Let the Stars Get in Your Eyes," "I'll Be There (If You Ever Want Me)," "My Shoes Keep Walking Back to You," "City Lights," and the massive hit "Crazy Arms"—and led a band that featured, at various times, such musicians as Willie Nelson, Johnny Paycheck, and Roger Miller. Price and his band were talented enough to make weak material, which helps make this exhaustive set interesting; after all, there's bound to be a few lesser cuts in a box that runs over 260 tracks. Though the strict chronological session order is occasionally tedious, the quality of the music far outweighs the flaws in presentation. For serious listeners and musicologists, *The Honky Tonk Years* is an essential purchase, since it offers a complete picture of one of the biggest figures in country music. Neophytes and casual listeners, however, are advised to stick with the single-disc collection *The Essential Ray Price*, simply because it is far easier to digest. —*Stephen Thomas Erlewine*

16 Biggest Hits / Aug. 10, 1999 / Columbia ✦✦✦✦

16 Biggest Hits may be missing some noteworthy songs, but it does provide an excellent summary of Ray Price's Columbia recordings between 1956 and 1973. Since it does contain the majority of his best-known songs—"Crazy Arms," "I've Got a New Heartache," "City Lights," "Heartaches By the Number," "The Same Old Me," "Make the World Go Away," "For the Good Times," "You're the Best Thing that Ever Happened to Me," "She's Got to Be a Saint"—at a mid-line price, it's an excellent introductory collection. —*Stephen Thomas Erlewine*

In a Honky Tonk Mood / Apr. 18, 2000 / Jasmine ✦✦✦✦

A set of excellent and inspired '50s transcriptions featuring Price & the Cherokee Cowboys at their very best. Before Price moved into a countrypolitan sound in the early '60s, he was a honky tonk cowboy of the highest order and tracks like "I'll Be There (If You Ever Want Me)," "You Done Me Wrong," "I'll Sail My Ship Alone," and "Don't Let the Stars Get in Your Eyes" showcase this sound to great effect. The Cherokee Cowboys are spotlighted on two instrumentals, "Steel Guitar Jubilee" and "Back Up and Push," while Price sings two great gospel hymns, "Peace in the valley" and "The Old Rugged Cross," ably backed by the Jordanaires. Another pure winner in this series and highly recommended. —*Cub Koda*

Prisoner of Love / May 16, 2000 / Buddha ✦✦✦

Prisoner of Love is the first release from Ray Price since 1992's *Sometimes a Rose*. Here the Cherokee Cowboy continues his mixture of lush string arrangements with his outstanding ability to project melancholy lyrics. These 12 tracks are divided between the country side of his repertory "I've Got a New Heartache" and "Better Class of Losers" along with standards like "Fly Me to the Moon" and "Body and Soul." —*Al Campbell*

Time / Aug. 27, 2002 / Audium ✦✦✦

Time gathers together the surviving members of Price's *Night Life*-era band, including steel guitarist Buddy Emmons, for an all-star album of sorts that plays out as a near-perfect revisitation of the singer's classic era. Price is in excellent voice, astonishingly so at times, and it's a genuine pleasure to hear how well his talent has endured, even well into his seventh decade. —*Jim Smith*

☆ **Burning Memories/Touch My Heart** / Jun. 24, 2003 / Audium ✦✦✦✦✦

The Audium reissue of these two Columbia albums by country great Ray Price is a godsend. *Burning Memories*, from 1964, is the first recording Price employed the liberal use of strings on; the album brought him the timeless hits "Release Me," the title track, and "Make the World Go Away." This was a blatant attempt, two years in the making, to cross over into the pop world for Price, and it worked. While country critics were scathing and many of the genre's fans were wondering is he had sold out, Price's profile was on the rise with mainstream pop music consumers. *Burning Memories* was a gamble that paid off big-time, though some concessions were made initially, and *Touch My Heart* from 1966 was one of them. Johnny Paycheck, a former bandmember of Price's, wrote the title track; it showcased Price straddling the honky tonk and pop worlds with more balance. Strings were not as prevalent as fiddles, and the steel guitar made a big-time return to the center of the Price sound. But the songs were something else again; they could be interpreted either way. Hard country examples were Merle Haggard's "Swingin' Doors" and Hank Cochran's "I Lie a Lot," with the title track and Dallas Frazier's "There Goes My Everything" showcasing the new balladic style with a rough-hewn grace and silky aplomb, making for the last country rave-up in Price's catalog until the late '80s. Here are 23 tracks—presenting the latter album first—that offer an astonishing portrait of an artist in transition. The sound is good if not excellent, and the liner notes by Nick Shaffran offer an inside portrait of the recording sessions. This is the only way to get either of these albums on CD, and is priced right to move. —*Thom Jurek*

Charley Pride

b. Mar. 18, 1938, Sledge, MS

Vocals, Guitar / Traditional Country, Country-Pop

With 36 number-one hits under his belt, Charley Pride, who is black, has helped prove how little race matters to the majority of country music fans. It's taken a longtime to understand that, though. His first single, "Snakes Crawl at Night," was released without publicity photos, as some in the industry feared listeners would automatically reject a black country singer. Since then, Pride's 12 gold albums in the U.S., combined with 30 gold and four platinum internationally, place him in the Top 15 all-time country record sellers. His easygoing singing style and easy-to-listen-to voice show why these honors have come his way. From picking cotton in his native Mississippi, Pride ended up working in a smelting plant in Montana after a stint as a semipro baseball player. At the suggestion of Red Sovine, Pride moved to Nashville, where he was signed by Chet Atkins of RCA. In 1966, "Just Between You and Me" brought Pride a Grammy nomination and national fame. At the end of the '60s and the early part of the '70s, he had five number-one singles in a row, including "All I Have to Offer Is Me" and "Is Anybody Goin' to San Antone." Numerous awards came in 1971 and 1972, with many more hits following, among them "She's Too Good to Be True," "Kiss an Angel Good Mornin'," and "Night Games." Pride's warm baritone voice and relaxed style made him the highest-selling act for RCA since Elvis Presley.

Pride was born on a cotton farm in Sledge, MS. His father was a sharecropper on the farm at a time. When he was 14 years old, Charley bought a guitar from Sears Roebuck and proceeded to learn how to play by listening to country music on the radio. Two years later, he turned his attention to baseball. He joined the Negro American League, playing with the Memphis Red Sox. After playing ball for two years, Pride joined the U.S. Army, where he served for two years. Upon his discharge, he intended to return to baseball, but he sustained injuries that affected his throwing arm. Discouraged that he couldn't qualify for the major leagues, Pride began working construction in Helena, MT, while he still played in the minors. Eventually, he earned a tryout for the California Angels in 1961, but they turned him down; the following year, the New York Mets rejected him as well.

Following his rejection in baseball, Pride turned his attention to music, and in 1963, he sang "Lovesick Blues" for Red Foley and Red Sovine backstage at one of Sovine's concerts. The veteran musicians were impressed and told Charley to go to Nashville. Heeding their advice, he traveled to Music City, but he couldn't break into the industry. However, both of the Reds and Webb Pierce kept recommending the fledgling singer to their associates and eventually helped him secure a management deal with Jack Johnson. Through Johnson, Pride met Jack Clement, who sent a demo tape of Pride's to Chet Atkins at RCA, who signed the vocalist in 1966. Later that year, Pride's debut single, "The Snakes Crawl at Night," was released but was issued without a publicity photograph, since the label was afraid that radio programmers would be reluctant to lend support to a black country singer. Both "The Snakes Crawl at Night" and his second single, "Before I Met You," gained a small audience, but it wasn't until "Just Between You and Me" that Charley became a star.

Released at the end of 1966, "Just Between You and Me" climbed to number nine and began a virtually uninterrupted streak of Top Ten singles that ran until 1984; out of his 54 singles released during those 18 years, only three failed to crack the Top Ten. However, Pride's success didn't arrive as easily as it may seem. Though he was praised upon the release of "Just Between You and Me" and won a Grammy award for the single, there remained resistance in certain quarters of the country audience to a black performer. Nevertheless, the consistent quality of Pride's music and the support from his fellow musicians helped break down doors. And the doors began to open very quickly—on January 7, 1967, he became the first black artist to perform on the *Grand Ole Opry* since DeFord Bailey in 1925. Over the next two years, his star steadily rose, and between 1969 and 1971, he had six straight number one singles: "All I Have to Offer You (Is Me)," "I'm So Afraid of Losing You Again," "Is Anybody Goin' to San Antone," "Wonder Could I Live There Anymore," "I Can't Believe That You've Stopped Loving Me," and "I'd Rather Love You." All of those singles also charted in the lower regions of the pop charts, giving evidence of his smooth, country-pop crossover appeal. "Let Me Live," taken from his gospel album, *Did You Think to Pray?*, temporarily broke his streak of number-one singles in the spring of 1971, but it won a Grammy for Best Gospel Performance. Directly after "Let Me Live," two of his biggest hits—"I'm Just Me" and "Kiss an Angel Good Mornin'"—arrived, earning him his greatest success on both the country and pop charts. Throughout the '70s, he continued to chart in the upper regions of the country charts, earning number-one singles like "It's Gonna Take a Little Bit Longer" (1972), "She's Too Good to Be True" (1972), "A Shoulder to Cry On" (1973), "Then Who Am I" (1975), "She's Just an Old Love Turned Memory" (1977), and "Where Do I Put Her Memory." During this entire time, he never changed his country-pop style, though he promoted new performers and songwriters like Ronnie Milsap, Gary Stewart, and Kris Kristofferson.

Pride's success continued during the first half of the '80s, as he continued to have number-one hits like "Honky Tonk Blues" (1980), "Mountain of Love" (1982), "You're So Good When You're Bad" (1982), and "Night Games" (1983). During 1984 and 1985, however, he grew frustrated with RCA Records, who began to promote newer artists at the expense of veteran performers like Pride himself. He left the label at the end of 1986, signing with Opryland's 16th Avenue label, where he returned to working with his old producer, Jerry Bradley. Pride had a number of minor hits for the label, highlighted by 1988's number five "Shouldn't It Be Easier Than This," before it collapsed. Pride moved on to Honest Entertainment in the early '90s, where he released *My 6 Latest & 6 Greatest*, where he dueted with the likes of Marty Stuart and Travis Tritt. Pride didn't record much after that album, yet he continued to be a popular concert attraction. On each of his shows, he was supported by his son Dion, who played lead guitar. In 1994, Pride was given the Academy of Country Music's Pioneer Award.—*David Vinopal*

Country Charley Pride / 1966 / RCA ✦✦✦

The Country Way / 1967 / RCA ✦✦✦✦✦

The Pride of Country Music / 1967 / RCA ✦✦✦✦✦
Charley Pride returns to the studio with another collection of edifying songs. The hit "Just Between You and Me" is included, as is "Apartment #9," which was also recorded by Tammy Wynette. Pride seems to have begun gaining his confidence in the recording studio, and is more willing to experiment a bit with his vocal style.—*Michael B. Smith*

Make Mine Country / 1968 / RCA ✦✦✦✦
Years before Freddy Fender scored a number-one hit (1975) with "Before the Next Teardrop Falls," and Charley Pride recorded an admirable version of the song for *Make Mine Country*. Other outstanding tracks include "I Guess Things Happen That Way," and "Lie to Me."—*Michael B. Smith*

Songs of Pride . . . Charley, That Is / 1968 / Koch ✦✦✦
Songs of Pride . . . is a straight CD reissue of a 1968 album by Charley Pride, and the hit on this record was "The Easy Part's Over," which went to number two the same year. Produced by Chet Atkins, Felton Jarvis, and Jack Clement, *Songs of Pride . . .* features love songs and hurtin' tunes with more fiddle and steel than might be expected. None of these tracks overlap with the *Essential* disc, providing fans with a mid-priced opportunity to delve more deeply into the work of Pride. —*Greg Adams*

The Sensational Charley Pride / 1969 / RCA ✦✦✦✦✦

In Person / 1969 / Koch ✦✦✦✦✦
Recorded live at Panther Hall in Fort Worth, TX, *In Person* gained Charley Pride a gold record in 1969, thanks in part to the abundance of early RCA hits included, like the highlight "Kaw-Liga."—*John Bush*

● **Best of Charley Pride** / 1969 / RCA ✦✦✦✦
The career of Charley Pride is worthy of record collecting beyond the confines of a greatest-hits set, but a listener who went out shopping for this type of item alone might find himself buried by a variety of volumes, few of which have any duplication. The first of several chapters' worth of retrospective collections released by RCA, this is a fine example of Pride's performing style. Some of the trademarks are his superb voice, often enveloped by background singers as if he were trying to hide from the producer, dead-on accompaniment that basically sticks to the roots sound of country & western, and an emotional depth that makes the country artists of later decades sound like they are scribbling in the margins of greeting cards. The Pride live album *In Person* has long been considered one of his masterpieces, especially for fans of hot pedal steel playing. The radio hit "Kaw-Liga" was originally on that record, and was wisely chosen as part of this collection, demonstrating not only Pride's flair for Hank Williams but his relaxed delivery. The casual feeling extends to the production, and it would be indeed hard to conceive of a country radio hit of today in which the singer would toss off a comment along the lines of "have a good time!" in the direction of the audience, right in the middle of a song. The Mel Tillis song "The Snakes Crawl at Night" is a cold-chills affair, and other great tracks include "Just Between Me and You" and "Gone, on the Other Hand." "The Day the World Stood Still" reveals the baritone side of Pride's vocalizing. Some nice production touches are evident courtesy of Jack Clement, who is also writer or co-writer of a good chunk of the tunes here. —*Eugene Chadbourne*

Just Plain Charley / 1970 / RCA ✦✦✦
In 1970, Charley Pride was well-enough established that RCA no longer had to put "country" in the title of his albums to reassure buyers that, yes, this black man you see on the cover is in fact singing country music. And sing country music he does on *Just Plain Charley*, from his second number-one hit, "(I'm So) Afraid of Losing You Again," to his usual assortment of heartbroken ballads. Pride was often in danger of being perceived as novelty act, but his expressive way with a ballad should have put that thought to rest right away. Pride demonstrates his aptitude for country crooning on "A Good Chance of Tear-Fall Tonight" and "Gone, Gone, Gone" (not to be confused with Lefty Frizzell's "She's Gone Gone Gone") , and covers some recent hits like "Me and Bobby McGee" and "I'm a Lonesome Fugitive." "It's All Right" shows how Pride continued to connect country music with rurality and poverty, thereby proving himself to be one of the more traditional singers of his era. *Just Plain Charley* isn't plain at all—it's a fine album from one of the greats. —*Greg Adams*

Charley Pride's 10th Album / 1970 / RCA ✦✦✦✦
The cardigan-clad man beaming through a trellis on the cover of *Charley Pride's 10th Album* doesn't look like a standard-bearer for traditional country music, but Pride's

allegiance to songs about rambling, poverty, and trains is commendable. Releasing ten albums in four years wasn't an unusual feat at the time, and Pride accomplished it by covering scads of well-known hits. This album breaks with the formula for only the second time (*Songs of Pride*, from 1968, is similar) and offers a plate of new songs by assorted Nashville songwriters. "This Is My Year for Mexico" was later a hit for Crystal Gayle, but it was unknown when Pride recorded it. "Is Anybody Goin' to San Antone" deservedly went to number one, but the remaining tracks are likewise very good. With "Able Bodied Man," "Special," and "A Poor Boy Like Me," Pride continues to mine country music's association with the working class and economic hardship at a time when the genre was increasingly moving toward glamour and the pop mainstream. Several of Pride's affecting ballad performances also grace an album that stands above the average of his consistently good catalog. —*Greg Adams*

Christmas in My Home Town / 1970 / RCA ✦✦✦✦✦

From Me to You / 1971 / RCA ✦✦✦
From Me to You, Charley Pride's 12th album, contains the number-one hits "I Can't Believe That You've Stopped Loving Me" and "Wonder Could I Live There Anymore." The latter invokes rustic imagery while adopting an implicitly urban pose, but most of *From Me to You* is willfully anachronistic. Everything on the album sounds like it could have come from the '60s, particularly "Sweet Promises," which could have been made ten years earlier. The Cajun theme of "Piroque Joe" and faux Lefty Frizzell phraseology of "Today Is That Tomorrow" likewise make overt connections with country music's past. Pride's nearly unique status as an African-American country artist may have spurred RCA to constantly reinforce his identity as a country singer with backward-looking repertoire, but the results are hard to fault. —*Greg Adams*

Did You Think to Pray? / 1971 / RCA ✦✦✦✦✦
Nobody can sing a Southern gospel song any better than Charley Pride, which is why *Did You Think to Pray?* became a staple of Sunday Christian radio stations for many years to come. Every song on the album is excellent, from the traditional "I'll Fly Away" to the clasic "Church in the Wildwood." Pride puts his heart and soul into each of these songs, which makes the record quite special. —*Michael B. Smith*

I'm Just Me / 1971 / RCA ✦✦✦

Charley Pride Sings Heart Songs / 1971 / RCA ✦✦✦✦✦
Not only did *Charley Pride Sings Heart Songs* yield Pride's biggest hit of his career, it also featured an array of country favorites including "You'll Still Be the One," "Anywhere," and the moving "Pretty Houses for Sale." This is the album that took Pride out of the Top 40 and put him into the Top Ten. —*Michael B. Smith*

A Sunshine Day With Charley Pride / 1972 / RCA ✦✦

The Best of Charley Pride, Vol. 2 / 1972 / RCA ✦✦✦✦✦
Perhaps because RCA wanted to leave no doubts about Pride's country heritage, his early career mined the standard three-chord structure almost exclusively. As with the first volume, this set does that, but in "Kiss an Angel Good Mornin'" and "Is Anybody Goin' to San Antone?," his performance is a notch or two above the previous package. —*Tom Roland*

Songs of Love By Charley Pride / 1973 / RCA ✦✦✦
Building on the success of 1971's *Charley Pride Sings Heart Songs*, RCA released *Songs of Love By Charley Pride*, featuring ten more "heart" songs. While this one fared a little less successfully than its predecessor, it still measures up pretty well, with several elite tracks. Among the best are "Good Hearted Woman" and "Too Weak to Let You Go." —*Michael B. Smith*

Sweet Country / 1973 / RCA ✦✦✦

Amazing Love / 1973 / RCA ✦✦✦

Pride of America / 1974 / RCA ✦✦

Country Feelin' / 1974 / RCA ✦✦✦✦

Charley / 1975 / RCA ✦✦

The Happiness of Having You / 1975 / RCA ✦✦

Sunday Morning with Charley Pride / 1976 / RCA ✦✦

She's Just an Old Love Turned Memory / 1977 / RCA ✦✦✦✦

The Best of Charley Pride, Vol. 3 / 1979 / RCA ✦✦✦✦✦
To be honest, Pride sounds a bit bored with some of this material. But "Mississippi Cotton Pickin' Delta Town" is practically a page out of his life. By the way, the cover art, with its rope script and blue-jeans-and-patches sports suit, is so '70s it's camp. —*Tom Roland*

Someone Loves You Honey / 1978 / RCA ✦✦✦✦

Burgers and Fries / 1978 / RCA ✦✦✦✦

You're My Jamaica / 1979 / RCA ✦✦✦

There's a Little Bit of Hank in Me / 1980 / RCA ✦✦✦
Charley Pride salutes Hank Williams on this fine collection by covering Williams' songs such as "I Can't Help It (If I'm Still In Love With You)," "Honky Tonk Blues," "I'm So Lonesome I Could Cry" alongside an original tribute tune, "There's a Little Bit of Hank in Me." —*James Chrispell*

Roll on Mississippi / 1981 / RCA ✦✦✦

Greatest Hits / 1981 / RCA ✦✦✦✦✦
Greatest Hits is a brief eight-track collection, but it does contain many of Charlie Pride's biggest RCA hits from the '70s, including "Burgers and Fries," "She's Just an Old Love Turned Memory," "When I Stop Leaving (I'll Be Gone)," "A Whole Lotta Things to Sing About" and "You're My Jamaica." Several of his biggest hits, including "Kiss an Angel Good Mornin'," "I'm Just Me," "I'm Gonna Take a Little Big Longer," and "She's Too Good

to Be True" are missing, so this *Greatest Hits* can't be called definitive, but it remains a good sampler. —*Stephen Thomas Erlewine*

Charley Sings Everybody's Choice / 1982 / RCA ✦✦✦✦✦
Dumb title, but it's an excellent album. Producer Norro Wilson revitalized Pride's career by bringing out the Memphis soul that rests in the shadows of his country veneer. —*Tom Roland*

Night Games / 1983 / RCA ✦✦

Power of Love / 1984 / RCA ✦✦✦

The Best of Charley Pride / 1991 / Curb ✦✦✦✦✦
Pride sang in a Hank Williams-influenced voice that yielded some of the best country performances of the late '60s and early '70s. —*Mark A. Humphrey*

My 6 Latest & 6 Greatest / 1994 / Honest ✦✦✦
Charley Pride seemed unstoppable in the 1960s and 1970s, when he enjoyed one number-one hit after another, but when he signed with Honest Entertainment in the mid-'90s, he was among the many veteran country legends who had lost a lot of ground to the younger country stars Nashville was pushing. Pride joined Honest with *My 6 Latest & 6 Greatest*, a likable country-pop effort demonstrating that the years certainly hadn't robbed him of his charm and charisma. This CD's 12 offerings fall into two categories: new versions of six of Pride's hits, and six songs employing young country artists. The Mississippi native is in good form on new solo versions of "Kiss an Angel Good Mornin'," "Roll on Mississippi," and "Is Anybody Goin' to San Antone," as well as selections that find him joined by Travis Tritt, Marty Stuart, Joe Diffie, or Hal Ketchum. Unfortunately, most of them aren't really duets, for most of Pride's guests don't have nearly enough room and end up serving as little more than background singers. An exception is the nice spot Tritt has on "Burnin' Down the Town." The album's strengths do outweigh its shortcomings, and it's good to see Pride back in the studio. —*Alex Henderson*

Platinum Pride: Greatest Hits, Vol. 2 / 1994 / Honest ✦✦✦
What was true of *Platinum Pride: Greatest Hits, Vol. 1* is also true of *Vol. 2*—Charley Pride revisits his classic RCA hits using the original arrangements. The results are enjoyable but not essential, and those getting into Pride for the first time would be better off hearing the original RCA recordings. *Vol. 2* focuses on hits Pride had between 1975 and 1982, most of which reached number one on the country charts—including "Hope You're Feelin' Me (Like I'm Feelin' You)," "Where Do I Put Her Memory," "Mountain of Love" and "She's Just an Old Love." A number-one hit in 1977, "I'll Be Leaving Alone" is a poignant account of a married man who is tempted to cheat but resists the urge. This was one of four CDs that Pride recorded for the Nashville-based Honest label in the 1990s. —*Alex Henderson*

Platinum Pride: Greatest Hits, Vol. 1 / Apr. 16, 1995 / Honest ✦✦✦
Some buyers assumed that this collection contained original versions of Charley Pride's major hits on RCA, but, in fact, both volumes of *Platinum Pride* offer new versions, although all of them use the original arrangements and sound a lot like the old RCA versions. This CD's focus is on the hits he had between 1966-1974, and when the singer revisits "I'm Just Me," "I'm Afraid of Losing You Again," "Is Anybody Goin' to San Antone," and other gems that went to number one on the country charts, it's obvious that his voice had held up well. Another high point of the disc is Hank Williams' amusing "Kaw-Liga," which had been a number-three hit for Pride in 1969. But as enjoyable as *Platinum Pride, Vol. 1* is, novices would be much better off starting out with a collection of his RCA recordings. This is for completists and for Pride's more devoted fans only. —*Alex Henderson*

36 All-Time Greatest Hits / 1996 / Collectors' Choice Music ✦✦✦✦✦
Available only through mail order, the three-disc *36 All-Time Greatest Hits* contains the majority of Charley Pride's greatest hits, including "I Can't Believe That You've Stopped Loving Me," "Just Between You and Me" and "Kiss an Angel Good Mornin'." Though the packaging is somewhat haphazard—there are only 12 songs on each disc, and there is a lack of liner notes—no other compilation contains as many hits in one place. —*Thom Owens*

Super Hits / Oct. 15, 1996 / RCA ✦✦✦✦
Super Hits is a budget-priced compilation that features ten of Charley Pride's biggest hits for RCA Records, including "Is Anybody Goin' to San Antone," "I'm So Afraid of Losing You Again," and "Where Do I Put Her Memory." Though the album isn't comprehensive, it nevertheless is an excellent collection by budget-line standards. —*Stephen Thomas Erlewine*

★ **The Essential Charley Pride** / Apr. 29, 1997 / RCA ✦✦✦✦✦
Charley Pride's significance in the history of country music isn't entirely tied to the quality of his music, although his warm baritone and adherence to "tradition" certainly provided the listening public with a wealth of enjoyable music. But his immense popularity with what is often assumed to be a conservative (read racially-intolerant) country audience in spite of (or because of) his skin color, will provide country music scholars with points to ponder for years to come. Beyond the curious phenomenon, though, is the music, which is often simply great. "Kiss an Angel Good Mornin'" and "Is Anybody Goin' to San Antone" are enduring classics, and his live version of Hank Williams' "Kaw-Liga" demonstrates the rural charm that helped make Pride a star. This 20-song collection is a good distillation of hits from the late '60s through the late '70s, including the aforementioned tracks as well as a number of other hits. Charley Pride had too long and too successful a career to sum up with a single disc, but until he is granted his deserved and overdue box set, *The Essential Charley Pride* will do. —*Greg Adams*

30 Years of Pride / Dec. 28, 1999 / BMG International ✦✦✦✦
30 Years of Pride is a showcase for the majority of Charley Pride's RCA hits from the late '60s through the '80s spread out over two discs, including "Kiss an Angel Good Mornin'," "Is Anybody Goin' to San Antone," "Mississippi Cotton Picking Delta Town," and "Mountain of Love." Those wanting only Pride's biggest hits would be better-served by the single-disc *RCA Country Legends*. —*Al Campbell*

Legendary Charley Pride / Sep. 5, 2000 / BMG International ✦✦✦✦✦
Charley Pride was always the odd man out in Nashville, and not just because of his race. The cat was a professional baseball player in the Pioneer League, and he was a good one. His sound was far more country than many of his peers with big whining steel guitars, huge gospel choruses, and deep mountain melodies entrenched in his popular mode of singing. Chet Atkins knew exactly what he was doing when he signed him, and Willie Nelson knew even better when he brought Pride to the *Grand Ole Opry* in the late '60s. Pride's particular gift was that he was a deep link between the countrypolitan sound of the time and the music's rich history that was brought into being by the Carter and Stoneman families. Nowhere is the evidence more clear than on this triple-CD package put out by RCA Australia (and budget priced). There are 50 tracks on this comp (as is customary for this series) that cover Pride's career from his first single, "Mississippi Cotton Picking Delta Town," to his first Grammy nomination in 1967 with "Just Between You and Me" to his first number-one single in 1969 with "All I Have to Offer You Is Me" to the rest of his 29 number-one singles (country charts), as well as interesting overlooked items, B-sides, and more. The final track listed here is Pride's last charting single, "Crystal Chandeliers." This is an awesome introduction to a major, if not cited often enough, country music powerhouse, and a solid compilation that bests anything released in the U.S. There is a lack of documentation in terms of years and related albums, but this is a small complaint when compared to the treasure trove of fine material here. —*Thom Jurek*

★ **RCA Country Legends** / Nov. 7, 2000 / Buddha ✦✦✦✦✦
Don't think of this as a definitive hits compilation. Instead, think of it as a perfect introduction to Charley Pride at his peak, proof that he was a genuine country talent, not just a hitmaker. He had a powerful baritone that worked equally well with hard country and country-pop, which may be the reason why he leaned toward the latter as his career progressed. This, however, captures him at the peak of his powers, concentrating primarily on the harder material but adding some pop for balance. This may dilute the portrait of his career somewhat, but it does a terrific job in summarizing his skills and importance. Yes, some familiar items are missing, but for the curious listener looking for confirmation of Pride as a country singer, this is the compilation to get. —*Stephen Thomas Erlewine*

A Tribute to Jim Reeves / May 15, 2001 / Music City ✦✦✦✦
Few artists would even dare attempt to cover the music of the legendary Jim Reeves, but country mainstay Charley Pride does so with admirable vocal prowess in *Charley Pride: A Tribute to Jim Reeves*. Pride's rich, mellow tone captures the essence of the man that fans called "Gentleman Jim." A number of Reeves' hits are here, including his signature hit "He'll Have to Go," a successful pop crossover in Reeves' day. Perhaps this common pop crossover thread is why Pride is able to deliver such a convincing tribute; Pride himself is a crossover act. Besides a warming vocal performance, this album has an extraordinary instrumental arrangement going for it. The same soft, airy Nashville sound throughout that closely matches original Reeves albums. When Charley Pride croons "Welcome to My World," it is clearly a world he shares, at least musically, with Jim Reeves. —*Rick Cohoon*

Jeanne Pruett (Norma Jean Bowman)

b. Jan. 30, 1937, Pell City, AL

Vocals / Traditional Country, Country-Pop

Best known for her chart-topping smash "Satin Sheets," Jeanne Pruett was a country-pop singer and songwriter who enjoyed a measure of success in the '70s and early '80s. Born Norma Jean Bowman in Pell City, AL, in 1937, she started singing in high-school and moved to Nashville in 1956 with her husband Jack Pruett, who went on to become Marty Robbins' guitarist. Pruett herself began writing songs while raising the family, and Robbins signed her to his publishing company in 1963 and recorded several of her songs (1966's "Count Me Out" being the biggest). In the meantime, Pruett also tried her hand at recording, cutting a few singles for RCA beginning in 1963 and giving it another shot with Decca in 1969. "Hold On to My Unchanging Love" (1971) was her first chart single, and after moving to MCA, 1973's "I'm Your Woman" took her into the country Top Ten for the first time. That same year, she scored her first and only number one with "Satin Sheets," whose accompanying album of the same name also topped the charts.

She continued to record and release singles through the rest of the '70s, but none duplicated that success, and while she enjoyed singing, she always made domestic life a priority. Pruett enjoyed a brief commercial resurgence in 1980, when she signed with the smaller IBC label and landed three straight Top Ten hits: "Back to Back," "It's Too Late," and "Temporarily Yours." A few more albums followed in the early '80s, none with similar results, and Pruett returned to domestic life, winning prizes for her cooking and gardening skills and authoring her own cookbook. —*Steve Huey*

● **Love Me** / 1972 / Decca ✦✦✦✦

Satin Sheets / 1973 / Decca ✦✦✦

● **Satin Sheets: Greatest Hits** / Sep. 22, 1998 / Varese ✦✦✦✦
In the beginning of Jim Bessman's liner notes for Varese's 1998 collection *Satin Sheets: Greatest Hits*, Jeanne Pruett remembers that producer Owen Bradley signed her to Decca on the spot, saying "This girl's got a 'housewife' sound that will sell millions of records!" Bradley's words proved to be true, as she turned out a steady string of country hits during the '70s and early '80s, highlighted by her breakthrough 1973 number one "Satin Sheets" and its successor, "I'm Your Woman." His words were also true because she did have a sound appealing to housewives—something based in Loretta Lynn's pure country (appropriate, considering the Bradley connection), but also with a distinct pop undercurrent, creating a sound that was at once country and crossover. Most importantly, it also fit her

adult themes of romance, cheating, and children, making for a good, solid body of work summarized thoroughly on this 18-track CD. All of her big hits for Decca and MCA are here, along with four sides she did for IBC at the start of the '80s (including the Top Tens "Back to Back," "Temporarily Yours," and "It's Too Late") as well as duets with Marty Robbins waxed for Audiograph (including the previously unreleased "Walking Piece of Heaven"). That housewife side of Pruett means that she sings sweetly, but not always memorably; it's a good voice, to be sure, but it's a little generic, which does suit this music, since it's also on the generic side. But that's not a *bad* thing necessarily—it's good generic music because it fits the genre, and it's very enjoyable on that level. There may not be many flat-out standouts, but there are no dogs, and even if it doesn't make the case for Pruett being more than a footnote in country history, it is nevertheless an enjoyable collection, and one that fans of '70s country would do well to explore. *—Stephen Thomas Erlewine*

Riley Puckett

b. May 7, 1894, Alpharetta, GA, **d.** Jul. 14, 1946, East Point, GA

Guitar, Vocals, Banjo / Old-Timey, String Bands

Riley Puckett was one of the pioneers of country music, a singer whose output both as a solo performer and as a member of the supergroup the Skillet Lickers left an indelible mark on the work produced in his wake. He was born George Riley Puckett on May 7, 1894, in Alpharetta, GA; though at birth he had the ability to see, a medical mishap during his infancy left him blind. He attended the Macon School for the Blind, where he learned to read Braille and began playing the banjo, followed by the guitar, developing a unique, arhythmic style of playing bass-note runs to bridge chord changes. He also attracted attention at regional fiddling contests.

Puckett made his radio debut with Clayton McMichen's Hometown Band on WSB Atlanta in 1922. He soon became one of the station's most popular performers, and began appearing as a soloist. The next year, he joined with mandolinist Ted Hawkins and fiddler Lowe Stokes to form the Hometown Boys, where his smooth vocal style and yodeling abilities earned the group a devoted following among WSB listeners, who began calling the singer "the Ball Mountain Caruso." In 1924, Puckett accompanied James "Gideon" Tanner to Columbia Records' New York City studios, where he cut his first sides, including a cover of Fiddlin' John Carson's "The Little Old Log Cabin," "Steamboat Bill," and "Rock All Our Babies to Sleep," believed to contain the first-ever appearance of yodeling on a country record. The results proved highly successful, and later in the year a second session followed; accompanying himself on banjo, Puckett recorded, among others, "Oh Susannah" and "You'll Never Miss Your Mother Till She's Gone."

In 1925, Columbia introduced their 15000-D Hillbilly Series, and Puckett quickly became one of the imprint's most successful acts; only Vernon Dalhart sold more records. A year later, he joined the Skillet Lickers, which also featured Gid Tanner and Clayton McMichen, and remained with the group through 1931. In 1927, he also joined high tenor Hugh Cross for the very first recording of "Red River Valley." The duo went on to cut two more sessions together, generating songs like "Gonna Raise a Ruckus Tonight" (released under the name Alabama Barnstormers), "Call Me Back Pal o' Mine," and "My Wild Irish Rose."

While the onset of the Depression did not crush Puckett's career, as it did to so many of his contemporaries, it did force him to curtail his prolific recording schedule. The records he did cut appeared under a variety of group names and aliases, the most successful being 1931's "My Carolina Home," issued as McMichen's Melody Men. After the demise of the Skillet Lickers, Puckett performed with McMichen's Georgia Wildcats; in 1932, the Skillet Lickers began anew, and Puckett also signed on with Bert Layne's Mountaineers. In addition, he recorded a number of duets with Red Jones, including "I Only Want a Buddy, Not a Sweetheart" and "St. Louis Blues."

By 1936, he was touring with former Mainer Mountaineer "Daddy" John Love and also performed again with Bert Layne. After organizing his own tent show to tour throughout the South, he returned to New York to record with Red Jones, duetting on "Altoona Train Wreck," "Take Me Back to My Carolina Home," and "The Broken Engagement." Puckett did not record again until 1940, when he cut the pop-oriented "Oh, Johnny, Oh," "Little Sir Echo," and "South of the Border." In 1941, he entered the studio one last time, performing "How Come You Do Me Like You Do," "Railroad Blues," and "Peach Picking Time in Georgia." Puckett continued performing on radio with the Stone Mountain Boys until 1946, when on July 14 he died from blood poisoning as a result of a boil on his neck which was left untreated. *—Jason Ankeny*

Old Time Greats, Vol. 2 / 1978 / Old Homestead ✦✦✦✦

Old Time Greats, Vol. 1 / 1978 / Old Homestead ✦✦✦✦✦

Several different labels took cracks at releasing collections by this fine old-timey music artist during the '70s, and this is perhaps the best one for an interested listener to try and track down, as it provides the most complete span of Riley Puckett's career. It contains work from two different prolific recording periods, the late-'20s Columbia sides and the mid-'30s Bluebird era. Liberated from his sideman role in the old-timey group Gid Tanner & the Skillet Lickers, Puckett lets loose with his own guitar style here as it had never been heard before. He has his own peculiar sense of humor and outlook on life, and some of the opinions he expresses may not be politically correct to the hearts and minds of later eras, so watch out. This entire package was previously released on the GHP label, with the exception of two scintillating guitar solos. Early cowboy and country singer Hugh Cross shows up on two tracks. Those trying to emulate the unique Puckett guitar style should heed the title of one of the best numbers here, "Don't Try It for It Can't Be Done." *—Eugene Chadbourne*

Waitin' for the Evening Mail / 1978 / County ✦✦✦✦

A wonderful performer from the heyday of old-time music, Riley Puckett really came into his own once he stopped being a sideman in various bands and began releasing sides on his own, many of them recorded for the Bluebird label during that company's revolutionary and fabulously successful marketing of various traditional American genres in the '30s. It was then that this performer's eccentric style of keeping time was able to function effectively and expressively without having to cater to the sound of a larger group. Ragtime, sarcastic, or sentimental material was Puckett's forte. In the '70s there was something of a stampede on the part of various independent labels to get long-lost old-time sides out on the marketplace, and this album does overlap slightly with a release on the Homestead label entitled *Old Time Greats, Vol. 1*. One of his most famous songs, "Ragged but Right," kicks off the first side and even though this was a composition of Carson Robinson, it is the Puckett version that has set the standard for performing this song, later done by many modern country & western artists such as George Jones and Johnny Paycheck. (Authorship is sometimes mistakenly credited to Jones.) Unhappily married listeners may particularly enjoy the tragic but hilarious "I Wish I Was Single Again." Puckett's guitar lines are beautiful, matched by his exquisite vocal delivery. *—Eugene Chadbourne*

● **Red Sails in the Sunset** / 1988 / Bear Family ✦✦✦✦✦

Here are 16 songs recorded by Puckett between August 1939 and October 1941 for Victor's Bluebird imprint, accompanied by his own guitar and mandolin (possibly played by his long-ago partner, Ted Hawkins) and accordion. The sound and performances are impressive, even if the repertory is on the nostalgic side, consisting mostly of material made popular during the first three decades of this century. Much of it is from the mid-'20s through the mid-'30s, including "Red Sails in the Sunset" (written by the same English composing team responsible for "South of the Border," which is also here), "Tie Me to Your Apron Strings Again," the jazz-band favorite "Margie," the dark-toned "Nobody's Business," the 1930-vintage standard "Get Out and Under the Moon" (first cut by Gene Austin in 1925), and "Oh, Johnny, Oh," which goes back to World War I. These journeys into the musical past were broken up by the presence of a Puckett original, the delightful "When I'm Back in Tennessee," and the then-new Saxie Dowell novelty tune "Playmates" (most familiar to rock & roll fans in the version sung by Sandy Stewart in the movie *Go Johnny Go*). Worth owning just for his version of "Walking My Baby Back Home." *—Bruce Eder*

Pure Prairie League

f. 1971, Cincinnati, OH, **db.** 1987

Group / Country-Rock, Soft Rock

Despite significant personnel changes, Pure Prairie League maintained itself as a successful country-rock band during the 1970s and early '80s, releasing ten albums and enjoying hits with different configurations of the group that included "Amie" and "Let Me Love You Tonight." Pure Prairie League was formed in Columbus, OH, in 1969 by singer/songwriter/guitarist Craig Fuller (born July 18, 1949, in Portsmouth, OH), singer/guitarist George Powell, bass player Jim Lanham, and drummer Tom McGrail, who gave the band its name, which was the name of a women's temperance group in the 1939 Errol Flynn movie *Dodge City*. Pure Prairie League built up a following in Ohio, playing around Cincinnati for a year before earning a record contract with RCA Victor. By that time, McGrail had left and been replaced by Jim Caughlin, though Billy Hinds had also drummed with the band for a time. Adding steel guitar player John David Call, the group went into the studio and recorded its self-titled debut album, which was released in March 1972 with a cover depicting a Western character named Luke, an illustration drawn by famed naturalist painter Norman Rockwell that had first appeared on the cover of *the Saturday Evening Post* in 1927. Luke would turn up on all the band's subsequent album covers, giving them a distinctive visual conception.

Pure Prairie League did not sell well enough to reach the charts, and the group fragmented. Lanham, Caughlin, and Call left, and remaining members Fuller and Powell brought back Hinds, who in turn recruited a friend, keyboard player Michael Connor, to play on the second album, *Bustin' Out*, and subsequently become a full-fledged band-member. Among the other session musicians on the album was David Bowie associate Mick Ronson, who played guitar and arranged the strings. Though later considered a landmark in country-rock, *Bustin' Out* initially suffered disappointing sales upon release in September 1972, and RCA dropped the group. But they added a second friend of Hinds', bassist Michael Reilly, and continued to play around the Midwest. During this period, Fuller encountered legal difficulties over his claim of conscientious objector status to avoid the draft, eventually serving two years in a hospital instead. (He was later pardoned by President Ford.) This forced him to leave the group, and he was replaced by Larry Goshorn. Call also rejoined.

In late 1974, Pure Prairie League's touring began to pay off as radio stations started playing "Amie," a song from *Bustin' Out*, leading RCA to issue the song as a single, reissue the album, and re-sign the band. *Bustin' Out* entered the charts in February 1975, nearly two and a half years after its release, and rose into the Top 40, eventually going gold. "Amie" charted in March 1975 and became a Top 40 hit. Of course, the song had been written and sung by Fuller, who was no longer in the band. (He would resurface in 1976 in the band American Flyer.) Instead, the sextet of Call, Connor, Goshorn, Hinds, Powell, and Reilly made Pure Prairie League's third album, *Two Lane Highway*, joined by the country stars Chet Atkins, Emmylou Harris, and Johnny Gimble. It was released in the spring of 1975. The title track became a minor chart entry, and the album reached the Top 40.

Pure Prairie League's fourth album, *If the Shoe Fits*, was released in early 1976 and was another Top 40 hit, spawning a minor country chart entry in a cover of the Buddy Holly hit "That'll Be the Day." The band's fifth album, *Dance*, followed in the fall of 1976. It was a disappointing seller, only getting into the Top 100 of the pop charts, though it became Pure Prairie League's first album to reach the country charts. A similar level of success greeted the two-LP concert recording *Live!! Takin' the Stage*, released in the summer of 1977. After that album was released, Call left the band and was replaced by Goshorn's brother, Tim. Pure Prairie League's seventh album, *Just Fly*, was released in the spring of 1978 and was another modest seller. At this point, the band fragmented again. The Goshorn brothers decamped to form their own band, and Powell retired to spend more time with his family, depriving the group of its last original member. The remaining trio of friends Hinds, Connor, and Reilly were left in possession of the band's name but in need of a new frontman. They held extensive auditions that resulted in the hiring of Vince Gill (born April 12, 1957, in Norman, OK) as lead singer and guitarist, followed by reeds player Patrick Bolin. This quintet released Pure Prairie League's eighth album, *Can't Hold Back*, in the spring of 1979. Its sales were disappointing, and the group left RCA and signed to Casablanca Records, a label better known for disco than country-rock. In early 1980, Bolin was replaced by Jeff Wilson, a singer and guitarist, and Pure Prairie League recorded its Casablanca debut, *Firin' Up*. The album was preceded by the single "Let Me Love You Tonight," which became a Top Ten hit, pulling *Firin' Up* into the Top 40 in the LP charts. A second single, "I'm Almost Ready," made the Top 40, and a third single, "I Can't Stop the Feelin'," also made the charts.

Pure Prairie League returned with its tenth album, *Something in the Night*, in the spring of 1981, prefaced by the single "Still Right Here in My Heart," which made the Top 40, followed by the chart entry "You're Mine Tonight." The album didn't do as well as its predecessor, but it did chart in the Top 100. Unfortunately, this marked the end of Pure Prairie League's national prominence, as Casablanca went bankrupt and Gill left the band, eventually becoming a successful country solo artist. Songwriter Gary Burr became the lead singer in 1982, remaining until 1985, when Fuller rejoined, remaining until 1987 and then moving on to the reformed Little Feat, where he replaced the late Lowell George. At that point, Pure Prairie League dissolved. In 1998, however, Reilly and Fuller launched a new edition of the band. The lineup also included Connor, Rick Schell, Fats Kaplan, and Curtis Wright. — *William Ruhlmann*

Pure Prairie League / Mar. 1972 / RCA ✦✦✦✦✦
For all those who think the Eagles are the be all and end all of country-rock, you owe it to yourself to search out this album. Any track here (or on the follow-up, *Bustin' Out*) holds up as well, if not better than, anything by the Eagles. This album also proves that Craig Fuller is a grossly underrated songwriter. A country-rock must! — *Jim Worbois*

★ **Bustin' Out** / Aug. 1972 / RCA ✦✦✦✦✦
The songwriting team of Craig Fuller & George Powell was one of the finest in the business, and on *Bustin' Out* they made an album that is unequaled in country-rock. The songs are meditative portraits of relationships that aren't running smoothly but are still alive, and they sound autobiographical rather than something contrived to sell records. These tunes are presented with grace and unusual taste, the country guitars and vocal harmonies backed with astonishingly sympathetic string arrangements by Mick Ronson. Both lyrical and musical themes carry over from song to song—"Falling in and out of Love" and "Amie" are really two halves of one suite, and there are echoes of that suite throughout the rest of the album. Despite the extraordinary beauty and intelligence of the music on this album, it was not immediately successful, and the already troubled band broke up after it was released. Nevertheless, the influence of *Bustin' Out* was profound, and one song in particular became a staple for bar bands everywhere. RCA re-released "Amie" as a single more than two years after the album came out, and it was a Top 30 hit. The revival of interest in Pure Prairie League led RCA to re-sign the group, alas without Craig Fuller. That hit status also led to a rediscovery of the merits of the rest of *Bustin' Out*, which is acknowledged to be one of the artistic high points in country-rock history. — *Richard Foss*

Two Lane Highway / 1975 / RCA ✦✦✦
With the departure of Fuller, the face (and sound) of Prairie League changed considerably. Larry Goshorn (ex-Sacred Mushroom) has replaced Fuller as the main songwriter in the band. And, while the overall album isn't up to its predecessors, there are still some nice moments including the title track, "Runner" and a humorous tribute to country music legend, Merle Haggard. — *Jim Worbois*

If the Shoe Fits / 1976 / RCA ✦✦✦
PPL continues in the same vein as the last LP with only a couple of George Powell tunes bearing any resemblance to the sound of the first two records. Not a bad record, but it's becoming harder to find any traces of what made this band so special. — *Jim Worbois*

Dance / 1976 / RCA ✦✦
It's getting more difficult to find positive things to say about the band's records by this time. Aside from some fine playing by Andy Stein (ex-Lost Planet Airman), J.D. Call's superb pedal steel work, and the track "All the Way," there isn't much to recommend this album. — *Jim Worbois*

Live!! Takin' the Stage / 1977 / RCA ✦✦
Live, PPL fairly accurately re-created their studio sound. Which makes one wonder, why buy this record if you have all the previous albums? The band doesn't seem to feel they have anything to prove so they walk through these tracks adding nothing. If you already like these songs, stick with the studio versions since nothing is added on this one. — *Jim Worbois*

Just Fly / 1978 / RCA ✦✦

Can't Hold Back / 1979 / One Way ✦✦
Another shake-up finds Goshorn and longtime steel player, J.D. Call, gone. Goshorn has been replaced by future modern country star Vince Gill as both main writer and leader of the group. By this time, they are PPL in name only as there is no resemblance between this and the original band. In fact, if you play "Rude Rude Awakening" next to the Eagles' "One of These Nights," it would be difficult to distinguish between the two bands. — *Jim Worbois*

Firin' Up / 1980 / Casablanca ✦
Producer John Ryan worked with a number of bands from different genres—the Allman Brothers, Santana, Rare Earth, Iron Butterfly, and Styx as well as techno-pop group Animotion—and his stamp helps steer a veteran group into a new decade. Though there are no original members from the first Pure Prairie League disc, this is the most significant album by the group since their second, *Bustin' Out*, which featured the hit "Amie" as well as new mainstays drummer Billy Hinds and keyboardist Michael Connor. Vince Gill's second outing with the group lands two Top 40 hits, the exquisite "Let Me Love You Tonight," which hit Top Ten as well as number-one adult contemporary, and the driving "I'm Almost Ready," which went Top 35 five months later. Gill writes 60 percent of the material here and shows a talent for crafting pop that ventures out of his country roots. On a non-group composition, the Flower/Sanderfur "I Can't Stop This Feeling," they sound like they've cloned Ambrosia's "Biggest Part of Me," or at least its aura—and that song was released at this same moment in time. On other titles they've retained (or lifted) the vibe of Firefall and the Eagles to good effect. While the slickness might turn off purists who believe Pure Prairie League was the second coming of the Flying Burrito Brothers, it would be a mistake to generalize and write this important outing off. *Firin' Up* is a country-pop album that was truly Gill's breakthrough, and outside of its historical importance is highly entertaining. "Janny Lou" is sweet and David Sanborn's brilliant sax work enhances Gill's tender love song, just as it was the frosting on the cake for "Let Me Love You Tonight." "I'm Almost Ready" embraces the Eagles, like their "Already Gone" meeting "Heartache Tonight." Outside of a 1995 hit with Amy Grant, Gill's major mainstream success and crossover appeal is found on this album. Just listen to "Give It Up" to see how he, and Pure Prairie League, could have climbed to even greater heights had they stayed on this pop/country path. There's not a bad track on *Firin' Up*, an album that's a fine example of adult contemporary, rock, and country formats all merging in the 1980s. More of a classic than it's been given credit for. — *Joe Viglione*

Amie & Other Hits / 1981 / RCA ✦✦✦✦
At eight tracks, this is really skimpy, but *Amie & Other Hits* nevertheless does offer a nice sampler of Pure Prairie League's RCA recordings. This does mean that their biggest hit, "Let Me Love You Tonight," is missing, along with anything else from their time at Casablanca, but this does give a basic overview of their earliest material, when they were led by the fine singer/songwriter Craig Fuller. — *Stephen Thomas Erlewine*

The Best of Pure Prairie League / Aug. 8, 1995 / Mercury Nashville ✦✦✦✦
As one of country-rock's most appealing groups, Pure Prairie League contributed to the late-'70s and early-'80 era of musical interbreeding which made them firm FM radio staples, as well as country music mainstays. Their highest charted single, "Let Me Love You Tonight" at number ten in 1980, was where country superstar Vince Gill began singing lead for the band and was their third vocalist. Sounding slightly more country than rock, Pure Prairie League's music gained popularity by churning out jangly guitar strummed tunes that imitated the Eagles recipe of sturdy country love songs. This collection of their best material is a superb rundown of all their hits, with an extra two bonus tracks at the end. "Amie," their first Top 40 entry, sung by Craig Fuller, kicks off this album and represents the early stages of the band's career with its light, breezy sound. Other stand-outs on this 14 song compilation include the number-34 hit "I'm Almost Ready" and the sincere sounding "Still Right Here in My Heart," with its timeless chorus and free-range melody. Mike Reilly sings the Buddy Holly classic "That'll Be the Day" with a modest country feel, and even the semi-edgy "Don't Keep Me Hangin'" holds up well amidst the other more countrified tracks on this best-of. Although Pure Prairie League weren't given quite the amount of attention they deserved, the music they produced befriended fans of both country and AOR. — *Mike DeGagne*

● **Greatest Hits** / Sep. 28, 1999 / RCA ✦✦✦✦✦
RCA's 1999 compilation *Greatest Hits* is the definitive portrait of Pure Prairie League at their peak. Although it contains none of their Casablanca recordings, and therefore it's missing their biggest hit, "Let Me Love You Tonight," it does have a comprehensive chronicle of the group's first four albums, including their breakthrough hit "Amie," the non-LP "She Darked the Sun," and nearly all of their best album, *Bustin' Out*, albeit not in sequence. It would have been nice to have "Let Me Love You Tonight" added to this collection, but it's hard to argue with what's here, since it is the best of the best years of the Pure Prairie League. — *Stephen Thomas Erlewine*

Eddie Rabbitt

b. Nov. 27, 1941, Brooklyn, NY, **d.** May 7, 1998
Guitar, Vocals / Country-Pop, Urban Cowboy, Soft Rock

One of country music's most innovative artists during the late '70s and early '80s, Eddie Rabbitt has made contributions to the format that have often gone overlooked. Especially in songs like the R&B-inflected "Suspicions" and the rockin' "Someone Could Lose a Heart Tonight," Rabbitt challenged the commonly recognized creative boundaries of the idiom. Hailing from Brooklyn and New Jersey, Rabbitt moved to Nashville in 1968. Though it took a few years to get his recording career off the ground, he paid the rent through songwriting, authoring Elvis Presley's "Kentucky Rain" and Ronnie Milsap's "Pure Love." Eddie continued to write professionally until 1975, when he signed with Elektra Records' newly established country division. Initially, Rabbitt made recordings that were decidedly country—mostly uptempo material, like "Two Dollars in the Jukebox" and "Drinkin' My Baby (Off My Mind)"—with thick, inimitable harmonies, most of them overdubbed by Rabbitt himself. However, with the assistance of his then-associates David Malloy and Even Stevens, Rabbitt's records became "progressively progressive."

In 1976, he started a string of Top Ten hits that ran uninterrupted until 1989. During that time, he had 16 number-one singles, including "Drinkin' My Baby (Off My Mind)" (1976), "You Don't Love Me Anymore" (1978), "Every Which Way But Loose" (1979), "Drivin' My Life Away" (1980), "I Love a Rainy Night" (1980), "Step By Step" (1980), and "You and I," a 1982 duet with Crystal Gayle. In the late '80s he returned to more traditional sounds, as his country shuffle "On Second Thought" demonstrates, but it was too late for Rabbitt to return to the top of the country charts, since he had already been supplanted by a newer generation of artists. The terminal kidney ailment of his son also factored in his decision to only sporadically record and perform during the '90s. In 1997, Rabbitt was diagnosed with lung cancer; the disease claimed his life on May 7, 1998. The LP *From the Heart* was issued posthumously. *—Tom Roland*

Eddie Rabbitt / 1975 / Elektra ◆◆◆

Rocky Mountain Music / 1976 / Elektra ◆◆◆◆

Rabbitt / 1977 / Elektra ◆◆◆◆

Variations / 1978 / Elektra ◆◆◆◆

Loveline / 1979 / Elektra ◆◆◆

Fellow reviewers will cringe at this choice, but it displays Rabbitt at his most daring. Lots of R&B influence—even a bit of a "disco" feel on a couple of tracks—inspired melodies and unusual chord progressions throughout. Lyrically lightweight, but hey, this is music not poetry. *—Tom Roland*

The Best of Eddie Rabbitt / 1979 / Elektra ◆◆◆◆◆

Strong melodies are enhanced by Rabbitt's searing harmonies. The instruments are "hotter" in the final mix than in other productions from the same period, so even the mainstream country fare is a little different from that of his mid-'70s contemporaries. *—Tom Roland*

Horizon / 1980 / Elektra ◆◆◆◆

This is Rabbitt's rockabilly release. "I Love a Rainy Night" and "Drivin' My Life Away" set the pace for side one: Sun-inspired, guitar-based productions, heavy on the echo. Side two is a bit ballad-heavy, though most of the tracks standup well individually. "That's Just the Way It Is" is something of a forerunner for "Someone Could Lose a Heart Tonight." *—Tom Roland*

Step By Step / 1981 / Liberty ◆◆◆◆◆

Radio Romance / 1982 / Liberty ◆◆◆

Rabbitt Trax / 1986 / RCA ◆◆◆

I Wanna Dance With You / 1988 / RCA ◆◆

Jersey Boy / Apr. 9, 1990 / Liberty ◆◆◆◆

Singer, songwriter, and guitarist Eddie Rabbitt completed this notable album in the spring of 1990. Country music lovers had no idea at the time that they only had a short eight years left to spend with him. At least the songs he recorded during his more than two-decade long career are here for the enjoying. *Jersey Boy* carries ten country tracks by this great artist. One of the songs, "American Boy," found its way into the hearts of many American soldiers and their families during the Gulf War. Other tunes on the album that Eddie Rabbitt fans might especially enjoy are "Only One Love in My Life," "Feel Like a Stranger," and "Tennessee Born and Bred." *—Charlotte Dillon*

Ten Years of Greatest Hits / Aug. 27, 1990 / Liberty ◆◆◆

This features "I Love a Rainy Night," "Two Dollars in the Jukebox," "Suspicions," and other hits. *—AMG*

Greatest Country Hits / 1991 / Curb ◆◆◆

Greatest Country Hits offers a few of Rabbitt's bigger hits, including "Drinkin' My Baby (Off My Mind)," "You Don't Love Me Anymore" and "I Just Want to Love You." However,

much of the remaining material is filler, and Rabbitt's top sellers—"Every Which Way But Loose" and "I Love a Rainy Night," to name just two—are nowhere to be found. *—Jason Ankeny*

● **All Time Greatest Hits** / Mar. 12, 1991 / Warner Bros. ◆◆◆◆◆

Warner's 1991 collection *All Time Greatest Hits* was the first CD-era compilation of Eddie Rabbitt's hit singles and, as such, it suffers from a lot of flaws common to first attempts— namely, it's way too short at ten songs, doesn't have all the hits it should, and is harmed by a narrow focus on just his Elektra recordings. That said, it's still a good sampling of his hits of the late '70s and early '80s, containing no less than nine Top Ten singles, including the number ones "Drivin' My Life Away," "I Love a Rainy Night," "Gone Too Far," and "Suspicions." All four of those songs are also featured on the latter-day 2003 compilation *Essentials*, which also includes other numbers ones missing here: "Every Which Way But Loose," "Drinkin' My Baby (Off My Mind)," "You Don't Love Me Anymore," and "I Just Want to Love You," all of which could arguably have been here (not to mention that this contains no big Liberty hits, like "Step by Step," "Someone Could Lose a Heart Tonight," and "You and I"). That said, this does boast five big hits that did not show up on that collection—"Rocky Mountain Music," "Two Dollars in the Jukebox," "Do You Right Tonight," "Pour Me Another Tequila," "Hearts on Fire"—along with "I Can't Help Myself (Here Comes That Feelin')," which makes it necessary if not as a first stop, at least as a way to get the rest of Rabbitt's prime-period Elektra hits until a truly comprehensive collection comes along. *—Stephen Thomas Erlewine*

Greatest Hits / Jun. 16, 1995 / Cema Special Markets ◆◆◆◆◆

CEMA Special Market's 1995 Eddie Rabbitt collection, *Greatest Hits*, may be a budget-line collection released as part of their Ten Best Series, but don't let that stop you from picking up this collection, since it is the only way to get his Liberty hits from the early and mid-'80s on CD. Warner has issued two collections of his Elektra recordings—one of which, 2003's *Essentials*, contained two of the songs here, "The Best Year of My Life" and the Crystal Gayle duet "You and I"—but the great majority of these songs have not been easily available on CD. In the case of the number one hits "Step by Step" and "Someone Could Lose a Heart Tonight," their absence has been nearly criminal, since they're two of his very best songs and singles, but there are several other big hits here: "You Can't Run From Love," "B-B-B-Burnin' Up With Love," "Warning Sign," and "She's Comin' Back to Say Goodbye." It's not a complete selection of his hits for the label—which makes the inclusion of the OK non-hits "Runnin' With the Wind" and "Years After You" a little puzzling— but it's far better than nothing, and until somebody releases a comprehensive Eddie Rabbitt retrospective, this has to stand as not just the best CD of these Liberty recordings, but the only way to get this material at all. For any fan, it's necessary until something better comes along. *—Stephen Thomas Erlewine*

Beatin' the Odds / Sep. 23, 1997 / Intersound ◆◆◆◆

The title of this album says more than many fans may realize. Eddie Rabbitt recorded *Beatin' the Odds* after having surgery to remove part of one of his lungs because of cancer and during the time in which he was enduring chemotherapy for the malevolent disease. Don't let his illness during the making of this album lead you to believe it isn't up to his normal standards. His vocal talent shines as brightly in this full-length offering as in any of the many others he completed during his long career—a career that saw his songs earn him more than two dozen country hits and eight pop hits. *Beatin' the Odds* carries 12 songs. Six of these were new songs he put together for the recording, and six were well-known fan favorites like "Drivin' My Life Away," "I Love a Rainy Night," and "I'll Make Everything Alright." Just those three songs alone are enough to make this a perfect addition to any country music collection. Sadly, the title of the album didn't become a self-fulfilling prophecy, and eight short months after *Beatin' the Odds* hit the store shelves, Eddie Rabbitt lost his battle to lung cancer. *—Charlotte Dillon*

● **Essentials** / Apr. 22, 2003 / Warner Strategic ◆◆◆◆◆

Eddie Rabbitt's catalog is in a bit of a mess, lacking a definitive greatest-hits collection that encompasses the hits he had for Elektra, Liberty (originally distributed through Warner, now available through EMI), and RCA. Since his peak period as a recording artist stretched from 1976-1988 as he hopped between the three labels, this is a little bit of a problem, since it can't all be contained on one disc without cross-licensing, which no label appears to want to do as of this writing in 2003. Without that cross-licensed collection, listeners have to either acquire no less than three collections to get the great majority of the hits, or choose which of the three has the right number—and the right selection—of hits. Of the three, Warner Strategic Marketing's 2003 collection, the 12-track *The Essentials*, may be the best, although it is in stiff competition with the 1991 ten-track collection *All Time Greatest Hits*, which also concentrates on his late-'70s and early-'80s recordings for Elektra. The two share four songs—"Drivin' My Life Away," "I Love a Rainy Night," "Gone Too Far," and "Suspicions"—and this has ten top hits, while *All Time Greatest Hits* has nine, which gives them a similar hits ratio. However, *The Essentials* has a bit better song selection, containing such necessary items as "Every Which Way but Loose," "You Don't Love Me Anymore," the Crystal Gayle duet "You and I," his first number one, "Drinkin' My Baby (Off My Mind)," and the Liberty-era "The Best Year of My Life," plus his own version of his original "Kentucky Rain," which Elvis made into a hit. None of these are on *All Time*, and they're all reason enough to choose this over the other collection, even though it is missing such big tunes as "Rocky Mountain Music," "Pour Me a Tequila," and "Hearts on Fire," not to mention the superb Liberty number ones "Step By Step" and "Someone Could Lose a Heart Tonight," both only available on CEMA's budget-line *Greatest Hits*. All of this reiterates that none of these collections are perfect, and all are necessary in order to get his hits, but if you were to choose just one—or to choose one to start with—*The Essentials* gets the nod. *—Stephen Thomas Erlewine*

Marvin Rainwater

b. Jul. 2, 1925, Wichita, KS

Songwriter, Vocals / Traditional Country, Rockabilly, Nashville Sound/Countrypolitan

In the current climate of political correctness, it's amazing to think that a scant few decades ago, a quarter-Cherokee country singer named Marvin Rainwater would shamelessly trade on his Indian pedigree to make himself a name on the country music circuit. But backing up this ridiculous charade was some very solid music from an artist who could work and create in a multiplicity of styles. Few artists in country music ever made music as quirky and just plain weird as that of one Marvin Rainwater. His recorded cannonade—featuring his strong, rumbling baritone—showed that he was equally adept at Western ballads and pop confections with breathtaking go-for-broke forays into rockabilly.

He was born Marvin Percy Rainwater in 1925. After a stint in the Navy during World War II serving as a pharmacist's mate, he turned to music full-time. He had originally been a classically trained pianist, but after an accident had removed part of his right thumb, he turned to country music and soon learned to strum a guitar proficiently enough to accompany his singing and compose songs on it. After putting down roots in nearby Virginia, Rainwater quickly became a fixture on the Washington, D.C., area honky tonk circuit, putting together his first band featuring a young Roy Clark on lead guitar and himself decked out in buckskin jacket and Indian headband. His first recordings came through the auspices of Bill McCall at 4-Star Records. Picturing himself as a songwriter first and performer second, Rainwater was hooked up through McCall with Ben Adleman, a songwriter with a small studio. Rainwater recorded several song demos to be pitched to other artists through Adleman's and McCall's publishing concerns, only to see the demos poorly overdubbed and released at the height of his later fame on a myriad of dime-store budget labels like Crown and others too microscopic to mention.

But McCall also took three completed masters from other sessions ("I Gotta Go Get My Baby," "Hearts' Hall of Fame," and "Albino Stallion") and had them pressed on a custom promotional 45, then promptly sold the masters to Coral Records. Rainwater's recording of "I Gotta Go Get My Baby" was promptly handed over to Teresa Brewer, who covered and had a hit with it in the pop market. But what propelled Rainwater up the show business ladder was a successful television performance on *Arthur Godfrey's Talent Scouts*, the early-'50s equivalent of *Star Search*. Godfrey had a top-rated morning show as well, and after his win, Rainwater made frequent guest spots on it, reaching a national audience for the first time. Rainwater responded in kind by recording a composition in his honor, "Tea Bag Romeo," a reference to Godfrey's sponsor, Lipton Tea. By late 1955 he was a full-time member of Red Foley's Ozark Jubilee television and touring show, relocating to Springfield, MO. On one package show, he was introduced backstage to a precocious little girl who wanted to sing that night on the show. After hearing the moppet belt out part of a tune, Rainwater was convinced and introduced young Brenda Lee Tarpley to Red Foley, and the rest—as they say—is both country and rock & roll history.

Shortly after signing with Foley, Rainwater started recording for MGM Records, his longest lasting label affiliation. The recordings are as scatter-gunned of an approach to commercial recording as you can possibly imagine. Solemn Americana recitations ("Pink Eyed Stallion") sat alongside novelty fluff like "Tennessee Hound Dog Yodel," which were B-sided by straight-ahead country weepers rife with down-home sentiments. Suddenly at his next recording session in March 1956, Rainwater shifted gears again, deciding to cast his lot with the emerging rockabilly sound. The result was a two-sided blast of tonal mayhem, coupling the out-of-control "Hot and Cold" with the slightly less frenetic "Mr. Blues." Though both sides kicked up sufficient noise, it cost him big time in the country fan department, the members of his fan club confused that this former folk balladeer had suddenly become an apostle for the big beat.

But rockabilly was a way for country artists to achieve pop stardom and, with the first successful attempts at crossover appeal already in place, Rainwater didn't have to wait long to find his song. That tune was "Gonna Find Me a Bluebird," a tune that went to number three on the country charts while simultaneously climbing to number 18 on the pop charts. Suddenly flush with success, Rainwater quit the Ozark Jubilee and moved his base of operations to New York City, ready to take on the world. But the follow-ups to "Gonna Find Me a Bluebird" were as diverse and quirky as his pre-hit output (one included a duet with Connie Francis) and his slide from the charts, coupled with one bad business deal after another, was swift and sure. In order to keep his slippery footing on *any* kind of chart, Rainwater had taken on a personal appearance schedule that would reduce lesser individuals to babbling protoplasm. By 1961, with his days on the pop charts largely behind him, Rainwater showed up for several recording sessions with his voice so burned out from show dates that he was unrecordable. His final MGM sessions not only remained unissued, but most of them appear to have been either lost or destroyed. In Rainwater's own words, "I had no voice and no money."

After a nine-month layoff, he signed with Warwick Records and with Link Wray & the Raymen backing him, put out a pair of singles that were as fine as anything he had recorded in his heyday. But the marketplace in both pop and country had changed a lot since 1957, and the sides fell stillborn at the presses. Going for it one more time, Rainwater and new partner Bill Guess built a studio in Chicago and started up Brave Records, solely devoting its catalog to new songs from the singer. Aside from a brief stay with United Artists in 1964 and a one-off session for Warner Bros. in 1969, the Brave singles document Rainwater's last commercial sides. Since the '70s—aside from an occasional appearance on a European rockabilly revival—Rainwater has been living in a house trailer in northern Minnesota on an undeveloped tract of land, spending most of his time ruminating on what might have been. He may not have become a big name, but he left behind a great number of sides that showed real musical depth and originality. And that's got to count for something. *—Cub Koda*

Classic Recordings / 1992 / Bear Family ♦♦♦♦♦

This four-CD set puts Marvin Rainwater's recording career from 1953 through 1969 into sharp relief, most notably his inability to fix on a sound, either country or rockabilly, and stick with it. In a fairer world, he wouldn't have had to decide, because he was good at both. Disc one opens with his earliest officially released sides, which ran the gamut from rockabilly to faux-western to upbeat comic country-pop to country blues, and one good dog song ("Tennessee Hound Dog Yodel"). Rainwater's best numbers here, however, may be the raucous rocker "Hot and Cold" and the only slightly more restrained "Mr. Blues," both of which show off Roy Clark's lead guitar in the strongest light. Disc two is more consistent, with fewer of the pop efforts of the prior years. The rockabilly sides, especially "(There's Always) A Need for Love," really spark this disc and provide the real drive around more convention pop/rock & roll numbers like "I Dig You Baby." Disc three has its great moments, such as "It Wasn't Enough," amid a series of duets with singer Bill Guess that present Rainwater at his most commercial and accessible. Disc four contains Rainwater's earliest sides, cut as demos in 1953 and 1954, and while the quality of the sound is a little shaky, the stuff goes to the core of Rainwater's music-making, free-wheeling studio performances without looking for the next big hit or trying to catch the wave of public fancy. The real joy here, however, are five live numbers recorded in 1962—Rainwater, already gone from MGM and disillusioned, still loved playing to an audience, as these sides show, and the only pity is that there isn't more of this stuff, especially since the sound is unexpectedly good. *—Bruce Eder*

● **Whole Lotta Woman** / 1994 / Bear Family ♦♦♦♦♦

A superb single disc of Rainwater's most rocking sides, 26 in all, although inexplicably leaving off his biggest hit, "Gonna Find Me a Bluebird." But there's much here to love, including the chugging "Mr. Blues" and "Hot and Cold" featuring explosive guitar from Roy Clark and "Boo Hoo," "Tough Top Cat," and "There's a Honky Tonk in Your Heart," which features backing from Link Wray & the Raymen. Marvin at his quirkiest and if you can live without his big hit, this is the package to grab. *—Cub Koda*

Rock Me: The Westwood Recordings / Jun. 12, 2001 / Bear Family ♦♦♦

Marvin Rainwater recorded two albums for the Westwood label while visiting England in the mid-'70s, only one of which was released at the time. This CD collects the complete recordings from those sessions, which find Rainwater revisiting a few hits, unveiling new originals, and interpreting a handful of cover songs while backed by a competent if sometimes ramshackle band. The title track, "Rock Me," is a remake of his MGM recording "Dance Me Daddy" with minor lyric changes. His attempts at "Proud Mary" and "Old Rivers" (on the latter of which Rainwater does a cheesy impression of Walter Brennan) were simply bad ideas, and far below the level of the surrounding cuts in terms of quality. Some of the new originals are excellent, and Rainwater still sounds pretty great at this late stage of his career. Despite the title, these are country rather than rock or rockabilly recordings, and even the remakes of his older songs are given more of a straight '70s country treatment. For those who hoped against all odds that someone would reissue Rainwater's '70s recordings, the minor flaws will be irrelevant. *—Greg Adams*

Bonnie Raitt

b. Nov. 8, 1949, Burbank, CA

Guitar, Vocals, Slide Guitar / Blues-Rock, Singer/Songwriter, Adult Contemporary, Pop/Rock, Slide Guitar Blues, Album Rock

Long a critic's darling, singer/guitarist Bonnie Raitt did not begin to win the comparable commercial success due her until the release of the aptly titled 1989 blockbuster *Nick of Time*; her tenth album, it rocketed her into the mainstream consciousness nearly two decades after she first committed her unique blend of blues, rock, and R&B to vinyl. Born in Burbank, CA, on November 8, 1949, she was the daughter of Broadway star John Raitt, best known for his starring performances in such smashes as *Carousel* and *Pajama Game*. After picking up the guitar at the age of 12, Raitt felt an immediate affinity for the blues, and although she went off to attend Radcliffe in 1967, within two years she had dropped out to begin playing the Boston folk and blues club circuit. Signing with noted blues manager Dick Waterman, she was soon performing alongside the likes of idols including Howlin' Wolf, Sippie Wallace, and Mississippi Fred McDowell and in time earned such a strong reputation that she was signed to Warner Bros.

Debuting in 1971 with an eponymously titled effort, Raitt immediately emerged as a critical favorite, applauded not only for her soulful vocals and thoughtful song selection but also for her guitar prowess, turning heads as one of the few women to play bottleneck. Her 1972 follow-up, *Give It Up*, made better use of her eclectic tastes, featuring material by contemporaries like Jackson Browne and Eric Kaz, in addition to a number of R&B chestnuts and even three Raitt originals. *Takin' My Time* (1973) was much acclaimed, and throughout the middle of the decade she released an LP annually, returning with *Streetlights* in 1974 and *Home Plate* a year later. With 1977's *Sweet Forgiveness*, Raitt scored her first significant pop airplay with her hit cover of the Del Shannon classic "Runaway"; its follow-up, 1979's *The Glow*, appeared around the same time as a massive all-star anti-nuclear concert at Madison Square Garden mounted by MUSE (Musicians United for Safe Energy), an organization she'd co-founded earlier.

Throughout her career, Raitt remained a committed activist, playing hundreds of benefit concerts and working tirelessly on behalf of the Rhythm and Blues Foundation. By the early '80s, however, her own career was in trouble—1982's *Green Light*, while greeted with the usual good reviews, again failed to break her to a wide audience, and while beginning work on the follow-up, Warners unceremoniously dropped her. By this time, Raitt was also battling drug and alcohol problems as well; she worked on a few tracks with Prince, but their schedules never aligned and the material went unreleased. Instead, she finally released the patchwork *Nine Lives* in 1986, her worst-selling effort since her debut. Many had written Raitt off when she teamed with producer Don Was and recorded *Nick of Time*; seemingly out of the blue, the LP won a handful of Grammys, including Album of the Year, and overnight she was a superstar. *Luck of the Draw* (1991) was also a smash, yielding the hits "Something to Talk About" and "I Can't Make You Love Me." After 1994's *Longing in Their Hearts*, Raitt resurfaced in 1998 with *Fundamental*. *—Jason Ankeny*

Bonnie Raitt / 1971 / Warner Bros. ♦♦♦♦

The astounding thing about Bonnie Raitt's blues album isn't that it's the work of a preternaturally gifted blues woman, it's that Raitt doesn't choose to stick to the blues. She's decided to blend her love of classic folk blues with folk music, including new folk-rock tunes, along with a slight R&B, New Orleans, and jazz bent and a mellow Californian vibe. Surely, *Bonnie Raitt* is a record of its times, as much as Jackson Browne's first album is, but with this, she not only sketches out the blueprint for her future recordings, but for the roots music that would later be labeled as Americana. The reason that *Bonnie Raitt* works is that she is such a warm, subtle singer. She never oversells these songs, she lays back and sings them with heart and wonderfully textured reading. Her singing is complemented by her band, who is equally as warm, relaxed, and engaging. This is music that goes down so easy, it's only on the subsequent plays that you realize how fully realized and textured it is. It's a terrific debut that has only grown in stature since its release. *—Stephen Thomas Erlewine*

Give It Up / Sep. 1972 / Warner Bros. ♦♦♦♦♦

Bonnie Raitt may have switched producers for her second album *Give It Up*, hiring Michael Cuscuna, but she hasn't switched her style, sticking with the thoroughly engaging blend of folk, blues, R&B, and Californian soft rock. If anything, she's strengthened her formula here, making the divisions between the genres nearly indistinguishable. Take the title track, for instance. It opens with a bluesy acoustic guitar before kicking into a New Orleans brass band about halfway through—and the great thing about it is that Raitt makes the switch sound natural, even inevitable, never forced. And that's just the tip of the iceberg here, since *Give It Up* is filled with great songs, delivered in familiar, yet always surprising, ways by Raitt and her skilled band. For those that want to pigeonhole her as a white blues singer, she delivers the lovely "Nothing Seems to Matter," a gentle midtempo number that's as mellow as Linda Ronstadt and far more seductive. That's the key to *Give It Up*: Yes, Raitt can be earthy and sexy, but she balances it with an inviting sensuality that makes the record glow. It's all delivered in a fantastic set of originals and covers performed so naturally it's hard to tell them apart and roots music so thoroughly fused that it all sounds original, even when it's possible to spot the individual elements or influences. Raitt would go on to greater chart successes, but she not only had trouble topping this record, generations of singers, from Sheryl Crow to Shelby Lynne, have used this as a touchstone. One of the great Southern California records. *—Stephen Thomas Erlewine*

Takin' My Time / 1973 / Warner Bros. ♦♦♦♦

This album is an overlooked gem in the catalog of Bonnie Raitt. On *Takin' My Time*, she wears her influences proudly in an eclectic musical mix containing blues, jazz, folk, New Orleans R&B, and calypso. Although she did not write her own material for this album, she demonstrates an excellent ear for songs and chooses material from some of the best songwriters of the day. She is a great interpreter, and her renditions of Jackson Browne's "I Thought I Was a Child" and Randy Newman's "Guilty" from this album are the definitive versions of these songs. The highlights of this album are the romantic ballads "I Gave My Love a Candle" and "Cry Like a Rainstorm," where Raitt adds an emotional depth to the performance unusual for such a young woman. (Perhaps that's a result of her spending time with elder statesmen of the blues community such as Mississippi Fred McDowell and Sippie Wallace.) Although the faster-paced songs like the calypso "Wah She Go Do" seem a little out of place, the playful tune is welcome among an album filled with the heartache of the slower tunes. Despite being a relative newcomer, Raitt had already earned the respect of her mentors and her peers, as evidenced by the musical contributions of Taj Mahal, and Little Feat members Lowell George and Bill Payne on the album. This is the last consistent album she would make until her comeback in the mid-'80s. *—Vik Iyengar*

Streetlights / 1974 / Warner Bros. ♦♦♦♦

Bonnie Raitt had delivered three stellar albums, but chart success wasn't forthcoming, even if good reviews and a cult following were. So, she teamed with producer Jerry Ragovoy for *Streetlights* and attempted to make the crossover record that Warner so desperately wished she'd release. Over the years, the concessions that she made here—particularly the middle-of-the road arrangements (as opposed to the appealingly laid-back sounds of her previous records), the occasional use of strings, but also some of the song selections—have consigned *Streetlights* to noble failure status. There's no denying that's essentially what *Streetlights* is, but that makes it out to seem worse than it really is. It winds up paling to the wonderful ease and warm sensuality of her first three albums—she only occasionally hits that balance—but it's still undeniably pleasant, and there are moments here where she really pulls off some terrific work, including the opening cover of Joni Mitchell's "That Song About the Midway," a good version of John Prine's "Angel From Montgomery," and the much-touted take on Allen Toussaint's "What Is Success." It may be easy to lament the suppression of the laid-back sexiness and organic feel of Raitt's earlier records, but there's still enough here in that spirit to make this worthwhile. *—Stephen Thomas Erlewine*

Home Plate / 1975 / Warner Bros. ♦♦♦

Homeplate takes Bonnie Raitt even further down the path toward mainstream production than the unjustly maligned *Streetlights*, but, ironically, it works better than its predecessor. Perhaps that's because producer Paul A. Rothchild has helped Raitt craft a record that's unapologetically pitched at the mainstream, where *Streetlights* often seemed to be torn between two worlds. The great thing about that is, regardless of the production, the essentials of Raitt's music have not changed. It remains a wonderful hybrid of American music, built on a thoroughly impressive set of songs, all delivered with Raitt's warm, expertly shaded, and undeniably sexy singing. She's such an accomplished singer, she sells these songs through productions that are much slicker than those that graced her earlier records, plus with a supporting crew of studio musicians. This production will undoubtedly dismay listeners that just like the earthiness of *Give It Up*, but *Homeplate* is still a success because, even though the recording is glossier, Raitt and her music remain the same and, if you're looking for that, it's still irresistible. *—Stephen Thomas Erlewine*

Sweet Forgiveness / Apr. 1977 / Warner Bros. ♦♦

Since *Home Plate* brought Bonnie Raitt within shooting distance of the Top 40, thereby being the greatest chart success she yet attained, it made sense that she re-teamed with its producer Paul A. Rothchild for its follow-up, *Sweet Forgiveness*. Rothchild's *modus operandi* remains slickness, but he has backed away from his fondness for studio musicians, letting Raitt record the majority of the record with her touring band (who only were spotted occasionally throughout *Homeplate*). All this means is that the near-hit "Runaway" is almost a ringer, largely because it's a poor choice for Raitt's sweetly funky Californian rock that was obviously designed as a bid for a single, therefore it was slicked up more than the rest of the record (which remains slick, but not glossy). *Sweet Forgiveness* is actually looser than *Homeplate*, a little less constrained. Then why isn't it quite as successful, artistically? That comes down to a selection of songs that aren't quite as effective as those Raitt usually picks—and, in that sense, "Runaway" was a good indicator of the album. However, the selection of material isn't bad. If the tunes don't happen to form into a whole, it's still filled with great moments, from Earl Randall's opener "About to Make Me Leave Home" to Karla Bonoff's closer "Home." *Sweet Forgiveness* may not be one of Raitt's unqualified successes (despite its hit status), it's still a solid record, one that's hard to deny if you're already a Raitt fan. *—Stephen Thomas Erlewine*

The Glow / 1979 / Warner Bros. ♦♦♦

Bonnie Raitt enjoyed critical success and blues/folk credentials with her self-titled debut, *Give It Up*, and *Takin' My Time*. By 1975, Raitt's style began to be defined by producer Paul Rothchild. *Home Plate* and *Sweet Forgiveness* were uncomfortable overtures to commercial propositions where Raitt's persona and sense of fun got lost. Produced by Peter Asher, *The Glow* was released in 1979 and includes great players like Danny Kortchmar, Bill Payne, and Waddy Wachtel. During this time, sales might have been a consideration as well as Raitt's tough image. If anything, Asher accentuated Raitt's rough edges and provided his customary production polish. Like many Asher productions of the period, *The Glow* gets its strength from its covers. Raitt takes on "I Thank You," "Your Good Thing (Is About to End)," and "Bye Bye Baby," and struts through them all with ease. "The Boy Can't Help It" doesn't fare as well. Robert Palmer's "You're Gonna Get What's Coming" makes for a great fit. Surprisingly, her take on Jackson Browne's "Sleep's Dark and Silent Gate" doesn't dig as deep as the great original. *The Glow* isn't a perfect album, but it's a great example of the music she was doing during a make-or-break time in her career. *—Jason Elias*

Green Light / 1982 / Warner Bros. ♦♦♦♦♦

Since 1975's *Homeplate*, Bonnie Raitt has veered closer to the mainstream than she has to the organic, sexy funk of her early-'70s records. This bothered many listeners, who chose to concentrate on the surface instead of the substance, but Raitt retained many of the same special qualities she demonstrated on those records into the '80s—namely, her excellent taste in material, fondness for blurring folk, blues, country, and rock, and her wonderfully subtle, always engaging, interpretations. *Green Lights* may suffer a bit from a production that clearly pegs it as a 1982 release, but strip away its production and it's yet another satisfying collection of roots rockers and bluesy ballads from the always reliable Raitt. Producer Rob Fraboni's recording may be a little bit too mainstream, lacking the new wave spark of, say, Dave Edmunds' similar-sounding recordings of this era, but Raitt nevertheless rises above the limitations of the recording and delivers a tight, enjoyable collection of amiable mainstream rockers with just a hint of roots. This isn't nearly as sexy as even *Sweet Forgiveness*, and it doesn't have much grit, but it has spirit and is fun, and it's a nice, smooth ride for those that like the direction Raitt's going. *—Stephen Thomas Erlewine*

Nine Lives / 1986 / Warner Bros. ♦♦♦

Bonnie Raitt's ninth and final album for Warner Bros. Records was a star-crossed affair that began in 1983 in a session with producer Rob Fraboni, which was a typical Raitt mixture of different genres and songwriters, from Jerry Williams ("Excited") and Eric Kaz ("Angel") to reggae star Toots Hibbert ("True Love Is Hard to Find") in a style similar to her 1982 album *Green Light*. This record seems to have been rejected by Warner, but three years later Raitt returned to the studio with Bill Payne (Little Feat) and George Massenburgh and cut a group of commercial-sounding songs by the likes of Bryan Adams and Tom Snow. *Nine Lives* splits the difference between the two sessions, with four tracks rescued from 1983, and five added from 1986, plus the theme from a forgotten Farrah Fawcett movie ("Stand Up to the Night" from *Extremities*). The result is predictably scattered and strained, and it was Raitt's lowest-charting album since her debut. Not surprisingly, it was also the last straw in her relationship with Warner. — *William Ruhlmann*

● **Nick of Time** / Mar. 1989 / Capitol ✦✦✦✦✦

Prior to *Nick of Time*, Bonnie Raitt had been a reliable cult artist, delivering a string of solid records that were moderate successes and usually musically satisfying. From her 1971 debut through 1982's *Green Light*, she had a solid streak, but 1986's *Nine Lives* snapped it, falling far short of her usual potential. Therefore, it shouldn't have been a surprise when Raitt decided to craft its follow-up as a major comeback, collaborating with producer Don Was on *Nick of Time*. At the time, the pairing seemed a little odd, since he was primarily known for the weird hipster funk of Was (Not Was) and the B-52's' quirky eponymous debut, but the match turned out to be inspired. Was used Raitt's classic early-'70s records as a blueprint, choosing to update the sound with a smooth, professional production and a batch of excellent contemporary songs. In this context, Raitt flourishes; she never rocks too hard, but there is grit to her singing and playing, even when the surfaces are clean and inviting. And while she only has two original songs here, *Nick of Time* plays like autobiography, which is a testament to the power of the songs, performances, and productions. It was a great comeback album that made for a great story, but the record never would have been a blockbuster success if it wasn't for the music, which is among the finest Raitt ever made. She must have realized this, since *Nick of Time* served as the blueprint for the majority of her '90s albums. — *Stephen Thomas Erlewine*

The Bonnie Raitt Collection / Jun. 28, 1990 / Warner Bros. ✦✦✦

Since Bonnie Raitt didn't score any big hits during her nine-album tenure at Warner Bros., compiling a best-of from those records is largely a matter of taste, and after Raitt's commercial breakthrough on Capitol with *Nick of Time* in 1989, Warners decided to trust her own taste in choosing songs for this compilation. The artist's input is usually considered a good thing, but in this case it has resulted in an idiosyncratic selection that fails to be representative or to cull the real highlights from Raitt's Warners catalog. Basically, that catalog breaks down into three sections—the first three solid albums, the second three good but uneven albums, and the last three mediocre, compromised albums. Raitt has opted to try to find at least a couple of tracks from each album, which means she necessarily slights her best work in favor of her weakest. Even by choosing four tracks from *Give It Up*, she still misses "Been Too Long at the Fair," and by restricting herself to two tracks from *Takin My Time*, she misses "Cry Like a Rainstorm" and "I Gave My Love a Candle." On later albums, the problem is more about selection than quantity. Why "Sugar Mama" from *Home Plate* and not "Run Like a Thief" and "I'm Blowin' Away"? Why "(Goin') Wild for You Baby" from *The Glow* and not the Grammy-nominated "You're Gonna Get What's Coming"? Why "Willya Wontcha" from *Green Light* and not "Me and the Boys"? Even taking into account differences in taste, Raitt's choices run in the face of the preferences of fans and critics to the point that the album fails to make the case for her Warners recordings as true expressions of her talents, a case that could have been made decisively with a better selection. — *William Ruhlmann*

Luck of the Draw / Jun. 1991 / Capitol ✦✦✦✦✦

Nick of Time not only was an artistic comeback for Bonnie Raitt, it brought her largest audience yet, so there was no reason to mess with success for its sequel, *Luck of the Draw*. And sequel is the appropriate word, since *Luck of the Draw* is nothing if it isn't "Nick of Time, Pt. 2." True, there's a heavier reliance on original material this time around, but the sound and feel of the record is identical to its predecessor. There is one slight difference—several of the songs appear tailor-made for crossover success, where *Nick of Time* felt organic. Nevertheless, *Luck of the Draw* is an unqualified success, filled with strong songs—including the hits "Something to Talk About" and "I Can't Make You Love Me," plus the Delbert McClinton duet "Good Man, Good Woman"—appealing productions, and just enough dirt to make old-school fans feel at home. — *Stephen Thomas Erlewine*

Longing in Their Hearts / Mar. 14, 1994 / Capitol ✦✦✦✦✦

On the follow-up to the follow-up (and another million-selling number-one hit), Bonnie Raitt contributes more than her usual share of original songs, writing four songs herself and setting a lyric of her husband's to music for a fifth. Elsewhere, she draws on such strong writers as Richard Thompson and Paul Brady, all for a collection devoted to devotion. Song after song expresses passion, usually with happy results—this is not the album of a woman with the blues. Even when she's dressing down a parent in her own "Circle Dance," Raitt offers forgiveness and understanding. There, and in other songs, the object of her emotions rarely seems to be perfect, but she takes that in and loves him, anyway. Co-producer Don Was provides a detailed production in which single elements—an accordion, a harmony vocal by Levon Helm or David Crosby—effectively color arrangements and complement Raitt's always soulful singing. — *William Ruhlmann*

Road Tested / Nov. 7, 1995 / Digital Sound ✦✦✦✦✦

In a 24-year recording career, Bonnie Raitt had not previously released a live album, so this concert set was overdue. Coming off three multi-platinum studio albums, Raitt and Capitol pulled out all the stops, compiling a 22-track, double-disc package from dates recorded in July 1995 in Portland and Oakland. Raitt ranged over her career, reaching back to her early folk-blues days and forward to the pop/rock songs that finally made her a big star in the late '80s and early '90s. She also shared the spotlight with such guests as Bruce Hornsby, Ruth Brown, Charles Brown, Kim Wilson of the Fabulous Thunderbirds, Bryan Adams, and Jackson Browne. But that didn't keep an artist who has spent the bulk of her career pleasing live audiences rather than cutting hits from displaying her personal warmth along with her singing and playing skills. She also introduced half a dozen songs new to her repertoire, including a surprising cover of Talking Heads' "Burning Down the House" and a few that had potential to help promote the album as singles, including "Never Make Your Move Too Soon" and "Shake a Little." Inexplicably, Capitol (which probably wished the album had been a more reasonably priced single-disc) failed to bring

the record home to consumers. The company's choice for a single was the anonymous Adams rocker "Rock Steady," done as a duet with him—apparently, they were confusing Raitt with Tina Turner. As a result, the album stopped at gold, spending less than six months in the charts. Despite that commercial disappointment, it will be for many Bonnie Raitt fans an example of her at her best that effectively bridges the two parts of her career, and also a good sampler for first-time listeners. — *William Ruhlmann*

Fundamental / Apr. 7, 1998 / Capitol ✦✦✦

Apparently in an attempt to find new sounds that would appeal to a new audience, Bonnie Raitt severed her ties with her comeback producer, Don Was, for *Fundamental*, hiring those masterminds of experimental adult pop, Mitchell Froom and Tchad Blake. Although Froom and Blake have worked with a number of singer/songwriters and roots musicians—including Elvis Costello, Suzanne Vega, Richard Thompson, Los Lobos, and Crowded House—they often emphasize the production over the song, pouring on layers of effects and novelty instruments that tend to obscure the songs and performances. While they don't go overboard on *Fundamental* like they did on Los Lobos' *Colossal Head*, they have pushed too much of their own style on Raitt. There are good songs scattered throughout the record, but it's hard to pick them out underneath the gauzy, murky production. Eventually, the album becomes a bit of a chore, since the sounds wear on the ears. That's too bad, because Raitt remains a vital artist—it's just that Froom and Blake haven't allowed her to rely on her talents here. — *Stephen Thomas Erlewine*

Silver Lining / Apr. 9, 2002 / Capitol ✦✦✦✦

With her road band laying the groundwork and with production responsibilities reverted primarily to her own hands, Raitt delivers varied and vivid performances throughout *Silver Lining*. Jon Cleary, an addition to the lineup, plays the pivotal role; his piano drives the steaming New Orleans groove on "Fool's Game," the posturing street funk of "Monkey Business," and the dusty blues tread on the acoustic-textured "No Gettin' Over You." The material, culled from American and African songwriters, along with a few Raitt originals, lends itself more to vocal interpretation than to straight-ahead blowing. Raitt's singing has never been more finely tuned, especially on the introspective title cut and on the final track, "Wounded Heart," a breathtaking duet recorded in one take with keyboardist Benmont Tench; after nailing it, Raitt reportedly fled the studio, moved to tears; any second attempt proved both undoable and unnecessary. On these performances Raitt exceeds her own standards for interpreting a lyric without compromise to her full-throated timbre. To balance these reflective moments, there are plenty of hotter ones; these also focus on the vocal, but with some exceptional guitar accompaniment as well, including Steve Cropper's licks on the low-key, Memphis-flavored "Time of Our Lives" and the greasy rhythms that push the band throughout "Gnawin' on It." Incendiary slide guitar work heats up parts of that track and several others, with another slide legend, Roy Rogers, joining in on the lascivious "Gnawin' on It." Still, *Silver Lining* is ultimately a showcase for exceptional singing and riveting backup work. It is also a likely milestone in Raitt's ongoing transition from blues guitar whiz to an artist of wider focus. The fires of her youth still blaze, though now they illuminate a more complex weave of techniques and a much greater depth of emotion. — *Robert L. Doerschuk*

Best of Bonnie Raitt on Capitol 1989–2003 / Jun. 3, 2003 / Capitol ✦✦✦✦✦

Willis Alan Ramsey

Vocals, Guitar / Singer/Songwriter, Country-Rock, Soft Rock, Folk-Rock

Singer/songwriter Willis Alan Ramsey is a cult legend among fans of Americana and progressive Texas country. Blending folk, country, and pop with witty, introspective lyrics, Ramsey recorded a critically acclaimed debut album for Leon Russell's Shelter label in 1972. It was one of the first albums by the new school of Austin singer/songwriters that would come to be tagged "progressive country" (Guy Clark and Townes Van Zandt among them). However, Ramsey subsequently disappeared from music, owing to conflicts with his label and a general distaste for the business. Countless artists covered material from *Willis Alan Ramsey*, most notoriously the Captain & Tennille, who took "Muskrat Candlelight" into the pop Top Five under the new title "Muskrat Love." That's no indicator of the respect Ramsey commanded in the country world, with artists like Jerry Jeff Walker ("Northeast Texas Women"), Waylon Jennings ("Satin Sheets"), Jimmy Buffett ("The Ballad of Spider John"), and Jimmie Dale Gilmore ("Goodbye to Old Missoula") all cutting versions of Ramsey's songs.

Ramsey spent most of the '80s living in the U.K. and studying Celtic music but enjoyed something of a rediscovery thanks to Lyle Lovett, who praised the songwriter to the skies. He and Ramsey co-wrote "North Dakota" for Lovett's 1992 album *Joshua Judges Ruth* and teamed up again for "That's Right (You're Not From Texas)" on 1996's *The Road to Ensenada*. Meanwhile, Shawn Colvin re-recorded "Satin Sheets" for her *Cover Girl* album, and Lovett later tapped the new song "Sleepwalking" for his own covers album, *Step Inside This House*. In 2001, Ramsey appeared on *Austin City Limits*, performing nine new songs as well as some older material; he also mounted a tour and reportedly worked on a new record. — *Steve Huey*

Willis Alan Ramsey / 1972 / Koch ✦✦✦✦✦

In many ways, Willis Alan Ramsey's debut album makes him sound like the archetypical Texas singer/songwriter; there's more than a little Guy Clark in his approach, a healthy dose of Townes Van Zandt, a dash of Jimmie Dale Gilmore, and one can hear the echoes of what Steve Earle and Lyle Lovett would draw from this music. But Ramsey's style—an engaging mixture of cowboy poetry, post-hippie wit and wonder, and singer/songwriter introspection—burst forth fully formed in 1972, while Van Zandt was still barely a rumor outside the Lone Star State, and Clark had yet to make himself heard on vinyl; Ramsey was at once a contemporary of the first wave of Texas songwriters, and one of the artists who blazed the trail for what would become one of the most fruitful tributaries of American roots music. While a number of artists covered material from *Willis Alan Ramsey* (the Captain & Tennille most famously with "Muskrat Candlelight"—retitled

"Muskrat Love"—though Waylon Jennings, Jerry Jeff Walker, and even Jimmy Buffett faired better creatively), one listen to the album is enough to convince anyone Ramsey was as much a performer as a songwriter. The bluesy drawl and frayed edges of Ramsey's voice convey a road-worn maturity that betrayed his youth (he was in his early 20s when he cut these sessions), and his production (in collaboration with Denny Cordell) is remarkably intelligent and imaginative for someone with so little experience in the studio. From the tragic road story of "The Ballad of Spider John," the weary nostalgia of "Goodbye to Old Missoula," and the Woody Guthrie tribute of "Boy From Oklahome" to the horny twang of "Geraldine and the Honeybee" and the goofy music-biz meditation of "Satin Sheets," Ramsey hardly makes a false move or a poorly considered gesture through the course of the album's 40 minutes. Part of the mystique that has sprung up around Willis Alan Ramsey's debut album is that he dropped from sight after recording it (due to differences with his record company and a lack of enthusiasm for the realities of the music business), and has yet to release a follow-up; while it's hard to imagine anyone whose heard it not hoping there's more where this came from, if your recording career was to be contained in a single album, you'd be very fortunate if it were as good as *Willis Alan Ramsey*. *—Mark Deming*

Ranch Romance

f. 1989, Seattle, WA

Group / Alternative Country, Western Swing Revival

Taking their name from a Western pulp magazine published in the 1930s, the genre-hopping swing band Ranch Romance formed in the late '80s. In the Seattle-based group's initial incarnation, Ranch Romance was an all-female quartet featuring singer/guitarist Jo Miller, bassist Nancy Katz, fiddler Barbara Lamb, and mandolinist Lisa Theo; in 1989, they issued their debut LP, *Western Dream*. After touring in support of k.d. lang, Theo left the band in 1991 and was replaced by accordionist Nova Karina Devonie and David Keenan on guitar, mandolin, and banjo. Lamb departed to attempt a solo career prior to the release of the second Ranch Romance effort, *Blue Blazes*; *Flip City* followed in 1993. *—Jason Ankeny*

● **Western Dream** / 1990 / Sugar Hill ✦✦✦✦✦

With their retro-swing-country style and all-girl harmonizing, Ranch Romance was one of the best country bands you've never heard of. Although it fails to capture the energy the band generated in concert, *Western Dream* does a great job of summarizing the band's many qualities: singer Jo Miller yodels her pants off on showcase numbers like "When the Bloom Is on the Sage" and "Western Dream," and the group takes an irreverent, almost bossa nova-ish approach to the Hank Williams standard "Lovesick Blues." There are also fine versions of potboiler material like "St. James Avenue" and "Ain't No Ash Will Burn." Fiddler Barbara Lamb provides the center of gravity in instrumental terms, but Miller's rich, bell-toned voice is always the main attraction. (*Western Dream* was originally released on the band's own Ranch Hand label in 1989; the Sugar Hill reissue adds three tracks.) *—Rick Anderson*

Blue Blazes / 1991 / Sugar Hill ✦✦✦✦

The sophomore album from this great retro band found them slowing things down a bit and paying more attention to arrangements and production. The results are more fully realized this time out, but not quite as much fun. There's a cooler, more laid-back feel to songs like the very swingy "What's Wrong With You" and the very country "Heartaches," and even the title track and "Racin' Burnin' Bridges" seem a little bit reserved. The romantic numbers are the ones that work best: "Arizona Moon" is a little bit clichéd, but it should be; "Babydoll" partakes of a Buddy Holly vibe to nice effect; and "Lucky One" is a good road lament. "Indeed I Do" is singer Jo Miller's attempt at a torch song, and it works pretty well. The album's only genuine misstep is "Buckaroo," a bizarre and nasty man-killing fantasy that seems out of place in the band's otherwise good-natured repertoire. *—Rick Anderson*

Flip City / 1993 / Sugar Hill ✦✦✦✦

On this, their third album, Ranch Romance recovered some of the energy that was missing from *Blue Blazes*. The program opens with the defiant "Wheatfield Annie" and then proceeds to the high-octane rockabilly of "Baby' s Gonna Come Back Home," and though things slow down with the prairie lament "Sweet Comfort in the Blues," they pick up immediately afterwards with a Cajun stutter-step on "Happy to See You." Guitar whiz David Keenan, who had had an on-and-off relationship with the group since its first album, is finally a fully-acknowledged member of the band at this point, and his rapid-fire licks enliven "Yes, Yes, Yes" and the jazzy instrumental "Swing Twain." (He also takes over the lead vocal slot on the forgettable "Have I Ever Let You Down . . . Completely.") The album ends with a lovely Tex-Mex ballad entitled "Can You Really Let Go of Columbia?" Very nice. *—Rick Anderson*

Jon Randall

b. Dallas, TX

Guitar / Contemporary Country

Contemporary country singer/songwriter Jon Randall was born in Dallas, TX. He relocated to Nashville as a teenager and by the age of 20 was supporting Emmylou Harris on guitar. His work with Harris' band the Nash Ramblers on the live *At the Ryman* earned him a Grammy, and in 1995, RCA issued his solo debut, *What You Don't Know*. The album was a mild success, but his Elektra/Asylum follow-up was held up and eventually shelved in the fallout from an internal label shakeup. Around the same time, Randall's marriage to country star Lorrie Morgan also fell apart. But Randall was undeterred. He left Asylum and re-emerged in 1999 with *Willin'*, a rootsy, bluegrass-flavored album that followed in the footsteps of "honest" country troubadours like Steve Earle. *—Johnny Loftus*

What You Don't Know / 1995 / RCA ✦✦✦

● **Cold Coffee Morning** / Sep. 22, 1998 / Elektra ✦✦✦✦

Jon Randall's *Cold Coffee Morning* displays not only his love for traditional country, but his own personalized take on it. Randall's backround as one of Emmylou Harris' Nash Ramblers, and the pedigrees of his sidemen—who have also worked with Patty Loveless, Hal Ketchum and Dwight Yoakam—give *Cold Coffee Morning* a rich heritage of its own, which includes ballads like "I Don't Go There" and "She Reminds Me of Texas." Willie Nelson and Lorrie Morgan duet with Randall on "Reno & Me" and "Knowing You're There," respectively, adding yet another distinctive touch to an accomplished album. *—Heather Phares*

Willin' / Sep. 21, 1999 / Eminent ✦✦✦✦

Duncanville, TX, native Jon Randall has paid his music-biz dues, performing with Emmylou Harris & the Nash Ramblers, as well as touring with the likes of Vince Gill, the Dixie Chicks, Alan Jackson, and the Sam Bush Band. All that work on behalf of others has paid a major dividend for Randall as well. *Willin'*, his third album (the third one to be released, anyway—another album sits in a closet at RCA Nashville, unreleased), is a dazzling collection of tunes. Randall's principal influences are bluegrass and country. When combined, the resulting vibe is a tasty bit of eclecticism that probably fits as readily into the Americana category as it does in country. Much in-demand as a backing vocalist, it's no surprise that Randall's singing is exceptional. His voice conveys a wealth of emotional depth, but then, the material on this album conjures Randall's intense vocal performances, so, as is so often the case, great songwriting is the bottom line. From the graceful "Sweet Loretta" to the growl of "Walk the Line" to the loping country backbeat of "Mountain of Regret" to the expansive heart of "Breakin' the Rules" and the breathtaking ballad "Afraid of the Dark," this album has a cumulative effect that's more penetrating than any single track. No matter how you break this down, *Willin'* is a superior piece of work. *—Philip Van Vleck*

Boots Randolph (Homer Louis Randolph III)

b. 1925, Paducah, KY

Saxophone, Trombone / Instrumental Rock, Nashville Sound/Countrypolitan, Country-Pop, Instrumental Country

Tenor saxophonist Boots Randolph was an important contributor to the Nashville Sound, the set of pop-flavored textures that dominated country music in the late '50s and early '60s. He was born in Paducah, KY, but grew up in small-town Cadiz, in Trigg County. Born Homer Louis Randolph III, he acquired the nickname "Boots" in childhood from his brother Bob. Randolph began playing the trombone in school and learned several other instruments, but by the time he was 16 he had begun to focus seriously on the sax. He honed his chops as a member of the U.S. Army Band during World War II.

After the war, Randolph returned home and performed semi-professionally for some years around Indiana, Kentucky, and Illinois. In the late '50s, Jethro Burns heard him play and suggested he move to Nashville. Burns introduced Randolph to Chet Atkins, who signed him to the RCA label. Randolph also quickly made the acquaintance of Atkins rival Owen Bradley and performed on many recordings Bradley helmed as producer. Nashville's new corps of session musicians spent its leisure time in the Printer's Alley section of the city's downtown, an actual alley (between First and Second avenues) that offered entrance to various basement barrooms, and Randolph became one of the group. Like other Nashville players, he took enthusiastically to jazz and rock & roll in addition to country music.

One single, the 1963 instrumental "Yakety Sax," showed Randolph putting all these influences together and delivering an extremely catchy tune; it became his only real hit. But Randolph was a consistent seller of LP albums (with 13 charted releases) in the 1960s and 1970s; offering pleasant saxophone covers of material from various genres of music, he became a counterpart to Atkins on guitar and Floyd Cramer on piano. He moved from RCA to the Monument label in 1966. For well over a decade, in addition, he averaged 200-300 studio sessions a year on recordings made by others. The saxophone heard on Elvis Presley's later records is likely to be Randolph's. In 1977, Randolph opened a successful club of his own in Printer's Alley; it endured into the 1990s and spawned another club in the Opryland U.S.A. area. Randolph remained active as an entertainer into the 2000s, and in 1994 the original *Yakety Sax* album was admitted into the unofficial country canon; it was reissued by Germany's Bear Family label. *—James Manheim*

Yakety Sax / 1960 / Monument ✦✦✦✦✦

Boots Randolph's Yakety Sax / 1963 / Monument ✦✦✦✦✦

Nashville session tenor saxman doing what he does best on a rocking set. *—Bill Dahl*

The Yakin' Sax Man / 1964 / Camden ✦✦✦

In the case of some artists, part of the package that comes with commercial success is to have their archive of material turned into a sloppy mess by a confusing jumble of business interests. RCA made loads of moolah off innovative artists coming out of the country & western scene and the studio empire presided over by Lord Chet Atkins, one of the big breadwinners being tenor sax honker Boots Randolph, whose instrumental hits exploded on radio and jukeboxes for a while. The label owes these artists enough that it is insulting no serious effort has been made to create well-produced, comprehensive collections of some of them, a problem that will hopefully be rectified eventually. In the meantime, listeners have the work of the low-budget Camden line, which siphoned off anything remotely commercial from parent company RCA for repackaging purposes as if it was cheap gas. These are albums that are stingy on playing time, as if some overlord had looked at a quality Boots Randolph album and ordered it cut in half. The packaging is generic and brings to mind a designer hustling toward a lunch break. The Pickwick International conglomerate also got involved in licensing the low-budget line, exporting in and out of Canada with apparently only one goal: the creation of an even shoddier product, the vinyl an imitation of a Shakey's pizza crust. Someone might pipe in at this point and say "It's still pizza!" and yes, it is still Boots Randolph, meaning if you put this record on at a party, for example, there would be a series of people asking who this is and making comments such as "Oh, how cool!" Some listeners may perceive the last decade of the 20th century as the era when instrumental music began crashing through genre barriers, but the much less pretentious work of Randolph and his unidentified associates goes in many of the same directions. The musicianship is tops, allowing the players to smoothly fool around on the perimeters of funk, swing, R&B, balladry, Cajun, Italian, and Latin. This collection contains both "Sleep" and "Sleep Walk," which can't be a bad thing. [The Pickwick version has a different playing order.] *—Eugene Chadbourne*

Sweet Talk / 1965 / Camden ♦♦♦

This is a quick taste of the country & western saxophonist's work from the initial phase of his career; the tunes go by in a snap not only because of their listener-friendly, unpretentious, and relaxed attitude, but because the record itself only features enough material for one side, not two. With a few hits under his belt, Boots Randolph was probing into new areas as well as trying to provide the type of material that had already won him a solid fan base well outside the cowboy hat crowd. Completely devoid of any information about the sessions or the other players involved, this album contains two of Randolph's better originals, the funky "Red Light" and "Little Big Horn," the latter tune possessing a groove so catchy it might have even turned General George Custer into a dancer rather than a fighter. The album title might be trying to indicate some kind of development from the "Yakety Sax" or more extreme "Cacklin' Sax" sound to something more mellow, a direction that works best on the pretty "Estrellita." RCA studio honcho Chet Atkins helps out with a tune entitled "Difficult," which could be a summation of the chances of getting someone else other than him to play guitar on your RCA session back then. "Greenback Dollar," a cornball folky number that was absolutely ruined by the Kingston Trio, is revitalized nicely by the honking saxman and his studio crew. "The Happy Whistler" is completely corny, and thus most likely to be the first track to get worn out from overplay. *—Eugene Chadbourne*

Sunday Sax / 1968 / Monument ♦♦♦

Boots Randolph With the Knightsbridge Strings / 1968 / Monument ♦♦

With the help of the Knightsbridge Strings, Boots Randolph reprises ten of the '60s' most famous songs, including "Moon River," "The Shadow of Your Smile," "Days of Wine and Roses" and "You've Lost That Lovin' Feelin'." *—Keith Farley*

Country Boots / 1972 / Monument ♦♦♦

Sentimental Journey / 1973 / Monument ♦♦♦♦

Greatest Hits / 1976 / Monument ♦♦♦♦

Tenor saxophonist Boots Randolph released numerous instrumental country-pop albums on the Monument label throughout the '60s and '70s. Think of him as the Percy Faith of Nashville. Much like Mr. Faith, Randolph's choice of instrumentals were geared toward both the country and easy listening audience and included tunes like "Gentle on My Mind," "Hey Jude," "Stardust," and "Proud Mary." His earliest and biggest hit was "Yakety Sax," a takeoff on the Coasters' R&B smash of 1958, "Yakety Yak." Even those who don't know the name Boots Randolph will more than likely recognize his version of "Yakety Sax" as the theme to the BBC comedy *the Benny Hill Show.* If you're looking to buy one Boots disc, this would be the one. *—Al Campbell*

● **Yakety Sax** / Jun. 27, 1994 / Bear Family ♦♦♦♦♦

Tenor saxophonist Boots Randolph released numerous instrumental country-pop albums throughout the '60s and '70s. Randolph's choice of instrumentals were geared toward both the country and easy listening audiences. This Bear Family compilation focuses on Randolph's early recordings, featuring "Hey Elvis," "Blue Guitar," and "Estrellita," and his biggest chart-topper, "Yakety Sax." At 23 tracks, *Yakety Sax* is probably more than the casual Boots Randolph listener will need. If you're looking to buy only one Randolph disc, check out *Greatest Hits* on Monument. *—Al Campbell*

Wayne Raney

b. Aug. 17, 1921, Wolf Bayou, AR, **d.** Jan. 23, 1993

Harmonica, Vocals / Traditional Country

Known above all for his 1949 number-one single "Why Don't You Haul Off and Love Me," Wayne Raney had a durable career in country music that reflected many of the tradition's most important influences at mid-century. In addition to his singing, Raney was well known for his harmonica playing. He and his longtime stage partner Lonnie Glosson sold millions of harmonicas through the mail and did much to establish the harmonica as an instrument accessible and popular everywhere. Born on a farm near Wolf Bayou, AR, he suffered from a foot deformity that prevented him from doing heavy farm work. He heard a street person "choke" a harmonica and was inspired to learn the instrument himself. By the time he was 13, he had headed for Piedras Negras, Mexico, across the river from Eagle Pass, TX, to perform on the powerful "border radio" station XEPN. In 1936 he met Glosson, and the two teamed up in 1938 to play on a radio station in Little Rock. They moved on to Cincinnati's WCKY and later to wide syndication; perhaps the heavy mail-order emphasis of the border radio enterprises, which sold everything from piano lessons to monkey-gland-implant impotence treatments, inspired Raney to think in terms of marketing the harmonica to listeners who enjoyed what he and Glosson played on the air.

After World War II Raney played briefly on the radio in Memphis and then teamed up with the Delmore Brothers, whose wry boogie numbers, punctuated with jovial blasts from Raney's harmonica, became national hits. In 1948, he went solo and hit the charts with two Top 15 singles, "Lost John Boogie" and "Jack and Jill Boogie." In 1949 he topped country charts with "Why Don't You Haul Off and Love Me," which also featured Glosson. The song crossed over to the pop Top 25 and was his biggest hit. Raney subsequently recorded novelty songs in the Little Jimmy Dickens vein, such as "Pardon My Whiskers" and "I Love My Little Yo Yo." He played on the *Grand Ole Opry* for one year, spent a few months touring with Lefty Frizzell in 1953, and performed on the *California Hayride* and WWVA *Jamboree* radio programs. In the late '50s he worked as a DJ, opened a recording studio, and started the bluegrass-oriented Rimrock label, on which he released several albums of his own; the King label collected many of his singles on the rather inaccurately named *Songs of the Hills* LP in 1958, and that record had a long life in the countless reissues that repackaged the King catalog.

He recorded a few singles in the late '50s and early '60s and continued to sell harmonicas until 1960, when the craze passed. Raney then returned to Arkansas and recorded a gospel album, *Don't Try to Be What You Ain't.* He also ran a chicken farm for a time, and he appeared occasionally on *Hee Haw* in the '70s. Eventually his health began to fail; he lost his voicebox in the late '80s and in 1990 published a brief autobiography, *Life Has Not Been a Bed of Roses.* He died of cancer in 1993 and was inducted into the Country Music Disc Jockey Hall of Fame. *—James Manheim*

● **Songs of the Hills** / 1958 / King ♦♦♦♦♦

One of the great country harmonica players, Raney also qualifies as as one of the most important harmonica players in the history of American pop, as he was one of the first musicians of any sort to fuse country and blues. This 16-cut collection in effect functions as a best-of, including the big hits "Why Don't You Haul Off and Love Me," "Lost John Boogie," and "Jack and Jill Boogie." Despite what the title might lead you believe, it's not exactly rural country-folk—it's hard-driving early country boogie with a decidedly urban influence. With the Delmore Brothers on backup, "Jack and Jill Boogie" in particular sounds like proto-rockabilly, with lengthy back-and-forth guitar exchanges that are about as close to white rock & roll as anyone got in 1948. Despite the no-frills package (even a bit of historical information and liner notes would have been nice), it's the best available anthology of this somewhat overlooked country and pop pioneer. *—Richie Unterberger*

Wayne Raney and the Raney Family / 1960 / Starday ♦♦♦♦

Don't Try to Be What You Ain't / 1964 / Starday ♦♦♦

That Real Boogie Boy: The King Anthology / Nov. 15, 2002 / Ace ♦♦♦♦♦

Wayne Raney's considerable legacy hadn't been well served by the CD era at the time of this 2002 release. This 25-track anthology is a good if imperfect start to correcting that imbalance. It's imperfect because it doesn't by any means have every significant King side waxed by this important country-boogie singer and harmonica player. In fact, it hardly renders the best prior CD compilation of Raney's work (*Songs of the Hills*) redundant, since about half of the songs on that budget-looking disc don't appear here. Still, it's a good survey of material that Raney cut at King in the late '40s and early '50s, including his big hit "Why Don't You Haul Off and Love Me" and such galvanizing hillbilly harmonica boogies as "Fast Train Through Arkansas," "Catfish Baby," and the great "Jack and Jill Boogie" (which clearly anticipates the riff exchanges of rock & roll). There are some nice close harmony ballads like "Lonesome Wind Blues" with clearer roots in old-time music. But there are a surprising number of tamer, more country-oriented performances that aren't nearly as raw and exciting as his hot harmonica boogies, particularly the later the year of recording, and Raney's voice is much less effective when he isn't bolstered by harmonizing singers. Yet it's a valuable package overall, boosted by liner notes giving a thorough overview of Raney's career. The CD has a previously unissued, undubbed version of his 1952 single "Undertakin' Daddy" (the overdubbed version from the released single is also included). *—Richie Unterberger*

The Rankin Family

f. 1989, Mabou, Cape Breton Island, Nova Scotia, **db.** 1999

Group / Contemporary Folk, Contemporary Celtic

Canada's Rankin Family got their start singing and dancing in their hometown of Mabou, Cape Breton Island, Nova Scotia. Pianist/fiddler John Morris, guitarist/vocalist Jimmy, and singers Raylene, Carol Jean (aka Cookie), and Heather developed a unique blend of Celtic traditionalism and contemporary folk and pop, dominated by the effortless harmonies of the Rankin sisters. In 1989 the combo recorded and self-released its debut and traveled throughout Eastern Canada, promoting it with performances at folk festivals and the like. A year later they issued their second recording, *Fare Thee Well Love.* The Rankin Family signed with EMI in 1992 and re-released their first two recordings. *North Country* followed a year later. The album was the best representation yet of the Rankins' mix of folk and traditional Gaelic songs and arrangements.

After 1995's *Grey Dusk of Eve* EP, *Endless Seasons* appeared. Produced by John Jennings (Mary-Chapin Carpenter), the album was a much more polished affair and incorporated a significant amount of original songwriting. *Uprooted* followed in 1998. Recorded principally in Nashville, the album included country-tinged material as well as experiments with expanded instrumentation and spoken word. The Rankin Family ceased performing as a unit in September 1999. Cookie went on to a solo career, Heather dabbled in acting, and Jimmy continued to work as a songwriter (he would go on to release *Song Dog* in 2001). Just a few months after the announcement, John Morris was killed in a traffic accident in Sydney, Nova Scotia. He was 40 years old. *—Johnny Loftus*

Fare Thee Well Love / 1990 / EMI ♦♦♦♦

Originally released independently, *Fare Thee Well Love* turned the Rankin Family into household names in Canada. Although traditional maritime music was something that many Canadians had *heard* about, *Fare Thee Well Love* was one of the first albums to successfully bring the tradition into the homes of people too embarrassed to pick up an Irish Rovers album. Most of the material is fairly traditional (some of it is even sung in Gaelic), but with more of a skew to the country music crowd than the pop crowd. Oddly enough, some of the album's best moments are those when the sound is colored a bit by keyboards and smoother production, like on the beautiful title track. Four of the Rankins take turns at vocals, with the women's voices blending crisp and clear. Although it may be a bit too traditional for fans of the more pop-oriented maritime music, it's noteworthy as one of the key albums in Canada's Celtic music resurrection. *—Sean Carruthers*

North Country / 1993 / EMI ♦♦♦♦

North Country solidifies the group's wholesome reputation. You can always count on the Rankins for at least one exquisite, stand-out pop melody per recording; that one here is the title track's tribute to Canadian wilderness. The voices of Cookie, Heather, and Raylene Rankin blend effectively with an intuitive sense of harmony. These are pure, attractive voices, but with a certain lack of emotional depth that parallels Jimmy and John Morris Rankin's sometimes over-sweetened, keyboard-dominated instrumentation. Three tracks rendered in Gaelic are pleasant, while Lisa Brown overdoses on the group's sugary, "golly-gee" side. For those who prefer eating the icing off the cake. *—Roch Parisien*

● **Rankin Family Collection** / 1996 / Rounder ✦✦✦✦✦
As one of the key groups to set the Celtic music revolution rolling in Canada, the Rankin Family definitely has their place in the country's musical tapestry. As a compilation of the band's early years, the *Collection* contains pretty much all the hits, and a fairly good sampling of all the aspects of the band: pop/country, original/traditional, male/female vocals, acoustic/lush. To be fair, the compilation tends to lean away from the more overtly Celtic material that the band does and more toward the polished pop numbers. The CD also contains bonus multimedia material on an enhanced CD program. *—Sean Carruthers*

Endless Seasons / Feb. 1996 / EMI ✦✦✦
While the Rankins have always been well-received by the country music fans in Canada, *Endless Seasons* is an album that's actually more focused to that crowd. This time out, the album was recorded in Nashville with country music bigwig John Jennings and a number of musical guests (including Mary-Chapin Carpenter and Sam Bush). Despite that, the album is painfully short on the things that endeared the group to listeners in the first place. The group's energy seems to have been sanded off in production, and while the album sounds gorgeous, it's really not a lot of fun apart from the upbeat "You Feel the Same Way Too," and even that is a bit staid in comparison to some of the group's previous output. *—Sean Carruthers*

Uprooted / Jun. 1998 / Rounder ✦✦✦
The Rankins, having now officially dropped the "Family" from their name, seemed to attempt an image change with this CD, both in their presentation and the music itself. The formerly Celtic/roots/folk band has turned in their tin whistle for a more "new country" sound. This shift of style has been building over the past few releases. The problem is, quite honestly, it does not really work. The music tends to be bland, with no sound that clearly distinguishes this band from any other new country band. This is a shame, since they had built their career on turning traditional tunes into their own. And, sadly, they seem to be revisiting old ground. The opening track, "Movin' On," is nothing more than a rewrite of "You Feel the Same Way Too" (from 1996's *Endless Seasons*), only it isn't as good, as it lacks the energy and excitement once found in the Rankin Family's music. The good news is that while Jimmy Rankin, the main writer for the band, attempts to modernize their sound, Cookie and Heather Rankin seem content to return to form, and produce some wonderful sounds, utilizing the band's almost innate talent for harmonizing. Cookie's "Maybe You're Right" is the clear highlight of the CD, a bouncy country-pop tune that really stays in the listener's head. Jimmy Rankin does shine with the somewhat bitter, but very interesting "Long Way to Go," featuring Heather Rankin spitting out the lyrics. Also, the Rankins do toss in some old traditional favorites at the end of the CD, just to remind listeners of their origin, and also what they are capable of performing. The problem is that there is not enough of what the band does best. *—Aaron Badgley*

Do You Hear . . . Christmas With Heather, Cookie & Raylene Rankin / Oct. 20, 1998 / EMI ✦✦

The Rarely Herd

f. 1989, Albany, OH
Group / Progressive Bluegrass, Traditional Bluegrass
The Rarely Herd were among the finest contemporary bluegrass bands to come out of Ohio, and became quite popular on the festival circuit. Playing a wide variety of progressive and traditional bluegrass along with their own unique compositions and adaptations from other genres, the Rarely Herd were especially noted for their close vocal harmonies and energetic performances. Their lineup included guitarist and lead singer Jim Stack; his brother, fiddler/mandolinist/vocalist Alan Stack, a former child prodigy; and bassist Jim Weaver.

A 1992 showcase at the International Bluegrass Music Awards established the Ohio band as a force in contemporary bluegrass. That same year, Pinecastle issued their debut, *Midnight Loneliness. Heartbreak City* followed in 1994; two years later, the gospel-flavored album *What About Him* was released to widespread acclaim. The Rarely Herd continued to win awards and win over audiences with their energetic mix of bluegrass prowess and on-stage antics. *Coming of Age* appeared in 1998, and *A Part of Growing Up* followed closely on its heels. *—Sandra Brennan & Johnny Loftus*

Midnight Loneliness / 1992 / Pinecastle ✦✦✦

Heartbreak City / 1994 / Pinecastle ✦✦✦

● **Pure Homemade Love** / 1995 / Pinecastle ✦✦✦✦✦

What About Him / Apr. 22, 1997 / Pinecastle ✦✦✦

Coming of Age / Oct. 27, 1998 / Pinecastle ✦✦✦✦
As the title suggests, *Coming of Age* is a sign that the Rarely Herd have matured into one of contemporary bluegrass' finest acts. Returning to mostly secular material, the group welcomes guest banjoist Don Wayne Reno. *—Steve Huey*

Part of Growing Up / 2000 / Pinecastle ✦✦✦

Rascal Flatts

Group / Contemporary Country
Rascal Flatts, a country trio known primarily for their pleasing harmony, is comprised of Gary Levox, Jay DeMarcus, and Joe Don Rooney. DeMarcus and Levox, both from Columbus, OH, founded the group and later added Rooney, a Picher, OK, native. The blend now known as Rascal Flatts came together when second cousins DeMarcus and Levox invited Rooney to sit in as a substitute guitar player at a *Printer's Alley* gig in Nashville. DeMarcus and Rooney were also playing in country star Chely Wright's band at the time. The rest is history. After landing a record deal with Lyric Street Records, the trio recorded an eclectic mix of country, pop, R&B, and more with their debut self-titled album. "Prayin' for Daylight" became the group's first smash single. "This Everyday Love" soon followed, with almost as many accolades. The band's second album, *Melt*, appeared in October 2002. With the success of first single "These Days," *Melt* had sold a million copies in eight weeks. *—Rick Cohoon*

● **Rascal Flatts** / Jun. 6, 2000 / Hollywood ✦✦✦✦
Rascal Flatts are three average, nice guys. They make contemporary country-pop that's nice, but ever so slightly and satisfyingly a cut above average. Nothing on their eponymous debut deviates from the norm—it's squarely down the center of the mainstream, edging closer to pop than it does to real country—but it's sweetly endearing and unassuming. Take the lead song and single, "Prayin' for Daylight," for example. It's almost defiantly square, but the trio doesn't ever realize that it's not hip to be square—the very quality that makes it so much fun. They revel in their warm harmonies, bright production, catchy midtempo pop tunes, and ballads of heartbreak and love that always seem happy. Rascal Flatts never really changes their approach at any point during the album—many of the zippier songs sound a lot like "Prayin' for Daylight" and the slower numbers are just slower variations of that tune—but that doesn't matter, since this is an amiable, well-crafted, professional record. Are there some slow moments? Well, yes, but they pass by easily, thanks to the surface gloss and the boys' cheerful attitude. *Rascal Flatts* may not be weighty, but it's not supposed to be. It's designed to be a sunny, pleasing modern country-pop album, and that's exactly what it is. *—Stephen Thomas Erlewine*

Melt / Oct. 29, 2002 / Hollywood ✦✦✦✦
Gary Levox has amazing vocal ability unsurpassed by any other male country singer heard on the charts today. That's why the best songs from *Melt* are the ballads—he sings them with such a fiery zeal that you can't help but be transfixed by the titanic sound coming out of the speakers. But that certainly doesn't mean that the uptempo and quicker songs aren't worth listening to. In fact, the whole 11-song collection is worth listening to over and over. A platinum-selling debut album with a follow-up sophomore album that's as brilliant as the first—if not more so—doesn't happen all that often in an industry subject to dozens of newcomers a minute. Their harmonies are musically superior and their songwriting efforts continue to be original and fresh. Rascal Flatts is a band that deserves more than its due. *—Maria Konicki Dinoia*

Ole Rasmussen

Bandleader / Western Swing
One of the more original bands from the postwar era, Ole Rasmussen & His Nebraska Cornhuskers produced a series of Western swing hits in the '40s and early '50s. With a sound that took a lot from the music from Bob Wills, the band was not based out of Nebraska as their name would seem to indicate, but instead was from California. Rasmussen was not much of a musician, but he was an excellent businessman and bandleader. He also knew a talented musician when he saw one and assembled one of the finest bands in the L.A. area. Teddy Wilds, and later Virgil Lee, provided vocals, Tex Atchison and Rocky Stone were on fiddles, Billy Tonnesen was on steel guitar, and Earl Finley was on electric guitar. The band's most prolific period came from 1950-1952, when they were signed to the Capitol label. After that period, their career quickly declined, and they had no more major hits. *—Stacia Proefrock*

● **Sleepy Eyed John** / Oct. 19, 1999 / Bear Family ✦✦✦✦
Bob Wills imitator Ole Rasmussen had a few years of success with the Nebraska Cornhuskers in the early '50s, the last years of Western swing's broad popularity. Although Rasmussen's worship of Wills' sound can be simply overbearing, his music is attractive today because of the songwriting contributions of fiddler Tex Atchison, especially the classic tongue-twister "Sleepy Eyed John" and "Which-A-Way Will You Go." After Atchison's departure in 1951 the best songs are collaborations between Rasmussen and various bandmembers. Of these, "You Were My Dream Last Night" is pretty great, but otherwise the collection is thoroughly average, with the excellent sound quality being an unexpected bonus. *—Jim Smith*

Leon Rausch

b. Oct. 2, 1927, Springfield, MO
Guitar, Vocals / Traditional Country, Western Swing
Known as "the voice" of Bob Wills & His Texas Playboys, Leon Rausch was born October 2, 1927, in Missouri. Edgar Leon Rausch was raised in a musical family and began playing guitar with his father at local dances as a child and continued through his high-school years. Upon graduation, Rausch joined the military and played off and on with local bands until he moved to Tulsa in 1955. Rausch received his first big break with an appearance on the *Louisiana Hayride* the following year, and on St. Patrick's Day 1958 he was asked to join Bob Wills & His Texas Playboys, replacing vocalist Glynn Duncan. Rausch's stint with Wills lasted into the early '60s. He then briefly joined Johnnie Lee Wills' band before forming his own group, the New Texas Playboys, in Fort Worth, TX. By the late '60s the band had appeared on *Cowtown Jamboree* and released a few singles without much fanfare. In 1973, an ailing Wills contacted Rausch about rejoining his Texas Playboys on what would be Wills' final record, *For the Last Time.*

Following Wills' death in 1975, Rausch and the original Texas Playboys continued to record and play gigs, including a high-profile appearence on *Austin City Limits.* In 1983 Rausch had slowed down his working pace but continued to take part in projects that interested him, including Asleep at the Wheel's *Tribute to the Music of Bob Wills* with the group that became the Playboys II. Since then, Rausch has written a book co-authored by

Dr. John E. Perkins Jr. titled *Leon Rausch... The Voice of the Texas Playboys* about his time with Wills. *—Al Campbell*

From the Heart of Texas / 1966 / Kapp ♦♦♦

She's the Trip That I've Been On / 1967 / Derrick ♦♦♦

● **For the Last Time** / 1974 / United Artists ♦♦♦♦

Live and Kickin' / 1978 / Capitol ♦♦♦

Eddy Raven (Edward Garvin Futch)

b. Aug. 19, 1945, Lafayette, LA

Vocals / Urban Cowboy, Country-Pop, Zydeco

Born Edward Garvin Futch, it's no wonder that his name was changed by a record executive to Eddy Raven on his very first single, released on tiny Cosmos Records in the late '60s. Numerous influences have made his music almost indescribable: the Cajun sounds of his native Louisiana, the blues influence from working with Johnny Winter, the rock & roll of his idol, Elvis Presley, and the pure country of the *Grand Ole Opry.* Befriended by Jimmy C. Newman, Raven made the first of many trips to Nashville in 1970, though he didn't move permanently for a couple of years. Signed to a publishing deal with Acuff-Rose, he wrote songs for Don Gibson and Roy Acuff, among others, and started making records himself in 1974. Despite the acclaim of his peers, Raven didn't actually earn a hit record as a recording artist until 1981, with the release of his *Desperate Dreams* album. After he lost his recording contract in a 1983 consolidation involving Elektra and Warner, Raven took the next year to realign his business. The Oak Ridge Boys earned a hit at that time with his song "Thank God for Kids," and Raven came out of his forced vacation strong, signing with RCA and gaining his first number-one single with "I Got Mexico." For the next half-dozen years, Raven remained a consistent staple of country radio: frequently adventurous, always listenable.

Raven began playing music when he was a child in Lafayette, LA, joining a garage rock band when he was 13 years old. Three years later, his family moved to Georgia, where Raven landed a job working in a radio station. He also managed to cut his own song, "Once a Fool," for the local independent label Cosmo. The record was released under the name "Eddy Raven," and Edward Futch used that moniker as his stage name from that day forward. In 1963, the family moved back to Lafayette, and Raven began working in a record shop called La Louisianne. The store's owner had a label of the same name, and Raven cut several records for the label, including his 1969 debut album, *That Cajun Country Sound.*

Jimmy C. Newman happened to hear *That Cajun Country Sound* and was impressed enough to land Raven a publishing deal with Acuff-Rose. Following the record's release, Raven began singing for Jimmie Davis' band. By 1971, other artists had begun recording Raven's songs, with Don Gibson taking "Country Green" into the Top Five; Gibson also recorded "Touch the Morning," while Jeannie C. Riley covered "Good Morning, Country Rain" and Roy Acuff sang "Back in the Country." Soon, Raven had gained a reputation as a songwriter and a performer within Nashville, and once Don Gant of Acuff-Rose became an A&R man for ABC Records, Eddy had a record deal of his own in 1974. For the next two years, he had a series of minor hits for the label, highlighted by the number 27 "Good News, Bad News" in 1975. He left the label in 1978, staying with Monument for one year before signing with Dimension the following year. None of his singles for either label were big hits, and he left Dimension in 1981.

Later in 1981, he signed with Elektra, where he had his first big hit with the number 13 "I Should've Called." Over the next two years, Raven had three Top 20 singles for Elektra, setting the stage for his breakthrough into the Top Ten in 1984. After spending 1983 resolving legal and managerial problems, Raven signed with RCA Records, releasing "I Got Mexico" in the spring. The single was a big hit, becoming not only his first Top Ten single, but his first number-one hit. For the remainder of the decade, he had a string of Top Ten hits for the label, including the number-one singles "Shine, Shine, Shine" (1987), "I'm Gonna Get You" (1988), and "Joe Knows How to Live" (1988). He left RCA for Universal in 1989, and he had two number one singles for the label—"In a Letter to You" and "Bayou Boys." Once Universal collapsed in 1989, he moved to their parent company, Captiol, but his records for the label were largely ignored because radio was beginning to program newer artists instead of veterans like Raven. During the '90s and 2000s, Raven lacked a record label, but he continued to tour and perform successfully. *—Tom Roland*

Desperate Dreams / 1981 / Elektra ♦♦♦

Raven had more creative control than in previous efforts and developed a tough-sounding album. It's heavy on rhythm guitar, long on bravado. *—Tom Roland*

● **The Best of Eddy Raven** / 1988 / RCA ♦♦♦♦♦

The ten-track *Best of Eddy Raven* collection covers Eddy Raven's most successful RCA records, released in 1988 after he left the label for Capitol. These original hits include "I Got Mexico," "Shine, Shine, Shine," "Sometimes a Lady," and "I'm Gonna Get You." *—Al Campbell*

Temporary Sanity / 1989 / Liberty ♦♦♦♦

Temporary Sanity is a mixed bag highlighting Raven at his best (the moody ballad "Island") and worst (the ham-fisted Cajun stylings of "Bayou Boys"). *—Jason Ankeny*

Greatest Country Hits / 1990 / Curb ♦♦♦♦♦

Greatest Country Hits is the most comprehensive collection of Raven's hits; it features three of his chart-toppers—"I Got Mexico," "Shine, Shine, Shine" and "I'm Gonna Get You." *—Jason Ankeny*

Greatest Hits / 1990 / Warner Bros. ♦♦♦

Greatest Hits these aren't; only one cut, "She's Playing Hard to Forget," even made the country Top Ten. *—Jason Ankeny*

Cookin' Cajun / Aug. 1996 / K-Tel ♦♦♦♦

Cookin' Cajun isn't strictly a duet album—although Raven and Sonnier play together, a good portion of the disc is devoted to solo tracks from both of the artists. It doesn't really matter that *Cookin' Cajun* is a piecemeal effort—the thing sounds good, no matter who is playing at whatever moment. Raven and Sonnier are two of the finest contemporary Cajun/zydeco players and while this disc isn't either artist's finest moment, it's a good-natured record that is a lot of fun while it's playing. Unfortunately, it doesn't provide quite enough sparks to make it worth returning to frequently. *—Stephen Thomas Erlewine*

The Best of Eddy Raven / 1997 / Curb ♦♦♦

Liberty's *Best of Eddy Raven* package is short at only ten cuts, but it does include the majority of his number one hits from the '80s, including "Joe Knows How to Live," "I Got Mexico," "Shine, Shine, Shine," and "I'm Gonna Get You." Though the album isn't comprehensive, it's a decent collection by budget-line standards. *—Al Campbell*

20 Favorites / Jan. 27, 1998 / Capitol Nashville ♦♦♦

20 Favorites is an entertaining summary of Eddy Raven's latter-day recordings for Universal and Capitol Nashville, featuring such hits as "In a Lettter to You," "Bayou Boys," "Sooner or Later," "Island," "Zydeco Lady," "Rock Me in the Rhythm of Your Love" and "Too Much Candy for a Dime," plus a selection of album tracks. It's not a definitive career overview, but it certainly a definitive overview of his work for Capitol Nashville, and it should interest fans of that era. *—Stephen Thomas Erlewine*

Live at Billy Bob's Texas / Apr. 27, 1999 / Live at Billy Bob's Texas ♦♦♦♦

While it's been far too long since a new Eddy Raven studio LP, *Live at Billy Bob's Texas* is an excellent showcase—without any glossy Nashville-style production, his music returns to its raw, rock & roll-influenced roots, lending an edge to hits like "I Got Mexico" and "Bayou Boys" that the originals lacked. *—Hank Small*

● **I Got Mexico: The RCA Victor Singles A's & B's** / Nov. 14, 2000 / WestSide ♦♦♦♦♦

I Got Mexico: The RCA Victor Singles A's & B's includes 21 Eddy Raven tracks from the '80s, featuring the number-one hits "Joe Knows How to Live," "I Got Mexico," and "Shine, Shine, Shine." Lesser tracks like "I Wanna Hear It from You," the Cajun-influenced "I'm Gonna Get You," and "You Should Have Been Gone By Now" make this U.K.-based WestSide compilation fairly comprehensive for the casual fan and worth the search. *—Al Campbell*

Living in Black and White / Mar. 6, 2001 / Row Music Group ♦♦♦

Eddy Raven's *Living in Black and White* conveys a cheerful, mellow tone through its bittersweet songs of heartbreak and hard work. Tracks like "Don't Worry About Me" and "Blue Cajun Moon" show that, after more than 30 years in the music business, Raven can still combine heartfelt lyrics with an inventive mix of country, rock, blues, and zydeco. *—Stacia Proefrock*

Live in Concert / Jul. 23, 2002 / Row Music Group ♦♦♦♦

In the 1980s, Eddy Raven enjoyed a string of number one hits such as "I Got Mexico," "Shine, Shine, Shine," and "In a Letter to You," establishing the Louisiana native as a bona fide country and Cajun singer/songwriter. Since then, Raven has kept busy writing songs, recording, and touring, though virtually none of his new material has broken through on country radio. Raven's *Live in Concert* album breathes new life into the hits that put him on the chart and reaffirms his talent as a showman. The singer offers 22 songs, almost all of which were either number one hits or easily recognizable as Eddy Raven trademark songs. Raven and RMG Records seem to have navigated the tricky business of pulling off a live album while keeping the integrity of the music. With numerous hits under his belt, Raven only includes one medley of "I Should Have Called/Who Do You Know in California," where many others would have shortened old favorites to promote the new. A pleasant extra comes at the end of the concert, when Raven sings "Other Than Montreal," a wistful story of new love that rivals only the singer's love of the Canadian city. Classic country fans will find *Live in Concert* an agreeable reminder of country's heyday before modern pop-infiltrated country became the order of the day. *—Rick Cohoon*

Wade Ray (Lyman Wade Ray)

b. Apr. 13, 1913, Evansville, IN, **d.** Nov. 11, 1998

Fiddle, Vocals / Traditional Country, Western Swing

Fiddler Wade Ray made his name playing traditional country and Western swing from a very young age but made very few recordings of his own over his lengthy career. Born Lyman Wade Ray in Evansville, IN, in 1913, he grew up in Boynton, AR, and at age four began playing a homemade fiddle his father fashioned from a cigar box. Just a year later, he was touring the vaudeville circuit as the World's Youngest Violin Player; he also learned to play tenor banjo and remained a vaudeville regular until his 18th birthday in 1931. He then moved to St. Louis and spent the next 12 years as the fiddler, singer, and musical director for Pappy Cheshire's Western swing group, the National Champion Hillbillies, until he was called to serve in the Army in 1943. Upon his return, he joined Patsy Montana's group the Prairie Ramblers for several years, also recording with the Ozark Mountain Boys.

He moved to Los Angeles in 1949, where he became a regular on *the Rex Allen Show* and appeared in the film *Hollywood.* He signed with RCA and released a total of 23 singles from 1951 to 1957, none of which charted ("Idaho Red" is perhaps the best known). However, he made a good living performing residencies in Los Angeles and played frequent gigs in various Nevada resort towns; he also appeared regularly on *the Roy Rogers Show* and *the Ernest Tubb Show.* He moved to Nashville and did session work in the mid-'60s and also recorded his first solo album, *A Ray of Country Sun*, for ABC-Paramount in 1966. RCA Camden released *Walk Softly (And Other Country Songs)* later that year, and in 1967 Ray collaborated with the likes of Homer & Jethro, Sonny Osborne, and Hargus "Pig" Robbins on *Down Yonder: The Country Fiddlers.* He continued his session work until 1979, when he retired to Sparta, IL, and performed with a local radio station's road show until health problems made it impossible. He passed away on November 11, 1998. *—Steve Huey*

A Ray of Country Sun / 1966 / ABC/Paramount ♦♦♦

A Ray of Country Sun may be slightly uneven, but it has enough strong moments—"Within Your Crowd," "A Penny for Your Thoughts," "Any Old Arms Won't Do" and "Too Many Rivers" among them—to make it an enjoyable LP. *—Thom Owens*

- **Walk Softly (And Other Country Songs)** / 1966 / RCA Camden ✦✦✦✦✦

Down Yonder: the Country Fiddlers / 1967 / RCA Victor ✦✦✦

Collin Raye (Floyd Collin Wray)

b. Aug. 22, 1959, DeQueen, AR

Vocals / Contemporary Country, New Traditionalist

Contemporary country star Collin Raye burned up the sales charts in the '90s, thanks to a blend of country-rock and smooth balladry, and a willingness to record socially conscious material in between the dance and romance tunes. Raye was actually born Floyd Collin Wray in DeQueen, AR, in 1959, and his mother, Lois, was a locally popular singer who opened concerts for various Sun Records stars in the '50s. She sometimes brought Collin and his older brother Scott on-stage to harmonize with her, and so Collin first performed publicly at the age of seven. As teenagers, he and Scott formed a country-rock outfit called the Wray Brothers Band, and Collin adopted the stage name Bubba Wray. They first played in Texas roadhouses and honky tonks and later found regular gigs in Portland, OR, and Reno, NV; the group also recorded several independent-label singles starting in 1983.

Shortening their name to the Wrays, they signed with Mercury in 1986 and released two singles over the next two years, but nothing came of them, and the group broke up. Raye contemplated leaving music in favor of a factory job that would support his new family but elected to stick it out, changing the spelling of his name and ultimately landing a deal with Epic in 1990. Raye released his debut album, *All I Can Be*, in 1990 and it really took off with the release of the second single, "Love, Me." A tearjerker about the death of a loved one, "Love, Me" zoomed to the top of the country charts in early 1992, becoming a popular funeral song among fans. The follow-up single, "Every Second," went to number two, and *All I Can Be* went platinum—as did its follow-up, 1992's *In This Life*, whose title track became Raye's second number-one hit and a popular wedding ballad. *In This Life* also spun off three additional Top Ten hits in "I Want You Bad (And That Ain't Good)," "That Was a River," and "Somebody Else's Moon."

Raye notched his third straight million-selling album with 1994's harder-rocking *Extremes*, whose number-two hit "Little Rock" was Raye's first big message song, taking on the subject of alcohol abuse. He also hit the Top Ten with "That's My Story," "Man of My Word," and "If I Were You" and landed another number one with "My Kind of Girl." *I Think About You* (1995) returned to his trademark ballad-heavy style and became his fourth platinum album in a row, helped by the Top Five hits "One Boy, One Girl," the anti-domestic-violence title track, the anti-racism "Not That Different," and "On the Verge."

Having cranked out hits for the last four years, Raye relaxed a little bit, issuing only the holiday album *Christmas: The Gift* in 1996 and the compilation *The Best of Collin Raye: Direct Hits* the following year; the latter's newly recorded "What the Heart Wants" and "Little Red Rodeo" both went Top Five. Finally, Raye issued another full album of new material, *The Walls Came Down*, in 1998. "Someone You Used to Know" and "Anyone Else" both made the Top Five, and "I Can Still Feel You" became Raye's fourth number-one hit; the album also contained an anti-child-abuse statement in "The Eleventh Commandment." Perhaps Raye's recent divorce had turned his attention to children even more than usual, for he followed that with an album of lullabies for kids, *Counting Sheep*, in 2000. Later that year, he issued the proper album *Tracks*, which featured the Top Five hit "Couldn't Last a Moment" but didn't produce the usual number of massive singles. The follow-up, 2001's *Can't Back Down*, confirmed that Raye was hitting a sales slump, as it became his first album to miss the country Top Ten. *—Steve Huey*

All I Can Be / Dec. 1990 / Epic ✦✦

Many people compared Raye to Vince Gill, especially since Gill sang harmony on the album's lead track and first single, "All I Can Be (Is a Sweet Memory)." Raye hit the top of the charts with the three-hankie "Love, Me," which his fans sometimes play at funerals. *—Brian Mansfield*

In This Life / Aug. 25, 1992 / Epic ✦✦✦

The soft-focus, yet rugged, album art helps establish Raye as the heartthrob his silky smooth tenor makes him out to be. Inside, it's an even smoother mix than *All I Can Be*, with Raye indulging his tendencies at every turn, including a revival of the Everly Brothers' make-out classic "Let It Be Me." The hit "I Want You Bad (And That Ain't Good)" put some sweat and muscle into Raye's image, but even the trucker song, "Latter Day Cowboy," sounds like it was written for the women back home. The album also includes "In This Life," a number-one hit; "Somebody Else's Moon;" and "That Was a River." *—Brian Mansfield*

Extremes / 1994 / Epic ✦✦✦✦✦

Tired of the balladeer image "Love, Me" and "In This Life" had tagged him with, Raye set out to show that he was made of stronger material. The first single, the rollicking "That's My Story," was a Lee Roy Parnell tune that Raye roared through. *Extremes*, as its title suggested, caromed recklessly from that type of song to, of course, ballads—but "Little Rock," about a recovering alcoholic, and "Dreaming My Dreams With You," earlier cut by Waylon Jennings, were two of the most powerful recordings of Raye's career. *—Brian Mansfield*

I Think About You / 1995 / Epic ✦✦✦✦

After attempting a somewhat rougher approach with *Extremes*, Collin Raye returned to his smooth ballad stylings on *I Think About You*. Though he still sings the occasional honky tonk raver, the high points on his fourth album come when he slows the pace down. *I Think About You* does suffer from a few bland tracks, but the album does demonstrate why Raye was one of the most popular country singers of the mid-'90s. *—Stephen Thomas Erlewine*

Christmas: The Gift / Oct. 29, 1996 / Sony ✦✦✦

Collin Raye's holiday album *Christmas: The Gift* contains the his versions of Christmas classics like "The First Noel," "Silent Night," "Away in a Manger," and "The Christmas Song." Raye delivers all the songs competently and the music is pleasant, yet there is no spark to the album. Only dedicated fans need pick up this *Gift*. *—Thom Owens*

- **The Best of Collin Raye: Direct Hits** / Mar. 11, 1997 / Epic ✦✦✦✦✦

The Best of Collin Raye contains all of the contemporary country singer's biggest hits and best-known songs—including "Every Second," "That Was a River," "Little Rock," "One Boy, One Girl," "Not That Different," and the number-one singles "Love, Me," "In This Life," and "My Kind of Girl"—making it an excellent introduction to the popular vocalist. *—Thom Owens*

The Walls Came Down / Jul. 14, 1998 / Epic ✦✦✦

Collin Raye waited three years to deliver an official studio follow-up to his hit 1995 album *I Think About You*. That record was dominated by ballads, as is its successor, *The Walls Came Down*. Certainly, Raye's smooth country tenor is ideal for country-pop ballads like "In This Life," but he runs the risk of sounding a little too samey, which is what happens on *The Walls Came Down*. There are a number of very good songs here, including the ballad "I Can Still Feel You," but since the record offers no surprises, it winds up sounding a little like a holding pattern instead of a step forward, even with bold message songs like the anti-child abuse "The Eleventh Commandment"—and after three years out of commission, it isn't unreasonable to expect a move forward. Nevertheless, the album is impeccably crafted and Raye's voice sounds as rich and smooth as ever, which makes *The Walls Came Down* a solid record, especially for fans. *—Thom Owens*

Tracks / May 2, 2000 / Epic ✦✦✦

Collin Raye's sixth conventional album continued his mainstream country-pop approach. "I Couldn't Last a Moment," which was on its way to the country Top Ten as the album was released, was a song of romantic regret that was typical of the album as a whole. The music sounded about as country as the Eagles, no more, no less, and Raye himself could have been mistaken for Don Henley in one of his smoother moments. "A Long Way to Go" was another song in which a man confessed his unhappiness at a romantic breakup, while several others expressed romantic devotion; "Landing in Love" concerned new love; "She's All That" was a romantic fantasy full of exaggerated praise of a woman. Taken together, you'd have to say that this was an album of songs aimed at pleasing Raye's female constituency, especially when you added in "Harder Cards," a story song about a patrolman who aids a victim of domestic violence by making her murder of her husband look like suicide, and "She's Gonna Fly," about an aging mother. Raye included the usual number of ballads, varying the formula now and then with an uptempo change of pace such as "A Long Way to Go." "Loving This Way," a breakup duet with Bobbie Eakes, also added diversity. Raye sang earnestly, as usual, but the material, while consistent, never rose above typical Nashville fodder, which kept the album from being anything more than another Collin Raye record, much like his others. Fortunately, that was all anybody expected from him. *—William Ruhlmann*

Love Songs / Sep. 26, 2000 / Sony ✦✦✦

Collin Raye built his career on romantic ballads, and a couple of his most popular ones—"Love, Me" and "In This Life"—are included on this ten-song budget anthology. But for the most part, the compilers have steered clear of Raye's country chart hits, no doubt fearing to cannibalize sales from his full-priced *The Best of Collin Raye: Direct Hits* collection. Instead, he is heard on album tracks that were hits for others, such as "Let It Be Me" (the Everly Brothers) and "Dreaming My Dreams With You" (Waylon Jennings). He has also cut one new cover just for this release, Don McLean's "And I Love You So" (Perry Como). Raye is, as ever, achingly sincere, but this is more a sampler than a real selection of his best love songs. *—William Ruhlmann*

Can't Back Down / Oct. 30, 2001 / Epic ✦✦✦

Since his debut on the charts with 1991's "Love, Me," Raye founded his career with songs that blend social issues with sentiment. *Can't Back Down* is in much the same vein, alternating between broken hearts and perseverance. In this visceral collection, fans will find such timely songs as "Ain't Nobody Gonna Take That From Me," about holding memories, pride, and feelings deep inside our hearts, and "What I Need," about a man who prays for strength, courage, and faith, but gets them by overcoming pain, fear, and emptiness. The tenor vocalist also includes some rhythmic grooves and country-rockers on this fluctuating album. "Gypsy Honeymoon" is reminiscent of "I Think About You," and "Young as We're Ever Gonna Be" is an ode to the fountain of youth. Fans will come to love and appreciate this eighth album, co-produced by James Stroud and Raye himself. *—Maria Konicki Dinoia*

Super Hits / Apr. 30, 2002 / Epic ✦✦✦

16 Biggest Hits / Sep. 24, 2002 / Sony ✦✦✦✦

Susan Raye

b. Oct. 8, 1944, Eugene, OR

Vocals / Traditional Country, Country-Pop, Bakersfield Sound

Best known for her work in conjunction with mentor Buck Owens, singer Susan Raye was born October 8, 1944, in Eugene, OR. She first began singing with a high-school rock group, but after the band called it quits, she auditioned for a local country station. Not only did she begin performing on the radio, she also landed work as a disc jockey, eventually becoming the host of a Portland TV program called *Hoedown*. It was at one of Raye's performances at an area nightclub where she met Jack McFadden, Owens' manager. McFadden was so impressed with her vocal talents that he persuaded Owens to fly her to his home in Bakersfield, CA, for an audition. Owens immediately offered Raye a slot on an upcoming tour, and in 1969, she cut her first record, "Maybe If I Close My Eyes (It'll Go Away)." Her next record, a cover of Jackie DeShannon's pop smash "Put a Little Love in Your Heart," was also her first Top 30 hit. At about the same time, she began a nine-year stint as a featured performer on the program *Hee Haw*.

Raye issued her first solo LP, *One Night Stand*, in 1970; the single "Willy Jones" became her first Top Ten hit, lending its name to the title of her follow-up album the next year. Also in 1970, she released two duet records with Owens, *We're Gonna Get Together* and *The Great White Horse*. Her biggest year as a solo artist came in 1971, when she issued three consecutive Top Ten hits—"L.A. International Airport," "Pitty, Pitty, Patter," and "(I've Got A) Happy Heart." The title track of 1972's *My Heart Has a Mind of Its Own* also reached the Top Ten. After hitting number nine in 1974 with "Whatcha Gonna Do With a Dog Like That" and scoring a success with Owens on a cover of the Mickey & Sylvia classic "Love Is Strange," Raye's hitmaking days were largely over; after issuing the 1976 LP *Honey, Toast and Sunshine*, she left Owens' tutelage to release a self-titled album in 1977. A year later, she retired in order to raise her six kids and returned to college to pursue a degree in psychology. In 1985, she came out of exile to release the album *Susan Raye: There and Back*, which generated the minor hit single "I Just Can't Take the Leaving Anymore." —*Jason Ankeny*

One Night Stand / 1970 / Capitol ✦✦✦

We're Gonna Get Together / Apr. 6, 1970 / Capitol ✦✦✦

Willy Jones / 1971 / Capitol ✦✦✦✦

Pitty, Pitty, Patter / 1971 / Capitol ✦✦✦✦

● **L.A. International Airport: 25 Great Hits** / 1971 / Capitol ✦✦✦✦

Wheel of Fortune / 1972 / Capitol ✦✦✦
Susan Raye's country version of "Wheel of Fortune," a number-one hit for Kay Starr in 1952, dispensed with the original's roulette wheel sound effects and reached the country Top 20 in 1972. That song forms the foundation of the album *Wheel of Fortune*, which contains mostly new material rather than the raft of covers heard on typical country albums of the period (although, to be fair, that practice was on the wane in the '70s). Raye was an artist with Buck Owens Enterprises and recorded several hit duets with Owens, and while none are included on the album, he features heavily on it. The recordings were made at Owens' Bakersfield studio, he wrote (or, in one case, co-wrote) half of the material, and his son, Buddy Alan, contributed the lovely ballad "I've Never Had a Dream Come True Before." In fact, Owens—not Capitol—has retained ownership of Raye's master tapes through the years. Raye's roots in rock & roll seemingly made her a strong candidate to become a crossover country singer but, perhaps due to Owens' influence, she cleaved to an identifiably country sound that is heard most pronouncedly on the banjo accompaniment of "Hide and Watch Me Go." —*Greg Adams*

Love Sure Feels Good in My Heart / 1972 / Capitol ✦✦✦

My Heart Has a Mind of Its Own / 1972 / Capitol ✦✦✦✦

(I've Got A) Happy Heart / 1972 / Capitol ✦✦✦

Cheating Game / 1973 / EMI ✦✦✦
"Cheating Game" was a Top 20 country hit for Susan Raye in 1973 and provided the title for this album from the same year. Raye blended adult pop and country music in a style similar to that of Crystal Gayle, years before Gayle became a big-name entertainer. Evidence of Raye's professional alliance with Buck Owens is all over the album, from the songs written by him and his son, Buddy Alan, to what sounds like uncredited background vocals by Alan on a couple of tracks. Owens had a hand in writing over half of the songs on the album, from his old favorite "Love's Gonna Live Here" to "The Kansas City Song," which he composed with frequent collaborator Red Simpson. Professional associations notwithstanding, the hard country names on the jacket can't be heard in the grooves of this smooth, contemporary-sounding country-pop album. —*Greg Adams*

● **16 Greatest Hits** / Sep. 7, 1999 / Varese ✦✦✦✦
Varese Sarabande's *16 Greatest Hits* is the first CD compilation of Susan Raye's country-pop hits of the early '70s—in fact, it's one of the first compilations of her work in years. *16 Greatest Hits* covers nearly all of Raye's hits, all but one produced by Buck Owens. His trademark Bakersfield sound is apparent throughout the collection, and not only on songs like "One Night Stand," "Willy Jones," and "When You Get Back From Nashville," which he wrote himself. However, Owens gave Raye a distinct pop sheen, taming the barroom beats of Bakersfield with sweet arrangements and gentle rhythms. This is perfect for Raye's sugary voice, which simply wouldn't have sounded convincing in Owens' normal, stripped-down sound. Raye's singles were of varying quality, yet even the weaker tunes sounded good thanks to the production and her fine performances. They were among the better country-pop of the early '70s that didn't come out of Nashville or was produced by Billy Sherrill or Owen Bradley, and *16 Greatest Hits* is the definitive collection of them. —*Stephen Thomas Erlewine*

The Red Clay Ramblers

f. Chapel Hill, NC
Group / Neo-Traditional Folk, Old-Timey, String Bands
One of the most authentic of the string band revival groups, the Red Clay Ramblers performed traditional Appalachian folk music and contemporary compositions, and mixed genres with such talent and authority that for years they were considered among the best of the modern revivalists of string band music. The Chapel Hill, North Carolina-based quintet included Tommy Thompson (banjo, vocals), Jim Watson (guitar, mandolin, vocals), Mike Craver (piano, harmonium, vocals), Jack Herrick (bouzouki, guitar, harmonica, bass, cello, flute, harmonium, vocals) and Clay Buckner (fiddle, harmonica, vocals). The Ramblers reached their widest audience through their work scoring and performing in off-Broadway productions; one of their most highly acclaimed albums was their score from Sam Shepard's *A Lie of the Mind*. —*David Vinopal and Sandra Brennan*

The Red Clay Ramblers / 1972 / Smithsonian Folkways ✦✦✦✦

Stolen Love / 1976 / Flying Fish ✦✦✦✦
Some listeners may prefer this group's later albums, which are more ambitious and stake out greater expansions of stylistic territory. This was their second venture, basically recorded live although not in front of an audience, and is one of the best examples of their mastery of the straight-ahead down-home music idiom. This was a smaller version of the group, without a regular bassist. In the quartet version the group still had quite a full sound, able to pull off enjoyable versions of Irish pieces and smooth things out here with a fairly moving ballad or a shape-note hymn. Things get off to an immediate kick with a version of "Yellow Rose of Texas" that is influenced greatly by the fiddle playing of Tommy Jarrell, the original melody tucked neatly away behind ornamentation and reharmonizing. Nicely warmed up, original Red Clay Ramblers fiddler Bill Hicks then presents a superb version of the standard "Big Sciota." This track at least has something in common with later Ramblers epistles, in which the earthy fiddling of this player would be used to recapture the listener after the group had perhaps strayed a bit too far from their home ground. "Abe's Retreat" shows the entire group's instrumental versatility, with Tommy Thompson reinforcing the cyclical rhythm with just the right snap. Other highlights include a lovely "Wind and Rain," a funny cover of a sometimes controversial Blind Alfred Reed song, and a climactic version of the fiddle workhorse "Forked Deer." The group recorded the tracks in the media center at the Duke University campus, playing together in live takes. It is a marvelous production, capturing the group's sound in a way which sometimes eluded them as subsequent productions became more complex. In the manner of their mentors in the New Lost City Ramblers, the liner notes credit the original performers of each of these pieces. —*Eugene Chadbourne*

Twisted Laurel / 1977 / Flying Fish ✦✦✦✦
Standing at a crossroads of old-timey music and the kind of progressive thought patterns and creativity that emerge in college towns such as the band's home base of Chapel Hill, the Red Clay Ramblers created a discography that is as much about making records as it is making music. The two biggest influences on this project seem to be the culturally rich results of pioneer recording efforts in American music in the '20s and '30s and the much later explosion of musical creativity in the '60s, when every garage band got to make a big artistic statement. As much as *Twisted Laurel* would never have been possible without old-time hillbilly music, it also could not exist without the example of albums such as the Band's *Music From Big Pink* or the refined album efforts of John Prine. It is a meticulously crafted piece of work which, if anything, could use a bit more looseness and edge in its occasional stuffy moments. Sometimes the good-timey numbers will prompt a listener to turn the volume down; it can be just too much hyper energy, despite the brilliance of the recorded sound. Yet the band seems to know when to pull back, following up the overdone pseudo-swing of "The Corrugated Lady" with a marvelous solo vocal and fiddle *tour de force* by Bill Hicks. The instrumental numbers such as "Flying Cloud Cotillon" are masterful, the piano playing of Mike Craver an absolute delight. The recording date is listed as 1967 on some copies of the album; however, be assured that even the nervous Flying Fish label wouldn't have waited nearly a decade to release this. —*Eugene Chadbourne*

Merchants Lunch / 1977 / Flying Fish ✦✦✦✦
The first track establishes the ground rules for this record featuring the classic lineup of the Red Clay Ramblers, with both pianist Mike Craver and the superb fiddler Bill Hicks. "Merchant's Lunch" is one of several originals that banjoist and vocalist Tommy Thompson either wrote or co-wrote for the project, and these songs reveal a deepening of the group's repertoire. For old-time music fanatics, this might have been the cause of discomfort, but it certainly can be said that the group created a terrific blend of its different material for this baker's dozen of tracks. Listeners looking for old-time numbers that kick up a rumpus will be able to dig right into "Molly Put the Kettle On" and Uncle Dave Macon's outrageous "Rabbit in the Pea Patch," although in the latter case the Red Clay Ramblers push a good thing by folding in too-cute diggi-diggi-di vocals of the sort Doug Kershaw used to come up with. The album is a luscious studio recording, with the fiddle tune medley on the second side one of the best-sounding tracks of this sort the group has ever recorded. The blend of mandolin, banjo, fiddle, bass, and piano is as rich as the aroma of a simmering stew that has had the benefit of a gourmet cook sprinkling spices into it. Group vocals are another aspect that shine on this production. "I've Got Plans" is an ambitious Thompson ballad that gets a nicely relaxed treatment, its profound effect on the flow of music providing a good example of the treasury this group had going in terms of repertoire. "Henhouse Blues" begins with exciting clawhammer banjo, followed by expert fiddle and mandolin solos. Many listeners will be up dancing even before the vocal comes in. In other words, a typical moment with the Red Clay Ramblers. Only the final track, a Fats Waller cover, doesn't come off as much more than a perfumed whiff of this master stylist, not much better than the efforts swing revival groups a few decades later. —*Eugene Chadbourne*

Chuckin' the Frizz / 1979 / Flying Fish ✦✦✦✦✦
When asked to name a favorite Red Clay Ramblers album, fans of the long-running North Carolina string band inevitably seem to pick this live album, recorded over three days in a home away from home, Chapel Hill's Cat's Cradle club. This was back in the days when this club was a small, intimate listening room with an adjoining, glassed-in bar and not the bowling-alley size venue it eventually evolved into. It is pretty easy to see why this record would be a favorite. It captures what is without question the best lineup of this group, and this is not to disparage other members nor to question why talents such as Bill Hicks and Mike Craver would have moved on to solo careers eventually. Having them all together here in such a happy live setting is a real treat. Yet this isn't simply the equal of any cassette machine that might have gotten clicked on during any Red Clay Ramblers gig during this period. This is a superbly produced set with a superior recorded sound, fully capturing the rich overtones in the blend of stringed instruments

and piano. Craver has never sounded better, and neither has Tommy Thompson, whose voice and banjo playing are adept and gorgeous. His ballad "Hot Buttered Rum" is wonderful, and this moving performance is one of the Red Clay Ramblers' best recorded moments. There is plenty of their snappy traditional string band material, tempos brisk and unfaltering—there is no weak link in this band messing up the tempos in a live setting. There are also some complicated originals that really demonstrate the versatility of the players, as well as suggesting a rehearsal schedule stained in blood and sweat. To play Craver's song "Thoroughly African Man" with all its twists and turns live and have it come out with so few glitcheroonies is quite an accomplishment. That said, it must be admitted that there are listeners who don't really like this side of the band's material, despite the fact that its roots in old-time music forms are just as valid. Nonetheless, it might be an acquired taste. This is not the case for "Aragon Mill," a tremendously powerful protest songs by Charlotte's Sy Kahn, representing another superb choice in material, or a Bill Boyd cover that swings like crazy. Yes, this is the ultimate Red Clay Ramblers souvenir, the cover art featuring two examples of the photographic medium's ability to completely capture the personality of an entire band, frozen in time and attitude. —*Eugene Chadbourne*

Hard Times / 1981 / Flying Fish ✦✦✦
Falling just a bit short of being one of this group's best, this album presents the Red Clay Ramblers of North Carolina in transition between what had been a classic lineup of players and the changing process of the group's later years, in which, one by one, these original members would drop out to either pursue solo careers or for health reasons. Fiddler Bill Hicks was the guy on the way out the door here, and still was enough of a bandmember to contribute fiddling on a few of the tracks. His replacement Clay Buckner gets his face on a Red Clay Ramblers album cover for the first time here. A great fiddle player, Buckner surely changed the political balance in the group as it dealt with the conflicts between old-time music and the new music being written by pianist Mike Craver and pianist Tommy Thompson. Buckner knows his way around the old-time fiddle repertoire, but also seemed to be one of the first members of this group to step forward when any mission was proposed that would take the band out of the Appalachian hills. When the influence of songwriters such as Stephan Foster and George Gershwin are taken into account, a Craver tune such as "Matinee Idol" might serve to expand a listener's concept of the Red Clay Ramblers from being simply an old-time revival outfit to something like masters in the overall field of musical Americana. But that's only if one likes the song or this type of material, and if that is not the case the album will completely crawl to a hault like a British taxi cab in the traffic situation known as "choc-a-bloc." Thompson gets things going again with the hilarious "The Face in the Mirror," which makes use of everything the band is good at, beginning with beautifully recorded old-time picking and continuing with bits of swing and Craver's pretty music hall-style obligatto. Uncle Dave Macon's "Chicken" gets the raunchy treatment it deserves, no surprise, but the lovely version of "The Wind and the Rain" is a really impressive deepening of the group's ability to project the combination of sentimentality and sadism that makes old-time music so enduring. The Irish material gets an extra boost by the guest shot from Triona Di Dhomhnail on bodhran. —*Eugene Chadbourne*

It Ain't Right / 1986 / Flying Fish ✦✦✦
It Ain't Right is an ambitious record, demonstrating the Red Clay Rambler's ability to meld all sorts of string band music, from celtic to folk, adding elements of folk and pop to the mixture. The album is augmented by cameos from trombonist Chris Frank and an occasional rhythm section. —*Thom Owens*

A Lie of the Mind / 1986 / Rykodisc ✦✦
The presence of playwright Sam Shephard must have the same effect on some people that mothballs are supposed to have on moths. Eyes glaze over, backs stiffen, and a sense of being totally uncomfortable sets in. As much as North Carolina's Red Clay Ramblers have expressed enthusiasm for their collaborations with Shephard, the soundtrack recording to his play *A Lie of the Mind* does not display the group at their most relaxed or lively. In fact, the band has been Shephard-ized beyond question. It is all perfectly respectable music, the songwriting drawn not only from the band's usual blend of the traditional and originals, but also including some Lefty Frizzell with a tasty country piano solo from Mike Craver. Most of what the band attempts—honky tonk, serious singer/songwriter material, cornpone rural humor—comes across as if someone had dropped an enormous and sopping wet blanket on top of it. The instrumental medley that closes the first side is an exception; it represents the totally rousing sound of this band at their best, bringing to mind students in a campus pub discovering old-timey music for the first time. "Light Years Away" is also a beautiful ballad, effectively followed by the romping "Cumberland Mountain Deer Chase." Hovering over the old-timey music atmosphere, however, is the Shephard rain cloud. One cringes in apprehension of what kind of awkward, uncomfortable drama is wed to this music. It is an inevitable difficulty for any music group doing a soundtrack album, since the house a group may build for their current family of songs is bound to be more relaxed than the hotel room offered by a playwright using a live music group for dramatic effect. Furthermore, Shepard obviously hopes the rich dramatic content and emotion of the old-timey music or the Skip James blues will rub off on his play. It is not a transaction one should bank on, since the formality of the dramatic process strips away much of this music's intensity. In only one sense is this album a necessary addition to a collection of recordings by this group. That is the excellent little bits of incidental music, much of which gets into interesting areas that these musicians are more than capable of dealing with, but have tended to avoid on their own recordings. Recorded sound is indeed good, but a little too clean overall. —*Eugene Chadbourne*

Far North / 1989 / Sugar Hill ✦✦✦

● **Twisted Laurel/Merchants Lunch** / 1991 / Flying Fish ✦✦✦✦✦
Two of the Red Clay Ramblers' best albums—*Twisted Laurel* (1976) and *Merchant's Lunch* (1977)—are collected on this outstanding two-fer CD. This is the sound of the band coming into its own. —*Thom Owens*

Rambler / 1992 / Sugar Hill ✦✦
Rambler is a latter-day recording by the Red Clay Ramblers, made over 20 years after their formation, but the group shows very few signs of wear and tear. The Ramblers runthrough a number of classic songs—not only bluegrass, but Celtic, gospel, folk, and pop classics, as well. If anything, the diversity of the material and the effortlessness of the group's performance only proves that the Red Clay Ramblers are getting better and more assured with age. —*Thom Owens*

Yonder / Aug. 14, 2001 / WWW.RCR.COM ✦✦✦

Live / Sep. 11, 2001 / WWW.RCR.COM ✦✦✦

Red Dirt Rangers

f. Stillwater, OK
Group / Country-Rock
As their name suggests, alt-country upstarts the Red Dirt Rangers are practitioners of the hard-to-define blend known as "red dirt music" (named for the reddish-brown soil of central Oklahoma and pioneered by folks such as Jimmy LaFave and Bob Childers). The group met at Oklahoma State University in Stillwater, and their country-rock-folk sound can fuse the disparate strands of Texas swing, Woody Guthrie, Bakersfield country, and the Grateful Dead during one performance. The Red Dirt Rangers released their debut, *Red Dirt*, in 1993, and throughout that decade exhaustively crisscrossed their home state. They have also released a children's album, *Blue Shoe*, and have appeared on the compilations *Pastures of Plenty: An Austin Celebration of Woody Guthrie* and *The Songs of Route 66*. With production help from veteran Lloyd Maines, the albums *Oklahoma Territory* and *Ranger's Command* followed in 1996 and 1999, respectively. —*Erik Hage*

Oklahoma Territory / 1996 / Ranger ✦✦✦
This is a band that fits not into any particular genre, but belongs in many. There is very much a country feel to the vocals and harmonies, and the instrumentation (notice the mandolin and pedal steel), yet they know how to rock the place. Listen to the fun they have rocking out on "Be My Baby" and "Dog on a Chain," and then the homage in the love song "Blue Diamond," with its slow honky tonk weepy country pedal steel guitar. They are greatly helped in their effort by the fine production work and clean sound that is typical of Lloyd Maines. This is a fun disc with good harmonies and a bonus track. —*Bob Gottlieb*

Ranger's Command / 1999 / Lazy S.O.B. ✦✦✦
In a just world, every album coming out of Nashville's pop-country hit factories would sound just like *Ranger's Command*. A seamless blend of straight country, honky tonk, Western swing, '70s country-rock, and even Native American sounds, this album seems as if it was made solely for the love of music, yet remains completely accessible. The Red Dirt Rangers' ace musicianship is always in service of the song, so much so that even their Charlie Daniels Band-style cover of Prince's "1999" sounds completely natural. In fact, it's really pretty astounding how many different influences the band manages to incorporate without ever sounding inconsistent; there are bits of everything from Bob Wills and the Band to C.W. McCall and Firefall here, all played with a smooth, tight-but-loose rootsiness that at times recalls Flatt & Scruggs. Special mention should also be made of the Red Dirt Rangers' excellent songwriting, which has all the craft of top Nashville writers, yet is loads more substantive and interesting. —*Pemberton Roach*

● **Starin' Down the Sun** / 2002 / Ranger ✦✦✦✦
Stillwater, OK's, Red Dirt Rangers have long been the banner carriers for the crazy stew that is the Oklahoma sound. Here, the rambling folk melodies of Woody Guthrie; the tough country swing of Bob Wills and Spade Cooley; the shambolic rootsy rock of Bob Dylan; and the freewheeling-fury freakdom of the Grateful Dead all come to roost is a steaming bath of Red Dirt Okie soul. The Rangers get help on this set—recorded in Leon Russell's old studio in Tulsa—from guitarist Terry "Buffalo" Ware and fiddler Byron Berline, to name just two. The solid rock & roll leanings of the Rangers are everywhere in evidence here. The opener, "We Don't Have to Say Goodbye," takes the country sound of Wills and strips it through with Doug Sahm's Tex-Mex border rock and the vocal harmonies of the Everly Brothers on the refrains. Then there's the "I Know You Rider" guitar sprawl of "Kite Fliers" that follows. While all of the Rangers songs, written by the exceptionally talented and good-natured Brad Piccolo, evoke the ghosts of some other musical era or artist, that's what they are supposed to do. Piccolo isn't interested in forging a place on the fringes of American music, but choose to be deeply implanted somewhere in the central roots of its sprawling tree. First and foremost, *Starin' Down the Sun* is a rock & roll album; it comes blazing out of the speakers with both barrels on stun—even on "Good Morning Maryanne," a greasy rocksteady reggae number! "Dwight Twilley's Garage Sale," on which the elusive rocker guests, is a sweet, shimmering country song that offers a catalog of everything in the sale; the lyrics are clever, funny, and bittersweet. "Elvis Loved His Mama" would be a throwaway in any other band's repertoire, but the Rangers turn it into a steaming, wooly rockabilly track with a moral. The disc closes with the gorgeous cowboy-flavored bluegrass of "Each Step You Take," which is a zen dictum on the revelation in everyday life as witnessed by a quartet of cats who should know. And this gorgeous song sums up the Red Dirt Rangers: They claim to be authorities on nothing and no one; they play their music, offer it on recordings and in person, and go about their business of making more. Consequently, this approach, combined with a steadfast dedication to musical excellence is winning them a fan base far outside of their Oklahoma homeland, though they'd keep doing it just the same if it didn't. —*Thom Jurek*

Blind Alfred Reed

b. 1880, Floyd, VA, **d.** Jan. 17, 1956

Fiddle, Vocals / Old-Timey, Traditional Country, Traditional Folk

This West Virginia singer/songwriter and fiddler was one of Ralph Peer's discoveries on the legendary 1927 Bristol field trip that unearthed both the Carter Family and Jimmie Rodgers. Reed was one of those uniquely Southern contradictions, both reactionary and progressive in his songs. "How Can a Poor Man Stand Such Times and Live?" echoed the sentiments of the rural poor (who tasted none of the Roaring Twenties prosperity), while "Why Do You Bob Your Hair, Girls?" invoked Biblical sanctions against flappers. Topical commentary of this sort was rare in early hillbilly recordings: Reed's contemporaries usually pruned a branch from the folk tree or swiped a page from Mom's Victorian songbook. Incongruously, Reed was a protest singer/songwriter out of time and place. Ry Cooder revived a couple of his songs in the '70s, the decade of Rounder's reissue of several Reed performances, *How Can a Poor Man Stand Such Times and Live? — Mark A. Humphrey*

● **How Can a Poor Man Stand Such Times and Live?** / 1920 / Rounder ✦✦✦✦✦

How Can a Poor Man Stand Such Times and Live? is '20s hillbilly social commentary, both reactionary ("Why Do You Bob Your Hair, Girls?") and progressive ("How Can a Poor Man Stand Such Times and Live?") from this West Virginia singer and fiddler. It's austere and engaging. *—Mark A. Humphrey*

Complete Recorded Works / Mar. 2, 1998 / Document ✦✦✦✦

Jerry Reed (Jerry Reed Hubbard)

b. Mar. 20, 1937, Atlanta, GA

Guitar, Vocals, Session Musician / Traditional Country, Progressive Country, Country-Pop, Rockabilly, Instrumental Country

Known throughout country music as "The Guitar Man," singer/songwriter Jerry Reed gained recognition not only for a successful solo career but also as an actor and ace session player. Jerry Reed Hubbard was born in Atlanta, GA, on March 20, 1937; after picking up the guitar as a child, he was signed by publisher and producer Bill Lowery to cut his first record, "If the Good Lord's Willing and the Creeks Don't Rise," at the age of 18. He continued releasing both country and rockabilly singles to little notice until rocker Gene Vincent covered his "Crazy Legs" in 1958.

After a two-year tenure in the military, Reed moved to Nashville in 1961 to continue his songwriting career, which had continued to gather steam even as he was in the armed forces thanks to Brenda Lee's 1960 cover of his "That's All You Got to Do." He also became a popular session and tour guitarist. In 1962, he scored some success with the singles "Goodnight Irene" and "Hully Gully Guitar," which found their way to Chet Atkins, who produced Reed's 1965 "If I Don't Live Up to It." In 1967, he notched his first chart hit with "Guitar Man," which Elvis Presley soon covered. After Presley recorded another of Reed's songs, "U.S. Male," the songwriter recorded an Elvis tribute, "Tupelo Mississippi Flash," which proved to be his first Top 20 hit.

After releasing the 1970 crossover hit "Amos Moses," a hybrid of rock, country and Cajun styles, Reed teamed with Atkins for the duet LP *Me & Jerry*. During the 1970 television season, he was a regular on *the Glen Campbell Goodtime Hour*, and in 1971 issued his biggest hit, the chart-topper "When You're Hot, You're Hot," which was also the title track of his first solo album. A second collaboration with Atkins, *Me & Chet*, followed in 1972, as did a series of Top 40 singles, which alternated between frenetic, straightforward country offerings and more pop-flavored, countrypolitan material. A year later, he scored his second number one, "Lord, Mr. Ford." In the mid-'70s, Reed's recording career began to take a backseat to his acting aspirations, and in 1974, he co-starred with his close friend Burt Reynolds in the film *W.W. and the Dixie Dancekings*. While he continued to record throughout the decade, his greatest visibility was as a motion picture star, almost always in tandem with headliner Reynolds; after 1976's *Gator*, Reed appeared in 1978's *High Ballin'* and 1979's *Hot Stuff*. He also co-starred in all three of the *Smokey and the Bandit* films; the first, which premiered in 1977, landed Reed a number two hit with the soundtrack's "East Bound and Down."

In 1979, he released a record comprised of both vocal and instrumental selections titled, appropriately enough, *Half Singin' & Half Pickin'*. It was followed a year later by *Jerry Reed Sings Jim Croce*, a tribute to the late singer/songwriter. In 1982, Reed's career as a singles artist was revitalized by the chart-topping novelty hit "She Got the Goldmine (I Got the Shaft)," followed by "The Bird," which peaked at number two. His last chart hit, "I'm a Slave," appeared in 1983. After an unsuccessful 1986 LP, *Lookin' at You*, Reed focused on touring until 1992, when he and Atkins reunited for the album *Sneakin' Around* before he again returned to the road. *—Jason Ankeny*

The Unbelievable Guitar and Voice of Jerry Reed / 1967 / RCA ✦✦✦✦✦

Nashville Underground / 1968 / RCA ✦✦✦✦✦

Alabama Wild Man / 1968 / RCA ✦✦✦✦

Actor, singer, and guitar man Jerry Reed blurred the line between country and pop music from the late '60s through the '70s while occasionally throwing in the odd novelty record for good measure. Released in 1968, *Alabama Wild Man* was one of the earliest examples of his crossover appeal. Reed played what he liked, had a good-time doing it, and made records strictly to entertain. However, that didn't mean he was creating one-dimensional music, proven here by the contemplative lyrics of "Today Is Mine" and "Losing Your Love," the Jimmy Reed-inspired instrumental "Twelve Bar Midnight," and the autobiographical title track featuring punchy boogaloo horns with country pickin'. As a side note, the addition of Reed's laid-back version of the Monkees' hit "Last Train to Clarksville" was recorded three decades before Cassandra Wilson would do the same for the song in the jazz world in 1995. *—Al Campbell*

Jerry Reed Explores Guitar Country / 1969 / RCA ✦✦✦✦

Jerry Reed Explores Guitar Country is an overlooked 1969 concept album that updated traditional folk and country tunes with modern pop-country arrangements. Classics like

"St. James Infirmary," "Blue Moon of Kentucky," "In the Pines," and "John Hardy" were assembled utilizing unconventional combinations of organ, banjo, congas, and jazz guitar. Much of the exploratory credit goes to the pop-country hybrid production mastery of Chet Atkins. *Jerry Reed Explores Guitar Country* is quietly influential in helping to map out the area where many alternative country artists now reside. [*Explores Guitar Country* is available with *Alabama Wild Man* on a One Way two-fer CD.] *—Al Campbell*

Better Things in Life / 1969 / RCA ✦✦✦

Cookin' / 1970 / RCA ✦✦✦

Cookin' was Jerry Reed's sixth RCA album, released in 1970 just prior to his first hit, "Amos Moses." While this disc doesn't include any hits, it is a good showcase for his stylistic dynamics, mixing country ("Just to Satisfy You"), crossover pop ("How Many Tomorrows"), and his guitar prowess (the instrumental "Gomyeyonyo"). All in all, *Cookin'* is a solid Jerry Reed disc. *—Al Campbell*

Ko-Ko-Joe / 1971 / RCA ✦✦

A largely eclectic and overproduced work, *Ko-Ko-Joe* isn't a great Jerry Reed album. From the loose Creedence Clearwater Revival meets the Charlie Daniels Band boogie of the title cut, to the countrified Tom Jones-like quality of the more pop-oriented "You'll Never Walk Alone" and "A Stranger to Me," the set lacks consistency. A four-minute mock anti-smoking dialogue, which appears to be more of a comedy piece than anything, is followed by a dead-serious cover of Gordon Lightfoot's "Early Morning Rain." Anthemic pop songs, straight country, and more blues-oriented songs are also included, making this a rather confusing and difficult listen. *—Matt Fink*

Me & Jerry / 1971 / RCA ✦✦✦✦

Me & Jerry is the first of Jerry Reed's collaborations with mentor and label mate Chet Atkins. While Reed would usually include an instrumental or two on his early RCA albums (after all, he was "the Guitar Man"), it was risky to release an exclusively instrumental disc, especially coming off the success of his previous set, *Georgia Sunshine*. The risk was worth it, as the fans responded positively to these two friends kickin' back and having fun making music together. Both *Me & Jerry* and the follow-up, *Me & Chet*, hold up well, and collectors of Chet Atkins especially should seek out these good-natured sessions. *—Al Campbell*

When You're Hot You're Hot / 1971 / RCA ✦✦✦✦

The release of "When You're Hot, You're Hot" found Jerry Reed topping the charts for the first time in 1971. Reed's early albums were consistently good as a whole, in part because of Reed's refusal to be anything but eclectic. Occasionally this skewed defiance manifested itself through an odd choice of pop-oriented cover versions, in this case, Lennon and McCartney's "Thank You Girl" and Bob Dylan's "Don't Think Twice It's All Right." The highlights of the album include his second hit, "Amos Moses," the instrumental "Turned On," and "Ruby Don't Take Your Love to Town," which sounds tailor-made to his delivery. *—Al Campbell*

I'm Movin' On / 1971 / Harmony ✦✦

Following the years he spent dabbling in rockabilly on Capitol in the '50s, but before he found fame as a guitarist and recording personality on RCA, Jerry Reed recorded for Columbia. The two or three years he spent on the label were transitional ones during which he began recording guitar instrumentals (very different from his later "claw"-style exhibitions) and experimenting with a wide variety of styles. Reed placed a couple of minor hits on the pop charts during his Columbia years, but neither of those hits are included on *I'm Movin' On*, a budget reissue containing nine of Reed's Columbia recordings. "Love and War" and "Too Old to Cut the Mustard" are nascent examples of the novelty approach that Reed later perfected, and the latter also shows early evidence of his propensity for drastically reworking well-known material. "I'm Movin' On" is presented as a rock-oriented instrumental and "Hit and Run" is a grisly song of tragedy very unlike anything he recorded before or after. This is fascinating stuff, but only for devoted fans. *—Greg Adams*

Me & Chet / 1972 / RCA ✦✦✦✦

The second time around, with the names reversed, Jerry Reed and Chet Atkins turn in another brilliant session of instrumental guitar interplay. This time, most of the songs are country tunes, and both include originals, with Reed's leadoff track, "Jerry's Breakdown," giving the pickers a chance for a display of speed, while his "Good Stuff" is slow and swampy. The highlight may be a spirited take on "Mystery Train," but there isn't a bad track, as the two pickers trade licks gleefully, sparking each other. *—William Ruhlmann*

Smell the Flowers / 1972 / RCA ✦✦✦

With the release of Jerry Reed's ninth RCA album, *Smell the Flowers*, his material was beginning to suffer and sound forced. For someone who had previously shown a talent for a variety of different, yet appropriate, material for his audience, it lacked Reed's personal touch. The only thread here is the overall good-natured "isn't it great to be alive!" theme that dominated the album with songs like "Don't Get Heavy," "Smell the Flowers," "Don't Let the Good Life Pass You By," and "Pave Your Way into Tomorrow." While no hit singles were generated from this 1972 album, it is interesting that the following year Mac Davis had the chart-topping "Stop and Smell the Roses," which sounded an awful lot like "Smell the Flowers." *—Al Campbell*

Hot A' Mighty / 1973 / RCA ✦✦✦✦✦

Hot A' Mighty is one of Jerry Reed's finest records—which means it's also one of his most fun. Featuring the smash single "You Took the Ramblin' Out of Me," it also contains a number of other stunners. The opener, Leadbelly's "Goodnight Irene," is such an item. Funked up, pickin' savvy, and greasy as hell, Leadbelly would have been proud of this white boy tearing it up like this while remaining sensitive to the song's original meaning. The chorus of backing vocalists gives it a real Muscle Shoals feel, too. There's a live medley of Chuck Berry tunes here that would normally seem like a way to fill an album but not for Reed, who worships Chuck. Reed is deeply moved by Berry's poetry and lays it out like the prophetic street life stuff it is. And of course there's Reed's picking, but he sticks close to Chuck's text rather than use his own funky style. He roars through portions of five tunes, including "The Promised Land," "Maybellene," "Johnny B. Goode," "School Day," and "Memphis Tennessee"—not in that order. Reed's version of "Sweet Memories" is from outer space for him in that it is such a straight-laced honky tonk version, but his deep baritone pulls off the tune. The single is pure country-funk, rollicking from front to back with popping guitar strings that sound like an electric banjo. And then there's Tennessee Ernie Ford's "Sixteen Tons," which has been radically reinvented to be a guitar jam-cum-funky soul tune, and Reed pulls it off without a hitch. Forget Tom Jones' version; this one tears it up. [*Hot A' Mighty* is available on CD as part of a two-fer with *Lord, Mr. Ford.* It's highly recommended.] —*Thom Jurek*

Lord, Mr. Ford / 1973 / RCA ✦✦✦✦✦
Lord, Mr. Ford is a fairly typical Jerry Reed album, which is to say it's filled with jaw-dropping guitar playing, excellent songs, and warm, rugged vocal performances. As usual, Reed alternates between countrypolitan ballads which showcase his smooth baritone vocal style and the ultra-funky swamp pop hybrid that he virtually created. Of course, those who know Reed's music well understand that he is equally at home with both these genres; his unwillingness to be pigeonholed has always at once somewhat limited his mainstream appeal and won him the undying devotion of a particularly loyal core fan base. The big hit here was the title track, a semi-political song written by the great hippie country songwriter Dick Feller. Reed's version is appropriately crotchety considering the song's "simple working man" theme, but it's amusing to hear notorious bad boy Reed forced to substitute the word "trick" for the original version's "bitch." The vocalist completely reinvents the Johnny Cash standard "Folsom Prison Blues" by employing an intensely rhythmic, New York City-style disco beat (several years before that craze hit), complete with Latin percussion. To top it off, Reed rips into a *Discipline*-era Robert Fripp-esque repeating guitar figure that sounds almost exactly like an African thumb piano. In addition, the album contains two of Jerry Reed's most beautiful guitar instrumentals and "One Sweet Reason," (another Feller composition), which features one of his most sensitive vocal performances. Overall, though Jerry Reed doesn't offer a lot of surprises here considering his always-varied output, *Lord, Mr. Ford* stands as one of the high points of his catalog and is a must-have for anyone interested in left-of-center country music. —*Pemberton Roach*

The Uptown Poker Club / 1973 / RCA ✦✦✦

The Best of Jerry Reed / 1973 / RCA ✦✦✦
The Best of Jerry Reed was the first compilation released by the Guitar Man's record label, RCA, in 1973. While the early hits are here—"When You're Hot, You're Hot," "Amos Moses," and "Georgia Sunshine"—it doesn't include anything post-1973, like "East Bound and Down," "The Bird," or "She Got the Goldmine (I Got the Shaft)." The better purchase is *RCA Country Legends: Jerry Reed*, released in 2001. —*Al Campbell*

Tupelo Mississippi Flash / 1974 / RCA Camden ✦✦✦✦✦

A Good Woman's Love / 1974 / RCA ✦✦✦

Paper Roses / 1974 / RCA ✦✦✦

Live at Exit Inn / 1974 / RCA ✦✦✦

Mind Your Love / 1975 / RCA ✦✦✦

Red Hot Picker / 1975 / RCA ✦✦✦

Jerry Reed in Concert / 1975 / RCA ✦✦✦

Alabama Woman / 1976 / RCA ✦✦✦

Both Barrels / 1976 / RCA ✦✦

East Bound & Down / 1977 / RCA ✦✦
Cobbled together to capitalize on the success of *Smokey and the Bandit*, *East Bound & Down* contains three of Jerry Reed's contributions to the soundtrack of that film along with odds and ends from previous albums. The title track is the big attraction, being a number two country hit and an infectious trucking song, while the other two soundtrack cuts are ephemeral and corny. The remaining tracks offer a little of everything, from a Coasters cover ("Framed") to a Bob Dylan cover ("Don't Think Twice, It's All Right") to the sappy "Rainbow Ride." *East Bound & Down* might be an adequate stand-in for the *Smokey and the Bandit* soundtrack for those fans who are only interested in Reed's contributions, but it is otherwise a shoddy piece of make-do product. —*Greg Adams*

Jerry Reed Rides Again / 1977 / RCA ✦✦✦
When Jerry Reed cut the 1977 album *Jerry Reed Rides Again*, he could have had no idea that after three years of minor hits, he would soon be riding high with "East Bound and Down," his contribution to the *Smokey & the Bandit* soundtrack. That commercial triumph was still months away when the two singles from *Jerry Reed Rides Again* met their comparatively lesser fates: the slick "Semolita" barely cracked the Top 20 and the novelty "With His Pants in His Hands" stalled well below the Top 40. The album is a typically fine effort, though, with superior material tucked away between the so-so hits. "(I'm Just A) Redneck in a Rock and Roll Bar" later became the flip side of "East Bound and Down," and the boastful "The Phantom of the Opry" is a more clever novelty than "With His Pants in His Hands." "The Bully of the Town" is one of Reed's trademark reinterpretations of classic material and another of many highlights on this strong album. —*Greg Adams*

Sweet Love Feelings / 1978 / RCA ✦✦✦

Reedology / 1978 / RCA ✦✦✦

Half Singin' & Half Pickin' / 1979 / RCA ✦✦✦
Half Singin' & Half Pickin' is split evenly between Reed's vocal performances and his instrumental guitar workouts. —*Jason Ankeny*

Jerry Reed Sings Jim Croce / 1980 / RCA ✦✦✦

Texas Bound and Flyin' / 1980 / RCA ✦✦✦✦

Dixie Dreams / 1981 / RCA ✦✦✦

The Bird / 1982 / RCA ✦✦✦
The last of Jerry Reed's major hits are included on *The Bird*, an album that encompasses his usually variety of novelties, love songs, and uniquely slick, funky country. His remake of Creedence Clearwater Revival's "Down on the Corner" falls into the the latter category, while "She Got the Goldmine (I Got the Shaft)" is a quintessential Jerry Reed novelty and his final number-one hit. "The Bird" was also a substantial hit and features decent impressions of Willie Nelson and George Jones, and "I'm a Slave"—sort of a sequel to his "Another Puff" from 1972—gave Reed his final Top 100 charter. When Jerry Reed is hot, he's hot, and despite some lesser moments, about half of *The Bird* really smokes. —*Greg Adams*

☆ **The Man With the Golden Thumb** / 1982 / RCA ✦✦✦✦✦
Though producer Rick Hall was infamous for producing Mac Davis' *Forty 82* debacle, possibly the worst album recorded in the history of country music, Jerry Reed and RCA retained him for *The Man With the Golden Thumb*. And it turned out exceptionally well. And while the title track is as much a novelty tune as Charlie Daniels' "The Devil Went Down to Georgia," which it resembles in some ways, it works and, over 20 years later, still sounds fresh and new, and the reason is simply that Reed is that man. There are few guitar players with more grit, grease, soul, and humor. Only Tony Joe White can be considered his peer in terms of pure musical talent, iconoclastic originality, and who-gives-a-damn guts. This is in many ways the soul album Reed always wanted to make. Recorded at Muscle Shoals with Johnny Sandlin in the engineer's chair, it's got the sound of R&B drenched through and through, from "Love Is Muddy Water," with Reed singing like Sam Moore. So take the rest of side one: There's "Shu Doo Pa Poo Pop, I Love Being Your Fool," with its Otis Redding phrasing and stinging guitars behind a pumping bass and B-3. Then, let it slip into the slow soul of "The Best I Ever Had" as sung by a fine country singer and end it with a thoroughly reverential and deeply felt reading of the Memphis R&B classic "Patches," the big hit by Clarence Carter, and you can go home satisfied. But there's more. Side two kicks it with "She Got the Goldmine (I Got the Shaft)." Then there's the funky-fried Dixie craziness of "44" and the Dan Penn-Spooner Oldham wrencher "It Tears Me Up." There are a couple of other cuts too, but you get the idea. This disc is a classic, and it's up to you to go and get your mind blown listening to it. —*Thom Jurek*

Ready / 1983 / RCA ✦✦✦

● **The Essential Jerry Reed** / Aug. 1, 1995 / RCA ✦✦✦✦✦
The Essential Jerry Reed contians over 20 of the singer/songwriter's greatest hits, from "Amos Moses" to "East Bound and Down," hitting the number ones "When You're Hot, You're Hot," "Lord, Mr. Ford," and "She Got the Goldmine (I Got the Shaft)." In addition to the hits, there's a handful of obscurities, but it remains the best single overview of Reed's career. —*Thom Owens*

Guitar Man / 1997 / Camden ✦✦✦✦✦
Guitar Man is a 22-song U.K. import that consists mainly of album tracks from the late '60s through the early '80s, as opposed to hit singles. There are a few hits in the mix, including "Amos Moses," "When You're Hot, You're Hot," and Jerry Reed's 1983 cover of Creedence Clearwater Revival's "Down on the Corner," but listeners in search of a greatest-hits package should look elsewhere. That said, *Guitar Man* offers a more balanced view of Reed's music than the *Essential* disc, since there is less of a focus on his novelty hits and a broader sampling of the ballads, instrumentals, and otherwise serious material that made up a large portion of his catalog. For fans, the real appeal of this set is the wealth of material that is otherwise difficult—if not impossible—to find on CD, including versions of "500 Miles Away From Home," "Sixteen Tons," and "The Devil Went Down to Georgia," which Reed recasts as a guitar duel with the devil. —*Greg Adams*

Super Hits / Jun. 3, 1997 / RCA ✦✦✦
Super Hits is a fine budget-price collection of Jerry Reed's biggest hits from the late '70s, including "When' You're Hot, You're Hot," "Lord, Mr. Ford," "(I Love You) What Can I Say," "The Bird," "East Bound and Down," and "She Got the Goldmine (I Got the Shaft)." —*Thom Owens*

When You're Hot, You're Hot/Ko-Ko-Joe / Jul. 1, 1997 / Collectables ✦✦✦
Sometimes appearing in listings under the title *Golden Classics Edition*, this two-fer collects two early-'70s albums by Jerry Reed, including the hits "When You're Hot, You're Hot," "Ko-Ko-Joe," "Another Puff," and "Lord, Mr. Ford." These are all available on BMG's *Essential Jerry Reed* disc, but what makes this package so appealing are the album tracks, which give a better indication of the breadth of Reed's talents than does the *Essential* collection. Reed's version of Dylan's "Don't Think Twice It's All Right" and John Loudermilk's should-have-been-a-hit "Big Daddy" feature some great guitar pickin', and his talents as a balladeer are demonstrated on several tracks, including his own "She Understands Me." Also present are the standard covers of others' hits, which might be regarded as filler if not for the novelty of Reed's unique style; The Coasters' "Framed" gets a humorous reading while he plays it straight on Gordon Lightfoot's "Early Morning Rain" and the Mel Tillis-penned "Ruby, Don't Take Your Love to Town." While not every track is a keeper, there is plenty of quality material here to enjoy. —*Greg Adams*

Pickin' / Feb. 16, 1999 / Southern Tracks ✦✦✦
This 1998 session finds the fingerpicking and songwriting joking genius producing himself along with help from Thom Bresh and Randy Goodman on a tune each. The album finds him running through ten funky and patented Reed grooves, playing his nylon string for the majority of the tunes, switching to electric for "Reed's Rag," "Talk the & Walk the Walk," and "Case of the Blues." It's a disc that holds up well with his best RCA hits. —*Cub Koda*

Here I Am / Sep. 15, 1999 / Bear Family ✦✦✦✦

Many fans of Jerry Reed may not realize that his recording career began in the mid-'50s when, as a teen, he signed to Capitol records. *Here I Am* collects his complete recordings for Capitol (30 songs), most of which were originals. "If the Good Lord's Willing and the Creek Don't Rise" was later covered by Johnny Cash during his tenure at Sun, and a few of the other tracks here occasionally surface on rockabilly compilations, but many of these recordings have been unavailable since they were originally waxed (and a few are previously unreleased). Reed's music at this stage was stylistically varied, from rockabilly to honky tonk to teen pop, and he had yet to develop the unique fingerpicking style that characterized his later recordings. Although the quality of the material is inconsistent, *Here I Am* chronicles the earliest phase of an important artist's career. Fans of Reed as well as those with a broad interest in rockabilly and '50s pop and country will likely enjoy this set. *—Greg Adams*

Alabama Wild Man/Jerry Reed Explores Guitar Country / May 9, 2000 / One Way ✦✦✦✦

One Way blessed Jerry Reed fans with five two-fers in 2000, each containing a pair of his RCA albums from the late '60s and early '70s. The introductory installment reissues *Alabama Wild Man* and *Jerry Reed Explores Guitar Country*, the first of which yielded a minor hit (twice) in the title track and gave the Georgia-born Reed an evocative but inaccurate nickname. The album tracks include several of Reed's fine ballads, one of many country versions of "Last Train to Clarksville," and a laid-back instrumental, "Twelve Bar Midnight." The only novelty besides the title track is "Broken Heart Attack," which humorously incorporates medical terminology. *Jerry Reed Explores Guitar Country* is one of Reed's best albums, a mostly vocal effort that strips away the horns and chorus to concentrate on his idiosyncratic fingerpicking style. The traditional songs in the set are transformed by Reed's hyperactive guitar and busy percussion tracks, resulting in a truly original sound. "Bluegrass (With Guts)" and "Swarmin'" add a banjo to the mix, and "Are You From Dixie (Cause I'm From Dixie Too)" receives an energetic, electrified reading that nearly reached the country Top Ten. Reed's blend of instrumental virtuosity, an irreverent approach to country tradition, and a wild sense of fun make for a delightful listening experience. *—Greg Adams*

Better Things in Life/Cookin' / May 9, 2000 / One Way ✦✦✦

The two albums collected on this CD were made before Jerry Reed began his run of popular novelty hits in the early '70s, but his comedy persona was already well-formed: the raunchy cover of Nat Stuckey's "Plastic Saddle" and camp reading of "Alabama Jubilee" are cases in point. The lazy funk of "Oh What a Woman!" gave Reed a minor hit, and "I'm a Happy Man" is one in a long line of originals that suggests that Reed is a genuinely contented guy. "Aunt Maudie's Fun Garden" and "The Semi-Great-Predictor" are products of their time; the latter in particular, with its sitar and vocal effects, sounds like the Monkees. Overall, *Cookin'* is an unusual, experimental album, while *Better Things in Life*, with the exception of "Johnny Wants to Be a Star" (essentially another "Guitar Man") and the jaunty, tack piano number "There's Better Things in Life," leans toward ballads. Some of the most unusual items in Reed's catalog are here, but relatively few showcases for his guitar playing. *—Greg Adams*

Georgia Sunshine/Oh, What a Woman! / May 9, 2000 / One Way ✦✦✦

"Amos Moses" was a turning point in Jerry Reed's career—it was his first gold record and a major crossover hit that set the tone for his subsequent hits. From then on, certain stylistic trademarks—novelty material, country-funk rhythms, his cackling laugh, and frequent exclamations of "son!"—became so strongly associated with Reed's name that they often eclipsed his reputation as a guitarist and his talent as a writer and singer of ballads. *Georgia Sunshine* shows the many faces of Jerry Reed, from "Amos Moses" and the similarly styled "The Preacher and the Bear" to the easy-swinging hit "Georgia Sunshine" and pop ballad "Dream Sweet Dreams About Me." Reed's guitar-based renditions of "Mule Skinner Blues" and "Eight More Miles to Louisville" are highlights that hearken back to the sound of his *Jerry Reed Explores Guitar Country* album. *Oh, What a Woman!* is a brief budget compilation that reprises the hit title track and "Roving Gambler" from the album *Better Things in Life*, along with the 1967 hit "Guitar Man" and album tracks from the late '60s. *Georgia Sunshine* is a fine effort, but it's too bad it wasn't paired with another original album for this reissue. *—Greg Adams*

Smell the Flowers/Jerry Reed / Jul. 25, 2000 / One Way ✦✦✦

Smell the Flowers/Jerry Reed pairs two early-'70s albums on one CD. Following a string of novelty singles, "Smell the Flowers" was a completely straight and characteristically upbeat Jerry Reed original that made the country Top 25 in 1972. Reed wrote nearly half the songs on the album of the same name, which is a mostly serious affair that spotlights Reed's pop side. Like Roy Clark, Reed is a phenomenal country guitar picker with a pop streak, and "If I Ever (Love Again)" mines the same easy listening territory that gave Clark crossover success with "Yesterday (When I Was Young)." "My Guitar and My Song" has a "Gentle on My Mind" vibe, while "It Ain't Home, but It Ain't Bad" and "Take It Easy (On Your Mind)" provide a little of the funky attitude that sells Reed's novelty songs. The self-titled album has Reed's re-recording of "Alabama Wild Man," which nearly reached the Top 20 four years after the original made a minor dent in the charts. This album offers a more typical program with plenty of uptempo songs, from the wah-wah guitar workout of "Almost Crazy" to a drastic reworking of "Misery Loves Company," a Reed original that was a number one hit for Porter Wagoner in 1962. *Jerry Reed* is quite varied and, though it lacks a guitar instrumental, offers a little of everything he does. *—Greg Adams*

Hot A' Mighty/Lord, Mr. Ford / Jul. 25, 2000 / One Way ✦✦✦✦

The two albums from 1972-1973 that appear on this CD are notable for the many remakes of standards and well-known country hits, which are often among the most enjoyable items in Jerry Reed's repertoire because of the way he radically reinterprets familiar material. Reed's rendition of "Sixteen Tons" on *Hot A' Mighty* is even funkier than Tom Jones' version, while "Goodnight Irene" and Mitchell Torok's "Caribbean" become

springboards for some inventive guitar picking. "I Just Don't Understand" sticks close to the arrangement of Ann-Margret's version, and "You Took the Ramblin' Out of Me" became the album's hit. The highlight is a live (or live-sounding) Chuck Berry medley that really rocks, while illuminating the similarities between the two artists' guitar-driven story-songs. The title track of *Lord, Mr. Ford* gave Reed a number one hit, but "Rainbow Ride" is its polar opposite—an example of the syrupy pop Reed cranked out at regular intervals. Enthusiasts of his guitar playing will appreciate the instrumentals "Two-Timin'" and "Pickie, Pickie, Pickie." Despite a few weak spots, this is one of the strongest discs in One Way's Jerry Reed reissue series. *—Greg Adams*

★ **RCA Country Legends** / Feb. 20, 2001 / Buddha ✦✦✦✦✦

Buddha's *RCA Country Legends* may miss a hit or two, but it winds up being the closest thing to a definitive Jerry Reed retrospective assembled in the CD era. The key is, while it samples liberally from his goofy (yet surprisingly tough) hits of the early '70s, it has its foundation in his '60s recordings, and follows that musical direction through his hit-making peak to the classic *Smokey & the Bandit* theme, "East Bound and Down." Yes, some may wish that it leaned a little heavier on the late-'70s recordings, but for hardcore country listeners, this is the compilation to get. *—Stephen Thomas Erlewine*

Del Reeves (Franklin Delano Reeves)

b. Jul. 14, 1933, Sparta, NC

Songwriter, Vocals, Guitar / Traditional Country, Nashville Sound/Countrypolitan, Truck Driving Country

Del Reeves enjoyed a run of success on the country charts during the latter half of the '60s, often penning his own material as well. He was born Franklin Delano Reeves in Sparta, NC, in 1933; the youngest of 11 children, he learned guitar by borrowing his brothers' instruments while they were serving in World War II. He was a local radio star by age 12 and later attended Appalachian State College and served in the Air Force, which led to a relocation to Sacramento. There he became a regular on *the Chester Smith Show* from 1958-1961, after which he moved to Nashville and began recording for Decca (his first chart single was 1961's "Be Quiet Mind"). He and his wife also became a professional songwriting team, contributing material to Carl Smith, Rose Maddox, Roy Drusky, and Sheb Wooley. Short stints at Reprise and Columbia preceded Reeves' signing with United Artists, where he landed his first number-one hit, "Girl on a Billboard," in 1965. Its follow-up, "The Belles of Southern Bell," made the Top Five, and "Women Do Funny Things to Me" reached the Top Ten in early 1966.

Three more songs—"Looking at the World Through a Windshield," "Be Glad," and his signature tune, "Good Time Charlie's"—made the Top Five over 1968-1969, and he cut a series of duets with Bobby Goldsboro and Penny DeHaven over the next several years. He also returned to the screen, hosting *Del Reeves' Country Carnival* on television and appearing in several feature films during the late '60s. His last big Top Ten hit came with 1971's "The Philadelphia Fillies," but he continued to record for United Artists through the '70s, cutting some more duets with Billie Jo Spears in 1976. He departed in 1979 and later became a music executive, playing a role in the signing of Billy Ray Cyrus. *—Steve Huey*

Del Reeves Sings Girl on the Billboard / 1965 / United Artists ✦✦✦

Del Reeves Sings Jim Reeves / 1966 / United Artists ✦✦✦

Santa's Boy / 1966 / United Artists ✦✦

Gettin' Any Feed for Your Chickens? / 1966 / United Artists ✦✦✦

Special Delivery / 1966 / United Artists ✦✦✦

Songwriter Hank Mills wrote Del Reeves' number one country hit "Girl on the Billboard," as well as later hits for other artists like Jim Ed Brown ("Angel's Sunday") and Robert Mitchum ("Little Ole Wine Drinker Me"). Since Reeves enjoyed so much success with one of Mills' songs, he turned to the writer for nearly half of the material on his 1966 album *Special Delivery*, including the album's single, "One Bum Town." Unfortunately, the plan was a bust, and "One Bum Town" broke Reeves' streak of major hits. The album has a number of notable tracks, however, including Mills' anachronistic historical song about Christopher Columbus, "Voyage of Ole Chris," and Larry Kingston's wordplay novelty "Wood Would." The country standard "Make the World Go Away" is incongruously thrust into the middle of these quirky songs to show that Reeves can play it straight. The weak sales of *Special Delivery* must have been a disappointment for Reeves, but it's an entertaining if obscure album. *—Greg Adams*

Struttin' My Stuff / 1967 / United Artists ✦✦✦

Six of One, Half-A-Dozen of the Other / 1967 / United Artists ✦✦✦

The Little Church in the Dell / 1967 / United Artists ✦✦

The Best of Del Reeves / 1967 / United Artists ✦✦✦✦✦

The Best of Del Reeves, Vol. 2 / 1970 / United Artists ✦✦✦✦✦

Baby I Love You / 1987 / Bear Family ✦✦✦✦✦

● **His Greatest Hits** / Sep. 15, 1994 / Razor & Tie ✦✦✦✦✦

Although brief (under 30 minutes), *His Greatest Hits* has been the only readily available collection of Del Reeves' '60s and '70s hits for United Artists, including his best-known song "Girl on the Billboard." Ten of the 12 songs on this collection made the country Top 20, and the remaining two charted in the lower reaches. More material would have been nice, but *His Greatest Hits* offers the essential tracks and is an otherwise fine anthology. *—Greg Adams*

Goebel Reeves

b. Oct. 9, 1899, Sherman, TX, d. 1969, California

Vocals / Traditional Country, Traditional Folk

Goebel Reeves was a singer/songwriter who eschewed his middle-class upbringing to become a hobo known as "the Texas Drifter" and sometimes as "George Riley, the Yodeling

Rustler"; he penned one of Woody Guthrie's signature tunes, "Hobo's Lullaby" (drawing the melody in turn from a Civil War song, "Just Before the Battle, Mother"), and according to legend and his own claims, he taught Jimmie Rodgers to yodel. They are thought to have traveled and performed together in the early '20s. Reeves was born in Sherman, TX, and grew up in Austin after his father was elected to the Texas state legislature. In 1917, he joined the U.S. Army and while fighting overseas was shot while on the front lines. He was discharged in 1921 and apparently chose to become a vagabond, temporarily earning a living as a singer. He did a stint as a seaman before making his recording debut for OKeh in 1929 and began using the above-mentioned monikers the next year.

Through the 1930s he cut about 35 sides for various labels; they followed the Rodgers mold in their mix of freedom-of-the-road yodeling numbers, comic pieces (such as a mother-in-law-joke parody of "St. James Infirmary"), and sentimental ballads, but Reeves specialized in reflective hobo-philosopher recitations that were quite distinct from Rodgers' hobo pieces. He composed virtually all of his own recorded material. His last recordings were made in 1938 for a radio-transcription company in Hollywood; they were mostly recitations and poems. Occasionally Reeves appeared on radio in both the U.S. and Canada, doing brief stints on the *Rudy Vallee Show*, the *National Barn Dance*, and the *Grand Ole Opry*. Later in the '30s, he returned to his seafaring career and spent time in Japan. During World War II, he entertained U.S. troops and then, because he spoke some Japanese, worked for the U.S. government in Japanese-American internment camps. Reeves died in a veterans' hospital in Long Beach, CA, in 1959. Several LP reissues in the 1970s reintroduced the almost forgotten Reeves to country collectors, and his complete studio recordings were collected on the 1994 Bear Family release *Hobo's Lullaby*. *—Sandra Brennan & James Manheim*

● **Hobo's Lullaby** / 1994 / Bear Family ✦✦✦✦✦

Hobo's Lullaby contains all the studio recordings Goebel Reeves made during his lifetime, including "The Drifter," "The Tramp's Mother," "The Wayward Son," "The Drifter's Buddy (The Drifter's Prayer)," and "When the Clock Struck Seventeen," among 21 other tracks. *—Thom Owens*

Jim Reeves

b. Aug. 20, 1923, Galloway, Panola County, TX, **d.** Jul. 31, 1964, Nashville, TN

Vocals, Guitar / Country-Pop, Nashville Sound/Countrypolitan

Gentleman Jim Reeves was perhaps the biggest male star to emerge from the Nashville sound. His mellow baritone voice and muted velvet orchestration combined to create a sound that echoed around his world and has lasted to this day. Detractors will call the sound country-pop (or plain pop), but none can argue against the large audience that loves this music. Reeves was capable of singing hard country ("Mexican Joe" went to number one in 1953), but he made his greatest impact as a country-pop crooner. From 1955 through 1969, Reeves was consistently in the country and pop charts—an amazing fact in light of his untimely death in an airplane accident in 1964. Not only was he a presence in the American charts, but he became country music's foremost international ambassador and, if anything, was even more popular in Europe and Britain than in his native America. After his death, his fan base didn't diminish at all, and several of his posthumous hits actually outsold his earlier singles; no less than six number-one singles arrived in the three years following his burial. In fact, during the '70s and '80s, he continued to have hits with both unreleased material and electronic duets like "Take Me in Your Arms and Hold Me" with Deborah Allen and "Have You Ever Been Lonely?" with his smooth-singing female counterpart of the plush Nashville sound, Patsy Cline—who also perished in an airplane crash—in 1963. But Reeves' legacy remains with lush country-pop singles like "Four Walls" (1957) and "He'll Have to Go" (1959), which defined both his style and an entire era of country music.

Reeves was born and raised in Galloway, TX, where he was one of nine children. Tragically, his father died when Jim was only ten months old, forcing his mother to farm and raise her family. At the age of five, he was given an old guitar, and shortly afterward, he heard a Jimmie Rodgers record through his older brother. From that moment on, Reeves was entranced by country music and Rodgers in particular. By the time he was 12 years old, he had already appeared on a radio show in Shreveport, LA. Though he was fascinated with music, Reeves also was a talented athlete and during his teens he decided he was going to pursue a career as a baseball player. Winning an athletic scholarship to the University of Texas, Reeves enrolled at the school to study speech and drama, but he dropped out after six weeks to work at the shipyards in Houston. Soon, he had returned to baseball, playing in the semiprofessional leagues before signing with the St. Louis Cardinals in 1944. He stayed with the team for three years before seriously injuring his ankle and thereby ruining his chances of a prolonged athletic career.

For the next few years, Reeves went through a number of blue-collar jobs while trying to decide on a profession. During this time he began singing as an amateur, appearing both as a solo artist and as the frontman for Moon Mullican's band. In 1949, Reeves cut a number of songs for the small independent Macy label, none of which were particularly successful. In the early '50s, Reeves decided that he would make broadcasting his vocation, initially working for KSIG in Gladewater, TX, before establishing himself at KGRI in Henderson. Over the next few years, Reeves was a disc jockey and newscaster at KGRI, moving to KWKH in Shreveport, LA, in November of 1952, becoming host of the popular *Louisiana Hayride*. Late in 1952, Hank Williams failed to make an appearance on the show, and Reeves sang in his place. His performance was enthusiastically received, and Abbott Records immediately signed him to a record contract. "Mexican Joe" was Reeves' debut single for Abbott, and it quickly climbed to number one in the spring of 1953, spending nine weeks at the top of the charts. It was followed by another number-one hit, "Bimbo," later in 1953, establishing that Reeves was not a one-hit wonder; later that same year, he was made a full-time member of the *Louisiana Hayride*. During 1954 and 1955, he had four other hit singles for Abbott and its parent company, Fabor, before RCA signed him to a long-term deal in 1955; that same year, he joined the *Grand Ole Opry*. At RCA, Reeves began to develop the distinctively smooth, lush, and pop-oriented style of country that made him a superstar and earned him the nickname Gentleman Jim. Peaking at number four, "Yonder Comes a Sucker" was his first Top Ten hit for RCA in the summer of 1955. It kicked off a remarkable streak of 40 hit singles, most of which charted in the Top Ten. Many of his singles also became pop crossovers, which indicates exactly how much of a pop influence there was on his music. Indeed, Reeves' vocal style derived from the crooning of Frank Sinatra and Bing Crosby, and early in his career he abandoned cowboy outfits for upscale suits. In the process, he brought country music to a new, urban audience.

Throughout the '50s and early '60s, Reeves racked up a number of major hits and country classics like "Four Walls" (number one for eight weeks, 1957), "Anna Marie" (1958), "Blue Boy" (number two, 1958), "Billy Bayou" (number one for five weeks, 1959), "He'll Have to Go" (number one for 14 weeks, 1960), "Adios Amigo" (number two, 1962), "Welcome to My World" (number two, 1964), and "I Guess I'm Crazy" (number one for seven weeks, 1964). "Four Walls" was the turning point in his career, proving to both Reeves himself and his producer, Chet Atkins, that his main source of success would come from ballads. As a result, Reeves became an even bigger star, not only in America but throughout the world. Reeves toured Europe and South Africa, building a strong following in countries that rarely had been open to country music in the past.

Reeves was at the height of his career when his private plane crashed outside of Nashville on July 31, 1964. The bodies of Reeves and his manager, Dean Manuel, were found two days later and were buried in his homestead of Texas. Though Reeves had died, his popularity did not vanish—in fact, his sales increased following his death. Throughout the late '60s, RCA released a series of posthumous singles, many of which—including "This Is It" (1965), "Is It Really Over?" (1965), "Distant Drums" (1966), and "I Won't Come in While He's There" (1967)—hit number one. The previously unissued songs were frequently mixed in with previously released material on album releases, making his catalog confusing but profitable for RCA. The flow of unreleased Reeves material did not cease during the '70s or '80s—in fact, there wasn't a year between 1970 and 1984 when there wasn't a Reeves single in the charts, either at the top or in the lower regions. Reeves was inducted into the Country Music Hall of Fame in 1967, and two years later, the Academy of Country Music instituted the Jim Reeves Memorial Award. Though the flood of unreleased material ceased in the mid-'80s, the cult surrounding Reeves never declined, and in the '90s, Bear Family released *Welcome to My World*, a 16-disc box set containing his entire recorded works. *—David Vinopal*

Bimbo / 1957 / RCA ✦✦✦✦✦

He'll Have to Go & Other Hits / 1960 / RCA ✦✦✦✦✦

There may have been other country crooners as smooth, but no one else in his era had the hand-in-glove marriage of great songs and appropriate "countrypolitan" production. This brief collection doesn't contain all of his biggest hits, but the most essential singles—"He'll Have to Go," "Four Walls," Billy Bayou," and "Anna Marie," among others—are included. *—Mark A. Humphrey*

The Country Side of Jim Reeves / 1962 / Pair ✦✦✦✦

The second side begins with a song entitled "Most of the Time." There is the usual flawless Chet Atkins-produced setup, and then comes a voice, a man who sounds so smooth and totally in control, and he sings "I just burned the picture of you that was on my wall." The contrast between the helpless emotion of the lyrics and the image of a crooner such as Jim Reeves makes for a classic country & western moment. When they call this album *The Country Side*, the label implies more of a country direction than some of the Reeves country-pop material. In point of fact Reeves may never be country enough for some listeners, but there is definitely some genre-specific content, including piercing pedal steel licks sopping wet with reverb and echo, and some excellent songs, including the artist's own "Yonder Comes a Sucker." As a country singer, though, he is a crooner, make no mistake. Every "o" he pronounces comes out "oooh." *—Eugene Chadbourne*

We Thank Thee / 1962 / RCA ✦✦✦

We Thank Thee is an inspirational album Jim Reeves released in 1962. Though it is pleasant—Reeves' voice is in good shape and the country-pop productions sound nice—nothing on the album particularly stands out, yet it is nice record for dedicated Reeves fans. The compact disc reissue includes four bonus tracks: "An Evening Prayer," "Treach Me How to Pray," "How Long Has It Been," and "The Padre of Old San Antone." *—Thom Owens*

Have I Told You Lately That I Love You? / 1964 / RCA Camden ✦✦✦

The album that was in the charts when Jim Reeves' plane went down on July 31, 1964, *Have I Told You Lately That I Love You?* is a solid slice of relatively pure country, largely free of the "countrypolitan" strings and choirs that were coming into fashion by 1964 and which would usually be dubbed onto Reeves' posthumous hits for the rest of the '60s and well into the following decade. Three hits are included: the title track (one of Reeves' very best weepers), "Your Old Love Letters," and "Each Time You Leave." The highlight among the album tracks is an absolutely terrific, faithful rendition of Woody Guthrie's "The Oklahoma Hills," proof that Reeves had deeper folk and pure country roots than many of his contemporaries. *—Stewart Mason*

Kimberley Jim / 1964 / Soundies ✦✦✦✦

Kimberly Jim is the soundtrack to the film in which Jim Reeves starred shortly before his death. The music runs the gamut, from rousing Broadway-style show tunes with a vocal chorus to a version of "Roving Gambler" that is one of the best and most country-sounding recordings of Reeves' late career. Other selections, including "Kimberly Jim" and "I Grew Up," are big-band vocal numbers that demonstate Reeves' versatility, and perhaps give further evidence of his continual drift toward the pop end of the spectrum. In fact, this music prompts the question as to whether *Kimberly Jim* is an anomaly or an indication that Reeves might have become a pure pop or easy listening vocalist had he lived. The songs on this collection don't crop up on greatest-hits packages, which makes *Kimberly Jim* an interesting oddity for those who wish to explore Reeves' catalog in greater depth. *—Greg Adams*

The Jim Reeves Way / 1965 / RCA ✦✦✦

Released in 1965, *The Jim Reeves Way* is a strong reminder of Reeves' classic "Nashville Sound," with the standards "Make the World Go Away" and "I Can't Stop Loving You" beside more obscure tracks like "There's That Smile Again" and "A Nickel Piece of Candy." The beautiful ballad "Maureen" is included as well. Reeves was very popular in South Africa and the rarities "Bolandse Nooientjie" and "Ek Verlang Na Jou," which are sung completely in Afrikaans, are included. It's somewhere during those two tracks that the listener, unless fluent in Afrikaans, realizes that Reeves could sing random syllables and it would still sound great. —*Matt Fink*

Distant Drums / 1966 / RCA ✦✦✦
Distant Drums produced several hit singles for Jim Reeves, including the title track, "Is It Really Over?," "This Is It," "Losing Your Love," "I Missed Me," and "Overnight." —*Steve Huey*

Greatest Hits: Jim Reeves & Patsy Cline / 1966 / RCA ✦✦
This album includes a duet made up by recording engineers after the deaths of both artists, plus individual recordings of some of their best songs. —*AMG*

The Legendary Jim Reeves / 1986 / RCA Special Products/Heartland ✦✦✦✦✦
For the classic country music fan that is not concerned with extensive documentation, deep minutiae such as track release dates, the albums certain songs came from or extensive biographical details, Australia's wing of RCA has issued a series of "*Legendary*" releases for many of the biggest stars in its vaults. This three-CD collection of the work of Jim Reeves is one stellar example. Priced to move (a triple disc for the price of a little more than a single), a punter can get virtually every one of Reeves' hits for the label in one package, as well as a few surprises. Here are 50 tracks, compiled according to aesthetic rather than strict chronology, that give a well-rounded portrait of the man who changed the face of country music with his golden mellifluous baritone. For those familiar with Reeves, everything you could ever want is here: "Welcome to My World," "Is It Really Over," "The Followers, the Sunset, the Trees," "Am I Losing You," "Partners," "Blue Side of Lonesome," "I Guess I'm, Crazy," "There's a Heartache Following Me," "Anna Marie," and many more. The story it tells is how in developing his vocal style, and reaching out to embrace the popular music of the era, Reeves—and RCA president Chet Atkins—brought country music itself into the mainstream, and, in doing so, insured its future with millions of Americans, as well as spreading Reeves' appeal all over the globe. Without incurring the expense of a Bear Family box set or getting ripped off for a single disc with as much obscure as familiar material, this is literally the best a consumer can do when it comes to getting a solid portrait of the voice, Jim Reeves. —*Thom Jurek*

Live at the Opry / 1987 / Country Music Foundation ✦✦✦
While it may seem strange that a live album offers a nearly complete introduction to an artist as important as Jim Reeves, *Live at the Opry* fits that bill. A compilation of radio performances recorded at the *Grand Ole Opry* between 1953 and 1960, the music on *Live at the Opry* is uniformly excellent, demonstrating Reeves' talent for country-pop as well as his command of a live audience. Most of his biggest hits are here, as well as a handful of unfamiliar numbers, and all are delivered with style by either his backing band Blue Boys or an *Opry* pick-up band. For both dedicated fans and neophytes, there's plenty to treasure on *Live at the Opry*. —*Thom Owens*

Gentleman Jim: 1955–1959 / 1989 / Bear Family ✦✦✦✦✦
This four-disc set, which contains 110 tracks, has Reeves' first ventures into pop as well as some of his best country performances of such favorites as "Am I Losing You?," "Just Call Me Lonesome," "According to My Heart," and others. A discography accompanies the set. —*AMG*

☆ **Four Walls: The Legend Begins** / Aug. 1991 / RCA ✦✦✦✦✦
Four Walls—The Legend Begins collects 20 songs Jim Reeves recorded between 1953 and 1957, including his earliest hits, "Mexican Joe," "Bimbo," "According to My Heart" and "My Lips Are Sealed." —*Stephen Thomas Erlewine*

The Very Best of Jim Reeves, Vol. 2 / Sep. 23, 1991 / BMG International ✦✦✦

★ **Welcome to My World: The Essential Jim Reeves Collection** / Mar. 1993 / RCA ✦✦✦✦✦
Welcome to My World: The Essential Jim Reeves Collection is a double-disc box set that offers an overview of his entire career, even if its balance is a bit uneven. Beginning with his early '50s hit, the box runs through most of his biggest hits, concentrating on his smooth countrypolitan '60s hits. Though fans of his early honky tonk material will feel that side of Reeves is overlooked, *Welcome to My World* is the best overall Reeves retrospective available. —*Stephen Thomas Erlewine*

★ **The Essential Jim Reeves** / Aug. 1, 1995 / RCA ✦✦✦✦✦
The Essential Jim Reeves runs through 20 of Reeves' biggest hits, throwing a couple of rarities along the way. It's by no means definitive, but it offers a good introduction to his countrypolitan sound. —*Stephen Thomas Erlewine*

The Intimate Jim Reeves / 1996 / BMG ✦✦✦
As the title indicates, *The Intimate Jim Reeves* emphasizes the ballad stylings of the countrypolitan singer, highlighted by the hit single "I'm Gettin' Better." Like most of Reeves studio albums, it suffers from an uneven selection of material, but his performance is smooth and convincing, as is the stylish production. Together, they make the album an enjoyable listen, even if its appeal is limited to dedicated Reeves fans. [The CD reissue includes four bonus tracks, including the hits "I Missed Me" and "Am I Losing You."] —*Stephen Thomas Erlewine*

Welcome to My World / 1996 / Bear Family ✦✦✦✦✦
This massive collection by the German Bear Family label is the most intimidatingly thorough collection of Jim Reeves' work. Basically, it's virtually everything from his recording sessions, and there are two separate boxes of his radio transcriptions besides! But this one is unwieldy enough—it's 16 CDs covering all of Reeves' recordings from his earliest in 1949 for the Macy label to his move to Abbott in 1952, including ten unissued alternate takes and rejected masters, a single side issued by Fabor, and then back to Abbott. These sides make up the first two discs of the collection and offer what most

folks have never heard in Reeves—his hillbilly records that reflect a beautiful fusion of the Western swing, honky tonk and cowboy traditions; Reeves' songwriting was also in full flower at this early period in Texas. The early crooning style that hinted at his later pop recordings came in the latter period of his association with Abbott. These songs are all revelatory in that they reveal without doubt what it was RCA heard in Reeves and why he stood out: His relaxed, smooth full-throated baritone delivery transcended country & western music. Beginning with disc three and going all the way though disc 13 are Reeves' complete recordings for RCA. The earliest of them are still very much in the country and Western swing tradition, but in the production the sound is a bit more lush, where the instruments begin to balance with Reeves' honeyed delivery. The fiddles play more like strings and so does the pedal steel. "I'm Hurtin' Inside" slips along without seam or stitch, and is a perfect example of where Reeves would go with his style. And it didn't take him long to get there. By the time Reeves recorded "Am I Losing You" in 1956, the mature ballad style was already in his voice, and producer Chet Atkins was aware of where it could go; still, it would be the recording of "Four Walls" in 1957 that the real transition was in full swing. And 1957 was a big year. The Jordanaires and Floyd Cramer became integral to the Reeves sound and the roots of countrypolitan were dug. They would begin to sprout on "Everywhere You Go," from that same year, which was as much Nat King Cole as it was Reeves: a brushed jazzy four on the drums, Cramer comping with beautiful—if a tad rigid—jazz chords, and the Jordanaires singing a near scat chorus behind Reeves. By December, with "I Love to Say I Love You" with the Anita Kerr Singers backing him, the transition was complete. The story is well-known from here beginning on the fifth disc; Reeves' prolific output as the king of country crooners was already evidenced by his chart success internationally. Even after the Beatles changed everything in 1963, Reeves was charting in England. From "He'll Have to Go" to "Welcome to My World" to "Missing You" and "Maureen," his last two sides before dying in a plane crash, it's all here. There's an entire disc dedicated to the (in)famous charted overdub recordings from 1966 and 1967, as well as two discs of demo recordings—59 tracks in all—that make this set not only a definitive document, but a testament to a legacy of genius, both Reeves and Atkins. As per usual, there is a full-size book with an authoritative essay by Colin Escott, exhaustive discographical documentation, and pages upon pages of photographs. Only fanatics will want it, but if you are one, you will not be disappointed. —*Thom Jurek*

Best of the Best of Jim Reeves / Jan. 6, 1998 / Koch ✦✦✦✦
There are more extensive Jim Reeves collections available than *Best of the Best of Jim Reeves*, but it does make a nice, budget-priced introductory sampler. —*Steve Huey*

Radio Days, Vol. 1 / Jan. 26, 1999 / Bear Family ✦✦✦✦✦
If you are a country music fan, especially classic country music fan, than you no doubt have a strong opinion on Jim Reeves. He's either the Caruso of the genre or a pop sellout who brought about the ruin of the original, raw honky tonk music, along with Chet Atkins, in favor of the countrypolitan sound. For those in the latter group, one listen to these radio transcriptions will change your mind forever. They were recorded for a show called "Country Music Time" for the U.S. Air Force over a period of a decade or so. These shows have long been buried in the Reeves vault, and were released to the folks at Bear Family by Mary Reeves, Jim's widow. Here's the rub: most of the tunes here will be well known to Reeves fans. There are classics such as "Am I Losing You," "Yonder Comes a Sucker," "Evening Prayer," "Have I Told You Lately That I Love You," "Four Walls," "Blue Boy," "Til the End of the World," and dozens of others. But there are also songs that even fans don't associate with Reeves that make their debuts here, many of them not on his recordings. The stunningly beautiful version of Woody Guthrie's "Oklahoma Hills" is one, and also his versions of Jimmy Rodgers' tunes, like "Waitin' for a Train," and Leon Payne's "Pride Comes Before a Fall." There are often two or three versions of a single tune like "Am I Losing You" or Roger Miller's "Billy Bayou," and two of "Evening Prayer." But in the different versions, recorded over the years, what becomes readily apparent is the change in Reeves' singing style—it become a gorgeous strolling country baritone that effortlessly glides from one place to the next without jumping for a note. These latter performances are deeply moving for their range and diversity, but also for their considerable soulfulness. Another myth the box dispels is that Reeves was a studio construct. All of these sessions were recorded live, with cats who weren't usually part of his regular band. Literally, these shows were made with Nashville session men learning the music on the fly, or performers who were familiar with it from some other source. Live Reeves is devastating in his originality and in his ability to communicate even the corniest lyric, such as Fred Rose's "Roly Poly." And on the ballads that were later layered in syrup by Atkins on studio recordings, such as "Anna Marie," and "Am I Losing You?," Reeves reaches deep into his gut for the right inflection to make the song authentic. Also, on "He'll Have to Go" and "Making Believe," the artist, according to Johnny Cash, had the servicemen silent and on the edge of their seats. Here too, these performances may just be the definitive recorded ones. An added bonus to the Reeves performances is the appearance of special guests on the radio programs, such as the Louvin Brothers, Atkins, Jean Shepard, Wanda Jones (singing the hell out of Tompall Glaser's "You're Making a Fool out of Me"), pedal steel giant Del Wood, Tommy Jackson, Archie Campbell, and many others, including, of course, the Blue Boys. Given that the song repetition isn't a nuisance—and it cannot be stressed enough what a boon it actually is—the only sticking point on the set is the continued use of the intro and outro of the theme to mark each new show. This does indeed get old, hearing the traditional "Beaumont Rag" throughout the set. That's what a remote control is for, however, and the skip button becomes a handy tool. But this is a small annoyance when the listener gets nearly 100 stellar Reeves performances, a couple of handfuls of other rare country classics, priceless documentation by Larry Jordan, and a slew of photographs on four pristinely mastered CDs. —*Thom Jurek*

★ **Singles: 1953–1960** / May 2, 2000 / BMG International ✦✦✦✦✦
Jim Reeves helped to popularize the Nashville sound, which brought a decidedly pop influence to country music. Reeves chalked up numerous hits for RCA using this formula, and 40 of those tracks recorded between 1953-1960 are included on this two-disc compilation from BMG. Like Marty Robbins, Jim Reeves was a favorite among both hardcore country fans and pop listeners alike due to quality singles such as "Mexican Joe," "Bimbo," "Four Walls," "Billy Bayou," "He'll Have to Go," and "Am I Losing You." This compilation is highly recommended, especially if you're just getting familiar with Gentleman Jim Reeves. —*Al Campbell*

The Unreleased Hits of Jim Reeves / Jun. 27, 2000 / Soundies ✦✦✦
Between 1967 and 1975, Jim Reeves' widow collaborated with Harold Bradley, Chet Atkins, and others to overdub new instrumental arrangements over existing studio and demo recordings Reeves made in the '50s and '60s. The idea was to perpetuate Reeves' posthumous career with a steady stream of potential "new" hits, but these 13 overdubs remained in the vaults until now. While it's hard to get overly excited about a batch of overdubs, some of which were recorded more than a decade after Reeves' vocal tracks were made, the new arrangements were directed by talented people and skillfully applied. Reeves sounds great as always, and a few of the tracks (the historical folk song "Ballad of '96," the countrified "Sand in My Shoes") are pretty interesting. Certainly listeners who followed Reeves enough to invest in Bear Family's mammoth *Welcome to My World* box set will want to augment their collections with this curious artifact. —*Greg Adams*

Legendary / Sep. 5, 2000 / BMG International ✦✦✦✦
Radio Days, Vol. 2 / Jun. 12, 2001 / Bear Family ✦✦✦✦
Greatest Hits / Aug. 28, 2001 / BMG International ✦✦✦✦✦
RCA Country Legends / Feb. 19, 2002 / RCA ✦✦✦✦
As part of RCA's *Country Legends* series, this set highlights country-pop crooner Jim Reeves' biggest hits from the late '50s to the early '60s. Among the 16 tracks are the number one singles "Mexican Joe," "Bimbo," "Four Walls," "Billy Bayou," "He'll Have to Go," and "I Guess I'm Crazy." This collection serves as an excellent career overview. —*Al Campbell*

Ronna Reeves

b. Sep. 21, 1958, Big Spring, TX
Vocals / Contemporary Country
Singer/songwriter Ronna Reeves spent most of her life in the music industry and was one of the more promising female singers to emerge in the 1990s. She was raised in Big Spring, TX, and began singing along with the radio and phonograph at age six. She won the Little Miss Big Spring competition at age eight; the judges' enthusiastic reaction to her singing in the show's talent segment inspired her parents to take her to a local guitar/fiddle teacher to evaluate her abilities, and he ended up adding Reeves to his band. By age 11, she had her own group, which played in Fort Worth nightclubs. There she met Ron and Joy Cotton, two promoters working out of Waco. A few years later, when she was 17, the Cottons invited her to open for his client George Strait, a gig she performed for the next 18 months. She went on to open for Ronnie Milsap, Randy Travis, Garth Brooks, the Judds, and Reba McEntire, among others. Her 1991 debut album, *Only the Heart*, was released with little notice. Her second album, *The More I Learn*, produced three minor hits, including "The More I Learn (The Less I Understand About Love)." *What Comes Naturally* (1992), although receiving critical praise, failed to produce any chart hits.

Reeves returned in 1995 with a new label (River North Records) and a new album, *After the Dance*. Her exposure had also been raised, thanks to a chance touring and recording turn with adult contemporary crooner Peter Cetera. That same year, she and Cetera scored a minor hit with a soft-focus cover of the ABBA hit "S.O.S." (The song appeared on Cetera's 1995 album *One Clear Voice*.) The collaboration proved to be fruitful, as Cetera helmed the production of Reeves' next album, 1998's *Day 14*. Instead of country, the album was a collection of straight-ahead rock and pop. Unfortunately, the album's promotion was delayed when Reeves was diagnosed with cancer in early 2002. The vocalist opted out of her River North contract, underwent chemotherapy, and tried to concentrate on writing songs. —*Johnny Loftus*

Only the Heart / 1991 / Mercury ✦✦✦
Only the Heart includes Reeves' cover of Ernie Ashworth's "Talk Back Trembling Lips," as well as contributions from noted Nashville songwriters like Dickey Lee and Bob McDill. —*Jason Ankeny*

● **The More I Learn** / 1992 / Mercury ✦✦✦✦✦
Reeves' second effort features "There's Love on the Line," her duet with Sammy Kershaw. —*Jason Ankeny*

What Comes Naturally / Dec. 1992 / Mercury ✦✦✦
Ronna Reeves / Nov. 7, 1995 / River North Nashville ✦✦✦
Rednex became an international sensation with their campy country-disco stomp "Cotton Eye Joe," a stupid, silly European view of American white trash culture. It was certainly a fun, guilty pleasure, but that can't be said for the rest of the album. *Sex & Violins* is filled with songs that sound like "Cotton Eye Joe" but not as infectious, funny, or catchy. For fans of the manic Euro-dance sound, it might provide some thrills, but most listeners will find the record tedious. —*Stephen Thomas Erlewine*

After the Dance / Nov. 7, 1995 / Polygram ✦✦✦✦
Like its predecessors, *After the Dance* is a well-crafted and rootsy album of modern country, that displays just a bit too much grit for contemporary country radio and too much polish for fans of alternative-country. Which means, *After the Dance* never found the audience it deserves. It may suffer from a couple of undistinguished songs, but Reeves' voice

is powerful and graceful throughout the album, giving weight even to the weaker material. *After the Dance* is not a perfect album, yet it demonstrates that Ronna Reeves should have a bigger audience than she does. —*Thom Owens*

Mike Reid

b. May 24, 1947, Altoona, PA
Songwriter, Vocals, Keyboards / Contemporary Country
A former defensive tackle for the NFL's Cincinnati Bengals, Mike Reid was one of the most sensitive writers of romantic songs in contemporary country music. He was born in Altoona, PA, the son of a railroad worker. Although he was a piano player from age six, Reid's real passion was sports; in 1969 he won the Outland Trophy as the best collegiate defensive lineman in the country. Reid also began to develop his musical talents, playing with local bands and graduating with a degree in music. He was drafted in the first round, and became the league's Defensive Rookie of the Year in 1970.

In addition to playing football, Reid also played music with local bands. While recovering from an injury, he met Larry Gatlin, who encouraged Reid's music and admired his song "Time Runs Away." In the off-season, Reid performed as a classical pianist with symphony orchestras in Dallas, Cincinnati, and Utah. In 1975, after undergoing knee surgery, Reid left football, joined the Apple Butter Band, and began playing Colorado ski resorts. As a songwriter, he was inspired by Leonard Cohen and Randy Newman. One of his songs was recorded by Jerry Jeff Walker in 1978, spurring him to pursue a solo career. He signed to ATV Publishing in 1980 and remained there for a year and a half. After meeting the head of Milsap Music, Rob Galbraith, Reid moved to the label and penned a few songs which appeared on Ronnie Milsap's 1982 album *Inside*, providing Milsap with a number one single, "Stranger in My House." Sylvia also scored a major hit with one of Reid's songs.

He continued as a successful songwriter for other artists as well, including Mark Gray, Marie Osmond, Tanya Tucker, and Conway Twitty, who had a major hit with "Fallin' for You for Years." Through the '80s, Reid penned 11 number-one hits. In 1990, he began his recording career, signing to Columbia and releasing *Turning for Home*, which contained the number one hit "Walk on Faith." Reid appeared on the charts three more times in 1991 with songs such as "As Simple as That." His most successful year was 1992, when he wrote several number-one hits for others, including Collin Raye's "In This Life." —*Sandra Brennan*

● **Turning for Home** / 1991 / CBS ✦✦✦✦
Turning for Home is Mike Reid's most consistent release, demonstrating not only his talent for crafting a fine contemporary country song, but also his ability to deliver it. Reid had long been known for writing terrific commercial songs, but with *Turning for Home*, he showed that he could sing them with emotion as well as any other singer. Though there are a couple of mediocre songs scattered throughout the record, the best moments—such as the surging hit singles "Walk on Faith"—make a convincing argument for Reid's talents as a vocalist. —*Thom Owens*

Twilight Town / 1992 / CBS ✦✦✦
While *Twilight Town* was not a commercial success, it does feature Reid's gem "I Can't Make You Love Me," later covered by the likes of Bonnie Raitt, Prince, and George Michael. —*Jason Ankeny*

Reno & Smiley

f. 1951, **db.** 1964
Group / Bluegrass, Traditional Bluegrass
Don Reno, Red Smiley, & the Tennessee Cut-Ups were a bluegrass band of such high quality that they gave serious competition to Flatt & Scruggs in the '50s. Reno, an unsurpassed master of the banjo, played for Bill Monroe in 1948, replacing Earl Scruggs. With a smooth and mellow baritone, Smiley made a perfect partner to Reno, singing lead to his high harmony part. Reno's incredible talent carried over to guitar playing and songwriting. Among his compositions are the exquisite "Emotions" as well as "Feuding Banjos," the unforgettable song in the film *Deliverance*, co-written with Arthur "Guitar Boogie" Smith. You don't know the five-string banjo if you haven't heard Reno.

Reno & Smiley both grew up in different rural sections of North Carolina and both played with the Morris Brothers at different times in their formative early years. After both men served in separate divisions of the Army during World War II, and after they were discharged they played in a variety of country bands—Reno even did a stint with Monroe after Scruggs left the Blue Grass Boys in 1948—before they met each other in December 1949. Both musicians were recruited by fiddler Tommy Magness to play in his band the Tennessee Buddies. In the summer of 1950, the pair began playing duets together. After cutting a few singles with Magness for King Records (which were eventually released on Federal) in the spring of 1951, they left the fiddler and began working with Toby Stroud's Blue Mountain Boys in Roanoke, VA. In the fall of that year, the pair finally formed their own band, the Tennessee Cut-Ups.

Initially, Reno & Smiley found it difficult to land jobs in Virginia and South Carolina. Nevertheless, they cut several sides for King early in 1952. Before those singles were issued, the duo had already split up, simply because they couldn't find work. Once the records did appear, they sold fairly well, and King's owner, Syd Nathan, convinced the duo to continue recording, even if they weren't actively performing. For the next three years, they made assorted records for King while Reno played with Arthur "Guitar Boogie" Smith and Smiley worked as a mechanic. On the first batch of recordings, they were supported by musicians like Jimmy Lunsford and Tommy Faile. By November 1954, they were allowed to use their longtime backing musicians, fiddler Mack Magaha and bassist John Palmer.

In the spring of 1955, Reno & Smiley reunited as a performing duo and soon landed a regular gig on WRVA's *Old Dominion Barn Dance*. Within a year, they were secured a daily morning television show in Roanoke as well as various shows for a station in Harrisonburg, VA. The pair made a handful of recordings for Dot in 1957, but they continued their relationship with King until 1964, recording a wealth of material. At the end of 1964, Reno & Smiley parted ways. Smiley had been slowly suffering from diabetes and no longer wanted to travel; consequently, he continued to do the television show in

Roanoke, but only occasionally toured. By spring 1968, he had completely retired. Reno played with a few bands before teaming up with Bill Harrell in 1966—Harrell would be his first true partner since Smiley, but he wouldn't be his last. For nearly two decades, Reno remained active in the bluegrass community, cutting numerous records and playing with a variety of collaborators. *—Stephen Thomas Erlewine & David Vinopal*

Instrumentals / 1958 / King ♦♦♦♦

● **Good Old Country Ballads** / 1959 / King ♦♦♦♦♦
Good Old Country Ballads is an original King album from 1959 that collects several singles that the bluegrass Reno & Smiley recorded durign the '50s. There's not any weak tracks on the record, and several songs, including "Country Boy Rock 'n' Roll," rank among their very best. It would have been nice to see the compact disc reissue fleshed out with bonus tracks, liner notes or even credits, but it's nice to have the music in any form. *—Thom Owens*

Variety of Country Songs / 1959 / King ♦♦♦♦♦
Like *Good Old Country Ballads, A Variety of Country Songs* is an original King album from 1959 that contains several singles Reno & Smiley recorded during the '50s. Where the predecessor concentrated on midtempo numbers, the songs on *A Variety* are generally speedier and more infectious, whether it is straightforward bluegrass or country gospel. Taken together with *Good Old Country Ballads, A Variety of Country Songs* gives a good idea of the depth of Reno & Smiley's talents. *—Stephen Thomas Erlewine*

Folk Songs of the Civil War / 1961 / King ♦♦♦

16 Greatest Gospel Hits / 1987 / Rounder ♦♦♦♦
16 Greatest Gospel Hits is a solid collection of traditional country gospel tunes—"How I Miss My Darling Mother," "There's a Highway to Heaven," "My Mother's Bible"—as performed by Reno & Smiley. While these perofrmances aren't breathtaking, they're sturdy and engaging and make a nice addition to any comprehensive bluegrass collection. *—Stephen Thomas Erlewine*

Early Years 1951-1959 / 1994 / King ♦♦♦♦♦
Early Years: 1951-1959 is a four-disc box set that presents all of Reno & Smiley & the Tennessee Cut-Ups' recordings for King Records in chronological order, as well as four sides they recorded for Federal as supporting musicians for Tommy Magness. The set contains many of Reno & Smiley's finest and most influential moments, most of which feature the support of bassist John Palmer and fiddler Mack Magaha. As a historical recording, *Early Years: 1951-59* is invaluable, since it documents the greatest recordings from one of the best bluegrass groups in history. However, it is difficult listen—this is educational listening, and is not intended for entertainment. For musicologists and dedicated fans, it's a necessary purchase, but country and bluegrass fans intending to build a basic bluegrass collection don't need to purchase this set. *—Thom Owens*

On Stage / May 14, 1996 / Copper Creek ♦♦♦♦♦
This collection of live performances, recorded July 21, 1957, at *New River Ranch* in Rising Sun, MD, and March 25, 1958, at Sunset Park in Oxford, PA, is a great companion to Reno & Smiley's established catalog of studio recordings. The performances are excellent, featuring the two stars backed by the Tennessee Cut-Ups, consisting of future Porter Wagoner alumnus Mack Magaha on fiddle and John Palmer on bass, and include nine numbers that the duo never recorded officially. The only flaw is the somewhat restricted acoustics, a product of the era in which these shows were taped—it sounds slightly more compressed than one would like, and sometimes Palmer's upright bass is slightly too obtrusive, at other times not sufficiently present. On the other hand, this is the listener's big chance to hear the duo's versions of "Billy in the Low Ground" (a dazzling showcase for Red Smiley and Mack Magaha), "When You and I Were Young, Maggie" (a great Don Reno banjo showpiece), and "Don't Stop Now," the latter highlighted by Smiley's glittering guitar runs, not to mention Don Gibson's "I Can't Stop Loving You" and the Stanley Brothers' "Big Ball in Brooklyn" (some of the fastest banjo playing you'll ever hear). And the live version of "Bonaparte's Retreat," illuminated by Reno's banjo pyrotechnics (and vocal clowning), coupled with their vocal acrobatics on the gospel "He Will Set Your Fields on Fire" are by themselves just about worth the price of the album. *—Bruce Eder*

Reno Brothers

Group / Traditional Bluegrass
The Reno Brothers—Ronnie, Dale and Don Wayne—were the sons of legendary banjo picker Don Reno; like their father, they focused their careers on string band and bluegrass music. Ronnie entered the music business around 1956, playing mandolin with his dad and Red Smiley on Roanoke, VA's *Top o' the Mornin'* TV show. Ronnie and his father kept hosting the show after Smiley left, and during the late '60s, he began playing bass with the Osborne Brothers. He remained with the Osbornes through the early '70s and then became the frontman for Merle Haggard's Strangers. Reno made his first solo entry on the charts in 1983 with "Homemade Love," three years after making his feature film debut in the Clint Eastwood film *Bronco Billy*. While Ronnie was forging his own career, his brothers joined their dad's Tennessee Cut-Ups and played with them long after he and his partner Bill Harrell split in the mid-'70s.

The brothers finally came together after their father died in 1984 to play music that was a cross between bluegrass and country. Their first recordings included their cover of "Yonder Comes a Freight Train" and "Love Will Never Be the Same." The trio also began hosting a regular TV show for the Americana cable network in 1993 which in its day was the only nationally broadcast television program to focus on bluegrass music. *—Sandra Brennan*

20 Bluegrass Originals / 1987 / Deluxe ♦♦♦

● **Three Part Harmony** / Feb. 25, 1998 / Pinecastle ♦♦♦♦♦
The Reno Brothers are a modern bluegrass/acoustic country music group with emphasis on vocal harmonies. Their harmonization tends to be very close, providing a rich vocal texture as opposed to an intricate one. Such music often sets up a cozy world shining with love for a woman and a love for God. While both shades are present on *Three Part Harmony*, excellent variety also appears with the "swinggrass" "Movie Time Blues" and the three instrumental cuts spread out over the album. Even the songs provide stunning instrumental breaks largely due to Don Wayne and Dale Reno (banjo/lead guitar and mandolin, respectively). Third brother and son to bluegrass legend Don Reno, Ronnie mostly takes the lead vocal. He displays the same exquisite Americana/country expression that won him acclaim with his father, Red Smiley, the Osborne Brothers, and Merle Haggard. Don Wayne takes the lead on the one quartet arrangement and sole gospel piece, "Let in the Guiding Light." *—Thomas Schulte*

Don Reno

b. Feb. 21, 1927, Spartanburg, SC, **d.** Oct. 16, 1984
Banjo, Vocals / Progressive Bluegrass, Traditional Bluegrass
Virtually unrivalled among his contemporaries for his mastery of the five-string banjo, Don Reno teamed with Red Smiley to create some of the finest bluegrass recordings of the postwar era—a superb tenor vocalist and songwriter, Reno also proved crucial to the emergence of the guitar as one of bluegrass' lead instruments, and ranks alongside the likes of Bill Monroe among the genre's true pioneers. Reno was born in Spartanburg, SC, on February 21, 1927, and raised primarily in rural North Carolina; at age five he built his first banjo, and as a teen backed the Morris Brothers and Arthur "Guitar Boogie" Smith. He also recorded with Woody Guthrie and was asked to join Monroe's Blue Grass Boys before serving in the military from 1944 to 1946. Upon returning from duty Reno fronted a local South Carolina band before replacing Earl Scruggs in the Blue Grass Boys, where like his predecessor he was key in popularizing the three-finger roll technique of banjo playing.

Reno left Monroe in 1949 to join Tommy Magness & His Tennessee Buddies; among his bandmates was guitarist Smiley, and while cutting a 1951 session with Magness for King Records subsidiary Federal, label owner Syd Nathan was so impressed by Reno and Smiley's interplay that he soon arranged for the duo to record under their own names. A marathon 16-song studio date the following January launched their career as headliners, with the Reno-penned hit "I'm Using My Bible for a Road Map" proving so successful it reportedly pulled King Records back from the brink of bankruptcy. Despite the popularity of their records, the duo proved unable to keep together their touring band, the Tennessee Cut-Ups, so in between sessions for King they worked independently, which allowed Reno to reunite with Smith; together they recorded the classic 1955 instrumental "Feuding Banjos," which was later retitled "Dueling Banjos" for its unauthorized use in the 1972 film *Deliverance*.

In May of 1955 Reno and Smiley organized the definitive lineup of the Tennessee Cut-Ups, including fiddler Mack Magaha and bassist John Palmer; a regular gig at Richmond, VA, station WRVA's *Old Dominion Barn Dance* finally afforded the group the opportunity to continue full-time, and over the next nine years they recorded a series of influential sides for King including "I Know You're Married," "Don't Let Your Sweet Love Die," and "Please Remember That I Love You." At the peak of their popularity, the duo also hosted *Top of the Morning*, a hit daily television show which ran for some seven years. However, in 1964 diabetes forced Smiley to retire from the road, and in late 1966 Reno began a new partnership with singer/multi-instrumentalist Bill Harrell which continued for a decade, a period which coincided with a resurgence in public interest in bluegrass as a result of a growing festival circuit. A much briefer liaison with fiddler Benny Martin also launched the country chart hit "A Soldier's Prayer in Vietnam."

During the early '70s Reno & Harrell recorded a series of LPs for labels including Monument, Dot, and CMH; on occasion Smiley returned to the fold as well, making his final live appearance just months before his death on January 2, 1972. After Reno & Harrell went their separate ways in autumn 1976, the former settled in Lynchburg, VA, where he began performing alongside sons Don, Wayne, Dale, and Ronnie; in 1979, he also again re-teamed with Smith for the album *Arthur Smith and Don Reno Feudin' Again*. Reno died October 16, 1984; his sons later recorded as the Reno Brothers. *—Jason Ankeny*

● **The Golden Guitar of Don Reno** / Jan. 25, 2000 / King ♦♦♦♦

Founding Father of the Bluegrass Banjo / Nov. 13, 2001 / CMH ♦♦♦♦

Restless Heart

f. 1984
Group / Country-Pop, Contemporary Country, Adult Contemporary
Playing a pop-friendly brand of country-rock indebted to the Eagles, Restless Heart was one of the most popular country bands of the late '80s and early '90s, scoring numerous hits on the country charts and a few major successes on adult contemporary radio as well. The band first got together in 1984 at the behest of producer/songwriter Tim DuBois, who wanted some musicians to demo a batch of material that walked the line between country and pop. Drummer/vocalist John Dittrich, pianist Dave Innis, bassist/vocalist Paul Gregg, and guitarist Greg Jennings were initially joined by singer Verlon Thompson, and the demo sessions went so well that the group decided to stay together and pursue a record deal. They signed with RCA in 1983, at which point Thompson was replaced by lead singer Larry Stewart, a demo vocalist Innis knew from Belmont College in Nashville.

Restless Heart's self-titled debut album was released in 1985 and contained three Top Ten hits: "I Want Everyone to Cry," "(Back to The) Heartbreak Kid," and "Til I Loved You." The 1986 follow-up, *Wheels*, was their true breakthrough release, topping the country charts and producing four number-one hits: "That Rock Won't Roll," the ballad "I'll Still Be Loving You" (also a number-three adult contemporary hit), "Why Does It Have to Be (Wrong or Right)," and "Wheels." *Big Dreams in a Small Town* (1988) was a successful follow-up, giving the band six consecutive chart-toppers thanks to its first two singles, "A Tender Lie" and "The Bluest Eyes in Texas"; its title track and "Say What's in Your Heart" also went Top Five. The title of 1989's *Fast Movin' Train* was an apt metaphor for the band's career, as it spawned two more Top Five hits in the title track and "Dancy's Dream."

Stewart left the group for a solo career in 1990; he later scored a big hit with "Alright Already," but never quite matched it. Meanwhile, Gregg and Dittrich split lead vocal duties on 1992's *Big Iron Horses*, which gave them another crossover smash with "When She Cries"; it went Top Ten country, hit number-two adult contemporary, and just missed the pop Top Ten. Innis left the band in 1992, and the remaining trio watched "Tell Me What You Dream" become their first adult contemporary chart-topper in 1993. However, after 1994's *Matters of the Heart*, they decided to disband. Jennings joined Vince Gill's band, while Dittrich worked with the Buffalo Club. There was a 1988 Restless Heart reunion—minus Innis—that resulted in four new tracks for that year's *Greatest Hits* compilation, as well as a tour with Gill. *—Steve Huey*

Restless Heart / 1985 / RCA ♦♦♦
The band's debut includes the hits "Let the Heartache Ride," "I Want Everyone to Cry," and "(Back to The) Heartbreak Kid." *—Jason Ankeny*

Wheels / 1986 / RCA ♦♦♦♦♦
The guys found their niche with this project. Big, overpowering sound, heavy backbeats, and very tight harmonies are here. In contrast, the ballads "I'll Still Be Loving You" and "New York (Hold Her Tight)" are incredibly sensitive. *—Tom Roland*

Big Dreams in a Small Town / 1988 / RCA ♦♦♦
BMG Special Products' *Big Dreams* may not be a strict hits collection, but it's a good budget-priced sampler that offers a nice snapshot of Restless Heart's peak hit-making years. There are a number of hits here—"Big Dreams in a Small Town," "That Rock Won't Roll," "Long Lost Friend," "Say What's In Your Heart," "I Want Everyone to Cry"—that are balanced by solid album tracks. If it's not a comprehensive collection, at least it is consistently entertaining and is a good bargain, considering its budget price. *—Stephen Thomas Erlewine*

Fast Movin' Train / 1989 / RCA ♦♦♦

Big Iron Horses / 1992 / RCA ♦♦♦
Down to a quartet, the guys in Restless Heart still have the highest Eagles rating in country music—they get the vocals right almost every time, and "Blame It on Love" evokes memories of the likes of "Witchy Woman." Musically, not much changed for the members of the band: They still like a good train song, and they're more likely to show the influence of Bruce Hornsby ("Meet Me on the Other Side") and Creedence Clearwater Revival ("Born in a High Wind") than any of country's honky tonk heroes. Another song, "When She Cries," became one of the biggest crossover hits of 1992. Paul Gregg, John Dittrich, and Dave Innis (who left the group after the album's release, reducing Restless Heart to a trio) trade lead vocals; they blend well from song to song, though Dittrich sounds the most like Don Henley, but it's definitely those harmonies that make *Big Iron Horses* run smooth. *—Brian Mansfield*

Matters of the Heart / May 24, 1994 / RCA ♦♦

Greatest Hits / May 19, 1998 / RCA ♦♦♦♦♦
An improvement over the Restless Heart best-of collection that RCA issued in 1991, *Greatest Hits* compiles 13 of the group's most popular songs, and also adds on three brand-new cuts. Containing five country chart-toppers—"That Rock Won't Roll," "I'll Still Be Loving You," "Why Does It Have to Be Wrong," "Bluest Eyes in Texas," and "A Tender Lie"—the set also includes pop radio smashes like "When She Cries" and "Tell Me What You Dream." *—Jason Ankeny*

● **RCA Country Legends** / Mar. 4, 2003 / RCA ♦♦♦♦♦
As part of RCA's *Country Legends* series, this set highlights Restless Heart's biggest hits from the mid- to late '80s. Among the 16 tracks are the number-one singles "That Rock Won't Roll," "I'll Still Be Loving You," "Why Does It Have to Be (Wrong or Right)," "Wheels," "A Tender Lie," and "Bluest Eyes in Texas." This collection serves as an excellent career overview. *—Al Campbell*

Billy Ray Reynolds

b. 1943, Saratoga Springs, MS
Vocals, Guitar / Outlaw Country, Honky Tonk, Traditional Country
Billy Ray Reynolds is a singer, songwriter, guitarist, and actor who, after a long career behind the scenes in the music business, finally came to the forefront in 2002 with his first solo album, *Whole Lot of Memories*. Reynolds was born in Saratoga Springs, MS, in 1943; when he was nine years old, he joined his parents for a trip to a *Grand Ole Opry* touring show in nearby Jackson, where he saw Hank Williams perform, sparking Reynolds' lifelong passion for country music. In time, Reynolds picked up a guitar, and after a brief stint playing bass with the Yankee Dollar, a folk-rock band who cut one album for Dot in 1968, he hooked up with Waylon Jennings and signed on to play guitar in his band. Reynolds spend several years playing live dates with Jennings and appeared on such albums as *Honky Tonk Heroes* and *Ladies Love Outlaws*.

Reynolds also took up a career as a songwriter, penning tunes that were recorded by artists such as Johnny Cash, Tompall Glaser, Dickey Betts, Tanya Tucker, and Johnny Rodriguez. However, while Reynolds remained in demand as a songwriter and sideman, a pair of singles for Epic in the mid-'70s failed to yield a label deal. Undaunted, Reynolds continued working with artists such as Ian Tyson and John Hartford and eventually added acting to his resumé, scoring small roles (often as villains) in movies and television projects; he also developed a passionate interest in the Civil War and self-distributed an album of folk songs concerning the War Between the States. In 2002, the independent Compadre label finally gave Reynolds a deal to record a solo album, and the 59-year-old singer released *Whole Lot of Memories* later that same year. *—Mark Deming*

Whole Lot of Memories / 2002 / Compadre ♦♦♦♦
Billy Ray Reynolds saw Hank Williams play the *Grand Ole Opry* when he was only nine; spent close to ten years playing guitar with Waylon Jennings' band; wrote songs for the likes of Johnny Cash, Tompall Glaser, and Tanya Tucker; and even penned a tune for the Allman Brothers Band (the band never cut it, but "Atlanta's Burning Down" became the title track of one of Dickey Betts' solo albums). Given his background, you might expect that Reynolds' belated solo debut, *Whole Lot of Memories*, doesn't sound much like a contemporary country album, and that's the best thing about it. Billy Ray Reynolds' voice is a strong honky tonk instrument, buffed by years of bourbon and nicotine, and like his old buddy Waylon, he knows how to sound soulful and sensitive when he isn't busy raising hell. Reynolds' tunes are top-notch, whether he's making time with the ladies ("Whatever Turns You On"), earning the wrath of his wife ("She's Cleaning the House"), rescuing his true love during the Civil War ("Atlanta's Burning Down"), or just singing the honky tonk blues ("Tumbleweed"). Reynolds also rounded up some great pickers for these sessions, and Merle Haggard stops by for a welcome cameo on "Two Step Me." While it's tempting to say *Whole Lot of Memories* is the sort of country album Nashville doesn't make any more, the truth is even in the good old days, they rarely turned out LPs as consistently pleasurable as this, and it's nice to know that Reynolds finally got to make a great solo album after close to 40 years in the business. I sure hope he doesn't have to wait as long to make another. *—Mark Deming*

Kimmie Rhodes

Vocals / Progressive Country, Singer/Songwriter, Alternative Country, Americana
The singing career of Lubbock, TX, native Kimmie Rhodes kicked off at the age of six, when she first performed with her family gospel trio. During her teens she began learning guitar and writing songs, and in 1979 moved to Austin, where she met her future husband and producer Joe Gracey. Two years later, Rhodes released her debut LP, *Kimmie Rhodes and the Jackalope Brothers*, followed in 1985 by her second effort, *Man in the Moon*. She recorded her third album, 1989's *Angels Get the Blues*, at Sun Studios in Memphis. While commercial success continually eluded Rhodes, her music proved popular with other performers; her song "I Just Drove By" was covered by Wynonna on the *Tell Me Why* album, and the duet pairing of Trisha Yearwood & Willie Nelson recorded "Hard Promises to Keep" for Yearwood's *The Song Remembers When*. Rhodes herself also cut a pair of duets with Nelson for his *Just One Love* LP; Nelson returned the favor for Rhodes' 1996 effort *West Texas Heaven*, on which she also teamed with Waylon Jennings and Townes Van Zandt. *Rich From the Journey* followed in the spring of 2000. *—Jason Ankeny*

Angels Get the Blues / 1989 / Heartland UK ♦♦♦

West Texas Heaven / Apr. 1996 / Justice ♦♦♦♦
Kimmie Rhodes, may not be so well-known outside of her home state, but she has been recording for the last 15 years, getting attention from European audiences and writing songs that have been recorded by stars like Willie Nelson, Wynonna Judd, and Trisha Yearwood. Rhodes' album, *West Texas Heaven*, is a melodic and dreamy, sweet and sad work of dryland, lonesome road beauty. Her voice is folksinger pretty and brings to mind Nanci Griffith and Iris DeMent, but she tastefully avoids the cute and quaint in her writing and subtle arrangements. Highlights are a series of duets with Nelson, Waylon Jennings, and Townes Van Zandt (who delivers one of his best vocal performances in years). *—Kurt Wolff*

Jackalopes Moons & Angels: A Collection, 1985-1990 / Nov. 4, 1997 / Last Call ♦♦♦♦
Between 1985 and 1989, Kimmie Rhodes lead a series of hard-working, hard-touring country ensembles and aggregations through a broad range of country & western styles, all the while developing her songwriting muse. She also recorded three albums, and *Jackalopes, Moons & Angels* collects 12 tracks from those three releases. As such, it documents three distinct eras of Kimmie Rhodes songcraft and acts as an audible record of sorts, charting the rapid growth of her compositional skills. It also captures some pretty hot musicians. The three songs included from the first record (*Kimmie Rhodes and the Jackalope Brothers*) can best be described as juvenilia, yes, but they are nevertheless rollicking and infectious recordings. "Contrabandistas" is a swaying Tex-Mex border song and "Sweetheart You're a Lot Like Texas" is a Lone Star barnyard polka-cum-square-dance number, while the swinging rock & roll beat of "I'm His Little Chevrolet" is pure Sun Studios with great electric picking and the band playing the hell out of the song as Rhodes howls like a honky tonk Emmylou Harris. The songs from the second album, *Man in the Moon*, reflect their dancehall genesis in the sing-song basslines and quick country pacing, from the title track's frenetic swing workout to the almost bluegrass "Daddy's Song." On the other hand, "1000 Magicians" is a heartbroken ballad, and "It'll Do" perhaps marks the first true flowering of Rhodes mature songwriting. She peppers the song with wonderful wordplay snapshots of a nowhere Texas town and its inhabitants, living broke but not broken with a nostalgic sweetness. Some of the earliest songs have an unexpected, amusing sense of humor, partly grounded in the moonlit gazebo lilt of pre-rock pop. It masks a slight tentativeness in the writing, but the songs are nonetheless accomplished and romantic. The third album, *Angels Get the Blues*, was recorded live, no overdubs, by Rhodes' Austin band at the legendary Sun Studios, with Joe Ely lending a hand and voice. The songs collected here from that album are gorgeous, fully mature country-folk tunes—including "I Just Drove By" later recorded by both Wynonna Judd and Willie Nelson—full of delicate lyrical insight. It proves an aural spreading of the wings as well, even moving into moody piano jazz on "Bad Times for Me" and straight soul-descending electric blues on "Trying for My Heart." The collection may not be entirely representative of Rhodes' sound or indicative of the full breadth of her abilities (that would occur on her fourth and fifth albums), but since all three of those original albums remain out of print, it is not only the most accessible but also the only way to hear her earliest efforts. It beautifully captures the budding seeds of an artist that would become one of the most acclaimed country-folk songwriters of the 1990s and beyond. *—Stanton Swihart*

● **Rich From the Journey** / Mar. 28, 2000 / Sunbird ♦♦♦♦♦
Her songs had been recorded by a passel of huge country and gospel stars and she had received bushels full of enthusiastic reviews and responses, but even after her acclaimed previous effort, 1996's *West Texas Heaven*, the spotlight had largely bypassed Kimmie Rhodes despite a phenomenal songwriting talent frequently mentioned alongside such

giants as fellow Texans Townes Van Zandt and Guy Clark. Her fourth album of new material (and fifth overall) continues her streak of exquisite singer/songwriter albums, but it is also a work of significant personal and musical growth. *Rich From the Journey* is humble and full of gentle, hushed praise, a thankful album in the sense that Rhodes' lyrics sparkle with gratefulness and joy for life's many aesthetic beauties, the outward ones that we can see, but also the internal ones that we must search ourselves to find. The album is suffused with a sunny, spiritual calm that is soft and absorbent, like a foot sinking into the wet beach sands of an ocean. The production (by son Gabe) is so subtle that it initially seems almost nonexistent, but it is actually what gives the album its airy, dreamlike quality. The sound may seem more Laurel Canyon than Texas, but regardless of its sonic lineage, it is a ceaselessly absorbing work graced by songwriting of genuine revelation and insight. Rhodes' delicate melodies float across the album's dozen tracks like beautiful feathers, but each one sparks an emotional response that does anything but dissolve or flutter away. She writes songs that grow more substantive the longer they marinate in your head. Previously her songs had tended to be grounded in the country-folk tradition, but *Rich From the Journey* finds Rhodes moving toward a more expansive, inclusive, and less easily ghettoized sound. "Yellow Sand" even has a moody, almost ambient cast that approaches wistfully pretty Portishead and Sarah McLachlan territory, but with far more resonance, and a hint of country lilt. The album is, in a sense, a step away from the roots vibe that characterizes much of Rhodes' catalog, but there is still plenty of rural, Americana gems, such as the petal steel-imbued shuffle, "I'm So Amazed," and the outstanding "God's Acre," which features Gillian Welch and David Rawlings. *Rich From the Journey* is an album at peace with itself, worldly but angelic, with a ringing sense of place. *—Stanton Swihart*

Love Me Like a Song / Jun. 2002 / Sunbird ✦✦✦✦✦

There was a time when Kimmie Rhodes was comfortably ensconced in the country genre. In fact, her early music was downright honky tonk at times, occasionally making further diversions into Tex-Mex and Western swing—about as hardcore country & western as it gets, in other words. But that phase had long since passed by the time the sumptuous *Rich From the Journey* was released. The album was country in only the most tangential way, and only if you coerced it into the category. Rhodes does sonically inch back toward the country fold somewhat on *Love Me Like a Song*, which should more than satisfy those who missed that aspect of the singer/songwriter's music on the previous effort. Fellow mavericks and spiritual forebears Willie Nelson and Emmylou Harris even make a pair of guest spots apiece, each wonderful, particularly the former's turn on the gorgeous "We've Done This Before" and the latter's on the gospel-flecked "Send Me the Sun," also featuring Beth Nielsen Chapman. And yet rigidly labeling her sound no longer does Rhodes' art justice. More than anything, she is about songs, plain and simple, and this album contains a tremendously well-written set of them. Although there are fewer atmospheric washes of electric keyboards, there is healthy carryover from *Rich From the Journey*, particularly in the delicate, airy melodies and the sense of rebirth and contentment that imbues the lyrics, most affectingly so on "Darkness Lifting" and "The One to Walk You Home" (another duet, this time with Benmont Tench). Nevertheless, the overall sound, again produced by son Gabe Rhodes, has a shade more punch and transparency, a bit more of the Austin lope here (the worldly-wise "Witness to the Crime") and a return to electrically bluesy sass there ("Midnight Song"). The songwriter also strikes out into enchanting new landscapes with "Play Me a Memory," an honest to goodness show tune done Broadway style, and the Eastern European eccentricities of "Louis' World" and "November December." All further evidence of why Kimmie Rhodes is one of the secret treasures of Texas song. *—Stanton Swihart*

Red Rhodes (Orville J. Rhodes)

b. Dec. 30, 1930, East Alston, IL, **d.** Aug. 5, 1995

Guitar (Steel) / Traditional Country, Country-Pop

Red Rhodes was one of the most versatile steel guitarists in country music. Born Orville J. Rhodes in East Alston, IL, his mother taught him to play the dobro when he was only five; at 15, he switched to the lap steel guitar, using a homemade stand. He played his first professional gig alongside his stepfather before moving to L.A. in 1960 to do session work. Eight years later, he was one of the most in-demand session men on the West Coast, and played with artists like the Byrds. Rhodes and his band played at the Palomino in L.A. during the late '60s and even worked on several Monkees sessions, which led to work as a steel player for Michael Nesmith's First National Band in 1969. He remained with Nesmith through both incarnations of the group, and continued his session work throughout the '70s, appearing with James Taylor, John Phillips, the Carpenters, Carole King, Chilli Willi & the Red Hot Peppers, and Seals & Crofts.

He has released a few solo albums, including, *Red Rhodes' Steel Guitar*, (1979) and *Fantastic Steel Guitar* (1980). Rhodes' playing was limited in the '80s and early '90s by the rheumatoid arthritis which affected the use of his hands. He devoted his time instead to his amp shop, occasionally making appearances at the International Steel Guitar Festival. In 1995, he played on Nesmith's Tropical Campfires album and went on tour with him. Shortly after he completed the tour he fell ill, succombing to interstitial lung fibrosis on August 5, 1995. *—Sandra Brennan*

Once a Day / 1961 / Crown ✦✦✦

Blue Blue Day / 1962 / Crown ✦✦✦

● **Steel Guitar Rag** / 1963 / Crown ✦✦✦✦

Velvet Hammer in a Cowboy Band / 1973 / Countryside ✦✦✦

Larry Rice

Mandolin, Vocals / Traditional Bluegrass

Larry Rice, a renowned mandolin player, began his bluegrass career by playing in his father's band, the Golden State Boys. He later formed his own band (the Haphazards) with brothers Tony and Ronnie. In the '70s, he co-founded the New South, with J.D. Crowe, Doyle Lawson, Red Allen, and Bobby Slone. After leaving the band in 1976 (Ricky Skaggs replaced him), Rice toured with Dickey Betts. His first solo album, *Hurricanes and Daydreams* (1985), was followed by *Time Machine. Notions and Novelties* appeared in 1996. *—John Bush*

Hurricanes and Daydreams / 1985 / Rebel ✦✦✦

● **Artesia** / 1990 / Rebel ✦✦✦✦✦

Notions and Novelties / Oct. 8, 1996 / Rebel ✦✦✦

Time Machine / Oct. 8, 1997 / Rebel ✦✦✦✦

Rice, Rice, Hillman & Pedersen

f. 1997

Group / Contemporary Country, Progressive Bluegrass

Although their name has been likened to a law firm, Rice, Rice, Hillman & Pederson are anything but a stodgy bunch of bookworms. The seeds of the acoustic country/newgrass group were planted in September 1963 when brothers Larry & Tony Rice, Chris Hillman, and Herb Pedersen all performed at a bluegrass festival in Pasadena, CA. The four came together, 33 years later, on the loose sessions of *Out of the Woodwork* on Rounder Records in 1997. Former Byrd Hillman plays guitar and mandolin, acoustic guitar hero Tony Rice (who was the original guitarist for J.D. Crowe & the New South) also sings, Tony's brother Larry plays mandolin and guitar, and former Laurel Canyon Rambler Herb Pedersen picks the banjo and the occasional guitar.

In addition to all of this instrumentation, each member takes turn on vocals, making for a diverse shift from song to song, as well as some rich overall harmonies. Their self-titled second album appeared in 1999, and another two years later, they released the warm acoustic *Running Wild*. *—Zac Johnson*

Out of the Woodwork / Jan. 14, 1997 / Rounder ✦✦✦

● **Rice, Rice, Hillman & Pedersen** / Oct. 5, 1999 / Rounder ✦✦✦✦

With a country and bluegrass music pedigree as long as your right arm, Tony & Larry Rice team up again with Chris Hillman and Herb Pedersen for another musical go-round that finds them all at the top of their game. On the other hand, despite the formidable musical chops of all the players involved, this is not an album full of flashy soloing, but rather a laid-back, reflective session of superlative music that draws from a multitude of sources. Hillman provides a quartet of new compositions and Larry Rice weighs in with "The Side Effects of Life" and "The Year of El Niño," but just as telling are the covers, roping in such diverse sources as the Grateful Dead, Delaney & Bonnie, and Flatt & Scruggs. Every bit as in the pocket as their first outing (1997's *Out of the Woodwork*), this second go-round is solid American music every note of the way. *—Cub Koda*

Running Wild / Oct. 30, 2001 / Rounder ✦✦✦

Billing themselves as an anti-supergroup, Rice, Rice, Hillman & Pederson have decades of talent under their belts, but their ego-free attitudes allow for the exchange of some genuine American music. Their third release as a group, Chris Hillman, Herb Pedersen, and brothers Larry & Tony Rice perform a unique blend of progressive bluegrass and earthy contemporary country, sharing vocal duties on a combination of new songs and country classics. Highlights include former Byrd Hillman's take on "4 + 20," written by his folk-rock contemporary and former Manassas bandmate Stephen Stills, and some truly inspired steel guitar accents from guest Jay Dee Maness, particularly on "Two of a Kind." With the addition of drums and additional instrumentation on many of the tracks, the band has expanded beyond the strictly acoustic sound of its earlier albums, but still retains a warm intimacy. The band's interpretations of classics, like Jim & Jesse's "Hard Hearted," the Beatles' "Things We Said Today," and the title track made popular by the Louvin Brothers work better than some of the originals (like the positively maudlin "The Mystery That Won't Go Away," which recounts the death of Jon Benet Ramsey). The album's high points outweigh its faults and make for a solid listen overall. *—Zac Johnson*

Tony Rice

b. Jun. 8, 1951, Danville, VA

Guitar (Acoustic), Guitar, Vocals / Progressive Bluegrass

Tony Rice is one of bluegrass' most inventive flatpicking guitar players. Although he's displayed a mastery of the genre's traditions, Rice set the standard for more contemporary styles. A former member of the Bluegrass Alliance, the David Grisman Quintet, J.D. Crowe's New South, and the Bluegrass Album Band, Rice has continued to reflect his eclectic approach on solo recordings, two albums with flatpicking guitar ace Norman Blake, and two albums, recorded with his brothers Larry, Ron, and Wyatt, as the Rice Brothers. In 1996, Rice joined with Chris Hillman, Herb Pedersen, and his brother Larry to record a tradition-rooted album, *Out of the Woodwork*.

Raised in Southern California, Rice inherited his musical skill from his father, who played with several West Coast bluegrass bands and was heavily influenced by California-based bluegrass groups, including the Dillards and the Kentucky Colonels, which featured influential guitar picker Clarence White. Moving temporarily to Kentucky in 1970, Rice became a charter member of the Bluegrass Alliance, one of the earliest contemporary bluegrass groups. As a member of J.D. Crowe's New South in the early '70s, along with Ricky Skaggs and Jerry Douglas, he continued to promote a new approach to the music of the hill country. After meeting imaginative mandolin player David Grisman during a jam session in 1975, Rice returned to California and helped to form the David Grisman Quintet. During the five years that he played with the group, Rice helped to lay the foundation for the "new grass" style that Grisman dubbed "Dawg Music."

Leaving the Grisman Quintet, Rice formed a bluegrass supergroup, the Bluegrass Album Band, with J.D. Crowe, Bobby Hicks, Doyle Lawson, and Todd Phillips. Although only a part-time venture, the group produced five memorable albums. Rice's albums as a soloist and with his band, the Tony Rice Unit, have ranged from the jazz-tinged *Mar West*, which included bluegrass-style treatments of tunes by Miles Davis and John Coltrane, to singer/songwriter-oriented albums, including *Cold on the Shoulder, Native American*, and *Me & My Guitar*, which featured his virtuosic guitar picking and soulful vocalizing of songs by Ian Tyson, Phil Ochs, and Gordon Lightfoot.

Rice released an album-length collection of Lightfoot's songs, *Sings Gordon Lightfoot*, in 1996. Rice has continued to interpret the traditional bluegrass repertoire as well, releasing an album of old chestnuts, *Plays and Sings Bluegrass*, the same year. Although he's recently experienced vocal problems that have prevented him from singing, Rice continues to amaze audiences with his masterful guitar playing. *—Craig Harris*

California Autumn / 1975 / Rebel ♦♦♦

Rice splits the material on *California Autumn* between vocal numbers and instrumentals while resurrecting old-time songs including "Billy in the Lowground," "Beaumont Rag" and "Red Haired Boy." *—Jason Ankeny*

Tony Rice / 1977 / Rounder ♦♦♦♦

This eponymous release was the first of Tony Rice's many albums for the Rounder label, and hardcore bluegrass fans will probably consider it his best. Joined by an impressive roster of sidemen representing both the old and new schools of bluegrass playing (including David Grisman, J.D. Crowe, Jerry Douglas, and Darol Anger), Rice runs through a program consisting primarily of bluegrass standards but also including a number of forward-thinking modern compositions, such as David Nichtern's "Plastic Banana" and Grisman's swinging "Rattlesnake." This album is one of the early landmarks in the development of what came to be called new acoustic music, an instrumental genre that drew almost equally on bluegrass, jazz, and classical traditions and came to be championed by Rice, Grisman, Anger, and a few others in their circle. But as Rice's warm singing on "Hills of Roane County" and "Banks of the Ohio" and his fiery flatpicking on "Big Mon" and "Farewell Blues" attest, this is also a very fine straight bluegrass album. It's difficult to pick out highlights, but the joyful "Eighth of January" and the wonderful twin fiddle arrangement on "Big Mon" are both definite showstoppers. *—Rick Anderson*

Manzanita / 1979 / Rounder ♦♦♦♦♦

Comprised of both traditional songs and contemporary numbers, *Manzanita* was the third record in a row to demonstrate Tony Rice's considerable instrumental talent, and this album he is backed by a band featuring Sam Bush, Ricky Skaggs, and Jerry Douglas, who give him incredibly sympathetic and nuanced support. *—Thom Owens*

Acoustics / 1979 / Rounder ♦♦♦♦

Acoustics was released in 1979, some two years after Tony Rice's involvement with the David Grisman Quintet's debut album. Like the Grisman recording, *Acoustics* proved to be a groundbreaking album for progressive bluegrass musicians. The music on *Acoustics* is all instrumental and features an incredible group of musicians including Sam Bush, Richard Greene, Mike Marshall, Todd Phillips, and, on one cut, David Grisman. Perhaps the first thing a listener will notice is that an instrumental like "Swing 51" has very little to do with bluegrass. The essence of "Swing 51" is—as the title suggests—swing jazz. This is a romantic music, inspired by the spirit of Stephane Grappelli and Django Reinhardt and perfectly suited for acoustic instruments. "Blues for Paradise" is a lovely melody, set in motion by Rice's subtle flat-picking and brought to full beauty by Sam Bush's violin. Bush and Greene share violin duties on *Acoustics*, proving especially apt at defining melodies and setting the mood. The highlight of this disc is the quick paced "So Much," a piece bursting with vitality. "So Much" was written by Rice and, like the other songs on *Acoustics*, features open structures with fascinating chord progressions. Emphasis throughout this album is placed on instrumental dexterity, with each musician given the chance to build and develop each lead at length. The musicians also provide unadorned accompaniment, leaving lots of quiet space around the lead player. The glue holding this project together is Rice, who also played a primary role in the original David Grisman Quintet. On this album Rice expands the role of the guitar, building each lead faultlessly through intricate succession. *Acoustics* gives notice that acoustic musicians, like jazz musicians, possess the skills required to create spontaneous and vital music. *—Ronnie D. Lankford Jr.*

Guitar / 197 / Rebel ♦♦♦

On *Guitar*, Rice focuses on instrumental renditions of songs like "Lonesome Reuben" and "Faded Love." Among the guests are J.D. Crowe and Bobby Slone. *—Jason Ankeny*

Mar West / 1980 / Rounder ♦♦♦

Mar West is the third recording by the Tony Rice Unit and like their other recordings, it features some of the best acoustic musicians on the scene. *Mar West* showcases music closely resembling swing jazz, and if it seems less inspired than an earlier effort like *Acoustics*, it is nonetheless a good instrumental album. Compare it to a lesser effort by Stephane Grappelli and Django Reinhardt: Perhaps the song choice is less than perfect and the musicians less inspired than usual, but who would want to miss it? Sam Bush, Richard Greene, Mike Marshall, and Todd Phillips join Rice for eight instrumentals. The title cut, which opens the album, also reveals its shortcomings. "Mar West" is one of those fast, open-chorded instrumentals that Rice enjoys writing. Rice kicks the piece off with quick-paced flat-picking that is technically perfect, but the solo continues for too long and is lacking in feeling. More successful is the measured "Waltz for Indira" with a nice mandolin part by Bush, and "Neon Tetra" with an inspired violin solo by Greene. Perhaps the best cut on the album is "Nardis," written by Miles Davis. "Nardis'" colored textures evoke a romantic mood and challenge the musicians to create distinctive, longing solos. Like the other Tony Rice Unit albums, emphasis remains focused on the skills of the individual musicians involved. Each instrumental provides the violin, guitar, and mandolin room for lengthy solos while Phillips' bass keeps everyone grounded. Both Rice fans and lovers of good acoustic music will enjoy *Mar West*. *—Ronnie Lankford Jr.*

Still Inside / 1981 / Rounder ♦♦♦♦♦

Still Inside is the fourth recording by the Tony Rice Unit and like their previous recordings, it is all acoustic and all instrumental, with emphasis centered on the skill of the individual musicians involved. *Still Inside* features some of the best acoustic musicians on the scene, including mandolin player John Reischman, violinist Fred Carpenter, and bassist Todd Phillips. The strength of the Tony Rice Unit albums also depend on the quality of the material, and on *Still Inside*, Rice draws on more diverse sources than he had on 1980's *Mar West*. This variety spices things up. Standouts include Earl Klugh's "Vonetta," a Latin-tinged instrumental with superb bass work by Phillips, and a relaxed-paced "Tzigani," a David Grisman piece that begins playfully slow, then flies into high gear. Rice's own material, as on the relaxed "Delvin" and the beautifully tender "Moses Sole," is stronger than on the previous album. Another difference this time is that Carpenter and Reischman are new to the group. Carpenter's violin adds a warm tone while defining melodies, and Reischman follows in the giant footsteps of Sam Bush and Mike Marshall without faltering. Reischman also adds his songwriting talents to the mix on "Birdland Breakdown," creating an odd but rewarding blend of Eastern European and bluegrass music. Rice's flat-picking thrives on the variety of melodies present on *Still Inside*, creating fresh expressions and romantic coloring at his usual swift pace. This album will please Rice fans as well as fans of acoustic music. *—Ronnie Lankford Jr.*

Bluegrass Album / 1981 / Rounder ♦♦♦♦

☆ **Backwaters** / 1982 / Rounder ♦♦♦♦♦

Is it jazz? Is it bluegrass? Is it early new age? At the time of *Backwaters*' release, Rounder Records was lumping it into a category called "new acoustic music." Call it whatever you choose, this is excellent music, impeccably played by a group of guys who are all virtuosos on their respective instruments. Even the most die-hard jazz cop would appreciate the playing, but one needn't be a critic to simply enjoy this collection. Tony Rice may be the finest acoustic guitar picker on the planet, and he also has written some beautiful pieces for this recording. Accompanied by Fred Carpenter and Richard Greene on violins, John Reischman on mandolin, with support from Todd Phillips on standup bass and brother Wyatt Rice on rhythm guitar, Rice takes his music to a whole new place. Every note sounds right, and each member of the ensemble plays with exceptional taste and class. Dave Grusin's "A Child Is Born" is absolutely gorgeous, and the quintet's bluegrass-paced take on "My Favourite Things" is an obvious, but reinvigorating, string-picker's nod to John Coltrane. "On Green Dolphin Street" is reminiscent of Stephane Grappelli and Django Reinhardt on their *Hot Club of France* recordings. After this release, Rice returned to more traditional-sounding folk and bluegrass music, but *Backwaters* is his masterpiece. So, what label can you place on this genre-defying music? How about Rice's own term, "spacegrass." *—Jim Newsom*

Bluegrass Album, Vol. 2 / 1982 / Rounder ♦♦♦♦

Church Street Blues / 1983 / Sugar Hill ♦♦♦♦♦

Church Street Blues is essentially a solo album by Tony Rice, demonstrating his musical eclecticism—the record features everything from contemporary folk to traditional country and blues—as well as his nimble instrumental grace. *—Thom Owens*

Bluegrass Album, Vol. 3: California Connection / 1983 / Rounder ♦♦♦♦

Bluegrass Album, Vol. 4 / 1984 / Rounder ♦♦♦♦

Cold on the Shoulder / 1984 / Rounder ♦♦♦♦

Béla Fleck, Vassar Clements, and Jerry Douglas are just a few of the guests on *Cold on the Shoulder*, on which Rice performs songs by Bob Dylan, Randy Newman, and Rodney Crowell. *—Jason Ankeny*

Me & My Guitar / 1986 / Rounder ♦♦

Me and My Guitar sports several Gordon Lightfoot compositions, including "Fine as Fine Can Be" and "Early Morning Rain." *—Jason Ankeny*

● **Devlin** / 1987 / Rounder ♦♦♦♦♦

Newgrass guitarist Tony Rice's work for Rounder Records is showcased on the mesmerizing *Devlin*. Pulling the best new acoustic tracks from his 1980 album, *Mar West*, and 1981's *Still Inside*, this compilation highlights Rice's fluid playing and progressive composition as he is backed by players like Sam Bush, Mike Marshall, Todd Phillips, John Reischman, and others. Alternately warm and crisp, comforting and energizing, his startlingly clean playing twirls and waltzes with the other instruments—one stepping out while another comes to the spotlight, often culminating in tightly locked passages with interwoven harmonies. These 15 instrumentals are lyrical without words, poetic without stanzas, and a brilliant glimpse into the soul of one of progressive bluegrass' most inventive players. *—Zac Johnson*

Native American / 1988 / Rounder ♦♦

Like its predecessor *Me and My Guitar, Native American* features a song about the assassination of Abraham Lincoln; this time out, it's "John Wilkes Booth," penned by Mary-Chapin Carpenter. *—Jason Ankeny*

Bluegrass Album, Vol. 5: Sweet Sunny South / 1989 / Rounder ♦♦♦

Plays and Sings Bluegrass / 1993 / Rounder ♦♦♦

Crossings / Dec. 6, 1994 / Mountain Home ♦♦♦♦

This Tony Rice CD is a little different from his typical fare, as it focuses exclusively on old-time hymns and spirituals, all featuring his unique style of picking that can't be mistaken for anyone else but the incredible guitarist himself. Accompanied by David Johnson (who plays mandolin, banjo, viola, fiddle, harmonica, bass, and banjotar), drummer Tony Creasman, and either Tim Surrett or Ben Isaacs on bass, Rice brings out the best in all of these time-tested melodies in this strictly instrumental disc. "Swing Low, Sweet Chariot" is an upbeat romp with a nod toward traditional bluegrass, while the inspirational hymn "Holy, Holy, Holy" is very subdued, with Rice prominently featured in the foreground. An elegantly improvised introduction to "Amazing Grace" may keep many listeners guessing. Although this CD may not be of much interest to strictly secular fans of Tony Rice, they owe it to themselves to give it a hearing, though it may be hard to acquire since this 1994 release seems to have lapsed from print. *—Ken Dryden*

River Suite for Two Guitars / 1995 / Sugar Hill ♦♦♦

For lovers of acoustic guitar, few things are more enjoyable than having two guitar heroes like Tony Rice and John Carlini record together. The music on *River Suite for Two Guitars* is performed by the two guitarists with no accompaniment, creating an intimate setting that is relaxed, while remaining professional. Only when the tempo picks up on songs like "It Takes a Thief" and "Fishscale" do Rice and Carlini really cut loose. In "Big Mang," one lead overlaps the other in an intense rush, while Miles Davis' "Nardis" finds Rice revisiting a song recorded by the Tony Rice Unit. It's amazing how much lead work these two guitarists can fit into a two minute song like "Banister River." Stereo allows Rice's guitar to appear on the left speaker, Carlini's on the right, but even without this convenience both guitarists' styles are easily discernible. The lead often changes every verse, keeping even quieter songs varied and layered; both players also provide tasteful and complex accompaniment to each other. The production is straight forward, allowing the music to stand on its own. Fans of both guitarists from their stint in the David Grisman Quintet will find this music quieter and less experimental, but will enjoy the eclectic song choices and the inspiration shared between two musicians. Certain slower songs like "Send in the Clowns" and "Summertime" are almost too quiet and familiar, but this is a minor complaint. *River Suite for Two Guitars* is the collaborative effort of equals who love to play guitar. Fans of both artists, and fans of good guitar music, should enjoy this one. *—Ronnie Lankford Jr.*

Tony Rice Sings Gordon Lightfoot / May 28, 1996 / Rounder ♦♦♦♦♦

Bluegrass singer/guitarist Tony Rice has been recording songs written by Gordon Lightfoot throughout his career, and this 17-track compilation gathers them together, adding a previously unreleased version of "Whispers of the North" that was cut for Rice's *Me and My Guitar* album. Included are tracks Rice recorded as part of J.D. Crowe & the New South, the Tony Rice Unit, the Rice Brothers, in a duo with Norman Blake, and as a solo artist. That means that on the various tracks he's joined by a newgrass who's who that includes Jerry Douglas, Ricky Skaggs, Sam Bush, Vassar Clements, and Béla Fleck, among others. The selections include "Wreck of the Edmund Fitzgerald" and "Early Morning Rain," but for the most part Rice eschewed Lightfoot's better known compositions, and the collection serves to illustrate the overall quality of the songwriter's catalog. Rice did not just use the songs as platforms for picking sessions, either. His singing clearly influenced by Lightfoot's, he brought a strong interpretive ability to the lyrics. Of course, the picking is pretty hot, too. *—William Ruhlmann*

Sings Gordon Lightfoot / Jun. 1996 / Rounder ♦♦♦

When one estimable musician covers another, two criteria invariably surface: Was it a fresh interpretation? Was some semblance of the original emotion retained? On *Sings Gordon Lightfoot*, it's fair to say Tony Rice meets both. Simply stated, Rice takes Lightfoot's catalog of rugged, Northern folk ballads and transposes them to Appalachian soil. Obviously, there is a distinct bluegrass undercurrent, but this is no real stretch considering the sparse, rural qualities of the originals. The track listing includes some familiar Lightfoot fare, including "Wreck of the Edmund Fitzgerald," "Bitter Green," and "I'm Not Sayin'," although Rice tends to dig well below the commercial surface for the meat of the album. Tracks like "You Are What I Am" and the previously unreleased "Whispers of the North"—which distinguishes itself as the most memorable song by a country mile—demonstrate both his familiarity and appreciation of the Canadian troubadour's canon. Instrumentally, Rice delivers his trademark: clean and tasteful acoustic pyrotechnics. He also employs a who's who cast of bluegrass pickers, including Jerry Douglas, Béla Fleck, and Vassar Clements to underscore Lightfoot's placid and literate songbook. The liquor here is sweet, but don't expect to blow any dust from the bottle. The production is rather distilled and slick—much like the pose Rice strikes on the album cover. *—Brian Kelly*

Unit of Measure / Oct. 31, 2000 / Rounder ♦♦♦

The Tony Rice Unit's last album of new material, *Backwaters*, was released in 1982. In fact, most of the lineup of the band, with fiddle player Rickie Simpkins, guitarist Wyatt Rice, mandolinist Jimmy Gaudreau, and bassist Ronnie Simpkins, formed in the mid-'80s, a few years after *Backwaters* was released. They had never recorded together. *Unit of Measure* is perhaps more traditional than previous Tony Rice Unit albums, with Bill Monroe's "Gold Rush" played as straight bluegrass. The eight-minute live version of "Sally Goodin" is a flatpicking, fiddle sawing bluegrass jam, and "Beaumont Rag" continues in this vein. Standouts on *Unit of Measure* include the now jazzgrass standard "Swing 42" and a new version of Rice's "Manzanita (1st Variation)." Both instrumentals capture the band at its spontaneous best, bringing a joy to the music that made the original Tony Rice Unit so exciting. Rickie Simpkins' fiddle work is outstanding throughout this album, immediately accessible with its romantic air and warm tone. As good as these musicians are though, the material leaves something to be desired. "Shenandoah," "An Olde Irish Aire (Danny Boy)," and worst of all, "House of the Rising Sun," sound like a typical set list for an all-night jam with friends, not material for a fresh recording. The listener's attention, at some point, will probably drift away. Oddly, much of this material was recorded way back in 1996, with only "Danny Boy" recorded in 1999. There is also the mysterious absence of tunes written by Rice (with the exception of "Manzanita" that had been written in the '70s). All of these factors give the impression that the band, as good as it is, is only going through the motions. One can only hope that *Unit of Measure* is just the starting point for the second life of the Tony Rice Unit. *—Ronnie Lankford Jr.*

Wyatt Rice

Guitar / Progressive Bluegrass, Traditional Bluegrass

The brother of Tony Rice, guitarist Wyatt Rice played in his brother's bluegrass band before forming his own group in the late '80s. The Wyatt Rice band has since recorded two albums in two different incarnations. The first version of the group was a sextet featuring violinist Rickie Simpkins and mandolinist Ray Legere; they released *New Market Gap* in 1989. By the mid-'90s, the group had become a quintet, and this lineup released *Picture in a Tear* in 1996. *—Stephen Thomas Erlewine*

New Market Gap / Feb. 1989 / Rounder ♦♦♦♦

On a leave of absence from his brother's Tony Rice Unit, Wyatt's put together a sextet featuring the talents of violinist Rickie Simpkins and mandolinist Ray Legere. Most of their material is made up of traditional compositions or Bill Monroe songs, but the record has a surprisingly modern sound that's as much folk as it is traditional bluegrass. *—Jason Ankeny*

● **Picture in a Tear** / Oct. 8, 1996 / Rounder ♦♦♦♦♦

Wyatt Rice's progressive bluegrass quintet shines on *Picture in a Tear.* Relying primarily on original material, Rice and his band pulls out energetic, vibrant performances out of each song on the record, even the weaker material. Fortunately, there isn't too much weak material here—the Wyatt Rice combo sounds like they've been playing together for years. *—Thom Owens*

Charlie Rich

b. Dec. 14, 1932, Colt, AR, **d.** Jul. 24, 1995, Hammond, LA

Piano, Vocals / Traditional Country, Progressive Country, Country-Pop, Rockabilly, Nashville Sound/Countrypolitan, Country-Soul

Charlie Rich was simultaneously one of the most critically acclaimed and most erratic country singers of post-World War II era. Rich had all the elements of being one of the great country stars of the '60s and '70s, but his popularity never matched his critical notices. What made him a critical favorite also kept him from mass success. Throughout his career, Rich willfully bended genres, fusing country, jazz, blues, gospel, rockabilly, and soul. Though he had 45 country hits in a career that spanned nearly four decades, he became best-known for his lush, Billy Sherrill-produced countrypolitan records of the early '70s. Instead of embracing the stardom those records brought him, Rich shunned it, retreating into semiretirement by the '80s.

Rich began his professional musical career while he was enlisted in the U.S. Air Force in the early '50s. While he was stationed in Oklahoma, he formed a group called the Velvetones, which played jazz and blues and featured his fiancée, Margaret Ann, on lead vocals. Rich left the military in 1956, and he began performing clubs around the Memphis area, playing both jazz and R&B; he also began writing his own material. Rich managed to land a job as a session musician for Judd Records, which was owned by Judd Phillips, the brother of Sun Records founder Sam Phillips. Around this time, saxophonist and Sun recording artist Bill Justis heard Rich play at the Sharecropper Club and asked the pianist to write arrangements for him. Sam saw Rich perform with Justis at a club gig and asked him to record some demos at Sun Studios. Phillips rejected the resulting demos, claiming they were too jazzy. After absorbing some Jerry Lee Lewis records Justis gave him, Rich returned to Sun quickly and became a regular session musician for the label in 1958, playing and/or singing on records by Lewis, Johnny Cash, Justis, Warren Smith, Billy Lee Riley, Carl Mann, and Ray Smith. He was also writing songs, including "Break Up" for Lewis, "The Ways of a Woman in Love" for Cash, and "I'm Comin' Home" for Mann, which was later cut by Elvis Presley.

In August of 1958, Rich released his first single, "Whirlwind," for the Sun subsidiary Phillips International. Throughout 1959, he recorded a number of songs at Sun, though only a handful were actually released. Rich didn't have a hit until 1960, when his third Phillips International single, "Lonely Weekends," became a Top 30 pop hit. However, none of its seven follow-up singles were a success, though several of the songs would become staples in his set, including "Who Will the Next Fool Be?," "Sittin' and Thinkin'," and "Midnight Blues." In the early '60s, Rich's career remained stalled. He left Sun Records in 1964, signing with Groove, a newly established subsidiary of RCA. His first single, "Big Boss Man," was an underground, word-of-mouth hit, but its Chet Atkins-produced follow-ups all stiffed. On Groove, he jazzily interpreted standards, but he also performed a handful of originals, including "Tomorrow Night" and "I Don't See Me in Your Eyes Anymore." Groove went out of business by the beginning of 1965, leaving Rich without a record contract.

Under the direction of Shelby Singleton, Smash Records signed Rich early in 1965. Singleton and Rich's producer, Jerry Kennedy, encouraged the pianist to emphasize his country and rock & roll leanings. The first single for Smash was "Mohair Sam," an R&B-inflected novelty number written by Dallas Frazier. "Mohair Sam" became a Top 30 pop hit, but none of its follow-ups were successful. Again, Rich changed labels, moving over to Hi Records, where he recorded straight country, but none of his singles for the label made any impression on the country charts.

Despite his lack of consistent commercial success, Epic Records signed Rich in 1967, mainly on the recommendation of producer Billy Sherrill. Sherrill helped Rich refashion himself as a Nashville-based, smooth, middle-of-the-road balladeer. At first, the singles were only moderately successful—"Set Me Free" and "Raggedy Ann" charted in the mid-40s in 1968—but persistence paid off in the summer of 1972, when "I Take It on Home" rocketed to number six. "I Take It on Home" set the stage for Rich's big breakthrough into the mainstream, 1973's *Behind Closed Doors* album. The title track from the record became a number-one hit early in 1973, crossing over into the Top 20 on the pop charts. Following the success of "Behind Closed Doors," RCA re-released "Tomorrow Night," which reached the Top 30, but it was "The Most Beautiful Girl," the proper follow-up to his first number one single, that established him as a star. "The Most Beautiful Girl" spent three weeks at the top of the country charts and two weeks at the top of the pop charts. *Behind Closed Doors* won three awards from the Country Music Association that year: Best Male Vocalist, Album of the Year, and Single of the Year for the title track. The album was also certified gold, Rich won a Grammy for Best Country Vocal Performance, Male, and he also took home four ACM awards.

After "The Most Beautiful Girl," number-one hits came quickly—"There Won't Be Anymore" (re-released from his RCA sessions), "A Very Special Love Song," "I Don't See

Me in Your Eyes Anymore" (also from RCA), "I Love My Friend," and "She Called Me Baby" (RCA) all topped the country charts, and several of the songs also crossed over into the pop charts. Mercury began re-releasing his Smash recordings, and two of them—"A Field of Yellow Daisies" and "Something Just Came Over Me"—became minor hits. All of this success led the CMA to name him Entertainer of the Year in 1974.

Rich didn't quite dominate the charts in 1975 as he did the previous year, but he did have three Top Five hits: "My Elusive Dreams," "Every Time You Touch Me (I Get High)," and "All Over Me," plus the Top Ten "Since I Fell For You." Even though he was at the peak of his popularity, Rich had begun to drink heavily, causing considerable problems offstage. His destructive behavior culminated at the CMA ceremony for 1975, when he presented the award for that year's Entertainer of the Year. Instead of reading the name of the winner, he set fire to the certificate that named the new winner, who happened to be John Denver. Fans and industry insiders were outraged, and Rich had trouble having hits throughout 1976—none of his singles cracked the Top 20.

The slump in his career couldn't be completely attributed to Rich's behavior. His records had begun to sound increasingly similar, as he and Sherrill were working over the same territory they began exploring in 1968. There were exceptions—such as 1976's acclaimed gospel record, *Silver Linings*—but it took Rich until 1977 to break back into the Top Ten with the number one "Rollin' With the Flow." Early in 1978, he signed with United Artists and throughout that year had hits on both Epic and UA. Rich worked at United Artists with Larry Butler, a producer who had a similar style to Sherrill. Epic continued to have hits, as "Beautiful Woman" reached the Top Ten in the summer and a duet with Janie Fricke, "On My Knees," became his last number-one hit that fall. "I'll Wake You Up When I Get Home," taken from the Clint Eastwood movie *Every Which Way but Loose*, was a number-three hit early in 1979; it would be his last Top Ten single.

Rich struggled to have a big hit throughout 1979, but none of his singles were anything more than a minor success. In 1980, he switched labels to Elektra, resulting in the number 12 single "A Man Just Don't Know What a Woman Goes Through" in the fall of that year. One more Top 40 hit followed—"Are We Dreamin' the Same Dream" early in 1981—but Rich decided to remove himself from the spotlight. For over a decade, Rich was silent, living in semiretirement and only playing the occasional concert. He returned in 1992 with *Pictures and Paintings*, a jazzy record produced by journalist Peter Guralnick and released on Sire. *Pictures and Paintings* received positive reviews and restored Rich's reputation, but it would be his last record. Rich died from a blood clot in his lung in the summer of 1995, when he was travelling to Florida with his wife, Margaret Ann. *—Stephen Thomas Erlewine*

Lonely Weekends / 1960 / Sun ✦✦✦✦

Lonely Weekends is 11 tracks of Charlie Rich at his piano-pumpin' best. Unlike his Sun label mate, Jerry Lee Lewis, Rich and Sam Phillips were able to come to a balance of power and finesse. Rich wasn't only a fine piano player, he was a great writer who knew how to arrange his own material. Phillips was looking for the commercial angle with Rich and got close more than a few times. This set—besides the rockin' and rollin' title track with the astonishing female backing chorus—has hints of the *Silver Fox* to come, in the slow, New Orleans-stroll read of the North/Zaret classic "Unchained Melody." The beautiful and unholy alliance of country, pop, and doo wop in Rich's own "Stay" is only eclipsed by his bona fide treasure "C.C. Rider." While many have covered it, no one has come close to achieving the perfect balance of rhythm & blues-flavored rock, high-lonesome honky tonk swagger, and gospel wail. "Rebound," co-written with Bill Justis, takes a Buddy Holly-style staggered vocal and puts it into Jerry Lee overdrive. Side two is even better, in that other than "Big Man," Rich wrote everything on it: "Who Will the Next Fool Be," covered by everyone from teen pop stars to soul groups to country artists; the searing "I Need Your Love"; and the smoking piano blitz of "Break Up," covered lamely by Elvis. Here it veers, like Lewis' material; it's out of control, with Rich jumpin' and poppin' all over the keyboard. The set ends with another Rich nugget that scored for many other artists, the honky tonk gem "Sittin' and Thinkin'." Rich's version is a tad sweeter—due, no doubt, to Phillips adding strings to the mix—but it's still plenty poignant. In all, this is a fine overview of what Rich brought to Sun—plenty. *—Thom Jurek*

The Many Sides of Charlie Rich / 1965 / Smash ✦✦✦

Charlie Rich Sings Country and Western / 1967 / Hi ✦✦✦

Rich interpreted 12 songs written by or associated with Hank Williams for this middling 1967 album, including "Hey Good Lookin'," "Cold Cold Heart," "I'm So Lonesome I Could Cry," and less celebrated tunes. [It's been reissued with 13 blue-eyed soul cuts that Rich recorded for Hi around the same time on the British import CD *Charlie Rich Sings the Songs of Hank Williams Plus the R&B Sessions*, which is the recommended alternative to searching for the out-of-print vinyl release.] *—Richie Unterberger*

☆ **Set Me Free** / 1968 / Koch ✦✦✦✦✦

Set Me Free was Charlie Rich's first album for Epic Records and the first record he ever cut with Nashville producer Billy Sherrill. Previously, Rich's producers hadn't known what to do with his eclectic style, although his sessions for Smash came close to capturing all sides of his personality. With Sherrill, Rich had a producer whose musical tastes were nearly as eclectic as his own, and that is captured on the freewheeling, diverse sounds of *Set Me Free*. Purists may be uncomfortable with Sherrill's lush production—he sets Rich's voice in a bed of strings, keyboards, horns, and backing vocals. Consequently, the sound of *Set Me Free* is laid-back and relaxed; occasionally, Rich sounds *too* relaxed, as if he didn't connect with the material. Although there are a handful of poor songs and half-hearted performances on the record, *Set Me Free* has an overall tone lacking on Rich's previous records that makes up for its assorted weaknesses. The songs come from a variety of sources, ranging from country and blues to jazz and pop, but they're all given a cohesive Nashville production by Sherrill, which is what makes *Set Me Free* one of Rich's best, most consistent albums. *—Stephen Thomas Erlewine*

☆ **The Fabulous Charlie Rich** / 1969 / Koch ✦✦✦✦✦

The Fabulous Charlie Rich follows the same formula as its predecessor, *Set Me Free*, but to more successful results. For starters, the record has a more consistent set of material—these are songs that Rich can really sink his teeth into, as evidenced by the beautiful, melancholy "Life's Little Ups and Downs" (written by his wife, Margaret Ann) and his own "Sittin' and Thinkin'." Furthermore, the core of each song—from the bluesy "July 12, 1939" and "Bright Lights, Big City" (which is done essentially as a Jimmy Reed medley, performed in the style of Ray Charles) to the soulful "I Almost Lost My Mind" and the country-pop stylings of "San Francisco Is a Lonely Town" and "Love Waits for Me"—is more apparent, thanks to Billy Sherrill's relatively trimmed-down production. There are still strings, vocal choruses, and horns throughout the album, but Sherrill has incorporated them into Rich's style more effectively. Occasionally, there is a fairly uninspired number, but *The Fabulous Charlie Rich* does capture the eclectic nature of Rich's music better than the great majority of his albums, even if the sumptuous production will make it less palatable for country purists. *—Stephen Thomas Erlewine*

Boss Man / Aug. 1970 / Koch ✦✦✦✦✦

Charlie Rich and Billy Sherrill reached a peak with *The Fabulous Charlie Rich*, creating a perfect middle ground between Rich's rootsier tendencies and Sherrill's country-pop leanings. Like many of Rich's records, it didn't sell, and that might have been one of the reasons its follow-up, *Boss Man*, was their weakest effort to date. Although there are quite a few high spots and the album essentially follows the same formula as their previous efforts, the material isn't consistent, alternating between bluesy shuffles and country weepers; both styles range from the brilliant to the boring. What's even worse is the fact that Rich himself sounds uninspired, giving competent but unenthusiastic performances. There's enough prime material to make *Boss Man* an enjoyable listen, particularly for Rich fans who know that he rarely comes up with consistent albums. However, it didn't have the spark of *The Fabulous Charlie Rich*, nor did it have the immaculate sheen of *Behind Closed Doors*, the country-pop masterpiece that followed *Boss Man*. Nevertheless, *Boss Man* had enough fine songs to make it an essential purchase for true Rich fans. *—Stephen Thomas Erlewine*

The Best of Charlie Rich / 1972 / Epic ✦✦✦

This album was released before Rich actually had any hits on this label. Fans will recognize some of the titles from earlier releases on other labels ("Big Boss Man," "Sittin' and Thinkin'"), but none of these versions could be considered a hit. That aside, there are still some good songs on here. Don't be put off just because the title isn't accurate. *—Jim Worbois*

☆ **Behind Closed Doors** / 1973 / Epic/Legacy ✦✦✦✦✦

Charlie Rich finally had a genuine hit with *Behind Closed Doors*, an exceedingly lush expansion of the sound he had essayed with producer Billy Sherrill on his first Epic albums. Here, Sherrill ups the ante considerably by adding layers of strings and choirs, and the two move the material toward the mainstream. The key to the record's success, is that Rich's signature blend of country, jazz, blues, rock, and pop retains its character throughout it all, resulting in an album that's a twin peak—the pinnacle of Sherrill's countrypolitan sound, while standing as one of Rich's great albums. The hit singles—"Behind Closed Doors," "The Most Beautiful Girl," "I Take It on Home"—deservedly receive most of the attention, but the record is filled with great songs, including two from his wife Margaret Ann ("A Sunday Kind of Woman," "Nothing in the World (To Do With Me)") that stand as highlights. Throughout it all, Rich delivers the kind of shaded, nuanced performances that earned him a devoted cult—a cult that might not cherish *Behind Closed Doors* as much as some of his other records because of its lushness, but if that lushness introduced a new audience to the wonders of Charlie Rich, it can't be bad at all. [The 2001 CD reissue contains four bonus tracks, culled from the 1972 album *We Love Each Other*.] *—Stephen Thomas Erlewine*

There Won't Be Anymore / 1974 / RCA ✦✦✦

While the issue date on this album is 1974, the material was recorded much earlier during the RCA years, which dates it to the late '60s. With Chet Atkins listed as producer, the album was licensed to PowerPak originally, but when *Behind Closed Doors* broke, RCA put it out themselves a year later. The obvious cash-in factor aside, there's not a damn thing wrong with the material here. Recorded by famed Nash Vegas engineers Bill Porter and Chuck Seitz, these two cats understood Rich's subtleties and strengths. The songs range from countrypolitan to slightly more pop-oriented material, with Rich's gorgeous and fullest baritone voice that is reminiscent in places of Elvis Presley's at its level best. Side one has a couple of Rich classics in "I Don't See Me in Your Eyes Anymore," "Too Many Teardrops," and "Turn Around and Face Me." Side two boasts the title cut and "It's All Over Now," with that lazy honky tonk piano. "No Room to Dance" is a nod back to the Sun years with its teen idol melody and mariachi backing band, which makes the track surreal. "Nice 'n' Easy" sounds like it could have been produced by Lee Hazlewood, but Rich's own signature croon moves it nearly into Bacharach/David territory. Not a great record, but certainly a good one and worth it to anyone who is interested in Rich's pre-Columbia material. *—Thom Jurek*

The Silver Fox / 1974 / Epic ✦✦✦✦✦

Charlie Rich's runaway success with "Behind Closed Doors" and "The Most Beautiful Girl" prompted media attention he could never have anticipated. Given that by the early '70s Rich had been in the business almost 20 years and had sold some records, nothing could have prepared him for what happened. *The Silver Fox* is an unprecedented album by a country and pop singer. Issued in 1974, it features a sidelong medley of Rich talking about his musical development and playing—along with a host of Nashville's finest and producer Billy Sherrill—examples indicative of his journey: a classical rondo, a steaming version of "Don't Put No Headstone on My Grave," a swing instrumental, a stomping version of his Sun Records classic "Break Up," the previously released version of "Behind

Closed Doors," and one of his most undeniable classics, "I Feel Like Goin' Home." Not as stirring as the version on *Pictures and Paintings* with the Memphis gospel choir, but with the Nashville Edition he pulls off a stunner that raises goosebumps; it can bring tears to the most hardened eyes. The flip side is filled with inspired covers of songs written by Sherrill and others, but the most notable tracks are Rich's own "Your Place Is Here With Me," with its Ray Charles-inspired gospel and blues swing, and "Whatever Happened," composed by Rich's wife, Margaret Ann. A sweet and lilting country ballad, it evokes nostalgia, bittersweet regret, and glimpses of time's passage. Laden with Sherrill's trademark string arrangements, a backing chorus, and Hargus "Pig" Robbins' honky tonk piano, in Rich's baritone, the tune becomes a gentle elegy of disappearance of innocence and first love. This is one of, if not the, finest of Rich's '70s recordings. *—Thom Jurek*

Very Special Love Songs / 1974 / Epic ♦♦♦♦

Making every effort to strike while the iron was hot, Epic sent Charlie Rich and Billy Sherrill back into the studio to keep his profile in the public eye. What should have been a haphazard dash-off slab of re-dos and hastily chosen tracks instead turned out to be one of the most pleasant surprises of Rich's monumental run in the 1970s. *Very Special Love Songs* is almost entirely comprised of cover versions and showcases the close, nearly symbiotic partnership Rich and Sherrill had developed. While more on the country tip than many of his recordings from the period, it's still country with a grand twist. The title track is layered with a huge string section and chorus that has Rich crooning like Richard Harris in "MacArthur Park." "Why Don't We Go Somewhere and Love" is more straight-ahead but has odd textures like Sherrill bringing in a barely audible harpsichord to play beneath the acoustic guitars and Hargus Robbin's honky tonk piano. The chorus is straight out of Mac Davis and hits home hard. Other tracks, such as "Take Time to Love," "A Field of Yellow Daisies," and "Why, Oh Why," are offerings of such soulful vulnerability they transcend every country music stereotype that existed at the time. Re-recordings of "He Follows in My Footsteps" and "There Won't Be Anymore" blow away the originals. Rich's voice is stronger, even if it is a bit more worn from cigarettes and whiskey, and it's so much more honest emotionally. Side one is the optimistic and hopefully side while the flip is a shade darker, sadder, more melancholy, but in true Rich fashion, "Pretty People" opens the glimmer of possibly, the barely glimpsed sliver of hope on the horizon that the sad times will end eventually and that the song's protagonist will be able to embrace that time with gratitude. The strings and piano carry the tune all the way out with the vocal ending barely a second before the track does, leaving its exhortations out in the ether hanging for the listener to take inside and contemplate. It's a wonderful release despite the rush. *—Thom Jurek*

Every Time You Touch Me (I Get High) / 1975 / Epic ♦♦♦♦♦

The 1970s were a magical time for Charlie Rich and producer Billy Sherrill. Sherrill was the first producer who not only understood how gifted Rich was musically—he knew virtually no bounds when it came to popular music styles—but could comprehend and deliver Rich's vision to record buyers. On the title track, restrained bass notes and minimal, jazzy pianism coast into a space where strings glide into Rich's verse. Shimmering trills in the piano's mid-range accent the end of each line, as do the female vocalists of the Nashville Edition. It's dreamy and ethereal and the listener encounters quite literally what the song's protagonist is describing. And "All Over Me" is a country tune with Rich's honky tonk accents caressed by Sherrill's strings and Pete Drake's pedal steel in a broken paean to love gone awry. This is the album that pointed to all the various directions Rich wanted to explore musically. Like Ray Charles' *New Sounds in Country and Western Music*, Rich extended it to include new textures and sounds in pop and country. A stunning example is "Since I Fell for You," where Rich treats the melody like a rhythm & blues crooner and takes it to the breaking point of its country root. Side two holds a surprise in the dark, film noir-ish beauty of Margaret Ann Rich's "Pass on By." Again, the deep R&B strains meet doo wop, soul, and early rock in a setting provided by Sherrill that could have been in a 1950s thriller sung in a smoky lounge. And while the rest of the side is terrific as well, Rich's own "Midnight Blues" walks the edge of rock and soul à la the Memphis sound. Shimmering strings in glissandi, stinging lead guitar, a trio of female verses echoing Rich's lines, and Hargus "Pig" Robbins' honky tonk piano make the track swagger and shimmy, carrying the listener out on a rough and rowdy, darkly tinted note. Whew! *—Thom Jurek*

Too Many Teardrops / 1975 / Pickwick ♦♦♦

When Charlie Rich broke through in 1973 with "Behind Closed Doors," his former labels, RCA and Mercury, released a flurry of singles containing recordings from the mid-'60s, and they sold incredibly well, reaching number one on the country chart in some cases. Few country artists' decade-old recordings would still be so marketable, but Rich's soulful country sound was far enough ahead of its time to sound contemporary years later. Rich's RCA recordings lack the funkiness of the Smash recordings he made a couple of years later, and some of the arrangements are pure pop, but the quality is high throughout. The budget label Pickwick reissued nine of these old RCA cuts on the album *Too Many Teardrops* in 1975 while Rich was still a hot artist, and although none of his freak '70s hits are included, the package gives collectors an affordable opportunity to hear more music from Rich's RCA period without having to find the more collectible original albums from the '60s. *—Greg Adams*

☆ **Silver Linings** / 1976 / Epic ♦♦♦♦♦

In 1976 Charlie Rich was still riding the charts on the heels of *Every Time You Touch Me (I Get High)* to be able to record whatever the hell he wanted to, and his label, Epic, wasn't about to argue. Produced by Billy Sherrill, *Silver Linings* is a collection of traditional spirituals done as only the Silver Fox could, melding country, rhythm & blues, jazz, and pop together to come up with something wholly original, adding depth and dimension to songs that have been worn lifeless by overuse. Usually artists close an album with "Will the Circle Be Unbroken," but Rich had balls enough to kick off the set with it—before moving into a hard-swinging read of "Down By the Riverside" that rivals Ray Charles' version for heart-stirring spiritual intensity and pure Saturday-night swagger. Whether backed by the Jordanaires or the Nashville Edition, Rich gets his choirs to deliver enough from the gut to allow him to work his magic. On "Why Me?" Rich sounds like a man at the end of his rope, and the choir serves to try to lift him above his despair. Side two is where the disc moves into overdrive with one of the finest-ever renditions of "Swing Low, Sweet Chariot" by a country artist. Rich's voice, with all its smoke and sweetness, blends well with the choir before kicking into a bluesy country stomp with whining pedal steel and snare drums popping in the margins. "Amazing Grace" is done as a cross between Jerry Lee Lewis' rock & roll and Meade "Lux" Lewis' boogie-woogie—it's unadulterated, sanctified sinner's music. Rich sends it all out on a spooky note with "Sometimes I Feel Like a Motherless Child," which is part original Negro spiritual and part late-night blues. Amazing from start to finish, *Silver Linings* is one of the Top Ten country gospel records of all time. *—Thom Jurek*

Greatest Hits / 1976 / Epic ♦♦♦♦♦

This focuses on his biggest hits ("Behind Close Doors," "The Most Beautiful Girl") though not necessarily the most representative work. Ignore the cheesy production, however, and you'll hear his vocals as utterly sublime. *—Dan Cooper*

Take Me / 1977 / Epic ♦♦♦

Rollin' with the Flow / 1977 / Epic ♦♦

Classic Rich / 1978 / Sony ♦♦♦

Once a Drifter / 1980 / Elektra ♦♦♦

American Originals / 1989 / Columbia ♦♦♦

These were the Epic hits that propelled Charlie Rich beyond the realm of just another country singer. Several classic country/pop crossover hits are included, such as "The Most Beautiful Girl," "Behind Closed Doors," and "My Elusive Dreams," but other tracks of equal importance, like "Every Time You Touch Me (I Get High)," "I Love My Friend," and "A Very Special Love Song," are omitted. Sony's *16 Biggest Hits* is still the best single package highlighting '70s-era Charlie Rich. *—Al Campbell*

☆ **Pictures and Paintings** / 1992 / Sire ♦♦♦♦♦

Despite a career that lasted over four decades, no record he ever made came as close to capturing the totality of Charlie Rich's musical persona as *Pictures and Paintings*. Ironically, it was to be his last recording; Rich died less than three years later in a motel in Florida of a blood clot in his lung. While Rich came into the public eye in the 1950s writing for Jerry Lee Lewis and with his own '60s hit "Mohair Sam," and became a superstar known as the Silver Fox in the early '70s for his Billy Sherrill-produced hits like "Behind Closed Doors," none of these records came close to capturing the complex essence of who Rich was as a songwriter, arranger, and pianist. *Pictures and Paintings* offers 11 slices of Rich the public had rarely, if ever, seen. Produced by Scott Billington with help from writer Peter Guralnick and Joe McEwen, Rich developed his material from informal jam sessions held over a couple of years with friends. The music ranges from jazz and blues to swing to country and gospel. Rich's own tunes, which make up the majority of the album, cut across genres and time lines. His radical reworking of "Every Time You Touch Me (I Get High)" (co-written with Sherrill) becomes a Latin-tinged samba worthy of being interpreted by the early Tamba 4 or Sergio Mendes. His reading of the title track, a co-write of the Doc Pomus/Dr. John collaboration, is a smoky, jazzy tune rather than a New Orleans-flavored R&B number. Michael Toles' shimmering chromatic shapes and colors on guitar, accented by Rich's tastefully placed piano fills, de-center the rhythm of the track and make it a steamy little swinging, midtempo ballad. Either Dean Martin or Conway Twitty could have recorded "You Don't Know Me" in their prime. Rich's own version has more soul than both of them put together, though. Rich's reading of Duke Ellington's "Mood Indigo" is no novelty number, but a serious revisioning of the harmonic extrapolations Ellington and Barney Bigard built into its chromatic architecture. Nothing can prepare the listener for the album's final track, however. "Feel Like Going Home" is a gospel tune of such desperation and disappointment, such a plea for deliverance, that it shatters the listener's composure. This writer defies anyone to be unmoved by it—if you aren't, you must have sawdust instead of blood in your veins. Rich begins with a simple country gospel motif, which he builds upon with each passing verse as the band enters the first into the background and then into the body of the tune, with a Hammond B-3 floating above it all. By the time the choir enters, the effect is devastating and the listener feels the crack in Rich's voice and spirit, but the choir buoys him and adds the hope that makes grace possible. It goes out soaring with promise and possibility, summing up an astonishing and extremely complex journey through American music so thorough, so masterfully executed, it could have only been navigated by someone of Rich's unparalleled abilities. To record an album of diverse and difficult material is one achievement, to make that material accessible to a wide range of listeners is yet another. Rich succeeded on both counts, and given that his life ended after this session, that final track is all the more powerful, eerie, and profound. On *Pictures and Paintings*, Charlie Rich saved the very best, his magnum opus, for last, and we are all the richer for it. For fans, this is as essential; for the beginner, this is as fine an introduction as there is. *—Thom Jurek*

☆ **The Complete Smash Sessions** / Aug. 4, 1992 / Mercury ♦♦♦♦♦

The Complete Smash Sessions contains everything that Charlie Rich recorded and released for Smash during the mid-'60s. Many of these songs forshadows the music Elvis Presley would make during his comeback in 1968, as well as the country-pop of the early '70s. Skillfully mixing rock, blues, R&B, country, and soul, Rich was at the top of his form when he made this music. He may have only had one hit during this period—"Mohair Sam" reached number 21 in 1965—but his tenure at Smash remained one of his most fruitful and creative periods. *—Stephen Thomas Erlewine*

Charlie Rich Sings the Songs of Hank Williams Plus the R&B Sessions / 1994 / Diablo ✦✦✦

Why the tongue-twisting title? Because this British import CD reissues his 1967 Hi LP *Sings Country and Western*, which consisted entirely of songs written by or associated with Hank Williams, adding 13 R&B/soul-oriented tunes he cut for the Hi label (some unreleased at the time) around the same era. The Hank Williams numbers are about what you would expect, or a little less. Rich offers competent updates of a dozen of Hank's tunes, and while the singing is good, the arrangements are pretty conservative, in a sort of take-no-risks crossover fashion. Far more interesting are the R&B sides, which bolster Rich's strong case as one of the great White soul singers. The backing is suitably funk/bluesy, and Rich's vocals are great. Some of the material may have been too jazzy or offbeat to stand much of a chance for commercial success at the time, but there's some notable buried treasure here, including a couple of Hayes-Porter covers. The Rich original "I'll Shed No Tears" is as close as soul and country come to mating, and "Pass On By" (written by Charlie's wife Margaret Ann) is blue-eyed soul at its jazziest and most sophisticated. —*Richie Unterberger*

☆ **Lonely Weekends: Best of the Sun Years** / Mar. 19, 1996 / AVI ✦✦✦✦✦

While the casual fan will only remember Charlie Rich for his later country MOR hits, if you really want to get in on the ground-floor and experience some of the wide variety and depth of the man's prodigious talents, here's exactly where you go to get straight. Sam Phillips pretty much let Rich do whatever he wanted to do at 706 Union, making a "Complete Sun Sessions" a real unlikely vote-getter on the reissue horizon simply because Rich had so much talent in so many different directions (jazz vs. country, blues vs. crass banality) that putting it all out almost makes no sense at all. Which is why this compilation is so refreshing; no filler, no dumb stuff, just the hits and the best tracks from a five- or six-year period when Rich was one of the last glimmers of hope for the label. All the early hits like "Lonely Weekends," "Sittin' and Thinkin'," and "Who Will the Next Fool Be" are aboard, along with several stereo tracks remixed from the original multi-track masters for the first time ever with sparkling sound. Charlie Rich was one talented man and here's where you find some of his best. —*Cub Koda*

☆ **Sun Sessions** / Mar. 26, 1996 / Varese Vintage ✦✦✦✦✦

One of the most misunderstood artists in popular music was Charlie Rich. He was also one of the most gifted; his talent was virtually boundless. While many artists showcased some of their best years on the Sun label, including Carl Perkins, Bill Justis, Jerry Lee Lewis, and countless others, Rich's body of work during and after Sun showcases a musical mind and piano stylist virtually unequaled. The Sun recordings originally appeared on a subsidiary Sam Phillips set up in 1957 called Phillips International. The 18 tracks included here represent the nine singles Rich cut for the label. And while most folks who've followed Rich's career even casually know he cut "Break Up," "Lonely Weekends," "Who Will the Next Fool Be," "Everything I Do Is Wrong," and "No Headstone on My Grave" (all of which he authored), they only know one side of the story. The true scorch of Rich's rock & roll years is here too, in a track such as the opening "Whirlwind," his first single cut in August of 1958 with a killer boogie-woogie piano line under a doo wop chorus backing Rich's rockabilly hiccup. Though he didn't write it, he wrote the flip and virtually everything else he recorded for Sun. "Philadelphia Baby" is down in the tough and raw R&B mode that sounds like the Big Bopper crossed with Big Joe Turner. "Rebound," with its heartbroken vocal and furious piano-pumpin' tempo, is one of the most mysterious moments in a career full of them. "Break Up" was originally written for Jerry Lee Lewis, but given his untimely marriage to his 13-year old cousin, Rich's version feels completely different. Elvis should have cut this one. Of course, in 1959 when he hit with "Lonely Weekends," everyone knew who Rich was but they weren't prepared for his eclecticism, though Phillips clearly was. "Gonna Be Waiting," issued in 1960, was an R&B shouter in the same vein as Ray Charles' music of the time. But the ballads work too, such as the country/doo wop fusion tune called "Caught in the Middle," with its teen idol melody line and honky tonk piano, and "Who Will the Next Fool Be," which Rich failed to score with but Bobby "Blue" Bland did. Rich's version kicks its ass all over the street. Also here is the original single version of "Midnite Blues" and the tough in the groove blues of "There Won't Be Anymore," in its original setting, with Rich growling and crooning his way through it, tearing the seams from the genres and opening up the world of heartache to a boundless world of sound that comes from the ether. This purchase is not debatable for anyone interested in rockabilly, blues, great country, or Rich. —*Thom Jurek*

★ **Feel Like Going Home: The Essential Charlie Rich** / Jan. 28, 1997 / Columbia/Legacy ✦✦✦✦✦

Though it bypasses his late-'70s and early-'80s records for United Artists and Elektra, the double-disc, 36-track set *Feel Like Going Home: The Essential Charlie Rich* covers Rich's best (and best-known) work for Sun/Phillips, Groove, Smash, and Epic, making it the first cross-licensed compilation ever assembled on the idiosyncratic vocalist and pianist. The multi-label approach works wonders in illustrating the depths of Rich's talents, since the compilation showcases all of his stylistic detours and his rich musical eclecticism. The song selection also helps showcase his versatility. While *Feel Like Going Home* contains all of his best-known songs in their original hit versions ("Lonely Weekends," "Who Will the Next Fool Be," "Sittin' and Thinkin'," "Big Boss Man," "Mohair Sam," "I Washed My Hands in Muddy Waters," "Set Me Free," "Don't Put No Headstone on My Grave," "Life's Little Ups and Downs," "Behind Closed Doors," "The Most Beautiful Girl"), it overlooks several big country hits from the mid-'70s in favor of lesser-known '60s and early-'70s recordings, which are stronger performances. As a consequence, *Feel Like Going Home* is the only compilation that truly shows the scope of Rich's talent, and it works both as an introduction and as a definitive retrospective. —*Stephen Thomas Erlewine*

Big Boss Man: The Groove Sessions / 1998 / Koch ✦✦✦✦✦

After a sporadic career at Sun Records in the late '50s, Charlie Rich hooked up with Nashville sound architect Chet Atkins in 1963 to record for RCA's R&B subsidiary, Groove. Rich proceeded to cut his usual mix of country, rockabilly, blues, and pop sides but with added, Nashville-sound touches like choral backing and strings; it was a style that landed somewhere between the raw sound of his Sun hits ("Rebound") and the pop-crossover tone of his Epic smashes ("Behind Closed Doors"). Fortunately, the glossier elements of the Groove sides collected on *Big Boss Man* are neutralized by Rich's powerful tenor voice and solid, jazz-tinged piano work. The mixed set includes blues-rockers like "Big Boss Man" and "Big Jack," as well as swinging, lounge treatments of "River Stay Away From My Door" and "Ol' Man River." Rich also applies his varied musical approach to many excellent originals here, like the driving, shuffle-beat tune "The Ways of a Woman in Love," the sanctified ballad "Rosanna Now," and the straight-pop song "Are You Still My Baby." Throw in a fine, Ray Charles-style number like "Tomorrow Night" and the touching country ballad Rich co-wrote with wife and tune-smith Margaret Ann Rich, and you have a completely satisfying set. Multifaceted artists are usually not tended to by a record industry comfortable with distinct categories, and this certainly explains why it took Rich so long to achieve stardom. Rich's fans, though, love his ability to forge a very distinct sound out of all kinds of music; this excellent Koch reissue of many of his Groove sides certainly proves the point. —*Stephen Cook*

Lonely Weekends: The Best of the Sun Years, 1958–1962 [Box Set] / Mar. 25, 1998 / Bear Family ✦✦✦✦✦

16 Biggest Hits / Feb. 2, 1999 / Sony ✦✦✦✦

Charlie Rich reached the country charts 45 times between 1968 and 1981 with recordings released on six different labels, though 25 of them were on Epic Records. This compilation presents the 15 highest charting of the Epic singles, including some of Rich's most successful ones—"The Most Beautiful Girl," "A Very Special Love Song," "Behind Closed Doors"—plus a non-hit recording of "Amazing Grace" to close the album. Since many of Rich's hits on labels like RCA Victor and Mercury came a decade after they were recorded, this album contains all the big hits of Rich's late maturity as a highly produced country crooner in the 1970s. But the buyer should realize that these are his biggest hits on Epic, not his biggest, period. —*William Ruhlmann*

Lonely Weekends: The Very Best of Charlie Rich / Feb. 2, 1999 / Collectables ✦✦✦

This is a great collection for anyone interested Charlie Rich's early career at Sun Records. The ardent fan may opt for Bear Records' mammoth, 90-song *Complete Charlie Rich Sun Collection*, but the 23 tracks on Collectables' *Lonely Weekends: The Very Best of Charlie Rich* also provides an effective overview of Rich's varied repertoire from the late '50s and early '60s. Rich was, in many ways, the most talented member of Sam Phillips' Sun roster, which also included "Million Dollar Quartet" icons Elvis Presley, Carl Perkins, Jerry Lee Lewis, and Johnny Cash. Rich not only furnished hits for Lewis ("Breakup") and Cash ("The Ways of a Woman in Love") but also was an accomplished jazz pianist and able to demonstrate his unmatched vocal prowess on many original gospel, pop, blues, and country numbers. Rich's swinging, rockabilly hits "Lonely Weekends" and "Rebound" are included in this collection along with lesser-known gems like the solo, boogie-woogie number "Donna Lee" and his version of Perkins' "Blue Suede Shoes." Other highlights include Rich's honky tonk blues "Who Will the Next Fool Be" (a minor country hit on its early-'70s re-release) and the autobiographical, alcoholic's lament "Sittin' and Thinkin'." Rich is best remembered for his later countrypolitan hits like "Behind Closed Doors," but, along with his solid sides for the Groove, Smash, and Epic labels in the '60s, the work he did for Sun should not be overlooked. Start with *Lonely Weekends: The Very Best of Charlie Rich* and work your way from there for a grand tour of the career of one of the unsung heroes of early rock & roll. —*Stephen Cook*

Early Years: Memphis Sound / Oct. 12, 1999 / Collectables ✦✦✦✦

Lonely Weekends/Time for Tears / Oct. 12, 1999 / Collectables ✦✦✦✦

Before Charlie Rich became "The Silver Fox," recording a slew of country-pop hits in the early '70s, he cut numerous rockabilly sessions for Sun Records in the '50s and early '60s. *Lonely Weekends/Time for Tears* combines two original LPs for the first time on one CD. Rich soulfully tears through favorites, including "Who Will the Next Fool Be?," "Lonely Weekends," "Sittin' and Thinkin'," and "Midnight Blues." You can't go wrong with this set reissued on the Collectables label. —*Al Campbell*

Ultimate Collection / Mar. 28, 2000 / Hip-O ✦✦✦✦

Tapping into Universal Music's incredibly deep vaults, the people at Hip-O have seen fit to include Charlie Rich in their ongoing *Ultimate Collection* survey series. Rich, of course, became a top-selling country singer in the early '70s, scoring crossover gold with chart-toppers like "Behind Closed Doors" and "The Most Beautiful Girl in the World." In addition to those pop smashes, this 18-track set takes in many other highlights from Rich's long and varied career, which stretched from his early days at Sun Records in the late '50s to an incredible final session (*Pictures and Paintings*) cut a few years before his death in 1995. Chronologically taking in his Sun, Groove, Smash, Epic, and Sire sides, the disc includes such Rich landmarks as "Lonely Weekends," "Mohair Sam," and "Feel Like Going Home." A fine retrospective of one of country music's most talented, versatile, and honest figures. —*Stephen Cook*

Love Songs / Sep. 26, 2000 / Epic ✦✦✦

This ten-song budget compilation gathers some of Charlie Rich's biggest hits, some minor chart entries, and some album tracks in its aim to sample the singer's ballad work. "Behind Closed Doors" is included, as is another country number one, "A Very Special Love Song." In concert with the latter hit, Rich made an album called *Very Special Love Songs* in 1974, and that's an obvious source for selections, with such tunes as "Why Don't We Go Somewhere and Love" and "Satisfied Man" plucked from it. Thus, not every song will be familiar to the casual fan, but as the title suggests, this is a mood collection, and Rich was often at his best in this smoldering mode. *—William Ruhlmann*

The Complete Charlie Rich on Hi Records / Oct. 17, 2000 / Hi ✦✦✦✦
The Hi recordings of Charlie Rich are in many ways the most reckless and adventurous of his career. In 1966 and 1967, Hi, a small Memphis label that hosted acts such as Willie Mitchell (and later Al Green) and the Bill Black Combo believed, like Sun, RCA, and Mercury before them, in Rich's prodigious talent but had no idea where to put him categorically. On this set of 28 tracks there is everything from killer Memphis soul à la the David Porter/Isaac Hayes collaborations "When Something Is Wrong With My Baby" and "Love Is After Me," to strutting pop-oriented country-soul such as "I'll Shed No Tears" and the downright funky "Can't Get It Right," with a burning female backing chorus. There are also versions of tracks Rich originally cut for RCA such as "Who Will the Next Fool Be" and "Hurry Up Freight Train." Most are the songs associated with Hank Williams that make up the second half of the disc. They are revelatory in that they reveal just how wide-ranging Rich's vision was. Beginning with Williams' own "My Heart Would Know," Rich takes the songs deep into his own musical soul and, like Ray Charles before him with *Modern Sounds in Country and Western Music*, makes them his own, turning them into timeless pop classics. Among Rich's recordings, these 11 songs are some of the most enduring. There is "You Win Again," where the pedal steel becomes an instrument of timbral control and coloration and the lyric becomes a shimmying doo wop-framed melody; "Hey Good Lookin'" sounds as if Rich is backed by Booker T. & the MG's and the Meters simultaneously. The cool Hammond B-3 run at the beginning of "Nobody's Lonesome for Me" takes a honky tonk tune and turns it inside out, making it a rousing party anthem. As for Williams "I'm So Lonesome I Could Cry," Rich's version is among the most beautiful and emotionally naked ever recorded. The set closes with Leon Payne's "They'll Never Take Her Love Away From Me." As pedal steel guitar winds out the sang lines, Rich pours virtually everything he has into Payne's deeply moving lyric. This isn't merely a sad song, it's a devastating one; it's a suicide note; but the tenderness evoked by Rich makes it among the most beautifully twisted love songs ever performed. This collection is essential for Rich fans, and something to consider for any fan of timeless, restless country-soul from the 1960s. *—Thom Jurek*

Kim Richey

b. Dec. 1, 1956, Dayton, OH

Guitar, Vocals / Contemporary Country, Progressive Country

Ohio might not seem like a hotbed of music, but when you have an aunt who owns a record shop, you've certainly got a leg up. That's how Kim Richey got hooked on what would become her chosen path—digging through bins of 45s and listening to everything she could, from Janis Joplin to the Lovin' Spoonful. In high-school, she started playing guitar but didn't rack up much stage time until in college. That was when she started a band and sang a lot of harmony. After college, she did a lot of moving, to and through Colorado, Washington, South America, Boston, Europe, and occasionally Nashville. Serving a stint as a cook at the Bluebird Café didn't do much harm to pull her into the singer/songwriter fold. In 1988, Richey planted her roots in Nashville to really test that fold and hone her own songwriting craft. She built a reputation as a singer who could interpret a lyric and harmonize with the best of them, all the while writing songs with an optimistic melancholy quality that is unusual and alluring. Before too long, Richey was signed to PolyGram Records, releasing her eponymous debut in 1995. *Bitter Sweet* and *Glimmer* followed in two-year increments. All three albums were tagged as contemporary country but actually fall in step pretty close to John Hiatt's brand of music making. Comparisons to Shawn Colvin have also run rampant over the years, due to Richey's cleverly twisting lyrical phrases and beats. By the time she made 1999's *Glimmer* with producer Hugh Padgham, her sound leaned even further toward the pop end of the spectrum. Cut to 2002 and the release of *Rise*. Teaming up with producer Bill Bottrell, Richey fleshed out her sound with worldly flavors of instrumentation, atypical for a so-called contemporary country artist. The result was mesmerizing and her most masterful work to date. *—Kelly McCartney*

● **Kim Richey** / 1995 / Mercury Nashville ✦✦✦✦
Kim Richey had managed some success on the Nashville songwriting scene by the time she released her eponymous debut in 1995. With it, Richey proved that she had the goods as a performer and musician, as well. Featuring some of Nashville's best studio musicians and most talented pop misfits, *Kim Richey* is a sterling delight. It would be easy to compare her to fellow folk-tinged artists like Shawn Colvin, but there's also more than a dose of Springsteen and Hiatt on here, too. Lyrically, Richey knows her way around a clever turn of phrase, as she explores the more unpleasant results of relationships. But she is no woman broken: Just check out the resilience on the gorgeous "You'll Never Know" or the unbridled optimism of new-found love on "Good." She also possesses a deliriously angelic voice, which is given plenty of room to roam on the hushed ballad "Let the Sun Fall Down." A stunning debut by a gifted artist. *—Tom Demalon*

Bitter Sweet / Mar. 4, 1997 / Polygram ✦✦✦✦
Kim Richey's second album avoids any sophomore slump and moves her toward a more pop oriented sound than heard on her debut. The southern California sound of the late '70s looms large; the most obvious point of reference, both musically and thematically, is Karla Bonoff's self-titled first album, the one that Linda Ronstadt mined for her, *Hasten Down the Wind*. This means that on contemporary terms, *Bitter Sweet* falls somewhere between Rosanne Cash's country and Shawn Colvin's folk. Richey's songs are intimate examinations of romantic relationships between women and men, more often than not ones that have gone awry. But Richey sings even the most broken-hearted of the songs with a sense of optimism, and thus avoids sinking into maudlin self-pity. Best of all, Richey is a fine lyricist, capable of taking a cliché and twisting it or reinvesting everyday language with meaning. One such example is the single "I'm Alright," which starts with the throwaway line, "After all was said and done," followed by the abrupt, "There was nothing left to do." Throughout *Bitter Sweet*, Kim Richey makes it plain that she was one of the most gifted songwriters working out of Nashville in the late '90s. *—Martin Monkman*

Glimmer / 1999 / Mercury ✦✦✦
Kim Richey's third album, *Glimmer*, continues her evolution toward a mainstream pop sound. Unfortunately, this evolution doesn't represent any artistic growth; in fact, the album in some ways is a step backward. Producer Hugh Padgham (best-known for his work with Genesis, the Police, and Sting and chosen by Richey because of his production of XTC's *English Settlement*) bathes the songs in a rather bland wash of sound, a significant change from the crisp production that characterized her first two albums. The production matches the lyrics, however, which are burnished to the point that little character remains. The concise and insightful lyrics that appeared on *Bitter Sweet* have given way to innocuous phrases that skirt dangerously close to cliché. Given the great music that characterized her first two albums, *Glimmer* is a disappointment. Let's hope that *Glimmer* is merely a sidestep for Kim Richey, and that she regains her footing for her next outing. *—Martin Monkman*

Rise / Oct. 1, 2002 / Lost Highway ✦✦✦✦✦
There's a lot about Kim Richey's *Rise* that is intriguing. All of it seems to circle around the balancing of playful and contemplative moods. The lyrics, the instrumentation, the arrangements—all are means to that intriguing end. She sits a song that reminisces about the greatest show on Earth ("The Circus Song") right next to a haunting ballad that struggles peacefully to hold on to the memories of a love affair ("Fading.") The mood shifts dramatically between the two, but it's OK. It's real. It's so much how a heart beats and how a mind thinks that you don't really notice. The timing of an album's release is always interesting to watch as well. In the same way Sheryl Crow's *C'mon C'mon* was a perfect spring/summer listen, *Rise* hitting the streets in October can't have been a coincidence. The crisp air and shimmering colors of autumn bleed into the quietude and introspection of winter in the same seamless way these songs flow into one another. The really cool thing is that these tunes are a total grab-bag of styles, rhythms, and attitudes, like a game of musical Tetris being played from track to track. Producer Bill Bottrell guides the pieces with a careful and creative hand, making each song excitingly unpredictable, both individually and as part of the collective soundscape. If you've never heard Richey's work, come on in, the water's perfect. If you have heard her previous efforts, forget what you know (no matter what that is) and dive in too. *Rise* is sure to please even the most fickle listener. *—Kelly McCartney*

Ricochet

f. 1993

Group / Contemporary Country

Ricochet emerged in the spring of 1996 to become one of the most successful new country groups, spending the better part of the year in the Top 40 of the country charts. The band formed in 1993, when drummer Jeff Bryant invited singer/guitarist Heath Wright to join his group Lariat, which also featured Bryant's brother Junior (fiddle/mandolin). Lariat disbanded soon after Wright joined, but he and the Bryants decided to try again under the name Ricochet. They held auditions to complete the band, and several members floated through it in the ensuing months. By the beginning of 1994, the final lineup had fallen into place with the addition of Greg Cook (bass, backing vocals), Teddy Carr (steel guitar), and Eddie Kilgallon (keyboards, rhythm guitar, saxophone, backing vocals). For the next two years, Ricochet toured the South and the West Coast, building up a fan base and developing its energetic, edgy neo-traditional sound. They often spent their downtime rehearsing and writing songs.

The group's original manager was friends with record producer Ron Chancey, who was known for his work with the Oak Ridge Boys. Chancey heard the group and arranged for them to cut a demo. He directed the tape to his son Blake, A&R director for Columbia Records in Nashville. After hearing Ricochet live, Blake Chancey and a handful of other Columbia executives decided to sign the band to a development deal under the direction of producer Ed Seay (Martina McBride, Collin Raye). In early 1995, the deal turned into a full-fledged record contract, and during the spring, the group recorded their first album. For the rest year, they toured the country as a supporting act for Merle Haggard, Doug Stone, and Charlie Daniels.

Ricochet's eponymous debut album, produced by Ron Chancey and Ed Seay, was released in early 1996. Preceded by the Top Five hit single "What Do I Know," the album was a hit and stayed on the charts for more than a year as "Daddy's Money" hit number one and "Love Is Stronger Than Pride" reached the Top Ten. The follow-up album, *Blink of an Eye*, was released the very next year, but it was a commercial disappointment, even though it produced three minor chart singles. Ricochet charted modestly with another three songs in 1998-1999, tracks intended for an album to be called "What a Ride" that was not released. In the meantime, the band underwent personnel changes. Jeff Bryant, suffering from carpal tunnel syndrome, left the drum chair, succeeded by Tim Chewning in August 1999, and Shannon Farmer replaced Teddy Carr on steel guitar. Meanwhile, Richochet retooled its third album, finally releasing it in September 2000 as *What You Leave Behind*. *—Stephen Thomas Erlewine*

● **Ricochet** / Jun. 1996 / Columbia ✦✦✦✦
This is the self-titled debut for Ricochet. It was released under the Sony/Columbia label in 1996. The album went on to be certified gold. Songs like "Daddy's Money," "What Do I Know," and "Love Is Stronger Than Pride" are all listed in the tracks, and all landed in Top Ten spots on the *Billboard* music chart. The same year the debut was released, Ricochet's music earned it awards such as top new vocal group from the Academy of Country Music, top new country artist from *Billboard* magazine, group of the year from the *Radio & Records* reader's poll, and favorite new group or duo by the *Country Weekly* Golden Pick awards. *Ricochet*—the group and the album—offers contemporary country

fans some great harmonies that are showcased on ballads like "What Do I Know." There are also some great uptempo numbers with plenty of guitar action. Overall, the debut is a pretty impressive contribution. Members of the country group are fiddler and guitarist Junior Bryant, bass guitarist Greg Cook, steel guitarist Shannon Farmer, drummer and harmonica player Keith Mellington, keyboardist Steve Paxton, and lead guitarist Heath Wright. All members serve vocal duties, but Wright is the lead singer. Some of the members also handle songwriting. The country band tours a lot, even doing USO shows for the armed services. —*Charlotte Dillon*

Blink of an Eye / Jun. 17, 1997 / Sony ✦✦✦
Ricochet's second album *Blind of an Eye* is similar to their eponymous debut, finding the group running through a selection of restrained country-rockers and earnest, polished ballads. Only a handful of tracks truly connect—such as the singles "He Left a Lot to Be Desired" and "Don't Forget to Feed the Jukebox (While I'm Gone)"—but the group is skilled enough to make the filler sound pleasant, even though it's not quite enough to make the record consistently enjoyable. —*Thom Owens*

What You Leave Behind / Sep. 12, 2000 / Sony ✦✦✦
It's been a long, tortuous road to a third album for Ricochet. After scoring a gold-selling hit and three Top Ten country singles with its self-titled debut in 1996, the group returned in 1997 with *Blink of an Eye*, which spawned three country chart entries, none of which got higher than the Top 20. They seemed poised for a third album in the fall of 1998 that even acquired a title, *What a Ride*, and a Columbia Records catalog number, 69198, but as a series of singles intended as advance tracks, "Honky Tonk Baby," "Can't Stop Thinkin' 'Bout That," and "Seven Bridges Road," failed to break into the Top 40, the release date somehow never arrived. Meanwhile, drummer Jeff Bryant and steel guitarist Teddy Carr were replaced. Finally, in the summer of 2000, a new single, "She's Gone," emerged and began climbing the country charts, and Columbia 69198, now called *What You Leave Behind*, got a firm release date, hitting record stores in the second week of September. As such a complicated history suggests it might, *What You Leave Behind* sounds like a collection assembled to find the band a hit single and stem its career decline. Ricochet's cover of Steve Young's "Seven Bridges Road," performed in a vocal harmony arrangement similar to the Eagles' 1981 hit version, has been retained, along with many of the Ron and Blake Chancey-produced tracks probably intended for *What a Ride*. ("Honky Tonk Baby" and "Can't Stop Thinkin' 'Bout That" are not included.) But a new producer, David Malloy, was brought in for a trio of songs, "She's Gone," "Do I Love You Enough," and "I Can't Believe (You Let Her Go)," which are sequenced first, second, and fourth, respectively, on the album. All three are light pop-country tunes with lyrics intended to please female listeners. Not that that constitutes a big change of direction for Ricochet, but it does put them squarely in the Lonestar mold, and it's striking that the closest thing to an aggressive, honky tonk tune on the album, the cover of Mickey Newbury's "Why You Been Gone So Long" (which was a 1969 country hit for Johnny Darrell), doesn't turn up until the seventh slot in the track listing. The overall result is a sweet, but fairly toothless effort. You can only hope that Ricochet will make a less bland, homogenous album next time; this time, their challenge was that if they didn't come up with a hit, there wasn't going to be a next time. —*William Ruhlmann*

Riders in the Sky

f. 1977
Group / Traditional Country, Cowboy, Western Swing Revival
Beginning each performance with their trademark greeting, "Mighty fine and a great big Western 'Howdy,' all you buckaroos and buckarettes," Riders in the Sky simultaneously paid tribute to and poked gentle fun at the classic cowboy songs of the 1930s and 1940s, particularly the work of the Sons of the Pioneers, Roy Rogers, and Gene Autry. During the 1980s and 1990s, the group was notable for its ability to attract fans both firmly within the country tradition (the Riders are members of the *Grand Ole Opry*) and from outside. Riders in the Sky are made up of lead singer Ranger Doug (born Douglas B. Green), Woody Paul (born Paul Chrisman) on fiddle and vocals, Too Slim (string bass and guitar), and since the mid-'90s, "Cowpolka King" Joey Miskulin on accordion. Before forming the band, the Michigan-born Ranger Doug was a member of Bill Monroe's Blue Grass Boys and was also a country music journalist, working at the *Country Music Foundation Press* as editor of the *Journal of Country Music*. Prior to joining the Riders, Woody Paul, a formidable swing fiddler, played with Loggins & Messina, and Too Slim was a member of Dickey Lee's band in addition to being a songwriter. The trio formed in the mid-'70s, playing a weekly gig at a Nashville nightclub that led to a slot on *Tumbleweed Theater* on cable television's Nashville Network (TNN).

Riders in the Sky made their recording debut in 1979 on the Rounder label with *Three on the Trail*, which set the pattern for their mix of classic and newly composed sentimental western numbers, parodies (like "The Legend of Palindrome," in which a figure resembling television's Paladin is described exclusively in sentences that read the same backwards and forwards), crack swing instrumental work, and Sons of the Pioneers-style harmony singing. They released five albums on MCA in the 1980s, and in 1985 they appeared in *Sweet Dreams*, the film biography of Patsy Cline. The group returned briefly to MCA in 1987, releasing *Riders Radio Theater* a year later. The success of that album led to the program *Riders Radio Theater* on National Public Radio, where the group was already well known from performances on Garrison Keillor's *Prairie Home Companion* program. In 1991 the Riders moved to CBS for the children's album *Harmony Ranch*, which led to a short-lived CBS-TV Saturday-morning television show. Riders in the Sky continued recording for Rounder and other labels into the 2000s, offering a *Great Big Western Howdy!* in 1998 and *Christmas the Cowboy Way* a year later. In 2000, *Woody's Roundup: A Rootin' Tootin' Collection of Woody's Favorite Songs* was released, and 2002's *A Pair of Kings* showcased the increasingly impressive instrumental talents of Miskulin and Paul. As Riders in the Sky approached their

25th anniversary they were known as an unfailing concert draw: Their shows featured such novelties as rope tricks in addition to music and humor. —*Sandra Brennan & James Manheim*

Three on the Trail / 1979 / Rounder ✦✦✦✦✦
Three on the Trail, the Riders in the Sky's debut album, established their tongue-in-cheek tribute to cowboys and western music. Though the humor is piled on a little thicker here than on their later releases, the music is often quite good and they never deviated from this formula—slightly ironic covers, affectionate jokes and made-to-order originals—on any of their subsequent records. They also rarely did it any better. —*Thom Owens*

The Cowboy Way / 1982 / MCA ✦✦✦

Prairie Serenade / 1982 / Rounder ✦✦✦

New Trails / 1986 / Rounder ✦✦✦

● **The Best of the West** / 1988 / Rounder ✦✦✦✦✦
The Best of the West contains 25 highlights from the Riders in the Sky's first five albums for Rounder Records, including such western standards as "Tumbling Tumbleweeds," "Here Comes the Santa Fe," "Don't Fence Me In," "Blue Montana Skies," and the group's namesake, "Ghost Riders in the Sky." —*Thom Owens*

Radio Theatre / Jun. 27, 1988 / MCA ✦✦✦
This contains 18 digitally recorded selections such as "Trail Traffic Report" and "Bio Feed-bag." Known for their odd outlooks, these three cowboys are some of America's favorites. —*AMG*

Weeds & Water / 1989 / Rounder ✦✦

Saturday Morning with Riders / 1992 / MCA ✦✦
Saturday Morning with Riders in the Sky collects favorites like "Back in the Saddle Again," "That's How the Yodel Was Born" and the group's eponymous theme song. —*Jason Ankeny*

Live / Mar. 15, 1992 / Rounder ✦✦✦
This square-but-hip comedy has songs crooned in lush Sons of the Pioneers-style Western harmony. —*Mark A. Humphrey*

Cowboys in Love / 1994 / Epic ✦✦✦✦✦
Putting the skits aside for the time being, the Riders focus largely on their underrated musical ability. Ranger Doug shows off his sublime baritone on several Western-style love songs, including an exquisite duet with Emmylou Harris on "One Has My Name, the Other Has My Heart." The instrumentals, especially Woody Paul's expert fiddling, are superb, as is the spirited take with guests Asleep at the Wheel on "I'm a Ding Dong Daddy From Dumas." —*Michael McCall*

Always Drink Upstream from the Herd / Oct. 31, 1995 / Rounder ✦✦✦✦
As they get older, Riders in the Sky sound more accomplished and, more importantly, they sound more sincere. Like any of the group's albums, *Always Drink Upstream From the Herd* combines standards with original material but the what makes it noteworthy is that sincerity—they still make jokes, but they can deliver the material more gracefully and skillfully than ever before, making it one of their most enjoyable efforts. —*Thom Owens*

Public Cowboy #1: The Music of Gene Autry / Oct. 22, 1996 / Rounder ✦✦✦✦✦
The Riders in the Sky cut this record in the wake of their performing a Gene Autry medley in a television appearance with Autry himself in the audience. The songs are done reverently but with a real sense of fun, essentially the same balancing act that has made them a success on-stage and television. Their main innovations are the harmony singing, which works well throughout, and a jazzy approach to Jimmie Rodgers' "Can't Shake the Sands of Texas From My Shoes." Autry's versions have held up magnificently well, but this loving tribute album is a necessary addition to any fan's collection. —*Bruce Eder*

The Best of the West Rides Again / 1997 / Rounder ✦✦✦✦✦
Picking up where the first compilation left off, *The Best of the West Rides Again* contains many of the best-known and most popular songs from the campy Western revival band, Riders in the Sky. —*Stephen Thomas Erlewine*

Great Big Western Howdy! / Jul. 14, 1998 / Rounder ✦✦✦✦
On the big scale you can call this album Western music, but on individual cuts it throws you some curveballs. It has harmonies and rhythms reminiscent of the Sons of the Pioneers, and it also has stretches of country—and they sure can yodel. With the Irish-flavored "Sidekick Jig," and the beautiful "A Border Romance," and "One More Ride" being main highlights, *Riders in the Sky* covers wide territory. Fine vocals are contributed by everyone, but enhanced by the addition of Marty Stuart's cowbilly voice. There is also some of the finest three-part yodeling to be heard. Then, as if this isn't enough, there is the absolutely smoking mandolin break contributed by Stuart, after a fine fiddle break contributed by Woody Paul. This is a great release for one and all. —*Bob Gottlieb*

Christmas the Cowboy Way / Oct. 5, 1999 / Rounder ✦✦✦
With *Christmas the Cowboy Way*, the modern torchbearers of the cowboy singing tradition, Riders in the Sky, deliver an interesting mix of the sublime and the goofy. "Corn, Water and Wood" is a sweet and touching adaptation of the story of the Advent, in which three cowboys bring regionally appropriate gifts to the newborn babe. Ranger Doug's "Virgen Maria" is also very affecting. On the lighter side, there's a great swing arrangement of "Let It Snow, Let It Snow, Let It Snow" that segues into "The Last Christmas Medley You'll Ever Need," which incorporates the first lines of about 20 Christmas songs. The group's cowboy adaptation of "The Twelve Days of Christmas" is also lots of fun. But "Side Meat's Christmas Stew" and "The Prairie Dog's Christmas Ball" are both just a bit too hokey, even though the hokiness is obviously part of the joke. Fans will definitely want this one, but newcomers may want to begin elsewhere. —*Rick Anderson*

Woody's Roundup: A Rootin' Tootin' Collection of Woody's Favorite Songs / Aug. 29, 2000 / Disney ✦✦✦

Inspired by *Toy Story 2, Woody's Roundup* features songs about everyone's favorite toy cowboy, as well as some country classics, as performed by Riders in the Sky. The "Woody's Roundup" theme, "Jessie, the Yodelin' Cowgirl," and "The Ballad of Bullseye" are among the best Woody-themed tracks, and the Riders' renditions of "Act Naturally," "Home on the Range," and "You've Got a Friend in Me" are just as charming as their children's album *Harmony Ranch*. Like *Toy Story 2* itself, *Woody's Roundup* is a creative, entertaining album for *Toy Story* fans of all ages. *—Heather Phares*

A Pair of Kings / Feb. 19, 2002 / Oh Boy ✦✦✦

Western swing revivalists Riders in the Sky have long been known for their engaging brand of Prairie Home Companion-style traditional cowboy music and their we're-having-a-great-time-and-so-should-you attitude, so their 2001 release, *A Pair of Kings*, comes pleasantly with no shocking surprises. The "pair of kings" referenced in the album's title are featured Riders Joey "the Cowpolka King" Miskulin and Woody Paul, King of the Cowboy Fiddlers. These members of nouveau Western swing royalty are ably backed by longtime Riders Ranger Doug and Too Slim on 12 songs that range from traditional Bob Wills-esque romps like "You Stole My Wife You Horsethief" and Johnny Mercer's "I'm an Old Cowhand," to more contemporary interpretations like their "Celtic Medley" and the jazzy "Bunkhouse Race." These four diehards are one of the few acts still making records in the traditional cowboy style, and their releases each deserve all of the recognition they get. *—Zac Johnson*

Billy Lee Riley

b. Oct. 5, 1933, Pocohontas, AR

Bass, Guitar, Harmonica, Vocals, Drums / Rockabilly

Billy Lee Riley is a rockabilly singer and multi-instrumentalist. An alumnus of Sun Records, he was one of the most crazed, unabashed rockers that label had to offer—in the company of Jerry Lee Lewis, Carl Perkins, and Sonny Burgess, that's saying a lot. Proficient at harmonica, guitar, bass, and drums, Riley contributed as a sideman to many a classic Sun session, and his combo, the Little Green Men (most notably guitarist Roland Janes and drummer J.M. Van Eaton), in time became the Sun house band. Riley recorded for a number of labels in a variety of styles, especially effective with blues. Though never commercially successful, Riley's Sun recordings of "Flyin' Saucers Rock 'n' Roll" and "Red Hot" (both covered in wooden renditions by Robert Gordon) remain landmarks of the genre. *—Cub Koda*

Twist and Shout! / 1968 / Cowboy Carl ✦✦✦

Recorded live at an Atlanta club on December 28, 1966 (although it wasn't released until 1968), this shows Riley trying to adapt to the trends of the day with a set comprised mostly of '60s rock and soul covers: "Twist and Shout," "In the Midnight Hour," "Poor Side of Town," "Nowhere Man," and "Barefootin'." It's more vital than you might suppose, because Riley is in fine, committed voice, with a decent band. It's kind of reminiscent of those Johnny Rivers live Whiskey-A-Go-Go albums, except Riley is a considerably better singer and performer, with a fiery spirit not unlike Bobby Fuller (whose own live-in-L.A. album, incidentally, is not as good as this one is). Only a couple of Riley originals in the program (the "Secret Agent Man"-type "Speed Lovers" is cool), but this is a pretty enjoyable release, though not a very important one. It was, incidentally, first put out on the Mojo label in 1968, but the 1981 Cowboy Carl reissue is easier to find. *—Richie Unterberger*

Classic Recordings, 1956–1960 / Jul. 1990 / Bear Family ✦✦✦✦✦

All the classic Sun sides, plus later Memphis recordings in a brilliant two-CD set. Raw rockin' at its finest. *—Cub Koda*

Blue Collar Blues / 1992 / Hightone ✦✦✦✦

Hot Damn / May 13, 1997 / Capricorn ✦✦✦

Billy Lee Riley sounds surprisingly sprightly for a veteran rockabilly performer on his 1997 comeback, *Hot Damn!* Conceived as tribute to his musical roots and family, *Hot Damn!* is a fairly engaging set of traditional rockabilly and country, punctuated by effective detours into the blues. Riley might not have the energy he did in the '50s, yet this album proves there's still a bunch of life in the old boy. *—Thom Owens*

● **Red Hot: The Best of Billy Lee Riley** / Feb. 2, 1999 / Collectables ✦✦✦✦✦

Billy Lee Riley never made a hit before scraping the bottom of the charts in 1972, but you'd never know it from his reputation as one of the top artists of the original rockabilly era. His classics "Red Hot" and "Flyin' Saucers Rock 'n' Roll" are included on this 22-track anthology of Riley's Sun recordings, which is the most affordable and readily available alternative to Bear Family's two-disc set *Classic Recordings 1956-1960*. Collectors should note that the last four cuts on this collection are from Riley's 1969-1970 return to Sun Records. Buyers wanting Riley's '50s material would have been happier with four more early rockabilly cuts in place of these mediocre country and rock recordings from the downside of Riley's career, but others may enjoy hearing the evolution of his sound. *—Greg Adams*

The Sun Years / Oct. 23, 2001 / Original Sun ✦✦✦✦

This is an excellent compilation featuring 25 Billy Lee Riley original Sun recordings from 1956-1962. His classic Sun sides feature hot rockabilly along the lines of Jerry Lee Lewis and Warren Smith at their most frantic. Besides Riley's essential songs, "Red Hot" and "Flyin' Saucers Rock 'n' Roll," this collection includes "Trouble Bound" (covered by the Blasters in 1985), "Let's Talk About Us," "Searchin'," and "Your Cash Ain't Nothin' but Trash." Also recommended is the single-disc *Classic Recordings, 1956-1960* on Bear Family. *—Al Campbell*

Jeannie C. Riley (Jeanne Carolyn Stephenson)

b. Sep. 19, 1945, Anson, TX

Vocals / Country-Pop, CCM

Best known for her international crossover hit "Harper Valley P.T.A.," Jeannie C. Riley was born Jeanne Carolyn Stephenson in Anson, TX, where she developed a love of country music as a girl. When she was a teenager, she made her first public performance, appearing on her uncle's jamboree show. Soon after high-school graduation, she married Mickey Riley; she wanted to become a professional musician, so she and her new husband moved to Nashville, where she performed secretarial work at Passkey Music. She also made a few demos as Jean Riley that led to the single "What About Them," which wasn't successful. Then, in 1967, her manager Paul Perry hooked Riley up with producer Shelby Singleton, with whom she recorded "Harper Valley P.T.A." The song became an instant hit, reaching number one on both the pop and country charts.

Later in 1968, Riley debuted on the *Grand Ole Opry* and released "The Girl Most Likely," which reached number six on the country charts. During the early '70s, she had a string of minor hits and five other Top Ten singles, including "Country Girl," "Oh, Singer" and "Good Enough to Be Your Wife." Around 1974, Riley became a born-again Christian and formed a new band, Red River Symphony, which had a minor hit in 1976, "The Best I've Ever Had." Following its release, Riley founded and began recording on the God's Country label. In 1981, she recorded the gospel album *From Harper Valley to the Mountain Top*. Throughout the '80s and '90s, she continued to be a popular contemporary Christian recording and performing artist. *—Sandra Brennan*

Harper Valley P.T.A. / 1968 / Sun ✦✦✦✦✦

The album based on the multimillion-selling title track is a fine recording that goes beyond the obvious attraction to the Tom T. Hall classic. It comes across nearly as a concept album that mirrors life in a small town in all its faults and tribulations, though not all songs make direct reference to Harper Valley. At the center of all this is the under-rated voice of Jeannie C. Riley, which has the right combination of strength, sass, and vulnerability to make the songs come alive. The listener is treated to songs detailing the characters mentioned in the hit title song, such as Mr. Harper, Widow Jones (who comes across as the worst of the three), and Shirley Thompson. Musically, many of the songs seem almost a copy of "Harper Valley P.T.A," but they usually work because each has its own distinct story to tell, and the sincerity of Riley's voice reinforces the tales well. "No Brass Band" is a welcome change from the formula, and paints the detailed story of a family's dreams that go unfulfilled. There is also fine dobro work by "Jerry Kennedy," and the production of "Shelby Singleton" keeps to a harder country sound that avoids the pitfalls of strings and unnecessary vocal backgrounds. *—Michael Ofjord*

The Best of Jeannie C. Riley / Oct. 22, 1996 / Varese ✦✦✦✦✦

Here is a 15-song compilation concentrating on her late-'60s/early-'70s prime; everything's from 1968-1971, except for a couple of inessential '80s cuts tacked onto the end. Sometimes thought of as a one-shot artist, Riley was one of the better unsung country singers of her era, with a far saucier delivery than was the norm. The material, much of it penned by the songwriting team of Myrna Smith & Margaret Lewis, is almost schizophrenic in its reach. "The Rib" could be heard as an early, dignified plea for women's rights; "The Generation Gap" had some muted anti-establishment undertones; and of course Tom T. Hall's "Harper Valley P.T.A." poked fun at small-town hypocrisy. At the same time, she also released bathetic ballads like "Things Go Better with Love"; "There Never Was a Time" is as corny an ode to family, God, and honest struggle as you can find in the country field. At any rate, the anthology as a whole is above average, also including the hits "Oh, Singer," "Good Enough to Be Your Wife," "Country Girl," and "The Girl Most Likely." *—Richie Unterberger*

Harper Valley PTA: The Very Best of Jeannie C. Riley / Feb. 2, 1999 / Collectables ✦✦✦✦✦

Known mostly for the number-one pop and country hit "Harper Valley P.T.A.," Jeannie C. Riley made it big in Music City right when the Nashville sound starting showing a few crossover signs smacking of the psychedelic '60s. With a voice somewhere in the vicinity of Ann-Margret after years of booze and cigarettes, Riley offers up her own youth culture statement on "The Generation Gap" and sings of being down and out to the tune of an imitation electric sitar on "Backside of Dallas." Fat rock beats abound on cuts like "The Girl Most Likely" while the liberal revivalism of the Doobie Brothers' "Jesus Is Just Alright with Me" gets prefigured on the hilariously titled "Will the Real Jesus Please Stand Up." Of course this a country collection, so Riley finds her trad voice on the pedal steel weeper "Duty Not Desire" and the updated honky tonk cut "Macon Georgia Bad Girl." Most impressive, though, are her forays into swamp country à la Bobbie Gentry's "Ode to Billie Joe": look out for standouts like "He Made a Woman Out of Me" and a version of Kris Kristofferson's chestnut "Help Me Make It Through the Night." And there are 15 more equally enjoyable tracks on this Collectables collection, making it the best of the few compilations of Riley's prime cuts from 1968-1974. For those still a little unsettled at the thought of investigating later born-again titles like *From Harper Valley P.T.A. to the Mountain Top*, this ones for you. *—Stephen Cook*

● **The Very Best of Jeannie C. Riley** / May 21, 2002 / Varese ✦✦✦✦✦

Varese Sarabande's 18-track 2002 collection *The Very Best of Jeannie C. Riley* replaces the company's previous 15-track 1996 compilation, *The Best of Jeannie C. Riley*. All but two of the songs from the older collection carry over to this disc, and the two that are left behind were '80s recordings that gave that CD a sour aftertaste, so they're hardly missed. The five songs on *Very Best* that weren't on *Best*—"Am I That Easy to Forget," "Games People Play," "Okie From Muskogee," "If You Could Read My Mind," "Help Me Make It Through the Night"—are all from her 1968-1971 peak, so this is a better collection in every way, showcasing one of the best, yet unheralded, country singers of her time. *—Stephen Thomas Erlewine*

LeAnn Rimes

b. Aug. 28, 1982, Jackson, MS

Vocals / Contemporary Country, Adult Contemporary

In 1996, LeAnn Rimes burst out of nowhere with her debut single, "Blue," which immediately captured the attention of country fans across America. It wasn't just the fact that her rich, powerful vocals were remarkably similar to Patsy Cline—it was the fact that Rimes was only 13 years old. Like Tanya Tucker and Brenda Lee before her, she had a hit with her debut single and was barely a teenager at the time. It was quite an auspicious way to begin a career. Born in Jackson, MS, but raised in Garland, TX, Rimes (born August 28, 1982) began singing as a child, performing at local talent contests. At the age of 11, she released her first album on an independent record label called Nor Va Jak. That same year, Bill Mack, a Dallas disc jockey and record promoter, met Rimes, and impressed by her talents, he took her under his wing and began cultivating a plan to break her into the mainstream. The cornerstone of Mack's plan was a song called "Blue," which he had written in the '60s. Mack claimed that he had written the tune for Cline, but she had died before she was able to record the song.

Throughout 1995, Rimes' career continued to gain momentum, as she performed more than 100 concerts and appeared on television shows across Texas. After Mack arranged a record contract for Rimes with Curb Records, the label sent out a release with the single of "Blue" that claimed the DJ had been waiting over 30 years to find the right vocalist to sing "Blue." The story was an exaggeration: "Blue" had been recorded by no less than three different artists, including Bill Mack and Kenny Roberts, who both released versions on Starday in the '60s, and in 1993, Kathryn Pitt released the record as a single in her native Australia. Nevertheless, the story was repeated throughout the country and mainstream music press, adding to the growing myth that Rimes was the successor to Cline's tradition. "Blue" and its accompanying album of the same name became major hits in the summer of 1996.

Blue debuted at number three on the pop charts, selling over 123,000 copies within its first week of release—the largest figure to date in the history of the SoundScan tracking system. Rimes was nominated for the Country Music Association Horizon award and the CMA Best Country Singer, becoming the youngest singer in the history of the CMA awards to receive a nomination; she won neither award. After two quickie 1997 releases—*Unchained Melody: The Early Years* and *You Light Up My Life: Inspirational Songs*—she issued her second proper LP, *Sittin' on Top of the World*, in 1998. Her self-titled third album followed a year later and *I Need You* appeared in early 2001. The next year, Rimes emerged with a sexy flair for the pop-oriented *Twisted Angel*. *—Stephen Thomas Erlewine*

● **Blue** / 1996 / Curb ✦✦✦✦

With this fabulous record that brought joy and fun to all avid listeners of country music, LeAnn Rimes arrived just in the nick of time, when country needed it most, amidst all the regulars of the scene such as Garth Brooks, Holly Dunn, etc. The record is a delightful free-for-all of sassy pick-me-up country that spells GOLD in many sorts of ways. Of course, the sleeper hit is "Blue," Rimes' radio-friendly airplay single that landed her a Grammy at the tender young age of 15. "Blue"—both the song and the record as a whole—certainly should and does affect listeners in a charismatic and lighthearted way. At the time, since she was still a teen herself, this collection of songs meant so much to Rimes and her adoring fans; it inspired thousands of teens then and continues to inspire them through to this day. Perhaps people of any age or style of interest will feel youthful again after a good listen and a half. This record of songs written by the best songwriters in country music served as a stepping stone for Rimes, and was deservedly a breakthrough album for the country music scene. *—Shawn M. Haney*

Unchained Melody: The Early Years / Feb. 11, 1997 / Curb ✦✦✦

Following the success of *Blue*, the album *Unchained Melody: The Early Years*, a collection of recordings made prior to her breakthrough, was issued. Considering LeAnn Rimes was only 13 when "Blue" became a hit makes the whole notion of "early years" a tad bizarre, but, in fact, they were recorded when the gal was in her preteen post-moppet stage. The recordings on this collection, which range from a note-for-note remake of the Whitney Houston version of Dolly Parton's "I Will Always Love You" to Bill Monroe's "Blue Moon of Kentucky" to the Beatles' "Yesterday" and a countrified version of the title track, cover a wide of array of styles, and are all covers, save for the 1980s-sounding "Share My Love." This album is essentially a LeAnn Rimes vocal showcase, as though the young lass had been set loose in a karaoke booth, which results in a record without any sort of real emotion or depth. Still, it works as something of an oddity, and the vocal chops, considering the source, are nothing less than astounding. *—Jose F. Promis*

You Light Up My Life: Inspirational Songs / Sep. 9, 1997 / Curb ✦✦✦

As the official sequel to *Blue* (*Unchained Melody* was a collection of early recordings), *You Light Up My Life: Inspirational Songs* carried a lot of expectations. It was a record that should have consolidated LeAnn Rimes' status as contemporary country's brightest new star, but instead it does a curious thing—it positions her as an adult contemporary crossover artist. *You Light Up My Life* has as much pop as country, relying on such easy listening standards as the title track, "The Rose," and "God Bless America." As a result, the album has a bit of a bland, homogenous quality—it certainly could have used a bit of country grit. Rimes sings well throughout *You Light Up My Life*, but she often doesn't seem to connect completely with the material—it's telling that a remix of her previous hit "How Do I Live" stands out as one of the finest cuts here. *You Light Up My Life* is far from disastrous—Rimes has too much natural talent to be sunk by poorly chosen material—but it isn't the great leap forward it could have been. *—Thom Owens*

Sittin' on Top of the World / May 5, 1998 / Curb ✦✦✦

Truth be told, the "country" label doesn't quite fit LeAnn Rimes. True, her debut single, "Blue," sounded like a lost honky tonk classic, but *You Light Up My Life* suggested that she wanted to be an adult contemporary crooner. Her third album (and, in many ways, the official follow-up to *Blue*), *Sittin' on Top of the World*, may be called country, but it's an adult contemporary album by any other name. Only three songs have any country feel to them, and they just barely fit that description—there may be steel guitars on "These Arms of Mine," and "Rock Me" may shuffle, but they hardly feel country. Most of the record consists of overarranged midtempo pop songs, as produced by her father, Wilbur. There's no denying that Rimes is quite talented and, given the proper guidance, could definitely make some great music, but Wilbur has selected a batch of material that's either inappropriate (really, Prince's "Purple Rain"?) or faceless. He's also pushed her to oversing, in hopes that it would sell the songs, but the truth of the matter is, she sounds best when she's relaxed and natural. And that's what's so frustrating about *Sittin' on Top of the World*—Rimes' gifts and personality surface just often enough to make you realize that this blandly pleasant album could have been much, much better. *—Stephen Thomas Erlewine*

LeAnn Rimes / Oct. 26, 1999 / Curb ✦✦✦✦

Essentially, *LeAnn Rimes* is a covers album, with one new song ("Big Deal") tacked onto the end, which makes it a return to her roots—which, in turn, means that it's sort of a salute to her main influence, Patsy Cline. Rimes tackles no less than five songs from Cline's *12 Greatest Hits*, plus "Lovesick Blues," which Cline also recorded. It's a tricky situation for a singer pegged as a Cline soundalike with her first hit single, "Blue." If those comparisons bother Rimes, it's impossible to tell from her performance, since she sings these six songs *exactly* like Cline does. As it turns out, imitation is a crutch Rimes uses quite often, since she mimics Janis Joplin on "Me and Bobby McGee" and pretty much uses Marty Robbins as a guide vocal on "Don't Worry." Since she has a good voice and these are, by and large, great songs, it's hard to complain—given the best set of songs of her career, she delivers good, professional performances, stumbling only on "Me and Bobby McGee" with Joplin-like histrionics. So, *LeAnn Rimes* winds up being one of her better efforts, even if her vocals are fairly mannered and the arrangements are fairly predictable. But the most curious thing about this covers album is that Rimes turns in her best performance on the lone new track. She sounds loose, confident and exciting on "Big Deal," and even more importantly, she never sounds like one of her idols—she sounds like herself. And since it comes at the end of the record, you can't help but wish she'd recorded an album of new, pure country songs as good as "Big Deal" instead of a collection of covers, no matter how well she sang those covers. *—Stephen Thomas Erlewine*

I Need You / Jan. 30, 2001 / Curb ✦✦✦

LeAnn Rimes had been inching toward pop as the '90s grew to a close, but she truly lunged at the pop charts with the soundtrack to *Coyote Ugly*, providing the voice for Piper Perabo's star-struck, fledgling singer/songwriter. This was a prelude to 2001's *I Need You*, her first full-fledged pop album—a crossover affair with more in common with Faith Hill's *Breathe* than Shania Twain's *Come on Over*. That means that its footing is squarely within adult contemporary pop, and it's heavy on ballads. Even when the tempo is kicked up a notch, as on "You Are" with its percolating drum machines, it's still midtempo AC pop. This isn't necessarily a bad thing, especially since she has a couple of good songs here (notably "I Need You," "But I Do Love You," and the *Coyote* leftover, "Can't Fight the Moonlight"), but it's not the most natural move in the world, either. Rimes' impressive voice sounds restrained in this setting, too self-consciously mature. In a nutshell, that's the problem with *I Need You*—it's a teenager attempting to make a thirtysomething album. That she occasionally succeeds is a testament to her vocal talents and the skills of her producers, but it shouldn't be surprising that it also feels awkward for large stretches, never quite becoming as alluring as *Breathe*, because this is a sound that she needs to grow into to be totally convincing. *—Stephen Thomas Erlewine*

God Bless America / Oct. 16, 2001 / Curb ✦✦✦

With all the American flag imagery on the packaging, it's a good bet that this post-September 11, 2001, compilation benefited the disaster recovery—even though no such promise is made on the insert. It does say, "These classic recordings were made while America was first discovering LeAnn Rimes." The obvious intention was to gather some of Rimes' inspirational and love songs that would uplift and encourage during the national crisis, and also make a nice little stocking stuffer that fits the patriotic mood. It's a nice cross section of American classics (her version of "God Bless America" is a show-stopper), Christian-themed gems ("The Sands of Time," "Middle Man"), and even a soft-spoken country-pop version of "The Lord's Prayer." "Put a Little Holiday in Your Heart" is the one tune that actually goes beyond the heartfelt and into the truly fun. Her a cappella version of "Amazing Grace" is also an impressive showcase for her well-known vocal chops. *—Jonathan Widran*

Twisted Angel / Oct. 1, 2002 / Curb ✦✦✦

Freed from her lawsuits, separated from the managerial control of her father, and now an adult, LeAnn Rimes redefines herself as a mainstream pop vocalist with *Twisted Angel*. If the title and the tarted-up sultry photographs didn't offer a clue that Rimes is no longer a country vocalist, the very first cut immediately offers proof that she's positioning herself somewhere between grown-up dance-pop and youthful adult contemporary. This is music for the hip middle of the road, then, which isn't a bad career move at all, since there's a void there with the absence of Whitney Houston, the breakdown of Mariah Carey, and Christina Aguilera's bizarre insistence to strip instead of sing. Rimes certainly has the voice for the crossover she desires, and the production is commercial, glossy, and ready for the radio, often appealingly so. All the basics are in place, but there are a couple of stumbling blocks on the road to success. First, there may not be an audience for it: even though this is well done, it is so pop it will alienate her older fans, and she needs to win over an older audience that may not be taken with her newly sexualized image. Second, the songwriting is a little uneven; often, it's very good workmanlike mainstream pop, but there are a couple of duds (namely, the irritating chorus on the "sassy" "Trouble With Goodbye"), and even the best material is melodic without being hooky or memorable.

But the biggest problem is that the production and attitude on *Twisted Angel* kind of fall through the cracks in 2002, when teen pop is dead and mainstream pop is veering away from divas and toward quirkier, friendlier singers like Vanessa Carlton, Avril Lavigne, and Michelle Branch. *Twisted Angel* is far from that attitude—it sounds like a holdover from 1996, and it's not bad at all according to those standards. But it does sound dated. This isn't a bad direction for LeAnn Rimes by any means, but next time around, she'd be better served by less Desmond Child and a sharper set of songs, plus a production that would ease her onto the modern mainstream radio where she so desperately wants to be. —*Stephen Thomas Erlewine*

Jason Ringenberg

b. Nov. 22, 1959, Illinois

Vocals, Guitar (Acoustic), Harmonica, Guitar / Country-Rock, Roots Rock, Country-Folk, Alternative Country, Singer/Songwriter, Alternative Country-Rock

While Gram Parsons may have the distinction of being the granddaddy of the ill-named "alt-country" genre, Illinois farm boy Jason Ringenberg is certainly the man who brought it to the stages of the world with a vengeance. Born in 1959 and raised on a pig farm in southern Illinois, Ringenberg moved to Nashville in 1981 to try his luck as a songwriter. He formed an acoustic country-punk band with drummer Jack Emerson called Jason & the Scorchers and released one EP in 1982 on the defunct Praxis label called *Restless Country Soul*. With additional members such as guitar slinger Warner Hodges and bassist Jeff Johnson, the band was re-christened Jason & the Nashville Scorchers, with Perry Baggs replacing Emerson on the drum kit. In 1983 the band recorded its debut mini-album, *Fervor*, which caused a stir among American critics. But it was Jason & the Nashville Scorchers' live show, with its embodiment of old-time rock & roll energy, punk swagger and grit, and country music's elegant excesses, that won them fans worldwide.

After *Lost & Found* was issued in 1985, Ringenberg had won enough celebrity to be berated publicly by country music's Ed Sullivan, Ralph Emery, on live television and become a major concert attraction all over the globe. The band disbanded in 1990 and Ringenberg became a solo performer. His debut, *One Foot in the Honky Tonk*, was met with critical praise but after being dismally promoted sank without a trace. The Scorchers reunited in the mid-'90s, issuing five studio albums and a live recording. Ringenberg did not give up his solo career, however, and recorded the simple, haunting acoustic masterpiece *A Pocketful of Soul* on his own label in 2000 as well as 2002's rollicking *All Over Creation*, featuring a boatload of guests, while continuing his touring and recording activities with the band. Ringenberg continues to be a very successful solo act when not playing with the Nashville Scorchers; he's toured the world three times in the 21st century alone. In October of 2003, Ringenberg tossed everyone a curve ball, recording and releasing his first children's record on the Yep Roc label, entitled *A Day at the Farm With Farmer Jason*. —*Thom Jurek*

One Foot in the Honky Tonk / 1992 / Liberty ✦✦✦

One Foot in the Honky Tonk is the first solo album from Jason Ringenberg, the leader of Jason and the Scorchers. On his own, Jason sticks closer to country than he does to rock & roll, delving deep into honky tonk and the twang of Bakersfield, turning out a tough but poignant set of stomping, rocking country. A couple of cuts miss the mark, but the best songs on *One Foot in the Honky Tonk* equal his work with Jason & the Scorchers. —*Stephen Thomas Erlewine*

A Pocketful of Soul / Jul. 4, 2000 / Jason Ringenberg ✦✦✦✦

After almost 20 years cranking out high-voltage cowpunk with Jason & the Scorchers, lead singer/songwriter/auteur Jason Ringenberg takes a trip back—way back—to his roots on his sophomore solo album, and first for his own label. Freed from the electrified confines of his band, Rigenberg's pure, yearning, high-lonesome voice rings out clearly in this 12-song set of acoustic country, hillbilly, and Appalachian music. Whether he's covering Guadalcanal Diary's "Trail of Tears," Johnny Horton's "Whispering Pines," or singing his own songs, Ringenberg's plaintive voice and bare but appropriate instrumentation gives this album a simple, sparse, bucolic feel. It's as if he's recorded these songs around a flickering campfire out on the open prairie. In fact, the opening track features the sound of wind and rain leading into a waltz-time acoustic guitar. The lilting "For Abbie Rose" written for his daughter and most of the other nostalgic tunes here would be totally out of place on a Scorchers release, but theywork beautifully in this homey context. Rudimentary string bass, accordion, fiddles, banjo and Ringenberg's mournful voice, often frighteningly close to Hank Williams Sr.'s evocative warble, combine to fashion an album that might have been recorded in the '50s rather than 2000. It's that authentic, timeless sense of place that creates the shimmering, unpretentious atmosphere here that is as rooted in classic Americana as Woody, the Carter Family, or the Band. While this may be too rudimentary and earthy for wilder Scorchers' fans, Ringenberg proves he's as comfortable, sincere, and unaffected singing these desolate songs of loneliness, religion, love, and wide-open spaces as he is with the whip-cracking punkabilly of his gruff rocking band. —*Hal Horowitz*

● **All Over Creation** / Jun. 18, 2002 / Yep Roc ✦✦✦✦

In his liner notes to *All Over Creation*, Jason Ringenberg writes that touring as a solo act behind *A Pocketful of Soul* caused him to spend a lot more time jamming with other musicians in his off hours than he ever had before, which led to this album, which finds him sharing each track with a different act (except for Kristi Rose and Fats Kaplin, who pop up twice). While *A Pocketful of Soul* focused on the traditional country side of Ringenberg's musical personality, *All Over Creation* is, well, all over the place, spinning between frantic rockabilly ("Honky Tonk Maniac From Mars" with Hamell on Trial), old-school country (a gender-reversed "Don't Come Home a Drinkin' (With Lovin' on Your Mind)" cut with BR5-49), balls-out rock & roll (the Wildhearts sit in on "One Less Heartache"), and subtle acoustic ballads ("I Dreamed My Baby Came Home," with Rose & Kaplan). If *All Over Creation* lacks the tighter focus of *A Pocketful of Soul*, its

eclecticism certainly mirrors the embrace of country and rock in all their forms that fueled Ringenberg's music with Jason & the Scorchers, and there are more than a few truly stellar tracks here: a new version of "Bible and a Gun" featuring superb vocals from Steve Earle, a masterful tune about the Irish emigration; "Erin's Seed," recorded with Lambchop; a striking bluegrass version of the Gun Club's "Mother of Earth"; and a beautiful lament for the changing south and the ravages of time, "Last Train to Memphis." Despite the many talented guest stars on hand, this is Jason Ringenberg's show, and *All Over Creation* proves once again as both a singer and a tunesmith, he's a talent to be reckoned with. It's great stuff. —*Mark Deming*

Jim Ringer

b. Feb. 29, 1936, Yell County, AR, **d.** Mar. 17, 1992

Guitar, Vocals / Progressive Bluegrass, Progressive Country, Contemporary Folk

At one time, it appeared as though singer/songwriter Jim Ringer would be a major star; instead, he wound up as a cult figure with a small but devoted following. He was born in Yell County in the Arkansas Ozarks; during the Dust Bowl years of the 1930s, his family migrated to California's Central Valley. It was a rough life, and by 18, Ringer was serving a three-year prison sentence. For a few years afterward, he was a transient hopping freight trains from job to job until 1969, when he became a professional musician. Two years later, he was a hippie in Berkeley, where he and 12 other friends bought a 1948 Chevy school bus and formed the Portable Folk Festival; the group spent 1971 touring the country and performing. Near the end of the year, Ringer began performing with Kenny Hall & the Sweet's Mill String Band; he cut an album with them in 1972. That year, he also cut his first solo album, *Waitin' for the Hard Times to Go*, for Folk-Legacy Records.

After meeting singer Mary McCaslin in 1972, Ringer teamed up professionally and personally with her, but continued to play individually too. In 1973, Ringer signed to Philo and released *Good to Get Home*. Two more albums followed in the subsequent three years. After he and McCaslin were married, they recorded a duet for Philo called "The Bramble and the Rose." Ringer signed to Flying Fish in 1981 and recorded *Endangered Species*, which produced the highly touted "Whiskey and Cocaine" and featured performances by the Dillards, the Burrito Brothers, and the Hot Band. He and McCaslin split up in 1989, and three years later, Ringer died on St. Patrick's Day. —*Sandra Brennan*

Waitin' for the Hard Times to Go / 1972 / Folk Legacy ✦✦✦

● **Good to Get Home** / 1973 / Philo ✦✦✦✦✦

Any Old Wind That Blows / 1975 / Philo ✦✦✦

Tramps & Hawkers / 1977 / Philo ✦✦✦✦

Endangered Species / 1981 / Flying Fish ✦✦✦✦

● **The Best of Jim Ringer: The Band of Jesse James** / Jul. 16, 1996 / Philo ✦✦✦✦✦

Riptones

f. 1990, Chicago, IL

Group / Neo-Traditionalist Country, Alternative Country, Roots Rock, Rockabilly Revival

Melding rockabilly, retro-country, and blues styles into a rollicking dance-friendly cocktail, the Riptones are one of the more traditionally oriented bands on Chicago's wild-and-woolly alt-country scene. Led by guitarist, singer, and songwriter Jeb Bonansinga, the band formed in 1990, with Bonansinga joined by his brother Tod Bonansinga on vocals and rubboard, Earl Carter on bass, Andon T. Davis on guitar, and Tom Harmon on drums. After several years of steady gigging around Chicago and building up a loyal following, the group recorded their first self-released album, *Cool Hand*, in 1994; the same year, a track by the Riptones appeared on the compilation *Insurgent Country, Vol. 1: For a Life of Sin*, the first release from the influential Bloodshot Records label. In 1996, the Riptones recorded a second album on their own dime, *World Renowned*, before they signed on with Bloodshot in 1997 and released their third album, *Extra Sauce*. The Riptones stripped back their style to a leaner and more rocking approach in 1999, while paring the lineup down to a trio; Tod, Andon T. Davis, and Harmon all left the group, and Kurt Wiesend came on board as drummer. (Davis, however, did make a guest appearance on the Riptones' 1999 album *Cowboy's Inn*.) In 2001, the band unveiled their fifth album, *Buckshot*, and another new lineup; Wiesend bowed out and drummer Perry LaFine stepped in to replace him, while Michael Krasovech joined as lead guitarist. In 2003, the group was putting the finishing touches on *Slant 6*, an all-instrumental album. —*Mark Deming*

● **Extra Sauce** / Aug. 5, 1997 / Bloodshot ✦✦✦✦

Splitting the difference between old-school country and high-attitude rockabilly, the Riptones work up a healthy twang on *Extra Sauce*, their first nationally distributed album (after a pair of hard-to-find self-released sets). While at times it sounds as if the band isn't sure just how hard they want to rock, guitarist Andon T. Davis and lead singer/ second axeman Jeb Bonansinga know how to make their six-strings work together as a unit, while bassist Earl Carter and drummer Tom Harmon set 'em up nicely whether in third gear or fifth. And Jeb Bonansinga's songwriting really sets this band apart; the straight-ahead honesty of his more C&W-oriented tunes ("How Mean You Really Are," "The Meanest Man in the World") suggests he could have a solid career as a Nashville tunesmith, and even when he's singing about such perennial roots rock themes as spicy food and equally spicy women, there's a light and un-selfconscious tone to his lyrics which is welcome. (And thankfully, "Motorcycle Man" doesn't celebrate biker culture so much as it casts a bemused glance at a lawyer playing hog rider on weekends.) Not quite perfect, but *Extra Sauce* shows the Riptones were a strong band with good ideas they would work out on future releases. —*Mark Deming*

Cowboy's Inn / Feb. 9, 1999 / Bloodshot ✦✦✦✦

The Riptones pared back the frills from their retro-country/rockabilly fusion on their 1999 album *Cowboy's Inn*, doubtless due to the fact that the band had been stripped down to a trio (singer and guitarist Jeb Bonansinga, bassist Earl Carter, and drummer

Kurt Weisend) from the five-piece edition which recorded their previous album. And the opening cut, "I Can't and I Won't," suggests that some pruning was just what the band needed; a hot-rodded bit of updated rockabilly with some hot guitar from briefly returning guitarist Andon T. Davis, "I Can't and I Won't" is one of the most exciting things the band has ever cut; and if the rest of the album never quite hits the same level of energy, the other tunes show that a simpler approach serves Bonansinga's songs quite well. "Hey You're Gonna Pay" and "Go Be and Do" reflect an admirably unclichéd approach to rockabilly, "Jack's Last Time" is an old-school cowboy ballad given a sharp modern twist, and "Big Timber" discovers the lost link between roots rock and surf music. *Cowboy's Inn* offers intelligent and muscular proof that the Riptones are one band who've been able to find a niche within the alt-country scene while creating an approach that's all their own, and it captures the group at their best. —*Mark Deming*

Buckshot / Aug. 22, 2000 / Bloodshot ✦✦✦
If *Buckshot* stylistically picks up where the Riptones left off with their previous album, *Cowboy's Inn*, it also finds the band refining their formula for the better. While the album favors the leaner sound that the three-piece edition of the Riptones brought to *Cowboy's Inn*, the addition of Michael Krasovech on lead guitar gives the arrangements some needed spark while letting frontman Jeb Bonansinga put his full attention on his vocals, which is where his greatest strength lies. But even though the band sounds fuller in this incarnation, the production still sounds tight and uncluttered, with a lean and muscular approach that fits the songs like a glove. And unlike most roots rockers who can't find much to sing about except cars 'n' girls, Bonansinga manages to write cool songs about radioactive fallout ("Rebel Rock Armageddon"), getting your life in order ("Get Me a Job"), and struggling to make it through an economic downturn ("Getting By"); it's rare to hear a rockabilly-influenced band actually deal with real life problems in their songs, and Bonansinga pulls it off pretty well. While the album falls a bit short on capturing this band at their best, *Buckshot* makes it clear the Riptones do what they do very well indeed, and anyone who finds their mixture interesting should enjoy it. —*Mark Deming*

Tex Ritter (Maurice Woodward Ritter)

b. Jan. 12, 1907, Marvaul, TX, d. Jan. 2, 1974, Nashville, TN
Vocals, Guitar / Traditional Country, Cowboy

Singing cowboy Tex Ritter stood as one of the biggest names in country music throughout the postwar era, thanks to a diverse career that led him everywhere from the Broadway stage to the political arena. He was born Maurice Woodward Ritter in Marvaul, TX, on January 12, 1907, and grew up on a ranch in Beaumont. After graduating at the top of his high-school class, he majored in law at the University of Texas. During college, however, he was bitten by the acting bug and moved to New York in 1928 to join a theatrical troupe. After a few years of struggle, he briefly returned to school, only to leave again to pursue stardom.

Ritter was playing cowboy songs on the radio when he returned to New York in 1931 to act in the Broadway production *Green Grow the Lilacs*; during scene changes, he also performed on his guitar. Thanks to his success on the stage, he began hosting radio programs like *Tex Ritter's Campfire* and *Cowboy Tom's Roundup* before entering the studio with producer Art Satherley in 1933, where his deep, lived-in voice graced songs like "Rye Whiskey." He caught the attention of Hollywood producer Edward Finney, who was searching for a cowboy singer in the mold of the highly successful Gene Autry and was tapped to star in the 1936 Western *Song of the Gringo*. Over the next two years, Ritter starred in a dozen films, including 1937's *Trouble in Texas* (co-starring a young Rita Hayworth), before Finney's studio, Grand National Pictures, folded. Ritter then switched to Monogram Studios, for whom he made some 20 Westerns, including 1940's *Take Me Back to Oklahoma* with co-star Bob Wills; work at Columbia and Universal followed, and by the time of his movie swan song, 1945's *The Texas Rangers*, he had appeared in a total of 85 films.

As Ritter's Hollywood career went into decline, his music career began to blossom, and in 1942, he became the first country artist signed to Capitol Records, where he recorded everything from traditional folk tunes to patriotic material to sentimental songs. In 1944, Tex Ritter & His Texans topped the charts with the single "I'm Wastin' My Tears on You." The record's flip side, "There's a New Moon Over My Shoulder," peaked at number two, as did the follow-up "Jealous Heart." 1945's "You Two-Timed Me One Time Too Often" proved to be Ritter's greatest success, holding at number one for 11 consecutive weeks. Among his other successes in the 1940s were 1945's number one "You Will Have to Pay," 1948's "Rock and Rye," and 1950's "Daddy's Last Letter (Private First Class John H. McCormick)," based on the actual correspondence of a soldier slain during the Korean War.

Ritter recorded the theme to the Fred Zinneman classic *High Noon* in 1953, and the resulting single proved extremely successful with pop audiences, helping win him the job as the MC of the television program *Town Hall Party*, which he hosted between 1953 and 1960. In 1958, he issued his first full-length LP, *Songs From the Western Screen*, followed the next year by *Psalms*. After leaving *Town Hall Party*, he released the LP *Blood on the Saddle*, a dark collection of cowboy narrative songs, and in 1961, he returned to the country charts after an 11-year absence with the Top Five hit "I Dreamed of a Hillbilly Heaven." In 1963 Ritter began a two-year tenure as the president of the Country Music Association, and in 1965 he moved to Nashville to join the *Grand Ole Opry*. After an unsuccessful bid for the U.S. Senate in 1970, Ritter died of a heart attack on January 2, 1974; his son John Ritter carried on the family name as a popular actor in TV sitcoms like *Three's Company* and *Hooperman*. —*Jason Ankeny*

Songs from the Western Screen / 1958 / Capitol ✦✦✦
Here are Ritter's original recordings of "High Noon," "Wichita," "The Searchers," and other songs from 1950's westerns, some recorded for the original films and others covers of soundtrack songs. (out of print) —*Bruce Eder*

Psalms / 1958 / Capitol ✦✦
This is Ritter's first religious album, reading various psalms to musical accompaniment arranged by scholar/composer/harpist Kathryn Julye. (out of print) —*Bruce Eder*

Hillbilly Heaven / 1961 / Capitol ✦✦✦
In response to the success of "I Dreamed of a Hillbilly Heaven," Capitol had Ritter re-record "High Noon," "Green Grow the Lilacs," and "Jingle Jangle Jingle" as part of these album sessions, backed by the Ralph Carmichael Chorus and Orchestra. (out of print) —*Bruce Eder*

The Lincoln Hymns / 1961 / Capitol ✦✦✦
Here are more religious recordings by Ritter, backed by the Ralph Carmichael Chorus and Orchestra, from the same sessions that also yielded his last big country hit of the 1960s, his recording of Eddie Dean's "I Dreamed of a Hillbilly Heaven." (out of print) —*Bruce Eder*

Stan Kenton & Tex Ritter / 1962 / Capitol ✦✦
This was the record, made with Stan Kenton's orchestra, that convinced Ritter it was time to move from Hollywood to Nashville. At the time of the sessions, however, he received a standing ovation from the orchestra at the conclusion of the recording, and overall this wasn't the worst idea in the world. The public never bought it, however, and the album was quickly deleted. (out of print) —*Bruce Eder*

Border Affair / 1963 / Capitol ✦✦✦
Ritter recorded this album in Spanish, with Ralph Carmichael leading marimba and mariachi bands. (out of print) —*Bruce Eder*

The Friendly Voice of Tex Ritter / 1964 / Capitol ✦✦✦✦✦
More recordings with the Carmichael Orchestra, along with Glen Campbell, Johnny Bond, and Billy Strange on guitars, with the King Sisters doing the back-up singing. A mix of western and folk material, and Ritter's last recording in Hollywood. (out of print) —*Bruce Eder*

Sweet Land of Liberty / 1966 / Capitol ✦✦✦✦
Ritter chose to record this collection of patriotic songs (including Woody Guthrie's "This Land Is Your Land") and speeches his first Nashville sessions late in 1966, just about the time that a fault line appeared in American politics over the Vietnam War. The timing was good and it was not, as listeners found themselves choosing sides over gestures like this, rather than listening to it on its merits. Ritter's first Nashville-recorded album. (out of print) —*Bruce Eder*

The Best of Tex Ritter / 1966 / Capitol ✦✦✦✦
Cast in the mold of Gene Autry, Tex Ritter first gained fame starring in over 80 Westerns during the '30s and '40s. After his film career folded in the early '40s, Ritter became the first country artist to sign to Capitol Records. His run of hits on the label lasted through the '60s and included such classics as "High Noon," "There's a New Moon Over My Shoulder," and "Jealous Hearts." This early best-of roundup includes those and several other hits recorded between 1943-1966. With his deep and gravelly voice in fine form, Ritter (at times sounding like a mix of Autry and Tennessee Ernie Ford) also shines on the Autry-inspired "We Live in Two Different Worlds," comedic fare like "Rye Whiskey" and "Boll Weevil," the old-timey waltz "Green Grow the Lilacs," and the kitschy yet incredible remembrance of country luminaries, "I Dreamed of a Hillbilly Heaven." Topped off with fine narrative songs like "Deck of Cards" and everything from banjo and accordion numbers to choral backdrops, this Tex Ritter collection might be outdated, but it still serves as a fine bargain introduction to the country star's long career. —*Stephen Cook*

Just Beyond the Moon / 1967 / Capitol ✦✦✦
This is the album accompanying Ritter's last, modest hit (the title track) of the 1960s. (out of print) —*Bruce Eder*

Tex Ritter's Wild West / 1968 / Capitol ✦✦✦
Ritter returns to a well established format, with yet another recording (his fifth) of "High Noon," among other Western songs, among them Johnny Bond's "Conversation With a Gun." (out of print) —*Bruce Eder*

Bump Tiddle Dee Bum Bum! / 1968 / Capitol ✦✦✦
Ritter's tribute album to veteran songwriter Cindy Walker, including "Blue Canadian Rockies." His first recordings since 1951 not to be produced by Capitol veteran Ken Nelson. (out of print) —*Bruce Eder*

Chuck Wagon Days / 1969 / Capitol ✦✦✦
More western songs, including "The Old Chisholm Trail," "Get Along Little Dogies," and "Rounded Up in Glory." (out of print) —*Bruce Eder*

Green, Green Valley / 1970 / Capitol ✦✦✦
With a new producer (George Richey) aboard, Ritter tackles some contemporary country tunes, including "Okie From Muskogee," on his first record of the 1970s. (out of print) —*Bruce Eder*

Super Country Legendary Tex Ritter / 1972 / Capitol ✦✦✦
Backed by a top-flight Nashville band, Ritter goes back to "Green Grow The Lilacs" and "Froggy Went A-Courtin'" amid other country and western and drinking songs. (out of print) —*Bruce Eder*

An American Legend / 1973 / Capitol ✦✦✦✦✦
The best LP collection of Ritter's work, a triple album featuring most of his best songs from 1942 onward, in their original versions, complete with newly recorded reminiscences by the singer bridging each one. Released late in 1973, the album was withdrawn and repackaged in 1974 to include his posthumous hit "The Americans." (out of print) —*Bruce Eder*

The Best of the Cowboys / 1988 / Hollywood ✦✦✦
This budget-priced ($7) eight song CD isn't half bad, despite the fact that it contains Ritter's stereo re-recordings of his classics. Tex could still put "High Noon" over with a lot of forcefulness in the 1960s, albeit in a more showy and elaborate arrangement. If anything,

his voice had mellowed and improved with age, and he was able to convey emotion with even greater sincerity than on his old recordings, though the overall sound of these sides is more commercial. "Boll Weevil," "Green Grow the Lilacs," and even "Rye Whiskey" are also great fun here, and there are far worse ways to spend 22 minutes than listening to this material. *—Bruce Eder*

Greatest Hits / 1990 / Curb ✦✦✦✦✦
Virtually all of Ritter's hits from his years with Capitol Records are included in this 12-cut collection, including "I'm Wastin' My Tears on You," and his first chart-topper. Also featured: "You Two-Timed Me One Time Too Often," "Jealous Heart," and "You Will Have to Pay." *—Jason Ankeny*

Country Music Hall of Fame / 1991 / MCA ✦✦✦✦✦
This CD contains 16 of the 30 songs that Ritter cut for Decca between 1935 and 1939. It is not his best material—it was on Capitol that he had his hits—but it is, in many ways, his most interesting body of songs. The early material here is more rough-hewn than most Western songs of the era, and, in keeping with Ritter's stage success as a folk-type balladeer in the cast of the Broadway show *Green Grow the Lilacs*, draws from folk as much as Western material. His first single, "Sam Hall," was a traditional British folk ballad that Ritter had sung in the show. "(Take Me Back to My) Boots and Saddle" comes off almost like a field recording, with none of the guile or sophistication that one expected of singing cowboys, and Ritter's natural, untutored baritone voice seems to come right out of the bunkhouse rather than the theater or the Hollywood soundstage. By 1936, and "The Hills of Old Wyoming," "High, Wide and Handsome," and "Sing, Cowboy, Sing," he was already developing a more sophisticated sound in keeping with his cowboy movies, although Ritter always sounded grittier than Gene Autry or the Sons of the Pioneers—he sounded more like a real cowboy who was singing, rather than a singing cowboy, with a beautifully raw, honest quality that made him more realistic if not as overtly attractive as a singer. Some of the latest material here, such as "When Its Lamplighting Time in the Valley," is engaging Western pop, a match for any of Autry's records in sophistication but driven by Ritter's unique, mournfully expressive baritone voice. *—Bruce Eder*

● **High Noon** / 1992 / Bear Family ✦✦✦✦✦
The single best collection of Tex Ritter's Capitol recordings isn't quite complete, but it's a lot better than Capitol's own Collector Series release on Ritter, and it's the best listeners are likely ever to see on this extraordinary artist, at least until a boxed set is forthcoming. The 28 songs here include most of the important tracks that he cut for Capitol between 1942-1956, including the ultra-rare 1952 British recording of "High Noon" (bar none, the best version of the song that Ritter ever did, and one that has a very unusual history to it) as well as the undubbed (i.e., drumless) original Capitol release; "Blood on the Saddle," "Jingle, Jangle, Jingle," "Goodbye, My Little Cherokee," the pop-western "Boogie Woogie Cowboy," and Ritter's definitive 1946 version of "Rye Whiskey." The range of styles here is daunting, as Ritter moves from early-'40s pop with a western twang ("Jingle, Jangle, Jingle") through authentic folk material ("Rye Whiskey") and into the western screen mythos—"Gunsmoke" is unexpectedly beautiful, but so is "Wichita," and Ritter's version of "The Searchers" is the best recording ever done of that Stan Jones movie theme song. There's also one previously unreleased track, Ritter's gorgeous rendition of "When It's Springtime in the Rockies." The notes and the detailed sessionography are up to Bear Family's usual daunting standards of excellence. *—Bruce Eder*

Capitol Collectors Series / Feb. 17, 1992 / Capitol ✦✦✦✦
Now deleted, this 25-song collection is as close as Capitol has gotten so far to doing a definitive collection on one of the label's founding artists. Ritter spent 31 years on the label, with successful singles in each decade of his relationship with Capitol from 1942 until 1973, and one would think that Capitol could do someone with a record like that some justice. There are some classics here, including "Rye Whiskey" and "Blood on the Saddle," as well as the obligatory "High Noon," but, like the rest of the *Capitol Collectors Series*, this disc was unsatisfying to true fans, leaving out more than a few worthy album tracks, not to mention a single or two that should be represented, even as it was too ambitious for the casual listener. (out of print) *—Bruce Eder*

Conservation With a Gun / Jan. 1, 1996 / Richmond ✦✦
Conversation With a Gun is a brief, eight-song budget CD that consists of re-recordings of some of Ritter's best-known songs. Some of the tracks feature keyboards and are vastly inferior to the originals. Ritter is in fine voice, though, and "Green Grow the Lilacs" sticks close to the arrangement and instrumentation of his 1945 recording. The "Saginaw Michigan" that appears here is not a version of the Lefty Frizzell hit, but an answer to it told from the perspective of the father-in-law. The re-recording of "Boll Weevil" is a standout, benefiting from a faster tempo than Ritter's 1945 recording and an enthusiastic vocal performance that might actually set it above the original recording. The cheap packaging and complete lack of liner notes, songwriting credits or recording dates makes this an artifact of minor interest to fans, but neophytes should stick with a collection of original recordings such as Capitol's *Vintage Collections*. *—Greg Adams*

Tex Ritter: Vintage Collections / 1997 / Capitol ✦✦
This is Capitol's second try at a Tex Ritter collection, and the second time they've blown it. Bear Family's 28-song *High Noon* disc, though not perfect, is far preferable to this 15-song collection, which leaves out so many key songs that it would be an embarrassment if not for the two previously unreleased cuts here, "I Was Out of My Mind" and "Waitin' and A-Worryin'," both of which are better than some of the previously released stuff here. The main problem is that the producers have focused too much on Ritter's pop songs ("There's a New Moon Over My Shoulder," "I'm Wastin' My Tears on You") and a handful of non-hits, and left out his grittier and personal songs ("Rye Whiskey," etc.), ignoring large chunks of his career in the process. It's not even that what's here is bad as music ("Have I Told You Lately That I Loved You" is superb)—just so inadequate in scope as to be almost useless. And why the makers chose to use one of Ritter's re-recordings of "High Noon," rather than the 1952 original, is anyone's guess. One good thing is that there is so little overlap with the Bear Family *High Noon* disc that this one makes a good supplement to it. For a real introduction, get the Bear Family disc. (And what's with the 15 songs here, when the others in the series have 20 songs?) *—Bruce Eder*

Blood on the Saddle / Jun. 23, 1999 / Bear Family ✦✦✦✦✦
Blood on the Saddle is a deluxe four-disc box set which collects Tex Ritter's recordings from 1932 to 1947, including his complete ARC and Decca sides, and everything from his first five years at Capitol. Over this period, Ritter progressed from spare, folksy readings of cowboy material to his mellow take on Western swing. Perhaps the earthiest of the singing cowboys, Ritter's rich personality and flair for the dramatic come through on these classic recordings. Hits such as "Jealous Heart" and "There's a New Moon Over My Shoulder" are represented, as well as alternate takes, unreleased songs, and rarities, including a number of recordings for children with spoken intros in the style later adopted by Merle Travis for his folk albums. Tex Ritter's catalog has been under-represented in the CD era, so collectors and serious fans will no doubt be thrilled by this loving presentation of his earliest recordings. *—Greg Adams*

Country Music Hall of Fame 1964 / Nov. 9, 1999 / King ✦✦
Another burn in this up-and-down series, this is loaded with late-period stereo recuts of his best-known tunes. If you can put up with hearing "I Dreamed of a Hillbilly Heaven" and "High Noon" saddled with dime-store-sounding synthesized keyboards, then this one's right up your alley. But if you want a fine collection of his very best, then pass this one right by and go straight for his original Capitol recordings. *—Cub Koda*

The Very Best of Tex Ritter / Jul. 25, 2000 / Varese ✦✦✦✦
Exactly half of these recordings previously appeared on the Hollywood Records compact disc *Conversation With a Gun*, including excellent remakes of "The Boll Weevil" and "Green Grow the Lilacs," both of which were recorded by Ritter for Capitol in the '40s. These recordings are said to be from a 1964 session for overseas radio broadcast, and Ritter remakes a number of his well-known songs. An answer to Lefty Frizzell's "Saginaw Michigan" is included ("Son of a Saginaw Fisherman"), along with the Harlan Howard's "The Gallows Pole" and an instrumental treatment of Johnny Bond's "Cimarron." *The Very Best* isn't Tex Ritter's very best—not even close—but fans will greatly enjoy a number of these tracks. *—Greg Adams*

High Noon [Box Set] / Dec. 13, 2000 / Bear Family ✦✦✦✦
High Noon is the second four-disc box set in Bear Family's revival of Tex Ritter's complete recordings. Picking up where the previous set, *Blood on the Saddle*, left off, *High Noon* covers the years 1947-1954, and includes every recording Ritter made for Capitol during that period. The set contains all four versions of the song "High Noon" and the hits "Deck of Cards," "Pecos Bill," "Rock and Rye," and "Daddy's Last Letter." Rather than presenting the material in strict chronological order as Bear Family often does, the set is organized thematically, with Ritter's country, western, and pop recordings on the first two discs, patriotic and religious songs on the third, and children's songs on the fourth. The children's songs are entertaining for listeners of all ages, since Ritter's charismatic performances are funny and unique. The range of material on *High Noon* is extremely eclectic and not always western in orientation, but Ritter was a true original who richly deserves the deluxe treatment. *—Greg Adams*

Sing, Cowboy, Sing / Jul. 24, 2001 / ASV ✦✦✦✦✦
Covering Ritter's Decca recordings between 1935-1939, *Sing, Cowboy, Sing* features 15 of the 16 songs on the *Country Music Hall of Fame* collection, omitting only "My Brown Eyed Texas Rose," while adding an additional ten tracks. That alone makes it the better purchase, and the transfers are outstanding to boot, presenting most of these songs with barely a scratch. Once you've absorbed Bear Family's single-disc *High Noon* collection, this is the next place to go. *—Jim Smith*

Have I Stayed Away Too Long [Box Set] / Feb. 2003 / Bear Family ✦✦✦✦✦

Dennis Robbins

b. Hazelwood, NC

Guitar, Songwriter, Vocals, Slide Guitar / Contemporary Country
A slide guitarist and former member of the Detroit blues-rock band the Rockets, Dennis Robbins also performed with the country-songwriter supergroup Billy Hill; among the songs he wrote were Garth Brooks' "Two of a Kind, Workin' on a Full House" and Shenandoah's "Church on Cumberland Road." Robbins was born in Hazelwood, NC, and grew up listening to traditional bluegrass music as well as rock & roll music. He began playing different styles of guitar music as a teen. Following high-school, Robbins was a U.S. Marine, and eventually moved to Detroit, where he played in different bands before joining up with the Rockets as a slide guitar player. The band was quite popular and opened for the likes of ZZ Top, Kiss, and Bob Seger. Tiring of touring, Robbins returned to North Carolina and then moved to Nashville, where in 1986 he released his debut solo album *The First of Me*. His lack of success spurred Robbins to form Billy Hill, which broke up in 1990 after only one album. Soon afterward, he became the first country artist to sign to Giant's new country division. His first single for the label, "Home Sweet Home," became a minor hit, and later appeared on the album *Man with the Plan* (1992). *—Sandra Brennan & Brian Mansfield*

The First of Me / 1986 / MCA ✦✦✦

I Am Just a Rebel / 1989 / Warner Bros. ✦✦✦✦

● **Man With a Plan** / Jun. 16, 1992 / Giant ✦✦✦✦✦
Redneck rock that lives and dies by the slide guitar, think of Hank Williams Jr. with a sneakier sense of humor. Tracy Lawrence found "Paris, Tennessee" here, and Confederate

Railroad got "I Am Just a Rebel" (which Robbins had earlier recorded with Billy Hill). Robbins broke the Top 40 with the slice-of-life "Home Sweet Home." *—Brian Mansfield*

Born Ready / Jul. 19, 1994 / Warner Bros. ✦✦✦

Hargus "Pig" Robbins

b. Jan. 18, 1938, Spring City, TN

Piano, Keyboards, Session Musician / Traditional Country, Western Swing, Nashville Sound/Countrypolitan

Perhaps the greatest session pianist/keyboardist ever to grace a Nashville recording studio, Hargus "Pig" Robbins maintained an amazingly prolific career from the late '50s on into the new millennium. Robbins was born in Spring City, TN, in 1938; an accident with his father's knife resulted in the loss of an eye, and he went completely blind before the age of four. He started taking classical piano lessons at age seven, and as he advanced, he learned to play country music by ear, particularly that of his idol, Tex Ritter. Robbins played the Nashville club scene after graduating and got his first session gig helping a friend record his demo. He subsequently joined the musicians' union and got his first big-time exposure on George Jones' 1959 hit "White Lightning." Over the next few decades, Robbins played behind a who's who of country music, recording with Patsy Cline, Loretta Lynn, Dolly Parton, Connie Smith, Tanya Tucker, Crystal Gayle, Ernest Tubb, Waylon Jennings, Willie Nelson, Bobby Bare, the Statler Brothers, Gary Stewart, and Kenny Rogers. Additionally, his appearance on Bob Dylan's 1966 classic *Blonde on Blonde* created demand for his work among folk (Joan Baez, Peter, Paul & Mary) and pop/rock artists (John Denver, Doug Sahm, the Everly Brothers, Ray Charles, Tom Jones, et al.). Robbins recorded his first solo album, *A Bit of Country Piano*, in 1963 and issued three more solo records on the Chart label during the late '60s. Robbins later returned to solo recording for Elektra, issuing a trio of albums—*Country Instrumentalist of the Year, A Pig in a Poke,* and *Unbreakable Hearts*—over 1977-1979. Over the '80s and '90s, Robbins was able to maintain his standing as Nashville's top session keyboardist with a new generation of contemporary country stars, playing with Randy Travis, Alan Jackson, Travis Tritt, Mark Chesnutt, Vince Gill, and Reba McEntire, among others; he also backed alternative rock pranksters Ween on their *12 Golden Country Greats* album of 1996. *—Steve Huey*

Play It Again, Hargus / 1968 / Chart ✦✦✦✦

Hargus Robbins / 1969 / Chart ✦✦✦

● **Country Instrumentalist of the Year** / 1977 / Elektra ✦✦✦✦

A Pig in a Poke / 1978 / Elektra ✦✦✦

Unbreakable Hearts / 1979 / Elektra ✦✦✦

Alive From Austin City Limits / 1979 / Flying Fish ✦✦✦

Marty Robbins (Martin David Robertson)

b. Sep. 26, 1925, Glendale, AZ, **d.** Dec. 8, 1982, Nashville, TN

Guitar, Vocals / Traditional Country, Cowboy, Country-Pop, Rockabilly, Pop, Nashville Sound/Countrypolitan

No artist in the history of country music has had a more stylistically diverse career than Marty Robbins. Never content to remain just a country singer, Robbins performed successfully in a dazzling array of styles during more than 30 years in the business. To his credit, Robbins rarely followed trends but often took off in directions that stunned both his peers and fans. Plainly Robbins was not hemmed in by anyone's definition of country music. Although his earliest recordings were unremarkable weepers, by the mid-'50s Robbins was making forays into rock music, adding fiddles to the works of Chuck Berry and Little Richard. By the late '50s, Robbins had pop hits of his own with teen fare like "A White Sport Coat (And a Pink Carnation)." Almost simultaneously, he completed work on his *Song of the Islands* album. In 1959, Robbins stretched even further with the hit single "El Paso," thus heralding a pattern of "gunfighter ballads" that lasted the balance of his career. Robbins also enjoyed bluesy hits like "Don't Worry," which introduced a pop audience to fuzz-tone guitar in 1961. Barely a year later, Robbins scored a calypso hit with "Devil Woman." Robbins also left a legacy of gospel music and a string of sentimental ballads, showing that he would croon with nary a touch of hillbilly twang.

Born and raised in Glendale, AZ, Robbins (born Martin David Robertson, September 26, 1925; died December 8, 1982) was exposed to music at an early age. His mother's father was "Texas" Bob Heckle, a former medicine showman who told his grandson cowboy stories and tales of the traveling show. Robbins became enraptured by the cowboy tales and, once he became a teenager, worked on his older brother's ranch outside of Phoenix, concentrating more on his cowboy duties than his studies. Indeed, he never graduated from high-school, and by his late teens, he started turning petty crimes while living as a hobo. In 1943, he joined the U.S. Navy to fight in World War II, and while he was in the service, he learned how to play guitar and developed a taste for Hawaiian music. Robbins left the Navy in 1947, returning to Glendale, where he began to sing in local clubs and radio stations. Often, he performed under the name "Jack Robinson" in an attempt to disguise his endeavors from his disapproving mother. Within three years, he had developed a strong reputation throughout Arizona and was appearing regularly on a Mesa radio station and had his own television show, *Western Caravan*, in Phoenix. By that time, he had settled on the stage name of Marty Robbins.

Robbins landed a recording contract with Columbia in 1951 with the assistance of Little Jimmy Dickens, who had been a fan ever since appearing on *Western Caravan*. Early in 1952, Robbins released his first single, "Love Me or Leave Me Alone." It wasn't a success and neither was its follow-up, "Crying 'Cause I Love You," but "I'll Go on Alone" soared to number one in January 1953. Following its blockbuster success, Robbins signed a publishing deal with Acuff-Rose and joined the *Grand Ole Opry*. "I Couldn't Keep From Crying" kept him in the Top Ten in spring 1953, but his two 1954 singles—"Pretty Words" and "Call Me Up (And I'll Come Calling on You)"—stalled on the charts. A couple of rock & roll covers, "That's All Right" and "Maybellene," returned him to the country Top Ten in 1955, but it wasn't until "Singing the Blues" shot to number one in fall 1956 that Robbins' career was truly launched. Staying at number one for a remarkable 13 weeks, "Singing the Blues" established Robbins as a star, but its progress on the pop charts was impeded by Guy Mitchell's cover, which was released shortly after Robbins' original and quickly leapfrogged to number one. The process repeated itself on "Knee Deep in the Blues," which went to number three on the country charts but didn't even appear on the pop charts due to Mitchell's hastily released cover. To head off such competition, Robbins decided to record with easy listening conductor Ray Conniff for his next singles. It was a crafty move and one that kept him commercially viable during the peak of rock & roll. The first of these collaborations, "A White Sport Coat (And a Pink Carnation)," became a huge hit, spending five weeks at the top of the country charts in spring 1957 and peaking at number two on the pop charts, giving him his long-awaited breakthrough record. After "A White Sport Coat (And a Pink Carnation)," Robbins was a regular fixation on both the pop and country charts until the mid-'60s. The Burt Bacharach & Hal David composition "The Story of My Life" returned Robbins to the number-one country slot in early 1957 (number 15 pop), while "Just Married," "Stairway of Love," and "She Was Only Seventeen (He Was One Year More)" kept him in teen-pop territory, as well as the upper reaches of the charts, throughout 1958. In addition to his pop records, Robbins recorded rockabilly singles and Hawaiian albums that earned their own audience. During that time, he began a couple of business ventures of his own, including a booking agency and a record label called Robbins. He also ventured into movies, appearing in the Westerns *Raiders of Old California* (1957) and *Badge of Marshal Brennan* (1958), where he played a Mexican named Felipe. The films not only demonstrated Robbins' love for Western myths and legends, but they signalled the shift in musical direction he was about to take. Over the course of 1958 and 1959, he recorded a number of cowboy and western songs, and the first of these—"The Hanging Tree," the theme to the Gary Cooper film of the same name—became a hit in spring 1959. However, the song just set the stage for Robbins' signature song and biggest western hit, "El Paso." Released in the summer, the single spent six months on the country charts, including seven weeks at number one, while hitting the top of the pop charts. A full album of western songs, *Gunfighter Ballads & Trail Songs*, became equally successful, reaching number six on the pop charts, and by the mid-'60s, it had gone platinum.

"El Paso" began a very successful decade for Robbins. "Big Iron," another western song, followed its predecessor to the Top Ten of the country charts in 1960, but it wasn't until 1961 that he had another huge hit in the form of "Don't Worry." Fueled by a fuzz-toned guitar (the first country record to feature such an effect), "Don't Worry" spent ten weeks at number one and crossed over to number three on the pop charts. The following year, "Devil Woman" became nearly as successful, spending eight weeks at number one; it was followed by another number one, "Ruby Ann." Between "Don't Worry" and "Devil Woman," he had a number of smaller hits, most notably the Top Ten "It's Your World," and for the rest of the decade, his biggest hits alternated with more moderate successes. With his career sailing along, Robbins began exploring racecar driving in 1962, initially driving in dirt-track racing competitions before competing in the famous NASCAR race. However, car racing was just a hobby, and he continued to have hits in 1963, including the number one "Begging to You." The following year, he starred in the film *Ballad of a Gunfighter*, which was based on songs from his classic album.

Robbins' chart success continued throughout 1964, before suddenly dipping after he took Gordon Lightfoot's "Ribbon of Darkness" to number one in spring 1965. For the remainder of the year and much of the next, his singles failed to crack the Top Ten, and he concentrated on filming a television series called *The Drifter*, which was based on a character he had created. He also acted frequently, including the Nashville exploitation films *Country Music Caravan, The Nashville Story,* and *Tennessee Jamboree* and the stock-car drama *Hell on Wheels*. Though "The Shoe Goes on the Other Foot Tonight" reached number three in 1966, it wasn't until "Tonight Carmen" reached number one on the country charts in 1967 that his career picked up considerably. During the next two years, he regularly hit the Top Ten with country-pop songs like "I Walk Alone" and "It's a Sin." Robbins suffered from a heart attack while on tour in August 1969, which led to a bypass operation in 1970. Despite his brush with death, he continued to record, tour, and act. Early in 1970, "My Woman My Woman My Wife" became his last major crossover hit, reaching number one on the country charts and 42 on the pop charts and eventually earning a Grammy award.

Robbins left Columbia Records in 1972, spending the next three years at Decca/MCA. Though "Walking Piece of Heaven," "Love Me," and "Twentieth Century Drifter" all reached the Top Ten, most of his singles were unenthusiastically received. Nevertheless, he sustained his popularity through concerts and film appearances, including the Lee Marvin movie *A Man and a Train* and *Guns of a Stranger*. In March 1974, Robbins became the last performer to play at the Ryman Auditorium, the original location of the *Grand Ole Opry*; a week later, he was the first to play at the new Grand Ole Opry House. The honors and tributes to Robbins continued to roll out during the mid-'70s, as he was inducted into Nashville Songwriters International Hall of Fame in 1975. That same year, he returned to Columbia Records, and over 1976 and 1977 he had his last sustained string of Top Ten hits, with "El Paso City" and "Among My Souvenirs" reaching number one. Following this two-year burst of success, Robbins settled into a series of minor hits for the next four years. In October 1982, he was inducted into the Country Music Hall of Fame. Two months later, he suffered his third major heart attack (his second arrived in early 1981), and although he had surgery, he died on December 8. In the wake of his death, his theme song to Clint Eastwood's movie *Honky Tonk Man* was released and climbed to number ten. Robbins left behind an immense legacy, including no less than 94 charting country hits and a body of recorded worked that proved how eclectic country music could be. *—Hank Davis*

Rock'n Roll'n Robbins / 1956 / Columbia ✦✦✦✦

The Song of Robbins / 1957 / Columbia/Legacy ✦✦✦

The Song of Robbins presents Robbins in the mold of the popular troubadour, featuring the most famous songs he was performing at the time. With three Hank Williams covers and favorites by Gene Autry and Fred Rose, the record achieves a nice balance of pop and honky tonk that doesn't succumb to excess. Although he didn't have any lasting hits from this album, Robbins is in typically strong voice and the mix of ballads and gentle rockers makes for pleasant listening. *—Jim Smith*

Song of the Islands / 1957 / Columbia ✦✦✦✦✦

☆ **Gunfighter Ballads & Trail Songs** / 1959 / Columbia/Legacy ✦✦✦✦✦
Gunfighter Ballads & Trail Songs was Marty Robbins' first album to consist entirely of western and cowboy music. Containing the hit single "El Paso," the album was divided between originals, traditional cowboy songs, and contemporary western songs. The result was a successful and thoroughly entertaining celebration of cowboy songs and western movies, particularly since the songs are alternately idealistic and adventerous. Sure, *Gunfighter Ballads & Trail Songs* doesn't deal in reality, but it is grounded in myth. It just happens to be one of the most effective and romantic statements of the cowboy mythology recorded in the late '50s and early '60s. [The 1999 CD reissue contains three bonus tracks: "The Hanging Tree," "Saddle Tramp" and "El Paso."] *—Stephen Thomas Erlewine*

More Gunfighter Ballads & Trail Songs / 1960 / Columbia ✦✦✦✦✦
Marty Robbins' sequel to *Gunfighter Ballads & Trail Songs* followed the same formula as its predecessor, dividing traditional cowboy songs with original numbers by Robbins. Though the album didn't feature any hit singles, it was the equal to its predecessor—"San Angelo" is one of Robbins' best cowboy songs, while his version of "Streets of Laredo" boasts one of his finest vocals. *—Stephen Thomas Erlewine*

Alamo / 1961 / Columbia ✦✦✦

Just a Little Sentimental / 1961 / Columbia ✦✦✦

More Greatest Hits / 1961 / Columbia/Legacy ✦✦✦
More Greatest Hits is a straight reissue of the 1961 LP on Columbia. While classic material like "El Paso" and "Don't Worry" are included, the main focus of this set is Robbins' gunfighter ballads: "Red River Valley," "Streets of Laredo," and "Ballad of the Alamo." This is a short program at only 11 tracks, and considering the vast array of solid discs encompassing Marty Robbins' full spectrum of hits, this is recommended to completists only. *—Al Campbell*

Devil Woman / 1962 / Columbia ✦✦✦✦✦

Marty After Midnight / 1962 / Columbia ✦✦✦
It's arguable that no country singer ever came closer to straight jazz than Robbins. Released in 1962, this album of mostly jazz standards is somewhat of an anomaly in his catalog, jazz being one of the few styles he would dabble in but never fully embrace. It is part of his remarkably diverse late-'50s/early-'60s period, in which he recorded Hawaiian music, cowboy songs, honky tonk, and pop covers, all within a five-year span. Robbins was known to dive headlong into a style, and that's certainly true here—there's not a shred of country anywhere on this album, save for an ever-present Nashville chorus and a slightly rockabilly version of "On the Sunny Side of the Street." It's not nearly as interesting, though, as Ray Price's *Night Life*, which utilizes the same smoky setting to better effect, and Robbins' take on these songs isn't distinctive enough to be memorable, which is perhaps the reason that most latter-day compilations have chosen to ignore this album. *—Jim Smith*

Return of the Gunfighter / 1963 / Columbia ✦✦✦✦✦

What God Has Done / 1965 / Columbia ✦✦✦✦
Considering the excellence of this album, it's surprising that Robbins didn't record more gospel music. It's downright shocking, however, that save for "The Great Speckled Bird" on *Singin' the Hits*, none of these tracks have ever appeared on a Robbins compilation. Even the incredibly varied *Essential Marty Robbins: 1951-1982* ignores it completely, but oh well—that makes it worthy of reissue, and there's nothing wrong with that. This isn't classic stuff, but it's punchy and tender in all the right places, highlighted by a vivacious take on "When the Roll Is Called Up Yonder," a somber, beautiful "Almost Persuaded," and the delicate closer, "Have Thine Own Way, Lord." Robbins sings passionately throughout, and the background singers, who have ruined many a '60s country record, actually enhance this one, giving the songs a churchy feel. Its budget price makes it a nice addition to any library. *—Jim Smith*

The Drifter / 1966 / Koch ✦✦✦✦✦
Based of Marty Robbins' syndicated television series of the same name, *The Drifter* was one of the purest cowboy albums Robbins ever made. Though Robbins had made several cowboy albums before—indeed, his love of western music informed much of his music—the instrumentation and song selection on *The Drifter* was stripped-down and direct, concentrating almost entirely on epic western narrative sagas. The lack of concise songs resulted in a less successful album by commerical standards—only "Mr. Shorty" was a hit, while the "El Paso" sequel "Feleena" ran over eight minutes—but *The Drifter* was of Robbins' most artistically ambitious albums, as well as one of his most accomplished. *—Stephen Thomas Erlewine*

★ **All-Time Greatest Hits** / 1972 / Columbia/Legacy ✦✦✦✦✦
Released in 1972, the double-album/single-CD *All-Time Greatest Hits* remains one of the best compilations ever assembled on Marty Robbins. Featuring 20 tracks—including most of his big hits—there are very few essential tracks missing from the collection. As an introduction, this relatively concise compilation is a bit more managable than the double-disc *Essential Marty Robbins* and, therefore, is more attractive to neophytes. *—Stephen Thomas Erlewine*

All Around Cowboy / 1979 / Columbia ✦✦✦
All Around Cowboy is the final cowboy album Marty Robbins ever recorded and it stands out as one of the best of his latter-day records. Though many of his latter-day recordings were hampered by mediocre material and indifferent performances, Robbins sounds lively on *All Around Cowboy*, breathing life into the songs and assembling a collection of terrific western tunes. Though the production relies a little too heavily on contemporary late-'70s trends, the Robbins' convincing performances make those flaws easy to ignore. *All Around Cowboy* may pale slightly to his early cowboy classics like *Gunfighter Ballads and Trail Songs*, but it's heart-warming to hear him this committed at a time when it sounded like he was losing faith in the music. *—Stephen Thomas Erlewine*

No. 1 Cowboy / 1980 / TeeVee ✦✦✦
Obviously, the main focus of *No. 1 Cowboy* is Marty Robbins' classic gunfighter ballads and cowboy-themed songs from the '60s and '70s. Originally recorded for Columbia, these 20 tracks have a quality that can't be denied: "Red River Valley," "Streets of Laredo," "Ballad of the Alamo," and, of course, "El Paso" and "El Paso City." This release from the TeeVee label is fine, but Columbia offers a vast array of solid discs encompassing the full spectrum of Marty Robbins hits; these easily available discs provide better sound quality, liner notes, and graphics. *—Al Campbell*

Biggest Hits / 1982 / Columbia ✦✦✦✦✦
Biggest Hits covers Robbins' early years as a recording artist, and includes hits like "El Paso," "A White Sport Coat (and a Pink Carnation)," "Singing the Blues" and "The Story of My Life" as well as many lesser-known efforts. *—Jason Ankeny*

A Lifetime of Song (1951–1982) / 1983 / Columbia ✦✦✦✦✦
It's a mystery why Columbia has so many Robbins compilations in print, since they all cover roughly the same territory. *Lifetime of Song (1951-1982)* isn't as comprehensive as the *Essential Marty Robbins: 1951-1982* box, nor as concise as *The Story of My Life*; what it is, rather, is a kind of a follow-up to 1972's *All-Time Greatest Hits* collection, featuring a number of classics ("A White Sport Coat," "Singing the Blues," "Among My Souvenirs") that were omitted from the earlier record. It duplicates many tracks from the aforementioned sets, but it's still great listening on its own, even if it isn't necessarily the place to start. *—Jim Smith*

Rock'n Roll'n Robbins: Marty Robbins Sings / 1985 / Bear Family ✦✦✦✦✦
In Bear Family's typically exhaustive fashion, the label has gone to the vaults to track down all of Marty Robbins' pre-rock & roll sides from 1953 ("It's a Long Ride") and 1954 ("Call Me Up"), as well as four bluesed-out cuts from that year that remained shelved until after his death in 1982, to the 1955-1957 rockabilly material. There are 19 cuts here, and they are sequenced according to rock & roll aesthetic rather than chronologically. And this makes sense, as "It's a Long Long Ride" is as much a honky tonk and Western swing tune as it is a rockabilly number. What makes it rock & roll at all is the shivering, reckless energy in the vocal—something uncommon in a Robbins recording of any stripe. "Pain and Misery" from the long-lost session is a rollin' and strollin' blues with bent guitar strings and a solid rock & roll shuffle. But when Robbins recut "That's All Right Mama" a mere six months after Elvis in 1955, the wheels were off. And that's what spills from this compilation, the skipping, driving country-rockabilly from 1955 and 1956 in tracks like "Pretty Mama," "Long Tall Sally," "I Can't Quit," "Knee Deep in the Blues," "Tennessee Toddy," and "Mister Teardrop," among others. Robbins' delivery could hold a tune on the rails, even when it threatened to roll off with his deeply emotive yet silvery croon that would sound insincere coming from anybody else. This is a stellar collection of 19 tracks with nary a weak one in the bunch. *—Thom Jurek*

American Originals / 1989 / Columbia ✦✦✦
American Originals is one of many Robbins collections spilt between hits (here, "Singing the Blues," "Ruby Ann," "Tonight Carmen") and much less popular recordings. *—Jason Ankeny*

Singin' the Hits / 1990 / CBS Special Products ✦✦✦
The Hits referred to in the title of CBS Special Products' *Singin' the Hits* aren't necessarily hits that Marty Robbins had himself, even though he did burn up the charts with "Singing the Blues," "Don't Worry" and "Begging to You," which are all on this collection. Instead, *the hits* means songs that were hits, whether Robbins actually charted with the song or not. That may frustrate some fans looking for a budget-line collection of hits, but the disc remains a good listen, since Robbins was an excellent vocalist who could deliver engaging interpretations of such songs as "Lovesick Blues," "I Started Loving You Again," "Bouquet of Roses," "Kaw-Liga," "She Thinks I Still Care" and "The Great Speckled Bird." That's the reason why this collection is worth its budget price for casual listeners. *—Stephen Thomas Erlewine*

☆ **The Essential Marty Robbins: 1951-1982** / 1991 / Columbia/Legacy ✦✦✦✦✦
The double-disc set *The Essential Marty Robbins: 1951-1982* effectively presents an overview of Robbins' long, prolific career, taking in nearly every style he tried out during that time. There are honky tonk and hillbilly numbers and cowboy songs, country-pop, rockabilly and Hawaiian tunes—in all, there are 50 songs, including the great majority of his big hit singles. In short, it's the perfect place to begin exploring his long, prolific and varied career, and it's a necessary addition to any country music library. *—Stephen Thomas Erlewine*

Ruby Ann: Rockin' Rollin' Robbins, Vol. 3 / 1991 / Bear Family ✦✦✦✦✦

Country 1951–1958 / 1991 / Bear Family ✦✦✦✦✦
Listeners charmed by his pre-*El Paso* country have a motherlode to explore in this five-disc boxed set filled with dewy-eyed weepers (his earliest recordings), his rockabilly (he cut the first cover of "Maybellene"), ancient country-folk accompanied solely by acoustic guitar ("The Dream of the Miner's Chill"), Hawaiiana ("Aloha Oe"), and a handful of his country-pop outings arranged by Ray Conniff. *—Mark A. Humphrey*

Isle of the Golden Dreams / 1992 / Bear Family ✦✦✦✦

The Legendary Marty Robbins / 1992 / Sony Special Products ✦✦✦
Sony Music Special Products' *The Legendary Marty Robbins* shouldn't be thought of as a hits collection—after all, it's missing "El Paso," "Don't Worry," "Devil Woman," "The Story of My Life," and "Begging to You," among many others. Instead, think of the compilation

as a sampler of sorts, one that spotlights Robbins' ease with a song, whether it's Hank Williams ("I Can't Help It (If I'm Still in Love With You)," "Kaw-Liga"), "Singing the Blues," or "A White Sport Coat (And a Pink Carnation)." Some listeners may be frustrated that there aren't many hits here, but it's an enjoyable (albeit brief at under 25 minutes) sampler for listeners on a tight budget. *—Stephen Thomas Erlewine*

Lost & Found / 1994 / Columbia ✦✦✦
Included is previously unreleased material and a studio-manufactured duet with Michael Martin Murphey on "Big Iron." *—Dan Cooper*

Musical Journey to the Caribbean & Mexico / 1994 / Bear Family ✦✦✦✦
Bear Family's *A Musical Journey to the Carribean & Mexico* contains all of Marty Robbins' calypso, Jamaican, and Latin experiments, from "Calypso Vacation" and "Calypso Girl" to "Bahama Mama," "Tahitain Boy," "La Borrachita" and "Adios Marquita Linda." Robbins did have a flair for this material—indeed, the very best songs here are quite enjoyable—but he often is saddled with mediocre material. Furthermore, Bear Family's quest for completeness means there are three versions of "Girl from Spanish Two" and two versions of "Kingston Girl" on the single disc, which helps make the disc rather tedious listening for anyone but dedicated fans. Nevertheless, those dedicated fans will be delighted with the collection, since this music has rarely been in print since its original release. *—Stephen Thomas Erlewine*

Rock'n Roll'n Robbins [Bonus Tracks] / 1996 / Koch ✦✦✦✦✦
When rockabilly reared its ugly head in country music circles back in the mid-'50s, hillbilly artists generally took one of two approaches to it: ignore it or take a stab at it. One country singer who decided to test these uncharted waters was Marty Robbins, and as this 12-song package clearly shows, he was well-equipped to take on the new sound. This compilation combines the original cover and the half-dozen songs that comprised a ten-inch vinyl album issued in the 1950s, with six more tracks (five of which were Columbia singles) released during the same time period. While the accent is on the "billy" side of the rockabilly equation along with Music City's attempt to tame the style down for an audience more accustomed to Grandpa Jones than Gene Vincent, this is very credible music, indeed. Rather than just covering the hits of the day (he was the first to cover Elvis' "That's All Right"), Robbins also contributed solid self-penned ditties like "Tennessee Toddy," "Respectfully Miss Brooks," and "Mean Mama Blues," although his best-known rocking effort, "Sugaree," is curiously missing from this collection. That a ballad singer whose sobriquet was Mister Teardrop could jump into this music so wholeheartedly is one of the more interesting footnotes to this confusing period in country music's history. *—Cub Koda*

☆ **The Story of My Life: The Best of Marty Robbins** / 1996 / Columbia/Legacy ✦✦✦✦✦
This 18-track compilation covering the first half of Marty Robbins' recording career is almost an exact duplication of a chronological list of Robbins' biggest country hit singles of the period, the only exception being "I Can't Quit Her (I've Gone Too Far)," and which, while a Top Ten entry, was not as big a hit as "She Was Only Seventeen (He Was One Year More)," which has been left out. (No one seems to have told annotator Rick Kienzle, who mentions the missing track and not the included one.) That means Robbins' 11 chart toppers are here, from "I'll Go on Alone" to "Ribbon of Darkness," with such massive hits as "Singing the Blues," "El Paso," "Don't Worry," and "Devil Woman" in between. The songs, 11 of which were written by Robbins himself, are amazingly diverse, covering country, western, pop, and folk styles, but the set is held together by Robbins' warm, country-tinged voice. The only objection to this set is that, at only 49-plus minutes, it could have been longer by half. *—William Ruhlmann*

Gunfighter Ballads & Trail Songs/More Gunfighter Ballads & Trail Songs / 1996 / Collectors' Choice Music ✦✦✦✦✦
Two of Marty Robbins' very finest albums, *Gunfighter Ballads & Trail Songs* and *More Gunfighter Ballads & Trail Songs*, are combined on this excellent single disc. With his cowboy albums, Robbins helped keep western music alive during the late '50s and early '60s, and the warm, affectionate spirit of this music illustrates why. The disc contains such hits as "El Paso," "Big Iron" and "Five Brothers," as well as classic versions of "Streets of Laredo" and "Strawberry Roan," and other western standards. *—Stephen Thomas Erlewine*

Country (1960–1966) / 1996 / Bear Family ✦✦✦✦✦
Cutting away all of Marty Robbins' rock & roll, Hawaiian and cowboy recordings, Bear Family's four-disc box set *Country (1960-1966)* contains nothing but his straight country and country-pop recordings of the early '60s. During that era, Robbins was one of the most popular performers in country music, scoring an impressive series of Top Ten hits and pop crossovers like "Don't Worry" and "Devil Woman," which are all included on this set. Where many Bear Family sets are so thorough and complete, they merely wind up being exhausting, *Country (1960-1966)* is entertaining from start to finish, since it is sequenced in a logical, listenable order and doesn't dwell on the rarities. Any serious fan of Robbins will find the set an essential addition to their library, and it is arguably the finest Robbins box Bear Family has released. *—Stephen Thomas Erlewine*

Under Western Skies / Feb. 1996 / Bear Family ✦✦✦✦✦
Four CDs covering Marty Robbins' complete Western recordings, 99 songs in all from 1958 until 1979. As a concept, *Under Western Skies* is cohesive and enjoyable, largely because Robbins' music, regardless of the particular year in which it was recorded, is unified thematically. It's also a superb showcase for Robbins' voice, one of the most versatile in country & western—he was equally adept at rock & roll, traditional country, or Western ballads dating back 100 years or more, but he had a way of extending the latter genre's melodic beauty and lyricism without ever seeming repetitive. Thus, it wasn't just that Robbins was covering this repertory, but that he was doing it in ways that, as a solo artist of his era, were just about definitive. Disc one contains songs from *Gunfighter Ballads & Trail Songs* and parts of the follow-up record, *More Gunfighter Ballads & Trail Songs*. Disc two is devoted to songs from *Return of the Gunfighter* and the rest of *More Gunfighter Ballads*, filled out with songs that only appeared previously in 1984 on a Bear Family vinyl release. By the mid-'60s, Robbins' voice was even better, richer and more confident on this material, and disc three reflects this. Disc four extends up through 1979, and it's something of a tribute to Robbins' success with this repertory that precious little was left in the vaults for Bear Family or anyone else to unearth and issue for the first time. The accompanying booklet is 60 pages long, and while it does seem as though the essay is not as well organized as it might have been, it's interesting overall, highlighted with excellent photographs and accompanied by lyrics to each of the songs and a full sessionography. *—Bruce Eder*

16 Biggest Hits / Jul. 14, 1998 / Sony ✦✦✦✦✦
Since Marty Robbins scored 16 number-one country hits between 1952 and 1976, a list of them provides a good standard against which to measure an album called *16 Biggest Hits*. By that standard, the album scores 15 out of 16, presenting Robbins' number-one hits from 1952's "I'll Go Alone" to 1976's "Among My Souvenirs," with one exception. "El Paso City," a number one hit in 1976, is absent, and instead the album ends with "Some Memories Just Won't Die," Robbins' last Top Ten country hit before his death in 1982. As "El Paso City" is a sequel to the included "El Paso," such a substitution is understandable, and so *16 Biggest Hits*, which just about lives up to its name, is the best available collection of Robbins' most popular songs through the years. There are several lengthier Robbins compilations on the market, but this one was released with a discounted list price of $11.97, which makes it particularly appealing to the new fan. *—William Ruhlmann*

Hawaii's Calling Me / Dec. 25, 1999 / Bear Family ✦✦✦
Marty Robbins clearly felt great affinity for the music of Hawaii, and the 28 tracks on this collection contain some of his finest and most evocative singing. Although the venture wasn't commercially successful, and the music occasionally suffers the intrusion of schmaltzy Nashville production, Robbins performs beautifully, creating a breezy mood that marks one of pop music's better attempts at the genre. *—Jim Smith*

Live Classics from the WSM Grand Ole Opry / May 22, 2001 / Audium ✦✦✦✦
These 21 tracks are drawn from 1951-1960 performances at the *Grand Ole Opry*, starting from a time at which Robbins was a relative unknown, and ending at a time when he was not just a country but a pop superstar, performing his number-one hit "El Paso" in 1960. While this in no way equals the best studio material he cut from the period, for Robbins fans, it's a fine, well-assembled opportunity to hear him in a different context. The sound is thinner, of course, than his Columbia recordings of the 1950s were, both in terms of the actual fidelity and the more basic live arrangements. It's kind of nice to hear him in a less slick setting, though, and he performs well, the repertoire including familiar hits like "A White Sport Coat," "The Story of My Life," "Singing the Blues," "Knee Deep in the Blues," "I'll Go on Alone," and "The Hanging Tree." Of more note to specialists will be the less familiar songs, like his take (with fiddle) on the Arthur Crudup/Elvis Presley classic "That's All Right"; two songs on his maiden 1951 *Opry* appearance ("Ain't You Ashamed" and "Good Night Cincinnati, Good Mornin' Tennessee") that he never recorded in the studio; a couple of gospel songs; and the Hank Williams cover "I Can't Help It (If I'm Still in Love With You)." In its own way, this set illustrates his considerable development over the course of the 1950s as aptly as a 1950s Marty Robbins best-of would. *—Richie Unterberger*

Just a Little Sentimental/Turn the Lights Down Low / Feb. 5, 2002 / Collectables ✦✦✦
Along with Eddy Arnold, Marty Robbins managed to crossover between the pop and country charts throughout most of his career. *Just a Little Sentimental* and *Turn the Lights Down Low* were originally released on Columbia in 1961 and 1965, respectively, and had been out of print for years before Collectables reissued them in 2002. Romantic chestnuts like "Unchained Melody," "Are You Sincere?" "Too Young," and "Hurt" make up the majority of these discs. However Robbins also turns in beautiful renditions of two country classics from the Hank Williams songbook, "Half as Much" and "I Can't Help It (If I'm Still in Love With You)," that fit perfectly within the romantic theme. These reissues are recommended especially to those who only know the country side of Robbins. *—Al Campbell*

Kenny Roberts

b. Lenoir City, TN
Vocals / Traditional Country, Cowboy
Best-known for his 1949 hit "I Never See Maggie Alone," Kenny Roberts was one of the last country singers to specialize in the legendary vocal technique of the blue yodel. Inspired by Yodeling Slim Clark, Jimmie Rodgers, and several singing cowboys, Roberts first came to prominence in the late '40s, and over the next five years he built up a fan base through his recording, frequent tours, and his appearance at yodeling concerts. Though he never had many hits—he only charted four times, between 1949 and 1950—he nevertheless remained a popular concert attraction well into the '80s.

Roberts was born in Lenoir City, TN, yet he was raised on a farm outside of Greenfield, MA. As a child, he became fascinated by the music of Clark and began singing as a teacher, making his first radio appearance when he was 15. Soon, he became part of the Down Homers, a local group who had a regular gig at WKNE, a New Hampshire radio station. Eventually, the group made their way toward the Midwest, playing at radio stations in Iowa and later settling in Fort Wayne, IN, where they regularly played a show called the Hoosier Hop. In a short time, Roberts had developed a reputation as a first-rate singer and yodeler.

The Down Homers—who also featured Bob Mason, Guy Campbell, Shorty Cook, and Lloyd Cornell—cut a record released as a Vogue Picture Disc. When World War II arrived halfway through the '40s, Roberts decided to enlist in the U.S. Navy in early 1945. Once the war was over, he returned to Fort Wayne, where he began a solo career. After a few months, he moved to St. Louis, where he appeared regularly on several different shows on KMOX, as well as the CBS Saturday morning show *Barnyard Frolics*. Roberts released one single on Vitacoustic before signing to Coral Records in 1948.

Roberts' career took off in 1949, as his single "I Never See Maggie Alone" reached number four on the country charts in the summer. The flip side, "Wedding Bells," also was a hit, reaching number 15, while his second single, "Jealous Heart," reached number 14. In the spring of 1950, "Choc'late Ice Cream Cone" became his second Top Ten single; it would also prove to be his last charting single.

Following his chart success, Roberts moved to Cincinnati, where he had a show on WLW Cincinnati and appeared regularly on the *Midwestern Hayride*. For the remainder of the decade, he concentrated his efforts on the Midwest, becoming a big regional star through his television shows in Dayton, OH (which became his home in 1952), Indianapolis, IN, and Saginaw, MI. Roberts continued to appear regularly on daytime Midwestern television—and, as of 1962, WWVA's *Wheeling Jamboree*—until the mid '60s. Around that time, he released an EP on the independent label Essgee, which led to a contract with Starday Records in 1965. Over the next five years, he released four albums for the label. Once his deal with Starday expired, he recorded briefly in the early '70s for Nashville Records.

In the early '70s, Roberts moved back to Dayton and concentrated on working in the Midwest and Canada. During the mid-'70s, he made a pair of albums for the Canadian label Point. By the end of the decade, he had moved back to his home state of Massachusetts, where he began playing concerts across the East. Roberts released one album for Palomino around 1980, which was followed by Longhorn's *Then and Now*, which combined historical cuts with new recordings. A few years later, Roberts moved to a farm near his childhood home in Greenfield. Though he was essentially retired, he continued to give concerts around the Northeast throughout the decade. *—Stephen Thomas Erlewine*

Indian Love Call / 1965 / Starday ♦♦♦

Recorded well over a decade after Kenny Robert's big 1949 hit "I Never See Maggie Alone," *Indian Love Call* includes a remake of that song as well as a re-recording of "She Taught Me How to Yodel," which Roberts had recorded for Coral in 1953. Roberts' impressive yodeling is featured on a few tracks, and his cover of "Indian Love Call" is a fitting choice given his superficial similarities to Slim Whitman. The production on these recordings is denser than that of his hits, and the material is split between yodels, novelties, and weepers. *Indian Love Call* is a fine album and a perfect companion to Bear Family's *Jumpin' & Yodelin'*, which contains most of Roberts' hits. *—Greg Adams*

• **Jumpin' & Yodelin'** / 1996 / Bear Family ♦♦♦♦♦

Remembered for his 1949 hit "I Never See Maggie Alone," Kenny Roberts' true distinction is that he was one of the most spectacular yodelers in the history of country & western music. He made the country Top 40 only four times, and three of those hits are included on this 29-track import, which covers 1949-1957. The material ranges from boogies and novelties to teen-oriented pop and rock & roll, but the most impressive tracks are the yodeling showcases, particularly "She Taught Me How to Yodel." Although it would have been nice if Bear Family had squeezed Roberts' 1949 hit version of "Jealous Heart" onto this already-packed disc, *Jumpin' & Yodelin'* is unlikely to be surpassed in terms of quality and content, unless Roberts receives the box set treatment. *—Greg Adams*

Eck Robertson

b. Nov. 20, 1887, Delaney, AR, **d.** Feb. 17, 1975

Fiddle / Old-Timey

Eck Robertson can only be called the source of a hidden history of country music. Probably the first fiddler to record on record (and also probably the first country record commercially available), Robertson seems to be the pinnacle and the origin of the Fiddle Contest tradition, and at the very least, his records and contest appearances in Texas were an inspiration for a generation of fiddlers. Fiddlers were country music's first virtuosos, and that can largely be attributed to Robertson's deep and soulful playing. He swings before swing became institutionalized on record (his first record came a short two years after Mamie Smith's "Crazy Blues"), and his records became the standard by which fiddle players were (and are!) tested. His playing is ingenious and intuitive, the kind of work one would expect from the originator of style, rather than a follower of some folk tradition. His version of "Sallie Gooden" drones and saws its way to a powerful conclusion. Its power sounds timeless, and it feels as if it could last for 20 minutes, and one wishes that it would. Robertson's early recordings evoke a kind of forgotten age and some timeless futurity and, as such, is an essential part of any history of country music.

Robertson was born in Delaney, AR, in 1887. His family shortly moved to Texas, and he became forever linked with a "Texas Sound" of fiddling: intense, showstopping, vaudevillian skill. He only recorded around 16 commercial recordings in the years 1922 and 1929. His recordings effectively tell the history of old-time music in the 1920s: His recordings alerted record companies to the market for old-time music throughout the South, and his return to recording in 1929 signaled the end of the classic old-time string band sound that had dominated country music during its first decade. He recorded mostly solo or with his family: his wife, Nettie, his daughter Daphne, and his son Dueron. He also recorded with Nat Shilkret, one of the earliest popular music stars.

Robertson went on to record one of the great tragedies of country music's history. In the 1940s he recorded over 100 songs for radio which have never been found. Despite his relative obscurity, Robertson reaped a few benefits from the 1960s folk revival and recorded some documentary material. He died on February 17, 1975. County Records released an excellent retrospective of his early work in 1998. *—Matt Laferty*

• **Old Time Texas Fiddler 1922–1929** / Jun. 1, 1999 / County ♦♦♦

For most listeners, until the release of this CD, the easiest way to partake of Eck Robertson's fiddle playing was to catch his appearance in the documentary *Festival*, about *the Newport Folk Festival*, where he played in the mid-'60s. The 16 sides here include Robertson's history-making June 30, 1922 recording of "Arkansas Traveller," which made him the first country musician ever to cut a record, and the material follows on as late as October 1929. Those slightly scratchy 1922 acoustic recordings with Henry Gilliland are still the definitive performances of those works, 80 years after they were laid down, and they're augmented by the presence of four more cuts from those sessions, with the rest of the disc filled out by the products of his 1929 Dallas recording sessions, the next time he went before a microphone. Whether playing as a solo performer or backed by piano, guitar, or small string band, Robertson's playing reflects the extraordinary combination of dexterity and energy that kept audiences spellbound from the 1920s to the 1960s. Robertson, already in his 30s and a veteran performer when the first of these recordings was made, often sounds like two or more musicians at the same time, and the fidelity of even the acoustic-era recordings is more than sufficient to capture the elegantly nuanced, highly complex figures played by the legendary fiddle virtuoso. Among the "firsts" here is a medley of "Sally Johnson"/"Billy in the Low Ground," the earliest record of a piece (especially "Billy in the Low Ground") that was to become a bluegrass standard over the next half century; and the earliest known record of "Turkey in the Straw," sounding like it's being played on a pair of enchanted fiddles. The instrumental numbers outshine the pair of vocal recordings ("The Island Unknown" Pts. 1 and 2, sung by Robertson and his wife Nettie) featured here. Of course, the irony behind this whole CD is that Robertson was criminally under-recorded for much of his early career, going seven years between his first two sets of sessions—and those were his last commercial recordings of his career, despite his living and playing another four decades. *—Bruce Eder*

Bruce Robison

Vocals, Guitar (Electric), Guitar (Acoustic), Producer / Singer/Songwriter, Alternative Country, Americana, Alternative Country-Rock, Country-Rock, Country-Folk

The Austin, TX-based singer/songwriter Bruce Robison issued his self-titled debut LP in 1995. He also attracted notice thanks to his inclusion on several compilations, including 1995's *Austin Country Nights: Rising Stars From the Heart of Texas* collection and *True Sounds of the New West*. The full-length *Wrapped* followed in 1997, and his sophomore effort, *Long Way Home From Anywhere*, appeared two years later. *—Jason Ankeny*

• **Wrapped** / 1997 / Sony ♦♦♦♦

On this album, Bruce Robison proves himself to be one of Austin's outstanding up-and-coming country songwriters. He seems equally comfortable writing about his youth in small-town Texas and mature adult relationships. In "My Brother and Me," Robison describes his Grandpa Charlie and sings, "Nobody like him in all my kin until my brother and me." The song movingly describes the adventures of four generations of the singer's family. The album's hands-down best song, however, is "Angry All the Time." Married with four kids, the singer realizes that he has to leave to find something that's been missing from his life. Robison's achingly beautiful lyrics are perfectly framed by an accordion and wife Kelly Willis' background vocals. Robison's style covers the whole range of country music. A mandolin and fiddle drive the bluegrassy "Don't You Ever Call My Name," while "Go to Your Heart" is electrified country-rock. Robison plays barroom swing on "12 Bar Blues" and ultra-traditional country on "When I Loved You," a Louvin Brothers song that he sings with Willis. But the focus always comes back to what makes this album great: Robison's songwriting. His lyrics are sometimes catchy and sometimes touching, but never heavy-handed, and even after the CD is over, they continue to captivate the listener's mind. *—Brian Wahlert*

Long Way Home From Anywhere / Jul. 13, 1999 / Sony ♦♦♦

Bruce Robison is a competent singer and performer, but a very good songwriter, which tends to make his albums sound like publishing demos. This is certainly true of his third record, on which he wrote or co-wrote seven of the ten songs. Robison knows the universe of the country song-bars, trucks, love gone wrong-but his eye for detail and the subtlety of his plotting put his compositions a cut above the rest. In "Drivin' All Night Long," an apologetic lover contemplates a head-on collision but restrains himself in consideration of the other driver's own loved one. "Just Married" begins full of love and contentment and ends that way, too, but in between, life gets hard—"I feel the chill of the early fall / I see the picture on the wall"—until the singer reveals that his bride can't stand him anymore. A great singer could make more of these songs than the songwriter himself does, however, and so could a great producer (he produced the record, too). *Long Way Home From Anywhere* may not make a star out of Bruce Robison, but they should be listening to it on Music Row. *—William Ruhlmann*

Country Sunshine / Sep. 18, 2001 / Boar's Nest ♦♦♦

Carson Robison

b. Aug. 4, 1890, Oswego, Labette County, Kansas, **d.** Mar. 24, 1957, Pleasant Valley, NY

Guitar, Songwriter, Vocals / Novelty, Old-Timey, Cowboy, Country Comedy

Carson Robison, known in some circles as "the granddaddy of the hillbillies," has mysteriously missed the recognition that has come the way of such contemporaries as Vernon Dalhart, not to mention successors such as Gene Autry and Merle Travis. A singer, guitarist, whistler, and actor, the sheer diversity of his talent, coupled with the relatively early beginning of his recording career, may have harmed him in terms of posterity. Robison's father was a champion fiddler, while his mother was a singer and pianist, and by the time he was 14 years old, he was already playing guitar professionally. A year later he was playing in bands and singing and by his 20s was proficient on a range of instruments as well as an accomplished whistler. It was in the latter capacity that Robison first came into the recording studio, as part of backing groups behind Dalhart and Wendell Hall. Ultimately he teamed with Dalhart, and the two recorded and toured together from 1924 until 1928. Robison also worked with the Crowe Brothers and co-wrote songs with Frank Luther Crowe ("My Blue Ridge Mountain Home," "Barnacle Bill the Sailor"). Other artists with whom Robison performed and recorded include singers Gene Austin and Frank Crumit and guitarist Roy Smeck.

In 1931, Robison formed his own group, the Pioneers, later rechristened the Buckaroos, which included John & Bill Mitchell, Frank Novak, and Pearl Pickens. The first country & western group to tour England, they had a considerable recording and broadcast career abroad as well as in America before World War II. Robison had a hit in 1942 with the old standard "Turkey in the Straw" and wrote songs on behalf of the war effort, including "We're Gonna Have to Slap That Dirty Little Jap." As late as 1948, he had a chart entry with "Life Gits Tee-Jus, Don't It?" and the year before his death, he recorded the novelty rock & roll number "Rockin' and Rollin' With Grandmaw." A fine technician as well as a good judge of songs, Robison was perhaps too sophisticated to be grouped with hillbilly singers, cowboy singers, or country music in general. His music had a veneer of pop sophistication that, in some ways, made it at times closer in spirit to Bing Crosby or even Eddie Cantor (check out "Everybody's Goin' but Me") than to Autry, while also lacking the honest directness (as well as the extraordinary harmonies) of the Sons of the Pioneers. Under other circumstances, he might've made a name in movies providing musical backgrounds, but media exposure beyond the radio eluded him. —*Bruce Eder*

Life Gets Tee-Jus, Don't It / 1958 / MGM ✦✦✦✦

Just a Melody / 1981 / Old Homestead ✦✦✦

The Kansas Jayhawk / 1987 / Cattle [Germany] ✦✦✦

A Hillbilly Mixture / 1988 / Axis ✦✦

Home, Sweet Home on the Prairie / 1996 / ASV ✦✦✦✦
A mixed bag of cowboy, hillbilly, country, novelty, and pop songs covering Robison's career from 1928 until 1936, including "My Darling Clementine" (which segues into "Annie Laurie" and "Camptown Races"), the delightful "In the Cumberland Mountains," "I Was Born in Old Wyoming," "Ramblin' Cowboy," "Smokey Mountain Bill," "Texas Dan," and the sad horse song "There's a Bridle Hangin' on the Wall." Amazingly, a lot of the material on this 25 song collection was cut in London in the 1930s, where Robison & the Pioneers were based for a time. The sound is exceptionally good, and the mix of country, jazz, blues, and pop influences—while not to everyone's liking—makes this record a fine addition to any 1920s or 1930s music collection. —*Bruce Eder*

● **A Real Hillbilly Legend** / 2002 / Cattle ✦✦✦✦✦
A Real Hillbilly Legend spans the years 1928-1951 and contains recordings Carson Robison made for several different labels, well-mastered from vintage 78s. It plays like a random assortment of singles, but the anthology is notable for including many of Robison's previously uncollected World War II propaganda songs. Some of these songs are humorous recitations (the hits "Hitler's Last Letter to Hirohito" and "Mussolini's Letter to Hitler"), but others are so mean-spirited they make Vince Vance's "Bomb Iran" sound like "Where Have All the Flowers Gone." "A Hundred Years From Now," for example, imagines a future in which the few surviving Japanese people are kept in zoos, and the title of "We're Gonna Have to Slap the Dirty Little Jap (And Uncle Sam's the Guy Who Can Do It)" speaks for itself. The jarring mixture of sentimental songs and racist "humor" aside, the historical value of *A Real Hillbilly Legend* is immense. —*Greg Adams*

Charlie Robison

b. Houston, TX
Guitar (Acoustic), Producer, Vocals / Singer/Songwriter, Alternative Country, Americana, Country-Rock, Alternative Country-Rock
Texas singer/songwriter Charlie Robison was born in Houston and raised on his family's ranch in the town of Bandera; absorbing the music he heard on the local honky tonk scene, he and brother Bruce—later an acclaimed performer in his own right—were also brought up on artists ranging from Black Sabbath to Gram Parsons to Bruce Springsteen. After discovering the thriving music scene in nearby Austin at age 15, Robison began writing his own material, drawing equal influence from rock and country; stints in the bands Chaparral and Two Hoots & a Holler followed, and he also joined the Millionaire Playboys, an all-star Austin ensemble. After contributing to albums from Alejandro Escovedo and Kelly Willis, Robison made his solo debut in 1995 with *Bandera; Life of the Party* followed three years later. Teaming up with his younger brother, Bruce, and fellow Texan Jack Ingram, in 2000 the trio released the appropriately named *Unleashed Live.* A second studio effort, *Step Right Up*, was issued in spring 2001. —*Jason Ankeny*

● **Life of the Party** / Aug. 25, 1998 / Sony ✦✦✦✦
Charlie Robison is a strong branch on that ever-growing tree of Texas singer/songwriters. His brother, Bruce, and sister-in-law, Kelly Willis, also contribute to the strength of production that Charlie & Lloyd Maines bring forth on this project. But, overall, it is Charlie's raw emotion and exposed nerve endings that make this release on the independent Lucky Dog label so attractive. Devastating is his "Sunset Boulevard," just as his wry humor comes forth on the very honky tonk "Barlight." The border sounds of "Don't Call Me a Fool" are intoxicating, while the steel on the Bruce Robison tune "You're Not the Best" takes the listener back in time to 1959. Covering Damon Bramblett's tune "Waiting for the Mail" allows Robison to show his bluesy side. Softer is "Indianola," and finishing the set, which started off with rip and roar via "Poor Man's Son," is "Molly's Blues." Overall, Charlie Robison turns in a well-layered performance of material that expresses a wide variety of emotions, situations, and characters. The musicianship here is first-rate; Maines on steel is well worth the price of admission in any event. A good introduction to the work of Charlie Robison and Texas singer/songwriters who are following in the footsteps of the outlaws Van Zandt, Clark, and Billy Joe Shaver. —*Jana Pendragon*

Unleashed Live / Sep. 26, 2000 / Sony ✦✦✦
Lucky Dog labelmates Jack Ingram and Bruce and Charlie Robison provide a virtual label sampler on this equally divided concert album recorded at *Gruene Hall* in New Bruanfels, TX. The three constitute a kind of South Central Texas version of the Flatlanders, that occasional triumvirate of Joe Ely, Butch Hancock, and Jimmie Dale Gilmore from West Texas. Each is a singer/songwriter with a Southwest perspective and

an interest in bars, drinking, heartbreak, and working class life. Bruce Robison, who leads things off with four songs, comes off as the most sensitive and literate of the three, calling up his older brother to sing with him on "Rayne, LA" and performing the divorce song "Angry All the Time" as a duet with Kelly Willis. Charlie Robison, who takes the lead on the middle four songs, is a crowd pleaser, filling his songs with drug and drinking references and lacing them with humor and melodrama, especially "Sunset Boulevard," in which he fantasizes about the kind of fame and fortune in the entertainment business that would allow him to forget a recent heartbreak, and the lengthy story song "Loving County," with its images of violence and infidelity. Concluding things, Jack Ingram rocks harder than either of the brothers, but his songs are still rooted in the ambience of a Texas barroom. And it sounds like they're all playing in a Texas barroom, as the audience hoots and hollers and sings along. This is the kind of live album that makes you wish you were there, with a beer in your hand and another couple under your belt. —*William Ruhlmann*

Step Right Up / Apr. 10, 2001 / Sony ✦✦✦
There was once a time when one could easily identify the roots of country music. English, German, French, Irish, and even African-American influences came together to create this genre. Charlie Robison and his music reflect that time, but he is in no way merely referencing a purer time. He has learned lessons from his ancestors and has truly made his own sound. His rugged good looks and obvious intelligence could easily make him a poster boy for alternative country, but a deeper listen to his third release *Step Right Up* will reveal much more than a pretty face. The lyrics range from tender to biting to brutal and are delivered with an honesty and wit lost throughout today's country charts. Songs about murder, robbery, and stale love capture the imagination of the listener while always being thoughtful and compassionate. Robison collected a large and varied group of musicians to make this record. Notables include his brother Bruce Robison who contributes his words and his voice, session legend Jim Lauderdale who sings backing vocals, and Robison's wife Emily Robison (Dixie Chicks) who plays banjo on several tracks. Robison is telling stories in his songs more than he is conveying feelings or desires. This too is a lost tradition from what was country music. "Desperate Times" chronicles the life of a lost Texas youth, and "John O'Reilly" oozes Irish influence with the story of an immigrant in Depression-era America. The album also includes a funny yet sadly true duet with Dixie Chick Natalie Maines called "The Wedding Song." Ultimately, Charlie Robison's *Step Right Up* demonstrates that sometimes an alternative is where it started in the beginning. —*Michael Cusanelli*

Ted Roddy

b. Corpus Christi, TX
Harmonica / Singer/Songwriter, Roots Rock, Alternative Country, Americana
A staple of the Austin, TX, club scene, singer/songwriter/harmonica wizard Ted Roddy paid his dues alongside the likes of Dale Watson, the Reverend Horton Heat, and the Bad Livers. Born in Corpus Christi, Roddy played his first live shows in the late '70s, eventually moving to Dallas to form the Midnighters with blues guitarist Mark Pollock. After the group disbanded, he turned to rockabilly and in 1983 started a new outfit, Ted Roddy and the Talltops, with Jim Heath (later known as Horton Heat) and Danny Barnes (who went on to join the Bad Livers). After relocating to Austin, the Talltops began to build a strong fan base not only locally but abroad, releasing several records in Europe. After going solo, Roddy played on LPs by Watson and Chris Smither before releasing his 1995 debut, *Full Circle. Tear Time* followed five years later. —*Jason Ankeny*

● **Full Circle** / Oct. 1995 / Hightone ✦✦✦✦
Roddy's harmonica and vocal work is up to snuff on this cheerful set, though the production seems on the thin side, giving the end result a sense of lacking a little in energy. Other than that, though, good-time entertainment. —*Steven McDonald*

Tear Time / Dec. 12, 2000 / Music Room ✦✦✦✦

Channelin' E / 2002 / Continental ✦✦✦

Jimmie Rodgers

b. Sep. 8, 1897, Meridian, MS, **d.** May 26, 1933, New York, NY
Guitar, Songwriter, Vocals, Banjo / Traditional Country, Yodeling
His brass plaque in the Country Music Hall of Fame reads, "Jimmie Rodgers' name stands foremost in the country music field as *the man who started it all.*" This is a fair assessment. The "Singing Brakeman" and the "Mississippi Blue Yodeler," whose six-year career was cut short by tuberculosis, became the first nationally known star of country music and the direct influence of many later performers, from Hank Snow, Ernest Tubb, and Hank Williams to Lefty Frizzell and Merle Haggard. Rodgers sang about rounders and gamblers, bounders and ramblers—and he knew what he sang about. At age 14 he went to work as a railroad brakeman, and on the rails he stayed until a pulmonary hemorrhage sidetracked him to the medicine show circuit in 1925. The years with the trains harmed his health but helped his music. In an era when Rodgers' contemporaries were singing only mountain and mountain/folk music, he fused hillbilly country, gospel, jazz, blues, pop, cowboy, and folk; and many of his best songs were his compositions, including "TB Blues," "Waiting for a Train," "Travelin' Blues," "Train Whistle Blues," and his 13 blue yodels.

Although Rodgers wasn't the first to yodel on records, his style was distinct from all the others. His yodel wasn't merely sugar-coating on the song, it was as important as the lyric, mournful and plaintive or happy and carefree, depending on a song's emotional content. His instrumental accompaniment consisted sometimes of his guitar only, while at other times a full jazz band (horns and all) backed him up. Country fans could have asked for no better hero/star—someone who thought what they thought, felt what they felt, and sang about the common person honestly and beautifully. In his last recording session, Rodgers was so racked and ravaged by tuberculosis that a cot had to be set up in the studio, so he could rest before attempting that one song more. No wonder Rodgers is to this day loved by country music fans.

The youngest son of a railroad man, Rodgers was born and raised in Meridian, MS. Following his mother's death in 1904, he and his older brother went to live with their mother's sister, where he first became interested in music. Rodgers' aunt was a former teacher who held degrees in music and English, and she exposed him to a number of different styles of music, including vaudeville, pop, and dancehall. Though he was attracted to music, he was a mischievous boy and often got into trouble. When he returned to his father's care in 1911, Rodgers ran wild, hanging out in pool halls and dives, yet he never got into any serious trouble. When he was 12, he experienced his first taste of fame when he sang "Steamboat Bill" at a local talent contest. Rodgers won the concert and, inspired by his success, decided to head out on the road in his own traveling tent show. His father immediately tracked him down and brought him back home, yet he ran away again, this time joining a medicine show. The romance of performing with the show wore off by the time his father hunted him down. Given the choice of school or the railroad, Rodgers chose to join his father on the tracks.

For the next ten years, Rodgers worked on the railroad, performing a variety of jobs along the South and West Coasts. In May of 1917, he married Sandra Kelly after knowing her for only a handful of weeks; by the fall, they had separated, even though she was pregnant (their daughter died in 1938). Two years later they officially divorced, and around the same time, he met Carrie Williamson, a preacher's daughter. Rodgers married Carrie in April of 1920 while she was still in high-school. Shortly after their marriage, Rodgers was laid off by the New Orleans & Northeastern Railroad, and he began performing various blue-collar jobs, looking for opportunities to sing. Over the next three years, the couple was plagued with problems, ranging from financial to health—the second of their two daughters died of diphtheria six months after her birth in 1923. By that time, Rodgers had begun to regularly play in traveling shows, and he was on the road at the time of her death. Though these years were difficult, they were important in the development of Rodgers' musical style as he began to develop his distinctive blue yodel and worked on his guitar skills.

In 1924, Rodgers was diagnosed with tuberculosis, but instead of heeding the doctor's warning about the seriousness of the disease, he discharged himself from the hospital to form a trio with fiddler Slim Rozell and his sister-in-law Elsie McWilliams. Rodgers continued to work on the railroad and perform blackface comedy with medicine shows while he sang. Two years after being diagnosed with TB, he moved his family out to Tucson, AZ, believing the change in location would improve his health. In Tucson, he continued to sing at local clubs and events. The railroad believed these extracurricular activities interfered with his work and fired him. Moving back to Meridian, Rodgers and Carrie lived with her parents before he moved away to Asheville, NC, in 1927. Rodgers was going to work on the railroad, but his health was so poor he couldn't handle the labor; he would never work the rails again. Instead, he began working as a janitor and a cab driver, singing on a local radio station and events as well. Soon, he moved to Johnson City, TN, where he began singing with the string band the Tenneva Ramblers. Prior to Rodgers, the group had existed as a trio, but he persuaded the members to become his backing band because he had a regular show in Asheville. The Ramblers relented, and the group's name took second billing to Rodgers, and the group began playing various concerts in addition to the radio show. Eventually, Rodgers heard that Ralph Peer, an RCA talent scout, was recording hillbilly and string bands in Bristol, TN. Rodgers convinced the band to travel to Bristol, but on the eve of the audition, they had a huge argument about the proper way they should be billed, resulting in the Tenneva Ramblers breaking away from Rodgers. He went to the audition as a solo artist, and Peer recorded two songs—the old standards "The Soldier's Sweetheart" and "Sleep, Baby, Sleep"—after rejecting Rodgers' signature song, "T for Texas."

Released in October of 1927, the record was not a hit, but Victor did agree to record Rodgers again, this time as a solo artist. In November of 1927, he cut four songs, including "T for Texas." Retitled "Blue Yodel" upon its release, the song became a huge hit and one of only a handful of early country records to sell a million copies. Shortly after its release, Rodgers and Carrie moved to Washington, where he began appearing on a weekly local radio show billed as the Singing Brakeman. Though "Blue Yodel" was a success, its sales grew steadily throughout early 1928, which meant that the couple wasn't able to reap the financial benefits until the end of the year. By that time, Rodgers had recorded several more singles, including the hits "Way Out on the Mountain," "Blue Yodel No. 4," "Waiting for a Train," and "In the Jailhouse Now." On various sessions, Peer experimented with Rodgers' backing band, occasionally recording him with two other string instrumentalists and recording his solo as well. Over the next two years, Peer and Rodgers tried out a number of different backing bands, including a jazz group featuring Louis Armstrong, orchestras, and a Hawaiian combo.

By 1929, Rodgers had become an official star, as his concerts became major attractions and his records consistently sold well. During 1929, he made a small film called *the Singing Brakeman*, recorded many songs, and toured throughout the country. Though his activity kept his star shining and the money rolling in, his health began to decline under all the stress. Nevertheless, he continued to plow forward, recording numerous songs and building a large home in Kerrville, TX, as well as working with Will Rogers on several fundraising tours for the Red Cross that were designed to help those suffering from the Depression. By the middle of 1931, the Depression was beginning to affect Rodgers as well, as his concert bookings decreased dramatically and his records stopped selling. Despite the financial hardships, Rodgers continued to record.

Not only did the Great Depression cut into Rodgers' career, but so did his poor health. He had to decrease the number of concerts he performed in both 1931 and 1932, and by 1933, his health affected his recording and forced him to cancel plans for several films. Despite his condition, he refused to stop performing, telling his wife that "I want to die with my shoes on." By early 1933, the family was running short on money, and he had to perform anywhere he could—including vaudeville shows and nickelodeons—to make ends meet. For a while he performed on a radio show in San Antonio, but in February he collapsed and was sent to the hospital. Realizing that he was close to death, he convinced Peer to schedule a recording session in May. Rodgers used that session to provide needed

financial support for his family. At that session, Rodgers was accompanied by a nurse and rested on a cot in between songs. Two days after the sessions were completed, he died of a lung hemorrhage on May 26, 1933. Following his death, his body was taken to Meridian by train, riding in a converted baggage car. Hundreds of country fans awaited the body's arrival in Meridian, and the train blew its whistle consistently throughout its journey. For several days after the body arrived in Rodgers' hometown, it lay in state as hundreds, if not thousands, of people paid tribute to the departed musician.

The massive display of affection at Rodgers' funeral services indicated what a popular and beloved star he was during his time. His influence wasn't limited to the '30s, however. Throughout country music's history, echoes of Rodgers can be heard, from Hank Williams to Merle Haggard. In 1961, Rodgers became the first artist inducted into the Country Music Hall of Fame; 25 years later, he was inducted as a founding father at the Rock & Roll Hall of Fame. Though both honors are impressive, they only give a small indication of what Rodgers accomplished—and how he affected the history of country music by making it a viable, commercially popular medium—during his lifetime. —*David Vinopal*

Train Whistle Blues / 1957 / RCA Victor ✦✦✦✦

My Old Pal / 1989 / ASV ✦✦✦✦
This album contains rich and varied material in its 18 tracks, including three blue yodels, Rodgers' wife's tribute to her husband recorded three years after his death, and a duet with Sara Carter. —*AMG*

☆ **First Sessions** / Jan. 1991 / Rounder ✦✦✦✦✦
The opening volume in Rounder's mammoth eight-disc Jimmie Rodgers reissue series presents his earliest, and in some cases, most tentatively performed material from 1927 and 1928. Rodgers quickly makes the leap from raw, if engaging singer to emphatic, distinctive artist, and midway through has established a singular sound and riveting delivery, with his trademark yodel and mastery of blues inflection and sensibility in place. These cuts include the signature track "Blue Yodel," aplus other classics such as "In the Jailhouse Now," "Treasures Untold" and "Memphis Yodel," as well as "The Brakemen's Blues." Things would never be the same for Rodgers, and these were the songs that helped make him an institution. —*Ron Wynn*

☆ **Vol. 5: America's Blue Yodeler 1930–31** / May 1991 / Rounder ✦✦✦✦✦
This fifth set of vintage Jimmie Rodgers performances included some spectacular collaborations. While neither sounded fully comfortable, the meeting of Rodgers and Louis Armstrong on "Blue Yodel No. 9" is a landmark date in music annals, two immortals finding a way to make seemingly disparate styles mesh on a short tune. Armstrong's wife at the time, Lil Hardin, accompanied the pair on piano. Rodgers also teamed frequently with Lani McIntire's Hawaiians on this set, often on throwaway tunes that Rodgers' vocals made enjoyable. There's another collaboration with a blues artist, this time Clifford Gibson on "Let Me Be Your Side Track," a great bawdy/innuendo number. Rodgers was paired with the Carter Family on two wonderful classic country numbers, the heartbreak tune "Why There's a Tear in My Eye" and the gospel song "The Wonderful City." —*Ron Wynn*

☆ **The Early Years 1928–1929** / Feb. 1991 / Rounder ✦✦✦✦✦
The second disc in the Jimmie Rodgers series covers 1928 and 1929, the years in which Rodgers solidified his stature as a premier performer. These 16 tracks saw him doing both his brilliant solo yodeling blues and also working with bands on some cuts. "Desert Blues" featured Rodgers backed by a group with cornet, clarinet, tuba and piano among the instrumentation. Steel guitarist John Westbrook provided tingling accompaniment on "I'm Lonely and Blue," "My Carolina Sunshine Girl" and "Blue Yodel No. 4." But once more, it's such cuts as "Daddy and Home," "You and My Old Guitar" and "Never No Mo' Blues" that are the triumphs, with Rodgers simply wailing, singing and yodeling, displaying the emotional clout and memorable style that turned these numbers into anthems. —*Ron Wynn*

☆ **On the Way Up 1929** / Mar. 1991 / Rounder ✦✦✦✦✦
This third Jimmie Rodgers disc in the eight-CD line covers arguably his greatest year, 1929. Rodgers scored huge hits doing popular novelty cuts like "Frankie and Johnny" and railroad numbers like "Train Whistle Blues," and continued cutting yodeling tunes, as well as cowboy songs and bawdy blues. The 17 cuts include the marvelous "Everybody Does It in Hawaii," with Weldon Burkes on ukulele and Joe Kapo on steel, and the memorable "Hobo Bill's Last Rides." The session also contains alternate takes of "The Land of My Boyhood Dreams" and "Frankie and Johnny." Rodgers was now ably mixing identities and personas, alternating between yodeling blues singer, railroad narrator and carefree cowboy. —*Ron Wynn*

☆ **Riding High 1929–1930** / Apr. 1991 / Rounder ✦✦✦✦✦
Jimmie Rodgers was enjoying the fruits of his labors in 1929 and 1930, the years covered on this fourth CD in Rounder's historic eight-disc retrospective series. The 17 numbers highlighted here were done either during his final 1929 session or in Hollywood the next year. They're primarily yodeling blues tunes, with Rodgers backed by guitarist Billy Burkes. There are two versions of "Anniversary Blue Yodel (Blue Yodel No. 7)," "Mississippi River Blues" and "Why Did You Give Me Your Love?," as well as stark, marvelous numbers like "She Was Happy Till She Met You," "A Drunkard's Child" and "Why Should I Be Lonely." This set also includes Rodgers working with Lani McIntire's Hawaiians on two tunes and with Bob Sawyer's Jazz Band on the finale, "My Blue-Eyed Jane." —*Ron Wynn*

☆ **Vol. 6: Down the Old Road 1931–32** / Jun. 1991 / Rounder ✦✦✦✦✦
This CD features songs with Jimmie Rodgers working in fresh formats as producer Ralph Peer attempted to break a sales slump. Rodgers recorded with the Louisville Jug Band on "My Good Gal's Gone Blues" and teamed with the Carter Family again in both Kentucky and Texas in 1931. They made four songs together, but three were unissued until after Rodgers' death. They're pleasant and often nicely sung, but not among either artist's

finest. Rodgers teamed with steel guitarist Cliff Carlisle and guitarist Wilber Ball on three songs, with Rodgers added ukulele backing. The final four cuts saw Rodgers return to his trademark railroad numbers and yodeling blues in 1932. For the most part, these weren't great tunes, as they show Rodgers experimenting and finally opting to do comfortable, familiar material rather than try new things. *—Ron Wynn*

☆ **No Hard Times, 1932** / Jul. 1991 / Rounder ✦✦✦✦✦
Although he was nearing the end, Jimmie Rodgers kept going in 1932, turning out several sterling numbers; among them were the dynamic "Blue Yodel No. 10" and riveting "No Hard Times" and "Long Tall Mama Blues," with Oddie McWinders on banjo. Rodgers also displayed his affection for his mother on "Mother, the Queen of My Heart" and the interesting confessional number "I've Only Loved Three Women." Rodgers teamed effectively with guitarist Slim Bryant on "Prairie Lullaby," "Miss the Mississippi and You" and "In the Hills of Tennessee," and once more sang frankly and movingly about his illness on "Whippin' That Old T.B.," although it wasn't as triumphant as "The T.B. Blues." *—Ron Wynn*

☆ **Last Sessions, 1933** / Aug. 1991 / Rounder ✦✦✦✦✦
Illness ravaged Jimmie Rodgers during his final days, as he attempted to record as much as possible. There's an eerie quality to such tunes as "The Yodeling Ranger," "Years Ago" and "Somewhere Down the Line," as it's evident that Rodgers was far from top vocal form. But despite the shortness of breath, lack of range and weak quality, he could still deliver emotionally gripping performances. The earlier cuts on the disc, "Blue Yodel No. 13," "Dreaming With Tears In My Eyes" and "I'm Free (From The Chain Gang Now)" have a hypnotic finality and edge, even when his vocals falter. Rodgers died 48 hours after he finished his final song, not turning in a particularly great performance, as might be expected. But his accomplishments had long ago established him as one of the most memorable performers in American music annals. *—Ron Wynn*

The Singing Brakeman / 1992 / Bear Family ✦✦✦✦✦
The Singing Brakeman is a six-disc set that compiles every song that Jimmie Rodgers ever recorded. It covers the same ground as Rounder's eight-disc set, but Bear Family's set condenses the material into six CDs and adds a large booklet that features a thorough discography and biography. Although it essentially has the same material, adding a few alternate takes that weren't on the Rounder series, *The Singing Brakeman* has a more scholarly approach—the discs are designed not as a casual listening experience, but intense, concentrated listening. In the end, however, it's neither superior or inferior to Rounder's series. No matter how they are presented, Rodgers' recordings constitute essential listening. *—Stephen Thomas Erlewine*

Train Whistle Blues / Apr. 20, 1994 / ASV ✦✦✦✦✦
For fans who want an excellent but not overwhelming selection of Rodgers' music, there are two solid choices: RCA's single-disc *Essential Jimmie Rodgers* collection or ASV/Living Era's two-part retrospective, of which *Train Whistle Blues* is the first. Some of Rodgers' best songs are here, among them "Blue Yodel No. 4 (California Blues)," "Hobo Bills' Last Ride," "Waiting for a Train," and "My Rough and Rowdy Ways." Individually, the two discs aren't as brilliant as ASV collectors are accustomed to, but together they paint a more complete picture of Rodgers' art. There is one essential item missing in "Muleskinner Blues," but just about everything else is adequately covered. *—Jim Smith*

Memorial Album / Apr. 22, 1997 / Collectables ✦✦✦
Jimmie Rodgers' *Memorial Album* gathers 24 songs taken from the Singing Brakeman's short recording career for RCA Victor in the late '20s and early '30s. While the majority of Rodgers' signature tunes are here—including "T for Texas (Blue Yodel No. 1)," "Away out on the Mountain," "Waiting for a Train," and "Daddy and Home"—a few essential tunes—like "Mule Skinner Blues" and "In the Jailhouse Now"—are missing. *—Al Campbell*

★ **The Essential Jimmie Rodgers** / Apr. 29, 1997 / RCA ✦✦✦✦✦
As the first serious attempt at a single-disc Jimmie Rodgers retrospective in the CD-era, *The Essential Jimmie Rodgers* isn't bad at all. Over the course of 20 songs, nearly all of his best-known songs—including "Blue Yodel, No. 1," "In the Jailhouse Now" and "Blue Yodel, no. 8 (aka Mule Skinner Blues")—are featured, and while some good things remain in the vaults, it's hard to argue with what's here. After all, *Essential* isn't designed for historians or completists—it's for the curious, who are reluctant to invest in either Rounder's multi-volume series or Bear Family's comprehensive box. For those listeners, *The Essential Jimmie Rodgers* is an invaluable introduction. *—Stephen Thomas Erlewine*

Father of Country Music / Jun. 17, 1997 / Pearl ✦✦✦
This collection actually lives up to its title, assuming you believe that country music runs the gamut from the blues to the mawkishly sentimental—which seems a fair assessment. Rodgers, for a while America's most successful performer, had all those bases—plus many in between—covered. On his own "Gambling Bar Room Blues" he could be as gritty as any bluesman (understandable, as it was a bluesman who taught him to play), and on his version of the blues ("Frankie and Johnny") he pulled no punches, nor did he tone the song down for the sensibilities of his white audience. But he was equally capable of the overly sweet "I've Only Loved Three Women"—that's mother, sister, and wife—or "My Old Pal" to balance the pendulum. There are a couple of his famous signature "Blue Yodel" songs here, including the superb "Blue Yodel (T for Texas)," as well as the self-aggrandizing "Jimmie the Kid" and the lighthearted "Pistol Packin' Papa." In other words, Rodgers had the kind of range in his material that no one else at the time could match. While most of the songs were recorded with bare accompaniment, some offered plenty of popular diversity; "Looking for a New Mama," for instance, had the Louisville Jug Band complementing him, offering a broader instrumental palette than many achieved at the dawn of country music. And so the album, which doesn't attempt to be a greatest hits, makes its case very eloquently. By all standards he was the pioneer, the man who did everything first—his contemporaries, the Carter Family, were definitely old-time by comparison—and was not only the father of country music, but America's first real singer/songwriter star. *—Chris Nickson*

Yodelling Ranger / Feb. 24, 1998 / Empress ✦✦✦
If, as annotator Tony Middleton claims, this import CD of Jimmie Rodgers recordings contains "22 of his finest," it does not contain any of his best-known songs. In fact, Rodgers' records were as consistent as they were similar, so nearly any randomly chosen batch of them would be pretty good. Compiler Colin Brown, in addition to avoiding obvious choices, has also looked for more unusual ones, so that, for example, he includes Rodgers' duet with Louis Armstrong on "Standin' on the Corner (Blue Yodel No. 9)," as well as both sides of a record featuring Rodgers and the Carter Family in song and conversation. None of these performances is among Rodgers' best, but they don't turn up on disc very often. *—William Ruhlmann*

Brakeman's Blues / Apr. 24, 2001 / Catfish ✦✦✦✦✦
As a primary founder of country music, Jimmie Rodgers' name isn't often associated with the blues. The blues, however, were an essential ingredient of early country, and Rodgers' series of blue yodels can attest to his affinity with the form. *Brakeman's Blues* is a generous collection of his blues material, featuring 24 cuts and clocking in at over 70 minutes. "Gambling Bar Room Blues" tells the bizarre tale of a jealous man who shoots and kills his best friend for talking to his girl and then proceeds to get falling-down drunk with a policeman at a bar. "The T.B. Blues" carries the cheerful refrain, "Gee but the graveyard is a lonesome place/They put you on your back, throw that mud down in your face," while "Pistol Packin' Papa" equates sexual prowess with handgun ownership. Rodgers' lyrics can be raw, addressing death, lonesomeness, and love more directly than most contemporary singers would dare; they can also include thinly veiled sexual innuendos that would make Conway Twitty blush. These subjects, of course, make for great blues songs. There are also songs about infidelity ("Blue Yodel No. 10"), murder ("Gambling Bar Room Blues"), and traveling ("Travelin' Blues"). One also shouldn't miss classics like "Peach Pickin' Time Down in Georgia," "Muleskinner Blues," and "In the Jailhouse Now." *Brakeman's Blues* succeeds all around. It's the perfect introduction for those unfamiliar with their country roots, and it's a good collection for those interested in Rodgers' blues connection. *—Ronnie D. Lankford Jr.*

Classic Sides 1927-1933 / 2002 / JSP ✦✦✦✦✦
An expansive five-disc box set comprising nearly everything Jimmie Rodgers released between 1927 and his far-too-early death in May 1933, *Classic Sides 1927-1933* is not definitive; the mammoth Bear Family set *The Singing Brakeman* and Rounder's eight-volume series contain every single recorded note Rodgers ever yodeled on tape, while this set drops a few of the jazz tunes and almost all of the alternate takes. This less-scholarly approach might make *Classic Sides 1927-1933* more attractive to the committed but not die-hard fan who wants all the classics—"T for Texas," "Blue Yodel #4," and the rest—without trawling through too much else. Others would (convincingly) argue that Rodgers was as much a jazz singer as he was a country boy, and that the alternate takes reveal that he rarely sang the same song the same way twice; those folks should steer themselves to the complete works, while casual listeners might start with one of the literally dozens of single-disc best-ofs. *Classic Sides 1927-1933* is perfect for those walking the middle ground, however. *—Stewart Mason*

Standing on the Corner / Jan. 1, 2002 / Recall ✦✦✦✦✦
Both the track order and remastering on this collection are superb, but that alone isn't basis for an unqualified recommendation. There are significant songs missing, but at 40 tracks this is the best budget sampler of Rodgers' music available, if one judges strictly on the music. The liner notes provide only a skeletal view of his accomplishments, but by drawing attention to lesser-known performances, *Standing on the Corner* is an invigorating listen, even for those who have already digested other samplers. There is one major gripe to be directed at compilers who continue to disregard the value of his terrific first single, "The Soldier's Sweetheart," but since the market has yet to see an affordable, truly definitive Rodgers overview, this comes as highly recommended as any other that is available. *—Jim Smith*

★ **RCA Country Legends** / Sep. 10, 2002 / RCA ✦✦✦✦✦
Jimmie Rodgers is an icon of American music, and this volume in the *RCA Country Legends* series does a fine job of presenting his music for both newcomers to Rodgers and longtime fans alike. The 17 tracks contain some of his most well-known numbers, like "Blue Yodel (T for Texas)," "Train Whistle Blues," "Blue Yodel #9," and "Blue Yodel #8 (Mule Skinner Blues)," as well as a few rare songs and a previously unissued take of "My Good Gal's Gone Blues." Highly recommended. *—Tim Sendra*

Johnny Rodriguez

b. Dec. 10, 1952, Sabinal, TX

Vocals, Guitar / Progressive Country, Tex-Mex, Outlaw Country, Salsa, Traditional Country, Country-Pop

A reliable country hitmaker for much of the '70s, Johnny Rodriguez was born in Sabinal, TX, in 1952, growing up 90 miles from the Mexican border. His older brother Andres, a big country music fan, bought him a guitar when he was seven, and he was playing and singing by his teens. Rodriguez was captain of his high-school football team at 16, but when his father died of cancer, he spiraled out of control, racking up four arrests in two years. While Rodriguez was serving a jail term, Texas Ranger Joaquin Jackson heard him sing and introduced him to music promoter Happy Shahan, who booked Rodriguez to work as a singing stagecoach driver at the Alamo Village Amusement Park during 1970-1971. There he was discovered by Tom T. Hall and Bobby Bare, who brought him to Nashville to join Hall's Storytellers. Not long after, Rodriguez signed with Mercury, releasing his debut single, "Pass Me By (If You're Only Passing Through)," in early 1973. It climbed into the Top Ten and turned out to be the first of 14 consecutive Rodriguez singles to do so.

His next two, "Ridin' My Thumb to Mexico" and "You Always Come Back (To Hurting Me)," both hit number one.1974 brought the Top Five hits "Dance With Me (Just One More Time)" and "We're Over," plus the number one "That's the Way Love Goes." The following year was even better, as all three of his singles—"I Just Can't Get Her Out of My Mind," "Just Get Up and Close the Door," and "Love Put a Song in My Heart"—hit number one. More Top Five hits followed over 1976-1977 in "I Couldn't Be Me Without You," "I Wonder If I Ever Said Goodbye," and "Desperado," but he and Mercury parted ways in 1979, upon which point he signed with Epic. "Down the Rio Grande" went Top Ten that year, but Rodriguez subsequently endured a serious commercial slump.

He returned to the Top Ten in 1983 with a pair of hits, "Foolin'" and "How Could I Love Her So Much," which proved to be the last of his career; his final chart single came with 1988's Top 20 hit "I Didn't (Every Chance I Had)" on Capitol. He did record a couple of honky tonk-style records during the '90s, specifically *Run for the Border* (Intersound, 1993) and *You Can Say That Again* (Hightone, 1996). *—Steve Huey*

All I Ever Meant to Do Was Sing / 1973 / Mercury ✦✦✦
Johnny Rodriguez was an exciting development in the world of country music: a Hispanic artist with a classic country voice like Merle Haggard, who expressed his ethnic heritage within the context of traditional country music. *All I Ever Meant to Do Was Sing* has two of Rodriguez's three number-one hits from 1973, "That's the Way Love Goes" and the country radio favorite "Ridin' My Thumb to Mexico." Rodriguez sings the country standards "Release Me" and "I Really Don't Want to Know" half in Spanish—a trick he would return to again and again in his career. Rodriguez co-wrote the title track with Tom T. Hall and, unlike most of his later albums, composed fully half of the songs by himself, which makes *All I Ever Meant to Do Was Sing* a particularly revealing and personal album. *—Greg Adams*

Introducing / 1973 / Mercury ✦✦✦✦✦

Just Get Up and Close the Door / 1975 / Mercury ✦✦✦
The title track of *Just Get Up and Close the Door* was Johnny Rodriguez's fifth chart-topper, falling in the middle of his peak years as a country hitmaker. The album mixes the old and the new, with a Willie Nelson song and two Billy Joe Shaver compositions alongside classics like "Am I That Easy to Forget" and "Fraulein," both of which are sung partially in Spanish. "Fraulein," a classic country ode to a German lady sung here in Spanish by an Hispanic-American artist, is Johnny Rodriguez's musical melting pot in a nutshell. Chuck Willis' R&B classic "C.C. Rider" also gets the country treatment from Rodriguez, wrapping up a solid album that manages to be simultaneously traditional and progressive. *—Greg Adams*

● **Greatest Hits** / 1976 / Mercury ✦✦✦✦✦
Greatest Hits contains 14 of Johnny Rodriguez's biggest hits from the early '70s, including the number one hits "You Always Come Back (To Hurting Me)," "Ridin' My Thumb to Mexico," "That's the Way Love Goes," "I Just Can't Get Her Out of My Mind," "Just Get Up and Close the Door," and "Love Put a Song in My Heart." *—Stephen Thomas Erlewine*

Love Me With All Your Heart / 1978 / Mercury ✦✦✦
Love Me With All Your Heart finds Johnny Rodriguez moving further toward pop, with the Top Ten title track being a case in point; the lovely, string-laden Spanish performance of an old Ray Charles Singers hit sounds more like Julio Iglesias than Johnny Rodriguez. Barry Gibb and Randy Newman each contribute a song, and "Ramblin' Rose," though country, is associated with Nat King Cole. Rodriguez sprinkles straight country like "I Need It Now," in which he sings in a higher register than usual, between his crossover efforts, but such traditional fare is scarce. Despite the unflattering cover photo that makes Rodriguez's neck his most prominent feature, *Love Me With All Your Heart* is a good album, assuming the listener doesn't mind his stylistic departures. *—Greg Adams*

Rodriguez / 1979 / Epic ✦✦✦✦

Through My Eyes / 1980 / Epic ✦✦✦

Biggest Hits / 1982 / Epic ✦✦✦✦

Foolin' With Fire / 1984 / Epic ✦✦✦

Full Circle / 1986 / Epic ✦✦✦

Gracias / 1988 / Capitol ✦✦✦

Super Hits / Sep. 5, 1995 / Epic ✦✦✦

You Can Say That Again / Jul. 1996 / Hightone ✦✦✦✦
Quite possibly the strongest release Johnny Rodriguez has offered since his heyday of the late '70s and early '80s, *You Can Say That Again* captures his honky tonk roots perfectly. Rodriguez alternates between honky tonk standards and new tunes written in the tradition. Not all of the new songs are fit to stand in comparison to the classics, but Rodriguez's sweaty energy and gritty, soulful vigor make *You Can Say That Again* a joy. *—Thom Owens*

Hits / Aug. 26, 1997 / Mercury ✦✦✦

Desperado / Jan. 15, 2002 / Mercury ✦✦✦

Kenny Rogers

b. Aug. 21, 1938, Houston, TX
Vocals, Bass, Guitar / Country-Pop, Adult Contemporary, Soft Rock, Urban Cowboy
It took several tries before Kenny Rogers became a star. As a member of the First Edition (and the New Christy Minstrels before that), he shared in some million-sellers, among them "Reuben James" and "Ruby, Don't Take Your Love to Town," an excellent Mel Tillis song about a disabled veteran. But superstardom lay ahead for this Texan, and it arrived in the late '70s. His experience with the two previous pop groups had prepared him well: He knew the easy listening audience was out there, and he supplied them with well-done middle-of-the-road songs with a country flavor. Having gone solo, in 1976 Rogers charted with "Love Lifted Me." But it was with an outstanding song by writers Roger Bowling and Hal Bynum, "Lucille," that his star shot upward. The rest (as they say) is history: award-winning duets with Dottie West and Dolly Parton, 12 TV specials, another song-of-the-year with "The Gambler," "Daytime Friends," "Coward of the County," "We've Got Tonight," "Crazy," "Lady" (his first pop number one), etc., etc., etc. And that's just the *musical side* of Rogers. In 1980, the made-for-TV movie *The Gambler* blasted the competition, followed quickly by *Coward of the County*, then enough sequels to *The Gambler* to get him to Roman numeral IV. Throughout the '80s, Rogers remained a celebrity, even when his sales were declining. Even during the '90s, when he rarely charted, his name, face, and music were recognizable in a series of concerts, television specials, films, and even fast-food restaurants.

Like many country superstars, Rogers came from humble roots. Born in Houston, TX, Rogers and his seven siblings were raised in one of the poorest sections of town. Nevertheless, he progressed through high-school, all the while learning how to play guitar and fiddle. When he was a senior, he played in a rockabilly band called the Scholars, who released three singles, including "Kangewah," which was written by Louella Parsons. Following his graduation, he released two singles, "We'll Always Fall in Love Again" and "For You Alone," on the local independent label Carlton. The B-side of the first single, "That Crazy Feeling," was popular enough to earn him a slot on *American Bandstand*. In 1959, he briefly attended the University of Texas, but he soon dropped out to play bass in the jazz combo the Bobby Doyle Three. While he was with the group, Rogers continued to explore other musical venues and played bass on Mickey Gilley's 1960 single "Is It Wrong." The Bobby Doyle Three released one album, *In a Most Unual Way*, before Rogers left the group to play with the Kirby Stone Four. He didn't stay long with Stone and soon landed a solo record contract with Mercury.

Rogers released a handful of singles on Mercury, all of which failed. Once Mercury dropped the singer, he joined the New Christy Minstrels in 1966. He stayed with the folk group for a year, leaving with several other bandmembers—Mike Settle, Terry Williams, and Thelma Lou Camacho—in 1967 to form the First Edition. Adding drummer Terry Jones, the First Edition signed with Reprise and recorded the pop-psychedelic single "Just Dropped In (To See What Condition My Condition Was In)." The single became a hit early in 1968, climbing to number five. Within a year, the group was billed as Kenny Rogers & the First Edition, and in the summer of 1969, they had their second and final Top Ten hit, "Ruby, Don't Take Your Love to Town." The country overtones of the single hinted at the direction Rogers was taking, as did the minor hit follow-up, "Ruben James." For the next two years, the First Edition bounced between country, pop, and mild psychedelia, scoring their last big hit with Mac Davis' "Something's Burning" in early 1970. By the end of 1972, the group had their own syndicated television show, but their sales were drying up. They left Reprise the following year, signing to Rogers' new label, Jolly Rogers. None of their singles became major hits, though a version of Merle Haggard's "Today I Started Loving You Again" reached the lower regions of the country charts late in 1973. Rogers left the group in 1974, and the band broke up the following year.

At the time the band broke up, Rogers was severely in debt and Jolly Rogers was out of business. In order to jump-start his career, he signed to United Artists in 1975, and with the help of producer Larry Butler, he devised an accessible, radio-ready, and immaculately crafted take on country-pop that leaned toward adult contemporary pop, not country. "Love Lifted Me," his debut single for the label, was a minor hit early in 1976, but it took a full year for Rogers to have a genuine breakthrough hit with "Lucille." Climbing to number one early in 1977, "Lucille" not only was a major country hit, earning the Country Music Association's Single of the Year award, but it also was a huge crossover success, peaking at number five on the pop charts. For the next six years, Rogers had a steady string of Top Ten hits on both the country and pop charts. His crossover success is important—his lush, easy listening productions and smooth croons showed that country stars could conquer the pop audience, if produced and marketed correctly. During the late '70s and early '80s, much of country radio was dominated either by urban cowboy or country-pop in the vein of Rogers' own singles. Between 1978 and 1980, he had five straight number-one country singles—"Love or Something Like It," "The Gambler," "She Believes in Me," "You Decorated My Life," "Coward of the County"—most of which also reached the pop Top Ten. In addition to his solo hits, he had a series of Top Ten duets with Dottie West, including the number-one hits "Every Time Two Fools Collide" (1978), "All I Ever Need Is You" (1979), and "What Are We Doin' in Love" (1981). Not only did his singles sell well, but so did his albums, with every record he released between 1976's *Kenny Rogers* and 1984's *Once Upon a Christmas* going gold or platinum.

By the beginning of the '80s, Rogers' audience was as much pop as it was country, and singles like his cover of Lionel Richie's "Lady" confirmed that fact, spending six weeks at the top of the pop charts. Rogers also began duetting with pop singers like Kim Carnes ("Don't Fall in Love With a Dreamer," number-three country, number-four pop, 1980) and Sheena Easton ("We've Got Tonight," number-one country, number-six pop, 1983). Rogers also began making inroads into television and film, appearing in a number of TV specials and made-for-TV movies, including 1982's *Six Pack* and two movies based on his songs "The Gambler" and "Coward of the County." Late in 1983, he left United Artists/Liberty for RCA Records, releasing a duet with Dolly Parton called "Islands in the Stream" as his first single for the label. Written by the Bee Gees and produced by Barry Gibb, the record became one of his biggest hits, spending two weeks on the top of both the country and pop charts. Rogers stayed at RCA for five years, during which time he alternated between MOR, adult contemporary pop and slick country-pop. The hits didn't come as often as they used to, and they were frequently competing with releases from Liberty's vaults, but he managed to log five number-one singles for the label, in addition to "Islands in the Stream": "Crazy" (1984), "Real Love" (1985), "Morning Desire" (1985), "Tomb of the Unknown Love" (1986), and the Ronnie Milsap duet "Make No Mistake, She's Mine" (1987). Despite his country successes, he no longer had pop crossover hits. Nevertheless, Rogers' concerts continued to be popular, as did his made-for-TV movies. Still, the lack of blockbuster records meant that RCA failed to renew his contract when it expired in 1988. Rogers returned to his first label, Reprise, where he had one major hit—1989's Top Ten "The Vows Go Unbroken (Always True to You)," taken from the gold album *Something Inside So Strong*—before his singles started charting in the lower half of the Top 40.

Throughout the late '80s and '90s, Rogers kept busy with charity work, concerts, his fast-food chain Kenny Rogers' Roasters, television specials, movies, and photography, publishing no less than two books, *Kenny Rogers' America* and *Kenny Rogers: Your Friends and Mine*, of his photos. Rogers continued to record, releasing albums nearly every year, but they failed to break beyond his large, devoted fan base and only made a slight impact on the charts. With 1998's *Christmas From the Heart*, he established his own record label, Dreamcatcher; *She Rides Wild Horses* followed a year later, and *There You Go Again* was issued in mid-2000. *—David Vinopal & Stephen Thomas Erlewine*

The First Edition / 1967 / Reprise ✦✦✦

Ex-members of the New Christy Minstrels (with the exception of the drummer, Mickey Jones) run the fun gamut on *The First Edition*, and had they disappeared after this effort it would have been a huge collector's item. The cardinal sin of Lenny Kaye's masterpiece *Nuggets* collection is that "Just Dropped In (To See What Condition My Condition Was In)" did not follow the Electric Prunes as the second track on *Vol. 1* of that revered collection, or show up on it at all. Is something missing from this picture? The psychedelicized Top Five hit from the winter of 1968 produced by Mike Post and arranged by Al Capps might have a few lyrics that would make Bob Dylan blush, but the song's fuzz guitar, attitude, and hook are unstoppable. It is up there with the Seeds' "Pushin' Too Hard" and Strawberry Alarm Clock's "Incense & Peppermints" as an extraordinary '60s classic. The rest of the album is top-notch as well, sounding like the Mamas & the Papas meets early Jefferson Airplane with Signe Anderson on vocals. It's Thelma Camacho who never got the name change or the recognition she deserved, the producer unable to pull a "White Rabbit" out of the hat for the singer. Camacho sounds great on "I Get a Funny Feeling" and "Hurry Up Love," and the album benefits from her presence. "Shadow in the Corner of Your Mind" may be a title that conjures up images of Bob Lind and Ted Nugent hammering out a song over the dinner table, maybe because they still look like the New Christy Minstrels on the cover, and Tom Smothers gushing on the liner notes is unique, but it was television that was instrumental in launching this group into the mainstream and the hit song does well surrounded by this musical environment. Drummer Mickey Newbury performed with Dylan, Trini Lopez, Johnny Rivers, and others, giving the group some much needed hipness. Tunes like Mike Post's co-write "Dream On," a few years before Aerosmith would hit with a different song by the same name, rock out harder than "Green Green," "Saturday Night," and "Today," Christy Minstrel's hits prior to Rogers joining the group. "Home Made Lies" has that "someday I'll teach you real fine" riff from the Animals' "It's My Life," Mike Settle lifting from here and there, while "Marcia: 2 A.M. sounds like Peter, Paul & Mary jamming with Paul Kantner and "Hurry Up Love" wants desperately to be girl group. The album's one drawback is that the band and producer don't go all the way in exploring these different styles the way they did on the hit "Just Dropped In." "Just Dropped In" not only made Kenny Rogers' voice the most familiar first, it's an all-out assault on the senses, its wild abandon necessary but absent from the other aspects of this disc. "Church Without a Name" explores—or maybe toys with—the blues, just adding to the feel of a band looking for a sound. They eventually found that sound, their run of hits from early 1968 to late 1970 a good three-year run. But this debut is splendid and it is fun to hear them emulating Marty Balin right off the bat with the first track, "I Found a Reason." It's not the Lou Reed tune, though if it were that Velvet Underground classic this album would have gained the legendary status it deserves. A lost gem worth rediscovering. *—Joe Viglione*

Ruby Don't Take Your Love to Town / 1969 / Reprise ✦✦✦

Something's Burning / 1970 / Reprise ✦✦

There's not much to recommend this record. The title track was a hit but is on the *Greatest Hits* LP. The rest of the tracks aren't really that interesting. By the way, "Elvira" is the same song the Oak Ridge Boys had a hit with 11 years later. *—Jim Worbois*

Tell It All Brother / 1971 / Reprise ✦✦✦✦

Appearing on their sixth album, *Tell It All Brother*, are the last two hits from Kenny Rogers & the First Edition, their sixth and seventh Top 40 chart-climbing 45 rpm records. Deep vocals with a bass-heavy rock sound employing just a touch of country leanings are what resonate through the title track. Alex Harvey's "Tell It All Brother," a politically correct statement that went Top 20 in the summer of 1970, is followed by Kin Vassey's "Heed the Call," one of the three weakest of Rogers' 27 Top 40 hits released between 1968 and 1984 (it lingered in the Top 35 in November of 1970). But "Heed the Call" is a great song, more uptempo than "Ruby," "Reuben James," and "Tell It All Brother," and with undeniable charm. Vassey would sing backing vocals for such diverse artists as Frank Zappa, Lionel Ritchie, and Kim Carnes, while writing songs and playing guitar for the solo Rogers as well. "Heed the Call" begins with tambourine and has gospel First Edition vocals over handclaps, marching drumbeats, and a campfire feel. It is, along with being the band's final hit, one that displays individual talents working in unison perhaps better than any of their previous commercial efforts—giving a hint of what the album tracks held. It contrasts with the title song chant, which is all Rogers, his big voice over the bass drum and tambourine, with piano and bass taking a back seat and the guitars invisible. "Shine on Ruby Mountain" is a Kenny Young song, and it has the uptempo square dance drive that is present on many of the non-hit album tracks. Rogers' adaptation of the traditional "Camptown Ladies" continues the party atmosphere with a hootenanny vibe. Mike Settle gets only one composition here, a far cry from the nine songs Settle wrote on the first album and the four he composed on *First Edition '69*, perhaps indicating how settled in Rogers and producer Jimmy Bowen were at this point in time. "I'm Gonna Sing You a Sad Song Susie" isn't a bad song—it just sounds like the singer/songwriter was listening to Glen Campbell's 1969 hit, "Where's the Playground Susie," a little too much. Is it any wonder the First Edition members are absent from Settle's 1971 self-titled solo album on Uni? It's what they call a clean break. Rogers' sole original, "Long Woman," co-written with Douglas Legrand, is an uptempo country-rocker, with the direction of the group more defined—it is no longer just a band but a vehicle for an emerging major star. After "Heed the Call," things come down a bit on side two with Harvey's third composition on the album, the beautiful ballad "Molly." It should have been a hit, for it is Harvey's "Delta Dawn" slowed down and ready to become a part of Elton John's *Tumbleweed Connection* album. "After All (I Live My Life)" is a perfect showcase for Thelma Lou Camacho, and why she didn't climb the charts with this group is a mystery—she arguably has the best and most distinctive voice. It sure sounds like Camacho is the only backing vocalist on this particular number—if the others are singing with her they take a back seat while a big Jimmy Bowen/Rogers production works behind Camacho (markedly different from more of the country chanting found on "We All Got to Help Each Other"). The two hits on this album did not get on Rogers' 1977 *Ten Years of Gold* retrospective, and though they aren't his best-known songs, they show that this crew had no aversion to experimenting with the formula. Both tunes add an interesting dimension to the band's classic 1971 release, *Kenny Rogers & the First Edition's Greatest Hits*. *—Joe Viglione*

Transition / 1971 / Reprise ✦✦✦✦

And a big *Transition* it is from the psychedelic near hard rock of "Just Dropped In," produced by Mike Post in 1968, to mellow tunes by Mac Davis, Kris Kristofferson, Carole King, and Alex Harvey, among others, just three years later. Ex-New Christy Minstrels bandmate Kim Carnes contributes "Where Does Rosie Go," and the Jimmy Bowen and Kenny Rogers production is crystal clear, allowing the singer to develop the sound that would hit big six years after this release. In fact, it was six and a half years between the last hit from the First Edition, 1970's "Heed the Call," and Rogers' number-one country smash, "Lucille," which opened the floodgates to 19 subsequent chart songs. What is amazing about *Transition* is that it is so good, yet its sound took more than half a decade to get established, more than a lifetime in the record industry. Not only was co-producer Jimmy Bowen responsible for Delaney Bramlett's *Class Reunion* and a Kim Carnes album, he worked with Frank Sinatra and Glen Campbell, and was the guy who oversaw many a Kenny Rogers & the First Edition hit. Side one is gospel pop, beginning with a Kenny Rogers original, "Take My Hand," with heavy religious overtones, a strong chorus, and big keyboards. It is Rogers going to church, but it's a great original, and had Aretha Franklin performed a duet with Rogers, "Take My Hand" would've been a smash. The Carole King/Toni Stern number "What Am I Going to Do" has another very strong hook, a bit more subdued, but the chorus kicks in almost as powerfully as on the first song. The one-two punch of these tunes is amazing. Alex Harvey's "All God's Lonely Children" continues this adult contemporary and gospel-oriented slant, gearing the listener up for the country-pop of side two. Rogers is in great voice for the most part, and the book he wrote, *Making It With Music*, published in 1978, would help explain to those interested what happened to him in between the hits. Gene Thomas' "Lay It Down" sounds like a sequel to "Tell It All," the 1970 Top 20 hit by the First Edition, but lines like "self-made hell" and Rogers' voice showing signs of wear and tear on the high notes are cause for concern. Despite that, *Transition* is an album of immense depth, and is the bridge between the First Edition and his solo career. It is the album that displays Kenny Rogers as a serious artist, and is worthy of a special place. If Rogers were Lou Reed, this would be the great lost album fans would go bonkers over. The country-pop that Rogers would become so famous for is totally revealed on the second side, with Kristofferson's "For the Good Times" and Mac Davis' "Poem for My Little Lady." The album is well named, and the singer gives his audience a taste of things to come. Classic stuff. *—Joe Viglione*

Kenny Rogers & the First Edition Greatest Hits / 1971 / Reprise ✦✦✦✦

You can listen to every single track on *Kenny Rogers & the First Edition Greatest Hits*, but what is most striking about this collection of songs is the brilliance of two tracks, Mike Settle's "But You Know I Love You," followed here by their first hit single, "Just Dropped In" (as it is called on this collection's cover, the label on the vinyl has the lengthy "Just Dropped In (To See What Condition My Condition Was In)"). The band could have evaporated after releasing just those two titles and would have been revered as pop maestros; both compositions are not what one would expect from exiles of the New Christy Minstrels. This album puts it into perspective with the seven Top 40 hits the group accrued between 1968 and 1970, as well as "Love Woman," "Momma's Waiting," and the Mac Davis title "I Believe in Music," which Gallery hit with and which was covered by many others, including Helen Reddy. It's not chronological, and opening up with "Ruby, Don't Take Your Love to Town" (as Rogers does with his 1978 solo greatest-hits package, *Ten Years of Gold*) is probably more of a personal decision. The sizzling guitars on the neo-hard rock "Just Dropped In" are relegated to the middle of the disc, though a Mick Jagger would have opened the album up with his "always hit 'em hard at first" mindset. But regardless of the tracking, the First Edition truly is a band that racked up an impressive array of hits which do not get their fair share of play on classic rock stations, some major oldies stations also neglecting what is an amazing body of work. Kenny Rogers' career and fame in country and pop music eradicated the value of this group on the live circuit, something many of its contemporaries embraced. Sad to say, a reunion of the First Edition would not get the response it deserves,as those who want to hear this material do so when Kenny Rogers comes to town. It's a credit to his skills as a businessman and performer, but the body of work created by his late-'60s/early-'70s group was substantial, and spinning *The First Edition Greatest Hits* puts it into perspective. The inclusion of "Love Woman" and "Momma's Waiting" takes away some of the momentum of the more familiar tunes—and the album would've been better served by a performance where Thelma Lou Camacho was lead vocalist, or the addition of a song which showcased Mike Settle's talents. (This was, after all, a band.) The Alex Harvey composition "Molly" from the *Tell It All Brother* album would also have been a nice addition to this. But eight out of ten is not a bad batting average, and there are eight home runs here—that's more music recognizable to the general public than the Youngbloods and the Zombies had combined, and look at how many packages and repackages those two groups have been blessed with. The First Edition never got the respect it richly deserved and this album with its wonderful Jimmy Bowen and Mike Post production work is important and still fun to listen to. Rogers re-cut five of these titles for his *Ten Years of Gold* disc on United Artists six years later in 1977, and those solo renditions of First Edition music take up side one of his personal "Greatest Hits" collection. *The First Edition Greatest Hits* comes in two editions on vinyl, a slick silver/aluminum cardboard package with a classy large flap, and a more conventional gray album cover that opens on the side (the latter version also utilized by the mail order "record clubs"). *—Joe Viglione*

Planet Texas / 1972 / Reprise ✦✦✦

The Ballad of Calico / 1972 / Reprise ✦✦✦

Years before Michael Murphey began singing songs about cowboys as a recording artist, he wrote the material on this album as a tribute to a ghost town in the Mojave Desert called New Vegas. Though not all of the songs work, the concept and packaging (including the enclosed booklet with notes and lyrics) make this one worth having. *—Jim Worbois*

Love Lifted Me / 1976 / EMI America ✦✦✦

Kenny Rogers / 1976 / United Artists ✦✦✦✦✦

"Laura (What's He Got That I Ain't Got)" and "I Wasn't Man Enough" start off this 1976 self-titled album from the star of the First Edition gone solo. As chronicled in his book, *Making It With Music*, Rogers figured out how to capitalize on his many years in the recording industry, and these vignettes helped bring country-style story songs to the mainstream Top 40 and adult contemporary radio. While country fans might have had an issue with Aussie lass Olivia Newton-John infiltrating their world back in the day, Rogers' tenure in New Christy Minstrels certainly gave him credibility, as did the earthiness of these performances. Songs like "Mother Country Music" and "While I Play the Fiddle" have an authenticity no alleged carpetbagger could bring to the format. "Why Don't We Go Somewhere and Love" lifts note for note the intro to Harriet Schock's "Ain't No Way to Treat a Lady," the big number-one adult contemporary hit for Helen Reddy from the year before. While letting the melody veer off, the songwriters keep the flavor of the Schock masterpiece intact, and it's a good study in songwriters rewriting in a style they admire while giving a tip of the hat (or the hand) in the process. Tom Jones' 1967 hit "The Green Green Grass of Home" gets a more-mellow reading with a less-sweeping arrangement. The formula stretches Count Basie singer O.C. Smith's first hit, "The Son of Hickory Holler's Tramp," almost beyond recognition. Rogers' voice is at the peak of its powers, stronger than before and on par with the superb musicianship behind him. "Till I Get It Right," with its lush strings, becomes almost a theme song for the ups and downs of his previous musical endeavors. All this leads up to "Lucille," that breakthrough hit six and a half years after he charted seven popular songs with his group First Edition. "Lucille" has all the elements of greatness—a potential one-night stand evaporates and the singer trades sex for heart, becoming a hero in the process. The premise and its hook are unforgettable; simple music dresses up the melody and story by not getting in the way. "Son of Hickory Holler's Tramp" is the reverse of "Lucille," the guy leaving the girl with 14 kids rather than the girl leaving the guy with four. Interesting song order, smart enough to cross genres and open the door to Rogers' impending superstardom. "Lay Down Beside Me," "Puttin' in Overtime at Home," and "While I Play the Fiddle" may not have the genius of "Lucille," but they are consistent with stellar arrangements and can't be called filler. Kenny Rogers worked hard for all he achieved as an entertainer and this album provides any proof that might be needed to silence the skeptics. *—Joe Viglione*

Daytime Friends / 1977 / EMI America ✦✦✦

Ten Years of Gold / 1977 / EMI America ✦✦✦✦✦

Once upon a time, prior to the floodgates opening and multiple Kenny Rogers greatest-hits and best-of collections finding their way to market, there was *The First Edition Greatest Hits* on Reprise in 1971, followed six years later by *Ten Years of Gold*. Kenny Rogers unites his early-hit years with the first real solo songs that built the foundation of his superstardom. But here's what makes the package important: *The First Edition Greatest Hits* material is re-recorded for this LP. The first five of that band's seven hits get a new treatment for the new label, United Artists. It took seven years for the Grammy-winning "Lucille" to pick up the slack from where "Tell It All Brother" and "Heed the Call" left off, and those two songs *are* left off—left off of this compilation. In the new millennium most record labels think nothing of licensing their music to any and all takers, but the '70s were a different world. Some may consider remaking brilliant productions by Jimmy Bowen and Mike Post the same sacrilege others claim film colorization is, but to those purists the answer is simple—get the original record. Rogers does faithful renditions of "Ruby, Don't Take Your Love to Town," "Reuben James," "But You Know I Love You," "Somethings Burning," and a somewhat laid-back version of the psychedelic classic "Just Dropped In (To See What Condition My Condition Was In)." It's rather humorous seeing how the producers here softened up "Just Dropped In," and for fans of the song this "colorization" is a nice second look—but, as they say, the original is still the greatest. Keep in mind, though, "Just Dropped In" songwriter Mickey Newbury is a country artist, so it is not as much of a stretch as the rearranging of John Carter's "Incense & Peppermints" would have been. The Top Five hit "Lucille" was quickly followed by the Top 30 hit "Daytime Friends" and it was the harbinger of things to come. Both "Lucille" and "Daytime Friends" got to number one on the country charts, making the crossover for the star complete. It would be about a year before Rogers' first of 18 more hit records would start charting, so this collection summed up the activity from late 1967 to late 1977. Larry Butler co-produces the affair with Rogers and they add "While the Feeling's Good," "Love Lifted Me," and "Today I Started Loving You Again" to the mix. Though those songs weren't on the national Top 40, it is clear the duo wanted to balance out the new with the old by including five titles from both phases of the singer's career. Rogers was the first to really combine country, adult contemporary, and national Top 40 pop chart action over a long period of time with multiple songs. Dolly Parton, Tammy Wynette, Johnny Cash, and others may have found fans in all three worlds, but Kenny Rogers was to country what the Bee Gees were to the discos—a name from '60s hit radio finding attention and conquering new avenues in the '70s and '80s. With the Jordanaires, steel guitarist Pete Drake, engineer Billy Sherrill, bassist Tommy Allsup, and many others, the singer immediately capitalizes on past and future, utilizing stellar players. In 1978, Kenny Rogers and record exec Len Epand published a book, *Making It With Music: Kenny Rogers' Guide to the Music Business*; it is a substantial chronicle of how this music came to be. *—Joe Viglione*

Love or Something Like It / 1978 / United Artists ✦✦✦✦

Every Time Two Fools Collide / 1978 / United Artists ✦✦✦

The Gambler / 1978 / EMI America ✦✦✦✦✦

Kenny Rogers took a bit of a chance in releasing this loosly based concept album at the time, but boy, did it pay off! Sales for the album went through the roof, as the title track and "She Believes in Me" became pop crossover hits, with the latter reaching the pop Top Ten. Later, "The Gambler" was turned into a string of made-for-television movies. *—James Chrispell*

Kenny / 1979 / Razor & Tie ✦✦✦✦

Kenny took a more romantic approach with *Kenny*. Though it contained the hit character sketch "Coward of the County," the album was mainly comprised of love songs like "You Decorated My Life" and "She's a Mystery." With such strong singles, the album actually became a bigger hit than its predecessor, *The Gambler*. *—James Chrispell*

Classics / 1979 / United Artists ✦✦✦✦

Kenny & Dottie West team up to perform such great tunes as "Just the Way You Are," "You Needed Me," Buck Owens' "Together Again," the Righteous Brothers' "You've Lost That Lovin' Feelin'," as well as the chart topping "All I Ever Need Is You." Produced by Larry Butler, the album boasts the highly professional sound that came out of Nashville in the late '70s, and there is some fine listening enjoyment to be found here. *—James Chrispell*

Gideon / 1980 / United Artists ✦✦✦

Kenny Rogers has released some tremendous albums, so giving him the opportunity to stretch and explore his music through a concept project like *Gideon* is something the artist deserved. Unfortunately, it isn't the classic epic it could have been, though there are some fine moments here. Written entirely by Kim Carnes and her husband David Ellington, it's easy to see why a great vocalist like Carnes found her most lasting fame recording the timeless renovation of a Jackie DeShannon country-pop tune rather than as a songwriter. It's that essence of fun on "Bette Davis Eyes" that's missing here, as the album gets bogged down in seriousness. "Going Home to the Rock" is a terrific intro, but the title track is labored, and "No Good Texas Rounder" is forced, like much of this recording. Redemption comes in the form of the Top Five hit from 1980, "Don't Fall in Love With a Dreamer." This was a great moment, not only for Rogers, but for Carnes as a songwriter, as she duets with her friend from the New Christy Minstrels on the hit, garnering her second biggest of ten Top 40 entries, second only to the aforementioned "Bette Davis Eyes." The problem is the songwriting. "Call Me Up (The Phone Is in the Cradle)" has a decent hook but not much in the verses, relying heavily on the superb production from Larry Butler and Rogers, with engineering by the legendary Billy Sherrill. Songwriting should never rely solely on the production; it's like having all frosting and no cake. Ambitious, with a three-page fold-out insert featuring a photo of the cowboy-dressed Rogers and all the lyrics, the pity here is that all the participants had the talent to come up with a country music version of *Tommy*. They miss the mark, and it just feels like everyone was too comfortable and too self-conscious of the work. Had Rogers combined with Tommy James and re-recorded that pop artist's Nashville album from the 1970s, *My Head, My Bed & My Red Guitar*, it would have been a special moment. That gem fell under the radar screen, and Rogers' huge popularity could have given that material the chance to be heard. Instead there are OK compositions like "These Chains" and "Somebody Help Me," material that feels like Kim and Dave were sitting around the campfire with their old friend Kenny and trying to imagine what happened a hundred years before. "One Place in the Night" is decent pop, keyboards and production making it feel out of place on this experiment, and one of the better tracks. "Requiem: Going Home to the Rock" is also a nice touch, but face it, singles were the game for Rogers. In just two months he would have a hit from the film *Urban Cowboy*, and four months after that he would find phenomenal success with a Lionel Richie tune. *Gideon* served a great purpose during Rogers' heyday, but its promise was unfulfilled. *—Joe Viglione*

Greatest Hits / 1980 / EMI America ✦✦✦✦✦

This particular Kenny Rogers collection focuses on the singer's EMI America chart entries from the late '70s and early '80s. The 12-track sampling includes "Don't Fall in Love With a Dreamer," "She Believes in Me," "Coward of the County," "Lady," and "The Gambler." "Reuben James" and "Ruby, Don't Take Your Love to Town" are re-recordings by Rogers, not the versions he made popular in the late '60s with his group the First Edition. Still, this is a good set for those who only want the hits. *—Al Campbell*

Share Your Love / 1981 / Razor & Tie ✦✦✦

Share Your Love began a downturn in Kenny Rogers' popularity. Comprised almost entirely of Lionel Richie songs, the album is pleasant, yet its adult contemporary pop direction was quite a departure at the time and was not greeted well with Kenny's country fans. A miss after a long string of hits. *—James Chrispell*

Love Will Turn You Around / Sep. 1, 1982 / EMI America ✦✦✦

We've Got Tonight / 1983 / Razor & Tie ✦✦✦

When Kenny Rogers paired up with Scottish pop songstress Sheena Easton for "We've Got Tonight," the hit title track from this 1983 album, one could quibble about Easton's occasionally overwrought and bombastic performance, but there are a few moments of truly sublime vocal interplay. The album provides a little of Rogers' trademark storytelling with "Scarlet," and quite a bit of soaring balladry as heard on "All My Life," both of which were hits. You will be forgiven for thinking the albums sounds a bit like Lionel Richie in places, since Richie contributes the song "How Long." Rogers ends the album with "You Are So Beautiful," a loving tribute to his legions of female fans, but male listeners may want to cutout early. *—Greg Adams*

☆ **Eyes That See in the Dark** / 1983 / RCA ✦✦✦✦✦

This is a masterpiece of a pop recording from Kenny Rogers. It is clear that Barry Gibb, Maurice Gibb, and co-producers Karl Richardson and Albhy Galuten remembered Rogers' pop roots with the First Edition and, despite the country twang of "Buried Treasure," the slick musicianship and modulation are not your typical country & western. There are four tracks written by Barry & Maurice and five more by Barry, Maurice, & brother Robin Gibb, including the stunning number-one hit from September 1983, "Islands in the Stream." It hit number one across the board on adult contemporary, country, and the Top 40, and deservedly so—the melody is infectious, impeccable, and perfectly recorded. Keep in mind this was five years after they created Frankie Valli's biggest-selling solo record, "Grease"—the pairing of Dolly Parton with Rogers makes for an amazing vocal sound to carry the melody. "Living With You" features the Bee Gees—it is Rogers fronting the Bee Gees, and why they didn't seek out more artists, new as well as established, to work their magic on is a pity. It's a lush setting for the country superstar, and as Barbara Streisand and Dionne Warwick enjoyed success thanks to this creative team, *Eyes That See in the Dark* stands as an important piece of the Rogers catalog and a really timeless recording. The Gatlin Brothers add their magic to "Evening Star" and "Buried Treasure," and these elements bring the Barry Gibb/Richardson/Galuten thousand-tracks production down to earth. "Evening Star" doesn't have the complexities of Samantha Sang's "Emotion," the producers being very careful to keep it simple, something they just weren't doing on all their other records. There are only ten tracks on *Eyes That See in the Dark*, Jimmie Haskell's strings the major instrument next to Rogers' sympathetic vocal performance. "Midsummer Nights" is co-authored by Barry Gibb and Galuten, making Barry the catalyst and driving force, as he is the only person with a hand in every tune. "Midsummer Nights" brings things back up after "Hold Me," and it is more adult contemporary than country. It would have made a great single but, as it was, the opening track, "This Woman," went Top 25 in early 1984, and by the end of that year Rogers would post his 27th Top 40 hit, ending a string started 16 years earlier in 1968. It isn't clear why they didn't, but the pretty Barry & Maurice Gibb tune "I Will Always Love You" (not to be confused with Parton's hit of the same name) and the title track certainly should have found some chart action as well. *Eyes That See in the Dark* is not the definitive Kenny Rogers album but, outside of greatest-hits packages, it is absolutely one of his most consistent and one of his best. *—Joe Viglione*

Duets / 1984 / Capitol ✦✦✦

This was such a natural album for Kenny Rogers, a compilation culled from four different sources, but it works very well. The Top Five 1980 hit with Kim Carnes, her biggest chart song a year before "Bette Davis Eyes" would take the world by storm, and the number one country hit, Top Ten smash with Sheena Easton, the remake of Bob Seger's "We've Got Tonight," each open a side of this album, sides which are followed by Dottie West and Rogers performing eight more tunes. Fans of Kenny Rogers will love this despite the fact that the production style and sound of the West/Rogers material is dramatically different from what David Foster put on "We've Got Tonight" and what Rogers and Larry Butler poured over in "Don't Fall in Love With a Dreamer." Rogers & West's 1981 Top 15 hit together, "What Are We Doin' in Love," is missing in action, strange as that seems, but the pair is definitely having fun with this format and the other titles they explore here, songs taken from two different Dottie West LPs: 1978's *Every Time Two Fools Collide* and 1979's *Classics*. Both singers sound like the master Ray Charles on the chorus of the Buck Owens-penned "Together Again," copying Charles from his 1966 hit. They don't do the same with "All I Ever Need Is You," though, abandoning Sonny & Cher's stylings for their own. West might start off a little like Cher, but when the tune gets into gear it is pure Dottie West, while Rogers' personality doesn't need Sonny Bono's comedy; Rogers' sincerity does the trick very nicely on what was a huge country hit for the duo. Larry Butler provides competent backing tracks for the two stars to have an enjoyable time, and they do. Hearing a different rendition of "(Hey Won't You Play) Another Somebody Done Somebody Wrong Song" or David Gates' "Baby I'm a Want You" is entertaining—it's just too bad they couldn't have gotten B.J. Thomas or the Bread vocalist to come to the party that was the original sessions. Producer Larry Butler co-wrote "(Hey Won't You Play) Another Somebody Done Somebody Wrong Song" with Chips Moman, and both men produced B.J. Thomas, so Rogers meeting West was a perfect opportunity to bring this nugget back. "'Til I Can Make It on My Own" and "That's the Way It Could Have Been" are both touching Tammy Wynette numbers, respectful versions by friends of the songwriter. Dottie West, Sheena Easton, Kim Carnes, and Kenny Rogers put a lot into the vocal performances, and that's what truly lifts this album to a special place, no matter when and where it was all recorded. It's also a clever way to slide the material from West's catalog over to Rogers'. *—Joe Viglione*

They Don't Make Them Like They Used To / 1986 / RCA ✦✦✦

Kenny Rogers' *They Don't Make Them Like They Used To* album's title track does what one critic said of Neil Young's *Time Fades Away*: remove the word "time" and the album reviews itself—"Neil Young Fades Away." The Burt Bacharach/Carole Bayer Sager song and production feels forced—the only track sounding like classic Kenny and kicking in as it fades. With five producers total it may have been a case of too many cooks, the music here a far cry from the string of hits put together by Larry Butler on Liberty Records for the former lead singer of the First Edition. No, they don't make 'em like they used to, but that doesn't mean this is a bad record; in fact, it's a very good album from a country-pop singer trying his hand at the slick adult contemporary associated with Whitney Houston and Celine Dion. Either of those artists could have sang Dave Loggins' "Anything at All," and it may have hit, same with "You're My Love," which features El Debarge on backing vocals. For Rogers it is a wonderful experiment that sounds good but may have been too much of a paramorphism—there's just not the balance that the Bee Gees struck with Kenny on *Eyes That See in the Dark*. Not including songwriters, almost four dozen individuals lent their talents to this underrated and pretty much forgotten 1986 album, Jay Graydon picking up where his colleague David Foster and George Martin left off on other RCA releases. The label didn't seem to be the company to keep this artist at the forefront, despite its fine work with his friend Dolly Parton. You'll find Rogers' co-hort Kin Vassy singing backing vocals on "Life Is Good, Love Is Better," Mike Boddicker on the title track, and Steve Lukather on the tune he co-wrote with Randy Goodrum, "If I Could Hold on to Love," but somehow quasi-disco wasn't going to work for an adult contemporary/country artist. Despite Rogers' friend Kim Carnes' success with "Bette Davis Eyes" at the beginning of the decade, Jay Graydon's guitar work with Alice Cooper and proficiency on Earth, Wind & Fire albums are where the producer leans towards here rather than drawing from his skills with artists like Parton. Make no mistake, this is Graydon's baby and it is admirable, from the stunning portrait of the star surrounded by pastels on the cover to the superbly slick presentation. Rogers is a total professional and pulls it off somewhat, but he does feel out of place. A reunion of the First Edition or the New Christy Minstrels may have been more interesting for the mid-'80s. Those voices would be certainly able enough to bring the title track home, the song "They Don't Make Them Like They Used To" the biggest disappointment here as it has so much to offer. It feels like Bacharach and Sager were going through the motions, and that's the pity, as the success of that soundtrack tune might've given the rest of this adult contemporary work a better chance. *—Joe Viglione*

25 Greatest Hits / 1987 / EMI America ✦✦✦✦✦

This two-CD set includes much the same material as *Greatest Hits*, but also has "Daytime Friends," "Love or Something like It," and "Love Will Turn You Around." *—Dan Cooper*

Something Inside So Strong / 1989 / Reprise ✦✦✦

At Their Best / 1990 / Hollywood ✦✦

At Their Best is a 20-track collection of the First Edition's biggest hits (there's "Ruby Don't Take Your Love to Town," "Something's Burning," "Tell It All Brother," and "Heed the Call," but no "Just Dropped In (To See What Condition My Condition Was In)" or "Reuben James"), presented in a shoddy manner, with bad packaging and sound. The fact that it doesn't contain all the hits prevents it from even being an adequate collection for casual listeners, and that's a little funny, since it seems like it would be easy to put all of the First Edition's big hits on one 20-track collection. Evidently, that's not the case. *—Stephen Thomas Erlewine*

20 Great Years / 1990 / Reprise ✦✦✦

This contains the hits "Lady," "She Believes in Me," "Something's Burning," "The Gambler," "Lucille," and others. *—AMG*

Greatest Country Hits / 1990 / Curb ✦✦✦

Greatest Country Hits is an 11-track budget-priced collection that features some of Kenny Rogers' biggest hits, including "Lucille," "The Gambler," "Coward of the County," "Lady," "She Believes in Me," "Love Will Turn You Around," "We've Got Tonight" and "Reuben James." Although this isn't a bad budget-priced disc, there are better collections available, offering more songs and better sound for not much more money. *—Stephen Thomas Erlewine*

Back Home Again / 1991 / Reprise ✦✦✦

All Time Greatest Hits, Vol. 1 / 1992 / Universal Special Products ✦✦✦

MCA Special Products' *All Time Greatest Hits, Vol. 1* features 18 highlights and hits from Kenny Rogers & the First Edition's recordings. Only one of the group's biggest hits, "Just Dropped In (To See What Condition My Condition Is In)," is present, but the remaining 17 tracks are all fairly entertaining country-rock and pop, highlighted by "Where Does Rosie Go?," "For the Good Times," "Sunshine," "My Washington Woman," "She Even Woke Me Up to Say Goodbye," "Just Remember You're My Sunshine," "Sleep Comes Easy" and "Last Few Threads of Love." It's hardly a definitive collection, but it's enjoyable and, compared to other budget-price compilations, it offers the most music for the money. *—Stephen Thomas Erlewine*

All-Time Greatest Hits / 1996 / CEMA ✦✦✦✦✦

A budget-line, triple-disc set containing 36 tracks, *All-Time Gretest Hits* isn't necessarily a definitive Kenny Rogers collection—it doesn't contain the First Edition's "Just Dropped In (To See What Condition My Condition Was In)" nor "Islands in the Stream," it isn't presented in chronological order, it doesn't have any liner notes, and it all could have fit on two discs—but it does contain the bulk of his biggest hits, including "Lucille," "She Believes In Me," "You Decorated My Life," "Ruby, Don't Take Your Love to Town," "Lady," "Don't Fall in Love With a Dreamer," "Every Time Two Fools Collide," "Coward of the County," "We've Got Tonight," and "The Gambler." As a result, it is an excellent bargain, even if there are more thoughtfully-assembled packages on the market. *—Stephen Thomas Erlewine*

Greatest Hits / Sep. 24, 1996 / Hip-O ✦✦✦✦✦

Kenny Rogers & the First Edition's *Greatest Hits* contains all of the group's greatest hits, including "Ruby, Don't Take Your Love to Town" and "Just Dropped In (To See What Condition My Condition Is In)," plus a number of lesser-known singles. Though the group didn't have enough strong material to make the compilation consistently entertaining, this single-disc collection is nevertheless the definitive retrospective of Rogers' early years. *—Stephen Thomas Erlewine*

Decade of Hits / Mar. 25, 1997 / Warner Bros. ✦✦✦
With the exception of "Islands in the Stream," Rogers' chart-topping duet with Dolly Parton, this compilation of the singer's mid-1980s and 1990s work for RCA and Reprise concentrates primarily on forgettable, minor hits including "Morning Desire," "The Vows Go Unbroken (Always True to You)," "Tomb of the Unknown Love" and "What About Me?," recorded with Kim Carnes and James Ingram. *—Jason Ankeny*

● **Through the Years: A Retrospective** / Jan. 26, 1999 / Capitol ✦✦✦✦✦
Through the Years: A Retrospective doesn't take its duties lightly—it truly does attempt to present a full portrait of Kenny Rogers, from struggling musician to bona fide superstar. Helpfully, it breaks down his career into four easily digestible discs, containing 20 tracks each. The first disc is dubbed "The Vintage Years" and it doesn't just feature songs from the First Edition—it contains revelatory material from his early groups the Scholars, the Bobby Doyle Three, and the Kirby Stone Four. The second disc is what most casual fans will treasure—an entire disc devoted to "The Number One Hits." The third disc rounds up various singles, album tracks, and duets Rogers recorded during his late-'70s and early-'80s peak. Which, of course, leaves the fourth disc like any other final disc in a box set—a collection of highlights from the years when the artist faded away from the spotlight. Certainly, this results in a thorough and accurate overview of his career, but that doesn't mean it's entirely listenable. Yes, hardcore fans and collectors will be interested in the first disc, but for many listeners, only the First Edition tracks will be noteworthy. Similarly, the final disc is extraneous for most tastes, leaving this little more than a very good two-disc summary of Rogers' hitmaking years. Naturally, single- and double-disc retrospectives of the hits are available elsewhere, for less money and without two extra discs, and that's what most fans will want. Nevertheless, anyone wanting a thorough summary of Rogers' entire career can't go wrong with *Through the Years*. *—Stephen Thomas Erlewine*

A&E Biography / Jan. 26, 1999 / Capitol ✦✦✦
Released as a companion piece to A&E's insightful, entertaining hour-long documentary of the same name, *A&E Biography* is a concise, entertaining collection that balances hits ("Lucille," "The Gambler," "Lady") with lesser-known songs, including album tracks, smaller singles and duets, such as "Every Time Two Fools Collide," his chart-topper with Dottie West. There are not enough big singles for the disc to qualify as a true greatest hits, but it has enough high points and interesting detours to make it an engaging listen, one that comes close to capturing the ebb and flow of Rogers' career even if it doesn't provide a completely accurate summary. *—Stephen Thomas Erlewine*

She Rides Wild Horses / May 11, 1999 / Dreamcatcher ✦✦✦
Despite his best efforts, Kenny Rogers spent almost all of the '90s hitless. Toward the end of the decade, he formed his own label, Dreamcatcher, and began to spend more time constructing his albums, starting with the adult contemporary *Across My Heart*. Its follow-up, *She Rides Wild Horses*, continues in the same direction, albeit with a slightly stronger country influence than before. There aren't any of the All-4-One cameos that cluttered *Across My Heart*, and the song selection, while still a bit uneven, is stronger—enough to give the impression that *She Rides Wild Horses* is some sort of a comeback. And in a way, it is. It's been a while since Rogers has delivered an album with as many appealing songs as he does here—"The Kind of Fool Love Makes," "Love Don't Live Here Anymore," "Let It Be Me," "The Greatest," the title song—and the sound of the record is smoothly pleasurable, even if it can get a little bland. That doesn't mean it will be a hit—after all, this is basically a return to his hitmaking sound of the early '80s—but for fans awaiting an album that harks back to his classic period, this will be welcome. *—Stephen Thomas Erlewine*

The Islands in the Stream: The Greatest Hits 1983–1988 / Jun. 15, 1999 / Music Club ✦✦✦✦
Music Club's 1999 collection *Islands in the Stream: The Greatest Hits 1983-1988* concentrates on a very specific period of Kenny Rogers' career: the time after he had already been a superstar and was now concentrating on crossover success, fashioning himself as an adult contemporary MOR crooner. He inaugurated this phase of his career with 1983's *Eyes That See in the Dark*, a record written by the Bee Gees that was arguably the finest album of his career, if judged on a pure track-by-track level. This turned out to be a quick peak, as each successive record was a little slicker, a little more considered, and a little less interesting. This collection contains most of the highlights from these albums, including all the hits and a good portion of *Eyes That See in the Dark*. While that record is still essential to any Kenny Rogers collection and provides unquestionably the best material, this does round up the best from the uneven records—tunes that prove he was indeed a good adult contemporary singer—and is worthwhile if taken on those terms. *—Stephen Thomas Erlewine*

Best of Kenny Rogers / Apr. 15, 2003 / Collectables ✦✦✦
For a musician who's had a string of hits on the country, adult contemporary, and pop singles charts for 30-plus years, it seems as though it wouldn't be too difficult for Collectables to put together a really solid single-disc *Best of Kenny Rogers*. To be fair, anything after the mid-'80s isn't truly essential, and Collectables chose not to place any of the Kenny Rogers & the First Edition tracks here; however, that still leaves a decade's worth of choice material, affording plenty of great songs ("Daytime Friends," "Love Will Turn You Around," "Anyone Who Isn't Me Tonight," etc.) that could've fit in here and made this the definitive one-CD Kenny Rogers compilation. Instead, this Collectables budget-line collection sits next to a long line of similar collections that also missed the mark by offering up the same meager ten-track selection. It's a shame, because what Rogers' catalog needs the most is an excellent single-disc overview with in-depth liner notes (not offered here) that spans more than the skimpy 37 minutes offered here. *—Gregory McIntosh*

Roy Rogers (Leonard Slye)

b. Nov. 5, 1911, Cincinnati, OH, **d.** Jul. 6, 1998, Victorville, CA
Guitar, Vocals / Traditional Country, Cowboy, Country Gospel

When Cincinnati-born Leonard Franklin Slye headed west in the spring of 1931, it was as a would-be musician, working jobs ranging from driving a gravel truck to picking fruit in California's Central Valley. In less than two years, he'd co-founded the greatest Western singing group of all time, the Sons of the Pioneers, and barely four years after that, he'd started a career as a movie star under the new name Roy Rogers. Ultimately he found great fame as a movie and TV cowboy and even founded a very successful chain of restaurants.

He was born in Cincinnati, OH, the son of Andrew and Mattie Womack Slye. The entire household was musical, and by the time he was a teenager, Len could play the guitar and the mandolin. Although he later took on the role of a cowboy before the public, the closest he got to riding the range was working the family farm they had in a small town outside of Cincinnati. By age 19, he'd headed out to California, where chance led him to enter an amateur singing contest on the radio, resulting in an offer to join the Rocky Mountaineers. There he made the acquaintance of Bob Nolan. They developed a harmonious friendship that worked well within the group for several months, until Nolan exited in frustration over their lack of success. His replacement was Tim Spencer, and eventually Slye, Spencer, and another singer named Slumber Nichols quit the Rocky Mountaineers in the spring of 1932 to form a trio of their own, which never quite came off. Slye decided to push on, joining Jack LeFevre & His Texas Outlaws.

In early 1933, he got Spencer and Nolan together to form what was then known as the Pioneer Trio. Their mix of singing and yodeling, coupled with their good spirits, won them a job on radio. Within a few weeks, they were developing a large following of their own on LeFevre's show, with their harmony singing eliciting lots of mail. A fourth member, fiddle player Hugh Farr, was added to firm up their sound early in 1934. The group's name was altered by accident—on one broadcast the station's announcer introduced them as "The Sons of the Pioneers." The group sold large numbers of records from the very beginning, with the classic Nolan original "Tumbling Tumbleweeds" cut at their very first session. Two more new members, Lloyd Perryman and Hugh Farr's guitarist brother Karl, were added, and by the mid-'30s the sextet was one of the top-selling country acts, performing to sell-out audiences and sought by radio stations and sponsors eager to back them on the air.

During this period, Slye did occasional work as a movie extra and bit player in B-Westerns under the name Dick Weston at Republic Pictures, where the reigning king of Western movies was another singer, Gene Autry, whose records outsold even the Pioneers'. In 1938, Autry entered into a contractual dispute with Republic that resulted in his failure to report for his next movie. Republic, anticipating the dispute, had put out the word—apparently more as a ploy than a real attempt at replacing their top male star—that they were looking for a new leading actor for their Westerns. Slye tried sneaking onto the lot with a group of extras and was caught, but a sympathetic director permitted him to take a screen test. He tested extremely well and got the part. At the time, the Pioneers had just signed a contract with Columbia Pictures to appear in and play musical support to Charles Starrett in a series of B-Westerns, and he was forced to leave the group in order to sign his own contract at Republic.

A new name was required and "Roy Rogers" was selected, the "Rogers" coming from Will Rogers and "Roy" coming off of a list. He made his debut in *Under Western Stars*; not only did it introduce Rogers as a new star, but also his horse, Trigger. A long-term contract followed, and for the next 13 years, he was one of the studio's mainstays, rivaling and later surpassing Autry at the box office. By 1940, Rogers was successful enough to approach Republic with a request for a salary increase. The studio was notoriously reticent on such matters, and he was denied any raise. But in lieu of the request, he extracted a much more valuable concession—the rights to the name Roy Rogers and all merchandising that went with it. The early '40s saw Rogers turn into a national institution. His Westerns became even more popular and accessible once they were taken out of the "historic" West of the 19th century and moved into the modern West, which allowed for more freedom in plotting and dialogue. With director Joseph Kane helming his movies, Rogers became the undisputed "King of the Cowboys" after Autry joined the U.S. Army Air Force in 1942. By 1944, however, the movies and records represented only a small part of the success that Rogers had achieved. The merchandising of Rogers memorabilia and other items—not just toys, but cereals and electric ranges—coupled with a syndicated radio show made him one of the most familiar figures in popular culture throughout the war years.

In 1944, with his first teaming with featured actress Dale Evans, the next major element in his screen success was in place. Their relationship was, at first, purely professional, but their chemistry on screen was undeniable, and Republic was soon pairing them up regularly. With the return of master action director William Witney from service in the war during 1945, Rogers' film career was poised for success for years to come, as Witney toughened up the Rogers movies and elevated their action sequences. All of this success, and the whirlwind of activity surrounding it, was negated by the death of Rogers' wife, Arline, from an embolism following the birth of their son, Roy Jr., on November 3, 1946. Rogers continued making movies and recording, along with his personal appearances and radio broadcast. In the course of their work together in pictures, he and Evans (who had already been designated "The Queen of the West" by Republic's publicity office) became ever closer. Finally, on December 31, 1947, the two were married. They made movies together for the remainder of the 1940s, and when the market for B-Westerns began to disappear with the advent of television, Rogers followed the lead of Western star William ("Hopalong Cassidy") Boyd and devised a television series of his own. *The Roy Rogers Show*, starring Rogers and Evans and co-starring Roy's Pioneers replacement, Pat Brady, went on the air on NBC in December of 1951, beginning a seven-year network run that introduced his work to yet another generation of fans.

His first solo recordings featured backup by Hugh & Karl Farr and Bob Nolan, and the complete Pioneers supported him in most of his recording sessions for the remainder of

1937 and 1938. Later on, however, Rogers was backed by Spade Cooley & His Buckle-Busters as well as various anonymous studio orchestras, although Karl Farr would turn up on his sessions as well into the 1940s. On record as a solo artist, Rogers was never as successful as the Pioneers or Autry, although he did have one promising early hit in 1938 with "Hi-Yo Silver," which reached number 13 on the charts. Even Rogers' sessions on his own recordings with the Sons of the Pioneers, however, little resembled his earlier work as a member of the Pioneers, for his was now the lead voice. And where Bob Nolan and Tim Spencer (the principal songwriters within the group) never strayed too far from some contact with the reality of the West, Rogers' music quickly took on the aura of more typical Hollywood Western songs, pleasant but not generally profound. His covers of songs such as "Don't Fence Me In" are probably the best remembered versions, thanks to his movies, and as songs like "San Fernando Valley" or "Home in Oklahoma" reveal, he had an extremely appealing tenor voice, not as memorable as Autry's voice but very pleasing to the ear nonetheless. Perhaps the most well-known of all Rogers' songs was one written by Evans and (originally) recorded by them together, "Happy Trails," which became the theme of *The Roy Rogers Show*. From the 1950s onward, his repertory included country music as well as Western songs and spirituals, the latter often recorded with Evans. Rogers continued to record into the 1970s, and he scored a hit in 1972 with "Candy Kisses."

He and Dale continued making personal appearances, often in the context of religious broadcasts and gatherings, as well as television broadcasts, into the early '90s. Rogers' main influence was in keeping the image of the singing cowboy alive. Along with Autry, who retired from personal appearances at the end of the 1950s, he was one of the most popular Western stars ever to record and was an influence on an entire generation of country & western singers that followed. In 1988, Rogers was elected to the Country Music Hall of Fame, giving him a second spot (the first having come as a member of the Sons of the Pioneers, who had been elected some years earlier). Two years later, the next generation of country musicians, including Emmylou Harris and Randy Travis, participated in a most unusual record, *The Roy Rogers Tribute*, covering Rogers' best known songs with him, including an all-star rendition of "Happy Trails." Two years later, Rogers, his wife, and eldest son recorded a new album of spiritual songs. Rogers died at his home in Victorville, CA, on July 6, 1998. —*Bruce Eder*

The Bible Tells Me So / 1962 / Capitol ✦✦✦
This album features "Amazing Grace," "How Great Thou Art," "It Is No Secret," "Peace in the Valley," "Take My Hand," and other gospel standards. —*AMG*

16 Great Songs of the Old West / 1963 / Golden ✦✦✦✦

The Country Side of Roy Rogers / 1970 / Capitol ✦✦✦
Roy Rogers' first real country (as opposed to western) album, more than 35 years after his recording debut, marked a new artistic and commercial era for him, as he started charting singles in that market on a steady basis and found a new audience, just at the point when a lot of men his age would have been looking at retirement. The content consists mostly of working class anthems, including covers of Merle Haggard's then-recent "Okie From Muskogee" and "The Fightin' Side of Me," interspersed with a few ballads and some inspirational/topical material ("Vision at the Peace Table") that doesn't really work. The accompaniment is generally stripped down here, and Rogers' singing sounds supremely confident. Spurred by the presence of the hit single "Money Can't Buy Love," it was a success and led to the release of two more LPs for Capitol. —*Bruce Eder*

A Man From Duck Run / 1971 / Capitol ✦✦✦
Roy Rogers' second modern country album is a beautiful record. His voice was always better than he was given credit for, and the choice of material is ideal, especially since this was an effort to redefine Rogers, proving he had a lot more to offer than "Happy Trails." There are no western songs, but only country songs that play well off of Rogers' gentle tenor voice—from the playful "Lovenworth" (a Top 15 country hit), through the sentimental ballad "If I Ever Get That Close Again" and the working-class anthem "I Never Picked Cotton," the artist shows an earthy, robust side far removed from his singing cowboy image; it's countrypolitan, no question, but for Rogers that was a step forward, and he gives a bravura performance, carrying a song like "Everything Changes" with such sincerity that one really wants to cry midway through. —*Bruce Eder*

Columbia Historic Edition / 1984 / Columbia ✦✦✦✦✦

The Best of Roy Rogers / 1990 / Curb ✦✦✦
With the wealth of classic Roy Rogers material available, these 12 tracks are definitely not the cream of the crop. A few decent songs from the early '70s are included: "Candy Kisses," "Lovenworth," "Money Can't Buy Love," and "Happy Anniversary." However, most of the attempts at contemporary material just didn't work for an American hero like the Singing Cowboy. While Dean Martin's version of "Lay Some Happiness on Me" fit his boozy, happy-go-lucky persona, it sounds foolish and flat coming from Rogers. —*Al Campbell*

Tribute / 1991 / RCA ✦✦✦
At 79, Rogers' voice wasn't as sure as it was in his heyday. But Richard Landis gave him sympathetic production, and none of his guests sound like paid hands or hired guns. Everyone involved—from Rogers' son Dusty to the Kentucky Headhunters—sounds more committed to making a good record than to adding star power. The material has been chosen accordingly, a good blend of old and new. The tribute's best when young singers repay an obvious debt (the duets with Ricky Van Shelton, Clint Black, and Randy Travis), but even when K.T. Oslin and Restless Heart join in the Sons of the Pioneers' theme, "Tumbling Tumbleweeds," they bring new life to an old workhorse. And Rogers' yodel is still in great shape. —*Brian Mansfield*

Country Music Hall of Fame Series / 1992 / MCA ✦✦✦✦✦
When Gene Autry got into a contract dispute with Republic Pictures in 1937, the studio replaced him with Sons of the Pioneers member Len Slye, whose name they changed to

Roy Rogers. These Decca tracks, which range from 1934 to 1942, cover Rogers' output just before he became "King of the Cowboys" with the release of *Ridin' Down the Canyon*. Two of these cuts were recorded with the Sons of the Pioneers; the rest are solo. —*Brian Mansfield*

16 Great Songs of Old West / Jul. 14, 1998 / Drive Archive ✦✦✦
The recordings on *16 Great Songs of the Old West* were made by Roy Rogers and Dale Evans in the mid-'50s for Golden Records. Backed by vocal group the Ranch Hands and directed by Mitch Miller, the duo cover many of the best known songs of the West, including "Home on the Range," "Colorado Trail," "Cool Water," "Tumbling Tumbleweeds," and "Red River Valley." Rogers & Evans sound great as they negotiate this well-worn material, some of which they'd recorded before. *16 Great Songs* would be a fine introduction for newcomers who wish to explore Western music, while old timers will appreciate the solid performances even if the obvious choices of material hold no surprises. —*Greg Adams*

Songs of the Old West / Sep. 8, 1998 / Universal Special Products ✦✦✦
MCA Special Products' *Songs of the Old West* is an entertaining roundup of ten narrative country & western songs Roy Rogers recorded, highlighted by versions of "Home on the Range," "Whoopee Ti Yi Yo," "Colorado Trail," "Streets of Laredo," "Tumbling Tumbleweeds," "Cool Water," "Railroad Corral" and "Red River Valley." —*Stephen Thomas Erlewine*

King of the Cowboys / Jan. 19, 1999 / ASV ✦✦✦✦
A fine compilation of Rogers' early songs with the Sons of the Pioneers and his sessions from the following decade, in all covering 1936-1947. He's at his best when only accompanied by the Sons, such as in the classic wanderlust anthem "Tumbling Tumbleweeds" and the gleeful guitar riffs of "When the Golden Train Comes Down." The orchestral tracks often show a pop influence that pales next to the restless energy of the rawer early tracks, and numbers like "Make-Believe Cowboy" can be a bit too sugary, but the later tracks nonetheless have some keepers like "Don't Face Me In" and the moody harmonies of "Blue Shadows on the Trail." When combined with the Rhino *Happy Trails* compilation, the release makes for an ideal overview of his early career. —*Paul Collins*

● **Happy Trails: The Roy Rogers Collection 1937–1990** / May 18, 1999 / Rhino ✦✦✦✦✦
This box is a brilliant achievement, and all the more surprising for what it does to elevate Roy Rogers' musical reputation. Essentially, Roy Rogers had two distinct musical periods—the first, in the Sons of the Pioneers from 1931 to 1937, is considered the more important; the second, as the singing cowboy star, far less important even though he became a cultural icon. *Happy Trails: The Roy Rogers Collection* offers a complete reconsideration of Rogers' post-Sons of the Pioneers musical career, offering a vast selection of previously lost songs, which greatly expand the range of music with which he is associated. Rather than assembling a collection of his commercial recordings, which concentrated on the most marketable side of Roy Rogers, Rhino producer James Austin went to Rogers' own archives and retrieved dozens of radio broadcasts, rehearsal tapes and live performances by Rogers, Dale Evans, the Sons of the Pioneers, the Riders of the Purple Sage, Pat Brady, and Gabby Hayes, that have been unheard for 50 years. The repertory they performed on those shows was infinitely wider ranging than Rogers' official record releases: traditional country songs of the 19th century, established country hits, older Pioneer hits reprised, Tin Pan Alley, bluegrass, swing and jazz, and even classical elements get a hearing. The pacing of these performances is also marvelous—Rogers' solo material, often featuring his inimitable yodelling, is sandwiched between Rogers/Sons of the Pioneers performances that are a match for any of their classic '30s work. The notes give us not only the background of the particular recordings by Rogers and company, but also the history of the songs themselves. The booklet is well annotated and illustrated, and the sound is pretty much beyond reproach, especially considering the half-century age of much of the unissued material. —*Bruce Eder*

A Man from Duck Run/The Country Side of Roy Rogers / Dec. 28, 1999 / EMI ✦✦✦
This is 20 of the best solo country songs that Roy Rogers ever recorded make for an enjoyable 50 minutes of listening. The sound is very good, and the packaging re-creates the original cover art, but unfortunately with no new annotation. —*Bruce Eder*

Ride Ranger Ride / Sep. 25, 2001 / Fabulous ✦✦✦✦
If the silver-bullet man is your cup of rotgut, then this is the batch you've been waiting for. While there are numerous compilations of Roy Rogers' material out there, including the truly definitive Bear Family set, this compiles on a single disc all of Rogers' classics with the Sons of the Pioneers through his solo singing cowboy days, ranging from 1943 through 1980. There are 21 songs here, including the title track, the "I'm an Old Cowhand" standard, "The Hills of Old Wyomin'," "Don't Fence Me In," the requisite "Hi Ho Silver" (of course), and pretty much all of the hits in between. "Hits" may be overstating the case, though, since Rogers only placed two solo tracks on the charts in his entire career, compared to Gene Autry, who placed 25. Nevertheless, if you are after the cowboy's best-known obscurities, then this is yer bet—especially for the budget price. —*Thom Jurek*

Along the Navajo Trail 1945–1947 / Mar. 19, 2002 / Naxos ✦✦✦✦

Old Time Country: Portrait Of Roy Rogers / Apr. 2, 2002 / Columbia River ✦✦✦

Tammy Rogers

b. 1966, Tennessee
Fiddle, Violin, Viola, Vocals / Progressive Bluegrass, Progressive Country, Contemporary Country
Fiddler Tammy Rogers was born in Tennessee in 1966 and raised in Irving, TX. As an adolescent, she was taught classical music but also performed regularly with her family

at bluegrass festivals. After graduating college, she joined Patty Loveless' backing band, which she followed with a stint backing Trisha Yearwood. After leaving Yearwood, Rogers became a prominent session musician, supporting Kieran Kane on both his final record for Atlantic Records and on his subsequent tour. When Kane was dropped by Atlantic, he formed his own label, Dead Reckoning, and Rogers soon became one of the company's first signings. Her 1995 debut, *In the Red*, was a collaborative instrumental effort with noted session drummer Don Heffington; her next effort, an eponymously titled 1996 effort, featured both her songwriting and vocal skills. *—Jason Ankeny*

● **In the Red** / 1995 / Dead Reckoning ♦♦♦♦
It is natural but unfortunate that *In the Red* is generally reviewed and regarded as a Tammy Rogers solo release. It is the fate of percussionists to be underappreciated, but she gave credit where credit was due. This release is credited to both Tammy Rogers and Don Heffington, and with good reason. He wrote or co-wrote half the tunes here, and his tasteful playing adds color and depth to pieces that cross the sonic spectrum from Tex-Mex to country to Middle Eastern music. They are wonderful together, his bodhran playing the kind of melody lines usually reserved for the bass guitar on "Get Out While You Can" while she plays an Arabic-inspired fiddle line. Though she has been pigeonholed as a country artist, Rogers shows herself adept at a variety of instruments and styles. When the two do play country music here, they give it some delightful twists, as in "John's Tune," where she plays the Norwegian Hardanger fiddle and he plays Irish bodhran. It does sound like country music, albeit with undeniable and interesting influences. Rogers and Heffington each take one vocal turn, both on original gospel pieces, and though hers is by far the more accomplished, both are effective and sound heartfelt. *In the Red* has simplicity of theme and subtlety of execution, plus 11 great original tunes and one classic. This CD is a must-have for anyone who appreciates instrumental bluegrass and Americana. *—Richard Foss*

Tammy Rogers / Jun. 1996 / Dead Reckoning ♦♦♦

Linda Ronstadt

b. Jul. 15, 1946, Tucson, AZ

Vocals / Country-Rock, Country-Pop, Adult Contemporary, Soft Rock, Folk-Rock, Pop/Rock, Traditional Pop

With roots in the Los Angeles country and folk-rock scenes, Linda Ronstadt became one of the most popular interpretive singers of the '70s, earning a string of platinum-selling albums and Top 40 singles. Throughout the '70s, her laid-back pop never lost sight of her folky roots, yet as she moved into the '80s, she began to change her sound with the times, adding "new wave" influences. After a brief flirtation with pre-rock pop, Ronstadt settled into a pattern of adult contemporary pop and Latin albums, sustaining her popularity in both fields. While Ronstadt was a student at Arizona State University, she met guitarist Bob Kimmel. The duo moved to Los Angeles, where guitarist/songwriter Kenny Edwards joined the pair. Calling themselves the Stone Poneys, the group became a leading attraction on California's folk circuit, recording their first album in 1967. The band's second album, *Evergreen, Vol. 2*, featured the Top 20 hit "Different Drum," which was written by Michael Nesmith. After recording one more album with the group, Ronstadt left for a solo career at the end of 1968.

Ronstadt's first two solo albums—*Hand Sown Home Grown* (1969) and *Silk Purse* (1970)—accentuated her country roots, featuring several honky tonk numbers. Released in 1971, her self-titled third album was a pivotal record in her career. Featuring a group of session musicians that would later form the Eagles, the album was a softer, more laid-back variation of the country-rock she had been recording. With the inclusion of songs from singer/songwriters like Jackson Browne, Neil Young, and Eric Anderson, *Linda Ronstadt* had folk-rock connections as well. *Don't Cry Now*, released in 1973, followed the same formula to greater success, yet it was 1974's *Heart Like a Wheel* that perfected the sound, making Ronstadt a star. Featuring the hit covers "You're No Good," "When Will I Be Loved," and "It Doesn't Matter Anymore," *Heart Like a Wheel* reached number one and sold over two-million copies.

Released in the fall of 1975, *Prisoner in Disguise* followed the same pattern as *Heart Like a Wheel* and was nearly as successful. *Hasten Down the Wind*, released in 1976, suggested a holding pattern, even if it charted higher than *Prisoner in Disguise*. *Simple Dreams* (1977) expanded the formula by adding a more rock-oriented supporting band, which breathed life into the Rolling Stones' "Tumbling Dice" and Warren Zevon's "Poor Poor Pitiful Me." The record became the singer's biggest hit, staying on the top of the charts for five weeks and selling over three-million copies. With *Living in the U.S.A.* (1978), Ronstadt began experimenting with new wave. recording Elvis Costello's "Alison"; the album was another number-one hit. On 1980's *Mad Love*, she made a full-fledged new wave record, recording three Costello songs and adopting a synth-laden sound. While the album was a commercial success, it signalled that her patented formula was beginning to run out of steam. That suspicion was confirmed with 1982's *Get Closer*, her first album since *Heart Like a Wheel* to fail to go platinum. Sensing it was time to change direction, Ronstadt starred in the Broadway production of Gilbert & Sullivan's *Pirates of Penzance*, as well as the accompanying movie. *Pirates of Penzance* led the singer to a collaboration with Nelson Riddle, who arranged and conducted her 1983 collection of pop standards, *What's New*. While it received lukewarm reviews, it was a considerable hit, reaching number three on the charts and selling over two-million copies. Ronstadt's next two albums—*Lush Life* (1984) and *For Sentimental Reasons* (1986)—were also albums of pre-rock standards recorded with Riddle.

At the end of 1986, Ronstadt returned to contemporary pop, recording "Somewhere Out There," the theme to the animated *An American Tail*, with James Ingram; the single became a number-two hit. She also returned to her country roots in 1987, recording the *Trio* album with Dolly Parton and Emmylou Harris. That same year, Ronstadt recorded *Canciones de Mi Padre*, a set of traditional Mexican songs that became a surprise hit. Two years later, she recorded *Cry Like a Rainstorm—Howl Like the Wind*—her first contemporary pop album since 1982's *Get Closer*. Featuring four duets with Aaron Neville, including the number-two hit "Don't Know Much," the album sold over two-million copies. Ronstadt returned to traditional Mexican and Spanish material with *Mas Canciones* (1991) and *Frenesi* (1992). She returned to pop with 1994's *Winter Light*, which failed to generate a hit single, as did 1995's *Feels Like Home*. In 1996, she released the children's album *Dedicated to the One I Love*; *We Ran* followed in 1998. Two years later, Ronstadt delivered the holiday collection *A Merry Little Christmas*. *—Stephen Thomas Erlewine*

Hand Sown Home Grown / 1969 / Capitol ♦♦
Linda Ronstadt's debut album is a transitional effort, as the vocalist began to abandon the folk leanings of the Stone Poneys for a relaxed country-rock approach. Several of the songs are well performed, but the majority of the music is unfocused and Ronstadt occasionally sounds unsure of herself. *—Stephen Thomas Erlewine*

Silk Purse / 1970 / Capitol ♦♦♦
While it followed the same musical approach of the debut, *Silk Purse* was an improvement on *Hand Sown Home Grown*, featuring more confident vocals from Linda Ronstadt and a stronger selection of songs, including "Lovesick Blues" and "Long Long Time." *—Stephen Thomas Erlewine*

Linda Ronstadt / 1971 / Capitol ♦♦♦
Linda Ronstadt's self-titled third album captured the singer moving away from the rootsier charms of her first two albums, toward a more polished take on country-rock. Supported by the Eagles throughout the record, Ronstadt turns in a strong performance, aided by a fine selection of material, including "Rock Me on the Water," "Crazy Arms," "I Still Miss Someone," and "I Fall to Pieces." *—Stephen Thomas Erlewine*

Don't Cry Now / 1973 / Asylum ♦♦♦
Don't Cry Now expanded the poprock concessions of *Linda Ronstadt*, and the result was the singer's first genuine hit record, peaking at number 45 on the charts. *—Stephen Thomas Erlewine*

☆ **Heart Like a Wheel** / 1974 / Capitol ♦♦♦♦♦
Following the same formula as her early records, *Heart Like a Wheel* doesn't appear to be a great breakthrough on the surface. However, Ronstadt comes into her own on this mix of oldies and contemporary classics. Backed by a fleet of Los Angeles musicians, Ronstadt sings with vigor and passion, helping bring the music alive. But what really makes *Heart Like a Wheel* a breakthrough is the inventive arrangements that producer Peter Asher, Ronstadt, and the studio musicians have developed. Finding the right note for each song—whether it's the soulful reworking of "When Will I Be Loved," the hit "You're No Good," or the laid-back folk-rock of "Willing"—the musicians help turn *Heart Like a Wheel* into a veritable catalog of Californian soft rock, and it stands as a landmark of '70s mainstream pop/rock. *—Stephen Thomas Erlewine*

Different Drum / 1974 / Capitol ♦♦♦♦♦
Different Drum collects the highlights of Linda Ronstadt's first three solo albums, adding five Stone Poneys tracks, including the hit "Different Drum," for good measure. It misses some fine tracks from her solo records, but the album remains a fine introduction to her early years. *—Stephen Thomas Erlewine*

Prisoner in Disguise / 1975 / Asylum ♦♦♦♦♦
Linda Ronstadt followed the commercial and critical breakthrough success of *Heart Like a Wheel* with *Prisoner in Disguise*, a record that essentially repeated the formula of its predecessor. While it lacked the consistency of *Heart Like a Wheel*, it was thoroughly enjoyable, highlighted by sturdy remakes of the Motown classics "Tracks of My Tears" and "Heat Wave." *—Stephen Thomas Erlewine*

● **Greatest Hits, Vol. 1** / 1976 / Asylum ♦♦♦♦♦
Greatest Hits, Vol. 1 is a good 12-track collection of Linda Ronstadt's biggest hits from the early '70s, beginning with the Stone Poneys' "Different Drum" and running through "Tracks of My Tears," from 1975's *Prisoner in Disguise*. In between, all of her best-known songs—"You're No Good," "When Will I Be Loved," "Heat Wave"—are included, plus selected minor hits, making it an excellent overview of her peak years. *—Stephen Thomas Erlewine*

Hasten Down the Wind / 1976 / Asylum ♦♦♦
Again, Linda Ronstadt repeats her slick, Californian pop/country-rock formula on *Hasten Down the Wind*. When the material is first-rate—such as "That'll Be the Day" or "Crazy"—Ronstadt's performances are terrific, but on the subpar songs—such as the three Karla Bonoff numbers—she's dragged down with her material. *—Stephen Thomas Erlewine*

Simple Dreams / 1977 / Asylum ♦♦♦♦♦
Featuring a broader array of styles than any previous Linda Ronstadt record, *Simple Dreams* reconfirms her substantial talents as an interpretive singer. Ronstadt sings Dolly Parton ("I Never Will Marry") with the same conviction as the Rolling Stones ("Tumbling Dice"), and she manages to update Roy Orbison ("Blue Bayou") and direct attention to the caustic, fledgling singer/songwriter Warren Zevon ("Poor Poor Pitiful Me" and "Carmelita"). The consistently adventurous material and Ronstadt's powerful performance makes the record rival *Heart Like a Wheel* in sheer overall quality. *—Stephen Thomas Erlewine*

Living in the U.S.A. / 1978 / Asylum ♦♦♦
On *Living in the U.S.A.*, Linda Ronstadt made the ill-advised move to incorporate some current musical trends, such as new wave, into her successful formula. While some of the record sounds good, the majority of the album is poorly executed, particularly her take on Elvis Costello's "Alison." *—Stephen Thomas Erlewine*

Greatest Hits, Vol. 2 / 1980 / Asylum ♦♦♦♦♦
Picking up where the first volume left off, *Greatest Hits, Vol. 2* contains Linda Ronstadt's biggest hits from the late '70s, including such songs as "It's So Easy," "Hurt So Bad," "Blue

Bayou," "Back in the USA," "Poor Poor Pitiful Me," "Ooh Baby Baby," "How Do I Make You" and "Tumbling Dice." Since Ronstadt's late-'70s albums tended to be a little spottty, this is a very useful summation of their highlights. *—Stephen Thomas Erlewine*

Mad Love / 1980 / Asylum ✦✦✦

Released in 1980, *Mad Love* featured Linda Ronstadt taking on new wave with mixed results. At this point, her albums with producer Peter Asher became routine and repetitive. This album's predecessor, *Living in the U.S.A.*, hit the cutout bins, so a change was in order. While many may miss the customary Ronstadt here, most of *Mad Love* does indeed work. The insinuating "I Can't Let Go" and the playful "How Do I Make You" do help Ronstadt attain a certain cuteness and freshness. The biggest hit, the cover of Little Anthony & the Imperials' "Hurts So Bad," has a great vocal and is made even better by Danny Kortchmar's emotive guitar solos. While the originals and style of guitarist Mark Goldenberg did predominate, *Mad Love* is mostly known for its three Elvis Costello covers. Although the often pitch-perfect Ronstadt is more than antithetical to Costello's angst, she more than connects with "Party Girl." Costello's "Talking in the Dark" closes the album on an oddly sweet note. The strange thing about *Mad Love* is that it did include a lot of players from Ronstadt's previous albums. Kortchmar, Russ Kunkel, Andrew Gold, and Nicolette Larson's great backing vocals all appear here. For the most part, *Mad Love* stood the test of time and is certainly different from the Ronstadt albums that preceded and followed it. *—Jason Elias*

Get Closer / 1982 / Asylum ✦✦

Get Closer was another successful album for Ronstadt, even though it didn't perform up to her platinum standards. Part of the reason for the relative lack of success was the lackluster material, which again signals that Ronstadt had lost touch with the mainstream pop scene. *—Stephen Thomas Erlewine*

What's New / 1983 / Asylum ✦✦✦

Lush Life / 1984 / Asylum ✦✦

For Sentimental Reasons / Feb. 1986 / Asylum ✦✦

Round Midnight with Nelson Riddle and his Orchestra / 1986 / Asylum ✦✦✦

Canciones de Mi Padre / 1987 / Asylum ✦✦✦

Linda Ronstadt abandoned the pop audience in 1983, turning toward traditional pop music. She recorded three albums with Nelson Riddle before changing direction yet again, this time recording a set of traditional Mexican songs titled *Canciones de Mi Padre*. As the title suggests, the record is a fairly sentimental collection, since these are songs from her childhood and her heritage. Occasionally, Ronstadt oversells the songs but overall, the album is charming, affectionate, entertaining and more successful than her stilted Nelson Riddle collaborations. *—Stephen Thomas Erlewine*

Cry Like a Rainstorm—Howl Like the Wind / Sep. 1989 / Asylum ✦✦✦

Mas Canciones / 1990 / Elektra ✦✦✦

Mas Canciones is a thoroughly enjoyable collection of Spanish and Mexican songs that is arguably stronger than its predecessor, since Ronstadt sounds more comfortable with the material than ever before. *—Stephen Thomas Erlewine*

Frenesi / Aug. 25, 1992 / Elektra ✦✦

Winter Light / 1994 / Elektra ✦✦✦

Feels Like Home / Mar. 14, 1995 / Elektra ✦✦✦

Dedicated to the One I Love / Jun. 1996 / Elektra ✦✦✦

We Ran / Jun. 23, 1998 / Elektra ✦✦✦

Western Wall: The Tucson Sessions / Aug. 24, 1999 / Elektra ✦✦✦✦✦

Linda Ronstadt and Emmylou Harris have frequently collaborated over the course of their long careers. Their voices are made for each other in a yin-yang meeting of Ronstandt's rich velvet alto and Harris' songbird-sweet soprano. *The Tucson Sessions* takes their collaborations to new heights. A collection of covers and originals tracing various paths of love and loss, the performances seem to have breathed in the desert where they were recorded. Arrangements airy as the space between desert and sky are grounded by gritty guitars, splashed with color from folk instruments and filled with glorious harmonies. Well known singer/songwriters are covered—Patty Griffin, Andy Prieboy, Rosanne Cash, Leonard Cohen, and Bruce Springsteen. Traditional presentations of Cohen's "Sisters of Mercy" and Springsteen's "Across the Border" take on new dimensions as sung by women. The spare arrangement and delicate harmonies lend a wonderful wistfulness to Cash's "Western Wall." A surprising cover choice with beautiful results is Sinead O'Connor's "This Is to Mother You." The album's best track, "1917," was written by folksinger David Olney. It's impossible to imagine anyone else singing this haunting tale of soldiers and women in WWI. Fragile and breathtaking, Harris' voice is buoyed by the angelic harmonies of Ronstadt and Kate & Anna McGarrigle. Harris also contributes, along with some collaborators, three tracks to the album, notably the spirited "Raise the Dead." *—Theresa LaVeck*

The Linda Ronstadt Box Set / Nov. 16, 1999 / Elektra ✦✦✦✦

Linda Ronstadt's generically titled four-CD, five-hour, 86-track box set retrospective attempts with considerable success to encompass the many types of music she's sung from the mid-'60s to the late '90s. The album is divided into five unequal parts, with 31 tracks given over to an "Album Retrospective," followed by seven tracks from "The Nelson Riddle Sessions," her three albums of classic pop, then five songs "En Español," drawn from her three Spanish language albums. That takes up the first two discs, with the third disc consisting of 20 "Collaborations" and the fourth 23 "Rarities." It is significant that the first section is called "Album Retrospective," signaling to the listener that Ronstadt is not interested in presenting her hit singles as such. In fact, most of her chart hits do turn up somewhere on the set, but a whole chunk of them is missing. At the time that Ronstadt was peppering the singles charts in the late '70s, she caught flack for her covers of Motown and rock & roll standards, and she herself has disavowed her recordings of such work, so maybe it shouldn't be a surprise that she has chosen to forget "Heat Wave," "Tracks of My Tears," "That'll Be the Day," "It's So Easy," and even modern rock songs like "How Do I Make You," with "Back in the U.S.A." and "Tumbling Dice" included only in live versions. A critic can hardly object, but Ronstadt fans should note that, as a result, the box set will not allow them to throw their *Greatest Hits* albums away. Also, the omissions tend to make Ronstadt seem like more of a balladeer than she has been in her career. She is much more interested in emphasizing her non-rock work. The "Rarities" disc really only contains five previously unreleased songs, and they are hardly revelations, including outtakes of material written by the likes of J.D. Souther and Karla Bonoff, longtime Ronstadt favorites. But the disc does suggest the singer's range, from the art songs of Carla Bley and Philip Glass to theater songs from *The Pirates of Penzance* and *Randy Newman's Faust. The Linda Ronstadt Box Set* clearly had major input from the artist herself, and its contents may not be what a Ronstadt fan or chart researcher would have chosen. But it certainly makes the case for Ronstadt as a hard-working performer who constantly challenged herself by trying styles beyond the Southern California folk-rock for which she remains best known. *—William Ruhlmann*

● **The Very Best of Linda Ronstadt** / Sep. 24, 2002 / Rhino ✦✦✦✦✦

If Rhino had merely combined Linda Ronstadt's *Greatest Hits, Vol. 1* and *Vol. 2*, they would have a compilation that captured her at her peak. They didn't do that for 2002's *The Very Best of Linda Ronstadt*, but they did follow that basic blueprint very closely, with 16 of the 21 songs culled from her '70s heyday, with the remaining five drawing from her late-'80s/early-'90s adult contemporary comeback, including "Don't' Know Much" and "Somewhere out There." That these songs don't quite fit musically with the laid-back Californian soft rock of the '70s doesn't matter, nor does it matter that her excursions into other genres—her traditional pop albums with Nelson Riddle, her Mexican records, her country albums with Trio—are missing ("Different Drum" with the Stone Poneys is here), because this collection expertly delivers her biggest hits in an enjoyable fashion with very little fat. Those original hits records remain first-rate, but it's nicer to get all of these on one disc instead of two. *—Stephen Thomas Erlewine*

Peter Rowan

b. Jul. 4, 1942, Boston, MA

Guitar, Mandolin, Vocals / Neo-Traditional Folk, Progressive Bluegrass, Contemporary Folk

A major cult figure among progressive bluegrass aficionados, Peter Rowan participated in a number of adventurous projects in the late '60s and '70s before embarking on a highly productive solo career. Primarily a guitarist, Rowan also sang, yodeled, and played various members of the mandolin family. He was born in 1942 and grew up in Weyland, MA, near Boston; his parents and several relatives were musicians, and he and his brothers Chris and Lorin grew up playing both rock and bluegrass together. Rowan also formed a Tex-Mex band called the Cupids in high-school, and after college he sang and played mandolin in the folk group the Mother Bay State Entertainers, whom he joined in 1963. He also played with Jim Rooney and Bill Keith, and in 1964 he joined Bill Monroe's legendary Blue Grass Boys as a vocalist and guitarist. He departed in 1967 to team up with mandolin virtuoso David Grisman in the eclectic, progressive-minded folk-rock band Earth Opera, who released two albums and often opened for the Doors.

Rowan next moved to the San Francisco Bay Area and joined Seatrain, a bluegrass/rock hybrid outfit. He appeared on two albums over 1970-1971, then left to play with Jerry Garcia and Grisman in the bluegrass group Old & In the Way, also joining Grisman in Muleskinner. In 1975, Rowan teamed with his brothers Chris and Lorin in the progressive bluegrass unit the Rowans, who released several acclaimed albums over the next few years. Rowan also performed with Flaco Jimenez in Mexican Airforce and issued his first two solo albums—1978's *Peter Rowan* and 1980's *Medicine Trail*—on Flying Fish. He issued the Tex-Mex project *Texican Badman* on Appaloosa in 1981 as well as an album with his Nashville-based group, the Wild Stallions. *The Walls of Time* was released in 1982, the first in a long string of albums for the Sugar Hill label that lasted well into the '90s.

Among the more notable, 1985's *The First Whippoorwill* was an affectionate tribute to Monroe, while 1988's *New Moon Rising* became the signature album of Rowan's solo career, featuring some of his most popular material. 1990's *Dust Bowl Children* was a completely solo performance, while 1991's *All on a Rising Day* continued his creative hot streak. Several more albums followed through 1996, including one, 1994's *Tree on a Hill*, that reunited him with Chris and Lorin; another, 1996's *Yonder*, paired him with dobro king Jerry Douglas for a set of duets. Rowan took a break from his solo career for a few years but continued to guest on albums by other artists, including the Czech folk group Druha Trava. He returned in 2002 with *High Lonesome Cowboy*, a collaborative effort with Don Edwards for Shanachie that also featured Tony Rice and Norman Blake. *—Steve Huey*

Peter Rowan / 1978 / Flying Fish ✦✦✦

The solo debut album of this bluegrass vocalist features an original mixture of styles and backing from Flaco Jimenez, Richard Greene, and Tex Logan. *—AMG*

Medicine Trail / 1980 / Flying Fish ✦✦✦

Texican Badman / 1981 / Appaloosa ✦✦✦✦

The Walls of Time / 1982 / Sugar Hill ✦✦✦

Walls of Time is a fine slice of traditional bluegrass and country, performed by several of the finest newgrass performers, including Sam Bush, Ricky Skaggs, and the Rowan siblings. Though the album focuses on vocal material, not instrumental, it remains an enjoyable, heartfelt evocation of classic bluegrass by some of the very best progressive bluegrass musicians of the '70s and '80s. *—Thom Owens*

Red Hot Pickers / 1984 / Sugar Hill ✦✦✦

Joining Rowan on this 1995 release are the Red Hot Pickers, a group comprised of Richard Greene, Roger Mason, Andy Statman, and Tony Trischka. The record marks a reunion for Rowan and Greene, both of whom were Blue Grass Boys with Bill Monroe before joining forces in Earth Opera, Seatrain and Muleskinner. —*Jason Ankeny*

The First Whippoorwill / 1985 / Sugar Hill ✦✦✦

The First Wippoorwill is a tribute album by Peter Rowan to his mentor, Bill Monroe, and it is one of the most moving salutes ever recorded in country music. It isn't moving purely in sentimental terms, either—what makes the record so successful is how Rowan affectionately demonstrates his debt to Monroe with invigorating, lively performances instead of treating the music as a museum piece. Rowan assembled a crackerjack backing band—featuring Buddy Spicher, Sam Bush, Roy Huskey Jr., Bill Keith, and Richard Greene—which helps him make one of the best, most focused records of his career. —*Thom Owens*

● **New Moon Rising** / 1988 / Sugar Hill ✦✦✦✦✦

Ex-Blue Grass Boy and Seatrain member Peter Rowan is captured here at the very top of his game. Aided by the then-fledgling Nashville Bluegrass Band, Rowan sets out to create a quality, original yet traditional bluegrass record and creates a classic. Such a force was this album in bluegrass circles, that Rowan and the Nashville Bluegrass Band, by popular demand, performed many of these songs at bluegrass festivals for the next decade. Whatever song style the Rowan pen attempts the Rowan pen nails. Whether it is straight-ahead grass like "That High Lonesome Sound," unapologetic gospel such as "Jesus Made the Wine," or wistful ballads like "Meadow Green" and the extraordinary title track, his writing is hitting on all eight. The Nashville Bluegrass Band's harmony singing, always their specialty, is especially potent here. Their floating, shifting harmonies on the title track are nothing short of transcendent. In Pat Enright and Alan O'Bryant, NBB boasts two of the best singers in bluegrass. NBB's Stuart Duncan on fiddle has become the standard for bluegrass violin, and splits his time with NBB as probably the most in-demand fiddle session player alive. Non-NBB member Jerry Douglas, a frequent Rowan partner in later years, abets on sliding, snaking dobro. In the past 20 years, Douglas' dobro has become the pre-eminent voice in bluegrass instrumentation. —*Steve Cooper*

Dust Bowl Children / 1990 / Sugar Hill ✦✦✦

All on a Rising Day / 1991 / Sugar Hill ✦✦✦✦✦

Tree on a Hill / 1994 / Sugar Hill ✦✦✦

Rowan & Wild Stallions / Jan. 22, 1996 / Appaloosa ✦✦✦

Yonder / Apr. 1996 / Sugar Hill ✦✦

Bluegrass Boy / Sep. 24, 1996 / Sugar Hill ✦✦✦✦

High Lonesome Cowboy / Sep. 10, 2002 / Shanachie ✦✦✦✦

The four men gracing the cover of *High Lonesome Cowboy* look more like farmers than musicians. The black-and-white photography, desert surroundings, and the old truck the old timers are leaning against evoke the West circa 1940 or so. This spare environment of the cover, in fact, mirrors the lean setting of the disc within. Don Edwards, Peter Rowan, Tony Rice, Norman Blake, and Billy & Bryn Bright join together to sing a fistful of Western favorites like "Goodbye Old Paint" and "The Old Chisholm Trail." The beauty of the entire project is its simplicity and non-pretentiousness. Edwards can be flamboyant vocalist, a Caruso of the plains. Here, however, he tones things down a bit, opting for a mellower approach to match Rowan's off-the-cuff style. Indeed, their voices work very well together and the unadorned style of the album sneaks up on the listener, much in the way a Norman & Nancy Blake album does. Lovely versions of "Midnight on the Stormy Deep" and "The Night Guard" give the impression of a couple of old cowhands sitting around the Coleman lantern as bright stars dot the summer sky. One might guess that there would be a lot of fancy picking with Rice and Blake on board, but this isn't the case. Rice only shows up on a few cuts, and Blake's work is always integrated into the tapestry of tumbleweeds and cactus blossoms. *High Lonesome Cowboy* is a low-key effort filled with simple music that runs deep. Fans of spare Western fare will want to round up a copy. —*Ronnie D. Lankford Jr.*

The Rowans

f. 1972, Boston, MA, **db.** 1982

Group / Progressive Bluegrass

Progressive bluegrass group the Rowans consisted of harmonizing brothers Peter (guitar, most members of the mandolin family), Lorin (guitar), and Chris (guitar, flute). All three grew up in the small Massachusetts town of Weyland, near Boston, and played rock and bluegrass music together. Peter played with several folk bands in the New England area, joined Bill Monroe's band for a time, then teamed up with mandolin virtuoso David Grisman in the folk-rock outfit Earth Opera during the late '60s and early '70s. Lorin and Chris, meanwhile, teamed up as the folk/pop/country-rock duo the Rowan Brothers in the early '70s. With Grisman in tow, they relocated to the San Francisco Bay Area and scored a record deal with CBS, helped in part by an endorsement from Grisman's old cohort Jerry Garcia.

The Rowan Brothers' self-titled debut was released in 1972, with Grisman producing under the alias David Diadem, and they opened for the Grateful Dead. By 1975, brother Peter was between projects, and he joined his brothers as the renamed trio the Rowans. Their eponymous debut together was released on Asylum in 1975 and received highly positive reviews for its progressive, sometimes jazzy leanings and extended compositions. The 1976 follow-up, *Sibling Rivalry*, was equally acclaimed, but most critics agreed that 1977's *Jubilations* halted the trio's creative hot streak. They subsequently parted ways with Asylum and issued two more albums on the small Appaloosa label in 1980 before disbanding to pursue other projects. The Rowans reunited periodically for performances, particularly in the late '80s, and in 1994 (as Peter Rowan & the Rowan Brothers) recorded *Tree on a Hill* for the Sugar Hill roots label. —*Steve Huey*

The Rowan Brothers / 1972 / CBS ✦✦✦✦

Released in 1972, the Rowan Brothers' eponymous debut arrived with a great deal of hype, including an ad featuring a quote from Jerry Garcia in which he stated that Chris & Lorin Rowan "could be like the Beatles. They're that good." Produced by Bill Wolf and David Grisman (credited as David Diadem), the first effort from the Stinson Beach, CA, duo never even came close to living up to such lofty praise. Though it can give a young artist a boost, this sort of hype can quite often be devastating, and probably hurt the pair in the long run. *The Rowan Brothers* is a mix of country-rock, folk, and pop tunes with cosmic ("the universe is nothing but a fantasy/of life's illusions throughout eternity") and hippie ("we'll put on our costumes, bring the music along/come on friends we'll sing a happy song") underpinnings, which are often trite and very much artifacts of the time. Although they may lack lyrical muscle, Chris & Lorin are capable of pleasant, catchy tunes that can be light and spirited or lush and pretty. Ignored at the time and somewhat dated today, *The Rowan Brothers* is another forgotten relic from the late-'60s and early-'70s San Francisco music scene. —*Brett Hartenbach*

● **The Rowans** / 1975 / Asylum ✦✦✦

Joined by brother Peter, Chris & Lorin Rowan signed with Asylum Records for their second outing, this time as the Rowans. Peter injects a bit more substance into the material, although it follows the same folk and country-rock leanings of its predecessor. Once again, Chris & Lorin offer a collection of sincere, tuneful, albeit slight songs, while Peter delivers three of the album's best cuts, including "Beggar in Bluejeans," "Thunder on the Mountain" and the near-classic "Midnight, Moonlight" (also released that same year as part of the great bluegrass project *Old & In the Way* and a few years later on his solo debut). —*Brett Hartenbach*

Sibling Rivalry / 1976 / Asylum ✦✦✦

In 1976, following their somewhat tepid debut as a trio, brothers Peter, Chris, & Lorin Rowan put together their best record, *Sibling Rivalry*. Chris and Lorin show real growth as songwriters with this record, and along with Peter, concentrate on what each does best. Chris' light yet infectious folk-pop love song "If I Only Could" and the swinging "Ya Ba Da Ba" are his best tunes to date, while Lorin, who had developed into a fine guitarist, is at the top of his game with "Sword of Faith/Soldier of the Cross" as well as his collaborations with Peter. Peter, whose material was the highlight of the trio's previous record, delivers another fine batch of songs, including the folk narrative "Joaquin Murrieta," "No Desanimes Amor (Don't Disappoint Love)," and the understated Appalachian tale "Tired Hands" (co-written with Lorin). *Sibling Rivalry*, which has been deleted for years, is the one album to hunt down if you're interested in checking out the Rowans or just this phase of Peter's long and varied career. —*Brett Hartenbach*

Jubilations / 1977 / Asylum ✦✦

With 1976's *Sibling Rivalry*, the Rowans seemed to be hitting their stride collectively and individually, which makes the limp *Jubilation* all the more disappointing. Excursions into light R&B, world music and the jazz/swing of Stephane Grappelli (Grappelli guests on the album's best track, "Don't Say Goodbye") aren't enough to save the record, which is riddled with hackneyed ideas and clichés. Titles such as "Best of Friends," "Give Ya Good Lovin'" and "Makin' It Easy" pretty much tell you everything you need to know about these songs. Even Peter, who has always been at the very least an intelligent lyricist, is rather unimaginative here, although it's his "Don't Say Goodbye" and the lovely "Love's Secret Sighs" that are rare highlights. *Jubilation* was the group's last recording for Asylum. —*Brett Hartenbach*

Dave & Sugar Rowland

f. 1975

Group / Country-Pop

Dave & Sugar were one of the most popular vocal groups in country music from the mid-'70s through the early '80s. Lead singer Dave Rowland was the group's one constant, while the two females comprising Sugar were subject to frequent change. Rowland was the son of a minister who began his career singing with a dance band. He was drafted in the mid-'60s and became a trumpet player with an Army band, and also formed his own group while stationed at Fort Belvoir, Virginia. In 1970, Rowland graduated from the Stamps Music School in Texas and then headed for Nashville, where he joined the Stamps Quartet. In 1974 he left the Stamps to join the more country-oriented Four Guys, singing behind Charley Pride and appearing on the *Grand Ole Opry*. After leaving the group, he worked as a singing waiter at Papa Leone's in Nashville, later forming a country-rock band, Wild Oates. When Rowland learned that Pride and Tammy Wynette were looking for backup groups, he formed the first incarnation of Sugar with Jackie Frantz and Vicki Hackeman. It was Pride who helped Dave & Sugar sign to RCA in 1975; that year the trio released their first single, the Shel Silverstein-penned "Queen of the Silver Dollar," and had a Top 25 hit.

Over the next few years, the threesome had many hits, including "I'm Gonna Love You," "That's the Way Love Should Be," and "I'm Knee Deep in Loving You." In 1977, Frantz tired of touring and was replaced by Sue Powell; the following year, Hackeman was replaced by Melissa Dean, and Dave & Sugar had their first number-one hit, "Tear Time." They had their second number one with "Golden Tears" in 1979; after touring with Kenny Rogers in 1980, a regular succession of personnel turnovers began. Dave & Sugar's last bit of chart success came in 1981 with two Top 40 hits, including "It's a Heartache," and the Top Ten hit "Fool By Your Side." Later, Rowland's label Elektra talked him into recording the solo album *Sugar Free*, which produced two unsuccessful singles. He then reunited with Dean and Powell without much success, so he created a new Sugar with Cindy Smith and Lisa Alvey. The latest Sugar lineup included Regina Leigh and Lori Mason. —*Sandra Brennan*

Dave & Sugar / 1976 / Dot ✦✦✦✦✦

The debut album from "the country ABBA," *Dave & Sugar* contains all of the trio's biggest hits as well as several excellent album tracks. Leader Dave Rowland has a classically deep, weepy country delivery, at times sounding like a cross between Kenny Rogers and Gary Stewart. Sugar (singers Jackie Frantz and Vickie Baker, with help from Sue Powell and Melissa Dean) have voices ideally matched to Rowland's and weave lead, backing, and harmony parts into a seamless and cohesive whole. The uncredited Nashville studio cats do a fine job of providing steadily grooving and sympathetic backing throughout, particularly on the classic "The Door Is Always Open," which features some fine twangin' guitar. Producers Jerry Bradley and Charley Pride occasionally are a little too liberal with the schmaltzy strings and reverb-drenched piano, but for the most part, the album successfully straddles a fine line between Nashville sound heartache and '70s cheese-pop. The material here is generally first-rate (writers include Bob McDill, Shel Silverstein, Johnny Duncan, and several others from Nashville's A list), and when Rowland, Frantz, and Baker join forces on the inevitable big chorus, the effect is often spine tingling. *—Pemberton Roach*

That's the Way Love Should Be / 1977 / RCA ✦✦✦

Stay With Me/Golden Tears / 1979 / RCA ✦✦✦

New York Wine, Tennessee Shine / 1980 / RCA ✦✦✦

Pleasure / 1981 / Elektra ✦✦✦

Sugar Free / 1982 / Elektra ✦✦✦

Anthology / Oct. 13, 1998 / Renaissance ✦✦✦✦✦
The budget-priced *Anthology* is a definitive overview of Dave & Sugar's country-pop smashes of the late 1970s, its 23 tracks assembling all of the group's smash hits for RCA. In addition to the chart-toppers "The Door Is Always Open" and "Golden Tears," the set also includes the Top Ten smashes "I'm Gonna Love You," "Don't Throw It All Away," "I'm Knee Deep in Loving You" and "Gotta Quit Looking at You Baby"—an excellent collection for new listeners and longtime fans alike. *—Hank Small*

● **Dave & Sugar/Greatest Hits** / RCA ✦✦✦✦✦
Greatest Hits is a solid collection of Dave & Sugar's best moments and works both as a career overview and an introduction to their sound. *—Stephen Thomas Erlewine*

Billy Joe Royal

b. Apr. 3, 1942, Valdosta, GA
Vocals / Pop-Soul, Country-Pop
Best known for his country-flavored rock hit "Down in the Boondocks," Billy Joe Royal had a long career that saw him become one of the first pop performers to successfully revive his commercial fortunes by turning to straight country music. Although he never had another hit as successful as "Down in the Boondocks," he racked up about 15 singles that hit the country charts over the course of the 1980s. Royal was born into a family of musical entertainers in Valdosta, GA, and made his debut on his uncle's radio show at the age of 11. He learned to play steel guitar and joined the Georgia Jubilee in Atlanta at 14, performing with Joe South, Jerry Reed, and Ray Stevens, among several other artists. Royal had his own rock & roll band in high-school and was regularly singing around Atlanta by the age of 16. He also spent time in Savannah, where he was influenced by African-American vocal styles and began to develop his distinctive vocal sound. Performing at a nightclub that also booked Sam Cooke and other African-American stars, Royal observed their vocal moves and began to practice them on his own time.

In 1962, he recorded an independent single that went unnoticed. Royal and South roomed together for a time, and two or three years later South contacted him with a song he wanted Royal to sing as a demo, in the hope that Gene Pitney would record it. Royal flew from Cincinnati (where he was working at the time) to Atlanta and cut "Down in the Boondocks," whose churchy echo resulted from the use during recording of a large septic tank that had been dragged into the studio.The demo ended up at Columbia, and the label signed Royal to a six-year deal. The song became Royal's breakthrough single, reaching number nine on the pop charts and briefly making the vocalist into a teen idol. Following its success, Royal had a string of lesser hits, including the Top 40 pop singles "I Knew You When," "I've Got to Be Somebody," and "Cherry Hill Park."

By the end of the decade, Royal's star waned, and he became a regular performer in Las Vegas and around Lake Tahoe. He also did a bit of acting on television, in feature films, and in commercials. In 1978, he recorded a cover of "Under the Boardwalk" and scored a minor hit. The wrong-side-of-the-tracks theme of "Down in the Boondocks" was a familiar one to country audiences, and during the early '80s Royal worked on establishing himself as a country artist. In 1984, he broke through when he recorded the Gary Burr composition "Burned Like a Rocket"; it was picked up by the Atlantic label, which signed Royal to a contract. The single became a hit and reached the country Top Ten in early 1986. Over the next two years he had a string of Top 40 hits, breaking into the Top Ten in late 1987 once again with "I'll Pin a Note on Your Pillow." In 1989, Royal released the album *Tell It Like Is*; the title cut, a remake of the venerable soul standard, became his biggest hit, peaking at number two, while the album itself stayed in the Top 15 for over a year. By 1990, Royal's style of pop-inflected country had been replaced by neo-traditional honky tonk at the top of the charts, and his popularity began to decline.

He continued to have minor hits into 1992 and toured into the 2000s. Royal launched a comeback with the 1998 album *Stay Close to Home* on the Intersound label, following up with the independent release *Now and Then, Then and Now* in 2001. "I know exactly what George Jones feels. But I know exactly what Ray Charles feels, too," Royal once said, and by the beginning of the new century, a host of reissues of Royal's work testified to his status as a vocal craftsman whose success transcended genre. *—Sandra Brennan & James Manheim*

Down in the Boondocks / 1965 / Trace ✦✦✦✦
Albums in the early '60s were often put out only after an artist had a couple of hits which could be packaged with other tunes. This is what appears to have been the case with *Down in the Boondocks*, with the album containing the title hit, as well as "I Knew You When," but some of the other songs here showed promise as well. Produced by Joe South, the record is well worth seeking out. *—James Chrispell*

Cherry Hill Park / 1969 / Columbia ✦✦✦

The Royal Treatment / 1987 / Atlantic ✦✦✦

Looking Ahead / 1987 / Atlantic ✦✦✦
A very dated, sometimes rather slick, production of many good tunes is what awaits you on *Looking Ahead*. Billy Joe Royal did have hits with some of these tunes, too, and rightly so. While not his best, the record kept his name before the audience at a time when other long-established artists were falling by the wayside. *—James Chrispell*

Tell It Like It Is / 1989 / Atlantic ✦✦✦
Features include "He Don't Know," "'Till I Can't Take It Anymore," "Are We There Yet?," and others. *—AMG*

● **Greatest Hits** / 1989 / Columbia ✦✦✦✦✦
This is the first official Billy Joe Royal greatest-hits package, released by Columbia in 1989. All of his early soul/country/pop hits are included: "Down in the Boondocks," "Cherry Hill Park," "Yo-Yo," "Hush," and his final hit for the label, a cover of the Drifters' classic "Under the Boardwalk." As a companion piece, pick up Royal's *Greatest Hits* (Atlantic), covering his country hits from the '90s. *—Al Campbell*

● **Greatest Hits** / 1991 / Atlantic ✦✦✦✦✦
Not to be confused with the *Greatest Hits* collection that Columbia released in 1989, this 1991 CD focuses on Billy Joe Royal's Atlantic output of the 1980s. Although this pop and pop-country material on the whole is much too slick, hits like "Old Bridges Run Deep," "'Til I Can't Take It Any More," and "Burned Like a Rocket" are likable enough. The CD's excessive slickness doesn't erase the fact that Royal's voice has a highly soulful quality. Black R&B has had a major impact on his vocal style, and it's obvious that he's spent a lot of time listening to Aaron Neville (a major influence), as well as Sam Cooke and Al Green. In fact, one of the CD's high points is a cover of Neville's signature song, "Tell It Like It Is." (Royal and Simply Red leader Mick Hucknall may have gone down very different roads, but they do have a lot of common ground in terms of influences.) Not for country purists, this is a collection that pop and R&B fans will find to be a decent listen. *—Alex Henderson*

Greatest Hits / 1991 / Hollywood ✦✦✦

The Best of Billy Joe Royal / Dec. 1, 1995 / Sony Special Products ✦✦✦✦✦
Sony Music Special Products' *The Best of Billy Joe Royal* is a fine collection, containing all of his charting singles for Columbia—"Down in the Boondocks," "I Know You When," "I've Got to Be Somebody," "I Knew You When," "Heart's Desire," "Campfire Girls," "Hush," "Cherry Hill Park," "Tulsa"—plus two other fine cuts from his catalog. The end result is a near-definitive collection, one that works as both a retrospective and an introduction. *—Stephen Thomas Erlewine*

Down in the Boondocks/Cherry Hill Park / Jul. 1, 1997 / Collectables ✦✦✦✦
Billy Joe Royal's first two albums, *Down in the Boondocks* and *Cherry Hill Park*, were combined on this single-CD reissue by Collectables. Although the sound and the packaging could be a little better, this still is a fine way for collectors to pick up these two records on disc. *—Stephen Thomas Erlewine*

Super Hits / Sep. 19, 2000 / Atlantic ✦✦✦
As part of the Sony *Super Hits* series, these ten songs provide an adequate representation of singer Billy Joe Royal at a budget price. This collection includes the original '60s pop hits "Down in the Boondocks" and "Cherry Hill Park" along with his mid-'80s country comeback hits "I'll Pin a Note on Your Pillow," "Funny How Time Slips Away," and "'Till I Can't Take It Anymore." Royal's voice remained consistently strong throughout the years, making this a quality combination of his most successful output from two decades. *—Al Campbell*

● **The Very Best of: The Columbia Years 1965–1971** / Aug. 27, 2002 / Taragon ✦✦✦✦✦
The Very Best of: The Columbia Years 1965-1971 provides an adequate representation of singer Billy Joe Royal's pop/soul output prior to his mid-'80s country comeback. These 23 tracks include the original versions of his '60s hits "Down in the Boondocks" and "Cherry Hill Park," along with the lesser-known "I Knew You When," "I've Got to Be Somebody," and Joe South's tune "Yo-Yo" (which became a Top Five hit for the Osmonds in 1971). This a quality single-disc compilation highlighting Royal's output with Columbia. *—Al Campbell*

Run C&W

Group / Progressive Bluegrass, Contemporary Country, Country Comedy
As you might guess, Run C&W is a novelty country project, but it has nothing to do with the rap group its name comes from; instead, group members Crashen Burns, Wash Burns, Side Burns, and Rug Burns transform vintage soul classics into bluegrass-style twang. Of course, the Burns Brothers are fictional creations; the group is actually composed of ex-Eagle Bernie Leadon on banjo, ex-Amazing Rhythm Ace Russell Smith on lead vocals, and Nashville songwriting pros Vince Melamed and Jim Photoglo on various instruments. The group debuted for MCA in 1993 with *Into the Twangy-First Century*, concentrating mostly on humorous rearrangements but also offering the occasional parody, original song, and jokey lyrical aside. *Row Vs. Wade* followed in 1995, after which the group went their separate ways. *—Steve Huey*

● **Into the Twangy-First Century** / 1993 / MCA ✦✦✦✦
If you don't believe bluegrass versions of soul classics is an inspired gag, listen to the beginning of Run C&W's "Stop in the Name of Love" and imagine the possibilities. The quartet also rewrote Arthur Conley's "Sweet Soul Music" to poke fun and Lee Greenwood and Tanya Tucker, among others, and parodied Billy Ray Cyrus' "Achy Breaky Heart" with "Itchy Twitchy Spot." *—Brian Mansfield*

Row Vs. Wade / 1995 / MCA ✦✦✦
As the name suggests, Run C&W is a parody of rap and soul, taking standard hip-hop lingo and forcing them into a country format. Like most comedy records, it's vaguely

amusing at first and runs thin near the end of the disc. Fortunately, the group's instrumental acumen saves the record from ever being tedious, even when the jokes are sophomoric. —*Thom Owens*

Bobby Russell

b. Apr. 19, 1941, Nashville, TN, d. Nov. 19, 1992
Songwriter, Vocals / Country-Pop
Songwriter Bobby Russell was born on April 19, 1941, in Nashville. His country-pop songwriting abilities produced several hits of the '60s and '70s. His first song to make an impact on the charts was a pop tune, "The Joker Went Wild," recorded in 1966 by teen idol Brian Hyland. Two years later Russell struck again with "Little Green Apples." It was first recorded by Roger Miller and was a Top Ten country hit in 1968, followed by O.C. Smith's version, which became a huge crossover pop record. The next release, the tearjerking "Honey" recorded by Bobby Goldsboro, hit number one on both the country and pop charts. In 1968 Russell signed to Elf Records and released his first album, *Words, Music, Laughter and Tears*. He stayed with the label until the following year, when he signed with the New York-based Bell Records and released the album *Dial-a-Hit*.

In 1971 Russell moved back to Nashville and hooked up with United Artists, scoring the country-pop hit "Saturday Morning Confusion." In 1973 he signed on with Columbia and also married pop singer/actress Vicki Lawrence, who had a number-one hit with Russell's composition "The Night the Lights Went Out in Georgia." Russell continued writing songs throughout the '80s, but by that time his glory days were behind him. He passed away on November 19, 1992, after suffering a heart attack. He was posthumously inducted into the Nashville Songwriters Hall of Fame in 1994. —*Al Campbell*

Words, Music, Laughter and Tears / 1968 / Elf ✦✦✦

● **Dial-A-Hit** / 1969 / Bell ✦✦✦✦
A compilation of Bell Records' tracks with the Box Tops' two biggest: "Cry Like a Baby" and "The Letter" book ending the other selections. Between the blue-eyed soul you have "I'll Be Sweeter Tomorrow (Than I Was Yesterday)," by the O'Jays, and the Delfonics' mournful "Break Your Promise" and jubilant "La, La Means I Love You." Along with James & Bobby Purify's raucous "Shake a Tail Feather," and some grits and eggs soul from Al Green by way of "Back Up Train." Numbers by Merrilee Rush, Bobby Russell, and the Masqueraders adds to the albums' diversity. —*Andrew Hamilton*

Saturday Morning Confusion / United Artists ✦✦✦

Johnny Russell

b. Jan. 23, 1940, Moorehead, MS, d. Jul. 3, 2001, Nashville, TN
Songwriter, Sax (Tenor), Vocals / Traditional Country, Country-Pop
Active as a performer and recording artist in the 1970s and 1980s, Johnny Russell was remembered for "Rednecks, White Socks, & Blue Ribbon Beer," perhaps country music's quintessential blue-collar anthem. He had several other moderate hits, but his greatest legacy was as a successful country songwriter whose compositions were recorded by artists ranging in time from Jim Reeves to George Strait. Russell was born and raised in the Mississippi Delta's Sunflower County. He heard the *Grand Ole Opry* as a youngster and was influenced by the music of Ernest Tubb, Lefty Frizzell, and Roy Acuff. His family moved to Fresno, CA, when Russell was 11, and he began to dream of a performing career. As a high-school student he took steps to realize his dreams—he entered and won various talent contests, and he began writing songs. Soon after turning 18 he recorded his first song, "In a Mansion Stands My Love," in 1958. The single had little impact, but it caught the attention of RCA producer and A&R czar Chet Atkins. Atkins suggested to Jim Reeves that he record the song, and it became the B-side of Reeves' monster 1960 hit "He'll Have to Go." That helped establish Russell's reputation as a songwriter, although his recording career on the ABC label went nowhere.

Russell's next major triumph came in 1963, when Buck Owens recorded Russell's "Act Naturally" (co-written with Voni Morrison of Owens' backing band) and had a number-one hit. Two years later, the Beatles covered the tune with country enthusiast Ringo Starr on vocals. The song had its genesis when Russell broke a date with a girlfriend when he was offered a recording session in Hollywood. "They're gonna put me in the movies," Russell explained apologetically to the girlfriend—and then wrote "Act Naturally" in a few minutes. Russell landed a staff songwriter position at the Wilburn Brothers' publishing house in Nashville, penning several hits in the late '60s and early '70s. These included the Wilburn Brothers' own "Hurt Her Once for Me." In 1971, Russell renewed his effort to become a recording star in his own right, and Atkins signed him to RCA. His debut single, "Mr. and Mrs. Untrue," and its follow-up, "What a Price," both became mid-level hits. Russell had his first Top 20 hit in 1973 with "Catfish John," and later that year "Rednecks, White Socks, & Blue Ribbon Beer" peaked in the Top Five and became his biggest hit. He had six more hits through 1975, including "Hello I Love You."

In 1977, he finished his stint at RCA with six more mid-range hits, including "The Son of Hickory Holler's Tramp." He then switched to Mercury and had a Top 30 hit with "How Deep in Love Am I?" He had several more hits with label, including "Here's to the Horses," but none of them made it past the Top 50. He continued to find success as a songwriter, however, teaming once again with Morrison for the Porter Wagoner/Dolly Parton duet "Making Plans." Russell adapted his honky tonk themes to the MOR sound that flourished around 1980. With Wayland Holyfield he co-wrote the major Statler Brothers hit "You'll Be Back Every Night (In My Dreams)," and he wrote or had a hand in such familiar numbers of that era as Gene Watson's "Got No Reason Now (For Going Home)" and the young George Strait's "Let's Fall to Pieces Together." In the mid-'80s, Russell joined the *Grand Ole Opry* as a comedy and vocal act, and in his later years he was a familiar sight in live appearances and on television, his 300-pound girth contained by colorful suspenders. Russell teamed up with Little David Wilkins in 1987 to record the minor hit "Butterbeans." Before the year was out, Russell had a mild stroke, and the following year he underwent surgery to remove a blockage from his chest. Still, he continued to perform and tour as before, serving as MC when Garth Brooks joined the *Opry* in 1990. As his health problems worsened in 2001, younger performers he had mentored, including Brooks and Vince Gill, gathered

for a benefit concert at the Grand Ole Opry House in Nashville. His untimely death at the age of 61 was due to complications surrounding diabetes. —*James Manheim*

Mr. & Mrs. Untrue / 1972 / RCA ✦✦✦

Catfish John / 1972 / RCA ✦✦✦

● **Rednecks, White Socks & Blue Ribbon Beer** / 1973 / RCA ✦✦✦✦
Russell is probably better known for the songs he's written or his appearances on country music television programs than as an artist. But this record is fun. From the liner notes that parody his most famous composition ("Act Naturally") and his girth, to the title track which just invites you to singalong. Not a landmark record but fun to listen to. —*Jim Worbois*

She's in Love With a Rodeo Man / 1974 / RCA ✦✦✦

Here Comes Johnny Russell / 1975 / RCA ✦✦✦✦

All-Time Greatest Hits / Mar. 13, 2002 / K-Tel ✦✦✦

Leon Russell (Claude Russell Bridges)

b. Apr. 2, 1942, Lawton, OK
Bass, Guitar, Piano, Keyboards, Vocals / Country-Rock, Singer/Songwriter, Pop/Rock, Album Rock
The ultimate rock & roll session man, Leon Russell's long and storied career includes collaborations with a virtual who's who of music icons spanning from Jerry Lee Lewis to Phil Spector to the Rolling Stones. A similar eclecticism and scope also surfaced in his solo work, which couched his charmingly gravelly voice in a rustic yet rich swamp-pop fusion of country, blues and gospel. Born Claude Russell Bridges on April 2, 1942, in Lawton, OK, he began studying classical piano at age three, a decade later adopting the trumpet and forming his first band. At 14, Russell lied about his age to land a gig at a Tulsa nightclub, playing behind Ronnie Hawkins & the Hawks before touring in support of Jerry Lee Lewis. Two years later, he settled in Los Angeles, studying guitar under the legendary James Burton and appearing on sessions with Dorsey Burnette and Glen Campbell. As a member of Spector's renowned studio group, Russell played on many of the finest pop singles of the 1960s, also arranging classics like Ike & Tina Turner's monumental "River Deep, Mountain High;" other hits bearing his input include the Byrds' "Mr. Tambourine Man," Gary Lewis & the Playboys' "This Diamond Ring," and Herb Alpert's "A Taste of Honey."

In 1967, Russell built his own recording studio, teaming with guitarist Marc Benno to record the acclaimed *Look Inside the Asylum Choir* LP. While touring with Delaney & Bonnie, he scored his first songwriting hit with Joe Cocker's reading of "Delta Lady," and in 1970, upon founding his own Shelter Records imprint, he also organized Cocker's legendary Mad Dogs and Englishmen tour. After the subsequent tour film earned Russell his first real mainstream notoriety, he issued a self-titled solo LP, and in 1971 appeared at George Harrison's Concert for Bangladesh following sessions for B.B. King, Eric Clapton, and Bob Dylan. After touring with the Rolling Stones, Russell increasingly focused on his solo career, reaching the number two spot with 1972's *Carney* and scoring his first pop hit with the single "Tight Rope." While the success of 1973's three-LP set *Leon Live* further established his reputation as a top concert draw, response to the country inspired studio effort *Hank Wilson's Back* was considerably more lukewarm, as was the reception afforded to 1974's *Stop All That Jazz*. 1975's *Will O' the Wisp*, however, restored his commercial luster, thanks in large part to the lovely single "Lady Blue."

In June of 1975, Russell married singer Mary McCreary; the following year the couple collaborated on *The Wedding Album*, issued through his newly formed Paradise Records label. Also in 1976, the Russell penned "This Masquerade" earned a Grammy Award for singer George Benson. He and McCreary reunited for 1977's *Make Love to the Music*, and upon completing the solo *Americana*, Russell teamed with Willie Nelson for 1979's *Willie & Leon*. He then spent the next two years touring with his bluegrass band, the New Grass Revival, issuing a live LP in 1981; although Paradise shut down later that year, the label was reactivated for 1984's *Hank Wilson, Vol. 2* and *Solid State*. Russell spent the remainder of the decade largely outside of music and did not resurface until issuing the Bruce Hornsby produced *Anything Can Happen* in 1992. The album appeared to little fanfare, however, and another long period of relative inactivity followed prior to the 1998 release of *Hank Wilson, Vol. 3: Legend in My Time*. *Face in the Crowd* appeared a year later. —*Jason Ankeny*

Leon Russell / 1970 / The Right Stuff ✦✦✦✦✦
Leon Russell never quite hit all the right notes the way he did on his eponymous debut. He never again seemed as convincing in his grasp of Americana music and themes, never again seemed as individual, and never again did his limited, slurred bluesy voice seem as ingratiating. He never again topped his triptych of "A Song for You," "Hummingbird," and "Delta Lady," nor did his albums contain such fine tracks as "Dixie Lullaby." Throughout it all, what comes across is Russell's idiosyncratic vision, not only in his approach but in his very construction—none of the songs quite play out as expected, turning country, blues, and rock inside out, not only musically but lyrically. Yes, his voice is a bit of an acquired taste, but it's only appropriate for a songwriter with enough chutzpah to write songs of his own called "I Put a Spell on You" and "Give Peace a Chance." And if there ever was a place to acquire a taste for Russell, it's here. —*Stephen Thomas Erlewine*

Leon Russell and the Shelter People / 1971 / The Right Stuff ✦✦✦✦✦
Leon Russell's accolades are monumental in a number of categories, from songwriting (he wrote Joe Cocker's "Delta Lady") to session playing (with the Rolling Stones and Bob Dylan, just to name a few) to his solo work. Unfortunately, it's the last category that never really attracted as much attention as it should have, despite a multitude of blues-based gospel recordings and piano-led, Southern-styled rock albums released throughout the 1970s. *Leon Russell and the Shelter People* is a prime example of Russell's instrumental dexterity and ability to produce some energetic rock & roll. Poignant and expressive tracks such as "Of Thee I Sing," "Home Sweet Oklahoma," and "She Smiles Like a River" all lay claim to Russell's soulful style and are clear-cut examples of the power that he musters through his spirited piano playing, and through his voice. His Dylan covers are just as

strong, especially "It's All Over Now, Baby Blue" and "It Takes a Lot to Laugh," while "Love Minus Zero/No Limit" and "It's a Hard Rain Gonna Fall" have him sounding so forceful they could have been Russell's own. A hearty, full-flavored gospel sound is amassed thanks to both the Shelter People and the Tulsa Tops who back Russell up on most of the tracks, but it's Russell alone that makes "The Ballad of Mad Dogs and Englishmen" such an expressive piece and the highlight of the album. On the whole, *Leon Russell and the Shelter People* is an entertaining and, more importantly, a revealing exposition of Russell's music when he was in his prime. The album that followed, 1972's *Carney*, is an introspective piece which holds up a little better from a songwriting standpoint, but this album does a better job at bearing his proficiency as a well-rounded musician. *—Mike DeGagne*

Asylum Choir II / Nov. 15, 1971 / The Right Stuff ✦✦✦✦
Of all Russell's early work as an artist, this record is the weakest; in particular, songs like "Tryin' to Stay Live" and "When You Wish Upon a Fag" feel dated. Nevertheless, *Asylum Choir II* is still a pretty nice record. Especially noteworthy is Russell's own version of "Hello, Little Friend"; Joe Cocker would later record the definitive version of the song. [The 1995 CD reissue features five bonus tracks.] *—Jim Worbois*

Carney / 1972 / The Right Stuff ✦✦✦✦
"Tight Rope" leads off *Carney*, and it's not just his biggest hit, it offers an excellent introduction to an off-kilter, confused, fascinating album. In a sense, it consolidates his two extremes, offering a side of fairly straightforward roots rock before delving headfirst into twisted psychedelia on the second side. On the whole, the second side deflates the first side, since it's just too fuzzy—it's intriguing, at least in parts, but it never adds up to anything. Besides, the first side is already odd enough, but in a meaningful way; here, his fascination with Americana sideshows is married to songs that work, instead of just being vehicles for tripping in the studio. Of course, part of what makes *Carney* interesting is that it contains a bit of both, but interesting doesn't equal compelling, as the whole of *Carney* bears out. *—Stephen Thomas Erlewine*

Hank Wilson's Back / 1973 / The Right Stuff ✦✦✦✦✦
Leon Russell knows something about country music. Born in Oklahoma, virtually all of the country and blues made their way through Tulsa along with Bob Wills & His Texas Playboys. And while Russell is known primarily as a rock & roll performer, that doesn't mean jack. The 14 songs here offer a glimpse of where Russell's heart really lies. All classic country and bluegrass tunes, *Hank Wilson's Back* features Russell and a few dozen of his closest friends from both L.A. and Nashville tearing up the classics. With everyone from Melba Montgomery, Billy Byrd, Johnny Gimble, Bob Moore, Weldon Myrick, and Pete Drake to Carl Radle, David Briggs, Charlie McCoy, and fellow Okie J.J. Cale, Russell in his alter ego runs through standards such as Lester Flatt's "Rollin' in My Sweet Baby's Arms," Hank Williams' "I'm So Lonesome I Could Cry" and "Jambalaya," Bill Monroe's "Uncle Pen," Hank Thompson's "Six Pack to Go," Leon Payne's "Lost Highway," George Jones' "The Window Up Above," Jimmie Driftwood's "The Battle of New Orleans," and as a closer, Leadbelly's "Goodnight Irene," which that prick John Lomax took a co-write on. This is no idle affair. Russell's reads of these classic songs from the country and bluegrass canon are played with fire, verve, and reverence, and he uses every trick in the book to get at the bottom of their meaning, allowing his voice to do things it never did before or since this recording. The playing is well rehearsed and stellar, and since it is played straight, the arrangements are minimal, making Cale's production job that much easier. *Hank Wilson's Back* is raw, immediate, and full of the kind of drunken passion that only someone who loves the country music tradition could execute. It's highly recommended. *—Thom Jurek*

Leon Live / 1973 / The Right Stuff ✦✦✦
This is a solid concert offering that showcases Russell's strengths (and weaknesses) as a live performer, with A-1 support throughout. *—Cub Koda*

Stop All That Jazz / 1974 / The Right Stuff ✦✦

Will O' the Wisp / 1975 / The Right Stuff ✦✦✦

Live in Japan / 1975 / Shelter ✦✦

The Best of Leon Russell / 1976 / DCC ✦✦✦✦✦
Pianist/composer/arranger Leon Russell has a resumé that would be the envy of most musicians: as an L.A. session player, he's recorded and toured with Jerry Lee Lewis, the Rolling Stones, B.B. King, Eric Clapton, George Harrison, Glen Campbell, and Bob Dylan, among many others. In addition, Russell came through the ranks of Phil Spector's early-'60s crew at Gold Star studios. Unlike a good share of session musicians and producers, though, Russell was able to carve out a fairly high-profile solo career. Covering his prime in the first half of the '70s, this hits collection includes such Russell chart-toppers as "Tightrope" and "Roll Away the Stone," along with hits he penned for others like "Delta Lady" (Joe Cocker) and "This Masquerade" (George Benson). And on top of a handful of numbers that take in a heady mix of gospel, pop, country, blues, and New Orleans R&B (comparisons to Doctor John are common), the album also includes a healthy dose of Russell's torch song-caliber and jazz-inflected numbers, including such standouts as "Bluebird" and "Your Song" (later given a stellar reading by jazz vocalist Shirley Horn). For the newcomer, this greatest-hits package offers the best introduction to Russell's catalog. *—Stephen Cook*

Willie & Leon / 1979 / CBS ✦✦

Hank Wilson, Vol. 2 / 1984 / Paradise ✦✦✦
Leon Russell used his alter ego, Hank Wilson, to explore his love of country classics, and the songs here certainly qualify, be it the venerable "Wabash Cannonball" or "Tumbling Tumbleweeds," or a run-through the honky tonk "If You've Got The Money Honey (I've Got the Time)," Lefty Frizzell's hit tune. The real problem—if it really is one—is that everything here gets treated the same. So "Oh Lonesome Me" gets the same blithe rendering as "Waltz Across Texas," with the band banging away, albeit in very musical fashion, without much subtlety or thought about the lyrics. While that works very well on Harlan Howard's wonderful "Heartaches By the Number," it's less successful elsewhere, as with "On the Wings of a Dove." It's as if, though Russell's heart is in the right place and his ability is beyond question, his taste abandoned him during the making of the disc, and the (uncredited) sidemen just do what they're told. So, while none of that stops this being a pleasant listening experience, it can't be anything more. Russell doesn't have the greatest voice, an acquired taste, although happily he keeps it at its least grating, but all the parts contribute to a whole that's never more than background music for the evening rush at a truck stop. *—Chris Nickson*

● **Gimme Shelter: The Best of Leon Russell** / Nov. 12, 1996 / EMI ✦✦✦✦✦
It's a little problematic to put together a compilation of such an album-oriented artist. But unless you're very deeply into the Russell catalog, this two-CD, 40-track best-of will serve as a retrospective of all that you need, largely covering his work from the first half of the '70s (a couple of songs from his 1992 Virgin album are also included), and featuring his best-known hits, big and small. It's a well-done tour through his blend of swamp rock, gospel, and bits of blues and country, with material from eight of his Shelter LPs, including the one he recorded in 1969 as part of the Asylum Choir. Interesting rarities include a 1974 single of "Wild Horses," a 1970 cover of Dylan's "She Belongs to Me" that only showed up on a compilation, and a folk-rockish 1965 single for Dot. *—Richie Unterberger*

● **Retrospective** / Oct. 21, 1997 / The Right Stuff/Shelter ✦✦✦✦
Retrospective is an 18-track collection that features the bulk of Leon Russell's greatest hits ("Tight Rope," "Roll in My Sweet Baby's Arms," "Lady Blue," "Back to the Island"), plus many key album tracks. Since Russell was primarily an album artist, this approach doesn't necessarily do him justice, but for listeners who only want the hits, this will do. However, the double-disc *Gimme Shelter: The Best of Leon Russell* is a better, more thorough overview and is the one serious fans should acquire. *—Stephen Thomas Erlewine*

Hank Wilson, Vol. 3: Legend in My Time / Apr. 7, 1998 / Ark 21 ✦✦✦
Revising his Hank Wilson persona, Leon Russell has emerged once again as a county artist on this album. As the third volume in a series that started in the 1970s, this is one of the most well-produced country albums ever. *Legend in My Time* rocks too, with such covers as the searing "Sixteen Tons" and "Okie From Muskogee." On the ballad side, a version of Willie Nelson's "Night Life" pretty much blows every other version away. Leon Russell is one of the most gifted and versatile musicians of the past 50 years, and here is another reason why. *—Matthew Greenwald*

Face in the Crowd / Jan. 26, 1999 / Saga ✦✦✦
After a popular period in the first half of the 1970s, Leon Russell dissipated his commercial appeal making duet albums with his wife and country collections. He didn't release a regular studio album between 1979's *Life & Love* and 1992's Bruce Hornsby-helmed *Anything Can Happen*. That album was criticized for Hornsby's meddling and performed disappointingly. Seven years later (with another of his "Hank Wilson" country albums in between), Russell is back on a small label with a more characteristic set that he co-produced with his son Teddy Jack. The craggy voice, even craggier now that Russell is in his late 50s, is in place, and the songs are piano-based R&B in his familiar style. Some echoes are even explicit: "Betty Ann," for example, is a calmer re-write of "Delta Lady." More often, however, the songs simply are consistent with the swampy style Russell pioneered in the early '70s, especially "Message From My Baby," "Mean and Evil," and "Don't Bring the Blues to Bed." No doubt it is far too late for Russell to regain his commercial standing, but old fans will find this album a long-awaited return to form. *—William Ruhlmann*

The Best of Leon Russell / Mar. 13, 2001 / EMI-Capitol Special Markets ✦✦✦

Signature Songs / Aug. 21, 2001 / Leon Russell ✦✦✦

Guitar Blues / Aug. 21, 2001 / Leon Russell ✦✦✦

Rhythm & Bluegrass: Hank Wilson, Vol. 4 / Oct. 23, 2001 / Leon Russell ✦✦✦
The idea of combining Leon Russell—a rocker—with the New Grass Revival—a bluegrass band—probably seems like a screwy idea on the surface. But Russell knew a thing or two about country roots and the New Grass Revival loved to add pianos and electric guitars to traditional music. Russell & the New Grass Revival even toured for a time and produced a live album. On *Rhythm & Bluegrass: Hank Wilson, Vol. 4* this crossover powerhouse covers something old, something new, and everything in between with mixed results. Traditional pieces like "Footprints in the Snow" and "In the Pines" seem less than inspired, while Lester Flatt's "Bluebirds Are Singing for Me" seems merely perfunctory. Everything flows smoother when Russell and the boys fall back on their soulful vocals and rocking rhythms. "I've Just Seen a Face" is pretty snazzy, even if it's derivative of the Dillards' late-'60s version, but the true moment of glory comes shining through on Ray Charles' "I Believe to My Soul." An odd choice, perhaps, but Russell digs deep into the lyric and the New Grass Revival provide full-bodied backup vocals. The album is short—30 minutes—and fans of either artist may find this cross pollination a tad strange. Nonetheless, *Rhythm & Bluegrass: Hank Wilson, Vol. 4* succeeds as an unusual progressive bluegrass experiment. *—Ronnie D. Lankford Jr.*

Moonlight & Love Songs / Apr. 9, 2002 / Leon Russell ✦✦✦
Seems like doing an album of standards has become the benchmark of a long career and respectability for those who used to pride themselves on being the outlaws of music. Willie Nelson's done it (several times) and so have many others—and now Leon Russell joins the crowd. And the resultant *Moonlight & Love Songs* isn't bad at all, with graceful—albeit sometimes anonymous—arrangements. By its very nature, the material is familiar, maybe too familiar at times (do listeners need another version of "Smoke Gets in Your Eyes"?), although Russell does dig up "'Round Midnight" and offers a good, slightly

thumping version of "That Lucky Old Sun," with piano courtesy of Bruce Hornsby. Russell's in good, relaxed voice, the abrasive quality that had made him so distinctive in earlier decades largely rubbed away. And he works surprisingly well with orchestral accompaniment, leaving his rock & roll shoes outside the session. There's nothing to fault about this album—it's smoothly produced, arranged, and performed. The problem is, there's very little exciting about it, either. Russell fans will love it, but overall the songs have been done better by others. —*Chris Nickson*

Tom Russell
b. 1950, Los Angeles, CA

Guitar, Vocals, Composer / Contemporary Country, Singer/Songwriter, Contemporary Folk, Americana

Americana singer/songwriter Tom Russell was born in Los Angeles in 1950. Raised on the cowboy music of the American West, he grew up to be a talented songwriter, and began issuing albums under his own name in the early '70s. However, Russell's material was also recorded by such luminaries as Johnny Cash, Guy Clark, Dave Alvin, Doug Sahm, and k.d. lang, to name only a few. While much of Russell's work mined the country tradition, he was also known to flavor his work with Tex-Mex, folk, and the cowboy music of his youth. After an acclaimed career spanning two decades, Russell found another gear with 1999's *The Man From God Knows Where*. A concept album eight years in the making, the LP presented a song cycle inspired not only by America's pioneers, but by Russell's own immigrant ancestors. *Borderland*, a set inspired by Russell's newfound home in the Juarez border region of Texas, followed in 2001. *Modern Art* appeared in April 2003. —*Johnny Loftus*

Heart on a Sleeve / 1984 / Demon ✦✦✦✦✦

Road to Bayamon / 1988 / Philo ✦✦✦✦
Good luck trying to pigeonhole Tom Russell based on the fine *Road to Bayamon*, which manages to sound cohesive while wandering all over the musical map. "Home Before Dark," one of several numbers here that he later re-recorded with country-soul singer Barrence Whitfield, is a radio-ready rocker, with a great hook and prominent guitar; the vocal and guitar on the equally fine "U.S. Steel," on the other hand, sound something like early Johnny Cash. And then there's "Alkali," a great relic from Russell's folky days with Patricia Hardin; and a surprisingly strong, faithful-to-the-original cover of Bruce Springsteen's "Fire." Not everything scores a homer: The lackluster vocals on Tom Waits' wonderful "Downtown Train," the album's other cover, seem particularly weak when compared with Rod Stewart's definitive version. But this CD—which gets a big boost from the pedal steel, fiddle, and accordion of Fats Kaplin—contains far more highlights than disappointments. —*Jeff Burger*

Poor Man's Dream / 1990 / Philo ✦✦✦✦
One of Russell's best albums, *Poor Man's Dream* is dominated by inspired folk/rock performances and by songs that sound like classics that have been around forever. In fact, Russell wrote 11 of the dozen tracks within a few years of the disc's release (though he had help on a few numbers from the likes of Katy Moffatt, Nancy Griffith, and Ian Tyson). Picking standouts on an album this strong isn't easy, but if pressed you might name "Walkin on the Moon," awhich is about falling in love; the melancholy "Spanish Burgundy"; "Gallo del Cielo," about a man trying to win the money to buy back his father's land; and "Navajo Rug," a nostalgic look at old times and an old love. Today many of these songs sound like standards; someday, one suspects, they will be. —*Jeff Burger*

Hurricane Season / 1991 / Philo ✦✦✦✦
Tom Russell scores consistently as both performer and songwriter on this release, which is loaded with inventive lyrics, effusive vocals, and rich, exuberant instrumentation. Best tracks include "Black Pearl," awhich benefits from Fats Kaplin's accordion; "Chocolate Cigarettes," which Russell cowrote with folksinger Sylvia Tyson; and the poignant "Haley's Comet," about the comet-like rise and fall of rock & roll's Bill Haley. In the years following this album's release, Russell has re-recorded many of these songs, and it's easy to see why—when you've got material this good, it must be pretty tempting to keep taking it off the shelf. —*Jeff Burger*

Cowboy Real / 1991 / Philo ✦✦✦✦
Fans of folksinger Tom Russell won't be surprised to learn that his father was an Iowa horsetrader or that his brother is a rancher and cattle supplier; all of his albums leave little doubt that he has the cowboy spirit in his blood. This particular album leaves less doubt than most, though, since Russell focuses exclusively here on his favorite cowboy songs. His warm, evocative voice is in fine form throughout the all-acoustic collection of originals, covers, and adaptations, and the 11 tracks are just about all winners. Highlights include "Zane Grey," a song about a horse that Russell first recorded in the mid-'70s with then-partner Patricia Hardin; "Gallo del Cielo" and "Navajo Rug," both duets with Canadian folkie Ian Tyson; and "Claude Dallas," a tale of a real-life modern-day outlaw who shot two game wardens in Nevada in 1981. —*Jeff Burger*

Box of Visions / Dec. 1992 / Philo ✦✦✦
Tom Russell, whose roots are in folk and cowboy music, flirts a little bit with rock on this release, which features a full backup band—drums, assorted keyboards, sax, the whole bit—and even a few longer electric guitar solos. It's not Russell's best or most original-sounding album, and it's certainly not the one to buy first. But there are some lovely story-songs here, all written or co-written by Russell, who got songwriting help on several tracks from fellow folkies like Steve Young and Tom Pacheco. Russell's prominently mixed vocals are uniformly excellent, moreover, and the harmonizing by Rosie Flores and Katy Moffatt is a nice plus. —*Jeff Burger*

The Early Years (1975–79) / 1994 / Dark Angel ✦✦✦✦✦
The folk music world hasn't exactly been holding its breath waiting for this reissue, but it should have been. Recorded two decades ago by singer/songwriter Tom Russell and his

performing partner of the time, Patricia Hardin, the CD combines remastered versions of 1976's wonderful "Ring of Bone" with 1978's nearly as good "Wax Museum." (One track from each LP has been deleted to allow both albums to fit on one CD.) Expect melodically inventive music, heartfelt vocals, and memorable lyrics about everything from life and death in the Southwest to the Hindenburg. ("Wax Museum" ends with the actual radio broadcast of the Hindenburg going down.) "Ring of Bone," in particular, boasts a charming, homespun feel—not surprising, since it was recorded more or less live on a shoestring budget—and both albums make good use of a wide range of instruments, including sousaphone, trumpet, violin, and what's billed as a "'50s Guy Lombardo saxophone." —*Jeff Burger*

Beyond St. Olay's Gate (1979–1992) / Oct. 18, 1994 / Round Tower ✦✦✦
An excellent best-of collection culled from several Russell albums released between 1979-1992, the music on this disc is such a sublime, if unassuming, slice of pure alternative country, it suddenly makes the very existence of a band like Whiskeytown seem redundant. With his quietly honest vocal delivery and carefully honed arrangements, Russell might not appeal to fans of the chillingly raw, whiskey-soaked, directness of a Townes Van Zandt or Hank Williams Sr., but he more than makes up for any lack of intensity with the sheer beauty of his lyrics. With a novelist's eye for detail and a penchant for using such atypically country settings as Puerto Rico and Norway, Russell has never been afraid to follow his own road; *Beyond St. Olav's Gate* is a fine introduction to the path's most enjoyable twists and tuns. —*Pemberton Roach*

● **The Rose of the San Joaquin** / Oct. 1995 / Hightone ✦✦✦✦✦
Tom Russell has grown consistently in the course of his many albums into one of the most articulate singer/songwriters on the country side of the tracks. His efforts with Barrence Whitfield and earlier incarnations of the Tom Russell Band have guitar work by Tom's longtime partner Andrew Hardin. On this record, however, Russell has chosen, along with producers Dave Alvin and Greg Leisz, to create a more linear feel to the album, with each song set feeling like it takes place in the border town Russell has been so good at describing. Each song is a miniature film soundtrack, with characters clearly drawn. "The Sky Above and the Mud Below" is one of the key tracks that truly brings the listener a sense of despair in the middle of nowhere with its slow tempo and plain-spoken telling. It is ominous in the way it builds to the inevitable conclusion as potent after repeated listening as the tragic ending in Russell's earlier *Gallo del Cielo*. On the other hand, "Out in California" celebrates lust and longing of a different and no less universal loneliness, for that girl with the red dress, driven home by some high-octane playing. "Somebody's Husband, Somebody's Son" (with Peter Case and Dave Alvin) is a hobo's waltz. The album also has some soft lovers ballads. The liner notes include Russell's reminiscence about the appearance and subsequent disappearance of a long lost relative that is perfectly in keeping with the tone of the album's songs. He has carved out a place for himself as a compelling storyteller, and this is one of his strongest albums of the '90s. —*Richard Meyer*

The Long Way Around (Acoustic Collection) / May 5, 1997 / Hightone ✦✦✦✦✦
Tom Russell has been releasing terrific records without pause since the mid-'70s, and this acoustic, mostly live retrospective package may be the best of the bunch. In fact, after listening to its 17 tracks—which include duets with Nanci Griffith, Jimmie Dale Gilmore, and others—the only remaining question about Russell is: Why isn't this guy very, very famous? Sure, you can hear lots of influences here—everyone from Merle Haggard and Buck Owens to Ian Tyson (a sometime collaborator) and Bob Dylan. But the end product is an artist with an instantly recognizable, personal sound. It's a little bit country, a little bit folk, a little bit rock, with lots of great picking, lilting melodies, and consistently first-rate lyrics that sound like the result of experience and conviction, not the desire to impress or score hits—but he sure does impress. There isn't a clunker in the bunch, but if forced to pick highlights, one might list "Beyond the Blues," a duet with Gilmore; "U.S. Steel," with guitar and vocal reminiscent of early Johnny Cash; "Walkin' on the Moon," which Russell wrote and performs with Katy Moffat; and "Gallo del Cielo," an exuberant south-of-the-border excursion. —*Jeff Burger*

Song of the West: The Cowboy Collection / Sep. 9, 1997 / HMG ✦✦✦
Along with *The Long Way Around*, another acoustic package also released in 1997, *Song of the West* was Tom Russell's attempt to sum up the previous ten years of his career on two newly recorded CDs. This package, which he calls "our definitive cowboy collection," focuses on his best-loved covers and originals about life in the Southwest. Among the 15 tracks: a live version of "The Sky Above, the Mud Below," a deftly told tale of horse thieves in the old West; a great reading of "Navajo Rug," which Russell wrote with Ian Tyson; "Alkali," which he first recorded in 1976 with then-partner Patricia Hardin; and "Gallo del Dielo," a musically and lyrically marvelous original about a Mexican who tries to raise money to buy back land that had been stolen from his father. *The Long Way Around* probably offers the best introduction to Russell, but if you like that, by all means run out and get this album as well. —*Jeff Burger*

The Man From God Knows Where / Mar. 16, 1999 / Hightone ✦✦✦✦
Tom Russell had been releasing great records for about 25 years by the time he issued this album, but he outdoes himself here. Eight years in the making, *The Man From God Knows Where* is a song cycle inspired by America's pioneers and, particularly, Russell's own immigrant ancestors; but it probably comes at least as much from the artist's imagination as from historical fact. Be that as it may, he does a terrific job of conjuring up the hard realities faced by America's early immigrants. The performances, meanwhile, are even more adventurous than we've come to expect from Russell. Featuring guest spots by Iris DeMent, Dave Van Ronk and others, the album mixes music of the American West with that of Ireland and Norway and, somehow, it all holds together. A fine, fine collection. —*Jeff Burger*

Borderland / Apr. 17, 2001 / Hightone ✦✦✦✦

Tom Russell proves once again to be perhaps the finest American folk-roots artist that most Americans never heard of. The title of this latest collection reflects a focus on the El Paso-Juarez area, but also on emotional geography and the borders between a man and a woman. Some of the skillfully told stories are clearly autobiographical; all of them paint detailed, memorable portraits. Russell is singing and playing as well as ever here, but he gets an added boost on this disc from producer Gurf Morlix, who has filled the same role for Lucinda Williams and Robert Earl Keen. Morlix helped pick the songs and the band—which includes such standouts as accordionist Joel Guzman and longtime Russell cohort Andrew Hardin on guitar—and put them all to good use in a production that keeps Russell's world-weary voice front and center. —*Jeff Burger*

Modern Art / Apr. 22, 2003 / Hightone ✦✦✦

Modern Art has to be the most confounding recording in Tom Russell's catalog. That he is a songwriter of epic proportion there can be no doubt. His decision here to issue a recording of half originals/co-writes and half covers, three of which are basically epitaphs (including one of questionable taste), is just the beginning of what makes it problematic. First the good news: Russell's "The Kid from Spavinaw," the greatest song that has thus far, and probably ever will be, written about Mickey Mantle, is easily the most moving thing on the set (the other is "The Dutchman"). Told in the first person, it relates much of Mantle's upbringing and his regrets, with the glory years alluded to more than spoken of. Gurf Morlix's pedal steel playing floats through the melody like an Oklahoma wind, carrying Russell's lyrics into the same immortality that Mantle's myth exists in. It's one the greatest songs Russell has ever written—which is saying a lot. Emmylou Harris' "Ballad of Sally Rose" is one of three duets with Nanci Griffith (who adds little to the project—even on her own "Gulf Coast Highway"—except name recognition). It's tepid and feels devoid of focus. The story is not convincing in this reading. Russell's "Muhammad Ali" is downright embarrassing; written with a sub-basement Jimmy Buffett faux-Caribbean rhythm, its lyric sounds hackneyed and insincere, full of clumsy rhymes and a narrative that reveals nothing about the man or the myth. One of the two most troubling moments comes in a cover of "American Hotel" by the late songwriter Carl Brouse, a peer of Russell's in talent if not reputation. Brouse died a few weeks before the recording was made and Russell talks about Brouse, whose life eerily mirrored the subject of the song, Stephen Foster. Russell begins with a strange, non-committal spoken word introduction that talks about Brouse's imagining of Foster in his last days dying a penniless alcoholic in New York's American Hotel (and likens it to Toulouse-Lautrec's passing in the film *Moulin Rouge!*). First, this version is on no way in the same league with Brouse's own; it's devoid of emotion and commitment. Secondly, the question has to be asked, why didn't Russell—a longtime acquaintance of Brouse's—record this song when it mattered, while he was alive? Russell has played it in his live set from time to time, and appearing the way it does here is odd to say the least. Let's just say it doesn't feel like a "fitting" tribute to an artist who deserved better than he got. The other is on a narrated medley of a title taken from a book and poem by Charles Bukowski, "Crucifix in a Death Hand," crossed with a lackluster cover of Warren Zevon's "Carmelita." Again, at the time of this writing, Zevon was dying of lung cancer, and one has to wonder if this track would have made the album if Zevon weren't ill. These are questions, not accusations, that unfortunately the readings of the songs don't answer.

"Racehorse Haynes" and "Isaac Lewis," story-songs that Russell is peerless in writing, alternately offer both his first-person accounts and reporter's eye for detail in picaresque couplets that make the lyrics become images cut from history and serve as virtual allegories for our own time. Andrew Hardin's guitar playing adds swaths of textured shade and color to Russell's melodies. The two have played together so long it's as if they are one person. "Tijuana Bible" is a smoking story of an infamous Hollywood murder. Eliza Gilkyson's depth and soul add an entire dimension to Russell's narrative. The song is a rockabilly shuffle, and a horrific song of a murder and a grave robbery that is chilling, intense, mysterious, and out of Hollywood legend. *Modern Art* is an album that is not without rewards, but it has so many questions attached, it is like a cipher; at times it feels cynical, jaded, and lost, like a journey that turns back on itself instead of reaching a destination with purpose. —*Thom Jurek*

John Wesley Ryles

b. Dec. 2, 1950, Bastrop, LA

Guitar, Vocals / Country-Pop

Although singer/songwriter John Wesley Ryles had over 30 chart singles between 1968 and 1988, he never reached the heights of some of his contemporaries. He was raised in rural Louisiana and Texas in a family who entertained themselves in the evening by singing. A guitar player from age six, he made his radio debut the following year. His family formed the Ryles Family Singers and entertained on various local radio stations until accepting an invitation to become regulars on Fort Worth's *Cowtown Hoedown*, which led to joining the *Big D Jamboree* in Dallas. The whole family moved to Nashville in 1965, and Ryles decided to go solo. He began singing demos, gained experience working as a studio engineer, and frequently appeared with various local club bands. In 1968, he released the single "Kay," which gave the 18-year-old Ryles, billing himself as John Wesley I, a Top Ten country and crossover pop hit. He recorded two follow-ups in 1969 that only made it to the middle of the charts, but made it to the Top 20 in 1970 with "I've Just Been Wasting My Time." The following year he had a Top 40 hit with "Reconsider Me."

By this time, however, young Ryles had become disillusioned and discouraged, and left Music City to begin performing at various clubs. In 1976, he made another bid for stardom with two minor hit singles. In 1977, he recorded "Fool;" at first it did nothing, but four months after its release it became a Top 20 hit. He followed with his biggest hit, "Lifetime Thing," which reached the Top Five. After that, he had several mid-range hits through the end of the '80s before becoming a session musician and demo singer. —*Sandra Brennan*

Kay / 1969 / Columbia ✦✦✦✦

● **John Wesley Ryles** / 1977 / ABC/Dot ✦✦✦✦

Shine on Me / 1978 / MCA ✦✦✦

Let the Night Begin / 1979 / MCA ✦✦✦

S

Doug Sahm

b. Nov. 6, 1941, San Antonio, TX, **d.** Nov. 18, 1999, Taos, NM
Guitar, Songwriter, Violin, Vocals, Leader / Rock & Roll, Blues-Rock, Progressive Country, Country-Rock, Tex-Mex, Roots Rock, Americana

Guitarist, composer, arranger, and songwriter Doug Sahm was a knowledgeable music historian and veteran performer equally comfortable in a range of styles, including Texas blues, country, rock & roll, Western swing, and Cajun. Born November 6, 1941, in San Antonio, TX, he began his performing career at age nine when he was featured on a San Antonio area radio station, playing steel guitar. Sahm began recording for a procession of small labels (Harlem, Warrior, Renner and Personality) in 1955 with "A Real American Joe" under the name Little Doug Sahm. Three years later he was leading a group called the Pharoahs. Sahm recorded a series of singles for Texas-based record companies including "Crazy Daisy" (1959), "Sapphire" (1961), and "If You Ever Need Me" (1964). After being prompted in 1965 to assemble a group by producer Huey Meaux, Sahm asked his friends Augie Meyers (keyboards), Frank Morin (saxophone), Harvey Kagan (bass) and Johnny Perez (drums), if they would join him. Meaux gave the group the name the Sir Douglas Quintet. The group had some success on the radio with "The Rains Came," but Sahm later moved to California after the group broke up, where he formed the Honkey Blues Band. He reformed his Quintet in California and recorded a now-classic single, "Mendocino." The resulting album was a ground-breaking record in the then-emerging country-rock scene. The Sir Douglas Quintet followed *Mendocino* with *Together After Five*, another album that led them to a larger fan base.

But it was Atlantic Records producer Jerry Wexler who realized that country-rock sounds were coming into vogue (and there was no place in Nashville for people like Sahm), so he signed both Sahm and Willie Nelson. One of his greatest albums, *Doug Sahm and Band*, (1973, Atlantic) was recorded in New York City with Bob Dylan, Dr. John, and accordionist Flaco Jimenez, and a resulting single, "Is Anybody Going to San Antone?" had some radio success. The Sir Douglas Quintet got back together again to record two more albums, *Wanted Very Much Alive* and *Back to the 'Dillo*. Among Sahm's most essential blues records are *Hell of a Spell* (1980, reissued in 1999), a blues album dedicated to Guitar Slim, and his Grammy-nominated studio album for Antone's, *The Last Real Texas Blues Band*. For his other material, there are several good compilations, including *The Best of Doug Sahm* (Rhino). *S.D.Q. '98* followed. Sahm died November 18, 1999; the posthumous *The Return of Wayne Douglas* appeared the following summer. —*Richard Skelly*

Rough Edges / 1973 / Mercury ✦✦

Doug Sahm and Band / Jan. 1973 / Atlantic ✦✦✦✦✦
Since major label Atlantic signed Doug Sahm as a solo artist and put him in a New York studio with top-flight producers Jerry Wexler and Arif Mardin and star sidemen like Bob Dylan, Dr. John, and David Bromberg (not to mention old stalwarts like Augie Meyers, Flaco Jimenez, and Martin Fierro), you might expect that the resulting album would be Sahm's big career move, a swing toward professionalism and the mainstream, and that's how it was perceived when it was released. Maybe that's why it also was dismissed when it didn't become a big hit. Trouble is, the record isn't slick at all—it sounds as loose as any of the Sir Douglas Quintet albums, if a little more country-oriented. But the album remains a Bob Dylan curio; Dylan's otherwise unavailable composition "Wallflower" is included, and he sings it and "Blues Stay Away From Me" with Sahm. —*William Ruhlmann*

Groover's Paradise / 1974 / Warner Bros. ✦✦✦✦
Anyone who finds hippies irritating might want to throw this record across the room—and that's a good review right there, since it has been long established via intense scientific study that music which somehow motivates people to throw records across the room is usually quite good. No exception to this rule here, as fans of Doug Sahm often choose this as a personal favorite, while it is also one of the better side projects of the Creedence Clearwater Revival rhythm section. If Sahm was writing the review himself in 1974, he would have no doubt described the whole thing as some kind of "trip"; after all, this expression is used three times alone on the back cover of this album, actually less than one might expect considering the stoned-out nature of the accompanying comics. These black-and-white illustrations by Kelly Fitzgerald are a great part of the record's enduring charm, but the music itself is deeper than the coolie hippie vibe. This is simply a great roots rock album, and like much of Sahm's work it is loaded with complex details as well as loving interplay between the musicians. These tracks indicate a mastery of many basic forms such as blues, rhythm & blues, norteño, country, and Cajun and the players always seem to be probing beyond this to find something new. Creedence Clearwater Revival drummer Doug Clifford produced as well as played, and did a superior job, irrigating the proceedings with a range of available Sahm streams like some kind of master gardener. The use of horns is excellent, not only providing plenty of punch in the arrangements but memorable effects such as the spooky baritone sax solo on "Just Groove Me." A large section of the sonic spread is always reserved for

Sahm's lush guitar playing, including lots of rock, country, and blues licks, while bassist Stu Cook sometimes adds additional guitar, expertly mocking the patented hypnotic John Fogerty sound for an effect that is not unlike Sahm sitting in on a Creedence album. Of course, the range of that classic '60s and '70s rock group seems quite limited compared to Sahm, who whips off an expert version of the Tex-Mex instrumental "La Cacahueta," the only track here which he did not compose himself. The well-crafted yet daringly personal and unembarrassed songs include haunting country-influenced ballads such as "Her Dream Man Never Came," as well as really top-notch examples of good old rock & roll, the hilarious "For the Sake of Rock 'n' Roll" and the bewitchingly cooking "Devil Heart." The second side of the original vinyl is one of this artist's most perfect set of songs. The final track, "Catch Me in the Morning," is one of several on this album that benefits from a long, satisfying arrangement—hardly the kind of simple dirt that is often tossed off the shovel in the quest for roots rock. The band tends to move through these pieces with confidence, as if already expecting to have lost the attention of the simpletons in the crowd. At the same time, there are those listeners who will find it hard to believe a simple song, let alone such a magnum opus, could be created from the almost nonexistent message of this song. "Call me in the morning, I am too tired to talk right now," is just about all this song says, and it is one of the marvels of Sahm that he is able to parlay a near-operatic sense of importance into such a typical part of daily life. Giving him an instrumental credit for being a "dreamer"—nicely enough, it comes right after the credit for bajo sexto—is one of the most appropriate details, or "trips," on *Groover's Paradise*. —*Eugene Chadbourne*

Texas Rock for Country Rollers / 1976 / Edsel ✦✦✦
Upon original release, *Texas Rock for Country Rollers* was credited to Sir Doug & the Texas Tornados. Little did anyone know how much confusion this might eventually create when years later Sahm formed a new band called the Texas Tornados with a nucleus of himself and several other musical legends from that state, only one of whom appears on this album, other than Sahm himself. That would be Augie Meyers, a regular sidekick of Sahm's from the Sir Douglas Quintet, so what is the reason that this isn't simply identified as a Sir Douglas Quintet album? Only the fact that there are at least six players present on the tracks, but funny, simple math never stopped Sahm from doing anything sensible before. In terms of presentation, attitude, and musical direction, this is pretty much a Sir Douglas Quintet-type affair, is definitely not a record by what would become the Texas Tornados, and includes at least three genuine classics such as the beautiful "Give Back the Key to My Heart," later to be redone by the band Uncle Tupelo. Good playing and better vibes abound but there is the feeling that somebody was asleep at the wheel, in that some of the best tracks simply fade out right in the middle of an important chorus. Why would a producer do this, unless there was some problem in the track that they couldn't stand to let anyone hear? An album most Sahm fans will want to own, and one in the could-have-been-a-contender category. —*Eugene Chadbourne*

Live Love / 1977 / Texas ✦✦✦
One of several live recordings that first came out on Augie Meyers' own Texas label in the '70s, this CD is consistently engaging. Playing as relaxed as this is always worth a listen, as the musicians make sounding so tight seem so easy. The choice of cover versions also demonstrates a devil-may-care attitude, culminating in a convincing display of Doug Sahm's ability to make any type of material his own, even something as well-known as the dreary "My Girl" or Eddie Floyd's "Knock on Wood." At the same time, the presence of such covers means this is not a disc a listener should turn to when looking for an example of the Sir Douglas Quintet at its deepest creatively and philosophically. In fact, it is hard to call this the Sir Douglas Quintet exactly above and beyond the fact that anything Sahm touches becomes "Sir Doug-y," as Pee Wee Herman would say. Sure, the label puts a photo of the Sir Douglas Quintet in 1965 on the back cover of the booklet, but they might as well have put a picture of the Doors, since this is not the lineup heard on the recording itself. Other releases of similar live material from this period credit it to lineups such as Doug Sahm, Augie Meyers, and "assorted friends" or the Texas Tornados, although the all-star lineup of the latter group is not present either. Quibbling, all of it. By any name, this is a group of players who can feel each other's every move, and deliver the goods about as well as it can be done. While not essential, these live recordings are hardly boring. "Dynamite Woman" is a bubbly highlight. —*Eugene Chadbourne*

Way Back When He Was Just Doug Sahm / 1979 / Rockhouse ✦✦✦

Hell of a Spell / 1980 / Takoma ✦✦✦
This is a hell of a disc. From the opening riffs this disc is crammed with Sahm's typical rompin' and stompin' Texas blues/rhythm & blues mix. This also includes liberal dashes of the Tex-Mex and rockabilly he grew up cutting his teeth on. Rudy "Tutti" Grayzell used to go to his school when Sahm was 11, as legend goes, and pose as his uncle and

pull the musical prodigy out of school to play some of the gigs that required some travel. This compilation is dedicated to one of his heroes, Eddie Jones, better known as Guitar Slim. He does one of his tunes on the disc, but it is the horns and overall sound and feel of the disc that bring back the memories of Jones. Six of the 11 tunes were penned by Doug Sahm and they standup as some of the best things he has done. He manages to take that voice of his and put all the ache and pain that things gone sour can evoke and guide you along with him down this road without ever getting sappy or maudlin. Listen to the tone and feel of "Hangin' on By a Thread" and the smooth shift to the Brook Benton heartbreak tune "I'll Take Care of You." He shifts gears with the precision of a Grand Prix driver. This disc shows off some of the remarkable range of Sahm's abilities and genius. This becomes clearer when you think of his work with Dylan, the Texas Tornados, and the early rock hits, such as "Mendicino" and "She's About a Mover." Also, this disc is the only one that comes to mind on which his longtime compadre, Augie Meyers, isn't helping with his familiar organ sound; instead, Kelly Dunn is handling keyboards. Sahm is Texas-bred, but his influences are as broad as the sky is big down there. Here he is concentrating on the blues, and he gets some exciting things down on the disc. *—Bob Gottlieb*

Border Wave / 1981 / Chrysalis ✦✦✦✦
Back to the 'Dillo / 1988 / Edsel ✦✦✦
In the '70s Augie Meyers cranked up a label called Texas and released a string of albums. The catalog included several live recordings involving a group of musicians that could be credited as loosely as they are for this production, or might also be known as the Sir Douglas Quintet or the Texas Tornados. Anyway, it's Doug Sahm and his faithful sidekick Augie Meyers plus many of the usual cohorts, including a horn section that sounds as if it has been practicing unison statements after every meal for the last decade. The live recording sound is perfectly acceptable for a '70s rock date, and the only thing that might detract from the experience of reliving a night at the infamous Armadillo Ballroom is the almost ridiculous jukebox nature of the program. Sahm's sidemen often complained that the leader neglected his brilliant original material for the sake of playing as many different covers as possible, and if the matter ever came to a jury trial, this recording could be brought in as exhibit A. There is a Chuck Berry song, followed by pretty little "Susie Q," followed by "Crazy Arms"—well, it is like a frat party that gets crashed by an old redneck trucker carrying a boom box. The last two songs are a cover of "Purple Haze"—very nice, as could be expected—and five minutes of jazz, competent, unexpected, and a weird way to end the show. This last instrumental, "Outro Song," is credited to Sahm, and there are only three other examples of his songwriting performed, best of which is a romping version of "Nuevo Laredo." *—Eugene Chadbourne*

The Return of the Formerly Brothers / 1989 / Rykodisc ✦✦✦✦✦
Texan folk hero Sir Doug Sahm meets underrated guitarist Amos Garrett and ex-Blasters keyboardist Gene Taylor and they cook like an Austin barbecue. [Originally released on Stony Plain Records in Canada in 1988, *The Return of the Formerly Brothers* was released in the U.S. by Rykodisc in 1989.] *—Jeff Tamarkin*

Juke Box Music / 1989 / Antone's ✦✦✦✦✦
Supported by the Antone's house band, Doug Sahm runs through 15 R&B and doo wop classics for *Juke Box Music*. Oddly there's no Tex-Mex here, considering that Sahm is one of the defining figures of the genre, but that's just a minor complaint, since the music here is just terrific. There's a wonderful relaxed quality to the performances, and the song selection boasts a number of forgotten gems, resulting in a little treasure for fans of R&B and American roots music. *—Thom Owens*

• **The Best of Doug Sahm (1968–1975)** / 1991 / Rhino ✦✦✦✦✦
Doug Sham once sang, "You just can't live in Texas if you don't have a lot of soul," and, as a proud son of the Lone Star state, he seemed bent on proving that every time he stepped in front of a microphone. Whether he was playing roots rock, garage punk, blues, country, norteño, or (as was often the case) something that mixed up several of the above-mentioned ingredients, Doug Sahm always sounded like Doug Sahm—a little wild, a little loose, but always good company, and a guy with a whole lot of soul who knew a lot of musicians upon whom the same praise could be bestowed. Pulling together a single disc compilation that would make sense of the length and breadth of the artist's recording career (which spanned five decades) would be just about impossible (the licensing hassles involved with the many labels involved would probably scotch such a project anyway), but this disc, which boasts 22 songs recorded over the course of eight years, is a pretty good starter for anyone wanting to get to know Sahm's music. You get two almost-hits ("Mendocino" and "(Is Anybody Going To) San Antone"), a healthy portion of memorable album cuts, and even a few unreleased songs as Sir Doug and his pals (among them fellow future Texas Tornado Augie Meyers and Doug's pal Bob Dylan) swing through vintage blues, country weepers, rootsy hippie jams, and a few cuts that defy convenient description, all dominated by Sahm's warm, expressive drawl, distinctive guitar work, and the loose but emphatic sound he knew how to draw from a band. Put it this way—there's one guy in a million who could write and record a song called "You Never Get Too Big and You Sure Don't Get Too Heavy That You Don't Have to Stop and Pay Some Dues Sometime" and not sound like a fool. Doug Sahm was that man, and you get to hear him sing it on *The Best of Doug Sham*, along with 21 other equally cool tunes. *—Mark Deming*

The Last Real Texas Blues Band Feat. Doug Sahm / 1994 / Discovery ✦✦✦
S.D.Q. '98 / Oct. 20, 1998 / Watermelon ✦✦✦✦✦
Many fanatic music listeners feel an artist's greatest works are accomplished when they are young, and would thus go backward toward an early Sir Douglas Quintet record in order to capture the best of this legendary Texas artist. This release on an independent label hardly made a ripple in the late '90s, although musically there is enough here to

create a tidal wave. Everything comes together beautifully in the proposed combination of tracks by Sahm and some of his old-time cohorts from both the quintet and the Texas Tornados and a collaboration with a younger bunch of dudes, namely the Gourds. Highlights there are, galore. No Sahm record would be this good unless Augie Meyers was on hand, and the man gets lots of solo space on all his axes. Pedal steel guitar player Tommy Detamore has some nice moments on the country material, of which there is lots. Rhythm section partners from the past—such as bassist Speedy Sparks and the fine drummer Ernie Durawa—are around to give the tunes a solid feel. One of the great things about the CD is the way it suddenly takes on a whole new life as a historical, political project through the sequence of songs, starting with the wonderful Sahm-panned "Louis Riel," going through the hysterical version of "The Ballad of Davy Crockett," and winding up with "Sooner or Later." On a more romantic note, there is a new version of an older Sahm song, "Give Back the Key to My Heart," certainly welcome since the original recorded version had such an unfinished feel to it. "Goodbye San Francisco, Hello Amsterdam" is another Sahm classic and surely a song with the potential to become a favorite. There is also a rollicking rhythm & blues bonus track tossed in at the end for added fun. *—Eugene Chadbourne*

She's About a Mover: The Best of Crazy Cajun Recording / Oct. 26, 1999 / Edsel ✦✦✦✦
This differs from Music Club's package in that this set also includes tracks issued as Doug Sahm solo sides, giving us a time frame between 1964 and 1977 to hear Sahm's art unfold. Of course, the early SDQ sides are the big ticket here. Rough and raw, they include the two big hits "She's About a Mover" and "The Rains Came." Yet the solo sides that fill up the cracks here are also every bit as raw, sometimes disconcertingly so, like the bass and drums that lose track of each other in the middle of "Seguin" or the maracas that never quite catch up to the band track on "You've Got Your Good Thing Down." If you wondered what Huey Meaux had in the vault on Sahm, here's your chance to find out. *—Cub Koda*

San Antonio Rock: The Harlem Recordings 1957-1961 / Apr. 4, 2000 / Norton ✦✦✦✦
If you think Doug Sahm's career began with the Sir Douglas Quintet, guess again. This 18-track collection rounds up all of Sahm's early 45s and demos, as well as rarities with Doug playing sideman in various Texas combos, the majority of it issued on the Harlem label out of Fort Worth. It's raw Texas music, soaked in R&B and rock & roll, and Sahm goes through no less than seven different backing units on this set, not to mention his sideman work with Spot Barnett, Jimmy Dee, and Red Hilburn. Lots of alternate takes, great booklet with loads of information, all putting into historical perspective this missing chapter in the history of this modern Texas troubadour. *—Cub Koda*

The Return of Wayne Douglas / Jun. 20, 2000 / Tornado ✦✦✦✦
The Return of Wayne Douglas—the title comes from one of the aliases Doug Sahm used during country music gigs around Austin, TX—turned out to be Sahm's final studio album. It was recorded just before his heart gave out in a Taos, NM, motel room on November 18, 1999, but released posthumously in late 2000 by Tornado Records, a division of Birdman Recordings. Sahm's band—which includes fellow Texas Tornado organist Augie Meyers, Bill Kirchen (Commander Cody & the Lost Planet Airman) on guitar, Tommy Detamore (Moe Bandy, Ronnie Milsap) on steel guitar, Bobby Flores (Ray Price's Cherokee Cowboys) on fiddle, and son Shawn Sahm on background vocals—are the perfect support group, giving this "country as chicken-fried steak" material the stripped-down and soulful touch it requires. The album is almost an homage to the state of Texas. In addition to new songs like "I Can't Go Back to Austin" and "Cowboy Peyton Place"—his paean to an Austin that existed 25 years earlier—there are country-style arrangements of Sir Doug classics: "Dallas Alice" and the album's last track, "Texas Me," written in California during a bout of homesickness some 30 years earlier. "I wonder what happened to that man inside," Sahm moans in his gravel-hewn, throaty manner, "the real old Texas me." There are also two covers. Bob Dylan's "Love Minus Zero/No Limit" is sent up Sahm-style with great aplomb. Leon Payne's "They'll Never Take Her Love From Me" tells a little story about the time Sahm and his father paid a visit to Payne at the "Blind Balladeer"'s home in Bandera, TX. Sahm was reportedly surprised at how easily Payne seemed to be able to move around inside his house without stumbling over furniture. The liner notes by James "Big Boy" Medlin say it best: "Doug was a tornado. A true force of nature. I'll think of him every time I see a west Texas dust devil. Every time I drink a longneck. Every time I order a taco. Every time I see the skyline of Manhattan." Well, that's what they say. *—Bryan Thomas*

In the Beginning / Aug. 29, 2000 / Aim ✦✦✦
In the Beginning chronicles the earliest singles released by the late Texas renegade Doug Sahm. Recorded between 1958 and 1962, these 14 songs encompass Tex-Mex, R&B, doo wop, polka, and early rock & roll from Sahm's pre-Sir Douglas Quintet days on the Harlem, Cobra, and Renner labels. Rare regional singles "Crazy Daisy," "Why, Why, Why," "Slow Down," "Baby Tell Me," and "Just a Moment" are a few of the gems collected. *—Al Campbell*

Son of San Antonio: The Roots of Sir Douglas / Sep. 11, 2001 / Music Club ✦✦✦✦
Son of San Antonio: The Roots of Sir Douglas chronicles some of the earliest singles released by Doug Sahm fronting the Sir Douglas Quartet. Recorded between 1962-1966, these 15 songs encompass material originally released on Tribe Records. The majority of tracks are cover versions, including "Bacon Fat," "One Way Out (It's a Man Down There)," "In the Jailhouse Now, No. 2," and "Wolverton Mountain." Of course, an early take of "She's About a Mover" is also included. *—Al Campbell*

Juke Box Music/Last Real Texas Blues Band / Apr. 22, 2003 / Texas Music Group ✦✦✦✦
In 2003, Texas Music Group released *Juke Box Music/Last Real Texas Blues Band*, which contained two complete albums—*Juke Box Music* (1989, originally released on Antone's)

and *The Last Real Texas Blues Band* (1994, originally released on Antone's)—by Doug Sahm on one compact disc. *—John Bush*

Buffy Sainte-Marie

b. Feb. 20, 1941, Piapot Reserve, Saskatchewan, Can

Guitar, Vocals / Country-Pop, Folk-Pop, Singer/Songwriter, Folk-Rock, Contemporary Folk

Buffy Sainte-Marie has enjoyed a long career that has seen her rise to stardom on the folk circuit and try her hand at country, rock, soundtrack themes, acting, activism, and children's television. For most listeners, she remains identified with the material she wrote and sang for Vanguard in the mid-'60s. Her songs that addressed the plight of the Native American, particularly "Now That the Buffalo's Gone" and "My Country 'Tis of Thy People You're Dying," were the ones that generated the most controversy. Yet she was also skilled at addressing broader themes of war and justice ("Universal Soldier") and romance ("Until It's Time for You to Go"). She was also a capable interpreter of outside material, although her idiosyncratic vibrato made large-scale commercial success out of the question.

Sainte-Marie was born to Cree Indian parents and adopted by a white family. Signed to Vanguard, she was one of the folk scene's more prominent rising stars in the '60s, and certainly the only widely heard performer articulating Native American viewpoints in song. Much of her best material from this era, however, gained its greatest commercial inroads via cover versions. "Universal Soldier" was one of Donovan's first hits. "Until It's Time for You to Go," perhaps her best composition, was covered by numerous pop singers, and became a big British hit for Elvis Presley in the early '70s. "Cod'ine," one of the few '60s songs to explicitly address the dangers of drugs, was covered by Californian rock bands Quicksilver Messenger Service and the Charlatans.

Sainte-Marie didn't pigeonhole herself as a folky, though, recording in Nashville in the late '60s in attempts to break into the country market. In the 1970s, she would make some rock records, including one (1971's *She Used to Wanna Be a Ballerina*) with contributions from Ry Cooder and Crazy Horse. These country and rock outings were far less successful, both commercially and artistically, than her early folk efforts. But Sainte-Marie was never as reliant on selling units as most musicians. She kept busy with a long-running stint on *Sesame Street*, performing benefits for and organizing on behalf of Native Americans, and composing for movies (she won an Oscar for the theme to *An Officer and a Gentleman*, co-written with her husband, producer Jack Nitzsche). She hadn't made an album for 15 years before issuing *Coincidence & Likely Stories* in 1992. *—Richie Unterberger*

☆ **It's My Way!** / 1964 / Vanguard ✦✦✦✦✦

This is one of the most scathing topical folk albums ever made. Sainte-Marie sings in an emotional, vibrato-laden voice of war ("The Universal Soldier," later a hit for Donovan), drugs ("Cod'ine"), sex ("The Incest Song"), and most telling, the mistreatment of Native Americans, of which Sainte-Marie is one ("Now That the Buffalo's Gone"). Even decades later, the album's power is moving and disturbing. *—William Ruhlmann*

Many a Mile / 1965 / Fontana ✦✦✦

Sainte-Marie's second LP was most notable for the original version of her most famous composition, "Until It's Time for You to Go," which is her most melodic and memorable track. The rest of the album is more traditional and rough-hewn than some would expect, including a Child ballad with a "Greensleeves"-like melody ("Must I Go Bound"), the Bukka White blues "Fixin' to Die," the oft-done ballad "Lazarus," an Irish-American murder ballad, and a traditional tune accompanied only by mouthbow ("Groundhog"). Of more interest are Sainte-Marie's own compositions, including "Los Pescadores" (which has some of her most uncompromising vibrato) and "Welcome Welcome Emigrante." *—Richie Unterberger*

Little Wheel Spin & Spin / 1966 / Vanguard ✦✦✦✦✦

Sainte-Marie took some tentative steps toward a more contemporary sound here, with contributions from supporting musicians such as Bruce Langhorne, Patrick Sky, Eric Weissberg, and Felix Pappalardi, all of whom were noted New York folk and folk-rock players. It's an average collection of songs, not among either her best or worst work, including some covers of traditional ballads among a mostly original program. It was one of those originals, "My Country 'Tis of Thy People You're Dying," that caught the most attention and remains her most protest-oriented composition. *—Richie Unterberger*

Fire & Fleet & Candlelight / 1967 / Vanguard ✦✦✦

Fire & Fleet & Candlelight was ridiculously over-eclectic, so much so that it comes as a surprise when the 14 songs have finished to find that the total length of the album is a mere 37 minutes. That doesn't mean there's not some worthy material, but the arrangements and material are all over the place. Variety is a good thing, but only when the quality is extremely consistent, and this 1967 album is erratic. "The Seeds of Brotherhood" is so in line with the kind of utopian singalong common to the folk revival that it inadvertently sounds like a parody of itself. Yet songs with orchestral arrangement by Peter Schickele are entirely different, with "Summer Boy" and "The Carousel" going into the Baroque-folk that Judy Collins was mastering during the same era. Joni Mitchell's "The Circle Game" and "Song to a Seagull" both predate Mitchell's release of her own versions, and "The Circle Game" sounds like Sainte-Marie's shot at making it into a hit single, with more straightforward pop/rock production than anything else she cut at the time. "Song to a Seagull," by contrast, is quite close in arrangement and vocal delivery to the treatment Mitchell gave it on her 1968 debut album. Her interpretation of the traditional "Lyke Wake Dirge" verges on the creepy; her cover of Bascom Lamar Lunsford's "Doggett's Gap" goes way back to her earliest folk roots, complete with mouth-bow; "97 Men in This Here Town Would Give a Half a Grand in Silver Just to Follow Me Down" is her fling at good-timey rock. There are yet more cuts that catch you off-guard, like the French-language pop reworking of her "Until It's Time for You to Go"; "Reynardine—A Vampire Legend," a traditional song with only vocals and mouthbow; and "Hey, Little Bird," whose upbeat symphonic pop vaguely foreshadows her songs for *Sesame Street*. Though not without its rewards, on the whole it's an unnerving record. *—Richie Unterberger*

I'm Gonna Be a Country Girl Again / 1968 / Vanguard ✦✦

And, one hopes, she'll *never* be a country girl again. Sainte-Marie went to Nashville to record this album, with help from such session vets as Grady Martin, Floyd Cramer, and the Jordanaires. As expected, it doesn't jell that well, although it's not as poor as you might fear. Sainte-Marie's strengths, though, are best amplified by folk material; her vibrato isn't suited for Nashville country. Predictably, the best songs are the ones which most recall her early folkie work. "Now That the Buffalo's Gone," alike several of her better songs, touches upon Native American issues, and the stark, somber "Tall Trees in Georgia," a solo acoustic guitar piece, seems like a refugee from an earlier album. *—Richie Unterberger*

Illuminations / 1970 / Vanguard ✦✦✦✦✦

In the year 2000, *Wire* magazine picked this spaced out gem from Native American folksinger and activist Buffy Sainte-Marie as one the "100 Albums That Set the World on Fire." Released in 1969, and now on CD, as of 2001, it was reissued as an import on 180 gram vinyl with its original glorious artwork and package. Interestingly enough, it's a record Sainte-Marie doesn't even list on her discography on her website. It doesn't matter whether she cares for it or not, of course, because *Illuminations* is as prophetic a record as the first album by Can or the psychedelic work of John Martin on *Solid Air*. For starters, all of the sounds with the exception of a lead guitar on one track and a rhythm section employed on three of the last four selections are completely synthesized from the voice and guitar of Sainte-Marie herself. There are tracks whose vocals are completely electronically altered and seem to come from the ether—check out "Mary" and "Better to Find Out for Yourself" as a sample. But the track "Adam," with its distorted bassline and Sainte-Marie throwing her voice all over the mix in a tale of Adam's fall and his realization—too late—that he could have lived forever, is a spooky, wondrous tune as full of magic as it is mystery and electronic innovation. The songs here, while clearly written, are open form structures that, despite their brevity (the longest cut here is under four minutes), break down the barriers between folk music, rock, pop, European avant-garde music and Native American styles (this is some of the same territory Tim Buckley explores on *Lorca* and *Starsailor*). It's not a synthesis in any way, but a completely different mode of travel. This is poetry as musical tapestry and music as mythopoetic sonic landscape; the weirdness on this disc is over-exaggerated in comparison to its poetic beauty. It's gothic in temperament, for that time anyway, but it speaks to issues and affairs of the heart that are only now beginning to be addressed with any sort of constancy—check out the opener "God Is Alive, Magic Is Afoot" or the syncopated blues wail in "Suffer the Children" or the arpeggiated synthesized lyrics of "The Vampire." When the guitars begin their wail and drone on "The Angel," the whole record lifts off into such a heavenly space that Hans Joachim Rodelius must have heard it back in the day, because he uses those chords, in the same order and dynamic sense, so often in his own music. Some may be put off by Sainte-Marie's dramatic delivery, but that's their loss; this music comes from the heart—and even space has a heart, you know. One listen to the depth of love expressed on "The Angel" should level even the crustiest cynic in his chair. Combine this with the shriek, moan, and pure-lust wail of "With You, Honey" and "He's a Keeper of the Fire"—you can hear where Tim Buckley conceived (read: stole) the entirety of *Greetings From LA* from, and Diamanda Galas figured out how to move across octaves so quickly. The disc closes with the gothic folk classic "Poppies," the most tripped out, operatic, druggily beautiful medieval ballad ever psychedelically sung. That an album like *Illuminations* can continue to offer pleasure 32 years after it was recorded is no surprise given its quality; that it can continue to mystify, move, and baffle listeners is what makes it a treasure that is still ahead of its time. *—Thom Jurek*

● **The Best of Buffy Sainte-Marie** / 1970 / Vanguard ✦✦✦✦✦

Sainte-Marie pursued a variety of musical styles, from folk to country to experimental rock, and all are represented on this wide-ranging double-record compilation. It doesn't all work, but there are some terrific songs, among them the Native American lament "My Country 'Tis of Thy People You're Dying," and the romantic "Until It's Time for You to Go," and a musical adaptation of a passage from a Leonard Cohen novel, "God Is Alive, Magic Is Afoot." [Beware of the abbreviated version, Vanguard 73113.] *—William Ruhlmann*

She Used to Wanna Be a Ballerina / 1971 / Vanguard ✦✦✦

The Best of Buffy Sainte-Marie, Vol. 2 / 1971 / Vanguard ✦✦✦

Sainte-Marie's best-known and best songs were used on Vanguard's *The Best of Buffy Sainte-Marie*. This 24-song set features mostly original material, along with some traditional tunes and the odd cover, like Joni Mitchell's "Song to a Seagull." While not all of the songs are good, it does illustrate the considerable range of her early recordings—from traditional folk accompanied only by mouthbow to country and western, a truly odd version of "Lyke Wake Dirge," a psychedelic rock cover of Richie Havens' "Adam," a French-pop remake of "Until It's Time for You to Go," and more. There was a lot more to Sainte-Marie than the early acoustic folk recordings, although those are what she's most famous for (and justly so). Like several of Vanguard's anthologies, however, this is sequenced poorly, jumping all over the place chronologically. It makes for a far more uneven experience than would be the case if the sides were arranged more or less in the order in which they were recorded. *—Richie Unterberger*

Moon Shot / 1972 / Vanguard ✦

Quiet Places / 1973 / Vanguard ✦✦

You know you're in trouble when the first track roars in like a Tina Turner tune, as Buffy Sainte-Marie unsuccessfully plays her hand at ballsy bar-band rock & boogie. Actually, most of the rest of the album eschews that approach in favor of more expected singer/songwriter territory, but this still makes for an unimpressive effort, with unsuitably mainstream rock production values hovering over much of the content. Sainte-Marie mixes her own compositions with covers of songs by Joni Mitchell, Randy Newman, and Carole King, but the only real highlight of the record is the final tune, the reflective and haunting ballad "The Jewels of Hanalei." —*Richie Unterberger*

Native North American Child: An Odyssey / 1974 / Vanguard ✦✦✦

Coincidence & Likely Stories / 1992 / Chrysalis ✦✦✦
Native American activist and singer/songwriter Buffy Sainte-Marie makes an incredible comeback on this recording after 16 years away from the studio. Busting all myths about dippy folkies, Sainte-Marie takes on the still-hot topic of Indian oppression while exploring sonic ground that is completely unexpected: programmed keyboards with Laurie Anderson-style voice-over ("The Priests of the Golden Bull"). The entire work is a hard-hitting condemnation of corporate greed and dirty politics, masked in new-agey sounds—about as subversive as it gets. —*Denise Sullivan*

Up Where We Belong / Feb. 1996 / EMI Premier ✦✦✦
For *Up Where We Belong*, Sainte-Marie makes the dubious decision to re-record fan favorites like the title track, "Universal Soldier," "Until It's Time for You to Go," "Cripple Creek" and "Bury My Heart at Wounded Knee." —*Jason Ankeny*

Junior Samples (Alvin Junior Samples)

b. Apr. 10, 1926, Cumming, GA, **d.** Nov. 13, 1983, Cumming, GA
Harmonica, Vocals / Country Comedy, Stories
Much-loved country comedian Junior Samples was a long-running regular on the TV show *Hee Haw*, where he was best known for his shaggy-dog storytelling, nearly incomprehensible accent, and colorful misuse of the English language (not to mention his trademark overalls). Born Alvin Samples in Cumming, GA, on April 10, 1926, he was a sixth-grade dropout who became a comedian by accident in 1966. His son found a large fish head, and Samples told his friends it was from a 22-pound, 9-ounce bass he'd caught, which would have broken the world record. The state Fish and Game Commission interviewed him on the radio, and his story was clearly false, but the interviewer thought it was hilarious and played it repeatedly on his radio show, to tremendous response. A tape of the story was set to music by the Chart Records label and released as a single called "World's Biggest Whopper." It nearly made the country Top 50 in 1967, and Samples appeared on several radio and TV shows, also recording a full-length comedy album for Chart called *The World of Junior Samples*.

Bull Session at Bull's Gap followed in 1968, and the following year Samples signed on at *Hee Haw*, shortly after the show's premiere. He was a smash hit, supplementing his stories with harmonica performances, misreadings of cue cards, and a long-running used-car salesman character. Chart released another album, *That's a Hee Haw*, in 1970 to capitalize on Samples' new exposure, but he concentrated on television for the remainder of his career. He remained a cast member on *Hee Haw* until his death on November 13, 1983. —*Steve Huey*

● **The World of Junior Samples** / 1967 / Chart ✦✦✦✦

Bull Session at Bull's Gap / 1968 / Chart ✦✦✦

That's a Hee Haw / 1970 / Chart ✦✦✦

The Best of Junior Samples / 1971 / Nashville ✦✦✦
The storytelling of Junior Samples is an acquired taste. He landed a spot on the television show *Hee Haw* on the strength of a fish tale he first told in 1966, "World's Biggest Whopper." In the late '60s, Samples recorded a few albums for Chart Records which contained good-natured yarns like "The Insurance Man," "Jailbird," "Junior's Love Life," and "The Disorderly House." While this material retains a charming innocence, for most listeners a little bit of Junior Samples goes a long way. —*Al Campbell*

Junior Samples and Archie Campbell / 197 / Chart ✦✦✦
Junior Samples and Archie Campbell is a collection of ten cuts originally released on Chart Records. Only three are performed with Archie Campbell; the rest feature an uncredited Ralph Emery as Samples' foil. The comedy bits, such as they are, consist of humorous interview excerpts set to music. Samples was a natural comedian, and some of his off-the-cuff remarks are quite funny and surprising—like his disgusting account of kissing girls who dip snuff in "Junior's Love Life"—but much of the entertainment value comes from his wry descriptions of poverty and backwoods culture. As country music became more oriented toward the pop mainstream and less reflective of the rural, economically depressed population that created it, characters like Samples became museum pieces. Whether you laugh at him or with him probably depends on your socioeconomic background, but he's quite a character either way. Samples' most famous bit, "The World's Biggest Whopper," is not included. —*Greg Adams*

Ray Sanders

b. Oct. 1, 1935, St. John, KY
Vocals / Traditional Country
Singer/songwriter Ray Sanders had over 14 chart hits during his 20-year career, but was most popular on the club circuit. The Kentucky native started out as a DJ in Elizabethtown in 1950. In addition to live performances he spent there, he also appeared on the *Lincoln Jamboree* and the *Renfro Valley Barn Dance* through most of the 1950s. After graduating college in 1957, he made his recording debut, without chart success. He debuted on the *Grand Ole Opry* in 1959, which led to his big break in 1960 when he signed with Liberty and debuted with "World So Full of Love," which made the Top 20. The next year, "Lonelyville" also made it to the Top 20. Sanders didn't have another hit until the end of the decade, but in 1969, he appeared again on the country charts wih "Beer Drinkin' Music." The following year he had a Top 20 hit with "All I Ever Need Is You." In 1977, he became the house act at the White Sands in Riverside, California. —*Sandra Brennan*

Feeling Good is Easy / 1969 / Imperial ✦✦✦

● **Ray Sanders** / 1972 / United Artists ✦✦✦✦

Texas Dance Hall Music / 1980 / Hillside ✦✦✦

Tommy Sands

b. Aug. 27, 1937, Chicago, IL
Vocals / Rock & Roll, Rockabilly, Teen Idol
The multi-talented Tommy Sands was born August 27, 1937, in Chicago, IL, to show-business parents. His entry into the business was no mistake, surprise, or happenstance, but genetic and inevitable. His father played piano and his mother sang. He took guitar lessons when he was eight years old and became an adequate axeman. By this time the Sands had moved to Houston, TX, where Sands got the acting bug. He moved to Los Angeles after high-school and landed a job on Cliffie Stone's country & western television show. The exposure led to regular appearances on Tennessee Ernie Ford's weekly television program and nightclub gigs.

He got a big break in 1957 when he got the lead role in *The Singin' Idol*, a television drama on rock & roll. The producer's first choice was Elvis Presley but he wasn't available, so a search went on and Sands won. A single from the show *Teenage Crush* on Capitol Records went to number two on *Billboard*'s pop chart and Sands became an overnight sensation. He appeared on many *Kraft Theater* shows and nearly every network variety show on television. No one-hit wonder, he also hit the charts with "Goin' Steady," "The Worryin' Kind," "Blue Ribbon Baby," "Sing Boy Sing," "The Old Oaken Bucket," and "The Parent Trap." The release of "I'll Be Seeing You," marked a new musical direction for Sands. He cut two albums with Nelson Riddle and continue to release singles for a variety of labels, but none in the teen rock format that made him famous. From the late '50s to the '70s he appeared in more than 150 television programs, and many movies including *Sing Boy Sing* (his first), *Babes in Toyland, The Longest Day, Ensign Pulver, None but the Brave, Mardi Gras*, and *The Violent One*. He married Nancy Sinatra in 1960; the union lasted five years. Where is he now? Still performing and thrilling fans all over the world. What else? It's in his genes. —*Andrew Hamilton*

Steady Date with Tommy Sands / 1957 / Capitol ✦✦✦✦
A Steady Date With Tommy Sands omits his most enduring track, "The Worrying Kind," but otherwise presents an adequate glimpse at the music of this teen idol. The recordings range from teen-oriented novelties ("Ring My Phone") to quasi-big band vocal material. One of the best songs on the set, "Blue Ribbon Baby," Sands co-wrote with a young Rod McKuen. This collection is adequate and affordable for those who are curious about Sands' music, but the omission of "The Worrying Kind" means that Bear Family's expansive single-disc Tommy Sands anthology is still the preferred collection. —*Greg Adams*

● **The Worryin' Kind** / 1994 / Bear Family ✦✦✦✦✦

Leslie Satcher

Vocals (Background) / Country-Pop, Contemporary Country
Since early childhood, singer Leslie Satcher dreamed of a career in music, specifically, a life in country music. She moved to Nashville attempting to follow the route of her pioneers, but found herself as an established songwriter for Music City instead. For several years, this jaunt molded her songwriting craft, penning songs for some of the genre's biggest chart toppers: Vince Gill, Reba McEntire, LeAnn Womack, Randy Travis, and Lorrie Morgan, just to name a few. But Satcher's Texas roots also kept her grounded, never giving up on her own music deal, which finally came true at the turn of the new millennium. Inking a deal with Warner Bros., *Love Letters* marked her debut in early 2001. —*MacKenzie Wilson*

Love Letters / Nov. 14, 2000 / Warner Bros. ✦✦
Broken romance seems to be the fuel that lights the fire for many country songwriters, and Leslie Satcher is no different. In fact, it's a common theme on this telling debut album from an accomplished songwriter. Having penned songs for the likes of Vince Gill, Sara Evans, and Martina McBride, Satcher brings to life her own heartbreak (the man she had hoped to marry marries someone else) in ten of the 11 mostly gloomy tracks she wrote or co-wrote. Lyrics like "I've had lovers leave me and my own heart deceive me" in "I Will Survive" or "you hardly say more than how was your day" in "Look Who's Talking Now," or even "she'll wear your old boots to the mailbox and your name on the rest of her life" in "Love Letters From Old Mexico," continue the sentiment. Everybody likes a good cry every now and then, but, unfortunately, Satcher kinda just makes you feel sorry for her. Still, *Love Letters* is worth at least a listen. —*Maria Konicki Dinoia*

Art Satherly (Arthur Edward Satherley)

b. Oct. 19, 1889, Bristol, England, **d.** Feb. 10, 1986, Fountain Valley, CA
Producer / Traditional Country, Cowboy
Talent scout, producer, and A&R legend Art Satherley was born Arthur Edward Satherley on October 19, 1889, in Bristol, England. He came to America in his early 20s, initially settling in Wisconsin, where he worked in a factory that made cabinets for Edison phonographs. Satherley's first real job in the record industry was promoting 78 rpm records of Ma Rainey and Blind Lemon Jefferson on the Paramount label. By 1930, he began working for Columbia Records and soon became one of the leading A&R men in country music. Between 1938 to 1952, Art Satherley recorded numerous artists, including Gene Autry, Bob Wills, Hank Penny, Lefty Frizzell, Carl Smith, Marty Robbins, and his favorite: Roy Acuff. After Satherley retired from Columbia in 1952, he took life at a slower pace and occasionally got involved in projects he was passionate about. Satherley was elected to the Hall of Fame in 1971. He died on June 10, 1986, in Fountain Valley, CA. —*Al Campbell*

● **Uncle Art Satherley: Country Music's Father** / 1991 / Columbia ✦✦✦✦

Sawyer Brown

f. 1981, Nashville, TN

Group / Country-Pop, Contemporary Country

One of those rare acts who actually became stars directly from winning *Star Search*, country-rockers Sawyer Brown wound up enjoying a long, hit-filled career and remained commercially viable into the new millennium. The group originally grew out of country-pop singer Don King's touring band, with guitarist Bobby Randall and drummer Joe Smyth signing on in 1979, and bassist Jim Scholten, keyboardist Gregg "Hobie" Hubbard, and guitarist/future lead singer Mark Miller all arriving in 1980. King stopped touring in 1981, and the group decided to stay together, naming themselves after the Nashville street where they rehearsed. They spent the next two years on the road, and their agent landed them an audition for the popular syndicated talent show *Star Search*. Sawyer Brown won the grand prize of 100,000 dollars, and it wasn't long before Liberty/Capitol signed them up in 1984. Their self-titled debut album was released in 1985, and their debut single, "Leona," climbed into the Top 20; its follow-up, "Step That Step," went all the way to number one, and the album fell one spot short of that same position.

Their sophomore album, *Shakin'*, was another hit, producing the Top Five single "Betty's Bein' Bad." The band endured a singles-chart slump over 1986-1987, likely a result of their increasingly slick country-pop production, but they rebounded when "This Missin' You Heart of Mine" went to number two at the end of 1987. Another commercially disappointing period followed, lasting into 1991, but it was interrupted by the Top Five single "The Race Is On," which helped its accompanying album, *The Boys Are Back*, climb into the Top Five. Following 1991's *Buick* album, Sawyer Brown parted ways with Liberty and signed with Curb; around the same time, guitarist Randall departed and was replaced by Duncan Cameron. Through it all, they never stopped touring, which helped them maintain a following, and it paid off when "The Walk" went to number two in late 1991.

Their first Curb album, *The Dirt Road*, produced two big hits in the Top Five title track and the band's second number one hit, "Some Girls Do." Their follow-up, 1992's *Cafe on the Corner*, was acclaimed by many critics as their most consistent, fully realized album, and it gave them three Top Five hits in the title track, "All These Years," and "Trouble on the Line." *Outskirts of Town* (1993) continued their hot streak, producing two more Top Fives in "The Boys & Me" and "Hard to Say," plus their third number one in "Thank God for You." The band capped off their commercial resurgence with *Greatest Hits 1990-1995*, a Top Five-selling compilation whose two new tracks, "I Don't Believe in Goodbye" and "This Time," both made the Top Five themselves.

Released later in 1995, the Top Ten *This Thing Called Wantin' and Havin' It All* produced another Top Five smash in "Treat Her Right" and was followed by two albums in 1997: the live *Six Days on the Road* (another Top Ten seller) and the gospel/CCM record *Hallelujah He Is Born*. The Top Ten *Drive Me Wild* arrived in 1999, and its title cut was also a Top Ten hit. Following 2002's poppy *Can You Hear Me Now*, the group parted ways with Curb and signed a new deal with Disney's country subsidiary Lyric Street. *—Steve Huey*

Sawyer Brown / 1986 / Liberty ✦✦✦

Shakin' / Jul. 1986 / Liberty ✦✦✦

Out Goin' Cattin' / Feb. 26, 1987 / Liberty ✦✦

Somewhere in the Night / May 1987 / Liberty ✦✦

Wide Open / Jun. 1988 / Liberty ✦✦✦

The Boys Are Back / Jun. 1989 / Liberty ✦✦✦

Buick / Jan. 7, 1991 / Liberty ✦✦✦

More songs about girls and cars—or, better yet, girls in cars. "The Walk" did so well as a single, the group included it on the next album, too. *—Brian Mansfield*

The Dirt Road / Jan. 6, 1992 / Curb ✦✦✦

The band's robust work ethic makes it into these songs about simple life and small-town values, and Mark Miller controls a tendency to over-sing them, maybe because he believes them. Miller's heart is still filled with clichés like "Burning Bridges (On a Rocky Road)," but the sleaze in his voice is convincing on "Ruby Red Shoes," which has to be a song of lust for Judy Garland. *—Brian Mansfield*

Cafe on the Corner / 1992 / Curb ✦✦✦✦✦

By *Cafe on the Corner*, the members of Sawyer Brown had essentially (i.e., for recording purposes at least) given up on being rock & rollers and revealed themselves to be a pretty decent country band. "Cafe on the Corner" paints a graphic picture of small-town desolation, but these guys are smart enough to avoid preaching: most of the album reflects the marvels of love. The rock & roll sneaks back in on the last two cuts, but by then it's too late to matter. A album filled with good songs, it also includes a great one (Mac McAnally's "All These Years"). *—Brian Mansfield*

Outskirts of Town / Aug. 10, 1993 / Curb ✦✦✦

This Thing Called Wantin' and Havin' It All / 1995 / Curb ✦✦✦

● **Greatest Hits 1990–1995** / 1995 / Curb ✦✦✦✦

Greatest Hits 1990-1995 collects ten Sawyer Brown chart-toppers recorded for Capitol Records, and yes, it does include the slick country-pop band's biggest singles from those years: "Some Girls Do," "Dirt Road," and "Cafe on the Corner." Unfortunately, several key tracks recorded prior to 1990 are missing. So, if you're looking for "Step That Step," "Shakin'," "Betty's Being Bad," "Leona," or "This Missing You Heart of Mine," you won't find them here. *—Al Campbell*

Six Days on the Road / Apr. 15, 1997 / Curb ✦✦✦

Sawyer Brown's records are frequently hampered by undistinguished material, which is what makes the live album *Six Days on the Road* such a treat. By featuring the cream of the band's repertoire and capturing the group in its natural live setting, the album is more exciting and engaging than the majority of Sawyer Brown's releases, making it a live album that's not just for the dedicated—it's for all of their fans. *—Thom Owens*

Hallelujah He Is Born / Aug. 19, 1997 / Atlantic ✦✦✦

Most country acts choose to temper holiday sentimentality with a little religion. Sawyer Brown takes a different approach. As its title telegraphs, *Hallelujah He Is Born* is a distinctly religious Christmas album—only a handful of songs aren't explicitly religious, and even they have a religious underpinning. That is the saving grace of the album, the one element that makes *Hallelujah He Is Born* stand out from the pack. The album still has the slick country-pop atmosphere that marks not only Sawyer Brown's work, but contemporary country in general—but its religious conviction makes it one of the more original (and, actually, *better*) country-pop Christmas records of recent years. *—Thom Owens*

Drive Me Wild / Mar. 2, 1999 / Curb ✦✦✦

The Hits Live / Nov. 7, 2000 / Curb ✦✦

Can You Hear Me Now / Jun. 11, 2002 / Curb ✦✦✦

Sawyer Brown has never made any apologies for being a pop-oriented country-rock band, and throughout their career, they've often traded on the sounds and styles of the time to keep them sounding contemporary. Still, it's a little strange seeing frontman going post-Matchbox Twenty with his looks—all adult-alternative pop, complete with short goatee and a photo in the liner notes where he looks startlingly like R.E.M.'s Michael Stipe. These visuals are a slight clue to where the band is going with *Can You Hear Me Now*, their first album of new material in three years. Though there are some twangy guitars here and there, along with a few uptempo shuffles, this is more a pop album than a country album, aimed at the audience that listens as much to adult-oriented mainstream pop (like Matchbox Twenty) and contemporary, post-Shania and Faith Hill country. Some might carp about this, but they're likely to be those who never listen to Sawyer Brown in the first place, since the band has always been a bit like this and they've always done this pretty well, and *Can You Hear Me* is no exception. This does adopt contemporary mores, but in a professional, engaging way, and while not all of the ten songs are strong, there are certainly more hits than misses. It's a solid effort, not just for Sawyer Brown, but as contemporary crossover country-pop albums go. *—Stephen Thomas Erlewine*

True Believer / Apr. 8, 2003 / Curb ✦✦✦

Most contemporary country acts perform spiritual numbers on occasion, and over the course of a two-decade career, Sawyer Brown has recorded enough of them to fill an album—and the band has done just that with 2003's *True Believer*. Featuring three new tracks alongside seven tunes that have become established parts of Sawyer Brown's set list through the years, *True Believer* reflects the pop-friendly modern country style that's long been the group's hallmark. Since more than a few CCM artists follow a similar creative path, this collection should appeal not only to the group's fans, but to Christian music enthusiasts looking to broaden their horizons a bit. While Sawyer Brown's high degree of polish hasn't always endeared the group to the more honky tonk-oriented country fans, in this context the band's easy professionalism is just what the material calls for, and *True Believer* honors Sawyer Brown's talent and faith in equal measure. *—Mark Deming*

Don Schlitz

b. Aug. 29, 1952, Durham, NC

Songwriter, Vocals (Background) / Contemporary Country, Urban Cowboy

A 1993 inductee into the Nashville Songwriters Hall of Fame, Don Schlitz was one of Nashville's preeminent songwriters and the author of numerous chart-topping hits. He was a native of Durham, NC, and after a short stint at Duke University in the early '70s, he moved to Nashville to seek his fortune, working as a swing-shift computer operator for five years while honing his songwriting skills. Schlitz got his big break in 1978 when Kenny Rogers had a monster hit with his "The Gambler." The number-one smash not only became one of Rogers' signature songs, but also spawned a series of TV-movies; later, Schlitz recorded and released his own version of the hit on his debut album, *Dreamers Matinee*. During the '80s, many other prominent artists recorded his songs, including John Conlee, Alabama, Randy Travis, Tanya Tucker, and Keith Whitley.

Schlitz frequently co-wrote songs with Paul Overstreet; one of their most distinguished collaborations was "Forever and Ever Amen," which became an enormous hit for Randy Travis. In 1987, Schlitz wrote or co-wrote five number-one singles, including "On the Other Hand," another hit for Travis. He continued steadily churning out hit songs, and was even commissioned by then-President George Bush to compose a theme for his "Points of Light" campaign in the early '90s. *—Sandra Brennan*

● **Dreamers Matinee** / 1980 / Capitol ✦✦✦✦

Live at the Bluebird Cafe / Jan. 23, 2001 / American Originals ✦✦✦

Timothy B. Schmit

b. Oct. 30, 1947, Oakland, CA

Bass, Vocals / Soft Rock, Country-Rock, Pop/Rock

Although he delivered a number of solo records, Timothy B. Schmit earned his greatest fame as a vocalist with the Eagles and Poco, two of the era's most successful mainstream country-rock outfits. Born October 30, 1947, in Oakland, CA, Schmit joined Poco prior to recording the band's 1971 LP *Deliverin'* and remained with the group for nine more albums. After the release of the band's 1977 *Indian Summer*, he was invited to join the Eagles, signing on, ironically enough, as a replacement for another former Poco member, Randy Meisner. Schmit's arrival coincided with the sessions for the Eagles' final LP, 1979's *The Long Run*; his contribution, "I Can't Tell You Why," proved to be a tremendous hit.

After internal dissent triggered the Eagles' breakup in 1982, Schmit began a solo career, issuing three LPs: 1984's *Playin' It Cool*, 1987's *Timothy B.* and 1990's *Tell Me the Truth*. He rejoined Poco for 1984's *Inomorata* and was also a popular guest musician, appearing on dozens of records including solo projects from onetime bandmates like Don Henley, Don Felder, and Richie Furay as well as LPs from Crosby, Stills & Nash, Jimmy Buffett, and Bob Seger. In 1989, Poco again reunited for the album *Legacy*, and in 1992, Schmit joined Ringo Starr's All-Starr Band, performing his showcase number "I Can't Tell

You Why" on a live LP recorded in Montreux. Shortly after, the Eagles ended months of speculation by announcing a reunion of the band's *Long Run*-era lineup; the subsequent tour and live LP, both dubbed *Hell Freezes Over*, were incredibly successful, reaffirming the Eagles' status as one of the world's most popular artists. *—Jason Ankeny*

Playin' It Cool / 1984 / Asylum ♦♦♦

Timothy B. / 1987 / MCA ♦♦♦

● **Tell Me the Truth** / Jul. 24, 1990 / MCA ♦♦♦♦
The voice behind the Top Ten 1980 hit for the Eagles' "I Can't Tell You Why" should have been a big star after his third solo album. Everything that was wrong on Don Felder's *Airborne* effort goes right on Schmit's *Tell Me the Truth* album, his charming voice gliding over charming songs like "In Roxy's Eyes" and "Something Sad." Having Rita Coolidge and Siedah Garrett on backing vocals is part of the artistically successful formula here, but the other key is that six producers converge to manufacture a very smooth and very polished affair. Danny Kortchmar, John Boylan, Don Felder, and the singer all contribute to the album's sound, and all separately or in combinations on different tracks. It begins with "Tell Me the Truth," and that '80s ambience that permeated solo recordings by Glen Frey, Don Felder, and Don Henley is certainly present on the Henley/Kortchmar production. Side two gets a lot heavier, with a bent toward '90s techno, not only on "Let Me Go" but more so on "Perfect Strangers," both produced by David Cole and co-writer Bruce Gaitsch. Could the Eagles have been listening to Deep Purple? And borrowing Barry Manilow songwriter Will Jennings for three songs in the process? "All I Want to Do" has an immaculate production by Gaitsch and Timothy B. Schmit, an Everly Brothers-type folk number with flamenco-style leads that borrow heavily from a folky George Harrison. It's very pretty and very pleasant, and the kind of breakthrough that could appeal even to the detractors of the Eagles' homogenized sound. It's so innocent that another dimension is added to this unique music mix. "Tonight" is pure pop, somewhat removed from Poco, or maybe it's Poco meets the Raspberries. The jangling guitars and bouncy drums have keyboards slinking in and out while Timothy B. Schmit just knocks this one right on the head. Having landed in the Top 25 with 1987's "Boy's Night Out," this album should have had multiple hits. Schmit's sincerity comes through in a way that makes Henley's ten solo hits and Glen Frey's seven as overbearing as they were overplayed. "For the Children" is another revelation with a beautiful choir-type chorus closing out a superb effort which deserved so much more attention. Pretty amazing when one considers how big the Eagles are and how this one got away. *—Joe Viglione*

Feed the Fire / May 1, 2001 / Lucan ♦♦♦

John Schneider

b. Apr. 8, 1960, Mt. Kisco, NY
Vocals / Country-Pop, Urban Cowboy
Best known for playing Bo Duke on the hit TV series *The Dukes of Hazzard*, John Schneider also maintained a parallel secondary career as a country singer for much of the '80s. Born in Mt. Kisco, NY, in 1960, Schneider grew up in Atlanta and started acting at the age of eight; he also learned guitar, and as a teenager he entertained at parties and other social events. He loved auto racing and briefly attempted to become a professional, and that experience helped him land his co-starring role on *The Dukes of Hazzard* in 1979. He remained with the series until its cancellation in 1985, with a brief interruption due to a contract walkout in 1982, and also appeared in several films and TV-movies. Meanwhile, Schneider recorded a country album called *Now or Never* for Scotti Bros. in 1981. It was a Top Ten hit on the country charts, and the single "It's Now or Never" made the Top Five on both the country and adult contemporary charts, just missing the pop Top Ten.

The holiday album *White Christmas* followed, and Schneider went on to sign with MCA, issuing five albums from 1984-1987. He scored four number one-singles during that time: "I've Been Around Enough to Know" (1984), "Country Girls" (1985), "What's a Memory Like You (Doing in a Love Like This)," and "You're the Last Thing I Needed Tonight" (both 1986). He also managed five other Top Ten hits, and one of his LPs, 1986's *A Memory Like You*, topped the country charts. Schneider kept his acting career going with a variety of guest starring roles on television, plus a few films, and appeared in a couple of *Dukes of Hazzard* reunion projects. He returned to the spotlight in 2001, when he landed the role of Clark Kent's father on the popular WB series *Smallville*. *—Steve Huey*

● **Greatest Hits** / 1987 / MCA ♦♦♦♦♦
Greatest Hits is a thorough overview of Schneider's career; it contains all four of his number one records—"I've Been Around Enough to Know," "Country Girls," "What's a Memory like You (Doing in a Love like This)" and "You're the Last Thing I Needed Tonight"—as well as the other Top Ten hits from his tenure at MCA. *—Jason Ankeny*

Schramms

f. 1987
Group / Indie Pop, Alternative Country-Rock
Melding pop, folk-rock, and alt-country sounds with quirky wit and a keen intelligence, the Schramms were the brainchild of gifted guitarist, vocalist, and songwriter Dave Schramm, who debuted the group in 1987. Schramm, who had previously played with Human Switchboard and Jon Klages, left Yo La Tengo in 1986, following the release of their debut album, *Ride the Tiger*, and he soon began working up material with fellow Human Switchboard alumnus Ron Metz and drums and bassist Terry Karydes, who had played in an embryonic version of Yo La Tengo. After Karydes' bass was stolen, she moved over to keyboards, and Mike Lewis, another former member of Yo La Tengo, took over on bass, with guitarist Todd Novak and sax player Pete Linzell filling out the lineup. The band dubbed themselves the Walking Wounded and lined up a short tour only to discover a group in California was already using that name; as a joke, the band billed themselves as the Schramms for the duration of the tour, only to discover the name stuck. They opted to keep the moniker. The pocket-sized independent label Okra Records invited the Schramms to record an album, and they released *Walk to Delphi* in 1989. However, Okra's distributor, Rough Trade, went out of business a matter of weeks after the album came out, effectively stalling its release in the U.S. To the band's good fortune, the Schramms developed a strong following in Germany, and the European label Normal Records signed on to release the second Schramms album, *Rock, Paper, Scissors, Dynamite*, in 1992. By this time, Lewis, Novak, and Linzell had bowed out of the band; Al Greller signed on as the new bassist, and Schramm opted to go on without a sax or second guitarist. In 1993, Karydes also left the band, with George Usher taking over on keyboards; this edition of the Schramms recorded two albums, 1994's *Little Apocalypse* and 1996's *Dizzy Spell*. (*Little Apocalypse* was released in the U.S. by East Side Digital, who the following year reissued *Walk to Delphi* and gave *Rock, Paper, Scissors, Dynamite* its belated American debut; *Dizzy Spell* was distributed by the fledgling alt-country label Checkered Past.) In 2000, the Schramms returned to the recording studio with another new lineup—Andy Burton joined as keyboard player after the departure of Usher, and a second guitarist, Jon Graboff, who had often guested with the group, signed on full-time. *100 Questions* was the Schramms' first album which was not self-produced; J.D. Foster oversaw the sessions, and Syd Straw, Richard Buckner, and Jeb Loy Nichols contributed guest vocals. *—Mark Deming*

Walk to Delphi / 1990 / Okra ♦♦♦♦♦
Between Dave Schramm's stints in both Human Switchboard and Yo La Tengo, Ron Metz's years with Human Switchboard, and Al Greller's work with Peter Stampfel, the Schramms had plenty of miles under their collective belt when they recorded their first album, *Walk to Delphi*, and if the results suggest the band was still fine tuning their musical personality, there's no arguing they play with tremendous skill and authority on these sessions, and Dave Schramm leaves no doubt that he's an unusually gifted guitarist and songwriter. The striking balance of pop, rock, and folk that the band found on *Little Apocalypse* was still a few years down the road, and in many respects *Walk to Delphi* is lighter and hookier than much of what would follow from this band, though it manages to fall a bit short of "radio friendly"—as tuneful as Schramm's tunes are here, and as winning the performances may be, there's a dark undercurrent to songs like "Out of the Earth," "He Has Got a Gun," and "The Way Some People Die," which belies their seemingly upbeat surfaces. But for a band taking their first turn at bat, the Schramms sound remarkable confident on *Walk to Delphi*, and with good reason, given the quality of the material and the easy skill Schramm and his bandmates bring to these recordings. Like much of the Schramms' body of work, *Walk to Delphi* slipped through the cracks on its first release in the U.S. (the band would fare better in time in Europe), but it's certainly a record that demands rediscovery, and fully rewards the search. *—Mark Deming*

Rock, Paper, Scissors, Dynamite / 1992 / Normal Records ♦♦♦♦
The second album from the Schramms, *Rock, Paper, Scissors, Dynamite*, sounds like the sort of record most bands don't come up with until six or seven years into their recording careers, speaking with the clear voices of seasoned veterans in firm command of their powers. Dave Schramm's songwriting had already developed an easygoing maturity that displayed wit without forcing a laugh and conveyed bitterness without spite or overwhelming angst. The second edition of the Schramms plays with authority, grace, and good humor; while Schramm's fleet-fingered guitar leads are the highlight, Terry Karydes' keyboards offer splendid melodic counterpoints, and bassist Al Greller and drummer Ron Metz are a rock-solid, no-nonsense rhythm section. If *Rock, Paper, Scissors, Dynamite* has a flaw, it's that it goes on a bit too long and doesn't shift gears often enough; while the album starts out well with the brilliant "Welfare of Your Enemy" and rolls on with a string of fine songs, it starts to lose a bit of steam at about the halfway point, and stays in a midtempo rut that is just a bit wearying by the time the disc finally comes to a close. In short, this album makes clear that the Schramms already had a lot going for them in the way of chops and studio smarts, but pacing an album was one task they hadn't yet learned to master. *—Mark Deming*

Little Apocalypse / Sep. 20, 1994 / East Side Digital ♦♦♦♦
The Schramms already had intelligence and maturity to spare when they cut their second album, *Rock, Paper, Scissors, Dynamite*, but the two years of seasoning that preceded the recording of 1994's *Little Apocalypse* is audible from the first play. While the Schramms already sounded tight on their earlier recordings, they sound positively intuitive on these sessions (especially Ron Metz, whose drumming offers lots of subtle color without calling attention to itself), and Dave Schramm's guitar playing has, if anything, grown even more striking and inventive, confirming his status as one of America's greatest unsung guitarists. And while *Rock, Paper, Scissors, Dynamite* sounded like a set of great songs, *Little Apocalypse* is a great *album*, displaying a greater thematic unity and enough tonal variety to keep it compelling from start to finish. And *Little Apocalypse* is dark enough to live up to its title, full of casual murders, angry apparitions, songs of the sirens, and vengeful final words alongside Schramm's usual tales of romantic distress and emotional discombobulation, painting a vivid picture of a world where things aren't quite right made all the more familiar by Schramm's warm, well-worn voice. (For good measure, the band also offers up another of its stellar covers: in this case, an inspired reading of Lucinda Williams' "Side of the Road.") A striking mix of the comfortable and the troubling, *Little Apocalypse* is a superb album from a band just hitting the top of its form. *—Mark Deming*

● **Dizzy Spell** / Mar. 17, 1998 / Checkered Past ♦♦♦♦♦
If ever there was a band whose albums demanded more than a single listen, it's the Schramms. On first spin, *Dizzy Spell* sounds like a pleasant, well-crafted bit of folk-leaning pop; play it a few more times, let it sink in, and you'll find it's a remarkably intelligent, expressive, and compelling album that becomes more satisfying each time out. Dave Schramm was not blessed with the finest voice of his generation, but give his craggy, conversational timbre a chance to register and you'll be amazed at its range of nuances, and his lyrics manage to be both witty and genuinely poetic without sinking into

pretension. More importantly, he's a superb guitarist who knows when to gently support a song and when to reel off a solo that's full of dexterity and fire. And with George Usher on keyboards, Al Greller on bass, and Ron Metz on drums, Schramm has a band that's solid and expressive but knows their first responsibility is to serve the song. And on *Dizzy Spell*, the Schramms offer up a dozen songs well worth hearing, particularly the bizarre suburban romance of "Wild Season," the remembrance of lost love of "Tell Me Again and Again," and the wistful, reflective title cut. Evocative, compelling, and seasoned with plenty of great guitar work, *Dizzy Spell* is a superb, criminally overlooked album that was one of the most pleasurable releases of 1998. *—Mark Deming*

100 Questions / Sep. 12, 2000 / Madacy ✦✦✦✦✦
Schramms quietly made a handful of superb albums through the 1990s which offered all the proof you'd need that Dave Schramm was a top-shelf guitarist, songwriter, and bandleader. But with 2000's *100 Questions*, Schramm and his usual studio cohort Gary Arnold have handed over the production duties to someone else for the first time, and the result is the band's strongest album to date. Musically, there isn't much that's strikingly different about *100 Questions*: Schramm's songs are still as dour, slyly witty, and keenly intelligent as ever; his tastefully angular guitar solos are still a delight to hear; and his band is solid and fully in touch with the subtleties of the songs. But producer J.D. Foster has encouraged tighter and more concise arrangements for the musicians, which give them less space to drift than they displayed on *Dizzy Spell* (*100 Questions*' 11 cuts zip by in a snappy 38 minutes, while *Dizzy Spell*'s dozen take a more leisurely 57 minutes), and the songs gain a lot of punch in the process. And the album simply *sounds better*, Foster's production and mix are brighter, warmer, and more vivid than anything Schramms have enjoyed in the past, and it brings out the best in Ron Metz's drumming, Andrew Harris Burton's keyboards, and Schramm's guitar. And Schramm and company have certainly risen to the occasion for their fifth time at bat; "Torn in Two," "Deny You," and "Simple Arithmetic" are pop that's intelligent, engaging, and hooky as all get out, while "I'll Believe," "Mailbox," and "She Says" prove this band is no less exciting when they cut back the tempo. And it says a lot about how good the Schramms are on *100 Questions* that the guest spots from Syd Straw, Richard Buckner, and Jeb Loy Nichols never upstage the group. It's hard to say why the Schramms aren't widely regarded as one of America's best and most interesting bands at the dawn of the millennium, but one listen to *100 Questions* proves it's not because they don't have the goods. *—Mark Deming*

Schuyler, Knobloch & Bickhardt

f. 1986
Group / Contemporary Country, Country-Folk
Thom Schuyler, J. Fred Knobloch and Craig Bickhardt were three prominent Nashville songwriters who briefly got together to form a rather eclectic band that played a blend of country, folk and pop. Originally formed in 1986 as Schuyler, Knobloch & Overstreet (with songwriter Paul Overstreet), the trio signed with MTM Records. Their debut single, "You Can't Stop Love," made it to the country Top Ten and remained on the charts over six months. After a change of name to the more manageable S-K-O in 1987, Overstreet left the band to pursue his own songwriting career, and Craig Bickhardt replaced him. The title track of S-K-B's *No Easy Horses* hit the Top 20, and the trio's next cut, "This Old House," made it to the Top 25. When MTM folded, they found themselves without a contract and disbanded soon after. Schuyler has since become the Vice President of RCA's country division, while Knobloch and Bickhardt have continued to write excellent songs. *—Sandra Brennan*

No Easy Horses / 1987 / MTM ✦✦✦✦

Tracy Schwarz

b. Nov. 13, 1938, New York, NY
Fiddle, Vocals, Session Musician / Traditional Bluegrass
Tracy Schwarz is one of the greatest traditional fiddlers in America. His credits run from the New Lost City Ramblers and the Strange Creek Singers to recordings with other traditional musicians, his family, and in more recent years with many Cajun greats. New York City-born and raised, Schwarz first came to love country music from radio broadcasts of the late '40s. The music he heard inspired him to learn the banjo and guitar. While in college, Schwarz also mastered the mandolin and the bass fiddle. He soon began playing in assorted bluegrass bands around Washington, D.C. During the early '60s, Schwarz enlisted in the Army for two years and during that time learned to play the fiddle. He began working with the New Lost City Ramblers as a replacement for Tom Paley in 1962, and eventually became a full-time member for ten years; his involvement in the band later tapered off as he became more interested in spending time on his Pennsylvania farm. He continued to appear with other bands, most notably the Strange Creek Singers through the 1970s. He continues to perform and explore new areas of traditional music. *—Sandra Brennan & Don Stevens*

Tracy Schwarz Cajun Trio / 1993 / Swallow ✦✦✦✦
The Tracy Schwarz Trio dedicated themselves to traditional, uncompromising Cajun music with French lyrics, acoustic backing and little or no pop/crossover orientation, and don't stray from their mission here. The musical menu's churning two-steps and swaying waltzes are sung exclusively in French. The trio's singing, harmonizing and playing are joyous and delightful, and anyone who enjoys exuberant fare should find it attractive. *—Ron Wynn*

● **Home Among the Hills** / Bear Family ✦✦✦✦✦

Darrell Scott

Dobro, Guitar, Mandolin, Vocals / Singer/Songwriter, Alternative Country, Progressive Country, Progressive Bluegrass
Best known as a songwriter for Garth Brooks and other country artists, and as a sideman for performers like Guy Clark and Tim O'Brien, Darrell Scott is an equally accomplished singer and multi-instrumentalist in his own right. Based in Nashville, Scott's career focuses on his ability to write songs that blend bluegrass, country, zydeco, folk, jazz, and pop influences with personal lyrics. Scott's writing includes collaborations with friends like Tim O'Brien, songs for country stars like Garth Brooks (Scott and O'Brien wrote "When There's No One Around" from *Sevens*), and for his own albums: 1997's *Aloha From Nashville* and 1999's *Family Tree*.

Yet his talents as a singer and performer shouldn't be minimized; as a part of Guy Clark's and Tim O'Brien's bands, Scott's skill with the dobro, mandolin, and guitar added an extra flair to their releases and performances. Likewise, his singing takes center stage on his own albums but adds a certain something to all the releases on which he appears. Though his many facets make him difficult to classify, Darrell Scott stands out for that very reason. *—Heather Phares*

● **Aloha From Nashville** / Apr. 22, 1997 / Sugar Hill ✦✦✦✦
Darrell Scott's debut album is an ambitious fusion of various American roots musics, intercut with touches of jazz. Scott's songwriting isn't always fully formed, yet his music is rich and welcoming, featuring layers of guitars, banjos, dobros, trumpets, accordions and sighing steel guitars. Occasionally, it loses itself in the mist, but *Aloha From Nashville* is a fascinating and often compelling listen. *—Thom Owens*

Family Tree / Apr. 20, 1999 / Sugar Hill ✦✦✦✦
Darrell Scott's second solo album, *Family Tree*, picks up where his debut *Aloha From Nashville* left off—that is, it features more of Scott's great writing, singing and playing. The title track in particular captures the album's gritty, moving feel and creative blend of country, folk, bluegrass and jazz. *—Heather Phares*

Jack Scott (Jack Scafone Jr.)

b. Jan. 24, 1936, Windsor, Ontario, Canada
Vocals, Guitar / Rock & Roll, Traditional Country, Rockabilly
Jack Scott sounded tough, like someone you wouldn't want to meet in a dark alley unless he had a guitar in his hands. When he growled "The Way I Walk," wise men (and women) stepped aside. Despite his snarling rockabilly attitude, Scott hailed from Ontario, Canada, and grew up near Detroit, developing a love for hillbilly music along the way. His first sides for ABC/Paramount in 1957 exhibited a profound country-rock synthesis, and after moving to the Carlton label, Scott hit the charts the next year with the tremulous ballad "My True Love," backed by his vocal group, the Chantones. Flip it over, however, and you have the hauling rocker "Leroy," all about some wacked-out tough guy who's content to remain behind the bars of his local jail. Scott's pronounced emphasis on acoustic guitar distinguishes atmospheric rockers like "Goodbye Baby," "Go Wild Little Sadie," "Midgie," and "Geraldine." But his principal pop success came with tears-in-your-beer country-based ballads—"What in the World's Come Over You" and "Burning Bridges" were massive smashes on Top Rank in 1960, and he recorded an entire album's worth of Hank Williams covers for the firm the same year.

Born in Windsor, Ontario, Scott (born Jack Scafone Jr., January 24, 1936) moved to a town on the outskirts of Detroit, MI, when he was ten years old. At the age of 18, he formed the Southern Drifters and after leading the band for three years, he signed to ABC as a solo artist in 1957. Over the next year, he released a handful of singles for the label before moving to Carlton Records the following year. His double-A-sided debut for Carlton, "My True Love"/"Leroy," became a huge hit, with the first song peaking at number three and the latter at number 11; it also became a Top Ten hit in England. During the next two years, Scott had a number of minor hits for Carlton, highlighted by the number eight hit "Goodbye Baby" (fall 1958). On most of these tracks, the Chantones provided vocal support.

Late in 1959, he switched labels, signing with Top Rank. His first single for the label, "What in the World's Come Over You," became a number-five hit early in 1960. It was followed a few months later by another Top Ten hit, the number-three single "Burning Bridges." The pair of singles were his last major hits, and over the next two years, his singles progressively charted at lower positions than their predecessors. Early in 1961, he signed with Capitol Records, but none of his three singles made the Top 40. Scott continued to vacillate between cowboy crooner and rough-edged rocker throughout the remainder of the '60s and '70s, recording for a variety of labels, including Groove and Dot. In 1974, he managed to have a minor country hit with his Dot single "You're Just Gettin' Better." During the '80s and '90s, Scott occasionally turned up on the oldies circuit, still looking and sounding like a man you seriously didn't want to mess with. *—Bill Dahl*

Scott on Groove / 1989 / Bear Family ✦✦✦✦
The music on *Scott on Groove* was recorded after Jack Scott's hit-making era on Capitol was finished. Scott recorded for Groove in the early '60s. During this time, he was trying to refashion his sound into a rock & roll/rockabilly direction. Not all of the attempts were successful, but the set is interesting for dedicated fans, but they would probably rather acquire this material on the more comprehensive box set, *Classic Scott*. *—Stephen Thomas Erlewine*

● **Greatest Hits** / 1990 / Curb ✦✦✦✦✦
Curb's *Greatest Hits* was the only American Jack Scott compilation available in the mid-'90s, after Capitol pulled its *Collector's Series* from the market. Although *Greatest Hits* only has 11 tracks—including a recently recorded version of "Running Scared"—it has the essential big hits ("My True Love," "Goodbye Baby," "Burning Bridges," "Leroy," "The Way I Walk," "What in the World's Come Over You") and is a serviceable collection, even if it is frustratingly brief. *—Stephen Thomas Erlewine*

The Way I Walk / 1990 / Roller Coaster ✦✦✦
Jack Scott cut a couple of great rockabilly 45s for ABC/Paramount to begin his career, and Scott's two biggest hits, "What in the World's Come Over You" and "Burning Bridges," were recorded directly after his stay at Carlton Records. But it's generally conceded by rockabilly fans that the majority of his best and most lasting work was cut for that label between 1958 and 1960. This 26-track compilation makes a nice one-stop for the casual

Scott fan who doesn't want to opt for Bear Family's massive multi-disc box set, as it's loaded with great rockers like "The Way I Walk," "Leroy," "Goodbye Baby," and his first big hit, "My True Love." But the non-inclusion of his two biggest hits and his early rockabilly singles keep this one from being the definitive package, although it's great listening all the way. *—Cub Koda*

Capitol Collectors Series / Oct. 8, 1990 / Capitol ♦♦♦♦

Classic Scott / Jun. 27, 1994 / Bear Family ♦♦♦♦♦

With the exception of Roy Orbison and Elvis, no white rock & roller of the time ever developed a finer voice with a better range than Jack Scott, or cut a more convincing body of work in rockabilly, rock & roll, country-soul, gospel, country-pop, or blues. And it's all here on this five-CD set, which probably seems at first like more Jack Scott than most of us need. Its 134 tracks include very, very few songs that aren't worth hearing at least twice (and most a lot more) and have more than their share of surprises. Anyone who laments Scott's failure to remain a rockabilly artist will be surprised at just how much he brought to country ballads and gospel, as well as the convincingly bluesy approach to rock & roll that he maintained years into his recording career. The handful of rockabilly tracks here, confined to the first half of the first disc (with their stereo mixes appearing on the last one), show Scott as a potential rival to Elvis Presley and Gene Vincent. He found success as more of a ballad singer, however, and never returned to his rock & roll roots for more than a song at a time. At the end of the 1950s, he moved back into the haven of country music, where he'd started in his teen years. The fit wasn't an ideal one, although Scott was good enough to make an album's worth of Hank Williams songs a worthwhile venture. This box has it all, mastered about as well as it's ever likely to be. Moreover, good as everything else is, the producers of this box have saved the best for last—unissued, undated demos a few of which are worth the price of a CD themselves. *—Bruce Eder*

Best of Jack Scott (1958–1960) / Dec. 12, 1995 / Stardust ♦♦♦♦♦

The Very Best of Jack Scott / Sep. 26, 2000 / Collectables ♦♦♦♦♦

Although it runs 23 tracks and contains such classics as "What in the World's Come Over You" and "Burning Bridges," Collectables' *The Very Best of Jack Scott* is not a definitive overview of his career, since it lacks such classics as "The Way I Walk" and "Leroy." This does a good job of rounding up such lesser-known, late-'60s recordings, which are by and large fairly good, but they don't make up for the absence of those previously mentioned songs. Not a bad collection, but not as good as it could have been—especially considering its generous running time. *—Stephen Thomas Erlewine*

I Remember Hank Williams/What in the World's Come Over You? / Nov. 12, 2002 / BGO ♦♦♦

In 2002, BGO released *I Remember Hank Williams/What in the World's Come Over You?*, which contained two complete albums—*I Remember Hank Williams* (1960, originally released on Top Rank) and *What in the World's Come Over You?* (also originally released in 1960 on Top Rank)—by Jack Scott on one compact disc. *—John Bush*

Scratch Band

f. 1980

Group / Country-Pop

The Scratch Band was best remembered as Don Williams' backing unit, but in 1982, the quartet stepped into the limelight to record their own album, *The Scratch Band Featuring Danny Flowers*. Lead guitarist and frontman Flowers, a native of North Carolina, arrived in Nashville around 1971, where he worked as a session guitarist; he met Williams during one of these sessions. In addition to playing music, Flowers was also a songwriter; in 1973, Emmylou Harris recorded his "Before Believing." Flowers joined Williams' band in 1974. Four years later, he wrote "Tulsa Time" while stranded in that city during a snow storm, and it became a number-one hit for Williams; Eric Clapton later recorded the song as well.

Keyboard player and guitarist Biff Watson was born and raised in Virginia and he too came to Nashville in 1971, where he joined Tennessee Pulleybone and went on to work with Tracy Nelson and Crystal Gayle's band Peace and Quiet. He joined Williams in 1979. Bass guitarist Dave Pomeroy was raised in Alexandria, VA, and briefly studied history in college before dropping out to become a full-time musician. After playing with other bands, he toured with Sleepy LaBeef and came to Music City in 1978. He joined Williams in 1980 after working with Guy Clark and Billy Joe Shaver. Drummer Pat McInerney was born and raised in England. He earned a college degree in sociology and in 1974 became a full-time musician, playing with Jimmy James and the Vagabonds, a popular soul band. By 1976, he was playing in a rock band, Limey, and later subbed for Williams' drummer during a European tour in 1977. He ended up joining Williams' band the following year. After releasing their only album, Scratch went back to working with Williams until he stopped touring. *—Sandra Brennan*

● **The Scratch Band Featuring Danny Flowers** / 1982 / MCA ♦♦♦♦

Earl Scruggs

b. Jan. 6, 1924, Flint Hill, NC

Banjo, Guitar, Vocals, Leader / Traditional Bluegrass

Earl Scruggs is to the five-string banjo what Paganini was to the violin. After more than 20 years with the Foggy Mountain Boys, forming the most famous band in bluegrass history, Scruggs and Lester Flatt parted company in 1969 because of artistic differences, with Flatt pursuing more traditional sounds and Scruggs forming the Earl Scruggs Revue with his two sons. The Revue appealed more to a young and urban audience and, with dobro player Josh Graves, played rock and other non-country music. Scruggs has made many albums since his parting with Flatt (including *The Storyteller and the Banjoman* with Tom T. Hall in 1982) and is seen on TV, often for reunion appearances. *—David Vinopal*

Earl Scruggs: His Family and Friends / 1972 / Columbia ♦♦♦♦♦

Earl Scruggs was only two years out of his partnership with Lester Flatt when he did the public television special that yielded *Earl Scruggs: His Family and Friends*, an all-star effort that lives up to the promise of its big-name guests. Cut at the *Grand Ole Opry*, at the homes of Joan Baez and Doc Watson, the Doug Underwood Ranch (for the Byrds segment), the home of Willie Morris (for the Morris Brothers), at a private home in Carmel, NY (for Bob Dylan's performance), at the site of the 1969 Vietnam War Moratorium in Washington, D.C., and at Madison High School in Madison, TN, the album and the special presented many facets of Scruggs' life and music and was quite daring in its time. Baez was like a lightning rod for controversy in those days, and Dylan wasn't too much more well-liked by the more conservative members of Scruggs' audience; and publicly presenting his own sympathy with the anti-war movement didn't necessarily earn the banjo virtuoso many points back in Nashville. As with almost every other aspect of Scruggs' life, however, his music won over even the harshest critics of his political views. And the music here is glorious—not only is Scruggs, along with the Earl Scruggs Revue, in excellent form, but Baez is in impeccable voice for "Love Is Just a Four-Letter Word," in a rendition with Scruggs' band, one of her greatest moments on record and worth the price of the CD by itself. Dylan is only present for "Nashville Skyline Rag," but considering how rarely seen he was in those days, any appearance was welcome. The version of "Foggy Mountain Breakdown" done to gurgling, squawking synthesizer accompaniment could easily be dispensed with, but the Byrds' version of "You Ain't Going Nowhere" is priceless, and the Doc Watson material is as enjoyable as anything in his Vanguard Records output of the same period. *—Bruce Eder*

Live at Kansas State / 1972 / Columbia ♦♦♦♦

One of the best albums of Scruggs' solo career, *Live At Kansas State* is a mirror image of his best live work with Flatt & Scruggs from the earlier decade. Backed by the Earl Scruggs Revue, an electric band that includes his two sons (with bassist Gary Scruggs doing most of the singing), he brings his virtuosity intact into the electric rock age, and this is a rocking band as well as a bluegrass outfit, doing songs by Bob Dylan and Joni Mitchell, '40s standards, and Jimmie Rodgers material interspersed with good originals. It's all just as enjoyable as the best Flatt & Scruggs material, only different, with electric bass pumping away and electric guitar sharing the spotlight with the banjo. *—Bruce Eder*

Dueling Banjos / 1973 / Columbia ♦♦♦

A hit like "Dueling Banjos" had to attract Earl Scruggs, though not much else of what's here resembles the famed track from the score of Deliverance. *Dueling Banjos* is sort of bluegrass-rock, Scruggs' banjo accompanied by electric guitar (courtesy of Randy Scruggs) and electric bass (Gary Scruggs), with Vassar Clements on fiddle, Josh Graves on the dobro, Chip Young on rhythm guitar, and Jody Maphis on drums. The playing is spirited enough, and the music incorporates textures that will be familiar to fans of rockabilly as well as bluegrass, "Just Joshin'" and "John Hardy" being perfect hybrids of the two sounds. Not all of the material is as interesting as that, however, and not only is there a certain sameness to the tracks, but there aren't enough virtuoso showcases (such as "Flint Hill Special") present to carry the entire album. *—Bruce Eder*

● **Artist's Choice: The Best Tracks (1970–1980)** / May 5, 1998 / Edsel ♦♦♦♦♦

Dueling Banjos/Live at Kansas State / Nov. 14, 2000 / Collectables ♦♦♦

Putting together one of Scruggs' best albums (*Live At Kansas State*) with one of his less interesting (*Dueling Banjos*) made good marketing sense, but it makes for an uneven CD. Tracks 11-22 are the real treats here, off the live album, and the price is low enough that one can regard the other ten songs as a bonus, with some occasionally brilliant moments. *—Bruce Eder*

Earl Scruggs and Friends / Aug. 28, 2001 / MCA ♦♦♦

Earl Scruggs practically invented the word banjo, and perhaps because of that he can count some of the most elite musicians among his "friends": Elton John, Sting, Melissa Etheridge, Don Henley, Johnny Cash, John Fogerty, and the list goes on. In a career that spans 50 years, Scruggs' five-string banjo stylings have helped to define American music. Here, on this 12-track compilation produced by son Randy, those banjo stylings can be heard in the same folk-based music he's known for, and also combined with a fresh and unequaled range of material that comes with having so many varied and dissimilar artists involved. Every song has a unique story to tell, but is always brandished with that distinctive Scruggs polish. *—Maria Konicki Dinoia*

Classic Bluegrass Live: 1959–1966 / Aug. 13, 2002 / Vanguard ♦♦♦♦

While cobbled together from mostly previously released material, *Classic Bluegrass Live* nonetheless neatly captures banjoist Earl Scruggs on his arc through the folk revival of the 1960s. The disc is culled from three performances at the renowned Newport Folk Festival—one with Hylo Brown in 1959 and two with longtime partner Lester Flatt in 1960 and 1966, respectively. The performances from 1959 and 1960 are rightly legendary. For many of the young revivalists, it was their first chance to see Scruggs' blitzkrieg three-finger banjo style live. The audience was predictably blown away. The music, of course, lives mightily up to its history. The recordings are crystal clear, and Scruggs (and Flatt) pick away with fury, rightfully earning their places in bluegrass and folk music history. The band still kicks during its set from the 1966 festival, though not as much. There's something missing in their manic reading of the classic "Orange Blossom Special." It's still a riveting piece, almost formal in its beauty. Whatever had made it contemporary is gone, though. By then, the folk revival was effectively over: Bob Dylan had electrified the summer before, and nothing would be the same again. Flatt & Scruggs close their set with "Ballad of Jed Clampett (Theme From *the Beverly Hillbillies*)," their theme music for the popular television show. Within a year, "Foggy Mountain Breakdown" would be used on the soundtrack to *Bonnie and Clyde*. And, soon after that, bluegrass would fade into a novelty for the bulk of the record-buying public, at least until the revival spurred by the soundtrack to *O Brother, Where Art Thou?* in the early 21st century. *—Jesse Jarnow*

Randy Scruggs

Guitar, Producer / Contemporary Country

The son of the legendary Earl Scruggs, singer/songwriter Randy Scruggs was for several decades one of Nashville's most sought-after producers and session players, collaborating with everyone from Waylon Jennings to George Strait to Emmylou Harris during a prolific career dating back to the 1970 release of *All the Way Home*, a collaboration with his brother Gary. Finally, in 1998, Scruggs recorded his debut solo LP, the all-star *Crown of Jewels*. —*Jason Ankeny*

Crown of Jewels / Jun. 23, 1998 / Warner Bros. ✦✦✦✦

Randy Scruggs says that recording this CD was more like "directing a movie than actually making an album." He produced and played guitar on every track, wrote a few songs, arranged a couple, sang on a few more, and, most importantly, assembled the all-star cast that makes this album such a joy to listen to. Almost every song here is an outstanding example of a producer's clear vision perfectly executed. The pairing of Emmylou Harris and Iris DeMent on the Carter Family classic "Wildwood Flower" is a match made in heaven, and Travis Tritt sounds great backed vocally by Harry Stinson and Sam Bush on a mostly acoustic version of the Pure Prairie League's "Amie." Another highlight is the Steve Goodman song "City of New Orleans" with John Prine and an outstanding backup chorus. Bruce Hornsby sings his own song about a hard-luck beauty queen, "Crown of Jewels," and even Joan Osborne sings on the rocking "Passin' Through." It's a testament to Randy Scruggs' producing genius and acoustic guitar talent that this album is not just a collection of exceptional tracks, but a cohesive package. Maybe Scruggs isn't really a director but the host of a party—one of the greatest country parties held in a recording studio since *Will the Circle Be Unbroken, Vol. 2*. And Scruggs was the master of ceremonies that time, too. —*Brian Wahlert*

Scud Mountain Boys

f. 1991, Northampton, MA, **db.** 1997

Group / Indie Rock, Alternative Country-Rock

The cult popularity of Uncle Tupelo and its spin-off groups Wilco and Son Volt opened the doors for what's become an entire new generation of musicians who grew up in the punk rock generation but have found genuine connection with traditional country music—especially as interpreted through Gram Parsons, who's more or less the granddaddy of country-rock. The Scud Mountain Boys—Joe Pernice, Stephen Desaulniers, Bruce Tull, and Tom Shea—clearly fit into this camp. The band originally played electric rock & roll under the name the Scuds. Pernice, Desaulniers, and Tull formed the group in Northampton, MA, in 1991, and they gained a respectable local following. But the bandmembers soon tired of hauling equipment around and found they much more enjoyed the after-show get-togethers playing acoustic country songs around the kitchen table at home. Finally they decided to haul the kitchen table to a club. Finding the response positive, they've kept with the new format.

The band's debut album, *Pine Box* (originally just a cassette release), features slow, intensely quiet originals alongside covers of '70s pop-country songs such as "Gypsies, Tramps and Thieves" and "Please, Mr. Please." It was literally recorded live around the kitchen table. Their second album, *Dance the Night Away*—which added a couple of rock songs from their Scuds days into the mix again—came out on Chunk Records in 1995, and national interest in the band grew quickly. In early 1996 they were signed to Sub Pop, and the label released the band's third album in less than two years, *Massachusetts*. —*Kurt Wolff*

Pine Box / 1995 / Chunk ✦✦✦✦

Originally released only on cassette, the Massachusetts label Chunk made this album available on vinyl as well. Contains beautiful, delicate original acoustic songs as well as covers of "Gypsies, Tramps and Thieves," "Please, Mr. Please," and "Wichita Lineman" that are as fun in spirit as they are moving. Recorded with a single mike in guitarist Bruce Tull's kitchen in Northampton, MA. —*Kurt Wolff*

Dance the Night Away / 1995 / Chunk ✦✦✦✦

Dance the Night Away, one of two albums the Scud Mountain Boys released in 1995 (*Pine Box* was the other), is a quiet but immediately compelling collection of 13 original songs plus two covers—one being the Jimmy Webb pop classic "Where's the Playground, Susie," which is likely the most reverent version of the song this side of Glen Campbell's. (Chunk Records, Box 244, Easthampton, Mass.,01027) —*Kurt Wolff*

● **Massachusetts** / Apr. 1996 / Sub Pop ✦✦✦✦✦

In just a short time, the Scud Mountain Boys have risen from relative obscurity (two 1995 albums for indie label Chunk) to a well-earned spot on the Sub Pop roster. The Boys' new album, *Massachusetts*, is once again a quiet, mostly acoustic collection of soft-spoken songs based around spare country rhythms and laid-back, whisperlight melodies. *Massachusetts* is more down-to-earth than the faux-hillbilly ramble poems of Palace Music, but also far less Americana-ized than Son Volt or any of the No Depression hangers-on. The sudden national attention seems not to have spooked the Scuds, and so while *Massachusetts* feels better crafted than the band's previous two albums—more mature in terms of songwriting—it retains the easygoing, kitchen-table spirit that marked the band's earlier work. This is music that moves slowly but grows on you quickly. —*Kurt Wolff*

The Early Years: Pine Box & Dance the Night Away / Apr. 22, 1997 / Sub Pop ✦✦✦✦✦

Pine Box and *Dance the Night Away* were the Scud Mountain Boys' first two albums. Released on the tiny indie Chunk Records, neither album received wide distribution, so when the group signed with Sub Pop in 1997, the label negotiated for the release of the double-disc set *The Early Years*, which featured both albums plus a handful of rarities. While *Massachusetts* remains their most accomplished album, the music on *The Early Years* isn't much weaker, and most alt-country fans will find the collection necessary listening. —*Thom Owens*

Dan Seals

b. Feb. 8, 1948, McCamey, TX

Guitar, Vocals / Adult Contemporary, Soft Rock, Country-Pop

After scoring several hits as part of the soft rock duo England Dan & John Ford Coley, Dan Seals reinvented himself as a country-pop singer and enjoyed a tremendous run of success during the latter half of the '80s. Born in McCamey, TX, in 1948, his brother was Jim Seals, later of another successful soft rock duo, Seals & Crofts. Both brothers played with their parents in the Seals Family Band, with Dan learning string bass; however, after their parents divorced, Dan spent several years moving around with his mother. They eventually settled in Dallas in 1958, and Seals spent his teen years playing in garage bands, where he first met John Ford Coley. They worked together in a band called the Shimmerers, which recorded some demos in 1965 and became the Southwest F.O.B. two years later, scoring a chart single with "The Smell of Incense." Seals & Coley left to form a duo in 1969 and kicked around for a while, landing an early-'70s deal with A&M that went sour. They finally hit big in the late '70s, with soft rock touchstones "I'd Really Love to See You Tonight" and "Nights Are Forever Without You" ranking as their best-known singles.

Seals went solo in 1980, signing with Atlantic and keeping the name England Dan for his debut album, *Stones*. In 1981, he underwent a grueling battle with the IRS that cost him nearly everything he owned. His follow-up album, *Harbinger*, stiffed, and he turned his attention to country music, adapting his style to fit the demands of country radio while still keeping his signature soft sound. Signed to Liberty/Capitol, he scored a pair of Top Ten hits on the country charts in 1984 with "(You Bring Out) The Wild Side of Me" and "God Must Be a Cowboy." "My Old Yellow Car" and "My Baby's Got Good Timing" had similar success in 1985, and his next single, a duet with Marie Osmond called "Meet Me in Montana," went all the way to number one. It also kicked off a spectacular run of nine straight chart-toppers: 1986 brought "Bop" and "Everything That Glitters (Is Not Gold)"; 1987 saw "I Will Be There," "Three Time Loser," and "You Still Move Me"; 1988 featured "Addicted" and "One Friend"; and 1989 gave him one more in "Big Wheels in the Moonlight." Not only that, he managed two more number ones in 1990, thanks to "Good Times" and "Love on Arrival." However, the arrival of Garth Brooks abruptly changed the country landscape, and Seals found his style out of favor. He moved to Warner Bros. in 1991, without much success, and despite releasing a few recordings on smaller labels in the latter half of the '90s, he was effectively a touring artist for the remainder of the decade. —*Steve Huey*

Stones / 1980 / Atlantic ✦✦✦✦

John Ford Coley is long gone, except for a co-write on "When It's Over," but producer/engineer Kyle Lehning is still onboard, and the project sounds very much like an England Dan & John Ford Coley album, new and renewed, so the breakup was good for one of them, artistically anyway. This is more a pop album than country, and with Richie Zito, Steve Lukather, and Ray Parker Jr. on guitars, you know it is going to swing more to the radio-friendly sound England Dan was synonymous with from his success with the duo. The title track was written by Kenny Loggins' cousin Dave Loggins, of "Please Come to Boston" fame, who contributed to a previous album, *Some Things Don't Come Easy*, and he adds some backup vocals on this and another tune. "Stones," a cynical piano-based song concerning those who feel love is more about obtaining gems than romance, is the one departure from the music Dan Seals had become associated with, and it's intriguing enough. "Getting to the Point" is pure pop that sounds like the '70s hits Dan Seals enjoyed with his former partner, while Gene Page's arrangement of "How Do I Survive" is downright funky. Sure, there were transitions in country music in 1980, but this is flat out adult contemporary pop sliding in through the back door. Legendary songwriters Cynthia Weil and Tom Snow team up for the snappy "Holding Out for Love," with its ambiguous hook, and perhaps there was hope the song would cross over to the dance crowd. The singer is either pouring out his troubles to someone at a bar or singing to that individual. "Mister, this time I'm holding out for love" doesn't make it clear, but it does make you think. "When It's Over" was written by Seals, John Ford Coley, and Bob Gundry, and any of these titles could have fit on any album by the former pair. The formula producer Kyle Lehning helped create is in full force, it's just that the album material is stronger, though no one song is as memorable as England Dan's half-dozen hits from the mid- to late '70s. There's really not a bad track here; "Take You Home" could absolutely be mistaken for Livingston Taylor, who was back on the charts this same year, while "Lullaby" has fiddle and strings and concludes the album with a lush and mellow mood, finding the singer in fine form. *Stones* is reflective of the early '80s, and for Dan Seals is the first solo effort in a catalog of about two dozen titles, if you include best-of collections. —*Joe Viglione*

Harbinger / 1982 / Atlantic ✦✦✦✦

Rebel Heart / 1983 / Liberty ✦✦✦

San Antone / 1984 / Capitol ✦✦✦

Big Wheels in the Moonlight / 1986 / Capitol ✦✦✦

On the Front Line / 1986 / Capitol ✦✦✦

● **The Best of Dan Seals** / 1987 / Liberty ✦✦✦✦

The Best of Dan Seals contains 11 of Seals' smooth contemporary country hits from the mid- and late '80s, including the number-one singles "Three Time Loser," "You Still Move Me," "Bop," "Everything That Glitters (Is Not Gold)," "Meet Me in Montana," "I Will Be There" and "One Friend." A couple of hits are missing, yet every truly essential item is here, making it the best retrospective of Seals' hit-making peak. —*Thom Owens*

Rage On / 1988 / Liberty ✦✦✦✦✦

On *Rage On*, Seals tells stories woven around traditional country themes while rarely resorting to country clichés. "Addicted," "They Rage On," "Five Generations of Rock County Wilsons"—these are tales of quiet desperation, and the empathy in Seals' voice makes their impact devastating. Almost as good as his *Best*. —*Brian Mansfield*

Won't Be Blue Anymore / Oct. 25, 1990 / Capitol ✦✦✦

On Arrival / Nov. 1990 / Liberty ✦✦✦
This is the product of a man very much in touch with his emotions. In "Bordertown," "A Heart in Search of Love" and "Wood," he works the listener's heart with the skill of a surgeon. At the same time, "Good Times" and "Love on Arrival" are incredibly celebratory. *—Tom Roland*

Walking the Wire / 1991 / Warner Bros. ✦✦✦
It features "A Good Rain," "We Are One," and "Mason Dixon Line," among others. *—AMG*

Greatest Hits / 1991 / Liberty ✦✦✦
Greatest Hits contains Dan Seals' biggest contemporary country hits from the late '80s, including the number-one singles "Addicted," "Big Wheels in the Moonlight," "Bop," and "Everything That Glitters (Is Not Gold)," among four other hits. Though it is a good collection, *The Best of Dan Seals* edges *Greatest Hits* out slightly, due to its larger concentration of big hits. *—Thom Owens*

Early Dan Seals / 1991 / Liberty ✦✦✦✦
As the title indicates, this anthology draws from Seals' first several years as a country artist; although a few songs were hits, including "Three Time Loser," "My Baby's Got Good Timing" and "My Old Yellow Car," most never cracked the charts. *—Jason Ankeny*

The Songwriter / Apr. 27, 1992 / Liberty ✦✦✦✦✦
This album contains such hits as "One Friend," "Wood," "Love on Arrival," "Three-Time Loser," and others. *—AMG*

Fired Up / 1994 / Warner Bros. ✦✦✦
Dan Seals, Texas-born and raised, is a gifted songwriter and a commanding singer. He gets his musical talents honestly; his father was a musician, his uncle a hit songwriter. By the age of four, Seals could play the string bass and took a spot in the family band. In the '80s he won a number of country music awards, including Songwriter of the Year, Single of the Year, and Vocal Duet of the Year. This 1994 album, *Fired Up*, released under the Warner Bros. label, carries several superb tracks, like "A Good Place to Be," "Hillbilly Fever," "A Rose From Another Garden," "Gentleman of Leisure," and "Love Thing." Country fans who like a little pop beat added to their music will find this album a sure keeper. Even those who prefer their country served straight up will be pleased with the lyrics of most tunes. *—Charlotte Dillon*

The Best of Dan Seals / Jun. 14, 1994 / Curb ✦✦✦
The Best of Dan Seals is a ten-track budget-priced collection that features some of his biggest hits, including "Bop," "My Old Yellow Car," "Meet Me in Montana," "After You" and "You Really Go for the Heart." Although this isn't a bad budget-priced disc, there are better collections available, offering more songs and better sound for not much more money. *—Stephen Thomas Erlewine*

In a Quiet Room / Oct. 1995 / Intersound ✦✦
In a Quiet Room is an acoustic album featuring Dan Seals running through a number of his biggest hits, as well as two new songs, one of which—"The Healing Kind"—boasts a guest appearance by Alison Krauss. It's a pleasant album, yet it doesn't offer any new revelations or great performances, which means it's a record only hardcore fans need to pick up. *—Thom Owens*

In a Quiet Room II / Nov. 24, 1998 / TDC ✦✦✦✦
This is a follow-up to the 1995 album *In a Quiet Room*. Most of the songs on this second-part offering are just as mellow as the ones on the first. There are a few bounces too, including background vocals done by artists Alison Krauss and Pam Tillis—both very talented ladies of country who can sing like angels. You'll also hear plenty of acoustic guitar and great lyrics on this album. Songs like "Nights Are Forever Without You," "Three Time Loser," "We Are One," and "Love on Arrival" kind of take fans back to earlier works by Dan Seals. *In a Quiet Room II* is one of those recordings that is perfect to accompany a lazy, relaxing afternoon when you want to just sit back, close your eyes, and let the music and its words and meanings flow over you. *—Charlotte Dillon*

Certified Hits / Aug. 28, 2001 / Capitol ✦✦✦✦
Country singer and songwriter Dan Seals started his professional musical career in the '60s with a three-member band called the Southwest F.O.B.. The group's debut single, "The Smell of Incense," made it onto the pop charts. When the same success didn't come from other recordings, Seals and one of the other members moved on to become the pop-style duo England Dan & John Ford Coley. The popular team released their first album, *Fables*, in 1971. By 1980 Seals had walked away from the twosome to record his first solo offering, *Stones*. He served up his country tunes with a good helping of pop flavoring. Fans seemed to agree with the style and his songs earned him a number of awards and hits. A string of full-length albums followed throughout the '80s and into the '90s. Now, two decades after that debut solo, *Certified Hits* proves that some things only get better with the passing of time. This collection of tunes includes big radio hits like "Everything That Glitters (Is Not Gold)," "Addicted," "Big Wheels in the Moonlight," and "One Friend." This album makes it easy for new fans, or old fans, to get a number of hits from Dan Seals on one recording. *—Charlotte Dillon*

Jeannie Seely

b. Jul. 16, 1940, Titusville, PA
Vocals / Traditional Country, Country-Pop
Jeannie Seely was known primarily as a duet partner, but she managed a few country hits of her own during the late '60s and early '70s. A native of Titusville, PA, Seely was born in 1940 and first performed on the radio at age 11. She sang at local dances and talent shows as a teen and moved to Los Angeles in 1961, where she worked as a secretary for a record company and honed her songwriting in the meantime. A deal with Challenge Records went nowhere, but when Dottie West recorded one of her songs in 1965, she heeded the advice of songwriter Hank Cochran and moved to Nashville. Almost immediately, she caught a big break when she was hired to replace Norma Jean as Porter Wagoner's television and touring duet partner. She landed a solo deal with Monument in 1966 and scored a major smash with "Don't Touch Me," a number-two hit penned by Cochran, who later became her husband. The song also won Seely a Grammy for Best Female Country Vocal. She left Wagoner's show (to be replaced by Dolly Parton) and later caught on in a similar touring/TV capacity with Ernest Tubb, and also became the first woman to wear a miniskirt on-stage at the *Grand Ole Opry*. Seely had several Top 20 hits during the late '60s, including "It's Only Love," "A Wanderin' Man," and "I'll Love You More (Than You Need)."

In 1969, she found her most commercially successful duet partner in Jack Greene; the two cut a hit album together, and their single "Wish I Didn't Have to Miss You" was a number-two smash in 1970. Seely continued to record through the '70s, cutting material for Decca, MCA, and Columbia in addition to Monument, and landed her biggest solo hit of the decade with 1973's Top Ten "Can I Sleep in Your Arms," which she adapted from an old hobo tune. She also wrote songs for other artists, most notably "Leavin' and Sayin' Goodbye," a number-one smash for Faron Young in 1972. Seely recovered from a near-fatal car crash in 1977 and had her last chart single the following year; she continued to tour and perform and appeared in several stage musicals during the late '80s. *—Steve Huey*

Seely Style / 1966 / Monument ✦✦✦

Thanks, Hank! / 1967 / Monument ✦✦✦
The Hank in the title refers to Hank Cochran, not Hank Williams, because Jeannie Seely recorded as many of Hank Cochran's songs as Connie Smith did of Bill Anderson's. The album leads off with the hit "A Wanderin' Man" before covering a number of Cochran's songs that were hits for other artists, such as Burl Ives' "A Little Bitty Tear" and "A Funny Way of Laughin'." Side two bogs down a little with ballads, but closes with the ever-popular "Make the World Go Away." The Pennsylvania-born Seely helped set the pattern for contemporary country artists since she looked like a model and had a very pop-oriented voice, but today she seems like Kitty Wells compared to some of the pure pop that has since passed for country. [*Thanks, Hank!* was later reissued by Harmony, Columbia's budget label, with the title *Make the World Go Away*.] *—Greg Adams*

I'll Love You More / 1968 / Monument ✦✦✦

Little Things / 1969 / Monument ✦✦✦

Can I Sleep in Your Arms/Lucky Ladies / 1974 / MCA ✦✦✦

● **Greatest Hits on Monument** / 1998 / Sony Special Products ✦✦✦✦✦
"Don't Touch Me" was Jeannie Seely's first hit, and a major one at that; it spent months on the country charts, hovering for three weeks at number two and crossing over to the pop chart before winning a Grammy Award. All told, Seely had eight hits on Monument between 1966-1968, although only two cracked the Top Ten. *Greatest Hits on Monument* compiles all of her hits for the label plus a half-dozen album tracks (nearly all of which were written by Hank Cochran) and provides an excellent and inexpensive survey of her early years. Although "How Is He," her last hit from this period, is a pure pop ballad, her other recordings are more identifiably country in style, but distinctly pop-oriented. Her recorded output in general was heavy on ballads, and the midtempo hits "Wanderin' Man" and "Welcome Home to Nothing" provide a welcome change of pace in the context of an album-length set. *—Greg Adams*

The Seldom Scene

f. 1971
Group / Bluegrass, Progressive Bluegrass, Contemporary Bluegrass
"We try to find material that's a little bit different, and approach the music in a little bit broader way than most bluegrass bands do," said the Seldom Scene's Dudley Connell to *the Baltimore Sun* in 1998. Since its inception in 1971, the Seldom Scene has thrived on playing bluegrass a little differently than everyone else. If other bands used a fiddler, the Seldom Scene used a dobro; if others relied on old standards, the Seldom Scene played rock classics like J. J. Cale's "After Midnight." Through skilled musicianship and an urban approach to bluegrass, the Seldom Scene has become one of the most influential—if not the most influential—bluegrass band of the last 30 years.

In 1971, mandolinist John Duffey, banjo player Ben Eldridge, guitarist John Starling, bassist Tom Gray, and dobro player Mike Auldridge formed the Seldom Scene. The band derived its name from its once a week performances, first at the Red Fox Inn in Bethesda, MD, and later at the Birchmere Restaurant in Alexandria, VA. Early albums like 1973's *Act One* and 1975's *Live at the Cellar Door* set the pace for progressive bluegrass while defining a unique sound that included Starling's smooth vocals, Duffey's versatile tenor, and Auldridge's ringing dobro. The band's smooth harmonies, love of eclectic material, and Duffey's colorful stage antics further separated the band from its peers. In 1977, Starling left the group to return to his medical practice and was replaced by vocalist Phil Rosenthal. The addition of Rosenthal and a change of labels to Sugar Hill did little to alter the Seldom Scene's basic sound. 1978's *Act Four* and 1981's *After Midnight* continued to draw material from traditional sources like Jimmie Rodgers and contemporary ones like Eric Clapton. The later album included both "Lay Down Sally" and concert favorite "After Midnight." When performing live, the group enjoyed stretching out songs like "After Midnight," allowing Duffey and Auldridge to take extended solos that sounded closer to jazz than bluegrass. In 1986, after making five albums with the Seldom Scene, Rosenthal departed and was replaced by Lou Reid. Original bass player Gray also left, making room for T. Michael Coleman.

With the addition of two new bandmembers, the Seldom Scene recorded the appropriately titled *Change of Scenery* in 1988. Some fans objected to Coleman's electric bass, but despite this "progressive" change, albums like 1990's *Scenic Roots* proved to be more traditional than earlier efforts. The band also had a talent for turning pop songs like the Beatles' "What Goes On" into standard bluegrass material. In 1993, Reid left the band and was replaced with ex-member John Starling. Although Starling remained with the band for only a year, his return proved a real treat to fans of early-'70s lineup as did the Seldom Scene's 1994 recording *Like We Used to Be.* In 1995 and 1996 the Seldom Scene weathered more changes than several bands combined. In 1995, dissension came to surface within the Seldom Scene because of their light touring schedule and the feeling among certain members that the band had lost its progressive edge. Singer Mondi Klein, bassist Coleman, and original member Auldridge parted ways with the band to turn the progressive bluegrass band Chesapeake into a full-time project. The Seldom Scene's remaining members recruited dobroist Fred Travers, bassist Ronnie Simpkins, and former Johnson Mountain Boys' singer, Dudley Connell. Together, the re-formed band recorded 1996's *Dream Scene.*

Before the band could consolidate their new lineup, founder and spiritual leader Duffey died of a heart attack. "John was 80 percent of the Seldom Scene," Eldridge told *the Boston Herald*, and no one, not even the band, could picture continuing without him. "The last year has been real tough for the band," Connell admitted to *the Baltimore Sun* in 1998. "Because he [John] was not only a wonderful musician and singer, but also kind of the personality of the band." Still, many wanted the band to continue, and the year-old lineup wanted to carry on the work they had begun with Duffey, so they recruited ex-member Lou Reid to help out on vocals and play mandolin. While Eldridge is the only remaining original member, the band continues to carry the spirit set forth by the Seldom Scene in 1971. Their 2000 recording *Scene It All* features both ringing Dobro and tight harmonies, as well as covers by Chuck Berry, Bruce Springsteen, and Bob Dylan. The Seldom Scene continues to garner both critical acclaim and adoration from a legion of fans. As the new century begins, the Seldom Scene emerges at the forefront of progressive as well as traditional bluegrass bands, continuing to amaze fans and influence future generations of musicians. *—Ronnie D. Lankford Jr.*

Act One / 1972 / Rebel ✦✦✦✦

The Seldom Scene's first three studio albums for Rebel are impeccable. Along with performers like John Hartford and the New Grass Revival, the Seldom Scene created quite a stir in the early '70s. While *Act One* included traditional pieces like "Will There Be Any Stars in My Crown" and "Summertime Is Past and Gone," it also drew material from folk and a new breed of singer/songwriters. And although many bluegrass fans would not have objected to "Darling Corey" or "500 Miles," they were less comfortable with "Sweet Baby James" and "City of New Orleans." Amazingly, all of the Seldom Scene's trademark elements are on full display on their first album. John Starling's folkie lead contrasts beautifully with John Duffey's high tenor, while dobroist Mike Auldridge gives this fiddle-less quintet a distinct edge. Tom Gray's bass is forever present within the band's spacious sound, while Ben Eldridge's banjo reminds the listener that the Seldom Scene is indeed a bluegrass group. The highlight among highlights? "With Body and Soul." Here, the band brings their lovely harmony to bear on a Bill Monroe classic, crafting a gut-wrenching *tour de force. Act 1* still sounds fresh and vital, and progressive bluegrass never got any better. *—Ronnie D. Lankford Jr.*

Act Two / 1973 / Rebel ✦✦✦✦

The writing credits themselves tell an interesting story on an early Seldom Scene album. Names like Norman Blake, John Prine, Hank Williams, and Earl Scruggs show the eclectic nature of the band's repertoire. No matter what genre the song came from, however, the Seldom Scene put their distinct stamp on it. A bouncy "Hello Mary Lou," for instance, has almost nothing in common with the Rick Nelson version, while a high-spirited version of "Paradise" is played fast enough for a country flat-footing contest. Add to this John Starling's resonant lead, the group's three-part harmony, and the sweet sounds of Mike Auldridge's dobro, and this band is immediately recognizable. While few would object to the band's style or material today, rock songs, folk vocals, and dobro—as opposed to fiddle—made the band unwelcome in some bluegrass circles in the early '70s. Nonetheless, even the most tried-and-true traditionalist can appreciate pieces like "I've Lost You" and "House of Gold." The standout track among standout tracks? Duffey's rendition of "Small Exception of Me." His high tenor packs the song with lots of mountain soul, milking it for every possible drop of pathos. The Seldom Scene never played any better than they did on their early Rebel albums—new bluegrass bands did. A must-have for old fans, *Act Two* also provides an excellent introduction for newcomers and a fine place to indoctrinate oneself into the treasures of progressive bluegrass. *—Ronnie D. Lankford Jr.*

Act Three / 1973 / Rebel ✦✦✦✦

Seldom Scene's *Act Three* is a low-key but entertaining progressive bluegrass album, capturing several of the genre's best musicians—including John Duffey, Ricky Skaggs, Mike Auldridge, John Starting, Ben Eldridge and Tom Gray—at the very beginning of their career. None of the musicians over-emphasize their skills, even on the jam "Rider," and the result is a subtly impressive set of excellent harmonies and brief, enticing instrumental leads. *—Thom Owens*

Old Train / 1974 / Rebel ✦✦✦✦

By 1974, the Seldom Scene was one of the hottest progressive bluegrass bands on the D.C. circuit. Their fourth album, *Old Train*, shows why. The band confidently kicks off with the instrumental "Appalachian Rain" before delving into their trademark three-part harmony on Herb Pedersen's "Wait a Minute." On songs like "Wait a Minute" and "Different Roads," John Starling's lead vocals sound more folk than bluegrass. Only John Duffey's tenor, coming in loud and clear on the chorus, reminds the listener that he or she is listening to a bluegrass group. The Seldom Scene, however, also has a traditional side. Sparkling versions of "The Old Crossroads," "Traveling on and On," and "Working on a Building" hark back respectfully to classic bluegrass. A number of guests help the band fill out its sound on *Old Train.* Linda Ronstadt's vocals show up on Paul Craft's drinking classic, "Through the Bottom of the Glass," while Ricky Skaggs' fiddling adds a number of flourishes. The album may seem a bit short by CD standards, but with material like the title track and "C & O Canal," every minute will be prized. For anyone curious about how good the original lineup sounded, *Old Train* provides a snapshot of a band that had it all. *—Ronnie D. Lankford Jr.*

Live at the Cellar Door / 1975 / Rebel ✦✦✦✦✦

The Seldom Scene made a series of landmark albums in the early- to mid-'70s that climaxed with *Live at the Cellar Door*, a glorious set of 23 songs from the band's broad repertoire. To those familiar with the band's earlier albums, classic pieces like "Rider," "City of New Orleans," and "Small Exception of Me" will be familiar. The initiated will also know that these songs sound just as fabulous live, and that no one would want to miss the seven-minute version of "Rider." A number of tasty items also make their debut here. Mandolinist John Duffey sings a lovely version of Dylan's "Baby Blue," while guitarist John Starling offers a sterling take of Carter Stanley's "The Fields Have Turned Brown." The band's spacious sound, with Tom Gray's ever-present bass and Mike Auldridge's ringing dobro, reproduces well in a live setting. Likewise, the Seldom Scene's trademark three-part harmony looses nothing outside of the more rarified air of the studio. The group, it should be noted, also has a keen sense of humor. The band's old-timey parody of "Hit Parade of Love" is guaranteed to offend anyone addicted to the high-pitched, whiney brand of traditional bluegrass. As if to make up for such effrontery, respectful renditions of "Georgia Rose" and "Will the Circle Be Unbroken" are also offered. Arguably, the Seldom Scene never got any better than this. *Live at the Cellar Door* is a progressive bluegrass classic, and sounds as fresh and alive today as it did in 1975. *—Ronnie D. Lankford Jr.*

New Seldom Scene Album / 1976 / Rebel ✦✦✦✦✦

Act Four / 1978 / Sugar Hill ✦✦✦

Baptizing / 1978 / Rebel ✦✦✦

After Midnight / 1981 / Sugar Hill ✦✦✦

At the Scene / 1983 / Sugar Hill ✦✦✦

Highlighted by a cover of Jackson Browne's "Jamaica, Say You Will" and two original inspirational numbers, *At the Scene* is a typically impressive effort by the Seldom Scene that emphasizes their considerable instrumental and vocal skills. *—Thom Owens*

Blue Ridge / 1985 / Sugar Hill ✦✦✦✦

● **The Best of Seldom Scene, Vol. 1** / 1987 / Rebel ✦✦✦✦✦

The Best of Seldom Scene, Vol. 1 contains a sampling of the progressive bluegrass band's first four albums on Rebel Records. Among the 16 tracks are several cover versions, including "Sing Me Back Home" by Merle Haggard; "City of New Orleans" by Steve Goodman; "Sweet Baby James" by James Taylor; "Paradise" by John Prine; and they even manage to make the Ricky Nelson '50s hit "Poor Little Fool" sound as if it was written as a bluegrass tune. *—Al Campbell*

Change of Scenery / 1988 / Sugar Hill ✦✦✦

15th Anniversary Celebration / 1988 / Sugar Hill ✦✦✦✦✦

This all-star tribute to America's finest progressive bluegrass band took place at the Kennedy Center in November of 1986, and featured performances by artists as prominent as Emmylou Harris and Linda Ronstadt and as influential as Charlie Waller, Ricky Skaggs, and Tony Rice. The program is a delight from beginning to end, and includes the band's own renditions of classic material ("Workin' on a Building," "Rose of Old Kentucky") as well as a number of tribute performances by the guest artists. Ricky Skaggs and Sharon White deliver a gorgeous duet version of Townes Van Zandt's "If I Needed You," while Harris and Ronstadt team up on "The Sweetest Gift." Original lead singer John Starling joins the Scene on several songs, and the resulting sound will make longstanding fans of the band wistful for the old days; though mandolinist and tenor singer John Duffey is beginning to sound his age at this point, the old magic is still there on "You Don't Know My Mind" and "Rose of Old Kentucky." The band's rollicking rendition of the traditional gospel classic "Take Me in Your Lifeboat" is the perfect finale. *—Rick Anderson*

Scenic Roots / 1990 / Sugar Hill ✦✦✦

With *Scenic Roots*, Seldom Scene returned to their traditional bluegrass roots. Although the music occasionally sounds forced, much of it is lively and wonderful, making the disc a worthwhile purchase for longtime fans, even if it isn't the place to start with this perrenial bluegrass favorite. *—Thom Owens*

Scene 20: 20th Anniversary Concert / 1991 / Sugar Hill ✦✦✦

For their 20th anniversary, Seldom Scene held a concert and invited all of the former members of the group to join them on-stage. Everyone turned up and the results are captured on the splendidly entertaining *Scene 20: 20th Anniversary Concert.* Seldom Scene runs through a wide variety of material, playing everying from traditional bluegrass numbers to Wilson Pickett's "In the Midnight Hour." For fans of the group, this album is an unexpected and totally delightful treat. *—Thom Owens*

Like We Used to Be / 1994 / Sugar Hill ✦✦✦

John Starling re-joined the Seldom Scene in 1994 to record an album that recalled the groups first lineup from 1971-1977 (minus bass player Tom Gray). Starling's vocals on "Grandpa Get Your Guitar" and "Almost Threw Your Love Away" carry the same solid smoothness of the early years. He also sings his share of sad songs of love lost and lives wasted as in "Like I Used to Do" and "Cheap Whiskey." the Seldom Scene have always shown a willingness to choose material from folk, country, and rock. The difference here is that the songs are quieter, drawing equally from folk and traditional bluegrass. The biggest difference though between *Like We Used to Be* and an earlier effort like *Act One* is that the former seems conservative in comparison, and conservative was never a word associated with the Seldom Scene. Perhaps this is due to the quieter material chosen for *Like We Used to Be*; but it is also due to how much bluegrass has changed because of the influence of groups like the Seldom Scene. Duffey's lead vocals also seems weaker and less resonant than on past efforts. Little of this will matter for fans of the original line-up: Starling's return after 17 years has been greatly awaited. They will hear the sweet harmony of a uniquely structured song like "Some Morning Soon" and know that it sounds a whole lot like old times. For fans of the Seldom Scene as well as fans of good bluegrass, this recording will represent a solid, pleasing effort. — *Ronnie Lankford*

Dream Scene / Sep. 24, 1996 / Sugar Hill ♦♦♦
In 1995 the Seldom Scene split apart and three of its members left to form the progressive bluegrass band Chesapeake. The remaining members re-formed with dobro player Fred Travers, lead singer Dudley Connell, and bassist Ronnie Simpkins to record what would be John Duffey's last album. The album begins with the spirited "Dry Run Creek" which tips its hat toward traditional bluegrass. Connell's vocals have a more country flavor than earlier Seldom Scene vocalists like John Starling and Phil Rosenthal, and this quality helps create a more traditional effort from a band known for its progressive tendencies. Despite these changes, the band retains much of its trademark sound and a good deal of credit for this should be given to Fred Travers' excellent dobro playing. The song choice is also solid, including an excellent version of Jean Ritchie's "Blue Diamond" and "Creedence Clearwater Revival's "Bad Moon Rising." There are lovely moments as when Duffey sings lead on "The Boatman," though it should be noted that his voice lacks the range it once had. The harmony singing on "The Little Sparrow (Fair and Tender Ladies)" even recalls the earlier sound of Duffey's first group, the Country Gentlemen. It is perhaps tempting to use such comparisons to suggest that Duffey is looking back over his long career on *Dream Scene*; but it would be closer to the truth to say that Duffey and the re-formed Seldom Scene are only trying to make good music. Toward that end, they have succeeded. *Dream Scene* is a fine effort for both old and new fans. — *Ronnie Lankford*

Scene It All / May 16, 2000 / Sugar Hill ♦♦♦♦
With the gradual departure of most of its original members and the sudden and untimely death of mandolinist/singer/founder John Duffey in late 1996, one might forgive the Seldom Scene if it had just given up the ghost. But instead, the sole remaining original member (banjoist Ben Eldridge) gathered some of the more recent participants around him (guitarist Dudley Connell, mandolinist Lou Reid, bassist Ronnie Simpkins, and dobro player Fred Travers) and made one of the better Seldom Scene albums of the last 20 years. The band's reputation as a "progressive" bluegrass band remains intact, though now with a tighter focus: no synthesizers, no electric instruments. But the unusual song selections are still there, from Bruce Springsteen's "One Step Up" to Muddy Waters' "Rollin' and Tumblin'" and the Chuck Berry chestnut "Nadine." As it turns out, those are not the album's high points. Although the band's rendition of "Rollin' and Tumblin'" works very well, the Springsteen tune doesn't sit very comfortably in its arrangement, and "Nadine" is a disaster—the banjo has to play painfully slowly to support the song's rhythm. But the Bill Monroe ("Blue and Lonesome") and Jim & Jesse ("I Will Always Be Waiting for You") numbers are standouts, and the funky bluegrass-gospel of "You Better Get Right" is also superb. Maybe it's time for the Seldom Scene to go "acid grass" for good. — *Rick Anderson*

Ronnie Self

b. Jul. 5, 1938, Tin Town, MO, **d.** Aug. 28, 1981, Springfield, MO
Vocals / Rockabilly
Why Ronnie Self never made it as a performer is one of the great mysteries and injustices of pop music history. He had the look and the sound—a mix of country, rockabilly, and R&B that sometimes made him sound like a white Little Richard, but mostly like the young Elvis or Carl Perkins—and he wasn't lacking for good songs, which he mostly wrote himself. He should have been there, thought of in the same breath as Perkins or Jerry Lee Lewis; instead, he's a footnote in rock & roll history outside of Europe, where he's treated as a legend. Self was born in Tin Town, MO, on July 5, 1938, the first of five children of Raymond Self, a farmer-turned-railroad worker, and the former Hazel Sprague. Self had a reputation as a wild boy, with incidents of vandalism and assault in his background. He became interested in music while still a boy, and began writing songs while in his teens. He was always submitting demos, and in 1956, Self got hooked up with Dub Albritton, who managed Red Foley, among other artists, and owned a publishing house, and Self was signed to a songwriting contract. His first recording sessions were held in Nashville on behalf of ABC Records, which led to a contract and the release of a single, "Pretty Bad Blues"/"Three Hearts Later," both sides of which were written by Self. Issued in 1956, the record failed to chart—although ABC listed a second single release by Self, "Sweet Love"/"Alone," that disc has never been found, nor have the tapes for those two songs.

In January of 1957, Self was picked by Albritton to perform as part of the Phillip Morris Caravan. Most of the acts on the package show were country players, and Self was the resident rockabilly representative—he quickly began attracting attention with his wild and highly animated stage act, not to mention the nature of his songs, which combined the intensity of R&B with high-energy rockabilly. His success on the tour helped get him a contract with Columbia Records in February of 1957. Self was back in the studio that month with a session band that included Grady Martin and Hank Garland on guitars with the singer, Floyd Chance, on bass, Buddy Harman on drums, and Floyd Cramer at the ivories. The resulting single, "Big Fool"/"Flame of Love," failed to chart, and a third song, Self's own "Black Night Blues," was unissued until 1990. Four months later, he had another try with four numbers cut in June of that year, which fared no better than their predecessors. Then, in December, he went in for one more session that yielded a piece of rapid-fire, high-powered rock & roll called "Bop-A-Lena." The raw power of Self's singing, coupled with the frantic beat, has resulted in "Bop-A-Lena" being labeled as the first punk single in some quarters. That might be a bit extreme, but not too far off the mark—that record moves, and it's just anarchic enough to be

recognizable not only to modern rockabilly practitioners like the A-Bones, but lots of punkers as well.

Self's career kept rolling, and in 1958 he even got picked for a screen test for the movie *Rally Round the Flag, Boys*. Meanwhile, "Bop-A-Lena," issued in the spring of 1958, began climbing the charts and eventually made it to number 68—not too high, but at least a beginning, or so it seemed. The single's success was, of course, welcomed, but it could not have come at a worse time. Self had married immediately after the "Bop-A-Lena" session, and by the time the single started to break around the country, the birth of Self's first child was an imminent prospect. He pulled out of the Phillip Morris tour and never made the screen test because of the birth of his son. Self's dropping out of the package tour was understandable. Coupled with his established reputation as something of a wild man and being somewhat unreliable, however, it led to his being all but barred from any major engagements, just as "Bop-A-Lena" was getting airplay and starting to generate sales. No live television variety show (and almost all of them were live then) was willing to book him for fear that he wouldn't turn up, "Bop-A-Lena" stalled low on the charts and disappeared soon after. By the end of 1958, Self was dropped by Columbia Records.

It was a year of between his final Columbia session in March of 1958 and his next one, for Decca as part of a three-year contract, in the summer of 1959. He never charted a song as a recording artist during his time with Decca, but he did see some success as a songwriter when Brenda Lee covered "I'm Sorry." He had other songs covered by Lee, and also by Jerry Lee, among other artists, and it was his songwriting that gave Self what little solvency he had in those years. By the early '60s, the bottom had fallen out of his reputation, however, as his chronic alcoholism began taking its toll. Pressured by the twin responsibilities of taking care of a family and maintaining a career, he chose the career, but he couldn't keep that going properly either. He left Decca in 1962 without a hit or many prospects and was signed to the Kapp label, where he cut a pair of songs, "Houdini" and "Bless My Broken Heart."

An attempt to get Self onto the Amy-Mala-Bell labels fell apart in the mid-'60s. He continued writing songs and living out a chaotic personal life, which was characterized by increasingly bizarre and self-destructive episodes, some played out in public and many a product of his triple-threat addictions to alcohol, marijuana, and various pills. Self had some good moments and good-times as a performer later in his career—he was especially highly regarded in Europe, practically like visiting royalty. The violent moments began to outnumber the others, however, and he deteriorated physically and mentally later on in life. By the early '80s, his condition had deteriorated more severely so that he couldn't work any longer. On August 28, 1981, he died in Springfield, MO.

Self left behind some 30 songs, and what is amazing is their sheer quality. As a singer and recording artist, he was a triple threat, equally strong as a singer of country ballads, hot white (and white-hot) R&B, and some of the fastest, most bracing rockabilly heard this side of the Sparkletones. It's been said too many times about too many performers, but as a singer, Self could have been another Elvis Presley, and had the potential to be bigger—he lacked Elvis' dark, brooding, charismatic sexuality (although he had a dark side, to be sure), which translated well onscreen, but he could take a song and turn it into the hottest piece of Dixie-fried rock & roll this side of Perkins, and with a frantic Jerry Lee edge to it as well. He may have been a little too country-fried for the rock & roll market after 1956 (a problem that Perkins also ran into), but his songwriting had enough variety to keep his stuff fascinating, and the quality of his music was extraordinary. — *Bruce Eder*

● **Bop-A-Lena** / 1990 / Bear Family ♦♦♦♦♦
This is one Bear Family disc that's a bargain any way you slice it, containing 30 songs cut between 1956 and 1963, covering his sound from the hard, raspy rockabilly of the title track to slightly bluesier slow numbers like "I Ain't Goin' Nowhere." At his best (and he was always at his best in the recording studio), Self could rock as hard as Elvis in his wildest Memphis days, edging into Little Richard territory—"You're So Right For Me" is almost scary in its echoes of the latter—or handle a ballad with the kind of wistful innocence that Rick Nelson turned into a career. The stuff here is all good, not a weak song or track in the 30, and anyone who thinks they know early rock & roll or rockabilly and doesn't own this CD is kidding themselves. — *Bruce Eder*

Kevin Sharp

b. Dec. 10, 1970, California
Vocals / Country-Pop, Contemporary Country
Though Kevin Sharp has come to light in the country field, his music is heavily commercial and could easily fit in several different genres, considering his dance-inspired production, heavy emphasis on ballads, and his cover of the Tony Rich Project's "Nobody Knows." Born in 1970 in rural northern California, Sharp first hit the stage at age three, performing at church with his musical parents and seven siblings. At age seven, he and his family moved to Weiser, ID—the home of the National Fiddle Festival—to begin a restaurant. Learning much about music from the fiddlers who packed Weiser every year for the festival, Sharp sang in local musicals and choral groups while in high-school. The family moved back to California in 1985, but he stayed active in music, singing in choral groups and a Sacramento light opera company while excelling at sports as well. He dreamed of a college football scholarship, but began to experience periods of fatigue and dizziness in 1989. The doctors later diagnosed bone cancer, and gave Sharp little chance to recover. After intensive radiation treatments permanently balded him, his prospects began to look even worse. Encouraged by the Make-A-Wish Foundation, Sharp asked to meet Los Angeles producer/songwriter David Foster, long an idol of his. The two hit it off well and became fast friends.

After years of treatment, Kevin Sharp finally beat cancer by 1993. He began working at the Great America theme park in Santa Clara, pitching a demo tape to various talent shows in the meantime. With David Foster's name still in his Rolodex, he called the producer and sent him a tape. Foster was at first hesitant to force pity on the young singer, but changed his mind after one song. Sharp was introduced to several country A&R representatives, made another demo, and was signed by Elektra/Asylum in 1995. His debut solo album *Measure of a Man* was released in November 1996 and hit the Top 20 Country charts. *Love Is* followed in 1998. *—John Bush*

● **Measure of a Man** / Sep. 24, 1996 / Asylum ✦✦✦✦
Kevin Sharp's eponymous debut album is essentially a countrified take on middle-of-the-road adult contemporary pop. Under the direction of producer David Foster, Sharp runs through a number of power ballads—including a cover of the Tony Rich Project's "Nobody Knows"—and tame dance-oriented uptempo numbers. Sharp is a fine, if rather faceless, singer—he sounds good, but he brings no spark to these expertly crafted backing tracks. In other words, it's pleasant background music, but it never grabs your attention. *—Thom Owens*

Love Is / Jun. 23, 1998 / Asylum ✦✦✦
Kevin Sharp's second album, *Love Is*, continues the countrified adult contemporary pop direction that he began on his debut, *Measure of a Man.* Without producer David Foster in tow, Sharp's sound has become a little less slick, but producer Chris Farren keeps the sound clean and polished. There are still problems with material, but his singing is more confident than before, which makes the weaker songs more convincing. Nevertheless, Sharp really shines only on the singles, which do stand out from the remainder of the album. And, like any other singles artist, his album is pleasant, but ultimately not as memorable as the hits themselves. *—Thom Owens*

Billy Joe Shaver

b. Aug. 16, 1939, Corsicana, TX
Guitar / Progressive Country, Singer/Songwriter, Honky Tonk, Outlaw Country, Americana

Billy Joe Shaver never became a household name, but his songs—including "Good Christian Soldier," "Willie the Wandering Gypsy and Me," and "I Been to Georgia on a Fast Train"—became country standards during the '70s and his reputation among musicians and critics didn't diminish during the next two decades. One of the best synopses of Billy Joe Shaver's upbringing is his own song, "I Been to Georgia on a Fast Train." When he sings that "my grandma's old-age pension is the reason that I'm standing here today," he ain't kidding. The "good Christian raising" and "eighth grade education"—not to mention being abandoned by his parents shortly after being born, working on his uncles' farms instead of going to high-school, and losing part of his fingers during a job at a sawmill—are all part of his life story. "I got all my country learning," he sings, "picking cotton, raising hell, and bailing hay."

Shaver did a quick turn in the Navy and worked a series of nowhere jobs (including the one in the sawmill) before trying his luck in Nashville. After several back and forth trips between Texas and Tennessee that gained him no response, he appeared one day in 1968 in Bobby Bare's Nashville office, where he convinced Bare to listen to him play. Bare ended up giving him a writing job. Shaver recorded one song for Mercury, "Chicken on the Ground," which went nowhere, but soon his songs began to see the light thanks to Kris Kristofferson ("Good Christian Soldier"), Tom T. Hall ("Willie the Wandering Gypsy and Me"), Bare ("Ride Me Down Easy") and, later, the Allman Brothers ("Sweet Mama") and Elvis Presley ("You Asked Me To"). Shaver's real breakthrough, though, came in 1973 when Jennings recorded an album composed almost entirely of Shaver's songs, *Honky Tonk Heroes*—largely considered the first true "outlaw" album.

Shaver's debut album was *Old Five and Dimers Like Me*, produced by Kristofferson and released by Monument (Kristofferson's label) in 1973. Along with the title track, it contained the now-classic Shaver songs "Willie the Wandering Gypsy and Me" and the aforementioned "Georgia on a Fast Train." Shaver switched to MGM a year later, but no album materialized. "Raising hell" was, as he had sung, part of his lifestyle at the time, and it kept him out of sight for a couple years. In 1976 Shaver resurfaced with *When I Get My Wings* on Capricorn, and followed it up a year later with *Gypsy Boy.* Johnny Cash recorded Shaver's "I'm Just an Old Lump of Coal (But I'm Gonna Be a Diamond Some Day)" in 1978, a song Shaver wrote just after he chose to give up drugs and booze and turned to God for help. Religious references do crop up his songs (including "Chunk of Coal"), but they never dominate the emotions or get in the way of the earthy rhythms and melodies.

Shaver switched labels again, this time to Columbia, in 1980, and recorded three more albums during the next decade: *I'm Just an Old Lump of Coal... But I'm Gonna Be a Diamond Some Day, Billy Joe Shaver*, and *Salt of the Earth.* The latter was produced by Shaver with his son, Eddy, who has played on every Billy Joe record since *Old Chunk of Coal* (he also toured in Dwight Yoakam's band in the 1980s). After a few more years out of the spotlight, Billy Joe returned once again in 1993, this time recording under the name Shaver. *Tramp on Your Street*, released on Zoo/Praxis, featured Eddy on lead guitar and Billy Joe's own raspy but loveable voice, and coming out during a time when hunky hat acts where the new flavor in Nashville, it was quickly recognized as one of the strongest and hardest country records to hit the shelves in many years. Shaver toured regularly over the next couple of years, and recorded a live album for Zoo, *Unshaven*, in 1995, but was dropped by the label a year later. *Victory* followed on the New West label in 1998, with *Electric Shaver* appearing a year later. The rock-oriented *The Earth Rolls On* appeared in spring 2001. *—Kurt Wolff*

★ **Old Five and Dimers Like Me** / 1973 / Koch ✦✦✦✦✦
Billy Joe Shaver slipped onto the recording scene very quietly in 1973. He was already heralded a fine songwriter by Jerry Jeff Walker, Willie Nelson, and Waylon Jennings, but even they'd recorded one or two songs of his up to that point. After the issue of this debut album, however, the floodgates opened for Shaver with the aforementioned trio and Johnny Cash himself recording Billy Joe's songs—a trend that continued 30 years later. *Old Five and Dimers Like Me* reveals a songwriter at the height of his power, a songwriter who undersells his case via quiet melodic music steeped in Texas country, folk, and the blues. While the title track is best known and the most often recorded (Waylon based his entire *Honky Tonk Heroes* around that track as the basis for an album of Shaver's tunes), each of this CD's 14 songs are gems. "Fit to Kill and Going Out in Style" became an anthem of the outlaw movement, and "Black Rose" echoes the Band's "Cripple Creek" with its funky country shuffle. The old-time honky tonk blues of "Played the Game Too Long" features a Dixieland horn section in the middle, and "Willie the Wandering Gypsy and Me" became David Allan Coe's theme after "Long Haired Redneck." And "Low Down Freedom" is the most poignantly written song about what it costs others when a man decides he needs to be free. Shaver was a study in contradictions on this album and proved to be so in life as well. He was a big man on the cover, a rough and tumble farmer who liked his music hot and simple and wrote words like a poet laureate. His performances of his own songs have been derided in the past because of the supposed limitations in his voice. But though he may not produce the performance drama that some of his peers can, his versions of these songs are far more poignant than any cover version of them. Shaver has always possessed an elegant and humble sense of dignity; it's on this recording, and on each one that followed. *Old Five and Dimers Like Me* is a masterpiece not only as a genesis for outlaw country, but of American songwriting at its very best. *—Thom Jurek*

When I Get My Wings / 1976 / Capricorn ✦✦✦
Billy Joe Shaver's sophomore effort came three years after 1973's *Old Five and Dimers Like Me.* Issued on Phil Walden's Capricorn label, Shaver was in the company of some serious Southern rockers as well as a small crew of his own and recorded a program entirely comprised of his own songs. Like many things coming from Capricorn at the time, including some of Delbert McClinton's early records, production was a bit heavier than suited the material. Nonetheless, the power, grace, and elegance in Shaver's songwriting come through even when his voice is mixed a bit low. Some of the standout tracks here are the title track, with its awesome hook in the refrain; the down-and-out "There Ain't No God in Mexico," which has been covered by everyone from Waylon Jennings to Steve Young live; the nostalgic party anthem "When the Word Was Thunderbird"; and one of Shaver's most covered and beloved songs, perhaps his anthem, "Ride Me Down Easy." This track alone is worth the purchase price of the album in that it carries within its simple melody and burning, honest lyric the nature of Shaver's life as an artist: communicate as directly as possible, never lie, and say it as if you mean it. The entirety of *When I Get My Wings* is a testament to an artist who has found his way as a songwriter and is aspiring to make records as good as the gems he pens. *—Thom Jurek*

Gypsy Boy / 1977 / Capricorn ✦✦✦✦
For his second record on Phil Walden's Capricorn label, Billy Joe Shaver and Walden pulled out all the stops. Knowing that the material was there, it was just a question of bringing the right group of players and a production team to bring it out and present it to the public. Produced by Emmylou Harris' husband at the time, Brian Ahern, his version of the Nash Vegas new country mafia were all present: Emmylou herself; Rodney Crowell, then a member of her Hot Band; Ricky Skaggs; Nicolette Larsen; Neil Young's producer and pianist, David Briggs; his steel player, Ben Keith; legendary country guitarist James Burton; country harmonicat supreme Mickey Raphael; drummer Karl Himmel; bassist Norb Putnam; Randy Scruggs; and others. While Shaver wrote most of the tunes here, including one of his signature anthems, "Honky Tonk Heroes," "Silver Wings of Time," and his first-ever single, "Chicken on the Ground" (re-recorded here), it is some of the collaborations and covers that make the album a standout. Most notably is Crowell's "In Going Crazy in 3/4 Time," a masterpiece written for Shaver's style of slow, deliberate delivery that is so moving. Add to this Shaver's collaboration with Bobby Bare on "We Stayed Too Long at the Fair" and the album-closer "You Asked Me To" with Waylon Jennings and the evidence is plain to see that Shaver and his team had learned how to make a songwriter's album. This has the emotional depth of his Capricorn debut, but places Shaver at the center of his songs like the masterful storyteller he is. With the background singing and dynamite playing, *Gypsy Boy* really moves and stirs. It's one of Shaver's finest moments on record, but alas, has never been issued on CD. *—Thom Jurek*

I'm Just an Old Chunk of Coal / 1981 / Koch ✦✦✦✦✦
On his Columbia debut, Billy Joe Shaver took some insurance along to his first recording date. Along with being able to have Eddie Kilroy produce him, Shaver asked the producer to include a burgeoning young guitarist on the album who had never recorded before, Shaver's young son, Eddy. When he heard him playing his slash-and-burn style of country and blues, Kilroy agreed and a musical partnership was forged that would last 20 years, until Shaver the younger died of a drug overdose. Also in the guitar fold were stalwarts Dale Sellers and Bobby Thompson. Dave Kirby played bass, Marshall Chapman sang backup on the set, and a host of others filled in the country, gospel, and rock mix that Shaver had been cooking up in his songs. The material ranged from the wild and wooly outlaw country-rock of "Fit to Kill and Going out in Style," to the downtrodden "Mexico," to the delightfully rollicking "Ragged Old Truck." There is also a re-recording of "When the Word Was Thunderbird" that works better in this setting than it did on *Gypsy Boy.* In Kilroy's hands, Shaver's songs, seemingly overly simple, took on the true mystery of their complexity. In virtually every song was the war between the spiritual and the physical. The title track is Shaver's true anthem and has been covered by any left-of-center country singer worth her or his salt since that time. But it is on the closer, "The Road," with its opening words, "The road it never changes but the people always do/Tonight the time has come to tell you so/The path along the riverside is sprinkled now with you/Stretching out to where God only knows," that the high, lonesome harmonica kicks in and the words come falling from the singer's mouth in a font of loneliness and near despair. But it never quite gets there—there's a determination to see it all through that rescues the song and underlines what a redemptive work of art *I'm Just an Old Chunk of Coal* is. *—Thom Jurek*

Billy Joe Shaver / 1982 / Columbia ✦✦✦✦✦
On his third album for Columbia, Billy Joe Shaver went back to the basics. Issued in 1982, long after the sheen had faded on the outlaw movement, of which Kris Kristofferson called Shaver the most authentic of the bunch, and despite five albums, he remained a

figure in the shadows, though most folks knew his songs. Like Dan Penn a decade later, Shaver decided to record a set of his classics and put them out there for public consumption in a modern setting. While it didn't work commercially, it made for a hell of a record. Shaver's redos of "Been to Georgia on a Fast Train," "Ride Me Down Easy," "Lowdown Freedom," "Old Five and Dimers Like Me," "One Moving Part," "Tell Me Virginia," "How Many Hearts Must You Break," and others are delivered with the kind of humble yet burning passion that Shaver put into the songs in the first place. Here he sings them for all they're worth, wringing every ounce of spirituality, emotion, and Texas grit from the heart of them. Shaver comes across as a bigger-than-life Buddha, recounting both good-times and bad, all of them held in a kind of equanimity to be reflected upon, learned from, and imparted from his experience. This is a songwriter's album to be sure, but it is also a singer's album. Never had Shaver sounded so assured, so full in possession of his voice, or so sure of his direction as on this album from 1982. *—Thom Jurek*

Salt of the Earth / 1987 / Columbia ✦✦✦

The fourth and last of Billy Joe Shaver's Columbia Records albums of the 1980s, *Salt of the Earth* was the singer/songwriter's first album of all-new material in six years and his last recording for another six, making it by definition a pivotal album in his infrequent recording career. It effectively encapsulates his characteristic style, from the hard-rocking honky tonk of "Whiteman's Watermelon" to the gentle "Hill Country Love Song." Shaver's conflicted morality allows him to announce fervently that "You Just Can't Beat Jesus Christ," then follow that song with "The Devil Made Me Do It the First Time" (the inevitable punch line being, "the next time, I done it on my own"). In Shaver's world, men work hard and play hard, too, and faith is observed more in intention than practice. Self-referential, funny, and moving, Shaver's songs, sung with cracked-voice conviction and played with gutbucket force, define outlaw style, here as on his other recordings. [This album didn't get a lot of attention when it was first released in 1987, and Sony's Lucky Dog imprint did fans a service on September 19, 2000, by remastering and reissuing it as part of its "Pick of the Litter" series of deserving, underappreciated vintage albums.] *—William Ruhlmann*

Tramp on Your Street / Aug. 10, 1993 / Volcano ✦✦✦✦✦

Billy Joe Shaver's first recording in six years is a stunner. Partnering with his guitar-slinging son, Eddy, *Tramp on Your Street* is a rollicking yet intimate ride through the world Billy Joe-style. There are smoking country-rockers that are brazen, raw, and in-your-face, such as the sizzling remake of "Been to Georgia on a Fast Train" (which is now the definitive version), "The Hottest Thing in Town," "I'm Just an Old Chunk of Coal," and the blues-rock of "I Want Some More/TennTex Tear Down." There is the restless Bob Wills swing of "Good Old U.S.A." and the shuffling Texas stroll of "If I Give My Soul." And of course, in the title track, "When Fallen Angels Fly," and the Louvin Brothers-inspired "I'm Gonna Live Forever," there are the searing, completely naked lyrics of repentance, deliverance, and doubt that have been a part of Shaver's music form the beginning. Without them, the center would be missing. The big question for most is: Can Billy Joe rock at his age? The answer is that with Eddy beside him turning it up, he can not only rock, he can roll too. This is a partnership based on respect, tough love, and iconoclastic musical ideals. It's deep in the roots of the sill and even deeper in the Shavers' blood. *Tramp on Your Street* is a monumental return to recording for Billy Joe Shaver and a triumph of Eddy's musical direction and six-string skill. *—Thom Jurek*

Honky Tonk Heroes / 1994 / Bear Family ✦✦✦✦✦

Unshaven: Live at Smith's Olde Bar / Jun. 27, 1995 / Volcano ✦✦✦✦✦

Unshaven: Live at Smith's Olde Bar, Billy Joe Shaver's only live recording, is proof that you can't keep a talent such as his out of the spotlight. Coming off of the success of *Tramp on Your Street*, his first recording in many years and the first with Eddy and his own band, this disc is a historical event that captures not only the power of the performance, but also the subtle, gentle spirit that is the man. Kicking off with the sizzling "The Hottest Thing in Town," which shows off the tight band that supports Shaver, the stage is set. Working through some old and some new compositions, every song is a Shaver original. "Georgia on a Fast Train" and "Old Chunk of Coal," longtime favorites that were covered by other less capable artists, come across as fresh. The Waylon Jennings hit that set off the explosion that was known as the Outlaw Movement during the 1970s, "Honky Tonk Heroes," is more heartfelt than ever. Heartfelt and tender, the man who has been compared to Hank Sr. in terms of talent and skill, makes even the coldest heart feel again as he sings "Live Forever," joined by Eddy, and the definitive love song, "Because You Asked Me To." Obviously the centerpiece of the band, he is also gracious and humble, giving all the players their due and glowing in the success of the son he loves so well. This is one live recording that not only works, it is an important document commemorating a moment in time in the life of one of the world's most exalted artists. *—Jana Pendragon*

★ **Restless Wind: The Legendary Billy Joe Shaver 1973–1987** / Oct. 1995 / Razor & Tie ✦✦✦✦✦

While Bear Family, the famous German reissue label, had issued a 25-track collection of Billy Joe Shaver in 1994 called *Honky Tonk Heroes*, domestic independent Razor & Tie have released an 18-cut retrospective covering virtually all of Billy Joe Shaver's career until his re-emergence in the 1990s. The Razor & Tie set is (far) less-expensive, its notes are just as comprehensive and well-written, and despite what's not here, it may indeed be a better bargain. At the very least this serves as a fine introduction to Billy Joe Shaver the man, myth, and magical songwriting storyteller. Beginning with a pair of tracks from his 1973 debut, *Old Five and Dimers Like Me*, this collection takes you through the various stages of a career marked by virtual anonymity among the record-buying public, and yet revered by his peers and would-be followers. Chances are, if you've listened to country music at all in the 1970s or 1980s, you've heard some of these songs, such as "I've Been to Georgia on a Fast Train," "Ride Me Down Easy" (covered by Carlene Carter on her *Musical Shapes* album), "When I Get My Wings," "Sweet Mama" (covered by the Allman Brothers), "I'm Just an Old Chunk of Coal," "Low Down Freedom," "Fit to Kill and Goin' out in Style," "Restless Wind," "Ragged Old Truck," "Amtrak (Ain't Comin' Back)," and "You Asked Me To," written with Waylon Jennings. Given the difficulty in coming across most of Shaver's catalog from this period, this collection is a good bet. Musically, it's as good as it gets. If you want the original outlaw singer/songwriter model, put away your Willie Nelson, Jerry Jeff Walker, and Guy Clark records and give this cat a listen. *—Thom Jurek*

Highway of Life / 1996 / Justice ✦✦✦✦✦

This first disc on the prominent Texas label Justice Records is a thoughtful, more sensitive acoustic version of Billy Joe & Eddy Shaver. With a new lineup that includes California country fiddle phenomenon Brantley Kearns, *Highway of Life* is a poetic look back on the rough-and-tumble life that has been the fodder for Billy Joe's artistry. A poet as well as a bard and philosopher, Billy Joe is once again at the center of Shaver's performance and style. Starting off with "Yesterday Tomorrow Was Today," a wordsmith's delight, and ending with a love song, "The First and the Last Time," written especially for his loving wife, Brenda Joyce Shaver, this release is revealing. The upbeat "West Texas Waltz" is moving in that it transports the listener back in time with its infectious and swaying rhythms, creating a romantic picture about dancing arm in arm with a lover beneath a clear and star-studded west Texas sky. Never at a loss to find humor in even his most introspective moments, "You're Only as Young as the Woman You Feel" is outstanding and makes a clear statement about growing older from a man's perspective. A different side of Billy Joe, Eddy, and their band of merry men, but still a noteworthy project that adds new depth and scope to the legend of Billy Joe Shaver. *—Jana Pendragon*

Victory / Jul. 14, 1998 / New West ✦✦✦✦✦

This is almost a greatest-hits package by virtue of the fact that *Victory* contains several remakes of well-known Billy Joe Shaver compositions, including "Live Forever," "If I Give My Soul," "Old Five and Dimers," and "You Can't Beat Jesus Christ." New cuts include "Son of Calvary," "Cowboy Who Started a Fight," and "My Mother's Name Is Victory," the tune that so aptly gives this project its title. Spiritually based, *Victory* gives the listener a glimpse into the soul of Shaver through the songs he has written about his relationship with his Lord. A man of strong spiritual conviction, Shaver has lived a life that often put him in conflict with his religious beliefs. This conflict was at the center of his vast and seemingly never-ending well-spring of music and his need to write. Working with his talented son, Eddy Shaver, who co-produced this first-ever release from New West Records, has given Shaver a renewed sense of himself and his place in the music industry. Stark and basic, *Victory* contains immense emotional landscapes and the always-startling vocal performances of the only songwriter who could ever hope to stand toe-to-toe with Hank Williams. Satisfying and potent, Billy Joe & Eddy Shaver continue to walk their own path to victory. *—Jana Pendragon*

Electric Shaver / May 4, 1999 / New West ✦✦✦

The title says it all. After several years of acoustic-based country, Billy Joe Shaver and his son Eddy have decided to up the ampage and deliver *Electric Shaver.* Theoretically, this is a good concept, but too much of the record sounds forced, as if blues-rock licks were grafted onto outlaw honky tonk backing tracks. Such grandstanding tends to obscure the songs, but then again, the rocking tracks on *Electric Shaver* aren't particularly strong, either. The opening pair of "Thunderbird" and "Try and Try Again" are cliché-ridden and awkward, two things Shaver has never been. However, things start looking up around the charming shuffle "New York City." From that point on (with an exception or two), things are laid-back and natural. The songs resonate and the performances are organic, not forced. As the Cajun-flavored "Manual Labor," the honky tonk ballad "I'll Be Here," the swinging "Way Down Texas Way," and Eddy's sweet midtempo country-pop tune "Heart to Heart" indicate, the Shavers are at their best when they let things flow, since the results are un-selfconsciously eclectic and quite charming. *—Stephen Thomas Erlewine*

The Earth Rolls On / Apr. 10, 2001 / New West ✦✦✦✦

In the photos that accompany *The Earth Rolls On*, veteran country-rocker Billy Joe Shaver looks as if he's lived through some hard times, and indeed he has: His son Eddy, a key member of his band Shaver and the lead guitarist on this album, died suddenly on December 31, 2000. The year before, Bill Joe's lifelong love, Brenda, died after a lengthy illness. Shaver had divorced her twice over the years—and married her three times. Experiences like these are reflected throughout this album, which is perhaps the most powerful of Shaver's career. "Hearts a Bustin'" is about Brenda, and so is the moving title cut ("The earth rolls on/Even though you're gone/The earth rolls on, and on, and on . . .); several of the other tracks, including "You're Too Much for Me" and "Star in My Heart," concern Shaver's reportedly rocky relationship with his son. But don't get the idea that everything here is somber: "Blood Is Thicker Than Water," also about Eddy, will bring a smile, and "Leavin' Amarillo" gets downright silly. Musically, this is fine stuff, thanks to Shaver's singing, Eddy's spirited guitar, and sterling backup from the likes of the E Street Band's Garry Tallent and Wilco's Jay Bennett and Ken Coomer. *—Jeff Burger*

Freedom's Child / Nov. 19, 2002 / Compadre ✦✦✦

Billy Joe Shaver is a man who has long known more than a little about hard times, and he was certainly put to the test between 1999 and 2001—his wife and mother succumbed to cancer; his son and musical collaborator, Eddy Shaver, died of a drug overdose; and he came face to face with his own mortality after suffering a heart attack on-stage while touring behind his final album with Eddy, *The Earth Rolls On.* Combine all this with the national malaise which struck America in the wake of the September 11 terrorist attacks, and it seems appropriate that *Freedom's Child*, Billy Joe Shaver's 13th album, released in the fall of 2002, eases back on the flinty country-rock he crafted with his son and aims for a quieter, more traditional approach and a contemplative tone. On *Freedom's Child*,

Shaver's thoughts often turn to family, relationships, and home, and whether he's thinking back on a rugged but happy childhood ("Wild Cow Gravy"), the hometown he left behind ("Corsicana Daily Sun"), relationships that didn't quite work out ("We"), and one that might just pan out yet ("Hold on to Yours (And I'll Hold on to Mine)"), he sounds sentimental without being cloying, with just enough grit to make it clear it's the hard-won little victories that often make the difference. The less-explicitly self-referential songs, most notably "Honey Chile" and "Day by Day," prove that Shaver is still a master storyteller, and if the playful patriotism of "Good Ol' U.S.A." is just a mite overplayed, the blunt realities of "That's Why the Man in Black Sings the Blues" serve as a balance. (And "That's What She Said Last Night" is on hand to prove that Shaver still has plenty of rowdy roadhouse stomp left in him.) The primarily acoustic arrangements of *Freedom's Child* put the emphasis squarely on Billy Joe Shaver and his songs, and the gruff warmth of his delivery and the honest emotional heft of his lyrics are more than strong enough to carry the burden; it's a fine and moving album from one of country's least-appreciated major talents. [The CD version of *Freedom's Child* also includes as a bonus an unreleased performance from the late Eddy Shaver, a solo blues workout called "Necessary Evil."] —*Mark Deming*

Rick Shea

b. 1953
Vocals / Bakersfield Sound
The son of a career Air Force officer, Rick Shea was born in 1953 when his family was stationed at Annapolis. As a child, Shea and his family traveled wherever the Air Force sent them. The elder Shea retired to San Bernardino, CA, when Rick was in junior high. This really was the starting point for Rick's association with California's country music and the Bakersfield sound. An alumnus of *Vol. 3* of the *A Town South of Bakersfield* project, Shea's song "Foot in the Fire" continues to be a popular, requested favorite. However, before there was even an inkling of a project like the *TSOB* compilation series, Shea had to discover the guitar. He began to play around in bands and gigging from the time he was in seventh or eighth grade. By high-school he had discovered Merle Haggard. After high-school he did acoustic solo dates wherever he could. He also began learning the basics of recording. Hanging out in studios owned by friends and other players gave him the education he would need.

In 1989 Shea released his first project, which featured a striking duet with another California country singer who also scored with the *TSOB* project, Patty Booker. *Outside of Nashville*, produced with Wyman Reese and John Lee White III, was a good record of Shea's career progress. A popular player around L.A., he was often featured with Chris Gaffney and Brantley Kearns and recorded with Heather Miles. A steel player as well as a guitarist, his songs were often scooped up by other performers, as is the case with his "Bed of Roses," which was included on Cody Bryant's debut disc. A 1995 CD, *The Buffalo Show*, caught the attention of Americana radio and included story-songs like "The Rattlesnake Daddy's Daughter," "Georgia Pines," and several Tex-Mex numbers sung in Spanish. In 1997, Shea went into the studio to record his next project. He was also a member of the band 1000 Wedding, joining old friend Wyman Reese as well as former Plowboy Tracy Huffman. As a sideline, he was known to do a little journalism. His review of the George Jones bio was a success after it was published in the *L.A. Times* during the summer of 1996. —*Jana Pendragon*

Outside of Nashville / 1989 / Independent ✦✦✦✦
This first effort by Rick Shea, available only on cassette, establishes him firmly in the California country tradition. A follower of Merle Haggard, Shea's work here reflects that preference. Outstanding even in 1989, Shea makes a stunning debut and his Bonnie Owens-Merle Haggard-esque duet with Patty Booker on "A House Divided," speaks volumes about the potency of the duet as an art form. Also good is Shea's "Against My Better Judgement," "Guns That Blaze Like Thunder," and the Shea-Gary Brandlin tune, "Every Rose." —*Jana Pendragon*

● **The Buffalo Show** / 1995 / Major Label ✦✦✦✦✦
In the years since Shea's first release, *Outside of Nashville*, he has developed into a songwriter of uncommon talent. This sophomore release takes the listener on one sweet ride. Reflecting the culture of southern California as much as the honky tonk culture of which he is a part, Shea's work here is dark and moody as well as picturesque. "Georgia Pines" is a mountain tale that enchants the listener with its imagery, as does "Sycamore Grove." "Border Town Girl" is a cultural study revealing the clash that takes place when two different cultures meet in one place. Interestingly enough, the story could have been taken just as easily from Texas as California. Another song that stands out is "One More Night," a joint venture between Shea and Wyman Reese. With good production, again Shea is assisted by Reese, John Lee White III, and labelhead Gary Mandell. The musicianship is exceptional, with artists like Brantley Kearns, Chris Gaffney, Skip Edwards, Keith Rosier, and Reese filling up the band. Background and harmony vocals are handled by Jann Browne, Heather Miles, Lonesome Stranger Randy Weeks, Gaffney, and Reese. An all-star lineup results in a project that will remain a solid and sparkling representation of the artistry involved. —*Jana Pendragon*

Sawbones / 2000 / Wagon Wheel ✦✦✦✦
This is only Rick Shea's third solo album in a decade, but the first since becoming a full-fledged member of Dave Alvin's Guilty Men band. Consequently, there's a slightly tougher feel to this release, likely inspired by Alvin's approach, yet Shea remains a unique voice in Americana music. Using his acoustic guitars, mandolins, and pedal steel as a backdrop for an eclectic stroll though stripped-down country, folk, blues, and swamp rock, Shea exudes class, dignity, and a heartfelt devotion to this music, which exudes from every track. Twelve of the 13 songs are originals (the only cover is an unplugged version of Lefty Frizzell's "Saginaw Michigan"), and all are deeply ingrained in the honky tonk, hardcore country and low-key, ominous rock & roll that inspires Shea. The title track

rocks with an easygoing Stones' swagger, Dave Alvin lends his guitar to the bluesy "Piedmont Ridge," and the determined stomp-along with the catchy riff of "Black-Eyed Girl" are the album's most aggressive cuts. But it's on the crackling "Lonesome Cannonball" where the eclectic pieces fit together as a forlorn fiddle sneaks between Alvin's robust, wiry guitar, a determined simmering midtempo beat, and Shea's easygoing vocals. The artist's yearning, plaintive, George Jones-styled singing (which is a bit of an acquired taste) and strong storytelling songs are more effective on the slower, acoustic tracks that provide the basis for the bulk of the disc. In particular, the lilting Mexican strains of "Magdalena" (some of which is sung is Spanish) shimmer with Shea's nylon guitar and just a hint of South of the Border percussion. The production, arrangements, and especially sound is stunning throughout *Sawbones*. It's obvious that Rick Shea took his time and dedicated substantial thought and effort to every song here, producing an invigorating, thoughtful, and sometimes sad journey through the often dark highways and bumpy gravel roads of American music. —*Hal Horowitz*

Shaky Ground / Jan. 1, 2000 / Aim ✦✦✦

SHeDAISY

f. Magna, UT
Group / Contemporary Country
Sister trio SheDaisy (or SHeDAISY, if you're picky) rode in on the late-'90s wave of female country-pop, following in the stylistic footsteps of Shania Twain, Faith Hill, and the Dixie Chicks. Kristyn, Kelsi, and Kassidy Osborn grew up in the small Utah town of Magna, near Salt Lake City, and started singing together as young girls, often putting on shows for their neighborhood. As they grew older, Kristyn spent more time alone writing songs, while Kelsi and Kassidy performed locally as a duo. After graduating from high school, eldest sister Kristyn joined her sisters, making them a three-part harmony group. They adapted their name from a Navajo word meaning "my sisters" and started taking their act all over the western U.S. Eventually they moved to Nashville in search of a record deal, working at department stores to pay the bills, and caught on with the smaller, Disney-owned label Lyric Street.

Their debut album, *The Whole Shebang*, was released in 1999 and gave the group a breakthrough single in "Little Good-Byes," which went to number three on the country charts. "I Will…But" made number two, and "This Woman Needs" became the group's third Top Ten hit, helping *The Whole Shebang* go platinum. While the group readied their proper follow-up, they kept product on the market via a 2000 holiday album, *Brand New Year*, and a remixed version of the debut, *The Whole Shebang: All Mixed Up*, in 2001. Finally, their sophomore effort, *Knock on the Sky*, was released in the summer of 2002. While it reached number three on the country album charts, its singles didn't enjoy the same level of commercial success as before. —*Steve Huey*

The Whole Shebang / May 11, 1999 / Hollywood ✦✦✦
SHeDAISY is one of those contemporary country acts who are country in name only. Using the work of Faith Hill, Shania Twain, and the Dixie Chicks as a starting point, the three Osborn sisters—Kristyn, Kelsi, and Kassidy—have created an appealingly polished collection of modern country-pop, which means it sounds as much (if not more) like mainstream, radio-ready adult contemporary pop as it does contemporary country. For purists, that will be a problem, but the fact of the matter is, SHeDAISY does this music very well and their debut, *The Whole Shebang*, is every bit as winning as Hill's *Faith* and Twain's *Come on Over*, even if it doesn't quite match the Dixie Chicks' *Wide Open Spaces*. The key to the record's success is not only the sisters' harmonies, which are very good, but Kristyn Osborn's fine songwriting skills. She wrote or co-wrote every song on the album, and while there are a few tunes that feel like filler, most of them are well-crafted, melodic, memorable songs which are distinctive enough to give the group their own identity. *The Whole Shebang* may not be pure country, but its glossy pop sheen and big hooks, along with SHeDAISY's charismatic vocals, are enough to make it a winning debut. —*Stephen Thomas Erlewine*

● **Brand New Year** / Sep. 26, 2000 / Hollywood ✦✦✦✦
The Osborn sisters and producer Dan Huff put a new spin on holiday music and put some funk in Christmas. Anything but country, *Brand New Year* is truly a treat for all music listeners. The incomparable harmonies of Kristyn, Kassidy, and Kelsi grace every song on the 12-song collection of new and old holiday music. But the Osborn sisters give their own delicious sound to tradition. "Deck the Halls," "Jingle Bells," and "Sleigh Ride" have all been consecrated with the melodious sound that is uniquely SHeDAISY. And the girls give the Andrews Sisters a run for their money on "Santa's Got a Brand New Bag," sounding much like "The Boogie Woogie Bugle Boy." Although Christmas albums generally do little to further a career, SHeDAISY better be prepared—*Brand New Year* is sure to be under every tree, making them a household name. —*Maria Konicki Dinoia*

The Whole SHeBANG: All Mixed Up / Sep. 25, 2001 / Hollywood ✦✦
SheDAISY and Grammy award-nominated producer Dann Huff decided after two years that they needed to do something a little different. The result: *The Whole Shebang: All Mixed Up* is a collection of radio remixes derived from the group's 1999 debut, *The Whole Shebang*. *All Mixed Up* offers the same chart-topping songs as the original, and attempts to put a fresh spin on the Platinum-plus selling debut with cool re-mixes and interesting musical twists. Call it what you will, but simply stated, it's the first album, this time with an overproduced sound. Listeners may hear heavier guitars, digitized sound breaks, some funky echoes, and the occasional a cappella break out. But unless you're a hardcore SHeDAISY fan, there really isn't anything excitingly new here or that you haven't heard already. —*Maria Konicki Dinoia*

Knock on the Sky / Jun. 25, 2002 / Hollywood ✦✦✦✦
The exuberance of SHeDAISY practically leaps off this disc, thanks to a dream marriage of savvy, catchy writing, crisp instrumental backup, and inspired solo and harmony singing. There's a sense that the session veterans called in for this one went above and

beyond what was expected; on "Man Goin' Down" and the vamp at the end of "Get Over Yourself," for instance, Steve Brewster is all over the drums, never losing the beat yet never lapsing into formulaic patterns. There's imagination in the production too, with a very effective switch to an old-timey radio episode on the bridge of "I'm Lit," and a canny decision to record the vocals, like the fiddle accompaniment, with minimal sweetening on the power ballad "Rush." Which, of course, points to the fact that SHeDAISY has achieved such a fusion of stadium gesture and reference to tradition that they can put a power ballad into a country framework and make it work. In fact, cinematic touches—muffled voices, a touch of thunder before the melodramatic "Repent," the "I Am the Walrus" strings that gliss from hoedown to hi-tech effect on "Everybody Wants You"—turn *Knock on the Sky* into a concept album; despite essentially mundane lyrics, the music and vision is enough to spirit the listener far from the farm toward more visionary places. —*Robert L. Doerschuk*

Shenandoah

f. 1985, Muscle Shoals, AL

Group / Contemporary Country, New Traditionalist

Most country groups of the '80s favored a commercial pop-oriented approach that alienated many traditional listeners but captured the ear of the mainstream. Shenandoah was one of the first groups to rebel against the urban cowboy image of the '80s and lead the way to the new traditionalism of the '90s. Initially formed in 1985 as a house band in Muscle Shoals, AL, it comprised vocalist Marty Raybon, guitarist Jim Seales, keyboard player Stan Thorn, bassist Ralph Ezell, and drummer Mike McGuire. One night, McGuire invited his friend, songwriter Robert Byrne, to come and watch the MGM band. He was impressed enough to record the band and offer the tapes to CBS, who christened and signed Shenandoah.

The group's self-titled album, released in 1987, leaned a little close to the pop-schmaltz they later rebelled against, though they reached the country Top 30 early in 1988 with "Stop the Rain." The following year, *Road Not Taken* outlined the group's approach to traditional country and became their most successful album; six singles reached the country Top Ten, led by the number ones "The Church on Cumberland Road," "Sunday in the South," and "Two Dozen Roses." *Road Not Taken* reached gold status by 1991 and earned Shenandoah the Favorite Newcomer award from *Music City News*. The first single from third album *Extra Mile* (1990) continued—and even topped—Shenandoah's success. "Next to You, Next to Me" became Shenandoah's biggest hit, topping the country charts for three weeks. It was followed into the Top Ten during 1990-1991 by "Ghost in This House," "I Got You," and "The Moon Over Georgia." The group's streak of hit singles ended with the mere Top 40 "When You Were Mine" in September 1991.

Despite the success, trouble was brewing. Three other bands came forward in 1991 claiming the Shenandoah name, and the resulting court costs and legal fees bankrupted the group by the end of the year. To make it even worse, CBS—who had named Shenandoah in the first place—dropped the group from its roster. The band settled the differences by 1992 and returned to country music with a contract from RCA and the number-two hit "Rock My Baby" in April of that year. Shenandoah's fourth album, *Long Time Comin'*, also featured the Top 15 "Leavin's Been a Long Time Comin'." Their fifth album *Under the Kudzu* (1993) continued Shenandoah's popularity, with the Top Five single "I Want to Be Loved Like That" and the group's fifth country chart-topper in early 1994, "If Bubba Can Dance (I Can Too)." Shenandoah moved to Liberty/Capitol in late 1994 for their sixth album, *In the Vicinity of the Heart*. The album was released in January 1995 and featured the Top Tens "Somewhere in the Vicinity of the Heart" (with Alison Krauss) and "Darned If I Don't (Danged If I Do)." Shenandoah returned to its roots in 1996 for *Now and Then*, which combined re-recorded versions of CBS singles with four new songs. Four years later, *2000* was released. —*John Bush*

Shenandoah / 1987 / Columbia ♦♦♦

It contains "What She Wants," "She Doesn't Cry Anymore," "She's Still Here," and other songs. —*AMG*

The Road Not Taken / 1989 / Columbia ♦♦♦♦♦

The songs mix the day-to-day struggles of everyday-Joe with a steady respect for love, personal roots, and family. It doesn't hurt to have six bona fide hits on it, either. —*Tom Roland*

Extra Mile / 1990 / Columbia ♦♦♦

Long Time Comin' / 1992 / RCA ♦♦♦

This album contains such hits as "Same Old Heart," "Rattle the Windows," and "Rock My Baby." —*AMG*

Under the Kudzu / 1993 / RCA ♦♦♦

Super Hits / May 31, 1994 / Sony ♦♦♦♦♦

In the Vicinity of the Heart / 1995 / Liberty ♦♦♦

Now And Then / Apr. 1996 / Capitol ♦♦

Uh-oh. It is always a mistake when recording artists allows a new record company to talk them into re-recording their old hits. Not only is it a consumer ripoff, but it also sends the message that the artists are spent as a contemporary force. One would not have thought that Shenandoah, coming off the Top Ten, Grammy-winning hit "In the Vicinity of the Heart," was in such dire straits, but the departure of 40 percent of the band prior to the release of this album indicates otherwise. And the decision to put only five new songs on the record, along with nine re-recordings and a repeat of "In the Vicinity of the Heart" from last time give the impression that a stop-gap was thought necessary. One can only hope that the remaining trio rebounds from this misstep. —*William Ruhlmann*

● **15 Favorites** / May 18, 1999 / Capitol ♦♦♦♦♦

Although the title of *15 Favorites* isn't entirely accurate—there are 12 hit singles, plus three previously unreleased tracks ("Wooden Cross," "What Else You Got to Live For," "Her Love Is a Miracle")—the disc remains an effective, entertaining summary of

Shenandoah's peak, making it an ideal introduction for neophytes and an enjoyable stroll down memory lane for longtime followers. —*Stephen Thomas Erlewine*

2000 / Sep. 12, 2000 / Free Falls ♦♦

Certified Hits / Sep. 24, 2002 / Capitol ♦♦♦♦

Jean Shepard

b. Nov. 21, 1933, Pauls Valley, OK

Bass, Vocals / Traditional Country, Honky Tonk, Bakersfield Sound

Few country singers—let alone female country singers—working since the 1950s have produced a large body of work as enduring as Jean Shepard's. Her voice is pure country—accent on both words. Born in Oklahoma, she grew up in Southern California, where Hank Thompson discovered her. She had her first Top Ten hit in 1953, and her last almost exactly 20 years later. In between, she cut one great record after another, mostly on Capitol Records. Nearly all of them crackle, no matter the topic, with honky tonk angel spunk. Born in Oklahoma, Shepard grew up in the area surrounding Bakersfield, CA. As a teenager, she began her musical career by playing bass in the Melody Ranch Girls, an all-female band formed in 1948. Hank Thompson discovered Shepard a few years after the group formed. Impressed by her talents, he helped her set up a record deal at Capitol Records, where she worked with Thompson's producer, Ken Nelson.

Shepard's first chart appearance was in 1953 as a duet partner with Ferlin Husky, with "A Dear John Letter" and its sequel, "Forgive Me John." Shepard & Husky toured the country following their hit singles. In 1955, she had her first solo Top Ten single, "A Satisfied Mind," which was backed by the number-13 hit "Take Possession." Later in the year, she had another Top Ten hit with "Beautiful Lies"/"I Thought of You." Her streak of hit singles led to an invitation to join the *Grand Ole Opry* in 1956. That same year, she joined Red Foley's Ozark Jubilee (TV show) and recorded *Songs of a Love Affair*, arguably the first concept album in country music history. Its 12 songs—which were all written by Shepard—depict a marriage torn apart by a love affair; one side of the album is written from the dissolution of a romance.

For nearly ten years after the release of "Beautiful Lies," Shepard wasn't able to get a song into the Top Ten. In fact, she had only two Top 40 hits during that period—"I Want to Go Where No One Knows Me" (number 18, 1958) and "Have Heart, Will Love" (number 30, 1959). She continued to record and tour—she was even named the Top Female Singer of 1959 by *Cash Box*—but nothing was breaking through to the public. This was primarily because she was a hardcore honky tonk singer in a time that country-pop was ruling the charts. In 1963, her husband Hawkshaw Hawkins died in the same plane crash that killed Patsy Cline. The following year, she returned to the Top Ten with "Second Fiddle (To an Old Guitar)." The song began a string of hits for Shepard. Although many of them failed to chart in the Top 20, she racked up 15 Top 40 hits between 1965 and 1970, including the Top Ten hits "I'll Take the Dog" (a duet with Ray Pillow, 1966), "If Teardrops Were Silver" (1966), and "Then He Touched Me" (1970).

Shepard's hits continued throughout the '70s, though as the decade wore on she hit the Top 40 with less and less frequency. Her last single was 1978's "The Real Thing," which peaked at number 85. During the '80s and '90s, Shepard didn't record, but she continued to perform at the *Grand Ole Opry* and tour, particularly in the U.K., where she had a strong fan base. —*Dan Cooper & Stephen Thomas Erlewine*

Songs of a Love Affair / 1956 / Capitol ♦♦♦♦♦

This Is Jean Shepard / 1959 / Capitol ♦♦♦♦♦

One of her earlier LPs is strong on her voice and steel-friendly West Coast production. It includes her spry, proto-feminist "Two Whoops and a Holler." —*Dan Cooper*

Lonesome Love / 1959 / Capitol ♦♦♦♦

Got You on My Mind / 1961 / Capitol ♦♦♦♦

Heartaches and Tears / 1962 / Capitol ♦♦♦♦

The Best of Jean Shepard / 1963 / Capitol ♦♦♦♦

A good compilation of her first wave of hits ("A Dear John Letter," "A Satisfied Mind"), this is also the LP that shows up most often in used record bins. —*Dan Cooper*

Lighthearted and Blue / 1964 / Capitol ♦♦♦

It's a Man Everytime / 1965 / Capitol ♦♦♦

I'll Take the Dog / 1966 / Capitol ♦♦♦

Many Happy Hangovers / 1966 / Capitol ♦♦♦♦

Heart, We Did All That We Could / 1967 / Capitol ♦♦♦

Your Forevers Don't Last Very Long / 1967 / Capitol ♦♦♦♦

Heart to Heart / 1968 / Capitol ♦♦♦

A Real Good Woman / 1968 / Capitol ♦♦♦

Seven Lonely Days / 1969 / Capitol ♦♦♦

★ **Honky Tonk Heroine: Classic Capitol Recordings, 1952–1962** / Dec. 1995 / Country Music Foundation ♦♦♦♦♦

At a time when most of her contemporaries were heading down the country-pop route, Jean Shepard was one of the few female honky tonk singers to stay true to the genre in the '50s and '60s. The definitive *Honky Tonk Heroine: Classic Capitol Recordings, 1952-1962* is a terrific anthology of her peak years. Most of her biggest hits are included, as are a handful of rarities that should delight casual fans as much as dedicated fans. —*Stephen Thomas Erlewine*

The Melody Ranch Girl / 1996 / Bear Family ♦♦♦♦♦

The five-disc box set *The Melody Ranch Girl* collects all 151 tracks that Jean Shepard recorded for Capitol Records between 1952 and 1964. Shepard's recordings for Capitol were undeniably her best—by and large, this is fiery, passionate honky tonk. All of her hits from this era, from "A Dear John Letter" and "A Satisfied Mind" to "Beautiful Lies" and "Second Fiddle (To an Old Guitar)," are included, as are several rarities, outtakes, and complete albums, including *Songs of a Love Affair*, one of the first country concept albums. The set also includes a thorough discography and biography, as well as many rare photos. For casual fans, *The Melody Ranch Girl* is far too lengthy and detailed to be pleasurable listening, yet for dedicated followers, it's an essential purchase. *—Thom Owens*

Songs of a Love Affair/Heartaches and Tears / Dec. 28, 1999 / EMI ✦✦✦✦
In 1999, EMI released *Songs of a Love Affair/Heartaches and Tears*, which contained two complete albums—*Songs of a Love Affair* (1956, originally released on Capitol) and *Heartaches and Tears* (1962, originally released on Capitol)—by Jean Shepard on one compact disc. *—Jason Birchmeier*

T.G. Sheppard (William Neal Browder)

b. Jul. 20, 1944, Humboldt, TN
Vocals, Guitar / Country-Pop, Urban Cowboy
After working his way through the record industry, T.G. Sheppard emerged in the mid-'70s as one of the leading country-pop singers, bringing the music closer to the rock-influenced, cosmopolitan sounds of urban cowboy. A native of Humboldt, TN, Sheppard headed off to Memphis after high-school, getting involved in the record business on several different levels. He tried recording as a pop artist and even signed with Atlantic Records under the name Brian Stacy, opening shows for the Beach Boys. A few years later, he took a job with a Memphis record distributor, then ended up in record promotion, where the job entailed calling radio stations and trying to persuade them to play his company's records. In that capacity for RCA, he helped break Elvis Presley's "Suspicious Minds," Perry Como's "It's Impossible," and John Denver's "Take Me Home Country Roads." After "going independent," he came across a demo tape of "Devil in the Bottle." He tried to talk a number of artists into doing the song, and when no one was interested, he decided to do it himself on Motown's fledgling country division, Melodyland Records. Primarily a recitation, "Devil in the Bottle" became a number-one hit in 1975, but within three years, the company folded, and Sheppard's career was in limbo. Connecting with record producer Buddy Killen, he signed with Warner, and starting in 1979, the two churned out some of country's best-crafted singles over a four-year period. Sheppard gradually moved away from recitations and grew significantly as a vocalist, though the press often ignored his achievements. He changed producers several times in the mid-'80s and, after a divorce in 1987, took a couple of years off for personal reflection. When he returned, Sheppard found it difficult to regain his earlier momentum.

As the nephew of the *Grand Ole Opry* comedian Rod Brasfield, Sheppard (born William Neal Browder, July 20, 1942) was exposed to music at a young age, and throughout his childhood, his mother gave him piano lessons. At the age of 16 he ran away from his Humboldt, TN, home, arriving in Memphis where he became a back-up vocalist and guitarist in the Travis Wammack Band. During this time, he was billing himself as Brian Stacy, and that was the credit on his first singles for Sonic Records. The label dropped him after all of his records failed, and he moved to Atlantic's Atco divison, where he released the rock & roll single "High School Days" in 1966. Though it didn't break nationally, it was a hit in the South, and soon he was opening for the likes of the Beach Boys and the Animals, while befriending Elvis Presley.

Instead of leading him toward a performing career, the minor success of "High School Days" made Sheppard decide to work behind the scenes in the record industry, and later in 1966 he became a record promoter for Hot Line Distibutors. Initially, he worked for Stax, but he quickly became the Southern regional promoter for RCA, where he helped push records by his friend Presley, as well as John Denver. While he was working for RCA, he also founded his own production and promotion company, Umbrella Productions. While working at promotion for Umbrella in 1972, he discovered a song by Bobby David called "Devil in a Bottle." Every record company he directed it to over the next year and a half turned the song down, so he decided to record a version himself. Eventually, he convinced Motown's developing country subsidiary Melodyland to license the record. Deciding to use T.G. Sheppard as his performing name, the vocalist released the record in the fall of 1974. "Devil in the Bottle" unexpectedly climbed to number one early in 1975, followed shortly by another number-one single, "Tryin' to Beat the Morning Home." Later in the year, "Another Woman" reached number 14 and "Motels and Memories" peaked at number seven, establishing Sheppard as a promising artist. Shortly after the release of "Motels and Memories," Motown was sued by a Los Angeles church over the right to use the name "Melodyland," and the label had to change its name to Hitsville. Sheppard had four other hit singles on Hitsville—including a cover of Neil Diamond's "Solitary Man" and the number eight "Show Me a Man" (1976)—before Motown finally decided to shut the label down.

By the time Hitsville collapsed, Sheppard was on his way to becoming a star—*Cash Box* magazine named him Best New Male Artist of 1976—so he was immediately snapped up by Warner. Sheppard became a genuine country star at Warner, paritially because the label promoted him correctly and partially because his sound—a smooth fusion of R&B rhythms, pop production, and country songwriting—became the blueprint for the urban cowboy movement that became country's most popular genre of the late '70s. After having two number-13 singles ("Mister D.J.," 'Don't Every Say Good-Bye") early in 1978, Sheppard released "When Can We Do This Again" in the summer. The single started a streak of 15 straight Top Ten hits that ran for the next five years. During that time, he had no less than ten number-one singles: "Last Cheater's Waltz" (1979), "I'll Be Coming Back for More" (1979), "Do You Wanna Go to Heaven" (1980), "I Feel Like Loving You Again" (1980), "I Loved 'Em Every One" (1981), "Party Time" (1981), "Only One You" (1981), "Finally" (1982), "War Is Hell (On the Homefront Too)" (1982), and the Karen Brooks duet "Faking Love" (1982). Over those five years, his style rarely changed—every record was well-crafted, highly produced country-pop highlighted by Sheppard's smooth croon. Sheppard continued to chart well throughout the latter half of the '80s, and between 1986 and 1987 he had a number-one single and three number-two records in a row ("Strong Heart," "Half Past Forever (Till I'm Blue in the Heart)," "You're My First Lady," "One for the Money") after he switched labels and signed to Columbia. However, his audience dipped dramatically in 1988, when his radio-ready sound became unsurped by a number of new traditionalist performers like Dwight Yoakam, Randy Travis, and George Strait. Between 1989 and 1990, he didn't record at all, and he was dropped by Columbia. In 1991, he returned to the charts with the Curb/Capitol single "Born in a High Wind," but he didn't remain with the label long. For the remainder of the '90s, he continued to tour and play concerts across a country, all the time lacking a new record contract. *—Tom Roland*

Slow Burn / 1983 / Warner Bros. ✦✦✦
This album has its weak moments, but Sheppard's performance is stronger than in previous albums. He's more confident, probably understands the craft of singing a little better, and—this being his first outing with record producer Jim Ed Norman—the arrangements don't bury him. *—Tom Roland*

● **The Best of T. G. Sheppard** / 1992 / Curb ✦✦✦✦
The Best of T.G. Sheppard highlights the singer's country chart entries recorded between the late '70s and early '80s. These original Warner Bros. recordings include "Do You Wanna Go to Heaven," "Only One You," "I Loved 'Em Every One," "Slow Burn," "Devil in the Bottle," and the novelty hit featuring actor Clint Eastwood, "Make My Day," from the film *Sudden Impact*. *—Al Campbell*

Pure Country / Aug. 25, 1998 / Sony ✦✦✦✦
Sony Special Products' *Pure Country* is an effective sampler of T.G. Sheppard's country-pop work for Columbia Records in the '80s. In fact, in many ways it works as a hits compilation of his Columbia years, since six of the featured songs—"One for the Money," "In Over My Heart," "You're My First Lady," "Strong Heart," "Doncha?," "Half Past Forever (Till I'm Blue in the Heart)"—were Top Ten country hits, while a few of the remaining cuts ("Fooled Around and Fell in Love," "Don't Say It With Diamonds (Say It With Love)," "You Still Do") were lesser hits. Because of that, *Pure Country* is more than just a good bargain for a budget-line collection—it's a good bargain in general. *—Stephen Thomas Erlewine*

Super Hits / Oct. 3, 2000 / Warner Bros. ✦✦✦✦
Super Hits contains 12 well-chosen tracks taken mainly from T.G. Sheppard's early- to mid-'80s recordings on Warner Bros. Included are the country-pop hits "Party Time," "Slow Burn," "Only One You," and "Last Cheater's Waltz." This is a good place to start if you have any interest in the urban cowboy/country-pop of the era, and it's a budget disc to boot. *—Al Campbell*

Billy Sherrill

b. Nov. 5, 1936, Phil Campbell, AL
Songwriter, Producer / Country-Pop, Nashville Sound/Countrypolitan
As a producer, songwriter, and A&R man, Billy Sherrill was one of the most influential non-performing figures in country music of the '60s and '70s. Sherrill was responsible for shaping the lush countrypolitan sound that helped change the production styles of country music during the '70s. Instead of relying on standard country instruments like steel guitars and fiddles, he recorded with string sections and vocal choruses, often overdubbing parts to give the music a grandiose, epic sound; in essence, it was the country version of pop producer Phil Spector's famous Wall of Sound. Some critics complained that his style wasn't pure country, yet there is no denying that he helped bring country music to a pop audience with the recordings he made with George Jones, Tammy Wynette, Charlie Rich, and Johnny Paycheck, as well as many, many others. Sherrill also helped build up the Epic artist roster during the '60s, making it into a formidable country label. Furthermore, he wrote and co-wrote many songs that have since become country classics, including "Stand By Your Man," "Your Good Girl's Gonna Go Bad," "I Don't Wanna Play House," "We Can Make It," and "The Most Beautiful Girl."

For someone with such an important place in country music history, Sherrill ironically wasn't interested in the music at all as a child—initially, he was attracted to blues, R&B, and jazz. Born and raised in Alabama, Sherrill was the son of an evangelical preacher. He learned how to play piano when he was a child, and he often played at revival meetings and funerals his father held. When he was a teenager, Sherrill learned how to play saxophone and led a jump blues band that played R&B and jazz. Soon, he was touring the South, playing in R&B and rock & roll combos. Eventually, he was signed as a solo artists by a small independent label in the late '50s, but none of his singles made any impact. In 1962, Sherrill discovered that an unknown Nashville country artist cut one of his songs when a royalty check arrived in the mail. Encouraged by the royalties, he moved to Nashville to pursue a career in the country music industry. Upon his arrival in Nashville, Sherrill was hired by Sam Phillips to oversee Sun Records' Nashville studios. After Sun and Phillips went bankrupt the following year, Epic Records' Nashville hired him as an in-house producer, and he was assigned to record any artist that all of the label's other producers had already rejected.

Before he moved to Nashville, Sherrill paid no attention to country music, and by the time he was hired by Epic, he was still unfamiliar with many of its production techniques and musical conventions. Instead of heeding the advice of the studio musicians he was working with, Sherrill forged ahead and created his own style, telling the professional musicians what to play. Basing his sound on the work of Phil Spector, Don Law, and Chet Atkins, he began pushing the boundaries of the Nashville sound of the '50s by making the productions bigger and more sweeping. Sherrill also decided to select the songs that his artists would record, often co-writing the songs to suit the singer's style and his own production.

Sherrill's first major hit arrived in 1965, when he overhauled the sound and career of David Houston, who had a hit two years earlier with "Mountain of Love." Houston hadn't had another big hit since that single, but Sherrill gave him "Livin' in a House Full of Love," which reached number three late in 1965. The following year, Houston recorded the Sherrill/Glenn Sutton song "Almost Persuaded," which spent nine weeks at number one. "Almost Persuaded" quickly became a standard, winning the Grammy for Best

Country & Western Song and becoming the subject of cover versions by artists as diverse as Louis Armstrong, Louis Prima, and Etta James.

Throughout 1966, Sherrill continued working with Houston, and later in the year he discovered Tammy Wynette, an Alabama hairdresser and waitress who entered his office, unannounced, early that year. Wynette had previously approached several other record labels but had been rejected. Sherrill signed her, co-writing "Your Good Girl's Gonna Go Bad" with Sutton with her specifically in mind. The single became a hit upon its early 1967 release, launching a very successful career for Wynette. Over the course of 1967, Sherrill turned out several number-one singles by both Houston ("With One Exception," "You Mean the World to Me," which both were number-one hits) and Wynette ("I Don't Wanna Play House"), plus "My Elusive Dream," which was a duet between the two vocalists. Also in 1967, Sherrill released the instrumental *Classical Country* under the name the Billy Sherrill Quintet.

The following year, Sherrill continued to work on recordings by Houston and Wynette, and he signed Charlie Rich, who he had previously worked with at Sun, to Epic. Though the first handful of records that Sherrill made with Rich were unsuccessful, the pair would have some major hits during the early '70s. Sherrill's most successful artists for 1968 remained Houston and Wynette, as David's "Have a Little Faith" and "Already It's Heaven" and Tammy's "Take Me to Your World," "D-I-V-O-R-C-E," and "Stand By Your Man" all reached number one. Not only did he produce those tracks, he wrote or co-wrote the majority of the songs. Sherrill's success with Houston and Wynette continued through 1969 and 1970, with both artists racking up several more number one hits.

Sherrill signed Barbara Mandrell to Columbia in 1969, and the next year he wrote and produced her first Top 40 single, "Playin' Around With Love." Mandrell's career continued to build momentum for the next four years, before she left Columbia, and Sherrill had a hand in producing or writing most of her hits for the label. Though Mandrell would later emerge as a star, the most significant addition to Sherrill's roster of vocalists was George Jones, who left Musicor for Epic in 1971. At first, the producer and signer didn't hit it off—Jones was accustomed to Pappy Daily's loose, nearly lazy production technique, and it took some time for him to feel comfortable with Sherrill's painstaking, demanding style—but the relationship would prove to be the most fruitful collaboration either artist would have. Sherrill expanded Jones' classic ballad style, bringing an epic sweep to his ballads while remaining close to George's honky tonk roots. Their first hit single, "We Can Make It," arrived in early 1972, a year after Jones & Wynette's "Take Me" became a Top Ten hit. For the next five years, Jones not only recorded solo singles with Sherrill, but he also made a series of duets with Wynette, and their hits often reflected the turbulent nature of their romance.

Jones wasn't the only artist to occupy Sherrill's time in 1972. In addition to Jones, Wynette, Houston, and Mandrell, Sherrill worked with a wide variety of other singers, including Jody Miller, Sandy Posey, Freddy Weller, and the teenaged Tanya Tucker. Sherrill's career continued to gain momentum over the next two years, as his regular stable of artists continued to have hits, and Rich finally began to chart with singles from the album *Behind Closed Doors*. Rich's title track and "The Most Beautiful Girl" became huge hits, reaching not only the top of the country charts, but also the pop charts; the latter also became a number-one hit in England. Also that year, he began to write songs for Joe Stampley, who would sign to Epic within two years.

By the time Stampley joined the Epic roster in 1975, Sherrill had become the most reliable hitmaker in Nashville, and both established and developing artists clamored to work with him. Over the course of the latter half of the decade, he not only worked with his old favorites like Wynette, Jones, Rich, Mandrell, and Stampley, he also produced or wrote songs for Johnny Paycheck, Marty Robbins, Ronnie Milsap, Janie Fricke, Ray Charles, David Allan Coe, Johnny Duncan, Bob Luman, David Wills, and Kenny Rogers & Dottie West. As the '80s arrived, Sherrill's hitmaking skills began to slip somewhat. Though he was invaluable in Jones' early-'80s comeback—producing and/or writing hits like "He Stopped Loving Her Today," "I'm Not Ready Yet," "If Drinkin' Don't Kill Me (Her Memory Will)," and "Same Ole Me," among others—Sherrill's songwriting wasn't being covered quite as frequently. Nevertheless, his songs continued to reach the charts, as Moe Bandy, Johnny Cash, Johnny Rodriguez, and Lacy J. Dalton made his songs into hits. In addition to his Nashville connections, Sherrill produced Elvis Costello's country album, *Almost Blue*, in 1981.

By 1980, Sherrill had been named Vice President/Executive Producer of CBS in Nashville, and he stayed in that position for the first half of the decade. In the middle of the decade, he left CBS to become an independent producer, working on Charles' country duets album, *Friendship*, but he returned to the label in 1986. Though he was signed to CBS for that period of time, he worked infrequently and his productions didn't hit the charts as frequently as they did during the previous two decades, and he soon slipped into retirement. Still, Sherrill didn't need any new hits to confirm his status as one of country music's premier producers and songwriters—his endless string of hits stands as a testament to his talents. *—Stephen Thomas Erlewine*

Shivers

f. Austin, TX

Group / Alternative Country-Rock, Alternative Country, Americana

Husband and wife gothic country duo Carey Kemper and Kelly Bell issued albums for much of the early '90s under the Shivers moniker. Since Kemper & Bell were essentially nomads—they lived in an RV and home-schooled their two children—their albums would be recorded during brief stops on their walkabout. Their self-titled debut effort appeared on the Minneapolis imprint Restless in 1994. It was a low-key, sometimes gloomy mixture of folk, roots, and country. Vocal duties were split between Kemper & Bell. *Buried Life* appeared in 1996; however, nothing more was heard from the Shivers, and both their Restless releases were out of print by the early '00s. *—Johnny Loftus*

Shivers / 1994 / Restless ♦♦♦

● **Buried Life** / Jan. 16, 1996 / Restless ♦♦♦♦

An earthy collection of rootsy country and folk delivered with an unpracticed energy and raw emotion. Some of the songs are upbeat and pushed along by drummer Barry Haney, while others are presented in a stark fashion, with just acoustic guitar and voice or the added textures of accordion, dobro, fiddle, and lap steel. The lyrical content evokes dark imagery, as in Carey Kemper's "Cult 45," while the music is hauntingly beautiful, particularly in songs like Kelly Bell's "House of the Spirits," with guest musician Jacqueline Ferrier-Ulton adding the lone and sad cello part over a strumming acoustic guitar. Kemper and Bell are especially compelling when they're singing together, sometimes recalling the dual-octave vocal style of X, and there's a sensual quality to songs like "No Love Lost." Bell gives a wistfully unforgettable performance on her "Make a Wish," and Kemper sounds a little reminiscent of a young Johnny Cash on "Cannonball." *—Jack Leaver*

Paul Siebel

Guitar, Songwriter, Vocals / Country-Rock, Singer/Songwriter, Folk-Rock, Country-Folk, Contemporary Folk

Despite the undeniably high quality of his songs—which have been covered by the likes of Linda Ronstadt, Bonnie Raitt, Ian Matthews, and Waylon Jennings—Paul Siebel is far from being a household name. Within folk circles and among songwriters, however, his two albums—1969's *Woodsmoke and Oranges* and 1971's *Jack-Knife Gypsy*—are legendary.

Siebel was born in 1937 in Buffalo, NY. Inspired by Hank Williams and Hank Snow, he taught himself to play guitar while in his teens. By the early '60s, after serving in the military, he began playing folk clubs, eventually moving to Greenwich Village, where he found support in the coffeehouse circuit. In 1969, a collections of demos he made with David Bromberg caught the attention of Elektra Records owner Jac Holzman, who offered him a modest recording deal (reportedly he was only given enough money to finance four three-hour recording sessions). The resulting album, *Woodsmoke and Oranges*, was met with critical praise from the media, including *Rolling Stone* magazine. Despite the attention, the album and its equally praised follow-up, *Jack-Knife Gypsy*, sold disappointingly little. Aside from a live album released in 1981, *Live at McCabes*, Siebel hasn't released an album since. *—Chris Woodstra*

Woodsmoke and Oranges / 1970 / Elektra ♦♦♦♦♦

Fans of Linda Ronstadt, Bonnie Raitt, or Ian Matthews records from the '70s will know some of these tunes already. Let their interpretations stand only as your introduction to this fine songwriter. While his style may not be as polished or commercial as any of the people who covered him, this is a fine batch of songs and deserve to be heard. *—Jim Worbois*

Jack-Knife Gypsy / 1971 / Line ♦♦♦

The first record may have drawn listeners for the opportunity to hear Siebel originals of songs they knew from elsewhere. This record does not have that same kind of pull but is every bit as good. His strong sense of melody and storytelling style paved the way for such current songwriters as Butch Hancock and Robert Earl Keen. *—Jim Worbois*

Live at McCabes / 1981 / Rag Baby ♦♦♦♦♦

Recorded in an intimate concert setting, it includes some of his signature tunes, such as "Louise," and along with perennials like "I'm So Lonesome I Could Cry," and "In the Jailhouse Now." *—Richard Meyer*

● **Paul Siebel** / Oct. 31, 1995 / Philo ♦♦♦♦♦

Though known mainly through others' interpretations of his songs (Ian Matthews, Linda Ronstadt, Bonnie Raitt), Paul Siebel's first two albums for Elektra are prime examples of the New York folk scene of the early '70s and easily among the scene's finest moments. While these albums were sadly overlooked at the time by all but his singer/songwriter peers and critics, they have since reached near-legendary status. *Paul Siebel* is a long-overdue collection of the high points of both albums, featuring *Woodsmoke and Oranges* in its entirety and five tracks from the follow-up, *Jack-Knife Gypsy*. *—Chris Woodstra*

Red Simpson

b. Mar. 6, 1934, Higley, AZ

Vocals / Traditional Country, Bakersfield Sound, Truck Driving Country

Best known for his string of trucking songs, Red Simpson was raised in Bakersfield, CA, the youngest of a dozen children. At age 14, he wrote his first song—about chickens—and sang it to his family's fowl. During the Korean War, he served aboard a naval hospital ship, the *Repose*, where he found relief by forming the Repose Ramblers, who played any instruments they could scrounge up. He bought better ones in Japan and began to practice in earnest, and became a professional musician in California after his discharge. Simpson was working at the Wagon Wheel in Lamont when Fuzzy Owens saw him and arranged for Simpson to work at his Clover Club as a piano player. He then got a job replacing Buck Owens at the Blackboard Club on weekends. Simpson was influenced by Owens, Merle Haggard and Bill Woods, who asked Red if he would write a song about driving trucks. (By the time Simpson handed him four truck songs, however, Woods had stopped recording.) Simpson began writing songs with Buck Owens in 1962, including the Top Ten hit "Gonna Have Love."

In 1965, Capitol's Ken Nelson was looking for someone to record some songs about trucking. His first choice was Haggard, who wasn't interested, but Simpson readily agreed. His first, Tommy Collins' "Roll, Truck, Roll," became a Top 40 country hit and Simpson recorded an album of the same name. That year he offered up two more trucking songs, both of which made it to the Top 50 or beyond. As a songwriter, he scored his first number one hit with "Sam's Place," recorded by Buck Owens. After that, Simpson decided to become a full-time writer. He returned to performing in 1971 with his Top Five hit "I'm a Truck," which had been written by postman Bob Staunton. In 1972, he debuted on the *Grand Ole Opry* and had two more "truck" hits for Capitol. In 1976, Simpson signed to Warner Bros. and released "Truck Driver's Heaven." The following year, he teamed up with Lorraine Walden for a series of duets that included "Truck

Driver Man and Wife." In 1979, Simpson appeared for the last time on the charts with "The Flying Saucer Man and the Truck Driver." Haggard recorded his song "Lucky Old Colorado" in 1988; later that year Simpson was diagnosed with skin cancer and underwent surgery, but he fully recovered and continued his writing and performing career. —*Sandra Brennan*

☆ **Roll, Truck, Roll** / 1966 / Capitol ◆◆◆◆◆

Red Simpson's first album of truck songs is a classic, and a fresh, rousing, unpretentious look at the joy, adventure, and loneliness of the road. The title song, authored by Tommy Collins, is the best and most serious song here, with a lot of heart in the writing and in the performance by Simpson—who speaks part of it with an honesty that a lot of actors would kill to capture in their work—and it was a Top 40 country hit. Not everything here comes close to the complexity of that number—there might to one too many songs about drivin' big ol' trucks wherever—but numbers like "Nitro Express" and (natch) "Six Days on the Road" keep a good beat, and "Truck Driver's Blues," living up to its promise, is a slow honky tonk number. Hearing this record again after a lot of years, one is sort of sorry that Red Simpson never got together with, say, Commander Cody on an album. —*Bruce Eder*

The Man Behind the Badge / 1966 / Capitol ◆◆◆◆◆

A good thematic collection comprised of songs about the police and the job they do. It may seem strange, when at least a small but significant portion of the audience for country music professes to have no use for any law but their own; in 1966, to lots of people under the age of 30, this was a totally alien effort. But country audiences ate it up then, lofting the single "The Highway Patrol" high onto the country & western charts. Everything here is a good example of the so-called Bakersfield sound, melding the working-class ethos of Merle Haggard with the polished professionalism of Buck Owens. Simpson is very clever in his use of language and imagery—"(Mary, Oh Mary) I'm Turning in My Star" is presents the grim side of its subject in what, at first, threatens to be a country equivalent of a teen death song, but becomes, instead, almost a screenplay set to music. Ken Nelson gave him the best production possible, a crisp, lean, lively sound with a lot of energy and tension, especially in the rhythm section and the lead guitar, and the result is an album that has held up exceptionally well. —*Bruce Eder*

Truck Drivin' Fool / 1967 / Capitol ◆◆◆◆

Red Simpson Sings a Bakersfield Dozen / 1967 / Capitol ◆◆◆◆◆

Red Simpson was the king of concept-oriented albums long before anyone else. In fact, his first six albums were all concepts. This one centers on his infatuation with his residence in Nash Vegas West, where both Merle Haggard and Buck Owens lived and worked. The Bakersfield sound is a hard country, twang-heavy one. And Simpson, who wrote all but three of the songs here—two others were written with Owens and one by the unknown but amazing Cliff Crawford. There are no themes that have to do with Bakersfield specifically, but it's that pedal steel/fiddle-driven ambience that clues listeners in immediately. Simpson was absorbed by the themes of the mid-'60s such as "Mini Skirt Minnie" from Memphis, TN—and he being a California boy—and then there's the forlorn tunes such as "I'm Gonna Write Momma for Money" (so a country boy can leave the city because he's got the blues). "George for a Day" is one of the most ludicrous songs Simpson ever wrote, but he sings the hell out of it. He's talking about George Jones here folks, which should tell you something. "It's My Last Night in Town" is a barnburning honky tonker, as is "Jeannie With the Light Brown Cadillac." This one kicks it, and you should too with a beer or some other beverage and laugh your ass off at this glorious but goofy album. —*Thom Jurek*

☆ **I'm a Truck** / 1971 / Capitol ◆◆◆◆◆

Red Simpson has to be the first country—or otherwise—singer to perform a definitive song about truck drivers from the point of a semi. This is an album by Simpson the singer, not Simpson the writer. But that doesn't stop it from being his best record. This is sh*t-kicking country, bad mother truck-drivin' rollickin' thick black smoke and diesel rot music. Here is the Benzedrine, the coffee, and the overnight layovers in loading docks. The crazier tunes such as "Nitro Express," "Runaway Truck," "Roll, Truck Roll," and "Black Smoke A-Blowin' Over 18 Wheels" are anthems, pedal-steel-howling, telecaster-strutting, razor-wire singing odes to the danger and the adrenaline rush of the life. The personal tragedies are recorded as well in "Where Love Used to Be" and "Take Me Home." But the Simpson/Buck Owens tune, "Motivatin' Man," is the ultimate truck driver's coat of arms. If this didn't twang so hard it would be a rock & roll album. Simpson's baritone spits his words out with the conviction of a man who understands the nature of the biz—and that doesn't mean music. For those who love hard-drivin', road-trippin', or back-porch-sitting drinking music, this is one classic stack-o-wax. —*Thom Jurek*

The Very Real Red Simpson / 1972 / Capitol ◆◆◆

Trucker's Christmas / 1973 / Capitol ◆◆

The Best of Red Simpson / 1995 / King ◆◆◆

The Man Behind the Badge/Roll, Truck, Roll / 1999 / Capitol ◆◆◆◆◆

Red Simpson's two 1966 albums, *The Man Behind the Badge* and *Roll, Truck, Roll* (which gets misprint on the back cover of the CD), paired together on a neat 24-song CD from England, very cleanly mastered with the original artwork intact, but no further annotation. —*Bruce Eder*

★ **The Best of Red Simpson: Country Western Truck Drivin' Singer** / Aug. 24, 1999 / Razor & Tie ◆◆◆◆◆

Prior to Razor & Tie's 1999 compilation *The Best of Red Simpson: Country Western Truck Drivin' Singer* there was no CD compilation of one of the quintessential truck driving country singers, nor had there even been a good, comprehensive vinyl collection

covering Red Simpson's classic Capitol recordings of the '60s and early '70s. So, *any* collection of his work would have been welcome, but fortunately this 20-track disc does its job perfectly, containing six of his seven charting hits (the last, 1976's "Truck Driver's Heaven," arrived outside of the scope of this collection and isn't part of his prime), along with a generous selection of album tracks from some of the greatest Bakersfield country albums of the '60s. Some may complain that Simpson's material is a little narrow, focusing almost entirely on vehicles, the rules of the road, policemen, truck stops, highways, and other concerns of truckers, but that's like complaining that George Jones sang too much about affairs of the heart. Truck driving country was Simpson's milieu, and while he didn't start the genre or have hits as big as either Dave Dudley or Dick Curless, he produced consistently enjoyable, tremendously entertaining country. Plus, he took the genre seriously, never deviating from its subject and themes, while also having a lot of fun with it, singing good-natured, good-humored songs about the road. Then, there was the sound of the records—filled with twangy Telecasters, propulsive skipping rhythms, echoed vocals, and tinkling pianos, this is Bakersfield country at its leanest, catchiest, and best, practically the definition of how truck driving country should sound, particularly because although it all sounds similar, it never sounds the same. There is a wealth of great songs here: The wonderful pro-police anthem "Highway Patrol," the surprisingly tender "Roll, Truck, Roll," the gleefully silly "I'm a Truck," the outlaw travelogue "Give Me Forty Acres," the menacing, minor-key "Diesel Smoke, Dangerous Curves," and terrific renditions of the perennials "Truck Drivin' Man" and "Six Days on the Road" are just the tip of the iceberg on this stellar compilation. It's certainly the cornerstone of any basic truck driving country collection, but it's more than that—it's one of the best unheralded collections of '60s country on the market. And it's perfect for long trips on the open road. —*Stephen Thomas Erlewine*

Daryle Singletary

b. Mar. 10, 1971, Cairo, GA

Vocals / Contemporary Country, Neo-Traditionalist Country

Neo-traditionalist singer Daryle Singletary was among the brightest new stars to arrive on the contemporary country scene of the mid-'90s, winning fans with his simple, honest songcraft and distinctively gravelly vocals. Born and raised in Cairo, GA, he grew up singing gospel alongside his cousins and brother, and while attending high-school enrolled in a variety of vocal classes; after graduation, he worked at a tractor dealership before relocating to Nashville to pursue a career in music. In Music City, Singletary frequently shared open-mike stages and amateur showcases alongside fellow up-and-comers like Tracy Lawrence and Tim McGraw; he eventually found work as a demo singer, recording the track "Old Pair of Shoes" for an independent label. The song made its way to Randy Travis, who decided to record it himself while recommending Singletary to his management team. In a short time, Singletary signed to Giant Records, and in 1995 he released his self-titled debut LP, scoring the smash hit singles "I Let Her Lie" and "Too Much Fun." The follow-up, *All Because of You*, appeared in late 1996 and generated the hit "Amen Kind of Love." Singletary's third album, *Ain't It the Truth*, was released in early 1998. —*Jason Ankeny*

Daryle Singletary / 1995 / Giant ◆◆◆

● **All Because of You** / Oct. 8, 1996 / Giant ◆◆◆◆

Daryle Singletary's debut album was a fine slice of neo-traditional country, but his follow-up, *All Because of You* is even better, boasting a stronger set of songs—such as the single "Amen Kinda Love"—and a more confident performance by Singletary. There are still a couple of weak tracks, which suffer from underdeveloped songs or slick production, yet *All Because of You* remains a solid neo-traditional modern country record. —*Thom Owens*

Ain't It the Truth / Feb. 24, 1998 / Giant ◆◆◆◆

Although it doesn't quite match the peaks of *All Because of You*, Daryle Singletary's third album, *Ain't It the Truth*, is a solid neo-traditional country album. Singletary's performances are becoming more assured all the time, as is his songwriting. Nevertheless, he relies more on outside writers than his own songs. As a result, the record is arguably his most consistent yet, even if it doesn't quite have the spark of his earlier records. —*Thom Owens*

Now and Again / Jul. 11, 2000 / Audium ◆◆◆

In Nashville, where an artist is often only as good as their last hit song, the concept of greatest hits tends to be a jaded one, especially when they come out too early in an artists career. Daryle Singletary is a solid artist, with three studio albums to his credit and hit singles that include "You Ain't Heard Nothin' Yet" and the country radio staple "Too Much Fun." However, Singletary is by no means a household name and would be better off focusing on new material rather that touting his few hit singles. Still the compilation bodes well, although not differing from most artists who walk the line between neo-traditionalist and suburban pop country. —*Curtis Zimmermann*

That's Why I Sing This Way / Apr. 23, 2002 / Audium ◆◆◆

What do names like Buck Owens, George Jones, Conway Twitty, and Johnny Paycheck have in common besides being the rulers of traditional country music? They all have songs they originally recorded included on this exciting mix of country lore from the expressive baritone Daryle Singletary. Singletary's first album in two years brings tradition back into the spotlight with an album of mostly covers by such classic artists as Owens, Jones, Lefty Frizzell, and Merle Haggard. But what gives the album its appeal are the harmony and background vocal guests—Dwight Yoakam, bluegrass queen Rhonda Vincent, and Jones himself on his 1967 hit, "Walk Through This World With Me." The 12-track collection is like an ode to the '60s when the Bakersfield sound dominated country music. —*Maria Konicki Dinoia*

The Sir Douglas Quintet

f. 1964, **db.** 1972

Group / Tex-Mex, Rock & Roll

Arguably the greatest and most influential Tex-Mex group ever, the Sir Douglas Quintet epitomized Texas' reputation as a fertile roots music melting pot and established the career of Tex-Mex cult legend Doug Sahm. The Quintet mixed country, blues, jazz, R&B, Mexican conjunto/norteño music, Cajun dances, British Invasion rock & roll, garage rock, and even psychedelia into a heady stew that could only have come from Texas. Although they went largely underappreciated during their existence (mostly in the '60s), their influence was far-reaching and continues to be felt in Texas (particularly the similarly eclectic Austin scene) and beyond; afterward, Sahm embarked on a frequently fascinating solo career and reunited with the Quintet or its individual members several times over the years.

According to legend, the Sir Douglas Quintet was the brainchild of Houston producer Huey P. Meaux, who at the height of the British Invasion took a stack of Beatles records into a hotel room and studied them while getting drunk on wine. He found that the beats often resembled those of Cajun dance songs and hit upon the idea of a group that could blend the two sounds well enough to fool Beatles fans into giving a local band a chance. Doug Sahm, meanwhile, had been something of a childhood prodigy as a country artist—he turned down a spot on the *Grand Ole Opry* in order to finish junior high and performed on-stage with Hank Williams. Sahm had made Meaux's acquaintance while leading a series of bands around San Antonio in high-school and wanted to work with him. Meaux told Sahm his idea and Sahm quickly formed a band featuring childhood friend Augie Meyers on organ, bassist Jack Barber, drummer Johnny Perez, and percussionist Leon Beatty (who didn't stick around for too long); saxophonist Frank Morin was added after a short time. Meaux gave them the deceptively British-sounding name the Sir Douglas Quintet and released their debut single, "Sugar Bee," on his Pacemaker label in 1964; it flopped. However, their next single, the British Invasion/garage-flavored "She's About a Mover" (on a different Meaux label, Tribe), became a classic of Tex-Mex rock and an international hit, climbing into the U.S. Top 20 in 1965. Later that year, "The Rains Came" hit the Top 40 and Meaux assembled an LP from their singles sessions with the misleading title *The Best of the Sir Douglas Quintet*. The group toured the United States and Europe, but upon returning, they were arrested at the Corpus Christi airport for possessing a tiny amount of marijuana. Feeling targeted for his long hair and hippie image, Sahm decided to break up the band upon his release from jail, and moved to San Francisco in early 1966; Morin tagged along.

Once in San Francisco, Sahm formed a new version of the Sir Douglas Quintet featuring Morin, keyboardist Peter Ferst (who was quickly replaced by Wayne Talbert), bassist John York (later of the Byrds, soon replaced by Whitney Freeman), and drummer George Rains; most of them were Texas expatriates as well. The new Sir Douglas Quintet gigged regularly around the Bay Area and signed with the Mercury subsidiary Smash. Their first album, *Sir Douglas Quintet + 2 = Honkey Blues*, was recorded with several extra horn players as the Sir Douglas Quintet + 2 and released in 1968; however, it lacked Augie Meyers' signature organ sound. Rains and Talbert soon left to concentrate on other projects and Sahm convinced Meyers and Johnny Perez to move up from Texas; they brought Meyers' old bandmate Harvey Kagan with to be the bassist. With almost all of their original members, the Sir Douglas Quintet recorded one of their finest albums, 1969's *Mendocino*; the title track became a Top 40 hit and a Tex-Mex rock staple and the whole record fit in very well with the emerging country-rock hybrid. Moreover, it made the group extremely popular in Europe, where they would retain a fan base for many years to come.

Together After Five followed in 1970, after which the group switched to a different Mercury affiliate, Philips. Also released in 1970, *1+1+1=4* featured members of both the Texas and California lineups of the Quintet, plus new bassist Jim Stallings. It was perhaps a sign that much of the group was beginning to drift into other projects again. Without Sahm, the remainder of the Quintet recorded an album for United Artists called *Future Tense*; several members also backed Gene Vincent as the Amigos de Musica. A homesick Sahm finally returned to Texas in 1971 and the Sir Douglas Quintet officially disbanded in late 1972, though some of its members—Meyers in particular—would continue to work with Sahm frequently during his solo career.

After being ignored by Mercury, Sahm signed with Atlantic as a solo artist; in the wake of Atlantic's promotional push, Mercury issued an album of unreleased Sir Douglas Quintet tracks, called *Rough Edges*, in 1973. This was the last new Quintet album for some time, until Sahm, Meyers, and Perez re-formed the group at the dawn of the '80s, along with new guitarist Alvin Crow and new bassist Speedy Sparks. They signed with the Chrysalis subsidiary Takoma and released the album *Border Wave* in 1981, which fused their eclectic Tex-Mex rock & roll with the concise pop sound of new wave (as Joe "King" Carrasco had been doing). Crow left prior to the supporting tour to work with his own band and was replaced by Louie Ortega; once again, the Quintet proved more popular in Europe, especially Scandinavia, than in their own country. They recorded for the European Sonet label during the '80s and Takoma occasionally released Quintet material as well. They scored an enormous Swedish hit with "Meet Me in Stockholm," though the accompanying album wasn't released in the U.S.; by 1985, the group had broken up again. Sahm and Meyers formed the Tex-Mex supergroup the Texas Tornados with Freddy Fender and Flaco Jimenez at the end of the decade and in 1994 presided over a one-off version of the Sir Douglas Quintet that featured Sahm's sons Shandon (drums) and Shawn (guitar). In November 1999, Sahm died of a heart attack. *—Steve Huey*

The Best of the Sir Douglas Quintet / 1966 / Tribe ♦♦♦

The Sir Douglas Quintet discography is confusing, not in the least because their first album, in 1966, was entitled *The Best of the Sir Douglas Quintet*. What's more, the LP was reissued in the '70s on the Crazy Cajun label; an identically titled album, on Takoma, had entirely different (and inferior) contents that did not draw from their mid-'60s Tribe sessions; and a nearly identically titled compilation, *The Best of Doug Sahm and the Sir Douglas Quintet* (1991, Mercury), likewise offered entirely different contents than the original Tribe LP did, without any material from those Tribe sessions. So: is the original *The Best of the Sir Douglas Quintet* still *really* the best? Yes. Even though it *is* a hodgepodge of mid-'60s singles, Doug Sahm originals, and covers, it *does* include their only two mid-'60s hits, "She's About a Mover" and the equally fine, but unjustly obscure, "The Rains Came." There's plenty else to sink your teeth into as well: a moody Animals-like cover of the ancient folk song "It Was in the Pines," the heartbreaking swamp-pop of "Beginning of the End," the peppy Cajun two-step rock of "Please Just Say So," and the Rolling Stones-like "It's a Man Down There." This does (especially for a putative best-of) illustrate that for all their strengths, the Quintet's major weakness was a relatively shallow well of truly top-line material. "The Tracker," for instance, is a blatant rewrite of the "She's About a Mover" groove, and several other tracks (like a hectic cover of "Quarter to Three") don't have too much going for them but likable energy. In addition, some of their stronger mid-'60s Tribe tracks are not here, but on BeatRocket's companion volume of Tribe cuts, *The Sir Douglas Quintet Is Back!* Still, the group's blend of British Invasion, blues, country, soul, and Cajun music was unique in its time, and Doug Sahm was already proving himself to be one of the most versatile and soulful white rock singers. [The CD reissue is enhanced by the addition of two B-sides, the greasy "Bacon Fat" and the rare moody 1964 cut "Blue Norther," as well as historical liner notes.] *—Richie Unterberger*

Sir Douglas Quintet + 2 = Honkey Blues / 1968 / Smash ♦♦♦

It is hard to believe that this is the first entry in the extensive Sir Douglas Quintet discography, as it seems like the kind of experimental venture an artist might throw out after a handful of successful albums have already been released. The electic nature of bandleader Doug Sahm is undisputed, but this has got to be his album with the most experimental jazz leanings, again not something one would expect. The type of themes that Sahm would return to again and again in his songwriting are here, delivered by a grouping that lacks one of the essential sparkplugs in the Sir Douglas Quintet engine, keyboard man Augie Meyers. There is presumed to be compensation in the form of a total of five horn players, including Bay Area session whiz Mel Martin, but someone decided to record them with enough reverb to submerge a whale. A total of seven songs, none of them really extended enough to account for paucity of titles, get a loping, jamming treatment that gets the message across, although a little vaguely at times. Certainly a promising, original album well above the level of most rock-bands-with-horns experiments of this era, but not as inspiring as this band's music would soon become. *—Eugene Chadbourne*

Mendocino / Apr. 1969 / Smash ♦♦♦♦♦

Chart success for the title song led to a hurried release for this band's second album, although perhaps the most famous song, "She's About a Mover, originated a few years prior with another version. Listeners will probably be more familiar with the version heard here, the one with the freaky feedback guitar solo and fake fadeout that oldies disc jockeys like to yabber over. This and "Mendocino" are only two of the many nearly perfect tracks on this record, some of which give off the illusion (perhaps an accurate one) that they were simply tossed off without a whole lot of preperation. "Texas Me" is genius on triple levels: there is the poetry of the lyrics, the soulful delivery from the singer, and finally the haunting recording fat with echoey, multitracked vocal and fiddle. When the listener reaches the end, "Baby It Just Don't Matter" it is as if one has strolled through an old neighborhood searching for a lost sound in the air, only to find a good, friendly rock band is jamming in a garage right down the block. The players are the classic Sir Douglas Quintet lineup including Augie Meyer. *—Eugene Chadbourne*

Together After Five / 1970 / Smash ♦♦♦♦

A supreme example of the Doug Sahm sound and aesthetic is at work here in their third complete studio album. There is perhaps the best recorded version of the Augie Meyers "cheap organ" sound, a well from which many a garage rock organist hath drunken deep. And it is great the way this instrument emerges out of arrangements emphasizing stark interplay between acoustic guitar and drums. A real ringer but one of the highlights of the album is the instrumental "T-Bone Shuffle," which rivals the Art Ensemble of Chicago for raucous boogie on the edge of lunacy. The songs include some of Sahm's best lyrics and most heartfelt singing, although he goes a bit overboard at times and threatens to come across like a burn-out overstaying his welcome on an open stage. This and a few strange errors in judgement such as the song "Dallas Alice"—imagine something that sounds too close to "Honey" for comfort and also has a flute solo—are the only things preventing this from being one of the best Sir Douglas Quintet albums. *—Eugene Chadbourne*

1+1+1 = 4 / Jun. 1970 / Philips ♦♦♦♦

The Sir Douglas Quintet delivered two excellent records back to back in *Mendocino* and *Together After Five*, but success was hard to come by, and it was hard to tell what path was the right one for a band as talented and fuzzily focused as this. Their fourth Mercury/Smash record, 1970's *1+1+1=4* didn't solve that puzzle and by trying to touch on a little of everything, it didn't provide any clear direction for the band to follow, nor did it showcase the band at its best. Even so, the Sir Douglas Quintet on a bad day were better and more interesting than many of their peers, and part of the fascination behind this record is to hear the group—or, more accurately, its leader Doug Sahm—try to craft an identity by adhering to the band's signature Tex-Mex while expanding in such disparate directions as pure country and horn-drenched progressive pop/rock. The country comes from sessions Sahm held with legendary producer Jerry Kennedy in Nashville; intended to be released as a solo single under the name Wayne Douglas, Sahm's laid-back Texas attitude never translated to the professional aesthetic of Nashville, and the results—"Be Real" and "Pretty Flower"—wind up being a fresh southern breeze on this typically loose-limbed, unfocused, freewheeling record. A large part of the charm of Sahm with the Sir Douglas Quintet is that he was undisciplined; he had no compunction in bringing in what engaged him at a particular time, tying it into his signature blend of rock & roll, R&B, and country. Here, he lays on a little bit too much of a guitar fed through a Leslie rotating speaker, a little bit too much of the punchy, jazzy horn-laced arrangements of such pop progressives as Blood, Sweat & Tears, and he panders a little bit too much to the album-oriented audience. It was all in vain, of course—no matter what he did, he couldn't erase the nature of his music, he couldn't remove the all-encompassing, all-Texan aesthetic, so it still sounded too idiosyncratic for its own good. That, of course, is what makes the music so rich and fascinating years after the fact, because even if Sahm tried different sounds, it still wound up sounding like him, and that's why it's aged much better than other records from that same year. It's a little too hazy and unfocused to be a true lost classic, but once you're hooked on the Sir Douglas sound, this is absolutely necessary. [The 2002 reissue on Acadia/Evangeline contains four bonus tracks: "I Wanna Be Your Mama Again (Nashville Version)," "I Don't Want to Go Home," "Leaving Kansas City," and "Colinda."] —*Stephen Thomas Erlewine*

The Return of Doug Saldaña / 1971 / Philips ◆◆◆◆◆
Since the Sir Douglas Quintet's records were so consistently satisfying and worked such a similar territory—a loose-limbed, freewheeling eclecticism that encompassed rock & roll, blues, country, and R&B in unequal measures at varying times—it can be hard drawing distinctions between their records. Certainly, there was a leap in quality and consistency when they moved to Smash, particularly after their tremendous *Mendocino* record, but each followed similar territory, with subtle shifts in either tone, subject, or music. Even so, their final Smash record, 1971's *The Return of Doug Saldaña*, is a special record that leapfrogs over the competition and arguably stands as their best record—the best representation of their musical aesthetic, their richest collection of music, their best collection of songs. Part of its appeal is that it stretches beyond the signature Tex-Mex sound they laid down with *Mendocino*; there is no song that captures that wild, wide-open sound, complete with the simple chord changes and careening organ. No, here the Sir Douglas Quintet wind up emphasizing their musical roots—whether it's the roadhouse blues jam of "Papa Ain't Salty" or the '50s rock & roll pastiche of "She's Huggin' You, But She's Lookin' at Me," a cinematic pastiche that's the American equivalent of David Bowie's similarly romanticized "Drive-In Saturday"—while settling into the post-hippie hangover of the early '70s, as the dreams of the late '60s die. Witness how the raving opener, "Preach What You Live, Live What You Live," finds its counterpart in the sweetly resigned "Stoned Faces Don't Lie," and how it covers both spectrums of emotion, as Doug Sahm and his group embrace ideals while simultaneously finding them dwindling away. This is the subtext in an album that finds a surplus of great Texas music, from the breezy "Me and My Destiny" and a cover of "Wasted Days, Wasted Nights" to the folky narrative of "The Railpak Dun Done in the Del Monte" and the loose blues of "The Gypsy." No other record by the Sir Douglas Quintet has such a consistently great set of songs or captures their ambition and skill as well as this, which is why it is arguably not only their finest record, but also one of the great lost records of its era, holding its own with the best of such similarly minded groups as the Band. A fantastic record that's just waiting to be discovered. [The 2002 reissue on Acadia/Evangeline contains two bonus tracks, the typically wonderful "Michoacan" and "Westside Blues Again."] —*Stephen Thomas Erlewine*

The Best of the Sir Douglas Quintet / 1980 / Takoma ◆◆◆◆
The new wave craze of the early '80s put some journalists and producers on the trail of Doug Sahm & the Sir Douglas Quintet, coinciding with a decision by Takoma to release both old and new material by the group. While this label is not really known for its reissue compilations, it has come up with a series of them in a variety of genres and these productions are usually first-rate. This is no exception, so for once a greatest-hits set devoted to a '60s rock act presents a fairly good picture of what the group's music was all about. Perhaps the good-natured diversity of Sahm's art would allow this to happen in any case, yet this still seems like an especially thoughtful collection of Sir Douglas Quintet tracks off several different early Smash albums. The songs have a really moving flow to them, no easy thing considering that the material is taken from various well-assembled complete albums and skips all over the place from country to Cajun to R&B to strange psychedelic experiments. The hits are here, beginning with "Mendocino," moving through "She's About a Mover," and including songs that will be personal hits for all fans of this band, and really had the potential to be much bigger hits, such as the marvelous "Dynamite Woman." This album is superior to other Sir Douglas Quintet releases that go under the best-of moniker, so watch out, look for the psychedelic day-glo blue lettering across the front; the consumer will know it is the right album if a headache kicks in after three minutes of staring at the cover. —*Eugene Chadbourne*

Border Wave / 1981 / Takoma ◆◆◆◆◆
How someone as old wave as Doug Sahm hooked into the new wave of the '80s is not exactly so mysterious if one examines the rich stylistic makeup of the Sir Douglas Quintet repertoire, and how so many of these grooves were finding their way into the sounds of the so-called new wave era. This album was put together as a partial result of Sahm's efforts to revive his group during those times, one that led to an increased touring and release schedule. It all turns out better than expected in the case of this session, which is beautifully recorded and played and features not only good Sahm tunes—some old and some new—but a refreshing brace of cover tunes from Ray Davies to Butch Hancock. Needless to say, Sahm makes each tune his own and is in fine vocal form. The remake of "Revolutionary Ways" is terrific, but the real showstopper is "Old Habits Die Hard," another entry in the long list of cooking rock songs that sound like they should have been hits—and that in reality nobody has ever heard of. —*Eugene Chadbourne*

Crazy Cajun Recordings / Feb. 18, 1999 / Edsel ◆◆◆
Doug Sahm, aka "Sir Doug" of the Sir Douglas Quintet, rock & roll's first long-haired redneck, was a walking compendium of Texas music styles. Whether it was Texas blues, Tex-Mex rock & roll, garage, country, R&B, soul, singer/songwriter, and anything in between, Sir Doug could wail it and nail it. What's more, he would tell you so. Just the natural,

Texas facts, ma'am. Most of this two-disc collection is culled from the Sir Douglas Quintet's Tribe Records years, produced by "Crazy Cajun" Huey P. Meaux, when the SDQ burst upon a Beatle landscape with one of rock & roll's all-time anthems, "She's About a Mover." The trademark sound of Sir Doug's country-boy, blues/rock vocals and Augie Meyer's simple, driving Vox organ lines, evident on "She's About a Mover," is the original blueprint for garage rock. The majority of the rest of this collection is filled with less successful follow-ups and album cuts, which is not to say the material isn't choice. Even at this early stage, almost everything Sir Doug played was sure and tight. As a child prodigy of sorts, Sahm had played Texas nightclubs since his pre-teens. Hence, by the time (1965) "She's About a Mover" hit the charts, he was a veteran, steeped in country, blues, and R&B. This wasn't two-chord, we-can-record-in-my-uncle's-basement garage rock. This was a young group of pros drawing upon their experiences and creating a whole new sound. SDQ's not-so-successful follow-up to "She's About a Mover," "The Rains Came," is included. Written by a then-obscure Freddy Fender, it is a damn near perfect single and, in an ideal Top 40 world, would have been just as big a hit as its predecessor. The descending chorus "rain, rain, rain, rain/my pillow's soaking wet" is flawlessly punctuated by Meyer's timely organ punches. Of the generous 41 cuts on this set, there are some early "finds" no SDQ fan should be without. "Oh, What a Mistake," "The Tracker," "It's a Man Down Here," "She Digs My Love," "You've Got Your Good Thing Down," "She's Gotta Be the Boss Babe," and especially "In Time" could have been, at the very least, regional hits. They are the cave paintings for what would later evolve into such SDQ masterpieces as the *Mendocino* and *Together After Five* albums. Other cuts here are interesting but not essential (i.e., Sir Doug's takes of "Wolverton Mountain," "Image of Me," "Philadelphia Lawyer," and "Quarter to Three"). One glaring weakness of this compilation is the incongruous inclusion of much later 1970s material such as "Seguin," "Nuevo Laredo," and "Revolutionary Ways." All are fine songs and essential for an SDQ 1970s anthology, but out of place in this package. —*Steve Cooper*

● Prime of Sir Douglas Quintet / Oct. 19, 1999 / Music Club ◆◆◆◆◆
It is unfortunate that no one can seem to muster a definitive collection of Sir Douglas Quintet's early (pre-Smash) recordings. This 15-song disc is a pretty good try, and has very good music, but doesn't quite take the cigar. No original recording or release dates are given, and the liner notes are vague about the sources for the material. About half of the tracks did show up on Tribe singles (and their sole Tribe LP) in the mid-'60s. The rest are of more mysterious origin, some sounding like casual demos, and some sounding as if they may date from a later period. The important thing to note is that this *does* have the original versions of their mid-'60s hits "She's About a Mover" and the equally worthy, though lesser known, "The Rains Came." "In Time" is an awkward but appealing attempt to incorporate British Invasion influences; "Beginning of the End" has that special lazy Texas doo wop/pop feel typical of Meaux's early-'60s productions; "Please Just Say So" is top-drawer Tex-Mex rock; and "Bacon Fat" is an engagingly sloppy cover of the Andre Williams R&B dance tune. The more obscure selections have less of a "band" sound and more of a country/folk/blues-orientation that puts Sahm's great roots vocals at the fore. On some of the slow country tunes, he sounds uncannily like Elvis Costello *wants* to sound when doing country music. "Blue Pass Me By" sounds like a Tribe-era outtake with its smoky barroom feel, while Sahm's "I Don't Want to Go Home" and the cover of Dylan's "One Too Many Mornings" have a more mature folk-rock feel. Sahm's singing is cool throughout, and almost everything is a good listen; it's just that a significant group such as Sir Douglas deserves a more thorough, and more thoroughly documented, compilation. —*Richie Unterberger*

● Best of the Sir Douglas Quintet / Mar. 20, 2000 / Beat Rocket ◆◆◆◆◆
A more or less straight-up reissue of the group's Tribe album. When producer Huey P. Meaux released this disc in 1966, he probably though it was the end of the group, as they had hadn't hit the Top 40 in almost a year and a drug bust decimated their ranks. Cobbled together from their 1965 sessions, this brings together "She's About a Mover," "The Rains Came," and strong versions of "Bacon Fat," "Quarter to Three," and "It's a Man Down There." If you're going to slim the collection down to just one Sir Doug collection, this is the one to grab. —*Cub Koda*

Sir Douglas Quintet Is Back! / Mar. 20, 2000 / Beat Rocket ◆◆◆◆◆
This and Beat Rocket's companion reissue of the 1966 *The Best of Sir Douglas Quintet* album seem to gather most or all of what the group recorded for Tribe in the mid-'60s. Seems simple enough, but it's cause for rejoicing among '60s collectors, considering that this back catalog had somehow eluded the marketplace for more than 30 years prior to these two sets. If you're looking to choose one over the other, *The Best Of . . .* would get the nod for its inclusion of their only two Tribe hits: ("She's About a Mover" and "The Rains Came"). However, the various flop singles and outtakes comprising *The Sir Douglas Quintet Is Back!* are about equal in quality to the sister volume, with the same invigorating, erratic combination of British Invasion, Cajun, blues, soul, country, and even folk-rock. Certainly "In Time," a minor-key Sahm original with echoes of the Animals and the Zombies, and "Blues Pass Me By," a grand illustration of Sahm's stature as one of the finest white soul-rock vocalists ever, rate among their finer moments. Another Sahm original, "She Digs My Love," has astonishing fluttering blues-rock guitar licks that sound a hell of a lot like Jimi Hendrix—although Hendrix had yet to release records under his own name when it came out. According to the liner notes, their debut 1964 single "Sugar Bee" preceded the Beatles' "She's a Woman" by several months, boasting a *very* similar riff and rhythm. It does make you wonder whether some of rock's giants somehow managed to borrow some ideas from Sir Douglas Quintet singles that very few people heard. At times the material on this disc can be perfunctory, but the mix of so many elements in one band (and sometimes in one song) are seldom less than interesting. —*Richie Unterberger*

1+1+1=4/Return of Doug Saldaña / Sep. 24, 2002 / Raven ✦✦✦✦✦

Raven's two-fer of the Sir Douglas Quintet's *1+1+1=4* and *The Return of Doug Saldaña*, released in 1970 and 1971, respectively, appeared roughly around the same time Audium reissued the two albums separately with bonus tracks, but it's tough to complain about a sudden surplus of their Smash material when it was so very hard to find on CD for many years. Though one other album for Smash followed—1973's *Rough Edges*, consisting mainly of earlier sessions, three tracks of which are added as bonus tracks here (along with "Michoacan" from the soundtrack of the 1972 film *Cisco Pike*)—these two records effectively capped off their stunning string of LPs for the label and compliment each other very well. *1+1+1* is a little sunnier and a little more open, *Return* is a grittier roadhouse record, but both are wonderful examples of Doug Sahm's freewheeling, all-encompassing roots music, filled with great songs and great performances that sound effortless and timeless. As to whether you should get the individual reissues or this two-fer, it's really a toss-up since the bonus tracks on those aren't available here and vice versa—pick whichever is either cheaper or easier to find, just as long as you get this music in some form. *—Stephen Thomas Erlewine*

Ricky Skaggs

b. Jul. 18, 1954, Cordell, KY

Fiddle, Guitar, Mandolin, Vocals, Banjo / Bluegrass, Progressive Bluegrass, Traditional Bluegrass, New Traditionalist, Bluegrass-Gospel, Progressive Country

By the time he was in his mid 30s, Kentuckian Ricky Skaggs had already produced a career's worth of music. At age seven he appeared on TV with Flatt & Scruggs; at 15 he was a member of legendary Ralph Stanley's bluegrass band (with fellow teenager Keith Whitley). None of his '80s peers, male or female, had better musical credentials than Skaggs. The term "multi-talented" lacks the power to characterize this extraordinary singer and instrumentalist. Not only can he sing and pick with the best in progressive country, his broad and deep experience in traditional music separates him from the crowd. In the estimation of many, he is without peer as a combination vocalist and instrumentalist (guitar, mandolin, fiddle, banjo). After playing with Ralph Stanley for three years, Skaggs moved on to progressive bluegrass bands the Country Gentlemen and J. D. Crowe & the New South. With his own band, Boone Creek, he mixed the old and the new, adding Django Reinhardt. Skaggs took Rodney Crowell's place in Emmylou Harris' Hot Band in 1977, and the band's excellent *Roses in the Snow* album showcased Skaggs' versatility. Two number-one hits came out of his 1981 album *Waitin' for the Sun to Shine*, and the awards started arriving. Skaggs is largely responsible for a back-to-basics movement in country music. He showed many that a bluegrass tenor with impeccable taste and enormous talent could sell traditional country in the '80s, a time when pop music had invaded the land of rural rhythm.

Skaggs began playing music at a very early age, being given a mandolin from his father at the age of five. Before his father had the time to teach Ricky how to play, the child had learned the instrument himself, and by the end of 1959, he had performed onstage during a Bill Monroe concert, playing "Ruby Are You Mad at Your Man" to great acclaim. Two years later, when Skaggs was seven, he appeared on Flatt & Scruggs' television show, again to a positive response. Shortly afterward, he learned how to play both fiddle and guitar and began playing with his parents in a group called the Skaggs Family. In addition to traditional bluegrass, Skaggs began absorbing the honky tonk of George Jones and Ray Price and the British Invasion rock & roll of the Beatles and the Rolling Stones. In his adolescence, he briefly played in rock & roll bands, but he never truly abandoned traditional and roots music.

During a talent concert in his midteens, he met Keith Whitley, a fellow fiddler. The two adolescents became friends and began playing together, with Whitley's brother Dwight on banjo, at various radio shows. By 1970, they earned a spot opening for Ralph Stanley. Following their performance, Stanley invited the duo to join his supporting band, the Clinch Mountain Boys, and they accepted. Over the next two years, they played many concerts with the bluegrass legend and appeared on his record *Cry From the Cross*. Skaggs also appeared on Whitley's solo album *Second Generation Bluegrass* in 1972. Though he had made his way into the bluegrass circuit and was actively recording, Skaggs had grown tired of the hard work and low pay in the Clinch Mountain Boys and left the group at the end of 1972. For a short while, he abandoned music and worked in a boiler room for the Virginia Electric Power Company in Washington, D.C., but he returned to performing when the Country Gentlemen invited him to join in 1973.

Skaggs spent the next two years with the group, primarily playing fiddle, before joining the progressive bluegrass band J.D. Crowe & the New South in 1974. The following year, he recorded another duet album with Whitley, *That's It*, and then formed his own newgrass band, Boone Creek, in 1976. In addition to bluegrass, the outfit played honky tonk and Western swing. Boone Creek earned the attention of Emmylou Harris, who invited Skaggs to join her supporting band. After declining her several times, he finally became a member of her Hot Band once Rodney Crowell left in 1977. Between 1977 and 1980, Skaggs helped push Harris toward traditional country and bluegrass, often to great acclaim. Skaggs also pursued a number of other musical venues while he was with Harris, recording a final album with Boone Creek (1978's *One Way Track*), two duet albums with Tony Rice (1978's *Take Me Home Tonight in a Song*, 1980's *Skaggs & Rice*), and finally, his first solo album, *Sweet Temptation*, which was released on Sugar Hill. *Sweet Temptation* was a major bluegrass hit, earning the attention of the major label Epic Records. The label offered him a contract in 1981, releasing *Waitin' for the Sun to Shine* later that year. The album was a big hit, earning acclaim not only in country circles, but also in rock & roll publications. By the end of the year, Skaggs had become a star and, in the process, brought rootsy traditional country back into the consciousness of the country audience.

During 1982 and early 1983, he had five straight number-one singles—"Crying My Heart Out Over You," "I Don't Care," "Heartbroke," "I Wouldn't Change You If I Could," "Highway 40 Blues"—as well as earning numerous awards. Later in 1982, he was made the youngest member of the *Grand Ole Opry*. For the next four years, he was a major artistic and commercial force within country music, raking up a string of Top Ten hits and Grammy Award-winning albums. His success helped spark the entire new traditionalist movement, opening the doors for performers like George Strait and Randy Travis. Toward the end of the decade, Skaggs wasn't charting as frequently as he had in the past, but he had established himself as an icon. Each of his records sold well, and he collaborated with a number of musicians, including Rodney Crowell, the Bellamy Brothers, Johnny Cash, Jesse Winchester, and Dolly Parton.

During the early '90s, Skaggs and his traditional music were hit hard by the slick sounds of contemporary country, and consequently, his records ceased to sell as consistently as they had ten years earlier. Columbia Records dropped the musician from their label in 1992 due to poor sales. However, Skaggs continued to perform concerts and festivals frequently, as well as host his own syndicated radio program, *the Simple Life*, which hit the airwaves in 1994. The following year, Skaggs returned to recording with *Solid Ground*, his first album for Atlantic Records. *Life Is a Journey* followed in 1997, and two years later he released *Soldier of the Cross*. *Big Mon: The Songs of Bill Monroe* followed in 2000 and was re-released in 2002 on the Lyric Street label as *Ricky Skaggs and Friends Sing the Songs of Bill Monroe*. In 2003, Skaggs released *Live at the Charleston Music Hall* on his own Skaggs Family label. *—David Vinopal*

Sweet Temptation / 1979 / Sugar Hill ✦✦✦✦✦

With guest vocals by then-boss Emmylou Harris, Skaggs' first solo effort (not counting the Boone Creek project) is equal parts bluegrass and Harris-styled new traditionalism. *—Dan Cooper*

Skaggs & Rice / 1980 / Sugar Hill ✦✦✦✦✦

Skaggs & Rice is a lovely duet album between Ricky Skaggs & Tony Rice. The two musicians run-through a number of bluegrass classics, performing them in a spare, simple old-timey style, backed only by their guitar and mandolin. Not only are the performances breathtaking, but the song selection—featuring Bill Monroe classics like "Mansions for Me" and "Tennessee Blues," as well as other standards like "Talk About Suffering" and "Have You Someone in Heaven Awaiting." *—Thom Owens*

Waitin' for the Sun to Shine / 1981 / Epic ✦✦✦

His first album after signing with Epic Records, this one took Skaggs into the mainstream, in effect beginning the new traditionalist movement. It has a simple, mountain approach, with lots of remakes and Skaggs' mournful vocal tones. The best cut is the plaintive title track. *—Tom Roland*

Highways & Heartaches / 1982 / DCC ✦✦✦✦✦

On 1982's *Highways & Heartaches*, Ricky Skaggs had developed his bluegrass roots with new traditionalist sensibilities and catchy pop tunes that fuel this album, which is one of his best. Four of these tunes—"Heartbroke," "You've Got a Lover," "I Wouldn't Change You if I Could," and "Highway 40 Blues"—were chart-toppers. The remainder of the decade found Skaggs often at the top of both the country single and album charts. *—Al Campbell*

Family & Friends / 1982 / Rounder ✦✦✦

Skaggs' last breath of pure bluegrass was recorded with help from the Whites, guitarist Peter Rowan, dobroist Jerry Douglas, and others. Included are two songs by Carter Stanley, one by Bill Monroe, and some fine examples of Appalachian gospel, including a stunning a cappella trio vocal on "Talk About Sufferin'." *—Brian Mansfield*

Don't Cheat in Our Hometown / 1983 / Epic ✦✦✦

Ricky Skaggs maintained his status on the country charts in 1984 with *Don't Cheat in Our Hometown*. Skaggs' combination of bluegrass, honky tonk, and pop material reigned at the center of country music in the early to mid-'80s, unquestioned here given the presence of the chart-topping "Honey (Open That Door)," a cover of Bill Monroe's "Uncle Pen," and the title track originally made famous by the Stanley Brothers, to whom the album is dedicated. *—Al Campbell*

Country Boy / 1984 / Epic ✦✦✦✦✦

Without a doubt, the highlight of Ricky Skaggs' 1984 *Country Boy* disc has to be the title track. It shows off Skaggs' bluegrass pickin', at warp speed. Bill Monroe's tune "Wheel Hoss" features Monroe keeping up with the virile Skaggs, while Skaggs shows what he learned at the feet of the master of bluegrass mandolin. Other highlights among the ten cuts include "Brand New Me," "Baby I'm in Love With You," and a version of George Jones' honky tonk classic "Window Up Above." *—Al Campbell*

Favorite Country Songs / 1985 / Epic ✦✦✦

On numerous albums recorded during the height of Ricky Skaggs' domination of the country charts in the mid-'80s, he always recorded tunes written or influenced by the pioneers of country and bluegrass music. *Favorite Country Songs* is a ten-track compilation featuring many of those influential tunes, including two by the Stanley Brothers ("If That's the Way You Feel" and "I'll Take the Blame"), Bill Monroe's "Can't You Hear Me Calling," and "Your Old Love Letters," a hit in the early '60s for both Porter Wagoner and Jim Reeves. This is an interesting tribute to the music that greatly influenced Skaggs. *—Al Campbell*

Live in London / 1985 / Epic ✦✦✦✦✦

This is the one Skaggs album to own if you can only have one. Because it's a live recording, the picking is just that much more exciting, and the album serves as an unofficial best-of, its highlights including "Heartbroke," "Uncle Pen," and a version of "Don't Get Above Your Raising" that features noted country fan Elvis Costello. *—William Ruhlmann*

Love's Gonna Get Ya / 1986 / Epic ✦✦✦

Skaggs continued to inch closer to modern mainstream country on *Love's Gonna Get Ya*, which features the hit "Love's Gonna Get You Someday." *—Jason Ankeny*

Comin' Home to Stay / 1988 / Epic ✦✦✦

Comin' Home to Stay marks Skaggs' return to traditional country, and includes "I'm Tired," "Thanks Again" and "(Angel on My Mind) That's Why I'm Walkin'." *—Jason Ankeny*

Kentucky Thunder / 1989 / Epic ✦✦✦

My Father's Son / 1991 / Epic ♦♦♦
A concept album about families, *My Father's Son* is the Skaggs album that owes the least to bluegrass. Skaggs is concerned with the legacies fathers leave their sons, both the wisdom ("Father Knows Best") and the limitations ("My Father's Son"). He also sees materialism for the distracting, destructive force it is. His duet with Waylon Jennings on "Only Daddy That'll Walk the Line" fits neatly, though perhaps not the way the writer intended. And because Skaggs' background is bluegrass rather than honky tonk, every father image is inextricably bound to God. *—Brian Mansfield*

Super Hits / Aug. 24, 1993 / Epic ♦♦♦♦♦
Super Hits is a budget-priced ten-track collection that contains a selection of Ricky Skaggs' greatest hits ("Cajun Moon," "Highway 40 Blues," "Uncle Pen," "Country Boy") that are padded by album tracks. It's not bad for a budget-priced collection, but it's far from definitive. *—Stephen Thomas Erlewine*

Solid Ground / Nov. 7, 1995 / Atlantic ♦♦♦
Country's most amicable music maker made a comeback with *Solid Ground*, his first release for Atlantic, a label not known for its country artists. From the cover of Harry Chapin's "Cat's in the Cradle" to the title track's wry drive, the album is put together well. These tunes are all pretty fair and comforting, and there is no ground more solid for an album to build upon. *—James Chrispell*

Life Is a Journey / Jul. 29, 1997 / Atlantic ♦♦♦
If Ricky Skaggs' latter-day albums lack the surprise and excitement of his early records, his sheer skill and musicianship nevertheless ensure that the albums are rarely boring. *Life Is a Journey* is a textbook example of this. There's nothing new here, to be sure, but Skaggs performs with grace and good humor that gives the music an extra, endearing kick. It may suffer from some ill-chosen material, and it may be a little spotty, yet *Life Is a Journey* remains another solid addition to Skaggs' catalog. *—Thom Owens*

Bluegrass Rules! / Oct. 21, 1997 / Rounder ♦♦♦♦♦
Fifteen years after leaving bluegrass behind, Ricky Skaggs returned to his first love in 1997 with *Bluegrass Rules!* It may have taken him a while to make this record, but the wait was well worth it. *Bluegrass Rules!* is an energetic, invigorating listen, filled with joy and spirited playing. Backed by Kentucky Thunder (Bryan Sutton, Bobby Hicks, Dennis Parker, Paul Brewster, Marc Pruett, Mark Fain), Skaggs enlivens traditional bluegrass songs with unpredictable arrangements, unexpected licks and impassioned singing. It's one of Skaggs' very best records, proving that most bluegrass musicians just improve with age. *—Thom Owens*

★ **Country Gentleman: The Best of Ricky Skaggs** / Jan. 27, 1998 / Epic/Legacy ♦♦♦♦♦
Country Gentleman: The Best of Ricky Skaggs is a terrific double-disc set that traces Skaggs' years at Epic Records, which spanned from 1981 to 1991. All of his charting singles are featured on this 32-track collection, including the number-one singles "Crying My Heart Out Over You," "I Dont' Care," "Heartbroke," "I Wouldn't Change You If I Could," "Highway 40 Blues," "Uncle Pen" and "Cajun Moon," as well as the Mark O'Connor/New Nashville Cats duet "Restless." Skaggs was one of the few country artists of his era to make albums as good as his singles, but boiling his career down to his singles does him no disservice—in fact, it accentuates the consistant brilliance of his music, not to mention its depth. It's a definitive portrait of one of the most important country musicians of the '80s, capturing him at his peak. *—Stephen Thomas Erlewine*

Ancient Tones / Jan. 26, 1999 / Skaggs Family ♦♦♦♦♦
Ricky Skaggs has become an American musical institution. Sure, you don't hear his name as often as, say, Garth Brooks, but he is just as important on the musical landscape. As a multi-instrumentalist, Skaggs has worked with the best in the business, and now he brings it all back home with this, the follow-up to *Bluegrass Rules!* on his own Skaggs Family record label and a collection of some of the finest classic bluegrass tracks ever compiled on a single disc. Beginning with a track penned by the father of bluegrass, Bill Monroe, Skaggs and his band move through "Walls of Time" with nothing short of perfection. Skaggs also covers "Mighty Dark to Travel," "Boston Boy," and "I Believed in You Darlin'," all written by Skaggs' mentor, Monroe. Also covered are Carter Stanley's "Lonesome Night" and "How Mountain Girls Can Love," a full-speed-ahead bluegrass romp. Billy Joe Foster's "Give Us Rain" and the definitive song of the genre, written by Ralph and Carter Stanley, "Pig in a Pen," are fresh and alive with Skaggs' smooth vocals and fiery mandolin work. Skaggs saves one spot on the album to perform his own composition, "Connerma," and delivers an excellent arrangement of the traditional "Little Bessie." It is a rare thing to find an album that so clearly defines an entire genre of music the way *Ancient Tones* does. It is a gem of a record—a record to help carry the memory of folks like Bill Monroe, the Stanley Brothers, and, of course, Ricky Skaggs into the 21st century. *—Michael B. Smith*

Soldier of the Cross / Sep. 14, 1999 / Skaggs Family ♦♦♦♦♦
Ricky Skaggs continues to embody the very spirit of the late Bill Monroe on his latest release, a 14-song collection of gospel favorites, delivered with all the bluegrass precision you have come to expect from the multi-talented Skaggs. From the sounding of a ram's horn at the album's outset, perhaps as a spiritual call to arms, the CD delivers a moving set of tunes, beginning with the title track, "Soldier of the Cross," a Lorin Rowan composition, and moving into Bill Monroe's own "A Voice From on High." Ralph Stanley's "The Darkest Hour" is a special treat, and marks the second time Skaggs has recorded this particular tune. He played and sang backup for Emmylou Harris' version of the song in 1978, but his version shines brightly in and of itself. One of the true classics here is "Gone Home," the old Bill Carlisle tune made famous in the 1950s by Flatt & Scruggs. Anyone who grew up in the South is bound to have heard at least half-dozen versions of this one, but none more pristine that the version included here. Also outstanding is the somber "Seven Hillsides," an absolutely powerful lyric that tells the story of a life from a preacher's perspective, and "Are You Afraid to Die," which includes an actual audio clip from one of Billy Graham's crusades. Closing out the CD is an a cappella rendition of the traditional "Lead Me to the Rock." Skaggs' soaring tenor voice sends chills up the spine with this faith-inspired vocal, and it is the perfect end-cap for an outstanding bluegrass album, as well as an inspirational gospel recording, all rolled into one. *—Michael B. Smith*

Big Mon: The Songs of Bill Monroe / Aug. 29, 2000 / Skaggs Family ♦♦♦
Featuring an all-star lineup of country and rock's biggest names, Ricky Skaggs' heartfelt tribute to bluegrass pioneer Bill Monroe is well-intended but a little too slick. Featuring artists like Mary-Chapin Carpenter, the Dixie Chicks, Charlie Daniels, John Fogerty, Bruce Hornsby, Patty Loveless, Joan Osborne, Dolly Parton, Travis Tritt, Steve Wariner, the Whites, and Dwight Yoakam, it is made overwhelmingly clear that the music of Monroe has made an impact on many different musical genres. Unfortunately, the genre that this CD is lacking is bluegrass; the listener has to wait until the last track (the scattered "Big Mon") to hear some real pickers like J.D. Crowe and members of the Del McCoury Band perform traditional down-home music. There is no one else in the music industry today who works harder to bring traditional American bluegrass to the mainstream audience, but unfortunately the vehicle it arrives in usually ends up being a new Cadillac, not the sturdy 1943 Ford pickup it belongs in. [This album was rereleased on Disney's Lyric Street imprint with one aditional track under the title *Ricky Skaggs and Friends Sing the Songs of Bill Monroe*.] *—Zac Johnson*

● **16 Biggest Hits** / Sep. 12, 2000 / Epic/Legacy ♦♦♦♦♦
Does *16 Biggest Hits* really contain Ricky Skaggs' 16 biggest hits as measured in the country singles charts? No, it doesn't. It contains his 13 biggest hits, plus three other songs that have special significance for the artist and his audience. Among his top 16 singles are "You Make Me Feel Like a Man," "Love's Gonna Get You Someday," and "Let It Be You," none of which are included here. In their place are "Don't Get Above Your Raising," Skaggs' first Epic single and first significant hit; "You May See Me Walkin'," his first Top Ten hit; and "Wheel Hoss," an album track from his *Country Boy* album written by his mentor, Bill Monroe. It's hard to argue with such substitutions, except to note that they rob the album's title of strict accuracy. The music contained here helped define the new traditionalist movement in country music in the 1980s. Skaggs, a top instrumentalist steeped in bluegrass, found a formula at the start of that decade which combined a heavy emphasis on traditional playing with a fresh approach that didn't violate the old-time sound so much as extend it. Trends come and go, and after Skaggs' style passed from mass popularity he predictably returned to the traditional style from which he had emerged, but not before he had reinvigorated country music with the hits heard on this album, which stands as an excellent introduction to his most popular work. *—William Ruhlmann*

History of the Future / Sep. 11, 2001 / Hollywood ♦♦♦♦
Does the world really need another version of "Shady Grove"? Ricky Skaggs apparently thinks so; he opens *History of the Future* with his rendition of the bluegrass standard. But if there's any guy who can cover such an over-covered tune, and make it work, it's Skaggs. His version includes a slightly different arrangement, backed by rickety percussion and, of course, Kentucky Thunder's instrumental fireworks. Another step away from Skaggs' past as Nashville pretty boy and country-pop star is another step deeper into his bluegrass roots. His vocals are just as fresh as ever, and that creative mandolin playing transcends that of his hero Bill Monroe. Traditional tunes like "Dim Lights Thick Smoke" and "Rollin' in My Sweet Baby's Arms" are performed with more than ample respect for tradition, while more modern tunes such as "Too Far Down to Fall" and "Halfway Home Café" hint of Skaggs' Nashville career. Yet, like the previous bluegrass releases with Kentucky Thunder, he mixes both without sacrificing anything. From start to finish, this sounds like one band performing a variety of songs, none of which sound out of place. Add your token instrumental (the Irish-flavored "Road to Spencer") and a token waltz (the Stanley Brothers' "Your Selfish Heart") and you have a quintessential modern bluegrass release. Everything is just so perfect that it's easy to dismiss it as too slick, but Skaggs and Kentucky Thunder are able to make the music soulful too. Now that's perfect. *—Scott Cooper*

Sing the Songs of Bill Monroe / Feb. 26, 2002 / Hollywood ♦♦♦
Featuring an all-star lineup of country and rock's biggest names, Ricky Skaggs' heartfelt tribute to bluegrass pioneer Bill Monroe is well-intended but a little too slick. Featuring artists like Mary-Chapin Carpenter, the Dixie Chicks, Charlie Daniels, John Fogerty, Bruce Hornsby, Patty Loveless, Joan Osborne, Dolly Parton, Travis Tritt, Steve Wariner, the Whites, and Dwight Yoakam, it is made overwhelmingly clear that the music of Monroe has made an impact on many different musical genres. Unfortunately, the genre that this CD is lacking is bluegrass; the listener has to wait until the last track (the scattered "Big Mon") to hear some real pickers like J.D. Crowe and members of the Del McCoury Band perform traditional down-home music. There is no one else in the music industry who works harder to bring traditional American bluegrass to the mainstream audience, but unfortunately the vehicle it arrives in usually ends up being a new Cadillac, not the sturdy 1943 Ford pickup it belongs in. [This album was originally released on Skaggs' own Skaggs Family Records under the title *Big Mon*, and was re-released on Disney's Lyric Street imprint under the title *Sing the Songs of Bill Monroe* with one additional track.] *—Zac Johnson*

Uncle Pen / Mar. 26, 2002 / Music Mill ♦♦♦♦
Uncle Pen is in many ways a tribute album done by Ricky Skaggs for Bill Monroe, the man known as the father of bluegrass music. Monroe invented the style and name in the '40s. There are ten tracks on this 2002 release, including three that were written by Monroe: "Can't You Hear Me Callin'," "Wheel Hoss," and the title track, "Uncle Pen," a real toe-tapping bluegrass ride. In fact, all of the tunes on this offering are bluegrass numbers.

The songs were actually recorded by Skaggs in the '80s, and have only now been combined into one album by Music Mill. Multi-instrumentalist Ricky Skaggs might be a country singer, but he has deep bluegrass roots that come through on this album. He has always seemed as comfortable singing straight bluegrass as progressive country. He does both distinctively. This album is a keeper for both Ricky Skaggs and Bill Monroe fans. *—Charlotte Dillon*

Live at the Charleston Music Hall / Mar. 25, 2003 / Skaggs Family ♦♦♦
As Ricky Skaggs' career progressed, he steadily got more traditional in his aesthetic and approach. So, when he announces partway through his 2003 album, *Live at the Charleston Music Hall* (recorded over two dates in November 2002 in South Carolina), that the band is largely playing new songs, it may come as a bit of a shock to casual listeners, since everything sounds traditional—even Harley Allen's Internet-referencing "A Simple Life" sounds as if it was written years and years ago. Since traditionalism is celebrated, not shunned, by bluegrass musicians, this is hardly unexpected or a problem, even if it does give Skaggs' recent music a comfortable predictability. That familiarity is undercut slightly by kinetic energy on this record, since this superb band has enough energy to make the traditionalism sound energetic, even when it still sounds very familiar. All of which adds up to an enjoyable record that nevertheless embodies a paradox: It's nothing that the serious fan hasn't heard before, but only the serious fan will truly thrill on the nuances and interplay that make *Live at the Charleston Music Hall* worth a spin. *—Stephen Thomas Erlewine*

The Essential Ricky Skaggs / Apr. 1, 2003 / Epic/Legacy ♦♦♦
From 1981 to 1991, Ricky Skaggs recorded ten albums for Epic, the highlights of which have been culled for the collection *The Essential Ricky Skaggs.* While this is a great document of his new traditionalist recordings from this era, the title "*Essential*" is a little misleading; none of his really terrific work with the Country Gentlemen and J.D. Crowe & the New South from the '70s or his more recent work reviving authentic bluegrass music is featured. Still, songs like "Don't Cheat in Our Hometown," "Lovin' Only Me," and "Heartbroke" showcase a confident and talented honest to goodness country singer. During an era where slick instrumentation and presentation was the norm, Skaggs managed to be successful on country radio and still maintain a strong artistic integrity, all of which is readily evident here. *—Zac Johnson*

The Smith Brothers

Group / Traditional Country, Cowboy, Country Gospel
The Smith Brothers were active in both gospel and country music for over 25 years, and also appeared in a few Westerns during the '40s. John Onvia Smith and Aubrey Lee Smith were both born in the mountains of East Tennessee. They formed their first string band when they were children, and aspired to become country music performers. In 1938, they got a job at a Cincinnati radio station, where they met Milton "Ace" Richman. The three men teamed up and moved to Columbus, where they worked with Hank Newman's Georgia Crackers. In 1940, they went to Charleston, SC, and sang Western music as the Red River Rangers. They finally settled in Atlanta and were joined by Eddie Wallace. They billed themselves as the Sunshine Boys Quartet and sang a wide variety of songs ranging from gospel to Western swing to barbershop at assorted Atlanta radio stations. During the mid-'40s, they went to Hollywood periodically to appear in movies featuring cowboy stars like Lash La Rue, Charles Starrett, and Eddie Dean. They also recorded a single as the Sunshine Boys.

The Smith Brothers worked primarily as a duo after 1948 and appeared on a daily 75-minute program in Atlanta for nine years; they also had a 15-minute gospel show called *Camp Meeting.* As a duo, they made their recording debut in 1951 with the tearjerker "Happy Birthday in Heaven." Two years later, they signed to Capitol as a gospel duo. Among their best-known songs were "I Have But One Goal," "Working in God's Factory," and "God's Rocket Ship." The Smiths later moved to Pittsburgh, appearing on WWVA's *Wheeling Jamboree* on Saturday nights. They continued on at other stations and made one album for the Sing label before retiring from music in 1965. *—Sandra Brennan*

That's My Jesus / 1964 / Sing ♦♦♦

● **The Grass Section** / 1993 / Red Clay ♦♦♦♦

Smith's Sacred Singers

Group / Traditional Gospel, Country Gospel
Smith's Sacred Singers were an amateur "shape-note" singing group led by J. Frank Smith, a Methodist teacher based in Braselton, GA. Relatively little is known about this group, which endured many personnel changes in its decade-long recording career, with Smith serving as the main constant. At its first recording session in Atlanta on April 23, 1926, Smith's Sacred Singers recorded a coupling issued on Columbia 15090-D, "Picture from Life's Other Side" combined with "Where We'll Never Grow Old." This became the biggest selling Gospel item in the Columbia 15000-D series, and was the first record to touch off an interest in recording rural gospel music on the part of the major record labels. Smith's Sacred Singers continued with Columbia through 1929, and then moved to Bluebird for another round of records in 1934 and 1935. Altogether Smith's Sacred Singers made a little over a hundred sides, many of which sold well and introduced to the catalog sacred material that would be recorded again and again by subsequent generations of Southern gospel singers. *—Uncle Dave Lewis*

Arthur "Guitar Boogie" Smith

b. Apr. 1, 1921, Clinton, SC
Banjo, Guitar, Mandolin / Traditional Country, Nashville Sound/Countrypolitan, Country Boogie
A link between the Western swing of the 1940s and the rockabilly of the 1950s, Arthur "Guitar Boogie" Smith was one of country music's seminal figures. In addition to inspiring several generations of country musicians via his region television program, *the Arthur Smith Show,* which aired from 1951 to 1982 and was the first syndicated country music show, Smith wrote and recorded some of country music's most influential tunes. His fiery instrumental "Guitar Boogie," recorded with the Tennessee Ramblers, has been often cited as the first rock & roll song. Released on October 23, 1948, the single sold nearly three-million copies and reached number 25 on the *Billboard* pop charts. It was subsequently transformed into a Top Five hit, "Guitar Boogie Shuffle," by Frank Virtue & His Virtuoso Trio in 1959.

Smith composed more than 500 songs, including many other hits. "Feudin' Banjos," co-written in 1955 with bluegrass banjo player Don Reno was renamed "Deulin' Banjos" and featured in the film *Deliverance* without permission. Suing for rights infringement, he won the case. Additional songs by Smith were covered by such country artists as Johnny Cash and Randy Travis. Willie Nelson featured Smith's song "Red Headed Stranger" as the title track of one of his most successful albums. Smith first surfaced in the mid-'40s as the leader of a Dixieland-influenced group the Crackerjacks and a gospel group, the Crossroads Quartet. He supplemented his income as a musician by hosting a show on 100,000-watt radio station, WBT. The owner of a recording studio in Charlotte, NC, Smith oversaw recordings by such artists as James Brown and Johnny Cash. *—Craig Harris*

Original Guitar Boogie / 1964 / Dot ♦♦♦♦

● **Here Comes the Boogie Man: The Original Recordings** / Apr. 18, 2000 / Jasmine ♦♦♦♦
Here Comes the Boogie Man collects 22 late-'40s radio transcriptions, some of which were purchased by MGM and released as commercial singles. One of these was Smith's Top Ten country hit, "Guitar Boogie," which is included here along with another Top Ten entry, "Boomerang." Mastered from commercial 78s and/or transcription discs, the sound quality on this CD is so-so, but the anthology receives points merely for existing. Smith's jazzy style recalls both Django Reinhardt and Les Paul, but his participation in the hillbilly boogie craze puts him in a class by himself. All 22 of these tracks are acoustic guitar instrumentals with minimal accompaniment; each track is heavy on boogie riffing with occasional virtuoso solos. In 2001, Jasmine released a follow-up volume, *One Good Boogie Deserves Another. —Greg Adams*

One Good Boogie Deserves Another / Oct. 31, 2000 / Jasmine ♦♦♦
Anyone interested in Arthur Smith should first check out *Here Comes the Boogie Man,* but for the unsatisfied, this is a decent second volume. It duplicates "Guitar Boogie" and "Boomerang" from *Here Comes the Boogie Man*, but a significant improvement in sound quality (due to better source material) makes them welcome. There's a handful of pretty funny vocal performances by Smith and some nice moments in "Be Bop Rag" and the jazzy "Twelfth Street Rag." There's a couple of stinkers, too ("Banjo Boogie" in particular), but Smith's picking generally sounds good no matter what the situation. *—Jim Smith*

Have a Little Fun / Jul. 25, 2002 / Jasmine ♦♦♦♦♦

Cal Smith (Calvin Grant Shofner)

b. Jul. 4, 1932, Gans, OK
Guitar, Vocals / Traditional Country, Country-Pop, Honky Tonk
Singer Cal Smith emerged from Ernest Tubb's band and enjoyed several hits of his own between the late '60s and mid-'70s. His best-known song was the sentimental "Country Bumpkin," but his gritty baritone voice was equally suited to more acid material such as "The Lord Knows I'm Drinking," a sharp denunciation of small-town religious self-righteousness. Smith was born Calvin Grant Shofner in Oklahoma but grew up in the San Francisco Bay area. A guitar player since childhood, he spent time with rodeo performers as a teen and began to think about a show-business career. With the support of his parents, who believed he was less likely to get into trouble on-stage rather than in the audience area of a barroom, he began playing professionally when he was 15, at a bar called the Remember Me Cafe. He was paid a dollar and 50 cents a night plus dinner, and his listeners were mostly migrant California vineyard workers.

It was a longtime before Smith could make a living playing music, however, and he did jobs ranging from truck driver to bronco buster during the 1950s. He was briefly married, but when his wife made him choose between music and her, Smith chose the former. (He later married again, with more durable results.) Smith appeared on the *California Hayride* television program soon after its inception in the mid-'50s. He did a two-year stint in the military and returned to the Bay Area after his discharge, working as a DJ at San Jose radio station KEEN and performing around the area in a band whose membership included Bill Drake, the brother of one of Ernest Tubb's Texas Troubadors. Tubb heard him play and following an audition hired him as a rhythm guitarist and MC in 1961. Several of Tubb's '60s hits feature Smith's playing. At that time he was still using the name Grant Shofner; his stage name gained currency after Tubb helped him land his first solo recording contract with Kapp Records in 1966. That year he released his first single, "I'll Just Go Home." He made his first chart entry with his sophomore effort, "The Only Thing I Want," which made it to the Top 60, and when "Drinking Champagne" (1968) cracked the Top 40, Smith left Tubb to focus on his own career. During his several years with Kapp he had eight more moderate hits, including "Heaven Is Just a Touch Away."

In late 1970 Smith signed with Decca, and material from Nashville's top writers began to come his way. In 1972 made it to the Top Five with what might be called the anti-sentimental breakup song "I've Found Someone of My Own," and a few months later he scored his first number-one hit with the Bill Anderson composition "The Lord Knows I'm Drinking," which also crossed over to become a minor pop hit. His next few singles did not do as well, but in 1974 he scored his second number one hit with "Country Bumpkin," a Don Wayne-penned tune that became Smith's signature song and a radio staple for years to come. Later that year he had his third number one, "It's Time to Pay the Fiddler." He continued appearing on the charts through 1979, switching to the MCA label for such releases as "The Rise and Fall of the Roman Empire." After the main phase of his recording career ended, Smith became an investor in the Nashville Sounds minor-league baseball team. He re-emerged briefly in 1986 on the tradition-oriented Step One label with the album *Stories of Life by Cal Smith.* —*James Manheim*

Drinking Champagne / 1969 / Kapp ♦♦♦

● **The Best of Cal Smith** / 1971 / Kapp ♦♦♦♦♦

I've Found Someone of My Own / 1972 / Decca ♦♦♦

I've Found Someone of My Own is arguably the finest album from one of the most neglected vocalist of the late '60s and '70s, Cal Smith. On this record, he tackles both classic honky tonk tunes, new country cuts, pop songs, R&B and soul numbers, which are all given a contemporary, early '70s gloss. But its Smith, with his haunting, pure voice gives each cut country grit, bringing each song down to earth. It's a record that convinces you Smith, in a perfect world, would have been a star. —*Thom Owens*

Country Bumpkin / 1974 / Decca ♦♦♦

It's Time to Pay the Fiddler / 1975 / Decca ♦♦♦

Carl Smith

b. Mar. 15, 1927, Maynardsville, TN

Vocals, Guitar / Traditional Country, Honky Tonk, Western Swing Revival

Known as Mr. Country, Carl Smith was one of the most popular honky tonkers of the '50s, racking up over 30 Top Ten hits over the course of the decade. Smith was also able to sustain that popularity into the late '70s, during which time he had a charting single for every year except one. Smith had a talent for singing smooth ballads which polished the rough edges of hardcore country. Nevertheless, he could sing pure honky tonk with the best of them, and his hardest country was made tougher by the addition of a drum kit. Smith was one of the very first country artists to regularly perform with a drummer, and though it earned him criticism at the time, the hard-driving sound of those uptempo numbers proved to be influential. Smith also occasionally dabbled in Western swing, and as he continued to record, he delved deeper into the genre. Since he specialized in honky tonk ballads and Western swing, Smith rarely crossed over into the pop audience. Still, he was one of the most popular and best-known country singers of his era, recording several classics—including "Let's Live a Little," "Let Old Mother Nature Have Her Way," "This Orchard Means Goodbye," "Cut Across Shorty," "Loose Talk," "(When You Feel Like You're in Love) Don't Just Stand There," and "Hey Joe!"—appearing in a handful of movies, and hosting his own television show. By the time he retired in the early '80s, he had hit the country charts nearly 100 times.

Smith was born and raised in Maynardsville, TN, which was also the hometown of Roy Acuff. As a child, Smith idolized Acuff, Ernest Tubb, and Bill Monroe. When he was a teenager, he taught himself how to play guitar. According to legend, he bought his first guitar with money he earned by selling flower seeds. At the age of 15, he was singing in the San Francisco-based country band Kitty Dibble & Her Dude Ranch Ranglers. Two years later, he learned to play string bass and spent his summer vacation working at WROL, a radio station in Knoxville. After Smith finished high-school, he briefly served in the U.S. Navy before heading back home. Once he returned to Tennessee, he continued to perform at WROL, usually playing bass for Skeets Williamson and Molly O'Day. Eventually, he began singing as well, and one of his colleagues at the station sent an acetate of Smith's singing to WSM in Nashville. WSM signed Smith to a contract, and he began working for the station and singing at the *Grand Ole Opry.* By 1950, Columbia Records signed Smith to a recording contract. His first hit, "Let's Live a Little," arrived in 1951, climbing all the way to number two. Over the course of the year, he racked up no less than three other hits, including the classic "If Teardrops Were Pennies" and his first number-one single, "Let Old Mother Nature Have Her Way." Also that year, he married June Carter, the daughter of Maybelle Carter; the two would later divorce, yet they had a daughter named Carlene that would become a musician in her own right during the '70s.

Throughout the '50s, Smith was a consistent presence in the country charts, racking up no less than 31 Top Ten singles during the course of the decade. In addition to recording, he began appearing in Western movies, like 1957's *The Badge of Marshal Brennan.* In 1956, he resigned from the *Grand Ole Opry* and joined a package tour organized by Phillip Morris. In 1957, he married country singer Goldie Hill, best-known for the number one hit "I Let the Stars Get in My Eyes." As the '50s ended, Smith was no longer as dominant in the upper reaches of the country charts as he was earlier in the decade, but he never stopped having hits. During the '60s, he consistently charted in the Top 40, which was indicative of his status as a country music statesman. In 1961, he appeared on ABC's country television series, *Four Star Jubilee*, and a few years later, he began hosting *Carl Smith's Country Music Hall* for Canadian television; the series also was syndicated in America.

Throughout the '60s and early '70s, he began to incorporate more Western swing into his repertoire, especially on his albums. Smith continued to release albums and singles on Columbia Records until 1975, when he signed with Hickory. After having a handful of minor hits for the label—including several that were released on ABC/Hickory—he decided to retire in the late '70s. Though he recorded an album of his greatest hits in the early '80s, Smith retreated from the spotlight after his 1979 retirement. He and his wife, Goldie, lived on their horse farm outside of Franklin, TN, and the two began to show horses professionally during the course of the decade. —*Stephen Thomas Erlewine*

Carl Smith / 1956 / Columbia ♦♦♦♦

Softly and Tenderly / 1956 / Columbia ♦♦♦♦

Sentimental Songs / 1957 / Columbia ♦♦♦

Smith's the Name / 1957 / Columbia ♦♦♦♦

Sunday Down South / 1957 / Columbia ♦♦♦

Let's Live a Little / 1958 / Columbia ♦♦♦♦

The Carl Smith Touch / 1960 / Columbia ♦♦♦

Easy to Please / 1962 / Columbia ♦♦♦

Easy to Please is a 1962 LP that yielded no hits for Carl Smith, and finds him in transition between the experimentation that produced his last major hits and his return to pure honky tonk music. "Love While You Can" uses a banjo to replicate the sound of Smith's hits "Make the Waterwheel Roll" and "Ten Thousand Drums" from 1959-1960, while most of the other tracks adopt a shuffle beat and swingy style that is very close to the music he made later in the '60s. "After the Boy Gets the Girl," a sweet song that was recorded by hard country singers from Ernest Tubb to Webb Pierce, is one departure from the dancefloor formula, as is the mildly humorous title track. *Easy to Please* is an intriguing record even if it didn't set the charts on fire. —*Greg Adams*

Carl Smith's Greatest Hits / 1962 / Columbia ♦♦♦

This 1962 album offers re-recordings of many of Carl Smith's most famous hits, including "Let Old Mother Nature Have Her Way" and "Hey Joe." The new versions are very close to the originals, although Smith's singing is mellower and the playing less biting. The title notwithstanding, several songs are non-hits, particularly on side two, where the majority fail to conform to the album's billing. Of these, "Gettin' Even" is a great uptempo number and "I Overlooked an Orchid (While Searching for a Rose)" is a re-recording of one of the earliest songs Smith cut for Columbia. The remakes are serviceable, but the original versions are ultimately preferable, which leaves only a few songs on *Carl Smith's Greatest Hits* to interest his most ardent fans. —*Greg Adams*

Tall, Tall Gentleman / 1963 / Columbia ♦♦♦

The song "Tall, Tall Gentleman" was the B-side of Carl Smith's crossover hit "Ten Thousand Drums" in 1959, and mirrored that song's historical folk orientation with its use of banjo and narrative lyrics. Smith reprised "The Tall, Tall Gentleman" as the title track of this 1963 album, and the re-recording is very similar to the original. Smith remade a number of his hits the previous year on the album *Carl Smith's Greatest Hits*, and he does the same here, revisiting "Back Up Buddy," "This Orchid Means Goodbye," and "(When You Feel Like You're In Love) Don't Just Stand There." "Loose Talk" is followed by its answer, "No More Loose Talkin'," which is an interesting touch, and each side ends with an inspirational song. Two hits from 1962-1963 are included: "Air Mail to Heaven," a sad story with a twist ending that was one of Smith's biggest hits of the '60s, and "Live for Tomorrow." *Tall, Tall Gentleman* is hampered by the numerous unnecessary re-recordings, but the new material, particularly "Air Mail to Heaven," is worthwhile. —*Greg Adams*

There Stands the Glass / 1964 / Columbia ♦♦

Although it isn't billed as such, *There Stands the Glass* is a tribute album to Webb Pierce; all but one of the songs were hits for Pierce, and the remaining one ("So Used to Loving You") was the B-side of "That Heart Belongs to Me" (which is also included). It might seem redundant to have one major star of hard honky tonk music cover the material of another, but Carl Smith's sound and phrasing is so different from Pierce, the results are entirely dissimilar. The no-nonsense production and lack of original material points to the fact that *There Stands the Glass* was purely an album effort, but Smith re-recorded the title track for single release on Hickory Records in 1977. —*Greg Adams*

I Want to Live and Love / 1965 / Columbia ♦♦

Kisses Don't Lie / 1965 / Columbia ♦♦♦

"Kisses Don't Lie" was a Top Five hit for Carl Smith in 1955, but the album bearing that name appeared years later in his career and was mostly comprised of covers of classic and modern country hits. Buck Owens' "Together Again" and Merle Haggard's "My Friends Are Gonna Be Strangers" are rendered in Smith's no-frills honky tonk style, and he returns "You Don't Have to Be a Baby to Cry," a pop hit in 1963 for the Caravelles, to its country roots. The theme of the album is allegedly one of Smith performing the songs of all-time great country composers, but in reality it is no different from typical '60s country album fare. Carl Smith retained more of his hard honky tonk sound from the '50s than many of his contemporaries, so his albums were welcome oases of straight country in that context. —*Greg Adams*

Man With a Plan / 1966 / Columbia ♦♦♦

"Man With a Plan" didn't perform well as a single for Carl Smith, probably because it wasn't a honky tonk ballad of the sort for which he was known in the '60s. The song stalled shy of the Top 40, but it's one of his best efforts of the period—a playfully boastful number with Jimmy Dean-style production. The remainder of the album that shares its name offers more predictable fare, including covers of "Tragic Romance" and the Webb Pierce/Wayne P. Walker song "How Do You Talk to a Baby." There are some drinking and dancing songs, too, and Mel Tillis' inspirational composition "Beautiful Wings" closes the album. Don Law and Frank Jones produced the album and, with the exception of the title track, did their usual job, surrounding Smith with fiddles rather than strings and keeping the affair pointed in a more "traditional" direction. —*Greg Adams*

The Country Gentleman Sings His Favorites / 1967 / Columbia ♦♦♦♦♦

Country on My Mind / 1968 / Columbia ♦♦♦♦

Deep Water / 1968 / Columbia ♦♦♦

Carl Smith Sings a Tribute to Roy Acuff / 1969 / Columbia ♦♦♦♦♦

Faded Love and Winter Roses / 1969 / Columbia ♦♦♦

"Faded Love and Winter Roses" was one of the last half-dozen Top 30 hits of Carl Smith's career, reaching number 25 in 1969. Despite that minor distinction, the song is a comparatively bland and predictable Fred Rose ballad that pales beside Smith's other chart hits of the period. The album of the same name has 11 songs, including new versions of Western swing oldies "One Has My Name, the Other Has My Heart" and "Time Changes Everything," and the more recent hit "I'm a Lonesome Fugitive." Smith made it through the Nashville sound era relatively unscathed, and his sound remained constant from the early '60s through the early '70s. Producer Don Law took a "traditional" approach with Smith, surrounding him with pedal steel and fiddles, so that his shuffles and weepers remained oases of '50s-style honky tonk. The album would have benefited from a few livelier tunes, but the album is practically identical to his others of the period. *—Greg Adams*

Take It Like a Man / 1969 / Harmony ✦✦

I Love You Because / 1970 / Columbia ✦✦

Leon Payne's country classic "I Love You Because" was one of Carl Smith's last Top 20 hits in 1969. "Good Deal, Lucille," the Cajun song popularized by Al Terry, also made the Top 20 for Smith, and both songs are included on the album *I Love You Because.* The raucous twin-guitar attack of "Good Deal, Lucille" is a little uncharacteristic for Smith, but "I Love You Because" and the rest of the album is exactly in line with his established '60s sound: hard country music for the honky tonk hardwood floor. The album is practically a tribute to country music's past, with renditions of well-known songs like "Kaw-Liga," "This Cold War With You," and "Please Help Me I'm Falling." Don Gibson's "Blue, Blue Day" gets a complete overhaul in Smith's hands, but the highlight among the album tracks is the funny "Mister, Come and Get Your Wife." Smith's term at Columbia was winding down at this point, but he could still fire off a few good ones. *—Greg Adams*

★ **The Essential Carl Smith (1950–1956)** / 1991 / Columbia/Legacy ✦✦✦✦✦

This collection of 20 of Carl Smith's classic sides from the years 1950-1956 reveal him at the height of his popularity. It also reveals his strengths as a singer of Western swing, honky tonk, and even transitional pop ballads. Smith's voice is pure country and, while he loved hard honky tonk music such as "Does Your Conscience Bother You?" and Ernest Tubb's "Don't Just Stand There," he also had the distinction—some at the time would say negative—of using a drummer. He was the first country performer to do so and the drums can be heard on "I Just Dropped in to Say Goodbye," "Are You Teasing Me," "Dog Gone It Baby, I'm In Love," "Back Up Buddy," the rockabilly "Go Boy Go," and the amazing "Loose Talk." Smith, who was a contemporary of Hank Williams, came from the same hard country school, his voice carrying within it that same high lonesome edge, but his ideas about production removed him from the country mainstream. No one can argue with success, though, and Smith charted from 1950 through 1970 in all years but one. Some of those, like Boudleaux Bryant's "Hey Joe," and his reading of Leon Payne's "You Are the One," as well as Porter Wagoner's moving "trademark": are all stunning examples of Smith's amazing voice that could interpretive virtually any song as a country heartbreaker or a honky tonk two step. Of all the Smith collections issued over the years, this one, is definitive and easily the most representative of the singer at his most innovative and adventurous. There is no way one can listen to Buddy Holly with any intelligence or Gene Vincent and not hear Smith; that's as solid a testimony as there is that his music transcends genres. *—Thom Jurek*

Satisfaction Guaranteed / 1996 / Bear Family ✦✦✦✦✦

Every song that Carl Smith recorded during the '50s is included on *Satisfaction Guaranteed*, a five-disc, 143-track box set that stands as the most comprehensive retrospective of the honky tonk star's peak period. During the era that *Satisfaction Guaranteed* covers, Smith scored more Top Ten hits than either Hank Williams or Lefty Frizzell, and many of his best songs—"Loose Talk," "Let Old Mother Nature Have Her Way," "Hey Joe!," "Are You Teasing Me," and "(When You Feel Like You're In Love) Don't Just Stand There," among them—are stone-cold honky tonk classics. For serious Smith and honky tonk fans, the set is essential, but the sheer length of the box—not to mention its strict chronological sequence—is tedious for anyone that isn't willing to dedicate the time to plow through the abundance of material here. *—Stephen Thomas Erlewine*

The Sixties Hits of Carl Smith / 2002 / Collectors' Choice Music ✦✦✦✦✦

Carl Smith's legacy and reputation is built on the hardcore honky tonk he cut for Columbia in the '50s, which ranks among the purest and best of its era. Since the dawn of the CD reissue boom in the '80s, that has been the Carl Smith music that's been reissued, first on Columbia/Legacy's excellent *The Essential Carl Smith (1950-1956)* then on Bear Family's fine 1996 five-disc box set *Satisfaction Guaranteed*, which contained the entirety of his '50s recordings. So much emphasis was placed on this era that listeners who came to Smith late may have thought he didn't record or didn't have success in the '60s, when the opposite is true. He continued recording for Columbia in the '60s, and while he rarely broke the country Top Ten, he placed frequently in the Top 20 right into 1970, ranking as one of the most consistent, reliable singers of the decade. This material remained out of print until Collectors Choice's 2002 collection *The Sixties Hits of Carl Smith*, which rounded up 24 of his hits, including every side that charted in the Top 20, along with seven singles that charted in the Top 40 or beyond. Smith didn't play it as pure as he did during the '50s: his honky tonk became a little less gritty, his productions were a little smoother, occasionally adding sweet backing vocals, he dabbled in folk and pop inflections, and he generally streamlined his music to fit the times. These concessions read tougher than they sound because, no matter how he polished or refined his sound, he stayed true to straight-ahead country and honky tonk in particular, which is part of the reason why he charted so consistently in the middle reaches of the charts—he consistently reached the country faithful, those listeners who wanted real country, regardless of the trends, which also meant that none of his singles gained a big enough audience to push into the Top Ten (apart from 1959's "Battle of New Orleans"-aping "Ten Thousand Drums," which rode the historical song fad to the upper reaches of the charts). While it is true that there is no one song that stands out from the pack, it's also true that there are no dogs, either. It's a consistently satisfying collection displaying a little more variety than expected while still staying true to Smith's vision of pure country. This is a very welcome release not just for Smith's legions of fans, but for any serious country music listener, since this proves that he wasn't just one of the best honky tonk singers of the '50s, he was one of the best of the '60s, too. Hopefully, Bear Family will follow this superb disc with a box set of Smith's complete '60s recordings, because after hearing this, it's hard not to want more. *—Stephen Thomas Erlewine*

Connie Smith (Constance Meadows)

b. Aug. 14, 1941, Elkhart, IN

Vocals, Guitar / Country-Pop, CCM, Country Gospel

In less than a year, Connie Smith moved from being a small-town Ohio housewife to country stardom with a number-one single to her credit. Perhaps overly compared to and identified with Patsy Cline, Smith is still considered by many to be one of the best and most underrated vocalists in country history. Her lonely desperation came straight from the heart, also: Her father was abusive when she was a child, causing Smith to suffer a mental breakdown while she was in her teens.

Smith was born Constance Meadows on August 14, 1941, in Elkhart, IN, but spent her early life first in West Virginia and later in Ohio. She married and became a housewife in the early '60s, singing occasionally on local TV shows around her home in Marietta, OH. She was singing near Columbus in August 1963 when country star Bill Anderson heard her and offered his help in getting a contract. She signed to RCA after a few months and recorded several selections in July 1964 with Chet Atkins at the helm. "Once a Day"—written especially for her by Anderson—was released as a single in September and hit the top of the country charts, reigning as number one for eight weeks.

Smith's follow-up, "Then and Only Then," hit number four (even the flip side reached the Top 25), and her Top Ten streak continued unabated until late 1968, including the big hits "If I Talk to Him," "Ain't Had No Lovin'," and "The Hurtin's All Over." Meanwhile, her success began to take a toll; constant appearances on the road, in films, and on *the Lawrence Welk Show* pushed Smith to the brink of suicide in 1968. She credits her Christian faith with saving her from killing herself. After Smith recovered from the pressure of being a fawned-over female country star, she began to balance chart success with a lighter schedule. Though her country hits were rarer than in her mid-'60s heyday, she was a better performer—and person—for it. Smith still managed the Top Tens "You and Your Sweet Love" in 1969, "I Never Once Stopped Loving You" the following year, and "Just One Time" in 1971. Her most successful year during the '70s was 1972. She recorded three big hits: the number five "Just What I Am," the number seven "If It Ain't Love (Let's Leave It Alone)," and the number eight "Love Is the Look You're Looking For."

By 1972, Smith began to incorporate more gospel into her act. With the help of her third husband, evangelist Marshall Haynes, she turned her live show into a traveling gospel road show and signed with Columbia, which permitted her to record more straight gospel songs. Though the material didn't score as well on the charts as her secular singles had, she managed to stay in the Top 20 during much of the '70s. After she signed with Monument in 1977, most of her singles dropped out of the Top 40. Though she has not been a commercial force since the '70s, Smith continues to perform with the *Grand Ole Opry* and in 1998 returned with her first LP in many years, a self-titled effort issued on Warner Bros. *—John Bush*

Cute 'n' Country / 1965 / RCA ✦✦✦✦✦

☆ **Connie Smith** / 1965 / RCA ✦✦✦✦✦

Cut in Music City, Smith's first LP (which includes "Once a Day") features her blowing through the Nashville Sound production like a down-home Streisand fronting the Lennon Sisters. *—Dan Cooper*

The Other Side of Connie Smith / 1965 / RCA ✦✦✦

Great Sacred Songs / 1966 / RCA ✦✦✦✦✦

Miss Smith Goes to Nashville / 1966 / RCA ✦✦✦✦✦

Connie Smith Sings Great Sacred Songs / 1966 / RCA ✦✦✦✦

Born to Sing / 1966 / RCA ✦✦✦✦✦

Connie Smith Sings Bill Anderson / 1967 / RCA ✦✦✦

Downtown Country / 1967 / RCA ✦✦✦✦

I Love Charley Brown / 1968 / RCA ✦✦✦

Soul of Country Music / 1968 / RCA ✦✦✦

More of the same unearthly sound, but this has Smith covering—at times burying—other singers' hits. Her version of Rex Griffin's "The Last Letter" is almost literally to die for. *—Dan Cooper*

Back in Baby's Arms / 1969 / RCA ✦✦✦✦✦

If any Thomas ever doubted Smith's religious convictions (which are as much a part of her story as her voice is) one listen to this LP's "How Great Thou Art" should take care of that mistrust. *—Dan Cooper*

Connie's Country / 1969 / RCA ✦✦✦✦✦

Young Love / 1969 / RCA ✦✦✦

The Best of Connie Smith, Vol. 1 / Jan. 1992 / RCA ✦✦

The Best of Connie Smith is a much-too-brief sampling of Connie Smith's biggest hits. Though there are some classic performances here—"Once a Day," "Then and Only Then," "If I Talk to Him," "Ain't Had No Lovin'," "The Hurtin's All Over," and "I'll Come Runnin'"—there is no reason why this stops short at eight tracks. Furthermore, there is even less reason why *The Best of Connie Smith* was the only collection of Smith's material print during the '90s. As this proves, she was an excellent vocalist, one of the best country music had to offer in the '60s. *—Thom Owens*

Greatest Hits on Monument / 1993 / Sony ✦✦✦

It's easy to see why fans of pure country—the kind of music Connie Smith effortlessly made during the '60s—are not crazy about her late-'70s recordings for Monument. Once she signed with the label in 1977, country was pretty much a thing of the past for her, as she delved not just into country-pop, but into heavily produced adult contemporary ballads and big, shiny disco-influenced pop numbers—surely not the kind of thing to please purists. And it didn't please nearly as many fans, either, since the hits dried up not long after her relatively faithful cover of Barry Gibb's "I Just Want to Be Your Everything" went to number 14 on the singles charts. She had a few other hits—the straight disco "Lovin' You Baby" inexplicably went into the country top 40, but "Smooth Sailin'," "There'll Never Be Another for Me," "Don't Say Love," "Lovin' You, Lovin' Me," and "Ten Thousand and One," all charted outside of the country Top 40, in progressively smaller positions—but her albums all stiffed. It's not hard to see why they didn't get a bigger audience. This is commercial music that doesn't really *work*. It has a state-of-the-art production that dates instantly, walks the line between crossover pop and country-pop rather clumsily, and lacks good material. Smith still sings well throughout it, but it's not a very good showcase for her talents, nor is it very good as crossover pop—it's too square and middle of the road, making the urban cowboy bubbling up at the time seem risky and edgy. As an artifact of its time, it is rather interesting—this is what MOR radio sounded like at the time, even if none of these were hits—but even if the production is appealingly soothing and mellow, the songs simply aren't good enough to make this interesting to anybody outside of hardcore fans of *soft* soft pop (probably something that doesn't exist) or dedicated fans of Smith. Sometimes, purists can be right. *—Stephen Thomas Erlewine*

★ **The Essential Connie Smith** / Apr. 1996 / RCA ✦✦✦✦✦

Connie Smith is perhaps the only female singer in the history of country music who can truly claim to be the heiress to Patsy Cline's throne. It's not that there aren't many amazing vocalists in the field, and plenty of legends among them. But in terms of the pure gift of interpretation of taking virtually any song and making it a country song of class and distinction, Smith is it. This collection, which covers the first eight years of her career from 1964, when she was "discovered" by Bill Anderson, to the turn of that decade in 1972, includes 20 tracks of pure honey and silk. Smith, who hails from Ohio, may not have the pedigree of Loretta Lynn or Tammy Wynette, but she nonetheless possesses that mercurial "thing" that Cline did: the ability to take the most blatantly country & western song and turn it into a thing that does not betray itself, yet has plenty of urban pop appeal. Here are the hits, "Once a Day," "Cry, Cry, Cry," "Burning a Hole in My Mind," "Just One Time," "I Never Once Stopped Loving You," "The Hurtin's All Over," "If It Ain't Love (Let's Leave It Alone)," and the amazing "Ribbon of Darkness" among them. The set ends with the great standard "How Great Thou Art," which is mindblowing in its rousing spirit. With classic production by Anderson and Bob Ferguson, this is one of the best collections in the RCA *Essential* series to come down the pike. The only problem is that once heard, the listener will be scouring the bins of used vinyl stores for all of Smith's classics. *—Thom Jurek*

Super Hits / Jun. 3, 1997 / RCA ✦✦✦

The ten-track collection *Super Hits* covers Connie Smith's most commercially productive period in the mid-'60s. These original Top Ten country hits include "The Hurtin's All Over," "Louisiana Man," "Then and Only Then," "Where Is My Castle," "Nobody but a Fool (Would Love You)," "Just One Time," and her first number one from 1964, "Once a Day." *—Al Campbell*

Connie Smith / Oct. 6, 1998 / Warner Bros. ✦✦✦✦

Connie Smith is a bona fide country and gospel music legend; she is quite literally the only person who deserves to share a reputation with Patsy Cline—Tammy Wynette and Loretta Lynn notwithstanding. Considering that this album is her first in four years and only her second in 20, there were no stakes other than her own expectations. Her husband, Marty Stuart, and Justin Neibank were enlisted as co-producers. (Neibank, who also produced Stuart, is one of the finest engineers and sound-mix technicians in the business, having worked on 25 Top Ten records in one capacity or another.) There's a slew of her own newly written material with Stuart, Harlan Howard, and others; Smith co-wrote nine of the album's ten tracks. Stylistically, this is tough traditional honky tonk music with an edge that makes it very attractive as a rock & roll record. Neibank understands how important the balance of electric, pedal steel, and acoustic guitars is to counterbalance the vocal and fiddles. The ballads, such as "Looking for a Reason," feature Smith's lyrics as end-of-the-road desperation in seeking a truth that is elusive as the steels whine in the foreground and the acoustic guitars and electrics wind around one another and a lonesome fiddle slides around as a backdrop. "You Can't Take Back a Teardrop" has an opening similar to "Crazy Arms," but it's on the far honky tonk edge, with Stuart leading the band in a driving, rollicking shuffle where fiddles drive a pedal steel ever toward the center of the pathos in the center of the bridge. The shimmering country-rock foreground of "Lonesome" is deceptive in that it opens out onto a bluegrass ghost song about love in the ether. "How Long" takes Smith's and Ray Price's models for the honky tonk song and stitches them together so tightly that there isn't any place but the barroom dancefloor for them to go. "Just Let Me Know" is similar, but it's pure Smith—she keeps her vocal focused on enunciating those lyrics of hers and keeping the vibe focused on the heartache that strolls along the dancehall floor looking for relief. "When It Comes to You" is a bad-ass country tune led by a rockabilly mandolin played by Stuart; fiddles cover the middle and Smith rocks it up with a blue yodel worthy of Jimmie Rodgers. There are a couple of questionable cuts, but nothing to complain about; they're pleasant enough but just don't feel like they fit—the Celtic-flavored closer "A Tale from Tahrarrie" being one. In all, this is not only a solid effort; it stands head and shoulders over most of the stuff that's come out of Nash Vegas in over a decade. Even if it doesn't sell a copy, it's a triumphant return for Smith. She hasn't lost a whit of her gift as a singer or as a writer. *—Thom Jurek*

☆ **Connie Smith/Miss Smith Goes to Nashville** / Sep. 12, 2000 / WestSide ✦✦✦✦✦

Born to Sing / May 8, 2001 / Bear Family ✦✦✦✦✦

Darden Smith

b. Mar. 11, 1962, Brenham, TX

Guitar, Vocals / Americana, Blues-Rock, Contemporary Country

Named after a local rodeo rider, Darden Smith grew up in Austin, TX. In the 1980s, the rootsy singer/songwriter began building quite a following, and his independent 1986 debut was snapped up by Epic. Three of its cuts were re-recorded for 1988's *Native Soil*; the single "Little Maggie" placed on the country charts. *Trouble No More*—a collaboration with British songwriter Boo Hewerdine of the Bible—followed in 1990. Three years later, Smith distanced himself even further from his country roots with the pop-oriented *Little Victories*. While he was a critical favorite, drawing comparisons to such mature songwriters as John Hiatt, Epic found Smith unclassifiable (i.e., unmarketable) and dropped him from its roster. *Deep Fantastic Blue* (1996) appeared on the indie Plump; it was an accomplished collection of folk-tinged pop. *Extra Extra* followed in 2000. It was a collection of songs that Smith felt were most-loved by audiences over the years. The introspective, jazz-tinged *Sunflower* appeared in summer 2002. It was a far cry from the dusty roots of Smith's early work yet cut from the same songwriting cloth. *—Johnny Loftus*

Native Soil / 1986 / Watermelon ✦✦✦

● **Darden Smith** / 1988 / Epic ✦✦✦✦✦

Trouble No More / 1990 / Columbia ✦✦✦

Little Victories / Apr. 27, 1993 / Chaos ✦✦✦✦

Little Victories was recorded with pop producer Richard Gottehrer; while far removed from country music, it stands among Smith's most mature and ambitious work. *—Jason Ankeny*

Deep Fantastic Blue / Oct. 1, 1996 / Plump ✦✦✦✦

When CBS (now Sony) signed Darden Smith in 1987, they may have hoped they were getting another country-pop singer/songwriter like Rodney Crowell. By the time a couple of albums had suffered undeserved anonymity, however, they may have been hoping for a critics' favorite with a modest commercial breakthrough like John Hiatt. But major labels do not wait forever for even the most promising artist to start exceeding his advances, and with this, his fifth album, Smith is now recording for his manager's indie label. It turns out this is all for the better, artistically, anyway. Darden's well-written songs are sufficiently straightforward enough to answer to any one of several production ideas. A good country producer could take them in a Garth-like direction, and a good rock producer could find another Tom Petty. Instead, Stewart Lerman has assembled a stellar backup unit of relative unknowns—anchored by bassist Graham Maby from the old Joe Jackson Band, and guitarist Richard Kennedy and drummer Stanley John Mitchell from the late, lamented Drongos—for a restrained folk-rock treatment that emphasizes the songs. Smith's lyrics cover familiar ground, touching on restlessness, hopelessness, hope, despair, freedom, aging, and, oh, yeah, lust. But he often has unusual ways of putting things, and he sings with conviction. There may not be a place for him on a major anymore, but he continues to grow as a songwriter and performer, and perhaps an audience will find him yet. *—William Ruhlmann*

Extra Extra / Jul. 11, 2000 / Valley ✦✦✦✦

Sunflower / Apr. 23, 2002 / Dualtone ✦✦✦✦✦

People whose first exposure to Darden Smith is a listen to *Sunflower* will be surprised that he began as a country artist. The tone throughout this album is of a modern singer/songwriter—with a jazz-influenced backing group—who is very strong at both singing and writing. His lyrics here are lovely, and he has a warm, emotional voice that puts them across with power and delicacy. In particular, "Satellite" is aimed straight at the adult contemporary hit market, with intelligent, wistful lyrics about a lover who will never commit to a permanent relationship. *Sunflower* has several songs in this vein—not about delirious first love, but about the long-term consequences of decisions and the twists in relationships. Not surprisingly, such topics tend toward philosophical and poetic sentiments, and Smith delivers them with effortless grace. On "New Gospel," the sentiments are overtly and interestingly religious, with lyrics comparing epiphany to new love, offering the possibility of a whole new set of rules to suit new circumstances. This song is followed by the final cut, the most personal and immediate on the album. "Swept Away" is a catalog of sensual moments with a lover, brief touches and embraces that mean much more than any casual watcher might guess. This song, like most of the rest of *Sunflower*, is mature, passionate, and thoughtful. Such intelligent material is a rarity in American pop, and all the more welcome for it. *—Richard Foss*

Fiddlin' Arthur Smith

b. Apr. 10, 1898, Humphreys County, TN, **d.** Feb. 28, 1971

Fiddle / Traditional Bluegrass, Old-Timey

There are many, many people named Arthur Smith in the world. There are at least two famous Arthur Smiths in country music, and each of them seem to have decided to use their instrument to identify themselves. So besides Fiddlin' Arthur Smith there is also Arthur "Guitar Boogie" Smith. And if one really wants to get Smith-happy, there is also a famous banjo builder, Arthur E. Smith. But let's say one was hanging out in the corner of Tennessee formed by the Cumberland and Tennessee rivers. In that case, there would be one and only one Arthur Smith of any note, and that would be the one who fiddled. He was called the "king of the fiddlers" in this neck of the woods, and literally all one has to do is go for a drive to be reminded of it. One can hum "Chittlin' Cookin' Time in Cheatham County" while driving through Cheatham County; likewise Smith has documented "Dickson County Blues," "Indian Creek," "Sugar Tree Stomp." Oh, and Smith's "Paris Waltz" was hardly written while he chomped on a baguette. That's Paris, TN, the little town across the river.

Smith is the giant of fiddle in the Tennessee valley, certainly one of the most influential fiddlers from the old-time school whose tunes, approach, and innovation continued to be copied by progressive bluegrass players decades later. He played professionally for nearly a half of a century, with only a few lulls in his career. Smith was born on a family farm and had no formal education beyond fifth grade. As was common in this time in the Tennessee hills he married quite young, just after the outbreak of World War I. Smith was 16, his bride Nettie was only 15. Already music was a big part of his life, although researchers have been unable to pinpoint exactly when he started playing. As a youngster he was already a fiddler, and good enough to work in some local bands, mostly playing dances. His wife played guitar in one of these groups. Nettie Smith recalled selling chickens to buy her husband a fiddle. The original price of this instrument was six dollars and 50 cents, and decades later it would be worth at least 100 times that much. The neighbor who sold this instrument was the appropriately named fiddler Grady Stringer, who would have to have been the first main influence on Smith as a musician. Another early influence was the fiddler Walter Warden, whose tunes are still part of the old-time repertoire.

Smith continued performing in the area, working with his wife, his cousin Homer Smith, and a fiddler named Floyd Ethredge who went on to work with the early *Grand Ole Opry* stars the Crook Brothers. In 1921 Smith moved to Dickson and began a railroad career, first as a logger and then later a linesman. The job involved travel back and forth across the state. Smith would pack his fiddle and pick up music from people he met along the way. One of these musicians that recalls Smith from this time was Jack Jackson, the first country artist to record in Nashville. This era was the very beginning of that city's life as the world's country & western music capital. The radio station WDAD at first wouldn't touch country music, finding it undignified. That was until a fellow named George D. Hay was hired as station manager, and the wealthy Henry Ford decided to promote fiddle contests to "preserve authentic American values." This is where Smith could step in, as he was already winning fiddle contests across Tennessee.

Smith's first appearance on the *Opry* was on December 23, 1927, for a 30-minute solo fiddle set. At this stage of his career he was not singing, but just played unaccompanied fiddle in the style of so many rural players. His cousin Homer re-joined Smith after several weeks on the *Opry*. The two of them wound up appearing on the show 28 times that year, more than any other act except the harmonica player DeFord Bailey. Nonetheless, he carried on with the railroad job, as nobody could have survived on the *Opry* wages of five dollars per man per show, regardless of how much farther a buck might have gone back then. But the travel in and out of Nashville definitely had an effect on Smith's ability to be in the right place at the right time to score a recording date with companies that were actively documenting the work of fiddlers, many of whom were much less popular than Smith. Smith and his cousin split up their relationship in the early '30s, and a new band called the Dixieliners was formed with the very talented brothers Kirk & Sam McGee. In many ways this was one of the first supergroups, putting together three virtuoso string players. The three players all had a great deal of repertoire in common, all were in their mid-'30s, ambitious, determined, and energetic. It was, in short, a great match.

It was in this combination that Smith began singing, an event about which Kirk McGee recalled, "Once he finally got to singing, and then we couldn't stop him." For the most part the group divided up chores thusly: Smith did the fiddling, Sam did the comedy, and Kirk and Sam did the vocals. A pianist was added to the group in due course, and Smith looked no farther than his daughter Lavonne Smith, who began to tour with the Dixieliners while still a high-school student, picking up her five-dollar pay at the *Opry* like the rest of the country greats. Fans of dissonant country music have spent lifetimes searching for a tape of an early broadcast by this band in which Lavonne was so startled by a steam whistle being blown on-stage that she pounded out a harsh chord in the style of avant-jazz pianist Cecil Taylor. This didn't make Smith very happy. "It was a goof, and Daddy didn't like goofs," she said. The Dixieliners became more and more professional through the *Opry*, the sponsorship of a glue company, and the hiring of an all-purpose booker, manager, and advance man. The group toured through the region, playing in many small communities. Sometimes they would be part of a larger Grand Ole Opry package tour that would feature performers such as Uncle Dave Macon. Some of these tours also involved the famous Delmore Brothers.

Smith was working with both groups in various combinations through about 1934, then began working with the Delmores exclusively, and it was with this combination that he finally began recording a series of sides for the Gennet label. The first sessions were done in New Orleans, and it included two tunes that came to be known as Smith classics, "Blackberry Blossom" and "Red Apple Rag." On sessions for Victor the next year, Smith once again opened his mouth and recorded some vocal numbers, and according to Alton Delmore it was a matter of economics, not choice as the record label felt instrumental music wasn't going to sell. The first Smith vocal hit went on to become another standard repertoire number, as do so many country tunes that have such a basic philosophy included right in the title: "There's More Pretty Girls Than One." More than five sessions were cut with the Delmores in the next few years, the tracks coming out under the name of the Arthur Smith Trio rather than the Dixieliners, although later album reissues on County reverted back to the Dixieliners name. Listeners of the time would have no idea whether a new record was a Smith feature or a Delmore Brothers cut, so completely had their styles meshed. Corrupt business practices also added to the confusion, as the guys would sometimes cut a song for one label under Smith's name, then redo it for a competing label as the Delmore Brothers.

More than 50 different songs were cut during this period, the most famous of the batch being Smith's song "Beautiful Brown Eyes," which would later lead to court action when the artists behind a cover version decided the song was in the public domain. Fiddle contests continued to be popular in these years, with promoters presenting bigger and bigger showdowns between fiddlers such as Curly Fox, Clark Kessenger, Clayton McMichen, and the Native American fiddler Natchee the Indian. These players were all so hot it was often impossible to choose a winner, unless one of them happened to have organized the contest in which case he would sometimes present the first-place prize to himself. The railroad job was taking a back seat to touring, and sometimes the music on tour was taking a back seat to hard drinking. Smith fell in with a bunch of rowdies at a 1938 fiddle contest and didn't even show up to square off against a team of fiddlers that included the sponsor, a local sherrif. The lawman was so upset with the Smith no-show he tried to have him arrested. It did lead to an *Opry* suspension, and as was often the case this momentary vacancy helped someone else get his foot in the door, in this case a little curly-haired singer named Roy Acuff. In the late '30s Smith was hired by the Tennessee Valley Boys, a young band on the rise that needed a well-known, senior statesman on fiddle out front. By 1939 this band included three fiddlers: Smith, the young Howdy Forrester, and Georgia Slim Rutland.

In 1940 Smith moved to Shreveport, LA, to join the Shelton Brothers on radio station KWKH. This job didn't keep Smith's interest and after roaming around the Gulf Coast he rejoined Lavonne in Decatur, AL, putting together a local radio band that somehow ended up consisting of players that all had the first name "Arthur," except of course for Lavonne. But unsure of how well the Band of Arthurs would fare on a 1940 recording date, Smith instead threw together a collaboration with the young Bill Monroe. This session was in many ways historic. It was the first recording Monroe would do and the last of Smith's Bluebird sessions. In the early '40s, as the world's attention was focused more and more on tragic events in Europe, Smith joined the Bailes Brothers in West Virginia. He had several featured solos with this show, and is credited with helping to popularize the song "Orange Blossom Special" as a feature for fiddlers.

In 1943 Smith began emphasizing his singing and songwriting, and published two important songbooks, *Songs From the Hills of Tennesse* and *Arthur Smith's Original Song Folio No. 1.* Smith continued working with different groups during the '40s including a duo with his son Ernest Smith and a backup stint with the cowboy singer Rex Griffin. His flair backing up the increasingly popular western style of music led to gigs with Jimmy Wakely, a former backup singer to cowboy star Gene Autry. Smith rode this horse ride into Hollywood, where he wound up appearing with Wakely's band in a series of low-budget Monogram oaters such as *Oklahoma Blues*. But a cowboy Smith was not, and luckily his bowing arm wasn't injured when one director made the mistake of putting the fiddler on top of a horse without first attaching him to the saddle with a strong adhesive bond. His recording career continued while on the West Coast, leading to a contract with Capitol, where he recorded "Orange Blossom Special" "Crazy Blues" and other successful numbers. For the first time he ran abreast of the North Carolina guitar picker with the same name, and the sides were released as "The Original Arthur Smith & His Dixieliners" to avoid confusion with the Guitar Boogie man.

The next decade would be the low point of Smith's career. After backing several country singers including Billy Walker, he wound up in Nashville working as a carpenter rather than as a musician, a development that can be partially blamed on Smith's alcoholism, although its significance as a symbol of that city's cultural backwardness shouldn't be downplayed. In the middle of this low period, Smith had the pleasure of hearing Roy Acuff singing "Beautiful Brown Eyes," no doubt while he was sawing a board on some job. The song became so popular that there were scores of cover versions, but everyone followed Acuff's lead and declared the song "public domain," despite it having appeared in a published Smith song folio in 1943. Smith won the suit but it was settled for a lump sum rather than any actual account of royalties. By the mid-'50s rock & roll was on everyone's mind and it seemed a nadir for old-time music. But by 1956 Smith had been invited back to the West Coast by Wakely, where he struck up a new collaboration with the famous country guitarist Merle Travis.

In the meantime a new folk revival had begun with groups such as the New Lost City Ramblers, whose member Mike Seeger was combing the hinterlands looking for authentic old-time musicians to research and document. His efforts led to combining Smith with his old pals the McGee brothers for a 1957 recording session held in Kirk's livingroom. Seeger was originally unsatisfied with the results, released one album, and then held onto the outtakes for nearly eight years, hoping a new session could be arranged. Finally the balance of the material was released. Fans of old-time music find this reunion of old friends, playing casually and with growing excitement at every tune, to be one of the finest recordings ever done in this genre. Another helpful development during this time was the interest in Smith's music coming from the modern bluegrass camp, as Flatt & Scruggs' fiddler Paul Warren began introducing a whole series of features based on Smith's material into the act. More work for the *Opry* old timers turned up in 1963 with the Starday label inaugurated a series of releases devoted to this music. The Smith album *Rare Old Time Fiddle Tunes* features fiddle accompanied only by son Ernest on guitar, and is considered another of Smith's masterpieces. Seeger issued invitations for Smith and the McGees to join the new folk circuit including appearances at the Newport Folk Festival in 1965, where they received a thunderous ovation. The mainstream audience attraction for this type of music was shortlived, though, and Smith wound up in his later years travelling on the same old rural circuit that he had started out in, frequently performing for old friends who would go to trouble to record the event because they sensed Smith was on his way out. He made his last appearance in 1969 in Louisville in a group with Sleepy Marlin and Tommy Riggs. He was buried near McEwen, TN, just a few miles from where he had first learned to fiddle a tune. His music remains so strongly remembered, and completely influenced so much of the country fiddling that came after it, that it seems no exaggeration to say that he lives on in a form more like a part of the landscape than the legend of a man. *—Eugene Chadbourne*

Rare Old Time Fiddle Tunes / 1962 / Starday ♦♦♦

This is late-period material from the kingpin Tennessee fiddlin' man, Fiddlin' Arthur Smith, accompanied here solely by his son on guitar in a program strictly dedicated to old-time fiddle tunes, *Rare Old Time Fiddle Tunes*. This narrows Smith's usual range of subjects considerably and some listeners may miss the sentimentality or cornpone humor that livens up some of his other recordings. And some may miss his singing, although others may wish his old cohorts the McGee Brothers had never gotten him started singing and be grateful for the relief. What it here is marvelous, a completely clear recording of guitar and fiddle, father and son, engaged in a retelling of story after story in that uncanny fiddle tune language. Smith's instrument has a different voice suited to each tune rich with sharply edgy shadings and pitch so perfectly between the cracks that it would send a piano tuner scrambling for cover. Avant-garde violinists or fans of their playing should check out the performance of "Cumberland Waltz." *—Eugene Chadbourne*

Fiddlin' Arthur Smith & His Dixieliners, Vol. 1 / 1978 / Scotdisc ♦♦♦♦

If a consumer bought an album by John Lennon, and the cover pictured him with two other former Beatles, would it be disappointing to find out the latter two lads don't actually appear on the record? Such is the case with the foolish decision to put a photo of Fiddlin' Arthur Smith with the McGee Brothers on the front of this album. The McGees did play in the Dixieliners, sure, and the combination of those three talents made up for an old-time music supergroup easily comparable with the Fab Four in terms of influence, if not worldwide popularity. But the McGees do not play on this record, nor the second volume in this series, so be warned. Using their picture is just plain stupid, yet it hardly can cast a shadow over the music which is first-rate. Smith is one of the most influential fiddlers of all time; indeed it would be difficult for a country fiddler to play a piece without doing something that Smith thought up, or passed on from his years of travel and interaction with other country players. The wonderful Delmore Brothers are on hand, making up for the non-McGee factor with aplomb. Other fine players here include fiddler Tommy Magness, bold and brave enough to lock horns with Smith on the fine "K.C. Stomp," and guitarist Billy Byrd, known for his work with Ernest Tubb. A booklet jam-packed with historical material and great old photos accompanies both volumes. *—Eugene Chadbourne*

Fiddlin' Arthur Smith & His Dixieliners, Vol. 2 / 1978 / County ✦✦✦✦
The second volume in this series of early recordings from the Tennessee fiddle master grabs material out of the same set of mid- to late-'30s sessions. The tunes were recorded in several different settings with the lion's share of the backup coming from the talented and sympathetic Delmore Brothers, with whom Smith shared a strong stylistic affinity as well as a natural knack for music making. Some of the absolute top Smith hits are here, such as "There's More Pretty Girls Than One," "Red Apple Rag," and the hysterical "House of David Blues" which seems to have something to do with an old Jewish baseball team. Smith's fiddle comes flying out of the speakers with the sonic authority that only certain masters obtain. Other highlights include a haunting version of "In the Pines" (is there any other kind?) and the wild, toe-tapping "Sugar Tree Stomp." An extremely well printed booklet accompanies both volumes, and includes extensive information and historic photography, just about everything one needs as a background to this music except the first names of the Delmore Brothers. *—Eugene Chadbourne*

● **Fiddlin' Arthur Smith & His Dixieliners** / May 14, 2002 / County ✦✦✦✦✦
This well-produced overview covers the years 1937-1940 and includes "Weary Weary World," "Red Apple Rag," "Little Darling," and several other hits (although it strangely omits "Walking in My Sleep," "Love Letters in the Sand," and "Beautiful Brown Eyes," some of Smith's other hits of the time). One doesn't need to hear hits, though, to appreciate Smith's tremendous skill, and with the Delmore Brothers on hand for a number of songs, this is nothing short of terrific. The liner notes provide some of the best insight yet into Smith's life and career and show definitively why he was such a tremendous influence on the first generation of bluegrass musicians. *—Jim Smith*

Hobart Smith

b. May 10, 1897, Saltville, VA, **d.** Jan. 11, 1965
Fiddle, 5-string Banjo, Guitar, Vocals, Piano / Old-Timey, Ballads, Field Recordings, Appalachian Folk
One of the most sadly overlooked masters of Appalachian folk music, Hobart Smith may not be widely known outside of those who happened to either see him at a '60s folk festival or the nascent folkies who were directly influenced by his driving, energetic banjo and guitar styles, but he arguably remains one of the most virtuosic performers his genre and era produced. Known as a quiet man, he clearly enjoyed the spotlight, transforming into a foot-stomping showman with rousing tunes and carefully embellished tales that identified him as the genuine article for a generation of musicians obsessed with such a cultural pedigree. A precise player of his own intricate arrangements of traditional old-timey tunes, Smith was an amazingly eclectic artist. Whether turning out deeply soulful country blues on guitar, channeling Earl Scruggs-like energy on complexly nuanced banjo tunes, diving into hauntingly rhythmic fiddle tunes, or lightening the mood with jaunty piano tunes, his music is always stamped with an ear for fluid melody and hypnotic rhythms.

Born in 1897 in Saltville, VA, Smith was immersed in the authentic Appalachian musical culture, sharing a musical tradition seven generations old by the time he arrived. As such, Smith's father had him playing the banjo by the age of seven, the guitar by the age of 14, and the fiddle, mandolin, piano, and organ within a few years. By 1915, he was gaining employment on the minstrel show circuit and had started his own string band to play at a variety of social functions from auctions to prison camps. At an indeterminate point, the influence of the blues crept into Smith's musical vernacular, coloring his rendering of traditional tunes forever thereafter. By the time he befriended Clarence Ashley in 1918 (whom he greatly respected as a musician and was probably influenced by on some level), he was nearly earning a living as a musician, although he would still have to find employment as a farmer, wagoner, house painter, and butcher. By 1936, Smith had begun to play the day's commercial popular music and had gained such regional renown that he and his sister, Texas Gladden, were invited to play before Eleanor Roosevelt at the prestigious White Top Festival in Southwest Virginia, making such an impression on the first lady that the two would be invited to perform at the White House.

In 1942, Smith recorded 40 tracks for Alan Lomax and the Library of Congress, resulting in a set of English ballads; banjo, fiddle, and guitar pieces; and Virginia murder ballads, not to mention a relationship with Lomax that would prove beneficial in the coming years. Eventually, Lomax would introduce him to Moses Asch, resulting in the recording of a soon out of print album for Asch's pre-Folkways disc label. Even so, the album went on to become quite influential on the burgeoning folk revival scene in New York City and Smith was convinced to focus solely on his traditional repertoire. As the years wore on, Lomax continued to record Smith, introduce him to folk festivals, and conduct extensive interviews to present the depth of his musical legacy. As artists such as the New Lost City Ramblers' Tom Paley, John Cohen, and Mike Seeger, as well as Jody Stecher, Hank Bradley, and Fleming Brown took in his performances during the folk festival boom of the 1960s, Smith was finally embraced as the musical genius he was and would again enter the recording studio for Folk Legacy that fully indulged his love of odd and obscure traditional tunes. Still, by the time Smith seemed on the verge of capitalizing on his unique talents, his health began to fail him. In 1965, his status as a true giant of traditional music growing with each performance, he passed away without fully benefiting from his prodigious talents. Although his legacy has been carried on by those his music touched in his lifetime, renewed interest in Hobart Smith's music resulted in the excellent *Blue Ridge Legacy* release in 2001. *—Matt Fink*

● **Blue Ridge Legacy—The Alan Lomax Portait Series** / Jun. 19, 2001 / Rounder ✦✦✦✦✦
Those who have followed the remarkable career of Alan Lomax are likely already familiar with the work of Hobart Smith. Smith's virtuosity on a variety of folk instruments, including banjo, guitar, and fiddle, have graced many a Lomax collection, as has his salt-of-the-earth voice. Listeners may be familiar with his readings of "Ellen Smith" or "Railroad Bill." Smith's output was prodigious, but many of the records were made for companies that no longer exist. Finding his records has been a problem. What a joy then to have many of his songs collected here. Perhaps best known for his song "The Cuckoo Bird," Smith was a professional musician who performed across the country with his wife, and, as his profession demanded, could play just about anything on anything. This disc does an admirable job of summarizing his remarkable career, including both searing instrumentals and sardonic vocal performances to give the initiate some idea of the scope of this man's talent. This disc should revive interest in a man whose influence on the folk revival of the '60s cannot be underestimated. *—Rob Ferrier*

Sammi Smith (Jewel Fay Smith)

b. Aug. 5, 1943, Orange, CA
Vocals / Progressive Country, Country-Pop, Outlaw Country
In the tradition of Waylon Jennings and Willie Nelson, singer/songwriter Sammi Smith was considered a country music outlaw, unafraid to sing songs that reflected the sometimes gritty realities of modern life. She first came to fame singing Kris Kristofferson's "Help Me Make It Through the Night" and was noted for her husky voice, the result of spending many years singing in smoke-filled clubs. She was born Jewel Fay Smith in California, but spent her childhood living in different southwestern states. At age 11, Smith dropped out of school and the following year began singing professionally in clubs. She married at age 15 and produced four children. At songwriter Gene Sullivan's urging, a newly divorced Smith moved to Nashville in 1967.

A year later she had her first minor hit, "So Long, Charlie Brown, Don't Look for Me Around." In 1970, she had another minor hit, but it was not until the end of the year that she had her first major smash with "Help Me Make It Through the Night," which made it to the top of the country charts and also became a Top Ten pop hit. Later that year, she wrote "Cedartown, Georgia," which became a major hit for Waylon Jennings. In 1973, Smith moved to Dallas to join Jennings and Willie Nelson and become an "outlaw." Through 1975, she had several hits including "Then You Walk In" and "Today I Started Loving You Again." She moved to Elektra in 1975 and remained with them for three years. During that time, she had several chart entries with such songs as "Loving Arms," "Days That End in 'Y'" (both 1977) and "Norma Jean" (1978), a tribute to Marilyn Monroe. In 1979, she signed to the independent label Cyclone and had a Top 20 hit with "What a Lie," In 1980, she moved to Sound Factory and had one Top 40 and two Top 20 hits including "I Cry When I'm Alone." Her last hit came in 1986 with "Love Me All Over." *—Sandra Brennan*

Lonesome / 1971 / Capitol ✦✦✦✦

Something Old, Something New, Something Blue / 1972 / Mega ✦✦✦✦

The Toast of '45 / 1973 / Mega ✦✦✦✦✦

Today I Started Loving You Again / 1975 / Mega ✦✦✦

Help Me Make It Through the Night / 1976 / Mega ✦✦✦

As Long As There's a Sunday / 1976 / Elektra ✦✦✦✦

Mixed Emotions / 1977 / Elektra ✦✦✦✦
Sammi sounds great on this album. In addition to her 1977 hit on Tom Jan's "Loving Arms," she takes songs like "A Woman Left Lonely" and "I've Seen Better Days" and makes them so thoroughly her own, you can't imagine anyone else ever trying to tackle them. *—Jim Worbois*

New Winds-All Quadrents / 1978 / Elektra ✦✦✦
This is more pop than country but there are a couple nice moments. The standout is the song "You Were Gone Before You Had a Chance to Say Goodbye." *—Jim Worbois*

Girl Hero / 1979 / Cyclone ✦✦
This is a rather disappointing record with a good half the songs featuring what might pass as a disco beat. Sammi is the kind of singer who could have really done nice things with some of these tracks; especially, the Amazing Rhythm Aces' "Dancing the Night Away." *—Jim Worbois*

● **The Best of Sammi Smith** / Oct. 22, 1996 / Varese ✦✦✦✦✦
Sammi Smith was a difficult singer to categorize. Straddling the line between lush country-pop and idiosyncratic outlaw country, she didn't belong to either world, which didn't effect the quality of her music but at times could mean that she slipped through the cracks between critical acclaim and commercial sales. She didn't want either, but neither arrived at the level she deserved, as Varese Sarabande's excellent 1996 compilation *The Best of Sammi Smith* illustrates. Smith's big break came in 1971 with her rendition of Kris Kristofferson's "Help Me Make It Through the Night." The song had been kicking around for several years and had been recorded many times before Smith's aching, wearily sensual version finally made it a crossover smash, bringing it to number one on the country charts and within the sights of the top of the pop charts. Her version wasn't just a hit, its production—which managed to feel rich and opulent while retaining country grit and sexiness—provided the template for the rest of her work on Mega, where

she was given lush, layered arrangements that managed to place her husky yet nuanced vocals front and center. Which is right where they should be, since Smith's interpretations were original and unpredictable, finding new spins on familiar material (her take on "Long Black Veil" is one of the eeriest cuts; "City of New Orleans" doesn't sound shop-worn in her hands; she turns the tables on Merle Haggard's "Today I Started Loving You Again"; just when you think she's a little low-key, she cuts a mean rug on the Bob Wills standard, "My Window Faces the South") and cutting definitive versions of songs by writers like Kristofferson, Dallas Frazier, Wayne Carson, and Shel Silverstein, among others. As a vocalist, she was on par with anybody in the outlaw movement, but her music, as exploratory as it was, was closer to country-pop, which meant that some didn't give her the credit she deserved at the time. This collection restores her reputation by putting those Mega sides back in print (along with a couple of subpar singles cut for Cyclone in 1979) and proving that Smith was one of the most interesting female country voices of the '70s. —*Stephen Thomas Erlewine*

Warren Smith

b. Feb. 7, 1933, d. Jan. 31, 1980
Guitar, Vocals / Traditional Country, Rockabilly, Rock & Roll

For sheer, heartfelt vocalizing abilities, of all the folks who stood in front of the microphone at Sun studio, Warren Smith may have been the most talented. Equally adept at storming rockabilly and the most gut-wrenching of country ballads, Smith always sang it from the heart, without giving in to phony rasping or histrionics. Though typecast as strictly a rocker, Smith left Sun and achieved minor success in the '60s as a country singer, his first love. —*Cub Koda*

Call of the Wild / 1990 / Bear Family ✦✦✦✦✦

Warren Smith left Sun Records in 1959 and, after a brief stay with Warner Bros., signed with Liberty Records, where he looked forward to doing country music rather than the hybrid rockabilly that Sun had him recording. With Joe Allison managing his recordings, he began making records with a smooth Nashville sound, even though they were done in Hollywood. With Johnny Western on guitar, Ralph Mooney on steel guitar, and Bobby Bruce and Harold Hensley on fiddles, he got a very refined commercial sound that yielded a few hits ("I Don't Believe I'll Fall in Love Today" made it to number five and "Odds and Ends, Bits and Pieces" got to number seven) and a superb album, *The First Country Collection of Warren Smith*, which featured covers of songs associated with Patsy Cline, Buck Owens, Charlie Walker, Eddy Arnold, and Rose Maddox, among others, and a couple of duets with singer Shirley Collie. The music here—Smith's complete Liberty recordings, plus his two 1966 vintage songs for the tiny Skill label—is among the most accomplished and inspired of Smith's career, and was work he was clearly proud of. The only drawback is the conventional nature of the arrangements—Allison and Liberty were, understandably, trying for the most commercial sound possible, and the results are a little dullish in retrospect. Smith's expression is fine, however, expressive and strong throughout (only the Skill sides are weak), and the playing, especially in the 1959-1960 sessions, is first-rate. Highlights among the later songs include "Five Minutes of the Latest Blues," "A Hundred and Sixty Pounds of Hurt," and "That's Why I Sing in a Honky Tonk." The notes, as usual, are extremely thorough, covering Smith's career in considerable detail from 1959 until his death in 1980. —*Bruce Eder*

● **The Classic Recordings: 1956–1959** / 1992 / Bear Family ✦✦✦✦✦

Ask any rockabilly cat and they'll tell you that Warren Smith was one of the greats. He's somebody the hardcore love, not just because he produced the frenzied "Ubangi Stomp" and not just because he cut the definitive version of "Rock & Roll Ruby," but also because he was a passionate, powerful country singer, wrenching enough emotion out of the traditional "Black Jack David" to make it seem like his own. He also had great midtempo sides like "So Long, I'm Gone," written by Roy Orbison and Sam Phillips, and "Red Cadillac and Black Moustache." As great as these songs are—and, decades later, they retain their vitality, thanks to both Smith's performance and the spare, vibrant sound of Sun Studios—they were not big hits, with only "So Long, I'm Gone" scraping the bottom reaches of the Top 100; but they are among the finest rockabilly and country of the late '50s, as Bear Family's stellar *The Classic Recordings: 1956-1959* proves. This single-disc, 31-track collection contains everything Warren Smith cut at the studio, including several alternate takes and unreleased material. Instead of cluttering the disc, these rarities show Smith's depth and range, as he sounds equally comfortable with hardcore country as he does with down and dirty rockabilly. The remarkable thing about the disc is that the songs and performances are all of consistently high quality. Unlike many of his rockabilly peers, either at Sun or elsewhere, Smith cut almost no dross, and his sides for Sun rank among the finest at the studio, holding its own against the work of Johnny Cash, Carl Perkins, and Jerry Lee Lewis, which is high praise indeed. Needless to say, *The Classic Recordings: 1956-1959* belongs in the library of any serious fan of '50s country, rockabilly, or rock & roll. —*Stephen Thomas Erlewine*

Uranium Rock: The Best of Warren Smith / May 23, 1995 / AVI ✦✦✦✦

Uranium Rock: The Best Of . . . is a wonderful 24-track collection containing all of Warren Smith's essential Sun recordings, from "Rock 'n' Roll Ruby" and "Ubangi Stomp" to "Black Jack David," "Red Cadillac and a Black Moustache," and "Uranium Rock." It's a more concise and more effective compilation than Bear Family's *The Classic Recordings*, and therefore, it's arguably the definitive overview. —*Stephen Thomas Erlewine*

Ubangi Stomp / Feb. 2, 1999 / Collectables ✦✦✦

Jim Smoak

Banjo / Bluegrass-Gospel, Bluegrass, Traditional Bluegrass

The state of Louisiana is regarded as a hotbed of musical activity, but not bluegrass. Jim Smoak has been credited with being the first bluegrass banjo player to emerge from the land of crazy Cajuns and saints who go marching in. With so many other styles of music prevalent and popular, establishing an audience for bluegrass was no easy task and Smoak may have been worn out by the '50s, by which time he had headed north where his style of picking was more appreciated. In that decade, Smoak was a member of two top outfits in the genre. Off and on through 1952 and the following year, he worked with Bill Monroe & His Blue Grass Boys, graduating to working consistently with the group in 1954. Monroe's group was known as something of a school for players, and Smoak thus joined a long list of banjo players who have been in the group. In the late '50s, he was a member of Hylo Brown & the Timberliners, a well-loved bluegrass band although hardly on the level of Monroe and his boys. It does represent some of Smoak's hottest playing, as he was part of a small, happening group that also included the wonderful fiddler Tater Tate.

Smoak continued playing both bluegrass and country & western through the '60s, and in the '70s became one of the few musicians on his instrument to publish a book including both tablature and standard notation. He published three different banjo instruction books in the '70s, the last one a collaboration with fellow player and educator Jerry Tainaka. The Smoak volumes, *5-String Banjo Technique* and *5-String Banjo Songbook*, both published by Experience in 1972 and 1974, respectively, are considered some of the finest texts for banjo instruction. Smoak recorded a fine solo album in 1979 for the Blue River label, entitled *Moonshine Sonata*. The popular country band the Dixie Chicks covered the song "This Heart of Mine," co-written by Smoak and Steven Brines on the group's album *Thank Heavens for Dale Evans*. —*Eugene Chadbourne*

Bayou Bluegrass / Aug. 27, 2002 / Arhoolie ✦✦✦✦

While banjoist Jim Smoak isn't well-known in bluegrass circles, his credentials are excellent. Smoak played and recorded with Bill Monroe in the early '50s and, following a stint in the army, played with Hylo Brown. In 1960 Smoak returned to the South and put together the Louisiana Honeydrippers for a recording session with Harry Oster. One can immediately pick up the influence of Monroe and the more rustic strains of tradition on *Bayou Bluegrass*. Smoak's old-time vocals seem just right for folk tunes like "Liza Jane," "Old Dan Tucker," and "Mama Don't Allow," and the band's accompaniment, more reminiscent of 1946 than 1960, seems just right. The ingredient that separates these songs and instrumentals from other traditional albums, however, is the "Bayou" factor, which is provided alternately by fiddlers Dewey Edwards and Bucky Wood. Edwards' bow work on "Rabbit, Where's Your Mammy?" and "The Fisher's Hornpipe" gives these pieces a real Cajun flavor. Smoak reinforces this old-time Cajun feel by using claw-hammer and single-note style, respectively, on these pieces. Several songs, including "East Bound Train" and "Underneath the Weeping Willow," are smoothed out a bit by J.C. and V.J. Meyers' fine harmony. *Bayou Bluegrass* is a vital disc, full of inspired performances and lots of deft picking. [The 2002 reissue includes four previously unreleased bonus cuts.] —*Ronnie D. Lankford Jr.*

Smokin' Armadillos

Group / Bakersfield Sound, Alternative Country-Rock, Americana

An energetic and wildly spirited country-rock sextet hailing from Bakersfield, the Smokin' Armadillos amazed the record industry by selling an astounding 150,000 copies of their independently released EP before they ever laid eyes on a recording contract. Comprised of Scott Meeks (guitar, vocals), Rick Russell (lead vocals), Darrin Kirkindoll (drums), Arron Casida (bass, vocals), and fiddle champion Jason Theiste, the band formed during the summer of 1992, with four of the group's six members knowing each other from high-school. They developed a huge following regionally, and on the advice of a friend who worked for a major label, they began to release singles and send them to radio stations. Oddly enough, even with stiff competition for airplay slots, some reporting stations began playing the singles and soon a demand was created for their music. The band released a five-song EP and shipped copies from an office in Bakersfield, as well as sold units at their popular live shows. The Smokin' Armadillos released three singles—"My Girlfriend Might," "I'm a Cowboy," and "Red Rock"—which took them to the top of the independent charts before they signed with MCG/Curb in 1994. They released their debut album in 1995, along with a reissued version of the EP. They returned in 2003 with Strike the Match on Housekeeping records. —*Jack Leaver*

Out of the Burrow / 1995 / Gramac ✦✦✦

● **Smokin' Armadillos** / Mar. 12, 1996 / MCA/Curb ✦✦✦✦

The Smokin' Armadillos' debut is pumped-up country music with a heavy lean toward power rock influences. This sextet from Bakersfield—ranging in age from 19-26—plays with an unbridled enthusiasm that serves the material well. Nine of the 12 tracks were written by the band, and most of them are driven by the burning championship fiddle playing of the youngest Armadillo, Jason Theiste. Although none of the tracks here are likely to change the world, original songs like "Thump Factor" and "Too Hot to Handle" exude a youthful charm and show some songwriting potential. Southern rock king Charlie Daniels makes an appearance on a cover of his spooky '70s hit "The Legend of Wooley Swamp," and the boys include reworked versions of a couple of their independent singles—the ones that started all the commotion. "My Girlfriend Might" is a catchy, lighthearted tune, but the country rap and probable live favorite, "I'm a Cowboy," borders on the ridiculous. But hey, these guys are still young. —*Jack Leaver*

Strike the Match / Aug. 19, 2003 / Housekeeping ✦✦✦

Todd Snider

b. Oct. 11, 1966
Guitar, Vocals / Singer/Songwriter, Roots Rock, Alternative Country, Americana

Singer/songwriter Todd Snider first garnered attention for his timely alternative rock satire "Talkin' Seattle Grunge Rock Blues," a folk-rock song which struck a chord with younger people fed up with angry alternative rock bands, and at the same time, appealed to aging rockers who grew up with the folk revival of the 1960s. Snider was born in

Portland, OR, and grew up in Santa Rosa, Austin, Houston and Atlanta. After moving to Memphis in the mid-'80s and establishing residency at a local club named the Daily Planet, he was discovered by singer/songwriter Keith Sykes, a member of Jimmy Buffett's Coral Reefer Band. Sykes began to work with Snider to help advance his career, and after passing on demo tapes of Snider to Buffett, he was signed to the star's Margaritaville Records.

Snider's debut album *Songs for the Daily Planet* was released in the fall of 1994; "Talkin' Seattle Grunge Rock Blues" was added to the album as an afterthought only after intense lobbying by a Canadian music critic, and ultimately became a minor hit. On his second effort, 1996's *Step Right Up*, Snider and his band the Nervous Wrecks (comprised of lead guitarist and multi-instumentalist Will Kimbrough, bassist Joe Mariencheck, drummer Joe McLeary and keyboardist David Zollo) continued blending bluegrass, blues, folk-rock and country-rock to forge their own distinctive sound. *—Richard Skelly*

Songs for the Daily Planet / 1994 / MCA ♦♦♦♦♦

It's ironic that Todd Snider's first radio exposure would come from a song included on his debut as an afterthought and contained as a "hidden" track. "Talking Seattle Grunge-Rock Blues" is reminiscent of early Dylan, hilarious in its satire as a clever dose of good-natured pokes at the industry hype surrounding the Seattle music scene (including references to Eddie Vedder and Nirvana). Although he is a very talented songwriter with a keen wit, at times Snider is just a little too consciously contrived for his own good, threatening to reduce his art to novelty. For instance, the extremely countrified "My Generation, Pt. 2" and the Mellencamp-esque "Alright Guy" are very humorous observations, but dangerously close to sounding trite, especially when compared to the seriousness of the chilling "You Think You Know Somebody," which deals with the ramifications of child abuse. A rootsy record that combines country and folk elements with a genuine rock & roll sensibility, *Songs for the Daily Planet* also features some cutting fretwork by one of Nashville's finest young guitarists, Eddy Shaver, the son of country outlaw Billy Joe Shaver, one of Snider's heroes. Overall a fine introduction to a remarkable voice. *—Jack Leaver*

● **Step Right Up** / Apr. 1996 / MCA ♦♦♦♦♦

Picking up where he left off with his exceptional debut *Songs for the Daily Planet*, Todd Snider continues his ragged-but-right blend of folk, country and rootsy rock & roll on this 14-song release. At times brilliant, Snider's songwriting talent is still intact, as is his passionate voice and the superb instrumental backing by his band the Nervous Wrecks. The first single "I Believe You" is a hopeful testament of the singer's faith in human nature. Keen observations of social and political issues are honestly presented, using wit and humor as in "Side Show Blues," "Tension," and with kick-in-the-gut seriousness—"T.V. Guide," "24 Hours a Day." It's not all weighty stuff though—the swampy "Moon Dawg's Tavern" and the Chuck Berry-esque rocker "Late Last Night" are just plain fun. Hear him out; he's got a lot to say. *—Jack Leaver*

Viva Satellite / Apr. 7, 1998 / MCA ♦♦♦♦

It may not be Tom Petty & the Heartbreakers, but the third studio release from southern rocker Todd Snider sure sounds like it. There are plenty of suspended and liberated guitar breaks here, plus a gentle country twang, and despite the annoying imitation of Tom Petty on several tracks, *Viva Satellite* has enough of a good-ol'-boy honky tonk feel, that it can stand well on its own merit. With a distinctive bluegrass/pop country slant, Todd Snider has produced a collection of familiar sounding melodies that will win you over. The reverence paid to the masters of countrified blues-rock Arlo Guthrie and Neil Young may be a bit on the heavy side, however on cuts like "Rocket Fuel," and the gospel-tinged "Godsend," Todd Snider proves he has a signature style all his own. *—Roxanne Blanford*

Happy to Be Here / Apr. 18, 2000 / Oh Boy ♦♦♦

Snider is amiable enough on his first album for John Prine's label, but he's taken his literal move to Nashville figuratively as well—becoming a more conventional singer/songwriter in the process, downplaying the quirks that got him noticed initially. There are some nice things here (the horns are a particular welcome blast of fun), but nice doesn't quite cut it musically. *—Michael Gallucci*

New Connection / 2002 / Oh Boy ♦♦♦

New Connection—Todd Snider's fifth album and the second for John Prine's Oh Boy label—finds the singer riding atop a warm band featuring Jason Wilber and David Jacques (both of Prine's touring unit), Paul Griffith, and Will Kimbrough. Like Kevn Kinney, Snider's voice alternates between a drawl and a scratch, occasionally dropping into Jim White-like whispers. It is in these cracks that Snider finds a wry strength, which he hangs on his almost traditional singer/songwriter wares. There are humorous tunes—"Vinyl Records," "Beer Run," and "Statistician's Blues"—but they're rarely anything more than cute. "Broke," meanwhile, sounds like a Nashville version of Lou Reed's "Goodnight Ladies." Snider gets a few elegiac beauties into the mix, too, including the subtly produced "Easy" and the almost heartbreaking "Class of 85." These are fine songs. Prine takes a guest turn on his own "Crooked Piece of Time," which fits in with the rest of the record almost too well. *—Jesse Jarnow*

Near Truths and Hotel Rooms Live / May 13, 2003 / Oh Boy ♦♦♦♦

Todd Snider's first live album, on which he accompanies himself on guitar and harmonica in folky style, conveys a stage personality only glimpsed in the more humorous of his songs on his previous five studio recordings. Snider performs his share of sensitive, reflective tunes, but they are overwhelmed by the funny ones and by his offbeat, spacy persona, which is equally laugh-provoking. Snider's similarity to John Prine, the head of his record label, is accentuated in songs like "I Can't Complain," which is full of cracked aphorisms and employs a fingerpicking style that seems borrowed from Prine. But elsewhere, Snider displays his own alcohol-drenched sense of humor, giving off a scatterbrained impression that sometimes recalls Arlo Guthrie, but is a bit less goofy (if equally wily) and a bit more like that of a drug casualty. "The Story of the Devil's Backbone Tavern," not a song but a lengthy introduction to a song called "The Ballad of the Devil's Backbone Tavern" (itself featuring a lot of talking), presents Snider's autobiography, which makes him sound like more of an inebriated good ol' boy than he could possibly be, but it is amusing. "Talking Seattle Grunge Rock Blues," which passes for his greatest hit, is dated by now, but still imaginative. *Near Truths and Hotel Rooms* may be closer to a comedy act than a concert, but if so, it's got most of the country comedians beat and assures that Snider has a career to fall back on if the music gig doesn't pan out. *—William Ruhlmann*

Hank Snow (Clarence Eugene Snow)

b. May 9, 1914, Liverpool, Nova Scotia, Canada, **d.** Dec. 20, 1999

Guitar, Vocals / Traditional Country, Cowboy, Honky Tonk, Country Boogie

Canada's greatest contribution to country music, Hank Snow was famous for his "traveling" songs. It's no wonder. At age 12 he ran away from his Nova Scotia home and joined the Merchant Marines, working as a cabin boy and laborer for four years. Once back on shore, he listened to Jimmie Rodgers records and started playing in public, building up a following in Halifax. His original nickname, the Yodelling Ranger, was modified to the Singing Ranger when his high voice changed to the great baritone that graced his hit records. In 1950, the year he became an *Opry* regular, his self-penned "I'm Moving On" (the first of his many great traveling songs) became a smash hit, reaching number one and remaining there for 21 weeks. "Golden Rocket" (also 1950) and "I've Been Everywhere" (1962), two other hits, show his lifelong love for trains and travel. But he was as much at home with two other styles, the ballad and the rhumba/boogie. Among his many great ballads are "Bluebird Island" (with Anita Carter of the Carter Family), "Fool Such as I," and "Hello, Love," a hit when Snow was 60 years old. Snow appeared regularly on the *Opry* into the '90s, proving that his incredible voice suffered no loss of quality over the last half-century, as well as what a tasteful, understated guitar stylist he is. With small stature and huge voice, Snow was a country traditionalist who gave much more to the business than he took.

Born and raised in Nova Scotia, Snow (born Clarence Eugene Snow) moved in with his grandmother when he was eight years old, following the divorce of his parents. Four years later, he re-joined his mother when she re-married, but his stepfather was an abusive, violent man who frequently beat Hank. Tired of the abuse, Snow ran away from home when he was 12 years old, joining a fishing boat. For the next four years, he served as a cabin boy, often singing for the sailors onboard. When he was 16, he returned home, where he began working odd jobs and trying to launch a performing career. His mother had given him a stack of Rodgers records which inspired him greatly. Within a few weeks of hearing Rodgers, Snow ordered a cheap, mail-order guitar and tried to learn his idol's trademark blue yodel. For the next few years, he sang around Nova Scotia before finally mustering the courage to travel to Halifax in 1933. Snow landed a weekly unpaid appearance on CHNS' Down on the Farm, where he was billed as both the cowboy Blue Yodeller and Clarence Snow & His Guitar. The following year, CHNS' chief announcer, Cecil Landry, suggested to Snow that he should change his name to Hank, since it sounded more Western.

Snow continued to perform in Halifax for the next three years, often struggling to get by. The severity of the financial situation was compounded when he married Minnie Aaiders in 1936, but the couple was soon relieved when he landed a regular paid program on the network *Canadian Farm Hour*, billed as Hank the Yodelling Ranger. By the end of the year, Snow had signed a deal with RCA Victor's Montreal branch and recorded two original songs: "The Prisoned Cowboy" and "Lonesome Blue Yodel." The songs were hits, beginning a string of Canadian-only hit singles that ran for the next ten years; during that time, he recorded nearly 90 songs. In the early '40s, he had a regular show on CBC, based in Montreal and New Brunswick. In 1944, he switched to CKCW in New Brunswick. Around that time, he switched his stage name to Hank the Singing Ranger, since his voice had deepened and he could no longer yodel.

Though he had become a star in Canada, the American market remained untapped. Snow tried to break into the U.S.A. several times, playing *the Wheeling Jamboree* in West Virginia, briefly moving to Hollywood, and performing concerts with his trick pony Shawnee, but he was having no luck finding fans. The problem partially lies with the fact that he was trying to find an audience that wasn't there, since most citizens were concentrating on World War II. Another stumbling block was RCA Records themselves, who refused to let Snow release records in America until he was well-known in the country. By 1948, Snow was singing on *the Big D Jamboree* in Dallas, TX, where he befriended the honky tonk legend Ernest Tubb. ET pulled enough weight at the *Grand Ole Opry* to get Snow a slot on the show in early 1950, and by that time, RCA had agreed to record him for the American audience.

Snow's American debut single, "Marriage Vow," became a minor hit at the end of 1949, but it fell off the charts after a week. Similarly, his debut appearance on the *Grand Ole Opry* in January was not well-received, prompting him to consider moving back to Canada. However, those ideas were soon abandoned when his breakthrough arrived in the summer of 1950. That July, "I'm Moving On" began its remarkable ascent up the charts, eventually landing at number one and staying there for a full 21 weeks. In the year after the release of "I'm Moving On," "The Golden Rocket" and "The Rhumba Boogie" both hit number one (the latter staying there for eight weeks), establishing Snow as a genuine star. Between 1951 and the end of 1955, Snow had a remarkable 24 Top Ten hits, including the massive hit single "I Don't Hurt Anymore," which spent 20 weeks at number one in 1954. Snow not only played his trademark traveling songs, but also country boogie, Hawaiian music, rhumbas, and cowboys songs. By the middle of the decade, he was a star not only in the U.S. and Canada, but throughout the world, gaining a particularly strong following over the years in the U.K.

Around 1954, Snow formed a booking agency with Colonel Tom Parker, who would later become infamous for being Elvis Presley's manager. Indeed, Snow played a formative role in Presley's early career, convincing the *Grand Ole Opry* to give the singer a chance in 1954. Though Elvis' appearance at the *Opry* was ill-received, Snow continued to push Presley to move toward country, and Hank was quite upset when Parker took complete control of Elvis' management around 1955. Still, Snow found a way to combat rock & roll—he recorded some light rockabilly singles himself. "Hula Rock" and "Rockin', Rollin' Ocean" were attempts to capture the beat of rock & roll but diluted with the rhumbas and boogie that made his singles hits during the early '50s. Though he was experimenting with the new genre, he hadn't abandoned country and he continued to regularly chart in the country Top Ten until 1965 with hits like "Big Wheels" (number seven, 1958), "Miller's Cave" (number nine, 1960), "Beggar to a King" (number five, 1961), "I've Been Everywhere" (number one, 1962), and "Ninety Miles an Hour (Down a Dead End Street)" (number two, 1963).

During the latter half of the '60s, Snow's career slowed down considerably, as he wasn't able to make the transition to the new, heavily orchestrated country-pop sounds, nor was he able to keep pace with the twangy roll of Bakersfield. Instead, his singles placed in the lower reaches of the charts, while his concerts and *Grand Ole Opry* appearances continued to be quite popular. It wasn't until 1974 that another monster hit arrived in the form of "Hello Love," which unexpectedly climbed to number one. Instead of sparking a revival, "Hello Love" proved to be a last gasp; between its release in 1974 and 1980, Snow had only two other Top 40 hits, which both arrived the same year as "Hello Love." Despite his declining record sales, his profile remained high through his concerts and several lifetime-achievement awards, including his induction to the Nashville Songwriters International Hall of Fame in 1978 and the Country Music Hall of Fame in 1979.

In 1981, Snow's recording career ended when RCA dropped him after a 45-year relationship. Snow was very upset with the label's treatment of him, as well as the direction that country music was taking, claiming that "80 percent of today's country music is a joke and not fit to listen to." He was equally angry that country's roots were being diluted by pop and rock production values. Though he never recorded again, Snow remained active in the *Grand Ole Opry* into the '90s, and he spent a lot of time working for his Foundation for Child Abuse. In the late '80s, Bear Family began a lengthy retrospective of several multidisc box sets that chronicled his entire recording career. In 1994, Snow published his autobiography, *The Hank Snow Story.* Late the following year, he was stricken with a respiratory illness, yet he recovered in 1996, returning to the *Grand Ole Opry* in August of that year. Snow died December 20, 1999, at the age of 85. *—David Vinopal*

Hank Snow Sings / 1952 / RCA ✦✦✦✦✦

Hank Snow Sings Jimmie Rodgers Songs / 1960 / RCA ✦✦✦✦✦
Jimmie Rodgers was one of Hank's greatest influences and this record is a work is made of pure love. Snow doesn't just "sing" these songs, as the title suggests. He gets inside them, lives them and makes them his. *—Jim Worbois*

The Southern Cannonball / 1961 / Camden ✦✦✦✦
Hank Snow might not have been quite at the commercial height of his career when he released *The Southern Cannonball,* but he certainly wasn't giving up on making consistently engaging albums. (Containing two classic Jimmie Rodgers' songs with the ballad "My Blue Eyed Jane" and the railroad tale of "The Southern Cannonball" is proof enough of that.) The instrumental "Under the Double Eagle" is another fine example of the guitar virtuosity for which Snow rarely receives sufficient credit. Snow's penchant for Spanish rhythms and melodies comes through once again in "Panamama," and the very strong ballad "There Wasn't an Organ at Our Wedding" help make this just another in the line of very listenable Hank Snow albums. *—Matt Fink*

Big Country Hits / 1961 / RCA ✦✦✦
A solid craftsman at work among a small group of Nashville superpickers, Hank Snow comes up with a program here that might be somewhat misunderstood from the album title of *Big Country Hits.* But it's easily explained by the album's humorous subtitle, "Songs I Hadn't Recorded Till Now"—naturally, because these are songs that were hits for other country artists, only a few of which have retained hit status over the nearly half a century that has ensued. While "Send Me the Pillow You Dream On" and "Mansion on the Hill" were still a solid part of the country repertoire in the new millennium, many of these other titles might come across more like unexpected discoveries, the valuable and often neglected work of '50s country songwriters such as Leon Payne and Don Gibson. The latter artist's "A Legend in My Time" confirms country music's status as the genre most likely to allow artists the opportunity to denigrate themselves in public. Snow might be a trifle soft around the edges for the outlaw country crowd, but he is the real deal and is in good form here, although there is a trifle of a hankering on his end to get back to his own material. The rhythm section of bassist Bob Moore and drummer Buddy Harmon is flawless throughout. *—Eugene Chadbourne*

I've Been Everywhere / 1963 / RCA ✦✦✦
BMG Special Products' *I've Been Everywhere: The Encore Collection* should not be confused with the 1963 Hank Snow album of the same name. Instead, it's a budget-priced collection of ten traveling songs Snow recorded at various stages in his career. Since *I've Been Everywhere* contains ten songs about places and travels, it turns out to be more consistent than many entries in *The Encore Collection,* yet it's not quite as coherent as a regular album. Nevertheless, it's a very good disc, as far as budget-priced collections go, featuring such songs as "Six Days on the Road," "El Paso," "When It's Springtime in Alaska," "Somewhere Along Life's Highway" and "I Went to Your Wedding." *—Stephen Thomas Erlewine*

Reminiscing / 1964 / RCA ✦✦✦

Songs of Tragedy / 1964 / RCA ✦✦✦
Songs of Tragedy is a follow-up to Hank Snow's much earlier RCA release, *When Tragedy Struck,* and continues Snow's homage to those who have endured life's heavy blows, focusing on prisoners praying for redemption and war-weary soldiers. The album's sound is more akin to easy listening than traditional country. Produced by Chet Atkins at "Nashville Sound Studio," it combines soft instrumentation, woozy backing vocals, and acoustic strumming behind Snow's marvelous voice. The songs themselves are less memorable than the album cover that features a full-size picture of hangman's noose. *—Jeff Schwachter*

More Souvenirs / 1964 / RCA ✦✦✦✦
Not exactly greatest-hits packages, the Hank Snow *Souvenirs* and *More Souvenirs* sets represent the repackaging possibilities that are possible once an artist has cut more than

100 titles for a particular record label. This guy was a rolling "Snow-ball" for sure by the mid-'60s in terms of accumulated masters, a literal avalanche of country music ranging from sentimental to humorous to honky tonk to all three combined, all of it recorded with fine Nashville backing bands. There seems to be no "yellow snow" amidst this material; any random selection of Snow RCA recordings of this sort will result in a country collection that could be placed under the microscope and studied by any manner of musician or artist attempting to create an authentic "roots" groove. On *More Souvenirs,* "Let Me Go Lover" kicks off the set with a swagger made all the more vivid by Ray Edenton's lead guitar twang and the fiddle licks of Chubby Wise. Snow forsakes the pedal steel on these recordings, going for a sound heavy on regular guitar, with odd highlights from both piano and the occasional trumpet solo. Side two starts off with two wonderful versions of haunting story-songs, "Miller's Cave" and "The Wreck of the Old '97." "Tangled Mind" and "One More Ride" both demonstrate Snow's knack for delivering a straightforward, unpretentious country song. *—Eugene Chadbourne*

Sings Your Favorite Country Hits / 1965 / RCA ✦✦✦
Hank Snow had three hits in 1965, but none of them are on *Sings Your Favorite Country Hits.* The album was aimed at Snow's fans, who would happily consume his versions of recent hits and older favorites because they enjoyed his voice and were familiar with many, if not most, of the songs. The then-"current" hit songs (all from 1963) include "Six Days on the Road," "Mary Ann Regrets," and "From a Jack to a King," while the oldies feature Marvin Rainwater's "Gonna Find Me a Bluebird"; the ever-popular "White Silver Sands"; and Jimmy Dean's first hit, "Bumming Around." This kind of album package, consisting of a name artist covering well-known songs, was common in the '60s, being easy to produce and a solid seller that pleased the artist's followers. The absence of original material would be seen as a fault by many latter-day critics, but *Sings Your Favorite Country Hits* was created for a certain purpose and, in that regard, is a success. *—Greg Adams*

Travelin' Blues / 1966 / Camden ✦✦✦✦
Having been off the country charts for a few years, Hank Snow decided to make an album of personal favorites that he hadn't yet recorded. The result is a fine album, including four Jimmie Rodgers covers and some excellent backup work from Anita Carter & the Rainbow Ranch Boys. *—Matt Fink*

Memories Are Made of This / 1970 / Camden ✦✦✦
It might be preposterous to assume any kind of thought or concern went into the production of this, a budget-line Hank Snow emission—one hesitates to glorify it with the word "release"—that is typical in its brevity but unusual in the collective implication of the songs chosen. Snow's own originals, sometimes good and sometimes just sentimental, are completely avoided in favor of a measly nine tracks smeared with loneliness, gambling, prisons, and memories of the past. The overall advice to read in these "Snow flakes" seems to be to "Just Keep A-Movin'," but what other advice can one expect from a songwriter whose surname is Walker? Albums with sides that are only about 11 minutes long have been known to inspire axe murders, so one might be cautious about introducing this particular release into one's home. Still, it is a little shot of straight-ahead country music, including a nifty Ernest Tubb cover. *—Eugene Chadbourne*

Lovingly Yours / 1980 / RCA ✦✦
While overall being comprised of mostly pleasant songs, *Lovingly Yours,* is not a standout recording in the Hank Snow catalog; it's probably about as middle-of-the-road as anything you'll find his name attached to. Sadly, it's also one of the last recordings he ever made. Though Snow is in fine form vocally, the material, mostly comprised of extremely mediocre pop balladry, is substantially overblown with rather trite overstatements fronting songs that contain little emotional punch. It's not that Snow can't deliver a fine ballad; it's just that tracks this overtly light, with breathy backup vocals and a hollow, atmospheric sound, just aren't characteristic of his best work. Plus, this is a true collaboration with Kelly Foxton, who possesses a pleasant, though nondescript voice, with the vocals being equally split between the two. The absence of both a solitary upbeat track and a sample of Snow's exemplary guitar playing is probably going to turn off hardcore fans as well. In the end, it seems that all of these factors made this album fade into obscurity about as quickly as Snow's duet partner did, and it appears few people have chosen to remember this effort at all. *—Matt Fink*

The Singing Ranger: 1949–1953 / 1989 / Bear Family ✦✦✦✦✦
Bear Family's *The Singing Ranger: 1949-1953* contains every song Hank Snow recorded for RCA in the beginning of his career. Not only are career-making songs like "I'm Movin' On," "Marriage Vow," and "The Rhumba Boogie" included, but so is a wealth of unreleased songs and alternate takes. For die-hard Hank Snow fans, this first volume of *The Singing Ranger* series is the most essential of the three. *—Stephen Thomas Erlewine*

★ **I'm Movin' On & Other Country Hits** / 1990 / RCA ✦✦✦✦✦
I'm Movin' On & Other Hits doesn't have all the hits Hank Snow had over the course of his career, but it has 20 essential tracks from the early '50s, including "The Rhumba Boogie," "Silver Bell," "The Wreck of the Old '97," "Marriage Vow," and the title track. These are the songs that made his career and while he had decades worth of other hits, this disc gives you an accurate sense of what Snow accomplished. *—Stephen Thomas Erlewine*

The Singing Ranger, Vol. 2 / 1990 / Bear Family ✦✦✦✦✦
Running from 1953 to 1958, the four-disc box set *The Singing Ranger, Vol. 2* contains everything Hank Snow recorded during those five years, including all the hits and a bevy of outtakes. Again, the set is not for the fairweather fan—there's plenty of brilliant music here, but its very scope makes it appealing only to completists, who will find much to treasure. *—Stephen Thomas Erlewine*

The Thesaurus Transcriptions / 1991 / Bear Family ✦✦✦✦
So what's to say about five CDs worth of unreleased Hank Snow material from 1950-1956, some of the artist's hottest years? Thesaurus was an RCA imprint that recorded nothing

but radio transcriptions. Snow recorded 138 tracks, none of which were ever released to the public, all of which are included here, completely remastered from master tapes and acetates. Snow is accompanied on the vast majority of these tracks by his Rainbow Ranch Boys, and some heavy company such as Chet Atkins, steel player Joe Talbot, and fiddler Curly Wise. Problem is, these details had to be fleshed out by the researcher who wrote the liner notes, Charles Wolfe. Most of the sessions say "Hank Snow, voice and guitar, other details unknown." It doesn't matter, though, fans of Snow will be able to readily recognize when guests appear and when the band is popping off many his classics, as well as many more obscurities. The sound quality on this set is astonishingly good considering the original condition of much of the source material. While it's true that RCA treasured Snow almost from the beginning for his earning power and his prestige in the country market, archival standards were not what they are today, and deterioration was inevitable. But the folks in the Bear Family lab painstakingly remastered these tapes, getting rid of most of the hiss, but leaving enough to include all the music. *The Thesaurus Transcriptions* are also not hindered in any way by the continuing practice of including intros and outros—like the *Jim Reeves & Friends set*. The honky tonk music flows fast, free, and passionately from Snow's deep Canadian folk-rooted voice. In listening to "Weary Blues" on disc one or "Then I Turned and Walked Away" from disc four, or "Do Right Daddy Blues" from disc five—and all of these are random examples, you could have chosen dozens of others—one can hear, in the grain of Snow's voice, what made him connect with people in the same way they connected with Hank Williams: simplicity and directness. Snow took care never to hide his voice and words behind arrangements or instrumental flourishes—even when a picking duel occurred in his songs—he went straight for the heart of the vocal and dragged it up to the top of the mix and let the story fall in front of the listener, bringing them into the song, whether it was a gospel tune; a Western swing blues; a somber, lovelorn ballad; or a honky tonk good-time dance tune. Snow sang them all the same way: to the listener. He could move from his lovely baritone to a lilting tenor as a device for getting a lyric, not an arrangement, across. What makes these tracks even more special is that since Snow wasn't bound by having to make records for sale, for commercial gain, he and his band felt no pressure in performing them. There is a relaxed, easy, strolling atmosphere present in all of the *Thesaurus* sessions; toward the end of 1952 and on until 1956, the sessions became sort of a social gathering for Snow and his musicians, a workshop for songs such as "Fire on the Mountain," "The End of the World," "Pins and Needles," "The Streamline Cannonball," "Blue Dreams," "The Sun Has Gone Down on Our Love," "Whispering Hoper," and literally dozens of others. Often the Thesaurus versions are superior to the more familiar commercially recorded ones for this very reason. It's not so much that they're so raw, because Snow was a consummate professional, but they are fresher, more immediate, without the usual distance between a recording set in time and space and the listener at the other end of the speakers. This is a set that will be of supreme interest not only to Snow collectors, but to those who collect vintage country music as well. There is nothing here that should have been discarded—except some of the corny photos in the booklet—and none of it rings the least bit contrived or untrue. This is one of the most important box sets that Bear Family has ever done. *—Thom Jurek*

☆ **The Singing Ranger, Vol. 3** / 1994 / Bear Family ✦✦✦✦✦

This is the third collection of Hank Snow's recordings issued by Bear Family, and covers a period not generally considered to encompass his biggest hit-making years (1958-1969, with some tracks from 1974 added for perverse measure). Yet he still managed to record some 320 songs, own two radio stations and two publishing companies, and open a music store and a music school! This third box set in the Snow legacy is staggering in scope. It contains 12 CDs, packed full, a book of rare interview dialogue with Snow, complete session works, and so many rare photographs they will leave the prospective buyer agape. The sound is pristine and painstakingly mastered, and the presentation is sublime. This is one of those sets that Bear Family does—like the other two—that makes a music fan wonder why other companies even bother to reissue archival material at all. As for the music itself, along with some of the most adventurous material Snow ever recorded, there are 14 completely unissued tracks —12 from the years that span the time frame of the box and two from a 1974 session added as a bonus. These were the years that Snow felt perhaps the most conflicted about the changes in Nashville, but nonetheless tried to ride the countrypolitan wave without selling his soul. By the sound of these masters, he was very successful. Along with his entire second tribute to Jimmie Rodgers called *Hank Snow Sings Jimmie Rodgers Songs* (with clarinet and trumpet to add to the author's jazz arrangements, from which, fantastically, no singles were ever issued), there are also two year's worth of material, from both 1959 and 1960, where Snow never recorded anything *but* singles! These tracks include Leon Payne's "I Heard My Heart Break Last Night," J.D. Loudermilk's "Father Time and Mother Love," Ted Harris' "Chasin' a Rainbow," "The Last Ride," "The Tramp's Story," and Cowboy Jack Clement's "The Man Behind the Gun," as well as some stunning instrumentals for B-sides, like "Hawaiian Sunset" and "Casey's Washerwoman Boogie" (with the Rainbow Ranch Boys). Also included is one of the most moving of Snow's originals, co-written with M.I. MacIntyre, called "My Nova Scotia Home." But it was in the year that Snow began recording albums again that things really got interesting for a number of reasons: first, his—and Chet Atkins'—choice in material for the period, and second, the variety of settings Snow found himself working in. Among the most satisfying and revelatory examples of his ability to put country-styled R&B across with a stripped-down band of just himself and Sleepy McDaniels on bass are "Life Time Blues" and "Sleepy Maple Leaves." The bigger-band material is also phenomenal, when one considers that Atkins was hiring people like Tompall Glaser, Velma Smith, Howard White, and Roy Huskey to play on Snow's sessions that early on. There are the usual barflies as well, among them Floyd Cramer, Chubby Wise, Gene Martin, and Doug Kirkham, too. Materially, from Payne's "I Love You Because" and Don Gibson's "A Legend in My Time" to "Fraulein," Marty Robbins' "I'll Go on Alone," and Webb Pierce's "That Heart Belongs to Me," Snow was deepening the grain of his country music background with slicker players. And it makes for an interesting dichotomy. But Snow was not immune to the 1960s. As the years roll on, listeners hear the sessions becoming more and more complex and the material expanding to include borderline pop songs. The rub is that Snow's voice was so fine in interpreting them, and in capturing their grain inside his own. There is Leiber & Stoller material here in "The Man Who Robbed the Bank at Santa Fe," as well as Billy & Bud Mize's "Call of the Wild," Marvin Rainwater's "Gonna Find Me a Bluebird," Buddy Knox's "Hula Love," Loudermilk's darkness-drenched "Break My Mind," John Hartford's "Gentle on My Mind" (a great version, too), an album of material by the poet Robert Service (!), a choogling little Christmas album, and the best train song album ever made. Along with these aberrations are the classic cowboy songs, train songs, love songs, geographical ballads and anthems, and historically sound country tunes that built the stature of the music. Snow was entrenched but had an open mind—more open than most, anyway. Ultimately, the '60s proved to be fertile for Snow, more fertile than he could have imagined at the time, partially because he was frighteningly engaged in living it, and partially because he didn't experience the same chart success he had in the '50s, though it was by no means a failed run commercially. These recordings help to fill out the portrait of one of the most vital artists to ever make it out of Nashville, and who remained true to his country roots to the end, no matter how adventurous and experimental his muse got. This is essential Snow, anyway you cut it. *—Thom Jurek*

Yodelling Ranger (1936–1947) / 1994 / Bear Family ✦✦✦✦✦

The Yodelling Ranger (1936-1947) is a five-disc box set containing all of Hank Snow's early recordings, including all of his material for RCA Canada and several unreleased songs, alternate takes and rarities. This material is primarily of interest to hardcore Snow fans—there aren't many well-known hits on the collection, but there are good versions of contemporary hits, as well as several answer records—but for those dedicated listeners, the set's comprehensiveness and loving liner notes are a worthwhile investment. Consumer warning: the fifth disc contains just four tracks—a two-part "Life Story" and two demos. *—Thom Owens*

The Singing Ranger, Vol. 4 / Apr. 4, 1995 / Bear Family ✦✦✦✦

My Early Country Favorites / 1996 / RCA Camden ✦✦

The material on this compilation isn't bad at all, featuring Snow on some of his more traditional performances. The problem is in the packaging—there are only ten tracks, there's absolutely no annotation, and the sound quality is substandard, with noticeable surface noise throughout. The music is all right, but there's got to be better ways to get it. *—Richie Unterberger*

Singing Ranger / Mar. 26, 1996 / RCA Camden ✦✦✦

Not to be confused with the Bear Family multi-disc set of the same name, this *Singing Ranger* disc is a handy 12-song collection of Snow material from Snow's early period (1949-53) on RCA-Victor, of which only one appeared on the out-of-print RCA best-of disc. The material includes fast-paced romantic numbers ("Honeymoon on a Rocket Ship"), bluesy numbers ("Mississippi River Blues"), sentimental ballads ("The Engineer's Child," "I Cried But My Tears Were Too Late"), and obligatory train songs ("Ben Dewberry's Final Run," which sounds a lot like the blues standard "Casey Jones," with the steel guitar mimicking a train whistle). There are no notes or any other information, and some of the sources betray surface noise, but most of this sounds pretty good. *—Bruce Eder*

★ **The Essential Hank Snow** / Apr. 29, 1997 / RCA ✦✦✦✦✦

In 1997, *The Essential Hank Snow* replaced *I'm Movin' On & Other Country Hits* as the one essential, single-disc retrospective of Snow's classic hits currently on the market. While it isn't quite as listenable as its direct predecessor, *The Essential* still captures all of Snow's styles, from Hawaiian music and country boogie to his famous traveling songs, featuring most of his best-known songs ("I'm Moving On," "The Rhumba Boogie," "Yellow Roses," "Silver Bell," "The Gal Who Invented Kissin'") along the way. *—Stephen Thomas Erlewine*

Yodelling Ranger: Young Hank Snow 1936–1943 / Mar. 16, 1999 / Bear Family ✦✦✦✦

Country Legends / May 15, 2001 / Buddha ✦✦✦

Wanderin' On—The Best of the Yodeling Ranger / Apr. 2003 / Bear Family ✦✦✦✦✦

Bear Family Records in Germany really like Hank Snow. They have done no less than six box sets totaling 39 CDs. And now number 40. These are the earliest of Snow's recordings, cowboy done in his native Montreal, Canada; they commence in a 1936 church recording session, and the last are from Victor's Montreal studios in 1947. Of the 25 tracks included here, Snow wrote all but six. The others are by legends like Bob Nolan and Roy Rogers. The most interesting aspect of these recordings—most of them feature Snow and his guitar only—is how much they push the envelope of the cowboy genre. There are many yodeling songs here, and songs of the range, but there are also some hard-rambling blues tunes in the tradition of Jimmie Rodgers, such as "San Antonio Mama," with killer slide work, and "Hobo's Last Ride," which is almost a Hank Williams ballad (as are "The Blue Velvet Band" and its sequel, "Answer to the Blue Velvet Band"). As for some of the earlier honky tonk material coming right out of the cowboy tradition, there is "We'll Never Say Goodbye, Just Say So Long" and Snow's amazing cover of the Walker/Sullivan classic "When My Blue Moon Turns to Gold Again." "Blue Ranger," with its lap steel, is a lonely cowboy lament that rings as true as anything that Gene Autry ever sang. And then there are the folk songs, like "The Night I Stole Old Sammy Morgan's Gin," with a 12-string. One can almost hear Phil Ochs singing this one at *Gertie's Folk City*. What this set proves is nothing less than that Snow was indeed every bit the innovator that Williams was, as both a songwriter and as a communicator. He may not have had Williams' voice, but Williams couldn't play guitar the way Snow could, either. This set is no less than amazing in that it reveals Snow arriving on the scene in full possession of his singular talent. You may not want six box sets of the man, but this is an album that historical country music fans should own. *—Thom Jurek*

Son Volt

f. 1994

Group / Alternative Country-Rock, Alternative Country, Americana

After touring in support of their 1993 masterpiece *Anodyne*, the seminal alternative country band Uncle Tupelo split up over long-simmering creative differences between co-leaders Jay Farrar and Jeff Tweedy. Tweedy recruited much of the band to form Wilco, while Farrar teamed up with original Tupelo drummer Mike Heidorn to form Son Volt, the more tradition-minded of the two Tupelo offshoots. Joined by brothers Jim (bass) and Dave Boquist (guitar, fiddle, banjo, fiddle, steel guitar), the band signed to Warner Bros. and released its debut album, *Trace*, in 1995. It was greeted with excellent reviews from most critics, offering a set of stark, subtle, mostly downbeat songs that drew from traditional country, folk, and roots rock. The single "Drown" was successful on both college and rock radio, and the band subsequently added unofficial fifth member Eric Heywood on mandolin and pedal steel for its second album. *Straightaways* (1997) mined territory similar to *Trace* and again received positive reviews, though some found Farrar's lack of creative progression troubling. *Wide Swing Tremolo* (1998) was a somewhat harder-rocking affair, but the erosion of critical support for the group continued. They ended up on an unofficial hiatus (rumors of their breakup were denied), and Farrar mounted a solo career with 2001's *Sebastopol*, putting the future of Son Volt in further doubt. —*Steve Huey*

● **Trace** / Sep. 19, 1995 / Warner Bros. ✦✦✦✦✦

Jay Farrar always provided the darkest, grittiest moments in Uncle Tupelo, so it comes as no surprise that Son Volt is a rawer record than *A.M.*, the first album by Wilco, a band led by his former partner Jeff Tweedy. Throughout Son Volt's debut *Trace*, the group re-works classic honky tonk and rock & roll, adding a desparate, determined edge to their performances. Even when they rock out, their is a palpable sense of melancholy to Farrar's voice, which lends a poignancy to the music. *Trace* isn't a great step forward from Tupelo's last album, the lovely *Anodyne*, but it is a fine continuation of the ideas Farrar has pursued over the course of his career. —*Stephen Thomas Erlewine*

Straightaways / Apr. 22, 1997 / Warner Bros. ✦✦✦✦

Although none of the songs on *Straightaways* immediately jump off the grooves, as was the case with the band's brilliant debut, *Trace*, repeated spins reveal a strong effort nonetheless. Whereas former Uncle Tupelo partner Jeff Tweedy and his band, Wilco, used its sophomore release to explore new territory, Son Volt leader and songwriter Jay Farrar keeps his band mining the same country-folk vein that Uncle Tupelo quarried. There are plenty of threads to connect *Straightaways* to *Trace*, such as the expressive playing of multi-instrumentalist Dave Boquist on guitars, fiddle, banjo, and lap steel, and Farrar's forlorn vocal delivery, which could give even the weakest song emotional power. On *Straightaways*, his songs live on the same late-night backwoods rural highways that *Trace* inhabited, with song titles like "Creosote" and "Cemetery Savior" conjuring up dark imagery. The album contains plenty of high points: the aforementioned songs, as well as the lonesome "Back Into Your World" and "Last Minute Shakedown." And the only place it comes up short is the lyrics—unlike *Trace*, whose songs "Windfall" and "Tear Stained Eye" stood by themselves and provided a universal feel and emotion that was easily grasped, much of the lyrical content of *Straightaways* seems open-ended and fragmented, with the intensity building on the haunting instrumental arrangements and Farrar's affecting vocal phrasing. —*Jack Leaver*

Wide Swing Tremolo / Oct. 6, 1998 / Warner Bros. ✦✦✦

While Son Volt's first two albums, *Trace* and *Straightaways*, received critical acclaim, they are both very restrained and sparse works underlain with languidness. These albums hinted, in their best moments, at Son Volt's potential to both write beautiful songs and rock out, but the band never seemed to completely let loose and turn it up to 11. Part of this may stem from their eclectic mix of musical influences. While the juxtaposition of styles ranging from country to bar-band rock & roll has been the key to Son Volt's sound, it has also been a point of contention for those who have criticized them for not knowing what sort of band they wanted to be. *Wide Swing Tremolo* represents an attempt to somewhat break the mold of the earlier releases, especially from the intensely sparse *Straightaways*. *Wide Swing Tremolo* is a wide-open, rocking album with precious little of the overt country influences found on previous Son Volt works. Instead, this album is driven by R.E.M.-like arpeggio guitar riffs and muscular, warm rhythms. It's a strong album. —*Matthew Hilburn*

Jo-El Sonnier

b. Oct. 2, 1946, Rayne, LA

Accordion, Vocals, Guitar / Americana, Traditional Cajun, Progressive Country

There have been better-known figures than Jo-El Sonnier within the Cajun music tradition of Louisiana. And there have been Louisiana musicians, such as Doug Kershaw, who have taken simplified versions of Cajun music to Nashville and experienced greater success in the world of country music. But no one has moved as easily between Cajun and country music as Sonnier, and no one is as well respected as a bridge between musical traditions. A fixture of the traditional Cajun scene, Sonnier has also reached the top levels of the country charts and brought his energetic accordion sounds to recordings by artists ranging from Bob Dylan to Steven Curtis Chapman.

Sonnier was born the son of French-speaking sharecroppers near Rayne, LA. He was raised in extreme poverty, often working in the cotton fields with his parents. Sonnier began playing his much older brother's battered accordion at age three and was soon known as something of a Cajun-music prodigy. He first performed on the radio when he was six (on Crowley, LA, station KSIG) and was recording by 11. As a teenager Sonnier became a well-established Cajun musician, recording four albums and at least a dozen singles on regional Louisiana labels. (Some were reissued in 2000 on the *Cajun Valentino* album, whose title referred to Sonnier's billing at the time.) He moved to California in search of wider fame in the early '70s, landing session work and making

friends among the Los Angeles music elite, and he seemed to have stardom within his grasp when he was signed to the Mercury label's Nashville division. Sonnier's Mercury releases attempted to make him into a Lousiana version of the wildly successful Freddy Fender, mixing his accordion with Nashville electric bass guitars and including French-language passages in some songs. Sonnier experienced little commercial success at the time, but his Mercury material continued to amass fans and was reissued in its entirety in 1992.

Meanwhile, Sonnier temporarily gave up on country music and returned to Lousiana, cutting the Grammy-nominated *Cajun Life* album for the Rounder label. Merle Haggard tapped Sonnier as an opening act in the early '80s, and renewed contacts with California musicians such as Albert Lee, who was then helping to spearhead Nashville's traditional-country revival as part of Emmylou Harris' Hot Band, led Sonnier to take another shot at recording in Nashville. Signed to RCA, he released the album *Come On Joe* in 1987. The album coincided with the crest of the late-'80s neo-traditionalist wave, and Sonnier soon was sharing country airwaves with the likes of Randy Travis as the album spawned two Top Ten singles, the ballad "No More One More Time" and a ferocious cover of British folkster Richard Thompson's Cajun-inspired "Tear-Stained Letter."

Sonnier moved to Capitol in the early '90s, but the new trend toward country music rooted in '70s rock left him behind. Although his country career never really recovered, Sonnier remained in heavy demand as a Nashville session player. Sonnier appeared on recordings by Alan Jackson and Harris and went far beyond country music with guest slots on releases by Elvis Costello and Edie Brickell & New Bohemians. He also had success as a songwriter; both Patty Loveless and George Strait recorded Sonnier's "Blue Is Not a Word," and he consistently placed songs on albums by other artists in the late '80s and early '90s. Sonnier also dabbled in acting, appearing in the films *Mask, They All Laughed*, and *A Thing Called Love*. Finally he returned to pure Cajun music and to the Rounder label, where he teamed with Beausoleil's Michael Doucet on several 1990s releases. A second Grammy nomination came Sonnier's way for the 1997 release *Cajun Pride*, and he joined fellow Louisianan Eddy Raven for the album *Cookin' Cajun*. Sonnier toured widely, performing at the New Orleans Jazz Festival and the *Grand Ole Opry* (in 1999) and visiting Europe and South America. His self-released album *Cajun Blood* won him a third Grammy nomination, one for the 2001 Best Traditional Folk Album award. By the early 2000s, Sonnier seemed to have found his niche: He was a true ambassador of French-descended Louisiana. —*James Manheim*

Cajun Valentine / 1979 / Goldband ✦✦✦

Hurricane Avory / 1979 / Goldband ✦✦

Scene Today in Cajun Music / 1979 / Goldband ✦✦

Cajun Life / 1984 / Rounder ✦✦✦

Jo-El Sonnier, like Jimmy C. Newman, has found a comfortable middle ground between traditional Cajun and contemporary country music, working both styles and achieving a measure of commercial and aesthetic success in each. This session accented the Cajun side, although it included competent pop/country material as well. Besides the autobiographical title track, Sonnier demonstrated his roots facilty on "Yes Yeux Bleu," "Jolie Blon" and "Les Grands Bois." Sonnier has gone on to become a bigger name in country, but this earlier date will appeal to both lovers of vintage material and those unaware of his solid Cajun skills and background. —*Ron Wynn*

● **Come on Joe** / 1987 / RCA ✦✦✦✦✦

Sonnier's French-Cajun accent brings new life to songs by Randy Newman, Richard Thompson, Moon Martin, and Dave Alvin. Steve Winwood takes an organ solo on a cover of Slim Harpo's "Raining in My Heart." Cajun-tinged contemporary country with a rock edge and intelligent songs, it is the best of Sonnier's Nashville work. —*Brian Mansfield & Mark A. Humphrey*

Have a Little Faith / 1990 / RCA ✦✦✦

The emphasis here lies more heavily on ballads, as Sonnier discovers John Hiatt and delivers penetrating versions of his "Have a Little Faith" and "I'll Never Get Over You." The album also includes a remake of Iry LeJeune's 1945 "Evangeline Special" and a straight-country single in "If Your Heart Should Ever Roll This Way Again." —*Brian Mansfield*

Tears of Joy / 1991 / Liberty ✦✦✦

The Complete Mercury Sessions / 1992 / Mercury ✦✦✦✦✦

Here are 15 fine '70s country songs, including the aching "Blue Is Not a Word." —*Mark A. Humphrey*

Hello Happiness Again / Sep. 28, 1992 / Liberty ✦✦✦

Cajun Roots / May 28, 1994 / Rounder ✦✦✦✦

Cajun Young Blood / Jul. 29, 1996 / Ace ✦✦✦✦✦

This is a cool collection of 28 sides recorded at Goldband Studios in Lake Charles, LA, in the late '60s and early '70s. Sonnier is an accomplished traditional Cajun accordionist and singer, and some of the sides here are in the straight-ahead Cajun mold. But this was also a time at which outside influences were creeping into the region, and this stuff is most interesting when it absorbs odd traces of rock, blues, and country. "Jump Little Frog," for instance, has an organ that wouldn't sound out of place on a Sir Douglas Quintet record; "Rolling Pin (Special)" has a fuzzy rock guitar; "Monkey on My Back" is a classy honky tonk-ish tune. He sure sounds like he's trying to replicate Norman Greenbaum's classic guitar riff from "Spirit in the Sky" on "Tasso Gumbo." That might sound too off-the-wall for Cajun purists, but for the general listeners that means that this is a far more diverse, and hence more enjoyable, Cajun anthology than most. —*Richie Unterberger*

Live in Canada / Oct. 1, 1996 / Stony Plain ✦✦✦

Cajun Pride / Apr. 8, 1997 / Rounder ✦✦✦

Among the ranks of great Cajun accordionists, Jo-El Sonnier stands tall. As a major purveyor of the traditional legacy of his culture, his records have won recognition with three Grammy nominations for Best Traditional Folk Album: with *Cajun Life* in 1984, *Cajun Pride* in 1997, and *Cajun Blood* in 1999. All of Sonnier's music speaks to the great pride that the Cajun people take in their culture. They have left countries to protect it, resisting oppressive attempts to interfere with their French language and religious practices. After fleeing first France and then Canada, the Acadian people settled in the wetlands of southwest Louisiana. Even in the land of the free, others were intolerant of Cajun folkways. They were persecuted and punished for them. They resisted and ultimately they prevailed. At last the world has come around to appreciating what the Cajun people have to offer, as their music, food, and *joie de vivre* are celebrated everywhere. So it is with a special feeling for the word that Jo-El Sonnier sings of *Cajun Pride*. Playing accordion and guitar on the album, Sonnier is joined by an array of fine musicians, including Michael Doucet and Tony Thibodeaux on fiddles, David Doucet on guitar, Junior Martin on steel guitar, David Egan on piano, Peter Schwartz on bass, and Danny Zeringue on drums. The play list on the CD reflects the Cajun reverence for tradition and love of dance, with old songs from the masters such as Nathan Abshire's signature tune, "Pine Grove Blues," and Lawrence Walker's "Midnight Waltz." There are plenty of traditional waltzes and two-steps, along with some tunes from the pen of Sonnier, including his "Jolie Fille." There is a fun-loving nod to the R&B genius of Chuck Berry: "Johnny B. Goode" goes Cajun in "Johnnie Fais Bien." The rest of the pieces are just great old Cajun favorites, the kind that young and old alike can dance to at the fais do do, proudly enjoying the cultural heritage that is uniquely their own. —*Rose of Sharon Witmer*

Cajun Blood / Nov. 16, 1999 / Sonnier International ✦✦✦
Cajun musician extraordinaire Jo-El Sonnier pays tribute to his heritage in his 1999 CD release *Cajun Blood*. The album is dedicated to his mother and father, who raised their family near Rayne, LA, deep in Cajun country. It was there that the young Jo-El Sonnier was steeped in the traditions of his culture and started playing the accordion at the age of three. Now a master of the instrument, Sonnier is a favorite of audiences all over the world who enjoy his special brand of traditional Cajun music. He is known for his singing as well as his playing—he was honored at the 1999 Golden Music Awards as male vocalist of the year. Sonnier brings those talents to bear on *Cajun Blood*, which was nominated for a Grammy in 2001 as Best Traditional Folk album. The recording opens with the title track, sung in French, and closes with another rendition of the song in English. Being bilingual is an option that Sonnier can now freely exercise. Cajuns have left behind the past oppression they endured, first in France, then in Canada, and finally in Louisiana, where they were shamed and punished for practicing their language and ways. Always, the proud Cajuns resisted attempts to destroy their culture. Today that culture is recognized for its unique contributions by mainstream society, affirming the pride Cajun people always have had in their heritage. Sonnier is ably assisted on the CD by musicians including Waylon Thibodeaux and Kenny Sears on fiddles, Brian Langlinais and Joe McMahon on guitars, and Joe Wright on pedal steel. Together, they perform traditional favorites, such as the "Allons a Lafayette"; standards, including D.L. Menard's signature tune, "The Back Door," Lawrence Walker's "Yo Yeux Noir," and Nathan Abshire's "Valse de Bayou Teche"; as well as songs penned by Sonnier himself. As the recording ends with the English version of "Cajun Blood," listeners are left knowing why those who carry Cajun blood are so proud of it. —*Rose of Sharon Witmer*

The Sons of the Pioneers

f. 1934, Central Valley, CA
Group / Traditional Country, Cowboy
The Sons of the Pioneers were the foremost vocal and instrumental group in western music, and the definitive group specializing in cowboy songs, setting the standard for every group that has come since. They were also one of the longest-surviving country music vocal groups in existence. More important than their longevity, however, the greatest achievement of the Sons of the Pioneers lay with the sheer quality of their work. Their superb harmonies and brilliant arrangements delighted three generations of listeners and inspired numerous performers.

The group's roots lay in the depths of the Great Depression, a time when the American spirit, and the spirits of millions of Americans, had nearly been broken by physical, economic, and emotional privation. Cincinnati-born Leonard Slye (born November 5, 1911) had headed out to California in the spring of 1931 from his native Ohio, working jobs ranging from driving a gravel truck to picking fruit for the Del Monte company in California's Central Valley. By sheer chance, he entered an amateur singing contest on a Los Angeles radio show called *Midnight Frolics* and a few days later got an invitation to join a group called the Rocky Mountaineers.

Slye played guitar, sang, and yodeled with the group, and before long they wanted an additional singer so they could extend their range. The man who answered the ad was Bob Nolan (born Robert Clarence Nobles, April 1, 1908, New Brunswick, Canada), from Tucson, AZ. Nolan had lived the life of an itinerant singer for a few years before settling down in Los Angeles, where he'd worked as a lifeguard as well as tried to make a living singing. Nolan joined the Rocky Mountaineers, and he and Slye developed a harmonious relationship that worked for several months, until he exited in frustration over the group's lack of success. Nolan was, in turn, replaced by Tim Spencer (born Vernon Spencer, July 13, 1908, Webb City, MO), who'd been earning his keep working in a Safeway Stores warehouse. Slye, Spencer, and another singer named Slumber Nichols quit the Rocky Mountaineers in the spring of 1932 to form a trio of their own, which never quite came off. Instead, Slye and Spencer spent a year moving in and out of the lineups of short-lived groups like the International Cowboys and the O-Bar-O Cowboys. The latter group broke up following a disastrous tour, and Spencer left music for a time. Slye decided to push on with an attempt at a career, joining yet another group, Jack LeFevre & His Texas Outlaws, who were fixtures on a local Los Angeles radio station.

In early 1933, things began looking up. Slye convinced Spencer to give up the security of a steady job once more, and also recruited Nolan, who was working as a caddy at a golf course in Bel Air. Weeks of rehearsals followed as they honed their singing hour after hour, while Slye continued to work with his radio singing group and Spencer and Nolan wrote songs. The group was called the Pioneer Trio and made its debut on KFWB radio, following an audition that included the Nolan song "Way Out There." Their mix of singing and yodeling, coupled with their good spirits, won them a job. Within a few weeks, they were developing a large following of their own on LeFevre's show, with their harmony singing eliciting lots of mail, and soon they were featured on the station's morning and evening lineups.

The group in its earliest form consisted of Slye, Nolan, and Spencer on vocals, with Nolan playing string bass and Slye on rhythm guitar. A fourth member was needed to firm up their sound, and early in 1934 he arrived in the form of fiddle player Hugh Farr (born Plano, TX, December 6, 1906), who also added a bass voice to the group and occasionally served as lead singer. The group's name was altered by accident on the eve of their going national. On one broadcast, the station's announcer introduced them as "The Sons of the Pioneers." Asked why he'd done this, the announcer gave the excuse that they were too young to have been pioneers, but that they could be sons of pioneers. The name seemed to stick, it fit well, and as they were no longer a trio, it made sense.

The Sons of the Pioneers' fame quickly spread well beyond the confines of Los Angeles, as a result of an informal syndication project undertaken by their station, which recorded the group in 15- and 30-minute segments for rebroadcast all over the country. It wasn't long before a recording contract with the newly founded Decca label (now part of MCA) was signed, and on August 8, 1934 (the same day that Bing Crosby made his debut for the label), the Sons of the Pioneers made their first commercial recording. The group would cut 32 songs with Decca over the next two years.

One of the songs cut at the first session was a Nolan original called "Tumbling Tumbleweeds," which he'd originally written on a rainy day in 1932 as "Tumbling Leaves." The group had introduced it on the radio as "Tumbling Leaves," but later changed it to "tumbleweeds" as more in keeping with their western image. It became their theme song and was quickly picked up by singers and bands all over the country. In 1935, the song was also licensed for use as the title of a Gene Autry Western, the first—but not the last time—that the paths of Autry and the Pioneers would cross. In 1935, a fifth member, Farr's brother Karl (born Rochelle, TX, April 25, 1909), who had played with Hugh on the radio during the 1930s, was added to the group on lead guitar, bringing the Pioneers' instrumental capabilities up to a par with their singing. Early that same year, they began appearing in movies for the first time, initially in short films and also providing the music for an *Oswald the Rabbit* cartoon, before making their first appearance in a full-length movie, *The Old Homestead*. Later that same year, they appeared in *The Gallant Defender*. They followed this with *Song of the Saddle* (1936), starring singer-turned-cowboy star Dick Foran, then with *The Mysterious Avenger* (1936) and the Crosby vehicle *Rhythm of the Range*. That same year, they appeared in a Autry movie, *The Big Show*.

Spencer left the group in September of 1936 and was replaced by Lloyd Perryman (born Ruth, AR, January 29, 1917), who was a fan of the Pioneers as well as a veteran of several singing groups, and who had already served as a "fill-in" Pioneer on occasion. Perryman was later to become a key member of the group, doing most of their vocal arrangements, serving as their on-stage spokesman, and handling the group's business affairs as well, and would remain with them longer than anyone, 41 years. Their broadcasts, concerts, and film appearances continued with work in the Foran-starring *California Mail* at Warner Bros. and Autry's *The Old Corral* at Republic. Finally, in late 1937, the group was signed by Columbia to work in Charles Starrett's Western films on a steady basis, beginning with *The Old Wyoming Trail*.

It was the movies that led to the next major change in the Pioneers' lineup. Slye had previously played bit acting parts in a handful of B-Westerns, including an appearance in a small role in an Autry film, under the name Dick Weston. But in 1938, Autry and the studio found themselves in a contractual dispute that they were unable to resolve, and the cowboy star failed to report for his next movie. Autry was placed on suspension while the studio began looking for a replacement that they could put into the picture. Slye auditioned and won the part and in the process was given a new name for his first starring film: Roy Rogers. *Under Western Stars*, as the film was eventually titled, was a hit, and Leonard Slye/Roy Rogers had a whole new career. In order to do the movie, however, he was forced to leave the Sons of the Pioneers, who were under exclusive contract with Columbia Pictures. To replace Slye, the group chose a friend of his, a singer and comic named Pat Brady, who played bass and handled much of the comedy within the group, although vocally he was weaker than the others, which forced the Pioneers to expand their lineup once more in 1938, with Spencer returning to fill out the harmony parts. The group continued to make movies with Starrett, appearing in 28 movies with him between 1937 and 1941.

The Sons of the Pioneers' recording career kept pace with their movie and radio work. They left Decca Records in 1936 to sign with the American Record Company (later part of Columbia Records) and appeared on that label's OKeh and Vocalion imprints on 32 songs in two sessions in late 1937. Although he'd officially left the group to pursue his film career, Rogers returned to sing with the Sons of the Pioneers on those sessions. The 1938-1942 version of the group, consisting of Nolan, Spencer, Perryman, the Farrs, and Brady, became the "classic" Pioneers lineup, the version of the group most familiar to audiences, largely because of their screen appearances.

In 1941, the group's contract with Columbia was up, and after years of Rogers' entreaties, Republic Pictures signed the Pioneers to appear in his movies, beginning with *Red River Valley* (1941), in which they were billed as Bob Nolan & the Sons of the Pioneers. The same year that they signed their contract with Republic, the group also signed with Decca Records. The American entry into World War II brought about the next change in their lineup. Perryman and Brady were both called up for the draft. Perryman was replaced by Ken Carson while he was fighting with the American forces in Burma, while Brady became a soldier in Patton's Third Army and was replaced by musician and comic Shug Fisher.

In 1944, the Sons of the Pioneers moved to RCA Victor, signed up by the head of company's country music division, Steve Sholes (who was also later responsible for bringing Elvis Presley to the label). They would be associated with RCA longer than to any other label, 24 years broken by a brief one-year stint elsewhere.

The change in labels resulted in the first major alteration in the Pioneers' sound since their founding. Previously, they'd been a self-contained outfit, providing virtually all of the sounds, vocal and instrumental, needed on their records. RCA, however, saw fit to provide the group's music with additional backup in the form of fuller instrumentation, including small-scale orchestration. At first, it worked reasonably well, as the Pioneers re-recorded several of their standards (including "Cool Water" and "Tumbling Tumbleweeds") with new arrangements that proved popular, and many fans regard their mid-'40s versions of their classic songs as the best of the many renditions that they recorded. They also recorded more gospel material as well as many pop-oriented and novelty songs. The Pioneers also provided backup for other performers throughout their time at RCA, including Rogers & Dale Evans, and Vaughn Monroe.

Amid all of this varied activity, which yielded hundreds of songs, they recorded a number of new western classics during their stay on the label, most notably Stan Jones' "(Ghost) Riders in the Sky" in 1949. Originally, Nolan had passed on doing the song, but after it became a hit for Monroe, the Pioneers covered it themselves. The group had ceased appearing onscreen in movies with the end of Rogers' B-Westerns at Republic in 1948, but two years later a new career opened up for them in movies courtesy of John Ford, who used their singing in three of his most acclaimed Westerns: *Wagon Master* (1950)—in which they had four songs, including "Wagons West"—*Rio Grande* (1950), and *The Searchers* (1956). Perryman was back in the lineup in 1946, although his interim replacement, Carson (who later became a well-known singer in his own right on *The Garry Moore Show*), continued to record with the group for another year. During this era, the group made some magnificent recordings; Spencer contributed more than his share of important songs, Fisher contributed as a songwriter, and Perryman took the lead vocals on some numbers. Brady also returned to the lineup later in 1946, and the group continued working in Rogers' Western movies through 1948.

These were golden years for the Sons of the Pioneers. Their hits on the country singles chart included "Stars and Stripes on Iwo Jima" (1945); "No One to Cry To" (1946); "Baby Doll," "Cool Water," and "Tear Drops in My Heart" (1947); "Tumbling Tumbleweeds" and "Cool Water" (1948); and "My Best to You" and "Room Full of Roses" (1949). It wasn't to last, however, as time and changing public tastes were to take their toll on the group. Spencer, who had written many of the group's more important originals, finally left the group in 1949, after several years of worsening problems with his voice. He was replaced by Ken Curtis (born Lamar, CO, July 2, 1916), a former singer with Tommy Dorsey and sometime actor who later became immortalized on television as Festus, Marshal Matt Dillon's grizzled backwoods deputy, on *Gunsmoke*. As a parting gesture, Spencer gave the group one of his best songs, "Room Full of Roses," which became Curtis' first lead vocal with the group. Soon after, Rogers began shooting his television series and recruited Brady as his comic relief sidekick. He was replaced by his wartime fill-in, Fisher. But it was the retirement of Nolan in 1949 that caused the biggest change in the group's lineup. Essentially, his exit came about purely for personal reasons. He was a very private individual to begin with, and 16 years with the Pioneers, although rewarding musically and financially, had begun to wear on him. He wanted more time to himself and more time to write songs. But the gap he left was huge—apart from having written many of the Pioneers' best known songs, Nolan had been the lead singer on many of their hits. He did continue to provide them with songs after his retirement and even rejoined them in the studio.

Perryman stepped into the breech opened by Nolan's exit. He had been taking a leadership role in the group over the previous few years and now took over leadership, recruiting a new sixth member, Tommy Doss (born Weiser, ID, September 26, 1920). Doss was an excellent singer, and his voice meshed beautifully with Perryman and Curtis, but within a year of his joining—through no fault of his—the group's record sales began to decline. There was an overall drop of interest in cowboy songs and western music, which resulted in RCA's attempts to push the Pioneers into the pop vocal market. These efforts failed and simultaneously lost them part of their country audience. Ironically, in 1952, the same year that the Pioneers got their first LP releases, the ten-inch discs *Cowboy Hymns and Spirituals* (made up of recordings from 1947) and *Cowboy Classics* (made up of material from 1945 and 1946), the group also left RCA in the wake of their declining sales figures. They didn't record at all in 1953, but at the end of the year the group signed once again to Coral Records. Simultaneously with the move, Curtis and Fisher both exited the lineup to go into television and film work. They co-starred on one television series, and Curtis would later serve as co-producer on a pair of low-budget horror films at the end of the 1950s, one of which, *The Giant Gila Monster* (1958), would feature Fisher.

They were replaced by Dale Warren (born Summerville, KY, June 1, 1925), a veteran of Foy Willing & the Riders of the Purple Sage, and Deuce Spriggens (born George R. Braunsdorf), a former member of Spade Cooley's band. The group's one-year stay at Coral proved no more successful than the last few years at RCA, however. By 1955 they were back with RCA, where they stayed for another 14 years. In a major change of strategy, RCA now wanted the old Nolan/Spencer sound. Nolan agreed to return to record with the group in the studio, but Spencer was no longer in good enough health or voice to be part of the group, and so Curtis was also asked to return as part of the studio version of the Pioneers. Brady also came back as bassist in the studio. The Sons of the Pioneers, in effect, became two groups—Nolan, Perryman, and Curtis were the studio vocal trio, backed by Brady, Hugh, and Karl Farr, recreating the group's classic sound on record, while Perryman, Doss, Warren, the Farrs, and Spriggens (who left soon after this arrangement began) played the concerts. It wasn't until 1958 that the touring version of the Pioneers began making their records as well.

By that time, more changes had overtaken the lineup. Nolan retired as a singer once and for all, and Hugh Farr, who felt that his fiddle playing wasn't appreciated by the other members, quit as well in 1958. Karl continued as a member, but on September 20, 1961, in the middle of a concert performance, he became agitated over a guitar string that had broken and suddenly collapsed and died of heart failure. The same month, Roy Lanham (born Corbin, KY, January 16, 1923), one of the busiest session guitarists on the West Coast, joined the group as Karl's successor. Brady was also back in the lineup by then, having rejoined to replace Fisher, who retired in 1959. Brady remained with the group until 1967. The next major change in the lineup came in 1963, when Doss retired from touring with the group, although he recorded with them until 1967. In 1968, Luther Nallie joined the group as lead singer and remained with the Pioneers until 1974. They were still very much a going concern, not only on the concert stage but in the recording studio—over a 12-year period from 1957 until 1969, RCA released 21 albums by the group. Nolan and Spencer were both elected the Nashville Songwriter Hall of Fame in 1971. A 1972 gathering at the Ambassador Hotel in Los Angeles brought together most of the surviving members of the Sons of the Pioneers except for Curtis, including a reunion of the original Pioneer Trio of Rogers, Nolan, and Spencer. And in 1976, the Sons of the Pioneers were inducted into the Country Music Hall of Fame.

This was a last hurrah for the original and early group members. Spencer died on April 26, 1976, and Perryman, who had been with the group since 1936, died on May 31, 1977. Farr, who had retired from the group in 1958, passed away on April 17, 1980, and Nolan died almost exactly two months later, on June 16, 1980. After Perryman passed away, the leadership of the Sons of the Pioneers was taken over by Warren, who had joined in 1952. He carried the group into the 1990s. They continued to perform in concert and recorded as well with a lineup that featured Rusty Richards (vocals), Doye O'Dell (guitar, vocals), Billy Armstrong (fiddle), Billy Liebert (accordion), and Rome Johnson (vocals). These Pioneers, along with younger country music groups such as the Riders in the Sky, were a constant reminder of the legacy of this much-loved western group. *—Bruce Eder*

Cowboy Hymns and Spirituals / 1952 / RCA ✦✦✦
The classic postwar Sons of the Pioneers, featuring Bob Nolan, Tim Spencer, Lloyd Perryman, Hugh & Karl Farr, and Pat Brady, doing gospel and spiritual songs. The material, cut in 1947, captures the devotional side of the Pioneers, which was an important alternate side to their songs of the trail. Since supplanted by 12-inch collections containing more songs, but a collectable disc. *—Bruce Eder*

Cowboy Classics / 1952 / RCA ✦✦✦
"Cool Water" and "Tumbling Tumbleweeds," in their 1945 and 1946 versions—often considered the best—with "Blue Prairie," "The Timber Trail," "Trees," and "Cowboy Camp Meetin'." These songs have been compiled elsewhere since, but this is a collectable disc as one of their first two LPs. *—Bruce Eder*

Western Classics / 1953 / RCA ✦✦✦
A second volume of western songs, including "Riders in the Sky," "Red River Valley," "Outlaws," and "Wind." The material covers 1946 through 1951, and the lineups range from Bob Nolan, Tim Spencer, Lloyd Perryman, Ken Carson, Hugh & Karl Farr, and Pat Brady ("Have I Told You Lately That I Loved You") through Nolan, Spencer, Perryman, the Farrs, and Pat Brady ("The Last Round-Up"), and Nolan, Perryman, Ken Curtis, the Farrs, and Brady ("Riders In the Sky"), up through Perryman, Tommy Doss, Curtis, the Farrs, and Shug Fisher ("Wind"). The different lineups are confusing, but this record was a good chance to compare the different postwar versions of the group at their respective bests. *—Bruce Eder*

How Great Thou Art / 1957 / RCA ✦✦✦
The Pioneers' second gospel collection, esentially an expanded version of *Cowboy Hymns and Spirituals*, comprised of recordings done in 1947 up through 1956, with Bob Nolan the common thread through most of it. *—Bruce Eder*

One Man's Songs / 1957 / RCA ✦✦✦
Here is the last new recording by the mid-'50s studio version of the Pioneers, led by Bob Nolan. *—Bruce Eder*

Wagons West / 1958 / RCA Special Music ✦✦✦✦
This is a wonderful sounding CD transfer of a 1958 compilation of some of the group's previously unanthologized (in 1958) songs, ranging from the 1950 vintage title track (which appeared on the soundtrack of John Ford's *Wagon Master*—the premiere of the network-TV series *Wagon Train*, based on the Ford movie, facilitated this release) to 1947's "The Whiffenpoof Song." The Nolan/Perryman/Spencer/Carson version of the group is featured (on "Cowboy Camp Meetin'"), as is the Perryman/Curtis/Doss lineup ("Wagons West"). The singing is impeccable throughout, the sound glowing and crisp, and the songs comprise a solid representation of material beyond the Pioneers' best known hits. The only flaw is a funny one involving the art work—on the 1996 CD reissue, someone at Special Music's art department accidentally had "Wagons East" (the name of John Candy's final film) printed on the jewelbox spine. *—Bruce Eder*

Cool Water / 1959 / RCA ✦
The title and cover art of the 1959 *Cool Water* LP were reused for this very unfortunate CD reissue, on which only half of the original's songs were included, without any notes—the compact disc was something of an insult to the intelligence of the modern listener. What is there sounds good, but the compact disc of *Cool Water* is still an abomination. *—Bruce Eder*

Cool Water (& 17 Timeless Favorites) / 1959 / RCA ✦✦✦✦✦
The LP version of this album—the Pioneers' first in stereo—was generally regarded as the best of the modern group's RCA albums. The first recording of the late-'50s touring lineup of the Pioneers (Lloyd Perryman, Tommy Doss, Dale Warren, and Karl Farr) was chock full of superb harmonies and exquisite arrangements, and became the best selling album in the Pioneers' history. *—Bruce Eder*

Room Full of Roses / 1960 / RCA ✦✦✦
This is a ten-song budget reissue of some of the Pioneers' '40s and mid-'50s songs, all in a romantic vein. *—Bruce Eder*

Lure of the West / 1961 / RCA ✦✦✦
More western material, recorded in November and December of 1960 by Perryman, Doss, Warren, and Karl Farr. Highlights include "Ragtime Cowboy Joe" and "Cimarron." This is rightfully considered one of the modern group's best harmony showcases. —*Bruce Eder*

Westwood Ho! / 1961 / RCA ✦✦✦
Here is a collection of earlier material by the group, covering the '40s and early 1952, through an entire side from 1957. —*Bruce Eder*

Tumbleweed Trails / 1962 / Universal Special Products ✦✦✦✦
This is the last recordings of the group with Karl Farr, from April of 1961, with the group in excellent voice, especially on the title track. —*Bruce Eder*

Good Old Country Music / 1963 / RCA ✦✦

Hymns of the Cowboy / 1963 / RCA ✦✦✦
Here is the modern group's only pure gospel album, recorded in November and December of 1962. —*Bruce Eder*

Our Men out West / 1963 / RCA ✦✦✦
This features solid harmony singing as usual, and some excellent songs, including modern covers of "South of the Border," etc. Recorded in August of 1962, this album featured the first appearance of guitarist Roy Lanham as a member of the Pioneers, and Wade Ray appears on backup fiddle. By this time, the group's arrangements were very slick and modern, and far more sophisticated than the original trio or their 1950's successors. Some of the material on this album later appeared on the compilation *San Antonio Rose*. —*Bruce Eder*

Trail Dust / 1963 / RCA ✦✦✦
The modern Pioneers—Perryman, Tommy Doss, Dale Warren, and Roy Lanham—cover Tim Spencer's songs. —*Bruce Eder*

Down Memory Trail / 1964 / RCA ✦✦✦
This is another nostalgic journey through the west, featuring "Bonaparte's Retreat," "Gone," "Left My Gal in the Mountains," and "Born to Lose," among others, performed by the then current group. —*Bruce Eder*

Country Fare / 1964 / RCA ✦✦✦✦
Here is a country album by the Pioneers, and one unusually strong on the instrumental side, featuring the most impressive guitar array in their history, Roy Lanham joining with guest musicians Neil Levang, and Glen Campbell. It's difficult to imagine that anyone could do an engaging version of a chestnut like "Listen to the Mockingbird," but these guys pull it off, despite the slickness of their arrangements by this time in their history. Some of this material appears on the budget compilation *San Antonio Rose*. —*Bruce Eder*

Tumbleweed Trails / 1964 / Vocalion ✦✦✦
This is a collection of the group's Coral Records material, including their cover of the title song from the Marilyn Monroe movie *River of No Return* from 1954, and a lot of early 1940's recordings ("Home In San Antone," etc.). There can be better collections than this done, unifying the Coral, Vocalion, and early Decca sides. —*Bruce Eder*

Sons of the Pioneers Best / 1964 / Columbia-Harmony ✦✦✦
This is a collection derived from the original Pioneers' short stay at the American Record Company in 1937. It's not the best work of the group, but a necessary addition for any completist. —*Bruce Eder*

Legends of the West / 1965 / RCA ✦✦✦
This features old songs about the West, and about the West's outlaws, including "Jesse James" and "Billy the Kid," "The Strawberry Roan," "O Bury Me Not on the Lone Prairie," etc. It's a powerful retro album by this most retro of western groups. —*Bruce Eder*

The Songs of Bob Nolan / 1966 / RCA ✦✦✦✦
This is a collection of Bob Nolan songs that are far less well known than, but only slightly less compelling than "Tumbling Tumbleweeds" or his other standards. Any real fan will want it, and RCA or Special Music should reissue it. —*Bruce Eder*

The Best of the Sons of the Pioneers / 1966 / RCA ✦✦✦✦
Here is part of RCA's same series with *The Best of Sam Cooke Vol. 2* etc. This release features the middle/late 1950s version of the group in their classic original singles, including "Tumbling Tumbleweeds," "Cool Water," "Riders In the Sky," "The Last Round-Up," and "San Antonio Rose." —*Bruce Eder*

Campfire Favorites / 1967 / RCA ✦✦✦✦
This has more romance of the range ("Don't Fence Me In"), as well as straight romantic ballads ("I Love You Truly") and country songs, as well as re-recordings of old standards. —*Bruce Eder*

San Antonio Rose & Other Country Favorites / 1968 / RCA Special Music ✦✦✦✦

South of the Border / 1968 / RCA ✦✦✦
This is the modern group's December 1967 recordings of more standards, this time in a Spanish/Mexican vein. These sessions also marked the end of Tommy Doss' and Pat Brady's recording careers with the group. —*Bruce Eder*

The Sons of the Pioneers Visit the South Seas / 1969 / RCA ✦✦✦
The final RCA lineup of the group—Perryman, Warren, Nallie, and Lanham—apply their considerable harmony skills to songs associated with Hawaii and other points in the Pacific ("Hawaiian Lullaby," "Tiny Bubbles," etc.), and do surprisingly well with this repertory. —*Bruce Eder*

Riders in the Sky / 1973 / RCA ✦✦
Like the rest of the albums in this RCA mid-priced reissue series, this was a nice idea badly executed. A paltry 18 songs spread over two long-playing discs, and featuring "Cool

Water" and "Riders in the Sky" from the 1940s, but no "Tumbling Tumbleweeds." Also included are "Cigareets, Whusky and Wild Women," "High Noon," "The Ballad of Davy Crockett," "Home on the Range," and "Blue Prairie," but none of this is done with much sense (modern stereo sides are juxtaposed with mid-'40s mono) of order or purpose, other than slapping a collection together. —*Bruce Eder*

☆ **Columbia Historic Edition** / 1982 / Columbia ✦✦✦✦✦
The Sons of the Pioneers' sides for the American Record Company are their least-known body of material—in contrast to their Decca and RCA Victor sides, which have been heavily exploited on CD at various times. This ten-song collection is still the only way to hear their work for the American Record Company, representing not a third of their output on the label. All sides of the group's output are represented, including cowboy and trail songs, gospel tunes and one hot instrumental. Although he'd officially left the group earlier, Leonard Slye (aka Roy Rogers) sang on several of the numbers recorded during the October and December 1937 sessions from which these songs were drawn. Bob Nolan's lead singing makes him a dominant presence (and he gets a solo vocal number here too), but Slye's singing and especially his yodeling on "The Devil's Great Grandson" and his solo number "Cowboy Night Herd Song" give him a chance to show off his abilities to great advantage. Hugh Farr and Karl Farr get to stand in the spotlight with their instrumental virtuosity as well, most notably on "When the Golden Train Comes Down" and "Cajun Stomp," which is essentially their number. The restoration job on these masters—held by the Country Music Foundation—is extraordinary, and the fidelity is a match for recordings made decades later. Columbia Legacy, which owns the American Record Company library, could find a way to be more generous in the programming, but this is one killer CD as it is. —*Bruce Eder*

Tumbling Tumbleweeds / 1986 / MCA ✦✦✦✦
This budget-priced ten-song CD is fairly enjoyable, and doesn't overlap with MCA's *Country Music Hall of Fame*. "I'm An Old Cowhand (From the Rio Grande)" is a great showcase for the guitar skills of Karl Farr and the fiddle virtuosity of Hugh Farr, and "Song of the Pioneers" is a great vehicle for Karl Farr, one of his best performances on guitar. Other songs include the late 1936 re-recording of "Tumbling Tumbleweeds" by the six-man Pioneers, which is otherwise unavailable on CD, "Cool Water," "Blue Bonnet Girl," "Empty Saddles," and "Blue Prairie." The singing, as always, is impeccable. —*Bruce Eder*

Tumbling Tumbleweeds / 1989 / RCA ✦✦✦
This is a mixed bag, combining the new Pioneers—Lloyd Perryman, Dale Warren, Luther Nallie, and Roy Lanham—their re-recording of the title track, "Song of the Land I Love," and "King of the Fools" from late 1968, with early '60s recordings by the previous line-up, including "Ramona," "Chant of the Wanderer," and "He Walks With the Wild and the Lonely." —*Bruce Eder*

★ **Country Music Hall of Fame** / 1991 / MCA ✦✦✦✦✦
Here is the most perfect collection of the Sons of the Pioneers' early work—which is their best work—available, 16 songs, half of which were recorded during the early and mid-'30s by the original group of Bob Nolan, Tim Spencer, Roy Rogers (then known as Leonard Slye), Lloyd Perryman, and Hugh & Karl Farr. No collection of theirs could open with anything stronger than the first two songs the Pioneers ever cut, "Way Out There" and the original, never-to-be-duplicated version of "Tumbling Tumbleweeds." They and the original version of "Cool Water" all rely on the Pioneers' three-part harmonies and their own instruments (acoustic guitars, fiddle, upright bass), sounding like musical gold pouring out of a portal from another age. Some of the songs are topical and, in their way, rather poignant reminders of the Great Depression, such as "When Our Old Age Pension Check Comes to Our Door." Other highlights include "There's a Round-Up in the Sky," "Ride Ranger Ride," "Private Buckaroo" (a topical song about World War II), "When the Moon Comes Over Sun Valley," and one previously unreleased gospel gem from their 1954 stay at Coral Records, "Somebody Bigger Than You and I." —*Bruce Eder*

Wagons West / 1996 / Bear Family ✦✦✦✦✦
Wagons West is a thorough four-disc box set containing 115 songs the Sons of the Pioneers recorded for RCA/Victor during the '40s, when the group was at the height of their popularity. Containing all of their best-known songs and hits like "Cool Water," "Stars and Stripes on Iwo Jima," and "Tumbling Tumbleweeds," plus several unreleased tracks and alternate takes, the set is the most complete portrait of the group's peak that has ever been drawn. Of course, the sheer length and weight of the set means that only musicologists and die-hard fans will find *Wagons West* consistently compelling, yet it still stands as one of the most essential—and comprehensive—western and cowboy box sets ever assembled. —*Thom Owens*

Songs of the Prairie / Nov. 25, 1998 / Bear Family ✦✦✦✦
The title of this stunning five-CD set is a bit misleading, for it contains gospel, Civil War, blues, square dance, and classic (19th century) popular tunes, as well as cowboy songs. And it's an extraordinary addition to the Sons of the Pioneers' output, 151 transcriptions done for Standard Radio of Los Angeles, between 1934 and 1936, the prime early years in the group's history—it's as though 151 Beatles songs from their first year of existence had suddenly turned up—and these have almost all been unheard for more than 60 years. The first four discs offer Sons of the Pioneers as a quartet, Bob Nolan, Tim Spencer, Len Slye, and Hugh Farr in their first flourish of success, beginning in August of 1934. The performances here are different from, and usually more spirited than, the group's Decca recordings. "Way Out There" is a number that the group cut commercially several times over as its lineup changed, but it never sounded fresher than the version here. Another joy of this set is the spotlight given to Hugh Farr—the violinist is showcased in a series of instrumentals, including "Milenburg Joys," "Fire in the Mountains," and "Whistlin' Rufus." And then there is the treat of the fourth and fifth discs, which feature the five-man group lineup, with guitar virtuoso Karl Farr; all of a sudden, the group's playing rises to the level

of its singing, from impressive to downright dazzling as the Farr brothers become a pair of dual sparkplugs in the instrumental mix. Some tracks are in slightly rough condition, but considering that these discs, according to the contracts under which they were licensed, were supposed to be destroyed at the end of their licensing term, just having them around to hear is something close to miraculous. *—Bruce Eder*

The Teleways Transcriptions / Jun. 22, 1999 / Soundies ✦✦✦
Enthusiasts of vintage radio as well as fans of the Sons of the Pioneers will enjoy *The Teleways Transcriptions*, a collection of four complete radio shows recorded in 1947, including intros, humorous between-song patter, and instrumental interludes for the reading of sponsors' messages, not to mention the accomplished playing and harmonies of the Sons. The material ranges from Western, sacred and sentimental songs to novelties and "ethnic" numbers. Unlike many radio transcriptions, on these shows the Sons perform complete songs rather than excerpts. The sound quality of the CD, mastered from transcription discs, is good but not on par with studio recordings, and each complete program is indexed as one track so that individual songs can be accessed only by scanning through the others. *The Teleways Transcriptions* offers an entertaining glimpse at a bygone era of American radio in addition to a wealth of rare recordings. *—Greg Adams*

Memories of the Range: Standard Radio / Jun. 7, 2001 / Bear Family ✦✦✦✦

Symphonies of the Sage / Oct. 23, 2001 / Bloodshot ✦✦✦✦
There's a fascinating mix of the old and new on *Symphonies of the Sage*, 25 radio transcriptions that the Sons of the Pioneers recorded in 1940. First there are the dreamy vocal harmonies of Tim Spencer, Lloyd Perryman, and Bob Nolan conjuring up images of lazy cattle, tumblin' tumbleweeds, and miles of endless prairie. Then there's the instrumental finesse of fiddler Hugh Farr and string-bending guitarist Karl Farr. Songs like the title cut and "Whoopee Ti Yi Yo" feature the Sons of the Pioneers' trademark vocals blending smoothly against a steady swinging beat. Instrumentals like "Cajon Stomp" up the ante on swing and share a common ground with Django Reinhardt and Stephane Grappelli's *Hot Club* work (with the exception being that Farr's guitar is electric on certain cuts). This dynamic combination of traditional harmonies and cutting-edge musicianship will get the blood of the oldest cowboy pumping. Classics like "Happy Cowboy" and "Cool Water" hold up well after 60 years, while the melancholy harmony of the Pioneers can still bring a tear to the eye of the most hardened ranch hand. Greg Adams' liner notes offer a nice historical backdrop to understand how a cowboy band blew into the Windy City in July of 1941. *Symphonies of the Sage* captures a number of dynamic performances by the Sons of the Pioneers and will be warmly welcomed by cowboys and cowgirls alike. *—Ronnie D. Lankford Jr.*

Cigareets, Whusky . . . And Cool, Cool Water / May 21, 2002 / ASV ✦✦✦✦✦
Depending on who you ask, the Sons of the Pioneers' RCA-Victor recordings (1944-1952) constitute either the group's best or second-best work. They enjoyed their greatest chart success during this time, but many rightly feel that these re-recorded versions of their early classics are inferior to the originals. Nonetheless, "Stars and Stripes on Iwo Jima," "No One to Cry To," "Teardrops in My Heart," and the title track were some of the group's biggest hits, and they're all here, although the omission of certain hits of this era (most notably "Baby Doll" and "My Best to You") makes this a somewhat scattershot collection. Still, it's about as good a sampler of the Pioneers' Victor recordings as one can currently find. *—Jim Smith*

★ **Ultimate Collection** / May 21, 2002 / Hip-O ✦✦✦✦✦
For really exhaustive coverage of the work of this groundbreaking cowboy harmony group, you'll want to invest in the Bear Family series; for a quick, budget-priced overview, try this label's *Tumbling Tumbleweeds* compilation. But for a more generously packed and lushly packaged overview collection (at full price), this is an excellent choice. It consists mainly, of course, of all the genre-defining hits you'll expect: "Cool Water," "I'm an Old Cowhand," "Riders in the Sky," "So Long to the Red River Valley," and more. Pre-1937 recordings feature the singing of founding member Roy Rogers, who is heard to particularly fine effect on the gorgeous "Blue Bonnet Girl," and one track (the jazzy "I'm an Old Cowhand") even features a guest vocal by Bing Crosby. The sound is of limited quality, but that's to be expected with vintage recordings. Highly recommended. *—Rick Anderson*

The Essential Collection / Mar. 4, 2003 / Varese ✦✦✦✦✦

Sons of the San Joaquin

f. 1987, California
Group / Cowboy
Joe & Jack Hannah grew up in the Great Central Valley of California, in the shadow of the Sierra Nevada Mountains. They were raised surrounded by cowboy lore and the Sons of the Pioneers songs that their father would sing around the family ranch. It was these early experiences that would later shape the Sons of the San Joaquin. In 1987, Joe's son Lon Hannah—himself an amateur singer—united with his father and uncle for an impromptu performance at his grandfather's birthday celebration. With that, the Sons were born. A chance appearance at the 1989 Elko, NV, Poetry Gathering sparked the interest of cowboy singer Michael Martin Murphey, who invited the trio to perform on his *Cowboy Songs* LP. The Sons signed with Warner Western (an imprint specializing in Western-themed music and poetry), and Murphey produced their 1992 debut, *A Cowboy Has to Sing*. The album was lauded for its effortless re-creation of the harmonies and storytelling that typified the Sons of the Pioneers' material.

Songs of the Silver Screen appeared a year later; the album revived B-movie Western soundtrack material that had originally been recorded by the Pioneers. Released in 1995, *From Whence Came the Cowboy* was the first Sons of the San Joaquin album to feature original material, the majority of which was written by Jack Hannah. For 1997's *Gospel Trails*, the Sons switched to the Western Jubilee Recording Company. The LP was a collection of favorite hymns, performed in the trio's distinctive three-part harmony. *Horses, Cattle & Coyotes* followed in 1999, and *Sing One for the Cowboy* was issued a year later. The trio continued to perform throughout the great American West and the rest of the world. *—Johnny Loftus*

A Cowboy Has to Sing / Jan. 1992 / Warner Bros. ✦✦✦✦
With *The Cowboy Has to Sing*, the Sons of the San Joaquin effortlessly re-create the classic western and cowboy sounds of the Sons of the Pioneers, which results in a thoroughly entertaining listen. *—Thom Owens*

Songs of the Silver Screen / Aug. 3, 1993 / Warner Bros. ✦✦✦✦
The second album released by Sons of the San Joaquin covers the best of Hollywood Westerns, including three songs by Bob Nolan ("Song of the Bandit," "Round Up Time Is Over," "He's Ridin' Home"), but not a complete deluge of familiar songs. As on their debut, the trio walk the line between respect and parody with aplomb, and the result is another delightful album. *—Keith Farley*

From Whence Came the Cowboy / Oct. 31, 1995 / Warner Bros. ✦✦✦✦
On their third album, *From Whence Came the Cowboy*, the Sons of the San Joaquin rely almost entirely on original songs, which are all written in the cowboy and western tradition. If the group wasn't able to write convincingly, the album would be a stilted paean to forgotten ways, but the group effortlessly captures the spirit of the West, making it an evocative and intriguing listen, and their best album to date. *—Thom Owens*

Gospel Trails / May 20, 1997 / Shanachie ✦✦✦

Horses, Cattle & Coyotes / Jan. 19, 1999 / Shanachie ✦✦✦

Sing One for the Cowboy / Oct. 10, 2000 / Shanachie ✦✦✦
The Sons of the San Joaquin aren't real cowboys; they don't even play real cowboys on TV. But they do know a thing or two about the cowboy song. Jack Hannah, Joe Hannah, and Lon Hannah craft a lonesome sound that harks back to the Sons of the Pioneers and other Hollywood rough riders from the '30s and '40s. The Sons of the San Joaquin aren't just a nostalgia act, though. Most of their songs have been written by Jack Hannah, who effortlessly captures the classic style. *Sing One for the Cowboy* gets a sprightly start with "Trail to San Antone," a song filled with dreamy harmony and Rich O'Brien's tasty guitar licks. Dale Morris and Richard Chon's twin fiddles adds a touch of Western swing to upbeat romps like "Texas Plains," while Ray Appleton's harmonica adds a forlorn note to "Rough String Rider." Even the titles of these songs evoke the open plains, mountain ranges, and endless skies of the west: "Sierra Nevada," "California," and "God Gave the Cowboy Montana." Fans will be happy to find no new surprises on *Sing One for the Cowboy*: some things, it seems, are better the way they used to be. *—Ronnie D. Lankford Jr.*

● **Fifteen Years: A Retrospective** / Oct. 8, 2002 / Shanachie ✦✦✦✦✦
If a group can stay together for 15 years, that's reason enough to celebrate. If that group, like the Sons of the San Joaquin, specializes in keeping music from a bygone era alive, the feat is even more special. *15 Years—A Retrospective* celebrates three singers' commitment to the wide-open plains, cattle roundups, and drinking coffee from a tin cup. As with the Sons of the Pioneers, the Hannahs—Jack, Joe, & Lon—fill their romantic odes with lots of close harmony and spare arrangements. Familiar fare—"Happy Cowboy," "Song of the Rover," and "Ghost Riders in the Sky"—mesh with a number of Jack Hannah originals to fashion an album as easy rolling as the prairie wind. The Hannahs' vision of the west is a romantic one: cacti, dusty trails, campfires, coyotes, and ponies litter the landscape. The cowboy might be punching cattle to the day he dies, as in "Utah," but he wouldn't have it any other way. If a song is titled "Anything but a Cowboy," one can be sure that the phrase will be qualified by, "That's why I'll never want to be." For anyone with an interest in '30s and '40s cowboy music, *15 Years—A Retrospective* offers an excellent introduction to one of the best Western revival bands. *—Ronnie D. Lankford Jr.*

The Sons of the West

f. 1936, Fort Worth, TX, **db.** 1942
Group / Traditional Country, Western Swing
The Sons of the West were a Western swing group who played mostly in Amarillo, TX, during the late '30s and early '40s, becoming the Panhandle area's first significant outfit working in that style. They were founded in 1936 by fiddler Son Lansford, a cousin of Bob Wills who'd performed with the Texas Playboys for a time. Lansford actually started the group in Fort Worth but moved them to Amarillo in search of a largely untapped market for music. The Sons ran through 11 members during the course of their brief existence: bassist/lead singer Jimmy Meek (who later assumed leadership of the group when Lansford departed), steel guitarist Billy Briggs (an innovative player who added a seventh string to his instrument in order to play chords), pianist Loren Mitchell, guitarists Freddie Dean and Jess Williams, banjoists Cliff Wells and Jess Robertson, and fiddlers Leonard Seago, Pat Trotter, and Buck Buchanan. They cut an album for Decca in 1938, which featured mostly pop standards, and recorded through 1941, when they scored their biggest hit with "Sally's Got a Wooden Leg" on Columbia. Most of the members were drafted into World War II in 1942, putting an end to the band. Briggs later played around the area with a band called the XIT Boys, which also featured Trotter and Williams, among others. *—Steve Huey*

Sons of the West / Texas Rose ✦✦✦

● **1938–1941** / Texas Rose ✦✦✦✦
This features "There's Evil in You Chillun," "Prairie Queen," "Am I Blue," "Spanish Cavalier," and more. *—AMG*

South Sixty-Five

Group / Contemporary Country
The country group known as South Sixty-Five—or later as South 65—offers boy band lovers a chance to go country, but not completely country. There's enough pop and rock flavor in the group's music to draw in fans of the Backstreet Boys, *NSYNC, and O-Town.

Members of South Sixty-Five are singers Brenton "Brent" Michael Parker, Jerimy Pat Koeltzow, Alfred "Doug" Douglas Urie, Lance Aaron Leslie, and Stephen Phillip Parker. The roots of South Sixty-Five can be traced to Delious Kennedy, one of the members of the R&B vocal quartet All-4-One. With the backing of Rick Blackburn, president of Atlantic Records Nashville, Delious hand-picked the first two members of the new country group, a pair of talented brothers, Stephen and Brent. A nationwide talent search was conducted to find the other three pieces to the puzzle: Jerimy, Doug, and Lance. By 1997, the act was together, polished, and already performing.

Brothers Brent and Stephen were born and raised in California. Brent on March 8, 1977, Stephen on January 31, 1970. They both began singing professionally when they were small children. It seemed the normal thing to do, since their family was a musical one, and performed as the Parker Gospel Group. The brothers went on separately to work with other groups before joining South Sixty-Five. Doug was born on June 27, 1976, in Claremore, OK. He spent his childhood singing along with the country greats he listened to on the radio. He followed more practical steps at first, working as an automobile mechanic, but his love for music was stronger than his need for financial security. It was a need his father understood well. Sadly, just before Doug signed his first recording contract, his father died.

Jerimy is from Hobart, OK. He was born on June 21, 1977. He grew up on a diet of country music television and dreams of stardom. At one time he worked as a construction worker. Besides being a singer, he can play the drums, guitar, and even piano. Lance is from Dallas, TX. He was born on November 14, 1976. His father's love for music was inherited by young Lance, who became a member of his first group when he was only in middle school. In high-school he was part of the choir. When that choir was picked to do backup singing for none other than Garth Brooks, Lance decided that music and performing were the things he wanted to turn into a career. He spent time polishing his skills and getting comfortable on-stage while working in musical revues in an amusement park in Texas. In 1998, South Sixty-Five recorded its self-titled debut album. Some critics thought the songs had a little too much pop style to them, but fans seemed to disagree. Still, when work on the sophomore album, *Dream Large*, started, the guys pulled in a little more country. The second album was released in 2001. In June of that same year, Doug Urie left the group to begin a solo career of his own. *—Charlotte Dillon*

● **South Sixty-Five** / Dec. 1, 1998 / Atlantic ✦✦✦✦

South Sixty-Five is the self-titled debut album from the group with the same name. Members Jerimy Koeltzow, Stephen Parker, Lance Leslie, Doug Urie, and Brent Parker all handle the singing duties on the recording. The music isn't what can be called pure country, bringing a lot of pop/rock and R&B flavor over the barbwire fence and into the pasture. If you think of what Backstreet Boys gone country would sound like, you'll get a good idea of what this revitalizing group has to offer music fans. Even the lyrics and style of songs are the classic boy band fashion of guy in love or guy hurting over the woman who did him wrong, mostly done in sweet harmonies sure to set young female hearts to fluttering. This debut album carries songs like "Baby's Got My Number," "Random Act of Senseless Kindness," "One of the Precious Few," "Love Will Last," and "No Easy Goodbye." Music videos made from the singles that spin off from the album earned South Sixty-Five plenty of exposure on CMT and other country music stations. *—Charlotte Dillon*

Dream Large / May 1, 2001 / Atlantic ✦✦✦✦

Dream Large is the sophomore full-length recording from the country-meets-boy-band group South Sixty-Five (also known as South 65). Members Jerimy Koeltzow, Stephen Parker, Lance Leslie, Doug Urie, and Brent Parker share harmonies on the album. This second full-length offering from the teen heartthrob group was produced by Bobby Huff, and carries tunes that lean a little closer to contemporary country than the debut album did, with its strong essence of pop and R&B. Some of the tracks on *Dream Large* are "Even If," "All I Ever Did," "I Swear to You," "One Moment," and "Only Perfect." After the album was completed, South Sixty-Five found itself dealing with two major changes that hadn't been expected. First, Atlantic Records Nashville, the label the group had signed its first recording deal with, went under, leaving them without a label. Second, Urie left the group, planning to start a solo career. Fans found themselves having to wait for a third album from the band to see what the end results of these changes would be. *—Charlotte Dillon*

Souther-Hillman-Furay Band

f. 1973, Los Angeles, CA

Group / Country-Rock, Soft Rock

Formed in 1973 at the urging of Asylum Records president David Geffen, Souther-Hillman-Furay was the offspring of just about every notable country-rock band. Richie Furay was a founding member of both Buffalo Springfield and Poco; Chris Hillman had been with the Byrds, the Flying Burrito Brothers, and Stephen Stills' Manassas; and J.D. Souther formed Longbranch Pennywhistle with Eagle Glenn Frey, as well as recording a solo record for Asylum and penning tunes for artists like Linda Ronstadt, Bonnie Raitt, and the Eagles. S-H-F's supporting cast also came with impressive credentials, including studio stalwart Paul Harris on piano, Al Perkins (Flying Burrito Brothers, Manassas) on pedal steel guitar, and former Derek & the Dominos drummer Jim Gordon (who also wrote the piano piece that concludes "Layla").

Although the band, which was meant to be a sort of country-rock version of Crosby, Stills & Nash, received a great deal of hype and promotion, things never really gelled. Their debut sold reasonably well, but the aptly titled *Trouble in Paradise* was poorly received. S-H-F broke up shortly thereafter with each member going on to solo careers. Souther released a couple of solo efforts, achieving a minor success with "You're Only Lonely"; Hillman recorded unsuccessfully for Asylum before teaming with former Byrd-mates Roger McGuinn and Gene Clark in McGuinn, Clark & Hillman, and then forming the popular country-rock Desert Rose Band; and Furay, who became a minister in Colorado, made three Christian-influenced albums, as well as re-joining Poco for their 20th-anniversary recording. *—Brett Hartenbach*

● **The Souther-Hillman-Furay Band** / 1974 / Asylum ✦✦✦✦

When David Geffen convinced Richie Furay, Chris Hillman, and J.D. Souther to join forces to form a country-rock supergroup, it seemed like an inspired suggestion. Crosby, Stills & Nash's folk-rock had scored big with a similar idea, while bands such as the Eagles, who recorded for Geffen's Asylum Records, had made some waves commercially in recent years. But despite high expectations along with the history of their members, the Souther-Hillman-Furay Band's 1974 eponymous debut never quite lived up to its promise. The trio, along with steel guitarist Al Perkins, drummer Jim Gordon, and Paul Harris on piano, delivers a collection of ten pleasant, if overall unremarkable tunes in the singer/songwriter, country-rock vein. There are glimmers of past glories by each, but only Furay really connects solidly. His "Fallin' in Love," which opens the record, is a winning, Poco-like rocker, while "Believe Me" is by far its most beautiful track. On the other hand, with the exception of a pair of modest successes, including the lightly funky "Border Town" and the straightforward rock & roll of "Safe at Home," Souther and Hillman's contributions are fairly lightweight. Even "Heavenly Fire," Hillman's heartfelt tribute to former bandmate Gram Parsons, who had died a few months earlier, is a bit lackluster and pales in comparison to the Eagles' "My Man" from the same year. Still, there should be enough here—thanks especially to the Furay tracks—that will at least be of moderate interest to most fans. [Originally released by Asylum in 1974, *The Souther-Hillman-Furay Band* was reissued domestically on CD by the Wounded Bird label in 2002.] *—Brett Hartenbach*

Trouble in Paradise / 1975 / Line ✦✦✦

With producer Tom Dowd, known for his work at Atlantic Records, at the helm, the Souther-Hillman-Furay Band seemed to be distancing itself a bit from its country-rock roots with its second release, the appropriately titled *Trouble in Paradise*. Here the band expands on the funkier aspects of its debut album, while at the same time slipping even closer to the middle of the road. On that record it was former Poco frontman Richie Furay who was responsible for the highlights, but this time out it's J.D. Souther, who penned four of the LP's nine tracks, who leads the way, with "Prisoner in Disguise" (recorded that same year by Linda Ronstadt) and the title cut the standouts. Still, Furay, whose two compositions were dominated by his recent conversion to Christianity, does connect with the lovely "For Someone I Love," which interestingly enough precedes the sleazy rationalizations of Souther's "Mexico." As was the case with the previous album, Chris Hillman's trio of selections, including "Love and Satisfy," which borrows the lyrics for the majority of its first two verses from his and Gram Parsons' "Train Song," are moderately successful, if in the long run somewhat forgettable. Before the recording of the album, original drummer Jim Gordon had left and was replaced by Ron Grinel (Souther also played drums on a couple of tracks), and what must have seemed like a great idea in 1973 was showing signs of unraveling. The band was finished by 1976 following *Trouble in Paradise*'s poor showing, with each of its primary members recording solo records for Asylum within the year. [Originally released by Asylum Records in 1975 and reissued on CD in 2002 by Wounded Bird.] *—Brett Hartenbach*

Southern Pacific

f. 1985, Los Angeles, CA, **db.** 1991

Group / Country-Rock, Contemporary Country, Roots Rock

Southern Pacific formed in 1983 around vocalist Tim Goodman, guitarist John McFee, drummer Keith Knudsen, bassist Jerry Scheff, and keyboardist Glenn D. Hardin. Both McFee and Knudsen were ex-Doobie Brothers; this rock & roll background would continue to tarnish for some the band's country-rock sound. Despite the adversity, Southern Pacific secured a deal with Warner, who issued its self-titled debut in 1985. A mixed bag, the album featured Tom Petty-penned rock songs alongside more countrified material from songwriters like Rodney Crowell. Former CCR bassist Stu Cook replaced Scheff after the first record; Kurt Howell, who had played with Crystal Gayle, took Hardin's place behind the keyboard. The refurbished Southern Pacific lineup issued *Killbilly Hill* in 1986, and the album's cover of Bruce Springsteen's "Pink Cadillac" was a minor hit.

Goodman departed then, to be replaced by vocalist David Jenkins. He was onboard for 1988's *Zuma*, which included Southern's biggest hit, "New Shade of Blue," but left soon after, leaving only McFee, Knudsen, Cook, and Howell. The quartet issued *County Line* in 1989, but it was Southern Pacific's last gasp. Warner released a final greatest-hits collection in 1991. McFee and Knudsen returned to the Doobies; Cook toured with Doug Clifford as Cosmo's Factory; and Howell formed a group called Burnin' Daylight. *—Johnny Loftus*

Southern Pacific / 1985 / Warner Bros. ✦✦✦

Southern Pacific tried to cross country and rock, sometimes with mixed results. Born from the ashes of the Doobie Brothers and Emmylou Harris' Hot Band, Southern Pacific's eponymous debut doesn't have a bad cut on it. Rock songs like Tom Petty's "Thing About You" and "Luann," which was written by Lou Gramm and Mick Jones of Foreigner, dovetail nicely with original cuts and more standard country fare from the likes of Rodney Crowell ("Bluebird Wine") and Chuck Pyle ("Jaded Lover"). In all, the album is a very promising first effort. *—James Chrispell*

Killbilly Hill / 1986 / Warner Bros. ✦✦✦✦

Instead of being weakened by changes in the band's membership, Southern Pacific actually grew stronger with the new lineup, as their second album *Killbilly Hill* demonstrates. Highlights on the record include the title cut and a cover of Bruce Springsteen's "Pink Cadillac" which was a sizable hit. The record is more country than their debut, which makes *Killbilly Hill* all the more highly recommended. *—James Chrispell*

Zuma / Jun. 21, 1988 / Warner Bros. ✦✦✦✦

County Line / 1989 / Warner Bros. ♦♦♦
Following the exit of vocalist/guitarist David Jenkins, *County Line* marked South Pacific's shift toward a more eclectic sound, as evidenced by guest appearances by Carlene Carter and the Beach Boys. —*Jason Ankeny*

● **Greatest Hits** / 1991 / Warner Bros. ♦♦♦♦
Southern Pacific included former members of the Doobie Brothers and Creedence Clearwater Revival who were dedicated to playing modern country music with just a hint of their rock roots. Although the band didn't last long, they did manage to make the country charts on several occasions between 1985-1989. Among the 13 hits included here are "Reno Bound," "New Shade of Blue," "Honey I Dare You," and "Thing About You," which adds Emmylou Harris on vocals. —*Al Campbell*

Killbilly Hill/County Line / Jul. 15, 2003 / Wounded Bird ♦♦♦

Southern Pacific/Zuma / Jul. 15, 2003 / Wounded Bird ♦♦♦

Southern Rail

Group / Traditional Bluegrass
Say the word "bluegrass" and the image in the minds of many will be Southern farmland and Appalachian hollows, but the fact is that there are hotbeds of bluegrass music all over the U.S., including outposts far north of the Mason-Dixon line. From their beginnings in the late '70s, and despite what might be presumed by their name, Southern Rail were a mainstay of the Boston bluegrass scene and were respected as one of the most consistently solid, traditionally oriented bands on the national scene. Formed in 1979, the continuing presence in the band, both artistically and in business dealings, was the husband and wife duo of singer/guitarist Jim Muller and bassist Sharon Horovitch. Both were products of immigrant families. Horovitch's grandparents came from Eastern Europe to Canada around the turn of the century, while Muller, born and raised in Richmond, VA, came from Italian stock on his mother's side and German on his father's. Muller's family was musical, and he gained his first exposure to bluegrass by listening to the *Old Dominion Barndance* show on Richmond's WRVA. He began playing guitar at 15 and got serious about bluegrass when he bought his first banjo around 1974.

While an undergraduate at McGill University in Montreal, where she was born and raised, Horovitch became involved in folk music, especially the French fiddle music of her native Quebec. She met Muller in 1975, when both were graduate students in Boston at MIT—Horovitch eventually earned a doctorate in molecular biology, while Muller's was in geophysics. Early in their relationship, Muller took Horovitch to see a show that featured the legendary Joe Val & the New England Bluegrass Boys as well as to her first bluegrass festival, and she was hooked—charmed especially by the on-stage personas of Val and his band. In 1977 Horovitch and Muller married. In 1978 Muller bought her a standup bass, began to write songs, and Southern Rail debuted as a band in 1979. As is often the case with bluegrass bands, the personnel changed frequently over the years, but Muller and Horovitch held the band together and logged thousands of miles playing music on a "semifull-time" basis in between their careers in science and other pursuits. In all its incarnations, the hallmark of Southern Rail's sound was the ability of Muller and Horovitch to hire first-class musicians to back up Muller's singing and songwriting, although the band also achieved a reputation for excellence in performing traditional material, especially gospel. Most importantly, though, Muller and Horovitch always emphasized the on-stage, entertainment aspect of their music, and this is something that a great many bands in all areas of music often overlook or discount. A Southern Rail show was always fun.

In 1994 the band signed with the respected Florida-based bluegrass specialty label Pinecastle Records, and their first release on that label, *Glory Train*, was nominated as Gospel Album of the Year by the International Bluegrass Music Association. In 1996, two members of the band left to pursue other projects, and Horovitch and Muller considered calling it a good run and folding the band. But, feeling they were having too much fun and had too much music left to play, they recruited Muller's brother Paul to play banjo and brought South Carolinian Bob Sachs in on mandolin. The result was a band that not only maintained its instrumental prowess, but with the combined singing of the Muller brothers, may have achieved its strongest vocal character to date. Another Pinecastle release, *Wasting My Time*, followed in 1998, but as they headed toward their 20th anniversary with six albums under their belts, Southern Rail were making pretty good use of their time. —*John Lupton*

● **Drive by Night** / 1991 / Turquoise ♦♦♦♦♦

Roadwork / 1992 / Turquoise ♦♦♦

Carolina Lightning / 1993 / Turquoise ♦♦♦

Glory Train / 1995 / Pinecastle ♦♦♦

Wasting My Time / 1998 / Pinecastle ♦♦♦

Red Sovine (Woodrow Wilson Sovine)

b. Jul. 17, 1918, Charleston, WV, **d.** Apr. 4, 1980, Nashville, TN
Vocals, Guitar / Traditional Country, Honky Tonk, Truck Driving Country
Though he had a long, distinguished career in country music, singer/songwriter and guitarist Red Sovine is best remembered for his earnest, funny, and at times highly sentimental recitations that took the cab of an over-the-road truck for their settings. Born Woodrow Wilson Sovine into an impoverished family in Charleston, WV, he was inspired as a child by WCHS radio musicians Buddy Starcher and Frank Welling. Sovine and his childhood friend Johnnie Bailes joined Jim Pike's Carolina Tar Heels and performed as "Smiley and Red, the Singing Sailors." They appeared briefly on the powerhouse WWVA *Jamboree* in Wheeling, but Sovine returned to Charleston to get married and took a factory job. He continued to sing on Charleston radio, but his friend Johnnie went on to greater renown as one half of the Bailes Brothers. Bailes continued to encourage Sovine's efforts, however, and in 1947 he assembled a band called the Echo Valley Boys.

After a year of performing in West Virginia Sovine moved to Shreveport, LA, where the Bailes Brothers were performing on KWKH. Sovine's own early morning show snared few listeners, but among his stagemates on the station's *Louisiana Hayride* show was Hank Williams, who steered Sovine toward a better time slot at WFSA in Montgomery, AL, and toward a contract with MGM Records in 1949. Over the next four years he recorded 28 singles, mostly following in Williams' honky tonk footsteps, that didn't make much of a dent on the charts but did establish him as a solid performer. Sovine continued to perform on the *Hayride* and made another valuable friend in fellow performer Webb Pierce, who in the early '50s was just at the beginning of a long string of Top Ten country hits. Pierce convinced Sovine to lead his Wondering Boys band and helped him along toward a contract with Decca in 1954. The following year Sovine cut a duet with Goldie Hill, "Are You Mine?," which peaked in the Top 15, and in 1956 he had his first number-one hit when he duetted with Pierce on a cover of George Jones' "Why Baby Why."

Sovine had two other Top Five singles that year and joined the cast of the *Grand Ole Opry*. After recording close to 50 sides with Decca by 1959, Sovine signed to Starday and began touring the club circuit as a solo act. In Montana in 1963 Sovine passed on the helping hand given him by older performers when he heard the singing of African-American minor-league baseball player Charley Pride and suggested that he move to Nashville. Sovine opened doors for Pride at Pierce's Cedarwood publishing house, but his own career hit a lull. "Dream House for Sale," which reached number 22 in 1964, came nearly eight years after his last hit. The genre of the spoken word truck driving song dated back to the late '40s, and Starday featured several specialists on its own roster, but it took several albums before Sovine's emotive baritone voice was paired with trucker material.

In 1965, Sovine at last found his niche when he recorded "Giddy-Up-Go," which, like most of his other trucker hits, was co-written (with Tommy Hill) by Sovine himself. That story of a father-son truck-stop reunion spent six weeks atop the country charts and even crossed over to become a minor pop hit. Subsequent truck driving hits included the ghost story "Phantom 309" and a tearjerker tale of a disabled child's CB-radio relationship with caring truckers, "Teddy Bear." The last-named song became Sovine's biggest hit since "Giddy-Up-Go," spending three weeks at the top of the country charts in 1976 and reaching number 40 on the pop charts. Sovine followed up "Teddy Bear" with "Little Joe," a tale of a blinded trucker and his devoted canine friend which became his last big hit. Sovine died in 1980 after suffering a heart attack while driving his van. —*James Manheim*

The One and Only Red Sovine / 1961 / King ♦♦♦♦
While *The One and Only Red Sovine* features honky-tonk classics like "Why Baby Why," the sound quality is dismal, rendering this otherwise comprehensive collection a disappointment. —*Jason Ankeny*

Giddy-Up-Go / 1966 / Starday ♦♦♦♦

Giddy-Up-Go / 1966 / Nashville ♦♦♦
Starday and its budget subsidiary, Nashville, both released albums by Red Sovine with the title *Giddy-Up-Go* in 1966, but they are completely different records. The one bearing the Nashville imprint does not contain the number one hit to which the title refers, but instead offers ten songs from only a handful of songwriters. Roger Miller's "Invitation to the Blues" is one of the few well-known songs, while three from the pen of George Jones dominate the second side. The instrumental "Trucker's Ramble" seems like a weak attempt to exploit the trucking theme of the song "Giddy-Up-Go," since there are no other trucking songs or recitations in the bunch. These recordings are unlike Sovine's hits, but aren't very different from the music he made for Decca in the '50s. —*Greg Adams*

Anytime / 1970 / Nashville ♦♦♦
Red Sovine is basically a dependable, middle-of-the-road country artist. Since he comes from the old school, he has mastered certain wonderful country grooves such as the so-called Ray Price shuffle, which drives along "More From Habit Than Desire." Of course, Sovine has been practically elevated to the status of a kitsch icon for his maudlin and sometimes bizarre song stories. "I Think I Can Sleep Tonight" is a letter from a young boy to his father, and it is this album's portion of this type of Sovine specialty. It is a sad and solemn discussion of this child's separation, and although some listeners may feel its power comes from sheer sentimentality, those with more experience in life will hear the lyrics as surprisingly realistic. It is followed by "Long Night," some of this artist's fine trucker country in the style of Dave Dudley, complete with grunting guitar licks. Then the Western swing is back for the superb "Don't Let My Glass Run Dry." This sequence is described to indicate just how much fun this album is, and it is pretty typical of the output of this artist. The fact that he is also a co-writer on a good share of the tunes adds to the growing respect. He doesn't create an irresistable aura of hopelessness or tear the walls down and his brand of country & western would never be considered deep philosophically. But he sings with great skill, over mystery session men tracks that are full of clean surprises. On "Too Much," a bass is subtly doubled on the piano, while on the hilarious "Nobody's Business," featuring an unidentified female vocalist, there is both a madly swinging beat played with brushes and Collins Kids-style electric guitar insanity. This label was an adjunct of Starday, one of the few labels country fans might buy just on the basis of so-called "label identity." On the back cover there is an offer to get an illustrated Starday catalog; that combined with the $3.00 sticker price from the used record pile could by itself inspire serious sentimentality about the good old days. Don't get too excited about the bargain aspect, since this entire album could have fit on one side of vinyl easily. —*Eugene Chadbourne*

Teddy Bear / 1976 / Deluxe ♦♦♦
Teddy Bear collects a few of Sovine's mid-'70s hits, including the title track, "Little Joe" and "Woman Behind the Man Behind the Wheel." —*Jason Ankeny*

The Best of Red Sovine / 1976 / Starday ♦♦♦♦
Although it doesn't have many tracks, *The Best of Red Sovine* contains all his big hits and is an excellent introduction to one of the kings of truck-driving songs. —*Thom Owens*

Gone But Not Forgotten / 1981 / Castle ♦♦♦
This is ultra-cheap budget compilation of tracks recorded at the tail end of Sovine's career. As such, it's still a nice blend of weepers in waltz time and classic three handkerchief

narrations, all couched in late-'70s, full-blown Nashville arrangements. Certainly not the place to start your Red Sovine collection, and even at bargain prices, something for the completist only. *—Cub Koda*

Sings Hank Williams / 1986 / Deluxe ✦✦✦✦✦
This album includes such songs as "The Funeral," "Everything's OK," "Just Waitin'," and "Men with Broken Hearts." *—AMG*

Phantom 309 / 1987 / Deluxe ✦✦✦
Besides the title track, *Phantom 309* offers none of Sovine's chart hits, and is for completists only. *—Jason Ankeny*

Famous Duets / 1989 / Hollywood ✦✦✦
Famous Duets is a misnomer; while these songs are duets, they're hardly famous—none of them even charted, and only those with Jean Shepard show any signs of life. *—Jason Ankeny*

Golden Hits / 1989 / Hollywood ✦✦✦✦
Golden Hits contains a handful of Sovine's biggest successes, including "Teddy Bear" and "Little Rosa." However, the rest of the songs—"Daddy's Girl," "Lay Down Sally," "Last Goodbye" and so forth—were minor hits if they even charted at all. *—Jason Ankeny*

Giddy-Up-Go / Aug. 12, 1994 / Hollywood ✦✦✦
Giddy-Up-Go title cut was Sovine's biggest hit; unfortunately, it's also the only hit on this collection, which is otherwise made up of filler. *—Jason Ankeny*

● **The Best of Red Sovine** / 1995 / TeeVee ✦✦✦✦
This is a true mixed blessing here. Oh, the packaging is an absolute disgrace, nothing past the gnarly photo of Red adorning the cover, no liner notes, recording, or publishing information to be found anywhere—just a cryptic listing of the 20 tracks on the back. But once you pop the disc into the player, you're rewarded with 20 of Red's best Starday sides, all presented in the most sparkling sound, the majority of them sporting vivid stereo mixes. If you run across this one in a budget bin somewhere, it's definitely worth the investment, crummy packaging and all. *—Cub Koda*

The Sovines

f. 1995, Columbus, OH
Group / Alternative Country-Rock, Truck Driving Country, Roots Rock, Alternative Pop/Rock

Among the Midwest's finest purveyors of diesel-fueled, honky tonk-approved roots rock, the Sovines blend lean but meaty twang-infused rock & roll with the glorious truck-obsessed heritage of country & western icons Red Simpson, Dave Dudley, and the king of truckin' country, Red Sovine, for whom the band was named. Proud sons of Columbus, OH, the Sovines were formed in late 1995 by guitarist Matt Benz, a former Bostonian who'd relocated to Ohio and played for a spell with the McGuires, and Bob Starker, a singer, guitarist, and sax player who was born in Ohio but had lived and worked in Boston in the 1980s before coming back home. Pooling their shared enthusiasm for Nick Lowe, the Who, and anyone who can convincingly play "Six Days on the Road," Benz and Starker joined forces with bassist Ed Mann, whose previous credits included the groups Ugly Stick and the Bush League All-Stars, and the Sovines were born; Pete English signed on to play drums, and in early 1998 the band released a cassette-only album, *Owner Operator*, on their own Semi-Tone label.

Lansing, MI's Kingpin Records released the band's second album (and first CD release), *Truckers Welcome*, later that same year. The band began touring some of the finer honky tonks around the Midwest and made an impression within the alt-country community after their first appearance at St. Louis' annual music festival, Twangfest. In late 1999, English left the band, and yet another former onetime Bostonian, Gene Brodeur, took over on drums. The band also began working with the Columbus-based indie label Oahu Records and released two more fine albums, 2000's *The Sad Last Days Of...* and 2001's live set *Comin' in Loaded!* In 2002, former Great Plains and One Riot One Ranger member Mark Wyatt joined the Sovines, playing keyboards and accordion, and later the same year they released their fifth album, *Stupefyin' Jones*. *—Mark Deming*

Owner Operator / 1998 / Semi-Tone ✦✦✦
The Sovines' first cassette-only release sounds like the work of a solid band who were still learning how to make their sound work in the recording studio...which makes sense, since that's pretty much what it is. Suffering from a shoestring budget and production that does little to flatter the band, *Owner Operator* is still fun to listen to; singer Bob Starker's strong pipes and boistrous personality carry the show (Matt Benz's guitar sounds fine when it manages to work its way through the murk), and the group's originals are good enough that you wish they'd recorded a few less covers (out of 13 songs, only five were written by the band). Not a bad debut, but it wouldn't take long for the Sovines to come up with something that did a much better job of capturing what makes them worthwhile. *—Mark Deming*

Truckers Welcome / 1998 / Kingpin ✦✦✦
Truckers Welcome was the first CD release from the Sovines, and in every respect it was a massive improvement over the group's previous cassette-only album, *Owner Operator*. If the production and mix isn't especially fussy, at least this time around everyone is loud, clear, and audible, and the performances are far more spirited, giving a much better picture of the band's overdriven live show. Matt Benz's guitars finally get a fair hearing here, and his blend of garage rock raunch and Bakersfield twang hits just the right note for these tunes; meanwhile, bassist Ed Mann and drummer Pete English are a tight-focused rhythm section, and vocalist (and occasional saxophonist) Bob Starker is clever, smart-ass, funny, and decisively rockin'. And while the 14 originals prove these guys know their truck tunes like nobody's business—top marks to the long-hauling "24-7-365 (Long Distance Man)" and the first song to combine 18-wheelers and Las Vegas, "Hi-Ballin' the Jack"—they've got plenty else to sing about too, such as the rockin' drunkards lament "Whiskey Bottle Now," the weird-ass spiritual vision "Jesus Dionysus," and the nostalgia gone bad of "So Much for History." In 1998, the Sovines were already one of the strongest bands to come out of the Midwest alt-country scene, and *Truckers Welcome* finally captured their glory on a piece of plastic; that's no small accomplishment, and the best part is that they got even better with time. *—Mark Deming*

The Sad Last Days Of... / 2000 / Oahu ✦✦✦✦
After figuring out how to make a good album with *Truckers Welcome*, the Sovines proceeded to get even better on their second CD release, *The Sad Last Days Of*.... Sounding every bit as potent as they do on-stage, but a few notches more precise (or less socially lubricated), the Sovines rock harder than ever on songs like "Just Got Back (In Town)," "Long Long Night," and "This Nite-Life," while at the same time digging even deeper into their country-souls with "Smoking in the Rain" and "40 Watt Night"; these guys not only keep growing as a band, but they get sharper as songwriters each time at bat. Bob Starker can sing roadhouse country just as well as he can shout "blamalama" on the rockin' numbers, guitarist Matt Benz can pick clean or crank out the power chords and not miss a trick on either side, and bassist Ed Mann and drummer Gene Brodeur hold down the big beat like they own it. Producer Tito Taylor does right by this band behind the board, giving them a beefier sound and making room for guest musicians without letting the sound get cluttered (hats off to Barry Hensley on pedal steel, Mark Wyatt on accordion, and Bob Hite at the piano). Points added for featuring the best song to date about peeing in a bottle while driving (and yes, I do remember Mike Watt's "Piss Bottle Man"). Great stuff from a band who, if the fates are just, will someday get a well-deserved hearing outside the Midwest. *—Mark Deming*

Comin' in Loaded! / 2001 / Oahu ✦✦✦✦
While they've made some fine studio albums, the Sovines' natural environment is on a stage, playing for a crowd ready to have a good-time, and this disc captures the band in their element, playing fast, loud, and loose for a vocally appreciative audience. Assembled from two shows recorded in the summer of 2001 at Little Brothers, a club in the Sovines' hometown of Columbus, OH, *Comin' in Loaded* pulls together songs from their previous albums as well as a few well-chosen covers (how many bands can cover Merle Haggard and the Runaways in the same set and make it work?), making it a sort-of "Sovines Greatest Should-Have-Been Hits." If the recording isn't as detailed as their studio work and the performances a shade less precise, this still captures the Sovines live experience with commendable accuracy, with Bob Starker in fine voice, Matt Benz's guitar leads sounding mighty fine, and Ed Mann and Gene Brodeur holding down the beat with unflagging energy. A spiffy souvenir of this band's live show, and a great inducement to check them out at a nightclub or drinking establishment near you. *—Mark Deming*

● **Stupefyin' Jones** / 2002 / Oahu ✦✦✦✦✦
While the Sovines' 2000 album, *The Sad Last Days Of*..., was a genuine improvement over 1998's *Truckers Welcome*, 2002's *Stupefyin' Jones* proved that these guys have it in 'em to top even their best stuff with a bit of hard work. The Sovines' fourth studio release, *Stupefyin' Jones* doesn't rock quite as hard as *The Sad Last Days Of*..., but in terms of songwriting, performance, and production, it sets a new standard for one of the Midwest's best alt-country outfits. "This Day in History" and "The Life of Your Party" prove Matt Benz can write breakup songs as well as anyone in Nashville these days (if not better), and slice-of-life numbers like Bob Starker's "Where to Put My Hands" and Ed Mann's "Mary Ann MacLeod" show that beyond this band's love of a good laugh (and a good song about trucks), they can also tell stories about real people with heart, soul, and intelligence. Don't get the idea that these guys have forgotten how to kick it out, though; "No Kinda Man" gets the album off to a good stompin' start, and "Crackin' Up" and "What Was Wrong" make it clear they know how and when to turn it up and hit it hard. And whether they're playing cry-in-your-beer weepers or snarling rock & roll, this band sounds tight, emphatic, and thoroughly committed on all 14 cuts. I'm not sure just how the Sovines are going to be able to top *Stupefyin' Jones*, but if they can keep working at this level, it'll put them way ahead of the vast majority of American bands treading the boards these days. *—Mark Deming*

Spanic Boys

f. 1986, Milwaukee, WI
Group / Roots Rock

The father and son team of Tom and Ian Spanic, of Milwaukee, WI, became the darling of the critics in the late '80s and early '90s, when they released three albums for Rounder Records. Known for their loud, intense, fiery guitar playing, their music could best be described as roots rock, complete with lots of references to blues and rockabilly thrown into their heavily guitar-laden mix. The father and son duo, whose harmonies are reminiscent of the Everly Brothers, got their first big break when they performed on *Saturday Night Live* in 1990, thanks to *SNL* bandmember and fellow guitarist G.E. Smith.

Both father and son, despite their 22-year age difference, share a passion for and count among their influences the Everly Brothers, Buddy Holly, Elvis Presley, Lonnie Mack, Merle Travis, Buck Owens, Ricky Nelson, and Chet Atkins. Although their influences may be some of the pioneers of rock & roll, they have the benefit of a range of effects and amplifiers with their guitar playing that late-20th century sound technology provides. Ian, an avid record collector and student of the sound of Buddy Holly, grew up a fish out of water of sorts in the 1980s, preferring roots rockers like Holly and Presley to more popular bands like Van Halen or Bon Jovi. On the other hand, Tom began playing guitar in 1956, when it all started. His playing speaks for itself, and coupled with his son's playing, the pair take the two-guitar rock & roll subgenre a step further, trading off on leads and delivering exquisite harmonies that you just don't hear a lot anymore. Their sound at times is country-rock, at other times rockabilly, and at other times blues-rock.

Before the pair began playing out together in local Milwaukee clubs in the mid-'80s, Tom's career had included a stint teaching classical guitar at the Wisconsin Conservatory.

He found he had more fun playing out with his son. He bought his son his first electric guitar, a reissued 1957 Buddy Holly Stratocaster, when Ian was 12. (The elder Spanic insisted that Ian just play an acoustic classical guitar until then.) The Spanic Boys cut their debut on a small Milwaukee label in 1988. After being invited to perform at the 1989 South by Southwest Music Festival by critic/NPR commentator Ed Ward, the pair secured their deal with Rounder Records, and the *Saturday Night Live* performance helped to establish their place on the musical map.

The Spanic Boys' self-titled debut was released in 1990 on Rounder and was followed by *Strange World* in 1991 and *Dream Your Life Away* in 1993, both also for Rounder. On their Rounder albums and at their South by Southwest performances, the pair were accompanied by Curt Lefevre, drums, Paul Schroeder, bass, or Mike Frederickson, bass. The Spanic Boys continue to perform around Wisconsin and the Northeast, but as of 1996, they weren't recording for Rounder anymore. However, given the ongoing renaissance of blues and roots rock music, that may change. A deal with Orchard surfaced during the new millennium, issuing *Spanic Family Album* and *Walk Through Fire* in 2000. *Torture* followed a year later. —*Richard Skelly*

Spanic Boys / 1990 / Rounder ✦✦✦✦✦

● **Strange World** / 1991 / Rounder ✦✦✦✦✦

Early Spanic Boys / 1992 / Rounder ✦✦✦

Dream Your Life Away / 1993 / Rounder ✦✦✦

The thing that draws most people to the Spanic Boys is the heartfelt and deft execution of roots rock, and for bands with such a following any experiment is risky. On *Dream Your Life Away* the band edged toward psychedelia and a harder sound, with disastrous results for their popularity. This isn't to say that the individual songs don't have merit, because many of them are very good. What is lacking is a sense of continuity and flow over the course of the album. The grim Byrds-esque guitar rave-up "What Was Is Gone" is preceded and followed by rockabilly pieces that are simple and sweet, and the discontinuity is a bit jarring. At times on this album the disparate elements do fuse into something brilliant, as proved by the edgy title cut. Unfortunately there are other points where you can hear good musicianship, good singing, and a good lyric, but the result just isn't compelling. Still, this album is worth having for such cuts as "Everything Not Right," which is as joyous a road song as any band has ever recorded. —*Richard Foss*

Spanic Family Album / 1996 / Orchard ✦✦✦✦✦

Released in 1996, *Spanic Family Album* is the fourth album by the father and son duo of Tom & Ian Spanic (not counting the 1992 compilation of early recordings called *Early Spanic Boys*). It's a departure for the Milwaukee-based roots rockers; earlier albums had featured the boys playing a loose and rockin' form of neo-rockabilly not too far removed from Chris Isaak's early albums. The lower-voltage *Spanic Family Album* (oddly, the Spanic Boys name appears nowhere on the packaging or disc) is largely acoustic, with minimal drums and no bass, and resembles albums like the Everly Brothers' late-'60s roots move *Songs Our Daddy Taught Us*, although with an all-original set list. Tom Spanic's cousin, Butch Westphal, joins the duo on this album, his high lonesome harmonies adding a more pure country edge to the proceedings. A relaxed, intimate set of simple and heartfelt songs, *Spanic Family Album* is an unpretentious gem. This album was released just as East Side Digital was closing its doors and transmogrifying into the folk and world music label Northside, and so it was in and out of the stores in no time at all. Orchard Records reissued the album in its original form in 2000. —*Stewart Mason*

Walk Through Fire / Aug. 8, 2000 / Orchard ✦✦✦

This independent 1998 release was Spanic Boys' first studio effort since 1993's *Dream Your Life Away*. It was issued partly due to the restlessness of avid fans clamoring for something new. It also demonstrated that this father/son duo was still active and fully capable of writing engaging roots rock. Like their early-'90s Rounder releases, *Walk Through Fire* mixes early rock & roll, country, and acoustic pop with catchy melodies and timeless vocal and guitar harmonies. However, unlike albums like *Strange World* and *Dream Your Life Away*, this offering lacks the overt psychedelic touches present on those records and more closely resembles their earlier recordings, *Spanic Boys* and *Early Spanic Boys*. —*Dave Sleger*

Torture / Feb. 20, 2001 / Checkered Past ✦✦✦

After vowing never to be at the mercy of label heads other than themselves, the members of this Milwaukee outfit took their act south to the independent Chicago-based Checkered Past Records for their seventh release, *Torture*. Aside from (perhaps) previous behind-the-scenes administrative decisions and roster priorities that didn't sit well with the Spanics, which led to their disenchantment with labels in general, their sound has remained remarkably constant throughout their recording history. The obvious exceptions were their early-'90s flirtations with psychedelic-laced roots rock and 1996's *Spanic Family Album*, which explored more of a twangy flavor—but the Spanic Boys' musical meanderings never seemed to obfuscate their overall sound. *Torture* incorporates all of their roots rock influences into a cohesive package. Produced by Ian Spanic, this album includes Beatles-esque pop, rockabilly, country, blues, and heartland rock in a manner not unlike Americana kingpin Steve Earle. And because of a professional partnership dating back to the mid-'80s and a father/son relationship dating back a bit further, their guitar and vocal interplay is tighter and smoother than ever before. While *Torture* doesn't necessarily cover uncharted territory for this duo, the maturity and comfort level displayed by Ian & Tom Spanic is apparent and, in an age when all of the original melodies seem to be taken, they can still churn out one irresistible three-minute song after another. —*Dave Sleger*

Larry Sparks

b. Sep. 15, 1947, Lebanon, OH
Guitar, Vocals / Bluegrass, Progressive Bluegrass, Traditional Bluegrass

Larry Sparks has said that he's the youngest old-timer around, and the self-description is an apt one. Emerging from the Stanley Brothers' Clinch Mountain Boys band, Sparks

carried on with the sounds created by bluegrass music's first generation. His style was no knock-off, however; it had a distinctively bluesy tinge anchored by Sparks' own guitar; a comparatively unusual lead instrument in bluegrass, where the triad of mandolin, banjo, and fiddle had defined the musical texture since the genre's early days. Sparks grew up in Lebanon, OH, in the southwestern part of the state that has produced several other top bluegrass artists. His parents came from Appalachian Kentucky, and one of his grandfathers was a fiddle contest champion. Sparks heard Cincinnati country star Wayne Raney on the radio when he was young and learned to play the guitar. His skills put him in demand not only for bluegrass but also for country and rock bands while he was in high-school, but after sitting in as lead guitarist with the Stanley Brothers as they toured Ohio in 1964, bluegrass took first place among his musical interests.

Sparks played increasingly often with the Stanley Brothers and made his recording debut in 1965 on a small Dayton, OH label. He spent three years as lead vocalist with Ralph Stanley & the Clinch Mountain Boys after Carter Stanley's death at age 41 in December 1966. Around 1970, Sparks formed his own band, the Lonesome Ramblers, and it's a rare bluegrass festival or concert series that hasn't played host to Sparks multiple times in the years since. Numerous younger bluegrass players have passed through the Lonesome Ramblers or appeared on Sparks' many recordings, Ricky Skaggs and fiddler Stuart Duncan being only two of the best-known examples. Sparks recorded for various labels in the '70s and early '80s, moving to Rebel in 1982 for the *Dark Hollow* LP. It was the first in a long string of recordings that sold steadily and won critical acclaim; most of Sparks' Rebel catalog remained in print in the early 2000s.

Along the way, Sparks made several songs into bluegrass standards. He unearthed an obscure folk-rock composition by Lawrence Hammond entitled "John Deere Tractor" and turned it into a perennial anthem of discontented rural folk adrift in the big city; the cover of the song by the Judds on their *Love Can Build a Bridge* album of 1990 was likely traceable to Sparks' own numerous performances. The Stanley Brothers' "Goin' Up Home (To Live in Green Pastures)" was one of several gospel pieces that every parking-lot pickup band wanted to learn after hearing Sparks sing it, and Sparks tended to focus on gospel in his own numerous compositions as well. Sparks and the Lonesome Ramblers barely slowed down in the 1990s, releasing several albums over the course of the decade, and 2003's *The Coldest Part of Winter* showed him in undiminished form. —*James Manheim*

Ramblin' Guitar / 1970 / Pine Tree ✦✦✦✦

New Gospel Songs / 1971 / Pine Tree ✦✦✦

Ramblin' Bluegrass / 1972 / Starday ✦✦✦✦

Bluegrass Old and New / 1972 / Old Homestead ✦✦✦✦

Larry Sparks Sings Hank Williams / 1977 / Rebel ✦✦✦✦✦

Larry Sparks expertly recasts several of Hank Williams' finest songs as bluegrass numbers in *Sings Hank Williams*, one of the finest records he ever released. Of special interest is the supporting band, which features a terrific performance from a young mandolinist named Ricky Skaggs. —*Thom Owens*

The Best of Larry Sparks / 1983 / Rebel ✦✦✦✦✦

The Best of Larry Sparks is an adequate collection for this fine traditional bluegrass singer. —*Mark A. Humphrey*

★ **Classic Bluegrass** / 1989 / Rebel ✦✦✦✦✦

Classic Bluegrass collects the highlights of Larry Sparks '70s and '80s albums, which were recorded for a variety of different labels. The compilation hits all the high points of the records, providing a definitive retrospective of his career, as well as an excellent, concise introduction to one of bluegrass' best singers. —*Thom Owens*

Silver Reflections / 1991 / Rebel ✦✦✦

Travelin' / 1992 / Rebel ✦✦✦

The Rock I Stand On / 1994 / Rebel ✦✦✦

Special Delivery / Oct. 10, 2000 / Rebel ✦✦✦✦

Larry Sparks has managed to remain within the fold of traditional bluegrass while also forming a unique style. This style includes hot flatpicking guitar, distinctive vocals, and a steady release of albums. *Special Delivery* finds Sparks with a good batch of songs and strong supporting players. The songs have been penned by a number of writers, but the themes are unified in outlook. Each lyric is imbued with a Southern, rural point of view, which includes championing the virtues of rural living, true love that transcends death (for a girlfriend or mother), and nostalgia for "the way things used to be." "Ghost Stories" tells of driving past abandoned farmhouses and overgrown gardens and leaves the listener with a sense of loss. This song, written by Bill Cook, Bo Jamison, and Jim Benson, captures something deep and elusive, much like Sparks' classic, "John Deere Tractor." "Timberline" is about having a quiet place to go and sort out one's thoughts, a place to "get it straight and head on home again." "Lovin' on Borrowed Time" is a defiant sendoff to a lover who's left for someone new (bluegrass musicians seem to lose women to other men almost as frequently as blues players do). Two instrumentals, "Around the Carousel" and "San Antonio Rose," give Sparks, mandolinist Scott Napier, and banjoist Josh McMurry room for a little picking and grinning. In fact, there really isn't anything bad to say about *Special Delivery*, though one should note its short length (33 minutes). Sparks is in good voice, his friends are in good form, and the 12 songs/instrumentals are good ones. This performance should be a real treat for lovers of traditional bluegrass. —*Ronnie Lankford Jr.*

The Coldest Part of Winter / Feb. 18, 2003 / Rebel ✦✦✦

It seems apt to release Larry Sparks' *The Coldest Part of Winter* in the middle of February. It's also an interesting coincidence that the Virginia-based Rebel released the album during the 2002-2003 season, one of the coldest Southern winters in recent history. One imagines a certain comforting warmth, however, in a new album by one of bluegrass' most steady hands. Listeners will not find anything radically different on Sparks' latest outing, and that is as it should be. Instead, listeners will find what they've come to expect: fine picking, vibrant vocals, and a lyrical emphasis on the values of the past. Mandolinist Scott Napier, banjoist Josh McMurray, bassist Matthew Madden, and fiddler Michael Cleveland join Sparks for a dozen traditionally based songs/instrumentals. Most of these pieces, like "Leavin' Me" and "This Old Road," only run for two to three minutes, meaning that the emphasis is placed on the songs themselves and that the instrumental accompaniment primarily works to underline the songs. This leaves Sparks' voice, which is as fine and steady as always, front and center on lovely pieces like "Winter in Miami" and "Let's Turn Back the Clock." For Southerners and traditional bluegrass lovers suffering from cabin fever, *The Coldest Part of Winter* should provide just the right tonic. —*Ronnie D. Lankford Jr.*

Minton Sparks

Speech/Speaker/Speaking Part, Vocals / Americana, Alternative Country
Nashville-based poet Minton Sparks proved there is some room for literary, arty fusions of spoken word with traditional folk in the oft-conservative Southern country-folk scene. Her laconic, sometimes sad and mordant, tales evoke quotidian country Southern life. For her 2001 *Middlin' Sisters* CD, she backed her radio-ready, storytelling-like delivery with low-key Appalachian-flavored folk music on guitar, mandolin, dobro, mandola, and banjo. —*Richie Unterberger*

● **Middlin' Sisters** / Apr. 10, 2001 / Dualtone ✦✦✦✦
Minton Sparks is a wonder. She's a performance poet from the Deep South that portrays Arkansas—and the South in general—in a way Bill Clinton either never knew or, if he did, never once dared mention. This is the South that Thomas Wolfe's Eugene Gant so desperately needed to leave. If you can picture Gillian Welch not being from L.A., and speaking rather than singing, you are beginning to get the picture. Better yet, Richard Buckner as a woman speaking clearly rather than mumbling, or even picture Flannery O'Connor as a performance poet without any of the pretentious New York Poetry Slam connotations that the word "performance" carries. *Middlin' Sisters* is a dark record, but not one without humor. Its 12 selections are reflections and observations of a life most of us could never know, or want to. With musical accompaniment by Marcus Hummon, Darryl Scott, and Rob Jackson, and no less than Waylon Jennings lending a hand as a fallen preacher on the album's last track. There are plenty of slide guitars and mandolins winding their way through a spare but riveting mix. Each of the selections are poignant, even scary in Sparks' plaintive delivery. In "Mississippi Moonshine," with a nasty dobro keeping her strolling, Sparks intones: "She'd a been the first issued a DUI on the Mississippi/My Gypsy used to say/out on the bow of a muddy Mississippi barge on a sweltering Delta night/Thelma anchored/Nipping hidden moonshine beneath a cloud of weary/Been cookin' in the kitchen since sun up/Ankles swollen beyond the banks of her shoes/The Dark drank the color from her yellow hair/As it fell oily in whiskey girls around her once beautiful face/Thelma was cursed by extremes: beauty, a penchant for strong anything, and barge kitchen men/Drunk, drivin' right down the middle of the muddy waters/She begged the sky a favor/The answer came on moonshine fumes written against the night/Being too much of oneself needs no forgiveness." There's also "Trella's Trash," with a claw hammer banjo. A story of "mama's" favorite aunt, told by the community whose "lies were told Arkansas style," about a woman who was 91 years old and left her husband after 65 years of marriage. This was a woman whose "Dark was the only hand she had left to hold." When Sparks moves from the gothic, she gets strangely philosophical, and its no less brutal, with "Words of Wisdom" imparted from Mee Maw, a crazy sage who paints a red circle on the wall of the barn every time her daughter marries another man. She says: "Time changes nothin' girl, but the size of your underwear/And hopefully your hairdo." After ranting about her daughter for a bit, Sparks says, "She turns her heavy prophecy on me: You girl, you'll end up in a double-wide sure as shootin'/with five at your feet/dust foggin' the white sheets you keep/hangin' out to dry." This record is short, most of its poems no more than a minute-and-a-half long, but it doesn't need to be; longer than it is—most of us couldn't take it. This is tough work, nearly unbearable in its rough-hewn beauty and tattered grace. This poetry is like Whitman's in that it sings, like Rosemary Danielle's in its disturbing revelations of a mysterious secret South, offered without judgment or cynicism, and like Wanda Coleman's in its toughness. The poems themselves resonate deeply within the listener, moving her from piece to piece on the edge of her seat, falling into reverie for the moment only to be yanked out of it again and again in wonder and sometimes disturbed at how beautiful some of these disturbing images are. Minton Sparks is a treasure whose imprint is only now being traced upon the culture; when the full weight of it comes to bear, don't say you weren't warned. *Middlin' Sisters* is the finest spoken word recording issued in America in more than ten years. —Thom Jurek

This Dress / Feb. 25, 2003 / Rural ✦✦✦✦
Why is it that Robert Altman hasn't made a film from the vignettes of Minton Sparks? Why is it that publishers aren't banging down her door in order to publish these small revelations of large truths? On her second full length, Minton Sparks is the greatest country singer who doesn't sing, a poet in a league with Lucinda Williams and Charles Williams, a storyteller as fine as Hazel Dickens; she's without without peer among her generation. On the follow-up to the remarkable, profound and quietly dazzling *Middlin' Sisters*, Ms. Sparks gives us 12 more tomes that are every bit as lean, every bit as tough as anything to come from Nuyorican Poets Café and come out of a timeworn tradition that has been documented in field recordings by Alan Lomax and others in earlier generations but left to the humid dirt in our own. Here, mothers, sisters, grandfathers, Waylon Jennings' playing cards, dogs, rusted trucks, trailers, houses dresses with stars wearing off them, bequeathed handbags, country dances where, in the hot, steamy Southern night, desire, excitement, and the desperate nature to hold on to this moment for all

its worth because there may not be another for a month. Mortality is everywhere on this record, underlining the feeling in the previous sentence. Sparks' stories have all the immediacy of a hip-hop narrative, and the emotional depth of a prayer for salvation. But there is also an acceptance: quiet, plaintive, unadorned by artifice. Sparks has some awesome help on this set: There's Maura O'Connell, whose Celtic restrained mournful wail adorns two tracks, the criminally under-appreciated Steve Conn plays bluesed-out piano and organ four more, Tammy Rodgers and her high lonesome fiddle lilt the fringes of a pair, Rob Jackson pulls out the fingerpicks on another couple, and Keb Mo' plays a gut-bucket bottleneck slide on another. There is nothing here that suggests anachronism, just a simpler truth mined for its meaning by the retelling of a story, a memory, real or imagined, in a poem. Ms. Sparks poetry has the same teeth Rebecca Wells' novels have, but the also offer a burning passion that smolders under a plain cotton dress, and a pair of pointy eyeglasses that know the secrets that lie in secrets. Once again, Ms. Sparks thrills us with her wisdom, humor and unflinching honesty that is so musical as to be as fierce and frightening as any punk ballad, yet as powerful as the lean, fine-sharpened lyrics offered by Sharon Olds and Eudora Welty. Ms. Sparks is singular, an outsider who offers far more than she receives; she instructs by trying to understand, and *This Dress* is an album for all of us no matter who we are or where we come from, the walk of life is offered here, step by step with roughshod grace a twinkle in the eye, and the passing of another day. Brilliant. — *Thom Jurek*

Billie Jo Spears

b. Jan. 14, 1937, Beaumont, TX
Bass, Vocals / Traditional Country, Progressive Country
Billie Jo Spears landed a few big country hits during the '70s, thanks to a sultry, bluesy voice that made her a perfect torch balladeer; while she never quite edged her way into stardom in the U.S., she earned a devoted following in Great Britain and toured there frequently. Spears was born in Beaumont, TX, in 1937, and made her professional debut at age 13 in an all-star country concert in Houston; not long after, she recorded the single "Too Old for Toys, Too Young for Boys" as Billie Joe Moore for Abbott Records. After high-school, she sang in nightclubs and looked for a record deal, recording some demos with producer Pete Drake. She got a contract with United Artists in 1964 and moved to Nashville, where she worked with producer Kelso Herston. Her initial singles fared poorly, and when Herston moved to Capitol two years later, Spears followed. Success continued to elude her until 1969, when "Mr. Walker, It's All Over" climbed into the country Top Five. She charted several more times through 1972 but was forced to have surgery on her vocal cords twice over the next two years in order to remove nodules and polyps that could have robbed her of her voice entirely.

Spears made a full recovery, however, and returned to United Artists in 1975. She scored her first number-one hit with the sensual "Blanket on the Ground" that year, and two of her 1976 singles—"Misty Blue" and "What I've Got in Mind"—reached the Top Five. She had several other minor hits that year and also cut an album of duets with Del Reeves. "If You Want Me" made the Top Ten in 1977, the last time Spears would visit that territory; several more singles reached the Top 20 by decade's end, but songs like "'57 Chevrolet" and "Lonely Hearts Club" were much bigger hits in Britain, and Spears began to devote more of her touring attention to the overseas market. Her last Top 20 single was 1981's "Your Good Girl's Gonna Go Bad," after which she and United Artists parted ways. Spears recorded sporadically for independent labels, usually based in the U.K. or Ireland, during the '80s and early '90s. She recovered from triple bypass surgery in 1993 and continued to tour, traveling regularly to the U.K. to perform for a still-affectionate fan base. —*Steve Huey*

The Voice of Billie Joe Spears / 1968 / Capitol ✦✦✦✦✦

Country Girl / 1970 / Capitol ✦✦✦✦

Blanket on the Ground / 1975 / United Artists ✦✦✦

I'm Not Easy / 1977 / United Artists ✦✦✦✦
Who were the queens of hard country music in the '70s? Loretta Lynn springs to mind, but Billie Jo Spears, too, was like an island in a sea of Barbara Mandrells and Janie Frickes. Spears' wonderful working-class Southern accent is a joy in itself, but the songs she interpreted fit perfectly with her sound and managed to be both traditional and modern. She defends her honor in "No Other Man" and the painfully forlorn title track, the latter of which was almost a Top Ten hit. "I Never Did Like Whiskey" is one of Spears' best cuts, a modern and commercial update of honky tonk music that should have been a much bigger hit than it was. Beyond those three songs, *I'm Not Easy* spotlights Spears' adeptness with ballads, as on the radically transformed cover of "Heartbreak Hotel" that transmits more heartbreak than Elvis Presley even attempted. A lot of big names contributed to this album in one way or another, but in the end it is the performances of Spears that elevate *I'm Not Easy* above the fray. —*Greg Adams*

Bille Jo Singles Album / 1979 / United Artists ✦✦✦✦✦

● **The Best of Billie Jo Spears** / 1992 / Razor & Tie ✦✦✦✦✦
The Best of Billie Jo Spears is a brief, slightly quirky 12-song collection of Spears' hits on Liberty and United Artists from the '70s and early '80s. The essential tracks are here, including the number-one hit "Blanket on the Ground" and lesser but excellent singles such as "Never Did Like Whiskey" and "Too Much Is Not Enough." Some bigger hits are omitted in favor of minor cuts (namely her cover of "What the World Needs Now Is Love," which charted in the lower reaches of the Top 100), but *The Best Of...* provides a good—if skimpy—look at a distinct and worthy vocalist. —*Greg Adams*

Billie Jo / United Artists ✦✦✦✦
Billy Jo is another fine effort from Spears and her producer Larry Butler, who penned several of the songs on the record, including the hit "(Hey Won't You Play) Another Somebody Done Somebody Wrong Song." Billie Jo's big hit this time around, however,

was "Silver Wings and Golden Rings," which topped country charts and made *Billie Jo* such a delight for easy-listening country music fans to enjoy. —*James Chrispell*

The Speer Family

f. 1921
Group / Southern Gospel, Country Gospel, Traditional Gospel

An important reference point in the appreciation of traditional Southern gospel quartet singing, the Speer Family emerged when there were countless Southern gospel quartets, but continued to perform into the 1990s. Although the Speer lineup had changed over the years, their music in the '90s was still true to the music they were making when the group was formed by patriarch G.T. in 1921. G.T. Speer was born in a rural community near Fayetteville, GA, and worked as a teacher at the Stamps-Baxter School of Music in Dallas. He also taught at the Vaughan School of Music, Lawrenceburg, TN. The first incarnation of the Speers was formed in 1921 with his wife Lena, his sister, and her husband. Until then, virtually every gospel group was made up of only males. G.T. persisted with his original lineup and, much to the surprise of gospel purists, became popular. He also strayed from the norm by having the Speers sing only gospel music, and soon other groups followed suit.

In 1925, his sister and brother-in-law left, so G.T. and Lena added their children Rosa Nell and Mary Tom to the lineup. They eventually left to raise their own children, but returned to become permanent members a few years later. Over the years, the Speer Family often contained other musicians, most notably Harold Lane, who spent two decades with them. Through the 1950s and '60s, the Speers were frequent guests on radio station WLAC Nashville. In 1966, G.T. suddenly died and became the first person inducted into the Deceased Category of the Gospel Music Hall of Fame; his wife Lena died the following year and became its second inductee in 1972. During their long career, the group has won numerous awards and honors, but one of the highest came in 1981 on the group's 60th anniversary: the Speers were entered into the Congressional Record and received a plaque that contained their first commercial record. To celebrate these events, the Benson Company distributed a commemorative anniversary album and packaged a multimedia presentation chronicling the distinguished family's history. In 1993, they released a new album, *A Beautiful Day*. —*Sandra Brennan & Bil Carpenter*

Hallelujah Time / 1990 / HB ✦✦✦

● **He's Still in the Fire** / 1990 / Homeland ✦✦✦✦✦

All Night Singing / 1991 / Starday ✦✦✦

Carl T. Sprague

b. 1895, Houston, TX, **d.** 1978
Vocals / Cowboy

Carl T. Sprague was one of the first cowboys on record, paving the way for such fine rangeland singers as Jules Allen, the Cartwright Brothers, and Harry McClintock. He was born in Houston and spent time as a youth involved in ranching and farming; the cowboy songs he performed were authentic, learned around late-night campfires. After graduating college in 1922, he began occasionally playing on radio, and was inspired to record after hearing Vernon Dalhart's "The Prisoner's Song." Sprague went to Camden, NJ, in 1925 and cut his debut recordings "When the Work's All Done This Fall" and "Bad Companions"; both of the cowboy tunes became quite successful, and he continued recording for Victor through 1929. In the '30s he worked several different jobs after settling down permanently in Bryan, TX, but did return to performing during the folk revival years. —*Sandra Brennan*

The First Popular Singing Cowboy / 1973 / Bear Family ✦✦✦✦

Cowboy Songs from Texas / 1975 / Bear Family ✦✦✦✦

● **Classic Cowboy Songs** / 1988 / Bear Family ✦✦✦✦✦

Cowtrails, Longhorns, and Tight Saddles: Cowboy Songs 1925–1929 / Jun. 2003 / Bear Family ✦✦✦✦

Jim Stafford

b. Jan. 16, 1944, Eloise, FL
Vocals, Banjo, Guitar, Keyboards / Country-Pop, Country Comedy, AM Pop

Best known for his humorous country novelty songs of the mid-'70s, multi-instrumentalist Jim Stafford also enjoyed a lengthy career as a television personality and live entertainer. Stafford was born in 1944 in the Florida town of Eloise, near Winter Haven, and learned guitar from his father. He started playing in local bands as a teenager, including one, the Legends, that included future country-rock legend Gram Parsons, as well as Kent LaVoie, who would later become singer/songwriter Lobo. After high-school, Stafford moved to Nashville and joined Jumpin' Bill Carlisle's backing band. He also worked on his songwriting and recorded some demos of his tunes, despite his distaste for his own singing voice. During one session, he developed the one-man band act that would later become part of his live performances, thanks to a drummer who abruptly walked out.

Stafford was performing in Clearwater, FL, when he ran into Lobo and asked if he would consider recording Stafford's original "The Swamp Witch." Lobo suggested that Stafford record it himself, and helped him land a contract with MGM; he would later produce many of Stafford's singles as well. "The Swamp Witch" scraped the bottom of the Top 40 in 1973, but it was the following year's "Spiders and Snakes"—a song co-written with David Bellamy of the Bellamy Brothers—that brought Stafford into the big time. The song peaked at number three on the pop charts, went gold, and helped make Stafford a household name. His sense of humor was also showcased on the follow-up hits "My Girl Bill" and "Wildwood Weed," the latter another Top Ten pop hit, and he charted in the Top 40 again in 1975 with "Your Bulldog Drinks Champagne" and "I Got Stoned and I Missed It."

By that time, Stafford was enough of a celebrity to get his own short-lived prime-time variety show, which ran during the summer of 1975. It was there that he met singer Bobbie Gentry, whom he married and later, in 1980, divorced. In 1981, Stafford appeared

in the Clint Eastwood movie *Any Which Way but Loose* and contributed his last chart single, "Cow Patti," to the soundtrack. The following year, he wrote three songs for Disney's animated feature *The Fox and the Hound*. He hosted two television programs, *Those Amazing Animals* and *Nashville on the Road*, in the early '80s and later in the decade served as a writer for the Smothers Brothers' return to prime-time television. In the meantime, he continued to tour and recorded a few one-off singles for various labels. In 1990, he settled in Branson, MO, which has since become a mecca for country music and family entertainment; he currently owns his own theater there and plays over 350 shows a year. —*Steve Huey*

Spiders & Snakes / 1974 / Polygram ✦✦✦

● **Jim Stafford** / 1974 / Polydor ✦✦✦

Jim Stafford's self-titled debut album gave him four Top 40 chart singles, with the school-boyish charm of "Spiders and Snakes" reaching the highest at number three in July of 1973. His friendly voice and novelty style of songwriting actually carried some well-deserved weight, especially throughout the lesson-teaching lightheartedness of "Swamp Witch," a well-crafted story song, and again on the laughable "My Girl Bill." "Wildwood Weed" sticks with Stafford's love of playing with words, and non-hits like "I Ain't Sharin' Sharon" and "16 Little Red Noses and a Horse That Sweats" carry on with the same type of innocent jocularity that ran amuck throughout the mid-'70s, bolstered by artists like Ray Stevens and C.W. McCall. Either this album or any of his hits packages will satisfy any interest. —*Mike DeGagne*

Not Just Another Pretty Foot / 1975 / MGM ✦✦

Greatest Hits / Jun. 6, 1995 / Curb ✦✦✦✦

One of the masters of the pun and the sharp quip, Jim Stafford gave novelty music some substance throughout his career, making a mark with "Spiders and Snakes" in 1973 and again a year later with "Wildwood Weed," both breaking the Top Ten. This greatest-hits package comprises ten of his best tracks, including the witty "My Girl Bill" and "Cow Patti," as well as droll little gems like "Don't Fool Around When There's a Fool Around" and "You Can Call Me Call Me Clyde." Many of Stafford's double entendres may seem a bit dated by today's standards, but there's still some attractive playfulness hidden in the simplicity of his songs. Two of Stafford's Top 40 singles, "Your Bulldog Drinks Champagne" and "I Got Stoned and I Missed It," both from 1975, are absent from Curb's compilation. —*Mike DeGagne*

Terry Stafford

b. Oct. 22, 1941, Hollis, OK, **d.** Mar. 17, 1996, Amarillo, TX
Vocals / Country-Pop, Pop

One-hit wonder Terry Stafford was known for his Elvis sound-alike single "Suspicion," which became a Top Five smash even at the height of Beatlemania in 1964. Stafford was born in Hollis, OK, on November 22, 1941, and grew up in Amarillo, TX. He moved to Los Angeles after high-school to pursue a singing career and performed at various local dances and social events. He got the chance to record a demo and chose "Suspicion," an album track from Elvis Presley's *Pot Luck* LP (1962). A local DJ took the song to Crusader Records, which remastered it and released it nationally in 1964. It went all the way to number three on the pop charts and did so during a week when the Beatles held every other spot in the Top Five. Stafford was never able to duplicate its success, though he did reach the Top 30 with his follow-up single, "I'll Touch a Star."

He continued to perform and also branched out into acting (the film *Wild Wheels*) and songwriting, penning Buck Owens' hit "Big in Vegas." In 1973, Stafford signed with Atlantic's newly formed country division and recorded a full-fledged country album, *Say, Has Anybody Seen My Sweet Gypsy Rose*. The title track edged into the country Top 40, and its flip side, the Stafford co-write "Amarillo by Morning," also enjoyed some regional popularity. It was later covered by George Strait for a major hit. Stafford recorded for Atlantic through 1974 then disappeared from the music scene. He died of liver problems in Amarillo on March 17, 1996. —*Steve Huey*

● **Suspicion** / 1994 / Ace ✦✦✦✦✦

Terry Stafford became one of only a few artists who managed to "steal" a hit from Elvis Presley by covering one of his album tracks—in this case "Suspicion" from Presley's album *Potluck*. You wouldn't necessarily realize from that track the extent to which Stafford is a Presley sound-alike, but he is in the same category of great Elvis imitators such as Vince Everett and Ral Donner. "Suspicion" was Stafford's biggest hit by far, but he enjoyed two other hits on the Crusader label in 1964. "I'll Touch a Star" was a big one on the adult contemporary charts, and "Follow the Rainbow" missed the Top 100 by one position. *Suspicion* is a reissue of Stafford's 1964 album, and it includes the title track and "I'll Touch a Star" along with a number of other compositions by songwriters from Presley's stable. The one quirky flourish that keeps these songs from sounding just like Elvis is the rinky-dink keyboard that plays throughout. —*Greg Adams*

The Best of Terry Stafford / Oct. 15, 1996 / Curb ✦✦✦✦✦

The Best of Terry Stafford, of course, contains his big hit single "Suspicion," but it also contains a number of other lesser-known singles, including his only other Top 40 hit, "I'll Touch a Star." Although the rest of the material on the compilation isn't the equal of "Suspicion," it is frequently entertaining. Stafford's voice is excellent and the '60s mainstream pop arrangements are usually engaging, even when the material is less than first-rate. —*Stephen Thomas Erlewine*

Joe Stampley

b. Jun. 6, 1943, Springhill, LA
Vocals / Traditional Country, Honky Tonk, Country Comedy, Urban Cowboy, Country-Pop

Joe Stampley has had a career that spans the genres and styles of music and entertainment. Born in Louisiana and raised on his father's Hank Williams records, Stampley began playing piano before the age of ten, and by the age of 15 he was recording demos with a local DJ named Merle Kilgore. The demos went nowhere, however, and neither did a 1961 session with the Chess label, but Kilgore was able to score a smooth R&B hit with a group he had formed called the Uniques. The song, 1966's "Not Too Long Ago," was a regional hit in the south, but the group was unable to capture any momentum and soon Stampley was changing gears again and making in-roads into the country music establishment. A Nashville publishing house, Algee Music, gave Stampley a contract and Algee head Al Gallico helped get the singer a recording contract with Paramount. Blending country and soul, Stampley had hits with 1971's "Take Time to Know Her" and "If You Touch Me You've Got to Love Me."

Though his smooth sound virtually defined the countrypolitan movement of the mid-'70s, Stampley changed gears once more when he started writing rougher, hard-edged honky tonk songs such as "Whiskey Chasin'." Yet Stampley still had other tricks up his sleeve, and in 1979 he teamed up with Moe Bandy to form a tongue-in-cheek comedy duo. The pair, known as Moe & Joe, had hits with songs such as "Just Good Ole Boys" and the ridiculous "Hey Joe (Hey Moe)" before falling off the cultural radar. *—Steve Kurutz*

Joe Stampley & the Uniques: Gold / Oct. 21, 1994 / Paula/Flyright ♦♦♦
Before his country career, Louisianan Stampley fronted the Uniques, a '60s roots rock band that probably needed its roots sunk a little deeper than they were. *—Dan Cooper*

● **The Best of Joe Stampley** / 1995 / Varese ♦♦♦♦♦
Here are 18 songs from the '70s, most of them big country hits, drawing primarily from his recordings for Dot in the early part of the decade (including his version of "The Most Beautiful Girl"). Also includes the number-one hits he cut after leaving Dot for Epic, "Roll on, Big Mama" and "Just Good Ol' Boys." *—Richie Unterberger*

● **Good Ol' Boy: His Greatest Hits** / 1995 / Razor & Tie ♦♦♦♦♦
Released the same year as Varese's *The Best of Joe Stampley*, Razor & Tie's *Good Ol' Boy: His Greatest Hits* complements the other label's collection. Where Varese's 18-track disc focuses on Stampley's early-'70s recordings for Dot/ABC, this concentrates on his late-'70s/early-'80s work for Epic. The two discs share a mere four tracks—the Dot singles "If You Touch Me (You've Got to Love Me)," "All These Things," and "Soul Song" and the Epic-era Moe Bandy duet "Just Good Ol' Boys"—so they have considerably different feels, and ironically enough, the album covers do not offer a clear indication of which era is covered where, since the Varese features a contemporary photo and it's all old material, while Razor & Tie boasts an older photo and new recordings. Phew! The two taken together provide a full picture of Stampley's career as a hitmaker, but as individual collections they can be problematic, since the Varese doesn't have as many big hits but does have better music (and, unfortunately, is now out of print), while the Razor & Tie has the big hits (including four duets with Bandy) but runs out of musical steam about halfway through, as the '70s give way to the '80s and Stampley turns toward slicker, pop-inflected production. That most of the limp singles are in fact "CD bonus tracks" doesn't matter because they slow down the flow of the record and their overly polished, heavily synthesized productions undercut Stampley's vocals, which are still good, along with the memory of the strong honky tonk and country-soul that comprise the first ten songs or so—and the Bandy duets that close the record hammer home that no matter how strongly Stampley started his stint at Epic, it ended up in a place that didn't showcase his talents. Nevertheless, those duets, combined with the first 11 tracks, help drive up the number of successful sides, and even if he slumped in the early '80s, his '70s Epic material—including "Roll on, Big Mama," "Dear Woman," "Red Wine and Blue Memories," "If You've Got Ten Minutes, Let's Fall in Love," and "Put Your Clothes Back On"—holds its own with the Dot recordings musically (plus, they were also bigger hits). Plus, that slump is an accurate reading of his career, as well, so *Good Ol' Boy* does its job well, summarizing the Epic recordings, warts and all. *—Stephen Thomas Erlewine*

Pure Country / Aug. 25, 1998 / Sony ♦♦♦♦
Sony Special Products' *Pure Country* is an effective sampler of Joe Stampley's country-pop work for Epic Records in the '70s. In fact, in many ways it works as a hits compilation, since five of the featured songs—"Roll on, Big Mama," "Red Wine and Blue Memories," "Do You Ever Fool Around," "If You've Got Ten Minutes (Let's Fall in Love)," "I'm Gonna Love You Back to Loving Me Again"—were Top Ten country hits, while the remaining cuts ("Whiskey Talkin'," "There She Goes Again," "I'm Goin' Hurtin'," "Poor Side of Town," "Brown Eyed Girl") all reached the Top 20. Because of that, *Pure Country* is more than just a good bargain for a budget-line collection—it's a good bargain in general. *—Stephen Thomas Erlewine*

The Stanley Brothers

f. 1947, **db.** 1966
Group / Traditional Bluegrass

If you even *think* you know bluegrass, you have to know Ralph (born 1927) and Carter Stanley (born 1925), the Stanley Brothers. Parallel to Flatt & Scruggs and Bill Monroe's Blue Grass Boys, though not with their renown, were Virginians Ralph & Carter, mountain boys who took those mountains and their traditions and their songs and wove them into a traditional bluegrass sound of utter purity, simplicity, and astonishing beauty. Their first band, formed around 1947, played more of a mountain/folk music reminiscent of the old string bands, changing to their style of ultra-traditional bluegrass when Monroe's band became popular. Even on their recordings in the early '50s, the Stanleys' unmistakable sound is there, with guitarist Carter singing lead and banjo player Ralph singing tenor harmony. In the opinion of many, Carter possessed the best lead voice in bluegrass history—rich, emotional, and (in the best sense of the word) lonely. He took a happy song and sang it sad; he took a sad song and sang it sadder. And Ralph's unworldly mountain tenor matched his brother's voice perfectly, soaring above and often lightening the emotional load of the lyrics, creating a duet unsurpassed in country history.

Ralph & Carter were born into a musical family—their father sang and their mother played banjo. As teenagers, the brothers began performing around their hometown. After graduating from high-school, the siblings both served in the Army during World War II. Carter was discharged before Ralph. When he returned to the U.S. he got a job singing in Roy Sykes' Blue Ridge Mountain Boys. He quit the group as soon as Ralph returned from the Army in October of 1946, and the brothers formed a band, the Clinch Mountain Boys. The Stanley Brothers had a regular gig at WNVA Norton for a few months. Then they moved to the Bristol, TN-based WCYB, where they appeared regularly on the *Farm and Fun Time* program. While they appeared on the show, they gained quite a following and soon signed a contract with the Rich-R-Tone label. The Stanleys made their first records early in 1947, the same year they began playing various radio stations in the South, including ones in North Carolina, Louisiana, and Kentucky. The Brothers and their five-piece Clinch Mountain Boys were developing their style, moving from traditional string band sounds to a Monroe-inspired bluegrass style. During the late '40s and early '50s, several well-respected musicians passed through the band, including Curley Lambert, Pee Wee Lambert, Chubby Anthony, and Bill Napier.

After recording ten songs for Rich-R-Tone, the Stanley Brothers were signed to Columbia in 1948. For the next three years, they stayed with Columbia, producing 22 songs during their stint at the label—these songs would become bluegrass classics. For a brief time in 1951, the Stanley Brothers broke up. Carter sang with Monroe and made a handful of records with the father of bluegrass. Ralph was sidelined for several months following a car crash. The break was brief and the band was back together before the end of the year. In the summer of 1953, they left Columbia for Mercury Records. During the mid-'50s, they made a series of recordings that expanded their boundaries, as they played gospel, honky tonk, instrumentals, and a number of original songs.

At the end of the decade, the Brothers left Mercury and signed to both Starday and King, moved to Live Oak, FL, and began playing the Swannee River Jamboree. In the early '60s, they played a number of television shows and concerts throughout the South and recorded numerous records. However, the duo began to suffer financial problems beginning in 1961, which meant they couldn't afford to retain a whole band. Nevertheless, the Stanley Brothers continued to tour, playing clubs and various bluegrass festivals. However, they rarely left the South and their career suffered because of this. They recorded for a number of smaller labels after leaving King, though none of the records sold much. In 1966, Carter became seriously ill. On December 1 of that year, he passed away. He was only 41 years old. Ralph continued performing with a new lineup of the Clinch Mountain Boys. For the next three decades, he performed with various new lineups of the band, playing festivals and clubs and recording numerous records. *—Stephen Thomas Erlewine & David Vinopal*

The Stanley Brothers & the Clinch Mountain Boys / 1959 / King ♦♦♦

Hymns and Sacred Songs / 1959 / King ♦♦♦
Hymns and Sacred Songs is an original album that the Stanley Brothers recorded for King Records in 1959. Comprised entirely of classic country gospel numbers, the music on the album is completely beautiful and haunting, thanks the brothers' extraordinary harmonies. *—Thom Owens*

Everybody's Country Favorites / 1959 / King ♦♦♦
Features "Sweeter than the Flowers," "Shenandoah," "I'm a Man of Constant Sorrow," and other hits. *—AMG*

Long Journey Home / 1961 / Rebel ♦♦♦♦
In the early 1960s, when the Stanley Brothers were between record labels, they spent a week playing at Johnny's Used Cars near Baltimore. Johnny Wilbanks loved bluegrass music and used it as a sales device, paying bands to play in his lot and sponsoring a radio show that broadcast from his office. He also ran the small Wango label, for which the Stanleys recorded four albums after their parking lot engagement. This is the second of those four, originally issued as Wango 104 and reissued on LP by County in 1972 and on CD by Rebel in 1990. The material is classic Stanley Brothers: "Pretty Polly," "Rabbit in a Log," and the well-known title track. The other three albums in the series focused on gospel material, but this one is strictly secular and prominently features Ralph Stanley's flying-ice-chips banjo style and, even better, the pioneering cross-picking of guitarist George Shuffler on excellent performances of "Wildwood Flower" and "Will You Miss Me." But, as always, the most powerful moments are those that find Ralph Stanley's melismatic mountain tenor taking center stage, as on "Pretty Polly." A must for Stanley fans. *—Rick Anderson*

Old Country Church / 1963 / Gusto ♦♦♦♦♦
A 1961 release of traditional gospel songs, this is among the Stanley Brothers' finest albums. The brothers were born and raised in the Clinch Mountain area of Virginia (also home to the similarly pioneering Carter Family), one of the most fiercely traditional areas of the Bible Belt, and the pair performed gospel music throughout their career. However, this album just has something special about it. Recorded in one brief session with Carter Stanley on guitar and lead vocals, Ralph Stanley on banjo and tenor harmonies, Curley Lambert on mandolin, Vernon Derrick on fiddle, and Chuck Stripling on bass, these ten simple, powerful songs are delivered with the righteous passion and enthusiastic sense of community of a real church service, where joy and devotion are inextricably intertwined. Even the most mawkish songs, like the ultra-maudlin "Mother's Only Sleeping," are delivered with sincerity and grace. The best tracks, like the title song, "My Sinful Past" and the closing "Kneel at the Cross," are as good as traditional gospel gets. Unusually for the Stanley Brothers, about half of the songs are sung in four-square harmony in the traditional gospel quartet style, with Lambert and Derrick filling in the vocal sound. *—Stewart Mason*

Stanley Series, Vol. 3 #3 / 1989 / Copper Creek ♦♦♦
The Stanley Series is a multi-volume series of live concerts from the Stanley Brothers. The 27-song *Vol. 3: #3* captures a 1958 show recorded with mandolinist Bill Napier, fiddler Ralph Mayo and bassist Jack Cooke. One of the highlights of the disc is "Going to

the Races," awhich the duo never recorded commercially; another is "No School Bus in Heaven," a contemporary folk song about a Kentucky school-bus crash. —*Thom Owens*

Stanley Series, Vol. 2 #1 / 1989 / Copper Creek ✦✦✦

The Stanley Series is a multi-volume series of live concerts from the Stanley Brothers. The 17-song *Vol. 2: #1* captures a 1956 show where the brothers were supported by fiddler Chubby Anthony, mandolinist Curley Lambert and bassist Doug Morris, who all shine on this cross-section of originals and standards. Of special note is Chubby's powerful fiddler, plus the group's excellent versions of Bill Monroe's "A Voice from on High" and the Stanleys' "Little Glass of Wine." —*Thom Owens*

The Stanley Brothers & The Clinch Mountain Boys 1949–1952 / 1991 / Bear Family ✦✦✦✦✦

This is it, the absolute perfect starting point for neophyte fans who want to discover the Stanley Brothers. The years between 1949 and 1952, when the Virginia brothers were signed to Columbia Records, are largely considered their most fruitful period. Certainly this lineup of their backing band, the Clinch Mountain Boys, was the strongest; besides Carter Stanley's assured leads and Ralph Stanley's heartbreaking tenor, these recordings introduced mandolin player Darrell "Pee Wee" Lambert and his one-of-a-kind high-baritone harmonies, the secret ingredient that made the Stanley Brothers' recordings from this era sound like nothing that had come before in bluegrass. As usual with Bear Family reissues, this set contains every note from the brothers' Columbia sessions, including previously unreleased alternate takes of "The Fields Have Turned Brown" and "Little Glass of Wine," along with full session notes and illuminating liner notes courtesy of historian Gary B. Reid. Yes, it has the original "I'm a Man of Constant Sorrow" for all of you *O Brother, Where Art Thou?* fans, but the 23 other tracks are every bit as vital, imaginative, and pure. This, in its purest and most graceful form, is what bluegrass is all about. —*Stewart Mason*

Early Starday-King Years 1958–1961 / 1994 / King ✦✦✦✦

The Early Starday-King Years: 1958-1961 is a 109-track, four-disc box set that compiles every track the Stanley Brothers cut for Starday and King during that era. At the time, the group were releasing albums both on Starday and King, so there was an immense amount of confusion between the releases; the box set helps clarify the matters, by gathering all of the music together and presenting it in chronological order. This way, it's possible to hear their progression, as well as the differences between the recordings for the two labels; on the King recordings, the Stanley Brothers tended to be more experimental, working in electric instrumentation. Though there is plenty of fine music on the set, *The Early Starday-King Years* is, overall, too thorough and extensive for anyone but bluegrass historians. —*Thom Owens*

☆ **Stanley Brothers & The Clinch Mountain Boys 1953–59** / 1994 / Bear Family ✦✦✦✦✦

Stanley Brothers & The Clinch Mountain Boys 1953-59 is a double-disc containing everything the group recorded during the latter half of the '50s for Mercury, Starday, and King Records. These recordings are generally considered to be among their best work and this set is the only one to make complete sense of the recordings. All of the group's best moments, plus many forgotten but equally fine gems, are included on the collection, making it a comprehensive retrospective. Nevetheless, it also functions as a good, if rather lengthy, introduction to the Stanley Brothers, since it showcases the richness and depth in their music. In short, it's an essential addition to any serious bluegrass collection. —*Thom Owens*

★ **Angel Band: The Classic Mercury Recordings** / 1995 / Mercury Nashville ✦✦✦✦✦

Angel Band collects the bulk of the Stanley Brothers' mid-'50s recordings, when they were expanding their sound slightly. Although it isn't always straight bluegrass, it shows how versatile and talented the Stanleys were. It's an essential purchase for a bluegrass collection. —*Thom Owens*

★ **Complete Columbia Recordings** / Mar. 1996 / Columbia/Legacy ✦✦✦✦✦

While this doesn't have the two alternate takes that surfaced on the nearly identical Bear Family collection *(1949-1952)*, this does have all 22 of the sides they officially released on Columbia, and will be much easier to find in the U.S. It's classic bluegrass of great historical importance, featuring mostly original compositions. —*Richie Unterberger*

Earliest Recordings: Complete Rich-R-Tone 78s (1947–1952) / Jul. 15, 1997 / Revenant ✦✦✦✦✦

This collection gathers the Stanley Brothers' earliest recordings: 78s they cut for the Rich-R-Tone label between 1947 and 1952. Included are traditional gospel songs, breakneck-paced bluegrass ("Molly and Tenbrooks"), and songs of their own that would later become staples ("Little Maggie"). There's some variation in the sound quality, but it isn't bad overall: a light hiss and some mild distortion of the high levels is as bad as it gets. Historic and wonderful, this Stanley Brothers release is a must-have for fans. —*Joslyn Layne*

Best of the Best of the Stanley Brothers / May 19, 1998 / Federal ✦✦✦✦

Bluegrass purists may quibble with the redundant album title—many believe that the brothers' 1948-1951 stint at Columbia Records is the pinnacle, not only of their career, but of traditional bluegrass itself—but it's impossible to argue with this material. Ten songs taken from the Stanley Brothers' 1958-1964 tenure recording for the King and Starday labels, this album does do an excellent job of pulling the very best material from the brothers' rather spotty later career. Opening with a sterling version of their signature song, the apocalyptic "Rank Strangers to Me," the album then moves through other gems like the standard "I'm a Man of Constant Sorrow," the frisky and sly "How Mountain Girls Can Love," and the chilling "Think of What You've Done." The Stanley Brothers flirted with country and even pop a bit during their King and Starday years, as evinced by the twangy "Love Me Darling, Just Tonight," but their drummerless traditional bluegrass sound remains the focus of this collection. A fine, inexpensive, but unfortunately brief introduction, this set is aimed primarily at those looking for an inexpensive entry point into the world of the Stanley Brothers. —*Stewart Mason*

Ridin' That Midnight Train: Starday King Recordings 1958–1961 / Sep. 28, 1999 / WestSide ✦✦✦✦✦

The Best of the Stanley Brothers: 20th Century Masters/The Millennium Collection / Oct. 1, 2002 / Mercury ✦✦✦

Although the Universal Music Group has been assembling discount-priced best-ofs for most of its catalog artists as part of its "20th Century Masters/The Millennium Collection" series and might have been expected to get around to the Stanley Brothers, who spent five years in the mid-'50s on the now-Universal-owned Mercury label, eventually, the inclusion of their 1955 recording of "Angel Band" on the Grammy-winning, multi-platinum soundtrack album to *O Brother, Where Art Thou?* is the immediate impetus for this collection. *O Brother, Where Art Thou?* has led record labels to scour their vaults for traditional bluegrass, under the impression that the success of the soundtrack has created a vast new audience for old-time mountain music. And indeed, anyone who liked hearing "Angel Band" likely will enjoy 11 more Stanley Brothers songs in their familiar style. But in a time when the most popular recording format, the CD, can hold up to 80 minutes of music, buyers are liable to be disappointed, even with the discount price, that the disc runs less than half an hour. The reason for this is hidden in music industry machinations and has to do with the fees record companies pay music publishers for the use of their songs. Any more than 12 songs, presumably, would lead to an economic sacrifice, since albums in the series never contain more tracks than that. But the Stanley Brothers' recordings are quite short, and as a result, so is this album. Therefore, even casual fans might be better advised to spring for the more extensive 1995 set *Angel Band: The Classic Mercury Recordings* for a sense of this five-year period in the Stanley Brothers' career. —*William Ruhlmann*

Ralph Stanley

b. Feb. 25, 1927, Stratton, VA

Banjo, Vocals / Bluegrass, Traditional Bluegrass, Bluegrass-Gospel, Contemporary Bluegrass, Truck Driving Country

Born in Stratton, VA, in 1927, Ralph Stanley and his older brother Carter formed the Stanley Brothers & the Clinch Mountain Boys. In 1946 Ralph and Carter were being broadcast from radio station WCYB in Bristol, VA. The music, which was inspired by their Virginia mountain home, was encouraged by their mother, who taught Ralph the clawhammer style of banjo picking that he and Carter became famous for. They recorded for such companies as the small Rich-R-Tone label and later Columbia, a relationship that lasted from 1949 until 1952. These classic sessions defined the Stanleys' own approach to bluegrass and made them as important as Bill Monroe. After leaving Columbia, the Stanleys were with Mercury, Starday, and King. Leaning towards more gospel at times, Carter and Ralph made a place for themselves in the music industry. In December of 1966, Carter Stanley died in a Virginia hospital after a steady decline in health. He was just 41 years old. After much consideration and grief, Ralph carried on without Carter. Already their haunting mountain melodies made them stand apart from other bluegrass bands, but Ralph expanded upon this foundation and took his own "high lonesome" vocals to a new plane.

Popular at bluegrass festivals, Ralph and each edition of the Clinch Mountain Boys grew to be one of the most respected outfits in bluegrass. As far as west as California and even up in the hollars of Kentucky, people were drawn to the poignant, mournful sound of Ralph Stanley's style. Different from all the rest, Ralph's ability to hit the right notes and chords made him a singer of trailblazing proportions. Ralph continued to record for a wide variety of labels, including Jalyn, Rebel, King Bluegrass, Blue Jay, Jessup, Stanleytone, his own label, and Freeland. A devoted family man, his constant touring took its toll on his first marriage, a union that produced daughters Lisa Joy and Tonya and oldest son Timothy. His second wife Jimmie, also a singer, gave him another son late in life; Ralph II followed in both his father's and uncle's footsteps and played in the Clinch Mountain Boys with his dad. A Bluegrass Hall of Fame member along with Carter, Ralph Stanley was an inspiration to Dwight Yoakam, Emmylou Harris, the late Keith Whitley and even Monroe acolyte Ricky Skaggs. With his raw emotions and Mother Stanley's three-fingered banjo technique, he helped bring the mountain style of bluegrass music to mainstream audiences. —*Jana Pendragon*

A Man and His Music / 1973 / Rebel ✦✦✦✦

This is Ralph Stanley in the early '70s, looking back on his inspirations and creating in one album a kind of distilled essence of his music, thus the title. The resulting picking sits well, more like aged scotch than the kind of stuff these bluegrass fiends cook up out in the woods. The music here is about as far away as one can get from the reputation this music sometimes gets as a bunch of super-fast, meaningless notes . The melodies of each piece are always coming to the forefront, the players taking delight in the many tonal perplexities that can be added while still maintaining that focus on simplicity. The clawhammer banjo style that Stanley demonstrates here is a wonder, passages of notes effortlessly rolling around on top of each other or articulated cleanly as if being spoken by a long, elegant forked tongue. The recording balance is really fun, instruments jumping out to solo as if the players were hiding behind one's sofa. The fiddler Curly Ray Cline pulls off a series of sizzling improvisations on "Bound to Ride," one of the many traditional tunes in the program, most of which get credited to Stanley due to his tremendously personal arrangements. Other highlights include the stomping banjo opener "Shout Little Lulu," the locomotivated instrumental "Train 45," and one of the best versions of "Rocky Island" ever recorded, rollicking and full of powerful harmonies that will be good for the listener's ears, if not their speaker system. —*Eugene Chadbourne*

I'll Answer the Call / 1987 / Rebel ✦✦✦

By 1988, when this album was originally recorded and released, Ralph Stanley had reverted to a mandolin-less instrumental lineup much like the one he and his brother had used early in their career as a band—a move originally designed to keep the group from sounding too much like a direct imitation of Bill Monroe's Blue Grass Boys. The material, too, harks back to the glory days of bluegrass-gospel music, and includes renditions of such staples as "Let the Church Roll On" and "In His Arms I'm Not Afraid" (which features some particularly spectacular tenor singing by Stanley). "Calling My Children Home" exemplifies the unaccompanied quartet singing that Stanley had done so much to popularize in the 1970s. But this album's emotional centerpiece is Stanley's solo vocal performance of the modal and vinegary "Daddy's Rose." All of that said, this is about an average Ralph Stanley album in terms of overall quality—which means, of course, that it stands head and shoulders above most other bluegrass-gospel records. *—Rick Anderson*

Pray for the Boys / 1990 / Rebel ✦✦✦

Classic Bluegrass / 1990 / Rebel ✦✦✦
Classic Bluegrass contains a cross-section of Ralph Stanley's recordings during the '70s, providing a good introduction to the trailblazing bluegrass artist. *—Thom Owens*

☆ **Bound to Ride** / 1991 / Rebel ✦✦✦✦✦
This disc collects 20 recordings made in the early '70s by the legendary Ralph Stanley with his Clinch Mountain Boys, who included, at various times, Ricky Skaggs, Roy Lee Centers, and even the late John Duffey. The fierce, elemental purity of Stanley's sound is captured beautifully on these sessions, many of which feature him playing clawhammer banjo in the style he learned from his mother. But though his banjo playing is very good, it's Stanley's singing that has always set him apart from the rest of the bluegrass pack: His piercing mountain tenor voice and his sanctified delivery almost sound like something from another world. When he sings "Pretty Polly," "Riding the Midnight Train," or especially, the hair-raising "Man of Constant Sorrow," the effect is visceral and spiritual at the same time. Listening to him blow out the microphone with Duffey and Centers on "The Lonesome River" is almost literally a religious experience. This is mountain music at its finest. *—Rick Anderson*

Almost Home / 1992 / Rebel ✦✦✦✦✦
Ralph Stanley, who is without a doubt the finest first-generation bluegrass singer still alive, here delivers 12 old-time gospel songs in a cappella quartet arrangements, and the result bears no more relationship to bluegrass than Gregorian chant does to a symphony. Though the cutting edge of Stanley's tenor voice has been ground down by decades of use, his mountain melisma has never sounded better. Rarely does he end a phrase on the single note you expect; instead he winds around it before landing gently, lending tremendous power to every cadence without ever raising his voice. His rendition of "God Put a Rainbow in the Clouds" is revelatory, almost on a par with his legendary performances of "Man of Constant Sorrow" and "Two Coats." "Village Church Yard" taps into a deep but stark vein of religious feeling and musical tone that borders on the medieval. And on "The Day Is Past and Gone" (actually a rearrangement of the shape-note hymn "Evening Shade"), he "lines out" each lyric before the other members of the quartet kick in with their parts. It's an approach he uses frequently throughout this program, despite the fact that everyone obviously knows the songs; he does it not because it's necessary, but because you're supposed to feel like you're in church when you listen to this music. If goose bumps could kill, possession of this album would be a felony. *—Rick Anderson*

● **Saturday Night & Sunday Morning** / 1992 / Freeland ✦✦✦✦✦
This 31-cut, two-disc project is a masterpiece reflecting both the secular and spiritual sides of Ralph Stanley's artistry. It is also a concept he mulled over in his mind for some time before executing it. The idea was to include performers from both the country and bluegrass worlds doing songs that somehow fit into the Stanley Brothers' tradition. With the inclusion of some Stanley originals as well as tunes written by Bill Monroe, Dwight Yoakam, Tom T. Hall, and Roy McMillan, this is not only a diverse compilation of material, but also one that never fails to interest the listener. Certainly the start-off number, McMillan's "Mountain Folks," which is done up just right by Ralph Stanley & the Clinch Mountain Boys, sets the tone. Followed by a duet between Stanley and Yoakam on the infectious "Down Where the River Bends," it quickly moves through to Stanley's final secular duet with fellow bluegrasser Bill Monroe. Their teamwork on "Letter From My Darling" is monumental. The spiritual numbers include Stanley and Tom T. Hall on the well-known gospel number "Rank Stranger" and Carter Stanley's sadly descriptive "The Fields Have All Turned Brown." But the most beguiling track is the fervent version of Yoakam's tribute song to his coal mining grandfather, Luther Tibbs. "Miner's Prayer" is given a gospel overhaul, making what was already a brilliant creation into an even more ageless tune that will be played, loved, and remembered for many generations to come. Ralph Stanley's high lonesome sound fits in perfectly here and is endlessly effective. Outstanding performances in both categories come from Patty Loveless, Alison Krauss, George Jones, Jimmy Martin, and Emmylou Harris, to name just a few. A concept that works well for Ralph Stanley and his many friends, this is certainly a project that belongs in every bluegrass or gospel collection. *—Jana Pendragon*

Back to the Cross / Aug. 15, 1992 / Freeland ✦✦✦
Like Bill Monroe, Ralph Stanley maintained his skills and spirit into the 1990s, still singing and picking classic bluegrass. He joined Freeland in 1992, and appropriately made his label debut a gospel session with the Clinch Mountain Boys. You wouldn't expect any surprises, and there weren't any; nor were there low points. The CD contained 12 wonderful renditions of traditional hymns and praise songs performed with the humility, grace and down-home artistry that has always characterized Ralph Stanley's music. *—Ron Wynn*

Saturday Night / Apr. 15, 1995 / Freeland ✦✦✦✦✦
This 31-cut, two-disc project is a masterpiece that reflects both the secular and spiritual sides of Ralph Stanley's artistry. It is also a concept he mulled over in his mind for sometime before executing it. The idea was to include performers from both the country and bluegrass worlds doing songs that somehow fit into the Stanley Brothers' tradition. With the inclusion of some Stanley originals as well as tunes written by Bill Monroe, Dwight Yoakam, Tom T. Hall, and Roy McMillan, this is not only a diverse compilation of material, but also one that never fails to interest the listener. Highlights include a duet between Stanley and Yoakam on the infectious "Down Where the River Bends," and it quickly moves through to the final secular duet between Stanley and fellow bluegrasser Bill Monroe. Their team work on "Letter From My Darling" is monumental. The spiritual numbers include Stanley and Tom T. Hall on the gospel number "Rank Stranger" and Carter Stanley's sadly descriptive "The Fields Have All Turned Brown." But, the most beguiling track is the fervent version of Yoakam's tribute song to his coal-mining grandfather, Luther Tibbs. "Miner's Prayer" is given a gospel overhaul that actually makes what was already a brilliant creation into an even more ageless tune that will be played, loved, and remembered for many generations to come. Ralph Stanley's *High Lonesome* sound fits in perfectly here and is endlessly effective. A concept that works well for Stanley and his many friends, this is certainly a project that belongs in every bluegrass or gospel collection. *—Jana Pendragon*

1971–1973 / Jul. 11, 1995 / Rebel ✦✦✦✦✦
This four-CD set is a collection of the entire output of Ralph Stanley & the Clinch Mountain Boys during an astonishing three-year period in the early '70s. The albums collected here include the first appearance of Stanley's signature a cappella bluegrass-gospel, and feature the outstanding lead singing of the late Roy Lee Centers. The strong incarnation of the Clinch Mountain Boys features Curly Ray Cline on fiddle, Jack Cooke on bass, and Ricky Lee on lead guitar. Teenage Stanley disciples and future country stars Keith Whitley and Ricky Skaggs make their first recorded appearances here also, and Country Gentleman John Duffey stops by to max out the needles on the Stanley Brothers classic *The Lonesome River.* The band runs through straight bluegrass, gospel, old-time banjo songs, fiddle tunes, and Stanley Brothers classics, all with great confidence and style. Songs are pulled from multiple and diverse sources, including the Carter Family, old country, Bill Monroe, and even a beautiful Jesse Winchester song, "Brand New Tennessee Waltz." This set is for purists more than bluegrass neophytes, but no fan of Ralph Stanley or the Stanley Brothers should be without it. These albums broke new stylistic ground at a time when there was some concern whether Ralph Stanley could continue in the wake of Carter Stanley's death. *—Ben O'Connor*

My All and All / Jun. 3, 1997 / Rebel ✦✦✦✦
Now that Bill Monroe has passed away, only one great voice left from bluegrass music's first generation remained, Ralph Stanley. And though he and Monroe were both staunchly traditional high-tenor singers, beyond that surface similarity you could hardly find two voices more different. Monroe's style was informed by the coal mines first and by the church second; though he could sing gospel convincingly, he was more likely to deliver a Jimmie Rodgers blue yodel than a hymn, and he played mandolin with a proud virtuosity that spoke wordless volumes about his fierce personality. Stanley, on the other hand, always has the church in his voice. He hardly ever yodels, and he rarely sings about muleskinners or coal mines. Instead he sings about God and sin and the resurrection, and his voice cuts like a whipsaw and echoes like a stainless-steel bell. Or it used to. Now that he's 70 years old, his voice doesn't really cut anymore. But it has lost none of its power to raise the hair on your neck—though it quavers and cracks, it is never off-pitch, and Stanley's palpable religious fervor is undiminished. *My All and All* is an all-gospel album, featuring several hot young players and singers (notably banjoist Steve Sparkman and the young Ralph Stanley II), all of whom consecrate their prodigious chops to the work of the Lord on tunes both old ("Jesus on the Mainline," "The Uncloudy Day") and new ("While Eternal Ages Roll," the title track). Stanley sings lead about half the time and plays banjo, unfortunately, very little; though Sparkman acquits himself beautifully, fans might miss the flying ice-chips sound of Stanley's picking. But even in the absence of his banjo playing and in the relative weakness of his voice, the power of the music here is both visceral and spiritual. *—Rick Anderson*

Songs My Mother Taught Me & More: Clawhammer Style Banjo / May 12, 1998 / Freeland ✦✦✦✦
Ralph Stanley is one of very few bluegrass banjo players who still take off the steel fingerpicks occasionally and play in the older, more traditional clawhammer (or "frailing") style. It's a more percussive, less intricate approach, one that carries with it the rough-hewn charm of old-time string band music rather than the flashier, more commercial appeal of bluegrass. This disc collects 18 live and studio recordings in that mode by Stanley, some made just a few years prior to this album's 1997 release and others dating as far back as the early '70s. Many of the tunes will be familiar to Stanley fans—he's recorded "Shout Little Lulie" and "Little Birdie" many times—but others are more obscure. While all of these performances are a delight, it's the live ones that work the best, partly because he sings more on those; the live performance of "Little Birdie" may be definitive. And the disc ends with an on-stage interview in which an unidentified MC gets Stanley to explain his technique in detail. Musician credits would have been helpful to those interested in this recording as a historical document, but the music couldn't be better. *—Rick Anderson*

Clinch Mountain Country / May 19, 1998 / Rebel ✦✦✦✦✦
The two-disc set *Clinch Mountain Country* is a treasure that amazes and inspires at every turn. Ralph Stanley is one of the true greats of American music. Kicking off with an all-time favorite, "How Mountain Girls Can Love," the set features Stanley's signature clawhammer banjo style and the distinctive mountain harmonies perfected by himself and his brother, the late Carter Stanley. Other guests from the music world include Dwight Yoakam, Marty Stuart, Bob Dylan, Patty Loveless, BR5-49, Rhonda Vincent, Gillian Welch, Laurie Lewis, Junior Brown, Vern Gosdin, Vince Gill, and many others.

One of the most poignant tracks is Stanley, the Clinch Mountain Boys, and country & western master George Jones singing "The Window Up Above." The meeting of Stanley & Jones is a monumental moment in music history. Together their voices blend effortlessly on a song that Jones wrote so many years ago. Also significant is the prominence of Ralph II, the man who will carry on the legacy his father and uncle began in the mountains of Virginia. Stanley's high lonesome vocal style is unlike any other sound, and he is without peer in the world of bluegrass music. This collection of tunes, many written by Carter and/or Ralph, is evidence of the heartfelt, soul-nourishing music the Carters brought out of the western Virginia Highlands and gave to the world. It's a worthy follow-up to the 1992 two-CD release *Saturday Night & Sunday Morning*. *—Jana Pendragon*

Man of Constant Sorrow / Jan. 23, 2001 / Rebel ✦✦✦✦✦
This collection was released to coincide with the release of Joel & Ethan Coen's film *O Brother, Where Art Thou?*, which features Ralph Stanley's a cappella rendition of "Oh, Death" and a number of other traditional bluegrass songs long associated with Stanley, including the immortal "Man of Constant Sorrow." This album brings together 13 classic tracks from the Stanley catalog; highlights include the title track, the absolutely hair-raising "Oh, Death," and a stirring version of "I've Just Seen the Rock of Ages." That last song, recorded in the early '70s, has never been released on CD before and features the lead singing of a very young Keith Whitley, who would later go on to significant success as a country singer. The only quibble one could make with this excellent collection is its length, which, at 33 minutes, is pretty skimpy for a best-of collection. But as an introduction to Ralph Stanley's singular brand of mountain music, you couldn't do better than this album. *—Rick Anderson*

Echoes of the Stanley Brothers / Mar. 13, 2001 / Varese ✦✦✦
Ralph Stanley is the elder statesman of bluegrass, both a link to the past and a living reminder of the music's relevance. *Echoes of the Stanley Brothers* is comprised of two albums, *Michigan Bluegrass* from 1971 and *Gospel Echoes of the Stanley Brothers* from 1973. The first album covers faithless women and murder, the second, faith and redemption. The bluesy "Another Song, Another Drink" will probably inspire anyone who's ever lost their love due to a bottle problem to hit the bars once again. Like some of Stanley's best music, there's a sense of fatalism that saturates lyrics like, "I realize how much I loved you/but it's too late for you to care." The end, it seems, is near. The plot-heavy "River Underground" carries the same determinism. The narrator marries a woman, she runs around with other men, he murders her and leaves no evidence, and, because he misses her, decides to commit suicide. (One wonders what might have happened had the song been extended another minute.) The best thing about both songs is the deep feeling that accompanies the vocals; the haunting harmonies hark back to the old-time music of the Appalachians and the lyrics seem to have been carved in stone. The jingoistic "Are You Proud of America" and "Let's Keep Old Glory Waving" remind one of the type of the flag-waving anthems that occasionally turn up during times of crisis (perhaps Vietnam here). These songs also don't age well—unless they are reissued during another crisis. The second album begins with the lovely "Let Me Walk Lord By Your Side," offers a heartfelt "The Darkest Hour Is Just Before Dawn," and presents a bluesy version of "White Dove." *Echoes of the Stanley Brothers* captures Stanley's new band, featuring Keith Whitley and Ricky Skaggs, respectfully paying tribute to their roots. Fans of the Stanley Brothers and of Ralph Stanley should enjoy this one. *—Ronnie Lankford Jr.*

Clinch Mountain Gospel / May 15, 2001 / Rebel ✦✦✦✦✦
Originally recorded in a single all-day session in the spring of 1977 and released later that year, this remains the best of the three albums made by Ralph Stanley's band during the brief period between the untimely demise of singer Roy Lee Centers and the beginning of Charlie Sizemore's nine-year tenure with the band. During those few months, Stanley's former singer Keith Whitley returned to take the lead vocal slot, and this stunningly beautiful set of old-time and bluegrass-gospel songs was one of the results. The program is predictable: Chestnuts like "Over in the Gloryland," "Beautiful Star of Bethlehem," "Amazing Grace," and "Mother's Not Dead" are all here, as are a couple of favorite hymn arrangements ("Amazing Grace," "Jesus Savior Pilot Me"). And for fans of the film *O Brother, Where Art Thou?*, there's an absolutely hair-raising rendition of "Oh, Death"; unlike the a cappella version that Stanley sings in the movie, this one features both Stanley & Whitley with a full-band accompaniment, but it's no less stark and powerful. This is one of the most powerful bluegrass-gospel albums ever made—never syrupy, never cheaply emotional, it grabs you by the scruff of the neck and fairly dares you not to get right with God. *—Rick Anderson*

Cry From the Cross / May 22, 2001 / Rebel ✦✦✦✦✦
Originally released on LP in 1972, this was the first album Ralph Stanley recorded with what many still consider the best band he ever had, one that included not only lead singer Roy Lee Centers (whose vocal similarity to Stanley's late brother, Ralph, was positively eerie), fiddler Curly Ray Cline, and bassist Jack Cooke, but also the young mandolinist Ricky Skaggs and guitarist Keith Whitley. Stanley had discovered Skaggs and Whitley playing old-timey brother duets in a club and was so taken with them that he invited them to tour with him, thus creating one of bluegrass history's legendary lineups. The material on *Cry From the Cross* is rendered expertly, but without any slickness; Stanley's rough-edged tenor voice dominates, as always, and the instrumental backing tends to be minimal. "Bright Morning Star" and "Sinner Man" are both performed a cappella, and the gripping "Two Coats," which would go on to become a staple of the Stanley repertoire, is here given a sharp-edged modal delivery that perfectly complements the song's stern moral message. This album is clearly a must for Stanley fans and will also serve as a good introduction for newcomers. *—Rick Anderson*

Clinch Mountain Sweethearts / Sep. 25, 2001 / Rebel ✦✦✦
Clinch Mountain Sweethearts can be thought of as a bluegrass version of John Prine's *In Spite of Ourselves*. Like Prine, Stanley is joined by a number of female singers, both later and classic, on 16 bluegrass gems. In fact, several names—Iris DeMent, Lucinda Williams, and Melba Montgomery—show up on both collections. Maria Muldaur cuts loose and gives it her all on the bluesy "The Memory of Your Smile." When Stanley joins her, the sound is oh so lonesome. DeMent joins the fray on "Ridin' That Midnight Train" and "Trust Each Other," and while both cuts work pretty well, the country inflections in her voice get lost in the uptempo material. One surprising cut features Chely Wright who, believe it or not, offers a good old-time vocal on "Angel Band" that has almost nothing in common with her trendy Nashville work. Montgomery delivers a gutsy take on Hank Williams' "You Win Again," which is a tad more believable coming from a female point of view. The Clinch Mountain Boys sound great as always. Combining bluegrass and old-time, they find the right groove for each piece and never hurry a song. *Clinch Mountain Sweethearts* works better than the Prine collection, mostly because Stanley is well-matched with most of his co-singers. When their voices don't match, they stay out of each other's way. Once again, *Clinch Mountain Sweethearts* finds Stanley making good music by adding a few contemporary touches to mountain traditions. *—Ronnie D. Lankford Jr.*

Live at McCabe's Guitar Shop 2-11-01 / Feb. 12, 2002 / DCN ✦✦✦
On February 11th, 2001, an intimate group of lucky people crammed into tiny McCabe's Guitar Shop to experience 55 years of bluegrass legacy firsthand when Ralph Stanley held court at the ripe age of 74 years young. Supported heavily by his Clinch Mountain Boys, Stanley acts initially as an MC, introducing the members of his band to each come up and take his turn on vocals and featured instrumentals, and during the second set takes center stage himself performing recent favorites like "Man of Constant Sorrow" and "Oh Death." The sparing use of the patriarch of bluegrass is by no means surprising, nor is it even a detraction. The able vocals of his son Ralph Stanley II and the superlative banjo picking of Steve Sparkman leave the elder Stanley to supply the piercing tenor harmonies that he perfected with his brother Carter in the '40s and '50s. The band turns in a searing "Daybreak in Dixie," expert clawhammer-style banjo playing on "Rocky Island," and an astounding a cappella rendition of "I'll Wear a White Robe" during this second set. The loose, intimate setting makes for a real authentic hills-and-hollers feel, and the appreciative (and fortunate) crowd seems genuinely awed at this rare opportunity to see a true musical legend in his element. While this is by no means the definitive Ralph Stanley album, or even a great starting point for listeners intrigued by what they found in the film *O Brother, Where Art Thou?*, it is a terrific document of how the music of the mountains can become more valuable as it ages. *—Zac Johnson*

Ralph Stanley / Jun. 11, 2002 / Columbia ✦✦✦
The undisputed modern patriarch of bluegrass, Ralph Stanley is presented starkly and honestly on this self-titled 2002 album. Similar in sound and execution to Johnny Cash and Rick Rubin's *American Recordings*, *Ralph Stanley* presents the 75-year-old vocalist in a bare-bones environment with only minimal musical accompaniment, highlighting his careworn voice without any studio trickery or noticeable overdubs. Assisted by the incomparable Norman Blake on guitar, Stuart Duncan on banjo, Mike Compton on mandolin, and bassist Dennis Crouch, the arrangements are never intrusive on Stanley's voice, allowing his natural tenor to creak and crag through ten classic ballads and one new original. Highlights include the gritty murder ballads "Henry Lee" and "Little Mathie Grove," and the bright harmonies from members of the Cox Family on the Hank Williams gospel number "Calling You." Country musicians may have lined up around the block to be involved with this project, but luckily, producer and folk aficionado T-Bone Burnett kept the raw power of Stanley's voice unencumbered by chorus after chorus of guest vocalist, making for a more straightforward and powerful final work. Unfortunately for some listeners, the years of performing have worn deep lines not only in his face, but in his voice as well. Anyone expecting the sharp, high-lonesome sound of "How Mountain Girls Can Love" and "Roll in My Sweet Baby's Arms" may be disappointed at the sound of the septuagenarian's old bones croaking together, but anyone who can appreciate the stark purity of honest American folk music will hold this album close to their hearts. *—Zac Johnson*

The Very Best of Ralph Stanley / Nov. 12, 2002 / Audium ✦✦✦
The title of Audium's 2002 release, *The Very Best of Ralph Stanley*, is a little misleading, and while it is not a genre-spanning, all-encompassing collection of everything the godfather of bluegrass recorded, it does grab 16 very nice recordings from the early to mid-'70s, with one recording jumping out from the year 2000. Stanley's most recognized songs ("Little Maggie," "Rank Stranger," "Man of Constant Sorrow," "O Death") are all represented, as well as some lesser-known gems like "Clinch Mountain Backstep," and the underrated "Katie Daley" (featuring performances by the very youthful Ricky Skaggs on mandolin and Keith Whitley on guitar). Roy Lee Centers, who acted as partner to Ralph Stanley's high-lonesome tenor after Carter Stanley's death ended the Stanley Brothers' career in 1966, features prominently on the album, ably taking lead vocals on nearly half of the songs. The highlight of the album is one of the warmest and most beautiful renditions of the song "Rank Strangers" available in the Stanley catalog, and it alone is worth the price of the disc. *—Zac Johnson*

John Starling

b. Mar. 26, 1940, Durham, NC
Guitar, Vocals / Progressive Bluegrass
A U.S. Army surgeon, guitarist, and singer, Starling played with the Seldom Scene progressive bluegrass band from 1971 until 1977. After playing with various other groups in the '80s, he rejoined Seldom Scene in the early '90s. *—David Vinopal*

● **Long Time Gone** / 1990 / Sugar Hill ✦✦✦✦✦
Clear-voiced John Starling puts aside his progressive bluegrass leanings and crafts a more straight-ahead country sound on his 1990 solo debut, *Long Time Gone*. Well-placed

appearances by Emmylou Harris, Tony Rice, Mike Auldridge, Herb Pedersen, Ricky Skaggs, and some slide work from producer Lowell George all add to the crisp, clean feel of Starling's voice. Composed of mostly classics and traditional tunes, the album culminates in a strong version of Gram Parsons' "Sin City," accented beautifully by Emmylou Harris' harmony vocals. Fans of Starling's work with the Seldom Scene will be more than pleased with his solo releases, *Long Time Gone* being the best of the bunch. —*Zac Johnson*

Waitin' on a Southern Train / 1995 / Sugar Hill ✦✦✦

Lucille Starr (Lucille Marie Raymonde Savoie)

b. St. Boniface, Canada

Vocals / Traditional Country, Country-Pop

Canadian singer/songwriter and yodeler Lucille Starr (born Lucille Marie Raymonde Savoie) was one of Canada's most popular country performers. She started her career singing with a British Columbia choir, Les Hirondelles, and then became the female lead with the Keray Regan Band. Eventually she and bandmember Bob Regan left to tour the country as Lucille & Bob. The duo had several successful singles in both the U.S. and Canada, including "No Help Wanted." With her powerful voice and vibrant performances, Starr soon attracted notice from several label executives, one of whom dubbed the act the Canadian Sweethearts. While in California, the two frequently appeared on local country music shows and on ABC's *Country America* show, where they appeared regularly for two years. They also appeared on the *Grand Ole Opry*, and toured North America with Hank Snow, Wilf Carter and Little Jimmy Dickens.

Both Starr and the Canadian Sweethearts signed to A&M Records in 1963, the latter reaching the Top 50 with "Hootenanny Express." They also had two top-rated hits in Canada, including "Looking Back to See." Starr went solo with *The French Cut*, which was produced by Herb Alpert and featured his Tijuana Brass. The title cut became a chart-topper, and the album produced five more hits. In 1967, the Canadian Sweethearts recorded in Nashville with producer Billy Sherrill. She appeared regularly on the charts through the mid-'70s. In 1977, she put an end to the Sweethearts partnership and cut another solo album, *The Sun Shines Again*, and it did quite well. Her subsequent album, *Back to You*, did very well in Canada and produced three hits, including a number one. —*Sandra Brennan*

Back to You / 1978 / Quality Canada ✦✦✦

Lucille Starr / A&M ✦✦✦

Lonely Street / Columbia ✦✦✦

Side By Side / Columbia ✦✦✦✦

● **Mississippi** / Koch ✦✦✦✦✦

The Statler Brothers

f. 1955, Staunton, VA

Group / Traditional Country, Country-Pop, Country Gospel

Named after a brand of tissues, the four members of the Statler Brothers did not in fact share a fraternal bond; what they did share, however, was the distinction of being one of the most successful vocal harmony groups in the history of country music. Formed in the group's home base of Staunton, VA, in 1955, the Statlers were originally a church trio comprised of bass vocalist Harold Reid (born August 21, 1939), baritone Phil Balsley (August 8, 1939), and tenor Lew DeWitt (March 8, 1938). In 1960, Reid's younger brother Don (born June 5, 1945) signed on to take the lead vocal reins, and the quartet performed gospel music under the name the Kingsmen. After arranging a meeting with the promotional department for a local Johnny Cash concert, the Kingsmen were asked to open the performance. Cash was so impressed that he invited the group to join the tour, and after changing their name to the Statler Brothers, they remained on the road with Cash from 1963 to 1971. The Statlers signed to Columbia Records in 1964 and a year later scored a huge country and pop hit with DeWitt's "Flowers on the Wall," which also lent its name to their 1966 debut album. *The Statler Brothers Sing the Big Hits* (1967) held true to its title's promise, generating a pair of Top Ten singles in "Ruthless" and "You Can't Have Your Kate and Edith, Too."

In 1969, the quartet moved to Mercury Records, where they remained for over two decades; their first single for the label, 1970's "Bed of Rose's," was a Top Ten hit. In the same year, they held their first Fourth of July picnic; for decades, the celebration remained an annual holiday spark, drawing tens of thousands of fans each summer. Throughout the first half of the 1970s, the Statlers remained fixtures on the Top 40 charts thanks to a string of nostalgic singles like 1972's "Do You Remember These" and "The Class of '57," 1973's "Carry Me Back," and 1974's "Whatever Happened to Randolph Scott." Their LPs of the period were often concept records: 1972's *The Statler Brothers Sing Country Symphonies in E Major* was whimsically formatted like an orchestral performance (complete with side-break "intermission"), while 1975's joint release *Holy Bible/Old Testament* and *Holy Bible/New Testament* fulfilled a long-standing dream to record a gospel project. 1973's *Alive at the Johnny Mack Brown High School*, on the other hand, was a tongue-in-cheek effort recorded under the group's comic alias Lester "Roadhog" Moran & the Cadillac Cowboys.

The sentimental "I'll Go to My Grave Loving You" was a Top Five hit in 1975 and was included on the Statlers' first best-of compilation, released later in the same year. After a series of Top Ten hits that included 1977's "The Movies" (another recurring Statler theme) and "I Was There," they earned their first chart-topper in 1978 with "Do You Know You Are My Sunshine," from the album *Entertainers…on & off the Record*. In 1980 the Statler Brothers celebrated their first decade on Mercury with *10th Anniversary*, which featured the smash "Charlotte's Web," taken from the film *Smokey and the Bandit, Pt. 2*, in which the group also co-starred. After 1982's *The Legend Goes On*, DeWitt was forced to leave the group as a result of Crohn's disease; the illness ultimately killed him on August 15, 1990. The remaining Statlers tapped Jimmy Fortune as his successor, and immediately Fortune earned the group its second number one with his "Elizabeth" (an homage to actress

Elizabeth Taylor), from the album *Today*. Their next two LPs, 1984's *Atlanta Blue* and 1985's *Pardners in Rhyme*, were credited to simply the Statlers; each record generated a number-one hit—"My Only Love" and "Too Much on My Heart," respectively—again composed by Fortune. They returned as the Statler Brothers for the 1986 inspirational release *Radio Gospel Favorites*, followed later in the year by *Four for the Show*. *Maple Street Memories* (1987) produced the Top Ten single "Forever"; 1989's "More Than a Name on the Wall," which peaked at number six, was their last significant hit. They continued releasing albums, however, and in addition to remaining a popular touring act in the 1990s, the Statler Brothers also hosted a long-running variety show on TNN. —*Jason Ankeny*

Flowers on the Wall / 1966 / Columbia ✦✦✦✦✦

When their 1966 crossover hit "Flowers on the Wall" was used in the 1994 movie *Pulp Fiction*, the Statler Brothers enjoyed a deserved career resurgence. The song's ironic denial ranks with George Jones' "She Thinks I Still Care" as one of country music's most vivid descriptions of a bitter reject trying to convince himself of his indifference toward his ex-lover. As *Flowers on the Wall* aptly demonstrates, the Statler Brothers' influence on country music extends to nearly every vocal harmony act that followed them. The Oak Ridge Boys are often cited as the most prominent disciples, and it's easy to trace the inspiration for their bass-vocal-hooked signature song, "Elvira," to the precedent of Harold Reid's deep, robust instrument. Equally adept at country, gospel, and pop, the voices of Phil Balsley, Lew DeWitt, and brothers Harold & Don Reid soar gracefully above diverse arrangements which run the gamut from near-a cappella minimalism to a rollicking mix of banjo, ukulele, and piano. Unlike many '60s albums, wherein the featured single is surrounded by inappropriate, lackluster remakes of the current hit parade, *Flowers on the Wall* balances its well-chosen cover material with original compositions that match the quality of the title smash. Having reached national prominence with the assistance of Johnny Cash, it's fitting that the group pays tribute by recording a lovely, mariachi-flavored version of Cash's "I Still Miss Someone." Roger Miller is another obvious influence, and the group not only revitalizes his "King of the Road" with their trademark harmony vocals, but also offers their own charming, Miller-inspired novelty entitled "The Doodlin' Song" (sample lyric: "does a stink weed really stink/and how far down does a kitchen sink?"). From the painful melancholy of "My Reward" to Tom T. Hall's cautionary tale of "Billy Christian," the Statler Brothers display remarkable versatility, especially for a debut album. Highly recommended, *Flowers on the Wall* is one of those rare musical treasures which bridges the gaps between several genres and generations. —*Vince Ripol*

Oh Happy Day / 1969 / Columbia ✦✦✦

Bed of Rose's / 1971 / Mercury ✦✦✦✦✦

In addition to the hit title track, the Statlers' Mercury debut *Bed of Roses* features the quartet's takes on Kris Kristofferson's "Me and Bobby McGee" and Ernest Tubb's "Tomorrow Never Comes." —*Jason Ankeny*

Pictures of Moments to Remember / 1971 / Mercury ✦✦✦✦

Country Music Then & Now / 1972 / Mercury ✦✦✦✦✦

This is from the early '70s. A bit rougher and less slick than some '80s dates. —*Ron Wynn*

The Statler Brothers Sing Country Symphonies in E Major / 1972 / Mercury ✦✦✦

The Statler Brothers Sing Country Symphonies in E Major is a concept album of sorts, formatted like an orchestral performance (there's even an "intermission" instead of a side break); with the exception of the occasional string performance, however, this is an otherwise straightforward Statlers effort, featuring the minor hits "Monday Morning Secretary" and "Woman Without a Home." —*Jason Ankeny*

Country Symphonies / 1972 / Polygram ✦✦✦

Innerview / 1972 / Polygram ✦✦✦

In addition to the nostalgic smash "Do You Remember These?," *Innerview* features the Statlers' renditions of "She Thinks I Still Care" and "Take Me Home, Country Roads." —*Jason Ankeny*

The World of the Statler Brothers / 1972 / Columbia ✦✦✦

Do You Love Me Tonight / 1973 / Harmony ✦✦✦

Carry Me Back / 1974 / Mercury ✦✦✦

Thank You World / 1974 / Mercury ✦✦✦

Holy Bible/Old Testament / 1975 / Mercury ✦✦✦✦✦

The Statlers realized a long-held dream with this collection of country gospel songs, the first of two records celebrating the band's Christian upbringing. —*Jason Ankeny*

Holy Bible/New Testament / 1975 / Mercury ✦✦✦✦✦

Released in tandem with its companion piece *Holy Bible: The Old Testament*, the Statlers spent more than eight years in preparation for this collection of country gospel. —*Jason Ankeny*

☆ **The Best of the Statler Bros.** / 1975 / Mercury ✦✦✦✦✦

The Statlers' first decade of recording is recalled in their initial *Best Of* collection. The compilation includes all of the quartet's biggest Mercury hits from the first half of the 1970s, including "Do You Remember These," "I'll Go to My Grave Loving You," and "Bed of Rose's." However, only one song from their late-'60s tenure at Columbia—the classic "Flowers on the Wall"—makes the cut. —*Jason Ankeny*

Harold, Lew, Phil & Don / 1976 / Mercury ✦✦✦

Country America Loves / 1977 / Polygram ✦✦

The Statlers scored a trifecta of Top Ten hits with the *Country America Loves* singles "Thank God I've Got You," "I Was There" and the nostalgic "The Movies." Additionally, this album includes renditions of Dolly Parton's "All I Can Do" and "Blue Eyes Crying in the Rain." —*Jason Ankeny*

Short Stories / 1977 / Mercury ♦♦♦♦♦

Entertainers . . . On & Off the Record / 1978 / Mercury ♦♦♦
Entertainers . . . On & Off the Record was one of the Statlers' most successful efforts from the 1970s, courtesy of their first number-one hit, "Do You Know You Are My Sunshine" as well as "Who Am I to Say" and "The Official Historian on Shirley Jean Berrell." *—Jason Ankeny*

The Best of the Statler Bros. Rides Again, Vol. 2 / 1980 / Mercury ♦♦♦♦♦
Released just four years after their first hits collection, *The Best of the Statler Bros. Rides Again Volume 2* collects their biggest singles from the bottom half of the 1970s. In addition to "Do You Know You Are My Sunshine," and the group's first number one, the collection features "Who Am I to Say," "How to Be a Country Star," and "The Official Historian on Shirley Jean Berrell." *—Jason Ankeny*

10th Anniversary / 1980 / Mercury ♦♦♦♦
The Statlers celebrated their first decade as members of the Mercury Records roster with this collection, which includes the hit "Don't Forget Yourself" as well as "Charlotte's Web," taken from the motion picture *Smokey and the Bandit II*. *—Jason Ankeny*

Years Ago / 1981 / Mercury ♦♦♦
Prior to recording *Years Ago*, the Statlers purchased their old grammar school in their hometown of Staunton, VA, renovating the building to serve as their offices. (On the album cover, the group is photographed on the auditorium's stage.) Perhaps as a result, the record is even more nostalgic and sentimental than most of the Statlers' efforts, as evidenced by the song titles alone, including "Memories Are Made of This" and "Today I Went Back." Among the record's hits were "Don't Wait on Me" and "You'll Be Back (Every Night in My Dreams)." *—Jason Ankeny*

Today / 1983 / Mercury ♦♦♦♦♦
Following the departure of Lew DeWitt, who left the group due to health problems, *Today* marked the addition of new tenor vocalist Jimmy Fortune, who immediately proved his worth by penning the Statlers' second chart-topper, "Elizabeth." Among the other hits: a cover of the Four Knights' "Oh Baby Mine (I Get So Lonely)," and "Guilty." *—Jason Ankeny*

Atlanta Blue / 1984 / Mercury ♦♦♦♦♦
After replacing founding member Lew DeWitt with Jimmy Fortune in the early '80s, the Statler Brothers made a considerable commercial comeback, which culminated with the *Atlanta Blue* album. What makes *Atlanta Blue* noticeably stronger than its predecessor or successor is the uniform excellence of the material—including the hit singles "Atlanta Blue," "One Takes the Blame" and the number one "My Only Love"—and the gorgeous harmonies of the Statler Brothers. *—Thom Owens*

Pardners in Rhyme / 1985 / Mercury ♦♦♦♦♦
The Statlers notched three consecutive Top Ten hits from *Pardners in Rhyme*, including the chart-topping "Too Much on My Heart," "Sweeter and Sweeter," and a cover of Ricky Nelson's "Hello Mary Lou." *—Jason Ankeny*

Four for the Show / 1986 / Mercury ♦♦♦

Radio Gospel Favorites / 1986 / Mercury ♦♦♦
Radio Gospel Favorites is a mixed bag of covers and original spirituals recorded directly for the project, rounded out with other similarly-themed songs ("One Size Fits All," "Sweet By and By," and "Amazing Grace") culled from previous LPs. *—Jason Ankeny*

Maple Street Memories / 1987 / Mercury ♦♦♦♦♦

The Greatest Hits / 1988 / Mercury ♦♦♦
A recycled greatest/best-of, including such Statler favorites as "Elizabeth," "Atlanta Blue," and "Guilty." *—Ron Wynn*

Live & Sold Out / Jun. 1989 / Mercury ♦♦♦
Live & Sold out is a satisfying live show from 1989 that features the Statler Brothers running through 11 of their biggest hits and most familiar songs, including "I'll go to My Grave Loving You," "Walking Heartache in Disguise" and "This Ole House." Though many favorites are missing—there's no "Flowers on the Wall" or "The Class of '57," for instance—the group sounds very good, and the record is an enjoyable, if inconsequential, listen. *—Thom Owens*

Music, Memories & You / 1990 / Mercury ♦♦
Music, Memories & You features the Statlers' last chart single to date, "Small Small World." *—Jason Ankeny*

All American Country / 1991 / Mercury ♦♦
Released on the downslope of the Statlers' popularity as recording artists, *All American Country* generated no chart singles, ending the group's run of 25 consecutive years with Top 100 hits. *—Jason Ankeny*

Home / 1993 / Mercury ♦♦
As the title indicates, *Home* is another of the Statlers' periodic reminiscences about their lives in small-town Virginia. There's also another of the group's occasional tributes to Chet Atkins, "Chet, You're the Reason." *—Jason Ankeny*

Today's Gospel Favorites / Jun. 22, 1993 / Mercury ♦♦♦
Today's Gospel Favorites is a collection of contemporary inspirational material, capably performed by the Statler Brothers. While the music is impeccably produced and the group is in fine voice, the disc doesn't provide many distinguished moments, even though the entire album is pleasant. *—Stephen Thomas Erlewine*

30th Anniversary Celebration / Nov. 21, 1995 / Mercury ♦♦♦♦♦
A 30th Anniversary Celebration is three-disc compilation covering the Statler Brothers' entire career, from their early days at Columbia to their hit-making peak at Mercury. Over the course of 62 tracks, all 27 of their Top 10 hits—including "Flowers on the Wall," "Do You Remember These," "The Class of '57," "Do You Know You Are My Sunshine," "Who Am I to Say," "Oh Baby Mine (I Get So Lonely)," "Elizabeth," "My Only Love" and "Too Much on My Heart"—are featured, as are a handful of lesser-known gems. For any fan of the group, this is an essential purchase, since it is a lovingly-produced, definitive retrospective of the Statlers' best-known material. In fact, it may be all the Statlers most listeners will ever need to own. *—Thom Owens*

★ **Flowers on the Wall: The Essential Statler Brothers** / Mar. 1996 / Columbia/Legacy ♦♦♦♦♦
The Statler Brothers started their recording career at Columbia Records and cut eight albums for the label in five years, scoring eight country singles chart entries, including the Top Ten hits "Ruthless," "You Can't Have Your Kate and Edith, Too," and the pop Top Ten crossover "Flowers on the Wall." This 18-track compilation includes all those hits, along with standards like "The Wreck of the Old '97," "Green Grass," and the gospel pop song "Oh Happy Day," and one previously unreleased track, "Half a Man," which, despite having been recorded two years later, sounds like the logical follow-up to "Flowers on the Wall." The influence of the Statlers' employer, Johnny Cash, is apparent, especially on "Hammer and Nails," on which he appears. At this early stage, without losing the sound of the classic country quartet, the Statlers also sang pop, folk, and gospel well. The only complaint to be made about this set is that, in the CD age, a running time of 42:15 is short for a compilation (if typical of country music). But nothing essential is missing. *—William Ruhlmann*

Red Steagall (Russell Steagall)

b. December, 22, 1937, Gainesville, TX
Vocals, Guitar, Mandolin / Traditional Country, Cowboy, Country-Pop, Honky Tonk, Bakersfield Sound, Nashville Sound/Countrypolitan, Truck Driving Country

Red Steagall has had three overlapping careers in the space of little more than 30 years and can take credit for discovering one great country talent, Reba McEntire. As a songwriter he's been responsible for over 200 compositions, several of which have become hits in the hands of other performers. As a Nashville-based artist, Steagall had his share of chart action in the 1970s and a few major hits. And as a singer of western songs as well as an author of poetry about the West, he is one of modern music's cowboy balladeers. Steagall was born Russell Steagall in Gainesville, TX, on December 22, 1937. He became a bull rider at rodeos while he was still a teenager, but at the age of 15 Steagall was stricken with polio and took up the guitar and the mandolin as therapy to recover the strength and dexterity of his arms and hands. He attended West Texas State University, and while he was there he formed his first group, a country band. Steagall went to the West Coast, where he had some success playing the folk clubs in the area around Los Angeles and had his first success as a songwriter in 1967, at age 30, when Ray Charles recorded his "Here We Go Again," which was later covered by Nancy Sinatra.

Steagall was signed to Dot Records in 1968, but after three years he moved over to Capitol, where he had his first country hit, "Party Dolls and Wine," in 1972 under the name Steagall. Soon after, he had a Top 20 country hit with "Somewhere My Love." He moved to Nashville in 1973 and followed up these two singles with two more hits, "True Love" and "If You've Got the Time." Steagall was a regular guest at rodeos, and while he was performing at the National Rodeo Finals in Oklahoma City in 1974, he spotted a young singer named Reba McEntire who was appearing with her family. He got her to record a demo and made sure that it was heard by anyone who could do McEntire some good, which resulted in her being signed to a recording contract while still in her teens.

Steagall continued to have hits, including "I Gave Up Good Morning Darling" and "The Finer Things in Life," both of which made the Top 20, and scored a Top 15 single with "Lone Star Beer and Bob Wills Music" in 1976. His recording of "I Left My Heart in San Francisco" made the charts as well. In the late '70s, he began moving toward western music as much as country. Steagall moved to Elektra Records in 1979, and in 1980, he decided to leave Nashville and took up residence at his ranch near Fort Worth.

His western recordings began yet another phase to Steagall's career. With his band, the Coleman County Boys, he became singularly popular at rodeos, and his records achieved a major following among fans of cowboy songs. His poems "Ride for the Brand" and "Born to This Land" were also extremely popular, and during the 1980s Steagall also had acting roles in several films, including *Benji the Hunted*, *Dark Before Dawn*, and *Big Bad John*. In 1991, the Texas legislature voted Steagall the Official Cowboy Poet of Texas. Soon after, he began recording for the Warner Western imprint, issuing *Born to This Land* in 1993. Steagall recorded steadily throughout the decade, releasing *Faith and Values* in 1995, *Dear Mama, I'm a Cowboy* in 1997, and *Love of the West* in 1999. *—Bruce Eder*

Party Dolls and Wine / 1972 / Capitol ♦♦♦♦

Somewhere My Love / 1973 / Capitol ♦♦♦
Somewhere My Love is two albums in one. Half of the songs are Western swing remakes of '40s-'60s pop songs like "Mona Lisa," "Love Letters in the Sand," and "Careless Hands." The album's singles were drawn from this category: the modestly successful title track (from *Dr. Zhivago*) that became one of Red Steagall's biggest hits, and Cole Porter's "True Love" (also a minor chart item). The other half of the album is comprised of Steagall's originals, which are straight country songs with little foundation in Western swing. "Something Nice and Easy" and "The Hard Times Will Be the Best Times" show a trace of George Jones creeping into Steagall's vocal, but the country songs are so different from the swing tracks that one wishes the album had gone entirely in one direction or the other. Turning pop oldies into Western swing seems to have had commercial potential, and Steagall continued to exploit this formula on occasion throughout his career even though it never yielded spectacular results at the retail level. *—Greg Adams*

If You've Got the Time / 1973 / Capitol ♦♦♦

The Finer Things in Life / 1974 / Capitol ♦♦♦

Lone Star Beer & Bob Wills Music / 1976 / MCA ♦♦♦♦
From the opening track to the closing note on side two, this is one fine example of Texas swing/honky tonk music, created at a time when America was rediscovering Bob Wills

and this type of music. Even old chestnuts like "Someday You'll Want Me," or "Truck Drivin' Man," with Johnny Gimble's smoking fiddle break are hot. *—Jim Worbois*

Texas Red / 1976 / ABC ✦✦✦

For All Our Cowboy Friends / 1977 / MCA ✦✦✦

Hang on Feelin' / 1978 / ABC/Dot ✦✦✦

● **Born to This Land** / Jan. 1993 / Warner Western ✦✦✦✦

Superb album of contemporary cowboy songs, mostly originals, by a man best known for having discovered Reba McEntire. Steagall looks and lives the part of a Western sage, and his voice has a depth that gives the illusion that he was actually there for a lot of the stories he sings about (he also tells a story or two, with a modern sensibility to some old western themes). The production by Steve Gibson is lean and unobtrusive, the album filled with gorgeous acoustic guitar and mandolin sounds, and the entire record is a worthy successor to the best of Marty Robbins, Tex Ritter, or the Sons of the Pioneers. The booklet includes an explanation of certain 19th and early 20th century Western and cowboy jargon. *—Bruce Eder*

Faith and Vaules / Aug. 8, 1995 / Warner Bros. ✦✦✦

Dear Mama, I'm a Cowboy / Jul. 15, 1997 / Warner Bros. ✦✦✦

Love of the West / Aug. 24, 1999 / Warner Bros. ✦✦✦

At the end of the '90s—at the end of the 20th century, actually—Red Steagall stands as an individual. There really isn't anyone like him. Nobody else is keeping the sound of traditional western music or cowboy songs alive, and nobody plays it straight like Red. That would be noteworthy even if he were simply a straight revivalist, but he's much more than that; along with some select collaborators, he keeps the tradition alive by adding new songs and ideas to it. That much is evident by *Love of the West*, a brief, ten-song salute to cowboy romance. It's a warm, endearing album, filled with warmth and humor. Most impressively, the new songs—and it's all new songs and stories, most of them at least co-written by Steagall—sound like campfire classics, not newly written tunes. It is true that if you view Steagall as a fuddy-duddy, this won't change your mind, but anyone who's enjoyed his previous album will certainly be charmed yet again by *Love of the West*. *—Stephen Thomas Erlewine*

Lone Star Beer & Bob Wills Music/For All Our Cowboy Friends / Feb. 22, 2000 / Koch ✦✦✦✦

Honky tonk bandleader Red Steagall had his '70s releases *Lone Star Beer & Bob Willis Music* and *For All Our Cowboy Friends* released on this one CD by Kock in 2000. *—Chris True*

Wagon Tracks / Oct. 8, 2002 / Shanachie ✦✦✦

When most Americans think of the west, they think of Wyoming, or Colorado, or California. The *Wagon Tracks* of Red Steagall's westward journey, however, begin in Ireland, where thousands left in search of a dream or simply a bite to eat. Many never stopped moving ("Through the Cumberland Gap") while others settled until conflicts, like the invasion of the south by carpetbaggers following the Civil War, pushed them onward ("Gone to Texas"). While Steagall's musical vision of the West doesn't abandon the romance of chasing the setting sun, he does remember the displacement of the Native American and the genocide of the buffalo ("The Last Buffalo"). After a long stop in Texas ("Out on the Texas Plains" and "Texas Bein' Texas"), *Wagon Tracks* heads for Nebraska ("My Nebraska Homestead") and up the Oregon Trail ("We Danced on the Oregon Trail"). Steagall & the Boys in the Bunkhouse rely on fiddles, acoustic guitars, and light percussion to deliver spare, tasteful arrangements. They reach the end of their 6,000 mile trek with "My America," a nice variation on "This Land Is Your Land." *Wagon Tracks* offers an in-depth portrait of westward expansion and will be warmly embraced by lovers of the open plains. *—Ronnie D. Lankford Jr.*

Keith Stegall

b. Nov. 1, 1955, Wichita Falls, TX

Guitar, Songwriter, Keyboards, Vocals / Country-Pop, Urban Cowboy

Country singer/songwriter/producer Keith Stegall was born in Wichita Falls, TX, in 1955 and started playing the piano at age four. He later learned guitar and formed a country band called the Pacesetters at age 12; during his early teen years, he also picked up the drums, started listening to R&B, and joined a rock band. At 15, he moved on to a folk group called the Cheerful Givers, in which he played guitar. After finishing school, he moved to Shreveport, LA, where he sang in a local lounge and also worked as the musical director of a Methodist church. In the meantime, he practiced his songwriting and was encouraged by Kris Kristofferson to try his luck in Nashville. He moved there in 1978 and had two minor chart singles in 1980, including his debut, "The Fool Who Fooled Around." He reached the Top 30 in 1983 with "I Want to Go Somewhere" and the Top 20 with its follow-up, "Whatever Turns You On." A self-titled album for Epic came out in 1985, which brought him his only Top Ten hit in "Pretty Lady." Nonetheless, Stegall found the going easier behind the scenes. His compositions were recorded by Mickey Gilley and pop singers like Al Jarreau and Helen Reddy, and he became an in-demand producer following his work on Randy Travis' *Storms of Life*. He was Alan Jackson's producer of choice right from the beginning and also worked with the likes of Tracy Byrd, Terri Clark, Sammy Kershaw, Lorrie Morgan, and Mark Wills, among others. In 1996 Stegall completed another album, *Passages*, which produced a minor chart single in "1969." *—Steve Huey*

Keith Stegall / 1985 / Epic ✦✦✦✦

● **Passages** / Feb. 27, 1996 / Polygram ✦✦✦✦

Tommy Shane Steiner

b. Austin, TX

Guitar, Vocals / Country-Rock, Progressive Country, Contemporary Country

Country singer Tommy Shane Steiner grew up surrounded by overachievers. His grandfather T.C. "Buck" Steiner was a champion rodeo rider and a member of the Cowboy Hall of Fame next to Pancho Villa and Annie Oakley. His parents were also rodeo entertainers: his father, Bobby, was a bull rider while his mother, Joleen, was a barrel-racing frontrunner. Even Tommy's kid brother, Sid, went on to chase the cowboy dream of becoming a steer wrestler, however it was never a part of Tommy's plan. He wanted to be a singer. He was a Rodeo Hall of Fame member as well, but an earnest 22-year-old with a vision. He went on to play the Texas club circuit in the late '90s. He made a name for himself and RCA Records took notice. Tommy Shane Steiner defined his own country-rock for his debut album *Then Came the Night*, issued in spring 2002. "What If She's an Angel" went Top Ten on the country charts. *—MacKenzie Wilson*

Then Came the Night / Apr. 9, 2002 / RCA ✦✦✦

Tommy Shane Steiner sure is good looking, as the cover pictures amply illustrate, and he makes pretty country music—smooth, clean, tuneful, catchy, polished. He protests that he's a bit of a ruffian on the opening track, "That Just Wouldn't Be Me," and he has a duet with Randy Travis, but his sweet singing is clear indication that he's not made for honky tonks, he's made for breaking hearts. Appropriately, his debut album, *Then Came the Night*, follows the lead of that voice, offering a collection of 11 radio-ready tunes ripe for crossover. This a mainstream pop album with a little bit of country dressing, and while that will inevitably upset some purists, that's what's good about this record. It's a solid, appealing mainstream pop record, a little bit square perhaps, but endearingly so, since he's a modest, likable singer. After this, Steiner could go either way—he could dive into pop and become a male Faith Hill—or he could try to strengthen his country roots and toughen up a bit. He currently leans toward the former, but the nice thing about this record is that it positions him for both directions. *—Stephen Thomas Erlewine*

Stevens Sisters

Group / Neo-Traditionalist Country, Contemporary Country, Progressive Bluegrass

Beth & April Stevens compose the country duo the Stevens Sisters. They've been performing together since their early childhood, but made music their career during their early 20s. Growing up in a musical family in Tennessee also allowed the Stevens Sisters to explore various genres apart from traditional country. Their father, Douglas, was a fiddle player and encouraged the girls to pick up instruments. Beth Stevens was playing banjo by age 12, while April mastered the mandolin. The fiddle, upright bass, and additional string instruments came later, shaping the Stevens Sisters into a matured pair of musicians in the Stevens Family Band. In 1996, the pair released the crossover bluegrass album *Sisters* on Rounder. Two years later and free from family reign, the Stevens Sisters were opening shows for Waylon Jennings, Merle Haggard, and the neo-traditionalist country act BR5-49. Their second album, *Little By Little*, was released in 2002. This time around, the Stevens Sisters were seasoned and smart, allowing *Little By Little* to take on a sophisticated tone compared to their first record. *—MacKenzie Wilson*

Little By Little / Apr. 23, 2002 / Rounder ✦✦✦

Once upon a time, women were more rare than drum kits on the bluegrass scene. Slowly, though, Laurie Lewis and Alison Krauss showed that they could sell records and win over the critics as well as the boys could. *Little By Little* represents April & Beth Stevens' adventurous follow-up to 1996's somewhat conservative *Sisters*. They both sing well, but since they are sisters working as a duo, their specialty is cutting loose in unison. Building on the shoulders of artists like Rhonda Vincent, the sisters put a contemporary spin on a dozen bluegrass tunes. It's difficult, after all, to imagine tradition-oriented singers like Dr. Ralph Stanley or Lester Flatt singing Lynyrd Skynyrd's "Tuesday's Gone." The country-flavored vocals on pieces like "Lonesome Wind" likewise owe more to Nashville acts like the Judds than to mountain music. Crisp acoustic arrangements on the jazzy "Love Every Time" and the high-stepping "Those Words We Said" provide the perfect backdrop for the sisters to launch their fine harmony. A number of well-known players show up for guest spots, including Rob Ickes, Sam Bush, and Dolly Parton, and all of the supporting musicians are excellent. Anyone who has enjoyed albums by Vincent or Dolly Parton will probably want to add the Stevens Sisters' *Little By Little* to their collection. *—Ronnie D. Lankford Jr.*

Jeff Steven

b. 1975, Alum Creek, WV

Main Performer, Vocals, Vocals (Background) / Country-Pop, Contemporary Country

Jeff Stevens & the Bullets were a family vocal trio formed in Alum Creek, WV, in 1975 consisting of brothers Jeff & Warren Stevens and cousin Terry Dotson. Jeff was born in Alum Creek and was influenced as a child by the music of Johnny Cash. He and Warren entered their first talent contest when Jeff was nine; he sang lead and his brother played bass. They won first prize, and Jeff knew he wanted to be a country performer. Early in their career, the band opened for such big-name acts as George Jones, Tammy Wynette, Johnny Cash, and Conway Twitty. In the early '80s, Jeff and Dotson became a songwriting team and provided Atlanta with two major hits, "Atlanta Burned Again Last Night" and "Sweet Country Music." In 1986, Stevens & the Bullets released a cover of Bruce Springsteen's "Darlington County" as their debut single. It made the Top 70, and their debut album followed.

They released their second album in 1987 and had their biggest hit with a cover of Michael Martin Murphey's "Geronimo's Cadillac." The trio disbanded in 1990, and Jeff tried to forge a solo career. In 1991 he made an album for Atlantic, but it was never released. With producer Keith Stegall's help, he began working with such established writers as Roger Murrah and Jim McBride. In 1993, Stevens co-authored "I Fell in the Water" with Jerry Salley and provided John Anderson with a Top Ten hit; working with Michael Clark, he later wrote Alabama's number one hit "Reckless." *—Sandra Brennan*

● **Jeff Stevens & the Bullets** / 1975 / Atlantic ✦✦✦✦

Bolt Out of the Blue / 1986 / Atlantic ✦✦✦

Ray Stevens (Harold Ray Ragsdale)

b. Jan. 24, 1939, Clarkdale, GA

Vocals, Piano / Novelty, Country-Pop, Country Comedy, AM Pop

One of the most popular novelty artists of all time, Ray Stevens enjoyed a remarkably long career, with a stretch of charting singles—some of them major hits—that spanned four decades. Unlike parody king Weird Al Yankovic, Stevens made most of his impact with original material, often based on cultural trends of the day. Yet his knack for sheer silliness translated across generations, not to mention countless compilations and special TV offers. Stevens was a legitimately skilled singer and producer who also performed straight country and pop, scoring the occasional serious hit. But in general, comic novelty songs were his bread and butter, and his brand of humor somehow managed to endure seismic shifts in popular taste and style.

Stevens was born Harold Ray Ragsdale on January 24, 1939, in the small town of Clarkdale, GA. He started piano lessons at age six and formed a band at 15 called the Barons, which played at local venues and social events. At 17, he moved to Atlanta and caught on with radioman Bill Lowery's music publishing company; one of his songs, "Silver Bracelet," got him a shot at recording for Capitol subsidiary Prep, but the single never hit outside of Atlanta. Stevens enrolled at Georgia State University to study classical piano and music theory and in the meantime continued to record for Lowery's NRC label. One of his earliest novelty songs, 1960's "Sgt. Preston of the Yukon," was building a national buzz until a copyright infringement suit took it off the racks. Stevens began performing regularly on a radio show called *The Georgia Jubilee*, which helped lead to a job with Mercury Records as a session musician, arranger, and A&R assistant. Meanwhile, in 1961, he landed his first Top 40 hit with the novelty (obviously) song "Jeremiah Peabody's Poly Unsaturated Quick Dissolving Fast Acting Pleasant Tasting Green and Purple Pills."

Once Stevens joined the Mercury staff, he recorded several more novelty singles. "Ahab the Arab," released in early 1962, was a smash hit, reaching the Top Five on the pop charts and even crossing over to the Top Ten on the R&B side. The follow-up, "Santa Claus Is Watching You," just missed the Top 40, but 1963's "Harry the Hairy Ape" returned him to the Top 20. Still, Stevens wasn't planning on a singing career; he concentrated more on learning the ropes in the studio. He worked with artists like Brenda Lee, Patti Page, and Brook Benton and sometimes sang as a substitute vocalist with the Jordanaires. In 1963, he played with Elvis Presley himself on the sessions for the *Fun in Acapulco* soundtrack. With no hits of his own on the way, however, Stevens wound up moving to the Monument label, where he signed on as a producer and arranger. There he worked with a young Dolly Parton and B. J. Thomas, among others, and formed a friendship with producer Bill Justis (best known for his Sun Records classic "Raunchy").

Stevens began recording again for Monument in 1968, delving into surprisingly pointed social commentary with the Top 30 pop hit "Mr. Businessman." Comedy was still in his blood, though, and Justis gave him an idea for a song called "Gitarzan." Stevens wrote the lyrics and voiced the characters, and in 1969 "Gitarzan" became his first Top Ten pop hit in seven years. His follow-up, a version of the Coasters' "Along Came Jones," reached the Top 30. Stevens also recorded "Sunday Mornin' Comin' Down," a song by a young up-and-comer named Kris Kristofferson. He was so pleased with the result that he turned down a chance to record Burt Bacharach's "Raindrops Keep Falling on My Head," which of course hit number one for Thomas. Unfortunately, Stevens' version of "Sunday Mornin' Comin' Down" flopped, but his instincts were right on, as Johnny Cash scored a major hit with it not long after. An appearance on Andy Williams' variety show led to Stevens signing with the singer's Barnaby label in 1970. He hit immediately with a straight pop song, the relentlessly cheery "Everything Is Beautiful," which displayed his heretofore unseen sentimental streak. "Everything Is Beautiful" was an enormous hit, climbing to number one on the pop charts and winning Stevens a Grammy. Follow-ups included the serious-minded pop song "America, Communicate With Me" (1970), the novelty song "Bridget the Midget (Queen of the Blues)" (1971), and the gospel-styled "Turn Your Radio On" (1972), the latter of which was his first Top 20 country hit. It was, of course, a novelty song that would give Stevens his next big success.

"The Streak," a 1974 ditty about the new fad of (what else?) streaking, zoomed up the charts to become Stevens' second number-one pop hit and also made the country Top Five. In the years that followed, Stevens' singles began to chart higher on the country side. His bluegrass-style rearrangement of "Misty" made the pop Top 20 in 1975, but it was a number-three country hit and won him another Grammy. His country Top 40 hits over the next several years included "Indian Love Call," "Honky Tonk Waltz," and a version of the pop perennial "You Are So Beautiful"; during this period, he switched over to Warner Bros. In 1977, he took a breather from country music to record an utterly bizarre version of Glenn Miller's swing classic "In the Mood," clucking all the instrumental parts like a choir of chickens (the single was credited to the Henhouse Five Plus Too). "I Need Your Help Barry Manilow," (1979) a takeoff on the MOR superstar's trademark style, was his last charting pop single.

Stevens switched labels again, this time to RCA, and promptly had a Top Ten country hit with the humorous "Shriner's Convention" in 1980. Several more singles failed to duplicate its success, and in 1984 he departed RCA for the greener pastures of MCA. Over the next few years, he enjoyed a period of renewed popularity. Songs like "It's Me Again, Margaret" (about an obscene phone caller), "The Mississippi Squirrel Revival," "The Haircut Song," "Would Jesus Wear a Rolex," and "I Saw Elvis in a U.F.O." may not have been his highest-charting (only "Squirrel" made it to the country Top 20), but they all became audience favorites and signature songs. Moreover, his albums sold better than they ever had before; 1985's *He Thinks He's Ray Stevens* reached number three on the country charts, and the 1986 follow-up, *I Have Returned*, actually hit number one. Both went gold, as did 1987's *Crackin' Up*, and Stevens issued several other albums for MCA up through 1991, when he charted for what appeared to be the last time with "Working for the Japanese."

In 1991, Stevens opened his own theater in Branson, MO, and played regularly there until 1993, when he sold the building to take a break. In 1992, he assembled a video collection of some of his best-known material and began a direct marketing campaign via television; the tape wound up selling over three-million copies, and Stevens has since released other videos through his own company. He also recorded new material occasionally, returning in 1997 with *Hum It* and the holiday album *Ray Stevens Christmas: Through a Different Window*. In the wake of the September 11 attacks, Stevens returned with the new single "Osama-Yo' Mama," which became his first charting country single in ten years, reaching the Top 50. It was followed in early 2002 by *Osama-Yo' Mama: The Album*, which climbed into the country Top 30. *—Steve Huey*

Gitarzan / 1969 / Varese ♦♦♦

Stevens plies his stock-in-trade pop novelties on this 1969 album, replete with hayseed monologues, skilled mimicry of various voices (spoken and sung), and Vegas-soul female backup singers. It sounds hokey now—and probably sounded hokey then—but not to everyone, as the title track made the Top Ten, and the remake of the Coasters' "Along Came Jones" made the Top Thirty. The rest of the album's divided between Stevenized covers of vintage rock novelties ("Yakety Yak," "Alley Oop") and satirical originals that ensured his stature as the Top 40's answer to *Hee Haw*. The CD reissue adds three bonus tracks, including "Bridget the Midget," a small hit from 1970, and "The Streak," his number-one single from 1974. Better than anything else on the disc, though, is his 1974 single "The Moonlight Special" (included here). This satire of DJ Wolfman Jack's TV show is actually genuinely funny in places, complete with spot-on send-ups of Jerry Lee Lewis and a Gladys Knight-type soul group. *—Richie Unterberger*

Greatest Hits / 1971 / Curb ♦♦♦

Curb's *Greatest Hits* is a ten-track budget-priced collection that features some of Ray Stevens' biggest hits, including "Everything is Beautiful," "Misty," "Indian Love Call," "Isn't It Lonely Together," "Would Jesus Wear a Rolex" and "There's a Star Spangled Banner." Although this isn't a bad budget-priced disc, there are better collections available, offering more songs, more hits and better sound for not much more money. *—Stephen Thomas Erlewine*

Greatest Hits / 1983 / RCA ♦♦♦♦

Greatest Hits collects Stevens' novelty songs like "The Streak," "Ahab the Arab," and "Everything Is Beautiful." *—Jason Ankeny*

Greatest Hits / 1987 / MCA ♦♦♦

The ten-track *Greatest Hits* collection covers three decades of Ray Stevens' most successful novelty records. These original hits include "The Streak," "It's Me Again, Margaret," and "The Mississippi Squirrel Revival," along with his straight country hits "Everything Is Beautiful," "Misty," and "Turn Your Radio On." *—Al Campbell*

Greatest Hits, Vol. 2 / Sep. 7, 1987 / MCA ♦♦♦

The ten-track *Greatest Hits, Vol. 2* collection covers Ray Stevens' most successful novelty records of the '80s. These are the original hit versions that received massive airplay on the Doctor Demento radio show along with a decent amount of country radio exposure, including "Would Jesus Wear a Rolex," "The Ballad of the Blue Cyclone," "The Haircut Song," and a ridiculous version of "In the Mood," in which instruments and vocalists are replaced with the sound of clucking chickens. *—Al Campbell*

His All-Time Greatest Comic Hits / 1990 / Curb ♦♦♦

His All-Time Greatest Comic Hits contains ten of Ray Stevens' most popular novelty numbers from the '70s and '80s, including "The Streak," "Shriner's Convention," "Gitarzan," "In the Mood," "It's Me Again, Margaret," "Ahab the Arab" and "Would Jesus Wear a Rolex." Though it doesn't have country-pop hits like "Everything is Beautiful" and "Misty," the record nevertheless remains a defintive collection. After all, nearly every listener identifies Stevens' with his novelties and for those listeners that want more funny stuff than what is on *Greatest Hits, His All-Time Greatest Comic Hits* is the only place to go. *—Thom Owens*

Collection / Feb. 2, 1993 / MCA ♦♦♦♦♦

Ray Stevens' *Collection* is a comprehensive single-disc overview of the cornball comedy jester. Original crossover hits from the '60s and '70s, like "Ahab the Arab," "Gitarzan," and "The Streak," are paired up with his country radio hits from the '80s, "Mississippi Squirrel Revival," "Shriner's Convention," and "It's Me Again, Margaret." Closing out the disc is "Everything Is Beautiful," the Stevens-penned international chart-topper from 1971. *—Al Campbell*

Classic Ray Stevens / Jun. 15, 1993 / Curb ♦♦♦

Classic Ray Stevens isn't an accurate title for this nine-track collection. There are no hits here, only re-recorded versions of such novelties as "If Ten Percent is Good Enough for Jesus (It Oughta Be Enough for Uncle Sam)," "The Higher Education of Ole Blue," "Super Cop," "If You and Yo' Folks Like Me and My Folks," "The All-American Two Week Summer Family Vacation," and "The Motel Song." Some fans may find this a little amusing, but there are better collections available, offering more songs and better sound for not much more money. *—Stephen Thomas Erlewine*

20 Comedy Hits Special Collection / Nov. 7, 1995 / Curb ♦♦♦

20 Comedy Hits Special Collection mixes original versions with re-recordings of such classic Ray Stevens songs as "The Streak," "Gitarzan," "Ahab the Arab," "Bridget the Midget (The Queen of the Blues)" and "Shriners' Convention," adding some new songs for good measure. There are a couple good chuckles here and there, but on the whole, there are other Stevens collections that cover the same territory better. *—Stephen Thomas Erlewine*

● **The Best of Ray Stevens** / Sep. 16, 1997 / Rhino ♦♦♦♦

Rhino's *The Best of Ray Stevens* is a thorough overview of the vocalist/comedian's peak, containing 20 tracks recorded between 1961 and 1977. All of his best-known songs, from "The Streak" to "Everything Is Beautiful," are included on this single disc, making it the one definitive Ray Stevens compilation. *—Stephen Thomas Erlewine*

Misty: The Very Best of Ray Stevens / Dec. 7, 1999 / Music Club ✦✦✦✦

This affordable import offers 22 of Ray Stevens' late '60s and early to mid-'70s recordings, including his biggest hits "The Streak" and "Misty," as well as several other charting singles. The collection offers a good balance between Stevens' comedy—which combines the silliest aspects of Roger Miller's and Jerry Reed's novelty records—and his straight material. The serious songs, including "Raindrops Keep Falling on My Head," "A Mama and a Papa," and the original recording of "Sunday Morning Coming Down," demonstrate Stevens' skill as a balladeer, a talent that is often overlooked in the face of his popular comedy recordings. The novelties are something that most listeners will either love or hate depending on their affinity for dumb humor, with Stevens' remake of "Along Came Jones" being one of his better comedy efforts. *Misty* hits all the high points and has more tracks than most domestic collections without being more expensive, which makes it a superior anthology. *—Greg Adams*

All-Time Greatest Hits / Apr. 3, 2001 / Varese Vintage ✦✦✦✦

This suffers from a major drawback that prevents it from being a definitive Ray Stevens greatest-hits compilation: It doesn't have his early-'60s Mercury hits. (The versions of "Ahab the Arab" and "Harry the Hairy Ape," his two biggest singles for the label, are not the Mercury originals, but re-recordings from the 1969 *Gitarzan* album.) Other than that, this covers the major bases of his recording career, including his Monument hits from the mid-'60s to the mid-'70s, such as "Mr. Businessman," "Gitarzan," "The Streak," "Misty," and "Everything Is Beautiful." The appearance of his 1960 single "Sergeant Preston of the Yukon"—which bubbled under the Top 100 before the company that owned the rights to the Sgt. Preston television character had it taken off the market—is a bonus. That song is rare and, like "Ahab the Arab," it's a Coasters-like novelty with more of a mainstream novelty approach than the Coasters used. Otherwise, this dwells on Stevens' commercial prime, when he alternated between novelty/comedy songs and sentimental, middle-of-the-road pop tunes with a country flavor. It's an odd and not wholly integrated mixture, and plenty of his low-charting singles in both idioms are represented, from "Freddie Feelgood (And His Funny Little Five Piece Band)" to "Unwind" and his covers of the Coasters' "Along Came Jones" and Kris Kristofferson's "Sunday Mornin' Comin' Down." *—Richie Unterberger*

Osama-Yo' Mama: The Album / Feb. 12, 2002 / Curb ✦✦✦

"When September 11th came, we were all horrified, outraged and we all just wanted to do something. Our president said, 'We need to go on with out lives and all of us need to do what we normally do.' I write songs and make records, so that's what I did. It was just my natural response. Maybe my doing what I do will help others focus some of their frustrations or have an appropriate way to laugh in these times when there's not that much to laugh about."—Ray Stevens, in his liner notes for his February 2002 release, *Osama-Yo' Mama*. Or, to put it another way, if Ray Stevens hadn't released an album after the worst attack on the U.S. in history, then the terrorists would have won. Nevertheless, Stevens didn't lie in his liner notes—with this record, he does exactly what he's always done, which is to turn everything from the trivial to the profound to either a novelty song or treacly pop. Both are in display here, with most of the copyrights dating from 2000, suggesting that this album wasn't just in the pipeline before the world stopped turning, it was pretty much completed and only three songs were added once we all slowly returned to normalcy—the 2002 copyright "The Lady on the Radio," a version of "United We Stand," and, of course, the title song. And, of course, if anybody pays any attention to this record, it's because of "Osama-Yo' Mama," which is pretty much exactly what you'd think it would be, but a little bit worse since it crawls along on a sub-"Little Egypt" rip with backing vocals out of the Hollywood Argyles, with no jokes outside of, "Osama, yo Mama didn't raise you right/She must have wrapped your turban too tight." Hardy har har. It's a novelty that's timely in its topic but pretty backward in its approach, sounding as if it came out of the late '50s, which may be why it didn't really take off (unlike Alan Jackson's ubiquitous "Where Were You When the World Stopped Turning" or Charlie Daniels' priceless piece of deliberately offensive redneck rage, "That Ain't No Rag, It's a Flag"). The rest of the album is typical latter-day Stevens—immaculately produced, bouncy, midtempo numbers that are mildly catchy but not memorable, outside of titles like "Hang Up and Drive" and "Freudian Slip," which are about what you think they're about. It's one of those albums that's not good but not bad, either, and nobody would be paying attention if it wasn't for the grab for attention in the title song. *—Stephen Thomas Erlewine*

12 Hits: Five Star Collection / Sep. 10, 2002 / Varese ✦✦✦

12 Hits: Five Star Collection is a budget-priced, single-disc overview of the king of country novelty records, Ray Stevens. His biggest early hits—"Ahab the Arab," "Gitarzan," and "The Streak"—are included along with his straight country chart hits, "Misty," "Turn Your Radio On," and his 1971 international chart-topper "Everything Is Beautiful." The combination of silly and sedate material provides a rare glimpse of Stevens' full range as a songwriter and vocalist. *—Al Campbell*

Classic Masters / Apr. 1, 2003 / Capitol ✦✦✦

While not as definitive an overview as Rhino's *Best of Ray Stevens*, *Classic Masters* is still a solid introduction to the unique work of Ray Stevens. Featuring 12 of the singer/songwriter/comedian's best songs and humorous skits recorded between the late '60s and the mid-'70s, the collection gives the schizophrenic impression of Stevens as both melodic social commentator and variety show-style cutup. However, given the high quality of Brill Building-style tracks like "Everything Is Beautiful," "Mr. Businessman," and "All My Trials"—which reveal Stevens to be a songwriter on par with Todd Rundgren with the chops of a Righteous Brother—it is unfortunate that Capitol didn't simply forgo the comedic bits for the more melancholy, serious stuff. *—Matt Collar*

B.W. Stevenson (Louis Stevenson)

b. Oct. 5, 1949, Dallas, TX, **d.** Apr. 28, 1988

Guitar, Vocals / Country-Pop, Soft Rock, AM Pop, Country-Rock

Best remembered for his 1973 smash "My Maria," singer/songwriter B.W. Stevenson (the "B.W." reportedly stood for "Buckwheat"—his real first name was Louis) was born October 5, 1949 in Dallas, TX. As a teen he played in a variety of local rock bands before attending college, eventually joining the U.S. Air Force; upon returning from duty Stevenson settled in the Austin area, where he became a frequent attraction on the city's thriving club circuit. Upon signing to RCA he was marketed primarily to country listeners, enjoying little success with either his 1972 self-titled debut or its follow-up *Lead Free*; the title track of 1973's *My Maria*, however, became a Top Ten pop favorite, although ironically it missed the country charts altogether. Stevenson never again recaptured the single's success, and after 1974's *Calabasas* he landed at Warner Bros. to issue *We Be Sailin'* a year later. "Down to the Station," from 1977's *Lost Feeling*, was his last chart hit, and after 1980's *Lifeline* his recording career was over. Sadly, Stevenson died on April 28, 1988 shortly after undergoing heart surgery; he was just 38 years old. *—Jason Ankeny*

● **The Very Best of B.W. Stevenson** / Feb. 8, 2000 / Collectables ✦✦✦✦✦

Collectables' *The Very Best of B.W. Stevenson* doesn't cull highlights from all of Stevenson's career. Instead, it focuses on two albums—it contains the entirety of 1973's *My Maria* (which, of course, brought him his big hit in the title track, plus a version of "Shambala" that eclipses Three Dog Night's version), then adds as bonus tracks to the end highlights from its 1974 follow-up *Calabasas* and assorted singles. Instead of being frustrating, this approach is actually rather ingenious since it shines the spotlight on Stevenson's easy-rolling, post-hippie country-rock peak. Some of this has dated, but charmingly so, since it's always warm, melodic, and engaging, while the best of it—the aforementioned tunes, plus cuts like "Be My Woman Tonight" and "A Good Love Is Like a Good Song"—has aged very well, still sounding both friendly and sturdy. This is a small gem, actually—a really nice, relaxing poppy country-rock album from the '70s, one that follows through on the sound of the single and delivers something satisfying (which can't be said of most artists perceived as one-hit wonders). *—Stephen Thomas Erlewine*

Gary Stewart

b. May 28, 1945, Letcher County, KY

Guitar, Vocals, Bass, Piano / Progressive Country, Country-Rock, Honky Tonk, Traditional Country

While much of what passes for contemporary country music in the '90s and 2000s sounds like reheated Eagles and Lynyrd Skynyrd, what's really annoying is what a youth-driven market it has become, leaving many great country performers of the '60s and '70s out in the cold. This is especially irritating when considering the career of Gary Stewart, one of the greatest of the hardcore-honky tonk school who, at his peak in the mid- to late '70s, could write and sing circles around just about any contemporary country star you could mention. A native of Florida, Stewart escaped a lifetime of working in an airplane factory in the late '60s by pitching some songs he'd written to soon-to-be RCA country label honcho Jerry Bradley. At the time, Stewart (who was composing with his friend Bill Eldridge) didn't aspire to more than being an in-demand Nashville songwriter, but after a couple of years writing with some success, and through Bradley's continued intercession, he was given the opportunity to record on his own. With his huge, vibrato-laden tenor voice (which sounds a bit like Jerry Lee Lewis'), Stewart, with the inestimable help of songwriter Wayne Carson, released 1975's *Out of Hand*, one of the finest honky tonk records of all time. Paced by the hit "She's Actin' Single (I'm Drinkin' Doubles)," Gary Stewart was quickly becoming a country music star.

Although he composed songs for traditional *Grand Ole Opry* stars (Cal Smith, Hank Snow), Stewart himself never emulated the traditional values espoused by the Nashville establishment; as one of his song titles stated, he was more of a "flat natural-born good-timin' man." He hung out (and caroused plenty) with Southern rock musicians, using them on his albums at a time when this was still considered radical. He was a renegade, unwilling to play the Nashville game, and his increasing success provided him with the autonomy he needed to do his own thing. However, this generally meant conspicuous excess, especially when it came to substance abuse. Still, from 1975 through 1980, Stewart's recorded work is mostly excellent, with a conspicuous high point coming in 1977 with the release of *Your Place or Mine*. A hard-driving slice of aggressive honky tonk, it was a rollickingly good piece of work, not the equal to *Out Of Hand*, but as important an assertion of Stewart's independence from the machinations of country music's star-making machinery. There were problems, however: Stewart was too country for rock audiences and too rock for country audiences, and that limited any stab at broader appeal.

In 1980, he released *Cactus and a Rose*, with considerable help from Southern rock vets Gregg Allman, Dickey Betts, Mike Lawler, and Bonnie Bramlett. It was a fine record, but attracted only Stewart's core audience, and at this point in his career, that simply wasn't enough. Suddenly it seemed as if his desire and creativity vanished. He hooked up with Dean Dillon and made a couple of terrible two-good-ol'-boy records that made the redneck rowdiness of Hank Williams Jr. sound philosophical by comparison. Not long afterwards, Stewart returned to Florida and stopped recording. After his alcoholism and drug use pretty much canceled out a large part of the '80s, Stewart returned, clean and sober, with a strong comeback record, *Brand New*, in 1988. It wasn't the Gary Stewart of old, but it was a respectable record, and it was enough to propel a comeback that continued with *I'm a Texan*. Considering that most folks had given him up for dead, this was a remarkable turn of events. His heyday was in the '70s, but Gary Stewart deserves to be celebrated for his considerable talent, tenacity, and influence. *—John Dougan*

You're Not the Woman You Used to Be / 1973 / MCA ✦✦✦

MCA put this album out in an attempt to capitalize on Gary's RCA success. Except for two tracks, all this material had been released while he'd been signed with Kapp and, in most cases, shows that Stewart hadn't yet found his voice or his style. The title track, though, is nearly as good as anything he did at RCA. *—Jim Worbois*

★ **Out of Hand** / 1975 / Hightone ♦♦♦♦♦
Along with Merle Haggard's *Back to the Barrooms* and Joe Ely's *Honky Tonk Masquerade*, this is the separate but equal third element of honky tonk's unholy trinity. While the album is called *Out of Hand*, it could just as easily have been named after its first cut, "Drinkin' Thing." Released in 1975 at the height of outlaw country's boom and the Texas songwriters' heyday, Stewart was in Nash Vegas cutting one of the most amazing collections of unruly drinking songs in country music history. From the opening "Drinkin' Thing" to an absolutely rocking version of Hank Williams' "Honky Tonkin'," the pace is set to go and the joint is set to blow. And whether it's a ballad like "I See the Want to in Your Eyes" or "Backslider's Wine," or a raw-bone stomper like the title track or "Sweet Country Red," the performance is inspired by a deep hedonism that only the most recklessly astute musicians would be sensitive enough to pull off. Add to this the greatest drinking song title ever, "She's Actin' Single (I'm Drinkin' Doubles)," and you have a recording that is indispensable for roots-music fans of any stripe. A strong case could be made for *Out of Hand* as one of the Top 100 country records of all time. *—Thom Jurek*

Steppin' Out / 1976 / RCA ♦♦♦
Not one of Stewart's strongest efforts but worth the price of admission just to hear him cover Willie Nelson's "I Still Can't Believe You're Gone." The original album came with an iron-on patch featuring Gary playing his guitar. *—Jim Worbois*

Your Place or Mine / 1977 / RCA ♦♦♦♦♦
Following by two years *Out of Hand*, one of the three greatest honky tonk records ever made, Gary Stewart had a tall order to fill. And while it's true it's not the same achievement that *Out of Hand* was, it nonetheless is a must-own for serious country fans. Put together three tried-and-tough Rodney Crowell tunes—"I Had to Get Drunk Last Night," "Rachel," and "Ain't Livin' Long Like This"—Stewart's own "Dancing Eyes," and Guy Clark's "Broken Hearted People," along with Willie Nelson's "Pretend I Never Happened," and you already have a strong recipe, especially with a crackerjack country-rock band like Stewart's. In direct opposition to Nashville's "wisdom," Stewart created an album where each track moved into another that was stronger. So, as good as the title track is, by the time you reach Stewart's "Dancing Eyes" at the end, you've gone up the escalator of quality to honky tonk heaven. The first three tracks on side two are enough to slay even the most unwaveringly cold, sand-for-blood-in-their-veins country fan and get 'em outta the chair or off the stool, to the dancefloor, and then back to weep in their beer. In addition to his own band, Stewart has some help from Emmylou Harris, Crowell, the late Nicolette Larson, Sue Richards, Jerry Wallace, and the Jordanaires on backing vocals. Yeah, not bad eh? This album is a bad mother and you need it. Find it—get to a used-record store or your favorite Japanese connection for a CD copy. What are you sittin' there reading for? *—Thom Jurek*

Little Junior / 1978 / RCA ♦♦♦
Gary Stewart is pure country. No Nashville strings or other countrypolitan accessories infiltrate his homegrown sound, and he makes no crossover concessions with his quavering cowboy vocals. As a result, Stewart is able to elevate the genre's clichés and stereotypes to a genuinely affecting level rarely attained by many country stars who simply manipulate proven formulas. *Little Junior* is by no means his best effort, but even average Stewart is a cut above the greatest triumphs of lesser artists. While covering the expected topics of drinking, gambling, and rambling, Stewart's aching warble adds new dimensions to shopworn generalizations, often evoking compassion for decidedly unsympathetic characters. He proves to be a capable songwriter on both the title track and "Single Again," in which he claims "the only thing I'm running from is the alimony man." Stewart also possesses an astute ear for outside material; by covering Hank Williams' "Honky-Tonkin'," Stewart concisely reveals both an early influence and a preferred musical style. He also transforms the Marshall Tucker Band's "Can't You See" into a bluegrass extravaganza complete with banjo, fiddle, dobro, and mandolin. Aside from occasional keyboards and acoustic guitar, Stewart wisely trusts his superb sidemen to actualize his musical visions, and their performances are consistently outstanding, especially Hal Rugg on steel guitar and Terry McMillan on harmonica. Above it all, Stewart's unique voice remains the undeniable highlight, and he invests every composition with his individuality. Those who prefer the dulcet tones of professionally trained singers or the slick studio creations of more commercial artists may not appreciate Stewart's relatively unsophisticated sound, but they could certainly learn from it. *—Vince Ripol*

Gary / 1979 / RCA ♦♦♦♦
The body of work Gary Stewart recorded for RCA in the 1970s and 1980s is singular in its quality and in its criminal neglect. Stewart's A&R man should get some kind of lifetime achievement award for keeping him on the label as long as he did, given how out of time Stewart's brand of honky tonk country and rock were. Recorded in 1979, *Gary* was issued at the dawn of the *Urban Cowboy* debacle, the beginning of the wane of the disco era, and the first light of new wave on American airwaves. Too early for Dwight Yoakam's neo-traditionalism and too late for the classic honky tonkers like Haggard and Jones et al., Stewart's vision was single-pointed: simply to perform, write, and record the best songs he could with the best group of musicians he could. Produced by Roy Dea, *Gary* features ten killer tracks ranging from gorgeous rough-hewn love songs such as "Shady Streets" to piano-pumpin' Jerry Lee Lewis-styled rockers such as "Mazelle" to the loungy barroom 4/4 of "The Blues Don't Care Who's Got 'Em." In addition, the Roger Miller-flavored read of Leon Payne's "Lost Highway" evokes the ghost of Hank Williams, who played the tune as a drinking anthem. Closing it out with the stunning "One More" is a coup; Stewart sings a rounder's confessional with all the regret of a sinner at the altar, but with the hopelessness of a convicted man. As the pedal steels whine in the background and Hargus "Pig" Robbins' piano moves the melody on, Stewart's protagonist becomes the essence of rawhide, unapologetic and unforgiving of himself or anyone else. It's simply a stunning conclusion to a very fine, very consistent album. Why Stewart isn't regarded in the same way as Merle Haggard and Kris Kristofferson is beyond comprehension. *—Thom Jurek*

Cactus and a Rose / 1980 / RCA ♦♦♦
This is not the kind of record most people would associate with Gary Stewart, one of the finest honky tonk singers ever. For this effort, he has teamed up with people like Allman Brother members Gregg Allman and Dickey Betts as well as Bonnie Bramlett (ex-Delaney, Bonnie & Friends) and Randy Scruggs. And, what do we learn? That Stewart could have easily fronted the Allman Brothers or Marshall Tucker or, vocally kicked Charlie Daniels' Southern rock butt from here to Pascagoula as a great honky tonk singer. *—Jim Worbois*

Gary's Greatest-17 Original Hits / 1981 / Hightone ♦♦♦♦♦
Featuring material recorded from 1973 to 1990—including songs from both his RCA and Hightone days—*Gary's Greatest* has 17 of Stewart's best songs and is an excellent introduction to the under-appreciated singer/songwriter. *—Thom Owens*

Brotherly Love / 1982 / RCA Victor ♦♦♦♦
Issued at the end of his tenure with RCA, Gary Stewart teamed up with songwriter Dean Dillon to release this odd little collection of honky and love songs. First, there are only four duets included with the album's ten selections, with the rest being divided up three each between Stewart and Dillon. It's hard to tell if the pair didn't have an album's worth of material each and combined their talents, if this was always set up as a collaboration, or what. No matter, as a collection of songs it works well. Stewart does his usual classic thing, burns down the house with hard-rocking country songs that belong in a barroom with thick smoke, bright light, and hillbilly music. Dillon's the more sensitive of the two and was obviously swinging for the Nash Vegas fences. The problem is, of course, his songs are too good. The standouts are the duets by far because they combine each man's strengths that make for a healthy tension—"Honky Tonk Crazy" and "Firewater Friends" are the best of the lot. But Dillon's "Let's Start a War" with its old-timey feel and poignant lyric works extremely well, as does Stewart's "Body Shop," which combines Jerry Lee Lewis, Hank Williams, and Chicago blues. The band includes longtime Stewart companions Weldon Myrick on steel, Bobby Thompson on guitar, Jerry Chook on bass, lead guitarist Dale Sellers, and harmonicat Terry McMillan, among others. They provide the loose, rowdy backdrop for these songs that seem to jump out of the speakers. The one duet ballad, "Suburban Life," is a charm of soulful countrypolitan honky tonk with Myrick's whinnying steel and the pair singing about walking out to take up residence in a bar and deciding it's not all it's cracked up to be. There are few questions in music like this other than why there so many songs like this on one record—on any Stewart record for that matter? Though Dillon's not that different. So here is a pair of reprobates doing what they do best, singing about drinking, working, women, and hassle. This is drinkin' country: aimless, unwavering, and true. *—Thom Jurek*

Gary Stewart's Greatest Hits / 1982 / RCA Victor ♦♦♦
A little on the short side (ten tracks), but with 50 percent of them coming from either *Out of Hand* or *Your Place or Mine*, this is as filler-free and succinct a career summation of this great artist available. Ironically, much of this sounds similar to what has made Garth Brooks and his ilk millionaires many times over, and Stewart (who was truly ahead of his time) was nearly forgotten. No one ever said life (especially in the music business) was fair, but a few spins of this and you will soon understand that nearly 20 years later, Stewart still stands taller than virtually all of the country performers making a mint from imitating his style. A perfect place to start. *—John Dougan*

Brand New / 1988 / Hightone ♦♦♦
After a six-year break, Gary Stewart returned to recording for the Hightone label in Oakland, CA. Other than rocking a bit harder—courtesy of guitar players Dale Sellers on lead and Allman Brother Warren Haynes on slide—Stewart is not a shadow of his former self, but himself, period: namely, a bad-assed honky tonk singer/songwriter who delivers drinking songs better than anyone except Merle Haggard. And like the days of yore when albums like *Out of Hand*, *Your Place or Mine*, and *Gary* were released on RCA, *Brand New* is a collection of bar-slammin' good-time rowdy honky tonk songs and broken, screwed-up love songs seen from the bottom of a glass. "Brand New Whiskey" feels like a Stewart rewrite of Guy Clark's "Take Me to a Barroom," and is every bit as good; "I Owe It All to My Heart" is a sad country song in the best sense of the word. "Lucretia" is a rocker with echoes of Derek & the Dominos' "Layla," done pub-style. Haynes is especially effective with his deliberate guitar histrionics. "Rainin' Rainin' Rainin'" is classic Gary Stewart, high, lonesome, the morning after, and recounting the tragedy to whoever will listen accompanied by a barroom piano and cut-time rhythm. "Looking for Some Brand New Stuff" and "Son of a Honky Tonk Woman" come out of the Jerry Lee Lewis fake book, with all the passion, psychosis, and dark piano-pumping fury. Ah, the classic country music; "I Get Drunk" is a track George Jones would have been proud to record first, but Stewart's delivery is actually more believable. The set ends with "Murdered By Love," a romper-stomper blues jam with Haynes and Sellers tearing each other up and Stewart singing his ass off. Sending the listener into an oblivion of drink, lost love, and regret—all recipes for a good night of wild partying you'll regret the next day. A fine return. *—Thom Jurek*

Battleground / 1990 / Hightone ♦♦♦
Battleground focuses on Stewart's Southern rock leanings on tracks like "Nothin' but a Woman" and "Let's Go Jukin'." *—Jason Ankeny*

I'm a Texan / Oct. 15, 1993 / Hightone ♦♦♦
More impassioned than ever, Stewart continues to excel at raw-boned honky tonk and revved-up country-rock. The songs don't all live up to his treatment, but when they do, as on "Honky Tonk Hardwood Floor" or the inviting "Come on In," he reveals the timidity that undercuts the new traditionalists of the modern country era. *—Michael McCall*

The Essential Gary Stewart / Jan. 28, 1997 / RCA ✦✦✦✦✦
Gary Stewart's *Essential* is an excellent cross-section of hit singles, rarities, and album tracks that demonstrates his talents as a songwriter and as a gritty honky tonk performer. *Gary's Greatest* remains a better way to become acquainted with Stewart's entire catalog, but *Essential* is still a fine sampler. *—Thom Owens*

Gary/Cactus and a Rose / Oct. 17, 2000 / WestSide ✦✦✦✦

☆ **Out of Hand/Your Place or Mine** / May 8, 2001 / Koch ✦✦✦✦✦
This two-fer, which pairs up Stewart's best album (1975's *Out of Hand*) and a decent similarly themed outing from two years later, serves as a fine intro to both Stewart's mildly outlaw country and one of the best genre albums of the '70s. *Your Place or Mine* sounds a little tame, as well as a bit flashy, in retrospect, but *Hand* is a seminal work, traditional in approach and style but with just enough rock & roll attitude to complement the honky tonking. *—Michael Gallucci*

The Best of the HighTone Years / Jan. 15, 2002 / Hightone ✦✦✦
If you're thinking this might include "She's Actin' Single (I'm Drinkin' Doubles)" or tracks from the wonderful *Your Place or Mine*, you're going to be disappointed. This is the post-rehab, dried-out Gary Stewart, somewhat mellower, with the vibrato in his voice more apparent than ever. Taken from the three albums he recorded for Hightone between 1988 and 1993, there are still some good songs on here—"Brand New Whiskey" approaches the real honky tonk rowdiness of his best work—but there are also some stinkers; except for the vocals, "An Empty Glass" could almost have come off an Eagles album, something that could *never* have been said about Stewart's earlier work; in fact, it stands as a condemnation, and "Nothin' Cheap About a Cheap Affair" never rises about cheap country cliché. But when Stewart doesn't sound like he's simply going through his paces, as on "Delia," which might have all the accouterments of old country (chiming steel, etc.), but is performed with a little passion, and "Let's Go Jukin'," co-written with Dickey Betts, which is pure rock & roll (all that's missing is the Chuck Berry guitar riff) in a honky tonk disguise, and proof that at the times old Gary Stewart does still shine through, even if, on the evidence of this set, he's really just a shadow of his former self. *—Chris Nickson*

Live at Billy Bob's Texas / Feb. 11, 2003 / Image ✦✦✦✦✦
Other than reissues and best-of releases, *Live at Billy Bob's Texas* is Gary Stewart's first new album in a decade, and his first-ever live recording—which seems odd for a performer whose songs seem to be tailor-made for live performance. In the 1970s, Stewart defined what was left of the true honky tonk tradition, and into the '80s and '90s continued to write and record quality material, but his style of country music had long fallen out of fashion and he fell into nearly complete obscurity. This is the album Stewart should have cut in the late '70s—it's full of 16 stunning examples of what he does best: write and perform hardcore honky tonk country flawlessly with all the piss, vinegar, and passion that much younger men only wish they could muster. There are many Stewart-penned classics in this bunch, including "She's Actin' Single (I'm Drinkin' Doubles)," "Flat Born Good Timin' Man," "Single Again," and "An Empty Glass (That's the Way the Day Ends)." Of the covers, Stewart's choices are impeccable: Wayne Carson's "Drinkin' Thing," Sterling Whipple's "In Some Room Above the Street," and one of the most moving versions of Danny O'Keefe's "Quits" ever captured on tape. Stewart's voice has actually gotten better with age, slightly lower and full of pathos, brokenness, and sheer hell-raising abandon. His band, though unforgivably not credited anywhere in the liner notes, is obviously rooted deep in Stewart's style of honky tonk country; pianos and pedal steel guitar dominate the proceedings and the rhythm section lays just behind the beat to let the guitars and voices fill the entirety of the space in the middle. The pedal steel player, whoever he is, deserves all the work he can handle for his tasteful, emotionally revealing fills that give Stewart that added ledge to step out on. Despite the fact that has been over 30 years since Stewart first appeared in Nashville, this debut live album numbers among his best. This is essential for fans and serves as a more-than-worthy primer for beginners. *—Thom Jurek*

John Stewart

b. Sep. 5, 1939, San Diego, CA
Guitar, Vocals / Singer/Songwriter, Adult Contemporary, Soft Rock, Folk-Rock, Contemporary Folk
John Stewart first gained recognition as a songwriter when his songs were recorded by the Kingston Trio. In 1960, he formed the Cumberland Three, which recorded three albums for Roulette. The following year, he joined the Kingston Trio, replacing Dave Guard, and stayed with them until 1967. His song "Daydream Believer" was a number-one hit for the Monkees at the end of that year. Stewart traveled with Senator Robert Kennedy on his 1968 Presidential campaign, an experience that affected him deeply. In 1969, he released his classic album *California Bloodlines*, the first of seven solo albums to reach the charts through 1980. Stewart found his biggest commercial success with the Top Ten album *Bombs Away Dream Babies* and its single "Gold" in 1979. He released several of his albums and albums by others on his own Homecoming label starting in the 1980s. *—William Ruhlmann*

Signals through the Glass / 1968 / Capitol ✦✦✦
Stewart's first album after leaving the Kingston Trio wasn't precisely a solo endeavor, as it was billed to both him and his wife, Buffy Ford, who often sings both harmony and lead vocals on the LP. Still, Stewart wrote all of the songs, and it's his singer/songwriter vision that dominates the record. It's an interesting but curious effort, very much a transitional one, mixing echoes of his troubadour folkie past with orchestrated California sunshine pop, the more darkly pensive aspects of the early singer/songwriting movement, and even whiffs of trendy psychedelic influence. The Americana narrative flavor that would color much of his work was prominent on songs such as "Lincoln's Train" (inspired by Abraham Lincoln's corpse's ride to his funeral), yet "Holly on My Mind" was rather luscious dreamy orchestrated pop. "July, You're a Woman" (re-recorded by Stewart on his next album, *California Bloodlines*) had enough Glen Campbell/Bob Lind-ish mainstream appeal to attract cover versions by Pat Boone, John Davidson, and Robert Goulet. Yet in contrast, "Draft Age" was almost chilling in its singsong vérité snapshot of the day in the life of a young man on the very day he becomes eligible for military service (i.e., for death in Vietnam). "Nebraska Widow" almost gets into funky folk-blues in its portrait of lonesomeness, and "Mucky Truckee River," if only inadvertently, seems to reflect the awakening of a folk circuit veteran such as Stewart to the contemporary social confusion of America in 1968. Rare and seldom discussed, it's worth checking out despite its unevenness, for fans of both Stewart and overlooked late-'60s folk-rock and singer/songwriter albums in general. *—Richie Unterberger*

California Bloodlines / 1969 / Capitol ✦✦✦✦✦
Issued in 1969, *California Bloodlines* is regarded by many to be singer/songwriter John Stewart's finest work. That's debatable, but it is a hell of an album. Stewart who had finally left behind the Kingston Trio to pursue a solo career, solidified it here. Well known as the guy who wrote "Daydream Believer" for the Monkees and "Gold" for Fleetwood Mac, Stewart proved to be a credible, sometimes even enigmatic performer in his own right. Nick Venet produced *California Bloodlines*. He took Stewart to Nash Vegas and enlisted a host of studio cats who existed largely outside of Chet Atkins' countrypolitan mafia: drummer Kenny Buttrey, bassist Norbert Putnam, harmonicat Charlie McCoy, Lloyd Green on pedal steel, and others including the most sought-after upright pianist in country music history, Hargus "Pig" Robbins. Incidentally, many of these same musicians played on Bob Dylan's *Nashville Skyline* session. Musically, *California Bloodlines* is a study in contradictions. Texturally thin like Stewart's voice, the songs are romantic visions of people and places that come out of a present which is already in the past and a past inhabited by ghosts. But this is also where Stewart excels lyrically. His portraits of spirits are made nearly flesh in his songs, which are ambitious lyrically if not musically, such as the title track, "The Pirates of Stone County Road," "Razor-Back Woman," "Some Lonesome Picker," "July You're a Woman," and "You Can't Look Back," with Green's pedal steel dancing throughout the melody and filling in each line. But perhaps the most beautiful track on the album is the elegiac "Missouri Birds," with its lilt and slow-stepped observations about space and time. And while generally regarded as a folk artist, Stewart's country roots are displayed here are as deep as Mickey Newbury's, even if he wasn't born in Texas. This is a glorious recording which kicks off an erratic yet never dull career with a bang. *—Thom Jurek*

☆ **Willard** / 1970 / Capitol ✦✦✦✦✦
John Stewart's follow-up to the unprecedented success of *California Bloodlines* stuck close to the same formula. Recorded in Hollywood with many of the same musicians from the earlier record—Norb Putnam, Kenny Buttrey, Charlie McCoy, among them—Stewart also employed other country musicians such as banjo boss Bobby Thompson and fiddle player Doug Kershaw as well as a host of his peers—from Russ Kunkel and Carole King to Danny "Kootch" Kortchmar, James Taylor, and Bryan Garofalo—at the suggestion of producer Peter Asher—later known for his schlock work with Linda Ronstadt and Carly Simon among others. Nonetheless despite Asher's best attempts at taming the thin, reedy wildness in Stewart's voice, it wasn't to be. Stewart is a songwriter with a rambling vision, and the best of his rambling songs are included here, and as such, he draws inspired performances from all of his bandmembers. The feel of the album is somewhat stripped of the California crap that was in so many records from that time. A listen to "Belly Full of Tennessee," with Kershaw's fiddle and Putnam's bass driving the tune, colored elegiacally with Thompson's banjo, makes it a Louisiana bayou dance tune. It's raw, tough, and full of unbreakable spirit. "Back in Pomona" is a country-rocker in the purest sense of the word. Stewart's uncompromising lyrical vision that relates the past as if it were a living, breathing present drives a band eager to carry those words through to the listener. *Willard* is a romantic record in the same way that *California Bloodlines* was, but its romanticism is well intentioned in that it poetically preserves a time period in America that was quickly disappearing. In the title track, Stewart's romanticism centers on a character, a hobo, who embodies everything that is free and wild, untamed, and often tragic, but there are no apologies, no sentiments other than the fact that this unlikely icon is everyone and everyone is him, separated only by circumstance. Likewise "Golden Rollin' Belly," about the need for a woman's sexual company, with Chris Darrow's fiddle and Thompson's banjo riding well inside a big fat Garofalo bassline. *Willard* is a country record in all the best ways; it just might be Stewart's master opus. *—Thom Jurek*

Sunstorm / 1971 / Warner Bros. ✦✦✦
When John Stewart moved to Warner Bros. in 1971, his first album for the label, *The Lonesome Picker Rides Again*, stuck closely to the formula his Capitol albums did, but with a boatload more energy. Continuing to record in California, *Sunstorm* uses many of the same musicians who appear on Stewart's previous records, but there are some notable differences in its sound. *Sunstorm* was the first record where Stewart and producer Michael Stewart moved into the direction of an album that was assembled as much as it was recorded, and the sound is lusher, fuller. In addition, piano maestro Glen D. Hardin handled the musical arrangements. This can be heard from the delicate balance struck between acoustic guitars, pianos, and basslines on "Kansas Rain." The way the choruses fall in the backdrop just above the string section makes an evocative soundscape for Stewart's poignant lyrics. "Cheyenne" is a classic folk ballad cum country rambler with killer crescendos and pedal steel and fiddle solos. But it's not until "Bring It on Home" that the rollicking country-rock comes whistling in for the strike. With the handclaps (some of them done by Billy Mumy, aka Will Robinson from *Lost in Space*), large singalong chorus, and honky tonk piano that make Hardin's arrangements take full effect, Stewart's production makes the set feel live. Guitar legend James Burton plays not only guitar and dobro but sitar on the title track. There's a touching moment of Stewart

with his father on "An Account of Haley's Comet." John Sr. recounts the personal story of his encounter with Haley's Comet, and Hardin assembles the musical accompaniment, with John Jr. and chorus singing the refrain. "Light Come Shine" is a cross-pollination of country-rock and gospel that is, with its grandiose chorus, corny at best, but it is redeemed by the Travis-style picking country of "Lonesome John." Like Jerry Jeff Walker and Guy Clark, Stewart could spin a yarn from the present as if it were a conversation that takes place in front of the listener. Pedal steel player Jerry Scheff's bass drives the tune from below, and the twin guitars of Burton and Mike Deasy roll in the lyric before giving way to the closer "Drive Again," which is a dead cross between Gram Parsons, Dave Dudley, and Delaney & Bonnie filtered through Stewart's lyrical perspective. It's not perfect, but it's a damned fine album, one that stands the time test even if its production sound is dated. *—Thom Jurek*

Lonesome Picker Rides Again / 1971 / Warner Bros. ♦♦♦

Sunstorm Live 1972 / 1972 / Bear Family ♦♦♦

Cannons in the Rain / 1973 / RCA Victor ♦♦♦♦

After recording a pair of records each for Capitol and Warner Bros., John Stewart moved over to RCA, where he remained a bit longer. Issued in 1973, *Cannons* was released just about the time the outlaw movement was cracking it in Austin with Willie Nelson, Jerry Jeff Walker, Waylon Jennings, Billy Joe Shaver, Guy Clark, Townes Van Zandt, Kris Kristofferson, and the rest. Stewart's music could not have sounded more out of place with the Texans. This was California country music that had been drenched in Stewart's folk influences and his love of West Coast production. To that end, Nick Venet, who had produced his records at Capitol, returned to Stewart's side. He enlisted some of old friends such as banjo boss Bobby Thompson, drummer Russ Kunkel, harmonicat Charlie McCoy, pianist Hargus "Pig" Robbins, and backing vocalist Buffy Ford. Some of the newer faces are what make the difference, however, and these include Pete Drake on pedal steel and dobro, the Nashville Edition on backing vocals, and guitarists Waddy Wachtel and Kelso Herston. The laid-back feel of the disc is a Venet trademark, but Stewart's in fine voice and lyrical form. The loopy melody of "Easy Money" that straddles the line between soft rock and honky tonk is an example as is the forlorn folky country of "Chilly Winds." "Road Away" is southern California country at its finest. The title cut with its tender chorus and gentle melody line is gorgeous here but would have been better served if cut by Marty Robbins or even Conway Twitty. This is like Jimmy Webb without the acid. "Lady and the Outlaw" is a nod to what was happening in Austin despite its high-on-weed spoken word intro. But here it is, Stewart rolling out a tune that could have been written by Jerry Jeff and sung by either Steve Young or Waylon. It's a hell of a way to close an album and makes the listener long for an entire record of tunes like this—which came with *Wingless Angels* the very next year. *—Thom Jurek*

Phoenix Concerts / 1974 / One Way ♦♦♦♦♦

John Stewart' *Phoenix Concerts* is regarded as one of the classic live records of the folksinger/songwriter genre, and it's easy to see why. It's obvious that Stewart has an adoring audience at the peak of his popularity in 1974. Taken from a few concert sessions, the bands range from the artist in a trio setting to being in a full on septet with pedal steel guitar and backing vocalists. Besides Stewart himself, the only notable performer on the sets is legendary drummer Jim Gordon. Many of Stewart's classics are here, including a very inspired "Wheatfield Lady" and "Kansas Rain." The music hearkens back to a much more innocent time that many at this concert no doubt longed for—as did the artist himself perhaps after 1968, when his dreams were shattered with the death of Robert Kennedy (Stewart toured with Kennedy on the campaign trail). Other gems here are "California Bloodlines," "Mother Country," "The Last Campaign Trilogy," which is so moving it's almost unbearable. With "Roll Way the Stone," "July, You're a Woman," and "Cody," Stewart hits his stride and goes over the top, and the gigs shift into a whole different gear. His stories are endearing and predate what Garrison Keillor did by a decade. The set officially closes with a stunning rendition of "Never Goin' Back (To Nashville Anymore)," that makes you forget the studio version and wonder why it wasn't covered by Townes Van Zandt or Mickey Newbury. That said, there are two bonus tracks on the CD from the same shows, "Freeway Pleasure" and "Let the Big Horse Run," that make this an essential set for anyone interested in Stewart or the roots of the singer/songwriter movement in America that is populated by many of this artist's pupils, Jerry Jeff Walker, Guy Clark, and Tom Russell among them. *—Thom Jurek*

Complete Phoenix Concerts / 1974 / Bear Family ♦♦♦♦♦

Fire in the Wind / 1977 / RSO ♦♦

Fire in the Wind marked the first of ex-Kingston Trio member John Stewart's three albums for RSO. The vastly underrated singer/songwriter had played record-company roulette ever since going solo in the late '60s, and he often worked with top Nashville session musicians in the middle of the 1970s. With this 1977 release, Stewart clearly embraced a more pop/rock approach while maintaining his folk roots and love of acoustic guitar. "Fire in the Wind" shows Stewart's skill with strong, simple melodies and irresistible choruses; catchy guitar fills and leads illustrate the album's more mainstream direction. His rich voice carries the country/folk number "Rock It in My Own Sweet Time." The clean acoustic and electric guitars ring brightly on the buoyant "On You Like the Wind." Stewart's lyrics often invoke images of nature; "Morning Thunder" is about a woman running naked in the sunshine. "Promise the Wind" is another pleasant number with a great chorus. Fans who've seen Stewart in concert know he has a sly sense of humor, but "18 Wheels" is one of the few times it's displayed on record. It's about the solitary existence of a truck driver, but the artist's protagonist looks down to see a couple in a car he's passing on the highway and fires off a hysterical line about the woman with a beehive hairdo "laying with her head in his lap/I don't believe she was takin' a nap." *Fire in the Wind* has a few strong songs, but it's more notable for laying the musical foundation for the hit album *Bombs Away Dream Babies* and single "Gold" two years later. *—Bret Adams*

Bombs Away Dream Babies / 1979 / Razor & Tie ♦♦♦♦♦

After departing the Kingston Trio and struggling for more than a decade to find success with his critically acclaimed folk albums, John Stewart finally reached his commercial peak with 1979's *Bombs Away Dream Babies*. It hit the Top Ten and temporarily turned him into a "new" pop star at age 40. Stewart's folk leanings are evident on this album, but it's mostly a straightforward pop/rock affair. The guest performances by Fleetwood Mac's Lindsey Buckingham on guitar and Stevie Nicks on background vocals certainly helped, especially since they were still riding high on the success of *Rumours*. "Gold" was a thinly veiled criticism of the music business set to a smooth shuffle beat. Ironically, it became a Top Five hit. The bittersweet "Lost Her in the Sun" and the darkly dramatic "Midnight Wind" also hit the Top 40. *—Bret Adams*

Dream Babies Go Hollywood / 1980 / RSO ♦♦♦♦

After folk-based Kingston Trio veteran John Stewart had a Top Five single with "Gold" from the Top Ten album *Bombs Away Dream Babies* in 1979, he largely repeated the pop/rock formula the next year with *Dream Babies Go Hollywood*. This time, Stewart didn't have the assistance of Fleetwood Mac's Lindsey Buckingham and Stevie Nicks (who were likely concentrating on *Tusk* hubbub). However, Linda Ronstadt and Nicolette Larson helped out and sang background vocals on most *Dream Babies Go Hollywood* cuts. "Hollywood Dreams" is a bright, easygoing pop tune. "Wind on the River," a dreamy, folk-pop ballad, is enriched by Stewart's warm, supple vocals. "Wheels of Thunder" is a pleasant surprise here because it's a straightforward rock & roll song; heavily distorted electric guitar licks cut through the warm keyboards, the crisp acoustic guitar, and the fast rhythm section. "Odin (Spirit of the Water)" is boldly dark and brooding; Stewart's lead vocals and the background vocals are fiercely energetic. "The Raven" is another highlight thanks to Stewart's ethereal, urgently whispered vocals and the female harmony vocals in the chorus. *Dream Babies Go Hollywood* marks Stewart's last sliver of solo mainstream success to date—a shame because his music is criminally underrated. Fortunately, a die-hard core of Stewart cultists have kept his name alive by packing his club and theater concerts and buying the albums he released on smaller independent labels as well as on his own Homecoming imprint. *—Bret Adams*

Trancas / 1984 / Affordable Dreams ♦♦♦

The Last Campaign / 1985 / Homecoming ♦♦♦♦♦

The Last Campaign, issued in 1985 on John Stewart's Home Records label, is an album of songs written during and about the presidential campaign of Robert Kennedy that ended in his assassination. Stewart and Buffy Ford traveled with Kennedy, playing on flatbed trucks from the backs of trains, on-stages at rallies, anywhere they could. Some of the songs, like "Pirates of Stone Country Road," have appeared before, but these are re-recordings of all of them, thematically linked to the promise and devastation that went along with Kennedy's death. California friends like Linda Ronstadt, Lindsey Buckingham, Chuck McDermott, and Fred Koch were on board as well as a few others. By and large this is a simple but beautiful recording that Stewart produced by himself, wrapped deeply in reverie and the romanticism of a time that perhaps never existed. But to the listener, no matter what questions exist beforehand—or after the albums closes with a reprise of the title song, and dreams are shattered, left in the dust, or embittered—this is all heartfelt and real. Not real in the sense that Stewart is necessarily right, but real in that he truly believes what he has written here. For the generation that came of age in the 1960s, 1985 might have seemed like a dark time—though it was streamline bright compared to what America at the beginning of the 21st century looks like. Folk music that says you can't go back to Kansas, offers you the (unintentionally) false promise of "Dreamers on the Rise," the desperate wishes of "Hearts and Dreams on the Line," and "Spirit-Survivors," and the exhortation to continue to dream despite the acknowledgement of tremendous loss and the passage of history. This is Stewart at his most brazen, lost, and honest, looking for answers that are ciphers in sand, scattered to the winds, and the realization of promises that were never really madder, let alone kept. The ghost in the grain of his voice on this record is one of the most chilling things in American music. *The Last Campaign* is indeed a last of its kind, a journey through time and the human heart where brave souls get tired and long for solace even if there isn't any to be had. It is in that hope, or in the spectre that disguises itself as such, that great art is born, and *The Last Campaign* is nothing if not great art. *—Thom Jurek*

Secret Tapes '86 / 1986 / Homecoming ♦♦♦

Secret Tapes II / 1986 / Homecoming ♦♦♦

Punch the Big Guy / 1987 / Shanachie ♦♦♦♦♦

If there was justice in the music world, *Punch the Big Guy* would have been a huge commercial success. John Stewart took his songwriting prowess to its zenith, brought in a stellar cast of musical compatriots, and put together his finest three-quarters of an hour. His lyrics here are fired with anger, righteous indignation, political awareness, compassion, and, ultimately, love. The arrangements, built around Stewart's fingerpicked electric guitar, are mesmerizing, and his muscular baritone provides the perfect delivery van for sharing these observations, memories, questions, and vows. One cannot come away from this music unaffected. On "Midnight of the World," Stewart asks, "Will you always be my girl?" while simultaneously pondering the last days of the world. "Runaway Train" later became a number-one country hit for Rosanne Cash, who contributes eerie vocal harmonies to "Price of the Fire" and "Angels With Guns." Throughout, however, Stewart expresses the sense of faith and hope outlined in "Ticket to the Stars": "There are forces to guide you/spirits beside you/Rivers to ride you home to the stars." John Stewart achieves a genuine merger of the personal, the spiritual, and the political on *Punch the Big Guy* and wraps it all up in a darkly colored but accessible package. The mix of ballads and upbeat rockers holds the attention of even a casual listener, but for those who invest a little of themselves in the depth of its songs, this album offers a chest full of rare musical treasure. *—Jim Newsom*

California Bloodlines/Willard / 1989 / Bear Family ✦✦✦✦✦

Deep in the Neon: Live at McCabe's / Jun. 1991 / Homecoming ✦✦✦

Cannons in the Rain/Wingless Angels / Jun. 27, 1994 / Bear Family ✦✦✦✦

Airdream Believer / 1995 / Shanachie ✦✦✦✦

Airdream Believer started out as a career retrospective and reconsideration by John Stewart, devoted to his own songs plus a few he really dug (like Johnny Cash's "Get Rhythm" and Billy Edd Wheeler's "The Reverend Mr. Black"), before it turned into something more. The music dates back, in some cases, to his days with the Kingston Trio, performed with Johnny Cash, Rosanne Cash, Nanci Griffith, Sara Hickman, and his former Kingston Trio bandmates Nick Reynolds and Bob Shane. Stewart is in excellent voice throughout, a husky baritone closer in spirit to Bruce Springsteen than to the Kingston Trio; the mix of songs is quirky enough, and the reconsiderations of the songs fresh enough, to prevent this from being a mere exercise in nostalgia. "Lost Her in the Sun," "Midnight Wind" (with Rosanne Cash on the harmonies), and a moody "Daydream Believer" (with Griffith) are major highlights, but the entire recording is worthwhile, and the presence of the guest artists is not just a gimmick. *—Bruce Eder*

• **Turning Music Into Gold: The Best of John Stewart** / 1995 / Polydor ✦✦✦✦✦

The title of 1995's *The Best of John Stewart: Turning Music Into Gold* is actually a misnomer. This German release is actually two complete albums—1979's *Bombs Away Dream Babies* and 1980's *Dream Babies Go Hollywood*—and two previously unreleased bonus tracks collected on one CD. *Bombs Away Dream Babies* has been the biggest commercial success of Stewart's critically acclaimed solo career. This Top Ten effort included the Top Five hit "Gold" and two other Top 40 singles, "Midnight Wind" and "Lost Her in the Sun." Fleetwood Mac's Lindsey Buckingham and Stevie Nicks were featured prominently on the album. *Dream Babies Go Hollywood* was the less successful follow-up. It duplicated the pop/rock leanings of its predecessor and its notable tracks include "Hollywood Dreams," "Wind on the River," "Odin (Spirit of the Water)," and "Lady of Fame." "Hard Time Town" and "Children of the Morning" are the acoustic guitar-based bonus cuts. The former is driven by bright strumming while the latter, written by Stewart's wife Buffy Ford, is based on sweet fingerpicking. The liner notes were assembled by Peter O'Brien, who compiled insightful Stewart quotes from various interviews conducted between 1977 and 1984. *The Best of John Stewart: Turning Music Into Gold* is invaluable for die-hard fans because *Dream Babies Go Hollywood* was still not available individually on CD as of mid-2000. *—Bret Adams*

Rough Sketches / Apr. 22, 1997 / Folk Era ✦✦✦✦✦

Stewart's voice is as rough as his pencil sketches and worn as Route 66 itself. It speaks of lonely, distant places with more than just words. This is brought further to light through the contrast with his sweet voiced wife Buffy Ford in "Interview With an Angel." Another Folk Era album, *Live at the Turf Inn, Scotland*, presents the two together. This prolific songwriter wrote "Molly Dee" for Kingston Trio, joined the trio for much of the '60s for 12 albums. He then left to write "Daydream Believer" for the Monkees. A very American singer/songwriter more than deserving of his Phoenix-based cult following. *—Thomas Schulte*

Bandera / Jan. 13, 1998 / Folk Era ✦✦✦

Backed by the Scottish band Lies Damn Lies, Stewart turns in a typically heartfelt performance on the fine *Bandera*, one of his grittiest folk-rock efforts to date. *—Jason Ankeny*

John Stewart & Darwin's Army / Feb. 16, 1999 / Appleseed ✦✦✦

Contemporary folk master John Stewart organized the quartet John Stewart & Darwin's Army, and the group's self-titled 1999 album became the singer/songwriter/guitarist's first band effort since leaving the Kingston Trio more than three decades earlier. Joining Stewart are his wife, vocalist Buffy Stewart, vocalist/guitarist John Hoke, and vocalist/guitarist Dave Crossland. The goal of the *John Stewart & Darwin's Army* album was to record great folk songs, ranging from traditional standards to modern songs, and even a few originals. Hoke sings a pleasant rendition of Bob Dylan's "My Back Pages." A rollicking version of "Darlin' Corey," popularized by the Weavers and Pete Seeger, features Stewart on banjo. Crossland's original, "Blood in the Fields," blends well with the classics. "Santy Anno/Coal Tattoo" is a driving medley, and Buffy Stewart's strong singing anchors the "Santy Anno" portion; both songs had been performed by the Kingston Trio in the past. Heavenly vocal harmonies and slow acoustic guitar lines highlight Merle Haggard's "Silver Wings." Buffy Stewart sings a beautiful a cappella version of "Somewhere Over the Rainbow" (aka "Over the Rainbow"), popularized by Judy Garland in *the Wizard of Oz*, of course. Other covers included are Joe South's "Don't It Make You Want to Go Home," Tim Hardin's "Reason to Believe" (a hit for Rod Stewart), Paul Simon's "Boy in the Bubble," "They Call the Wind Mariah" from the musical *Paint Your Wagon*, and Leadbelly's "Goodnight Irene" (another favorite recorded by the Weavers). The liner notes feature an interview with John Stewart talking about the *John Stewart & Darwin's Army* project in detail. *—Bret Adams*

Gold: Best of John Stewart / Apr. 18, 2000 / Wrass ✦✦✦✦✦

John Stewart's *Gold* is a spectacular two CD, 41 song best of compilation. It is perfect for the casual fan . . . if there is such a thing. Stewart has a diehard cult of fans who probably have every LP or CD they can get their hands on anyway, and that's quite a task considering the bulk of the former Kingston Trio member's early solo output is shamefully either out of print or only available as expensive imports. *Gold* collects everything from Stewart's singer/songwriter acoustic work to his rock-oriented songs, including his only three Top 40 hits, all from 1979's *Bombs Away Dream Babies*: "Gold," "Lost Her in the Sun," and "Midnight Wind." The 1969 critical favorite *California Bloodlines* is represented by five remarkable songs including the title track, "Mother Country," and "July You're a Woman." "Durango," "All Time Woman," and "Cannons in the Rain" are other fine examples of early Stewart, but "Armstrong/Spirit" is the best illustration. This poignant song about Neil Armstrong's moon landing and its unifying effect on problem-filled Earth is resonant in its dignified simplicity. "Hung on the Heart" and "Runaway Train" are highlights of disc two, but of particular note are "Sweet Dreams Will Come and "I Remember America." The former is a joyous bluegrass/folk/rockabilly duet with Nanci Griffith while the latter, although a tad curmudgeonly, recalls America's pre-JFK-assassination promise and laments modern society's breakdown. *Gold* includes an essay by John Tobler, but it lacks musician credits, which would document the caliber of "anonymous" session aces—particularly those in Nashville—and high-profile stars who have worked with Stewart over the years. *—Bret Adams*

Wires From the Bunker / Oct. 10, 2000 / Appleseed ✦✦✦

There is quite a tale concerning how these "lost tapes" of John Stewart, recorded from 1983 to 1985, came to the light of day. The liner notes tell the saga of a dusty box of dusty tapes in a dusty garage, being very poorly duct-taped by Stewart, and then mailed to his friend Tom Delisle in 1991. Stewart, a humble sort of musical celebrity, was merely trying to clear out his garage. The recordings were made just after Stewart lost his third big-label contract, this time with RSO, where he had released the 1978 hit "Gold." Two albums and a declining sales demographic later, Stewart was shopping for a label, but still writing and recording. Hence, the fabled box of recordings. The musical modus employed on these 18 songs is a mix of Stewart's earlier folk and singer/songwriter styles on Capitol Records and RCA, both solo and with the Kingston Trio, and his echo-y, hypno-rock style from his RSO days. Of the latter style, especially choice is "American Way," a pumping rocker featuring friend and Fleetwood Mac alumnus Lindsey Buckingham on backing vocals. It is a compelling, hook-driven song that would not have been out of place on Stewart's hit RSO album *Bombs Away Dream Babies*. In his folkier mode, "The Escape of Old John Webb," a tune earlier recorded by the Kingston Trio, is a standout. Ex-Trio mates Dave Guard and Nick Reynolds even assist on backing vocals. The worth of this collection depends on how one feels about Stewart and garages. For the converted, it is an unexpected treasure "box." Of the 18 cuts, a good dozen are album-ready, major-to-minor gems. Even the demo-ish curios are never less than interesting. For those uninitiated to the pleasures of Stewart's music, a better place to start would probably be 1969's classic *California Bloodlines* on Capitol Records or 1979's *Bombs Away Dream Babies* on RSO. Of course, neither of these recordings was once held together by duct tape. *—Steve Cooper*

Willard/California Bloodlines / Mar. 9, 2002 / BGO ✦✦✦✦

In 2002, BGO released *Willard/California Bloodlines*, which contained two albums—*Willard* (1970, originally released on Capitol) and *California Bloodlines* (1969, also originally on Capitol)—by John Stewart on one compact disc. *—Tim Sendra*

Havana / Mar. 25, 2003 / Appleseed ✦✦✦✦

Havana ranks among John Stewart's best albums, which is saying a good deal, since he has released more than 40—many of them excellent—in a career that dates all the way back to 1961. His first new studio recording in five years, *Havana* features an eclectic mix of 15 folk-tinged ballads and spirited rockers, all but one by Stewart. (The sole non-original is the standard "Lucky Old Sun," which proves a perfect match for the singer's world-weary baritone.) The lyrics—some personal, some political—hit their marks more often than not and are frequently poignant ("Waiting for Castro to Die" and the terrific "Cowboy in the Distance") or funny. ("Attention Kmart shoppers," Stewart begins one song, "Do you really need all of that crap?") Not every lyric works: While clearly heartfelt, a tribute to Stewart's wife ("Miracle Girl") is cliché ridden; "Davey on the Internet" is fun but nonsensical; and songs about rock & roll and Princess Diana all fall short in their effort to say something profound. But the melodies and vocals are consistently strong on this CD. So is the instrumentation, which is mostly by Stewart, who plays guitars, banjo, bass, keyboards, percussion, and harmonica. Even when a lyric occasionally falls short, therefore, the music is strong enough to keep you well entertained. *—Jeff Burger*

• **The Earth Rider—The Essential John Stewart 1964–1979** / May 20, 2003 / Raven ✦✦✦✦✦

If ever there was an enigma in American music, John Stewart is it. How many people can claim to have been the last member of the Kingston Trio and become its frontman, to have been the official musician for the Robert Kennedy campaign, to write hits for the Monkees and Fleetwood Mac, to be admired by Johnny Cash, Merle Haggard, Kinky Friedman, Emmylou Harris, and the entire L.A. Jackson Eagles studio mafia? Just one: John Stewart, who continued to still kick them out, record after record, albeit on smaller labels than Capitol or A&M. While there are plenty of reasons to seek out Stewart's Kingston Trio material, this anthology on Raven doesn't do so, partially because that material is so well documented elsewhere and in part because as a solo artist Stewart was his own enigma. Like the Byrds, the Mamas & the Papas, the Grateful Dead, the Eagles, Jackson Browne, Warren Zevon, Jefferson Airplane, the Beach Boys, and Buffalo Springfield, Stewart embodied a particular tract of California's musical terrain and its mystique. In Stewart's music, like "California Bloodlines," "Razorback Woman," "Some Lonesome Picker," "Willard," and other songs, his folk met country and the expanding textures of pop; his stories entered the listener without force but left their mark nonetheless. "Daydream Believer" is Stewart's voice in a real folk song, kissed by the brightness of pop and graced with California's sunshine. From "Anna on a Memory" to "Chilly Winds," Stewart seemed unaffected by the changing times. He was still looking under the surface for the places in memory and in emotions that make listeners experience things in common. Most of the material here is from the late '60s and early to mid-'70s, but as late as *Fire in the Wind*, Stewart may have been using updated production techniques but was still writing paeans to truckers. Only on the material from *Bombs Away Dream Babies* with its smash "Gold" and "Midnight Wind" do the sounds embrace the modern day—yet even here the lyrics don't. With Fleetwood Mac kicking behind him (and turning his questions into the very things he was begging the answers to), Stewart is still looking at society with bemusement and a wonder that expresses disillusionment at why others don't notice the glory and the grace in people who work in gas stations. Raven has done a fantastic job of revealing how large the myth of Stewart is and how great his enigma remains with this 24-track anthology. For the curious, dubious, and faithful, this is a fine way to spend your hard-earned money. *—Thom Jurek*

Larry Stewart

b. Mar. 2, 1959, Paducah, KY
Vocals / Contemporary Country
Best known as the frontman for the vocal group Restless Heart, singer Larry Stewart first came to Nashville with hopes of a career in baseball, not music; the recipient of an athletic scholarship to Nashville's Belmont College, he quickly found himself drawn to the music business instead and decided to pursue a career as a performer. After working a series of menial industry jobs, his vocals on a series of demo recordings helped win him the lead spot with Restless Heart. After leaving the group, Stewart issued his solo debut, *Down the Road*, in 1993. *Heart Like a Hurricane* followed a year later, and in 1996 he returned with *Why Can't You*. Although his albums had usually contained a straight-up pop tune or two, Stewart made a more pronounced step in that direction with 1999's *Learning to Breathe*. *—Jason Ankeny*

● **Down the Road** / Apr. 27, 1993 / RCA ♦♦♦♦
Yeah, Restless Heart had its biggest success after he left. Judging from *Down the Road*, though, the split was one of those situations where the parts are greater than the sum. Just when "Alright Already" and "I'll Cry Tomorrow" convince you Stewart has made a country record, he tosses off a pop gem like "We Can Love." He also cut Kevin Welch's "I Came Straight to You," a definite plus. *—Brian Mansfield*

Heart Like a Hurricane / 1994 / Columbia ♦♦♦

Why Can't You / Sep. 3, 1996 / Sony ♦♦♦
Larry Stewart's third album suffers from an uneven selection of material and production that plays it too close to the vest, but the singer manages to salvage about half the songs with a convincing, powerful performance, making *Why Can't You* a marginal improvement over its predecessor, *Heart Like A Hurricane*. *—Thom Owens*

Learning to Breathe / May 18, 1999 / Windham Hill ♦♦♦
After leaving Restless Heart, Larry Stewart spent several years trying to carve out a place in contemporary country for himself. Finally, he decided to make a move toward adult contemporary pop with his 1999 album, *Learning to Breathe*. Truth be told, Stewart's pop move doesn't sound all that different from Shania Twain and Faith Hill's allegedly country albums, but that isn't a bad thing at all. He has a smooth, robust voice that fits well into the smooth, contoured textures of adult contemporary pop. And if he doesn't always have the material to make *Learning to Breathe* a totally engaging record, he and his collaborators and guest stars—including producer Michael Omartian, Michael McDonald and Vince Gill—have created an album that sounds pleasing even on the filler, although it's singles like "Still in Love" that remain memorable. Which means that he's delivered a genuine adult contemporary album. *—Stephen Thomas Erlewine*

Wynn Stewart

b. Jun. 7, 1934, Morrisville, MO, **d.** Jul. 17, 1985, Hendersonville, TN
Vocals / Traditional Country, Bakersfield Sound
Wynn Stewart was one of the leading figures of West Coast country music, developing in the early '50s the style that would later become known as the Bakersfield sound. Along with Tommy Collins and Buck Owens, Stewart stripped down the sound of honky tonk, taking away the steel guitars and relying on electric instruments, a driving beat, and loud, energetic performances. For most of the late '50s and early '60s, Stewart released a series of independent singles that performed respectably yet failed to break him into the mainstream. By the end of the '60s, he had modified his sound slightly, bringing himself closer to country-pop territory. The shift in style was successful, resulting in his lone number-one hit single, "It's Such a Pretty World Today," but Stewart wasn't able to become a genuine country star, despite his steady stream of records during the '70s and '80s. At the time of his sudden death in 1985, he was preparing for another comeback, which may have resulted in some long-overdue critical and popular acclaim. Even though he never received those accolades while he was alive, his early singles like "Wishful Thinking" and "Big, Big Love" clearly inspired contemporaries like Owens and Merle Haggard, as well as '80s neo-traditionalists and alternative country musicians like Dwight Yoakam and k.d. lang, which guarantees him a place in the history of contemporary country music.

Stewart was born in Morrisville, MO, and spent most of his childhood moving around the country with his sharecropping family. Following World War II, he spent a year working for KWTO in Springfield, MO, before moving to California in 1948 with his family. Originally, Stewart wanted to become a professional baseball player, but he suffered from a hand disease and was too short to play ball professionally, so he concentrated on a musical career. While he was still in high-school, he formed a band and began playing clubs around California. Eventually, he met steel guitarist Ralph Mooney, who joined Stewart's band; rounding out the group's lineup were guitarist Roy Nichols and bassist Bobby Austin. In 1954, Stewart signed a contract with the independent label Intro, where he released "I've Waited a Lifetime" and "Strolling." The second single drew the attention of Stewart's idol, Skeets McDonald, who had arranged an audition at Capitol Records for him. By the summer of 1956, Stewart had signed with Capitol and released his first single for the label, "Waltz of the Angels," which spent one week at number 14 on the country chart; the song was later a hit for George Jones and Margie Singleton. Subsequent singles were released on Capitol, but none of the records made any impact, and Stewart left the label.

With the help of Harlan Howard, Stewart signed with Jackpot, a subsidiary of Challenge Records, in early 1958. Occasionally employing Mooney on steel guitar, Stewart made a series of singles that explored a number of different styles, from rockabilly and pop to pure honky tonk. In late 1959, he finally had a hit with "Wishful Thinking," which climbed to number five early in 1960. Shortly after the success of "Wishful Thinking," he moved to Las Vegas, where he hosted a local television show and opened the Nashville Nevada Club. By the early '60s, Stewart's reputation, if not his sales, was considerable, and he continued to have a string of moderate hit singles, including the Jan Howard duet "Wrong Company," "Big, Big Love," and "Another Day, Another Dollar." In 1962, Haggard joined Stewart's band as a bassist, and Wynn eventually gave him "Sing a Sad Song" for his debut single.

After his Vegas ventures went bankrupt, Stewart headed back to California in 1965, re-signing with Capitol Records. Early in 1967, he had his first significant hit for the label, "It's Such a Pretty World Today," which spent two weeks at number one. Following its success, Stewart concentrated on softer, more commercially acceptable material, and the result was a string of hit singles that ran into the early '70s. By 1972, his sales were beginning to decrease, and Stewart switched record labels, signing with RCA. Over the next three years he released a number of singles, none of which cracked the Top 40. In 1975, he signed with Playboy Records, scoring a comeback single with the Top Ten "After the Storm" the following year. He stayed with Playboy for two more years, which resulted in only one other hit single: his own version of "Sing a Sad Song."

Stewart launched his own independent label, WIN, in 1978, and his first single, "Eyes Big as Dallas," scraped the bottom of the Top 40. Though the musical climate of the '70s was changing rapidly, leaving Stewart behind, he also wasn't able to achieve more success because of his developing alcoholism. Eventually, he decided to step back from performing in the early '80s, using the time away from the spotlight. During the mid-'80s, Stewart decided to launch a comeback with an extensive tour and a new album on his Pretty World record label when he died suddenly of a heart attack on the eve of the tour. Following his death, the posthumous "Wait Till I Get My Hands on You" became a minor hit. *—Stephen Thomas Erlewine*

★ **California Country: The Best of the Challenge Masters** / 1995 / AVI ♦♦♦♦♦
This masterful collection is the best of Wynn Stewart, the early years. Included here are 29 cuts that range from the hits to some of the more obscure numbers he recorded in California while signed to both Jackpot and Challenge: "Come On," a rockabilly tune; "Wishful Thinkin'"; and two of the three big Challenge hits, "Big, Big Love" and "Another Day, Another Dollar." As good as anything recorded since, Wynn Stewart's voice was always notable. Best described as a "rolling chord style," Stewart continues to be praised as one of the outstanding vocalists of the genre. His contribution to the West Coast country scene and to the Bakersfield sound makes him one of the founding fathers of that musical ilk. Tunes that demonstrate this include "Playboy," "Falling for You," a Ralph Mooney tune, and "Heartaches for a Dime." His duets with Jan Howard, then married to Harlan Howard, convinced the young woman to pursue a singing career. "How the Other Half Lives," "Wrong Company," and "We'll Never Love Again" continue to set a standard for couple's duets. Ending with the bleak "The Black Limousine" seems fitting since Stewart's career was cut short in 1985 when he died of a heart attack just as he was about to make another bid for success. Underappreciated, especially in the U.S., Wynn Stewart and the songs he wrote and recorded continue to draw attention to a talent and a career that never quite took off, yet is more remarkable than most of the artists who find themselves sitting at the top of the charts with their pockets full of gold. This is an exceptional introduction to Wynn Stewart as well as a remarkable collection for Wynn Stewart fans to savor and enjoy. *—Jana Pendragon*

Wishful Thinking / Aug. 22, 2000 / Bear Family ♦♦♦♦♦
Bear Family's *Wishful Thinking* compilation gathers virtually everything that Bakersfield sound pioneer Wynn Stewart ever recorded, summarizing his three-decade career over the course of ten discs. "Keeper of the Keys," "It's Such a Pretty World Today," "Sing a Sad Song," "Waltz of the Angels," and the title track are some of the many highlights from this 279-song collection, which traces Stewart's evolution from his hard-driving, rockabilly tinged sound in the '50s to a more pop-oriented country style in the '60s, '70s, and '80s. His complete works for labels such as Jackpot-Challenge, Copre, Playboy, and his own Win and Pretty World imprints are also included. As with all Bear Family releases, *Wishful Thinking* also includes extensive liner notes, and the first full-length Wynn Stewart biography is part of the package as well. Though the *California Country: The Best of the Challenge Masters* collection is probably still the best introduction to Stewart's work, *Wishful Thinking* is a treasure for his longtime fans. *—Heather Phares*

★ **The Very Best of Wynn Stewart 1958–1962** / Jun. 5, 2001 / Varese ♦♦♦♦♦
It may pale next to the 29-track *California Country*, but this is the finest extant single-disc collection on Wynn Stewart, gathering most of his best cuts for Challenge and three of his early Jackpot singles, including the lost classics "How the Other Half Lives" and "Above and Beyond (The Call of Love)." Fans might be disappointed at what isn't here, but *Very Best of* does feature two good songs ("One Way to Go" and "Don't Look Back") missing from *California Country*, and is a thoroughly enjoyable collection of one of the finest voices ever to slip under the country music radar. *—Jim Smith*

Lowe Stokes

Fiddle / String Bands
This classic old-time fiddler is a bit of a mystery man, showing up as the senior member of a band formed in 1918 by fellow fiddle genius Clayton McMichen, one of the regular sidekicks of Lowe Stokes over the years. At first called the Lick the Skillet Band, then the Old Hometown Band, this double-fiddle group eventually morphed into Gid Tanner & the Skillet Lickers, one of the most famous and well-loved of old-time groups from this era that managed to be recorded. But if the saga of Stokes is to be believed, life on the road with this band was more about licking one's wounds than licking skillets. On one tour,

the trouble-bound Stokes was stabbed perilously near the heart as the nasty consequence of a love triangle, then was shot in the hand in a drunken altercation a few days later while still healing from the earlier wound. This was something of a gory preliminary to the next Skillet Lickers tour, where the poor Stokes would have his hand shot off completely. Luckily, a fellow fiddler in the outfit was a skilled engineer and was able to design a special hook that allowed Stokes to hold his bow despite the injury. This was something of a distinction obviously, with old-time music fans decades later still commenting on the wonders of seeing "a photograph of Lowe Stokes, playing one-handed" on fiddle chat rooms in cyberspace.

Stokes was mostly known as a sideman. In the Skillet Lickers, he played alongside guitarist and singer Riley Puckett and mandolinist Ted Hawkins, fiddlers Bert Layne and Gid Tanner, as well as the aforementioned McMichen. He also worked in the group Seven Foot Dilly & His Dill Pickles, led by fellow North Georgia fiddler John Dilleshaw. There was a series of recordings Stokes did as frontman for his band, the North Georgians, including titles such as "I Wish I Had Stayed in the Wagon Yard," "Home Brew Rag," "Wave That Frame," and "Take Me to the Land of Jazz." Many of these recordings were collected for a series of reissues on the Document label. He also recorded with cowboy singer Hugh Cross. In 1925, poet Stephan Vincent Benet wrote a poem, entitled "the Mountain Whipporwill," which was based on seeing Stokes win a fiddle contest in Atlanta the year before. Not quite as timeless as a piece of poetry, Stokes nonetheless was feeling fit enough to fiddle at the 1982 Brandywine festival, leaving ecstatic fans still guessing about his exact age. He remains one of the classic icons of old-time fiddling, an important influence to all new generations of players taking on this genre. *—Eugene Chadbourne*

- **Lowe Stokes, Vol. 1: 1927–1930** / Sep. 7, 2000 / Document ♦♦♦♦

Cliffie Stone (Clifford Gilpin Snyder)

b. Mar. 1, 1917, Burbank, CA, **d.** Jan. 17, 1998

Bass / Traditional Country

A native of California, Cliffie Stone was born Clifford Gilpin Snyder in Burbank on March 1, 1917. The son of entertainer, comedy star, and banjo picker Herman the Hermit, Stone was known for his struggle to bring California's country & western music into favor in post-World War II America. He began playing bass in big bands with Freddie Slack and Anson Weeks as well as with other bands around Hollywood and Pasadena, but it was his work on radio stations KFUD and KFWB that brought him respect. Shows such as *Covered Wagon Jubilee* and *Lucky Stars,* broadcast out of Los Angeles, allowed him to show off his numerous skills. Working as a DJ, comedian, performer, and host, Stone won fame doing 28 radio shows a week between 1943 and 1947. As a featured performer on the *Hollywood Barn Dance,* he made a place for himself in country music history. In 1946 he accepted a position with Capitol Records, who were gearing up for the still as yet undefined Bakersfield movement. An A&R executive with Capitol for 20 years, Stone discovered Tennessee Ernie Ford, whom he managed from 1947 to 1957, Molly Bee, Hank Thompson, and others who were flocking to L.A. to record.

In spite of his success at Capitol, Stone was best remembered for his radio work. His show on Pasadena radio station KXLA, *Dinner Bell Roundup,* was a daily variety presentation that brought large numbers of country & western entertainers into the homes of his listeners. In 1944 the show picked up and moved to El Monte. The new location brought with it a new name, *Hometown Jamboree.* Recording six albums of his own he earned co-writing credits on hits "Divorce Me C.O.D.," "So Round, So Firm, So Fully Packed," and in 1947, "Silver Stars, Purple Sage, Eyes of Blue." He recorded with various versions of his own band, including Cliffie Stone & His Orchestra, Cliffie Stone & His Barn Dance Band, as well as Cliffie Stone's Country Hombres.

Concentrating on the business side of things, the 1960s saw Stone's publishing company, Central Songs, flourish. He even headed up a label, Granite, for a time. The father of Curtis Stone, one of the founding members of Highway 101, Stone wrote several books, including *Everything You Always Wanted to Know About Songwriting but Didn't Know Who to Ask,* published in 1991. He died of a heart attack on January 17, 1998. *—Jana Pendragon*

- **The Grunt Song and Other Country Classics** / Jan. 21, 2003 / Jasmine ♦♦♦♦

Doug Stone

b. Jun. 19, 1956, Newnan, GA

Vocals / Contemporary Country, New Traditionalist

Contemporary country star Doug Stone made his name as a lonesome baritone balladeer, though he's also adept at hard uptempo country. Stone was born and raised in Newnan, GA, and learned guitar from his mother—also a country singer—starting at age five. As a teenager, he performed in skating rinks in his hometown and later moved on to playing area bars while working long hours as a mechanic during the day. Stone was already several years past 30 when a Nashville-based manager saw his act and helped him finally land a record deal with Epic. His self-titled debut was released in 1990 and broke him in a big way with the despairing lead single "I'd Be Better Off (In a Pine Box)," which shot into the country Top Five. Stone landed three more Top Ten hits from the album, including "Fourteen Minutes Old," "These Lips Don't Know How to Say Goodbye," and his first number one, "In a Different Light." He quickly completed a follow-up album, *I Thought It Was You,* for release in 1991, which confirmed his downtrodden persona and became his second straight million-seller on the strength of three Top Five hits: the title track, "Come in Out of the Pain," and a second number one in "A Jukebox With a Country Song."

Shortly before the release of his third album, *From the Heart,* in 1992, Stone underwent quadruple bypass surgery; he recovered in time to issue the holiday album *The First Christmas* by year's end. Meanwhile, *From the Heart* kept spinning off one hit after another: "Warning Labels" and "Made for Lovin' You" went Top Ten, and both "Too Busy Being in Love" and "Why Didn't I Think of That" topped the charts. Stone continued his frantic hitmaking pace with 1993's *More Love,* which contained three Top Ten smashes in "Addicted to a Dollar," "I Never Knew Love," and the title track. Like *From the Heart, More Love* went gold, and Stone followed it in 1995 with the compilation *Greatest Hits, Vol. 1,* whose newly recorded "Little Houses" went Top Ten. Later in the year, Stone returned with *Faith in Me, Faith in You;* while it featured hits in the title track and "Born in the Dark," nothing reached the Top Ten. To make matters worse, his health problems continued: in December 1995, he suffered a near-fatal heart attack, and the recuperation time put the recording of his next album on hold. In 1997, Stone was nearly killed in a plane crash, and all the near-death experiences led him to slow down his touring and recording pace. He eventually parted ways with Columbia and went to Atlantic for 1999's *Make Up in Love,* his most pop-oriented offering to date. Thanks to declining sales, it was his only album for the label, and he subsequently moved to the independent Audium label for 2002's *The Long Way. —Steve Huey*

Doug Stone / 1990 / Epic ♦♦♦♦♦

"I'd Be Better Off (In a Pine Box)" is a towering expression of self-pity that most singers could spend a career trying to top. If Stone never bested his performance on his debut, he came close with ballads like "In a Different Light" and "My Hat's off to Him," becoming a genuine heartthrob in the process. *—Brian Mansfield*

I Thought It Was You / 1991 / Epic ♦♦♦

Self-pity has always played an integral role in country music, but it's more effective a song at a time, not spread over an entire album. Unlike some harder-voiced honky tonkers who funnel their emotions into cathartic country blues, Stone seems to wallow in sorrow. His ex is showing him up; his kid's growing up too fast; his new wife's walking out on him and telling him to shut up as he slams the door. This guy's favorite honky tonk even gets turned into a fern bar. *—Brian Mansfield*

From the Heart / 1992 / Epic ♦♦♦♦♦

Song for song, Stone's third album is his strongest, lacking the peak-and-valley terrain of his debut and the incessant self-pity of *I Thought It Was You.* Stone's voice is at its pain-wracked best with "Warning Labels" and "This Empty House," and if you think he pulls the heartstrings with the sad songs, wait'll you hear what he does with "Made for Lovin' You" and "Too Busy Being in Love." The heart references take on a special meaning given the open-heart surgery that preceded this album: in "Warning Labels," Stone gives a first-hand account of the serious damage those country tearjerkers can do. And here we figured it was all that Southern-fried food. *—Brian Mansfield*

The First Christmas / Apr. 1992 / Epic ♦♦♦

Given the number of songwriters in Nashville, it's surprising the town hasn't produced more Christmas songs. *The First Christmas* gets a bunch of them, though. Songs like "An Angel Like You" play off Stone's romantic-balladeer image, and "When December Comes Around" would sound great any time of year. "Sailing Home for Christmas" depicts the irony of soldiers celebrating the coming of "peace on earth" while stationed on a battleship. *—Brian Mansfield*

More Love / Nov. 16, 1993 / Epic ♦♦♦

With "Addicted to a Dollar," balladeer Stone stakes his claim for "hot country" status alongside all his Nashville peers. *—Dan Cooper*

Greatest Hits, Vol. 1 / 1995 / Epic ♦♦♦♦

Greatest Hits, Vol. 1 is a decent overview of Doug Stone's country ballads recorded for Epic in the early '90s. Among these Top Ten hits are "I'd Be Better Off (In a Pine Box)," "I Thought It Was You," "Come in Out of the Pain," and his first number one, "In a Better Light." While a few favorites are missing, the mid-line pricing makes this worth picking up. *—Al Campbell*

Faith in Me, Faith in You / 1995 / Columbia ♦♦♦

- **Super Hits** / Mar. 4, 1997 / Columbia ♦♦♦♦♦

Super Hits is a brief but strong compilation of Doug Stone's biggest hits, including "These Lips Don't Know How to Say Goodbye," "Faith in Me, Faith in You," "Fourteen Minutes Old," "I'd Be Better Off (In a Pine Box)," "Come in Out of the Pain," "More Love," "In a Different Light" and "Why Didn't I Think of That." *—Stephen Thomas Erlewine*

Pure Country / Aug. 25, 1998 / Sony ♦♦♦

Sony Special Products' *Pure Country* is a sampler of Doug Stone's country-pop recordings for Epic Records in the '90s. Where most volumes of *Pure Country* function as effective hits compilations, this disc only contains one big hit—"A Jukebox with a Country Song"—which makes it of less interest to its target audience of casual fans. Nevertheless, there is enough strong material here to make it worth its budget price for some budget-conscious listeners. *—Stephen Thomas Erlewine*

Make up in Love / Sep. 7, 1999 / Atlantic ♦♦♦

Somewhere along the way, Doug Stone traded relatively straightforward honky tonk balladeering for mainstream country balladeering that leaned heavily toward country-pop. Since his voice has always been rich and sweet, not heavily country, the transition makes sense, but it's still sort of surprising how slick and radio-ready his sixth album, *Make Up in Love,* is. It's country in name only, simply because it has prominent acoustic guitars, steel guitars, and a bit of a twang, but the songs and performances are all adult contemporary pop—it's quite remarkable that a cover of R.B. Greave's kitschy pop-soul classic "Take a Letter, Maria" is the closest this comes to hardcore country. Since Stone's voice is pleasant, the music is often pleasant, but it's hardly memorable. Perhaps if he had taken the leap into straight adult pop and worked with stronger material, *Make Up in Love* would be more than simply pleasantly forgettable, but as it stands, it's inoffensive, professionally made country-pop. Stone is capable of more than that, as his earlier records prove, but he does sound in his element here, even if the music isn't as effective as his albums from the early '90s. *—Stephen Thomas Erlewine*

The Long Way / Sep. 24, 2002 / Audium ♦♦♦

After Doug Stone's career was curtailed for nearly seven years by health problems coupled with a pair of less than successful major-label releases in the mid-'90s, Stone came back on the new-country indie Audium Records with 2002's *The Long Way,* a somewhat scattershot but promising retrenchment. It's a bit disappointing for longtime fans, as over half of the ten songs here are re-recordings of previously released material, including acoustic remakes of Stone's biggest country radio hits and four re-recorded tracks from a barely released abortive attempt at a comeback from 1999, *Make Up in Love.* The arrangements this time out seemingly have an ear cocked toward the alt-country scene, as they're not nearly so suffocatingly slick as Stone's previous albums. However, Stone's vocal style, which mixes George Strait's quaver and Randy Travis' twang, is pure Nashville, as is his penchant for big ballads like the war-themed "POW 369." *The Long Way* shows that Doug Stone is pretty much back on top of his game, but unfortunately, his primary skills are out of step with what's successful both in alt-country and in post-Shania Twain country-pop Nashville. *—Stewart Mason*

Ernest V. Stoneman

b. May 25, 1893, Monorat, VA, **d.** Jun. 14, 1968

Guitar, Vocals / Traditional Country

Ernest "Pop" Stoneman was one of the first, and most popular, early country artists. He was born in Carroll Country, VA, and raised by his father and three cousins, who taught him traditional Blue Ridge Mountain songs. He married as a young man and, when not working various odd jobs, played music for friends and neighbors. After hearing a Henry Whitter record and swearing he could do better, in 1924 he set off to New York to get a recording contract and prove it. His first single, "The Sinking of the Titanic," came out on the OKeh label later that year and became one of the biggest hits of the 1920s. At first he was accompanied only by his autoharp (his best-known instrument) and harmonica, but later switched to guitar; Stoneman was also adept at playing the jew's-harp and the clawhammer banjo. In 1926, he surrounded himself with a full string band, mostly composed of relatives and neighbors. His career reached its peak in 1927, when he became the top country artist at Victor and led the Bristol sessions, which helped the Carter Family and Jimmie Rodgers gain renown. Stoneman continued to record through 1929, setting down over 200 songs.

When the Great Depression hit in the early '30s, Stoneman lost everything and moved his wife and nine children to Washington, D.C. They remained there in desperate poverty while Stoneman worked odd jobs and tried to re-establish his career, finally finding work at a munitions plant. At the end of the 1940s, he and his talented clan began performing as the Stoneman Family. By 1956, he had earned the moniker "Pop" and appeared on the NBC television game show *The Big Surprise*, where he won $10,000. Later, his children's band, the Blue Grass Champs, became the Stonemans, which Pop himself joined after retiring from the plant in the late '50s. He continued appearing with them and singing lead vocals through the early '60s. In 1965, the Stonemans signed with MGM in Nashville and hosted a syndicated TV show. In 1967, Stoneman's health began to deteriorate; he continued recording and performing through the spring of 1968, until his death in June. *—Sandra Brennan*

Old-Time Tunes of the South / 1957 / Folkways ♦♦♦♦

Cool Cowboy / 1959 / Capitol ♦♦♦

Ernest Stoneman & the Blue Ridge Corn Shuckers / 1970 / Rounder ♦♦♦

A historic collection such as this deserves something more in the way of liner-note documentation than the five paragraphs of text this album comes with. A sense of time and place is soaked through and through these recordings, however, and may be more than enough to transport listeners to times long ago and far away. In terms of recording technology, this might have been the stone age: These are muddy, lo-fi recordings in which individual instruments are often hard to discern. Some of the pressings of this record were mastered so low that listeners may experience problems with hum as they crank their amplifiers up. The music is more of an antique version of country & western than the often instrumentally oriented old-time string band sound. Vocals are featured prominently, usually done in harmonies with the high voice of fiddler Kahle Brewer particularly striking. The material contains many standards of the repertoire, such as "Sourwood Mountain" and "Old Joe Clark," and many moments of great sentimentality. In the lesser hands of some old-time music revival groups, some of this material would just be over the top. Stoneman & His Blue Ridge Corn Shuckers, including guitar plus several fiddles and banjos in the instrumental lineup, have no such negative impact. The songs are played with skill and an instrumental tightness that sometimes combines the efforts of the players into a pleasant sound that rolls along like a calliope. The highlights include "All Go Hungry Hash House," which has to be the best restaurant review ever to come disguised as an old-time tune. *—Eugene Chadbourne*

• **Ernest Stoneman: 1928 Edison Recordings** / 1996 / County ♦♦♦♦

1928 Edison Recordings contains all 22 tracks that Ernest Stoneman recorded for Edison in 1928. On these sessions, he was backed by a string band, which gave him and his autoharp a fuller sound, yet this music remains pure, direct and rural—his versions of traditional numbers like "The Prisoner's Lament," "I Remember Cavalry" and "Fallen By the Wayside" are startling in their openness. *—Thom Owens*

Stoney Lonesome

Group / Traditional Bluegrass

Stoney Lonesome consists of Kate MacKenzie (guitar, vocals), Chris Kaiser (mandolin, lead guitar, vocals), Kevin Barnes (banjo, dobro, vocals), Brian Wicklund (fiddle, vocals), and Patty Shove (bass). The group first gained attention by appearing frequently on Prairie Home Companion during the '80s. In the early '90s, the quintet began releasing albums on Red House Records, starting with *Lonesome Tonight* in 1991 and followed by *Blue Heartache* the next year. *—John Bush*

Lonesome Tonight / 1991 / Red House ♦♦♦

Stoney Lonesome frequently appeared on the radio series *A Prairie Home Companion.* On this album he plays some of his own compositions plus traditional music from Ola Belle Reed and the Stanley Brothers. *—AMG*

• **Blue Heartache** / 1992 / Red House ♦♦♦♦

On their second album *Blue Heartache*, Stoney Lonesome's music gelled, thanks in particular to Kate MacKenzie's powerful, emotional singing. The album is splt between originals and covers of classic country and bluegrass songs; often, the originals hold their own with the classics. *—Thom Owens*

Carl Story

b. May 29, 1916, Lenoir, NC, **d.** Mar. 30, 1995, Greer, SC

Fiddle, Vocals / Bluegrass, Traditional Bluegrass, Country Gospel

Guitarist, fiddler, and vocalist Carl Story became known as "The Father of Bluegrass Gospel Music" over his decades-long career. Though less well known than Bill Monroe, Ralph Stanley, and other bluegrass pioneers, he was present as the genre took shape and was for many years a highly influential figure whose band served as a training ground for many younger musicians. Story was born to musically inclined parents who played for square dances, and he learned both the fiddle and guitar when he was young. String band music snared his attention when he was in his teens, and he was active on radio in Lynchburg, VA, in the early '30s. Around 1935, Story and teenage banjoist Johnnie Whisnant moved to Spartanburg, SC, to play in a band called the Lonesome Mountaineers, which eventually spawned the Rambling Mountaineers. The band performed on radio around the South until Story left to become a fiddler for Bill Monroe & his Blue Grass Boys in 1942, replacing fiddler Howdy Forrester after Forrester was drafted. In 1943, Story, too, was drafted into the U.S. Navy.

Following his discharge, Story reassembled the Rambling Mountaineers with Jack and Curley Shelton, Hoke Jenkins, and Claude Boone. The band's membership changed over the years, and many members, such as Tater Tate and Red Rector, went on to become important bluegrass figures. Story and his group began recording both secular and gospel songs for the Mercury label in 1947, and remained with the label until 1952. He moved to Columbia the following year and recorded over a dozen singles. The pure bluegrass phase of his career, merging the "high lonesome" Monroe sound with gospel harmony vocals and skilled picking from Story and his sidemen, began with the band's signing to Starday in the late '50s. Over some ten albums between then and the early '70s, Story tended almost exclusively toward gospel. Such albums as 1963's *Mighty Close to Heaven* featured upbeat material ("You Don't Love God (If You Don't Love Your Neighbor)") mixed with numbers that employed the poetic qualities of bluegrass songwriting in the service of intense professions of faith (the title track, in which Story sings that he came "mighty close to heaven with my tears"). Story and his band became fixtures on the bluegrass festival circuit, and he toured consistently even after he entered semi-retirement in Greer, SC, outside of Greenville, where he worked as a disc jockey. His funeral in 1995 was attended by bluegrass royalty, from Bill Monroe on down. *—Sandra Brennan & James Manheim*

The Best of Country Music / 1967 / Scripture ♦♦♦

The Best of Country Music is the most unusual album in Carl Story's catalog. The track list on the back cover is comprised of sacred songs such as one would expect from the Father of Bluegrass Gospel, but the front cover advertises a completely different set of secular songs. The album actually contains the latter, and—despite the title—includes bluegrass renditions of surprising selections like the Singing Nuns' "Dominique" and the String-a-Longs' 1961 instrumental rock & roll hit "Wheels." "Step It Up and Go," with its hyperactive boogie beat, is one of Story's most driving performances, and "I Overlooked an Orchid" is performed as straight country with bluegrass instrumentation, à la Jim Eanes. An energetic run-through of "Stoney Lonesome" is one of a few moments of traditional bluegrass on the album, but elsewhere *The Best of Country Music* (which inexplicably pictures a church on the cover) is an entirely atypical effort. *—Greg Adams*

• **16 Greatest Hits** / 1976 / Starday ♦♦♦♦♦

Late and Great Carl Story / 1995 / Kingdom ♦♦♦

The Late and Great Carl Story features 14 bluegrass renditions of such gospel standards as "Old Time Religion," "Cry Holy Unto the Lord," and "Unclouded Day." A cover of "Daddy Sang Bass" displays a sense of humor, and the performances in general are spirited and affecting. The packaging offers minimal liner notes and no recording information, so it is difficult to say when these recordings were made, but the collection is an otherwise pleasing anthology of recordings by an under-recognized bluegrass heavyweight. *—Greg Adams*

Somebody Touched Me / Jan. 25, 2000 / King ♦♦♦♦

George Strait

b. May 18, 1952, Pearsall, TX

Guitar, Vocals / Contemporary Country, New Traditionalist, Western Swing Revival

Out of all the new country singers to emerge in the early '80s, George Strait stayed the closest to traditional country. Drawing from both the honky tonk and Western swing traditions, Strait didn't refashion the genres; instead, he revitalized them for a new decade. In the process, he became one of the most popular and influential singers of the decade, sparking a wave of neo-traditionalist singers from Randy Travis and Dwight Yoakam to Clint Black, Garth Brooks, and Alan Jackson. Strait was born and raised in Texas, the son of a junior high-school teacher who also owned and operated a ranch that had been in the Strait family for nearly hundred years. When George was a child, his mother left the family, taking her daughter but leaving behind her sons with the father. During his childhood, he would spend his weekdays in town and his weekends on the ranch. Strait began playing music as a teenager, joining a rock & roll garage band.

After his high-school graduation in the late '60s, Strait enrolled in college but soon dropped out and eloped with his high-school sweetheart, Norma. In 1971, Strait enlisted in the Army; two years later, he was stationed Hawaii. While in Hawaii, he began playing country music, initially with an Army-sponsored country band called Rambling Country. They played several dates off the base under the name Santee. Strait left the Army in 1975, returning to Texas with the intent of completing his education. He enrolled in Southwest Texas State University at San Marcos, where he studied agriculture. While he was studying, he formed his own country band, Ace in the Hole.

Ace in the Hole made a few records for the independent Dallas-based label D in the late '70s, but they never went anywhere. Toward the end of the decade, Strait attempted to carve out a niche in Nashville, but he failed since he lacked any strong connections. In 1979, he became friends with Erv Woolsey, a Texas club owner who had formerly worked for MCA Records. Woolsey had several MCA executives come down to Texas to hear Strait. His performance convinced the company to sign him in 1980. "Unwound," Strait's first single, was released in the spring of 1981 and climbed into the Top Ten. The follow-up, "Down and Out," stalled at 16, but "If You're Thinking You Want a Stranger (There's One Coming Home)" reached number three in early 1982. The song sparked a remarkable string of Top Ten hits that ran well into the '90s. During that time he had an astonishing 31 number-one singles, beginning with 1982's "Fool Hearted Memory."

Throughout the '80s, he dominated the country singles charts, and his albums consistently went platinum or gold. Strait rarely abandoned hardcore honky tonk and Western swing—toward the beginning of the '90s, his sound became a little slicker, but it was only a relative change. Strait was also one of the few '80s superstars to survive the generational shift of the early '90s that began with the phenomenal success of Brooks. In 1992, he made his first movie, *Pure Country*, which featured him in the lead role. Strait released a four-disc box set career retrospective, *Strait Out of the Box*, in 1995. By the spring of 1996, it had become one of the five biggest-selling box sets in popular music history. *Blue Clear Sky*, his 1996 album, debuted on the country charts at number one and the pop charts at number seven. In 1997, he released *Carrying Your Love With Me*, following it with *One Step at a Time* in 1998. *Always Never the Same* appeared a year later, as did the seasonal effort *Merry Christmas Wherever You Are*. The simply titled *George Strait*, featuring the hit single "Go On," hit the shelves in late 2000. *—Stephen Thomas Erlewine*

Strait Country / 1981 / MCA ✦✦✦✦

☆ **Strait From the Heart** / 1982 / MCA ✦✦✦✦✦

George Strait may have landed his first number one in 1982, making him an "overnight sensation," but he'd been working for it since 1976. *Strait From the Heart* boasts "Fool-Hearted Memory," a perfect slow two-step that raged in all the dancehalls in America for half a year and sent folks to the bins in droves seeking out Strait's records. What they found was a singer of uncommon vitality who could sing honky tonk, countrypolitan, and the new traditional sounds that were just beginning to assert themselves after the first wave of "new country." The new Strait fans were interested in the ballads such as "Marina del Rey" and "A Fire I Can't Put Out," but they are hardly the best cuts on the set. In fact, when Strait lets it get on the raw side is when he is at his best. Tracks such as "Honky Tonk Crazy," his cover of Guy Clark's "Heartbroke," the Western swing of his original "I Can't See Texas From Here," and the strutting barroom anthem "The Steal of the Night" offer a portrait of Strait as a man who can do it all. His work is not over-produced, and his voice rings clear and true, offering only what the song needs to reveal itself to the listener. *Strait From the Heart* may not be the exact beginning of the story, but it is the first part of the legend. *—Thom Jurek*

Right or Wrong / 1983 / MCA ✦✦✦

The title track is vintage Bob Wills, and much here draws from similar swinging Southwestern roots. *—Mark A. Humphrey*

Strait Country/Strait from the Heart / 1983 / MCA ✦✦✦

Two early albums appear in one. The first and arguably the best of the '80s crop of Haggard-indebted hats, Strait has never much wavered from a Western swing-tinged, honky tonk base. *—Mark A. Humphrey*

☆ **Does Fort Worth Ever Cross Your Mind** / 1984 / MCA ✦✦✦✦✦

Two years after his breakthrough album, *Strait From the Heart*, George Strait was riding the charts again with perhaps his finest recorded moment. *Does Fort Worth Ever Cross Your Mind*, both the album and the song, were, along with Dwight Yoakam's *Guitars, Cadillacs, Etc., Etc.*, the only real traditional country records on the radio in 1984. And Strait is not a "new traditionalist." He came out of Texas a country singer, and album after album he proved that he was a traditional country singer. The title cut, written by Sanger and Darlene Shafer is one of four they placed on the album, and another, "Honky Tonk Saturday Night," charted as the disc's second single. Jimmy Bowen staggered the tunes here to reflect all of Strait's considerable strengths—there are hot and jumpy Western swing numbers such as "Any Old Time" and ballads like "You're Dancin' This Dance All Wrong," along with honky tonk weepers such as "I Should Have Watched That First Step." But there are a few barroom ravers as well as the swinging honky tonk of "Love Comes From the Other Side of Town" and the smoking closer "The Fireman." This is the tightest selection of tracks, perfectly sequenced and gorgeously sung by an earthy country singer who was at the very top of his powers. *Does Fort Worth Ever Cross Your Mind* is an enduring classic two decades later and is timeless in its appeal. *—Thom Jurek*

Something Special / 1985 / MCA ✦✦✦✦✦

Something Special is another excellent George Strait record from the mid-'80s, featuring new traditionalist classics like "Left's Gone" and "The Chair." Occasionally, the album wanders into softer, more sentimental territory than Strait has explored in the past, yet that only makes the straight country more effective. *—Thom Owens*

★ **Greatest Hits** / 1986 / MCA ✦✦✦✦✦

A good overview of Strait's first round of MCA chartbusters from the early '80s, it includes "Right or Wrong," "Amarillo by Morning," "You Look So Good in Love," "Fool Hearted Memory," "A Fire I Can't Put Out," "Let's Fall to Pieces Together," and several other hits. *—Mark A. Humphrey*

Merry Christmas Strait to You / 1986 / MCA ✦✦✦

Ocean Front Property / 1987 / MCA ✦✦✦✦✦

This excellent album went triple platinum for country-singing great George Strait. It was a sure success with songs like "Am I Blue," "All My Ex's Live in Texas," "Burning Flames," "My Heart Won't Wander," and the fun title track, "Ocean Front Property"—which hit the *Billboard* music charts with a firm number-one debut holding spot. In today's country music world, Strait, a native Texan and one-time rancher, has served as a strong role model for many young artists hoping to follow in his impressive footsteps. His music seems able to reach both critics and fans, either with emotion or simple toe-tapping swing rhythm, offering modern country that doesn't forget its roots. *Ocean Front Property* is one of those albums that you'll want to keep close at hand, since it's a perfect replayer, and great if you like to singalong. *—Charlotte Dillon*

#7 / 1987 / MCA ✦✦✦

☆ **Greatest Hits, Vol. 2** / 1987 / MCA ✦✦✦✦✦

Greatest Hits, Vol. 2 picks up George Strait's string of hits in 1984 and includes ten of his biggest singles from the mid-'80s, including "Does Fort Worth Ever Cross Your Mind," "The Fireman," "The Chair," "Nobody In His Right Mind Would've Left Her," "It Ain't Cool to Be Crazy About You," "Ocean Front Property," and "All My Ex's Live in Texas." *—Stephen Thomas Erlewine*

If You Ain't Lovin' (You Ain't Livin') / 1988 / MCA ✦✦✦

Included is a great cover of the old Faron Young title song, and other swingin' tonkers. *—Mark A. Humphrey*

Beyond the Blue Neon / Feb. 6, 1989 / MCA ✦✦✦

Beyond the Blue Neon doesn't really alter George Strait's formula at all, but it is remarkable for its consistent quality. Over the course of its ten tracks, nothing on the album rings false. Strait's voice is pure and gorgeous, while the material—particularly "Ace in the Hole," "Hollywood Squares," and "Baby's Gotten Good at Goodbye"—is first-rate. In short, it is one of his finest albums ever. *—Thom Owens*

Livin' It Up / May 15, 1990 / MCA ✦✦✦

Chill of an Early Fall / 1991 / MCA ✦✦✦

Strait holds his own on this hit album despite a plethora of new hats in the decade since his debut. *—Mark A. Humphrey*

2 Ten Strait Hits / Dec. 31, 1991 / MCA ✦✦✦✦✦

Ten Strait Hits covers ten straight Top Ten singles (including eight number-one hits) that George Strait had between 1988 and 1990, all of which are presented in chronological order. Several of his most popular songs—including "Famous Last Words of a Fool," "Ace in the Hole," "Baby Blue," "Baby's Gotten Good At Goodbye," "I've Come to Expect It From You" and his biggest hit, "Love Without End, Amen"—are featured on this collection. Though Strait did make very good albums, his singles compilations remain excellent albums in their own right, showcasing some of the very best country music made in the '80s and '90s. *—Thom Owens*

Holding My Own / 1992 / MCA ✦✦✦

This features "Faults and All," "Here We Go Again," and "Gone As a Girl Can Get," among others. *—AMG*

Pure Country / 1992 / MCA ✦✦✦

Easy Come, Easy Go / 1993 / MCA ✦✦✦✦

Popular country singer George Strait once again does what he does so well on this late-1993 album, *Easy Come, Easy Go*. He mixes the standards of traditional country, a bit of good ol' honky tonk, along with just a tiny little taste of pop and Texas swing to offer up some really worth-a-listen tunes, including "Stay out of My Arms," "I'd Like to Have That One Back," "Without Me Around," and "That's Where My Baby Feels at Home." He also adds in his own take on an old George Jones cover, "Lovebug." The songs on this recording cover the basics: heartbreak, loving, drinking, and cheating. A fantastic addition to any country collection, especially a George Strait one. *—Charlotte Dillon*

Lead On / Nov. 8, 1994 / MCA ✦✦✦

Award-winning singer George Strait's 1994 album, *Lead On*, went double platinum—and for good reason. The songs on this superb country recording showcase the artist's smooth Texas baritone along with the expected honky tonk fiddle cries and steel guitar twangs. Though *Lead On* doesn't have an enormous runaway hit in its tracks, many of the songs found their way onto the music charts. Some of the offerings on this release include "I'll Always Be Loving You," "What Am I Waiting For," and "You Can't Make a Heart Love Somebody." The album's liner notes carry the lyrics for those who can't resist the urge to singalong but need a little help with the words. *—Charlotte Dillon*

★ **Strait Out of the Box** / Sep. 12, 1995 / MCA ✦✦✦✦✦

A truly comprehensive four-CD compilation covering the years 1976-1995, including all 31 of his number-one hits, 11 more chart singles of great musical significance, 19 LP tracks, and 11 more rare tracks, plus a brace of unreleased songs that are anything but leftovers. The opening three tracks, all written by Strait and dating from 1976-1979, show a lot of potential on his part as a singer fronting a competent band. 1981's "Unwound" was where his career lifted off, and his singing takes on serious depth and range. Beyond "Unwound," there's a lot here that could've done well as singles, displaying his early sound as a mix of traditional country and country-pop. Strait ultimately rebelled against the latter, but the songs off of his first two LPs show a prodigious talent in any milieu he'd have chosen to work. Disc two opens with the Bob Wills number "Right or Wrong," which became central to Strait's sound and image and, in the early '80s, was a reminder that as smooth as those early MCA songs had been, Strait had a genuine commitment to Western swing and traditional country music. Disc three divides its space between ballads and honky tonk numbers, with some comedy and some bracing Western swing. Disc four is all '90s material, right up through April 1995. The cut that helped sell this set is Strait's never-issued 1993 duet with Frank Sinatra on "Fly Me to the Moon," which never should have been left off the *Duets* album—the two singers' voices sound right together, and the song works as is. The producers have provided a booklet with an extensive biographical essay, a full sessionography, and comments from Strait himself on each of the songs included. *—Bruce Eder*

Blue Clear Sky / Apr. 1996 / MCA ✦✦✦✦✦

Country's most consistent traditionalist, George Strait, scores again with *Blue Clear Sky*, one of the best albums of his 15-year career. *Blue Clear Sky* shows off Strait's range with a well-chosen sweep of material. "Rockin' in the Arms of Your Memory" and "I'd Just as Soon Go" prove that well-written, mainstream adult ballads can carry an insinuating strength when performed with the subtle grace of a master. On "Need I Say More," Strait reveals again that he's also a wonderful jazz-tinged crooner. "I Ain't Never Seen No One Like You" swings with the joyful ease of a youngster on a backyard set, and "Do the Right Thing" gives Strait the chance to show casually that he can navigate an eccentric meter, masking how difficult the inventive arrangement might have been for a lesser vocalist. Strait, an experienced calf-roping competitor, also includes "I Can Still Make Cheyenne." Instead of creating a deadly, dramatic situation or joking about the macho manner of the lifestyle, the song uses a telephone call between a struggling rider and his lover to convey the dreams, the fears, the financial hardships, and the difficulties of life on the road that surround the sport. Just like the singer, the song relies on quietly reserved emotion to convey enormously important sentiments. *—Michael McCall*

Carrying Your Love with Me / Apr. 22, 1997 / MCA ✦✦✦

Blue Clear Sky was a defining moment in George Strait's career, illustrating that he could still deliver a masterpiece in the latter half of his career. Its follow-up, *Carrying Your Love With Me*, isn't quite as strong, yet it still has a number of very nice moments, making it a worthwhile endeavor for fans, even if it lacks its predecessor's resonance. *—Thom Owens*

Very Best of, Vol. 2: 1988–1993 / 1998 / MCA Nashville ✦✦✦✦

One Step at a Time / Apr. 21, 1998 / MCA ✦✦✦✦

One Step at a Time continues the hot streak George Strait began with *Blue Clear Sky*. It's not on par with that latter-day masterpiece, yet equals its follow-up, *Carrying Your Love With Me*, by offering a uniformly excellent set of songs that are all delivered with conviction from Strait. If anything, Strait is getting better with age, as he's able to give even mediocre material nuanced, impassioned performances, which is a trick younger country artists need to learn if they're ever going to have a catalog as rich and consistently rewarding as his. *—Thom Owens*

Always Never the Same / Mar. 2, 1999 / MCA ✦✦✦

The problem with George Strait is this: His albums are so consistently good that a fine effort like *Always Never the Same* runs the risk of getting overlooked simply because it's not a masterwork like 1996's *Blue Clear Sky* (to pick but one). Of course, we should wish that all artists could have such a problem. With his smooth, emotive voice, George Strait continues to show the rest of the pack how country music can (and should) be done. *Always Never the Same*, like the rest of his albums, never panders to the latest trend that happens to be sweeping Nashville at the time. Strait has always remained true to his country roots, and here they are in evidence once again. Songs like "Meanwhile," "What Do You Say to That," "That's the Truth," and the title track are classic Strait songs, building on the 20 years of success he's had as a pure neo-traditionalist. *Always Never the Same* doesn't offer anything new from George Strait, just the same great voice put to work singing solid songs in a pure country style. *—Martin Monkman*

Merry Christmas Wherever You Are / Sep. 21, 1999 / MCA ✦✦✦

Latest Greatest Straitest Hits / Mar. 7, 2000 / MCA ✦✦✦✦✦

With a career that spans nearly 20 years, 26 albums that have been certified platinum or multi-platinum, and countless number-one and Top Ten hits, it's probably easy for George Strait to gather some songs for a greatest-hits album. The cream of the crop turn up here, drawn from his four most recent studio albums. "Carrying Your Love With Me," "Adalida," "Blue Clear Sky," and "Today My World Slipped Away" are just a few of the celebrated songs that grace this prodigious 15-song anthology. But no country artist's greatest-hits album is complete without the obligatory addition of at least two new songs, and Strait fulfills this obligation with a slightly appealing duet with fellow country artist Alan Jackson, crooning about "Murder on Music Row," and "The Best Day," which has filled the airwaves of country radio. It takes only one listen to *Latest Greatest Straitest Hits* to remind listerners that George Strait continues to hit them out of the park and will go down in history as one of the top country entertainers of all time. *—Maria Konicki Dinoia*

George Strait / Sep. 19, 2000 / MCA ✦✦✦

George Strait continues his foray into the neo-traditionalist country style that he helped to pioneer on his 24th album, the simply titled *George Strait*. His voice has deepened over the years but he sounds just as alive as he did on his 1981 debut, and his songs hold just as much pain. The stark "If It's Gonna Rain" and the rich "She Took the Wind From His Sails" are testaments to the years that Strait has put into his craft and his unique ability to infuse a song with honest heart and soul. While some fans of "young country" might wonder where the screaming guitar solos and distorted fiddles are, fans of traditional country will no doubt be able to tell them where to go. *—Zac Johnson*

The Road Less Traveled / Nov. 6, 2001 / MCA ✦✦✦

Industry icon George Strait is obviously still "countrified" in *The Road Less Traveled*, but the country traditionalist has a few out of the ordinary tricks up his sleeve this time. After 25 platinum albums flavored mainly with Texas swing and grassroots country, Strait is now playing the experimentalist. Though the album does touch upon traditional Strait material with songs such as "She'll Leave You With a Smile" and "Don't Tell Me You're Not in Love," the singer employs uncharacteristic synthetic vocal enhancement à la Cher's (mentioning Cher in the same sentence with George Strait never seemed possible before) "Do You Believe in Love" remix on his Cajun tune "Stars on the Water." The mix may make you check the CD case to make sure it's Strait you're playing, but doesn't come across as that distracting. The irony comes two cuts later, when Strait calls for "The Real Thing," referring to the music of artists such as Johnny Cash and Carl Perkins. The arrangement of the album's first single, "Run," is also a bit of a change for Strait, though the song's idea is undeniably country. *The Road Less Traveled* finishes out with a song written by Merle Haggard and Terry Gordon that Strait calls "the soundtrack to his life." "My Life's Been Grand" seems like a suitable message to fans after 57 million records sold and, as Strait points out in another cut from this fascinatingly diverse album (contradiction and all), that's the difference between "Living and Living Well." *—Rick Cohoon*

20th Century Masters—The Millennium Collection: The Best of George Strait / Mar. 26, 2002 / MCA ✦✦✦

George Strait himself chose the 12 number-one country hits included in this midline-priced compilation, which presents digitally remastered tracks. The hits ranged from "You Look So Good in Love," which topped the charts at the start of 1984, to "Easy Come, Easy Go," a number one in October 1993. During this period, an additional 11 Strait singles also reached the country summit, so this is just a sampling. Some of his biggest hits (i.e., ones that stayed at number one longer)—such as "Love Without End, Amen" and "I've Come to Expect It From You"—are included, while others—such as "You Know Me Better Than That" and "If I Knew Me"—are not. In the less easily quantifiable category of signature songs, again some are included, notably "All My Ex's Live in Texas," while others, such as "Ocean Front Property," are missing. So Strait easily could come up with a second volume for *20th Century Masters—The Millennium Collection* without even getting too far into the 1990s. And he probably will. *—William Ruhlmann*

For the Last Time: Live From the Astrodome / Feb. 11, 2003 / MCA ✦✦✦

The "For the Last Time" in the title does not refer to the last concert George Strait ever gave, nor does this suggest that this is a farewell to live albums; in fact, it's the first live album Strait has ever released. The "last time" refers to the last concert of the Houston Livestock Show and Rodeo ever given in the Houston Astrodome, a show that Strait headlined, breaking records by drawing 68,266 people, the largest audience the venue ever saw (for the record, he top-lined the first Livestock Show at its new home, Reliant Stadium). This was a big, big occasion—highlighted by an on-stage guest spot by former President George Herbert Walker Bush, where number 41 proclaimed that "everyone in Texas loves him and everyone across this country loves his music"—so it makes perfect sense that it would be commemorated with an audio souvenir, and *For the Last Time* isn't bad at all on those terms. Its biggest problem is its nature: it captures a big-stage, big-sound production, where it's about the spectacle as much as the music, so when it's presented as a CD, it's not as exciting as the concert, nor is it as exciting as many of his straight studio records. It's professional, well-performed, and enjoyable without being dynamic, surprising, or lively; it never feels as lived-in or real as the best of Strait's music. Part of the reason for that is the song selection, which is heavy on ballads and midtempo numbers, de-emphasizing harder country and Western swing. When they do go for purer country, such as on the death-of-country-music lament "Murder on Music Row," it sounds great, but this is not about gritty country, this is a soundtrack to spectacle. It's fine as that, but it's not the great live George Strait album it could have been. *—Stephen Thomas Erlewine*

Honkytonkville / Jun. 10, 2003 / MCA ✦✦✦✦✦

The release of *Honkytonkville* should make anyone who harbored insane thoughts about George Strait having his best years behind him certifiable. While it may be his 27th album—not counting greatest-hits and Christmas records—Strait sounds hungrier than ever here. Produced by Strait and Tony Brown, the tough barroom ballads and breakneck dance tracks are back with a vengeance, and the material, written by the more imaginative tunesmiths in Nash Vegas, is his strongest in a decade. A quick for-instance is the jukebox-breaking opener, "She Used to Say That to Me," penned by Jim Lauderdale and John Scott Sherrill. Done is a slick 4/4 with a Wynn Stewart-esque melody line and a lyric that's as tender as it is tough, Strait wraps that voice of his around all the pain in it and comes out still standing. The title track, written by Buddy Brock, Dean Dillon (who is well represented here), and Kim Williams, is a fiddle-laden traditionalist anthem to the ghosts of people and places gone yet ever present. "Look Who's Back in Town," with its gorgeous piano lines (reminiscent of a Billy Sherrill production) sounds like a country version of Johnny Rivers' "Poor Side of Town," while everybody had better watch it because "Cowboys Like Us" could signal a return to outlaw country. The weepers work too, such as "Tell Me Something Bad About Tulsa," the Guy Clark-inspired "Desperately" by Bruce Robison and Monte Warden, and the soul-country of "Heaven Is Missing an Angel." But the barnburner on this one is "I Found Jesus on the Jailhouse Floor." It may be a gospel song, but it'll have the honky tonky line dancers pounding the beer before sweating it out on the dancefloor on the Saturday night before Sunday morning. It is completely conceivable to hear this song being done by Merle Haggard's Strangers in 1967 or by Buck Owens in 1969. "Honk if You Honky Tonk," another Dillon joint, is harder rocking than anybody but Montgomery Gentry—and they will kick themselves for not recording it first. If the DJs at country radio can hear, they'll be playing the hell out of this one—it's got five or six singles if it has one. Not that Strait was ever anything but country; this is the first hard country album of 2003, and he's got the torch burning bright for the tradition while not giving up an inch of his modernity. *—Thom Jurek*

Mel Street (King Malachi Street)

b. Oct. 21, 1933, Grundy, WV, **d.** Oct. 21, 1978, Hendersonville, TN

Vocals / Traditional Country, Progressive Country, Honky Tonk

Before his career ended in tragedy, Mel Street was a talented hard country singer whose emotional style harked back to the honky tonk of yesteryear. He was born King Malachi

Street in Grundy, WV; most sources list his birthdate as 1933, but his family claims 1935. The son of a coal miner, Street first performed publicly on a radio show at age 16. He married, had a family, and moved around Ohio for a few years working as an electrician on radio transmission towers. He started performing in Niagara Falls clubs in 1960 and simultaneously learned auto repair, which led to his moving back to West Virginia to open a body shop in 1963. He continued to sing, however, and eventually landed his own half-hour Saturday night show on a local TV station, which ran from 1968-1972.

He released his first single, "Borrowed Angel," in 1970 on the small Tandem label, which was owned by cable TV company heads Jim & Jean Prater. It managed some airplay and was licensed for wider release by Royal American Records, which helped it become a Top Ten nationwide hit in 1972. Street signed to Metromedia and had his first and only Top Five hit with the follow-up, "Lovin' on the Back Streets," in 1973. Now adopting a rigorous touring schedule, Street moved to GRT Records in 1974, where he had two Top 20 hits with "You Make Me Feel More Like a Man" and "Forbidden Angel." Another Top Ten in "I Met a Friend of Yours Today," arrived in 1976, after which he moved over to major label Polydor. Two albums followed in 1977 and 1978, and he had two more hits with "Barbara, Don't Let Me Be the Last to Know" and "If I Had a Cheating Heart." He was rewarded with a lucrative new contract with Mercury, and stardom appeared to be just around the corner. However, Street had been battling depression and alcohol problems for some time, and as his touring schedule took more and more of a toll on his family life, he became increasingly unable to cope. On October 21, 1978 his birthday he committed suicide. He had a couple of posthumous chart singles with "Just Hangin' On" and "Tonight Let's Sleep on It Baby," but sadly, his tremendous potential was never fully tapped. *—Steve Huey*

● **Greatest Hits** / 1976 / Deluxe ✦✦✦✦✦

This brief, ten-song budget CD collects five of Mel Street's Top 40 hits, including the posthumous hit "Tonight Let's Sleep on It Baby" and five others. Three of the hits here reached the Top Ten. Street was a talented singer in the direction of Moe Bandy who enjoyed several years of chart success, but a career-spanning anthology might be difficult to assemble since he recorded for so many different labels. *Greatest Hits* is too brief and passes over a lot of hits, but it's one of the few Mel Street CDs on the market, and at least offers some solid music at a bargain price. *—Greg Adams*

Strength in Numbers

Group / Progressive Bluegrass, Traditional Bluegrass

Strength in Numbers was an all-star side project comprised of Sam Bush (fiddle/mandolin), Jerry Douglas (dobro), Béla Fleck (guitar/banjo), Mark O'Connor (guitar/mandolin), and Edgar Meyer (bass). The artists were familiar with one another, having performed in the same circles for years, as well as on the same stage—in numerous incarnations—at the annual Telluride Bluegrass Festival. Strength in Numbers grew out of appearances by the group as sort of the *de facto* house band at the Colorado festival; *The Telluride Sessions*, its only album, documented the easygoing newgrass fusion that Strength in Numbers would often perform there. Accomplished bluegrass musicians all, the members of Strength in Numbers were also steeped in the jazz and classical traditions, which found their way into the arrangements on *The Telluride Sessions*. Most of the bandmembers said there would never be another Strength in Numbers album after the first. But since each musician continued to play on the others' albums and appear at festivals such as Telluride, the potential for more genius was there. *—Johnny Loftus*

The Telluride Sessions / 1989 / MCA ✦✦✦✦✦

The Telluride Sessions, the only album from the bluegrass supergroup Strength in Numbers, is an off the cuff set of newgrass that demonstrates the considerable instrumental skill of each member. Fluctuating between jazzy experiments and straightforward bluegrass, the music on *The Telluride Sessions* is adventurous and unpredictable, revealing more levels upon each listen. *—Thom Owens*

Stringbean (David Akeman)

b. Jun. 17, 1915, Annville, KY, **d.** Nov. 10, 1973, Nashville, TN

Banjo / Traditional Bluegrass, Old-Timey, Traditional Country, Country Comedy

To millions of younger country music fans, David Akeman, better known as Stringbean, was one of the comedy powerhouses of the *Grand Ole Opry* and television's *Hee Haw*, of which he was one of the original cast members. As a banjo player, however, his work goes back to the 1940s and a three-year stint with Bill Monroe. Akeman was born to a farm family in Annville, in Jackson County, KY, and he became interested in music at an early age—no surprise there, since not only did his father play the banjo at local dances, but he was surrounded by players of considerable skill in his local community, from all of whom he learned the banjo. He built his first homemade instrument at age seven out of a shoebox and thread borrowed from his mother, and by the time he was 12 he traded a pair of prize bantams he had raised for a real banjo. He was already making the rounds of local dances and developing a reputation on the instrument, but not earning a living. Akeman spent time working for the Depression-era Civilian Conservation Corps, building roads and planting trees.

Then he entered a talent contest that was being judged by singer-guitarist-musical saw player Asa Martin, and won. He joined Martin's band, and during one performance the bandleader stumbled over Akeman's name and, unable to remember it, introduced him to the crowd as "String Beans." With his tall, lanky frame, the name was a natural and it stuck. At first, Akeman only played banjo in the group, but when another performer failed to turn up for a show, he was pressed into service as a singer and comic, and the act caught on. From that day forward, Akeman divided his time between comedy and music, along with some success as a semipro baseball player. He also broadcast on WLAP out of Lexington, KY, and played with various groups during the late '30s. At the time, the banjo had virtually disappeared from country music, and it was old-time players like Akeman who helped keep it alive.

Curiously enough, it was as a sandlot ballplayer—and not a banjo player—that Akeman first came to the attention of Monroe, who fielded a private semipro team. It wasn't too long before Monroe learned of Akeman's other talents, and in the early '40s David became a full-fledged member of Bill's group, where he remained from 1943 until 1945, playing on such recordings as "Goodbye Old Pal." Akeman also spent some of his time during this period teamed with Willie Egbert Westbrook as "String Beans and Cousin Wilbur," a comedy duo, who often worked on the same bills with Monroe's outfit. Akeman left Monroe in 1945—his replacement was Earl Scruggs, a banjo player with a radically different technique. That same year, he married Estelle Stanfill. During 1946, he first began working with Grandpa Jones (Louis Marshall Jones), a fellow old-time banjo player with a penchant for comedy. During the late '40s, Akeman also formed a team with Lew Childre and became a regular performer on the *Grand Ole Opry*. By this time, he'd adopted the costume by which he became best known to the public, a nightshirt and pants that made him look like a very tall man with very short legs. This kind of costume had many antecedents, including Slim Miller, a onetime stage comedian who was said to be Akeman's direct inspiration.

After the war, Akeman also became a protégé of Uncle Dave Macon, one of the biggest stars of the *Grand Ole Opry*. Macon, who died in 1952, was a banjo-player/comic and one of the *Opry*'s most beloved performers. He took Akeman under his wing, telling him stories and jokes and playing him songs, and toward the end of his life he gave Akeman one of his own banjos. Akeman was known by this time as Stringbean, and he was one of the *Opry*'s top stars throughout the 1950s. Oddly enough, he didn't begin recording on his own until the early '60s, when he signed to the Starday label. By that time, Scruggs had emerged as the dominant figure in banjo playing, especially among younger listeners, but Akeman still had an audience for his older style of playing and his mixture of cornball comedy and song. He had hits with "Chewing Gum" and "I Wonder Where Wanda Went" and recorded seven albums between 1961 and 1972. The first of those albums, *Old Time Pickin' & Grinnin' with Stringbean* (1961), was one of the best of these, representing his repertory of the era—folk songs (especially humorous animal songs), tall stories, jokes—although several of his subsequent albums are also worth hearing, most notably *Salute to Uncle Dave Macon* (1963) and *Old Time Banjo Picking and Singing* (1964). Akeman and Jones became the two biggest exponents of old-time banjo playing during this era.

Akeman remained a star of the *Opry* for the rest of his life, and in 1969 he and Jones became founding members of the cast of the television series *Hee Haw*. He became an instant hit, his lanky figure and bewildered expression, coupled with self-deprecating one-liners, making Akeman one of the most popular members of the cast. All of this ended tragically for Akeman and his wife, Estelle, on November 10, 1973. They returned home from a performance at the *Opry* and surprised a pair of burglars who shot the banjoman dead on the spot and pursued and killed his wife. It was Jones who found the bodies the next day, and the murders sent shock waves through the Nashville community. The subsequent capture and life sentences imposed on the killers—two brothers—did little to assuage the anger that Akeman's colleagues and friends felt. His memory lives on in the Monroe songs on which he played and the relative handful of his own recordings that have surfaced. *—Bruce Eder*

● **Old Time Pickin' and Grinnin' with Stringbean** / 1961 / Starday ✦✦✦✦✦

Stringbean / 1962 / Starday ✦✦✦✦

Salute to Uncle Dave Macon / 1963 / Starday ✦✦✦✦✦

The most serious and carefully thought out album in Akeman's career, a funny, moving, lively tribute record to the most beloved banjo-player/humorist in country music. *—Bruce Eder*

Old Time Banjo Picking and Singing / 1964 / Starday ✦✦✦

Way Back in the Hills of Old Kentucky / 1964 / Starday ✦✦✦

Here is another look at Akeman's past, and the banjo styles that he grew up with in Kentucky. *—Bruce Eder*

Hee Haw Cornshucker / 1971 / Nashville ✦✦✦

Akeman's television stardom led to this, his first album in seven years, with its requisite quota of funny songs and jokes, all a bit more forced than his earlier records. *—Bruce Eder*

Front Porch Funnies / Jan. 1, 1996 / King ✦✦✦

The only David Akeman CD to date, 15 minutes of good-time comic songs ("Run Rabbit Run"—which will remind one of Chuck Berry's "Maybelline"—and "Good Ol' Mountain Dew"), funny story songs ("I'm the Man That Rode the Mule Around the World"), and dog songs ("Here Rattler Here"). The sound is crisp, the collection is too short, and a lot of it with remind listeners of Grandpa Jones (who has more material out), but it also represents a brand of banjo-playing and humor that country audiences devoured insatiably for decades. And it captures a brand of old-time banjo playing that has all but disappeared. *—Bruce Eder*

The Stripling Brothers

f. Alabama

Group / String Bands

Between 1928 and 1936, the Stripling Brothers—fiddler Charlie and guitarist Ira—recorded 42 tunes, the first 18 for the Brunswick label, and the remainder for Decca. The sides they released reflect the rich (and otherwise un-recorded) fiddle traditions of their home in West Alabama; they also showcase the unique abilities of that area's most accomplished fiddler. Charlie Stripling was born in Pickens County, AL, in 1896; Ira was born in 1898. As a teenager, Charlie picked up the fiddle and, accompanied by his brother's guitar, won first prize at his first fiddle contest. For the rest of his career, Charlie dominated all of the competitions he entered. Encouraged by their success, the brothers auditioned for Brunswick Records at a studio in Birmingham, where they cut two sides. They recorded again for Brunswick in 1929 in Chicago; in 1934 and 1936 they recorded for Decca in New York and New Orleans, respectively. Their 42 recordings include a number of breakdowns, waltzes, and other dance pieces, many of Charlie's own composition or adapted from traditional and popular sources; the brothers only recorded two numbers with vocals, "Weeping Willow" and "Railroad Bum." Their later recordings incorporated increasing pop influences, reflecting the evolution of dance styles and musical tastes. Though the Striplings may have asserted a mostly regional influence, the number of recordings they made—on both sides of the Depression—and the virtuosity of the playing attest to their stature as performers.

After the 1936 session, economic necessity forced Ira to focus on his business as a store owner, and he ceased playing at dances and competitions. Charlie, who worked as a sharecropper, continued to play and was often accompanied by his young sons, Robert and Lee Edwin (of his nine children, all were proficient on at least one instrument). Though he never returned to commercial recording, Charlie Stripling continued to fiddle professionally through the '50s, when failing health finally forced him to stop. He died in 1966; his brother Ira died the following year. *—Burgin Mathews*

- **Complete Recordings, Vol. 1 (1928–1934)** / Sep. 23, 1997 / Document ✦✦✦✦

Complete Recorded Works, Vol. 2: 1934–1936) / Sep. 23, 1997 / Document ✦✦✦

Marty Stuart

b. Sep. 30, 1958, Philadelphia, MS

Guitar, Mandolin, Vocals / Bluegrass, Traditional Bluegrass, Contemporary Country, New Traditionalist, Country-Rock

One of country's most historically minded new traditionalists, Marty Stuart was also one of the most eclectic, moving between honky tonk, rockabilly, country-rock, traditional country, and bluegrass. He was also one of the more flamboyant showmen, supporting his party-hearty image with a wardrobe of rhinestone-laden Nudie suits. Stuart was born in Philadelphia, MS, in 1958 and grew up obsessed with country music. He learned guitar and mandolin as a child and by age 12 was performing with the bluegrass group the Sullivans. He soon met Lester Flatt bandmember Roland White, which led to an invitation to play a Labor Day gig in Delaware with the band in 1972. Flatt invited Stuart to join the band permanently and took responsibility for overseeing the teenager's continued education.

Stuart stayed with Flatt up until the legendary bluegrass master broke up his band in 1978 for health reasons; he passed away the following year. Stuart moved on, playing with fiddler Vassar Clements and guitarist Doc Watson while doing session work, and was invited to join Johnny Cash's backing band in 1980. In 1982, he stepped out to record his first solo album, *Busy Bee Cafe*, an informal jam session for Sugar Hill with guest spots by Cash, Watson, and Earl Scruggs, among others. The following year, he married Cash's daughter Cindy. He left Cash's band in 1985 to pursue a solo career. He signed with Columbia and released a self-titled debut album in 1986. Despite a Top 20 country hit in "Arlene," the record didn't sell very well, and Columbia refused to issue his completed follow-up, *Let There Be Country*. Stuart's marriage also broke up in 1988, and he returned home to Mississippi to gather his wits. Jerry Sullivan invited him to rejoin the Sullivans as mandolinist, which recharged Stuart's confidence for a return to Nashville.

Stuart landed a deal with MCA in 1989 and released his label debut, *Hillbilly Rock*, later that year. This time he was more successful, landing a Top Ten hit with the title track and earning positive reviews from critics, who compared his sensibility to that of Dwight Yoakam. *Tempted* (1991) was successful critically and commercially as well and spawned three Top Ten hits in the title cut, "Little Things," and "Burn Me Down." In the wake of Stuart's breakthrough, Columbia finally released *Let There Be Country* in 1992. Stuart also completed his official follow-up, *This One's Gonna Hurt You*, which featured a Top Ten hit in the title duet with Travis Tritt and became his first gold album. Though he'd earned a fervent following, Stuart found these successes hard to duplicate—1994's *Love and Luck* saw his sales slipping, and perhaps in response, MCA issued the hits and rarities compilation *The Marty Party Hit Pack*. That in turn led to a series of "Marty Party" concert specials on The Nashville Network.

Honky Tonkin's What I Do Best (1996) however, failed to win the wide critical acclaim of its predecessors. Stuart was already moving on to other concerns as well. He'd acquired an extensive collection of country memorabilia by that point and in 1996 won his first term as president of the Country Music Foundation (which oversees the Country Music Hall of Fame); he would serve in that capacity through 2002. He also remarried in 1997, to fellow country singer Connie Smith (who'd first made an impression on him during his teen years). When he returned to recording, it was in 1999 with *The Pilgrim*, a concept album based in country tradition, yet with a distinct progressive inclination. Despite strong reviews, it didn't sell well, and Stuart later parted ways with MCA. He went on to sign with Sony's Nashville division and released his label debut, simply titled *Country Music*, in the summer of 2003. *—Steve Huey*

Busy Bee Cafe / 1982 / Sugar Hill ✦✦✦

Busy Bee Cafe is a loose, jam-oriented record with guest appearances from Johnny Cash, Earl Scruggs and Doc Watson. *—Jason Ankeny*

Marty Stuart / 1986 / Columbia ✦✦

A former bluegrass picker and Johnny Cash sideman, Stuart burst on the scene with this largely rockabilly flavored album. Not a great album, but made somewhat more interesting by some of the people appearing on the record and the inclusion of two Steve Forbert songs. *—Jim Worbois*

Hillbilly Rock / 1989 / MCA ✦✦✦✦✦

Hillbilly Rock is the epitome of what the adult Marty Stuart is all about. With a new groove that runs just left of center, while still retaining a classic country & western-bluegrass flair, *Hillbilly Rock* is a wild ride to what surely must be honky tonk heaven. On par with Dwight Yoakam's debut, *Hillbilly Rock* sets the tone for a whole new faction of neo-traditionalists. Opening with the title cut, an infectious romp that demands your attention, and ending on a high note with a love song, "Since I Don't Have You," crafted by Stuart and another tragically overlooked supernova, Mark Collie, this is one heck of an album. "Western Girls," a favorite of the numerous cowgirls who follow his career, and the Merle Kilgore-Tillman Franks tune "The Wild One" all demonstrate how effective Marty Stuart is. "Cry, Cry, Cry," a Johnny Cash hit, is made new again. While this release displays more of Stuart's own songwriting skills, it also displays how deeply involved he is with the music he plays. *—Jana Pendragon*

Tempted / 1991 / MCA ✦✦✦✦✦

Equal in scope and purpose to Dwight Yoakam's sophomore release, *Hillbilly Deluxe*, *Tempted* is still a wild and wonderful adventure into hillbilly territory. With a slight tempering of Marty Stuart's sharp edge and abandon, there is still plenty here to rave about. Stuart kicks country-pop in its well-defined hindquarters with his take on the always popular Hank Sr.-Bill Monroe number "I'm Blue, I'm Lonesome." More than just infectious, this is one song you can't get enough of. "Little Things," "Burn Me Down," and "Paint the Town Tonight" all capture the spirit of honky tonk. But Stuart is just as deadly when he slows things down and does a ballad. "Till I Found You" and "I Want a Woman," written with Montana's most notable resident, Kostas, are a delight. Another winner from the man who said, "You can't really be in country music unless you've spent a few nights in the parking lot of the Palomino" (use your imagination). An experienced night owl, Stuart brings all those nights at the Pal and many other bars, dives, and dancehalls to good use here. Very authentic. *—Jana Pendragon*

Once Upon a Time / 1992 / CMH ✦✦✦

This is certainly a special compilation that records the importance of Lester Flatt, Roland White and the band the Nashville Grass to a budding 12-year-old who played a burning mandolin. That boy would grow up to be Marty Stuart. With performances featuring Marty on mandolin and guitar, it is apparent from the start that Lester Flatt saw something special in Marty and made a place for him in his band. Mentoring is what it was called, it is not as common as it once was, but because of Flatt's interest, country and roots music has been doubly rewarded. Marty Stuart's connection to the past, his interest in the old timers who still play and his own talent make him a true musical treasure. This release documents the early years and provides a glimpse into the development of an artist of character and quality. *—Jana Pendragon*

This One's Gonna Hurt You / 1992 / MCA ✦✦✦✦

With a snappy duet of the title with his buddy Travis Tritt, and an interesting prologue that explains how Stuart and Hank Sr. got together somewhere in outer space, this is a fun experience. "High on a Mountain Top" is outstanding as is "Hey Baby." His paean to country music, "Now That's Country" explains why this is a gold album. But, Stuart's edge is verging on the pedestrian in places. *—Jana Pendragon*

Let There Be Country / Aug. 18, 1992 / Columbia ✦✦✦✦✦

This early recording gives a clear idea of just who Marty Stuart is. Without all the hype and over production of many of the MCA recordings, *Let There Be Country* displays Stuart's traditional hillbilly bent. Only his 1982 Sugar Hill debut, *Busy Bee Cafe*, defines him better. Self-produced, it is obvious that the artist knows what he is doing in terms of material and performance. With the inclusion of only two original songs, the rest of the tunes are strong statements by Stuart concerning country music. Merle Haggard's "Mirrors Don't Lie" is strong evidence of Stuart's affiliations. Also good is Bill Monroe's "Get Down on Your Knees and Pray." Stuart's version of the Johnny Horton hit "One Woman Man" is priceless and the sincere sweetness he reflects on the Harlan Howard-Max D. Barnes number "I'll Love You Forever (If You Want Me To)" is stunning. A worthy addition to any Stuart collection. *—Jana Pendragon*

Love and Luck / 1994 / MCA ✦✦✦

On *Love and Luck*, Marty Stuart's fourth album for MCA, he balances some of the requisite country-pop/rock cuts with more traditional honky tonk numbers. Stuart himself either wrote or co-wrote seven of the 11 tracks, and with the exception of "That's What Love's About," where the schmaltz factor unfortunately cancels out some of the interesting harmonic moments of the composition, they are uniformly strong. The rock-influenced title track and the haunting "Oh, What a Silent Night" are some of his strongest efforts, but they pale in comparison to the centerpiece of the record, a moving version of the excellent Billy Joe Shaver song "If I Give My Soul." Also particularly nice is Stuart's version of the Byrds' "Wheels," which perfectly captures the song's bittersweet feel. Stuart is one of that rarest of all commodities: a superstar country vocalist who also has enough instrumental chops to make the services of even Nashville's cadre of virtuosos unnecessary. He demonstrates this on the instrumental "Marty Stuart Visits the Moon," where the singer gets to flash his mandolin chops on a catchy, uptempo track. This is not to say that the studio band isn't top-notch, because they are, and they include such notables as Randy Scruggs, John Jorgenson, John Barlow Jarvis, Paul Franklin, and Béla Fleck. There are some clunkers on *Love and Luck*, like the repetitive and boring "Shake Your Hips," but overall this is a fine effort from Stuart, and shows his range nicely. *—Daniel Gioffre*

- **The Marty Party Hit Pack** / 1995 / MCA ✦✦✦✦✦

This is a hits package that shows off Marty Stuart's hard-earned success with tongue firmly planted in cheek. The man is a precious commodity and the songs presented here include his contribution to the Mercury tribute album to Elvis, *It's Now or Never*. "Don't Be Cruel" is handled expertly and given a little panache by the Don Was Band and the Jordanaires. The Staple Singers join Stuart for a gospel version of "The Weight," produced by Was. As for the known hits, they are all here, including the Tritt-Stuart duet that appeared on Tritt's album of the same name, "This One's Gonna Hurt You (For a Long, Long Time)," another classic from the man who also penned "The Whiskey Ain't Workin'" with Ronny Scaife. "Western Girls," "Hillbilly Rock," and two previously unreleased cuts, "If I Ain't Got You" and "The Likes of Me," round things out. Hoopin' it up Marty style is whole lot of fun. *—Jana Pendragon*

Honky Tonkin's What I Do Best / Jun. 18, 1996 / MCA ✦✦✦

There is something missing here that is an important element of Marty Stuart's artistry: unadulterated enthusiasm. While you get a strong glimpse of it when he performs "The Mississippi Mud Cat and Sister Sheryl Crow," a song he wrote specifically for the pop diva, the only time it really takes control is on the title cut, another duet with Travis Tritt.

Honky Tonkin's What I Do Best is not as much a honky tonk album as a reflection of lethargy. The production is oftentimes over the top or too soft and takes away from what you know is intrinsically Stuart. In a mellow mood, Stuart writes or co-writes all the tunes. He and Kostas come up with "You Can't Stop Love." Also included here are "Shelter From the Storm," "Sweet Love," "Rocket Ship," and "Thanks to You." "Country Girls" is too much like an earlier tune that worked, "Western Girls," to really make a splash. Overall, this is not a good representation of the great talent that is Marty Stuart. Perhaps he's been in that factory town too long, working with too many of the same factory clones to continue to reach beyond that tiny pin point of light they consider to be country music. Stuart has always stood apart from this crowd. Perhaps it's time to get out, find a new stake of ground to honky tonk on, and a new producer or two who won't fence him in. This 1996 release falls too far short to be placed among his other works. *—Jana Pendragon*

The Pilgrim / Jun. 15, 1999 / MCA ♦♦♦

20th Century Masters—The Millennium Collection: The Best of Marty Stuart / Jan. 8, 2002 / MCA ♦♦♦♦

The Marty Stuart entry in the mid-priced *20th Century Masters—The Millennium Collection* series is the best compilation of Stuart's work yet released. It shares seven tracks with the 1995 set *The Marty Party Hit Pack*, a best-of that is more imaginative, but less complete. This onc contains Stuart's ten biggest country solo hits on MCA between 1990 and 1996, plus "This One's Gonna Hurt You (For a Long, Long Time)," one of his three hit duets with Travis Tritt, and the final track from his ambitious but commercially marginal 1999 concept album, *The Pilgrim.* An outspoken advocate of country's long-standing traditions, Stuart has nevertheless tried to transform those traditions in his recordings, and you can hear that on these hits, especially "High on a Mountain Top," which features a prominent mandolin part and bluegrass-style harmonies, but is still driven by a twangy electric guitar. That balance of old and new made Stuart a significant Nashville hitmaker between 1990 and 1992, and though that period of his career passed, he continued to try to forge a new, authentic country sound on *The Pilgrim.* This compilation provides a thumbnail sketch of his most popular work, and it will serve casual fans as an excellent and inexpensive *précis.* *—William Ruhlmann*

Country Music / Jul. 1, 2003 / Columbia ♦♦♦♦♦

Marty Stuart's *Country Music* is not, as some have said a radical departure from his already eclectic body of work. As to whether it's "the album of his life," is up for debate too, since Stuart doesn't sound here like he's slowing down. Stuart has given us one of the most consistent catalogs in the country genre since 1980. He has few peers in terms of quality—George Strait, Dwight Yoakam, and a few others are in his league. But *Country Music* is different and may arguably be the finest recording he's ever issued. This is his first full-on country-rock record with no apologies. Teamed with grand master engineer and producer Justin Niebank (Widespread Panic, the Subdudes, etc.), Stuart & His Fabulous Superlatives turn old nuggets such as "A Satisfied Mind," Johnny Cash's "Walls of a Prison" (that open and close the album respectively) into wooly country-rockers with killer three- and four-part harmonies and burning guitars, Hammond B-3s, mandolins, pedal steels and rockin' drums. On the other hand, newer songs by the performer and a handful of others are already revved up and cut to fly. This is a rock & roll record cut from the man vein of honky tonk country. And the country that it comes from is pure—give a listen to "Farmer's Blues," a sweet slow, two-step drenched in pedal steel with a duet vocal by Merle Haggard, or the burning-down blues-rock with dobro and banjo of "Tip Your Hat," with Uncle Josh Graves and Earl Scruggs. But even the straight up rockers such as "Sundown in Nashville," "By George" (which has dumb lyrics but kicks ass anyway), "Wishful Thinkin'," and "Too Much Month," feel as if they could have been played by a rowdier version of Rockpile, while the midtempo tracks—"Fool for Love," "Here I Am," "If You Wanted Me Around"—only serve to underscore the influences of Messrss. Dave Edmunds and Nick Lowe. Ultimately, this album is relentless, in both its attack and in the pleasure it provides the listener. There are hot licks everywhere, great songs and vocals and a tapestry of moods, textures and shades that serve to leave one impression: that Stuart's radical experimentation of the last ten years has resulted in this, his finest moment thus far: offering a prolonged look at how inseparable country and rock & roll are from one another. This may be the summer album of 2003 and, if there is any justice at all end up on the Ten Best list of virtually ever critic worth her salt. —Thom Jurek

The Sullivan Family

f. 1949, Alabama

Group / Traditional Bluegrass, Country Gospel

The Sullivan Family, a bluegrass/gospel group who have played extensively on the festival circuit, were known for their distinctive, driving beat and the robust singing of Margie Sullivan. The trio was founded by Enoch & Emmett Sullivan, both of whom were born in the Tombigbee Valley in southern Alabama. The sons of a minister, the brothers grew up with a love of gospel music; they also liked string band music and were influenced by Bill Monroe and Johnnie & Jack. Born in northern Louisiana, Margie also grew up influenced by the traditional bluegrass singers she heard on the radio. In addition to Monroe's music, she was also influenced by such female singers as Wilma Lee Cooper and Molly O'Day. After touring with evangelist Hazel Chain, she met Enoch at a revival in 1949; they married and bought a farm near St. Stephen, Alabama.

As a group, the Sullivans started out playing in local churches and then appeared on a local radio station in Picayune, MS. In 1950, they moved to a station in Jackson, AL, and six years later moved to Thomasville. In 1959, they made their recording debut for Revival and later that year were befriended by Walter Bailes, on whose Loyal Records they recorded for many years. The Sullivans primarily performed at churches, on television, and on radio. Longtime friends of Bill Monroe, the Sullivans began playing at his various bluegrass festivals in 1968 and soon gained a whole new following. Over the years, the band has included other family members, including father Arthur, uncle Jerry, and Margie's youngest daughter Lisa. The band continued to perform and record on different American and Canadian labels through the '80s up to the mid-'90s. *—Sandra Brennan*

- **Get on Board** / Old Homestead ♦♦♦♦

Doug Supernaw

b. Sep. 26, 1960, Bryan, TX

Vocals / Contemporary Country, New Traditionalist

Doug Supernaw was a singer/songwriter from Houston, TX, influenced mainly by Gene Watson, Keith Whitley, and George Jones. He briefly attended college on a golf scholarship but soon gave in favor of swinging on-stage in clubs throughout Texas. His freewheeling style incorporated as much of Willie Nelson's solemnity as it did Jimmy Buffet's energy, and fans loved it. Supernaw arrived in Nashville in the mid-'80s and soon secured work writing songs for a publishing house. But it was a bad situation, and soon Supernaw was back on-stage in Texas, perfecting his take on new traditionalist country.

Supernaw's first appearance on wax was 1993's *Red and Rio Grande*, which appeared on the indie BNA. It spawned three charting hits, including "Reno" and the smash "I Don't Call Him Daddy." But an impossibly long string of bad luck stalled his rise. Supernaw broke his neck while surfing; shortly after his neck brace was removed, he was in a head-on auto collision. To compound matters, all of his band's gear was stolen in Ohio, and then Supernaw nearly died from a case of food poisoning. Despite all of the catastrophes, he survived and in 1994 issued his delayed BNA follow-up, *Deep Thoughts From a Shallow Mind.* It was followed a year later by *You Still Got Me. Fadin' Renegade* appeared in early 2003. *—Johnny Loftus*

- **Red and Rio Grande** / Apr. 27, 1993 / BNA ♦♦♦♦♦

Included are his initial mainstream country hits, "Reno," and the anthem for divorced fathers, "I Don't Call Him Daddy." *—Michael McCall*

Deep Thoughts from a Shallow Mind / Sep. 13, 1994 / BNA ♦♦♦

You Still Got Me / Nov. 1995 / Giant ♦♦♦

Swampwater

f. 1969, **db.** 1971

Group / Country-Rock

Outside of Europe, where their music found a serious following, Swampwater remains best remembered as Linda Ronstadt's late-'60s backing group, her first post-Stone Poneys band. Formed by John Beland (guitar, dobro, piano), Gib Gilbeau (fiddle, guitar), Stan Pratt (drums), and Eric White (bass)—Clarence's brother, and an ex-member of the Kentucky Colonels—in 1969, Swampwater specialized in a then unique Louisiana-based style of rock & roll. White left the lineup after their first national tour backing Ronstadt and was succeeded by Thad Maxwell, who had previously played with Beland in One Man's Family. Early in 1970, the group cut an album for Starday/King Records that was originally intended as a Gilbeau solo vehicle, but it evolved into a group effort with a unique sound, not as smooth as Poco or Rick Nelson's Stone Canyon Band or as spaced out as the Flying Burrito Brothers. Their main influences—Gilbeau's country and Cajun roots and Beland's admiration of harmony-based acts such as the Byrds, the Beach Boys, and the Everly Brothers—were reflected in the 11 songs that were finished over a two-day period, and then went unreleased for 25 years.

Theirs was a brand of well-sung Cajun rock, straight out of the Louisiana bayou (except for the harmonies, which would've done credit to the Byrds). They had no prior equivalent in rock music, and the group's singing was considered so unusual that they got a fair amount of session work just singing backup to other acts, including Pete Seeger, Arlo Guthrie, Joan Baez, Country Joe McDonald, and Odetta. It was Guthrie who finally lured them away from Ronstadt in 1971. Her next backing band was the Eagles. Swampwater did a second self-titled album for RCA with Herb Pedersen added on guitar and vocals, and then went their separate ways. While the Eagles, Firefall, and other country-rock groups made regular runs up the charts and embedded themselves in the popular consciousness, Swampwater was largely forgotten except in Los Angeles and by dedicated early Ronstadt fans. After the breakup, Gilbeau joined the Burrito Brothers, and Beland performed on a number of session dates before going solo. Maxwell played with Guthrie before hooking up with Gilbeau again and "Sneaky" Pete Kleinow in a group called Sierra; he later played guitar with Mac Davis for some time before becoming a teacher. *—Bruce Eder*

- **Swampwater** / 1970 / One Way ♦♦♦♦♦

No, not Swampwater's RCA album, but the never-released Starday/King record from 1970. As beautiful, lyrical, and unpretentious an album as ever surfaced out of the L.A. country-rock scene, the sounds run the gamut from swamp rock like "Workin' on a Tugboat" to elegant country-rock like "Louisiana Woman" and "Look out Your Window," resplendent in soaring harmonies and a lush mix of acoustic and electric guitars and dobro. There's also the Merle Haggard-style "It's Your Game Mary Jane," the Creedence Clearwater Revival-style "River People," and even one Everly Brothers homage, "Desperation's Back Again." The overall quality of the songs is extremely high and a match for the best country-style albums of the Byrds or the best work Poco ever issued. And it may just beat the Burrito Bros. out, apart from their first three albums. It's all a must-own body of work for anyone who likes the Byrds, Crazy Horse, the Burritos, or the Eagles. *—Bruce Eder*

Billy Swan

b. May 12, 1942, Cape Girardeau, MO

Bass, Guitar, Vocals, Keyboards, Producer / Rock & Roll, Country-Rock, Pop/Rock

Best remembered for his 1974 neo-rockabilly smash "I Can Help," Billy Swan had a long and varied career in the music biz, with a large percentage of it spent behind the scenes. Swan was born in Cape Girardeau, MO, in 1942 and grew up listening to country music until he discovered rock & roll as a teenager. He learned drums, piano, and guitar and also began writing songs. "Lover Please," a song he wrote at age 16, was recorded by a local group he played with called Mirt Mirly & the Rhythm Stoppers; later, when Swan's friends traveled to Memphis to record with Elvis bassist Bill Black, Black wound up cutting the tune himself. Not long after, "Lover Please" found its way to R&B star Clyde McPhatter, who turned it into a Top Ten hit in 1962. Swan stayed in Memphis to write for Black's combo and also worked as a guard at Graceland for a time. He soon moved to Nashville, where he worked as a janitor at the Columbia studios (later handing the job over to a young Kris Kristofferson) and later as a roadie for Mel Tillis; he also wrote songs recorded by Tillis, Conway Twitty, and Waylon Jennings.

An association with Monument Records led to Swan's first gig as a record producer, in which he oversaw Tony Joe White's 1969 Top Ten smash "Polk Salad Annie." The following year, Swan joined Kristofferson's backing band as the bass player and toured with him for the next year and a half. He next served as a sideman for Kinky Friedman and Billy Joe Shaver, and shortly after his return to Kristofferson's band, he got a recording deal of his own with Monument. Tossed off in the studio during sessions for Swan's first album, "I Can Help" was a bouncy, rockabilly-styled number that featured Swan's distinctive electric organ work. It went to number one on both the pop and country charts in 1974, and the accompanying album of the same name also topped the country list. Swan never came close to duplicating its success, but he did reach the country Top 20 with a 1975 single, "Everything's the Same (Ain't Nothing Changed)," and cut three more albums for Monument.

He later recorded an album for A&M in 1978 and another for Epic's country division in 1981. He also continued to play in Kristofferson's touring band and worked with T-Bone Burnett frequently during the '80s as well. In 1986, Swan teamed with Randy Meisner in the country-rock band Black Tie, which released the album *When the Night Falls*. Taking time out from his still-active career as a session and backup musician, Swan recorded a new album at the original Sun studios, *Like Elvis Used to Do*, in 2000. In 2002, he teamed up with Meisner again, as well as Alan Rich, on a self-titled album from the aptly named Meisner, Swan & Rich. *—Steve Huey*

I Can Help / 1975 / Monument ✦✦✦✦✦

Billy Swan / 1975 / Monument ✦✦✦✦

At a little under 26 minutes in length, Billy Swan's self-titled album (on CD combined with the LP *Four*) is nonetheless a testament to the fact that he was more than just a one-hit wonder. The band of musicians gathered is impressive, including Bobby Wood on piano, the Jordanaires on backup vocals, and Carl Perkins on two numbers written by the man himself, "Your True Love" and "Blue Suede Shoes." What also makes the recording a cut above is the tightness of the band and Swan's ability to write and play in a rockabilly-country-soul style that is true to the roots of the music yet retains an individual stamp. Swan's voice isn't particularly strong, but it has an eager-to-please, slightly nervous but friendly quality. This fits in very well with the song themes, which often deal with some aspect of insecurity in a love relationship. One of the best cuts, "Vanessa," certainly outrocks "I Can Help"; it is in contention as one of Swan's best songs. "Ms. Misery" includes a blazing sax solo, and "Your True Love," featuring Perkins on guitar, actually outstrips the original. On half of the cuts the Jordanaires add their wonderful, patented Elvis-style backup vocals, sounding retro and contemporary at the same time. All in all, this album stacks up well against those artists who tried to keep the spirit of rockabilly alive, such as Dave Edmunds or, later, the Stray Cats. Though Swan is generally seen as a minor artist, this album proved that he has had at least one top record up his sleeve. *—Michael Offord*

Rock 'n' Roll Moon / 1976 / Monument ✦✦✦

Four / 1977 / Monument ✦✦✦

Billy Swan / 1977 / CBS ✦✦✦

Billy Swan's Best / Aug. 31, 1993 / Red Baron ✦✦✦✦✦

Listeners expecting tuneful updated rockabilly along the lines of "I Can Help" (which leads off this collection) may be disappointed by this CD. There's nothing as instantly compelling as the big hit (only "Vanessa" approaches its energy), much of the material lies closer to country than rock, and there are a few tame covers of '50s oldies. Nonetheless, Swan ranks among the more interesting country-pop/rock hybrids, as you could guess from the song title "(You Just) Woman Handled My Mind," and his thin, wavering voice is oddly memorable. Most of the material on this best-of is written by Swan, with occasional assistance from notables Guy Clark, Buddy Emmons, and Kris Kristofferson. *—Richie Unterberger*

I Can Help/Rock 'n' Roll Moon / Apr. 8, 1997 / See for Miles ✦✦✦

See For Miles reissued Billy Swan's first two albums, *I Can Help* and *Rock 'n' Roll Moon*, on a single disc in 1997. Although the records are spotty, they have enough strong songs to prove that "I Can Help" was not a fluke, and they are worth the time of any serious fan of that or any of Swan's other songs. *—Stephen Thomas Erlewine*

Billy Swan/Four / Apr. 8, 1997 / See for Miles ✦✦✦

See For Miles reissued Billy Swan's third and fourth albums, *Billy Swan* and *Four*, on a single disc in 1997. Although the records are spotty, they have enough strong songs to satisfy fans who liked Swan's hit singles. *—Stephen Thomas Erlewine*

● **Best of Billy Swan** / Jan. 27, 1998 / Epic/Legacy ✦✦✦✦✦

Epic/Legacy's *The Best of Billy Swan* is a fine 16-track collection that features highlights from his recordings for Monument, Columbia, and Epic in the '70s and '80s. Swan's unexpected crossover hit, "I Can Help," is here, but the remaining 15 songs veer closer to country, bearing just a slight resemblance to the bouncy pop/rock of the hit. Among the remaining songs are the country hits "Everything's the Same (Ain't Nothing Changed)," "You're the One," "Shake, Rattle and Roll," "I Just Want to Taste Your Wine," "Do I Have to Draw a Picture," "I'm Not Lovin' You," "Stuck Right in the Middle of Your Love," "With Their Kind of Money and Our Kind of Love," and "Your Picture Still Loves Me (And I Still Love You)," as well as "Lover Please," the Clyde McPhatter song Swan wrote when he was in high-school. Not all of the songs meet the standards of "I Can Help" and "Lover Please," but many of them are interesting and are among the better country-pop of their era. *—Stephen Thomas Erlewine*

Like Elvis Used to Do / Apr. 11, 2000 / Koch ✦✦✦

Recorded at the original Sun studios in Memphis, this turns into an Elvis tribute album from Swan. But rather than just replicate Elvis' old Sun sound and arrangements, Swan puts his own spin on these tracks and despite the historic surroundings, the session has a modern sound to it that's not at all reverential. Instead, Swan simply has a good-time with these old war-horses, changing them around to suit his needs and vocal timbre. The result is a loose session that captures some real rock & roll feeling, without becoming a mundane retro exercise. Definitely worth a listen. *—Cub Koda*

Meisner, Swan & Rich / Dec. 3, 2002 / Rev-Ola ✦✦✦✦

Jimmy Swan

b. Nov. 18, 1912, Cullman County, AL

Bandleader, Vocals, Guitar / Traditional Country, Honky Tonk

Jimmy Swan rose from dirt farmer's son to bandleader, giving jobs to Hank Locklin and Hank Williams in the bargain. At one point, Swan was seen as a potential successor to Williams, but his musical sensibilities, spawned in Birmingham, AL, before World War II and at the honky tonks around Hattiesburg, MS, immediately after the war, failed to match the public's changing taste. As a hillbilly and honky tonk singer, he was initially one of the very few white artists on the tiny Trumpet label (best remembered as the early recording home of Sonny Boy Williamson II), where he had some success in the early '50s, but he later found his music too out of style to sell in serious numbers.

Swan was born into a farm family, but his father abandoned them before he was old enough to walk, and he was raised in Birmingham, AL, where he sold newspapers and shone shoes on the street to help make ends meet, living at near-starvation level after the death of his mother in the late '20s. Among his clientele during the shoe-shining phase of his life was Jimmie Rodgers, the Singing Brakeman, whom the young Swan encountered in a pool hall, and who also influenced Swan as an aspiring singer. By 1928, when the 15 year old won a singing contest at a local radio station, he began thinking that he might have a future in music. Swan ended up living the life of a hobo when things got really bad, riding the rails and ending up in Mississippi just about the time that the stock market crash of 1929 ushered in the Great Depression. By then he was 17, married, and working on various farms—this and the birth of several children was to keep him out of music professionally until early in the 1940s, when he formed his own band. By that time he was living near Mobile, and the guitarist he chose for that first band in 1944 was another Alabama shipyard worker named Hank Locklin. Swan also occasionally availed himself of the services of another guitarist with a future as a singer, Hank Williams, who was knocking around Mobile at the time.

After World War II, living in Hattiesburg, MS, Swan got regular radio gigs on several stations, weeknight shows at various honky tonks, and Saturday night shows at the Hattiesburg Civic Center. By 1948, however, he'd given up music because he didn't like playing the honky tonks and witnessing their drunkenness and violence, and instead became a radio disc jockey. Apart from his Saturday night shows at the Civic Center, he left music and didn't return full-time until 1952, when Swan become one of a tiny handful of white artists signed to Lillian McMurry's Trumpet Records label. Swan's first record, the hillbilly ballad "I Had a Dream," was a reasonable success nationally, eliciting covers by several other singers. He also saw some sales in early 1953 with "The Last Letter," a Williams tribute song issued in the wake of the country legend's death that New Year's Day. Suddenly, Swan was in demand over at MGM as a potential successor to Williams, but his contract at Trumpet prevented this hookup with the late singer's label from happening for several years. In the interim, he kept making records for McMurry and even managed an appearance in a low-budget 1954 color Western *Jesse James' Women*, starring (and directed by) Don Barry and Peggy Castle, which was shot on location in Mississippi.

By the mid-'50s, when he was finally in the hands of MGM, however, Swan found that the label was looking for a sound different from the one that he was interested in making. The public had started abandoning the hard-country, hillbilly sound that he favored and was buying more lushly produced pop-oriented records. Locklin, who'd begun a recording career of his own in 1948, was to find success with this softer sound. Swan, however, wanted no part of anything that didn't sound like he did when he played onstage, and he was enough his own man to reject this for himself. He was still doing hillbilly type music late in the 1950s, and even into the mid-'60s, he was making records that could have come out of the 1940s.

By then, Swan had various business ventures working for him, including part-ownership of a radio station, and was becoming concerned with matters beyond music. As a white Southerner born early in the 20th century, he'd never accepted the notion of big government as espoused by the Democratic Party, at least in the absence of a crisis on the scale of the Great Depression, or the liberal social policies that increasingly drove the National Party. Swan had already run for sheriff locally in Hattiesburg in the mid-'60s. In 1966, seeking to emulate country singer-turned-Louisiana governor Jimmie Davis, and anticipating a similar effort by Tex Ritter, Swan entered statewide politics, standing for governor of Mississippi as an opponent of President Lyndon Johnson's Great Society program. He lost, coming in third in the primary, and failed in his subsequent bids for elective office. By that time, he was retired permanently from music as well, having recorded two abortive sides for a small Mississippi-based label. His music was largely forgotten by then, being hopelessly out of style in the slick, Nashville-dominated world of modern country music. In 1993, nearly 25 years after Swan's retirement from music, Bear Family issued the first comprehensive collection of his music. *—Bruce Eder*

● **Honky Tonkin' in Mississippi** / 1994 / Bear Family ✦✦✦✦✦

Here are 30 songs covering 16 years, Jimmy Swan's complete output from 1952 through 1968/69, that any serious fan of Hank Williams ought to own already if they're really serious. Swan's twangy hillbilly intonation and stripped-down band sound went from being hot stuff on the radio and in the honky tonks around Hattiesburg to commercial poison in little more than three years, from 1952 to 1955, but he kept right at it until the end of the 1960s. It didn't sell much after 1955, but it sure is good listening. —*Bruce Eder*

Sweethearts of the Rodeo

f. 1973, California
Group / Contemporary Country, New Traditionalist
Sister duo the Sweethearts of the Rodeo scored a series of Top Ten country hits during the late '80s with a blend of contemporary country-rock and traditional bluegrass. Janis (born November 28, 1995) and Kristine Oliver (born March 1, 1957) grew up in the Los Angeles suburb of Manhattan Beach and started singing harmony together while still in elementary school. As teenagers, they performed together in garage bands and, later, acoustic bluegrass groups and also played by themselves in coffeehouses as the Oliver Sisters. In addition to bluegrass, they also took a strong liking to country-rock groups like Poco and the Byrds and eventually renamed themselves the Sweethearts of the Rodeo after the latter group's classic country-rock album. Their music took a similar turn, and after high-school they performed at clubs and festivals around southern California.

Emmylou Harris took a liking to them, and soon the Sweethearts were opening for prominent country acts and occasionally singing backup session vocals; after a while on the scene, they found husbands in Pure Prairie League lead singer Vince Gill (Janis) and Blue Steel guitarist Leonard Arnold (Kristine). In 1983, the Gills moved to Nashville for the sake of Vince's budding solo career, and the Arnolds followed suit several months later. While supporting their husbands and raising their families, Gill & Arnold started singing again, and in 1985 they won a high-profile talent competition that resulted in a deal with Columbia. Their self-titled debut album was released the following year, and their first single, "Hey Doll Baby," just missed making the country Top 20. The follow-up, "Since I Found You," turned out to be the first of seven consecutive Top Ten hits as well as the first songwriting success for Foster & Lloyd, who would land a record deal of their own in the wake of the song's breakthrough. Both *Sweethearts of the Rodeo* and its 1988 follow-up, *One Time, One Night*, sold well on the strength of singles like "Chains of Gold," "Gotta Get Away," "Midnight Girl/Sunset Town," "Blue to the Bone," "Satisfy You," and a bluegrass reworking of the Beatles' "I Feel Fine."

Buffalo Zone (1990) wasn't as commercially successful, and although the sisters wanted to experiment with their sound, the label pushed for more of what had made their initial singles hits; additionally, Columbia was frustrated with their reluctance to tour extensively, owing to their family commitments. After the disappointing sales of 1992's *Sisters*, Columbia dropped them, and they signed on with the roots label Sugar Hill, which allowed them much greater creative control. Their first effort was 1993's *Rodeo Waltz*, and it marked a return to their roots in acoustic bluegrass, folk, and classic country. Gill & Arnold subsequently opened their own clothing store in their Tennessee hometown of Franklin. They returned to recording with 1996's *Beautiful Lies*, an even rootsier offering that blended rock covers with bluegrass classics and old-time country tunes. The Sweethearts also continued to tour, both alone and with a backing band. —*Steve Huey*

Sweethearts of the Rodeo / 1986 / Columbia ✦✦✦✦✦
These California sisters gone to Music City feature good vocal harmony on contemporary, rock-tinged country. —*Mark A. Humphrey*

One Time, One Night / 1988 / Columbia ✦✦✦
One Time, One Night includes the group's hit remake of the Beatles' "I Feel Fine." —*Jason Ankeny*

Buffalo Zone / 1990 / Columbia ✦✦✦
More melancholy than the Sweethearts' earlier work, *Buffalo Zone* includes the hit "This Heart." —*Jason Ankeny*

Sisters / 1992 / Columbia ✦✦
Sisters is a subtle, sweet album of introspective folk-laced country, highlighted by the lovely harmonies of the Sweethearts of the Rodeo. —*Thom Owens*

Rodeo Waltz / 1993 / Sugar Hill ✦✦✦
When a record starts off with a classic Johnny Cash tune like "Get Rhythm," you know you're on the right foot. When it also includes Tex Ritter's "Long Time Gone," Jesse Winchester's "Brand New Tennessee Waltz," and Gordon Lightfoot's "Steel Rail Blues," you know, at the very least, the artist has good taste in songs. And when that artist is Sweethearts of the Rodeo, you know the voices will sure be pretty and the harmonies aplenty. You could just about consider these two ladies, Janis Gill and Kristine Arnold, to be the Everly sisters. They are sisters, after all, who have been singing together since the early '60s and they cover a lot of the same musical ground that Phil & Don Everly covered. And it never hurts to have Roy Huskey Jr. on bass and Vince Gill on guitar for you, even if you're married to one of them. In an age when country and pop are almost indistinguishable, it's nice to have a few artists dusting off some good, old tunes and offering them up to a new generation of fans. —*Kelly McCartney*

Beautiful Lies / Aug. 20, 1996 / Sugar Hill ✦✦✦
Sneaking through the herd of slick, contemporary country artists who are basically singing pop (if not for the occasional fiddle or pedal steel) must not be an easy task. But every now and then comes the rare traditionalist with a twang and a swagger and a bucket full of heartache to sing about. Enter Sweethearts of the Rodeo. They are country even when (or if) country isn't cool. And thank goodness. Because even legendary stalwart Dolly Parton tiptoes over to the bluegrass side of the pasture half the time. Not these gals. With harmonies galore, they sing and sing. And they aren't separatists either, tossing in covers of Donovan's "Catch the Wind" and Bob Dylan's "One More Night." They work because those tunes hold that simple, heartfelt beauty—missing in so many of Nashville's hitmakers—that is the essence of good country music. *Beautiful Lies* is a decent little record. Nothing terribly earth-shattering, but that's just fine. —*Kelly McCartney*

● **Anthology** / Apr. 4, 2000 / Renaissance ✦✦✦✦✦
Anthology collects many of Sweethearts of the Rodeo's finest moments, from their first single "Hey Doll Baby" to subsequent hits like "Midnight Girl," "Satisfy You," "Chains of Gold," and "Blue to the Bone." The sisters' sweet harmonies also soar on "Since I Found You," "This Heart," and "A Woman Can Tell Every Time." This 20-track compilation is a welcome overview of the Sweethearts' pop-tinged country sound. —*Heather Phares*

Sweethearts of the Rodeo/One Time, One Night / Nov. 14, 2000 / Collectables ✦✦✦
This two-fer from Collectables features a pair of out of print Sweethearts of the Rodeo LPs: *Sweethearts of the Rodeo* and *One Time, One Night*, both originally issued on Columbia in 1986 and 1988. Highlights among the 22 tracks include "Midnight Girl/Sunset Town," "Hey Doll Baby," and "Satisfy You," which provide a perfect combination of country-rock and traditional bluegrass. —*Al Campbell*

The Swinging Steaks

f. 1990
Group / Roots Rock
Paul Kochanski (vocals, bass) and Jamie Walker (vocals, guitar) first played together in the early '80s for a Boston-based band named the Drive. Local acclaim and a first-place finish on MTV's *the Basement Tapes* didn't prevent the band from breaking up in 1989. The Swinging Steaks were formed soon after, when Kochanski and Walker recruited Tim Giovanniello (vocals, guitar) and Jim Gambino (vocals, piano, organ); they later picked up the Del Fuegos' drummer, Joe Donnelly, when that band folded. The group pursued a roots rock style, using soul, honky tonk, gospel, and pop in addition to straight-ahead rock & roll. After an album was released on the band's own Thrust label, 1992's *Suicide at the Wishing Well*, Capricorn signed the band and released *Southside of the Sky* (1993). —*John Bush*

● **Suicide at the Wishing Well** / 1992 / Thrust ✦✦✦
Members of Boston's the Drive reinvented themselves with this very strong 1992 release on their own Thrust label, and the departure from the slick pop the Drive was known for is immediate. Imagine if you will a band that sounds like the Rolling Stones when they transform themselves into their "Country Honk," "Moonlight Mile," and "Dead Flowers" persona to have a good idea of what the Swinging Steaks are all about. Some of these tracks appear on the band's Capricorn debut, but this powerful collection of 15 tunes and two hidden tracks is classic and it landed them the deal after garnering airplay on Boston's WBOS. "Bone Bag" features Rich Gilbert on pedal steel, but the song has more crunch than you'd expect for a country/pop disc. "Beg, Steal or Borrow" has a Byrds kind of vibe with intensity that shows the maturity and development the guys garnered on the Boston scene. That artistry culminates in track 15; the late Jimmy Miller steps in with a rare re-creation of one of his classic Rolling Stones productions as "Live With Me" is covered—allegedly with Keith Richards guitar lines played by the Steaks, riffs that Miller pulled from the original version. It is exquisite and a tribute to Jimmy's genius, recorded just a few years before his passing. Highlights on this CD are the sublime "Circlin'," written by vocalist/guitarist Tim Giovanniello, its tentative riff and eerie ambience are just perfect for the melancholy vocal. Jamie Walker's title track is the exact opposite, but equally as strong. And that is the secret of the Steaks' success. Rather than hit you with Lennon/McCartney or Jagger/Richards co-writing, the two identities give this group its identity. —*Joe Viglione*

Southside of the Sky / 1993 / Capricorn ✦✦✦
When the Swinging Steaks were signed to Capricorn Records, the label produced seven tracks and lifted five more from their 1992 debut *Suicide at the Wishing Well*. "Do Me a Favor" and "Circlin'" were taken as is, while the songs "Beg, Steal or Borrow," "Right Through You," and the title track "Suicide at the Wishing Well" were remixed by producer Gary Katz and engineer Wayne Yergellun. For their major label debut, the failure to include Jimmy Miller's superior production of the Mick Jagger/Keith Richards composition "Live With Me" was a definite oversight, but maybe Phil Walden's label was interested more in the country-pop side of this group. "Do Me a Favor" still sounds like a distant cousin to Jackson Browne's "Redneck Friend," while "Circlin'" is the best overall track—a masterpiece by Tim Giovanniello. Jamie Walker's new title track, "Southside of the Sky," opens the album for 45 seconds, and then is reprised with the nearly three-minute full version at the album's close. It's a good song one expects from these highly consistent journeymen. Their debut contained 17 songs, and this now out of print album featured seven new tracks; compiling both as a single unit of their music from 1992-1993 would be advisable. —*Joe Viglione*

Shiner / 1995 / Thrust ✦✦✦
Shiner is a little less country inflected than some of Swinging Steaks' other albums, reducing the twang and maintaining the fiery roots rock performances of their sharply crafted, hook-laden songs. The band is particularly adept at balancing the immediacy and authenticity of acoustic instrumentation with well-placed jolts of electricity. The high-watt chorus of the opening "All in This Together," for instance, explodes out of the laid-back verses, linked by a catchy electric guitar riff and a (strangely) uncredited harmonica solo. Likewise, "This Kind of Love" benefits from a ringing acoustic rhythm guitar foundation embellished with catchy electric licks and warm Hammond organ. "Lonely Man" is even more effectively produced, throwing in a mandolin performance by co-frontman Jamie Walker. As usual, Walker shares songwriting, guitar playing, and lead vocal duties with Tim Giovanniello. The two are extraordinarily compatible, though Giovanniello's songs on *Shiner* tend to be a little less mature and consistent than his partner's. "Roadside" and "Standin' Alone" are particularly weak offerings, bogged down respectively by swagger and sentimentality. Giovanniello's "Wait 'Til the End" and "Come My Way," however, are two of the best songs on the album. *Shiner* was co-produced by Chris Lannon, and this, too, seems to be a winning partnership; the recordings and arrangements are generally

crisp and effective. A few songs would have benefited if the producers had toned down the electric firepower, but fans who want to hear more of the Steaks' unplugged virtuosity can find it on their next album, *Bare. —Evan Cater*

Bare / 1997 / Thrust ✦✦✦✦
Bare is a sort of "when in Rome" project for the Boston-based roots and country-rock outfit Swinging Steaks. The band's high-energy electric firepower and their slight Nashville twang has always made them a bit of an anomaly in a town that has acquired a reputation as the nation's capitol of contemporary folk music. So it's tempting to speculate that their fourth album—a virtually unedited recording of an unplugged, wholly acoustic live performance at one of Boston's many folk clubs, the Olde Vienna Kaffeehaus—might be an attempt to demonstrate that the Steaks are just as adept as their mellow neighbors at exciting an audience without any 20th century technology. Which isn't to say that they've toned things down any. Introducing the band at the beginning of the concert, the Olde Vienna's Robert Haigh effuses "it is a real pleasure to welcome these guys to our stage 'cause [with them] things tend to get a little rowdy and in a folk club that's a nice change of pace." Things do indeed get rowdy. The singing and songwriting duo of Tim Giovanniello and Jamie Walker lead the Steaks on a crackling acoustic romp through many of their best numbers—"Saddle Up," "Own Worst Enemy," "This High," "Suicide at the Wishing Well"—as well as a spirited rendition of Tom Van Zandt's "White Freight-liner Blues" that takes full advantage of Jim Gambino's red hot honky tonk piano playing. This record is naturally a little less polished than the Steaks' studio recordings, but they make up for the occasional fits of over-singing and the odd missed note with heaping doses of good old-fashioned fun. *—Evan Cater*

Kicksnarehat / Aug. 29, 2000 / Thrust ✦✦✦✦
The cover art for Swinging Steaks' fifth album, *Kicksnarehat*, proudly proclaims their hometown: "Swinging Steaks Boston, MA." But listeners who haven't seen the cover could easily be excused for mistakenly thinking that this is Austin, not Boston. There is a distinct country-rock shading to the album, replete with a rootsy power twang reminiscent of the Jayhawks and Uncle Tupelo and flashes of Cracker-esque goofiness. But the Steaks are even more consistent than some of their influences in their ability to build sharp, memorable hooks on solid roots rock foundations. The opening "Freeman," a highly charged anthem centered around muscular electric guitar and hammond organ power chords, would sound right at home alongside many of the biggest AOR hits of the '80s and '90s. It has the feel of a surefire single, but the band's best work comes later on the record. Songs like "Heart Will Take You Home" and "Win Again" and the irresistibly quirky "Bugs" demonstrate that the four accomplished musicians are just as comfortable in mellower settings, balancing the amp-busting thrust of their rock tunes with acoustic guitars, mandolin, and banjo. The band concludes the record with a foot-stomping Chuck Berry-esque cover of Bob Seger's "Get out of Denver" that gives pianist Jim Gambino a chance to show off his chops. It's a perfect ending for an enormously spirited album that exhibits impressive polish and skill without diminishing its infectious good ole boy charm. *—Evan Cater*

Sylvia (Sylvia Jane Kirby)
b. Dec. 9, 1956, Kokomo, IN
Vocals / Country-Pop, Soft Rock, Urban Cowboy
Growing up in Kokomo, Indiana, Sylvia moved to Nashville around Christmas of 1975 with a definite gameplan: get a job as a secretary, get to know influential people in town, and build a career as a recording artist. The plan worked. She picked up a job as the receptionist for Pi-Gem Music, headed by record producer Tom Collins. She started singing on demo sessions, and Collins helped her secure a recording contract with RCA. Since she'd never performed live before, Sylvia ended up learning to do concerts at the same time she was making hit records. With an engaging voice, a bubbly personality, and a beautiful appearance, Sylvia was practically a marketing dream, and Collins built her sound around catchy melodies and strong backbeats. Songs like "Drifter" (number one, 1981), "The Matador" (1981), "Nobody" (number one, 1982) and "Like Nothing Ever Happened" (1982) became big hits; "Nobody" even crossed over into the pop Top 40.

The material was often lyrically shallow, however, and Sylvia grew increasingly frustrated. She left Collins and recorded a pair of albums with record producer Brent Maher. The second was never released. Sylvia, instead, was dropped by RCA in 1987. She used the opportunity for personal growth (she toured almost constantly during the height of her career and was emotionally drained) and to develop as a songwriter. In 1992, she re-emerged as a touring artist and pursued a recording deal with self-penned material that was inner-directed and uplifting. *—Tom Roland*

Drifter / 1981 / RCA ✦✦✦

Just Sylvia / 1982 / RCA ✦✦✦✦
Producer Tom Collins plays around with her vocals a lot, altering them electronically for effects that range from ever-so-slight to overbearing. But the material's predominantly sassy, and as catchy as a virus. The honesty in "You Can't Go Back Home" really hurts. *—Tom Roland*

Snapshot / 1983 / RCA ✦✦✦

Surprise / 1984 / RCA ✦✦

One Step Closer / 1985 / RCA ✦✦

● **Anthology** / Nov. 18, 1997 / Renaissance ✦✦✦✦
Renaissance's 1997 collection *Anthology* is easily the most comprehensive collection assembled on early-'80s smooth country-pop singer Sylvia. Weighing in at 24 tracks, this contains all 18 of her charting hits and runs from the start of her career in 1979 to 1989, when she effectively retired from active recording. Although the quality of some of the smaller hits and the non-hit material is a little erratic—five years later, the *RCA Country Legends* disc did a far better job of sorting through the non-hits material (even if it was at the expense of some genuine hits)—this nevertheless showcases Sylvia at her best. After all, she was an artist who targeted the charts and aimed for crossover success, so she makes the most sense when distilled to her singles, and while the packaging might leave a little to be desired, *Anthology* couldn't present those singles better. *—Stephen Thomas Erlewine*

RCA Country Legends / Sep. 10, 2002 / RCA ✦✦✦✦
It's easy to see why hardcore country listeners expressed nothing but disdain for Sylvia during her hitmaking peak in the early '80s. At a time when country music already trending toward light, sweet pop music, Sylvia's records were the aural equivalent of cotton candy, so light they nearly floated in the air. Add her good looks to the equation, and she seemed like a model marketed as country to the legions of country purists. And they did have a point, since Sylvia's music was only marginally country. There was a bit of twang here and there, some traditionally country themes and song structures, but it was sugar-coated and polished to a gloss, fitting in better aurally with the soft rock of the time instead of even the country-pop. All this is evident on her 16-track installment of BMG Heritage's *RCA Country Legends* series. What makes this series interesting is that it doesn't use the *Billboard* charts as the sole guideline for compilation; instead, it takes the biggest hits and expands them with album cuts, B-sides, and rarities intended to draw a clearer picture of the artist's depth as a country artist. Usually, this has produced some very interesting, revealing collections, but it's an approach that's kind of odd for Sylvia, since her entire career only makes sense in terms of the charts, and this comes up short on hits. Of the 16 tracks, only six were hits, leaving 12 charting hits behind, including big ones like "Fallin' in Love," "Snapshot," "Sweet Yesterday," and "Like Nothing Ever Happened." For a chart-oriented artist, that's a lot of missing material, but *RCA Country Legends* still works—and, in fact, functions as a nice counterpoint to Renaissance's comprehensive 1997 hits package *Anthology*—because it's sequenced well, contains the biggest and best hits, while digging up a few choice cuts like "Cry Baby Cry," "No News Is Good News," "Tonight I'm Gettin' Friendly With the Blues," and "Eyes Like Mine" that prove that Sylvia did depth outside of the charts. That said, *RCA Country Legends* won't change any minds about her musical attributes—this is still *very* soft country-pop, and even condensed to a collection, there are a few dull moments here and there—but for those that like Sylvia or early-'80s soft rock, this is quite enjoyable and nearly as an effective an introduction to her as the hit-laden *Anthology —Stephen Thomas Erlewine*

T

James Talley

b. Nov. 9, 1944, Mehan, OK

Guitar, Vocals, Producer / Country-Pop, Singer/Songwriter, Electric Memphis Blues, Progressive Country, Country-Rock

James Talley is a man of many roles—singer/songwriter, guitarist, and recording artist. He can sound like a rival to Stevie Ray Vaughan on numbers like "Bluesman," or a genuinely soulful John Denver on numbers like "Alabama Summertime," and has also crossed swords with Steve Goodman on "Everybody Loves a Lovesong"—and he's written one romantic masterpiece, "Up From Georgia," one of the most achingly beautiful love songs to come out of modern country music. Anyone not having heard of him, however, can be forgiven, for although he's an American and has played throughout the U.S., his work mostly appears on the German-based Bear Family label. He's represented by live albums, a couple of studio releases, and one expensive box set concept album, *The Road to Torreon*, for which he wrote songs to accompany a group of photographs from the American Southwest. *Nashville City Blues* was released in 2000. —*Bruce Eder*

Got No Bread, No Milk, No Money, But We Sure Got a Lot of Love / 1975 / Capitol ◆◆◆◆

James Talley's 1975 debut for the Capitol label was perhaps unnoticed by the country music establishment, deemed not sophisticated enough and too inside the hillbilly tradition for the outlaws; nonetheless, it is an unqualified artistic achievement. Featuring 12 of his own songs, this album of Talley's music comes from the rural country blues and from Bob Wills' Western swing, and his songs are rooted in the everyday lives of folks, whether working-class or living in poverty, who make the best of difficult situations without too much complaining. The title track, with its blues riffing and sweet hillbilly abandon, tells the story of a woman loved enough to break a man without malice because she loves him too. "Red River Memory" is an update of the "Red River Valley" legend set to the same melody with a shimmering pedal steel in the background just under the acoustic guitars. "Give Him Another Bottle" inhabits the terrain where honky tonk, bluegrass, and the blues all meet and converse. The rodeo queen at the heart of "Calico Gypsy" is classic Talley, where people are evoked not only as memories but as reflections of the natural world from the color of the sky to the blooming of summer flowers. Side one closes with the lone cover on the album, Johnny Gimble's "Big Taters in the Sandy Land," on which the author plays fiddle. The rest of the disc—such as tracks like "No Opener Needed," a Merle Haggard-esque bluesy love song, or "Take Me to the Country," a rambling country poem where the elegiac and the prosaic commingle inside the desperation of a broken heart—make Talley a master of the ordinary. Talley can tell a story plainly without the use of extended metaphors and framework artifices, and when he communicates this directly, he can touch even the hardest and most cynical heart. This is as auspicious a debut as there is. —*Thom Jurek*

Tryin' Like the Devil / 1976 / Capitol ◆◆◆◆◆

On *Got No Bread, No Milk, No Money, But We Sure Got a Lot of Love*, James Talley established himself as a songwriter of true substance and a purveyor of relative truth. There was no cynicism in his vision, and like Mickey Newbury, he understood that the image in a song communicates everything and all language should be directed to conveying it. On *Tryin' Like the Devil*, Talley digs deeper into his blues roots, and deeper into his portrayal of the image, so that the listener gets an actual picture in her or his mind. The rambling, pastoral "Deep Country Blues," with its whining dobro, lonesome harmonica, and Travis-style guitar picking, offers a tale of simple backcountry love amid the plenitude of the land and the absence of money. But like all innocence, it breaks down into a reality not expressed here, yet referred to as a gazer through the past where the scar on the heart is plainly visible. The waltz that is "Give My Love to Marie" comes from the mouth of a black-lung miner on his deathbed, who recounts his inability to resolve the fact that there are "millions in the ground, but not a penny for me." Economics is also the theme of "Are They Gonna Make Us Outlaws Again?," not Willie and Waylon. Here is Woody Guthrie's ghost speaking through the mouth of fellow Okie Talley with a dobro, a thumping standup bass, and an acoustic guitar leading the séance. The title track, with its electric guitars and modern honky tonk riff, is a snapshot of pot-bellied truckers, whiskey, red-headed waitresses, and lonely midnights all engaged in reconciling broken dreams yet not giving up on life. They're all separate, all inseparable: "A lot of lonely people just like me." Johnny Gimble's fiddle solo soars in the bridge. "Nothin' But the Blues" is one of Talley's most covered songs, but its easy-swinging Bob Wills-style execution in his gorgeous tenor makes it a late-night lounge lizard's anthem full of wheel-spinning-in-a-rut blues. The set ends on the up though, with "You Can't Ever Tell." It's a strutting honky tonker with Talley exhorting his lover to say the hell with everything in order to go out on the town and raise some hell. This is a fitting end, considering this has been an album about the tough side of the working and loving life, and this small bit of relief is all

anyone has a right to expect after all. *Tryin' Like the Devil* is a masterful work by one of country music's most profound and empathetic of talents. —*Thom Jurek*

Blackjack Choir / 1977 / Capitol ◆◆◆◆◆

Blackjack Choir is ultimate expression of all that James Talley is as a songwriter and performer. *Blackjack Choir*, his third album for Capitol, was released in 1977 at the dawn of the *Urban Cowboy* hype, the beginning of the wane of the outlaws, the kicked-open door of punk, and the cocaine heights of disco. Oh yeah, and the period in which mainstream pop and rock sucked more than at any other time in their history up to that point. In other words, it's a miracle the album was made at all by a major label. Talley used basically the same band he'd employed on his previous outings, but added Reggie Young on guitar and a cello and tuba for texture on a couple of songs. The depth was already there, but *Blackjack Choir* also had dimension. "Bluesman," the opener, kicks it off with Young kicking in on electric, Talley in his smooth tenor riding above a horn section that slips and slides through his lyrics, which are, of course, about the workmanlike side of being a bluesman. "Alabama Summertime" is a country song with pretty steel guitars, but inside its sunny disposition is an ache, a blues, a looking back, a longing. "Everybody Loves a Lovesong" could have been written by Mickey Newbury with its beautiful Dixieland blues and jazz feel, with a tack piano and tuba framing the rhythm section. Talley's command of Southern musical styles and voices is encyclopedic. "Daddy Just Called It the Blues," a funky urban blues tune that brings a New Orleans second line up against the funk and Chicago blues, sounds like the music Ray Wylie Hubbard and Waylon Jennings were trying to make at the time—but this stuff has way more soul. But as in all of Talley's works, the words count at least as much as the music. Talley never milks his words for emotion; he just tells his stories in the first or third person, and the worker is the teller of all truth. For prime evidence, check "Migrant Jesse Sawyer," a story so weighty and full it's a shame it wasn't the album's closer. But that comes two track later, after a working-class love song: "When the Fiddler Packs His Case" features Johnny Gimble tearing it up along with dobro boss Josh Graves on a bluegrass stomper that carries the album out on its highest note. *Blackjack Choir* carries the listener through the many sides of the working life, and all the moods and textures of that experience. It's a masterpiece. —*Thom Jurek*

Ain't It Somethin' / 1978 / Capitol ◆◆◆◆◆

By the time James Talley issued his fourth album for Capitol, his sound had been transformed from a simple fusion of folk, country, and blues to a hotbed of steaming R&B, funky New Orleans second-line rhythms, country, and even rock. These 11 tracks suggest that Talley was moving honky tonk and folk music into a new era, one that would explode just a few years later. But Talley was ahead of his time and *Ain't It Somethin'* didn't even chart. Ultimately it doesn't make a difference, because Talley went on to do alright for himself as Nashville's number one real-estate broker and developer and has continued to record. Despite the changes in arrangement and style, Talley's songs are still about the same people he wrote about on his first record: the poor, working class, day laborers, farmers, factory men and women just doing everything they can to make a life for themselves. The only politics in Talley's songs come from his experience as a social worker, a farmer, and growing up in Torreon. Check the beautiful piano lines and melody in "We Keep Tryin'," where he sings: "Me and Mattie, we ain't got no influential friends/Just tryin to beat them blues." Or the soft, jazzy overtones in "Dixie Blue," with Billy Puett's clarinet easing the piece in before Randy Scruggs slips his banjo into the mix and Steve Hostak fills in with an electric on top of Josh Graves' dobro and Jerry Shook's acoustics. "Nine Pounds of Hashbrowns" is Nashville funky strut at its finest and Talley doesn't even have to stretch to get there: "Nine pounds of hashbrowns and a rock & roll degree/Will take me anywhere you might want to see," with horns, James Brown-style, punching the margins and a pair of dueling greasy guitars riffing outside the melody. And right from here it's the simple folk music of "Richland Washington," about a father who made plutonium. Here the echoes of Roscoe Holcomb and Bascom Lamar Lunsford fall in with Talley's melody, while his story comes right out of Woody Guthrie. The last two tracks on the set are Talley at his best, the poignant ballad "The Poets of the West Virginia Mines" and "What Will Be There for the Children?" Both are folk songs done in the modern vernacular, both tender and empathetic beyond anything being written today. Talley's eye was never journalistic; it was the observation of the neighbor, allowing the spare instrumentation to help him impart to another neighbor what he sees and feels about it all as a way of communicating and extending the dialogue of life, particularly life as witnessed by the heart. In the 1970s, Talley issued four masterpieces in a row. —*Thom Jurek*

● **Got No Bread, No Milk, No Money/Tryin' Like the Devil** / 1989 / Bear Family ◆◆◆◆◆
Got No Bread/Tryin' Like the Devil combines James Talley's 1975 and 1976 albums for Captiol Records on one disc. Talley had a gift for writing detailed, bluesy folk songs that

were aimed directly at working-class audience. Of course, it was the kind of venture that worked on a cerebral level more than a visceral one, so critics—and even President Jimmy Carter—celebrated these songs, while very few people ever bought either album. Still, both of these records hold up remarkably well, and there's a number of understated gems scattered throughout this compact disc. —*Thom Owens*

Blackjack Choir/Ain't It Somethin' / 1989 / Bear Family ♦♦♦
This has 22 songs, electric and acoustic, mostly in a bluesy vein, although the gorgeous folk-style ballad "Up from Georgia" is also here. Talley is good with electric backing, but his acoustic country blues ("Magnolia Boy," etc.) sounds fresher and more distinctive. B.B. King puts in a welcome appearance on "Bluesman" to kick off the set, but the rest has a quiet power that's equally appreciated. The main difference between the two bodies of songs (originally off of two separate albums) is the absence of a trio of female backup singers on the last 12 songs from the later session. A solid midtempo country album in a very deep shade of blue. —*Bruce Eder*

Woody Guthrie & Songs of My Oklahoma Home / Jan. 4, 2000 / Cimarron ♦♦♦
Oklahoma-born James Talley gives stirring accounts of most of the 21 Woody Guthrie songs on this 70-minute CD. Richard Hardy's mandolin adds considerable color to the timbre of these well-arranged recordings, which are dominated by Talley's suitably emotive and pleasing voice. Talley evidently identifies deeply with much of this repertory and invests a lot of himself in each piece, and the backup singing melds nicely with his lead vocals. The recording quality is exceptionally good, bringing out the delicate timbre of the playing, and only the availability of Guthrie's versions (and those by contemporaries such as Pete Seeger) makes this a less-than-obvious choice, though it is an excellent assembly of many of the composer's most famous songs (with "Goodnight Irene" used as the music for the poem "Red Wing," and the Jack Guthrie co-authored "Oklahoma Hills" also present). —*Bruce Eder*

Nashville City Blues / Jul. 11, 2000 / Cimarron ♦♦♦♦
For the uninitiated, placing an album like *Nashville City Blues* in the CD player will be a pleasant surprise. Pleasant because it is a country album that, despite its title, has nothing to do with Nashville, and pleasant because James Talley's approach to country is shot through with the blues. There are no retro-honky tonk songs in sight, and while Talley does wear a hat on the CD cover, it isn't a cowboy hat. The album kicks off with the title cut, a rocking kiss-off to Nashville and all it's cookie-cutter sameness. "I've Seen the Bear" is a long-running narrative with a late-night feel and insightful observations, while "Workin' for Wages" lays down a few honest words about the blue-collar life. "You Can't Get There From Here" and "House Right Down the Road" are fun rockers that give Talley a chance to cut loose with some nice guitar work. A number of songs like "Don't You Feel Low Down" and "If It Wasn't for the Blues" emphasize the "blues" in the album's title. The arrangements throughout *Nashville City Blues* are pure country, meaning guitar, mandolin, steel, dobro, and an occasional piano. The instruments blend well together, and the overall production is spare. Talley, who has penned all of the songs, writes intelligent lyrics and has a pleasant singing voice. He remembers and celebrates country music's working-class roots. For fans of "real" country music, *Nashville City Blues* will be an ear-opening experience, leaving them anxious for upcoming reissues of Talley's earlier work. —*Ronnie Lankford Jr.*

Touchstones / Apr. 23, 2002 / Cimarron ♦♦♦♦
James Talley is that rarest of things these days, a true country singer. Not "new country," not "alt-country," but the real thing. He writes beautifully about real people and the problems of their everyday lives, and sings his songs in a voice that could belong to Willie Nelson's brother (indeed, "Not Even When It's Over" could have been written for Nelson, so perfectly does it suit his style). He can go from a tender family ballad like "Richland, Washington" or "Give My Love to Marie" to a wonderful little slice of history ("W. Lee O'Daniel and the Light Crust Dough Boys") and make it all flow perfectly. A pretty stellar cast helps out, including accordionist Ponty Bone and Texas singer Joe Ely, but it's always Talley who's at the heart of things, remarkable perhaps even more for the perceptiveness of his writing and the poetic lyricism to lines like "Hand of amber, soul of gold/There's a story to be told," which might seem silly from someone else but make perfect sense coming from his lips. He's someone to be experienced when you're tired of all the inanities that often masquerade as lyrics, and want to revel in the quiet joy of his performance. American classics, true American classics, are a rarity, but James Talley is one, and *Touchstones*, like all his other records, is a gem to be discovered. —*Chris Nickson*

Gid Tanner

b. Jun. 6, 1885, Thomas Bridge, GA, **d.** 1960, Dacula, GA
Leader / Old-Timey, String Bands
The Skillet Lickers were one of the most important and influential string bands of the '20s and '30s. Led by fiddler Gid Tanner, the band combined old-timey country music with a wacky sense of humor and showmanship that made the group one of the most popular country bands in America. The original lineup of the band featured the dexterous and stunning interplay of Tanner, guitarist Riley Puckett, fiddler Clayton McMichen, and banjoist Fate Norris. From 1926 to 1931, the Skillet Lickers were the most popular country band in the country. Following the original band's dissolution, Puckett and latter-day fiddler Bert Layne led various bands called the Skillet Lickers, but the group wasn't relaunched until 1934, when Tanner formed a new lineup that recorded one final session that yielded their biggest hit, "Down Yonder."

Tanner did have the right to the Skillet Lickers name; after all, he was the musician that sparked Columbia Records A&R representative Frank Walker to assemble the entire band in 1925. Prior to the formation of the Skillet Lickers, Tanner had worked his way up through the conventional circuit of festivals and traveling shows that fiddlers frequented. His first great success arrived in the middle of the 1910s, when he began to regularly win fiddling conventions in Atlanta. In addition to playing, Tanner was also an accomplished comedian, which meant he was an all-around entertainer, capable of winning audiences easily. Eventually, Columbia asked him to record for their label, and in early 1924, he traveled to New York with his longtime friend and accompanist, Puckett, and made a handful of singles.

The following year, Walker traveled to Atlanta with the intentions of forming a string supergroup. Remembering Tanner and his records, he asked the fiddler and Puckett to be the core of this group, adding McMichen and Norris to the lineup. Choosing the name the Skillet Lickers (a tribute to the Lickskillet Band, a string band that used to play fiddler contests), the band recorded and released their first singles in 1926. The Skillet Lickers were an immediate hit, shooting to the top of the charts with the double A-sided single "Bully of the Town"/"Pass Around the Bottle and We'll All Take a Drink." The single was followed quickly by "Watermelon Hanging on the Vine"/"You," which confirmed their status as hillbilly stars. With their third single, the Skillet Lickers released their first comedy record with "A Corn Licker Still in Georgia," which alternated music with a comic dialogue about backwoods moonshiners. The record was their biggest single yet, equalled by their second comedy hit, "A Fiddler's Convention in Georgia." Not only did the comedy records sell better than the straight instrumental fiddling records. Any single featuring Puckett singing became a huge hit.

Along with the success came internal tension within the band. All of their records were credited to "Gid Tanner & His Skillet Lickers," which became a source of irritation to Puckett and McMichen, both of whom felt that they were more integral to the sound of the band than Tanner. A compromise was reached, and the records bore the convoluted credit "Gid Tanner & His Skillet Lickers With Clayton McMichen and Riley Puckett." However, that didn't put an end to friction within the group, who had by then included several new, younger members like fiddlers Lowe Stokes and Bert Layne. The new members want to move the Skillet Lickers toward Western swing music. McMichen sided with the newer members, but the remaining trio wanted to stay true to their folk roots. By 1930, the members had begun to part ways and had stopped touring regularly. In addition to working with the Skillet Lickers, McMichen became a studio musician for Columbia and played with Jimmie Rodgers. Finally, he formed a new string band called the Georgia Wildcats. McMichen nevertheless participated in all of the studio sessions for the Skillet Lickers, which came to a halt in 1931.

Following the disbandment of the Skillet Lickers in 1931, Puckett and Layne both toured and recorded with groups called "the Skillet Lickers," but the name was officially reclaimed by Tanner in 1934, when he signed to Victor's Bluebird label. Tanner assembled a new group of Skillet Lickers—including Puckett, mandolinist Ted Hawkins, guitarist Mike Whitten, guitarist Hoke Rice, guitarist Hugh Cross, and his sons Arthur and Gordon, on banjo and fiddle respectively—and recorded over 30 songs in San Antonio. It was the final time Tanner ever entered a studio. The sessions produced "Down Yonder," which became Tanner and the Skillet Lickers' last big hit. Following the 1934 session, the Skillet Licker name was retired, and not long after that, Tanner retired himself. Puckett, McMichen, and Layne all pursued solo careers. Following Tanner's death in 1960, his son Gordon continued fiddling, preserving the tradition of his father and the Skillet Lickers. —*Stephen Thomas Erlewine*

Gid Tanner and His Skillet Lickers / 1973 / Rounder ♦♦♦♦

Kickapoo Medicine Show / 1988 / Rounder ♦♦♦♦♦
When it comes down to it, and record collectors are hanging off a cliff deciding to grab at a tree root or a particular side, a record like this is going to make the difference between life and death. "Once you've heard this you've heard everything," was the way this record was described by one collector, whose outstretched arms were meant to encompass a collection of thousands of records from different genres, all of which are apparently rendered obsolete by the collective playing of Gid Tanner, Clayton McMichen, and Riley Puckett. It is true that as far as super trios go, this one leaves them all in the dust, from Cream to the Three Stooges. And this is not mere hyperbole. The musical invention is way beyond Clapton, and in between segments of instrumental virtuosity the band actually pulls off little comedy skits, such as the nonsense which opens up the album. Turned up loud enough, a listener might be able to convince neighbors that deranged hillbillies have moved in, perhaps resulting in a new-neighborhood buffer space. Perhaps it is more desirable that the neighbors come over and start dancing, hooting, and hollering like folks did back at the house parties in the day when these pieces were recorded. That could certainly be possible as well, because these tracks have incredible spirit. The music literally jumps up and down. The guitar style of Puckett is wonderful, the notes so fat and provocative its ridiculous. Wimpy bluegrass pickers who philosophize about chromatic runs should go back to these records and listen to the way Puckett played over the chords. The fiddling is beyond belief, McMichen teaming up with his rowdy partner, Lowe Stokes, for glorious passages, voices sometimes chiming in with the fiddle in odd harmony. The version of "You Gotta Quit Kicking My Dawg Around" is a knockout, while other listeners are sure to be fond of "You Gotta Quit Drinkin' Shine." "Rake and Rambling Boy" has a lovely vocal and an elegant tempo. "Mississippi Sawyer" is quite an effective ending track and would have been hard to top. "New Dixie" is a fast-moving anthem and one of several tracks in which someone's falsetto vocal creates an atmosphere that borders on surreal. The recording quality is primitive, but fans of scratchy vinyl will absolutely adore some of the stuff that gets passed along from the original discs these tracks were transferred from. Parts of this stuff sound like the high tide at Carolina Beach, but it all adds to the delicious atmosphere. Liner note information is way on the slim side, a bit of a letdown considering the detail this label has gone to on other occasions. —*Eugene Chadbourne*

● **The Skillet Lickers** / 1996 / County ♦♦♦♦♦
The single-disc compilation *Skillet Lickers* contains 16 tracks that the hillbilly musical comedy group recorded between 1926 and 1931, including "Ride Old Buck to the Water," "Dixie," and "Leather Breeches." The Skillet Lickers were one of the most popular groups of their time, and although their music and humor has dated considerably in the decades

since, the musical talents of fiddler Gid Tanner remain impressive, and this compilation is the best way to hear him and his group. *—Thom Owens*

Tarnation

f. 1992, San Francisco, CA

Group / Alternative Country-Rock, Dream Pop

The country art band Tarnation was essentially a vehicle for Paula Frazer, a talented singer and songwriter who returned to roots music only after a successful foray into 1980s post-punk. Frazer was born and raised in Sautee Nacoochee, GA, a tiny community located in the foothills of the Smoky Mountains, where as a child she sang in her father's church choir, developing a remarkably adept soprano. At the age of 14, the Frazers moved to Arkansas, where she began performing with local jazz groups. After graduating high-school, Frazer relocated to San Francisco, where she followed a stint in a Bulgarian women's choir with tenures in a number of area punk groups, most notably the all-female Frightwig.

In 1992, she formed Tarnation with former S.F. Seals members Lincoln Allen and Michelle Cernuto, along with steel guitarist Matt Sullivan. Setting their dark ballads and love songs against a stark, ominous backdrop dominated by reverb-soaked guitars, Tarnation debuted in 1993 with *I'll Give You Something to Cry About*. In 1995, they issued *Gentle Creatures*, their first LP for the arty British label 4AD. Shortly after the record's release, Allen, Cernuto, and Sullivan left the group and were replaced by guitarist Alex Oropeza, drummer Joe Byrnes, and bassist/lap steel player Bill Cuevas. *—Jason Ankeny*

● **Gentle Creatures** / Aug. 22, 1995 / 4AD ✦✦✦✦✦

Given that Tarnation's frontwoman Paula Frazer is best known for her work with the L.A. post-punk band Frightwig—and since *Gentle Creatures* is, after all, a product of the arty 4AD label—the absolute-torch-and-twang authenticity that defines the record is a wonderful surprise; ethereal yet earthy, the album's strength derives from all of its seeming contradictions. Powered by Frazer's deft songwriting and smoky vocals, *Gentle Creatures* is melancholy and gorgeous, its love songs and ballads cloaked in reverb and gothic imagery. What Tarnation shares with its 4AD stablemates is an uncanny knack to build and maintain a rich, dense atmosphere; the record is dusky and otherworldly, haunted by the spirits of failed relationships, late-night radio transmissions, and other ghostly presences. *—Jason Ankeny*

Mirador / Apr. 8, 1997 / Reprise ✦✦✦✦✦

As of *Mirador*, Tarnation became, for all intents and purposes, the Paula Frazer band, both for better and for worse. Frazer certainly dominated *Gentle Creatures*, and Matt Sullivan is not missed anywhere on *Mirador*, but the second album doesn't have the brilliant highs of the debut. That said, it is a more consistent record, and her new developments are quite intriguing. Frazer has created a dark, neo-Spanish feel that owes as much to spaghetti Westerns as it does to traditional country, and while her songwriting has improved, it's distressing that the cover of the Nightcrawlers' "Little Black Egg" stands out on the initial listen. Subsequent plays reveal the depth and subtlety of her songs, which her rich, powerful voice makes all the more effective. If *Mirador* is a stumble, it's only a slight one—Tarnation are still one of the most provocative bands dream pop and alt-country have yet produced. *—Stephen Thomas Erlewine*

Carmol Taylor

b. Sep. 5, 1931, Brilliant, AL, **d.** Dec. 5, 1986

Songwriter, Vocals / Traditional Country, Honky Tonk

Carmol Taylor was best known as a honky tonk songwriter, but he was also a talented performer. He was born in Brilliant, AL, and began playing professionally in his early teens. When he was about 15, Taylor teamed up with Billy Sherrill to form Carmol Taylor & the Country Pals. The group stayed together for over 20 years, and between 1954 and 1974 played on a number of Southern radio stations. He launched his recording career in 1955, and in the early '60s he and the Pals began hosting a television show out of Columbus, MS, where they performed for nine years.

Sherrill went on to become one of the most influential record producers in country music, and he helped Taylor break into professional songwriting by getting him a job at Al Gallico Music. In 1965, Charlie Walker had a Top Ten hit with Taylor's "Wild as a Wildcat." Soon after, Taylor began collaborating with Sherrill, Norro Wilson and George Richey. Together, they produced several major hits during the 1970s, including "He Loves Me All the Way," "My Man," "The Grand Tour," and "There's a Song on the Jukebox." Although he had been recording since the mid-'50s, Taylor didn't appear on the charts until the mid-'70s, with such songs as "Play the Saddest Song on the Jukebox" and "I Really Had a Ball Last Night." In 1980, Taylor himself became a producer, and in 1985, he and Gary Lumpkin provided George Jones and Lacy J. Dalton with a Top 20 hit, "Size Seven Round (Made of Gold)." Taylor died of lung cancer the following year. *—Sandra Brennan*

Song Writer / 1976 / Elektra ✦✦✦

I Think They Call It Homesick / 1984 / Country International ✦✦✦

● **Honky Tonk Two Steppin' Beer Drinkin' Saturday Nite** / 1987 / Password [UK] ✦✦✦✦

Chip Taylor (John Wesley Voight)

b. 1940, New York, NY

Guitar, Vocals / Country-Rock, Singer/Songwriter, Folk-Rock

Chip Taylor probably will always be known as the songwriter who wrote "Wild Thing" and "Angel of the Morning." Born John Wesley Voight (the actor Jon Voight is his older brother), Taylor began playing country music while still in high-school in Yonkers, NY. After finishing high-school, he briefly took up his father's occupation, becoming a professional golfer. But he suffered a wrist injury and turned back to music. In 1962, he signed to Warner Bros. Records, and his single "Here I Am" "bubbled under" the *Billboard* Hot 100 in November. He became more successful, however, as a songwriter, scoring his first hit with "I Can't Let Go" (co-written with Al Gorgoni), which was recorded by the Hollies for a chart entry in March 1966. (Linda Ronstadt revived the song for a Top 40 hit in 1980.) Then came the simplistic, but unforgettable "Wild Thing," recorded by another British group, the Troggs, who topped the charts with it in July, creating a much-covered standard. A parody by "Senator Bobby" (comedian Bill Minkin) hit the Top 40 in January 1967, and the Jimi Hendrix Experience performed the song at the Monterey Pop Festival in June.

Meanwhile, Taylor continued to write hits: "Make Me Belong to You" (co-written with Billy Vera) hit the Top 40 for Barbara Lewis in August 1966; "I Can Make It With You" was cut by both the Pozo-Seco Singers and by Jackie DeShannon, with the Pozo-Seco Singers' version winning out and hitting the Top 40 in October 1966; the American Breed recorded "Step Out of Your Mind" for a Top 40 hit in July 1967; and Billy Vera & Judy Clay hit the Top 40 with "Country Girl City Man" (co-written with Ted Daryll) in March 1968. But Taylor's second standard was "Angel of the Morning," a ballad about pre-marital sex that pushed the boundaries of acceptable subject matter in pop music. Merrilee Rush & the Turnabouts recorded the song, and it reached the Top Ten in June 1968; Juice Newton revived it in 1981 for a second Top Ten hit and a gold record. With Gorgoni, Taylor wrote "I'll Hold Out My Hand," recorded by the Clique for a Top 40 hit in December 1969. Also in 1969, Janis Joplin recorded Taylor and Jerry Ragavoy's "Try (Just a Little Bit Harder)" and released it as the leadoff track on her debut solo album, *I Got Dem Ol' Kozmic Blues Again Mama!*

Taylor had not given up his ambition to be a recording artist himself. He and Gorgoni recorded together under the name Just Us, then Taylor cut a series of solo albums in the 1970s, including *This Side of the Big River*, which reached the country charts in 1975, as did five Taylor singles between 1975 and 1977. His songwriting efforts also found favor in Nashville, with "Sweet Dream Woman" (co-written with Gorgoni) reaching the country Top Ten for Waylon Jennings in 1972 and Anne Murray's recording of "Son of a Rotten Gambler" in the country Top Ten in 1974. Nevertheless, Taylor gave up the music business and became a professional gambler, not returning to music until 1993 when he joined a national songwriters' tour. He released a new album, *The Living Room Tapes*, in 1997, followed by *Seven Days in May* in 1998, *The London Sessions Bootleg* in 2000, *Black and Blue America* in 2001, and a collaboration with Carrie Rodriguez, *Let's Leave This Town*, in 2002. *—William Ruhlmann*

Gasoline / 1971 / Buddah ✦✦✦

Chip Taylor's Last Chance / 1973 / Warner Bros. ✦✦✦

Some of Us / 1974 / Warner Bros. ✦✦✦

This Side of the Big River / 1975 / Warner Bros. ✦✦✦✦

● **Hit Man** / Sep. 17, 1996 / Gadfly ✦✦✦✦

There's something about singer/songwriters doing their own material, and while Chip Taylor is one of the greats (and produced one of the greats, Neil Diamond), he is in an industry where his legacy puts him a few steps ahead of P.F. Sloan in terms of success, but far short of the name recognition enjoyed by a Carole King (a status she deserves, as does Taylor). This is a great—but incomplete—collection of songs that were and still are highly influential. "Try Just a Little Bit Harder" might not be as notorious as "Wild Thing" or "Angel of the Morning" but, being a Janis Joplin signature, it sure got into a lot of homes. When Clive Davis played a rare Joplin performance on *the Midnight Special* television program, he chose a version of "Try" where Pearl just exploded across the stage. Taylor's version here is more laid-back, but so absolutely essential for two reasons—because it was so vital to Joplin's solo career, and because it is such a tremendous song on its own. Not the biggest hit in Linda Ronstadt's career, "I Can't Let Go" is one of her more exciting ones, and it's great to hear the creator take it on, as well as "Any Way That You Want Me," a song covered by Evie Sands and the Troggs. Gadfly Records does a good job here, and the liner notes have chart information as well as anecdotes from Taylor on how and why some of the tunes were written. His performances are excellent and deserving of chart action on their own, or at least some serious adult alternative radio airplay. There are 13 selections and, though some important compositions are missing—the American Breed's "Step Out of Your Mind," the Clique's "I'll Hold Out My Hand" from the album that launched their Tommy James hit "Sugar on Sunday," and Taylor's own 1962 minor chart entry "Here I Am"—the sincerity in delivery and the historic importance make this a textbook you can learn from and enjoy. *Hit Man* is an excellent resumé of a vital creative force in music, and could keep young minds focused if used in classrooms to teach the art of painting a song. Apart from that, it is a monster album that truly deserves platinum success. *—Joe Viglione*

The Living Room Tapes / Mar. 25, 1997 / Gadfly ✦✦✦

The Living Room Tapes is a modest, engaging collection of unassuming, catchy country and folk-rock songs from Chip Taylor. Supported by two guitarists, Jon Stolle and David Mansfield, Taylor turns in a modest performance which only accentuates the subtle charms of his songs. Not every cut on the record is memorable, but the best moments confirm his talent for constructing sturdy, melodic, and provocative songs. *—Thom Owens*

The London Sessions Bootleg / Jan. 25, 2000 / Train Wreck ✦✦✦✦

Chip Taylor's early resumé as the author of such '60s hits as "Wild Thing" and "Angel of the Morning" is a poor preparation for his '90s career as a singer/songwriter; a better indication is his country music from the early '70s, like the Waylon Jennings hit "Sweet Dream Woman." He may be a born-and-bred New Yorker, but listening to Taylor's idiosyncratic recent work, you would swear he was from Texas; the closest approximations are people like Jimmie Dale Gilmore and Guy Clark. Following a 1998 European tour, Taylor entered a London recording studio to cut a bunch of new songs and decided he liked the results enough to release them on his own record label, Train Wreck Records. Before he could do so, however, he cut another session of newly written songs in New York and liked those, too. The result is this sprawling two-disc set, running over an hour and 45 minutes. It's appropriate that Taylor has given it the relatively undefined *London*

Sessions title, and that he has referred to it as a bootleg. There are some wonderful individual songs here, but they do not cohere into an album, and the off-the-cuff, live-in-the-studio performances are unpolished, sounding not so much like a bootleg as a collection of demos. What's great about the set, however, is the oddball, but often impressive material. Some songs are misfires, but by the time such tracks play, the listener is willing to accept the hit-or-miss quality of Taylor's songwriting, since the good ones are so imaginative. The whole thing comes to an appropriate end with a hidden track that finds Taylor, just having woken up from a dream in which Kris Kristofferson gave him the first line, singing an improvised song into his bedside tape recorder. One could bet that wasn't the only song that came to him in a dream. —*William Ruhlmann*

Black and Blue America / Aug. 7, 2001 / Train Wreck ✦✦✦✦
Chip Taylor has turned into the philosopher of country music, not to mention its social historian. With each track introduced by a soundbite that seems to act as a springboard for his lyrical musings, Taylor tracks the way America lost its innocence ("Black and Blue America"), relationships ("In Your Weakness"), the carefree young life ("For Worth Thursday Night," which gets extra points for a gratuitous mention of Robert Earl Keen), and alcohol and faith ("Dance With Jesus"). So, by its nature, this isn't an album for casual listening, although on one level listeners can let it float along, with a sound that ranges from alt-country to gospel. It's largely stripped-down, but that suits him. When the band swells behind him, Taylor's voice takes on neo-operatic tones that simply don't work. What's really passion sounds merely like too much effort. But the songs definitely do work, and duets with Lucinda Williams, John Prine, and former soul diva P.P. Arnold sparkle, even when they're as bleak as Williams' contribution to "The Ship." Over the years Taylor's work has turned introspective, but this might be his deepest yet, a plumbing of what life, America, and its people has become. His future releases will probably have the same warm humor, compassion, and hope for the future as *Black and Blue America*. —*Chris Nickson*

Let's Leave This Town / Sep. 3, 2002 / Texas Music Group ✦✦✦
This new release by this legendary Texas songwriter is a far piece from the Troggs' *Wild Thing*, but it is still the same person who has worked his way around the music business. This is his teaming with up-and-coming fiddler/singer Carrie Rodriguez to bring a slew of new songs to the public, some of which are destined to become hits in the country & western music scene. He wrote, or co-wrote, ten of the 12 tunes here, and there isn't a wormy one in the package. Before the focus turns too much to this legend, take a listen to the stellar and sensitive fiddling this budding new singer is capable of producing. "There's a Hole in the Midnight" has a feel to it that calls back the best of sad country songs without being disgustingly maudlin; oh, it's a weeper all right—however, that line of gush is not crossed. There is a good mix in the tempos of the tunes and this disc never gets stuck in any rut. They have a remarkable group of musicians playing with them that go a long way to bring out the best in his music, including former Van Morrison stalwart John Platinia on electric guitar and Fairport Convention's Dave Mattacks handling the drums. However, this is their disc and it is they who make it dazzle as a bright star in that lonesome Texas prairie night. —*Bob Gottlieb*

Les Taylor

b. Dec. 27, 1948, Oneida, KY
Guitar, Vocals / Contemporary Country
Vocalist Les Taylor grew up in central Kentucky. He caught his big break when, in 1980, fellow Kentuckians Exile—fresh off their number-one hit "I Want to Kiss You All Over"—tapped him as their new contributing lead singer and rhythm guitarist. Taylor performed with the group for most of the decade but left in 1989 to pursue a solo career. He had some success with his solo debut, "Shoulda, Woulda, Coulda." The album *That Old Desire* followed and was a minor hit. Taylor followed it up with 1991's *Blue Kentucky Wind*, which featured a duet with Shelby Lynne, but the album didn't kick up much interest. Taylor eventually reunited with Exile founder J.P. Pennington during the mid to late '90s, and the two tackled the nostalgia circuit with a rehashed backing band. —*Johnny Loftus*

That Old Desire / 1990 / Epic ✦✦✦
That Old Desire features the minor hits "Shoulda, Coulda, Woulda Loved You" and "Knowin' You Were Leavin'." —*Jason Ankeny*

● **Blue Kentucky Wind** / 1991 / Epic ✦✦✦✦
"I Gotta Mind to Go Crazy" and "The Very First Lasting Love," a duet with Shelby Lynne, are the highlights of *Blue Kentucky Wind*. —*Jason Ankeny*

Tut Taylor

b. 1923, Milledgeville, GA
Dobro, Guitar / Traditional Bluegrass, Old-Timey
A musician's musician, Tut Taylor never achieved widespread popularity, but was highly respected and emulated by his peers. He was born in Milledgeville, Georgia and started out playing banjo as a child before learning mandolin. His lifelong passion for the dobro began at age 14, when he heard Brother Bashful Oswald play. After writing to Roy Acuff to learn the name of the instrument, he bought one and taught himself to play it using the same flatpicking style he used on his mandolin. In the early '60s, Taylor, Glen Campbell and the Dillards teamed up to form the Folkswingers, and through 1964 released three albums, including *12 String Dobro!* Taylor made his debut solo album *Dobro Country* in 1964. In the late '60s, he joined the Dixie Gentlemen, and in 1969, he and fiddler Vassar Clements became the core of John Hartford's backup band. In 1970, Taylor co-founded GTR, a noted instrument shop in Nashville, and recorded with such artists as David Bromberg.

He didn't record another solo album until 1972's *Friar Tut*; he and Randy Wood then teamed up with Ginger Boatwright and Norman Blake to created the popular nightclub and music store the Old Time Pickin' Parlor, which became a favorite haunt of the

Nashville elite. The following year, he appeared on the album *Hank Wilson's Back*. Taylor released another solo effort in 1975, *The Old Post Office*, followed in 1976 by *Dobrolic Plectoral Society*. From the rest of the decade until his retirement, he also ran Tut Taylor's General Store in Nashville. —*Sandra Brennan*

12 String Dobro / 1964 / World Pacific ✦✦✦

● **Friar Tut** / 1972 / Rounder ✦✦✦✦✦
The steel strings sing on this disc of original songs from the dobro guitar master. Taylor served in John Hartford's Aereo-Plain band, and is joined here by fellow bandmate Norman Blake and mandolinist Sam Bush on a string-bending feast. —*Tim Sheridan*

Dobro Country / 1975 / United Artists ✦✦✦

The Old Post Office / 1976 / Flying Fish ✦✦✦
Here, Taylor plays old and new tunes on the dobro with guests Butch Robbins and Norman Blake. —*AMG*

Dorbrolic Plectoral Society / 1976 / Takoma ✦✦

Chalee Tennison

b. Apr. 11, 1969
Vocals / Contemporary Country
Before arriving in Nashville, contemporary country singer Chalee Tennison worked as a prison guard with the Gatesville Unit and Mountainview Unit of the Texas Department of Criminal Justice; among her wards was death row inmate Karla Faye Tucker. Concurrently cutting her teeth performing with a series of bands throughout the central Texas region, Tennison eventually relocated to Music City, singing on a series of demos which caught the attention of producer Jerry Taylor and ultimately resulted in a contract with Asylum; heralded by the single "Someone Else's Turn to Cry," her self-titled debut LP was released in mid-1999. *This Woman's Heart* followed a year later. —*Jason Ankeny*

Chalee Tennison / Jun. 8, 1999 / Elektra ✦✦✦✦
Just about every one of Chalee Tennison's songs on her self-titled debut album, including her first release, "Someone Else's Turn to Cry," reek of heartbreak. From the effervescent "Handful of Water," the solemn "Just Because She Lives There," to the heartfelt "Leave It at That," one can tell this woman's had some experience with romances gone sour. But there's nothing sour about Tennison's first foray into country music. With so many country artists making the cross over to pop, Chalee Tennison reminds you of the reasons you started listening to country music in the first place. —*Maria Konicki Dinoia*

● **This Woman's Heart** / Oct. 10, 2000 / Asylum ✦✦✦✦✦
Chalee Tennison doesn't have to worry about the sophomore jinx. Her self-titled debut album met with little more than critical acclaim, so one can only hope that album number two, *This Woman's Heart*, garners greater commercial success for this talented artist. Whether it's a ballad or a song with an upbeat tempo, Tennison sings it with wild abandon. Maybe there are too many female country artists on the charts to give Tennison her due, but what separates her from the pack is her own brand of country music—it's soulful and pure. Her voice is so appealing and original and it makes every one of her songs worth listening to. Whether she's singing about being a fool and making mistakes in "Yes I Was" or prayers that have been answered in "We Don't Have to Pray," she brings a welcome and refreshing sound to country music fans and, hopefully, finds herself in a welcome place on country radio and on the charts. —*Maria Konicki Dinoia*

Gordon Terry

b. Oct. 7, 1931, Decatur, AL
Fiddle, Vocals / Traditional Bluegrass
Gordon Terry was one of the finest fiddlers in bluegrass. The Decatur, AL, native first gained national exposure when he joined the *Grand Ole Opry* at age 19. He remained there for eight years and during that time recorded a few solo singles for different labels as well as played with Bill Monroe's Blue Grass Boys. In 1957, he had his most popular single with "Wild Honey." He made his film debut in the Western *Hidden Guns* and moved to L.A. in 1958 to continued his solo career. Terry also turned up on different television shows, including the *Sky King* series. He returned to Tennessee in the late '60s to do side and session work and in 1977 released *Disco Country*. In 1981, Terry issued *Rockin' Fiddle*. That same year, he and Bob Wills were inducted into the Fiddlers Hall of Fame. —*Johnny Loftus*

Liberty Square Dance Club / 1962 / Liberty ✦✦✦
Gordon Terry's *Liberty Square Dance Club* is one of countless albums released in the '50s and early '60s to provide music for square dancing. It is a utilitarian record in that sense, issued in two versions, with and without Homer Garrett's instructional calls. What makes *Liberty Square Dance Club* more interesting than the typical square dance album is that Terry is such a respected and talented fiddler, and he tackles a dozen traditional fiddle tunes like "Fire on the Fiddle," "Cotton Eyed Joe," and "Black Mountain Rag." For those whose interest concerns Terry's playing rather than square dancing, look for the version that omits the calls. —*Greg Adams*

Square Dance Party / 1962 / RCA Victor ✦✦✦
For many, square dancing only brings back painful elementary school memories of forced contact with the opposite sex and embarrassing missteps on the gym floor; for others, it conjures up fond recollections of nights out on the town. Luckily, for the latter group, there are plenty of square-dancing clubs and competitions across the country, not to mention a few callers' associations. And for those who like to do their swinging at home, there's this 1962 square-dance record (complete with calls) to take the place of a live band and caller. From a strictly musical standpoint, one also gets to hear the fine fiddle work of bluegrass veteran Gordon Terry. Known for later marginalia like his *Disco Country* and *Rockin' Fiddle* albums, Terry joined the *Grand Ole Opry* when he was 19 and made several sides with Bill Monroe's Blue Grass Boys. In the '50s, he had a few solo hits and

acted in some Westerns, eventually making his way to L.A. While not spending days at the studio, Terry was cutting albums like this one. So don your hat and boots, and listen closely to caller Al Gottlieb reel off classics like "Single Couple Hash," "Little Red Hen," and "Split the Ring." *—Stephen Cook*

● **Lotta, Lotta Women** / 1995 / Bear Family ✦✦✦✦✦
Bear Family's single-disc, 30-track *Lotta, Lotta Women* compilation showcases the bulk of Gordon Terry's early '60s recordings, including "It Ain't Right," "Trouble on the Turnpike," "Queen of the Seasons," "Lonely Road," "For Old Time's Sake," "You Remembered Me," "Long Black Limousine," "Slow Down Old World," "I Don't Hurt Anymore," "All By My Lonesome" and the title track. *—Thom Owens*

Texas Instruments

f. 1983
Group / Roots Rock
A product of the same vibrant Austin roots rock scene which produced the True Believers, the Reivers, and the Wild Seeds, the Texas Instruments were formed in 1983 by guitarist David Woody, bassist Ron Marks, and drummer Steve Chapman. Combining their mutual interest in punk with an affection for heartland music, the group issued their debut EP, *More Texas Instruments!*, in 1985; a self-titled full-length album appeared two years later. After the release of 1988's *Sun Tunnels*, the Texas Instruments added second guitarist Clay Daniel to their lineup. In 1991, the group completed its third album, *Crammed into Infinity*; before the record's release, however, their longtime label, Rabid Cat, declared bankruptcy, and the disc spent many months in limbo, eventually seeing the light of day in 1990. *Magnetic Home* followed three years later. *—Jason Ankeny*

More Texas Instruments! / 1985 / Longhead ✦✦✦
The Texas Instruments' debut EP offers a glimpse of the group's fusion of post-punk and electric roots music in its earliest stages of development. *—Jason Ankeny*

Texas Instruments / 1987 / Rabid Cat ✦✦✦

Sun Tunnels / 1988 / Dr. Dream ✦✦✦✦
The first of the Texas Instruments' records cut with noted underground producer Spot, this full-length debut offers heartfelt roots rock blasted through with punk abandon; in addition to clear debts to country and garage rock, the band salutes its folk heritage by closing out the disc with covers of Woody Guthrie's "Do-Re-Mi" and Bob Dylan's "A Hard Rain's Gonna Fall." *—Jason Ankeny*

● **Crammed into Infinity** / 1991 / Rockville ✦✦✦✦✦
Expanding into a quartet for their third full-length, the Texas Instruments continue to explore their musical roots on *Crammed Into Infinity*. Even with the fuller sound, the music is gloriously ragged country-rock, influenced as much by the Minutemen as by Hank Williams; along with new, post-punk material like "World's Gotten Smaller," they cover the traditional "Standing Here Wondering Which Way to Go." *—Jason Ankeny*

Magnetic Home / Jan. 1993 / Doctor Dream ✦✦✦

Speed of Sound / Apr. 16, 1995 / Doctor Dream ✦✦✦
The Texas Instruments closed their career with this gritty, soulful disc in 1994. The quartet of drummer Steve Chapman, bassist Ron Marks, and guitarists Clay Daniel and David Woody assembled a ten-track epic, with some of the best songs of their career. Woody's confident and poetic vocal style is the highlight of *Speed of Sound*. The band's simple musical style really comes together on "Big Machine," harmonies and chords melding together in a terribly brilliant way. The band's Texas roots are really evident on "Life 'Til Now" and "One From the Other," which combine scorching guitars and a pounding rhythm section to create two of the disc's most remarkable songs. It's on "One From the Other" that Woody's vocals begin to sound vaguely similar to Tom Petty. The graceful instrumental "Sidewalk Museum" is a choppy and brazen song, while the title track closes the disc with modest instrumentation and Woody's effortlessly smooth vocals leading the attack. *Speed of Sound* was recorded with Jim Monroe at For the Record Studio in Orange, CA. *—Stephen Cramer*

Texas Tornados

f. 1989
Group / Conjunto, Tex-Mex, Roots Rock, Americana
The ultimate Tex-Mex supergroup, Texas Tornados were composed of some of the genre's most legendary figures: Doug Sahm, Augie Meyers (Sahm's bandmate in the groundbreaking Sir Douglas Quintet), Hispanic country star Freddy Fender, and accordion virtuoso Flaco Jimenez. The group's infectious, party-ready sound blended country, early rock & roll, Mexican folk music, R&B, blues, and whatever other roots musics crossed their paths. The Tornados first assembled in 1989 at a concert in San Francisco, billing themselves as the Tex-Mex Revue. They enjoyed the collaboration so much they decided to stick with it and generated far more publicity together than they would have solo; Jimenez had released several acclaimed albums by that point, but Sahm had recorded only sporadically during the '80s, and Fender hardly at all.

Their self-titled debut album was released on Reprise in 1990—in both English and Spanish versions—to rapturous reviews and also sold pretty well, reaching number 25 on the country charts. The group toured extensively behind it and issued the Grammy-nominated follow-up album *Zone of Our Own* in 1991, again to hugely positive reviews. By the time of 1992's *Hangin' on By a Thread*, the group's primary audience was Latino, and Jimenez accordingly took more and more of the spotlight. After more touring, the group went their separate ways to concentrate on other projects and work on new material; most notably, Sahm and Meyers formed a new version of the Sir Douglas Quintet. In the meantime, Reprise issued a compilation, *The Best of Texas Tornados*. The Tornados reconvened in 1996 for the album *4 Aces*, which didn't attract quite as much attention or acclaim as their previous work. The group's late-1998 concert at Antone's in Austin was recorded and released the following summer as *Live From the Limo, Vol. 1*; unfortunately, it would prove to be the only volume, as Sahm died of a heart attack in late 1999. *—Steve Huey*

The Texas Tornados [Spanish Version] / Mar. 1990 / Reprise ✦✦✦✦✦
Some of the original *Texas Tornados* album was already sung in Spanish, but this is an all-Spanish edition of the record. *—William Ruhlmann*

The Texas Tornados / Aug. 1990 / Reprise ✦✦✦✦✦
Predictably, this debut album by a sort of Tex-Mex Traveling Wilburys is a delight. Forty percent of the Sir Douglas Quintet—Doug Sahm and Augie Meyers—is represented, along with Freddy Fender and accordionist Flaco Jimenez. The album reflects the differing strains that each brings to the music, from the more pop/country approach of Sahm and Meyers to Fender's bluesy singing and Jimenez's Mexican playing. An all-star project that brings out the best in its members, *Texas Tornados* is a landmark Tex-Mex album. (The track "Soy De San Luis" won the 1990 Grammy Award for Best Mexican/American Performance.) [*Texas Tornados* was also released in an all-Spanish edition.] *—William Ruhlmann*

Zone of Our Own / 1991 / Reprise ✦✦✦✦✦
Even if the Texas Tornados had picked a different name, it would be pretty hard to imagine them coming from anywhere besides the Lone Star State; their high-spirited mixture of Tex-Mex, norteño, garage rock, blues, and hardcore honky tonk flavors brands them as proud sons of a place all these sounds and more happily co-exist on a regular basis. *Zone of Our Own*, the second album from the all-star quartet of Freddy Fender, Flaco Jimenez, Augie Meyers, and Doug Sahm, isn't quite up to the same level as their superb self-titled debut, but it sure doesn't miss by much. Sahm gets to rave up on Sir Doug-style rockers like "I Ain't That Kat Anymore," Fender sings sad and soulful on "Oh Holy One," Jimenez burns up the squeeze box on "La Mucura," and Meyers gets to show off his bluesy side on "Did I Tell You." For all the sonic diversity of the Texas Tornados, *Zone of Our Own* still sounds like it's all of a piece, like the play list of some blessedly eclectic radio station beaming out along the border, as the four frontmen bounce off each other with joyous aplomb. If you're looking for some aural seasoning for your next barbecue, *Zone of Our Own* is just the bottle of hot sauce you need. *—Mark Deming*

Hangin' on By a Thread / 1992 / Reprise ✦✦✦✦✦
Album number three from the Texas Tornados (and the last until a short-lived reunion four years down the line) followed the same path as their first two entries—which is to say, if it was fun and came somewhere from the great state of Texas, you'll find a taste of it here. With "Guacamole," Augie Meyers finally penned a fitting follow-up to "(Hey Baby) Que Paso"; Freddy Fender shows off his strong but silky pipes on the uptempo "A Mover El Bote" and the weepy "I'm Trying"; Flaco Jimenez celebrates both the accordion and the bottle on the heartbroken "Ando Muy Borracho"; and Doug Sahm serves up a lot of rock and a little reggae on the title cut and "La Grande Vida." While the Tex-Mex influences dominate more strongly on *Hangin' on By a Thread* than they had on the first two albums, the album also sounds a bit more cohesive as a result, and Sahm's more rock-oriented material still displays a strong sense of the aural and cultural cross pollination that makes Texas music (and the Texas Tornados) so great. While it hardly sounds like a final gesture, curtain calls were not what this band was about, and *Hangin' on by a Thread* did make a better final chapter to the Texas Tornados' story than their 1996 reunion album, *4 Aces*. *—Mark Deming*

● **The Best of Texas Tornados** / Feb. 8, 1994 / Reprise ✦✦✦✦✦
Featuring material from all of their albums, *The Best of Texas Tornados* is a terrific compilation of one of the best Tex-Mex bands of the last two decades. *—AMG*

4 Aces / Jul. 9, 1996 / Reprise ✦✦✦
Despite a few good moments—like the rollicking "Clinging to You"—*4 Aces* is a bit too predictable of a good-time from the Texas Tornados. Certainly, all of the ingredients that made their previous recordings delightful are present, but the problem is the album doesn't ever quite catch fire with the goofy fun that distinguished their best music. *—Thom Owens*

Live from the Limo, Vol. 1 / Jul. 13, 1999 / Virgin ✦✦✦
It's hard to imagine a better place for the Texas Tornados to record a live album than Antone's in Austin, Texas, where the Tex-Mex superstar act performed in December 1998. The group draws heavily on its 1990 debut album, performing six of its ten tracks. Since they never really improved on that set, that's fine, and they add to it by including member Freddy Fender's hit "Wasted Days, Wasted Nights" and members Doug Sahm and Augie Meyers' Sir Douglas Quintet hit "Mendicino." The club atmosphere is perfect for the group, which exhorts the enthusiastic crowd to singalong, a request that is lustily satisfied. *—William Ruhlmann*

B.J. Thomas (Billy Joe Thomas)

b. Aug. 7, 1942, Houston, TX
Vocals / Country-Pop, Soft Rock, Pop, Pop/Rock, CCM
B.J. Thomas (born Billy Joe Thomas) straddled the line between pop/rock and country, achieving success in both genres in the late '60s and '70s. At the beginning of his career, he leaned more heavily on rock & roll, but by the mid-'70s, he had turned to country music, becoming one of the most successful country-pop stars of the decade. Thomas began singing while he was a child, performing in church. In his teens, he joined the Houston-based band the Triumphs, who released a number of independent singles that failed to gain any attention. For the group's last single, Thomas and fellow Triumph member Mark Charron wrote "Billy and Sue," which was another flop. After "Billy and Sue," Thomas began a solo career, recording a version of Hank Williams' standard "I'm So Lonesome I Could Cry" with producer Huey P. Meaux. Released by Scepter Records in early 1966, the single became an immediate hit, catapulting to number eight on the pop charts. Although he had a series of moderate follow-up hits, including a re-release of "Billy and Sue,"

Thomas failed to reenter the Top Ten until 1968, when "Hooked on a Feeling" became a number-five, gold single. The following year, he scored his biggest hit with Burt Bacharach & Hal David's "Raindrops Keep Fallin' on My Head," taken from the hit film *Butch Cassidy and the Sundance Kid.* It was followed by a string of soft rock hits in the next two years, including "Everybody's Out of Town," "I Just Can't Help Believing," "No Love at All," and "Rock and Roll Lullaby," which featured guitarist Duane Eddy and the vocal group the Blossoms.

After "Rock and Roll Lullaby," Scepter Records went out of business and B.J. Thomas headed to Paramount Records. At Paramount, Thomas had no hits, prompting the singer to pursue a new country-pop direction at ABC Records. "(Hey Won't You Play) Another Somebody Done Somebody Wrong Song," his first single for ABC, became his second number-one record on the pop charts, as well as establishing a country career for the vocalist. For the next decade, he continued to have hits on the country charts, with a couple of songs—most notably "Don't Worry Baby"—crossing over into the pop charts. During this period, he switched record companies at a rapid pace, but it did nothing to slow the pace of his hits. Thomas hit his country peak in 1983 and 1984, when he had the number-one hits "Whatever Happened to Old Fashioned Love" and "New Looks From an Old Lover," as well as the Top Ten hits "The Whole World's in Love When You're Lonely" and "Two Car Garage." Throughout the '80s, B.J. Thomas recorded a number of hit gospel records for Myrrh concurrently with his country hits. At the end of the '80s, the hits began to dry up for Thomas, but he continued to tour, and put out the occasional country and gospel record in the '90s. *—Stephen Thomas Erlewine*

Tomorrow Never Comes / 1966 / Scepter ✦✦✦

Tomorrow Never Comes had the kind of mid-'60s music that's never gotten too much critical attention, perhaps because it was simultaneously so mainstream in tone yet too eclectic to easily classify. Still recording in Texas under the production of Huey P. Meaux, B.J. Thomas sang diverse material that blended varying degrees of pop, rock, country, soul, and swamp pop. Stylistically it's an impressive mixture, and Thomas' voice is pleasantly strong though not remarkably expressive or distinctive. However, none of the songs—largely written by his early associate Mark Charron (who also helped with the arrangements)—were all that special, though they were OK. None of them were hits, either, though "Daddy" is a dripping-sentimental gender rewrite of his mid-1966 hit single "Mama." That's a somewhat strange cut, as is "Plain Jane," a song about a girl who commits suicide after a prank fake invitation to the prom. So is "The Rains Came," which is the same Meaux song that the Sir Douglas Quintet had a raucous Tex-Mex stomping hit with, but which here gets an unrecognizably slow ballad arrangement that changes the melody substantially as well. *—Richie Unterberger*

I'm So Lonely I Could Cry / 1966 / Scepter ✦✦✦✦✦

Is he a country singer? Is he a soul singer? Those questions are never really answered as he goes from covering two Hank Williams songs to copying Tom Jones' arrangement of "It's Not Unusual" and singing "Midnight Hour." Either way, he doesn't quite pull it off. *—Jim Worbois*

On My Way / 1968 / Scepter ✦✦✦

This album features two of Thomas' biggest hits, both written by Mark James, who later wrote "Suspicious Minds" for Elvis. They are the most interesting tracks on this record, as most of the others are covers that add nothing to the original. *—Jim Worbois*

Young and in Love / 1969 / Scepter ✦✦✦

The move to Memphis results in a more cohesive sound for Thomas and a more satisfying album. Even though there were no hits on this record, it's more interesting than some of the records that did have hits. *—Jim Worbois*

Greatest Hits, Vol. 1 / 1969 / Scepter ✦✦✦

This *Greatest Hits* collection was compiled only three years into a career that was to span decades. As a result, it doesn't provide much of a retrospective of B.J. Thomas' career, and it was released just a bit too early to include his signature song, "Raindrops Keep Fallin' on My Head," which was released the same year. But it does a nice job of encapsulating his first three records, *Tomorrow Never Comes*, *I'm So Lonely I Could Cry*, and *On My Way.* Those albums, recorded between 1966-68, consisted of pop standards rendered in Thomas' resonant Texas baritone and backed by strings, piano, and guitar. A few of the songs on the record were made famous by Thomas, such as the catchy Mark Charron songs "Billy and Sue," "Mama," "Bring Back the Time," and "Plain Jane," but most had already been recorded before Thomas came along. There are two old Elvis Presley tunes, "Love Me Tender" and "Crying in the Chapel," as well as two by Hank Williams: "I Can't Help It If I'm Still in Love With You" and "I'm So Lonesome I Could Cry," which was Thomas' first big hit. The record, with its straightlaced lyrics and guy-next-door photos, projects a wholesome image that could as easily have been marketed in 1959 as 1969. *—Evan Cater*

Billy Joe Thomas / 1972 / Scepter ✦✦✦

This 1972 album shows B. J. Thomas in good form, capable of intelligently handling a lyric, especially when given worthy material. One of the highlights of the album and Thomas' career is the hit "Rock and Roll Lullaby," which approximates some heavenly Beach Boys-type harmonies to give a subtle yet powerful reading to the tale of a young unwed mother. Adding some fine touches to the well-thought-out production is Duane Eddy on guitar and the Blossoms on backup vocals. Another cut worthy of special mention is Jimmy Webb's "A Song for My Brother." Thomas delicately sings about the lost innocence of youth, accompanied only by Webb's classically inspired piano playing. It is an intelligent, evocative song, and both singer and player complement each other perfectly. "The Stories We Can Tell," written by John Sebastian, is also an excellent number given special treatment by Pete Drake's subtle and effective steel guitar. There are a few weak moments on the album, such as the beginning of "Happier Than the Morning," a Stevie Wonder tune that starts off dangerously close to MOR until being paradoxically saved by a Wonder harmonica solo. "Are We Losing Touch" also comes close to schmaltz territory, without much lyrical variation on the obvious theme. However, most of the songs are first-rate and arranged skillfully. Thomas himself has a gift for singing soulfully without apparent effort, swirling around lyrics with emotion yet rarely overstating or becoming excessively dramatic. That talent, along with the high quality of material and musicians presented here, makes for a highly listenable pop album. *—Michael Ofjord*

Greatest Hits / 1972 / Curb ✦✦✦

Curb's *Greatest Hits* is an 11-track budget-priced collection that features some of B.J. Thomas' biggest hits, including "Raindrops Keep Fallin' on My Head," "(Hey Won't You Play) Another Somebody Done Somebody Wrong Song," "Hooked on a Feeling" and "I'm So Lonesome I Could Cry." Although this isn't a bad budget-priced disc, there are better collections available, offering more songs, more hits and better sound for not much more money. *—Stephen Thomas Erlewine*

B.J. Thomas / 1977 / MCA ✦✦✦

After releasing two albums in 1975 produced by the legendary Chips Moman, one including his second chart-topping hit, "(Hey Won't You Play) Another Somebody Done Somebody Wrong Song," B.J. Thomas would change direction with two Chris Christian-produced albums in 1977, *Home Where I Belong* on the Christian label Myrrh and this self-titled release on MCA. A cover of the Beach Boys' "Don't Worry Baby" went Top 20 around the time of Thomas' 35th birthday in August of 1977, pleasant pop and the last of his 14 Top 40 hits that began 11 years earlier. Thomas looks a mess on the cover photo, and Christian should've known better than to prop up a recovering man and make him look so... desolate. Thomas looks more dead than alive on the album jacket, extinguished rather than born again, but the voice is still very much intact and sounding great. Of the 11 tunes in this collection, the three covers of established hit recordings are the most memorable. There's a great rendition of Barry Mann/Cynthia Weil's "Here You Come Again" (a few months before that tune would launch Dolly Parton into the pop charts) and a passable cover of Randy Goodrum's "It's Sad to Belong," which hit for England Dan & John Ford Coley two months before the version of "Don't Worry Baby" included here. Despite the singer being in great voice, the rest of the album has too many contrived moments that interrupt the flow. The neo-gospel of "Our Love Goes Marching On" feels out of place, and Christian's co-write, "Plastic Words," is a much too plastic song, even copping the "I love you mommy" line that worked so well for Helen Reddy in 1974 on her gem "You and Me Against the World." The "I love you daddy" here is so forced it adds insult to injury; perhaps the producer never heard the commandment "thou shalt not steal." Christian does redeem himself (pun intended) with "Still the Lovin's Fun," a superior middle-of-the-road track, of which there are not enough here. The result is an album that would have made a terrific EP, the influence of the born-again mafia having a much too negative effect on Thomas' career. Linda Hargrove's "Impressions" works well, as does the Troy Seals/Donnie Fritts number "We Had It All" and Mac Davis/Mark James' "Play Me a Little Traveling Music," but the shifting from pure adult contemporary to country to faith occurs so abruptly that it leaves this album uneven. As an interpreter, B.J. Thomas is one of the best in the business, and this was the perfect time for an entire album of covers of popular tunes to further establish the star in the mainstream. *—Joe Viglione*

B.J. Thomas in Concert / 1980 / MCA ✦✦✦

This album was recorded live at the Dallas Convention Center Little Theater on July 21, 1980. The concert took place not long after two key conversions for B.J. Thomas: his conversion to Christianity and his conversion to country music. The first is evident throughout the record, in the selection of songs like "Doctor God," "Hallelujah Thank You Jesus," and "Jesus Hearted People" and in his four minute "Testimony," which reveals that being born again helped him beat a drug habit. The second conversion is more or less undetectable on this recording. The music here tends more toward traditional gospel, not only in lyrical content and the piano, organ, and brass arrangements, but in Thomas' unusually flamboyant gospel vocals. The album demonstrates a level of versatility in Thomas' vocals that has rarely been heard on his studio recordings. The only song that makes a break from gospel is "Raindrops Keep Fallin' on My Head," the Burt Bacharach tune for which Thomas is most remembered. (Other than, perhaps, the theme song for the Kirk Cameron sitcom *Growing Pains.*) In his "Testimony," Thomas reveals that he's "not as well known as I'd like to be." Anyone who has been in the business as long as Thomas had to know that evangelical gospel music was not the fastest road to superstardom. Records like *B.J. Thomas in Concert* were a career risk that he was willing to take to be able to share his faith. Whatever you think of his music or his beliefs, that courage has to respected. *—Evan Cater*

Love Shines / 1983 / Epic ✦✦

Love Shines was one of the gospel records B.J. Thomas recorded after his conversion to Christianity. The Christian label Priority was undoubtedly thrilled to enlist the rangey mellifluousness of Thomas' voice, already famous for songs like "Raindrops Keep Fallin' on My Head" and "Hooked on a Feeling." The album was released in 1983, just as Thomas' country western career was taking off, and *Love Shines*, while not overtly country, makes ample use of steel guitar, harmonica, and other Southwestern conventions. The sound is best described as country-flavored Texas gospel pop. Lyrically, the album focuses on typical evangelical themes: the desire to lead a godly life, the difficulty of living faithfully in a fallen world, and the anticipation of the second coming. "That's What's Wrong With the World Today"—which was co-written by B.J.'s wife Gloria Thomas—features some of the most clever (if heavy-handed) lyrics, with lines like "No one stops to hear the prophet speak/Meanwhile in the alley the salesman holds a crowd/Putting artificial comforts in their hand/A profit the salesman understands." But *Love Shines* isn't really a songwriter's album. It's meant to serve two purposes: to win souls and to show off Thomas' considerable talents as a singer. *—Evan Cater*

● **Greatest Hits** / 1990 / Rhino ✦✦✦✦✦
Rhino's *Greatest Hits* is a definitive collection, chronicling Thomas' peak of popularity in the late '60s and early '70s. All of his big hits are here—"I'm So Lonesome I Could Cry," "Hooked on a Feeling," "Raindrops Keep Fallin' on My Head," "I Just Can't Help Believing," "No Love at All," "Rock & Roll Lullaby," "(Hey Won't You Play) Another Somebody Done Somebody Wrong Song"—along with a generous selection of lesser-known singles and album tracks. The end result may not change anybody's mind about Thomas—he was simply a good mainstream pop singer, which pleases some listeners but not others—but there's no denying that this is the ultimate Thomas collection. *—Stephen Thomas Erlewine*

Golden Classics / Sep. 1, 1995 / Collectables ✦✦✦

More Greatest Hits / Sep. 12, 1995 / Varese ✦✦✦✦✦
Picking up where Rhino's *Greatest Hits* collection left off, Varese's *More Greatest Hits* doesn't have any of the big hit singles, but it is ideal for those listeners that want to dig a little deeper into B.J. Thomas' extensive catalog. *—Thom Owens*

The Very Best of B. J. Thomas / Aug. 12, 1997 / Varese ✦✦✦✦✦
The "very best" in the title of this 17-track collection is somewhat debatable on a number of accounts. There are still more hits that could been crammed into this package, as six of the entries are non-chart (usually) album tracks. The non-inclusion of "Billy and Sue," "Mama" and "I'm So Lonesome I Could Cry" seems almost criminal, and while the album tracks are interesting and show his vocal prowess to great effect, when a compilation banners itself to be a "very best-of," it should be *just* that. Next time, save the album cuts for a rarities package somewhere down the reissue road. *—Cub Koda*

New Looks and Old Fashioned Love: The Best of B. J. Thomas / Jan. 25, 2000 / Razor & Tie ✦✦✦✦
Razor & Tie's 18-track *New Looks and Old Fashioned Love: The Best of B.J. Thomas* concentrates on B.J. Thomas' country-pop work for Columbia and Cleveland International Records in the '80s. Not every hit he had during this era is here but all the big hits are: "Whatever Happened to Old Fashioned Love," "New Looks From an Old Lover," "Two Car Garage," "The Whole World's in Love When You're Lonely," "The Girl Most Likely To," and "Night Life." The first half of the disc eases on by on its slick commercialism—which is a compliment. This is well-constructed, contemporary country-pop, melodic and polished tunes about modern concerns. They do sound a little dated, thanks to the synths and production techniques, but they're entertaining, unabashedly commercial period pieces from the early '80s. The second half of the record draws heavily from Thomas' 1986 covers album *Night Life*, which may have been more straight-ahead than its immediate predecessors, yet the production was too sterile (the drums are entirely too big) to give it the country grit it needs. Still, these covers lend credence to Thomas' skills as an interpretative singer, and they help make this a strong retrospective of the third act of his career. The last song—"As Long as We Got Each Other (theme from *Growing Pains*)," which happens to be a duet with Dusty Springfield—doesn't really fit the rest of the collection, aside from the fact that it was also cut in the '80s, but it's enjoyable and it's nice to have it included on a hits compilation. *—Stephen Thomas Erlewine*

Greatest Hits, Vol. 1 / Apr. 4, 2000 / Varese ✦✦✦✦
Greatest Hits, Vol. 1 was originally released in 1969, not in time to have B.J. Thomas' first number-one single, "Raindrops Keep Fallin' on My Head," be included on the collection. Other than that significant omission, the compilation is an excellent overview of Thomas' first few years of hit-making, made even better on Varese Sarabande's 2000 reissue, which includes the three charting singles that didn't make the original release—"Tomorrow Never Comes," "It's Only Love," and "Pass the Apple Eve." If you can overlook the absence of "Raindrops Keep Fallin' on My Head," this is a really nice compilation of his '60s work, but many casual fans might want to seek out Rhinos' *The Very Best of B.J. Thomas*, which covers all of his Scepter recordings up until 1972, not just the '60s cuts. *—Stephen Thomas Erlewine*

Love Songs & Lost Treasures / Jan. 30, 2001 / Varese ✦✦✦✦
Love Songs & Lost Treasures collects B.J. Thomas singles, album cuts, and previously unreleased tracks from the mid-'60s to the early '70s. Thomas delivers heartfelt renditions of the Carpenters' "Hurting Each Other," Brook Benton's "Rainy Night in Georgia," "Heartbreak Hotel," and "Smoke Gets in Your Eyes"; unreleased songs such as "I Just Don't Know What to Do With Myself" and "This Is a Love Song" reaffirm Thomas as a mellow, amiable country-pop singer. *—Heather Phares*

Benny Thomasson

Composer, Fiddle / String Bands, Bluegrass, Traditional Bluegrass, Progressive Bluegrass
This man is one of the legends of Texas fiddling, and beyond that a musician of such great power and scope that he is often compared to luminaries such as Charlie Parker for jazz or Isaac Stern for classical music. Meaning that just the sound of his instrument, instantly recognizable from the first few bars he plays, creates an immediate sense of intensity in the music that lesser players would have to take a few moments working up a sweat to create, if they could. His musical reach is as big as the state he came from, extending out in the development of Western swing as well as providing a historical background of traditional fiddling. He is one of the best examples of so-called "fiddlers," who despite technical and musical differences are violinists just like anyone else, playing the violin in a virtuoso manner without the benefit of classical training. Without the standard he set, there would surely be no players of the Mark O'Connor variety. In fact, the white instrument the latter hotshot fiddler plays was given to him by Thomasson himself.

He was one of ten children in a music-loving family. Both his father, Luke Thomasson, and uncle, Ed Thomasson, were well-known area fiddlers, and Benny has often recalled in interviews a memory of his father practicing a new tune, which eventually became the fiddle standard "Midnight on the Water." Local musicians hung around the house jamming and the way Benny tells it, back then a musician didn't have to look around for gigs. Anywhere Luke went, for example, somebody would ask him to play his fiddle. Keeping appointments or sticking to any kind of schedule would be impossible, because one never knew how long one of these spontaneous fiddle fests might last. Benny started playing fiddle at the age of three, but he did need his father's help to hold the instrument at the edge of a bed to lay the neck down on. Still, this early start gave him plenty of time to get ready for the musical career awaiting him. By the age of 19, he was eager to make his mark at a local fiddle contest. Believing he was one of the greatest players alive, he got up and gave it his all. No, this story does not end with him capturing all of the top honors and being acknowledged as one of the great geniuses of music. He was in fact ignored because he had yet to develop his powerful personal sound and concept. But the event was a kick in the rear, the musical wake-up call that often makes a young player decide that five or six hours of each day could be spent practicing instead of whatever else one might have been doing. He went to work on a repertoire of fiddle tunes, developing his own variations in sections without making any too drastic changes.

The approach worked for him and he began to finally be noticed by other musicians and the public alike. He went on to win the Texas State Fiddling Championship 15 times, plus three consecutive wins in the worldwide event held in Crockett, TX, and many other competitions. His ability to mow down opponents with a wave of his bow partially came from the superb repertoire he developed, which included two-part pieces he had learned from his dad, Canadian and Irish reels learned by ear, and also from published fiddle collections and the modern Texas breakdown style. The musical philosophy of Texas fiddling also tied in with the sometimes verbose or exaggerated nature of goings-on in that state, since a fiddle tune that might only have two parts to it in Virginia would appear in Texas with five different sections. Again, this was an aspect that might give a fiddler some extra artillery in a showdown. He further enhanced the sound and resonance of his instrument by utilizing a variety of interesting fiddle tunings. But perhaps one of the finest features of his playing was the technique he had learned from relatives, all of whom played in an older style of fiddle in which the bowing hand makes a larger turn than what would come to be considered the proper fiddling technique in later generations. This allows the player to bring in more notes with that hand, although it can limit the amount played with the other. This fiddler's bowing hand was once said to look like a pendulum swinging.

Musicians of Thomasson's generation were helped mightily in their career endeavors by the advent of radio. Thomasson and his brothers were in a variety of groups that played on broadcasts, including an old-time music program sponsored by the Sears Roebuck company, also one of the great sources for mail-order banjos, fiddles, and guitars. This particular show afforded excellent exposure and Thomasson and his brother, guitarist Lewis Thomasson, got the job just because they happened to show up for a random audition one afternoon when the show's producers still had no idea what music they were going to use to start the new show. The popularity of old-time music on the air eventually became understood by various record companies who sent their scouts literally all over the country in the '20s and '30s. Although many great old-time players left recorded documents because of these activities, listeners are not so lucky in the case of Benny Thomasson because the results of a 1929 recording session he did for OKeh with another brother, Jim Thomasson, have disappeared. It could have been the birth of the song "I Fall to Pieces," since apparently somebody with butterfingers dropped the wax master somewhere in the process of it being shipped back off to the big city. Nonetheless, the fiddler made up for the recording debacle later in his career. In the late '60s, he recorded for the County label with great results. His *Country Fiddling From the Big State* is practically a fiddle contest without the hoopla because within its grooves the fiddler presents a selection of both old-time and Western swing numbers such as might be presented in a contest event. In fact, the concept of a fiddler preparing a series of pieces to be performed in competition is credited to Thomasson, and has become the accepted norm for participants in such events.

In the '70s, Thomasson relocated to Washington state, where he struck up musical relationships with many of the young local regional players who were involved in a resurgence of interest in old-time music and various other traditional American styles. A young guitarist named Dudley Hill, who was totally enamored with Thomasson's recordings on the County label, approached the great master in the halls of a high-school where a Washington state fiddle contest was being held. "Can I play with you?" Hill asked with probably something of a tremble in his voice. The two went on to form a musical and personal bond, playing on several of each other's records, the results released on Voyager albums such as Thomasson's *Say Old Man Can You Play the Fiddle* or Hill's *From a Northern Family*. The former release contains some marvelous examples of the fiddler's work with backup in informal jam sessions. Being on the West Coast even gave Thomasson access to Hollywood. The younger disciple Byron Berline managed to arrange an on-screen appearance in the early Arnold Schwarzenegger film *Stay Hungry*, long before the tough guy created an image where he would be more comfortable smashing a banjo over someone's head then picking it. Thomasson and his family reportedly walked out of the screening when they realized there was going to be a nude love scene.

Despite the possibilities of concluding on such an entertaining note, it should be mentioned that recordings and oral legend are not the only means through which the music of this fiddler survives. The Seattle-based Petimer Press has published a book, entitled *Benny Thomasson Fiddle Transcriptions* for those brave enough to try this at home. *—Eugene Chadbourne*

● **Country Fiddling From the Big State** / 1970 / County ✦✦✦✦✦
There are several solo fiddle releases on this label that are out and out masterworks, and this is one of them. It is aptly titled, bringing to mind the many definitions of "big" Texans like to bring up, all of which suit Thomasson's music to a big T. Producer Charles Faurot begins his liner notes with a discussion of Thomasson's success in Texas fiddle contests. Apparently there are three major categories in these contests, and Thomasson is a regular winner in two of them, old-time tunes and Western swing. Both styles are represented here, but the latter might cause confusion for listeners wanting something with a Bob Wills feel. Remember, this is a solo fiddle record and Western swing becomes more

of a state of mind, involving lots of improvisation. "In Western swing you try and fiddle yourself into a tight spot…and then get out of it," Faurot quotes one fiddler. Although it is hard to imagine a tight spot in the state of Texas, at least geographically, Thomasson has the ability to maneuver where he wants to with a gorgeous tone that owes part of its robust flavor to the tunings used. Tempo is also striking; Thomasson has a way of creating drive while keeping the basic beat relaxed. This is music that is big even by Texas standards. Most of the tunes are traditional, although the title of one is a link to a tradition many listeners would most likely rather forget. Perhaps those offended can pretend "Nigger in the Woodpile" is a rap tune. It would have been interesting to have had at least some information about the recording session. —*Eugene Chadbourne*

Hank Thompson (Henry William Thompson)

b. Sep. 3, 1925, Waco, TX

Guitar, Vocals / Traditional Country, Western Swing, Honky Tonk, Bakersfield Sound
Hank Thompson was perhaps the most popular Western swing musician of the '50s and '60s, keeping the style alive with a top-notch band, tremendous showmanship, and a versatility that allowed him to expand his repertoire into romantic ballads and hardcore honky tonk numbers. Born September 3, 1925, in Waco, TX, Henry William Thompson was the son of immigrants from Bohemia and grew up idolizing Western swing and country musicians like Bob Wills, Jimmie Rodgers, and Gene Autry. He began learning harmonica and guitar as a child, and appeared in local talent shows as a teenager, which eventually led to his own local radio program (billed as Hank the Hired Hand). After graduating from high-school in 1943, Thompson joined the Navy as a radio technician and often wrote songs to entertain his fellow soldiers. Following his discharge, Thompson studied electrical engineering at Princeton through the G.I. Bill, but eventually decided to pursue music as a career. He returned to Waco and to the radio business, and set about putting together a band he dubbed the Brazos Valley Boys. They quickly became a popular live act around the area and recorded their first single, "Whoa Sailor" (a song Thompson had written in the Navy) for the Globe label in 1946. A few more singles followed for Bluebonnet, by which time Tex Ritter had become a Thompson admirer. Ritter helped Thompson land a record deal with Capitol in 1947, an association that would last for the next 18 years.

Thompson scored his first major hit for Capitol in 1949 with the smash "Humpty Dumpty Heart," the biggest of his six charting singles that year. In 1951, he hooked up with producer Ken Nelson, who would helm many of his most successful records. Those records included "The Wild Side of Life," a monster hit from 1952 (over three months at number one) that became Thompson's signature song. Its cynical attitude inspired an answer record by Kitty Wells called "It Wasn't God Who Made Honky Tonk Angels," which made her the first female artist in country music history with a million-selling record. Thompson continued to score hit after hit during the '50s, including 21 songs that reached the Top 20 on the country charts and five Top Tens in the year 1954 alone. A savvy promoter, Thompson devised a number of ways to make himself stand out from the crowd (even past his suave cowboy wardrobe): his early-'50s television show in Oklahoma City was the first variety show broadcast in color and he was the first country artist to tour with a sound and lighting system (put together using his Navy and collegiate experience), the first to receive corporate sponsorship, and the first to record in high-fidelity stereo. He also gave early breaks to musicians like guitar legend Merle Travis and female rockabilly pioneer Wanda Jackson. Toward the end of the '50s, Thompson began to create LPs that were more cohesive than just mere collections of singles plus filler; 1958's *Dance Ranch* and 1959's *Songs for Rounders* were Western swing/honky tonk masterpieces, especially the latter, which stirred up controversy with its groundbreakingly adult (some said decadent) lyrical content. In 1961, Thompson recorded the first live album ever released in the history of country music, the classic *At the Golden Nugget*.

After that burst of inspired creativity, Thompson's luck began to change: the public's taste was moving toward slick country-pop and the electrified Bakersfield sound and despite several more fine records, Thompson's relationship with Capitol ended in 1965. He first moved to Warner Bros., then ABC/Dot in 1968 (which became part of MCA in 1970). Thompson continued to record and tour and his singles charted regularly during the '70s all the way up to 1983, though he never matched the level of success he'd enjoyed in the '50s and early '60s. Even after the hits dried up, Thompson maintained a demanding concert tour schedule, playing all over the world. He was elected to the Country Music Hall of Fame in 1989 and continued to tour through late 2003 when he chose to retire from the road. —*Steve Huey*

Songs of the Brazos Valley / 1956 / Capitol ✦✦✦✦
Thompson's first album is an entertaining combination of fast-paced novelty tunes ("Rub-a-Dub-Dub"), slow romantic ballads ("Yesterday's Girl"), covers of numbers by Jimmie Rodgers ("Mother, The Queen of My Heart") and Bob Nolan ("At the Rainbow's End"), and surprisingly brisk adaptations of traditional material ("John Henry," with a killer solo by Billy Raymond Carson). A very solid ten-inch long-player. —*Bruce Eder*

North of the Rio Grande / 1956 / Capitol ✦✦✦
Thompson's second album employs the services of Merle Travis, who had hooked up with Thompson a few months earlier, and the lead guitar now has a wonderfully fluid quality, as graceful as it is swift. The album has more folk adaptations ("This Train"), a Bob Wills cover ("Big Beaver"), and some sentimental ballads ("The Little Rosewood Casket"), but the emphasis is mostly on romance, including slow pieces ("Gloria") and mid- and uptempo dance numbers ("Baby I Need Lovin'"). —*Bruce Eder*

New Recordings of Hank's All-Time Hits / 1956 / Capitol ✦✦✦
Here are re-recordings of older Thompson songs by the newest version of the Brazos Valley Boys, including "Swing Wide Your Gate of Love," "Humpty Dumpty Heart," "Whoa Sailor," "I'll Be Your Sweetheart For a Day," along with some new numbers. All of it is tight and hot. —*Bruce Eder*

Hank! / 1957 / Capitol ✦✦✦✦
This is a surprise, with Thompson and company covering swing standards ("Don't Be That Way") as well as adding their own parts of the repertory ("Prosperity Special,"

featuring Merle Travis on steel guitar). Also included is a cover of Bob Wills' "Hang Your Head In Shame" and Ernest Tubb's "Don't Look Now (But Your Broken Heart Is Showing)." The band was nearing its peak from this point in its history. —*Bruce Eder*

☆ **Dance Ranch** / 1958 / Capitol ✦✦✦✦✦
This is one of the group's best albums, filled with Western swing standards ("Bubbles in My Beer," "Drivin' Nails in My Coffin"), honky tonk ("Lawdy, What a Gal"), and originals by Thompson. The Brazos Valley Boys also contribute four instrumentals, including numbers associated with Bob Wills ("Beaumont Rag"), Artie Shaw ("Summit Ridge Drive"), and Woody Herman ("Woodchopper's Ball"). —*Bruce Eder*

Favorite Waltzes / 1959 / Capitol ✦✦✦
This is a sort of novelty album, and not an entirely successful one, consisting of waltz-tempo pieces, backed by chorus, including "Let Me Call You Sweetheart," "What Will I Do On Monday," and "Shenandoah Waltz." Not Thompson's most exciting record, but it makes for pleasant enough listening, and the musicianship is very solid. —*Bruce Eder*

☆ **Songs for Rounders** / 1959 / Capitol ✦✦✦✦✦
This is maybe Thompson's best LP, made up of songs about the rougher, raunchier sides of life, including "Cocaine Blues," "Little Blossom," "Deep Elem" (a real hot rocking number), and "Rovin' Gambler." This record was considered very controversial within conservative country music circles at the time, and in many ways broke a lot of ground within the field. This was also his first stereo album. —*Bruce Eder*

Most of All / 1960 / Capitol ✦✦✦

This Broken Heart of Mine / 1960 / Capitol ✦✦✦
It was a year between *Songs for Rounders* album and *Most of All*, owing to the backlog of sides he had built up, but the results of the Thompson band's first stereo album were so encouraging that they were back in the studio to do more in stereo. The songs are very solid, including a re-recording of "Rock In the Ocean." —*Bruce Eder*

An Old Love Affair / 1961 / Capitol ✦✦✦✦
Here are covers of Jimmie Davis ("I Dreamed of an Old Love Affair"), Marty Robbins ("Sing Me Something Sentimental"), and Floyd Tillman's "I Gotta Have My Baby Back," along with a bunch of Thompson originals. —*Bruce Eder*

☆ **At the Golden Nugget** / 1961 / Capitol ✦✦✦✦✦
At the Golden Nugget was not only the first live album ever recorded for commercial release by a single country artist, but is arguably Hank Thompson's best album, representing his amalgam of honky tonk and Western swing better than any other long-player in his history. Most country artists of his generation responded better to the enthusiasm of an audience than to the cold, usually tense, often retake-laden ambience of a studio, and Thompson had a very satisfied audience that night in March of 1961. The record is made all the more alluring by the presence of Merle Travis (who had played on Thompson's recordings since 1953) on lead guitar, and two numbers out of Travis' repertory ("Nine Pound Hammer," "John Henry") are included among the 13 songs here. The CD transfer, from 1995, is state of the art, and the historical notes are an extra treat. Along with Capitol's 1996 *Vintage Collections* compilation, this is essential to own, and not just for country music fans—rock & rollers (and not just Flying Burrito Bros. aficionados) can also learn a few things from Thompson. —*Bruce Eder*

Cheyenne Frontier Days / 1962 / Capitol ✦✦✦✦
Thompson's second live album in one year isn't nearly as successful as *At the Golden Nugget*, lacking the latter's near-perfect acoustics, although the performances are quite good. The songs include not only a bunch of Thompson standards, including "Rose City Chimes" and "You're Walking on My Heart," but the real highlight is a Thompson-sung version of Merle Travis' "Cincinnati Lou" with the songwriter on guitar. —*Bruce Eder*

The Number One Country and Western Band / 1962 / Capitol ✦✦✦
This is a hot all-instrumental album, featuring numbers drawn from a multitude of sources, including established country standards like "Under The Double Eagle" and even adaptations of German folk song ("Westphalia Waltz"). —*Bruce Eder*

The Best of Hank Thompson / 1963 / Capitol ✦✦✦

Live at the State Fair of Texas / 1963 / Capitol ✦✦✦✦
It took serious effort, against genuine sonic adversity, to get a usable album from these October 1962 live dates, but the effort was worth it—the group sounds really good, the choice of material is perfect, and if the *Golden Nugget* album didn't exist, this wouldn't be a terrible substitute. Needless to say, many of the songs dwell on the Lone Star State, including a cover of Ernest Tubb's "There's A Little Bit of Everything In Texas." The fiddle playing by Jimmy Belkin, Roddy Bristol, and Billy Jack Saucer is especially dazzling, and Merle Travis and Billy Gray acquit themselves well on guitar as well. —*Bruce Eder*

Breakin' in Another Heart / 1965 / Capitol ✦✦✦
At a glance, *Breakin' in Another Heart* looks like a half-hearted effort, since the title track is a re-recording of one of Thompson's decade-old hits and the album was recorded at the end of his long tenure with Capitol Records, but it is not a throwaway. The dozen songs are split 50/50 with ballads on side one and Thompson's originals on side two. On the ballad side, "There's No You" is a beauty that demonstrates the ease with which Thompson negotiated sophisticated melodies, and the other songs are nearly as good. The originals tend toward ballads, too, which makes this a very laid-back affair overall. "I'd Have Never Found Somebody New" is an echoey waltz, and the remake of "Breakin' in Another Heart" is a near replica of the original but perhaps a bit mellower, since Thompson's voice had deepened. Thompson remained on the charts for decades without ever updating his sound much, which proves the enduring appeal of his style. —*Greg Adams*

The Luckiest Heartache in Town / 1965 / Capitol ✦✦✦✦

☆ **A Six Pack to Go** / 1966 / Capitol ♦♦♦♦♦
1965 was the year Hank Thompson & His Brazos Valley Boys began a run of drinking records, and this was the first. *A Six Pack to Go* is a classic by any country music standard: It is full of honky tonk songs, heartbreak songs, a couple of polkas, and a few Western swing tunes to boot. With all of the songs centering around drinking—the title track, "Drunkard's Blues," "Hangover Heart," the Bob Wills/Tommy Duncan classic "Bubbles in My Beer," "Honky Tonk Town," and the downright depressing "Hangover Tavern" among others. The delivery Thompson gives them is all but depressing, however. He is a bouncy singer with a band that always plays on the right side of honky tonk and has Western swing in the heart of everything they play. But what sets *A Six Pack to Go* apart from many of Thompson's other recordings is the playing of guitar icon Merle Travis kicking it on the lead. He bends and turns notes no matter how laid-back the track. Thompson's effortless delivery stands in sharp contrast to this and makes for a startling kind of intensity in the proceedings. Each song is a furthering of the journey into alcoholism, its cause—usually women—and no cure. While the songs have a cherry feel to them, this is one dark record, and there is no redemption anywhere present. A classic. *—Thom Jurek*

Breakin' the Rules / 1966 / Capitol ♦♦♦

Where is the Circus (And Other Heart Breakin' Hits) / 1966 / Warner Bros. ♦♦

Just an Old Flame / 1967 / Capitol ♦♦♦

The Countrypolitan Sound of Hank's Brazo Boys / 1967 / Warner Bros. ♦♦♦

The Best of Hank Thompson, Vol. 2 / 1967 / Capitol ♦♦♦♦

☆ **On Tap, in the Can, or in the Bottle** / 1968 / Dot ♦♦♦♦♦
Where 1965 saw Hank Thompson & His Brazos Valley Boys start a cycle of drinking albums that offered, in cheery fashion, the dark side of the bottle, that cycle came to an end after a ton of touring and three years later with one of the, if not the, finest Thompson recordings of all time. *On Tap, in the Can, or in the Bottle* features 12 tracks of Thompson's best songwriting either solo or with partners, all centered around a moving set of Western swing, honky tonk, and country boogie melodies that features subjects of loss, grief, alcoholism, and its costs. These songs are sad, dark, and fermented in heartbreak and tragedy, yet along with Merle Travis helping out on lead guitar on cuts such as "He's Got a Way With Women," the title track, "Here Is the Circus," "Where Is the Clown," "I've Got a Date With a Teardrop," "No. 1 on the Hurt Parade," and "Love Walked Out Before She Did," darkness never sounded so bright and as a result so pathological. In addition, Thompson knew how to construct the country song in such a way that it left the listener wanting always more. There isn't a cut here over three minutes, and virtually by today's standards, every cut could have been a single. A masterpiece of writing, playing, sequencing, and overall honky tonk bravado, *On Tap, in the Can, or in the Bottle* is one of the greatest country records of all time. *—Thom Jurek*

Hank Thompson Salutes Oklahoma / 1969 / Dot ♦♦♦

Smoky the Bar / 1969 / Dot ♦♦♦♦♦
On the back cover of Hank Thompson's 1969 classic *Smoky the Bar*, Carol Ehler calls Thompson "The Poet Laureate of beer drinkers." No sh*t. With titles like "Let's Get Drunk and Be Somebody," "Pop a Top," "What's Made Milwaukee Famous (Has Made a Loser Out of Me)," "Drunkard's Blues," as well as a few sidewinders like "Cocaine Blues" and Jimmie Rodgers' "My Rough and Rowdy Ways," you get the picture. This is honky tonk music made for the people who frequent them. Thompson may have changed his topic by the late '60s to almost exclusively drinking songs, but his unique musical vision hadn't. The hard Ernest Tubb honky tonk and the gorgeous swing of Bob Wills and the vocal harmonies of the early cowboy songs meld perfectly in Thompson's relaxed croon, and with a host of whining fiddles, strummed guitars, and barely audible percussion all covered by a tinkling upright piano. In fact, his approach to his material is so laid-back, lyrics like "through these bloodshot eyes the whole world looks rosy..." sound perfectly natural. There are some interesting sonic textures and ambiences here added by producer Joe Allison, especially the film noir-ish backdrops created by the pedal steel and the Nashville sounds in "Drunkard's Blues." But if Thompson had an anthem, it was "Pop a Top," a song so perfectly suited to the foolish drunk who's lost everything except the ability to drink. The hard Western swing with elements of country boogie is laced inside a barroom midtempo romp laced with fiddles (not strings). This and "Six Pack to Go" were the man's anthems, and in the refrain: "Pop a top again/I think I'll have another round/Another one my friend/And then I'll be gone and you can let/Some other fool sit down." Thompson's drinking songs are tremendous for the way they chronicle both the good-time aspect and camaraderie of drinking and the dark side caused by its excess. This is one of Thompson's finest works from top to bottom and should be sought out by every fan of great 1960s country music. *—Thom Jurek*

Next Time I Fall in Love, I Won't / 1971 / Dot ♦♦♦

Cab Driver: A Salute to the Mills Brothers / 1972 / Dot ♦♦♦
Hank Thompson's 1972 tribute to the Mills Brothers is an interesting idea: ten country and Western swing versions of songs associated with the popular black vocal group. Thompson's own compositions were often melodically sophisticated, so he has no trouble negotiating these songs that have become, in many cases, pop and jazz standards. The repertoire suggests that Thompson followed the Mills closely since "Cab Driver" was a late, minor hit for the group in 1968. Thompson charted higher with that song than the Mills did, and also enjoyed modest success with his version of "Glow Worm." The Mills Brothers, in a fitting turnaround, recorded country music in the '70s, so Thompson's unusual enterprise makes an odd sort of sense in retrospect. *—Greg Adams*

25th Anniversary Album / 1972 / Dot ♦♦♦
In the late '60s, Hank Thompson started recording for Dot Records after a long and successful run at Capitol. It was at Capitol where he scored many of his biggest hits, such as "Wild Side of Life," "Whoa! Sailor," and "Humpty Dumpty Heart." These and many other of his chart-toppers from the '40s and '50s can be heard on Capitol's *Vintage* collection. Dot's *25th Anniversary Album* contains the same songs, but in re-recorded versions from the late '60s and early '70s. These new renditions are decent, but are mired in cloyingly sweet harmony vocals, roller-rink guitar solos, and stilted rhythm tracks; this sound is a far cry from the hard-swinging and somewhat rough-hewn backing his longstanding band, the Brazos Valley Boys, provided him with during the '50s. There are some of Thompson's original Dot hits here, like "On the Tap, in the Can, or in the Bottle," but they are more novel than memorable. *25th Anniversary Album* is fun to listen to, but if you want a solid collection of Thompson's prime recordings, get the Capitol collection and leave this one for completists and curio seekers. *—Stephen Cook*

Kindly Keep It Country / 1973 / Dot ♦♦

A Six Pack to Go / 1974 / Dot ♦♦♦♦♦

20 Greatest Hits / 1986 / Deluxe ♦♦
For the most part, *20 Greatest Hits* offers re-recordings of Thompson chestnuts like "Wild Side of Life," "A Six Pack to Go" and "Humpty Dumpty Heart." *—Jason Ankeny*

Capitol Collectors Series / 1989 / Capitol ♦♦♦♦♦
Hank Thompson's *Capitol Collector's Series* contains a good cross-section of his big hits and lesser-known singles, making it an excellent single-disc introduction to one of the finest honky tonk vocalists of the late '40s and early '50s. *—Thom Owens*

Country Music Hall of Fame Series / 1992 / MCA ♦♦♦
While MCA's *Country Music Hall of Fame Series* is usually a good place to check out country stars for the first time, this edition featuring Hank Thompson doesn't quite make the grade. But, if you are impressed with Capitol's *Vintage* disc, which collects most of his classic work from the '50s ("The Wild Side of Life," "Whoa!, Sailor"), it's not such a bad idea to come back to this latter-day collection afterwards. Even with some extra rinky-dink arrangements, Thompson still shines through with a honky tonk-lite mix of drinking sides ("On Tap, in the Can, or in the Bottle"), sentimental gems ("Just an Old Flame"), and life chronicles ("Money, Trouble and Love"). It's a fine, if nonessential roundup. *—Stephen Cook*

Hank Thompson & His Brazos Valley Boys / 1996 / Country Routes ♦♦♦
The French LP *Hank Thompson & His Brazos Valley Boys* is a compilation of live radio performances Thompson and his band gave in 1952, just as his career was beginning to take off with the massive success of "The Wild Side of Life." Even though neither that song, or any of his earlier, lesser hits, are included on this collection, the album doesn't suffer as a result. Thompson & the Brazos Valley Boys sound tough and inspired, bringing a considerable amount of grit to his swinging honky tonk. The record remains an item for collector's only, but for those willing to seek it out, it is an enjoyable and fascinating historical artifact. *—Stephen Thomas Erlewine*

★ **Vintage** / 1996 / Capitol ♦♦♦♦♦
Here are 20 songs, containing nearly all of the essential items from Thompson's history with Capitol Records from 1947 through 1961, from "(I've Got A) Humpty Dumpty Heart" through "Oklahoma Hills." In addition to containing all of the expected hits, such as "The Wild Side of Life," there are a few nice bonus tracks, such as the Brazos Valley Boys' instrumental "Big Beaver," and excellent notes, depicting Thompson's arrival at the label, the founding of the Brazos Valley Boys, the beginning of his long and profitable relationship with producer Ken Nelson, and the background on each song's recording and history. *—Bruce Eder & Thom Owens*

Hank Thompson & His Brazos Valley Boys (1946–1964) / 1996 / Bear Family ♦♦♦♦♦
It's 12 CDs, 321 tracks, and lists for over $300, but for those with the budget or the discipline to save up for it, this box set is it—not only every record that Hank Thompson cut for Capitol between 1947 and 1964, but also his ultra-rare, never-before-reissued sides for Globe and Blue Bonnet from 1946 and 1947. Disc one opens with those early jewels—there's not a less-than-first-rate recording on this 30-song CD, and the playing, while a little crude compared to Thompson's later work, is a match for anything being recorded at the time. Disc three begins Thompson's history as an album artist, and the character and quality of the material changes somewhat—there are a few more slow numbers, and some slight sameness begins to intrude into the music, but the quality of the performances is undiminished. Disc four has the major part of his second album along with a ton of singles, and the latter are generally more brisk and upbeat than the LP material. Disc five includes the first extensive re-records of Thompson's older stuff, and also includes Thompson's brief foray into rock & roll, as well as lots of Western swing standards. Disc seven opens real hot, with the stuff off of *Songs for Rounders*, and a bunch of instrumentals that round out the 1958 material, then jumps ahead a year to his next session. Discs nine and ten jump ahead a bit to Thompson's last studio work for Capitol, released through 1965. Discs 11 and 12 are devoted to Thompson's live albums from the early 1960s. And to top it off, this set comes with an oversized *hardcover* book, featuring not only a biography and sessionography, but recollections by Thompson about every recording session. *—Bruce Eder*

The Best of Hank Thompson: 1966–1979 / Oct. 22, 1996 / Varese ♦♦♦♦♦
Hank Thompson didn't stop recording or having hits when he left Capitol Records, although given the lack of attention paid to his Warner and Dot albums (along with their scarcity on CD), it sometimes seems that way. Fact of the matter is, Thompson continued to chart steadily into the early '70s and as late as 1979 he had a Top 30 country hit. Also, he continued to deliver satisfying music, as Varese's terrific 1996 collection *The Best of Hank Thompson: 1966-1979* proves. Spanning 16 tracks, this covers his brief time at Warner (he signed with them shortly after leaving Capitol in 1965 and was gone by 1968) and his decade stint at Dot (which eventually became ABC, then MCA); there are four

Warner cuts, including a duet with Merle Travis, with the remaining 14 drawn from Dot/ABC. While it is true that his backing bands weren't quite as stunning as they were during the peak of his Capitol recordings and his material was a little inconsistent, with the productions being considerably more polished and streamlined, these are relative assessments—compared to other straight-ahead country from the same era, Thompson's Warner and Dot material ranks very high indeed, and it's aged very well. Thompson's gifts as a writer, singer, and bandleader were so prodigious it would have been shocking if they had disappeared completely just because a few years passed and he switched labels, yet it's still a nice surprise to hear how flat-out fun this collection is. Thompson remains a sharp, clever songwriter—he's great finding small, funny truths and twisting commonplace phrases, as on "He's Got a Way With Women" (which is followed up with "and he's just got away with mine")—and a great judge of material, finding songs that suited his warm, friendly voice and his similarly wide open-hearted band. Even when a song gets a little silly—such as "I See Them Everywhere," when Thompson starts seeing little green men when the bottle empties—his delivery is so charming and the band so good, it's easy to roll along and just enjoy the sound of the band. Not all of his charting hits for Dot are here, but most are and it's a great summary of the latter half of Thompson's active recording career, offering substantial proof that when he was at his best, he was still as good as ever was. Hopefully, more of this material—either reissues of actual albums or a box set—will see eventually see the light of day. *—Stephen Thomas Erlewine*

Radio Broadcasts (1952) / Aug. 19, 1997 / Flyright ♦♦♦♦

From one standpoint, a disc of single-take radio performances from Hank Thompson is superfluous, because Thompson recorded three official live albums for Capitol Records. On the other hand, this stuff—cut for the U.S. government's Office of Price Stabilization in 1952—is a good deal earlier than any of Thompson's official live LPs, and so it captures his band and his sound at a choice point in their history. The sound is fairly clean, but raw and loud throughout this 16-song collection. The micing is close and the volume is high, so that one gets a sense of what Thompson's live sound of the period was like, rougher and crunchier than his studio sides. Dusty Stewart's steel guitar and Billy Gray's lead guitar are especially impressive, and Thompson's singing is extraordinary. The songs include "Shotgun Boogie," which Thompson had yet to record officially, as well as numbers by Hank Williams ("I Can't Help It"), Floyd Tillman ("I Gotta Have My Baby Back"), and others whom Thompson admired. It all greatly expands the range of available Thompson recordings, a welcome event in any case. *—Bruce Eder*

Hank World: The Unissued World Transcriptions / Aug. 24, 1999 / Bloodshot ♦♦♦

Hank Thompson is in the Country Music Hall of Fame, and few artists deserve to be there more than he does. Since 1948, he's made the country music charts nearly 80 times. He wrote "The Wild Side of Life" (the tune that Kitty Wells answered with "It Wasn't God Who Made Honky Tonk Angels," thus launching her career) and was the first country artist to record a live album and to be recorded in stereo. He brought Western swing into the '50s with a flourish, using a warm, folky style that was equal parts Bob Wills and Merle Travis, but with a fingerprint all its own. *Hank World* stems from recordings Thompson made in the early '50s in a studio set up in his house. These sides were separate from the commercial recordings he was making for Capitol, so there's a wealth of unissued material to delve into, giving a much bigger picture of what the Hank Thompson band would have sounded like in a honky tonk on a hot night back then. This is country with a "western" appended to it. And since there simply isn't enough of the real thing around anymore, these performances are worth their weight in gold. Tracks like "New Deal of Love," "My Front Door Is Open," and "When You're Lovin', You're Livin'" make excellent additions to Thompson's lengthy discography; they're full of inventive wordplay and Thompson's honeyed vocals. And band instrumentals like "Texas Playboy Rag" and "Don't Be That Way" show that his Brazos Valley Boys could tackle everything from Bob Wills to Benny Goodman with a finesse that combined true swing with a tight ensemble sound. Next to any of Thompson's classic Capitol recordings, this is your next stop—an excellent purchase if you want to amass a collection of the real stuff. You can dance, drink, and cry in your beer to it—all still major prerequisites if the music is to stay true to its roots. And the roots on this set are very deep indeed. *—Cub Koda*

☆ **Dance Ranch/Songs for Rounders** / Sep. 21, 1999 / Koch ♦♦♦♦♦

Koch's *Dance Ranch/Songs for Rounders* combines two of Hank Thompson's greatest albums on one disc. Recorded in 1957, *Dance Ranch* is one of Thompson & the Brazos Valley Boys' best albums, filled with Western swing standards ("Bubbles in My Beer," "Drivin' Nails in My Coffin"), honky tonk ("Lawdy, What a Gal"), and originals by Thompson. The Brazos Valley Boys also contribute four instrumentals, including numbers associated with Bob Wills ("Beaumont Rag"), Artie Shaw ("Summit Ridge Drive"), and Woody Herman ("Woodchopper's Ball"). Released in 1959, *Songs for Rounders* may be Thompson's best LP, made up of songs about the rougher, raunchier sides of life, including "Cocaine Blues," "Little Blossom," "Deep Elem" (a real hot rocking number), and "Rovin' Gambler." This record was considered very controversial within conservative country music circles at the time, and in many ways broke a lot of ground within the field. This was also his first stereo album. *—Bruce Eder*

☆ **A Six Pack to Go/Breakin' in Another Heart** / Dec. 28, 1999 / EMI ♦♦♦♦♦

In 1999, EMI released *A Six Pack to Go/Breakin' in Another Heart*, which contained two complete albums—*A Six Pack to Go* (1966, originally released on Capitol) and *Breakin' in Another Heart* (1965, originally released on Capitol)—by Hank Thompson on one compact disc. *—Jason Birchmeier*

In the Mood for Hank / Jul. 11, 2000 / Jasmine ♦♦

These 26 radio transcription recordings from the '50s include a number of remakes of Thompson's own hits, as well as other weepers, novelties, and instrumentals. The liner notes don't reveal where these recordings were derived, but it is probably World Transcriptions, the source of material that has appeared on CDs from a couple of other labels, too. The sound quality could be better—Jasmine's mastering from vintage transcription discs seems a little indifferent at times—but many of the performances are fine. There are better packages available if you are in the market for a collection of Hank Thompson's transcriptions, but this one will do in a pinch. *—Greg Adams*

Seven Decades / Jul. 18, 2000 / Hightone ♦♦♦♦

Seven Decades is an impressive album any way you look at it: Thompson sounds almost as good as ever, he's still writing some great material (the album is more than half original), and the songs he chose to cover are interesting and even ambitious. "Condo in Hondo" and "Lobo the Hobo" indulge Thompson's trademark wordplay, while "Medicine Man" celebrates the bygone days of the medicine show. Tex Williams' hit "The Night Miss Nancy Ann's Hotel for Single Girls Burned Down" gets an entertaining run-through, while "Dinner for One, Please James" and the Kingston Trio's "Scotch and Soda" are smoky sounding and ready-made for the supper club. Thompson even breathes some fire into such well-worn covers as "In the Jailhouse Now" and "Wreck of the Old '97." With crystal clear sound, tasteful production, and lots of great Merle Travis-style picking by Thom Bresh, *Seven Decades* is sturdy enough to stand alongside Thompson's best. *—Greg Adams*

Hayden Thompson

Vocals / Rockabilly

Thompson made his recording debut with "I Feel the Blues Coming On" on the Von label in 1954. He signed with Sun in 1956 and recorded the Junior Parker song "Love My Baby" with support from Billy Riley's band and Jerry Lee Lewis. Held back for several months, the single failed to become a hit when it was finally released in 1957; none of his other Sun recordings yielded a hit either. Disappointed by his lack of success, Thompson moved to Chicago in 1958 and recorded for several labels, including B.E.A.T., Arlen, and Kapp. His country-tinged recordings for Kapp enabled him to make a guest appearance on the *Opry*, but he never achieved the stardom he desired. *—Todd Kristel*

● **Rockabilly Guy 1954–1962** / Charly ♦♦♦♦

Joe Thompson

b. Dec. 9, 1918, Mebane, NC

Vocals, Fiddle / Old-Timey

Some memories last a life time, especially sweeter memories of the forbidden. For old-timey North Carolina fiddler Joe Thompson, some of his fondest and earliest memories revolve around music and more specifically around his father's fiddle, which was forbidden to him when he was a boy. Well into his eighth decade, Thompson liked to recall the days of his childhood when his farmhouse was quiet and the adults were occupied elsewhere. He'd make his way into his parents' bedroom, intent on getting his six-year-old hands on his daddy's fiddle. All the while, he'd do his best to ignore the warnings from his father that replayed in his head predicting that he'd break the instrument because he was too young. Determined, Thompson found the fiddle and played it. He'd never had a lesson, but simply learned by keeping his eyes on his father's deft playing. His mother, Rosie, wise to her boy's desire to make music as magically as her husband Walter, covered his tracks so he wouldn't get into trouble. The boy soon owned his own child-sized fiddle, thanks to a neighbor who raised money by selling seeds. Unfortunately, the new fiddle lacked strings, but Thompson didn't let that fact deter him. He promptly devised his own strings out of a wire screen.

When not taking care of their farms, Walter Thompson and his brother, John Arch Thompson, frequently played for local square dances and the duo proved a popular attraction. Joe Thompson joined the act when he was about seven years old, still so small that when he sat to play he wasn't able to put his feet flat on the floor. John Arch's son, Odell Thompson, also played his banjo for the local dances. Joe Thompson continued to perform through the 1930s at Southern dances. His cousin Odell, however, turned to the blues guitar, although he never completely gave up old-timey fiddle music. The Thompson cousins often played such songs as "Hook and Line" and "Cindy Gal" for family and friends. With the renewed awareness of folk music during the 1970s, including that of African Americans, Thompson and his fiddle entered the spotlight. He and his cousin played at a number of festivals, the prestigious Carnegie Hall, and traveled to Australia. In 1991, the North Carolina Folk Heritage Awards honored the cousins. Unfortunately, Odell Thompson passed away in 1994 as the result of a car crash. Joe Thompson continued on performing with the support from the likes of Clyde Davis and Bob Carlin up until he suffered a stroke in the fall of 2001, which nearly ended his illustrious career. Thompson's determination to play overcame the doctor's prediction that he would never perform again when Thompson returned to the stage in the spring of 2003. *—Linda Seida*

Family Traditions / Jul. 27, 1999 / Rounder ♦♦♦

Thompson's fiddle playing is raw and honest and this disc captures him in an informal setting. While he plays all too familiar tunes on the disc, such as "Old Joe Clark" and "Soldier's Joy," his style does put some life back into them. *—Tim Sheridan*

Sue Thompson (Eva Sue McKee)

b. Jul. 19, 1926, Nevada, MO

Fiddle, Vocals, Guitar / Traditional Country, Nashville Sound/Countrypolitan

Best known for her breathy, little-girl singing voice, Sue Thompson had several novelty pop hits in the early '60s before reinventing herself as a more mature country singer in the mid-'70s. Thompson was born Eva Sue McKee in Nevada, MO, in 1925 and was singing cowgirl songs and playing guitar on-stage by the age of seven. After her family moved to San Jose, she appeared on the local *Hometown Hayride* TV show during her teens. She worked in a defense plant during World War II, then married and had a daughter at age 20; however, the marriage lasted only three years, and she subsequently returned to performing in northern California clubs. Her winning performance at a San Jose talent contest caught the attention of singer Dude Martin, who was also a bandleader and radio/TV host. Martin invited her to join his band and became her husband not long after; the two recorded some duets, and "If You Want Some Lovin'" helped Thompson land her first solo deal with Mercury. Meanwhile, Martin added singer/comedian Hank Penny to his revue in 1952; within a year, Thompson divorced Martin and married Penny, and the two hosted a TV show in Los Angeles for two years before moving to Las Vegas to work the casinos. They recorded separately and together for Decca but failed to land any major hits.

Thompson signed with Hickory Records in 1960 and landed two Top Five pop hits the following year with the John D. Loudermilk-penned novelty tunes "Sad Movies (Make Me Cry)" and "Norman." Two more Loudermilk numbers, 1962's "James (Hold the Ladder Steady)" and 1965's "Paper Tiger," brought her further success. During this era, Thompson played effectively to the teen audience thanks to her cute, extremely young-sounding voice, despite the fact that she was pushing 40. She recorded sporadically through the remainder of the '60s, without finding similar success. In 1972, she teamed up with country singer Don Gibson for three duet albums over the next two years; some of their songs charted respectably, in particular "I Think They Call It Love" and "Oh, How Love Changes." Thompson also managed a few solo hits during this period, the biggest of which was "Big Mable Murphy." Her last chart single came in 1976 with "Never Naughty Rosie," and she subsequently concentrated on the Las Vegas casino circuit. She remarried once again and later moonlighted as an MC at North Hollywood's famed *Palomino Club* for a time. She settled in Las Vegas permanently and performed from time to time in the '90s. *— Steve Huey*

Meet Sue Thompson / 1962 / Hickory ◆◆◆
A quick read-through of the song titles and writers' credits might give one the impression of a country album in the offing, but in reality this is a pleasant honky tonk-pop hybrid. With its doo wop beats and relentlessly burbling baritone sax, the album brings to mind a jukebox, a chocolate milkshake, and an early '60s-style cute blonde, which in this case would be Sue Thompson, a talented musician and singer. Her version of "Oh, Lonesome Is Me" is among the best of quite a bunch of recordings of this song, which she accomplishes due to the strength of her voice and plenty of sparkle. Her choice of songwriters is tasteful, as there are several numbers here from John D. Loudermilk as well as songs by Don Everly and the brothers Bryant and Kershaw. *— Eugene Chadbourne*

Greatest Hits / 1974 / Curb ◆◆◆◆◆
Curb's *Greatest Hits* is a 12-track budget-priced collection that features some of Sue Thompson's biggest hits, including "Sad Movies (Make Me Cry)," "Paper Tiger," "Candy and Roses," "Never Naughty Rosie," "She Reminds Me of Me" and "Tennessee Waltz." Although this isn't a bad budget-priced disc, there are better collections available, offering more songs, more hits and better sound for not much more money. *— Stephen Thomas Erlewine*

Golden Classics / Sep. 1, 1995 / Collectables ◆◆◆◆◆
The combination of Sue Thompson's Betty Boop voice and songwriter John D. Loudermilk's cutesy material (which was pure bubblegum before such a term existed) produced two major pop hits in the early '60s, "Norman" and "Sad Movies Make Me Cry." Thompson placed ten other minor hit singles on the charts through the mid-'60s before pairing up with Don Gibson for a series of minor-to-moderate country hits in the '70s. *Golden Classics* has all of Thompson's Top 100 pop hits plus several non-hits, most of which were written by Loudermilk or the team of Felice & Boudleaux Bryant. A couple of Thompson's singles that "bubbled under" the Top 100 are omitted, but *Golden Classics* is otherwise a thorough anthology of this singer's early pop hits. *— Greg Adams*

● **The Very Best of Sue Thompson** / 2003 / Varese ◆◆◆◆◆

Cyndi Thomson
b. Oct. 19, 1976, Tifton, GA
Vocals / Country-Pop, Contemporary Country
Cyndi Thomson grew up in Tifton, GA, the last of four sisters. Following in her older siblings' footsteps, Thomson started singing in church, and later in high-school and at talent pageants. She moved to Atlanta to attend college, but soon felt drawn to Nashville, and decided to try and make it in Music City. Like any young Nashville hopeful, Thomson got a few small breaks here and there, but they came in between lots of heartache and struggle. She enrolled in Belmont University's music business program, waitressed, and did a bit of modeling until she was able to catch a real break. Eventually, the young singer met songwriter Tommy Lee James, and the two began writing songs together. A recording contract with Capitol Nashville followed, as did a management agreement with Simon Renshaw (Dixie Chicks). Thomson's debut, *My World*, appeared in July 2001, and the album went gold behind the number-one single "What I Really Meant to Say."

However, in October 2002, Thomson announced that she was quitting the entertainment business. In a statement, Thomson cited overwhelming personal demands as reason for her departure. "The next step in my career would be to make a new album … with the many obligations that go along with it," she said. "I have now realized that I cannot commit to those obligations." Industry reaction was mixed. Capitol Nashville chief Mike Dungan said he "cried several times" when Thomson told him she was quitting, but he was also matter-of-fact, remarking "[she] was a big part of my business plan." *— Johnny Loftus*

● **My World** / Jul. 31, 2001 / Capitol ◆◆◆
At 24, Cyndi Thomson's deepest country music influence is current diva Trisha Yearwood, who herself was only a third-generation pop-country singer who transcended the genre's limitations with a rich voice and killer songs. But Thomson's youth shouldn't be held against her. For in the field of curtain-shirted rock & roll wannabes and Brooks & Dunn clones and Shania Twain-esque glamor queens who couldn't sing a lick if there weren't pitch levelers in recording studios, Thomson is a rarity. As a singer she posses a genuine slippery, smoky alto that reaches deep inside the heart for the lyric rather than in the trembling upper registers of her instrument. She has the songs too, given that her

producer and co-writer is none other than Tommy James. Lastly, she's a country singer first and a pop singer second. *My World* will, hopefully, lay claim to a slot on the country chart near the top, which would mean there was hope for Nash Vegas (not a lot, but a smidge anyway—which is more than there is now). Sure, there are the requisite fiddles on her record, but there are also banjos and flat-picked guitars, as well as recorders, Hammond B-3s (as on the single "What I Really Meant to Say"). The single is clearly meant to put the album in the hands and minds (not like they really have them, but we'll give them the benefit of the doubt on this set) of country music radio station programmers. Once said single charts, the label digs into the disc for further material, hopefully to the title track or "Hope You're Doing Fine," with its ringing mandolin and pedal steel whine. Ultimately, *My World* has some concessions to the pop market: it's slickly produced; there are some taut, pop sheeny arrangements and a few drum machines here and there. But compared to the absolute crap being cranked out of Nash Vegas, this is a bona fide country record in the same tradition as Thomson's mentor Yearwood. And there are a lot lower sights (especially now) to set your eyes on. *— Thom Jurek*

Paul Thorn
Vocals, Guitar / Singer/Songwriter, Alternative Pop/Rock, Roots Rock, Alternative Country, Americana
Tupelo, MS's Paul Thorn was a prizefighter and skydiver before becoming a rootsy singer/songwriter. As a boxer, Thorn once fought against Roberto Duran and as a musician, he has toured and collaborated with Sting, Paul Carrack, Joe Diffie, Tanya Tucker, Ronnie Milsap, and Carole King. He released his debut album, *Hammer & Nail*, in 1997 and followed it with *Ain't Love Strange* two years later. *— Heather Phares*

Hammer & Nail / Jun. 17, 1997 / A&M ◆◆◆

Ain't Love Strange / Jul. 27, 1999 / Perpetual Obscurity ◆◆◆
Paul Thorn's second album *Ain't Love Strange* features more of the singer/songwriter's quirky, confessional, roots-based songs, including "Liberace & Fabio," "Where Was I," "Burn down the Trailer Park," "Help Me out, Hook Me Up," and "That's All I Know Right Now." While it may not have the immediate impact of his debut *Hammer & Nail, Ain't Love Strange* is another worthwhile effort from Thorn. *— Heather Phares*

● **Mission Temple Fireworks Stand** / Aug. 13, 2002 / Back Porch ◆◆◆◆◆
Paul Thorn's second studio full-length and his debut for Virgin's Back Porch Records is a wild, wooly, roots-drenched voyage into the dark, conflicted, yearning heart of America. A Tupelo, MS, native and the son of a Church of God minister, Thorn knows the boundaries—where they can be stretched and where the paradoxes with no answers lie. His job is to puzzle over the questions and to seek to illuminate them by means of narratives, exhortations, and humor that is rooted in gritty garage rock, Southern blues and gospel, and honky tonk music. Thorn's life experience has been rich; along with being a singer and songwriter, he has been an artist in the Howard Finster tradition, a boxer who fought Roberto Duran once, and a factory worker. All of these elements come into play on this deeply spiritual look at both the sacred and profane. There is no ethereal posturing here—just spit, vinegar, and a rugged toughness that knows that the soft side of things needs attention. To get a mental and aural picture of this sound, try to look at Greg Brown's gritty-voiced wit and Lyle Lovett's melodic sense, teamed with the rock sensibility of Lynyrd Skynyrd, the steamy soul and funk of Delaney Bramlett, and the rough-hewn ballad approach of Steve Earle. Thorn's approach features an army of electric guitars behind him, and he needs them because he tells big stories. The second track, "Rise Up," is a single mom's anthem; come to think of it, with it's crunching, transcendent major-chord riff, "Rise Up" is for anybody who wants to make changes wholesale. The drums crack just enough to carry Thorn's big voice over the top, to ride the guitars and underline his chorus. There is also the title track, which holds one of the most powerful metaphors ever for taking a good, hard look at how we live and how we view others: "I saw a black man with a bible and a sparkler in his hand/He was holding a tent revival and running a fireworks stand/He said the end of the world is coming so you better get on your knees/Today bottle rockets are two for one/ But salvation is always free." One of the more poignant cuts is "Even Heroes Die," a ballad with a gorgeous piano slipping underneath the brushed drums before the organ and guitars come in a gently cresting wave. Thorn tells the story of Elvis becoming not only a parody of himself in life, but a cartoon character in death; Presley is a homeboy from Tupelo. But he juxtaposes it with the story of a street preacher who dies alone in a shelter. "Sister Ruby's House of Prayer" is an elemental rock track with Southern boogie guitars that could have come from a .38 Special hit, layered with sitars and a big drumbeat. While some would draw surface comparisons to another minister's son and visual artist-cum-musician Jim White, all that it adds up to is life circumstance. Thorn's music is big, loud, and full of an in-your-face attitude. His humor is not wry or effete, nor does he present himself as an outsider in any way—just a songwriter with a curious vision of the world, heaven, and, of course, hell. Highly recommended. *— Thom Jurek*

Thrasher Shiver
Group / Contemporary Country
Thrasher Shiver was a contemporary country duo known for evocative vocal harmonies. Neil Thrasher came from a family of singers. His father Joe played with the country gospel group the Thrasher Brothers. Neil got his start as a singer with his father's band, and eventually moved on to demo and background vocal work in Nashville. Before he united with Thrasher, Kelly Shiver led a contemporary bluegrass combo called County Line. He also was involved in Nashville's thriving demo and songwriting circuits. The two performers eventually met through influential country impresario Bob Doyle, whose Doyle & Associates managed Garth Brooks. After meeting in Doyle's office one day, Thrasher & Shiver began writing and recording together, and it was immediately apparent that their voices meshed perfectly. In 1995, they signed to Asylum, and the label issued their self-titled debut in September 1996. Thrasher and Shiver wrote the majority

of the record themselves, and were lauded for their traditional approach to modern country. Their version of the Delmore Brothers' classic "Blues Stay Away From Me" appeared on the Asylum-released soundtrack to the 1997 film *Traveller*. They continued to write songs for the Nashville crowd—both as a duo and separately—throughout the rest of the '90s. —*Johnny Loftus*

Thrasher Shiver / Sep. 9, 1996 / Elektra ♦♦♦
Thrasher Shriver's eponymous debut album is polished but impassioned country-rock that touches on honky tonk, barroom weepers and modern country barn-burners. Although the band sometimes suffers from trying to hard to avoid Nashville clichés, resulting in underdeveloped songs, they manage to create a classy, rootsy sound that gives their best songs a bracing directness that cuts quite deeply. Moments like "Goin' Goin' Gone" and "All the King's Horses" suggest that the band will be able to develop into something quite special, given just a little more time. —*Thom Owens*

Sonny Throckmorton

b. Apr. 2, 1941, Carlsbad, NM
Songwriter, Vocals / Traditional Country
Sonny Throckmorton started out as a performer, but instead he became one of the most successful songwriters in country music, with over 1,000 of his songs recorded by such artists as Tanya Tucker, Dave & Sugar, Merle Haggard, Jerry Lee Lewis, the Oak Ridge Boys, Doug Stone and even comedian George Burns. He was born James Fron Sonny Throckmorton in Carlsbad, NM, and spent much of his childhood traveling the Southwest before his family finally settled in Wichita Falls, TX. After college, Throckmorton moved to San Francisco and played rock & roll in area clubs. At the urging of guitarist and publisher Pete Drake, he switched to country music and moved to Nashville in 1964, working as a bass player for Carl & Pearl Butler for two years. He then wrote for and managed Drake's publishing company. In 1965, Bobby Lewis had a Top Five hit with Throckmorton's "How Long Has It Been." He remained in Nashville for a few more years as a song promoter and staff writer for different companies before landing a job as a staff writer for the prestigious Tree Publishing. Unfortunately, none of the young writer's songs became hits, and he was fired.

In 1975, Throckmorton moved to Texas because he had promised himself that he would quit music if he didn't succeed by age 35. His fellow songwriters continued trying to sell Throckmorton's songs, however, and six months later he returned and was rehired by Tree. In nine months, over 150 of his songs were recorded, including "Thinking of a Rendezvous," Johnny Duncan's first number-one hit. Another of his songs, "Knee Deep in Love with You," became a country standard. Between 1976 and 1980, a Throckmorton song appeared on the charts almost every week. His 1978 hit for Jerry Lee Lewis, "Middle Age Crazy," even became the basis of a major movie, and he was named Songwriter of the Year by the Nashville Songwriters Association three years in a row starting between 1978 and 1980.

In 1976, Throckmorton tried recording his own songs, first for Starcrest and then for Mercury, but the biggest hit he had, "Last Cheater's Waltz," only reached the Top 50. Fortunately, his stature as a major songwriter flourished and in 1980, he was named BMI Songwriter of the Year. Seven years later, with innumerable hits under his belt, Throckmorton was inducted into the Nashville Songwriters Hall of Fame. He recorded *Southern Train* for Warner in 1986 and then retired to his Texas farm to be with his family. —*Sandra Brennan*

● **The Last Cheater's Waltz** / 1978 / Mercury ♦♦♦♦♦

Southern Train / 1986 / Warner Bros. ♦♦♦♦

Mel Tillis (Lonnie Melvin Tillis)

b. Aug. 8, 1932, Tampa, FL
Guitar, Vocals / Country-Pop, Traditional Country
In light of all the attention given Mel Tillis' infamous speech impediment—he even named his autobiography *Stutterin' Boy*—the polished, sincere vocal delivery and songwriting skills that first earned him fame were often lost in the shuffle; nonetheless, throughout the course of his many decades in country music, Tillis remained one of Nashville's most enduring personalities. Born Lonnie Melvin Tillis in Tampa, FL, on August 8, 1932, it is believed that his stuttering was the result of a bout with malaria at the age of three. As a child, he learned guitar, and in high-school studied both the violin and the drums. At the age of 16, he first performed publicly at a local talent show, and after graduation he entered the military. While stationed in Okinawa, Japan, he formed a group called the Westerners, which played local clubs.

After exiting the service in 1955, Tillis went to college and held odd jobs until moving to Nashville the following year. He found little success as a writer or performer there and soon returned to Florida; then, in 1957, Webb Pierce reached number three with Tillis' composition "I'm Tired," earning the aspiring artist a songwriting contract with Pierce's Cedarwood Music. After playing with the likes of Minnie Pearl and Judy Lynn, Tillis cut his first single, a cover of the standard "It Takes a Worried Man to Sing a Worried Song," in 1957; the B-side, the self-penned "Honky Tonk Song," quickly became a chart-topper for Pierce. After a few excursions into rock & roll territory, Tillis earned his first Top 40 hit with 1958's "The Violet and a Rose."

While Tillis continued to chart singles like 1959's "Finally" and a pair of duets with Bill Phillips, "Sawmill" and "Georgia Town Blues," his greatest success at the turn of the decade remained as a songwriter. He continued supplying Pierce with hit after hit, including the 1959 smashes "I Ain't Never" and "No Love Have I" along with 1962's "Crazy Wild Desire" and 1963's "Sawmill." Also covering Tillis' songs were Bobby Bare ("Detroit City"), Ray Price ("One More Time," "Burning Memories," "Heart Over Mind"), Stonewall Jackson ("Mary Don't You Weep"), and Little Jimmy Dickens ("The Violet and a Rose," also covered by Wanda Jackson). In 1962, Tillis released his first LP, *Heart Over Mind*; a year later, he teamed with Pierce for the hit "How Come Your Dog Don't Bite Nobody but Me."

In 1965, Tillis recorded his first Top 15 hit, "Wine." A string of successes followed, including 1966's "Stateside," "Life Turned Her That Way" (the title cut from his 1967 album), and his first Top Ten, 1968's "Who's Julie." At the same time, his stature as a songwriter continued to grow thanks to hit covers of his "Ruby, Don't Take Your Love to Town" (by both Johnny Darrell and Kenny Rogers & the First Edition) and "Mental Revenge" (Waylon Jennings). At the end of the 1960s, Tillis and his esteemed new backing band the Statesiders came into their own as performers; after two 1969 Top Ten hits, "These Lonely Hands of Mine" and "She'll Be Hanging Around Somewhere," he scored back-to-back Top Five hits in 1970 with "Heart Over Mind" and "Heaven Everyday." In 1971, he began a successful string of duets with Sherry Bryce which included "Take My Hand" and "Living and Learning," and he released the album *Live at the Sam Houston Coliseum*.

"I Ain't Never" (1972) became his first chart-topper, and the remainder of the decade which followed was Tillis' most fertile period as an artist, as evidenced by a series of Top Five smashes like "Neon Rose," "Sawmill," "Midnight, Me and the Blues," "Stomp Them Grapes," and "Memory Maker." Between 1976 and 1980, he scored five more number ones—"Good Woman Blues," "Heart Healer," "I Believe in You," "Coca Cola Cowboy," and "Southern Rains." He also appeared in a number of films, including 1975's *W.W. and the Dancekings* (with Burt Reynolds and Jerry Reed), 1977's *The Villain* (starring Kirk Douglas and Arnold Schwarzenegger), Clint Eastwood's *Every Which Way but Loose* in 1979, and 1980's all-star *Smokey and the Bandit II*. Albums of the period included 1976's *Love Revival* and 1980's *M-M-Mel Live*, in addition to a series of hits compilations.

In 1981, Tillis recorded a duets album with Nancy Sinatra called *Mel and Nancy*, but like most of his work throughout the 1980s, it failed to repeat the success he had previously enjoyed. Although he continued to work in films (co-starring in both *Cannonball Run* pictures) and notched the occasional Top Ten hit (like 1981's "A Million Old Goodbyes" or 1983's "In the Middle of the Night"), his days as a superstar were over. Still, he remained a popular songwriter, especially among younger artists; his "Honey (Open That Door)" and "Diggin' Up Bones" were number-one hits for, respectively, Ricky Skaggs and Randy Travis. Tillis also continued as a successful road act, and in the early '90s, his daughter Pam became one of country's biggest stars. —*Jason Ankeny*

Life's That Way / 1967 / Kapp ♦♦♦♦
Mel Tillis' recording of the classic Harlan Howard composition "Life Turned Her That Way" barely missed the country Top Ten and bubbled under the pop charts, becoming one of his most successful singles during his late-'60s term on Kapp. The album *Life's That Way* contains that song and several notable originals by Tillis, including his version of "Ruby (Don't Take Your Love to Town)," which is excellent except for the audible residue of a reference vocal or scrapped vocal take. That song became a hit for Johnny Darrell, and "Unmitigated Gall," which is presented here in a driving, bass-heavy performance, was a hit for Faron Young. Tillis may have repaid Faron Young for recording his song by covering the 1958 hit "Alone With You" (which Young co-wrote) for this album. Tillis didn't usually devote much space on his LPs to covers of recent hits, but he picked two good ones on *Life's That Way* with Kenny Price's "Walking on New Grass" and Nat Stuckey's "Sweet Thang." "That's Where My Money Goes" is practically a sequel to Tillis' hit "Sawmill." *Life's That Way* is a typical Mel Tillis album in that it features a respectable percentage of originals and maintains an above-average level of quality while showing everyone that even when his own records weren't selling a million, his songs were definitely going places. —*Greg Adams*

Something Special / 1968 / Kapp ♦♦♦
Something Special contains two of Mel Tillis' hits from 1968—the ballads "Destroyed by Man" and "Something Special"—the latter of which reached the Top 20. Tillis wrote only four of the 11 songs on this album, which will be a disappointment to those who appreciate his tremendous but undervalued songwriting talent. "I Haven't Seen Mary in Years," a good graveyard weeper, was recorded by Bill Monroe in 1969, but Tillis' version is arguably more effective. The highlight on *Something Special* is the album's closer, "I've Lived So Fast and Hard," a Dolly Parton composition that sounds exactly like something Tillis could have written. Tillis' career had started to really take off when he left Kapp for MGM, where he made some of his biggest hits, but his Kapp albums are very consistent and more similar in style to his popular '70s recordings than his early rock-oriented sides for Columbia. —*Greg Adams*

Would You Want the World to End / 1972 / MGM ♦♦
After more than a decade of professional songwriting and recording, Mel Tillis finally broke through in the '70s to become a major country star. On the basis of chart hits, he was one of the Top Ten country artists of the decade. *Would You Want the World to End* was made during his peak years and yet is as unremarkable a record as you will find in his catalog. The title track was a hit, but the album cuts work the same slow shuffle beat over and over again on a lineup of forgettable songs. The problem is almost certainly a hyperactive record release schedule; a popular artist could put out four albums a year in this era, and it was understandably difficult to maintain a high level of quality. Although Tillis is a very talented songwriter, he contributed only one song to the album, "Gonna Burn Some Bridges." The monochromatic cover art fittingly reflects the music on this serviceable but slight effort. —*Greg Adams*

Best Way I Know How / 1975 / MGM ♦♦♦

Welcome to Mel Tillis Country / 1977 / MGM ♦♦
Mel Tillis left MGM for MCA in 1976, and *Welcome to Mel Tillis Country* was his last original album for MGM. The album feels like it was cobbled together together to fulfill a contractual obligation, but Tillis had hit his stride at this point and could do no wrong. The re-recordings of his Kapp hit "Heart Over Mind" and "Ruby, Don't Take Your Love to Town" (which wasn't a hit for Tillis, although he wrote and recorded it in the '60s) are pleasant enough, but Tillis' take on the Johnny Cash rockabilly classic "Rock and Roll Ruby" is pretty exciting. "Come on Home" and "Always Just a Memory Away" were issued on a single but were eclipsed by Tillis' new MCA efforts to such a degree that the single didn't even chart. It's a testament to Tillis' talent that even his half-baked efforts are so worthwhile. —*Greg Adams*

Night Train To Memphis / 197 / Hilltop ♦♦♦
Train to Memphis gathers nine tracks from various albums Mel Tillis recorded for Kapp Records between 1966-1970. None of the songs were hits for Tillis, but "Lonely Girl" was a hit for Carl Smith, and "Night Train to Memphis" has been widely recorded. "Tom Dooley" is the song Pam Tillis first sang on the *Opry* as an eight-year-old, which may have inspired her father to cut his own version. "Okeechobee Ocean," one of several songs written by Tillis, was also recorded by Burl Ives. These album tracks are better heard on the original albums with the hits than cobbled together on a budget LP. *—Greg Adams*

M-M-Mel Live / 1980 / MCA ♦♦♦

Mel and Nancy / 1981 / Elektra ♦♦♦
Mel and Nancy is a collection of duets from Tillis and Nancy Sinatra. It includes the minor hits "Play Me or Trade Me" and "Where Would I Be." *—Jason Ankeny*

American Originals / 1989 / Columbia ♦♦♦♦♦
American Originals compiles material from Tillis' brief time at Columbia Records. He was with the label at the beginning of his career, and while he was there, he primarily recorded his own material. *American Originals*, though too brief at ten tracks, gives a good sense of his developing talents. *—Thom Owens*

Greatest Hits / 1991 / Curb ♦♦♦♦♦
Featuring a selection of his late '70s and early '80s hits—including the number-one "Coca Cola Cowboy," "Lying Time Again," "Southern Rains," "Your Body Is an Outlaw," "New Patches," and "Blind In Love"—Curb's *Greatest Hits* is a servicable, but not thorough, retrospective that does work as an effective introduction to Mel at the height of his popularity. *—Thom Owens*

● **Memory Maker** / 1995 / Mercury ♦♦♦♦♦
Although he reached his commercial peak in the latter half of the decade, Tillis hit his creative stride in the early 1970s, the period compiled on *The Memory Maker.* Leading off with "I Ain't Never," and his first number one, the collection also features "Sawmill," "Mental Revenge," "Neon Rose," and "Midnight, Me and the Blues." *—Jason Ankeny*

The Best of Mel Tillis / Jul. 8, 1997 / Curb ♦♦♦
Curb's *The Best of Mel Tillis* is a pretty good budget-priced, ten-track collection, but in no way is this definitive. This is a cost-effective way of obtaining Tillis' most popular songs from the '80s, including "A Million Old Goodbyes," "I Ain't Never," "New Patches," and "Texas Cowboy Night," which features Nancy Sinatra. For a more thorough investigation of the classic Mel Tillis country/pop sound, pick up the single-disc, 16-track RCA *Country Legends* collection. *—Al Campbell*

Pam Tillis

b. 1957, Plant City, FL
Vocals / Country-Pop, Urban Cowboy, Contemporary Country
The daughter of country legend Mel Tillis, Pam Tillis made her own way in the music business, eventually becoming a contemporary country star in the '90s. Tillis was born on July 24, 1957, in Plant City, FL, but raised mostly in Nashville and started taking piano lessons at age eight. She switched to guitar at 12 and played in talent contests during her teenage years. Somewhat wild and rebellious, she survived a near-fatal car crash at age 16 that required extensive facial reconstruction. Fortunately, she recovered fully and pursued music aggressively at the University of Tennessee, singing with the High Country Swing Band (which played country-rock and jug-band music) and in a folk duo with Ashley Cleveland. She quit school in 1976 and worked at her father's publishing company, placing her composition "I'll Meet You on the Other Side of the Morning" with Barbara Fairchild. She also formed her own backing band, which soon relocated to the San Francisco Bay Area and renamed themselves Freelight; they developed an adventurous style based on jazz and rock, not country.

Tillis returned to Nashville in 1979, though, and sang backup for her father while raising her first child as a single parent, fronting an R&B band, and continuing to write songs, a couple of which were recorded by Gloria Gaynor and Chaka Khan. Tillis performed regularly at Nashville's Bluebird Cafe with several other female singer/songwriters and landed a deal with Warner Bros. in the early '80s. She released one album, the pop-oriented *Above and Beyond the Doll of Cutey*, in 1983 and had her first chart single the following year with "Goodbye Highway." Several more singles were released through 1987, but none even managed to make the Top 50; even so, Tillis was making her name as a songwriter for Tree Publishing, with compositions recorded by Highway 101 and Conway Twitty, among others. In 1989, the same year she acted in a Tennessee production of *Jesus Christ Superstar*, she landed a new deal with Arista. Tillis released her label debut, *Put Yourself in My Place*, in 1991, and the lead single, "Don't Tell Me What to Do," raced into the Top Five, giving Tillis her long-awaited breakthrough. Of the album's five total singles, "One of Those Things" and "Maybe It Was Memphis" also made the Top Ten (as did the album). *Homeward Looking Angel* (1992) was an equally successful follow-up, with "Shake the Sugar Tree" and "Let That Pony Run" both making the Top Five.

Tillis co-produced her third Arista album, 1994's *Sweetheart's Dance*, which proved to be her most successful yet and earned her the ACM's award for Female Vocalist of the Year. "Spilled Perfume," "When You Walk in the Room," and "In Between Dances" all went Top Five, and "Mi Vida Loca (My Crazy Life)" became her first ever number-one hit. Released in late 1995, *All of This Love* was the first album Tillis produced by herself, and gave her Top Tens in "Deep Down" and "The River and the Highway." Two new songs from 1997's *Greatest Hits* compilation, "All the Good Ones Are Gone" and "Land of the Living," both went Top Five as well. *Every Time* (1998) reflected her recent divorce from songwriter Bob DiPiero and gave her a near-Top Ten hit in "I Said a Prayer." A reshuffling at Arista delayed the release of *Thunder and Roses* until 2001, so in the meantime, Tillis performed on Broadway in the Leiber & Stoller tribute production *Smokey Joe's Cafe. Thunder and Roses* found Tillis' commercial momentum slowing down, and she and Arista subsequently parted ways. She caught on at Epic's roots subsidiary Lucky Dog and debuted for them in 2002 with *It's All Relative: Tillis Sings Tillis*, a collection of her father's material that finally found her embracing his legacy on her own terms. *—Steve Huey*

Put Yourself in My Place / 1991 / Arista ♦♦♦♦♦
The album that established Tillis as a performer in her own right has a traditional country base cut with bluegrass, folk and rock. It all creates the same sort of mixed breed she sings about in "Melancholy Child": "You take a black Irish temper, some solemn Cherokee, a Southern sense of humor, and you got someone like me." Her characters are the awkward dancers of "I've Seen Enough To Know": bruised, tentative, and needing to be cajoled back to love. Even the throwaway songs are of a high standard; the best ones ("Maybe It Was Memphis," "Don't Tell Me What to Do") are truly enticing. *—Brian Mansfield*

Homeward Looking Angel / 1992 / Arista ♦♦♦
Tillis had an enviable challenge with *Homeward Looking Angel*—topping *Put Yourself in My Place*, which spawned four top-ten singles, including "Don't Tell Me What To Do." Tillis' pure, full-bodied country voice can be both a boon and a burden. Some track on *Angel* reek with cliché, her twang exaggerated to the verge of annoyance, for instance, on the retro "Do You Know Where Your Man Is." Others work an original magic, including the sly and sexy "Shake the Sugar Tree" and the wry and telling "Cleopatra, Queen of Denial." These songs, along with "Let That Pony Run," had no trouble finding their way to the chart heights of their predecessors. *—Roch Parisien*

Pam Tillis Collection / Feb. 1, 1994 / Warner Bros. ♦♦♦♦♦
Before hitting big with Arista Records and "Don't Tell Me What to Do," Tillis had recorded rock-influenced country for Warner Bros. She had minor success with the likes of "There Goes My Love" and "These Memories of You," but what makes *Collection* interesting is early versions of "One of Those Things" and "Maybe It Was Memphis" as well as a version of "Five Minutes," later a hit for Lorrie Morgan. *—Brian Mansfield*

Sweetheart's Dance / Apr. 26, 1994 / Arista ♦♦♦♦♦
Producing herself for the first time (along with Steve Fishell), Tillis found the magic blend of Nashville Sound, California country-rock and post-Beatles pop. She released the heady "Spilled Perfume" as her first single, but the riches of *Sweethearts Dance* go much deeper: the Bo Diddley/Tejano rhythms of "Mi Vida Loca (My Crazy Life)," the lilting waltz of "In Between Dances," and a playfully romantic title cut. A charming album without a bad cut, *Sweethearts Dance* ranks with the best of Trisha Yearwood, Wynonna Judd and Carlene Carter. *—Brian Mansfield*

All of This Love / Nov. 7, 1995 / Arista ♦♦♦

● **Greatest Hits** / Jun. 3, 1997 / Arista ♦♦♦♦♦
Greatest Hits contains all of Pam Tillis' biggest singles, including the Top Ten country hits "Don't Tell Me What To Do," "One of Those Things," "Maybe It Was Memphis," "Shake the Sugar Tree" and "Let That Pony Run," plus two new songs, "Land of the Living" and "All the Good Ones Are Gone." *—Thom Owens*

Every Time / Jun. 30, 1998 / Arista ♦♦♦♦
Pam Tillis is in possession of a fine country voice, and on this particular project she displays her talent proudly, twang and all. While there is the usual overproduction that characterizes Nashville in the '90s, and some material that seems more in line with the pop world, Tillis has the strength to break through and shine. Especially good is the Leslie Satcher tune "Whiskey on the Wound," which seems to demonstrate just how deep Tillis' traditional roots run inspite of all the nonsense. Jamie O'Hara's composition "Lay the Heartache Down" also allows Tillis to spread her wings and fly, but the most breathtaking cut is the Thompson/Cunningham co-write "A Whisper and a Scream"; the performance here is unsurpassed, heartbreaking, soul-shaking, and chilling. For this track alone, *Every Time* is bound to be counted as one of Tillis' most distinctive projects. *—Jana Pendragon*

Super Hits / Jul. 18, 2000 / Warner Bros. ♦♦♦
Sony's *Super Hits* collection is a decent budget-priced, ten-track collection containing some of Pam Tillis' most popular songs, including "Maybe It Was Memphis" and "One of Those Things." Also included are a few "pre-Memphis" hits from the mid-'80s, "Those Memories of You" and "Goodbye Highway." To be definitive, this disc would have to include "Don't Tell Me What to Do," "Cleopatra, Queen of Denial," and "Shake the Sugar Tree," which it doesn't. For a more thorough single-disc summary of her hits, check out *RCA Country Legends. —Al Campbell*

Thunder and Roses / Mar. 6, 2001 / Arista ♦♦♦
The Tillis name is a staple in country music. Pam's dad, Mel Tillis, has graced country since the '50s, and Pam's been in the business since prior to 1979 either as a songwriter, backup singer, or club performer. She hasn't had a big career or even an exceptionally huge hit, but she has maintained a consistent career by keeping herself on the charts with songs like "Maybe It Was Memphis" and "All the Good Ones Are Gone." She continues her consistency on this 11-track collection of respectable, just-decent songs. Album number seven doesn't really offer anything new in terms of what you usually get from Pam, except for a first-time duet together with dad Mel. The bonus track, "Waiting on the Wind, is a thoroughly likable rendition of a song they've previously performed live together. "Jagged Hearts," the album's first track is also worth a mention. *Thunder and Roses* would make a fine addition to your Pam Tillis collection. *—Maria Konicki Dinoia*

● **RCA Country Legends** / Apr. 9, 2002 / RCA ♦♦♦♦♦
Pam Tillis' *Country Legends* is a good 16-track collection that contains most of Pam Tillis' hits—all of those that most listeners want—along with a handful of album tracks, all taken from her recordings for Arista. It's a good, solid collection, the best yet assembled on Tillis, and is an expert introduction. *—Stephen Thomas Erlewine*

It's All Relative / Sep. 3, 2002 / Epic/Lucky Dog ✦✦✦✦

Best known as an engaging and often humorous performer, and secondarily as Nashville songbird Pam Tillis' father, Mel Tillis deserves greater recognition as one of country music's more enduring and consistent songwriters. This oversight is addressed in *It's All Relative*, as Pam joins with a cast of Music City luminaries to interpret some of his better-known works. Her performance is right on the money from start to finish. On uptempo tracks, whether honky tonk excursions like "Unmitigated Gall" or a brisk rockabilly sprint with Ray Benson through "Honey (Open That Door)," she's expressive, though somewhat restrained. It's at slower tempos that her abilities are most evident, as she exploits the interpretive room that ballads allow. An exceptional harmony singer, she knows how to play off of the unique timbre and phrasing contributed by Dolly Parton on a lacelike rendition of "Violet and a Rose" and Emmylou Harris in a more Daniel Lanois-influenced treatment of "Heart Over Mind." On her own, Tillis is even stronger; she turns "Detroit City" into an intimate journal, with misty memories of home and the weary grind of life in the city made equally vivid by her reading. Yet on "Emotions," backed by jazz pianist Beegie Adair, Tillis eases smoothly into a torchier style that has nothing to do with rural idylls. The last track, "Come On and Sing," brings Dad into the picture, along with a gaggle of his grandkids; it's a predictable cameo, but irresistible nonetheless and a perfect dessert for this rich repast. —*Robert L. Doerschuk*

Floyd Tillman

b. Dec. 8, 1914, Ryan, OK, **d.** Aug. 22, 2003, Bacliff, TX
Guitar, Vocals / Honky Tonk, Traditional Country

Floyd Tillman is probably best known for writing "It Makes No Difference Now," a country classic that he sold to Jimmie Davis for $300 in 1938, only to watch it become a hit for Davis, Cliff Bruner, Bing Crosby, Gene Autry, and others. That song was one of the first to tap the bitter acceptance of romantic dissatisfaction that was to set the tone for so many later country songs. He was a major performer in his own right and one of the creators of honky tonk country music, repeatedly cited as an influence by Willie Nelson and other Texas performers.

Tillman was born in Ryan, OK, but raised in Post, TX, in a sharecropper family. He began playing guitar and mandolin, performing as a backing musician for local fiddlers while he was still a child. In 1933, at age 19, Tillman joined Adolph & Emil Hofner's house band at Gus' Palm Garden in San Antonio. Two years later, he became the leader of the Blue Ridge Playboys, a Houston band that spawned several of the most innovative country musicians of the pre-World War II era. In 1936, he began singing and playing electric guitar, mandolin, and banjo with the Mack Clark Orchestra, a Houston pop ensemble. Through these varied experiences, Tillman absorbed a whole range of 1930s music and got a good taste of the rhythmic freedom of jazz. He also began writing songs and taking lead vocals occasionally; one of his early compositional efforts, co-written with Blue Ridge Playboy Leon Selph, was "It Makes No Difference Now." Late in life, he succeeded in regaining rights to the song.

With jukeboxes spreading across the industrializing Southwest and the market for recordings rebounding as the Depression waned, Tillman began a solo recording career of his own on the Decca label in the late '30s. Joining the Army during World War II, he remained in Texas and continued to compose and perform. It wasn't long before his trademark delivery, sometimes described as a cross between Ernest Tubb and Frank Sinatra, began to emerge; he combined the low-volume vocal inflections of the crooner with tight country voice production. He had his first number-one hit in 1944 with "They Took the Stars Out of Heaven," and his songwriting, inspired by wartime themes of separation, continued to develop along with his vocal style. He notched two Top Five hits, "G.I. Blues" and "Each Night at Nine," that lamented the soldier's distance from loved ones even as they began to forge postwar country music's language of loneliness. Reportedly these songs were often aired by Japanese propaganda broadcaster Iva Toguri, known as Tokyo Rose, in an attempt to encourage American soldiers to desert.

Tillman continued to perform around Houston after the war, and in the late '40s he had two more major hits with songs he himself he had composed: 1947's "I Love You So Much It Hurts" showcased Tillman's individualistic country-jazz vocals to the fullest, and 1949's "Slippin' Around," one of the first country songs to take cheating as its theme, was covered by Jimmy Wakely and Margaret Whiting and became as well known among pop fans as in the world of country. Tillman continued to find inspiration in current events with such songs as the much-covered "This Cold War With You." He enjoyed solo success as late as 1960 with "It Just Tears Me Up," and he continued to write songs and to appear around Texas occasionally. He was inducted into the Country Music Hall of Fame in 1984. He passed away on August 22, 2003 after a protracted struggle with leukemia. —*James Manheim*

☆ **Columbia Historic Edition** / 1985 / Columbia ✦✦✦✦✦

The 11-track *Columbia Historic Edition* contains the bulk of Floyd Tillman's hits from the late '40s, including "Drivin' Nails in My Coffin," "I Love You So Much, It Hurts," and "Slippin' Around," plus a number of lesser-known songs that rival the hits in quality. Certain songs, like his Decca hits and "I'll Never Slip Around Again" and "I Gotta Have My Baby Back," aren't included but *Columbia Historic Edition* remains the best compilation of Tillman's peak. —*Stephen Thomas Erlewine*

Country Music Hall of Fame Series / 1991 / MCA ✦✦✦✦✦

Tillman had his biggest hits in the late '40s while recording for Columbia, but these World War II-era sides for Decca show him as a leader of a Texas dance band that's not afraid to mix it up with some jazz playing. Moon Mullican plays piano on a number of these sides. —*Brian Mansfield*

Crazy Cajun Recordings / Feb. 23, 1999 / Edsel ✦✦✦

Floyd Tillman's *Crazy Cajun Recordings* features 26 tracks for Huey P. Meaux's Houston-based label. These are re-recordings of such Tillman classics as "Drivin' Nails in My Coffin"; "Slipping Around" and its follow-up, "I'll Never Slip Around Again"; and "Battle of the Bottle." The only non-original tune is a version of Ernest Tubb's "Walking the Floor

Over You." Die-hard Tillman fans will want this, but new listeners should start with *The Best of Floyd Tillman* on Collector's Choice. —*Al Campbell*

★ **The Best of Floyd Tillman** / Apr. 20, 1999 / Collectors' Choice Music ✦✦✦✦✦

Country Music Hall of Famer Floyd Tillman finally gets a fair showing on this, a 24-track anthology of his greatest recordings for Columbia from 1946-1954, including such classics as "Drivin' Nails in My Coffin" and "Slipping Around" (plus its follow-up, "I'll Never Slip Around Again"). All of Tillman's hits for the label are included and much more, offering a thorough picture of *Tillman* at his peak. *The Best of Floyd Tillman* is an excellent and essential anthology of this influential artist's smooth, Western swing-inflected honky tonk. —*Greg Adams*

Country Music Hall of Fame 1984 / Nov. 9, 1999 / King ✦✦

Part of King's *Country Hall of Fame* series, this brings together 12 tracks from this artist's heyday at the label. Although the booklet is nonexistent, there's a nice bio on Tillman on the tray card, and the transfers are decent, featuring biggies like "I Love You So Much It Hurts," "Drivin' Nails in My Coffin," and "Empty Glass." This is real honky tonk, circa the late '40s, and these tracks capture a sound that left country decades ago. —*Cub Koda*

The Best of Floyd Tillman / Columbia ✦✦✦✦✦

It contains his classics, such as "Slippin' Around" and "Gotta Have My Baby Back." Wait for this one; with Columbia reissuing much of its vintage country material, this stuff has got to appear on CD in some form. —*Richard Lieberson*

Aaron Tippin

b. 1958, Pensacola, FL
Vocals / Contemporary Country, New Traditionalist

Aaron Tippin was part of the commercial explosion of new traditionalist country in the early '90s, making his name with a mixture of macho, rowdy honky tonkers, sentimental ballads, and patriotic working-man's anthems. Tippin was born in Pensacola, FL, in 1958, and grew up mostly on a family farm near Greer, SC, where he first started singing to pass the time while doing chores. He started playing guitar at age ten but also inherited a love of flying from his father, who'd worked as a pilot prior to becoming a farmer. Tippin himself earned his pilot's license at 15 and began flying professionally before the age of 20. He was studying to become a commercial airline pilot when the industry took a major downturn, which convinced him to return to music. He played the local honky tonk circuit and worked on his songwriting while holding a series of blue-collar day jobs. Unfortunately, his marriage broke up, and with nothing to lose, he finally moved to Nashville in 1986. He landed a job as a staff songwriter at the legendary Acuff-Rose firm, where his compositions were recorded by the likes of Charley Pride, Mark Collie, and David Ball, among others. In 1990, his demo tape landed him a contract with RCA.

Tippin's debut album, *You've Got to Stand for Something*, was released in 1991; its title cut became a Top Ten smash in the wake of the Persian Gulf War, and Tippin was invited along on Bob Hope's *USO* tour. His second album, 1992's *Read Between the Lines*, was a million-selling Top Ten smash, producing three Top Ten singles in "I Wouldn't Have It Any Other Way," "My Blue Angel," and his first number one, "There Ain't Nothing Wrong With the Radio." *The Call of the Wild* (1993) underlined Tippin's penchant for rabble-rousing anthems like "Honky Tonk Superman," the Top Ten "Working Man's Ph.D.," and the Top 20 title cut. The following year's *Lookin' Back at Myself* was less successful, but 1995's *Tool Box* returned him to the top of the singles charts with "That's as Close as I'll Get to Loving You." Tippin also remarried that year.

When Tippin's follow-up singles failed to duplicate their predecessor's popularity, his relationship with RCA began to fray. They eventually parted ways, and it wasn't until 1998 that Tippin managed to score another deal, this time with Disney subsidiary Lyric Street Records. He co-produced his label debut, *What This Country Needs*, which was released later that year and returned him to the Top Ten via the single "For You I Will." The follow-up, 2000's *People Like Us*, became the first Tippin album to make the country Top Five, thanks to the number-one smash "Kiss This," a song co-written by Tippin's wife Thea. The Christmas album *A December to Remember* followed in 2001, and Tippin returned with a proper follow-up, *Stars & Stripes*, in 2002. The post-September 11 anthem "Where the Stars and Stripes and the Eagle Fly" was a crossover smash, not only reaching number two on the country charts but also climbing into the pop Top 20. —*Steve Huey*

You've Got to Stand for Something / 1991 / RCA ✦✦✦✦✦

This exciting hardcore country comes from a man whose previous blue-collar experience as a farm hand, welder, pilot, and truck driver made him a publicist's dream. It includes the singles "You've Got to Stand for Something," "I Wonder How Far It Is over You, " and "She Made a Memory out of Me." —*Brian Mansfield*

Read Between the Lines / 1992 / RCA ✦✦✦✦

A good follow-up by this popular hatless hillbilly contains "There Ain't Nothin' Wrong With the Radio," "I Wouldn't Have It Any Other Way," "My Blue Angel," and more. —*Mark A. Humphrey*

Call of the Wild / Aug. 1993 / RCA ✦✦✦

Though he was still capable of singing up a storm and cranking out great grooves, some of Tippin's song choices were hillbilly silly. Of course, they were also the singles, which had names like "Honky Tonk Superman" and "Working Man's Ph.D." —*Brian Mansfield*

Lookin' Back at Myself / Nov. 8, 1994 / RCA ✦✦✦✦✦

Lookin' Back At Myself has a good cross-section of Aaron Tippin's biggest hits and best songs, making it an excellent introduction. —*Thom Owens*

Tool Box / Nov. 21, 1995 / RCA ✦✦✦

Aaron Tippin's *Tool Box* ranks among his finest work, as the singer explores slightly new territory. In addition to his trademark honky tonk, barroom ravers, there are a number of soulful ballads that demonstrate the full range of Tippin's talents. —*Stephen Thomas Erlewine*

● **Greatest Hits. . . and the Some** / Mar. 25, 1997 / RCA ✦✦✦✦
Greatest Hits and Then Some contains all of Aaron Tippin's best-known songs and biggest hits from the early '90s, including "I Wouldn't Have It Any Other Way," "My Blue Angel," "Working Man's Ph.D.," "I Get It Honest," and the number-one singles "You've Got to Stand for Something" and "That's as Close as I'll Get to Loving You." —*Thom Owens*

Super Hits / Mar. 24, 1998 / RCA ✦✦✦
Super Hits contains ten hits from the peak of Aaron Tippin's career, including "Without Your Love," "That's as Close as I'll Get to Loving You," "Honky Tonk Superman," "I Got It Honest," "There Ain't Nothin' Wrong With the Radio," "My Blue Angel," "I Wonder How Far It Is Over You," "She Made a Memory Out of You" and "You've Got to Stand for Something." Ultimately, this collection isn't as good as his *Greatest Hits* compilation, but it's still a good bargain for the budget-conscious. —*Thom Owens*

The Essential / Jun. 2, 1998 / RCA ✦✦✦✦
Aaron Tippin was an important contributor to the traditionalist movement in the '90s. Tippin approached country music with a honky tonk attitude, leading to some of the era's rootsiest tunes on country radio. These 16 tracks include his debut hit, "You've Got to Stand for Something," "The Man That Came Between Us (Was Me)," "Working Man's Ph.D.," and his first number-one hit, "There Ain't Nothing Wrong With the Radio." The disc closes with an above-average version of Billy Swan's "I Can Help." —*Al Campbell*

What This Country Needs / Oct. 6, 1998 / Hollywood ✦✦✦✦
For those who always thought Aaron Tippin was wasting that fantastic voice on his many trademark, but somewhat contrived "working-man" anthems, *What This Country Needs* is the first confirmation of his true potential for greatness. This record, his first after leaving RCA, surpasses his previous work in nearly every respect. His voice is even more sublime than before, sometimes even achieving the extraordinary richness of '70s-era Waylon Jennings. What really make this album a whole different animal, though, are the songs. Tippin's finest moments have always been his heart-on-the-sleeve ballads, like "I Promised You the World" (from 1994's *Call of the Wild*). There are several excellent tunes in that vein here, particularly the lump-in-the-throat-prompting "I'm Leaving," but even the uptempo material always smartly avoids the common new-country problem of emphasizing clever turns of phrase over emotional content. The album's production, although replete with honky tonk steel guitars and fiddles, is thoroughly modern without being cheesy. Some songs even sound a little like the best work of the Eagles, except with a truly kick-ass real country singer. Whether it was increased artistic control (Tippin co-produced the album), a new label, or perhaps the birth of his child, something apparently lit a serious fire under Aaron Tippin, as this album stands head and shoulders above anything he recorded prior. Accessible, yet substantial and moving, *What This Country Needs* is that rare record that should appeal to mainstream country and alt-country lovers alike. —*Pemberton Roach*

People Like Us / Jul. 25, 2000 / Lyric Street ✦✦✦
Aaron Tippin's first album with Lyric Street, *What This Country Needs*, released in 1998, met with modest success. Almost two years later, *People Like Us* is sure to bring even greater success to country's "hard-working," "honest," and "strong" Tippin, the man who gave us the colossal hit, "That's as Close as I'll Get to Loving You" from 1995's *Tool Box*. Keeping traditional country alive with acoustic and steel guitars and fiddles, *People Like Us* breathes new life into a category of music that's been in a vegetative state. The 11 songs on this album are a welcome listen, including the animated "Kiss This" and "The Best Love We Ever Made" with Tippin's wife Thea providing sweet vocals on lead and harmony. Sounding "too country" sure hasn't killed this career. —*Maria Konicki Dinoia*

A December to Remember / Sep. 18, 2001 / Hollywood ✦✦
The first ever full-length Christmas album from Aaron Tippin isn't bad. He puts his own "working man" spin on popular holiday fare like "Jingle Bell Rock," "Blue Christmas," "Silent Night," and "Away in a Manger," sung as a charmingly winsome duet with wife Thea. And no country Christmas album would be complete without some new songs, so Tippin and Thea wrote or co-wrote seven newbies including standout originals "It's a Good Thing Santa Ain't Single" and "The Year That Santa Never Came." Even Scrooge himself would have a hard time not enjoying this sweet little album. —*Maria Konicki Dinoia*

RCA Country Legends / Jun. 11, 2002 / RCA ✦✦✦✦
The new traditionalist movement in the early '90s brought about a shift in the country establishment, away from a glossy pop sound and back to the roots of the music. Aaron Tippin was one of the singers who weren't afraid to be more influenced by Hank Thompson and Lefty Frizzell than by Kenny Rogers. He signed with RCA in 1990, released *You've Got to Stand for Something*, and had a big hit on the country charts with the title track. Since then he's had lots of hit records, including two number one smashes: "There Ain't Nothing Wrong With the Radio" and "That's as Close as I'll Get to Loving You." This 16-song set collects all his hits and many key album tracks, including songs from his out-of-print debut. Fans of Aaron Tippin and good solid country music will find this set a worthwhile addition to their collection —*Tim Sendra*

Tony Toliver (Charles Anthony Toliver)
b. Richards, TX
Piano, Vocals / Contemporary Country, New Traditionalist
Born on the Fourth of July, Tony Toliver (born Charles Anthony Toliver) grew up in the small town of Richards, TX. In his early teens, Toliver played bass and sang in the Piney Woods Quartet, a family gospel group that gigged all across southeast Texas. By 18, he had heard Ronnie Milsap and was so taken with his music that he began playing piano. After putting a band together, Toliver gigged around Huntsville until deciding at the age of 25 that a move to Nashville was mandatory. Toliver held several day jobs, while playing anywhere he could at night. While working at the Hall of Fame Motel, singer Dottie West heard Toliver and offered him a job. Toliver's first gig with West was at the White

House, when President Ronald Reagan threw a 75th birthday party for Lady Bird Johnson. Toliver continued to work with West for the last four and a half years of her life. After West died, Toliver kept the band together and in 1995 cut his self-titled debut album for Curb/Capitol. The following year he released his second disc, *Half Saint, Half Sinner*. —*Al Campbell*

Tony Toliver / 1991 / Curb ✦✦✦

● **Half Saint, Half Sinner** / Sep. 24, 1996 / Rising Tide ✦✦✦✦
Tony Toliver's third solo album *Half Saint, Half Sinner* is a terrific set of rootsy contemporary country, driven by his pounding piano. —*Thom Owens*

George Tomsco
b. Apr. 24, 1940
Guitar / Rockabilly
Heard most often in the Fireballs, George Tomsco's nimble guitar work was influenced by rockabilly, country & western, and Latin music. Although few fans would recognize his name, he was one of the most popular and influential instrumentalists of Tex-Mex styled rock music, finding particular favor in Britain with the Shadows, who covered some Fireballs songs. In addition to playing with the Fireballs (who also recorded with vocalist Jimmy Gilmer), Tomsco played on numerous sessions in the late '50s and 1960s, often working at the Clovis, NM, studios of Norman Petty, famous for producing several Buddy Holly hits. Although he was most frequently heard as a session player on instrumental records that bore some similarity to those of the Fireballs, or with vocalists who were trying to imitate Holly, he was versatile enough to also contribute to sides by folksinger Carolyn Hester and soul artist Arthur Alexander. He didn't record on his own often, but a 30-song anthology consisting mostly of tracks he did with the Fireballs and as a session musician, *The Tex-Mex Fireball*, was issued under his name in 1998. —*Richie Unterberger*

● **The Tex-Mex Fireball** / Nov. 24, 1998 / Ace ✦✦✦
A 30-song anthology of Tomsco's career, culling together tracks by the Fireballs (including their first hit, "Torquay," and a raw previously unissued demo cover of Little Richard's "Rip It Up"), scattered cuts he did in the 1960s under his own name and as half of "George & Babs," and a wealth of items from the late '50s and '60s on which he worked as a session guitarist. The scope of this material is impressive; as a listening experience, it's inconsistent. At the top of the pile are Buddy Holly classics like "Crying, Waiting, Hoping" (the Fireballs posthumously overdubbed some Holly demos), Jimmy Gilmer's number-one 1963 hit "Sugar Shack," Arthur Alexander's superb 1965 soul lament "You Don't Care," and a 1964 track by Carolyn Hester, "That's My Song," that was co-written by Tomsco and his wife. Much of this, however, is slight if inoffensive early-'60s style Tex-Mex vocal and instrumental rock. As for the highlights among the material that's hard to find otherwise, Jimmy Craig's "Oh Little Girl" (from 1959) is a close Buddy Holly soundalike, and George & Babs' "Come On Home" is a pretty decent mid-'60s-style pop/rocker. Everything here is from 1958-1969, with the exception of three tracks done by a reunited Fireballs in 1989. —*Richie Unterberger*

The Tractors
Group / Contemporary Country, Neo-Traditionalist Country
The Tractors were one of the country-rock bands to benefit from the modern country boom of the early '90s. With their good-time boogie and rootsy country-rock, the Tractors were able to send their eponymous debut to platinum status. Although based in Tulsa, all of the members of the Tractors—guitarist Steve Ripley, bassist Ron Getman, vocalist Casey Van Beek, keyboardist Walt Richmond, and drummer Jamie Oldaker—were well-known Nashville session musicians before they came to prominence in the early '90s. The group landed a contract with Arista Records and released their self-titled debut album in the summer of 1994. Supported by the hit single "Baby Likes to Rock It," the record became a Top Ten country hit, eventually selling over two-million copies.
Instead of following the debut with a standard second record, the band released a holiday album, *Have Yourself a Tractors Christmas*, in the fall of 1995. Like its predecessor, the Christmas record was a hit, although it didn't come close to replicating the chart status of *The Tractors*. The band took most of 1996 off, spending time with their families and working on side projects, as lead songwriter Steve Ripley prepared material for their third album, *Farmers in a Changing World*, which was finally released in the autumn of 1998. —*Stephen Thomas Erlewine*

● **Tractors** / 1994 / Arista ✦✦✦✦✦

Owner's Manual / Aug. 2, 1994 / Arista ✦✦✦

Have Yourself a Tractors Christmas / Oct. 10, 1995 / Arista ✦✦✦
Country Christmas gets wrapped up boogie blues-rockin' style thanks to the Tractors' *Have Yourself a Tractors Christmas*. A little manipulative, perhaps, to redo their hit single "Baby Likes to Rock It" under the guise of "Santa Claus Is Comin' (In a Boogie Woogie Choo Choo Train)" but, with the exception of a coupl'a slow cookers, this blend of originals and trads rolls right on down the track. —*Roch Parisien*

Farmers in a Changing World / Nov. 3, 1998 / Arista ✦✦✦✦
Four years after their acclaimed debut, the Tractors finally delivered their full-fledged follow-up, *Farmers in a Changing World*, in late 1998. (A holiday album, *Have Yourself a Tractors Christmas*, appeared in 1995, but that doesn't count as a sequel to *The Tractors*). During that time, contemporary country became even more infatuated with the pop-country crossover, as the success of Shania Twain and Faith Hill proved. The title of the album hints at that situation, but the Tractors ignore such trends, choosing to synthesize a plethora of American roots musics into a distinctive sound—they're farmers in a changing world. Sure, they remain rooted in country, but they try a bunch of other things, including soul, New Orleans R&B, and rockabilly with "The Elvis Thing," backed by no less than Scotty Moore, James Burton, and D.J. Fontana. What ties it all together is

Steve Ripley's fine songwriting and the band's excellent taste in covers; the material is so good that the eclecticism doesn't seem jumbled—it makes sense. It may have taken a while for the album to have been recorded, but the wait was worth it. —*Stephen Thomas Erlewine*

Fast Girl / Apr. 24, 2001 / Audium ✦✦✦✦
A fine slab of NRBQ/Dave Edmunds-style country-inflected rock & roll, 2001's *Fast Girl* is another typically enjoyable album from the Tractors. Like their namesake farm equipment, the Tractors are never flashy, and they're built more for comfort than speed. Goofy rockers like "Babalou" (nothing to do with Desi Arnaz, of course), two-step ballads like "It's a Beautiful Thing," and honky tonk covers like the Tractors' version of Moon Mullican's classic "Don't Ever Take My Picture Down" blend into an eclectic but never scattershot blend of country, R&B, and early rock influences. In these surroundings, even stylistic experiments like the extended jam that closes the otherwise ultra-poppy "Ready to Cry" make perfect sense. *Fast Girl* is not the Tractors' best album, but coming as it did after a nearly four-year layoff, it shows that the group hadn't lost anything in its downtime. —*Stewart Mason*

Big Night / Oct. 8, 2002 / Audium ✦✦✦

Diana Trask

b. Jun. 23, 1940, Warburton, Australia
Vocals / Traditional Country, Country-Pop
Australian singer Diana Trask was a popular performer in the U.S. during the '60s and '70s. She was born in Warburton, a small logging town near Melbourne, to a musically talented family. She first gained attention in Australia at age 16 after winning a nationwide talent contest, and began playing on television. Later, she was a part of a pop group which opened for such American stars as Sammy Davis Jr., who liked her music and suggested she come to the U.S. In 1959, Trask did, but didn't find much success until she spent a week guesting on Don McNeil's *Breakfast Club*, which led to a contract with Columbia and a regular spot on the TV show *Sing Along with Mitch*. Both of her initial albums were pop-oriented.

After marrying in the early '60s, Trask returned to Australia, but by 1966, she and her family were living in New York, where she continued trying to further her pop career. After visiting the CMA DJ Convention in Nashville, she decided to focus on country music instead. She debuted on the country charts in 1968 with the low-ranked "Lock, Stock and Teardrops," but later that year she reached the Top 60 with "Hold What You've Got." In 1969, Trask released her debut album *Miss Country Soul* and toured with Hank Williams Jr. Although she continued to have modest hits, her popularity didn't take off until 1972, when she had a Top 30 hit with "We've Got to Work It Out Between Us." In 1973, she made the Top 20 twice with "Say When" and "It's a Man's World (If You Had a Man Like Mine)." The following year, she had a Top 15 crossover hit with "Lean on Me." She returned to Australia during the mid-'70s and earned a few gold records there. Trask returned to the U.S. in 1981 to record a pair of singles, but then retired for the remainder of the decade. During the 1990s she again resumed performing. —*Sandra Brennan*

Diana Trask on TV / 1961 / Columbia ✦✦✦
● **Diana Trask's Greatest Hits** / 1974 / ABC/Dot ✦✦✦✦✦
The ABC Collection / 1977 / ABC ✦✦✦✦✦

Merle Travis

b. Nov. 29, 1917, Rosewood, KY, **d.** Oct. 20, 1983, Tahlequah, OK
Guitar, Guitar (Electric), Vocals / Traditional Country, Country Boogie, Instrumental Country
Merle Travis was virtually without peer as a guitarist and songwriter. A unique stylist, he was respected and prominent enough to have an instrumental style ("Travis picking") named after him, and only Chet Atkins even comes close to the influence that Travis had on the way the guitar is understood and played in country music. (Indeed, Atkins was initially signed to RCA to be that label's Merle Travis.) As a songwriter, he wasn't far behind, with originals such as "Sixteen Tons" crossing over as popular standards in the hands of other artists. He even played two different vital and indirect roles in the development of rock & roll, and was no slouch as a recording artist, with his own share of chart hits and novelty songs.

Merle Robert Travis was born on November 29, 1917, in Rosewood, KY. His father was a coal miner, and the family lived on the bare edge of poverty; eventually this experience, coupled with a phrase that Travis' father used to describe their lives, became the basis for the song "Sixteen Tons." His very first instrument was a five-string banjo, but when he was 12 year old his older brother gave him a homemade guitar. Travis was lucky enough to have as neighbors Ike Everly, later the father of Don and Phil, and Mose Rager, who played in a unique three-finger guitar style that had developed in that area of Kentucky. Travis learned this approach as a teenager and grew astonishingly proficient in a repertory that included blues, ragtime, and popular tunes. It wasn't enough to earn a living, and he survived by working in the Civilian Conservation Corps as a teenager.

His first break came during a visit to his brother's home in Evansville, IN, in 1935, where his chance to entertain at a local dance resulted in membership in a couple of local bands and a chance to appear on a local radio station. By 1937, he was a member of Clayton McMichen's Georgia Wildcats, and a year later he'd moved on to the Drifting Pioneers, who found a permanent broadcasting gig at Cincinnati's WLW. The *Boone Country Jamboree* radio show kept the group busy until World War II came along and forced it to disband. While a member of the Drifting Pioneers, Travis acquired a national following, and also began playing with Grandpa Jones and the Delmore Brothers in a gospel quartet called the Brown's Ferry Four. He later teamed up with Jones as "the Shepherd Brothers" as the first artists to record for the newly founded King Records label in 1943. He and Jones even exchanged songs and found the sources for a few songs together—it was while out with Jones one day at a black church in Cincinnati that Travis heard the sermon that became the song "That's All."

Travis spent a short stint in the Marines, but was quickly discharged and returned to Cincinnati. During the late winter of 1944, he headed for Los Angeles, where he began making appearances in Charles Starrett's Western movies and playing with Ray Whitley's Western swing band. With guidance from Tex Ritter and bassist Cliffie Stone, in 1946 he released the topical song "No Vacancy"—dealing with the displacement of returning veterans—along with "Cincinnati Lou," and earned a double-sided hit. His next major project was a concept album, *Folk Songs of the Hills*, which was intended to compete with Burl Ives' successful folk recordings. The record, released as a set of four 78-rpm discs, was a failure at the time it was released in 1947 (it wasn't even transferred to long-playing disc until nearly ten years later). However, it yielded several classics, among them the Travis originals "Sixteen Tons," "Dark as a Dungeon," and "Over By Number Nine," as well as introducing such standards as "Nine Pound Hammer"; it also became a unique document, depicting a beautiful all-acoustic solo guitar performance by this master virtuoso.

The initial failure of the folk album aside, 1947 began a boom period in Travis' career. In addition to writing the million-selling hit "Smoke! Smoke! Smoke!" for his friend Tex Williams, he had a half-dozen Top Ten records himself, including "Divorce Me C.O.D.," "So Round, So Firm, So Fully Packed," and "Three Times Seven." Travis also devised the first solid-body electric guitar, coming up with a model which, when perfected by Leo Fender, would become a key element in early rock & roll. The string of hits didn't last, but Travis' career continued uninterrupted, with performances on-stage, television, and record. Beginning in 1953, he landed a fairly visible movie role in one of the biggest films of the year, *From Here to Eternity*, where he performed "Re-Enlistment Blues," and it was around that same time that he began playing on all of his friend Hank Thompson's records. In 1955, Tennessee Ernie Ford had his crossover hit with "Sixteen Tons," and it was around that same time that Travis acolytes such as Atkins were making a major impact on music themselves. Scotty Moore, who'd first been influenced by Travis from his radio performances, had become Elvis Presley's lead guitarist, and a year after Elvis hit nationally, the Everly Brothers (themselves Atkins disciples) started topping the charts.

Travis was one of those musical figures who was referred to constantly, either musically or literally, by dozens of major figures, but he was never able to ascend the charts himself again. Much of the problem lay in his personal life. Along with a reputation as one of country music's top axemen, Travis also became known as a wildman, especially when he drank. He was arrested more than once for public intoxication and drunk driving—on his motorcycle—and in 1956 there was a highly publicized report of police surrounding his home after he assaulted his wife. Then, during the early '60s, he was hospitalized briefly after being arrested while driving under the influence of narcotics. He managed to pull his professional life together in the mid-'60s to do one new folk-style album, *Songs of the Coal Mines*, which, like its predecessor *Folk Songs of the Hills*, failed to sell on its original release. His other albums—mostly instrumental, such as *Walkin' the Strings*—proved much more significant and influential at the time as standard acquisitions for aspiring guitarists. He still played occasionally and became something of a star on the college folk circuit, teaming with Atkins for the Grammy-winning *Atkins-Travis Traveling Show* in 1974. Travis finally seemed to settle down after he married his fourth wife, Dorothy—the former wife of his longtime friend Hank Thompson—and focused once again on music. He recorded tribute albums to the Georgia Wildcats and began working again with old associates like Grandpa Jones, and it looked like Travis was to enjoy a resurgence of musical and public acclaim. At age 65, however, he suffered a massive heart attack and died the following morning. —*Bruce Eder*

The Merle Travis Guitar / 1956 / Capitol ✦✦✦✦
Merle Travis' first instrumental long-player is a guitar masterpiece, encompassing originals ("Black Diamond Blues," "Walking the Strings"), covers of other people's old hits ("The Waltz You Saved For Me"), and a few antique pop songs ("On a Bicycle Built For Two," "The Shiek of Araby"). In its time, this album was considered as significant as any Chet Atkins album, and an important showcase for the electric guitar, in particular, though Travis would do even better than this a couple of years later on his all-acoustic *Walkin' the Strings*. —*Bruce Eder*

Back Home / 1957 / Capitol ✦✦✦✦✦
A reissue of his eight-song 1947 album *Folk Songs of the Hills*, with four additional cuts from the Capitol *Electrical Transcription* series. [The LP has been reissued in its entirety on the 1996 CD version of *Folk Songs of the Hills*, with the addition of a song that was previously unreleased in the U.S.] —*Richie Unterberger*

Walkin' the Strings / 1960 / Capitol ✦✦✦✦✦
Although originally issued on LP in 1960 (it was reissued on CD in 1996), these 22 songs were actually recorded in the late '40s and early '50s for Capitol's *Electrical Transciption* series. This showcases Travis' fingerpicking abilities at their best, on unaccompanied acoustic vocal and instrumental numbers; most of the material is original, with a few standards by the likes of Stephen Foster and Georgia Tom Dorsey. —*Richie Unterberger*

Songs of the Coal Mines / 1963 / Capitol ✦✦✦✦
Travis recorded this concept album over a period of three days in March 1963, consisting of 12 originals dealing with the lives of coal miners, a subject that Travis knew well, as the only male member of his family to have escaped a livelihood earned underground. The material consists of folk and blues ("Pay Day Comes Too Slow" is one of the best pieces of white blues you'll ever hear, regardless of how many Eric Clapton albums you may own already), all very vivid in its textures and sensibilities, and it's a crying shame that the album never made the charts, as this was obviously a project very close to Travis' heart. The cover is also something of a classic, though it hardly emphasized this as a Travis album, consisting of drawings that might've come out of any miner's family album. —*Bruce Eder*

Great Songs of the Delmore Brothers / 1969 / Capitol ✦✦✦✦✦

Travis Pickin' / 1981 / CMH ✦✦✦✦✦
Until his Capitol Records instrumental recordings become available again, this is one for guitar buffs to go for. —*Richard Lieberson*

Country Guitar Thunder (1977-1981) / 1983 / CMH ✦✦✦✦✦
Merle Travis recorded his portion of this album in association with veteran flatpicker Joe Maphis (maybe the fastest guitarist that ever lived) during 1977 and 1981 in Nashville, TN, Albuquerque, NM, and Charlotte, NC. It's an all-instrumental album made up of duets and Maphis solo-featured numbers, and material ranging from traditional pieces like "Irish Washerwoman," "L'il Liza Jane," and "John Henry" to movie and television theme music ("Ballad of Thunder Road," "Bonanza"). The sound is crisp and vivid, as well as surprisingly warm, and these guys knew how to make the stereo separation work for them. Six of the 16 tracks are Maphis numbers, but the rest is a dazzling interweave of playing by two of the greatest country guitarists that ever lived. And it's budget priced, to boot. *—Bruce Eder*

Merle Travis Story—24 Greatest Hits / 1989 / CMH ✦✦✦✦✦
Although *The Merle Travis Story—24 Greatest Hits* consists of re-recordings from the late '70s, it gives a better sense of why Travis was important than Rhino's *The Best of Merle Travis*. Unlike Rhino's set, CMH concentrates on Travis' guitar playing, which is why he was an important musician. Therefore, it gives a far better sense of why the guitarist was a revered, influential artist than the vocal hits of Rhino's collection, even if the music was recorded late in his career. *—Thom Owens*

The Best of Merle Travis / 1990 / Rhino ✦✦✦✦✦
Rhino's *The Best of Merle Travis* may contain all of his big chart hits, but it's a misleading collection. Instead of focusing on Travis' revolutionary playing, the set runs through his hits and novelty songs, which all emphasize his vocals. Therefore, it isn't quite as comprehensive—or essential—as it initially appears. The album hints at his greatness, but never shows why Travis' playing was so groundbreaking. *—Thom Owens*

The Radio Shows, 1945–1946 / 1990 / Country Routes ✦✦✦

Unreleased Radio Transcriptions 1944–1949 / 1991 / Rounder ✦✦✦
This album contains 22 tracks of performances originally broadcast on such shows as *Hollywood Barn Dance*, *Melody Roundup*, and the *Grand Ole Opry*, among others. *—AMG*

Merle Travis 1944-49 / 1991 / Country Routes ✦✦✦✦✦
A dazzling collection of 22 radio recordings by Travis, some solo and some done backed up by the likes of Johnny Bond, done for such shows as *Hollywood Barn Dance*, *the Melody Roundup* and *Dinner Bell Roundup*, the *Grand Ole Opry*, *the Country Barn Dance*, and *the Cliffie Stone Western Party*. The earliest of these sides date from immediately after Travis' 1944 discharge from the Marine Corps, and show him establishing himself in Los Angeles in association with producer/emcee Cliffie Stone, who later brought Travis to Capitol Records. The later stuff, from 1946 on, overlaps with Travis' early period at Capitol, including things like his *Grand Ole Opry* performance of "John Henry," which he had also cut for Folksongs of the Hills. Travis preferred the radio performances to his studio recordings because of radio's less-formal requirements and easier-going approach to music-making, which allowed him to improvise as he pleased within the time available—you could joke around on radio in ways that no one was allowed to in the studio. Among the notable songs is Travis' cover of "Old Rattler," a dog song that he learned from Grandpa Jones during their period playing together in the Brown's Ferry Four; his cover of Jimmie Rodgers' "T for Texas"; and "Roll on Mississippi," an old Boswell Sisters harmony number played by Travis in a subordinate position to Johnny Bond. Some of the stuff is very short, but all of it is worth hearing and owning by anyone who presumes to like Travis. The sound quality is uniformly good, and the notes are excellent. *—Bruce Eder*

Folk Songs of the Hills (Back Home/Songs of the Coal Mines) / Jun. 28, 1994 / Bear Family ✦✦✦✦
This German import—which goes for about double the cost of the U.S. CD *Folk Songs of the Hills* —contains not only *Folk Songs of the Hills/Back Home* (but *not* the previously unreleased "This World Is Not My Home"), but also an entire additional Travis album, the 1963 *Songs of the Coal Mines*, which deal with the lot and lives of coal miners. The songs include "Black Gold," "Harlan County Boys," "The Browder Explosion," and "Bloody Brethitt County," a song as savage as its title implies. The extra cost is worth it, in the absence of a separate U.S. CD release of *Songs of the Coal Mines*. Travis completists will want it, and any folk or blues enthusiast (check out "Pay Day Comes Too Slow") should want it. *—Bruce Eder*

☆ **Guitar Rags & A Too Fast Past** / Jul. 15, 1994 / Bear Family ✦✦✦✦✦
Containing five CDs and 141 songs, and runs nearly seven hours, this set is pure gold, whether you like Travis' instrumental string dazzlers or his novelty hits of the late '40s—and it's just about 100 percent indispensable to anyone who likes good folk, hillbilly, country, or blues. Disc one is worth half the cost by itself, 20 of its 28 tracks drawn from Travis' early/mid-'40s career on King, Capitol, and a handful of forgotten labels, in duets and group settings. This includes his recordings with Grandpa Jones (on guitar, no less) as the Sheppard Brothers from 1943, and his topical (anti-Axis) songs recorded under aliases. All of this stuff features not only Travis' superb guitar, but excellent harmony singing by him as well. The first Travis solo track as we would know it, "That's All," is worth the wait, and later selections find him slipping into the sound recognized from his familiar recordings. Part of disc two is given over to *Folk Songs of the Hills*, but Travis' full band sound is also well represented. Disc three contains more of Travis' full-band pop numbers, and a similar new discovery in an alternate take of "Merle's Boogie Woogie," the first multi-tracked country recording ever done. Disc four, with 31 tracks, covers 1950 to 1953, when Travis' sound became more varied—there were still full-band pop numbers; his group was stripped down, and there were fewer novelty numbers. Disc five is a mix of superb instrumentals and rousing pop numbers, along with some blues and a few reworked old standards. It may be the strongest of the five. The book is excellent—all 80 pages of it—and the sound on all but a handful of tracks is as good as being at the session. *—Bruce Eder*

Country Hoedown Shows & Films / Jan. 24, 1995 / Country Routes ✦✦
For collectors only, *Country Hoedown Shows & Films* contains 25 tracks drawn from radio transcriptions, soundies, and films. Although the outside packaging doesn't say so, several songs are solo performances by artists such as Ernest Tubb and Tex Williams, and some are ensemble vocal pieces or duets with Carolina Cotton, Judy Hayden, and others. The sound quality and performances on the transcriptions are good; the film tracks are very rough. On the transcriptions Merle Travis sometimes changed the arrangements or tempos of his well-known songs quite a bit, and performed some songs ("Midnight Special") that he did not record in the studio at the time. *—Greg Adams*

Unissued Radio Shows, 1944–1948 / Jan. 24, 1995 / Country Routes ✦✦✦✦
This features 28 radio broadcast transcriptions from the mid- to late '40s of Merle at arguably the peak of his strengths. These loose, Cliffie Stone-produced broadcasts capture Merle at his most relaxed and musically imaginative. His version of "Cannonball Rag," which features a bridge not found on the better-known Capitol version, is absolutely mind-boggling in its effortless technique, while his coughing spurt in the middle of a duet with wife Tex Ann is loaded with simplistic charm. In between the solo guitar pieces are a great a cappella "Churchy Time," some of the early band hits like "Divorce Me C.O.D.," and the trial run (from the *Grand Ole Opry*) of "When My Baby Double-Talks to Me." Transfer quality varies wildly, but nothing sounds horrible, and the performances are worth every nick and pop. It's a marvelous collection. *—Cub Koda*

Guitar Retrospective / Jul. 18, 1995 / CMH ✦✦✦✦

Folk Songs of the Hills [Expanded Edition] / 1996 / Capitol ✦✦✦✦✦
In 1946, Capitol approached Travis with the idea of cutting a folk album, and although he wasn't an especially folk-oriented artist, he agreed to give it a go. Although the resulting 1947 record (released as a 78 rpm album) didn't sell well, it was a respectable effort performed by Travis on solo acoustic guitar. Folksy introductions embellish the songs, which include standbys like "John Henry" and "Nine Pound Hammer." Travis added a few songs of his own penned in the folk style, and one of these, "Sixteen Tons," would prove to be his most famous composition, reaching number one when it was covered by Tennessee Ernie Ford in the 1950s. The CD reissue combines the eight songs from the 1947 release with four songs from the Capitol *Electrical Transciption* series that were added to the batch when the album was reissued as *Back Home* in 1957; it also adds a song from the 1946 sessions that was previously unreleased in the U.S., "This World Is Not My Home." *—Richie Unterberger*

Turn Your Radio On (1944–1965) / Jul. 14, 1998 / Country Routes ✦✦✦✦

★ **The Best of Merle Travis: Sweet Temptation 1946–1953** / Apr. 18, 2000 / Razor & Tie ✦✦✦✦✦
Covering a time frame from 1946 to 1953, here's a nice collection of Travis' biggest hits. As revered as Merle is as an innovative and influential guitarist, this set principally highlights his best-known tunes as a singer/songwriter, including the original "Sixteen Tons," "So Round, So Firm, So Fully Packed," "Divorce Me C.O.D.," "Kentucky Means Paradise," and the title track. But the picking side of Travis' talent is nicely highlighted on "Cannonball Rag," "Guitar Rag," and the closing "I'll See You in My Dreams." Not the perfect introduction to Merle's many talents, but a darn good cornerstone to any collection you might want to build off it. *—Cub Koda*

Sixteen Tons / Jun. 25, 2002 / ASV ✦✦✦✦✦
This isn't a definitive Merle Travis collection, but it does a good job of filling the gaps in Razor & Tie's *Sweet Temptation* compilation. It may omit "Cannonball Rag" and some other quintessential performances, but makes up for it by including the entire *Folk Songs of the Hills* album, with the original versions of "Nine Pound Hammer" and "Dark as a Dungeon." The bulk of this material was recorded during Travis' late-'40s peak, which means, unfortunately, that there is nothing from *Walkin' the Strings*, but then, anyone lucky enough to find a copy of that album should have a contractual obligation to pick it up. *—Jim Smith*

The Very Best of Merle Travis / Sep. 17, 2002 / Varese ✦✦✦

Merle Travis in Boston 1959 / May 20, 2003 / Rounder ✦✦✦
This warm live recording from 1959 finds Merle Travis all alone on his acoustic six-string, the perfect accompaniment to his robust voice. Splitting time between instrumentals and vocal numbers like "Dark as a Dungeon," "John Henry," and the ubiquitous "Sixteen Tons," Travis' singing and legendary picking are pristinely recorded, alternating between being darkly chilling and joyously grinning. It may seem like a foot race to have 22 tracks in 43 minutes, but nearly every tune is introduced by Travis with a quick story or humorous anecdote, so the 16 actual songs are each given ample time. Blurring the line between country and folk, Merle Travis was never in better form, and his songs are as timeless in the 21st century as they were when they were written. *—Zac Johnson*

Randy Travis (Randy Bruce Traywick)

b. May 4, 1959, Marshville, NC
Vocals, Guitar / Contemporary Country, New Traditionalist, Neo-Traditionalist Country, Country Gospel
Like the Beatles in rock, Randy Travis marks a generational shift in country music. When his *Storms of Life* came out in 1986, country music was still wallowing in the post-urban cowboy recession, chasing elusive crossover dreams. Travis brought the music back to its basics, sounding like nothing so much as a perfect blend of George Jones and Merle Haggard. He became the dominant male voice in country until the rise of "hat acts" like Garth Brooks and Clint Black, releasing seven consecutive number one singles during one stretch. He won the CMA's Horizon Award in 1986 and was the association's Male

Vocalist of the Year in 1987 and 1988. Travis (born Randy Bruce Traywick, May 4, 1959, Marshville, NC) was born and raised in North Carolina, in a small town outside of Charlotte. His father encouraged his children to pursue their musical inclinations, as he was a fan of honky tonkers like Hank Williams, Jones, and Lefty Frizzell. Randy began playing guitar at the age of eight, and within two years, he and his brother Ricky formed a duo called the Traywick Brothers. The duo played in local clubs and talent contests.

Both of the brothers had a wild streak, which resulted in Ricky going to jail after a car chase and Randy running away to Charlotte at the age of 16. While he was in Charlotte, he won a talent contest at Country City U.S.A., a bar owned by Lib Hatcher. Hatcher was impressed by Travis and offered him a regular gig at her bar, as well as a job as a cook. For several years, he sang and worked at Country City. He still had trouble with the law in his late teens. At his last run-in with the police, the judge told him if he saw Travis again he should be prepared to go to jail for a longtime. Travis was released into the care of Hatcher. In a short time, Hatcher became Travis' manager, and the pair began to concentrate on his career. Joe Stampley helped Travis land a contract with Paula Records in 1978. The following year, Travis released two singles under his given name; one of them, "She's My Woman," scraped the bottom of the country charts.

In 1982, Travis and Hatcher moved to Nashville, where she managed the Nashville Palace nightclub while he sang and cooked. Within a couple of years, the pair independently released his debut album under the name Randy Ray; the record was called *Randy Ray Live* and sold primarily in the Nashville Palace. Thanks to Hatcher's persistent efforts and the *Randy Ray Live* album, Warner Bros. signed Travis in 1985 and suggested that he change his performing name to Randy Travis. "On the Other Hand," his first single for the label, was released in the summer of that year and climbed to number 67. Despite its lackluster performance, radio programmers were enthusiastic for Travis, as evidenced by the number six placing of "1982," which was released late in the year. "1982" was followed by a re-release of "On the Other Hand" in the spring of 1986. This time, the song hit number one.

Storms of Life, Travis' full-fledged debut album, was released in the summer of 1986 and became a huge success, eventually selling over three-million copies. Travis was the first country artist to go multi-platinum; before his success, most country artists had difficulty achieving gold status. With his mass appeal, he set the stage for country music's crossover success in the early '90s. However, Travis dominated the late '80s. The last two singles from *Storms of Life*, "Diggin' Up Bones" and "No Place Like Home," hit number one and two, respectively. "Forever and Ever, Amen"—the first single from his second album, 1987's *Always & Forever*—began a streak of seven straight number-one singles that ran through 1989. *Always & Forever* was more successful than his debut, reaching number 19 on the pop charts and going quadruple platinum; it also earned him the CMA's award for Male Vocalist of the Year. *Old 8x10* (1988) and *No Holdin' Back* (1989) weren't quite as successful as their predecessors, but they still spawned number-one singles and both went platinum.

Travis was still at the top of his form in the beginning of the '90s, starting the decade with his biggest hit, "Hard Rock Bottom of Your Heart." However, his hold at the top of the charts began to slip after Clint Black and, in particular, Garth Brooks. Nevertheless, Travis never fell away completely—his albums continued to gold and he usually could crack the Top Ten. *Wind in the Wire*, a soundtrack to his television special released in 1992, marked his first unsuccessful album—none of the singles broke the Top 40. *This Is Me*, released in 1994, was a successful comeback to the top of the charts, featuring "Whisper My Name," his first number-one hit in two years. In August 1996, Travis released *Full Circle*, his last album for Warner Bros. He left the label in 1997, signing with the fledgling "super" label DreamWorks. His first album for the label, *You and You Alone*, was released in the spring of 1998; *Man Ain't Made of Stone* followed a year later. Traveling the familiar country route, he released an album of traditional and contemporary religious songs, *Inspirational Journey*, which hit the stores in late 2000. The album went on to win two awards at The Gospel Music Association's 32nd Annual Dove Awards in 2001; *Inspirational Journey* took home honors for Country/Bluegrass Album of the Year and Country Recorded Song of the Year for "Baptism." Select songs from the album also made their way in the two-part finale for *Touched by an Angel*, which featured Travis in character. Two years later, Travis continued with his gospel fare with the release of *Rise and Shine*. *—Brian Mansfield & Stephen Thomas Erlewine*

☆ **Storms of Life** / 1986 / Warner Bros. ♦♦♦♦♦

His first and best album features astonishing Lefty Frizzell-style pipes, excellent material, and sympathetic production. Easily the most impressive country debut of the '80s, it includes "1982," "On the Other Hand," "Diggin' up Bones," and "No Place like Home." *—Mark A. Humphrey*

☆ **Always & Forever** / 1987 / Warner Bros. ♦♦♦♦♦

This one stayed at the top of the country charts for ten months and sold five-million copies. Well, of course he was huge. If you had songs as good as "Forever and Ever, Amen" you'd be a star too. *—Brian Mansfield*

Old 8x10 / 1988 / Warner Bros. ♦♦♦♦♦

Almost on a par with *Storms of Life*, *Old 8x10* lacks the monster hits of his debut but wears just as well. When Travis sings of love, he doesn't mean romance; there's a permanence in his voice that sounds like settling down. The album contains "Honky Tonk Moon," "Deeper than the Holler," and "Is It Still Over?" *—Brian Mansfield*

No Holdin' Back / 1989 / Warner Bros. ♦♦♦♦

Released in 1989, *No Holdin' Back* was an anomaly for a record coming from Nash Vegas at the turn of the decade: It's a very traditional country album. Period. Travis is a honky tonk singer who uses the entire scope of the music's history as his playground. He doesn't take a lot of chances, as this record proves, but then he doesn't need to. It's not about ambition on *No Holdin' Back*. Kyle Lehning's production is flawless, in that he allows Travis' big voice to be buoyed by his accompaniment. He sounds like he's dead center in the mix. The album begins with the Matraca Berg nugget "Mining for Coal," an elegiac love song. That's typical enough, but on the very next track, his cover of Melvin Endsley's "Singing the Blues," there is a straight-up honky tonk song complete with male backing chorus—à la the Jordanaires—vocals, plinky upright piano, harmonica, and a barroom tempo. But that's not all: Travis lets out a long Hank Williams-style yodel that will make the listener feel the master's ghostly presence. The single "He Walked on Water" by Allen Shamblin was a bad choice, though it sold well. It's a syrupy ballad that is so overly sentimental that there is no place in the song for Travis to go. The most notable cut on the set is Brook Benton's "It's Just a Matter of Time," and it should have been picked as the album's first single to radio and retail. First, coming almost in the middle, it's the hinge for the entire album. Secondly, this is Travis at his best, stretching to get to the heart of a music that has so little to do with country; like Ray Charles on the other side, he has to make this soul song his own. And he does. It's a country song like it was written that way. The other standout is "Hard Rock Bottom of Your Heart," a modern country shuffle reworked though the tradition. Travis goes after it like Merle Haggard would, slipping in under those verses to max out the emotion from the melody, and then driving that refrain home with a hammer as the pedal steel whines and the crisp drums accent the end of each beat. This is solid Travis, and it proves that at the end of the 1980s he was really just getting started. *—Thom Jurek*

Old-Time Christmas / Aug. 29, 1989 / Warner Bros. ♦♦♦

Of these ten Christmas songs, some are old, some are new, and one is by Travis ("How Do I Wrap My Heart for Christmas," written with Paul Overstreet). "God Rest Ye Merry Gentlemen" is outstanding. *—Brian Mansfield*

Heroes and Friends / 1990 / Warner Bros. ♦♦♦

This duets album includes the obvious influences (George Jones, Conway Twitty, Tammy Wynette) as well as a few surprises (B.B. King, Clint Eastwood). The Jones song, "A Few Ole Country Boys," and the title track were hit singles. *—Brian Mansfield*

High Lonesome / 1991 / Warner Bros. ♦♦♦♦

High Lonesome is a mature record by a seasoned, forward-thinking country artist. Randy Travis, like George Strait and Alan Jackson, saw the new young bucks heading his way up the charts with a watered-down version of the country music he held sacred. And Travis is a direct descendent of the greats like George Jones and Merle Haggard as well as Jim Reeves and Ernest Tubb. Travis wanted to articulate his vision of the music further and entrench it deeper in its roots, which were beginning to give way to the faux rock and pop styles of Garth Brooks and his dire ilk, who wore bachelor pad curtains for shirts. Travis co-wrote five of the album's ten tracks, including a trio with Jackson. Of those, "A Better Class of Losers" is the song that Brooks wishes he could have written. This is the angry side of the George Jones/Tammy Wynette version of "We're Not the Jet Set." Stinging dobros and pedal steels underline every one of Travis' indictments of yuppie culture. In addition, "I'd Surrender All" shows the pair digging deep into the territory Conway Twitty inhabited before he urbanized his sound, and their "Forever Together" is as fine a country love ballad as the 1990s produced; it's a song Hag would have been proud to record back in the day. Another highlight is the mandolin and fiddle-driven waltz that comprises the title track. Written by the criminally undersung Gretchen Peters, it's the long, slow ballad with dobros ringing in the background that was made for Travis' amazing voice. He expresses without stretching; each phrase rings as true as the last. Kyle Lehning's production is unobtrusive and clean, setting Travis in perfect balance with a band that feels live. Not to be outclassed in the honky tonk department, "Allergic to the Blues" is a politically incorrect swinging barroom anthem written by Jackson and Jim McBride. Keeping a woman hostage because of an unwillingness to experience pain and rejection is hardly tasteful, but this is a country song and the tongue is firmly placed in cheek in Travis' read. The set closes with "I'm Gonna Have a Little Talk," an awesome a cappella duet with Take 6. It's country gospel elevated by the 6 to high tension rather than to differing versions of rural gospel. Take 6 is thoroughly modern, sophisticated, and glossy. Travis is so country he couldn't be city if he tried to buy it. This wouldn't have worked anywhere near as well if he had recorded the track with the Blind Boys of Alabama, but in this context, it puts a slick finishing touch on a fine album. *—Thom Jurek*

Wind in the Wire / 1992 / Warner Bros. ♦♦

This album of western cowboy music, some old and some new, was made to go with a TV show of the same name. *—Brian Mansfield*

★ **Greatest Hits, Vol. 1** / Sep. 15, 1992 / Warner Bros. ♦♦♦♦♦

When Travis finally got around to releasing a greatest-hits collection, he realized he had almost enough material for two albums. So, adding two new songs to each, he put them out simultaneously. Volume one gets the edge for including those first two hits, "1982" and "On the Other Hand"; the best of the new songs, "If I Didn't Have You"; and the shattering "Reasons I Cheat," which proved as early as 1986 that Travis could write 'em as well as sing 'em. *—Brian Mansfield*

☆ **Greatest Hits, Vol. 2** / Sep. 15, 1992 / Warner Bros. ♦♦♦♦♦

Here are 11 more Travis classics are included, among them "Diggin' Up Bones," "Forever and Ever, Amen" and a fabulous remake of Brook Benton's "It's Just a Matter of Time." The new songs are "Look Heart, No Hands" and "Take Another Swing at Me." *—Brian Mansfield*

This Is Me / 1994 / Warner Bros. ♦♦♦♦

This Is Me, his first album in three years—after a pair of greatest-hits albums and a vanity project—shows that while Randy Travis may have been takin' care of other business, his talent hadn't gone anywhere. He kicks things off with a bang on "Honky Tonk Side of Town," which exploits all of Travis' strengths in one song, from its shuffling swinging honky tonk blues melody to his shifting and rolling vocal inflections to the burning guitars, singing fiddles, and Pig Robbins' unmistakable piano tinkling. Before a feminist listener can catch her breath, Travis jumps back in with another uptempo bluesy number that will have her laughing at "Before You Kill Us All." There are fine midtempo country ballads here too, including Trey Bruce's brilliant "Whisper My Name," among the greatest songs Travis has ever recorded. The backing vocals by Suzy Ragsdale, Darrell Scott, and Verlon Thompson set the tune apart and accent what a grateful love song this is. There are few of these in country music, and of the ones that do exist too many are overly sentimental. This one rings like the stone truth. Larry Gatlin's "Runaway Train" is given proper choogling treatment here, with acoustic guitars ushering in Travis' vocal before the band underlines it all with sheer momentum and gives the title and lyric ass-kicking honky tonk credence. Gatlin's gift for metaphor is nearly singular, and Travis exploits it to the fullest here. On the Kieran Kane-penned "Gonna Walk That Line," Travis runs through his best George Jones bass singing, and Mark O'Connor's fiddle lifts a modern Ernest Tubb-styled barroom tune to a sophisticated, swinging elegance. The set closes with "Oscar the Angel," the only overly sentimental song on the album and its weakest link. The message of the tune is fine, but it's pure corn. At least it's the last track. *This Is Me* is a better effort from Travis than anybody had any right to expect, and proves he is still a force to reckon with. *—Thom Jurek*

Forever & Ever . . . The Best of Randy Travis / 1995 / Warner Bros. ✦✦✦✦✦

Full Circle / Aug. 1996 / Warner Bros. ✦✦✦✦

Randy Travis' *Full Circle* is a return to form, of sorts. Although he never really left the country charts, his mid-'90s albums suffered from a tendency to sound a bit too similar too each other. *Full Circle* solves that problem by simultaneously reaching back into his hardcore honky tonk roots and moving toward more contemporary material, such as Mark Knopfler's "Are We in Trouble Now." Travis' exquisitely textured and weathered voice gives the new songs a gravity they might not have had if another vocalist had sung them. Furthermore, producer Kyle Lehning has once again assembled a top-notch backing band that manages to sound rootsy and professional simultaneously. With a fine band and an excellent set of material, Travis rises to the occasion with *Full Circle*, producing one of his finest albums of the '90s. *—Thom Owens*

You and You Alone / Apr. 21, 1998 / DreamWorks ✦✦✦

You and You Alone was a pivotal album for Randy Travis and his new label, DreamWorks. For Travis, it was designed to solidify his status as one of Nashville's new elders; for DreamWorks, it would have gotten their foot in the door of the notoriously insular Nashville music establishment. While *You and You Alone* doesn't quite fulfill either goal, it still is a sturdy record that makes Travis' many talents abundantly clear. It lacks the focus and consistent songwriting of its predecessor, *Full Circle*, which was his finest record in years, but individual moments shine just as brightly as the best from that album. Furthermore, producers James Stroud and Byron Gallimore (Travis also had a hand in producing) have given the record a clean, appealing sound that accentuates Travis' strengths. There are enough fine songs and good moments—including cameos from Alison Krauss, Melba Montgomery, and Vince Gill—to make this a solid entry in Travis' catalog, but it doesn't have enough flair to make it the big splash DreamWorks desired. Still, the small pleasures are as important as the big ones in Travis' music, and that's what makes *You and You Alone* a modest success. *—Thom Owens*

Greatest #1 Hits / Aug. 25, 1998 / Warner Bros. ✦✦✦✦✦

When you have as many number one hits as Randy Travis, it's possible to have a collection called *Greatest #1 Hits*—you can select the best of the best. And, despite the presence of "1982," which never went past number six, that's pretty much what this is—a selection of ten (nine, if you discount "1982") songs that are the best of his best. Which means that "On the Other Hand," "Diggin' Up Bones," "Forever and Ever, Amen," "Too Gone Too Long," "I Told You So," "Deeper Than the Holler," "It's Just a Matter of Time," "Hard Rock Bottom of Your Heart" and "Look Heart, No Hands," are on one disc. Which means in turn that it's a bargain for most casual fans. *—Stephen Thomas Erlewine*

A Man Ain't Made of Stone / Sep. 21, 1999 / DreamWorks ✦✦✦

Randy Travis has always been a traditionalist, which was fine in the late '80s, when he brought straight-up, hardcore country back into the charts, but a decade later, he was out of step with the charts. After spending his career at Warner, he switched to DreamWorks, adopting a new production team (James Stroud and Byron Gallimore) along the way. Ironically, *You and You Alone*, his 1998 debut for the label, wasn't up to the standard of *Full Circle*, his last for Warner, and *A Man Ain't Made of Stone*, his second effort for DreamWorks, isn't either. Much like its predecessor, *A Man* is a sturdy, solid affair that takes a couple of chances that don't quite work, while offering several good, no-frills traditionalist numbers. All those are packed toward the front end of the album, and by the sixth song, "No Reason to Change," the record feels like a modest latter-day masterstroke. Things go a little haywire on the second half, beginning with "Where Can I Surrender," a turgid ballad with a gospel choir supporting him. From that point on, Travis isn't on secure ground, as even promising numbers are undone by weird quirks: the enjoyable rocker "I'll Be Right Here Loving You" is undone by a chanted litany of modern conveniences/hassles in the verse, "Once You've Heard the Truth" takes a weirdly anthemic turn in the chorus. Travis retains his dignity throughout it all, and the record is redeemed by the nice closer "Thirteen Mile Goodbye," but by that point, *A Man Ain't Made of Stone* has revealed itself as nothing new, simply a solid Randy Travis record. Much of it sounds fine, but it doesn't have the character of his earlier records, which proves that it's possible to stay traditionalist and still be memorable. *—Stephen Thomas Erlewine*

Super Hits, Vol. 1 / Feb. 8, 2000 / Warner Bros. ✦✦✦

Plucking tracks from throughout Randy Travis' decade-long tenure at Warner Bros., *Super Hits, Vol. 1* is an entertaining but, naturally, incomplete budget-priced sampler containing ten of Travis' biggest hits. While it contains material from albums not covered on the two volumes of *Greatest Hits*, as well as a couple tracks from the old days that didn't make those collections either, it's a little too scattershot to be satisfying as a hits compilation. Still, what's here makes for a good listen, and budget-minded Travis fans may find it worth their while to pick this up; most, however, are advised to stick with the two *Greatest Hits* volumes. *—Steve Huey*

Inspirational Journey / Oct. 31, 2000 / Warner Bros. ✦✦✦

Released during Travis' tenure with Warner Bros. but held for release until 2000, *Inspirational Journey* is the singer's first religious album. In earlier decades, Tennessee Ernie Ford and B.J. Thomas made second careers by recording specifically for the Christian market. Other country singers would record occasional gospel albums, not to sell records, necessarily, but out of love for the music and perhaps a sense of obligation. Consequently, gospel albums by Loretta Lynn, Johnny Cash, Tammy Wynette, Merle Haggard, and Dolly Parton ranked among those artists' most satisfying efforts. And such is the case here. Kyle Lehning under-produces almost to the point of this sounding like a Don Williams album. The voice is way out in front and the instruments and background vocalists provide a bed of support. There's occasional seasoning by bluegrass instruments including banjo, fiddle, and Jerry Douglas' dobro. (One exception is "The Carpenter," which features co-lead and harmony vocals by Waylon Jennings and Jessi Colter.) Fact is, if it weren't for the lyrics, *Inspirational Journey* would sound like any of the other good Randy Travis albums that Lehning produced. Which means that some listeners may find Travis' Lefty Frizzell-derived singing a bit on the sleepy side, despite the occasionally moderate-tempo change of pace from the ballads that constitute most of the album. But the singer's fans will appreciate his warmth, sincerity, and taste. Complete lyrics and musicians' credits are included, though tiny type against a dark background renders them all but unreadable. *—Todd Everett*

Live: It Was Just a Matter of Time / Aug. 28, 2001 / Image ✦✦✦

★ **Trail of Memories: The Randy Travis Anthology** / Jul. 16, 2002 / Rhino ✦✦✦✦✦

Trail of Memories: The Randy Travis Anthology is a welcome, needed addition to his catalog. Although he's had hits collections before, nothing has come close to offering as much music as this two-disc, 44-track collection, nor has anything else made as strong a case for his musical accomplishments—in this light, he truly sounds like the heir to such classic country singles as Merle Haggard, Lefty Frizzell, and George Jones. Part of the reason that might not have been apparent to some listeners during the '80s is that even a new traditionalist like Travis was recorded according to the state-of-the-art standards of the time. So, even his grittiest material has a clean, sparkling surface; big drums; and a lot of instrument separation, all the hallmarks of mainstream production in the '80s. Years later, it's easier to listen past the production and hear the songs and Travis' singing which, as this collection proves, is remarkably sturdy and consistent throughout his career. And *Trail of Memories* touches on each aspect of his career, from his first hit "Diggin' Up Bones" to his late-'90s recordings for DreamWorks. Throughout it all, what's surprising is how little Travis has changed—the best of his songs are always strong, simple, memorable, sung in a similar fashion, while dressed in pretty, clean production that disguises how close to classic late '50s/'60s hardcore country this really is. He was heralded as a keeper of the flame in the '80s and, in 2002, when this collection was released, his music sounds purer than ever. Needless to say, this is an essential cornerstone in any contemporary country collection. *—Stephen Thomas Erlewine*

Rise and Shine / Oct. 15, 2002 / Warner Bros. ✦✦✦✦

In his second gospel album, Travis professes his faith within a traditional/contemporary Nashville setting. As steel guitars keen and fiddles whine, he delivers the message clearly, in his familiar unforced, relaxed style. Aside from "Everywhere We Go," a rousing call to resist secular efforts to "take your Commandments off the schoolhouse walls," these songs generally stick to the rusticities long associated with country Christianity, with evocations of Mama and fishin', a whiff or two of brimstone, and unsubtle wordplay ("The Son/sun's gonna rise and shine"). The music is appropriately sentimental, though the slow-drag, saloon shuffle of "I'm Ready" sounds a lot more like Saturday night than Sunday morning. It adds up to a strong performance, presented with flawless studio clarity and persuasive, understated feeling. *—Robert L. Doerschuk*

● **The Essential Randy Travis** / Mar. 25, 2003 / Warner Bros. ✦✦✦✦✦

Following less than a year after Rhino's splendid double-disc retrospective *Trail of Memories*, Warner's budget-line collection *The Essential Randy Travis* covers the same territory, albeit in a much more concise fashion. Boasting a mere 12 songs, this disc has no pretense of being exhaustive or comprehensive, but rather just presents the cream of the crop of his Warner years. And even if it is missing a couple of heavy-hitters such as the superb "1982," it fulfills its goal very well, presenting most of the really big songs and hits, all in an affordable package. *Trail of Memories* remains the definitive anthology and the Warner-era *Greatest Hits* packages remain excellent in their own right, but this has a sharp, wide-ranging song selection and presents Travis at his finest, giving it the edge for those listeners who only want one, concise collection of his best. *—Stephen Thomas Erlewine*

Buck Trent (Charles Wilburn Trent)

b. Feb. 17, 1938, Spartanburg, SC

Banjo, Vocals / Traditional Country

Buck "Mr. Banjo" Trent was not only one of the finest players in country music, he was also the inventor of the electric banjo. Born Charles Wilburn Trent in Spartanburg, SC, he began playing steel guitar at age seven, and debuted professionally on an Ashville, NC television station at age 17. He joined the *Bill Carlisle Show* near the end of the 1950s and soon afterward made his first appearance on the *Grand Ole Opry*. In 1962, he joined Porter Wagoner's Wagon Masters and designed the electric banjo, an instrument shaped something like a steel guitar which featured a mobile bridge used to change the pitch. Trent remained with Wagoner through 1973 and then spent the next seven years as the opening act for Roy Clark; he also appeared regularly as a featured musician on the long-running TV show *Hee Haw*. He began recording in 1962, initially under the name Charles

Trent; during the '70s, he recorded several albums, including *Bionic Banjo* (1976). He began recording on his own Buck Trent label in the 1980s and two years later recorded an eponymous album on MCA/Dot. During the 1990s, he was a regular performer in Branson, MO. —*Sandra Brennan*

- **The Best of Buck Trent** / MCA ✦✦✦✦✦

Justin Trevino

Vocals / Neo-Traditionalist Country, Honky Tonk

Texan Justin Trevino hasn't let his blindness stand in the way of fulfilling his musical dreams. Picking up the guitar at age seven, Trevino discovered that the only way to utilize the chords he was learning was to sing songs along with them. Trevino's father convinced local club owners to let his teenage son perform and he worked his first professional gigs at 13, playing in juke joints and honky tonks in the Austin area. Performing with his hero, Johnny Bush, Trevino was pushed into the spotlight at age 16 and worked steadily as a member of Bush's Bandoleros as well as backing country legends like Hank Thompson, Kitty Wells, and Wanda Jackson. The young musician's home demos were the basis of his independently released debut album *Texas Honky-Tonk*, followed by *Loud Music & Strong Wine*, recorded with members of Johnny Bush's Bandoleros and the Pure Texas Band as well as steel guitarist Jimmy Day. Lone Star Records released his third album *Traveling Singing Man* in early 2001. Calling in Cajun singer Jimmy C. Newman and rockabilly mainstay Wanda Jackson, Trevino released his fourth record, *The Scene of the Crying*, in 2002. —*Zac Johnson*

Loud Music & Strong Wine / Aug. 22, 2000 / Neon Nightmare ✦✦✦

Justin Trevino is a singer with a fine sense of country's dramatic flair, and he likes countrypolitan-flavored histrionics just as much as he goes for straight honky tonk. He has a classic country heart and a young singer's pipes, and on *Loud Music & Strong Wine*, you can sense that '50s and '60s country (particularly of the Ray Price variety, though Trevino clearly has a reverence for Ernest Tubb as well) is embedded in his DNA. "One More Drink and Then I'll Go" finds the golden-throated Trevino squeezing every ounce of pathos out of the track, as does "I Only Make You Happy When I Cry," a Trevino original. Country music, with its rugged principles, has made plenty of room for raw vocalists, but Trevino is a singer's singer. He has a vibrato-laden voice that would serve him well across genres, but it's a distinct treat to hear him work his way around a trad-minded country number. —*Erik Hage*

- **Traveling Singing Man** / Feb. 20, 2001 / Texas Music Group ✦✦✦

Justin Trevino, who released his debut LP in 1998, is a fan of the kind of country music that ruled Nashville from the late '50s through the early '70s—and it shows. He's a darn fine practitioner of that classic brand of music, from the opening shuffle of Mel Tillis' "All Right I'll Sign the Papers" to the sophisticated production of the title track, which was written by the late Justin Tubb (who happens to be Trevino's namesake). The version calls to mind the unabashed cornball beauty of countrypolitan at its best, like George Jones' "Good Year for the Roses" and Roy Clark's "Yesterday, When I Was Young." Trevino's neo-traditionalism stems from country artists who can really sing, and it's clear that folks like Ray Price have inspired him. This Texan is a country singer in the loveliest sense... the way it used to be. —*Erik Hage*

The Scene of the Crying / Nov. 12, 2002 / Texas Music Group ✦✦✦

Few contemporary artists have a feel for heart-piercing classic country like Justin Trevino; his ability to understand and appreciate a good shuffle or two-step is akin to a wine connoisseur's understanding of his chosen delicacy. Trevino stays the course of previous efforts on *The Scene of the Crying*, offering a few originals but primarily focusing on covers of classics and more obscure tracks by other artists. As usual, Trevino includes a song by his namesake and friend (until his death), Justin Tubb, with "You'll Never Get a Better Chance." He also duets with idols Jimmy C. Newman and rockabilly star Wanda Jackson on the album. (The latter on a version of her "What Have We Done.") He enlists a fine crop of musicians for support here, including the well-heeled Bobby Flores (fiddle) and Dickie Overby (pedal steel). Some well-known highlights include takes on Mel Tillis' "Old Faithful" and Connie Smith's "Then and Only Then" (written by Country Music Hall of Famer Bill Anderson). As usual, though, what truly startles the listener is Trevino's pipes: He's a silky sweet country warbler in the tradition of such golden-throated predecessors as Marty Robbins, Ray Price, and Johnny Bush. —*Erik Hage*

Rick Trevino

b. May 16, 1971, Austin, TX

Vocals / Contemporary Country, Tex-Mex, Tejano

During the mid-'90s, Rick Trevino emerged as one of the first popular Hispanic singers in country music since the mid-'70s, when Freddy Fender and Johnny Rodriguez were having hits. Beginning with "She Can't Say I Didn't Cry" in 1994, Trevino racked up several hits over the next few years with his Garth Brooks-inspired blend of new country and album rock. Trevino was born into a musical family—his father was a member of a local Tejano group. Both of his parents fostered his musical interests, and as a child, he listened to a variety of music, including Tejano, country, classical pianist Van Cliburn, and mainstream pop/rockers like Elton John and Billy Joel. Soon, he was taking classical piano lessons and studying the clarinet. After graduating from high-school, he was offered a baseball scholarship to Memphis State University, but he declined the offer to study music.

In 1993, he released his first album, the Spanish-language *Dos Mundos*. It was accompanied by a single release of "Just Enough Rope," which was released in English, Spanish, and a bilingual version; it was the first traditional country single to be released in both Spanish and English. The English version was a moderate hit, reaching number 44. In 1994, Trevino released an eponymous album, which featured English versions of most of the songs from *Dos Mundos*, plus a few new cuts. *Rick Trevino* became a hit, producing the Top 40 "Honky Tonk Crowd" and the Top Ten singles "She Can't Say I Didn't Cry" and "Doctor Time." Trevino's second album, *Looking for the Light*, was released in 1995; it was accompanied by a Spanish version. Like its predecessor, *Looking for the Light* was a hit, albeit not as big as the debut—it only spawned one Top 40 hit, the number six "Bobbie Ann Mason." *Learning as You Go*, Trevino's third album, was released in 1996; *Changing in Your Eyes* followed two years later, and *Mi Son* was released in spring 2001. —*Stephen Thomas Erlewine*

Dos Mundos / Sep. 1993 / Sony Discos ✦✦✦

Rick Trevino / 1994 / Columbia ✦✦✦✦

- **Looking for the Light** / 1995 / Columbia ✦✦✦✦✦

Un Rayo de Luz / 1995 / Sony ✦✦✦

Learning as You Go / 1996 / Columbia ✦✦✦

Learning As You Go, Rick Trevino's third English album, isn't quite as consistent as its two predecessors, but songs like "Learning As You Go" demonstrate that this is only a slight slump for the singer, not the end of the road. —*Thom Owens*

Super Hits / Sep. 14, 1999 / Sony ✦✦✦✦

Trick Pony

f. 1996

Group / Neo-Traditionalist Country, Contemporary Country

Contemporary country trio Trick Pony drew heavily from the sounds of the '70s, particularly outlaw country and country-rock. The group was formed by guitarist Keith Burns and bassist Ira Dean in 1996; the two had known each other for five years and were both working as sidemen for established artists—Joe Diffie and Tanya Tucker, respectively. They decided on a two-man, one-woman format in which lead vocals would be shared, and Burns' wife at the time discovered a perfect fit in California-born singer/guitarist/harmonica player Heidi Newfield, who quickly joined the band. Trick Pony spent several years honing their sound on the Southern club circuit and gradually incorporated more and more original material into their sets. They landed a deal with Warner Bros. in 2000 and issued their self-titled debut the following year. Their first single, "Pour Me," narrowly missed the country Top Ten, and its follow-up, "On a Night Like This," climbed into the Top Five; third single "Just What I Do" was another near-Top Ten. *Trick Pony* was certified gold within a year of its release, and in 2002 they followed it up with *On a Mission*, whose title track made the Top 20. —*Steve Huey*

- **Trick Pony** / Mar. 13, 2001 / Warner Bros. ✦✦✦✦

Elvis-style rock meets contemporary country music on Trick Pony's rollicking first single release, "Pour Me," from the band's self-titled debut. The song explodes right out of the starting gate and sets the stage for the rest of the 13-track disc, which is raucous country-rock music. Heidi Newfield, the trio's sassy lead singer, offers a powerhouse of a vocal delivery on *Trick Pony*, and her sound is reminiscent of Dolly Parton and Bonnie Raitt. Such songs as "Party of One" and "One in a Row," with its calypso-type flavor, offer up good old-fashioned bar fare. Elsewhere, anyone who has ever been broke before will truly appreciate the tongue in cheek "Spent," which genuinely describes the state of only having nickels and dimes as collateral. Johnny Cash and Waylon Jennings guest on the band's redo of Cash's "Big River." And the midtempo "Just What I Do," sung by bassist Ira Dean, and "Can't Say That on the Radio," sung by guitarist Keith Burns, have great pop-adult contemporary crossover potential, like many country artists have enjoyed in the early 21st century. While there a few ballads on the album, the most moving is the swaying "Stay in This Moment," which effectively captures the essence of wanting to stop time during a perfect instance shared between lovers. *Trick Pony* is an ideal listen for those who go to a bar to drink, dance, and forget about their problems. It's also a good pick for people who enjoy music that is real, carefree, sometimes melancholy, as well as rousing. What an impressive first effort by a group that promises to have more shots of whiskey and good songs up their sleeve. —*Liana Jonas*

On a Mission / Nov. 5, 2002 / Warner Bros. ✦✦✦

Performances are spirited, songs are catchy, and the good-time vibe is unavoidable throughout Trick Pony's sophomore release. What distinguishes this trio from their colleagues on the Music City assembly line are the rough edges they leave in their vocals. Even on their tightest harmonies they project a spontaneity that feels far more genuine than cultivated. The material, most of which is their own, provides plenty of catchy hooks and down-home wordplay, though none of it leaves much of an aftertaste. Willie Nelson makes a predictably informal appearance in a cover of his old "Whiskey River" hit; its thrown-together quality feels pretty much like everything Nelson has done these past several decades. —*Robert L. Doerschuk*

The Trio

Group / Traditional Country, New Traditionalist

This contemporary country superstar trio was comprised of Dolly Parton, Linda Ronstadt, and Emmylou Harris. In 1987 they recorded an album of country music and did a concert tour in support of it. The long-awaited sequel to the project, titled simply *Trio II*, finally appeared in late 1998. —*Bil Carpenter*

- **The Trio** / 1987 / Warner Bros. ✦✦✦✦✦

Bringing together Emmylou Harris, Dolly Parton, and Linda Ronstadt for the album *Trio* was a truly inspired idea, and not simply because they were three of the finest voices in country and pop music at the time. While a gifted entertainer, Parton is also a business-savvy professional who will willingly set aside her gifts as a pure country singer if she thinks her audience would rather hear something like "Nine to Five." However, give her a stage for old-school country material, and she will always rise sublimely to the occasion. Similarly, some of Linda Ronstadt's finest work was on her early country-rock albums (especially *Heart Like a Wheel*), but she seems to operate best with strong collaborators; left to her own devices, she's just as likely to pick wrong-headed material in styles not comfortable to her, but in the right settings her gifts still dazzle. And while

Emmylou Harris had as strong a track record as anyone in Nashville in the 1980s, it's obvious she loves to collaborate with others, and sings harmonies with the same rich and affecting beauty that she brings to her headlining gigs. So you take two gifted artists who need proper direction, team them up with an excellent collaborative artist, and the results should fall neatly into place. In truth, that's a formula as likely as not to fail, but on *Trio* the experiment works brilliantly. The three vocalists display an obvious affinity and respect for one another's talents, inspiring superb performances in one another, and while they all shine in their solo spots, some of the album's most pleasurable moments are when the three harmonize, with their distinct but equally impressive voices melding into a whole that's more than the sum of its parts. Harris, Parton, and Ronstadt also make the most of a set of fine songs (certainly a better program than Parton or Ronstadt had taken on in the studio in a while), and producer George Massenburg lined up a wonderfully subtle and intuitive backing group, with Ry Cooder, David Lindley, and Albert Lee picking gloriously without calling undue attention to themselves. In short, *Trio* is that rare example of an all-star collaborative effort that truly shows everyone involved to their best advantage, and it ranks with the best of all three headliners' work. *—Mark Deming*

Trio II / Nov. 17, 1998 / Elektra ✦✦✦

Widely agreed upon as technically perfect, this five-year-in-the-making collaboration among these Oprytown divas should be a diamond—or three diamonds: a *Trio II* tiara. But this album, for all its harmonic, sopranic vibrato perfection, is not a glassy ride across the entire lake. Let Linda Ronstadt covet the tracks for her own album projects as much as she reportedly had—Dolly Parton walks all over this record in true Dollywood fashion, with Emmylou Harris and Ronstadt chirping deliciously behind her. There are plenty of exceptions to this, as "Feels Like Home" is really Ronstadt's, and Harris treats "You'll Never Be the Sun" with crystal, bitter prayer-book reverence. Even contributing fiddles and pedal steel guitars drop by to accompany Parton without a flaw. It isn't her fault her voice, as distinct as the rarest and loudest bird in a forest populated by rare and loud birds, outsculpts the tone and impact of any song she sings with others. She and the gals score a soaring version of the old Carter Family classic "Lover's Return" in a heartbreaking three-parter; the baffling choice to include a Parton-heavy Neil Young standard about the survival and solitude of the dope-drenched '60s, "After the Gold Rush," is, well, baffling. Parton changes his lyrics to say, "I felt like I could cry," instead of voicing the song's former urge to procure some mind-altering substances. In general, a gem along the beautiful lines of cubic zirconium, from the most well-intended and loving of real-deal songbird girlfriends. *—Becky Byrkit*

Tony Trischka

b. Jan. 16, 1949, Syracuse, NY

Banjo / Progressive Bluegrass, Contemporary Bluegrass

The avant-garde banjo sylings of Tony Trischka inspired a whole generation of progressive bluegrass musicians; he was not only considered among the very best pickers, he was also one of the instrument's top teachers, and created numerous instructional books, teaching video tapes and cassettes. A native of Syracuse, NY, Trischka's interest in banjo was sparked by the Kingston Trio's "Charlie and the MTA" in 1963. Two years later, he joined the Down City Ramblers, where he remained through 1971. That year, Trischka made his recording debut on *15 Bluegrass Instrumentals* with the band Country Cooking; at the same time, he was also a member of Country Granola. In 1973, he began a two-year stint with Breakfast Special. Between 1974 and 1975, he recorded two solo albums, *Bluegrass Light* and *Heartlands*. After one more solo album in 1976, *Banjoland*, he went on to become musical leader for the Broadway show *The Robber Bridegroom*. Trischka toured with the show in 1978, the year he also played with the Monroe Doctrine.

Beginning in 1978, he also played with artists such as Peter Rowan, Richard Greene, and Stacy Phillips. In the early 1980s, he began recording with his new group Skyline, which recorded its first album in 1983. Subsequent albums included *Robot Plane Flies Over Arkansas* (solo, 1983), *Stranded in the Moonlight* (with Skyline, 1984) and *Hill Country* (solo, 1985). In 1984, he performed in his first feature film, *Foxfire*. Three years later, he worked on the soundtrack for *Driving Miss Daisy*. Trischka produced the Belgian group Gold Rush's *No More Angels* in 1988. The following year, Skyline recorded its final album, *Fire of Grace*. He also recorded the theme song for *Books on the Air*, a popular National Public Radio Show, and continued his affiliation with the network by appearing on Garrison Keillor's *Prairie Home Companion*, *Mountain Stage*, *From Our Front Porch*, and other radio shows. Trischka's solo recordings include 1993's *World Turning*, 1995's *Glory Shone Around: A Christmas Collection* and 1999's *Bend*. *—Sandra Brennan*

Bluegrass Light / 1973 / Rounder ✦✦✦

Bluegrass Light is Tony Trischka's debut album and demonstrates how the banjoist pushed the boundaries of the genre by incorporating jazz, folk and country elements. Though some of his ideas sound a little unformed, the album remains one of the most exciting records in his catalog. *—Thom Owens*

Heartlands / 1975 / Rounder ✦✦✦

Fiddle Tunes for Banjo / 1981 / Rounder ✦✦✦✦

What unites these three banjo players—Tony Trischka, Bill Keith, and Béla Fleck—is their shared status as stylistic innovators on an instrument that, to most people, embodies strict traditionalism. There's still debate as to whether Trischka or Keith originated the "melodic" style of bluegrass banjo playing, one which tends to follow the melody exactly and fill in the spaces with scalar embellishments, rather than hitting occasional melody notes from within cascades of arpeggios, as is the practice in traditional, Scruggs-style picking. Neither Trischka nor Keith has proved willing to claim precedence over the other, so the debate may never be settled. At the time of this recording, Fleck (who would later go on to great fame playing a sort of banjo-based jazz fusion) was a young player expanding the boundaries of the Trischka/Keith school. On most of the program, the banjoists take turns leading separate groups through bluegrass standards such as "Black Mountain Rag" and "Fiddler's Dream" (as well as unusual fare like the Irish tune "Paddy Kelly's Jig"), but on the two bonus cuts provided on this CD reissue, the three team up for barnstorming trio arrangements of "Bill Cheatham" and "John Hardy." Needless to say, the playing is amazing, but you don't have be a banjo player to enjoy the rapport these guys share or the music they make. *—Rick Anderson*

Robot Plane Flies Over Arkansas / 1983 / Rounder ✦✦✦✦

It is funny to listen to *Robot Plane Flies Over Arkansas* and look back on the reviews that ran in conservative publications such as *Old Time Music* at the time the album came out. From the comments at the time, one would think this was a recording of the bombing of Dresden or instruments being smashed along the I-40. And 30 years later, the solo banjo piece "Avondale," short as it is, would no doubt start a fistfight were it to be played backstage at a banjo-picking contest. This is one of the most famous albums of what came to be known as progressive bluegrass, and while it is in the nature of many musicians to be progressive in their thinking, they sometimes find themselves caught in styles of music that don't encourage such an attitude. This is the situation Trischka found himself in when he and his cohorts started stretching many of the ideas of what might be appropriate to play in a combo whose instrumentation had been handed down from traditional bluegrass bands (i.e., mandolin, banjo, acoustic guitar, and so forth). Many of the sort of chord progressions and arrangements heard here have been copied shamelessly *ad nauseum* ever since, sometimes by second-rate hacks and sometimes by the participants themselves. There is an exciting dimension to hearing these ideas being presented for what is often nearly the first time, and anyone familiar with bluegrass and its conventions can feel twinges of panic at some of the choices of notes, similar to how a frightened camper reacts to each successive weird noise from the forest. And many later recordings of this type of music don't quite strike such a perfect balance of the best aspects of the related musics of bebop and bluegrass. One thing is for sure: This is one of the finest recordings of acoustic instruments ever made, and the consistency is amazing considering that the tracks originate from several different sessions on both the East and West Coasts. Pickers heard here at their absolute best include Andy Statman, Matt Glaser, Darol Anger, David Grisman, Tony Rice, and Barry Mitterhoff. *—Eugene Chadbourne*

Hill Country / 1985 / Rounder ✦✦✦✦

Bluegrass fans may want to zero in on this particular album, as it was banjo whiz Trischka's first shot at paying tribute to his traditional roots, done at a time when his reputation had been clearly established as an avant-garde or progressive bluegrass player. His former student Béla Fleck helped produce some of the sessions, and put together a lineup of players that would require several vans to haul around. The recordings are done to a turn, with the sound of the acoustic instruments positively shimmering. Actually, most of the tunes are Trischka originals, with only one traditional number, and the effort to create tunes in a more standard bluegrass vein pays off with what has proven to be some of his most memorable composing efforts. "New York Chimes" is delightful. *—Eugene Chadbourne*

Skyline Drive / 1986 / Flying Fish ✦✦✦✦

With *Skyline Drive*, Tony Trischka injects progressive bluegrass techniques into the smooth, post-Urban Cowboy country-pop. While Trischka isn't as technically skilled as Béla Fleck or Ricky Skaggs, he is more accessible to a mainstream country audience on this album. For most bluegrass fans, of both traditional and progressive persuasions, the pop concessions are a bit hard to swallow, yet there are some very strong—mainly instrumental—that make it a worthwhile listen. *—Thom Owens*

● **Dust on the Needle** / 1988 / Rounder ✦✦✦✦✦

Fire of Grace / 1989 / Flying Fish ✦✦✦✦

Solo Banjo Works / Jul. 15, 1992 / Rounder ✦✦✦✦✦

World Turning / 1993 / Rounder ✦✦✦

One man's exploration of the history of the banjo, *World Turning* is not for the bluegrass purist. The styles here vary as widely as the guests, from the dusty afternoon of William Burroughs' voice narrating the simple playing of "The Boatman's Dance/Over the Mountains" to the Violent Femmes helping out on "Down in the Cider House," which sounds remarkably like the Velvet Underground at times. In such an ambitious project, there are bound to be moments not to an individual's taste, but on the whole, this experiment is a success, with Trischka's grasp of his instrument complete. *—Jeff Crooke*

Glory Shone Around: A Christmas Collection / Oct. 1995 / Rounder ✦✦✦

Traditional folk fans will want to snap up Tony Trischka's *Glory Shone Round*, a diverse, highly textural seasonal collection in which Trischka's acclaimed banjo work ranges from raw bluegrass to delicate classical, with such guests as Pete Seeger and the Turtle Island String Quartet. *—Roch Parisien*

Early Years / Oct. 27, 1998 / Rounder ✦✦✦✦

Bend / May 4, 1999 / Rounder ✦✦✦

Listeners that can't deal with the banjo for anything other than a "Foggy Mountain Breakdown" will be the ones forced to "bend" in order to accept that Tony Trischka has put together a good fusion-jazz band with Southern rock overtones, and seems pretty serious about it. The young "jam band" audience of the early 21st century definitely gravitates toward music such as this, and with Mike Gordon of Phish giving a thumbs-up in the liner notes, Trischka might not have to care about older fans that would rather hear him play bluegrass or banjo pieces from the minstrel era. He doesn't play a note on this CD that doesn't sound beautiful. The younger fellows backing him up have a tall order trying to play on his level, with as much originality and innovation, and in some ways it is too much to expect. Half the excitement of Trischka is that he is playing like this on a banjo, not just for the sake of novelty but because it is a beautiful instrument, and all styles of music sound great on it, including this. Follow-up solos on electric guitar or tenor sax, though fluent, can't help but be an anti-climactic. There's more to these players than just their improvisational skills. The leader utilizes compositions by several of the bandmembers to balance out the program, and the writing is consistently fine. Those that view themselves as totally opposed to fusion-jazz should give this CD a chance, as this is a fusion band with an important difference besides the leader's instrument—the group has a bluegrass influence! Try finding that on your *Return to Forever* discs. —*Eugene Chadbourne*

New Deal / Mar. 4, 2003 / Rounder ✦✦✦✦
Tony Trischka has been a banjo innovator since his earliest recordings in the 1970s. He is widely credited—usually in tandem with fellow pioneering stylist Bill Keith—with inventing the "melodic" style of bluegrass banjo playing, an approach which focuses on chromatic lines rather than the rhythmic arpeggios of Scruggs-style picking. On *New Deal*, Trischka continues to push the envelope, gathering around himself a band that includes saxophone, electric guitar, electric bass, and drums, and playing tunes that range from jazzy adaptations of bluegrass standards (such as the group's arrangement of "Earl's Breakdown") to original blues compositions that prominently feature slide banjo ("Hand Me My Banjo Down") and even a sort of faux-Pacific Rim fusion ("Quasi Qoto"). The most technically impressive number is saxophonist Michael Amendola's "Miracle Man," a fiery workout written specifically for Trischka, but the most musically revelatory moments come during "Hand Me My Banjo Down," on which Trischka plays a resophonic banjo and demonstrates once and for all that the five-string banjo is a natural blues instrument. (Note also Loudon Wainwright's fine vocal cameo on that track.) Bluegrass purists will find much to sniff at on this album, but this is a treasure trove for roots music aficionados with adventurous tastes. —*Rick Anderson*

Travis Tritt

b. Feb. 9, 1963, Marietta, GA
Guitar, Vocals / Contemporary Country, New Traditionalist
Travis Tritt was one of the leading new country singers of the early '90s, holding his own against Garth Brooks, Clint Black, and Alan Jackson. He was the only one not to wear a hat and the only one to dip into bluesy Southern rock. Consequently, he developed a gutsy, outlaw image that distinguished him from the pack. Throughout the early '90s, he had a string of platinum albums and Top Ten singles, including three number-one hits. Tritt fell in love with music as a child, teaching himself how to play guitar when he was eight and beginning to write songs when he was 14. Travis was determined to have a musical career, but his parents didn't encourage him to follow his instincts. His mother didn't mind that he wanted to perform, but she wanted him to sing gospel; his father was afraid there was no money in singing. When he was 18, he tried to settle down, work, and have a family but was unsuccessful—he was married and divorced twice before he was 22. He continued to play music while working various jobs, including one at an air-conditioning company. The company's vice president was a guitarist who gave up hopes of a musical career and urged Tritt to follow his dreams. Tritt quit his job and began pursuing a career full-time.

In 1982, Tritt began his pursuit by recording a demo tape at a private studio which was owned by Danny Davenport, who happened to be an executive at Warner Bros. Davenport heard the vocalist's songs and was impressed, deciding to take Tritt under his wing. For the next several years, the pair recorded demo tapes while Tritt played the honky tonk circuit. The singer was developing a distinctive sound, adding elements of country-rock and Southern rock to his honky tonk. Partway through in 1989, Warner Bros.' Nashville division signed Tritt, and his debut album, *Country Club*, appeared in the stores in the spring 1990. It was preceded by the Top Ten hit, "Country Club." Upon the release of his debut album, Tritt entered the first ranks of new country singers. His next two singles, "Help Me Hold On" and "I'm Gonna Be Somebody," hit number one and two respectively. "Put Some Drive in Your Country," which had a clear rock & roll influence, stalled at number four, since radio programmers were reluctant to feature such blatantly rock-derived music.

Despite his success, the Nashville music industry was hesitant to embrace Tritt. His music and stage show owed too much to rock & roll, and his image didn't conform with the behatted legions of new male singers. Nevertheless, Tritt had a breakthrough success with his second album, 1991's *It's All About to Change*. Prior to its release, he had hired manager Ken Kragen, who also worked with Lionel Richie, Trisha Yearwood, Kenny Rogers, and We Are the World. Kragen helped market Tritt in a way that appealed to both country fans and a mass audience, sending *It's All About to Change* into multiplatinum territory. *T-r-o-u-b-l-e*, Tritt's third album, was released in 1992. Although it didn't match the success of *It's All About to Change*, it had the number-one single, "Can I Trust You With My Heart," and went gold. Tritt bounced back in 1994 with *Ten Feet Tall & Bulletproof*, which went platinum, spawned the number-one single "Foolish Pride," and marked his highest position, number 20, on the pop charts. His 1995 compilation *Greatest Hits: From the Beginning* went platinum within six months of its November release. *Restless Kind* was released in 1996, followed two years later by *No More Looking Over My Shoulder*, *Down the Road I Go* was issued in fall 2000. —*Stephen Thomas Erlewine*

Country Club / 1990 / Warner Bros. ✦✦✦
Tritt proclaimed his influences early with "Put Some Drive in Your Country," which paid homage not only to Roy Acuff and George Jones but to Hank Williams Jr. and Duane Allman as well. It was the lowest-charting single off Tritt's debut, but it sold him a ton of albums. Radio programmers preferred the ambitious "I'm Gonna Be Somebody" and the ballads "Help Me Hold On" and "Drift off to Dream." —*Brian Mansfield*

It's All About to Change / 1991 / Warner Bros. ✦✦✦✦✦
Better production means ballads like "Anymore" sound bigger and rockers like "Bible Belt" (with Little Feat) and a cover of bluesman Buddy Guy's "Homesick" rock harder.

Tritt brought in Marty Stuart for a duet on "The Whiskey Ain't Workin'" and revived "Here's a Quarter (Call Someone Who Cares)" as a catchphrase. —*Brian Mansfield*

T-r-o-u-b-l-e / 1992 / Warner Bros. ✦✦✦
Tritt's covers of Buddy Guy ("Leave My Girl Alone") and Elvis Presley ("T-R-O-U-B-L-E") are nice touches and show deeper roots than the Gary Rossington cowrite ("Blue Collar Man") or the last album's Little Feat remake. Beyond that, *T-r-o-u-b-l-e* is almost indistinguishable from *It's About to Change*: a good novelty song masquerading as more, a couple of ballads with big flourishes, and a large helping of Southern. That's a good formula, granted, but it still sounds like a formula. —*Brian Mansfield*

A Travis Tritt Christmas—Loving Time of the Year / Sep. 29, 1992 / Warner Bros. ✦✦✦
The harder Tritt rocks on *Loving Time of the Year*, the better he sounds. His Southern-boogie versions of "Winter Wonderland" and "Silver Bells" make a perfect antidote to sleigh-bell burnout. When he tries to be an "interpretive singer" on "Have Yourself a Merry Little Christmas," he falls flat on his face. Elsewhere, Tritt writes the title track while covering two by Buck Owens and one by Sonny James. —*Brian Mansfield*

Ten Feet Tall & Bulletproof / 1994 / Warner Bros. ✦✦✦✦
Tritt's most personal album is the one in which he feels most comfortable with his Southern rock/outlaw mantle. ("Outlaws like Us," in fact, features the voices of Hank Williams Jr. and Waylon Jennings.) Tritt poked fun at his own foibles in the title track and co-wrote "Wishful Thinking" and "No Vacation from the Blues" with Lynyrd Skynyrd's Gary Rossington. "Wishful Thinking" and "Foolish Pride" are ballads that rival "Anymore" for power and Skynyrd and Bob Seger for production values. —*Brian Mansfield*

● **Greatest Hits: From the Beginning** / Sep. 12, 1995 / Warner Bros. ✦✦✦✦✦
Greatest Hits—From the Beginning features 15 of Travis Tritt's biggest hits, including "Country Club," "Help Me Hold On," "Here's a Quarter (Call Someone Who Cares)," and "Tell Me I Was Dreaming." Although there are a couple of hits missing, nothing essential has been overlooked and it's a first-rate introduction. —*Stephen Thomas Erlewine*

Restless Kind / Aug. 27, 1996 / Warner Bros. ✦✦✦✦✦
Under the direction of Don Was, Travis Tritt turns in one of his leanest and easily his grittiest country record yet with *Restless Kind*. Cutting back the country-rock flourishes that have always distinguished his sound, Tritt opts for twangy guitars, wailing fiddles, dobros, and unaffected guts vocals. Mirroring the stripped-down instrumentation, the song selection is straight-ahead honky tonk, rockabilly and traditional country. Tritt benefits immeasurably from this approach—he has never sounded so alive. Actually, he has never sounded so purely country. —*Thom Owens*

No More Looking over My Shoulder / Oct. 13, 1998 / Warner Bros. ✦✦✦
On his eighth album of roughed-up country (kind of a cross between '70s Southern rock and sparkling, modern Nashville), Travis Tritt plugs in his amps and commands his group of industry vets to play loud. And in his single-minded quest to bring back the aural joys of Lynyrd Skynyrd and Molly Hatchet (as well as a bit of pre-*Hotel California* Eagles, the peaceful, easy feelin' guys), Tritt proceeds to kick down the barn doors of any great commercial crossover and then stirs up a ball of dust that sounds conspicuously way out of time. The few times he plays the Nashville game (and Tritt's not as far removed from all the big-hat cowboys as he thinks he is) are actually the moments where *No More Looking Over My Shoulder* finds a comfort zone (the plaintive ballad "If I Lost You" is the best thing here). Someone should tell him that his redneck heroes weren't all that revolutionary, and that they certainly don't transcend all that well in the '90s. —*Michael Gallucci*

Super Hits, Vol. 2 / Feb. 8, 2000 / Warner Bros. ✦✦✦
Travis Tritt's *Super Hits, Vol. 2* collects more of his best-selling singles, including "Can I Trust You With My Heart," "Put Some Drive in Your Country," "Here's a Quarter (Call Someone Who Cares)," and "Ten Feet Tall & Bulletproof." With only ten tracks, it's not as comprehensive a set as 1995's *Greatest Hits—From The Beginning*, but it does include later singles such as "If I Lost You" and "More Than You'll Ever Know." An adequate overview of Tritt's biggest hits and a fair introduction to his work. —*Heather Phares*

Down the Road I Go / Oct. 3, 2000 / Columbia ✦✦✦
One word describes Travis Tritt and his music: consistent. Since his first release in 1989, Tritt has been adding bluesy Southern rock to his country honky tonk roots, creating a sound all his own. Having written or co-written seven of the album's 11 tracks, Tritt says *Down the Road I Go* does have a purpose: "I want to continue to connect with my female audience, but I want to include songs that come from a more male perspective. If country is going to have a resurgence, we are going to have to get the men listening again." Male and female fans alike will enjoy this solid effort from a man who hasn't lost his touch even after eight dependable albums. —*Maria Konicki Dinoia*

Lovin' Side / Feb. 5, 2002 / Rhino ✦✦✦✦
In February of 2002, Warner/Rhino offered up two Travis Tritt compilations, one spotlighting his "Rockin' Side," the other his "Lovin' Side." Titles don't come much clearer than that, so it shouldn't come as a surprise that both compilations deliver on their promise without straying from their template. Because they stick to a theme, neither has all of his hits, but that's not a problem since the selected hits—in this case, tunes like "Help Me Hold On" and "More Than You Will Ever Know"—are surrounded by sharp selections from his albums, giving each compilation a surprisingly well-rounded feel. If *The Lovin' Side* isn't as successful as *The Rockin' Side*, it's because Tritt sounds more engaged on uptempo material, and his ballads often aren't as compelling as his rockers, but it has to be said that this does sustain a smooth, romantic mood quite well. Note that this really does take "lovin'" seriously, meaning that honky tonk numbers (and big hits) like "Country Club" and "Here's a Quarter (Call Someone Who Cares)" are entirely absent, but

those looking for either the "Rockin' Side" or "Lovin' Side" of Travis Tritt will find either volume satisfying. —*Stephen Thomas Erlewine*

Rockin' Side / Feb. 5, 2002 / Rhino ✦✦✦✦✦

In February of 2002, Warner/Rhino offered up two Travis Tritt compilations, one spotlighting his "Rockin' Side," the other his "Lovin' Side." Titles don't come much clearer than that, so it shouldn't come as a surprise that both compilations deliver on their promise without straying from their template. Because they stick to a theme, neither has all of his hits, but that's not a problem since the selected hits—in this case, tunes like "T-R-O-U-B-L-E" and "Ten Feet Tall & Bulletproof"—are surrounded by sharp selections from his albums, giving each compilation a surprisingly well-rounded feel. Of the two, *The Rockin' Side* is superior because Tritt sounds livelier, freer, truer in this setting than he does crooning ballads, and the material is also far more consistent. Note that this really does take "rockin'" seriously, meaning that honky tonk numbers (and big hits) like "Country Club" and "Here's a Quarter (Call Someone Who Cares)" are entirely absent, but those looking for either the "Rockin' Side" or "Lovin' Side" of Travis Tritt will find either volume satisfying. —*Stephen Thomas Erlewine*

Strong Enough / Sep. 24, 2002 / Columbia ✦✦✦

After the disappointing performance of 1998's *No More Looking Over My Shoulder* and his departure from Warner Bros. Records, Travis Tritt mounted a surprising comeback with his Columbia Records debut, 2000's *Down the Road I Go*. *Strong Enough*, that album's follow-up, similarly tones down the Southern rock aspect of Tritt's musical palette in favor of a more straight-ahead country sound more acceptable to country radio programmers. In the opening track, the self-written "You Can't Count Me out Yet," Tritt addresses the premature rumors of his commercial demise as well as his return to form. "Some thought I was finally gone for good," he sings, "but those doubters just got rattled/ 'Cause I'm back in the saddle/Doing better than a body should." If so, it's because he has gotten better at playing the Nashville game, and while the album is not devoid of uptempo honky tonk material, notably "If You're Gonna Straighten up (Brother Now's the Time)," "Time to Get Crazy," and "I Can't Seem to Get Over You" (each of which Tritt co-wrote), there are many sentimental ballads that look back regretfully on changing times, particularly "County Ain't Country," or treat romantic subjects. Tritt's composition "Strong Enough to Be Your Man," the album's advance single, is an affirmative answer record to Sheryl Crow's 1993 song "Strong Enough," which asked, "Are you strong enough to be my man?" Another good singles choice would be "Can't Tell Me Nothin'," and "You Really Wouldn't Want Me That Way," which also touts the singer's independence, could find a home on radio, too. The irony is that in such songs, Tritt is actually conforming to Nashville's dictates: using standard formulas or co-writing with music row pros, recording with the usual session men. So far, it appears he can have it both ways. —*William Ruhlmann*

The Essentials / Apr. 22, 2003 / Warner Strategic ✦✦✦✦

Released in the spring 2003, *The Essentials* is the third compilation of Travis Tritt's Warner material in 14 months and the fourth of any note. Since the two 2002 releases were thematically based, separated into one disc of love songs and one disc of rockers, this leaves 1995's *Greatest Hits: From the Beginning* as *The Essentials'* real competition, since they both cover the same ground—namely, his recordings between 1989 and 1995/1996, with the newer comp extending just a yearlonger than its predecessor. *Greatest Hits* is three songs longer than *The Essentials*, and all but two of the 12 songs— "More Than You'll Ever Know" and "Lord Have Mercy on the Working Man"—on *The Essentials* are on *Greatest Hits*, and that record had a couple of songs that maybe should have made the cut, including "Put Some Drive in Your Country" and "Ten Feet Tall & Bulletproof." So, *Greatest Hits* winds up with a slight edge, but it is only a slight edge, since this is a budget-priced collection and it does, after all, have the basics—"T-R-O-U-B-L-E," "The Whiskey Ain't Workin'," "More Than You'll Ever Know," "Here's a Quarter (Call Someone Who Cares)," "Country Club," among them—for a good price. On that level, *The Essentials* easily satisfies. —*Stephen Thomas Erlewine*

Greg Trooper

b. New Jersey
Guitar, Vocals / Singer/Songwriter, Americana

Born and raised in New Jersey, Greg Trooper's songs have been recorded by the likes of Steve Earle, Rosanne Cash, and Vince Gill. In the early '70s, Trooper left the folk clubs of Greenwich Village for the music scene of Austin, TX, before moving to Lawrence, KS, where he entered college and continued to hone his guitar, singing, and songwriting skills. He returned to New York for the '80s and part of the '90s, where he recorded his first two records: *We Won't Dance* and the critically acclaimed *Everywhere*. The records caught the attention of Earle—who recorded Trooper's "Little Sister." In the early '90s, Trooper met fellow New Jerseyite and ex-E Steet Band bassist Garry Tallent, who like Trooper would settle in Nashville. Tallent produced Trooper's 1996 album *Noises in the Hallway* and released it on his D'Ville Records. *Popular Demons* followed in 1998. After the release of that album, he signed with famed Nashville indie Eminent Records, which released *Straight Down Rain* in 2001. —*Jack Leaver*

We Won't Dance / 1986 / Wild Rags ✦✦✦

Everywhere / 1992 / Black Hole ✦✦✦✦

Songwriter Greg Trooper's independent CD with his band the Flatirons contains great examples of his thoughtful commercial style, which is not so much folk as folk-rock, with its ringing guitars and catchy hooks. Key tracks here are: the title cut, a haunting World War II memoir co-written by Sid Griffin; the rollicking, country-tinged "Ireland" (which may or may not be about the nation); and "Blind Spot," an acid-tinged romantic tribute with harmony vocals by Rosanne Cash. The 1999 KOCH Records reissue contains two bonus tracks, "Too Bad For You," a bouncy, fingerpicking showcase with a rueful lyric

recorded in 1998, and "A Train Runs By My Door," recorded in 1996. —*Richard Meyer & William Ruhlmann*

Noises in the Hallway / Jan. 30, 1996 / D'Ville ✦✦✦✦

Singer/songwriter Greg Trooper has been covered by artists as diverse as Billy Bragg, Steve Earle, and Maura O'Connell, which gives an idea of the wide range of styles on *Noises in the Hallway*. Working from a basic folk-rock base, Trooper adds stylistic flourishes that makes the album compelling not only lyrically, but musically as well. —*Stephen Thomas Erlewine*

Popular Demons / Sep. 15, 1998 / Koch ✦✦✦

● Straight Down Rain / Mar. 20, 2001 / Eminent ✦✦✦✦✦

Greg Trooper has built a reputation as a solid singer/songwriter whose works have been covered by everyone from Billy Bragg to Steve Earle and Vince Gill. Though he hails from New Jersey, he's lived between Nashville and Austin long enough to be considered a local in both places. He's recorded four previous albums, and has written the single greatest remembrance song in history—"Every Single Day"—and is loved by pretty much everybody who plies his craft. In other words, the guy has developed his talent over time and his previous recordings to finally deliver the album he always dreamed he'd record. That record is *Straight Down Rain*. Trooper gets to the root of what he has always been yet never completely accepted: a rock & roll songwriter who likes the raw, stinging tone of a Fender Telecaster and the punch of a drum kit to go with occasional pedal steel guitars and fiddles. Produced by Phil Madiera and starring drummer Kenny Blevins, guitarist David Jacques, and a host of guests that include Julie Miller, Bill Lloyd, Fats Kaplan, and Maura O'Connell, the set opens with "Nothin' but You," a rocker in the East Coast tradition with twin ringing guitars, a solid if jazzed up backbeat by Blevins, and a B-3 to pump the groove along. It's a lovelorn road song, which is only fitting on a rock record. But when he gets to the line "I've got more fear than wisdom/I've got fences to mend/You've got an ocean of reasons/To let this chapter end/When I pull in tomorrow/And I reach for your hand/Will you turn away and wonder/What's the point in starting this thing over again," you can feel his doubt and confusion. Still, he rises to a simple but staggering truth in the refrain: "I saw absolutely nothin', absolutely nothin' but you." The humility and simplicity in this statement tears down all the divisions that exist between the lover and the loved. They both want the same thing, though the cost is high. This is followed by a genuine 21st century rock & roll anthem. No, there is no contradiction between "rock" and "anthem" in the 21st century, and this track proves it. "Staring Down the Night" is a track where in the mirror you face your desolation and shortcomings and wear them like colors on the sleeve. There are swaggering guitars to be sure, but there is also a layered, triggered drum loop. Trooper has a knack for taking huge emotions, ambiguous life and love situations, and presenting them in a manner simple and crafty enough to be songworthy, yet free enough from artifice to remain honest. He's mature enough to let the crap slide to the other end of the bar and curious enough to let it come near him in the first place. The sequencing of this is stunning. The third track is "Real Like That," a bona fide country-rock love song with Miller's gorgeous voice shining through on the refrain. Trooper employs many facets of the rock & roll terrain on *Straight Down Rain*. He can be greasy, funky, and swaggering ("Doghouse"), folksy ("You Love Your Broken Heart"), and straight-ahead ("Sometimes It Takes a Hurricane"), but he always comes off as the real thing. There isn't a forced moment on this set. His songs find a crack in their spines and turn in on themselves to touch a side of the story previously unconsidered. As a songwriter, this makes Trooper courageous. He is not merely a confessionalist, nor is he an idealist: His protagonists are nagged by doubt and the contradictions they find within themselves. Yet, they have no choice but to see it through another day with the sliver of hope necessary to find, if not redemption, then another sliver to make it greater than the sum of that doubt, and to narrow the space between those contradictions. This is real songwriting by a writer who takes life as it is and makes no attempt to turn it into something greater than it already is. Why? Because he knows just how great it is already. *Straight Down Rain* is a watermark Trooper will be judged against from now on. It is inspired, emotionally foolhardy, roadwise, chock full of amazing hooks and melodies, and reflects the stuff of life with the consideration of a man *and* the swagger of a kid looking for a Saturday night thrill. *Straight Down Rain* is awesome. —*Thom Jurek*

Floating / May 13, 2003 / Sugar Hill ✦✦✦✦✦

So finally Greg Trooper gets a deal on what amounts to a real label. And while it's a label normally associated with bluegrass and superpickers, that's fine. Sugar Hill has issued records by Guy Clark, too. It's about time. On *Floating*, Trooper reveals once again that he is an artist of the old school, one for whom development is a journey, not a destination. Each album stronger than the last—which is saying something when you've never released a bad one—is an exercise not only in the language of lyric writing and melody sculpting but also in the intimate communication that is supposed to occur between singer and listener. Trooper's songs on *Floating* are the musical equivalent of the poetry of somebody like Kenneth Patchen. His eye is keen, looking for the smallest, seemingly most insignificant detail in a shadowy street-corner scene, and his ear is even keener, picking up the whispers and silent conversations kept within but held in common experience and spoken, laughed, and cried from. The title track is a slow country song that addresses the sight and feel of a river with all of its pastoral memories for the protagonist, until one day the dead and bloodless body of a young girl floats up and rests on its banks. There is no judgment, just the question and the witness, as also in the two tracks that open the album, "The Road Is Long" and "Where My Tears Break Through" (written with Buddy Mondlock). The former, set to a shuffling country-rock beat and ringing guitars, states in passionate form the simple fact that, despite devastation by love, there is nothing left but to move along a step at a time to some unforeseen destination. On the latter— a country song with Buddy Miller guesting alongside members of the 77's, a fine rock band—the protagonist bears witness to the fact that life is tough, with murder, environmental ruin, and horrific news abounding, and that one can only remain steady and hold his ground. But it's in the moment of a lover's assurance, in the gesture of a glance, a kiss, the promise of meeting the next day, or being told that one is loved that the tears come to the surface, because they cannot be contained by the joy and searing admittance of need in the human heart. But Trooper is not sentimental, nor is he cheerless. "Lucky That Way" is a humorous acknowledgment that love can be out of reach despite one's good fortune in many areas. There is a little bit of rock & roll in all of Trooper's country tunes, and in his most rocking cuts the feel of a laid-back Sunday country song is a ghostly presence ("Hummingbird"). But he's not limited here, either. "Apology" is a soul tune worthy of anything Willy DeVille ever cut. But it is on "Muhammad Ali (The Meaning of Christmas)"—not to be confused with Tom Russell's—that the totality of Trooper's gift is revealed. In waltz tempo, he tells the story of Ali teaching by his example, first as a man broken by Parkinson's and lastly as a champion who overcame all odds to become one, that the sum total of humanity is generosity. And Trooper's voice rings with the lines: "... But listen when this old warrior speaks/'I am the greatest,' he said with a grin/But he was talking about you/Not about him/And was teaching me the meaning of Christmas." The impression, the eye of Ali as a trembling man in whom dignity still reigns and for whom generosity is a way of life, is borne out by a tune simple and elegant enough not to get in the way of such a profound and moving lyric. Steve Earle writes in his liner notes that Trooper is one of the few songwriters whose songs he covers when playing live. That's a compliment to be sure, but Trooper is easily as honest and searing as any of his peers, Earle notwithstanding. *Floating* is as fine a country-rock record as you are likely to come across—ever. *—Thom Jurek*

Ernest Tubb

b. Feb. 9, 1914, Crisp, TX, **d.** Sep. 6, 1984, Nashville, TN

Guitar, Vocals / Traditional Country, Honky Tonk

The incomparable Ernest Tubb ("E.T." to all who knew him) became a legend as much for what he was personally as for the half-century career that stretched from his first radio date in 1932 to his death in 1984. Though other singers with better voices and more raw musical talent have come and gone, none has inspired greater love from fans over six decades. Along with such performers as Jimmie Rodgers, Roy Acuff, Bill Monroe, Hank Williams, Lefty Frizzell, and George Jones, Tubb is country music personified. He was among the first of the honky tonk singers and the first to achieve national recognition. His first recording was "The Passing of Jimmie Rodgers," a tribute to his hero. His long association with Decca began with "Blue Eyed Elaine" in 1940. Three years later his self-penned "Walkin' the Floor Over You," a country classic, was a hit, leading to the *Opry*, movie roles, and stardom. In 1947 he opened his Nashville record store and began the *Midnight Jamboree*, which followed the *Opry* on WSM and advertised the shop while showcasing stars and those on the rise. By that time, he had become one of the most recognizable musical stars in the world, bringing country music to the widest audience it had ever seen. Over the years, Tubb toured widely with His Texas Troubadours, pressing the flesh with fans after shows that featured his many hits, including "Slippin' Around," "Two Glasses Joe," "Tomorrow Never Comes," "Drivin' Nails in My Coffin," "Rainbow at Midnight," "Let's Say Goodbye Like We Said Hello," and "Driftwood on the River." In 1975, after 35 years with Decca/MCA, he was let go, the allegiance of company executives not matching that of his multitude of fans. Because of a lung disease Tubb had to rest in pain on a cot between takes, ending his career just as his hero, Rodgers, had 50 years earlier. Quoting one of his album titles, Tubb left a legend and a legacy.

The youngest of five children, Tubb was born in Ellis County, TX, but his farming parents moved across the state to Benjamin when he was six years old. By the time he was in his pre-adolescence, his parents had divorced, and he spent his teens traveling between his two parents, working odd jobs. Early in his adolescence, Tubb was attracted to the music of Rodgers. By his late teens, Tubb had picked up the guitar on the advice of a friend and fellow guitarist named Merwyn Buffington. Following Rodgers' death in May of 1933, Tubb decided that he wanted to pursue a musical career and emulate his idol. He moved to San Antonio, where he again hooked up with Buffington, who was currently playing with the Castleman Brothers on a local radio station. The guitarist convinced his employers to let Tubb sing as a guest vocalist, and soon Ernest had his own regular early-morning show.

At this point in his career, Tubb sounded very similar to Rodgers and was still obsessed with his idol. Eventually, he tracked down and met Rodgers' widow, Carrie, and she was quite taken with Tubb, loaning him one of Jimmie's guitars and convincing RCA to sign the young singer. The first singles he recorded were quite similar to Rodgers (including two tributes to the Singing Brakeman), but the records failed to sell and he was quickly dropped from the label. Ernest continued to plow ahead, playing a variety of small clubs and radio stations, without gaining much attention. A major point in Tubb's musical development was the removal of his tonsils in 1939. With his tonsils gone, he could no longer yodel, which meant he developed his own distinctively twangy, nasal singing style. Decca Records agreed to record him in April of 1940, and one of the resulting singles, "Blue Eyed Elaine," became a minor hit. Decca agreed to sign him to a longer contract by the end of the year, by which time he had also had a regular radio show on a Fort Worth station, KGKO, sponsored by the flour company Gold Chain.

Early in 1941, he cut several new songs, this time backed by Fay "Smitty" Smith, a staff electric guitarist for KGKO. The first single released from these sessions was "Walking the Floor Over You." Over the next few months, the single became a massive hit, eventually selling over a million copies. "Walking the Floor Over You" was the first honky tonk song, launching not only Tubb's career but also the musical genre itself. Tubb sang the song in the Charles Starrett movie *Fighting Buckeroos* (1941), which led to another film appearance in Starrett's *Ridin' West* (1942). By the end of 1942, he was popular enough to gain a release from his Gold Chain contract, and he headed to Nashville. Upon his arrival in January of 1943, he joined the *Grand Ole Opry* and became the first musician to use an electric guitar in the *Opry*.

Between 1942 and 1944, Tubb made no recordings because of a strike within the recorders' union, yet he continued to tour, often with Pee Wee King and Roy Acuff. Ernest returned to recording in 1944, releasing the number two "Try Me One More Time" early in the year, following by his first number-one single, "Soldier's Last Letter," that summer. The two singles kicked off a nearly 15-year streak of virtually uninterrupted Top Ten singles (only four of his 54 singles of that era failed to crack the Top Ten, and even then they made the Top 15). In 1946, he began recording solely with his band, the Texas Troubadours, and he became one of the first country artists to record in Nashville. Between the end of 1945 and the conclusion of 1946, he had a number of huge hits, including "It's Been So Long Darling," "Rainbow at Midnight," "Filipino Baby," and "Drivin' Nails in My Coffin." The singles cemented his reputation in the U.S. and won him new fans around the world.

Early in 1947, he opened the Ernest Tubb Record Shop in Nashville, which he promoted through the *Midnight Jamboree*, a radio program he designed to fill the post-*Opry* slot on the radio. That year, he became the first country star to play Carnegie Hall in New York, signalling how much he had done to increase country music's popularity across the U.S.; a few years before, it would have been unthinkable to have such rural music play in such an urban venue. During 1949, he hit the height of his popularity, charting an astonishing 13 hit singles during the course of the year—which is even more remarkable considering that the chart only had 15 positions each week. Most of those songs were classics, including "Have You Ever Been Lonely? (Have You Ever Been Blue)," "Let's Say Goodbye Like We Said Hello," "I'm Biting My Fingernails and Thinking of You" (a collaboration with the Andrews Sisters), "Slipping Around," and "Blue Christmas." The following year, he had 11 hit singles, including "I Love You Because" and "Throw Your Love My Way," plus several hit duets with Red Foley, including "Tennessee Border No. 2" and the number one "Goodnight Irene." Tubb also demonstrated his influence by helping Hank Snow appear on the *Grand Ole Opry* and supporting Hank Williams.

Throughout the '50s, Tubb recorded and toured relentlessly, racking up well over 30 hit singles, the majority of which—including the classics "Driftwood on the River" (1951) and "The Yellow Rose of Texas" (1955)—reached the Top Ten. By the end of the decade, his sales dipped slightly, which only meant he wasn't reaching the Top Ten, only the Top 20, with regularity. Nevertheless, he stopped having big hits in the early '60s, as rock & roll and newer, harder honky tonk singers cut into his audience. Even with the decline of his sales, Tubb was able to pack concert halls, and his television show was equally popular. While the quality of his recordings was rather uneven during this time, he still cut a number of classics, including "Thanks a Lot," "Pass the Booze," and "Waltz Across Texas." Beginning in 1964, Decca had him record a series of duets with Loretta Lynn, and over the next five years he made three albums and had four hit singles: "Mr. and Mrs. Used to Be," "Our Hearts Are Holding Hands," "Sweet Thang," and "Who's Gonna Take the Garbage Out."

In 1966, Tubb was diagnosed with emphysema and in spite of the doctors' warnings, he continued to tour and record actively into the early '70s. During that time, he continued to rack up a number of minor hits, as well as lifetime achievement awards. In 1965, he became the sixth member to be inducted to the Country Music Hall of Fame. In 1970, he was one of the first artists inducted to the Nashville Songwriters International Hall of Fame. Shortly after receiving the last reward, his hits slowed down drastically—over the next five years, he only had one minor hit, 1973's "I've Got All the Heartaches I Can Handle." Decca and Tubb parted ways in 1975, and he signed with Pete Drake's First Generation label, where he had one minor hit, "Sometimes I Do," in early 1978. The following year, Drake developed an all-star tribute to Tubb, *The Legend and the Legacy*, which featured stars like Willie Nelson, Merle Haggard, Chet Atkins, and Charlie Daniels overdubbing their own work on original recordings Ernest had made. Released on Cachet Records, the album produced two minor hits with "Waltz Across Texas" and "Walkin' the Floor Over You" before being pulled from the market due to contractual reasons.

The Legend and the Legacy would be the last time Tubb reached the charts. In the three years following its release, he continued to tour, but in late 1982 he was forced to retire due to his health. During the last days of his final tours, he had to take oxygen and rest on a cot between shows, eerily resembling the circumstances of Rodgers' last recording sessions. Tubb succumbed to emphysema on September 6, 1984, leaving behind an enormous legacy that helped shape the face of contemporary country music. *—David Vinopal*

Old Rugged Cross / 1951 / Decca ✦✦✦✦✦

Jimmie Rodgers Songs / 1951 / Decca ✦✦✦✦✦

Ernest Tubb Favorites / 1956 / Decca ✦✦✦

It's not really a new LP, but compilation album consisting of old singles drawn from Tubb's 1940s material. *—Bruce Eder*

The Daddy of 'Em All / 1957 / Decca ✦✦✦✦✦

The Daddy of 'Em All was Ernest Tubb's first actual LP (not just a collection of pre-existing singles), was cut in mid-1956 and released a year later, and was one of the great honky tonk long-players of its era. Among the surprises is Tubb's tour back through his own history—required to deliver a dozen finished tracks, Tubb made the most of the opportunity, reaching back to songs that he'd written and never recorded, or tried without success to record in prior years, including "When a Soldier Knocks and Finds Nobody Home," "Mississippi Gal," and "I've Got the Blues for Mammy." Those, plus his excellent recordings of the old Tommy Duncan/Bob Wills standard "I Knew the Moment I Lost You" and Rex Griffin's "My Hillbilly Baby" make this an amazingly strong debut album (and a "debut" LP for an artist with a solid string of hits who'd been recording since 1936!). The backing band includes Billy Byrd on electric lead guitar, Tommy Jackson on the fiddle, and Owen Bradley and Floyd Cramer sharing the piano chores. *—Bruce Eder*

The Importance of Being Ernest / 1959 / Decca ✦✦✦✦

Ernest Tubb's fourth LP release and second album of new recordings was a sort of concept album, with side one consisting of numbers new to his repertory, including Cindy Walker's "I Wonder Why I Worry Over You," the rollicking "Educated Mama" (with its "Folsom Prison Blues" beat), and Justin Tubb's "That, My Darlin', Is Me," and older songs, among them Hank Williams' "I'm a Long Gone Daddy" and "Your Cheatin' Heart," and the old Bob Wills standard "San Antonio Rose." These were also Tubb's first stereo releases, and he took well to the new configuration. His voice had softened and mellowed somewhat by this time and, if anything, had a more attractive quality for this material. "Your Cheatin' Heart" doesn't come off as well as "I'm a Long Gone Daddy," although Tubb sings it very smoothly and sweetly. The Texas Troubadours backing him up now included steel player Buddy Emmons and Johnny Johnson on rhythm guitar. —*Bruce Eder*

The Ernest Tubb Story [With the Texas Troubadours] / 1959 / Decca ✦✦✦✦
A double album of 24 new recordings, in stereo, of older songs, with the Anita Kerr Singers and the Jordanaires on hand backing Tubb for some of it, such as the gorgeously mellow Tubb-co-authored "Let's Say Goodbye Like We Said Hello" and "Tomorrow Never Comes," where the Jordanaires take the choruses. Some of the best work here, however, is on the Tubb solo vocal tracks such as "Blue Christmas." By this time, Tubb's voice had mellowed and softened to a rich, highly flexible baritone, more expressive than it had ever been before. Billy Byrd's playing adds sparkle to the performances, and overall they're comparable to the originals, if not as desirable in historical terms. These versions supplanted the originals on many of the subsequent Decca compilations. Alas, by early 1959, Byrd would leave the Texas Troubadours after a decade of brilliant work for a solo contract with the fledgling Warner Bros. Records. (out of print.) —*Bruce Eder*

Ernest Tubb Record Shop / 1960 / Decca ✦✦✦
Is this the only album ever named after a record store? There really ought to be more, considering how important record stores are in the history of recordings. Of course, the fact that the artist owns the shop probably helped with the titling decision, a savvy bit of self-promotion from a guy who was pretty good at that sort of stuff. Cut during four sessions spread over about a week in the spring of 1960, this is a superbly produced session with the stamp of Owen Bradley all over it. The sound is luscious and fat, sporting exciting trademarks such as tandem lead guitars. Drumming by Murrey Harman could be considered a textbook example of fine country & western timekeeping. Hint to drummers: he uses brushes most of the time. Terrific piano playing by Floyd Cramer sends some of the tracks over the edge into the realm of the sublime. Bobby Garrett supplies the required country ambience on pedal steel, while the lead guitar duties are doubled up between Grady Martin and Buddy Emmons, the latter more famous as a pedal steel man but certainly not a lazybones on the smaller axe either. By this period in his career, Tubb was hardly writing songs anymore. Instead he would choose from stacks of material that was being offered to him, as well as putting together cover versions of hits. Here we actually have something of a concept album, in which he is supposedly performing songs by other artists that are best-sellers in his shop. This includes several numbers that have certainly received more than their share of cover versions, such as "He'll Have to Go" and the classic Hank Williams testament to powerlessness, "You Win Again." Tubb makes these numbers all his own, sometimes apparently effortlessly and sometimes by hitting a note nobody else can, such as the way he handles the line "I'll tell the man to turn the jukebox way down low" in the former song. "Who Will Buy the Wine" by Billy Mize, a stinging portrait of a drunken floozy, is a classic honky tonk number. It is in some ways amazing that Tubb can deliver a tawdry number such as this so convincingly, while at the same time putting across such a wholesome personality. The Western swing shuffle beat gets a good workout on "Pick Me up on Your Way Down," and again if the "down" refers to musical pitches, one isn't going to find too many other singers to pick up hanging around in this basement part of the vocal range. There are records by this artist that are a bit more inspired and feature even better instrumental lineups. But this one really should satisfy any kind of fan of country music, and Tubb-thumpers will certainly want it for the cover alone, which features him posing in front of a record rack in his store. This illustration joins the interesting list of record jackets in which artists put albums by other performers on view, but a closer look in this case will reveal mercenary intentions. All the albums in the racks happen to be ones that are also on the Decca label. —*Eugene Chadbourne*

Midnight Jamboree / 1961 / Decca ✦✦✦
This isn't really an Ernest Tubb album but, rather, a showcase—recreating the radio show of the title that he did out of the Ernest Tubb Record Shop—featuring various artists. Kitty Wells, Webb Pierce, Patsy Cline, and the Wilburn Brothers are featured doing one song each. Ernest Tubb & His Texas Troubadours provided five songs, complete with fake applause dubbed on. The performances are suitable lean and convincing, and the material includes new songs by Justin Tubb, as well as new versions of old 1940s country standards. (out of print) —*Bruce Eder*

☆ **All Time Hits** / 1961 / Decca ✦✦✦✦
Tubb covers mostly (though not entirely) older songs here, that were (or had been) hits for others, including A. P. Carter's "Wabash Cannonball," and George Morgan's "Candy Kisses," Floyd Tillman's "I Love You So Much It Hurts," his old friend Hank Snow's first big hit, "I'm Movin' On," and Johnny Cash's "I Walk the Line." The mere existence of these songs makes them priceless, as documents of Tubb's style, even if they lack the urgency of his "own" songs. (out of print) —*Bruce Eder*

Golden Favorites / 1961 / Decca ✦✦✦

Thanks a Lot / 1964 / Decca ✦✦✦

Good Year for the Wine / 1970 / Decca ✦✦✦✦
The gospel of the Tubbites decrees that this wasn't his absolutely number-one best band—not quite—but the well-oiled machine that had become the Texas Troubadours was running perfectly well at this point. And when it came to putting together albums, there had usually been more than enough recent sessions, all featuring current bandmembers often augmented by one or two guest guitarists or a session pianist. There would be plenty of good material, between all the songs that were being offered to Tubb and all the ones

he had picked out himself as sounding interesting with his big ears and yen to help up-and-coming country artists. This is a vintage Tubb bottle to be sure, despite the presence of a song entitled "It's America (Love It or Leave It)" by one Jimmie Helms. The first side of the album is among the most perfect sides of country music ever recorded. —*Eugene Chadbourne*

Greatest Hits, Vol. 2 / 1974 / MCA ✦✦✦✦
Packaged in a color gatefold cover, the MCA reissue of what had formerly been a Decca greatest-hits set is a fine example of this historic country artist in action. Tubb fans will certainly like all the photos that are included, although printing and color registration is so out of focus it's as if whoever was responsible had been at one of those all-night poker and drinking bouts Tubb & His Texas Troubadours were so famous for. The music itself has no such blurry hangover. For the most part the tracks come from the '50s, although there is one piece that dates from only a few years before this set first saw the light of the day in the mid-'60s. These performances are as sharp as the barbed-wire tips protecting a Texas ranch from intruders, the circle of players drawing in a variety of legendary pickers as well as Tubb's most cherished and most reliable sidemen. "Warm Red Wine" is a memorable track originating at a session where Tubb experimented with the band's sound by adding the rich timbre of an acoustic mandolin. A less-impressive collaboration is the 1951 track with the Anita Kerr Singers, a vocal group who blends far less cohesively with the booming, sometimes even tuneless voice of Tubb than the Andrews Sisters did back when the country artist was a young man. He was most assuredly not young anymore when he hit the final 1964 recording date, and had also not been such a factor in "hit" country radio for a few years. So like many second volumes in a greatest-hits series, there are songs here that are only hits in the artistic sense of the word. The fact that all these tracks were just business as usual for Tubb makes it all the more impressive. For the most part, Tubb was an artist whose every side could be regarded as an artistic hit, especially when the ranks of the Troubadours were packed with clever soloists or the rhythm section of bassist Jack Drake and drummer Murrey Harman. The 1947 "Seaman's Blues" presents the feeling of the artist in transition. The material harkens back to Tubb's idolatry of Jimmie Rodgers and the band meshes in only a tentative way, the steel licks of Jerry Byrd racing past the efforts of temporary lead guitarist Tommy Paige. Jump ahead a dozen years and the band is like a brand new touring bus that's just been tuned up by an expert mechanic. It is country & western heaven, a concept that has even been sung about by the likes of Dolly Parton. Hearing Tubb singing with Billy Byrd and Grady Martin ricocheting twin lead guitars, Buddy Emmons on pedal steel, and Floyd Cramer on piano is an experience to be found well past the pearly gates and into the glorious honky tonk inner sanctum. Martin switches to six-string bass for a 1960 session, the lead guitar now in the capable hands of Leon Rhodes while Cramer provides another constellation's worth of stellar twinkling. The producers wisely included plenty of material from sessions with players such as these, the fine pedal steel player Buddy Charleton finally relieving Emmons when it was time to "Pass the Booze." —*Eugene Chadbourne*

The Legend and the Legacy / 1979 / Edsel ✦✦✦
☆ **The Legend and the Legacy, Vol. 1** / 1979 / Cachet ✦✦✦✦✦
The highest possible rating for this project reflects its brilliance as a grand statement about country & western music, especially the incredible loyalty its artists have toward historic figures in the genre. In this case, the giant being saluted is Ernest Tubb, a colossus who had such vast influence on country music that they probably had to barricade the studio doors just to keep every performer in Nashville from trying to get in and pay their respects. In terms of an Ernest Tubb record, this is a very, very good one, although one certainly could argue that albums he cut in his prime with the finest versions of his bands should stand as the high points in his career. Yet again, the power of this album extends beyond the Tubb career and includes performances by many big names in country music, all done on the sly. The history of these sessions and their subsequent releases, reissues, and repackagings is long and confusing. At the center of it all is guitarist and producer Pete Drake, another country music giant who really loved Tubb. He got his idol to record a bunch of his old songs in the late '70s, during a period when the aging Texan was beginning to think his career was about over. Figuring it to be a solo project, Tubb about went through the roof with excitement when he heard the finished mixes. Suddenly there was Willie Nelson, singing the second verse of "Waltz Across Texas." Then there was the surprising presence of Loretta Lynn, Tubb's singing partner from years back. As the playbacks rolled on, each song revealed an exciting guest shot, including performances by Johnny Cash, Johnny Paycheck, and many others. The listener who has never heard a bit of country & western except for whatever got through the radio scan can be directed to this album as an example of the genre's great qualities. It is all here, from the stellar instrumental playing done in a confident yet relaxed manner to the many different vocal styles, each soaked through and through with personality. The production itself achieves its various glories through a rare combination of traditional musical approaches and relationships and the modern studio art of overdubbing, which allows artists who weren't even in the same room together at one time the chance to sing a duet. The contents of this particular set represent a shortened version of the entire session output, thus the "*Vol. 1.*" However, this pressing on the Canadian Cachet label joins the list of album releases that were given a first volume number, only to never be followed by a subsequent edition. As well as Drake did with the artistic production, he appears to have floundered with the business of this album, resulting in a variety of pressings and more confusion than there are potatoes in a Texas breakfast burrito. There was at first a long delay in release as Drake begged for a major label to put out the project, all in vain. Tubb was considered too old for the big-shots in the country music industry by this time. The initial self-produced album that came out was badly distributed, and, in fact, when Cachet got a Canadian option on this material, there were many consumers in the U.S. who found it easier to get the release from Up North than the domestic issue. In the '90s, the

material was finally repackaged in its entirety, meaning suckers who had the first volume and had been waiting for the second had to buy everything all over again. One repackaging from Intercontinental includes just enough of the first volume and the other material to irritate anyone attempting to complete their collection. The Cachet set may be a case where less is more, as some Tubb fans feel the best material from these sessions was all packed onto this first volume. *—Eugene Chadbourne*

Honky Tonk Classics / 1983 / Rounder ✦✦✦✦✦
There is an enormous amount of material available by this artist. If someone is being selective, an argument could be made either way in the case of this interesting set assembled by Rounder from Decca masters. It isn't just a greatest-hits package, though it has that aspect. It isn't just an outtakes and rarities collection, though more than half the tracks had not been released on album in the U.S. Most assuredly what it also isn't is a full-album's worth of material by the best versions of His Texas Troubadours. Tubb was an artist who had a firm hand on the studio process, picked the best musicians with care, and put together strong album collections of his material while he was alive. Most importantly, his albums often involved a thematic exposition of various emotions. Since country music is so much about sentimentality and feelings, obviously a recording put together with this intent is going to be more meaningful to most listeners than attempts at historic perspective, especially in a format too brief to really be thorough. Listeners newly seeking out his material should be directed to Tubb's own productions. What will probably happen, however, is that interest will develop in his complete history once one is exposed to the prime stuff. The Rounder collection makes for something of a history lesson, though the perspective is a bit blurred. He was not an artist who had his musical vision totally together right out of the front gate, to be sure. He is heard with sparse backing on the early tracks of this set, and he sounds unaware of where he is going to go and what he is going to do. The excellent biography of this Texas country legend by Ronnie Pugh is a good companion for this album. Reading about these early sessions, practically done on-the-run in hotels, will fill out the sound of the music recorded that day. The same author is responsible for the liner notes here; considering his enthusiasm for the different Texas Troubadours in his book, it is flabbergasting that he makes so little effort to identify the sidemen on this album, although a name is dropped here and there. As the sequence of tunes jump forward, sometimes skipping a couple of years, the listener will hear Tubb building up his band sound piece by piece. It isn't a revolving door of musicians by any means. A picker will join up and stay for several years, and the tracks cut after the recording ban of World War II find him still playing with pretty much the same guys as before the hostilities started. A bassist is shifted over to rhythm guitar; the rhythmic feel of the band solidifies like Texas hardwood once bassist Jack Drake comes on board. By then we are approaching the end of the first side, but he plays on every track but one after that. With drums not added to the lineup until 1950, the band's rhythmic propulsion was provided by a combination of the bass and different percussive comments from the string players. The rhythm guitarists were of extreme importance, often working in tandem beautifully. The chattering of steel guitar and lead guitar was something that Tubb watched grow in importance to his own musical concept. The selections start to sound like totally vintage Tubb once steel players such as Don Helms, who played on all the Hank Williams records, are on board. When lead picker Billy Byrd joins the lineup, the sound of the band becomes instantly distinctive, like a well-known product trademark seen at a distance. This guitarist deserves a stellar place in any and all musical halls of fame for having both the audacity and good taste to end every single one of his solos with the same lick. As side two reaches a climax, Tubb is now recording in Nashville and producer Owen Bradley is collaborating. The productions become more lavish, but Tubb was not an artist who was sent packing to the cosmopolitan part of town behind a lot of strings and oohing and aahing choirs. Bradley sets up twin lead guitar pickers—Byrd battling Grady Martin—and increases the heaviness of the steel, resulting in tracks country fans will cherish. *—Eugene Chadbourne*

Ernest Tubb With T. Texas Tyler / 1983 / Radiola ✦✦
Ernest Tubb With T. Texas Tyler is a major find—the complete November 23, 1946, Checkerboard Jamboree radio show featuring Ernest Tubb & the Texas Troubadours playing live before an audience, in astonishingly good, clean sound. The music isn't continuous (there are some sponsor plugs and comedy, including some racially offensive stereotype humor by an Amos & Andy-type act called Jam Up & Honey); Tubb isn't the only artist included (Vic Willis tries to anticipate Jimi Hendrix's act—on the accordion; Dot & Smokey do "You Go to Your Church and I'll Go to Mine," the Oklahoma Wranglers do "Daisy Mae," and Wally Fowler sings "John Hendricks' Vision"); and ideally, Radiola would have indexed the songs, which include Tubb's "You Brought Sorrow to My Heart," "Forgive Me," "I'm Walkin' the Floor Over You," "Divorce Me C.O.D.," and "I Told Them All About You" (the latter sung by Troubadours Jimmy & Leon Short). Still, this is what country music on the radio was like, which is how listeners have almost any live material from this era to enjoy in the first place, and it shows off the people it was made by even better than official records do, as well as their tastes and interests, and in that regard this disc is a must-own for any serious country music fan. Also included is a complete *T. Texas Tyler & His Western Dance Band* radio show—his first, from January 11, 1950—and, as an extra bonus, a complete *Eddy Arnold Purina Show* from October of 1954. *—Bruce Eder*

★ **Country Music Hall of Fame** / 1987 / MCA ✦✦✦✦✦
Boasting 16 tracks, *Country Music Hall of Fame* is the most complete single-disc Ernest Tubb compilation available. All of the songs—which range from "Walking the Floor Over You" in 1941 to "Waltz Across Texas" in 1965—are the original hit versions, not the remakes that tend to flood the budget-line collections. That alone would make *Country Music Hall of Fame* a necessary purchase, but the compilers have also done an excellent job of whittling down Tubb's extensive career to 16 tracks that show neophytes exactly how and why the vocalist was important. Not every one of Tubb's biggest hits are included on *Country Music Hall of Fame*, to be certain, but many of the most important—"Soldier's Last Letter," "You Nearly Lose Your Mind," "Seaman's Blues," "It's Been So Long Darlin'," and "Letters Have No Arms"—are present, making the disc an essential addition to any basic country record collection. *—Stephen Thomas Erlewine*

Retrospective, Vol. 1 / 1987 / Universal Special Products ✦✦✦

Retrospective, Vol. 2 / 1987 / MCA ✦✦✦
This second volume contains such favorites as "Mr. & Mrs. Used to Be," "Waltz Across Texas," "Too Old to Cut the Mustard," and others. *—AMG*

Live 1965 / 1989 / Rhino ✦✦✦✦✦
Live 1965 wasn't intended to be a special show, but in a way that's why it is. The album was recorded in 1965 on one of Ernest Tubb's many concerts that year and it captures him in his element, joking with the audience and running through a selection of his greatest hits. Though the performance certainly isn't raucous, it's engaging and the disc functions as a valuable historical document. *—Stephen Thomas Erlewine*

Let's Say Goodbye Like We Said Hello / 1991 / Bear Family ✦✦✦✦✦
These 119 songs over five CDs represent Ernest Tubb at the very peak of his career musically and commercially, from 1947 until 1953. Disc One is filled with winners; Tubb's voice on these and the rest of the songs in this collection is at its richest and most expressive, not exactly soaring (it never did that) but never straining into the top of his range, and the results, coupled with Jerry Byrd's steel guitar and Tubb's and Jimmie Short's guitars, are exceptionally satisfying, crisp and well-articulated playing bringing out his singing at its best. Disc two is highlighted by the presence of several duets featuring Tubb with the Andrews Sisters, which work beautifully, the Andrews Sisters crossing over from pop to country rather than Tubb moving in the other direction; here also is Red Foley, along with an album of religious songs and some great solo numbers. (By itself, this disc would have made a great single-platter release.) Disc three features a bunch of duets with Red Foley, and even a pair of cuts with the trio of Tubb, Foley, and Minnie Pearl. Disc four has more work with Foley, all of it worthwhile, and also includes Tubb's tribute records to Hank Williams and Jimmie Rodgers, as well as his topical Korean War songs and his first covers of compositions by his son Justin. Disc five is a mixed bag, nearly half of it comprised of good duets with Red Foley and a few prime solo numbers, and the other half dominated by a dozen religious songs and Christmas numbers recorded for a theme album. The notes are informative and nicely thorough, though the booklet also has a few more photos than is typical on these sets. *—Bruce Eder*

Yellow Rose of Texas / 1993 / Bear Family ✦✦✦✦✦
This five-CD/150-song collection, covering the end of 1954 up through 1960, is the only way to hear any of this material, other than finding his old albums (which isn't such a bad idea). By 1955, Ernest Tubb was one of the most popular and beloved country artists in Nashville, adored by the public and revered by his fellow musicians. His work as host and player on the radio (and short-lived television) broadcasts of the *Grand Ole Opry* and the *Midnight Jamboree*, made him a familiar figure to millions, his genial presence punctuated by an easygoing sense of humor. Disc one of this set includes numerous highlights in a wide range of styles. The second disc is more consistent in tone and content, mixing blues and midtempo ballads, most of which are compiled here for the very first time, including four priceless cuts pairing Tubb off with the Wilburn Brothers. By this time, Tubb's backing band included Hank Garland sharing electric lead guitar chores with Grady Martin, with Tommy Jackson still on the fiddle and Floyd Kramer at the piano, and all of it is among the best-played country music of its era. By the fourth disc, Tubb is settling comfortably into musical middle age; the settling down comes not a moment too soon for a man whose second marriage produced its fourth child in 1958, about the same time his first grandchild was born. Disc five opens with Tubb at his most mature and sophisticated, freely moving between honky tonk, country-pop, and modern country sounds, his voice at its richest. His band, however, is lacking its edge, with lead guitarist Billy Byrd replaced by Leon Rhodes, and the later songs from this period show Tubb slackening off as well, a somewhat less interesting singer and interpreter. *—Bruce Eder*

Thanks a Lot [Compilation] / 1995 / Country Skyline ✦✦✦
Not to be confused with Ernest Tubb's 1964 LP *Thanks a Lot*, this *Thanks a Lot* is a collection of duets that Pickwick's Country Skyline label assembled in 1995. The duets were recorded in the 1960s and 1970s, when Decca united the country icon with some of the younger country stars of the day—most of whom were young enough to be his sons or daughters. This British release is full of songs that were major hits for Tubb in the 1940s and 1950s—however, Country Skyline doesn't provide the original or the definitive versions, but rather, offers likable remakes. Some of the collection's highlights include Tubb getting together with Conway Twitty on "It's Been So Long, Darlin'," Johnny Cash on "Soldier's Last Letter," son Justin Tubb on "Blue Eyed Elaine," and Loretta Lynn on "Thanks a Lot." Meanwhile, "Don't Just Stand There" finds Tubb joining forces with Leon Russell in the early '70s—an interesting combination—and "Have You Ever Been Lonely" is a duet with Mel Tillis. These recordings fall short of essential, and the CD isn't recommended to novices, who would be better off starting out with an anthology of Tubb's definitive 1940s and 1950s hits. Nonetheless, *Thanks a Lot* is enjoyable and is worth having in your collection if you're a seasoned Tubb fan. *—Alex Henderson*

Family Bible / Jan. 1, 1995 / MCA ✦✦✦✦✦
It contains the title track plus "Stand by Me," "The Wings of a Dove," "I Saw the Light," and others. *—AMG*

Walking the Floor over You [Box Set] / 1996 / Bear Family ✦✦✦✦✦
OK, it's eight 70-minute-plus CDs and over $200 retail, and that would dissuade even loyal fans from springing for this set. But there's not a bad cut here, nor more than a dozen tracks that have been heard in 50 years, or are ever likely to be heard elsewhere. And

most of the 200+ songs, covering 1936 until early 1947, never showed up on LP. The first six songs on disc one are of special interest, since they feature Tubb with only his own guitar as accompaniment—since his voice is the dominant instrument, before age and smoking hardened it, the stuff is all worthwhile. The first Decca sessions from 1940 are also of extraordinary interest—the playing is sharper and anticipates his later recordings with a band, and Tubb's newly narrowed, deeper voice has a freshness that his later singing gradually lost. His subsequent sessions were even more successful, accompanied by Dick Ketner on electric guitar, which gave Tubb a more assertive sound and a backing against which his voice worked even better—here are the roots of honky tonk music. Disc two is where honky tonk comes into the world fully formed, with a comparatively loud, jaunty backup and Tubb's vocals acquiring the smooth, deep, emotive quality that characterized his peak performance. This disc is Ernest Tubb lean and mean, creating a popular music genre as he goes along. Disc three and the three that follow are made up of the rarest, largest body of work in Tubb's entire career—the World Broadcasting Service recordings, made during the musicians' strike. Disc seven returns to Tubb's formal Decca recordings, while disc eight contains 26 previously unreleased cuts. The notes, photos, and sessionography on this volume are as overwhelming as the musical contents. *—Bruce Eder*

Ernest Tubb: Vol. 1 (1942–1949) / 1996 / Australian Import ✦✦✦✦✦
Ernest Tubb, Vol. 1 (1942-1949) is a 22-track disc that covers E.T.'s biggest early hits for Decca, including "Drivin' Nails in My Coffin," "Filipino Baby," and "Have You Ever Been Lonely." For listeners that want a more comprehensive single-disc introduction than the *Country Music Hall of Fame* collection, this Australian-only collection and its companion volume are worth tracking down, even though it is missing his signature song, "Walking the Floor Over You." *—Stephen Thomas Erlewine*

Ernest Tubb: Vol. 2 (1949–1951) / 1996 / Australian Import ✦✦✦✦✦
Ernest Tubb, Vol. 2 (1949-1951) is a 20-track disc that covers the second wave of hits that Tubb had for Decca in the late '40s and early '50s, including "I Love You Because," "My Filipino Rose," "Slipping Around," "Warm Red Wine," "Driftwood on the River," "Letters Have Nor Arms" and "I'm Biting My Fingernails and Thinking of You." For listeners that want a more comprehensive single-disc introduction than the *Country Music Hall of Fame* collection, this Australian-only collection and its companion volume are worth tracking down. *—Stephen Thomas Erlewine*

The Best of Ernest Tubb / Oct. 29, 1996 / Curb ✦✦
The Best of Ernest Tubb contains re-recorded versions of several of Tubb's biggest hits, including "Walking the Floor Over You," "Soldier's Last Letter" and "It's Been So Long Darling." Though these versions aren't particularly bad, E.T. doesn't sound as strong as he did on the original recordings, so musically they offer no revelations. Historically, they're of no importance, since the original recordings were the groundbreaking work. In other words, this budget-priced *Best Of*... is no bargain, and is most definitely not the place to start. *—Stephen Thomas Erlewine*

Complete Live 1965 Show / Dec. 15, 1998 / Lost Gold ✦✦✦✦✦
This 29-song set is the place to start listening to Ernest Tubb; this concert ranges freely across Tubb's history in the course of a single set, covering a quarter century of songs, and also captures the warmth, the humor, and the majesty of the "Texas Troubador." Camelot's 1999 release of the *Complete Live 1965 Show* is an expanded, newly remixed version of the same show from the Magic Castle Ballroom near Seattle, WA, that Rhino had out as a 20-song single disc ten years ago. The nine additional tracks include four numbers by Jack Greene and Cal Smith, plus instrumentals by the band, Tubb's "Seaman's Blues," and another rendition of "Walking the Floor Over You." Tubb was always defensive about his singing, especially after the mid-'50s, when his range narrowed even further. He was completely in his element on-stage, however, and his sense of timing and his control compensate for any lack of range. Moreover, he's backed by a tight band; a solid country outfit with a twist—Greene rode the drums harder than most outfits of this kind ever allowed anyone to do, and the result is a country band with one great beat. One ends up forgiving Tubb's seriously flattened high notes on "Slipping Around" and "Mississippi Gal," and marveling at his smooth style of delivery and the rock-solid backup; and on most of what's here, he excels as a singer (it's hard to imagine anyone doing as fine a job on "Pass the Booze"), as long as he doesn't reach too high—and on quite a few, including "Thanks a Lot," Tubb's baritone is downright perfect for the number. *—Bruce Eder*

Waltz Across Texas [Box Set] / Jan. 26, 1999 / Bear Family ✦✦✦✦✦
Not to be confused with any other collection using the same title, Bear Family's five-CD *Waltz Across Texas* continues the label's comprehensive release of Ernest Tubb's complete recordings. The highlights for most fans will be the dozen 1964-1965 duets with Loretta Lynn, which are considered essential listening, but there's a lot more here worth owning. Tubb's vocal range had narrowed considerably in the ten years or so leading up to the 1960s, but he and producer Owen Bradley had worked out recordings that made his range sound greater than it was. For a lot of real fans, the highlights on disc one will be the raw studio performances of cuts that were later mixed with applause for release as the fake "live" *On Tour* album, which might have been a cheat but did present Tubb and the band playing loose and freewheeling. Disc three has a generally jauntier selection of material, including a dozen songs by the Texas Troubadours; its last two songs mark the beginning of the Ernest Tubb-Loretta Lynn collaborations. The quality of Tubb's music held steady even coming up on his 30th year in the recording business, mostly by virtue of his continuing to find good songs and Owen Bradley's way of recording him to the best advantage—his voice on much of his mid-'60s output sounds like a finely aging instrument, and far more comfortable and pleasing than some of his late '50s material. Disc five presents the balance of the early Lynn duets, as well as the title track, Tubb's last major hit. The sound throughout is state-of-the-art, and the annotated booklet is worth owning by itself, for what it tells us about the man and the band. *—Bruce Eder*

Another Story [Box Set] / Sep. 16, 1999 / Bear Family ✦✦✦✦✦

20th Century Masters—The Millennium Collection: The Best of Ernest Tubb / Feb. 8, 2000 / MCA ✦✦✦✦
Part of Universal's massive *20th Century Masters/The Millennium Collection*, this 12-song budget set draws on a cross-section of recordings pulled from his salad days with Decca. Highlights include "Walking the Floor Over You," "Have You Ever Been Lonely," "Waltz Across Texas," "Slippin' Around," and a duet with Loretta Lynn on "Sweet Thang." Together, the songs make a wonderful introduction to the music of this country legend. *—Cub Koda*

Early Hits of "The Texas Troubadour" / Jul. 11, 2000 / ASV ✦✦✦✦
Unfortunately, sloppy budget CDs are not uncommon in the country market. The price might seem right, but in many cases, the buyer is subjected to inferior sound quality (due to inferior remastering) as well as a lack of liner notes and recording dates. And quite often, country budget labels conveniently forget to mention the fact that they're offering re-recordings of the artist's hits—not the better-known original versions. There are plenty of poorly assembled Ernest Tubb collections floating around, but this British release isn't one of them. From fine digital remastering and first-rate material to informative liner notes, *Early Hits of "The Texas Troubadour"* gets it right. The focus of this 72-minute CD is Tubb's '40s hits; the disc, which spans 1941-1949, doesn't get into his pre-Decca recordings of the '30s or his post-'40s triumphs. But while *Early Hits of "The Texas Troubadour"* isn't the last word on Tubb's legacy, it does tell part of his story impressively well. All 25 of the songs on this disc were major hits for the influential honky tonker, and that includes "Walking the Floor Over You" (his breakthrough hit of 1941) and "Blue Christmas" as well as "It's Been So Long, Darling," "Have You Ever Been Lonely?," and the moving "Soldier's Last Letter" (a tear-jerker about a mother who receives a letter that her young son wrote shortly before he was killed in battle during World War II). Occasionally, Tubb makes some pop moves; the 1949 hit "Don't Rob Another Man's Castle" features the Andrews Sisters and has as much to do with traditional pre-rock pop as it does with country. But 90 percent of the material is pure, unadulterated honky tonk. Anyone who is seeking an introduction to Tubb's '40s hits can't go wrong with this nicely assembled collection. *—Alex Henderson*

★ **The Definitive Ernest Tubb Hits Collection** / Jul. 10, 2001 / Collectors' Choice Music ✦✦✦✦✦
Ernest Tubb is one of the all-time greats—a Jimmie Rodgers devotee who built upon the style of his idol to forge one of the most instantly recognizable sounds in the history of country music. Despite his towering stature as a pioneer and a hit-maker, Tubb has been poorly represented domestically on CD. This two-disc collection, with 40 original recordings, remedies that oversight by offering the most comprehensive overview available short of investing in Bear Family's series of complete recordings box sets. All but one of these tracks were hits, and duets with the Andrews Sisters, Red Foley, and the Wilburn Brothers add a little variety to Tubb's basic sound. Spanning the years 1941-1965, the *Definitive Ernest Tubb Hits Collection* is a must for serious students of country music, and a generous anthology of major hits for more casual listeners. *—Greg Adams*

Walking the Floor Over You (The Hits, Vol. 1) / 2003 / Proper ✦✦✦✦

Slippin' Around (The Hits, Vol. 2) / 2003 / Proper ✦✦✦✦

Blue Eyed Elaine (Tubb the Songwriter) / 2003 / Proper ✦✦✦✦

Time After Time (Writers Galore) / 2003 / Proper ✦✦✦✦

Justin Tubb

b. Aug. 20, 1935, San Antonio, TX
Vocals / Traditional Country, Honky Tonk
A fixture on the *Grand Ole Opry*, singer/songwriter Justin Tubb, the eldest son of the legendary Ernest Tubb, had a style all his own; but for one duet version of "Blue Eyed Elaine" on his 1985 album *The Legend and Legacy*, he always recorded independently of his famous father. Justin was born in San Antonio, TX, and spent most of his life in the Lone Star State with his mother Elaine, who separated from Ernest in 1948. He got his professional start in local clubs during college, and eventually moved to Nashville. At his father's suggestion, Tubb got a job working as a DJ in Gallatin, TN, where he occasionally performed some of the songs he had written, and made his recording debut in 1953 with "Ooh-La-La." Throughout the 1950s, Tubb recorded steadily, but had only moderate success with his solo efforts. He did a little better singing novelty duets with Goldie Hill; in 1954, they reached the Top Five with their version of Jim Ed & Maxine Brown's "Looking Back to See," followed with the Top 15 "Sure Fire Kisses." In 1955, he joined the *Opry*, and in 1956, he had his first solo success with the Top Ten hit "I Gotta Go Get My Baby."

Tubb signed to Starday in the early '60s, released a few albums, and toured so much that he was temporarily dropped from the *Opry* for not appearing often enough. After 1963, he signed with RCA and released two duets with Lorene Mann, including "We've Gone Too Far Again." He had one more minor hit with "But Wait There's More," his last chart appearance. He continued to record, tour and appear on the *Opry* through the '70s. He also continued to write songs, and his "Lonesome 7-7203" was a number-one hit for Hawkshaw Hawkins while "Be Glad" became a major hit for Del Reeves. Additionally, his "What's Wrong with the Way We're Doing It Now" became a popular song with fans of the traditional country sound. Tubb also wrote and recorded songs paying tribute to his father, including "Thanks, Troubadour, Thanks" and "Just You and Me, Daddy." He died January 24, 1998. *—Sandra Brennan*

The Star of the Grand Ole Opry / 1962 / Starday ✦✦✦
The songs on *The Star of the Grand Ole Opry*, mostly about unrequited love, include "Five Minutes of the Latest Blues" (along with "How's It Feel," the best song here), as well as

his remake of his own mid-'50s cover of the Browns' "Looking Back to See," and a similar re-recording of "I've Gotta Go Get My Baby," also from his Decca years. Unfortunately, the material, while pleasant and competent, doesn't represent Justin Tubb anywhere near his prime (he was only on Starday for two albums, both issued the same year) or at his best. And the songs and index numbers on the back of the jewel case don't match the order on the CD. —*Bruce Eder*

● **The Best of Justin Tubb** / 1965 / Starday ✦✦✦✦

What's Wrong With the Way We're Doing It Now / Oct. 12, 1999 / First Generation ✦✦✦

Tanya Tucker

b. Oct. 10, 1958, Seminole, TX
Vocals / Country-Pop, Country-Rock, Contemporary Country

Tanya Tucker had her first country hit in 1972, when she was just 13 years old. Over the succeeding decades, Tucker became one of the few child performers to mature into adulthood without losing her audience, and during the course of her career, she notched a remarkable streak of Top Ten and Top 40 hits. Born in Seminole, TX, much of Tucker's childhood was spent moving throughout the Southwest as her father pursued construction jobs. At the age of six, she began taking saxophone lessons; two years later, she decided she wanted to sing, and made an auspicious debut with Mel Tillis, who was so impressed by her talents that he invited her on-stage to perform. In 1969, Tucker and her family moved to Las Vegas, where she regularly performed. Eventually, she recorded a demo tape that gained the attention of songwriter Dolores Fuller, who sent it to producer Billy Sherrill. At the time, Sherrill was the head of A&R at CBS Records, and he was so impressed with the demo tape that he signed the teenaged vocalist to Columbia Records. Sherrill initially planned to have Tucker record "The Happiest Girl in the Whole USA," but she passed on the tune, choosing "Delta Dawn"—a song she heard Bette Midler sing on *The Tonight Show*—instead.

Released in the spring of 1972, the song became an instant hit, peaking at number six on the country charts and scraping the bottom of the pop charts. At first, Columbia Records tried to downplay Tucker's age, but soon word leaked out and she became a sensation—her second single, "Love's the Answer," also became a Top Ten hit later in 1972. Tucker's third single, "What's Your Mama's Name," became her first number-one hit in the spring of 1973. Two other number ones—"Blood Red and Goin' Down" and "Would You Lay With Me (In a Field of Stone)"—followed, establishing Tucker as a major star. In 1975, she signed with MCA Records, where she had a string of hit singles that ran into the late '70s. In 1978, she decided to radically change her image and cross over to rock with her *T.N.T.* album. Despite the controversy over the record and its sexy cover, it went gold the following year.

By the end of the '70s, her sales were declining—in 1980 she only had two hits. Also in 1980, she recorded a few singles with Glen Campbell, with whom she was romantically linked. In addition to recording, she also made her feature film debut in *Hard Country*. She switched to Arista Records in 1982, where she had several hits, highlighted by the Top Ten "Feel Right." In 1984 and 1985, she had no hits and signed with Capitol Records. In early 1986, she returned with "One Love at a Time," which rocketed to number three. For the rest of the decade, she scored a constant stream of Top Ten singles, including four number-one hits. Her success continued in the early '90s, even though her sales began slumping as the decade wore on. By the new millennium, Tucker was still in the game. Several retrospectives and various hits collections were released; In 2002, Tucker issued her 31st album, her most personal album to date, *Tanya*. —*Sandra Brennan*

Delta Dawn / 1972 / Columbia ✦✦✦✦

This is the album that started it all. Tanya Tucker was 13 when she struck pay dirt with her debut single, "Delta Dawn" by Larry Collins. To say that in the 21st century Tucker would still be considered a major force in country music over 30 years later would have been considered laughable at the time. But nonetheless, Tucker has joined Loretta Lynn, Tammy Wynette, and Dolly Parton as one of country music's true divas and has had a longer-lasting time in the spotlight than any of them. "Delta Dawn" is one of the greatest songs in country's canon, both in terms of Tucker's performance and Larry Collins' songwriting. But there is more to this debut album than that track. "New York City Song" by Larry Hargrove feels like Harry Nilsson wrote it. The cover of Hank Williams' "I'm So Lonesome I Could Cry" is not only credible, it's deeply moving. Tucker's second single is here too, "The Jamestown Ferry," and the Jerry Reed classic "Smell the Flowers." Rounding out the collection—in an era where, with the exception of Merle Haggard's records, country albums were singles with lots of filler—are George Richey's fine "Soul Song" and "He's All I Got." Tucker at 13 was in full possession of her throaty voice, though producers hadn't yet learned how to make it work to its fullest capacity. Nonetheless, this is one of the most auspicious debuts in popular music history. —*Thom Jurek*

The Sound of Tanya Tucker / 1972 / CBS ✦✦

☆ **What's Your Mama's Name** / 1973 / CBS ✦✦✦✦✦

In 1973, Columbia Records wisely turned the production of Tanya Tucker's sophomore effort over to senior producer Billy Sherrill. There was a lot at stake considering the kind of backlash country critics were infamous for. Tucker and Sherrill proved she was no fly-by-night child star with *What's Your Mama's Name*. They put the songwriting team of Montgomery & Frazier on the map with the title track, which was almost as catchy and certainly as lyrically deep as "Delta Dawn." When Tucker sang "Horeshoe Bend," about a young woman losing her virginity to a rounder, people were captivated—though not as much as they would be when she issued David Allan Coe's "Would You Lay With Me (In a Field of Stone)" a year later. In other words, the prurient interests of the country music public were piqued, but it didn't matter because Tucker's voice kicked ass and the material was top-notch. Sherrill's experimenting in the studio certainly paid off: even songs like "California Cotton Fields" and "Teddy Bear Song" balanced out the risqué tunes. It also didn't hurt that Tucker is pictured on the back cover sitting on a porch swing in a

coat holding a puppy. The mixture of a young woman's budding yet brazen sexuality and innocence combined with the voice of a fully developed artist were too much to resist, even for cynics. Her traditional chips were unquestionable given her Hank Williams cover on her debut and "California Cotton Fields" (also by Montgomery & Frazier) here, which slotted her in the mainstream for good. While the second side is as strong as the first, it is marked by the genius read of Curly Putnam's "Blood Red and Goin' Down," a tragic story of a father relating the story of his unfaithful wife to his daughter before taking homicidal action on the illicit lovers. Given that it was the second single, it proved that Tucker's story songs were exactly what the public wanted from her. With the Nashville Edition and the Jordanaires behind her, the song is bigger than life. "Song Man" was a small taste of the kind of country-rock and pop that Tucker would pioneer later in her career, making for an album every bit as—and more—satisfying than her debut. —*Thom Jurek*

☆ **Would You Lay With Me (In a Field of Stone)** / 1974 / CBS ✦✦✦✦✦

Tanya Tucker's third album accomplished two things. First, it cemented her position in country music as a young singer of power, taste, and artistic excellence. Secondly, thanks to the title cut, she brought David Allan Coe out of obscurity and into the country mainstream—at least as far as he would ever come into it. "Would You Lay With Me (In a Field of Stone)" was a bit beyond Tucker's years in terms of subject matter. She was just 15 when she cut it, and in the grain of her voice listeners hear an erotic yearning that goes far beyond the dictates of an innocent love song. Billy Sherrill, who produced the single and the album, understood this implicitly, and his crossover production drew people in by appealing to the image of the young singer versus the maturity of the song; hence, the prurient interests of the country and pop-buying public ensured the single a number-one position on the *Billboard* charts. The challenge was to come up with an album that could support its opening track. And Sherrill did it. From Harold Reid's awesome "Bed of Roses" to Ed Bruce's "The Man That Turned My Mama On" to Lobo's paean to infidelity, "How Can I Tell Him," to Kris Kristofferson's "Why Me Lord," Sherrill and Tucker constructed an album of smoldering sensuality and gloriously wrought performances. Unlike many performers, Tucker arrived two years earlier a fully developed artist. No matter what song she was presented with, she sang the hell out of it with equal conviction, and in her reedy yet throaty wail, the voice of a woman existed in the body of a young girl. Whether it's a somewhat kitschy number like Bobby Braddock's "I Think the South's Gonna Rise Again" or John Rostill's hymn to commitment and undying love, "Let Me Be There," or the tough gospel of "The Baptism of Jesse Taylor," Tucker handles the lyrics and melodies with so much control and aplomb that it's difficult to believe how young she is here. This is also the album that finally convinced everybody that Tucker was no fluke; the cynics liked her first record but credited it to luck, the second they grudgingly accepted, and they embraced this one wholeheartedly and a new superstar was born in country music. The funny thing is, by listening to this record—now available as part of a two-fer with *What's Your Mama's Name* on Collectables with fine sound—you would know Tucker had no doubts from the beginning. Her story has proved her right. —*Thom Jurek*

Tanya Tucker / 1975 / MCA ✦✦✦

Tanya Tucker was to the 1970s what Brenda Lee was to the early '60s and LeAnn Rimes was to the 1990s—the country-pop teenager who could sing with a maturity that belied her youth. When Donny Osmond and Michael Jackson were being marketed as teen idols, Tucker avoided having a cutesy, teeny bopper image and came across as an artist who was insightful beyond her years. Tucker was only 16 when she recorded this self-titled LP, which was her first album for MCA and boasted the major hits "Lizzie and the Rainman" and "San Antonio Stroll." The rest of the album is also decent and occasionally excellent. Even though Tucker wasn't old enough to vote in 1975, she's convincing when she tackles Jessi Colter's "I'm Not Lisa" as well as Dusty Springfield's "Son of a Preacher Man" and the Linda Ronstadt smash "When Will I Be Loved." And on "The King of Country Music," Tucker provides a moving, bittersweet description of an aging, world-weary country star who has spent a longtime in life's trenches. Tucker, of course, was never a hardcore honky tonker, but if you like your country laced with a lot of pop, this album is certainly enjoyable. —*Alex Henderson*

★ **Greatest Hits** / 1975 / Columbia ✦✦✦✦✦

No matter how far Tucker's come the last 20 years, it all comes back to "Delta Dawn," "What's Your Mama's Name?," and the other hillbilly-gothic hits of her youth. Producer Billy Sherrill is best known for his work with George Jones & Tammy Wynette, but how he turned an underage, waifish Southwest homegirl into a singer to make old boys sweat is surely his most notable, if unsettling, career achievement. —*Dan Cooper*

Here's Some Love / 1976 / MCA ✦✦✦

At the age of 18, Tanya Tucker had nothing left to prove to anyone. She'd been consistent in quality and chart power since 1972's *Delta Dawn* and its following string of singles and successful albums. This effort was issued when she was 16 during the middle of the 1970s. It was recorded at the height of outlaw fever, and in true Tucker fashion, she wasn't following any trends. Now on MCA, Tucker and producer Jerry Crutchfield sought to continue the crossover appeal she had established on previous recordings. Hence, *Here's Some Love* is perhaps the most uncharacteristic record of Tucker's early career, as it features her first real forays into pop territory yet retains some of the most rootsy country songs she'd recorded up to that point—most notably, "Round and Round the Bottle Goes," "You Just Loved the Leavin' Out of Me," "The Gospel Singer," "I Use the Soap," and "Take Me to Heaven." These are delivered with Tucker's mature voice, full, less-grainy, and more disciplined. But it's the title track, with its soft rock sensibilities; and the country-rocker "I'm Gonna Love You Anyway," with its ultra-modern-sounding drums and near-funky guitars; and Dave Loggins' "Comin' Home Alone," with its sweeping string arrangements and torch song arrangement, that come across more like Brenda Lee than Loretta Lynn. "Holdin' On" is arranged to sound like a cross between Charly McClain and Jimmy Buffet. What all this counts for is not clear until we consider records like *T.N.T.* and those she made later—that Tucker was restless and wanted to break her own mold. *Here's Some Love* is her very first attempt. And while it may not be as compelling as her earlier—or many of her later—records, it nonetheless has more than enough moments to keep it satisfying. —*Thom Jurek*

Greatest Hits Encore / 1976 / Liberty ✦✦✦
This contains "The Jamestown Ferry," "Pecos Promenade," "Delta Dawn," "Here's Some Love," and other hits. —*AMG*

T.N.T. / 1978 / MCA ✦✦✦
In the pumped-up disco era of the late '70s, Tanya Tucker, a full six years after her debut—and all of 19 years old—was still tearing up the charts and exploiting her now-fully developed womanhood. Hooking up for the first time with Jerry Goldstein, who was about as far from Billy Sherrill as you could get, Tucker issued a mostly uptempo, steamy record that rocked as hard or harder than it twanged. Opening with Phil Everly's rocker "Lover Goodbye," complete with synth drums, and following it with the torch and twang of "I'm the Singer, You're the Song," co-written with Goldstein, it was pure eros wrapped in strings and electric guitars. But the real tale of the tape is told beginning with track three: a cover of Buddy Holly's "Not Fade Away," with Mickey Raphael on blues harmonica, which funked almost as much as it rocked. Cross this with a riveting read of John Prine's "Angel From Montgomery" that rivals Bonnie Raitt's and a scorching "Heartbreak Hotel," and you have a side that can be played over and again ad infinitum. But side two is charged on with a scorching, sensual "Brown Eyed Handsome Man." While it never gains the same momentum as that track, the ballads and honky tonk numbers are steeped in a pop sound that wears surprisingly well over two decades later. Oh yes, on the beautiful midtempo ballad "The River and the Wind," Seals & Crofts help on the backing vocals; it's probably the best thing they ever did given how awful their own records are. —*Thom Jurek*

Greatest Hits / 1978 / MCA ✦✦✦✦✦

Tear Me Apart / 1979 / MCA ✦✦✦

Ridin' Rainbows / 1979 / MCA ✦✦✦

Dream Lovers / 1981 / MCA ✦✦✦

Should I Do It / 1981 / MCA ✦✦✦

The Best of Tanya Tucker / 1982 / MCA ✦✦✦
This is later '70s material for the blooming of a belter, honky tonk style. —*Mark A. Humphrey*

Live / 1982 / MCA ✦✦✦

Changes / 1983 / Arista ✦✦

Love Me Like You Used To / 1987 / Liberty ✦✦✦✦✦
This fully mature artist is uncompromisingly gritty in the sanitized new Nashville. —*Mark A. Humphrey*

Strong Enough to Bend / 1988 / Liberty ✦✦✦

Greatest Hits / 1989 / Liberty ✦✦✦✦
This particular collection of Tanya Tucker's *Greatest Hits* is pulled from her revamped career, recorded between 1986-1991 for Liberty. Many of these songs appealed to both pop and country audiences, achieving crossover popularity. Some of the highlights from this ten-cut, budget-priced collection include "One Love at a Time," "Strong Enough to Bend," "Love Me Like You Used To," and "If It Don't Come Easy." —*Al Campbell*

Tennessee Woman / 1990 / Liberty ✦✦✦
For some mysterious reason, Tanya Tucker's *Tennessee Woman* sounds out of time for its 1990 year of release. Some of this disc has the feel of a late-'70s outlaw recording with those guitars popping all over the place, pianos dropped in all the right spots, and tempos ranging from the hardcore 4/4 two-step to the rock & roll waltz. But that's not a bad thing. Tucker is in great voice here, turning in a deck of fine songs with a couple of real standouts. In fact, starting with the first two tracks, Paul Overstreet's "Take Another Run" and the Garvin/Shapiro-penned "Shotgun," the set is off with a real bang. In particular, the latter has an old Western feeling in the refrains and minor-key signature that is deceptively ushered in with a near classical piano line before the acoustic guitars and Telecasters come flowing through the middle of a true cowgirl's love song. There's a duet with T. Graham Brown on the cover of Foster & Lloyd's "Don't Go Out." On it, two singers grittily plead with one another not to betray one another. It's a duet with plenty of country-soul despite the outrageously slick production. The medley of the Tucker/Gary Stewart-scripted title track with "Ben's Song" is one of those killer honky tonk love songs made regal by the cascading guitars and rim shots. The hottest track, though, is "It Won't Be Me," which is Tucker doing her best (albeit reinterpreted) Dwight Yoakam. It kicks and makes the listener move. Paul Kennerley's "Walking Shoes" is another neo-trad outlaw song; with its road theme, slippery guitar feel, and cut-time honky tonk beat, it's more rock & roll than country, but it never leaves the country idiom. It wouldn't be hard to imagine Waylon Jennings or Hank Williams Jr. recording this one. It's a fine effort. —*Thom Jurek*

What Do I Do With Me / 1991 / Liberty ✦✦✦
Ballads ("Down to My Last Teardrop," "Trail of Tears") are belted by the best female country singer of her generation. —*Mark A. Humphrey*

Greatest Country Hits / 1991 / Curb ✦✦✦
Greatest Country Hits highlights a combination of songs from Tanya Tucker's earliest chart entries in the '70s—"Lizzie and the Rainman," "San Antonio Stroll," and "Texas

(When I Die)"—along with those recorded for Liberty in the '80s, "One Love at a Time," "I'll Come Back as Another Woman," and "Love Me Like You Used To." For the complete rundown of Tanya Tucker's hits, invest in the double-disc set *The Upper 48 Hits 1972-1997*. —*Al Campbell*

Collection / 1992 / MCA ✦✦✦✦
This particular Tanya Tucker *Collection* focuses on the singer's MCA chart entries from the late '70s. The 14-track sampling includes "Lizzie and the Rainman," "San Antonio Stroll," "Texas (When I Die)," "Here's Some Love," "Can I See You Tonight," and "Delta Dawn." These early examples of crossover success would be experienced a second time around in the late '80s when Tucker signed with Capitol and released a whole new slew of hits. For the complete rundown of Tanya Tucker's hits encompassing both MCA and Capitol, invest in the double-disc set *The Upper 48 Hits 1972-1997*. —*Al Campbell*

The Best of Tanya Tucker / 1992 / TeeVee ✦✦✦✦✦
While the title of this CD may be true, it is a bit misleading. Rather than a greatest-hits collection, this CD compiles Tanya Tucker's first two Columbia LPs in their entirety. There are plenty of hits, including "Would You Lay With Me (In a Field of Stone)," "Blood Red and Goin' Down," and "What's Your Mama's Name" (all of which reached number one on the C&W charts), and, in fact, half of the 20 songs on this CD cracked the country Top 40. The remaining album tracks are uniformly fine, including Tucker's versions of contemporaneous hits such as "Teddy Bear Song" and "The Happiest Girl in the Whole U.S.A.," as well as "Almost Persuaded" and Jerry Reed's "Smell the Flowers." This disc is a treasure trove for those interested in the earliest—and often best—recordings Tanya Tucker ever made. —*Greg Adams*

Can't Run From Yourself / Sep. 28, 1992 / Liberty ✦✦✦
Edgier and more consistent than *What Do I Do With Me*, *Can't Run From Yourself* runs the range of Tucker's abilities, from the slow-blues burn of Marshall Chapman's "Can't Run From Yourself" to the wistful melancholy of Hugh Prestwood's "Half the Moon." A rollicking duet with Delbert McClinton on "Tell Me About It" is matched by the fine romance of "Two Sparrows in a Hurricane"; which one you like best will depend strictly on personal preferences. Switch one song on each side, and you've got a side of rockers and a side of ballads. —*Brian Mansfield*

Greatest Hits / 1993 / Capitol ✦✦✦
Tanya Tucker returned to the top of the charts with her late-'80s records for Capitol Records. Though it is a budget-line collection and, by nature, too brief, *Greatest Hits* nevertheless has several of her best songs from this era and is worthwhile acquiring as a sampler. —*Thom Owens*

Greatest Hits 1990–1992 / Apr. 20, 1993 / Liberty ✦✦✦✦✦
As the title says, *Greatest Hits 1990-1992* contains all of the biggest hits Tanya Tucker had in the early '80s, including the number-two singles "Down to My Last Teardrop," "(Without You) What Do I Do With Me," "Some Kind of Trouble," and "Two Sparrows in a Hurricane," among others. —*Stephen Thomas Erlewine*

Soon / Oct. 11, 1993 / Liberty ✦✦
Soon dips into some average material and over-synthesized production. Fortunately, Tucker pulls out of the dive thanks to two ballads—"Soon" and "Silence is King"—strong enough to rise above the treatment, and a pair of toothy tracks—"Sneaky Moon" and "A Blue Guitar"—that get back to the resonating riffs of the opener. —*Roch Parisien*

Girls Like Me / 1994 / Capitol ✦✦✦✦
Given her predilection for switching record labels, it's more than interesting to look at the debut albums Tanya Tucker issued for each. They are always undeniably strong, consistent, and soulful. *Girls Like Me* is no exception, produced by Jerry Crutchfield and featuring a tight collection of songs that reflects Tucker's considerable experience as a vocalist and a country music icon. From the Paul Overstreet & Paul Davis-penned opener, "One Love at a Time," which could almost be interpreted as autobiographical, to the beautiful swanky pop of Davis' "Fool, Fool Heart," Tucker shows both sides of her complicated amorous life. But it's when the shimmering synthesizer introduces the Karen Brooks/Matraca Berg-authored title track that Tucker turns in her most inspired performance on the set. Beginning slow and sultry as an "other side of the tracks" story, it shimmers with a desperate but simmering passion that reflects the dreams and wreckage of "passion on the beach" through the eyes of a "paperback dreamer." Again, as she relates the tale of finding a love whose intensity she couldn't sustain, Tucker is baring her own soul. She seeks the "long and lonely streets" before the bridge and screaming guitar usher in a moment of hope, a desperate one that in fact refuses to say die. And then there's Marshall Chapman's tough "Daddy Long Legs," which cuts deeply in Tucker's interpretive groove. The track is part Bobbie Gentry, part Tucker, and part Delbert McClinton; it drips funky blues and steamy honky tonk. *Girls Like Me* is a winner from end to end and one of the best efforts of the '80s for Tucker. —*Thom Jurek*

Fire to Fire / 1995 / Liberty ✦✦✦
Considering that even at 13 years old, Tanya Tucker sounded like a world-weary adult, it's no surprise that in 1994, firmly ensconced in middle age, her vocals had gained a profound sense of life experience that few other singers of any genre can approach. Thankfully, on *Fire to Fire* Tucker doesn't even bother with the sort of boot-scootin' modern fluff that would underutilize her wonderfully sandpapery voice. Rather, she concentrates primarily on tear-jerking country ballads and mature pop, wringing so much emotion out of each word that she often recalls late-'70s/early-'80s era George Jones. Producer Jerry Crutchfield wisely keeps the music minimal throughout, allowing Tucker's voice to carry the tunes. Occasionally, Crutchfield's pop side gets the best of him (resulting in songs that sound like they'd be a bit more comfortable on a Don Henley album), but luckily the music never overwhelms the message. Standouts include "Come in Out of the World," the title track (a duet with Willie Nelson), and "Love Will," which moves jauntily along with

a nice Muscle Shoals-inspired groove. *Fire to Fire* is an adult album in the best sense of the word. There are no barnburners or instant chart classics here, just thoughtful song-writing, flawless (if sometimes uninspired) musicianship, and one of the all-time greatest voices in country music. —*Pemberton Roach*

Love Songs / Aug. 20, 1996 / Capitol ✦✦✦
Love Songs is a budget-priced collection of Tanya Tucker's most popular love ballads from the late '80s and early '90s, as well as a few rarities ("I'm in Love and He's in Dallas" and "Your Love Amazes Me") that were previously only included on her eponymous box set. It's a nice collection, even if it is a little brief. However, it isn't a true hits compilation, so it's not as valuable or useful as some of her other collection. Casual fans should stick with the greatest hits sets, but for the budget-minded, *Love Songs* is a fun sampler. —*Stephen Thomas Erlewine*

Complicated / Mar. 25, 1997 / Capitol ✦✦✦✦
On her 30th album, Tanya Tucker turns in an inspired, tough performance that offers a series of songs reflecting her life's many travels and travails. A musical firebrand on record since she was 14, Tucker has ridden out the scandals, the glories, and the excesses to become one of country music's true jewels. Produced by Gregg Brown to coincide with the issue of her autobiography, *Nickel Dreams*, *Complicated* is a cleanly produced record of fine songs and great musical performances from some bona fide studio legends, such as Hargus "Pig" Robbins, Pat Buchanan, Reggie Young, Billy Joe Walker, and the incomparable Fats Kaplin. What matters most, of course, is Tucker's performance, and she is in devastatingly fine voice here. The material ranges from the sublime to the merely adequate, but it's all delivered so passionately it doesn't matter. A true standout is the Dulaney & Jones-penned "Little Things," with its gorgeous guitar fills and Tucker's completely convincing delivery about not needing the finer things in life. The opener, "Ridin' Out the Heartache," by Cathy Majeski, has slide guitars and fiddles cascading around Robbins' piano in the opening bars before Tucker enters with an acoustic guitar, delivering an anthem of independence and leaving nowhere for parts unknown to get past the blues. The Allen/Jones ballad "It Hurts Like Love" contains Tucker's finest gritty vocal in a ballad. It seemingly is at odds until she gets to the refrain and it all becomes clear. And then there's her read of Harlan Howard's singing two-step mariachi-infused "I Don't Believe That's How You Feel," which should erase any doubt that Tucker can still sing traditional music with verve, originality, and passion. "Love Thing" is funky backbeat-driven country, with Tucker just behind the beat making it come out like that "feeling inside" with slide guitar underlining every phrase. Of course, it should sound this way—Delbert McClinton wrote it. Nice and greasy. And then there's the bluesy country-rock of the title track, written by Pat McLaughlin, that is equal parts honky tonk and rockin' blues. In all, this is a dynamite record, full of all the right stuff; with Tucker in full-on gritty voice over all that slick production, it's a study in country contradiction that works in spades. —*Thom Jurek*

Super Hits / Feb. 17, 1998 / Sony ✦✦✦
Included are ten of 's greatest hits, from "Delta Dawn" and "The Man That Turned My Mama On" to "You Are So Beautiful." Though there would've been plenty of room for additional hits, this disc isn't a bad value when bought at a cheap price. —*John Bush*

★ **What's Your Mama's Name/Would You Lay With Me (In a Field of Stone)** / Nov. 9, 1999 / Collectables ✦✦✦✦✦
At first glance, this might seem to be a strange pairing. *What's Your Mama's Name* and *Would You Lay With Me (In a Field of Stone)* are Tanya Tucker's second and third albums, begging the question as to why *Delta Dawn* and *What's Your Mama's Name* weren't issued together on a single disc. There are complex reasons to be sure, but one of them is simply that these two recordings are more suited to one another for a number of reasons; the first is that they prove that *Delta Dawn* was no fluke, and even that her next two efforts, as albums, were even stronger than her debut. Part of the reason is that Columbia Records turned Tucker's recording career over to its finest staff producer, Billy Sherrill. Here, the title tracks from each recording would be hits, and given the presence of "California Cotton Fields," "Blood Red and Goin' Down," "The Man That Turned My Mama On," "How Can I Tell Him," "Let Me Be There," "The Baptism of Jesse Taylor," and others, there's nary a weak moment over two albums—with the possible exception of "I Think the South's Gonna Rise Again." This is one of the best two-fers Collectables has ever issued, with excellent sound. —*Thom Jurek*

20 Greatest Hits / Sep. 26, 2000 / Capitol ✦✦✦✦✦

20th Century Masters—The Millennium Collection: The Best of Tanya Tucker / Oct. 31, 2000 / MCA ✦✦✦✦
Given that it features just 11 songs, *20th Century Masters—The Millennium Collection: The Best of Tanya Tucker* actually does a pretty good job at covering the highlights of her mid-'70s to mid-'80s work. Singles like "San Antonio Stroll," "Here's Some Love," "Texas (When I Die)," and "Can I See You Tonight" trace her development from a purely country artist into a country-rock crossover star. Though best-ofs like *20 Greatest Hits* offer a deeper and more comprehensive look at Tucker's music, *The Millennium Collection* is more than adequate for the most casual fans. —*Heather Phares*

★ **The Upper 48 Hits: 1972–1997** / Sep. 24, 2002 / Raven ✦✦✦✦✦
Tanya Tucker wasn't just a great country singer—she was a great country *story*, growing up in the public eye from her first Top Ten single, "Delta Dawn" in 1972, to her last, "Little Things" in 1997. In between, she racked up numerous hits and tabloid headlines, causing controversy at the outset of her career with her sexiness and provocative material that sounded even riskier in the hands of a 14-year-old singer. Soon, the country Lolita image gave way to a wild young woman who had an affair with Merle Haggard and a broken engagement with Glen Campbell; musically, the pure progressive country of her early recordings gave way to a flirtation with pop and rock, before she swung back to country.

Then, she cleaned up and straightened out her music, turning toward a mature country-pop that brought her through the '90s. It was a hell of a ride, with a hell of a lot of good music, all chonicled on Raven's double-disc, 48-track *The Upper 48 Hits: 1972-1997*, the most comprehensive and best overview of her career ever likely to be assembled. This collection is so good not just because the music is generally excellent, but because the sequencing has a real narrative drive, mirroring the ups and downs, triumphs and turmoil of Tucker's career. When she hit a low point in her career, this collection does too—there is a bit of a dip somewhere after the early '80s, when her music became a little bit too streamlined, but she comes tearing back with a series of sexy, husky-voiced, rowdy singles that propel her to the successful, tasteful material of the '90s. Yes, it's the earliest material that is the most distinctive—her early-'70s breakthroughs "Delta Dawn," "What's Your Mama's Name, Child?," "Blood Red and Goin' Down," "Would You Lay With Me (In a Field of Stone)," "The Man That Turned My Mama On," and "Lizzie and the Rainman" among them—because the songs were risky and strong, the productions adventurous, and the performances shockingly mature. That was music in a class of its own, but Tanya Tucker herself was in her own class too—she was a survivor, and while her career did see a few valleys, she pulled through and wound up with a terrific body of work, best heard on this stellar collection. —*Stephen Thomas Erlewine*

The Tune Wranglers

f. 1935, San Antonio, TX
Group / Western Swing
The honky tonky scene of Texas in the '30s would have hardly been sympathetic to a milquetoast; the last thing one would want to have in a Western swing band of that era would have been a coward for a frontman. Then again it worked out fine for the mighty Tune Wranglers of San Antonio, whose guitarist and singer was none other than Buster Coward. Other original members of the group, which was founded in the mid-'30s, included banjoist Eddie Fielding and the fiddler and singer Charlie Gregg. The former man's eventual replacement would become one of the group's hot attractions: the banjoist Joe Barnes, hiding behind the stage name of Red Brown, sported a rapid soloing style that has influenced a wide range of musicians from heavy metal fuzz boxers to the makers of the Indian film music. The players apparently never went full-time with their musical pursuits, keeping a hand and a lasso or two in play as cowboys. Nonetheless, time was made to cut some 80 sides, some of them in Spanish, and to do gigs in some 200 different towns annually, traveling more than 100,000 miles to get there and back.

The group's repertoire was quite similar to many other Western swing outfits of the time, mixing together cowboy songs, sometimes gimmicky enough to border on pop novelties, with traditional old-time country music. "Texas Sand" was the group's most well-known song, and the normally macho Texas music fans seem to have forgiven the song for being written by a Coward. The band's popularity wandered over the border into Mexico courtesy of the frequent broadcasts over WOAI and other regional radio outfits. This airplay dramatically increased when the Tune Wranglers released their side entitled "El Rancho Grande." The Bluebird label honchos liked the Mexican angle well enough to begin an entire series, promoting Tune Wranglers sides under the band name of Tono Hombres.

The group first began recording for the firm in 1936, shortly before adding steel guitar legend Eddie Duncan to the band. Vocal chores tended to be divided up within the band based on the genre of the song, with the steel guitarist picking up pop ditties and the Coward singing the blues, which figures. Revard's Playboys was another band from the same time that was considered quite similar, and with good reason; many of the same guys were on-stage in a series of revolving door hirings and firings. Eddie Whitely was out of the Tune Wranglers to sing on the early Revard's Playboys sides, for example, then he went back to his original band. Meanwhile, his replacement switched places with him in the second band. One of the Tune Wranglers fiddlers, Leonard Seago, also quit to join the other band at one point. The band's third and final recording session consisted mostly of Hawaiian numbers including the romantic "Hawaiian Honeymoon" By then bandmembership had swollen to include the musical twins Neal & Beal, handling banjo and reeds, respectively. —*Eugene Chadbourne*

● **1936–1938** / Aug. 22, 2000 / Texas Rose ✦✦✦✦✦
One of the earliest and most entertaining Western swing groups, the Tune Wranglers specialized in both cowboy music and raucous, 1920s-style jazz and blues. Concerning the latter, they were among the greatest groups of their day, turning out exciting, swinging material that was the equal of Bob Wills in daring if not quality. The group's rowdy banter and call-and-response harmonizing are immensely entertaining, reminiscent of the Maddox Brothers & Rose and early Bill Monroe. This is especially true of the sides featuring pianist Eddie Whitley, a master of barrelhouse jazz who could turn any old song into a hard-swinging good-time. All told, this is a fairly astonishing listen featuring the group's only hit, "Texas Sand," and other splendid moments such as "El Rancho Grande," "Red's Tight Like That," and the twisted novelty "Sarah Jane." —*Jim Smith*

Zeb Turner (William Grishaw)

b. Jun. 23, 1915, Lynchburg, VA, **d.** Jan. 10, 1978
Guitar, Songwriter, Vocals / Boogie-Woogie, Traditional Country, Honky Tonk
Born as William Grishaw, honky tonk guitarist Zeb Turner took his name from his best-loved composition, the "Zeb Turner Stomp." Turner first turned up on wax as a member of the Hi Neighbor Boys on the American Record Label in 1938, but he soon left the group to join forces with his brother James who took the stage name of Zeke Turner. The Turner brothers played guitar on many sessions shortly after WWII, turning up on records by Red Foley and Hank Williams and writing Eddy Arnold's 1947 hit, "It's a Sin." In addition to lending his country boogie guitar work to others, Zeb Turner often recorded in his own right on small, regional labels such as Nashville's Bullet Records and, later, Cincinnati's King Records. Though he never enjoyed mainstream success, Turner did have a long career, eventually ending up as a folksinger in Montreal. —*Steve Kurutz*

● **Tennessee Boogie & Jersey Rock** / Mar. 7, 2000 / WestSide ✦✦✦✦✦
Zeb Turner played proto-rock & roll and country boogie in addition to the standard honky tonk fare. Making his mark first as a studio guitarist (he added the sparkle to Hank Williams' "Mind Your Own Business"), he soon signed with King Records and from 1949 to 1953 cut these pioneering sides for the label. These 24 tracks are the sound of country music in transition, chock-full of Turner's hot guitar and heartfelt singing. There are highlights aplenty, including "Boogie Woogie Lou," "Why Don't You Haul Off and Get Religion," "Rag Man Boogie," "I Got Loaded," "Crazy Heart," and "Jersey Rock," which predates the Bill Haley sound by a full year. A wealth of great music by an artist who deserves a much wider hearing. —*Cub Koda*

Wesley Tuttle

b. Dec. 30, 1917, Lamar, CO
Guitar / Western Swing, Traditional Country, Cowboy
The brevity of the 1940s and '50s country charts did a disservice to artists like Wesley Tuttle, who enjoyed wide exposure on radio, television, and film but had few chart hits. If country music's Top 100 had been compiled in those early days, Tuttle's popularity would be more apparent to present-day chart perusers. Tuttle was an important figure in the West Coast country music scene, but his retirement from secular music in 1957 contributed to the low profile from which he suffers, even though he remained active in sacred music throughout the '60s. Born Wesley LeRoy Tuttle in Lamar, CO, on December 30, 1917, he gained an early exposure to phonograph records in the cafe where his parents worked. The Tuttles relocated to San Fernando, CA, just before Tuttle's fifth birthday, and there he learned to play the ukulele and acquired an interest in singing and performing. At the age of eight he lost the middle three fingers of his left hand in an accident at his father's butcher shop, which forced him to chord his ukulele (and eventually, guitar) with his right hand.

While recovering from the accident, Tuttle received a radio as a gift and took an interest in Jimmie Rodgers, who inspired Tuttle to learn how to yodel. By the age of 12 Tuttle could play guitar, sing, and yodel with enough proficiency to earn a spot on KNX in Los Angeles. In the early '30s he caught the ear of Stuart Hamblen, who invited Tuttle to appear on his radio show, "The Family Album," the most popular country music program in southern California at the time. From there Tuttle obtained other radio and film work, such as performing Dopey's yodel in the Walt Disney film *Snow White & the Seven Dwarfs*. Success emboldened Tuttle to quit high-school and pursue a music career in earnest. In 1939, Tuttle moved to Dayton, OH, and worked at WLW in Cincinnati, where he married his first wife and met Merle Travis. Tuttle returned to California after a dispute with WLW, resuming radio work and meeting Johnny Bond. Through Bond's connections, Tuttle joined the Jimmy Wakely Trio and, in 1944, backed Tex Ritter on the recording session that yielded the hit "Jealous Heart." Tuttle also appeared in a number of Western films starring Jimmy Wakely, Charles Starrett, and Tex Ritter. The success of "Jealous Heart" led to a contract with Capitol Records, and Tuttle cut his first sessions in 1944.

Tuttle brought in Merle Travis, who had moved to California, as his guitarist and backing vocalist—a role that Travis would fill for several years. Tuttle made a handful of significant hits, including the chart-topping "With Tears in My Eyes" in 1945 and one of four hit versions of "Detour" in 1946. The demands of Tuttle's career contributed to the breakup of his marriage, and in 1946 he married Marilyn Meyers, who became his duet partner. As Wesley & Marilyn Tuttle, the couple made Tuttle's final chart hit, "Never," in 1954. In the '50s Tuttle worked as a writer and host on the country music television program *Town Hall Party*, but he quit television and canceled his contract with Capitol in 1957 after converting to Christianity. He enrolled in a Christian college to become a minister, and in 1959 made his first gospel album for Sacred Records. Tuttle served as Sacred's musical director and recorded a number of religious albums—with and without Marilyn—through 1969 before retiring from music altogether. —*Greg Adams*

Sings / 1969 / Sacred ✦✦✦
Wesley Tuttle's final album for Sacred is an appealingly homespun collection of gospel songs performed simply with piano, an occasional guitar, and two uncredited background vocalists (one may be Tuttle's wife, Marilyn) who form a harmony trio on the choruses. Tuttle refurbishes "Detour," the country classic he introduced on Capitol Records in 1946, with new religious lyrics, and does the same with "Tumbling Tumbleweeds." (The latter, curiously, is not credited to Bob Nolan even though Tuttle had a long-standing personal and professional relationship with the Sons of the Pioneers.) The music is pure gospel in presentation, even on the remakes of secular songs, and Tuttle's delivery is plain and sincere. *Sings* is a far cry from the yodels, boogies and Texas swing of Tuttle's early days, but is an honest expression of this country legend's religious convictions. —*Greg Adams*

● **Detour** / May 21, 2002 / Bear Family ✦✦✦✦✦
Detour takes a look at the career of Wesley Tuttle, a nearly forgotten player in the West Coast country music scene of the '40s and '50s. The set contains four CDs, a DVD, and an 86-page book packaged in an LP-sized box. The first two discs hold most of Tuttle's Capitol recordings, including all of his hits and the early sides that prominently feature Merle Travis on guitar and background vocals. The remaining two audio discs are packed with rare radio transcriptions from the '40s. The DVD has a handful of telescriptions (early music videos) and a Jimmy Wakely film, *Song of the Sierras*, in which Tuttle co-stars. As for the music, Tuttle is similar in style to his confederates—Jimmy Wakely, Johnny Bond, and Merle Travis—but with much less novelty material than the latter two, and very little western music. Tuttle favored slow and medium tempos, and his accomplished yodeling is heard on only a few cuts. *Song of the Sierras*, mastered from a good print, is an average singing cowboy western with a ridiculous plot, but happily features a lot of music. The mere existence of a Wesley Tuttle box set practically precludes any criticism, but there are a couple of problems. One is that *Detour* omits an entire disc's worth of Capitol and Coral recordings; since Bear Family has a reputation for offering complete recordings sets, and their releases carry a premium price, the omission is puzzling. Most

buyers would probably have preferred a fifth disc of music instead of, or in addition to, a DVD. Another puzzler is that the usual licensing information for the Capitol cuts is missing, which raises questions as to what was used as source material—the original masters or commercial 78s? The sound is excellent but with noticeable surface noise in places, and the matter wouldn't be an issue if not for Bear Family's well-established reputation and high price. Many collectors would have been thrilled with a single-disc anthology, so, nitpicks aside, a multi-disc Wesley Tuttle set is a welcome thing. —*Greg Adams*

Shania Twain

b. Aug. 28, 1965, Windsor, Ontario, Canada
Vocals / Country-Pop, Pop/Rock, Contemporary Country, Adult Contemporary
Emerging in the mid-'90s, Shania Twain (pronounced shu-NYE-uh) became the most popular country music artist since Garth Brooks. Skillfully fusing mainstream, AOR rock production with country-pop, Twain and her producer/husband Robert John "Mutt" Lange created a commercial juggernaut with her second album, *The Woman in Me*. The record became a multi-platinum phenomenon, peaking at number five on the pop charts and eventually selling over nine-million copies in the U.S. alone. Twain might have sold a lot of records, but like other mega-selling acts before her, she earned few good reviews—most critics accused her of diluting country with bland, anthemic hard rock techniques and of shamelessly selling her records with sexy videos. Fans ignored such complaints, mainly because her audience was comprised of many listeners that had grown accustomed to such marketing strategies by constant exposure to MTV. And Twain, in many ways, was the first country artist to fully exploit MTV's style. She created a sexy, video-oriented image—she didn't even tour during the year when *The Woman in Me* was on the top of the country charts—that appealed not only to the country audience, but also to pop fans. In turn, she became a country music phenomenon.

Twain was born in Windsor, Ontario, and raised in the small, rural town of Timmins, Ontario. As a child, she learned to play guitar at an early age and would spend much of her time singing, writing, and playing. Early on in her musical development, her parents pushed her on-stage, making her perform frequently around their little town; often, she would be pulled out of bed around one in the morning to sing at local bars, since as a child she could only appear in the clubs after they had stopped serving alcohol. In addition to bars, she sang on local radio and television stations and community events. When she was 21 years old, both of her parents died in a car crash, forcing her to take responsibility for her four younger brothers. In order to pay the bills and keep food on the table, she took a job singing at a resort in Deerhurst. With the money she earned at the resort, she bought a house and had the family settle down.

At the resort, she sang show tunes, from George Gershwin to Andrew Lloyd Webber, as well as a little country. Twain stayed there for three years, at the end of which all of her siblings had begun lives of their own. When she was finally independent again, she assembled a demo tape of her songs, and her manager set up a showcase concert in Canada. Twain caught the attention of a few insiders with the concert, and within a few months, Mercury Nashville had signed her to their roster. Her eponymous debut album was released in 1993, and although it wasn't a major hit, it performed respectably in the U.S., launching two minor hit singles, "What Made You Say That" and "Dance With the One That Brought You"; in Europe, the album was more successful and Country Music Television Europe named her Rising Video Star of the Year.

Shortly after the release of *Shania Twain*, the singer met and fell in love with Robert John "Mutt" Lange, a hard rock producer known for his work with AC/DC, Def Leppard, Foreigner, and the Cars. Lange had been wanting to move into country music for a while, and after hearing Twain's debut album, he decided to get in contact with her with the intention of working on an album. By the end of the year, the pair had married and begun working on her second record. The two either wrote or co-wrote the material that eventually formed *The Woman in Me*.

The Woman in Me was released in the spring of 1995. Its first single, "Whose Bed Have Your Boots Been Under?," went to number 11 early in the year, quickly followed by "Any Man of Mine," which became her first number-one single in the spring. The album's title track went to number 14 in the fall, while the fourth single, "(If You're Not In It for Love) I'm Outta Here!," rocketed to number one toward the end of the year; early in 1996, "No One Needs to Know" became her third number-one hit. By the beginning of 1996, *The Woman in Me* had sold over six-million copies and broken the record for the most weeks spent at number one on the country charts. During the course of 1996, it would rack another three million in sales. *Come On Over* followed in 1997. She spent the next two years touring the globe in support of the album; by the end of 1999, *Come On Over* had sold 36-million copies.

Twain took a sabbatical and returned to her Swiss home for some down time with her husband. The next summer, she and Lange welcomed their first child. A son, whom they named Eja, arrived August 21, 2001. During this time, Twain brainstormed for a fourth album. While balancing a domestic life and a career, the end result was *Up!*, which appeared in November 2002. —*Stephen Thomas Erlewine*

Shania Twain / Apr. 20, 1993 / Mercury ✦✦✦
Shania Twain's eponymous debut album is a bland set of contemporary country that demonstrates her considerable vocal abilities but none of the spark that informs her breakthrough, *The Woman in Me*. Part of the problem is that none of the songs are well-constructed and each leans toward soft rock instead of country or country-rock. By and large, the songs lack strong melodies, so they have to rely on Twain's vocal skills, and although she is impressive, she is too showy to make any of these mediocre songs stick. It's a promising debut, largely because it showcases her fine vocal skills, but it isn't engaging enough to be truly interesting outside of a historical context. —*Thom Owens*

The Woman in Me / 1995 / Mercury ✦✦✦✦✦
Shania Twain's second album broke down the doors of stardom for the singer, selling over four-million copies by the beginning of 1996. Like many country artists of the mid-'90s, Twain's music combined country conventions with mainstream rock flourishes, creating a sound that appealed to both audiences. *The Woman in Me* isn't necessarily flawless

product—the material is a bit inconsistent, and the music plays it a bit too safe—but it all sounds convincing, thanks to the dynamic charisma of Shania Twain. *—Stephen Thomas Erlewine*

★ **Come on Over** / Nov. 4, 1997 / Mercury ✦✦✦✦✦

Shania Twain's second record, *The Woman in Me*, became a blockbuster, appealing as much to a pop audience as it did to the country audience. Part of the reason for its success was how producer Robert John "Mutt" Lange—best-known for his work with Def Leppard, the Cars, and AC/DC—steered Twain toward the big choruses and instrumentation that always was a signature of his speciality, AOR radio. *Come on Over*, the sequel to *The Woman in Me*, continues that approach, breaking from contemporary country conventions in a number of ways. Not only does the music lean toward rock, but its 16 songs and, as the cover proudly claims, "Hour of Music," break from the country tradition of cheap, short albums of ten songs that last about a half-hour. Furthermore, all 16 songs and Lange-Twain originals and Shania's sleek, sexy photos suggest a New York fashion model, not a honky tonker. And there isn't any honky tonk here, which is just as well, since the fiddles are processed to sound like synthesizers and talk boxes never sound good on down-home, gritty rave-ups. No, Shania sticks to what she does best, which is countrified mainstream pop. Purists will complain that there's little country here, and there really isn't. However, what is here is professionally crafted country-pop—even the filler (which there is, unfortunately, too much of) sounds good—which is delivered with conviction, if not style, by Shania, and that is enough to make it a thoroughly successful follow-up to the most successful country album by a female in history. *—Stephen Thomas Erlewine*

☆ **Come on Over: The International Version** / Nov. 23, 1999 / Mercury ✦✦✦✦✦

The week the *Come on Over: The International Version* appeared in the U.S., *Come on Over* was still in the Top 20 after spending over two years on the charts and selling over 14-million copies. That is massive success and it's all the more remarkable because the hits on pop radio were not on the album. Each single was remixed and refurbished—most notably the dance reworking of "That Don't Impress Me Much"—with an eye on Top 40 and adult contemporary radio, plus foreign markets that wanted Shania the pop diva, not Twain the country crooner. Actually, the original versions weren't all that country to begin with; they were adult contemporary pop tunes with the occasional violin or steel guitar—enough to make *Come on Over* seem like country on the surface, but at its heart, it was pop music. That's why the single remixes were so successful—they revealed the true nature of the song. Similarly, *The International Version* feels more genuine than the original, since it has no qualms embracing the gaudy thrills of pop. Every cut on *Come on Over* has been remixed for this version and the sequencing has changed. Each track benefits from this tinkering, since these versions are giddily infectious and present Shania as the pop diva she really is. In this incarnation, *Come on Over* stands as the best pop diva album of the late '90s—playful, funny, tuneful, catchy, amusing, sexy. No diva has delivered a record this consistently fun in years—not Mariah, not Whitney, not Madonna (who abandoned the whole idea of fun during the '90s, anyway). Sure, almost all of its best qualities are on the surface but that's precisely why it's irresistible. *—Stephen Thomas Erlewine*

Beginnings: 1989–1990 / Dec. 14, 1999 / Jomato ✦✦✦

The songs on this album, *Beginnings: 1989-1990*, are just what the title indicates: the beginnings—tunes that were recorded between late 1989 and early 1990. These tunes were really only intended to be used as demos to help draw attention to a young and struggling singer who who would become hot as fresh-cooked griddle cakes, country diva Shania Twain. These 12 remastered and remixed songs are more rock, power pop, and adult contemporary than country, fitting into the late '80s just as they should have when they were done. Many of the numbers on this 1999 album were written by both Paul Sabu and the young Twain. All of the songs aside from "For the Love of Him" can be found on another album called *The Complete Limelight Sessions*, along with five other songs from the same time period. If you buy this album instead, though, you have the pleasure of knowing that part of the purchase price will go to worthwhile charities like the Make a Wish Foundation in Phoenix and Kids' Cafe/Second Harvest in Chicago. *—Charlotte Dillon*

The Complete Limelight Sessions / Oct. 23, 2001 / Limelight ✦✦✦

The Complete Limelight Sessions by Shania Twain is put together from early demo songs that were remastered and polished up a bit for this 2001 album. The 17 tracks on this offering were recorded during 1989 and into 1990. This was before Mercury Records had signed Twain to a contract, when she was still pretty much an unknown, working hard to provide a suitable living for herself and her orphaned siblings. The songs on this album are a little different than the country tunes fans are used to from Twain. These are more dance or pop/rock, but still the daring and heart of the young star shine through. There are a number of bootlegs out there that carry these songs, but they don't match the better quality of this recording—not that the quality of this one is way up there. "It's Alright," "Send It With Love," and "For the Love" are a few of the highlights from *The Complete Limelight Sessions*. All in all, this is a decent collection of Shania Twain's early work, and her most loyal fans will find it worth having in spite of more than a few flaws. It also comes with the bonus of a few rare photos of Twain from those early days. *—Charlotte Dillon*

Up! / Nov. 19, 2002 / Mercury ✦✦✦✦✦

When *Up!* was released in November 2002, Shania Twain revealed in one of many promotional interviews that she writes far more songs than can fit on her records and that she hides any personal, introspective songs she pens, not even playing them for her husband and collaborator Robert John "Mutt" Lange. Now, this is certainly a psychological quirk worth exploring, but it also suggests why Twain's albums are such brilliant pieces of mainstream pop. Anything that doesn't fit the mold is discarded, so the album can hum along on its big, polished, multipurpose hooks and big, sweeping emotions. This is Super-Size pop, as outsized and grandiose as good pop should be. And, unlike the work of most pop divas, where the subject matter is firmly about the singer, none of the songs on *Up!* are remotely about Shania Twain, the person—let's face it, she's never faced a situation like "Waiter! Bring Me Water!," where she's afraid her guy is going to be stolen away by their hot waitress. No, these songs have been crafted as universal anthems, so listeners can hear themselves within these tales. Just as cleverly, the songs are open-ended and mutable—always melodic, but never stuck in any particular style, so they can be subjected to any kind of mix and sound just as good. (Indeed, *Up!* was initially released in no less than *three* different mixes—the "Red" pop mix, the "Green" country mix, and the "Blue" international mix; sometimes the differences in mixes were so slight, it sounded like nothing was changed, but each mix revealed how sturdy and melodic the structure of each of the 19 songs was, and how they were designed to sound good in any setting.) True, the sheer length of the album could be seen as off-putting at first, since these 19 tracks don't necessarily flow as a whole. Then again, part of the genius of *Up!* is that it's designed as a collection of tracks, so the album is durable enough to withstand years on the charts, producing singles with different textures and moods every few months. Time revealed *Come on Over* as a stellar pop album, and the same principle works for *Up!* Upon the first listen, singles seem indistinct, and it seems like too much to consume at once, but once you know the lay of the land, the hooks become indelible and the gargantuan glossiness of the production is irresistible. In other words, it's a more than worthy follow-up to the great mainstream pop album of the late '90s, and proof that when it comes to shiny, multipurpose pop, nobody does it better than Shania Twain. *—Stephen Thomas Erlewine*

Conway Twitty (Harold Lloyd Jenkins)

b. Sep. 1, 1933, Friars Point, MS, **d.** Jun. 5, 1993, Branson, MO

Guitar, Vocals / Traditional Country, Country-Pop, Rockabilly, Nashville Sound/ Countrypolitan

Originally a '50s rock & roll singer, Conway Twitty became the reigning country superstar of the '70s and '80s, racking up a record 40 number-one hits over the course of two decades. With his deep, resonant down-home voice, Twitty was one of the smoothest balladeers to work in Nashville during the country-pop era, but he was also one of the most adventurous. More than any other singer, he was responsible for selling country as an "adult" music, slipping sexually suggestive lyrics into his lush productions, yet never singing misogynist lyrics—by and large, his songs were sensitive and sensual, which is part of the reason why he achieved such a large success. Once Twitty reached the top of the country charts in the late '60s, he stayed there for years on end, releasing a consistent stream of Top Ten hits that both defined and expanded the limitations of country-pop by adding subtle R&B, pop, and rock & roll influences. Though he had some pop success, Twitty remained country to the core—occasionally, his song titles were simply too corny—which was why he retained his popularity until his death in 1993.

The son of a riverboat captain, Twitty (born Harold Lloyd Jenkins, September 1, 1933; died June 5, 1993) was born in Mississippi and raised in Helena, AR, where he learned to love not only country, but also blues and gospel. When he was ten years old, he joined his first group, the Phillips Country Ramblers, who occasionally performed on local radio. Despite his interest in music, he originally planned to become a professional baseball player. Jenkins was talented enough to be offered a contract by the Philadelphia Phillies, but he was unable to join the team, since he was drafted into the Army during the Korean War. While he was serving in the Far East, he sang with a country band called the Cimarrons. Returning to America in 1956, Jenkins still had an open offer to join the Phillies, yet he decided to pursue a musical career after he heard Elvis Presley.

With dreams of recording for Sun Records, Jenkins headed to Memphis, where Sam Phillips did indeed sign him to a recording contract, but none of the tracks he cut were ever released; Jenkins' biggest contribution to the label was writing "Rock House," a minor hit for Roy Orbison. Leaving Sun in late 1956, he set out on a rockabilly package tour, during which he invented the stage name of Conway Twitty by combining the names of an Arkansas and Texas city, respectively. At the beginning of 1957, he signed to Mercury Records, where he released a handful of singles that didn't make much of an impact, though "I Need Your Lovin'" scraped the very bottom of the pop charts. In 1958, he moved to MGM Records, where he finally achieved success with "It's Only Make Believe," a song he had written with Jack Nance. Recorded with vocal support by Presley's back group, the Jordanaires, "It's Only Make Believe" became a major hit, spending two weeks at number one and going gold. Over the course of 1959 and 1960, Twitty released a number of singles, the most popular of which were the Top Ten "Danny Boy" and "Lonely Blue Boy," and appeared in the B movies *Sex Kittens Go to College, Platinum High School*, and *College Confidential*.

Twitty's rock & roll fame arrived suddenly and it went away just as quickly. By the beginning of 1961, his singles had stopped entering the Top 40. Nevertheless, he continued to tour, but soon MGM dropped him from their roster. Signing with ABC-Paramount, he began to add more country songs to his repertoire, yet he was still primarily recording pop material. Once Ray Price took Twitty's "Walk Me to the Door" to the country Top Ten, Conway decided he wanted to become a country singer, but he didn't actively pursue that avenue until 1965, when he walked out in the middle of a concert at a New Jersey nightclub. By the end of 1965, Twitty had begun a collaboration with record producer Owen Bradley, one of the cornerstones of the Nashville sound, and had signed to Decca Records. In the spring of the following year, he released his first country single, "Guess My Eyes Were Bigger Than My Heart," which peaked at number 18. For the next two years, he had a steady stream of four minor hits, finally breaking into the Top Ten with "The Image of Me" in the spring of 1968, followed a few months later by his first number-one hit, "Next in Line." For the next four years, he had a string of 12 Top Five singles for Decca, eight of which—including "I Love You More Today," "To See My Angel Cry," "Hello Darlin'," "Fifteen Years Ago," and "How Much More She Can Stand"—were number-one hits. In late 1970, he began a professional relationship with Loretta Lynn, releasing their first duet, "After the Fire Is Gone," early in 1971. The record became the first of five straight number-one country hits, which also included "Lead Me On," "Louisiana Woman, Mississippi Man," "As Soon as I Hang Up the Phone," and "Feelins'." Over the course of the decade, Twitty and Lynn continued to work together, releasing one album a year and racking up a total of 14 Top Ten hits; they also won four Duo of the Year awards from the Country Music Association, three Vocal Group of the Year honors from the Academy of Country Music, and one Grammy for Best Vocal Performance by a Group ("After the Fire Is Gone").

Twitty's solo career continued to thrive alongside his duets with Lynn. In 1973, Decca became absorbed by MCA Records, and all of his new records were released on MCA. The changeover in labels happened to coincide with an increased suggestiveness in much of his material, including the major hit single "You've Never Been This Far Before," which spent three weeks at number one during the summer of 1973, despite being banned by several radio stations. Not all of his songs were as explicitly sexual, yet they all had an adult theme and their layered, string-laden production was designed for more mature audience, who bought Twitty records in droves. Until 1983, he had a remarkably consistent string of Top Ten singles for Decca, most of which hit number one. Among his best-known hits from this era were "I See the Want To in Your Eyes," "Linda in My Mind," "Touch the Hand," "After All the Good Is Gone," "I've Already Loved You in My Mind," "Happy Birthday Darlin'," "Tight Fittin' Jeans," and "Red Neckin' Love Makin' Night." As he continued to rule the charts, Twitty expanded into other business ventures, including banking, property, a booking agency, and ultimately, a theme park called Twitty City. The size of his international popularity was confirmed when he re-recorded "Hello Darlin'" in Russian for a joint American/Soviet space mission.

In late 1981, he briefly moved to Elektra, where he released several hit singles, many of which were pop covers like the Pointer Sisters' "Slow Hand" and Bette Midler's "The Rose." Twitty signed with Elektra in 1983, where he had a string of hits over the next three years. Again, he covered several pop songs—the Eagles' "Heartache Tonight," the Commodores' "Three Times a Lady"—but he kept recording country songs, including the number ones "Somebody's Needin' Somebody," "I Don't Know a Thing About Love (The Moon Songs)," "Don't Call Him a Cowboy," and "Desperado Love," a 1986 chart-topper which proved to be his last number one.

Twitty returned to MCA in 1987, releasing the back-to-back number two hits "Julia" and "I Want to Know You Before We Make Love." Though he continued to have Top Ten hits through the end of the decade, his success began to slip slightly in the early '90s, once new country forced older performers off the top of the charts. Nevertheless, he remained quite popular, selling both records and concert tickets, until his sudden death from an abdominal aneurysm in the summer of 1993. Immediately following his death, he was praised and mourned from all quarters of the public, not just country music fans, and his record of over 40 number one hits remains unlikely to be surpassed. *—Stephen Thomas Erlewine*

Conway Twitty's Greatest Hits / 1960 / MGM ✦✦✦

These are the songs that helped make Conway Twitty a household name (and inspire the character Conrad Birdie in the musical *Bye Bye Birdie*.) This stuff still holds a thrill more than 30 years later. Also, the liner notes, while not entirely accurate, are still a lot of fun. Check out Twitty's Vital Statistics. *—Jim Worbois*

Conway Twitty Sings / 1965 / Decca ✦✦✦

Conway Twitty / 1965 / MGM ✦✦✦✦✦

Look into My Teardrops / 1966 / Decca ✦✦✦

Here's Conway Twitty & His Lonely Blue Boys / 1968 / Decca ✦✦✦✦

Next in Line / 1968 / Decca ✦✦✦

Darling, You Know I Wouldn't Lie / 1969 / Decca ✦✦✦✦

I Love You More Today / 1969 / MCA ✦✦✦

You Can't Take Country Out of Conway / 1969 / MGM ✦✦✦

Hello Darlin' / 1970 / Decca ✦✦✦✦✦

To See My Angel Cry/That's When She Started to Stop Loving You / 1970 / Decca ✦✦✦

How Much More Can She Stand / 1971 / Decca ✦✦✦

I Wonder What She'll Think About Me Leaving / 1971 / Decca ✦✦✦

We Only Make Believe / 1971 / MCA ✦✦✦

When two of the biggest country stars joined forces, the result was instant success. "After the First Is Gone," Loretta Lynn & Conway Twitty's first duet single, soared to number one and crossed over to the pop charts, inaugurating a professional association that would yield over a decade of hits. *We Only Make Believe*, their first duet album, plays on the title of Twitty's first big solo hit, "It's Only Make Believe," which the pair reinterprets as a country duet with steel guitar. "After the Fire Is Gone" is here, and Lynn and Twitty each contribute an original song. Lynn's composition, "Don't Tell Me You're Sorry," is reminiscent of the playful sparring songs of Porter Wagoner and Dolly Parton and ends with some strained ad libs (they'd get better at that as time went on). Nothing on the album approaches the excellence of "After the Fire Is Gone," but *We Only Make Believe* is a good starting point for one of the archetypal duos in country music. *—Greg Adams*

Lead Me On / 1971 / MCA ✦✦✦

The title track of Conway Twitty & Loretta Lynn's second duet album, *Lead Me On*, was the pair's second single and gave them their second number-one hit. If they seemed charmed at this point, they would soon appear invincible as they hit the top spot again and again. The interesting thing about *Lead Me On* is that there is so much steel guitar on these cuts it sounds as though they didn't even try to make another crossover contender like "After the Fire Is Gone." Some of the material has a country-pop pedigree, namely Freddie Hart's "Easy Loving" and Bobby Edwards' "You're the Reason," but the presentation is pure country. There are a few old-fashioned cheating songs of the sort at which Twitty and Lynn excel, a bow to honky tonk heritage with Webb Pierce's "Back Street Affair," and one bit of modern slang wrapped in straight country music (Billy Edd Wheeler's "You Blow My Mind"). As with their first duet album, the two conclude with a playful number, the frisky "Get Some Loving Done." *—Greg Adams*

Greatest Hits / 1971 / MGM ✦✦✦

Despite the fact that the stage name Conway Twitty obviously demonstrates a complete sense of confidence and determination, the recording career of this artist took off in extended fits and starts, kind of a slow-motion version of a teenage girl changing outfits several times before finally stepping outside. In each period he was prolific, so thus one can have a greatest-hits package on Conway Twitty that only includes material from one of his images. This album repackages his MGM material, to whom in the late '50s and early '60s he was signed on as a kind of mutation of Elvis Presley and Perry Como in every way one can imagine, musically and physically. Unlike either of these guys, he was hands-on musically, co-writing a batch of the material. So when the frighteningly overheard "It's Only Make Believe" begins side one, the listener should put aside the anguish of experiencing yet another version of this song and concentrate instead on putting a chalk mark on the wall of Twitty for being one of the writers. Now most fans of this singer would agree that his final personification as a sturdy Nashville type was where it was really at. With fortitude, he took on the impossible task of stepping in as a proper-age romantic substitute for Ernest Tubb in hit country vocal duets with Loretta Lynn. The only problem with him going country was that he completely abandoned the reckless, gimmicky rockabilly singing that had been part of his earliest personification as a rockin' daddy. This album has really very little country presence and too much unfortunate crooning that no amount of pitch control diddling is going to put right, but it does have wonderful examples of the el warpo rockabilly mentality inserting itself in the midst of shlock. Is there such a thing as shlockabilly? This is it. Take the example of "Danny Boy," where Twitty masterfully judged the exact point when listeners would snap, thinking it was going to be a long, serious version of the song. That's when the whole group starts rocking with the perfect touch of bad taste that only the masters seem to have at their fingertips. "It's a Blue Bird Blue" combines the vocal delivery of a moonshine-soaked hillbilly with twangy electric guitar and the kind of pristine string section MGM had on tap. Some of the rockabilly singing is really fantastic, plus tracks such as "The Hurt in My Heart" contain weird passages where he stops singing completely and just makes grumbling sounds in his throat. "Mona Lisa" is the same song that Nat King Cole croons, but this arrangement is a medium-tempo rocker with snare drums loud enough to be heard in New Orleans, background singers, and a Chuck Berry-style guitar solo. Ludicrous and a waste of a good ballad, but it works. As the album winds toward its conclusion, the listener will gratefully accept everything that is passed forward because Twitty, after all, is a charming host. *—Eugene Chadbourne*

Conway Twitty / 1972 / Decca ✦✦✦

Conway Twitty Sings the Blues / 1972 / MGM ✦✦✦

I Can't See Me Without You / 1972 / Decca ✦✦

☆ **Conway Twitty's Greatest Hits, Vol. 1** / 1972 / Decca ✦✦✦✦✦

This artist has as many greatest-hits packages as some artists have hits. This particular set actually does have his greatest hit and greatest song ever, the fantastic "Hello Darlin'," which he can certainly take pride in having written himself. Twitty has been responsible for his own material off and on through his career, but the amount of interest he has shown in his various recording projects wavers greatly. The image he projects in the photos that accompany this set is that of the serious, studio artist, composing a new song whenever a pad and paper is handy. He actually only wrote two of the songs on is set. Still, most songwriters would like to be Twitty on the front cover, an eye cocked in concentration while seated on the black leather couch in his own studio, album covers mounted all around him. OK, the red jumpsuit he is wearing is horrifying, and the little girl whose face is lodged in between "Twitty's" and "Greatest" in the title even more so. Some of these songs are taken from less-than-inspired recording sessions, even though for awhile just about anything with the Twitty name would get ample airplay. That is perhaps one of the reasons that all of these songs were number one hits, when some of them don't sound like they really should be. There is also a similarity in the romantic theme to the tracks that can be wearing on the listener. In this case it could be better hearing these tracks in the context of their original album releases, where they were no doubt surrounded by more complimentary material. This is the drawback of a greatest-hits set for an artist like this, whose public seemed to only expect one sort of record out of him. It is true that between the opening song and the Merle Haggard number that follows, Twitty definitely puts his best foot forward. Other highlights include "I Can't See Me Without You" and "The Image of Me." *—Eugene Chadbourne*

She Needs Someone to Hold Her / 1973 / MCA ✦✦✦✦

You've Never Been This Far Before / 1973 / MCA ✦✦✦✦

In 1973, Conway Twitty was still among the handful of kings of the countrypolitan sound. The title track of this set had some problems at country radio due to what was supposedly the suggestive nature of its title. Too bad radio missed out on a great song and a very fine Twitty album. He wrote both singles on the album, the other being the wondrously sad "Baby's Gone." In typical fashion, Twitty's voice was still in fine shape after almost 20 years of belting it out on records and stages. This is Twitty at his most country-fried, and there is still that rockabilly sheen to his delivery such as on "Bring It On Home to Your Woman." But the gift of Twitty's interpretive singing is felt best on cuts like Wiley Smith's "Til the Pain Outwears the Shame." He stays in the honky tonk groove and takes it to the bridge of pure sorrowful wail with a backing chorus boosting him up into the stratosphere. On "Baby's Gone," it becomes clear that Elvis Presley listened to a lot of Twitty in the late '60s and early '70s. His phrasing reflects it. And Twitty was so much more honest emotionally. And when he gets into the upper registers as he does on Jack Dunham's "When the Final Change Is Made," the spine tingles. And yet, he can turn a classic like Harlan Howard's "Above and Beyond (The Call of Love)" into a Buck Owens-styled Bakersfield honky tonk stomper. *You've Never Been This Far Before* is a remarkable album that contains within it all the magic that Twitty brought to country music. —*Thom Jurek*

Clinging to a Saving Hand / 1973 / MCA ✦✦✦

Steal Away / 1973 / MCA ✦✦✦

Honky Tonk Angel / 1974 / MCA ✦✦✦

I'm Not Through Loving You Yet / 1974 / MCA ✦✦

Linda on My Mind / 1975 / MCA ✦✦✦✦✦

Linda on My Mind is one of Conway Twitty's finest moments on wax. For a man who could sing the contents on a soup can and make it emotionally compelling, that is saying something. Twitty was such a badass as a persona and as a vocalist—not too mention as a songwriter, as through the '70s he wrote virtually all of his singles—he was bigger than life. The title track is an example where the honky tonk beer-weeper is transformed into a real-life drama complete with visuals and a backing chorus to underline the song's most poignant moments and a pedal steel ringing above it all to pierce the air. And while it's true that Twitty was making albums full of these songs in the 1970s, it was because he could always do it convincingly. But that didn't keep him from throwing a few surprises onto each album and this one is no exception. His version of the Flatt & Scruggs standard "Rollin' in My Sweet Baby's Arms" is done not as a bluegrass tune but as a honky tonk song for the first half and then as an electric bluegrass rocker! There's also Twitty's read of Kris Kristofferson's "Why Me" that reinvents the original by turning it into a prayer rather than an accusation. And, of course, it has to be mentioned that the infamous "I" trilogy is on this album: In a row, Twitty laces "I'll Get Over Losing You," "I Just Can't Get Over You (Getting Over Me)," and "I'm Getting Tired of Losing You." Twitty wrote the first and last part of this unholy trinity of barroom weepers. And man, does he sing the hell out of them. Despite the obvious humor at their placement, not only on the same album but also in succession, these songs are devastating in their emotional brokenness and helplessness. Twitty ends the album a few tracks later with another of his songs that comes to the conclusion that "Only Love Can Make Her Stay." Oh yeah, this is the stuff. Find it, get it, play it to death; you may become enlightened. —*Thom Jurek*

Feelins' / 1975 / MCA ✦✦✦

This Time I've Hurt Her More / 1975 / MCA ✦✦✦✦

High Priest of Country Music / 1975 / MCA ✦✦✦

United Talent / 1976 / MCA ✦✦

Conway Twitty's Greatest Hits, Vol. 2 / 1976 / MCA ✦✦✦✦✦

Greatest Hits, Vol. 2 is a great summation of Conway's early '70s hits, including "You've Never Been This Far Before," "There's a Honky Tonk Angel (Who'll Take Me Back In)," and "I See the Want To in Your Eyes," among others. —*Thom Owens*

Play, Guitar Play / 1977 / MCA ✦✦✦

I've Already Loved You in My Mind / 1977 / MCA ✦✦✦✦

Georgia Keeps Pulling on My Ring / 1978 / MCA ✦✦✦✦

Conway / 1978 / MCA ✦✦✦

Cross Winds / 1979 / MCA ✦✦✦

Not a great Twitty album, it still has it moments. This album does feature two hits ("Don't Take It Away" and "Happy Birthday Darlin'"), as well as "Heavy Tears," a fine John Hiatt song which Hiatt has yet to release. —*Jim Worbois*

Heart & Soul / 1980 / MCA ✦✦✦

Rest Your Love on Me / 1980 / MCA ✦✦✦

Two's a Party / 1981 / MCA ✦✦✦

Two's a Party may not have been one of Conway & Loretta's very best records—there is a bit too much pop here, not enough country—but the two singles, "Lovin' What You Lovin' Does to Me" and "I Still Believe in Waltzes," were good, and there were enough strong album tracks, such as "I'd Rather Have What We Have" and "The State of Our Union," to make it worthwhile for dedicated fans. —*Stephen Thomas Erlewine*

Number Ones / 1982 / MCA ✦✦✦✦✦

After moving from rock & roll to country, Twitty remained sensitive to criticism he might not be serious, rarely deviating from the standard three-chord country song for about his first decade in the format. This package, which selects material almost randomly from 1975-1981, does a good job of showing a Twitty more willing to experiment, particularly with the soulful "Don't Take It Away" and the dramatic "I May Never Get to Heaven." —*Tom Roland*

Southern Comfort / 1982 / Elektra ✦✦✦

Dream Maker / 1982 / Elektra ✦✦✦

Conway's #1 Classics, Vol. 2 / 1983 / Elektra ✦✦✦✦

By Heart / 1984 / Warner Bros. ✦✦✦

Chasin' Rainbows / 1985 / Warner Bros. ✦✦✦

Don't Call Him a Cowboy / 1985 / Warner Bros. ✦✦✦

Borderline / 1987 / MCA ✦✦

Borderline includes the hits "Julia," "I Want to Know You Before We Make Love," and "That's My Job." —*Jason Ankeny*

☆ **20 Greatest Hits** / 1987 / MCA ✦✦✦✦✦

20 Greatest Hits contains every one of Loretta Lynn & Conway Twitty's hits from the '70s, including the number-one singles "After the Fire Is Gone," "Lead Me On," "Louisiana Woman, Mississippi Man," "As Soon as I Hang Up the Phone," and "Feelins'." In addition

to the obvious hit singles, there are a number of lesser-known album tracks which are, with only a few exceptions, the equal of the hits. In short, *20 Greatest Hits* presents the very best of perhaps of the greatest country duet team of the '70s and is a necessary addition to any country record collection. —*Stephen Thomas Erlewine*

Still in Your Dreams / 1988 / MCA ✦✦✦

The Top Ten hits "Goodbye Time," "Saturday Night Special" (with harmonies by Vince Gill), and "I Wish I Was Still in Your Dreams" are among the featured cuts on *Still in Your Dreams.* —*Jason Ankeny*

Making Believe / 1988 / MCA ✦✦✦

A reunion of early '70s hitmakers (Twitty & Loretta Lynn) proves they're still in fine form. —*Mark A. Humphrey*

#1's: The Warner Brothers Years / 1988 / Warner Bros. ✦✦✦

This greatest-hits set shows (with the exception of "The Rose") an artist in command of his own performance, with a clear grasp on quality material and a strong sense of powerful arrangements. —*Tom Roland*

House on Old Lonesome Road / 1989 / MCA ✦✦

House on Old Lonesome Road leads off with "She's Got a Single Thing in Mind," the energizing hit which reaffirmed Twitty's standing among the era's country's giants. —*Jason Ankeny*

Crazy in Love / 1990 / MCA ✦✦

Crazy in Love generated a pair of Top Three hits, "I Couldn't See You Leavin'" and the title cut. —*Jason Ankeny*

Greatest Hits, Vol. 3 / 1990 / MCA ✦✦✦

Greatest Hits, Vol. 3 runs through Conway Twitty's big hits from his second stint at MCA Records in the late '80s. The collection includes the Top Ten hits "Julia," "I Want to Know You Before We Make Love," "That's My Job," "Goodbye Time," "Saturday Night Special," "I Wish I Was Still in Your Dreams," and "She's Got a Single Thing in Mind." —*Stephen Thomas Erlewine*

☆ **Silver Anniversary Collection** / 1990 / MCA ✦✦✦✦✦

Here are 25 hits from Twitty's work for MCA and Warner Bros. contained on this album, from "Guess My Eyes Were Bigger than My Heart" (1966) to "She's Got a Single Thing in Mind" (1989). It's an excellent introduction to one of the most popular singers in country music history. —*AMG*

Even Now / 1991 / MCA ✦✦✦

"She's Got a Man on Her Mind" and "Who Did They Think He Was" are the hits included on *Even Now.* —*Jason Ankeny*

The Best of Conway Twitty, Vol. 1: The Rockin' Years / 1991 / Mercury ✦✦✦✦✦

The Best of Conway Twitty, Vol. 1: The Rockin' Years contains all of the recordings he made for Mercury Records in the late '50s, when he was trying to follow in the footsteps of Elvis. Naturally, there's a lot of rockabilly on this collection—which he did very well—as well as some ballads that hint at his future country career. In between are some of his very best moments, including "It's Only Make Believe," "Mona Lisa," "Is a Bluebird Blue," and "Lonely Blue Boy." —*Stephen Thomas Erlewine*

Final Touches / 1993 / MCA ✦✦✦

Produced by Don Cook, *Final Touches* has its moments, but seems a less fitting swan song for Twitty than his princely duet with Sam Moore on the *Rhythm Country & Blues* album. —*Dan Cooper*

Rockin' Conway: The MGM Years / Oct. 19, 1993 / Mercury ✦✦✦✦✦

At a mere ten songs, it's too brief, but includes "It's Only Make Believe," and a rocked-out version of "Danny Boy," and "Is a Blue Bird Blue?," the first major cut for songwriting-legend Dan Penn. —*Dan Cooper*

☆ **The Conway Twitty Collection** / 1994 / MCA ✦✦✦✦✦

The Conway Twitty Collection is a stellar four-disc box set that contains every essential track he ever recorded. Beginning with some early recordings—including a cut from when he was a pre-teen—the set runs through every hit from 1958's "It's Only Make Believe" to 1993's "I'm the Only Thing (I'll Hold Against You)." Several rarities are scattered throughout, but the true treasure of the compilation is the simple fact that it contains the great majority of his Top Ten hits, including his duets with Loretta Lynn. It is a lasting testament to his considerable talents. —*Stephen Thomas Erlewine*

Country Classics / Oct. 15, 1996 / Critique ✦✦✦

Country Classics is a budget-priced collection that features a few of Conway Twitty's biggest hits—including "It's Only Make Believe" and "You've Never Been This Far Before"—plus a specially-written personalized tribute to Twitty himself, which is only available on this compilation. Though there are a few hits here, the fidelity isn't very good, the selection is scatter-shot and missing several big hits, and the packaging is a little cheap. In short, it's all right for the budget-minded, but there are far better collections on the market. —*Stephen Thomas Erlewine*

Rock 'n' Roll Years / Jun. 24, 1997 / Bear Family ✦✦✦✦

Fans of Conway Twitty's pre-country recordings will rejoice with this massive eight-disc, 192-track collection, collecting every track from an eight-year period encompassing 1956 to 1964. Here's Conwayfrom his start as a scrapping rockabilly to his early hit-making triumphs right up to the cusp of his even more popular change in direction. The first disc collects his 1956 recordings for Sam Phillips in Memphis. Although Conway, with his band, the RockHousers never saw a release on Sun Records, it certainly wasn't for lack of trying. The disc kicks off with his original recording of the band's theme, "Rockhouse," which became Roy Orbison's second Sun single. Although few titles seemed to survive, several full sessions featuring multiple takes did, and they're here. Disc two is where the hits begin, kicking off with "It's Only Make Believe." With a career-making tune under his belt, Twitty quickly moved in to a groove of recording teen ballads like "The Story of My Love" while still cutting growly rockers like "I Vibrate (From My Head to My Feet)." Discs three and four continue the trend with the hits "Mona Lisa" and "Danny Boy." The next two discs find Twitty exploring the 1950s rock & roll catalog, but Conway's move to country is presaged with the inclusion of "Walk on By." There's also a nice duet with Roy Orbison on "I'm in a Blue, Blue Mood." The final two discs show Twitty trying on R&B and blues numbers for size, plus rockers like "The Pickup," whose beat and storyline presaged Orbison's "Oh, Pretty Woman" by a couple of years. Glossy, uptown versions of "City Lights," "Faded Love" and 17 raw demos of hard country material close the set. Those who only know Conway's later, lacquer-haired country period will find this massive box a major revelation. *—Cub Koda*

The Ultimate Collection / Aug. 10, 1999 / Hip-O ✦✦✦✦✦
The Ultimate Collection may be missing some big hits—after all, Conway Twitty ruled the country charts throughout the '70s and '80s—but it comes surprisingly close to fulfilling the promise of its title. Many of his best-known songs are here—"It's Only Make Believe," "Lonely Blues Boy," "Hello Darlin'," "You've Never Been this Far Before," "Louisiana Woman, Mississippi Man," "Linda on My Mind," "I'd Love to Lay You Down," "Tight Fittin' Jeans," "That's My Job"—and they date from all eras of his career. A collection that spotlights his prime years in the '70s is still the better introduction, since it contains nothing but great songs, but this is nevertheless a good sampler of his entire career that would be very useful for neophytes. *—Stephen Thomas Erlewine*

20th Century Masters—The Millennium Collection: The Best of Conway Twitty / Sep. 14, 1999 / MCA ✦✦✦
Spanning his first hit "Make Believe" to early-'80s singles such as "Tight Fittin' Jeans," Conway Twitty's *20th Century Masters—The Millennium Collection* does a decent job of presenting his career highlights in a dozen songs. "Hello Darlin'," "You've Never Been This Far Before," and "After the Fire Is Gone" are some of the other highlights from this somewhat abbreviated collection; *The #1s Hits Collection* provides a far deeper look into Twitty's body of work, but this album will probably satisfy most casual fans. *—Heather Phares*

20th Century Masters—The Millennium Collection: The Best of Conway Twitty & Loretta Lynn / May 9, 2000 / MCA ✦✦✦✦
20th Century Masters—The Millennium Collection: The Best of Conway Twitty & Loretta Lynn is an excellent overview of the two singers' work together during the 1970s, containing 12 of their Top Ten country duets (five of which topped the country charts). It was an incredible run that made Twitty and Lynn the most commercially successful country duet partners of all time, in spite of the fact that they were never romantically linked (a rarity in the world of male-female country duets). Digitally remastered sound and liner notes by Todd Everett cinch this as a package well worth picking up. *—Steve Huey*

★ **The #1 Hits Collection** / Sep. 12, 2000 / MCA Nashville ✦✦✦✦✦
Judging an artist on the basis of what hit the top of the charts can occasionally be a risky business, since it's not always true that the best material is the most popular. In the case of Conway Twitty, however, it's an excellent criteria, since over the course of nearly 30 years, the great majority of his singles did indeed reach the top of the chart, so winnowing down his catalog to just number-one singles still gives an excellent overview of the scope and quality of Twitty's music, even if it leaves behind such classic sides as "I Wonder What She'll Think About Me Leaving," which peaked at a mere four. In fact, even though MCA Nashville/Decca's double-disc collection *The #1 Hits Collection* has 33 tracks, it doesn't even have all of his number-one hits, largely because it cuts off in 1981, the last year he recorded for MCA, so even though this is quite extensive, it doesn't even have *all* of his chart-toppers! That said, it does have all the number ones from his late-'60s/'70s peak, when he was produced by Owen Bradley and dominated the country charts with his lush romantic ballads and duets with Loretta Lynn, four of which are included here. Yes, 1994's four-disc box set *The Conway Twitty Collection* fills in some gaps this leaves behind, but those are minor. All the major hits and songs are here, providing both an excellent summary and introduction to this country giant. *—Stephen Thomas Erlewine*

Love Songs / Jan. 23, 2001 / MCA ✦✦✦
Contrary to the back cover's claim, Conway Twitty did record quite a lot of love songs over the years—they might not have been romantic, but most of his songs were about romantic relationships, which could be easily labeled love songs—but this 14-track collection does a fine job of capturing romantic highlights from his decades at MCA-associated labels. There are several hits here, such as "I'd Love to Lay You Down" and "Kiss an Angel Good Mornin'," yet this isn't designed as a hits album—it's mood music, and on that level, it succeeds quite well. Twitty's warm baritone was quite seductive, and he had usually had fine material, which means this collection of highlights is quite alluring, even seductive, in its own way. *—Stephen Thomas Erlewine*

20th Century Masters—The Millennium Collection: The Best of Conway Twitty, Vol. 2 / Aug. 7, 2001 / MCA ✦✦✦
This 12-track addition to the *20th Century Masters* series has a couple of Conway Twitty's biggest hits—"Red Neckin' Love Makin' Night," "That's My Job," the Loretta Lynn duet "Louisiana Woman, Mississippi Man"—but, for the most part, it avoids the iconic in favor of the hits from the time. As such, the pop trainspotter won't find this enormously satisfying, but for anyone who followed the charts at the time, or in retrospect, this is a fine choice. *—Stephen Thomas Erlewine*

20 Classics / Oct. 16, 2001 / Varese ✦✦✦✦
Conway Twitty's *20 Classics* is a fairly straightforward best-of featuring the chart-toppers and nothing but the chart-toppers. Pick out any song here, and it was a big hit in its time. Therefore, this collection highlights exactly why Twitty's acknowledged as such a legend in the country community. In addition to being straightforward, *20 Classics* is fairly nondescript—nothing too fancy about it. And that's somewhat of an issue, since you come to expect extraordinary Rhino-style packaging with your best-ofs nowadays. Still, if you don't care about the extras and just want the chart-toppers and nothing but the chart-toppers, *20 Classics* shouldn't disappoint. *—Jason Birchmeier*

Looking Back: The Very Best of the MGM Years / Dec. 3, 2002 / RPM ✦✦✦✦✦
For those who lack the cash or incentive to invest in Bear Family's mammoth eight-CD *Rock 'n' Roll Years* box set, this two-CD, 40-song overview of Conway Twitty's 1958-1963 MGM sides is a fine summary of his early career. All his Top 100 chart hits are here, as are numerous flops, B-sides, and LP tracks. It's true that these were the most rock-oriented years of Twitty's long career, and also that many of these sides are derivative of early Elvis Presley. But it can also be said that of the singers who owed much to Elvis, Twitty was one of the best—not just on hits like "It's Only Make Believe," "Lonely Blue Boy," and "Danny Boy," but also lesser-known items like the growling rockabilly-pop of "Make Me Know You're Mine" and "Trouble in Mind," the "Mystery Train" imitation "The Long Black Train," and the ballad "Heavenly." Twitty was also one of the few sub-Elvis singers equally capable of summoning decent rockabilly-pop and slow deep-voiced ballads. It's not all pop/rock, either, with his incipient country-pop leanings coming to the fore on some early-'60s tracks like "What a Dream" and "Looking Back" (which sound a little like Brenda Lee's productions of the era), "A Man Alone" and "She Ain't No Angel" (both not far in mood from Roy Orbison's harder-rocking early-'60s cuts), and the melodramatic "The Flame." He didn't cultivate as strong an identity as any of his reference points, Elvis and otherwise, and some of these tunes are generic if spiritedly performed late-'50s/early-'60s period pieces, but overall it's a quite worthy anthology. *—Richie Unterberger*

Two Dollar Pistols

Group / Alternative Country-Rock, Alternative Country
After spending over a decade playing drums in various rock bands, singer/songwriter John Howie Jr. eventually exchanged his kit for a six-string acoustic guitar and a handful of broken-hearted, whisky-drinking country ballads to form Two Dollar Pistol. Taking a cue from old-time country-folk from the Sun Records era of the 1950s, Merle Haggard and George Jones, Howie remained in his home state of North Carolina rather than jumping ship to the carbon-copy, commercialized country of Nashville. With the accompaniment of guitarists Greg Hawks and John Prince, drummer Chris Phillips (who can also be found behind the set in the Squirrel Nut Zippers), bassist Jack Campbell, fiddler Jon Kemppainen and steel guitarist Steve Watson, Two Dollar Pistols' constant gigging was eventually rewarded with a deal on Hep-Cat Records, who put out their debut *On the Down Time* in 1997.

Their follow-up *Step Right Up* was released the next year on Yep Roc. An EP with Tift Merritt of duets became a fan favorite, prompting Howie to make lineup changes. Guitarist Scott McCall, bassist Neal Spaulding, and drummer Mark Weaver joined the band and hit the road to promote the album. This lineup lasted into 2002, when the group recorded and released *You Ruined Everything*. *—Mike DaRonco*

On Down the Track / Aug. 12, 1997 / Hep-cat ✦✦✦

Step Right Up / Sep. 1, 1998 / Yep Roc ✦✦✦
On this live album, the Two Dollar Pistols kick off their set with the old George Jones "tears & beer" tune "Heartaches and Hangovers," which not only nicely sets up their musical themes, but also firmly establishes the sound they're shooting for: hard-edged, traditional honky tonk. While their music is a step back into country music's past, this North Carolina band avoids the traps of studious revivalists and kitschy retro country groups. They play with a vital spiritedness that injects their sincerity with some playfulness. With his robust, twangy vocals, John Howie Jr. would have sounded natural on the same stage alongside Jones, Merle Haggard, or Ernest Tubb. Similarly, his original songs, like "Me, Myself & Wine" and "Bring the Heartache," contain the elements—hooks, heartbreak, and some clever wordplay—found in classic honky tonk tunes. In fact, it's hard to differentiate the originals from old school tunes "A Wound Time Can't Erase" and "Wine Me Up" made famous by Stonewall Jackson and Faron Young, respectively. Also, helping matters are the strong performances by the other bandmembers. Lead guitarist Steve Howell, pedal steel player John Neff, and fiddler Jon Kemppainen, in particular, bring an authentic honky tonk feel to the music. This live recording provides all the "dim light, thick smoke, and loud, loud music" (although the group doesn't do that Joe Maphis classic) that you'd want to hear in a honky tonk band. *—Michael Berick*

● **Two Dollar Pistols with Tift Merritt** / Oct. 12, 1999 / Yep Roc ✦✦✦✦✦
Chapel Hill, NC, musicians the Two Dollar Pistols, led by John Howie Jr., team up with singer Tift Merritt of the Carbines for a real alt-country explosion, on this, their first-ever collaboration. This EP features seven cuts—two originals and five cover tunes—and every track is as smooth and tight as you could hope for. Howie's deep vocal strains complement the exquisite country singing of Merritt, and the music that results sounds great. Among the tunes covered are Charley Pride's "I'm So Afraid of Losing You Again," George Jones & Melba Montgomery's "Suppose Tonight Would Be Our Last," Willie Nelson & Emmylou Harris' "One Paper Kid," and Porter Wagoner & Dolly Parton's "Just Someone I Used to Know." "We Had It All," written by Donnie Fritts, and previously recorded by both Ray Charles and Waylon Jennings, is given the duet treatment, and it works very well. The pair of Merritt/Howie originals fit perfectly into the mix. Merritt may be the best hope for a return to traditional country music. She is no doubt one of the finest female vocalists singing country today, and Howie ranks right up there at the top of the male vocalist category himself. The CD is only about 25 minutes long, but there isn't a wasted minute on it. There hasn't been this much honesty in country music since the day

Gram Parsons met Emmylou Harris. We can only hope that the guys decide to return to the studio and cut a full-length work of art soon. Better yet, how about a live album? Just one listen and you'll be a fan. *—Michael B. Smith*

You Ruined Everything / Aug. 13, 2002 / Yep Roc ✦✦✦
Although this might as well have been a John Howie Jr. solo release (all the musicians except the singer/songwriter have been replaced since the last album), the Two Dollar Pistols continue to refine their pure roots honky tonk on their third full album. Not as polished or commercially appealing as the debut from old crony Tift Merritt, with whom they recorded a sublime EP, Howie continues to mine heartbreak, loss, and the dejected misfortune of love's more crestfallen side that proved successful for George Jones, one of Howie's obvious role models. Certainly, this music is well-written and produced with plenty of emotion, as well as the requisite amount of pedal steel and reverbed guitar. Yet the songs—all of which are Howie originals—blend together before the album is half over. Subtle organ on "You've Grown Tired of Me," one of the disc's many ballads, adds a classy touch of R&B, and the Roger McGuinn-style chiming guitar on "Gettin' Gone" provides a nifty folk-rock kick. But the album needs a few more melodic hooks like those in the title track to click with anything other than an already-dedicated honky tonk audience. Falling somewhere between the traditional revivalism of Dwight Yoakam—but with less sex—and the more commercial boom of Randy Travis' baritone vocals—but less calculated—Howie is the real deal. With some more hummable songs that work off his core country & western, he might be a twang force to be reckoned with. Although this album has highlights and is a consistently satisfying listen, there are too few tracks jumping out of the pack of the down-home honky tonking that remains at the center of Howie's uncompromising approach. *—Hal Horowitz*

T. Texas Tyler (David Luke Myrick)

b. Jun. 20, 1916, Mena, AR, **d.** Jan. 28, 1972, Springfield, MO
Vocals / Traditional Country
Charismatic singer/songwriter T. Texas Tyler was a successful figure from the late '40s through the mid-'50s, often credited with helping to popularize the sentimental country "recitation"—a storytelling composition partly or completely spoken by the performer—with his massive 1948 hit "Deck of Cards." He was born David Luke Myrick in Mena, AR, and from childhood aspired to become a country performer. As a young man, Tyler moved to Rhode Island to live with his brother, who was stationed there while serving in the Navy. He got his start working in radio in the early '30s and then spent much of the decade touring and performing on the radio, creating his stage name by combining the names of cowboy crooners Tex Ritter and Tom Tyler. His travels took him as far as Newport, RI, and Los Angeles. While performing in Charleston, WV, in 1939, Tyler teamed up with fiddler Clarence Clere to form Slim & Tex. They remained together playing radio stations in West Virginia until 1942, when Tyler landed a spot on the Shreveport, LA, radio station and consistent talent incubator KWKH. Tyler served in the U.S. Army during World War II.

Following his discharge in 1946, Tyler went to southern California and began appearing daily on the radio in Long Beach and Los Angeles. His proximity to the new record labels that were springing up in southern California helped his career along, and he signed with the small but growing Pasadena label Four Star. Soon he had moderate hits with several covers of widely performed country songs of the day: "Filipino Baby" (1946), followed by "Remember Me" and Jack Guthrie's "Oklahoma Hills." Tyler had his biggest single in 1948 with the enormously popular "Deck of Cards," which peaked in the Top Three, continued to sell for years, and spawned numerous imitations. The piece had perhaps an older pedigree than any other in the country repertoire; similar poems in which a soldier uses a deck of cards as a set of religious symbols have been found dating back to the medieval era.

Tyler followed up that smash with another recitation: the tear-wrenchingly sentimental Mary Jean Shurtz composition "Dad Gave My Dog Away." His popularity resulted in a booking at New York City's Carnegie Hall, and in 1949 he sang a song in the Western *Horsemen of the Sierras*. Later that year, he had a Top Five hit with a cover of Hank Williams' "My Bucket's Got a Hole in It." Tyler was given his own television show, *Range Round Up*, in Los Angeles, and in the early '50s he favored an upbeat, folksy style in which sung phrases were frequently introduced by a hearty, guttural swoop. He had two more major hits in 1953, "Courtin' in the Rain," and then went into a personal and professional slump with the advent of rock & roll. A marijuana possession arrest in Texas slowed his career, but many of his recordings were collected in the newly popular format of the LP album. He signed with the Starday label and performed several times on the *Grand Ole Opry*. In the '50s he became a gospel singer and Assembly of God minister, recording the all-gospel album, *The Great Texan*, for King in 1960. Tyler spent the bulk of the 1960s touring and preaching; he also recorded a gospel album for Capitol, a secular country album for Starday (*Sensational New Hits of T. Texas Tyler*, 1964), and three independently produced gospel albums that he sold at his revivals. Following the death of his first wife, Claudia, in 1968, Tyler remarried and settled down in Springfield, MO, where he preached to a local congregation and also performed occasionally. "The man with a million friends" died in early 1972 of stomach cancer. *—James Manheim*

The Best of T. Texas Tyler / Sep. 15, 1998 / Collectors' Choice Music ✦✦✦✦✦
Tyler's growled vocals were his trademark, but otherwise he trod similar ground as Ernest Tubb. This CD collects 18 recordings made for the Four Star label between 1945 and 1954, including seven Top Ten C&W hits, two of which are recitations (the oft-covered *Deck of Cards* and the groan-inducing *Dad Gave My Dog Away*). It's too bad Collectors' Choice didn't cross-license *Bumming Around*, his one Top 40 C&W entry for the Decca label, but otherwise this disc is a perfect collection of Tyler's most important recordings. The sound quality is sometimes rough, but *The Best of T. Texas Tyler* is a welcome anthology of this nearly forgotten artist. *—Greg Adams*

Ian Tyson

b. Sep. 25, 1933, Victoria, British Columbia, Canad
Guitar, Vocals / Cowboy, Contemporary Folk, Americana
Half of the early-'60s folk group Ian & Sylvia, Ian Tyson retreated from performing and recording after the duo disbanded in the mid-'70s to become a rancher in the foothills of Southern Alberta, Canada. He quietly returned to music-making in the 1980s, releasing a series of albums that focused on detailed songs about the concerns of the working cowboy. Tyson was born in Victoria, British Columbia. As a child he was involved in rodeo, not music—he didn't learn to play the guitar until he was recovering from rodeo-related injuries. In the late '50s, he began performing as a folksinger. In 1961, he met singer/songwriter Sylvia Fricker and the two musicians began performing together; they also married three years later. Ian & Sylvia and their band, Great Speckled Bird, became popular on the folk scene and released their self-titled debut album in 1962.

In 1963, they released *Four Strong Winds*; the title track, written by Tyson, became a folk standard. Ian & Sylvia successfully recorded together through the mid-'70s. The duo also began hosting a television show, *Nashville North*, which became the *Ian Tyson Show* when the couple split up in the middle of the decade. After Ian & Sylvia's break-up, Tyson recorded *Ol'Eon*. He temporarily retired from recording in 1979 to work his ranch, but returned with *Old Corrals & Sagebrush* in 1983. In 1984, he toured with Ricky Skaggs and also released an eponymous album. Tyson released a third album, *Cowboyography*, two years later, and in 1991, he released another popular Canadian album, *And Stood There Amazed*, which contained the hits "Springtime in Alberta" and "Black Nights." Subsequent releases include 1994's *Eighteen Inches of Rain*, 1996's *All the Good 'Uns* and 1999's *Lost Herd*. *—Sandra Brennan & Michael McCall*

- **Greatest Hits, Vol. 1** / 1969 / Vanguard ✦✦✦✦✦

Greatest Hits, Vol. 2 / 1969 / Vanguard ✦✦✦✦

One Jump Ahead of the Devil / 1978 / Stony Plain ✦✦✦

Ian Tyson / 1984 / Stony Plain ✦✦✦✦

Cowboyography / 1987 / Vanguard ✦✦✦
One of the few Ian Tyson albums to be released in the U.S., *Cowboyography* is also one of his best records, demonstrating his skill for melding traditional western musical and lyrical themes with contemporary arrangements, productions and sensibilities. *—Thom Owens*

I Outgrew the Wagon / 1989 / Stony Plain ✦✦✦✦✦
This is the best of his series of homegrown album on what he calls "cowboy culture." Included are simple, unadorned songs affectionately yet unromantically examining rural life on the Canadian plains, as well as a couple of philosophical offerings. *—Michael McCall*

And Stood There Amazed / Feb. 1991 / Stony Plain ✦✦✦

Eighteen Inches of Rain / 1994 / Vanguard ✦✦✦✦✦
He's been absent from the U.S. of A. for a while since the dissolution of Ian & Sylvia, but he certainly hasn't been idle—Tyson is quite a success in Canada, and Vanguard, a label he's been associated with previously, is taking a chance on repeating that success here. *Eighteen Inches of Rain* is the latest in Tyson's "Cowboy Culture" series (Vanguard is also reissuing *Cowboyography*), and it's a damn fine collection of songs about contemporary cowboys, ranchers and just plain folks, beautifully performed and sung, elegantly designed, and equipped with excellent lyrics. Many cuts are above the run of country music—songs like "Horsethief Moon" and "Rodeo Road" are songs that transcend boundaries. *—Steven McDonald*

Old Corrals & Sagebrush & Other Cowboy Culture Classics / 1994 / Stony Plain ✦✦✦✦
Old Corrals & Sagebrush & Other Cowboy Culture Classics is a CD reissue of Ian Tyson's 1983 album *Old Corrals & Sagebrush*, plus all but three tracks from his self-titled album from 1984. *Old Corrals* was Tyson's first album devoted entirely to western material, and includes classics such as "Whoopee Ti Yi Yo" and "I Ride an Old Paint" (as "Leavin' Cheyenne"). The original composition "Alberta's Child" pays tribute to Canadian country star Wilf Carter, and "Gallo de Cielo" is an epic story-song written by the likeminded Tom Russell. "Night Rider's Lament," later revived on Nanci Griffith's *Other Voices, Other Rooms*, ends with a demonstration of Tyson's yodeling skills on the fade-out. The songs from Ian Tyson are similarly Western in theme, including the traditional "Colorado Trail." The electric guitar and pedal steel throughout give some of the songs a pure country rather than Western flavor, but the former folk artist (who started out as a rodeo rider) handles both styles convincingly. Tyson's contribution to the Canadian country music tradition may come as a surprise to those who remember him from his Ian & Sylvia days, but the world of Western music should be glad to have him. *—Greg Adams*

All the Good 'Uns / 1996 / Stony Plain ✦✦✦✦✦
Ian Tyson is the undisputed master of traditional cowboy culture music and *All the Good 'Uns*, drawn from his five *Cowboyography* releases, removes any possible excuse for those who even casually appreciate roots music from being converted. Here are 19 distinctive narratives of wide-eyed wonder, love of the land, and sagebrush wisdom conveyed through good, honest songs performed with integral simplicity. *—Roch Parisien*

Lost Herd / Mar. 23, 1999 / Vanguard ✦✦✦✦
Ian Tyson's *Lost Herd* paints nine musical portraits of life in the West. Recorded in Toronto, Calgary, and Nashville with those cities' finest musicians, the album captures the loneliness of the plains, long days of summer, and dreams of the Canadian landscape. Songs like "La Primera" and "Brahmas & Mustangs" represent true cowboy culture, while Tyson's cover of "Somewhere Over the Rainbow" adds a rustic dreaminess to the classic tune. *Lost Herd* is a welcome blend of cowboy traditions from yesterday and today. *—Heather Phares*

Live at Longview / Feb. 5, 2002 / Vanguard ✦✦✦

Calling an artist a living legend is a loaded proposition. Sometimes, it's a nice way of saying that one still respects an artist—even though his or her best days are far behind. Ian Tyson is a living legend, but one wouldn't want to assign him or his music to the dustbin. While *Live at Longview* returns to classics like "Navajo Rug" and "Fifty Years Ago," he also continues to explore Western terrain with new material. He's joined by a small group of musicians, featuring guitarist Gord Matthews, bassist Gord Maxwell, and fiddler Myran Szott. An intimate mix of hot licks and good harmony leaves lots of space—like an open range—for this music to breathe. In many ways, *Live at Longview* resembles Guy Clarks' *Keepers*: a solid set nicely delivered to a friendly audience. There are good versions of "M.C. Horses" and "Magpie," and a relaxed, jazzy take on the '50s standard "Blue Moon." It's particularly interesting to hear Tyson sing "Someday Soon," especially if one is only familiar with the Suzy Bogguss or Judy Collins version. His rough-hewed pipes give the song a down to earth quality, as though it really had something to do with a wild rodeo man. "Jerry Ambler" is probably the oddest and most enjoyable piece on the album, combining the drums of Thom Moon with Tyson's cowboy rap. Of course, no matter how good, *Live at Longview* could never reach the heights of catching a Tyson show. Nonetheless, it's easy to play the disc and imagine being in one's favorite watering hole, drinking one's favorite beverage, and listening to one's favorite Canadian folky. —*Ronnie D. Lankford Jr.*

Uncle Tupelo

f. 1987, Belleville, IL, **db.** 1994
Group / Alternative Pop/Rock, Alternative Country-Rock, Alternative Country, Americana
With the release of their 1990 debut LP, *No Depression*, the Belleville, IL, trio Uncle Tupelo launched more than simply their own career—by fusing the simplicity and honesty of country music with the bracing fury of punk, they kick-started a revolution which reverberated throughout the American underground. Thanks to a successful online site and subsequent fanzine which adopted the album's name, the tag "No Depression" became a catch-all for the likeminded artists who, along with Tupelo, signalled alternative rock's return to its country roots—at much the same time, ironically enough, that Nashville was itself embracing the slick gloss associated with mainstream rock and pop.

Uncle Tupelo was led by singers/songwriters Jay Farrar and Jeff Tweedy, lifelong friends born in the same Belleville hospital in 1967. During high-school, the pair formed a punk cover band called the Primitives along with drummer Mike Heidorn and Farrar's older brother Wade. After Wade enlisted in the Army, the Primitives broke up, but in 1987, the remaining trio reunited, changed their name to Uncle Tupelo, and began incorporating elements of country into their music as well as writing original material. Touring constantly throughout the Midwest, the bandmembers eventually quit school as their music became more and more successful, and in 1989 they signed a contract with the small independent label Rockville.

Taking its name from the A. P. Carter gospel song covered therein, *No Depression* reflected the band's disparate influences, ranging from everyone from Hank Williams to bluesman Leadbelly through to the famed post-punk trio Hüsker Dü. The most rock-centric of Uncle Tupelo's releases, its songs were meditations on small-town, small-time life, candid snapshots of days spent working thankless jobs and nights spent in an alcoholic fog. After the release of "I Got Drunk," a brilliant single backed with a cover of the Flying Burrito Brothers' "Sin City," 1991's *Still Feel Gone* struck a finer balance between their rock and country aims. While Farrar's contributions—sung in his reedy, Neil Young-like voice—were often informed by a rootsy, scorched-earth mentality, Tweedy's, with their grittier vocals, delved deeper into the trio's punk origins, as typified by the song "D. Boon," a tribute to the late frontman of the legendary Minutemen.

A year later, Uncle Tupelo released *March 16-20, 1992*, an acoustic record which saw the group plunging fully into country and folk. Recorded live in the studio with producer Peter Buck (of the band R.E.M.), the album drew heavily on painstakingly authentic covers of standards like "Moonshiner" and "Satan, Your Kingdom Must Come Down" along with a fitting rendition of the Louvin Brothers' "The Great Atomic Power" and Farrar's and Tweedy's originals, which maintained the record's spare, haunting ambience. Shortly after its release, Heidorn left the group to devote time to his family and was replaced by drummer Ken Coomer, formerly of the group Clockhammer. Multi-instrumentalists Max Johnston and John Stirratt also signed on as part-time members.

In 1992, Uncle Tupelo signed to major label Sire/Reprise and in 1993 issued the LP *Anodyne*. Widely regarded as the group's definitive statement, it was a true country-rock hybrid which accented the power of both musical forms; the album even featured a cover of the song "Give Back the Key to My Heart" sung with its writer, roots rock pioneer Doug Sahm. After a tour in support of the album, however, the long-standing relationship between Farrar and Tweedy dissolved in bitter acrimony, and Uncle Tupelo disbanded; shortly thereafter, Tweedy recruited Coomer, Johnston, and Stirratt to form the band Wilco, while Farrar reunited with Heidorn in Son Volt. —*Jason Ankeny*

No Depression / 1990 / Rockville ♦♦♦♦
Uncle Tupelo's landmark opening salvo is the group's most rock-oriented album, steeped more in breakneck speed, punk crunch, and guitar dissonance than any of their subsequent efforts. Indeed, despite the presence of mandolins, fiddles, and banjos—as well as inclusion of the title track, a faithful cover of the A. P. Carter classic—the trio's vaunted country leanings are less musical than thematic on *No Depression*, thanks in large part to singers/songwriters Jay Farrar and Jeff Tweedy's acute depictions of rural, blue-collar life. Like the Replacements—never more obvious an influence than on this LP—Uncle Tupelo's songs paint grim, unrelenting portraits of aimless Midwestern existence, split between days working on the opening cut's "Factory Belt" and nights spent blurry-eyed and wasted ("Whiskey Bottle," "Before I Break"). Still, for all of the record's doleful cynicism—virtually every cut nods toward dashed hopes, broken promises, and paralyzing fear—there's an undeniable electricity afoot as well; by channeling the mournful clarity of country into the crackling fury of punk, *No Depression* brings new life to both musical camps. —*Jason Ankeny*

Still Feel Gone / Sep. 17, 1991 / Rockville ♦♦♦
Still Feel Gone is Tupelo's transitional record; while it goes far in fusing the band's rock origins with their country aspirations, the alliance is often an uneasy, even schizophrenic, one. Writers Jay Farrar and Jeff Tweedy are rarely in synch; while the former's contributions embrace roots music wholeheartedly, Tweedy's songs journey more deeply into rock

than ever before—his opening track, "Gun," is the most straightforward pop number the trio ever recorded, while "D. Boon," a tribute to the fallen leader of the legendary post-punk trio the Minutemen, borders on thrash. Still, while *Still Feel Gone* lacks the consistency of its predecessor *No Depression*, it's a more wide-ranging record, deeper in maturity, subtlety and texture—all clear evidence of things to come. —*Jason Ankeny*

March 16-20, 1992 / Aug. 3, 1992 / Rockville ♦♦♦♦♦
Produced by R.E.M.'s Peter Buck, *March 16-20, 1992* represents Uncle Tupelo's full evolution into a true country unit; with the exception of the eerie squalls of guitar feedback which haunt Jeff Tweedy's mesmerizing "Wait Up," there's virtually no evidence of the trio's punk heritage. Instead, the all-acoustic album—a combination of Tupelo originals and well-chosen traditional songs—taps into the very essence of backwoods culture, its music rooted in the darkest corners of Appalachian life. An inescapable sense of dread grips this collection, from the large-scale threat depicted in the stunning rendition of the Louvin Brothers' "The Great Atomic Power" to the fatalism of the worker anthems "Grindstone" and "Coalminers"; even the character studies, including a revelatory "Moonshiner," are relentlessly grim. A vivid glimpse at the harsh realities of rural existence, *March 16-20, 1992* is a brilliant resurrection of a bygone era of American folk artistry. —*Jason Ankeny*

Anodyne / May 1993 / Sire ♦♦♦♦♦
Uncle Tupelo never struck a finer balance between rock and country than on *Anodyne*, their major-label debut and parting shot. For all of the ill well undoubtedly simmering throughout these sessions, Jay Farrar and Jeff Tweedy have never before been more attuned to each other musically; where earlier records often found the band's twin forces moving in opposing directions, *Anodyne* bears the full fruits of their shared vision. Recorded live in the studio, the album encompasses and reinterprets not only country-rock (evidenced by the group's pairing with Doug Sahm on his "Give Back the Key to My Heart") but also traditional country (the tribute to the songwriting legacy of "Acuff-Rose"), rock (the churning "The Long Cut," "Chickamauga") and folk ("New Madrid," "Steal the Crumbs"), the band's reach never once exceeding its grasp. —*Jason Ankeny*

● **89/93: An Anthology** / Mar. 19, 2002 / Columbia/Legacy ♦♦♦♦♦
Uncle Tupelo wasn't the first band to merge the soulful twang of country music with the passionate roar of punk rock (that honor would probably go to either the Meat Puppets, Jason & the Scorchers, or X), but in 1989 the Minutemen-meets-Gram Parson clatter of Uncle Tupelo's debut album, *No Depression*, took what some then called "cowpunk" in a new and decidedly different direction. From the start, Uncle Tupelo's music was smart, muscular, emotionally compelling, and played the punk and country sides of the band's musical personality for all the heartfelt sincerity that marked the best music of both genres—and refused to make a joke out of either. Making music that people didn't simply enjoy, but believed in, Uncle Tupelo was the sort of band that attracted an unusually devoted fan following, and while it's inaccurate to trace the entire 1990s "alt-country" movement back to the group, one could certainly argue that Uncle Tupelo was as crucial to that scene as Black Flag was to '80s punk. Though a combination of hard work, fine music, and setting a peerless example of honesty and integrity, Uncle Tupelo blazed a trail that dozens of other fine bands would follow. It's difficult to sum up a band as important as Uncle Tupelo—and its four-album recording career—with one 72-minute CD, and *89/93: An Anthology* is hardly the final word on the group or its music, but it *is* a fine and thoughtfully compiled introduction to the band's work. *89/93: An Anthology* features representative cuts from all four Uncle Tupelo albums—*No Depression*, *Still Feel Gone*, *March 16-20, 1992*, and *Anodyne*—as well as a few non-LP single sides, compilation tracks, demos, and live takes from radio broadcasts. The collection often favors the band's quieter, more contemplative side over the louder stuff (though there are plenty of high-octane rockers on hand, with the rare single "I Got Drunk" and a charging cover of the Stooges' "I Wanna Be Your Dog" especially notable), and while Jay Farrar's songwriting tended to dominate the group's albums, this compilation strives to give equal time to his then-partner Jeff Tweedy, most likely to make the disc equally appealing to new fans of Son Volt and Wilco, Farrar and Tweedy's post-UT groups. But while longtime fans are the most likely to quibble about what is or isn't on *89/93: An Anthology*, the truth is you could hardly ask for a better beginner's guide to Uncle Tupelo and its music—the best-known tunes are all here, the sequence gracefully replicates the arc of the band's career, the hard-to-find single tracks and unreleased tunes give even loyal fans something new and interesting, and whether picking quietly on the front porch or bashing their Les Pauls into submission, Uncle Tupelo serves up powerful, timeless, and joyous music on each of these 21 cuts. A splendid trip down memory lane for those who were there and a revelation for the uninitiated, *89/93: An Anthology* offers tangible proof that Uncle Tupelo was a group that truly mattered—and still matters nearly a decade after the bandmembers called it a day. —*Mark Deming*

Still Feel Gone [Bonus Tracks] / Mar. 11, 2003 / Columbia/Legacy ✦✦✦
Uncle Tupelo clearly defined their nervy Gram Parsons-meets-the Minutemen sound on their debut album, 1990's *No Depression*, and their 1991 follow-up, *Still Feel Gone*, found them branching out into new variations of their previously established themes. While *No Depression* was dominated by breakneck tempos with the occasional slow, contemplative number thrown in for variety, *Still Feel Gone* found Uncle Tupelo taking a closer look at the middle ground, as evidenced by the high-strung acoustic guitars of "Still Be Around," the measured but powerful Crazy Horse stomp of "Looking for a Way Out," the lonesome shuffle of "True to Life," and the stark atmospherics of "If That's Alright" (the latter of which in retrospect sounds like the first dawning of the ideas Jeff Tweedy would explore with Wilco). But plenty of what made *No Depression* so impressive is still on view here, including the brutal stutter-step of "Gun," the simple but powerful declaration of "Watch Me Fall," and the heartfelt tribute to an obvious influence, "D. Boon." And if anything, the band sounds even more powerful this time out, and the broader picture of their abilities only confirms how strong a combination Jay Farrar, Jeff Tweedy, and Mike Heidorn really were. Columbia/Legacy's 2003 reissue has been newly remastered, which gives the audio noticeably greater detail and punch, and five bonus tracks have been included—two hard-to-find single sides ("Sauget Wind" and a cover of the Soft Boys' "I Wanna Destroy You"), and early demos of three cuts from the album which differ significantly from the final versions ("Watch Me Fall," "Looking for a Way Out," and "If That's Alright"). If *Still Feel Gone* isn't as immediately impressive as *No Depression*, a few plays confirms it's still the work of a gifted band at full strength, and this reissue gives the album the special treatment it deserves. *—Mark Deming*

No Depression [Bonus Tracks] / Mar. 11, 2003 / Columbia/Legacy ✦✦✦✦
Within what would come to be known as the "alt-country" scene, Uncle Tupelo's first album, 1990's *No Depression*, was the shot heard around the world; they most certainly weren't the first band to fuse the heartache of country with the brains and brawn of punk rock, but they managed to bring the two styles together without camp or gimmicks, in a manner that truly honored both genres and allowed their shared celebration of passion and belief above all else to shine through, and its example would be followed by literally thousands of musicians across the country. Over a dozen years after it first hit the racks, *No Depression* still sounds like a truly inspired bit of record-making; Jay Farrar's songs carry the bulk of the album, and great songs they are, especially the charging "Graveyard Shift" and "Factory Belt" and the mournful "Whiskey Bottle" and"Life Worth Living." It would take a bit longer for Jeff Tweedy to start playing on an equal level, but the realistic yet impressionistic snapshots of "Train" and "Screen Door" made it clear the man had the goods, and as a team Tweedy, Farrar, and Michael Heidorn sound all but unstoppable here, tight as a drum and investing each song with a life-or-death level of emotional force. Columbia/Legacy's 2003 reissue actually manages to improve one of the most impressive debut albums of the 1990s; the remastering is sharp and well-detailed, and this version tacks on six bonus tracks (seven if you count "John Hardy," which Rockville Records tagged onto the original CD release of the album, but left off the LP), including the previously unreleased "Blues Die Hard" (from a four-track home recording), the hard-to-find "Won't Forget," terrific covers of "Left in the Dark" and "Sin City," and stripped-down demos of "Whiskey Bottle" and "No Depression." If you're a longtime fan, upgrading to this edition of *No Depression* is well-worth your time and money, and if you're not all that familiar with the group, this album will show you why Uncle Tupelo was a band who mattered so much to so many. *—Mark Deming*

March 16-20, 1992 [Bonus Tracks] / Mar. 11, 2003 / Columbia/Legacy ✦✦✦✦✦
While Uncle Tupelo's first two albums occasionally nodded toward the quieter side of traditional country music, they were dominated by tough, guitar-driven rock & roll which stylistically split the difference between the Minutemen and Neil Young. So Uncle Tupelo's third album, *March 16-20, 1992*, came as a bit of a surprise to their fans when it first hit the racks; almost entirely acoustic, the album stripped the group's sound to the bone and focused at once on the framework of Jay Farrar and Jeff Tweedy's songwriting and the traditional folk music which had contributed to their musical (and political) world view. Seven of the album's 15 tunes were covers, and with the exception of the Louvin Brothers' much-covered "Atomic Power," all were traditional Appalachian ballads, some of which dealt with the politics of rural poverty ("Coalminers"), while others documented the everyday tragedies of life along America's margins ("Lilli Schull," "I Wish My Baby Was Born"). As for the group's originals, the different songwriting approaches of Farrar and Tweedy were becoming more telling on *March 16-20*; while Farrar's tunes were solid, somber, and resonant, Tweedy began investigating more angular melodic approaches and stylized lyrics (most notably on "Black Eye" and "Wait Up"). However, if the passion and belief which informed Uncle Tupelo's music was presented in quieter and more subtle form on *March 16-20, 1992*, it was still very much in evidence, and this album helped to reaffirm the importance of acoustic music and folk's roots in the growing alt-country movement. Columbia/Legacy's 2003 reissue boasted new mastering which boosts the clarity and transparence of these sessions, while including six bonus tracks, including the previously unheard instrumental "Take My Word," covers of "I Wanna Be Your Dog" (different from the version on *89/93: An Anthology*), and the theme from *the Waltons*, and homemade demos of three tunes which later appeared on the album. *—Mark Deming*

Anodyne [Bonus Tracks] / Mar. 11, 2003 / Rhino ✦✦✦✦✦
This 2003 reissue of Anodyne on Rhino adds five bonus tracks: three previously unreleased tracks and two live songs that were only available on a promo-only disc issued in 1994 called The Long Cut + Five Live. The three studio cuts are a mixed bag. "Stay True" is a fairly tuneless hard rock tune penned by Jay Farrar that features thundering riffs and ham-handed soloing, "Wherever" is a heartbroken and lovely ballad written by Jeff Tweedy that easily could have fit on the album proper, and "Are You Sure Hank Done It This Way" is a rollicking stab at one of Waylon Jennings' best tunes with Joe Ely joining in on vocals and guitar. The two live cuts—a raw take on the truck driver's anthem "Truck Drivin' Man" and a long workout on Dale Hawkins' "Suzie Q"—are fun and full of energy. Too bad Rhino didn't include the other three songs that were on the The Long Cut + Five Live. Still, with the comprehensive liner notes, improved sounds, and mostly worthwhile bonus tracks, this is a great document for fans of the band. *—Jason Ankeny*

Uncle Walt's Band

f. Spartanburg, SC, **db.** 1983
Group / Progressive Country, Contemporary Folk, Americana
Uncle Walt was Walter Hyatt, his band was Champ Hood and David Ball. The group became a legend on an Austin music scene already crowded with legends and the three members can certainly be considered to have similar status. Hyatt's death in the 1997 ValuJet plane crash in the Florida Everglades was kind of a grisly gilding of his already respected name. Death will do that to a musician, especially if the circumstances are shocking. Too bad good old Uncle Walt wasn't around to write a song about what happened; maybe he would have looked at it from the point of view of the alligators, like the Ted Hughes about the hawk.

Uncle Walt's Band actually formed in Spartanburg, SC, not Austin. The group was assembled while Hyatt was still going to high-school, with Hood playing guitar and bassist Ball having a ball on the bottom end. From the beginning, the trio developed a lovely blend of vocal harmonies that, combined with skilled picking, was just the stuff to attract a loyal following. Touring, of course, was the ticket since Spartanburg played the same part in the Uncle Walt's Band members' lives that it did for every musician from there; as in, the town is a good place to get out of. After graduating in 1971, the trio moved to Nashville. Over the next year, Uncle Walt's Band worked many Nashville clubs for the average pay in the 20-dollar range, and "that ain't each," as the stingy bar owner with bad English used to explain it. The group decided to try its luck in Austin, which had a much more progressive country music scene.

Lyle Lovett was one of the many young Texas college kids who was a fan of the band in its hungry days, part of an audience that always included a large number of musicians whose tongues were hanging out of their ears. A relationship developed between the band and Lovett, who would become into an extremely talented country singer/songwriter and actor. Lovett did an opening act for Uncle Walt's Band as he began his career and a decade later would turn the tables, hiring Hyatt as his opening act on national tours. The group's progress in the music business was just as up and down as Hyatt's solo career would be. At first, it seemed like Uncle Walt's Band was going to be one of those combos that called it quits right after its first album hits the streets. Yet this first album, the result of finally making some industry contacts in Nashville, slowly bubbled rather than doing a quick fade. There seemed to be a lot of new fans as a result, encouraging the bandmembers to give it another or try. The group continued bouncing between Nashville and Austin, finally settling in the latter town for good in 1978.

It finally seemed as if things were going to work out, especially from the point of view of the group's packed live shows. There were never any changes in membership, but it was the leadership potential of each of the three that created the band's final breakup in 1983. Ball, Hood, and Hyatt pursued solo careers from then on out, but there have been a few Uncle Walt's Band reunions. The three got together to sing backup on the track "Once Is Enough" from Lovett's 1989 Grammy-winning album *Lyle Lovett & His Large Band*. Hyatt's solo album, *King Tears*, produced by Lovett for MCA, can also be considered sort of a band album since all three members play together on it. A second Hyatt solo effort, on the other hand, features his old bandmates, but never all three at the same time, so it's not really a reunion. The Antone's label released the tribute collection, entitled *Uncle Walt's Band & Friends Celebrate the Songs of Walter Hyatt*, following Hyatt's demise. Hood and Ball are featured, naturally, along with several van loads of Austin musicians. While the band's original album pressings would be considered a mother lode if found in a used record pile, the Sugar Hill label has released a fine pair of compact discs compiling tunes from these recordings. *—Eugene Chadbourne*

● **An American in Texas Revisited** / 1980 / Sugar Hill ✦✦✦✦✦

The Girl on the Sunny Shore / 1980 / Sugar Hill ✦✦✦

Keith Urban

b. Oct. 26, 1967, New Zealand
Producer, Guitar (Electric), Vocals, Guitar / Contemporary Country, Alternative Country-Rock, Contemporary Singer/Songwriter
Born in New Zealand, Keith Urban learned to play guitar as a six-year-old in Australia, after a young woman asked to place an ad in his dad's shop window offering guitar lessons. His parents made a deal with her that they would advertise in return for lessons for their young son. The boy had natural ability. By the time he was eight, Urban was winning talent shows. He also was involved in a youth acting company which required him to sing, dance, and memorize lines, all of which led to the ease on-stage which would serve him well in his music career. With his father deeply interested in American culture and country music, it was also natural that Keith would gravitate towards country music early on, when he was influenced by the singing of Glen Campbell, Dolly Parton, and Don Williams, and the songwriting of Jimmy Webb ("Galveston"). Urban added his own dimension to those influences when he discovered Dire Straits, and became interested in the guitar playing of Mark Knopfler and Fleetwood Mac's Lindsey Buckingham, embarking on in-depth study and endless practice of their techniques.

At the start of the '90s, Australian country music was primed for a revolution. Keith Urban—young, brash, blonde, rock-ish—was part of that revolution. His first album saw him win several major awards. Throughout his rise Urban always had his eye on Nashville, TN, USA. That's where the music in his heart was born and still lived. Almost from the beginning he made periodical pilgrimages to Nashville, forging valuable career bridges.

In 1997 Urban decided to base himself in Nashville. With his Australian bandmate, drummer Peter Clarke, he formed the three-piece band the Ranch. Their original bass player soon returned to Australia, but West Virginian Jerry Flowers quickly fit in. Their live shows, featuring Urban's standout lead guitar playing led to a record deal with Capitol Nashville and a management contract with I.R.S. Records founder/Police manager

Miles Copeland. The group's debut album, *The Ranch*, was released to critical acclaim in 1997. Critics raved about the album's unique take on country music and Urban's guitar playing. Other artists also took notice, and when the Ranch disbanded, other artists called on Urban to add some of his fleet-fingered magic to their records. Garth Brooks asked Urban to play on *Double Live*. The Dixie Chicks invited him to play on their second album. Matt Rollings, one of Nashville's top musicians, hired Urban as a session player on an album he was producing and the two immediately clicked.

Impressed by Rollings' knowledge of Nashville's session players, Urban asked him to produce his next record, another solo album. His tour in support of that album included opening for such major acts as Dwight Yoakam, Faith Hill, and Tim McGraw, as well as headlining his own shows. Ten years on he was doing to Nashville what he'd done to Tamworth. The result was American country hits for "It's a Love Thing" and "Your Everything," and a Grammy award nomination for Best Country Instrumental Performance for "Rollercoaster." *—Ed Nimmervoll*

1991 / 1997 / EMI ✦✦✦

Keith Urban / Oct. 19, 1999 / Capitol ✦✦✦

Keith Urban looks too fresh-faced to be in country music. Where's the gruff, scraggly cowboy? He must be buried beneath that fair Australian exterior, because, upon first listen, the contemporary cowboy is everywhere in such infectious, uptempo songs like "It's a Love Thing" and "I Wanna Be Your Man" and in endearing ballads like "But for the Grace of God" and "Your Everything." Urban's unmatched prowess with a guitar can be specifically heard in "Rollercoaster," a rare instrumental gem, generally unheard of on a country music album. Urban's signature style and distinctive take on country music, a fusion of rock-style guitar with seemingly radio-friendly songs, is a formula that will take him from newcomer status to superstar. *—Maria Konicki Dinoia*

● **Golden Road** / Oct. 8, 2002 / Capitol ✦✦✦

Keith Urban's live shows are something to be reckoned with, and this sophomore release from Capitol Records captures some of that excitement. His famously cool guitar slinging can be heard in abundance on such songs as "Who Wouldn't Wanna Be Me," "Jeans On," and "You Look Good in My Shirt." Urban seems naturally comfortable experimenting with different instruments, melodies, and influences. He evolves into a respectable songwriter on this collection, having penned eight of the album's 12 tracks, including an upbeat yet deliciously sweet song about his dad called, originally enough, "Song for Dad." Album number two scores high marks—lots of contagious rhythms, irresistible lyrics, and pleasing melodies. *—Maria Konicki Dinoia*

The V-Roys

f. 1994, Knoxville, TN, **d.b.** 1999
Group / Adult Alternative Pop/Rock, Roots Rock, Power Pop
Formed in Knoxville, TN, the V-Roys began to walk the fine line between rootsy country and cutting-edge alternative rock with their formation in 1994, comprising vocalist/guitarist Scott Miller, lead guitarist John Paul Keith, bassist Paxton Sellers, and drummer Jeff Bills. The quartet signed to Praxis Records, but the label folded soon after, prompting Steve Earle to sign the V-Roys to his E-Squared Records. He also produced the band's debut album, *Just Add Ice*. Just before the album was released in September 1996, Keith left the band and was replaced by Mic Harrison. In 1998, the V-Roys issued their sophomore effort, *All About Town*, again co-produced by Steve Earle. Two years later, *Are You Through Yet?* was released. —*John Bush*

Just Add Ice / Sep. 10, 1996 / E Squared ✦✦✦
The liner notes of the V-Roys' *Just Add Ice* contain an endorsement from the album's co-producer and alt-country's favorite hardcore troubadour, Steve Earle, hailing the Tennessee quartet as "an important band, believe that." Earle's comments should come as no surprise since the V-Roys deliver the same jangling, melancholy country-rock that he himself has perfected over the years, though without his rebellious edge. The album is a little rough around the edges compared to its 1998 follow-up, the more subtle, but endlessly melodic *All About Town*. Here the band exerts plenty of energy, pumping out some good old rock & roll on tracks such as "Guess I Know I'm Right," "Cry," and "Sooner or Later." When the guys do slow down the tempo, the remind the listener that country music was never meant to be pretty, with songs like "Goodnight Loser" and "Lie I Believe." Finally, the band shows its playful side with the closing track "Cold Beer Hello," which sports a swaggering rhythm and an air of spontaneity. Time will tell if the V-Roys are as important as their mentor claims them to be, but *Just Add Ice* is certainly a step in the right direction. —*Michael Frey*

● **All About Town** / Aug. 25, 1998 / E Squared ✦✦✦✦
All About Town is the latest reason to praise the V-Roys. They have put out 12 concise songs that swing from the Creedence-ish "Window Song" to the country-folk of "Mary" to the sounds of Appalachia in "Virginia Way" to the great highway tune of "Strange." On this, as on their last disc, the V-Roys ply their talents without a single bad moment. Helped out by the Twangtrust, they can be mighty proud of *All About Town*. —*James Chrispell*

Are You Through Yet? / Nov. 7, 2000 / E Squared ✦✦✦
The Knoxville based V-Roys were one of the more promising groups (along with such acts as Wilco, Whiskeytown, and the Old 97's) to emerge out of the mid-'90s alternative country-rock scene. Their commercial success, however, never matched up with their critical acclaim. Calling it quits at the end of 1999, the band released this live album as their going-away present. Recorded at the Down Town club in Johnson City, TN, this disc serves up a dozen originals drawn from the band's two full-lengths, along with a handful of covers. The band's strengths are well-displayed in this boisterous set, which ranges from punchy twang rockers like "Cry" to the more bucolic "Virginia Way." Not surprisingly, these live renditions reveal a rawer, more energetic sound than the album versions. The moody "Sorry Sue" gets revved up with more biting guitar work and "Wind Down," which winds up the album, turns into a set-closing blowout. While their standout tune "Over the Mountain" lacks the studio touch of a gentle Celtic tin whistle, it becomes transformed into a roots rock jig. One can triangulate three of this disc's cover tunes (Neil Young's "Motion Pictures," the La's' "There She Goes," and the Replacements' "IOU") and get a good sense of the V-Roys' sound: countrified bar rock with some pop hooks and a scrappy attitude. *Are You Through Yet?* ends up serving not only as a marvelous send-off, but it also provides a fine introduction to the group for those who missed them the first time around. Singer/guitarist Scott Miller moved on to a solo career, while guitarist Mic Harrison founded the Faults, who originally included the band's rhythm section of bassist Paxton Sellers and drummer Jeff Bills. —*Michael Berick*

Joe Val (Joseph Valiante)

b. Jun. 25, 1926, Everett, MA, **d.** Jun. 11, 1985
Mandolin, Leader, Vocals / Traditional Folk
Singer/songwriter Joe Val was a prominent traditional bluegrass musician and leader of the New England Bluegrass Boys. A native of Everett, MA, he was born Joseph Valiante, and his interest in bluegrass started in his early teens. He was influenced by fiddler Tex Logan, who had come north to study at M.I.T. and wound up giving the young performer his stage name. Val started out as a guitar player, but also mastered the banjo and mandolin. He got his professional start playing with the Radio Rangers, and later joined the Berkshire Mountain Boys; with the progressive Charles River Valley Boys, Val recorded a distinguished album of bluegrass-adapted Beatles songs in 1967. Although Val played with progressive groups, he himself continued to favor a more traditional

bluegrass sound; to this end, he founded the New England Bluegrass Boys in 1970 with guitarist Herb Applin, banjo player Bob French and bass player Bob Tidwell. The following year, they made their debut album. Although the group underwent many personnel changes over the next decade, Val was able to produce a remarkably consistent sound over the course of numerous albums. Sadly, Joe Val was stricken with cancer in the 1980s just as his band was beginning to achieve wider recognition; his last performance was in late 1984, and he died on June 11, 1985. —*Sandra Brennan*

● **Diamond Joe** / Oct. 17, 1995 / Rounder ✦✦✦✦✦
For over 25 years, Joe Val was, in the words of Peter Rowan, the voice of bluegrass in New England. It didn't matter that he was a short, skinny Italian (his last name was really Valiante) from a blue-collar Boston suburb, nor did it matter that his renditions of Bill Monroe and Jimmie Rodgers standards were often tinted by a decidedly Yankee inflection. On-stage he was an unassuming, bespectacled, quietly smiling presence until he opened his mouth to sing, at which point he filled the entire hall. His high tenor voice had the clarity and heft of a ten-pound icicle, and no less an authority than Del McCoury is on the record expressing wonderment at its power. Val, who worked at a day job as a type-writer repairman until his death in 1985 and who had to ask for time off from work in order to tour with his band, blazed the way for Boston's nascent folk and bluegrass scene with the Lilly Brothers in the early '60s, and later surrounded himself with the cream of that city's musical crop, including banjo legends Don Stover and Bill Keith and the less well-known members of the New England Bluegrass Boys (notably the criminally unknown guitarist and singer Dave Dillon). His mandolin playing was good, though nothing to write home about; it was that voice that set him apart from all the competition, and still does. This collection of tracks from Val's various Rounder albums, though not as nice as a wholesale reissue of his back catalog would be, is still an excellent overview of his work and includes such spine-tingling highlights as "T for Texas," "Goodbye Old Pal," and the hair-raising "Poor Ellen Smith." The chorus to "A Voice From on High" still reverberates around one's skull, and his yodeling on "Sparkling Brown Eyes" still sets a standard of soul and accuracy that is rarely matched. This disc is essential to any bluegrass collection. —*Rick Anderson*

One Morning in May / 1996 / Rounder ✦✦✦✦
One Morning in May dates from the early days of the New England Bluegrass Boys, when Joe Val's razor-sharp tenor voice was matched almost eerily by that of guitarist Herb Applin; though you can argue that later lead singers (in particular the mighty Dave Dillon) complemented him better, there was an undeniable power in the classic high, lonesome sound that Applin and Val generated together. "One Morning in May" was recorded in 1971, when Val's voice was at its peak strength—bluegrass standards like "Sparkling Brown Eyes" and "Dark Hollow" are perfect showcases for the power and range of that spectacular voice. The program also includes a few fine gospel numbers, a decent Val-penned instrumental, and the requisite tear-jerking, poor-child-dying-in-the-snow song ("The Little Paper Boy"). It's too bad Val's and Applin's voices weren't recorded a bit more cleanly, but the band sounds great—Bob French was one of the best meat-and-potatoes banjo players around, and Herb Applin's guitar playing is unassuming but solid. Val himself, staunch traditionalist though he was, had an endearing tendency to get a bit too bouncy and syncopated with the mandolin backbeats, but this edition of the New England Bluegrass Boys was as solid as any that followed. Here's hoping the rest of Val's back catalog finds its way onto CD, the sooner the better. —*Rick Anderson*

Leroy Van Dyke

b. Oct. 4, 1929, Spring Fork, MO
Songwriter, Vocals / Traditional Country, Country-Pop, Nashville Sound/Countrypolitan
Singer/songwriter Leroy Van Dyke was best known for penning the country novelty standard "The Auctioneer" and the country-pop smash "Walk on By," his biggest hit. Born in Missouri, Van Dyke originally wanted to be a farmer. He earned a degree in agriculture and journalism at the University of Missouri, where he first began playing guitar. His uncle had been an auctioneer, and Van Dyke himself studied livestock auctioneering and worked as an auctioneer for a time. Following graduation, Van Dyke worked as a newspaper reporter. Sent to Korea during the Korean War, he began performing for his peers and wrote "The Auctioneer," which recalled Van Dyke's uncle and was dedicated to his cousin. The song contains passages of actual auction calls. Following military service, Van Dyke returned to journalism in Chicago but kept up his performing career, appearing on Red Foley's *Ozark Jubilee* television show. In 1956, he entered a talent contest on Chicago radio station WGN, performing "The Auctioneer." DJ Buddy Black signed up as Van Dyke's manager and slipped in a document giving himself co-writing credits and half the royalties for the song. Released as a single on the Dot label, the song hit the pop charts in late 1956 and appeared on the country charts in early 1957, where it climbed to the Top Ten.

In 1961, Van Dyke went to Nashville and signed with Mercury. One of his early releases on the label was "Walk on By," which went right to the top of the country charts and remained there for 19 weeks; it also crossed over to the Top Five on the pop charts. Van Dyke contributed his distinctive smooth tenor to what became one of country music's quintessential cheating songs, a fast two-step number with a certain sly veneer of sophistication. "Walk on By," which gained a Grammy nomination for Van Dyke, was followed up with another major crossover hit, "If a Woman Answers (Hang Up the Phone)," and the Top 40 "Black Cloud." In 1962, Van Dyke began appearing on the *Grand Ole Opry*. His next few Mercury releases gained only middling success, and in 1965 he signed to Warner Bros. and had Top 40 success with "Roses From a Stranger."

In 1967, Van Dyke appeared in the film *What Am I Bid?* He recorded throughout the decade but hit the charts only with "Louisville" in 1968. Nevertheless, he remained a strong draw in Las Vegas (where he was among the first country performers to package and deliver his own self-contained show) and other upscale concert locales; as a performer Van Dyke mastered the art of combining a rural persona with countrypolitan sheen; he offered what he called "city-style country music" on the album *the Leroy Van Dyke Show*. In 1977, he notched one final minor hit, "Texas Tea." Later that year he also released two albums, *Gospel Greats* and *Rock Relics*, both produced by old friend Shelby Singleton. He performed often in Branson, MO, after that town emerged as a country music tourist mecca, and he continued to appear at the agricultural trade shows and livestock auctions whence his music had sprung. *—Sandra Brennan & James Manheim*

Walk on By / 1962 / Mercury ✦✦✦✦

The Leroy Van Dyke Show / 1965 / Warner Bros. ✦

Leroy Van Dyke had few substantial hits after his 1961 smash "Walk on By," which is probably why he felt the need to reinvent himself in the late '60s. *The Leroy Van Dyke Show* is a studio album that strives to convey the feel of Van Dyke's nightclub show, complete with spoken introductions and a theme that is reprised at the end of the "concert." Van Dyke described the sound of this album as "city-style country music" for people who like pop versions of country songs without realizing their origins, and his show was accordingly tailored to suit nightclub audiences who had little appreciation for rural or working class music. Consequently, the program includes pure pop songs like "Stay With Me" (a minor hit for Frank Sinatra) and Petula Clark's "I Know a Place," while the country songs are turned into Cheez Whiz with Van Dyke's heretofore unimaginable lounge-style vocal antics. The album's intro, "Big, Wide Wonderful World of Country Music," was ostensibly conceived to promote the genre but sounds like an advertising jingle. Despite a few moments of unintended hilarity, *The Leroy Van Dyke Show* is a painful stylistic experiment that must have worked better live than on record. *—Greg Adams*

Lonesome Is / 1968 / Kapp ✦✦

Lonesome Is was recorded during Leroy Van Dyke's label-hopping period, when the Top 40 was slipping farther and farther from his grasp. After the debacle of his Vegas-style Warner Bros. album, *The Leroy Van Dyke Show*, his attempt to woo the pop audience continued with *Lonesome Is*, his first album for Kapp. Side one is exclusively pop (notwithstanding the fact that Bobby Goldboro's "Honey" also reached number one on the country charts), and includes a rare example of a country artist doing a song by Rod McKuen. The two songs that are identifiably "country," namely the minor hit "You May Be Too Much for Memphis, Baby" and John Hartford's "A Simple Thing as Love," are cast in the Glen Campbell mold. Van Dyke's identity crisis—being marketed as a country artist while aspiring to become a tuxedoed easy listening vocalist—pushed his later recordings into a dismal stylistic never-never land. *—Greg Adams*

Leroy Van Dyke's Greatest Hits / 1969 / Kapp ✦✦✦✦✦

Leroy Van Dyke: The Original Auctioneer / 1988 / Bear Family ✦✦✦✦✦

● **Walk on By [Bear Family]** / 1994 / Bear Family ✦✦✦✦✦

While *The Auctioneer* contained the highlights of Leroy Van Dyke's '50s hits for Dot, *Walk on By* concentrates on his early '60s singles for Mercury, including "If a Woman Answers (Hang Up the Phone)," "Black Cloud," "Happy to Be Unhappy" and the title track, which spent an extraordinary 19 weeks at the top of the country charts. By and large, the material on *Walk on By* is stronger than that on *The Auctioneer*, making it an excellent introduction to this talented singer. *—Thom Owens*

Ricky Van Shelton

b. 1952, Danville, VA

Guitar, Vocals / Contemporary Country

Ricky Van Shelton was one of country music's biggest male stars during the late '80s and early '90s, prior to the emergence of crossover sensations like Garth Brooks. Van Shelton's smooth baritone croon made him especially popular as a country-pop ballad stylist, but elsewhere he incorporated elements of rock, gospel, and classic honky tonk. Van Shelton was born in Danville, VA, in 1952 and grew up in the small town of Grit. He learned to sing at church and discovered country music as a teenager, performing at local gatherings whenever he could. After high-school, he played the area club circuit and worked a series of day jobs, and in late 1984 he finally made the move to Nashville to make it in the business. He performed in nightclubs until a local newspaper columnist heard his demo and helped arrange a showcase that landed Van Shelton a deal with CBS in 1986.

Van Shelton released his debut album, *Wild-Eyed Dream*, in 1987, and his first-ever single, "Crime of Passion," hit the country Top Ten. Its follow-up, "Somebody Lied," went all the way to number one; so did the album, and so did another single, "Life Turned Her That Way." Van Shelton quickly recorded a follow-up album, *Loving Proof*, which appeared in 1988 and also topped the country charts; it spun off three number-one hits in "I'll Leave This World Loving You," "From a Jack to a King," and "Living Proof," while "Hole in My Pocket" made the Top Five. While readying his third proper album, Van Shelton also completed two specialty projects: the 1989 holiday album *Ricky Van Shelton Sings Christmas* and the 1990 gospel record *Don't Overlook Salvation*. Meanwhile, his official follow-up to *Loving Proof*, *RVS III*, was released in 1990 and became his third number-one album. "I've Cried My Last Tear for You" gave him another number-one single, while "I Meant Every Word He Said" and "Statue of a Fool" both topped out at number two; "Life's Little Ups and Downs" also made the Top Five.

In 1991, Van Shelton teamed up with Dolly Parton for the chart-topping duet "Rockin' Years" and subsequently issued another album, *Backroads*. Though it just missed the top of the country charts, *Backroads* kept his hit streak going strong, producing two more number ones in "Keep It Between the Lines" and "I Am a Simple Man" (giving him a total of nine) and a number-two hit in the title track. Musical tastes can shift quickly, and by the time Van Shelton conquered the alcohol abuse that had begun to take a toll on his personal life, Garth Brooks was completely altering the contemporary country landscape. To hold fans over, he released *Greatest Hits Plus* in 1992, and its newly recorded track, "Wild Man," hit the Top Five. He returned in 1993 with *A Bridge I Didn't Burn*, but the album didn't spawn any huge hits, as had been expected; it went gold, but it was the only Van Shelton album to date that ultimately failed to go platinum.

Love and Honor (1994) continued his commercial downturn, and tensions with Columbia led Van Shelton to part ways with his label a couple years later. He busied himself with, among other projects, a series of children's books centered around the character Quacker the Duck that he'd begun several years earlier. He also formed his own label, RVS, and recorded an album on his own called *Making Plans*, which he distributed via an exclusive agreement with the Wal-Mart store chain in 1997. The following year, Vanguard stepped in to give the record a wider release. Van Shelton subsequently signed with the Audium label, home to many veteran country artists, and recorded a new album, *Fried Green Tomatoes*, in 2000. *—Steve Huey*

Wild-Eyed Dream / 1987 / Columbia ✦✦✦

This debut from this country hunk balladeer, with occasional thumpin' at the hop contains "Working Man Blues," "Crime of Passion," and more. *—Mark A. Humphrey*

Loving Proof / 1988 / Columbia ✦✦✦✦✦

Here are stabs at rockabilly alongside the ballads at which Shelton excels. Some of the songs on the album are "From a Jack to a King" and "Hole in My Pocket."*—Mark A. Humphrey*

Ricky Van Shelton Sings Christmas / 1989 / CBS ✦✦✦

Ricky Van Shelton Sings Christmas was released in 1989, after his first two albums made him a very popular country musician. It may have been a little quick to release a holiday record, but Van Shelton was at a peak of popularity, so it made sense to release a record at that point. And *Sings Christmas* wasn't a bad album, even if it wasn't particularly distinctive. He is in good voice throughout the record and does a nice job with the standards, even if the newer songs are somewhat weak. Ultimately, *Sings Christmas* is the kind of record only hardcore fans will need to hear, but they should be pleased with it. *—Thom Owens*

RVS III / 1990 / Columbia ✦✦✦

The third album puts out more sounds in the winning Shelton formula, such as "I Still Love You," "I've Cried My Last Tear for You," "Oh Pretty Woman," and more. *—Mark A. Humphrey*

Don't Overlook Salvation / Jun. 1990 / Columbia ✦✦

Featured are "The Old Rugged Cross," "To My Mansion in the Sky," "Just as I Am," and others. *—AMG*

Backroads / 1991 / Columbia ✦✦✦✦✦

When he's not trying to be Roy Orbison (as he did on 1990's *RVS III*), it's easy to see that Van Shelton's a fine singer. And this is a fine record—so fine it's tempting to hunt for signs of listener manipulation. But Van Shelton balances the self-pity of songs like "After the Lights Go Out" with the uptempo punch of stuff like "Call Me Up." So even though Van Shelton recycles "Rockin' Years," the duet from Dolly Parton's *Eagle When She Flies*, just call it good taste, sit back, and enjoy. *—Brian Mansfield*

Greatest Hits Plus / 1992 / Columbia ✦✦✦✦✦

Despite rocking hits like "Wild Man" and "I Am a Simple Man" (or even the new cover of Elvis Presley's "Wear My Ring Around Your Neck"), Ricky Van Shelton's greatest-hits collection shows that he's made his best records as a balladeer raised on stone-country gospel. For proof, just listen to "Just As I Am," "I'll Leave This World Loving You" or "Keep It Between the Lines." *—Brian Mansfield*

A Bridge I Didn't Burn / 1993 / Columbia ✦✦✦✦

In 1992 singer Ricky Van Shelton earned a couple of awards and a lot of attention with the hit duet, "Rockin' Years," that he did with one of the queens of country music, Dolly Parton. By that point in his career Shelton was used to both the awards and the spotlight. He had come a long way in less than a decade, going from playing at Nashville clubs as a fill in to watching many of his songs climb the charts to earning a spot as a member of the renowned *Grand Ole Opry*. He had reached his dream, won his battle with alcoholism, found himself still in one piece, and was nowhere near ready to toss in the towel. A year after his hit duet with Parton, Shelton completed the album *Bridge I Didn't Burn*—a fitting title after his victories. The album went gold with the help of outstanding songs like "If They Turn off Our Lights," "Still Got a Couple of Good Years Left," "I Know the Way by Broken Heart," and "Roses After the Rain." This is a really impressive album by a talented artist. *—Charlotte Dillon*

Love and Honor / Nov. 1, 1994 / Columbia ✦✦✦✦

Ricky Van Shelton fans know the artist for his new traditionalist sound, mostly with no sparkle or flash, just modern country that hasn't forgotten its roots. On this 1994 album, *Love and Honor*, you'll get to sample more of the same. Sometimes, though, getting just what you expect is a plus, and this album doesn't fail to please, offering songs like "Wherever She Is," "Love Without You," and "Where the Tall Grass Grows." Van Shelton has a magnificent baritone voice that fits perfect with country ballads. By the time he had completed *Love and Honor*, he had already had more than a dozen number-one hits, several albums that went platinum, and walked away with awards for Vocal Collaboration, Video of the Year, Male Artist of the Year, Male Vocalist of the Year, Entertainer of the Year, and others. One listen to this hard-to-find recording and country music lovers will see why his career has been so successful. *—Charlotte Dillon*

Super Hits / 1996 / Columbia ✦✦✦✦
Super Hits is a budget-priced ten-track collection that contains a re-recorded selection of Ricky Van Shelton's greatest hits ("Life Turned Her That Way," "I Am a Simple Man," "From a Jack to a King") which are padded by album tracks. It's not bad for a budget-priced collection, but it's far from definitive. *—Stephen Thomas Erlewine*

Super Hits, Vol. 2 / 1996 / Sony ✦✦✦✦
Super Hits, Vol. 2 is a nice budget-line collection that features six of Ricky Van Shelton's Top Five hits among its ten tracks, as well as rare covers of "Oh Pretty Woman" and "Wear My Ring Around Your Neck." For the very casual fan, *Super Hits, Vol. 2* may be satisfactory, but it'll leave many listeners craving more material. *—Thom Owens*

Pure Country / Aug. 25, 1998 / Sony ✦✦✦✦
Sony Special Products' *Pure Country* is an effective sampler of Ricky Van Shelton's country-pop recordings for Columbia Records in the '80s and '90s. In fact, in many ways it works as a hits compilation, since many of the featured songs—"From a Jack to a King," "Just as I Am," "A Couple of Good Years Left," "Hole in My Pocket," "Life's Little Ups and Downs"—were charting hits. Because of that, *Pure Country* is more than just a good bargain for a budget-line collection—it's a good bargain in general. *—Stephen Thomas Erlewine*

Making Plans / Oct. 27, 1998 / Vanguard ✦✦✦✦
This album is filled with heartfelt ballads that showcase the superb vocal talents of country singer Ricky Van Shelton. After years under major-label contract to Columbia Records, *Making Plans* was recorded under a new label, one financed and owned by Shelton. This high-quality album carries 12 tracks, all of which are really good songs, making it hard to pick out the top few from the 1998 offering. Some of the numbers that seem to have gotten the best word-of-mouth reviews from fans include "She Needs Me," "The Best Is Yet to Come," and "I Wish You Were More Like Your Memory." "Borrowed Angel" was written by Mel Street and "When the Feeling Goes Away" was penned by the legendary Merle Haggard. *—Charlotte Dillon*

● **16 Biggest Hits** / Feb. 2, 1999 / Columbia/Legacy ✦✦✦✦✦
Ricky Van Shelton scored 16 Top Ten country solo hits between 1987 and 1993, and they are all on this appropriately named compilation, which is sequenced in hit order: first the ten number ones, then the three number twos, and so on. Van Shelton came in on the neo-traditionalist wave of the mid-'80s, and his hits spotlight such veteran country songwriters as Harlan Howard, Roger Miller, and Boudleaux & Felice Bryant and include revivals of standards like "From a Jack to a King." They also exhibit the sentiment and wordplay typical of the country songwriting craft on such newly composed works as the philosophical "Keep It Between the Lines" and the romantic twist of "I Meant Every Word He Said." As country veered toward pop in the Garth-and-Shania era of the '90s, sturdy talents like Van Shelton struggled, but this thorough collection of his most popular material confirms his veneration of traditional country and his status as one of its latter day masters. *—William Ruhlmann*

Fried Green Tomatoes / May 23, 2000 / Audium Entertainment ✦✦✦✦
The album *Fried Green Tomatoes* is standard Ricky Van Shelton fare, a delectable serving of the kind of songs that earned him so many country music awards during the '80s and '90s. Maybe he has taken that old saying to heart about if something isn't broken, don't fix it. Of course that doesn't mean this artist is afraid to add a little dash of new spice on songs like "From the Fryin' Pan." Not every tune of this 2000 Audium Entertainment album is the best Shelton has to offer, but his striking voice can help cover a few weak lyrics. Most of the songs, though, need no such help, and Ricky Van Shelton fans will really enjoy popping this one into the stereo often. A couple of the best tunes are this album are "Call Me Crazy" and the touching "Your One and Only." *—Charlotte Dillon*

Blue Christmas / Oct. 10, 2000 / Audium ✦✦✦

Townes Van Zandt (John Townes Van Zandt)

b. Mar. 7, 1944, Fort Worth, TX, **d.** Jan. 1, 1997, Smyrna, TN
Guitar, Songwriter, Vocals / Progressive Country, Country-Rock, Singer/Songwriter, Contemporary Folk, Americana

Townes Van Zandt's music doesn't jump up and down, wear fancy clothes, or beat around the bush. Whether he was singing a quiet, introspective country-folk song or a driving, hungry blues, Van Zandt's lyrics and melodies were filled with the kind of haunting truth and beauty that you knew instinctively. His music came straight from his soul by way of a kind heart, an honest mind, and a keen ear for the gentle blend of words and melody. He could bring you down to a place so sad that you felt like you were scraping bottom, but just as quickly he could lift your spirits and make you smile at the sparkle of a summer morning or a loved one's eyes—or raise a chuckle with a quick and funny talking blues. The magic of his songs is that they never leave you alone.

Despite his warm, dusty-sweet voice, as a singer Van Zandt never had anything resembling a hit in his nearly 30-year recording career—he had a hard enough time simply keeping his records in print. Nonetheless, he was widely respected and admired as one of the greatest country and folk artists of his generation. The long list of singers who've covered his songs includes Merle Haggard and Willie Nelson (who had a number-one country hit with "Pancho & Lefty" in 1983), Emmylou Harris, Jimmie Dale Gilmore, Nanci Griffith, Hoyt Axton, Bobby Bare, the Tindersticks, and the Cowboy Junkies.

Van Zandt was a Texan by birth and a traveler by nature. His father was in the oil business, and the family moved around a lot—Montana, Colorado, Minnesota, Illinois, among other places—which accounted for his sometimes vague answers to questions of where he "came from." Van Zandt spent a couple years in a military academy and a bit more time in college in Colorado before dropping out to become a folksinger. (Van Zandt often returned to Colorado in subsequent years, spending entire summers, he said, alone in the mountains on horseback.) Van Zandt moved to Houston and got his first paying gigs on the folk music circuit there in the mid-'60s. He played clubs like Sand Mountain and the Old Quarter (where in 1973 he recorded one of his finest albums, *Live at the Old Quarter*, released four years later), and he met singers such as Guy Clark (who became a lifelong friend and frequent road partner), Jerry Jeff Walker, and blues legend Lightnin' Hopkins, who had a large influence on Van Zandt's guitar playing in particular.

Another Texas songwriter, Mickey Newbury, saw Van Zandt in Houston one night and soon had him set up with a recording gig in Nashville (with Jack Clement producing). The sessions became Van Zandt's debut album, *For the Sake of the Song*, released in 1968 by Poppy Records. The next five years were the most prolific of Van Zandt's career, as Poppy released the albums *Our Mother the Mountain*, *Townes Van Zandt*, *Delta Momma Blues*, *High, Low, and In Between*, and *The Late Great Townes Van Zandt*. These included such gems as "For the Sake of the Song," "To Live's to Fly," "Tecumseh Valley," "Pancho & Lefty," and many more that have made him a legend in American and European songwriting circles. Van Zandt moved to Nashville in 1976 at the urging of his new manager, John Lomax. He signed a new deal with Tomato Records and in 1977 released *Live at the Old Quarter*, a double album—and the first of several live recordings—that contained many of his finest songs. In 1978 Tomato released *Flyin' Shoes*; the long list of players on that album included Chips Moman and Spooner Oldham.

Van Zandt didn't record again for nearly a decade, but he continued to tour. He moved back to Texas briefly, returning again to Nashville in the mid-'80s. During the early '80s, both "If I Needed You" and "Pancho & Lefty" became country radio hits. In 1987, Van Zandt was back in business with his eighth studio album, *At My Window*, which came out on his new label, Sugar Hill. By this time, Van Zandt's voice had dropped to a lower register, but the weathered, somewhat road-weary edge to it was as pure and expressive as ever. Two years later, Sugar Hill released *Live & Obscure* (recorded in a Nashville club in 1985), and two more live albums (*Rain on a Conga Drum* and *Rear View Mirror*) appeared on European labels in the early '90s. In 1990, Van Zandt toured with the Cowboy Junkies, and he wrote a song for them, "Cowboy Junkies Lament," which appeared on the group's *Black Eyed Man* album (along with a song the Junkies wrote for him, "Townes Blues").

Sugar Hill released *Roadsongs* in 1994, on which Van Zandt covered songs by Lightnin' Hopkins, Bruce Springsteen, the Rolling Stones, and others, all recorded off the soundboard during recent concerts. At the end of that same year, Sugar Hill released *No Deeper Blue*, Van Zandt's first studio album since 1987. Van Zandt recorded it in Ireland with a group of Irish musicians. Van Zandt sang every song but only played guitar on one. A year and a half after the release of *No Deeper Blue*, Van Zandt died unexpectedly on January 1, 1997; he was 52 years old. Posthumous releases included collections like *Last Rights: The Life & Times of Townes Van Zandt* and *Anthology: 1968-1979*, as well as albums like 1998's *Abnormal* and the following year's *A Far Cry From Dead*, which featured previously unreleased songs.

The early 2000s saw a resurgence of interest in Van Zandt's music and enigmatic life; three book projects and two films entered production, and features on the musician appeared in such tastemaking rags as *Mojo*. But perhaps the greatest gem was the discovery of a collection of Van Zandt demos dating from 1966, a full two years before his proper debut. The ten previously unreleased recordings were issued by the Houston imprint Compadre in April 2003 as *In the Beginning*.... Included in the release were liner notes written by John Lomax III, grandson of the troubadour's manager. *—Kurt Wolff*

For the Sake of the Song: First Album / 1968 / Rhino ✦✦✦
Produced by Jack Clement, Townes' debut is unfortunately marred by inappropriate arrangements. Includes the first recordings of the title song and "Tecumseh Valley" along with obscure songs like "The Velvet Voices" and "Talkin' Karate Blues." Re-released by Rhino in 1993 as *For the Sake of the Song: First Album*. *—Kurt Wolff*

Our Mother the Mountain / 1969 / Tomato ✦✦✦✦
Townes Van Zandt's second album, issued in 1969, is one of the strangest sounding in his catalog. While Kevin Eggers is listed in the prime spot as producer, the string arrangements and other flourishes have the Nash Vegas trademark of Cowboy Jack Clement. Backed by a string section, flutes (that actually solo), a standup bass, and organic hand percussion, as well as acoustic and electric guitars, Van Zandt offered listeners one of his least-recognized but finest collections of songs. Along with the sweet and plaintive "Be Here to Love Me" is the hunted, stark, and poetically unnerving "Kathleen." Van Zandt's simple fingerpicking style is augmented by a string orchestra filling the spaces between lines and underlining his phrases; the track has a stark yet cinematic quality that makes it all the more chilling. The title track is a blues in the tradition of Bob Dylan's "Ballad of Hollis Brown," augmented by a lonely flute and Van Zandt's lyrics, which come from somewhere beyond space and time: "She tells me she comes from my mother the mountain/Her skin fits her tightly and her lips do not lie/She silently slips from her throat a medallion/Slowly she twirls it in front of my eyes/Singing' Tura Lura-Li-O/I watch her, I love her and I long for to touch her/The satin she's wearin' is shimmerin' blue/And outside my window her lady's a sleepin' my dogs a gone huntin' their howlin' is through/Singin' Tura Lura-Li-O/So I reach for her hand and her eyes turn to poison/And her hair turns to splinters and her thair turns to brine/She leaps 'cross the room and stands in the window/And screams that my firstborn will surely be blind/Singin' Tura Lura-Li-O." There is a rupture in the narrative here, as Van Zandt confesses that "Our Mother the Mountain" is an apparition from his unconscious made into flesh. It's spooky, spare, and so rich in imagery that it's tempting to turn the record off after this. To do so would be to miss other Van Zandt gems like "Tecumseh," "Snake Mountain Blues," and "St. John the Gambler." As the record comes to a close with "Why She's Acting This Way," it becomes clear that Eggers, Clement, and Van Zandt were emulating, or at least attempting to come up with, the same kind of texture and ambience that Van Zandt's friend and influence, Mickey Newbury, had on his recordings. And while it's true only Newbury could pull of what he did on his own records, *Our Mother the Mountain* stands out in

Van Zandt's oeuvre as his most ornate, but as a result adds a warm, abstract, and hauntingly beautiful dimension to his poetic vision as a singer/songwriter. *—Thom Jurek*

Townes Van Zandt / 1969 / Tomato ✦✦✦✦
On his third album, Townes Van Zandt recut three crucial tracks from his debut album, "For the Sake of the Song," "Waiting Around to Die," and "I'll Be Here in the Morning." It was some indication of the obscurity in which he remained enveloped, but no indication of the quality of his work. (Actually, Van Zandt re-recorded songs from his first album on his later ones because he disliked the earlier recordings.) As usual, his closely observed lyrics touched on desperate themes, notably in the mining ballad "Lungs," but they were still highly poetic, especially the album-closing "None But the Rain," which reflected on a failed relationship. Van Zandt's fingerpicking was augmented by spare arrangements, usually featuring one added instrument for color, such as a fiddle or flute. [Originally released by Poppy Records in 1969, *Townes Van Zandt* was reissued by Tomato Records in 1989.] *—William Ruhlmann*

Delta Momma Blues / 1971 / Tomato ✦✦✦
Townes Van Zandt's dour viewpoint found more expression on his fourth album, its most characteristic song being "Come Tomorrow," on which he looked forward to how lonely life would be when his lover left. Even "Brand New Companion," which hailed the arrival of a lover, was done as a blues. "Here's to feeling good," he sang in "Only Him or Me," then added, "Here's to feeling bad." But, as usual, what made Van Zandt so compelling was that, in songs like "Rake" and "Nothin'," the painted despair so vividly. [Originally released by Poppy Records in 1970, *Delta Momma Blues* was reissued by Tomato Records in 1989.] *—William Ruhlmann*

The Late Great Townes Van Zandt / 1972 / Tomato ✦✦✦✦✦
If there were a stranger title for an album by a man who was—at the time—still alive, I'd like to hear it. Originally released by Poppy Records and reissued by Tomato first in 1989 and again in 2003, *The Late Great Townes Van Zandt* was a crucial point for the singer and songwriter. His productivity had been waning as he slacked off the album-a-year pace and was about to fall off entirely—after this, Van Zandt wouldn't record for another six years. Despite the slowdown and the lack of all originals, some of Van Zandt's greatest work is contained on this album. Among the originals are two of his most enduring and most-often-covered classics, the outlaw/hobo legend "Pancho & Lefty" and one of the greatest love songs of the late 20th century, "If I Needed You." Also here are the haunting "No Lonesome Tune," "Snow Don't Fall," and "Sad Cinderella." In addition are two more obscure tracks that deserve more exposure: the stunning and visceral "Silver Ships and Andilar" and the rollicking "Heavenly Houseboat Blues." Van Zandt could pick a cover as well and did in the form of Hank Williams' "Honky Tonkin'," done in a completely original way; Guy Clark's "Don't Let the Sunshine Fool Ya"; and the old standard "Fraulein." Van Zandt's sixth album was more than a collection of songs, it was a signpost of a fork in the road for him both as a songwriter and as a performer, and perhaps that is why decades later this album, among his early ones, holds up as well as it does; it was not about settling for anything for Van Zandt on *The Late Great Townes Van Zandt*, it was about looking for something other than what was in front of him. *—Thom Jurek*

High, Low, and In Between / 1972 / Rhino ✦✦✦✦✦
While Townes Van Zandt was still recording for the Poppy label, he decided to open his sound up to more of the influences that helped to make him a songwriter in the first place. One was gospel, the other was the blues. *High, Low, and In Between* was issued in 1972, and in typical fashion, outside of Texas and a few hip New York critics, the record sold next to nothing. It's a miracle in retrospect that Van Zandt was able to record at all. The same perfectionist, high-quality performances are evident here as they were on earlier records, and five of Van Zandt's classics are included on this set. First there's a filled-out country version of "You Are Not Needed Now." With a drum kit, a Hargus "Pig" Robbins-styled piano, and a punchy bassline, Van Zandt delivers the lyrics in a relaxed, almost casual style. Then there's the spooky outlaw folk song "The Highway Kind." This is the heart ballad of the itinerant wanderer. The easy honky tonk strut of "No Deal" became one of Van Zandt's most-loved story songs. And perhaps one of the finest songs ever written is next, the stellar exercise in empathy and tenderness "To Live Is to Fly." An acoustic guitar picked Travis-style, a piano, snare drum, and a simple bassline frame Van Zandt's poetry in such a way that it hovers above and the words fall from his mouth as certain as the sun in the summertime. It's wistful, full of longing and detachment. It's also an excellent epitaph for the most misunderstood artist of our generation. "Mr. Gold and Mr. Mud" is another "Pancho & Lefty," although faster, like Bob Dylan's "Idiot Wind," a morality tale that offers no answers, only more questions in a minor key. Aside from these, the title track and the two gospel tracks, "Two Hands" and "When He Offers His Hand," are new exercises in expansion for Van Zandt and they work well as inspiration pieces and even better as ironic ones. Van Zandt's band included guitarist Larry Carlton, Donnie Owens, and David Cohen and a host of others. Tomato reissued this set in 1989 after it had been dormant on vinyl for a while, and by Rhino it got the complete remastered treatment in 2003, supervised by Van Zandt's widow, Jeanene. This, along with Van Zandt's previous four albums as well as *Live at the Old Quarter*, are essential parts of any country fan's library and for those interested in the Van Zandt myth. There was nothing musical about the music, as evidenced here. *—Thom Jurek*

★ **Live at the Old Quarter (Houston, Texas)** / 1977 / Tomato ✦✦✦✦✦
Townes Van Zandt is one of the most impressive songwriters to emerge in the '70s, and his extensive catalog is sufficiently consistent to be recommended in its entirety, once the listener has acquired a taste for his spare, dry delivery and gallows humor. The place to get that taste is on this live disc (originally a two-LP set), which features the best of Van Zandt's early songs, including "If I Needed You" and "Pancho & Lefty." *—William Ruhlmann*

Flyin' Shoes / 1978 / Rhino ✦✦✦
Some critics have been known to document their children's reactions to certain records as a way of making a point. The device can be tedious, but at least the reaction of a seven-year-old Molly Chadbourne to a live performance by Townes Van Zandt will never be preserved for posterity in these pages due to censorship problems. What caused an otherwise quite polite young girl to burst into a critical tirade of obscenity would have be the Van Zandt tendency to play one downer song after another. In a round-robin setting, Van Zandt is even able to follow-up the performance of an anguished Scottish tragic death ballad with an original song that once again makes it seems like the Texas singer/songwriter has it worse than anyone else in the world, which may actually be true considering how much money he lost playing poker at this particular folk festival. This depressed attitude and the entire album full of morose ballads that could result is perfectly alright if delivered with confidence. On this particular album, this artistic territory is staked out and in several cases presented brilliantly. But the balance of the album is padded out with lesser tracks, some of which seem like jam filler. A four-minute version of "Who Do You Love" is not what buyers of Townes Van Zandt records are looking for, and while the prospect of howling lead slide guitar combined with his music is also not really a pleasant one, even that could be done with more polish than what listeners get here. With this many musicians involved in the sessions there really ought to be a stronger presentation of the material. It sounds as if Van Zandt was unable to finish what he started in terms of leading the musicians through enough varied, strong material to create a memorable album. The best tracks include "No Place to Fall," the type of track that confirms this artist's individuality on the country music scene. He stands in direct contrast to the typical image of the male country singer as being some kind of infallible individual, a stereotype that even Willie Nelson wags his ponytails to. Van Zandt has more in common with the confessional, vulnerable singer/songwriters of the James Taylor ilk, a comparison that unfortunately extends to his musical backing. The incredible pedal steel player Jimmy Day really leans on his country licks throughout, as if shouting out directions to the rest of the musicians. Van Zandt is in good voice and lyrically continues to walk the tightrope that makes his songs so fascinating. One moment he delivers a very simple line—such as, "all my friends are leaving and you say its OK"—and makes it sound like meaningful poetry; the next moment he is dropping his own friend's names as if that really meant something, which it doesn't. [A 1994 reissue added four bonus tracks.] *—Eugene Chadbourne*

At My Window / 1987 / Sugar Hill ✦✦✦
Steve Earle once said "Townes Van Zandt is the best songwriter in the whole world, and I'll stand on Bob Dylan's coffee table in my cowboy boots and say that." To make such a bold statement, Earle must have had some evidence to back him up. *At My Window* will suffice as some of that evidence, no doubt. Whether in sweetly tender ballads or honky cowboy ditties, Van Zandt truly wrote of heartache and heartbreak with the best of them. And though his voice lacks the warm honey feel of Lyle Lovett's, he has a down-home, melancholic charm all his own. You need not strain to hear the lonely in his voice. You can so easily picture him sitting by a fire out on a prairie somewhere serenading the full moon. For Van Zandt was of a different breed. In "Buckskin Stallion Blues" he sings "If three and four were seven only, where would that leave one and two?" That's a contemplation for the ages. More a kindred spirit to Hank Williams than Lovett, his life was in his songs. And the world is all the better for that. *—Kelly McCartney*

Live & Obscure / 1989 / Sugar Hill ✦✦✦
Townes Van Zandt played to a standing room-only crowd in Nashville on April 19, 1985, when he recorded *Live & Obscure* at 12th and Porter. The show was billed as "the return of the lost sheep of the songwriting fold." The rambling Texas troubadour did not disappoint his fans, peers, and colleagues that night (or any other). In this intimate setting, Van Zandt's aw-shucks charm comes through not just his songs, but his in-between banter. Luckily, he failed to heed his mother's advice to not talk, just play and sing. Another beauty that appears in a raw setting such as this is of the songs themselves. No one will argue that a stunning performance by a great singer can make any song seem transcendent. That phenomenon has certainly played a part in Van Zandt's career. But when the author stands on-stage with little musical support to deliver the goods in their truest, original form and they still shine, well that's what separates the men from the boys. That's the moment when legends are made or broken. For Van Zandt was certainly no great singer, but his songs were no less transcendent when sailing on his voice. Though Janis Joplin, Willie Nelson, and Merle Haggard made some of these tunes famous, it was Van Zandt that gave them life. *—Kelly McCartney*

The Nashville Sessions / 1993 / Tomato ✦✦✦
When Poppy Records went bankrupt in 1973, it left Townes Van Zandt with two unreleased albums. One was *Live at the Old Quarter, Houston, Texas*, which was released by Tomato, Poppy's successor, in 1977. The other was a studio recording that languished for 20 years until being issued by Rhino/Tomato in 1993 under the title *The Nashville Sessions*. By that time, Van Zandt had put ten of its 12 songs on such albums as *Live at the Old Quarter*, *Flyin' Shoes*, *At My Window*, and *Live & Obscure*. Since six of them turned up on his next studio album, *Flyin' Shoes*, *The Nashville Sessions* acted as a kind of rough version of that album. Otherwise, one might have suspected that the songs came from before Van Zandt's sixth album, *The Late, Great Townes Van Zandt*, since they seemed to have more in common with his fifth album, *High, Low, and In Between*. One of the two previously unheard songs, "Upon My Soul," was similar to the uptempo gospel tunes on that album. One also might have suspected that the songs could be outtakes from the fifth and sixth albums, since they were not quite up to the quality of those records. *—William Ruhlmann*

Rear View Mirror / 1993 / Sundown ✦✦✦
In 1990, Townes Van Zandt was working on a three-CD retrospective for which he was rerecording much of his repertoire. That album never appeared, but in 1993, the tiny

Austin-based Sundown label released *Rear View Mirror*, a 17-track album running nearly 58 minutes and containing newly recorded versions of Van Zandt songs dating back to 1968. "Unique Instrumentation," and a cover note read, though that seemed to consist of the occasional second guitar and a fiddle. (Sparse applause indicated the recording had been made in a club.) Many of Van Zandt's best-known songs were included—"Pancho & Lefty," "If I Needed You," "To Live Is to Fly," "Tecumseh Valley," and others—and while this was not the best set of recordings of those songs, the tendency of Van Zandt's albums to go out of print might mean this was the only one you would find in your nearest record bin, in which case the album was highly recommended. —*William Ruhlmann*

Roadsongs / 1994 / Sugar Hill ✦✦✦
The liner notes of *Roadsongs* alone are worth the price of admission, or sticker price, as the case may be. The music is simply the cherry on top. Townes Van Zandt recorded the tracks heard here on his travels over the course of a few years. His band came and went, but that didn't seem to matter. It's always a curious matter when a songwriter as amazing and noted as Van Zandt chooses to tip his 24-gallon hat to his own musical heroes. That's what *Roadsongs* is, a nod to other songwriters. Lightnin' Hopkins scores four tunes, Bob Dylan two. A couple of traditionals make the cut, as well as pieces by Bruce Springsteen, Joe Ely, and Mick Jagger and Keith Richards. It's an interesting array of talent, brought together by Van Zandt in all of his good-old-boy glory. A snapshot of a true American troubadour doing what he does best: singing about heartbreak in some joint somewhere to folks who know about such things. Van Zandt was quoted once as saying "The world's got enough blues that nobody needs to hear." Thank goodness he kept on singing anyway. —*Kelly McCartney*

No Deeper Blue / 1995 / Sugar Hill ✦✦✦
Van Zandt's subject matter had not changed much in the seven years between recordings, as was apparent only a few lines into the leadoff track, "A Song For," when Van Zandt spoke-sang, "I'm weak and I'm weary of sorrow." In fact, he wasn't weary of enumerating the causes of sorrow, as was proven especially in "Marie," sung in the voice of a derelict whose life gets worse and worse until his pregnant girlfriend dies. Songs like that were typical of Van Zandt, but this time he also displayed an unusual range, from the scary, calypso-like song of temptation "The Hole" to the weird tall tale of "Billy, Boney and Ma" in which a man and a skeleton turn to a life of crime, demonstrating Van Zandt's humorous side. Van Zandt even found room for two lullabies. Musically, the album, which was recorded in Ireland and produced by Philip Donnelly, who also played guitar, benefited from an unusually varied group of styles, from the Chicago blues of "Goin' Down to Memphis" to the Memphis rockabilly of "Gone Too Long," with a strong complement of Irish-flavored tunes played on such traditional instruments as uilleann pipes and tin whistle. The diverse musical styles made the album Van Zandt's most listenable, even when the lyrics were at their most desperate. By 1994, after a stream of live re-recordings of his older material, Van Zandt had begun to seem like a songwriter whose best songs, good as they were, were behind him. *No Deeper Blue* demonstrated that the muse was still with him. —*William Ruhlmann*

Rain on a Conga Drum: Live in Berlin / Nov. 7, 1995 / MMS ✦✦✦✦
This 18-track, 63-minute import disc was Townes Van Zandt's third live album, recorded in October 1990. It shared eight selections with his first, *Live at the Old Quarter, Houston, Texas*, and five with his second, *Live & Obscure*. Distinguishing this set were some interesting covers, including Lightnin' Hopkins' "Short-Haired Woman Blues" and the Rolling Stones' "Dead Flowers," a long, funny story concerning the composition of Van Zandt's most famous song, "Pancho & Lefty," and the otherwise unrecorded original "Catfish Song," a typically poetic and downcast Van Zandt composition. And, if you didn't have any of Van Zandt's other albums, discovering material like "If I Needed You," "To Live Is to Fly," and "Tecumseh Valley" would be a revelation. —*William Ruhlmann*

Pancho / Feb. 7, 1996 / Edsel ✦✦✦

High, Low, and In Between/The Late Great Townes Van Zandt / Oct. 1, 1996 / Capitol ✦✦✦✦✦
High, Low, and In Between and *The Late Great Townes Van Zandt*, Townes Van Zandt's two classic records from 1972, were reissued on a single CD from Capitol in 1996. *High, Low, and In Between*, Van Zandt's fifth album, was different from his first four starting with the first few notes. The leadoff track "Two Hands" was an uptempo gospel number featuring piano and backup vocals. Van Zandt returned to religion in the country waltz "When He Offers His Hand," sang rock & roll with a harmony vocal on "Standin'," tried a martial beat worthy of Johnny Cash on the gambling story song "Mr. Gold and Mr. Mudd," and even turned to comedy in "No Deal." The musical variety made *High, Low, and In Between* a more interesting listen than Van Zandt's previous work, but what made it his best album since his debut was the quality of the songs, especially "You Are Not Needed Now" and "To Live Is to Fly." By *The Late Great Townes Van Zandt*, his sixth album in five years, Van Zandt seemed to be getting less prolific, but his songwriting craft only improved. Van Zandt re-recorded yet another track from his debut album, "Sad Cinderella," and did three cover tunes, including one by main influence Hank Williams. But among the remaining seven new originals were "Pancho & Lefty," a sly Western story-song about two outlaws, and "If I Needed You," among his most telling romantic statements. The two songs would become valuable copyrights for Van Zandt, and they made this oddly titled album one of his best—which was good, since, as it happened, it would be his last release for five years. —*William Ruhlmann*

The Highway Kind / Mar. 18, 1997 / Normal Germany ✦✦✦
Judging by the number of live albums credited to him, Townes Van Zandt must have lived his life on the road. Or perhaps he simply recorded every show he did, just in case, always ready to make Alan Lomax proud. Nevertheless, another result of this steadfast dedication to documentation is *The Highway Kind*. Again, Van Zandt wanders through honky

tonks and cowboy bars across America and Europe, band in tow, heart on sleeve. This collection of tunes is comprised of a mixed bag of originals and covers, all with that ever-present common thread of lonesomeness figuring prominently, in one fashion or another. It's yet another piece of the musical landscape that was Van Zandt's life, work, and talent. And luckily there are so many. —*Kelly McCartney*

Abnormal / Aug. 11, 1998 / Normal ✦✦✦
Abnormal was released one year after the 1997 death of Townes Van Zandt. *Abnormal* is a live acoustic release featuring songs recorded throughout Europe, and showcasing songs from throughout his career. Many fans prefer this stripped-down setting for Van Zandt's music: intimate, personal, and palpable; there is no hiding the sorrow that exudes from these songs. These are sad songs, folks, and Van Zandt doesn't dress them up as anything else. Delivered through his troubadour-weary voice and guitar, even the light-hearted "Shrimp Song" sounds like a eulogy. The disc ends with "Old Shep," a song so sad that Van Zandt says it "takes the cake." He barely gets through the song, stopping every few lines to regain his composure. Even though most of his music is sad, it is not sentimental. You get the sense that, like Hank Williams before him, Van Zandt means what he sings, and that honesty is why fans gravitate toward him. *Abnormal* is not the best Townes Van Zandt album by far, but it will not disappoint those who already love him. With Van Zandt gone, these stray recordings are all we have left. —*Dan Lee*

Anthology: 1968–1979 / Aug. 25, 1998 / Charly ✦✦✦✦✦
Singer/songwriter Townes Van Zandt has become a legendary cult figure for a combination of things: for writing some of the most honest, heartfelt countrified pop ballads since Gram Parsons, and for dying young due to a combination of alcoholism and hard living. Like his idol Hank Williams and the aforementioned Parsons, Van Zandt's music has served as inspiration to the next generation of gritty, personal songwriters, and the reasons why can be found in Charly's thorough *Anthology: 1968-1979*. Beginning with Van Zandt's early forays into sparse, folky confessions and moving through his darker, even more personal country arrangements, this two-disc collection supplies the listener with an excellent introduction to his "hits" ("If I Needed You," "For the Sake of the Song," "Pancho & Lefty"), as well as a look at some of his lesser-recognized gems ("Come Tomorrow," "High, Low and In Between," "No Lonesome Tune"). His voice was never hailed as being flawless, and he never claimed to be a guitar virtuoso, but his songwriting has proven to be an inspiration to artists throughout the last quarter century. Van Zandt kept recording throughout the '80s and '90s, continuing to tour until his death in 1997, and while there are certainly worthwhile moments in those 20 years, the majority of his truly noteworthy output is represented here. Anyone curious about this legendary cult figure will find this anthology an eye-opening introduction, while longtime Townes fans will delight in having all of these classics on one collection. [The same songs delivered with different packaging were released through Varese Sarabande records with the identical title in 2001]. —*Zac Johnson*

A Far Cry From Dead / Jun. 29, 1999 / Arista ✦✦✦
Called the greatest songwriter ever by Nashville rebel Steve Earle, *A Far Cry From Dead* is a collection of the sharp, insightful writing that led Earle to make such a bold claim about Van Zandt. Included are the songs that became hits for others, such as "Pancho & Lefty" (which Willie Nelson made into a 1983 hit), as well as the material that made Townes a revered songwriter and performer in his own right. More than anything though, the album showcases just how honest and revealing Townes' words are. The blunt reality of the aborted relationships in "Many a Fine Lady," for example, and the exalted freedom of "To Live's to Fly" do more to broadcast his mastery than the magazine covers he always seemed to be overlooked for. —*Steven Kurutz*

In Pain / May 9, 2000 / Normal Germany ✦✦✦
Culled from the same European tour dates as *Abnormal* and *The Highway Kind*, this set of minimal live performances features a number of true Van Zandt classics, including "Snowin' on Raton," "To Live's to Fly," "Mr. Mudd and Mr. Gold," and "You Are Not Needed Now." The man's in fairly decent voice, too, given how many of his later recordings betrayed the ravages of his hard-scrabble life. But even with his voice on his side, Van Zandt sounds as if he's trying to fend off death with a joke and a song—and not necessarily succeeding. Though hardly the place for neophytes to begin, *In Pain* is a fitting and aptly named epitaph for this beloved singer/songwriter. —*Brian Beatty*

The Anthology: 1968–1979 / Jul. 17, 2001 / Varese ✦✦✦✦✦

Texas Rain / Oct. 23, 2001 / Tomato Music ✦✦✦✦
The only thing wrong with this album is its title. *Texas Rain* (with the subtitle "The Texas Hill Country Recordings") doesn't suggest anything about the contents. To be useful, the name of this album would be "Townes Van Zandt and Friends Sing the Songs of Townes Van Zandt," because that describes the contents accurately. In the early '90s, as he frequently told interviewers, Van Zandt was at the Fire Station recording studio in San Marcos, TX, recording what was supposed to be a 60-song box set of his material. That project did not appear before his death at the start of 1997, but these 12 tracks derive from the sessions. On them, Kevin Eggers—who produced Van Zandt's early Poppy/Tomato albums of the late '60s and early '70s, on which many of these songs got their first recorded performances—puts together sympathetic, filled-out arrangements and brings in a series of sympathetic duet partners for Van Zandt. These include Emmylou Harris, who scored a hit with Van Zandt's "If I Needed You" and joins him on it here, and Willie Nelson, who, with Merle Haggard, hit with Van Zandt's "Pancho & Lefty" and here performs "No Lonesome Tune" and "Marie." ("Pancho & Lefty" itself gets a Tex-Mex treatment courtesy of three-quarters of the Texas Tornados—Freddy Fender, Doug Sahm, and Augie Meyers—along with Rubin Ramos and the Texas Revolution.) But Van Zandt himself is never overwhelmed by the assistance. He is in good voice and dominates the proceedings with his matter-of-fact phrasing, which emphasizes the dry wit and detail of the lyrics. There has

been a glut of Van Zandt releases since his death, and this one doesn't present any new material, so it can't be considered essential. But there are some terrific performances of the songwriter's better songs. — *William Ruhlmann*

Live at McCabe's / Nov. 27, 2001 / Return to Sender ◆◆◆

The Best of Townes Van Zandt / Mar. 12, 2002 / Tomato Music ◆◆◆◆◆

After a number of short-lived compilations, it seems that *The Best of Townes Van Zandt* is finally going to be the album that definitively represents Van Zandt's classic Tomato recordings. That's good and bad, actually, for a number of reasons. On the plus side, it is generally agreed that Van Zandt's music is best heard in an intimate acoustic setting, and *The Best of Townes Van Zandt* leans heavily toward that supposition, featuring "Tecumseh Valley" and "White Freightliner Blues" from the concert album *Live at the Old Quarter* and the second recorded version of "For the Sake of the Song" that Van Zandt preferred to the 1968 original. There's nothing from his debut record, however, and even if Van Zandt may have wanted it that way, some listeners may miss the youthful vigor of those first versions. And it's certainly true that Tomato didn't pick the best versions of all these songs; "Waitin' Around to Die," for example, the Calvin Russell duet version from *Texas Rain*, is far inferior to almost every other version Van Zandt recorded. (It's one of two duets, the second with Willie Nelson, that seem to have been included merely for the sake of seeming stylish rather than presenting a true best-of.) In general, though, this collection is pretty good, featuring most of the songwriter's classics plus latter-day favorites such as "Dead Horses" and interesting album tracks like "Who Do You Love" and "Tower Song." People are going to cry out over some of this stuff, asking where's this and that, but such omissions ensure that people will continue to buy Van Zandt's proper records, and that is essential. — *Jim Smith*

The Very Best of Townes Van Zandt: The Texan Troubadour / Jun. 25, 2002 / Metro ◆◆◆

While there has been a real glut of Townes Van Zandt "greatest-hits" collections of late, *The Texan Troubadour* relies heavily on his story-songs, recounting tales of drunken hoboes and ill-fated outlaws mixed in with his Dylan-esque love songs. The chronological format works well, and it is fascinating to listen as he really comes into his own on the second disc, abandoning the bizarre orchestration and incongruous string sections of his early recordings and relying more heavily on his gentle voice and appropriately sparse accompaniment. The one thing that becomes evident is how bone-crushingly depressing most of these tunes are, especially combined with the knowledge of his troubled later life and untimely death at the age of 52. Still, there are flickers of hope in these modern tragedies, leaving the listener with the faint but clear hope of the human spirit surviving all of the broken hearts and empty bottles that Van Zandt can hand out. This collection is unfortunately missing some of his really great recordings like "Tower Song," "You Are Not Needed Now," and (unforgivably) his cover of "Dead Flowers," but what fun would a best-of compilation be if there were nothing for music geeks and scholars to debate? — *Zac Johnson*

Absolutely Nothing / Oct. 1, 2002 / Normal ◆◆◆

Singer Songwriter / Oct. 1, 2002 / EMI Plus ◆◆◆◆

Singer Songwriter, released in Europe by EMI's EMI Plus reissue imprint, consists of recordings licensed from Charly Records that were, in turn, obtained from Tomato Records in the U.S. The 16 tracks come from Townes Van Zandt's studio albums of 1968-1978: *For the Sake of the Song*, *Our Mother the Mountain*, *Townes Van Zandt*, *Delta Momma Blues*, *High, Low, and in Between*, *The Late Great Townes Van Zandt*, and *Flyin' Shoes*. The 16 selections, running 56 minutes, constitute a best-of compilation, beginning and ending with Van Zandt's best-known compositions, "Pancho & Lefty" and "If I Needed You," which were country hits for others, and including many of the other songs that he played frequently in his shows, such as "Waiting Around to Die," "Tecumseh Valley," and "To Live Is to Fly." Since Van Zandt's death in 1997, many compilations and concert recordings of his work have been released. This one, which includes a lyric sheet and is offered for a modest price, is a good basic primer. — *William Ruhlmann*

Texas Troubadour / Nov. 5, 2002 / Snapper ◆◆◆◆

In the Beginning ... / Apr. 22, 2003 / Compadre ◆◆◆◆

In the Beginning is, unlike so many posthumous recordings or rip-off collections of sub-par material by major artists, the real thing. These ten songs feature Van Zandt, already developed as a considerable songwriting talent, in his debut Nashville session produced by none other than Cowboy Jack Clement. Some can debate the quality of these songs against his others, but to this critic it doesn't make a whit of difference. In 1966, two years before the issue of *For the Sake of the Song*, Van Zandt was already deeply entrenched in his rambling tales of losers, gamblers, ne'er-do-wells, and restless drifters who somehow made up his ethos. His poetry, like Bob Dylan's or any great bluesman's, could stand apart from the music. While the material recorded with a band is steeped sonically in the rock sound of the time, it is nonetheless timeless. Anybody whose first couplet on track one is, "I got a black widow for a mama, Lord/I got a Diamond back rattler for a Pa," backed by a driving, lonesome guitar a two-note bassline and garagey 4/4 drumbeat, is already in the pocket of his art. "Black Widow Blues" and "Hunger Child Blues" are out-and-out rockers, with Van Zandt's voice like an Old-Testament prophet abandoned by God roiling above the din. But there's the sparse beauty of his solo material, too. "Gypsy Friday," with its restless, wandering spirit, is summed up in one line: "If you want to call me friend/The friend you best begin/Blowing secrets to the winds of gypsy Friday." "Waitin' for the Day" is deeply influenced by Hank Williams' forlorn waltzes, with Van Zandt's turnarounds built into the country lines. "Black Jack Mama" is a blues in the same way Dylan's "Subterranean Blues" is, except for one thing—Van Zandt gets the same effect with just a guitar. But Van Zandt's greatest gift was his empathy, rooted firmly in a lonesome tenderness that could take brokenness into his songs, even at this early date, and turn them into stories that were not only descriptive and honest emotionally, but

psychologically instructive. In "Maryetta's Song," with his slow, flatpicked run carrying the outlines of his melody, he sings: "She stands all alone with her sorrow/Like a bird that's afraid to sing/She lives for the pain tomorrow will bring/Will she call if she starts to go/Or will she silent go?" That same question could have been asked of Van Zandt, and sadly, we know the answer. The plaintive "When Your Dream Lovers Die" is one of the most stunning love songs in his catalog. "In the Beginning" offers time-tested proof that Van Zandt existed as an artist, to bring the song the life it deserved apart from time and space—and perhaps even his own authorship. *In the Beginning* is a necessity for any fan; the packaging is gorgeous, with paintings of Van Zandt, photographs, and lyrics. The sound is pristine and the music is as necessary as anything in his oeuvre. — *Thom Jurek*

Phil Vassar

b. Lynchburg, VA

Vocals, Piano / Contemporary Country, Contemporary Singer/Songwriter

Contemporary country singer Phil Vassar made his name as a chart-topping songwriter before landing a record deal and becoming a hitmaking artist in his own right. Vassar was born in Lynchburg, VA, and won a track scholarship to James Madison University, where he first began to take music seriously. He moved to Nashville, learned to play piano, and sang his original material in clubs. One club patron and fan brought Vassar's demo tape to his father, crooner Engelbert Humperdinck, and Humperdinck wound up recording "Once in a While," a song Vassar had co-written with a bartender friend, in 1996. Vassar's songwriting career blossomed from there, as he landed a publishing contract with EMI and penned hits for Collin Raye ("Little Red Rodeo"), Alan Jackson ("Right on the Money"), Tim McGraw ("For a Little While"), Jo Dee Messina ("Bye Bye," "I'm Alright"), and BlackHawk ("Postmarked Birmingham").

He signed a record deal of his own with Arista in 1998 and was named ASCAP's Country Songwriter of the Year in 1999. His self-titled debut album was released in 2000, and the lead single, "Carlene," shot into the country Top Five; its follow-up, "Just Another Day in Paradise," went all the way to number one. "Six-Pack Summer" also reached the Top Ten, and yet another single from the album, "That's When I Love You," became Vassar's third Top Five hit in early 2002. *Phil Vassar* was certified gold for sales of half a million copies, and its follow-up, *American Child*, was released later in 2002. The title track gave Vassar yet another Top Five single. — *Steve Huey*

● **Phil Vassar** / Feb. 22, 2000 / Arista ◆◆◆◆

Phil Vassar established himself as a top country songwriter by penning vigorous, rock-influenced romps for Tim McGraw and Jo Dee Messina. On his own, Vassar is an enthusiastic vocalist, a skilled pianist, and a gifted composer of spirited, nostalgic tales. Like Tom T. Hall, Vassar has a talent for chronological storytelling, squeezing big emotions out of small-town details. The boisterous "Carlene," an immediate hit, details the rediscovery of a high-school valedictorian who blossomed into a fashion model. "Joe & Rosalita" follows a similar blueprint, commemorating the journey of two childhood sweethearts from senior prom to domestic bliss. Subsequent hits like "Just Another Day in Paradise" and "That's When I Love You" benefited from the album's good-time piano and guitar vibe, and launched Vassar as a distinctive recording artist. Various country music awards may have solidified his reputation among his peers, but no accolade validates Vassar's talent more than a song like "Didn't You Know She's Gone," in which Vassar speaks through various inanimate objects before admitting the truth to himself. As the dialogue progresses, echoes of '60s pop give way to heartbreaking guitar until his revelation surmounts poetic denial. It is one of many highlights on *Phil Vassar*, an imaginative debut that suggests he has a wealth of future material for himself and others. — *Vince Ripol*

American Child / Jul. 2002 / Arista Nashville ◆◆◆

What makes Phil Vassar a true find in today's Nashville climate is his rock-solid ability to pen a convincing song and then turn around and sing it in an equally convincing manner. His writing has been embraced by everyone from Alan Jackson to Cledus T. Judd to Engelbert Humperdinck. Vassar's sophomore album on Arista Records, *American Child*, is exactly what he wants it to be: 12 songs that he had a hand in writing and knew he could convey to his audience. That translates into some catchy lines, a few unconventional choruses, and Vassar's fervent belief in every note. The album offers both powerful ballads like "I Thought I Never Would Forget" and "Stand Still" tempered with the humor of "Athens Grease," the story of a Georgia mechanic Vassar dubs the "redneck Picasso of the manual transmission." The title cut is probably some of Vassar's best songwriting, with plenty of good ole' American imagery. On the downside, some of the cuts just don't merit space on this album. That's no slap to Vassar's songwriting; the best of the best can't write top quality every time they pick up the pen. Here, it's more a question of weeding out and replacing tunes such as the generically bland "I'll Be the One" that ends the album or the confusing "Forgettin's So Long." That said, *American Child* is a solid, enjoyable effort with a few flaws. — *Rick Cohoon*

Ben Vaughn

Guitar, Vocals / Rock & Roll, Singer/Songwriter, Roots Rock, Retro-Rock

Retro-rocker Ben Vaughn attracted attention for his faithful re-creations of pre-Beatles rock & roll, pop, and roots music, all of which were filtered through his quirky sense of humor. Vaughn grew up in Philadelphia and played drums in the local punk band the Sickidz in 1980. Two years later, roots rockers the Morells recorded his composition "The Man Who Has Everything" on their acclaimed *Shake and Push* album. Vaughn began playing around Philadelphia with a band dubbed the Ben Vaughn Combo, gradually branching out into other parts of the Northeast. His first album, *The Many Moods of Ben Vaughn*, was released in 1986 on the U.K. imprint Making Waves and shortly thereafter was licensed for American release by Restless. It received enthusiastic reviews, and Marshall Crenshaw covered its "I'm Sorry (But So Is Brenda Lee)" on his *Downtown* album. The follow-up, *Beautiful Thing*, appeared in 1987, again to positive response, and Vaughn signed a permanent deal with Restless; after its release, the Combo elected to disband, and Vaughn became a true solo artist. *Blows Your Mind* was released in 1988, and its 1990 follow-up, *Dressed in Black*, featured guest appearances by Crenshaw, John Hiatt, the Violent Femmes' Gordon Gano, Alex Chilton, and country duo Foster & Lloyd.

In the meantime, Vaughn's interest in musical history led to some side gigs as a compiler and producer. He contributed to retrospective releases on Johnny Otis and Joe South and produced albums by cult legends Charlie Feathers and Arthur Alexander, among others. He also scored two documentary films, *Favorite Mopar* (about muscle cars) and *Wild Girls Go Go Rama*, and spent some time in Nashville writing songs with Rodney Crowell and Bill Lloyd. In the meantime, Restless issued the compilation *Mood Swings* in 1992. Vaughn's next recording was a covers album, *Mono USA*, which appeared on Bar/None in 1994. He followed it in 1995 with *Instrumental Stylings*, an eclectic album that incorporated bits of his film scores, and a collaborative effort with Kim Fowley dubbed *Kings of Saturday Night*. Thanks in part to *Instrumental Stylings*, he was tapped to compose the surf-style theme song for the TV sitcom *Third Rock From the Sun* and wound up winning a composer's award from BMI for it. Most of the music from *Instrumental Stylings* was ultimately featured on the show at one time or another. Vaughn went on to serve as music director for *That '70s Show* as well and returned with a new album in 1997; *Rambler 65* was recorded on an eight-track studio set up in Vaughn's vintage car of the same name. —*Steve Huey*

● **The Many Moods of Ben Vaughn** / 1986 / Restless ✦✦✦✦✦
With a backing that includes bass, drums, and accordion, guitarist and singer Vaughn deadpans his way through a collection of his comic songs ("I Dig Your Wig," "Wrong Haircut"), most of which are played in a country/rockabilly style. —*William Ruhlmann*

Beautiful Thing / 1987 / Restless ✦✦✦
"I feel like Jerry Lewis in France/When you hold me tight," sings Vaughn as the band recreates a Bob Dylan-in-1965 sound. How can you not love a smart, funny guy like that? —*William Ruhlmann*

Blows Your Mind / 1988 / Restless ✦✦✦

Dressed in Black / 1990 / Restless ✦✦
Vaughn's fourth effort features cameos by Alex Chilton, Marshall Crenshaw, John Hiatt and Gordon Gano. While the opening track, "Big Drum Sound," 'tis a jab at modern recording technology not unlike the Dead Milkmen's "Instant Club Hit (You'll Dance to Anything)," the remainder of the album fits snugly into Vaughn's usual retro style. —*Jason Ankeny*

Mood Swings / 1992 / Restless ✦✦✦

Mono USA / 1994 / Bar/None ✦✦✦✦✦
Who knew that artists as disparate as Fred Neil, the Ventures, and Alan Vega were actually spiritual kin? Ben Vaughn knew all along and he proved it on this album of covers. Vaughn has always been part musicologist, and he probably thumbed through a record collection the size of two rooms to rescue the songs (and in some instances, the artists themselves) featured on *Mono USA* from the gutters of rock history in which they had lay forgotten. The album was a labor of love, collecting four years worth of eight-track home recordings from Vaughn's basement studio, each of them lovingly recorded in mono ("It was good enough for Phil Spector and Brian Wilson...," the liners intone) with Vaughn playing all the instruments himself. The result is a trip to the wrong side of the early-pop-music tracks—trashy surf, adrenalized rock & roll, unhinged rockabilly, blues both rollicking and brooding, beer-soaked honky tonk, galloping cowboy tunes, weepy pop ballads, country, and R&B nuggets—with nary a roots genre bypassed. Some of the names covered on *Mono USA* are familiar (Dion, Link Wray, Willie Nelson), some are cult artists (Lee Hazlewood, Neil), some have remained obscure despite having a measure of success (Lobo, Henson Cargill, Tom T. Hall), and some are just plain obscure (Jody Chastain, Ersel Hickey). No matter what each artist's legacy is, however, each of the 18 songs is stellar. The album plays like an old, half-imagined AM radio station, and it inspires the same sort of excitement that a teenager must have felt listening at night to an old scratchy signal in his or her bedroom during the '50s and '60s. Vaughn's intent was neither to dramatically alter nor exactly mimic the original versions, just to resurrect some lost classics and have some fun doing so, and the joy shines through. This is not, however, exactly a conventional cover album. It is neither a genre exercise nor a vanity project, and it is not a throwaway. Instead, it is Vaughn's lifeblood, the music that made him, and the same cloth from which he is cut. Vaughn's own original songbook is filled with tunes that aspire to the same heights (or lows, as the case may be) and the same spirit as his archival selections. The album is ultimately held together by his inimitable charm and his audible love for these songs, as well as his skill as a musician and interpreter. One gets a distinct feeling after listening to *Mono USA* that Vaughn is among like-minded artists, that decades from now one of his own lost classics will appear on an album just like this one. —*Stanton Swihart*

Instrumental Stylings / 1995 / Bar/None ✦✦✦
Instrumental Stylings sort of seemed like Vaughn's resumé for a Hollywood scoring career. Sure enough, following the release of the album, he contributed the award-winning theme song to the television series *Third Rock From the Sun*, and much of the music from *Instrumental Stylings* was subsequently featured on the show. In fact, a couple of the album cuts were originally written for a 1991 muscle car documentary, *Favorite Mopar*, and a few others originally appeared in Vaughn's score to the documentary *Wild Girl's Go Go Rama*, so scoring is a function that he had already proven himself primed to tackle. *Instrumental Stylings* is not a soundtrack album, but it certainly tackles its fair share of instrumental touchstones. Vaughn shies away from no genre: bone-crunching surf, spaghetti western, drag-strip stompers, country blues boogie, Italian soundtrack, breezy bossa nova, Tex-Mex cowboy ballads, noir Indian music, and numerous mix-and-match hybrids thereof. One of the most surprising aspects of the album is his ability to evoke a wildly eclectic array of sources and styles and create a palpable mood and atmosphere

with each one using virtually the same basic instrumentation. The constants on the album are Vaughn's crazily reverbed guitar and rock-steady drumming. He also douses many of the songs with simplistic organ runs and a bevy of alien effects. Amazingly—and it is a testament to his estimable skills—Vaughn manages to make the album sound like a compilation of the finest camp sounds from exploitation flicks of the '50s and '60s. He is as gifted at replicating B-movie styles as Todd Rundgren is at reproducing pop/rock ones. It is virtually impossible to be put off by the retro stance of the music because it exudes such a joyous quality and is crafted so impeccably. It may have been created as incidental music, but it doesn't play as such. Instead, it hangs together as a tribute that is often better than the music it is meant to acknowledge. —*Stanton Swihart*

Kings of Saturday Night / Mar. 21, 1995 / Sector 2 ✦✦✦

Rambler 65 / Feb. 18, 1997 / Rhino ✦✦✦
Ben Vaughn has always been an excellent roots rocker and *Rambler '65* is another worthy addition to his catalog. Vaughn recorded the entire album in his old 1965 Rambler, cramming himself and an eight-track tape-recorder into the car, which functioned as a makeshift studio. While the car studio is nothing more than a gimmick, designed to snag a few magazine articles, the music is hardly trivial, demonstrating his ability to recreate the sound of '50s and '60s rock & roll and country with ease, as well as his talent for clever, memorable hooks that keep tradition alive without being enslavened to the past. —*Thom Owens*

The Vidalias
f. Atlanta, GA
Group / Alternative Country
One of the most promising bands of the insurgent country movement of the '90s, the Atlanta five-piece the Vidalias—named for Georgia's famous onions—blended country, rockabilly, bluesy rock, and occasional swing, deriving a sound that recalls the country-rock of the Flying Burrito Brothers and at times hints at the Western swing of Asleep at the Wheel. Led by the vocal, guitar, and songwriting talents of Charles Walston, the group also included Henry Bruns on pedal steel guitar, bassist Jim Johnson, guitarist Page Waldrop, and David Michaelson—of the original Georgia Satellites—on drums. —*Jack Leaver*

Melodyland / 1995 / Upstart ✦✦✦✦
The debut album from this Georgia-born quintet manages to capture both the essence and spirit of classic country and the soulful rawness of early rock & roll. Throughout the 11-song set, fun tunes like the catchy Western swing/rockabilly opener "Faking It" are mixed with sad ballads, such as the second song, "Tokens of Affliction." The latter begins with the lonesome wail of a harmonica, and builds with the haunting and mournful cry of Henry Bruns' superb pedal steel guitar. When Charles Walston opens his mouth, it's a classic and earnest country delivery, reminiscent of Gram Parsons. Walston is a remarkable songwriting talent, able to indulge in wordplay without sounding trite, and to supply melodies that sound instantly familiar, while remaining highly original. —*Jack Leaver*

● **Stayin' in the Doghouse** / Sep. 17, 1996 / Upstart ✦✦✦✦✦
The Vidalias' Charles Walston possesses a singing voice that bears an uncanny, almost frightening resemblance to his fellow Georgian Gram Parsons. At a time when it seemed that everybody and their brother was dropping the country-rock pioneer's name as an influence, being saddled with the comparison could be considered more a curse than blessing. Walston and the other four Vidalias, however, need not worry. There's enough originality here to put to rest any notion that Walston and company are merely an imitation of a novelty. *Stayin' in the Doghouse*, the Vidalias' second album is a 12-song collection, continuing the great musicianship and first-rate songwriting of 1995's *Melodyland*. If anything, this record is slightly more consistent than that effort, with the band's sound more focused, due largely to the fact that Walston's songwriting has just gotten better. With a tip of the hat to country-era Byrds, the original Flying Burrito Brothers, and a straight-ahead roots rock sensibility, *Stayin' in the Doghouse* is a pleasure throughout. Once again, pedal steel guitarist Henry Bruns demonstrates he's a force to be reckoned with, whether it be lightning-quick picking or weeping crescendos. Song highlights include the country-rockin' swagger of "Misery Loves Company," and the minor-keyed "Whose Side Are You On?" with Bruns copping a snippet of melody from the Western movie theme "The Good, the Bad & the Ugly" for effect. —*Jack Leaver*

Gene Vincent
b. Feb. 11, 1935, Norfolk, VA, d. Oct. 12, 1971, Los Angeles, CA
Guitar, Vocals / Rock & Roll, Rockabilly
Gene Vincent only had one really big hit, "Be-Bop-A-Lula," which epitomized rockabilly at its prime in 1956 with its sharp guitar breaks, spare snare drums, fluttering echo, and Vincent's breathless, sexy vocals. Yet his place as one of the great early rock & roll singers is secure, backed up by a wealth of fine smaller hits and non-hits that rate among the best rockabilly of all time. The leather-clad, limping, greasy-haired singer was also one of rock's original bad boys, lionized by romanticists of past and present generations attracted to his primitive, sometimes savage style and indomitable spirit. Vincent was bucking the odds by entering professional music in the first place. As a 20-year-old in the Navy, he suffered a severe motorcycle accident that almost resulted in the amputation of his leg, and left him with a permanent limp and considerable chronic pain for the rest of his life. After the accident he began to concentrate on building a musical career, playing with country bands around the Norfolk, VA, area. Demos cut at a local radio station, fronting a band assembled around Gene by his management, landed Gene Vincent & His Blue Caps a contract at Capitol, which hoped they'd found competition for Elvis Presley.

Indeed it had, as by this time Vincent had plunged into all-out rockabilly, capable of both fast-paced exuberance and whispery, almost sensitive ballads. The Blue Caps were one of the greatest rock bands of the '50s, anchored at first by the stunning silvery, faster-than-light guitar leads of Cliff Gallup. The slap-back echo of "Be-Bop-A-Lula," combined with Gene's swooping vocals, led many to mistake the singer for Elvis when the record first hit the airwaves in mid-1956, on its way to the Top Ten. The Elvis comparison wasn't entirely fair; Vincent had a gentler, less melodramatic style, capable of both whipping up a storm or winding down to a hush.

Brilliant follow-ups like "Race With the Devil," "Bluejean Bop," and "B-I-Bickey-Bi, Bo-Bo-Go" failed to click in nearly as big a way, although these too are emblematic of rockabilly at its most exuberant and powerful. By the end of 1956, the Blue Caps were beginning to undergo the first of constant personnel changes that would continue throughout the '50s, the most crucial loss being the departure of Gallup. The 35 or so tracks he cut with the band—many of which showed up only on albums or B-sides—were unquestionably Vincent's greatest work, as his subsequent recordings would never again capture their pristine clarity and uninhibited spontaneity.

Vincent had his second and final Top Twenty hit in 1957 with "Lotta Lovin'," which reflected his increasingly tame approach to production and vocals, the wildness and live atmosphere toned down in favor of poppier material, more subdued guitars, and conventional-sounding backup singers. He recorded often for Capitol throughout the rest of the '50s, and it's unfair to dismiss those sides out of hand; they were respectable, occasionally exciting rockabilly, only a marked disappointment in comparison with his earliest work. His act was captured for posterity in one of the best scenes of one of the first Hollywood films to feature rock & roll stars, *The Girl Can't Help It.*

Live, Vincent continued to rock the house with reckless intensity and showmanship, and he became particularly popular overseas. A 1960 tour of Britain, though, brought tragedy when his friend Eddie Cochran, who shared the bill on Vincent's U.K. shows, died in a car accident that he was also involved in, though Vincent survived. By the early '60s, his recordings had become much more sporadic and lower in quality, and his chief audience was in Europe, particularly in England (where he lived for a while) and France. His Capitol contract expired in 1963, and he spent the rest of his life recording for several other labels, none of which got him close to that comeback hit. Vincent never stopped trying to resurrect his career, appearing at a 1969 Toronto rock festival on the same bill as John Lennon, though his medical, drinking, and marital problems were making his life a mess, and diminishing his stage presence as well. He died at the age of 36 from a ruptured stomach ulcer, one of rock's first mythic figures. *—Richie Unterberger*

☆ **Bluejean Bop!** / Aug. 13, 1956 / Capitol ♦♦♦♦♦

Gene Vincent's very first album, cut in June 1956, was a rushed affair—which is obvious from the haphazard song selection—but manages to be one of the most exciting LPs to come out of the early rock & roll era, rivaling Elvis Presley's first two albums, which date from the same period. Its virtues, which is to say, the virtues of Gene Vincent & His Blue Caps as high energy rock & rollers, transcend the lack of quality songs on the album—the title hit is joined by some rocked up standards ("Lazy River," "Peg O' My Heart," and "Ain't She Sweet," which the Beatles picked up in their early repertory by way of Vincent, and made their first vocal recording five years later), a country ballad ("Wedding Bells") or two, and some hastily written rave-ups ("Jumps, Giggles and Shouts," etc.), little of it high-grade rock & roll material in and of itself. As it turned out, Vincent and his band didn't need first-rate songs to produce great rock & roll—they rise to the occasion here, throwing the hard rocking numbers into the air like the musical equivalent of jitterbug dancing, or stretching out elegantly on the handful of ballads, and the result is one of the few truly virtuoso rock & roll albums of the era. What sets *Bluejean Bop!* apart from Elvis' albums, in particular, and most other white rock & roll of the period, is that it has the tight sound of an actual working band, where Elvis' (and most other white rock & rollers') albums, in particular, almost inevitably featured session players whose presence helped make for an idealized recording, but not a good representation of how they sounded on-stage—which is what rock & roll was really about. Vincent and company, by contrast, were playing shows virtually every night during the period of these sessions. The sessions themselves were done in a hurry, without any help from studio musicians; and they were conducted with minimal input from producer Ken Nelson, who pretty much let the band do what came naturally. The result is a lean, tight sound, akin to a live recording—which this practically was—in terms of minimal retakes, lots of spontaneity, and no overdubbing. [*Bluejean Bop!* was reissued in 1998 by Collectables Records, paired off with Vincent's next album, *Gene Vincent & His Blue Caps*, on the same CD, as *Bluejean Bop/Gene Vincent & His Blue Caps*.] *—Bruce Eder*

☆ **Gene Vincent & His Blue Caps** / Mar. 4, 1957 / Capitol ♦♦♦♦♦

Gene Vincent & His Blue Caps, cut in October 1956, only four months after its predecessor, came about under slightly less favorable circumstances than the *Bluejean Bop!* album. Cliff Gallup, whose lead guitar had been so central to the group's original sound, and rhythm guitarist Willie Williams, who was only somewhat less important to their sound, had been gone from the band for nearly two months when producer Ken Nelson decided it was time to cut material for more singles and a second album. Gallup was persuaded to rejoin temporarily for the sessions that yielded this album, and with him he brought not only a hot-sounding instrument but one first-rate original song, "You Better Believe," alongside a few other notable band originals ("Cruisin'," "Hold Me, Hug Me, Rock Me") that are among the best songs Vincent and his band ever recorded. The sound ends up similar to the *Bluejean Bop!* album, with a little more depth in places and Vincent showing more maturity and confidence, which is how he gets away with "Unchained Melody," the most challenging ballad he'd cut up to that time—Gallup's trilled, mandolin-like playing (which turns up on "I Sure Miss You" as well) also serves to make this one of the more unusual and memorable of the many good versions of this song. Vincent's singing also stands out on his dark, moody, ominous rendition of the Delmore Brothers' "Blues Stay Away From Me." And the band runs circles around virtually every other white rock & roll outfit of the period. Unfortunately, *Gene Vincent & His Blue Caps* would also be the last time that this version of the band would turn up on record with Vincent—Gallup soon left again, and in less than three months, every member of the group except drummer Dickie Harrell would be gone. [In 1998, Collectables Records reissued this album, paired with *Bluejean Bop*, on *Bluejean Bop/Gene Vincent & His Blue Caps*.] *—Bruce Eder*

Gene Vincent Rocks! And the Blue Caps Roll / Mar. 18, 1958 / Capitol ♦♦♦♦

By the time of the December 1957 sessions that made up this, his third album, Gene Vincent's band had changed radically from its original lineup, with drummer Dickie Harrell the only original member (and even he wasn't long for the lineup). Johnny Meeks was the lead guitarist, and while he was a good player, he wasn't the kind of wildly inventive talent that Cliff Gallup had been; Meeks also had a cleaner sound, with none of the dark, almost dirty, blues-style licks that Gallup traded in. New rhythm guitarist Max Lipscomb (who later changed his professional name to Scotty McKay) doubled on piano, the first time that instrument was heard on a Gene Vincent record; Bobby Jones played bass, and former rhythm guitarist Paul Peek shifted to backing vocals alongside Tommy Facenda (collectively the two came to be known as the Clapper Boys). The changes resulted in a somewhat less frantic sound. The music was beautifully played and exciting, but a little bit tamer overall; the occasional wild shouts that punctuated the old band's playing were absent, and Vincent was indulging increasingly in softer pop and ballad material, which worked but also served to tone down the impact of the album. The music was still lively, but much more a creation of the studio than an offshoot of intense, raucous stage performances. *—Bruce Eder*

Shakin' Up a Storm / Oct. 1964 / EMI-Columbia ♦♦♦

Virtually everything on Gene Vincent's final EMI album, *Shakin' Up a Storm*, is superb, representing some of his best rock & roll from a decade in which he went years between albums. Cut with the backing group the Shouts and released only in England, *Shakin' Up a Storm* is an unusual record, containing elements of the burgeoning Merseybeat sound and soft-rock covers of country songs. The album (which has been reissued as part of EMI's *100th Anniversary* series, in glittering 24-bit sound) starts off well with a raucous "Hey Hey Hey," fueled by the fiery saxwork of Jim Field. It then switches gears on "Lavender Blue," a soft ballad that was more Elvis Presley's speed (though Vincent does surprisingly well, singing as softly as he knows how), before launching into the rockabilly-style "Private Detective," on which Tim Bates' lead guitar shines. "Shimmy Shammy Shingle" is a thumping number that, with a heavier bass sound, could've passed for a Liverpool-style rocker, and "Someday (You'll Want Me to Want You)" is a decent cover of a pop standard. Vincent's abilities as an R&B singer—showcased on his magnificent 1963 single "Where Have You Been All My Life"—are highlighted several times on *Shakin' Up a Storm*, most notably on a cover of Sam Cooke's "Another Saturday Night," on which Vincent's voice is richly expressive and the mix of rhythm guitar and organ accompaniment adds a nice, new wrinkle to the song. "Slippin' & Slidin'," featuring Bates' rippling lead guitar and a great vocal performance from Vincent, is a stomping rocker that could've passed for a first-rate Merseybeat track. Vincent also does well with "Send Me Some Lovin'," which allows him to stretch out vocally in front of a sax and rhythm guitar arrangement. "Love Love Love," with its multi-tracked vocals and bouncy rhythm guitar part, sounds like a direct attempt to emulate the Merseybeat sound. It opens a series of songs that ought to have given Vincent's detractors pause; he might not have charted a record in a couple of years when this album was issued—even in England—but he could still generate exciting music in almost any rock & roll idiom. "Baby Blue," co-authored by Vincent and featuring pounding support by the Shouts, sounds like it was snatched straight out of one of Gene's 1957 sessions. The producers could've ended *Shakin' Up a Storm* with the blazing "Suzie Q," but instead they threw on one more number, a hard-rocking rendition of Jimmie Davis' "You Are My Sunshine." Featuring Victor Clarke's heavy drumming, Field's honking sax, and a hot performance by organist Erik Baker, the song nonetheless belongs to Vincent, who transforms this country-pop classic into a serious rock & roll screamer. *—Bruce Eder*

Bop That Just Won't Stop / 1974 / Capitol ♦♦♦♦♦

This is a good distillation of 12 of Vincent's best early tracks. Subsequent compilations have included this material and much more. But this is one of the most consistent of the lot, eliminating a lot of the average stuff and focusing exclusively on tracks cut with the band's first and best lineup (with guitarist Cliff Gallup). Beware of later editions of the LP that, inexcusably, eliminated a couple of the better songs. *—Richie Unterberger*

Greatest Hits / 1982 / Onyx Classix ♦♦

The bare bones of Vincent's best work, with ten tracks including "Be-Bop-A-Lula," "Lotta Lovin'," "Bluejean Bop," and "Race With the Devil." It gets a comparably low rating not for the quality of the music (which is good), but its brevity. There's a much more thorough, slightly more expensive Gene Vincent best-of available (on Capitol) that can be found with a minimum of effort. *—Richie Unterberger*

The Capitol Years 1956–63 / 1987 / Charly ♦♦♦♦

While Vincent recorded a fair number of overlooked gems during his prime, he also cut a greater number of uninspired tracks. This lavishly packaged and exhaustively annotated ten-album set inadvertently charts the rapidly plummeting quality of his recordings, even as it unearths worthy obscurities. It does manage to gather all of his classic 1956 sessions with guitarist Cliff Gallup in the same place, but Gene's subsequent efforts could have easily been boiled down to a supplementary disc or two. *—Richie Unterberger*

The Last Session / 1987 / Dutch East India ♦♦♦

Rockabilly pioneer Gene Vincent never heard the fruits of his final in-studio labors, which Britain's state-run BBC station broadcast in November 1971. The timing was bittersweet, following his death at 36 from a bleeding ulcer, while he was hounded by creditors, ex-wives, and the gradual erosion of his professional fortunes. Vincent recorded these songs on October 1, 1971, shortly after arriving in Britain, which remained in his corner after other territories had fallen by the wayside. His biggest American hits, "Be-Bop-A-Lula" and "Say Mama," are naturally represented here, as is Chuck Berry's "Roll Over Beethoven." Vincent sounds much wispier than at his '50s peak, but he gamely drives himself along, while the band crackles beneath him; lead guitarist Richard Cole and keyboardist Dave Bailey prove to be the standouts. The most interesting track here is "Distant Drums," which the band hadn't played before; it's low-key, haunting, and perfectly suits Vincent's reduced vocal firepower. Vincent played his final gigs on October 3-4, 1971, after which he fled to the U.S. His death there barely a week later ensured his journey into legend, and the tradition of excavating any squeak of tape remotely associated with him. Liner notes and packaging are excellent, while the performance makes an interesting one-off addition to the canon, although for completists only. *—Ralph Heibutzki*

Into the Seventies . . . Plus / 1989 / See for Miles ✦✦✦
Gene Vincent's last albums—*If Only You Could See Me Today* and *The Day the World Turned Blue*—found him bidding to revive a status he'd achieved with his mid-'50s hit "Be-Bop-A-Lula." These releases tackled different styles to varying success, with inconsistent material being the main problem. The oddest and worst tracks are "Slow Times Comin'" and "Tush Hog," which take nearly 16 minutes between them; they're decently sung, but overwhelmed by clichéd, meandering wah-wah guitar solos. "Danse Colinda" is an equally ill-advised stab at Cajun music, while "Our Souls"' title gets twisted into a venomous dig at former manager Don Arden. Off-kilter arrangements spoil other tracks, such as the eccentric monologue shoehorned between the verses of "There Is Something on Your Mind" or the abrupt collapse of Vincent's galloping country-rock original, "The Woman in Black." The least-contrived moments work best; his aching remake of "500 Miles Away From Home" suggests that Vincent could have carved out a niche in country music, had he wanted it. Though less vocally powerful than his mid-'50s peak, Vincent was still a forceful interpreter of R&B (Brook Benton's "Looking Back on My Life") and his beloved rockabilly (Carl Perkin's "Boppin' the Blues"). And, though he only wrote or co-wrote 20 tracks, Vincent wasn't a bad songwriter, either. Five of them are on these albums, including "Geese," a sorrowful look at life behind bars, while "The Day the World Turned Blue" is a bittersweet salute to fallen rock & roll pioneer Buddy Holly. With better material and production choices, Gene Vincent's twilight era could have ended on a more upbeat note; this compilation supports the old adage of talent shining through regardless of setting. *—Ralph Heibutzki*

Capitol Collectors Series / 1990 / Capitol ✦✦✦✦✦
Gene Vincent may have been one of rock & roll's first great Dixie-fried wild men, but consistency was not his strong suit, and for every work of lunatic genius in his catalog (such as "B-I-Bickey-Bi, Bo-Bo-Go" and "Woman Love"), there are a few failed ballads and novelty tunes foisted upon him by clueless A&R men back in the day. This compilation from Capitol Records' fine *Collectors Series* line represents a noble and largely successful attempt to skim off the cream from his Capitol masters; while the material has been remixed for compact disc release, the new versions honor the sound and spirit of the original (though the mono versions have a shade more punch), and the track listing offers plenty of meat with little filler. While Razor & Tie's later collection *The Screaming End: The Best of Gene Vincent* rocks harder, *Capitol Collectors Series* in many ways offers a more accurate look at Vincent's career, with the wildness starting to seriously fade near the end of the disc without skidding into his really dire material. Even on the lesser tunes, Vincent's gloriously prurient vocals are upfront throughout, and the superb fretwork of Cliff Gallup, Paul Peek, and John Meeks prove the guy had *great* taste in guitar players. Added bonus: an instrumental take of "Rocky Road Blues" that will help make you the coolest person at karaoke night. *—Mark Deming*

Gene Vincent Box Set / 1994 / EMI ✦✦✦✦✦
Six CDs containing the complete Capitol and EMI-Columbia recordings by Vincent, from 1956 through 1964. The 151 tracks may seem excessive, but the sound glitters, and since most of the post-1962 material was never issued in the U.S., this stuff could be revelatory to serious fans. And the booklet is filled with detailed notes, sessionographies, and great photos. *—Bruce Eder*

The E.P. Collection / Mar. 19, 1996 / See for Miles ✦✦✦
This Gene Vincent import set on See for Miles collects several of the singer's U.K. EPs. Many of Vincent's lesser chart entries are present, including "Five Feet of Lovin'," "Baby Blue," "Lovely Loretta," and "Dance to the Bop." That's not saying this set doesn't contain enjoyable material ("Race With the Devil," for instance, is here), but it's not the cream of the crop. If you're looking for Vincent's biggest hit, "Be-Bop-A-Lula," it's included on *The EP Collection, Vol. 2.* A better purchase would be the single-disc *Screaming End: The Best of Gene Vincent* on Razor & Tie. *—Al Campbell*

★ **The Screaming End: The Best of Gene Vincent** / Jan. 21, 1997 / Razor & Tie ✦✦✦✦✦
The Screaming End: The Best of Gene Vincent & His Blue Caps contains 20 of Gene Vincent's very best songs, including all of his hit singles ("Be-Bop-A-Lula," "Race With the Devil," "Lotta Lovin'," "Wear My Ring," "Dance to the Bop") and several lesser-known but equally exciting singles and album tracks ("Bluejean Bop," "Crazy Legs," "Cruisin'," "Cat Man," "Who Slapped John," "Jump Back, Honey, Jump Back," "B-I-Bickey-Bi, Bo-Bo-Go," "Red Blue Jeans & a Ponytail"). *The Screaming End* may have one less song than *Capitol Collectors Series,* but it contains a stronger selection of material and the original mixes, plus a more infectious, listenable sequence, making it the defintiive single-disc overview of this rock & roll pioneer. *—Stephen Thomas Erlewine*

Bluejean Bop!/Gene Vincent & His Blue Caps / Apr. 7, 1998 / Collectables ✦✦✦✦
The first two Gene Vincent albums (which together run under an hour) paired on one CD are a real treat, chronicling a ferocious array of talent—not just Vincent as a singer, who started strong and improved dramatically between the two albums' songs, but Cliff Gallup and Willie Williams' hot lead and rhythm guitar pairing on the first dozen tracks, and some great virtuoso lyrical flourishes by Gallup on the second dozen tracks. Dickie Harrell's playing, heavy but always memorable on the snare, was also a sound that a lot of drummers (especially in England) sought to emulate, and Jack Neal and the original recording engineer managed to get one of the cleanest upright bass sounds to be found on rock & roll records of this period. See reviews of the individual LPs for the other virtues of this essential CD. *—Bruce Eder*

Gene Vincent Rocks! And the Blue Caps Roll/A Record Date with Gene Vincent / Apr. 7, 1998 / Collectables ✦✦✦✦
In 1998 Collectables reissued Gene Vincent's original Capitol LPs from 1957-1960 as a series of three two-fers, giving buyers an opportunity to hear most of Vincent's Capitol recordings without going to the trouble and expense of tracking down an import box set. The two 1958 LPs reissued on this CD contain no hits but lots of solid rockers and ballads in Vincent's characteristic style. The hits "Be-Bop-A-Lula" and "Race With the Devil" are included as bonus tracks for the convenience of anyone who doesn't already own a greatest-hits collection. If you like Gene Vincent, you'll enjoy practically everything here. *—Greg Adams*

Sounds Like Gene Vincent/Crazy Times / Apr. 7, 1998 / Collectables ✦✦✦✦
These two albums, from 1959 and 1960, respectively, find Gene Vincent staying the rock & roll course in the face of adverse trends. Teen idols—with their injection of classic pop arrangements and melody into rock music—increasingly held sway, while the style of Elvis Presley circa 1956 was in sharp decline. Vincent, unperturbed, kept cranking out excellent rockers in his established style as though the '50s would never end. To be fair, *Sounds Like Gene Vincent* reveals a little evolution; a couple of the soft ballads make use of a fairly lush vocal chorus, and the influence of Buddy Holly can be heard in places. But these developments are fleeting, and *Crazy Times* is a return to no-nonsense rock & roll. Wonderful music, although, from a commercial standpoint, Vincent was doomed. [Three hits are appended as bonus tracks: "Lotta Lovin'," "Wear My Ring," and "Dance to the Bop."] *—Greg Adams*

Lost Dallas Sessions 1957–1958 / May 19, 1998 / Dragon Street ✦✦✦✦
A major find in rockabilly history, the tapes and acetates comprising *The Lost Dallas Sessions 1957-1958* provide a missing piece of the puzzle to one of the genre's most inspired and prolific performers, Gene Vincent. After a year of whirlwind touring behind his hit, "Be-Bop-A-Lula," Vincent moved his band from Norfolk, VA, to Dallas, TX, and hooked up with the *Big D Jamboree* and Ed McLemore as his new manager. Ace guitarist Cliff Gallup had already left the fold, and Vincent was also assembling a new revamped version of the band. Replacing Gallup was guitarist Johnny Meeks, and these demo recordings from Sellers Company Recording Studio in Dallas feature him and the new Blue Caps lineup. The original version of "In My Dreams" is aboard, along with original stabs at "The Night Is So Lonely," "Lady Bug," and "Lonesome Boy." There are also home recordings of Vincent & His Blue Caps taking three swipes at "Lotta Lovin'" and another one of "In My Dreams," buttressed with demo versions of "On My Mind" and "Nervous," the latter two featuring only Vincent and Meeks. To flesh things out, there's a rip-roaring live performance of Vincent & His Blue Caps on the *Big D Jamboree* from the same period doing "Bluejean Bop," "Whole Lot of Shakin' Going On," "Dance to the Bop," and "Lotta Lovin'." As if this wasn't enough, there's also material from other '50s Vincent-connected artists who also left unreleased material behind at the Sellers studio, with tracks from Norton Johnson, Darrell Glenn, Bob Kelly, and Grady Owen completing this very essential package for the true rockabilly fanatic. *—Cub Koda*

EP Collection, Vol. 2 / Jul. 28, 1998 / See for Miles ✦✦✦✦
This Gene Vincent import set on See for Miles collects several of the singer's U.K. EPs. Many of Vincent's chart-topping entries are present, including "Bluejean Bop," "Woman Love," "B-I-Bickey-Bi, Bo-Bo-Go," and the number-one hit "Be-Bop-A-Lula." While this is a better-than-average set, it does omit a few titles that most fans want. A better purchase would be the single-disc *Screaming End: The Best of Gene Vincent* on Razor & Tie. *—Al Campbell*

The Legend at His Best / Apr. 4, 2000 / Collectables ✦✦✦
Gene Vincent recorded some of the hottest rockabilly during his short claim to fame in the late '50s, including the number one Elvis sound-alike "Be-Bop-A-Lula." By the early '60s, however, much like Presley, Vincent began recording material geared specifically toward a pop audience. On this 53-track box set of Capitol material, Vincent's rockabilly tracks—"Teenage Partner," "Race With the Devil," and "Bluejean Bop"—are essential, while his versions of "By the Light of the Silvery Moon," "You'll Never Walk Alone," "Hey, Good Lookin'," and "Summertime" aren't. This is recommended to Vincent fanatics. The average fan will be satisfied with the single-disc *Screaming End: The Best of Gene Vincent* on Razor & Tie. *—Al Campbell*

☆ **Gene Vincent & His Blue Caps [Bonus Tracks]** / Sep. 17, 2002 / Capitol ✦✦✦✦✦
Gene Vincent & His Blue Caps had a little more time to prepare their second, self-titled album than they had had for their first, *Bluejean Bop!* As a result, there were none of the ballad standards that had filled up the track list of that disc, alternating with the rockabilly tunes. *Gene Vincent & His Blue Caps* rocked more consistently than its predecessor, the only real exception being a cover of the much-recorded 1955 torch song "Unchained Melody." The rest of the time, Vincent and the band rocked out. Guitarist Willie Williams had been replaced by Paul Peek, and guitarist Cliff Gallup, although he had also left, had returned just for this recording, making the LP the final sessions by a near-original version of the Blue Caps. Gallup brought along a couple of songs, "You Told a Fib" and "You Better Believe," while others were contributed by Vincent and his partner, Tex Davis. But the material was less important than the approach, which was raucous rockabilly bop.

"Hold Me, Hug Me, Rock Me," for instance, was an example of unfettered rocking, with the band raging and Vincent howling. [The 2002 reissue adds five tracks to the album, but still brings the running time to only just over 40 minutes. The added tracks include both sides of Vincent's fifth single, "Bi-I-Bickey-Bi, Bo-Bo-Go" and "Five Days, Five Days," plus the first takes of "Important Words," "Teenage Partner," and "Five Feet of Lovin'," making an already excellent rockabilly workout even better.] *—William Ruhlmann*

☆ **Bluejean Bop! [Bonus Tracks]** / Sep. 17, 2002 / Capitol ✦✦✦✦✦
Gene Vincent & His Blue Caps' debut album, *Bluejean Bop!*, was rushed out in August 1956 just after his first and biggest single, "Be-Bop-A-Lula," had peaked in the Top Ten. The speed with which it had been assembled was apparent in the song selection. Vincent and Tex Davis had penned "Be-Bop-A-Lula" (or obtained it, anyway), but the songwriters turned up, together or in combination with others, on only four tracks of the LP (which did not feature the hit, an oversight corrected by the 2002 reissue), the title song, "Who Slapped John?," "Jumps, Giggles and Shouts," and "Bop Street." Augmenting the original material were some surprising covers, including the 1951 Frankie Laine hit "Jezebel," the 1920s Tin Pan Alley standards "Ain't She Sweet" and "Wedding Bells (Are Breaking Up That Old Gang of Mine)," the 1947 Roy Acuff country hit "Waltz of the Wind," Hoagy Carmichael's 1931 composition "Lazy River," and the *Ziegfeld Follies* song "Peg o' My Heart" from 1913. Such material served to broaden Vincent's appeal, demonstrating that he was more than just the hiccuping rockabilly cat of "Be-Bop-A-Lula," that he could handle ballads in his breathy, emotive voice in the manner of, say, Johnnie Ray. Nevertheless, it was the bop tunes that most appealed, especially because of the Blue Caps' spare, propulsive accompaniment. [The 2002 reissue expands the brief original album with half again as many bonus tracks, among them Vincent's second single, "Race With the Devil," and his fourth, "Crazy Legs." (His third single was the album's title song, so it was already present.) As such, the disc now contains Vincent's 1956 recordings, and they show him, if lacking the cocky authority of Elvis Presley, to possess an emotional commitment his Memphis rival never matched.] *—William Ruhlmann*

Rhonda Vincent

b. Jul. 1962, Kirksville, MO
Vocals, Mandolin, Fiddle / Contemporary Bluegrass, Progressive Bluegrass
Bluegrass vocalist and fiddler Rhonda Vincent began her professional music career at the age of five, playing drums with her family's band the Sally Mountain Show. She picked up the mandolin at eight and the fiddle at ten, performing with the family band at festivals on weekends. After appearing on TNN's nationally televised *You Can Be a Star* program in her mid-20s, Vincent struck out on her own, singing with the *Grand Ole Opry's* Jim Ed Brown, eventually leading to a deal with Rebel Records.

Her work with Brown and her Rebel recordings caught the attention of Giant Nashville's president James Stroud who signed Vincent to record two contemporary country albums. After her time at Giant, she moved to Rounder Records, and demonstrated her passion for the traditional music she grew up with on *Back Home Again.* A car accident in December 1999 kept her from a planned trip to Nashville for auditions, so she hired her band (unusually named the Rage) through the Internet. Rhonda Vincent and the Rage have been gaining popularity at bluegrass festivals since their formation, playing hard-driving, high energy contemporary bluegrass music. Her 2001 album *The Storm Still Rages* was nominated for seven International Bluegrass Music Association awards, including female vocalist of the year, while fiddle player Mike Cleveland and banjo player Tom Adams earned nominations in their respective instrumental categories. A three year unbroken string of IBMA "Female Vocalist of the Year" awards led to the 2003 release of *One Step Ahead*, another tour and another well-deserved showering of critical praise. *—Zac Johnson*

Dream Come True / 1990 / Rebel ✦✦✦✦

Timeless and True Love / 1991 / Rebel ✦✦✦✦✦

New Dreams & Sunshine / 1991 / Rebel ✦✦✦
On *New Dreams & Sunshine,* Vincent moves closer to the Nashville mainstream due to its emphasis on country ballads and slicker production values. *—Jason Ankeny*

Bound for Gloryland / 1991 / Rebel ✦✦✦

Written in the Stars / Oct. 26, 1993 / Giant ✦✦✦

● **Trouble Free** / 1996 / Warner Bros. ✦✦✦✦✦
Rhonda Vincent is a bluegrass prodigy who has been a favorite on the string band festival circuit for years. Her 1994 album for Giant Records found her being pushed a little too forcibly toward the country mainstream; still, on occasion, the specialness of her hard-country twang shined through. With *Trouble Free*, she fulfills her promise with soaring beauty. Co-producer (and Giant Records chief) James Stroud backs off and allows Vincent to explore a traditional country terrain that encompasses the fierce, severe magnificence of bluegrass and the sorrowful whine of honky tonk heartbreak. Vincent excels at both, showing the same kind of hard, soulful splendor that Keith Whitley displayed when he evolved from bluegrass to traditional country. Vincent's guests pretty much define her tastes: She performs a duet with Randy Travis—in his best performance in years—and, elsewhere, enjoys harmony support from Alison Krauss and Dolly Parton. Vincent and Krauss have been linked for years (Vincent was one a runner-up in a bluegrass contest that Krauss won). Krauss' commercial success certainly helped renew Giant's belief that Vincent, too, could attract a larger mainstream audience. But the two aren't that similar as vocalists. Where Krauss' voice is sweet and pure, Vincent's is twangy and aggressive. What they share is a commitment to musical integrity. *—Michael McCall*

Back Home Again / Jan. 11, 2000 / Rounder ✦✦✦
Rhonda Vincent's 17 albums have seen her journey from bluegrass to country and back to bluegrass again over the course of a career that began when she was just five. *Back Home Again* solidifies here position in the bluegrass community, which is where she truly belongs—her voice and musical skill never really fit well into the world of commercial country music. Vincent's greatest talent is as a vocalist, and her twangy sound is right at home on this album. On *Back Home Again*, she also plays mandolin on most tracks. She chooses her songs well, coming up with a collection of faith-tinged tunes about love and struggle, but at times her rendition of them seems a little fast and frantic. Bluegrass has a history of lightning-fast solos and chaotic jumbles of strings, but there are places on this album where a little more clarity could be achieved by simplification or a slight slow-down. Still, though, there are many highlights on the album: the touching "Little Angels," a cover of the great Dolly Parton song "Jolene," and "Out of Hand," which is performed with her father, Johnny, and brother, Darrin, recreating the sound that they had when they performed together during Rhonda's childhood as the Sally Mountain Show. *—Stacia Proefrock*

The Storm Still Rages / Jun. 5, 2001 / Rounder ✦✦✦✦
After spending several years languishing in Nashville, Rhonda Vincent made an unusual career move: she returned to bluegrass and recorded *Back Home Again* for Rounder in 2000. Garnering positive responses from critics and fans, Vincent knew she had made the right move. A cross between traditional and contemporary bluegrass, *The Storm Still Rages* features superb accompaniment and a handful of well-chosen songs. Vincent has also penned or co-penned several of the songs, including the opening cut, "Cry of the Whippoorwill." Her expressive vocal on the heartbreaker "Don't Lie" is lovingly underlined by Stuart Duncan's fiddle and Bryan Sutton's mandolin. Bassist Darrin Vincent, Rhonda's brother, adds harmony on a number of cuts, perfectly bringing each chorus into focus. There's a nice version of "I'm Not Over You," the song that inspired the album's title, with guest Rob Ickes on the Resophonic guitar, and a bluesy take on Hank Williams' "My Sweet Love Ain't Around." Although the arrangements vary quite a bit from song to song, banjoist Tom Adams and guitarist Sutton provide a steady base to work from. Complaints? Only that certain old-hoary classics like "Drivin' Nails in My Coffin" clash with Vincent's attractive vocals. It may be difficult for the listener to believe that this pretty voice is halfway to the grave from drinking rotgut. This aside, *The Storm Still Rages* should allow Vincent to take her place beside contemporary bluegrass alumni like Alison Krauss and Laurie Lewis. *—Ronnie D. Lankford Jr.*

My Blue Tears / Sep. 24, 2002 / Rebel ✦✦✦

One Step Ahead / Apr. 29, 2003 / Rounder ✦✦✦✦
Rhonda Vincent has so adeptly incorporated the sparkling production of the best contemporary bluegrass recordings with the heartfelt songwriting and passionate playing of the classic era of traditional bluegrass that her third album for Rounder hits that almost perfect balance: updated enough to not sound stuffy, but faithful enough to still sound honest. The leadoff track, "Kentucky Borderline," is an ol' fashioned train song along the lines of "Orange Blossom Special" or "Wabash Cannonball," and the title track (a duet with guest vocalist Alison Krauss) takes reverent cues from the Del McCoury Band in its tight harmonies and laid-back, bluesy solos. In context, the divorce-through-the-eyes-of-a-child song "Caught in the Crossfire" is only slightly maudlin, and the blistering trucker tribute "Ridin' the Red Line" is sung with such amphetamine-fueled conviction that very few female country singers could pull it off convincingly, but Vincent has the range (and the Rage) to perform both the dewy-eyed "Crossfire" and the fiery "Red Line" back to back. The group's warm, a cappella rendition of "Fishers of Men" is reminiscent of Doyle Lawson & Quicksilver's best gospel work, and their 20-second rip through the Martha White Flour song is a sly nod to Flatt & Scruggs and any other picker who has exchanged their music for a quick sponsorship to all of the "Health and Happiness" tonics throughout the years. Highlighted throughout by breakup waltzes, makeup stompers, '40s train songs, '70s trucker songs, and up-to-the-minute acoustic folk numbers, *One Step Ahead* is all over the place thematically, but right on the money stylistically. *—Zac Johnson*

The Volebeats

f. 1988, Detroit, MI
Group / Roots Rock, Alternative Country
Born in and around the Motor City in 1988, the Volebeats formed due to a mutual boredom of and displeasure for trendy bands and music. Starting as an acoustic outfit, lead guitarist/vocalist Matthew Smith and vocalist/guitarist Jeff Oakes began writing songs with Terry Rohm and Jeff's brother Al. With Keir McDonald (from Detroit's Medusa Cyclone) on drums, the Volebeats began performing on street corners throughout the Detroit suburbs. For the first few years of its existence, the band had a revolving group of musicians that included another Oakes brother, Brian, on upright bass, drummer Mike Murphy and guitarist Mark Niemenski (both from another Detroit band Hysteric Narcotics), drummer Bill Peterson, and Rebecca Kaplan on fiddle. Fusing hardcore country and folk music with a melodic pop flair and rock & roll sensibility, the Volebeats released their debut *Ain't No Joke* on Relapse Records in 1989, with current guitarist and songwriter Bob McCreedy—who had played with Oakes in the Frames in 1981—joining the group shortly thereafter.

Over the next few years they recorded a single for Icon Records and could be found on various compilations. Then in 1994, the Volebeats signed with the Safe House label, releasing their second full-length, *Up North*, which garnered the group critical acclaim. A six-song EP, *Bittersweet*, was released in 1995 and featured a cover of Barry White's "I'm Gonna Love You Just a Little More, Baby." With drummer Scott Michalski and bassist Russell Ledford joining the band, the Volebeats' lineup was solidified as the group entered the studio to record its 1997 release, *The Sky and the Ocean.* Two years later, the group issued *Solitude*, and their 2001 release, *Mosquito Spiral*, featured pop and psych influences that recalled Medusa Cyclone and Smith's other band, Outrageous Cherry. *—Jack Leaver*

Ain't No Joke / 1989 / Gadfly ✦✦✦
The CD reissue of the Volebeats' debut album (originally released on the Relapse label in 1989) will probably be most appealing to those who already love the band. The

production is scrappy, more like a demo than a professional recording, and the same is unfortunately true of the singing. The danger of making twangy country-rock is that unless you play really, really well, your music is going to be received as parody, and that's exactly what the uncertain vocals and clumsy two-step rhythm of "And You Know It" sounds like. Ditto for "Fool's Castle" and the plodding "Magic Town." "Everytime I Smoke a Smoke" is both better sung and better played, and "Halfway to Nowhere" is even better. Two of the three bonus tracks, however, are even worse than the missteps on the original program. Recommended for completist fans only. —*Rick Anderson*

Up North / 1994 / Safe House ✦✦✦✦

A folky, country record that's inviting and likable in its simple and uncomplicated presentation. Songs of longing, such as "Back in Your Heart," are driven with the locomotive shuffle of brushes on a snare, and garnished with the lonesome cry of a lap steel or Smith's single tremolo lead guitar lines. But what really elevates this record is songwriting that is ripe with memorable melodic content and an acute sense of lyrical phrasing. But just as important is the way in which the two principle writers and singers Jeff Oakes and Matthew Smith work off of each other vocally. Whether in unison or tight harmony, together or in counterpart fashion, their voices, backed by the low-key instrumentation, create a mood that captivates and brings these deceptively simple songs to life. —*Jack Leaver*

Bittersweet / 1995 / Third Gear ✦✦✦✦

A six-song EP, *Bittersweet* contains well-written and pleasing country/folk songs with Oakes and Smith's vocals delivering the same pure and unpretensious charm that made *Up North* such a great record. The arrangements are simple, but affecting; plus, you get a intriguing and darkly seductive cover of Barry White's "I'm Gonna Love You Just a Little More, Baby." —*Jack Leaver*

● **The Sky and the Ocean** / Mar. 7, 1997 / Safe House ✦✦✦✦✦

Detroit's Volebeats' third full-length album is a standout effort, demonstrating that their songwriting chops just continue to improve with each album. Once again bandmembers Jeff Oakes (vocals), Matthew Smith (lead guitar, vocals) and Bob McCreedy (guitar, vocals), serve up unforgettable melodic hooks with thoughtful lyrical content. The Volebeats' arrangements are uncluttered and the laid-back, acoustic-based country/folk grooves are embellished mainly by Smith's haunting Shadows-style lead guitar. And that style is particularly gripping on the stunning title track, underscoring artful lyrics with a eerie musical vibe that resembles a '60's movie theme. The band steps it up on an uncharacteristic, although fittingly welcome, rockabilly-tinged number "Warm Weather," which features some rollicking, ivory-tickling by one-time bandmember Keir McDonald. Although any of

the group's records would be a worthwhile choice, *The Sky and the Ocean* showcases an extremely ear-pleasing and talented band that has hit its stride. —*Jack Leaver*

Solitude / May 4, 1999 / Safe House ✦✦✦

Detroit's Volebeats specialize in a sort of classic pop (à la the Walker Brothers) form of north woods country music. Each record is a statement of bittersweet longing couched in lovely harmonies, ringing guitar waves, and bountiful tides of reverb. However, if not the "bitter" half of bittersweet, *Solitude* may at least be the road map toward the dark side of Middle America. The album is bookended by the instrumentals "Desert Song" and "Music Box"—the latter an exercise in collapsing wide open spaces, the former a muslin-wrapped sepia-toned portrait of a Main Street dime store gone ghost town. In between, the Volebeats work in their familiar palette of dual vocals (the angelic twang of Jeff Oakes and the plaintive '60s-tinged croon of Matthew Smith, both in fine, subdued form here), echo chamber sonics worthy of any pipeline-riding surf outfit (but at quarter speed and recorded in the depths of February), and the muted wallop of Scott Michalski's drumming (itself a main character in many of the songs' casts of sounds). The Volebeats often border on bleak but never give in to the darkness, even when exploring the maddening inner dialogue of traitorous love lost, as on "Back in a Minute," amidst the backdrop of "cold nights and scattered stars." There's always the comfort in sadness. And, when the suburbs of Detroit with their bleak, seemingly interminable winters and endless, intertwining highways are the environment in which your psyche is formed and your songs are crafted, borderline bleak is totally honest. There are moments of instrumental joy here, or at least nods toward rocking out for fun and frolic—such as the Link Wray-esque "Speed Boat." But on *Solitude*, the prevailing winds blow toward the kind of sentiments expressed on "Just as You Are Beautiful"—unrequited love observed with painful detail. No depression? The Volebeats may have redefined the term with *Solitude*. —*Chris Handyside*

Mosquito Spiral / 2000 / Third Gear ✦✦✦✦

New country sounds not found on the FM dial hold the interest of both the converted and ears from the alternative rock, indie, and singer/songwriter streams. Often lumped into this category, the Volebeats strive as much for affinity with classic Canadian pop. Blurring distinctions, their excellent release *Mosquito Spiral* is quintessential song-oriented craft. To ears raised on pop and rock there will be something rural about these unpretentious songs that achieve so much success through delicate harmony vocals and acoustic arrangement. The Volebeats transform each simple theme of lost love, nostalgia, and more to heart-inscribing sonic memorabilia that could be the unforgettable piece playing during the credits of that worldview-changing film of character transformation you saw last summer. —*Tom Schulte*

The Waco Brothers

f. Chicago, IL

Group / Indie Rock, Alternative Country-Rock, Alternative Country, Americana

The Waco Brothers were one of many projects spearheaded by Jon Langford, the frontman of the seminal British punk band the Mekons. An alternative country outfit based in Langford's adopted home of Chicago, the Waco Brothers essentially grew out of mid-'80s Mekons records like *Fear and Whiskey* and *The Mekons Honky Tonkin'*, which explored the group's interest in roots music. After the Mekons eventually returned to a more straightforward, punk-flavored sound, the Waco Brothers emerged over a decade later as a vehicle for Langford's long-dormant country leanings; fusing honky tonk and rockabilly with Langford's typically political lyrics, they issued their debut, *To the Last Dead Cowboy*, in 1995. *Cowboy in Flames* followed in 1997 and *Electric Waco Chair* was issued in fall 2000. *—Jason Ankeny*

To the Last Dead Cowboy / Sep. 5, 1995 / Bloodshot ✦✦✦

Give Jon Langford four hours with nothing to do and chances are good he'll create another side project, and at first the Waco Brothers sounded like yet another way for Langford and his drinking buddies to pass the time while the Mekons got it together to make another album. (Langford himself has said the Waco Brothers were originally put together to play gigs for beer at their favorite Chicago watering holes.) But *To the Last Dead Cowboy* also made it clear Langford was in inspired form writing in a more explicitly country style than he'd managed during the Mekons' twangy period; if "Sometime I Wonder" and "Bad Times (Are Comin' Round Again)" don't exactly sound like the stuff of current Nashville hits, that's exactly the point, and they cut deeper to the heart of C&W's dark and reckless soul than anything Garth Brooks or Shania Twain could ever dream of (and "Plenty Tuff, Union Made" is one of the few really great labor anthems of the 1990s). Also, Langford had collaborators who could pull their weight in the songwriting department—Dean Schlabowske contributes several winners, including "Harm's Way" and "If You Don't Change Your Mind," and Tracy Dear turned in "Too Sweet To Die" and "K.T. Tennessee." *To the Last Dead Cowboy* has a looser, more casual sound than later Waco Brothers releases, and at this point they sounded a bit more like goof than a real band. But they were already a truly inspired goof, and it set the stage for the great work they would record soon afterward. *—Mark Deming*

● **Cowboy in Flames** / Jan. 28, 1997 / Bloodshot ✦✦✦✦

On *To the Last Dead Cowboy*, the Waco Brothers sounded like one of Jon Langford's better side projects; on *Cowboy in Flames*, they sounded like a real band, and a damn good one at that, and that made all the difference in the world. A year and a half of gigging around the Midwest had given substance to the Wacos claim of being "the World's Tuffest Country Band," while the full-time addition of Mark Durante on steel guitar reinforced the twang in their tone as Langford and Dean Schlabowske kicked up the wattage on their guitars. The working-class rage that bubbled under the surface of the first album came to a full boil on *Cowboy in Flame*, and that passion fueled the sweaty, urgent rage of the best cuts, especially "See Willy Fly By," "Take Me to the Fires," and the title cut. At the same time, the band proved the could slow things down and still make their music connect, as "Dollar Dress" and "Dry Land" eloquently testify. The inspired covers (supercharged arrangements of "White Lightning" and "Wreck on the Highway") make clear the band's nitro-fueled take on classic country comes from a place of love and respect, and the final cut, "Death of Country Music," speaks volumes about what's wrong with the current state of mainstream C&W (and, by extension, American culture). Some wag once described the Waco Brothers as "half Cash, half Clash," and, on *Cowboy in Flames*, they sound strong enough to make good on both halves of that equation. A triumph, and one of the finest albums to emerge from the Chicago alt-country scene. *—Mark Deming*

Do You Think About Me? / Sep. 9, 1997 / Bloodshot ✦✦✦✦

Listening to *Do You Think About Me?* is like riding a mechanical bull. It doesn't last very long, but it makes you hold on for dear life. Clocking in at just over 30 minutes, *Do You Think About Me?* features the the Waco Brothers' exhilarating and indescribable hybrid of country and punk. Some of the tracks on the album remain from their previous acclaimed albums, *To the Last Dead Cowboy* and *Cowboy in Flames*, but they don't feel like refried leftovers. "South Bend" and "Got to Be Someone" sound like tributes to Keith Richards. The group also pay homage to the Clash in their blistering cover version Neil Young's "Revolution Blues." Lest you think the group is forgetting its country roots, they pull out quaint ditties like the steel-pedaled "Hard Times" and "Arizona Rose." The result is an album that's impossible to classify. Whatever it is, if you're going to listen to it, make sure to hold on to something that's bolted to the floor. *—Jon Azpiri*

Wacoworld / Feb. 23, 1999 / Bloodshot ✦✦✦

Jon Langford's punk roots are showing more than usual on this uneven disc (after all, he also fronts the Mekons). But while the rock edge of "Pigsville" is nice to hear, his obsession with all things cowboy begins to sound silly after a time with his Manchester accent. While the Mekons' "Honky Tonkin'" was a charming tip of the hat, it sounds like the English cowboy gag is wearing thin. *—Tim Sheridan*

Electric Waco Chair / 2000 / Bloodshot ✦✦✦✦

As the Waco Brothers mature into a real band rather than just another of Jon Langford's many side projects, Dean Schlabowske and Tracy Dear have tried to carry a greater amount of the songwriting weight, and their sound has taken on a more individual personality, rather than the "Mekons-with-a-twang-and-faster-tempos" sound of their debut. This didn't work out so well on 1999's *Waco World*, a somewhat muddled set that lacked the fire and focus of the group's best work, but *Electric Waco Chair* finds the Wacos firmly back on track; Schlabowske and Dear are learning to deliver material just as strong as Langford's always top-shelf work (especially "Jamaican Radio Obituary" and "Fox River"), and the band sounds tighter, stronger, and more expressive than ever before (the three live cuts also testify to the Wacos undeniable strength on-stage). If *Electric Waco Chair* offers a bit less pure fury than the Waco Brothers' high-water mark, *Cowboy in Flames*, from a musical standpoint it finds this band sounding better than ever before, and their rabble-rousing anger is still very much in evidence if you're looking for it; the Waco Brothers are one of the very best bands to emerge from the alt-country scene, and this album proves they're only getting better with time. *—Mark Deming*

New Deal / Oct. 22, 2002 / Bloodshot ✦✦✦✦

The Wagoneers

Group / Alternative Country

The Wagoneers came out of Austin, TX, during the 1980s with a sound that quickly attracted a following among traditionalists as well as the rockabilly crowd. Made up of Austin favorite Monte Warden on lead vocals and rhythm guitar, Brent Wilson playing lead and contributing backing vocals, Craig Allan Pettigrew on bass, and drummer Thomas A. Lewis Jr., the Wagoneers opened the floodgates for what was to be known as alternative country. Throwing a fist in the face of Nashville's manufactured hat-act syndrome, the Wagoneers created a very loud buzz. With a first successful release on Herb Alpert's A&M Records, *Stout & High*, they filled a void that had been overlooked. After making a big splash, the Wagoneers followed up with a second CD that quickly vanished from memory. However, their contribution to the never-ending search for real country music places them in the history books alongside other bands like the Lonesome Strangers, the Georgia Satellites, the Derailers, and another Texas act, High Noon. The band eventually disintegrated and Warden went on to a solo career that depended more on pop music rather than the traditional country & western that fit his vocal style so well. *—Jana Pendragon*

● **Stout & High** / 1988 / A&M ✦✦✦✦✦

An exceptional debut from the Wagoneers, an Austin-based quartet that combined edgy country and rockabilly. Led by lead singer and principle songwriter Monte Warden, the Wagoneers' sound borrowed heavily from the country leanings of Buddy Holly and his teenage collaboration with fellow Texan Bob Montgomery. Warden has a magnetism which jumps from the grooves, and lead guitarist Brent Wilson adds tight harmony à la Bob to Buddy, or Phil to Don Everly, and capably sings lead on his own "Lie and Say You Love Me." Aficionados of pedal steel guitar will delight in the understated but expressive playing by veteran Katon Roberts. There really isn't a weak cut here, and co-label head and legendary trumpet player Herb Alpert even lends his legendary trumpet—in a magnificent Tex-Mex solo flourish—at the intro of the title track, a story song about the historic fall of the Alamo. Although the band had a minor hit with "I Wanna Know Her Again," the band broke up after two albums and Warden went on to a solo career and followed more of a rootsy/pop muse, but he sounds the most natural singing the country stuff. The first country album released by A&M, the Wagoneers were a precursor to kindred but more successful bands like the Mavericks. Produced by notable Nashville producer Emory Gordy Jr., if this record had been released three or four years later, it might have stood a better commercial chance. *—Jack Leaver*

Good Fortune / 1989 / A&M ✦✦

Coming on the heels of their premiere hit CD, *Stout & High*, this second release is more than just disappointing. The band that had taken traditional country & western music by the boot straps and brought it back into the limelight failed miserably to repeat their hat trick a second time. While the talent is there, the energy and enthusiasm are not. At best, this is a third-rate recording that appears to have been done in a hurry with little or no concern for the end result. Sadly, the production is more in tune to pop music, and lead singer Monte Warden's leanings in that direction are killing to the original spirit of the Wagoneers. As if an omen of what was to come, the album starts off with a Warden-Mas Palermo co-write that seemingly reflects Warden's plans for a solo career. Still, there are moments when the band comes around. Ahead of their time and making every cut count on *Stout & High*, they recapture their foresight on "Por Favor Senior," which foreshadows the early sound of future Nashville hitmakers the Mavericks. An all-star lineup of talent makes the failure of this project all the more baffling. Sleepy LaBeef, Glen Duncan, Glen D. Hardin, and pedal steel provided by Kayton Roberts should add up to success. Warden, always the main songwriter, exhibits some of the old zest when he joins six-string bassist Craig Pettigrew in the writing of "Take Me." The predecessors of the likes of Big Sandy and His Fly-Rite Boys, High Noon, and the Lucky Stars will always be regarded as pioneers who point back to tradition, substance, and real country & western music the way it's supposed to be done in spite of their drastic plunge into oblivion. —*Jana Pendragon*

Porter Wagoner

b. Aug. 12, 1927, West Plains, MO

Songwriter, Vocals / Traditional Country, Country-Pop, Nashville Sound/Countrypolitan
Porter Wagoner, the Thin Man from West Plains, MO, is a case of an artist often ahead of his time who has always appeared hopelessly behind the times. He's among the most immediately recognizable figures in country music, largely due to his exploiting TV—and flashy costumes—a good 20 years before the video boom. And while he's forever perceived as the man who tried to hold Dolly Parton back from pop success, he was also responsible, in many ways, for putting her in a career position where the issue could even arise. As for his music, since signing with RCA in 1952 he has produced a wealth of superb hard country, and just as much of the most wretchedly oversentimentalized tripe you'll ever want to hear. The latter, of course, is half the reason we love him.

Wagoner was born in West Plains, MO. As he grew up, he fell in love with the country music he heard over the radio, teaching himself guitar so he could sing and play along with them. When he was a teenager, he landed a job at a local market, where he would frequently sing when business was slow. The owner believed that Porter's singing was actually helping the store's reputation, so he arranged to sponsor a local radio show that would feature the fledgling vocalist. Throughout the late '40s, Wagoner was singing on the local West Plains radio station. Eventually, a Springfield radio station called KWTO offered Porter a show in 1951. Around the same time, Red Foley was beginning his *Ozark Jamboree* program, which was based in Springfield and broadcast both on KWTO and national television. Foley brought Wagoner onto his show, which helped the young vocalist land a record contract with RCA Records. In 1954, his ninth single "Company's Comin'" hit the Top Ten. It was followed in the spring of 1955 with "A Satisfied Mind," which stayed at number four for four weeks. At the end of the year he released "Eat, Drink, and Be Merry (Tomorrow You'll Cry)," which climbed to number three in early 1956. In 1957, he joined the *Grand Ole Opry* and moved to Nashville, where he formed his backing band, the Wagonmasters.

For the rest of the '50s, Porter continued to record, but he never broke the Top Ten again. It would take another television show for him to return to the top of the charts. In 1961, he began hosting his own television show, which was syndicated out of Nashville. It was the most popular country show of the '60s, growing from 18 stations in 1961 to over a hundred stations in the early '70s. Wagoner often sang with Norma Jean, a new female singer he introduced to the country audience, on these programs. The look of Porter's television show defined country music for much of America's general public during the '60s, although his music rarely departed from traditional country. In 1967, Norma Jean was fired from the show and replaced by Dolly Parton, who was then an unknown singer. Not only did exposure on Wagoner's program kick-start Parton's career, it provided a boost for Porter's as well. Parton was enormously popular on the show and their first joint single, "The Last Thing on My Mind," rocketed to number seven at the beginning of 1968. The song launched a string of Top Ten hits that ran more or less uninterrupted until 1975, when the duo stopped working together. In 1968, the Country Music Assocaition named the duo the Vocal Group of the Year; the CMA would award them Vocal Duo of the Year in 1970 and 1971, as well.

Although the duo of Wagoner & Parton was successful, it wasn't stress-free. Porter continued to have solo hits during the late '60s and early '70s, though none of them were as big as his songs with Parton. Furthermore, he resented her attempts at a solo career; on her part, she felt musically restrained by him. The tensions culminated in late 1974, when she parted ways with Wagoner. RCA issued two singles in 1975 and 1976, and both of the songs—"Say Forever You'll Be Mine" and "Is Forever Longer Than Always"—hit the Top Ten. The pair would continue to duet sporadically over the next decade, highlighted by the number two hit, "Making Plans," from 1980. After Parton and Wagoner separated in 1975, Porter continued to film his TV show and to chart singles, but all of his hits were minor. In 1976, he retired from touring, choosing to concentrate on producing a his own studio, Fireside. Wagoner sued Parton in 1979 over various contractual problems; the suit was settled out of court the following year. For the first few years of the '80s, Porter had several minor hits, but he stopped recording in 1983.

In 1981, Wagoner and RCA Victor parted ways after nearly 30 years, and his television show went off the air. He mounted a minor comeback in 1982, appearing in the Clint Eastwood film *Honkytonk Man* and recording an album, *Viva Porter Wagoner*, for Eastwood's label imprint at Warner Bros. Records, Viva, that made the country charts and produced a couple of minor country singles chart entries. After that, he only made occasional recordings for small labels. He toured with the Right Combination, an all-girl band, for several years. In the late '80s and early '90s, he became increasingly active on the Nashville Network, to the point that Opryland named him its "Goodwill Ambassador" and he was a regular host of the *Grand Ole Opry* radio and television programs. In July 2000, he released his first new album in many years, *The Best I've Ever Been*. —*Dan Cooper & Stephen Thomas Erlewine*

Satisfied Mind / 1956 / RCA Victor ✦✦✦✦✦
This is a common vinyl sampling of Porter's raw-boned early sound. The title cut, from 1955, was his first number-one hit. It also has "Company's Comin'," in which he makes the arrival of dinner guests sound as exciting in the current context as logging onto the Internet. —*Dan Cooper*

Slice of Life—Songs Happy 'n' Sad / 1962 / RCA Victor ✦✦✦✦✦

Sing Duets / 1962 / RCA Victor ✦✦✦

The Porter Wagoner Show / 1963 / RCA Victor ✦✦✦✦✦

Porter Wagoner in Person / 1964 / Koch ✦✦✦✦
One of the earliest live LPs released by a country musician, *In Person* documents a rousing Porter Wagoner show direct from his hometown of West Plains, MO. Produced for release by Chet Atkins and also featuring Norma Jean on several songs, the album includes favorites like "Foggy Mountain Top," "An Old Log Cabin for Sale" and "Come on In (And Make Yourself at Home)." —*John Bush*

The Thin Man From West Plains / 1965 / RCA Victor ✦✦✦✦✦

An Old Log Cabin for Sale / 1965 / RCA Camden ✦✦✦✦
Though it doesn't have any major hits, *An Old Log Cabin* contains several excellent performances from Porter Wagoner, including "Everything She Touches Gets the Blues," "Dear Lonesome" and the title track. —*Thom Owens*

Confessions of a Broken Man / 1966 / RCA Victor ✦✦✦✦
Not the coolest of the cool among you can hear the aformentioned "Skid Row Joe" without a lump rising in your throat to interrupt your laughter. —*Dan Cooper*

The Best of Porter Wagoner / 1966 / RCA ✦✦✦✦✦
The Wagonmasters could drive as hard as any backup band of the day, and this set shows it on cuts like "Y'all Come (You All Come)." Meanwhile, good ol' Porter could be as morbid as any singer of his day. Witness "Misery Loves Company," "Green, Green Grass of Home," and "Skid Row Joe." —*Dan Cooper*

Your Old Love Letters & Other Country Hits / 1966 / RCA Camden ✦✦✦
Your Old Love Letters features several excellent country ballads, including the title song and "Out of Sight Out of Mind." It also has its share of filler, but there's enough fine moments to make the LP a worthwhile bargain-bin purchase. —*Thom Owens*

Live on the Road / 1966 / RCA Victor ✦✦✦

Soul of a Convict & Other Great Prison Songs / 1967 / RCA Victor ✦✦✦✦✦

The Cold Hard Facts of Life / 1967 / RCA Victor ✦✦✦✦
Good, straight-ahead country is one reason to hunt for this LP. The other reason is the album cover—a near-consensus choice as the hillbilly graphics howler of all time. Write to your congressman to get this back in print as is. —*Dan Cooper*

More Grand Old Gospel / 1967 / RCA Victor ✦✦✦

Porter Wagoner Sings Ballads of Heart & Soul / 1967 / Camden ✦✦✦

The Silent Kind / 1967 / Camden ✦✦✦
Preserving the cover photo of Porter with a blond pompadour and wearing a psychedelic print shirt, *The Silent Kind* is a budget CD reissue of the original 1967 album of the same name. In addition to "The Cold Hard Facts of Life," a tale of adultery and murder that reached number two on the C&W charts, *The Silent Kind* includes a few notable tracks, including "One More Dime" and a version of Bill Monroe's "Uncle Pen." The remainder of this brief album is heavy on recitations, which slow things down considerably. For fans and completists, *The Silent Kind* has its modest charms; for others, its rewards may be too slight. —*Greg Adams*

The Bottom of the Bottle / 1968 / RCA Victor ✦✦✦✦

Just Between You and Me / 1968 / RCA Victor ✦✦✦

The Carroll County Accident / 1969 / RCA Victor ✦✦✦

Me and My Boys / 1969 / RCA Victor ✦✦✦✦

Always, Always / Aug. 16, 1969 / RCA Victor ✦✦✦

You Got-ta Have a License / 1970 / RCA Victor ✦✦✦✦
In 1970, Porter Wagoner still sounded a lot like he did in 1965. Behind Bob Ferguson's production, Wagoner embraced the countrypolitan ethic to the nth degree, but there was something in his voice that couldn't be cosmopolitan—it was too country, a bit too hayseed and backwoods. The way he wrote songs and performed them was singular. His particular brand of psychobilly presented as sentimental country songs—"Roses Out of Season," "Stranger's Story," "Little Boy's Prayer"—is genuinely off the rail. They are done without a hint of humor or distance and Wagoner is committed to the music, to these lyrics, and most of all to his delivery of them, as he comes across as authentic, unwavering, and scary as hell—remember "Rubber Room"? Wagoner's willingness to accept the role of downtrodden yet innocent outsider is eclipsed only by his pride in it. "Southern Bound," a rambling honky tonk song, reflects a country boy's determination to get home to a sweetheart after working in the city for a day too long. "My Special Prayer" is one of the most twisted songs about alcoholism and neglectful parenting ever written. The dark side is where Wagoner goes when he wants to feel comfortable. But he's always on optimism's glimmering side. The title cut by Tommy Collins is hilarious in that it combines rockabilly, honky tonk, and calypso music in a tale of a fishing expedition gone wrong. All of Wagoner's albums from the period beginning in 1962 through 1974 are consistently amazing for their brutal honesty, corniness, and commitment to the country sh*tkicker ethic. Amazing. —*Thom Jurek*

Skidrow Joe—Down in the Alley / 1970 / RCA Victor ✦✦✦✦
This LP is worth seeking out—as so many of Porter Wagoner's are—just for the cover, which shows him with reverse Grecian formula in his hair, dressed in skid row clothes, standing outside the old Ryman circa 1970, with an empty pint bottle behind him, hat in hand, looking insane. It's funnier than hell. Like "The Rubber Room" from the mid-'60s, this is a theme album on the horrors, reasons, and solutions for drinking. As Skid Row Joe himself puts it in the liner notes: "Here are some thoughts and sights that go on in a wino's mind—a man that drinks to ease the pain." There are the amazing spoken word dialogues such as Wagoner's own "The Silent Kind," delivered in the first person, or

"The Sidewalks of Chicago" written by Dave Kirby, which was a minor hit for Merle Haggard in the '60s. There's also a stunning version of Dolly Parton's gem "The Alley" that Wagoner delivers without irony or humor, but stark, blistering emotion. On the flip Wagoner does justice to two more Parton songs, "One More Dime" and the closer, which is the most devastating thing on the set, "When I Drink My Wine." Charlie Alridge's "Mama" restates the alleged reason for Skid Row Joe's existence—or lack of—with "Mama" and the unlikely choice of Tom Paxton's "Bottle of Wine," later covered by the rock band the Fireballs, and Johnny Mullin's "I Judged a Man" is the album's best morality play. In all, Wagoner succeeds again on another of his concept albums. He lends both humor and pathos to his subject and delivers all of it without a trace of irony or cynicism. This is honky tonk music all right, but it may make you think twice about hanging out in them so often. *—Thom Jurek*

Porter Wagoner & Dolly Parton / 1970 / RCA Victor ✦✦✦✦✦

Two of a Kind / 1971 / RCA Victor ✦✦✦✦
Whereas *The Essential Porter Wagoner and Dolly Parton* collects 20 of the pair's Top 40 C&W hits, *Two of a Kind* includes only nine. The rest of the songs on this 20-track CD are lesser hits and album tracks that do not overlap with the *Essential* disc. Consequently, fans of Porter and Parton's feudin' and fightin' duets may find it worthwhile to add this disc to their collection for the 11 exclusive tracks. Of these songs, "Fight & Scratch" is alone worth the price of the disc. As an anthology for the curious, *Two of a Kind* is too idiosyncratic to be definitive, but the obscurities make it worthwhile. *—Greg Adams*

Simple as I Am / 1971 / RCA Victor ✦✦✦

Porter Wagoner Country / 1971 / Camden ✦✦
Porter Wagoner's adherence to rural themes and hard country music in the Nashville sound era made him a hero for those who take their country straight. The notes accompanying *Porter Wagoner Country* theorize about what makes a Wagoner song (it comes "straight out of the country music tradition") before offering ten songs spanning Wagoner's career from the '50s through the late '60s. "I've Enjoyed as Much of This as I Can Stand" is the only hit, but the moody "Out of the Silence (Came a Song)" is an intriguingly dark number about being grateful for what you've got, and "I Haven't Seen Mary in Years" is similarly melancholic. Two early cuts, "I Guess I'm Crazy" and "Tricks of the Trade," are stylistically dissimilar—particularly where Wagoner's singing is concerned—and are unfortunately muffled from the reprocessed stereo effect. *Porter Wagoner Country* is a disposable item in Wagoner's catalog, but has several worthwhile cuts for those who don't already own the original albums from which they're drawn. *—Greg Adams*

What Ain't to Be, Just Might Happen / 1972 / RCA Victor ✦✦✦
During the boom years of the Nashville sound, country veteran Porter Wagoner was riding high with his popular TV variety show, scoring hits and releasing bizarre solo efforts like *What Ain't to Be, Just Might Happen.* Dating back to 1968's *Bottom of the Bottle* and 1970s *Skid Row Joe,* Wagoner's taste for loose concept albums finds fresh legs with this record's gallery of insane drifters. While the town loon is given the humanistic treatment on "Wally the Weirdo," those really beyond the pale are found running into walls and conjuring rhymes in the "Rubber Room." Peopling the equally strange, psychedelic-light music are bits of insanity-inducing echo, some cartoonishly avant-garde vocal harmonies, and Wagoner's melodramatic soliloquies. Completing the picture on "I Found a Man," Wagoner himself loses it by mistaking his soul for a catatonic man in the streets. Taking a break from these vaudevillian freakouts, "Wagoner" sets aside a few songs to chronicle country's garden-variety nutters losing it over lost love and crazed relationships; the quaintly bizarre backdrops of earlier numbers are soon replaced by straight country. An oddly satisfying mix of pedal steel toe-tappers and high-grade kitsch. *—Stephen Cook*

The Thin Man From West Plains: The RCA Sessions 1952–1962 / 1989 / Bear Family ✦✦✦✦✦
From a cover of "Settin' the Woods on Fire" in September 1952 to "Blue House Painted White" in August of 1962, this four-CD set is a priceless overview of the best part of Porter Wagoner's career. Disc one features his earliest stuff, most of which is solid honky tonk material sung in Hank Williams' style. Most of it disappeared without a trace at the time, but it's all extremely enjoyable and shows some of Wagoner's versatility. His own sound, as it developed on the later songs on disc one and all of disc two, is more backwoods, with a strong folk component, but also beautifully harmonized. Wagoner's most striking attribute was the sheer joy evident in his singing and playing, whether he was doing a deeply religious number ("What Would You Do") or a loving tribute to Bill Monroe ("Uncle Pen"). He was equally comfortable with bluegrass and also country blues, as is clear from the previously unissued "My Brand of Blues," where he sounds a lot like Johnny Cash. Disc three shows Wagoner working in a smoother, more sentimental and commercial country-pop-oriented vein, but as late as 1959, he was still doing wonderfully exuberant numbers. Disc four covers the early '60s, the period during which Wagoner continued to merge the stripped-down country of his roots and the smooth Nashville sound. Among the outtakes released for the first time is "Private Little World," featuring a killer guitar solo totally unexpected in a romantic number like this. The accompanying book is informative, though not as well organized as the usual Bear Family notes. *—Bruce Eder*

Porter's Pure Gold / 1991 / RCA ✦✦✦✦✦
This low-budget-produced CD is the pick title until RCA sees fit to give him a legitimate reissue set. Actually, it's a pretty decent glimpse at the many moods of career-peak Wagoner. And yup, its got "Skid Row Joe." *—Dan Cooper*

★ **The Essential Porter Wagoner and Dolly Parton** / Jun. 1996 / RCA ✦✦✦✦✦
The Essential Porter and Dolly contains all of Wagoner and Parton's Top Ten hits, including "The Last Thing on My Mind," "Holding on to Nothin'," "Just Someone I Used to Know," "If Teardrops Were Pennies," "Please Don't Stop Were Pennies," and "Say Forever You'll Be Mine." In addition to the hits, a handful of interesting obscurities are included, making this the definitive retrospective of Porter & Dolly's partnership. *—Thom Owens*

★ **The Essential Porter Wagoner** / Apr. 29, 1997 / RCA ✦✦✦✦✦
The Essential Porter Wagoner is the first thorough CD-era collection of his greatest hits, and while it misses a few items, all of the essential songs—from "Company's Comin'" and "A Satisfied Mind" to "The Carroll County Accident" and "Uncle Pen"—are here, making it a necessary addition to any country collection. *—Stephen Thomas Erlewine*

The Best I've Ever Been / Jul. 4, 2000 / Shell Point ✦✦✦
Notwithstanding the press materials accompanying this CD that claim it is Porter Wagoner's first new album in 20 or 25 years, he has continued recording, fitfully, since parting company with RCA Victor in 1981 after close to 30 years on the label. But his releases have been largely on his own labels and have consisted largely of rerecordings of his old hits. *The Best I've Ever Been* (an unfortunate title that gives the incorrect impression that this is another hits collection), the second release on the independent Nashville label Shell Point Records, is the 72-year-old's treatment of a group of songs written by Damon Black, a former Missouri farmer who turns out to have a true sense of what makes a good country song. Black is especially strong on the leadoff track, "Brewster's Farm," a song about the plight of farmers that deserves to be the theme song of *Farm Aid,* even if it does rhyme "farm" with "foreign." Black can also write a country song with a twist, such as the saga of a May-December romance, "I Knew This Day Would Come." And he specializes in story songs filled with family reminiscences and homespun philosophy. Wagoner, who is still in good voice, renders the material well, backed by a crack band that includes such Nashville veterans as pianist Hargus "Pig" Robbins. This is an album that for the most part could have been made in 1960 as easily as 2000, and that's not accidental. Shell Point, which previously released the original version of the controversial "Murder on Music Row" as performed by its author, Larry Cordle, is dedicated to promoting traditional country, and there is no greater symbol of traditional country left standing than Porter Wagoner. *The Best I've Ever Been* furthers the argument that old-time country, like Wagoner, is alive and well in the new millennium, even if it concludes with a "bonus track" on which the singer looks forward to his heavenly reward. *—William Ruhlmann*

A Rare Slice of Country / Jul. 11, 2000 / Jasmine ✦✦✦
A Rare Slice of Country collects 26 radio transcriptions from programs recorded several years apart in the early and mid-'50s. The early tracks predate Wagoner's stardom and find him hewing more closely to the sound of Hank Williams. The later recordings offer more instrumental variety and some pretty elaborate vocal arrangements for transcription recordings, particularly on the excellent "Pay Day." Jim Reeves and Red Foley appear as MCs, and their banter with Wagoner and song introductions are included. Renditions of several of Wagoner's hits appear, including "A Satisfied Mind," "Eat, Drink and Be Merry (Tomorrow You'll Cry)," and "Uncle Pen." Entertaining and interesting, *A Rare Slice of Country* will please collectors and casual listeners. *—Greg Adams*

★ **RCA Country Legends** / Mar. 5, 2002 / RCA ✦✦✦✦✦
The *RCA Country Legends* series—previously on the reactivated Buddha label, but as of 2002, showing up on BMG Heritage, since Buddha no longer exists—stands out because the compilers don't open up Joel Whitburn's *Billboard* chart books and copy down the 16 biggest songs. Instead, they alter their choices slightly, skewing it to a particular sound or style, usually telling a better story about the actual sound and intent of the artist than if they were just concerned with hits. That's even true with Porter Wagoner's volume of *RCA Country Legends*—it may be missing a number of big hits (how could it not be; he was one of the biggest stars of his era, continually hitting the charts for year upon year), but it has the biggest hits, surrounded by selections that give a good idea of who Wagoner was as an artist and entertainer. No, not every big song is here, but no other CD-era compilation gives a better idea of what Porter Wagoner was all about than *RCA Country Legends,* which is why it's an essential addition to any comprehensive country library. *—Stephen Thomas Erlewine*

Unplugged / Sep. 10, 2002 / Shell Point ✦✦✦

Frank Wakefield

b. Jun. 26, 1934, Emory Gap, TN
Mandolin, Vocals / Progressive Bluegrass, Traditional Bluegrass, Instrumental Country
One of the chief innovators on the mandolin, Frank Wakefield played straight bluegrass with a number of well-known bands, including Red Allen and the Greenbriar Boys. Born into a musical family in Emory Gap, TN, by age eight he already knew how to play harmonica, guitar and bass. In 1950, his family moved to Dayton, OH, and soon afterward, he took up the mandolin and formed the gospel-oriented Wakefield Brothers with sibling Ralph, who played guitar. In 1951, the brothers made their first radio appearance in Dayton. After the duo split up, Frank teamed with Red Allen in 1952 to form Red Allen & Frank Wakefield and the Kentuckians. They remained partners through 1972, occasionally pursuing side projects as well. It with Allen that Wakefield mastered the banjo and dobro, and when he moved with Allen to Washington, D.C. in 1960, he began offering private mandolin lessons; his star pupil was a young David Grisman. Wakefield joined the Greenbriar Boys in 1965 and remained with them through 1970. He also founded the Good Ol' Boys, and in 1971 recorded *The Frank Wakefield Band.* He cut *Pistol Packin' Mama* in 1974 with Don Reno, Jerry Garcia, Dave Nelson and Chubby Wise. He also continued to teach, and released an instructional video. *—Sandra Brennan & David Vinopal*

Red Allen and Frank Wakenfield—Bluegrass / 1964 / Folkways ✦✦✦✦

The Frank Wakefield Band / 1971 / Rounder ✦✦✦✦

● **Frank Wakefield With Country Cooking** / 1972 / Rounder ✦✦✦✦✦

Pistol Packin' Mama / 1974 / Round ✦✦✦✦✦

Frank Wakefield and the Good Old Boys / 1992 / Relix ✦✦✦

She's No Angel / 1992 / Relix ✦✦✦

Frank Wakefield / Flying Fish ✦✦✦

Jimmy Wakely

b. Feb. 16, 1914, Mineola, AR, **d.** Sep. 25, 1982, Mission Hills, CA

Vocals, Guitar, Piano / Cowboy

Jimmy Wakely was one of the last vocalists to make it in movies as a singing cowboy or transform a movie contract into a successful recording career. A protégé and discovery of Gene Autry, he was never remotely as successful as Autry in movies, nor did his record sales approach those of his mentor, but Wakely was successful as a crossover act, his voice and repertoire attractive enough to find favor with pop as well as country & western audiences.

James Clarence Wakely was born in Arkansas on February 16, 1914, but was raised in Oklahoma, where he spent much of his early life in a succession of odd jobs while he nursed his ambitions for a career in music. Eventually he joined up with Dick Reinhardt and Johnny Bond to form the Jimmy Wakely Trio in 1937. Their main influence was the Sons of the Pioneers, and their singing and playing proved attractive enough to land them a regular broadcasting gig in Oklahoma City. Having achieved some recognition locally, they managed to parlay that into a meeting with Autry when he toured Oklahoma in 1940, and the singer was impressed enough with their work to invite them to California. Wakely and company became regulars on Autry's Melody Ranch radio show, and also began appearing in his films for Republic Pictures. Strangely enough, despite Wakely's later success, Johnny Bond became the first member of the trio to get a recording contract in 1941. Wakely got his own recording deal in 1942, shortly after he left the Autry fold, and had his first hit a year later with a cover of country yodel star Elton Britt's wartime anthem, "There's a Star-Spangled Banner Waving Somewhere."

At the time, despite—or perhaps because of—the omnipresence of World War II in peoples' lives, the singing cowboy image that Gene Autry established in movies was still thriving. On the home front, the public (especially the kids) liked the movies, and there was money to be made. Autry was serving in the U.S. military, but Roy Rogers and Tex Ritter both continued riding and singing their way through screen adventures, and other small studios were in the market for their own singing cowboys. Monogram Pictures, Republic's major competitor among B-movie studios, approached Wakely with a contract in 1944, and his first picture, *Song of the Range*, was a modest success, leading to a five-year stint in front of the cameras. Wakely was never as natural an actor as Autry or Roy Rogers, but his voice was attractive and his 28 Westerns were reasonably successful in their time. Amid Wakely's work in B-Westerns, his recording career thrived, as he began recording a uniquely sophisticated array of country, cowboy, and pop songs. His string began with his own "Song of the Sierras," a richly atmospheric ballad that presented his voice in a deep, serious light. His first major crossover hit followed a year later in 1948 with "One Has My Name (The Other Has My Heart)," a touching song about a tragic romantic triangle that reached the top spot on the country & western charts and the Top Ten on the pop charts. Wakely became especially closely associated with the music of honky tonk songwriter Floyd Tillman, and one cover, "I Love You So Much It Hurts," spent five weeks at the number-one spot on the country charts in 1949.

It was producer Lee Gillette who thought of teaming Wakely up with songstress Margaret Whiting in what proved to be a very successful partnership. Their first song together, the infidelity story "Slippin' Around," set the pattern for their partnership, the effervescent Whiting and the smooth, laid-back Wakely—who, by that time, was becoming known as the Bing Crosby of country & western music—balancing each other perfectly. "Slippin' Around" spent 17 weeks at the number-one spot on the country charts and a week at the number-one pop chart position, and the two had nine subsequent hits together, including "Wedding Bells" and "When You and I Were Young Maggie Blues." It was inevitable from all of this success that Wakely would become a media star. In 1952, he became the star of *the Jimmy Wakely Show* on the CBS radio network. After co-hosting the ABC television network series *Five Star Jubilee* in 1961 with Tex Ritter, he continued to record for his own Shasta Records label, which he founded as a mail-order distribution company in the mid-'60s. He continued to perform live in an act that included his son and daughter, and remained popular during the 1970s, until age and health problems began taking their toll. Wakely died of emphysema in 1982. *—Bruce Eder*

Santa Fe Trail / 1956 / Decca ✦✦✦✦✦

Santa Fe Trail is a late-'50s album of western favorites performed by silver-screen cowboy Jimmy Wakely with the Jud Conlon Singers and the Three Rays. Several years had passed since Wakely's last hit when this was recorded, but the atmospheric production and Wakely's Bing Crosby-influenced singing created a mesmerizing evocation of twilight on the trail. "Red River Valley," "Take Me Back to My Boots and Saddle," and "Blue Shadows on the Trail" are a few of the well-worn western standards Wakely tackles, but his versions are so lovely it's impossible to complain. The instrumental arrangements are understated, with simple accordion, harmonica, and acoustic guitar, but purists may object to the lush vocal chorus, which makes the proceedings sound like western mood music at times. It's an undeniably beautiful collection of recordings, though, and a nice return to Wakely's western roots after years of making crossover hits. *—Greg Adams*

Vintage Collections Series / Aug. 7, 1996 / Capitol ✦✦✦✦✦

The 20-track *Vintage* compilation contains nine of Jimmy Wakely's biggest hits, including "One Has My Name (The Other Has My Heart)," "I Love You So Much it Hurts," "Till the End of the World," "I Wish I Had A Nickel," "Mona Lisa," plus three of his most popular duets with Margaret Whiting: "Slipping Around," "Wedding Bells," and "When You and I Were Young Maggie Blues." The remainder of the collection consists of lesser-known, but equally good, selections, as well as five unreleased cuts designed to lure in hardcore collectors. Fortunately, the unreleased songs are worthwhile, and help to add to the image of Wakely as one of the great singing cowboys of the late '40s and early '50s, which, in turn, makes *Vintage* a first-rate retrospective. *—Thom Owens*

Jimmy Wakely Collectors Edition / Feb. 24, 1998 / Simitar ✦✦✦✦

Jimmy Wakely Collectors Edition contains a dozen 1940s sides by one of the last men to join the ranks of the movies' singing cowboys. Wakely's sound is less ornate than that of Gene Autry, his idol from the same period—Autry was already moving in the direction of popular music, while Wakely was still evolving a sound of his own. Most of the songs are sentimental ballads: "(Take Me Back to My) Boots and Saddle," a cowboy movie theme if there ever was one, is the best song here, and nothing else would seem out of place in one of Wakely's movies, except his cover of Kokomo Arnold's "Milk Cow Blues" and his own jaunty "Oklahoma City Blues," which are effective accounts of life's joys and troubles and add some extra spark to the collection. Wakely, whose own band included future country star Johnny Bond, was a good judge of talent and had been in backing bands for any number of stars before hitting it big himself. He gets first-rate backing here from Pete Martinez on steel guitar and lead guitarist Jack Rivers (author of this album's "Don't Lay the Blame on Me," a good Western swing style number)—their playing on "In the Hills of Wyoming," guitars echoing Wakely's phrasings on the chorus, is delightful. Wakely's first hit, "I'm Sending You Red Roses," isn't here, and some of the sound quality is a little rough—the sources on this collection weren't perfect—but otherwise, this is a good representation of Wakely's early output. *—Bruce Eder*

● **The Very Best of Jimmy Wakely** / Jul. 25, 2000 / Varese ✦✦✦✦✦

The Very Best of Jimmy Wakely includes singles like "Slippin' Around," "Beautiful Brown Eyes," "I Love You So Much It Hurts," and "One Has My Name (The Other Has My Heart)" along with 12 other hits. "I'll Never Let You Go, Little Darlin'" and "Too Late" are also featured on this worthwhile collection from one of the '40s and '50s most popular singing cowboys. *—Heather Phares*

Christmas Collection / Oct. 17, 2000 / Varese Vintage ✦✦✦

Jimmy Wakely was one of the last big screen movie cowboys drawing on the success of Roy Rogers and Gene Autry. These Christmas recordings were initially released on Wakely's Shasta label in the late '50s. Along with traditional Christmas favorites—like "Winter Wonderland," "Frosty the Snowman," "Joy to the World," and "Rudolph the Red-Nosed Reindeer"—are original compositions "Swingin' Jingle Bells" and "That's Santa Claus." If you find yourself reaching for the *Gene Autry Christmas* record every December, you should own the *Jimmy Wakely Christmas Collection*. *—Al Campbell*

Singing Cowboy / 2002 / Varese ✦✦✦✦

From Cowboy to Country / Jan. 21, 2003 / Jasmine ✦✦✦✦✦

The Melody Kid / Apr. 8, 2003 / ASV/Living Era ✦✦✦✦

The Walkabouts

f. 1984, Seattle, WA

Group / Indie Rock, Alternative Country-Rock, Alternative Pop/Rock

Despite their background (punk), geography (Seattle), and label affiliation (Sub Pop), the Walkabouts were anything but a grunge band; dark, haunting, and elegiac, their work instead sprung forth from the storytelling traditions of American roots music and the kinetic excitement of rock & roll. The Walkabouts were formed in 1984 by Chris Eckman and his brothers Curt and Grant, all of whom had previously played together in a number of punk-pop outfits, along with singer Carla Torgerson, a veteran of folk and street singing. The group's lineup proved fluid, although Chris Eckman and Torgerson remained the Walkabouts' driving forces; a later roster including bassist Michael Wells, multi-instrumentalist Glenn Slater, and drummer Terri Moeller did hang together for a number of years.

After issuing a self-titled cassette in 1984, the Walkabouts released the EP *22 Disasters* a year later. A full-length LP, *Weights and Rivers*, was planned for 1987, but the record was never released—a harbinger of music industry problems to come. Instead, the group offered *See Beautiful Rattlesnake Gardens* in 1988, which not only marked the continued maturity of Eckman and Torgerson's songwriting but also earned the Walkabouts a contract with the fledgling Sub Pop label. The deal resulted in upgraded production values, as evidenced by 1989's *Cataract* and its follow-up, the next year's six-song EP *Rag & Bone*, which featured the keyboard work of the newly added Slater.

Released in 1990, *Scavenger* proved to be the last Walkabouts record issued in their native land for some time; however, while the deal with Sub Pop's American division went sour, the label's European division, Glitterhouse, hung on to the Walkabouts, where the band's following had been steadily growing. Between 1993 and 1995, the group issued a staggering seven full-length records in Europe—three by the full band, a limited-edition live collection, and three more released by the duo of Chris & Carla. Finally, in 1995 the three aforementioned Walkabouts albums—the double-LP set *New West Motel*, the all-covers *Satisfied Mind*, and the more rock-oriented *Setting the Woods on Fire*—all appeared domestically. A year later, the band issued two more albums, the all-new *Devil's Road* (recorded with the Warsaw Philharmonic Orchestra) and *Death Valley Days: Lost Songs and Rarities, 1985-1995*, a collection of odds and ends. In November 1996, Wells left the Walkabouts to devote himself to his side project, Pluto Boy; he was replaced by bassist Baker Saunders. *Trail of Stars* followed in 2000. *—Jason Ankeny*

22 Disasters / 1985 / Necessity ✦✦

See Beautiful Rattlesnake Gardens / 1987 / Pop Llama ✦✦✦

On the Walkabouts' debut, the band's sound is still in its embryonic stages; the focus is on jangly, electric folk-rock, with few traces of the country, blues and roots music from which their later work would draw. Still, the songwriting of Chris Eckman and Carla Torgerson is already strong, and Torgerson's vocals are lovely. *—Jason Ankeny*

Cataract / 1989 / Sub Pop ✦✦✦

The band's first Sub Pop LP is a diverse affair sewn together from an ever-expanding array of influences and passions, highlighted by such haunting roots meditations as "Hell's Soup Kitchen," "Long Black Veil" (an original composition, and not the standard), and "Whiskey XXX." *—Jason Ankeny*

Rag & Bone/Cataract / 1990 / Sub Pop ✦✦✦

The addition of keyboardist Glenn Slater fleshes out the Walkabouts' sound on the six-song *Rag & Bone* EP, texturing typically strong efforts like the honky-tonk rave-up "The Anvil Song" and the gentle "Medicine Hat" with even greater color and dimension. —*Jason Ankeny*

Scavenger / Oct. 1990 / Sub Pop ✦✦✦

Like its predecessors, *Cataract* refines the Walkabouts' sound even as the band's scope broadens—the further afield their fascination with music's backroads takes them, the more remarkably assured they grow. —*Jason Ankeny*

● **Satisfied Mind** / 1993 / Creative Man ✦✦✦✦✦

Like Yo La Tengo's *Fakebook*, the Walkabouts' *Satisfied Mind* is a definitive artistic statement masquerading as a loose-knit collection of acoustic covers. Sometimes a group's selection of cover material, combined with their ability to make the songs their own, winds up revealing as much about their craft as their original music, and such is the case here; mining the work of diverse artists like the Carter Family, Gene Clark, Mary Margaret O'Hara, John Cale, and Nick Cave, *Satisfied Mind* represents the purest evocation to date of the Walkabouts' aesthetic and its standing at the crossroads of country, rock, folk, and punk. By casting well-known songs in an entirely new light—Patti Smith's "Free Money" becomes an ominous waltz, while Charlie Rich's "Feel Like Going Home" is renewed as an epic dirge—the album makes explicit all of the implicit connections in the Walkabouts' work. By extension, it underlines the connections binding the spectrum of roots music as well; *Satisfied Mind* doesn't simply suggest that diverse sounds can coexist together—it proves that they always have. —*Jason Ankeny*

New West Motel / 1993 / Glitterhouse ✦✦✦✦

The double-album *New West Motel* bears more than a passing similarity to the work of Neil Young (whose "Like a Hurricane" gets covered here), thanks to its edgy juxtaposition of blistering guitar workouts and plaintive acoustic cuts. —*Jason Ankeny*

Setting the Woods on Fire / 1994 / Cargo ✦✦✦✦

Despite taking its title from a Hank Williams song, *Setting the Woods on Fire* ranks among the Walkabouts' most rock-based efforts. A sweeping, stately record, it owes a great deal to the Stones' *Exile on Main St.*, particularly on the boogie shuffle "Old Crow" and the horn-powered, R&B-flavored "Hole in the Mountain." —*Jason Ankeny*

Devil's Road / Jan. 1996 / Virgin Schallplatten ✦✦✦✦✦

Half of the tracks comprising *Devil's Road* feature the string arrangements of the Warsaw Philharmonic Orchestra, giving greater depth to a sound that's already impossibly rich. Recorded in Berlin, the album is dark and soulful, the work of a band at the peak of its powers. —*Jason Ankeny*

Death Valley Days: Lost Songs and Rarities, 1985–1995 / Nov. 1996 / Glitterhouse ✦✦✦

Death Valley Days is a fragmentary collection reining in scattered tracks drawn from demos, B-sides, unreleased albums, compilations and tribute records, along with a few covers left off the domestic reissue of *New West Motel*. —*Jason Ankeny*

Nighttown / 1997 / Virgin ✦✦✦✦✦

The Walkabouts continue to deepen their exploration of diverse arrangements to good effect on *Nighttown*. Many of the songs employ string orchestration, but in a manner opposite from almost every other rock act—the violins and cellos are used to darken the atmosphere, not to sweeten it. The lyrical tone is dark (though not unremittingly gloomy) as well, exuding world-weariness, ambiguity, and guarded optimism in varying degrees; not for nothing is there a reference to "Scott Walker Street" in "Tremble Goes the Night." The Walkabouts are one of the few groups around effectively delving into disturbing themes without bludgeoning the message to death with metallic guitar assaults and cord-shredding vocals. Nor do they, like (say) Mazzy Star, retreat into druggy numbness and mantra-like repetitiveness. This, of course, does not make them at all trendy, and the failure of most of their '90s albums (including this Europe-only release) to even get issued in the U.S. does not make one proud to be an American. —*Richie Unterberger*

Trail of Stars / Apr. 4, 2000 / Glitterhouse ✦✦

While it has been a few years since a Walkabouts record has been readily available in the United States, the band has enjoyed significant success in Europe. *Trail of Stars*, released on Germany's Glitterhouse Records and distributed by Seattle's Innerstate, finds the band still mixing the cold and faceless Euro-tones they have absorbed through relentless overseas touring with American lyrical images. Drenched in John Cale-like soundscape washes and heavy strings, *Trail of Stars* comes off as morose and dirge-like. Only "Straight to the Stars" doesn't feel like a death march. This is frustrating, since the instrumentation of the record is expertly crafted and lovingly played. The Walkabouts are a band seriously committed to the quality of their music, and one slightly skunked release is no big deal. Their output is tremendous, and as regrettable as *Trail of Stars* may be, it is still considered a criminal offense that the Walkabouts are so underappreciated and poorly distributed in the U.S. —*John Duffy*

Train Leaves at Eight / Aug. 22, 2001 / Glitterhouse ✦✦✦✦

The Walkabouts' second collection of covers comes with a quite definite theme, a musical tour of Europe, ranging from Greece in the South all the way up to Norway. And it's most definitely a journey, one which suits the darker, more introspective, and very literate nature of this Seattle band. But the ground covered is more than geographic; not many bands could move from Greek icon Mikis Theodorakis to Krautrockers Neu! on the same record. But the Walkabouts, whose career has largely happened in Europe, handle it with aplomb, throwing up plenty of changes in arrangements and working hard to penetrate to the core of a song, even the enigmatic "Solex in a Slipshod Style," on the face of it an odd choice, coming from Dutch sampling queen Solex. A few of the writers might be

familiar to Americans, like Jacques Brel and Scott Walker, but the majority of the names will be unknown—a good thing, since the music can be judged on the interpretation, not the original version. A few famous friends, like R.E.M.'s Peter Buck and Los Lobos sax man Steve Berlin add contributions, but it's the band who make it special, with Carla Torgerson's velvety voice caressing the lyrics while Chris Eckman worries his way into others. It might not be the most relaxing journey on offer, but it's one of the most rewarding, a night train across a Europe, not only through the countries, but also the hearts, minds, and souls. —*Chris Nickson*

Drunken Soundtracks / 2002 / Glitterhouse ✦✦✦✦

The second Walkabouts rarities compilation, following *Death Valley Days*, *Drunken Soundtracks* is a mighty fine plunge into the obscurer side of the band—admittedly already obscure enough in its home country—during its end-of-the-'90s days. The group's eternal transformation into something new is captured wonderfully from the start—the title track, sung by Carla Torgerson and recorded in 2001, sounds next to nothing like anything from even eight years ago aside from her wonderful voice. But rather than rural country atmospheres or classic rock fire, the song is supple and smoky with tinges of jazz and blues—piano and drums are more prominent than anything else—not to mention ambient techno here and there. It's a good summation of albums like *Nighttown* and *Trail of Stars* and more besides, but that said, it's hardly a case of abandoning their past (as the stunning "Death's Black Train" makes clear), more one of incorporating it and finding new settings. A number of cover versions help make this clear, starting with a strong take on Mickey Newbury's "How Many Times (Must the Pipe Be Paid for His Song)." Other songs that perhaps shed a clearer light on the Walkabouts' more recent obsession include Serge Gainsbourg's "Sorry Angel" and Scott Walker's "Cowbells Shakin'," but the former gets the brew spiked with a clattering breakbeat after being through Tom Waits' wringer. Gainsbourg takes another bow as well with a cover of "Bonnie and Clyde" originally released on a limited-edition live album—with full backing from an orchestral string section and a dramatic arrangement with a killer false ending, it could well be the definitive English-language take. The touch of regular producers and engineers Phill Brown and Kevin Suggs can be heard throughout, bringing out the dark beauty of the songs excellently. —*Ned Raggett*

Ended Up a Stranger / Apr. 23, 2002 / Innerstate ✦✦✦✦✦

For the past 17 years, Carla Torgerson, Chris Eckman from the Northwest corner of the United States, and a revolving cast of players have crafted albums of fine, independent gothic (as in Flannery O'Connor and William Faulkner, not Bauhaus) American music and have influenced countless bands along the way, many of whom are too foolish to acknowledge their influence. Counting bootlegs and mail-order issues, they have issued no less than 15 albums and countless singles and EPs for labels such as Virgin, Glitterhouse, Sub Pop, and others, without receiving a whit of popular acclaim. Yeah, critics love them, so what—they can't make a living on what critics write. The bottom line is that this band crafts exquisite songs from the shadowy side of the American experience, and *Ended Up a Stranger* offers evidence aplenty. The opener is the gorgeous "Lazarus Heart," where a string quartet and a skittering drum kit usher in a weary protagonist who cannot even recount her stories in full, but instead just gives impressions, like flashes of light along a boulevard at night: "I keep crashin'/Into parked cars/Waitin' for a horse/And it's blue rider/Followed you that night/You tasted lucky/We staggered blessed/Your scars they ... matches, my dress/Never mind/The happy ending ... Lazarus heart, Lazarus heart/ We forget/We risk/We're tired/We're true/Veils and whispers/Rivers of ether." Torgerson is haunted and resigned; she's been here before and knows that tomorrow the cycle begins again without the hint of a different direction, but she holds out, like Beckett, for that one glimmer where everything can change on a dime. But as the songs droop from their structures like a lazy, dark weeping willow in August, the sadness and shadows grow deeper. On songs such as "More Heat Than Light," Eckman sings, "There are moments of grace in the heat of the chase/But it's more heat than light." Guitars shimmer in the distance and an organ crawls in from the margins as Eckman becomes more weary than Leonard Cohen, yet is just as determined to hold on to the song. As the drums and electric guitars come in waves, he struggles to hold the seam where his resignation and his cursed optimism hold him hostage. On "Fallen Down Moon," a slippery folk song touches the trace edge of an old, Spanish flamenco melody in stutter-step 4/4 time: "There's a love that will cut us in two/First we're wild/And then we drink ... Makin' out with Judas/Just to make your bail/We do sh*t like that/Just before we crack/But there's splendor in the cracks/And gold in the darkest blue/I dreamed you're comin' back/I dreamed I'd wait for you/But I'm getting' tired of dreamin'/Fallen down moon/Everything goes wrong ... We lose for our own good ... We break the best when nothin's left." The strings hold up her vocal, carrying it over Eckman's guitar solo and the ceremonially played drum kit. There it is, the moment of defeat that continues inside a life, or inside of lives. Rock & roll meets the place where the crossroads offer nothing more than a choice between nothing and nowhere. But in music like this, beauty lies in the willingness to make that choice anyway, to choose the poetry and confession and sordid revelation rather than suffer it alone for no purpose. Guitars, drums, strings, organs, pianos, and horns braid together in a weave that accurately reflects back the jagged shards of pain and shimmering, heat-mirage shadows of lives passing at the margins of the abyss, as in the R&B swagger that infects "See It in the Dark"; it doesn't matter where the roads lead as much as that they head down to somewhere and are traveled by a gang that includes the musicians, their protagonists, and their listeners. The album ends with the title track, and here the double-edged sword reveals the fineness of the slash once again, because it's the only thing left worthy of praise. In a slow, sparse, plodding tempo—in fact, one that almost doesn't exist—Eckman reveals the sum total of a night spent restlessly roaming through his own space, a ghost in the house of his own life as he records the sounds of his stomping grounds through a microphone out the back window of his car: "Lord, I've become a stranger… in my old haunts." The moment the last syllable drops from his lips, a screaming, slow electric guitar punches the space though; it's a wail of pain buffered only by an accordion holding the bottom space. And though the seam of the track is broken and glass is falling everywhere, he continues: "Hello desire/And what your spooky name/Implies/In you, I found my silk/And swagger/The calm before the prize/And though I, once was warned/You'd be the grave in which I'd lie/With you, I was no stranger… in my old haunts/Someday I'll hit the turnpike/Speed past a truck stop burnin'… and I'll listen to these tapes I've made/My symphony of phantoms." Another guitar screams here, with strings and drums and bass and an almost unrestrained wail cutting through the mix without such a clean slash, leaving tears and bloodlines everywhere and the sound of ghosts to fade it to black. While the Walkabouts have never made a weak record, nor even a mediocre one, *Ended Up a Stranger* may be their magnum opus, a record so fine, so darkly beautiful and intoxicatingly forlorn and shadowy in its streaked grays and blues, that it almost defies praise. —*Thom Jurek*

Watermarks / Nov. 19, 2002 / Innerstate ✦✦✦

Billy Walker

b. Jan. 14, 1929, Ralls, TX
Guitar, Vocals / Traditional Country, Western Swing, Honky Tonk
A native of west Texas who was active on the *Grand Ole Opry*, Billy Walker emerged from the talent-rich Dallas scene of the late '40s and early '50s. After a brief stint on Capitol, he was signed to Columbia in 1951 at almost exactly the same time as Ray Price. For a while, Walker, Price, and Lefty Frizzell were all recording at the legendary Jim Beck studio in Dallas, which did for '50s honky tonk what Sun Studio in Memphis did for rockabilly. Nevertheless, Walker enjoyed his greatest success ten years later in Nashville, where the studio sound was perhaps more suited to his smooth tenor voice. —*Dan Cooper*

● **Billy Walker's Greatest Hits** / 1963 / Columbia ✦✦✦✦✦
Early-'60s Nashville Sound, though always with Walker's voice agreeably front and center, it contains "Charlie's Shoes" and a 1961 take on Willie Nelson's "Funny How Time Slips Away." —*Dan Cooper*

Billy Walker's Greatest Hits, Vol. 2 / 1969 / Columbia ✦✦✦✦
It's noteworthy for "Cross the Brazos at Waco," and Walker's 1964 quasi-sequel to Marty Robbins' "El Paso," and a terrific version of the Harlan Howard/Walker tune "Down to My Last Cigarette." —*Dan Cooper*

Cross the Brazos at Waco / 1993 / Bear Family ✦✦✦✦✦
Here's the usual exhaustive, prestigious, and expensive package (six CDs and a book) from Germany's Bear Family, the best roots-music reissue company in the world. Covering the years 1949 to 1965, the set chronicles Walker's career from his initial, tentative Capitol cuts through his entire career on Columbia. —*Dan Cooper*

Greatest Hits on Monument / Mar. 9, 1993 / Columbia ✦✦✦
Greatest Hits on Monument collects 15 of Billy Walker's recordings for Monument from 1966-1970, including all of his Top 40 C&W hits for the label. "A Million and One" was his biggest hit during this period, reaching number two. Other notable tracks include the airy, Gordon Lightfoot-esque "Sundown Mary" and the Tex-Mex flavored "In Del Rio." The material often tends toward string-laden balladry, although the disc offers a fair amount of variety within its bounds. Compositions are featured by such heavyweights as Kris Kristofferson, Harlan Howard, and Dallas Frazier, among others. —*Greg Adams*

Charlie Walker

b. Nov. 2, 1926, Collins County, TX
Vocals / Traditional Country, Cowboy, Country-Pop, Honky Tonk
Country singer Charlie Walker had a sporadic career with one major highlight, his 1958 classic hit release of Harlan Howard's "Pick Me up on Your Way Down." Texas-born Walker began in the early '40s as a vocalist in the Cowboy Ramblers. After several years singing with the Bill Boyd-led group, Walker briefly retired from the performing side of the business to work as a DJ. A recording contract with Columbia brought him back to performing, though, and it was then that he scored with Howard's classic composition. Minor hits followed, including a trilogy of honky tonk-inspired tunes, "Close All the Honky Tonks," "Honky Tonk Season," and even a cover of the Rolling Stones' "Honky Tonk Women." After the hits dried up, Walker moved to the land of mediocre performers, Las Vegas, and sang there for several years before attempting an unsuccessful comeback with MCA in 1986. —*Steve Kurutz*

Charlie Walker's Greatest Hits / 1961 / Columbia ✦✦✦
Close All the Honky Tonks / 1965 / Epic ✦✦✦✦✦
Born to Lose / 1965 / Epic ✦✦✦✦
Wine, Women & Walker / 1966 / Epic ✦✦✦✦✦
Don't Squeeze My Charmin / 1967 / Epic ✦✦✦✦
Charlie Walker Recorded Live in Dallas, Texas / 1969 / Epic ✦✦✦✦
He Is My Everything / 1969 / Epic ✦✦✦
Honky Tonkin' / 1971 / Epic ✦✦✦✦

● **Pick Me Up on Your Way Down** / Feb. 23, 1999 / Bear Family ✦✦✦✦✦
Charlie Walker is remembered for his 1958 hit "Pick Me Up on Your Way Down," but he charted over two dozen hits in his long career that included stints with Imperial, Decca, Columbia, Epic, RCA, and Capitol. *Pick Me Up on Your Way Down* is a five-disc box set that collects Walker's complete recordings from his earliest, tentative efforts for Imperial through the end of his tenure with Epic in the late '60s. Walker was a honky tonker in the Texas dancehall tradition second only to Ray Price in his use of the shuffle beat, but he varied his approach enough so that a set of this length doesn't become tedious. His early

recordings were sometimes sung uncertainly, but Walker improved with age to the point where the last recordings on this box set are some of the best. Walker's late-'60s efforts were surprisingly adventurous (including an incredible hard-rocking cover of the Rolling Stones' "Honky Tonk Women") and much better than his declining fortunes on the charts would suggest. —*Greg Adams*

Clay Walker

b. Aug. 19, 1969, Beaumont, TX
Guitar, Vocals / Contemporary Country, New Traditionalist
With his first two singles reaching number one upon their release, Clay Walker immediately established himself as a commercial success. Unlike most of his new country contemporaries of the mid-'90s, he was able to sustain that success over a couple of years, racking up no less than five number-one singles in the first three years of his career. Clay Walker (b. August 19, 1969) was born and raised on a farm in Beaumont, TX, the hometown of George Jones. Walker fell in love with country music at an early age, when his father gave him a guitar when he was only nine years old. After he graduated from high-school, Walker pursued a musical career full-time, playing concerts across the South, the Midwest, and Canada. For over three years, he toured and went to school, taking courses about the music business. During this time, he acted as his own manager. Eventually, he became the house singer at the Neon Armadillo bar in Beaumont. While performing at the club, producer James Stroud heard Walker and offered to work with the singer. Stroud helped Walker secure a contract with Giant Records, and the pair began working on the vocalist's debut album.

"What's It to You?" became a number-one hit upon its release in August of 1993, with "Live Until I Die" following it into the pole position later that same year. Both singles were featured on his debut album, *Clay Walker*, which was released in the fall of 1993. "Where Do I Fit in the Picture," the third single from the album, became a number 11 hit in early 1994. "White Palace" was a flop, failing to crack the Top 40, but "Dreaming With My Eyes Open" became his third number-one hit in the summer of 1994, helping make his debut record a platinum album. *If I Could Make a Living* was not quite as successful as his debut, yet it still yielded the number-one title track. *Hypnotize the Moon*, Walker's third album, appeared in the fall of 1995, preceded by the number-two single "Who Needs You Baby." He followed with *Self Portrait* in 1996 and *Rumor Has It* in 1997. A *Greatest Hits* collection appeared in 1998 and a new album, *Live, Laugh, Love*, was released in 1999. *Say No More* followed two years later. —*Stephen Thomas Erlewine*

Clay Walker / 1993 / Giant ✦✦✦✦✦
Clay Walker is another country music product from Beaumont, TX (others include George Jones, Mark Chestnutt, Doug Supernaw, and Tracy Bird) who has broken into the Nashville music scene. Walker has a high-energy voice and a growl that reminds you of Conway Twitty. The highlights of his first album include "What's It to You?," his first number-one hit, and "Live Until I Die." Other featured songs include "The Silence Speaks for Itself" and "White Palace." —*Larry Powell*

If I Could Make a Living / Sep. 27, 1994 / Giant ✦✦✦✦✦
Hypnotize the Moon / Oct. 17, 1995 / Giant ✦✦✦✦
Clay Walker's *Hypnotize the Moon* is his most assured, cohesive album to date. Walker shines on both polished, contemporary ballads and gritty traditional country, and his consistently excellent performance is what carries the album over the weak spots. —*Stephen Thomas Erlewine*

Self Portrait / Oct. 15, 1996 / Nu Millennia ✦✦✦
Self Portrait is a CD-ROM that is divided between interview footage of Clay Walker, music videos, and exclusive shots of Walker's Houston ranch. Most of Walker's hits—plus a previously unheard version of "Nobody's Darling"—are featured on the disc, but this is a disc designed for a fan of Clay Walker the personality, not Clay Walker the musician. Most of the information is trivial and unrelated to the construction of his music or progression of his career. Still, Walker fanatics will find certain segments of the CD-ROM of use, even though the interface could have been a little more user-friendly. —*Thom Owens*

Rumor Has It / Apr. 8, 1997 / Giant ✦✦✦
By *Rumor Has It*, Clay Walker had settled into a comfortable formula of radio-ready country-pop and honky tonk, and he had ceased to experiment with his music. Which isn't a bad thing, because Walker is a consummate professional able to make even mediocre material sound good. *Rumor Has It* may not be among his very best, yet there are enough strong moments to make it worthwhile for most fans. —*Thom Owens*

● **Greatest Hits** / Jun. 9, 1998 / Giant ✦✦✦✦✦
This greatest-hits package contains 14 of Clay Walker's biggest hits from his first four albums on Giant Records. Walker's output in the '90s included the hits "Dreaming With My Eyes Open," "Who Needs You Baby," "Live Until I Die," and his first number one, from August of 1993, "What's It to You?" If you're looking for Walker's hits, this collection contains them all. —*Al Campbell*

Live, Laugh, Love / Aug. 24, 1999 / Giant ✦✦✦
Clay Walker is a good journeyman singer. He has a strong voice, knows how to twist clichés to his advantage, and knows that straying too far from the clichés will lose his wide audience. In turn, that means that he's enjoyable, but a little predictable, which is an accurate assessment of *Live, Laugh, Love*, his fifth album. The album never really distinguishes itself from its predecessors. Like those records, it's a safe blend of pop ballads, mild rockers, and polished honky tonk, all delivered in Walker's twangy tenor. Even if the ballads occasionally touch on adult contemporary (witness "Once in a Lifetime Love"), it's considerably more country than, say, Tim McGraw, but the music doesn't show enough imagination and isn't organic enough to stand apart from the neo-traditionalist pack. That said, it's hardly bad—the material may be uneven, but "She's Always Right" has a good sense of humor and "Lose Some Sleep Tonight" is quite good, while the title track is an amusing twist on Faron Young's "Live Fast, Love Hard,

Die Young," a calypso-ish number that is designed for yuppies into hat music. Ultimately, *Live, Laugh, Love* drags a bit too much to rank among Walker's best, but it has its moments. *—Stephen Thomas Erlewine*

Say No More / Mar. 27, 2001 / Warner Bros. ✦✦✦
Of Clay Walker's first six albums, four went platinum and two went gold. *Say No More*, lucky number seven, seems destined for the same fate. This 11-track collection of inspirational prose about life and love covers everything from dreams to regret to tough times, but the common thread is love. In fact, the sensitivity on this album is so expressive that it makes you want to run right out and hug the one you love. The album's title track is an awesome song about falling out of love. "Could I Ask You Not to Dance" is a formidable song about losing someone you love and regretting it. "You Deliver Me" is a great track about feeling complete with your partner. Walker said, "I haven't ever put this much time or this much heart into an album, not even the first one. There's emotion in every single cut." There sure is. He adds some spice with a remake of Richie Valens' 1959 hit "La Bamba," as well as the pulsating "Texas Swing." Produced by Byron Gallimore, Blake Melvis, and Brent Mason, *Say No More* is a fine album from an artist who has proved his staying power time and time again. *—Maria Konicki Dinoia*

Jerry Jeff Walker (Ronald Clyde Crosby)

b. Mar. 16, 1942, Oneonta, NY
Guitar, Vocals / Progressive Country, Singer/Songwriter, Outlaw Country
Jerry Jeff Walker is strongly associated with the progressive ("outlaw") country scene that centered around Austin, Texas, in the 1970s and included such figures as Willie Nelson, Guy Clark, Billy Joe Shaver, the Lost Gonzo Band, Waylon Jennings,and Townes Van Zandt. Ironically, however, Walker is not a native Texan. He was born Ronald Clyde Crosby in upstate New York and recorded his first several albums while living in New York City. He didn't move to Austin until 1971, but he's remained a major figure in the area ever since. Walker has been quoted as saying, "the first time I set foot in Texas, particularly in Austin, I knew I was home."

Walker first recorded with the folk-rock group Circus Maximus for Vanguard in 1967. The band split after its second album, and Walker signed with Atco and released his first solo album, *Mr. Bojangles*, in 1968. He is, for better or worse, best known as the writer of "Mr. Bojangles," an enduring pop classic he wrote at the after meeting a street singer named Bill "Bojangles" Robinson in a New Orleans drunk tank. His version of "Bojangles" never hit it big, but the Nitty Gritty Dirt Band's rendition made the Top Ten of the pop charts in 1971. In 1972 Walker signed with Decca/MCA and released a self-titled album that included his version of Guy Clark's "L.A. Freeway," and "That Old Time Feeling," along with his own "Hill Country Rain," his reputation for being a "gypsy songman" found its roots in this outing. His best-known album from the period, however, however, is *Viva Terlingua*, which he recorded in 1973 in the tiny Texas town of Luckenbach with the Lost Gonzo Band. The album went gold, and it's his biggest-selling album to date. His subsequent recordings of the 1970s, particularly *It's A Good Night For Singin'*, *Ridin' High*, and *A Man Must Carry On* solidified Walker's reputation for being not only a great songwriter, but a wonderful interpreter of the work of his peers, and for being the greatest example of the living embodiment of "cosmic cowboyism."

Walker was a hard partier throughout much of his career (his friends called him "Jacky Jack"), and this reputation became part of his identity. He's since cleaned up his act—in part thanks to his wife, Susan, whom he married in 1974—and he's continued to record into the 2000s. He released a couple albums on Elektra/Asylum in the late '70s, but remained mostly with MCA until his 1982 album *Cowjazz*—a record that became his last for any major label. The Elektra recordings, *Jerry Jeff* and *Too Old To Change* were undervalued during their heyday, and have been proved to be among his most adventurous and enduring recordings thanks to a Wounded Bird two-fer reissue on CD in 2003. Walker, as evidenced by these recordings, was the only one of his peers—with the possible exception of *Willie Nelson*—who unrelentingly sought change and development in his sound. It didn't help with a country music industry completely hoodwinked by (sub)urban cowboyism and a pop market less receptive to organic American music than at any time in its history.

In 1985, however, he showed the industry he could live without their help and released the first of a series of self-made cassettes, *Gypsy Songman*, many of which he sold via a mailing list that has grown to more than 40,000 strong. In 1987, Walker worked out a deal with Rykodisc that released his CDs until 1996 when their partnership ended. He has since continued to market his material on True & True through his website and live shows. While Walker's Tried & True issues have not been as critically regarded as his earlier work, they are compelling, occasionally brilliant, always written from the perspective of where his gypsy songman is at this particular musical moment.

In 1991 and 1992 Walker hosted the weekly TV show, *the Texas Connection*, on TNN. In 1993, he returned to Luckenbach for an anniversary recording that became the album *Viva Luckenbach!* Walker's birthday is a major celebration in Austin every March, when he plays several shows in different local clubs and theaters. In 1999 he published an autobiography, *Gypsy Songman*, accompanied by an LP of the same name. Walker's most recent release, *Jerry Jeff Jazz* showcases him singing jazz pop and swing standards in front of a small tightly knit combo. While his voice has lost of its pliability in recent years, it nonetheless suits the gorgeous, homey quality of this recording; it is his finest moment on record in over a decade. Apparently this old coyote still has plenty of tricks up his sleeve. *—Kurt Wolf & Thom Jurek*

Mr. Bojangles / 1968 / Rhino ✦✦✦✦✦
Walker's debut introduced his dry vocals and narrative songwriting style, with support from many session musicians, the most notable of whom were Ron Carter and David Bromberg. The influence of Dylan and other singer/songwriters of the time is felt fairly strongly on this extremely low-key release (especially on the seven-minute "Desolation Row"-like "The Ballad of the Hulk"), but Walker favored the country and folk side of folk-rock much more than the rock side. The title track, taken into the Top Ten by the Nitty Gritty Dirt Band, remains his most famous song. [The CD reissue includes the original mono single version of "Mr. Bojangles" and its flip side, as well as liner notes with comments on the songs by Jerry Jeff himself.] *—Richie Unterberger*

Driftin' Way of Life / 1969 / Vanguard ✦✦✦✦✦
A beautifully simple album of country-flavored original songs, mostly from the point of view of the sentimental roustabout, this great record sounds as though the players just went in, knocked it off, and hit the road. *—Richard Meyer*

Five Years Gone / 1969 / Line ✦✦✦✦
Five Years Gone, originally released on Atco in 1969, might be one of the oddest albums from the '60s you will find in the country section of your local record store. More in line with contemporary singer/songwriters such as Danny O'Keefe, John Stewart, and even Neil Diamond, *Five Years Gone* is a forward-looking album rooted in late-'60s folk and folk-rock rather than popular country. Certainly the poetic but sometimes inscrutable lyrics owe more to Bob Dylan than any Nashville tradition, even though Nashville heavyweights including Weldon Myrick, Hargus "Pig" Robbins, and Charlie McCoy make up the band. Myrick in particular shines here, turning in some wonderfully haunting steel guitar lines. The late '60s and early '70s were an interesting time during which Atco released a number of seemingly uncommercial but ultimately enduring singer/songwriter albums, of which *Five Years Gone* is a prime example. *—Greg Adams*

Bein' Free / 1970 / Line ✦✦✦
After his minor hit "Mr. Bojangles" and strange 1969 sophomore solo album *Five Years Gone*, Jerry Jeff Walker made the (moderately) more bluesy and countrified *Bein' Free*, a strong album on which he wrote nine of the 11 songs. "I'm Gonna Tell on You," a funny anti-hypocrisy singalong, kicks things off, and the album moves from there into the sorts of poetic singer/songwriter creations that could just as easily have landed Walker's records in the folk or rock bins. "A Secret" makes good use of Michael Utley's organ, "Vince Triple-O Martin" and the stripped-down "Harmonica Talk" are blues-based stompers, while most of the remainder is comparatively hushed and introspective. *Bein' Free* is a freewheeling and fun affair from one of country music's most original Yankee practitioners. *—Greg Adams*

Jerry Jeff Walker / 1972 / Decca ✦✦✦✦✦
The self-titled *Jerry Jeff Walker* issued on Decca in 1972 completed Walker's transition from New York folkie to Texas singer/songwriter. He left New York a decade earlier, but with all of his rambling around, he didn't make Austin his home until 1971, and everywhere in this record's grooves is the city's famed funkiness, good-time, laid-back, tacit-as-it-comes feeling—even on the tracks recorded in New York. The organic feeling in the original versions of "Hill Country Rain" and "Charlie Dunn" are virtually peerless among his contemporaries. Add to this a pair of Guy Clark's finest songs—"That Old Time Feeling" and "L.A. Freeway"—"Curly & Lil," and "When I Had You," and already you have the makings of one of the classics of the outlaw period in American country music. Walker is at the peak of his powers here, and this began a string of records that wouldn't run out until the mid-'80s. Walker is surrounded here by what would become the Lost Gonzo Band—Robert Livingstone, Gary P. Nunn, and crew—Michael Murphy, David Bromberg, Joanne Vent, and Ellen Kearney on vocals, Mickey Raphael, and about a dozen others who recorded 14 miles of tape with no board—it was mixed by Walker and Michael Brovsky in New York later. "Her Good Lovin' Grace" sums up the entire ambience of these sessions with its false beginning that becomes a real one and the whole band slipping and sliding their way through a song that's being written as they go. Amazing. Like *It's a Good Night for Singin'*, *Walker's Collectibles*, and *Viva Terlingua*, this is a spotless masterpiece, full of amazing songs, great playing, a sound that defines the era yet is timeless, and enough passion and good-time spirit to liven up even a funeral. *—Thom Jurek*

Viva Terlingua / 1973 / MCA ✦✦✦✦✦
Viva Terlingua, recorded live in Luckenbach, TX, on a hot August night in 1973, is among the most legendary of "live" singer/songwriter albums ever released. It's the *Live at the Fillmore East* of redneck Texas folk-rock. Essentially, it's Jerry Jeff fronting the Lost Gonzo Band at the beginning of their long run together playing, living it up, having a ball, giving everybody the impression that life was a party, and to be sure, it was for a while. Given the loose, inspired performance on this set, Walker was every bit the equal of Willie, Waylon, and Billy Joe Shaver at the time. The material is terrific. Half of it is from Jerry Jeff's catalog: "Sangria Wine," "Gettin' By," "Little Bird," "Get It Out," and "Wheel." The rest? Can't possibly do better: Guy Clark's "Desperados Waiting for the Train," Ray Wylie Hubbard's "Up Against the Wall, Redneck Mother," Michael Murphy's "Backslider's Wine," and Gary P. Nunn's *Austin City Limits* anthem, "London Homesick Blues." It doesn't sound anything like it was recorded in front of an audience, but it does sound live as hell. These folks were partyin' it up and layin' down the tracks at white heat. This record was made in a night and it feels like it was made in your living room. It's guaranteed to lift any dark mood within 15 minutes. This record asks no questions and there are no hidden meanings in Walker's or anybody else's lyrics; it's all there for the taking. And that's what makes it the enduring classic it is. *—Thom Jurek*

Walker's Collectibles / 1974 / MCA ✦✦✦
Following up *Viva Terlingua* with a studio record was a tall order for Jerry Jeff and the Lost Gonzo Band, but true to form as they were until the late '70s, they rose to the occasion with an inspired set of songs. Walker wrote six of the album's ten tracks, the Lost Gonzo Band's Gary P. Nunn wrote two more, Billy Callery wrote one, and David Cohen wrote another. It was all in the family. It's an uptempo, rockin' country record with "Salvation Army Band" kicking everything off; it's followed by a drunken, barely pulled-off "Will There Be Any" a cappella. There are the tough outlaw love songs like "She Left Me Holdin'" and the long, moving ballad "My Old Man," which follows the wild Dixieland ride of "I Like to Sleep Late in the Morning." There's Gary P. Nunn fronting

the band on a live version of "Rock Me, Roll Me" and the brass band feel of "The First Showboat." This is where Stephen Foster meets Louis Armstrong's Hot Fives meets Jerry Jeff's lazy, drawling Texas bass voice on the Mississippi. The album's high point is a ballad, Walker's version "Well of the Blues" by Nunn. It's simply arranged: a piano, a bass drum, a brushed snare, Walker's deep voice, and a backing chorus with a B-3 easing in the background very slowly and faintly. What can you say? It's another winner. *—Thom Jurek*

Ridin' High / 1975 / MCA ✦✦✦✦✦

The mid- to late '70s were good to Jerry Jeff Walker. He recorded a string of absolutely endearing classics of the outlaw singer/songwriter genre of country music: *Viva Terlingua, Walker's Collectibles, Jerry Jeff Walker, It's a Good Night for Singin'*, the live *A Man Must Carry On*, and this one, *Ridin' High* from 1975. Most Walker fans will argue like hell about which is best, but they are interchangeably great and stand the test of time in the same way Guy Clark's and Billy Joe Shaver's albums do. In any case, *Ridin' High* is pure Texas country drunk & roll with some Nash Vegas players added to the Lost Gonzo Band for some truly Cosmic Cowboy yammering. The material here is top-notch: Willie Nelson's "Pick Up the Tempo," Bob Livingston's "Public Domain," and Guy Clark's "Like a Coat From the Cold"—and they're the first three tracks on the album! Walker has a way of delivering drunken anthems and tender ballads in his deep bass voice that brings you into the song so far you feel as if he's singing it just for you and your friends. He does this consistently on this album, backed by a star cast of players including not only the Gonzos but also Johnny Gimble, David Briggs, Norbert Putnam, and others. And the gorgeous horn touches added by Michael Brovsky are stunning. Two of Walker's own best songs are here, "I Love You," written for his then new wife Susan, and the rowdy man's good-time anthem "Pissin' in the Wind." The album is rounded out by Jesse Winchester's "Mississippi You're on My Mind," Mike Burton's oft-covered nugget "Night Rider's Lament," and a few others. The album feels like a solid stream of hippie cowboy music fed by cold Lone Star, lots of pot, and the occasional line. To listen closely is to miss the point. This is an album to be experienced with the senses, entering into the free flow of Walker's good-time world even for the 40 minutes it takes to listen to the album. But that's far better than nothin', ain't it? *—Thom Jurek*

It's a Good Night for Singin' / 1976 / MCA ✦✦✦✦✦

While *It's a Good Night for Singin'* is usually as highly regarded as *Viva Terlingua, Ridin' High*, or *Jerry Jeff Walker*, it is not only the equal of those recordings, but perhaps, in its own way, more consistent than all of them—or therefore their superior. Released in 1976, it has the strongest opening side of any record in Walker's career. It includes a stomping cover of Tom Waits' "Lookin' for the Heart of Saturday Night," reinvented as a rock & roll song with B-3s and Fender Rhodes pianos underneath a throbbing bassline (and replaces Waits' own version as definitive), and an urbanized honky tonk read of Butch Hancock's "Standin' at the Big Hotel" that blows away Joe Ely's and sounds a lot more like L.A. than Dallas—which was the original intent of the song—just to name two. In addition, Walker rounds out side one with the Gary P. Nunn/Karen Brooks classic "Couldn't Do Nothin' Right," a ballad of resignation and brokenness at leaving a lover who always expected more than there was to give; it also features Lee Clayton's greatest love song, "Won't You Give Me One More Chance," Bob Livingstone's "Head Full of Nothin'," and a stirring, good-timey take on Billy Joe Shaver's classic "Old Five and Dimers Like Me." What is most notable here is what a great interpreter Walker is on other writers' songs, rather than as a songwriter making them his own in the process. There is only one original on the set, and that's the immortal "Stoney," which proves Walker hadn't lost it, but was going for something else entirely. There are a couple of Keith Sykes' tunes on side two, including "Someday I'll Get out of These Bars" (which Walker hasn't yet, over 27 years later), Billy C. Farlow's "Leroy," and Bob Livingstone's title track, all of which prove, like the first side, that this was indeed an album for singing, not writing, and as such, it stands as one of Walker's water marks; it endures far better than some of his other material from the same period. *—Thom Jurek*

A Man Must Carry On / 1977 / MCA ✦✦✦✦

When issued on LP, *A Man Must Carry On* was a double set sold for a special price. On CD it is two separate volumes at full-list price. What the hell? OK, OK, the music. *A Man Must Carry On* is Jerry Jeff Walker with the Lost Gonzo Band and some poet friends, Willie Nelson, and a bunch of folks. Some of it is live in front of an audience, some of it is in the studio, and some of it is a mess. And thank goodness. Released at the dawn of punk rock—though most folks had no idea until 1980 or so—*A Man Must Carry On* was Jerry Jeff and producer Michael Brovsky doing what they did best, throwin' stuff at the wall to see what stuck. Most of this does. The live material is truly fine, wooly and free-flowing. It's worth the purchase price for side four alone: "Mr. Bojangles; "L.A. Freeway"; a rock & roll medley of "Sea Cruise," "Johnny B. Goode," and "Peggy Sue"; a version of Dylan's "One Too Many Mornings"; and rounded off with the profane and the sacred: Ray Wylie Hubbard's anthem "Up Against the Wall Redneck Mother," which gives way to the Carters' "Will the Circle Be Unbroken." Talk about immediacy, spontaneity, and energy... screw the Sex Pistols. Other treasures include deeply moving renditions of "Honky Tonk Music" and "Railroad Lady" by Walker and Jimmy Buffett. The latter was actually cut by Merle Haggard! But the uncovering of it all is the place near the end of side three when Hondo Crouch, an infamous mayor of a small Texas town, gets up and reads his cowboy poetry in his unwavering, aged voice. Where else but on a Jerry Jeff Walker record could you get hillbilly music, live rock & roll, and performance art along with spirituals? Highly recommended. *—Thom Jurek*

Contrary to Ordinary / 1978 / MCA ✦✦✦

Contrary to Ordinary was the beginning of a shift in Jerry Jeff Walker's music that would forever take him away from the simple songwriting and production style that had created such a magical run of albums from 1970-1977. It would also be his last album for MCA. Does that mean this isn't a fine recording? Hardly. In fact, it might be the last of his consistent records, but it brings huge production into his material as well as his deep love of the Caribbean, as evidenced by the opener, "Tryin' to Hold the Wind Up With a Sail," with its faux-calypso rhythms and synthed steel-drum sounds. "Saturday Night Special" has Walker working with a fretless bass player and covering the Lee Clayton tune with a full horn section and funky backbeat. But it works like a mother; the Jerry Lee Lewis-meets-Albert Ammons boogie-woogie of "Suckin' a Big Bottle of Gin" doesn't. But there is a true classic here—Walker's reading of Rodney Crowell's "Til I Gain Control Again" closes side one, and it's one of the finest versions of the song ever cut. Walker is totally believable as a character who is just barely hanging on to life by a thread because of his brokenness and being ravaged by love. The title cut is a Walker anthem and here it comes off purely and without artifice. Ultimately, this is a fine album, but it feels unsure of itself and very self-conscious. The songs don't feel linked thematically as they did on previous records. But it holds up well over time, unlike a lot of other albums from the period. *—Thom Jurek*

Jerry Jeff / 1978 / Elektra ✦✦✦✦

The close of the 1970s saw Jerry Jeff Walker quickly approaching the second major crossroads in his career. The first happened when he moved to Texas and left behind his shuffling folk music ways. The second occurred when he was with Elektra, on this album in particular. Walker was moving in directions where enormous sounds and big-time rock & roll crescendos as well as a steady stream of jazz influences were entering his work, and he was writing less and less. Here, the first two tracks are startling in their contrast, as is the first half of the album to the second. The opener, "Eastern Avenue River Railway Blues," begins with the familiar, slow, meandering good-time Walker telling a story in song in his inimitable fashion. That is dressed in overlaid piano tracks and jazz scatting and still retains its essential Walker flavor. Lee Clayton's "Lone Wolf" is given a Neil Young and Crazy Horse treatment with grungy guitars screaming and huge drums popping all over the mix. Contrast this with the bluesy "Bad News," with its New Orleans R&B-cum-honky tonk country flavor, full of horns and upright piano and raucous guitars, and you have something of an anomaly for Walker. This continues through "Boogie Mama," which sounds like Bob Seger in Texas, and the easy Dixieland swing of "I'm Not Strange," a big Walker singalong with electric guitars backing a brass section. And then comes the shift where Walker's growing fascination with the Caribbean becomes entrenched in his sound on "Good Lovin' Grace." But on Guy Clark's "Comfort and Crazy" and "Follow," Walker leans into a love song in a way that only he can, despite the rhythmic invention. They are tender, full of his rich bass voice, and sweet in the same way an old sweater is. The album ends with Rodney Crowell's classic ballad "By the Banks of the Old Bandera," a song that may not have been written for Walker, but after recording it, no one else should be allowed to. In all, *Jerry Jeff* is a far better album than it seemed to be in its day. It was simply ahead of its time, and those in the music press who criticized it just didn't quite know what listeners were hearing. [Both *Too Old to Change* and this one are Walker classics that have stood the test of time, and both are available on one fine-sounding CD from Wounded Bird Records. Apologies to *Jerry Jeff* and crew for misunderstanding the first time around, and thanks for this one.] *—Thom Jurek*

Too Old to Change / 1979 / Elektra ✦✦✦✦

Musically, this is a restless, adventurous album. Walker left his Austin gang behind for the most part, with the exception of drummer Freddie Krc. Reese Wynans jumped aboard on acoustic piano, Dave Perkins played lead guitar, and Bobby Rambo played rhythm. Musicologist and jazz musician David Amram played French horn on a couple of cuts, and on Susanna Clark's "Ill Be Your San Antone Rose," Carole King sings a duet with Walker—one of the album's high points, along with the title track—and there is also a garage rock version of Rodney Crowell's "Ain't Livin' Long Like This." Side two boasts a few gems as well, such as Willis Alan Ramsey's "Northeast Texas Women," Paul Siebel's "Then Came the Children," and a weird but satisfying version of Kris Kristofferson's "Me and Bobby McGee." With conga drums, marimbas, subtle French horns, and clarinets, Walker was going after something else in his music. He was searching for a way to open up his brand of Texas country music to the world, and on *Too Old to Change* it works like a charm. *—Thom Jurek*

The Best of Jerry Jeff Walker / 1980 / MCA ✦✦✦✦✦

The Best of Jerry Jeff Walker is a concise, ten-track collection of tunes from his years on the MCA label. It includes all the Jerry Jeff favorites while never being anything more than a straightforward greatest-hits compilation, thereby making it a fine record for those wishing an overview of his career. *—James Chrispell*

Reunion / 1981 / MCA ✦✦✦

Cowjazz / 1982 / MCA ✦✦✦

Gypsy Songman / 1988 / Rykodisc ✦✦✦✦✦

Gypsy Songman is a very good 28-song overview of Jerry Jeff Walker's career, concentrating on his lesser-known songs. The compilation is divided between originals and eight covers, all of which are performed with his signature laid-back style. *—Thom Owens*

Live from Gruene Hall / 1989 / Rykodisc ✦✦✦

Live from Gruene Hall is an excellent return to form from Jerry Jeff Walker. Running through a selection of new songs, Walker is accompanied by a tight version of the Lost Gonzo Band, who help turn these performances into little gems. The hit singles "I Feel Like Hank Williams Tonight," "The Pickup Song" and "Trashy Women" only are the tip of the iceberg. It's may be a live album, but *Live from Gruene Hall* is arguably one of the best records Walker ever made. Of special note is a brief vocal cameo by Willie Nelson. *—Thom Owens*

● **Great Gonzos** / 1991 / MCA ✦✦✦✦✦
Great Gonzos is a good cross-section of 14 of Jerry Jeff Walker's best-known songs, including "Mr. Bojangles," "Old Five and Dimers Like Me," "Desperados Waiting for the Train" and "Sangria Wine." It's not necessarily definitive—several of his actual charting hits did not make the collection, including "Jaded Lover," "It's A Good Night for Singing," and "Got Lucky Last Night"—but it cuts to the essence of Walker, making it an excellent introduction. —*Thom Owens*

Navajo Rug / Aug. 1991 / Rykodisc ✦✦✦
Navajo Rug offers Walker's tribute to aging athletes, "Nolan Ryan (He's a Hero to Us All)." —*Jason Ankeny*

Hill Country Rain / 1992 / Rykodisc ✦✦✦✦
After *Too Old to Change*, Jerry Jeff Walker went into a creative slide—albums like *Cowjazz* and *Reunion* were embarrassing for an artist of his stature—that existed until he signed with Rykodisc, and even then on *Gypsy Songman*, and this set has Walker playing some of his older tunes redone with modern production. But on both records, particularly here, Walker is clearly in the midst of a creative renaissance. *Hill Country Rain* kicks off with a stunning freewheeling anthem in "Rock & Roll My Baby" in which he restates his claim to the outlaw throne. Walker's obsession with fusing his brand of country with his adopted home in the Caribbean drenches "So Bad Last Night," but it works better than anything Jimmy Buffett has written in the same vein for over two decades. The plaintive cover of Steven Fromholz's "Singin' the Dinosaur Blues" blows away the original and could have been written by Walker himself. In any case, Fromholz should never play it again after this. The place of pan pipes feels a bit strange but adds immeasurably. But it's Walker's own songs that ring the truest. Accompanied by the Lost Gonzo Compadres—Gary P. Nunn is missing, but Lloyd Maines is present—plainly put, Walker writes his ass off here, from "Time to Stay Home," with its moving account of wisdom gained from a lifetime of being a gypsy songman, to the moving and tender "Last Night I Fell in Love Again" and on into "To the Artist." Walker's decades of war stories have evolved into a bittersweet wisdom. Even the recordings of "Curly and Lil" and the title track are fresh and new, wringing new truths from the old words. This is a record about songs, not about Walker's myth; here is a place where art and the truth converge, and listeners are lucky to encounter them both in his work once again. —*Thom Jurek*

Christmas Gonzo Style / 1994 / Rykodisc ✦✦✦

Viva Luckenbach! / 1994 / Rykodisc ✦✦✦
If you like sappy songs, honky tonk humor and a Texas twang, this is the album for you. Far too regional to have ever reached a popular audience, this 1994 Rykodisc CD captures live a band having a good-time. If you can get past the overdone sentimentalism of songs like "Keep Texas Beautiful," you should have no problem listening to the fun tracks on the CD, like "Movin' On." —*Jeff Crooke*

Night After Night / Dec. 28, 1995 / Rykodisc ✦✦✦

Man Must Carry On, Vol. 1 / Jan. 28, 1997 / MCA ✦✦✦✦✦
The first in a series compiling the songs of the legendary Texas singer/songwriter Jerry Jeff Walker, *The Man Must Carry On, Vol. 1* includes "Don't It Make You Want to Dance," "Roll on Down the Road," "Leavin' Texas," "Honky Tonk Music" and "Ro-Deo-Deo Cowboy." —*Jason Ankeny*

Man Must Carry On, Vol. 2 / Jan. 28, 1997 / MCA ✦✦✦✦✦
A Man Must Carry On, Vol. 2 features sly Walker favorites like "Up Against the Wall, Redneck Mother," the Guy Clark-penned "L.A. Freeway," "Will the Circle Be Unbroken" and "Mr. Bojangles." —*Jason Ankeny*

Lone Wolf: The Best of Jerry Jeff Walker / 1998 / Warner Archives ✦✦✦
This compilation draws seven tracks each from the two albums Jerry Jeff Walker released on Elektra Records: *Jerry Jeff* (1978) and *Too Old to Change* (1979). Walker moved to Elektra after a successful run on MCA and promptly got lost. While that can in part be attributed to record company convulsions, it's also apparent listening to the performances of these songs of dissolution that their singer was taking their themes to heart—he sounds hung over most of the time. Of course, that's an appropriate condition for titles that include Guy Clark's "Comfort and Crazy," Keith Sykes' "I'm Not Strange" and Rodney Crowell's "I Ain't Living Long Like This." Sometimes on these songs, Walker recalls the easygoing hedonism of Jimmy Buffett, but unlike Buffett, he sounds like he was still living the life he was singing about and is the worse for wear. It's good to have this material back in print, and it is a significant chapter in Walker's history, but it isn't Walker at his best. —*William Ruhlmann*

Cowboy Boots & Bathin Suits / Apr. 14, 1998 / Tried & True ✦✦✦

Best of the Vanguard Years / Mar. 23, 1999 / Vanguard ✦✦✦✦
Jerry Jeff Walker's *Best of the Vanguard Years* collection includes some of his finest songwriting for Circus Maximus as well as his early solo efforts. This album features two versions of his ballad "Fading Lady," one recorded with Circus Maximus and one with the players Walker worked with in Nashville while recording his solo album *Driftin' Way of Life. Best of the Vanguard Years* also features songs like "Trying to Live Right," "Negative Dreamer Girl" and "No Roots in Ramblin'," which hint at the influence Walker would have on country and folk-rock groups for years to come. —*Heather Phares*

Gonzo Stew / May 8, 2001 / Tried & True ✦✦✦

Ultimate Collection / Aug. 28, 2001 / Hip-O ✦✦✦✦✦
Ultimate Collection is the most lengthy and comprehensive anthology yet assembled on Jerry Jeff Walker, with tracks licensed from three different labels spanning the late '60s through the late '70s. His classic "Mr. Bojangles" is here with other crowd pleasers such as "Hairy Ass Hillbillies," "Pissin' in the Wind," and "Up Against the Wall Redneck Mother." Walker had a poetic side, too, but *Ultimate Collection* focuses mainly on his ram-

bunctious singalongs, and entirely skips some of his early albums. All but one of his hits from the '70s is included, but none of his '80s hits made the cut. In sum, *Ultimate Collection* is an imperfect survey of Walker's first decade or so, but has plenty of popular appeal. —*Greg Adams*

20th Century Masters—The Millennium Collection: The Best of Jerry Jeff Walker / Sep. 10, 2002 / MCA ✦✦✦✦
Unforgivably, it does not say this *anywhere* on the CD packaging, but this is a compilation of material from Walker's MCA releases of the early to late '70s. This was one of his stronger periods as both a commercial and artistic presence, so what's the harm in putting release dates on the track listings? At any rate, it's a fair run-through a dozen tracks from half a dozen albums, at a time when Walker was among the foremost singer/songwriters fusing country, rock, Americana, and a little pop. Focusing on story-songs with the somewhat humorous yet world-weary tone common to numerous Texas-based singer/songwriters of this ilk, this includes some of Walker's better works, like "Sangria Wine," "Pissin' in the Wind," and "Hairy Ass Hillbillies." Also it reflects the role he took as an interpretive artist to popularize some songs by Guy Clark ("L.A. Freeway," "Desperadoes Waiting for a Train"), Ray Wylie Hubbard ("Up Against the Wall, Redneck Mother"), and Billy Joe Shaver ("Old Five and Dimers Like Me"). Note that the version of "Mr. Bojangles" here is not Walker's original recording, but a live one from the *A Man Must Carry On* album. —*Richie Unterberger*

Too Old to Change/Jerry Jeff / May 20, 2003 / Wounded Bird ✦✦✦✦
While it's inexcusable that MCA hasn't done this with some of the best of Jerry Jeff Walker's catalog—titles such as *It's a Good Night for Singin', Jerry Jeff Walker*, and a single-package version of *A Man Must Carry On* come immediately to mind—Wounded Bird has accomplished something quite special in releasing this pair of his Elektra sets. Generally considered to be inferior to his MCA material, hearing them in the context of this time period reveals just how consistent the material and performances are, and secondly, it is revelatory to see just how visionary and musically restless Walker had become when he began to produce himself. Here is the Walker fans had come to know and love, singing songs about rounders and everyday folks in their joys and struggles—as well as a tune or two about having too much of a good-time—placed in musical settings that contained everything from hard rock, Caribbean rhythms, Dixieland jazz, bluegrass, outlaw country, folk, and even soul. *Too Old to Change* is the first chapter, with Walker sticking close to what he knew—great songs, good players, fine performances, and stretching it by using conga drums, marimbas, and a whole slew of musicians not associated with Austin at all (including Carole King on one track). Then he took it to the limit on *Jerry Jeff*, with a nearly divine sonic cacophony of great dynamics, a killer collection of songs, musically genre-bending instrumentation and performances, and a *joie de vivre* fans hadn't heard since his earliest country records. The remastering job is fabulous on these titles, giving fans a chance to hear this period in Walker's career in a whole new light. The only complaint is the lack of credits that were on the original albums, but then sometimes you can't have everything, and this will do quite nicely. —*Thom Jurek*

Chris Wall
b. Newport Beach, CA
Guitar, Harmonica, Vocals / Singer/Songwriter, Alternative Country, Americana
Any guy could put on a Stetson hat and pretend he is a country singer, but Chris Wall is the real thing, a songwriter who knows about honky tonks and country clichés. Wall is alternately humorous ("Something to Shoot" from *Honky Tonk Heart*) and personable, relating little stories showing that he wears his honky tonk heart on his sleeve. Born in Newport Beach, CA, Wall was the son of a singer who collaborated with the Sons of the Pioneers' Bob Nolan. Wall also spent time at his uncle's cattle ranch, growing to love the country more than his usual surroundings. He later moved to Montana and began writing country songs; he met Guy Clark in 1987 and, after the two swapped songs, Clark recommended the young singer to Jerry Jeff Walker, who caught his show in Jackson Hole, WY. Impressed by what he saw, Walker invited Wall down to Austin in 1988 to record with him. After a few sessions, he moved there and released his debut tape in mid-1989. Rykodisc signed the back-to-basics country guitarist after hearing the tape and seeing his support slot for Walker. Remixed and remastered, *Honky Tonk Heart* appeared in 1990. *No Sweat* was released the following year. A long hiatus preceded the release of *Tainted Angel* in 1998. —*John Bush & Dennis MacDonald*

● **Honky Tonk Heart** / 1991 / Rykodisc ✦✦✦✦✦
Though it could use a more distinguished instrumental backing, *Honky Tonk Heart* is a fine neo-traditional country album, demonstrating that Chris Wall is a vocalist of considerable promise. —*Thom Owens*

No Sweat / Sep. 27, 1991 / Rykodisc ✦✦✦

Tainted Angel / Oct. 6, 1998 / Cold Spring ✦✦✦✦
Backed by the members of the band Reckless Kelly, Chris Wall returns from a long studio hiatus with the fine *Tainted Angel*, a record which balances the dark, poignant intimacy of songs like "Turns to Tears," "I Never Got Over Losing You" and "The Empty Seat Beside Me" with raucous, neo-honky tonk performances. —*Jason Ankeny*

Any Saturday Night in Texas—Live / Oct. 20, 1998 / Cold Spring ✦✦✦✦
Joined by guests including Dale Watson, Kelly Willis, Mary Cutrufello and Bruce Robison, Chris Wall is at the top of his game throughout *Any Saturday Night in Texas—Live*; the wit at the heart of all his songs really blossoms in the concert setting, as does his skill as a storyteller—the man's a true raconteur. —*Hank Small*

Cowboy Nation / Mar. 9, 1999 / Cold Spring ✦✦✦✦
Cowboy Nation remains Chris Wall's most poignant record, an honest and heartfelt song cycle capturing the gradual erosion of the western lifestyle and its accompanying mythos.

Produced by the legendary Lloyd Maines, the album is tough but tender, its most reflective moments tempered by Wall's cynical wit—its centerpiece, "I Feel Like Hank Williams Tonight," is a lost classic. —*Hank Small*

Jerry Wallace

b. Dec. 15, 1933, Kansas City, MO

Guitar, Vocals / Country-Pop, Nashville Sound/Countrypolitan

Considered a pop act during the late '50s with a pair of huge hits, Jerry Wallace successfully migrated to the country field during the '60s and '70s. Wallace began recording in 1951 and burst onto the pop charts in 1958 on the Challenge label with "How the Time Flies" and the even bigger "Primrose Lane" a year later. His focus became more country-oriented with "Shutters and Boards" and "In the Misty Moonlight" in 1963-64, and he made a full-fledged switch in 1965 after switching to the Mercury label. A move to Liberty in 1968 didn't pay off, but in 1972, soon after he began recording for Decca, "If You Leave Me Tonight I'll Cry" topped the country charts (as did the LP *To Get to You*). During the next year, "Do You Know What It's Like to Be Lonesome" and "Don't Give Up on Me" both reached the Top Five, but Wallace only managed one more Top Ten, 1974's "My Wife's House" (for MCA). He charted continually until the end of the decade, though, while recording for MGM, 4-Star, BMA, and Door Knob. —*Bill Dahl*

Greatest Hits / 1990 / Curb ✦✦✦✦✦

Curb's *Greatest Hits* is an ten-track budget-priced collection that features some of Jerry Wallace's biggest hits, including "Primrose Lane," "How the Time Flies," "To Get to You," "Don't Give Up on Me" and "If You Leave Me Tonight I'll Cry." Although this isn't a bad budget-priced disc, there are better collections available, offering more songs, more hits and better sound for not much more money. —*Stephen Thomas Erlewine*

● **Primrose Lane: The Very Best of Jerry Wallace** / Jul. 28, 1998 / Collectables ✦✦✦✦✦

Although the packaging and remastering could have been a little sharper, *Primrose Lane: The Very Best of Jerry Wallace* remains the best available collection of his pop hits from the '50s and '60s, all of which were recorded for Challenge. Country fans will want a collection that spotlights his Liberty, Decca, MCA and MGM recordings, but fans of his pop hits will be pleased with this generous, 24-track collection—even with its small handful of imperfections. —*Stephen Thomas Erlewine*

Don Walser

b. Sep. 14, 1934, Brownfield, TX

Vocals / Alternative Country, Americana, Western Swing Revival, Yodeling

Even in Texas folk and country music circles, singer and guitarist Don Walser is regarded as unique. The songs Walser specializes in aren't exactly current; he sings classic old Western swing tunes. In a sense, he's a man on a mission: keeping the old Texas country songs alive. Songs like "Cowpoke," "Tumbling Tumbleweeds," and "Mexicali Rose" are signature tunes for Walser, who is also one of the country's premier yodelers. Songs penned and popularized by Bob Wills, the Sons of the Pioneers, Hank Williams, Faron Young, Merle Travis, and Johnny Horton are all part and parcel of what you're likely to hear in the course of a typical Walser show.

Walser's mother died when he was 12 and his father worked nights, so to keep himself company, he listened to the radio in his childhood home of LaMesa in West Texas. He formed his first band at 16, and a year later, he was playing the few clubs and roadhouses around LaMesa. At the same time Walser was playing country music, a west Texas neighbor of his, Buddy Holly, was raising the roofs at local roadhouses playing rock & roll. As rock & roll came into fashion in the late '50s, Walser and other country musicians were nearly run out of business. With the rise of rock & roll, Walser put his budding music career on hold in 1957 and joined the National Guard. Through a procession of day jobs with the National Guard, Walser's musical adventures remained an avocation. Most recently, he worked as an internal auditor for the state Adjutant General's office in Austin. But through the 39 years with the National Guard, he always played music with various bands, mostly as a hobby. He retired in 1994 and picked up where he'd left off in his youth, taking his act on the road full-time.

Walser's albums for Watermelon Records include a few of his originals, like "Rolling Stone from Texas." Many fans are awestruck upon first hearing Walser's unique voice. His albums for Watermelon include *Texas Top Hand*, *Rolling Stone From Texas*, and *Down at the Sky-Vue Drive-In*. Walser tours around Texas and the U.S. with a group called the Pure Country Band, and he's also quick to credit Ray Benson's group, Asleep at the Wheel, with helping to keep old, often obscure Western swing tunes alive. Now in his late '60s, Walser has lived in Austin since 1984, where he's found legions of supportive fans who believe in and understand the "real country" music he performs. —*Richard Skelly*

● **Rolling Stone From Texas** / 1994 / Watermelon ✦✦✦✦

Once upon a time, a Texas label called Watermelon released country music that was as honest as the latest fare from Nashville was plastic. When Watermelon went belly up, a number of artists like the Derailers and Don Walser were out of luck. Now, thanks to the Texas Music Group, a few of these gems are being reissued. Western swinger Walser cut his first album, *Rolling Stone From Texas*, for Watermelon in 1994. This debut still shimmers, whether Walser is yodeling, singing an original, or offering a fresh take on Jimmie Rodgers' "California Blues." There's a fine version of Tennessee Ernie Ford's treatise on the dangers of courtship, "Shotgun Boogie," and an authentic rendering of Stan Jones' classic, "Cowpoke." Marty Robbins' "Don't Worry (About Me)" and Willie Nelson's "Three Days" also make noteworthy appearances. The arrangements vary a bit from song to song, but Western swing staples like pedal steel, lap steel, dobro, and lots of fiddle are prominent. Walser's fun and self-assured vocals on "(The Party Don't Start) 'Til the Playboys Get Here" convince the listener that he isn't just mimicking an old style: he loves and personifies western music. Like Don Edwards, Walser also convinces listeners that older styles of country can be just as relevant and enjoyable today. *Rolling Stone From Texas* is a fine introduction to Walser and a fine introduction to contemporary Western swing. —*Ronnie D. Lankford Jr.*

The Archive Series, Vol. 1 / 1995 / Watermelon ✦✦✦✦

The Archive Series, Vol. 2 / 1995 / Watermelon ✦✦✦✦

Texas Top Hand / Mar. 19, 1996 / Watermelon ✦✦✦✦✦

After decades of playing Texas dancehalls, Don Walser enjoyed his first national recognition in 1994, thanks to the gleeful celebration of his unmistakable vocal talent in *Rolling Stone From Texas*. *Texas Top Hand* finds him enjoying the fruits of his success by taking a few songs uptown. Working again with producer Ray Benson of Asleep at the Wheel, Walser again yodels with unabashed acrobatic delight and soars with nimble, full-throated joy through country classics and old-sounding new tunes. He sings with a robustly happy spirit, as his sky-high trills convey, and this time he occasionally leads a brassy big band with the same homespun clarity that he lends to steel-driven, peanut-shell dancehall tunes. —*Michael McCall*

Down at the Sky-Vue Drive-In / Apr. 21, 1998 / Watermelon ✦✦✦✦

While *Down at the Sky-Vue Drive-In* might not match the heights of *Texas Top Hand* and *Rolling Stone From Texas*, it still is an axcellent set of of direct, no-nonsense progressive country from the remarkably talented Don Walser. Whether they're new songs or covers of classics like "Cherokee Maiden" and "Please Help Me I'm Falling," the songs are first rate, and the lean production from Ray Benson brings out the best. Among the highlights on the album are his two duets with Mandy Barnett ("I'm Leaving It Up to You," "Hearts of Stone") and "Rose Marie," a surprisingly successful collaboration with the Kronos Quartet. —*Thom Owens*

Here's to Country Music / Sep. 21, 1999 / Sirc ✦✦✦✦

Don Walser's *Here's To Country Music* runs contrary to most of the albums by contemporary country music artists, eschewing rock & roll antics and pop polish for genuine country music. Honky-tonk, Western swing, cowboy yodeling and other traditional country music styles get their due on songs like "Sugar Moon," "Oakie Boogie," "Polka Dot Blues," "Paper Rosie" and eight others. Crystal Gayle and Teddy Wilburn also make appearances on *Here's to Country Music*, giving the album even more of a traditional, generational feel. —*Heather Phares*

I'll Hold You in My Heart / Sep. 26, 2000 / Valley ✦✦✦✦

It's fitting that around the time of this release Don Walser won a National Heritage Award, for this man's voice is a national treasure and qualifies as high Texas folk art. Walser's been doing this for a half-decade, and many of those years as an avocation, so obviously he has not seen the rewards and recognition of many of his classic country peers. The new millennium finds him still keeping swinging country music alive, however—and in good throat, as *I'll Hold You in My Heart* attests. He's made his mark with his unparalleled yodeling, and the album kicks off with his unearthly stylings all over the yodeling showcase "Yodeling the Blues." The title track places Walser in ballad mode, and when he punctuates his lonesomeness by shooting glibly up into falsetto, it'll raise the hair on your arms. The Walser composition "El Paso Cowboy" finds Walser alternating between straight, low-histrionic honky tonk singing and short, sweet flourishes of yodeling. He also tackles Merle Haggard's "Hungry Eyes" in a lower register and pays tribute to Haggard and co-icon Buck Owens with the Bakersfield-flavored "Buck & Merle." When it comes to evocative, classic country music, it doesn't get much better than this. —*Erik Hage*

Dare to Dream: The Best of Don Walser / Oct. 30, 2001 / Texas Music Group ✦✦✦✦✦

Don Walser is Texas, it's really as simple as that. He epitomizes the state's music even more than the legendary Willie Nelson. For years he toiled the honky tonks and bars while holding down a day job, and didn't record his first album until 20 years after his first single in 1964. But since he began recording, he's unleashed a series of classic Texas country tunes, starting with his signature piece, "Rolling Stone From Texas," represented, as it should be, in two versions: one the polished album edition, the other a rawer live version from 1964, the year it appeared as a single. What they bookend is nothing less than a series of marvels, like "The John Deere Tractor Song," a wonderful ode to farmers; a glorious version of "Whispering Pines" that shimmers, with Walser's soft yodel bumping it along; his own "Hot Rod Mercury," car nostalgia in four honky tonk minutes; and a very strange version of "Rose Marie," performed with the Kronos Quartet. There are tracks collected from soundtracks, compilation albums, and a couple of unreleased pieces, and they're all sung with the same easy grace that's Walser's trademark. He has a big voice (he's been called the Pavarotti of the plains), and while relaxed, there's sometimes a formality about it that harks back to the '30s and '40s, which suits songs like Felice Bryant's "We Could You and I," as well as his own wonderful material, which has brought him deserved success. Walser deserves a greatest-hits set, and this collection serves him very well indeed. —*Chris Nickson*

Sings Pure Country / Bear Family ✦✦✦

Monte Warden

Vocals / Alternative Country, Americana

Monte Warden combines rockabilly roots rock with honky tonk and blue-eyed soul ballads. He first caught the eyes of his native Austin, TX's scene in 1983. At the age of 15, Warden's trio, Whoa Trigger!, won Best New Band at a local awards show. Five years later, his band, the Wagoneers, won the award again and became a "young country" favorite with two albums on A&M, *Stout & High* and *Good Fortune*. His first solo album (self-titled) appeared in July of 1993, and the follow-up, *Here I Am*, was released in July 1995. *A Stranger to Me Now* followed in 1999. His solo backing band, the Lonesharks, includes guitarist Brent Wilson (formerly of the Wagoneers), bassist Brad Fordham, and drummer/co-producer Mas Palermo. —*John Bush*

● **Monte Warden** / 1993 / Watermelon ✦✦✦✦✦
Imagine finding a long-lost Buddy Holly album—not outtakes, but the real thing. Then start playing *Monte Warden* just about anywhere—"Don't Know a Thing," "It's Amazing," "All I Want Is You," or even the ballad "Just to Hear Your Voice." You won't feel let down. *—Brian Mansfield*

Here I Am / 1995 / Watermelon ✦✦✦
Monte Warden's second album for the Austin, Texas-based Watermelon label, *Here I Am* is a fine example of the kind of country/roots rock hybrid for which the label's home city is so well known. Although there are few surprises, the musicianship is top-notch with that incredibly tight, but relaxed, feel that only the most experienced pros can pull off. All of the album's ten tracks were written or co-written by Warden and, as the cover photo of Warden clutching a Rickenbacker 360 would indicate, are closer to the pop side of the roots rock fence. In fact, much of the music here would not seem out of place on Rockpile's *Seconds of Pleasure*, or any of that band's members' (particularly Dave Edmunds) rootsier solo efforts. In addition, there are echoes of other purveyors of pure pop like Marshall Crenshaw and T-Bone Burnett (and, on the beautiful "Do You Remember," Warren Zevon). Warden's voice, while not particularly distinctive, has a pleasant, unaffected quality and a surprisingly clear upper-register tone that sometimes recalls Roy Orbison. Unfortunately, Warden never seems particularly involved emotionally in the music. Although some songs are almost saved by the snappy lead guitar work of David Murray, and it's obvious that Warden is a very capable artist, the album as a whole comes off more as an exercise in proficiency, or a songwriting demo, than as a fully realized work. *—Pemberton Roach*

A Stranger to Me Now / Mar. 9, 1999 / Elektra ✦✦✦

Steve Wariner

b. Dec. 25, 1954, Noblesville, IN

Guitar, Vocals, Bass / Contemporary Country, Neo-Traditionalist Country, Western Swing Revival, Country-Folk

One of country music's most versatile performers, Steve Wariner grew up in suburban Indianapolis, interested in the Beatles on the radio, as well as Chet Atkins and George Jones, the artists his father listened to most frequently. He started playing music in his dad's band, and by his high-school years, he was playing local clubs. At age 17, he caught the ear of Dottie West, who persuaded him to join her band, and in that position he ended up playing bass on her classic 1973 single "Country Sunshine." He moved on to work as a sideman for Bob Luman and signed a singles deal with RCA Records in 1976. His career developed slowly, and in the beginning, the low-tuned guitars and wide range of his singles brought frequent comparisons to the early Glen Campbell hits. His first really successful single was "Your Memory," which peaked in the country Top Ten in early 1981, followed by "By Now" and "All Roads Lead to You," which topped the country charts in December. RCA released another couple of singles before finally issuing his debut album, *Steve Wariner*, in the fall of 1982. He returned to the country Top Ten in 1983 with "Midnight Fire," which became the title track of his second album, and "Lonely Women Make Good Lovers."

Wariner's career really took off when he left RCA for MCA in late 1984. His first single for the new label, "What I Didn't Do," made the country Top Five in early 1985, setting off a string of 18 consecutive Top Ten hits that included the chart-toppers "Some Fools Never Learn," "You Can Dream of Me," "Life's Highway," "Small Town Girl," "The Weekend," "Lynda," "Where Did I Go Wrong," and "I Got Dreams" (the last two Wariner compositions). This run took him into 1990, when he switched to Arista Records. He had considerable initial success on the new label, with his first Arista album, *I Am Ready*, going platinum (none of his previous albums had even gone gold) and his first three Arista singles making the Top Ten. And he shared a 1991 Grammy Award for Best Country Vocal Collaboration with Ricky Skaggs and Vince Gill for "Restless," a track on Mark O'Connor's album *The New Nashville Cats*.

Wariner scored a country Top Ten hit with "If I Didn't Love You" in the summer of 1993, but his record sales were declining. His 1996 instrumental album, *No More Mr. Nice Guy*, his first release in three years, did not chart, but that year he joined the *Grand Ole Opry*. In 1997, he sang with Anita Cochran on "What If I Said," and the single topped the country charts in early 1998, just after Garth Brooks' recording of Wariner's composition "Longneck Bottle" had gone to number one. This twin success reinvigorated his career. He signed to Capitol Records, Brooks' label, and released "Holes in the Floor of Heaven," which made the country Top Five, winning the Country Music Association's awards for Song of the Year and Single of the Year. *Burnin' the Roadhouse Down*, his debut album for Capitol, reached the country Top Ten, went gold, and crossed over to the Top 50 of the pop charts. He followed it with 1999's *Two Teardrops*, which also went gold; the same year, he shared his second Grammy for Best Country Instrumental for the Asleep at the Wheel track "Bob's Breakdown." His third Capitol album, *Faith in You*, was released in May 2000. *—William Ruhlmann and Tom Roland*

● **Steve Wariner** / 1982 / Buddha ✦✦✦✦✦
By the time of his debut album in 1982, guitarist, songwriter, and vocalist Steve Wariner's sophisticated country-pop sound was already perfected, and it showed by the quality of the material. While the album only contained ten tracks, over half ended up on the country charts: "All Roads Lead to You," "Kansas City Lights," "By Now," "Your Memory," "Don't It Break Your Heart," and "Don't Plan on Sleepin' Tonight." The original album is out of print, but these songs can be found on any number of Wariner best-of collections. *—Al Campbell*

Midnight Fire / 1983 / RCA Victor ✦✦✦

Life's Highway / 1985 / MCA ✦✦✦
Life's Highway was Steve Wariner's third album for RCA and showed him moving into a more mature musical direction. The best moments here outshine anything Wariner had recorded up to that point, including three hit singles: "She's Crazy for Leaving," "Starting Over Again," and the album's philosophical centerpiece, "Life's Highway." It's odd that someone with Wariner's songwriting stature didn't contribute to any of the album's hits. *—Al Campbell*

One Good Night Deserves Another / 1985 / MCA ✦✦✦

It's a Crazy World / 1987 / MCA ✦✦✦✦✦
Wariner's in charge vocally, and seems to glide through the album effortlessly. He's received more responsibility for his own direction, and—with one or two exceptions—has upgraded every aspect of his record, particularly in song selection and musicianship. *—Tom Roland*

Greatest Hits / Sep. 7, 1987 / RCA ✦✦✦✦✦
Many of Steve Wariner's best moments were his singles and *Greatest Hits* contains many of his best and biggest hits, including the number ones "Some Fools Never Learn," "You Can Dream of Me," and "Life's Highway." *—Thom Owens*

I Should Be with You / Mar. 7, 1988 / MCA ✦✦✦

I Got Dreams / 1989 / MCA ✦✦✦

Laredo / 1990 / MCA ✦✦✦
After nine years and nine number-one singles, Wariner had basically established himself as Mr. Consistency. *Laredo* proved, again, that he could sing any type of country well—swing ("L-O-V-E, Love"), rock ("The Domino Theory"), and heartbreak ballads conveying genuine pain ("She's in Love," "There for Awhile"). *—Brian Mansfield*

Greatest Hits, Vol. 2 / 1991 / MCA ✦✦✦
This second volume of Steve Wariner's output for the RCA label includes the number one hits "I Got Dreams," "Where Did I Go Wrong," "Hold On (A Little Longer)," and "I Should Be With You." For a more thorough summary of Wariner's hits from this era on one disc, check out *The Ultimate Collection* on Hip-O. *—Al Campbell*

I Am Ready / 1991 / Arista ✦✦✦✦
Wariner, a master of the subtle touch, builds this album's impact quietly and methodically, with songs like Bill Anderson's "The Tips of My Fingers" and Wariner's own "Like a River to the Sea." "Leave Him out of This" is a masterpiece of smoldering intensity, its raging anger and pain barely held in check. The only time Wariner lets it loose is at the end, where he locks his guitar in mortal combat with Mark O'Connor's fiddle in the cathartic "Crash Course in the Blues." *—Brian Mansfield*

Drive / Jul. 27, 1993 / Billboard Singles ✦✦✦

No More Mr. Nice Guy / Mar. 12, 1996 / Arista/BMG Special Products ✦✦✦

Burnin' the Roadhouse Down / Apr. 21, 1998 / Capitol ✦✦✦✦
Burnin' the Roadhouse Down finds Steve Wariner in typically fine form. It may have been five years since his last vocal album, *Drive* (there was an instrumental album, *No More Mr. Nice Guy*, in the meantime), but all that time off has revived Wariner, resulting in an album that's the equal of his 1991 high-water mark, *I Am Ready*. His music may not be as fresh as it was in the early '80s, when he was at the the beginning of his career, but he's become a masterful craftsman, and that's why the album shines. From the affecting ballad "Holes in the Floor of Heaven" to the Garth Brooks duet on the title track, *Burnin' the Roadhouse Down* is a terrific contemporary country record that finds a journeyman at the top of his form. *—Thom Owens*

The Hits / Oct. 6, 1998 / MCA ✦✦✦✦
With mentors like the late Dottie West, singer Bob Luman, and fellow guitar great Chet Atkins, Wariner has managed to remain vital in the music business since 1977. His deal with MCA, signed in 1984, has resulted in a career of some stature. An excellent technician, his guitar playing makes him a standout. Known for his soft touch in selecting material, songs like "The Weekend," "Can I Come Over Tonight" and "The Domino Theory," his most country country hit, built his reputation. Less obvious is his ability to pull out the stops, as he does on "Lynda," showing off his first recorded guitar solo, and "Life's Highway." *—Jana Pendragon*

Two Teardrops / May 4, 1999 / Capitol ✦✦✦
Burnin' the Roadhouse Down was a glorious comeback for Steve Wariner, proof positive that he could still deliver the goods after several years out of the spotlight. Its sequel, *Two Teardrops*, doesn't reach those same heights, but that doesn't mean that the album is a failure. As a matter of fact, the best moments on *Two Teardrops* equal those on its predecessor—it just that the material on this record isn't quite as consistent. That said, even the filler is engaging due to Wariner's lively performances, which help keep the record's momentum going throughout the 15 tracks. It may not be the stunner *Burnin' the Roadhouse Down* was, but *Two Teardrops* proves that Wariner can continue to make winners. *—Thom Owens*

Faith in You / May 9, 2000 / Capitol ✦✦✦
Steve Wariner's third Capitol album, *Faith in You*, is another consistent, craftsman-like effort from an artist who has made the most of his second chance in country music. Wariner has had the advantage that he is, at heart, a player more than a frontman, and his abilities as a guitarist, understated but always apparent in the style of his mentor, Chet Atkins, provide a basic level of enjoyment no matter what else is going on. Wariner is also a formalist who can write and perform a Western swing tune, like "I Just Do," and make it sound authentic. *Faith in You* contains several such genre exercises, as the singer/songwriter/guitarist picks his way through everything from the rock & roll sound of "Katie Wants a Fast One" (featuring Garth Brooks) to the gospel style of "Blinded," along the way standing toe to toe with Clint Black on "Been There," and coaxing a typically expressive effort from co-writer Rodney Crowell with the Mexican-tinged "Longer Letter Later." His "Holes in the Floor of Heaven" set a standard for sentimental, philosophical story songs in recent country music, and Wariner comes up with several

of them here, the most obvious winner being "Turn in the Road," though "Waiting in the Wings" and "I Wish I Were a Train" also fit the bill, and any of the three would make good singles. "Traditionalist" is a term with a specific meaning in country music, so it can't really be used to describe Wariner, who is a master of a variety of country subgenres, each of which has its own tradition. His approach may not be as admirable as that of a truly original artist, but country is a music that rewards adherence to its heritage, and country has no more faithful servant than Steve Wariner. *—William Ruhlmann*

Ultimate Collection / Aug. 29, 2000 / Hip-O ♦♦♦♦

Steve Wariner's *Ultimate Collection* gathers some of the best sides he recorded for RCA, MCA Nashville, and Arista Nashville, including number one country hits like "All Roads Lead to You," "Some Fools Never Learn," "Where Did I Go Wrong," and "Small Town Girl." The collection also includes his duets with Nicolette Larson ("That's How You Know When Love's Right") and Glen Campbell ("The Hand That Rocks the Cradle") as well as hit singles such as "The Tips of My Fingers," "I Should Be With You," and "Life's Highway." The most complete collection of Wariner's work available, *The Ultimate Collection* emphasizes both the depth and diversity of his enduring career. *—Heather Phares*

Steal Another Day / Feb. 4, 2003 / SelectOne ♦♦♦♦♦

Steve Wariner is one of Nashville's most mild-mannered and soft-spoken artists, but beyond this simple humility lies a talent that continues to evolve and to create beauty. Indeed, Wariner is just as at ease penning the profound as he is crooning it. Not only that, he'll pick the song on his acoustic guitar with the skill of his mentor, Chet Atkins. Simultaneously piloting his new Selectone Records label, Wariner proves with his latest release, *Steal Another Day*, that his thumb is still on the pulse of what fans want. The most remarkable aspect of the new release is the artist's faithfulness to the traditional Steve Wariner sound on cuts such as "Snowfall on the Sand" and "Steal Another Day" while showcasing a new Steve Wariner on the Latin-flavored "Kiss Me Anyway" and "Carmelita." This sensational talent just continues to evolve in all aspects of his music. Wariner seems to want his listeners to realize this evolution by including new recordings of previous hits like "Where Did I Go Wrong" and "Small Town Girl." *Steal Another Day* is an impressive package from a major player in the Nashville music market. *—Rick Cohoon*

The Hits Collection / Mar. 25, 2003 / Capitol ♦♦♦

The ten-track *The Hits Collection* covers Steve Wariner's most commercially productive period for Capitol Records. While Wariner had numerous chart-toppers for RCA throughout the '80s, his reign on the country charts fizzled shortly thereafter until he moved to Capitol Records in the late '90s. Wariner co-wrote the majority of his comeback hits featured here, including "Burnin' the Roadhouse Down" featuring Garth Brooks, "Holes in the Floor of Heaven," and "Every Little Whisper." *—Al Campbell*

Paul Warren

b. May 17, 1918, Lyles, Hickman County, TN, **d.** Jan. 12, 1978

Fiddle, Guitar, Vocals, Session Musician / Progressive Bluegrass, Traditional Bluegrass

Paul Warren was an extraordinary bluegrass sideman who played fiddle on scores of radio and television shows and recording sessions; although he was in the music business over 35 years, he never made a solo studio album. Warren was born and raised in Hickman County, TN; his earliest influences were his father, who played clawhammer banjo, and Fiddlin' Arthur Smith. He got his start playing high-school dances with partner Emory Martin in the mid-'30s. In 1938, he joined Johnnie Wright's band; by 1940, they had become successful enough to abandon their day jobs and focus full-time on music. He remained with Wright and his Tennessee Hillbillies until entering the Army in 1942, where legend has it that he survived capture and two years in a German POW camp because he entertained the guards by playing "Under the Double Eagle" on fiddle. After his discharge, Warren returned to Wright's band. After Wright formed Johnnie & Jack with Jack Anglin, Warren played behind them until 1953, and also spent a year playing on Kitty Wells recordings like "It Wasn't God Who Made Honky-Tonk Angels" and "Release Me."

In 1954, he began his long association with Lester Flatt & Earl Scruggs when he replaced Benny Martin in their Foggy Mountain Boys; he appeared on all of their recordings between 1954 and 1969. When Flatt & Scruggs broke up in the late '60s, Warren played in Flatt's Nashville Grass through early 1977 when his health began to fail and he was forced to retire; he died the following year. Although he never recorded by himself, a collection of tunes featuring his work was posthumously gathered by Lance Le Roy, who released them a tribute album in 1979. *—Sandra Brennan*

● **America's Greatest Breakdown Fiddle Player** / 1957 / CMH ♦♦♦♦

Dale Watson

b. Oct. 7, 1962, Alabama

Guitar, Vocals / Alternative Country, Americana

A staunch adherent of old-style honky tonk and Bakersfield country, Dale Watson positioned himself as a tattooed, stubbornly independent outsider who was only interested in recording authentic country music. As a result, he never sold many records, but his music was championed by numerous critics and alternative country fans. Watson was born in Alabama in 1962 but spent his teenage years near Houston, and he grew to think of Texas as his true home state. His father and brother were both musically inclined, and he began writing his own songs at age 12, making his first recording two years later. After graduating from high-school, he spent seven years playing local clubs and honky tonks. He moved to Los Angeles in 1988 on the advice of Rosie Flores and soon joined the house band at North Hollywood's now-legendary alt-country venue the Palomino Club. He recorded two singles for Curb in 1990, "One Tear at a Time" and "You Pour It On," and appeared on the third volume of the compilation series *A Town South of Bakersfield* in 1992. Not long after, he moved to Nashville and spent some time writing songs for the Gary Morris publishing company.

Watson didn't find commercial country much to his taste, and he relocated to the more progressive-minded scene in Austin, TX, where he formed a backing band called the Lonestars. He scored a deal with Hightone and released his debut album, *Cheatin' Heart Attack*, in 1995. It was greeted with enormous acclaim for the vitality Watson brought to his vintage-style material and performances and also featured a witty dig at mainstream country in "Nashville Rash." Follow-up *Blessed or Damned* appeared in 1996 and continued in a similar vein, as did 1997's *I Hate These Songs*. His next release, *The Truckin' Sessions*, appeared on Koch in 1998 and was devoted entirely to that distinct country subgenre of truck driving songs. Unfortunately, it was almost his last. In 2000, Watson's fiancée was killed in an automobile accident; devastated, he attempted to drown his sorrows in booze and drugs and nearly died of an overdose shortly after Christmas. He wound up checking himself into a mental institution to recover and re-emerged later in 2001 with the deeply sorrowful tribute *Every Song I Write Is for You*, which appeared on Koch's new country imprint Audium. A couple of lower-key releases followed, the holiday album *Christmas in Texas* (2001) and *Live in London, England* (2002). *—Steve Huey*

● **Cheatin' Heart Attack** / 1995 / Hightone ♦♦♦♦♦

Watson's hearty, down-to-earth honky tonk makes *Cheatin' Heart Attack* one of the most exciting country debuts this side of Junior Brown's *12 Shades of Brown*. Watson and his band Lonestar burn through 14 no-nonsense songs that prove the genre can be vital and fun at the same time. Watson's voice is pure, deep, and strong, and his songs feature guitar and pedal steel prominantly. He's a veteran of the Texas honky tonk circuit, which shows in his sharp arrangements on songs like "List of Reasons," "Holes in the Wall," and "Nashville Rash"—the latter mixing heartfelt commentary on the current country market with a smart sense of humor. *—Kurt Wolff*

Blessed or Damned / 1996 / Hightone ♦♦♦♦

Blessed or Damned pretty much picks up where Watson's 1995 debut, *Cheatin' Heart Attack*, left off. He pines for "A Real Country Song" on modern radio, sings praises for his adopted state on "That's What I Like About Texas" (a good-natured duet with Johnny "Whiskey River" Bush), and wonders at the fate of his chosen musical genre on the moving title track. Watson may have no surprise ace in the hole on *Blessed or Damned*, but it's nonetheless a solid hand of fresh, invigorating material. *—Kurt Wolff*

I Hate These Songs / Jun. 10, 1997 / Hightone ♦♦♦

Dale Watson's third album, *I Hate These Songs*, is a little tamer than *Blessed or Damned* or *Cheatin' Heart Attack*, but it remains a solid collection of neo-honky tonk. Watson writes sturdy, memorable songs in the tradition of Merle Haggard and Waylon Jennings, and he delivers them with conviction and humor that compensate for his resistance to move the form forward. *—Thom Owens*

The Truckin' Sessions / Aug. 18, 1998 / Koch ♦♦♦♦♦

Dale Watson is one of the strongest country & western vocalists around. As always, he is very convincing, and his tribute to truckin' tunes is a delight. All originals, the 14 cuts presented here would make Bakersfield bard Red Simpson proud. Mostly upbeat, Watson manages to tip his hat to his home state of Texas with some swing on "You've Got a Long Way to Go" and the Bakersfield sound on the humorous "I'm Fixin' to Have Me a Nervous Breakdown." Straight-down-the-pike truckin' songs like "Have You Got It On," "Makin' Up Time" and "...Loose Nut Behind the Wheel" keep this project moving along at a nice pace. A more melancholy Watson displays his soft center on the touching "Big Wheels Keep Rollin'." All in all, a great ride. *—Jana Pendragon*

Every Song I Write Is for You / Jul. 24, 2001 / Audium ♦♦♦

Watson puts together a collection of songs about grief and loss for his fifth release, which is dedicated to his fiancée, who died in an automobile accident. The album is pining and remorseful and features string accompaniment on most of the 14 tracks. On it Watson still harbors a deep appreciation for the Merle Haggard-perfected Bakersfield sound, but here he does so without the usual honky tonk grit that he has when he's accompanied by his band, Lonestar. This is a quiet set dripping with romantic longing that's elevated occasionally by the upbeat "Your the Best Part of Me" and the swing-inflected "Money Can't Buy Her Love," but that's anchored in the deep despair that led Watson, who nearly lost his own life during a drug and alcohol binge brought on by the loss, to write these songs. *—Travis Drageset*

The Best of the HighTone Years / Jan. 15, 2002 / Hightone ♦♦♦♦♦

Dale Watson is more than the spiritual heir of Merle and Buck—his music has all the dim lights and beer mugs of the best honky tonk. This compilation creams the best work of his three Hightone discs, all of which sound as if they should have been recorded in the '50s or '60s rather than the '90s; if there was ever a man out of time, it's Dale Watson. He can write some classic cheating songs, like "Caught"; truckers' anthems, such as "Hey Driver" and "Truckstop in La Grange" (which might be the only song to celebrate La Grange, KY, and romanticize I-71); and condemn modern country on "Nashville Rash," which also pays tribute to his heroes. His deep voice and style (which can easily become a sing-speak) owes plenty to Merle Haggard and a little to George Jones, while his players, including the great Jerry Donahue, can twang like there's no tomorrow. About the only place where it comes unstuck is on "Blessed or Damned," which tries to step outside the musical and lyrical boundaries where Watson is comfortable to bad effect—it sounds pretentious, boring, and sloppy, a far cry from the tightness of his other work. If you think honky tonk died, then you need this. It's not alt-country (whatever that is); it's nothing but dyed-in-the-wool heartbreak diesel, although you need to bring your own beer to cry into. But if you get a hankering for that classic country sound, unrepentant, then Dale Watson's your man—and he always will be. *—Chris Nickson*

Live in London, England / Jun. 25, 2002 / Audium ♦♦♦

Doc Watson (Arthel Watson)

b. Mar. 2, 1923, Deep Gap, NC

Guitar (Acoustic), Banjo, Guitar, Harmonica, Vocals / Old-Timey, Traditional Country, Traditional Folk

In the latter half of the 20th century there were three preeminently influential folk/country guitar players: Merle Travis, Chet Atkins, and Arthel "Doc" Watson, a flatpicking genius from Deep Gap, NC. Unlike the other two, Watson was in middle age before gaining any attention. Since 1960, though, when Watson was recorded with his family and friends in Folkways' *Old Time Music at Clarence Ashley's*, people have remained in awe of this gentle blind man who sings and picks with a pure and emotional authenticity. The present generation, folkies and country pickers alike, including Ricky Skaggs, Vince Gill, the late Clarence White, Emmylou Harris, and literally hundreds of others, acknowledge their great debt to Watson. Watson has provided a further service to folk/country by his encyclopedic knowledge of many American traditional songs. While Travis and Atkins started on acoustic guitars and moved to electric, before Watson's "discovery" during the folk revival in the early '60s, he played electric in a local all-purpose band that played current rock, swing, country, and of course folk music. He gained recognition gradually, first from the *Clarence Ashley* album, which led to a rave performance at the Newport Folk Festival in 1963. Folkways soon recorded an album of Watson, followed in 1964 by a series of albums by Vanguard, nearly one a year through the decade.

No sooner had interest in folk music waned than Watson was back in great demand because of the three-disc *Will the Circle Be Unbroken*, a watershed album in 1972 that was created by the Nitty Gritty Dirt Band. It featured Watson, Travis, Roy Acuff, and a who's who of country greats. Merle, Watson's son and a talent in his own right, began appearing with his father regularly. The result was good enough for them to win two Grammys for traditional music, in 1973 and 1974. Father and son played beautiful music together for over 15 years, until Merle died tragically on the family farm in 1985. Following his son's death, Doc continued with his appearances, showcasing his beautiful voice, his great instrumental talent, and his mastery of traditional material. He is an American treasure.

Early in his childhood in Deep Gap, Watson was struck by an illness that restricted the bloodflow to his eyes, resulting in his blindness at an early age. As a child, he was surrounded by music and was given a new harmonia every Christmas. When he was ten, his father gave him a homemade fretless banjo, which Doc played consistently for the next three years. Around the same time he picked up the banjo, Watson began attending the School for the Blind in Raleigh, NC. At the age of 13, Doc began playing guitar after being introduced to the instrument by his cousin. Six months after receiving his guitar, Doc and his older brother Linney began busking on street corners, singing traditional numbers. By his late teens, Watson had learned how to fingerpick from his neighbor Olin Miller.

In 1941, Watson joined a band that had a regular radio program in Lenoir, NC. It was at this show that he earned his nickname, once one of the announcers referred to the guitarist as "Doc" during the broadcast. For the next six years he played around North Carolina. In 1947, he married Rosa Lee Carlton, the daughter of fiddler Gaither W. Carlton. Though his father-in-law taught him a number of traditional songs, Doc didn't play any traditional material publically during the '40s, preferring to concentrate on country instead; to pay the bills, he also worked as a piano tuner. Watson joined the supporting band of a local pianist and railroad worker named Jack Williams in 1953. With Williams, Doc played electric guitar and perfromed a variety of music, from country to rock and pop. After staying with Jack for eight years, Watson joined the Clarence Ashley String Band and traveled with the group to New York in order to appear at a Friends of Old-Time Music concert. His performance at the concert was a resounding success, and he was invited to perform at Gerde's Folk City in Greenwich Village.

The invitation to perform in New York was an indication that the folk boom of the early '60s was beginning to gain momentum, and Doc became one of the major benefactors of the revival. Young college students began to follow his music and he soon switched to acoustic guitar on the advice of Ralph Rinzler. During 1961, Watson made his recording debut on Clarence Ashley's *Old Time Music at Clarence Ashley's*, a performance which earned him considerable acclaim. Two years later, his solo spot at the Newport Folk Festival stole the show; that same year he released his first solo album, *Doc Watson & Family*. In 1964, Doc began giving concerts accompanied by his son Merle on second guitar. From that point on, Doc and Merle were constant collaborators and one of the most popular performers on the folk and traditional music circuit. Even when the folk boom of the '60s died down toward the end of the decade, Watson retained his audience, and when he was spotlighted on the Nitty Gritty Dirt Band's breakthrough 1972 album *Will the Circle Be Unbroken*, he earned another generation of new fans. In 1974, his album *Then and Now* won the Grammy for Best Ethnic or Traditional Recording; the following year, he and Merle took home the same award for their *Two Days in November*.

Doc and Merle continued to perform and record successfully during the early '80s, giving numerous successful concerts each year and earning many awards, including another Grammy in 1979 (Best Country Instrumental Performance for "Big Sandy"/"Leather Britches"). In 1985, Merle tragically died in a tractor accident on his home farm. Following his son's death, Doc stopped performing for a short time, yet he made a comeback supported by guitarist Jack Lawrence and bassist T. Michael Coleman, who had played with Watson since 1974. Throughout the '80s and '90s, Doc continued to perform and record to enthusiastic audiences. During that time he won two more Grammys—Best Traditional Folk Recording for both 1986's *Riding the Midnight Train* and 1990's *On Praying Ground*—as well as a North Carolina Award in Fine Arts. *Home Sweet Home* followed in 1998 and *Third Generation Blues* in 1999. *—David Vinopal*

Old Time Music at Clarence Ashley's, Vol. 1 / 1961 / Folkways ♦♦♦

This comfortable and sometimes haunting set of old-timey music involves a patchwork of players from the Appalachians quilt. One of the most interesting parts of the extended booklet that is enclosed, and one of the parts that is least likely to strain one's eyes due to the miniscule typeface of the text, is a blow-up map of the area where Virginia, West Virginia, Kentucky, Tennessee, and North Carolina close in on each other. The participating players all hail from different parts of this region, the resulting diagram resembling those charts detectives put up on the wall in order to trace where a suspect might live in a certain part of a city. There are great performances here, such as "God's Gonna Ease My Troublin' Mind," in which the slightly strained vocals of Tom Ashley have a great appeal and the amusing bass vocal part from Doc Watson is just the right touch. Elsewhere, Watson's performances are a bit perfunctory, material he has continued to do for the decades subsequent to the release of this set, and with not much variation. "The Louisiana Earthquake" is an unaccompanied vocal by Stella Walsh Gilbert, the recording so intimate that one can hear a door being slammed at one point. This is one of two such performances on this set. The other, "The Haunted Woods," is an a cappella song story by Eva Ashley Moore which is not a good idea for a bedtime lullaby choice. Gaither Carlton, Watson's father-in-law, equips himself well on both banjo and fiddle, while the work of Fred Price on the latter instrument is never less than absorbing. Vocalist Tommy Moore pulls off a memorable "True Lovers," backed by the sympathetic guitar tickling of Watson and Clint Howard. Moore was only 13 when this was recorded, meaning his voice was in the process of changing. This is not to suggest this performance is similar to that of a boy soprano. Yet it sounds remarkably feminine yet as far away from the ethos of the slick country & western female star as a mansion in Nashville is from a rambling shack in the hills around Deep Gap. Howard also gets plenty of chance in the spotlight, bringing the set to a rousing conclusion with a "Pretty Little Pink" that is a direct hit of the old-time vibe, complete with clawhammer banjo from Jack Johnson and Moore getting his teen thimbles on a washboard. Ashley is absolutely charming on "Honey Babe," Price harmonizing on the melody line with his sweet fiddle. *—Eugene Chadbourne*

Jean Ritchie and Doc Watson at Folk City / 1963 / Smithsonian Folkways ♦♦♦

According to reissue annotator Joe Wilson, Doc Watson and Jean Ritchie had never heard of each other before they got together for a concert at Folk City in 1963, which says something about the 40-year-old Watson's obscurity at the time and about his limited knowledge of other performers, since 39-year-old Ritchie had been recording for more than a decade. The two had a lot in common, however, the North Carolina-born guitarist and banjo player sharing a repertoire of traditional material with the Kentucky-born dulcimer player. During their set (actually featuring only six songs performed together, with seven solos by Watson and four by Ritchie), they mixed murder ballads with spirituals and dance tunes. The titles included many songs that were familiar to country fans, and that would become familiar to folk fans as well: "Pretty Polly," "Wabash Cannonball," and "Amazing Grace." Especially interesting were "Go Dig My Grave," "Hiram Hubbard," and "House Carpenter," on which Watson played banjo and Ritchie sang. This was very much a joint appearance rather than a real duo outing, but the performers were sufficiently strong and complementary enough to make it work. [The 1990 Smithsonian Folkways reissue added three tracks—"East Virginia," "Blue Ridge Mountain Blues," and "Pretty Saro"—to the original 1963 release.] *—William Ruhlmann*

★ **Doc Watson** / 1964 / Vanguard ♦♦♦♦♦

Watson's arrival on the folk scene of the '60s was a major event in American music, due mostly to his appearance at the 1963 Newport Folk Festival and the release of this self-titled album the following year. Not only did it revolutionize folk guitar picking, but it set the standard for the rest of his career with its mix of old-timey numbers, blues, gospel, and adapted fiddle tunes. The album is incredibly varied, from the stark, banjo-driven "Country Blues" to the humorous "Intoxicated Rat," and many of these songs became Watson standards, especially his signature song "Black Mountain Rag." His incredible flat-picking skills may have been what initially wowed his audiences, but it was Watson's complete mastery of the folk idiom that assured his lasting popularity. *—Jim Smith*

Treasures Untold / 1964 / Vanguard ♦♦♦♦♦

Treasures Untold is comprised of unreleased performances recorded at the 1964 Newport Folk Festival. At the concert, Doc Watson and his family were in fine form, breathing life into a number of old-timey songs, ranging from ballads to folk songs to gospel. It's an exciting, affectionate performance, highlighted by four duets by Clarence White. *—Thom Owens*

Doc Watson & Son / 1965 / Vanguard ♦♦♦♦

Merle Watson's debut with father Doc Watson was recorded shortly after they performed their first concerts together in California, and it shows the duo's musical partnership already in full flower, an incredible fact considering that Merle had only been picking guitar for eight months! The best songs here turned up on later Vanguard best-ofs, but there's a fair amount of greatness in the astonishing instrumental medley "Fiddler's Dram/Whistling Rufus/Ragtime Annie" and "Little Stream of Whiskey," an old Irish drinking song transformed into a hobo ballad with a bouncy fingerpicked melody. Perhaps most astonishing is the solo harmonica workout "Mama Blues," in which the elder Watson imitates the sound of a child crying, showing off yet another facet of his incredible musical skill. *—Jim Smith*

Home Again! / 1966 / Vanguard ♦♦♦

Watson's fourth Vanguard album is his most affecting folk-style record, with unexpectedly warm vocals matched to the quiet virtuosity of his playing. With only a couple of instrumentals on this 14-song collection, the rest features Watson performing lively, achingly beautiful renditions of popular folk standards ("Katie Morey," "Georgie," "Froggie Went A-Courtin'," "Matty Groves"). There isn't a weak number here, although highlights include the haunting "Winter's Night," and "The F.F.V.," the latter a grim but lively song in memory of a train wreck and a dead engineer. All are played with very imposing dexterity by Watson, joined by his son Merle and Russ Savakus on upright bass. This album was a great showcase for Watson's voice—vaguely similar to but rougher-hewn than Burl Ives—which is often overlooked in the aura of his playing. *—Bruce Eder*

☆ **Southbound** / 1966 / Vanguard ✦✦✦✦✦

Southbound was a pivotal record for Doc Watson. Upon its 1966 release, it demonstrated that Watson was capable of more than just dazzling interpretations of folk songs, but that he could also write excellent original material and rework new country songs in a fascinating manner. *Southbound* also marked the recorded debut of Merle Watson, Doc's astonishingly talented son. —*Thom Owens*

Ballads From Deep Gap / 1967 / Vanguard ✦✦✦✦✦

The largely overlooked *Ballads From Deep Gap* features a great song list and some of Doc & Merle Watson's best early playing. This is a jaunty, exciting record, highlighted by "The Cuckoo," Doc's take on a version made famous by neighbor Clarence Ashley. There's nothing routine about anything here, though: "Stack-O-Lee" (featuring Merle on lead guitar), "Roll in My Sweet Baby's Arms," and "Travelin' Man" are imbued with warm, rolling energy that is as invigorating as anything the pair recorded. In the end, *Ballads*, ironically, plays like a dance—it's fast, fun, and slightly reckless compared to some of Doc Watson's other albums of the time. That atmosphere, though, makes it an inspired effort. —*Jim Smith*

Old-Timey Concert / 1967 / Vanguard ✦✦✦✦

Although Doc Watson, Clint Howard, and Fred Price were giving similar concerts at the beginning of the '60s, this performance for the Seattle Folklore Society wasn't recorded until 1967. Nonetheless, it gives a good sense of the state of Watson's art before he went solo, finding him in cahoots with neighbors and friends and singing old-time material in an intimate setting. This album features a few solo performances by Watson and terrific, cheerful interplay among all three men. "Sunny Tennessee," "Walking in Jerusalem," "Crawdad," and "Will the Circle Be Unbroken" are highlights, but this is a highly entertaining concert throughout, with a few songs like "Mountain Dew" containing guitar breaks that are fast even by Watson's standards. As a side note, this album's track data are off slightly—track one is given to Howard's spoken introduction, while "I Saw a Man at the Close of the Day/Cackling Hen," supposedly track 19, takes up tracks 20 and 21, bringing the total count to 24, not 22 as listed on the cover. —*Jim Smith*

Doc Watson in Nashville: Good Deal! / 1968 / Vanguard ✦✦✦

The early and mid-'60s were good for Doc Watson in folk circles, but by the end of the decade, the folk boom was fading, and he gravitated back toward country audiences (even Joan Baez was cutting records in Nashville). This pleasant but unexceptional album was one result. Watson does genially sung, beautifully played covers of songs by Roy Acuff ("Streamline Cannonball"), Jimmie Rodgers ("Peach Pickin' Time in Georgia"), A.P. Carter ("I'm Thinking Tonight of My Blue Eyes"), and even Blind Boy Fuller ("Step It Up and Go"), scattered among a handful of original and traditional numbers. The playing is more impressive than the arrangements, which have that trademark Nashville smoothness, bolstered by Merle Watson and Grady Martin on guitars, Tommy Jackson and Buddy Spicher on fiddles (they get a workout on "June Apple"), Floyd Cramer at the piano, and Buddy Harman on the drums. —*Bruce Eder*

Doc Watson on Stage (Featuring Merle Watson) / 1971 / Vanguard ✦✦✦✦

One of Doc Watson's finest later records, *On Stage* is a virtual travelogue of his entire career in one record, almost a greatest hits record, live. Assisted by Merle Watson, the program flows from lightning fast hoedowns such as "Brown's Ferry Blues," where Watson picks lightning fast with a dexterity that is almost unbelievable. His feel and command of the instrument is truly incredible. "Open Up Them Pearly Gates for Me" has a similar effect. There are also numerous stories and patter (mostly about the songs) in between the cuts, and it guides you through the performance. Watson also shines on this album as well, especially his exquisite fingerpicking on "Banks of the Ohio." A timeless slice from one of the fathers of modern country music. —*Matthew Greenwald*

Doc & Merle Watson's Guitar Album / 1972 / Flying Fish ✦✦✦

Like *Pickin' the Blues*, *Guitar Album* features Doc and Merle Watson supported by a small band and playing blues. Both guitarists play with deft, nimble grace, spinning out surprisingly hard-edged lines that are simultaneously fluid and gritty. —*Thom Owens*

The Elementary Doctor Watson! / 1972 / Sugar Hill ✦✦✦✦

This was Watson's first album after leaving Vanguard, and it nicely showcased his new "country" sound, featuring mellow but terrifically played traditional and contemporary material. Particularly nice are the versions of "Going Down the Road Feeling Bad," Tom Paxton's "The Last Thing on My Mind," and "More Pretty Girls Than One." With Norman Blake (on dobro) and Vassar Clements contributing, this is a great Sunday morning record, a genuine pleasure from start to finish. —*Jim Smith*

☆ **The Essential Doc Watson** / 1973 / Vanguard ✦✦✦✦✦

It's a measure of how succinct Doc Watson's interpretations of traditional music are that this 26-song collection is one of the few Vanguard double-LP compilations to make it onto CD completely intact, with no songs eliminated, and it still clocks in at under 70 minutes. It's also one of the better sounding of the Welk Music Group's mid-'80s CD reissues from the Vanguard catalog, and one only wishes that the label could have included a set of liner notes about the performer. The first half of this disc (and the first LP of the original double album) is made up of studio recordings that feature Watson working solo, in a small-group setting, and also accompanied by a full band of top Nashville session musicians, including Grady Martin, Tommy Jackson, and Buddy Spicher; tracks 13-26 were recorded live at the Newport Folk Festival in 1964 and 1965, and feature a relaxed, outgoing Watson accompanied by no more than a pair of musicians. As for the music itself, it's about as wide and varied a body as one could wish for—from Watson's very stylized versions of "Tom Dooley," "Shady Grove," and "Rising Sun Blues" (his rendition of "House of the Rising Sun") to gospel numbers, all of it beguiling in its musicianship as well as its content. Watson's singing and playing are sweeter on the studio sides, but the live tracks show him in a relaxed, outgoing mood. Although it's not as thorough an

account of his musicianship as the four-CD *Vanguard Years* compilation, this disc does give any neophyte a good look at what he's about, and the music is excellent on its own terms. —*Bruce Eder*

Two Days in November / 1974 / Poppy ✦✦✦✦

Although Arthel "Doc" Watson had been a central figure in the folk and acoustic music that was native to the Appalachian southeastern U.S. since the late '50s, significant success came later in his life. By the mid-'60s, Doc Watson (vocal/guitar/harmonica) had been joined by his son Merle Watson (guitar/banjo), and together they were responsible for scores of releases featuring their inimitable brand of infectious and honest acoustic folk and traditional country music. The title *Two Days in November* (1974) refers to the length of time it took to document this ten-track album. However, that certainly didn't deter it from scoring a Grammy for Best Ethnic or Traditional Recording—the duo's second in as many years. Doc Watson's amplified approach to traditional melodies as well as the reworking of cover material is decidedly modern, yet the interpretations directly hark back to their acoustic counterparts with sides such as the talking blues of "Walk on Boy," also recorded by a wide range of talents including the blue-eyed doo wop of the Belmonts to the song's co-author, Mel Tillis. The hot-steppin' good-time rag "Kinfolks in Carolina" has been gleefully adapted from one of the senior Watson's most revered contemporaries, Merle Travis. Precise picking from both men often weave seemingly effortless dual leads, such as the breakneck speed of "The Train That Carried My Girl From Town" or the sunny disposition of "Doc's Rag." Several of the musicians from this long-player also contributed to the previous Grammy winner *Then and Now* (1973), including Jim Isbel (drums/percussion), Joe Allen (bass), Kenny Malone (percussion), and Chuck Cochran (piano). Seasoned as well as developing enthusiasts of bluegrass, newgrass, traditional country, and Americana agree that Doc & Merle Watson developed and created some of their finest music in the early to mid-'70s—many, like *Two Days in November*, were initially only available on the regional Poppy Records label. This meant that the international circulation was practically unheard of. [In the 1990s, Sugar Hill reissued a majority of these titles onto CD for the first time—with splendid results. Although some of the discs are now out of print, they are worth the search as well as highly recommended for inclined parties.] —*Lindsay Planer*

Memories / 1975 / Sugar Hill ✦✦✦✦✦

Here are 22 songs originally recorded by Doc Watson (with Merle Watson producing in association with Chuck Cochran) for Capitol/EMI in the mid-'70s, a life-retrospective including traditional numbers like "Shady Grove" and A.P. Carter's "Wabash Cannonball," Jimmie Rodgers' "In the Jailhouse," and the old jug band standard "Mama Don't Allow No Music," among others. Apart from the fact that some of the songs were apparently overdubbed (Watson plays more than one instrument on certain numbers) and the presence of a more or less full country/bluegrass band (with unobtrusive electric piano and bass on a few tracks), there's nothing here to distinguish these recordings from Watson's Vanguard and Folkways stuff of the mid-'60s—not only is Watson's playing as fine as, or better than, on the earlier records, but the voice is still there, so much that maybe the best track on this record is the a cappella "Wake Up, Little Maggie," maybe the most beautiful song Watson has ever recorded. Notes might have been nice, but the recording credits and song histories are thorough, and the sound is superb, right down to the exquisite harmonies on numbers like "Keep on the Sunny Side." —*Bruce Eder*

Lonesome Road / 1977 / EMI America ✦✦

Doc does the country blues as well as anything else he does and this record is filled with some fine performances. From "Stone Wall" (on which Doc sings harmony with himself) to the hot picking on songs like "Minglewood Blues" and "I Ain't Going Honky Tonkin' Anymore" this is quite a good record. —*Jim Worbois*

Tradition / 1977 / Rounder ✦✦✦✦

The greatest recordings are often ones that include periods of complete rejection in their histories. These tapes were made in 1964 but not made available to the public until more than a dozen years later, when the music was finally released in U.S. and the U.K. by Rounder and Topic, respectively. The Watson in question is indeed Doc Watson, and while this huge presence in American folk music dominates the proceedings like the Jolly Green Giant looking out over the vegetable fields, this album completely stands out from that artist's discography. Listeners who find Doc Watson's recordings a trifle on the slick side will want to give this collection a listen. While the man has become a highly acclaimed international performer and has graced the most important stages in the world, he comes from a tradition of music that was originally made at home for the entertainment of family and neighbors. A great old-time fiddler may have enjoyed being the hero of his county, but he did not aspire to play at Carnegie Hall or do solo sellout nights at a slick nightclub such as the Bottom Line. Performing music in such venues inevitably is the domain of highly polished entertainers who can hold large audiences in the palms of their hands, giving the types of performances that tend to be several worlds away from those featured here. Members of the extended Watson family—father-in-law, distant cousin, what have you—get involved here in a series of solos and small groupings, the recorded sound as rough as a chunk of whittling wood and the tunings sometimes even rougher. It is the real thing, and an album that by itself could serve as a fine introduction in every way to the charming world of old-time music, including diverse examples of its harmonic and melodic structures as well as the typical subject matter of songs such as "I Heard My Mother Weeping." All the instruments associated with this genre are here in full force, including banjo, fiddle, guitar, and the unaccompanied vocal. There are several performances that are incredibly powerful, particularly "Am I Born to Die?," sung by Doc Watson accompanied only by Gaither Carlton on fiddle. —*Eugene Chadbourne*

Red Rocking Chair / 1981 / Flying Fish ✦✦✦

Down South / 1984 / Rykodisc ✦✦✦

Pickin' the Blues / 1985 / Flying Fish ✦✦✦✦

Son Merle Watson gets top billing along with his dad on this superior release of acoustic mountain music, but it is really a group effort in which the smooth mastery of Doc Watson serves as a kind of a picture frame for each of the musical canvases included. The album title might indicate some limitation in the material, but the concept of "blues" has always been a bit more open in the white, Appalachian tradition than in African-American music. For example, one of the chord changes in "Freight Train Blues" would have probably made Muddy Waters want to jump out in front of one. Of course, a great amount of work has gone into segregating black and white music throughout the U.S., with the Appalachian area absolutely no exception. Jesse Helms would no doubt be proud of how much energy has gone into making it seem like the black and white musicians of his home state of North Carolina had absolutely nothing to do with each other over the years. What we have here is really a delightful blend of several different blues traditions, transcending the stupid questions of race as if it were a bit of dust that can be blown off a the phonograph needle. Some of the music is quite swinging, such as "Carroll County Blues," the fiddle playing of Sam Bush evoking more the clean sound of jazz violinists than the rugged tone of old-time fiddlers. "Stormy Weather" comes from the catalog of vocal jazz classics that are strongly influenced by blues, but actually have their own harmonic structure that is quite different from typical blues. Watson is such a fine vocalist that he is able to make a number such as this sound relatively fresh, no doubt helped by a blend of acoustic instruments not normally associated with this type of tune. But whatever style the players take on, everything is performed beautifully with deep feeling, comfortable tempos, and inspired picking that is never simply grandstanding. Fans of acoustic guitar will love this record—the instruments are recorded beautifully, especially in that warm, sonorous mid-register. *—Eugene Chadbourne*

Riding the Midnight Train / 1986 / Sugar Hill ✦✦✦

This bluegrass album has Nashville super-pickers Sam Bush, Mark O'Connor, and Béla Fleck. These are the last recordings of Merle Watson. *—Mark A. Humphrey*

Portrait / 1988 / Sugar Hill ✦✦✦

On this album, Watson is joined by such guest artists as Sam Bush and Mark O'Connor. *—AMG*

On Praying Ground / 1990 / Sugar Hill ✦✦✦

The Doc Watson Family / 1990 / Smithsonian Folkways ✦✦✦✦✦

Doc Watson, grandfather of the folk revival movement, has had a profound influence on American traditional music. Not only did he pioneer the playing of fiddle tunes on a flattop guitar, but through his incessant touring has brought traditional music to a larger audience. This Smithsonian Folkways release captures not only Doc Watson, but almost a dozen family members at the height of their power and has been deservingly hailed as a classic recording. Right from the opening track, "Old Groundhog," Watson and family send the listener on an amazing journey into the American musical past and present. Incidentally, their performance of "Old Groundhog" is certainly the equal of Bascom Lamar Lunsford's "I Wish I Was a Mole in the Ground," in terms of surreal country, capturing as it does race relations, commentary on shoe strings, as well directions for catching a groundhog. On "The House Carpenter," a weepy tale of that conflates religious and personal love, a haunting female voice sings almost off-key accompanied only by a fiddle that doubles on the melody. On the instrumental "Bonaparte's Retreat," Watson offers a droning, sea shanty-influenced version of this song staple of Mississippi river communities. Some of the family's best work is found in the spirituals scattered about the album. "When I Die" features a beautiful, uplifting three-part harmony, as does "The Lost Soul," which contains the wickedly abject refrain, "I'm paying now/the penalty." A fabulous record that's a must-listen for any serious fan of American music. *—Brian Whitener*

My Dear Old Southern Home / 1991 / Sugar Hill ✦✦✦

My Dear Old Southern Home is one of Doc Watson's best latter-day records, boasting an affectionate collection of old time and traditional country songs. Watson pay attention to the standards by the Carter Family and Jimmie Rodgers, but he also digs deep into the old-timey songbook and comes up with gems from more obscure acts like the Delmore Brothers and Bonnie Dodd. For some fans, *My Dear Old Southern Home* will seem like it lacks Watson's signature guitar work, but it's a wonderful, warm listen. *—Thom Owens*

Remembering Merle / Jun. 1992 / Sugar Hill ✦✦✦✦✦

Remembering Merle is an affectionate tribute to Doc Watson's deceased son, featuring several songs—which were all recorded live between 1970 and 1976—that showcased his work. Doc & Merle touch on a number of different genres, from folk and blue to rockabilly, all the while demonstrating the younger Watson's considerable talent. *—Thom Owens*

Original Folkways Recordings: 1960–1962 / 1994 / Smithsonian Folkways ✦✦✦✦

This important release documents the rediscovery of banjoist and comedian Clarence (Tom) Ashley in the early '60s, and the simultaneous introduction of a young and then-unknown guitar picker, the astounding Doc Watson. Ashley was one of the many musicians of the '20s and '30s whose early work appeared briefly on Harry Smith's 1952 *Anthology of American Folk Music*, the legendary collection that provided inspiration for much of the subsequent folk revival; as well as fueling up-and-coming urban "folk-singers" with a wealth of material, Smith's anthology ultimately led to the rediscovery and re-recording of such musicians as Dock Boggs, Mississippi John Hurt, and Ashley, who himself initiated the discovery of his neighbor, Doc Watson. At the time of the earliest recordings in this two-disc set, Ashley was some 20 years out of practice, while Watson's only outlet for performance was as an electric guitar player in a nearby rockabilly band; Watson did not own an acoustic guitar, nor Ashley a banjo. Over the course of these initial field recordings and later concert performances, however, Watson & Ashley demonstrate remarkable familiarity with local traditions, repertoire, and styles,

showcasing and continually sharpening their profound skills and aesthetic senses. They are joined on various performances by a handful of fine local musicians, including Clint Howard, Fred Price, and Gaither Carlton. For much of the '60s, this loose ensemble toured colleges and festivals, also producing material for the Folkways LPs *Old Time Music at Clarence Ashley's, Vol. 1* and *Vol. 2*. This 1994 reissue includes material from those albums along with 20 additional selections from the period and excellent notes by folklorist Ralph Rinzler. Included are the very first commercially released recordings by Doc Watson, who emerges here as a formidable soloist; also featuring some of the last recordings by veteran Clarence Ashley, the set is required listening for Watson fans and for enthusiasts of old-time music, its entertainment value as strong as its historical significance. The surprising offspring of the urban revival's intersection with a traditional musical community, Watson & Ashley's *Original Folkways Recordings* reveals a bottomless well of tradition and a music as fresh and exciting today as it was to the college kids and festival followers of the early '60s. *—Burgin Mathews*

Songs From the Southern Mountains / Oct. 19, 1994 / Sugar Hill ✦✦✦

This contains previously unreleased material from the early '60s as well as three tracks recorded in 1973. It has a scattershot feeling about it that comes from the material being recorded at different times, but it digs up some good stuff along the way. Particularly nice are Watson's performances of Blind Boy Fuller's "My Little Woman, You're So Sweet" and "Just a Friend," in which he duets with mother Rosa Lee. The liner notes by Watson's daughter Nancy are a treat, recalling memories of grandpa Gaither Carlton, the first Watson Family recording session, and the April night that Merle Watson began playing guitar. *—Jim Smith*

Docabilly / 1995 / Sugar Hill ✦✦✦

While he made his reputation as an acoustic guitar bluegrass flatpicker, the album title correctly implies there's another kind of music here. Helped by some hotshot players, including Marty Stuart and Duane Eddy, this album delivers some joyous, rollicking rockabilly, mixing early rock & roll classics with some country comforts. Although his singing strains a bit on the slow numbers, this American treasure comes through in grand style on the upbeat tunes. "That's Why I Love You Like I Do," "Heartbreak Hotel" and "Shake Rattle and Roll" are particularly good. *—Mark Allan*

Vanguard Years / Nov. 14, 1995 / Vanguard ✦✦✦✦✦

This is four-CD, 64-song collection drawn principally from Doc's Vanguard releases of the 1960s and early 1970s (tapped his solo LPs and performances at the 1963 and 1964 Newport Folk Festival). This was Doc's best period recording-wise, and certainly you couldn't hope for a better document of his virtuosity, as the guitarist covers all manner of American folk and blues styles over the course of the set. It's too much, however, for listeners who aren't big fans; Vanguard's *Essential Doc Watson* is a more economical survey. If you *are* a big fan, though, you'll be especially interested in the 16 previously unreleased performances. Comprising the whole of disc four, these are mostly taken from live duets with Merle Travis or Doc's son, Merle Watson. *—Richie Unterberger*

Then and Now/Two Days in November / 1996 / Sugar Hill ✦✦✦✦

Beat Goes On reissued *Then & Now* and *Two Days in November*, two albums Doc & Merle Watson recorded for Poppy Records in the early '70s, on one CD in 1996. Both records are excellent, laid-back collections of traditional folk, country and bluegrass and are worth the time of any Watson fan. *—Stephen Thomas Erlewine*

Watson Country / Jun. 1996 / Flying Fish ✦✦✦✦

This collection is drawn from the albums Watson recorded for Flying Fish between 1980-1984. As the title implies, it features a selection of traditional country tunes and newer songs done in a country style. It has the smooth Nashville production characteristic of his albums of the time, but that's not really a flaw—even if it takes some of the leather out of his playing, having a full backing band extends his appeal beyond the hillbilly curtain, and to many ears, that's a good thing. Everyone sounds comfortable and plays great, with Mark O'Connor and Sam Bush being a few of the musicians contributing. A nice range of writers are covered here too, including Jimmie Rodgers, Merle Travis, Tom Paxton, the Delmore Brothers, and Dan Fogelberg. Doc recorded many albums in this style, but for newcomers this is a nice sampler of his middle years. *—Jim Smith*

Elementary Doctor Watson!/Then and Now / Mar. 25, 1997 / Collectables ✦✦✦

Two of Doc Watson's albums from the early '70s, *Elementary Doctor Watson* and *Then & Now*, were combined on this single-CD reissue by Collectables. Although the sound and the packaging could be a little better, this still is a fine way for collectors to pick up these two records on disc. *—Stephen Thomas Erlewine*

Doc & Dawg / Aug. 19, 1997 / Acoustic Disc ✦✦✦✦

Flatpicking legend Doc Watson and mandolin virtuoso David Grisman have been playing together periodically for more than 30 years. In 1997, Grisman compiled some of the gems from these informal sessions and released them on his Acoustic Disc label. The 14 cuts were recorded mostly at Grisman's home in California between 1987 and 1991. The tracks are mainly traditional country and bluegrass tunes played lovingly and often with great restraint. On songs like the George Gershwin classic "Summertime," Grisman in particular makes every note count. Watson's voice is still strong and soulful. But, it is the instrumental duets that really shine, especially the two Bill Monroe tunes "Bluegrass Stomp" and "Kentucky Waltz" and the title track, "Doc & Dawg." This is an intimate collaboration between two men at the top of their craft who share a passion for acoustic music. It is a pleasure to listen in. *—S. Colby Miller*

Home Sweet Home / Sep. 15, 1998 / Sugar Hill ✦✦✦✦✦

Originally recorded in 1967 with additional material recorded in 1998, this is a tribute to the vast talent of Merle Watson, whose life was cut short in a tractor accident in 1985. These recordings are even more impressive when it is understood that they were made just five months after Merle started playing banjo. Expert even then, he was a delight to his father, Doc. With this release, Merle Watson's place in traditional American music is defined and assured. Along with Marty Stuart, Sam Bush, Alan O'Bryant and T. Michael Coleman, Doc Watson gives these early recordings of his son's mastery a new life. Songs like "Girl in the Blue Velvet Band," "Old Joe Clark" and "Little Maggie" carry the listener away. Ending with "I Wonder How the Old Folks Are at Home" and "Home Sweet Home" gives this release a poignant twist. It's highly recommended. *—Jana Pendragon*

Third Generation Blues / Apr. 20, 1999 / Sugar Hill ♦♦♦♦

Nobody plays a flat-top guitar quite like the versatile Doc Watson, and with *Third Generation Blues*, Watson teams with his son Richard to present a collection of 14 exquisite blues, country-folk, and gospel covers, each one as unique as a fingerprint. They perform the tunes on guitar, accompanied only by T. Michael Coleman on bass. From the down-home blues of Bubba White's "Honey Please Don't Go" and the country blues of Jimmie Rodgers' "Train Whistle Blues," to the uptempo rendering of the classic "House of the Rising Sun," the Watsons again provide the smooth vocals and seamless guitar work for which both men have become known and respected. "If I Were a Carpenter" and "Milk Cow Blues" are both incredible, and the duet dishes up the gospel music with a huge dose of spirit, from "Uncloudy Day" to "Precious Lord Take My Hand," and the folk music fires burn brightly on "Gypsy Davey" and "Moody River." The blues make their way around again with "Columbus Stockade Blues" and "Walk on Boy," and the Watsons' reading of "Summertime (And the Living Is Easy)" is simply intense. There has always been something just plain enjoyable about Doc—perhaps it is his easygoing demeanor or his undeniably easy-to-digest vocal style, or maybe it's the fact that he's one of the hottest flatpickers this side of Chet Atkins. *Third Generation Blues* offers prime examples of all of these traits, accompanied by the astounding picking of Richard to create an album that sets itself apart from the rest as a diamond in the rough. This is a collection of some of the most loved blues, gospel, and folk tunes of the 20th century, performed by some of the best minstrels of the century. *—Michael B. Smith*

The Best of Doc Watson: 1964–1968 / Apr. 20, 1999 / Vanguard ♦♦♦♦♦

Boasting 23 tracks (three unreleased) culled from six of Watson's classic Vanguard albums, *The Best of Doc Watson: 1964-1968* is a great summing up of the music he made during that period and a perfect testament to his standing as a true American musical treasure. Showcasing the amazing depth of ability that Watson has made his trademark, this collection covers all the bases, including outstanding examples of his virtuosic flat-picking guitar work in great instrumentals like "Dill Pickle Rag," "Windy and Warm" and the amazingly dexterous "Beaumont Rag." A perfect synthesis of country, blues and folk, Watson bounces from haunting murder ballads like "Omie Wise" and the solemn "Tom Dooley" to lighthearted numbers like "Muskrat" and "Intoxicated Rat." Faithful covers of Jimmie Rodgers' "My Rough and Rowdy Ways" and the Carter Family's "The Cyclone of Ryecov" show the reverence with which Watson tackles the work of the masters who have inspired his music. No fan of flat-top guitar picking should be without this one in their collection. *—Matt Fink*

Foundation: Doc Watson Guitar Instrumental Collection, 1964–1998 / Jul. 25, 2000 / Sugar Hill ♦♦♦♦

On first listen, this short 16-track collection seems like it has to be missing a great deal, but on further inspection, one finds that it really isn't. Of course, it omits large chunks of Watson's instrumental albums, but then, there weren't many of those to begin with. That said, what *Foundation* presents is a good variety that spans most of his career and includes many of his best traditional transcriptions ("Black Mountain Rag"), as well as some of his best originals ("Nashville Pickin'"). The set is nicely remastered as well, and although one misses Watson's vocals from time to time, this is a very pleasant listening experience. *—Jim Smith*

Doc Watson at Gerdes Folk City / Sep. 11, 2001 / Sugar Hill ♦♦♦

This album documents Doc Watson's first solo public appearance; it finds him in front of an appreciative West Village crowd at the height of the early-'60s folk music craze, playing a borrowed acoustic guitar (at the time the only guitar he owned was the electric Les Paul with which he had been making a living as a member of a North Carolina rockabilly band) and performing a varied set of tunes that range from traditional ballads like "Little Sadie" and "The Roving Gambler" to traditional blues and Merle Travis-style guitar showcases. He's joined at various times by local folk luminaries John Herald, Ralph Rinzler, and Bob Yellin, but what is consistently striking is his mastery of the stage and the warmth and gentle virtuosity of his playing—attributes that would later come to define his art, but which are remarkable in an artist performing solo for the first time. Highlights include an excellent arrangement of "Milk Cow Blues," an a cappella rendition of "The Lone Pilgrim," and an all-too-brief performance of the Travis classic, "Cannonball Rag." It's highly recommended. *—Rick Anderson*

'Round the Table Again / Apr. 2, 2002 / Sugar Hill ♦♦♦

Performances by Doc Watson with Frosty Morn have become a high point at Merlefest, the annual gathering launched in memory of Doc's son and collaborator, Merle Watson. The band, formed by Merle shortly before his death in 1985, plays impeccably on this Merlefest recording, but Doc opens alone with two traditional performances, playing banjo behind his own vocals on "Lynchburg Town" and singing a cappella on the haunting ballad "Coo Coo Bird." Gradually, the rest of Frosty Morn takes the stage, one song at a time; as each member comes out, Watson steps back a little further until he is integrated fully into the group. Understandably though, he holds the spotlight more than anyone else, telling a few folksy preacher jokes, urging his colleagues to "play it, son," even yodeling in classic fashion on "Jimmie's Mean Mamma Blues." The younger guys on the gig seem eager too, but to a fault; they whoop and yelp a little excessively after "On a Monday" and turn "Show Bizness" into a somewhat silly exercise. Watson, in contrast, tempers his enthusiasm with an almost anachronistic dignity. He does overreach at times, most awkwardly on an uncomfortable rendition of the R&B chestnut "Sincerely." Though his voice has worn a bit, it still animates more congenial material with his combination of warmth and stoic detachment. This is evident especially in his reading of "Nights in White Satin," which raises spirits that would doubtless have startled the Moody Blues. In the end, all of these tracks only echo the introduction that opens the disc: "A national treasure... Doc Watson." *—Robert L. Doerschuk*

Legacy / Apr. 9, 2002 / High Windy ♦♦♦♦♦

Anyone who has developed a deep love for Doc Watson will be elated by this three-disc biographical journey through his life and music. Two discs are devoted to conversations between Watson and longtime friend David Holt, in which Doc recalls his youth, his early career, and his tours with son Merle. Scattered throughout the interview are intimate performances of songs that Watson has played throughout his career, including "Deep River Blues," "Tom Dooley," and a version of "Tennessee Stud" that ranks among the most thrilling ever heard. The set's 72-page booklet, a detailed biography full of reminiscences, song notes, and rare photographs, is an absolute treasure, as fascinating as anything that is ever likely to be assembled on the man. Disc three is devoted to an excellent concert recorded at the Diana Wortham Theater in Asheville, NC, in 2001. Packed with favorites as well as some songs that Watson has never recorded, it proves that, at nearly 80, he is every bit as captivating as he was at Gerdes Folk City in the early '60s. It's a pity there aren't more sets like this around, but it seems fitting that the great Doc Watson should be among the first to have one. *—Jim Smith*

Lonesome Road/Look Away! / Sep. 24, 2002 / Southern Music ♦♦♦♦

Doc Watson's United Artists Records catalog (long-since acquired by EMI) was tapped for two compilations in the fall of 2002, this two-fer combining his 1977 album *Lonesome Road* and his 1978 album *Look Away!*, licensed by Southern Music Distribution, and *Songs From Home* on EMI's Capitol Records label. The flurry of activity can be traced to the success of the *O Brother, Where Art Thou?* soundtrack, with its traditional country and bluegrass music. That's ironic, given that Watson's tenure at UA in the 1970s came due to the success of an earlier traditional country collection, the Nitty Gritty Dirt Band's *Will the Circle Be Unbroken* album, on which he appeared. The record business is nothing if not trendy, but if that's what it takes to bring two albums as enjoyable as *Lonesome Road* and *Look Away!* back into print, so be it. Watson is, of course, joined by his son, Merle Watson, on both releases, as well as by small bands that give the tracks a rocking punch. He essays a variety of country and folk standards, including Mississippi John Hurt's "My Creole Belle" (the only track that overlaps with *Songs From Home*) and Bob Dylan's "Don't Think Twice, It's All Right." The disc ends with two previously unreleased bonus tracks, "New Born King" and "Peace in the Valley," both of them gospel songs on which Watson is joined by an orchestra and choir. The tracks are not consistent with the feistier material from the original LPs, but they are warmly and sincerely performed and provide a reverent coda to an excellent collection. *—William Ruhlmann*

Songs from Home / Oct. 22, 2002 / Capitol ♦♦♦♦

After stints on Folkways and Vanguard Records in the '60s and early '70s, Doc Watson contracted with the independent Poppy label, which earned a distribution deal with United Artists (UA) in the wake of the success of the Nitty Gritty Dirt Band's 1972 UA album *Will the Circle Be Unbroken*, on which Watson appeared. Having released *Elementary Doctor Watson!* on Poppy in 1972, followed by *Then and Now* in 1973 and *Two Days in November* in 1974 (all of these albums actually co-credited to Doc & Merle Watson), he next issued the double-LP *Memories* directly on UA in 1975, following with 1976's *Doc and the Boys* and then three more Doc & Merle albums, 1977's *Lonesome Road*, 1978's *Look Away!*, and 1979's *Live and Pickin'*. Four of those eight albums made the country charts, and one, *Memories*, even made the pop charts, but that was the end of Watson's sojourn with a large national label; by 1981, he was back to recording for the small folkie independent Flying Fish. This 49-minute, 17-track compilation draws on the Poppy/UA catalog, long since acquired by Capitol Records. Just as Watson's pact with UA was a response to the success of the traditional *Will the Circle Be Unbroken*, this release, part of a series of Capitol country and bluegrass compilations, is a response to the success of the traditional *O Brother, Where Art Thou?* Fine, if that's what it takes. The team of Watson, father and son, is in fine form on these recordings, which include covers of material by Mississippi John Hurt, Jimmie Rodgers, and others, plus traditional tunes. "Big Sandy/Leather Britches" was a deserving recipient of the 1979 Grammy Award for best country instrumental performance. The recording quality is high and the performances are stellar, making this an excellent sampler of Watson's music. *—William Ruhlmann*

Trouble in Mind: Doc Watson Country Blues Collection / Apr. 8, 2003 / Sugar Hill ♦♦♦♦

Trouble in Mind makes an interesting argument: Doc Watson, long deified in bluegrass and traditional folk circles, is also a fine country blues player. Perhaps the misunderstanding comes from the long tradition of dividing blues and folk players into different genres, or the mistaken assumption that black musicians (who often played the blues) didn't influence white musicians (who usually played folk). Watson, as this collection shows, included pieces like "Country Blues" at the very beginning of his career in 1964. For the next 34 years he repeatedly returned to the blues well, drawing on favorites like "Worried Blues," "Never No More Blues," and "Memphis Blues." Watson's eclectic approach uses a variety of instruments to render these traditional and public domain pieces fresh. On "Rain Crow Bill" he plays solo harmonica; on "White House Blues" he plays banjo. Most of the arrangements are simple, often augmented by his son Merle Watson on a second guitar or banjo. Another reason that many have never identified Watson as a blues player also has something to do with his guitar style. His fingerpicking method has more in common with the Piedmont style of John Hurt than the more familiar Delta style of Robert Johnson. The less-bluesy Piedmont style, in fact, seems much closer to folk.

Trouble in Mind makes a convincing argument for Watson's ability as a purveyor of the blues. In its fine selection of songs and well-executed performances, though, the collection is no different than other Watson collections: good music, regardless of genre, is good music. —*Ronnie Lankford Jr.*

Doc and the Boys/Live and Pickin' / Jun. 10, 2003 / Southern Music ◆◆◆

Gene Watson

b. Oct. 11, 1943, Palestine, TX
Bass, Vocals, Guitar / Country-Pop, Honky Tonk, Traditional Country

Though he can sing honky tonk, Gene Watson built a reputation for soulful ballads in the classical country tradition. Born one of seven children in Palestine, TX, Watson married early and was working as an auto-body man when he began frequenting the clubs in Houston. He recorded for a few small-time regional labels during the early '70s like Wide World and Stoneway. Watson finally had success in 1974, when a steamy single for Resco—"Love in the Hot Afternoon"—was picked up for national distribution by Capitol Records, igniting a firestorm of national hits: "Where Love Begins," "Paper Rosie," "Farewell Party," "Should I Come Home (Or Should I Go Crazy)," and "Nothing Sure Looked Good on You." In 1982, shortly after moving to MCA, Watson recorded his only chart-topper, "Fourteen Carat Mind." A parade of Top Ten entries followed during the early '80s, including "Speak Softly (You're Talking to My Heart)" and "You're Out Doing What I'm Here Doing Without." Watson is a vocal stylist of considerable talent, and still owns his own body shop. —*David Vinopal*

Love in the Hot Afternoon / 1975 / CEMA ◆◆◆

Because You Believed in Me / 1976 / Capitol ◆◆◆

Paper Rosie / 1977 / Capitol ◆◆◆

Reflections / 1978 / Capitol ◆◆◆

Beautiful Country / 1978 / Capitol ◆◆◆

The Best of Gene Watson / 1978 / Liberty ◆◆◆◆

Old Loves Never Die / 1981 / MCA ◆◆◆

Between This Time & The Next Time / 1981 / MCA ◆◆◆

The Best of Gene Watson, Vol. 2 / 1981 / Capitol ◆◆◆

This country singer lacks the mega-star status of a George Jones or a Merle Haggard but he has talent, a beautiful voice, and is fairly good at choosing songs. Still, a listener can wonder why the subject of a second volume of such an artist's so-called "best" recordings even comes up, especially when the playing time is so short that it seems like Watson is going out the back door only a moments after he has come in the front, to paraphrase a Haggard song. What is classic here is, of course, the great "Nothing Sure Looked Good on You," a song that literally rapes the notion of a typical country & western song with its eyes. Songwriter Joe Allen's indecisive ditty "Should I Go Home, or Should I Go Crazy" was a hit for several artists, but what is even better is another song by the same writer, "Pick the Wildwood Flower," which has both catchy chord changes and a pleasingly sentimental lyric. —*Eugene Chadbourne*

This Dream's on Me / 1982 / MCA ◆◆◆◆◆

Sometimes I Get Lucky / 1983 / MCA ◆◆◆

Little by Little / 1984 / MCA ◆◆◆

Greatest Hits / 1986 / MCA ◆◆◆◆◆

MCA's *Greatest Hits* collection fills in the gaps left by Curb's *Greatest Hits* collection, featuring such '80s hit singles as "What She Don't Know Won't Hurt Her," "Fourteen Carat Mind," and "You're Out Doing What I'm Here Doing Without." —*Thom Owens*

Back in the Fire / 1989 / Warner Bros. ◆◆◆

Gene Watson's music was always traditionalist, so it is no surprise that his 1989 comeback album *Back in the Fire* fits directly within the new traditionalist movement that began dominate country music at the time of the record's release. What separates Watson from the pack of singers that followed him is how closely he sticks to the roots—despite a relatively slick contemporary production, the album is straightforward, hard country, highlighted by a clutch of remarkable ballads. What distinguishes *Back in the Fire* is the first-rate song selection and the exceptional performances from Watson, who continually demonstrates his talent for pure, unaffected country singing. —*Thom Owens*

● **Greatest Hits** / 1990 / Curb ◆◆◆◆◆

This is a solid collection of '70s hits by this unpretentious, terribly underrated country singer. The key track is "Farewell Party," a deceptive, near-trance-inducing honky tonk number that delivers an emotional knockout at precisely the moment many country songs wimp out. —*Dan Cooper*

At Last / 1991 / Warner Bros. ◆◆◆

Well, on the album cover he doesn't dress like a lounge country singer, but that's sure the way the man sings. *At Last* doesn't sink completely into the schmaltzy stuff, but it comes close—a lot of the album sounds like Jim Reeves having a bad day, and there's very little serious country music going on ("You Can't Get Arrested in Nashville" is downright embarrassing.) —*Steven McDonald*

The Best of Gene Watson / Feb. 27, 1996 / Curb ◆◆◆

Best of Gene Watson is a ten-track budget-priced collection that culls highlights from his recordings for Curb in the mid-'80s, including the two hit singles "Got No Reason Now for Goin' Home" and "One Hell of a Heartache." Watson wasn't at his commerical or artistic peak during these years, and as a result *Best of Gene Watson* shouldn't be seen as a definitive overview of his career, or even a worthwhile introduction to his music. Instead,

it's a sampler of a brief period of his career that may appeal to fans who want a collection from each stage of Watson's career. —*Stephen Thomas Erlewine*

18 Greatest Hits / Nov. 9, 1999 / TeeVee ◆◆◆

This is an enjoyable budget sampler highlighting Gene Watson's Capitol honky tonk hits. These 18 tracks include his earliest chart-toppers from the mid- to late '70s, including "Love in the Late Afternoon," "Farewell Party," "Cowboys Don't Get Lucky All the Time," and "Nothing Sure Looked Good on You." For a collection that combines the best of Watson's Capitol and MCA material, pick up *The Ultimate Collection* on Hip-O. —*Al Campbell*

From the Heart / Sep. 11, 2001 / Row Music Group ◆◆◆

Not much has changed musically from the 1970s/1980s Gene Watson to the 2001 Watson who has released *From the Heart* on RMG Records. He has been recording for nearly three decades, and it is perhaps his stylistic consistency and raw talent that keeps him afloat in the ever-changing tide of Nashville. Like the albums that contained hits such as "Love on a Hot Afternoon" and "Memories to Burn," this album is highly vocal and unmistakably traditional. It should come as no surprise that some of the most impressive material on the album are Watson's characteristically sincere love ballads, such as "When You're Not Looking Back" and "Would It Be Cheatin'," which isn't about cheating at all. As if to acknowledge the spirit of the country greats before him, Watson even includes the sorrowful "I Never Go Around Mirrors," written by the late, great Lefty Frizzell. Lovers of the traditional country scene will find that *From the Heart* lives up to its title—that's where all of Gene Watson's music comes from. —*Rick Cohoon*

Ultimate Collection / Nov. 20, 2001 / Hip-O ◆◆◆

This is an enjoyable budget sampler featuring 23 of Gene Watson's Capitol and MCA honky tonk hits. These original recordings include his first hit from 1975, "Love in the Late Afternoon," "Got No Reason for Goin' Home," and "Memories to Burn." Besides the omission of the classic "Farewell Party," *Ultimate Collection* is recommended for those just getting familiar with Watson's mellow and soulful take on traditional country music. —*Al Campbell*

Love in the Hot Afternoon/Paper Rosie / 2002 / Hux ◆◆◆◆

This CD reissue pairs Gene Watson's first and third albums together on a single disc. From 1975, Watson's debut, *Love in the Hot Afternoon*, included the hits "Love in the Hot Afternoon," "Where Love Begins," and "You Could Know as Much About a Stranger." Relying wholly on outside material, there wasn't much distinctive to Watson's approach to set him aside as a major talent. But his understated brand of country-pop with a honky tonk flavor was pleasing enough, and he was savvy enough to take material by some superior writers, like "Bad Water" (which was co-written by Jackie DeShannon), "Through the Eyes of Love" (by Jack Clement), and "For the First Time" (by Jessi Colter). Much of this mix of romantic ballads and moderately uptempo tunes was routine in melody and lyrical focus, though "This Is My Year for Mexico" added a nice Tex-Mex touch. But Watson did bring an unfettered sincerity to the proceedings, and the production, featuring top Nashville session cats like Charlie McCoy and Hargus "Pig" Robbins, didn't try to lay on too much. *Paper Rosie*, from 1977, featured the title track, an involved story-song with flutes, steel guitar, and soothing background choral vocals. It was a big hit for the singer, and set the mood for an album of low-key, indeed a little sluggish, Nashville country by a singer suited for songs with a resigned tone. He took on "If the Shoe Fits, Wear It" by Ray Griff, author of his mid-'70s hit, "Where Love Begins," and also covered numbers by Marty Robbins ("You Gave Me a Mountain"), Dolly Parton ("Most of All Why"), and Porter Wagoner ("Tennessee Sunshine"), cutting a little loose in a hoedown fashion for the Wagoner tune. —*Richie Unterberger*

Dallas Wayne

Bass / Honky Tonk, Contemporary Country

From Springfield, MO, Wayne sings straight-up honky tonk that's too plain-spoken and realistic to stand a chance of getting marketed by Nashville. His 2000 HMG/Hightone release, *Big Thinkin'*, was co-produced by Robbie Fulks, who also contributed acoustic guitar and harmony vocals; the backing band consisted of members of Springfield band the Skeletons. A sophomore effort *Invisible Man* was issued in spring 2001. —*Richie Unterberger*

Big Thinkin' / Sep. 12, 2000 / HMG ◆◆◆

Wayne plays good-natured, low-key honky tonk country, singing in a low and gruff, though not gravelly, voice. There's not much to make this stand out from the pack of earthy honky tonk discs from the past, present, and most likely future, but he does have an affable manner and, sometimes, a good sense of humor. That especially comes to the fore on "If That's Country," in which he really sticks it to all those Nashville pseudo-urban cowboys singing MOR pop and trying to pass themselves off as real country singers, with a tune not far removed from Nancy Sinatra's "These Boots Are Made for Walkin'." "You can kick my Ozark ass if that's country," he pronounces, and as a native of Springfield, MO, he's entitled. Elsewhere there's some sad balladry ("I'm Back (And Lonelier Than Ever)"), nearly rockin' uptempo stuff, hoe-down near-bluegrass ("The Temptress's Smile"), a pretty good title phrase for "We Never Killed Each Other (But Didn't We Try?)," and a drawn-out narrative of drawn-out love on the six-and-a-half-minute "Ralene Wheeler." —*Richie Unterberger*

Invisible Man / Apr. 10, 2001 / Texicalli ◆◆◆

● **Here I Am in Dallas** / Aug. 21, 2001 / Hightone ◆◆◆◆

This album's opening track, "Bouncin' Beer Cans off the Jukebox" (one of the seven Dallas Wayne originals here), throws down the gauntlet on Wayne's own style by evoking the names of those Bakersfield giants Buck and Merle. Wayne plays reverent, hardcore honky tonk, and this is another strong release chock-full of classic country instrumentation. All of the originals are quite strong, but worth particular mention are the countrypolitan-flavored tearjerker "The Stuff Inside" (which stirs thoughts of George Jones' "Good Year for the Roses"), the lively and gorgeous "If These Walls Could Cry," and the fiddle-driven roadhouse anthem "I'm Going to Break Some Promises Tonight." Wayne also has an ear for which tunes to cover—no more evident than on the title track (once a Faron Young single), on which he manages to sound at once bewildered, grumpy, and heartbroken. Dallas Wayne makes country music that doesn't just nod to, but seems to inhabit that wonderful time between the late '50s and early '70s. It's genuine stuff indeed. *—Erik Hage*

Jimmy Wayne

b. Oct. 23, 1972

Vocals / Contemporary Country

By all Nash Vegas accounts, North Carolina singer and songwriter Jimmy Wayne comes from the wrong side of the tracks. Born in 1972, he was abandoned by his father at a young age and raised by a troubled mother and/or in a series of foster homes when she was in prison. On his 15th birthday he saw his stepfather shoot his stepsister three times, paralyzing her, and survived a murder attempt by the same man. He entered, and then ran from, a county home and became a homeless youth who did what he had to to survive on the street. His encounter with a neighborhood couple led them to give him a job, a place to live and created the pillars of his final foster family. With Bea and Russell Costner Wayne was able for the first time to indulge his love of music, which include Hall & Oates, Alan Jackson, Lionel Ritchie, Ronnie Milsap, Iron Maiden, Queensryche, and Judas Priest. He formed his first band, called Fantasyche, and began taking music seriously. When Beatrice died, Wayne finished high-school and became a prison guard at the Gaston Correctional Facility. An inmate who made an anti-drug presentation using a guitar during a school assembly influenced him greatly. Wayne visited the inmate for songwriting advice and went to work at the prison while studying criminal justice at a local community college. After finishing his associate's degree, he left North Carolina for Nashville.

For three years, he worked at Acuff-Rose writing songs alongside Dean Dillon and Whitey Shafer, while polishing his playing and singing skills. During this time he co-wrote Tracy Byrd's Top Ten smash "Put Your Hand in Mine," with Skip Ewing. Wayne signed his own deal with DreamWorks Nashville in 2001, after being courted by producer Chris Lindsey and James Stroud. His debut was issued in June of 2003 and placed a single in the Top Ten before release. "Stay Gone," was a *Billboard* country hit. It was followed by "Paper Angels," a narrative of Wayne's own life in the street and those he encountered there; "Blue and Brown," about an encounter with a foster brother who became an inmate at the prison where Wayne worked; and a devastatingly honest revenge fantasy entitled "The Rabbit." Given the timing of its release, Wayne's album turned a small industry buzz into a wildfire of publicity and speculation about the new directions he was using in country music and pop, which the industry glommed onto with desperate hope. Nashville's identity problems in the early part of the millennium created a crisis at radio and on CMT, leading the industry into a tailspin due to cookie-cutter artists singing mediocre songs. Wayne may be pretty, but he is substantive and presents an entirely new twist on the entire country tradition. *Billboard*, country music and even the Country Music Foundation took an early and large interest in his career. *—Thom Jurek*

Jimmy Wayne / Jun. 24, 2003 / DreamWorks ♦♦♦♦

Despite the fact that he was signed during Nashville's most serious identity crisis, Jimmy Wayne may not be a "pure country artist" (whatever that phrase means anymore, and who needs pure anything?), but he does possess two things that the great singer songwriters in any genre do: passion and honesty. Wayne writes edgy life and love songs that come from his own autobiography, much of it spent surviving a broken family and homelessness. His tunes are informed by influences ranging from Steve Earle to Daryl Hall to Don Henley. Wayne's darkness, and it is considerable, is tempered by the openness in the grain of his voice and his vulnerability. His youth is not ashamed to sing straight about the weight of his brokenness and yet his willingness to endure it because love in any guise is better than its alternative. The album's first single, "Stay Gone," despite his protagonists plea to remain apart—out of sight because of the pain—is nonetheless an invitation for the rest of us to remember our own experiences. "Paper Angel," talks about the forgotten, the lost, the taken, children who Wayne knows well; in fact, as the power chords and mandolin entwine around his reaching vocal and cascading acoustic guitar, we come to understand that he can understand that he can sing this way because he's been these children. When he sings the refrain, with more yearning and determination to convince than in a thousand Steve Earle songs, it's because he knows the other side: "Paper Angels/You're in my thoughts and prayers/No matter where you are remember God's right there/he's asking all of us to help take care/of paper angles everywhere." The production team of Chris Lindsey and James Stroud has added a lot to songs that are in essence very simple and powerful in and of themselves. It's obvious they want this kid to be a star, but he would have gotten there without all this. The music biz in Nash Vegas has dug its own cookie cutter grave by signing look-alikes who are pretty on TV and giving those models songs by hacks to record. Then there are the creeps who run country radio and have consciously done everything to ruin country music and its rich heritage; they deserve their fate. However, as a result of folly and greed and arrogance, the entire biz there needs to look at virtually everything that comes their way since they don't know what it is people want, and that's definitely a positive. Programmers actually have to do their jobs, A&R men have to listen to tapes instead of looking at 8x10 glossies to debate whether they'll look good on CMT. Wayne's the real thing. He could make a hard country record, he could make a pop record, a solid rock album; he could even cut a solid soul record with his voice. As a result he could deliver the goods in a more chancy setting, but it's a small complaint. This album may be a tad slick but the substance far outweighs the polish. This is a young man for whom the sky is the limit. He can write, sing and yeah, for a guy who spent so much of his life living outdoors and in shelters, he's a handsome devil too. But the grain of truth that's in his voice outstrips any image or sonic trappings that may be placed upon him from outside. Keep your ears open; this young man is no flash in the pan. *—Thom Jurek*

Jim Weider

b. Woodstock, NY

Guitar / Roots Rock, Retro-Rock

Born in Woodstock, NY, infamous sideman Jim Weider jumped into the music industry as soon as he could. The area was a hotbed for national talent, with acts like Bob Dylan and the Band recording there. He began recording and hiring himself out to songwriters for backup, eventually gathering up enough money to move to Nashville. He joined Johnny Paycheck's touring band, and supported himself through session work and playing local concerts. By the early '80s, Weider moved back to his hometown and began a tour with Robbie Dupress. When 1983 rolled around, he met former Band drummer Levon Helm, who invited him to join his touring band. Helm was very impressed by Weider, so when the Band was ready to reunite in 1985, Weider took Robbie Robertson's spot when Robertson declined the reunion. He continued to perform with the Band as the decade went on, eventually playing with the group at Roger Waters' recreation of *The Wall* at the Berlin Wall.

In 1993, he also played with the group at Bob Dylan's tribute concert in Madison Square Garden and at Bill Clinton's Inaugural Ball. On top of these performances, he also kept himself busy playing on albums by Robbie Dupree, Artie Traum, Paul Burlison, Rick Danko, and many others. His membership in the Band actually lasted longer than Robbie Robertson's original tenure, as he stayed with the band throughout the '90s, even performing with them at Woodstock '94. When he had time off from the group, he released several best-selling instructional videos for guitar, and finally released his own solo album with the Honky Tonk Gurus entitled *Big Foot* in 1999. *—Bradley Torreano*

Big Foot / Jun. 6, 2000 / Paras Recording ♦♦♦

Sessioncat, Johnny Paycheck sideman, and recent inductee into the Band, Jim Weider, his Honky Tonk Gurus, and a role call of top musicians (Tony Levin, David Sancious, Garth Hudson, et al.) take on Weider's roots rock guitar instrumentals and tunes as disparate as Jimi Hendrix's "Little Miss Lover," Chuck Berry's "Deep Feeling," Bobby Womack's "I'm in Love," and the Jimmy Cliff standard "Many Rivers to Cross." With Weider's unquestionable ability to give rock, blues, and R&B the full guitar-athon treatment, the results should find him fans among contemporary blues freaks and jam-band followers. *—Denise Sullivan*

Gillian Welch

b. 1968, California

Guitar, Vocals, Banjo / Neo-Traditional Folk, Singer/Songwriter, Alternative Country, Americana

A young singer/songwriter armed with a voice and sensibility far beyond her years, Gillian Welch drew widespread acclaim for her deft, evocative resurrection of the musical styles most commonly associated with rural Appalachia of the early 20th century. Welch was born in 1968 in California and grew up in West Los Angeles, where her parents scored the music for the comedy program *the Carol Burnett Show.* It was as a child that she became fascinated by bluegrass and early country music, in particular the work of the Stanley Brothers, the Delmore Brothers, and the Carter Family.

In the early '90s, Welch attended the Berklee School of Music in Boston, MA, where she began performing her own material, as well as traditional country and bluegrass songs, as part of a duo with fellow student David Rawlings. After honing their skills in local open mike showcases, the duo began performing regularly throughout the country. While opening for Peter Rowan in Nashville, they were spotted by musician and producer T-Bone Burnett, who helped Welch and Rawlings land a record deal. With Burnett producing, they cut 1996's starkly beautiful *Revival*, an album split between bare-bones duo performances—some even recorded in mono to capture a bygone sound—and more full-bodied cuts featuring legendary session men like guitarist James Burton, upright bassist Roy Huskey Jr., and drummers Buddy Harmon and Jim Keltner.

Her sophomore album, *Hell Among the Yearlings*, followed in 1998. The years following her second release found Welch involved in several soundtracks (*O Brother, Where Art Thou? Songcatcher*), tribute albums (*Songs of Dwight Yoakam: Will Sing for Food, Return of the Grievous Angel: A Tribute to Gram Parsons*), and guest spots on other artists' albums (Ryan Adams' *Heartbreaker*, Mark Knopfler's *Sailing to Philadelphia*). Following the success of *O Brother*, Welch & Rawlings found themselves in the center of a traditional American folk revival and released their third album, *Time (The Revelator)*, in mid-2001. Steady touring, guest appearances, and the release of a DVD (*The Revelator Collection*) kept the pair busy, but in 2003 they found time to record *Soul Journey*, their second release on their own Acony Records label. *—Jason Ankeny*

● **Revival** / Apr. 1996 / Almo Sounds ♦♦♦♦♦

After looking at the cover of Gillian Welch's debut album, *Revival*, and listening to the first two cuts, "Orphan Girl" and "Annabelle," you'd be tempted to imagine that Welch somehow stumbled into a time machine after cutting some tunes at the 1927 Bristol, TN, sessions and was transported to a recording studio in Los Angeles in 1996, where T-Bone Burnett was on hand and had the presence of mind to roll tape. It takes a closer listen to *Revival* to realize that Welch and her partner, David Rawlings, are not mere revivalists in the old-timey style; Welch's debts to artists of the past are obvious and clearly acknowledged, but there's a maturity, intelligence, and keen eye for detail in Welch's songs you wouldn't expect from someone simply trying to ape the Carter Family. What's more, the subtle, blues-shot menace of "Pass You By" and "Tear My Stillhouse Down" and the jazzy undertow of "Paper Wings" point to the breadth and depth of Welch's musical vision, which encompasses a spectrum broader than the rural musics of the 1920s and '30s. If Welch and Rawlings often reach to sounds and styles of the past on *Revival*, they do so with an unaffected sincerity and natural grace, and the album's best moments ("Orphan

Girl," "One More Dollar," and "Tear My Stillhouse Down") are the work of a gifted singer and songwriter who knows how to communicate the sounds of her heart and soul to others, and producer Burnett gets those sounds on tape with unobtrusive skill. A superb debut. —*Mark Deming*

Hell Among the Yearlings / Jul. 28, 1998 / Acony ✦✦✦✦

Lacking some of the focus that made her debut album so stunning, *Hell Among the Yearlings* is nevertheless a thoroughly satisfying second album from Gillian Welch. Instead of backing away from the rustic folkiness of *Revival*, Welch deepens her bleak, clear-eyed worldview, which makes her spare, old-timey arrangements all the more powerful. On occasion, the performances and songs are a bit too studied to be truly effective, but those moments are fleeting—*Hell Among the Yearlings* offers ample proof that Welch is a talented, individual songwriter and that her debut was no fluke. —*Thom Owens*

Time (The Revelator) / Jul. 31, 2001 / Acony ✦✦✦✦

Gillian Welch's third album, *Time (The Revelator)*, finds the folk vocalist and musician shifting her attention from achingly beautiful mountain ballads to achingly beautiful pop/rock ballads. Regarding this album, Welch states: "As opposed to being little tiny folk songs or traditional songs, they're really tiny rock songs. They're just performed in this acoustic setting. In our heads we went electric without changing instruments." This philosophy is most evident in songs like "I Want to Sing That Rock and Roll" and "Elvis Presley Blues," with her longtime collaborator David Rawlings accompanying her on Louvin-esque high harmonies and vintage guitar. Fans of the duo's neo-old-timey sound will be happy to hear a few of their familiar, intimate dust bowl folk songs peering through the fence posts. The banjo-driven "My First Lover" could've been recorded on Alan Lomax's back porch, while the title track aches and moans along with the best of her two previous albums. Rawlings' production on the album remains warm and intimate throughout, capturing the subtleties of the acoustic instruments and earthy harmonies. Highlights include the passionate romp "Red Clay Halo," which includes the best elements of time-honored folk stylings and their newfound passion for rock & roll, and the hushed awe that captures the audience in the Ryman Auditorium during the live recording of "I Want to Sing That Rock and Roll." *Time (The Revelator)* ends with an unprecedented 15-minute track called "I Dream a Highway," which drifts lazily through the album's final moments, sweetly dozing in the current like Huck and Jim's Mississippi River afternoons. Welch and Rawlings are at the top of their form and continue to make the best Americana recordings without resorting to drenching their albums in guest stars, but by writing and performing heartfelt songs that speak with a clear and undeniable honesty. —*Zac Johnson*

Soul Journey / Jun. 3, 2003 / Acony ✦✦✦

Gillian Welch and David Rawlings may, in fact, shock and appall folk purists with their fourth album, *Soul Journey*. "Are those drums?" "Is that an organ?" "Wait a minute, is that an electric bass?!?" The album uses these musical elements to drive home a living-room, lazy-summertime jam-session feel that hasn't really shown itself on Welch's previous releases. The album's opener, "Look at Miss Ohio," evolves into her toughest rocker since "Pass You By" on her debut, *Revival*, and the whole album culminates in the relative cacophony of "Wrecking Ball," a drunked-up barroom stumble highlighted by Ketcham Secor's loping fiddle lines and Rawlings' fuzzed-out guitar solo. Between these bookends is a mixed bag of traditional folk songs ("Make Me a Pallet on Your Floor," "I Had a Real Good Mother and Father"), loose blues phrasing ("Lowlands," "No One Knows My Name"), and a number of trademark Welch/Rawlings near-whispered murder ballads and orphan love songs. The thing that shines through most clearly is that the group had a lot of fun making *Soul Journey*, but that doesn't necessarily translate into a terrific album. Aside from a handful of real solid honest-to-gosh gems, the whole album feels a little too casual and off-the-cuff to stand on equal footing with her other recordings. The choruses often become just repeated phrases over and over again ("Lowlands," "No One Knows My Name," "I Made a Lovers Prayer," and the unfortunate "One Monkey"), and the songwriting seems less developed, as if the initial construction of the song has taken a back seat to the sheer enjoyment of performing it. That being said, it is a wonderful, dusty summertime front-porch album, full of whiskey drawls and sly smiles, floorboard stomps and screen-door creeks. While it does not exactly meet the impeccable standards that her previous three releases set, it is still a fine addition to her discography and well worth listening to all summer long. —*Zac Johnson*

Kevin Welch

b. Aug. 17, 1955, Long Beach, CA

Guitar, Songwriter, Vocals / Singer/Songwriter, Alternative Country, Americana

Americana singer/songwriter Kevin Welch left his Oklahoma home at age 17 to pursue a life in music, settling in Nashville in 1978 after years of traveling. He soon signed on as a staff writer at Sony/Tree, over the decade to follow authoring songs for artists including Waylon Jennings, Roger Miller, Trisha Yearwood, Ricky Skaggs, and the Highwaymen; Welch's self-titled solo debut finally appeared on Reprise in 1990, followed two years later by the acclaimed *Western Beat*. Country radio remained resistant to his downbeat, acoustic style, however, and in 1995 he teamed with fellow Nashville renegades Kieran Kane, Tammy Rogers, and Harry Stinson to form his own independent label, Dead Reckoning. Welch's first album for the label, *Life Down Here on Earth*, followed soon after, and in 1999 he returned with *Beneath My Wheels*. Between 1999 and 2001, Welch recorded the *Millionaire* album with friends from Denmark called the Danes, and released it in the U.S. on Dead Reckoning. —*Jason Ankeny*

● **Kevin Welch** / 1990 / Reprise ✦✦✦✦✦

Welch's songs sprawl out like great, open flatlands, mixing elements of folk, country, and rock in a captivating way. Welch himself—half-singing, half-speaking songs such as

"Hello, I'm Gone" and "Some Kind of Paradise"—comes off as a cross between a renegade storyteller and a heartland romantic. —*Brian Mansfield*

Western Beat / 1991 / Reprise ✦✦✦

The title of *Western Beat* signals what kind of music Kevin Welch plays—it's western music, but with a heavy, urban beat. It's a fresh, lively sound, supported by a number of first-rate songs, including "Sam's Town," "Train to Birmingham," and "Early Summer Rain." —*Thom Owens*

Life Down Here on Earth / 1995 / Dead Reckoning ✦✦✦

Kevin Welch is a card-carrying member of the Texas school of songwriting, and it is easy to reel off the names of some of his classmates: If you like Guy Clark, Lyle Lovett, Steve Earle, Joe Ely, or any one of a dozen or so other literate singer/songwriters with a Southwest sensibility who have been in and out of Nashville since the 1960s, then you'll like Kevin Welch, too. Welch's obvious talents brought him a contract with Warner Bros., but despite the regard in which the school is held by aficionados, its members rarely sell records in numbers significant enough to interest a major label for long, and *Life Down Here on Earth* finds him on an artist-owned indie. Of course, that means he got to make the record he wanted to, and with four years between releases he had plenty of songs, not having to rely on covers as he did to an extent on 1991's *Western Beat*. Over familiar-sounding folk-rock and country-rock arrangements, he sings world-weary, older-but-wiser lyrics about life's travails, the doomed search for love, and the joys of kicking back now and then. The album's philosophy is contained in its opening and closing tracks. "Pushing Up Daisies" talks about how hard things can be, but concludes that "it's better than pushing up daisies," while the album's title song notes that, while your tombstone will have two dates, it's what happens in the dash in between that matters. Although Welch is worthy of comparison with the best in his field, he is also somewhat generic, which may explain why he isn't better known. His reedy voice is a ringer for T-Bone Burnett's, and his songs, while always craftsmanlike, would benefit from stronger performances. Maybe that's why he makes most of his money from song publishing. —*William Ruhlmann*

Beneath My Wheels / Jun. 22, 1999 / Dead Reckoning ✦✦✦

Kevin Welch's 4th album *Beneath My Wheels* features more of the expansive songwriting for which he has become known in alt-country and folk circles. Tracks like "Everybody's Gotta Walk" and "Full Moon Over Christiania" weave folk, country and rock together, telling compelling stories of love and life. —*Heather Phares*

Millionaire / Jul. 9, 2002 / Dead Reckoning ✦✦✦

Backed by a Copenhagen-based band he dubs the Danes, Kevin Welch rocks out a little more than usual on his fifth album, *Millionaire*. This unit has mastered the kind of rock shuffle for which the Rolling Stones are known; you get the feeling they could encore with a good version of "Honky Tonk Women." The arrangements make a good basis for Welch's songs, a typically high-quality collection of tunes that reflect on life and love. Welch's characters, who usually speak in the first person, are among life's losers, particularly the unhappy participant in the Witness Protection Program who narrates "Witness," but many of them are redeemed by love. Indeed, there are quite a few outright love songs, including the title song, "Choose to Believe," and "I Can Sure Love You," with an excellent cover of Van Morrison's "Queen of the Slipstream" joining them. It's good there's so much true love, since life seems desperate without it, especially on "Killing Myself." These songs are more impressive than the symbolic ones, such as "Long Cold Train" and "The Sun King and the Winter Moon," but the band's performances make interesting listening even of tunes with somewhat muddled lyrics. Welch, meanwhile, is becoming a better and more expressive vocalist, which also helps put across his material. On earlier records, you yearned to hear what a real singer could do with his compositions, but on *Millionaire* he has come into his own as a performer. —*William Ruhlmann*

Freddy Weller (Wilton Frederick Weller)

b. Sep. 9, 1947, Atlanta, GA

Guitar, Songwriter, Vocals / Country-Pop, Traditional Country

Guitarist and songwriter Freddy Weller had a successful behind-the-scenes career in pop/rock before finding solo success as a country singer. Born Wilton Frederick Weller in Atlanta in 1947, he started playing both banjo and mandolin at age eight and soon moved on to the guitar as well. During his teen years, Weller performed regularly on the local radio show Georgia Jubilee, where he shared time with the likes of Jerry Reed, Joe South, and Billy Joe Royal. He soon became a regular session guitarist in the area, most notably playing on Royal's 1965 hit "Down in the Boondocks"; while in Royal's touring band, Weller met Paul Revere & the Raiders, who offered him their lead guitar slot in 1967. Weller spent the next four years as a member of the Raiders, and in 1969 he worked with pop singer Tommy Roe in a songwriting capacity, co-writing the smash hits "Dizzy" and "Jam Up Jelly Tight." Later that year, Raiders frontman Mark Lindsay offered Weller the chance to return to his first love, country music, when the group canceled a recording session. Weller took the studio time instead, and his version of Joe South's "Games People Play" went to number two on the country charts that year; moreover, the follow-up single, South's "These Are Not My People," reached number five. Weller departed the Raiders to focus on his solo career in 1971, the same year he scored three straight Top Five hits on the country charts with "Another Night of Love," "Indian Lake," and "The Promised Land."

Weller reached the country Top 20 three times over 1972-1973 with songs he either wrote or co-wrote: "The Roadmaster," "She Loves Me (Right Out of My Mind)," and "The Perfect Stranger." He also penned Bob Luman's country smash "Lonely Women Make Good Lovers" in 1972, and it was later covered for another hit by Steve Wariner. Weller's final Top Ten hit was a 1973 cover of Chuck Berry's "Too Much Monkey Business," and he reached the Top 20 twice more in 1974 with "I've Just Got to Know (How Loving You Would Be)" and "You're Not Getting Older (You're Getting Better)." In 1975, he left Columbia to record an album for ABC/Dot but subsequently returned to Columbia and continued to record for them through the early '80s. He couldn't duplicate his earlier run of commercial success as a singer but kept up his songwriting; when a few small-label efforts in the '80s failed to attract much attention, he supplied material to stars like Reba McEntire ("They Asked About You"), John Michael Montgomery ("She Don't Need a Band to Dance"), and George Jones ("What I Do Best"), among others. — *Steve Huey*

Games People Play/These Are Not My People / 1969 / Columbia ✦✦✦✦

Another Night of Love / 1971 / Columbia ✦✦✦✦

The Promised Land / 1972 / Columbia ✦✦✦

The Roadmaster / 1972 / Columbia ✦✦✦

Too Much Monkey Business / 1973 / Columbia ✦✦✦✦

Sexy Lady / 1974 / Columbia ✦✦✦

Freddy Weller / 1975 / ABC/Dot ✦✦✦

Freddy Weller's Greatest Hits / 1975 / Columbia ✦✦✦✦

Liquor, Love and Life / 1976 / Columbia ✦✦✦

Love Got in the Way / 1978 / Columbia ✦✦✦

Go for the Night / 1980 / Columbia ✦✦✦

Freddy Weller rides into the '80s with *Go for the Night*, a record that sounds like slick, countrified versions of songs Jimmy Buffett passed on. Nothing here on the record stands out like on his previous efforts, but there is a certain charm which pervades this release. Weller is too much a professional to make a bad record, but this isn't one of his best. — *James Chrispell*

- **The Very Best of Freddy Weller** / Mar. 11, 2003 / Collectors' Choice Music ✦✦✦✦
Freddy Weller was a member of Paul Revere & the Raiders who launched a solo career as a country singer at the end of the '60s, just as he started having success as a songwriter when his collaborations with Tommy Roe led to Roe having hits with their co-written numbers "Dizzy" and "Jam Up Jelly Tight." Clearly, Weller was not one to be pigeonholed, and as his career rolled on during the '70s, he continued to not quite follow a straight path. Although he was known as a songwriter, he had his biggest country hits with covers of pop and rock tunes from the '60s, taking Joe South's "Games People Play" to number one, Chuck Berry's "The Promised Land" to three, the same placing achieved by his cover of the Cowsills' "Indian Lake." He opened up his sound with a little bit of soul and mellow grooves, resulting in a stretch of smooth romantic hits. He dabbled in funny, tongue-in-cheek songs that gently lampooned '70s pop culture fads, such as "Fantasy Island" and "Bar Wars." Throughout it all, his music flowed easily and his warm, simple voice sold it convincingly, leading to 19 country Top 40 hits, all of which are collected on Collectors Choices' 22-track 2002 release *The Very Best of Freddy Weller*, which is surely the definitive overview of his career as a hitmaker. Weller's music is enjoyable if probably a little too relaxed and unassuming for its own good to be truly memorable, which may be why this is the first comprehensive overview ever assembled on him. His hits are easy-rolling and friendly, walking a line between traditional country and sweeter country-pop while taking a couple unexpected but related detours. It's very pleasant to hear, but it also sounds very much like its time. With that in mind, *The Very Best of Freddy Weller* can be recommended not just as a comprehensive overview/introduction of his music, but also as a period piece of sweet, pop-inflected '70s country that may not transcend its time but nevertheless evokes it nicely. — *Stephen Thomas Erlewine*

Kitty Wells (Muriel Deason)
b. Aug. 30, 1918, Nashville, TN
Vocals, Guitar / Traditional Country, Honky Tonk, Nashville Sound/Countrypolitan
One of the few country stars born in Nashville, Kitty Wells (born Muriel Deason) had a string of hits from the '50s to the early '70s that earned her the title Queen of Country Music. She made her radio debut on Nashville's WSIX, where she met her future husband, Johnnie Wright of Johnnie & Jack. She began touring as part of Johnnie & Jack's show; Wright gave her the stage name, taken from an old folk ballad called "I'm A-Goin' to Marry Kitty Wells." Wells recorded unsuccessfully for RCA before switching to Decca, where she hit with 1952's "It Wasn't God Who Made Honky Tonk Angels," a response to Hank Thompson's "The Wild Side of Life." Its controversial pre-feminist lyrics, which blamed unfaithful men for creating unfaithful women, paved the way for Loretta Lynn and Tammy Wynette and established Wells as the first major female country star. Wells recorded a number of answer songs and remakes, but she has top-notch original material as well, including some of Harlan Howard's earliest hits.

Wells began singing as a child, learning guitar from her father. As a teenager, she sang with her sisters, who performed under the name the Deason Sisters, on a local radio station. The group began singing on the station in 1936. The following year, she married Johnnie Wright. Shortly after their marriage, Wells & Wright began performing together along with his sister, Louise Wright; they called themselves Johnnie Wright & the Harmony Girls. Jack Anglin, Louise's husband, joined the group in 1939, and they renamed the band the Tennessee Hillbillies, which would eventually evolve into the Tennessee Mountain Boys.

Anglin was drafted into the Army in 1942. Following his departure, Wright & Wells performed as a duo; it was at this time that she adopted the Kitty Wells stage name. When Anglin returned from the Army, he and Wright formed the Johnnie & Jack duo. Wells would tour with the duo, occasionally performing backup vocals. In 1946 and 1947, the duo had a regular spot at the *Grand Ole Opry*, and Wells rarely performed with them. However, she did sing with the pair when they joined the *Louisiana Hayride* in 1948. The *Louisiana Hayride* helped Johnnie & Jack land a record contract with RCA Records in 1949. That same year, Wells recorded some gospel tracks—featuring Johnnie & Jack as instrumental support—for RCA, but they were unsuccessful. Following those recordings, Wells was more or less retired for the next few years. In 1952, Paul Cohen, an executive at Decca Records, approached Wells to record "It Wasn't God Who Made Honky Tonk

Angels." Wells recorded the song and it became a smash hit, reaching number one in the summer and staying in that position for six weeks. Later in 1952, she joined the *Grand Ole Opry*.

"It Wasn't God Who Made Honky Tonk Angels" was followed by "Paying for That Back Street Affair," a response to Webb Pierce's "Back Street Affair." The single reached number six in the spring of 1953, helping to establish a permanent place at the top of the charts for Wells. For the rest of the '50s, she hit the Top Ten with regularity, racking up a total of 23 Top Ten hits. In the early '60s, her career dipped slightly, but she continued to have Top Ten hits frequently. During the late '60s and '70s, Wells' streak of hits evaporated, but she managed to have a string of minor hits and remained a popular concert attraction. In 1974, Wells was inducted into the Country Music Hall of Fame, and with good reason. Kitty Wells broke down the doors for female country singers, paving the way for artists like Patsy Cline, Tammy Wynette, and Loretta Lynn. During the '80s, her activity slowed—in addition to running a museum outside of Nashville, she toured with her husband, Johnnie, and frequently appeared on the *Grand Ole Opry*. In 1991, Kitty Wells was given a Lifetime Achievement Award from the Grammys. — *Brian Mansfield & Stephen Thomas Erlewine*

Country Hit Parade / 1956 / Decca ✦✦✦✦
Kitty Wells was a major influence on Dolly Parton, Linda Ronstadt, Emmylou Harris and so many other women who crossed over from country to pop. "Too many times married men think they are single" is the sentiment displayed in "It Wasn't God Who Made Honky Tonk Angels"—which is 1950s male bashing, and Wells' perfect vocal cuts through the violin and accompaniment. It's pure country music that is far removed from the slick pop Nashville began manufacturing decades after this groundbreaking disc. "Paying for That Back Street Affair" is one of three Billy Wallace titles, featuring the lyrics "you gambled and I lost/now I must pay with hours of despair." The songs are full of someone having done someone wrong, and though there is a sameness throughout, vocally and instrumentally, the purity of Wells' performance and sincerity makes the 12 short stories very appealing. "I don't claim to be an angel, my life's been full of sin" is her statement, and she's sticking to it. Wells covers Roy Acuff, Zeke Clements, and J.B. Miller, and the work is consistently high. The passion in the opening track, Jimmy Work's "Making Believe," is powerful stuff, but it's her performance on the Eddie Miller/Dube Williams/Robert Yount classic "Release Me" which is the album's high point, as influential as the hit "It Wasn't God Who Made Honky Tonk Angels." This track may have helped establish Engelbert Humperdinck's career as he took the song to the Top Five in 1967. Jimmy Heap had a country hit with the "Release Me" in 1955, and Esther Phillips took it to the top of the R&B charts in 1962 (as well as Top Ten on the Top 40), but Kitty Wells adds something extra to it here, and her performance of the tune is timeless. Release Me doesn't have "your lips are sweet as honey" lines, but "There's Poison in Your Heart" lines, and maybe that's what makes it so effective. Still, Kitty Wells can take corny country lyrics and deliver them with total sincerity. *Kitty Wells Country Hit Parade* is a classic of the genre and gave inspiration to decades of male and female vocalists who went on to inspire others. It is entertaining beyond its historical importance. — *Joe Viglione*

Winner of Your Heart / 1956 / Decca ✦✦✦✦

Dust on the Bible / 1959 / Decca ✦✦✦✦✦
Dust on the Bible is a moving set of country gospel performed with affection and honest by Kitty Wells. The material on the album ranges from standards to contemporary classics like "The Great Speckled Bird," and not a single cut on the record fails to raise the hairs on the back of your neck. In the late '50s, country gospel albums didn't come much finer than *Dust on the Bible*. — *Thom Owens*

After Dark / 1959 / Decca ✦✦✦

Seasons of My Heart / 1960 / Decca ✦✦✦✦
Seasons of My Heart is an excellent LP collection of country ballads highlighted by the title track, Hank Thompson's "Most of All," and Marty Robbins' "The Hands You're Holding Now," Hank Locklin's "Send Me the Pillow You Dream On," John D. Loudermilk's "If I Had the Right to Do You Wrong," Kitty's original "I'll Be All Smiles Tonight," and the hit singles "Fickle Fun," "The Other Cheek" and "Amigo's Guitar." — *Thom Owens*

Kitty's Choice / 1960 / Decca ✦✦✦✦✦
Kitty's Choice is comprised almost entirely of contemporary country classics like "Sugartime," "Your Cheatin' Heart," "Half As Much," "Tennessee Waltz," "Jambalaya," and "My Happiness," adding a couple of obscurities for good measure. All of the songs are performed with gusto by Wells, making it one of her most enjoyable records of the early '60s. — *Thom Owens*

Kitty Wells' Golden Favorites / 1961 / Decca ✦✦✦✦✦
Despite the title, *Kitty Wells' Golden Favorites* isn't strictly a greatest hits collection. Though most of the LP is comprised of big hits—"Hey Joe," "(I'll Always Be Your) Fraulein," "Jealousy," "Mommy for a Day," "Amigo's Guitar," "Left to Right"—it is padded out by tracks that were either lesser hits ("All the Time") or songs that were never released as singles (an excellent version of Don Gibson's "I Can't Stop Loving You," "Your Wild Life's Gonna Get You Down"). All of the cuts that weren't hits are nearly equal in quality to the popular singles, making *Golden Favorites* one of Wells' best early '60s records. — *Stephen Thomas Erlewine*

The Queen of Country Music / 1962 / Decca ✦✦✦
It's ironic that an LP called *Queen of Country Music* would contain covers of pop songs like "Moody River" and "What Am I Living For," but it's a testament to Kitty's talent that she can make the songs sound like genuine country numbers. Furthermore, the rest of the record consists of excellent cuts like "Hello Walls," "Am I That Easy to Forget," and "Pick Me Up on Your Way Down," making the record a thoroughly enjoyable listen—even if it doesn't include any hit singles. — *Thom Owens*

Singing on Sunday / 1962 / Decca ✦✦✦

Relying on traditional gospel songs, *Singing on Sunday* is an enjoyable but unexceptional early '60s gospel LP from Kitty Wells, highlighted by excellent takes on "The Wings of a Dove" and "That Glory Bound Train." —*Thom Owens*

The Kitty Wells Story / 1963 / Decca ✦✦✦✦✦

The Kitty Wells Story was the first vinyl collection of Kitty's biggest hits ("It Wasn't God Who Made Honky Tonk Angels," "Paying for That Back Street Affair," "Whose Shoulder Will You Cry On," "Makin' Believe") and it remains a strong compilation. Not all of her biggest hits are present on the set and it was later replaced with stronger collections, but the compilation remains entertaining and it has a couple of gems that never found their way onto any other set (with the notable exception, of course, of Bear Family's gigantic, multi-disc box set). —*Thom Owens*

Especially for You / 1964 / Decca ✦✦✦

Though the production occasionally leans too heavily toward the pop direction and there are a few awkward covers such as "Busted," and *Especially for You* remains an exceptional mid-'60s LP from Kitty Wells, highlighted by the hit singles "Unloved Unwanted," "Will Your Lawyer Talk to God," and "We Missed You," plus strong versions of "Act Naturally," "Make the World Go Away," and "Ring of Fire." —*Thom Owens*

Country Music Time / 1964 / Decca ✦✦✦

Despite a handful of undistinguished songs, *Country Music Time* remains a strrong mid-'60s album from Kitty Wells, highlighted by the hit singles "This White Circle on My Finger," "Password," and "I've Thought of Leaving You." —*Thom Owens*

Burning Memories / 1965 / Decca ✦✦✦

Though it has a few strong tracks, particularly the hit single "I'll Repossess My Heart," the LP *Burning Memories* is too uneven in terms of material and is burdened by too many overdubbed vocal chorus and strings to be consistently enjoyable. —*Thom Owens*

The Kitty Wells Family Gospel Sing / 1965 / Decca ✦✦✦

The Kitty Wells Family Gospel Sing is a good, but unremarkable, country gospel LP from the mid-'60s, largely comprised of contemporary songs that fail to make a lasting impression. —*Thom Owens*

Lonesome, Sad and Blue / 1965 / Decca ✦✦✦

A loosely constructed concept LP about loneliness and heartbreak, *Lonesome, Sad and Blue* is a typically enjoyable set of country ballads and weepers from Kitty Wells. Though the production and song selection occasionally veers to close to country-pop territory (witness the version of Henry Mancini's "Dear Heart" and the Jordanaires' vocal accompaniment), Wells' powerful voice keeps the album's footing firmly in country, especially when she belts out "Oh, Lonesome Me," "The Race is On," "Welcome to My World," "Cheatin' is Catching," and "You're the Only World I Know." —*Thom Owens*

Lonely Street / 1965 / Decca ✦✦✦

Lonely Street is a slightly uneven but enjoyable mid-'60s LP that alternates between country-pop ballads and honky tonk. Among the highlights are "If Teardrops Were Pennies," "Sweeter Than the Flowers," "The Waltz of the Angels," and the title track. —*Thom Owens*

Country All the Way / 1966 / Decca ✦✦✦

Country All the Way is a strong mid-'60s LP from Kitty Wells, featuring supportive, not overbearing, vocal accompaniment from the Jordanaires, as well as an excellent selection of songs highlighted by the hit singles "A Woman Half My Age," "A Woman Never Forgets," and "Meanwhile Down at Joe's," plus excellent album cuts like "Too Many Rivers," "Together Again," "Cryin' Time," and "Nobody But a Fool (Would Love You)." —*Thom Owens*

Guilty Street / 1966 / Decca ✦✦✦

Kitty Wells was past her prime in 1969, but she still had her voice and could still put a song on the charts, at least the lower reaches thereof. She would never again have a hit as big as *Guilty Street*'s "Happiness Hill," and even that didn't reach the Top 40. The title track charted as a single, too, but Wells' nasal voice was an artifact of the '50s and primarily appealed to the loyal remnants of her old audience. It is fascinating to hear Wells attempt pop songs like the Chordettes' "Born to Be With You" and Roy Orbison's "Only the Lonely (Know the Way I Feel)," but "Stand By Your Man" and "Daddy Sang Bass" are better suited to her sound. Jim Anglin from the Anglin Brothers wrote two of the album's songs, which will interest listeners who also follow the doings of Wells' husband, Johnny Wright. —*Greg Adams*

The Kitty Wells Show / 1966 / Decca ✦✦

The Kitty Wells Show is an entertaining LP documenting a mid-'60s concert headlined by Wells. Kitty only performs four songs—"You Left Your Mark on Me," "It's All Over But the Crying," "Love's Enough for Me" and her trademark song "It Wasn't God Who Made Honky Tonk Angels"—with the rest of the album taken over by her fellow country vocalists Bill Phillips, Bobby Wright, and Johnny Wright, plus instrumentalists Paul Yandell and Odell Martin. Though it would have been nice to hear a complete concert from Kitty, the record is fun; nevertheless, it isn't really the kind of album that holds up on repeat listens. —*Thom Owens*

Kitty Wells Sings Songs Made Famous by Jim Reeves / 1966 / Decca ✦✦✦

Songs Made Famous by Jim Reeves is an enjoyable LP collection of Kitty singing songs associated with Reeves including "Four Walls," "Billy Bayou," "She'll Have to Go," "Welcome to My World" and "Bimbo." —*Thom Owens*

Kitty Wells / 1966 / Vocalion ✦✦✦

Released on Decca's Vocalion subsidary, *Kitty Wells* is a fitfully entertaining LP collection of odds and ends that ranges from sublime ("Thou Shalt Not Steal," "You'll Never Be Mine

Again," "A Heartache for a Keepsake") to the merely average ("The Life They Live in Songs"). —*Thom Owens*

Love Makes the World Go Around / 1967 / Decca ✦✦✦

For most Kitty Wells fans, *Love Makes the World Go Around* is a bit of a frustrating listen. The LP does boast a handful of fine songs, particularly the Dallas Frazier covers "Baby's Coming Home" and "There Goes My Everything," but the production is too lush for Kitty's honky tonk roots, as the minor hit singles "Only Me and My Hairdresser Know" and "Love Makes the World Go Around" indicate. —*Thom Owens*

Queen of Honky Tonk Street / 1967 / Decca ✦✦✦

Though the material is slightly uneven and the album only has one hit single (in the form of the title track), *Queen of Honky Tonk Street* is still a very good late-'60s LP by Kitty Wells. Occasionally, the production is a bit too heavy for Wells' honky tonk inclinations, but her gutsy voice always makes the songs worth hearing. —*Thom Owens*

Together Again / 1967 / Decca ✦✦✦

Together Again is a very entertaining reunion album from Kitty Wells & Red Foley. From the hit singles "Happiness Means You," "Hello Number One," and "Living As Strangers" to album tracks like "Together Again," "My Wall Came Tumblin' Down," "Have I Told You Lately That I Love You?" and "My Happiness," there isn't a weak song on the LP, and the two vocalists sound terrific together. —*Thom Owens*

Country Heart / 1969 / Vocalion ✦✦✦✦

The fiddle is heavy, the voice is distinctive, and the Benny Martin/Jim Denny tune "Each Day" starts off this compilation of music from Kitty Wells' past releases on Decca Records. There's a beautiful black-and-white of the younger Wells on the back cover, while an older color photo of the star sitting on a white fence in a pink polka dot dress adorns the front of the *Country Heart* album. Cindy Walker's "Dancing With a Stranger" and Johnny Master's "Stubborn Heart" show Wells at the peak of her powers, the voice full and vibrant gliding over precise arrangements. The entire album is in "simulated stereo" but, thankfully, it still sounds like mono and the label didn't ruin the beauty of the original tracks. Ray Crisp joins in on the vocals for "Broken Marriage Vows," but it's only for the chorus, as the "Queen of Country Music" stays center stage where she belongs. There's a beautiful rendition of the Fred Rose/Hank Williams tune "A Mansion on the Hill," and all ten songs are strong examples of the singer's work, though the album could have been a bit more informative—there's no mention of who the musicians are or from which albums this music was compiled. Still, hearing Wells performing "Beside You" is a treat, and you don't need the flowery liner notes that are here to enjoy it. As a collection of ten top-notch performances by Kitty Wells, *Country Heart* works. —*Joe Viglione*

Singin' 'Em Country / 1970 / Decca ✦✦✦

Singin' 'Em Country is a slightly uneven but thoroughly enjoyable LP from 1970, boasting excellent versions of Felice Bryant's "We Could," and Don Gibson's "Don't Take All Your Loving," and Carl Perkins' "Rise and Shine." —*Thom Owens*

Sing Heartwarming Gospel Songs / 1971 / Decca ✦✦✦

Husband and wife Johnny Wright & Kitty Wells didn't record as a duo very often relative to the length of their careers, but made at least a couple of albums for Decca in the late '60s and early '70s. *Sing Heartwarming Gospel Songs* is the second such album, and finds the pair treading familiar ground on a platter of sacred songs backed by the Wright Family, a vocal group comprised of their semi-famous offspring, Bobby Wright and Ruby Wright. Old-time religious music like "God Put a Rainbow in the Clouds" joins more contemporary material such as Merle Haggard's "Jesus Take a Hold" and Don Gibson's "There's a Big Wheel," performed with presence and abundant country gospel appeal by these veteran performers. —*Greg Adams*

Forever Young / 1974 / Capricorn ✦✦✦

Country Spotlight / 1991 / K-Tel ✦

Country Spotlight does not feature the original, classic versions of Wells' greatest hits; it's full of decidedly inferior rerecordings. Besides that, it is woefully short at 25 minutes, making this disc a complete ripoff. —*Stephen Thomas Erlewine*

☆ **Country Music Hall of Fame Series** / 1991 / MCA ✦✦✦✦✦

Country Music Hall of Fame contains 16 of Kitty Wells' best songs, giving a reasonably thorough overview of her career by combining big hits like "It Wasn't God Who Made Honky Tonk Angels" with minor hits like "A Woman Half My Age." The songs on this single disc were recorded for Decca Records between 1952 and 1965, so it naturally touches on many of the highlights from her artistic heyday, including "Release Me," "Making Believe," "I Can't Stop Loving You," "Mommy for a Day," and "Heartbreak, USA." It's an excellent retrospective, even though several important cuts—including most of her uptempo material—is missing. Nevertheless, it's collects many of her most important songs and provides a terrific introduction to one of the most important vocalists in country music history. —*Stephen Thomas Erlewine*

Queen of Country Music / Jun. 28, 1994 / Bear Family ✦✦✦✦✦

Bear Family, the venerable German label that does reissue boxes better than any American label—with the possible exception of Mosaic—of U.S. artists, has taken the cream of Kitty Wells career and issued one of the most historically important collections in the history of country music. The *Queen of Country Music* is a four-CD box, with exhaustive biographical and session notes by Charles Wolfe that documents in their entirety, nine years of Ms. Wells career, from its inception through to its turning point and superstardom, the years 1949 to 1958; there are 114 tracks in all. Along with every major hit and B-side from the eras including classic original versions of "It Wasn't God Who Made Honky Tonk Angels," "Hey Joe!," "I Hear the Jukebox Playing," "Lonely Side of Town," "Making Believe," "Dust on the Bible," "The Place That Kills," "Right or Wrong," "Just When I Needed You," "The Great Speckled Bird," "Jealousy," and many others. There are plenty of alternate takes, unissued tracks and as the session notes attest, Wells was the beginning for many, including the legendary producer Owen Bradley who worked with her and Patsy Cline, simultaneously. Box sets such as this one, while geared to the collector and fanatic, have it would seem limited appeal, but the Queen of Country Music can be looked at in a different light entirely. The story of Wells ascent to stardom also accurately reflects the changing tides in Nashville and the changing popular attitudes toward country music. Like Don Gibson, Wells, while remaining firmly a country roots and honky tonk vocalist, nonetheless because of Bradley's production techniques and marketing changes ushered in by Chet Atkins at RCA, experienced a certain amount of crossover success due to massive jukebox play in barrooms and lounges all over the North, As in the Gibson set, this one offers a real view of Nashville's evolution into its real glory years from 1955-1970, *—Thom Jurek*

Honky Tonk Angel / 1996 / ♦♦♦♦♦

Honky Tonk Angel is a 19-track, single-disc import compilation of the majority of Kitty Wells' Top Ten hits from the '50s and the early '60s. Featuring such classic honky tonk hits as "Makin' Believe," "Release Me," "Heartbreak U.S.A.," "Jealousy," "Searching (For Someone Like You)" and "It Wasn't God Who Made Honky Tonk Angels," the disc is first-rate, yet it doesn't offer enough different material from *Country Music Hall of Fame* to make it worth an extensive search. *—Stephen Thomas Erlewine*

★ **God's Honky Tonk Angel: The First Queen of Country Music** / Aug. 15, 2000 / Edsel ♦♦♦♦♦

No one ever sang a cheatin' song better than Kitty Wells, and this collection of her peak-period material (25 songs recorded for Decca between 1952 and 1965) is as good an introduction as one could ask for to one of country & western's seminal artists. Wells was one of Nashville's first major female stars, and if she often sang as a wife who strayed, she also gave a voice to every woman who had been led into shame by a no-good man, and her strong, rich voice was the perfect instrument for a gal wrestling with the shame, remorse, and anger of infidelity. And while Wells could take the grief, she could also dish it out; "Will Your Lawyer Talk to God," in particular, is possessed of a righteous wrath the Louvin Brothers would have envied. The earlier sides on this disc (especially her first hits "It Wasn't God Who Made Honky Tonk Angels" and "Paying for That Back Street Affair") are tough, flinty honky tonk at its best, with Wells' superb vocals buoyed by great (though unfortunately uncredited) fiddle and steel guitar accompaniment, and while the later selections are arranged and produced in a manner more befitting the countrypolitan slant of the day, Wells' performances are as tough and pure as ever, and she's a joy to listen to throughout. While the sheer breadth of Kitty Wells' career would prevent any single-disc collection from being definitive, as an overview of her most important period, *God's Honky Tonk Angel* is an ideal starting place. *—Mark Deming*

20th Century Masters—The Millennium Collection: The Best of Kitty Wells / Jun. 4, 2002 / MCA ♦♦♦♦

20th Century Masters—The Millennium Collection: The Best of Kitty Wells is a decent primer of her best years with Decca, collecting such definitive singles as "It Wasn't God Who Made Honky Tonk Angels," "Makin' Believe," "Heartbreak U.S.A.," "Mommy for a Day," and "Release Me." Tracks like "Will Your Lawyer Talk to God" reflect the strong, proto-feminist feeling of her work, which not only influenced further generations of female country artists but also echoed the sentiments of many women in the '50s and '60s. At only a dozen tracks long, *20th Century Masters—The Millennium Collection: The Best of Kitty Wells* is no match for the Bear Family box or even more extensive single-disc collections like *God's Honky Tonk Angel*, but it's a concise collection of songs from country music's first queen. *—Heather Phares*

Peter Wernick

Banjo / Progressive Bluegrass, Instrumental Country

Banjo player Pete Wernick started his recording career back in 1971, when he belonged to the instrumental group Country Cooking. Before the decade was over, he established Hot Rize, a progressive bluegrass outfit. He went on to record as a solo artist, and his 1993 Sugar Hill release, *On a Roll*, spawned the hit "Ruthie." In addition to recording and performing, Wernick, aka "Dr. Banjo," served the International Bluegrass Music Association (IBMA) as president. He also writes songs, teaches banjo, and is an author. Wernick first became interested in the banjo during his teen years, when he paid close attention to the playing of Earl Scruggs. While attending Columbia University in New York City, where he earned a doctorate in sociology, he kept his hand in music by playing with local outfits. During the 1960s, he also hosted a regional bluegrass-based radio program. With degree in hand, he headed to Ithaca, where he was a Cornell University sociologist. It was during his time at Cornell that he founded Country Cooking. Wernick left New York for Colorado during the mid-'70s, and once there he put together an album for Flying Fish, *Dr. Banjo Steps Out*. Not long after, he pulled together Hot Rize, a band that also included Nick Forster, Charles Sawtelle, and Tim O'Brien. The group went to the number one bluegrass spot with "Just Like You," a song written by Wernick.

In 1990, the banjoist and his pals in Hot Rize took home the title of Entertainer of the Year, which was bestowed by the IBMA. When group members went their separate ways in 1990, Wernick continued to perform and record with such artists as Chris Thile, Jody Stecher & Kate Brislin, Jerry Douglas, Peter Rowan, and Jeff White. His band, the Live Five, plays a mix of Dixieland and bluegrass, and first appeared on his *On a Roll* album. Wernick also performs in a duo called Dr. & Nurse Banjo, which features wife Joan Wernick, who plays the guitar and sings. Instructional materials put out by Wernick include *How to Make a Band Work* and *the Bluegrass Songbook*. *—Linda Seida*

● **Dr. Banjo Steps Out** / 1978 / Flying Fish ♦♦♦♦♦

Dr. Banjo really steps out on this one. Introducing flute, synthesizer, and a whole host of trippy studio effects into a bluegrass album was pretty progressive for the mid-'70s (even in an era where John Hartford and New Grass Revival were pushing the boundaries), and Pete Wernick uses the emerging technology to progress even further. Excellent players like Tim O'Brien, Andy Statman, Tony Trischka, and Russ Barenberg (to name just a few) shift the sound from retro to futuristic, often within the same song. Although the phase-shifting banjo feels a little like a gimmick after the first few times it appears, that still does not detract from the musical sparks that fly from the main collaborators. Soon after this release, Wernick and O'Brien went on to form Hot Rize, a band that pushed the edges of what was thought to be bluegrass even further out, and the glimmers of those future explorations are what make *Dr. Banjo Steps Out* one of those uniquely listenable historical documents. *—Zac Johnson*

On a Roll / 1993 / Sugar Hill ♦♦♦

I Tell You What / Jul. 23, 1996 / Sugar Hill ♦♦♦

Up All Night / 2002 / Niwot ♦♦♦♦

Ever since he first ran his banjo through a phase shifter in the 1970s, banjo wizard Peter Wernick has been something of a maverick. Though he's never turned his back on bluegrass, he branches out happily and promiscuously into genres where five-string banjo players have rarely ventured before. With his band the Live Five—which includes clarinet, vibes, drums, and electric bass in addition to his banjo—Wernick explores bebop, traditional swing, bluegrass, and original compositions that walk the various lines separating those genres. The result is an album that will certainly not please bluegrass purists but will be greatly enjoyed by anyone who cares more about fun than categories. Highlights include the band's tight but not uptight performances of the Wernick originals "Owensboro Hop" and "On a Roll," as well as a joyful rendition of "Sweet Georgia Brown" and an absolutely perfect adaptation of the Earl Scruggs classic "Foggy Mountain Special." With its boogie-woogie rhythms and bluesy chord progression, that tune was really meant more for a jazzy setting like this one than for a traditional bluegrass arrangement. It's highly recommended. *—Rick Anderson*

Dottie West (Dorothy Marie Walsh)

b. Oct. 11, 1932, McMinnville, TN, **d.** Sep. 4, 1991, Nashville, TN

Vocals, Guitar / Country-Pop, Nashville Sound/Countrypolitan

Dottie West was one of the most successful, and controversial, performers to rise to popularity during the Nashville sound era; like her friend and mentor Patsy Cline, West's battles for identity and respect within the male-dominated country music hierarchy were instrumental in enabling other female artists to gain control over the directions of their careers. Born Dorothy Marie Walsh outside McMinnville, TN, on October 11, 1932, she was the oldest of ten children; after her abusive, alcoholic father abandoned the family, her mother opened a small cafe. Dottie began appearing on local radio just shy of her 13th birthday and went on to study music at Tennessee Tech, where she also sang in a band; the group's steel guitar player, Bill West, became her first husband in 1953. After graduation, the Wests and their two children moved to Cleveland, OH; there, Dottie began appearing on the television program *Landmark Jamboree* as one half of a country-pop vocal duo called the Kay-Dots alongside partner Kathy Dee. At the same time, West made numerous trips to Nashville in the hopes of landing a recording deal; in 1959, she and Bill auditioned for Starday's Don Pierce and were immediately offered a contract. Although the resulting singles West cut for the label proved unsuccessful, she nonethless moved to Nashville in 1961. There, she and her husband fell in with a group of aspiring songwriters like Willie Nelson, Roger Miller, Hank Cochran, and Harlan Howard; they also became close friends with Cline and her husband Charlie Dick.

West earned her first Top 40 hit in 1963 with "Let Me Off at the Corner," followed a year later by the Top Ten "Love Is No Excuse," a duet with Jim Reeves (who had scored a major success with her "Is This Me?"). Also in 1964, she auditioned for producer Chet Atkins, the architect of the Nashville sound, who agreed to produce her composition "Here Comes My Baby"; the single made West the first female country artist to win a Grammy Award, leading to an invitation to join the *Grand Ole Opry*. In Atkins, West found the perfect producer for her plaintive vocals and heart-wrenching songs; after releasing the *Here Comes My Baby* LP in 1965, they reunited for the following year's *Suffer Time*, which generated her biggest hit yet in "Would You Hold It Against Me." In 1967, the West/Atkins pairing issued three separate albums— *With All My Heart and Soul* (featuring the smash "Paper Mansions"), *Dottie West Sings Sacred Ballads*, and *I'll Help You Forget Her*, she also appeared in a pair of films, *Second Fiddle to a Steel Guitar* and *There's a Still on the Hill*.

After the 1968 LP *Country Girl*, West teamed with Don Gibson for a record of duets, 1969's *Dottie and Don*, featuring the number-two hit "Rings of Gold." The album was her last with Atkins, and she followed it with two 1970 releases, *Forever Yours* and *Country Boy and Country Girl*, a collection of pairings with Jimmy Dean. Around the time of 1971's *Have You Heard... Dottie West*, she left Bill and in 1972 married drummer Bryan Metcalf, who was a dozen years her junior. Suddenly, West's image underwent a huge metamorphosis; the woman who once performed dressed in conservative gingham dresses and refused to record Kris Kristofferson's "Help Me Make It Through the Night" because it was "too sexy" began appearing in skin-tight stage attire. As the sexual revolution peaked, so did West's career; after the 1973 success of the crossover smash "Country Sunshine," written for Coca-Cola, her material became far more provocative and, much to the chagrin of country purists, more commericially successful as well.

After the release of *House of Love* in 1974, West notched a number of Top 40 hits like "Last Time I Saw Him," "When It's Just You and Me," and "Tonight You Belong to Me." In 1977, she was recording the song "Every Time Two Fools Collide" when, according to legend, Kenny Rogers suddenly entered the studio and began singing along. Released as a duet, the single hit number one, West's first; the duo's 1979 "All I Ever Need Is You" and 1981 "What Are We Doin' in Love" topped the charts as well, and a 1979 duets album titled *Classics* also proved successful. As a solo artist, West notched a pair of number ones in 1980—"A Lesson in Leavin'" and "Are You Happy Baby?"

As the 1980s progressed, West's popularity began to slip; she appeared in a revealing photo spread in the men's magazine *Oui* and toured with a production of the musical *the Best Little Whorehouse in Texas*. In 1983, she married for the third time, to soundman Al Winters, who was some 23 years younger than she was; a year later, she appeared in the play *Bring It on Home*. Her last chart hit, "We Know Better Now," reached only number 53 in 1985. Although she remained a popular touring act, West's financial problems mounted, and in 1990, after divorcing Winters, she declared bankruptcy, culminating in the foreclosure of her Nashville mansion. After a car accident and a public auction of her possessions, she began making plans for a comeback, including an album of duets and autobiography. But en route to a September 4, 1991, appearance at Opryland, the car she was riding in flipped, and a few days later West died of her injuries. A made-for-television biography followed a few years later. *—Jason Ankeny*

A Legend in My Time / 1971 / RCA ✦✦✦✦✦

Special Delivery / 1980 / United Artists ✦✦✦

With her career revitalized by the duets with Kenny Rogers, West takes a new tack. Her "Country Sunshine" is replaced with country-funk and a touch of melancholy. *—Tom Roland*

● **The Essential Dottie West** / Jan. 30, 1996 / RCA ✦✦✦✦✦

This Dottie West collection is truly overdue. Most of these tracks have been long out of print even prior to the CD revolution. The set opens with a smooth duet between crooner Jim Reeves & West on "Love Is No Excuse." It must have been difficult to decide on 20 songs for what will probably be the only release on West in this series. In addition to recording several big original hits, she left a body of excellent cover songs, such as her haunting rendition of Don Gibson's "A Legend in My Own Time," which is sadly absent here. Two upbeat but so-so Gibson duets are presented here, "There's a Story (Goin' Round)" and "Rings of Gold." Barring those couple of tracks, the song selection is flawless. Hank Cochran's slightly honky tonk "Me Today and Her Tomorrow" is featured, as is a warm duet with Jimmy "The Sausage King" Dean on "Slowly." There are three songs from what may well be West's best album, 1966's *Suffer Time*. Two superb B-side singles show up—the quiet "Childhood Places" and the uptempo "Reno," which carries a storyline similar to Linda Ronstadt's "Desperado" or Judy Collins' "Someday Soon." West's stellar rendition of "His Eye Is on the Sparrow" is simple and seemingly divinely inspired. When she pays homage to her rural roots on "Country Girl" or bemoans her role of absentee mother on "Six Weeks Every Summer (Christmas Every Other Year)" it's hard to imagine West ever topping these records in substance or passion. *—Bill Carpenter*

Are You Happy Baby: Collection (1976–1984) / Nov. 18, 1997 / Razor & Tie ✦✦✦✦

There are all kinds of country music: hillbilly, bluegrass, honky-tonk, etc. Dottie West is the queen of Spandex country: a slickly produced Nashville brand of country-pop. For those who do not know her work, it is most telling that she shares vocal duties on six of the 20 tracks here with Kenny Rogers. This best-of collection is filled with juke box weepers, and it should be said that there is some fun music here. But traditional country purists should steer well clear. *—Tim Sheridan*

RCA Country Legends / Sep. 25, 2001 / Buddha ✦✦✦✦

Like other volumes in Buddha/BMG Heritage's *RCA Country Legends*, the Dottie West disc contains a mixture of big hits, album tracks, and singles that didn't make the upper reaches of the charts, all compiled with the intention of capturing the purest country of her recordings for RCA. West was with RCA from 1963-1976, but this doesn't attempt to chronicle all 13 years (and, of course, it overlooks her urban cowboy hits of the late '70s and early '80s for United Artists and Liberty). In fact, it bypasses her first hit, the Jim Reeves duet "Love Is No Excuse," and goes no further than 1973's "Country Sunshine." There are other singles that are missing, most of which are featured on the previous CD-era compilation, 1996's *The Essential Dottie West*, which was out of print by the time this was released in 2001. There is a good deal of overlap between the two collections, actually, as they share eight tracks, all hits: "Here Comes My Baby," "Would You Hold It Against Me," "What's Come Over My Baby," "Paper Mansions," the Don Gibson duet "There's A Story (Goin' Round)," "Country Sunshine," "Country Girl," and the Jimmy Dean duet "Slowly." There are two minor *Billboard* hits here not on that collection—"Careless Hands" and "If It's All Right With You"—but if hits are what you're looking for, *The Essential* is what to find, since all but two of the songs were charting hits. Here, there are ten hits and six interesting also-rans, ranging from the heavily echoed reading of Willie Nelson's "Night Life," another Gibson duet on "Lock, Stock and Teardrops," another Dean duet with "Sweet Thang," and excellent sides like "Let Me off at the Corner," "The Cold Hand of Fate," and "Before the Ring on Your Finger Turns Green," all of which prove that West was one of the most reliable straight-ahead female country singers of the '60s. That's why this *RCA Country Legends* is a good overview and introduction, even if it doesn't have all the hits. *—Stephen Thomas Erlewine*

Absolutely the Best / Sep. 27, 2002 / Fuel 2000 ✦✦✦✦

Elbert West

Vocals / Neo-Traditionalist Country, Contemporary Country

New traditionalist country singer Elbert West had a strong taste of success in the early '90s when he penned Tracy Lawrence's first two big hits, "Sticks and Stones" and "Can't Break It to My Heart." But subsequent years of spending all his royalties and trying to eke out a living as a songwriter in Nashville—a town that, throughout the '90s, increasingly turned its back on the classic brand of country he writes—led to him becoming a recording artist himself. West released his debut album, *Livin' the Life*, in 2001. The effort serves up the kind of country once put to vinyl by folks like Merle Haggard and George Jones (both of whom provide good reference points for West's baritone). Many of the themes penned by West, who was raised in the coal fields of West Virginia, revolve around defiance, and there's a real rock & roll spirit at work in his performances. The first single from *Livin' the Life*, "Diddley," exemplifies that spirit with its rollicking energy and in-your-face lyrics. *—Erik Hage*

● **Livin' the Life** / 2001 / Broken Bow ✦✦✦✦

Classic country, energetic playing, and rock & roll spirit is at the heart of this release. Back in the early '90s, Elbert West penned the first two hits for Tracy Lawrence. On this release, his debut, West moves into the spotlight as an artist in his own right. It's an old story that the music coming out of Nashville throughout the '90s and beyond has been weak (and "un-country"). But an effort like this reminds us what the genre should be—and what it was in the grand old days of Merle Haggard, George Jones, and others. Elbert West is country-rock in the way that Haggard was country-rock (let's pause to remember that Haggard brought a rock & roll spirit to country long before Gram Parsons was old enough to dip into his trust fund; that's why guys like Parsons and Chris Hillman idolized him). West has a big, husky baritone, a keen songwriting ability, a defiant attitude, and is a major country talent. Highlights of *Livin' the Life* include the title track, "Diddley," the beautiful "Robin Loves to Hear Me Sing," and "Crawling Time." *—Erik Hage*

Shelly West

b. 1958, Cleveland, OH

Vocals / Country-Pop, Urban Cowboy

The daughter of the legendary Dottie West and her first husband Bill, a noted steel guitar player, Shelly West was a popular singer of pop-flavored country tunes during the 1980s. Shelly got her start at age 17 touring with her mother's show; she started out singing backup, but was soon given lead vocal chores. While touring, she fell in love with her mother's lead guitarist Allen Frizzell; they married and left the band in 1977 to move to California. Allen was the little brother of Lefty and David Frizzell, the latter of whom had a regular gig in a neighboring town. The newlyweds soon joined his band and played with him for a few months. They toured the Southwest, and upon their return, David began looking for a record label. A demo of the duet "Lovin' on Borrowed Time" featuring West and her brother-in-law impressed record producer Snuff Garrett, who signed them both to Casablanca West. Unfortunately, Polygram took over the label and dumped the duo, who unsuccessfully tried their luck in Nashville.

Garrett still believed the two had potential and eventually played their song and its follow-up "You're the Reason God Made Oklahoma" to actor Clint Eastwood, who had just founded his own record label, Viva. Eastwood liked the latter song and added it to his film *Any Which Way You Can*, and the song hit number one on the country charts in early 1981. Their next four songs, beginning with the Top Ten hit "A Texas State of Mind," were also successful, and the duo's considerable success continued through 1985, when they split up. (They cited a lack of good duet songs as their main reason; the fact that West and her husband had just divorced may also have been a factor). West made her solo debut in 1983 with "Jose Cuervo," which hit number one and provided a sales boost for the tequila company. Her solo follow-up "Flight 309 to Tennessee" made the Top Five. Between 1984 and 1986, West had a string of solo successes that included "Somebody Buy This Cowgirl a Beer" and "Don't Make Me Wait on the Moon." Later that year she had one more mid-range hit, "Love Don't Come Any Better Than This," and then faded from the charts. She basically stopped recording after remarrying, but did reunite with David Frizzell for a few shows in the late '80s. *—Sandra Brennan*

Red Hot / 1983 / Viva ✦✦✦

● **West by West** / 1983 / Warner/Viva ✦✦✦✦

Don't Make Me Wait on the Moon / 1984 / Warner/Viva ✦✦✦

Speedy West

b. 1924, Springfield, MO

Pedal Steel, Guitar (Steel) / Traditional Country, Instrumental Country

One of the greatest virtuosos that country music has ever produced, Speedy West bridged the Western swing and rockabilly eras with eye-popping steel guitar. Besides contributing to literally thousands of country sessions, West cut many of his own instrumentals, as a solo act and with his guitarist partner Jimmy Bryant. Adept at boogie, blues, and Hawaiian ballads, West played with an infectious joy and daring improvisation that, at its most adventurous, could be downright experimental. It's doubtful whether anyone could collect all of Speedy's solos under one roof, but it was his sessions of the 1950s and early '60s—especially those with Jimmy Bryant—that found his genius at its most freewheeling and dazzling. *—Richie Unterberger*

Two Guitars Country Style / 1954 / Capitol ✦✦✦✦

West of Hawaii / 1958 / Capitol ✦✦✦

Steel Guitar / 1960 / Capitol ✦✦✦✦

Along with partner and guitarist Jimmy Bryant, pedal steel virtuoso Speedy West played on several thousand sides and worked with hundreds of vocalists including Ernest Tubb, Loretta Lynn, Frank Sinatra, Jim Reeves, Tennessee Ernie Ford, and Bing Crosby. West's sometimes histrionic and cartoon-like playing is easily recognizable and comes out of his total command of the instrument. In fact, due to their wild flights and seamless interplay, many observers have labeled West and Bryant the Charlie Parker and Dizzy Gillespie of country. West's innovative use of bebop licks and phrasing is certainly heard often on this 1960 solo record for Capitol. In particular, cuts like "Caffeine Patrol" and "Flippin' the Lid" find him in a briskly swinging mood and even trading fours with his guitarist (no credits are listed for the album). Of course, considering his vast studio resumé, West delves into a variety of genres and styles here, including Western swing, Hawaiian music, sentimental cowboy ballads, and blues. And thankfully, West never overdoes the guitar pyrotechnics; his occasional zinger and slinky-toy flourishes are always dropped strategically. Maybe not as crucial a first disc purchase as one of the two fine compilations on Razor & Tie (which also feature Bryant), but still a very fine album. *—Stephen Cook*

Guitar Spectacular / 1962 / Capitol ♦♦♦

Steel Guitar from Outer Space / 1989 / See for Miles ♦♦♦♦♦

Together with the 1960 *Steel Guitar* LP, this is West at his peak. This compilation gets the nod not because of superior quality, but because of sheer quantity—24 tracks, half from rare '50s singles, the other half comprising the entirety of his 1963 album *Guitar Spectacular.* The appeal of these skyrocketing boogies and swing tunes is not at all limited to country fans; even in the 1990s, it sounds quite advanced and cutting-edge. *—Richie Unterberger*

For the Last Time / 1990 / Step One ♦♦♦

• **Stratosphere Boogie: The Flaming Guitars of Speedy West & Jimmy Bryant** / 1995 / Razor & Tie ♦♦♦♦♦

Fans of country and jazz guitar will discover two new idols after delving into this 16-track collection, which features the best of the genre-shattering sessions recorded by this legendary duo. Between Bryant's jazzy, lightning-fast leads and West's brash, ground-breaking pedal steel work, the two recorded some of the most astounding instrumental country music of all time. Whether it's the hilarious "Sleepwalker's Lullaby" or top-fuel classics like "Old Joe Clark" and "Arkansas Traveler," the pair's 1950s records were among the most experimental music being made anywhere in America. It doesn't hurt to add that they were extremely influential, and one spends nearly as much time laughing along with these songs as they do trying to figure out how the hell anyone ever got this good. *—Jim Smith*

Flamin' Guitars / May 6, 1997 / Bear Family ♦♦♦♦

Perhaps the most difficult thing in writing about a box set like this is how to convey in words—few or many—the magic, wonder, and intimidating musicianship that is contained on these recordings. Over four CDs, the seeds, roots, branches, and trees of a musical partnership were formed and lived out on the public stage, and remain all but unknown to those who were not country music fans during the era. While one Speedy West & Jimmy Bryant compilation has appeared on Razor & Tie, as a single disc it only begins to offer the legend of this pair of musical innovators. For starters, Speedy West was the first picker to use a *pedal* steel guitar in the business in 1948—and he was doing it in L.A., not Nashville. It's true that Leon McAuliffe had played the steel guitar earlier while playing with Bob Wills, but none of those instruments had pedals. The partnership with Jimmy Bryant was forged in a barroom one night after Speedy's set, and it became of the most prolific and enduring in music history, ending only with the death of Bryant in 1980. The mutant, futuristic kind of Western swing that had extrapolated from Bob Wills' creation is enduring, still forward-looking, and truly out of time and space. As for partners who were undaunted, the adversity these cats encountered with their space age country bachelor pad music—especially from the fascists in Music City—was formidable. But they succumbed not a bit, used not one sound effect that wasn't already installed in the volume knob or reverb pedals, and ended up making dozens of records and playing sessions with everybody from Bing Crosby to Spike Jones to Jean Shepard to Merle Travis to the Billy May Orchestra. The Bear Family box begins with the earliest solo sides in late September 1949, when Bryant cut four tracks with Corky Carpenter on vocals. They include "Just Remember," "Jelly Bean's Daddy," "Boogie Barn Dance," and "Gamblin' Money." These are unadulterated Western swing tunes with Bryant's penchant for tossing in Django Reinhardt chord voicings into the breaks. Next up is "Steel Strike," a single Speedy cut for Capitol as a sideman for an Eddie Kirk session. It's the beginning, here in 1950, of where he wants to go with his own music—and that finally happens in September of that same year when he and Bryant cut "Bryant's Boogie" and "Red Headed Polka," two scathing instrumentals that put the focus on the strings to sing. It's still a mutation of Bob Wills' Western swing, but it also prefigures rockabilly and slips bebop lines into its breaks to bring all the music of the day firmly into view. Over the course of 12 years, the pair cut an astonishing 91 sides—and these are just the master takes—with producer Ken Nelson in the Capitol studios. These do not include any of the work the pair did as sidemen for other artists, which would make up an entire box set of its own. Bear Family has been judicious enough to include one CD of this work, which ranges from their earliest work in 1949 with Merle Travis to a session in 1954 with Tennessee Ernie Ford. There are a number of alternate takes and unreleased masters included, copious liner notes by Rich Keinzle, and virtually every session detail available. But the main thing is the music, as the pair's innovative, fiery style begins to take shape and turns everything once thought of as "instrumental country music" on its head; listeners can hear the glee and surprise of the musicians themselves at their creations. Licks are played and runs are executed that neither man could have anticipated before his partner had spun off his own skittering skein of notes. The music drives as hard as the best rock & roll and contains the knotty, full-blown improvisation one would expect from a hard bop group in full swing. And the arrangements are stellar; whether they were written by Nelson, guitarist Billy Strange, or Bryant & West, they prefigure and overstep everything else that was going on during those years. One listen to disc three's Hawaiian music—beginning with track seven, "Hawaiian War Chant," and culminating some 20 tracks later in "Sunset at Waikiki"—is enough to make anyone laugh, cough, stutter, and finally just shut up in disbelief at what has just transpired. And as if that weren't enough, the disc begins with a Western medley of classics such as "On the Alamo" and "The Night Rider," which thunders with a steel string fury so unruly, yet so completely precise, that it's a wonder it was executed by human beings—but thank God it was. The staggered arpeggio sequences on the Western swing material in the mid-'50s has never been touched either for its pure musicological sophistication or it's pure fun quotient. And perhaps that's the most astonishing thing of all: No matter how outside the music of West & Bryant got, you could always dance to it. Try hanging that on the superchoppers of today—in any genre—and see what hind of hellish steps result! This set isn't for everybody, but it most definitely warrants the attention of the steel guitar freaks as well as Speedy & Jimmy fans. It should also nudge the curiosity of Western swing fans to look further west for inspiration and, finally, it should interest serious early rock & roll and bebop fans for its temperament and musical genius. In other words, this set is indispensable for anyone seriously interested in the history and development of American music. *—Thom Jurek*

Swingin' on the Strings: The Speedy West & Jimmy Bryant Collection, Vol. 2 / Mar. 9, 1999 / Razor & Tie ♦♦♦♦♦

Speedy West & Jimmy Bryant recorded a wealth of quality material in the 1950s, in enough quantity to dispel any notions of regarding them as a novelty act. Those who want more West/Bryant instrumentals after hearing their *Stratosphere Boogie* collection (also on Razor & Tie) but don't want to spring for *the Bear Family* box set will be happy to own this second volume of 1951-1956 tracks. The caliber of these 20 selections is almost uniformly high, whether it's the blazing leads and slightly dissonant accents of "Frettin' Fingers," the faster-than-bejesus run-through of Rodgers/Hart's "Lover" (one of five cuts previously unavailable in the U.S.), the pre-exotica jungle/bird noises created on West's steel for "West of Samoa" or the six-minute "China Boy," on which Bryant disregarded the producer's gestures to "cut." The slow numbers tend to impress less than the flashier workouts, but even on those they can throw in some head-spinning licks, like the steel guitar facsimile of a train whistle that opens "Railroadin'." *—Richie Unterberger*

There's Gonna Be a Party / Nov. 14, 2000 / Jasmine ♦♦

The 30 tracks on this inexpensive import are mostly steel guitar instrumentals taken from 1950s transcriptions discs of Tennessee Ernie Ford's radio show. Tennessee Ernie introduces nearly all of the selections and sometimes banters with West, and guitarist Jimmy Bryant appears on a half-dozen tracks. The sound quality is a little flat, and the performances not as sprightly and engaging as Speedy West & Jimmy Bryant's Capitol recordings, but *There's Gonna Be a Party* provides an entertaining program of rarities for true believers. *—Greg Adams*

Johnny Western

b. Oct. 28, 1934, Two Harbors, MN

Guitar, Vocals / Cowboy

A lover of the Old West and its mythos from childhood, Johnny Western was one of the finest and most impassioned exponents of cowboy songs; a successor to both Gene Autry and Marty Robbins whose career paved the way for the work of Michael Martin Murphey, Ian Tyson, and the Riders in the Sky, all of whom owed him a debt for carrying cowboy music into and beyond the 1960s. He was born in Twin Harbors, MN, on October 28, 1934, and raised at various Civilian Conservation Corps camps (where his father was an officer and instructor) and Indian reservations along the Canadian border. The turning point in his life came on his fifth birthday, when his parents took him to see a 1936 Western called *Guns and Guitars* starring Gene Autry; Johnny knew then and there that he wanted to be exactly like the man on the horse, strumming a guitar and singing a song.

For his 12th birthday, Western was given a guitar; hardly a year had gone by when he was invited to turn professional. He'd been recorded at the local 4-H Club singing Gene Autry's "Riding Down the Canyon" and other songs, which resulted in an invitation to join a collegiate singing trio. He mostly played rhythm guitar, but also got to sing, and when the group recorded an audition tape for KDHL in Faribault, MN, Johnny was asked to sing one solo number. He chose "(Ghost) Riders in the Sky," and ended up getting a weekly radio spot, which then became three days a week, and finally six days each week. In addition to singing, he acted as a DJ and host, introducing live and recorded country & Western music. He also earned a mention in *Billboard* magazine as the youngest DJ and singer on American radio. By the age of 16, he was playing on bills with his one-time idols the Sons of the Pioneers.

Soon after graduation, he made the jump from radio to television, becoming a singing cowboy on KMMT-TV, and landed a recording contract with a small Minnesota-based record label called JOCO. He and his fellow guitarist John Fields cut a handful of singles, including "The Violet & the Rose" and "Let Old Mother Nature Have Her Way," which received good airplay locally and in Iowa, Wisconsin, and the Dakotas. Johnny Western's television show, which allowed him to sing to his young audience before introducing the day's Western movie, lasted for two years. During this period, he got to play concerts with Western stars such as Rex Allen and Tex Ritter, and had them as guests on his show. In 1954, however, he gave up the program, heading for Hollywood to pursue his real goal to be a movie cowboy.

This was the hardest jump of all, because they weren't making many Westerns in Hollywood anymore, or looking for singing cowboys. It was years before he got to work in front of a movie camera; in the meantime, he earned a place in Gene Autry's band, replacing Johnny Bond as a guitarist and singer. After Autry retired from performing, Western did a pilot for a series called *Pony Express* which, in turn, led to appearances in more than 30 other television shows (including *Gunsmoke*) and several feature films, including *The Dalton Girls, Fort Bowie,* and *Gunfight at Dodge City.* In 1957, a new series called *Have Gun, Will Travel* went into production; Western was cast in a small role in one episode, and while working on the show he composed a song about the series' hero, Paladin. "The Ballad of Paladin" was adopted as the show's closing theme, and Johnny Western was signed to the CBS network's record division, Columbia Records.

He was soon either acting in or singing on the music tracks of several series, including *Pony Express, Boots and Saddles, Tales of Wells Fargo,* and *Bat Masterson,* and his performing and singing careers were suddenly revived. Under Columbia Records producer Don Law (who also produced Johnny Cash), he recorded dozens of sides, including the singles "Only the Lonely" (1959), "Della's Gone" (1960), "Darling Corey" (1961), "Gunfighter" (1962), and "Kathy Come Home," along with an album, *Have Gun, Will Travel* (1962). He was also asked by Johnny Cash to join his band as a singer/guitarist. He remained a member of Cash's band for six years, playing rhythm guitar on recordings such as "Johnny Yuma, The Rebel," "The Little Drummer Boy," and "Lorena," among many others. During his years at Columbia, Western was also befriended by Marty Robbins, who later participated in Western's recordings of "(Ghost) Riders in the Sky" and the redone "Ballad of Paladin." When he wasn't on tour with Cash, Western was playing shows on his own and working with ex-members of Ernest Tubb's and Porter Wagoner's bands.

At the end of 1963, he left Columbia Records and moved to Philips, where he had a very brief, unsuccessful stay. Johnny Western was a popular draw in Las Vegas, however, and also began making the rounds of Western shows. He continued to record for various labels, including Hep ("The Violet & The Rose," 1967), and he made the acquaintance of Waylon Jennings, then a songwriter and aspiring country star. He recorded "The Streets of Dodge City" for the 1970 film *Dodge City, Kansas*, and also wrote the music for a documentary film, *Rodeo—A Matter of Style*, released in 1976 as part of the country's Bicentennial celebration. Western also recorded numerous sides for Johnny Cash's House of Cash label, which became the basis for a retrospective album. During most of this period, he played 200 shows a year. In 1986, he resumed his radio career with a series in Wichita, KS. In 1993, Western began work on a new album, a sort of cowboy supersession, with the Sons of the Pioneers, Rex Allen, Rex Allen Jr., Red Steagall, and Michael Martin Murphey, entitled *Johnny Western and the Sons of the Pioneers and Friends*. Health problems intervened, however, when Western was incapacitated by a bypass operation, and the album went unreleased. *—Bruce Eder*

Have Gun, Will Travel / 1962 / Columbia ✦✦✦✦

Johnny Western's only album for a major label wasn't recorded until he'd been with Columbia Records for three years, so it's a fully mature work, replendant in the lore and lure of the west. In addition to his third version of "The Ballad of Paladin," and the album features "The Lonely Man," one of Western's finest and most introspective vocal performances, the gallows ballad "Hannah Lee," the standard "The Streets of Laredo" (done with a bit too much drama), Stan Jones' hauntingly beautiful "Cowpoke" and "The Searchers," and "The Last Round-Up." The production is fairly elaborate at times, but, except for "The Streets of Laredo," never excessive, and Western's baritone sounded beautiful in those days. (out of print) *—Bruce Eder*

Johnny Western / 1980 / Bear Family ✦✦✦✦

The Gunfighter / 1981 / Bear Family ✦✦✦✦

● **Gunfight at O.K. Corral** / 1989 / Bear Family ✦✦✦✦

Johnny Western as he sounded in 1984, which is good—the voice is still a rich, enveloping baritone, rougher and not as flexible as it was in the early '60s but still pleasing and memorable. His rendition of "Gunfight at O.K. Corral" won't displace Frankie Laine's, but it has a drive and power all of its own. Stan Jones' "Ghost Riders in the Sky" gets a beautiful workout, as flamboyant vocally as Johnny Cash's was instrumentally—Jones is also represented by "The Searchers," "Hannah Lee," "Lillies Grow High," and "Cheyenne." Bob Nolan's poignant "Song of the Bandit" (adapted from the English ballad "The Highwayman") is also here, sung with great affection, sincerity, and intensity. Western also covers his own "The Gunfighter," which he wrote for Marty Robbins, and Johnny Cash's "Don't Take Your Guns to Town"—at this point in his career, Western's voice lacked the expressive range of Cash's. There are also lots of covers of television themes, including two very upbeat medleys of "Johnny Yuma—The Rebel" (originally a Johnny Cash song on which Western played rhythm guitar), "Bonanza," and "The Ballad of Paladin"; "Bat Masterson" and "Wyatt Earp"; and the theme from "Rawhide." The personnel includes Billy Strange, Art Sparer, Jack Clement (who also produced), and Western on guitars. *—Bruce Eder*

Heroes and Cowboys / 1993 / Bear Family ✦✦✦✦✦

This is as good as it gets for Johnny Western fans. And, in the absence of a single-disc collection from Columbia or Rhino, it's also the only route to go to get any Johnny Western material other than "The Ballad of Paladin." The three-CD set with 200 minutes of music, which retails for a whopping $85, has everything that Western recorded from 1952 for JOCO up through his '70s sides for House of Cash, and a ton of rare radio transcription recordings. Disc one contains some unreleased Columbia sides, and the JOCO sides from 1952 and 1953, nicely restored, with John Field showing himself a great one-man western combo with the use of Les Paul-style overdubs. Disc two features more Columbia sides from the late '50s and early '60s, as well as Western's 1964 Philips sides and his songs cut for the Hep label in 1966. The Columbia material includes Western's attempts to crack the folk market, which may not have succeeded commercially but are great listening anyway. The Hep sides are the most interesting, however, for the sheer restraint that they show—Western's later sides for Columbia and Philips showed a certain degree of excess on the production side, while the Hep sides benefit from a slightly leaner, more delicate backup. The House of Cash recordings featured on disc two also show off Western in a leaner setting, doing new performances and superb covers. Disc three consists of rare radio transcription performances done for the syndicated shows *Country Style, USA* and *Country Music Time* circa 1960, with Western doing sharp, lean renditions of numerous songs, backed by a band that included Marty Robbins on the piano. The material was a mix of country and folk standards, along with western material that he was directly associated with, and some fascinating covers. The sound on this material has held up exceptionally well, and it is exclusive to the Bear Family release. *—Bruce Eder*

Billy Edd Wheeler

b. Dec. 9, 1932, Whitesville, WV

Songwriter, Vocals / Traditional Country, Country-Pop

Known for writing several major country hits that showed the influence of the folk-pop music with which he began his career, Billy Edd Wheeler was also a versatile performer who notched hits of his own, recorded a series of innovative albums in the 1960s, and extended his creative activities into poetry, painting, nonfiction writing, and acting. Perhaps he was the only Yale Drama School student to go on to a career in country music. Wheeler was born in Boone Country, WV. He attended Warren Wilson College in North Carolina and Berea College in Kentucky, where he earned a B.A. in 1955. After college, he worked as a magazine editor and then served two years as a Navy pilot. He taught at Berea for several years, performing folk music on the side and at one point landing a pops concert slot with the Lexington Symphony Orchestra (now the Lexington Philharmonic). Spurred by the attention, he recorded country and bluegrass songs (later collected on two LP albums) on the Monitor label, beginning in 1959.

He made some appearances on *the Today Show* and other network television programs and performed on *the WWVA Jamboree* in Wheeling, WV. Wheeler then moved east, studying playwriting at the Yale Drama School for one year and trying his luck as a playwright in New York. (By 2003 he had written 16 plays.) He also began writing songs, two of which, "The Reverend Mr. Black" and "Desert Pete," became pop hits for the Kingston Trio. "The Reverend Mr. Black," a vivid portrait of a country preacher, was later covered by Bill Anderson and other country artists. Hank Snow ("Blue Roses") and Rex Allen were among the country singers who recorded early Wheeler songs, but he also placed songs with folk artists such as Judy Collins and Richie Havens.

In 1963, Wheeler began recording more or less as a folk artist for Kapp Records, but as that New York-based label soon made a move into country music, Wheeler found the transition a natural one. The following year, he made his debut on the charts with "Ode to the Little Brown Shack Out Back," a lament for the vanishing outhouses of the rural south that hit number three on the country charts. No more hits were forthcoming, but Wheeler's albums on Kapp fell well outside the '60s country mainstream; 1967's *Paper Birds* showed the influence of psychedelia. Wheeler continued to circulate songs in Nashville, and several of them were recorded; Johnny Cash and June Carter Cash reached number two in 1967 with Wheeler's *Bickersons*-like dialogue song "Jackson." Cash also recorded Wheeler's torrid love song "Blistered." Wheeler found his own way back to the charts one year later, though "I Ain't the Worryin' Kind" stalled at number 63 (it was covered by pop singer O.C. Smith). He signed with United Artists in 1969 and had minor success with "West Virginia Woman" and "Fried Chicken and a Country Tune."

During the '70s, he recorded for RCA Victor and Capitol but charted only occasionally. Nevertheless, his songwriting provided a consistent income. Elvis Presley had a Top Five hit with Wheeler's "It's Midnight," and in 1980 he hit it big when he and Roger Bowling penned Kenny Rogers' smash hit "Coward of the County." It spent three weeks at number one on the country charts. By the early 2000s, Wheeler estimated the total sales of recordings containing his songs at 57 million units, with various Rogers compilations constituting a sizable portion of that total.

With his wife and two children, Wheeler moved back to Swannanoa, NC, where he had attended college. He continued to write poetry, having published his first volume, *Song of a Woods Colt*, in 1969, and accelerated his playwriting activities. Wheeler has also authored a compilation of Appalachian humor and has created paintings in a folk-art style. He continued to write songs and to perform at festivals, played the banjo on several bluegrass albums, held songwriting workshops in his home, and recorded occasionally. Wheeler returned to folk music with the 1979 album *Wild Mountain Flowers*, released on the Flying Fish label. *—James Manheim*

Billy Edd / 1961 / Monitor ✦✦✦

Bluegrass Too / 1962 / Monitor ✦✦✦✦

New Bag of Songs / 1964 / Kapp ✦✦✦

Memories of America/Ode to the Little Brown Shack out Back / 1965 / Kapp ✦✦✦

Wheeler Man / 1965 / Dapp ✦✦✦

Goin' Town & Country / 1966 / Kapp ✦✦

Paper Birds / 1967 / Kapp ✦✦

I Ain't the Worryin' Kind / 1968 / Kapp ✦✦✦✦

● **Wild Mountain Flowers** / 1979 / Flying Fish ✦✦✦✦✦

Some Mountain Tales About Jack / Spoken Arts ✦✦✦

Cheryl Wheeler

b. Jul. 10, 1951, Timonium, MD

Guitar, Vocals / Country-Folk, Contemporary Folk, Contemporary Singer/Songwriter

Known for her comic as well as her emotionally intense songs, folksinger/songwriter Cheryl Wheeler was raised in Timonium, MD, and began playing the guitar and ukulele as a child. She first performed professionally at a local restaurant, but soon graduated to clubs in the Baltimore and Washington, D.C., areas. In 1976, she moved to Rhode Island, where she became a protégée of country-folksinger/songwriter Jonathan Edwards, for whom she initially served as bass player. Her first recording, a four-song EP called *Newport Songs*, was released in 1983. Edwards produced her first full-length album, *Cheryl Wheeler*, released on North Star Records in 1986. One of the songs on the album, "Addicted," was covered by Dan Seals and became a number-one country hit in September 1988.

North Star licensed her second album, *Half a Book* (1988), to the short-lived Cypress imprint of A&M Records. She then signed to the Nashville division of Capitol Records and released *Circles & Arrows* in 1990; Suzy Bogguss' cover of "Aces" from that album was a Top Ten Country hit in 1992. (Subsequently, her songs were covered by Bette Midler, Juice Newton, Maura O'Connell, Linda Thompson, and others.) In 1993, Wheeler moved to the Philo imprint of the independent Rounder label for her fourth album, *Driving Home* (Rounder reissued *Circles & Arrows* in 1994). She followed it with *Mrs. Pinocci's Guitar* (1995) and *Sylvia Hotel* (1999). *—William Ruhlmann & Jason Ankeny*

● **Cheryl Wheeler** / 1986 / North Star ✦✦✦✦✦

Circles & Arrows / 1990 / Philo ✦✦✦✦

Half a Book / 1991 / Cypress ✦✦✦

Driving Home / 1993 / Philo ✦✦✦

On *Driving Home*, Cheryl Wheeler has finally got the natural sounding production that her material needs. Her melodies are highly ornamented and shine through. The distinctive nature of her voice is never overshadowed by synthesized sound as on previous albums. As in the past the material is often humorous, as in "Don't Forget the Guns," commercially romantic; "Silver Lining" and heart-warmingly beautiful; "Arrow." This is an excellent album. *—Richard Meyer*

Mrs. Pinocci's Guitar / Oct. 17, 1995 / Philo ♦♦♦

"Is It Peace or Is It Prozac?," asked Cheryl Wheeler on the funniest song of her fifth album, *Mrs. Pinocci's Guitar.* But a listen to the whole album belied the humor of that tune and its comic companions, the anti-television diatribe "TV" and the lambasting of right-wing attitudes "Makes Good Sense to Me." If Wheeler had once been on mood enhancers, she seemed to be off them for most of this album, which had a melancholy tone with its slow tempos and minor keys. Romantic dissolution seemed at the bottom of this sadness, on songs like "Does the Future Look Black," "School Girls," "So Far to Fall," and "Piper," but it extended to natural threats on "The Rivers" and "The Storm," and to the threat of aging in "Time Taketh Away," to the point on "Howl at the Moon" that the singer was wishing she was an animal who didn't have to do much more than eat and sleep. Wheeler seemed to be struggling against such depression, filling the CD booklet with family snapshots, opening the album with the warm-hearted title song, and concluding it with a rough demo performance of the uncertainly hopeful "One Love." But the overall theme of the record was dour enough to suggest that peace through Prozac might not be such a bad idea. *—William Ruhlmann*

Sylvia Hotel / Jan. 26, 1999 / Philo ♦♦♦

Though the topics on her sixth album include farmers, gun control, potatoes, cats, and, on a hidden track, even banking, Cheryl Wheeler spends most of her time singing about a first-person character who travels extensively around the country ("Lighting Up the Mighty Mississippi," "Rainy Road to Atlanta," and the title track) smoking, drinking too much, and trying to get over heartache. Longtime listeners will recognize this person with her unrelieved self-pity and her interests in nature and pets, but some may be beginning to wonder whether the songwriter really suffers more romantic trouble than the rest of us, or whether it just fascinates her as a songwriting subject. The tone always seems to suggest that the breakup happened recently and that the singer is in the early stages of recovery. She seems hurt, vulnerable, confused, and depressed. But that's exactly how she sounded more than three years ago on her last album. Wheeler's other witty, wordy songs, such as "If It Were Up to Me," a list song speculating on the reasons for violence that concludes, "If it were up to me, I'd take away the guns," and the comic "Potato," set to the tune for "The Mexican Hat Dance," provide some relief, even though they have a somewhat desperate edge to them. "Unworthy," another list song about what the singer should be doing, and the untitled bank song, which ends in an expletive, are humorous only in form; they have very serious points to make. It has been said with some justification that unhappy romance makes for good songwriting (and Tolstoy once wrote that all happy families are alike), but one wishes that Wheeler would try writing a few songs when she is on the upside of one of her romances, not just when they're falling apart. *—William Ruhlmann*

Different Stripe / Jan. 28, 2003 / Philo ♦♦♦♦

After a short stint at Capital in the late '80s, singer/songwriter Cheryl Wheeler found a more permanent home at Philo, where she recorded albums like *Driving Home* (1993) and *Mrs. Pinocci's Guitar* (1995). *Different Stripe* offers a lengthy retrospective of her impressive musical career, and although it has been released by Philo, it contains several selections from her work with Capitol. Wheeler is an introspective songwriter with a contemporary folk sensibility. On "Moonlight and Roses" she poetically describes the end of a relationship, adding poignantly, "There's nothin' you'd ask me that I wouldn't try/Please don't let this love go by." "Gandhi/Buddha" takes a more contemplative turn as she imagines that she must have accomplished great deeds in a former life to deserve true love. Wheeler is also a master of description, using details of weather and the seasons to reflect a particular mood. The picturesque "When Fall Comes to New England" captures the subtle changes of cooler nights, geese flying south, and squash ripening on the vine. "75 Septembers" considers a grandmother and the tremendous changes that occurred during her lifetime. "Are you more amazed at how things change, or how they stay the same?," Wheeler asks. The production varies from piece to piece, but the singer and the song remain the focal point of this collection. For anyone unfamiliar with Wheeler's work, *Different Stripe* is the place to start. For those already familiar with her formidable talents, the disc serves as a reminder of a long and productive career. *—Ronnie D. Lankford Jr.*

Onie Wheeler

b. Nov. 10, 1921, Senath, MO, **d.** May 26, 1984

Harmonica, Vocals / Traditional Bluegrass, Traditional Country, Rockabilly

Born in Senath, MO, on November 10, 1921, Onie Wheeler recorded traditional country, bluegrass, and rockabilly (for Sun) in a career that stretched from a small radio show in Missouri all the way to the *Grand Ole Opry.* He played guitar and harmonica as a child, but never performed professionally until after service in World War II. Beginning in 1945, he worked radio broadcasts in Missouri, Arkansas, Michigan, and Kentucky. Wheeler formed the Ozark Cowboys five years later with Ernest Thompson and brothers A.J. and Doyal Nelson. The Cowboys played clubs in Texas in 1952, and were encouraged to travel to Nashville by Little Jimmy Dickens.

After reaching Music City, Onie Wheeler and the Cowboys found a deal with Columbia. He recorded in 1953, and though his material wasn't successful, Lefty Frizzell reached the Country Top Ten a year later with Wheeler's "Run 'Em Off." By the mid-'50s, his repertoire began to lean toward rockabilly; he signed to Sun Records in 1957, and toured with Elvis Presley, Jerry Lee Lewis, and Carl Perkins. He spent some of the late '50s in California, but returned to Nashville to record for Epic, Starday, United Artists, and Musicor during the '60s. Wheeler toured with the bands of George Jones and Roy Acuff, and finally hit the charts himself when "John's Been Shucking My Corn" placed modestly in 1973. He even watched his daughter Karen place three singles on the charts during the mid-'70s. Wheeler owned and operated a guitar repair shop during the late '70s and early '80s, working occasionally with Acuff on the *Grand Ole Opry.* He was playing at the *Opry* with Rev. Jimmie Snow in May 1984 when he collapsed and died on-stage. *—John Bush*

● **Onie's Bop** / 1991 / Bear Family ♦♦♦♦

Onie's Bop combines 31 tracks that represent Onie Wheeler's honky tonk and rockabilly recordings from the '50s for both Columbia and Sun Records. While Wheeler recorded for other labels in the '60s and '70s, this Bear Family collection gathers his early rockin' sides, including "Run 'Em Off," "Little Mama," "She Wiggled and Giggled," and "Onie's Bop." *—Al Campbell*

Whiskeytown

f. 1994, Raleigh, NC, **db.** 1999

Group / Alternative Country-Rock, Americana, Alternative Pop/Rock

A band with as turbulent an existence as Whiskeytown was bound to implode sooner or later, but by the time they did, they had one of the largest cult followings of any alt-country band. Most accounts traced the source of all the turmoil to bandleader Ryan Adams, a gifted young songwriter whose flashes of brilliance came hand in hand with a volatile temper and an appetite for alcohol. Adams became notorious for his outbursts and erratic performances, and countless disputes with bandmates (some of them on-stage) inevitably led to frequent personnel changes. Yet during their five-year lifespan, Whiskeytown made some undeniably compelling music that only increased the mystique around their *enfant terrible* leader.Whiskeytown was formed in 1994 in Raleigh, NC, by singer/guitarist/banjoist Adams, a 20-year-old ex-punk rocker who'd discovered the country-rock of Gram Parsons. The band's other charter members were fiddler/occasional lead singer Caitlin Cary, guitarist Phil Wandscher, bassist Steve Grothmann, and drummer Eric "Skillet" Gilmore. They cut a seven-song EP called *Angels* for the local indie Mood Food in 1995 and quickly followed it with their full-length debut, *Faithless Street,* in early 1996. Strongly indebted to Parsons, Uncle Tupelo, and the Replacements, the album earned rave reviews from the alt-country press (*No Depression* magazine in particular), and a performance at that year's South by Southwest music festival helped net them a deal with the Geffen roots affiliate Outpost.

Mood Food issued *Rural Free Delivery,* a compilation of early recordings, in 1997, the same year Whiskeytown completed their major-label debut, *Stranger's Almanac.* There was already a new rhythm section, in the person of bassist Jeff Rice and drummer Steven Terry, and Wandscher left not long after the album was released that summer.The supporting tour for *Stranger's Almanac* was a stormy one, doing much to earn Adams his bad-boy reputation, and by the time the dust settled, Adams and Cary were the only members standing. They added multi-instrumentalist Mike Daly, who not only played keyboards, guitar, pedal and lap steel, mandolin, mandocello, and dulcimer, but also co-wrote a great deal of material with Adams for the band's next album.

Supporting musicians came and went at a furious pace, including onetime fIREHOSE member Ed Crawford and original drummer Gilmore. Somehow, a semistable studio lineup coalesced long enough to complete *Pneumonia,* the third official Whiskeytown album, in 1999. However, a series of label mergers shelved the record indefinitely, during which time it was heavily bootlegged and acquired a strong underground reputation. With the album in limbo, Whiskeytown gave up the ghost. Adams released his solo debut, *Heartbreaker,* in 2000, and Cary issued her own solo EP, *Waltzie,* that year as well. *Pneumonia* was finally released in 2001 on the Universal roots subsidiary Lost Highway and earned some of the group's strongest reviews yet for its eclectic approach. Adams' second solo album, *Gold,* appeared in 2002, and Cary released the solo albums *While You Weren't Looking* and *I'm Staying Out* in 2002 and 2003, respectively. *—Steve Huey*

Faithless Street / 1996 / Outpost ♦♦♦♦

Faithless Street serves as an interesting document in the history of alt-country upstarts Whiskeytown, showing 20-year-old bandleader and chief songwriter Ryan Adams' head-first leap from member of a high-school punk band into an emotionally charged, alcohol-fueled, traditional-minded country singer. The majority of the album was recorded in the summer of 1995 near Whiskeytown's hometown of Raleigh by Chris Stamey (dB's) and overflows with beer bottle, front porch, sun-drenched country anguish. Of the recording, Adams recalls: "All I remember is what we had to drink and Skillet and Ray Duffy's pre-occupation with fireworks... the Roman candles and black cats sounded a lot like I'd hope we'd one day sound—pretty little things all set on fire waiting to get destroyed." Looking back on this statement, the band's history of lineup changes and well-documented on-stage fights seems to fit into Adams' five-year plan perfectly. The music itself is often sparse and gritty, brutally honest, and quite beautiful, especially in the introspective "If He Can't Have You," "Desperate Ain't Lonely," and the achingly gorgeous "Excuse Me While I Break My Own Heart Tonight." For all of the attention surrounding Adams' songwriting and Gram Parsons-like self-destructive bluster, one of the album's highlights comes from violinist and vocalist Caitlin Cary's "Matrimony," sung with a fierce independence that is a far cry from Tammy Wynette's "Stand By Your Man," although with a similar heartfelt enthusiasm. Regarding his songwriting in the *Faithless Street* era, the lead singer later confided: "In retrospect, I knew that was the last optimism I was gonna have for a longtime," which sounds implausible regarding most of the album's subject matter, but later proved to be true. Overall, the album (re-released in 1998 by Outpost Recordings with several bonus tracks) stands as a terrific recording on its own, and also foreshadows many of the forthcoming troubles and achievements in the arc of the band's life span. *—Zac Johnson*

Rural Free Delivery / May 6, 1997 / Mood Food Records ♦♦♦

Independently released, *Rural Free Delivery* finds Whiskeytown in a bit of a transition from local heroes to national spotlight. Rockin' country pervades *R.F.D.,* especially on "Take Your Guns to Town," while the acoustic side comes to the fore on "Tennessee

Square." While not essential, "Rural Free Delivery" is a fine batch of tunes that fans of Whiskeytown will love to hear. It's well worth seeking out. —*James Chrispell*

● **Stranger's Almanac** / Jul. 29, 1997 / Outpost ✦✦✦

Whiskeytown's first major label release, 1997's *Stranger's Almanac*, brought a lot of critical attention, particularly to the band's young singer and songwriter Ryan Adams. His world-weary drawl is pervasive throughout the album, with an honesty that belies his age (Adams was 22 at the time of recording, but many of the songs were written well before then). Credit must also be given to violinist and vocalist Caitlin Cary, whose good old-time fiddle sings above the rest of the band's crash and swagger, and whose vocal harmonies help to soothe Adams' gritty yowls and croons. The radio single "16 Days" is one of the stronger tracks, starting forlorn but quickly accelerating through the chorus, and "Everything I Do" pulls in some understated Hammond B-3 organ and a Memphis-style horn section. Unfortunately, the album also drags in spots and often sounds like a studio creation, heavy with reverb and overdubs (unlike their collection of demos and indie release *Faithless Street*). One sure indicator of the notorious volatility of the band lies in the liner notes that read "This time Whiskeytown were as follows…," showing the signs of unrest that quickly burned out those around Adams' lifestyle and temperament. Alejandro Escovedo appears on three tracks, sounding rough and unprepared on a chorus of the otherwise sublime "Excuse Me While I Break My Own Heart Tonight," but adding subtle acoustic textures to "Dancing With the Women at the Bar." Overall, *Stranger's Almanac* is a good listen and a fine introduction to both the band's brash muscle and Adams bitterly tender songcraft. Listeners looking for something grittier might try their collection *Faithless Street*, and those in need of music on a grander pop scale should investigate *Pneumonia*, the band's third and final album. —*Zac Johnson*

Pneumonia / May 22, 2001 / Lost Highway ✦✦✦✦

Whiskeytown had ceased to be a band in the truest sense by the time they recorded their third (and final) full-length album, *Pneumonia*; the group began to collapse during the touring following *Strangers' Almanac*, with members coming and going at a remarkable pace, and for the *Pneumonia* sessions, the only musicians on hand who had appeared on *Faithless Street* three years earlier were lead vocalist and songwriter Ryan Adams and violinist and backing vocalist Caitlin Cary. Multi-instrumentalist Mike Daly and percussionist/producer Ethan Johns dominated the sessions' sprawling cast of players, with James Iha and Tommy Stinson popping up on some tracks. Ultimately, *Pneumonia* sounds more like a Ryan Adams solo project than anything else, and it walks a decidedly different path than the Whiskeytown albums that preceded it—there are no charging rockers in the manner of "Drank Like a River" or "Yesterday's News," and the country twang of "Too Drunk to Dream" or "Someone Remembers the Rose" has receded into the background (though Cary's violin and occasional mandolin or steel guitar lines from Daly do add a high-lonesome undertow to several songs, especially the plaintive "Sit and Listen to the Rain" and "My Hometown"). This is easily Whiskeytown's most ambitious and eclectic work, and the sparkling pop of "Don't Be Sad" and "Mirror Mirror," the lovely faux-tropicalia of "Paper Moon," the haunting tape-loop reverie of "What the Devil Wanted," and low-key power balladry of "Crazy About You" all prove that, despite his reckless public persona, Ryan Adams had gained a wealth of maturity and intelligence (at least as a songwriter and recording artist) since the last time he'd entered a recording studio. *Pneumonia* was recorded in 1999, but the closing of Outpost Records in the wake of that year's Polygram/ Universal merger put the album on the shelf for two years; in the meantime, *Pneumonia* developed an underground reputation as a lost classic, and while that description is going a bit far to make a point, it is an undeniably striking and beautifully crafted set of songs, and it's interesting to imagine where this music would have taken Whiskeytown if the album had met its original release date—assuming that Whiskeytown was still a band by the time the record was finished. —*Mark Deming*

Bryan White

b. Feb. 17, 1974, Lawton, OK

Vocals / Contemporary Country

With his big voice, easygoing manner, and streamlined mainstream country-pop, Bryan White easily fit into the post-Garth Brooks climate of the mid-'90s. His first album, *Bryan White*, began a string of number-one hits that ran into 1996. White was born and raised in Oklahoma City, where he became involved in music in an early age. Both of his parents were professional local musicians and when Bryan was five, his father taught him how to play drums. As a teenager, he played drums in both of his mother and father's band—his mom sang rock & roll, his father country—which gave him a broad musical knowledge and skill. Eventually, he formed his own trio. At first, he only drummed but during a sound check his mother heard him sing "Stand By Me." After the song was over, his mother was in tears and she encouraged him to become a vocalist himself. In no time, he learned how to play guitar and began writing songs.

Following his graduation from high-school, White headed to Nashville, where he hooked up with Billy Joe Walker Jr., a family friend who happened to be a session musician in the Music City. Over the next two years, Walker helped White hone his act and helped him land a job as a demo singer. Eventually, producer Kyle Lehning, who worked with Randy Travis and Dan Seals in the past, began working with Walker and White. The three crafted Bryan White's debut album and landed the singer a record contract with Asylum. The self-titled debut appeared in 1994.

The first two singles from the record—"Eugene You Genius" and "Look At Me Know"—didn't gather much attention, with the latter peaking at number 24. However, in the spring of 1995, "Someone Else's Star" rocketed to number one, followed by "Rebecca Lynn" in the fall. In the spring of 1996, his second album, *Between Now and Forever*, was released, accompanied by the number-one single "I'm Not Supposed to Love You Anymore." "So Much for Pretending" became his fourth number-one single in a row in the fall of 1996. Also in the fall, he won the Country Music Association's 1996 Horizon Award, as well as their award for Best New Touring Artist. *The Right Place* followed in

1997, and two years later White resurfaced with *How Lucky I Am*. His first seasonal release, *Dreaming of Christmas*, appeared in 1999. Warner Bros. pulled together his four number-one hits and a handful of Top 20s for a *Greatest Hits* album, released in late 2000. —*Stephen Thomas Erlewine*

Bryan White / 1994 / Elektra ✦✦✦

Between Now and Forever / Mar. 26, 1996 / Elektra ✦✦✦✦

Sounding like a cross between a young Bobby Vinton and early Johnny Tillotson, Bryan White could also be called a '90s Glen Campbell, someone he often refers to in his stage act. While not everything on *Between Now and Forever* is top-notch, most songs are high-quality Nashville fare. Throughout the album, White brings us songs of experience with an air of undeniable cleanliness and the result is a record that is not bad at all. —*James Chrispell*

The Right Place / Sep. 23, 1997 / Elektra ✦✦✦

Bryan White doesn't shake things up on his third album, *The Right Place*, but he doesn't need to. He found his perfect formula on *Between Now and Forever*, now, he's simply seeing where it takes him. White has a nice, easygoing style that may only be marginally country by hardcore standards, but it's undeniably fine country-pop. Like many modern country records, *The Right Place* comes up a little short, clocking in with only ten songs, too many of which are filler, but the very best moments, like "Love Is the Right Place" and "Leave My Heart Out of This," are quite good indeed. —*Thom Owens*

How Lucky I Am / Aug. 24, 1999 / Elektra ✦✦✦

On the surface of things, it's hard to see why Bryan White is taken more seriously than some contemporary country-pop singers, since it sounds as slick and polished as some artists that are frequently derided by critics. Upon closer inspection, it becomes clear that the difference is material. Along with producers Derek George and Dann Huff, he knows how to select good material, even if that means sacrificing the number of original tunes on the record. Then, they give the solid songs clean crisp production. True, that production is more suited for adult contemporary stations than contemporary country—if it wasn't marketed as country, most listeners wouldn't label this as such—but it's not bad on those terms. White's voice can be a little thin and uncharismatic, which is a bit of a problem over the long haul, but taken in small doses (such as on singles), *How Lucky I Am* works. —*Stephen Thomas Erlewine*

Dreaming of Christmas / Oct. 26, 1999 / Elektra ✦✦✦

● **Greatest Hits** / Oct. 31, 2000 / Elektra ✦✦✦✦

As demonstrated on this compilation, which contains his ten biggest hits and two new tracks, Bryan White never made really compelling country music. In fact, the music is only country-flavored pop, the real antecedents for which lie in early '70s folk-rock. When White performs a ballad like "I'm Not Supposed to Love You," it sounds like the Eagles doing "Desperado"; when he turns to a rhythm song like "So Much for Pretending," it recalls Stephen Stills' "Love the One You're With." Clearly, White is more pop than country, and he has paid the price by apparently becoming a has-been before his 25th birthday. The two new songs, "How Long" and "The Way You Look at Me," are typically pleasant, but they don't sound like what's needed to turn things around. As it stands, *Greatest Hits*, which manages to encapsulate all of White's popular material without including anything from his 1999 album *How Lucky I Am*, sums up a representative career in the pop-oriented country music of the '90s with no indication that that career will flourish in the future. —*William Ruhlmann*

Clarence White

b. Jun. 7, 1944, Lewiston, ME, **d.** Jul. 14, 1973, Palmdale, CA

Guitar, Vocals / Bluegrass, Progressive Bluegrass, Traditional Bluegrass, Progressive Country, Country-Rock

Clarence White was a gifted guitarist who was one of the pioneers of country-rock in the late '60s. Although died young, his work with the Byrds and the Kentucky Colonels, among others, remained celebrated among country-rock and bluegrass aficionados in the decades following his death. Born in Maine but raised in California, White began playing the guitar at an early age, joining his brothers' band, the Country Boys, when he was just ten years old. The band eventually evolved into the Kentucky Colonels. Clarence left the Colonels in the mid-'60s, becoming a session musician; he played electric guitar on many rock and pop albums. He also began playing with the duo of Gib Gilbeau and Gene Parsons in local California clubs. Gilbeau and Parsons frequently worked with the Gosdin Brothers, so the duo was able to land a cameo appearance for White on the *Gene Clark With the Gosdin Brothers* album. Around the same time, Clarence recorded a solo album for Bakersfield International which the label didn't release.

In 1968, White joined Nashville West, which also featured Gene Parsons, Gib Gilbeau, "Sneaky" Pete Kleinow, Glen D. Hardin, and Wayne Moore. Nashville West recorded an album for Sierra Records, but the record didn't appear until 1978. White was invited to join the Byrds in the fall of 1968. Roger McGuinn was rebuilding the Byrds' lineup after the departure of Chris Hillman and Gram Parsons, who went on to form the Flying Burrito Brothers. Clarence White fit into the revamped Byrds' country-rock direction. He played on the group's untitled album, which spawned the single "Chestnut Mare." While he was with the band, he continued to work as a session musician, playing on Randy Newman's *12 Songs* (1970), Joe Cocker's eponymous 1969 album, and the Everly Brothers' *Stories Would Could Tell* (1971), among others.

Once the Byrds disbanded in 1973, Clarence White continued his session work and joined Muleskinner, which also featured David Grisman, Peter Rowan, John Guerin, Bill Keith, John Kahn, and Richard Greene. Muleskinner only released one album, which appeared later in 1973. After the Muleskinner record was finished, White played a few dates with the Kentucky Colonels and began working on a solo album. He had only completed four tracks when he was killed by a drunken driver while he was loading equipment onto a van; he died on July 14, 1973. Following his death, several posthumous albums of his work with the Kentucky Colonels and the Byrds appeared, as did various albums that featured his playing, including Jackson Browne's *Late for the Sky* and Gene Parsons' *Kindling*. *—Stephen Thomas Erlewine*

Kentucky Colonels: Live in Sweden (1973) / 1976 / Rounder ♦♦♦♦

● **Clarence White & the Kentucky Colonels** / 1980 / Rounder ♦♦♦♦♦
Clarence White & the Kentucky Colonels includes 1964-1967 live performances that are musts for bluegrass guitar enthusiasts. White was a member of the Byrds and a session player for Linda Ronstadt and the Everly Brothers. *—Richard Lieberson*

33 Acoustic Guitar Instrumentals / 2000 / Sierra ♦♦♦♦♦
Clarence White's guitar playing was captured on a number of albums and in a variety of styles between the mid-'60s and his early death in 1973. Still, one cannot help but listen to the Kentucky Colonels *Appalachian Swing!* and want to hear more of White's fine acoustic work. Now, on *33 Acoustic Guitar Instrumentals*, one can. These recordings were captured on a home tape during 1962, featuring no more than White's lead guitar with Roger Bush playing rhythm. This album, recorded two years before *Appalachian Swing!*, shows just how far his flatpicking had advanced. Most of the instrumentals are short—from 44 seconds to a little over two minutes—and feature well known tunes such as "Sugarfoot Rag," "Nine Pound Hammer," and "Sally Goodin." Some material—"In the Pines" and "I Am a Pilgrim"—is shot through with bluesy, soulful playing. Even on straightforward material like "Banks of the Ohio" and "Old Joe Clark," White shows an incredible sense of rhythm, timing, and melody. The oldest of warhorses, "Wildwood Flower," sounds fresh here, and perhaps it is because there is always a sense of openness and intelligence in White's playing, something that is absent from contemporary flatpickers who trade style for speed. The liner notes replace the normal biographical information with testimonials of acoustic players influenced by White, including Jerry Garcia, Tony Rice, and Doc Watson. For those who are already familiar with White, this album is a must have; for the unfamiliar, this is a great place to start. *33 Acoustic Guitar Instrumentals* is a lovely album from a master flatpicker captured in rare form. *—Ronnie Lankford Jr.*

Tuff and Stringy Sessions 1966-68 / Apr. 15, 2003 / Ace ♦♦♦♦
Though this is by no means the best of Clarence White's guitar work—or even necessarily the best of his session work from 1966-1968—it's an important document of no less than 26 rare tracks predating his joining the Byrds. These recordings, often but not always released on the Bakersfield International label (in fact a few were previously unreleased), find White perfecting his transition to the electric guitar and country-rock from bluegrass. The confusing aspect of this phase of his career, on record anyway, is that White's presence is the only real thread running through these recordings, most (though not all) of which feature him only as a session man, rather than as the billed or featured artist. It's quite a crazy quilt of disparate tracks, combining, in varying degrees, country, pop, rock & roll, folk, and folk-rock, with some blues, R&B, Byrds, Beatles, and Cajun licks thrown in. That might not make it the easiest listen in the world, but the variety also makes it fascinating, as White fishes around numerous mixtures of country and rock on obscure recordings by Gary Paxton, Wayne Moore, the Sanland Brothers, Darrell Cotton, Gib & Jan, Jan & Clarence, Jack Reeves, Dennis Payne, the Great Love Trip, and other names known to very few, even in the record-collecting world. Alongside these are eight tracks credited to White himself, some of them previously unreleased. White and the artists explored an almost zany range of tangents, occasionally using sitar, Mellotron, and guitar through a Hammond organ Leslie unit, not to mention nut pulls for bending strings. What keeps this from being as good as it is historically interesting is the material, which is only average (if often ear-perkingly quirky) for the most part. Some of the tracks rise above that level, though, like the Byrds-like country-rock-psychedelia of the Spencers' "Make Up Your Mind," with some great fuzz effects, the blunt Dylan-ish folk-rock of Darrell Cotton's "Don't Pity Me"/"If We Could Read" single, and the beautiful country ballad "She's Gone" by Gib & Jan (though another recording of the song from the same era, by the Gosdin Brothers, is better). Especially worthy of note are a couple of previously unissued circa-1966 electric rock recordings by White's just-ex-bluegrass band the Kentucky Colonels, particularly the Beatles-influenced folk-rock of "Made of Stone" (co-written by Eric Weissberg); these might be the first studio tapes of White playing electric guitar. The lengthy liner notes by compiler Alec Palao do a great deal to chart White's progress during this particularly blurry and hard-to-follow juncture in his career. It should be noted that this is not a complete overview of White's session work during the time, which also included tracks with the Byrds, the Everly Brothers, Rick Nelson, Gene Clark, and others not represented on this compilation. *—Richie Unterberger*

Joy Lynn White

b. Arkansas
Vocals / Contemporary Country, Americana
Joy Lynn White was born in Arkansas, but raised in Mishawaka, IN. At the seasoned age of five, White began singing with the White Family Band, led by her father, Gene White. After high-school, she headed to Nashville, where she worked as a demo singer before landing a recording contract with Columbia, who issued her debut as Joy White in 1992. *Between Midnight & Hindsight* showcased White's fiery vocal delivery and flair for cutting, freewheeling honky tonk. However, the album's three singles found only moderate success, and the album quickly faded. Undeterred, White added a middle name and returned in 1994 with the barreling *Wild Love*. But despite White's undeniable vocal style and the presence of a crack studio band, the album wasn't a success. Columbia dropped her, and she took some time off to refocus.

White re-emerged in 1997 with a new label (Polygram) and a new album, *Lucky Few*. Recorded with Dwight Yoakam's West Coast production team, the album featured songwriting contributions from such notables as Lucinda Williams and Jim Lauderdale, and toned down White's powerful delivery, tempering it with arrangements that fell somewhere between mature Nashville pop-country and the more grassroots approach of outsider country acts like Nanci Griffith. The album met with critical acclaim, but still didn't break White into the mainstream. After *Lucky Few*, White continued to collaborate as a singer with artists like Yoakam and the Mavericks, and worked as a staff writer for Nashville's *Welk Music*. She contributed songs to Lucinda Williams' 2001 album, *Essence*, and found success in Europe's thriving country & western scene. In 2000, the Lucky Dog imprint reissued *Between Midnight & Hindsight* in a remastered version as part of its "Pick of the Litter" series. Two years later, White self-released *On Her Own*, a collection of solo demo recordings, through her website. *—Johnny Loftus*

Between Midnight & Hindsight / Apr. 1992 / Columbia ♦♦♦♦
Joy White (who became Joy Lynn White on her second album, *Wild Love*, in 1994 and was so named on the 2000 reissue of her first, *Between Midnight & Hindsight*) certainly seemed like a budding country star when her debut album was released in 1992 and spawned three chart singles, "Little Tears," "True Confessions," and "Cold Day in July." Possessed of a powerful voice that cut through honky tonk tunes such as "Wherever You Are" and caressed ballads like "It's Amazing," White clearly was the real thing, a country performer steeped in the subgenres of the style, from country blues ("Hey Hey Mama") to Cajun ("Let's Talk About Love Again"). She could wring depths of feeling from the plot twists of the tearjerker "Why Do I Feel So Good" and barnstorm through the stomping "Wishful Thinking" with equal effectiveness. Maybe she was a little too convincing on the honky tonk material, though, in a field that often prefers women to flaunt their femininity rather than their feistiness. In any case, none of the singles really took off, the album didn't chart, and neither did its two follow-ups. Eight years later, the Lucky Dog imprint remastered and reissued *Between Midnight & Hindsight* as part of its "Pick of the Litter" series of underappreciated catalog recordings, an act of benevolence that deserved to inspire a reassessment of Joy Lynn White, whose music sounded just as good as ever. *—William Ruhlmann*

● **Wild Love** / 1994 / Columbia ♦♦♦♦♦
White added a middle name, but didn't change her sound much. On the Springsteenian rave-up "Wild Love," her hillbilly vibrato left the impression of passion about to spin out of control. Her version of the redneck-pride anthem "I am Just a Rebel" (earlier recorded by Billy Hill, Dennis Robbins and Confederate Railroad) added toughness to her image (as though she needed it), and the likes of "Too Gone to Care" and "On and on and On" showed she could rock out even while singing hard country. *—Brian Mansfield*

Lucky Few / Apr. 8, 1997 / Polygram ♦♦♦♦♦
There are few female artists who can vocally compete with Joy Lynn White. Her two previous Nashville projects set her aside from all the cute girlie-girls the pop-slop country format manufactured. This, her first project with top West Coast producers Dusty Wakeman and Pete Anderson, provides more evidence of her vocal talent. Recorded in Los Angeles and with songs written by the likes of Lucinda Williams, Jann Browne, and Jimmy Lauderdale to ensure the high caliber of the material and musicians like Lauderdale, Scott Joss, Larry Mars, Tom Brumley, and Marty Stuart providing musical support, there is no reason why *The Lucky Few* should not be added to the annals of country & western history as an outstanding event. A duet with Dwight Yoakam on the Lauderdale tune, "It's Better This Way," is the project's crowning glory. The title track and both Williams' cuts, "I Just Wanted to See You So Bad" and "I Lost It," are highlights. Surprisingly, White's honky tonk edge seems less biting, and her in-your-face power is somewhat muted. For many, these qualities made her all the more appealing in an age when runnin' with the honky tonk crowd was frowned upon. Obviously White is aiming for the crossover audience here. Still, the lady has the chops. *—Jana Pendragon*

Lari White

b. 1966, Dunedin, FL
Vocals / Contemporary Country
Most contestants on televised talent shows never are able to forge a lasting career, but Lari White is the exception that proves the rule. After winning on the Nashville Network's *You Can Be A Star*, White went on to become one of the most popular female new country singers of the mid-'90s, breaking through into the big time in 1994. Born and raised in Dunedin, FL, Lari White began performing when she was a child, singing in a gospel group with her parents and brother. The group, called the White Family Singers, sang at local church and community gathering. After a while, the children began working pop music into the act, most notably Elvis Presley. As a teenager, Lari sang show tunes at talent contests and sang with a local rock & roll band. She earned a scholarship to the University of Miami, where she studied vocals and music engineering. After a while, she began writing her own songs, singing in local clubs at night and taking professional singing jobs. Upon graduating from college, she travelled around the United States, looking at various local music scenes. In 1988, she decided to move to Nashville and try to become a professional.

Later in 1988, she appeared on the Nashville Network's *You Can Be a Star* and won the first prize. The award led to a record contract with Capitol. Before the end of the year, she had released a single on Capitol, "Flying Above the Rain," which became a regional hit in the South but failed to break into the big time. Later that same year, she joined Ronnie Milsap's publishing house and began taking acting lessons. For the next few years, White continued in this vein, choosing to hone her talent, sing in local dinner theaters and wait for another break. That break arrived in 1991, after an ASCAP showcase revived interest in her talents. Following the showcase, Rodney Crowell asked her to sing backup vocals in his live band. In 1992, White signed a record contract with RCA and Crowell produced her debut album, *Lead Me Not*, which was released the following year.

Lead Me Not received strong reviews and produced three minor hit singles: "What a Woman Wants," "Lead Me Not," and "Lay Around and Love You." *Wishes*, White's second album, became her breakthrough release, producing the Top Ten singles "That's My Baby," "Now I Know," and "That's How You Know (When You're in Love)." *Don't Fence Me In*, White's third album, wasn't quite as successful as its predecessor, but it continued her success. *Stepping Stone* followed in 1998. *—Stephen Thomas Erlewine*

Lead Me Not / Apr. 27, 1993 / RCA ✦✦✦✦✦
White's ambitious debut covered a lot of musical territory, from straight country ("Where the Lights Are Low") to torch ballad ("Just Thinking"), from Latin-flavored pop ("Made to Be Broken") to fervid gospel ("Good Good Love"). The breadth of her talent turned out to be something of a problem. Since nobody could get a handle on her, none of the album's three singles ("What a Woman Wants," "Lead Me Not," and "Lay Around and Love on You") broke the Top 40. *—Brian Mansfield*

Wishes / Jun. 1994 / RCA ✦✦✦✦✦
Produced by Garth Fundis (Trisha Yearwood, Keith Whitley), *Wishes* focused White's abilities into something more palatable to the country mainstream. The first single, "That's My Baby," asounded like a companion piece to Yearwood's breakthrought "She's in Love With the Boy." But where Yearwood turned her back on that kind of those kind of small-town, teen-passion songs, White made a whole album of them. *Wishes* is filled with charm, playfulness, and nifty hooks, especially on "That's How You Know," a thrilling duet with Hal Ketchum. *—Brian Mansfield*

Don't Fence Me In / Feb. 13, 1996 / RCA ✦✦✦

● **The Best of Lari White** / Jan. 28, 1997 / RCA ✦✦✦✦✦
Lari White didn't have that many big hits—she didn't begin having Top Ten singles until 1995—but that doesn't mean she didn't record a wealth of strong music, as *The Best of Lari White* proves. By selecting the highlights from her three albums, the compilation helps neophytes get up to speed with her past, but *Lead Me Not* and *Wishes* remain terrific albums in their own right. *—Thom Owens*

Stepping Stone / Jul. 28, 1998 / Hollywood ✦✦✦✦
Lari White has one of the finest voices in popular music. Her ability to bring the strength of her gospel background to anything she sings makes her talent a real treasure. Sadly, she has been misused and abused by the factory system in Music City and has not attained the success she should have. But quality can't be overlooked; like cream, it rises to the top. And while most of the material on this project is not worthy of her talent, she still makes a good showing all across the board. Perhaps the most stunning performance this time out is "You Can't Go Home Again," a traditional tune that allows White to show off the prowess in her vocal style. Just as good is the Deborah Allen-Chuck Jones tune "On a Night Like This," which showcases White's ability to rock. The thing about Lari White is that no matter the caliber of material, for better or worse, she makes you believe every word she sings. *—Jana Pendragon*

Tony Joe White

b. Jul. 23, 1943, Oak Grove, LA
Guitar, Harmonica, Songwriter, Vocals / Pop-Soul, Country-Pop, Rock & Roll
Tony Joe White has parlayed his songwriting talent into a modestly successful country and rock career in Europe as well as America. Born July 23, 1943, in Goodwill, LA, White was born into a part-Cherokee family. He began working clubs in Texas during the mid-'60s, and moved to Nashville by 1968. White's 1969 debut album for Monument, *Black and White*, featured his Top Ten pop hit "Polk Salad Annie" and another charting single, "Roosevelt and Ira Lee (Night of the Moccasin)." That same year, Dusty Springfield reached the charts with White's "Willie and Laura Mae Jones." Brook Benton recorded a version of White's "Rainy Night in Georgia" that hit number four early in 1970; the song has since become a near-standard with more than 100 credits. White's own "Groupie Girl" began his European success with a short stay on the British charts in 1970.

White moved to Warner Bros. in 1971, but success eluded him on his three albums—*Tony Joe White*, *The Train I'm On*, and *Homemade Ice Cream*. Other stars, however, continued to keep his name on the charts during the 1970s: Elvis charted with "For Ol' Times Sake" and "I've Got a Thing About You Baby" (Top Five on the country charts), and Hank Williams Jr. took "Rainy Night in Georgia" to number 13 on the country charts. White himself recorded *Eyes* for 20th Century Fox in 1976, but then disappeared for four years. He signed to Casablanca for 1980's *The Real Thang* but moved to Columbia in 1983 for *Dangerous*, which included the modest country hits "The Lady in My Life" and "We Belong Together."

Tony Joe White was inactive through much of the '80s, but worked with Tina Turner on her 1989 *Foreign Affair* album, writing four songs and playing guitar and harmonica. He released *Closer to the Truth* a year later for his own Swamp label, and toured with Eric Clapton and Joe Cocker to very receptive French crowds (*Closer to the Truth* has sold 100,000 copies in that country alone). His 1993 album, *Path of a Decent Groove*, was released only in France, though Warner's *The Best of Tony Joe White* earned an American release the same year. *Lake Placid Blues* (1995) and *One Hot July* (1998) were Europe-only efforts until 2000, when Hip-O Records brought out *One Hot July* in the U.S., giving White his first new major label domestic release in 17 years. *—John Bush*

Black and White / 1969 / Monument ✦✦✦
When "Polk Salad Annie" blared from transistor radio speakers in the summer of 1969, the first thought was of Creedence Clearwater Revival, for Tony Joe White's swamp rock bore more than a passing resemblance to the sound John Fogerty whipped up on *Bayou Country* and *Green River*. But White was the real thing—he really was from the bayou country of Louisiana, while Fogerty's bayou country was conjured up in Berkeley, CA. Plus, White had a mellow baritone voice that sounded like it had been dredged up from the bottom of the Delta. Besides "Annie," side one of this album includes several other White originals. The best of these are "Willie and Laura Mae Jones," a song about race relations with an arrangement similar to "Ballad of Billie Joe," and "Soul Francisco," a short piece of funky fluff that had been a big hit in Europe in 1968. "Aspen, Colorado" presages the later "Rainy Night in Georgia," a White composition popularized by Brook Benton. The second side consists of covers of contemporary hits, with the funky "Who's Making Love" and "Scratch My Back" faring better than the slow stuff. Dusty Springfield had a minor hit with "Willie and Laura Mae Jones," and White's songs were recorded by other performers through the years, but "Polk Salad Annie" and the gators that got her granny provided his only march in the American hit parade. *—Jim Newsom*

. . . Continued / 1969 / Monument ✦✦✦

Tony Joe / 1970 / Monument ✦✦✦✦

Tony Joe White / 1971 / Warner Bros. ✦✦✦✦✦
Tony Joe White's self-titled fourth album, *Tony Joe White*, finds the self-proclaimed swamp fox tempering his bluesy swamp rockers with a handful of introspective, soul-dripping ballads and introducing horn and string arrangements for the first time. The album—White's 1971 debut for Warner Bros.—was recorded over a two-week period in December 1970, in two different Memphis studios (one was Ardent Studios, where Big Star later recorded their influential power pop albums). His producer was none other than London-born Peter Asher, who had just produced James Taylor's early hits for the label (he would continue to produce hits for Taylor and Linda Ronstadt on his way to becoming one of the most successful producers of the '70s). One can surmise that Warner Bros. may have put White and Asher together as a way for the producer to work his magic with an artist who had much promise. White had already scored big with 1969's "Polk Salad Annie" for Monument, and he was having success as a songwriter too: "Rainy Night in Georgia" was a huge hit for Brook Benton in 1970. As you might expect, there aren't really too many surprises here, despite the addition of the Memphis Horns and other Muscle Shoals sessioners. The songs are fairly standard and straightforward, nothing too out of place or experimental, and White's husky Southern warble remains the album's key focus. Many of the songs will remind the listener just how turbulent the cultural climate of the late '60s and early '70s was in the U.S. White's soulful Southern-tinged spoken drawl introduces "The Change" (as in a "change is gonna come"), then a potent theme and oft-spoke clarion call that, indeed, the times they were a changin'. "Black Panther Swamps" and "I Just Walked Away" (the album's first single) are also successful at what they attempt. Meanwhile, over on the more sentimental side, "The Daddy" concerns itself with the generation gap between father and son, and mentions the son cutting his long hair ("a little respect will never hurt you"). The mawkish "Five Summers for Jimmy" will appeal to fans who liked Bobby Goldsboro's "Honey." On a more positive note, "A Night in the Life of a Swamp Fox" was White's somewhat-frustrating look at what was going on in his life, playing his sole hit for fans but wanting something more out of his career. Unfortunately, this album never did bring him the success he craved, although it deserves another listen. In 2002, *Tony Joe White* was reissued for the first time in the U.S. on CD by the Sepia Tone label. *—Bryan Thomas*

The Train I'm On / 1972 / Warner Bros. ✦✦✦✦✦
Tony Joe White's second Warner Bros. album is an awesome, exquisite musical jewel and a departure from most of the attributes for which he is best known, from songs like "Polk Salad Annie." Acoustic textured for much of its length and built on a close, intimate sound overall, *The Train I'm On* is permeated with the dark side of White's usual swamp rock sound, filled with songs about unsettled loves and lives, and men caught amid insoluble situations. Betraying surprising vulnerability for much of its length, even on songs like "If I Ever Saw a Good Thing" and "300 Pounds of Hongry" (among the few full band numbers here, with a gorgeous sax solo by Charles Chalmers on the former), he shows off an emotional complexity that wasn't always obvious on his earlier work, only really cutting loose boldly on "Even Trolls Love Rock and Roll" and a tiny handful of other cuts. The rest is dark, pensive, soulful bluesy rock, highlighted by some bristling acoustic guitar work (check out "As the Crow Flies") and superb singing throughout ("The Migrant" is worth the price of admission by itself). [The album was reissued in 2002 by Sepia Tone with new annotation, in a beautifully remastered mid-price edition.] *—Bruce Eder*

Homemade Ice Cream / 1973 / Warner Bros. ✦✦✦

Eyes / 1976 / 20th Century ✦✦
Three years after leaving Warner Bros., Tony Joe White returned with *Eyes*, released on 20th Century. His record label wasn't the only thing that changed. Abandoning the idiosyncratic, bluesy country-rock that made his name, White turned to smooth disco, creating a late-night seduction record closer to Boz Scaggs than Tony Joe White, but that's not necessarily a bad thing, since White's voice suits the stylish groove well and it's appealing on the surface. This is an album made for romance. Six of the ten songs have some conjugation of "love" in the title, and if that wasn't clear enough, there was the swinging cover photo, finding Tony Joe in a wide-open, wide-collared shirt, chatting up a lovely blond woman. If that belabors his point a little much by not offering much subtlety, it does at least deliver a swank seduction sound that is thoroughly late '70s, sounding more tied to its time than White's music usually does. That might be why many White fans don't dig this album—it's such a smooth affair that when he returns to the swamp, as on "Texas Woman," it's disarming—but it's enjoyable for what it is. *—Stephen Thomas Erlewine*

Real Thang / 1980 / Casablanca ✦✦

Dangerous / 1983 / Columbia ✦✦

● **Polk Salad Annie: The Best of Tony Joe White** / 1994 / Warner Archive ✦✦✦✦✦
Here are 20 tracks from 1969-1973, the period of White's greatest success, including "Polk Salad Annie" and White's own version of his composition, "Rainy Night in Georgia." Most of this is quality swamp-rock with pop-soul-conscious production; on cuts like "High Sheriff of Calhoun Parrish," it sounds very much like he was trying to achieve a groove in the mold of Bobbie Joe Gentry's "Ode to Billie Joe." Sometimes he gets real down-home in a stomping backwoods blues style that makes him sound a little like a White

counterpart to John Lee Hooker, as on "Stockholm Blues." If there's any criticism to be levied against this music, it's in its occasional lack of variety, White mining staple swamp rock boogie riffs for all they're worth. However, few, if any, performers and writers were as skilled as White in doing so, and he has a fine knack for sharp storytelling lyrics. *—Richie Unterberger*

One Hot July / Oct. 6, 1998 / Polygram ✦✦✦
Tony Joe's first U.S. release since 1983 finds the swamp-rocker in rare form. Produced by Roger Davies—Tina Turner's manager/producer, and the one responsible for her '80s breakthrough—this is the most cohesive album he's made since his early Monument LPs with Billy Swan. Tony Joe is kept tightly focused with a small combo (Hammond organ, bass, drums), and the rest of the space in the mix is occupied by the star's funky guitar, harmonica, and breathy vocals, recorded so close he sounds like he's two inches from the listener's face. It also helps that Tony Joe's songwriting skills have only sharpened over the years; the disc is simply loaded with great songs, including "Crack the Window Baby," "Gumbo John," "I Want My Fleetwood Back," and the moody "Cold Fingers," "I Believe I've Lost My Way," and "Across From Midnight." One of his very best, and as highly recommended as they come. *—Cub Koda*

Beginning / 2001 / Swap ✦✦✦✦✦
It's something to contemplate when an artist of Tony Joe White's stature waits until his 29th record to make the album he's been dreaming about for most, if not all, of his career. It's the mark of a visionary artist to nurture deep within the smoldering coal of a flame that needs room to burn hot and true, until the conditions are right for its creation and unveiling. It doesn't matter how long it took, however, what makes a difference is that the Swamp Fox is heard unadorned and unfettered by studio embellishments or safety nets. This is TJW raw and direct, full of grit, truth, and an unsettling sensuality. This is the sound of the night, where the bullfrogs, snakes, hungry 'gators, broken dreamers, haunted desperadoes, lonesome travelers, and wild-eyed seekers of the unspeakable all come together in one man's musical dreams to speak. *Beginning* is the sound of the dirty, funky, hot, and muggy blues. The setting could be a juke joint out in the swamp or a sitting room with a handful of couples slithering in the darkness or a noisy barroom reduced to a hush by the subtle power and gripping conviction of the stomp in Tony Joe's foot, his chunky, percussive snake-charming guitar, and the forbidding whisper and moan that's in the grain of his voice. This is untamed, unrelenting seduction and instruction music fashioned from country, blues, and rock & roll. From the deep bottom of "Rich Woman's Blues" to the desolate, broken weekday-after poetry in "Going Back to Bed" and the mournful, slinky, folk-gospel of "Raining on My Life," White lets one image fall down on another, with the riffs and hooks to anchor them in his own personal mythology and iconography of life and love that translates from the grooves through the speakers and into our hearts. One of White's particular gifts is, even when singing in the first person, he offers an empathetic view so close to the bone that we not only know the people in these songs, we've *been* them. In addition to all this we are presented with, also included are the heartbreakingly desolate folk tune "The Drifter" and the mariachi-flavored "Down By The Border," a love song so broken, that nothing is ever resolved, no wound is ever closed; there's only the song and its ghostly echoes ringing out over the empty miles and abandoned years. In White's voice, the listener can hear the want calling her name over time and tide. That said, it remains true that White takes his principal inspiration from the deep, greasy, low-down, funked-up blues. It's the same blues that offers the hint of forbidden fruit fulfills seductive promises and gets to the root of the emotions that sear and transform and/or bring people together for the common cause of celebrating in order to forget. Finally, it's the same blues that makes a man sit alone with a guitar in a cabin to moan and sing out his life into the welcoming midnight sky. Tracks like "The Ice Cream Man," with its backbone slipping, in-between-the-sheets groove, the dark, Delta tragedy folk blues of "Clovis Green," the malevolence and resignation in the right-hand boxy strum on "More to This Than That" (where the listener can imagine the screaming electric guitars and shuffling drums, though the acoustic version is what makes it possible), and the slippery, backwoods six-string stomp and slip of "Who You Gonna Hoo-Doo Now." The songs on *Beginning* add up to a cipher of a record; it's so fully Tony Joe White that we wonder why it took so long, yet, so out of step, time, and place with everything else that's going on out there it has no place to dwell except its own. It is mercurial and deeply mysterious, it may speak plainly but it gives up its secrets slowly. All of this is told on "Rebellion," the closest thing to a manifesto that White has ever issued. In its knotty blues wrangling, White lays out the truth and the challenge. He makes his own way because he has to—he's an artist possessed with the same kind of restless vision that drove every real one, from Stephen Foster to Ray Charles, from Louis Armstrong to Hank Williams, and from Chuck Berry to John Lennon, to make his mark—no matter the cost. This new issue is a precious commodity, because in it, one can hear his entire history as it has played itself out on those 28 previous records, and how the foundations he's built will provide a home for that now brightly burning flame to shine for decades to come. Given an honest listen, it will provide something like that for others as well. *—Thom Jurek*

Snakey / Nov. 5, 2002 / Swamp ✦✦✦✦
Why Tony Joe White isn't spoken of in the same revered tones as J. J. Cale is a mystery as well as a crime. White invented a brand of greasy, funky, deeply soulful Louisiana bayou rock that's been quoted by everyone from the Neville Brothers and the Meters to Marvin Gaye to the Red Hot Chili Peppers to ZZ Top to Funkadelic to the Cramps to the Gun Club to the White Stripes. Mark Knopfler owes his entire guitar playing approach to White. OK, enough bitching. *Snakey* is the most aptly titled Tony Joe record in some time. Here that shadowy guitar style, with its serpentine leads and chunky, syncopated chords, catches a groove that is echoed by Little Troll Forrest's basslines punching through the pocket just ahead of Boom Boom Cohen's drumming. The songs—whether it be "Feeling Snakey," with its screaming leads and soulfully regretful message about leaving the booze alone to uncoil the body and mind to boasting about how your woman knows how to make the crawfish boil, or the driving, fuzzed-out high-wire act that is "Bayou Blues" (ZZ Top got the entire *Eliminator* album from this sound)—are timelessly nasty in the best rock & roll sense of the word, with wickedly sly humor tossed in between lines for measure. Then there's the coolest, most ominous song ever written about hanging out in a health-food store in "The Organic Shuffle," which bleeds into the overdriven swamp-box guitar funkery of "Livin' off the Land." This doesn't mean that Tony Joe isn't capable of tenderness; far from it. "Rico," a gorgeous, slinky, mariachi-tinged country song, is subtitled "(14) Field Worker." It's an empathetic portrait of a migrant worker who accepts his situation while trying not to lose sight of his dreams, which have nothing to do with money. The balls-out funk of "Tastes Like Chicken" is White at his best, letting all of the country, soul, funk, blues, rock, and folk contradictions fall into one another. Lyrically the song is as hilarious as it is spooky, capping off yet another Swamp Fox masterpiece. Oh yeah, not only are there no bad Tony Joe White records, there aren't any mediocre ones, either; this man has the most remarkably consistent track in modern music, beginning in the late '60s and continuing to this day. *—Thom Jurek*

Eyes/Dangerous / Feb. 25, 2003 / Raven ✦✦
Raven released Tony Joe White's 1976 album *Eyes* and his 1983 record *Dangerous* as a two-fer early in 2003 (on the front and back cover, it's rather ingeniously called *Dangerous Eyes*, but the spine lists it as a straight two-fer, complete with *Eyes* arriving first in proper chronological order). *Eyes* was released on 20th Century and has never appeared on CD prior to this; *Dangerous* was released on CD in the U.S. in 2001. Even though seven years separate these two records and even though his 1980 release for Casablanca, *Real Thang*, is skipped, the pairing still makes some sense, since both records find White stretching out from his trademark sound and delving headfirst into disco. *Eyes*, in particular, is an anomaly, a largely disco album that sounds closer to Boz Scaggs than Tony Joe White, but that's not necessarily a bad thing, since White's voice suits the stylish groove well and it's appealing on the surface. *Eyes* is deliberately a love album—the word appears in half of the song titles—and if that belabors his point a little much by not offering much subtlety, it does at least deliver a swank seduction sound that is thoroughly late '70s, sounding more tied to its time than White's music usually does. That might be why many White fans don't dig this album—it's such a smooth affair that when he returns to the swamp, as on "Texas Woman," it's disarming—but it's enjoyable for what it is. *Dangerous* is in the same vein, but it breathes a little more, offering a stronger dose of the swamp pop that made his name. That and disco make for strange bedfellows—including song titles like "Hold on to Your Heiney"—and the album sometimes seems unsure of its identity, but it's usually enjoyable, even it doesn't offer many distinctive songs. So, in total, *Eyes* and *Dangerous* are detours in White's career, which makes them a perfect pairing for a two-fer. It might not be something that the die-hard fans of the early albums love, but completists will be glad that both of these records are on disc, and listeners who prefer soulful, stylish disco-rock to funky, gritty swamp rock might find that they like this more than the music he's traditionally associated with. *—Stephen Thomas Erlewine*

The Whites

f. 1971

Group / Progressive Bluegrass, Traditional Bluegrass, Contemporary Country, Country Gospel

One of the longer-lived family harmony groups in country music, the Whites started out as a bluegrass group, enjoyed a period as country hitmakers in the '80s, and later concentrated on gospel music. Buck White (vocals, piano, mandolin) and his daughters Sharon (vocals, guitar) and Cheryl (vocals, bass) officially comprised the group, but their roots dated back to Buck's first band in 1947. He went on to play bluegrass, honky tonk, and Western swing with a variety of bands in the '50s, most notably the Blue Sage Boys, and moved his family to Arkansas in 1961. Not long after, he and his wife Pat formed the Down Home Folks with another musical couple, Arnold & Peggy Johnston. Later on, Sharon and Cheryl started performing with the Johnstons' two sons as the Down Home Kids, and when the family moved to Nashville in 1971, they were integrated into the regular Down Home Folks lineup. The Down Home Folks recorded five bluegrass albums during the '70s, with Pat retiring from the group in 1973. They caught a break when Emmylou Harris featured them on her 1979 album *Blue Kentucky Girl* and brought them out on tour with her as an opening act.

Changing their name to the Whites to emphasize their family ties, Buck, Sharon, and Cheryl turned their attention to the country mainstream and had their first charting single in 1981 with a version of "Send Me the Pillow That You Dream On." They scored a Top Ten country hit in 1982 with "You Put the Blue in Me," the same year Sharon married Ricky Skaggs. The next year, they issued their first album as the Whites, *Old Familiar Feeling*, on Warner Bros. and welcomed dobro virtuoso Jerry Douglas into their backing band. "Hangin' Around" and "I Wonder Who's Holding My Baby Tonight" both went Top Ten in 1983, as did "Give Me Back That Old Familiar Feeling" and "Pins" the following year. The Whites moved over to MCA and issued three albums from 1984-1987, just missing the Top Ten with the single "If It Ain't Love (Let's Leave It Alone)." In 1988, they made the switch to gospel music with *Doing It By the Book*, which appeared on the Word label. They spent much of the '90s without a record deal but returned in 1996 with *Give a Little Back* on the small Step One label. Another Whites album, *A Lifetime in the Making*, appeared on Skaggs' Ceili imprint in 2000. *—Steve Huey*

● **Greatest Hits** / 1987 / Curb ✦✦✦✦✦
Although the Whites (Buck White and his daughters Sharon and Cheryl) were primarily a gospel bluegrass group, they recorded several country hits for Warner and Curb Records, beginning with "Hangin' Around" in 1983. These ten tunes showcase their unique blend of bluegrass instrumentation and harmony with modern country production on other

chart-toppers, including "Hometown Gossip," "Pins and Needles," and "If It Ain't Love (Let's Leave It Alone)." —*Al Campbell*

Doing It By the Book / 1988 / Word ♦♦♦

Poor Folks Pleasure / Nov. 17, 1995 / Koch ♦♦♦

Give a Little Back / Feb. 6, 1996 / Rock Bottom ♦♦♦

A Lifetime in the Making / Aug. 15, 2000 / Ceili Music ♦♦♦♦
Ricky Skaggs' Ceili label has quickly gained a reputation for quality recordings, and the Whites' *A Lifetime in the Making* is no exception. The stars of this disc are vocalist and guitarist Sharon White, vocalist and bass player Cheryl White, and vocalist and mandolinist Buck White. This album offers what listeners have come to expect from the Whites: beautiful harmony, good song choices, and great acoustic accompaniment. Jerry Douglas has produced this album with a steady hand, and also adds his always tasteful dobro playing. Songs like "Before the Prairie Met the Plow" and "Always Coming Home" will probably be described as bluegrass, but the smooth harmonies and relaxed pace seems to share more with country and folk. This folk connection is strengthened by the inclusion of songs like "Fair and Tender Ladies." This song has a lovely arrangement and includes harmony and lead vocals by Emmylou Harris. While a melancholy air occasionally enters songs like, "I Miss Who I Was (With You)," *A Lifetime in the Making*, like all of the Whites' music, is filled with joy. "Key to the Kingdom" and "Jesus is the Missing Piece" are cheerful, swinging gospel songs, more likely to inspire hand clapping than religious reflection. It should be noted that while the Whites are often listed as a gospel group, religious songs only represent one aspect of this recording. *A Lifetime in the Making* is a fine album, sure to please old and new fans alike. —*Ronnie Lankford Jr.*

Keith Whitley

b. Apr. 1, 1955, Sandy Hook, KY, **d.** May 9, 1989, Nashville, TN
Guitar, Vocals / Progressive Bluegrass, New Traditionalist, Progressive Country
Keith Whitley's legacy loomed large over the country music landscape of the '90s. A talented new country singer and songwriter, Whitley was just beginning to emerge as a superstar at the time of his death in 1989. Throughout the next decade, his reputation as both a performer and writer continued to grow, as other artists had hits with his songs and posthumous recordings climbed into the Top Ten. Born and raised in Kentucky, Whitley began singing as a child, winning a talent contest at the age of four. When he was eight years old, he learned how to play guitar and within a year he was singing on a Charleston, WV-based radio station. Whitley formed his first band at the age of 13, playing nothing but straight bluegrass. A few years later, he formed the Lonesome Mountain Boys with his high-school friend, Ricky Skaggs. The Lonesome Mountain Boys primarily played Stanley Brothers songs and soon became a popular attraction.

In the late '60s, Ralph Stanley was looking to re-form his band after the death of his brother and partner, Carter. He was so impressed with Whitley and Skaggs, he asked them to join his Clinch Mountain Boys group. The duo accepted the offer immediately and began appearing with the band in 1970. Whitley stayed with the Clinch Mountain Boys for two years, recording a total of seven albums, including 1971's *Crying From the Cross*, which was named the Bluegrass Album of the Year. In 1973, Whitley left the group. For two years, he drifted through various other bands, including acts that played country, not bluegrass. He returned to the Clinch Mountain Boys in 1975 and stayed with them for another two years. During his second tenure with the band, he made five albums. In 1978, Keith joined J.D. Crowe's band the New South. Whitley recorded three albums with the New South between 1978 and 1982, which vacillated between bluegrass and straight country (the highlights of this era were re-released on CD as *Sad Songs & Waltzes* in 2000).

Whitley began a full-fledged solo career after leaving the New South in 1982. Signing with RCA Records, he released his debut album, *Hard Act to Follow*, in 1984. A record of pure honky tonk, it didn't attract much of an audience. The following year, he released *L.A. to Miami*, a more commercial affair which spawned the number-14 single "Miami, My Amy." After that single peaked early in 1986, he had three back-to-back Top Ten hits: "Ten Feet Away," "Homecoming '63," and "Hard Livin'." Late in 1986, he married Lorrie Morgan. Although *L.A. to Miami* was a success, its slick production didn't please Whitley. In 1987, he recorded a follow-up to the record that sounded exactly the same as its predecessor. Unsatisfied with the musical direction of his new effort, Whitley convinced RCA to shelve the completed album and have him work on another record with a new producer, Garth Fundis. *Don't Close Your Eyes* was the result. Released in the spring of 1988, the album solidified Whitley's commercial standing. The first three singles from *Don't Close Your Eyes*—"Don't Close Your Eyes," "When You Say Nothing at All," and "I'm No Stranger to the Rain"—were all number-one hits.

Things may have been going smoothly on the surface for Keith Whitley, but behind the scenes he was being torn apart by alcoholism. On May 9, 1989, he suffered from a fatal case of alcohol poisoning; he was 34 at the time of his demise. Just before his death, he completed his fourth album, *I Wonder Do You Think of Me*. The record was released shortly after his death and its first single, which was the title track, reached number one, as did its follow-up, "It Ain't Nothin'"; another single from the album, "I'm Over You," reached number three in 1990. During the '90s, RCA repackaged and re-released many of Whitley's recordings—including several unreleased songs—in various compilations. Lorrie Morgan recorded an electronic duet, "'Til a Tear Becomes a Rose," with her late husband in 1990; it peaked at number 13. In 1994, a tribute album to Whitley was released. —*Stephen Thomas Erlewine*

Hard Act to Follow / 1984 / RCA ♦♦
In 1984, *Hard Act to Follow* was Keith Whitley's first record for RCA. While the material doesn't match up with the tremendous success he would achieve on his next three albums for the label, you can hear Whitley making the transition from bluegrass-based material into mellow country-pop with a bit of honky tonk. Among the highlights include "Turn Me to Love," "A Hard Act to Follow," "If A Broken Heart Could Kill," and "If You Think I'm Crazy Now (You Should Have Seen Me When I Was a Kid)." —*Al Campbell*

L.A. to Miami / 1985 / RCA ♦♦
L.A. to Miami was Keith Whitley's breakthrough album. While it contains several chart-topping hits, including "Homecoming '63," "Hard Livin'," "Love at Ten Feet Away," and "Miami, My Amy," the album suffers as a whole from a lack of tempo change. The consistent laid-back approach becomes a bit too mellow, tending to drag the album down. Even though there was a lack of honky tonk material on the album, Whitley would adjust that on his follow-up release, *Don't Close Your Eyes*. By the way, the album also includes "On the Other Hand," which became Randy Travis' first minor hit, also released in 1985. —*Al Campbell*

Don't Close Your Eyes / 1988 / RCA ♦♦♦♦♦
Don't You Close Your Eyes was more successful than Keith Whitley's two previous albums and it's easy to see why. Though the record still suffered from a handful of mediocre songs and a slightly soft production, the overall album was leaner and more direct than Whitley's earlier solo work, showcasing his talent for heartfelt honky tonk singing and his skill for crafting excellent barroom ballads. "Don't Close Your Eyes," "When You Say Nothing At All," and "I'm No Stranger to the Rain" were the hits, but there's a wealth of excellent material here, including a haunting version of Lefty Frizzell's "I Never Go Around Mirrors." The sheer strength of the best numbers make the handful of weaker songs perfectly excusable. After all, country in the late '80s rarely got better than *Don't You Close Your Eyes* at its best. —*Thom Owens*

★ **I Wonder Do You Think of Me** / 1989 / RCA ♦♦♦♦♦
Though Keith Whitley displayed his immense talents on his previous albums, it was only in small measures. It wasn't until *I Wonder Do You Think of Me*, his fourth and final album, that he truly came into his own. The difference between this album and its predecessors is focus. The essential style remains the same, but Whitley has decided to concentrate only on a heart-tugging, gritty honky tonk and to give the record an appropriately straightforward, simple production. The direct approach gives more weight to the sad tales of lost love and drinking and when Whitley died shortly before the record's release, these songs gained even more gravity. Still, *I Wonder Do You Think of Me* stands as an excellent testament—songs like "It Ain't Nothin'," "I'm Over You" and the title track only begin to suggest the depth and appeal of this album. —*Thom Owens*

☆ **Greatest Hits** / 1990 / RCA ♦♦♦♦♦
Assembled shortly after Keith Whitley's death, *Greatest Hits* contains nine of his biggest hits—including the Top Ten singles "Ten Feet Away," "Don't Close Your Eyes," "When You Say Nothing at All," "I'm No Strangter to the Rain," "I Wonder Do You Think of Me," "It Ain't Nothing," and "I'm Over You"—plus two unreleased songs: a duet with wife Lorrie Morgan on "'Til a Tear Becomes a Rose" and a demo of "Tell Lorrie I Love Her." It's an excellent compilation, but it is a bit unbalanced, drawing almost entirely from *Don't Close Your Eyes* and *I Wonder Do You Think of Me*. Granted, those are his two best albums, but it would have been nice to have collected the highlights from his uneven first two solo records as well as the obvious hits. Nevertheless, *Greatest Hits* is the perfect record for fans that just want the hits. —*Thom Owens*

Kentucky Bluebird / 1991 / RCA ♦♦♦
Kentucky Bluebird is a posthumous album of unreleased Keith Whitley material that was issued a year after his 1989 death. This is a documentary of sorts, including Whitley's early appearance on *the Buddy Starcher Show*, a duet recorded with Earl Thomas Conley called "Brotherly Love," and live versions of favorites like "I Never Go Around Mirrors" and the title track. Especially interesting for dedicated fans are the interview segments included throughout. This is definitely not a first-purchase disc, but a recommended curio. —*Al Campbell*

The Essential Keith Whitley / Jun. 18, 1996 / RCA ♦♦♦♦♦
The Essential Keith Whitley is an excellent single-disc retrospective of the late country singer/songwriter, including such classic songs as "I Wonder Do You Think of Me," "If You Think I'm Crazy Now," "I'm Losing You All Over Again," and "Miami, My Amy." Although it concentrates on his earlier recordings, it is stil the best, most comprehensive collection assembled on the tragically short-lived country star. —*Thom Owens*

Sad Songs & Waltzes / 2000 / Rounder ♦♦♦♦
The origins of Keith Whitley's "new traditionalist" roots are readily evident on *Sad Songs & Waltzes*, a collection of some of classic country's most prolific songwriters' grittiest contributions. Available for the first time on CD, this album pulls together tracks from Whitley's work on J.D. Crowe's 1982 LP *Somewhere Between* and adds five previously unreleased songs, each filled with twang and heartache. Tastefully remixed by J.D. Crowe, the 15-song CD features Alison Krauss, Carl Jackson, and Diamond Rio's Gene Johnson and really captures the essence of Keith Whitley not only as a performer, but also as a true fan of country music. —*Zac Johnson*

RCA Country Legends / Mar. 5, 2002 / RCA ♦♦♦♦
This is an enjoyable sampler from one of the leaders of the new traditionalist movement, Keith Whitley. The 16 tracks stem from his mid- to late-'80s RCA material, including the hits "When You Say Nothing at All," "I'm No Stranger to the Rain," and "Ten Feet Away." Whitley's widow, Lorrie Morgan, appears on "'Til a Tear Becomes a Rose," which was released posthumously following Whitley's accidental death from alcohol poisoning in 1989. —*Al Campbell*

Ray Whitley

b. Dec. 5, 1901, Atlanta, GA, **d.** Feb. 21, 1979, California
Vocals / Cowboy
Singer/songwriter Ray Whitley was one of Hollywood's first cowboy crooners. Unlike Gene Autry, he remained a supporting actor and never starred in his own series of feature films, although he did make many musical film shorts during the mid-'30s. In tandem

with Fred Rose, he also co-penned some of Autry's best-loved songs, including "Back in the Saddle Again" and "Ages and Ages Ago." Whitley, born in Atlanta, initially played music only occasionally at community gatherings until discovering Jimmie Rodgers in the late '20s. He finally turned to professional performance when the Depression forced him into prolonged unemployment; his first gigs were with the Range Ramblers, later renamed the Six Bar Cowboys, who played the World Championship Rodeo up through the 1960s.

Ray Whitley made his recording debut in 1933, and finally came to Hollywood in 1936, where he made his feature film debut co-starring with William Boyd in *Hopalong Cassidy Returns.* Between 1938 and 1942, he made a series of short films for RKO, and also played the sidekick in a few Tim Holt films. His final film appearance came in 1956, playing the ranch manager in the James Dean classic *Giant.* During the 1950s, he briefly managed the Sons of the Pioneers and Jimmy Wakely. Whitley recorded through the late '70s and was a popular performer at cowboy film festivals, where he sang and demonstrated his considerable prowess with a bullwhip. He died in 1979 on a fishing trip to Mexico. *—Sandra Brennan*

Ray Whitley Sings His Favorite Songs / Circle D Video ♦♦♦♦

Slim Whitman (Ottis Dewey Whitman Jr.)

b. Jan. 20, 1924, Tampa, FL

Vocals, Guitar / Traditional Country, Cowboy, Folk-Pop, Country-Folk, Country-Pop

Though he was once known as "America's Favorite Folksinger," Slim Whitman was, for the majority of his career, more famous in Europe than in the United States. Best remembered for his early-'50s hit singles like "Love Song of the Waterfall," "Indian Love Call," and "Singing Hills," Whitman was an excellent yodeler known for singing mellow, romantic and clean-cut songs. As a child, Slim Whitman (born Ottis Dewey Whitman Jr.) became infatuated with music and learned to yodel listening to Montana Slim and Jimmie Rodgers records. At age 17, he married 15-year-old Geraldine Crist, a preacher's daughter. The newlyweds moved to a 40-acre farm south of Jacksonville, FL, where Whitman worked as a meat-packer. While working in the plant, he suffered an accident and lost two fingers on his left hand. After the accident, he began working in a Tampa shipyard. During World War II, Whitman served in the U.S. Navy, where he learned to play guitar.

Following the war, he returned to the shipyard and also joined a local minor-league baseball team, the Plant City Berries. Whitman remained with the team through 1948, but then began building a singing career at several Tampa radio stations, eventually creating a back-up band, the Variety Rhythm Boys. Slim Whitman got his first big break after Colonel Tom Parker—who was managing Eddy Arnold at the time—heard him singing on radio station WFLA. Parker landed a contract with RCA for Whitman by the end of 1948. After reluctantly complying with the label's request to change his first name to "Slim," he released his first single, "I'm Casting My Lasso Towards the Sky"—eventually to become his theme song. He made his national debut on the Mutual Network's *Smokey Mountain Hayride* in the summer of 1949, and the following year joined the *Louisiana Hayride.* Despite his national exposure, Whitman's career wasn't making much of an impact and he was forced to take a job as a part-time mailman.

In the early '50s, he released a cover of Bob Nolan's "Love Song of the Waterfall," which became his breakthrough hit, peaking at number ten on the country charts; the follow-up single, "Indian Love Call," made him a star, peaking at number two on the country charts and crossing over into the pop Top Ten. Both sides of his next single—"Keep It a Secret" / "My Heart Is Broken in Three"—were also major hits and he continued to have a string of Top Ten hits into the mid-'50s. In 1955, his title song for the film *Rose-Marie* became a smash on both sides of the Atlantic; following its success, Whitman joined the *Grand Ole Opry,* and then went to Britain in 1956 as the first country singer to play the London Palladium. Throughout the late '50s and early '60s, he had a string of British hits, including "Tumbling Tumbleweeds," "Unchain My Heart," and "I'll Take You Home Again Kathleen."

Although he was experiencing great success in the U.K., Whitman's career was in neutral in the U.S. After 1954's "Singing Hills," he had only two Top 40 hits in the course of a decade. In 1965, he bounced back into the country Top Ten with "More Than Yesterday." For the next few years, he had a series of minor country hits, including "Rainbows Are Back in Style" (1968), "Happy Street" (1968) and "Tomorrow Never Comes" (1970). Throughout the early '70s, he continued to have minor hits, but in 1974, he retired from active recording. In 1979, Whitman filmed a television commercial to support Suffolk Marketing's release of a collection of his greatest hits. On the strength of the commercials, *All My Best* sold four-million records and became the best-selling television-marketed album in history. After its success, the label released *Just for You* in 1980 and *The Best* in 1982. Between 1980 and 1984, Whitman had a small run of minor hits, highlighted by 1980's number-15 hit, "When." In the late '80s, he returned to television-marketed albums, releasing *Slim Whitman—Best Loved Favorites* in 1989 and *20 Precious Memories* in 1991. During the '90s, Whitman recorded infrequently but continued to tour successfully, particularly in Europe and Australia. *—Sandra Brennan*

I'm a Lonely Wanderer / 1963 / Bear Family ♦♦♦

Greatest Hits / 1990 / Curb ♦♦♦

Curb's *Greatest Hits* is a 12-track budget-priced collection that features some of Slim Whitman's biggest hits, including "Indian Love Call," "Secret Love," "Rose-Marie," "It's a Sin to Tell a Lie," "The Cattle Call" and "I Remember You." Although this isn't a bad budget-priced disc, there are better collections available, offering more songs, more hits and better sound for not much more money. *—Stephen Thomas Erlewine*

● **The Best of Slim Whitman (1952-1972)** / 1990 / Rhino ♦♦♦♦♦

Over its 17 tracks, *The Best of Slim Whitman (1952-1972)* runs through all of his Top 10 hits—from "Love Song of the Waterfall" to "Something Beautiful (To Remember)"—adding significant hit singles like "Cattle Call," "The Twelfth of Never," and "Rainbows Are Back in Style." Out of all the Whitman collections, nothing surpasses this one for selection and sound—it's the definitive compilation. *—Thom Owens*

Best Loved Favorites / 1991 / Vanguard ♦♦♦♦♦

Rose Marie / 1996 / Bear Family ♦♦♦♦♦

Rose Marie is a six-disc, 162-track box set containing all of Slim Whitman's recordings between 1949 and 1959, including all of his early sides for RCA Victor and his classic singles ("Singing Hills," "Indian Love Call," "Rose-Marie," "Love Song of the Waterfall") for Imperial Records. For any dedicated Slim Whitman fan, this lovingly assembled collection is necessary, though, due to its size, it is probably only of interest to devoted fans. Nevertheless, the box stands as the most comprehensive set ever assembled on Whitman's heyday, and it is unlikely to ever be surpassed in terms of sheer quantity and comprehensiveness. *—Stephen Thomas Erlewine*

Vintage Collections Series / Mar. 11, 1997 / Capitol ♦♦♦♦

For fans, *Vintage Collections* offers a concise view of Slim Whitman's hits; for the uninitiated, here is a chance to experience his otherworldly falsetto at a mid-level price. Although Capitol's *Vintage Collections* discs typically offer 20 tracks, the volume devoted to Whitman compiles only 15 songs. This compilation features all of his Top 40 hits (including "Indian Love Call" and "Rose-Marie"), two tracks previously unreleased in the U.S., and a few later hits from the '60s and '70s. *—Greg Adams*

Legendary / Apr. 11, 2000 / Castle ♦♦♦♦

Pure Country / Jan. 1, 2001 / Sony ♦♦♦

The Whitstein Brothers

f. Pineville, LA, **db.** Nov. 14, 2001

Group / Close Harmony, Traditional Country

The classic harmonies of the Whitstein Brothers evoked the brother duets that flourished in country music from the 1930s through the 1950s, especially resembling those of the Louvin Brothers. Robert & Charles Whitstein were born one year apart in Pineville, LA, to farmer R.C. Whitstein, who sang and played guitar on his own radio show in nearby Alexandria. The brothers grew up with seven other siblings, and their first exposure to harmony singing came from hearing their parents sing gospel music on Sundays. They learned music early, and before reaching their teens they had appeared on the television show *Country Time* and won local talent shows. They made their first recordings in their early teens; their debut single, "Louisiana Woman," became a local hit in 1962. Its success inspired the brothers to head for Nashville, where they billed themselves as the Whitt Brothers and toured with Faron Young, Porter Wagoner, and Little Jimmy Dickens. Both Whitsteins were drafted in the early '60s, and Robert served in Vietnam.

In 1969, after being discharged from the military, they returned home and recorded *The Whitstein Brothers Sing Gospel Songs of the Louvin Brothers* (their name was spelled "Whitstine" on the original release, but was corrected when Rounder released the album on CD in the 1990s). The album, a neglected classic in the brother-duet tradition, gained little attention, but the brothers continued to perform around Louisiana while working at other jobs; Robert Whitstein was a lumber contractor. Finally, in 1980, one of their concerts caught the ear of longtime Louisiana songwriter and talent spotter Tillman Franks, who had shepherded the career of Johnny Horton, among others. Dazzled by their virtuoso harmonies, Franks encouraged the brothers to move to Nashville.

Their pure duet sound, with mandolin and guitar in the foreground, made quite a splash among lovers of traditional country music, but it took them several years to land a recording contract—and when they did, it was with Massachusetts-based Rounder Records. Their 1984 debut for the label, *Rose of My Heart,* paid tribute to their forebears in the brother-duet tradition, mixing classic songs like "Kentucky" with original compositions in the same style and featuring top bluegrass players as sidemen. The Whitstein Brothers followed up *Rose of My Heart* with 1989's Grammy-nominated *Old Time Duets.* The brothers split up in the early '90s, and Charles Whitstein teamed up with Charlie Louvin in 1992 to record *Charlie Louvin and Charles Whitstein: Hoping That You're Hoping,* followed a year later by a live album recorded in Holland. In 1994, the Whitstein Brothers reunited and resumed recording together. They returned to Rounder for the 1996 album *Sweet Harmony,* which compromised their traditional sound not a bit even as its song selection included contemporary material such as Paul Simon's "The Sound of Silence." The brothers became major festival attractions and toured internationally, but their partnership was severed by Robert Whitstein's death on November 14, 2001. *—James Manheim*

● **Rose of My Heart** / 1984 / Rounder ♦♦♦♦♦

Trouble Ain't Nothin' but the Blues / 1987 / Rounder ♦♦♦

Old Time Duets / 1990 / Rounder ♦♦♦♦♦

On *Old Time Duets,* the Whitstein Bros. returned to pure traditional country, recording many songs that influenced them to begin playing country music. The Whitsteins play songs by the Louvin Brothers, the Blue Sky Boys and the Delmore Brothers, bringing these classic songs to life. It's an album that firmly establishes the duo as the heirs to the tradition of close harmony brother duets. *—Thom Owens*

Charlie Louvin and Charles Whitstein: Hoping That You're Hoping / 1992 / Copper Creek ♦♦♦

Sweet Harmony / Feb. 1996 / Rounder ♦♦♦♦

While no one can be expected to follow in the footsteps of the Louvin Brothers, arguably the greatest of country music's long history of brother acts (which also includes the Delmores, the Blue Sky Boys, and Charlie & Bill Monroe), the Whitstein Brothers are nonetheless keeping the tradition of harmonizing siblings very much alive—and creating wonderful music in the process. *Sweet Harmony* is Robert and Charles Whitstein's fifth album for Rounder Records, and it's a beautiful, acoustically-based mix of traditional (Roy Acuff, Louvin Brothers) and contemporary (David Olney, Paul Simon) material, lovingly rendered by the brothers' sweet, steady voices. *—Kurt Wolff*

The Wilburn Brothers

f. 1953

Group / Traditional Country

As members of the larger Wilburn Family group (mother, father, elder brothers, sister), nine-year-old Teddy (b. 1931) and ten-year-old Doyle (1930-1982) appeared on the *Opry* in 1940; 13 years later, when they had grown up, they became part of the *Opry*'s regular cast. With Jim & Jesse McReynolds and Bobby & Sonny Osborne, the Wilburns continue the tradition of brother duets in country music. Their wide choice of material is shown by the traditional "Knoxville Girl," a hit in 1959, and the more modern sound of "Hurt Her Once for Me" (1966). —*David Vinopal*

The Wilburn Brothers / 1957 / Decca ✦✦✦✦✦

The Big Heartbreak / 1960 / Deluxe ✦✦✦

The Wonderful Wilburn Brothers / 1961 / King ✦✦✦✦

Before signing to Decca, the Wilburns made some recordings for King Records, and 12 of those sides are collected here. The packaging offers no recording dates, session info, or liner notes, and the sound quality is poor. These tracks are unavailable elsewhere, though, which gives this disc a certain historical cache. The music is less polished and more acoustic than their later recordings, and there are a few standout tracks, including "Down in Dixie (Where They Say You-All)" and "Will You Be Ready (To Wear a Golden Crown)." Those with a specific interest in the Wilburn Brothers may enjoy these tracks despite the abysmal sound quality, but general listeners are advised to beware. —*Greg Adams*

Carefree Moments / 1962 / VL ✦✦✦

Trouble's Back in Town / 1963 / Decca ✦✦✦✦✦

This 18-track collection is the best one-stop overview of the brothers' biggest hits as well as their guest appearances with Webb Pierce and Ernest Tubb. As down-home country as their TV show and live appearances were, these tracks, in contrast, head straight for Music City, U.S.A. more and more with the passage of time, with the Anita Kerr Singers becoming a second chorus on their biggie "Trouble's Back in Town," a honky tonk tune of no little import. The early sides like "I Wanna Wanna Wanna" and "I'm So in Love With You" capture Doyle and Teddy at their exuberant best; their voices harmonize empathetically like all brothers acts do. With great notes and excellent transfers to recommend it, until a larger retrospective shows up, this is your best buy. —*Cub Koda*

The Wilburn Brothers! / 196_ / Design ✦✦✦

The ten cuts on this budget album are drawn from the Wilburn Brothers' early King recordings. All of these songs (plus two others) are reissued on the King CD *The Wonderful Wilburn Brothers*, but the Design album has better sound quality in spite of the reprocessed stereo effect. Not surprisingly, the Wilburns' arrangements on these early cuts are more old-fashioned than on their later Decca hits, with mandolin and what would be a '30s-style brother duo approach if not for the pervasive steel guitar. The material ranges from novelties ("Goose Pimples") to covers of recent hits like Tennessee Ernie Ford's "Anticipation Blues" and Hank Williams' "Long Gone Lonesome Blues." "Anticipation Blues" sounds more like Emmett Miller than Tennessee Ernie, which again shows how much of a throwback the Wilburns were at this point. These aren't their best performances but, for the traditionally minded, may be preferable to their later Nashville sound-era hits. —*Greg Adams*

● **Retrospective** / 1987 / MCA ✦✦✦✦✦

This nice overview of the Wilburn Brothers' smooth Decca hits of the '50s and '60s features 12 songs. —*Mark A. Humphrey*

Wilburn Brothers: Stars of Grand Ole Opry / Sep. 14, 1999 / First Generation ✦✦✦

This ten-song budget set draws on a cross section of recordings from the brothers of the *Grand Ole Opry*, the Wilburn Brothers. Highlights include "I Know a Goodbye When I See One," "Roll Muddy River," "Knoxville Girl," and "I'm Gonna Tie One on Tonight." While much of the Wilburn Brothers' material is out of print, this is a satisfactory introduction until their catalog on the Decca label is reissued. —*Al Campbell*

Wilco

f. 1994

Group / Alternative Pop/Rock, Alternative Country-Rock, Adult Alternative Pop/Rock

The alternative country band Wilco rose from the ashes of the seminal roots rockers Uncle Tupelo, who disbanded in 1994. While Jay Farrar, one of the group's two singer/songwriters, went on to form the band Son Volt, his ex-partner Jeff Tweedy established Wilco along with the remaining members of Tupelo's final incarnation, which included drummer Ken Coomer as well as part-time bandmates John Stirratt (bass) and Max Johnston (mandolin, banjo, fiddle, and lap steel). Guitarist Jay Bennett rounded out the group, which in 1995 issued their debut album, *A.M.*, a collection of spry country-rock tunes that followed the course established in Tweedy's earlier work. Wilco's sophomore effort, 1996's two-disc set *Being There*, marked a radical transformation in the group's sound; while remaining steeped in the style that earned Tweedy his reputation, the songs took unexpected detours into psychedelia, power pop, and soul, complete with orchestral touches and R&B horn flourishes. Shortly after the release of *Being There*, which most critics judged to be among the year's best releases, Johnston left the group to play with his sister, singer Michelle Shocked, and was replaced by guitarist Bob Egan of the band Freakwater. At the same time, while remaining full-time members of Wilco, Stirratt, Bennett, and Coomer also began performing together in the pop side project Courtesy Move. In 1998, Wilco collaborated with singer/songwriter Billy Bragg on *Mermaid Avenue*, a collection of performances based on unreleased material originally written by Woody Guthrie.

Their stunningly lush third album, *Summer Teeth*, followed in 1999 and met with critical acclaim but only average sales, initiating tensions with their label, Warner Bros. 2000 saw the release of *Mermaid Avenue, Vol. 2*, which featured more selections from the

band's collaborations with Bragg on Woody Guthrie's unfinished songs. Following this release, longtime drummer Ken Coomer decided to amicably leave the band and was replaced by the Chicago-based Glenn Kotche. The band then focused on recording their fourth album, *Yankee Hotel Foxtrot*, which ultimately led to the departure of guitarist Jay Bennett, and further tensions with their label. Unwilling to change the album to make it more "commercially viable," Wilco bought the finished studio tapes from Warner/Reprise for a reported $50,000 and left the label altogether. Leaked tracks from the album surfaced on the Internet in late 2001, and the stripped-down lineup of Tweedy, Kotche, Stirratt, and multi-instrumentalist Leroy Bach embarked on a small tour to support—or drum up support for—their unreleased album. Nonesuch Records picked up the album and the official release came out in early 2002 to widespread critical acclaim. Meanwhile, an independent film documenting the drama surrounding the album entitled *I Am Trying to Break Your Heart* followed in the fall of 2002. During the down time after the album was recorded, Tweedy composed and recorded the film score to the Ethan Hawke film *Chelsea Walls*, which ended up being released around the same time as *Yankee Hotel Foxtrot*. —*Jason Ankeny & Zac Johnson*

A.M. / Mar. 28, 1995 / Sire/Reprise ✦✦✦

Not surprisingly, Wilco's debut album, *A.M.*, isn't a great departure from Uncle Tupelo. Wilco's music rocks in a more conventional way than Uncle Tupelo, rolling along with a loping beat that swings more than it rocks. "Casino Queen" is a shambling, bluesy honky tonk number that's boozier than anything Tupelo recorded, which is indicative of the major difference between the bands. Wilco wears its heart on its sleeve, writing songs that fit into the conventions of country-rock, not ones that rework the rules. "Box Full of Letters" doesn't deviate from the standard midtempo country-rock number, yet it's done so well it doesn't matter. Still, the opener, "I Must Be High"—a clever love song that subtly tweaks both lyrical and musical clichés, as well as featuring a killer melody—casts a shadow over *A.M.*, offering the knowledge that Wilco can subvert the genre without losing its accessibility. In its light, all the very good songs that follow seem somewhat disappointing. —*Stephen Thomas Erlewine*

● **Being There** / Oct. 29, 1996 / Sire/Reprise ✦✦✦✦✦

While Wilco's debut, *A.M.*, spread its wings in an expectedly country-rock fashion, their sophomore effort, *Being There*, is the group's great leap forward, a masterful, wildly eclectic collection shot through with ambitions and ideas. Although a few songs remain rooted in their signature sound, here Jeff Tweedy and band are as fascinated by their music's possibilities as its origins, and they push the songs which make up this sprawling two-disc set down consistently surprising paths and byways. For starters, the opening "Misunderstood" is majestic psychedelia, built on studio trickery and string flourishes, while "I Got You (At the End of the Century)" is virtual power pop, right down to the hand-claps. The lovely "Someone Else's Song" borrows heavily from the Beatles' "Norwegian Wood," while the R&B-influenced boogie of "Monday" wouldn't sound at all out of place on *Exile on Main Street*; and on and on. The remarkable thing is how fresh all of these seeming clichés sound when reimagined with so much love and conviction; even the most traditional songs take unexpected twists and turns, never once sinking into mere imitation. "Music is my savior/I was named by rock & roll/I was maimed by rock & roll/I was tamed by rock & roll/I got my name from rock & roll," Tweedy sings on "Sunken Treasure," the opener of the second disc, and throughout the course of these 19 songs he explores rock as though he were tracing his family genealogy, fervently seeking to discover not only where he came from but also where he's going. With *Being There*, he finds what he's been looking for. —*Jason Ankeny*

Summer Teeth / Mar. 9, 1999 / Warner Bros. ✦✦✦✦

Jeff Tweedy once blazed the trail for the American rock underground's embrace of its country and folk roots, but as the decade draws to its close he's spearheading the return of classic pop; simply put, what once were fiddles on Wilco records are now violins—the same instrument, to be sure, but viewed with a radical shift in perception and meaning. While lacking the sheer breadth and ambition of the previous *Being There*, *Summer Teeth* is the most focused Wilco effort yet, honing the lessons of the last record to forge a majestic pop sound almost completely devoid of alt-country elements; the lush string arrangements and gorgeous harmonies of tracks like "She's a Jar" and "Pieholden Suite" suggest nothing less than a landlocked Brian Wilson, while more straightforward rockers like the opening "I Can't Stand It" bear the influence of everything from R&B to psychedelia. Still, for all of the superficial warmth and beauty of the record's arrangements, Tweedy's songs are perhaps his darkest and most haunting to date, bleak domestic dramas informed by recurring themes of alienation, adultery, and abuse—even the sunniest melodies mask moments of devastating power. If *Summer Teeth* has a precedent, it's peak-era Band; the album not only possesses a similar pastoral sensibility, but like Robbie Robertson and company before them, Wilco seems directly connected to a kind of American musical consciousness, not only rejuvenating our collective creative mythology, but adding new chapters to the legend with each successive record. —*Jason Ankeny*

Yankee Hotel Foxtrot / Apr. 23, 2002 / Nonesuch ✦✦✦✦

Few bands can call themselves contemporaries of both the heartbreakingly earnest self-destruction of Whiskeytown and the alienating experimentation of Radiohead's post-millennial releases, but on the painstaking *Yankee Hotel Foxtrot*, Wilco seem to have done just that. In early 2001, the Chicago-area band focused on recording their fourth album, which ultimately led to the departure of guitarist Jay Bennett and tensions with their record label. Unwilling to change the album to make it more commercially viable, the band bought the finished studio tapes from Warner/Reprise for $50,000 and left the label altogether. The turmoil surrounding the recording and distribution of the album in no way diminishes the sheer quality of the genre-spanning pop songs written by frontman Jeff Tweedy and his bandmates. After throwing off the limiting shackles of the alt-country tag that they had been saddled with through their 1996 double album *Being There*, Wilco experimented heavily with the elaborate constructs surrounding their simple melodies on *Summer Teeth*. The long-anticipated *Yankee Hotel Foxtrot* continues their genre-jumping and worthwhile experimentation. The sprawling, nonsensical "I Am Trying to Break Your Heart" is as charmingly bleak as anything Tweedy has written to date, while the positively joyous "Heavy Metal Drummer" jangles through bright choruses and summery reminiscences. Similarly, "Kamera" dispels the opening track's gray with a warm acoustic guitar and mixer/multi-instrumentalist/"fifth Beatle" Jim O'Rourke's unusual production. The true high points of the album are when the songwriting is at its most introspective, as it is during the heartwrenching "Ashes of American Flags," which takes on an eerie poignancy in the wake of the attacks at the World Trade Center. "All my lies are always wishes," Tweedy sings, "I know I would die if I could come back new." As is the case with many great artists, the evolution of the band can push the music into places that many listeners (and record companies for that matter) may not be comfortable with, but, in the case of Wilco, their growth has steadily led them into more progressive territory. While their songs still maintain the loose intimacy that was apparent on their debut *A.M.*, the music has matured to reveal a complexity that is rare in pop music, yet showcased perfectly on *Yankee Hotel Foxtrot*. —*Zac Johnson*

Honey Wilds (Lee David Wilds)

b. 1902

Vocals / Old-Timey, Traditional Country, Country Comedy, Minstrel

Revisionist history has largely erased the name of Honey Wilds from country music lore. His importance to the music's evolution remains unassailable: a Southern humorist and regular performer on the *Grand Ole Opry* between 1932 and 1952, Wilds was the creative force behind the *Opry*'s first tent tours, which were instrumental in bringing rural music to mass audiences. His recorded legacy was less substantial, resulting in only a handful of songs. Regardless, the reason why Wilds' name is frequently omitted from the official record is a simple—yet infinitely complex—one: he was a minstrel singer who performed in blackface for white audiences during the segregation era. Rather than serving as a painful reminder of America's past, he instead fell prey to the nation's notoriously selective memory, and has essentially vanished.

Although many of the details of his life remain sketchy, it is known that Lee David Wilds was born into abject poverty in southeastern Texas in 1902. His father, the owner of a brickyard, died of pneumonia at the age of 32. Wilds grew up in a racially mixed community, learning to play the blues from the black musicians who performed at a nearby theater. He also took up the ukelele. In the mid-'20s, he joined a minstrel show, forming a duo with Lasses White, a blackface comedian and veteran of vaudeville. White, who had earned his nickname as a child because of his sweet tooth, was known for giving his partners complementary stage names, and so Honey Wilds was born.

Although music accounted for a large share of Lasses and Honey's act, the two men were primarily comedians. They performed novelty songs, often parodies of current hits. Like Al Jolson and Emmett Miller before them, their act consisted of material appropriated from African-American culture, allowing white audiences the opportunity to experience, albeit secondhand, a form of entertainment which the society at large otherwise deemed wholly inappropriate. (There also existed a parallel circuit where black performers appeared in whiteface, again as a means of crossing color lines.) Most blackface performers insisted that their work sprung not from racism but from a deep admiration for black popular culture; the validity of such statements is debatable, although in Wilds' case it appears to be true, especially given his background and adult friendships with the likes of DeFord Bailey, one of country music's few black acts.

In 1932, Lasses and Honey were offered a six-week contract to perform at the *Opry*. Wilds ended up staying on for over two decades, his tenure broken only by a brief 1939 foray into Hollywood; although he soon returned to the *Opry*, both White and their mutual friend Chill Wills remained in California. Instead of going solo, Wilds formed another duo, Jam-Up and Honey, in 1940. Following his return from the West Coast, he also began pondering methods of improving the existing touring network, which consisted typically of two or three acts hitting the road together. With the *Opry*'s endorsement, he bought an 80-by-200 foot tent, assembled a road crew and a wide variety of entertainers, and began promoting the tour throughout the country. The *Opry* tent shows proved highly successful, running annually from early April to Labor Day between 1940 and 1949.

Despite close friendships with Hank Williams (according to legend, it was Wilds who nicknamed Hank Jr. "Bocephus"), Roy Acuff, Ernest Tubb, Red Foley, and other *Opry* staples, Wilds rarely wrote or recorded his own material, focusing instead on live performances. Among his few existing recordings include "Alabamy Bound," a traditional country blues, and "De Lion's Cage," an old Emmett Miller routine cut with producer Owen Bradley. In 1952, Jam-Up and Honey left the *Opry* to accept an offer in Knoxville; by that time, the duo no longer performed in blackface, and their act gradually fell out of favor. In 1957, the team split, and Wilds dropped out of music, running a service station until 1960, at which time he began hosting a local children's television program. By 1967, he had retired permanently, and died several years later. —*Jason Ankeny*

The Wilkinsons

Group / Contemporary Country, Country-Folk, New Traditionalist, Neo-Traditionalist Country

Belleville, Ontario's Steve, Amanda, and Tyler Wilkinson have enjoyed tremendous success since the release of their first single, "26 Cents." The Wilkinsons' debut album, *Nothing But Love*, gained them some momentum and notoriety while projecting a wholesome, family image of father, daughter, and son. Award nominations began pouring in, including CMA's Horizon Award and Vocal Group of the Year and the Academy of Country Music Awards' nomination for Single of the Year. The 2000 release of *Here and Now*, their second album, won the trio accolades with the Canadian Country Music

Association for Best Album. The smash single "Jimmy's Got a Girlfriend," featuring the vocals of a maturing Tyler, was the album's biggest success. *Shine* appeared in spring 2001. —*Rick Cohoon*

Nothing But Love / Aug. 11, 1998 / Warner Bros. ✦✦✦

● **Here and Now** / Apr. 4, 2000 / Warner Bros. ✦✦✦

This singing family delighted country music fans with their 1998 debut, *Nothing But Love*, which put "26 Cents" on the country charts and the Wilkinsons on the map. In less than a year's time, daughter Amanda, younger brother Tyler, and dad Steve earned an amazing 22 award nominations from the Academy of Country Music, the Country Music Association, the Canadian Country Music Association, and the Grammys. Their follow-up, *Here and Now*, mixes things up over the course of its 11 tracks, with Tyler on lead vocals for five songs. The Wilkinsons are truly a family collaboration, as Steve wrote six of the songs and Amanda and Tyler penned "It Was Only a Kiss." Amanda's vocals, Tyler's harmonies, and Steve's writing all contribute to one of the finest sophomore outings by a country group in a longtime. —*Maria Konicki Dinoia*

Jess Willard

d. May 26, 1959

Vocals / Traditional Country, Honky Tonk

Although his career as a recording artist lasted less than ten years, Jess Willard, a self-described "plain country boy," is remembered fondly for his cheerful personality as well as "Honky Tonk Hardwood Floor," which became a minor rockabilly standard. Born in 1916 four months after his namesake took the heavyweight championship from Jack Johnson, he hooked up with cowboy singer Jack Guthrie in the '40s, who became Willard's chief musical influence. After Guthrie died of TB in 1948, Willard vowed to carry on his name and music. He traveled to L.A. in 1949 and it was there that Capitol A&R man Lee Gillette heard him sing Guthrie's "Oklahoma Hills" while sitting in with Ole Rasmussen's band. Gillette signed Willard and on June 14, 1950, he had his first recording session with a hand-picked band that included Jimmy Bryant, Cliffie Stone, and Tex Atchison. After over two years at Capitol, (where he scored no hits), Willard toured the Far East with Eddie Hazlewood. In 1955, he toured with Eddie & Hank Cochran (the Cochran Brothers) and joined them for a number of *California Hayride* shows. He recorded his final single in 1959 before dying of a heart attack on May 26, 1959, aged 43. —*Jim Smith*

● **Honky Tonk Hardwood Floor** / Dec. 13, 2000 / Bear Family ✦✦✦✦✦

Jess Willard's Capitol recordings comprise one of the best obscure catalogs Bear Family has released. He was blessed to have an excellent assortment of material to sing— these songs sparkle both musically and lyrically—and Willard's irresistible, untrained delivery is a true delight. *Honky Tonk Hardwood Floor* covers his complete sessions from 1950-1952, as well as a pair of songs from the *California Hayride* shows with the Cochran Brothers in 1955. As great stuff unfolds and continues to unfold, it becomes clear that Willard was a genuine talent, and even though many of these songs bear the strong influence of Hank Williams and Lefty Frizzell, there are some excellent country boogies and proto-rockabilly numbers ("Honky Tonk Hardwood Floor" became a minor rockabilly standard). "Turn That Gun Around," in particular, is a hoot, full of dark humor and lucid imagery, and "My Mail Order Mama" and "Slippin' Around With Jole Blon" are terrific. There's a loose, cheerful sway to everything here, so much so that it's hard to believe how uncelebrated Willard has been to the community at large. That's the standard response from Bear Family aficionados, but let's face it, even their best finds don't always yield a whole album's worth of strong material. That's happily not the case here, and this is a disc that can be recommended unreservedly. —*Jim Smith*

Slim Willett (Winston Lee Moore)

b. Texas, **d.** 1966

Vocals / Traditional Country

Slim Willet was best known for writing "Don't Let the Stars Get in Your Eyes," a smash hit not only for himself but also Skeets McDonald and Ray Price. He was born Winston Lee Moore in Texas, and started out working in the aircraft industry in the late '40s. Near the decade's end, he became a regular on KRBC Abilene. In 1950, Willett founded the Hired Hands and made his recording debut with "Tool Pusher from Snyder." Before the year's end he had become a regular on WFAA Dallas' *Big D Jamboree*; he also joined Shreveport's *Louisiana Hayride* in 1951 and continued working on all three shows through the mid-'50s. Willet and his band debuted on the *Grand Ole Opry* in 1954, the year he launched his own label and released four singles, including "Star Light Waltz." By 1956, the band had split up, and Willet began working on KNIT Abilene, where he remained until 1964. Willet later purchased part of KCAD Abilene, where he worked until he died of heart failure in 1966. —*Sandra Brennan*

● **Slim Willett** / 1959 / Audio Lab ✦✦✦✦

Old Patch Songs / 1962 / Winston ✦✦✦

Don Williams

b. May 27, 1939, Floydada, TX

Guitar, Vocals / Traditional Country, Country-Pop

With his laid-back, straightforward vocals and large, imposing build, Don Williams came to be known as "the Gentle Giant." That nickname was bestowed on him in the early '70s, when he began a string of countrypolitan hits that ran into the early '90s. Williams was never known as an innovator, but his ballads were immensely popular; in the course of his career, he had a total of 17 number-one hits. Williams began playing guitar when he was child, learning the instrument from his mother. As a teenager, he played in a variety of country, rockabilly, folk, and rock & roll bands. After completing high-school, he formed his first band with a friend called Lofton Kline. Williams and

Kline recruited another singer, Susan Taylor, and formed the Pozo-Seco Singers, a folk-pop group, in 1964. The following year, the band signed a contract with Columbia Records. In 1966, the Pozo-Seco Singers had a pop hit with "Time," which climbed into the Top 50. For the next two years, they had a series of minor hits, highlighted by two Top 40 hits in late 1966, "I Can Make It With You" and "Look What You've Done." The group stayed until 1971.

After the Pozo-Seco Singers disbanded, Williams decided to pursue a career as a songwriter in Nashville, since he wasn't convinced that he was suited for a solo career. He signed with Jack Clement's Jack Music, Inc., initially just as a songwriter. By the end of 1972, he had signed with JMI as a solo artist, releasing "Don't You Believe" as his debut. The song went nowhere, but "The Shelter of Your Eyes" climbed to number 14 at the beginning of 1973. For the next year, Williams scored a string of minor hits before he had his 1974 breakthrough, "We Should Be Together," which reached number five. The single led to a contract with ABC/Dot.

"I Wouldn't Want to Live If You Didn't Love Me," his first single for ABC/Dot, reached number one in the summer 1974. The single launched a string of Top Ten hits that ran more or less uninterrupted until 1991; between 1974 and 1991, only four of his 46 charting singles didn't make the Top Ten. Instead of reaching the top of the charts with his original material, most of his big hits were covers of other songwriters, including John Prine, Bob McDill, Dave Loggins, and Wayland Holyfield. During the '70s, Don Williams became the most successful country artist in the world. His country-pop not only crossed over into the American pop mainstream, it also gained him a large following in England and Europe. In addition to his Top Ten hits, Williams won several country music awards, highlighted by the Country Music Association naming him Male Vocalist of the Year in 1978, the same year his number-one single "Tulsa Time" was named Single of the Year. In the late '70s, he began acting, appearing primarily in the films of his friend Burt Reynolds, including *W.W. and the Dixie Dancekings* and *Smokey and the Bandit II*.

In the early '80s, Williams slowed down the pace of his career slightly, as he was suffering from back problems. Nevertheless, the hits continued to come and many of his singles reached number one. In 1986, he left MCA Records—who had acquired the ABC label while he was recording for it—signing with Capitol. The change in labels didn't affect his career at all, as he continued to hit the Top Ten with regularity. In 1987, he underwent back surgery, which cured his problems. Williams signed with RCA Records in 1989. Initially, he continued to have hits, but his streak came to an end in early 1992, following his last Top Ten single, "Lord Have Mercy on a Country Boy." Although he continued to perform in the mid-'90s, he had effectively retired to his Nashville farm, returning to recording in 1998 with *I Turn the Page*. *—Stephen Thomas Erlewine*

Time / 1966 / Columbia ♦♦♦

I Can Make It with You / 1967 / Columbia ♦♦♦

Don Williams, Vol. 1 / 1973 / MCA ♦♦♦♦♦

Don Williams' first album as a country singer was originally released on Cowboy Jack Clement's JMI label before being snapped up by ABC-Dot the following year. There were four hits on this record; not a small feat for any artist much less on the first try. Over the years Williams has made some fine records but none better than this. *—Jim Worbois*

Don Williams, Vol. 2 / 1974 / JMI ♦♦♦♦

Don Williams, Vol. 3 / 1974 / MCA ♦♦♦♦

By the time he released *Don Williams, Vol. 3*, Williams had found his laid-back style and knew exactly what songs would exploit that sound to its fullest. That may mean that *Vol. 3* doesn't feel as immediate or fresh as *Vol. 1*, but that also doesn't necessarily mean that it's a lesser album. If anything, it's more consistent. From beginning to end, there's hardly a bad track on *Vol. 3*, with a number of songs—such as "The Ties That Bind," "Goodbye Isn't Really Good At All," "I Wouldn't Want to Live If You Didn't Love Me" and "I've Turned You to Stone"—qualifying as real gems. This is the record that catapulted Williams to stardom, and after just a cursory listen, it's easy to see why. *—Stephen Thomas Erlewine*

Greatest Hits / 1975 / MCA ♦♦♦♦♦

This compilation of hits from the first three albums represents only the tip of the Don Williams musical iceburg. While there is not a bad song on this collection it will only serve to make the listener anxious to find the records from which these songs came. *—Jim Worbois*

Greatest Hits, Vol. 1 / 1975 / MCA ♦♦♦♦♦

Greatest Hits, Vol. 1 contains 12 of Don Williams' biggest hits from the mid-'70s, including "Amanda," "Come Early Morning," "The Shelter of Your Eyes," "I Wouldn't Want to Live if You Didn't Love Me," "We Should Be Together" and "The Ties That Bind." In addition to the hits, the compilation contains first-rate album tracks like "Ghost Story" and "I Recall a Gypsy Woman," making it an excellent retrospective of Williams' early career. *—Thom Owens*

You're My Best Friend / 1975 / Dot ♦♦♦

Harmony, Vol. 3 / 1976 / MCA ♦♦♦♦♦

By the time *Harmony* came out, Eric Clapton and Pete Townshend were singing Don's praises and covering his songs. Williams had also begun to stretch out musically, making this the more interesting of the two albums. On *Vol. 3*, Williams continues in the vein of his first record. There's lots of good stuff, but it's not quite on par with the first album. *—Jim Worbois*

Greatest Country Hits / 1976 / Curb ♦♦♦

Greatest Country Hits only covers Williams' late-'80s chart successes, like "Heartbeat in the Darkness," "Then It's Love," and "We've Got a Good Fire Goin'." *—Jason Ankeny*

Country Boy / 1977 / MCA ♦♦♦♦

In retrospect, it's easy to see what a creative tear Don Williams was on when he was with ABC. It wasn't so much that he was able to draw great material from songwriters, but that he knew his strengths and weaknesses better than anyone else, he could produce his own records, and he drew on both of those things to make one fine album after another. With his partner, Garth Fundis, as engineer and in backing vocals, there was virtually nothing he couldn't accomplish. And while Williams is best known for his love songs, pro and con and broken, his reach extends to other themes as well. *Country Boy* is one of those extended reaches. The title track, a love song fantasy, is quickly followed up by the Bob McDill classic "Louisiana Saturday Night," a hit for Mel McDaniel a few years later. And Williams keeps turning these themes around one another for the entire album with his own crack band and a nine-piece string section. "Overlookin' and Underthinkin'" is a fractured love song, and it's followed by the consequences of a rural fool who is "Sneakin' Around." It happens again on side two with the celebratory "I've Got a Woman in You," immediately followed by "Rake and Ramblin' Man," with a character who is turned inside out by the possibility that he's not just the redneck he thinks he is. Williams is in full control of his destiny, but he lets the listener discover that the characters in his songs are not and they often make it up as they go. He's a magician with a silver voice who is pure country-soul, and on *Country Boy* that soul is bared for all to hear. *—Thom Jurek*

Visions / 1977 / ABC ♦♦♦

Visions isn't earth-shattering, but it is a standard Don Williams record, which means solid songwriting, spot-on phrasing, and the most laid-back vocal style to ever come out of Nashville. "Time on My Hands" and "Some Broken Hearts Never Mend," in particular, with their easy bounce juxtaposed against a melancholy lyric, are both classic examples of the Williams style of singing. *—Steve Kurutz*

Expressions / 1978 / ABC ♦♦♦♦♦

It's been said many times, but it's worth saying for eternity: There is no one with a voice like Don Williams. In its gentle, slow, and airy baritone drawl, it transfers emotions to a listener that perhaps the songwriter never even thought were in his tune. Williams had a very good year in 1978. *Expressions* is like a summing up of everywhere he'd been since the Pozo-Seco Singers and the places he was journeying to. Recorded at Cowboy Jack Clement's studio and produced by Williams with Garth Fundis, the album features a crack band that includes Johnny Gimble on fiddle and underground pedal steel ace Lloyd Green. On the opener, "I Would Like to See You Again," when Williams' voice enters over a mandolin strummed between the acoustic guitar's fingerpicking changes, the listener realizes that this is a Don Williams love song. Despite the fact that the beloved is nowhere in sight and hasn't been for some time, Williams delivers the wish as if it were a poem in her presence. The mood is followed by "You've Got a Hold on Me," with a killer country hook as Williams sings, "You're not even here/I'm in love with a memory...," and the truth in the lyric dawns on the listener. But it's not all love songs. Williams' read of the gem "Livin' on Tulsa Time" is a downright funky cowboy tune and uncharacteristically dirty and nasty. And then there's the second side, which opens with "Lay Down Beside Me," one of the most tender and moving songs Williams ever delivered. In fact, it becomes clear that this album is appropriately titled in that its ten tracks are *Expressions* on the state of the artist as an artist. The songs hold no bounds. All are stripped down to the essence of the emotion they communicate, whether it is joy, brokenness, loneliness, celebration, or quiet reflection and the touch of pain in the heart at old memories; they are all expressed as simply as possible by a singer whose empathy is unlike any other. "Give It to Me" is a track Johnny Lee wishes he's recorded first, and then "Not a Chance" is one of those sad songs where Williams' protagonist blames himself for his loneliness, his tenderness and love too deep to blame the one who wronged him. As the album closes with another sparsely orchestrated song on "When I'm With You," it becomes clear that the old cliché "it's the singer, not the song" is dead-on when it comes to Williams in particular and this devastatingly great record in general. *—Thom Jurek*

The Best of Don Williams, Vol. 2 / 1979 / MCA ♦♦♦♦♦

Most performers warrant a single-volume greatest-hits package. Legends sometimes get two depending on whether or not there was a major division in their career or they switched labels. Don Williams has three and he needs it. Here's the kicker: *Vol. 2* is a better collection than *Vol. 1* was. There are 11 tracks here, and they capture Williams at the absolute peak of his powers, the mid- to late '70s. While it's easy to complain that a track or two were left off or one was included that shouldn't have been, Williams satisfies all the arguments here by issuing the cuts that sold the best as singles, from "Love Me Tonight" and the Williams/Wayland Holyfield classic "'Till the Rivers All Run Dry" to "Some Broken Hearts Never Mend," "Rake and Ramblin' Man," "Falling in Love," "I've Got a Winner in You," "Say It Again," "Tulsa Time," "She Never Knew Me," and others, all but one produced by Williams ("Tulsa Time" is Williams and Garth Fundis). In sum, this is the sound Williams would patent and others would work so hard to copy in the 1980s. Cats like Johnny Lee, David Frizzell, Ronnie McDowell, and countless others ended up sounding like crummy pop singers while Williams never sounded like anything but a country singer. In the CD era it's possible to get all three best-ofs on a single two-disc collection, but whatever way they're available, find them. You won't be sorry. *—Thom Jurek*

☆ **I Believe in You** / 1980 / MCA ♦♦♦♦♦

Don Williams, whose star had been on the rise for nearly a decade, hit his pinnacle in 1980. *I Believe in You*, both single and album, were the best-selling recordings Williams had ever had—and this man had sold more than a few. From the mid-'70s on, Williams continued to refine a formula that didn't feel like one—choose the best songs from a proven stable of writers for your particular laid-back style of delivery, use the same musicians in the studio, and, along with your former engineer, produce the record yourself. It worked like a charm at ABC, and on MCA it worked even better. *I Believe in You* is the most seamlessly beautiful album Williams recorded since *Expressions*, and in terms of the quality of the material, maybe even eclipsed it, though it's a tough call. The free-flowing easy stroll of Williams' singing underscored by dreamy yet simple country arrangements on these ten songs is wondrous. Bob McDill wrote half this record, which includes such Williams staples as the faux Caribbean-flavored "I Want You Back Again," the shimmering "Falling Again," the folk-flavored outlaw country of "Simple Song," and side two's opening kicker, "Ain't It Amazing," as well as the closer, the airy and impressionistic "Slowly But Surely." He didn't pen the smash, though; a lilting country song dipped in early-'60s Bobby Darin rock that was authored by Roger Cook and Sam Hogin. In many ways it's far from the best song on the record, but it does have that slowpoke hook that sucked in virtually everybody who heard it. In sum, the album is solid track to track, without a weak moment, and gives Williams fans what they desired most: a collection of tunes that were all love songs no matter how they were framed, because no one, no one, sings a love song like Don Williams, even now. *—Thom Jurek*

Especially for You / 1981 / MCA ✦✦✦✦
A year after his biggest-selling record ever, the pressure was on Don Williams to deliver, and he did. While *Especially for You* didn't sell quite as well as *I Believe in You*, it sold plenty. Economics aside, it is—like all of Williams' work from the mid-'70s through the early '90s—remarkably consistent, full of great songs and the now trademark production sound of Williams and Garth Fundis. There are some new twists here as well. While the song catch this time out was as good as any, with contributions from Bob McDill, Rick Beresford, Roger Cook, Dave Hanner, and other cats in the band such as Dave Kirby and Charles Cochran, there are two covers here of a very special nature. The first is the album's opener, "Fair Weather Friends." Written by Joe Allen and Johnny Cash, the song feels as if it were written for Williams despite the steady but muted Cash rhythm that is ever present in the song. One can hear Cash's voice singing it too, as he has for years, but this version doesn't sound so much like a proclamation or exhortation, but like a fireside chat from an elder to a younger. The other is a duet with Emmylou Harris on a read of Townes Van Zandt's jewel "If I Needed You," which kicks off side two. Astonishingly faithful to the original and so ghostly in its slow, shimmering approach that it's almost not even there, it has the wallop of an emotional train wreck. Perhaps this track should have closed the set instead of opened its second half, because the voices of Harris and Williams move toward each other so effortlessly, so full of elegiac passion, that the other cuts can't complete, though they are excellent works. Oh well, at least the material is here and as an album it sticks up. *—Thom Jurek*

Prime Cuts / 1981 / Capitol ✦✦✦✦✦
Williams released four greatest-hits albums for MCA, so this is the fifth of his career. The R&B flavor of "Heartbeat in the Darkness" shakes up his approach. Much of the remainder is a thing of sparsely scored beauty. *—Tom Roland*

Listen to the Radio / 1982 / MCA ✦✦✦

Yellow Moon / 1983 / MCA ✦✦✦

Cafe Carolina / 1984 / MCA ✦✦✦
Williams has a very identifiable core sound, but occasional subtle differences can seem like major alterations. Here he recruits sax player Jim Horn, and while Horn doesn't play on every track, his mere presence provides a fresh change. *—Tom Roland*

The Best of Don Williams, Vol. 3 / 1984 / MCA ✦✦✦✦

Greatest Hits, Vol. 4 / 1985 / MCA ✦✦✦

New Moves / 1986 / Capitol ✦✦✦
In between MCA and RCA, Don Williams spent a few minutes at Capitol Records, where he, Garth Fundis, and the band put together a new collection of songs that had the most radical sounds for Williams on it. *New Moves* is Williams moving more consciously into a more pop-directed sound. In 1986 country was coming out of its most confused period. The new traditionalists were making waves led by Dwight Yoakam's razor-sharp return-to-Bakersfield charge and anchored by George Strait and Randy Travis. Garth what's-his-name (you know, the guy who wears department-store-bought curtains for shirts) was barely a blip on the screen at that moment. Williams, who had always been a mostly traditional country singer, decided it might be the time to investigate pop. While his sound is not radically different, there are some lovely highlights added to Williams' normally sparse yet elegant arrangements—a soulful horn section complete with saxophone solo and soul-styled bass riffing on the opener, "Heartbeat in the Darkness," which proved to be a big single. But experiment is all it was, because Williams remained a firmly committed country singer, as tracks like Bob McDill's "Shot Full of Love" and "We Got Love" attest to. Pat McLaughlin's hoedown jumper "Send Her Roses" is about the closest Williams had come to honky tonk since he began his career, and there is also the mariachi-flavored "Senorita" and Williams' own stunner, "The Light in Your Eyes," a love ballad so fraught with emotion and genuine tenderness it's amazing it could be captured in a recording studio. With a lilting viola and floating pedal steel sidling up next to a spare dobro and acoustic guitar, Williams comes shining through in the verses and is followed by a piano immediately after laying single notes and simple chords as texture. And then it happens: Williams sings a genuine—if modern—honky tonk tune that could have been recorded by Jerry Jeff Walker in Dennis Linde's "Then It's Love." These were new moves indeed, and though some critics had a tough time with them, the public loved the album and its singles. *—Thom Jurek*

☆ **20 Greatest Hits** / 1987 / MCA ✦✦✦✦✦
The best thing about Don Williams is that it's so hard to peg him against this, that or the other country music era. Hits like "Amanda," "You're My Best Friend," "I Believe in You," and "Good Ole Boys like Me," all present in this collection, are so understated it's as if they float on top of Nashville history. *—Dan Cooper*

One Good Well / 1989 / RCA ✦✦✦✦
Nine years after his biggest-selling album, *I Believe in You*, Don Williams was still racking up the hits, and would for a few more years yet. *One Good Well* was Williams' first album for RCA, and sold reasonably well, in part because the formula he and Garth Fundis had been using for the past 15 years worked with listeners, and in part because Williams' laid-back country sound is timeless. The years and cigarettes had taken some of the silk off of his voice, but he could still deliver a love song better than anybody on the block, younger or older. While "I've Been Loved By the Best" and "Just as Long as I Have You" were the biggest singles off the album, they aren't necessarily the album's finest cuts. The title track, written by the team of Kent Robbins & Mike Reid, is nearly a country gospel song sung as a rousing love anthem. Uncharacteristically, Williams himself contributed a song to the set, and "Cryin' Eyes" is one of the best things here, tempered with beautiful slow and elegant guitar solos and strings arranged by Charles Cochran. Another standout is Beth Nielsen Chapman's "Maybe That's All It Takes," with its nearly classical intro that seemingly floats into a stunning pop song arranged as such and colored texturally by pedal steel and strings. Williams is at his most restrained and precise here, but it feels like an intimate conversation, exactly the way Chapman herself writes and performs. *One Good Well* contains only nine tracks, and it leaves the listener wanting more; it also proves that, although slightly more scuffed, Williams' gift had retained its quiet power and majesty. *—Thom Jurek*

True Love / 1990 / RCA ✦✦✦
True Love includes the hits "Back in My Younger Days" and "Lord Have Mercy on a Country Boy." *—Jason Ankeny*

Currents / 1992 / RCA ✦✦✦✦
This contains such hits as "Catfish Bates," "The Old Trail," "Too Much Water," and more. *—AMG*

Lord I Hope This Day Is Good / 1993 / MCA ✦✦✦

Evening With Don Williams: Best Live / Jun. 28, 1994 / Unity ✦✦✦
Recorded live in Great Britain, *An Evening with Don Williams* is a very decent, if unnecessary, collection of live recordings that stray very little from the originals. Williams' smooth baritone is wrapped around each of the instantly endearing country hits, like "Good Ole Boys Like Me," "'Till the Rivers All Run Dry," "It Must Be Love" and "Lord, I Hope This Day is Good." No new ground is covered, but hardcore Williams fans will definitely want to check out *An Evening with Don Williams* if, for nothing else, the extensive interview at the end. *—Matt Fink*

Don Williams, Vol. 1/Don Williams, Vol. 2 / Mar. 25, 1997 / Edsel ✦✦✦
In 1996, Edsel released *Don Williams, Vol. 1/Don Williams, Vol. 2*, which contained two complete albums—*Don Williams, Vol. 1* and *Don Williams, Vol. 2*, both originally released on JMI in 1974—by country legend Don Williams on one compact disc. *—Tim Sendra*

I Turn the Page / Oct. 27, 1998 / Warner Bros. ✦✦✦
Don Williams' first major release after toiling around indieville for a half-decade is a real winner, a honky tonk reverie by a weathered cowboy turning his own page of life (this album was recorded when Williams was 59 years old). Wide-open stories of friendship, love, morality, and, yes, home on the range grace *I Turn the Page* with an elegance and sparkle that only a seasoned vet could bring to them. And while hints of his Nashville hit-making machinery from a couple decades past pops up occasionally (in the somewhat canned production and playing of the usual sidemen), Williams himself keeps the album in a relaxed mood, riding the rails of his heart and home with an emotional conviction that's soaked in ever-glowing sunshine. And his voice, once among country's most emblematic, has become an imperative tool, infused with gratitude and devotion to his life and everything it touches. *—Michael Gallucci*

20th Century Masters—The Millennium Collection: The Best of Don Williams, Vol. 1 / May 9, 2000 / MCA ✦✦✦✦
20th Century Masters—The Millennium Collection: The Best of Don Williams, Vol. 1 is a decent but not really necessary compilation of Williams' recordings for MCA, featuring 12 of his biggest hits from the '70s and early '80s. The problem is, nearly all of the songs are included on *20 Greatest Hits*, which offers a more thorough overview of Williams' career at a price that really isn't much more expensive than *The Millennium Collection*. The remastered sound is quite nice, but *20 Greatest Hits* remains the Williams compilation to get. *—Steve Huey*

★ **Anthology** / Oct. 17, 2000 / Hip-O ✦✦✦✦✦
Spanning two discs, 20 years, and 40 songs, Hip-O's *Anthology* is a definitive overview of Don Williams' hit-making peak, containing the cream of his chart-topping country smashes. It's neatly divided, with the first disc devoted to his '70s work, the second to his '80s, and if the first is a bit stronger, it's only because it's more interesting to hear an artist hit his stride than settling into a signature sound. Still, there are great moments throughout both discs, all offering definitive proof that Williams' laid-back, warm country-pop was as good as mainstream country-pop got—it was lush and accessible, but with real country roots, unlike many of his peers. *—Stephen Thomas Erlewine*

Live Greatest Hits, Vol. 2 / Apr. 17, 2001 / Row Music Group ✦✦✦
Country stalwart Don Williams provides a live set of his greatest hits on the aptly titled *Live Greatest Hits, Vol. 2*. The group he's assembled, including Mike Nobel and Billy Sanford on guitar, Charles Cochran on keyboards, drummer Brian Barnett, and bassist Dave Pomeroy, all turn in note-perfect renditions of Williams' hits, including "'Til the Rivers All Run Dry," "Back in My Younger Days," and the album's highlight, "I Believe in You." Recorded at different locations, Williams' voice sounds as smooth as it did in the '70s, and the live environment gives a new life to the songs. *—Zac Johnson*

20th Century Masters—The Millennium Collection: The Best of Don Williams, Vol. 2 / Sep. 25, 2001 / MCA ✦✦✦✦
The most iconic of Don Williams' songs, namely his '70s hits, were on his first volume of *20th Century Masters—The Millennium Collection*, leaving the second installment as a bit of "more of the best" as it draws on his biggest hits from the late '70s and, particularly, the '80s. This should not be taken as some sort of judgment on the quality of the material since it is quite high, even if it isn't terrific, like it was on the first volume. Don Williams was having hits for a longtime for a reason—his warm voice was perfectly suited for the laid-back country-pop of his era (indeed, he helped define its very sound), and even the second-tier, latter-day material is very, very good indeed, as this collection proves with hits like "I've Got a Winner in You," "Lay Down Beside Me," "It Must Be Love," and "Listen to the Radio." Hip-O's double-disc *Anthology* remains the best choice for serious listeners, but this is a fine choice for budget-minded fans looking for '80s hits from Williams. *—Stephen Thomas Erlewine*

Silver Turns to Gold / Jul. 23, 2002 / Row Music Group ✦✦✦✦✦
Silver Turns to Gold is an aptly titled CD for legend Don Williams; though age is bringing silver to his hair, his music is still solid gold. The album is exquisitely produced, and Williams' James Taylor-like vocals make the listener feel as if he/she is floating on a cloud. The liner notes of this quasi-tribute reveal that each of the songs holds special meaning for Williams, which is certainly why each one is crooned to perfection. The Nashville sound of "Pretend" is captivating, while the versatility of other album cuts, such as the cover of Rod Stewart's "Reason to Believe," prove Williams as one of country's top vocalists. As always, the songs are simple and to the point. Material from top industry songwriters Gordon Lightfoot and Carole King share disc space with Williams' own material and that of son Tim Williams. Altogether, this is some of the most sincere Don Williams music to date. *—Rick Cohoon*

Hank Williams

b. Sep. 17, 1923, Mount Olive, AL, **d.** Jan. 1, 1953, Oak Hill, WV
Guitar, Vocals / Traditional Country, Honky Tonk
Hank Williams is the father of contemporary country music. Williams was a superstar by the age of 25; he was dead at the age of 29. In those four short years, he established the rules for all the country performers that followed him and, in the process, much of popular music. Williams wrote a body of songs that became popular classics, and his direct, emotional lyrics and vocals became the standard for most popular performers. Williams lived a life as troubled and reckless as that depicted in his songs.

Hank Williams was born in Mount Olive, AL, on September 17, 1923. When he was eight years old, Williams was given a guitar by his mother. His musical education was provided by a local blues street singer, Rufus Payne, who was called Tee Tot. From Tee Tot, Williams learned how to play the guitar and sing the blues, which would come to provide a strong undercurrent in his songwriting. Williams began performing around the Georgiana and Greenville areas of Alabama in his early teens. His mother moved the family to Montgomery, AL, in 1937, where she opened a boarding house. In Montgomery, he formed a band called the Drifting Cowboys and landed a regular spot on a local radio station, WSFA, in 1941. During his shows, Williams would sing songs from his idol, Roy Acuff, as well as several other country hits of the day. WSFA dubbed him "the Singing Kid" and Williams stayed with the station for the rest of the decade.

Williams met Audrey Mae Sheppard, a farm girl from Banks, AL, in 1943 while he was playing a medicine show. The following year, the couple married and moved into Lilly's boarding house. Audrey became Williams' manager just before the marriage. By 1946, he was a local celebrity, but he was unable to make much headway nationally. That year, Hank Williams and Audrey visited Nashville with the intent of meeting songwriter/music publisher Fred Rose, one of the heads of Acuff-Rose Publishing. Rose liked Williams' songs and asked him to record two sessions for Sterling Records, which resulted in two singles. Both of the singles—"Never Again" in December 1946 and "Honky Tonkin'" in February 1947—were successful and Williams signed a contract with MGM Records early in 1947. Rose became the singer's manager and record producer.

"Move It on Over," released later in 1947, became Hank Williams' first single for MGM. It was an immediate hit, climbing into the country Top Five. By the summer of 1948, he had joined the *Louisiana Hayride*, appearing both on its tours and radio programs. "Honky Tonkin'" was released in 1948, followed by "I'm a Long Gone Daddy." While neither song was as successful as "Move It on Over," they were popular, with the latter peaking in the Top Ten. Early in 1949, he recorded "Lovesick Blues," a Tin Pan Alley song initially recorded by Emmett Miller and made popular by Rex Griffin. The single became a huge hit upon its release in the spring of 1949, staying at number one for 16 weeks and crossing over into the pop Top 25. Williams sang the song at the *Grand Ole Opry*, where he performed an unprecedented six encores. He had become a star. Hank and Audrey Williams had their first child, Randall Hank, in the spring of 1949. Also in the spring, Hank Williams assembled the most famous edition of the Drifting Cowboys, featuring guitarist Bob McNett, bassist Hillous Butrum, fiddler Jerry Rivers, and steel guitarist Don Helms. Soon, he and the band were earning $1,000 per concert and were selling out shows across the country. Williams had no fewer than seven hits in 1949 after "Lovesick Blues," including the Top Fives "Wedding Bells," "Mind Your Own Business," "You're Gonna Change (Or I'm Gonna Leave)," and "My Bucket's Got a Hole in It"; in addition to having a string of hit singles in 1950 including the number ones "Long Gone Lonesome Blues," "Why Don't You Love Me," and "Moanin' the Blues"; as well as the Top Tens "I Just Don't Like This Kind of Livin'," "My Son Calls Another Man Daddy," "They'll Never Take Her Love From Me," "Why Should We Try," and "Nobody's Lonesome for Me." That same year, Williams began recording a series of spiritual records under the name Luke the Drifter.

Williams continued to rack up hits in 1951, beginning with the Top Ten hit "Dear John" and its number one flip side "Cold Cold Heart." That same year, pop vocalist Tony Bennett recorded "Cold, Cold Heart" and had a hit, leading to a stream of covers from such mainstream artists as Jo Stafford, Guy Mitchell, Frankie Laine, Teresa Brewer, and several others. Williams had also begun to experience the fruits of crossover success, appearing on the Perry Como television show and being part of a package tour that also featured Bob Hope, Jack Benny, and Minny Pearl. In addition to "Dear John" and "Cold, Cold Heart," Williams had several other hits in 1951, including the number one "Hey, Good Lookin'" and "Howlin' at the Moon," "I Can't Help It (If I'm Still in Love With You)," "Crazy Heart," "Lonesome Whistle," and "Baby, We're Really in Love," which all charted in the Top Ten.

Though his professional career was soaring, Hank Williams' personal life was beginning to spin out of control. Before he became a star, he had a mild drinking problem, but it had been more or less controlled during his first few years of fame. However, as he began to earn large amounts of money and spend longtimes away from home, he began to drink frequently. Furthermore, Hank's marriage to Audrey was deteriorating. Not only were they fighting, resulting in occasional separations, but Audrey was trying to create her own recording career without any success. In the fall of 1951, Hank was on a hunting trip on his Tennessee farm when he tripped and fell, re-activating a dormant back injury. Williams began taking morphine and other pain killers for his back and quickly became addicted. In January of 1952, Hank and Audrey separated for a final time and he headed back to Montgomery to live with his mother. The hits were still coming fast for Williams, with "Honky Tonk Blues" hitting number two in the spring. In fact, he released five more singles in 1952—"Half As Much," "Jambalaya," "Settin' the Woods on Fire," "You Win Again," and "I'll Never Get Out of This World Alive"—which all went Top Ten. In spite of all of his success, Hank turned completely reckless in 1952, spending nearly all of his waking hours drunk and taking drugs, while he was frequently destroying property and playing with guns.

Williams left his mother in early spring, moving in with Ray Price in Nashville. In May, Audrey and Hank were officially divorced. She was awarded the house and their child, as well as half of his future royalties. Williams continued to play a large number of concerts, but he was always drunk during the show, or he missed the gig altogether. In August, the *Grand Ole Opry* fired Williams for that very reason. He was told that he could return once he was sober. Instead of heeding the *Opry*'s warning, he just sank deeper into his self-destructive behavior. Soon, his friends were leaving him, as the Drifting Cowboys began working with Ray Price and Fred Rose no longer supported him. Williams was still playing the *Louisiana Hayride*, but he was performing with local pickup bands and was earning reduced wages. That fall, he met Billie Jean Jones Eshlimar, the 19-year-old daughter of a Louisiana policeman. By October, they were married. Hank also signed an agreement to support the baby—who had yet to be delivered—of one of his other girlfriends, Bobbie Jett, in October. By the end of the year, Williams was having heart problems and Toby Marshall, a con-man doctor, was giving him various prescription drugs to help soothe the pain.

Hank Williams was scheduled to play a concert in Canton, OH, on January 1, 1953. He was scheduled to fly out of Knoxville, TN, on New Year's Eve, but the weather was so bad he had to hire a chauffeur to drive him to Ohio in his new Cadillac. Before they left for Ohio, Williams was injected with two shots of the vitamin B-12 and morphine by a doctor. Williams got into the backseat of the Cadillac with a bottle of whiskey and the teenage chauffeur headed out for Canton. The driver was stopped for speeding when the policeman noticed that Williams looked like a dead man. Williams was taken to a West Virginia hospital and he was officially declared dead at 7:00 AM on January 1, 1953. Hank Williams had died in the back of the Cadillac, on his way to a concert. The last single released in his lifetime was "I'll Never Get Out of This World Alive."

Hank Williams was buried in Montgomery, AL, three days later. His funeral drew a record crowd, larger than any crowd since Jefferson Davis was inaugurated as the President of the Confederacy in 1861. Dozens of country music stars attended, as did Audrey Williams, Billie Jean Jones, and Bobbie Jett, who happened to give birth to a daughter three days later. "I'll Never Get Out of This World Alive" reached number one immediately after his death and it was followed by a number of hit records throughout 1953, including the number ones "Your Cheatin' Heart," "Kaw-Liga," and "Take These Chains From My Heart." After his death, MGM wanted to keep issuing Hank Williams records, so they took some of his original demos and overdubbed bands onto the original recording. The first of these, "Weary Blues from Waitin'," was a hit but the others weren't quite as successful. In 1961, Hank Williams was one of the first inductees to the Country Music Hall of Fame. Throughout the '60s, Williams' records were released in overdubbed versions featuring heavy strings, as well as reprocessed stereo. For years, these bastardized versions were the only records in print and only in the '80s, when his music was released on compact disc, was his catalog restored to its original form. Even during those years when only overdubbed versions of his hits existed, Hank Williams' impact never diminished. His songs have become classics, his recordings have stood the test of time, and his life story is legendary. It's easy to see why Hank Williams is considered by many as the defining figure of country music. *—Stephen Thomas Erlewine*

Honky Tonkin' / 1957 / MGM ✦✦✦
A posthumous Hank Williams collection that's diametrical opposite of the *Luke the Drifter*, opening with "Jambalaya (On the Bayou)" and rolling through 11 more hot numbers, all about men and women who enjoy having a good-time. There's nothing not to love about this album as far as it goes, although, as with most of his other LPs, it has been supplanted many times by various CD releases. *—Bruce Eder*

Hank Williams as Luke the Drifter / 1962 / MGM ✦✦✦✦✦
An expanded version of a ten-inch LP from 1955, this album features a dozen songs cut by Hank Williams in a gospel/reverential vein in the guise of *Luke the Drifter*. For those unfamiliar with them, the songs are all well-chosen and they work within the context of devotional and cautionary songs, Williams easily slipping into this mode of performance, usually with a gospel organ accompaniment and very understated steel guitar—the one mood-breaker, much closer to Williams' secular material, is the upbeat, dark-humored, almost comical "Everything's Okay," which basically holds that "we're still a-livin'/so everything's okay." [As with most of MGM Records' posthumous Hank Williams releases, this album has been supplanted by the Polydor CD reissues of his work.] *—Bruce Eder*

On Stage! Hank Williams Recorded Live / 1962 / MGM ✦✦✦
One of MGM Records' countless posthumous albums of Hank Williams' music, *On Stage!* was of interest during the LP era for assembling 31 minutes of material from the October 1949 "Health and Happiness Show" broadcasts. Like the rest of Williams' LP catalog, this album has been supplanted by Polydor's late '90s release of the complete "Health and Happiness Show" recordings. At the time, however, it offered a glimpse of the Drifting Cowboys—Don Helms on steel guitar, Jerry Rivers on fiddle, Hillous Butrum playing bass, and Bob McNett on guitar—in their early days, and a look at what Williams was like in performance, although Audrey Williams is also present in these performances, sharing the stage with him. The annotation by Grant Turner is also very thorough, indicating that someone at MGM took Williams' legacy very seriously in those days. *—Bruce Eder*

Beyond the Sunset / 1963 / Mercury ✦✦✦✦
This is a classic session with Hank Williams assuming the role of Luke the Drifter. These stunning narratives will surely conjure up images of campfires and Sundays at the chapel. The selections are backed by organ, steel guitar, or his own acoustic guitar strumming, which has always been overlooked. Old favorites such as "Men With Broken Hearts," "I've Been Down That Road Before," and "Beyond the Sunset" are all treated with special care, but "The Funeral" is the session's most stirring moment. It is hard to believe that Hank Williams was still in his 20s (he died when he was 29) when this music was recorded. He is an American treasure and this is one of his most enduring recordings. Essential. *—Robert Taylor*

Kaw-Liga and Other Humorous Songs / 1965 / MGM ✦✦✦✦✦
Though humor probably isn't the first thing that comes to mind when remembering the music of Hank Williams, he probably should receive more credit for his rather sharp wit, finding the tragic irony in the lives of the characters in his songs. That being said, this collection, despite having some classic material like "Move It on Over," "Honky Tonk Blues," and "Mind Your Own Business," contains too many of Williams' spoken recitations like "Just Waitin'," "Everything's Okay," and "I've Been Down That Road Before" to be considered a real quality collection; plus, it's not always that easy to hear the real humor in songs like "I'll Never Get Out of This World Alive" and "Nobody's Lonesome for Me" in the first place. *—Matt Fink*

The Legend Lives Anew (Hank Williams with Strings) / 1966 / MGM ✦✦

24 of Hank Williams' Greatest Hits / 1970 / MGM ✦✦✦✦✦
24 of Hank Williams' Greatest Hits was originally released as a set of overdubbed recordings, where the spare original recordings were augmented by a fuller band and, occasionally, strings. In the '80s, Mercury reissued the album with the original, undubbed versions of the songs and this version stands as an excellent retrospective of Williams' finest moments, containing a wealth of tremendous, timeless songs like "Your Cheatin' Heart," "I'm So Lonesome I Could Cry," "Honky Tonk Blues," "Cold, Cold Heart," "Mind Your Own Business," "Hey Good Lookin'," and "Jambalaya," among others. It's an excellent introduction, but *40 Greatest Hits* offers a deeper selection and, therefore, is an even better starting point. *—Stephen Thomas Erlewine*

24 Greatest Hits, Vol. 2 / 1976 / Polygram ✦✦✦✦
When compared with *40 Greatest Hits* (which came out the following year), this record is light on both tracks and liner notes. Adding insult to injury, these tracks are also offered in simulated stereo. OK, but there are better packages. *—Jim Worbois*

★ **40 Greatest Hits** / 1978 / Mercury ✦✦✦✦✦
Hank Williams' body of work is so large and has been repackaged so many times in so many forms that the notion of creating a definitive compilation almost seems like an impossible goal. However, as a one-stop shopping place for Hank's basic repertoire, *40 Greatest Hits* is as good as it gets. While it doesn't include everything, practically every memorable hit is here, and thankfully every cut appears in its original form (that means in mono, with no string overdubs or artificial duets with his family members). The track sequence subtly reflects the arc of Williams' short but vitally important career, and there's enough good music and great songs here to make a fan of anyone with even a passing interest in American music. If you care about country music, you need some Hank Williams in your collection, and there isn't a better introduction to his rich body of work on the market than *40 Greatest Hits*; begin here, then start exploring. *—Mark Deming*

☆ **I Ain't Got Nothin' But Time (December 1946–April 1947): Vol. 1** / Jan. 1985 / Mercury ✦✦✦✦✦
I Ain't Got Nothin' But Time (December 1946-April 1947): Vol. 1, kicked off Polydor's eight-volume reissue series of Hank Williams' complete recorded works. Though the series did eventually leave several demos, radio performances, and live tracks in the can, those were later issued in a variety of other formats. The eight-volume series did contain all of Williams' studio recordings, plus the bulk of his home recordings and live tracks. What makes the series especially interesting is how his great songs are placed in context with the large variety of material Williams also performed. For instance, on *I Ain't Got Nothin' But Time*, "Honky Tonkin'," "Move It on Over," and "I Saw the Light" sit next to a batch of gospel recordings ("Battle of Armageddon," "Wealth Won't Save Your Soul") as well as home versions of Western and Western swing songs ("Cool Water," "Roly Poly"). It's an endlessly fascinating listen, especially for Williams fans who only know *40 Greatest Hits*, or even *The Complete Singles Collection*. A wealth of hidden gems, as well as several lesser, but still enjoyable, songs are on each volume, and each collection is essential for any serious Williams fan, or any country music historian. Since it contains his very first recordings, *I Ain't Got Nothin' But Time* is sparse and direct, which gives the songs—largely comprised of gospel numbers—more weight. Highlights including "Calling You," "My Love for You Has Turned to Hate," "(Last Night) I Heard You Crying in Your Sleep)," and the non-session "Alone and Forsaken" in addition to the aforementioned hits. *—Stephen Thomas Erlewine*

☆ **Lovesick Blues (August 1947–December 1948): Vol. 2** / Feb. 1985 / Mercury ✦✦✦✦✦
Among the material on *Lovesick Blues (August 1947-December 1948): Vol. 2*, the second volume of Polydor's series of Hank Williams' complete recorded works, is "Lovesick Blues"; the single that made him a star and that song illustrate the difference between this volume and its predecessor, *I Ain't Got Nothin' But Time*. By and large, the secular music on *Lovesick Blues* is lighter than the gospel that dominated the first volume—the majority of the songs are pure honky tonk, whether its the rollicking boogie of "Rootie Tootie" and "Fly Trouble," the gritty "Honky Tonkin'" and "I'm a Long Gone Daddy," or the wrenching ballad "A Mansion on the Hill." Among the other highlights of a disc filled with uniformly excellent songs are the session recordings "I'm Satisfied With You" and "I'll Be a Bachelor 'Til I Die," the overdubbed nonsession recording "We Live in Two Different Worlds," and the non-session recordings "Please Don't Let Me Love You" and "Weary Blues From Waitin'." *—Stephen Thomas Erlewine*

☆ **Lost Highway (December 1948–March 1949): Vol. 3** / Jan. 1986 / Mercury ✦✦✦✦✦
Though "Lovesick Blues" made Hank Williams into a star, it didn't become successful until March of 1949, which means the material that comprises *Lost Highway (December 1948-March 1949): Vol. 3* was all recorded before he knew it was a hit. As a result, the music on *Lost Highway* is a bit uneven, since the future of Williams' recording career was uncertain; he wasn't sure whether his records would sell, and he consequently performed a couple of his most unfocused sessions. The session recordings on *Lost Highway* do contain several classics—"Honky Tonk Blues" (presented in a rocking alternate take), "Mind Your Own Business," and the title track—but there are also several awkward duets with his wife Audrey ("Lost on the River," "I Heard My Mother Praying for Me"). The true gems on *Lost Highway* arrive in the non-session recordings. The overdubbed non-session recordings contain the excellent "A Teardrop on a Rose," "I'm Going Home," and "The Angel of Death," while the undubbed non-session recordings contain "Singing Waterfall," "I'm Free at Last," and "Alabama Waltz." *—Stephen Thomas Erlewine*

☆ **I'm So Lonesome I Could Cry (March 1949–August 1949): Vol. 4** / Feb. 1986 / Mercury ✦✦✦✦✦
With much of the material on *I'm So Lonesome I Could Cry (March 1949-August 1949): Vol. 4*, Hank Williams began to reveal his personal demons through his songs—"I'm So Lonesome I Could Cry," "I Just Don't Like This Kind of Living," "You're Gonna Change (Or I'm Gonna Leave)," "A House Without Love," and the initial, non-hit version of "My Son Calls Another Man Daddy" all cut close to the bone. Ironically, his career was riding high at the time, with songs like "Wedding Bells," "You're Gonna Change (Or I'm Gonna Leave)," and "My Bucket's Got a Hole In It" peaking in the upper reaches of the country Top Ten. The aforementioned songs comprise the bulk of the session recordings on *I'm So Lonesome I Could Cry* and the non-session recordings are just as strong as the official recordings. Most of the overdubbed non-session songs on the compilation are first-rate gospel ("Are You Building a Temple in Heaven," "How Can You Refuse Him Now"), while the undubbed tracks contain such gems as a demo of "Fool About You," "No One Will Ever Know," "If You'll Be a Baby (To Me)," and "We're Getting Closer to the Grave Each Day." *—Stephen Thomas Erlewine*

☆ **The Collector's Edition** / 1987 / Mercury ✦✦✦✦✦
After completing an excellent, comprehensive reissue of every recording Hank Williams made during his life, Polygram and Mercury packaged the eight discs together in the indispensable box set *The Collector's Edition*. Since it is difficult to buy one installment in the series without wanting the remaining volumes, the box is the best way to purchase the series. However, during the mid-'90s, *The Collector's Edition* became difficult to find, since Polygram/Mercury inexplicably took the set, as well as the eight individual discs, off the general market. The record company made a deal with Tower Records, and the chain became the only retailer to sell Williams' complete recordings as of the mid-'90s. And, Tower only sells the eight discs as *The Collector's Edition* box, which means that the set is the only way to purchase the complete recordings of country music's most important artist. It may take a little time to track it down, but for any serious country fan, *The Collector's Edition* is worth the effort. *—Stephen Thomas Erlewine*

☆ **Long Gone Lonesome Blues (August 1949–December 1950): Vol. 5** / Jan. 1987 / Mercury ✦✦✦✦✦
Among the highlights of the studio recordings on *Long Gone Lonesome Blues (August 1949-December 1950): Vol. 5* are the hit singles "Long Gone Lonesome Blues," "Why Don't You Love Me?," "My Son Calls Another Man Daddy," "They'll Never Take Her Love From Me," "Nobody's Lonesome for Me," "Moanin' the Blues," and "Cold, Cold Heart"—in fact, out of the eight studio sessions on the collection, only "Why Should We Try Anymore?" failed to chart. The rest of the compilation consists of a handful of overdubbed non-session recordings and live tracks, as well as several excellent undubbed non-sessions songs ("Low Down Blues," "It Just Don't Matter Now," "There's No Room in My Heart for the Blues," "Last Night I Dreamed of Heaven"), and the first Luke the Drifter recordings (including "Too Many Parties and Too Many Pals," "The Funeral," and "Everything's Okay"). *—Stephen Thomas Erlewine*

☆ **Hey, Good Lookin' (December 1950–July 1951): Vol. 6** / Feb. 1987 / Mercury ✦✦✦✦✦
Out of the ten studio recordings on *Hey, Good Lookin' (December 1950-July 1951): Vol. 6*, no less than six—"Dear John," "I Can't Help It (If I'm Still in Love With You)," "Howlin' at the Moon," "Hey Good Lookin'," "(I Heard That) Lonesome Whistle," and "Crazy Heart"—were hits, while two of the four remaining cuts ("My Heart Would Know," "I'd Still Want You") were nearly as strong as the well-known songs. The other two, "The Pale Horse and His Rider" and "A Home in Heaven," were duets with Williams' wife, Audrey, and while they were better than most of their collaborations, her voice remains tuneless and painful.

The pair of live tracks are engaging, but the undubbed non-session recordings are the real hidden gems; all three songs ("The Angel of Death," "I Can't Escape From You," "Message to My Mother") are haunting and evocative. The remainder of *Hey, Good Lookin'* is comprised of six Luke the Drifter recordings, and while they are strong (particularly "Ramblin' Man," "A Picture From Life's Other Side," and "I've Been Down That Road Before"), they pale slightly to the rest of the compilation. *—Stephen Thomas Erlewine*

☆ **Let's Turn Back the Years (July 1951–June 1952): Vol. 7** / Mar. 1987 / Mercury ✦✦✦✦✦
Hank Williams' life was beginning to unravel during the time he recorded the material on *Let's Turn Back the Years (July 1951-June 1952): Vol. 7*, yet that didn't mean his music suffered. In fact, much of *Let's Turn Back the Years* ranks among his best work. Among the hits on the ten studio tracks included on the disc are "Crazy Heart," "Half As Much," "Baby, We're Really in Love," "Honky Tonk Blues," "Jambalaya (On the Bayou)," and "I'll Never Get out of This World Alive." The studio tracks also include the fine "I'm Sorry for You, My Friend," "Window Shopping," and the title track. While the overdubbed and group non-session recordings are good gospel, the true gems of the non-session material arrive in the undubbed recordings, which include such simple and affecting performances as "Thank God," "Someday You'll Call My Name," "How Can You Refuse Him Now?," "When You're Tired of Breaking Other Hearts," and "A Teardrop on a Rose." *—Stephen Thomas Erlewine*

☆ **I Won't Be Home No More (June 1952–September 1952): Vol. 8)** / Apr. 1987 / Mercury ✦✦✦✦✦
The music on *I Won't be Home No More (June 1952-September 1952) Vol. 8*, is the last that Hank Williams recorded, and his inner demons and personal traumas are evident throughout the compilation. There are a couple of lighthearted songs on *I Won't Be Home No More*, namely "Settin' the Woods on Fire" and "Kaw-Liga," and they stand out among the unflinching despair and sorrow that comprises the remainder of the collection. In addition to the two previously mentioned songs, the studio recordings feature "You Win Again," "I Won't Be Home No More," "I Could Never Be Ashamed of You," "Your Cheatin' Heart," and "Take These Chains From My Heart." While the studio tracks are all chilling in their emotional immediacy, the remaining live cuts, Luke the Drifter sides, and non-session recordings are even more haunting, with "Mother Is Gone," "A House of Gold," "Ready to Go Home," and "Why Don't You Make Up Your Mind" ranking as some of the highlights. *I Won't Be Home No More* is supremely affecting, containing some of the finest music Hank Williams ever recorded. *—Stephen Thomas Erlewine*

Rare Demos: First to Last / 1990 / Country Music Foundation ✦✦✦✦✦
Rare Demos: First to Last compiles all 24 publisher's demos that the country Music Foundation originally released as *The First Recordings* and *Just Me and My Guitar*. These are stark, moving recordings that cut to the core of each songs. Though the master takes are masterpieces in their own right, the demo versions are equally essential for dedicated fans, since they offer new insights to Williams' songwriting, as well as his performance technique. *—Stephen Thomas Erlewine*

Greatest Hits / Oct. 17, 1990 / Polygram ✦✦✦✦

☆ **Original Singles Collection . . . Plus** / 1992 / Mercury ✦✦✦✦✦
The title of *The Original Singles Collection . . . Plus* is slightly misleading. Although PolyGram marketed the three-disc, 84-song set as a complete collection, it doesn't feature all of the singles Hank Williams released during his lifetime. Several singles Williams released under the pseudonym "Luke the Drifter" as well all of the duets he cut with Audrey Williams aren't present. Despite these handful of songs, *everything* else is included in their original, undubbed versions and are presented in the best sound possible. For a fan that wants all the essential songs without springing for the eight disc series of complete recordings, *The Original Singles* collection is invaluable. *—Stephen Thomas Erlewine*

Health & Happiness Shows / 1993 / Mercury ✦✦✦✦✦
The double-disc set *Health & Happinesss Shows* collects eight complete radio shows that Hank Williams recorded in 1949, when his career was just taking off. Throughout the collection, Williams sounds energetic and vibrant, even during his between-song stage patter which is nearly fascinating as the music. It's a set that is designed for collectors, but even casual Williams fans will find much to treasure on the *Health & Happiness Shows*. *—Stephen Thomas Erlewine*

Alone & Forsaken / Apr. 25, 1995 / Mercury ✦✦✦
Even the most casual music fan should be able to scrape together the cash for the still-unbeatable *40 Greatest Hits*, if not the three-disc *Original Singles Collection . . . Plus More* or the monumental ten-CD *The Complete Hank Williams*. The unrepentant cheapskate, however, could do worse than this strange 17-track compilation. The songs were chosen by The The frontman Matt Johnson (he contributes written comments to the liner notes and a spoken introduction to the album). Johnson's morose sensibilities clearly influenced the choice of songs; upbeat classics like "Hey Good Lookin'" are nowhere to be found. There are enough genuine essentials ("Lost Highway," "I Saw the Light," "I'm So Lonesome I Could Cry"), though, to satisfy those whose curiosity is limited, and the four non-session demos that round out the set may help collectors with light pockets forget about all the rare treasures included in more expensive packages. The idiosyncratic track selection makes this both less and more than a traditional greatest-hits album. A cynic might question whether it will reach the college rock hipsters whom Johnson intends to lure, but only a fanatic could argue that it is a less-than-satisfying listen. *—Daniel Browne*

Low Down Blues / Aug. 20, 1996 / Polygram ✦✦
Low Down Blues is a mid-priced compilation of Hank Williams' bluesiest material. The 16-track collection features classics like "Honky Tonk Blues," "Lovesick Blues," "Moanin' the Blues," and "Long Gone Lonesome Blues," as well as five demo recordings. As a sampler, *Low Down Blues* is fine—it offers a different perspective on Hank than most other collections and it was thoughtfully compiled—but serious collectors will want to stick with the more complete compilations and casual fans will be better-served by either *40 Greatest Hits* or *24 Greatest Hits*. And that means *Low Down Blues* essentially doesn't have an audience. It's a nice collection, but it essentially purposeless. Only collectors who enjoying hearing the subtle differences in different sequencing will find *Low Down Blues* essential. *—Stephen Thomas Erlewine*

☆ **The Complete Hank Williams** / Sep. 22, 1998 / Mercury ✦✦✦✦✦
Between 1986 and 1987, Mercury launched its first effort to chronicle Hank Williams' complete recorded works, releasing a series of eight double albums/single CDs which were later collected as a box set. Both the individual compilations and the box set were pulled from the market in the '90s, clearing the way for *The Complete Hank Williams*, a ten-disc box set which purported to contain all of Williams' recordings. Mercury, however, played it a little loose with their terms, deciding that "complete" covers the studio recordings, demos, and selected live performances, leaving overdubbed tracks and many live cuts (including much of *The Health and Happiness Shows*, which was released as a separate collection) in the vaults. This is bound to frustrate some collectors, but it makes for a better listen, actually. Instead of piling all the recordings into an impenetrable chronological trawl through Williams' recording life, the compilers logically devoted specific discs to the studio sessions, live cuts, and demos. In particular, the studio discs are quite compelling, but for hardcore fans, the previously unheard live performances (including several songs that Williams only performed in concert) are the real treasures. Then again, only hardcore fans will invest in such a lavish, extensive box set as *The Complete Hank Williams*, and there's little question that they'll be quite pleased with it. *—Stephen Thomas Erlewine*

There's Nothing as Sweet as My Baby / 1999 / Mount Olive ✦✦✦
There's Nothing as Sweet as My Baby is a documentation of a 1951 radio transcription that features rowdy, exciting takes of several country classics, as well as Hank's versions of contemporary songs. There might not be many of his big hits, but listeners buying this album aren't looking for hits, they're looking for revelations and *There's Nothing as Sweet as My Baby* is full of them. Williams turns in terrific versions of "Cherokee Boogie," "Blue Eyes Crying in the Rain," "Lonely Tombs," and "I Can't Help It (If I'm Still In Love With You)," and there is a brief interview, as well as a song by his wife, Audrey Williams. It's an excellent addition to a comprehensive Hank Williams collection, and perfect for fans of the double-disc set *Health & Happiness Shows*. *—Stephen Thomas Erlewine*

Live at the Grand Ole Opry / Sep. 28, 1999 / Mercury ✦✦✦
This two-disc set brings together every extant performance from Hank Williams' brief hookup with the *Opry*. The first disc collects 21 performances, both musical and in the company of *Opry* comedy regulars Minnie Pearl and Rod Brasfield. To give a sense of how his presence worked in the format of the show, the second disc is a complete *Opry* broadcast from 1950 with Williams as part of the cast that also features Red Foley, Wally Fowler and the Oak Ridge Quartet (forerunners of today's Oak Ridge Boys), Minnie Pearl, Claude Sharpe and the Old Hickory Singers, and blackface comedians Jamup and Honey. Whether he's singing one of his famous hits or an old gospel favorite, or playing straight man to Brasfield or Pearl, it's obvious that here was a performer with personality aplenty, and it comes across on these old acetates with amazing impact. *—Cub Koda*

20th Century Masters—The Millennium Collection: The Best of Hank Williams / Oct. 19, 1999 / Mercury ✦✦✦
The Hank Williams volume of *20th Century Masters: The Millennium Collection* is a good, basic compilation of Williams' highlights, featuring such timeless tunes as "Hey, Good Lookin'," "Jambalaya," "Move It On Over," "Honky Tonk Blues," "Why Don't You Love Me," "Honky Tonkin'," "I Saw the Light," and "Lovesick Blues." Yes, there are some major songs missing—"I'm So Lonesome I Could Cry," "You Win Again," "A Mansion on the Hill," "My Bucket's Got a Hole in It," "Half as Much," and "My Son Calls Another Many Daddy," among others—but this is fine as a budget-line sampler for casual fans. It's not the best compilation in his catalog, but it doesn't have a bum track on it, and it's a mighty fine listen. *—Stephen Thomas Erlewine*

Alone with His Guitar / Sep. 19, 2000 / Mercury ✦✦✦
A real treat for Hank-o-philes who really drooled over the few gritty demo recordings that appeared on the extensive box set *The Complete of Hank Williams*. Leading off with the previously unreleased "Tennessee Border," ten of the 18 cuts here come from early 1949 appearances on Shreveport, Louisiana's KWKH; and the rest are demo recordings made to pitch songs to his label. These provide a warm, intimate look at a man playing songs on his guitar that would change the world. *—Zac Johnson*

I Saw the Light / Feb. 27, 2001 / Mercury ✦✦✦✦✦
Every bit as essential as his country hits, *I Saw the Light* is an excellent testament to the songwriting genius of Hank Williams. A very spirited and, at times, utterly beautiful collection that has to rank with the best country-gospel albums ever made; these perfectly crafted songs might take Williams out of the honky tonk, but they can't take the honky tonk out of Williams' sound, as the tracks sound contemporary to anything else in his catalog. Standout harmonies on "How Can You Refuse Him Now" and "Jesus Remembered Me" to the just plain frightening "Angel of Death" and the poignant "Wealth Won't Save Your Soul" rank with Williams' best work. Overall, a truly essential piece in the viewing of Hank Williams' entire body of work. *—Matt Fink*

Blues Come Around / Jun. 26, 2001 / Catfish ✦✦✦✦✦
Certain historical figures, like country music legend Hank Williams, loom so large they are difficult to write about. What can be said that hasn't already been offered by another writer? Likewise, how can a record label justify another collection by an artist whose music has been so frequently repackaged and reissued? The answer, apparently, is quite

simple: concentrate on an aspect of Williams' style that has been under-recognized. *Blues Come Around* does just that, emphasizing his connection—and country music's connection—to the blues. The titles alone—"Moanin' the Blues," "Blues Come Around," and "Lovesick Blues"—go a long way toward convincing the listener that this man had a bad case of the you-know-whats. Certain songs, like "I'm So Lonesome I Could Cry" and "Move It on Over," retain a blues structure as well as typical blues subject matter. In fact, the characters that inhabit most of Williams' songs live sad lives. They cheat on their women, and their women cheat on them; they make the wrong choices and know they're bound to hell; they attend weddings, but only to watch their true love marry someone else. Songs about these low-down lonesome characters couldn't help but be partially tinged with the blues. The string bending of the steel guitar and lonesome moan of the fiddle add a dusty-Delta atmosphere to these proceedings. *Blues Come Around* serves to remind country fans just how important the Piedmont and Delta sounds were to the formation of their music. It also succeeds by emphasizing a number of lesser-known gems and ignoring Williams' more familiar hits. *Blues Come Around* is a fine collection. *—Ronnie D. Lankford Jr.*

★ **The Ultimate Collection** / Jul. 23, 2002 / Universal ✦✦✦✦✦

Mercury/UTV Records' 2002 release *The Ultimate Collection* does not follow a strict chronological running order over the course of 42 songs and two discs, but that's not a problem, since the sequencing flows easily and is logical to the ear. Besides, the other "best introduction/summary" to Hank Williams—1978's *40 Greatest Hits*—didn't run chronologically, either. That collection still is the best choice for an introduction, even if it doesn't have the re-mastered sound this boasts, because it has a better song selection. True, all of the stone-cold essentials are here, but there are lot of songs that really should have been here—"My Son Calls Another Man Daddy," "Nobody's Lonesome for Me," "Dear John," "Baby, We're Really in Love," for instance—that aren't, since the compilers favor a slight revisionist bent that will appeal to alt-country fans (more gloom-&-doom, not as much fun). It should be noted that this complaint is a minor one, applicable to those who already have a lot of Hank Williams, and, overall, this is an excellent summary of his greatest work, one that will satisfy most listeners, or will convert those who have yet to realize why Hank is a legend. *—Stephen Thomas Erlewine*

Hank Williams Jr.

b. May 26, 1949, Shreveport, LA

Guitar, Vocals / Southern Rock, Outlaw Country, Urban Cowboy, Traditional Country

The offspring of famous musicians often have a hard time creating a career for themselves, yet Hank Williams Jr. is one of the few to develop a career that is not only successful, but markedly different from his legendary father. Originally, Hank Jr. simply copied and played his father's music, but as he grew older, he began to carve out his own niche and it was one that owed as much to country-rock as it did to honky tonk. In the late '70s, he retooled his image to appeal both to outlaw country fans and rowdy Southern rockers, and his makeover worked, resulting in a string of Top Ten singles—including the number one hits "Texas Women," "Dixie on My Mind," "All My Rowdy Friends (Have Settled Down)," "Honky Tonkin'," and "Born to Boogie"—that ran into the late '80s. Hank Jr. never was above capitalizing on his father's name, yet his tributes and name-dropping often seemed affectionate, not crass. Also, "Bocephus"—as his father nicknamed him when he was a child—was a passionate cheerleader for patriotic American values; he even wrote a pro-Gulf War song during 1991. All of these actions helped make him an American superstar during the '80s, becoming one of the most recognizable popular culture figures of the era. As new country took over the airwaves in the '90s, Williams slowly disappeared from the charts and his concerts stopped selling as well as they did ten years earlier, yet he retained a devoted core audience throughout the decade.

The son of Hank and Audrey Williams, Hank Williams Jr. was born in Shreveport, LA, in 1949. Less than four years later, his father died, leaving behind a huge legacy. When Hank Jr. was eight years old, Audrey decided to push her son into the spotlight, positioning him as the rightful heir to his father's legacy. Dressed in a white Nudie suit, he would sing Hank Sr.'s biggest hits on package tours, and by the time he was 11, he had made his first appearance on the *Grand Ole Opry*. After a few years of touring, Hank Jr.'s voice broke in 1963. As soon as his voice changed, Audrey had her son sign a contract with MGM Records. Hank Jr. recorded his father's "Long Gone Lonesome Blues" as his debut single, and the record was a hit upon its early 1964 release, climbing to number five. Later that year, he sang all the material for the Hank Williams Sr. bio pic *Your Cheatin' Heart* and starred in the film *A Time to Sing*. Though he immediately had a hit, he wasn't able to follow it up with another Top Ten hit until 1966, when his self-penned "Standing in the Shadows" reached number five. By that time, he had begun to grow tired of his reputation as a Hank Williams imitator and was trying to create his own style, as "Standing in the Shadows" proved. Following that single, he began to explore rock & roll somewhat, occasionally performing under the name Rockin' Randall.

Despite his half-hearted rock & roll attempts, Williams continued to concentrate on country music, turning out a string of hit singles, including the number one "All for the Love of Sunshine" and a number of inspirational cuts released under the name "Luke the Drifter Jr.," a reference to his father's alter-ego. Though his career was doing well, Hank Jr. began falling into drug and alcohol abuse after he turned 18 years old. His personal life became progressively more complicated, culminating in a suicide attempt in 1974. Following the attempt, Williams moved to Alabama where he not only got his life together, but he changed his musical direction as well. Hooking up with Southern rockers like Charlie Daniels, Marshall Tucker, and Toy Caldwell, he recorded *Hank Williams Jr. & Friends*, which fused hardcore country with rock & roll. Though he wasn't scoring as many hits as he had in the early '70s, his music was becoming more original and focused. Just as his career was being revived, tragedy beset Williams. While he was climbing a mountain in Montana in 1975, he fell 442 feet down the side of the mountain. His injuries were serious—his skull was split and his face was crushed—but he survived. Following extensive reconstructive cosmetic surgery, he had to relearn how to speak and sing. Williams' recovery period lasted a full two years. When he re-emerged in 1977, he aligned himself the outlaw country movement, as Waylon Jennings produced Hank Jr.'s comeback effort, *The New South*. It took several years before Williams began to have hits again—his biggest hit in the late '70s was a cover of Bobby Fuller's "I Fought the Law," which reached number 15—but in the final six months of 1979, he had two Top Ten singles, "Family Tradition" and "Whiskey Bent and Hell Bound," which began a virtually uninterrupted streak of 29 Top Ten hits that ran into 1988.

Throughout the '80s, Hank Williams Jr. was one of the most popular, and controversial, figures in country music. Following his image makeover, he appealed primarily to young, and rowdy crowds with his hell-raising anthems and jingoistic ballads. Though he had established his own distinctive style, he continued to name check and pay tribute to his father, and these salutes became as much a part of his act as his redneck rockers. Both the wild music and the party-ready atmosphere of his concerts made Hank Jr. an immensely popular musician and helped him crossover into the rock & roll audience. Williams' career really began to take off in 1981, when he had three number-one hits—"Texas Women," "Dixie on My Mind," and "All My Rowdy Friends (Have Settled Down)"—and *Rowdy* began a streak of 15 gold or platinum albums that ran until 1990. During that time, he won several awards, including back-to-back Country Music Association Entertainer of the Year in 1987 and 1988.

By the end of the decade, Hank Jr.'s persona was becoming a little tired, especially in light of the new breed of clean-cut new country singers that had taken over Nashville. Williams could still have a hit—such as "There's a Tear in My Beer," which was an electronic duet between him and his father—but by the end of 1990, he was no longer hitting the Top Ten and by the middle of the decade he had trouble reaching the Top 40. Despite his declining record sales, Hank Jr. remained a popular concert draw into the latter half of the '90s, ending an uncharacteristically long studio hiatus in 1999 with *Stormy*. *—Stephen Thomas Erlewine*

Songs of Hank Williams / 1963 / MGM ✦✦✦✦✦

Sing Great Country Favorites / 1964 / MGM ✦✦✦

Your Cheatin' Heart: Hank Williams' Life Story / 1964 / MCA ✦✦✦

When Hollywood made its biopic of the Hank Williams story in the mid-'60s, *Your Cheatin' Heart*, the vocals were supplied by a 15-year-old Hank Williams Jr. (though George Hamilton played Williams in the film). Hank Jr. did a creditable job, sounding older and more polished than you'd expect considering his tender age, on Hank Sr. standards like "Your Cheatin' Heart," "I Saw the Light," "Cold, Cold Heart," and "I'm So Lonesome I Could Cry." The arrangements are sometimes anachronistically modern, as though Williams Sr. was suddenly backed by Nashville Sound arrangements; listen to those sweet strings and backup vocals on "Cold Cold Heart," for instance, or the Boots Randolph-type sax on "Jambalaya." [Rhino's 1998 CD reissue adds a heap of bonus tracks, including no less than eleven "unplugged" acoustic outtakes that are both truer to the spirit of the originals, and an interesting context in which to hear Hank Jr.'s emerging voice. There are also detailed, entertaining liner notes of the genesis of the film and Hank Jr.'s soundtrack contributions.] *—Richie Unterberger*

Country Shadows / 1966 / MGM ✦✦✦

Country Shadows is an album from the days before Hank Williams Jr. found his own sound. Consequently, he attempts a number of styles, from his crossover hit "Endless Sleep" to straight country and country-pop. A trucking song, "Ten Ton Load," and "Pecos Jail" show him dealing in the working class and outlaw themes with which he would come to be identified in the '70s. "Standing in the Shadows" is a moving composition that inspires sympathy for the constant comparisons to his father Hank Williams Jr. suffered early on, as do the ambivalent liner notes that essentially beg the listener to give the poor boy a chance. In reality *Country Shadows* is a fine album for those who like (or even prefer) early Hank Williams Jr., in that it contains three of his first four hits and an uncommon selection of material that diverges from the typical covers-laden formula of '60s country albums. *—Greg Adams*

Blues My Name / 1966 / MGM ✦✦✦

In My Own Way / 1967 / MGM ✦✦✦

Songs My Father Left Me / 1969 / MGM ✦✦✦✦✦

Luke the Drifter Jr. / 1969 / Polydor ✦✦

Live at Cobo Hall, Detroit / 1969 / Polygram ✦✦

Living Proof: The MGM Recordings 1963–1975 / 1974 / Mercury ✦✦✦✦✦

Living Proof is a double disc set that chronicles Hank Williams Jr.'s recordings between 1964 and 1975. During this time, he was still developing his own style and began moving out of his father's shadow. Nearly all of the worthwhile tracks he recorded in this period are included on this set and while they aren't as forceful as his later, rowdier hits, many of the songs are almost as memorable. *—Thom Owens*

Bocephus / 1975 / MGM ✦✦✦✦

☆ **Hank Williams Jr. & Friends** / 1976 / Polydor ✦✦✦✦✦

"And Friends" is right. Hank Williams Jr.'s first step off the Hank Sr. bandwagon—against all counsel from his mother and managers—is a doozy of a record. Teaming with Toy Caldwell, Charlie Daniels, Pete Carr, and producer Dick Glasser, among others, Bocephus turned in one of the most inspiring performances of his career. First there is his read of Marshall Tucker's classic "Can't You See" that is wrought with so much emotion it literally spills from the band toward his tortured vocal. Next there are two of Hank Jr.'s own classics, "Stoned at the Jukebox," which has been covered by any country star worth his or her salt, and his personal anthem, "Living Proof." He dared fate on this one, coming off an attempted suicide and preceding a fall 600 feet down a mountain. But he was indeed "Living Proof" that he could survive his father's legend and do something noteworthy of his own. On top of all this are amazing renditions of

"Brothers of the Road" and his own "Montana Song." Though it's brief, it smokes; *Hank Williams Jr. & Friends* stands as a personal watermark for Bocephus; it is one of the best country-rock albums ever made and stands with the best of the outlaw recordings of the era. —*Thom Jurek*

14 Greatest Hits / 1976 / Polydor ✦✦✦✦✦
Williams was a good, if conventional, country singer during the early years covered in this anthology (1966-1974). It includes 11 of his first 12 Top Ten hits, among them the number ones "Eleven Roses" and "All for the Love of Someone." —*William Ruhlmann*

The New South / 1977 / Warner Bros. ✦✦✦✦
After the unqualified success of *Hank Williams Jr. & Friends*, which included members of the Allman Brothers, the Marshall Tucker Band, Charlie Daniels, Waylon, Willie, and plenty of others, Hank Jr. had found his voice. *The New South* is part two of Williams' outlaw saga, one that would take him from being a great writer and interpreter of other people's songs to being a self-parody. Waylon is on board on this set as a guitarist, a backing vocalist, and, most importantly, as co-producer with Richie Aldright. The song selection is amazing. Opening with the original "Feelin' Better," Williams states his case for leaving his old stage persona behind convincingly with Jennings underlining every line on the refrain. The cover of Steve Young's classic "Montgomery in the Rain" is full of pathos and emotion and features some killer guitar work from Leon Sherrill. Williams also covers Young's "Long Way From Hollywood" to close the set. But the confidence Williams displays here is uncanny as he tackles with great tenderness Gordon Lightfoot's "Looking at the Rain," his pop's "You're Gonna Change (Or I'm Gonna Leave)" as a rock & roll song, and Bill Monroe's "Uncle Pen" pretty much straight up. Williams contributes two more songs to the set in the ballad "Once and for All," which spells out the wages of a life spent rambling, and the title track, a modern cracker anthem complete with fiddles, a pedal steel, and a slow- to midtempo strut. The highlight of the latter part of the set is Williams' read of Jessi Colter's "Storms Never Last," the most pure and simple country song on the entire album. And Williams sings the hell out of it. "Tennessee" is a poignant song considering Williams Jr.'s struggles with Nashville up to that point in wanting to get away from recording programs solely of his father's songs. The mold was broken on *Hank Williams Jr. & Friends*, and this is a bit of comeuppance that sounds a bit like Toy Caldwell's "Can't You See." Like its predecessor, this is a winner all the way through, full of stomping outlaw music and beer-swilling ballads. —*Thom Jurek*

One Night Stands / 1977 / Warner Bros. ✦✦✦
One Night Stands was the album released just prior to Hank Williams Jr.'s breakthrough onto the country charts with "Whisky Bent and Hell Bound." You can hear Hank Jr. shedding the last of his famous father's legacy and developing his own outlaw persona. *One Night Stands* utilizes modern Southern rock-oriented arrangements that emphasized Bocephus' interest in the Allman Brothers, ZZ Top, and the Marshall Tucker Band. While the album didn't generate any hits, it does include some very personal songwriting in the Kris Kristofferson vein, including "She's Still the Star (On the Stage of My Mind)" and "It's Different With You." —*Al Campbell*

Whiskey Bent and Hell Bound / 1979 / Warner Bros. ✦✦✦✦✦
The Jimmy Bowen/Hank Williams Jr. team kicked up the tension a couple of notches on 1979's *Whiskey Bent and Hell Bound*. Since Nash Vegas didn't seem to give a damn one way or the other, the pair leaned on the rockin' side of country even harder. Utilizing Waylon and cats like James Burton, David Briggs, Larry Londin, Buddy Spicher, Kieran Kane, Reggie Young, and the Muscle Shoals Horns, they took the outlaw boogie into the stratosphere. From the first four tracks, Hank Jr. feels like he's auditioning to be a member of Black Oak Arkansas or Molly Hatchet on the outside and the Allmans, Lynyrd Skynyrd, and Marshall Tucker on the inside. "The Pressure Is On" is one of those moody Southern rock ballads that feels like it may explode at any time. "Tired of Bein' Johnny B. Goode" is a redneck call to arms, "Outlaw Women" has been sung by every motorcycle club from coast to coast since 1979, and "I Don't Have Any More Love Songs" is one of the finer divorce songs written during that decade. But it's a divorce song of remorse and regret, not bitterness or clever one-upmanship. It's honest, true, and painful. Williams is not one to wallow and his disappointments come right back with a slash-and-burn cover of the nugget "White Lightnin'," most closely associated with George "Thumper" Jones. And before allowing all that good-time fun to go to waste, Williams and band weigh in with one of his most notorious macho outlaw tomes, "Women I've Never Had." It's sexist as hell, and Hank wanted it that way. It's an in-your-face to political correctness and feminism. The set cooks up to here and after, and the track feels out of place on the album, though it is exceptionally well-crafted as a song. It's easy to see why he complained later that it wasn't a single, though he is out of his mind for doing so. "OD'd in Denver" is its own dark reward and the band digs into the groove deep and greasy. The album closes with three covers, the most notable and soulful of which is Gregg Allman's "Come and Go Blues," which is not played by the band so much as attacked, and Williams' vocal does Allman's example proud. *Whiskey Bent and Hell Bound* is the mother of Williams Jr.'s outlaw records and it rocks harder than anything in his catalog. —*Thom Jurek*

Family Tradition / 1979 / Warner Bros. ✦✦✦✦
Family Tradition followed *The New South* by a couple of years and delved deeper into Hank Williams Jr.'s spirit of adventure in reinventing his music to fit him as an individual. Far from giving a damn about what Nash Vegas thought of him at this point, Williams worked with three different producers on this set: Jimmy Bowen, Ray Ruff, and Phil Gernhard. While it's true that this set doesn't have the grit that *Hank Williams Jr. & Friends* or *The New South* had, it does showcase Williams as a singer of real distinction and his love of soul and R&B music. An example of how willing he was to experiment was on the opening track, where he covers the Bee Gees' "To Love Somebody" with a cho-

rus of backing vocalists. And he pulls it off in spades. It's moving, it swings, and it has that gospel feel that the hint of this song always contained but which had never been brought out before. He follows the R&B tip on "Old Flame, New Fire," an Oskar Soloman song that fuses country and Memphis-style R&B—again, with the female chorus raining down all around him. On Steve Young's dark and tenuous love song "Always Loving You," Charlie Daniels fiddles his way through the background in his inimitable style and Reggie Young's electric guitar can be heard trading fills with Brad Felton's steel. A notable cover on the set is a funky-butt read of Bobby Fuller's "I Fought the Law." There's a country feel in the phrasing, but that was there in the original tune; Williams brings a popping bass and honky tonk piano to the proceedings. It's not the best version of the tune, but it is an interesting one. The latter half of the set is chock-full of Hank Jr. compositions, with the notable exception of Ivy J. Bryant's "Only Daddy That'll Walk the Line," a song closely associated with Waylon Jennings. But Williams' version rocks harder than any other on record. Williams' own personal outlaw anthem is present as well, the infamous and wonderful "Family Tradition," with Daniels laying out a laid-back but gorgeous fiddle solo in the bridge. There's also the redneck manifesto "I've Got Right" and the killer "Paying on Time." In all, this is a slick, over-the-top-production album, but the quality of the songs and the arrangements, along with Williams' dynamite singing voice, make this set a necessity. —*Thom Jurek*

Habits Old and New / 1980 / Warner Bros. ✦✦
Habits Old and New is a standard Hank Williams Jr. album from the early '80s, containing several covers of his father's classics ("Kaw-Liga," "Move It On Over"), a tribute to his father (Kris Kristofferson's "If You Don't Like Hank Williams"), plus several rabble-rousing redneck rockers ("All in Alabama," "American Way"). —*Thom Owens*

The Pressure Is On / 1981 / Warner Bros. ✦✦✦✦
Still hanging out with producer Jimmy Bowen, Hank Williams Jr.'s *The Pressure Is On* continued his streak of winners that began back in the 1970s with *Hank Williams Jr. & Friends*. Williams concentrated more on his songwriting here and nailed two of his most famous compositions, both of which were Top Five singles that flew in the face of a Nash Vegas establishment that, while it had co-opted the outlaw movement (Mel Tillis released an album called *I'm an Outlaw*—yeah, right) couldn't quite get with Williams, despite the fact that he sold tons of records and had a host of young fans the Music Row think tanks should have been happy to cultivate. But like Steve Earle, Williams wasn't interested in any sort of compromise; he'd had enough during his lifetime. The two tracks that garnered the most airplay and notice from this set are "A Country Boy Can Survive," its own redneck anthem of rugged individualism during the Reagan years, and "All My Rowdy Friends Have Settled Down," a tale of the aging and settling of the outlaw generation from Waylon to Kristofferson to Willie. (Funny, David Allan Coe isn't mentioned.) But there are other amazing tracks here as well: the title track with its bluesy front end and in-the-dark shadow vocal; the silly but poignant, rocking bluegrass stomper "The Coalition to Ban Coalitions"; the metaphorically astute "Weatherman"; and "I Don't Care if Tomorrow Never Comes." In addition, the cover of Jimmie Driftwood's "Tennessee Stud" here rivals Johnny Cash's version more than a decade later, and the Emerson/Emerson rocker "Ramblin' in My Shoes" is tougher than leather and sharper than a Buck knife. It's another rock & roll country album from Williams, and a good one to boot. The man is on a roll. —*Thom Jurek*

Rowdy / 1981 / Warner Bros. ✦✦✦
In 1981, Hank Williams Jr was one of the hottest acts in country music, starting the year with this album, which spawned the number one hits "Texas Women" and "Dixie on My Mind" and the striking "Are You Sure Hank Done It This Way." —*William Ruhlmann*

High Notes / 1982 / Warner Bros. ✦✦
Containing his hit cover of his father's "Honky Tonkin'" as well as an intriguing version of the Beatles' "Norwegian Wood," *High Notes* is a typically entertaining early '80s record from Hank Williams Jr., featuring a handful of excellent redneck country-rockers—"Whiskey on Ice," "Heaven Ain't a Lot Like Dixie," "South's Gonna Rattle Again,"—mixed with a little filler and the odd soul-searching cut like "If You Wanna Get to Heaven." —*Thom Owens*

★ **Hank Williams Jr.'s Greatest Hits** / 1982 / Warner Bros. ✦✦✦✦✦
This was the first single package highlighting the outlaw hits of Hank Williams Jr. These are the tunes that metamorphosed Hank Jr. from being "the singing son of a country legend" to becoming a legend in his own right. All of the early-'80s hits are here: "Family Tradition," "Whiskey Bent & Hell Bound," "Women I've Never Had," "Texas Women," "Dixie on My Mind," "A Country Boy Can Survive," and "All My Rowdy Friends (Have Settled Down)." This is Hank Jr. as Southern rock/country outlaw, not shy about letting his feelings or personal tragedies shine through. —*Al Campbell*

Man of Steel / 1983 / Warner Bros. ✦✦✦
Man of Steel is a bit of a disappointing album from Hank Williams Jr. Even though the record contains a few hits, including the title cut and his father's classic "Queen of My Heart," the majority of the material lacks the *Bocephus* edge. Songs like "The Air That I Breathe" by the Hollies or the Allman Brothers' "Midnight Rider" may have been too well-known in their original incarnations to allow Williams to really add anything new to them. It's not a failure, but not one of his best from the '80s. —*Al Campbell*

Major Moves / 1984 / Warner Bros. ✦✦✦
Williams topped the country charts with this album, largely on the strength of the raucous "All My Rowdy Friends Are Coming over Tonight," though the title track and the caustic "Attitude Adjustment" were also hits. —*William Ruhlmann*

Five-O-Five / 1985 / Warner Bros. ✦✦
Five-O-Five finds Hank Williams Jr. scoring big with three hit singles: "I'm for Love," "This Ain't Dallas," and the standard "Ain't Misbehavin'." The album does tend to rely

heavily on outlaw country anthems, including "The Nashville Scene," "Something to Believe In," "Outlaw's Rewards," and a version of Warren Zevon's "Lawyers, Guns and Money." —*Al Campbell*

Greatest Hits, Vol. 2 / 1985 / Warner Bros. ✦✦✦✦✦

A well-chosen hits collection covering 1983 to 1985, including "Leave Them Boys Alone" and "All My Rowdy Friends Are Coming Over Tonight." —*William Ruhlmann*

Montana Cafe / Feb. 1986 / Warner Bros. ✦✦✦

By the time of 1986's *Montana Cafe*, Hank Williams Jr. had established himself as a singular hitmaking country artist, long out of his father's shadow. This allowed Bocephus to loosen up his outlaw image a bit, making this is a happier album because of it. Among the ten tracks are plenty of upbeat hits, including "Country State of Mind," "Mind Your Own Business" featuring Reba McEntire and Willie Nelson, and what would become Hank Jr.'s signature song, "My Name Is Bocephus." —*Al Campbell*

Born to Boogie / 1987 / Warner Bros. ✦✦✦✦✦

Born to Boogie is Hank Williams Jr. claiming his reign as elder statesman over the burgeoning young-country movement of the late '80s. This is heavy on uptempo rock tunes, including the title cut, the Rolling Stones' "Honky Tonk Women," and "Keep Your Hands to Yourself," originally by the Georgia Satellites. The album's centerpiece is the anthemic "Young Country," in which Williams and his likeminded musicians/friends (including Highway 101, T. Graham Brown, and Marty Stuart) engage in a singalong declaring their love for not only the classic country of Hank Williams, but equal admiration for the Rolling Stones, ZZ Top, and Van Halen. —*Al Campbell*

Hank Live / 1987 / Warner Bros. ✦✦✦

Fans of Hank Williams Jr. will get a kick out of this sloppy, rockin' live set from 1986. It's no secret that Hank Jr. has a love of Southern rock, and on *Hank Live* he lets loose. These are the Bocephus songs that won over the attention of rock fans, including "My Name Is Bocephus," "I Really Like Girls," "La Grange," and the king of all Southern rock anthems, "Sweet Home Alabama." Even his straight country material comes across with a definite kick that doesn't transfer to the studio albums. The ultimate Hank Jr. party record. —*Al Campbell*

Wild Streak / Jun. 21, 1988 / Warner Bros. ✦✦

Greatest Hits, Vol. 3 / 1989 / Warner Bros. ✦✦✦✦✦

This chronicles Williams' ongoing '80s success, 1985-1989, featuring the number-one hits "I'm for Love," "Ain't Misbehavin'," "Mind Your Own Business," and "Born to Boogie." —*William Ruhlmann*

America (The Way I See It) / 1990 / Warner Bros. ✦✦✦

Williams plays political commentator on this, a collection of his best revenge fantasies, reasons for America's problems, and the theme from Monday Night Football. The album includes the survivalist anthem "A Country Boy Can Survive" and "Don't Give Us a Reason," an open letter to Saddam Hussein. —*Brian Mansfield*

Lone Wolf / 1990 / Warner Bros. ✦✦✦

Pure Hank / 1991 / Warner Bros. ✦✦✦

Pure Hank generated two minor hits, "If It Will It Will" and "Angels Are Hard to Find." —*Jason Ankeny*

Maverick / Oct. 1991 / Capricorn ✦✦✦

Williams' first album for the revived Capricorn label rocks harder than usual, even while he's evangelizing for country music. A good chuck of *Maverick* sounds like a cross between a roaring drunk and a *Penthouse* letter. There's also a great ghost story ("Cut Bank, Montana") and a really dumb novelty song ("Fax Me a Beer"). There's probably not a soul on earth who could pull off "Come on Over to the Country" but Hank—it's corny and obvious about everything country music wishes it was. But every time the slide guitar kicks in, he makes it all come true. —*Brian Mansfield*

The Best of Hank Williams Jr., Vol. 1: Roots and Branches / Aug. 4, 1992 / Mercury ✦✦✦✦✦

The title is a bit of a ringer here, as these are the songs Hank Jr. charted with through the mid-'60s to mid-'70s, before his reincarnation as Bocephus, the outlaw country-rocker, brought him mega-success. However, this 20 track compilation makes for interesting listening to hear how he evolved to his present style. —*Cub Koda*

Out of Left Field / 1993 / Warner Bros. ✦✦✦

Williams had been making the same rowdy records over and over again for so long that the aptly-titled, ballad-oriented *Out of Left Field* amounts to a small revelation. Not only does Williams turn down the guitars here, he turns down the Southern rebel persona as well; the songs are reflective and fairly sensitive, mournful ballads invested with real emotion. *Out of Left Field* doesn't completely toss out the rockers, but its the quiet, melancholy hues which make this Williams' best effort in quite some time. —*Jason Ankeny*

Tribute to My Father / Sep. 21, 1993 / Curb ✦✦✦

Greatest Hits, Vol. 1 / Sep. 21, 1993 / Curb ✦✦✦

Greatest Hits, Vol. 2 / Feb. 22, 1994 / Curb ✦✦✦✦

Even though this second Hank Williams Jr. *Greatest Hits* package is a bit lighter than the first, this is still an enjoyable sampler of Bocephus tunes from the mid- to late '80s. The ten tracks include a few staples in Hank Jr.'s catalog: "All My Rowdy Friends Are Coming Over Tonight," "Attitude Adjustment," and "Honky Tonkin'." Also featured are several duets, including two with Waylon Jennings ("The Conversation" and the similarly themed "Leave Them Boys Alone") and one each with Ernest Tubb and Tanya Tucker, as well as the single "Two Old Cats Like Us" with Ray Charles, which was not available on any other album at the time. —*Al Campbell*

The New South, Vol. 2 / 1995 / Curb ✦✦✦

American Legends: The Best of the Early Years / Sep. 1, 1995 / Polygram Special Markets ✦✦

Truth be told, Hank Williams Jr. wasn't particularly popular during the period covered by Polygram Special Markets' *American Legend: The Best of the Early Years*, nor was he at the peak of his creativity. He was simply trying to find his sound in the '60s, occasionally succeeding and occasionally failing. There's some good material to be found in his numerous recordings, and *American Legend* does a nice job of rounding them up, giving space to his four Top Ten singles of the time—"Standing in the Shadows," "It's All Over But the Crying," "Cajun Baby," "I'd Rather Be Gone"—plus selecting six other solid entries. All told, it's a worthy overview of Williams' first decade of recording and worth its budget price. —*Stephen Thomas Erlewine*

20 Hits Special Collection, Vol. 1 / Nov. 7, 1995 / Curb ✦✦

20 Hits Special Collection, Vol. 1 is an odd collection of hits, re-recordings and also-rans. There are certainly some fine moments here, but it isn't as comprehensive or well-executed as a 20-track greatest-hits collection should be. —*Stephen Thomas Erlewine*

Three Generations of Hank / Sep. 17, 1996 / Curb ✦✦

Hank Williams Jr. has never been above tampering with his father's recorded works—an overdubbed version of "There's a Tear in My Beer" was a Top Ten hit in 1989—but there was no precedent for *Three Generations of Hank*, which features overdubbed, electronic trio recordings of Hank Sr., Hank Jr. and Hank Williams III. There might be a lot of wonderful songs on this record, but it's hard to get beyond the weird, morbid sensation of hearing these pieced together electronic duets. Even though Hank Jr. is the blood heir to his father's legacy, *Three Generations of Hank* is one of the strangest and most unnecessary tributes to that legacy yet recorded. —*Thom Owens*

Hank Williams Jr. Sings Hank Williams Sr. / Apr. 17, 1998 / Rhino ✦✦✦✦

At the time *Hank Williams Jr. Sings Hank Williams Sr.*—the soundtrack to the MGM film *Your Cheatin' Heart*—was released, it wasn't certain if Hank Jr. would be able to separate himself from his dad. Of course, he was able to become his own artistic entity, making records that surpassed this, but *Hank Williams Jr. Sings Hank Williams Sr.* remains an enjoyable, straightforward collection of sympathetic treatments of such Hank classics as "Your Cheatin' Heart," "I Saw the Light," "Jambalaya," "Cold Cold Heart," "Hey Good Lookin'," "I'm So Lonesome I Could Cry," and "You Win Again." The original productions were somewhat slick and overproduced, boasting saxophones and electric guitars that may upset purists. For them, this Rhino reissue is ideal, since it contains no less than 12 bonus tracks, including two alternate mixes of "Jambalaya" and "I Saw the Light," and ten acoustic mixes that prove even more than the finished mixes that Hank Jr. was a talented singer and a true heir to his dad's legacy. —*Stephen Thomas Erlewine*

Early Years, Vol. 1 / Oct. 6, 1998 / Curb ✦✦

Early Years, Vol. 1 contains material released just prior to Hank Williams Jr.'s breakthrough onto the country charts. The ten tracks are pulled from two of his earliest sessions for Elektra Records, *One Night Stands* and *New South*. Both albums utilized modern Southern rock arrangements, a direction that would lead Hank Jr. to the top of the country charts in the '80s. Most of the material on this compilation still sounds great with the exception of an awful cover version of Eric Carmen's lush and weepy pop hit "All By Myself." Bocephus just couldn't pull that one off! —*Al Campbell*

Early Years, Vol. 2 / Oct. 6, 1998 / Curb ✦✦

Early Years, Vol. 2 contains material released just prior to Hank Williams Jr.'s breakthrough onto the country charts. The ten tracks are pulled from two of his earliest sessions for Elektra Records, *One Night Stands* and *New South*. Both albums utilized modern Southern rock arrangements, a direction that would lead Hank Jr. to the top of the country charts in the '80s. Most of the material on this compilation still sounds great especially Steve Young's "Montgomery in the Rain," and Gordon Lightfoot's "Looking at the Rain." The one dud here is an awful cover version of Jackson Browne's "You Love the Thunder." —*Al Campbell*

The Complete Hank Williams Jr / Apr. 6, 1999 / Curb ✦✦✦

To be fair, the title of *The Complete Hank Williams Jr.* is disingenuous, since three discs are hardly enough space to cover his complete recordings or even his complete recordings for Curb Records. So, forget the title and concentrate on the music, which is a distillation of his decade-long stint at Curb. Granted, these ten years found Williams coasting to a certain extent, relying more on his superstar status than pushing his music forward, but that doesn't mean that the music itself is weak. There are a few cuts that don't quite measure up with the best of his work, but there's little arguing that the compilers have done an excellent job of rounding up the highlights from these uneven years, resulting in an exhaustive survey of Williams' latter-day work that will be useful for fans that want to dig deep yet don't want to invest in his entire catalog. —*Stephen Thomas Erlewine*

Stormy / Aug. 31, 1999 / Curb ✦✦✦✦

At a certain point, Hank Williams Jr.'s act became pure schtick. On record, it probably can be narrowed down to 1990, when he released *America (The Way I See It)*. A decade and half prior to that, he had perfected his rowdy, rockin' rebel sound, but with *America*, his outlaw attitude blended with reactionary redneck politics, jingoistic slogans, football anthems, and sendups of contemporary U.S. life. From that point on, each album got progressively sillier, relying on near-parodies like "Fax Me a Beer" and "Don Juan D'Bubba" as his voice started to fade away. With 1999's *Stormy*, his first album in three years, he turns this all to his advantage. Plenty of stars have larger than life personas, but Hank Jr.'s is so large it can be perceived as both genuine and self-parody. Make no mistake, *Stormy* will play well to his legions of fans, simply because it delivers. It's been a while since he's created an album so lean and hard, filled with strong rockers, honky tonkers, and ballads. Hank Jr. also knows that his audience loves fights, football, and partying because he is his audience—a good-old boy out for a good-time. *Stormy* is the ideal soundtrack for that because he gives them exactly what they want. To an outsider, though, the album could be seen as a big joke, as titles like "I'd Love to Knock the Hell Out of You," "Where Would We Be Without Yankees," "Naked Women and Beer," "Hank Hill Is the King," and "Sometimes I Feel Like Joe Montana" (a ballad, nonetheless) suggest. Hank Jr.'s whole act may be schtick, but it's schtick that works because it's genuine and heartfelt. You may laugh with or at him, and *Stormy* is fun either way. *—Stephen Thomas Erlewine*

★ **The Bocephus Box** / Aug. 29, 2000 / Curb ♦♦♦♦♦
The years covered on Curb's *The Bocephus Box (1979-1999)* are the 20 years where Hank Jr. was an American icon, the larger-than-life rowdy man of country. His rise began in the early '80s, when he hit upon a terrific blend of honky tonk, Southern rock, blues, and country that appealed to rock and country audiences alike—rednecks of all persuasions, as less charitable critics would say. Throughout the '80s, he ruled the country charts, as every single one of his new albums went gold. For some observers, he slipped into self-parody halfway through that reign, but as this three-disc box set proves, the best of his music was remarkably consistent. Yes, the individual albums sagged somewhat (especially in the mid-'90s), but he remained true to his vision and had a good choice of material, whether it was newly written songs or rock covers. Early on in *The Bocephus Box*, it dawns on you that while some have replicated his style—and while he has spent a longtime working the same ground—nobody really did this rowdy, rockin' country before Hank, and nobody has done it better since. Country purists may deny it, but he was a distinctive stylist, and while he got a little silly even when he was good, he usually delivered, especially in a concentrated setting like this. During those two decades, he released an album almost every year, which were distilled to 65 songs and three discs with almost no duds—which means he must have been doing something right. For doubters and fans alike, this is the place to really absorb Hank Jr. at the height of his powers. *—Stephen Thomas Erlewine*

Essential / Oct. 30, 2001 / Polygram International ♦♦♦♦
This is Hank Williams Jr. of the '60s and early '70s, before his outlaw makeover. Originally recorded for MGM Records, these songs are good, but not essential. They are especially flat compared to his Elektra output. Hank Jr. covers a variety of straight country material, including a version of "A Rainy Night in Georgia," his father's classic "Your Cheatin' Heart," and two early tunes that hint at his future transformation, "Stoned at the Jukebox" and the autobiographical "Living Proof." *—Al Campbell*

The Almeria Club Recordings / Jan. 8, 2002 / Curb ♦♦♦♦
The words self, parody, and Hank Williams Jr. have been inextricably tied for such a longtime—nowhere more so than in his 1999 album, *Stormy*, where he seemed like he was auditioning for a sketch comedy, competing with Bob Odenkirk's send-up on *Mr. Show*—that the spare, gritty, compelling 2002 release, *The Almeria Club Recordings*, comes as a bracing surprise. It's not that Williams Jr. has left all of his silly self-mythologizing behind, or that he's now developed a disdain for the ridiculous—witness "Big Top Women," who "sure do bounce around," or how he's decided that he's "X-Treme Country," or how he mentions hanging with Kid Rock and Hank III on "The 'F' Word"—but all that is part of his character, and it's much more acceptable now that he's reclaimed the other thing that's defined him—namely, a talent for raw, hardcore honky tonk that's genuine, so genuine that it gives the rockers passion and the ballads a real melancholy streak. This, according to the man himself, may have been inspired by the location of the recording—*The Almeria Club*, allegedly the site where a Hank Williams Sr. performance was interrupted by a gun-toting man looking for his cheating wife—and if that's so, he should continue to record there, because he hasn't sounded this committed, this alive, in years. Even when the album gets silly, which it does frequently, it's buttressed by a crackerjack band at the top of their game and a set of really good songs. More than that, Williams Jr. clearly has some emotional stake in the songs, whether it's his salute to dead friends "Cross on the Highway," the post-September 11, 2001 "America Will Survive," "Last Pork Chop," the second of two tributes to Kansas City Chiefs linebacker Derrick Thomas here, or "Tee Tot Song," dedicated to the man who taught Hank Williams Sr. how to play guitar. The end result is a stripped-down, fun, gutsy, and even moving album that offers a welcome musical reminder that Hank Williams Jr. is indeed his father's son (something that he's never stopped reminding us verbally throughout the years). *—Stephen Thomas Erlewine*

Hank Williams III

b. Dec. 12, 1972, Nashville, TN
Guitar (Acoustic), Vocals / Contemporary Country, Honky Tonk, New Traditionalist, Americana
Shelton Hank Williams III was born December 12, 1972, in Nashville, TN. As the grandson of Hank Williams and the son of Hank Jr., he was country music royalty before he ever sang a note. But he didn't immediately follow his forebears musically, choosing instead to bang around the Southeast, playing drums in punk and hardcore combos and smoking prodigious amounts of weed. It was the outlaw spirit of his lineage, alive and unwell and floating in the bong water. By 1996, steep child support payments and his thirst for Mother Nature had forced Hank III onto to the straight and narrow, and he signed a contract with Music City giant Curb. The label issued *Three Hanks: Men With Broken Hearts*, which brought the voices of all three generations of Williams men together via the ghastly miracles of modern technology. It was about as far from what Hank III wanted as he could get and signaled the beginning of his stormy relationship with Curb.

Williams was in a tight spot. While his name, face, and uncanny vocal resemblance to his grandfather almost guaranteed him a thriving country audience, he had no patience for Nashville's squareness and rigid control. He and his Damn Band could wow a crowd with a spot-on set of gorgeous country balladry and spirited honky tonk. But III could just as easily shift gears into screeching, Black Flag-style punk rock with his hard-rocking combo AssJack. He was the kind of anomaly enormous record companies couldn't stand—eminently marketable, yet defiantly unpredictable. Curb issued Hank III's proper debut in September 1999. Entitled *Risin' Outlaw*, it presented 13 rough-hewn country numbers colored by Hank's honky tonking vocals. And while he played his share of "country" gigs to support it, Williams also appeared at the 2001 *Vans/Warped Tour* alongside punks like Rancid. The irascible III also dismissed *Outlaw* as a label-controlled fiasco almost immediately after its release.

After a few years of touring and trying like mad to be released from his Curb contract, III returned to wax in early 2002 with *Lovesick, Broke & Driftin'*. While *Outlaw* had featured material from outside writers, the new LP was all Hank III but for a previously released cover of Bruce Springsteen's "Atlantic City." He also produced, recorded, and mixed it by his lonesome in just two weeks. At this point Hank's relationship with Curb became even more strained. The label refused to release his appropriately named *This Ain't Country* LP, which featured songs like "Life of Sin" and "Hellbilly." At the same time, it refused to grant Hank III the rights to issue it on his own. He and the record company reached an impasse, which III only exacerbated with the "F*** Curb" T-shirts he sold through his thriving website. *Thrown Out of the Bar*, his third honky tonk album, was scheduled for release in 2003, as was the long-awaited *This Ain't Country*. Additionally, III issued extremely limited-edition releases through his website (often in quantities of 100 or less) and continued to play bass in Superjoint Ritual, the brutal side project of Pantera frontman Phil Anselmo. *—Johnny Loftus*

Risin' Outlaw / Sep. 7, 1999 / Curb ♦♦♦♦
Hank Williams III's debut album *Risin' Outlaw* presents 13 tracks that show Williams' affection for authentic, rough around the edges country. From the catchy, driving album opener "I Don't Know" to his honky tonk vocals on "You're the Reason," Hank III blends his famous heritage with his own musical outlook. Ballads like "Lonesome for You" and uptempo tracks like "If the Shoe Fits" show off Williams' ability to be purely country as well as original. *—Heather Phares*

● **Lovesick, Broke & Driftin'** / Jan. 29, 2002 / Curb ♦♦♦♦
Hank Williams III has repeatedly made it clear that he was unsatisfied with his debut album, 1999's *Risin Outlaw*. So this time around he took matters into his own hands, producing *Lovesick, Broke & Driftin'* himself and recording and mixing the release in a truncated span of two weeks. This appears to have been a good decision for the DNA marvel known as Hank Williams III, for the album is a much less-forced, more organic effort than his debut. This time around he relies primarily on his own songwriting chops—with the exception of a questionable version of Bruce Springsteen's "Atlantic City," which trades the stark power of the original for bouncy honky tonk—and not on contributions from folks such as Wayne Hancock. The effort revels in the paradox of being a Hank Williams; "Calling Your Name" finds him reaching out to the Lord, while "Mississippi Mud" and "Nighttime Ramblin' Man" are fiercely unrepentant, glorying in the allure of long drinking bouts and pot smoking. (The latter being Hank Williams III's updated spin on the Williams mythology of debauchery.) The title track is the kind of downtrodden, whiskey-soaked number for which his grandpa was known, while "Lovin' and Huggin'" is more in line with the good-time party anthems his dad has ridden to success. The biggest surprise here, however, is going to be the emotional range of the album; *Lovesick, Broke & Driftin'* makes it clear that Hank Williams III is not content to sit back and trade on legacy. He has emerged as a songwriter to be taken dead seriously. *—Erik Hage*

Leona Williams (Leona Belle Helton)

b. Jan. 7, 1943, Vienna, MO
Vocals / Progressive Country, Traditional Country, Contemporary Country
Leona Williams was born Leona Belle Helton January 7, 1943, in Vienna, MO. She sang in her family band as a child and by 1958 had landed her own radio show on Kansas City's KWOS called *Leona Sings*. This outlet brought her to the attention of Loretta Lynn, who asked Williams to join her touring band as a bassist and backup vocalist. Williams signed as a solo artist with Hickory in 1968 and cut a few minor hits for the label, including "Once More" and "Country Girl With Hot Pants On." She bounced from Hickory to MCA, where she recorded the landmark *San Quentin's First Lady* in 1976. (It was the first country album recorded by a female inside a prison.) Williams had joined Merle Haggard's backing band in 1975, but she soon replaced his estranged wife Bonnie Owens as featured vocalist.

Her and Haggard's professional and private lives were merged for several years. While their brief marriage was stormy, the duo were more successful as a songwriting team. 1978's "Bull and the Beaver" cracked the country Top Ten; "We're Strangers Again" charted in 1983, but the song also marked the dissolution of her relationship with Haggard. Williams continued to record and contributed vocals to albums by Vince Gill and Johnny Bush. She released the solo effort *Melted Down Memories* in 1999 and appeared as part of the *Us Girls!* music variety show in Branson, MO. *—Johnny Loftus*

Old Loves Never Die / Jul. 8, 2001 / Bear Family ♦♦♦

Lucinda Williams

b. Jan. 26, 1953, Lake Charles, LA
Guitar, Vocals / Singer/Songwriter, Alternative Country-Rock, Contemporary Folk, Americana, Heartland Rock, Alternative Folk
The object of cultish adoration for years, singer/songwriter Lucinda Williams was universally hailed as a major talent by both critics and fellow musicians, but it took quite some time for her to parlay that respect into a measure of attention from the general public. Part of the reason was her legendary perfectionism: Williams released records only infrequently, often taking years to hone both the material and the recordings thereof. Plus, her early catalog was issued on smaller labels that agreed to her insistence on creative

control but didn't have the resources or staying power to fully promote her music. Yet her meticulous attention to detail and staunch adherence to her own vision were exactly what helped build her reputation. When Williams was at her best (and she often was), even her simplest songs were rich in literary detail, from her poetic imagery to her flawed, conflicted characters. Her singing voice, whose limitations she readily acknowledged, nonetheless developed into an evocative instrument that seemed entirely appropriate to her material. So if some critics described Williams as "the female Bob Dylan," they may have been oversimplifying things (Townes Van Zandt might be more apt), but the parallels were certainly too strong to ignore.

Williams was born in Lake Charles, LA, on January 26, 1953. Her father was Miller Williams, a literature professor and published poet who passed on not only his love of language, but also of Delta blues and Hank Williams. The family moved frequently, as Miller took teaching posts at colleges around Louisiana, Mississippi, Georgia, Arkansas, and even Mexico City and Santiago, Chile. Meanwhile, Lucinda discovered folk music (especially Joan Baez) through her mother and was galvanized into trying her own hand at singing and writing songs after hearing Dylan's *Highway 61 Revisited*. Immersed in a college environment, she was also exposed to '60s rock and more challenging singer/songwriters like Leonard Cohen and Joni Mitchell. She started performing folk songs publicly in New Orleans and during the family's sojourn in Mexico City. In 1969, she was ejected from high-school for refusing to say the Pledge of Allegiance, and she spent a year working her way through a reading list supplied by her father before leaving home. Williams performed around New Orleans as a folk artist who mixed covers with traditional-styled originals. In 1974, she relocated to Austin, TX, and became part of that city's burgeoning roots-music scene; she later split time between Austin and Houston, and then moved to New York. A demo tape got her the chance to record for the Smithsonian's Folkways label, and she went to Jackson, MS, to lay down her first album at the Malaco studios. *Ramblin' on My Mind* (later retitled simply *Ramblin'*) was released in 1979 and featured a selection of traditional blues, country, folk, and Cajun songs.

Williams returned to Houston to record the follow-up, 1980's *Happy Woman Blues*. As her first album of original compositions, it was an important step forward, and although it was much more bound by the dictates of tradition than her genre-hopping later work, her talent was already in evidence.However, it would be some time before that talent was fully realized. Williams flitted between Austin and Houston during the early '80s, then moved to Los Angeles in 1984, where she started to attract some major-label interest. CBS signed her to a development deal in the mid-'80s but wound up passing since neither its rock nor its country divisions knew how to market her; around the same time, a short-lived marriage to drummer Greg Sowders dissolved. Williams eventually caught on with an unlikely partner—the British indie label Rough Trade, which was historically better known for its punk output. The simply titled *Lucinda Williams* was released in 1988, and although it didn't make any waves in the mainstream, it received glowing reviews from those who did hear it. With help from guitarist/co-producer Gurf Morlix, Williams' sound had evolved into a seamless blend of country, blues, folk, and rock; while it made perfect sense to roots-music enthusiasts, it didn't fit into the rigid tastes of radio programmers. But it was clear that she had found her songwriting voice—the album brimmed with confidence, and so did its assertive female characters, who seemed to answer only to their own passions.

Many critics hailed *Lucinda Williams* as a major statement by a major new talent. Rough Trade issued a couple of EPs that featured live performances and material from *Lucinda Williams*, and Patty Loveless covered "The Night's Too Long" for a Top 20 country hit. However, it would be four years before Williams completed her official follow-up. She signed with RCA for a time but left when she felt that the label was pressuring her to release material she didn't deem ready for public consumption. Instead, she went to the small Elektra-distributed label Chameleon, which finally released *Sweet Old World* in 1992. A folkier outing than *Lucinda Williams*, *Sweet Old World* was an unflinching meditation on death, loss, and regret. Even its upbeat moments were colored by songs like the title track and "Pineola," two stunning, heartbreaking accounts of a family friend's suicide (poet Frank Stanford, *not*, as many listeners assumed, Williams' own brother). Needless to say, the record won rave reviews once again, and Williams toured Australia with Rosanne Cash and Mary-Chapin Carpenter. On that tour, Carpenter decided to record "Passionate Kisses," the key track and statement of purpose from *Lucinda Williams*. It shot into the country Top Five in 1993 and won its writer a Grammy for Country Song of the Year.

Other artists soon started mining Williams' back catalog for material: avowed fan Emmylou Harris recorded "Crescent City" on 1993's *Cowgirl's Prayer* and cut "Sweet Old World" for her 1995 alternative country landmark *Wrecking Ball*; plus, Tom Petty covered "Changed the Locks" for 1996's movie-related *She's the One*. As the buzz around Williams grew, so did anticipation for her next album. With Chameleon having gone under, she signed with Rick Rubin's American Recordings label and began sessions with Morlix again co-producing. Dissatisfied with the results, Williams' rigorous retouchings led to Morlix's departure from the project and her backing band.

In 1995, she moved into Harris' neighborhood in Nashville and through Harris hired Steve Earle and his production partner Ray Kennedy. At first, she was so enamored with their work that she re-recorded the entire album from scratch. When it was finished, she decided that the results sounded *too* produced, and took the record to Los Angeles, where she enlisted Roy Bittan (onetime E Street Band keyboardist) to co-produce a series of overdub sessions that bordered on obsessive. During the long wait for the album, the media began to pay more attention to Williams; some of the coverage was fairly unflattering, painting her as a neurotic control freak, but she always countered that it was unfair to criticize the process if the results were worthwhile.Rubin mixed the final tracks, but the album was further delayed when he entered into negotiations to sell the American label. Mercury stepped in to purchase the rights to the album, which was finally released in 1998 under the title *Car Wheels on a Gravel Road*. Boasting a bright, contemporary roots rock sound with strong country and blues flavors, not to mention major-label promotional power, the album won universal acclaim, making many critics' year-end Top Ten lists and winning *the Village Voice*'s prestigious Pazz & Jop survey. It also won Williams a Grammy for Best Contemporary Folk Album (despite being the least folk-oriented record in her catalog) and became her first to go gold, proving to doubters that she was not just a songwriter, but a full-fledged recording artist in her own right.

After a merger shakeup at Mercury, Williams wound up on the Universal-distributed roots imprint Lost Highway. She was the subject of an extensive, widely acclaimed profile in *the New Yorker* in 2000, written by Bill Buford, who was nominated for a National Magazine Award for his work; however, Williams and some of her supporters took issue with some of his more objective-minded analysis.Williams delivered her next album, *Essence*, in 2001, after a relatively scant wait of just three years. An introspective collection, it often found Williams taking a simpler, more minimalistic lyrical approach and was greeted with rapturous reviews in most quarters. The track "Get Right With God" won Williams her third Grammy, this time for Best Female Rock Vocal, which further consolidated her credibility as a singer, not just a songwriter. Paring down the time between album releases even further, Williams returned in 2003 with *World Without Tears*, which became her highest-charting effort to date when it debuted in the Top 20. *—Steve Huey*

Ramblin' on My Mind / 1979 / Smithsonian Folkways ✦✦

A collection of blues and country standards by Robert Johnson, Memphis Minnie, Hank Williams, and others. Williams is accompanied only by guitarist John Grimaudo. [Re-released by Smithsonian/Folkways in 1991 as *Ramblin'*.] *—Kurt Wolff*

Happy Woman Blues / 1980 / Smithsonian Folkways ✦✦✦✦

Williams' first collection of original material—recorded with a full band—is stunning for its mixture of blues, folk, and country traditions with her captivating, complex, and visceral approach to writing and singing. Songs like "Lafayette," "King of Hearts," and "Sharp Cutting Wings" are classics: structurally solid and emotionally intense. A gutsy, refreshingly rootsy album. [Re-released by Smithsonian Folkways in 1990.] *—Kurt Wolff*

Lucinda Williams / 1988 / Koch ✦✦✦✦✦

Lucinda Williams took eight years to write and record her second album of original songs. While some producers and record executives have said that she is difficult to work with, one can never argue with the finished product. She crafts each song meticulously and deftly blends country, blues, and folk to create a unique sound that cannot be pigeonholed into any particular format. Her voice contains a heartache comparable to Emmylou Harris, but she has a darker side and a toughness that allows her to live inside the blues or rock with abandon. Re-released with bonus tracks after receiving long overdue commercial acclaim for *Car Wheels on a Gravel Road*, *Lucinda Williams* is an album that has been long been recognized as a classic. It has been mined for hit songs over the years by such artists as Mary-Chapin Carpenter, who turned "Passionate Kisses" into a country hit, and Tom Petty, who included "Changed the Locks" on his soundtrack album *She's the One*. In addition to writing strong melodies, Lucinda Williams is an amazing songwriter with a knack at writing a lyric that acknowledges the complicated nature of relationships while cutting right to the heart of the matter. Every song packs an emotional punch line and rewards the listener each time with something new. The bonus tracks mostly feature Williams accompanied only by her guitar, and it adds emotional weight to the album's highlight, "Side of the Road," which expresses the delicate balance of giving up oneself in a relationship without losing one's own identity. A must-own for country and blues fans that appreciate great songwriting. *—Vik Iyengar*

Sweet Old World / Aug. 25, 1992 / Chameleon ✦✦✦✦✦

After seemingly coming out of nowhere to be hailed as a major songwriter and roots-music stylist, it took Lucinda Williams four years to prepare the follow-up to her masterful 1988 eponymous album. When it finally arrived, *Sweet Old World* proved to be every bit the equal of its predecessor, if not even better. Although *Sweet Old World* isn't really a concept album, it often feels like one. Its first half is dominated by the title track and "Pineola," two stunning meditations on suicide. Their sense of tragedy is reinforced with the closing cover of Nick Drake's "Which Will," and their shadow hangs heavy over the rest of the album. Several character portraits ponder where and why their subjects' lives went wrong; in this context, the dead-end situations seem that much more tragic and final. Moreover, when Williams offers an emotionally complex love ballad or a sexy blues strut, it's hard to take them as truly celebratory; here, the singer sounds as though she wants to appreciate who she has while she still can. That's also why "Little Angel, Little Brother" doesn't come off as remotely sentimental; the affectionate tribute works so well that, sandwiched between "Sweet Old World" and "Pineola," Williams' brother sounds like the suicide victim (it was actually a family friend). Williams' voice glows with the same warmth, for although it's limited in range, it's also a gorgeous instrument that Williams has learned to manipulate for maximum impact. Stylistically, *Sweet Old World* is similar to *Lucinda Williams*, juggling both the sounds and instruments of country, folk, blues, and rock & roll. It might not explode with confidence in the manner of *Lucinda Williams*, but *Sweet Old World* is no less vital; it's a gorgeous, elegiac record that not only consolidates but expands Williams' ample talents. *—Steve Huey*

★ **Car Wheels on a Gravel Road** / Jun. 30, 1998 / Mercury ✦✦✦✦✦

It isn't surprising that Lucinda Williams' level of craft takes time to assemble, but the six-year wait between *Sweet Old World* and its 1998 follow-up, *Car Wheels on a Gravel Road*, still raised eyebrows. The delay stemmed both from label difficulties and Williams' meticulous perfectionism, the latter reportedly over a too-produced sound and her own vocals. Listening to the record, one can understand why both might have concerned Williams. *Car Wheels* is far and away her most produced album to date, which is something of a mixed blessing. Its surfaces are clean and contemporary, with something in the timbres of the instruments (especially the drums) sounding extremely typical of a late-'90s major-label roots rock album. While that might subtly alter the timeless qualities of Williams' writing, there's also no denying that her sound is punchier and livelier. The production also throws Williams' idiosyncratic voice into sharp relief, to the point where it's noticeably separate from the band. As a result, every inflection and slight tonal alteration is captured, and it would hardly be surprising if Williams did obsess over those small details. But whether or not you miss the earthiness of *Car Wheels'* predecessors, it's ultimately the material that matters, and Williams' songwriting is as captivating as ever. Intentionally or not, the album's common thread seems to be its strongly grounded sense of place—specifically, the Deep South, conveyed through images and numerous references to specific towns. Many songs are set, in some way, in the middle or aftermath of not-quite-resolved love affairs, as Williams meditates on the complexities of human passion. Even her simplest songs have more going on under the surface than their poetic structures might indicate. In the end, *Car Wheels on a Gravel Road* is Williams' third straight winner; although she might not be the most prolific songwriter of the '90s, she's certainly one of the most brilliant. —*Steve Huey*

Essence / Jun. 5, 2001 / Lost Highway ✦✦✦✦

Between her well-documented determination to retail full control of her music and the plain-spoken willfulness of her best-known songs, Lucinda Williams is practically the working definition of a strong woman you do not want to mess with, but she reveals a very different side of her musical personality on her sixth album, *Essence*. Subtle and often stark, *Essence* is an unusually quiet and frequently downbeat set that depicts a fragile emotional vulnerability which rarely makes its presence felt in Williams' music; there's an unadorned longing in songs like "Blue" and "Lonely Girls" that's new and deeply affecting, and the leaf-in-the-breeze quaver of Williams' voice on "I Envy the Wind" is as heart-rending as anything she's ever committed to tape. But while a blue mood dominates *Essence*, this isn't an album about the blue funk of heartbreak, but a chronicle of the search for transcendence over sorrow in our lives, as her characters look for a path out of isolation ("Out of Touch"), try to find answers through faith ("Get Right With God"), or reconcile love with the desires of the flesh ("Essence"). As a songwriter, Williams has long shown a knack for charting the human heart and mind with intelligence and economy, and *Essence* finds her at the peak of her form; the delicacy of this music does not speak of weakness, but of the passion and bravery it takes to bare one's soul. And while Williams has gained a certain infamy for her obsessive perfectionism in the studio, the quality of her work speaks for the wisdom of her decision-making process, and *Essence* proves how well she understands the art of recording; producing in collaboration with Charlie Sexton (Tom Tucker and Bo Ramsey also contributed), *Essence* sounds full and rich even in its quietest moments, and her sweet-and-sour voice blends with the arrangements with subtle perfection. Those hoping for another dose of the bluesy roots rock of *Car Wheels on a Gravel Road* may be disappointed, but if you want to take a deep and compelling look into the heart and soul of a major artist, then you owe it to yourself to hear *Essence*. —*Mark Deming*

World Without Tears / Apr. 8, 2003 / Lost Highway ✦✦✦✦✦

While many considered *Car Wheels on a Gravel Road* and *Essence* as definitive statements of arrival for Lucinda Williams as a pop star, she "arrived" creatively with her self-titled album in 1984 and opened up a further world of possibilities with *Sweet Old World*. The latter two records merely cemented a reputation that was well-deserved from the outset, though they admittedly confused some of her earliest fans. *World Without Tears* is the most immediate, unpolished album she's done since *Sweet Old World*. In addition, it is simply the bravest, most emotionally wrenching record she's ever issued. It offers unflinching honesty regarding the paradoxes inherent in love as both a necessary force for fulfillment and a destructive one when embraced unconsciously. Fans of her more polished, emotionally yearning material may have a hard time here because there isn't one track—of 13—that isn't right from the gut, ripped open, bleeding, and stripped of metaphors and literary allusions; they're all cut with the fineness of a stiletto slicing through white bone into the heart's blood. *World Without Tears* is, among other things, predominantly about codependent, screwed-up love. It's about relationships that begin seemingly innocently and well-intentioned and become overwhelmingly powerful emotionally and transcendent sexually, until the moment where a fissure happens, baggage gets dumped in the space between lovers, and they turn in on themselves, becoming twisted and destructive—where souls get scorched and bodies feel the addictive, obsessive need to be touched by a now absent other. The whole experience burns to ashes; it becomes a series of tattoos disguised as scars. The experience is lived through with shattering pain and bewilderment until wrinkled wisdom emerges on the other side. Most of Williams' albums have one song that deals with this theme, but with the exception of a couple of songs, here they *all* do. Musically, this is the hardest-rocking record she's ever released, though almost half the songs are ballads. Her road band—on record with her for the first time—cut this one live from the studio floor adding keyboards and assorted sonic textures later. The energy here just crackles. Sure, there's gorgeous country and folk music here. "Ventura," with its lilting verse and lap steel whining in the background, is a paean to be swallowed up in the ocean of love's embrace. In fact, it's downright prosaic until she gets to the last verse: "Stand in the shower to clean this dirty mess/Give me back my power and drown this unholiness/Lean over the toilet bowl and throw up my confession/Cleanse my soul of this hidden obsession." The melodic frame is still moving, but the tune reverses itself: It's no longer a broken-hearted ballad, but a statement of purpose and survival. "Fruits of My Labor" is a straight-ahead country song. Williams shimmers with her lyric, her want pouring from her mouth like raw dripping honey. Her words are a poetry of want: "I traced your scent through the gloom/Till I found these purple flowers/I was spent, I was soon smelling you for hours . . . I've been trying to enjoy all the fruits of my labor/I've been cryin' for you boy, but truth is my savior." One can hear the grain of Loretta Lynn's voice, with an intent so pure and unadorned. But the muck and mire of "Righteously," with its open six-string squall, is pure rock. It's an exhortation to a lover that he need not prove his manhood by being aloof, but to "be the man you ought to tenderly/Standup for me." Doug Pettibone's overdriven, crunching guitar solo quotes both Duane Allman and Jimi Hendrix near the end of the tune. "Real Live Bleeding Fingers and Broken Guitar Strings" is a Rolling Stones-style country-rocker with a

lyric so poignant it need not be quoted here. "Over Time," a tome about getting through the heartbreak of a ruined relationship, could have been produced by Daniel Lanois with its warm guitar tremolo and sweet, pure, haunting vocal in front of the mix. "Those Three Days" may be the most devastating song on the record, with its whimpering lap steel and Williams' half-spoken vocal that questions whether a torrid three-day affair was a lie, a symbolic sacrifice, or the real thing. The protagonist's vulnerability is radical; she feels used, abused—"Did you only want me for those three days/Did you only need me for those three days/Did you love me forever just for those three days." Yet she holds out hope that there is some other explanation as the questions begin to ask themselves from the depth of a scorched heart and a body touched by something so powerful it feels as if it no longer owns itself. Pettibone's solo screams and rings in the bridge to underline every syllable and emotion. "Atonement" is something else altogether; it's a punkish kind of blues. If the White Stripes jammed with 20 Miles in a big studio it might sound like this, with Williams singing from the depths of a tunnel for a supreme megaphone effect. She growls and shouts and spits her lyrics from the center of the mix. And Taras Prodaniuk's fuzzed-out basement-level gutter bass is the dirtiest, raunchiest thing on record since early Black Sabbath. "Sweet Side" is almost a poem in song, attempts to inspire someone who's been broken by life to accept his goodness. It is *not* a rap song despite what's been written about it so far. It's more in the tradition of Bob Dylan's early talking blues, but with a modern organic rhythm played by Jim Christie instead of drum loops. In addition, there is the gorgeously tough "People Talking," the most straight-ahead country song Williams has written since "Still I Long for Your Kiss" (from the *Horse Whisperer* soundtrack, not the version that appears on *Car Wheels*, which is dull and lifeless by comparison). Here again, Pettibone's guitar and the slippery, skittering shuffle of Christie's drumming carry Williams' voice to a place where she can sing her protagonist's personal, soul-searing truth without restraint. *World Without Tears* is a work of art in the Henry James sense; it is "that which can never be repeated." It is as fine an album as she could make at this point in her life—which is saying plenty. While she has never strayed from her own vision and has made few compromises, this album risks everything she's built up to now. The audience she's won over time—especially with her last two records—may find it over the top, which would be too damn bad; it'd be their loss. Hopefully, history will prove that *World Without Tears* sets a new watermark for Williams, and is an album so thoroughly ahead of its time in the way it embraces, and even flaunts, love's contradictions and paradoxes—the same way the human heart does. It is this writer's hope that people will be listening to and learning from it for years to come. —*Thom Jurek*

Robin & Linda Williams

f. 1973

Group / Progressive Bluegrass, Singer/Songwriter, Country-Folk, Contemporary Folk, Americana

The sounds of rural America are explored through the warm vocal harmonies and acoustic guitar-driven arrangements of Virginia-based husband and wife duo Robin & Linda Williams. Accompanied by the appropriately named Their Fine Group, featuring dobro ace Kevin Maul and ex-Red Clay Ramblers bassist Jim Watson, the Williams blend a mixture of bluegrass, folk, and acoustic country music. As semi-regular performers on Garrison Keillor's nationally-broadcast radio show *A Prairie Home Companion*, the duo and their band developed a solid international following. In addition to being featured on the duo's 12 albums, the Williams' songs have been covered by many artists including Tom T. Hall, Mary-Chapin Carpenter, Emmylou Harris, George Hamilton IV, Tim & Mollie O'Brien, the Nashville Bluegrass Band, the Seldom Scene, Boiled in Lead, and Holly Near.

Although they launched their musical collaboration in Nashville, the Williams first met in Myrtle Beach at the home of Linda's parents in 1971. Robin grew up in North and South Carolina and had already begun performing as a soloist, while Linda attended high-school and college in Michigan and had dabbled in guitar and banjo. Performing at open mikes and songwriters' workshops in Nashville in 1972 and 1973, Robin & Linda Williams developed their musical talents. Their first break came in 1975 when they phoned Keillor at the suggestion of multi-instrumentalist and fellow bandmember Peter Ostroushko. For the next five years, the duo appeared on Keillor's radio show whenever they were in Minneapolis. They continued to appear on the show up to 12 times a year after *A Prairie Home Companion* went national in 1980. The Williams also toured and recorded two albums with Keillor's group, the Hopeful Quartet.

The Williams' had their greatest success during the 1990s. Their first album with Their Fine Group, *Live*, was recorded in Holland in 1992. In the summer of 1993 they did a 16-city tour with Mary-Chapin Carpenter and later sang harmonies on Carpenter's Grammy Award-winning album *Stones in the Road*. Their 1996 album, *Sugar for Sugar*, spent 11 weeks in the top 20 of Gavin's Americana Chart and was followed by an all-gospel recording called *Good News*. In January 1998, they released *Devil of a Dream*, which featured songs co-written with Jerome Clark; *In the Company of Strangers* followed two years later. —*Craig Harris*

Harmony / 1981 / June Appal ✦✦✦✦

● **Close As We Can Get / 1984 / Flying Fish ✦✦✦✦✦**

Close as We Can Get/Nine 'Til Midnight / 1984 / Flying Fish ✦✦✦✦

The two albums that Robin & Linda Williams recorded in the mid-'80s for Flying Fish were eventually combined onto a single cassette or compact disc. —*Sean Westergaard*

Nine 'Til Midnight / 1985 / Flying Fish ✦✦✦

All Broken Hearts Are the Same / 1988 / Sugar Hill ✦✦✦✦✦

Rhythm of Love / 1990 / Sugar Hill ✦✦✦

Turn Toward Tomorrow / 1993 / Sugar Hill ✦✦✦

Produced by John Jennings, this collection of primarily Robin & Linda songs is held together by great economical band arrangements. Weepers like "When the Last Tear

Falls" and "Chain of Pain" are given an uptempo treatment so we don't have to get to torn up about life's hardships. "Lying to the Moon" brings the CD to a peaceul close. *—Richard Meyer*

Robin & Linda Williams & Their Fine Group Live / 1994 / Sugar Hill ♦♦♦
Recorded while on tour in Holland, this album finds Robin & Linda Willams in a more basic band setting. It lets the strength of their vocals come through better than on some of their slicker studio records. The high point comes with "The Devil Is a Mighty Wind." *—Richard Meyer*

Sugar for Sugar / Apr. 1996 / Sugar Hill ♦♦♦

Devil of a Dream / Jan. 20, 1998 / Sugar Hill ♦♦♦
Beautifully crafted work from Robin & Linda Williams, who have a knack for blending American folk music with some very familiar elements from country music—the end result is equally acceptable to folk or country fans. The strength here is in the songs, which move from storytelling mode to emotional explorations to low-key humor. The Williamses perform mostly in duet mode, though some songs will bring one voice out more than the other; both of them have a pleasantly worn-in sound, if a relatively limited range. Their in-studio musical support is more than adequate, though not spectacular—which is a plus, as it never threatens to overwhelm the songs. *—Steven E. McDonald*

In the Company of Strangers / Jan. 25, 2000 / Sugar Hill ♦♦♦
Whenever they perform on *A Prairie Home Companion*, this husband-and-wife team is always the best element on the program—with their powerful, sinewy voices (both grew up on gospel music) and instrumental chops (she's a great clawhammer banjo player, he's a very fine guitarist) they take every song they perform firmly by the throat and squeeze every drop of emotion from it, and they always do so in a way that manages to direct your attention to the song itself, rather than to their performance of it. They have a vocal blend as perfect in its way as that of the Stanley Brothers; when Linda's singing lead and Robin's belting out a low harmony it will raise the hairs on the back of your neck. But somehow their albums are often a disappointment. It's tempting to blame it on the studio environment or some other metaphysical factor, but the painful fact may simply be that the songs they write aren't as good as the ones they often sing on-stage, which are likely to be old gospel or other traditional material. Lyrically, this stuff is all great; there just aren't many memorable tunes. It's telling that on *In the Company of Strangers* the only really memorable original song is the title track (which is outstanding) and the best song of the program is a Hank Williams number. Their version of "Cold, Cold Heart" rivals Williams', frankly. If only they could write like he did. *—Rick Anderson*

Visions of Love / Feb. 5, 2002 / Sugar Hill ♦♦♦
Robin & Linda Williams take a chance on their latest album by opening with a cornerstone from the Carter Family's canon, "I'll Twine 'Mid the Ringlets" (aka "Wildwood Flower"). Unlike the original, the pace is slackened to give the deep emotion of the song room to breathe. The pace, combined with Linda Williams' sensitive vocal, gives this classic a fresh face. Interestingly, the Williams concentrate on covering other artist's songs this time around. Taking turns on vocals and accompanied by spare, tasteful arrangements, they survey great songwriters like Hank Williams, Merle Haggard, and Bruce Springsteen. As with "I'll Twine 'Mid the Ringlets," Linda's version of "Hungry Eyes" and Robin's "Ramblin' Man" slow the pace, allowing room to concentrate on soulful vocals. Linda trades pure folk for the jazzy flavors of Tin Pan Alley pop on "Wasting My Time, Wasting My Love on You" and the album ends on the solemn notes of "If I Should Fall Behind," a song that takes on a personal note when sung by a married couple. While the selection of material is fine, a certain sameness in style and approach makes one wish that the Williams would let their hair down and kick out the acoustic jams now and again. It's as though their careful craftsmanship removes the spark necessary to bring these tunes to life. Fans of past efforts, however, will appreciate the duo's eclectic choice of covers and their professional approach on *Visions of Love*. *—Ronnie D. Lankford Jr.*

Tex Williams

b. Aug. 23, 1917, Ramsey, IL, **d.** Oct. 11, 1985
Vocals, Guitar / Western Swing, Traditional Country

Although not nearly as well-known as figures like Bob Wills, the Maddox Brothers, and Merle Travis, Tex Williams was an important Western swing performer. Like all of the aforementioned musicians, he helped develop country music from its rural, acoustic origins to a more danceable, city-fied, and electrified form with a much wider popular appeal. At his peak in the late '40s, he also recorded some of the most enjoyable country swing of his time, distinguished by his talking-blues vocal delivery. Much of his style can be heard in the Western swing-influenced recordings of revivalists like Asleep at the Wheel, Commander Cody, and Dan Hicks.

The singer and guitarist caught his first big break after moving to Los Angeles in 1942. At that time California was populated by many former Texans and Oklahomans working in the defense industry, creating a need for Western swing entertainment in a region not noted for country music. One of the musicians on this circuit was fiddler Spade Cooley, who employed Jack Williams as his singer, nicknaming him "Tex" to ensure easy identification by the many Texans in their audiences. Several of Cooley's mid-'40s Columbia singles featured Tex on vocals. Capitol offered a contract to Williams as a solo artist, which strained the relationship between Tex and the tempestuous Cooley to the breaking point. Cooley fired Williams in June 1946, a move which backfired badly, as most of Cooley's band opted to follow Tex rather than remain with their difficult boss. Cooley achieved his greatest subsequent notoriety when he was convicted of beating his wife to death in a drunken fit in 1961.

Tex's renamed backing band, the Texas Caravan, was one of the best units of its kind. Numbering about a dozen members, it attained an enviable level of fluid interplay between electric and steel guitars, fiddles, bass, accordion, trumpet, and other instruments (even occasional harp). At first they recorded polkas for Capitol, with limited success. They found their true calling when Williams' friend Merle Travis wrote most of "Smoke! Smoke! Smoke! (That Cigarette)" for him, emphasizing Tex's talking-blues delivery and heavier boogie elements. The song was a monstrous commercial success in 1947, and indeed one of the biggest country hits of all time, making number one on the pop charts. That set the model for several of Williams' subsequent hits: hot Western swing backup, over which Tex would roll his deep, laconic, easygoing narratives of humorous, slightly ridiculous situations. As enjoyable as these were, they were just one facet of the Texas Caravan's talents. The outfit was also capable of generating quite a heat on boogie instrumentals and more straightforward vocal numbers in which Williams actually sang rather than spoke.

Williams' commercial success began to peter out in the early '50s, and he left Capitol in 1951. He continued to record often in the 1950s, mostly for Decca, without much success; in 1957, the Western Caravan disbanded. He pressed on, however, returning to Capitol in the early '60s, and recording a live album that included Glen Campbell on guitar. He had one final country hit, the memorably titled "The Night Miss Ann's Hotel for Single Girls Burned Down," which entered the Top 40 in 1971. *—Richie Unterberger*

★ **Vintage Collections Series** / Jan. 23, 1996 / Capitol ♦♦♦♦♦
This has Tex's late-'40s peak, with the late-'40s smashes "Smoke! Smoke! Smoke! (That Cigarette)," "Never Trust a Woman," "Suspicion," and "That's What I Like About the West." It also includes some lesser-known items from radio transciption discs, and a couple of songs from an early '60s live album with Glen Campbell on guitar. *—Richie Unterberger*

The Very Best of Tex Williams / Jul. 25, 2000 / Varese ♦♦♦
The Very Best of Tex Williams collects 13 of the Western swing star's most memorable songs and includes three previously unreleased performances: "Love Carefully," "Giddy-Up Go," and "Shakespeare Cha-Cha." "The Battle of New Orleans," "I'll Hold You in My Heart," "Little Ol Wine Drinker Me," and "Yankee Go Home" are some of the entertaining songs included on this collection, but its lack of definitive tracks like "Smoke! Smoke! Smoke! (That Cigarette)" and "Never Trust a Woman" makes it a less than ideal starting point. *—Heather Phares*

That's What I Like About the West / Jan. 22, 2002 / ASV ♦♦♦♦♦
Now that Capitol's *Vintage Collection* is out of print, this is the best available Tex Williams compilation. Actually, it's the best of them all, as it features his biggest hits not only with the Western Caravan, but also with Spade Cooley's orchestra, making it about as definitive as you could hope for. The sound quality is as good as it gets (the Cooley tracks actually sound better than Columbia's *Spadella!* re-mastering) and it restores excellent songs like "Miss Molly" and "Birmingham Bounce," as well as experimental fare like the jazzy, exotic "Artistry in Western Swing," which had been cutout of previous collections. Diehards may have some qualms about the track selection, but all the biggies are here, and even the more obscure songs are generally excellent. *—Jim Smith*

Tex Williams & His Western Caravan: 1946–1951 / Feb. 26, 2002 / Country Routes ♦♦♦♦♦

Victoria Williams

b. Dec. 23, 1958, Shreveport, LA
Guitar, Vocals / Singer/Songwriter, Folk-Rock, Alternative Country-Rock, Contemporary Folk, Alternative Folk, Adult Alternative Pop/Rock

Despite a successful career as a idiosyncratic country-folk performer, Victoria Williams was perhaps best known as a songwriter; thanks, ironically enough, to a tribute album recorded in her honor. Born in Louisiana in 1959, Williams taught herself to play the guitar while still in her teens, and soon began composing songs. In college, she joined her first band, the G.W. Korners. After spending some time on the road, she ended up in California in 1979, where she was a regular at Los Angeles' famed Troubadour Club's "Hoot Nights." After first returning to Louisiana with the intent of forming a band, she moved back to L.A., where she performed on Venice Beach and ultimately signed a recording contract which proved fruitless.

Soon after, Williams met musician Peter Case, formerly of the Plimsouls. Not only did they form an act together—a jug band-like trio named the Incredibly Strung Out Band—but the couple also married. Finally, Williams made her solo recording debut in 1987 with *Happy Come Home*, a collection showcasing her vivid songcraft as well as her off-kilter, squeaky vocal style. After the record was released, Williams starred in a documentary by the filmmaker D.A. Pennebaker. In 1989, she and Case divorced; a follow-up record, *Swing the Statue!*, appeared in 1990.

In 1992, while opening for Neil Young, Williams began experiencing a numb feeling in her hands which made it increasingly difficult to play her guitar. Upon visiting a doctor, she was diagnosed with the degenerative neurological disorder multiple sclerosis. The medical bills quickly piled up, and like many musicians, she was not covered by health insurance. In response, her manager began assembling friends and fans to record Williams' songs for a benefit album; the result, 1993's *Sweet Relief: A Benefit for Victoria Williams*, featured the likes of Pearl Jam, Lou Reed, Matthew Sweet, the Jayhawks, and Soul Asylum, whose rendition of "Summer of Drugs" was the record's first single. Due to its all-star lineup, *Sweet Relief* far outsold any of Williams' own efforts, raising not only funds for her medical treatment but her visibility within the musical community as well. Additionally, the record's success enabled Williams to establish the Sweet Relief Fund, created to assist other musicians with health problems; in 1996, a second tribute record, honoring the partially paralyzed singer/songwriter Vic Chesnutt, was released.

In 1994, Williams issued *Loose*, a varied collection featuring duets with Soul Asylum's Dave Pirner and the Jayhawks' Mark Olson, Williams' second husband. A year later, she and her Loose Band released *This Moment in Toronto*, a live career overview which also offered a handful of standards ("Smoke Gets in Your Eyes," "Imagination") as well as one new song, "Graveyard." Her fourth solo album, *Musings of a Creek Dipper*, was released in 1998. Two years later, Williams issued her strongest effort date with *Water to Drink*. In

2002, she recorded an album of standards entitled *Sings Some Ol' Songs*. Her renditions of "Moon River," "Someone to Watch Over Me," and "My Funny Valentine" breathed new life thanks to Williams' impeccable touch. —*Jason Ankeny*

Happy Come Home / 1987 / Geffen ◆◆◆◆

It is indeed a rarity when a debut album is able to distil the essence of any artist. However, Victoria Williams is considerably more than just any artist and *Happy Come Home* is the personification of the word *eclectic*—just like Williams herself. She wasn't alone in creating her eponymous masterpiece, either. A cavalcade of pop and rock music's elite congregated with Williams in the celebration of the varied music on the album. The simple folk tales, sage-like observations, and just plain good advice that she writes about are personified by an unbelievably delicious cast of characters both in the studio as well as in between the lines. There is an undeniable strength and maturity in Williams' songwriting. Like few artists or albums, *Happy Come Home* reveals an artist fully developed with a style and persona that is uniquely American and arguably irresistible. Another musician fitting that description is Van Dyke Parks—whose contributions to this disc are almost immediately evident. His signature orchestral flourishes are unmistakable throughout the string arrangements for "TC," "Main Road," and the opening cut, "Shoes." Sonically, his pallet blends the humor and whimsy of Mark Twain with the noir romanticism of George Gershwin. These hues ideally suit Williams' folk-tinged songs. In the case of "TC"—a legitimate pocket symphony—there are also a few well-placed nods to Prokofiev's "Peter and the Wolf." The rock & roll pieces—notably "Animal Wild" and the trippy "Merry Go Round"—are best described as late-'80s alternative or college rock. A quick rundown of the personnel might best give an idea of the direction Williams found herself and her music in, as it was being somewhat moulded by producer Anton Fier. Among the luminaries are: Syd Straw, Bernie Worrell, T-Bone Burnett, Carla Bley, Peter Blegvad, and Hugh McCracken. Their various—and unspecified—contributions are at times typical, but never predictable. It would be futile to attempt a list of all the disparate musical styles that unify *Happy Come Home*. They range from gospel ("I Will Do His Will") to acoustic folk ("Happy Come Home" and "Lights") and hit upon more subtle influences such as jazz ("Big Fish") and even a sort of bayou travelogue "Opelousas." Concurrent with the release of the album, Williams was the subject of a 28-minute documentary by legendary filmmaker D.A. Pennebaker. The video—also titled *Happy Come Home*—features nine of the 13 tracks from the disc, including a few performed spontaneously for the camera. Originally aired on MTV, it was briefly available on VHS at Williams' live shows. —*Lindsay Planer*

● Swing the Statue! / 1990 / Mammoth ◆◆◆◆◆

On the follow-up to her landmark debut, *Happy Come Home* (1987), Victoria Williams' skills as a multi-faceted songwriter become increasingly stronger and more distinct. The lack of aural opulence—such as Van Dyke Parks' string arrangements—reveal a less-forced approach, resulting in a giant leap forward in terms of the development of Williams' own voice. Likewise, her rich Louisiana bayou roots increasingly influence her music and act as a strong motif throughout not only *Swing the Statue*, but her future releases as well—most notably her contributions to the Original Harmony Ridge Creekdippers. Perhaps drawing upon her own experiences, *Swing the Statue* has an air of melancholia wafting throughout much of the album. Both "Boogieman" and "I Can't Cry Hard Enough"—while divergent in terms of musical style—speak directly to the feelings of loss and abandonment. These aptly juxtapose against the innocence and youthful awe of "Look at That Moon" and "Wobbling" as well as the spiritual guidance found in "Lift Him Up" and "Weeds." Unlike *Happy Come Home*, *Swing the Statue* is exceedingly more reserved and somewhat stark—with an emphasis on acoustic instrumentation. These aptly inhabit Williams' remarkably jazzy arrangements. While examples are abundant, most specifically are the easy and lethargic "Clothesline," as well as the freewheeling "On Time" or "Vieux Amis"—the latter of which is also sung in the French-derived Cajun dialect. The wholly diverse collection of sounds and styles explored on the disc would continue to inform Williams' work, although it would be another four years before her international breakthrough album, *Loose* (1994), would be released. While she would ultimately retain much of the momentum gained on *Swing the Statue*, the dissolution of her record label, Rough Trade, left Williams very little in the way of national or international publicity or promotion. A much more devastating blow was dealt while on the road supporting this album when Williams was diagnosed with the degenerative neurological disorder multiple sclerosis. Her ultimate triumph/co-existence with the disorder gave birth to much of the celebratory tone on her follow-up, *Loose*. —*Lindsay Planer*

Loose / 1994 / Mammoth ◆◆◆◆◆

Sometimes one has to wonder just where great records come from; when something comes out of the factory spotless, full of brightness, life and love, grit and suffering, all offered as a gift to the listener. *Loose* is Victoria Williams' comeback record after her two amazing but misunderstood Geffen records, *Happy Come Home* and *Swing the Statue!* In the interim she was diagnosed with multiple sclerosis and had no health insurance. The Sweet Relief Foundation was set up and helped to take care of her—and other uninsured musicians'—expenses and restore her health. *Loose* is the evidence of that health and the final proof for all the naysayers that Williams is among the most gifted singers and songwriters of her generation. With a cast of musicians that includes the Jayhawks, Van Dyke Parks, the Tower of Power Horns, Tammy Rodgers, Dave Pirner, Greg Leisz, Don Heffington, Doug Wieselman, and a ton of others, the music ranges from the blue-eyed R&B of "You R Loved," with its punchy horns and passionate declaration of redemption, to the jazzy Ben Sidran-esque "Harry Went to Heaven," to the beautiful country duet "When We Sing Together" between Williams and soon-to-be husband Mark Olson that comes across as a Gram Parsons/Emmylou Harris duet. There is joy and more joy in the proceedings. But it is more than that. Inside the sound of Williams' unusual yet glorious voice is the sound of gratitude. In the musical accompaniment there is an excitement

that something is unfolding here that will perhaps never be experienced again, that music is being made without ego, showcases, excesses, or even specific direction. Everything is spontaneously created and then disciplined in its final execution. Check out the loopy off-the-beat "Polish Those Shoes" with its orchestral accompaniment behind the beat of the rock band. Then there's Williams' absolutely astonishing read of "What a Wonderful World." Like Louis Armstrong's—and this is not a comparison between versions but a likeness of emotional transference—Williams expresses not only wonder but folksy wisdom in each line. Likewise, so does the cover of Spirit's "Nature's Way," a duet with Soul Asylum's Dave Pirner. The feeling is almost prayer-like, but it's a prayer of acceptance rather than one of supplication. But it is in Williams' own songs that the truth of her accomplishment lies, such as "Sunshine Country," organic yet psychedelic yet as hooky as any fine pop song, the loopy "Happy to Have Known Pappy," the tender folk song "My Ally," the shambolic rock & roll of "Get Away," and the concluding gospel track, "Psalms," which with its tenderness and reverence, expresses a simple faith and profound dedication. Paul Fox's production is ingenious, culling virtually anything he could afford to make each song a piece in a lush yet easily accessible tapestry of texture, ambience, and pop majesty. This is a comeback record that brought an artist back into the public eye—however briefly—and created a masterpiece that transcends genre by blurring all the lines in the name of excellence, emotional honesty, and visionary creativity. —*Thom Jurek*

This Moment: In Toronto With the Loose Band / Nov. 7, 1995 / Atlantic ◆◆◆

Victoria Williams' first international tour as a headliner— supporting her 1994 release *Loose*—yielded *This Moment: In Toronto With the Loose Band*, her first concert recording. Williams (guitar/vocals) is supported by a six-piece band centering around the Williams Brothers (no relation to Victoria), David (vocals) and Andrew (guitar), as well as Tim Ray (keyboards)—all of whom had participated in the creation of *Loose*. Joining them are neo-folk session heavyweights Joey Burns (bass/vocals) and David Mansfield (violin/dobro/pedal steel guitar/mandolin). As an ensemble, they animate choice selections from Victoria's previous studio efforts—*Happy Come Home* (1987) and *Swing the Statue* (1990)—with an emphasis on material from *Loose*. As a songwriter, Victoria Williams conjures exquisite images weaved around an ethereal folk/jazz delivery—which is more often than not also saturated in down-home psychedelia, examples of which abound throughout *This Moment*. Primary among them is "Graveyard," which was renamed "Blackbirds Rise" on her follow-up studio release *Musings of a Creek Dipper* (1998), as well as the achingly beautiful reading of the Jimmy Van Heusen/Johnny Burke pop standard "Imagination." The undemanding and comfortably intimate environs that Williams create during performance are punctuated by the spontaneous on-stage arrival of her traveling companion and puppy, Molly—inspiring Victoria to ad-lib "Oh its good to have a dog. It's good to see their smile. It's good to have your arms around 'em when it's been a long while"—during the opening to what develops into a rousing "Crazy Mary." Another endearing moment catches Victoria interacting with the audience and spontaneously performing requests—most notably "TC." Although accompanied by her own solo piano, she lovingly re-creates Van Dyke Parks' breathtaking string arrangements. *This Moment* is a precious and rare gift from a flower to her audience. —*Lindsay Planer*

Musings of a Creek Dipper / Jan. 13, 1998 / Atlantic ◆◆◆

Abandoning the lush orchestral backdrops that dominated most of *Loose*, Victoria Williams expands her musical skills on *Musings of a Creekdipper*, finding an original, eclectically rural sound that enhances the off-center originality of her songs. Producing the album with Trina Shoemaker, Williams has found a collection of sounds and styles that makes the record her most ambitious so far. For the most part, her experiments work, whether it's the cellos and coronets of "Periwinkle Sky" or Wendy & Lisa's drum loops on "Train Song (Demise of the Caboose)." What really holds the album together is Williams' songwriting, which remains consistently impressive, both in lyrical and musical terms. There are a few numbers that don't quite work, but they only illustrate that Williams' best efforts are quirky but graceful folk-rock gems. —*Stephen Thomas Erlewine*

Water to Drink / Aug. 15, 2000 / Atlantic ◆◆◆◆

Williams is an innovative and adventurous songwriter and performer, but many find her folky antics and unique voice to be a bit much. Certainly *Water to Drink*, her first solo album since 1998's critically acclaimed *Musings of a Creek Dipper*, will add quite a few new souls to each camp. Here Williams stretches herself artistically and scores more than a few creative triumphs, but her personal mannerisms color their share of songs as well. The opening song swings along in somewhat self-indulgent ramblings about personal freedom, forgiveness, and her grandmother's hat pin, backed up by an instrumental soup of buzzy psychedelic guitars and Carole King-inspired piano. The result is a muddy mess that doesn't seem to go anywhere in particular. The rest of the album truly is a joy, however. The hippie vibe works better on "Joy of Love," where a breezy chorus seems more like a rallying cry than a repetitive drone. The title track "Water to Drink" is even better. An English version of Antonio Carlos Jobim's "Agua de Beber," the song allows Williams a fun vehicle for her vocal creativity. Here her voice seems more in its element, gaining a kind of Betty Boop coy sexiness instead of the croony qualities that seem to pervade elsewhere. Indeed, two of the other strongest performances on the album, on "Until the Real Thing Comes Along" and "Young at Heart," are standards, proving that Williams may be strongest when interpreting the songs of other people. Perhaps her lyrical quirkiness and eccentric tone and phrasing is a little too much all at once and the constraints of performing another composer's songs tone down the blur of her ideas, giving her space where she can spread out and share her immense talent. —*Stacia Proefrock*

Sings Some Ol' Songs / Aug. 6, 2002 / Dualtone ◆◆◆

Victoria Williams is a storyteller of her own kind who possesses a matchless whimsicality. On her fifth album, *Sings Some Ol' Songs*, Williams' peculiar vocal beauty comes alive in an exciting collection of traditional standards. It's a great fit, too. Williams is delightfully intelligent in giving some of these songs new life, but doesn't miss out on the initial grace behind them all. Williams soaks herself in light jazz sounds on the blushing rendition of Henry Mancini's "Moon River." Richard Rodgers & Lorenz Hart's classic "My Funny Valentine" is vocally sleek, while the old-timey good-time of "Keep Sweeping Cobwebs Off the Moon" and the sassy salsa beats of "And Roses and Roses" are fashionably more her style. The obscuro fun of Eden Ahbez's "Mongoose" is equally playful. *Sings Some Ol' Songs* is essentially a reverie of traditional pop and its musical roots. The production is clear and concise, allowing the dreamlike quality of *Sings Some Ol' Songs* to simply arrive. Williams keeps things innocent in a natural way in keeping listeners interested. With this particular album, she's introducing swan songs of yesteryear to a new audience. It's absolutely lovely. *—MacKenzie Wilson*

Foy Willing (Foy Willingham)

b. 1915, Bosque County, TX, **d.** Jun. 24, 1978, Nashville, TN
Vocals / Cowboy
Singer, songwriter, and actor Foy Willing was best known as the founder of the Riders of the Purple Sage, a popular cowboy band known for their harmonies and appearances in low-budget Westerns from the '40s and '50s. Born Foy Willingham in Bosque County, TX, he began as a soloist and member of a gospel group on local radio. In 1933 he began appearing on a radio show in New York City but left in 1935 to work as a radio announcer back in Texas. In 1940, Willing moved to California and had established a version of the Riders there (the band had actually been founded in 1936 by Buck Page and a few others). Willing's Riders included Patti Page on vocals, fiddler Johnny Paul, and accordionist Ken Coopern. World War II call ups caused the lineup to fluctuate during this period, but the group did have some success on the charts, including the country Top Tens "Texas Blues" (1944) and "Have I Told You Lately That I Love You" and "Detour," both from 1946. Willing and his band also appeared on radio shows and even dabbled in film. In 1944, they made their feature film debut in *Cowboy From Lonesome River*, a Western featuring Charles Starrett. The following year, the band began appearing regularly on the All Star Western Theater. They continued appearing in films through the decade and in 1948 became Roy Rogers' new backup band after the Sons of the Pioneers left. The Willing-led Riders disbanded in 1952, though he continued to use the name for a number of years after his semi-retirement from performing. During the late '50s and early '60s, the group occasionally reunited to record and perform, and Willing went on to appear at Western festivals during the 1970s. Willing died July 24th, 1978, in Nashville, TN. He was 63. *—Johnny Loftus*

Riders of the Purple Sage / 1950 / Varsity ✦✦✦

Cowboy / 1958 / Roulette ✦✦✦✦

The New Sound of American Folk / 1962 / Jubilee ✦✦✦

Collectors Edition / Feb. 24, 1998 / Simitar ✦✦✦✦
These dozen 1940s-vintage recordings by Foy Willing & the Riders of the Purple Sage range in sound quality from decent to good. The origins aren't indicated, although they seem to be radio transcriptions. The songs are core western repertory: "Cool Water," "Home on the Range," "Red River Valley," "The Last Round Up," "Tumbling Tumbleweeds," and "Jack O' Diamonds" (aka "Rye Whiskey"). Traditional folk material is represented by "Blue Tail Fly" and "Big Rock Candy Mountain." Willing and company owed a lot to the Sons of the Pioneers, and in the overall scheme of things the original Pioneers' renditions of much of this repertory would be preferable, but Willing and his group, featuring Al Sloey, Jimmy Dean (not the future sausage king), and Scotty Harrell on vocals, had more of a Western swing approach to music. The group's version of "Blue Tail Fly" is a real treat, and the yodel-version of "She'll Be Comin' Round the Mountain" (which features an ocarina solo) done in a similar swing version is one of the CD's highlights. On the opposite end of the spectrum, "The Old Chisholm Trail" is done in a basic, stripped-down version that sounds not too different from a trail recording, with minimal instrumental backing. And "Oh Bury Me Not on the Lone Prairie" is worth the price of the disc by itself. The rendition of "Mexicali Rose" featured here is almost entirely instrumental, which makes it a bit unusual, especially in the exceptionally prominent twangy dobro flourishes, which makes one wonder if it was done in the wake of Anton Karas' zither-laden score to Carol Reed's *The Third Man*. *—Bruce Eder*

● **Cowboy/The New Sound of American Folk** / Aug. 17, 1999 / Soundies ✦✦✦✦✦
This CD collects two albums made late in Foy Willing's career, *Cowboy* (1958) and *The New Sound of American Folk* (1962). *Cowboy* is comprised mostly of popular Western songs ("Red River Valley," "Cool, Cool Water") and Western swing ("Rose of San Antone," "Have I Told You Lately That I Love You"). The group harmonies are lovely, and the pop/rock flourishes, including a female chorus and an occasional hot electric guitar solo, add delightful textures. Even better is *The New Sound of American Folk*, which takes a folk-pop approach similar to that of ('50s) Jimmie Rodgers, whose "Kisses Sweeter Than Wine" is covered. Mary Ford provides some vocals, and the resulting blend recalls the Browns' flirtations with folk music. The material is varied and the arrangements interesting and sometimes surprising, making *The New Sound of American Folk* a forgotten gem that deserves to be rediscovered. *—Greg Adams*

The Willis Brothers

f. 1932, **db.** 1995
Group / Traditional Country, Western Swing
James "Guy" Willis, Charles "Skeeter" Willis, and John "Vic" Willis started playing music on their family farm as kids. As teenagers in 1932, the Willis Brothers formed the Oklahoma Wranglers, formed as a band, playing a blend of Western swing and cowboy. Skeeter Willis sang and fiddled; Guy sang lead and played guitar; and, in the original lineup, eldest brother Joe played along. The Willis Brothers played on Shawnee, OK's KGEF throughout the '30s. In 1939, Joe married and left, and Vic, who played accordion, piano, and sang, joined. The brothers moved to Kansas City to appear on *Brush Street Follies* until 1942, when they disbanded to fight in the war. Reunited in 1946, they joined the *Grand Ole Opry* and signed to Sterling Records, and had the distinction of backing Hank Williams on his first recordings.

After leaving the *Opry* in 1949, the Willis Brothers toured with Eddy Arnold until 1957 and appeared in the films *Feuding Rhythm* and *Hoe Down*. In an attempt to play to an audience beyond just Western fans, the Oklahoma Wranglers name was dropped for the Willis Brothers. The band recorded steadily with Mercury, RCA, and Coral before signing with Starday and finally charting with the truck-driving country hit "Give Me 40 Acres (To Turn This Rig Around)" in 1964. Back at the *Opry*, the Willis Brothers remained there until Vic died at 73 in a 1995 car crash. *—Ron DePasquale*

● **24 Great Truck Drivin' Hits** / Mar. 11, 1994 / Deluxe ✦✦✦

Kelly Willis

b. Oct. 2, 1968, Annandale, VA
Vocals / Contemporary Country, New Traditionalist
Although the work of new traditionalist singer/songwriter Kelly Willis earned widespread critical acclaim, she found little in the way of comparable commercial success; her sound, a smart hybrid of *country* and rock, simply assimilated both musical styles too well to gain acceptance in either camp. Born in Oklahoma and raised in the Washington, D.C., area, she began performing in her boyfriend (and future husband) Mas Palermo's band at the age of 16. Her powerhouse vocals were so popular with club audiences that soon the group was renamed Kelly & the Fireballs in her honor. After Willis graduated high-school, the band moved to Austin, TX, only to break up six months later.

As a result, Willis began learning to play guitar while drummer Palermo honed his songwriting chops. The duo started a new band, Radio Ranch, with guitarist David Murray, steel player Michael Hardwick, and bassist Michael Foreman. One of Radio Ranch's performances so impressed singer Nanci Griffith that she began lobbying her label, MCA, to sign to group, leading to Willis' 1990 debut *Well Travelled Love*. In an attempt to capitalize on Willis' stunning looks, she was marketed as a girl-next-door type, and despite the presence of the full band, only her name appeared on the album jacket. Despite the glowing reviews, the LP fared poorly; and so, for her 1991 sophomore effort *Bang Bang*, she was depicted as a coquettish pin-up. Again, however, the good publicity the record received did not translate to radio airplay nor chart sales, and to top it all off, Willis and Palermo separated.

For her third album, comprised largely of her own songs, Willis joined forces with pop producer Don Was; the self-titled 1993 effort suffered the same fate as its predecessors, however, and she was dropped by MCA shortly after its release. Following a few years of relative inactivity, she resurfaced in 1995 duetting with Son Volt's Jay Farrar on the *Red Hot & Bothered* compilation, and after issuing a 1996 independent label EP, *Fading Fast*, announced plans for a 1997 LP on A&M. In late 1996, she married fellow Austin musician Bruce Robison. While the '90s drew to a close, Willis inked a deal with Rykodisc. Her fourth album, *What I Deserve*, appeared in 1999 and it was a breakthrough hit for Willis. *Time Magazine* hailed the album as "the smartest, most consistently worthwhile *country* CD" to have been released that year. Three years later, Willis returned to the scene with *Easy*, which included collaborative efforts with Vince Gill, Union Station's Dan Tyminski, and Nickel Creek's Chris Thile. *—Jason Ankeny*

Well Travelled Love / 1990 / MCA ✦✦✦
On her debut, this Austin country-rocker sings Texas-steel tunes and roisterous rockers with spirited assurance, but there's a natural tremble in her voice that makes her sound dangerous yet vulnerable. Willis is one of the few country singers with the disarming beauty to become a true sex symbol, and if she's the feminine response to all the hat acts, that's fine. *—Brian Mansfield*

Bang Bang / 1991 / MCA ✦✦✦✦✦
Willis' idea of country comes from female rockabillys like Janis Martin and Wanda Jackson and from the blues-influenced Texas crowd she runs with in Austin. *Bang Bang* reflects that influence in the blistering tempos of "Too Much to Ask" and "Standing By the River," the Tex-Mex groove of "The Heart That Love Forgot," and an absolutely incendiary version of Joe Ely's "Settle for Love." *—Brian Mansfield*

Kelly Willis / 1993 / MCA ✦✦✦✦✦
Where Willis' first two albums occasionally turned into showcases for her musicians, *Kelly Willis* emphasizes concise, twangy pop songs over barn-burners. Willis sings a mandolin-propelled cover of Marshall Crenshaw's "Whatever Way the Wind Blows" and blends her voice with two members of Jellyfish on "One More Night." She also dips into Nashville's back catalog with a version of the Kendalls' 1977 "Heaven's Just a Sin Away." *—Brian Mansfield*

Fading Fast / 1996 / A&M ✦✦✦✦
Originally released as a promotional item to coincide with the inclusion of the song "Fading Fast" on the *Boys* soundtrack, collectors' frenzy to obtain this four-song EP led to its commercial release—but only in Texas. The excitement generated by the EP is easy to understand; this is simply the best music Kelly Willis has ever made. Joined by Son Volt's Jay Farrar on three tracks and the band *16 Horsepower* on a fourth, Willis turns in impeccable performances on some of her strongest songwriting efforts yet (Willis wrote or co-wrote three songs; the fourth was penned by husband Bruce Robison). The loose, country-rock vibe doesn't detract from her viability as a commercial country artist, but boosts her appeal to the No Depression crowd considerably. Every song here is an absolute gem, and it's shameful to think that three-fourths of these tracks were nearly doomed to obscurity on a promotional CD. *Fading Fast* offers an excellent and inexpensive introduction to Kelly Willis, and it's a must for her fans. *—Greg Adams*

What I Deserve / Feb. 23, 1999 / Rykodisc ✦✦✦
This effort from country singer Kelly Willis has a number of important things going for it. First of all, there's her voice, which is an almost archetypally perfect blend of sweetness

and grit. Then there are her backing musicians—in particular guitarist Mark Spencer, who makes a recognizably country sound without overdoing it or descending into bathos and stereotype. Last, and very importantly, there's producer Dave McNair, who has crafted a beautifully balanced and full-bodied sound for the album without allowing things to get too slick and prettified. What's lacking, for the most part, are melodies strong enough to grab your interest and hold it. There are some hooks—"Take Me Down" is quite singable, and there's a great version of Nick Drake's "Time Has Told Me"—but they're relatively few and far between, and scarcity of hooks can be death for a country album. In this case the lack is far from fatal, but it's noticeable. Recommended with reservations. —*Rick Anderson*

● **One More Time: The MCA Recordings** / Sep. 12, 2000 / MCA Nashville ✦✦✦✦✦
MCA Nashville's *One More Time: The MCA Recordings* was released on the heels of the independent success Kelly Willis enjoyed in 1999 with *What I Deserve*. Though it may have appeared after a success, the compilation isn't really a cash in. It's really quite useful, as a matter of fact, since it summarizes her three MCA albums—1990's *Well Travelled Love*, 1991's *Bang Bang*, and 1993's *Kelly Willis*—while adding "Little Honey," her contribution to the *Thelma & Louise* soundtrack. For anyone looking to catch-up after *What I Deserve*, this is an excellent place to go (especially since two of her three MCA albums were out of print at the time of *One More Time*'s release), and it's a satisfying listen in its own right. —*Stephen Thomas Erlewine*

Easy / Aug. 20, 2002 / Rykodisc ✦✦✦✦
Austin, TX, sure has it good—a lot of amazing musicians are calling it home: Shawn Colvin, Patty Griffin, and the Dixie Chicks, to name a few. Add Kelly Willis to the list, because with *Easy* she has earned, or at least kept, her place in amazing-ville. Funny thing is, Willis is almost the perfect synthesis of the above-mentioned artists. She has a tender, romantic way in her songcrafting not at all unlike Colvin. Her voice has an rich, expressive ache, as does Griffin's. And she incorporates the best of country and bluegrass music into her own sonic foundry à la the Dixie Chicks (it certainly doesn't hurt much that she and Dixie Chick Emily Robison are sisters-in-law via the Robison brothers, Bruce and Charlie). With *Easy*, Willis offers up a half-dozen original compositions and a few very tasteful covers that are, well, easy— easy on the ear, easy on the heart, easy on the mind. She's one of those gals who can say she was country when country wasn't cool, if only for her dignified and much-appreciated adherence to a real, organic, rooted sound that's as much Americana as anything else. This framework suits her well. The record would have been great without them, but it should also be noted that some very talented folks contributed a little something along the way. Alison Krauss, Chris Thile, Vince Gill, Dan Tyminski, and Ian McLagan all get a tip of the hat on this one, too. —*Kelly McCartney*

Billy Jack Wills

b. Feb. 26, 1926, Memphis, TX, **d.** Mar. 2, 1991
Bass / Western Swing
Perhaps the most underrated Western swing bandleader ever was Billy Jack Wills, the youngest brother of Bob, whose Western Swing Band broke new ground for the genre in the early '50s. Born February 26, 1926, in Memphis, Hall County, TX, Billy Jack was exposed at an early age to the music of his famous brother, as well as his father, champion fiddler John Wills. After beginning his professional career in brother Johnnie Lee Wills' Tulsa band in the early '40s, Billy Jack went to California to work as a bassist and drummer for the Texas Playboys. In that group, he played a significant role both as a vocalist and songwriter, lending his bluesy voice to "Cadillac in Model A" and providing lyrics to the massive hit "Faded Love."

After six years as a member of the Texas Playboys, Billy Jack got his chance as a leader when Bob moved his base of operations from the *Wills Point Ballroom* in Sacramento to Oklahoma City. Tired of touring, mandolinist Tiny Moore stayed behind to manage Wills Point. Needing a new band to fill the void left by Wills' departure, Moore suggested Billy Jack. Bob agreed, and Moore and Billy Jack assembled a band that included trumpeter and bassist Dick McComb, fiddler/bassist Cotton Roberts, rhythm guitarist Kenny Lowery, and steel guitarist Tommy Varner. The group, dubbed Billy Jack Wills & His Western Swing Band, began broadcasting over Sacramento's KCRA radio in 1950, soon moving to the considerably larger KFBK. The band truly came into being, however, after the start of the Korean War. Looking to replace the drafted Varner, Wills hired a local teenager named Vance Terry, a disciple of Noel Boggs whose crisp, driving style added the final element to the group's adventurous sound.

The enormous age difference (20 years) between Billy Jack and Bob meant that the younger's musical interests were considerably more advanced. While Bob had drawn inspiration from the primitive blues and jazz of the 1910s and '20s, Billy Jack's muse lay in the developing genres of jump blues, R&B, and bebop. These fixations gave his group a progressiveness that was found nowhere else, characterized by its hard-swinging jazz rhythms and bluesy, shouted vocals, which drew heavily from the styles of Wynonie Harris and Roy Brown. Between 1950 and 1954, the group enjoyed a strong Northwest following, touring and building up an eclectic repertoire of radio transcriptions. They covered many of the popular black hits of the time, including Ruth Brown's "Teardrops From My Eyes" and Larry Darnell's "For You, My Love." In 1953, the group cut a version of Roy Brown's "There's Good Rocking Tonight"; later that year, they turned in a rollicking arrangement of Bill Haley's first hit, "Crazy, Man, Crazy."

The group's success, however, was short-lived. In 1954, Bob Wills disbanded the Texas Playboys and returned to Sacramento to perform with Billy Jack. The idea was to increase business at Wills Point, but the results were disastrous. Bob quickly took charge of the group and against the wishes of most involved, immediately set off on tour, at which point Tiny Moore quit to host a children's television show. Out on the road, energies were soon sapped. Under Wills' control, the boldness that had characterized the band's radio broadcasts began to fold, channeled into what was by now the rather stale sound of the Texas Playboys. That and the emerging television craze effectively ended the group. Vance Terry quit to enroll in college; he later joined Jimmie Rivers & the Cherokees. Tiny Moore went on to play with Merle Haggard & the Strangers. Billy Jack struggled on without success until 1960, when he retired from music. He died on March 2, 1991. —*Jim Smith*

● **Billy Jack Wills & His Western Swing Band** / 1952-1954 / Western ✦✦✦✦✦
One of the most underrated (and generally overlooked) Western swing bands ever was the outfit that Billy Jack Wills (younger brother of Bob Wills) led in the early- to mid-'50s. A favorite in northern California at the time but largely forgotten since then, the band is heard performing 16 selections on this album that were recorded at a radio station in Sacramento. In addition to Wills (who just takes one vocal and is primarily in a supportive role), the group consists of the great electric mandolin player Tiny Moore (who also has six vocals), steel guitarist Vance Terry, trumpeter Dick McComb, guitarist Kenny Lowery and bassist Cotton Roberts (who occasionally switches to fiddle). The swinging material (which is highlighted by "Johnson Rag," "Air Mail Special," "Tuxedo Junction," "Twin Guitar Special" and "Summit Ridge Drive") is consistently memorable. —*Scott Yanow*

Crazy Man Crazy / 1952-1954 / Western ✦✦✦✦✦
The second of two Billy Jack Wills albums put out by Mutual Music in their Western swing series is the equal of the first. Wills (Bob's younger brother) led one of the last great Western swing bands, a mighty outfit which on this LP features the leader taking four vocals, the great electric mandolin player Tiny Moore (who also pays a bit of fiddle and has five vocals of his own), steel guitarist Vance Terry, trumpeter Dick McComb, Kenney Lowery on rhythm guitar, Cotton Roberts on bass and fiddle, and the supportive drummer Tommy Perkins. The radio transcriptions featured on the two albums showcase the group at the height of its power; the second LP's highlights include "Skiddle Dee Boo," "Stardust," "Sweet Georgia Brown," "Jazz Me Blues," and "Steel Guitar Stomp," but all 16 selections are enjoyable. In addition to combining country music and swing, Wills' band was open to the influence of bebop and early R&B. It's highly recommended. —*Scott Yanow*

Crazy Man Crazy / Mar. 9, 1999 / Joaquin ✦✦✦✦✦
Joaquin's second collection of Billy Jack Wills' music, like the first, reflects his R&B roots, particularly in jump blues and the early jazz of Louis Armstrong. The liner notes portray his band as a "missing link" between Western swing and rock & roll, and that's a good judgment: Wills' vocals were deeply influenced by R&B shouters like Wynonie Harris, making him among the first country artists to overtly combine the two genres. "For You, My Love" and "Milk Cow Blues" are two of his greatest pre-rock & roll fusions. "Stardust" is terrific, generating fantastic solos from Dick McComb and Tiny Moore. The sound quality flits, but the songs are strong and Vance Terry's steel guitar is crisp and perfect. Excellent stuff. —*Jim Smith*

Bob Wills

b. Mar. 6, 1905, Kosse, TX, **d.** May 13, 1975, Fort Worth, TX
Fiddle, Songwriter, Leader, Vocals / Traditional Country, Western Swing
Bob Wills' name will forever be associated with Western swing. Although he did not invent the genre single handedly, he did popularize the genre and changed its rules. In the process, he reinvented the rules of popular music. Bob Wills & His Texas Playboys were a dance band with a country string section that played pop songs as if they were jazz numbers. Their music expanded and erased boundaries between genres. It was also some of the most popular music of its era. Throughout the '40s, the band was one of the most popular groups in the country and the musicians in the Playboys were among the finest of their era. As the popularity of Western swing declined, so did Wills' popularity, but his influence is immeasurable. From the first honky tonkers to Western swing revivalists, generations of country artists owe him a significant debt, as do certain rock and jazz musicians. Bob Wills was a maverick and his spirit infused American popular music of the 20th century with a renegade, virtuosic flair.

Bob Wills was born outside of Kosse, TX, in 1905. From his father and grandfather, Wills learned how to play mandolin, guitar, and eventually fiddle, and he regularly played local dances in his teens. In 1929, he joined a medicine show in Fort Worth, where he played fiddle and did blackface comedy. At one performance, he met guitarist Herman Arnspiger and the duo formed the Wills Fiddle Band. Within a year, they were playing dances and radio stations around Fort Worth. During one of the performances, the pair met a vocalist called Milton Brown, who joined the band. Soon, Brown's guitarist brother Durwood joined the group, as did Clifton "Sleepy" Johnson, a tenor banjo player.

In early 1931, the band landed their own radio show, which was sponsored by the Burris Mill and Elevator company, the manufacturers of Light Crust Flour. The group re-christened themselves the Light Crust Doughboys and their show was being broadcast throughout Texas, hosted and organized by W. Lee O'Daniel, the manager of Burris Mill. By 1932, the band was stars in Texas but there was some trouble behind the scenes; O'Daniel wasn't allowing the band to play anything but the radio show. This situation led to the departure of Milton Brown; Wills eventually replaced Brown with Tommy Duncan, who he would work with for the next 16 years. By late summer 1933, Wills, aggravated by a series of fights with O'Daniel, left the Light Crust Doughboys and Duncan left with him. Wills and Duncan relocated to Waco, TX, and formed the Playboys, which featured Wills on fiddle, Duncan on piano and vocals, rhythm guitarist June Whalin, tenor banjoist Johnnie Lee Wills, and Kermit Whalin, who played steel guitar and bass. For the next year, the Playboys moved through a number of radio stations, as O'Daniel tried to force them off the air. Finally, the group settled in Tulsa, where they had a job at KVOO.

Tulsa is where Bob Wills & His Texas Playboys began to refine their sound. Wills added an 18 year-old electric steel guitarist called Leon McAuliffe, pianist Al Stricklin, drummer Smokey Dacus, and a horn section to the band's lineup. Soon, the Texas Playboys were the most popular band in Oklahoma and Texas. The band made their first record in 1935 for the American Recording Company, which would later become part of Columbia Records. At ARC, they were produced by Uncle Art Satherley, who would wind up as Wills' producer for the next 12 years. The bandleader had his way and they cut a number of tracks which were released on a series of 78s. The singles were successful enough that Wills could demand that steel guitarist Leon McAuliffe—who wasn't on the first sessions due to ARC's abundance of steel players under contract—was featured on the Playboys' next record, 1936's "Steel Guitar Rag." The song became a standard for steel guitar. Also released from that session was "Right or Wrong," which featured Tommy Duncan on lead vocals.

Toward the end of the decade, big bands were dominating popular music and Wills wanted a band capable of playing complex, jazz-inspired arrangements. To help him achieve his sound, he hired arranger and guitarist Eldon Shamblin, who wrote charts that fused country with big band music for the Texas Playboys. By 1940, he had replaced some of the weaker musicians in the lineup, winding up with a full 18-piece band. The Texas Playboys were breaking concert attendance records across the country, filling out venues from Tulsa to California; and they also had their first genuine national hit with "New San Antonio Rose," which climbed to number 11 in 1940. Throughout 1941 and 1942, Bob Wills & His Texas Playboys continued to record and perform and they were one of the most popular bands in the country. However, their popularity was quickly derailed by the arrival of World War II. Tommy Duncan enlisted in the Army after Pearl Harbor and Al Stricklin became a defense plant worker. Late in 1942, Leon McAuliffe and Eldon Shamblin both left the group. Bob Wills enlisted in the Army late in 1942, but he was discharged as being unfit for service in the summer of 1943, primarily because he was out of shape and disagreeable. Duncan was discharged around the same time and the pair moved to California by the end of 1943. Wills revamped the sound of the Texas Playboys after World War II, cutting out the horn section and relying on amplified string instruments.

During the '40s, Art Satherley had moved from ARC to OKeh Records and Wills followed him to the new label. His first single for OKeh was a new version of "New San Antonio Rose" and it became a Top Ten hit early in 1944, crossing over into the Top 20 on the pop charts. Wills stayed with OKeh for about year, having several Top Ten hits, as well as the number ones, "Smoke on the Water" and "Stars and Stripes on Iwo Jima." After he left OKeh, he signed with Columbia Records, releasing his first single for the label, "Texas Playboy Rag," toward the end of 1945. In 1946, the Texas Playboys began recording a series of transcriptions for Oakland, CA's Tiffany Music Corporation. Tiffany's plan was to syndicate the transcriptions throughout the Southwest, but their goal was never fulfilled. Nevertheless, the Texas Playboys made a number of transcriptions in 1946 and 1947, and these are the only recordings of the band playing extended jams. Consequently, they are close approximations of the group's live sound. Though the Tiffany transcriptions would turn out to be important historical items, the recordings that kept Wills & the Playboys in the charts were their singles for Columbia, which were consistently reaching the Top Five between 1945 and 1948; in the summer of 1946, they had their biggest hit, "New Spanish Two Step," which spent 16 weeks at number one.

Guitarist Eldon Shamblin returned to the Playboys in 1947, the final year Wills recorded for Columbia Records. Beginning in late 1947, Wills was signed to MGM. His first single for the label, "Bubbles in My Beer," was a Top Ten hit early in 1948, as was its follow-up, "Keeper of My Heart." Though the Texas Playboys were one of the most popular bands in the nation, they were beginning to fight internally, mainly because Wills had developed a drinking problem that caused him to behave erratically. Furthermore, Wills came to believe Tommy Duncan was demanding too much attention and asking for too much money. By the end of 1948, he had fired the singer.

Duncan's departure couldn't have come at a worse time. Western swing was beginning to fall out of public favor, and Wills' recordings weren't as consistently successful as they had been before; he had no hits at all in 1949. That year, he relocated to Oklahoma, beginning a 15-year stretch of frequent moves, all designed to find a thriving market for the band. In 1950, he had two Top Ten hits: "Ida Red Likes the Boogie" and "Faded Love," which would become a country standard; they would be his last hits for a decade. Throughout the '50s, he struggled with poor health and poor finances, but he continued to perform frequently. However, his audience continued to shrink, despite his attempts to hold on to it. Wills moved throughout the Southwest during the decade, without ever finding a new home base. Audiences at dance halls plummeted with the advent of television and rock & roll. The Texas Playboys made some records for Decca that went unnoticed in the mid-'50s. In 1959, Wills signed with Liberty Records, where he was produced by Tommy Allsup, a former Playboy. Before recording his first sessions with Liberty, Wills expanded the lineup of the band again and reunited with Tommy Duncan. The results were a success, with "Heart to Heart Talk" climbing into the Top Ten during the summer of 1960. Again, the Texas Playboys were drawing sizable crowds and selling a respectable amount of records. In 1962, Wills had a heart attack that temporarily debilitated him, but by 1963, he was making an album for Kapp Records. The following year, he had a second heart attack which forced him to disband the Playboys. After the second heart attack, he performed and recorded as a solo performer. His solo recordings for Kapp were made in Nashville with studio musicians and were generally ignored, though he continued to be successful in concert.

In 1968, the Country Music Hall of Fame inducted Bob Wills and the following year the Texas State Legislature honored him for his contribution to American music. The day after he appeared in both houses of the Texas state government, Wills suffered a massive stroke, which paralyzed his right side. During his recovery, Merle Haggard—the most popular country singer of the late '60s—recorded an album dedicated to Bob Wills, *A Tribute to the Best Damn Fiddle Player*, which helped return Wills to public consciousness and spark a wide-spread Western swing revival. In 1972, Wills was well enough to accept a citation from ASCAP in Nashville, as well as appear at several Texas Playboy reunions, which were all very popular. In the fall of 1973, Wills and Haggard began planning a Texas Playboys reunion album, featuring Leon McAuliffe, Al Stricklin, Eldon Shamblin, and Smokey Dacus, among others. The first session was held on December 3, 1973, with Wills leading the band from his wheelchair. That night, he suffered another massive stroke in his sleep; the stroke left him comatose. The Texas Playboys finished the album without him. Bob Wills never regained consciousness and he died on May 13, 1975, in a nursing home. Wills was buried in Tulsa, the place where his legend began. —*Stephen Thomas Erlewine*

The Best of Bob Wills, Vol. 1 / 1967 / MCA ♦♦♦

☆ **Bob Wills Anthology** / 1973 / Columbia ♦♦♦♦♦
This two-LP set gives listeners a very good overview of the highly influential recordings of Bob Wills & the Texas Playboys. Many of Wills' best-known recordings of his prime years are included among the 24 selections with highlights including "Spanish Two Step," "Maiden's Prayer," "Steel Guitar Rag," "New San Antonio Rose," and "Twin Guitar Special." Programmed loosely in chronological order, the music is split fairly evenly between the 1935-1938 and 1940-1941 period with two later performances wrapping up the compilation. Wills was the most famous of the Western swing bandleaders, leading a very strong outfit that featured the steel guitar of Leon McAuliffe, guitarist Eldon Shamblin, fiddlers Jesse Ashlock and Louis Tierney, and vocalist Tommy Duncan, among others; some selections also include horns. Wills' band found the perfect blend between country music and swing-oriented jazz, and this set can serve as an excellent introduction to his enjoyable music. —*Scott Yanow*

For the Last Time / 1974 / United Artists ♦♦♦♦♦
For the Last Time documents two historic moments in American music: The last time Bob Wills would ever attend or participate in a recording session—he never made the final day of the session, having suffered a severe stroke the night before—and the reunion of the great Texas Playboys, who began in the 1930s and recorded and toured together through the beginning of World War II. All living members were present, as well as Texas Playboy-for-a-day Merle Haggard, who drove all night from Chicago to make the session (he literally begged Wills to be a part of the sessions). These sessions took place on December 3 and 4, 1973, in Dallas, a short ride from Wills' home, with most of the '30s and '40s band in place, including Leon McAuliffe and Leon Rausch acting as vocalists for the lion's share of the material, with Wills singing on six tracks and Haggard guesting on three and playing fiddle as part of the string section. Haggard's singing on "Texas Playboy Theme" is particularly moving, and one can hear the pride in his voice as Wills gives his patented "ahhhhhh-haaaaaaawwwww!" to show his own pleasure with the proceedings. Wills was seated in the center of the band and actually directed it from his wheelchair. What is most remarkable is that on certain cuts—such as "Blue Bonnet Lane," a track recorded for a movie in 1942 and not performed since—the band nailed it on one take. Tommy Allsup's production is flawless in that it is so minimal it's almost as if the band were playing in the listener's living room. He captures the warmth, immediacy, and overwhelming emotion in the proceedings as they happen on such Texas Playboy classics as "San Antonio Rose," "Faded Love," "What Makes Bob Holler," "Big Ball's in Cowtown," "Bubbles in My Beer," "That's What I Like About the South," "Milk Cow Blues," "Twin Guitar Boogie," and "When You Leave Amarillo," just to name a few. Fiddle great Hoyle and son Jody Nix actually guest on a couple of tracks in the vocal seat, and Wills gives them his approving nod with his drawling yodel. In all, this is far from the lame tribute record we see so frequently these days; this is a deeply moving and inspiringly executed presentation of Bob Wills as not only a bandleader, but as an innovator and mentor. In other words, it is the only fitting tribute possible, with the man still very much alive sitting among his bandmates for the very last time. —*Thom Jurek*

Columbia Historic Edition / 1982 / Columbia ♦♦♦
Columbia Historic Edition is a ten-track compilation of material Bob Wills and the Texas Playboys recorded for Columbia Records in the late '30s and '40s, with eight of the tracks dating before 1941. Many of Wills' greatest songs, such as "Right or Wrong" and "Cherokee Maiden," are included, as are a handful of lesser-known songs like "Lyla Lou" and the instrumental "Cowboy Stomp." Though there are several more comprehensive collections available on the market, *Columbia Historic Edition* is a thoroughly entertaining and concise sampling of Wills' classic period. —*Stephen Thomas Erlewine*

☆ **Tiffany Transcriptions, Vol. 1** / 1982 / Rhino ♦♦♦♦♦
The first of ten volumes (produced for CD by Jeff Alexson and Tom Diamant) of radio transcriptions done by Bob Wills and his band in the mid-'40s is the strongest of the bunch. Done for the Tiffany Music Company—a concern formed by Wills, songwriter Clifford Sundin, and radio personality Clifton Johnson (Cactus Jack)—between 1946 and 1947, these recordings were intended as the basis for a syndicated radio series, but soon after the initial distribution of some of the recordings, the company was dissolved and the music withdrawn. Sundin had possession of the recordings, along with the relevant business files and promotional materials, until his death in 1981, after which the release of the music became possible through Kaleidoscope Records (which also handles records by Kate Wolf, Tiny Moore and Jethro Burns, the Bobs, the Sundogs, and the Zazu Pitts Memorial Orchestra), distributed by Rhino. The music features Wills and his band performing in a freer atmosphere than the typical recording session, not trying for a perfect take as much as a lively flow to each of the songs that would make the radio listener continue to tune in each week. The music is closer to a live performance than anything else Wills and his band ever recorded, with the members very informal and obviously enjoying themselves. *Tiffany Transcriptions, Vol. 1* gives a good idea of the entire ten-disc set, a mix of country, dance, jazz, folk, and blues standards (including a version here of "What's the Matter With the Mill," a song equally well known in versions by Moon Mullican and Muddy Waters), with vocalist Tommy Duncan at the top of his form. The sound is astonishingly good as well, given the age of the masters and the fact that they were never intended to be preserved for posterity. —*Bruce Eder*

★ **Tiffany Transcriptions, Vol. 2** / Sep. 1986 / Rhino ♦♦♦♦♦
Subtitled "The Best of the Tiffanys," and this 14-song collection is made up of live-in-the-studio radio transcription versions of some of Wills' most popular numbers, including "Take Me Back to Tulsa," "Cherokee Maiden," "Steel Guitar Rag," "Ida Red," and "San Antonio Rose." Essentially a live best-of, the performances and the material are unique, with some superb spontaneous jamming and experimentation and overall good spirits. —*Bruce Eder*

☆ **Tiffany Transcriptions, Vol. 3** / Sep. 1986 / Rhino ◆◆◆◆◆
With the unofficial title "Basin Street Blues," and this collection is devoted to Wills' covers of jazz and blues standards. In addition to the free-spirited version of title track, we get covers of Kokomo Arnold's "Milk Cow Blues," Lee Pockriss' "Crazy Rhythm," Phil Baxter's "I'm a Ding Dong Daddy," and eight previously unissued numbers among the 14 included here. Sort of the group's jazz standard showcase, with lots of prominent piano work from Millard Kelso, dazzling steel from Noel Boggs, Roy Honeycutt, and Herb Remington, plus Wills' and Joe Holley's usual excellence on the fiddles, and some sizzling electric mandolin from Tiny Moore, matched by electric guitar from Eldon Shamblin and Lester Junior Barnard. The version of "Milk Cow Blues" alone, one of Tommy Duncan's best blues performances, makes this worth owning, and Lester Junior Barnard's guitar solo is icing on the cake. —*Bruce Eder*

☆ **Tiffany Transcriptions, Vol. 4** / Sep. 1986 / Rhino ◆◆◆◆◆
"You're From Texas" is the subtitle of this volume, which more or less tells the story of the content—all songs from or having to do with Texas, including Cindy Walker's "You're From Texas" and "Blue Bonnet Lane," N. Howard "Jack" Thorp's "Little Joe the Wrangler" (one of the earliest cowboy songs ever put down on sheet music), the anonymous "Beaumont Rag," and the traditional "Red River Valley." The music is country, but the approach is a mix of jazz and dance band, and the beat, along with the richness of the arrangements, is infectious. Anyone with a special appreciation for the jazz or country sides of Western swing will love this volume. —*Bruce Eder*

☆ **Tiffany Transcriptions, Vol. 5** / 1986 / Rhino ◆◆◆◆◆
The Tiffany Transcriptions, Vol. 5 contains a number of radio transcriptions recorded between 1946 and 1947. Though there are several songs on *Vol. 5* that were on earlier editions of *The Tiffany Transcriptions*, the key to the whole series is how Wills & the Playboys stretch out musically, soloing with abandon and grace. —*Thom Owens*

☆ **Tiffany Transcriptions, Vol. 6: Sally Goodin'** / 1987 / Rhino ◆◆◆◆◆
Subtitled "Sally Goodin," *Tiffany Transcriptions, Vol. 6* is a volume of mostly traditional songs, some of dealing with life in Oklahoma, which isn't so far from Texas that a Texas-based swing band couldn't rightfully do them. Two versions of the title track, one a rollicking instrumental and the other a rendition with lyrics by Bob Wills and Tommy Duncan, are included, along with a performance of Jack and Woody Guthrie's "Oklahoma Hills" (recorded in May of 1946, when Jack was still alive) that one wished lasted about a minute longer, and even Irving Berlin's "I'm Putting All My Eggs in One Basket." Maybe the most unusual track here, other than the Berlin number, is "Playboy Chimes," written by Wills and Herb Remington, which features some dazzling string playing by about half a dozen guys in the band. Their version of Jimmie Rodgers' "Never More Hard Times Blues," with its prominent yodeling, also makes for an unusual change of pace for the group. —*Bruce Eder*

☆ **Tiffany Transcriptions, Vol. 7: Keep Knockin'** / 1987 / Rhino ◆◆◆◆◆
With the title "Keep Knockin'," this volume has some of the roots of rock & roll (as in "Keep Knockin' But You Can't Come In"), and also intersects with jazz by way of Duke Ellington's "C-Jam Blues" and old-time pop numbers like "Tea For Two." The group in its different incarnations ripples through these and 11 other numbers, mostly dance pieces with some blues thrown in. —*Bruce Eder*

The Golden Era / 1987 / Columbia ◆◆◆
A perfect complement to *The Bob Wills Anthology*, this two-LP set from 1987 does not duplicate any of the earlier compilation's performances. Bob Wills' Texas Playboys were the most influential of all Western swing bands, setting the standard for other groups to follow. This very interesting collection has 32 lesser-known but rewarding performances including 13 previously unissued selections (many of which are alternate takes). Drawn from Wills' prime years, the spirited renditions feature such top musicians as fiddlers Jesse Ashlock and Louis Tierney, the great steel guitarist Leon McAuliffe and pianist Al Stricklin in addition to singer Tommy Duncan and Wills himself on fiddle. This is highly recommended, at least until Columbia gets around to having a more complete series on CD. —*Scott Yanow*

Fiddle / 1987 / Country Music Foundation ◆◆◆
As the title suggests, *Fiddle* concentrates on Bob Wills' sometimes neglected Western fiddle style. Over the course of 20 tracks, which were recorded between 1935 and 1942, Wills and his colleagues—including Jesse Ashlock, Louis Tierney, Joe Holley, Clifton Johnson and Art Haines—run-through a number of styles, ranging from direct fiddle and guitar duets to Cajun and jazzy big band numbers. For dedicated fans, it's an excellent addition to a library, even if it is a bit specialized for some tastes. —*Stephen Thomas Erlewine*

☆ **Tiffany Transcriptions, Vol. 8: More of the Best** / 1988 / Rhino ◆◆◆◆◆
Song for song one of the best parts of this series, without a slow or uninspired moment anywhere in its 38-minute running time. The bouncy "Twinkle Twinkle Little Star" will surprise all listeners with its beat as well as the rippling solos on fiddle, steel guitar, and electric guitar, and the stomping "Sun Bonnet Sue" is worth the price of the CD. This volume also has Bob Wills & His Texas Playboys stretching out on an old blues, "Sitting on Top of the World" (yes, the same number later played by Cream), and roaring through the guitar and fiddle showcase "Big Beaver," which gets into some scintillating pyrotechnics all around the band. This is very much the country side of Western swing, but dressed up in the kind of virtuoso playing that one more often associated with light jazz, and the fidelity is astoundingly good for mid-'40s transcription discs. —*Bruce Eder*

Tiffany Transcriptions: For Collectors Only / 1990 / Rhino ◆◆◆◆◆
The least known part of the this series of releases, mostly because it falls outside the numbered body of titles. The hook here is the McKinney Sisters, Dean & Evelyn, who were usually subordinate to lead singer Tommy Duncan on most of Wills' best-known recordings. On these 22 tracks, however, they're out front as a vocal duet, singing, yodeling,

and generally filling the jaunty, jazzy sound of their songs with some very sweet, very Western tones, all different in texture from the Tommy Duncan-sung numbers. The effect is rather startling, given the familiarity of Duncan's voice in this context, and allows even longtime fans to redefine their perceptions of the group. Among the familiar fare here, done in unfamiliar versions, are "Tumbling Tumbleweeds," "Blue Skies," and "All By Myself." —*Bruce Eder*

☆ **Tiffany Transcriptions, Vol. 9: 1946–1947** / 1991 / Rhino ◆◆◆◆◆
The last entry in this nine-volume set caps a triumphant reissue series that reveals, perhaps better than any other currently available recordings, the genius of Bob Wills and his band in the mid-'40s, while they were at the peak of their skill and popularity. As always, a major attraction is the smooth but robust singing of Tommy Duncan on such crowd-pleasing tunes as "My Life's Been a Pleasure" and "Milk Cow Blues." And, as always, the exuberant yelps and catcalls of Wills himself are either charming or irritating, depending on your personal inclination. The band's irresistible blend of swinging jazz and stomping Texas two-step country is showcased on instrumentals like "12th Street Rag" and "Texas Playboy Rag," and even a couple of big band potboilers: "In the Mood" and "Sentimental Journey." In a gesture of inspired kitsch, the band also struts and bounces its way through an uptempo rendition of "What Is This Thing Called Love." Like the other eight volumes in this series, this one should be considered an essential part of any country music collection. —*Rick Anderson*

★ **Anthology 1935–1973** / 1991 / Rhino ◆◆◆◆◆
The only comprehensive retrospective of Bob Wills & the Texas Playboys, the double-disc set *Anthology 1935-1973* contains material from every label the Playboys recorded for and features the hit version of each of Wills' most famous songs, including "Right or Wrong," "Time Changes Everything," "Corrine, Corrina," "New San Antonio Rose," "Take Me Back to Tulsa," "Cherokee Maiden," "Roly-Poly," "Stay a Little Longer," "Big Beaver," "Bubbles in My Beer," "Faded Love," and many others. It's the rare compilation that functions both as a definitive overview and an excellent introduction. —*Stephen Thomas Erlewine*

Country Music Hall of Fame Series / 1992 / MCA ◆◆◆◆◆
This set contains Western swing recordings made by Wills from 1955-1967, including such hits as "With Tears in My Eyes," "Cornball Rag," "Texas Two Step," and many more. —*AMG*

The Essential Bob Wills & His Texas Playboys / Aug. 25, 1992 / Columbia/Legacy ◆◆◆◆◆
A basic 20-track primer to some of the Western swing master's best sides. Acknowledged classics like "Steel Guitar Rag," "Take Me back to Tulsa," and "Stay a Little Longer" are all here, with the players and arrangements that made Wills and his Texas Playboys legends in country music. —*Cub Koda*

Longhorn Recordings / 1993 / Bear Family ◆◆◆◆◆
These mid-'60s Dallas sessions feature Wills in both large band and small rootsy combo settings. —*Dan Cooper*

Classic Western Swing / 1994 / Rhino ◆◆◆
Rhino's budget-priced, ten-track *Classic Western Swing* contains the hit versions of such Bob Wills staples as "San Antonio Rose," "Time Changes Everything," "Faded Love," "Roly-Poly," "Steel Guitar Rag," "My Window Faces the South," "Take Me Back to Tulsa," "Stay a Little Longer," "Big Beaver" and "Cherokee Maiden." There isn't any historical perspective on the disc, nor does it give a true sense of Wills' greatness, but for any casual listener who just wants the big hits—or the neophyte reluctant to spend more than eight dollars on a disc—this works just fine. —*Stephen Thomas Erlewine*

Encore / 1994 / Liberty ◆◆◆
As its title implies, *Encore* is a collection of late Bob Wills recordings, made after his primary work was done. In 1960, Wills reunited with singer Tommy Duncan, who had left his band in 1948, for the Liberty Records LPs *Together Again* (1960) and *Living Legend* (1961). Naturally, the two recorded many early Wills favorites, such as "Take Me Back to Tulsa" and "San Antonio Rose," but also included was "Heart to Heart Talk," which became Wills' first country Top Ten hit in a decade, and his last. In 1963, Liberty recorded a "solo" Wills album, *Bob Wills Sings and Plays*, on which the bandleader, while still accompanied by a group, was prominently featured both on fiddle and vocals. Ten years later, United Artists Records recorded what turned out to be the final Bob Wills album, *For the Last Time*, when Wills suffered a stroke following the first session. This three-CD set, which, with a running time of two hours and 35 minutes, might have just fit onto two discs, draws from all these recordings as well as some live radio transcriptions from 1963-1964 for a comprehensive portrait of Wills' last two decades. The box, which features a cover photograph of Wills in his prime and gives no indication of when the tracks were recorded, could be deceiving, and the lavish 40-page booklet, containing an extensive essay by Wills biographer Charles R. Townsend, tends to suggest that these recordings have more importance than they actually do in Wills' discography. As Townsend writes, the set contains "fifty-seven of the best recordings Wills made in his later years," but, while entertaining and constituting a coda to his greatest work that is of historical interest, these recordings are not among Wills' best overall. —*William Ruhlmann*

The King of Western Swing: 25 Hits (1935–1945) / Apr. 21, 1998 / ASV ◆◆◆◆
As singer, fiddler, and bandleader of the Texas Playboys, Bob Wills played the same fatherly role to western swing that Bill Monroe did to bluegrass. No one is sure if he invented the music itself, but it's clear that the recordings of his Texas Playboys have since come to define the genre. As a musical hybrid, western swing introduced blues and country music to big band jazz and swing, polishing the results to achieve an urban sophistication necessary for broad appeal. *The King of Western Swing* is a fine overview of Wills' first decade as a recording artist. It begins (after an introductory "New San Antonio Rose")

at his first session in 1935 with "Osage Stomp" and ends in 1945 with the dates that produced "Roly Poly," "Stay a Little Longer," and "New Spanish Two-Step." In between, Wills and his 13- to 18-piece band swing through some of their most popular songs. Early recordings drew most heavily from country and blues. In the tradition that brought this rural music into the city in refined form, the Texas Playboys recorded sweet-coated material like "Never No More Hard Times Blues," "Fan It," and "Sugar Blues." As the group grew in size, it developed a fuller big band sound that embraced both popular material (Leon Huff's quivering croon on "We Might as Well Forget") and conventional swing ("Whoa Baby," "Big Beaver"). The atmosphere they create on these early recordings is contagiously carefree. Steel guitars and fiddle solo over hopping, swing tempos alongside trumpets and slide trombones. The smooth voice of Tommy Duncan (one of Wills' vocal mainstays) delivers the dry humor of "Roly Poly" ("daddy's little fatty") and the melancholy of the sublime "Dusty Skies" with the same straight face. Overseeing all of this is Wills himself. When not lending his golden fiddle to a song, he's shouting encouragement, commentary, and praise ("Aaaaah ha! Swing it on out, boys!"). *The King of Western Swing* is one of the most satisfying single-disc collections of Bob Wills and his band in their prime. Blending the worlds of country, blues, and jazz, the 25 cuts bring together stomping instrumentals, novelty numbers, and the Playboys' biggest hits from the period. *—Nathan Bush*

Harmony Airshots 1953 / Feb. 23, 1999 / Country Routes ♦♦♦

It's pretty difficult to find a Bob Wills recording that doesn't please. Although there are some flaws with this CD, it is no exception to the rule. Because the source material was recordings from the radio, sound quality is not as good as one would want. The flip side of this is chance to hear the spontaneity and banter of the band playing "live." Even the excellent *Tiffany Transcriptions* don't capture that as fully as this recording. An added plus is the chance to hear the band work out on "Mama Inez," which is pretty far afield from the usual soil the Texas Playboys tilled. One hears the band late in its career and the absence of Tommy Duncan in particular is keenly felt, but you can still witness the power of Bob Wills & the Texas Playboys in this recording. *—Megan Lynch*

20th Century Masters—The Millennium Collection: The Best of Bob Wills / Feb. 8, 2000 / MCA ♦♦♦

Part of Universal's massive *20th Century Masters/The Millennium Collection*, this 12-song budget set draws on a cross-section of recordings pulled from his tenures with MGM, Kapp, and Decca. Highlights include "Bubbles in My Beer," "Cadillac and a Model A," "Milk Cow Blues," and "New Spanish Two Step." This is a good blend of early sides with later recordings of the Texas Playboys, giving a nice overview of his career. *—Cub Koda*

Hall of Fame / Apr. 4, 2000 / DCC ♦♦♦

Hall of Fame collects 22 songs from Bob Wills & His Texas Playboy's Liberty years, and includes Billboard chart hits like "San Antonio Rose," "Stay a Little Longer," "Hang Your Head in Shame," "Bubbles in My Beer," and "Ida Red Likes the Boogie." It's a good collection of the group's late-'50s/early-'60s recordings. *—Heather Phares*

☆ **San Antonio Rose** / Dec. 13, 2000 / Bear Family ♦♦♦♦♦

This box set of 11 CDs and one DVD, issued by the Bear Family label in Germany, features all the recordings Bob Wills did from 1932 until 1947. In effect, perhaps more than any other Bear Family boxes (which are admittedly for fanatics), this collection—with its changing lineups, painstaking documentation, and phenomenal performances—offers a stunning portrait in sound, images, and words of the true crossroads of American music. On these CDs one can hear the sound of antiquity, the present popular styles of the day, and a solid and well-executed vision of the future integrated into a gloriously rowdy, swinging whole. From the first recordings Wills did with Milton Brown & His Brownies in 1932 to the first finished take of "Osage Stomp" in Brunswick's Dallas warehouse by Wills' own Texas Playboys, a remarkable change is heard. With Wills, the emphasis was on music as a whole entity. It began with ancient fiddle tunes taught to him by his father and grandfather and came to include virtually every style of American pop music—and a few polkas—that emerged from the beginning of the century, wrapped into one seemingly loose, joyous brew for massive public consumption courtesy of the Southwest. And it was massively consumed and influenced virtually all of the country, pop, big-band, swing, and rock & roll music that came after it, whether the creators of that music acknowledge it—or today's idiot generation even heard of Wills—or not. Virtually all of the ARC and Columbia recordings—including all of their subsidiary labels such as Vocalion, Brunswick, etc.—and all of the great vocalists are here: Tommy Duncan performs on the majority of these tracks, but also Leon McAuliffe, Dean & Evelyn McKinney, Laura Lee Owens, and of course Wills, among others. Remarkable too are how many songs here, now regarded as beloved American standards, were first cut by the Texas Playboys; among them are "San Antonio Rose," "Steel Guitar Rag," "Take Me Back to Tulsa," "Trouble in Mind," "Miss Molly," "New San Antonio Rose," "Spanish Two Step," and many others. All of them are infused with the bristling energy, sizzling intent, and good humor and charisma of the bandleader. As if it weren't enough to release all of the previously issued material from these years, Bear Family includes every surviving alternate take, completely unreleased material, studio banter, airchecks, and more. The progression of the band and Wills' musical restlessness grow right until the end of these recordings, when the Texas Playboys left Columbia. In fact, because of the origin, performances and period of the material, and amazing sound quality, this is the only Wills set worth owning. The DVD in the package is the 1940 film of *Take Me Back to Oklahoma* starring Tex Ritter, with Ritter fronting the Texas Playboys. The complete and exhaustive notes and Rich Kienzle's book-length biographical and critical essay, combined with hundreds of photographs in a hardbound book, make this the only package that has ever done Wills' legacy and influence justice—and there are more boxes to come. *—Thom Jurek*

Take Me Back to Tulsa: The Original Columbia Recordings, Vol. 1 / Apr. 24, 2001 / Rounder ♦♦♦♦

Bob Wills & His Texas Playboys were the pacesetting Western swing band of 1935-1945, mixing together the instrumentation and flavor of country music with swinging jazz. This sampler has 16 of the Playboys' better recordings, including the rollicking "Ten Years," "Beaumont Rag," "Blue Yodel No. 1," "Spanish Two Step," and "San Antonio Rose." The music is not in chronological order (skipping around quite a bit) and completists will not be satisfied, but as an introduction to this important's band's music, this CD fits the bill quite well. *—Scott Yanow*

Boot Heel Drag: The MGM Years / Jul. 10, 2001 / Uptown/Universal ♦♦♦♦♦

Wills' peak is usually reckoned as the late '30s to the mid-'40s. His slightly later recordings, dating from the time his popularity began to slip, have received comparatively little attention. However, you really can't detect much of a drop in quality, on record anyway, on this double-CD compilation of 50 tracks he did for MGM from 1947-1954. This was not a total dry spell for him hit-wise, and all five of his Top Ten country charters (all from 1948-1950) during that span are here: "Ida Red Likes the Boogie," "Thorn in My Heart," "Keeper of My Heart," "Bubbles in My Beer," and "Faded Love." True, it was not a time of great stability for the Texas Playboys. No less than nine different lineups are heard on the record, and their most famous vocalist, Tommy Duncan, left in 1948 (and appears on only about a third of the songs on this compilation). Still, overall they still ground out top-notch Western swing on disc, the commendably diverse repertoire drawing on blues, boogie, jazz, pop, and novelty humor. The material and production get a little slicker than his earlier recordings occasionally, but there's plenty of exuberant vocal and instrumental interplay. *—Richie Unterberger*

Faded Love / Sep. 25, 2001 / Catfish ♦♦♦♦

Bob Wills may be the king of Western swing, but he's perhaps less well-known than other pivotal country music figures like Hank Williams or Jimmie Rodgers. Unlike Williams and Rodgers, he was a bandleader, not a front-and-center singer. The Texas Playboys were as likely to play an instrumental as a song, and when they did play a song, Tommy Duncan usually took over. Wills' association with the great state of Texas also put him outside of the Nashville loop. But one look at the long list of great songs—among the greatest—by Wills and company, and the listener recognizes that he or she knows this Western swinger better than he or she had imagined. For starters, there's "New San Antonio Rose," "Stay a Little Longer," and "Take Me Back to Tulsa," which are cornerstones in classic country repertoire. Add to this Duncan's silky-smooth vocals and a group of top-notch fiddlers, steel players, and guitarists, and Wills couldn't miss. The only possible complaint one might have against the king of Western swing is his—dare one say it?—irritating habit of shouting out, "Sing it Tommy!," among other things, in the middle of a song. Perhaps such outbursts were exciting when the group played live, but on record they're mostly interruptions. *Faded Love* serves as a good intro to the Texas swinger & his Playboys. It lets the listener know that Bob Wills put the western in country & western, and that he, like Rodgers and Williams, belongs at the very top of country greats. *—Ronnie D. Lankford Jr.*

Stay a Little Longer: The Original Columbia Recordings, Vol. 2 / Jan. 22, 2002 / Rounder ♦♦♦♦♦

Containing 16 cuts from the mid-'30s to the mid-'40s, this compilation of Wills' Columbia sides is a little quirky in that it doesn't present itself as a best-of or a thematic anthology. It's just a dip into his massive body of 1930s and 1940s recordings, including some of his better-known tracks—"Steel Guitar Rag" (described in the liner notes as "the less familiar take, in which Bob doesn't holler 'Domino!' at the end"), "Stay a Little Longer," "Home in San Antone"—but by no means the ones that many Wills fans would select. So it's more useful for someone who's not collecting Wills systematically, rather than the specialized Wills or Western swing fan. What's here is a decent enough cross-section of the territory Wills ploughed in his early recording career, from all-out hoedowns and bluesy tunes to waltzes and vaudeville-influenced numbers, the latest recording (1945's "Stay a Little Longer") showing a bop jazz influence. *—Richie Unterberger*

Take Me Back to Tulsa / Apr. 8, 2002 / Proper Box ♦♦♦♦♦

Everyone who's ever explored Western swing knows that Bob Wills' music was revolutionary, but any fan who hasn't listened to the music on disc one of this collection probably doesn't realize how revolutionary it really was. Most modern retrospectives concentrate on music that Wills made after his signature sound was firmly established, but the earliest (and seldom heard) sides here are fascinating in that they reveal the specific foundations for Wills' great synthesis. Old-timey fiddle tunes, primitive jazz, blues, gospel—the breadth of his repertoire was staggering, and his bands not only played those myriad disparate genres, but mastered them utterly. There are dozens of seldom-heard gems throughout this four-disc set, but none more exciting than those found early on: "Get With It," with Leon McAuliffe's jazzy, astonishingly dissonant guitar solo that predates Scotty Moore's rockabilly licks by nearly 20 years, Tommy Duncan's brilliant, jazzy yodeling on "I Ain't Got Nobody," the beautiful gospel ballad "There's No Disappointment in Heaven," "Basin Street Blues," and on and on. The accompanying 50-page booklet contains a nice historical essay and rare photographs, but may be problematic to researchers in that its session notes are sometimes inaccurate. In terms of the music, however, nothing but good words can be said. Many of these songs have probably never been heard by CD-era fans, being previously available only on Bear Family's massive box set, and every single one of Wills' hits are included, as well as many of the classic *Tiffany Transcriptions*. And all for under $25. *—Jim Smith*

The Great Bob Wills/Remembering . . . The Greatest Hits of Bob Wills / Apr. 15, 2003 / Collectables ♦♦♦

This two-fer from Collectables unites two Bob Wills records that were originally issued as compilations in the first place: *The Great Bob Wills* was issued in 1965 on the Harmony

HL label and *Remembering… The Greatest Hits of Bob Wills* was issued three years after Wills' death in 1975 as a greatest-hits set by Columbia. What the two have in common are the earliest years and maturing years of the Texas Playboys' recordings; the Harmony HL collection dates almost exclusively from the 1940s, when the band was kicking between 1945-1947. The last cut is an instrumental by Wills called "Bob Wills Special" from 1940, and "Fat Boy Rag" dates from 1938. The Columbia album dates from Wills' first recording session in 1935 through a recording of Fred Rose's "Roly Poly" in 1945. The sound quality is more than acceptable, if not fantastic, and the performances on both albums included are nothing less than stellar. As is typical with Collectables' material, there are no musician credits, though certain tracks cite vocal credits. There is a neat little essay by Don Law—the man who signed Wills to his first contract with Columbia—in the booklet which details the 1935 session. For beginners, this is a pretty good place to start at a decent price; for collectors, there probably isn't anything here you haven't heard before.
—*Thom Jurek*

Johnnie Lee Wills

b. Sep. 2, 1912, Jewett, TX, d. 1984

Banjo, Fiddle, Leader / Traditional Country, Western Swing

Fiddler Johnnie Lee Wills led the most popular prewar Western swing band around the Oklahoma area; that is, after older brother Bob moved his Texas Playboys to California in 1940. He was born in Jewett, TX, on September 2, 1912, the second of four musical sons and seven years behind Bob. Johnnie Lee learned about music from his father, and began playing banjo with Bob when the Texas Playboys moved to KVOO-Tulsa in 1934. He formed the Rhythmairs in 1939, but returned to the fold the following year when Bob split the Playboys into two groups. Johnnie Lee took over the second unit (switching from banjo to fiddle), with younger brother Luther Jay on bass. A few months later, Bob moved to California and left Johnnie with his own band, christened Johnnie Lee Wills & His Boys. The brothers remained close though, and when Bob needed a substitute as leader, he called Johnnie.

Johnnie Lee Wills & His Boys signed with Decca in 1941, and recorded ten initial sides. The group played on another session when a recording ban was lifted after World War II, but moved to Bullet Records in 1949. Wills' Bullet recordings proved to be the most popular of his career. Early in 1950, "Rag Mop" spent five weeks at the number-two spot in the country charts, and crossed over to the popular Top Ten; though a version by the Ames Brothers did even better. Later that year, "Peter Cotton Tail" also hit the country Top Ten. He moved to RCA Victor in 1952, but none of his recordings sold very well. Western swing's popularity was declining, though Wills' regional fame remained unchanged and he continued to appear regularly on KVOO until 1958. Wills recorded several albums for Sims in the early '60s, but his band broke up in 1964. He continued to work occasional shows and dances, and opened a Western clothing store in Tulsa with his son, John Thomas Wills. By the late '70s, the Western swing revival took notice of Johnnie Lee Wills, and releases of his early-'50s material appeared on Rounder and Bear Family. He also recorded reunion albums for Flying Fish and Delta with many former Texas Playboys.
—*John Bush*

Where There's a Wills, There's a Way / 1962 / Sims ✦✦✦

Johnnie Lee Wills at the Tulsa Stampede / 1963 / Sims ✦✦✦

Reunion / 1978 / Flying Fish ✦✦✦✦✦
Bob Wills' brother remained in Tulsa in the '30s and led a band that became a training ground for dozens of Western swing sidemen; many of the best are reunited here, in what were to be his last recordings. —*Charles S. Wolfe*

Tulsa Swing / 1978 / Rounder ✦✦✦
Tulsa Swing is culled from a variety of live radio transcriptions Johnnie Lee Wills & His Boys recorded between 1950 and 1951, during the group's heyday. Relying more on standards than on Wills' own hits "Rag Mop" and "Peter Cotton Tail," *Tulsa Swing* nevertheless offers a good idea of Wills' standard concert repertoire, as well as the band's loose, freewheeling sound, particularly that of fiddler Curly Lewis and vocalist Leon Huff.
—*Stephen Thomas Erlewine*

Dance All Night / 1980 / Delta ✦✦✦

Rompin' Stompin' Singin' Swingin' / 1983 / Bear Family ✦✦✦✦✦

● **Band's A-Rockin'** / Nov. 19, 1996 / Krazy Kat ✦✦✦✦✦
Band's A-Rockin' includes 27 songs—70-plus minutes—of radio transcriptions dating between 1941 and 1951, and some of the hottest Western swing you're ever going to hear. The title track is pretty cool, but then Johnnie Lee Wills kicks it into high gear with "Boogie Woogie Highball," a jazzy, swingin' instrumental that could've been part of Benny Goodman's repertory if that band had only come from Texas instead of Chicago. Curly Lewis' and Henry Boatman's fiddles contend with Don Harlan's clarinet and a bunch of talented guitarists who passed through the lineup—this band was a multiple-threat in the solo department, with Clarence Cagle and Bob Booth both in there pitching on the piano and trumpet, respectively, as well. There's not a bad song here, and some of the stuff here was important at the time—by some estimates, Johnnie Lee's cover of "Rag Mop" kept the Bullet label afloat nearly a year longer than it otherwise would have survived. Their version of "Milk Cow Blues" may be the best cover by any white musicians this side of Darby & Tarlton. Some of the 1941-vintage tracks ("Whatcha Know Joe," "Keep a Light in Your Window Tonight") have a fair amount of noise in the background, but it not serious enough to detract from the music in any major way. Anyone seeking to own a Western swing CD recorded by someone other than Bob Wills should make this a first pick. —*Bruce Eder*

Mark Wills (Mark Williams)

Vocals / Contemporary Country

Although he didn't quite achieve the fame or sales of new country contemporaries as Tim McGraw or Clay Walker, Mark Wills earned a respectable following and strong reviews

following the release of his eponymous 1996 debut album. As a teenager in the small town of Blue Ridge, GA, Mark Wills (b. Mark Williams) was fond of pop-metal bands like Poison and Bon Jovi, and throughout his teens he played in metal garage bands. But as he became an adult, his tastes shifted toward country-pop and new traditionalist country. Considering that he grew up around country music, singing it both at home and in church as a small boy, this wasn't surprising.

At the age of 17, he entered a talent show at the Buckboard Country Music Showcase in nearby Marietta. He won the contest, which quickly led to weekly performances at the Buckboard. For five years, he played at the club five nights a week. In addition to his regular shows, he began singing on demo tapes in the Atlanta area, eventually working his way into the Nashville demos circuit. At one of his Buckboard shows, he was spotted by Carson Chamberlain and Keith Stegall, who helped him secure a contract with Mercury Nashville. Chamberlain and Stegall produced Wills' eponymous debut album, which was released in the fall of 1996. The record became a moderate country hit, peaking at number 38 on the country charts. *Wish You Were Here* followed in 1998, and in early 2000 Wills returned with *Permanently*. —*Stephen Thomas Erlewine*

● **Mark Wills** / 1996 / Mercury Nashville ✦✦✦✦

Wish You Were Here / May 5, 1998 / Mercury Nashville ✦✦✦
Wish You Were Here isn't quite as consistently engaging as Mark Wills' eponymous debut, yet the very best moments, such as the ballad "I Do (Cherish You)," offer proof that he's a fine, nuanced singer capable of great things. He achieves great things only occasionally here, but that's often enough to make it a successful second album from this young vocalist. —*Thom Owens*

Permanently / Jan. 11, 2000 / Polygram ✦✦✦✦
With a reputation for music and songs that speak to people's hearts, Mark Wills' *Permanently* doesn't disappoint. With songs like "In My Arms" about being a dad to a brand-new baby daughter (a tribute to his little girl) and "Rich Man" about being rich in love, Wills' has a penchant for appealing to fans' sensitive sides. But whether he's singing about love, loss, fear, joy, or hope, Wills delivers a rock-solid third album with ease and confidence. No doubt that comes from working with producer Carson Chamberlain for the third time and singing about the things he knows best. Mixing things up just a bit, Wills recorded "Almost Doesn't Count," a song made popular by pop star Brandy, with his very own brand of soulful country. —*Maria Konicki Dinoia*

Loving Every Minute / Aug. 21, 2001 / Mercury Nashville ✦✦✦
Album number four continues the Wills tradition of telling a story with his voice. He clearly possesses a natural ability to hone his vocal stylings to narrate songs that listeners can identify with because they are about real feelings. Like wanting to leave a small town or a dead-end job in "One of These Days," or hating a place because your ex moved there with a new squeeze in "I Hate Chicago," or wondering if you'll ever meet someone to spend your life with in "Somebody." There are the standard you-take-my-breath-away love ballads, as well as the grand tear-jerker "The Balloon Song," which is about a boy who misses his mother who has passed away. *Loving Every Minute* is different in that it fuses some pop production touches, not normally typical for Wills, with his earthy country vocals, but in a career of chart-topping singles and platinum status, it certainly has the same fate. —*Maria Konicki Dinoia*

Jesse Winchester

b. May 17, 1944, Shreveport, LA

Guitar, Keyboards, Vocals / Singer/Songwriter, Contemporary Folk, Folk-Rock

Jesse Winchester was the music world's most prominent Vietnam War draft-evader, though his renown came from a body of wry, closely observed songs. After growing up in Memphis, Winchester received his draft notice in 1967 and moved to Montreal, Canada, rather than serve in the military. In 1969, he met Robbie Robertson of the Band, who helped launch his recording career. In the same way that James Taylor's history of mental instability and drug abuse served as a subtext for his early music, Winchester's exile lent real-life poignancy to songs like "Yankee Lady," which appeared on his debut album, *Jesse Winchester* (1970). He became a Canadian citizen in 1973. Despite critical acclaim, his inability to tour in the U.S. prevented him from taking his place among the major singer/songwriters of the early '70s, but he made a series of impressive albums—*Third Down, 110 to Go* (August 1972), *Learn to Love It* (August 1974), *Let the Rough Side Drag* (June 1976), and *Nothing but a Breeze* (March 1977)—before President Jimmy Carter instituted an amnesty that finally allowed him to play in his homeland. By that time, the singer/songwriter boom had passed, though Winchester continued to record (*A Touch on the Rainy Side* (July 1978), *Talk Memphis* (February 1981), *Humour Me* (1988)) and even scored a Top 40 hit with "Say What" in 1981. His most prominently covered songs include "Yankee Lady" (Brewer & Shipley), "The Brand New Tennessee Waltz" (Joan Baez, Ian Matthews), "Biloxi" (Tom Rush, Jimmy Buffett), "Mississippi, You're on My Hind" (Jerry Jeff Walker, Stoney Edwards (for a Top 40 country hit)), "Defying Gravity" (Jimmy Buffett, Emmylou Harris), "Rhumba Girl" (Nicolette Larson (for a pop chart entry)), "Well-A-Wiggy" (the Weather Girls (for an R&B chart entry)), and "I'm Gonna Miss You, Girl" (Michael Martin Murphey (for a Top Ten country hit)). In 1999, Winchester returned from a long recording hiatus with the new album *Gentleman of Leisure*. —*William Ruhlmann*

Jesse Winchester / 1970 / Stony Plain ✦✦✦✦✦
Jesse Winchester first gained notice as a protégé of the Band's Robbie Robertson, who produced and played guitar on his debut album and brought along bandmate Levon Helm to play drums and mandolin. The album had much of the rustic Southern charm and rollicking country-rock of the Band. Winchester's other immediate appeal was a certain sense of mystery. A Southern American expatriate living in Canada, he was unable to appear in the U.S. to promote the album, which was released in a fold-out LP jacket that featured the same sepia-toned portrait (which looked like one of those austere Matthew Brady photos from the Civil War era) on each of its four sides. Winchester

emphasized the dichotomy between his Southern origins and his Northern exile in songs like "Snow" (which Robertson co-wrote), "The Brand New Tennessee Waltz" ("I've a sadness too sad to be true"), and "Yankee Lady." *Jesse Winchester* was timely: it spoke to a disaffected American generation that sympathized with Winchester's pacifism. But it was also timeless: the songs revealed a powerful writing talent (recognized by the numerous artists who covered them), and Winchester's gentle vocals made a wonderful vehicle for delivering them. — *William Ruhlmann*

Third Down, 110 to Go / 1972 / Stony Plain ♦♦♦♦♦

If Jesse Winchester's debut album was an auspicious introduction to a powerful new songwriting talent, his two-and-a-half-years-in-the-making follow-up was in some ways even more impressive. Without the influence of Robbie Robertson, Winchester, who produced most of the album himself (three tracks were handled by Todd Rundgren), gave it a homemade feel, using small collections of acoustic instruments, an appropriate setting for a group of short, intimate songs that expressed a deliberately positive worldview set against an acknowledgment of desperate times. Winchester found hope in religion and domesticity, but the key to his stance was a kind of good-humored accommodation. "If the wheel is fixed," he sang, "I would still take a chance. If we're skating on thin ice, then we might as well dance." The album was littered with such examples of aphoristic folk wisdom, adding up to a portrait of a man, cut off from his very deep roots and yet determined to maintain his dignity with grace and even occasionally a goofy sense of humor. — *William Ruhlmann*

Learn to Love It / 1974 / Stony Plain ♦♦♦

As the title suggests, making a virtue of necessity had always been a goal of Jesse Winchester's, and by the time of the release of his third album, the American expatriate had gone ahead and assumed Canadian citizenship. This seemed to free him to comment explicitly on his anti-war exile in "Pharaoh's Army" and especially a version of the old campaign song "Tell Me Why You Like Roosevelt" updated with new lyrics: "In the year of 1967, as a somewhat younger man, the call to bloody glory came, and I would not raise my hand." Elsewhere, Winchester continued to write love songs to his lost South ("L'Air De La Louisiane," "Mississippi, You're on My Mind") and, to a lesser extent, to pursue the wistful philosophizing found on *Third Down, 110 to Go* ("Defying Gravity"). The sense that he was repeating himself was inescapable, however, and with one-third of the album written by others and two of the originals in French Canadian, it was also obvious that Winchester was straining to come up with material. Interestingly, the two Russell Smith songs included, "Third Rate Romance" (which Smith sang uncredited) and "The End Is Not in Sight," went on to become Top 40 country hits for Smith's group, the Amazing Rhythm Aces, in the next two years. Stoney Edwards took "Mississippi, You're on My Hind" into the country Top 40 in 1975. — *William Ruhlmann*

Let the Rough Side Drag / 1976 / Stony Plain ♦♦♦

At his best, Jesse Winchester is an inspired songwriter with a unique worldview. But even at less than his best, he is a craftsman, capable of turning out an album's worth of well-written songs like those here that, now and then, suggest his personal viewpoint. The title track, another of Winchester's reflections on the importance of persevering under difficult circumstances, and "Damned If You Do," which suggests that you might as well follow your heart because you're in trouble either way, are up to his usual standard. But even slight songs like "Everybody Knows But Me" are clever and enjoyable, and overall, *Let the Rough Side Drag*, with its accomplished mixture of country and R&B, was Winchester's most accessible album so far, even if it was his least ambitious. — *William Ruhlmann*

Nothing But a Breeze / 1977 / Stony Plain ♦♦♦

Jesse Winchester regularly took two years between record releases, but he brought in his fifth album, *Nothing but a Breeze*, a mere nine months after its predecessor, *Let the Rough Side Drag*. The impetus for such speed seems to have been the potential commercial bonanza to be gained by Winchester's first U.S. appearances since he moved to Canada to avoid the draft in 1967, due to President Jimmy Carter's amnesty program. Winchester also used a real producer, Brian Ahern (known for his work with Emmylou Harris), for the first time, and augmented his usual backup band with session stars such as Ricky Skaggs and James Burton, plus supporting vocalists like Harris and Anne Murray. The result was an Ahern-style country-pop album, but, perhaps predictably, a rather light effort for Winchester, who performed three covers among the ten tracks and included among the originals such comic trifles as "Twigs and Seeds" and "Rhumba Man." The title track, which became his first singles-chart entry, and "My Songbird," which Harris later covered, were effective songs, but the significance of *Nothing but a Breeze*, which enjoyed a media buzz and became Winchester's highest-charting album (which isn't saying much), was in inverse proportion to the attention it received. — *William Ruhlmann*

A Touch on the Rainy Side / 1978 / Stony Plain ♦♦♦

With American recording studios open to him for the first time, Jesse Winchester traveled to Nashville and enlisted producer Norbert Putnam, who assembled the elements of the Nashville Sound, with its strings and horns and backup choruses, to make an album that moved him more toward lush country and especially R&B. Winchester's flexible voice, capable of gliding into a sweet falsetto, made the latter more successful than might have been expected. What kept the album from being one of his better collections was not the slick production, it was the material. A year after a media blitz had failed to make him a star, Winchester was starting to show signs of strain. He led the album off with the title track, an explicit expression of devotion to his wife, who he mentioned by name. This was followed by a sour on-the-road song, "A Showman's Life," and later on there were tributes to driving and drinking. In fact, the most heartfelt song was "Little Glass of Wine," an alcoholic's love song. None of this was up to his songwriting standard. — *William Ruhlmann*

Talk Memphis / 1981 / Stony Plain ♦♦♦

Having rushed to make *Nothing But a Breeze* and *A Touch on the Rainy Side* and getting his two least impressive albums for his trouble, Jesse Winchester spent two and a half

years woodshedding before returning to the record racks with *Talk Memphis*. For the album, he returned to his hometown and worked with producer Willie Mitchell, best known for his Al Green records. It wasn't as unlikely a matching as might be imagined; Winchester had always had a soulful, flexible voice as ready as Green's to take off into the upper registers to express emotion. And Memphis-style R&B had always been an element, along with country, folk, pop, and gospel, in Winchester's sound. On his early albums, his lighthearted style had been in the service of an embattled vision, but gradually that darkness gave way, to the point that he began to seem lightweight. *Talk Memphis* put his effervescence and musicality to good use, resulting in his first Top 40 hit, the catchy "Say What," and the rest of the album was just as easy on the ears, with the title track providing a suitably gritty Memphis-soul sendoff. But that wasn't enough to break the album beyond the bottom rungs of the charts, and after seven albums in 11 years, Winchester left the world of major-label record-making. — *William Ruhlmann*

Humour Me / 1988 / Sugar Hill ♦♦♦

After seven years, Jesse Winchester returned to record stores with a well-crafted pop album made up of new originals in his familiar, winning style. He mixed elements of folk, rock, country, R&B, and gospel on the songs, employing a first-rate backup group featuring New Grass stars Sam Bush, Jerry Douglas, Béla Fleck, Edgar Meyer, and Mark O'Connor, plus saxophonist Jim Horn. These pros were able match Winchester's forays into light gospel ("Let's Make a Baby King") and R&B ("Well-A-Wiggy," which had been a hit for the Weather Girls), as well as the straightforward romantic pop songs that made up the bulk of the record. *Humour Me* lacked the depth of Winchester's best work, but it was easily on a par with his substantial body of craftsmanlike music of the mid-'70s. His voice remained warm and supple, so that his own versions of the songs were effective, and the album also served as a demo for other singers in search of good pop material. — *William Ruhlmann*

● **The Best of Jesse Winchester** / 1989 / Rhino ♦♦♦♦♦

Jesse Winchester wrote and recorded more than enough great songs for Bearsville to fill a single-disc compilation, which means that some of them were bound to be left off. The trick was to balance the material from the brilliant first two albums with a careful selection from the subsequent five albums, each of which had its virtues. This 14-track album chooses four from *Jesse Winchester*, including the essential "Yankee Lady," "Biloxi," and "The Brand New Tennessee Waltz," and three from its follow-up, *Third Down, 110 to Go*. There are three from *Learn to Love It*, one each from *Nothing But a Breeze* and *A Touch on the Rainy Side*, and two from *Talk Memphis*. Lesser material such as "Tell Me Why You Like Roosevelt" and "Rhumba Man" could have been excised in favor of more from *Third Down*, but the selection is good enough to give a reasonable representation of Winchester's seven Bearsville albums, which contain some of the most impressive songwriting of the 1970s. — *William Ruhlmann*

Gentleman of Leisure / Jun. 22, 1999 / Sugar Hill ♦♦♦♦

From the opening vocals of the almost rockabilly "Club Manhattan," the undeniably excellent songwriting of Jesse Winchester makes its way back into our collective psyche. Backed by an unparalleled group of musicians, and with guest appearances from such musical dignitaries as the Fairfield Four, Jerry Douglas, Steve "The Colonel" Cropper, and Vince Gill, Winchester has assembled a highly enjoyable album, filled with the same magic his past releases all possessed. The kind of musical and lyrical genius that has caused dozens of artists to record his music gets into some funky blues territory with "Sweet Little Shoe," and downright beautiful with "That's What Makes You Strong," featuring the lap steel guitar work of Jerry Douglas, who also acts as producer for the album. The title track is a rocking blues number with some out-in-front drums from John Gardner and more of Jerry Douglas' excellent lap steel. "Wander My Way Back Home," a gospel tune, backed by the fabulous Fairfield Four, is one of the album's best tracks, and is reprised at the very end of the record. "Just Because I'm in Love With You" brings some Roy Orbison feeling, with flawless harmonies from country superstar Vince Gill. "Sweet Loving Daddy" features some fine dobro picking from Douglas, but the absolute finest track on the album has to be the final cut, "I Wave Bye Bye." *Gentleman of Leisure* is an album 11 years on coming, and it was well worth the wait. — *Michael B. Smith*

Jesse Winchester Live From Mountain Stage / Oct. 23, 2001 / Blue Plate ♦♦♦

Jesse Winchester started his career as a singer/songwriter with his self-titled debut way back in 1970, and many will at least be familiar with his work through other singers. Jimmy Buffett sang the lovely "Biloxi," Jimmie Dale Gilmore the dreamy "Defying Gravity," and Emmylou Harris the pensive "Songbird." All of these songs show a careful attention to capturing and holding fragile moments, pregnant with emotion. Winchester's *Live From Mountain Stage* performance is barebones: just a guy, his guitar, and a fistful of gems. While this setup may lack the dynamism of a studio album like 1999's *Gentleman of Leisure*, it has the quiet intimacy one might expect from catching a favorite singer at a local club. Songs like "Yankee Lady" and "Brand New Tennessee Waltz" harken back to his debut, while "Just Like New" and "That's What Makes You Strong" represent his '90s work. Winchester's subdued, sensitive vocals caress each phrase, filling delicately constructed pieces like "Songbird," "Eulalie," and "Little Glass of Wine" with deep feeling. To prevent an overdose of sentiment, "Just Like New" and "Gentleman of Leisure" throw in a bit of gentle humor. While *Live From Mountain Stage* never attempts to deliver the "Best of Jesse Winchester," it does offer a nice place to familiarize oneself with this first generation singer/songwriter. — *Ronnie D. Lankford Jr.*

Chubby Wise (Robert Russell Wise)

b. Oct. 2, 1915, Lake City, FL, d. Jan. 6, 1996
Fiddle, Session Musician / Western Swing

Most closely associated with Western swing and early bluegrass, Chubby Wise was one of the greatest fiddlers in country music. Born Robert Russell Wise in Lake City, FL, he didn't begin playing the fiddle until age 15, and got his start working nightclubs in

Jacksonville before becoming a full-time musician in 1938, when he joined the Jubilee Hillbillies. In 1942, he joined Bill Monroe's Blue Grass Boys and began playing at the *Grand Old Opry.* He performed and recorded with the band through 1948, and also worked with other performers such as Clyde Moody, with whom he co-wrote the "Shenandoah Waltz." He and Moody worked together until late 1949, when Wise returned to the Blue Grass Boys for another brief stint. Later, Wise performed with the York Brothers, Flatt & Scruggs, and Connie B. Gay's band. In 1954 he went to Nashville and joined Hank Snow's Rainbow Ranch Boys on the *Opry,* remaining with the band through 1970. When not touring, Wise did session work with such performers as Mac Wiseman, Red Allen and others, and began recording solo fiddle albums in 1969. He also played at the occasional bluegrass festival. In 1984, he moved to Florida and cut back on his workload, although in 1992 recorded with the Bass Mountain Boys. Wise passed away in 1996. *—Sandra Brennan*

● **An American Original** / 1995 / Pinecastle ✦✦✦✦

Although traditional fiddler Chubby Wise had appeared on hundreds of recordings by everyone from Hank Snow to Hank Williams, the best place to find his skipping and aching bow work is on the 1995 recording *An American Original.* Expertly recorded by Sonny Osborne of the Osborne Brothers in late 1994, the nearly 80-year-old fiddler tears through some real barnburners, like "Cotton Eyed Joe" and "Little Liza Jane," but still slows it down for the weepers, "I Can't Stop Loving You" and a great cover of Hank Williams' "I'm So Lonesome I Could Cry." Instrumental bluegrass at its finest, Chubby Wise's *An American Original* truly lives up to its name. *—Zac Johnson*

Mac Wiseman

b. May 23, 1925, Crimora, VA

Guitar, Vocals / Bluegrass, Progressive Bluegrass, Traditional Bluegrass, Contemporary Bluegrass, Truck Driving Country

Famed for his clear and mellow tenor voice, Mac Wiseman recorded with many great bluegrass bands, including those of Molly O'Day, Flatt & Scruggs, Bill Monroe, and the Osborne Brothers; his command of traditional material made him much in demand by bluegrass and folk fans alike. Wiseman was born in Crimora, VA, and grew up influenced by traditional and religious music and such radio stars as Montana Slim Carter. Wiseman started out working as a radio announcer in Harrisonburg in 1944. At the same time he worked as a singer with Buddy Starcher. He later formed his own group and continued performing with others, including Molly O'Day and Flatt & Scruggs, through the '40s. In 1949, he recorded a single, "Travelin' Down This Lonesome Road," with Bill Monroe. By the 1950s, Wiseman was again leading his own band.

Possessing one of the best tenor voices in bluegrass, Wiseman differed from Monroe and Flatt & Scruggs in that he usually sang alone, with little or no harmonizing. His band also employed two fiddles to play contemporary songs such as Speedy Drise's "Goin' Like Wildfire" as well as adaptations of standards such as the Carter Family's "Wonder How the Old Folks Are at Home" and Mac and Bob's "'Tis Sweet to Be Remembered." With the Country Boys, a band that featured such pioneering musicians as Eddie Adcock and Scott Stoneman, Wiseman recorded many popular local singles, and had his first national Top Ten hit with his version of "The Ballad of Davy Crockett." The song's success steered Wiseman away from bluegrass and more towards pop and country. In 1957, Wiseman began recording for Dot; he had a few major successes for the label with such songs as "Jimmy Brown the Newsboy" before moving to Capitol in 1962, where he recorded both country and bluegrass tunes. He began working for Wheeling's WWVA *Jamboree* in 1965, and also began to play at bluegrass festivals; over the next three decades, he became one of the most popular performers on the circuit.

Wiseman moved to Nashville in 1969 and signed with RCA Victor. His first—and only—hit for the label was the Top 40 novelty tune "If I Had Johnny's Cash and Charley's Pride." While at RCA, he also recorded three well-received bluegrass albums with Lester Flatt. From the mid-'70s on, Wiseman concentrated on bluegrass, becoming a fixture at festivals and releasing a series of records on independent records that ran into the '90s. In 1992, Wiseman narrated the documentary *High Lonesome,* a chronicle of bluegrass music, and in 1993 was inducted into the Bluegrass Hall of Fame. *—Sandra Brennan & David Vinopal*

The Mac Wiseman Story / 1976 / CMH ✦✦✦✦✦

Mac Wiseman Sings Gordon Lightfoot / 1979 / CMH ✦✦✦✦

A classic of bluegrass and country crossover, 1977's *Mac Wiseman Sings Gordon Lightfoot* masterfully matches Wiseman's famous country croon with Lightfoot's old-time country-folk tunes, all with a great backing band including Eddie Adcock on banjo and Clay Smith on acoustic guitar. Wiseman has a real knack for combining down-home flavor with vintage Vegas or Hollywood panache—as on the Willie Nelson-meets-Neil Diamond "Rainy Day People." "Summertime Dream" has a rollicking but pretty arrangement and features Wiseman really belting it out. "For Lovin' Me" and "Early Morning Rain" maybe aren't as deep and emotive as Lightfoot's versions, but Wiseman turns them into shuffling, thoughtful bluegrass tunes with a little more levity than the originals. Finally, "Ribbon of Darkness" is the real winner here—it's Hank Williams, Marty Robbins, and Willie Nelson all wrapped up in a nostalgic two and a half minutes of country and bluegrass. Fans who bought this LP in 1977 are sure to be delighted to find this slice of memory on CD, and for those—whether country or bluegrass fans—who are new to Mac Wiseman, *Mac Wiseman Sings Gordon Lightfoot* will make a great entry into his canon. *—Charles Spano*

Classic Bluegrass / 1987 / Rebel ✦✦✦

Classic Bluegrass captures a 1976 recording session where Mac Wiseman re-recorded many of his earlier hits, plus a handful of new material. Instead of being tired retreads, these new versions nearly equal the originals, since Wiseman's voice has matured and is rich with nuance. *Classic Bluegrass* may not be the definitive Mac Wiseman album, yet it comes very close to fulfilling that bill. *—Thom Owens*

24 Greatest Hits / 1987 / Deluxe ✦✦✦

Early Dot Recordings, Vol. 2 / 1988 / Rebel ✦✦✦✦✦

Early Dot Recordings, Vol. 2 picks up where the first volume left off, featuring some of the best early recordings Mac Wiseman made, including the hit "Jimmy Brown the Newsboy." *—Thom Owens*

Greatest Bluegrass Hits / 1989 / CMH ✦✦✦✦

Greatest Bluegrass Hits showcases ten recordings featuring "the voice with a heart," Mac Wiseman. The set includes songs the mellow-voiced tenor recorded between 1958-1963, playing alongside the Wilburn Brothers. Although this compilation contains first-rate performances of "I Wonder How the Old Folks Are at Home," "Jimmie Brown, the Newsboy," and "'Tis Sweet to Be Remembered," there is nothing new here for the die-hard collector. *—Al Campbell*

Grassroots to Bluegrass / 1990 / CMH ✦✦✦

● **Early Dot Recordings, Vol. 3** / 1992 / Rebel ✦✦✦✦✦

Early Dot Recordings, Vol. 3 highlights Mac Wiseman's late-'50s tenure with that label. At 16 tracks, this is far from complete, but it does contain a fine array of great performances, including "Don't Let Your Sweet Love Die," "You're Sweeter Than Honey," "Four Walls Around Me," and "I Saw Your Face in the Moon." *—Al Campbell*

Rare Singles and Radio Transcriptions / 1992 / Cowgirlboy [Germany] ✦✦✦✦

Teenage Hangout / 1993 / Bear Family ✦✦✦

Fans of Mac Wiseman's bluegrass might not know what to make of this batch of Dot recordings from the mid-'50s/early '60s. These 30 ultra-commercial sides consist of tight, precise performances of teen pop, rock & roll, and country-pop numbers, including many covers of contemporary hits. Wiseman's versions of hits such as "Tom Dooley," "Sixteen Tons," and "The Three Bells" benefit from arrangements that differ from the originals, while performances of less obvious material such as "Teen Age Hangout" and "Step It Up and Go" have become third-string rock & roll classics. Only "I Like This Kind of Music" even recalls bluegrass or hillbilly music—Wiseman was obviously going for the commercial gold with these tracks. *Teenage Hangout* documents an odd detour in Wiseman's career while offering some '50s fun for the rock & roll crowd. *—Greg Adams*

20 Old-Time Country Favorites / Jul. 22, 1997 / Rural Rhythm ✦✦✦

The 20 tracks on this CD (recorded in the mid-'60s) aren't bluegrass, but rather mostly-acoustic country with drums and occasional flourishes such as electric guitar leads with effects. As the title suggests, the songs include standards such as "Corina Corina," "Rovin' Gambler," and "Turkey in the Straw" in brief renditions; most tracks are under two minutes in length, and a few songs are barely over a minute long. The performances are interesting and entertaining, and will certainly please those who don't get too worked up over modern influences creeping into "old time" music. *—Greg Adams*

Mac, Doc & Del / 1998 / Sugar Hill ✦✦✦✦

Joined by Alison Krauss, Jerry Douglas, and Rob & Ronnie McCoury, among others, this is a treasure created by three of very recognizable voices from the world of bluegrass music. And these Groovegrass Boyz never sounded better! An exciting adventure that includes some pretty fancy fiddle work by Jason Carter. The senior McCoury, Del, is bright and meaningful on "The Old Accent" and solidly traditional on "Speak to Me Little Darlin'." Mac Wiseman is superb vocally on "When a Soldier Knocks." These three masters blend their voices effortlessly throughout, as "Live and Let Live" displays. The McCoury family is unstoppable as they join Carter and bass man Mike Bubba to perform an energetic rendition of "I've Endured." Don Reno's notable tune "Talk of the Town" is a masterpiece, when McCoury, Wiseman, and Doc Watson team up to create a stunning moment. The standard "I Wonder Where You Are Tonight" is exceptional as their clear harmonies rise and fall magically. Emotionally satisfying, this is a special project within the scope of traditional American music. *—Jana Pendragon*

Most Requested / Mar. 6, 2001 / CMH ✦✦✦

Combining the setup and general feel of a bluegrass band with the heartbreaking arrangements of traditional country, Mac Wiseman's *Most Requested* is a reflection of his success at both styles of music. Wiseman pulls off his blend by using his most powerful attribute—his voice. His sad tenor howl floats effortlessly over the picking and strumming, making for not only a beautiful combination of styles but something that has his distinctive stamp on it. On standards like "In the Pines" and "House of the Rising Sun," Wiseman's arrangements make them into lazy country ballads, with hints of bluegrass coming through. But then on tracks like "The Bluebirds Are Singing for Me," the banjos and chugging rhythms are out in full force and the country is only suggested through Wiseman's voice. The only real problem with the album is that at times the production robs the music of some of its power, making the affair sound more like a mainstream '80s country album. For example the first track, "Did She Mention My Name," is a good country song that is devoid of the grit it needs because of the polished studio sound. Fans of Wiseman or even just fans of good roots music may find this to be very a good listen, but this probably will not sway those not enamored with the genre. *—Bradley Torreano*

Johnny Wolfe

b. Alice, TX

Vocals / Bakersfield Sound

Johnny Wolfe was born in Alice and raised in Alvin, TX. Raised on the Bakersfield country of Merle Haggard and Buck Owens, Wolfe had soon learned guitar and rounded up a few pals to form the Sundowners. The band toured the juke joints and roadhouses of the Southwest, and Wolfe used the time to hone his songwriting skills. When the Sundowners eventually dissolved, Wolfe had a stockpile of songs. Together with collaborator Davin James, Wolfe's solo debut began to take shape and, in 2001, *Bad Tonight* was issued by the independent Bullnettle. The album featured some high-profile guests, including Hank Williams Jr.'s Bama Band, and was lauded for its trad country, rough-and-tumble sound. —*Johnny Loftus*

● **Bad Tonight** / Oct. 30, 2001 / Bullnettle ✦✦✦✦✦

Johnny Wolfe slings a mean Telecaster, has a golden voice, and writes songs that often sound like trad country classics. All of which is to say that *Bad Tonight* is a great achievement. "Say Ya Do" is pure old-time rock & roll, while "No Angels Down Below" bears the influence of the Bakersfield sound. Wolfe also occasionally mixes things up nicely with some pop inflections here and there, such as with the rolling organ and melodic touches on "Check Engine Light." Wolfe's singing particularly shines on the ballad "Tell Me True," which he hunkers down into like Ray Price or George Jones. The bluesy title track is a great showcase for Wolfe's guitar chops; however, it uncannily echoes Chris Isaak and therefore wouldn't be a good representative track for a new listener. With folks like Wolfe, Dallas Wayne, and Wolfe's good friend, Davin James, making albums like these, it seems there's strong hope for reverent, real, good-time country music. —*Erik Hage*

Lee Ann Womack

b. Jacksonville, TX

Vocals, Vocals (Background) / Contemporary Country, Neo-Traditionalist Country, Adult Contemporary

After spending several years as a professional songwriter, Lee Ann Womack became one of the breakout contemporary country stars of 1997 with her eponymous debut album. Born and raised in Jacksonville, TX, Womack became infatuated with music at an early age, which is appropriate for the daughter of a disc jockey. Her father often took her to work, where she picked out records to play on the air. Following high-school graduation, she attended South Plains Junior College in Levelland, TX. The school was one of the first in the country to offer degrees in country and bluegrass music, and Womack soon became a member of the college's band, Country Caravan. She traveled throughout the South and California with Country Caravan and stayed with the group until she left South Plains to study music business at Belmont University in Nashville. That led to an internship in MCA's A&R department.

By 1990, she had settled in Nashville, where she married and became a mother. She continued to attend Belmont, as well as write songs. Soon, she began singing on songwriting demos and performing her own showcase concerts. Eventually, Womack was spotted by Tree Publishing at one of her showcases. In 1995, the company signed her after listening to one of her original demos. While she was a staff writer at Tree, she co-wrote songs with Ed Hill, Bill Anderson, Sam Hogin, and Mark Wright. Her songs were recorded by Anderson and Ricky Skaggs.

Within a year after signing to Tree, Lee Ann Womack signed to Decca Records as a recording artist. Wright was hired as the producer for Womack's debut album, which was comprised of both original material and songs written by professional songwriters. Mark Chesnutt, Ricky Skaggs, Sharon White, and Tony Brown all appeared on the record, which created a buzz in the industry. Lee Ann Womack's eponymous album was released in May of 1997, and shortly after its release, it reached the Top Ten on the country chart. *I Hope You Dance* followed in mid-2000. *Something Worth Leaving Behind* appeared in mid-2002 and it was a sure fit for Womack to move into country mainstream for good. *A Season for Romance* was released before the year's end, but Womack was itching for the stage. In early 2003, Womack earned a small part on the CBS drama *The District*. She also earned two Grammy nods: one for Best Female Country Vocal Performance for *Something Worth Leaving Behind* and Best Vocal Collaboration (Country) for her duet with Willie Nelson on "Mendocino County Line." —*Stephen Thomas Erlewine*

Lee Ann Womack / May 13, 1997 / MCA Nashville ✦✦✦

Lee Ann Womack's eponymous debut showcases a promising country vocalist who is more comfortable with ballads and pop than down-home honky tonk. The slick, professional production helps make the album a pleasant listen, despite the fairly uneven songwriting, and Womack certainly has a voice that can make the mediocre sound appealing, which results in a winning debut. —*Thom Owens*

Some Things I Know / Sep. 22, 1998 / MCA ✦✦✦

On Lee Ann Womack's self-titled debut album, she moved effortlessly from traditional country balladry to honky tonk to country-pop, but on this second effort, her varied styles have melded into a prosaic Nashville sound for the '90s. To be sure, Womack's voice, an achingly sweet instrument not unlike Dolly Parton's, is still one of the best in country music, but stylistically, there's little here to hold the listener's interest. "A Little Past Little Rock" is a prime example. Lyrically, the song is predictable: "I'm a little past Little Rock and a long way from over you." The strings from the Nashville String Machine and the "ooh"s and "ah"s in the background contribute to the blandness of the track, and even such studio stars as Brent Mason on electric guitar and Jelly Roll Johnson on harmonica only play tastefully and without inspiration. The album's hilarious highlight, "I'll Think of a Reason Later," sounds like anything else on the radio in the late '90s, but on this album it stands out from the too laid-back sound of the rest of the songs. It seems that producer Mark Wright has made an effort to soften Womack's sound to make it more palatable to country radio, but in the process he has removed the soul of her music. Hopefully, next time out they'll return to the style that brought her a CMA Female Vocalist of the Year nomination in 1998. —*Brian Wahlert*

● **I Hope You Dance** / May 23, 2000 / MCA ✦✦✦✦

After a platinum-selling self-titled debut and a gold follow-up with *Some Things I Know*, Lee Ann Womack just keeps getting better. *Billboard* calls it "a career record." *I Hope You Dance* is one of the finest albums to hit country music post Shania Twain. Womack possesses such a sweet, melodious voice and its distinctiveness graces every one of the 12 tracks like they were chosen just for her vocals. But it's the album's title track, a dedication to Womack's daughters (and featuring the Sons of the Desert) that will leave you feeling swept away. (Her daughters, Aubrie and Anna Lise, who were ages 9 and 1, respectively, at the time, appear in the video with her.) "Don't let some hardened heart leave

you bitter/When you come close to selling out, reconsider/Give the heavens above more than a passing glance/And when you get the choice to sit it out or dance, I hope you dance." Listeners will undoubtedly dance to *I Hope You Dance*. —*Maria Konicki Dinoia*

Something Worth Leaving Behind / Aug. 20, 2002 / MCA ✦✦✦✦

I Hope You Dance garnered so much critical acclaim that it naturally would be a tough act to follow. But album number four lives up to its predecessor with 13 tracks that calm the soul. Womack's voice is so soothing that the whole listening experience is rather tranquil, peaceful, and serene. It's also pretty ballad-heavy, with Womack pushing her vocal talents to the limit on "Orphan Train" (about feeling like a misfit) and "You Should Have Lied" (about cheating). There does exist a place for a little bit of toe-tapping, uptempo music on "I Need You" and "Surrender." Otherwise, what you have here is a quiet yet determined album that packs a full punch. Go Lee Ann. —*Maria Konicki Dinoia*

The Season for Romance / Oct. 29, 2002 / MCA ✦✦✦

Cardinal rule number one for introducing new holiday songs amidst a sea of newly arranged classics: Make them compelling! No doubt she hopes that listeners will slow dance to the title track of her first holiday offering, but, despite its sweet sentiment, it's one of the handful of bland tracks amidst many that are far more interesting. The most unique choice Lee Ann Womack makes is moving away from her comfy country roots and doing a traditional jazz/big band-flavored party for the season at hand. Her wry duet of "Baby It's Cold Outside" with Harry Connick Jr. is fully of sultry cool and sassy personality—qualities the disc's other ballads could use more of. The medley of "Let It Snow/Winter Wonderland" is rendered in a classic '50s crooner fashion, with rising splashes of horn section complementing her lush vocals. That same tenderness serves her well on a sparse, folksy arrangement of "Silent Night," a mood she balances with sassy swingers like "The Man With the Bag." Even if there's some unevenness here, the disc in general lives up to its title concept. —*Jonathan Widran*

Jeff Wood

b. May 10, 1968, Oklahoma City, OK

Vocals, Bass, Keyboards / Contemporary Country, Americana

A graduate of Oklahoma State University who also attended two years of law school, Jeff Wood knew mega-star Garth Brooks from college and used to watch him perform at a Holiday Inn there. When Wood was thinking of moving to Nashville to pursue a music career, Brooks was the first one to show him around town. Getting his first publishing deal in 1994 with EMI Publishing, Wood wrote "Cowboy Love," which was cut by John Michael Montgomery. After a short-lived and fruitless deal with Liberty Records, Wood signed with Imprint Records and recorded his debut album in 1996. —*Jack Leaver*

● **Between the Earth and the Stars** / 1997 / Imprint ✦✦✦

Most of Jeff Wood's debut is of the '70s sensitive singer/songwriter fare, although a couple of cuts stand out and help to establish him as a viable country artist. The opening track "You Call That a Mountain," and is the strongest track in this collection and could almost sell the album on its own merit. Wood's style and delivery are worthwhile, and he cowrites five of the ten songs here. Also noteworthy is the Don Schlitz/Vince Gill contribution "You Just Get One," and Wood's uptempo "Long Way from OK." A mostly mellow set, heavy with pop-ish power ballads that should appeal to fans of the Dave Loggins-meets-John Berry school of country-pop. —*Jack Leaver*

Wooden Leg

Group / Alternative Country-Rock, Americana

After the breakup of the electric bluegrass band the Blood Oranges, the group's mandolinist Jim Ryan and guitarist Mark Spencer reunited to form the more rock-oriented Wooden Leg, which issued its self-titled debut LP in 1996. —*Jason Ankeny*

● **Wooden Leg** / Apr. 1996 / East Side Digital ✦✦✦✦

Blood Oranges founder Jimmy Ryan has come back around to rurally inspired rock & roll with Wooden Leg, whose self-titled debut also features former Oranges guitarist Mark Spencer (now a regular in Freedy Johnston's band) and drummer Keith Levreault. Ryan's mandolin is placed up front in the mix, but this is not a bluegrass album: The guitars and rhythms keep the songs balanced. —*Kurt Wolff*

Bob Woodruff

b. Mar. 14, 1961

Guitar (Acoustic), Vocals / Country-Rock, Singer/Songwriter, Americana

Bob Woodruff played in rock & roll bands as a kid growing up in New York City and New York state, but when he started writing songs, country music was where he found his vehicle for expression. While attending college in New York, Woodruff started writing country-oriented songs and formed a band called the Fields, which developed a loyal following regionally and was offered a recording contract with Restless Records. The Fields recorded a low-budget record, but Restless went bankrupt before the album could be released, so at that point Woodruff decided to pursue music as a solo act.

He started playing gigs by himself and as his songwriting became more country, his lawyer was sending tapes to Nashville. In the meantime, Restless solved its bankruptcy problems and offered Woodruff another deal, but he ended up signing with Asylum Records' Nashville division in late 1992. His debut album, *Dreams & Saturday Nights*, was released in 1994 to critical acclaim, but his melding of R&B, country, and rock didn't go over at country radio and Woodruff ended up parting ways with the label after one album. Woodruff found a new home for his music at Imprint Records and released his second album, *Desire Road*, in 1997. —*Jack Leaver*

● **Dreams and Saturday Nights** / 1994 / Asylum ✦✦✦✦

A wonderful, but mostly overlooked debut from this talented native-New York singer and songwriter. The album's leadoff track, "Bayou Girl," garnered some airplay, but unfortunately did very little to gain Woodruff any substantial audience in country music.

Woodruff's songs deal with typical country music subject matter: failed romance, broken dreams, and more. But what makes these stories and characters so believable is the yearning and a hint of vulnerability in which Woodruff emotes, both in his lyrics and vocal delivery. Whether it's a musician's dreams worn down by rejection ("Hard Liqour, Cold Women, Warm Beer") or the trapped feeling of becoming a father too soon ("Poisoned at the Well"), Woodruff's words paint unforgettable pictures of everyday longing and frustration. To convey a feeling, he's even willing to leave clever wordplay and convention at the door and simply wear his heart on his sleeve. Musically, *Dreams and Saturday Nights* is roots country with sharp rock & roll sensibility; the lack of contemporary-Nashville production slickness is refreshing. The legendary James Burton plays lead guitar on almost every cut and an album highlight is a duet with Emmylou Harris on the lonesome ballad "I'm the Train." —*Jack Leaver*

Desire Road / 1997 / Imprint ✦✦✦✦

With a change of record labels, Woodruff returns with a strong follow-up to his 1994 debut, *Dreams and Saturday Nights*. Taking a decidedly more roots rock and pop approach in the production, these songs are still more country than most of the modern stuff, and *Desire Road* isn't likely to alienate anyone who was grabbed by Woodruff's excellent debut. Hook-laden melodies abound, driven along with jangly 12-string guitars that still have a lot of meat to them and merge a Beatles/Byrds melodic sense with a Creedence-like earthiness. In fact, the album kicks off with Fogerty's "Almost Saturday Night," a country-rockified version that doesn't have too far to stretch. Woodruff continues with potent original songs, such as "That Was Then," a song about an aging musician who just has to keep playing, which sounds like a continuation of the character he introduced with "Hard Liquor, Cold Women, Warm Beer," the unforgettable song from his first album. "All That Love Has Worn Away" takes a delicious guitar figure à la British Invasion and sets it off against a Spanish-sung chorus with an intoxicating melody, which makes the song as wonderfully unusual as it is compelling. Throw in a couple of Arthur Alexander R&B gems (including "Everyday I Have to Cry" and "If It's Really Got to Be This Way") handled with loving care, and you have a record you'll want to visit again and again. —*Jack Leaver*

Sheb Wooley

b. Apr. 10, 1921, Erick, OK, d. Sep. 16, 2003, Nashville, TN
Vocals / Novelty, Traditional Country, Cowboy, Country Comedy

Among pop-culture scholars, Sheb Wooley is best remembered for his late-'50s rock & roll/comedy hit "Purple People Eater," which sold over three-million copies. But among country music aficionados, especially fans of cowboy songs, Sheb Wooley is the real article, or as near as one gets to it in modern times. A rodeo rider from the time that he was a boy, he was making a living on the circuit as a teenager, before he ever turned to music as a career. He turned to music and then acting, appearing in such Westerns as *High Noon*, before he was ever well-known as a singer, and later spent six seasons playing cowhand Pete Nolan on the television series *Rawhide*, even as he pursued a career in country music. In addition to cowboy songs, his repertory includes traditional country music and hillbilly tunes, along with the ubiquitous "Purple People Eater." Later on in the 1960s, he also developed a drunken comic persona named Ben Colder, whose success in satirizing various elements of country music, its audience, and its sensibilities actually threatened to eclipse Sheb Wooley.

Sheb Wooley was born in Erick, OK, on April 10, 1921. An avid rider from an early age, he was competing in local rodeos before he was ten years old, and by the time he was a teenager was one of the best young riders on the circuit. Music was also one of his interests, and Wooley got his first guitar when his father swapped a shotgun for the instrument. The family was poor, and living was very tough during the 1930s; more than once their crops were virtually blown away by the dry dust bowl winds. Wooley led his own country band in high-school, but music didn't offer the prospect of a living, and he made his living for a time working the oil fields of Oklahoma as a welder. As with many Oklahomans looking for a better future, Wooley headed to California in the late '30s and nearly earned a living at a packing plant, moving crates of oranges. By then Wooley was married to Melba Miller, the older sister of future country music star Roger Miller. When World War II broke out, Wooley found himself labeled 4-F (ineligible for military service) because of injuries he'd suffered as a rodeo rider, and he spent much of the war working in defense plants.

In 1945, he made his first records for the Bullet label in Nashville, and began appearing as a singer/guitarist on WLAC; the job paid nothing, but allowed him to get paid work elsewhere. His Bullet sides were cut at WSM, home of the *Grand Ole Opry*, but they saw almost no play or exposure of any kind. A year later he moved to Fort Worth, TX, and got a regular spot on radio there, sponsored by Calumet Baking Powder. Finally, in 1949, at the suggestion of a friend at WSM, Wooley decided to take the plunge and head for California in hope of getting some movie work. Around this same time, he was signed as a songwriter to Hill & Range, the publishing company, which, in turn, led to his being signed by the newly founded MGM Records in 1950. MGM already had a legendary figure in its roster, in the person of Hank Williams, but country music was booming, and there was room for as many worthwhile talents as the label could find.

He also took acting lessons in the hope of getting some work on the screen. Wooley succeeded more than he could have hoped in this capacity, appearing in small parts in 40 feature films, beginning with *Rocky Mountain*, Errol Flynn's final Western, in 1949. His most notable screen came two years later in the classic *High Noon* (1952), in which he played Ben Miller, the leader of the outlaw gang gunning for town marshal Gary Cooper. He also played an important supporting role in the historical drama *Little Big Horn* (1951), starring Lloyd Bridges and John Ireland, and was seen in *The Man Without a Star* (1955), *Giant* (1956), and *Rio Bravo* (1959), starring John Wayne.

Amid all of his film work, Wooley continued recording and writing songs. It wasn't until 1958, however, that he had a hit of any consequence, and it was a most unexpected song. Wooley had written several songs that were hits for other singers, most notably "Are You

Satisfied," which got to number 11 on the country charts as recorded by Rusty Draper in 1955. Wooley had always displayed a gift for parody, and the song he finally scaled the pop charts with was "Purple People Eater," a parody of various pop culture crazes including monster movies (some people at the time suggested—incorrectly—that the sci-fi/horror classic *The Blob*, starring Steve McQueen, which was released at around the same time as Wooley's song, was virtually a film of the song). Wooley had to fight to get the song released, and it ultimately became one of the biggest hit singles in the history of MGM Records.

He was unable to follow-up the success of "Purple People Eater," however, and it wasn't until 1962 that he had another hit, this time a country chart-topper called "That's My Dad." In 1958, Wooley was cast in the role of Pete Nolan in the television Western *Rawhide*, starring Eric Fleming and Clint Eastwood, which premiered in January of 1959. He later wrote some scripts for the series as well, and in 1959, in order to fulfill public demand for a recording of the series' title song, he recorded his own version of the *Rawhide* theme song and an entire album of Western songs, which failed to chart. He later recorded an album of folk-style material that was released in the wake of the MGM wide-screen epic blockbuster movie *How the West Was Won*, but this also failed to catch on with the public.

His film work continued during this time, and it was because of movie and television commitments that he was unable to record the song "Don't Go Near the Indians." Instead, former movie cowboy/singer Rex Allen recorded it and had a hit with it. In response to his bad luck, Wooley cut a joke parody follow-up to the song, entitled "Don't Go Near the Eskimos," and created a new, inebriated comic persona to present it. "Ben Colder" was born with "Don't Go Near the Eskimos," and for the rest of his career Wooley—in a manner anticipating the lot of David Johansen/Buster Poindexter—had to split his time between appearances as "straight" country/cowboy singer Sheb Wooley and drunken comic Ben Colder. (Some of the other names that Wooley had considered for this persona, according to one source, were "Ben Freezin'" and "Klon Dyke"). In 1969, when the country music showcase *Hee Haw* went on the air, Wooley became the show's resident songwriter, providing the series' comic musical numbers. Ben Colder went on to have several more hits, including "Almost Persuaded No. 2," and in 1968 the Colder persona was voted Comedian of the Year. Wooley continued recording under both guises into the 1980s, although his last chart single in either persona dated back to 1971.

In 1998, Wooley was diagnosed with leukemia and spent the next few years in and out of hospitals battling the condition. On September 16, 2003 Sheb Wooley passed away at the age of 82. The previous year Wooley had been honored by Tennessee Senator Fred Thompson, who referred to the singer/songwriter/actor as an "American treasure." —*Bruce Eder*

Songs from the Days of Rawhide / 1960 / MGM ✦✦✦

Wooley's singing lacks sufficient variety to carry off this collection of a dozen songs, most of them (apart from the Dimitri Tiomkin *Rawhide* theme) originals. They aren't bad, but they're also not terribly ambitious. "The Goodnight-Living Trail" is a fascinating piece of history set to music, and works better than most of the album. "Indian Maiden" is closer in spirit to Wooley's comedy songs, and draws its melody from the Merle Travis classic "Smoke! Smoke! Smoke! (That Cigarette)." Tex Owens' old hit "Cattle Call" also gets a loving treatment. The playing (featuring the likes of guitarist Billy Strange and drummer Earl Palmer) is good, but there are better albums in this vein available from Marty Robbins and Johnny Cash, among others. —*Bruce Eder*

Tales of How the West Was Won / 1963 / MGM ✦✦✦✦

A masterful concept album, and an oddity, built around a movie. MGM had the blockbuster *How the West Was Won* out on screen, and their record division asked Wooley to record an album to tie-in with the film. The result is a superb collection of folk and western-style songs that tie in with various sequences in the movie, including excellent spoken word tracks ("Wagonmaster's Diary"), fine sentimental ballads ("Papa's Old Fiddle"), and even a brilliant cover of the Alfred Newman-Ken Darby title track from the movie. Two years after the release of this album, Darby added the song "Big Land," and MGM re-released it with the new track (but without the Newman-Darby movie song) as *It's a Big Land* (MGM 4325). —*Bruce Eder*

● **The Very Best of Sheb Wooley** / 1965 / MGM ✦✦✦✦✦

Rawhide/How the West Was Won / Feb. 1996 / Bear Family ✦✦✦✦

This isn't an ideal compilation, in the sense that none of the material on it was ever a hit, so the general public might not care for it—and people looking for anything like "Purple People Eater" or the Ben Colder material will be disappointed. But Bear Family has gathered together Wooley's two early-'60s country & western albums, and they're very fine, even including a few originals that are quite good. He does a good job with the *Rawhide* title song and also deeply evocative pieces like "Enchantment of the Prairie" and "The Story of Billy Burdell," backed by the likes of Earl Palmer on drums. *How the West Was Won* includes numbers such as "High Lonesome" and "Plowin' in the New Ground," and the sentimental "Papa's Old Fiddle," all of which come off well in the manner of Gene Autry/Johnny Western/Sons of the Pioneers-style Western songs. The backing musicians include Charlie McCoy on harmonica and Earl Palmer on drums. —*Bruce Eder*

The Purple People Eater / 1997 / MGM ✦✦✦

Inspired by the success of David Seville's "Witch Doctor," Sheb Wooley decided to work up his own tape-manipulation novelty and created "The Purple People Eater," a huge number-one hit in 1958. This CD is a companion to Bear Family's *That's My Pa* box set and two other single discs which, in combination, account for most of Wooley's recordings. *The Purple People Eater* concentrates on novelty songs, including the instrumental EP *The Purple People Eater Plays Earth Music*, a couple of sequels to "The Purple People Eater," and the unbelievable "Pygmy Love." Other recordings are merely pop-oriented (Wooley's first hit from 1955, "Are You Satisfied") or uptempo country, but for the most part, this is the wackiest music in Wooley's catalog. Bear Family usually organizes its reissues in a more sensible manner than Sheb Wooley received with his haphazard thematic packages, but lovers of novelty music will appreciate this one. —*Greg Adams*

- **Wild and Wooley, Big Unruly Me** / Nov. 5, 1997 / Bear Family ✦✦✦✦

Sheb Wooley is best known to American novelty song fans as the cat who recorded "Purple People Eater" in 1958, a number-one smash, and "That's My Pa" from 1962. Still others know him as the character Pete Nolan in the TV show *Rawhide*, or Ben Wilson in the film *High Noon*. But only collectors know about the astonishingly varied career Wooley created between roughly the end of 1956 and 1971. This is the second volume of his work issued by Bear Family. The first, *Purple People Eater*, concentrated mostly on hits and all of the novelty songs that scored in an even minor way. *Wild and Wooley, Big Unruly Me* fixes its sites on the more obscure recordings, a couple minor hits, and rare unissued tracks and B-sides from 1957-1970. Few tracks on either set concentrate on Wooley's voluminous country music catalog, which is now the subject of a BF four-CD box set. Here is the near doo wop "Recipe for Love" juxtaposed against the rockabilly/calypso (?) mishmash that is "I'm Too Young." But there's also the wacky "Sweet Chile," which is part Cajun, part Bo Diddley, and part Pat Boone! There's an absolutely dreadful rendition of "'Til The End of the World," which was a hit for Jim Reeves, and a knockout rock & roll tune called "Mississippi Twist" that went unreleased until this volume appeared. Ultimately there are a few of the nuttier novelty numbers here, such as "Buba Hoo, Baba Dee," the title track in a different version than the one that appears on *Purple People Eater*, "One of Them Roarin' Songs," and "Little Bitty Bilbo Abernathy." The only thing the tracks seem to share is the warm baritone Wooley effortlessly displayed in his younger years—that and his restlessness for any kind of song. Highly recommended as one of pop & roll's true oddities. —*Thom Jurek*

- **That's My Pa** / Mar. 25, 1998 / Bear Family ✦✦✦✦✦

This box and its 113 songs cover the years 1945 through 1972, and the least known side of Sheb Wooley's career, but the one where he started out—as a country singer and songwriter, first fronting a Western swing-style band and later working in the straight commercial Nashville style. Warning to casual Sheb Wooley fans—there's no "Purple People Eater" here, or any sign of Wooley's "Ben Colder" comedy alias. Most were never on LP, and only a handful have been available in decades. The first ten cuts on this box, dating from 1945 and 1947, reveal him as a talented, smooth Gene Autry-type singer with more depth and range, with a good Western swing band behind him. On the MGM sides, beginning in 1948, the music is more polished, and the mix of songs is weighted more toward sentimental ballads. The middle section of this box shows us a fascinating set of possibilities—starting at the dawn of the 1950s, Wooley began merging Western swing with some components of R&B; his music could easily have moved toward rock & roll, but Wooley evidently wasn't comfortable making that jump. The material from the 1960s and early 1970s is utterly polished, and some of it is beautiful, commercial country music, using all of the smooth Nashville techniques. The assembly of the discs is also strange, mostly owing to the fact that after 1961, a huge amount of Wooley's studio time was given over to comedy tracks as "Ben Colder," leaving big gaps in his "straight" output for years at a time. The accompanying booklet contains a finely detailed account of Wooley's career. —*Bruce Eder*

Jimmy Work

b. 1924, Akron, OH

Vocals, Composer / Traditional Country, Country-Pop, Honky Tonk

Jimmy Work isn't a name that most country music fans are familiar with, even though as a songwriter he was responsible for "Tennessee Border," "Making Believe," and "That's What Makes the Jukebox Play." Like a handful of performers, he worked happily at music for many years but felt privileged simply to have had the opportunity to record and perform, and gladly kept his day job as a millwright. Jimmy Work was born in Akron, OH, in 1924. Two years later, his parents moved to a farm in Dukedom, TN. He began playing guitar when he was seven years old after he picked up a guitar his father had originally bought for his mother. His two biggest influences at that point in his life, and for many years after, were Gene Autry and Roy Acuff, and one can safely include Jimmie Rodgers on the list as well. He was in a band in high-school, and was a good enough fiddle player to win contests on that instrument as well. He began writing songs before he was in his teens, and was encouraged by reactions to his music.

By 1945, he was playing country music in Pontiac, a suburb of Detroit, MI; and while things started slowly for Work, playing country music in a northern industrial area, they got better in the years immediately as Southerners, white as well as black, moved there to take defense plant jobs and stayed on afterward as part of the automobile and related industries. Players like Jimmy Work were a welcome reminder of home for many of these newly transplanted country listeners. By the mid-'40s, Work had a big enough audience from his local radio appearances to justify the publication of a songbook, as he later cut his first two singles for a tiny label called Trophy. Those first two singles, featuring Work on acoustic guitar and a single electric guitar backup, were highly derivative of Jimmie Rodgers, and even featured Work yodeling in the manner of the Singing Brakeman. His third single, "Tennessee Border," was his first version of the song, cut for the tiny Alben label. His record didn't sell, but a year later, "Tennessee Border" was picked up by five different artists—Red Foley, Bob Atcher, Jimmie Skinner, Tennessee Ernie Ford, and Hank Williams—and became a hit for four of them, all at once. Foley's led the pack, peaking at number three on the country charts, with Ford's following at number eight, Atcher's at number 12, and Skinner's bringing up the rear at number 15; ironically, it was Hank Williams' version that failed to chart.

The success of those records got Jimmy Work his first major-label contract with Decca Records in 1949, and "Tennessee Border" also got him invited to appear on the *Grand Ole Opry*; Work also played at the *Ernest Tubb Midnight Jamboree*. By the time of his second session for Decca in August of 1949, Work was being backed by Red Foley's Pleasant Valley Boys, which included Jerry Byrd and Delmore Brothers veteran Zeke Turner on guitars, Ernie Newton on bass, and the legendary Tommy Jackson on fiddle. Unfortunately, despite the quality of the players and the momentum imparted by the success of "Tennessee Border," Work never had any hits from his Decca work, and by 1950 he was

released from the label. After a short stay with the tiny Bullet label in 1950, Work jumped to the London label in 1951, which yielded "Pickup Truck," his witty slice-of-Southern-life song, and "Do Your Honky Tonkin' at Home."

During this period, Work's music, mostly by virtue of the bands he was using for backup, was heavily influenced by the honky tonk style of Lefty Frizzell. It may have been the derivative nature of his sound, coupled with the indifferent nature of the material, that left Work out in the cold where sales of his own records were concerned during this period. Still without a hit of his own to his credit, Jimmy Work signed with Capitol Records in 1952, and although his first four songs yielded no hits, the label stuck with him. It was only after a second round of sessions that he was dropped from the label's roster in 1953. He then moved to the Dot label, and it was there that he cut two of his most popular songs, "Making Believe" and "That's What Makes the Jukebox Play." "Making Believe," issued in 1955, rose to number 11 for Work, but it was Kitty Wells, releasing a rival version, who saw the lion's share of record sales with a number-two single.

"That's What Makes the Jukebox Play" became a number-six single for Work in the summer of 1955. Work's success boosted his concert activity during the mid-'50s, and he happened to share a number of concerts in 1955 with Elvis Presley, who was still a regional phenomenon. His future with Dot Records was secure for the time being, with two major hits behind him, and Work continued playing dates, recording, and writing songs; occasionally he would experiment with new sounds, as with his rockabilly-style cover of "Rock Island Line," issued in the wake of English skiffle king Lonnie Donegan's hit version (which charted in America).

Work wasn't a rockabilly player or a rock & roller, however, and the rise of the new music took away just enough of the impetus from country music in general that he eventually was forced to give up the music business. He sold real estate and cut some singles (including yet another version of "Tennessee Border") for the All label, based in Whittier, CA. By 1959, it was all over, and Work knew it; the music had passed him by, and the honky tonk style wasn't even in favor among the country audience that did remain. He returned to the job he was trained for and knew best, a millwright, on the farm in Dukedom, TN, near the border with Kentucky. Jimmy Work kept his hand in songwriting, signed with the Acuff-Rose organization, and some of his past glories were revisited in later years. Emmylou Harris brought "Making Believe" back into the Top Ten with a new version in 1977, and Moe Bandy, that diehard honky tonk enthusiast, brought "That's What Makes the Jukebox Play" to number 11 on the country charts a year later.

A prodigious talent with an ear for songwriting that would be the envy of most country players, and a smooth-yet-jaunty honky tonk style, Jimmy Work was unjustly forgotten and overlooked for many years by too many people. Even on those occasions when the songs were less than first-rate, or the backing band wasn't what it might have been, his delivery saved the record. He was never too bothered by the obscurity into which he fell in the 1960s, satisfied that he'd had the chance to make music, and having settled into a comfortable living. In 1986, Bear Family Records issued the first LP of Jimmy Work's songs, which was followed by a second vinyl disc, and later by a double-CD set from the same label, tying up all the loose ends of Work's career. —*Bruce Eder*

- **Making Believe** / 1994 / Bear Family ✦✦✦✦✦

Here are 48 songs that make up Jimmy Work's combined output for Decca, Capitol, Triumph, Album, Dot, and so on. Much of what's here on *Making Believe*, apart from those early yodel-style numbers, is some of the most pleasing and rousing honky tonk music you can find, unique in sound and style despite the similarities to Lefty Frizzell in the early '50s. The support personnel vary considerably (some of the better bands aren't even recorded for posterity), from complete unknowns to the likes of Grady Martin and Tommy Jackson, but Work's singing is remarkably consistent and attractive regardless of who's playing behind him. Among the highlights from the previously unreleased tracks are two different versions of "Puttin' on the Dog (Tom Cattin' Around)," both of which were considered too risqué to be issued at the time. The released stuff includes the original and re-recorded versions of "Tennessee Border," "Making Believe," and "That's What Makes the Jukebox Play" and the weirdly delightful "Do Your Honky Tonkin' at Home" and "Hospitality," among too many treasures to name. —*Bruce Eder*

Darryl Worley

b. Oct. 31, 1964

Vocals / Contemporary Country

Country singer/songwriter Darryl Worley grew up in Pyburn, TN, the son of a father who left his job at a local paper company to become a Methodist preacher and a mother who was a featured singer in the church choir. He became a hard-working yet rebellious young man—earning a degree in biology with a minor in organic chemistry while drinking bootlegged whiskey and partying at honky-tonks—who never gave up on making music his full-time pursuit. While holding various jobs, including a stint as a teacher, Worley played clubs on the weekends and occasional weeknights; finally, he signed a publishing deal with Fame in Muscle Shoals and began playing bars nearly every night of the week, and even broke his engagement to become a full-time performer and songwriter. He signed to DreamWorks Nashville in 1999 and released the single "When You Need Love" the following spring; his debut album, *Hard Rain Don't Last*, arrived in mid-2000. The album got a decent amount of play on radio and CMT, and after a successful tour of the U.S. Worley returned to the studio for his next album. *I Miss My Friend* arrived in the summer of 2002 at the top of the country charts, hitting number one in its first week. Before the year's end, Worley toured Afghanistan during Christmas time, spending time with American troops. The experience was overwhelming and mind-blowing for Worley; and he captured such emotion in his sophomore effort, *Have You Forgotten?* This album, which appeared on DreamWorks in May 2003, was a small tribute to the U.S. troops fighting for Iraqi Freedom as well as a great musical progression for Worley. —*Heather Phares*

Hard Rain Don't Last / Jul. 18, 2000 / DreamWorks ✦✦✦✦

Darryl Worley was born and raised in Tennessee. He has mentioned being influenced by country greats like Hank Williams, George Jones, Willie Nelson, and Merle Haggard.

Hints of those influences show through in Worley's own music, but without taking over. *Hard Rain Don't Last* is his debut full-length offering. He co-wrote many of the tunes on this first album, including "When You Need My Love," "Feels Like Work," "If I Could Just Be Me," "A Good Day to Run," and "Too Many Pockets," as well as the impressive title track. A number of the tunes made their way onto the Top 20 charts. The songs on *Hard Rain Don't Last* move from slow and soft ballads to toe-tapping Western swing filled with the sound of the expected steel guitar and fiddle, and are all enjoyable. Though a lot of country music seems caught somewhere closer to pop or rock than country, this recording proves that traditional doesn't have to be outdated. *—Charlotte Dillon*

● **I Miss My Friend** / Jul. 16, 2002 / DreamWorks ✦✦✦✦

This Merle Haggard/Randy Travis sound-alike oozes natural talent. Worley is a standout in a sea of country-pop wannabes. Words like "good ol' boy," "honky tonk," and "down home" can be used to describe this straight-shooting album. The buoyant "Tennessee River Run," the first cut, sets the tone, letting listeners know that for the next 41 minutes they would be in for a hootin' and hollerin' ride. And they are with songs like "Callin' Caroline" and "Spread a Little Love Around." Notables include the bluesy "Family Tree" and the jazz-infused "Opportunity of a Lifetime." Worley's skill as a songwriter is not to be overlooked, either. *I Miss My Friend* is a gratifying listen. *—Maria Konicki Dinoia*

Have You Forgotten? / Apr. 15, 2003 / DreamWorks ✦✦✦

Darryl Worley started to gain a larger audience in 2002 when his second album, *I Miss My Friend*, brought him to the top of the country charts. So, even if he was on a career upswing prior to the release of *Have You Forgotten?* in 2003, it doesn't make this album and its title song feel any less than an opportunistic stab at riding war fever and patriotism toward superstardom. Consider this: *Have You Forgotten?* contains a seemingly generous 16 songs, but when the details are dissected, it becomes apparent that there are six songs apiece from Worley's first two albums, 2000's *A Hard Rain Don't Last* and 2002's *I Miss My Friend*, which constitute half of each record. That means that there are merely *four* new songs here, three of which are war-related (the other finds the singer stating "I Need a Breather," wishing he was wasting away in a Margaritaville, since he needs a break from "this angry boss man"—he sure does "got some ways that the world don't agree with," apparently). Worley goes out of his way to align himself with the red, the white, and the blue, standing in front of the stars and stripes on the front cover and posing with troops on the back. Then, of course, there's "Have You Forgotten?," where Worley cheerfully flaunts his ignorance of international politics in a flag-waving fervor. If Toby Keith's "Courtesy of the Red, White & Blue" made Alan Jackson's "Where Were You When the World Stopped Turning" seem complex and nuanced, Worley makes Keith seem worldly and wise. Worley twists every piece of logic and emotion regarding the War on Iraq and 9-11, treating the two as if they were interchangeable. First, he claims that "this war" is about fighting for "this piece of ground," something that is simply untrue. Then, he forgets that Osama Bin Laden and Saddam Hussein are *not* the same person (then again, polls indicate that a *majority* of the American population believe there were Iraqis on the 9-11 planes, when there were not), then makes a ludicrous leap in logic in claiming that protesters against the Iraqi War are saying we "shouldn't worry 'bout Bin Laden," an argument that has *never* been made. Worley is attempting to fuse the anger of Keith with the tear-jerking Jackson, and he's come up with an utter mess, something that feels calculated, not heartfelt. So, perhaps it's only appropriate that it is the title song on this disc, which is more compilation than proper album, where the song itself—and the haphazard, thrown-together, opportunistic nature of the record—overshadows the material from his first two records, the material that suggests he's a neo-traditional country singer with some real promise. Unfortunately, all that is overshadowed by his sour patriotic hucksterism on *Have You Forgotten?* *—Stephen Thomas Erlewine*

Chely Wright (Richelle Renee Wright)

b. Oct. 25, 1970, Kansas City, MO

Vocals / Contemporary Country, Neo-Traditionalist Country

After several years of hard touring, Chely Wright broke through to become a chart-topping star on the contemporary country scene. Born Richelle Renee Wright in Kansas City in 1970, she grew up in the small town of Wellsville, KS, and fell in love with country music before she'd even started school. She took piano lessons starting at age four and began singing in groups at 11, also playing trumpet in her school band. At 14, she started performing in local clubs with a backing band called County Line, which featured her father on bass. The summer after her junior year of high-school, she performed in the long-running Ozark Jubilee show, and as a senior, she successfully auditioned for a job impersonating female country stars at Nashville's Opryland theme park. She moved there permanently in 1989 and spent the next three years working at Opryland and an assortment of day jobs. Eventually, she landed a publishing deal on the strength of her songwriting, and a record contract with Mercury/Polydor followed.

Wright's debut album, *Woman in the Moon*, was released in 1994 and attracted positive notice from some critics and the country music community, earning her a Top New Female Vocalist award from the ACM. Unfortunately, neither it nor its follow-up, 1996's *Right in the Middle of It*, sold very well. Wright asked for her release from Polydor and moved over to MCA, where she had the opportunity to work with the commercially savvy producer Tony Brown. Though it wasn't a smash, Wright's 1997 label debut, *Let Me In*, did make the country Top 40 and gave the singer her first Top 20 hit in "Shut Up and Drive." Moreoever, her constant touring was paying off in the form of a growing fan base, setting the stage for her breakthrough with 1999's *Single White Female*. The album's title track became Wright's first number one hit, and the following year, she and Brad Paisley duetted on their co-composition "Hard to Be a Husband, Hard to Be a Wife." Her next album, *Never Love You Enough*, became her first to break the country Top Ten, and she reached the Top 30 with the title track and "Jezebel." *—Steve Huey*

Woman in the Moon / 1994 / Mercury ✦✦✦

● **Right in the Middle of It** / Feb. 1996 / Polydor Nashville ✦✦✦✦

This 1996 album, *Right in the Middle of It*, is the sophomore offering from award-winning country singer Chely Wright. The recording is filled with both ballads and fast-paced numbers, and features plenty of natural country twang. Wright has enough vocal talents to handle the ballads and enough energy to carry the toe-tappers. This might only be her second album, but she's had plenty of singing experience, starting with family get-togethers when she was a small child, where singalongs with fiddles and guitars were the norm. Before she hit her teens she had already formed a country band of her own. Early on Wright was exposed to music greats like Loretta Lynn, Buck Owens, Connie Smith, and Conway Twitty. Many of those influences can be heard in the songs on *Right in the Middle of It*. Wright, also a gifted songwriter, penned three of the tunes on this album: "The Other Woman," "Gotta Get Good at Givin' Again," and the title track. *—Charlotte Dillon*

Let Me In / Sep. 9, 1997 / MCA ✦✦✦✦

For her third album, Chely Wright switched record labels and teamed up with producer Tony Brown, who helmed the boards for records by George Strait and Reba McEntire, among others. Brown stripped Wright's music down to the core—for much of *Let Me In*, she's singing over clean acoustic arrangements; only a few cuts are adorned with pop/rock instrumentation. Wright benefits from the spare arrangements, which only emphasize her lovely voice and charisma. The result is her most accomplished and arguably best album to date. *—Thom Owens*

Single White Female / May 18, 1999 / MCA ✦✦✦✦

Chely Wright reunited with producer Tony Brown—the man behind hit records by George Strait and Reba McEntire, as well as Wright's own *Let Me In*—for her fourth album, *Single White Female*. The record picks up where its predecessor left off, offering a selection of ten songs with clean, tasteful arrangments that place Wright in the forefront. If the songs aren't always immediately grabbing, they're all classy, well-written tunes that slowly work their way into memory. Even when Wright and Brown shoot for the charts, such as on the big chorus of "The Love That We Lost," they pull it off, since Chely never oversings and the instrumentation is never bombastic. She still sounds her best on ballads, but her uptempo numbers—including the clever title track and "The Fire"—are equally convincing, which is one of the main reasons that *Single White Female* is a welcome addition to an already impressive catalog. *—Stephen Thomas Erlewine*

Never Love You Enough / Sep. 25, 2001 / MCA ✦✦

Personable and traditional, Wright is the bland new face of country. On 1999's *Single White Female*, she struck a feminist pose for all 21st century Dixie chicks, taking the voice of the modern everywoman on a cycle of songs detailing the little parts of working and non-working relationships. This more conservative follow-up finds her back on the farm, still tracking the ins and outs of love, but accompanied by a shrugging indifference. Ultimately, it orbits around the concept of love as an unquestionable force, even something to fall back on. *Single White Female* was all about breaking from tradition; *Never Love You Enough* is about getting it all back. Sometime at the turn of the century, Wright got the idea that being a single female is no way to spend the new millennium. *—Michael Gallucci*

Johnnie Wright

b. May 13, 1914, Mt Juliet, TN

Vocals / Traditional Bluegrass, Traditional Country

Singer/songwriter Johnnie Wright spent much of his career working with Jack Anglin in the popular duo Johnnie & Jack, and was also the husband of Kitty Wells. He was born in Mount Juliet, Tennessee, and first performed with Anglin in 1936. They teamed up full-time in the 1940s and, except for the time Anglin spent overseas during the war, remained together for over two decades. In 1952, the duo and Wells were invited to join the *Grand Ole Opry*, where they remained for 15 years. Following Anglin's death in 1963, Wright continued performing and making records. In 1964, he & His Tennessee Mountain Boys had a Top 25 hit with "Walkin', Talkin', Cryin', Barely Beatin' Broken Heart." The following year, he had success with "Hello Vietnam," a number-one hit. In 1968, he and Wells recorded an autobiographical duet, "We'll Stick Together," and continued playing live shows together through the early '80s, when they left music to run a souvenir shop. In 1992, the couple and their son Bobby began playing together again. *—Sandra Brennan*

Hello Vietnam / 1965 / Decca ✦✦✦

Country Music Special / 1966 / Decca ✦✦✦

Country, The Wright Way / 1967 / Decca ✦✦✦

● **Johnny Wright Sings Country Favorites** / 1968 / Decca ✦✦✦✦

Michelle Wright

b. Jul. 1, 1961, Morpeth, Ontario, Canada

Vocals / Country-Pop, Contemporary Country

Vocalist Michelle Wright was born in Morpeth, Ontario, where she began singing as a child. She took after her father, a performer in a country & western group; and her mother, who sang with the Reflections for over a decade. Wright joined a band in college and was in and out of combos for the next three years until she formed her own group in 1983. After five years with that group, Wright went solo and issued *Do Right By Me* in Canada. The LP garnered Wright widespread acclaim and led to a contract with Arista in Nashville. *New Kind of Love* was her first release for Arista; it dropped July 17, 1990. She followed it with the decidedly more slick *Now & Then*, which featured the hit singles "Take It Like a Man" and "He Would be 16" ("Take It" also hit number one in Canada). By 1996's *For Me It's You*, Wright was an established superstar in her native country but was still merely a critical favorite in the U.S. She issued *The Reasons Why* in 1997 and a greatest-hits collection in 2000. Wright returned in 2003 with the poppy "Shut Up and Kiss Me." *—Johnny Loftus*

Do Right By Me / 1988 / Savannah ♦♦♦

● **Michelle Wright** / 1990 / Arista ♦♦♦♦
With her husky, cigarette-deep voice, Wright sounds like nothing so much as a young Lacy J. Dalton on her American debut. There's some straight country here ("The Dust Ain't Settled Yet"), but more often than not, Wright's singing R&B material with steel guitars. Not only does she sing the stuff, she knows how: drop her voice two octaves on "Not Enough Love to Go 'Round," and she's Barry White. *—Brian Mansfield*

New Kind of Love / Jul. 17, 1990 / Arista ♦♦♦

Now & Then / 1992 / Arista ♦♦♦
Wright made a mainstream move with *Now & Then*, downplaying the R&B and remaking herself as a sleek, sultry version of Lorrie Morgan. It paid off, too: she had her first real hits in the U.S. with "Take It Like a Man" and "He Would Be 16," a tear-jerking ballad dealing with the regrets of giving an illegitimate child up for adoption. Her Nudie jackets and black bodysuits made her a video favorite, too. The music's not as distinctive here as on *Michelle Wright*, but the hits hold up nicely. *—Brian Mansfield*

For Me It's You / Aug. 27, 1996 / Arista ♦♦♦♦
For Me It's You continues Michelle Wright's streak of winning albums. Featuring songs from writers as gifted as Rodney Crowell and Pam Tillis, the album has a rich selection of material that is alternately gritty and soulful and always powerful. Wright blesses each song with her powerful pipes, singing the songs with conviction—even when the songs border on lightweight country-pop, she sings them as if they were pure country. The result is a terrific little album, one that makes you wonder why Wright isn't a star in America like she is in her native Canada. *—Thom Owens*

The Reasons Why / 1997 / Arista ♦♦♦

● **Greatest Hits** / Jan. 25, 2000 / Arista ♦♦♦♦

Wylie & the Wild West Show

f. 1989

Group / Yodeling, Western Swing Revival, Alternative Country-Rock, Alternative Country
After moving to Los Angeles from his native Montana, Wylie Gustafson formed the Wild West Show in 1989. Influenced by his father, a Montana rancher who also played guitar and sang cowboy songs, and an older brother, whom he was once in a band with, Gustafson is an accomplished yodeler, who blends West Coast honky tonk with Western music. Landing in Nashville in 1992, Wylie & the Wild West Show released several videos that received regular airplay on both CMT and TNN; and although the tall, bespectacled redhead failed to break ground on radio, he makes regular appearances at the *Grand Ole Opry*. The high-energy performer and his band also tour extensively, having played throughout the U.S., as well as Australia, Canada, and Europe. In 1996, Wylie & the Wild West Show were signed to Rounder Records; *Total Yodel!* followed two years later, and in early 2000 the group returned with *Ridin' the Hi-Line*. *—Jack Leaver*

● **Wylie & the Wild West Show** / 1992 / Cross Three ♦♦♦♦♦
The jumpin' debut from Wylie & the Wild West Show, the tall bespectacled redhead from Montana and his band. About as good as modern roots rockin' country and Western swing can get, this is wild fun, with Wylie and his band supplying plenty of dance-inspiring tracks. Wylie has an encyclopedic ear for the aforementioned styles and is blessed with a golden voice that falls somewhere between his obvious hero, Marty Robbins, and maybe a young Merle Haggard. Lead guitarist Will Ray's string bending is superb, as well as Marty Rifkin's steel playing. Check out Wylie's masterful yodeling on "The Yodeling Fool" and "All Hat, No Cattle," a humorous indictment of "hat" singers. This is true-to-form stuff, with memorable songs that sound traditional, without coming off as cheap retro knockoffs. And Wylie and company mix up the grooves enough to keep things interesting, as in the swampy "Talkin' About My Baby" and the blues-tinged "Wishful Thinking." *—Jack Leaver*

Get Wild / 1994 / Cross Three ♦♦♦
Evoking the spirit of the singing cowboy and mixing Western swing—Bob Wills-style—with a traditional country and old fashion rock & roll sensibility, Wylie's brand of music is as wide open as the Northern plains of Montana, the state from which he hails. Fans of the late Marty Robbins will delight in the heartfelt homage Wylie pays his musical hero, by including two of Robbins' classics: "Devil Woman" and "I'm Gonna Be a Cowboy." Wylie's original tunes are also shadowed by Robbins' influence. Check out the Spanish-flavored "Hey Maria." A guest spot by Merle Haggard on the humorous ode to rejection "Ugly Girl Blues" is lots of fun and "Too Late," co-written by the Mavericks' Raul Malo is truly great rockabilly. *—Jack Leaver*

Way Out West / 1996 / Rounder ♦♦♦♦
The third album from Wylie & the Wild West Show can do nothing but gain the lanky redhead more of an audience. *Way Out West* contains a little bit of everything that made his first two records so enjoyable—honky tonk shuffles, traditional swing country, great ballads, a yodel tune, and plain ol' rockin' roots country. An album highlight is when Wylie and his band rip through the Del Reeves truckin' classic "Girl on the Billboard." And if there was ever a doubt of his singing talent, Wylie demonstrates his powerful falsetto, reinventing the much-covered pop standard "I Remember You," while also impressively yodeling his way through the Tex-Mex frolic of "Give Me a Pinto Pal." As with his other records, musicianship is superb, making this album a must for old fans as well as anyone who appreciates traditional country styles injected with a youthful verve. *—Jack Leaver*

Total Yodel! / Aug. 18, 1998 / Rounder ♦♦♦♦
Where *Way Out West* impressed the listener with wild rockers and stratospheric yodeling, *Total Yodel!*, ironically, is a fairly low-key affair, heavy with high lonesome ballads and cowboy songs. Indeed, we hear more of Wylie's yodeling skills here, but rather than knocking our socks off, they are a subtle part of the music in the style of Jimmie Rodgers, and a number of covers (including three by Rodgers) confirm that Wylie values tradition over gimmickry. Infectious in its simplicity, *Total Yodel!*'s sincerity and energy set the tone for its masterful follow-up, *Ridin' the Hi-Line*. *—Jim Smith*

Ridin' the Hi-Line / Feb. 8, 2000 / Rounder ♦♦♦♦♦
Wylie hits his stride full-on here, turning in not only his best collection of original songs, but some of the purest, sincerest music to grace the genre in years. If *Way Out West*'s unsaddled energy left a gimmicky (but ecstatic) impression, and *Total Yodel!* was reverent almost to the point of irrelevance, *Ridin' the Hi-Line* takes the best elements of both and transforms them into an album that stands alongside the best country records of all time. It's not just that Wylie's songwriting hits its peak here, but the production is nuanced and enriching in all kinds of ways, from the addition of clarinets and vocal harmonies to the crisp reverb of dancefloor swingers like "Jitterbug Boogie" and "Ol' Coyote." He's also helped immensely by the addition of two new and outstanding guitarists, Ray Doyle and Duane Becker, whose effortless musical rapport fleshes out every detail. Wylie's love for cowboy life really comes into its own here as well, as self-penned songs like the gorgeous "Ridin' the Hi-Line" transcend nostalgia to the point of becoming modern classics. *—Jim Smith*

Paradise / 2001 / Rounder ♦♦♦♦
Paradise doesn't quite match the high-standard set *Ridin' the Hi-Line*, but it's hard to deny that Wylie and company have turned out another excellent album. Gone are the joyous whooping clarinets, and although one misses their energy, there are many fine moments here, especially Wylie's adaptation of an old Badger Clark cowboy poem, which he sets to music for the lovely "To Her." Other highlights include Dylan's "Girl From the North Country," the Latin shuffle of Hank Snow's "The Gal Who Invented Kissin'," and a return to country-rock for "Hooked on Honky Tonk" and "Yodel Boogie." Elsewhere, though, the album is reminiscent of *Total Yodel!* in its simplicity and lulling melodies. There is enough spice and gallop to keep his dancers moving, but the overall impression is a slower, gentler album. *—Jim Smith*

Tammy Wynette

b. May 5, 1942, Itawamba County, MS, **d.** Apr. 6, 1998

Vocals, Guitar / Traditional Country, Country-Pop, Honky Tonk, Nashville Sound/ Countrypolitan
In many ways, Tammy Wynette deserves the title of "the First Lady of Country Music." During the late '60s and early '70s, she dominated the country charts, scoring 17 number-one hits. Along with Loretta Lynn, she defined the role of female country vocalists in the '70s. After her father, who was a musician, died when she was just eight months old, Wynette was raised on her grandparents' home in Mississippi; her mother moved to Birmingham, AL, to do military work. As a child, Wynette taught herself to play a variety of instruments left behind by her father. When she was a teenager, she moved to Birmingham to be with her mother. At 17, she married her first husband, Euple Byrd, and set to work as a hairdresser and beautician. The marriage was short-lived, but it produced three children within three years. By the time her third child was born, the couple were divorced.

Wynette's third child had spinal meningitis, which meant she had several expensive medical bills to pay. In order to gain some extra money, she began performing in clubs at night. In 1965, she landed a regular spot on the television program *the Country Boy Eddie Show*, which led to appearances on Porter Wagoner's syndicated show. The following year, she moved to Nashville, where she auditioned for several labels before producer Billy Sherrill signed her to Epic Records. "Apartment #9," Wynette's first single, was released late in 1966 and almost broke the country Top 40 early in 1967. It was followed by "Your Good Girl's Gonna Go Bad," which became a big hit, peaking at number three. The song launched a string of Top Ten hits that ran until the end of the '70s, interrupted by three singles that didn't crack the Top Ten. After "Your Good Girl's Gonna Go Bad" was a success, "My Elusive Dreams" became her first number one in the summer of 1967, followed by "I Don't Wanna Play House" later that year.

During 1968 and 1969, Wynette had five number-one hits—"Take Me to Your World," "D-I-V-O-R-C-E," "Stand By Your Man" (all 1968), "Singing My Song," and "The Ways to Love a Man" (both 1969). In 1968, she started a relationship with George Jones, which would prove to be extremely stormy. Beginning in 1971, Wynette and Jones recorded a series of duets—the first was the Top Ten "Take Me"—which were as popular as their solo hits. However, the marriage was difficult and the couple divorced in 1975; they continued to record sporadically over the next two decades. Throughout the '70s, Tammy Wynette racked up number one hits. In the early '80s, her career began to slow down. Although she still had hit singles, she didn't reach the Top Ten as easily as she did in the previous decade. That trend continued throughout the rest of the decade and into the '90s. Even though she didn't have as many hits as she had in the past, Wynette remained a respected star and a popular concert attraction. In the '80s, Wynette began suffering a variety of health problems, including inflammations of her bile duct. She was hospitalized several times during the mid-'90s before her death on April 6, 1998. *—Stephen Thomas Erlewine*

☆ **Your Good Girl's Gonna Go Bad** / Apr. 1967 / Epic/Legacy ♦♦♦♦♦
Wynette's 1967 debut album is still one of her best. Having secured the services of countrypolitan producer Billy Sherrill and an Epic contract in 1966, she cut her first single, "Apartment #9," and first big hit, "Your Good Girl's Gonna Go Bad," both of which are included here. And while some of the other material here doesn't quite match the quality of those gems, the album still contains enough solid sides, like "Walk Through This World With Me" and "Send Me No Roses," to ensure its essential status. Add to that stellar covers of the David Houston hit "Almost Persuaded" and Loretta Lynn's "Don't Come Home a Drinking (With Loving on Your Mind)," and you have one of the classic debuts in country music. *—Stephen Cook*

D-I-V-O-R-C-E / Dec. 1967 / Koch ♦♦♦♦♦
Tammy Wynette's third album, *D-I-V-O-R-C-E* features the number one C&W hit by the same name in addition to a bevy of album tracks, including covers of "Gentle on My Mind," "The Legend of Bonnie and Clyde," and the Beatles' "Yesterday." Amazingly, Wynette's version of "Yesterday" actually succeeds, and it's far less cloying than might be expected. Other tracks include "Kiss Away," co-written by producer Billy Sherrill, and "Honey (I Miss You)," an answer to Bobby Goldsboro's "Honey." The vocal performances are excellent even on the more disposable material, and although nothing here approaches the level of the title track, the album is ultimately rewarding for those whose interest in Tammy Wynette extends beyond her greatest hits. *—Greg Adams*

☆ **Stand By Your Man** / 1968 / Epic/Legacy ♦♦♦♦♦
"Stand By Your Man" became a number one C&W hit as well as Tammy Wynette's signature song, and the album that shares its name topped the C&W album chart and crossed over to the pop chart, achieving platinum sales status along the way. Others in the music industry must have been paying attention, considering that two album tracks, "I Stayed Long Enough" (written by Wynette) and "Forever Yours," soon became hits for Billie Jo Spears and Dottie West respectively. Unlike Wynette's previous album, *D-I-V-O-R-C-E, Stand by Your Man* does not rely heavily on material associated with other artists, the most notable exception being a recording of Webb Pierce's 1957 hit "It's My Way." Although the result is a consistent album by '60s standards, the commercial importance of *Stand By Your Man* is more significantly tied to the strength of the title track than to its overall quality. [Two years after Koch's CD-release of *Stand By Your Man*, Sony Legacy reissued it with bonus tracks.] *—Greg Adams*

Take Me to Your World/I Don't Wanna Play House / Jan. 5, 1968 / Koch ♦♦♦♦
Built around the two big hits comprising the title, this was a strong outing from Wynette, sensitively and sparely produced by Billy Sherrill (who co-wrote those two hits and one of the other better tracks, "Good"). Wynette is in good plaintive voice throughout the record, showing her interpretive skills to good effect on her version of Johnny Ray's "Cry," although the reading of "Ode to Billie Joe" is too jaunty (especially when compared with Bobbie Gentry's magnificent original). "It's My Way," with its sad melody, multi-tracked vocals, and spare steel guitar, is a standout. [The CD reissue on Koch adds historical liner notes.] *—Richie Unterberger*

Inspiration / 1969 / Epic ♦♦♦
At the turn of the 1960s, when everything felt like it was coming apart at the seams in the U.S., it seemed like a natural thing for the reigning queen of country music to record an album that brought everything back to its basics—at least in her perception. And it sounds like it was the right thing to do as well. *Inspiration* is an album of spirituals and gospel tunes from the age-old canon of Protestant Christianity and one or two that could be. There are 11 tracks on an album that begins with "You'll Never Walk Alone." Hearing it once is enough to make you take the record off just to be able to absorb its power. It transcends the element of a hymn and becomes a killer country song that transcends country music and becomes a universal anthem. But it gets better. While Tammy Wynette's versions of "Just a Closer Walk With Thee," "I Believe," and "He's Got the Whole World in His Hands" are fine and stirring, they pale in comparison to the opener. However, "Battle Hymn of the Republic" and "How Great Thou Art" are awe-inspiring as well—enough (almost) to make a Buddhist reconsider. Most of these songs are not done straight. They are contemporized (courtesy of the great Billy Sherrill in the producer's chair) for a modern pop-country audience with plenty of pedal steels, fiddles, and honky tonk upright pianos, but they are no less reverent for their rearrangements. Quite the contrary; they are in fact more relevant to the day, perhaps in the same way—during that same year—that Jimi Hendrix's playing of the "Star Spangled Banner" at *Woodstock* re-interpreted the old anthem for an entirely new generation who was ready to forsake it. This album may not appeal to everyone, but for those willing to consider it on its own terms, it's a gem. *—Thom Jurek*

The Ways to Love a Man / 1969 / Epic ♦♦♦♦

☆ **Tammy's Greatest Hits** / 1969 / Epic ♦♦♦♦♦
This follows Wynette's trail of tears right out of the chutes on classics like "Stand By Your Man" and "D-I-V-O-R-C-E." Producer Billy Sherrill's less-than-light touch never found a better instrument to work with than her voice. *—Dan Cooper*

Tammy's Touch / 1970 / Epic ♦♦♦

The World of Tammy Wynette / 1970 / Epic ♦♦♦

The First Lady / 1970 / Epic ♦♦♦
The country music on this record moves along with the elegance of a deer cautiously approaching a riverbank. The songstress seems at the height of her powers, able to orchestrate each phrase and establishing a near alter ego relationship with the pedal steel guitar. What might keep listeners from returning over and over to this particular bottle of country wine would be the repetitious nature of the songs. This album gives the impression that producer Billy Sherrill decided to somehow follow or even top "Stand By Your Man" in terms of having a female singer either cooing in submissiveness or pleading to be let back into the arms of a particular man. It proves too daunting a task for the producer in his second role as author or co-author of a good chunk of these songs. Nothing has the rip-roaring thematic grandeur of "Stand By Your Man," and boredom sets in. The second side provides a too-brief glimpse of the glory that could have been with "Sally Trash," a wonderful song that easily ranks among Wynette's best recordings. *—Eugene Chadbourne*

Christmas with Tammy Wynette / 1970 / Epic ♦♦♦
Tammy Wynette was at her commercial peak in 1970 when she released her Christmas disc. A typical Nashville album of the time (containing only ten tracks and running a mere 26 minutes), it featured country treatments of the usual sacred seasonal favorites—"O Little Town of Bethlehem," "Away in a Manger"—and secular evergreens like "Blue Christmas" and "White Christmas." "Merry Christmas (We Must Be Having One)" and "One Happy Christmas" were new songs in Wynette's standard country style. Wynette and producer Billy Sherrill were playing it safe, which is not a bad thing in a Christmas album, but that meant that the album's appeal would be to fans who just wanted to hear Wynette sing these familiar songs. [As an LP, the album went out of print in the 1980s; it was reissued on CD in 1998 shortly after Wynette's death.] *—William Ruhlmann*

We Sure Can Love Each Other / 1971 / Epic ♦♦♦

Tammy's Greatest Hits, Vol. 2 / 1971 / Epic ♦♦♦♦♦

Bedtime Story / 1972 / Epic ♦♦♦
Tammy Wynette possessed one of the most distinct and powerful voices in country music. On several albums cut during her late-'60s and early-'70s peak, she seamlessly combined the raw twang of vintage honky tonk with the vocal suppleness that the pop-friendly and slick-sounding countrypolitan style demanded. As was the case with many of her prime releases, Billy Sherrill produced 1973's *Bedtime Story*, deftly showing his widescreen touch with a fetching blend of strings, vocal harmonies, and a variety of crisp instrumental textures. Wynette is in fine form as well, delivering heartbreak and determination in equal measure. Besides the hit title track (later found on her divorce concept album, *Kids Say the Darndest Things*), there are several top-notch tracks like "I'm Gonna Keep on Loving Him" and "Tonight My Baby's Coming Home." Along with such other fine original albums as *Stand By Your Man* and *D-I-V-O-R-C-E, Bedtime Story* is a sure bet for fans seeking something beyond the slew of Wynette retrospectives. *—Stephen Cook*

My Man / 1972 / Epic ♦♦

Kids Say the Darndest Things / 1973 / Epic ♦♦♦
Wynette and Sherrill join forces for a concept album, including "Listen, Spot," "My Daddy Doll," "Buy Me a Daddy," and "Too Many Daddies." Sound funny? It is. Except "Too Many Daddies" will still rip your heart out. *—Dan Cooper*

The First Songs of the First Lady / 1973 / Epic ♦♦♦♦♦

Another Lonely Song / 1974 / Epic ♦♦♦

Woman to Woman / 1974 / Epic ♦♦♦

I Still Believe in Fairy Tales / 1975 / Epic ♦♦
The sound of this Billy Sherrill production conjures up images: a screened in porch on a summer night, and music designed to be played at any volume without disturbing the neighbors. A country session band strained through a filter until all the bottom disappears. And then there's country queen Wynette, known for her wailing, but here sounding downright submissive. In fact, this is country music that might have been written as the background for the signing of a surrender treaty. "I'll Take What You Can Give Me (When You Can)" is the opening track on side two, but might have been a memo from Wynette to Sherrill concerning the songs selected for this album. The two created many, many recordings together and so it isn't such a shock that they might rest on their laurels now and then. The idea of a striking, energetic arrangement that jumps out of the speakers is the fairy tale here, even though Wynette and Sherrill have surely created just that at other times, at other studio sessions. Wynette comes out of the kitchen with the dish everyone has been waiting for right near the end, in the form of several of her original songs, which try a little harder and even have some pedal steel that hasn't been mixed out of the picture. *—Eugene Chadbourne*

Greatest Hits, Vol. 3 / 1975 / Epic ♦♦♦
The best reason to include this package is to simply say that one greatest-hits album from Wynette just isn't enough. The lyrical and musical themes here are much the same as in the first package, but the quiet determination of "'Til I Get It Right" and the pure celebration of "My Man (Understands)" help broaden the picture of Wynette just a little. *—Tom Roland*

'Til I Can Make It On My Own / 1976 / Epic ♦♦♦♦

You and Me / 1976 / Epic ♦♦♦

One of a Kind / 1977 / Epic ♦♦♦♦♦
The team of Tammy Wynette and Billy Sherrill was incomparable. In 1977 at the dawn of the urban drugstore cowboy phenomenon, Wynette was still making classic countrypolitan records with Sherrill and would continue to until they parted company and she began working with future husband-producer George Richey. *One of a Kind* is of those classy classic records they made together. Wynette was, at that point, a true diva and country music's reigning queen—and for good reason. With her inspired performances on songs of virtually every stripe, from the simple acoustic-flavored rags to the wished-for love story of "That's the Way It Could Have Been," to the soaring, regal citified country of "Love Survived" with its cascading strings, transcendent chorus, and shattering crescendos, to the wondrous honky tonk innuendo of "Heaven Is Just a Sin Away," and the brazen and beautiful "I'll Be Your Bridge (Just Lay Me Down)," the performances are just awe inspiring. After these two tracks the album closes with a typical Sherrill cipher: the slightly corny "Dear Daughters," which features mom having a spoken heart-to-heart with four girls whose lives she's either missed or is missing because of being on the road. There is no apology, but it's implied and it's a completely owning of the life Wynette had chosen. There's real regret here no matter how couched in lush strings and the Nashville Edition's sweet, wordless backing vocals, and that somehow makes the entire album make a different kind of sense, one that recognizes that even though there are dire consequences made for some decisions they often need to be made anyway. 1977 was the year the Sex Pistols screamed onto the scene with a whole, bleak new way of looking at the world; it was also the year Wynette released one of her finest albums and kept the spirit of the old one firmly in mind. *—Thom Jurek*

Let's Get Together / 1977 / Epic ✦✦✦

Womanhood / 1978 / Epic ✦✦✦

Just Tammy / 1979 / Epic ✦✦✦

Only Lonely Sometimes / 1980 / Epic ✦✦✦

You Brought Me Back / 1981 / Epic ✦✦

Soft Touch / 1982 / Epic ✦✦✦

Good Love & Heartbreak / 1983 / Epic ✦✦

Even the Strong Get Lonely / 1983 / Epic ✦✦✦

Biggest Hits / 1983 / Epic ✦✦

Biggest Hits is a good budget-priced collection that contains several of Tammy Wynette's biggest hits, including "I Don't Wanna Play House" and "Stand By Your Man." There are better Wynette collections available, ones that offer more songs for only a little more money, but this isn't bad, considering that it is a budget-line collection. —*Stephen Thomas Erlewine*

★ **Anniversary: 20 Years of Hits** / 1987 / Epic ✦✦✦✦✦

"Stand by Your Man" and "D-I-V-O-R-C-E" speak for themselves. But not to be overlooked are the less honored likes of "Apartment #9," her debut hit, written by Johnny Paycheck; and "Your Good Girl's Gonna Go Bad," in which her freedom (instead of little J-O-E's tears) are at stake. Also included are three duets with George Jones. —*Dan Cooper*

Tears of Fire: The 25th Anniversary Collection / Nov. 3, 1992 / Epic ✦✦✦✦✦

Tears of Fire: 25th Anniversary, a three-disc box set covering Wynette's entire career, contains most of her hits as well as rarities and oddities like her lead vocal on KLF's "Justified and Ancient." It's hard to fault a collection that includes such classics as "Stand By Your Man" and "D-I-V-O-R-C-E," but casual fans might want to stick with the single-disc *Anniversary—20 Years of Hits* collection. —*Thom Owens*

Super Hits / Mar. 19, 1996 / Epic ✦✦✦✦✦

A no-frills, ten-song disc running under 29 minutes, *Super Hits* should be purchased only at a discount price by a newcomer to Tammy Wynette who wants to get an idea of her music. That said, the set contains her three biggest hits, "I Don't Wanna Play House," "D-I-V-O-R-C-E," and "Stand By Your Man," five other number-one hits, and two more that made the Country Top Ten between 1967 and 1976. Strictly speaking, these are not Wynette's ten biggest hits, but they constitute a good sampling of her most popular work. —*William Ruhlmann*

Super Hits, Vol. 2 / Oct. 13, 1998 / Sony ✦✦✦

Tammy Wynette's best-known songs, "Stand By Your Man" and "D-I-V-O-R-C-E," were included on her first *Super Hits* collection in 1996, but since she scored 20 number-one country hits and the *Super Hits* albums only have ten tracks, there were obviously many more selections for *Vol. 2*. In fact, eight of the songs here topped the country charts, the most successful of them being "He Loves Me All The Way." The two non-chart-toppers are "Apartment #9," Wynette's first record, and "Your Good Girl's Gonna Go Bad," her first Top Ten hit. —*William Ruhlmann*

Collector's Edition / Oct. 13, 1998 / Sony ✦✦

The gimmick on this ten-song compilation is that each of these familiar recordings has been re-mixed and remastered from the original session tapes and features a few seconds of studio chatter at the start. So, we get to hear laughter, count-offs, and false starts. Producer Billy Sherrill says things like, "Okay, take two." None of this tells us anything new about the recordings, and it's hard to think of this as anything but Epic's exploitation of tracks that have already been reissued many times before. "I'm gettin' tired of this song," Wynette comments before the start of "You Can Be Replaced." We couldn't agree more. —*William Ruhlmann*

16 Biggest Hits / Feb. 2, 1999 / Epic/Legacy ✦✦✦✦✦

Unlike "greatest" hits or "best-of" compilations, whose titles imply a qualitative element, *16 Biggest Hits* is measurable solely by commercial success. And by that measure, *Tammy Wynette's 16 Biggest Hits* is exactly what it says it is, presenting the singer's 16 number-one country hits from 1967 to 1976 in chronological order, from "I Don't Wanna Play House" to "You and Me," with standards like "D-I-V-O-R-C-E," "Stand By Your Man," and "'Til I Can Make It on My Own" in between. (Her chart-topping duets with David Houston and George Jones are not included.) Wynette was the queen of the plaintive heartbreak ballad on many of these tracks (five of which she co-wrote), though there were occasional expressions of domestic contentment such as "He Loves Me All The Way" and "My Man (Understands)," and more pieces of womanly advice in the tradition of "Stand By Your

Man," such as "Run, Woman, Run" and the cautionary "Good Lovin' (Makes It Right)." Released only a couple of months before her death, *16 Greatest Hits* was a fitting tribute to Tammy Wynette. —*William Ruhlmann*

Love Songs / Jan. 14, 2003 / Epic/Legacy ✦✦✦

Though it probably would've been easier to compile a collection of Tammy Wynette breakup songs, *Love Songs* does a good job of gathering some of the lighter and more optimistic songs from the '60s and '70s. The compilation's mood ranges from lovelorn but hopeful on songs like "Help Me Make It Through the Night" and the classics "Take Me to Your World" and "'Til I Get It Right"; deeply romantic on "No One Else in the World"; and devoted on "If You Think I Love You Now," "Walk Through This World With Me," and of course, "Stand By Your Man." Indeed, songs such as "Loving You Could Never Be Better" and "Right Here in Your Arms" are a welcome reminder that not all of her songs were about unhappy endings and surviving them. Granted, most of her definitive songs were about those topics, and as such, *Love Songs* doesn't feature as many of her absolutely essential moments as a more straightforward greatest-hits collection might, but even relatively lightweight tracks such as "The Twelfth of Never" and "The Hawaiian Wedding Song" reaffirm just how consistently well-crafted all the work she did in the '60s and '70s was. Including some of Wynette's duets with George Jones would've taken the collection's swoon factor to another level, but as it stands *Love Songs* is a refreshing and romantic collection of her work. —*Heather Phares*

Holly Wynnette

b. Columbia, SC

Vocals / Country-Pop, Contemporary Country

When country fans hear the name Holly Wynnette, they might wonder if she is related to Tammy Wynette, the late country-pop superstar who gave us major hits like "Stand By Your Man," "D-I-V-O-R-C-E," "I Don't Wanna Play House," and "The Ways to Love a Man." But, in fact, they are unrelated; and Holly Wynnette, unlike Tammy Wynette, spells her last name with two n's instead of only one. Favoring a waifish, sweetly girlish style of singing, Holly Wynnette is a country-pop/adult contemporary vocalist from South Carolina. She is far from a country purist; much of her material is country mixed with rock and pop, and her adult contemporary offerings are more pop than anything. Wynnette was born and raised in Columbia, SC, where she started singing at the age of five, in addition to studying piano, ballet, and tap dancing. Growing up, she entered various state beauty pageants and was crowned Little Miss South Carolina in 1989 and Teen Miss South Carolina in 1994. Wynnette also won various local talent contests, and she traveled to Nashville and Los Angeles in the hope of making connections in the music business.

In the early 2000s, Wynnette came to the attention of Ray Ruff, a veteran producer, arranger, and promoter who, over the years, had worked with everyone from Hank Williams Jr. to Pat Boone. Ruff was starting a new Los Angeles-based label called HitPros, and Wynnette became his first signing. In 2001, Ruff co-produced Wynnette's debut album, *My Future Ex-Boyfriend*. HitPros released the title song as a single in early January 2002, and the album itself came out the following month. —*Alex Henderson*

My Future Ex-Boyfriend / Feb. 5, 2002 / Hitpros ✦✦✦

No one will accuse Holly Wynnette of being a big-voiced belter. The country-pop/adult contemporary singer has a small, thin voice, and she brings a waifish approach to her debut album, *My Future Ex-Boyfriend* (which was co-produced by music industry veteran Ray Ruff). Nonetheless, she usually gets her points across, and when Wynnette has the right material to work with, her sweetly charming vulnerability serves her well. At times, Wynnette is saddled with inappropriate material. "Come Lay It on Me" and "You Can't Do That" are spunky country/rock/pop numbers that call for someone who has a bigger voice and a gutsier, more aggressive delivery—perhaps Patty Loveless, perhaps Shania Twain, perhaps Tanya Tucker, perhaps Trisha Yearwood—and Wynnette is simply too waifish to be convincing on this type of song. But elsewhere, her waifishness proves to be an advantage. "Spotlight" and "Love Where You Are" are the sort of sentimental ballads that allow Wynnette to fully embrace her sweet, girlish vulnerability; consequently, they work well for her. That isn't to say that she is only successful on ballads; one of the CD's best tracks is the catchy, uptempo title song. But whether she is singing at a slow, medium, or fast tempo, Wynnette is at her best when she has vulnerable lyrics to go with her waif-like voice. The singer fares well on a cover of Leiber & Stoller's "I (Who Have Nothing)" and would probably fare equally well if she covered Wanda Jackson's "Right or Wrong," but she would not be convincing on something as spunky as Twain's "Man! I Feel Like a Woman!" Although uneven, *My Future Ex-Boyfriend* has more ups than downs—and its best tracks make the listener want to keep an eye on Wynnette and see how she develops. —*Alex Henderson*

Trisha Yearwood

b. Sep. 19, 1964, Monticello, GA

Vocals / Country-Pop, Contemporary Country

One of the most popular female country singers of the '90s, Trisha Yearwood initially rose to fame as a protégée of Garth Brooks but quickly staked out her own identity as an assertive yet vulnerable modern woman. Yearwood was born in the small town of Monticello, GA, in 1964 and grew up on a farm owned by her father, who also worked as a prominent local banker. She loved Elvis Presley as a child and sang in musicals, choral groups, and talent shows while in school. She enrolled at the University of Georgia, but in 1985 she transferred to the music business program at Belmont College in Nashville. Yearwood served an internship with MTM Records and soon moved on to become an in-demand demo singer, which resulted in an up-and-coming Brooks hiring her as a backup vocalist. Yearwood appeared on Brooks' 1989 debut and its blockbuster follow-up, *No Fences*, and with the help of producer Garth Fundis, she staged a showcase performance in 1990 that landed her a record deal with MCA.

Yearwood's self-titled debut album was released in 1991, and the lead single, "She's in Love With the Boy," rocketed to the top of the country charts, making her an instant star. Three more singles from the record—"Like We Never Had a Broken Heart" (co-written by Brooks), "That's What I Like About You," and "The Woman Before Me"—all went Top Ten, and Yearwood toured as Brooks' opening act, gaining immense exposure. As a result, she became the first female country singer ever to sell a million copies of her debut album—and, a little bit later on, two million. Her follow-up was the acclaimed *Hearts in Armor*, which appeared in 1992 during the aftermath of a divorce. Two of its singles, "Wrong Side of Memphis" and the Don Henley duet "Walkaway Joe," reached the Top Five, and the record as a whole established Yearwood as an artist of creative ambition; like its predecessor, it also went platinum. The title track of 1993's *The Song Remembers When* went to number two, and she followed it with a Christmas album, *The Sweetest Gift*, in 1994; that year, she also married Mavericks bassist Robert Reynolds.

In 1995, Yearwood released her fourth proper album, *Thinkin' About You*, another hugely popular collection that featured her second and third number-one hits in "XXX's and OOO's (An American Girl)" and the title track, plus another Top Ten in "I Wanna Go Too Far." The record found her music hinting more at adult contemporary-style country-pop, a trend that continued on 1996's *Everybody Knows*. "Believe Me Baby (I Lied)" was another chart-topping smash, and the title track also made the Top Five. In 1997, Yearwood issued her first compilation, *Songbook: A Collection of Hits*, which became her first album to top the country charts and which also reached the pop Top Five. She also recorded the Diane Warren-penned ballad "How Do I Live" for the soundtrack of the movie *Con Air*, and it was nominated for a Best Song Oscar; it also reached number two on the country charts and nearly made the pop Top 20 as well (though this performance was hurt by a competing version from LeAnn Rimes). Two new singles from *Songbook* were also hugely successful: "In Another's Eyes," a long-awaited duet with Brooks, hit number two, and "Perfect Love" went all the way to the top.

Yearwood won Female Vocalist of the Year awards from the CMA and ACM in 1997 and 1998, respectively, and she also picked up her first solo Grammy for "How Do I Live," giving her a sort of country equivalent of the Triple Crown. Now settled into her role as a big-voiced, crossover-friendly diva, Yearwood released her next all-new album, *Where Your Road Leads*, in 1998, with Tony Brown producing in place of Fundis. "There Goes My Baby," "Powerful Thing," and "I'll Still Love You More" all went Top Ten, and another duet with Brooks on the title cut made the Top 20. Also in 1998, Yearwood made her first real foray into acting, taking a recurring role on the CBS military drama *JAG* that would last for the next few seasons. Unfortunately, her marriage to Reynolds broke up, and 2000's *Real Live Woman*—recorded with Fundis—was a more personal outing that reflected some of her heartbreak and turmoil. Perhaps as a result, it sold fairly well in spite of not producing any major hit singles. With new producer Mark Wright behind the boards, Yearwood returned in 2001 with *Inside Out*, which topped the country charts and produced the Top Five smash "I Would've Loved You Anyway." —*Steve Huey*

Trisha Yearwood / 1991 / MCA ✦✦✦✦

Hindsight being 20/20, when Trisha Yearwood's eponymous debut was issued in 1991, it was obvious a star had been born. From the choice of players, to Garth Fundis' snappy crisp production, to the songs written by the cream of the crop of Nashville's new generation—including a pair by Garth Brooks, Pat McLaughlin, Carl Jackson, and one by Kostas and Hal Ketchum. What set Yearwood apart is her enormous voice; coming from Georgia, there is no lilt in it—she can go from a whisper to a full-throated wail in a second, and her pitch is spot on every time. Fundis and MCA chose the kinds of songs Yearwood sings better than almost any of her peers—working-class love songs, from the opener, the simple midtempo rocker "She's in Love With the Boy," to the ballads such as "Like We Had a Broken Heart," written by Brooks with Pat Alger. Brooks sings backup here, and the pace of the song is slow. Its poetry is in the emotion her voice conveys rather than the lyrics, which aren't bad; they just aren't special. But it's "Fools Like Me" (by

Kostas and Ketchum), where Yearwood lets every bit of what's inside of her out. A slow rocker with a Hammond B-3 swirling gently in the background played by Al Kooper, this is the broken love song at its best. When Yearwood sings, "You go your way baby, and I'll go mine/I'll go crazy like the wind," the entire track just comes apart before she reaches the end of the verse. The vision of a goodbye said in some motel parking lot or suburban driveway is almost unbearable. Yearwood was the first female country singer of her generation that didn't try to be a sex symbol, and she didn't try to project anything other than the fact that she was a good singer. And she was and is a fine singer, and this is a very classy debut that stands the test of time. —*Thom Jurek*

● **Hearts in Armor** / Sep. 1, 1992 / MCA ✦✦✦✦✦

The leap Trisha Yearwood made as an artist between her debut in 1991 and *Hearts in Armor* in 1993 is remarkable. It remains one of her highest achievements. In addition, this one was wrought from conflict; it was released just after divorce and the record feels like an exorcism. As with her debut, producer Garth Fundis and Yearwood selected songs from the cream of Nashville's hit producers; "Wrong Side of Memphis," a tough, near spitting rocker tempered by honky tonk fiddles was written by Matraca Berg and Gary Harrison, opened the disc and may have thrown fans of her ballad style. But fears would have been unfounded as "Harrison's Nearest Distant Shore" was all ballad and then some. There's the R&B-flavored "You Say You Will," by Beth Neilsen Chapman, that's sassy and tough, full of funky piano and a killer acoustic guitar solo by Billy Walker Jr. and a killer backing vocal by Raul Malo (before anyone knew who the Mavericks were). Chapman also contributes a stunning ballad to this set, "Down on My Knees," that is wrenching in its pure intent. "Walkaway Joe" features a harmony vocal by Don Henley and dobro ace Jerry Douglass. Yearwood's telling the story she tells best, working-class love gone bad. But the finest moment on *Hearts in Armor* is Yearwood's cover of Emmylou Harris' "Woman Walk the Line," with Harris singing backup with Stuart Duncan on fiddle and Sam Bush on mandolin along with Yearwood's band; this is the ultimate testament about being woman cheated on who goes out to have a drink to hear some music and walk the line between marriage and dissolution. It's searing in its heartbreak and full of the tension that comes with the territory of loving someone who needs by his very nature to cheat. It's devastating, helped in part by Harris' unobtrusive but emotionally loaded backing vocal to Yearwood's open-throated wail. Henley also guests on the closer, which is the title track. If there is any speculation about whether Yearwood was airing her dirty laundry on the album, it becomes obvious in this song, that this is about her dealing with her own emotions, her own issues. Blame is useless in this ballad, there's nothing left but heartbreak and emptiness and the challenge of rebuilding a life haunted by the ghosts of another. *Hearts in Armor* is stunning; it's one of the best heartbreak records country music delivered in the '80s and '90s. —*Thom Jurek*

The Song Remembers When / 1993 / MCA ✦✦✦✦

The Song Remembers When is another chapter in the ongoing collaboration between Trisha Yearwood and producer Garth Fundis. Where 1992's *Hearts in Armor* was a cathartic masterpiece that broke Yearwood worldwide, this record is straighter down the contemporary country lane. As usual, the material is top-notch no matter where the pair get it from. Whether the tunes come from stalwarts like Kostas, Rodney Crowell, and Willie Nelson or relative unknowns like the phenomenal Kimmie Rhodes, this ten-song set delivers the same drama and tension with glorious transcendent singing from Yearwood. The title cut opener is a reverie of innocent love gone bad, recalled at a retail store counter while receiving change. Midtempo ballads are a Yearwood strength and she delivers tough and true. Next, "Better Your Heart Than Mine," by almost country chanteuse Lisa Angelle and pop washout Andrew Gold, is a beautiful twining of Bonnie Raitt-styled R&B, roots rock and neo-traditionalist\country with some killer guitar playing by the great Steuart Smith. Rodney Crowell backs Yearwood on his "I Don't Fall Love So Easy"; it's one of those beautiful country songs that almost isn't. Crowell has always been able to walk the pop-country borderline, and in Yearwood's voice he has found the perfect vocalist to execute his vision. She sings the hell out of a slick little down-tempo rocker by making it sound like it's the easiest song in the world to deliver honestly. Nelson not only contributes a tune here, but he guests both in duet and backing vocalist capacities on his own "One in a Row" and Rhodes' "Hard Promises to Keep." His presence adds real depth and dimension here because his thin, reedy voice stands in such sharp contrast to Yearwood's full-throated one. "Here Comes Temptation" by Kostas is one of those groovy little pop numbers that touches on the kind of '60s pop that came from Doc Pomus & Phil Spector crossed through the heart by contemporary Nash Vegas; it's glitzy surface covered by a sheen of sweet soul even if it is accompanied by a pedal steel. The disc closes with Matraca Berg's "Lying to the Moon." Accompanied only by her band, Yearwood takes a pop song and turns it into a country song with the ripped up heart that comes in the grain of her voice. It's poetry, this combination of singer and song. She couldn't sing it any better if she'd written it; the accents create tension and drama and images from every betrayed-lovers movie from the '40s on, washing through the mix. Only a real singer can deliver the image from the heart of the song. Yearwood here is the heart of the song itself. *—Thom Jurek*

Thinkin' About You / 1995 / MCA ✦✦✦

Although there are a couple of high points on *Thinkin' About You*, the record is weighed down with mediocre material and slick, commercially oriented prodcution. Occasionally, Yearwood's vocals save the day, but there are times where she oversings the songs, giving them emotion they don't deserve. In all, it's one of the few Trisha Yearwood albums that can be called a disappointment. *—Thom Owens*

Everybody Knows / Aug. 27, 1996 / MCA ✦✦✦

Trisha Yearwood firmly enters middle-age with *Everybody Knows*, a collection of ballads and country-pop. Even when she kicks the tempo into high-gear, Yearwood and her band lay back, easing the beat along instead of pushing it. Similarly, the country-pop is engaging and relaxed, gently winning you over. But the heart of the album lies in her ballads, which are appropriately theatrical and grandiose—it's big music with big melodies. The quality of the songs are a little uneven, but Yearwood continues to improve as a singer, which means she brings conviction even to the lackluster material on *Everybody Knows*. *—Thom Owens*

Songbook: A Collection of Hits / Aug. 26, 1997 / MCA ✦✦✦✦✦

(Songbook) A Collection of Hits is a terrific overview of Trisha Yearwood's hit singles of the early and mid-'90s, containing such songs as "She's in Love With the Boy," "Like We Never Had a Broken Heart," "The Woman Before Me," "Walkaway Joe," "The Song Remembers When," "XXX's and OOO's (An American Girl)," "Thinkin' About You" and "I Wanna Go Too Far." It's a near-definitive collection that shows why Yearwood was one of the most popular contemporary country vocalists of the '90s. *—Thom Owens*

Where Your Road Leads / Jul. 14, 1998 / MCA ✦✦✦✦

Trisha Yearwood is a pop diva who knows how to play her instrument, her voice. Perhaps one of the most gifted contemporary pop vocalists, Yearwood continues to explore the vast expanses of her talent. Displaying only traces of her early work as a country music artist, she sings with yearning on songs like "Powerful Thing." Buddy Miller's backing vocals on "Bring Me All Your Lovin'" are a highlight of this project. Yearwood's brilliance is adequately displayed on "I Don't Want to Be the One" and "I'll Still Love You More," a Diane Warren composition. She is at her best when she inhabits the world of emotional ballads and snappy, uptempo tunes about the emotional life of modern women. While she is no country singer by any stretch of the imagination, she is still an important element in pop music. *—Jana Pendragon*

Real Live Woman / Mar. 28, 2000 / MCA ✦✦✦

Once an artist like Trisha Yearwood enters her second decade of recording, it's easy to take her for granted. Why? Well, consistency doesn't make for quite as dramatic a story as dramatic swings between brilliance and failure. That may be unfair, but that's the way it is. Yearwood has never swung between such extremes. She has released some exceptional albums, plus a couple of sub-par efforts, but for the most part, she has remained an artist that is reliable—you pay your money, and you know you'll get something satisfactory. *Real Live Woman* is one of those records; it may not rock your world, but it will hardly disappoint. A little more mature and straight-ahead than even her latter-day efforts, *Real Live Woman* is a measured, deliberate record in the best possible sense. The tempo never gets too heated, but the songs never drift into laziness, either. The tunes are always melodic and always well-chosen. They don't just play to Yearwood's strengths, but they're solid songs in their own right, whether it's a new Matraca Berg and Al Anderson song ("I'm Still Alive"), an overlooked Springsteen tune ("Sad Eyes") or a Linda Ronstadt chestnut ("Try Me Again"). Yes, there are a couple of moments where the momentum drags ever so slightly, but as soon as they occur, the album perks back up with the next song. *Real Live Woman* isn't significantly better or worse than the average Trisha Yearwood album, but that's not a bad thing, since few people do this in mainstream country—meaning, by late-'90s/early-'00s standards, country music that still sounds country but is also melodic enough for pop—quite as well as this. *—Stephen Thomas Erlewine*

Inside Out / Jun. 5, 2001 / MCA Nashville ✦✦✦✦

Trisha Yearwood's full of a whole lotta love. Five of the album's 12 tracks have "love" in the title, and the seven others that don't are about love and relationships. But whatever Yearwood's singing about, she still manages to dazzle listeners even ten years and ten albums into her career. She's an artist who blossoms with every album and just keeps getting better. She's even managed to arrange a superior list of musical collaborators, including Don Henley (back for more after "Walkaway Joe") on the rhythmic title track; Roseanne Cash harmonizing on the classic song she originally composed, "Seven Year Ache"; and even Vince Gill lending his vocal talents to the blazing "I Don't Paint Myself Into Corners." With praiseworthy songs too numerous to mention, *Inside Out* is bound to inspire fans and fellow artists alike. Simply put, Trisha Yearwood is timeless. *—Maria Konicki Dinoia*

Dwight Yoakam

b. Oct. 23, 1956, Pikeville, KY

Guitar, Vocals / Bakersfield Sound, New Traditionalist, Alternative Country, Country-Rock, Country-Pop, Neo-Traditionalist Country

With his stripped-down approach to traditional honky tonk and Bakersfield country, Dwight Yoakam helped return country music to its roots in the late '80s. Like his idols Buck Owens, Merle Haggard, and Hank Williams, Yoakam never played by Nashville's roots; consequently, he never dominated the charts like his contemporary Randy Travis. Then again, Travis never played around with the sound and style of country music like Yoakam. On each of his records, he twists around the form enough to make it seem like he doesn't respect all of country's traditions. Appropriately, his core audience was composed mainly of roots rock and rock & roll fans, not the mainstream country audience. Nevertheless, he was frequently able to chart in the country Top Ten, and he remained one of the most respected and adventurous recording country artists well into the '90s.

Born in Kentucky but raised in Ohio, Yoakam learned how to play guitar at the age of six. As a child, he listened to his mother's record collection, honing in on the traditional country of Hank Williams and Johnny Cash, as well as the Bakersfield honky tonk of Buck Owens. When he was in high-school, Yoakam played with a variety of bands, playing everything from country to rock & roll. After completing high-school, Yoakam briefly attended Ohio State University, but he dropped out and moved to Nashville in the late '70s with the intent of becoming a recording artist. At the time he moved to Nashville, the town was in the throes of the pop-oriented urban cowboy movement and had no interested in his updated honky tonk. While in Nashville, he met guitarist Pete Anderson, who shared a similar taste in music. The pair moved out to Los Angeles, where they found a more appreciative audience than they did in Nashville. In L.A., Yoakam and Anderson didn't just play country clubs, they played the same nightclubs that punk and post-punk rock bands like X, the Dead Kennedys, Los Lobos, the Blasters, and the Butthole Surfers did. What Yoakam had in common with rock bands like X, the Blasters, and Los Angeles was similar musical influences; they all drew from '50s rock & roll and country. In comparison to the polished music coming out of Nashville, Yoakam's stripped-down, direct revivalism seemed radical. The cowpunks, as they were called, that attended Yoakam's shows provided an invaluable support for his fledgling career.

Yoakam released an independent EP, *A Town South of Bakersfield*, in 1984, which received substantial airplay on Los Angeles college and alternative radio stations. The EP also helped him land a record contract with Reprise Records. Dwight's full-length debut album, *Guitars, Cadillacs, Etc., Etc.*, was released in 1986 and was an instant sensation. Rock and country critics praised it and it earned airplay on college stations across America. More importantly, it was a hit on the country charts, as its first single, a cover of Johnny Horton's "Honky Tonk Man," climbed to number three in the spring, followed by the number four "Guitars, Cadillacs" in the summer. The album would eventually go platinum. *Hillbilly Deluxe*, Dwight's 1987 follow-up, was equally successful, spawning four Top Ten hits: "Little Sister," "Little Ways," "Please, Please Baby," and "Always Late with Your Kisses." In 1988, Yoakam had his first number-one hit with "Streets of Bakersfield," a cover of a Buck Owens song recorded with Owens himself. It was the first single off his third album, *Buenos Noches From a Lonely Room*, which continued his streak of Top Ten hits. "I Sang Dixie," the album's second single, went to number one, and "I Got You" reached number five. In 1989, Yoakam released a compilation album, *Just Lookin' for a Hit*, which went gold. "Long White Cadillac," taken from the collection, stalled at number 35 in the fall of 1989.

Although his 1990 album *If There Was a Way* didn't have as many Top Ten hits, it was a major success; it was his first album since his debut to go platinum. *This Time*, released in the spring of 1993, was an even bigger hit, spawning three number two singles—"Ain't That Lonely Yet," "A Thousand Miles From Nowhere," and "Fast as You"—and going platinum. After its release, Yoakam was silent for two years, returning in the summer of 1995 with *Dwight Live*, which didn't set the charts on fire. In the fall of that year, he released his sixth album, *Gone*, which went gold by the spring of 1996, although it didn't produce any major country hits. After 1997's *Under the Covers*, a collection of cover songs, Yoakam returned with the all-new *A Long Way Home* in 1998. Another compilation, *Last Chance for a Thousand Years: Greatest Hits From the '90s*, was released in 1999; its newly recorded version of Queen's "Crazy Little Thing Called Love" became Yoakam's biggest hit in six years, even hitting the lower reaches of the pop charts thanks to its exposure in a khakis commercial. Two albums followed in 2000: *dwightyoakamacoustic.net*, a bare-bones, all-acoustic revisitation of Yoakam's back catalog; and the more standard studio project *Tomorrow's Sounds Today*, which featured further collaborations with Buck Owens and a cover of Cheap Trick's "I Want You to Want Me." *—Stephen Thomas Erlewine*

Guitars, Cadillacs, Etc., Etc. / 1986 / Reprise ✦✦✦✦

Dwight Yoakam's *Guitars, Cadillacs, Etc., Etc.* began as an EP issued on the California Oak label. When Reprise signed him, they added four more tracks to the mix to round it out as an album. Yoakam, a Kentuckian, brought country music back into its own medium by reviving the classic Bakersfield sound with the help of his producer and lead guitarist, former Detroiter Pete Anderson. As a result, the "new traditionalist" movement was born, but Yoakam was always a cut or three above the rest, as this album displays in spades. *Guitars, Cadillacs, Etc., Etc.* kicks off with a smoking cover of Johnny Horton's "Honky Tonk Man," a song now so closely associated with Yoakam the original has all but been forgotten. But this is only the beginning. Yoakam's own songs such as "Bury Me," a duet with Maria McKee, and "South of Cincinnati" reference both the pastoral and dark sides of his native state. "South of Cincinnati" is a paean to those who left Kentucky for Ohio in search of jobs, and "Bury Me" celebrates the land itself. In addition, the title track, with Anderson's Don Rich-influenced guitar style, walks the Buck Owens line until the line extends to Yoakam. With fiddles and backing vocals, Yoakam's street poetry is both poignant and profound, built into a barroom anthem. In addition to this there is the gorgeous "Miner's Prayer," an acoustic number powered by dobro (courtesy of David Mansfield), flat-picked guitar, and Yoakam's singing of his grandfather and generations like him who lived and died in the mines of Kentucky. Here Bill Monroe meets Ralph Stanley meets Bob Dylan. In the grain of Yoakam's voice there isn't one hint of irony, only empathy and raw emotion. Yoakam also does a more than acceptable version of June Carter's "Ring of Fire," the "Cherokee" of country music—meaning that if you can play it and pull it off you're taken seriously by the veterans. The album closes with the Harlan Howard classic "Heartaches By the Number." Because of Ed Black's steel playing, Brantley Kearns' fiddle, and Anderson's guitar, the accompaniment is stronger and far edgier than the Ray Price version, but from Yoakam's throat comes an entirely different story than Price's. In Price's case the song was a plea, in Yoakam's it's a statement of fact. An astonishing debut, *Guitars, Cadillacs, Etc., Etc.* changed the face of country music single-handedly and remains one hell of a party record. —*Thom Jurek*

Hillbilly Deluxe / 1987 / Reprise ✦✦✦✦

Hillbilly Deluxe proves beyond the shadow of a doubt that Dwight Yoakam's *Guitars, Cadillacs, Etc., Etc.* was no fluke. There's no sophomore slump here, and while *Hillbilly Deluxe* may be seen as an extension of his debut, repetition 'taint necessarily a bad thing. In fact, it can be heard and viewed as Yokam and producer/guitarist Pete Anderson cementing the commitment to Bakersfield-styled honky tonk music. Yoakam's voice is a dead cross of Merle Haggard's early voice and Lefty Frizzell's—a fine cover of the latter's "Always Late (With Your Kisses)" is included here—and as such, it is one of the purest, most soulful voices in the music of this era. But as displayed on his debut, Yoakam is one hell of a songwriter as well. Cuts like "Little Ways," the album's first single, "Readin' Writin," "Rt. 23," and the amazing "Throughout All Time," with its dancing fiddles and lap steel guitars entwined with Anderson's lead, are worthy of serious consideration as among the finest country songs written in the preceding five years. An added bonus is a killer version of Doc Pomus' classic "Little Sister" that rivals Elvis Presley's—yeah, that's right—and blows Ry Cooder's tepid cover of it away. The only other cover here is the classic "Smoke Along the Track" by Alan Rose and Dan Helms, and in true hardcore troubadour fashion, Yoakam makes it his own, swinging it in the best Johnny Cash & Tennessee Three fashion rhythmically and with Haggard's winsome railroad vocal that he took from Jimmie Rodgers. While there can be no doubt about Yoakam's "hillbilly" roots in Kentucky, this disc is deluxe in virtually every way. —*Thom Jurek*

☆ **Buenos Noches From a Lonely Room** / 1988 / Reprise ✦✦✦✦✦

The third effort from Kentucky's Dwight Yoakam shows the first signs of beginning to stretch out and be comfortable with his unique approach to hard honky tonk music, Bakersfield-style. *Buenos Noches From a Lonely Room* features a number of variations on the themes Yoakam explores in his songs—mainly heartache. Not since Leon Payne has anyone gone from love that is so obsessive it cares not a whit for the most basic of life's needs ("I Got You"), to a murderous jealousy ("What I Don't Know"), to homicide ("Buenos Noches From a Lonely Room (She Wore Red Dresses)") in the first five songs. In addition, Yoakam and producer/guitarist Pete Anderson are exploring the colorations of other instruments in their mix such as the addition of the legendary Flaco Jimenez's accordion on the title track. The transition tracks between these three facets of human meltdown are the stunning melody in "One More Name" and a radical cover of Johnny Cash's "Home of the Blues." In addition, there's a read of J. D. Miller's "I Hear You Knockin' " as an alternate ending, though it's still plenty dark. After the murder in the title track, the cycle is complete, and the album shifts gears radically. It kicks off with a balladic elegy to a worn-out drunk called "I Sang Dixie," full of lilting fiddle and subtle singing leads from Anderson. It's a tearjerker in classic country fashion, its tone almost reverential. Track two is a duet with Yoakam's hero, Buck Owens, who came out of retirement—briefly—to record this song and a new album. There's only one song the pair could sing together, the anthem of lost but proud down-and-out ramblers, and that's Homer Joy's "Streets of Bakersfield." The other cover here is Hank Locklin's beautiful love song "Send Me the Pillow" with a return by Maria McKee on backing vocals (she sang a duet on "Bury Me" with Yoakam on *Guitars, Cadillacs, Etc., Etc.*). The pair are as natural together as Gram Parsons and Emmylou Harris were, though far more traditional in their approach. As chapter three in the Dwight Yoakam restoration of honky tonk music project, this is the best yet. —*Thom Jurek*

★ **Just Lookin' for a Hit** / 1989 / Reprise ✦✦✦✦✦

Released in 1989 just three years after his debut, *Just Lookin' for a Hit* may have been a bit premature for a greatest-hits album, but it did the trick and sold better than any album Dwight Yoakam had thus far issued. This set is chock-full of the definitive Dwight—at the time—from the opener, a hard rocking version of the Dave Alvin & the Blasters' "Long White Cadillac," to his self-penned honky tonk soul jam "Little Ways," before moving into hardcore barroom twang with Johnny Horton's "Honky Tonk Man" and the rockabilly country kicker "I Got You." Just how closely Yoakam walked the line between hard country and soulful rockabilly is nowhere more evident than it is on his cover of Doc Pomus' "Little Sister." Thankfully his theme "Guitars, Cadillacs" is here as is his duet with k.d. lang on Gram Parsons' "Sin City." Add "I Sang Dixie," "Please, Please Baby," and his duet with Buck Owens on "Steets of Bakersfield." When one considers that these are merely highlights—and some of them arguable choices—from his first three records, the true value of Yoakam as a recording artist who single-handedly revitalized traditional country music becomes evident. This is a smoking hits collection but is only a taste of the treasures that lie within the individual albums themselves. —*Thom Jurek*

☆ **If There Was a Way** / 1990 / Reprise ✦✦✦✦✦

If There Was a Way from 1990 is the first full display of Dwight Yoakam's doppelgänger on record. From the midtempo honky tonk of "The Distance Between You and Me" and the classic Bakersfield balladry of "The Heart That You Own" to the balls-out live 21st century rockabilly "It Takes a Lot to Rock You Baby," Yoakam shows his fragmented musical personality that somehow remains inside the framework of his own brand of country. Fans of the old heroes such as Ernest Tubb, Merle Haggard, George Jones, Buck Owens, Hank Thompson, Loretta Lynn, and so on dig Yoakam because he knows how to write and sing a good old country song. The kids and pop audiences love him because he seems to speak to them as much with his swagger as his electricity—guitarist Pete Anderson is like Don Rich, only from the rock side of the country music fence. "Nothing's Changed Here," written by Yoakam and master songwriter Kostas, is a nod to Tubb in that it refers to the master's "Walkin' the Floor Over You" in "Nothing's Changed Here," a barroom stroller with a gorgeous fiddle solo by Don Reed and a splendid use of reverb by Anderson. "Since I Started Drinkin' Again" is a bluegrass sh*tkicker, but it is one hell of a self-destructive broken-heart song that features some awesome fiddlework by Scott Joss and mandolin and backing vocals by Tim O'Brien. The bluesy, doo-woppy, Doc Pomus-inspired rock balladry of the title track is another move toward the margins for Yoakam—especially with the shimmering B-3 work by Skip Edwards. "It Only Hurts Me When I Cry," Yoakam's co-write with Roger Miller, who sings backing vocals on the track, is another rocker à la early Conway Twitty. Ultimately the duet with Patty Loveless on Kostas and Kathy Louvin's "Send a Message to My Heart" is a wrought and deeply moving love song. Loveless is the best of her generation. Not even Martina McBride with all her emotion and range can match the soul in the grain of her voice, nor does anyone possess as pure a country voice with the exception of Emmylou Harris perhaps. The bravest moment on the record is also its most fun. The closer is a truly hillbilly deluxe version of Wilbert Harrison's anthem "Let's Work Together." Anderson tears this mother up, raw and wooly, and Yoakam proves himself as fine a R&B singer as he is a country crooner. Here again the rock side of country, the soul side of rock, and the country side of soul are all wrapped here in Yokam's voice backed by a band who have a complete understanding of the tune. It's highly recommended. —*Thom Jurek*

La Croix D'Amour / 1992 / Reprise ✦✦✦✦✦

An international-only compilation, *La Crois D'Amour* is worth searching out for its rarities: two songs that appeared on other collections (Elvis Presley's "Suspicious Minds" and the Grateful Dead's "Truckin' ") and four new tracks, among them covers of the Beatles' "Things We Said Today" and Them's "Here Comes the Night." —*Brian Mansfield*

☆ **This Time** / 1993 / Reprise ✦✦✦✦✦

Six years after his monumental debut recording, *Guitars, Cadillacs, Etc., Etc.*, Dwight Yoakam is still delivering the goods. After inadvertently (and unwillingly) being credited with creating the new traditionalist movement, Yoakam takes his hard-edged country influences from Buck Owens, Johnny Horton, Ray Price, and Merle Haggard and expands them to include new instruments and textures as well as voices—one can hear in these broken love songs the voice of Gene Pitney as well—and come up with something new again. *This Time* is not a party record in the way his first pair of albums were. Take the first half of *Buenos Noches From a Lonely Room* and add a marvelously played Hammond B-3 courtesy of Skip Edwards and keep the downer flow going and you got it. Buck Owens' spirit appears on "This Time," a song that, while deep in the Bakersfield groove, has a more elegiac tone thanks to Yoakam's songwriting collaboration with country songsmith legend Kostas (who first worked with Yoakam on *If There Was a Way*); they wrote half the album together. Kostas' lush approach to melody is not alien to Yoakam's as demonstrated by the tunes Dwight penned himself—"Pocket of a Clown" (with a doo wop backing chorus in swing harmony) and the devastating ballads "A Thousand Miles From Nowhere" and "Home for Sale," among others. But in Kostas Yoakam found a writer as interested in textures as in unique ways to use his voice. "Two Doors Down" is a stunning example, as is the lone cover on the disc, by Kostas and James House, "Ain't That Lonely Yet," where Yoakam moves into Roy Orbison territory with strings and lush backdrops that meld Bakersfield with Pitney's conceptual mini-soundtracks and the arrangements on Jim Reeves' best records. With production help from Dusty Wakeman (Lucinda Williams' self-titled and *Sweet Old World* albums), Pete Anderson was able to add depth and dimension to an already full sound. The echoes of early rock and soul entwine the honky tonk tempos and instruments and become something wholly other. This album is a welcome addition to Yoakam's formidable catalog. *This Time* is no sell out; it's a new way to present the timelessness of hard, torn, wasted-love country love songs with less reckless sentimentality and more honest emotion. —*Thom Jurek*

Dwight Live / May 23, 1995 / Reprise ✦✦

A straight presentation of Dwight Yoakam playing his greatest hits in concert, *Dwight Live* is a solid record, highlighted by a long, intense take on "Suspicious Minds." Nevertheless, nothing on the album improves on the original recorded versions, making *Dwight Live* essential for devoted fans only. —*Stephen Thomas Erlewine*

Gone / Nov. 1995 / Reprise ✦✦✦✦

Gone is a startling moment in Dwight Yoakam's career. It's been a decade since the California Oaks six-track EP version of *Guitars, Cadillacs, Etc., Etc.* had been released (before Warner picked it up, added four cuts, and issued it as an album in 1986). It's been a helluva run thus far, and *Gone* marks it as a milestone. Given that record companies don't nurture artists over their first two or three albums anymore, Yoakam has managed ten years on the charts and a decade's worth of fine albums—with a couple of masterpieces among them. *Gone* fully integrates the early-'60s grooving rock and R&B of Doc Pomus and Leiber & Stoller with the hard honky tonk of the Bakersfield sound with regional touches that have become so prevalent on his records (example: note the opening track here, "Sorry You Asked?," with its mariachi horns in the refrains and bridge). Yes, and sometimes they all occur in the same song such as on the title track here where the Farfisa sound of Tex-Mex, Doug Sahm-style rock meets Chuck Berry's guitar riffing meets Buck Owens country, and all of it is Yoakam. Then there's "Gone" with its Hammond B-3 and string section that could be an early rock anthem from the New York street corners if it weren't for Yoakam's restless Kentucky voice crooning in the swinging Texas wind. Even the straight rock & roll of "Never Hold You," with its psychedelic guitar fills before its "C.C. Rider"—à la Mitch Ryder not Charlie Rich—refrain turns on a country-rock dime. Pete Anderson is a guitar slinger maximus who may have been schooled by the Buckaroos' Don Rich's style, but he plays with the razor-sharp intensity of the Detroit rocker he is. While it's true that those who long for Yoakam's pure honky tonk style may be lost a bit here, with a few spins they'll get it. Yoakam's music has been a thrill to witness as it has developed. *Gone* is the work of a singular talent with input from many different sources, from instrumentalists and horn and string sections to a dozen backing vocalists all used on different tracks. As the album closes with "Heart of Stone," a co-write with Kostas, you hear Yoakam go back to where modern country music came from in the first place: In the cascading strings that fall over the face of the mix, the band slide in behind them and the ghosts of Jim Reeves and Patsy Cline enter the singer and intone the kind heartbreak that can only be voiced in a country song. Chalk up another winner for Yoakam. *—Thom Jurek*

Under the Covers / Jul. 15, 1997 / Reprise ✦✦✦

Given how easily Dwight Yoakam makes the songs of others his own, including classics like "Sin City" and "Streets of Bakersfield" as well as the Doc Pomus nugget "Little Sister," it's a wonder it took him 11 years to record an album of covers. Yoakam had nothing left to prove as a songwriter, penning hit after hit and album after album of constantly evolving country music that remained true to the honky tonk tradition while stretching it sonically—without revisionism. Here, Yoakam interprets everyone from Roy Orbison to the Clash to the Beatles to Danny O'Keefe, often radically reworking these genuine enduring classics of popular music to bring out the hidden meanings rather than remake them in his own image, the near bluegrass version of "Train in Vain" being a prime example. The Orbison tune that opens the album, "Claudette," rocks with a country swagger the original never had and feels like more of a celebratory tome to a third party than it does a love song. The Raymond Douglas tune "Tired of Waiting" made a household radio favorite by k.d. lang is as far from a country song as can be with a full horn section—and this cut works the least—and is an oddity but entertaining when heard once. O'Keefe's "Good Time Charlie's Got the Blues" is less melodic than the writer's version, but it is far more desolate and haunting. The duet on Sonny Bono's "Baby Don't Go" with Sheryl Crow doesn't really work either, because Crow is not a country singer and there's enough countrypolitan in Yoakam's read that the two singers seem cold and at odds with each other. The lush, funky version of Jimmy Webb's "Wichita Lineman" may not replace Glen Campbell's, but it is a credible, even fine read with all of its textural embellishments (Pete Anderson, Yoakam's guitarist and producer is a genius), a B-3, layers of guitars, double-timed drums... awesome. "Here Comes the Night," with its ringing electric 12-string guitars and faux Caribbean rhythm is stunningly beautiful, and the Beatles' "Things We Said Today" is a psychedelic country jewel. While this set is not perfect, it's still damn fine and warrants repeated listens to come to grips with Yoakam's visionary ambition. *—Thom Jurek*

Come on Christmas / Aug. 26, 1997 / Warner Bros. ✦✦✦

Dwight Yoakam's *Come on Christmas* is a rollicking set of rocking holiday classics that is ironically highlighted by the title track, a haunting original that is one of Yoakam's best songs of the late '90s. The remainder of the album is comprised of high-spirited, entertaining country-rockers that may not add anything new to Yoakam's catalog, but they nevertheless make the record an enjoyable holiday album. *—Thom Owens*

A Long Way Home / Jun. 9, 1998 / Reprise ✦✦✦

As he entered his second decade of recording, Dwight Yoakam began to take more time between records. A three-year gap separated *A Long Way Home* from *Gone*—the last time he went that long between albums of new material was 1990's *If There Was a Way* and 1993's *This Time*. As it happened, *This Time* was a masterpiece, a breakthrough of sorts in that it expanded Yoakam's already large stylistic trickbag. *A Long Way Home* doesn't rank with *This Time*, probably because it is an outgrowth of that leap forward instead of the leap itself, but like *Gone*, it is a rich, diverse, continually impressive collection of timeless songs. Yoakam and his producer/guitarist Pete Anderson keep things interesting by never following conventions—"These Arms" has a Bakersfield foundation, but it's graced by sweeping Nashville strings that bring the song into new territory. That's just one of many unexpected touches that make *A Long Way Home* a rewarding listen, even if it doesn't consistently reach the heights of such previous masterstrokes as *Guitars, Cadillacs, Etc., Etc.*, *Buenos Noches From a Lonely Room*, and *This Time*. *—Stephen Thomas Erlewine*

☆ **Last Chance for a Thousand Years: Greatest Hits from the '90s** / May 18, 1999 / Reprise ✦✦✦✦✦

During the '90s, Dwight Yoakam settled into a weird role. No longer a representative of the cutting edge, the way he was in the '80s, he was nevertheless far too restless and young to become an elder statesman. Instead, he followed his own path, which resulted in a series of albums that were (arguably) every bit as rewarding as his '80s efforts. And, like his '80s recordings, his '90s albums stood as cohesive, individual entities that nevertheless boasted several great singles apiece. Which is a roundabout way of saying that Yoakam was as much a singles artist as he was an album artist, and that's why his second compilation, *Last Chance for a Thousand Years: Greatest Hits from the '90s*, is every bit as entertaining and revelatory as *Just Lookin' for a Hit*. It is true that the hits didn't arrive as fast and furious in the latter half of the '90s as they did in the first, but the quality of the singles didn't dip at all, as this terrific disc proves. All of the 11 singles—including "Turn It On, Turn It Up, Turn Me Loose," "It Only Hurts When I Cry," "A Thousand Miles from Nowhere," "Ain't That Lonely Yet," "Fast As You," "Sorry You Asked"—sound like modern classics, and the two previously unreleased cuts ("Thinking About Leaving," "I'll Go Back to Her"), plus his cover of Queen's stab at rockabilly, "Crazy Little Thing Called Love," nearly match that standard. And if it is true that country artists can be judged by their singles comps, as some have alleged over the years, then *Last Chance for a Thousand Miles* proves that Yoakam is one of the greats of the '80s and '90s. *—Stephen Thomas Erlewine*

dwightyoakamacoustic.net / May 30, 2000 / Reprise ✦✦✦

At first glance, *dwightyoakamacoustic.net* might look like a simple re-recorded greatest-hits album that's pleasant but unnecessary. However, the spontaneity and depth of these performances should give any Yoakam fan pause before dismissing it out of hand. Other than the fact that it has no discernible connection to the Internet, the album is exactly what the title promises: aside from one electric-guitar overdub, it's nothing but Yoakam and an acoustic guitar the whole way through. This ultra-stripped-down setting gives Yoakam a chance to establish an intimacy of performance that relies simply on the expressiveness of his voice and his ability to fill up space with compelling guitar work. To a certain extent, Yoakam could be handicapped by the familiarity of most of these songs, but revisiting one's back catalog is certainly not without precedent; outlaw country's biggest stars frequently re-recorded old favorites to reflect their changing sounds. Besides, he's generally successful at reinventing this selection of hits and top-notch album tracks for the album's solo format. Without much to concentrate on other than emotive power in Yoakam's voice, the heartbreaking ballads are that much more affecting, culminating in the a cappella, album-closing rendition of the once uptempo "Guitars, Cadillacs." The approach also helps evoke the wide-open spaces of songs like "Bury Me" and "A Thousand Miles From Nowhere." Not everything here is revelatory—in the end, some songs *are* merely pleasant—but overall, *dwightyoakamacoustic.net* is a left-field success, a testament to the richness of Yoakam's back catalog and his skill as an interpreter. *—Steve Huey*

Tomorrow's Sounds Today / Oct. 31, 2000 / Warner Bros. ✦✦✦✦

The title has to be a goof because this album, as well as Dwight Yoakam's entire catalog, should be dubbed "Yesterday's Sounds Today." The only connection Yoakam retains to the slick, cross-over, big hat crowd is the big hat, and these 14 tracks prove that even as country music continually evolves into glossy pop, this artist has entrenched himself in all things retro. The crying steel guitars, jaunty mandolins, and plaintive fiddles that drive this rootsy country & western could have been recorded in the 1950s, and only the tasty electric guitar licks of longtime producer/cohort Pete Anderson bring the music up to date. Further cementing his connection with the classic Bakersfield sound, Yoakam invites founding father Buck Owens to join the fold once more (their 1988 collaboration produced a number-one C&W hit with "The Streets of Bakersfield") and the resulting three tracks yield results just as winning. Yoakam goes the Hank Williams Sr. route on "A Promise You Can't Keep" and especially "The Heartaches Are Free," which sounds so similar to a Hank Sr. tune in melody and vocal inflection, you'll find yourself double checking the liner notes to be sure it's a Yoakam original. The singer dips into his '70s classic rock roots again too, as he follows up his wildly successful Queen remake with a cover of Cheap Trick's "I Want You to Want Me." Like his interpretation of "Crazy Little Thing Called Love," he makes it sound like an obscure barnstorming country track instead of the power pop nugget it is. Ten of the album's 14 tunes are self-penned and song titles like "A World of Blue," "A Place to Cry," "The Sad Side of Town," and "Time Spent Missing You" show that Yoakam is still drenched in the spilt tears, heartbroken brand of country that has proven to be so lucrative, artistically and commercially, in the past. Best of all, he makes it seems easy. Even though there's little stylistic maturation in his approach since his first release in 1986, Yoakam's songwriting craft keeps improving, and any track from this album could be a hit single. With *Tomorrow's Sounds Today*, Dwight Yoakam has fashioned a contemporary roots-conscious country album whose qualities, like the artist's distinctive style, are timeless. *—Hal Horowitz*

South of Heaven, West of Hell / Oct. 2, 2001 / Warner Bros. ✦✦

As country music's favorite antihero, Yoakam has built an impressive dossier as an actor in films like *Red Rock West*, *Sling Blade*, and *The Newton Boys*. *South of Heaven, West of Hell* was his poorly received debut as a writer/director. As far as the soundtrack to this ambitious film goes, there are plenty of the fine modern/vintage country tunes that Yoakam seems to produce so effortlessly. And though none stand out as classics, songs co-written with Billy Gibbons and Mick Jagger deserve a listen. But those little dialogue snippets bridging the songs add very little. They reveal nothing interesting about the film other than its obvious plot points, and don't do much on their own either. Bekka Bramlett guests on "Who at the Door Is Standing." *—John Duffy*

☆ **Reprise Please Baby: The Warner Bros. Years** / Nov. 12, 2002 / Rhino ✦✦✦✦✦

Randy Travis sold more records and George Strait was a purer country singer, but Dwight Yoakam was as influential as either on country music in the '80s. A Kentucky-born, Ohio-raised refugee from Nashville, he headed out to California where he managed to play Bakerfield country for L.A. punks, laying the groundwork for the Americana movement of the late '80s and '90s by not only revitalizing classic country from honky tonks to country-pop ballads through his traditionalist readings, but treating rock songs in a similar fashion. Nowhere is this more apparent than on Rhino's excellent four-disc box set *Reprise Please Baby: The Warner Bros. Years*, a superb chronicling of his time at Reprise/Warner Records. What makes this set so successful is that it doesn't focus simply on the hits, though they're all here. Instead of just the hits, they're interlaced with key album tracks, covers, duets, and songs cut for compilations, all necessary to understanding Yoakam's music and his influence. Take his superlative duet with Flaco Jimenez on Warren Zevon's "Carmelita" and how it blurs the lines between country, punk, classic rock, and singer/songwriters, creating the sound that would come to be known as Americana. Nearly every alt-country artist sought this expert balance of self-consciously classic instrumentation, contemporary subject matter, stylized yet sincere delivery, and clean production—a delicate balance many sought to replicate, yet few succeeded in capturing. It's a brilliant moment, but one that wasn't on any Dwight album, and this rightly presents it, among other rarities, as key parts of his legacy. Among the revelations on *Reprise Please Baby* is that Yoakam had this balance perfected from the beginning, from before he released his landmark debut, *Guitars, Cadillacs, Etc., Etc.*; his ten-track demo from 1981 is included here on the all-previously unreleased fourth disc, and it holds its own among his best albums in both its songwriting and performance. This entire disc—which also contains two fine duets with Kelly Willis and a string of covers, recorded anywhere from 1986 to 2002, all very good, with a nimble "Oh Lonesome Me" and a rip-roaring "My Bucket's Got a Hole in It" standing as particular highlights—makes it necessary for collectors, but the set wouldn't be much if it was just for the completists. What makes it such a success is that it presents Yoakam's full achievement through a sharp, thorough examination of his prodigious output, turning in a convincing case for his greatness while being a hell of an entertaining listen. He produced his share of great albums, but *Reprise Please Baby* tells everything country fans of any stripe need to know. —*Stephen Thomas Erlewine*

Population Me / Jun. 24, 2003 / Audium ✦✦✦✦

Dwight Yoakam returns on a new label with his first album proper in three years—the soundtrack to his directorial film debut, *South of Heaven, West of Hell* is just that, not an album of songs. And while one might wonder if this is more of the same brand of Bakersfield-styled honky tonk blues from Yoakam and be right, there are two arguments as to why it's a necessary purchase. First and foremost, the quality of Yoakam's material is the most consistent in country music since the outlaws of the mid-'70s—while kings Haggard and Jones released great records consistently in the '70s and '80s, neither streak was as long as Yoakam's, who arguably has never released a shoddy album. This one is no exception. Most importantly are the surprises, of which there are plenty. On the opener, "The Late Great Golden State," written by Mike Stinson, Yoakam does his best Jackson Browne-Eagles—and actually reveals why the L.A. drugstore cowboy sound is timeless when done right. Former Eagle Timothy B. Schmidt lends a hand on the backing vocals and gives it a solid "take it easy" rollicking roll. Elsewhere, as on the title track driven by guitar ace Pete Anderson and pedal steel, banjo, and dobro king Gary Morse, Yoakam weaves a perfect blend of driving rockabilly, Chuck Berry, and honky tonk. On a banjo-drenched cover of Burt Bacharach's "Trains and Boats and Planes," Yoakam sings his skinny butt off, while Anderson rides the mandolin down into the lost wail of Scott Joss' fiddle. They transform the pop song into a traditional country shuffle graced with the high lonesome sound of Earl Scruggs' electrifying banjo work, punching the fills and turnarounds with grease and grit. "If Teardrops Were Diamonds" is one of Yoakam's most beautiful ballads. Willie Nelson performs a duet with him, adding a gorgeous pop sensibility to Yoakam's hillbilly moan. Through the rest, Yoakam's songwriting continues to grow and transform itself into an accurate reflection of American culture as felt through the poetic heart of a country musician. The songs are right there: lean, tough, raw, and drenched with hooks as well as emotions—check out the honky tonk stroll of "I'd Avoid Me Too." This is stellar, kickin' impure country. —*Thom Jurek*

Yonder Mountain String Band

f. Nederland, CO

Group / Progressive Bluegrass

Although the Yonder Mountain String Band was formed in Nederland, CO, its origins go back to Urbana, IL, where college student and banjo player Dave Johnston met mandolin player Jeff Austin. Austin moved west and settled in Nederland. Johnston joined him there, and the two met bass player Ben Kauffman and guitarist Adam Aijala at a club called the *Verve*. In December 1998, they formed the Yonder Mountain String Band to open for a band at the Fox Theatre in Boulder. They developed a following among bluegrass fans and also among jam band fans as they played extensively and worked their way up the bar and club circuit in the West. In the fall of 1999, they released their debut album, *Elevation*, on their own Frog Pad Records label. By the fall of 2000, they were playing in larger venues, such as the Fillmore Auditorium in San Francisco. They released a live recording as their second album, *Mountain Tracks, Vol. 1*, in the spring of 2001, and followed with another studio set, *Town By Town*, in the fall of 2001. —*William Ruhlmann*

Elevation / 1999 / Frog Pad ✦✦✦

This Nederland, CO, band's brand of string band music is as steeped in the jam band tradition as it is in the high and lonesome bluegrass sounds originated by Bill Monroe. Though this isn't the first band to blend these influences, driving rhythms and exceptional picking make for an enjoyable debut, if not one without definite weaknesses. The band's vocals and songwriting talents (all four members sing and write) simply don't equal its instrumental abilities. Banjo player Dave Johnston's keening tenor sounds most believable floating above the band's rustic groove on "The Lonesome Heart" and the jukebox-ready alt-country weeper "Eight Cylinders." Jeff Austin is fast-fingered on the mandolin but sings too near the top of his limited vocal range. The Yonder Mountain String Band's chops put many of the album's weaker songs over anyway, suggesting that the band's live shows will make them wildly popular on the jam band and bluegrass festival circuits, where songwriting and singing are very often secondary to instrumental flash. Progressive bluegrassers Mike Marshall and Darol Anger make guest appearances. —*Brian Beatty*

● **Mountain Tracks, Vol. 1** / 2001 / Frog Pad ✦✦✦

Tie-dyed bluegrass for third-generation hippie jam band followers doesn't get much better than this band's sophomore release, a live album recorded over two nights at Boulder, CO's Fox Theatre. The band has fun with an unlisted rendition of Peter Tosh's "Legalize It" (hidden in the middle of their own "Keep on Going") and J.J. Cale's "If You're Ever in Oklahoma," but the opening cover of Carter Stanley's "Sharecropper's Son" sounds a tad too polished and buttoned-down to come across as a genuine tribute to an older musical tradition. Less a progressive bluegrass outfit than a jam band equipped with acoustic instruments and a vague sense of history, this band is at its best when it can stretch out and play off of each other during extended instrumental breaks. Though still unlikely to covert nonbelievers, *Mountain Tracks, Vol. 1* is probably a perfect tour memento for this young band's growing legion of neo-hippie fans. —*Brian Beatty*

Town By Town / 2001 / Frog Pad ✦✦✦

As its title implies, *Town By Town*, the Yonder Mountain String Band's second studio recording and third CD overall, is something of a concept album about life on the road, the reality for the quartet's members since the group's formation. Mandolin player Jeff

Austin's "New Horizons" concerns the rescue of a family from a flood, and guitarist Adam Aijala's "A Father's Arms" is a war story with a Vietnam-era tone, but even these two songs are about family and dislocation, and the rest of the songs are dominated by references to travel, with the necessary impact on the singers' love lives, resulting either in breakups or pleas for fidelity, a major factor. But the lyrics of these original songs penned by the bandmembers, sung in their uniformly reedy tenors, are less significant than the music underlying them, a familiar mixture of fast-picked guitar, mandolin, and banjo, with producer Tim O'Brien adding welcome fiddle and bouzouki lines here and there. In addition to three outright instrumentals ("Easy As Pie," "Wildewood Drive," and "Hog Potato"), "New Horizons" and "Peace of Mind" both contain extended instrumental sections that go beyond the term "breakdown" into the kind of loose improvisation typical of rock bands like the Grateful Dead, justifying the group's inclusion under the jam band umbrella. Nevertheless, there is plenty here to enthuse a traditional bluegrass fan. (After three minutes of silence at the end of "Peace of Mind" comes a six-plus-minute hidden track, probably titled "Dance, Boatman, Dance," which is taken at a sprightly square dance tempo and features O'Brien's fiddle extensively.) —*William Ruhlmann*

Mountain Tracks, Vol. 2 / Aug. 20, 2002 / Sci Fidelity ✦✦✦

The Grateful Dead's Jerry Garcia was known for his affection for bluegrass, which led him to form side bands like Old & In the Way, but his reputation as an acid rock guitarist always stood in the way of wide acceptance in the bluegrass community. The Yonder Mountain String Band, representing a new generation of bluegrass pickers, not only seems ready to admit Garcia to the bluegrass pantheon, but also wants to adapt the Dead's taste for meandering improvisation to what was previously a form of music devoted to speed and economy. The group is thus evolving a new form of bluegrass that has earned it kudos in the jam band category, and this tendency is nowhere more evident than in their two live albums. This second one, recorded in the fall of 2001, gives a good sense of the band's proclivities and talents. They're not afraid to take off on extended excursions, stretching a medley of mandolinist Jeff Austin's "Peace of Mind" and "Follow Me Down to the Riverside" past 26 minutes, and their choice of covers is revealing. The Rolling Stones' faux country "No Expectations" is played for real and extended to ten minutes; outlaws Waylon Jennings and Willie Nelson are recalled on "Good Hearted Woman"; and John Hartford's "Two Hits and the Joint Turned Brown" reeks of reggae and ganja. The Yonder Mountain String Band is to becoming to bluegrass what the Kronos Quartet is to chamber music; just as that classical outfit shakes things up by performing Jimi Hendrix's "Purple Haze" as an encore, so this bluegrass group does the unexpected by gathering around a single microphone on the album's hidden track, a soulful rendition of Pink Floyd's "Goodbye Blue Sky." Bill Monroe may be spinning in his grave, but the audience has a great time. —*William Ruhlmann*

York Brothers

Group / Traditional Country, Close Harmony

The York Brothers played together from the '30s through the '50s, developing a musical style which grew from traditional country into a more contemporary sound. Both George and Leslie York were born in Lawrence County, KY, and were heavily influenced by the Delmore Brothers. As a young man, George worked in coal mines and later began his music career in Denver, CO, playing in local clubs and on the radio in the evenings. Leslie, who was seven years younger, got his start after winning a talent contest in Lexington, KY. Not long afterward, the brothers teamed and played together on a station in Portsmouth, OH. They then moved to Detroit, where their music caught fire with the Southern transplants who had come to work in the burgeoning auto industry.

The Yorks made their recording debut in 1939 and had success with "Going Home" and the controversial, slightly racy "Hamtramck Mama," which was banned in the Polish-American Detroit suburb of the same name. The notoriety got the brothers signed to Decca in 1941, where they released six singles, including "Speak to Me Little Darling." Just as they were becoming popular, World War II erupted, and both Yorks served in the Navy until the war's end. They then joined the *Grand Ole Opry* and began recording for King in 1947, where they found success with such outspoken tunes as "Let's Not Sleep Again" and "Mountain Rosa Lee." They also became interested in rhythm and blues, a musical style that influenced some of their later songs like "Tennessee Tango" and "River of Tears."

George and Leslie returned to Detroit in 1950, where they stayed until 1953, moving to Dallas to work on local television. They recorded on King until 1956 and then started their own label. Around this time, George began having problems with his voice, so Leslie took over the lead parts. Eventually, the York Brothers went their separate ways; George ran a Dallas nightclub before his death in 1974, while Leslie worked different jobs until passing on a decade later. —*Sandra Brennan*

● **16 Great Country & Western Hits** / 1963 / King ✦✦✦✦✦

Detroit in the 40's & 50's, Vol. 1 / Mar. 14, 2000 / Collector ✦✦✦✦

Rusty York

b. May 24, 1935, Harlan County, KY

Banjo, Vocals / Traditional Bluegrass, Traditional Country, Rockabilly, Rock & Roll

Rusty York was born May 24, 1935, in Harlan County, KY. A 1951 concert appearance by Earl Scruggs & the Foggy Mountain Boys inspired the already musically curious York, who, after moving to Cincinnati, bought a five-string banjo and began to play out. His first collaborator was Willard Hale, and the duo gigged locally with acts like Jimmie Skinner and Hylo Brown. When Elvis Presley broke in 1957, York decided that an update in sound was necessary. He and Hale cut a version of Buddy Holly's "Peggy Sue" for King, which led to York's teaming with vocalist Bonnie Lout in a rockabilly project. 1959 saw the recording of two of York's most rollicking numbers, "Red Rooster" and "Sugaree." The rockabilly phase was a minor success, but by the 1960s, York had returned to bluegrass and country. He also began to cultivate an interest in the business end of country and in

1961 started building a studio in his garage. By the early '70s York had retired from performing to concentrate on his Jewel Records imprint/studio full-time. Jewel continued to operate out of Cincinnati throughout the 1980s and '90s, and into the 21st century. *—Johnny Loftus*

Rust York and the Kentucky Mountain Boys / 1960 / Blue Grass Special ♦♦♦

● **Dueling Banjos** / 1973 / Q.C.A. ♦♦♦♦

Rock 'n' Memories / 1981 / Jewel ♦♦♦

Faron Young

b. Feb. 25, 1932, Shreveport, LA, **d.** Dec. 10, 1996

Vocals, Guitar / Traditional Country, Country-Pop, Honky Tonk, Nashville Sound/ Countrypolitan

Originally known as "the Hillbilly Heartthrob" and "the Singing Sheriff," Faron Young had one of the longest-running and most popular careers in country music history. Emerging in the early '50s, Young was one of the most popular honky tonkers to appear in the wake of Hank Williams' death, partially because he was able to smooth out some of the grittiest elements his music. At first, he balanced honky tonk with pop vocal phrasing and flourishes. This combination of grit and polish resulted in a streak of Top Ten hits—including "If You Ain't Lovin'," "Live Fast, Love Hard, Die Young," "Sweet Dreams," "Alone With You," and "Country Girl"—that ran throughout the '50s. During the '60s, Young gave himself over to country-pop, and while the hits weren't quite as big, they didn't stop coming until the early '80s. Through that time, he was a staple at the *Grand Ole Opry* and various television shows, including *Nashville Now,* and he also founded the major country music magazine, *Music City News.* Most importantly, he continued to seek out new songwriters—including Don Gibson, Willie Nelson, and Kris Kristofferson—thereby cultivating a new generation of talent.

Faron Young was born and raised outside of Shreveport, LA. While he was growing up on his father's dairy farm, he was given a guitar, and by the time he entered high-school, he had begun singing in a country band. Following high-school, he briefly attended college, before he left school to join the *Louisiana Hayride* as a regular performer. While on the *Hayride,* he met Webb Pierce and in a short time, the pair were touring throughout the South, singing as a duo in various nightclubs and honky tonks. In 1951, he recorded "Have I Waited Too Long" and "Tattle Tale Tears" for the independent label Gotham. After hearing the singles, Capitol Records decided to buy Young's contract away from Gotham in 1952. That same year, he was invited to perform regularly on the *Grand Ole Opry.* Just as his career was taking off, Young was drafted into the Army to serve in the Korean War. Assigned to the Special Service division, he sang for the troops in Asia and appeared on recruitment shows; while on leave, he recorded his debut Capitol, "Goin' Steady." Upon its early 1953 release, it climbed to number two on the country charts and it was followed in the summer by "I Can't Wait (For the Sun to Go Down)," which hit number five. Young was discharged from the Army in November of 1954, releasing "If You Ain't Lovin'," his biggest hit to date, shortly after he returned. The single was quickly followed in the spring of 1955 by "Live Fast, Love Hard, Die Young," which became his first number-one hit, and the number-two single, "All Right."

As soon as he returned to the U.S., Faron Young began turning out singles at a very rapid pace, and most of them charted in the Top Ten. In addition to recording, he began appearing in films, starting with 1955's *Hidden Guns.* Over the next few years, he was in no less than ten films—including *Daniel Boone, Road to Nashville, Stampede, A Gun and a Gavel, That's Country,* and *Raiders of Old California*—and was featured in many television shows. Upon his first film appearance, Faron earned the nickname the Young Sheriff, which eventually metamorphasized into the Singing Sheriff. Young's career truly began to hit its stride in 1956, as "I've Got Five Dollars and It's Saturday Night" and "You're Still Mine" reached number four and three, respectively, during the spring, followed by the number two "Sweet Dreams" later that summer. "Sweet Dreams" not only was his biggest hit since "All Right," but it gave songwriter Don Gibson his first significant exposure. Soon, Young developed a reputation for finding promising new songwriters, bringing Roy Drusky's "Alone With You" to the top of the charts in the summer of 1958 and taking Willie Nelson's "Hello Walls" to number one in 1961; Young was one of the first artists to record a Nelson song.

Young continued to record for Capitol through 1962, when he switched labels and signed with Mercury. In general, Young's Mercury recordings were more pop-oriented than his Capitol work, possibly because "Hello Walls," his last number one for Capitol, reached number 12 on the pop charts. Throughout the early and mid-'60s, Young's music became more polished and produced, yet his audience didn't decline dramatically; he may not have been hitting the every top of the charts with the same frequency as he was during the '50s, but he was still a consistent hitmaker, and singles like "You'll Drive Me Back (Into Her Arms Again)," "Keeping Up With the Joneses," and "Walk Tall" climbed into the Top Ten.

Faron left the *Grand Ole Opry* in 1965, deciding that it was more profitable for him to tour as a solo artist instead of being restricted to the *Opry.* Following his departure from the *Opry,* Young began to explore a number of different business ventures, including a Nashville-based racetrack and helping to run the country music publication *Music City News,* which he co-founded with Preston Temple in 1963. By the end of the decade, he began to return to honky tonk, most notably with the hit "Wine Me Up," which reached number two upon its summer 1969 release. For nearly five years, Young continued to reach the Top Ten with regularity, including such hits as "Your Time's Comin'," "If I Ever Fall in Love (With a Honky Tonk Girl)," "Step Aside," and "It's Four in the Morning." During this time, Young continued to appear on television shows and he made the occasional appearance on the *Grand Ole Opry.* During the late '70s, his hits gradually began to fade away. In 1979, he left Mercury for MCA, but none of his singles for the new label reached the Top 40.

For most of the '80s, Young performed concerts, maintained his business interests, and appeared on television; in short, he was acting like the country music statesman he was. In 1988, he briefly returned to recording, signing with the small label Step One, and had two minor hits on the label. After that brief burst of activity, he retreated to semi-retirement, occasionally making concert appearances. During the '90s, Young was stricken with a debilitating emphysema. Depressed by his poor health, he shot himself on December 9, 1996, and passed away the next day. Though he was underappreciated toward the end of his career, Faron Young was a groundbreaking vocalist during the '50s, and he remains one of the finest honky tonkers of his time. *—Stephen Thomas Erlewine*

Sweethearts or Strangers / 1957 / Capitol ♦♦♦

Faron Young began recording in 1951, but *Sweethearts or Strangers* was his first album. Besides that distinction and the fabulous cover photo of Young in a brilliant turquoise western shirt, the album is standard fare. Sound-alike covers of Hank Williams' "I Can't Help It" and "Your Cheatin' Heart" join classic songs like Spade Cooley's "Shame on You" and Jimmie Davis' "You Are My Sunshine." Young's hard, Hank Williams-derived honky tonk sound is classic, but the menu of popular favorites is too predictable to be really interesting. None of the songs were hits for Young, but his country remake of the big '40s pop hit "You Call Everybody Darlin'" was a good idea. *—Greg Adams*

☆ **Hello Walls** / 1961 / Capitol ♦♦♦♦♦

Hello Walls is perhaps the best-known Faron Young album, largely because of Willie Nelson's stellar title track, which was a monster smash as a single. But despite the fact that it's the first track on the album, and that Nashville was already deeply entrenched in filling albums around singles with crap, Young wasn't so easily put down. His voice, his own songwriting, and his ideas about production in a studio were not to be taken lightly, and here they aren't. Along with "Hello Walls," a slew of other fine songs round out this collection, many of them being signposts for other artists: "There's Not Any Like You Left" proved to be an enormous influence on Buck Owens, "Big Shoes" on Merle Haggard, "Forget the Past" on Conway Twitty, and many more. Truth be told, of the 12 tracks here, only "Out of My Heart" and "Anything Your Heart Desires" are losers. The rest is Young at his best, coming out of the Hank Williams mold and creating a honky tonk sound that was amiable and full of clever lyrical tricks, with a backing band that was as good as any in the business. This is a great place to start any Faron Young collection. *—Thom Jurek*

This Is Faron / 1963 / Mercury ♦♦♦

The All-Time Great Hits . . . / 1963 / Capitol ♦♦♦♦♦

Country Dance Favorites / 1964 / Mercury ♦♦♦♦♦

Here's a stack of late-in-the-career recordings from Faron Young being recycled on this generic budget package. Faron is in good voice, the backing is strictly formulaic Music City, and the set list is loaded with crowd pleasers like "Release Me," "Faded Love," and "She Thinks I Still Care." No new ground broken here by a long shot, and not the place to hear Faron's honky tonk message; stick with his original Capitol recordings instead. *—Cub Koda*

Faron Young's Greatest Hits / 1965 / Mercury ♦♦♦

There are many greatest hits packages by this artist. In this case, the material is drawn from his Mercury output exclusively, and the most famous song is the immortal "Live Fast, Love Hard, Die Young." This tasty bit of rockabilly raving tends to show up on all of the Young hits collection—even if the labels involved had to steal it. Here, no such treachery is involved, but most of the other titles are not ones that have retained a great deal of hit status. Young was trying everything during his contract with this label, with some of the material better suited to the fragile ego he projects so sweetly. One thing there is aplenty is the slick "countrypolitan" sound of background voices and instrumental backup cleansed of much interpretive noodling, which generally makes for dull listening. Other touches in the arrangements are almost perverse, such as the strange percussion clinking in "I Miss You Already and You're Not Even Gone," a song that seems to suggest inaccuracies in the philosophy of "How Can I Miss You When You Won't Go Away." "You'll Drive Me Back (Into Her Arms Again)" and "Nothing Left to Lose" boast the marvelously catchy Ray Price Western swing boogie beat, the latter tune also springing to life via some anonymous steel guitar chirping. "Old Courthouse" is a good narrative of smalltown America, while "Nightmare" is Faron Young for fans of perverse, demented country & western, who will drool over the track. Kind of a go-go honky tonk beat goes on in the background, while Young sings lines such as "I dreamt I saw you in a foreign car/ A-neckin' with a movie star" in a voice that almost sounds like it has been sped up slightly. Several of the songs reveal what must have been an attempt to imitate Marty Robbins, and they are not the most successful moments on the disc. Careful selection when building up one's Faron Young collection could result in finding the top moments in this collection located elsewhere, perhaps alongside better company. *—Eugene Chadbourne*

I'll Be Yours / 1968 / Pickwick ♦♦♦

Pickwick's *I'll Be Yours* is a reissue of an excellent original Capitol LP by Faron Young, featuring such definitive Young performances as "Just Married," "When It Rains It Pours" and "You're Still Mine." Though there are a couple of weak tracks, the album remains a thoroughly engaging listen. *—Thom Owens*

Wine Me Up / 1970 / Mercury ♦♦♦

Faron Young was one of the hottest country stars in the land when he made *Wine Me Up,* an album that demonstrates his mastery of various country music forms and yielded two major hits. The title track, a clever drinking song, nearly topped the country chart, and "Your Time's Comin'" (written by Kris Kristofferson and Shel Silverstein) reached the Top Five. Unfortunately, Young spends a lot of time on songs that quickly became over-recorded and tiresome, like "Little Green Apples" and "Ruby, Don't Take Your Love to Town," but his uncommon arrangements and excellent performances redeem the uninteresting material. A pair of Glen Campbell hits ("Gentle on My Mind," "Galveston") show that this honky tonk stalwart can roll with the trends without succumbing to pop sweetness, and Young reassures lovers of hard country with straight-up country like "Painted

Girls and Wine." *Wine Me Up* goes in several directions at once, but Young's vocal skill ties it all together. *—Greg Adams*

Faron Young Sings This Little Girl of Mine / 1972 / Mercury ✦✦

"This Little Girl of Mine," a heartfelt expression of a father's love for his daughter, was a Top Five hit for Faron Young in 1972 and one of his last big hits even though he remained on the charts through the end of the '80s. The accompanying album, ponderously titled *Faron Young Sings This Little Girl of Mine*, begins with that hit before negotiating a list of mostly downcast songs that quickly dispel the sentimental glow of the title track. "Forever Was the Name of Our Sunshine" is an example of the kind of nonsense that crept into country music in the early '70s, although it at least serves as an upbeat buffer between the title track and later songs like the depressive's lament "One of My Sad Days" and the heartbroken torment of "A Woman's Touch." "Left to Right and Right to Wrong" is one of the then-new breed of sexually frank country songs that caused so much controversy at the time, and seems a little inappropriate on an album centered around a sweet song about a little girl. The album is a strange emotional rollercoaster of hard country songs, some of which are worthy of individual consideration even though they do not hold together as an album. *—Greg Adams*

The Best of Faron Young / 1979 / Impact ✦✦✦

There are so many best-of collections available from this type of country artist that one is tempted to try and create a "best of the best-ofs." If so, this one can be skipped entirely, since it adds nothing to the situation other than yet another low-rent knock-off. This label created its own best-of series of whatever was available for legal licensing, and in this area the Impact label is being given the benefit of the doubt. The only "impact" made here must have been cartons of these babies hitting the loading docks at truck stops. There is absolutely nothing wrong with any of the music, which includes some of this artist's greatest sides. Interested consumers could just do much better, either from the point of view of having some of the liner notes and photography that are available in other Faron Young collections or in terms of actual playing time. This album is over so fast one wants to retitle the great last song "Live Fast, Love Hard, Die Young . . . and Play Quickly." Young has a great voice and manner of delivery, but that is only part of what is going on here. He also had a real knack for finding and encouraging the most fascinating new songwriters, and was able to add a sense of the dangerous and demented to each interpretation he created. Compare "Hello Walls" as sung by Faron Young with the song as it is done by its writer, Willie Nelson. In the latter case, the image is of good ol' Willie Nelson, a red bandana wrapped around his hair, chilling out at home and maybe missing his girlfriend a wee bit. With Young, on the other hand, there is really the sense of a hopelessly lonely, tormented individual walking the floors and staring at the windows and ceiling until his brain starts to crack. It is not a comfortable feeling, and neither is the sense of possessiveness displayed in the swinging "Country Girl"—the way he sings the line "When you're on the dancefloor and he holds you soft and sweet/Does he ever wonder, who put the shoes on your feet?" is haunting, a great moment in country music. Needless to say, none of the sidemen are credited, rendering one impotent in the ability to praise the creators of such great touches as the pedal steel licks on "Wine Me Up" or the rollicking, rolling rhythms of "Riverboat." *—Eugene Chadbourne*

All-Time Greatest Hits / 1990 / Curb ✦✦✦✦✦

Curb's *All-Time Greatest Hits* is a nice, but too brief, collection of Faron Young's biggest hits: "Hello Walls," "Live Fast, Love Hard, Die Young," "Alone With You," "Sweet Dreams," and "Goin' Steady." It's hardly a definitive collection—classic early hits like "If You Ain't Lovin' (You Ain't Livin')," "I've Got Five Dollars," and "All Right" aren't included—but it's a good sampler for the budget-conscious. However, it shouldn't be thought of as a substitute for the more complete *Live Fast, Love Hard: Original Capitol Recordings, 1952-1962*. *—Stephen Thomas Erlewine*

The Classic Years 1952–62 / 1992 / Bear Family ✦✦✦✦✦

Swashbuckling Louisiana honky tonk, much of Faron Young's early work on Capitol is marked by an undertone of grinning lasciviousness. That's not a bad thing, given how many of his industry pals completely hid their wolfishness behind apple-pie lyrics. In any case, Bear Family has here collected the entirety of Young's Capitol output on five CDs. Besides the swaggering stuff ("If You Ain't Lovin'," "Live Fast, Love Hard, Die Young," and the amazing "Alone with You") one can hear the hit version of "Sweet Dreams" he cut seven years before Patsy Cline's. It comes with a beautiful 48-page book. *—Dan Cooper*

Golden Hits / 1995 / Mercury Nashville ✦✦✦✦✦

Golden Hits is part of Mercury's mostly-deleted *American Essentials* series. Presented here are 13 tracks from the '60s and early '70s, including "It's Four in the Morning" and the hit re-recording of "Goin' Steady." Everything on this collection was a Top Ten hit, but not all of Young's Top Ten hits from the period are represented. *Golden Hits* is a good companion to the Country Music Foundation's collection of his '50s honky tonk classics, although the brevity and lack of recording dates and substantial liner notes leaves open the possibility for a better anthology of this period. *—Greg Adams*

★ **Live Fast, Love Hard: Original Capitol Recordings,1952–1962** / Oct. 1995 / Country Music Foundation ✦✦✦✦✦

Given that the Country Music Foundation assembled this collection rather than Capitol Records, it's a far more representative example of Faron Young's understated honky tonk genius than anything else compiled on a single disc. For hardcore fans and collectors, there are the Bear Family sets. These 24 tracks represent all of the major moments in Young's career, from his early, raw, hard-driving barroom singles ("Tattle Tale Tears," "If That's the Fashion," and "I Got Five Dollars and It's Saturday Night") to the evolution of his singing style to a singing example of the pure countrybilly hedonist (the title track) to a pseudo-country crooner who still delivered in the pure Hank Williams style (unlike, say, Jim Reeves) in the late '50s ("I Miss You Already") to a near rockabilly ("That's The Way I Feel") to his late-period full-throated yet reedy baritone ("Hello Walls" and a live "Three Days" that rocks as hard as Elvis did in the '50s). In addition, the listener can also judge the quality of the material Young had to work with. Not a prolific songwriter, he utilized the likes of Tommy Collins (in the early '50s), Marvin Rainwater, Roger Miller, and Willie Nelson in addition to partnering with Bill Anderson, George Jones, and Roy Drusky for most of his own material—though Young did write "Tattle Tale Tears" and "Goin' Steady" by himself. This material also provides a snapshot of a different Nashville, the one that Hank Williams left and was quickly being fazed from existence. These recordings, even the latest of them, are raw, lean, tough; they swing hard, out of the Jimmie Rodgers blues tradition into honky tonk. By the '60s, only Merle Haggard and Hank Thompson were still doing this. The package is deluxe for a single disc, with killer, not often seen photographs and a fine historical and biographical essay by the CMF's Daniel Cooper. If having one great Faron Young collection is your goal, let this one be it. *—Thom Jurek*

The Hits / Mar. 31, 1998 / Mercury ✦✦✦

Mercury Nashville's *The Hits* is an interesting 11-track collection that selects highlights from Faron Young's recordings for Mercury Records between 1963 and 1978. It features several latter-day hits—including "It's Four in the Morning," "Wine Me Up," "If I Ever Fall in Love With a Honky Tonk Girl," "Yellow Bandana," "Your Time's Coming," and "This Little Girl of Mine"—which often don't make hits collections. They don't match his '50s hits, but it's nice to have them available. On the down side, the collection also features remakes of "Sweet Dreams," "I Miss You Already (And You're Not Even Gone)," "Keeping Up With the Jones," and "Live Fast, Love Hard, Die Young." Although these are fine re-recordings, four original singles from this era would have been preferable to the remakes. Still, *The Hits* has its purpose, offering seven hits that may be of interest to curious fans familiar with Young's classic period and wishing to explore his music a little deeper. It's far from a perfect collection, but it's acceptable as a budget-priced disc. *—Stephen Thomas Erlewine*

This Is Faron Young!/Hello Walls / Nov. 3, 1998 / EMI ✦✦✦

This British EMI reissue of two of Faron Young's legendary albums on one disc is a book for Young fans who have only been able to get compilations on CD before now. Between them, *This Is Faron Young!* and *Hello Walls* contain no less than six charting singles. The title track of the latter album and "Live Fast, Love Hard, Die Young" from the previous one are in the annals of the development of the music as prime examples of honky tonk-style country as an art form in and of itself. But also included here are "Goin' Steady," "If You Ain't Lovin' (You Ain't Livin')," "Big Shoes," "Forget the Past," and slew of others that are just as fine. Two weak tracks from *Hello Walls* make this collection a bit more human, but even these cuts are far better than the best work by lesser artists. Young's Hank Williams influence was most pronounced here, and these two albums also reveal that he and Williams developed the "Shreveport sound." This is music that sounds live even though it was made in a studio; it's raw, immediate, and full of an amiable good nature, deep blues feeling, and clever wordplay with buckets of steel guitars and fiddles wrapped around the singer. Awesome. *—Thom Jurek*

★ **The Complete Capitol Hits of Faron Young** / Oct. 17, 2000 / Collectors' Choice Music ✦✦✦✦✦

Collector's Choice has come up with another of their delectable double CDs of essential material by the country legend Faron Young. There are 41 tracks that document the ten years he spent with Capitol. During that time, Young went from being an opening act who recorded minor hits to an international superstar. Virtually all his major—and most secondary-choice—tracks are here, from his first hit, "Goin' Steady," to Tommy Collins' "If You Ain't Lovin' (You Ain't Livin')" to Joe Allison's anthemic "Live Fast, Love Hard, Die Young" to Willie Nelson's "Three Days." Young wrote most of the tracks here, either alone or in collaboration with other performing artists such as Marvin Rainwater ("I Miss You Already") and George Jones ("Let Him Know"). But the most revelatory aspect of Young's single sides for Capitol is their remarkable consistency, not only in quality but in sound, lyrical concerns, arrangement, and presentation. Young created a formula for himself and it worked, yet despite his uniform approach, he always sounded fresh and new. Like Hank Williams, Young's work, as documented here, is not only timeless but sounds right on time. All the passion, pathos, and melancholy of these honky tonk songs informed two—perhaps even three—generations of country music stars, though most would never acknowledge it. If you can only have one Faron Young collection, let this be it. *—Thom Jurek*

20th Century Masters—The Millennium Collection: The Best of Faron Young / Jul. 10, 2001 / Uptown/Universal ✦✦✦✦✦

The 1950s and the early '60s are viewed as the most crucial years of Young's recording career. Since this compilation covers only the years 1964-1972, it might not be fair to categorize these tracks as truly the "best" of Young. Nonetheless, it was certainly a successful period for him commercially, with all dozen of these songs making the country Top Ten, one of them ("It's Four in the Morning") heading all the way to the top. If it's not his best or earthiest material, it's certainly respectable straight country, and, with some exceptions toward the later end of that time scale, not as slickly produced as much country-pop from the era was. Young was also important for getting songs by several top county writers wide exposure, as heard on this disc via his hit interpretations of tunes by Justin Tubb ("Keeping Up With the Joneses," sung with Margie Singleton), Mel Tillis ("Unmitigated Gall"), Kris Kristofferson and Shel Silverstein (who co-wrote "Your Time's Comin'"), Tom T. Hall ("If I Ever Fall in Love (With a Honky-Tonk Girl)"), and Jeannie Seely ("Leavin' and Sayin' Goodbye"). *—Richie Unterberger*

Walk Tall: The Mercury Hit Singles 1963–1975 / Nov. 25, 2002 / Demon/WestSide ✦✦✦✦✦

When Faron Young left Capitol in 1962 after the expiration of his contract, he had, in ten years, racked 41 Top 40 country hits. Beginning in 1963, with a strange knockoff of Marty

Robbins' "El Paso," Young began a run of 39 more hits for Mercury over the next 12 years. In 22 years, Young had scored a total of 80 country hits—all but one in the Top 40. This set of Mercury material may not be as raw and hillbilly as the earlier Capitol stuff, but it does sound a bit more woolly than his final Capitol sides. Countrypolitan was all the rage in the 1960s, and remained so until outlaw music made its mark on the charts in 1974. Young, continuing to write his own songs and record only the choicest by other composers, offered a different voice than his early Hank Williams-inflected one. His baritone was rich and warm and full of sentiment and dreamy texture, as can be heard on "Yellow Bandana," "You'll Drive Me Back (Into Her Arms Again)," "This Little Girl of Mine," and "She Went a Bit Farther," as well as honky tonk stompers such as "Wine Me Up," "It's Four in the Morning," "Keeping Up With the Joneses" with Margie Singleton, "Here I Am in Dallas," and "Your Time's Comin'." Young never completely lost the hard country edge in his sound, despite the layers of strings and backing vocalists. His delivery remained passionate, direct, and soulful. And while this material may not have the raw punch some of the other music did, it has a breadth and depth few country singers with the possible exception of Robbins and Ray Price could get next to, let alone copy. This is an excellent representation of Young's time spent with Mercury, and for novices who are curious, *The Complete Capitol Hits of Faron Young* on Collector's Choice and this 24-track volume will provide virtually everything you will ever need. *—Thom Jurek*

Absolutely the Best / Mar. 25, 2003 / Varese ♦♦♦♦

Judging by the mere track listing, Fuel 2000's 2003 collection *Absolutely the Best* does indeed have many of Faron Young's absolute best songs. That doesn't mean it's the absolute best collection on the market, however—not when there's the Country Music Foundation's superb 24-track collection *Live Fast, Love Hard: Original Capitol Records, 1952-1962* or the even more exhaustive 2000 Collectors Choice release, *The Complete Capitol Hits of Faron Young* (not to mention the Bear Family box *Hello Walls*, which contains all of his Capitol recordings for those really serious fans). These are better than *Absolutely the Best*, which serves up 14 of those classic country hits, as compiled and annotated by Bill Dahl (whose liner notes are typically strong, even though it would have been nice to have separate track information as well). Since the previously mentioned collections are geared more toward collectors, there is a space for this disc, since it offers an expert selection of his biggest and best songs, but if you already know you want a serious, thorough collection, pass this by for either the CMF or Collectors Choice release. If you just want a sampling, this satisfies. *—Stephen Thomas Erlewine*

Neil Young

b. Nov. 12, 1945, Toronto, Ontario, Canada

Guitar, Harmonica, Piano, Songwriter, Vocals, Ukulele / Country-Rock, Singer/Songwriter, Hard Rock, Folk-Rock, Album Rock, Heartland Rock

After Neil Young left the Californian folk-rock band Buffalo Springfield in 1968, he slowly established himself as one of the most influential and idiosyncratic singer/songwriters of his generation. Young's body of work ranks second only to Bob Dylan in terms of depth, and he was able to sustain his critical reputation, as well as record sales, for a longer period of time than Dylan, partially because of his willfully perverse work ethic. From the beginning of his solo career in the late '60s, he never stopped writing, recording, and performing; his official catalog only represented a portion of his work, since he kept countless tapes of unreleased songs in his vaults. Just as importantly, Young continually explored new musical territory, from rockabilly and the blues to electronic music. But these stylistic exercises only gained depth when compared to his two primary styles: gentle folk and country-rock, and crushingly loud electric guitar rock, which he frequently recorded with the Californian garage band Crazy Horse. Throughout his career, Young alternated between these two extremes, and both proved equally influential; there were just as many simpy singer/songwriters as there were grunge and country-rock bands claiming to be influenced by Neil Young. Despite his enormous catalog and influence, Young continued to move forward, writing new songs and exploring new music in his fourth decade as a performing artist. That restless spirit ensured that he was one of the few rock veterans as vital in his old age as he was in his youth.

Born in Toronto, Canada, Neil Young moved to Winnipeg with his mother following her divorce from his sports-journalist father. Young began playing music in high-school. Not only did he play in garage rock outfits like the Esquires, but he also played in local folk clubs and coffeehouses, where he eventually met Joni Mitchell and Stephen Stills. During the mid-'60s, he returned to Toronto, where he played as a solo folk act. By 1966, he joined the Mynah Birds, which also featured bassist Bruce Palmer and Rick James. The group recorded a couple of singles for Motown, which were ignored. Frustrated by his lack of success, Young moved to Los Angeles in his Pontiac hearse, taking Palmer along as support. Shortly after they arrived in L.A., they happened to meet Stills, and they formed Buffalo Springfield, who quickly became one of the leaders of the Californian folk-rock scene. Despite the success of Buffalo Springfield, the group was plagued with tension, and Young quit the band several times before finally leaving to become a solo artist in May of 1968.

Hiring Elliot Roberts as his manager, Young signed with Reprise Records and released his eponymous debut album in early 1969. By the time the album was released, he had begun playing with a local band called the Rockets, which featured guitarist Danny Whitten, bassist Billy Talbot, and drummer Ralph Molina. Young renamed the group Crazy Horse and had them support him on his second album, *Everybody Knows This Is Nowhere*, which was recorded in just two weeks. Featuring such Young staples as "Cinnamon Girl" and "Down By the River," the album went gold. Following the completion of the record, he began jamming with Crosby, Stills & Nash, eventually joining the group for their spring 1970 album, *Deja Vu*. Although he was now part of Crosby, Stills & Nash, Young continued to record as a solo artist, releasing *After the Gold Rush* at the end of the year. *After the Gold Rush*, with its accompanying single "Only Love Can Break Your Heart," established Young as a solo star, and fame only increased through his association with CSN&Y.

Although Crosby, Stills, Nash & Young were a very successful act, they were also volatile, and they had split by the spring 1971 release of the live *Four Way Street*. The following year, Young had his first number one album with the mellow country-rock of *Harvest*, which also featured his first (and only) number one single, "Heart of Gold." Instead of embracing his success, he spurned it, following it with the noisy, bleak live film *Journey Through the Past*. Both the movie and the soundtrack received terrible reviews, as did the live album *Time Fades Away*, a record recorded with the Stray Gators that was released in 1973. Both *Journey through the Past* and *Time Fades Away* signaled that Young was entering a dark period in his life, but they only scratched the surface of his anguish. Inspired by the overdose deaths of Danny Whitten in 1972 and his roadie Bruce Berry the following year, Young wrote and recorded the bleak, druggy *Tonight's the Night* late in 1973, but declined to release it at the time. Instead, he released *On the Beach*, which was nearly as harrowing, in 1974; *Tonight's the Night* finally appeared in the spring of 1975. By the time of its release, Young had recovered, as indicated by the record's hard-rocking follow-up *Zuma*, an album recorded with Crazy Horse and released later that year.

Young's focus began to wander in 1976, as he recorded the duet album *Long May You Run* with Stephen Stills and then abandoned his partner midway through the supporting tour. The following year he recorded the country-rock-oriented *American Stars 'n Bars*, which featured vocals by Nicolette Larson, who was also prominent on 1978's *Comes a Time*. Prior to the release of *Comes a Time*, Young scrapped the country-rock album *Homegrown* and assembled the triple-album retrospective *Decade*. At the end of 1978, he embarked on an arena tour called *Rust Never Sleeps*, which was designed as a showcase for new songs. Half of the concert featured Young solo, the other half featured him with Crazy Horse. That was the pattern that *Rust Never Sleeps*, released in the summer of 1979, followed. The record was hailed as a comeback, proving that Young was one of the few rock veterans who attacked punk rock head-on. That fall he released the double album *Live Rust* and the live movie *Rust Never Sleeps*.

Rust Never Sleeps had restored Young to his past glory, but he perversely decided to trash his goodwill in 1980 with *Hawks & Doves*, a collection of acoustic songs that bore the influence of conservative, right-wing politics. In 1981, Young released the heavy rock album *Re-ac-tor*, which received poor reviews. Following its release, he left Reprise for the fledgling Geffen Records, where he was promised lots of money and artistic freedom. Young decided to push his Geffen contract to the limit, releasing the electronic *Trans*, where his voice was recorded through a computerized vocoder, later that year. The album and its accompanying, technology-dependent tour were received with bewildered, negative reviews. The rockabilly of *Everybody's Rockin'* (1983) was equally scorned, and Young soon settled into a cult audience for the mid-'80s.

Over the course of the mid-'80s, Young released three albums that were all stylistic exercises. In 1985, he released the straight country *Old Ways*, which was followed by the new wave-tinged *Landing on Water* the following year. He returned to Crazy Horse for 1987's *Life*, but by that time, he and Geffen had grown sick of each other, and he returned to Reprise in 1988. His first album for Reprise was the bluesy, horn-driven *This Note's for You*, which was supported by an acclaimed video that satirized rock stars endorsing commercial products. At the end of the year, he recorded a reunion album with Crosby, Stills & Nash called *American Dream*, which was greeted with savagely negative reviews. *American Dream* didn't prepare any observer for the critical and commercial success of 1989's *Freedom*, which found Young following the half-acoustic/half-electric blueprint of *Rust Never Sleeps* to fine results. Around the time of its release, Young became a hip name to drop in indie rock circles, and he was the subject of a tribute record title *The Bridge* in 1989. The following year, Young reunited with Crazy Horse for *Ragged Glory*, a loud, feedback-drenched album that received his strongest reviews since the '70s. For the supporting tour, Young hired the avant-rock band Sonic Youth as his opening group, providing them with needed exposure while earning him hip credibility within alternative rock scenes. On the advice of Sonic Youth, Young added the noise collage EP *Arc* as a bonus to his 1991 live album, *Weld*.

Weld and the Sonic Youth tour helped position Neil Young as an alternative and grunge rock forefather, but he decided to abandon loud music for its 1992 follow-up, *Harvest Moon*. An explicit sequel to his 1972 breakthrough, *Harvest Moon* became Young's biggest hit in years, and he supported the record with an appearance on *MTV Unplugged*, which was released the following year as an album. Also in 1993, Geffen released the rarities collection *Lucky Thirteen*. The following year, he released *Sleeps With Angels*, which was hailed as a masterpiece in some quarters. Following its release, Young began jamming with Pearl Jam, eventually recording an album with the Seattle band in early 1995. The resulting record, *Mirror Ball*, was released to positive reviews in the summer of 1995, but it wasn't the commercial blockbuster it was expected to be; due to legal reasons, Pearl Jam's name was not allowed to be featured on the cover.

In the summer of 1996, he reunited with Crazy Horse for *Broken Arrow* and supported it with a brief tour. That tour was documented in Jim Jarmusch's 1997 film *The Year of the Horse*, which was accompanied by a double-disc live album. In 1999, Young reunited with Crosby, Stills & Nash for the first time in a decade, supporting their *Looking Forward* LP with the supergroup's first tour in a quarter century. A new solo effort, *Silver and Gold*, followed in the spring of 2000. In recognition of his 2000 summer tour, Young released the live album *Road Rock, Vol. 1* the following fall, showcasing a spectacular two night account of Young's performance at the Red Rocks Amphitheater in Morrison, CO, in September 2000. A DVD version titled Red Rocks Live was issued that December, including 12 tracks initially unavailable on *Road Rock, Vol. 1*. *—Stephen Thomas Erlewine*

Neil Young / Jan. 1969 / Reprise ♦♦♦

On his songs for Buffalo Springfield, Neil Young had demonstrated an eclecticism that ranged from the rock of "Mr. Soul" to the complicated, multi-part arrangement of "Broken Arrow." On his debut solo album, he continued to work with composer/arranger Jack Nitzsche, with whom he had made "Expecting to Fly" on the *Buffalo Springfield Again* album, and together the two recorded a restrained effort on which the folk-rock instrumentation, most of which was by Young, overdubbing himself, was augmented by discreet string parts. The country & western elements that had tinged the Springfield's sound were also present, notably on the leadoff track, "The Emperor of Wymoning," an instrumental that recalled the Springfield song "A Child's Claim to Fame." Still unsure of his voice, Young sang in a becalmed high tenor that could be haunting as often as it was listless and whining. He was at his least appealing on the nine-and-a-half-minute closing track, "The Last Trip to Tulsa," on which he accompanied himself with acoustic guitar, singing an impressionistic set of lyrics seemingly derived from Bob Dylan's *Highway 61 Revisited*. But double-tracking and the addition of a female backup chorus improved the singing elsewhere, and on "The Loner," athe album's most memorable track, Young displayed some of the noisy electric guitar work that would characterize his recordings with Crazy Horse and reminded listeners of his ability to turn a phrase. Still, *Neil Young* made for an uneven, low-key introduction to Young's solo career, and when released it was a commercial flop, his only album not to make the charts. [Several months after the album's release, Young remixed it to bring out his vocals more and added some overdubs. This second version replaced the first in the U.S. from then on, though the original mix remained available overseas.] *—William Ruhlmann*

☆ **Everybody Knows This Is Nowhere** / May 1969 / Reprise ✦✦✦✦✦

Neil Young's second solo album, released only four months after his first, was nearly a total rejection of that polished effort. Though a couple of songs, "Round Round (It Won't Be Long)" and "The Losing End (When You're On)," shared that album's country-folk style, they were altogether livelier and more assured. The difference was that, while *Neil Young* was a solo effort, *Everybody Knows* marked the beginning of Young's recording association with Crazy Horse, the trio of Danny Whitten (guitar), Ralph Molina (drums), and Billy Talbot (bass) that Young had drawn from the struggling local Los Angeles group the Rockets. With them, Young quickly cut a set of loose, guitar-heavy rock songs—"Cinnamon Girl," "Down By the River," and "Cowgirl in the Sand"—that redefined him as a rock & roll artist. The songs were deliberately underwritten and sketchy as compositions, their lyrics more suggestive than complete, but that made them useful as frames on which to hang the extended improvisations ("River" and "Cowgirl" were each in the nine-to-ten-minute range) Young played with Crazy Horse and to reflect the ominous tone of his singing. Young lowered his voice from the near-falsetto employed on his debut to a more expressive range, and he sang with greater confidence, accompanied by Whitten and, on "Round Round," by Robin Lane. *Everybody Knows This Is Nowhere* was breathtakingly different when it appeared in May 1969, both for Young and for rock in general, and it reversed his commercial fortunes, becoming a moderate hit. (Young's joining Crosby, Stills & Nash the month after its release didn't hurt his profile, of course.) A year and a half after its release, it became a gold album, and it has since gone platinum. And it set a musical pattern Young and his many musical descendants have followed ever since; almost 30 years later, he was still playing this sort of music with Crazy Horse, and a lot of contemporary bands were playing music clearly influenced by it. *—William Ruhlmann*

☆ **After the Gold Rush** / Aug. 1970 / Reprise ✦✦✦✦✦

In the 15 months between the release of *Everybody Knows This Is Nowhere* and *After the Gold Rush*, Neil Young issued a series of recordings in different styles that could have prepared his listeners for the differences between the two LPs. His two compositions on the Crosby, Stills, Nash & Young album *Déjà Vu*, "Helpless" and "Country Girl," returned him to the folk and country styles he had pursued before delving into the hard rock of *Everybody Knows*; two other singles, "Sugar Mountain" and "Oh, Lonesome Me," also emphasized those roots. But "Ohio," a CSNY single, rocked as hard as anything on the second album. *After the Gold Rush* was recorded with the aid of Nils Lofgren, a 17-year-old unknown whose piano was a major instrument, turning one of the few real rockers, "Southern Man" (which had unsparing protest lyrics typical of Phil Ochs), into a more stately effort than anything on the previous album and giving a classic tone to the title track, a mystical ballad that featured some of Young's most imaginative lyrics and became one of his most memorable songs. But much of *After the Gold Rush* consisted of folk-country love songs, which consolidated the audience Young had earned through his tours and recordings with CSNY; its dark yet hopeful tone matched the tenor of the times in 1970, making it one of the definitive singer/songwriter albums, and it has remained among Young's major achievements. *—William Ruhlmann*

Harvest / Feb. 1972 / Reprise ✦✦✦✦✦

Neil Young's most popular album, *Harvest* employs a number of jarringly different styles. Much of it is country-tinged, although there is also an acoustic track, a couple of electric guitar-drenched rock performances, and two songs on which Young is accompanied by the London Symphony Orchestra. But the album does have an overall mood and an overall lyric content, and they conflict with each other: The mood is melancholic, but the songs mostly describe the longing for and fulfillment of new love. Young's concerns are perhaps most explicit on the controversial "A Man Needs a Maid," which contrasts the fears of committing to a relationship with simply living alone and hiring help. Over and over, he sings of the need for love in such songs as "Out on the Weekend," "Heart of Gold," and "Old Man," and the songs are unusually melodic and accessible; the rock numbers "Are You Ready for the Country" and "Alabama" are in Young's familiar style and unremarkable, and "There's a World" and "Words (Between the Lines of Age)" are ponderous and overdone. But the love songs and the harrowing portrait of a friend's descent into heroin addiction, "The Needle and the Damage Done," remain among Young's most affecting and memorable songs. *—William Ruhlmann*

Journey Through the Past / Nov. 1972 / Reprise ✦✦

Most soundtrack albums don't really contain the soundtracks to movies as they sound and as they are edited for the screen—a song heard in a snippet on a car radio in the film, for example, will be presented in its entirety and with good sound on the album. But the soundtrack to Neil Young's fantasy/documentary *Journey Through the Past* does contain an audio record of what's on screen: songs are cut off or fade out, to be replaced by fragments of something else, and the sound is not improved. So, *Journey Through the Past* doesn't work as well apart from the film as most soundtracks do. But the main problem with it is the same one that the film suffers: it doesn't make much sense. A mixture of TV footage of the Springfield, live footage of Crosby, Stills, Nash & Young, rehearsal footage of the *Harvest* sessions and news footage, it doesn't coalesce into a coherent movie or a coherent record; if some of this material were used as part of a box set, it would have historical value and be interesting to fans, but in this context it was baffling. *—William Ruhlmann*

Time Fades Away / Oct. 1973 / Reprise ✦✦✦✦

In his concerts of the early '70s, the prolific Neil Young frequently played new, unrecorded songs, sometimes for half the show or more. This tendency found its expression on his fifth album, *Time Fades Away*, a live record consisting of previously unreleased songs, most recorded during his national concert tour during the first quarter of 1973. The album also represented the culmination of Young's desire to present his music in as raw a state as possible: not only was it mastered direct to disc from the 16-track tape, but also the performances were anything but polished. The approach was consistent with the unvarnished nature of the songs: *Time Fades Away* was an album by a man who seemed to have lost something and was determinedly trying to regain it. Both its sound and its songs were alien to much of the mass audience Young had gained with "Heart of Gold" and *Harvest*. Ultimately, his escape from the commercial trap into which he had fallen would seem a healthy development in his career, and *Time Fades Away* was the first (mis)step. *—William Ruhlmann*

☆ **On the Beach** / Jul. 1974 / Reprise ✦✦✦✦✦

Following the 1973 *Time Fades Away* tour, Neil Young wrote and recorded an Irish wake of a record called *Tonight's the Night* and went on the road drunkenly playing its songs to uncomprehending listeners and hostile reviewers. Reprise rejected the record, and Young went right back and made *On the Beach*, which shares some of the ragged style of its two predecessors. But where *Time* was embattled and *Tonight* mournful, *On the Beach* was savage and, ultimately, triumphant. "I'm a vampire, babe," Young sang, and he proceeded to take bites out of various subjects: threatening the lives of the stars who lived in L.A.'s Laurel Canyon ("Revolution Blues"); answering back to Lynyrd Skynyrd, whose "Sweet Home Alabama" had taken him to task for his criticisms of the South in "Southern Man" and "Alabama" ("Walk On"); and rejecting the critics ("Ambulance Blues"). But the barbs were mixed with humor and even affection, as Young seemed to be emerging from the grief and self-abuse that had plagued him for two years. But the album was so spare and underproduced, its lyrics so harrowing, that it was easy to miss Young's conclusion: He was saying goodbye to despair, not being overwhelmed by it. *—William Ruhlmann*

☆ **Tonight's the Night** / Jun. 1975 / Reprise ✦✦✦✦✦

Written and recorded in 1973 shortly after the death of roadie Bruce Berry, Neil Young's second close associate to die of a heroin overdose in six months (the first was Crazy Horse guitarist Danny Whitten), *Tonight's the Night* was Young's musical expression of grief, combined with his rejection of the stardom he had achieved in the late '60s and early '70s. The title track, performed twice, was a direct narrative about Berry: "Bruce Berry was a working man/He used to load that Econoline van." Whitten was heard singing "Come on Baby Let's Go Downtown," a live track recorded years earlier. Elsewhere, Young frequently referred to drug use and used phrases that might have described his friends, such as the chorus of "Tired Eyes," "He tried to do his best, but he could not." Performing with the remains of Crazy Horse, bassist Billy Talbot and drummer Ralph Molina, along with Nils Lofgren (guitar and piano) and Ben Keith (steel guitar), Young performed in the ragged manner familiar from *Time Fades Away*—his voice was often hoarse and he strained to reach high notes, while the playing was loose, with mistakes and shifting tempos. But the style worked perfectly for the material, emphasizing the emotional tone of Young's mourning and contrasting with the polished sound of CSNY and *Harvest*, which Young also disparaged. He remained unimpressed with his commercial success, noting in "World on a String," "The world on a string/Doesn't mean anything." In "Roll Another Number," he said he was "a million miles away/From that helicopter day" when he and CSN had played Woodstock. And in "Albuquerque," he said he had been "starvin' to be alone/Independent from the scene that I've known" and spoke of his desire to "find somewhere where they don't care who I am." Songs like "Speakin' Out" and "New Hama" seemed to find some hope in family life, but *Tonight's the Night* did not offer solutions to the personal and professional problems it posed. It was the work of a man trying to turn his torment into art and doing so unflinchingly. Depending on which story you believe, Reprise Records rejected it or Young withdrew it from its scheduled release at the start of 1974 after touring with the material in the U.S. and Europe. In 1975, after a massive CSNY tour, Young at the last minute dumped a newly recorded album and finally put *Tonight's the Night* out instead. Though it did not become one of his bigger commercial successes, the album immediately was recognized as a unique masterpiece by critics, and it has continued to be ranked as one of the greatest rock & roll albums ever made. *—William Ruhlmann*

Zuma / Nov. 1975 / Reprise ✦✦✦✦✦

Having apparently exorcised his demons by releasing the cathartic *Tonight's the Night*, Neil Young returned to his commercial strengths with *Zuma* (named after Zuma Beach in Los Angeles, where he now owned a house). Seven of the album's nine songs were recorded with the reunited Crazy Horse, in which rhythm guitarist Frank Sampedro had replaced the late Danny Whitten, but there were also nods to other popular Young styles in "Pardon My Heart," an acoustic song that would have fit on *Harvest*, his most popular album, and "Through My Sails," retrieved from one of Crosby, Stills, Nash & Young's abortive recording sessions. Young had abandoned the ragged, first-take approach of his previous three albums, but Crazy Horse would never be a polished act, and the music had a lively sound well-suited to the songs, which were some of the most melodic, pop-oriented tunes Young had crafted in years, though they were played with an electric-guitar-drenched rock intensity. The overall theme concerned romantic conflict, with lyrics that lamented lost love and sometimes longed for a return ("Pardon My Heart" even found Young singing, "I don't believe this song"), though the overall conclusion, notably in such catchy songs as "Don't Cry No Tears" and "Lookin' for a Love," was to move on to the next relationship. But the album's standout track (apparently the only holdover from an early intention to present songs with historical subjects) was the seven and half-minute epic "Cortez the Killer," a commentary on the Spanish conqueror of Latin America that served as a platform for Young's most extensive guitar soloing since his work on *Everybody Knows This Is Nowhere*. *—William Ruhlmann*

Long May You Run / Sep. 1976 / Reprise ♦♦♦

Long May You Run is not a Neil Young solo album. It is credited to "The Stills-Young Band," which is to say, Stephen Stills and his band with Young added, and the two divide up the songwriting and lead vocals, five for Young, four for Stills. The pairing, though it proved short-lived and had, in fact, ended before this album was released, must have seemed commercially logical. Like Young, Stills had seen his record sales decline after a successful period following the 1970 breakup of CSNY. So had erstwhile partners David Crosby and Graham Nash, but they had returned to Top Ten, gold-selling status in the fall of 1975 with their *Wind on the Water* duo album. Why couldn't Stills and Young do the same thing? Maybe they could have (and, actually, this was the first gold album for either in two years) if they had made a better record together. Young's songs were pleasant newly written throwaways with the exception of the title track, a trunk song he had written as a tribute to an old car. Stills' compositions seemed more seriously intended, but still were not substantial. The playing, largely handled by the professional session man-types in Stills' band, was far smoother than what one was accustomed to in a Young album. The result was a listenable record, but not a compelling one, and thus well below Young's usual standard and Stills' best. *—William Ruhlmann*

American Stars 'n Bars / Jun. 1977 / Reprise ♦♦♦

Neil Young made a point of listing the recording dates of the songs on *American Stars 'n Bars*; the dates even appeared on the LP labels. They revealed that the songs had been cut at four different sessions dating back to 1974. But even without such documentation, it would have been easy to tell that the album was a stylistic hodgepodge, its first side consisting of country-tinged material featuring steel guitar and fiddle, plus backup vocals from Linda Ronstadt and the then-unknown Nicolette Larson, while the four songs on the second side varied from acoustic solo numbers like "Will to Love" to raging rockers such as "Like a Hurricane." Just as apparent was the album's unevenness: side one consisted of lightweight compositions, while side two had more ambitious ones, with "Will to Love," for example, extending the romantic metaphor of a salmon swimming upsteam across seven minutes. The album's saving grace was "Like a Hurricane," one of Young's classic hard rock songs and guitar workouts, a perennial concert favorite. Without it, *American Stars 'n Bars* would have been one of Young's least memorable albums, and since it turned up the following year on the compilation *Decade*, the LP was rendered inessential. *—William Ruhlmann*

★ **Decade** / Nov. 1977 / Reprise ♦♦♦♦♦

Given the quirkiness of Neil Young's recording career, with its frequent cancellations of releases and last-minute rearrangements of material, it is a relief to report that this two-disc compilation is so conventional and so satisfying. A 35-track selection of the best of Young's work between 1966 and 1976, it includes songs performed by Buffalo Springfield, Crosby, Stills, Nash & Young, and the Stills/Young Band, as well as solo work. In addition to five unreleased songs, *Decade* offers such key tracks as the Springfield's "Mr. Soul," "Broken Arrow," and "I Am a Child"; "Sugar Mountain," a song that had appeared only as a single before; "Cinnamon Girl," "Down By the River," and "Cowgirl in the Sand" from *Everybody Knows This Is Nowhere*; "Southern Man" and the title track from *After the Gold Rush*; and "Old Man" and the chart-topping "Heart of Gold" from *Harvest*. This is the material that built Young's reputation between 1966 and 1972, although he is more idiosyncratic with the later material, including the blockbusters "Like a Hurricane" and "Cortez the Killer" but mixing in more unreleased recordings as the set draws to a close. He seems intent on making the album a listenable one that will appeal to a broad base of fans, and he succeeds despite the exclusion of much of the harrowing work of 1973-1975. Nevertheless, the album is an ideal sampler for new listeners, and since there is no one-disc Young compilation covering any significant portion of his career, this lengthy chronicle is the place to start. *—William Ruhlmann*

Comes a Time / Oct. 1978 / Reprise ♦♦♦♦♦

Six and a half years later, *Comes a Time* finally was the Neil Young album for the millions of fans who had loved *Harvest*, an acoustic-based record with country overtones and romantic, autobiographical lyrics, and many of those fans returned to the fold, enough to make *Comes a Time* Young's first Top Ten album since *Harvest*. He signaled the album's direction with the leadoff track, "Goin' Back," and its retrospective theme augmented with an orchestral backup and the deliberate beat familiar from his number-one hit "Heart of Gold." Of course, Young remained sly about this retrenchment. "I feel like goin' back," he sang, but added, "Back where there's nowhere to stay." Doubtless he had no intention of staying with this style, but, for the length of the album, melodies, love lyrics, lush arrangements, and steel guitar solos dominated, and Young's vocals were made more accessible by being paired with Nicolette Larson's harmonies. Larson's own version of Young's "Lotta Love," released shortly after the one heard here, became a Top Ten hit single. Other highlights included the reflective "Already One," which treats the unusual subject of the nature of a divorced family, the ironic "Field of Opportunity," and a cover of Ian Tyson's folk standard "Four Strong Winds" (a country Top Ten hit for Bobby Bare in 1965). *—William Ruhlmann*

☆ **Rust Never Sleeps** / Jul. 1979 / Reprise ♦♦♦♦♦

Rust Never Sleeps, its aphoristic title drawn from an intended advertising slogan, was an album of new songs, some of them recorded on Neil Young's 1978 concert tour. His strongest collection since *Tonight's the Night*, its obvious antecedent was Bob Dylan's *Bringing It All Back Home*, and, as Dylan did, Young divided his record into acoustic and electric sides while filling his songs with wildly imaginative imagery. The leadoff track, "My My, Hey Hey (Out of the Blue)" (repeated in an electric version at album's end as "Hey Hey, My My (Into the Black)" with slightly altered lyrics), is the most concise and knowing description of the entertainment industry ever written; it was followed by "Thrasher," which describes Young's parallel artistic quest in an extended metaphor that also reflected the album's overall theme—the inevitability of deterioration and the challenge of overcoming it. Young then spent the rest of the album demonstrating that his chief weapons against rusting were his imagination and his daring, creating an archetypal album that encapsulated his many styles on a single disc with great songs—in particular the remarkable "Powderfinger"—unlike any he had written before. *—William Ruhlmann*

Live Rust / Nov. 1979 / Reprise ♦♦♦♦♦

Hawks & Doves / Nov. 1980 / Reprise ♦♦♦

Re-ac-tor / Nov. 1981 / Reprise ♦♦

Trans / Jan. 1983 / Geffen ♦♦

Everybody's Rockin' / Aug. 1983 / Geffen ♦♦

By following the hi-tech *Trans* after only seven months with a rockabilly album, Neil Young baffled his audience. Just as he had followed the sales peak of *Harvest* in 1972 with a series of challenging, uncommercial albums, Young had now dissipated the commercial and critical acceptance he had enjoyed with 1979's *Rust Never Sleeps* with a series of mediocre albums and inexplicable genre exercises. *Everybody's Rockin'*, credited to "Neil and the Shocking Pinks," represented the nadir of this attempted career suicide. Running less than 25 minutes, it found Young covering early rock evergreens like "Betty Lou's Got a New Pair of Shoes" and writing a few songs in the same vein ("Kinda Fonda Wanda"). If he had presented this as a mini-album at a discount price, it would have been easier to enjoy the joke Young seemed to intend. As it was, fans who already had their doubts about Young dropped off the radar screen; *Everybody's Rocking* was his lowest-charting album since his 1969 solo debut, and he didn't release another album for two years (his longest break ever between records). *—William Ruhlmann*

Old Ways / Aug. 1985 / Geffen ♦♦♦

In 1984, Geffen Records sued Neil Young on the grounds that he had submitted uncharacteristic, uncommercial records to the label. By the time a settlement had been reached, Young had been on the road with a country band called the International Harvesters for over a year and recorded a revamped version of *Old Ways*, a 1982 recording originally rejected by Geffen which was cut in the style of *Harvest* and *Comes a Time*, but with a stronger country leaning. Young depends heavily on friends, especially for vocals—Waylon Jennings sings harmony on six out of the ten tracks, and one of the others is a duet with Willie Nelson. Though populated by cowboys and country references, Young's take on the genre is typically idiosyncratic, including a reworked version of his autobiography in "Get Back to the Country," a cover of the 1956 Gogi Grant hit "Wayward Wind," and the uncategorizable "Misfits," which portrays astronauts watching Muhammad Ali fights on television in space. *Old Ways* is not a great Neil Young album and at the time of its release served to alienate him even further from his audience, but it has its moments.*—William Ruhlmann*

Landing on Water / Jul. 1986 / Geffen ♦♦

Life / Jul. 1987 / Geffen ♦♦♦

This Note's for You / Apr. 1988 / Reprise ♦♦♦

Eldorado / 1989 / Reprise ♦♦♦

Freedom / Oct. 1989 / Reprise ♦♦♦♦♦

Neil Young is famous for scrapping completed albums and substituting hastily recorded ones in radically different styles. *Freedom*, which was a major critical and commercial comeback after a decade that had confused reviewers and fans, seemed to be a selection of the best tracks from several different unissued Young projects. First and foremost was a hard-rock album like the material heard on Young's recent EP *Eldorado* (released only in the Far East), several of whose tracks were repeated on *Freedom*. On these songs—especially "Don't Cry," awhich sounded like a song about divorce, and a cover of the old Drifters hit "On Broadway" that he concluded by raving about crack-Young played distorted electric guitar over a rhythm section in an even more raucous fashion than that heard on his Crazy Horse records. Second was a follow-up to Young's previous album, *This Note's For You*, which had featured a six-piece horn section. They were back on "Crime in the City" and "Someday," though these lengthy songs, each of which contained a series of seemingly unrelated, mood-setting verses, were more reminiscent of songs like Bob Dylan's "All Along the Watchtower" than of the soul standards that inspired the earlier album. Third, there were tracks that harked back to acoustic-based, country-tinged albums like *Harvest* and *Comes a Time*, including "Hangin' on a Limb" and "The Ways of Love," two songs on which Young duetted with Linda Ronstadt. There was even a trunk (or, more precisely, a drunk) song, "Too Far Gone," which dated from Young's inebriated *Stars 'n Bars* period in the '70s. While one might argue that this variety meant few Young fans would be completely pleased with the album, what made it all work was that Young had once again written a great bunch of songs. The romantic numbers were carefully and sincerely written. The long imagistic songs were evocative without being obvious. And bookending the album were acoustic and electric versions of one of Young's great anthems, "Rockin' in the Free World," a song that went a long way toward restoring his political reputation (which had been badly damaged when he praised President Reagan's foreign policy) by taking on hopelessness with a sense of moral outrage and explicitly condemning President Bush's domestic policy. *Freedom* was the album Neil Young fans knew he was capable of making, but feared he would never make again. *—William Ruhlmann*

Ragged Glory / Oct. 11, 1990 / Reprise ✦✦✦✦✦

Weld / Oct. 1991 / Reprise ✦✦✦✦✦

Harvest Moon / Oct. 27, 1992 / Reprise ✦✦✦

The year of the 20th anniversary of the release of his most popular album, *Harvest*, Neil Young released a new album that harked back to that recording, employing many of the same musicians, again dubbed the Stray Gators, as well as arranger Jack Nitzsche and background singers Linda Ronstadt and James Taylor. He also used a similar folk-country acoustic style and sang songs that often had a personal, confessional tone. But the similarities were more of form than of content because, while *Harvest* was the statement of a confused, if earnest, 26-year-old, *Harvest Moon* embodied the ruminations of a somewhat regretful 46-year-old. Indeed, the greatest comparison to be made between the two records was that Young tried to use the passage of time as a confirmation of continuity. In the first several songs, he seemed to be trying to reconcile with his wife and revive their love, though he was uncertain that was possible. In "One of These Days," he regretted the loss of friendships over the years. "War of Man" and the long and ponderous "Natural Beauty" concerned environmental preservation, and even the rollicking banjo tune "Old King" was a lament for the death of a faithful dog. "I never tried to burn any bridges," sang an artist whose contradictory instincts to move on and to return found him, by the time of his 27th solo album, trying to get back to the feel of his fourth. If the attempt was not completely successful, nevertheless it was well and honestly made, and Young wasn't alone in his desire. As Hollywood has long-since learned, sequels have a built-in audience, and *Harvest Moon* became Young's best-selling album in 13 years. *—William Ruhlmann*

Lucky Thirteen / Jan. 5, 1993 / Geffen ✦✦✦

Unplugged / Jun. 15, 1993 / Reprise ✦✦✦✦✦

The virtue of the "unplugged" concept pioneered by MTV was that it provided a forum for rock musicians to re-interpret their work without using rock's favorite instrument, the electric guitar. But by 1993, the *Unplugged* sessions were serving as another way of creating product without coming up with anything really new, thus joining live albums, greatest hits albums, and covers albums. Neil Young, who has always alternated between rock and folk approaches to his music anyway, would not seem like an ideal candidate for an "unplugged" session, but in a few of the 14 selections in this 65-and-a-half-minute recording, he did give his audience new ways to listen to his repertoire. Particularly notable were a pump-organ and harmonica arrangement of his guitar rock classic "Like a Hurricane" and an acoustic guitar rendition of his Buffalo Springfield hit "Mr. Soul." For the most part, however, Young's *Unplugged* was simply an acoustic live album drawn from a show that was part of his *Harvest Moon* promotional tour. Songs like "Pocahontas" and "The Needle and the Damage Done" had been in his acoustic set lists for years, played exactly as they were here. While Young ranged across his career, picking songs from as far back as 1967 and including three *Harvest Moon* songs, the set did not function as a live acoustic greatest hits selection since favorites like "Heart of Gold" and "Old Man" were missing. The choices seemed nearly arbitrary: Popular songs like "Helpless" (first heard on the 1970 Crosby, Stills, Nash & Young album *Déjà Vu*) shared space with relatively obscure album tracks like "World on a String" (from *Tonight's the Night*) and the never-before released 20-year-old song "Stringman." It may be that a random selection of 14 Neil Young songs gives as accurate a representation of his work as a more carefully compiled one would, but it does not show Young off at his best. *Unplugged* is an enjoyable record that with greater care in arrangement, performance, and song selection could have been considerably better. *—William Ruhlmann*

Sleeps With Angels / Aug. 16, 1994 / Reprise ✦✦✦✦

Mirror Ball / Jun. 27, 1995 / Reprise ✦✦✦

Dead Man / Feb. 27, 1996 / Vapor ✦✦

Broken Arrow / Jul. 2, 1996 / Reprise ✦✦✦

Year of the Horse / Jun. 17, 1997 / Reprise ✦✦✦

Silver & Gold / Apr. 25, 2000 / Reprise ✦✦✦

Silver & Gold went through a number of incarnations before it was finally released in the spring of 2000. The endless delays raised hopes for the album, as did superstition—dedicated Neil Young fans believed he was creatively reborn at the end of each decade. *Everybody Knows This is Nowhere*, *Rust Never Sleeps*, and *Freedom* added credence to this theory, but those records were knocked out quickly, appearing a year after their predecessors. In contrast, *Silver & Gold* appeared four years after *Broken Arrow*. During those four years, all sorts of projects were in the works for Neil, including a 1999 reunion with Crosby, Stills & Nash. Young's three songs on their comeback *Looking Forward* were pleasant acoustic numbers that often seemed a little slight. It was easy to assume that Young was saving the real treasures for his solo record, but *Silver & Gold* doesn't confirm that theory. Instead, it's a continuation of his *Looking Forward* contributions, performed with the warm, amiable ramble of *Harvest Moon*. A pleasant sound, to be sure, but not exactly what Young followers were expecting. They also may be a little dismayed to realize that two of its best songs, "Silver & Gold" and "Razor Love," date from 1982 and 1987, respectively, suggesting that Neil may not be at the top of his game. Still, there are no truly bad songs here, although the light-hearted, light-headed reminiscence "Buffalo Springfield Again" treads close to the borderline. It's a low-key, charming, *comfortable* record, which is hardly a bad thing at all—it just doesn't quite live up to the abnormally high expectations. Fortunately, those expectations fade upon repeated plays, and *Silver & Gold* reveals itself as a nice Neil Young record. Nothing particularly special, but nice all the same. *—Stephen Thomas Erlewine*

Road Rock, Vol. 1: Friends & Relatives / Nov. 21, 2000 / Reprise ✦✦✦

Are You Passionate? / Mar. 26, 2002 / Reprise ✦✦

Steve Young

b. Jul. 12, 1942, Newnan, GA

Guitar, Vocals / Country-Rock, Singer/Songwriter, Alternative Country, Progressive Country, Outlaw Country, Alternative Country-Rock, Americana, Roots Rock, Rock & Roll, Folk-Rock, Honky Tonk, Country-Folk

A singer, tunesmith, and purveyor of what he dubbed "Southern music"—a brew of country, folk, rock, blues, gospel, and Celtic styles—Steve Young was a songwriter's songwriter, an acclaimed performer whose work found its greatest commercial success in the hands of other artists and earned him praise from the likes of Waylon Jennings, Townes Van Zandt, and Lucinda Williams. Born in Georgia and raised throughout the South, by his teens Young was already playing guitar and writing his own songs. In the early '60s, he moved to New York City and became affiliated with the burgeoning Greenwich Village folk music scene. After a brief return to Alabama, where he'd spent time growing up, he settled in California in 1964.

On the West Coast, Young found work as a postal carrier while striking up friendships with the likes of Stephen Stills and Van Dyke Parks. A tenure with the psychedelic folk unit Stone Country yielded an eponymous 1968 LP, and a year later, Young issued his solo debut *Rock Salt & Nails*, a country-rock excursion featuring cameos by Gram Parsons, Chris Hillman, and Gene Clark. He moved to Reprise in 1971, and with the title track of that year's *Seven Bridges Road*, he offered perhaps his best-known composition, popularized through a series of covers by artists like the Eagles, Joan Baez, Rita Coolidge, and Ian Matthews. He had another tremendous success when Waylon Jennings covered "Lonesome, On'ry and Mean" in 1973, turning it into a signature anthem of the outlaw country movement; later on, Hank Williams Jr. notched a hit with "Montgomery in the Rain." As for his recording career, Young released 1975's *Honky Tonk Man* on the tiny Mountain Railroad label before his songwriting success earned him a shot with RCA. The result was two excellent albums, 1976's *Renegade Picker* and 1978's *No Place to Fall*.

Despite his success as a songwriter, Young flirted with the charts but never rose beyond a devoted cult following. He spent the majority of the 1980s touring the world, garnering a reputation as a standout live performer, and released occasional records like 1982's *To Satisfy You*, 1987's *Look Homeward Angel*, and 1990's *Long Time Rider*, the latter two of which were recorded in the Netherlands. The trend continued into the next decade, and in 1991 he issued his first concert recording, *Solo/Live*, an acoustic collection summarizing his career to date along with pop and soul covers like "You Don't Miss Your Water" and "Drift Away." A second LP on Watermelon, *Switchblades of Love*, followed two years later and continued his creative renaissance, but he fell silent for much of the rest of the '90s. In early 2000, he finally returned with *Primal Young* on the Appleseed label. *—Jason Ankeny & Steve Huey*

Rock Salt & Nails / 1969 / Canyon ✦✦✦✦

Rock Salt & Nails is a highly regarded cult country-rock-folk record, in part because some of the supporting musicians are highly regarded pioneers of the form; Gram Parsons, Chris Hillman, and Gene Clark all appear on the album. While it is not among the very best of such late-'60s hybrids, it is pretty good, though too low-key to command the kind of wide interest (by cult standards, anyway) that someone like Clark or Parsons did. Young has an unusually convincing reedy voice, never overdoing the melodramatics, yet establishing a dramatic atmosphere that admits hints of blues, soul, and swamp pop. When distant, mournful strings are added to his more anguished and somber songs, like "7 Bridges Road," "Holler in the Swamp," and "Kenny's Song," there's an effective multi-dimensionality rare in early country-rock. Other songs, particularly the covers of old country tunes, are less striking. It's an interesting release, though, that's quite rewarding for fans of more adventurous country-rock fusions. *—Richie Unterberger*

Seven Bridges Road / 1972 / Rounder ✦✦✦✦✦

The Blue Canyon-label issue of Steve Young's classic *Seven Bridges Road* is actually a reissue of the Reprise version, which appeared two years earlier in 1971. Young bought the rights to the album and got it back into the public after Reprise unwisely deleted it. It has also been reissued by Rounder. What distinguishes the album—a follow-up to the well-received A&M album *Rock Salt & Nails*—is the appearance of Young's signature tunes: the title track; "Lonesome, On'ry & Mean," which was a smash for Waylon Jennings as an outlaw anthem and established Young as a songwriter for many other country stars; and the melodic jeremiad "Montgomery in the Rain." *Seven Bridges Road* is also the most purely "country" record Young ever issued. There is no rock & roll on this set, and there aren't any folk songs either. It's pretty much a honky tonk record in the Merle Haggard vein, with a voice equally influenced by the West Coast folk-rock sound. Nashville's session cats—including Pete Drake on pedal steel, fiddle ace Buddy Spicher, harmonica player Charlie McCoy, Elvis sideman D. J. Fontana, producer and pianist David Briggs, and more than a dozen others—contributed to the album. All but three tracks were written or co-written by Young; of the covers, his read of Haggard's "I Can't Hold Myself in Line" is a stunner. On the humorous side, "The White Trash Song"—performed with the Last Mile Ramblers—is a stomping electric bluegrass number that hints at the more rockist direction Young would be heading in on future recordings. But it is on the three bona fide classics that we encounter a fully developed Young, not only as a songwriter, but as a singer. In particular, "Seven Bridges Road" and "Montgomery in the Rain" offer a writer who has taken everyone from Thomas Wolfe to Hank Williams and turned them into something completely his own: prosaic, profound, and scathingly original. No matter which version you end up with, just end up with one; this is a bona fide masterpiece. *—Thom Jurek*

Honky Tonk Man / 1975 / Rounder ✦✦✦✦

The year, 1975, marked the return to the recording scene for Steve Young. *Honky Tonk Man*, released on Wisconsin's tiny Mountain Railroad Records, was his first recording since *Seven Bridges Road* in 1971 (which had been reissued in 1973). This is the most straight-up country record Young ever cut. He handles both lead and rhythm guitar chores with a band of fine session players, including Kamau Gravatt, who did double duty with Weather Report. Other than redos of Utah Phillips' "Rock Salt & Nails" and his own "White Trash Song," Young sticks somewhat close to the canon of classic country with a few surprises—at least on side one; side two is mostly his own material. The deep blues read of Bob Wills' "Brain Cloudy Blues" is radical and as far from Western swing as it gets, but it also showcases Wills' own roots in the blues. The title cut is a version of the Johnny Horton classic with swinging fiddles by Craig Ruble and Cal Hand's warbling pedal steel kept in line by Bill Petersen's electric bass. Young's vocal is a reedy baritone that gets to the heart of matter—that this is a drinking playboy's anthem. Side one eclipses with a high, lonesome take on Hank Williams' "Ramblin' Man" that is as cur-dog low as it is restless and a cover of Robbie Robertson's "The Night They Drove Old Dixie Down." Young's version is pastoral and slow; it's as mournful as a funeral song and comes across as a folk elegy for the Deep South at the end of the Civil War. Side two is marked by Young's own stunner, "We've Been Together on This Earth Before," "Vision of a Child," and two live cuts done with Doc Watson of the traditional "Sally Goodin'" and the spooky country of "Travelin' Kind." Like *Seven Bridges Road*, *Honky Tonk Man* is a fine outing from Young, though it is hampered a bit by somewhat shoddy recording. But the material and his performance of it are top-notch. [The remastered CD greatly improves the sonics and is worth the extra money the import costs.] *—Thom Jurek*

Renegade Picker / 1976 / RCA ✦✦✦✦

Renegade Picker, issued in 1976, is the first of a pair recorded for RCA—to date, Young's last major-label deal. *Renegade Picker* and its compatriot, *No Place to Fall*, issued two years later, are stellar examples of outlaw country at its best. Equal parts country, rock, blues, and gospel, the album is stocked like a trout pond with awesome songs. Young is his own best coach when it comes to recording material other than his own, and here he grabs the best. The title track is a stomping, choogling, cut-time anthem with Buddy Emmons' pedal steel and the popping electrics of Jerry Chock and Dale Sellers. As if to answer the question as to where the new hard-driving sound came from, Young follows it up with a moving cover of Merle Haggard's "I Can't Be Myself," a slow and deliberate honky tonk number full of restless country-soul. Side one's highlight is a rollicking version of J.D. Loudermilk's "Tobacco Road" driven by bluesed-out acoustic guitars, stomping feet, and Terry McMillan's harmonica. If side one is a primer on Young's country heritage and outlaw lineage, side two is his statement of purpose. The first cut is a re-recording of "Lonesome, On'ry and Mean," with a full-on band burning at the edges of his vocal. Buddy Emmons' steel drives the entire track just atop the drums. But it's Young's version of Guy Clark's "Broken Hearted People (Take Me to a Barroom)" with Tracy Nelson's backing vocals that brings the essence of the fissure between the tradition and new breed home. His reading of the song is more country than Clark's folky one, but Young can hear Hank Williams and Billy Joe Shaver in Clark's lyric; he holds the tension between the two inside the grain of his voice. [*Renegade Picker* and *No Place to Fall* have been reissued as a double-CD package on BMG in Europe, completely remastered for a budget price. No matter how you get these records, just get them. They sound as relevant as they did 25 years ago.] *—Thom Jurek*

No Place to Fall / 1978 / RCA ✦✦✦✦

Issued in 1978, *No Place to Fall* is, regrettably, the second and last album for RCA. Like its predecessor, *Renegade Picker*, Young's ever-evolving music is centered in the heart of outlaw country this time out, though there are, as usual, interesting twists and turns. The band is stellar, with Buddy Emmons and Buddy Spicher, Tracy Nelson, Jerry Shook, Dale Sellers, and a bunch of guitar pickers, as well as drummer Kenny Malone, among others. The material is noteworthy on many levels, not the least of which is Young's decision to record, for the third time, "Montgomery in the Rain" and "Seven Bridges Road." Once more, he reinvents both songs, fills them out, adds different textures and stresses, and as a result, in the grain of his voice the meanings widen and deepen. The title track was written by the late Townes Van Zandt, and Young's read is damn near definitive, with layers of guitars haunting the middle of the tune and his own voice carrying the lonely edge of Van Zandt's lyric into oblivion. In addition, Young delves deep into Okie blues with a barbed-wire-and-whiskey cover of J. J. Cale's "Same Old Blues," with stunning slide guitar work. But it is in the cover of Mentor Williams' composition "Drift Away"—the multi-million-seller recorded by Dobie Gray—that Young offers his greatest surprise. This is a soul song, performed by a soul singer originally, and here Young, while keeping the song's intent essentially the same, transforms it into a country prayer. The same can be said for his loose cover of Dylan's "Don't Think Twice It's Alright"; Young reworks the melody slightly while emphasizing different parts of the lyric as the band fills in the cracks to bring an entirely new light to the song. *No Place to Fall* failed ultimately to sell, but it did a great deal to bolster his confidence as both a bandleader and as a producer. Young is a survivor, albeit on the fringes; he is one of the few whose records are so consistent as to be essential listening for anyone interested in late 20th century country music and rock & roll. *—Thom Jurek*

To Satisfy You / 1981 / Rounder ✦✦✦

To Satisfy You is one of Steve Young's most curious recordings. Well-known as a songwriter's songwriter, there is only one original on the set ("The River and the Swan") and it's the last track on the album. In addition, for those who view Young—mistakenly—as a country artist, his cover of Buddy Holly's "Think It Over" that opens the disc will be a rude awakening. It rocks, rolls, slips, and strolls with Young digging into his blues voice for the heart of the lyric. It isn't cute; it's razor-wire sharp and brutal. His funky version of Waylon Jennings' "To Satisfy You," with its Mack Truck slide guitars, must have done Waylon proud. This is rock & roll that Ronnie VanZandt from Lynyrd Skynyrd would be proud of, given that Young is from Alabama. Walter Vinson's "Top of the World" is offered in a similar funky treatment before Young turns the Jagger/Richards nugget "No Expectations" into an outlaw country-rock anthem before finishing the side with Dave Olney's amazing tome "The Contender." The whole song is in overdrive; it's Jerry Lee Lewis meets Bob Dylan & the Band live. "Corrina Corrina" is given a fairly faithful treatment, though it's bright in the same way that latter-day outlaw country music is bright. There's plenty of swing and guts, but there's polish too. Jesse Winchester's "All Your Stories" is given a faithful low-key treatment, and Young makes the song his own. The biggest surprise here is the cover of Cat Stevens' "Wild World," completely reinvented from the ground up with ringing guitar solos bringing in the vocal a full two choruses in. The melody is close, but the tempo is up; the twin leads transform it into an indictment instead of a romantic swan song. W. T. Davidson's "They Call It Love" is too saturated in reverb to be very effective, despite the fact that it's a quality blues song. Finally, Young's own tune is a haunting love song of contradiction and epic proportion as seen through the eyes of the personal. It's a beautiful example of a love song that considers love for the sake of the other rather than as self-fulfillment. Young's voice is strong, ringing deep and wide, with the musical backing painting it for effect. A fine, if confounding, effort, *To Satisfy You* is one that Young's fans will embrace readily, but does not serve as an introduction to newcomers. *—Thom Jurek*

Seven Bridges Road / 1981 / Rounder ✦✦✦

Steve Young's career has been nothing if not confusing. This 1981 version of his classic *Seven Bridges Road* album (which was cut for and "secretly released" by Reprise in 1971 and then reissued on the independent Blue Canyon) is an interesting reissue on CD—as much as for what it does not do as for what it does. When Rounder put out *Seven Bridges Road*, they asked Young to recut the title track, which he did, and the version is a fine one, if not definitive. Subsequently, they used five more tracks from the original sessions—"Montgomery in the Rain," "Long Way to Hollywood," "My Oklahoma," "Ragtime Blue Guitar," and "Lonesome, On'ry and Mean." Rather than do a straight reissue, they added other tracks from those sessions that had never before been released: a killer version of Bob Dylan's "Down in the Flood" with a major-league slide solo by Ry Cooder, another Dylan tune done as only Young can perform it: "Days of '49" (meaning, yes, Dylan should just give him the song). A musical version of Steven Vincent Benet's "Ballad of William Sycamore" and Terry Gilkyson's "Wild Goose." These songs were left off the original for God knows what reason other than space perhaps or because publishing royalties would have been too expensive. What is so confounding, however, is that given the extended length of CDs and Rounder's sizable budget—no matter what they would have you believe—why didn't they just remaster the entire original album, with both versions of the title track, and re-add what they took out? Along with their dodgy artist contracts, this is what makes Rounder such a pain in the ass as a record company—laziness. If CD is your thing, this is the only way you can get the album. If you still possess a turntable, the original—which holds up far better as an album—can be found by rummaging auction and used websites online and hunting through the bins at used record stores. For Young fanatics like this one, both are necessary. *—Thom Jurek*

Old Memories / 1984 / Country Roads ✦✦✦

Look Homeward Angel / 1987 / Mill ✦✦✦✦

The late '80s saw Steve Young spending a lot of time in the Netherlands, recording and releasing two of his most enigmatic (and deeply satisfying) albums, *Long Time Rider* and this one. *Look Homeward Angel* was recorded with famed guitarist Jonas Fjeld, who along with Young produced the album. It features some of the songwriter's most poignant and rollicking material. From the opener, "Lonely Boy," where the shimmer of acoustic guitars are underscored by the atmospheric synthesizer work of Kjetil Bjornstadt and the ringing electric six strings of Fjeld and Brent Bnelesson, it tells a tale of hard-won maturity and acceptance of life for what it is while yearning all the same. "Ridin' Down the Highway" is Southern rock at its best; kicking the Waylon Jennings one-two, one-two rhythm to accompany a road-weary musician's testimony—"I've been cut by that old cocaine, boys/I've been cut by that old alcohol/I've been cut by some pretty women/But the deepest cut of all/Is ridin' down the highways/Goin' to do another show"—the glissandi synths usher in David Olney's gorgeous "If My Eyes Were Blind." Bjornstadt understands the commitment in this love song and he frames it rather than carries Young's sang lines. Cut-time rhythm shuffles through easily, allowing the lyric all of its power and majesty. Three roots rockers bordering on honky tonk, rockabilly, and straight-up '50s swagger follow the opening trilogy before the most powerful of love songs commences: Jubal Young's song written for Steve, his father, about his childhood as an itinerant songwriter and rambler's son. Young's own courage in even performing it is remarkable, but the performance is devastating in its searing honesty and raw acceptance amid the rings of acoustic and electric guitars accompanied by a hypnotic rhythm track: "Broken hearts will pass away/Love will find another way/Broken hearts will pass away, I know." The final track, the title, influenced by Young's own life and Thomas Wolfe's novel of the same name, is a hopeful song about dying and what death means in how people live in this moment. Lilting guitar lines, floating synths, and slow, spare lyrics underline Young's narrative obsession in trying to tell the truth about his own life, about what he sees and what he feels about death and what comes after. What a finish. It's like hearing a future Buddha sing. Like *Long Time Rider* and *Switchblades of Love*, *Look Homeward Angel* is simply far ahead of its time. *—Thom Jurek*

Long Time Rider / 1990 / Voodoo ✦✦✦✦✦

Along with *Look Homeward Angel*, *Long Time Rider* is Steve Young's most obscure and difficult-to-come-by recording. It is also one of the most lyrically adventurous, intimate, and musically minimal and moving albums he's ever committed to tape. Issued in 1990, this is a eight-cut, 45-minute album that deals with acceptance, willingness, and determination to forgive others and yourself, and ultimately to find compassion. While this may seem unlikely territory for one of American music's true outlaws, it is at least as "real" as the inner landscape of the man who wrote "Lonesome, On'ry and Mean" decades ago. A new age cowboy Young is not. "Behold the Stars" is a gorgeous acoustic guitar ballad that looks deeply into eternity as an expression of the moment: "Behold the stars/See how they haunt/The dreams we have behind these bars...." And then there's the devastatingly beautiful "War of Ancient Days," where the song's protagonist goes back to his former wife and adversary and commits to throwing down his sword: "I didn't come here to see who gets the best deal/You can have the stuff I will survive/But I came here to wage war on the poverty/That I see in our eyes/And I'm here to pay the tallest price/For now I'm willing to change my ways/And I'm here to lay the wreath of peace at your feet/And end this war of ancient days." "Have a Laugh" and "My Love" were later recut for the album *Switchblades of Love*, and these versions are significantly different. Virtually every cut here is an exhortation to inferiority, self-examination, letting go, and expressing the release of that baggage as a real life, hard-won kindness. "Only You" is a song Bruce Springsteen wishes he could have written. It has a loping rock & roll melody directness and an arrangement that makes Young's words come off as love for another accepted as a truth reborn everyday. The album ends with the title track, a blues disguised as a gospel song. Young offers recounts of his alcoholism, his surrender, and his new beginning full of weariness and gratitude. He expresses his willingness to sing for the others who "can't get no lower and they can't get no higher," and a vow to be a "Long Time Rider" if that is what his heart in response to the universe so requests. There are too few recordings that get to this depth, with this kind of attention to detail and honesty. It's simply a masterpiece of ravage and rebirth. — *Thom Jurek*

Solo/Live / Mar. 1991 / Watermelon ✦✦✦✦✦

In all likelihood, there will never be a Steve Young greatest-hits collection—all of his chart success has come courtesy of other artists' renditions of his material. In any case, at least there's *Solo/Live*, an intimate acoustic collection which serves as a fine overview of Young's career as well as a good introduction to his talents. Recorded in 1990 at Houston's Anderson Fair, the record includes most of his best-loved songs, including "Seven Bridges Road," "Montgomery in the Rain," and "Long Way to Hollywood." In addition, there are covers of "You Don't Miss Your Water," "Tobacco Road" and "Drift Away," as well as the traditional sea chanty "Go to Sea No More." — *Jason Ankeny*

Switchblades of Love / 1993 / Watermelon ✦✦✦✦✦

Steve Young's records are always exercises in paradox and *Switchblades of Love* is no exception; perhaps it creates the rule. This album—with a stellar cast that includes Benmont Tench, Katy Moffatt, Steven Soles, Van Dyke Parks, David Miner, and David Kemper, as well as Young's guitar-slinging son, Jubal—is the most realized and perfectly executed record of his career. Its songs are about confrontation with the falsehood of self; mortality and how it cycles into the eternal; and responsibility, love, and violence—oftentimes these themes collide within the same song, poetically, spiritually, and above all, humanly. There are few albums that kick into gear with the intensity that this one does. "Have a Laugh" is a mariachi-tinged folk song with an irresistible melody that philosophically spells out the importance of loving/exhibiting kindness toward ourselves by watching our minds and keeping a sense of humor about us at all times. Immediately after, he launches into the title track, a confrontation with the horrors and blessings we commit and give freely in the name of love. Young sends the song out to both victims and perpetrators as well as lovers, and ultimately turns the responsibility for change upon himself: "Me I think I'm gonna go out and put my switchblades down/Way on down in the ground/No applause, there won't be a sound/Just a rusty spade down in that honest

earth/I will bow down to the stars/And ask forgiveness for the scars/That I have made/In the name of love." With Jubal's razor-wire soloing (this kid smokes) scorching the body of the tune, this isn't merely a hymn of atonement, it is a prophetic anthem of the human condition. Other standouts include "Angel of Lyon," a song about a man who gives up everything to follow a vision and regrets nothing, despite the fact that he gives up his life in order to find it. There's also a fine cover of Dave Olney's "If My Eyes Were Blind" and "Midnight Rail," where Young makes his most autobiographical statement, yet tells the story of many more, "Well I am a midnight rider/I ride a midnight rail/And I've seen a glimpse of heaven/And at least half of hell," yet transforms this into a stunning paean to hope and goodwill. Soles' guitars and Crowley's keyboards (mimicking bagpipes) entwine with Young's baritone to create a textural grace. It needs to be said that like his other albums, *Switchblades* isn't an easy listen. As the critic and promoter Dave Brogren said: "Those looking for release here will be disappointed; they'll only be confronted with questions." That's about as fine an endorsement there is. — *Thom Jurek*

● **Lonesome On'ry & Mean** / Feb. 11, 1997 / Raven ✦✦✦✦✦

This collects the highlights from Young's first six albums, including the original versions of his three most famous songs: "Seven Bridges Road," "Lonesome, On'ry and Mean," and "Montgomery in the Rain." Although Young's earliest work is a curious (but enjoyable) mix of Steppenwolf and the Moody Blues, beginning about the time of his third album *Seven Bridges Road*, Young's original voice establishes itself, and from that point the writing, as well as the performances, are compelling. Young never enjoyed any commercial success himself, but this shows why he was considered with such high regard among his peers. — *Jim Smith*

Primal Young / Feb. 22, 2000 / Appleseed ✦✦✦✦

Steve Young has a big voice. It is the type of voice most shower dreamers wish they had, comprised of volume, sustain, range, and emotion. Young, however, is also an accomplished songwriter, though, typically, his albums tend to be half covers and half originals. This album, released 30 years into his career, finds Young's vocal pipes as strong as ever and his songwriting just as sharp as when he penned such classics as "Seven Bridges Road" and "Montgomery in the Rain." And, true to form, there are six originals to five covers. The opening cut, "Jig," is a Young song about the dance (jig) of life. The "jig" is universal and individual: "If you wanna get it on with me/you gotta listen to my tune/If you want me to get it on with you/you gotta play your tune, too." It is a subtle, solid beginning by a sure, old hand. Cut two, "Scotland Is a Land," is a Young-penned song anthemic enough to become Scotland's national song (or some such). Young's powerful baritone, accompanied by the erstwhile Van Dyke Parks on accordion, is hypnotic as he proclaims, "Scotland is a land/where I might want to die." For a cracker from North Georgia, Young sings of Scotland with the conviction of a native. And that is Young's strength as a songwriter—he is instantly, and naturally, believable. Of course, it doesn't hurt that his booming voice nails the listener to a wall. Young's take of "East Virginia" evidences another of his strong points—he can play an acoustic guitar as fast and deft as if playing a banjo. In fact, on uptempo burners, Young frequently plays banjo lines on the guitar, pumping like some crazed-though-on-the-one piston. The tempo of his vocal on "East Virginia" is only half the tempo of his breakneck picking, creating a unique tension and emphasis on what he is singing. It is as attention grabbing as a steady gaze across a bustling room. Young has successfully plied this technique in the past on such songs as "Travelin' Kind" and "The White Trash Song." Nothing misses on *Primal Young*. Other originals, such as "Heartbreak Girl," "Little Birdie," and "No Longer Will My Heart Be Truly Breaking," are so distinguished in composition and performance, one once again wonders why Steve Young has never been placed on an equal pedestal with the likes of Merle Haggard or Waylon Jennings. The covers, including a devil-may-care, shirttails-out rendition of Tom T. Hall's "The Year That Clayton Delaney Died" and a warbling, soul-drenched take of Lloyd Price"'s "Lawdy Miss Clawdy," are so splendidly bent to Young's style, he could easily be their composer. Thirty years in and Steve Young is still "primal." — *Steve Cooper*

Various Artists

... And the Answer Is: Great Country Answer Discs from '50s-'60s, Vol. 1 / 1995 / Bear Family ♦♦♦♦♦
Bear Family's three-volume *And the Answer Is: Great Answer Discs From the '50s and '60s* series documents the phenomenon of answer records, presenting both the original hit and the response to the single. These were songs designed to respond to hit singles, with the hopes that the second record would climb up the charts as well. Answer records were prevalent in pop and R&B as well as country, but on *And the Answer Is: Vols. 1 and 3*, Bear Family concentrates on country records. At their best, answer records became classics of their own—Kitty Wells' "It Wasn't God Who Made Honky Tonk Angels," and her response to Hank Thompson's "Wild Side of Life," arguably became even more famous than the record it was answering—but most of the singles were simply novelties. Consequently, the music here is for fetishists and collectors—after all, the average fan doesn't need to hear Jim Reeves' "Mexican Joe" followed by Carolyn Bradshaw's "The Marriage of Mexican Joe"—but for any country or pop music fan with an interest in the arcane and unusual, *And the Answer Is* is a very enjoyable series. Highlights of *Vol. 1* include Webb Pierce's "There Stands the Glass" / Betty Cody's "Please Throw Away the Glass," Hank Thompson's "Yesterday's Girl" / Goldie Hill's "I'm Yesterday's Girl," Skeets McDonald's "Don't Let the Stars Get in Your Eyes" / Goldie Hill's "I Let the Stars Get in My Eyes," Hank Williams' "Jambalaya" / Goldie Hill's "I'm Yvonne (From the Bayou)," and Hank Locklin's "Geisha Girl" / Skeeter Davis' "Lost to a Geisha Girl." —*Stephen Thomas Erlewine*

... And the Answer Is: Great Pop Answer Discs from '50s-'60s, Vol. 2 / 1995 / Bear Family ♦♦♦♦♦
Bear Family's three-volume *And the Answer Is: Great Answer Discs From the '50s and '60s* series documents the phenomenon of answer records, presenting both the original hit and the response to the single. These were songs designed to respond to hit singles, with the hopes that the second record would climb up the charts as well. Answer records were prevailant in country, pop and R&B, but on *And the Answer Is: Vol. 2*, Bear Family concentrates on pop/rock records from the '60s. Pop/rock answer records never produced a classic on the level of Kitty Wells' "It Wasn't God Who Made Honky Tonk Angels," and her response to Hank Thompson's "Wild Side of Life." Instead, most pop responses were simply novelties, which means *And the Answer Is: Great Answer Discs from the '60s* is designed for fetishists and collectors with a taste for the arcane and unusual. Anyone who has a passing interest in the bizarre side roads of pop music will find the compilation very entertaining. Highlights of *Vol. 2* include Marcie Blane's "Bobby's Girl" / Sherry Sisters' "Stay Away from Bobby," Jack Scott's "Burning Bridges" / Bobbie Jean's "You Burned the Bridges," Ray Peterson's "Tell Laura I Love Her" / Marilyn Michaels' "Tell Tommy I Need Him," Bobby Vee's "Please Don't Ask About Barbara" / Mike Regal's "Is It True What They Say About Barbara," Pat Boone's "Are You Lonesome Tonight" / Thelma Carpenter's "Yes, I'm Lonesome Tonight," and Barry Mann's "Who Put the Bomp" / Frankie Lymon's "I Put the Bomp." —*Stephen Thomas Erlewine*

... And the Answer Is: Great Country Answer Discs From '60s, Vol. 3 / 1994 / Bear Family ♦♦♦♦♦
Bear Family's three-volume *And the Answer Is: Great Answer Discs From the '50s and '60s* series documents the phenomenon of answer records, presenting both the original hit and the response to the single. These were songs designed to respond to hit singles, with the hopes that the second record would climb up the charts as well. Answer records were prevalent in pop and R&B as well as country, but on *And the Answer Is: Vols. 1 and 3*, Bear Family concentrates on country records. At their best, answer records became classics of their own but most of the singles were simply novelties. Consequently, the music here is for fetishists and collectors, but for any country or pop music fan with an interest in the arcane and unusual, *And the Answer Is* is a very enjoyable series. Highlights of *Vol. 3* include Johnny Cash's "Ballad of a Teenage Queen" / Tommy Tucker's "Return of the Teenage Queen," Jim Reeves' "He'll Have to Go" / Jeannie Black's "He'll Have to Stay," David Houston's "Almost Persuaded" / Donna Harris' "(He Was) Almost Persuaded," Kenny Rogers' "Ruby, Don't Take Your Love to Town" / Geraldine Stevens' "Billy, I've Got to Go to Town," Hank Locklin's "Please Help Me, I'm Falling" / Skeeter Davis' "(I Can't Help You) I'm Fallin' Too," and Billy Walker's "Charlie Shoes" / Jonic Mosby & Johnny's "The Answer to 'Charlie's Shoes.'" —*Stephen Thomas Erlewine*

15 Down Home Gospel Classics / Jan. 20, 1998 / Arhoolie ♦♦♦♦♦
Arhoolie, as is made plain in this 15-song sampler of their gospel catalog, does not favor slick modern spiritual music. (Or, as they say straight-up in the brief liner note, "The selections on this disc... are not by trendy, popular massed choirs.") Much of this is in fact gospel-blues: spiritually oriented numbers by major bluesmen Big Joe Williams, Mance Lipscomb, Robert Pete Williams, Jesse Fuller (a nice slide guitar treatment of "Amazing Grace"), and Fred McDowell, as well as more contemporary steel guitar-flavored gospel

by Aubrey Ghent. The arrangements are sparse (sometimes acoustic) and the vocals are soulful, not just by the aforementioned acts, but also by such relative unknowns as the Campbell Brothers, who work more in a contemporary electric vein. It's not being heretical to say that there's more passion and musical quality on this compilation than there is on innumerable glossily produced gospel recordings by feel-good ensembles with higher profiles. By the way, the track by steel guitarist Black Ace, "Farther Along," was previously unissued on CD. —*Richie Unterberger*

16 Down Home Country Classics / Jan. 20, 1998 / Arhoolie ♦♦♦♦♦
This is in effect a sampler of Arhoolie's country-related catalog, with cuts from 16 different releases. It's country of the old-timey and early honky tonk variety, not of the produced country-pop sort, though that's not a drawback. Highlights include the Maddox Brothers & Rose's raucous "George's Playhouse Boogie," the Carter Family's "Hello Stranger" (from a 1939 radio broadcast), the Strange Creek Singers' "No Never No" (with Alice Gerrard and Hazel Dickens duetting on vocals), and Toni Brown's "You Turned Your Back," a lost modern hillbilly classic of sorts (and also the rarest cut, previously issued on an Arhoolie 45-rpm single). Also including selections by Del McCoury, J.E. Mainer, the Any Old Time String Band, and many others, this may be too old-timey/Appalachian in nature for those with modern country tastes. —*Richie Unterberger*

19 Hot Country Requests / 1985 / Epic ♦♦♦
19 Hot Country Requests contains a selection of early-'80s mainstream country hits recorded by a variety of Columbia and Epic artists, including Merle Haggard ("Going Where the Lonely Go"), Mickey Gilley ("Talk to Me"), Willie Nelson ("Last Thing I Needed, First Thing This Morning"), George Jones ("I Always Get Lucky with You"), Ricky Skaggs ("Highway 40 Blues"), David Allan Coe ("Ride"), Janie Fricke ("He's a Heartache (Looking for a Place to Happen)"), Ronnie McDowell ("You're Gonna Ruin My Bad Reputation") and a duet by Haggard & Nelson ("Pancho & Lefty"). The track selection is a little uneven and there are a few dull moments, but on the whole, it's a very entertaining disc with a handful of classic songs. —*Stephen Thomas Erlewine*

20 Years of Stony Plain / 1996 / Stony Plain ♦♦♦♦♦
Twenty years is a remarkable track record for any independent label living in the modern age, let alone one that specializes in never-commercially-fashionable roots music while working from the industry Mecca of Edmonton, Alberta. As committed and timeless as keynote artists Ian Tyson, Cindy Church, Amos Garrett, Maria Muldaur, Dutch Mason, Long John Baldry, and Jr. Gone Wild, Stony Plain celebrates this anniversary milestone with a two-disc, 40-track collection that samples its 240-release roots rock, country, folk, blues, R&B, and alternative-pop repertoire. Disc one of *Twenty Years of Stony Plain* zeroes in on country/folk, including choice tracks from Tyson (a pair of duets with Tom Russell and Suzy Bogguss), Steve Earle, Grievous Angels, Doug Sahm with the Formerly Brothers, Bobby Charles, a Japan-only Garrett-Muldaur duet, a previously unreleased Rita Chirelli-Prairie Oyster collaboration, and splashes of alternative spice from Jr. Gone Wild and Spirit of the West. Disc two targets the blues, led by Mason, Duke Robillard, Jimmy Witherspoon, the Holmes Brothers, Jim Byrnes, Downchild Blues Band, Paul James with John Hammond, and harmonica legend Walter Shakey Horton—the first session ever produced (in 1972) by label founder and big-kid music fan Holger Petersen, who still captains the Stony Plain ship. From Stony Plain's reissues catalog, *20 Years* represents the likes of Winchester's and Great Speckled Bird's classic, eponymous debuts (folk-rock and country-rock landmarks respectively), King Biscuit Boy and Crowbar (look for upcoming compilations for each), and Ellen McIlwaine's "I Want Whacha Got"—the set's eye-popping, slide guitar/blues-belting scorcher. While the collection touches on the full 20 years, over half the selections are culled from 1990 to the present. As such, if something here catches your ear, it's likely to still be in print. In another astute bit of marketing, five tracks serve as teasers from upcoming Stony Plain releases by Long John Baldry, Roosevelt Sykes, Professor Longhair, Johnny Shines, and Lowell Fulson. —*Roch Parisien*

20th Century Masters—The Millennium Collection: Best of Bluegrass / Jul. 2, 2002 / Universal ♦♦♦♦
One of the first *Millennium Collections* to tackle a genre instead of an artist's work, *20th Century Masters—The Millennium Collection: Best of Bluegrass* does a respectable job of covering the style within a dozen songs. The collection ranges from bluegrass pioneers Bill Monroe & His Blue Grass Boys' "In the Pines" and "Blue Moon of Kentucky" to contemporary bluegrass sounds like Ricky Skaggs' "Hallelujah I'm Ready" and Vince Gill's "High Lonesome Sound." Lester Flatt's "Foggy Mountain Breakdown," Jimmy Martin's "Widow Maker," and the Osborne Brothers' "Ruby Are You Mad" are some of the collection's other highlights. While it would take a box set of Bear Family proportions to give a truly detailed bluegrass history, this collection is a good introduction to the style and how it's changed over the years. —*Heather Phares*

Ain't I'm a Dog: 25 More Rockabilly Rave-Ups / 2000 / Columbia/Legacy ♦♦♦♦
Like its simultaneously released companion volume *Whistle Bait!*, this rescues 25 obscure rockabilly tracks of the 1950s from the CBS vaults. Not that every name here is obscure: Carl Perkins, Marty Robbins, Link Wray, Rose Maddox, and Johnny Horton are pretty well known, while the Collins Kids, Ronnie Self, and Ronnie Dawson (heard here under the pseudonym Commonwealth Jones) have pretty sizable cult followings. When you get down to a previously unreleased 1956 tune by one Werly Fairburn, though, you're getting as arcane as any white-label European rockabilly bootleg comp. At any rate, this isn't quite as impressive as *Whistle Bait!*, but it has a similar mix of good crazed out-and-out rockabilly and country hillbillies trying to adapt, more or less, to the rockabilly sound. High points are Joe Maphis and Larry Collins' sizzling instrumental duet "Hurricane," Johnny Horton's two contributions (from the overlooked period when he was a nearly rockabilly honky tonker), Link Wray's typically overdriven instro "New Studio Blues," and Ronnie Self's "You're So Right for Me," where his hoarse vocals must have made the dignified major-label execs reach for the smelling salts. Talk about raw: Commonwealth Jones' 1961 single "Who's Been Here?"/"Do Do Do" (both songs are included) was likely the crudest slab of rock issued on a big label that year. Some of the rest is just OK, and Rose Maddox does sound like she would have rather been sticking with country swing than getting to grips with the new music on "Hey Little Dreamboat," with its odd combination of electric guitar and fiddles. *—Richie Unterberger*

Altamont: Black Stringband Music / 1989 / Rounder ♦♦♦
From the Library of Congress comes this compilation of works by black string bands. The black string band is something of a rarity, hailing from prior to the recording era in large part and pushed under the carpet by the rush of commercial labels to provide hillbilly music and blues, with the middle-ground black string bands (essentially black hillbilly music, in some sense) disappearing in the process. In the 1940s, a pair of bands was recorded in Tennessee with the help of the Library of Congress, eventually leading to this CD. The first seven cuts come from the Frazier/Patterson Band, using vocals, banjo, and fiddle. The second seven come from the John Lusk Band. In both sections, what one hears is in large part standard-sounding string band music. What is most notable here is potentially not the music so much as its origin. There are features that are specific to this substyle; primarily, the slight inflection of the blues mixed into the compositions. This might be something for a musicologist to enjoy, though beyond this small item there is little to note that is different from other string band recordings available. The music is performed well—not exceptional and not terrible. Pick it up as an interested scholar before you pick it up as an interested listener, but listen once either way. *—Adam Greenberg*

American Fiddle Tunes / 2000 / Library Of Congress ♦♦♦
American Fiddle Tunes presents 28 field recordings (most around one minute long) of usually unaccompanied fiddlers from the mid-'30s through the early '40s, with decent sound quality on most of the tracks. Included on this album that was originally issued in 1971, are many reels and other dance tunes, some of which date back to historical events such as Napoleon's career ("Bonaparte's Retreat") and the Virginia slave rebellion led by Nat Turner in 1931 ("Run Nigger Run"). These recordings from the Library of Congress' Archive of Folk Song come from across the U.S., including several performances each from fiddlers Leizime Brusoe (of Wisconsin), W.M. Stepp, Luther Strong (both from Kentucky), Patrick Bonner (Michigan) and one or two recordings each from ten other fiddlers. The liner notes are amazingly thorough, giving a detailed history of each song, followed by a list of early (often 18th & 19th century) manuscripts and other sources that printed the piece, as well as a list of published and unpublished recordings of the song and related variants. This and the sheer amount of solo fiddle heard here, can become an overwhelming amount of fiddling and information to absorb for those who just want some fiddle music! Yet the painstaking detail included here will bear repeated study and listening that is sure to satisfy dedicated fiddle fans and music historians. *—Joslyn Layne*

American Fogies, Vol. 1 / Feb. 20, 1996 / Rounder ♦♦♦♦
If you're looking to investigate the sheer variety of musical traditions in America, this is definitely the place to start, in large part because many of the artists involved aren't big names dipping their toe into different waters. These are people—many of whom have barely been heard nationally—for whom their particular musical style is life, like the Aux Cajunals, whose take on the blues "Baby Please Don't Go" is an accordion-driven stomp. Lee Sexton's "Rye Whiskey" is just banjo and voice in the best Roscoe Holcomb lineage (the two are actually related), while Wayne Henderson offers some Doc Watson-style picking on "Chow Time." But the album becomes far more satisfying when it casts its net wider to encompass more of the ethnic groups who've settled in America, such as the Pastatones' "Chitarra Romana"—Italian music from New Mexico—or "Pia Kuba," which comes from the Texas Polish community. And it would hardly be representative of the U.S. without a healthy sprinkling of Mexican music, such as "La Repetida" from Sabas Espinosa and Freddie Porras, which explores the burgeoning Tejano genre. But while the majority of these performers might not have big reputations (there are a few exceptions, like klezmer man Andy Statman and blues figures Corey Harris and Alvin "Youngblood" Hart), don't be fooled into thinking the playing is anything less than superb. Producer and compiler Ray Alden proves to have a shrewd ear for talent and the ability to coax something wonderful out of those he records, be it the Kentucky fiddle of Clyde Davenport or the unique Native American/Cajun hybrid of A-Machetah/Bayou Eclectico. From all corners of the U.S., and most especially its heartland, this is definitely the sound of America—and these people are far from fogies. *—Chris Nickson*

American Fogies, Vol. 2 / Apr. 1996 / Rounder ♦♦♦♦
On the first *American Fogies* disc, producer Ray Alden gave a glimpse of the range of acoustic traditional music being made in the U.S. On the second volume he narrows his focus a little, looking most intently at music made by women and also old-timey music—with the former members of the seminal New Lost City Ramblers featuring prominently in the latter. Of course, Alden doesn't limit himself exclusively to these two things; like a magpie, he gathers glittering music, like Michael Lightnin' Wells' "Crawling King Snake" with its lovely slide work, or Ralph Blizzard & the New Southern Ramblers. Perhaps surprisingly, a fair bit of the music comes from the Pacific Northwest, with artists like Laurie Andres, Hank Bradley, and Cathie Whitesides. But music knows no boundaries, as West Virginian Elaine Purkey reworks "Wayfaring Stranger" into a moving song about miners shows. So there's old-timey, cowboy songs, sizzling instrumentals ("Kansas City Kitty" from Gretchen Van Houten and Joyce Yoxall is one of the delights of this record), and even a track from the Heartbeats featuring Donna the Buffalo's Tara Nevins. Amazingly, it all fits together with remarkable internal logic, flowing gorgeously from cut to cut until it winds up with contributions from the people who helped revive old-timey music in the '50s, the New Lost City Ramblers. The Tracy Schwarz Cajun Trio hark back to the early, more formal days of bayou music and Mike Seeger offers an object lesson in banjo picking on "Down the Road," while John Cohen, along with daughter Sonya, becomes part of Last Forever on "Dillard Chandler," an interesting variation of "Little Saro." It makes for the perfect conclusion, paying tribute to those who helped ensure that this music, with its varied roots, remained healthy. *—Chris Nickson*

American Roots Music / Oct. 16, 2001 / Palm ♦♦♦♦
The successes of the breakthrough soundtrack from the film *O Brother, Where Art Thou?* and the in-depth PBS television series *Ken Burns' Jazz* seem to have combined in the 2001 production of Palm Pictures' four-part TV series *American Roots Music*. The series touches on the development of the distinctly American styles of traditional folk, country, blues, gospel, Western swing, bluegrass, cajun, zydeco, Tejano, and Native American music. Corresponding with the television event, Palm has released a four-CD box set soundtrack with a 48-page booklet covering the styles covered during the show. Much like a broadened version of the amazing *Washington Square Memoirs: The Great Urban Folk Boom, 1950-1970* CD set, *American Roots Music* has pulled together an impressive list of performers, including the Carter Family, Jimmie Rodgers, Bill Monroe, B.B. King, Hank Williams, Robert Johnson, Son House, Woody Guthrie, Leadbelly, the Staple Singers, Clifton Chenier, Flaco Jimenez, and Bob Dylan. The depth of the track selection is impressive, as is the breadth of the performers chosen. The producers have chosen to include some studio recordings, and some audio tracks taken from the film archives, making for a somewhat uneven sound quality. While the previously unreleased nature of these select tracks will appeal to collectors and die-hard fans, those just exploring these styles might be turned off by the rough quality of these performances. The discs span more than eight decades of music, acting as a good overview of these genres for new listeners, while Americana enthusiasts will view it as another great collection of the most influential American roots artists in music history. [Also available from Palm is a 19-song CD sampler entitled *American Roots Music: Highlights* and a video collection containing the entire television series on DVD and VHS.] *—Zac Johnson*

American Roots: A History of American Folk Music / Apr. 25, 2000 / Best Music Int'l ♦♦♦♦♦
Dutch discount reissue label Disky's four-CD box set *American Roots: A History of American Folk Music* is an ambitious undertaking, at least as far as sheer length is concerned. In other respects, it can be considered skimpy: the packaging is negligible; there are no annotations beyond song titles, artist and songwriter credits, and copyright dates; and the selections, probably mastered from records, often have a primitive sound quality. But the compilation still manages to be an exhaustive collection of vital American acoustic music. Three of the four discs consist of music that today would be referred to as "country," though in its day it was called "hillbilly," and for a period in the 1940s actually was known as folk music. Running from 1927 to 1948, the roughly chronological selections trace some of its earliest recorded manifestations to the beginnings of the modern country music industry. The major early names in country music are extensively represented, with many well-known songs included. Country music is not generally thought of in the same category as folk music in America, if only for political reasons. It may have taken a Dutch compilation to point out the musical similarities by devoting CD four to the urban folksingers of the 1940s (Woody Guthrie, Pete Seeger), who borrowed many of their tunes from hillbilly predecessors. After listening to the earlier discs, the concordances are inescapable; you can tell that the city-based folkies deliberately based their approach on rural forebears who wouldn't have thought much of their political views. It seems that, while American record labels continue to assert copyright claims on this material domestically, Europeans are free to consider anything more than 50 years old as in the public domain. But that doesn't explain why *American Roots* is being readily imported into the U.S., where it was sold for less than $30 by one mail-order firm beginning in 2000. At that price, it's a remarkable bargain, making available a wealth of vintage country and folk material that is difficult to come by in any form, much less gathered into one box set. On that basis, *American Roots* can be highly recommended. *—William Ruhlmann*

The Angels Are Singing: A Women's Bluegrass Gospel Collection / Aug. 20, 2002 / Rounder ♦♦♦
One of the primary distinguishing features of bluegrass music has always been the male voice—the fierce and otherworldly falsetto of Bill Monroe was as important to the establishment of bluegrass as a musical genre as were his hard-driving mandolin and the fiery banjo picking of Earl Scruggs. But although women have traditionally been regarded as peripheral in the history of bluegrass music, there are many who have made significant contributions, and they have done so throughout the music's history. From

the rough-hewn mountain laments of Hazel Dickens to the soulful smoothness of Alison Krauss, the distinctive sounds of women bluegrass singers have added a distinctive dimension to the music's development. This collection of bluegrass-gospel songs features women singing in a wide variety of bluegrass styles: the Stevens Sisters contribute the dark and bluesy "In My Time of Dying," Claire Lynch gets funky on a modern gospel composition called "Paul and Peter Walked," and Ola Belle Reed delivers a chilling a cappella rendition of "Six Feet of Earth Makes Us All One Size." Rhonda Vincent and Kathy Kallick both perform driving and rootsy numbers, while the Cox Family's contribution is, as usual for them, both gorgeous and slightly strange. Strict traditionalists might be put off by a few of these selections (the clarinet intro on "The Wayfaring Stranger" is especially startling), but everything here is very much worth hearing. *—Rick Anderson*

☆ **Anthology of American Folk Music, Vol. 1–3** / Aug. 19, 1997 / Smithsonian Folkways ✦✦✦✦✦

Originally released in 1952 as a quasi-legal set of three double LPs and reissued several times since (with varying cover art), *Anthology of American Folk Music* could well be the most influential document of the '50s folk revival. Many of the recordings that appeared on it had languished in obscurity for 20 years, and it proved a revelation to a new group of folkies, from Pete Seeger to John Fahey to Bob Dylan. The man that made the *Anthology* possible was Harry Smith, a notoriously eccentric musicologist who compiled 84 of his favorite hillbilly, gospel, blues, and Cajun performances from the late '20s and early '30s, dividing each into one of three categories: Ballads, Social Music, and Songs. Smith sequenced the three volumes with a great amount of care, placing songs on the Ballads volume in historical order (not to be confused with chronological order) so as to create an LP that traces the folk tradition, beginning with some of the earliest Childe ballads of the British Isles and ending with several story songs of the early 20th century. The cast of artists includes pioneers in several fields, from the Carter Family and Uncle Dave Macon to Blind Lemon Jefferson, Mississippi John Hurt, and the Alabama Sacred Harp Singers. Many of the most interesting selections on the *Anthology*, however, are taken from artists even more obscure, such as Clarence Ashley, Bascom Lamar Lunsford, and Buell Kazee. After the *Anthology* had been out of print for more than a decade, Smithsonian/Folkways reissued the set in a six-disc boxed set, with the original notes of Harry Smith, as well as a separate book of new reminiscences by artists influenced by the original and a wealth of material for use in CD-ROM drives. *—John Bush*

☆ **Anthology of American Folk Music, Vol. 4** / May 23, 2000 / Revenant ✦✦✦✦✦

The Harry Smith-compiled three-volume *Anthology of American Folk Music* set, originally released in the 1950s and reissued to much brouhaha in 1997, was one of the most important records in launching the folk revival. It was not well known, though, that Smith compiled a fourth volume that was unissued. Revenant finally put it out in 2000, and like its three predecessors, it contains classic pre-World War II American country, blues, and folk music, with some gospel and Cajun too. It does differ from the first three volumes in its focus on a slightly later period, with all the tracks culled from the years 1928-1940. Leadbelly, Robert Johnson, Joe Williams, Bukka White, Memphis Minnie, and John Estes are all major blues artists; the Monroe Brothers, the Carter Family, Uncle Dave Macon, and the Blue Sky Boys all giant country/bluegrass pioneers; and the Hackberry Ramblers are one of the pre-eminent Cajun groups. A few of these songs are archetypes that have burned their way into the American collective musical consciousness: John Estes' "Milk Cow Blues," the Carter Family's "No Depression in Heaven," Joe Williams' "Baby Please Don't Go," and the Monroe Brothers' "Nine Pound Hammer Is Too Heavy." Other less famous performances are quite intriguing, like Sister Clara Hudmon's "Stand By Me" (believed by some to be Bessie Smith recording under a pseudonym) and Jesse James' raw and rollicking piano blues "Southern Casey Jones." At 28 songs spread over two CDs, it's a little shorter than might be expected for a box set, though as compensation, it's enclosed in a pretty incredible 96-page liner-note-sized hardcover book with writing by Dick Spottswood and John Fahey. *—Richie Unterberger*

Anthology of Country Music: Early Country Harmony 1940s / ACM ✦✦✦✦✦

Here are 20 rare gems of early country harmony, including selections from the Blue Sky Boys, the Louvin Brothers ("I Love God's Way of Living" is a stone classic), Johnnie & Jack, the Carlisle Brothers, and names that are primarily known only to country scholars, like Molly O'Day & Lynn Davis, James & Martha, and Carl Butler. Four of the tracks were previously unissued, including a radio duet between Hank Williams & Little Jimmy Dickens. This is country music just down from the mountains, with a spiritual quality in both the gospel tunes and the secular ones. The only factors preventing this LP (and its companion volume covering the 1930s) from getting five-star ratings are the imperfect transfers from original copies (although the sound quality's fairly good), and the total lack of liner notes. Otherwise, they should be considered essential to any comprehensive collection of early country music. *—Richie Unterberger*

☆ **Appalachian Stomp: Bluegrass Classics** / 1995 / Rhino ✦✦✦✦✦

Like many Rhino compilations, this is geared more to the novice or the casual fan than the aficionado, but that's not a criticism. If someone wants a basic primer of the bluegrass sound past and present that manages to be accessible and avoid unduly clichéd track selection, this 18-song compilation fits the bill well. Most of the biggest names are here (Bill Monroe, Flatt & Scruggs, the Dillards, the Stanley Brothers, the Kentucky Colonels, J.D. Crowe, Ricky Skaggs, Alison Krauss), as are some of the genre's top standards ("Blue Moon of Kentucky," "Orange Blossom Special," "Uncle Pen," "Foggy Mountain Breakdown"). The inclusion of Flatt & Scruggs' "The Ballad of Jed Clampett," Eric Weissberg & Steve Mandell's "Dueling Banjos," and The Nitty Gritty Dirt Band's "Will the Circle Be Unbroken" may rankle purists, but it clears the path to listeners who are only familiar with the idiom through these songs, and may find a lot more that they'll like on the less overexposed performances on this anthology. *—Richie Unterberger*

Appalachian Stomp: More Bluegrass Classics / Apr. 20, 1999 / Rhino ✦✦✦✦

With some of the genre's most recognizable songs having already been used, *Appalachian Stomp: More Bluegrass Classics* isn't quite up to the level of the first *Appalachian Stomp* collection, which remains one of the best introductory bluegrass surveys available. However, it does maintain a similarly high standard of quality, featuring selections by legends like Bill Monroe, Flatt & Scruggs, Ralph Stanley, J.D. Crowe, Alison Krauss, the Stanley Brothers, and many others. It's a great way for bluegrass neophytes to sample more top-notch material after being hooked in by the first volume. *—Steve Huey*

Arkansas Shout / Nov. 6, 2001 / Jazz Oracle ✦✦✦

This is an intriguing CD for it features all of the music that the American Record Corporation (ARC) recorded during a field trip to Hot Springs Arkansas in March 1937 other than some gospel performers. The performances (originally released on the Vocalion, Melotone, and Perfect labels) range from big band swing to Western swing and blues. The 28 selections on this generous CD include cuts by the Range Riders (a solid Western swing band with a weak saxophonist), Fats Smith's Rhythm Kings, Three Fifteen & His Squares, the Original Yellowjackets, trumpeter Ike Ragon's Orchestra, Albert Gale's Orchestra, Tommy Settles, and Jazzbo Tommy's Lowlanders. Not all of the selections are of equal quality and some of the styles and songs were already several years behind the times, but overall the music is quite enjoyable. Best are the six selections from the Original Yellowjackets, an excellent no-name nine-piece group that could have gone much further if they had moved up North. Serious early jazz collectors will definitely want this CD. *—Scott Yanow*

The Art of Traditional Fiddle / Feb. 13, 2001 / Rounder ✦✦✦✦✦

If you're looking for an ideal introduction to fiddle playing as practiced in North America, look no further than this stuffed-full Rounder Heritage release, which serves up some 33 tracks of various vintages, many of them previously unreleased. This is traditional fiddle playing as you'll find it (or would have, in some instances) in sitting rooms, family kitchens, church halls, social halls, and on commons and greens—music with roots in England, Scotland, and Ireland, as well as in much of Europe and Scandinavia. An exciting, energetic collection to sit and listen to, and very distracting indeed when trying to read through the detailed notes (in very small type) by producer Mark Wilson. Rounder has certainly hit the bull's-eye here. *—Steven McDonald*

Banjo Jamboree / 1996 / Tradition ✦✦✦✦✦

If a diverse anthology of banjo-driven folk music is what you're after, this is an excellent choice. Besides folkies like Eric Weissberg, Marshall Brickman, and Mike Seeger, it has contributions by a few unexpected names like Roger McGuinn (who offers a "Banjo Cantata"), David Lindley, hot country and rock session man Joe Maphis, and Mason ("Classical Gas") Williams. Selections by less celebrated names like Jim Helms and Dick Weissman round out the collection, the major strike against it being the near-total lack of source information in the liner notes, which don't give any of the original session dates. *—Richie Unterberger*

Banjo Pickin' Girl, Vol. 1 / 1980 / Rounder ✦✦✦

An inappropriate album title weakens an otherwise quite interesting collection of material by early female country performers. It's the "banjo" in the title, accompanying a shot of an elderly woman playing an old-time banjo, that would obviously lead listeners to conclude that there is lots of banjo playing on this record. This is hardly the case. Most of the women actually accompany themselves on guitar, even Louisiana Lou when she dishonestly sings "With My Banjo on My Knee Blues." Furthermore, some of the recordings are so decrepit and fuzzy that one can't even tell a banjo is being played, which is the case with the opening track entitled "Big Eyed Rabbit," a good subject for a banjo tune if there ever was one. The program finally finds its way to heavy banjo territory, but not until close to the end of the second side. This is where one finds Lily May Ledford, one of the great banjo players, on several tracks recorded with her band, the lovable Coon Creek Girls. A booklet enclosed inside is full of interesting information, but could have used a staple to hold it together. Fans of vintage recordings of folk, Western, and cowboy songs will enjoy this collection, except for those that have trouble with political incorrectness. The track "All Night Long" by Roba Stanley, for example, contains lyrics about how bad black people supposedly smell. A nice job has been done remastering some of these recordings, bringing out all the lovely tones of the Blue Ridge Mountain Singers' harmony singing, for example. There are several nice, quite early tracks by cowboy lass Patsy Montana backed by the wonderful Prairie Ramblers, cut when she was still working under her real name, Rubye Blevins. Still, fans of banjo playing should look elsewhere for their kicks. *—Eugene Chadbourne*

Bayou Rockabilly Cats / May 2, 2000 / Ace ✦✦✦

Louisiana's Goldband label is perhaps best known for its Cajun and R&B recordings, but also did record a good deal of hillbilly and rockabilly sides in the '50s. *Bayou Rockabilly Cats* contains 26 of them, although when the most recognizable artists on a compilation are Al Ferrier, Hopeless Homer, and Goldband chief Eddie Shuler himself (with Eddie Shuler's All Star Reveliers), you know this is one for the specialists. Actually, much of this is not quite standard rockabilly, but country music in the process of making the transition to rockabilly. There are fiddles and steel guitars on plenty of the cuts, and the tempos are often more in the country boogie or two-step mold than they are in rock & roll. Truth be known, that makes this more interesting than many such compilations of obscure rockabilly (such as numerous ones on the Ace label itself), as the country-rockabilly bridge hasn't been documented and investigated with nearly as much depth as some other roots-of-rock genres have. (There are, for instance, appreciably more reissues of late-'40s—early-'50s R&B and jump blues on the cusp of turning into rock & roll.) In general the performers on this disc had more of a Southern swamp to their lilt, as well as some traces of Cajun rhythms (although those aren't that prevalent). There aren't major overlooked classic songs or amazing performers, but the style's done with a lot of panache and good-natured energy. It's not all hillbilly-rockabilly crossover either; some of the sides are just flat-out raw rockabilly, and Bee Arnold does piano-based work with more of an R&B flavor (even using a clarinet on "Plant You Know, Dig You Later"). Arnold's 1954 single "Way Down Under Blues," in fact, is pretty unusual for the time, and one of the earlier instances anywhere of a white musician recording in a hardcore R&B style that approached rock & roll. When Goldband records were reissued after the '50s, there were electric bass overdubs that Shuler was persuaded to use to make them sound more contemporary-sounding, to the vexation of collectors and historians that rightly prefer the originals. Those listeners will be glad to hear that this CD consists solely of the unoverdubbed original versions, marking in fact the first time the original singles have ever been reissued (although eight of the selections are not from vintage '50s 45s, but from '80s releases that contained previously unissued '50s performances). *—Richie Unterberger*

Best of Austin City Limits: Country Music's Finest Hour / 1996 / Columbia/Legacy ✦✦✦
From its inception in the mid-'70s until the late '90s, *Austin City Limits* was the premier country music television show in America. What distinguished the show from its competition was its emphasis on performance—each show spotlights one or two showcase artists, plus various guest artists, who are allowed to play whatever they want. The result was a series of freewheeling, eclectic and passionate music show unlike any other. *The Best of Austin City Limits: Country Music's Finest Hour* collects 16 highlights from the show's long, illustrious history and, as expected, some of the biggest name in country music are involved. From Merle Haggard ("Silver Wings," 1978) and George Jones ("He Stopped Loving Her Today," 1985) to Asleep At the Wheel ("Boogie Back to Texas," 1987) and Alison Krauss ("Baby, Now That I've Found You," 1995), the album has a wide selection of first-rate artists and stellar performances that hint at the rich legacy of the show. In fact, if there's anything wrong with the disc, is the fact that it feels incomplete, even though it includes such luminaries as Willie Nelson, Tammy Wynette, Waylon Jennings, k.d. lang, Mary-Chapin Carpenter, Dwight Yoakam, the Mavericks, the Judds, Charlie Daniels, and Patty Loveless. There's no fault with any of these selections, indeed, but after the disc is finished, you're waiting for the sequel. *—Thom Owens*

The Best of Bluegrass, Vol. 1 / 1953 / Polygram ✦✦✦
The Best of Bluegrass, Vol. 1 is an excellent 22-track sampler of the genre, containing most of the most famous songs in bluegrass, including the Country Gentlemen's "Can't You Hear Me Calling?," and the Lonesome Pine Fiddlers' "Blue Moon of Kentucky," Flatt & Scruggs' "Roll in My Sweet Baby's Arms" and "Foggy Mountain Breakdown," and the original version of "Duelin' Banjos," which was initially released under the title "Feudin' Banjos" by Arthur Smith & Don Reno. As a one-stop introduction, it's hard to beat this collection. *—Stephen Thomas Erlewine*

The Best of Bluegrass: Preachin' Prayin' & Singin' / Sep. 24, 1996 / Polygram ✦✦✦✦
Recorded between 1949 and 1960, this 18-track bluegrass collection culled from the Polygram vaults includes music from the Louvin Brothers, Flatt & Scruggs, the Stanley Brothers, Carl Story, and the Osborne Brothers. It also features Lowell Blanchard's "Jesus Hits Like the Atom Bomb," made famous by the film *Atomic Cafe*. *—Jason Ankeny*

The Best of Lin/Kliff Records: Rockabilly / Jun. 25, 1994 / Collectables ✦✦✦✦✦
This 18-song compilation is a good compromise for anyone who doesn't want to spend $100 on the Bear Family *Linn and Kliff Records* box. The music, by David Ray ("Jitterbugging Baby," "Lonesome Baby Blues"), Steve Wright ("Wild, Wild Woman," "Far and Distant Lands"), the Chuck-a-Lucks ("Disc Jockey Fever"), Buck Griffin ("Pretty Lou"), Andy Starr ("Dirty Bird Song," "Lover Man," "Do It Right"), the Jokers ("Dogfight"), Don Terry ("Knees Shakin'") et al., almost all rocks hard and fast, with hardly any let-up (apart from "Far and Distant Lands" and "Lover Man") in the pacing. And this is the easiest way for the curious to discover uncanny Buddy Holly soundalike Ray Ruff ("I Took a Liking to You"), who came to Lin Records after leaving Holly's former producer, Norman Petty. One minor drawback is the sound, which is decent but not remotely as impressive as the Bear Family material, and the notes, which are sketchy about most of the talent represented here. *—Bruce Eder*

Billboard Top Country Hits: 1959 / 1959 / Rhino ✦✦✦✦✦
The year is 1959 and the top of the country charts features a surprising mix of material. From the latter-day honky tonk of Webb Pierce ("I Ain't Never") to the latest pop crossover bid from Faron Young, this bargain disc spotlights some classic fare by future Hall of Fame figures like Johnny Cash, George Jones, and Buck Owens. And if you're game for a history lesson, Johnny Horton will provide it in fine kitsch style with his "Battle of New Orleans." A tidy way for country buffs to brush up on their *Billboard* archives. *—Stephen Cook*

Billboard Top Country Hits: 1960 / 1960 / Rhino ✦✦✦✦✦
Rhino's budget series honoring country music's biggest hits stops at 1960 and gathers up ten classics from that year. In addition to Buck Owens' "Excuse Me (I Think I've Got a Heartache)," Marty Robbins' "El Paso," and Ferlin Husky's immortal "Wings of a Dove," the set also features Jim Reeves' "He'll Have to Go," Ray Price's "One More Time," and Johnny Horton's "Sink the Bismarck." Selections from Skeeter Davis, Don Gibson, and Jeanne Black complete the collection. *—Cub Koda*

Billboard Top Country Hits: 1961 / 1961 / Rhino ✦✦✦✦✦
This budget set brings ten of 1961's biggest country recordings as part of Rhino's ongoing *Billboard* chart hit series. Big-ticket items include Buck Owens ("Foolin' Around"), Patsy Cline's "I Fall To Pieces," Jimmy Dean's "Big Bad John," George Jones' "Tender Years," and Johnny Horton's "North to Alaska." Hits from Faron Young, Don Gibson, Floyd Cramer, and Marty Robbins complete the set. *—Cub Koda*

Billboard Top Country Hits: 1962 / 1962 / Rhino ✦✦✦✦✦
The cream of Nashville is on hand for this, another of Rhino's roundups of the country charts. This time out 1962 is in the spotlight, and the perennial hitmaking likes of Jim Reeves ("Adios Amigos"), Patsy Cline ("Crazy"), and Marty Robbins ("Devil Woman") are in the mix. And lest you think there will be no classic samples of some kitsch-minded and topical fare, the disc includes Jimmy Dean's "P.T. 109" and Hank Snow's exhausting "I've Been Everywhere." A fine dose of vintage country at a bargain price. *—Stephen Cook*

Billboard Top Country Hits: 1963 / 1963 / Rhino ✦✦✦✦✦
Rhino's budget series honoring country music's biggest hits stops at 1963 and gathers up ten classics from that year. Besides a pair of Buck Owens biggies ("Act Naturally" and "Love's Gonna Live Here"), the set also features Johnny Cash's "Ring of Fire," Skeeter Davis' "The End of the World," Dave Dudley's "Six Days on the Road," and Bill Anderson's "Still." Selections from Ned Miller, Marty Robbins, George Hamilton IV, and Carl Butler complete the collection. *—Cub Koda*

Billboard Top Country Hits: 1964 / 1964 / Rhino ✦✦✦✦✦
This budget set brings ten of 1964's biggest country recordings as part of Rhino's ongoing *Billboard* chart hit series. Big-ticket items include a pair from Buck Owens ("Together Again" and "My Heart Skips a Beat"), a pair from Roger Miller ("Dang Me" and "Chug-A-Lug"), Lefty Frizzell's "Saginaw, Michigan," George Jones' "The Race Is On," and Johnny Cash's "Understand Your Man." Hits from Connie Smith, Jim Reeves, and Marty Robbins complete the set. *—Cub Koda*

Billboard Top Country Hits: 1965 / 1965 / Rhino ✦✦✦
The top of the *Billboard* charts country style. Rhino presents the best of country music from 1965, when the Nashville sound was in full swing, the likes of Buck Owens were bringing new sounds through the side door, and Jim Reeves was pining for those pop days of old. Besides two fine sides by Owens ("I've Got a Tiger By the Tail" and "Buckaroo"), the remainder here is mostly in the pop-weepie mode or cruising along trucker-song style. Listeners can look to Eddy Arnold's "Make the World Go Away" for a genuine classic of the former variety, while Dave Dudley and Roger Miller's cuts, respectively, represent the rough-hewn and chestnut take on the latter. Best purchased with no prior country music experience and at a rock-bottom price. *—Stephen Cook*

Billboard Top Country Hits: 1966 / 1966 / Rhino ✦✦✦✦✦
This volume includes David Houston's "Almost Persuaded," and Loretta Lynn's "You Ain't Woman Enough," and Jack Greene's "There Goes My Everything." *—AMG*

Billboard Top Country Hits: 1967 / 1967 / Rhino ✦✦✦
The year is 1967 and country music is heading toward its varied yet ultimately crossover-heavy future: The Nashville sound is at its apex, and Merle Haggard and Buck Owens are bringing rootsy good news from the West Coast. One of the best things, though, is the emergence of Tammy Wynette and her early domestic-saga hit, "I Don't Wanna Play House." Like this gem, Wynette's classic duet with David Houston, "My Elusive Dreams," was produced by the master of the late-Nashville sound, Billy Sherrill. So, with Owens and Haggard keeping the honky tonk flame lit with a song apiece and Sherrill guiding many of those production-minded sessions, George Jones finds the middle ground between the raw and pop ends of country with his slick yet rough-around-the-edges weepie "Walk Through This World With Me." Order another beer and dance that last slow one before closing time. *—Stephen Cook*

Billboard Top Country Hits: 1968 / 1968 / Rhino ✦✦✦✦✦
It's 1968 and Rhino has stepped in to help one and all relive the year's chart-topping country memories. The Nashville sound was in full swing and the mix took in honky tonk, pop, West Coast, and some kitsch. On the rawer, outlaw end, Merle Haggard ("Mama Tried") and Johnny Cash ("Folsom Prison Blues") find the Top 40 without too many concessions. On the other hand, Tammy Wynette and Glen Campbell expertly show the lush side of things with two veritable standards. And for a classic Nashville narrative, there's Jeannie C. Riley's "Harper Valley P.T.A." A fine and varied tour of country during the Aquarius years. *—Stephen Cook*

Billboard Top Country Hits: 1986 / 1986 / Rhino ✦✦✦✦✦
Rhino's most recent set of *Billboard* country anthologies begin at 1986 and show through its lineup just how much things have changed since then in country circles. Ricky Skaggs, John Conlee, Lee Greenwood, T.G. Sheppard and T. Graham Brown are not exactly factors in the 1990s, while Exile is hanging on for dear life. Both Tanya Tucker and Dan Seals have seen better days. Only Hank Williams Jr. and Steve Wariner currently matter, and Wariner is doing better tunes now than "Life's Highway." *—Ron Wynn*

Billboard Top Country Hits: 1987 / 1987 / Rhino ✦✦✦✦✦
The 1990s have seen country continue to evolve, and the second volume in Rhino's latest anthology line demonstrates the changes once more. There are cuts from The Forester Sisters, O'Kanes (defunct), Highway 101 (now with a new lead vocalist) and holdovers Hank Williams Jr. and Steve Wariner. But it also begins with Randy Travis' superb "Forever and Ever, Amen" and includes Rosanne Cash's sublime "This Is the Way We Make a Broken Heart." These compensate for another Exile song. *—Ron Wynn*

Billboard Top Country Hits: 1988 / 1988 / Rhino ✦✦✦✦✦
The third volume in Rhino's latest country series towers over the previous two, reflecting both improved songwriting and performance level. Only Earl Thomas Conley's "What I'd Say" dips slightly, while such songs as "Streets of Bakersfield" from the duo of Dwight Yoakam and Buck Owens, Keith Whitley's "When You Say Nothing at All" and Randy

Travis' "I Told You So" and "Set 'Em Up Joe" are all fabulous cuts, as are Tanya Tucker's "Strong Enough to Bend" and Highway 101's "Cry, Cry, Cry." *—Ron Wynn*

Billboard Top Country Hits: 1989 / 1989 / Rhino ✦✦✦✦✦

While country ranks as the number-one radio format and is arguably the nation's most popular adult form, Rhino's anthology series of number one hits certainly provides ample food for thought regarding what types of songs have been genuine hits: Eddie Rabbitt, Shenandoah and Eddy Raven had number-one hits in 1989. The disc's saving grace comes from Patty Loveless, Randy Travis, Keith Whitley, Highway 101, and Steve Wariner, while it is filled out by Ronnie Milsap and a decent Dolly Parton cut. *—Ron Wynn*

Billboard Top Country Hits: 1990 / 1990 / Rhino ✦✦✦✦✦

The fifth volume in Rhino's country anthology line concludes things in 1990. Once more, many of the number ones offer reason to stop and ponder the condition of contemporary country radio. Shenandoah, Paul Overstreet, Dan Seals, and Mike Reid are not bad, but all of them are as close to MOR and folk as country. Randy Travis, Patty Loveless, and Holly Dunn also scored number-one hits, as did Lorrie Morgan. Joe Diffie is a lot closer to country than many of these acts, and Alabama is almost hardcore honky-tonk next to Shenandoah. *—Ron Wynn*

Black & White Hillbilly Music: Early Harmonica Recordings from the 1920s & 1930s / 1996 / Trikont ✦✦✦

This is all pure country music, before there really was such a thing. This is the folk music of England, Ireland, and Scotland wrapped up in the Smoky Mountains of Tennessee and in the Appalachian plains, and was transformed into something so perversely American it was a freak show to the rest of the country when it finally was released on recordings. These recordings by the Crook Brothers, DeFord Bailey (the first black instrumentalist on the *Grand Old Opry* stage), the Jackson County Barn Owls, the Riverside Ramblers, Karl & Harty, the Pickard Family, Dr. Humphrey Bate & His Possum Hunters, Lonnie Glosson, and others were the sounds of people telling stories to one another in the confines of their communities, playing the old songs as if they had a secret code not decipherable outside the holler. Music was played by clans for other clans; many of them identifying their "turf" and placing the name "Ramblers" after it (there are four such acts on this disc). This is primarily string band music, unique because of the prominence of the harmonica in the ensembles themselves. Fiddle solos were replaced or at least augmented by harmonica. As an album, it doesn't have the power or the focus that other Trikont compilations have. It feels shoddily snapped together to meet a production deadline, with this theme as its only unifier. That said, it's of more than casual interest because of the material, which is very fine, and most of it is so obscure that it is seldom (if ever) referenced. Of particular note is the early swing flavor of the Nelstone's Hawaiians, formed during the brief national craze for Hawaiian guitar music. It seems there was contact beyond the mountain ridge after all. Glosson's "Lonnie's Fox Chase" is part Irish reel, part blues shuffle, part stomping bluegrass thunder. Using his voice to add percussion in and out of rhythm, Glosson had a few tricks up his sleeve as a harmonica player, but he used them very effectively, bending pitches that give the appearance that he's changing keys on the same harmonica, and then singing through the harmonica body as he blew into it, creating true microtones. This psycho track is worth the price of the entire compilation. There's supposedly a guitar on this cut as well but you can't hear it and it doesn't matter. The other solid jam is DeFord Bailey's "John Henry." This is a blues stomp from 1928. The polyrhythms created by Bailey's harmonica allowed for shifts and breaks in the melody in which the body of the tune changed from a country shuffle to a steamy blues while remaining recognizably the same song. Despite its flaws, this is still a worthy collection. *—Thom Jurek*

Black Banjo Songsters of North Carolina & Virginia / Jan. 20, 1998 / Smithsonian Folkways ✦✦✦

Here are 32 tracks of African-American banjo players from North Carolina and Virginia playing in the old-time folk style, recorded between 1974 and 1997. This is one of numerous releases illustrating that the roots of American music have more of a commonality than is often supposed. Many of the standards covered by the musicians on this record were (and are) in the repertoire of white folk artists, and it seems almost arbitrary to try to determine whether this is more of a country or a blues collection. Several of the players use odd tunings, and their instrumental skills outshine the vocals, which often sound like off-the-cuff afterthoughts. Although this is well-produced (with a booklet giving background on black banjo playing and the history behind the songs), it's really more of academic interest than something to play for entertainment; historical importance aside, it sounds like just another banjo collection. And "Coo Coo" is a classic song, but how many more versions do you want to hear? (There are three more here.) *—Richie Unterberger*

Blue Ridge Mountain Banjo / Nov. 4, 1997 / Pinecastle ✦✦✦✦

The fiery three-finger banjo picking style that was perfected (though not invented) by Earl Scruggs in the early '40s transformed the sound of country music and, when Scruggs joined the band of bluegrass pioneer Bill Monroe, became the signature sound of bluegrass, making it instantly recognizable to listeners all over the world. Scruggs-style banjo remains one of America's favorite musical sounds, and it has developed and branched out in various substyles: the "melodic" style developed by Tony Trischka and Bill Keith, the jazzy single-string style of Don Reno, and the even jazzier innovations of banjo wunderkind Béla Fleck, among others. This compilation of banjo showcases tunes from the catalog of the Pinecastle label and stays fairly close to traditional bluegrass styles, though the legendary Eddie Adcock does jazz things up with his Don Reno-on-caffeine performance of "Mangadang," and Scott Vestal's "Polka on a Banjo" is a novelty tune based on old polka melodies. Scruggs himself appears (performing with both Sonny Osborne and the late John Hartford) on a very nice arrangement of the A.P. Carter favorite "Foggy Mountain Top." But the most interesting performance of the program comes from Mark Johnson, who has successfully adapted the older clawhammer banjo style to bluegrass, dubbing his approach "clawgrass." This is a fine overview for lovers of America's only indigenous instrument. *—Rick Anderson*

Bluegrass Beginnings / Jun. 26, 2001 / Catfish ✦✦✦✦

Any album that includes bluegrass luminaries such as Bill Monroe, the Stanley Brothers, and Flatt & Scruggs looks promising. Add a few lesser-known performers like the the Lilly Brothers and the Lonesome Pine Fiddlers and the listener has *Bluegrass Beginnings*. Bluegrass has become more popular in recent years thanks to Alison Krauss and Dolly Parton, but to hardcore fans the first ten years—the mid-'40s to the mid-'50s—remain the golden era. *Bluegrass Beginnings* offers a blast from the mountain past for old-timers, a 60-minute program packed with classics. To the recent convert, the album offers a chance to look at the roots of this overcharged folk music. There are several lovely tracks by the Stanley Brothers including "The White Dove" and "I Love No One But You," and good selections, "Down the Road" and "My Cabin in Caroline," by Flatt & Scruggs. Phebel Wright offers up a rousing instrumental, "Lint Head Stomp" ("lint head" was used as a derisive name for cotton mill workers), while the Lonesome Pine Fiddlers deliver the lively "Lonesome Sad and Blue." It would have been helpful to have the origin of each track on the liner notes so that a listener could search out similar material. However, the quality music should offer the proper inspiration to seek out other recordings by these artists. *Bluegrass Beginnings* succeeds by offering a pure and pleasing dose of the real thing. *—Ronnie D. Lankford Jr.*

Bluegrass Breakdown / 1992 / Vanguard ✦✦✦

This album, which features the work of such artists as Bill Monroe, the Stanley Brothers, the Dillards, and the Greenbriar Boys, was recorded at the Newport Folk Festival in 1963-1965. *—AMG*

Bluegrass Class of 1990 / 1990 / Rounder ✦✦✦✦

This compilation album reads like a who's-who of the progressive bluegrass/new acoustic music movement: pros like mandolinist David Grisman, guitarist Tony Rice, dobro player Jerry Douglas and a pre-Flecktones Béla Fleck are all represented, as well as the (very) young Alison Krauss and many, many others. Though most of the guns are big, some of the album's best moments come from artists who were relative unknowns at the time of its release: the Whitstein Brothers offer a classic guitar-mandolin duo number in the prewar style of the Blue Sky Boys; Krauss delivers two modern bluegrass gems in a voice as bright and pure as an icicle melting in the sun. The album's highlight, though, is the rendition of "Old Home Place" by J.D. Crowe and the New South. It's a chestnut, all right, but the combination of Crowe's driving banjo and the ringing, bittersweet blend of Tony Rice and Ricky Skaggs' voices will make your hair stand on end every time you hear it. This album belongs on every bluegrass fan's desert island list. *—Rick Anderson*

Bluegrass Essentials / Apr. 7, 1998 / Hip-O ✦✦✦✦

This is an 18-track collection featuring selections from everyone from Bill Monroe to Vince Gill. With selections from Jim & Jesse, J.D. Crowe, Ricky Skaggs, Alison Krauss, Jimmy Martin, the Dillards (who played the Darlings on the *Andy Griffith Show*), Reno & Smiley, Flatt & Scruggs, the Stanley Brothers, Claire Lynch, Del McCoury, Jonathan Edwards, Chesapeake, and the Country Gentlemen, it's extremely hard to find fault with any of the artists or selections aboard. A great value in the midline field. *—Cub Koda*

Bluegrass Masters / 1996 / Vanguard ✦✦✦✦✦

The title doesn't lie—this disc has 21 tracks by three of the best acts in the field (Bill Monroe, Flatt & Scruggs, and Jim & Jesse McReynolds), recorded live at the 1965 and 1966 Newport Folk Festivals. The sound and performances are good, and each act presents some familiar favorites—the McReynolds offer "Dueling Banjos" and "Sugarfoot Rag," Monroe does "Shady Grove" and "Cotton-Eyed Joe," and Flatt & Scruggs play "Orange Blossom Special," "Foggy Mountain Chimes," and "The Ballad of Jed Clampett." A youthful Peter Rowan, then a guitarist with Monroe, does a duet vocal with the bandleader on "Walls of Time." *—Richie Unterberger*

Bluegrass Super Hits / Aug. 27, 1996 / Sony ✦✦

The good news is that, featuring Bill Monroe & His Blue Grass Boys, Lester Flatt and Earl Scruggs & the Foggy Mountain Boys, Roy Acuff, and Ricky Skaggs, among others, this compilation features some of the most accomplished artists in bluegrass and that they perform such classic songs as "Blue Moon of Kentucky," "Uncle Pen," and "Great Speckled Bird." The bad news is that very few of these tracks can accurately be called hits (much less super hits), in many cases they are not the original versions, and the disc contains only ten tracks at a running time of 29 1/2 minutes. Assuming you find it at a discount price and you're looking for only the most superficial sense of what constitutes bluegrass, however, the good may outweigh the bad. *—William Ruhlmann*

Bluegrass U.S.A. / Sep. 24, 2002 / CMH ✦✦✦

One might expect from the mood of the U.S. in 2002 that *Bluegrass U.S.A.* had something to do with patriotism, but it doesn't—at least not directly. Instead, the collection insinuates that bluegrass, like jazz, is an American art form, and that gathering a number of traditional favorites is by its very nature a patriotic act. A number of classic performers—Jim & Jesse, Grandpa Jones, and the Osborne Brothers—are on hand to offer nifty renditions of "Sleepy Eyed John," "Are You From Dixie?," and "Hillbilly Fever." The fun thing about a collection like this is having all of these songs in one place, as though one was listening to a 40-minute radio program of bluegrass favorites. There's fancy banjo and mandolin picking on Don Reno's "Charlotte Breakdown" and a nice bit of flatpicking on the Stonemans' version of "Under the Double Eagle." While there's much to recommend about *Bluegrass U.S.A.*, the collection also has a couple of downsides. While a number of well-known tunes appear, the artist who made them popular doesn't necessarily perform them. "Ballad of Jed Clampett," for instance, is performed by Lester Flatt & Nashville

Grass, not Flatt & Scruggs. For the bluegrass novice, there's also the problem that the liner notes fail to identify the source of each track. If a listener is unconcerned with these flaws, *Bluegrass U.S.A.* will prove the perfect disc to reacquaint oneself with a handful of traditional classics. —*Ronnie D. Lankford Jr.*

Bona Fide Bluegrass Mountain Music / Apr. 23, 2002 / RCA ✦✦✦
O Bandwagon, Where Art Thou? In the frenzied rush to capitalize on the unprecedented success of the film (oh, you know which one), many labels have cranked out one old-timey collection after another. Luckily in this case, the RCA labels have the archives to back up their compilation and what results is sort of a second primer on traditional country music from the likes of Bill Monroe, the Carter Family, Jimmy Martin, and the underrated Wade Mainer. Spanning from 1928 to 1956 in a roughly chronological order, *Bona Fide Bluegrass Mountain Music* documents the evolution of this American roots music into the modern recording era. While longtime bluegrass fans will be familiar with all of the big names, the deeper cuts from Jimmy Murphy, the Morris Brothers, and the Country Pardners should be worth the price of the disc alone. Those who enjoyed the rich textures and pure honesty of the best-selling soundtrack will certainly enjoy this second volume of old-timey goodness. —*Zac Johnson*

The Bottle Let Me Down: Songs for Bumpy Wagon Rides / Jun. 18, 2002 / Bloodshot ✦✦✦
Before any insurgent country diehards rush out to purchase this album, they should be forewarned: it's a collection of children's songs—though not necessarily an album for children. In fact, the results are just twisted and subversive enough to give mom and dad some listening pleasure (assuming that mom and dad went to college in the halcyon days of Uncle Tupelo and have a subscription to *No Depression* magazine). There aren't only tried-and-true kid's songs on this collection—such as Rosie Flores' wonderfully swinging "Red, Red Robin"—there are also, believe it or not, some fine originals. Examples include Alejandro Escovedo's touching birthday tune "Sad and Dreamy (The Big 1-0)" and a song that Cornell Hurd (leader of Austin, TX, Western swing revue the Cornell Hurd Band) originally wrote for his young sons called "Don't Wipe Your Face on Your Shirt." This compilation is a lot of fun and good listening without trekking down the novelty path. —*Erik Hage*

Brewed in Texas: The Original Texas Happy Hour / Mar. 19, 2002 / Compadre ✦✦✦
Ever since the day some nameless string band got the idea of playing in a beer joint, drinking has been one of the most enduring themes of country music, and *Brewed in Texas* is a compilation from Houston-based indie label Compadre Records that features 20 acts from the Lone Star state weighing in on the pros and cons of getting drunk. For the most part, this is top-drawer honky tonk stuff, and while a few well-known names are on board—most notably Jerry Jeff Walker, Wayne Hancock, Todd Snider and John Rich, formerly of the group Lonestar—many of the lesser-known acts shine just as bright, particularly Slaid Cleves on "Horseshoe Lounge," Beaver Nelson's "Forget Thinkin'," Roger Creager's inspired story song "The Everclear Song," and Tommy Alverson's "Un Mas Cerveza." *Brewed in Texas* also gives something close to equal time to songs celebrating the joys of getting plastered (such as Adam Carroll's "Ol' Milwaukee's Best") and others which concern themselves with getting loaded to drown out the sorrows of life and love gone wrong (most notably Chris Wall's "Turns to Tears"). *Brewed In Texas* is a super-sized portion of high-octane hard country the way they used to cut it back in the 1950s and '60s, and nearly every cut satisfies (and even the weakest cuts beat out the work of the hat-wearing lames Nashville coughs up like hairballs these days)—if this disc isn't on the juke at your favorite watering hole, then they just don't know what's good for business. —*Mark Deming*

☆ **The Bristol Sessions, Vol. 1** / 1991 / Country Music Foundation ✦✦✦✦✦
This volume is presumably the first in a series of discs dedicated to reviving and restoring the legendary Ralph Peer sessions which commenced in the summer of 1927 in Bristol, TN. Peer was certainly no stranger to the recording industry as it existed in the 1920s. However, it was his initial encounter with Atlanta, Georgia fiddler John Carson and the song "Little Old Log Cabin in the Lane"—which eventually sold over a million copies—that quietly sparked a revolution of Southern rural music. He set up shop in Bristol with top-of-the-line audio equipment (at least by 1927 standards) in the hopes of not only capturing some of the locals, but also cashing in on the copyrights of their primarily traditional material. He eventually documented the origins of bluegrass, mountain music and what is generally referred to as the sounds of Americana. All said, Peer's eventual haul garnered nearly 80 respective recordings—18 of which are included on this incipient volume. Indeed their value can not be overestimated as Johnny Cash so boldly proclaimed that "the *Bristol Sessions* is the single most important event in the history of country music." Material from seminal artists such as Jimmie Rodgers—whose "Soldier's Sweetheart" and "Sleep, Baby, Sleep" are included here—as well as the Carter Family, who are represented by the tracks "Single Girl, Married Girl" and The "Storms Are on the Ocean." There are also lesser-known, yet no less decisive cuts such as the Alcoa Quartet's "Remember Me O Mighty One" and the Teneva Ramblers "Miss Liza, Poor Gal." Although there are other compilations available that include many of these sides, few come close in as apt an historical context. Co-producer Rich Kienzle's liner notes essay dispels much of the mythology surrounding the material and the sound is arguably better than ever thanks to meticulous remastering and digital transfers from the best available sources. Here's hoping for many more installments in the *Bristol Sessions*. —*Lindsay Planer*

Cajun String Bands 1930's: Cajun Breakdown / Nov. 18, 1997 / Arhoolie ✦✦✦✦✦
Here are 25 Cajun tracks from the 1930s, reflecting the transition of Cajun music to arrangements that placed the fiddle at the fore and did away with the accordion. Almost half of the cuts belong to J.B. Fuselier, with four by Leo Soileau, one by the Dixie

Ramblers, and seven by Luderin Darbone, fiddler of the Hackberry Ramblers (who back him on the selections here). Fuselier sounds like early Western swing with a Cajun fiddle; Clifford Breaux has a rawer, lazier charm, particularly on "Continuez de Sonner." There's a lot of spontaneity in these sessions, with unpredictable calls that sound like cousins to the ones that dotted Bob Wills' arrangements, though it can get a little monotonous over the course of the CD. It's not as diverse or interesting as some other early Cajun comps, like *Cajun Dance Party*, but still of considerable value to enthusiasts of Cajun '30s music, or early roots music in general. —*Richie Unterberger*

Cat Music / Feb. 24, 1998 / HMG ✦✦✦✦✦
Another collection of retro and original rockabilly from Ronny Weiser's vault of his Rollin' Rock label from the 1970s. The highlights on this volume include tracks recorded in the 1950s by Groovey Joe Poovey ("Move Around"), Bob Luman ("That's All Right"), Whitey Pullens ("Walk My Baby Back Home"), Diana Wisdom ("Bop Cat Baby") and "Everybody's Gone But Me"), Jimmy Patton ("Let Me Slide"), Bob Edwards ("Blue Blue Baby" and "What'll I Do") and Alvis Wayne ("Lay Your Head on My Shoulder"). Equally fine are the inclusion of retro '70s recordings by Merle Travis and Ray Campi ("Lost John Boogie" and "Merle's Boogie Woogie"), Johnny Carroll, Mac Curtis and Jackie Lee Cochran, showing the connecting thread that kept the music alive through fads and fashion. —*Cub Koda*

Cattle Call: Early Cowboy Music and Its Roots / 1996 / Rounder ✦✦✦✦✦
The first of a four-volume history of cowboy music, this collection of 14 songs from 1925-60 was compiled with an eye for illustrating the roots of the style, as heard in songs from sources that date before the commercialization of the form. It covers a fair amount of territory, including stars like Jimmie Rodgers, Tex Ritter, Tex Owens, and the Sons of the Pioneers; early women performers in the style, Patsy Montana and the Girls of the Golden West; early cowboy film singers Ken Maynard and Ray Whitley; and even the Mexican sounds of Trio Los Pancho. Like the entire series, each track is annotated with thorough notes about the history of the songs and the performers. —*Richie Unterberger*

Chess Rockabillies / Phonogram Chess ✦✦✦✦
Although Chess Records' reputation firmly rests on their monumental achievements in the blues and rhythm & blues field (and rightly so), the label also recorded—or leased from other labels—a fair amount of high-quality rockabilly music. Much of this interest came from Chuck Berry's success in the pop market with "Maybellene," and followed by the leasing of Dale Hawkins' hit "Susie Q." This 20-track collection gathers up many of the singles that Chess issued during that flurry of activity, with the addition of a couple of unissued sides. "Sugaree" by Rusty York was originally cut for Note and appears here off the stereo master, a surprising audio development for a rock & roll record from 1959. The Jet Tones were a band brought in to record a hasty cover version of Wilbert Harrison's "Kansas City," but the wild instrumental flip, "The Jet Tone Boogie," is the side to be reckoned with here, a slab of real rockabilly with powerhouse drumming and guitar solos. Dale Hawkins' "Lovin' Bug," a previously unissued master, makes its first appearance on this collection and is a worthy addition to his early discography. Not many African-Americans were willing to adapt to the new shakin' music, but those that did usually came up with fine results, and West Coast bluesman Johnny Fuller's "All Night Long" and G.L. Crockett's "Look Out Mabel" featuring Earl Hooker on guitar are prime examples of the form. Later Nashville session stalwart Hargus "Pig" Robbins clocks in with two tracks of piano-pumping rock & roll, as does Russell Bridges (later to reincarnate as Leon Russell) with a very Jerry Lee like "All Right." Fans of guitar-driven Southern-style rockabilly will positively revel in the inclusion of Bobby Sisco's "Tall Dark Handsome Man" with its fine guitar solos, Billy Barrix rewriting "Baby Let's Play House" with his "Cool Off Baby," and "Love Me" by Jimmy Lee and Wayne Walker, the duo that gave the label its first hit in the country field. Other notable tracks include "Roses Are Blooming" by Bob Silva and the Silva Tones and Memphis rockabilly Gene Simmons' bluesy "The Shape You Left Me In." This is a fine compilation literally begging for an American release. —*Cub Koda*

Classic Country Music, Vol. 1 / 1990 / Smithsonian ✦✦✦✦
An absolutely indispensable series, Smithsonian's *Classic Country* line of discs covers the music with great care and historical savvy. This first volume kicks things off with 25 tracks ranging from early string band sides (Gid Tanner & His Skillet Lickers) and the first country classics (the Carter Family, Jimmie Rodgers), to the mountain genius of Roy Acuff and popular cowboy-centric hits by Gene Autry, Tex Ritter, and the Sons of the Pioneers. And hinting at things to come, the collection wraps things up with a taste of Bob Wills' Western swing and Ernest Tubb's early honky tonk. So, from the '20s through the '40s, and with a bevy of milestones to hear along the way, this ride through hillbilly history is not to be missed. —*Stephen Cook*

Classic Country Music, Vol. 2 / Smithsonian ✦✦✦✦✦
Classic Country Music, Vol. 2 has a good cross-section of honky tonk, cowboy and traditional country cuts from the '50s, including tracks from Hank Williams, Kitty Wells, Webb Pierce, Al Dexter, Moon Mullican, Gene Autry, Hank Thompson, Floyd Tillman, and Lefty Frizzell. —*Thom Owens*

Classic Country Music, Vol. 3 / 1990 / Smithsonian ✦✦✦✦
On par with their excellent jazz collection, Smithsonian's *Classic Country Music* series takes in the highlights from the early string band days of the Carter Family and the rise of honky tonk to the Nashville sound and the crossover sounds of the '80s. Spread over four discs with close to 25 tracks a disc, the series offers country newcomers an ideal place to start. The third installment takes up the story in the mid-'50s, as rock & roll was starting to make waves. The first half covers the latter days of honky tonk with hits by Ray Price and Johnny Horton, not to mention a few nods to the Sun Records milieu by way of some Jerry Lee Lewis and Johnny Cash. The disc proceeds to take in most of the '60s,

including early country-pop (Jim Reeves and Patsy Cline), the Bakersfield sound (Buck Owens), mega hits (Bobbie Gentry and Roger Miller), and two of the music's strongest female voices (Loretta Lynn and Tammy Wynette). A fine taste of country before the producers really started jockeying for the crossover dollar and lost sight of those honky tonk roots. *—Stephen Cook*

Classic Country Music, Vol. 4 / 1990 / Smithsonian ✦✦✦✦
This fourth and last volume in the Smithsonian's country series covers the music from the last days of the Nashville sound up through the nouveau honky tonk of the early '70s and the rock and pop-tinged, chart topping likes of Alabama, the Judds, and Charlie Daniels. Also included, the original alt country of Gram Parsons, a bit of honky tonk revival by Dwight Yoakam, and a genuine pop smash from Dolly Parton. As usual, the Smithsonian has produced a quality collection, in spite of the often conflicting demands of historical brevity and commercial recognition. And while some of the later material falls short, the disc mostly stays on track thanks to a little help from George Jones, Waylon Jennings, Lefty Frizzell, and Loretta Lynn. A history lesson for the tavern set. *—Stephen Cook*

Classic Country: 1960–1964 / Dec. 17, 1999 / Time-Life ✦✦✦✦
While Time-Life is not the first word in reissues, they have done a fine job here with this country overview from 1960-1964. Like other titles in their country series spanning 1950-1979, this two-disc, 30-track sampler skims the top of the charts for the day's country smashes. The period in question was one of Nashville's most transitional, as the rough-hewn sound of the honky tonk style (Hank Williams, Ray Price, Webb Pierce, Lefty Frizzell, etc.) gave way to the strings and pop flavors of the Nashville sound. With RCA leading the way, thanks to Chet Atkins' A&R work and Owen Bradley's production, the industry embraced a smooth and clean sound epitomized by the likes of chart-toppers like Jim Reeves, Patsy Cline, Roger Miller, Faron Young, Marty Robbins, and Skeeter Davis. This collection features all those acts doing their biggest hits (Miller's "Dang Me," Reeves' "Welcome to My World," Davis' "The End of the World"). As such, the collection proves a worthy introduction for the country newcomer. And lest one think it was all over-produced pop during this time, this edition of *Classic Country* also features the latter-day honky tonk of George Jones, Buck Owens, Johnny Cash, and Carl Butler. Gathering gems from a cross-section of labels, including Decca, Columbia, and RCA, this country roundup will be sure to please listeners itching to get their feet wet. *—Stephen Cook*

Classic Country: 1965–1969 / Dec. 17, 1999 / Time-Life ✦✦✦✦
Time-Life enters the country compilation sweepstakes with a somewhat slim yet still solid mix of late-'60s hits and misses. Spanning most of the big country labels, the 15-track set ranges from outlaw sides (Merle Haggard's "Mama Tried" and Waylon Jennings' "Only Daddy That'll Walk the Line") to a few slices of Nashville sound gloss (Eddy Arnold's "Make the World Go Away"). In between, there are plenty of other chart-toppers by Glen Campbell ("Wichita Lineman"), Jeannie C. Riley ("Harper Valley P.T.A."), Loretta Lynn ("Don't Come Home a Drinkin' [With Lovin' on Your Mind]"), and Roger Miller ("King of the Road"). And Elvis even makes an appearance, with his ethereal gospel stunner "Crying in the Chapel." Taken in tandem with the more bulky and focused *Columbia Country Classics: The Nashville Sound*, this varied sampler makes for a heady, late-night tavern soundtrack. *—Stephen Cook*

Cliffie Stone's Radio Transcriptions 1945–1949 / 1991 / Country Routes ✦✦✦✦
Cliffie Stone's Radio Transcriptions 1945-1949 contains 19 performances from several of the biggest names in country music of the late '40s. Stone was one of the best-known and most-popular record producers and radio hosts in California during that era, and was responsible for helping to promote many of the best performers on the West Coast during that time, as this compilation proves. *Radio Transcriptions* boasts an impressive array of styles and talents, ranging from the country-boogie of Tennessee Ernie Ford with Merle Travis and the hillbilly duets of the Armstrong Twins, to the swinging guitarist Red Murrell and the smooth croons of Jimmy Wakely. It's an entertaining and informative portrait of West Coast country in the postwar years, and many die-hard country fans will find it very worthwhile. *—Stephen Thomas Erlewine*

Close to Home: Old Time Music From Mike Seeger's Collection (1952–1967) / Jun. 17, 1997 / Smithsonian Folkways ✦✦✦
Collected by Mike Seeger from 1952 to 1967 as he roamed around the Appalachian Mountains, *Close to Home* is one of the better detailed sets of authentic old-time Southern American music to be found. Though mostly recorded at the musician's home on a single, hand-held microphone, the warmth and charm of the performances captured make up for any supposed lack of recording quality, as Seeger no doubt took great pains to document these archaic stylings before they died with their performers. Of the 38 tracks featured, some legends like Sara and Maybelle Carter of the Carter Family fame, Elizabeth Cotten, and fiddler Eck Robertson appear, though the majority are simply local legends or unknowns. As such, it might come as some surprise to hear the level of accomplishment reached by these common folks, as a few were even said to have been badly out of practice when recorded. A majority of the tracks are lively fiddle or banjo instrumentals, though a few harmonica workouts, gorgeous autoharp and dulcimer tunes, and a cappella tracks appear, as well. This is very honest music, without a hint of pretension, and one can only wonder how many similar talents lived and died without ever having shared their talents outside of their local community. Excellent liner notes composed by Seeger himself give a wonderfully detailed commentary on how he came about to record the featured artists, and also place the performers within their historical context. There might be more complete collections on the market, but for the single-disc price and the amount of quality music here, *Close to Home* is highly recommended. *—Matt Fink*

☆ **Columbia Country Classics, Vol. 1: The Golden Age** / 1990 / Columbia ✦✦✦✦✦
This five-volume set contains 128 of the greatest country music recordings in Columbia's vaults, which span the genre from its beginnings. Each volume (available separately or as a set) contains major country artists. This first volume contains 27 landmark recordings by the artists that made them famous, such as the late Roy Acuff's "Wabash Cannonball" and the Carter Family's "Will the Circle Be Unbroken"—16 artists in all. *—AMG*

Columbia Country Classics, Vol. 3: Americana / 1990 / Columbia ✦✦✦✦
Part of Columbia's excellent *Country Classics* survey series, this 25-track roundup of Americana-themed material takes in the vast landscape by way of geography, history, and patriotism. Ranging from early honky tonk-era sides to '80s roots, *Columbia Country Classics, Vol. 3: Americana* spotlights hits by Marty Robbins ("El Paso"), Johnny Horton ("North to Alaska"), Lefty Frizzell ("Saginaw, Michigan"), and the Charlie Daniels Band ("The Devil Went Down to Georgia"). Bookended by the picaresque likes of "The Ballad of Davey Crockett" (Fess Parker) and "Highwayman," the mix packs it in with more U.S. gold from Hawkshaw Hawkins, Johnny Cash, and Stonewall Jackson, among others. It's a rousing bit of old-timey fun. *—Stephen Cook*

Columbia Country Classics, Vol. 4: The Nashville Sound / Columbia ✦✦✦✦✦
The Nashville Sound picks things up in the mid-'50s, and chronicles the rise of country-pop (aka the Nashville sound). In 1955 Marty Robbins made number one on the country charts with a mixture of pristine honky tonk and smooth vocals in "Singing the Blues." This and many of the early tracks on this collection were produced by Columbia's own Nashville sound architect Don Law, who would bring honky tonk to its logical and streamlined extreme; Ray Price still sounds polished even without strings ("Night Life") and Hawkshaw Hawkins jumps into the fray with an appealing choral and country mixture ("I Can't Seem to Say Goodbye"). Law would reach his peak with Billy Walker's seamless, easy listening rendition of the Willie Nelson perennial "Funny How Time Slips Away." Producer Billy Sherrill took the reigns in 1965, and pushed the Nashville sound to its peak, with up-in-the-mix strings and choir, plenty of echo and reverb, and rhythm sections that sounded unobtrusively compact. Sherrill found quick success with David Houston's "Almost Persuaded," Tammy Wynette's career-defining hit "Stand By Your Man," and later with luxuriously arranged hits for George Jones. Charlie Rich's hugely successful crossover hits "Behind Close Doors" and "The Most Beautiful Girl in the World," though, would be Sherrill's watermark and come to represent the apex of the Nashville sound. Along with Rich's hits, Lynn Anderson's "I Never Promised You a Rose Garden," Barbara Mandrell's "The Midnight Oil," and Tanya Tucker's "Would You Lay With Me (In a Field of Stone)" would set the stage for country's transformation into the ultra-polished music it became during the '80s and '90s. *—Stephen Cook*

Columbia Country Classics, Vol. 5: New Tradition / 1988 / Columbia ✦✦✦
The final volume in the set contains music from today, both established artists and up-and-coming ones, like Larry Gatlin, Asleep at the Wheel, Willie Nelson, Sweethearts of the Rodeo, the O'Kanes, and more. *—AMG*

Common Thread: The Songs of the Eagles / 1994 / Warner Bros. ✦✦
In a benefit album for Don Henley's pet project, Walden Pond, a number of the biggest stars in contemporary country music come together to pay tribute to the influence the Eagles had on country and rock. Ironically, all of the interpretations on *Common Thread* are more pop/rock-oriented than the original versions, making the album a well-intentioned but pointless exercise. *—AMG*

The Complete Sun Singles, Vol. 1 / 1994 / Bear Family ✦✦✦✦
This is the first in a projected six-volume set chronicling the entire singles output of Sun Records, their subsidiaries Flip and Phillips International, run in strict chronological order. No alternate takes, no studio chitchat, no second-guessing decades after the fact—just the simple history of some of the greatest American music that ever came from one man's vision, label owner and production genius Sam Phillips. Each box features four CDs, and this first volume brings us the first 52 Sun singles—both A- and B-sides—plus both sides of all the singles on Flip, Sam's short-lived 1955 subsidiary. It takes us from the humblest of humble beginnings—when Sun was a raw blues label, cutting one early Memphis blues classic after another—through the first recordings of Elvis, Johnny Cash, and Carl Perkins, leaving us poised near Sun's golden rockabilly age. A great many record collectors got started because of their endless fascination with Sun. Seldom—if ever—has a label's minutiae been held to such scrutiny that even artists who only saw one or a handful of scant-selling releases have become cult heroes. And the first flowering of Elvis aside, that's really the big ticket here—hearing the story of a unique, maverick label unfold before your very ears. It's easy to see within the first half-dozen singles on disc one that Sam Phillips was gonna put out *exactly* what felt good to *him.* Maybe Phillips never mastered the art of the studio fade-out, but he could drill right into the heart and soul of an artist and capture mood and ambience on tape in a way that the Chess or Bihari brothers never could. For all the blues classics covered by disc two, the first white artists were also starting to appear on the little yellow label. Disc three is where the whole ball game starts to change with the arrival of Elvis, but his first four singles aren't the only great stuff on this disc. Disc four shows Phillips slowly moving away from the blues and heading his label into country music, with rockabilly still almost a sideline dalliance. Elvis' final Sun single is here, but many of the classics on this disc come from Sam applying his production expertise to a clutch of great country singles—some of his best and most unaffected records came out of this batch. Bottom line: this box is the first step to owning one of the great labels of all time, and some of the best blues, country and rock & roll you'll ever experience. There's also a 68-page bound booklet with label reproductions and photos galore, plus great notes from Sun researchers Hank Davis and Colin Escott. The price tag might

seem a tad hefty to some, but compared to what the original 78s and 45s are going for—all of them lovingly restored here when masters were missing, by the way—this thing's a steal. —*Cub Koda*

Complete Sun Singles, Vol. 2 / 1995 / Bear Family ♦♦♦♦

Vol. 2 of this series runs the label's output, both A- and B-sides, from Sun 229 ("Daydreams Come True" by Maggie Sue Wimberly) to 278 (Tommy Blake's rockabilly howler "Lordy Hoody"). At our starting point with this box, Elvis had moved on to RCA Victor and worldwide stardom, and the first million-seller for the label—Carl Perkins' "Blue Suede Shoes"—was looming on the horizon. By the end of it, we're in the midst of the original rockabilly revolution. This is truly Sun's golden age.

Vol. 1 in the series showed how Sun evolved from a blues label to the first recordings by Elvis, Carl Perkins and Johnny Cash, which firmly moved it into country territory, for this is how all three artists were originally marketed. Disc one picks up the thread nicely with the Carl Perkins spin of "Blue Suede Shoes" and "Honey Don't." Disc two hits paydirt in a big way with Johnny Cash's "I Walk the Line" and "Get Rhythm," Roy Orbison's "Ooby Dooby," "Go! Go! Go!," "Rockhouse," and "You're My Baby" (featuring Roy at his rockabilly guitar-picking best), Carl Perkins' "Boppin' the Blues," "Dixie Fried," and "All Mama's Children," Billy Riley's debut disc "Trouble Bound" and "Rock With Me Baby," and the twin-spin coolness of Warren Smith's "Ubangi Stomp" and "Black Jack David," two of the best sides ever cut at *706 Union Avenue.* More Johnny Cash is aboard disc three, with "Train of Love" and "There You Go," and right after that is the debut disc from the Ferriday Fireball himself, Jerry Lee Lewis, with "Crazy Arms" and "End of the Road" both amply demonstrating how fully formed his style was when he entered Sam's studio. Right after that is one of the best Sun records *ever,* Billy Riley's "Flying Saucer Rock & Roll," featuring the Killer on backup piano and guitarist Roland Janes whipping the tremolo bar on his Strat into a frenzy on the intro. Our final disc keeps the rockin' banner flying high with Jerry Lee's epochal "Whole Lot of Shakin' Going On" and its flip, "It'll Be Me," a number taken at a wild-ass breakneck tempo with a piano solo that ranks as one of his best. Special mention should also be made about the massive bound booklet that comes with this four-disc set; it is the epitome of cool, featuring photos that'll make your eyes get as big as 78s, while Hank Davis' notes are as spot on the money as anybody could ask for. Not just throwing together some photos you've seen a zillion times together with a scant recycled text, this book actually *enhances* the Sun Records experience. —*Cub Koda*

Complete Sun Singles, Vol. 3 / 1996 / Bear Family ♦♦♦♦

The third entry into this six-volume series chronicling the entire Sun singles catalog begins in the fall of 1957. The tiny label—which had been essentially a two-person operation in the beginning and through its early gestation—was now a major independent with national hits in (pop, country, and rhythm & blues. Sun was not only the little label that could, but also a major force in shaping rock & roll and the boundaries of pop music overall. Sun was no longer a regional label making strange, quirky music for a small chunk of the Southern demographic, but a part of the national marketplace. As this installment in the series clearly illustrates by its chronological end in the summer of 1959, Sun wanted to be a part of that marketplace and would change their trademark sound accordingly. Backup singers, tenor sax solos, overdubs, a taming of the raw excitement—these were all stylistic notions unthinkable of a Sun record only a couple of years back. But for every pop teen idol experiment gone awry, for every slick(er) concession to the marketplace, Sun Records still rocked harder than any label on the planet and made much original music in the bargain. In the A- and B-sides of these 50 singles, we hear the changes in Sun and, indeed, rock & roll itself. Disc one features one of the most cathartic moments in Sun history: Jerry Lee Lewis' two-sided classic, "Great Balls of Fire" and "You Win Again." Both sides of the Johnny Cash coin (the cool and the cloying) are well represented; Roy Orbison was being moved into similarly commercial fish-out-of-water territory, and Carl Perkins' last single for the label also appears. Disc two features sides from the man responsible for much of the new bent toward mainstream commercialism—producer/songwriter/musician Jack Clement, who wrote pop fluff like "Ballad of a Teenage Queen," played the acoustic guitar riff on "Big River," and produced sessions for Phillips. The third disc has numerous highlights from the first track to the last; the final disc takes us up to the summer of 1959, a fallow time for rock & roll, although there's still much great music to be heard. However, even the gradual taming of rockabilly and the sweetening of the hillbilly sounds the label was noted for couldn't possibly prepare the listener for 11-year-old chalk-on-a-blackboard moppet Sherry Crane; "Winnie the Parakeet" and its flip side "Willie Willie" is simply the worst Sun record of all time, no contest. Along with these 101 sides (including a Jerry Lee interview track) is a sumptuous, bound 68-page booklet, chock full of label photos, excellent track-by-track text from Hank Davis, and rare photos of everybody from Johnny Cash to the sickly sweet Sherry Crane. —*Cub Koda*

Complete Sun Singles, Vol. 4 / Mar. 18, 1997 / Bear Family ♦♦♦♦

By the time the singles on this four-disc set were released (1959 into 1962), Sun was a much different label than the one that discovered Elvis Presley just a few years earlier. Presley, Johnny Cash, Carl Perkins and Roy Orbison had moved to other labels, and Jerry Lee Lewis was in the middle of trying to reassemble the pieces of his career. Label owner Sam Phillips was in the midst of leaving his fabled *706 Union Memphis Recording Service* for a new studio across town, never again finding the warm intimacy that graced his early recorded efforts. The label also pursued trends that seemed to be selling at that moment, and largely gone was that anarchic spirit that made all the early Sun issues so legendary. But there was still a pronounced regional flavor and inherent sound to a Sun record—even the ones cut in Nashville during this period—that emerged from the grooves, no matter how much the original master tape was embalmed in chirping female choruses and syrupy strings. Disc one sports more than a few classic sides—including Rayburn Anthony's "Alice Blue Gown" and Tracy Pendarvis' double-sided blast from Sun's past, "A Thousand Guitars"/"Is It Too Late"—amid the commercial dross. There were other stray nods to Sun's rockin' past with Sonny Wilson's "The Great Pretender" (sporting one of the most confused guitar breaks ever released on the label) and "I'm Gonna Take a Walk," but perhaps even more interesting was the continual mining of the vaults for more Johnny Cash sides. Disc two follows this pattern, with a pair of Jerry Lee Lewis 45s and Cash singles standing alongside Tracy Pendarvis' "Is It Me" as musical high points, but these were severely undercut by the issuance of pop-inspired crossover material. Disc three kicks off with a major surprise, a two-sided Charlie Rich instrumental issued under the name Bobby Sheridan. More Cash material from the vaults is aboard, along with Jerry Lee's back-to-the-charts hit, "What'd I Say." The final disc illustrates what a hit record did to Jerry Lee's stock at the label, as Sun issued one single after another in its wake, scoring another hit with "Money" alongside "Sweet Little Sixteen," the last Sun chart entry. Harold Dorman's "Uncle Jonah's Place," Johnny Cash's "Blue Train" and Don Hosea's "Uh Huh Huh" (actually Willie Cobb's "You Don't Love Me") complete the list of listenable items on this set. Sun was nearing the end of the line as well as changing its musical direction, but there was still great stuff to be found in their release schedule, and this box nicely collects it all up in one place. —*Cub Koda*

Complete Sun Singles, Vol. 5 / Feb. 11, 1998 / Bear Family ♦♦♦♦♦

The fifth volume in Bear Family's exhaustive assembling of every single issued by Sam Phillips picks up the story of the end of Sun Records and the beginnings of its Phillips International subsidiary. This follows Sun releases from 1962 to 1968 and the first two years of the P.I. imprint, beginning in 1957. By the early 1960s, Sun was back to being a small, local label with little—if any—impact on the national scene. Its final 13 releases drifted out over a period of three years to scant acclaim and little promotion. Disc one kicks off with the pop stylings of teen idol wannabe Tony Rossini and instrumentals from the Four Upsetters. Other highlights include selections from Billy Adams, Bill Yates, Jerry Lee Lewis (including "Teenage Letter"), a reissue of Smokey Joe's "Signifying Monkey," and the final record from Johnny Cash. Disc two finds the label responding to the British Invasion in their own unique Memphian way with sides from Randy & the Radiants and the Jesters' "Cadillac Man" and "My Babe," possibly the last great Sun single. There are also diverse selections from Billy Adams, Bill Yates (including two issued under the pseudonym of Gorgeous Bill), Johnny Cash clone Dane Stinit, a reissue of David Houston's Phillips International single "Sherry's Lips," soul music from the Climates, gospel from Brother James Anderson, the final Sun issue from Load of Mischief and the final Sun record from Jerry Lee ("Carry Me Back to Old Virginia"). Disc three begins the chronicling of Sam's Phillips International label. Phillips International began in 1957 as somewhat of a "pop" alternative to the rockabilly fare that was the bread and butter of the Sun label, but quickly showed an all-over-the-road approach that eventually short-circuited the operation. Kicking off with the country-pop of Buddy Blake's "You Pass Me By," the first 11 singles in the catalog were a delightful collection of unreconstructed rockabilly, commercial rock & roll (including Bill Justis' mega-hit "Raunchy"), hot Memphis hybrid music and straight up pop/rockers. The final disc kicks off with Barbara Pittman's "Everlasting Love" and continues chronicling the rest of the label's output from 1958 and the first three singles from 1959. Among the many high spots are Ernie Barton's first single for the label ("Stairway to Nowhere"), a pair of great singles from Cliff Thomas, Ed & Barbara, Bill Justis searching for a follow-up to "Raunchy," Ken Cook's "Crazy Baby," and Charlie Rich's first single ("Philadelphia Baby"). —*Cub Koda*

Conmemorativo: A Tribute to Gram Parsons / 1993 / Rhino ♦♦♦♦

In his short recording career, Gram Parsons attempted to bridge the gap between country and rock music. Arguably the founder of country-rock, Parson's timeless influence on music is undeniable, and that is perhaps why this tribute works so remarkably well. A diversity of artists are included, with interpretations that range from reverent note-perfect readings, like the Musical Kings' (featuring Kevn Kinney and R.E.M.'s Peter Buck) version of the Flying Burrito Brothers' "Cody, Cody" to renditions that rework the songs, as in Finger's cover of "Still Feeling Blue," which takes straight honky tonk country and gives it a rockin' Rolling Stones feel. And although he recorded a number of cover versions, every song on this tribute was either written or co-written by Gram. Every phase of his career is also represented in the 17 tracks: from his folkie days in the mid-'60s—"November Nights" (Coal Porters) to his final recording session in 1973—"Return of the Grievous Angel" (Joey Burns and Victoria Williams). Noteworthy is the inclusion of Polly Parsons (Gram's daughter) & Eden performing "The New Soft Shoe." All in all, there really isn't a bad version, and some of them are superb, such as Uncle Tupelo ("Blue Eyes"), Steve Wynn ("Christine's Tune") and Stephen McCarthy("One Hundred Years From Now"). —*Jack Leaver*

Country All-Stars: Jazz from the Hills / 1994 / Bear Family ♦♦♦

Formed in the mid-'60s, the Country All-Stars is a supergroup comprised of in-demand Nashville session musicians. The group's *Jazz from the Hills* is an appropriately swinging set of country standards and original material. While the playing is tasteful and frequently engaging, it is a bit too slick for hardcore country fans, but fans of collegiate jazz and mainstream country-pop will find *Jazz from the Hills* entertaining. —*Thom Owens*

Country Classics, Vol. 4: The Nashville Sound / 1990 / Columbia ♦♦♦♦

Country Classics, Vol. 4: The Nashville Sound is a superb, 26-track collection that functions as a showcase for Billy Sherrill's lush, sweeping production. Few single discs capture the sound of '60s and early-'70s country-pop as well as this, and that's even more remarkable when you consider it's culled solely from the vaults of Columbia and Epic Records. Among the artists showcased are Johnny Cash ("I Still Miss Someone," "Ring of Fire"), Marty Robbins ("Singing the Blues," "Devil Woman"), June Carter ("Jackson"), Hawkshaw Hawkins ("I Can't Seem to Say Goodby"), David Houston ("Almost Persuaded,"

"My Elusive Dreams"), Sandy Posey ("Bring Him Safely Home to Me"), Johnny Paycheck ("She's All I Got"), Stonewall Jackson ("A Wound Time Can't Erase"), George Jones ("A Picture of Me (Without You)," "The Grand Tour"), Ray Price ("For the Good Times"), Lynn Anderson ("I Never Promised You a Rose Garden"), Barbara Mandrell ("The Midnight Oil"), Tanya Tucker ("Would You Lay with Me in a Field of Stone") and Charlie Rich ("I Take It on Home," "Behind Closed Doors," "The Most Beautiful Girl"). *—Stephen Thomas Erlewine*

Country Shots: Barroom Biggies / 1994 / Rhino ♦♦♦
Country Shots: Barroom Biggies celebrates one of country's most beloved song topics: drinking. Jerry Lee Lewis' "What's Made Milwaukee Famous (Has Made a Loser of Me)," Moe Bandy's "Barstool Mountain," and Loretta Lynn's "Don't Come Home a Drinkin' (With Lovin' on Your Mind)" all bemoan the perils of a few too many, while George Jones' "If Drinkin' Don't Kill Me (Her Memory Will)," and Eddie Rabbit's "Drinkin' My Baby (Off My Mind)" are tear-in-your-beer classics. Shelly West's "Jose Cuervo," Hank Thompson's "On Tap, in the Can or in the Bottle," and Mel Tillis' "Stomp Them Grapes," on the other hand, sing the praises of alcohol, beer, and wine. Mickey Gilley's "The Power of Positive Drinkin'" and Willie Nelson's "Whiskey River" are some of the other highlights of this collection, which makes the most of its thematic nature and delivers a cohesive, entertaining collection of country drinking songs. *—Heather Phares*

Country Shots: Gearjammin' Greats / 1994 / Rhino ♦♦♦
As its title suggests, *Country Shots: Gearjammin' Greats* features country songs devoted to the truck driving life, as songs like George Hamilton IV's "Truck Driving Man," Dave Dudley's "Truck Drivin' Son-Of-A-Gun," and Red Simpson's "I'm a Truck" attest. C.W. McCall's classic "Convoy," Del Reeves' "Looking at the World Through a Windshield," and Tom T. Hall's "Ravishing Ruby" are some of the album's other highlights. Though it might be a trucker-themed collection, *Gearjammin' Greats* will appeal to country fans of all persuasions. *—Heather Phares*

Country Shots: God Bless America / 1994 / Rhino ♦♦♦
Country Shots: God Bless America delivers patriotic country songs such as Ernest Tubb's "It's America (Love It or Leave It)" and Hank Williams Jr.'s "Don't Give Us a Reason." Bobby Bare's "God Bless America Again," Lee Greenwood's "God Bless the U.S.A.," and Glen Campbell's "God Must Have Blessed America" sing America's praises somewhat less stridently. Tex Ritter's "Americans (A Canadian's Opinion)" adds a bit of humor to the album, while Bill Anderson's "Where Have All Our Heroes Gone" and Autry Inman's "Ballad of Two Brothers" are poignantly patriotic. Though it's not the most diverse collection in the *Country Shots* series, *God Bless America* will please any country fans looking for the perfect soundtrack to their Fourth of July parties. *—Heather Phares*

☆ **Country: Nashville—Dallas—Hollywood—1927/1942** / 1994 / Frémeaux ♦♦♦♦♦
Old-time country compilations don't get any better than this dazzling 36-song double CD, made up of artists who are unrepresented (or barely represented) on CD, and genuine rarities by some who are well represented. The opening track, "Railroad Blues" by Sam McGee, heralds a brace of blues-based country songs by G.B. Grayson ("Omie Wise"), the Carolina Tarheels ("Peg and Awl"), Buster Carter and Preston Young ("Lazy Farmer Boy"), where black and white rural music meet and interweave inextricably—Dick Justice's "Brownskin Blues" and Jimmie Tarlton's "Slow Wicked Blues" (with some gorgeous yodeling) are as good fine examples of blues as anything you'll hear on the Yazoo or Document labels, and there's not a Gene Autry blues number even present! Old-style blues and old time banjo styles also link together in Buell Kazee's "Butcher Boy." The Williamson Brothers perform one of the earliest commercial recordings of "John Henry," entitled "Gonna Die With This Hammer in My Hand," and the Monroe Brothers and the Delmore Brothers are also present on this collection. It's also possible to hear records such as "The House Carpenter" by Clarence Ashley, which could easily have given Bob Dylan the direction to his early folk style (and I'm not willing to bet that he didn't know some of this stuff). Jimmie Rodgers is here ("Blue Yodel No. 8"), as is the Carter Family ("John Hardy," "Wildwood Flower"), but so is Tex Ritter in his ultra-rare 1935 recording of "Rye Whiskey, Rye Whiskey," the closest thing he had to a commercial success in that decade. The second disc does go further into performers who are remembered today, such as Milton Brown & His Brownies ("Hesitation Blues"), Patsy Montana ("I Wanna Be a Cowboy's Sweetheart"), Shelly Lee Alley & His Alley Cats ("Women, Women, Women"), Bob Wills ("Liza, Pull Down the Shades," "What's the Matter With the Mill"), and even one who's still around in 1997, Roy Rogers, on "Cowboy Night Herd Song." The sound is excellent, though the notes are a bit sketchy, given the sheer amount of material included here. (French import) *—Bruce Eder*

Country: The American Tradition / Oct. 12, 1999 / Sony ♦♦♦♦
Even when isolated from the gargantuan 26-disc box set *Sony Music 100 Years: Soundtrack for a Century*, the 51-track *Country: The American Tradition* is impressive. Columbia was one of the biggest labels in the early days of the record industry, as is evident from the beginning of this collection, which features cuts by Fiddlin' John Carson, Charlie Poole, Gid Tanner & His Skillet Lickers, and the Carter Family. What's more impressive is that the label—and later, its subsidiaries—captured the sound of each era. A glance at the featured artists—Gene Autry, Bob Wills, Bill Monroe, Johnny Cash, the Byrds, Tammy Wynette, Willie Nelson, George Jones, Mary-Chapin Carpenter, and the Dixie Chicks are among them—gives a sense of not only how the label developed, but how country music did as well. Some major artists are missing—they didn't sign everyone, after all—as are some trends, but the overall effect is overwhelming. This set traces the history of country music in the 20th century, offering a terrific educational experience while also being entertaining. It's a feat that's difficult to pull off, let alone by concentrating on one group of labels, which is why it's all the more impressive. *—Stephen Thomas Erlewine*

Cowboy Country: Shadows on the Trail / Jul. 11, 2000 / Jasmine ♦♦♦
Another entry in Jasmine's excellent series of vintage radio transcriptions, *Cowboy Country* collects 24 performances of Western material by Jimmy Wakely, Johnny Bond, Tex Ritter, Sons of the Pioneers, and others. One of the many highlights is the inclusion of five songs by the seldom-heard Cass County Boys, the Western vocal combo that accompanied Gene Autry on-stage and screen. Carolina Cotton appears on the stunning "Yodel Mountain Song," one of two great yodeling showcases on this disc (the other being Rex Allen's "Yodelin' Crazy"). The sound quality is rough in spots, but *Cowboy Country* is full of rare recordings that any Western music enthusiast will want to hear. *—Greg Adams*

Cowboy Hymns & Prayers / Jul. 29, 1996 / Warner Bros. ♦♦♦
Cowboy Hymns & Prayers features a good cross-section of contemporary cowboy singer/songwriters contributing originals and covers of Christian sprituals and inpirational songs. All of the material is drawn from the Warner Western vaults, with all but two of the tracks (Waddie Mitchell's "Cowboy Prayer" and Mark O'Connor's "Amazing Grace") featured on the label's official albums. Like many various artists collections, *Cowboy Hymns & Prayers* is slightly uneven, but the best of the songs on the record is moving, heartfelt and rustically poetic, as only real cowboys can be. *—Stephen Thomas Erlewine*

Cowboy Songs from Folkways / 1991 / Smithsonian Folkways ♦♦♦♦♦
This is a richly varied set, from Leadbelly to Woody Guthrie, drawn from the vast Folkways archives and dating from the early '40s to the '60s. It also has excellent annotations. *—Charles S. Wolfe*

Cowboy Songs, Ballads, and Cattle Calls from Texas / Library of Congress ♦♦♦
Recorded in the '40s by the Library of Congress (usually by John Lomax), all of this material was Texan in origin, and sung by Texans. That even holds true of the performance by Lomax (originally of Dallas) himself, who sings "The Buffalo Skinners." If, for instance, folkloric recordings of field hollers could be seen as several-steps-removed ancestors of the blues, these tracks are likewise several-steps-removed ancestors of cowboy and country music. All but two of the selections are a cappella solo vocals, and indeed one is not a "song" as such but a spoken conversation between Lomax and Sloan Matthews about cattle calls, with Matthews periodically demonstrating actual cattle calls. The slightly muffled fidelity and stark, unaccompanied performances make this unlikely to interest the general listener, but it's an important collection of tunes illustrating aspects of the roots of cowboy and Texan culture. *—Richie Unterberger*

The D Singles Collection, Vol. 1 / 1996 / Bear Family ♦♦♦♦♦
In the '50s, the landscape of the recording industry was profusely dotted with scads of tiny, independent labels recording blues, rock & roll, country and whatever on shoestring budgets hoping for a coast to coast biggie that would put them on the map. They were largely run by quirky, indomitable spirits and if you were looking for one in Texas, your man was Pappy Daily, who founded Starday Records and fostered the early careers of George Jones and Webb Pierce. Well versed in both the retail and juke box vendor ends of the business, Daily started up the D label from the ashes of Starday and this four disc complete run of the label's first 60 or so singles (plus alternates) makes for one mind boggling collection of regional music circa the late '50s. On the surface, there seems to be little to no rhyme or reason to the release schedule here; a dozen or so rock & roll wannabes, a million Tex Nobodies either sticking to their shrinking market country guns or straddling the fence trying to play some of that be-boppin' music, then suddenly whammo! here's the Big Bopper doing "Chantilly Lace"!! But as any independent record label owner would be the first to tell you, "records was cheap to make back then" and given Daily's penchant for pressing up sides for strictly Southern jukebox consumption (the reissues of the late-'40s Gold Star Harry Choates Cajun fiddle sides included here) and cheerfully proclaiming that he wanted to put out a record on every singing disc jockey in America, the crazy quilt of the catalog starts to become a bit clearer, stray polka and Mexican mariachi releases aside. Oh yeah, and for just plain weird (as in "what's *this* doin' here?") you just gotta check out Al Travis' "Mom & Dad Love You Too," which could easily win just about any award you'd like to give out for whitest sounding 45 on a box set. While there's no big names here to champion, there's also way too much fine music in this box set to let it go unnoticed. *—Cub Koda*

The Definitive Bluegrass Collection / Nov. 13, 2001 / CMH ♦♦♦
Calling any album *The Definitive Bluegrass Collection* is a bold statement for any record label, especially so for CMH. Luckily for them, they've got the rights to the definitive versions of a lot of bluegrass standards, like the Osborne Brothers' "Rocky Top," "Are You Missing Me" by Jim & Jesse, and "I'm Using My Bible for a Roadmap" by Don Reno, all of which are featured on this two-disc set. However, it is a bit of a misnomer to call the album "definitive" without any recordings by Bill Monroe, the Stanley Brothers, or Flatt & Scruggs (although Lester Flatt & Nashville Grass do appear on a couple of tracks). Nevertheless it is a solid collection of 30 great bluegrass songs, performed ably by a bunch of great artists. *—Zac Johnson*

Don't Fence Me In: Western Music's Early Golden Era / Feb. 1996 / Rounder ♦♦♦♦♦
The second volume of Rounder's cowboy music retrospective documents the form's coming of age in the late '30s and '40s, when the genre became part of the popular mainstream via both commercial recordings and films. The music was becoming more commercial via slicker arrangements and harmonies, but retained links to country and folk sources even as it widened its popular appeal. These 14 cuts include classics by some of the leading cowboy singers, including Gene Autry, the Sons of the Pioneers, Tex Ritter and Roy Rogers, as well as relative lesser-knowns like Louise Massey and Ray Whitley, and a track in the cowboy style by Western swing king Bob Wills. *—Richie Unterberger*

Don't Let the Bastards Get You Down: A Tribute to Kris Kristofferson / 2002 / Jackpine Social Club ✦✦✦✦

Kris Kristofferson is best known as a second-string actor whose resumé features two or three misfires like *Fire Down Below* and *Girls' Night* for every moment of genuine greatness, such as *Lone Star*. And even at the height of his career in music, his work was hampered by a voice that, to put it charitably, takes a bit of getting used to. But none of that changes the fact that at his peak, Kristofferson was one of the very finest songwriters to ever emerge from Nashville, possessing a literate intelligence that never slipped into pretension and a masterful feel for character and detail. While Kristofferson's songbook would seem perfectly suited for a tribute from a roster of alt-country all-stars, *Don't Let the Bastards Get You Down: A Tribute to Kris Kristofferson* takes a more ambitious approach, mixing electronic and indie rock artists in with a bunch of top-shelf roots rockers. While Polara and Oranger hardly offer a purist's approach to Kristofferson's tunes, their contributions prove how malleable his material really is (and that his melodies are just as strong as his lyrics), while Tom Verlaine's cool but passionate take on "The Hawk" and the alt-folk of Mark Kozelek and Hannah Marcus' "Lights of Magdala (which Kristofferson recorded but didn't write) demonstrate how much Kristofferson's work means to so many musicians. Elsewhere, the performances by Kelly Hogan and Paul Burch are as strong as you'd expect, Northern Lights and the Mother Hips sound great, and Jon Langford's duet with Chip Taylor finds him at the top of his game. In short, hipsters who don't know Kris Kristofferson's work as a songwriter (or longtime fans keen on hearing new interpretations of his stuff) are advised to check out *Don't Let the Bastards Get You Down* pronto. —*Mark Deming*

Dot Rock 'n' Roll / 1996 / Ace ✦✦✦

The Dot label recorded all kinds of pop in the 1950s; this 28-track compilation focuses on their hardest rocking sides, most of which are rockabilly or rockabilly-related. Dot didn't really have a "house" sound, and what you get here is a trail mix of obscure '50s, mostly white rock & roll, with only a couple of big hits (Sanford Clark's "The Fool" and Nervous Norvus' insane novelty, "Transfusion"). A number of these rarities will have considerable appeal to collectors, like the non-hits by one-hit wonders Robin Luke and Ray Sharpe; the raunchy white Little Richard sounds of Jimmie Dee's "Henrietta" (which was a small hit); a single by Ray Campi (who really didn't become well-known until he became a rockabilly revival artist decades later); a solo outing by ex-Cricket Niki Sullivan; a 1958 Jerry Lee Lewis-clone number by future country star Mickey Gilley; and a rockabilly cut by Mac Wiseman of the Foggy Mountain Boys. It's solid fodder for the most part, though rather middle-of-the-pack as far as vintage rockabilly goes. —*Richie Unterberger*

☆ **Doughboys, Playboys and Cowboys: The Golden Years of Western Swing** / Dec. 14, 1999 / Proper ✦✦✦✦✦

This four-disc box chronicles the development of Western swing from the Fort Worth Doughboys' 1932 recordings through its heyday in the late '40s. Along the way, the collection covers every major artist, from Bob Wills and Spade Cooley to pioneers like Milton Brown and Bill Boyd, who have been under-represented almost to the point of extinction in the CD era. It also includes Patsy Montana's groundbreaking hit single, "I Want to Be a Cowboy's Sweetheart," and other fascinating tracks such as the Tex-Mex stomper "El Rancho Grande" by the Tune Wranglers, "Bring It on Down to My House" by Derwood Brown & His Musical Brownies, and dozens of others. The accompanying 43-page booklet features bios on all the artists as well as song notes and rare photographs. Unfortunately, this doesn't include anything after 1947, but such is the nature of Proper boxes. Besides, this doesn't claim to be an exhaustive chronology—the subtitle, "The Golden Years of Western Swing," states the intent and, as such, this is magnificent stuff. Considering what's been included, it's hard to squabble over what's been left out ("Take Me Back to Tulsa," "Milk Cow Blues," and "Steel Guitar Rag" are notable examples), but pretend you don't know that and this set is perfect, containing every artist, every development, and every song that made Western swing a national phenomenon. —*Jim Smith*

Down From the Mountain: O Brother, Where Art Thou? / Jul. 24, 2001 / Uptown/ Universal ✦✦✦

Recorded at Nashville's historic Ryman Theater as a sort of a musical wrap party for the Coen Brothers' 2000 film *O Brother, Where Art Thou?*, this album offers live versions of several of the traditional American folk songs featured in the film, with a few additions along the same vein. Sounding almost like an all-traditional country episode of "A Prairie Home Companion," the guests (including Alison Krauss, Dan Tyminski, the Whites, the Fairfield Four, and the Cox Family, among others) amiably exchange songs on-stage, reveling in the atmosphere of warm country, bluegrass, and blues music. Highlights include two non-traditional tracks from Gillian Welch and David Rawlings, whose earthy compositions fit in seamlessly with the time-honored traditional songs, and Emmylou Harris' contribution "Green Pastures" (which originally appeared on *Roses in the Snow*, her own Americana revival album from some 20 years earlier). Some of the songs don't fare as well, unfortunately, with musician/actor Chris Thomas King's "John Law Burned Down the Liquor Sto' " sounding a bit too faux-traditional, but hometown favorites the Fairfield Four more than make up for it with their hair-raising rendition of the work song/spiritual "Po' Lazarus." Of particular note is fiddler and folklorist John Hartford's cheery rendition of the hobo fantasy "Big Rock Candy Mountain," which proved to be his last recorded performance before his death nearly a year later. The concert is recorded so well that it is occasionally surprising to hear applause at the end of the songs; the performances are so nearly flawless it is easy to forget that this was a live recording. Fans of traditional American folk music and those who have enjoyed the *O Brother* soundtrack will not be disappointed. —*Zac Johnson*

Down to the Promised Land: 5 Years of Bloodshot Records / Jun. 20, 2000 / Bloodshot ✦✦✦✦✦

As independent record labels go, five years is a lifetime. Half a decade and over 70 releases after a late-night drunken tirade against the music industry gave it life, Chicago's Bloodshot Records has proven itself to be perhaps the most important Americana-no Depression-alt-country heap. The label has always prided itself in merging punk and country in the most unholy of matrimonies, and *Down to the Promised Land* proves the marriage works. Within the two-disc set's 40 tracks are excellent rock tunes from the likes of the Yahoos, the Waco Brothers (doing the Who's "Baba O'Riley"), aggressive cowpunk from the Roughnecks, and Trailer Bride, straight-up honky tonk from the Cornell Hurd Band and Nora O'Connor, and speedgrass from folks like the Meat Purveyors and Split Lip Rayfield. But the biggest moment? Without a doubt the Unholy Trio's low-fi cover of Public Enemy's "Bring the Noise," complete with strains of "Dixie" thrown in for good measure. —*John Duffy*

Dressed In Black: A Tribute to Johnny Cash / Sep. 17, 2002 / Dualtone ✦✦✦✦

Few artists deserve tribute more than Johnny Cash, and none pose a greater challenge to those who would offer their homage. The problem is that his sound has been pounded so deep into America's soul that it's almost impossible to play his music without lapsing into imitation—and those who try to avoid that trap can sound a little misguided. Examples of both approaches abound throughout *Dressed in Black*, though even the bravest performers generally sing to a tack bass rhythm accompanied by those menacing low guitar licks that Cash patented long ago. Some do a pretty good job of evoking Cash, especially James Intveld, whose rendition of "Folsom Prison Blues" comes darn close to the original, and Chuck Mead on "There You Go." Damon Bramblett also has Cash's phrasing down; the fact that his voice is pitched about an octave higher, along with his Maybelle Carter style on guitar, makes "I'm Gonna Sit on the Porch and Pick on My Old Guitar" a special treat. Then there's Billy Burnette, whose playing comes closest to the essence of Cash but whose vocals completely miss the squint-eyed macho quality that "Ring of Fire" requires. Rarest of all are those artists who have found their own voice yet use this format to acknowledge their forebears; none does this more persuasively than Dale Watson, who turns "I Walk the Line" into something both powerful and original—the ultimate tribute that anyone can pay to the real icons in this business. —*Robert L. Doerschuk*

★ **Early Days of Bluegrass, Vol. 1** / 1974 / Rounder ✦✦✦✦✦

A brilliant performance of "Leavin' Tennessee" by the Kelleys kicks off the first side of the first volume of this landmark series of historic early bluegrass compilations, surely one of the best projects this sometimes overrated folk and roots-music label has ever undertaken. Who are the Kelleys? One of many important and innovative performers from the early years of this genre whose names and reputations might have fallen by the wayside—for awhile. A great side effect—or perhaps the main point—of such careful documentation of what was originally almost casual band activity on a purely regional basis is the distinct possibility of a kind of canonization of performers who have never basked in the glory of modern-day musical heroes, but whose efforts contain every bit as much feeling and vitality, if not a heck of a lot more. The Lilly Brothers are one of the groups here whose reputation did become massive in the bluegrass world, and their superb early tracks are on par with everything else on this great volume. But the tracks are just as often fascinating recordings by artists whose brilliance is as unquestionable as their obscurity. These are performances that in terms of bluegrass history are more like clues uncovered by a shrewd sleuth rather than the obvious important moments that everyone thinks they know about. Some of these tracks originate from custom pressings the artists shelled out for themselves or private recordings carried out by fanatic radio stations. Beginning with the opening track's status as a kind of phenomenal overture to the entire series, crystallizing the energy of bluegrass as if rows of dancers were kicking up their gams, this volume has enough masterpiece tracks to warrant a pick as perhaps the best set in the entire series. Some highlights include "Holston Valley Breakdown," a banjo showpiece for Baskell Rose of the type that would make an old-timey banjo player drop his few remaining teeth into his jar of homebrew, and "If You Don't Love Your Neighbor" by banjoist Shannon Grayson & His Golden Valley Boys, a song with a perfectly frank, hard-hitting, and righteous message—the bluegrass equivalent of tossing a bucket of ice water in the face of a hypocritical fundamentalist preacher, and required listening for anyone who thinks this genre produces nothing but reactionary songs of Americana. "Gonna Lay My Old Guitar Down" by the fine Floyd Lacewell is sure to be a favorite among types who carry their axes everywhere with them. This track is one of several that feature the instrumental handiwork of fiddler "Pappy" Sherrill and banjoist Snuffy Jenkins—fine stuff indeed. The Red Belcher material is a wonderful glimpse into the recording career of fiddler and vocalist Tex Logan, whose discography is unfortunately not as in focus as it deserves to be. An appealing part of the listening experience that is part of all these sets is the variety, the manner in which tracks slip back and forth between the worlds of slower-moving, more deeply sentimental old-timey and the rapidly moving, musically subversive bluegrass onslaught. It is also a long excursion in terms of time, including material from the beginning of the '40s with an extremely strong old-timey and string band influence as well as mid-'50s recordings in which the Nashville recording studio sound begins to dominate. It is a pleasant trip, like enjoying a slow-moving country road as well as the burst of energy when the man who has been driving his hay-bobber at 16 miles an hour finally gets off the road. The Hobo Jack Adkins tracks feature early use of electric guitar as well as legendary Appalachian sidemen such as banjoist Ray Goins and the Cline brothers—Ray Cline on fiddle and Ezra Cline on bass. In other words, most of the Lonesome Pine Fiddlers. —*Eugene Chadbourne*

● **Early Days of Bluegrass, Vol. 2** / 1976 / Rounder ✦✦✦✦

This is another trip up the river. For the second volume in its historical bluegrass series—all of which, it must be stressed, is a crucial part of any good bluegrass collection—Dick

Spottswood paddles his boat on a course typical of this series when it is in compilation mode. Some of these tracks represent tiny streams that historically wind up a dribble: artists who made only one record, regional labels started by people nobody can remember, sidemen whose identities are unknown who were brought in because somebody else in the band was drunk. Soon listeners are in deep water, with players whose prolific contributions were not only a delicious part of the bluegrass lardner, but highly influential in country & western music as well. The Brewster Brothers from Knoxville are heard on their own here, but would be familiar pickers to any listeners who have come across Carl Story albums on the Starday label. The latter artist went between bluegrass and country as if it was the North Carolina/Tennessee state line—which it might have been, actually. Red Allen is another of this sort of player who has a couple of marvelous tracks here. Thanks to these performers, the newly developing country & western music received a vital transfusion of bluegrass and old-timey feeling, which sometimes is all that has sustained the genre when drained by outside forces such as disco and Eagles-style country-rock. None of that kind of stuff here. "Island Creek Mine Fire" is a really dramatic track, a country hit in Cleveland that was yanked off the air when relatives of victims from the actual mine fire became offended. It doesn't get more real than that, but many of the artists here aren't even trying for that sort of emotional impact. Instead, it is off to the imaginary bluegrass world of hyper-tempos and in a sense totally abstract instrumental virtuosity, or a plunge into the stark melodrama to be found only on "Road of Shame." The excellent Dave Woolum, here heard in the company of Curley Tuttle & the Laurel County Boys, is responsible for that enjoyable track, but appears on another in name only. Toby Stroud's superior version of "Jesse James," featuring the Blue Mountain Boys, is another highlight, as is terrific playing from Frank Wakefield in two different contexts. One favorite of college radio bluegrass and old-timey programmers is "Another Old Dog in the Race" by the Country Pardners, a group who at one point was thought to have the hitmaking potential of Hank Williams. As usual, thorough liner notes accompany the project, the text sometimes consisting of amusing letters from the players involved. Information about the authors of the songs is hit and miss, however. *—Eugene Chadbourne*

Early Days of Bluegrass, Vol. 3: New Sounds Ramblin' from Coast to Coast / 1975 / Rounder ♦♦♦♦

There are some tracks on this set that are absolutely gems, as good as anything in any bluegrass collection. Looked at as an album, the diversity represented in this selection of pieces recorded over a decade and a half is supposedly part of the idea, but results in a volume that is best appreciated as part of the entire Rounder *Early Days of Bluegrass* series than on its own. And appreciate this series is something bluegrass fans definitely do, some of them establishing small altars to the albums in a corner of the listening room. This third volume does establish that groups and recordings were being formed and made in many different parts of the country as the '50s rolled along, not just Nashville and the Appalachians. Even the later tracks also demonstrate that not much of a rift existed between bluegrass and country & western at this stage of the game, with some of the music even venturing into the western cowboy song genre. There are also touches appropriate to country, but generally restricted from bluegrass, including electric guitar and piano. Bluegrass was still a new enough style that associating with it wouldn't make a country performer sound "old fashioned" —and this material was recorded at least 30 years before country performers would want to considered out of touch with the latest trends. Of the 16 tracks, a fourth are by the Lonesome Pine Fiddlers, a great band that made a series of albums with a revolving line-up. Collectors will find the work of the more obscure artists the most exciting to unearth, especially when the result is something as magnificent as the "Orange Blossom Special" performed by Jerry & Sky. This bluegrass warhorse, the subject of instrumental hamming both hideous and horrifying in the hands of a Doug Kershaw or Charlie Daniels, might just be a number listeners have sworn off experiencing ever again, unless made to by force. Well, sit tight, for this version features not only ferocious mandolin tweaking by Ralph Jones, but ends with train sound effects done by an unidentified violinist that are so vicious they would make avant garde noise violinist Polly Bradfield grind her teeth. Then there's Hack Johnson, certainly no hack. His version of "Home Sweet Home" with His Tennesseans proves that this standard makes a most perfect bluegrass number, and will never sound good any other way, be it ever so humble. Other great acts featured in this collection include the picking team of Rebe Gosdin and Rabe Perkins known as Rebe & Rabe and the superb Colwell Brothers, an example of early '50s Hollywood bluegrass. Terrific pickers such as banjoists Allen Shelton, Joe Maphis and Noah Crase, flatpicker Jimmy Martin and fiddler Nelson Young are all part of the action. Hillbilly jokes can be made about the Eubanks Brothers spelling the name of their peace song "Message For Piece," but maybe that's not "the kinda piece them boys is after," as they would say up in the hills. *—Eugene Chadbourne*

Early Days of Bluegrass, Vol. 5: Rich R Tone Story / 1974 / Rounder ♦♦♦♦

When the veteran North Carolina senator Jesse Helms began picking on the National Endowment for the Arts in the '80s, one wonders if he realized that the funding body had recently helped pay the bills for this incredible series of early bluegrass reissues, documenting much important music from Tennessee, Virginia, and North Carolina itself. Surely there is even material here that Helms could relate to, such as the threatening ditty "The Wicked Path of Sin" by Stoney & Wilma Lee Cooper. At any rate, this volume focuses on the Rich R Tone label, one of the most important companies to produce bluegrass recordings in the early days of that genre's development. While a variety of labels had been going around the country recording "race," "hillbilly," and "folk" records since the '20s, the outlook of Rich R Tone was more like the "D.I.Y" or doing-it-yourself ethic identified with generations down the line when punk groups put out their own records and various cooperatives were formed. The firm's owner and founder, James Stanton, began a mission in the '40s to record the music that was popular and being played at the time in the Appalachians, regardless of whether it was considered "folk" or not. And this music was bluegrass in its innovative and formative stages. Stanton drove around the countryside selling these albums out of the back of his car. The bluegrass bands that got their start through his enterprise include the Stanley Brothers, whose Ralph Stanley would finally pick up a Grammy in 2002. They are represented with the fine track "Little Glass of Wine." The 15 other tracks include one or two songs each by nine other bluegrass and/or rural gospel outfits, most of which are fairly obscure besides the aforementioned Stoney & Wilma Lee Cooper. Glenn Neaves & the Grayson County Boys kick things off with a terrific version of "The Old Swinging Bridge," while other highlights include the team of Pee Wee Lambert and Curley Parker energizing the "Weary Hobo" and recalling "Just a Memory." "Rattlesnake Daddy" is the single lively entry from a combination of the Bailey Brothers and the Happy Valley Boys, and will make listeners want to hear more by these players. A 1954 recording by the Caudill Family is a stunning example of four-part vocal harmonizing from the Appalachian gospel tradition. Frank Hunter and His Black Mountain Boys are also featured with two superb recordings, the heartfelt "Long Time No See" and a song that could be something of a tribute to Sir Stanton of Johnson City—"Tennessee Boy." The excellent documentation standard set by this series continues with this set, which includes a well-done booklet about the artists involved and the history of the label. *—Eugene Chadbourne*

El Primitivo American Rock'n'roll & Rockabilly / 1993 / Ace ♦♦♦

24 rockabilly tracks recorded in Nashville between 1956 and 1964 under the direction of Murray Nash, who ran the small Do-Ra-Me label. The title doesn't lie. This is raw, and rare; about half of the selections weren't even issued until this CD compilation. Mel Robbins is the most recognizable name here, as some of tracks were picked up for distribution by Chess, although you'd have a hard time finding anyone familiar with his work other than die-hard rockabilly collectors. Mick Farren's liner notes give the impression that you're about to hear a rockabilly *Gong Show* of sorts, but although the performances are more on the level of inspired amateurism than old Gene Vincent sides, it's rather enjoyable, rarely crossing into ineptitude. You shouldn't get these Elvis-Eddie Cochran-Carl Perkins-et al. derivations unless rockabilly's your main dish, but not everything has to be classic to be good clean fun. That's what's on tap here, offering infectious enthusiasm (if not much originality) and occasional bursts of memorability (as in the Imps' instrumental "Uh Oh," with fuzzy chords reminiscent of vintage Link Wray). *—Richie Unterberger*

The Fantastic Pickin' on Series Bluegrass / Oct. 15, 2002 / CMH ♦♦♦♦

The *Pickin' On* series of releases has a simple formula: Get together some hot bluegrass pickers and let them loose on an album's worth of songs by a huge rock band or artist. The series has proved quite popular and CMH keeps crankin' 'em out. This disc collects 12 highlights from past releases, including versions of the Rolling Stones' "Paint It Black," U2's "I Still Haven't Found What I'm Looking For," Jimi Hendrix's "Purple Haze," and Pink Floyd's "Wish You Were Here." Part of the fun of the series is hearing familiar AOR staples being deconstructed and rebuilt bluegrass style. It must have been a daunting task to arrange Bruce Springsteen's "Born to Run" or the Beatles' "Paperback Writer." Bluegrass purists no doubt find this concept to be a sellout of the worst kind, but more easygoing fans of the style and fans of weird concepts in general will find much to enjoy in both the *Pickin' On* series and in this sampler. *—Tim Sendra*

Fire on the Strings, Vol. 1: Ultimate Guitar and Banjo . . . / 1993 / CMH ♦♦♦♦

If red-hot banjo and guitar pickin' is your thing, then this one's right up your alley. With banjo and guitar hotshots like Eddie Adcock (an explosive "Goodbye Bluebelle"), Merle Travis (a beautiful solo rendition of "Silver Moon"), Sonny Osborne, Joe Maphis (great take on "Liebstraum"), and Don Reno and Arthur Smith (who also duets with Maphis on "Water Baby Boogie"), this acoustic-based feast for the ears doesn't let up for a second. It's simply top-heavy with spirited playing, and the recording quality has a perceptible presence that literally blossoms in headphones. If this set sounds exciting, it plays even better. *—Cub Koda*

From Where I Stand: The Black Experience in Country Music / Jan. 27, 1998 / Warner Bros. ♦♦♦♦♦

An ambitious three-CD mini-box that is not 100 percent successful in its attempt to document the history of black country music, *From Where I Stand* is quite worthy and admirable nonetheless. Each disc is assembled thematically: disc one concentrates on pre-World War II string band and folk acts, disc two has soul singers' interpretations of country material, and disc three spotlights black artists working more or less within the country mainstream from the late '60s onward. Disc one is interesting in its illustration of how early rural white and black musicians drew from such similar material that they could sound far closer to each other stylistically than historians might lead one to believe. Three of *Grand Ole Opry* harmonica player DeFord Bailey's rare cuts are here; other highlights are numbers by Leadbelly and artists (Peg Leg Howell, Bo Chatmon) who have been more commonly categorized into the blues idiom. Disc two has country-oriented material by Solomon Burke, Arthur Alexander, the Supremes, Ray Charles, Joe Tex, Etta James, and others, mostly from the golden age of soul. Disc three has cuts by modern black country acts, as well as outings into country by soul singers. Artistically, it's the least successful of the discs—a black singer doing faceless country-pop is just as boring as a white singer doing it. There are so many covers of country tunes by soul singers on the final two discs that one gets the sense the compilers stretched the definition of black country as far as they could simply to fill this out to the length of a box set, which isn't necessarily such a bad thing. The soul cuts are probably the best in the box, and the historical connections between the artists and their country influences are made clearer by a fine 60-page booklet. *—Richie Unterberger*

Georgia String Bands (1928–1930) / 1992 / Story of the Blues ♦♦♦
All 17 selections on this CD (music leased from the Austrian Document label) were recorded in Atlanta during 1928-1930. The string bands usually feature banjo and guitar with occasional violin and plenty of vocals. This disc has the complete output from the team of Pink Anderson & Simmie Dooley (four selections), Henry Williams & Eddie Anthony (two songs), Lonnie Coleman (also just two numbers), Macon Ed & Tampa Joe (eight selections), and the lone side (which was previously unreleased) by Brothers Wright & Williams (who may actually have been Macon Ed & Tampa Joe under a pseudonym). The music is mostly good-time with occasional low-down blues and plenty of spirit. There's nothing essential, but overall these performances give one a good flavor of what blues and country music sounded like in Atlanta in the late '20s. *—Scott Yanow*

Georgia Stringbands, Vol. 1 / May 2, 1998 / Document ♦♦♦
This unique collection highlights some of the lesser-known figures of Georgia's hillbilly industry. The Spooney Five, the Watkins Band, Theo and Gus Clark, and the Carroll County Revelers each offer lively dance pieces, most of them instrumental and of fine if unexceptional quality. The real stars of this album, meanwhile, are the Cofer Brothers, Paul and Leon, whose obscure career produced a handful of remarkable and unpredictable string band sides, showcasing a deeper connection with black musical styles than is evident in the mainstream string band recordings of the period. The brothers play fiddle and guitar duets in a ragged, earthy fashion, their utter lack of refinement constituting a distinct, often amusing, and genuinely entertaining sound. On the sentimental tune "Where the Morning Glories Glow," their shaky, comically pitiful voices warble feebly through romantic descriptions of childhood against Paul Cofer's equally uncertain violin accompaniment; their "All Go Hungry Hash House" is a very funny treatment of a tune which crops up also in the repertoires of Dave Macon and Charlie Poole, and in "The Great Ship Went Down" the brothers take on the popular theme of the Titanic. The Cofers also recorded six sides as the Georgia Crackers, with friend Ben Evans on guitar and Leon switching to banjo; on these tracks, the brothers' sound is markedly different: the vocals grittier, the rhythm more insistent, and the performances rendered overall bluesier, completely abandoning any remnants of gentility. Their "Georgia Black Bottom" is a marvelous reworking of the traditional "Deep Elem Blues," while "Riley the Furniture Man" is the rowdier, raunchier half-brother of a later Cofer Brothers creation, "Keno the Rent Man." The performances of the Cofers and the Crackers are immensely valuable revelations of the rawest and darkest outskirts of early white string band music, and, at least for some enthusiasts, should make up for the album's slower spots. *—Burgin Mathews*

Get Hot or Go Home: Vintage RCA Rockabilly '56–'59—Vols. I & II / Country Music Foundation ♦♦♦♦♦
Get Hot or Go Home: Vintage RCA Rockabilly, '56-'59 is an expertly assembled double-disc collection of rare rockabilly from the RCA vaults. After Elvis Presley became a star, RCA decided to sign a number of new acts to their label, as well as revamp some older country artists to fit the new rockabilly sound. It didn't matter that they bought out Elvis' contract from Sun—they didn't want to risk missing the next Elvis, so they signed anyone they could find. Of course, none of the artists on *Get Hot or Go Home* (including an early Roy Orbison) could have followed Presley's footsteps—they were either too hillbilly (Pee Wee King, Homer & Jethro, Tommy Black) or too slick to cut it. That doesn't mean that the compilation makes for bad listening; in fact, the unevenness of the material makes the set all the more appealing, because the failures are nearly as entertaining as the successful cuts. Out of all the artists on *Get Hot or Go Home*, only Joe Clay sounds as if he should have had a full-fledged career, but the also-rans, one-hit wonders, and the country guys trying to go rockabilly are all fascinating and frequently fun. It's a great purchase for avid rockabilly and country fans. *—Stephen Thomas Erlewine*

God Less America / Feb. 2, 1999 / Crypt ♦♦♦
Hats off to the bent folks at Crypt for unearthing some of the most primal and hilariously horrifying country & western songs recorded between 1955 and 1966. *God Less America* is not for the faint of heart and can only be compared to Leon Payne's mental illness opus "Psycho." Listening to these 15 tracks, you have to ask yourself why Horace Heller went to the trouble of releasing a song like "Ed's Place," which opens with the sound of a gun blast, revealing a jealous man who has just shot his wife at the local waterin' hole. What follows is a monologue taking the listener through his ensuing confusion and realization of the murder he has just committed. Or, in the case of "Please Don't Go Topless Mother" by youngster Troy Hess, a boy despairs over his single mother's topless go-go dancing occupation in order to support her son. It's hard to suppress a guilty laugh when he whines the lines, "Please don't go topless mother/My friends won't come to see me anymore/But their daddies do." This earnestly warbled plea by the young'un features the kind of syrupy country & western instrumental sludge one might expect to hear played between just those types of shows where mom bares it all. Did these would-be country crooners really think these tales of American debauchery could have made it into the jukeboxes of honky tonks throughout this great land? The probable answer is yes, and that's what makes *God Less America* so fascinating and somewhat scary. *—Al Campbell*

Goldband Rockabilly: Boppin' Tonight / Mar. 1, 1994 / Ace ♦♦♦♦
Culled from several vinyl albums, this brings together 22 of the best rockabilly sides from Louisiana's Goldband records onto one compact disc. Kicking off with Al Ferrier's "Let's Go Boppin' Tonight," this disc also features four more from Ferrier (including "Honey Baby" and "No, No, No"), five from Little Billy Earl (including "Couple in the Car," "I Never Had the Blues" and "Honey Baby-O"), seven from Larry Hart (including "Coffins Have No Pockets," "I'm Just a Mender" and snippets of three other tunes culled from audition demos), three from Johnny Jano ("Mabel's Gone" being a notable highlight), a pair from Bill & Carroll ("Bluff City Rock," "Hold Me Baby") and stray single entries from Jay Chevalier ("Castro reviously unissued "Standing at the Door"), Chuck Carbo ("Yes I Got You"), Calvin Spears ("Come On Home"), Gerri Hall (the previously unissued alternate take of "What I Learned About You"), Little Booker ("Teenage Rock") and Mac Rebennack doing business as Gene & Al's Spacemen ("Mercy"). A special bonus is also the inclusion of the original version of "Sea Cruise," with Huey Smith doing the vocals, and the original version of "New Orleans" by Big Boy Myles, a local hit before Gary U.S. Bonds covered it for the national market. *—Cub Koda*

The Golden Age of American Rock 'n' Roll, Vol. 10: Special Country Edition / May 7, 2002 / Ace ♦♦♦♦♦
As the fine series *The Golden Age of American Rock 'n' Roll* focused on rock & roll hits of all kinds from the mid-'50s to the mid-'60s, the title of this offshoot might be confusing. How can you have a country edition of a rock & roll anthology series? It might be better to think of this as a compilation of 30 country hits from 1956 to 1965 that crossed over, usually in a big way, to the pop charts: every one of the tracks made the country Top Ten and the pop Top 100, sometimes getting into the Top Ten of the pop listings as well. As such, a lot of rock & roll fans, and fans of just plain popular music, would be about as familiar with these as they were with rock smashes of the era. Not many anthologies focus on this notable subsection of country and pop, and as expected Ace does a fine job in mixing big and small hits by superstars, one-shots, and country stars who only occasionally crossed over in a big way. Several undisputed classics are here: Johnny Cash's "Ring of Fire," Marty Robbins' "El Paso," Patsy Cline's "I Fall to Pieces," Don Gibson's "Oh Lonesome Me," Bobby Bare's "Detroit City," and Dave Dudley's "Six Days on the Road," for instance. The more experienced collector might get more of a turn-on from the numerous additional items that have never really become staples of pop oldies radio, like Leroy Van Dyke's "Walk on By," George Hamilton IV's "Abilene," Wanda Jackson's "Right or Wrong," and George Jones' "White Lightning." If there's any slight drawback to this compilation, it's that though some of the songs were inarguably quite successful, there are some not-so-hot novelties, saga songs, and hits à la Jim Reeves' "He'll Have to Go" that were indicative of Nashville's drift toward stultifying mainstream pop coated with country frosting. But there's more good than bad here, and the 24-page liner notes are excellent, filling in a lot of career details for those who might not be country specialists. *—Richie Unterberger*

The Gospel Ship: Baptists Hymns & White Spiritual / 1994 / New World ♦♦♦♦
To 21st century city-dwellers, some of this music is going to sound downright creepy. Whether that tells us more about the religious culture of the Appalachians or about the secular culture of the modern American city is a question that could spawn 1,000 tedious seminars, but that question is musically beside the point: this is music that draws on scores of cultural influences and yet could only come from one place. The first five tracks consist of "testimonies" (brief homilies) by various mountain pastors followed by hymns sung by their congregations. These are not the sturdy foursquare hymns of Lutheran Germany or the lush polyphonic Latin incantations of the Catholic mass—this is weird, eerie music that snakes its way along strange modal pathwáys like mist drifting through a swamp or a snake slithering between bare-limbed trees on a cold autumn night. There is little good singing to be heard here. These are not singers; they are congregants and worshipers, and how good they sound is of little consequence to them. The melodies are not pretty; at times they are almost imperceptible. But there is a curious power in this music and in the preaching of the ministers. The remainder of the program consists of gospel songs performed mainly by solo singers; stylistically, they range from early country music in the style of the Carter Family ("Old Gospel Ship" by Ruby Vass) to blues-inflected eschatology ("When the Stars Begin to Fall" by Hobart Smith, Preston Smith, and Texas Gladden) and straight-ahead bluegrass (the Mountain Ramblers' gently swinging rendition of "My Lord Keeps a Record"). It's highly recommended. *—Rick Anderson*

The Gram Parsons Notebook: The Last Whippoorwill / Jun. 27, 2000 / Shell Point/Echomusic ♦♦♦
No doubt inspired by *Mermaid Avenue*, the album of Woody Guthrie lyrics set to music and performed by Billy Bragg and Wilco, John Nuese, a former musical associate of Gram Parsons, dug out a notebook of Parsons' with which he had been entrusted upon Parsons' death in 1973 and interested country performers Carl Jackson, Jim Lauderdale, and Larry Cordle in turning some of its contents into songs. The result is nowhere near the significance of the Guthrie album, if only because the posthumous collaborators only had a half-dozen lyric fragments to work with. In some cases, they wrote new lyrics, and in all cases they composed music in Parsons' country-rock style. That still wasn't enough material for an album, so the disc is filled out with covers of Parsons songs like "Hickory Wind" and "A Song for You," plus a couple of songs about Parsons and a cover of the Rolling Stones' "Dead Flowers" with bowdlerized lyrics. There are no lost masterpieces here, but a couple of the songs—"L.A. Customs Blues" and "Blurry Slurry Night"—do have some of Parsons' style to them. Featuring performances by the likes of Ricky Skaggs and Marty Stuart, the album is never unpleasant to listen to, but it constitutes a very minor, not to say compromised, addition to the Gram Parsons catalog. *—William Ruhlmann*

The Greatest Hits of Hickory Records, Vol. 2 / 1993 / Scotti Bros. ♦♦♦
Founded by Roy Acuff & Fred Rose (partners in the major country music publisher Acuff-Rose), Hickory had chart success for several decades running, but didn't have much in the way of a trademark sound. This collection of a dozen hit singles spans 1956-1978, including Acuff's 1965 cover of "Freight Train Blues" (his only track on the compilation), a couple of rootsy '50s sides from Wilma Lee & Stoney Cooper, and some odds and ends from Don Gibson (including a duet with Sue Thompson), Ernie Ashworth, Glenn Barber, and others. It's mostly OK pop-country, but not something that would exert a great pull on prospective buyers, although it collects a few singles that aren't so easy to find elsewhere. *—Richie Unterberger*

● **Guitar Player Presents: Legends of Guitar: Country, Vol. 1** / 1990 / Rhino ✦✦✦✦✦
Part one of an astutely compiled pair, it showcases the kings of country guitar from the '30s to the '70s and includes work from Jimmy Bryant, Speedy West, Chet Atkins, and Joe Maphis. It has good liner notes on both sets. *—John Floyd*

Guitar Player Presents: Legends of Guitar: Country, Vol. 2 / 1991 / Rhino ✦✦✦✦✦
Here is part two of this well-done collection. *—John Floyd*

Gulf Coast Grease: the Sandy Story, Vol. 1 / 1996 / Ace ✦✦✦
Based in Mobile, AL, the independent Sandy label recorded a bunch of rockabilly/early rock sides in the late '50s, though none of the acts on this 24-song compilation had anything close to a national smash. It's solid, often crudely recorded (in the positive sense of that description) material, perhaps with more of a honky-tonk/swamp flavor than the average rockabilly collection. The highlight may be Jackie Morningstar's "Rockin' in the Graveyard," one of the better overlooked early rock 'n' horror novelties. Ray Sawyer, later to lead Dr. Hook, appears here under his own name on a couple of respectably rockin' early-'60s singles. *—Richie Unterberger*

Heart Beats: Country Lovin'—Songs from the Heart / Jan. 14, 1997 / Rhino ✦✦✦
A collection of 15 romantic country tracks, "compiled by women at Rhino Records" (the feminine perspective of the compilation is emphasized/marketed prominently on the cover), all but one dating from 1983-1995. The one that doesn't, Dolly Parton's 1974 number one "I Will Always Love You," is probably the best song here. It's mainstream country—which, in latter days, has pretty much meant mainstream pop—with a likely substantial crossover audience in the soft-rock market. Tanya Tucker, Kathy Mattea, Patty Loveless, John Michael Montgomery, Collin Raye, Doug Stone, Shenandoah, Restless Heart, Crystal Gayle, and others check in with some of their more tender smashes. This is presented with far greater care than most anthologies of this type (i.e., there are in-depth, intelligent liner notes), but that doesn't change the fact that it's rather unexceptional musically. *—Richie Unterberger*

Heroes of Country Music, Vol. 1: Legends of Western Swing / Jun. 18, 1996 / Rhino ✦✦✦✦
The first volume in Rhino's excellent *Heroes of Country Music* takes on the original purveyors of Western swing with 18 tasty tracks. Cut during the prime years of the '30s and '40s, the material features both stars (Bob Wills, Hank Penny, Leon McAuliffe, Light Crust Doughboys) and the relatively obscure (Jesse Ashlock, Dickie McBride, the Fort Worth Doughboys?). The music and lyrics run the gamut, too, covering classics (Modern Mountaineers' "Everybody's Truckin'"), boogie-woogie (Spade Cooley's "Bogg's Boogie"), the depression (McAuliffe's "Panhandle Rag"), and even the raunchy side of the bedroom (Lightcrust's "Pussy, Pussy, Pussy"). Topped off with Hank Thompson's go at Woody Herman's "Woodchopper's Ball" and Tex Williams' aesthetes nod "Artistry in Western Swing," this Western swing sampler should work mighty fine for all those little doggies lookin' to break in to the big time. *—Stephen Cook*

Heroes of Country Music, Vol. 2: Legends of Honky Tonk / Jun. 18, 1996 / Rhino ✦✦✦✦
In many ways, the honky tonk years of the '40s and '50s represent the real golden era of country music. Fashioned from the early string band and hillbilly sound of Jimmie Rodgers and the Carter Family, honky tonk, with its more overt blues sensibilities, took country music to its rootsy extreme, before the lush production values of the Nashville sound arrived on the scene. Honky tonk also gave air to music's picaresque backbone: the tavern culture thriving on the outskirts of town. This Rhino roundup provides a fine sneak peak into that smoke-filled and beer-soaked world. Featuring many classics, the disc ranges from early cuts by Al Dexter ("Honky Tonk Blues"), Ernest Tubb ("Walking the Floor Over You"), and Ted Daffan ("Born to Lose") to some late-hour triumphs by Lefty Frizzell ("Just Can't Live That Fast (Any More)"), Charlie Walker ("Pick Me Up on Your Way Down"), and George Jones ("A Girl I Used to Know"). In between, there's more than just filler by the likes of Hank Thompson, Red Foley, and the grand honky tonker himself, Hank Williams. Along with Columbia's equally impressive *Honky Tonk Heroes* collection, this 18-track sampler is a great way to see what all the fuss is about. *—Stephen Cook*

Heroes of Country Music, Vol. 3: Legends of Nashville / Jun. 18, 1996 / Rhino ✦✦✦✦
Part of Rhino's multi-volume series chronicling different eras in country music, *Heroes of Country Music, Vol. 3* tells the story of Nashville's rise as a music powerhouse in the '50s. Thanks to established labels like RCA and Columbia and talented producers like Don Law, Chet Atkins, and Steve Sholes, the music shifted from the honky tonk sounds of the late '40s and early '50s to the crossover country-pop of Marty Robbins, Patsy Cline, and Faron Young. The 18 tracks here feature sides from these and many other stars of the decade, including Ray Price, Webb Pierce, Kitty Wells, Ernest Tubb, and Hank Williams. From the rough-hewn sound of tavern nights to the first rumblings of the Nashville sound, this disc takes you on a guided tour with a generous dose of the hits. *—Stephen Cook*

The Hickory Records Story, Vol. 1 / Nov. 6, 2001 / Audium ✦✦✦

The Hightone Records: The First 10 Years / 1994 / Hightone ✦✦✦✦
With 21 tracks, 74 minutes, rock, blues, country and Billy Wirtz—what else can you ask for? Well, it comes with a low sticker price, so you get a low-cost taste of the range of material issued by this Oakland-based label. And, yes, it's definitely a various-artists collection that's worth getting your hands on. The album opens with Robert Cray and closes with Chris Gaffney, and in between you get cuts from Dave Alvin, Dick Dale, Otis Rush, Billy Wirtz, Joe Ely and lots more. *—Steven McDonald*

Hillbilly Boogie / 1994 / Columbia/Legacy ✦✦✦✦✦
A find for fans of Western swing and honky tonk music, *Hillbilly Boogie*'s 20 selections from 1946-1954 mirror the carefree postwar years with a rousing blend of vocal numbers and instrumentals. The selections include everything from fiddle and pedal steel combo swingers like Paul Howard & His Cotton Pickers' "Drinking All My Troubles Away" to big-band country numbers like Al Dexter & His Troopers' "New Broom Boogie." Even the South's unsung Eastern European musical heritage is given its due on a handful of accordion-heavy polkas, including Spade Cooley's "Yodeling Polka" and Louise Massey & the Westeners' "Squeeze Box Polka." Plenty of boogie-woogie rhythm is also on hand with Curley Williams & His Georgia Peach Pickers' "Georgia Boogie" and Andy Reynolds & His 101 Ranch Boys' "Fiddlin' Boogie." Other fine cuts are contributed by country stars Bob Wills, Lefty Frizzell, and Little Jimmy Dickens. Topped off with excellent transfers from the original lacquers, plenty of humor ("Hamburger Hop"), and fine playing throughout, *Hillbilly Boogie* is a must for devotees of the golden era of pre-Nashville sound country music. *—Stephen Cook*

☆ **Hillbilly Fever, Vol. 1: Legends of Western Swing** / 1995 / Rhino ✦✦✦✦✦
Where most country various-artists collections are designed with dollars, not sense, in mind, Rhino's five-disc *Hillbilly Fever* series was thoughtfully compiled and intelligently executed. *Hillbilly Fever* concentrates on the classic era of recorded country music, running from 1933 to 1975, spotlighting nearly all the important artists (usually with one of their best-known songs) along the way. The first volume of the series, *Legends of Western Swing*, is an 18-track compilation that encapsulates the genre. Featuring cuts by the Fort Worth Doughboys, Milton Brown, the Light Crust Doughboys, Cliff Bruner, Johnnie Lee Wills, Bob Wills, Spade Cooley, Tex Williams, Leon McAuliffe, and Hank Thompson, the disc contains all of the most important musicians in the genre, as well as a handful of terrific obscurities. As a result, *Legends of Western Swing* functions as a definitive, essential introduction to one of the most infectious genres in country music. [None of the five discs in the *Hillbilly Fever* series sold in its initial release, probably because its title was too smug to appeal to either hardcore record collectors or casual country fans. A year after the release of *Hillbilly Fever*, Rhino reissued the entire series under the title *Heroes of Country Music*. Unfortunately, the second time around, they pulled several essential tracks from each disc. But even in its edited form, the series is worth getting.] *—Stephen Thomas Erlewine*

★ **Hillbilly Fever, Vol. 2: Legends of Honky Tonk** / 1995 / Rhino ✦✦✦✦✦
Hillbilly Fever, Vol. 2: Legends of Honky Tonk is an essential primer in country music's most enduring genre, boasting some of the greatest barroom tunes ever recorded during the genre's heyday. Beginning in 1937 with Al Dexter's "Honky Tonk Blues" and ending 30 years later with Jim Edward Brown's "Pop-A-Top," the disc contains definitive cuts from nearly all of honky tonk's major players, including Rex Griffin ("The Last Letter"), Ernest Tubb ("Walking the Floor Over You"), Floyd Tillman ("Drivin' Nails in My Coffin"), Hank Williams ("Honky Tonkin'"), Leon Payne ("I Love You Because"), Hank Thompson ("The Wild Side of Life"), Lefty Frizzell ("Just Can't Live That Fast (Any More)"), and George Jones ("A Girl I Used to Know"). Though several additional songs and artists could have been included, *Legends of Honky Tonk* is nevertheless an essential overview and introduction to country's defining genre. *—Stephen Thomas Erlewine*

☆ **Hillbilly Fever, Vol. 3: Legends of Nashville** / 1995 / Rhino ✦✦✦✦✦
"The Nashville sound" commonly refers to the lushly orchestrated country-pop sound also called countrypolitan, which came to prominence in the late '50s. *Hillbilly Fever, Vol. 3: Legends of Nashville* bypasses that era, choosing to concentrate on the classic days of the *Grand Ole Opry*. As a result, *Legends of Nashville* has a wide range of styles, from honky tonk to country-pop, but it all sounds unified because it captures the essence of pre-rock & roll country music (1945-1956). Though the collection doesn't have a story to tell like its two predecessors, *Legends of Nashville* is just as essential to any comprehensive country collection, simply because of the number of classics available on the disc: Eddy Arnold's "Bouquet of Roses," Ernest Tubb's "It's Been So Long Darling," Pee Wee King's "Tennessee Waltz," Hank Williams' "Lovesick Blues," George Morgan's "Room Full of Roses," Webb Pierce's "Wondering," Slim Whitman's "Indian Love Call," Kitty Wells' "It Wasn't God Who Made Honky Tonk Angels," Faron Young's "If You Ain't Lovin' (You Ain't Livin')," the Louvin Brothers' "I Don't Believe You've Met My Baby," Ray Price's "Crazy Arms," Marty Robbins' "Singing the Blues," and Patsy Cline's "Walkin' After Midnight." *—Stephen Thomas Erlewine*

☆ **Hillbilly Fever, Vol. 4: Legends of the West Coast** / 1995 / Rhino ✦✦✦✦✦
Hillbilly Fever, Vol. 4: Legends of the West Coast doesn't just cover the Bakersfield sound of the late '50s and early '60s, but also traces its development through the late '40s and '50s. The disc begins with a selection of cowboy songs (Jack Guthrie's "Oklahoma Hills," Gene Autry's "You Are My Sunshine," Sons of the Pioneers' "Cool Water"), before moving toward Western swing (Al Dexter's "Too Late to Worry," Spade Cooley's "Shame on You") and country-boogie (Tennessee Ernie Ford's "Mule Train"). By the end of the disc—after Skeets McDonald's "Don't Let the Stars Get in Your Eyes," Jimmy Wakely's "One Has My Name (The Other Has My Heart)," Tex Ritter's "High Noon (Do Not Forsake Me)," and Joe Maphis & Rose Lee's "Dim Lights Thick Smoke (And Loud, Loud Music)" have all been heard—the electrified honky tonk of Bakersfield begins to emerge in the form of Jean Shepard ("A Dear John Letter"), Tommy Collins ("You Better Not Do That"), Ferlin Husky ("Gone"), Wynn Stewart ("Wishful Thinking"), Buck Owens ("Second Fiddle"), and Merle Haggard ("Sing a Sad Song"). Since it covers so many different styles, *Legends of the West Coast* is a little inconsistent. Nevertheless, it tells its story well and contains a wealth of classics, making it another essential addition to any comprehensive country library. *—Stephen Thomas Erlewine*

☆ **Hillbilly Music: Thank God!, Vol. 1** / 1989 / Bug ✦✦✦✦✦
Hillbilly Music: Thank God!, Vol. 1 is a 24-track, double-LP/single-disc collection of proto-Bakersfield, hillbilly and honky tonk music from the Capitol Records vaults. All of the material on the compilation was recorded between the late '40s and the mid-'50, and most

of these artists are from the West Coast, which means this music has a different flavor than the Nashville-based honky tonk of the same era. *Hillbilly Music* is also filled with rarities from the likes of Buck Owens, Tommy Collins, Tennessee Ernie Ford, Hank Thompson, Jean Shepard, Merle Travis, Rose Maddox and Tex Ritter. Though there are a handful of lesser items on the compilation, *Hillbilly Music* is a historical document of the best kind—it's entertaining and educational. —*Thom Owens*

Hokum Blues (1924–1929) / Nov. 21, 1995 / Document ◆◆◆◆
Although this CD is titled *Hokum Blues*, all but two of the eight groups actually predate hokum (which came of age in the fall of 1928), although all have some aspects of the good-time music. The performances are quite obscure, with two titles apiece by Ukulele Bob Williams, the Two of Spades, Louise Ross, Feathers and Frogs, and Swan & Lee (the only recordings by any of these performers). In addition, there are four songs apiece from Ki Ki Johnson and the team of Danny Small & Ukulele Mays, plus seven numbers (including two instrumentals) by the Pebbles. Listening to this early acoustic music, the performances both look forward to hokum and even swing in spots, while hinting strongly at its early roots in string music and minstrel shows. Collectors will want this one. —*Scott Yanow*

Honky Tonk Boogie / Jun. 17, 1997 / Hip-O ◆◆◆
Another budget compilation in MCA's Hip-O line, this brings together 14 hard-stompin' favorites from country music's elite. Kicking off with Hank Williams Jr.'s anthemic "Born to Boogie," the twang is turned up to full blast on Steve Earle's "Guitar Town" and the Mavericks' "All You Ever Do Is Bring Me Down." Tracks include two number-one hits, the aforementioned Hank Jr. hit and Mark Chesnutt's "It's a Little Too Late" and Top Ten favorites from Marty Stuart ("Honky Tonk Crowd"), Waylon Jennings ("Honky Tonk Heroes"), George Jones ("Honky Tonk Song") and the Iguanas' "My Girlfriend Is a Waitress." The Cajun quotient in country music is also represented here with Jo-El Sonnier's "All American Saturday Night" and Joe Ely's roadhouse rendition of Hank Sr.'s "Honky Tonkin'." Selections from Lee Roy Parnell ("Oughta Be a Law"), Marty Brown ("Don't Worry Baby"), Delbert McClinton ("Before You Accuse Me") and Pirates of the Mississippi ("Honky Tonk Blues") complete the collection. —*Cub Koda*

Honky Tonk Heroes / Feb. 15, 2000 / FreeFalls Entertainment ◆◆◆
Scanning the cover and track listing of Pedernales/FreeFalls' *Honky Tonk Heroes* it's hard to tell what this collection credited to Billy Joe Shaver, Willie Nelson, Waylon Jennings, and Kris Kristofferson actually is. Is it a various-artist compilation, a live effort or re-recordings? Well, it's the closest to re-recordings, but that term implies a shoddy rip-off, which is certainly what this album is not. Released in 1999 but consisting primarily of recordings that were cut in Willie Nelson's studio, Pedernales, in 1989 when Shaver was recording with his son, guitarist Eddie. As the recording progressed, Shaver started hauling out such classic songs as "Ain't No God in Mexico," "You Asked Me To," "I'm Just an Old Chunk of Coal," and "Easy Come Easy Go (aka Ride Me Down Easy)," with first Willie sitting in, singing, and playing, then Waylon and Kristofferson as well. Each vocalist traded verses and Nelson and Eddie Shaver traded guitar solos. The recordings were easy and relaxed, but filled with nuance and passion. These are songs the musicians have played countless times, but it's clear that they still love the tunes and anyone that's come to love Shaver's songs, whether it's through his recordings or Willie, Waylon, or Kristofferson's, will likely find this to be quite charming. Not really a major album, but an enjoyable one for old five and dimers nonetheless. —*Stephen Thomas Erlewine*

Honky Tonk Super Hits / Mar. 19, 1996 / Epic ◆◆◆
In case there was any doubt that drinking and hanging around in bars continues to be a preoccupation in country music, this ten-song compilation should dispel it. From George Jones and James Taylor's 1978 hit "Bartender's Blues" to Rick Trevino's 1994 chart single "Honky Tonk Crowd," these singers proclaim the wonders of the nightlife and the joy of crying in your beer. The most successful are Doug Stone, whose "A Jukebox with a Country Song" topped the charts in 1992 by lamenting that the local watering hole had turned into a fern bar, and Vern Gosdin, who went to number one in 1988 with "Set 'Em Up Joe." But all these night owls have something to howl about. —*William Ruhlmann*

Hot Rod: Hot Rod Cowboys / May 5, 1997 / Right Stuff ◆◆◆
As compilations go, this is a decent 14-song collection of songs about cars, trucks, and the open road, some very familiar (Roger Miller's "King of the Road"), a few classics (Merle Haggard's "White Line Fever," Johnny Bond's re-recording of his 1960 hit "Hot Rod Lincoln"), some serious sides (Johnny Cash's "Highway Patrolman"), and lots of fun (George Jones' "The Race Is On," Asleep at the Wheel's "Route 66," Jimmy Dolen's "Hot Rod Race," Red Foley's "Travelin' Man"). There are, as usual with this series, no notes of any kind about the music, although there's lots of info about classic hot rods and their engines, in keeping with the disc's link to *Hot Rod* magazine. The sound is good, it's handy, and it has a couple of unique tracks. —*Bruce Eder*

I'm a Honky Tonk Daddy / Flyright ◆◆◆◆
I'm a Honky Tonk Daddy is a 20-track collection that features a good cross-section of material recorded for Flyright during the '50s. The compilation does feature Lefty Frizzell, but most of it is dedicated to obscure performers. For hardcore honky tonk fans, the very rarity of these artists makes *I'm a Honky Tonk Daddy* worthwhile, but for most country fans, the music on this collection will only be of passing interest. —*Thom Owens*

Imperial Rockabillies, Vol. 1 / 1993 / Imperial-Pathe ◆◆◆
As a pioneering West Coast rhythm & blues label, Lew Chudd's Imperial Records was well equipped to take advantage of the sweeping changes in the indie record market when Elvis Presley's Sun recordings suddenly changed the whole ballgame. Chudd had always recorded hillbilly music since Imperial started in 1947, but now actively scoured the South to find performers or records from small labels who could compete with Presley, Gene Vincent, Buddy Holly, and the host of talented Sun rockabillies dominating the

marketplace. This first of three volumes documents that pursuit and offers up some incredible recordings from that ground-floor period in rock & roll's history. How close Chudd had his ear to the ground is exemplified by the kickoff track, Bob Luman's version of "Red Hot." Featuring scorching guitar breaks from a young James Burton, this was a cover of Sun artist Billy Lee Riley's version, itself a cover of Sun bluesman Billy "The Kid" Emerson's original. But Chudd's nose for raw rockabilly led the company to several excellent outside master purchases, and Weldon Rogers' "So Long, Good Luck and Goodbye," The Strikes' "If You Can't Rock Me," and Billy Eldridge's crude "Let's Go Baby" all saw releases on tiny local Texas labels before being picked by Imperial for national consumption. Hillbilly artists already on the roster like disc jockey Bill Mack ("Play My Boogie") and country songwriter Merle Kilgore ("Everybody Needs a Little Lovin'") took a swipe or two at the new music, while artists like Warren Miller ("Everybody's Got a Baby But Me"), Lew Williams ("Bop Bop Ba Doo Bop"), Laura Lee Perkins ("Don't Wait Up") and Sammy Gowans ("Rockin' By Myself") came to the label and were recorded in Hollywood. Fans of wild, trebly rockabilly guitar work with revel in Dennis Herrold's raunchy "Make With the Lovin'," sporting a Telecaster sound that must have tested the limits of 45 RPM reproduction back then, and Johnny & Dorsey Burnette's "Warm Love" featuring a dynamite solo ride from country picker Joe Maphis. Rhythm and blues singer Roy Brown gets all echoed up on his "Hip Shakin' Baby" (one of several rockabilly sides he cut for the label) and the other can't-miss highlight comes with Bill Allen's reverberation screamer "Please Give Me Something." Although there are two other volumes in this set, this one features the highest number of classic, collectible tracks and alone would make a fine addition to any rockabilly collection. —*Cub Koda*

Imperial Rockabillies, Vol. 2 / 1993 / Imperial-Pathe ◆◆◆
This disc, like its predecessor, explores a wide range of blues and country-based music under the general heading of rockabilly, a genre that embraces everything from Elvis wannabes to aging hillbilly singers trying to reinvent themselves as rockin' daddy-o's. This collection includes no less than nine of the artists featured in the first volume with Johnny Burnette, the Strikes (featuring Andy Starr on lead guitar), Laura Lee Perkins, Lew Williams, Johnny Garner, Dennis Herrold, Roy Brown, Merle Kilgore and Roy Brown all returning with a bushelful of classics, including some incredibly rare sides. Burnette kicks things off with "Sweet Baby Doll," and a rocked-up version of "Swing Low, Sweet Chariot," while Laura Lee Perkins' excellent "Oh La Baby" and "Kiss Me Baby" stand as one of the few examples of female rockabilly, the latter track featuring an agitated guitar break from string wizard Joe Maphis. Texas band the Strikes are aboard with three tracks ("Baby I'm Sorry," "Rockin'," and "I Don't Want to Cry Over You" which has vocals listed on the original label as by the Three Pelves!) while Bob Luman's "All Night Long" showcases guitar work from a pre-Ricky Nelson James Burton, who also appears in a support role behind Johnny Burnette and Johnny Garner's "Kiss Me Baby." The hillbilly boogie side of things comes up for examination with the inclusion of "Ernie" and "Ride Jesse Ride" by Merle Kilgore, "Lies" by West Coast disc jockey Lee Ross, "Rockin' Baby" and "Diggin' 'n' Datin'" by Gene Henslee (both from 1954), and "Hey Baby" by Bill Lawrence, the latter inexplicably recorded in Hawaii. Lew Williams returns to this volume with a pair of his best, "Abracadabra" and "Cat Talk," the latter based on "cat music," rockabilly's original appellation in Texas. Roy Brown's "Be My Love Tonight" sounds more like a New Orleans version of a 1920s pop song, but the Louisiana side of rockabilly is well represented by Al Jones' smoking original, "Loretta," sounding for all the world like a lost Dale Hawkins band track. The collection closes with "Willa Mae" by guitarist Al Casey, best known for his work with Duane Eddy. It's not as hot as volume one, but still some great music aboard. —*Cub Koda*

Imperial Rockabillies, Vol. 3 / 1993 / Imperial-Pathe ◆◆◆
The third and final volume in this set exploring the rockabilly from the vaults of Imperial Records extends its view to include late rockers from 1960 with a backward glance to hillbilly boogie items going back to 1950 from the label's 8000 country music series of singles. Country boogie artist Billy Briggs appears here twice, with two different takes of his signature tune from that series, "Chew Tobacco Rag" from 1950. The four holdover artists from the previous two volumes are well represented here as well. Dorsey Burnette's demo version for Ricky Nelson of "It's Late" and the previously unreleased "I Only Came Here to Dance," Laura Lee Perkins' version of Hank Williams' "I Just Don't Like This Kind of Living," Lew Williams' "Gone Ape Man" and "Something I Said," Bob Luman's "Make Up Your Mind Baby" (featuring James Burton on guitar) and the Strikes' previously unissued "My Poor Heart" all add much-welcomed weight to their slender discographies. The Buddy Holly side of rockabilly's equation rears its head on this compilation with the inclusion of Clovis, New Mexico upstarts Jimmy Craig ("Oh Little Girl") and Ronny Smith ("Long Time No Love") as well as a tribute record of sorts ("Buddy") by a 14-year-old Jackie Dee, later to go onto songwriting fame as Jackie DeShannon. This compilation is also full of wonderful one-shots by totally obscure artists. There might not be much in the way of information on the likes of Jay Banks (the crudely played and sung "Get Off My Back"), Slick Slavin ("Speed Crazy," a sort of rockabilly Nervous Norvus), Bobby Lonero (the New Orleans rocker "Little Bit") or Jackie Walker ("Only Teenagers Allowed"), but all left great material behind as their calling cards. Another stunning Joe Maphis guitar solo surfaces on Nick Venet's (later producer of the Beach Boys) "Love In Be-Bop Time" and Andy Starr's crude but extremely effective break on the Strikes' "My Poor Heart" is another must hear. With no bottom-of-the-barrel scrapings here, this final volume is a worthy entry to the series. —*Cub Koda*

● Insurgent Country, Vol. 1: For a Life of Sin / 1994 / Bloodshot ◆◆◆◆
This is the first in a collection of compilations featuring artists that perform country and American roots music who are uncompromising in their dedication to each individual musical vision. The term "Insurgent Country" has been used to describe a growing faction of artists who reach back to traditional foundations, bringing them forward and injecting

their own personal feel. The first volume primarily focuses upon an already-established Chicago country and roots community that dates back to the 1920s when the WLS *National Barn Dance* began its reign. Although the first volume is the weakest of the three, it's definitely worth a listen, with a good cross-section of the current alternative country scene, which includes strong tracks by Robbie Fulks ("Cigarette State"), Freakwater ("Drunk Friend"), as well as the legendary Chicago stalwarts the Sundowners ("Rockin' Spot"). *—Jack Leaver*

Insurgent Country, Vol. 2: Hell-Bent / 1995 / Bloodshot ♦♦♦
With the second volume of the *Insurgent Country* series, Bloodshot Records broadens their scope to include bands from all over the country. The results give an inkling to just how many great country and roots artists exist—one's that are making remarkable music and out there with minimal, or no radio exposure at all. The quality of the performances are more even here than on the first volume and of the 17 artists and songs represented, there are many strong tracks. Once again, Chicago's country singer/songwriter Robbie Fulks highlights the set with "She Took a Lot of Pills (And Died)." Detroit's best kept secret the Volebeats turn in a typical low-key, but memorable song "One I Love," and Dallas' Old 97's contribute the rowdy, bluegrass-tinged rave-up "Por Favor." One of the collection's other standout tracks, "22," from San Francisco's Richard Buckner, is also the darkest. In chilling literary detail, Buckner's song character describes his suicide from unrequited love, casting a long but compelling shadow on the collection. *—Jack Leaver*

● **Insurgent Country, Vol. 3: Nashville—The Other Side of the Alley** / 1996 / Bloodshot ♦♦♦♦♦
The best and most consistent of the lot so far, *Vol. 3* concentrates on alternative country and roots acts based in and around Nashville. A wonderful way to get a good sampling of this exciting and growing music scene. Highlights of the 18-song set include: Tim Carroll's "Open Flame," mainstay forefathers Jason & the Scorchers "One Last Question," Kristi Rose & the Handsome Strangers "Rise & Shine" and the Wilco off-shoot Courtesy Move "Those I'll Provide." *—Jack Leaver*

Jamie/Guyden Story / 1995 / Bear Family ♦♦♦♦
The double-disc set *Classic Jamie Masters* contains a selection of highlights from the Jamie vaults, boasting 60 tracks from the late '50s and early '60s. Jamie didn't really have a signature sound, which means that *Classic Jamie Masters* is all over the place in terms of sound and style, flipping between rock & roll, country, pop and R&B in the blink of the eye. Furthermore, the set doesn't contain many hit singles. While there are a number of famous names, only two of them—Duane Eddy and Barbara Lynn—are represented by big hits. Nevertheless, the set is a quite entertaining, especially for listeners who are looking for rarities, obscurities and arcane items from big names. *Classic Jamie Masters* contains tracks by Duane Eddy ("Rebel Rouser," "Because They're Young," "40 Miles of Bad Road"), Barbara Lynn ("You'll Lose a Good Thing," "(I Cried At) Laura's Wedding"), Titus Turner ("Sound Off"), Barbara Mason ("Yes I'm Ready"), Bruce Channel ("Going Back to Louisiana"), Johnny Rivers ("Hole in the Ground"), Mac Davis ("I'm a Poor Loser"), Danny & the Juniors ("Oh-La-La Limbo"), Neil Sedaka ("Ring a Rockin'"), Maureen Gray ("Dancing the Strand"), Lee Hazlewood ("Words Mean Nothing"), Sanford Clark ("Son of a Gun"), Harold Melvin & the Blue Notes ("Get Out"), and Barbara Mason ("Oh How It Hurts"). *—Stephen Thomas Erlewine*

Jitterbug Jive: Hot Texas Swing 1940–1941 / Mar. 18, 1997 / Krazy Kat ♦♦♦
Subtitled "Hot Texas Swing, 1940-1941," this set brings together a nice cross-section of tracks from territory bands that sprang up in the wake of Bob Wills, Milton Brown, and the entire Western swing movement. Artists like Bill Mounce, the Bar X Cowboys, Modern Mountaineers, the Dixie Ramblers, and the Sons of Dixie may not be household names by any stretch of the imagination (although names like Bob Dunn, Leon Payne, Tiny Moore, Jimmy Wyble, Moon Mullican, and Cliff Bruner show up on these sides), but the music is top-notch, unfettered by commercial restraints, local music with a free and wild spirit. Loads of steel playing, twin fiddles and swinging rhythm sections coupled with jaunty vocals make these old Bluebird 78s come to life. Decent transfers of the material and extensive liner notes make this a package well worth the extra effort to find. *—Cub Koda*

Johnny Gimble's Texas Honky-Tonk Hits / CMH ♦♦♦
Johnny Gimble's Texas Honky-Tonk Hits is a two-album compilation of the fiddler's finest moments. The album does feature solo cuts from Gimble, but the real meat of the collection lies in the wonderful selection of songs that he recorded with other artists. Featuring tracks by the Wills Brothers, Mac Wiseman, Carl Butler, Johnny Bond, Rose Lee Maphis and Stuart Hamblen, all of the music on *Texas Honk-Tonk Hits* swings with the best of Western swing and tugs at the heart like the best honky tonk, and throughout it all, Gimble's fiddle soars. More than anything, *Texas Honky-Tonk Hits* offers convincing evidence that Johnny Gimble was the finest country fiddler to ever record. *—Thom Owens*

Jubilation, Vol. 3 (Country Gospel) / Mar. 1992 / Rhino ♦♦♦♦♦
While the first two volumes in the series spotlighted the history of African-American gospel, this volume peeks over the other side of the fence and sheds the light on six decades' worth of country gospel performances. It's all top-notch, too, with Hank Williams' "I Saw the Light" spearheading an 18-track collection that includes classics from Kitty Wells, Roy Acuff, Bill Monroe, Patsy Cline, Johnny Cash, the Carter Family, the Louvin Brothers, Webb Pierce, and Martha Carson. That gospel is a long-running tradition in country is exemplified by the inclusion of tracks from modern stars like Ricky Skaggs & Tony Rice, Doyle Lawson & Quicksilver, the Nitty Gritty Dirt Band, and old guard like Buck Owens, George Jones & Tammy Wynette, and Ernest Tubb. It's a delightful set. *—Cub Koda*

Jug & Washboard Bands, Vol. 2 (1928–1930) / 1992 / Story of the Blues ♦♦♦
Jug and washboard bands were quite popular in the late '20s. This disc has the complete recordings of the Tub Jug Washboard Band (four titles including "Washboard Rag" and "Lady Quit Her Husband Onexpectinly"), a pair of sermons by Rev. E.S. "Shy" Moore that are included because the backup rhythm section includes a jug, the vocal duo of Feathers & Frogs (also backed by a rhythm section with a jug), and eight selections by Phillips' Louisville Jug Band, a band that includes such odd instruments as the C-melody sax, the walking cane flute, and a jazzhorn. Overall, the music is spirited if not essential, casting some light on the rural music of the late '20s. *—Scott Yanow*

Kindred Spirits: A Tribute to the Songs of Johnny Cash / Sep. 24, 2002 / Sony ♦♦♦
The second of two Johnny Cash tribute discs released in September 2002 (the other is *Dressed in Black: A Tribute to Johnny Cash*) brings out the big guns in terms of marquee talent. As the album's coordinator, musician Marty Stuart has the background and contacts to pull this project off. Any collection with previously unreleased tracks from Bruce Springsteen, Bob Dylan, Dwight Yoakam, Emmylou Harris, and Steve Earle has built in credibility. All the participants are enthusiastic and dedicated, but the most stirring tracks inject a different spin to the originals. Unfortunately there aren't enough of those. Stuart's version of "Hey Porter" is respectful but doesn't deviate enough from Cash's boom-chika rockabilly to make it worth the effort. Yoakam's "Understand Your Man" even keeps the mariachi trumpets that added such an offbeat sound to Cash's '60s work. Daughter Rosanne's version of "I Still Miss Someone" is tender but lacks punch, as does Springsteen's solo acoustic "Give My Love to Rose," which sounds like an outtake from *Nebraska*. Dylan's spoken intro to "Train of Love" thanks Cash for standing up for him "way back when" before launching into one of the most emotionally stirring performances on this album. Little Richard does his best "Long Tall Sally" with a rock'em sock'em "Get Rhythm," but his voice isn't what it used to be and the song ends up sounding more like a Richard tune than a Cash one. Much better is Keb' Mo', who slows down "Folsom Prison Blues" to an ominous, swamp/bluesy crawl. Travis Tritt successfully re-arranges "I Walk the Line" into a slow but menacing honky tonk ballad similar to how George Jones might approach it. Though it's fraught with the best intentions and tries to deviate from the hits (where's "Ring of Fire"?), *Kindred Spirits* is disappointing because even with the high-profile talent, few add anything unique, enlightening, or inspirational to Cash's already timeless music. *—Hal Horowitz*

The King's Record Collection, Vol. 1 / Mar. 10, 1998 / Hip-O ♦♦♦
Here's a novel concept—a 14-track compilation of the original versions of tunes Elvis Presley made popular. In a nod to Presley's catholic tastes, this volume brings together artists as diverse as Bill Monroe ("Blue Moon of Kentucky"), the Shelton Brothers ("Just Because"), the Drifters ("Money Honey"), Leon Payne ("I Love You Because"), Little Junior Parker ("Mystery Train"), Smiley Lewis ("One Night"), Arthur "Big Boy" Crudup ("That's All Right") and Arthur Gunter ("Baby, Let's Play House"). The songs are sequenced chronologically and stop just prior to his induction into the U.S. Army in 1958. It's a fascinating look at the source material behind Elvis' rise to fame. *—Cub Koda*

The King's Record Collection, Vol. 2 / Mar. 10, 1998 / Hip-O ♦♦♦
Vol. 2 of this fascinating series delves into the tunes Presley recorded and covered after being inducted into the military in 1958 and finishing with his last Top 15 hit in the 1970s, Chuck Berry's "Promised Land." Sequenced chronologically, the highlights include Ketty Lester's "Love Letters," Hank Snow's "A Fool Such As I," Lowell Fulson's "Reconsider Baby," Tommy Tucker's "High Heel Sneakers," Jack Greene's "There Goes My Everything," Jimmy Reed's "Big Boss Man" and Jerry Reed's "Guitar Man." Another fascinating collection that shows off both Presley's wide-ranging tastes and his ability to jump between styles with consummate ease. *—Cub Koda*

The King-Federal Rockabillys / 197 / ♦♦♦♦♦
In the mid-'50s, perhaps spurred by the success of Elvis Presley and other country-oriented artists who were enjoying crossover success on the pop charts, Syd Nathan started issuing rockabilly recordings on his King and Federal labels. Although none of the artists compiled here ever achieved anything remotely resembling a hit for the label, these 14 tracks featuring the cream of the rockabilly sides from the King and Federal labels stand as a fine document to the burgeoning rockabilly sound. The big ticket here are four classic tracks from the legendary Charlie Feathers ("One Hand Loose," "Bottle to the Baby," "Everybody's Lovin' My Baby," and "Nobody's Woman") and five from King label mate Mac Curtis, "Granddaddy's Rockin'," "Say So," "If I Had a Woman," "Little Miss Linda" and the previously unissued "Goosebumps." Although seldom remembered today, the Texas-born Curtis was the more successful of the two artists, recording 16 sides for the label. Far and away, the strangest track aboard this collection is "Jungle Rock" by Hank Mizell. Strange simply because the record was a flop back in the '50s, only to become a freak hit in England in 1976, some 20 years after its release, bringing Mizell out of retirement to a hero's welcome abroad. Hillbilly boogie fans will love "Peg Pants" by Bill Beach and Joe Penny's "Bip a Little, Bop a Lot," both solid numbers with great soloing, especially the steel breaks on Beach's effort. Canada's answer to the Collins Kids, Bob & Lucille, come up with a great novelty rocker with "Eenie Meeny Miney Mo," complete with all the hiccuping and glottal shrieks that are emblematic of great classic rockabilly vocalizing. A borderline rocker (more rock & roll than real rockabilly if you're splitting hairs about such things) comes in the form of "Rockin' Up" by Ronnie Molleen. A wild rocker with a Little Richard-style vocal, this one definitely stands out against the guitar-driven tracks here, but is a fine addition regardless. *—Cub Koda*

Legacy: A Tribute to the First Generation of Bluegrass / May 20, 1997 / Sugar Hill ♦♦♦
This tribute album consists of previously released tracks by such modern bluegrass greats as Doyle Lawson, Tony Rice, the Seldom Scene, and Ricky Skaggs; all of the songs were either written by or closely associated with one of the foundational artists of early bluegrass: Bill Monroe, the Stanley Brothers, or Flatt & Scruggs. Fiddler Byron Berline opens the program with Monroe's "Rose of Old Kentucky," on which Berline's playing is perfect as always. Unfortunately, singer Vince Gill doesn't have anywhere near enough voice to

cover Big Mon, but just about everything else on this album is superb. Ricky Skaggs and Tony Rice perform "Memories of Mother and Dad" in the venerable "brother duet" style; the Laurel Canyon Ramblers do Flatt & Scruggs proud with their powerful rendition of "Preachin', Prayin', Singin'." Marty Stuart—something of a bluegrass prodigal—delivers a stark and powerful performance of Lester Flatt's "Get in Line, Brother" with the help of Johnny Cash and Alan O'Bryant. Though these performances could never take the place of the originals, this is a fine and heartfelt tribute to bluegrass music's pioneers. *—Rick Anderson*

Making Singles, Drinking Doubles / Dec. 10, 2002 / Bloodshot ♦♦♦♦
A more conventional label would simply round up their greatest hits in recognition of their 100th release, but not the gang at Bloodshot, the Chicago-based indie behind the likes of Kelly Hogan and Neko Case. As suggested by the title, *Making Singles, Drinking Doubles* is a well-balanced collection of out-of-print singles and unreleased tracks. If the selections aren't necessarily their "biggest hits," they still represent a handy introduction to the country's premier alt-country label—or *insurgent country*, as they would have it—as well as a boon for the collector. Although there are no duds, there are some definite standouts: the Meat Purveyors' bluegrass-flavored "Madonna Trilogy" ("Like a Virgin," "Lucky Star," and "Burning Up"), Rex Hobart and the Misery Boys' twangy take on Poison's "Every Rose Has Its Thorn," and Adams' previously unreleased charmer "Goodbye Honey" and an acoustic version of "To Be Young (Is to Be Sad, Is to Be High)." Although there are a few omissions, like the Old 97's and Robbie Fulks, both are already represented by their own Bloodshot compilations of obscurities and rare tracks. *—Kathleen C. Fennessy*

Man of Constant Sorrow and Other Timeless Mountain Ballads / May 21, 2002 / Yazoo ♦♦♦♦
Yazoo offers up another classic collection of mountain ballads and old-timey heartbreakers from the '20s and '30s on *Man of Constant Sorrow*. Chestnuts like "Ommie Wise," "John Hardy," "Darling Cora," and the title track are interspersed with lesser-known recordings from B.F. Shelton, Grayson & Whitter, Charlie Poole, and Ernest Stoneman. The Blue Sky Boys' contribution, "In the Hills of Roane County," is a chillingly beautiful high lonesome murder ballad highlighting Earl & Bill Bolick's fraternal harmonies, and the youthful Cousin Emmy's stark "Pretty Little Miss Out in the Garden" is accompanied intimately by her own gentle banjo picking. Surprisingly, the only clunkers on the album come from the usually spectacular Eck Robertson, whose singing fiddle is unusually out of tune and he spends both of the tracks competing with a female vocalist who shouts over the top of him (pre-dating Audrey Williams' offenses by a couple of decades). These 20 tracks were taken directly from rare old 78s, so some pops and crackles are to be expected, but anyone with a worn-out copy of *The Anthology of American Folk Music* won't mind a bit. *—Zac Johnson*

Memphis Ramble: Sun Country Collection, Vol. 1 / 1990 / Rhino ♦♦♦♦♦
Memphis Ramble: Sun Country Collection is an excellent, single-disc cross-section of hits and obscurities from the vaults of Sun Records, including prime cuts from the likes of Johnny Cash, Warren Smith and Jerry Lee Lewis. *—Thom Owens*

Memphis Rocks: Rockabilly in Memphis: 1954–1968 / 1992 / Smithsonian ♦♦♦
Here's the Smithsonian Institution's take on rockabilly; subtitled *Rockabilly In Memphis, 1954-1968*, this is a very fine collection of some of that city's best—and more obscure—practitioners. Although there's a fair smattering of Sun hits aboard—"Whole Lotta Shakin' Goin' On," "Mona Lisa," "High School Confidential," "I Walk the Line"—there's also a number of rare tracks on here to highly recommend it. Almost everything on here emanates from the Sun label, with the exception of Carl McVoy's "You Are My Sunshine" and Charlie Feathers' "Stuttering Cindy," the only track to be recorded past the 1950s in this set. If you collect enough Sun packages, you might get all the tracks that are on this collection, but any compilation that has Ray Harris' "Come On Little Mama" as its leadoff track has a wild rockin' agenda of its own that sets its apart from the others. *—Cub Koda*

Memphis Sanctified Jug Bands 1928–1930 / 1994 / Document ♦♦♦
The "sanctified" Church of God in Christ (COGIC) was and is formative in African-American gospel music far beyond its numerical strength, in part because it drew heavily from secular instrumental music when other groupings disapproved of guitars pianos and the rest. These sensational recordings by a handful of groups are similar to the secular jugbands, but outswing most of them three to two. *—John Storm Roberts*

Mercury Rockabillies: Louisiana Rock 'n Roll / 1993 / Big Tone ♦♦♦
Anyone who thinks that Sun Records had the market cornered on rockabilly music and Southern rock & roll will find something here to keep them busy for a few hours. Big Tone doesn't seem to have anything resembling official permission (like, there's no licensing information) and the source material seems to be derived from vinyl, albeit clean discs. But this collection of 30 songs issued by Mercury Records starts off in top gear and burns rubber until about halfway through, when it switches gears to the somewhat tamer and more stylized Louisiana portion of the disc. Artists range from Eddie Bond & His Stompers to Professor Longhair (working as Roy Byrd) & His Blues Jumpers, with J. P. ("Big Bopper") Richardson and Conway Twitty representing the most familiar stopping points. Others include: Thomas Wayne ("You're the One That Done It"), Billy Wallace ("Burnin' the Wind"), early Elvis soundalike Roy Moss ("You Nearly Lose Your Mind," "You're My Big Baby Now"), and Cookie & the Cupcakes ("Mathilde," "Got You On My Mind"). Twitty's "Born to Sing the Blues" and two numbers by balladeer Johnny "T" Talley (trying real hard to rock out, and 90 percent succeeding) are a little too slow and tame in some ways, next to the rockabilly material. The sound is good despite the slight compression and momentary traces of surface noise. The notes are extremely thorough as well. *—Bruce Eder*

Miami Rockabilly / Feb. 10, 1998 / Ace ♦♦♦
Miami is not the first, or even the tenth, city one associates with rockabilly, but there were a number of local artists recording for small labels there in the late 1950s. This compilation has 32 sides released on a slew of tiny companies, sometimes in press runs of only a thousand or so copies. Miami did not cultivate a distinct or interesting rockabilly sound, and although this is passably entertaining stuff (sometimes crudely recorded and clumsily performed), this is yet another one of those anthologies where the responsible critic strains for odds and ends to pick out from the overall flood of generic beats and riffs. Bobby Shane's outrageous "TV Mama," which has previously been compiled on albums of rare weird '50s rock, is certainly the highlight, with its contorted vocal moans and stutters. Kent Westberry, who would join Carl Perkins' band on bass and become a successful country songwriter, manages a sort of imitation Everly Brothers-"Bye Bye Love" sound on "No Place to Park"; Buck Trail gets some cool outer-space echo effects on "Knocked Out Joint on Mars." This also has Tommy Spurlin's "Heart Throb," which somehow showed up in the *Porky's* movie. *—Richie Unterberger*

Mississippi String Bands and Associates (1928–1931): Complete Recorded Works / 1991 / Document ♦♦♦♦
The music on this enjoyable CD of rarities features overlapping groups that recorded in Atlanta in 1928, Jackson, MS, in 1930, and Chicago during several sessions in 1931. All of the recordings released under the names of singer Alec Johnson, the Mississippi Mud Steppers, the Mississippi Blacksnakes, and Sam Hill From Louisville are here. Such notables as guitarist/violinist Bo Carter, Charlie McCoy on mandolin, guitarist Joe McCoy, and guitarist/singer Walter Vincson are prominent in supporting roles and it is interesting to hear these future blues stars this early in their careers. Blues historians will want this valuable set. *—Scott Yanow*

Monument Story / 1994 / Sony ♦♦♦
The Monument Story is a two-disc overview of the Monument label spanning the late '50s through the mid '70s. Monument had a number of left-field chart successes and had an impressive roster of talents, including Ray Stevens, Kris Kristofferson, Dolly Parton and Roy Orbison (all of whom are represented on this anthology). Although some may find Monument recordings intrinsically interesting, most listeners will be drawn to this collection by the many hard-to-find hits, including Henson Cargill's "Skip a Rope," the Dixie Belles' "(Down at) Papa Joe's," and Dick Flood's version of "The Three Bells." The 36 tracks include some rarities as well, notably Willie Nelson's "I Never Cared for You," one of a handful of sides he recorded for Monument before signing with RCA in the early '60s. *—Greg Adams*

Mobile Strugglers & Louis James' String Band / 1996 / American Music ♦♦
Two unrelated string band sessions are combined on this CD reissue. The Mobile Strugglers originally only had two numbers released from 1949 but on this set there are seven tunes (including five that have vocals). Comprised of violinists James Field and Charles Jones, guitarist Paul Johnson, bassist Wesley Williams and Lee Warren on mandolin and banjo, the primitive but charming performances capture a now-lost rural musical tradition; highlights inlcude "Memphis Blues," "Fattening Frogs for Snakes" and "Billboard March." The second half of this CD showcases violinist Louis James (who switches to clarinet for one number) in a 1965 trio with guitarist Ernest Roubleau and bassist August Lanoix. Although enjoyable if taken in small doses, James' limited ideas run thin after a while. Ironically his repertoire is pretty wide, ranging from swing tunes and the waltz "After the Ball," to an "Untitled Quadrille Tune" and "King Bolden's Song" (which sounds like an ancestor to "Up a Lazy River"). But overall, this CD is recommended more for historians than for casual listeners. *—Scott Yanow*

More Bona Fide Bluegrass and Mountain Music / Oct. 8, 2002 / RCA ♦♦♦♦♦
This single CD compilation is the companion volume to the BMG Heritage release *Bona Fide Bluegrass & Mountain Music* (2002)—both of which focus on the high and lonesome sound of traditional Americana from the 20th Century. The enormous success of Joel Cohen's *O Brother, Where Art Thou?* (2000) spawned not only a well-received soundtrack, but also collections such as this. *More Bona Fide Bluegrass and Mountain Music* (2002) includes one-and-a-half-dozen sides which, despite spanning over half a century, are undeniably united by common acoustic-based motifs and organic musical themes. RCA Victor was one of the first companies to fully embrace and take advantage of the field and on-location recordings. In particular, the label's artist and repertoire (A&R) man Ralph Peer has been credited for uncovering performers as far afield as Hoyt Ming ("Indian War Whoop (Country-Dance)") to Piedmont fiddle legend Arthur Smith ("Freight Train Moan") during various talent scouting excursions throughout the southeastern United States. In addition to Peer's various discoveries, this set includes original recordings of tunes which have remained in the traditional folk genre for decades. One specific case in point is the revelation "You Are My Sunshine." Although the track later became a signature song for two-term Louisiana Governor Jimmy Davis, the original—which is included here—features the Pine Ridge Boys' 1939 recording. No bluegrass collection could be considered complete without copious contributions from Lester Flatt who is highlighted in several different musical scenarios. Here, he is featured both as a solo artist on "Head Over Heels in Love" as well as with Bill Monroe as the pair present "My Little Cabin Home on The Hill" and "Will You Be Loving Another Man." More recent inclusions, from the early 1970s, pair Flatt with Mac Wiseman for seminal readings of "Over the Hills to the Poorhouse" and "The Bluebirds Singing For Me." While far from complete or definitive, this collection is certainly a worthy find for fans of authentic American folk/bluegrass and mountain music. *—Lindsay Planer*

Mountain Music of Kentucky / Mar. 19, 1996 / Smithsonian Folkways ♦♦♦♦♦
In 1959, John Cohen of the New Lost City Ramblers made field recordings in the mountains of Kentucky of Appalachian folk performers who were virtually unknown to the record-buying public. This is no-nonsense, sometimes raw stuff, with fiddlers, banjos,

a cappella singers, and Baptist church choirs presenting folk standards, blues-influenced numbers, stomping bluegrass, even the odd country song. It's got as much of the unadulterated American white folk feel as the older recordings on Harry Smith's *Anthology of Folk Music* box (to use a celebrated example), though the material here is of better fidelity. Although some of these artists would make other recordings, only Roscoe Holcomb—the most passionate and arresting of them—would gain anything like substantial recognition. This is too basic and unschooled, not to mention too long, to hold the attention of the average folk or bluegrass fan, but scholars and roots aficionados will value its no-frills authenticity. Originally issued as a single LP in 1960, the two-CD reissue adds an hour of previously unreleased material, and lengthy historical liner notes by John Cohen. *—Richie Unterberger*

The Music Never Stopped: Roots of the Grateful Dead / Nov. 1995 / Shanachie ✦✦✦
An interesting concept: a compilation of the original versions of 17 songs frequently covered by the Grateful Dead in concert. Thoughtfully assembled, it showcases several aspects of their eclectic roots, encompassing jugband folk, country & western, Appalachian mountain music, country blues, '50s Chicago electric blues, R&B, Dylan, Guthrie, Holly, Berry, and more. Some of the recordings are very famous (Dylan's "It's All over Now, Baby Blue," Holly's "Not Fade Away"); others are downright obscure (Obray Ramsey's "Rain and Snow," the rare original version of "Morning Dew" by little-known Canadian folkie Bonnie Dobson). If you're a Dead fan, this is a valuable, very listenable collection of some of their key influences. It may seem churlish to point this out to Deadheads, but if you're *not* a Dead fan, you'll find this to be a first-rate collection of roots music that's much more enjoyable than hearing the Dead's interpretations of the same tunes. *—Richie Unterberger*

The Music of Kentucky: Early American Rural Classics 1927–1937, Vol. 1–2 / 1995 / Yazoo ✦✦✦✦✦
Many rural fiddlers, guitarists, and banjo players from the state of Kentucky were taped while the recording industry was in its infancy. This interesting and valuable two-volume set, numbering 53 songs in all, presents a wide-ranging set of old-timey folk styles, by artists who are known only to scholars in the field. Much of the material is taken from the famed Bristol sessions of the late '20s, and late-'30s field recordings by renowned folklorist Alan Lomax. The roots of much modern country, folk, and even blues can be heard in these heartfelt, occasionally stirring performances of great conviction, religious or otherwise. It's not just a history lesson, and is a lot more accessible to modern-day listeners than many would assume. *—Richie Unterberger*

My Rifle, My Pony and Me / Jun. 28, 1994 / Bear Family ✦✦✦
There is astonishingly little overlap between this 26-song collection, consisting of songs from various western movie and television soundtracks, and other, rival domestic releases. As usual, Bear Family has done its best to gather together the best and most unusual of this material—a promotional-only single of Ricky Nelson and Dean Martin singing "My Rifle, My Pony and Me" from *Rio Bravo* (adapted by Dimitri Tiomkin from the title theme from a score he wrote for an earlier John Wayne/Howard Hawks movie, *Red River*); Merle Kilgore (sounding a lot like Tex Ritter) doing the title song from *Nevada Smith*; "The Legend of Shenandoah" by James Stewart, telling the plot of the fim while a chorus sings the title tune, as a sort of audio trailer for the movie *Shenandoah* (more of an eastern than a western); the Sons of the Pioneers doing the title theme from *The Searchers*; Marty Robbins' version of "The Ballad of the Alamo"; Tex Ritter's second (and best) recording of "High Noon"; and the Sons of the Pioneers performing "Song of the Wagonmaster" and "Wagons West" from *Wagonmaster*; Roy Rogers singing "The Yellow Rose of Texas" (to an utterly unfamiliar melody); Johnny Cash's "The Sons of Katie Elder" (a soundtrack never reissued on CD); and the only CD release of Dean Martin's "Rio Bravo." There are no notes, but everything else is first-rate about this disc. *—Bruce Eder*

Mystery Train: Classic Railroad Songs, Vol. 2 / Mar. 11, 1997 / Rounder ✦✦✦✦
The lure of the railroad is explored thoroughly in the second volume of Rounder's railroad compilations, with songs recorded from the '20s through to the '80s. The image of the railroad is burned into American history, representing just about anything you want it to represent—freedom, loss, greed, power, mystery, flight, mythology, integration, disintegration, growth… whatever symbol you need. The 14 songs here have as many themes to them, from the last fatal run of Casey Jones to men and women whose sweethearts waft away on long black trains. Most affecting when the songs come out of the bluegrass tradition, entertaining throughout. Artists include Johnny Cash, the Whitstein Brothers, Steve Goodman, the Carter Family, Bob Wills & His Texas Playboys (cutting the rug effectively with "Take The 'A' Train") and Mary McCaslin amongst others. *—Steven McDonald*

Nashville at Newport / Sep. 5, 1995 / Vangard ✦✦✦✦
Nashville at Newport chronicles the legendary folk festival's gradual acceptance of country music by gathering a total of 31 *Newport* performances by country artists from 1963 to 1968. The disc opens with one song apiece from Jimmie Driftwood, Mother Maybelle Carter, and Ramblin' Jack Elliott. Next come several songs each by Hazel Dickens and Kirk McGee. Then there are extended sets (at least six songs) by Ike Everly and his son Don (of the Everly Brothers), Roy Acuff & His Smoky Mountain Boys, and Johnny Cash. Although the recording quality is sometimes not quite up to par, the performances are excellent, and the historical value of the music is undeniable. *—Steve Huey*

Nashville Early String Bands, Vol. 1 / Oct. 10, 2000 / County ✦✦✦✦
Radio dealt a serious blow to the recording industry in the early '20s, bringing music into everyone's home for free. Radio came to Nashville in 1923, but it wasn't until 1925 when WSL started the *Grand Old Opry.* Early performers lived in the surrounding area and usually played the program free of charge. *Nashville Early String Bands, Vol. 1* captures the energy and wildness of those early days. A variety of known and lesser-known artists appear here, from Uncle Dave Macon to the Arthur Smith Trio. Dr. Humphrey Bates sings the hilariously outrageous "My Wife Died Saturday Night" that carries the refrain, "My wife died Saturday night, Sunday she was buried, Monday was my courting day, and Tuesday I got married." Sam McGee praises his favorite automobile in the bouncy "Chevrolet Car" (he tried unsuccessfully to interest Chevrolet in the song's advertisement value) and the Binkley Brothers' Dixie Clodhoppers sing the excellent "I'll Rise When the Rooster Crows" and "Give Me Back My Fifteen Cent." The Arthur Smith Trio's out of the ordinary "Stood on the Bridge at Midnight" finds the narrator at the bridge with the moon in the sky and the water rushing down below him. While the reason for his sorrow is never clear, the imagery catches his mood perfectly. The detailed liner notes provide good information about the performers and provide a sense of the early *Opry*'s history. While certain cuts on this collection are scratchy, the overall quality is very good. These recordings offer a fine look at country music's roots, complete with fiddles and banjos, untrained singers, and traditional songs. *—Ronnie Lankford Jr.*

Nashville Early String Bands, Vol. 2 / Oct. 10, 2000 / County ✦✦✦✦
Radio came to Nashville in 1923, but it wasn't until 1925 when WSL started the *Grand Old Opry.* In the beginning, the *Grand Old Opry*, overseen by George D. Hay, was a wild and rumpus program that utilized unpaid musicians who lived nearby. *Nashville Early String Bands, Vol. 2* captures the energy and wildness of those early days. DeFord Bailey offers fine versions of harmonica blues on "Muscle Shoals Blues" and "Alcoholic Blues," showing that early country music included a wide variety of instruments. Sam & Kirk McGee sing "Brown's Ferry Blues," a song made famous by the Delmore Brothers. While less polished than the Delmore Brothers, their more old-time version is filled with energetic banjo. Uncle Dave Macon's charisma shines through on "Over the Road I'm Bound to Go" and "Bake That Chicken Pie." Although many early string bands had singers, a singer was by no means necessary and many groups performed without one. Instrumental recordings like Theron Hale & Band's "Fire in the Mountain" and the fiddling of Uncle Jimmy Thompson on "Billy Wilson" are prominent throughout this album. Whatever these early recordings lack in "polish" they make up for in liveliness. These early recordings also prove widely eclectic, performing without the guidelines of a "country sound." Several cuts on *Nashville Early String Bands, Vol. 2* contain a few scratches, but the overall fidelity is very good. These recordings offer a fine look at country music's roots, complete with fiddles and banjos, untrained singers, and traditional songs. *—Ronnie Lankford Jr.*

The Nashville Sound: Owen Bradley / Feb. 1996 / Decca ✦✦
Producer Owen Bradley is undoubtedly one of the most important figures in Nashville country music. This skimpy ten-song sampler, however, is not the best way to appreciate his legacy. Certainly some of the performances are pivotal classics (Brenda Lee's "I'm Sorry," Patsy Cline's "Crazy"), but it's so short that it's virtually over as soon as it starts. Also, a couple of the standards here (Kitty Wells' "It Wasn't God Who Made Honky Tonk Angels," Red Foley's "Chattanoogie Shoe Shine Boy") are not the original versions, but remakes. *—Richie Unterberger*

National Geographic: Destination Appalachia / Oct. 9, 2001 / Sugo ✦✦✦
Another in *National Geographic*'s far-reaching Destination series, *Destination Appalachia* seems a lot closer than some of their exotic destinations, but the region is no less exotic and culturally enriching than their journeys to Spain and Africa. The CD comes complete with intriguing cultural facts and maps of each region included in the enclosed foldout. The album's subtitle, Bluegrass, Banjos & Smoky Mountain Tales, gives little insight as to what is contained within—mostly contemporary bluegrass artists like Ricky Scaggs and Tony Rice with a handful of classic bluegrass artists like the Osborne Brothers and the Bluegrass Cardinals. While this is a fine (even excellent) collection of newer bluegrass music, the assumption from the title and the cover photo is that it will be chock-full of old-time gritty field recordings from the likes of Roscoe Holcomb and Buell Kazee. The album on the whole is a cleanly recorded, well-planned, studio-produced collection of traditional folk songs, but part of what makes true traditional Appalachian folk so electrifying is the way it creaks and groans through the bones and souls of the players, as is demonstrated almost exclusively on the CD by rough fiddler Art Stamper's "Brushy Fork of John's Creek." Although performers like progressive bluegrass artist and Harvard graduate Alison Brown don't necessarily embody the age-old old-timey feel, the music she interprets is undoubtedly rooted in the mountains. *—Zac Johnson*

Newport Folk Festival: Best of Bluegrass 1959–1966 / Apr. 10, 2001 / Vanguard ✦✦✦✦✦
These three discs present 51 tracks recorded at the Newport Folk Festivals between 1959 and 1966, including some giants of the genre: Flatt & Scruggs, Jim & Jesse, Bill Monroe, and the Stanley Brothers. There's a generous portion of material by most of the acts featured, including seven 1965 songs by Monroe, ten (from 1960 and 1966) by Flatt & Scruggs, and 13 (from 1963 and 1966) by Jim & Jesse. The Newport Folk Festivals were important events for the popularization of all facets of folk or folk-based music, and this set effectively encapsulates their contributions to bringing bluegrass to a wider (and often white and Northern) audience. No less than 16 of the cuts were previously unreleased, although with the exception of a couple 1963 Jim & Jesse performances, these are by the least well-known acts on the set: Hylo Brown & the Timberliners (with Earl Scruggs), Don Stover, and the Lilly Brothers (with Don Stover and Tex Logan). As for the most recognizable "hit" of the package, Flatt & Scruggs do a version of their famous *Beverly Hillbillies* theme, "The Ballad of Jed Clampett"; and Jim & Jesse do an unexpected cover of Chuck Berry's "Memphis, Tennessee." Most interesting are the three tunes by Hazel Dickens and Alice Gerrard. These have a sense of reaching for something and hunger that

is not always heard in the always-accomplished, but flashily polished, performances on much of the rest of the package. *—Richie Unterberger*

O Christmas Tree!: A Bluegrass Collection for the Holidays / Nov. 5, 2002 / Rounder ✦✦✦

Sooner or later, every artist in every genre comes to a crossroads: to record or not to record holiday songs, that is the question. It might be easy to argue, from a critic's point of view, that the world doesn't really need another version of "Rudolph the Red-Nosed Reindeer" or "Winter Wonderland." But what about bluegrass versions of these songs by Lynn Morris and the Shankman Twins? Certainly Ron Stewart's take on "Silver Bells," backed by fiddle and acoustic guitar, brings something new to this perennial favorite, and it's doubtful that there's ever been a spunkier version of "O Come All Ye Faithful" than the one banjoist Tony Trischka lays down. The truth is, it's fun to hear these overly familiar songs get a fresh makeover. Doyle Lawson and Quicksilver's a cappella medley of "The First Noel/It Came Upon a Midnight Clear/Joy to the World" captures the simple beauty of these solemn carols, while Open Road's tradition-fueled "Blue Christmas" would have made Bill Monroe smile. *O Christmas Tree* also collects a few less familiar pieces (at least to city folks) like "Christmas Is Near," "Smoky Mountain Christmas," and "Call Collect on Christmas." With 18 songs/instrumentals and nearly an hour of music, this compilation will make a fine addition to one's holiday music collection. *—Ronnie D. Lankford Jr.*

O Sister! The Women's Bluegrass Collection / Oct. 30, 2001 / Rounder ✦✦✦✦✦

The latest in a lengthening string of releases designed to benefit from association with the Coen brothers film *O Brother, Where Art Thou?* is this all-girl bluegrass compilation, which features on its cover the requisite stubbly cornfield and archaic font style. Opportunistic as the packaging may be, there's no arguing with the quality of the content. Generously packed with outstanding performances by women as stylistically disparate as Hazel Dickens, Claire Lynch, and Kathy Kallick, *O Sister* is a delightful celebration of several generations of criminally unheralded female bluegrass artists. The highlights are many, but particular standout tracks include Rhonda Vincent's rocking "Lonesome Wind Blues," the hard-edged mountain sound of Phyllis Boyens (backed up by Hazel Dickens & the Johnson Mountain Boys), and the clawhammer banjo-powered "Comin' Down From God" by the relatively unknown Carol Elizabeth Jones. The usual suspects are here too, of course, including Alison Krauss (on the exquisitely gentle and sweet "Every Time You Say Goodbye") and the Cox Family (twice). You might buy this one because you feel guilty about the way women have been neglected in the bluegrass world, but you'll keep coming back to it because the songs are just so dang good. *—Rick Anderson*

O Sister 2: A Women's Bluegrass Collection / 2002 / Rounder ✦✦✦

In the wake of the success of *O Sister* in 2001, the Rounder label wisely decided to follow it up with another collection of bluegrass songs, old and new, performed by female singers and instrumentalists. Though the sound of hard-edged and high-pitched men's voices has almost defined bluegrass music from the beginning, women have made significant contributions as well, though those contributions have not always gotten the recognition they deserved. *O Sister 2: A Woman's Bluegrass Collection* continues the project of rectifying that oversight, and does so quite nicely by showcasing performances by relative unknowns like Carol Elizabeth Jones and Alecia McKnight alongside such usual suspects as Rhonda Vincent, Claire Lynch, Lynn Morris, and the inevitable Alison Krauss. Stylistically, this second collection ranges a bit further afield than the first one did; alongside strictly traditional material like "Poor Ellen Smith" (sung with reedy power by the gracefully aging Ola Belle Reed) and the Jimmy Martin classic "Pretending I Don't Care" (performed here by Rhonda Vincent), there are more pop-flavored delights, such as Carol Elizabeth Jones' sweetly tuneful original song "Someday" and even a downright avant-garde contribution from the Wayfaring Strangers, whose "Memories of You" features a klezmer clarinet. Everything here is worth hearing, though overall this collection doesn't pack quite as much punch as the first one did. *—Rick Anderson*

Ohio Rockabilly / Hamilton ✦✦✦

Seldom is the state of Ohio thought to be a mecca for rockabilly, but this 18-track collection clearly shows that there were several enthusiastic practitioners of the shakin' music working out of the Buckeye state. The majority of these artists ended up on myriad dime-sized labels like the one used for this reissue, and their brief time in pursuit of the solid gold Cadillac and the diamond pinky ring are documented here. Kicking off with the most "produced" sides on this collection, Billy Adams' "You Gotta Have a Ducktail," "That's My Baby," and answer novelty record "The Return of the All American Boy," there's a crude country-band feel to the majority of sides compiled here. The half-dozen sides from the anonymous Bobby Martin ("Jo Jo Rock & Roll," "Dood It," "Give Your Heart to Me," "Sleepy Time Blues," "I Ain't Gonna Rock," and "There Ain't No Nothin' Tonight") sound like demos that were all cut the same day—and probably were—with a local band running through a batch of tunes that nobody knows all *that* well. Nothing on these tracks has a glimmer of excitement attached to it, but the crudeness of the recordings nonetheless has a charm of its own. Amazingly enough, the five tracks of hillbilly boogie from Stan Johnson delivers the goods in a far more energetic manner than the previous six from rocker Bobby Martin. "Big Black Train" is in the Johnny Cash mode with a nod to Elvis' "Mystery Train," while "Six White Horses" (the only tune here that Johnson didn't write) is an uptempo blues with solid guitar breaks and lively drumming. "Shimmy and Shake" is a piano-driven boogie, while "Lonesome Man" features strong slappin' bass and great guitar solos, and "Baby Baby Doll" is so produced (electric bass, lots of reverb, perhaps a different band) as to almost sound like another artist. But it's back to the hill country with the two tracks from Emery Blades, "The Rock and Roll Carpenter" and "Look What You Done to Me," both rife with steel guitar solos and guitar playing closer to Chet Atkins than anything else. Hoyt Webb and Arnold Van Winkle close out the proceedings with a double dose of hillbilly boogie with the accent on the 'billy side of the equation with Webb's "Baby Won't You Slow It Down" and Van Winkle's "An Old Rusty Dime," both featuring ripping fiddle breaks. Billy Adams' "You Gotta Have a Ducktail" has long been a collector's favorite, but the rest of tunes on this collection are truly for completists only. *—Cub Koda*

OKeh Western Swing / 1982 / Epic ✦✦✦✦✦

The beginnings and evolution of Western swing are explored in colorful fashion on this definitive two-LP set. The 28 selections (programmed loosely in chronological order) start out with a couple of country-oriented singers performing in jazz settings (Al Bernard and Emmett Miller during 1927-28) before moving to the mid-'30s and performances by Roy Newman, the Blue Ridge Playboys, the Range Riders, W. Lee O'Daniel & His Hillbilly Boys and the Crystal Springs Ramblers. Seven selections from Bob Wills' Texas Playboys (dating from 1935-1941) are followed by numbers from the Saddle Tramps, the Sons of the Pioneers, the Light Crust Doughboys, the Hi Neighbor Boys, Hank Penny, the Swift Jewel Cowboys and the Sweet Violet Boys. Side four covers 1941-1942 with cuts by Ocie Stockard's Wanderers, the Hi-Flyers, Sons of the West, Adolf Hofner, and Slim Harbert before concluding with a 1946 performance by Spade Cooley and an obscurity from Leon McAuliffe in 1950. This two-fer serves as a perfect introduction to listeners (from both the country and jazz worlds) who are not that familiar with the joyous country/jazz fusion from the Depression years known as Western swing. It's recommended. *—Scott Yanow*

Old-Time Music From Southwest Virginia / Nov. 20, 2001 / County ✦✦✦✦

While many believe that country music started in the summer of 1927 when Ralph Peer recorded the Carter Family, a number of old-time musicians—including Dock Boggs—had already had their music committed to wax. *Old-Time Music From Southwest Virginia* collects instrumentals and songs released between 1924 through 1931, offering a historical snapshot of the fledging genre as it appeared in the Appalachians of Virginia. The oldest material originates from Fiddlin' Powers & Family, representing, as Charles Wolfe points out, the earliest recordings of a professional string band. A little-known guitarist named Emry Arthur sings several of the most intriguing songs on the album, including "She Lied to Me," "Reuben Oh Reuben," and "Careless Love." The guitar work on "Reuben Oh Reuben" has a mysterious, off-center quality of the kind that players like John Fahey would later develop. The most familiar artist on this anthology is banjoist/vocalist Dock Boggs, who delivers "Down South Blues," "Country Blues," "Pretty Polly," "Old Rub Alcohol Blues," and "Danville Girl." While Boggs' selections may be available on other collections, they provide a familiar voice between more obscure musicians. The sound quality varies from cut to cut, which is to be expected on recordings originating from worn 78s. Taking this into consideration, County has done a fine job transferring this material to compact disc. The album, at 76 minutes, is also quite a bargain. For anyone curious about early country music, *Old-Time Music From Southwest Virginia* offers a rich collection of traditional material before commercial considerations put a straightjacket on studio performances. *—Ronnie D. Lankford Jr.*

Old-Time Music From West Virginia (1927–1929) / Mar. 18, 1997 / Document ✦✦✦

Old-Time Music From West Virginia features the complete recordings of Dick Justice and the Williamson Brothers and Curry, along with eight sides by Frank Hutchison, whose earlier work is collected on Document's *Complete Recorded Works, Vol. 1 (1926-1929).* This set is consistently worthwhile, though only Hutchison is well known among the performers; the Williamson Brothers and Curry only produced six obscure records, but these sides reveal extensive performance experience and vintage string band style. Justice is an able guitarist who plays rags and ballads with equal skill, also producing a couple of decent waltzes with fiddler Reese Jarvis. Several of his sides demonstrate obvious familiarity with black musical styles: his "Brown Skin Blues" entirely transcends the conventions of racial classification, while the excellent "Cocaine" is clearly derived from an earlier recording of "Cocaine Blues" by black singer and fellow West Virginian Luke Jordan. Frank Hutchison was allegedly a friend of the Williamson Brothers and Curry as well as Justice, though his recorded output and subsequent influence far outweighed those of his associates. While in his earlier sessions Hutchison recorded with harmonica and guitar, these sides from July of 1929 only include the latter instrument, which the player gracefully leads through a range of genres. In "Cumberland Gap," his guitar skillfully evokes the sound and style of a claw-hammer banjo; for his two final performances, Hutchison adopts a slide and produces a couple of genuine blues. Though Hutchison's recordings provide a substantive closure to this set and to the career of a talented musician, his work is available elsewhere, and this is not the place to start a Frank Hutchison collection. What makes this CD most worth owning is instead the presence of the lesser-known figures. These men stand out on their own as able and experienced (if under-recorded) artists; their performances are additionally interesting for their insight into West Virginia's most engaging musical community on record. It's recommended to fans of the genre. *—Burgin Mathews*

The Other Side of the Mountain: Bluegrass, Newgrass and Beyond / Oct. 8, 2002 / Compass ✦✦✦✦

While the post-*O Brother, Where Art Thou?* craze has put a premium on old-time bluegrass in the Bill Monroe and Lester Flatt mold, another rich vein of acoustic music has been neglected. Born in the late '60s and early '70s, progressive bluegrass (often called newgrass) blends the old with the new to create an eclectic, constantly shifting hybrid. *The Other Side of the Mountain: Bluegrass, Newgrass and Beyond* offers a dozen progressive songs and instrumentals, providing a nice intro into the genre and a chance to check out Compass' impressive roster. Tim O'Brien delivers a fine vocal on "Handsome Molly," while Sam Bush converts Elvis Costello's "Every Day I Write the Book" into a catchy piece of acoustic new wave. Peter Rowan revisits "Rainmaker" with a little help from Drew Emmitt, while Judith Edelman delves into her trademark Americana on

"Good Day, There It Goes." *The Other Side of the Mountain* is also rich in lovely instrumental work. Both Darol Anger and Mike Marshall, veterans from the David Grisman Quintet, make a number of appearances, and hotshot mandolinist Matt Flinner is joined by guitarist David Grier and bassist Todd Phillips on "City Chickens" and "Dixie Hoedown." All of these divergent styles, from folk-jazz to acoustic funk, are brought together by a high level of musicianship and a love of innovation. For anyone curious about how things sound on *The Other Side of the Mountain*, this collection will more than suffice. *—Ronnie D. Lankford Jr.*

Ozark Folksongs / Nov. 27, 2001 / Rounder ✦✦✦
Possibly surfacing in response to the 2001 film *Songcatcher*, this collection of earthy and gritty Southern folk songs came to light on compact disc later that same year. The simply titled *Ozark Folksongs* is in a similar vein as Smithsonian/Folkways' many field recordings (*Close to Home*, *Mountain Music of Kentucky*) and Rounder's own Alan Lomax/*Southern Journey* compilations. These 1941-1942 recordings by Vance Randolph (one of the unsung folk song collectors of the 20th century) are just a sampling of the over 800 recordings he made in the rural American South. Unfortunately, the sound quality on these 35 tracks is below even the expected "pops and cracks" threshold of many archival recordings, but the stark honesty of the performers still shines through the hiss and click of Randolph's portable recorder. The spectacular liner notes detail each of the folksongs as well as giving a quick sketch of as many of the original performers as possible, making the package a complete archival resource, but casual folk fans may be less satisfied. It's still highly recommended. *—Zac Johnson*

The Pioneers of Bluegrass / Jun. 11, 2002 / CMH ✦✦✦✦
The subtitle of this compilation is "20 of Bluegrass Music's Greatest Hits," and it does not tell a lie. The producers might also have added that the performers were bluegrass music's greatest performers as well. Featured on the CD are musicians like Bill Monroe, Grandpa Jones, the Osborne Brothers, and Merle Travis, who made this music the exciting and heartfelt art form that people are constantly being bowled over by. A few of the classics collected here are "Great Speckled Bird" by Jim & Jesse, "Footprints in the Snow" by the Smith Brothers Bluegrass Orchestra, and "Will the Circle Be Unbroken" by Lester Flatt. If you were one of the multitudes who bought the *O Brother, Where Art Thou?* soundtrack and are looking for more authentic bluegrass, *The Pioneers of Bluegrass* is fine place to start. *—Tim Sendra*

Poor Man, Rich Man: American Country Songs of Protest / 1989 / Rounder ✦✦✦✦✦
Recorded between 1923 and 1936, these 16 country and old-timey songs comment upon the conditions of the time, particularly the struggles of workers, miners, and the Depression. The "protest" factor is muted in comparison with, say, 1960s folksingers or even Woody Guthrie; these are more like reflections of the difficulties of the common man than statements of anger or defiance. Whether you're in this for the social commentary or not, it's a pretty respectable collection of vintage country and folk on purely musical terms, with selections by major figures such as Uncle Dave Macon, Fiddlin' John Carson, Gene Autry, the Dixon Brothers, Ernest Stoneman, and Blind Alfred Reed, along with several less famed performers. *—Richie Unterberger*

Prayers From Hell: White Gospel & Sinner's Blues, 1927–1940 / Jan. 2000 / Trikont ✦✦✦✦
This compilation of hillbilly gospel music and twisted Southern white blues could have been taken from one of the discs in Harry Smith's *Anthology of American Folk Music*—there's even an essay included by Greil Marcus, a reprinted chapter from his *Invisible Republic* book. Normally, this would reek of copycat-ism and a cheap way to make a buck. Given that this is the Trikont label from Germany, you can be assured this isn't the case. Their notes and packages are superb, they make their records primarily for a European audience, where the Smith *Anthology* may not be available, and there is a different focus, one that is perversely curious in its approach to this very foreign—to them—music. Besides, they put some gems on here Smith didn't include because his anthology was based on only six years of recorded material. As for the music, it's stellar. This is solid, primitive, hillbilly gospel music and blues. The remastering is excellent and the material choice is wonderful. From the Carolina Ramblers Stringband's "That Lonesome Valley" to the Dixon Brothers' "Didn't Hear Nobody Pray" (covered recently by the Fairfield Four) and "When Gabriel Blows His Trumpet for Me" to Byron Parker & His Mountaineers, the Carter Family, and Bill Carlisle, we hear the sound of the hopeful pilgrims, assured of their place in the heavens with God. Some of these songs also plead for the one who is lost to turn from sin (the Carters' "Better Farther On"). The praise is definite but reserved, plaintively sung with the fear of God in their approach. There is a loneliness in these songs that speaks of everything from poverty to a sense of continual loss—it's whistling in the graveyard music. However, the coin flips on this disc several time when we hear Frank Hutchison's "Hell Bound Train" and "Stackalee," or the mad-dog glass-chewing howl of Dock Boggs' wailing through "Country Blues," "New Prisoner's Song," "Sugar Baby," and "Pretty Polly." Boggs and Hutchison even the score—they show the dark-as-death side of culturally enforced Christianity and refuse to be tamed or comforted. Joining them are Ledford & Daniel Nicholson's fiddle and banjo blues ballad "Ninety Nine Years" from 1932. It's a tale of love, betrayal. Gambling, love, and murder. All of these songs appear in the mirror of redemption, past it, out of its dimension and scope. But even here, rebellious as they are, Jesus wins. Just after Bogg's "Pretty Polly" sends chills down the spine for the coldness of its tale, its unrepentant bitterness and anger, we are led out of the entire compilation by Edith & Sherman Collins' "I Can't Feel at Home in This World Anymore." Something becomes obvious in the tune and both gospel and sinner's tunes turn back on themselves and meet the bridge where the title of this song is literally true in both cases, and the pitfalls of earthly existence is, too; it's just the attitude regarding departure from that place that's different. *—Thom Jurek*

Ragged But Right: 30's Country Bands / 1990 / RCA ✦✦✦✦✦
The little-known performances on this very interesting CD feature four separate quartets comprised of strings (including violin, banjo, guitar, mandolin and/or bass) and smaller collaborations from the same dates. There are selections from the final recording sessions of Gid Tanner & his Skillet Lickers and numbers from the Prairie Ramblers (a top Western swing group), the pioneer bluegrass group J.E. Mainer's Mountaineers and Ade Mainer's similar Sons of the Mountaineers. While one thinks of the 1930s as the big-band era, clearly there was a great deal of other music being performed at the same time and this CD sampler should greatly interest collectors of early country and Southern roots music. *—Scott Yanow*

Rarest Rockabilly & Hillbilly Boogie: The Best of Ace Rockabilly / Jan. 1, 1993 / Ace ✦✦✦✦✦
This compact disc combines two Ace Records vinyl compilations of choice 1950s material. *Rarest Rockabilly & Hillbilly Boogie* anthologizes rockabilly history through the prism of the vanity pressing. For a hundred dollars or so, an Elvis wannabe could cut a couple songs and get back a small pressing for their efforts. Once copies were distributed to nearby radio stations, promoters, and juke box operators, the remaining stash was given away to fans and relatives or sold at dances. Texas-based Starday Records was a hotbed for this; in a period of six years, they issued over 500 titles on their Dixie label or vanity labels, and these are this basis for this compilation. As primitive as some of these are, the music is just fine. Most of the artists collected here are just names on labels of a phonograph record company, yet the inclusion of two early rockin' sides from Jimmie Dale Gilmore are most illuminating. This compilation errs on the side of hillbilly boogie but if cowboy boots stand in for blue suede shoes, there's still pep aplenty in selections like Bill Mack's "It's Saturday Night" and Buddy Shaw's "Don't Sweep That Dirt on Me." *Best of Ace Rockabilly* returns to the classic sound and is loaded with collector's prizes. Sonny Fisher's "Rockin' Daddy" and "Sneaky Pete" are raw Texas style rockabilly at its best, while Louisiana is represented by Link Davis' "Trucker From Tennessee" and Jimmy Johnny's "I Can't Find the Doorknob." The big ticket items are two of George Jones' rare excursions into the deep waters of the big beat, "Rock It" and "How Come It." All in all, a superlative compilation that truly gives a sense of rock & roll's ground-floor incarnation in the wake of Elvis. *—Cub Koda*

Real: The Tom T. Hall Project / Oct. 20, 1998 / Sire ✦✦✦✦
Real: The Tom T. Hall Project assembles a wide variety of Nashville denizens, alt-country enthusiasts, and folky singer/songwriter types to pay tribute to the songs of Tom T. Hall. The result is that rare tribute album which sums up the strengths of its subject while introducing a fair number of legitimate interpretations of that artist's work. Not everything here hits the mark, but much of it does, and it handsomely illustrates the depth of Hall's writing and the versatility of his music. The performers vary widely not only in their preferred musical style, but also in their tactics of interpretation: Some strip the songs down to the barest musical bone in order to emphasize the lyrics, while others take new approaches to reinventing the songs, placing them in musical backdrops which reveal additional emotional facets behind the lyrics. Highlights include Johnny Cash's "I Washed My Face in the Morning Dew," Iris DeMent's "I Miss a Lot of Trains," Syd Straw's "Harper Valley P.T.A.," Ralph Stanley's "The Water Lily," Kelly Willis' "That's How I Got to Memphis," Whiskeytown's "I Hope It Rains at My Funeral," Mark Olson's "It Sure Can Get Cold in Des Moines" (featuring Victoria Williams), and Joe Henry's "Homecoming." *—Steve Huey*

Rebel Voices: Songs of the Industrial Workers of the World / 1992 / Flying Fish ✦✦✦
Flying Fish and Rounder are independent labels which started up in the '70s, specializing in various types of roots music. The former company was apparently started up by Bruce Kaplan, a dissatisfied member of the Rounder collective. One of the disagreements might have been about politics, an element that Rounder seems to avoid despite the strong presence protest songs have in many types of American folk styles. The label even went as far as to remove a controversial political song from a Hazel & Alice album, while Flying Fish, on the other hand, has actually released some product with a strong leftist bent, this compilation of labor songs among them. The most obvious audience for music such as this are people who are upset about their jobs; based on that perhaps faulty concept, this album should have sold millions. The presence of Utah Phillips looms large. He is a combination activist, organizer, songwriter, singer, and storyteller, and there are few performers who can put across a song such as "The Two Bums" as well as he can. The album also combines its participants into various small groupings and a big ensemble finale, an idea that works just as well in an album sequence as it has on many folk festival stages. There are several numbers originating with Joe Hill, needless to say, but also a grand Malvina Reynolds cover by Faith Petric and a terrific take on the classic "Hallelujah, I'm a Bum" by Bob Bovee. Besides delivering its intended messages, this collection also puts the spotlight on some fairly unknown performers in a context that brings welcome thematic strength and emotional power to their work. *—Eugene Chadbourne*

Red, White & Bluegrass / Feb. 13, 2001 / CMH ✦✦✦
Red White & Bluegrass is a compilation from CMH Records featuring a handful of bluegrass and country artists performing songs about America. While there are some instrumental versions of "The Star Spangled Banner" and "America the Beautiful," the real fun songs are the ones about places in America. Merle Travis' almost forgotten "There Ain't a Cow in Texas" and the Osborne Brothers' reworking of "Rocky Top" (here called "Georgia Piney Woods") stand out as highlights. The inclusion of the merely average "Pennsylvania Polka" and "Dixie in My Eye" makes it seem like the compilers may have been reaching a little bit to fill in the corners with anything remotely American, but on the whole it is a fun collection. *—Zac Johnson*

Return of the Grievous Angel: A Tribute to Gram Parsons / Jul. 13, 1999 / ALMO Sounds ✦✦✦✦✦

Although he's not as well known outside music circles as Jimi Hendrix or Kurt Cobain, the early death of Gram Parsons was arguably just as great a loss. Parsons' country-rock hybrid became a touchstone for artists from the Rolling Stones to Elvis Costello to the '90s "alternative country" giants Uncle Tupelo and the Jayhawks. In addition to his importance as a songwriter, Parsons gave Emmylou Harris her big break. Now, Harris and co-executive producer Paul Kremen have hand picked an all-star list of artists, including Costello and Tupelo & Jayhawks' descendents Wilco and the Rolling Creekdippers, for *Return of the Grievous Angel: A Tribute to Gram Parsons*. The songs, culled from Parsons' early days with the Byrds through his posthumously released solo album *Grievous Angel*, are uniformly excellent, or better. The best covers, like Lucinda Williams and David Crosby's "Return of the Grievous Angel" and the Rolling Creekdippers' "In My Hour of Darkness," feature the soaring, intertwined harmonies Parsons and Harris turned into magic on the originals. Harris herself joins the Pretenders ("She"), Beck ("Sin City") and Sheryl Crow ("Juanita") for songs Parsons did before he began recording with her. The resulting duets evoke why the original *Grievous Angel*, featuring Harris, was so stunning. *—Mark Morgenstein*

Rhythm Country and Blues / 1994 / MCA ✦✦✦

Rhythm Country & Blues is one of those various artists collections that always works better on paper than it does in practice. The intent behind the album was to demonstrate that there wasn't much difference between country and soul, either in terms of songwriting or performance. In order to prove this theory, the producers came up with a series of 11 duets featuring one country musician and one R&B musician, and had the duos sing classic songs. So, *Rhythm Country & Blues* is filled with duets like Conway Twitty & Sam Moore's "Rainy Night in Georgia," and Al Green & Lyle Lovett's "Funny How Time Slips Away," Clint Black & the Pointer Sisters' "Chain of Fools," Aaron Neville & Trisha Yearwood's "I Fall to Pieces," and George Jones & B.B. King's "Patches." Given all that talent, the album should have been a stunner. Instead, it's merely competent. It suffers from forced duets like Patti LaBelle & Travis Tritt, an overly-familiar selection of songs, and too-slick production. *Rhythm Country & Blues* sold well intially because a well-orchestrated publicity campaign but, in retrospect, that marketing plan was the most memorable thing about the entire project. *—Thom Owens*

Rig Rock Deluxe: A Musical Salute to the American Truck Drivers / Sep. 3, 1996 / Upstart ✦✦✦✦

The advantage *Rig Rock Deluxe* has over other tribute albums is that, for the most part, we either don't know the original versions of these songs, or they're new. That, combined with the genuine fun most of these artists seem to be having, makes *Rig Rock Deluxe* a hoot. Don Walser kicks things off inimitably with "Truck Driving Man." He's a tough act to follow, but artists including (but not limited to) Buck Owens, Red Simpson, Junior Brown, Shaver, Steve Earle, Son Volt, and the Bottle Rockets do their caffeinated best. Only a couple of songs don't make the grade: Kelly Willis' "Truckstop Girl" for not using a pocka-chicka backbeat and Nick Lowe's "I'm Coming Home" for being recorded in Stockholm. The whole shebang winds up with Dale Watson, Rosie Flores, Wayne Hancock, Toni Price, Kim Richey, and many others performing as Rig Rock Deluxe on "Six Days on the Road." Makes for a great ride. *—Brian Briscoe*

Rio Bravo & Other Movie and TV Themes / Apr. 25, 2000 / Bear Family ✦✦✦✦

If you've got a yen to add something different to the collection, here's an off the beaten trail delight that fills the bill. This 25-track collection features movie and TV theme songs that should be familiar to any baby boomer who remembers these pictures and TV shows when they were first out and about. From Dean Martin's "My Rifle, My Pony and Me" from *Rio Bravo* to Johnny Cash's "Bonanza" to Gene Autry's "Back in the Saddle Again" to Percy Faith's "The Virginian," this collection throws a wide net and yields a bunch of tracks that'll bring a smile to your face while you say, "hey, I remember that!" Well thought out, with the usual top-notch Bear Family quality in the sound and notes department; an offbeat delight. *—Cub Koda*

☆ **Rock This Town: Rockabilly Hits, Vol. 1** / 1991 / Rhino ✦✦✦✦✦

Rock This Town: Rockabilly Hits, Vol. 1 is a stellar, 18-track collection that contains such classic rockabilly singles as Johnny Burnette's "The Train Kept A-Rollin," Bill Haley's "Rock the Joint," Roy Orbison's "Ooby Dooby," Carl Perkins' "Blue Suede Shoes," Billy Riley's "Red Hot," Dale Hawkins' "Susie-Q," Buddy Knox's "Party Doll," Gene Vincent's "Lotta Lovin'," Buddy Holly's "Oh Boy!," Jerry Lee Lewis' "High School Confidential," and Ritchie Valens' "Come On, Let's Go." Not only does it contain those hits, but there are terrific obscurities from Jimmy Lloyd, Nicky Nelson, Sonnee West, Janis Martin, and Sanford Clark, making *Rock This Town* and its companion volume a definitive collection for the average listener. *—Stephen Thomas Erlewine*

☆ **Rock This Town: Rockabilly Hits, Vol. 2** / 1991 / Rhino ✦✦✦✦✦

For its first half, the second volume of *Rock This Town: Rockabilly Hits* is as strong as its predecessor, running through such classic singles as Eddie Cochran's "C'mon Everybody," Wanda Jackson's "Let's Have a Party," Conway Twitty's "Danny Boy," Ronnie Hawkins' "Mary Lou," Johnny Horton's "Honky Tonk Hardwood Floor," Jack Scott's "The Way I Walk," and the Rock-a-Teens' "Woo-Hoo." The latter half contains rockabilly revival numbers ranging from Commander Cody ("Hot Rod Lincoln"), Dave Edmunds ("I Hear You Knocking"), and Billy Swan ("I Can Help") to the Blasters ("Flattop Joint"), Robert Gordon ("Red Hot"), and Stray Cats ("Rock This Town"). While these latter-day recordings have merit, they would have been better heard on a third volume, leaving the second volume to additional cuts from the '50s and '60s. So, that does mean *Rock This Town* is an imperfect collection, but there's enough good stuff to make it necessary for anyone who purchased *Vol. 1*. *—Stephen Thomas Erlewine*

Rockabilly Bash, Vol. 1 / Bopalacious ✦✦✦✦

Rockabilly, the ground-floor music of white rock & roll, is a genre with a multiplicity of styles jammed within its narrow borders. This particular compilation features 14 tracks that cover the bases from the earliest uptempo honky tonk hillbilly boogie to flat out classic rockabilly to burgeoning teenage rock & roll. While everything here is taped off of scratchy 78s and 45s and the legality of this compilation is somewhat in doubt, this and its companion second volume nonetheless deliver some of the best of the obscure delights that permeate this genre. The hands-down big-ticket item on here is the compilation's closing selection, "She Said," from West Virginia one-man-band lunatic Hasil Adkins. If you've never experienced Hasil's music and had to sweat it down to one selection to experience your ordeal by fire by, this would probably be the one. Full of shrieks and whoops, a confused story line and a rubber band guitar hoedown beat, the end result is nothing short of the audio equivalent of Grandpa Jones on acid. The other selections in this collection will sound somewhat tame to this number, but almost anything would in comparison, such is the originality in Adkins' crude music. Norman Witcher's "Somebody's Been Rockin' My Boat" and its flip side, "Wake Me" both feature spitfire guitar pitted against alto sax solos, an unusual instrument and sound in rockabilly. Another two-sided entry comes from Art Adams and the Rhythm Knights. The top deck, "Dancing Doll," is a standard rockabilly celebration taken at a breakneck tempo that's ironically unsuitable for dancing. The flip, "She Don't Live Here No More," is a pounding bluesy shuffle with a recurring drum lick that drives the song's narrative along. For a classic example of high-octane hillbilly boogie, look no further than "Wore To A Frazzel" by Tony and Jackie Lamie. Over a pumped-upbeat, the song is merely a jump blues played by a hillbilly string band, but what a band! Earmarked with worked-out descending riffs, a vocal from Tony that constantly crosses bar lines in mid-verse, and wild steel guitar breaks and fills, this ultra-rare single is the sound of a band throwing down big time circa 1956. Duane Eddy's musical cohort Al Casey (the composer of "Ramrod") is aboard with a vocal effort, "Got the Teenage Blues," while the truly teenaged end of things is also admirably represented by the Kingbeats' prepubescent-sounding "I'll Tell My Mama On You." Honky tonk singing is well anthologized here as well, with Luke McDaniel doing business as Jeff Daniels on "Switchblade Sam," Cliff Davis & the Kentucky Playboys' "Hard Hearted Girl," Eddie and Chuck's "Boogie the Blues" and the positively geriatric-sounding Tim Dinkins and his Texas Cutups' "Cattin' Tonight" all documenting older country singers at odds with the new sound that was slowly moving them into obsolescence. Fans of the genre will want this one for the Adkins cut alone, but everything on here is grade-A material and well worth seeking out. *—Cub Koda*

Rockabilly Essentials / Aug. 25, 1998 / Hip-O ✦✦✦

This 18-track collection brings together some of the most highly prized and influential rockabilly recordings from the ground-floor days of rock & roll's history. You can't really fault the song selection here, starting with Jerry Lee Lewis ("Great Balls of Fire") and finishing up with Johnny Burnette & the rock & roll Trio's "Train Kept A-Rollin'." In between, this compilation is packed tight with classics from Gene Vincent ("Be Bop A-Lula"), Dale Hawkins ("Susie-Q"), Carl Perkins ("Blue Suede Shoes"), Eddie Cochran ("Summertime Blues"), Buddy Holly & the Crickets ("I'm Lookin' for Someone to Love") and Brenda Lee (Bigelow 6-200"). Even better is the inclusion of cult favorites like Warren Smith's "Rock'n'Roll Ruby," Joe Bennett and the Sparkletones' "Black Slacks," the Collins Kids' "Hoy Hoy," Rusty York's "Sugaree," Billy Lee Riley's "Red Hot" and the Phantom's 1:31 nutzo and chaotic "Love Me." Selections from Jack Scott, Wanda Jackson, Sanford Clark and Roy Orbison and the Teen Kings complete this fine package. It's an excellent first purchase and a wonderful introduction to this genre. For once, here is collection that truly lives up to its title.*—AMG*

Rockabilly From Tennessee, Vol. 2 / White Label ✦✦✦

In the wake of mega-success engendered by Sam Phillips' Sun label in Memphis, several small labels sprang up throughout the state of Tennessee, hoping lightning would strike their enterprises as well. One of these was Ernest Tucker's Linco label out of Fayetteville, right over the border from Alabama. Tucker's label output was far more rural than Sun's, and these 13 tracks reflect that approach and outlook. The set kicks off with Clyde Owens and his Moonlight Ramblers' "Swing It, Little Kitty" and the classic cry-in-your-beer ballad, "My Last Bouquet." Abetted with a mountain of tape echo and a 60-cycle hum that pervades both recordings, Owens' band is pure country right down to the rasping fiddle solos and Clyde's creaky old man vocals, but the music could not be less real or heartfelt. Clayton Hillis and the Rocket City Rockettes' "Rocket City Rock" and "Don't You Know I Love You" show a crude combo straddling between country and the new emerging rhythm style with semi-successful results. Curtis Long & the Rhythm Rockers' "Hootchey Cootchey" is probably the best known tune aboard as far as collectors as concerned, and is a four-square rocker despite its guitar lopsided mix, which is somewhat straightened out on the flip side, "After All." The Johnson Boys do double duty here, backing the Jay Dee's on "Mystic Madonna" and masquerading as the Four Sons on the twangy bongo-driven instrumental "Little Rock." Hollis Champion and the Secrets' minor key romp "Old Red Devil" belies a singer with only tenuous connections to the shakin' music, but the high-octane kick of the band makes such concerns minor ones. Perhaps the only big name here is Alton Delmore (half of the Delmore Brothers) with his "Good Times in Memphis," which sounds a lot older than its 1959 recording date would lead you to believe. The compilation closes with three tracks by the ultra-mysterious Marvin Moore, whose style skirts the boundaries of Western swing with "What's Going On," jump blues with "Jumping the Boogie," and the solo "I'm on This Rocket," which sounds like another singer entirely. A stellar collection of rarities that will whet the appetite of the hardcore collector and open up the ears of novices peeling back the layers of rock & roll's early days. *—Cub Koda*

Rockabilly Rarities, Vol. 1 / Aug. 13, 2002 / Yeaah ♦♦♦
Rockabilly Rarities, Vol. 1 plucks a big pile of rockabilly from scarce 45s that populated small-time record shops throughout the U.S. during the '50s and '60s. While this is a lovingly put-together compilation of rockabilly recorded during the style's peak, it's definitely something for longtime devotees and not newcomers. Some of the songs included are "Shaken and a Shuddern" by Jim Pike & the Kephart Rockers, "Rootie Tootie Baby" by Lee Mitchell & the Combo, "You Lied to Me Honey" by Junior Garvey & the Rock-N-Tones, "Boogie Woogie Country Girl" by Stephenson & the Four Kings, "I've Gotta Find Someone" by Tiny Tim & His Tornadoes, and "Go Girl Go" by Country GJs. These songs have been digitally remastered, and most of them are appearing on CD for the very first time. *—Andy Kellman*

Rockabilly Rarities, Vol. 2 / Sep. 3, 2002 / Yeaah ♦♦♦
In case the 32 tracks of obscure 1950s rockabilly offered on the first volume of this series weren't enough for you, here are 30 more. (And if you still want more, the series continues for another three volumes.) For those with a passing interest in the music itself, just the immensity of the archeological accomplishment represented by this series is enough to make the jaw drop. But for those with a deep love for this period of American musical history, these discs are a treasure trove. Obviously, not everything on offer here is a gem, and every one of the five densely packed anthologies in this series could have been reduced by about one-third without any regrettable loss of content. But the diamonds are all the more thrilling for the effort it takes to find them: "Red Hot Mama" by Wayne Williams & the Sure Shots is one such, as is the swinging "Enie Meanie Minie Moe" by Hoyt Johnson & the Four Recorders. On the other hand, the Braves' "Woodpecker Rock" is stupid even by rockabilly's relatively relaxed intellectual standards, and the paleosexism of Gene Norman & the Rocking Rockets' "Snaggletooth Ann" will be startling to most modern ears. Like the others in the series, this disc is more than just a historical document, but it probably won't convert anyone who needs to be converted. *—Rick Anderson*

Rockabilly Rarities, Vol. 3 / Sep. 3, 2002 / Yeaah ♦♦♦
This disc, like the other four in the series, might be most productively regarded as a sort of standardized test for aspiring rockabilly experts. Just about every name on this 32-track collection constitutes a genuine secret handshake for serious fans—start talking about the finer points of Jim Floey's unusually complex chord progressions or the jazz-influenced guitar solos on Sonny Cole's "Robinson Crusoe Bop" and you're guaranteed to be instantly welcomed into any sock hop in town. As for listening pleasure, well, these discs are a bit more spotty in that regard. There are some strangely brilliant moments on this one, like Glen Goza & the Damangos Impact's gleeful novelty number "Goshmody What a Body" and Jim Billington's equally ebullient "Love Bug Crawl." But many of these tracks (notably "How Can You Be Mean to Me" by Dale Vaughan & the Starnotes and Orangie Ray Hubbard's vaguely creepy "Sweet Love") are seriously marred by hideous sound quality, and a few of the featured artists are simply incompetent—Mel McGonnigle's valiant struggle to keep track of his song's basic rhythmic structure would be funny if it weren't so sad. Hardcore fans of vintage and obscure rockabilly shouldn't hesitate, but others should proceed with some caution. *—Rick Anderson*

Rockin' at Town Hall / 1961 / Country Routes ♦♦♦♦
The British-based Country Routes label (part of Interstate Music) is best known for its releases of radio transcriptions of country artists, and once upon a time the 13 artists represented here *could* have fit into the country category. But they're all really rock & rollers, performing live on radio's *Town Hall Party*, and doing some of the best rockabilly music that money can buy. In contrast to the relatively low-fi Elvis Presley *Louisiana Hayride* transcriptions, the stuff here is loud and generally cleanly mastered, and the lineup, apart from the absence of Elvis and Buddy Holly, is practically a who's-who of country-rockers recorded live between 1959 and 1961: Carl Perkins ("Blues Suede Shoes," "Matchbox/Boppin' the Blues"), the Collins Kids ("Shake Rattle & Roll"), Warren Smith ("Rock 'n Roll Ruby"), Bob Luman ("I Got a Woman," "Oh Lonesome Me," "I'm Walkin'," "Milk Cow Blues"), Larry Collins ("Ramrod," "Honky Tonk"), Wanda Jackson ("Real Cool"), and Amos Headrick ("Good Rockin' Tonight"). There are a few sloppy moments, and a couple of songs are incomplete, but by and large this collection really cooks on all burners all the way through, and gives a glimpse of what some of the best rockabilly players sounded like playing directly to an audience on some really good nights. The Bob Luman songs alone (backed by a band that includes James Burton on electric guitar) are worth the price of this disc, and the Larry Collins and Collins Kids stuff will astound the uninitiated. *—Bruce Eder*

Roots 'n' Blues: The Retrospective 1925–1950 / Jun. 30, 1992 / Columbia/Legacy ♦♦♦♦♦
Roots 'n' Blues: The Retrospective presents five hours of music over four discs, covering the traditional recordings made by Columbia Records and its associated labels from 1925 to 1950. As an all-inclusive survey of American roots music, this set is an invaluable library piece and a good reference, but where this collection really stands out is in its presentation. The collection does a better service than the more academic studies by including a variety of styles—including early string band recordings, spirituals, jugbands, blues, Cajun and country music, mixing the better known artists with the more obscure—in the end, the diversity makes for good listening as well as a good learning experience. *—Chris Woodstra*

Roots Music: An American Journey / Oct. 1, 2001 / Rounder ♦♦♦♦♦
Over the course of their 30-year career, Boston's Rounder Records has amassed an amazing catalog of recordings drawing on just about every American musical tradition you can think of. Known primarily as a bluegrass and folk label, Rounder has also released (both under their own imprint and through subsidiary labels like Heartbeat, Bullseye Blues, and Philo) numerous albums by Cajun, old-time, reggae, contemporary folk, zydeco, and blues artists. *Roots Music* is culled from the catalog of the Rounder imprint itself, and its four discs veer wildly from the hardcore fiddle tunes of Norman Blake and the old-timey singing of Suzanne Thomas to the raucous Cajun two-steps of the Balfa Brothers and D.L. Menard, and from there to the elegant conjunto stylings of Los Pregoneros del Puerto and the Texas country-rock of Jimmie Dale Gilmore. It's a pretty unusual compilation that has the old-time string band the Freight Hoppers rubbing right up against legendary New Orleans pianist James Booker, but then, that's the kind of label Rounder has always been. *Roots Music* is a fitting and aptly titled tribute to this American treasure. *—Rick Anderson*

The Rough Guide to Americana / Jul. 10, 2001 / World Music Network ♦♦♦
An alphabet soup of country-tinged musical idioms are ladled up on *The Rough Guide to Americana*. According to the CD's editor, British journalist Sylvie Simmons, this compilation includes examples of alternative country, country-rock, roots rock, paisley underground, lo-fi country, insurgent country, and no depression styles. Though this barrage of categories may sound confusing, all the tunes on *Americana* are supposedly influenced by rootsy country music and position themselves as a hearty alternative to watered-down country-pop. The CD kicks off with "Through the Trees," a melancholy tune by husband-wife duo the Handsome Family. With their backbeat nailed down by a drum machine, this outfit strums folksy progressions while reciting a cinematic narrative about suicide, weightlessness, and love. Another compelling cut on *Americana* is Split Lip Rayfield's "Kiss of Death." It's a tight little ditty that melds the intensity of Slayer with the acoustic twang of a bluegrass revival. Though the CD's editor touts the compilation as an example of grittier country music, many of *Americana*'s tracks lack depth. Like the city slicker who is terrified of getting their SUV dirty, some of the CD's less convincing tracks are timid and obsessively polished. Likewise, a number of Americana staples—such as Freakwater, Alejandro Escovedo, Gram Parsons, and Wilco—are conspicuously missing from the lineup. Regardless, the 20-song compilation of countrypolitan and singer/songwriterly music stands as a needed introduction to the growing Americana scene. *—John Vallier*

The Rough Guide to Bluegrass / Feb. 27, 2001 / World Music Network ♦♦♦
When fiddle-playing Scottish and Irish immigrants brought their jigs, reels, and airs with them to the U.S., the Celtic music that they played eventually evolved into what we now know as bluegrass and country. Over the years, some artists have blurred the lines between bluegrass and country; that frequently happens on *The Rough Guide to Bluegrass*. This compilation isn't for bluegrass purists—World Music Network takes an eclectic approach to the subject, and some of the tunes are closer to old-time country than bluegrass. But all of the selections have some type of Appalachian influence, which is the common denominator between the artists who provide hardcore bluegrass (Jim & Jesse and the Virginia Boys, Red Allen & the Kentuckians, Emerson & Waldron, the McCoury Brothers) and the artists who favor more of an old-time country approach (Hazel Dickens, the Johnson Mountain Boys). The CD even gets into country-pop; Claire Lynch's "Sweetheart Darlin' of Mine," for example, has a strong Dolly Parton influence, but minus the slick production values of modern Nashville. Meanwhile, banjo virtuoso Béla Fleck combines jazz and bluegrass on "Crossfire." Fusing jazz and hillbilly music isn't a new idea—back in the 1930s, Bob Wills and his colleagues embraced a hillbilly/jazz hybrid that came to be known as Western swing. But Fleck is an innovator who, on some of his other recordings, has brought rock and funk as well as bluegrass to his jazz foundation. This compilation is hardly the last word on bluegrass—how could it be without anything by the great Bill Monroe? But it does take an interesting and highly enjoyable look at some of the Appalachian and Appalachian-influenced sounds of recent decades. *—Alex Henderson*

Rough Stuff / Nov. 4, 1997 / Buffalo Bop ♦♦♦
Rough Stuff is a typical Buffalo Bop release, with some inventive and tragically forgotten rock & rollers sandwiched in between well-meaning, raucous but unexceptional examples of the genre. I don't know where Mirasonic Records was located, but based on Bob Hicks' "Rock, Baby, Rock," they seemed to have the Sun sound down just about perfect, and Hicks had a punky, slightly whiny edge that made him closer to Gene Vincent than Elvis Presley or Carl Perkins. Merle Matts, by contrast, needed a slightly heavier electric sound and maybe a more powerful player on the sax on "Pink Shoes"—Jack King runs into a similar problem with his soft, Ricky Nelson-like "Ready to Go Steady." The Accent are also relatively soft and lyrical, but they're so close in sound and spirit to Buddy Holly of "Peggy Sue" that they can be forgiven their melodic experiments, which, incidentally, mostly work. Jimmy Smith's "Pinch Me Quick" (off of Wonder Records) could be a Stray Cats demo, it's so sharp in execution and recording—he's a Carl Perkins-type singer, the guy on piano sounds like he's been listening to Jerry Lee Lewis, and only a lack of imagination in the lead guitar part prevents this from being one of the jewels in the Buffalo Bop treasure trove of singles. Chewing Ray may not have been going far with that name, to judge from the fact this his "Little Boogie Ding Dong" is off of an acetate, but his combination of incomprehensible single and the hyperactive drumming give the song a compelling lunatic edge. Bobby Martin & the Rhythm Rockers are two of the sub-Elvis artists here. *—Bruce Eder*

Sacred Steel Guitar / Jan. 21, 1997 / Arhoolie ♦♦♦♦
This is one amazing collection. Subtitled "Traditional Sacred African-American Steel Guitar Music in Florida," this multi-artist chronicling of this seldom-heard genre is a musical and emotional delight. The electric lap steel guitar has been the instrument of choice in both the Jewel Dominion and Keith Dominions (both African-American Holiness-Pentecostal churches) since the late '30s, replacing the traditional church organist. This collection showcases the pioneering work of five of its best known and most influential sacred steel practitioners: Willie Eason, Sonny Treadway, Glenn Lee,

Henry Nelson, and his son, Aubrey Ghent. Their individual approaches to this style range from crude blues-based slides and slurs (blues table steel master Hop Wilson is called to mind more than once here) to highly technical flourishes bordering on country pedal steel sounds, with all of it played with a sincerity and spirit indigenous to the music, which is nothing short of heartfelt and energetic. Split evenly between instrumentals and the instrument interfacing with the congregation and choir at live religious services, the music runs the gamut from still and beautiful (Sonny Treadway's instrumentals) to the wild and abandoned playing of Aubrey Ghent. This is 75 minutes of music that will appeal to blues and gospel and even retro-minded rock & roll fans willing to take the time to explore this fascinating genre. *—Cub Koda*

Saddle Up!: the Cowboy Renaissance / 1996 / Rounder ♦♦♦

Here are 14 songs performed by cowboy revivalists, spanning 1973-1992. As is the case with most records that aim to preserve and revive a style, it just doesn't compare to the earlier stuff, in passion or originality. It does, however, contain work by several of the most popular performers working the field, such as Ian Tyson, Michael Martin Murphey, and Riders in the Sky; there's also Willie Nelson, with his seminal "Red Headed Stranger." *—Richie Unterberger*

Small Screen Cowboy Heroes / 1994 / Sony ♦♦♦♦

The 1950s saw a revival of western songwriting in a popular vein, mostly sparked by the popularity of the western on television, where it was the dominant genre during the years 1957-1963 (at one point there were over two dozen western series running each week on the three networks, in addition to syndicated series). This 12 song collection draws from some of the most popular of them (Johnny Western's "The Ballad of Paladin," Frankie Laine's "Rawhide," "The Rebel-Johnny Yuma," sung by Johnny Cash, "Happy Trails" sung by Roy Rogers) and a number of rarities, such as Gail Davis (TV's Annie Oakley) singing "I'm Female Thru and Thru," and Robert Horton, star of the mid-1960's series *A Man Called Shenandoah* (precursor to *The Lazarus Man*) singing "Shenandoah." *—Bruce Eder*

Something Got a Hold on Me: A Treasury of Sacred Music / 1983 / RCA ♦♦♦♦♦

Country music has always had strong ties to Christianity, and this collection of RCA Victor country-gospel music from 1927-1941 demonstrates that heritage, starting with the Carter Family and continuing through the Monroe Brothers, Bill Monroe, the Blue Sky Boys, Uncle Dave Macon, and others. The standouts are A. P. Carter's title track and Dorsey Dixon's "I Didn't Hear Nobody Pray," but there is an outpouring of fervor for "the old-time religion" through every one of these performances. *—William Ruhlmann*

Song of the Hills: Instrumental Impressions of America's Heartland / Jan. 19, 1999 / Shanachie ♦♦♦♦

Featuring an all-star cast of traditional folk musicians including Eric Weissberg, Jay Ungar, Molly Mason, Tony Trischka, Norman Blake, and John Doan, *Song of the Hills* is composed of light and airy interpretations of old-time American music. Fiddle, flatpicked guitar, dobro, and subtle orchestration run-through most songs, giving a rich full sound on compositions ranging from spirituals to barn dances. Although the performances are clean and flawless, it is almost a shame to see such brilliant musicians slowed to a rather bland pace. While not for the most die-hard bluegrass and old-timey aficionados, the album is a gentle walk through pleasant versions of these comfortable tunes. *—Zac Johnson*

Songcatcher II: The Tradition That Inspired the Movie / May 7, 2002 / Vanguard ♦♦♦

The 2001 film *Songcatcher* told a semi-fictional story of a field musicologist who "discovers" authentic English and Scottish folk ballads being sung by people in the Appalachian region of the United States. The film (along with another popular film of the time) kindled interest in the old-timey music spotlighted in the movies, and due to popular demand Vanguard released a compilation of the original versions of the songs that ended up being re-recorded for the soundtrack. Legendary artists like Dock Boggs, Almeda Riddle, Doc Watson, and Roscoe Holcomb all contribute some of the best-known folk ballads of the era, including "Black Jack Davey," "Pretty Saro," "House Carpenter," and a gripping version of "Matty Groves." Although *Songcatcher* was set near the turn of the century, these gems from Vanguard's vaults are mostly from the '60s folk revival festival circuit, and although they offer crisp sound quality and strong presence, these artist's true golden recordings were done in the '20s and '30s. The 1927 recordings of the young and hungry Dock Boggs singing "Sugar Baby" blow away the versions of the same song 40 years later, as is the case with Clarence Ashley, Mother Maybelle Carter, and every other performer on this disc (with the exception of Watson, who will be equally astounding until the day he dies, and then beyond). Still, this is a spectacular folk revival collection, perfect for those who enjoyed the music in the movie but were disappointed with the contemporary updates on the film's soundtrack. *—Zac Johnson*

The Songs of Hank Williams Jr: A Bocephus Celebration / Feb. 11, 2003 / Warner Bros. ♦♦♦

In the ongoing effort to make sure everyone who has recorded more than a couple of albums is feted with a tribute disc, the folks at Warner Bros. and Curb have assembled a star-studded tribute to Bocephus himself, Hank Williams Jr. Drawing its participants from both the traditionalist wing of country and the long-in-the-tooth Southern rockers, the disc straddles the line between rock and country much as junior always has. On the country side, there is a nice mix of big names like Montgomery Gentry, Tracy Lawrence, and Alan Jackson, who turns in one of the disc's highlights with an aching version of the ballad "The Blues Man," and smaller stars who shine brightly: Andy Griggs weeps his way convincingly through "Old Habits"; Trick Pony, featuring the lone female to be found here, turns in a rollicking version of "All My Rowdy Friends Are Comin' Over Tonight"; and Chad Brock pulls off a coup by roping in John Anderson, George Jones, and Williams Jr. to help him sing "A Country Boy Can Survive." The rockers are represented by the current incarnations of bands that ruled the 1970s airwaves. These songs are generally less successful than the ones the country artists perform. The Marshall Tucker Band sound old and broke on "All My Rowdy Friends Have Settled Down," .38 Special tunelessly stomps its way over and through "If It Will It Will," and Lynyrd Skynyrd sounds pretty lame attempting a metal boogie version of "Born to Boogie" (they probably need to stop hanging out with Kid Rock). The only rock artist who sounds half decent is Dan Baird from the Georgia Satellites. He turns in a nasty version of "Whiskey Bent & Hell Bound" that actually sounds better than the original. Speaking of the original, Williams Jr. claims the last track of the disc for himself, performing a heartfelt version of "Outlaw's Reward" featuring many of the artists who appear on his tribute and also Stevie Wonder (!) on harmonica. *—Tim Sendra*

The Songs of Jimmie Rodgers: A Tribute / Aug. 19, 1997 / Sony ♦♦♦

Because it was assembled with more care than most tribute records, *The Songs of Jimmie Rodgers: A Tribute* is better than most tributes, yet it is still far from perfect. Bob Dylan assembled the record as the first release on his Egyptian record label, and his presence is felt. *The Songs of Jimmie Rodgers* is filled with A-level artists, including Dylan, Van Morrison, Mary-Chapin Carpenter, Bono, John Mellencamp, Willie Nelson, Steve Earle, Alison Krauss, Dwight Yoakam, and Jerry Garcia (in his last recorded studio performance). All these artists demonstrate affection for Rodgers, yet about half of the songs sound studied, not inspired. Still, the best moments—Earle rocking through "In the Jailhouse Now," Nelson's "Peach Pickin' Time Down in Georgia," Dylan's "Sweet Liza Jane"—do everything they should: they deliver a great performance that is enjoyable on its own terms, yet makes you want to go back to the original artist. *—Stephen Thomas Erlewine*

Songs of the West / 1993 / Rhino ♦♦♦♦♦

This "definitive collection of cowboy songs" covers both famous and obscure odes to the high lonesome plains by Gene Autry, Roy Rogers, Tex Ritter, Marty Robbins, Slim Pickens, Bob Wills, and others. Spanning the 1930s to the present, the 72-track, 4-CD collection is broken into four separate thematic discs. *Vol. 1* features "Cowboy Classics" like "Back in the Saddle Again," "Mule Train," and "Happy Trails." The real find here has to be the ultradramatic narrative by Walter Brennan describing the "Gunfight at the O.K. Corral." *Vol. 2*, "Silver Screen Cowboys," features tunes from Hollywood Westerns; *Vol. 3* is devoted exclusively to performances by the kingpins of the genre, Gene Autry and Roy Rogers. The final disc is perhaps the most fun of the batch, presenting movie and television themes like "Bonanza," "Gunsmoke," "The Good, the Bad, and the Ugly," and "Rawhide." The box comes with a 60-page color booklet that includes detailed essays, photos, and reproductions of movie posters. *—Richie Unterberger*

Stained Glass Hour: Bluegrass and Old-Timey Gospel Music / 1992 / Rounder ♦♦♦♦♦

Rounder Records is about as well-equipped as any label at providing a first-rate collection of old-time and bluegrass-gospel music, and that's exactly what they've done in this generous, 24-track disc. The stylistic range is about as broad as it possibly can be within the limits of the gospel genre—from Hazel Dickens' almost medieval mountain inflections on "Here Today, Gone Tomorrow" and "Beautiful Hills of Gallilee," to the countrified (and drum-enhanced) sound of J.D. Crowe & the New South on "Crying Holy." Ricky Skaggs and Tony Rice join forces for the brother-duet classic "Talk About Sufferin'," and the Louvin Brothers (one of the original brother duets) are represented by a 1952 recording of "Sinner You'd Better Get Ready." Banjo wizard Tony Trischka steps to the front of Del McCoury's band to sing his own "Looking for the Light," and Joe Val lends his unearthly tenor voice to a soaring rendition of "I Hear a Voice Calling." There are many other highlights as well on this exceptionally fine collection. *—Rick Anderson*

Stampede! Western Music's Late Golden Era / 1996 / Rounder ♦♦♦♦♦

The third installment of Rounder's four-volume cowboy music series contains the songs most likely to be familiar to the general listener: Tex Ritter's "High Noon," Vaughn Monroe's "Riders in the Sky," Marty Robbins' "El Paso," Johnny Western's "The Ballad of Paladin," Eddy Arnold's "Cattle Call." Taken from the years spanning 1945-1960, it presents the form at its most pop-oriented, but it's not less enjoyable for that. Filling out the 14-track set are numbers by the likes of Elton Britt, Jimmy Wakely, and the Sons of the Pioneers (one of whose tracks is the theme to one of the definitive cowboy western films, *The Searchers*). *—Richie Unterberger*

Starday Dixie Rockabilly, Vol. 2 / Jul. 11, 2000 / Ace ♦♦♦

Ace's second volume of rare rockabilly cuts for the Starday-Dixie operation in the late '50s focuses to a large degree on custom pressings, essentially pay-to-play vinyl with emerging artists paying for Starday to press a very small quantity of discs. When an archive compilation is entirely devoted to such material, the result is often something that is best left in the closet, but actually this 24-song disc is pretty respectable. Like much Starday rockabilly, it often has far more of a country hillbilly flavor than the well-known rockabilly of the era did. That's certainly the case with the most famous (by far) artist represented, Buck Owens, who did a couple of nice rockabilly numbers under the pseudonym Corky Jones on a 1957 single. He redid one of them ("Hot Dog"), in fact, in 1988 as a duet with Dwight Yoakam. As for other highlights, Joe Poovey's "Careful Baby" is like hillbilly with a Bill Haley rick-a-tick beat and (like "Hot Dog") is one of the relatively few items here that you could imagine having some commercial success. That accusation certainly could not be levied at Eddie Seacrist's "Dancing to the Rhythm of a Rock'n'Roll Band," with a moronic cowbell-anchored nonsense chorus and ham-fisted drums that make you wonder whether the performance was authentically comically inept or a deliberate rock & roll parody. As for other names you might actually recognize, Lucky Wray's slightly raw country-nearing-rockabilly 1956 single is by one of Link Wray's brothers, and Link himself plays on those two songs, with barely a trace of the wildman guitar rock for which he would become known. The anthology's fidelity is usually pretty good, and although some numbers are obviously mastered from wobbly sources, in this case that adds to the amateurish appeal. *—Richie Unterberger*

The Starday-Dixie Rockabillys, Vol. 1 / 197 / King ✦✦✦

In rock & roll's early days, Texas was one of the few Southern states where the new music truly flourished. Rockabilly singers and likeminded combos sprang up in the wake of Elvis and the other Sun rockabillies who played in the state, and venues that normally booked strictly country acts embraced the new sound as well. One of these cities was Dallas with its *Big D Jamboree*, which gave both visiting rockers and local bands a chance to shine. These 13 tracks from the vaults of the Dallas, Texas-based Starday label document that scene with a handful of singles from that label, along with several unreleased tracks. Label owner Pappy Daily seems to have tampered very little with the output on his label, as most Starday (and his Dixie custom press label) singles exhibit an unvarnished and unbridled passion in their performances. Link Davis' "Sixteen Chicks" and Rudy "Tutti" Grayzell's "Ducktail" kicked up enough noise regionally to get covered by RCA Victor rockabilly Joe Clay as both sides of his first single for that label. Sonny Fisher's contribution here is Texas rockabilly at its most elemental, full of swagger, menace and knife-edge guitar solos on tracks like "Rockin' and Rollin'" and "Pink & Black," an ode to the genre's official colors. Link Davis checks in again with the stomping "Don't Big Shot Me," a slice of Cajun rockabilly that's exceptionally fine. Many of the local artists Daily recorded or leased masters from were also disc jockeys, with Pappy releasing sides on them to take advantage of their local popularity and the airplay that they could provide for his other releases. The most notable of these was Bill Mack, who recorded for Imperial, Starday and other labels, and his "Kitty Kat" is a classic example of the hillbilly boogie sound. Other proto-rockabilly sides are aboard with "Rock Candy Rock" by Fred Crawford and "Get Off My Toe" by Cliff Blakely being especially noteworthy. Big-ticket rockabilly classics come in the form of Benny Joy's "Spin the Bottle" and Groovey Joe Poovey's ode to Jerry Lee Lewis, "Ten Long Fingers (On 88 Keys)," awith Poovey also represented by two unissued tracks, "Careful Baby" and the doo wop-styled "Luella." Although this compilation is somewhat hampered by its short running time and lack of detailed notes, what *is* here is nonetheless grade-A rock & roll from its ground-floor inception. *—Cub Koda*

Starday-Dixie Rockabillys, Vol. 2 / 197 / King ✦✦✦

The Starday family of labels has more in-laws than a hillbilly family has second cousins, apparently. The logos of no less than seven different labels are printed along the bottom of this album jacket, and the liner notes provide more information about various business transactions between Starday, King, and Houston's Gold Star studios than they do about the artists themselves. In fact, there is not a word included about any of these artists, let alone a line. There is also no information about who wrote the songs that are recorded, some of which sound like they were made up as the tape rolled. The late '70s and early '80s were something of a heyday for compilation reissues of this sort of material on vinyl, and as anyone familiar with country and rockabilly would know, there doesn't seem to be any end to the line of obscure, unknown artists who emerge from the shadows in the course of such projects. Here we have names such as Link Davis, Sonny Fisher, Thumper Jones, Benny Joy, and "Groovey" Joe Poovey, most of whom toiled in the confines of the previously mentioned Houston studios in order to come up with these rhythmically charged ditties. The "rockabilly" label was of course something that has often been attached to recordings such as these after that fact, and there are cases where one wonders why. While titles such as "Rock It," "Fat Woman," "Let's Get Wild," "Move Around," and "Rockin' Daddy" obviously are touchstones of the rockabilly philosophy, Poovey seems something of a fish out of water with "My Life's Ambition." Sound is pretty good overall despite the fact that some of the tracks were remastered from vinyl singles and sound like somebody first poured moonshine over them and then did a jig. Like its bastard offspring garage rock, rockabilly is an art form which no amount of garbage seems to be able to damage. Be it bad taste, shoddy equipment, or sloppy recording, it all just adds to the ambience, which is thick enough to thoroughly soak a slice of white bread on this collection. What is missing is a single artist whose inspiration takes them way above and beyond the norms of the genre. Die-hard rockabilly fanatics will no doubt want this stuff, but listeners who are attempting to touch base with geniuses of the genre should head for the trailers inhabited by types such as Hasel Adkins, Charlie Feathers, or Carl Perkins. This is also not a particularly generous collection, as listening to the entire set will take less than a half an hour. *—Eugene Chadbourne*

String Bands (1926–1929) / Jun. 2, 1994 / Document ✦✦✦✦

String Bands (1926-1929) has a few remarkable tracks: the hilarious, warbling vocals on the Kansas City Blues Strummers' "Broken Bed Blues" and a very rare cello solo on the Old Pal Smoke Shop Four's "Black Cat Blues" will single-handedly justify the purchase for some enthusiasts. The album is most recommended, however, for the light it sheds on the intersecting traditions of black-and-white rural musical styles in the early age of recording. Andrew and Jim Baxter, a fiddle-guitar duo from Georgia, demonstrate equal virtuosity at blues and country dance styles and are, deservedly, the best-known performers on the disc; Nap Hayes and Matthew Prater fuse Scott Joplin's ragtime with more traditional, country styles on their mandolin-guitar duets. Most interestingly, the compilation includes two racially integrated groups, a phenomenon otherwise absent in the 1920s recording industry: fiddler Andrew Baxter joins the otherwise all-white Georgia Yellowhammers on "G Blues," and Jim Booker, another black fiddler, joins Taylor's Kentucky Boys for four standard dance pieces, including "Soldier's Joy" and "Grey Eagle." The four tracks by the Alabama Sheiks which conclude the album—recorded, despite the title of this collection, in 1931—are fair duets by another guitar-fiddle duo obviously influenced by the great Mississippi Sheiks, whose "Sittin' on Top of the World" they imitate reasonably well. Although not highly recommended for casual listeners, this collection will be of great interest to many and provides a welcomed expansion of modern understandings of string band music. *—Burgin Mathews*

Sun Gospel / Mar. 14, 2000 / Bear Family ✦✦✦✦

Tapping into a side of the Sun catalog that seldom—if ever—comes up for air, this brings together 32 tracks combed from the issued and unissued sides of the vaults to present a wider and clearer picture of just about every type of gospel music Sam Phillips recorded back in the day. From the jam-session ramblings of Elvis, Jerry Lee, and Carl Perkins on "Just a Little Talk With Jesus," to the black gospel tradition of the Jones Brothers on "Gospel Train" and "Amazing Grace," to the country gospel of Howard Serratt ("Trouble-some Waters") and Cast King with the Miller Sisters (a beautiful alternate take of "Can't Find Time to Pray"), this set covers all of Sun's stylistic quirks, showing that there was always time for a gospel tune, sometimes right smack dab in the middle of a rock & roll session (Jerry Lee's "When the Saints Go Marching In"). The crowning touch is a recitation from Sam Phillips himself, entitled "Would Anybody Care?," a true tear jerker by any measure. It's one of the most interesting Sun collections you're likely to come across. *—Cub Koda*

☆ **The Sun Records Collection** / 1994 / Rhino ✦✦✦✦✦

There have been a lot of Sun compilations over the years; this three-CD, 74-song compilation strikes the medium ground between abridged single-disc highlights and overkill ten-album box sets. What this means is that you get virtually all the key sides of this vastly influential blues, country, and rockabilly label, including the biggest Sun hits cut by Elvis, Carl Perkins, Jerry Lee Lewis, Johnny Cash, Charlie Rich, and Roy Orbison. There's also a lot of the pioneering electric blues cut by label head Sam Phillips before he made rockabilly Sun's focus, including sides by Howlin' Wolf, B.B. King, Rufus Thomas, Junior Parker, and James Cotton. Then there are the interesting small hits and flops by minor rockabilly figures like Warren Smith, Billy Lee Riley, Malcolm Yelvington, Onie Wheeler, and Carl Mann. There aren't any previously unreleased songs, so the Sun specialist most likely already has everything here; it's a better buy for the avid, knowledgeable fan who isn't a completist. *—Richie Unterberger*

Sun Records: 25 Red-Hot Rockabilly Classics / Sep. 24, 2002 / Varese ✦✦✦✦

Although there is a lot of music on this CD, and a lot of it's good and none of it's bad, it's not the front line of the classic rockabilly produced by Sun Records in the 1950s. There's nothing by Elvis Presley, which is understandable given licensing hurdles, yet there are also no big hits by Jerry Lee Lewis, Carl Perkins, Carl Mann, Roy Orbison, Charlie Rich, or Johnny Cash, though at least all but Rich and Cash are represented by something on this disc. It's more like a potpourri of rockabilly from throughout the Sun roster, much of it obscure (and some of it unissued at the time), in Varese Sarabande's apparent design to issue a wealth of relatively unfamiliar material from the Sun catalog on the installment plan. If you're in the niche that wants more than Sun's greatest hits but doesn't want to go for the big import Sun box sets, it's a reasonable survey of Sun rockabilly that most likely doesn't yet reside in your collection for the most part. Really, only Carl Perkins' "Everybody's Trying to Be My Baby" and maybe Billy Riley & His Little Green Men's "Flying Saucer Rock and Roll" are fairly well-known to historically minded rock listeners. Also here are some little-traveled items by Perkins, Lewis (whose "Real Wild Child (Wild One)" is a highlight), and Orbison. The main diet, however, is work by the lower echelons of the Sun team who never got national exposure: Malcolm Yelvington, Luke McDaniel, Warren Smith (represented by the reasonably well-known "Ubangi Stomp"), Ray Harris, Sonny Burgess, Tommy Blake, Hayden Thompson, Johnny Carroll, Rudy Grayzell, Ray Smith, and Carl McVoy. And there's early work by some artists who did get national attention, but not on Sun: Harold Jenkins (later known as Conway Twitty), Gene Simmons, Dickey Lee, and Ed Bruce. Because the Sun house rockabilly sound was itself so good, this is above-average rockabilly, though often similar sounding, as is a pitfall of the genre. This might be underselling the compilation a little; it's pure and invigorating if not quite first-tier rockabilly that testifies to the depth of Sun's efforts. And some of the songs do make it into that first tier, particularly the aforementioned ones by Lewis, Perkins, and Riley. *—Richie Unterberger*

Sun Rockabilly: The Classic Recordings / Feb. 14, 1992 / Rounder ✦✦✦✦✦

Out of country and R&B came rockabilly. Sun Records covered all three styles with the likes of Johnny Cash, Little Milton, and Carl Perkins. Rock & roll also came out of the mix at Sun thanks to two of label head Sam Phillips' prized acts: Elvis Presley and Jerry Lee Lewis—not to mention Perkins. Fortunately, for fans of these heavy hitters, there are literally thousands of reissues on the market. But for those with an ear for Sun's rich store of early blues and R&B sides, as well as the company's many mid-'50s rockabilly singles, the pickings were slim for years. Now, thanks to labels like Rhino, Charly, and Rounder, a wealth of obscure early rock & roll sides produced in Memphis are getting released. This Rounder collection of 14 rockabilly obscurities certainly is welcome, with its mix of relatively well-known cuts (Gene Simmons, Billy Riley, and Conway Twitty) and truly marginal sides (Ernie Barton, Ray Harris, and Jack Earls). Highlights include Warren Smith's classic "Miss Froggie" ("I got a gal/She's shaped just like a frog"), Barton's "She's Gone Away" (the Cramps and X must have heard this one early on), Tracy Pendarvis' exemplary train song "Southbound Line," and Hayden Thompson's fine rendition of the Junior Parker side "Love My Baby." Topped off with informative liner notes by Sun specialist Colin Escott, this solid if somewhat slim collection will work just fine as a first-disc choice for the rockabilly-curious. *—Stephen Cook*

☆ **The Sun Story** / 1987 / Rhino ✦✦✦✦✦

Summing up the history of one of America's most important record labels in 20 songs is a task that borders on the impossible, and *The Sun Story* is hardly the final or definitive word on the subject of Sam Phillips and the nearly seismic impact his label wrought on popular music. While Sun Records is usually cited for (a) giving birth to rock & roll, (b) creating a home for rockabilly, or (c) bringing Elvis Presley into the recording studio for the first time, producer and label founder Sam Phillips had a broader vision than any of those descriptions would imply, embracing in one way or another the full range of the music of the American South—blues, R&B, hard country, gospel, and even a dash of pop. Rhino Records' original two-LP vinyl edition of *The Sun Story* offered a solid introduction to the superb and eclectic roster of talent that recorded for Phillips' little label; sadly, the current single-CD version shortchanges Phillips' vitally important R&B recordings (Jackie Brenston, Roscoe Gordon, and the Prisonaires) in favor of the better-known rock & roll performers who followed them. But as a convenient and affordable collection of Sun's best-known hits and better-known also-rans, *The Sun Story* more than fills the bill, packed to the brim with great, groundbreaking music from Elvis Presley, Jerry Lee Lewis, Carl Perkins, Johnny Cash, Billy Lee Riley, Roy Orbison, Charlie Rich, and many others. As is the norm with a collection from Rhino, the remastered audio is superb (something that hasn't always been the case with earlier Sun reissues), and the liner notes are informative, intelligent, and entertaining. *The Sun Story* is hardly the complete Sun story, but it's not bad as a starter, and if you're looking for a disc with some of the greatest and most satisfying American rock & roll ever committed to tape, this is just what you need. —*Mark Deming*

Swingwest!, Vol. 1: Bakersfield / 1999 / Razor & Tie ✦✦✦✦✦
Part one of Razor & Tie's three-part series of Bakersfield country from the '50s and '60s leans heavily (though not exclusively) on Ken Nelson-produced cuts for Capitol. Perhaps this 20-track overview is a bit too casual in its sweep for the country fanatic, but it's a good sampler of key sounds for most listeners. Many of the style's important figures are represented here, including Ferlin Husky, Jean Shepard, Tommy Collins, Wynn Stewart, Rose Maddox and Merle Haggard. The selections often dig past obvious hits to less obvious items, like Husky's 1952 recording of "Gone" with Speedy West on guitar (which he would re-record a few years later in Nashville for a big hit), Jan Howard's "I Wish I Was a Single Girl Again" (written by husband Harlan), the "Please Mr. D.J." 1964 B-side by Merle Haggard, and Bobby Austin's "Apartment #9" (covered with greater success by Tammy Wynette). There's also one of country's most ridiculous hit novelties, Red Simpson's "I'm a Truck." —*Richie Unterberger*

Swingwest!, Vol. 2: Guitar Slingers / 1999 / Razor & Tie ✦✦✦✦✦
Recorded between 1947 and 1972, with the accent on pre-1965 material, this 20-song compilation highlights the instrumental skills of country guitarists working on the West Coast in the heyday of the L.A.-Bakersfield country sound. Like the other *SwingWest!* volumes, it's largely drawn from the Capitol vaults, but that's no great drawback, as Capitol's roster included such ace pickers as Jimmy Bryant, Joe Maphis, Merle Travis, Roy Clark and Speedy West, not to mention odds and ends in the country style by James Burton, Glen Campbell and Les Paul. All of those names are found on this anthology, along with stellar work by sidemen on tracks bearing the name of star bandleaders Merle Haggard and Hank Thompson. To be honest, you'll get as much quality swinging country virtuosity, with considerably more daring and invention, on Razor & Tie's Speedy West-Jimmy Bryant compilations. But if you're looking for a wider historical perspective, this is a good disc. A previously unreleased 1965 version of "Caravan," credited to Ferlin Husky but probably a jam by session musicians between songs, is not extraneous but a real highlight. It, and the cuts by Joe Maphis and Joe Clark, boast dazzlingly fast yet tasteful playing. —*Richie Unterberger*

Swingwest!, Vol. 3: Western Swing / 1999 / Razor & Tie ✦✦✦✦✦
Although country swing originated in Texas and Oklahoma, by the '40s and '50s many of its best performers were playing and recording in southern California. In part, this was because many Texans and Oklahomans moved west during this time; in part, it was also because major record companies were starting to record country in Los Angeles. This is a first-rate collection of 20 Hollywood-recorded western swing, or heavily Western swing-derived, tracks from 1945-1964, mostly done for Capitol, and most done between 1954-55. There are fine cuts by Bob Wills, Spade Cooley, Tommy Duncan, Hank Thompson, Merle Travis and Tex Williams (the massive hit "Smoke! Smoke! Smoke! (That Cigarette)"). Of equal stature are selections by less famed names like boogying pianist Merrill Moore (with a version of "Down the Road Apiece"), Woody Guthrie's cousin, Jack Guthrie, early rockabilly-type music by Cliffie Stone, and steel guitar virtuoso Leon McAuliffe. This was a time at which country music was gracefully incorporating influences from a wide variety of genres: blues, swing jazz, pop, cowboy music and boogie. That eclecticism made this one of the most interesting points of country's evolution, and this compilation captures some high points of this phase well. —*Richie Unterberger*

Tangled Up in Bluegrass: A Tribute to Dylan / Feb. 13, 2001 / CMH ✦✦✦
Tangled Up in Bluegrass offers 12 instrumental versions of songs from the master of folk, Bob Dylan. The songs have been chosen from throughout Dylan's career, from the early "Don't Think Twice" to the recent "Love Sick." The arrangements are mostly acoustic, with an occasional organ or electric guitar thrown in. "Knockin' on Heaven's Door" begins with the same pacing as the original only to push itself into high gear, evoking a sound reminiscent of the New Riders of the Purple Sage. "She Belongs to Me" receives some nice jazz-grass fiddle by way of Richard Greene, while David West—the central player in this whole effort—adds some great guitar work to "Tangled Up in Blue." The upbeat version of "Love Sick" is one of the better cuts on the album, and it's refreshing that someone decided to do a new Dylan song instead of just relying on the classics. One of the revelations of this project is that Dylan's songs hold up very well as instrumentals; and to those who never appreciated the uniqueness of his vocals, this album shows that they really were good songs with good melodies. It is also curious how natural certain songs—"Don't Think Twice" or "Mr. Tambourine Man"—sound on a banjo. Could it be that Dylan's roots run deeper into the Appalachians than is commonly recognized? This may not be the most original approach to Dylan's oeuvre, but it will probably be of

interest to his fans and bluegrass aficionados searching for something a little different. —*Ronnie Lankford Jr.*

Ten Years of Collectors Records / White Label ✦✦✦✦
In the world of reissue labels, even reissues can beget reissues, and that's the case here, a 16-track distillation of the very best tracks from the first 40 compilations issued on the White Label and Collector label imprints. The Lonesome Drifters' "Eager Boy" and the more countryish "Teardrop Valley" start this compilation off and show a fine craft for lyrical construction, a rarity in this genre. Jimmy Roby's "Wait a Little Baby" and "Be Boppin' Baby (Pt. 2)" are classic bare-bones rockabilly, driven by a guitar, string bass, and drums kicking in all the right spots. Piano pounders Billy Wayne and Teddy Redell check in with Wayne & the Jackson Boys' "Walking and Strolling" and "I Love My Baby" while Teddy reinvents Jerry Reed's "Guitar Man" as "Piano Man." Benny Joy's classic "Spin the Bottle" and an alternate take of the Van Brothers' "Servant of Love" featuring even wilder guitar work than the original 45 are two big ticket highlights and other musical highlights abound in the crude-sounding recordings from the Dyersburg, TN, Benton label. Bobby Lollar's "Bad Bad Boy" and Charles Dean's "Train Whistle Boogie," "Itchy," and "Parking in the Dark" (the latter featuring full-blown rockabilly trombone playing) are as real as it ever gets on compilations such as these and are well worth the price of admission. As rockabilly compilations go, this one's a definite keeper for the collection. —*Cub Koda*

Texas Fiddle Bands, Vol. 1: 1925–1930 / Oct. 12, 1999 / Document ✦✦✦
Here are the complete recorded works of Captain M.J. Bonner, Smith's Garage Fiddle Band, the Red Headed Fiddlers, and Solomon & Hughes. These are crude, exciting sounds, sometimes bordering on frantic as the players get lost in the music. Texas fiddlers are well known for "double-stopping" (which gives the impression of two fiddles), and you'll hear lots of it from all the artists compiled here. It's a marvelous document of Texas string band music from the late '20s and early '30s. —*Cub Koda*

☆ **Texas Music, Vol. 2: Western Swing & Honky Tonk** / 1994 / Rhino ✦✦✦✦✦
Not just valuable to Texas music fans, but also to country music enthusiasts of all kinds, this 18-track compilation is heaviest on Western swing classics from the 1930s and 1940s, and also has a bit of 1950s honky tonk and Western swing revival from the 1970s. Bob Wills, Milton Brown, the Light Crust Doughboys, and Floyd Tillman are all represented with classics, and there are less expected highlights like Roy Newman's "Everybody's Trying to Be My Baby," which Carl Perkins would record (with considerable alteration to the music and the words) in the 1950s, providing in turn the basis for the Beatles' cover version. The Light Crust Doughboys' "Knocky-Knocky" and Cliff Bruner's "Milk Cow Blues" show how close blues could roam to the center of Western swing. Renowned tunes by Ernest Tubb, Lefty Frizzell, and Hank Thompson signify honky tonk's golden years; Ted Daffan offers the 1942 version of "Born to Lose," now a country standard; and zydeco even creeps in with Harry Choates' "Harry's Blues." Johnny Gimble, Asleep at the Wheel, and Alvin Crow bring the disc to a close with cuts from the 1970s. It's an excellent overview of the best in vintage Texas country sounds, with something to offer both the novice and the collector. —*Richie Unterberger*

Texas Rockabilly / Nov. 23, 1999 / Ace ✦✦✦
A pretty broad title for a compilation that is certainly not a survey of Texas rockabilly as a whole, but a 28-song overview (spanning 1956-1964) of the output of the tiny Sarg label, which operated out of Luling, TX (near San Antonio). Sarg never had a national hit, and indeed never had the expectation that the records would do more than get some regional airplay on Texas and Louisiana stations. None of these performers went on to make a bigger name, and the only one that might excite even a bit of name recognition is Link Davis, a veteran of country and Western swing who had a country hit with "Big Mamou" in the late '40s. If there's anything to distinguish this from some of the other small-time vintage rockabilly anthologies on the market, it's a larger-than-normal country influence on some of the material (indeed some of these musicians, such as Davis, were country & western swingers trying to cross over). On the other hand, some of the sides are not especially country-soaked, but plainly follow the path of Elvis, Jerry Lee, and even Little Richard; R&B saxophone also takes a front seat on some tracks, like Jimmy Farmer's "Long Black Train" and the Downbeats' "Come on Over." The recording quality is also considerably above the norm for small-label rockabilly comps (on both Ace and other labels). Otherwise, though, it's straightforward, derivative rockabilly that usually sticks to three-chord progressions in a manner that is both moderately enjoyable and thoroughly predictable. Glen Bland's moody "Mean Gene" is about the best of the lot. Cecil Moore's 1964 instrumental single "Diamond Back" has a little bit of Lonnie Mack about it; a regional hit that was picked up by Atco for national distribution, it was as close as Sarg came to getting a national hit. —*Richie Unterberger*

That'll Flat Git It!, Vol. 1 / 1992 / Bear Family ✦✦✦✦
That'll Flat Git It!, Vol. 1 contains 31 tracks of '50s rockabilly culled from the vaults of RCA Victor. Originally created with hopes of rivaling the success of Elvis Presley, RCA began releasing rockabilly-flavored material. Half of these tracks just don't cut it, like Lee Denson's "New Shoes" (a painfully obvious ripoff of "Blue Suede Shoes") and Jimmie Rodgers Snow's "Milk Cow Blues," entertaining but a bit too heavy on the country side of the fence. The other half of this disc is filled with gritty guitar twang and hiccup vocals that are absolutely wild, including Joe Clay's "Sixteen Chicks," Joey Castle's "That Ain't Nothing But Right," and Ric Cartey's ultra-primitive "Heart Throb" and "Oooh-Wee." —*Al Campbell*

That'll Flat Git It!, Vol. 2 / 1992 / Bear Family ✦✦✦✦✦
That'll Flat Git It!, Vol. 2: Rockabilly from the Decca Vaults isn't quite as consistent as its predecessor since Decca's roster wasn't as wild or engaging as RCA's, but there's a number of gems scattered throughout these 30 tracks—including Johnny Carroll's "Wild Wild

Women," Don Woody's "You're Barking up the Wrong Tree," Terry Nolan's "Ten Little Women," Buddy Covelle's "Lorraine"—and rarities to make it worthwhile for hardcore rockabilly fetishists. Anyone else will find much of this material a little tedious and repetitive. —*Stephen Thomas Erlewine*

That'll Flat Git It!, Vol. 3 / 1992 / Bear Family ♦♦♦♦♦
More raw rockabilly and country bop, this time from the vaults of Capitol Records. While the label had Gene Vincent and Esquerita, a quick listen to these will reveal rockabilly sounds with the accent on the 'billy. Skeets McDonald's "You Oughta See Grandma Rock" goes a long way toward defining the compilation's strengths, and Tommy Sands, long thought of as a teen idol singing pop mush, stokes the fires here with "The Worryin' Kind" and "Playin' the Field." While Ferlin Husky masquerading as Simon Crum on "Bop Cat Bop," The Rio Rockers' "Mexicali Baby" and Bobby Lee Trammell's "You Mostest Girl" show the length and breadth of the genre, perhaps the most fascinating earful of all is The Louvin Brothers testing the waters of rockabilly with "Red Hen Hop" and "Cash on the Barrelhead." —*Cub Koda*

That'll Flat Git It!, Vol. 4 / 1995 / Bear Family ♦♦♦
Like the previous three volumes of Bear Family's *That'll Flat Git It!*, the fourth installment contains a wealth of obscure, and frequently bizarre, rockabilly. For *Vol. 4*, Bear Family reached into the vaults of Festival Records, a label that had no stars or hit singles to speak of (although songwriter Otis Blackwell did record a handful of singles for the label). Almost all of this disc is solely of interest to fetishists—after all, it features seven tracks from Billy Barry, five cuts by Charlie Starr, two songs by Ronnie Dio, and "Motorcycle" from one Billy Balls—and even then, much of this music is only of passing interest. While *That'll Flat Git It, Vol. 4* does have a handful of good cuts (Barry's "The Wild One," Starr's "You Ain't My Number One," and Blackwell's "One Broken Heart for Sale"), it remains a lesser entry in the series. —*Stephen Thomas Erlewine*

That'll Flat Git It!, Vol. 5 / Jun. 24, 1997 / Bear Family ♦♦♦
That'll Flat Git It!, Vol. 5 mines the Dot Records vaults for rockabilly and rock & roll obscurities, and in so doing significantly overlaps with the Ace Records compilation *Dot Rock 'n' Roll* from the previous year. The two compilations have 20 tracks in common, but *That'll Flat Git It!, Vol. 5* succeeds where *Dot Rock 'n' Roll* failed by including the Phantom's notorious rockabilly single "Love Me," the master for which is owned by Pat Boone! Also unique to this collection is a rock & roll performance by country star Cowboy Copas (as Lloyd Copas) and a second early rocker by Mickey Gilley. Ray Campi, Sanford Clark, and Leroy Van Dyke are a few of the better-known artists featured on this excellent-sounding and well-annotated collection, made especially for serious collectors of '50s rock & roll. —*Greg Adams*

That'll Flat Git It!, Vol. 6 / 1994 / Bear Family ♦♦♦
That'll Flat Git It!, Vol. 6 is the second time Bear Family dipped into the vaults of Decca Records to assemble a collection of rare and arcane rockabilly (the first was *Vol. 2*), and while the results aren't quite as consistently entertaining as its predecessor, *Vol. 6* is nevertheless one of the finest installments of the series. The key to its success is how the bizarre backwoods rockers are juxtaposed with country singers like Red Foley, Justin Tubb, Rex Allen, and Red Sovine trying to ride the rockabilly wave. Not all of the songs are strong, but the best—Billy Harlan's "School House Rock," Lou Graham's "Wee Willie Brown," James Gallagher's "Crazy Chicken," Warner Mack's "Roc-A-Chicka," Eddie Fontaine's "One and Only," Billy Gray's "Tennessee Toddy," Baker Knight & Knightmares' "Bring My Cadillac Back," the Rockin' Saints' "Cheat on Me Baby" and Jerry Engler's "Sputnik (Satellite Girl)"—are pure fun. —*Stephen Thomas Erlewine*

That'll Flat Git It!, Vol. 7 / 1996 / Bear Family ♦♦♦
Culled from the vaults of MGM Records, *That'll Flat Git It!, Vol. 7* is very similar to the Decca volumes in Bear Family's arcane rockabilly series. The disc is divided between rock & rollers who sound like weirder versions of Elvis Presley and country artists trying to hitch their wagons to the rockabilly bandwagon. By and large, the MGM artists aren't as strong as those on Decca, although Marvin Rainwater handled rockabilly better than many of his country counterparts. For fetishists, the bizarre backwoods boogie of Jimmy Swan ("Country Cattin'"), Bernie Early ("Your Kisses Kill Me"), the Berry Kids ("You're My Teen Age Baby"), Ron Hargrave ("Drive-In Movie"), Bob Gallion's "My Square Dancin' Mama," Buck Griffin ("Stutterin' Papa") and Carson Robison ("Rockin' and Rollin' With Grandmaw") is prime material, but the best music on the collection arguably comes from Rainwater and Conway Twitty, who have stronger voices and material than most of their peers on this collection. —*Stephen Thomas Erlewine*

That'll Flat Git It!, Vol. 8 / 1996 / Bear Family ♦♦♦
That'll Flat Git It!, Vol. 8 is comprised of off-beat and obscure rockabilly from the Columbia vaults. Unlike their major label peers RCA, Decca and MGM, Columbia didn't push many of their country artists toward rockabilly, so the majority of the compilation is devoted to arcane vocalists like Bolean Barry ("Long Sideburns"), Bobby Lee Trammell ("You Mostest Girl"), Bonnie Guitar ("Frantic Party"), Alvadean Coker ("We're Gonna Bop"), Tom Tall ("That's Alright With Me"), Dickie Podolor ("I Love You Girl"), and Dusty Rose ("Rockin' Maraccas," "Hula Rock"). For the most part, this is the kind of twisted rockabilly that is fun in small doses, unless you're a fetishist, of course. Out of all the songs on *Vol. 8*, only Johnny Horton's pair of songs ("Bawlin' Baby," "Shotgun Boogie") are particularly strong musically—the rest is judged by a different scale, one where rarity and novelty are of greater value than musical worth. For any collector of arcane rockabilly, *Vol. 8* is just as enjoyable as the rest of the discs in the *That'll Flat Git It!* series, yet it doesn't offer any truly great rock & roll, which means that it will only appeal to that cult. —*Stephen Thomas Erlewine*

That'll Flat Git It!, Vol. 10 / Apr. 25, 2000 / Bear Family ♦♦♦♦

That'll Flat Git It!, Vol. 11 / 1998 / Bear Family ♦♦♦
Another entry in Bear Family's excellent label by label retrospective of rockabilly's best, this one featuring 30 tracks of ground-floor boppin' billies from the stable of Mercury Records. Unlike Sun records (and few others), there was no defined sound or production to the label's rockabilly output; masters came from Memphis, Chicago, Nashville, Houston, Fort Worth, and even New York City on this collection. Mercury never really had a strong commitment to their country division, and as rockabilly was the rhythm branch of that division, none of these records even remotely became hits. Eddie Bond and Roy Moss end up being the big names here, with each artist represented by four tracks each, accounting for over 25 percent of the album's content. But stellar one-offs by Thomas Wayne ("You're the One That Done It"), Rudy Grayzell ("Let's Get Wild"), Sleepy LaBeef ("All the Time"), Curtis Gordon ("Draggin'"), Billy Wallace ("That's My Reward"), the Hi-Liters (the explosive "Dance Me to Death") make the rest of this volume equally as noteworthy. Every volume in this series is a winner for quality content, but this one ups the ante and then some. Not rockabilly's greatest, just some of its very best. Excellent liner notes and information from Bill Millar top this stellar package. —*Cub Koda*

That'll Flat Git It!, Vol. 12 / Aug. 19, 1997 / Bear Family ♦♦♦
This entry in Bear Family's single-disc label retrospectives delving into various companies' rockabilly treasures lands this times at the doorstep of Imperial Records, which also houses the few stray masters that showed up on the United Artists and Liberty labels back in the 1950s. The lineup is as top drawer as you could ask for; Bob Luman with a young James Burton on lead guitar ("Red Hot," "All Night Long"), Weldon Rogers ("So Long, Good Luck and Goodbye"), Billy Eldridge ("Let's Go Baby"), Dennis Herrold ("Hip Hip Baby" and the mind-destroying "Make With the Lovin'"), the Burnette Brothers with Joe Maphis on lead guitar ("Warm Love"), the Strikes ("If You Can't Rock Me," "Rockin'," "Baby I'm Sorry," "I Don't Want to Cry Over You"), Sammy Gowans ("Rockin' By Myself") and the hillbilly boogie of Lew Williams and Bill Mack make for some of the best titles the music has to offer. After you assemble a nice collection of essential Sun, Elvis and Johnny Burnette sides, this should be your very next stop. —*Cub Koda*

That'll Flat Git It!, Vol. 14 / Aug. 19, 1997 / Bear Family ♦♦♦

That'll Flat Git It!, Vol. 18 / Dec. 14, 1999 / Bear Family ♦♦♦♦

That's Bluegrass!: CMH Records 20th Anniversary Collection / Jul. 11, 1995 / CMH ♦♦♦♦♦
Two discs, 40 cuts, 20 years of bluegrass selections from CMH. Just about every bluegrass style you can think of is represented here, with examples from Lester Flatt, the Stonemans, the Eddie Adcock Band, Joe Maphis, Mac Wiseman, Vassar Clements, Bill Monroe and more. It's a spectacular collection (to say the least), lots of fun, and a great introduction to the art and science of bluegrass. —*Steven McDonald*

This Is Americana, Vol. 1: A View From Sugar Hill / Oct. 8, 2002 / Sugar Hill ♦♦♦♦
Compilations are sometimes accompanied by ambitious titles like "Bluegrass Today" or "The Roots of Country," as though one collection could encompass the birth or current state of an entire genre. Occasionally, however, an album like *This Is Americana* actually delivers the goods. Drawn from the talented group of artists recording for Sugar Hill—including Rodney Crowell, Hot Rize, and John Cowan—this generous collection brings together 15 songs and one instrumental. The music runs the gauntlet of the hard-to-nail-down Americana genre, from the acoustic sounds of Baucom, Bibey & Blueridge to the eclectic, electric hodgepodge of the Gourds. There are old standbys like Doc Watson and Doyle Lawson along with new faces like Railroad Earth and Sean Watkins. *This Is Americana* also serves as an excellent introduction to all of these artists. "Two Quarts Low" gives ample evidence that ex-New Grass Revival singer John Cowan still has one of the best voices on the progressive bluegrass scene, while "Out Here in the Middle" finds James McMurtry digging deep to offer sharp observations on life in America. Of course, no Sugar Hill collection would be complete with out an appearance by Jerry Douglas, a dobro player so prolific that one might be tempted to think that he sleeps in the studio. "Patrick Meets the Brickbats" rolls along at a nice clip, giving Douglas a chance to combine good taste with speedy picking. *This Is Americana* is a fine collection that will remind one of listening to a good radio program without any commercials. —*Ronnie D. Lankford Jr.*

Totally Classic Country, Vol. 1 / Jul. 23, 2002 / Varese Vintage ♦♦♦
Totally Classic Country, Vol. 1 is a solid collection of country staples from the '50s, '60s, and '70s, including Johnny Cash's "I Walk the Line," Patsy Cline's "Walkin' After Midnight," and George Jones' "Walk Through This World With Me." Marty Robbins' "El Paso," Jimmy Dean's "Big Bad John," and Bobby Bare's "Detroit City" are some of the other songs that will be instantly recognizable to someone with only a passing knowledge of country music's heyday. Tracks by Wynn Stewart, Lynn Anderson, Nat Stuckey, and Cowboy Copas complete this enjoyable overview of some of the best songs from country's golden age. —*Heather Phares*

Totally Country / Feb. 5, 2002 / BNA ♦♦♦♦
Contemporary country's spinoff of the *Totally Hits* series, *Totally Country* gathers 17 of the style's recent hits, including the Dixie Chicks' "Without You," Brooks & Dunn's "Only in America," Billy Gilman's "One Voice," and Travis Tritt's "It's a Great Day to Be Alive." Other standouts include Montgomery Gentry's "She Couldn't Change Me" and Dwight Yoakam's cover of the Cheap Trick classic "I Want You to Want Me." Though it's probably not of much use to die-hard fans of contemporary country (unless they want to use it as a ready-made mix for their car stereos), *Totally Country* is an appealing collection of crossover singles that will please most people looking for "that song they heard on the radio." —*Heather Phares*

Totally Country, Vol. 2 / Oct. 29, 2002 / Sony ♦♦♦
The *Now* series of pop hit compilations, which began to be successful in the U.S. in 1998 after years of popularity overseas, led to other such collections, notably the rival *Totally*

Hits series, which has in turn spawned genre-specific "Totally..." collections, including *Totally Country*, and this is the second volume. Like its many predecessors, it is distinguished by the unusual cooperation of record labels, with all five major labels and two independents contributing. But one significant difference between the pop collections and this one has to do with the currency of the material. The compilers of the *Now* albums are careful to use songs still in the charts when the disc is released. But *Totally Country, Vol. 2* includes only four tracks that were active in the *Billboard* country singles chart on release day, only two of those, Montgomery Gentry's "This Town" and Tammy Cochran's "Life Happened," still on their way up the list. Although most of the rest of the selections are Top Ten country hits, they are past hits, in some cases dating back quite a ways. George Strait's number-one country hit "The Best Day," released in late 1999 and peaking in April 2000, may be the oldest, but many of these songs date back to 2000 or 2001. Of course, the country market moves much slower than the pop one, and it can take a track many months to reach its full chart potential; then that track may remain a "recurrent" on country radio for an equal number of months. Still, the cover of this album claims it contains "17 New Chart-Topping Hits," and that's just not true. Nevertheless, there are plenty of recent country hits here, and at a time when few of them were actually released as commercial singles, consumers may welcome the collection. *—William Ruhlmann*

Traditional Fiddle Music of Kentucky, Vol. 1: Up the Ohio and Licking Rivers / Jan. 14, 1997 / Rounder ✦✦✦

Recorded between 1972 and 1995 (though mostly in the 1970s), this set and its companion volume (*Traditional Fiddle Music of Kentucky, Vol. 2: Along the Kentucky River*) document folk fiddle styles in northeastern Kentucky, usually recorded by fiddlers born around the beginning of the 20th century. The fiddle tunes reflect and illustrate the variety of influences that found their way into Appalachian music, from Scots-Irish ballads to blues, waltzes, and hornpipes. To those without a deep or scholarly interest in the form, much of it will tend to run together and sound similar. For those who *do* want delve deep into the style, it's a valuable document including 39 tracks, 70 minutes of music, and voluminous liner notes about the fiddlers and the origins of the songs. *—Richie Unterberger*

Traditional Fiddle Music of Kentucky, Vol. 2: Along the Kentucky River / Jan. 14, 1997 / Rounder ✦✦✦

Like *Vol. 1* of this Rounder series, this compiles 1972-1995 field recordings of Kentucky old-time music fiddlers, mostly made in the 1970s. This is different from its predecessor in that it concentrates upon musicians who are closer to the central part of the state, while the first installment focused on ones from a more northeastern part. Musically it's not far removed from the earlier volume, though the presence of banjo and mandolin on some cuts makes the connection to bluegrass more audible. There are 38 songs here, but as some only last for a minute or so it adds up to only 54 minutes, and makes for a bit of a see-saw home listening experience. *—Richie Unterberger*

Travis County Pickin' / Jun. 10, 1997 / HMG ✦✦✦✦

This compilation (whose title comes from a combination of Travis pickin' and the fact that Austin, Texas—where this was cut—is in Travis County) features 15 tracks of original compositions by Austin guitarists, performed by the composers. The songs follow the country-jazz traditions laid down by artists like Speedy West, Jimmy Bryant, Merle Travis, Leon Rhodes, Chet Atkins, and Ernest Tubb's band, the Texas Troubadours. Produced by session picker Jim Stringer (who appears in some sort of guitar capacity on eight of the tracks) in his home studio, the project carries with it a down-home feel, with far more emphasis on the performances than on dazzling us with production hype, but sounds great nonetheless. Dave Biller—the initial inspiration for the project—kicks things off with a blisteringly fast "Austin-tatious," with top-notch turns from Rick "Casper" Rawls ("White Corn" and "Buckaroo 2002"), Brian Hofeldt ("The Creeper" and "Ellen"), Joel Hamilton's tribute to Danny Gatton ("Danny's Boogie") and Merle Travis acolyte Sean Mencher ("House of Cards" and "Your New Flame (Is Burning Me)") following close behind, making this one delightful album to listen for all the different styles involved. Great rhythm section support from Lisa Pankratz, Karen Biller, Terry Kirkendall and Donald Lindley on drums, Kevin Smith and Sharon Ward on string bass, and Jimmy Pettit on electric gives each of the soloists plenty of room to fly. With this much twang and jazz dynamite from the city's best picking aboard, this is one great example of what Austin's thriving music scene is all about. *—Cub Koda*

☆ **Truck Driver's Boogie: Big Rig Hits Vol. 1: 1939-1969** / May 22, 2001 / Audium ✦✦✦✦✦

Produced in conjunction with the Country Music Hall of Fame, this is probably the best compilation of country songs about trucks, truckers and trucking, a mini-genre onto itself. It's not a mere novelty: big names like Johnny Horton, Jim & Jesse, and Jimmy Martin are here, and the chronological and stylistic range is wide, from country blues laments of the early 1940s to the near-rockabilly of Horton's "I'm Coming Home" and the more standard Nashvillized pop-country of the 1960s. It could be that just one song, Dave Dudley's 1963 hit and perennial trucker's anthem "Six Days on the Road," will be instantly familiar to many listeners. A number of the 20 tracks never appeared on CD before this release, including some real goodies, like Doye O'Dell's creepy "Diesel Smoke (Dangerous Curves)," with its bleating horns and nerve-tingling fiddles and steel guitar; the Milo Twins' "Truck Driver's Boogie," a late-'40s release very much like the Delmore Brothers' boogie recordings; and Kay Adams' spunky "Little Pink Mack," the one song here by a woman and a rare tale of truck driving from a feminine perspective. The lengthy liner notes trace both the history of country truck driving songs and specific details about the material on the CD, capping a release that treats the style as worthy of historical enshrinement, but is quite fun too. *—Richie Unterberger*

True Life Blues: The Songs of Bill Monroe / Oct. 15, 1996 / Sugar Hill ✦✦✦✦

The 17 newly-recorded songs on this album comprise a loving tribute to the man generally considered to have invented bluegrass music, and the album was timed well, coming out just shortly before Monroe's death in 1996 at the age of 85. The songs are mostly pretty predictable. The program leads off with the Nashville Bluegrass Band's rendition of "Molly and Tenbrooks" (on which Alan O'Bryant does a pretty fair Monroe impression), and proceeds through a hair-raising rendition of "I'm on My Way Back to the Old Home" by the Del McCoury Band. Other classics by various lineups follow: Vassar Clements and Richard Greene team up for a bracing run-through of the instrumental "Scotland"; Laurie Lewis and Kathy Kallick do great job on the title track; and Tim & Mollie O'Brien give "Sitting Alone in the Moonlight" a suitably haunting performance. Peter Rowan may be overrated as a singer, but as a former Blue Grass Boy and a tireless champion of Monroe's work, he has certainly earned the right to sing "Travelin' This Lonesome Road" and "Letter From My Darlin'." Highly recommended. *—Rick Anderson*

Tulare Dust: Tribute to Merle Haggard / 1994 / Hightone ✦✦✦✦✦

If you've been paying any attention at all, you know Merle Haggard ranks among the best singers country music has ever produced. What you might not realize is that he's also one of the genre's finest songwriters. For evidence, just listen to this tribute album, which finds a motley crew of roots artists performing 15 of their favorite Merle tunes. Despite the absence of many of his best-known songs, the package leaves little doubt that, as the liner notes put it, "Haggard may be the last of a breed of great country songwriters that began with Jimmie Rodgers, and continued through Hank Williams and Lefty Frizzell." Every composition radiates with Haggard's honesty, eye for detail, and strong point of view, and every track has the feel of a classic. The vast majority of the performances are as impressive as the songs. Tom Russell, who co-produced with Dave Alvin, delivers the package's most Haggard-like vocal on a beautifully handled medley of dust-bowl stories, "Tulare Dust/They're Tearin' the Labor Camps Down," while Alvin turns in a haunting "Kern River." Among the many other highlights: Iris DeMent's "Big City," which Haggard reportedly loved; Rosie Flores' interpretation of "My Own Kind of Hat," one of Haggard's many declarations of independence; Barrence Whitfield's version of "Irma Jackson," which addresses race relations via the tale of an interracial romance; Steve Young's affecting "Shopping for Dresses"; and the melancholy "I Can't Be Myself," where Katy Moffatt hits thrilling high notes. Nobody sings Haggard quite like Haggard, but these recordings are classics in their own right. *—Jeff Burger*

Virginia Roots: The 1929 Richmond Sessions / 2002 / Outhouse ✦✦✦✦

From October 13 through October 19, 1929, OKeh Records recorded numerous roots musicians in various styles in Richmond, VA. This two-CD set presents 32 songs recorded during those sessions, as well as one cut in 1928 for the QRS label by the Richmond Starlight Quartet, who recorded four songs for OKeh at these 1929 sessions that were not issued. Just as a point of fact, this compilation does not include everything done at these sessions by any means; at least 93 songs by 30 groups were recorded, but only 36 songs by 13 groups came out. Four of those, on two singles by the Virginia Male Quartet, have never been discovered by collectors to the compiler's knowledge, so what we have here is about the most complete representation of these Richmond sessions that could be assembled. But on to the music, which is the real reason to be concerned about the contents. This is a sprawl of white and black Southern styles of the late '20s, from old-time fiddle music and black gospel to harmonica country blues, jug band, and even pseudo-Hawaiian music (by the Tubize Royal Hawaiian Orchestra). You wouldn't say this is the most historic or astonishingly good such music cut during the era; a compilation of the best such performers and songs from similar sessions throughout the south would be much better. It's just an interesting and eclectic document of heartfelt, from-the-gut roots sounds of all sorts from the time and place, sometimes memorably so, as in the Monarch Jazz/Jubilee Quartet of Norfolk's gospel blues "Pleading Blues" or "Don't Let the Blues Get You Down" by the Buck Mountain Band, who included Wade Ward (who'd become better known during the 1960s folk revival). Occasionally the fidelity's so crackly as to seriously inhibit listening pleasure (particularly on two sides by the Monarch Jazz/Jubilee Quartet of Norfolk), but in general it's pretty good, or as good as could be expected for material taken from ancient singles. The package includes copious notes about the sessions, songs, and performers. *—Richie Unterberger*

Wa-Chic-Ka-Nocka / Jun. 26, 2000 / Buffalo Bop ✦✦✦✦✦

Wa-Chic-Ka-Nocka is yet another installment in Buffalo Bop's long line of collections that compile obscure, usually independent-label rockabilly and rock & roll recordings of the '50s mastered directly from original 45s. The theme this time is music about Native Americans, or "Indians," as the era dictated. The songs are filled with ridiculous stereotypes and sometimes cringe-inducing insensitivity, but were recorded in the spirit of fun rather than hostility, for what that's worth. The package is interesting in that it shows the influence of Hollywood Westerns, television, and Western comic books on popular music, and also the unselfconsciousness and ease with which songwriters could tap into this particular formula. And it is definitely a formula—tom tom drums and war whoops are nearly ubiquitous, and there is a certain guitar riff that gets recycled endlessly. A number of instrumentals with thematically appropriate titles are included, as well as a couple of R&B numbers. *Wa-Chic-Ka-Nocka* is one of the strongest, if most politically incorrect, packages released by Buffalo Bop in terms of novelty and historical value. *—Greg Adams*

Wanted! the Outlaws / 1996 / RCA ✦✦✦✦✦

The term "outlaw" had been bandied about after Jennings' 1972 hit "Ladies Love Outlaws," but it didn't permanently gel until the release of the album *Wanted! The Outlaws* in 1976. The songs in this packaged product weren't new—the album contained previously released material by Nelson, Jennings, Glaser, and Jennings' wife, Jessi Colter, (who had hit the charts a year earlier with "I'm Not Lisa"). But it marked the industry's recognition of the changing times, and as the centerpoint of a campaign to publicize Nashville's new "progressive" breed it worked like a charm. It quickly became the first country album to sell more than a million copies, and it boosted the careers of all involved. In 1996, RCA re-issued *Wanted! The Outlaws* on CD for the first time, adding one new Waylon and Willie recording (a lively reading of Steve Earle's "Nowhere Road") and nine "lost" tracks. But "lost" isn't really correct: Like the original 11 selections, such songs as Waylon's "Slow Movin' Outlaws" and Willie's "Healing Hands of Time" have been previously released. They do, however, sweeten the package, making this 20th anniversary edition a decent (though by no means definitive) sampler of outlaw country. *—Kurt Wolff*

Western Swing / Jun. 27, 2000 / ASV/Living Era ♦♦♦
This compilation features over 72 minutes of Western swing remastered from the original recordings. Featured, among others, are Spade Cooley, Bob Wills & His Texas Playboys, the Hi-Flyers, and the Crystal Springs Ramblers. This budget-priced disc from the ASW/Living Era label is an attractive set. *—Al Campbell*

● **Western Swing, Vol. 1** / 1966 / Old Timey ♦♦♦♦♦
As genres of music go, Western swing has got to be one of the most fun. Instrumental dexterity abounds and there are lots of sparkling tunes and many aspects of what makes jazz so exciting without the heavy intellectual baggage that the latter form sometimes drags along behind it like a steamer trunk. The Old Timey subsidiary of Arhoolie began what would be a whole series of Western swing anthologies with this set. Early pressings do not indicate that this is *Vol. 1*, however, so perhaps initial plans were more modest. This collection is really quite unique. It includes a generous portion of Bob Wills, of course. There are also performances from the Lightcrust Doughboys and Milton Brown & His Brownies, both following a similar direction to Wills. The tracks by the Hackberry Ramblers, recorded in New Orleans, have much more of a Cajun influence and could have easily been included in an anthology from that genre. Bill Boyd & His Cowboy Ramblers don't quite have the virtuosity of the other groups, but provide an enjoyable example of the link between so-called cowboy music and this new, jazz-influenced style. The youngest track comes from the late '40s and fiddler Harry Choates. Fans of the late-period Merle Haggard album *If I Could Only Fly*, of which there are many, will be interested to hear the Choates track "Rubber Dolly"; it is the fiddle tune that is referred to both instrumentally and in the lyrics to that album's delightful song, "Thanks to Uncle John." Although some editors might have been tempted to program these tracks in chronological order, in this case Chris Strachwitz used a purely musical approach to sequencing that works wonderfully. This album is both a good introduction to Western swing for the novice as well as a collection that has plenty to offer the listener who have may have heard plenty already. Many of the hot-shot pickers associated with this music are on hand. There is no information provided about who might have composed the tunes on the record. *—Eugene Chadbourne*

☆ **When I Was a Cowboy, Vol. 1** / 1996 / Yazoo ♦♦♦♦♦
These are the records that gave everyone from Gene Autry through Marty Robbins the basis for their careers, bridging the gap between 19th century reality and 20th century nostalgia. These 23 songs are the real article from the mid-to-late 1920s, a time when the singers had ridden the range, and the events they sung of were often within living memory. This material is the white equivalent of recordings by Blind Lemon Jefferson, Papa Charlie Jackson et al., and anyone owning their records—even if they don't like cowboy songs—ought to own this as well; J.D. Farley's "Bill Was a Texas Lad," could even pass for blues. Alas, there is no information included about Farley, the Cartwright Brothers, Harry McClintock ("Sam Bass"), Edward L. Crain ("Bandit Cole Younger"), the Crowder Brothers, Taylor's Kentucky Boys ("The Dixie Cowboy"), Carl Sprague ("The Last Longhorn"), Billie Maxwell, Watts & Wilson, Lonesome Luke & His Farm Hands (who give us an authentic square dance), or Patt Patterson & His Champion Rep Riders, and the only name that will be recognizable to modern listeners is rider-actor Ken Maynard, whose "Lone Star Trail" is one of the best things here. All of it is stripped down, sometimes with no more than a guitar accompaniment; the singing is raw and unaffected, but some of it displays surprising virtuosity, most notably the Arkansas Woodchopper's dexterous guitar playing on "I'm a Texas Cowboy" and "Texas Ranger" by the Cartwright Brothers, with a droning fiddle accompaniment that emphasizes the British origins of the melodies behind some of these songs. The sound is also unusually good. *—Bruce Eder*

☆ **When I Was a Cowboy, Vol. 2** / 1996 / Yazoo ♦♦♦♦♦
Yazoo Records' second cowboy compilation has some of the same artists and a few others, like the Crockett Family ("Buffalo Gals Medley"), Paul Hamblin ("The Strawberry Roan"), Buell Kazee, and McGinty's Oklahoma Cowboy Band ("Cowboy's Dream"). The material is equally strong, and much of it, including Harry McClintock's "Jesse James," is absolutely priceless. As with the first volume, there's no biographical material on any of the artists, but the music speaks well for itself—Jules Allen's "The Girl I Left Behind Me" seems pretty much the basis for every version that has followed since, Rowdy Wright's "I'm a Wandering Bronco Rider" and "I'm a Jolly Cowboy" both have delightfully raw energy, and the Delmore Brothers' exquisitely harmonized "The Fugitive's Lament" is the thematic precursor to every record the Everly Brothers ever cut, especially "Take a Message to Mary." The real find, however, may be Buell Kazee's soaring banjo-driven "The Cowboy Trail," sung in a haunting nasal twang, which is one of the most honest *and* dramatic pieces among the 23 songs here. The sound is generally excellent, apart from distortion in the opening bars of "The Burial of Wild Bill" by Frank Jenkins & His Pilot Mountaineers, and some unavoidable surface noise evident on Dick Devall's otherwise gorgeous a cappella "Tom Sherman's Barroom." *—Bruce Eder*

Whistle Bait: 25 Rockabilly Rave-Ups / 2000 / Columbia/Legacy ♦♦♦♦
Culled from the CBS vaults, *Whistle Bait* is a very good anthology of 25 rockabilly numbers—or, if not quite rockabilly, tracks by country artists veering close to rockabilly—that for the most part will be unfamiliar to all but the most dedicated rockabilly collectors. Sure, there are some stars and cult faves here, like the Collins Kids, Link Wray, the post-Sun Carl Perkins, the post-Sun Johnny Cash, and Ronnie Self, whose "Bop-A-Lena" (included here) was one of the most certifiably insane rockers ever put out by a major label. You also get a generous helping of country artists trying to board the rockabilly wagon, and actually, they usually acquit themselves quite well. Don't believe it? Listen to Lefty Frizzell's "You're Humbuggin' Me," Rose Maddox's "Wild Wild Young Men," and Little Jimmy Dickens' "I Got a Hole in My Pocket" for evidence. Then there are the cats you've never heard of that managed to put out something quite hep, like Jaycee Hill on his 1956 single "Romp Stompin' Boogie." Johnny Horton draws from the best of both honky tonk and rock & roll on his two numbers, which are a far cry from the corny Americana that would land him big pop hits at the end of the '50s. Although there's undeniable aesthetic purity in collecting anthologies of crude rockabilly by no-hopers on some tiny label operating out of a small Texas oil town, the truth is that this big company vault-clearing exercise is way better than the average such rockabilly collection. It may not be too popular to say so, but one of the reasons is that major label production values usually delivered far better-sounding, tighter performances and secured better material. Put this on your shopping list if you want quality rare rockabilly. *—Richie Unterberger*

White Country Blues, 1926–1938 . . . / 1993 / Columbia/Legacy ♦♦♦♦
White Country Blues 1926-1938: A Lighter Shade of Blue is an excellent, revealing 48-track, double-disc collection culled from the Columbia, American, and OKeh vaults. All of the material on this double-disc set was recorded by country artists that drew heavily from the blues, whether it was incorporating the genre into their own compositions or covering blues and hokum songs. Though there are several stars, such as Roy Acuff, many of the performers on *White Country Blues* are obscure, especially for listeners whose knowledge of country music stops at Hank Williams. That is one of the many reasons why *White Country Blues* is invaluable. It's a thoughtfully compiled and thorough historical reissue that presents a wealth of rare, fascinating material. While it might not always be an easy listen, it's remains an essential purchase for any comprehensive country collection. *—Thom Owens*

The World of Crazy Cajun / Jul. 27, 1999 / Edsel ♦♦♦♦
This 22-track sampler brings together the wide array of music and musicians who recorded in the '60s and '70s for Huey Meaux's Crazy Cajun label. With 34 albums already in the series, this collection only represents a small sampling of the vast holdings in Meaux's master vaults. But it's all great stuff with stellar tracks from Doug Kershaw, Ronnie Milsap, B. J. Thomas, Roy Head, Delbert McClinton, Mickey Gilley, T-Bone Walker, Lowell Fulson, Rod Bernard, Johnny Copeland, Freddy Fender, Dr. John, the Sir Douglas Quintet, Barbara Lynn and many others. This is a nice introduction to this series chock full of American musical treasures. *—Cub Koda*

World's Greatest Bluegrass Banjos / 2002 / CMH ♦♦♦
When CMH named this collection, they decided to go for broke. Their collection wouldn't just include the best banjo picking from eastern Virginia, or the South, or even the entire U.S. Instead, it would be *World's Greatest Bluegrass Banjos*. To back up their assertion, CMH brought together recordings by banjoists like Vic Jordon, Sonny Osborne, and Grandpa Jones. There's a nifty version of "Limehouse Blues" by Eddie Addock that even includes some nifty guitar and a bouncy take on "Dueling Banjos" by Don Reno. Lester Flatt & the Nashville Grass deliver a charged-up rendition of "Roll in My Sweet Baby's Arms" with the help of Kenny Ingram's speedy banjo technique, while Arthur Smith and Don Reno cut loose on a funky piece titled "Memphis Five String," which sounds a little like a mountaineer's version of "Memphis." While *World's Greatest Bluegrass Banjos* sells itself on the strength of its five-string material, many of these pieces leave room for fiddle, mandolin, and guitar solos, sweetening the package. A number of these songs/instrumentals, like "Soldier's Joy," will be familiar, but there are also pleasant surprises like a banjo-infused "Tequila." For the banjo fanatic and casual bluegrass fan, this collection offers 45 minutes of fancy picking. *—Ronnie D. Lankford Jr.*

World's Hottest Bluegrass / Sep. 3, 2002 / CMH ♦♦♦
CMH has gone from issuing bluegrass versions of songs borrowed from the Who and the String Cheese Incident to issuing the occasional, down-home bluegrass compilation. *World's Hottest Bluegrass* has to be one of the most eclectic collections of mountain music ever released. Classic acts like Jim & Jesse and the Osborne Brothers share disc space with old-timers like the Stonemans and lesser-known pickers like Chubby Anthony. The songs and instrumentals live up to the album's title by keeping the pace upbeat and joyous. Grandpa Jones sings a rambunctious version of "Are You From Dixie?" while Joe Maphis lends his nifty guitar picking to "Liberty" and "Fiddle Pickin'." Wynn Osborne contributes "Bluegrass Breakdown," one of the odder pieces on the album, along with a fairly straight version of "Earl's Breakdown." The Osbornes show off their knack for sterling harmony on "Hillbilly Fever," while Jim & Jesse delve into novelty terrain with "Diesel on My Tail." The Stonemans' "Heartbreak Mountain" includes a tasty bit of dobro picking, as does Josh Graves and Bobby Smith's "Shiloh March." The collection ends with Anthony offering up a lively version of "Lee Highway Blues," a nice tune to end on. While the picture of the burning banjo on the cover of *World's Hottest Bluegrass* may frighten anyone who plays acoustic music, the disc itself should have a more soothing effect. *—Ronnie D. Lankford Jr.*

Yee-Haw!: The Other Side of Country / Mar. 13, 2001 / QDK Media ♦♦♦♦
Now here's an odd one: a compilation of very obscure country tunes from across America recorded between 1968-1975. Alt-country indeed. Seriously, the opening track, "Never

Trust a Woman," from 1969—by a band called Spur who wished they were the Byrds circa the Gram Parsons era—has lines in the refrains such as: "Never trust a woman with your dope/Don't ever Trust a woman with your hash/Don't ever trust a woman with your speed." Pedal steel guitars duel with four-part harmonies and gutbucket bass—weird. The next cut, "Tawney," one from Illinois semi-legend Arlie Neaville, comes right out of the 1966-1970 period of Roy Orbison—beautiful folky melodies woven with horns, jangling guitars, and Neaville's stunningly beautiful voice, full of deep emotion and wild abandon. Already the many-sided personality of this compilation is splitting at the seams. But it gets even more surreal with two tracks from Peter Grudizen's *Unicorn* album—folky and freaky with psychedelic effects. The titles? "White Trash Hillbilly Trick" and "The Lost World." Palmer Rocky checks in with an apocalyptic folk song worthy of Jandek or Bonnie "Prince" Billy. A lot of this is more on the folk side of country, but the songwriting is never less than interesting and sometimes, as in the case of William C. Beeley's "Galivanter" and Neaville's "Today Was the Time" (written by Jim Cuomo), it is downright astonishing. And with the exception of "Don't Ever Trust a Woman" and Grudizen's cuts—and perhaps "Kill the Pig" by Mother Tucker's Yellow Duck, which is nothing more than a psych workout disguised as country music—this is serious, very fine, and worthy of repeated listening. Germany's Normal label does it again. *—Thom Jurek*

Movie Soundtracks

All the Pretty Horses / Jan. 9, 2000 / ✦✦✦✦

Sure, the movie was no *Sling Blade*, even if directed by the one and only Billy Bob Thornton. But let's face it, they took two hours outta the thing! All the griping aside, the score, composed and performed by country music renaissance man Marty Stuart—and his collaborating bandmembers Kristin Wilkinson and Larry Paxton—is something else completely. Comprised of 23 tracks, Stuart's score does sound like soundtrack music, but no matter. He and his sextet have taken the drama of the film's text and created an aural theater of the American West. At the heart of each theme is a core of mandolin, viola, bass, guitar, accordion, piano, and percussion. Orchestrations ride ambiently in the background, highlighting tension and drama. In "Edge of the World," cornets play at the music's outermost edge, hinting at a red Sonoran sunset. In another place, guitars, both strummed and soloed upon, create an impressionistic picture of a campfire jam session. Elsewhere, "Strawberry Tango, Part One and Two" features a full horn and string section painting the atmosphere at a cantina dance from its wild beginnings until its sultry ending. Daniel Lanois, who scored Thornton's *Sling Blade* (well, it actually sounds as if he threw a bunch of leftover studio bits on a tape for the movie), makes a return appearance here with an actual song. The track "Porque" features the stirring vocals of Raul Malo of the Mavericks, who contributed the lyrics to the selection. It's a sad, romantic ballad. Lost love drips from the cowboy's hat, regret drapes itself in tears in his shaded eyes, and he stands out in the rain singing to no one. Also, homage is paid to Stuart's greatest influence and benefactor, the daddy of bluegrass music himself, Bill Monroe. His "My Last Days on Earth" is included here. (Everybody knows nobody was listening to bluegrass music in Texas or Mexico in the late '30s.) The only real complaint about this gorgeous score is its brevity. Clocking in at under 50 minutes, it's easy to hear where edits have been made out of longer tracks, though each piece flows into the next like water. It's a mirror image of the movie but doesn't suffer near as badly for it. Despite his already prodigious talents as a songwriter, singer, and musician who is almost single-handedly keeping the country music tradition alive in the modern idiom, Stuart has proven himself a capable and worthy composer of film music. Here's hoping there's more work of this kind in his future. —*Thom Jurek*

American and Italian Western Screen Themes / Apr. 19, 1994 / Milan ✦✦✦✦

Bad Day at Black Rock / 2001 / Rhino Handmade ✦✦✦✦✦

From the Internet-exclusive audio boutique Rhino Handmade comes this compilation of original motion picture music from noted composer André Previnand performed by the MGM Studio Orchestra. Not only does this single CD include the complete soundtrack to the Spencer Tracy epic *Bad Day at Black Rock* (1955), but also key selections from three additional scores as well—*Tension* (1949), *Scene of the Crime* (1949), and *Cause for Alarm* (1950). Notably, only the tracks from *Bad Day at Black Rock* are presented in stereo—which has been mixed with a nod toward aural widescreen (read: optimal stereo channel separation). As with most cinematic or "incidental" music, the underlying subtext is to represent the on-screen action. However, a large part of Previn's success was his seemingly innate ability to manufacture much more than musical backdrops or scenery. He deals in the realm of creating tension and release within his sonic dramas. Likewise, he shades the themes in different hues as they reoccur—intimating a visual foreshadowing or flashback—similar to that of many classical works. From the introductory notes to the various "Main Titles," the listener becomes engrossed with the instant attention demanded by the dynamics in the music. The immediacy and ominous—almost threatening—tonality that pervades the opening sequence of *Bad Day at Black Rock* is a motif which reveals itself throughout each of the film's subsequent scores—particularly during the "Medley: Smith Visits Sheriff/Doc Gets Mad." The remaining three films are noir dramas from Previn's earliest days at MGM when he was barely out of his teens. It is amazing the breadth of scope he possessed at such an early age. Even the background music—such as the epigrammatic jazzy cue titled "Billboard" from *Scene of the Crime* is shrouded in uncertainty and seemingly untoward intent. The disc is accompanied by a 20-page liner notes booklet containing still photos, plot synopses, as well as discographical details about each recording date and a fresh perspective from Turner Classic Movies music producer George Feltenstein. *Bad Day at Black Rock* is limited to an edition of 4,500 and is available exclusively at www.rhinohandmade.com. —*Lindsay Planer*

Bandolero! / 1968 / Project 3 ✦✦✦

Bonanza: A Ponderosa Party / 1962-1966 / Bear Family ✦✦✦✦

Bonanza was the quintessential Western television series. It told the story of a family led by ranch owner Ben Cartwright (Lorne Greene), who had sired three sons: introspective, intellectual Adam (Pernell Roberts), hulking, good-natured "Hoss" (Dan Blocker), and volatile, handsome Little Joe (Michael Landon). When *Bonanza* first went on the air, it was common practice to get the stars of hit series to expand into other areas, especially recording. Disc one opens with *Ponderosa Party Time*, the first *Bonanza* album, which is

contrived and sometimes silly but always lively. It features country and folk songs with Greene, Landon, Roberts, and Blocker all singing in character. The material here isn't far removed from the sort of records that Gene Autry used to make for his movies, except that none of these guys is as good a singer as Autry. *Lorne Greene's American West*, which makes up the first part of disc two, is a pretty good record; *Welcome to the Ponderosa* fills out the rest of the disc. Disc three is made up of Greene's *Portrait of the West* and *Lorne Greene: The Man* albums. These are more western songs, traditional pieces interspersed among modern songs, but both are more elaborately produced than the two previous records. Not all of it works, but it is fun, and livelier than *Welcome to the Ponderosa*. Pernell Roberts' *Come All Ye Fair and Tender Ladies* opens disc four; it's a pleasant folk album, using mostly traditional or traditional-type material. He sings in a pleasant, rich baritone that makes this the strongest of the eight albums included here. Dan Blocker's 1963 album *Our Heritage*, recorded with singer/actor John Mitchum, fills out disc four. This was a story-and-song celebration of American history, with the folksy, pleasing Blocker telling the stories and Mitchum singing. —*Bruce Eder*

Bound for Glory / 1976 / EMI America ✦✦✦

Dances with Wolves / Feb. 2, 1995 / Sony ✦✦✦✦✦

John Barry's fifth Oscar-winning score is a profoundly moving body of music, generally (though not entirely) elegiac in tone, very much like the movie for which it was written. It's also a bit of a mixed bag, occasionally falling back on material that will be familiar to fans of the James Bond movies that Barry scored during the early/mid-'60s. The main title theme uses some of those devices—dense, heavy string passages adjacent to trumpet calls—but it is hardly representative of the full score. The real heart of *Dances With Wolves* is the pensive, tragic "John Dunbar Theme," which is far closer in spirit to Barry's music for *Somewhere in Time* or *They Might Be Giants*, films (and scores) far removed from the Bond movies. It seems as though, when Barry is asked to write music for characters that are complex and troubled (of which Bond is neither), he delivers the goods in the guise of musical material that reflects those elements. Some elements familiar from the Bond films can be found scattered throughout this soundtrack, particularly the violin-driven "stings" that open "The Death of Timmons" and the horn calls that herald its closing; the string parts underneath the hyperactive percussion of "Pawnee Attack" might've been lifted right out of *From Russia With Love* and "Stands With a Fist Remembers," with its secondary violin part, in the upper register of the strings. Much of *Dances With Wolves*, however, shows a broadening of Barry's sound—he uses the vast canvas of Kevin Costner's movie and Dean Semler's cinematography as the basis for one of the most richly scored soundtracks of his career, working with some of the largest orchestras ever heard in one of his films; "Journey to Fort Sedgewick," "Kicking Bird's Gift," "Two Socks at Play," "The Death of Cisco," and "Journey to the Buffalo Killing Ground" have an almost Copland-like majesty about them, and "The Buffalo Hunt" is one of the finest pieces of music the man ever wrote. At times, it sounds as though Barry had every string player and hornist in Los Angeles present, and topped it all out with an oversized percussion section, but none of the music or the scoring here sound excessive. *Dances With Wolves* has appeared in several CD editions, some featuring bonus tracks, and in 2000 became the first soundtrack ever released as a Super Audio CD (with presence on the percussion and the horns that will knock the listener's socks off). —*Bruce Eder*

The Electric Horseman / 1979 / Columbia ✦✦✦

☆ **Faccia a Faccia (Face to Face)/La Resa Dei Conti (The Big Gundown)** / Mask ✦✦✦✦✦

A Fistful of Dollars / 1967 / RCA ✦✦✦✦✦

Sergio Leone and Ennio Morricone define the spaghetti Western style of film and music so squarely, the competition is barely considered. It was on the backs of films such as this 1967 smash, starring a pre-Dirty Harry Clint Eastwood, that their well-known reputation rests. The CD is more than you expect. Of course, Morricone has that unique style that he and older, less Italian-influenced Western film composers made synonymous with the action from St. Louis to the Rockies, and the deserts from there to the coast. There are the clip-clop beats similar to the trot of horses, the weary harmonica trill, and the peculiar whistling, that puckered sound of aloneness that still makes one think of solitary battles against the self as much as mounted foes. But Morricone also loves rustic, romantic orchestrations that use his whole orchestra. When a trumpet hits a solo on "Theme From Fistful of Dollars," backed by chilly strings and Spanish-strummed acoustic guitars, it's one of Byronic, beautiful, spacious solitude. Cymbals crash over a piano's bass keys, amidst rumbling trumpets and trombones, and the thump of timpani. Flutes and violins dart as much as thrust and parry, and background voices "Ahhh" in that everyman way, along with whip-cracks. It's all pretty prairie, rolling hills, grasslands and cattle, wagon wheels, and unshaven men with uncertain life spans. It's so mood-setting, you expect to see cactus or bison outside your door instead of an asphalt city. It's instrumental music that's a veritable co-star in a motion picture, not a pack of pre-recorded hit songs all wedged into a film like large square pegs into tiny round holes. This is authentic film scoring, and it is as alluring and inviting as Leone's movie itself. You can see it just to hear this. —*Jack Rabid*

For a Few Dollars More / 1971 / BMG International ✦✦✦
RCA Records faced a problem at the close of the 1960s, surrounding Ennio Morricone's music from Sergio Leone's "Man-With-No-Name" Westerns starring Clint Eastwood. The first one, *A Fistful of Dollars*, had yielded a successful soundtrack album when issued in America in 1967, despite the fact that Morricone had only recorded 14 minutes of music for it. There was demand for a soundtrack LP from the second movie, especially in the wake of United Artists Records' enjoying a substantial hit with its soundtrack release from the third movie in the trilogy, *The Good, the Bad & the Ugly*. Keep in mind that Morricone had only recorded 14 minutes of music from *For a Few Dollars More*. As a result, they assembled a soundtrack album on *For a Few Dollars More*, which included the six music tracks from that film and repeated the six original tracks from *A Fistful of Dollars*. It all sounds good, and it's interesting to hear the composer add the sound of an oboe to his distinctive use of trumpet, guitar, and whistling on a new and haunting melodic canvas of western musical landscapes. There are no notes, alas, and there's little other information printed, but the album is enjoyable as far as it goes. It should also be noted, however, that most of the key sections of this and *A Fistful of Dollars* are available at a lower price on RCA's Ennio Morricone collection, *Legendary Italian Westerns*, which is also well-annotated. —*Bruce Eder*

Francesco Demasi's Western Soundtracks / 1995 / Beat ✦✦✦

From Alamo to El Dorado, Vol. 2 / Jun. 24, 1997 / Bear Family ✦✦✦
While the first volume in this wonderful series focused on TV and movie themes in the Western vernacular, such as *Bonanza*, *Gunfight at the OK Corral*, et al., this second collection digs deeper into the American kitsch experience—as envisioned through the eyes of a German family's view of popular culture in the U.S. There are no less than 23 selections here that vary in range and quality from Nat King Cole and Stubby Kaye's bizarre rough-and-rowdy theme song for the Jane Fonda vehicle *Cat Ballou*, to Jose Feliciano's rockabilly singing of "Old Turkey Buzzard" from the film *MacKenna's Gold*, to Glen Campbell's gorgeous "A Man With True Grit" from the film *True Grit*. There's a vibe that runs through all of this seemingly disparate material, and that is how the Western theme song evolved from a simple Hollywood instrumental with lots of sound effects to the aftermath of Ennio Morricone's adaptations for spaghetti Westerns by Sergio Leone to the involvement of show tune composers such as Elmer Bernstein and Dan Black in the genre. There are traditional contributors of course, such as Tex Ritter with his theme to *Wichita*, the Sons of the Pioneers with "Sugarfoot," and Johnny Gregory with his theme from *Bronco*. But there was also an era when singers like Wayne Newton contributed his silky Vegas voice to the series *Stagecoach* and Andy Williams and his champagne throat sang on the soundtrack for the John Huston/Paul Newman vehicle *The Life and Times of Judge Roy Bean*. Thankfully, there is also a fine rendition here from the original released soundtrack to the television program *Wagon Train*, and Dean Martin weighs in with "The Wind, The Wind" from the film *Pardners*—yes, it was a comedy. The package, unlike other Bear Family packages, contains literally no liner notes, but the sound has been remastered expertly and the booklet includes literally dozens of reproductions of movie posters (mostly German versions!) and stills from both film and TV. This is every bit as essential as the first volume and even more off the beaten track. —*Thom Jurek*

Gettysburg / 1993 / Milan ✦✦✦✦✦
Randy Edelman's score to this epic (read: long) historical drama is intended to be majestic and stirring. It's full of grand themes and swelling string sections. But like that sea of pasted-on beards that dominated the proceedings of Ted Turner's creaky retelling of the Civil War's greatest battle, it all seems artificial. And, like the film, it's less likely to soar than to snore. —*William Ruhlmann*

☆ **Giant** / 1998 / Tsunami ✦✦✦✦✦
A straight reissue, out of Germany, of the out of print Capitol soundtrack album, in excellent sound. Tsunami has done a few like this and it is always surprising how the label manages to clean up its sources. In this instance, apart from the sweeping "Main Title" theme and the brilliant, lonely, sad, and exultant "Jett Rink Theme," the best moments come in "Road to Reata," an extended passage that mixes swirling strings and a haunting melody. At certain moments, "Road to Reata" recalls composer Dimitri Tiomkin's work on the movie *Portrait of Jennie* and his arrangements of Debussy's music from that score. The $20 U.S. list price for this European import may seem steep, but it is the only way to get the soundtrack as of the turn of the century. The artwork is also superior to the Capitol release, with great black and white photos inside, though there are no notes. —*Bruce Eder*

☆ **The Good, the Bad & the Ugly [Compilation]** / 1992 / RCA ✦✦✦✦✦
Certainly purists will prefer the versions of these classic Ennio Morricone spaghetti Western soundtracks conducted by Morricone himself to the ones on this compilation, which were arranged and conducted by Hugo Montenegro. Still, anyone who likes prime Morricone from that era will probably enjoy this CD quite a bit. Containing pieces from three of the most famous Morricone-scored films, all of the material was released in 1967, and it must be said that Montenegro didn't miss a trick, employing the low twangy guitars, weeping horns, and ghostly whistles that are usually identified as Morricone trademarks. Perhaps these are a tad more bombastic, orchestrated, and pop-slanted than Morricone's own versions but, if anything, Montenegro's touches enhance the grandiose sadness of the melodies. Contains the massive hit version of the theme from *The Good, the Bad & the Ugly*, which went to number two in 1968. —*Richie Unterberger*

The Good, the Bad & the Ugly/A Fistful of Dollars / May 23, 1995 / RCA ✦✦✦
Along with the James Bond, Pink Panther, and Peter Gunn themes, the title piece of *The Good, the Bad & the Ugly* is arguably one of the greatest themes ever written. The entire

score ties with those from *Midnight Express* and *Blade Runner* as the greatest soundtracks of all time. Many imitated the profoundly unique, deeply haunting style of composer Ennio Morricone, but none could attain his level of brilliance. Hugo Montenegro comes very close in a pop vein. His version of "The Good, the Bad & the Ugly" was a smash, and he weaves bells, marching chants, and myriad other sounds into a spaghetti tapestry that not only recalls the tension on the screen, but also makes for fine listening. The themes from *A Fistful of Dollars* and *For a Few Dollars More* also have several great moments. Get this too-brief comp for its excellence and historical significance, but get Morricone's originals because therein can be heard some of the best music ever created. —*Doug Stone*

☆ **Good, the Bad & the Ugly/The Big Gun Down** / Jun. 20, 1995 / Vivi Musica ✦✦✦✦✦

Gunsmoke / Jan. 1, 2001 / Cliffhanger ✦✦✦✦

Hang 'Em High / 1968 / RCA ✦✦✦

High Lonesome / Jun. 17, 1994 / CMH ✦✦✦✦
This companion album to the fine bluegrass documentary of the same name is a stirring collection of music. The presence of stalwart pioneers like Bill Monroe and Ralph Stanley sees to that, as does the inclusion of innovators like the Osborne Brothers and the Seldom Scene. To attempt to sketch the story of bluegrass music is a daunting (and impossible) task, but this collection takes a good crack at it with well-chosen tracks and interjected comments by the artists. Fittingly, the collection starts with the father of the genre, Monroe, and his "Body and Soul." The track epitomizes the "high lonesome" sound with Monroe's mournful, almost barking cries and the glorious twin fiddles. Monroe and Stanley are covered well—with recordings from the '50s (Ralph Stanley with the Stanley Brothers), '60s, '70s, and '80s—without forgetting important folks like Mac Wiseman and Jimmy Martin. Particularly amazing is Ralph Stanley's gospel number "Gloryland," done here a cappella with Ricky Skaggs and Keith Whitley. It is at once spiritual, gorgeous, and chilling. —*Erik Hage*

High Noon / RCA Victor Red Seal ✦✦✦✦

Honeysuckle Rose / 1980 / Columbia ✦✦✦

Honkytonk Man / 1983 / Warner Bros. ✦✦✦✦

The Horse Whisperer / Apr. 7, 1998 / MCA ✦✦✦✦
The soundtrack to Robert Redford's sweeping rural romance *The Horse Whisperer* is an excellent collection of contemporary country. The album favors alt-country singer/songwriters like Gillian Welch, Don Edwards, Steve Earle, Iris DeMent, Allison Moorer, Emmylou Harris and Lucinda Williams, but in this context, it becomes clear that such mainstream stars as Dwight Yoakam, Mavericks, and George Strait build from the same tradition. As a matter of fact, it's refreshing to the borders break down between the two extremes, since it reveals that aesthetically, they're not that far apart. But the real treat with *The Horse Whisperer* is the fact that none of the 12 tracks are weak. It's the rare soundtrack that works just as well as an individual as it does a souvenir. —*Thom Owens*

I Western / Aug. 1, 1995 / BMG Italy ✦✦✦✦

Johnny Guitar / 1954 / Varese Sarabande ✦✦✦✦✦

The Last Picture Show / 1971 / MGM ✦✦✦✦

Last Stand at Saber River / 1997 / Intrada ✦✦✦
A rousing, thundering Western score from David Shire, whose work usually tends toward the quieter and more reflective end of the film score spectrum. Here, the music is meant to accompany Tom Selleck on an adventure based on an Elmore Leonard novel. The orchestra has a strong, dense sound to it, though the music itself holds no real surprises. —*Steven McDonald*

☆ **The Legendary Italian Westerns** / 1990 / RCA ✦✦✦✦✦
These are the performances, more than any other, that Morricone's reputation was built upon. This 31-track, 73-minute collection draws highlights from nine of his 1960s Westerns, leaning especially heavily on *A Fistful of Dollars*, *For a Few Dollars More*, and *Once Upon a Time in the West*. Ranging from hysterical gunfighter ballads to contemporary classical chamber music, it is among the most dramatic and evocative music composed in any idiom. —*Richie Unterberger*

Lie of the Mind / 1990 / Sugar Hill ✦✦✦✦

Lonesome Dove / Oct. 20, 1998 / Sonic Images ✦✦✦

Lonesome Dove: Classic Wester Scores / Aug. 20, 1996 / Silva ✦✦✦
The soundtrack to the epic Western mini-series *Lonesome Dove* is as dramatic, heart-tugging and powerful as the series itself, capturing all of its grand splendor through its majestic score. —*Rodney Batdorf*

☆ **The Long Riders** / 1980 / WEA International ✦✦✦✦✦
Ry Cooder's soundtrack for *The Long Riders* received a top-notch treatment from Warner Bros. (Japan), who not only did an excellent remastering job, but backed it up with English lyrics to the songs, notes, and a Japanese insert. Cooder was in fine form with this score, using original material, unusual and anachronistic instruments (saz, tamboura, electric guitar), and elements of traditional songs from the Civil War period. As a result, the album can be appreciated as a unique entity, away from the film—and bonded to the film, the music provides grace and power to the onscreen events. —*Steven McDonald*

Louisiana / 1947 / Daywind ✦✦✦
Louisiana is billed as "the first commercial release of the first country & western soundtrack." The 12 songs are drawn from a promotional record sent out in conjunction with the release of Jimmie Davis' 1947 bio-pic *Louisiana*. Four songs appear in instrumental and vocal versions, including Davis' super-smash "You Are My Sunshine." "Bang Bang" and "There's a New Moon Over My Shoulder," both big hits for Davis, are likewise

included, although it should be emphasized that these are transcription recordings and not the original hit versions. The playing time, at just over 21 minutes, is too brief, but these sessions have historical value and at the very least provide a remedy to the dearth of Davis' music available domestically. *—Greg Adams*

☆ **Magnificent Seven** / Sep. 29, 1998 / Rykodisc ✦✦✦✦✦
Amazingly, this 1998 CD was the first release in any form of the original soundtrack music recordings from John Sturges' *The Magnificent Seven.* At the time of the movie's release, United Artists Records was a new label that, surprisingly, had not done well with its soundtrack albums, and Elmer Bernstein was known for only a tiny handful of scores, so a soundtrack album never appeared. Then the movie became a huge hit, and Bernstein's title theme was picked up for use in a generation of Marlboro cigarette commercials. UA didn't get anything resembling a soundtrack album out until 1966 when the sequel, *The Return of the Magnificent Seven*, reused much of Bernstein's key material. And as United Artists was a distributor, rather than a studio with a permanent lot and vault, the original music recordings were lost until the early '90s. The discovery of the recordings has led to this 65-minute CD, done in high-definition digital sound, which puts the thundering orchestra practically in your living room. Bernstein's music is some of the most lyrical and expressive of his career, resounding in the influences of the best of Copland, Mussorgsky, Stravinsky, and a half-dozen others swelling out of your speakers. Even the effects music is here, and it's all clean and close. The care with which the music has been treated is matched by the elegance of the packaging, which—in addition to full, detailed notes—includes a recreation of the original poster that unfolds to a big chunk of full size. Ironically, the package is so good, and the sound so vivid, that listening to the CD is a lot like watching the movie, which is what a soundtrack would have evoked in 1960, too. *—Bruce Eder*

☆ **The Magnificent Seven/The Hallelujah Trail** / Nov. 1993 / Koch International ✦✦✦✦✦
Elmer Bernstein's score for *The Magnificent Seven*, especially its title theme, was among the most popular Western movie music ever written (the title tune became the "Marlboro Cigarette Theme" and also turned up in the concert version of the Nice's recording of Bob Dylan's "She Belongs to Me"). But at the time of its release in 1960, Western movie scores weren't necessarily selling well, and United Artists failed to release an actual soundtrack album from the film. James Sedares and the Phoenix Symphony give a sweeping account of the music in this new digital recording, the fullest recording that the score has ever received. The new recording lacks some of the urgency of the movie's scoring, but makes up for it with a larger-than-life sound and a grand orchestral gesture, imparting to Elmer Bernstein's music the scope of a supremely bold concert suite. The notes are well-detailed and informative as well. And as a bonus, there is a performance of the seven-minute overture from *The Hallelujah Trail*, a film whose music was its best part. *—Bruce Eder*

Maverick / 1994 / Atlantic ✦✦✦✦✦
The soundtrack to *Maverick* doesn't feature Randy Newman's original score—it is a collection of ten contemporary country numbers, with a Newman song and a version of "Amazing Grace" thrown in for good measure. Though the album features many big stars—including Waylon Jennings, Clint Black, Vince Gill, Tracy Lawrence, Restless Heart and John Michael Montgomery—it doesn't have many terrific performances. Many of these songs sound like castoffs and throwaways, and while there are a handful of good cuts (Black's "A Good Run of Bad Luck" is particularly fine), the album is by and large a medicore collection. *—Thom Owens*

Maverick / 1994 / Reprise ✦✦✦
Maverick the movie mixes an old-fashioned Western setting with some modern-day comedy and action, and even a little sexual tension and romance. Stars in this film are Mel Gibson, Jodie Foster, and James Garner. It seemed only appropriate that during the making of it another big-name artist, Randy Newman, be called in to handle the musical score, along with Frank Wolf as producer. It was orchestrated by Don Davis and Jack Hayes. This country-styled musical score carries tracks that travel smoothly from dark and melancholy to energetic and humorous. Many Newman fans might find this album a little different than his normal offerings, but still worth a listen or two. Fans of the movie itself might enjoy the *Maverick* soundtrack also, with its list of songs done by top country singers such as Clint Black and Vince Gill. *—Charlotte Dillon*

Missouri Breaks / 1976 / MCA ✦✦✦

Music from "A Fistful of Dollars" & "For a Few Dollars More" / 1968 / RCA ✦✦✦✦✦

Music from "Songwriter" / Oct. 1984 / Columbia ✦✦✦✦
Willie Nelson was making so many records in the mid-'80s that it was easy for one to get lost in the shuffle, and that's what happened to this album. Tri-Star, the company that distributed Nelson's film *Songwriter*, gave it very little promotion, even though it was a good movie that contained one of the singer/actor's finest screen performances. He played Doc Jenkins, a country singer/songwriter who signs an onerous record deal and then finds a way out of it by enlisting the help of his friend Blackie Buck, played by Kris Kristofferson. Music filled the movie, much of it written and performed by the principals, and rather than release a soundtrack album, Columbia Records issued *Music From Songwriter*, an album billed to Nelson and Kristofferson. Each side of the LP began with a duet by the two performers, with the rest of side one given over to Nelson tracks and the rest of side two to Kristofferson tracks. The opening duet, "How Do You Feel About Foolin' Around," became a country singles chart entry, but the best material was Nelson's, including the title song and the caustic "Write Your Own Songs," addressed to "Mr. Music Executive" and "Mr. Purified Country," and sung in the character of Doc Jenkins, though it no doubt expressed the feelings of Nelson as well. Kristofferson hadn't made a solo album in four years, and his four solo tracks found him concerned with topical issues having to do with illegal immigration ("Crossing the Border") and war ("Under the Gun"). Such songs had little to do with the movie, but a lot to do with the singer/songwriter's own current concerns, and he delivered them with fervor over a rocking band. The album made the pop and country charts, and *Songwriter* earned an Academy Award nomination for best original song score, losing to *Purple Rain.* *—William Ruhlmann*

Music From Lonesome Dove: The Soundtrack Album / 1993 / Cabin Fever ✦✦✦

Music of Great Westerns / Pro Arte ✦✦✦✦

Nashville / 1975 / MCA ✦✦✦✦
Folks, let's get one thing straight. The at-times charmingly bad, humorous, or excellent soundtrack to Robert Altman's groundbreaking and influential *Nashville* isn't to be taken at face value throughout. There's a blizzard's chance in Tullahoma County that you'll get a proper grip of it without context of the film itself. The film is a vivid look at the cult of celebrity and power, tracing the actions of a couple dozen characters throughout five days in the country music capital. With numerous performances by these figures that go hand-in-hand with the environ, the film is just as much a musical as it is a realistic slice of southern America, circa 1974. As much of the performances captured in the film are by local amateurs, the material isn't always top level. That's why it succeeds—it's realistic. As the director himself assesses in the liner notes to the MCA Nashville reissue from 2000, "We weren't trying to write 'great' songs. We aimed to meet the spectrum of songs coming out of the Nashville scene." Spectrum is the key word here—the quality of the material and the range of emotions within are extremely broad. Lonesome lives on the road, extramarital affairs that need to be severed, romantic longings, national pride, self-assurance—just about any topic tackled within a typical country song is covered. Most of the songs were written by the actors with their characters in mind, which adds more of that necessary realism. The musicianship is excellent and fitting, including the work of legendary session hands like Vassar Clements, David Briggs, and Weldon Myrick. Convincing performances come from Henry Gibson, in the role of star Haven Hamilton. (Gibson is also well-known as a gravity-defying Illinois Nazi in *The Blues Brothers.*) He cuts his lover loose in "For the Sake of the Children," giving her three reasons—Jimmy, Kathy, and sweet Lorelei; "Cause Jimmy's been wishin' that I take him fishin'; his Little League pitchin' is somethin' to see." His "Keep A-Goin'" is a surefire mood lifter: "Ain't no use to sit and whine 'cause the fish ain't on your line; bait your hook and keep a-tryin'—keep a-goin'!" Other excellent performances are turned in by Karen Black and Keith Carradine, whose "I'm Easy" won an Academy Award for Best Song. *Nashville* is a fine elixir in an age of soundtrack-before-plot movies and and a hoot to boot. *—Andy Kellman*

O Brother, Where Art Thou? / Dec. 5, 2000 / Mercury ✦✦✦✦✦
The critical consensus at the end of 2000 was that it had been one of the weakest film years in recent memory. Which may have been true, despite *O Brother, Where Art Thou?*, the Coen brothers' delightfully warm and weird Depression-era re-telling of Homer's *Odyssey.* But for music lovers, 2000 was an amazing year at the movies, and it produced several excellent soundtrack compilations including *Almost Famous*, *Dancer in the Dark*, *Wonder Boys*, and *High Fidelity*. Even with such steep competition, the soundtrack album for *O Brother, Where Art Thou?* may be the best of the year. In order to capture the sound of Mississippi circa 1932, the Coens commissioned T-Bone Burnett, a masterful producer whose work with artists like Elvis Costello, Sam Phillips, Joseph Arthur, and Counting Crows has earned him a special place in the folk-rock hall of fame, to research and recreate the country, bluegrass, folk, gospel, and blues of the era. The Coens were so taken with Burnett's discoveries that the film became a unique sort of musical revue. There are no original compositions here (though Burnett is given a "music by" credit usually reserved for composers), and the characters do not generally break into stylized song and dance numbers (as they do in, say, *Everyone Says I Love You*). But nearly every scene in *O Brother* is set to a period song, and the music frequently drives and defines the action. With two exceptions—a stunning 1955 Alan Lomax recording of a black prison chain gang singing "Po Lazarus", and Harry McClintock's "Big Rock Candy Mountain"—every song was recorded for the film by an impressive assembly of old-time country veterans (Fairfield Four, Ralph Stanley, the Whites) and talented newcomers (Gillian Welch, Alison Krauss, Emmylou Harris). These recordings, which were made without the meddling clarity of digital technology, give the film much of its power and authenticity. A significant segment of the plot hinges on the (utterly plausible) notion that Dan Tyminksi's ebullient rendition of "I Am a Man of Constant Sorrow" could be a runaway hit. A memorable sequence involving three riverside sirens centers around an eerie version of "Didn't Leave Nobody But the Baby." And Stanley's a cappella performance of "O Death" sets a chilling tone for a climactic struggle at a Ku Klux Klan rally. Throughout, Burnett's steady guiding hand is evident. This soundtrack is a powerful tribute not only to the time-honored but commercially ignored genres of bluegrass and mountain music but also to Burnett's remarkable skills as a producer. *—Evan Cater*

Once Upon a Time in the West / 1968 / RCA ✦✦✦✦
Arguably a milestone for both director Sergio Leone and his musical cohort Ennio Morricone. After deconstructing the classic American western by way of *The Good, the Bad & the Ugly* and *A Fistful of Dollars*, Leone distilled his intentions with 1968's *Once Upon a Time in the West.* For his part, Morricone framed Leone's meditative camera work and mythic narrative with a mix of hauntingly spacious pieces and reconfigured snatches of old-timey tunes. Just within the stretch of the first four pieces here, Morricone evokes the endless expanse of the West with a Copland-esque aria (the main title theme), weaves some twisted grit into the showdown theme with loads of guitar fuzz ("As a Judgment"), ingeniously combines whistling and a clippity-clop rhythm for a respite piece ("Farewell to Cheyenne"), and conjures the surreal end of the cowboy mythos via a wonderfully disjointed serial-style number ("The Transgression"). And whether sounding upbeat or stark, Morricone informs it all with the dry and windswept vacancy of the West. It's beautiful and stunning. *—Stephen Cook*

☆ **Once Upon a Time in the West** / Jun. 6, 1988 / Import ♦♦♦♦♦

Once upon a Time in the West [Compilation] / Dec. 14, 1999 / Disky ♦♦♦♦

No, this is not a re-recording of composer Ennio Morricone's famed soundtrack—from the movie where Henry Fonda played the most evil man in the history of the world—this is a compilation of some of his more well known themes and interludes. And like any of other thousand or two other compilations of this sort, the astute music listener is asking themselves, "Why would anybody put this stuff together on a single disc like *this*?" Or, if you are a member of the music buying public who is looking for some Morricone to have in your collection, would this be a wise choice—especially for the price? The answer to the first question would be: aesthetics. The answer to the second would be: no. The manner in which this compilation is assembled is a strategy of beauty and grace, streaming together the opening theme from the title to "Chi Mai" to "The Mission" to "Cockney's Theme" from *Once Upon a Time in America.* Move from there to "Gabriele's Oboe," from *The Mission* to the theme from *Sacco and Vanzetti*, and you are beginning to grasp the seamless methodology of the unaccredited compiler's esthetic. This is a subtly illustrative picture of Morricone as a hopeless yet tasteful romantic—and that's not even the first half. The rest follow suit and becomes a glorious symphony of mood, nuance, and texture that the composer himself would be proud of—even "The Good, the Bad, and the Ugly" is handled in this manner as it is sandwiched between "The Falls," from *The Mission*, and "Baci Dopo Il Tramonto," from *La Venexiana.* As to why it wouldn't make a good Morricone disc for the novice, it's only because it leaves too many important things off in its quest to be a segueing portrait. There are others that are far more suitable, Like Rhino's two-disc Ennio Morricone *Anthology.* But for the connoisseur, this is an entirely new way of hearing Morricone's genius, and is thus indispensable. *—Thom Jurek*

The Outlaw Josey Wales / 1976 / Warner Bros. ♦♦♦

Paint Your Wagon / 1977 / MCA ♦♦

The movie *Paint Your Wagon* was an awkward attempt to update the plot of an old stage musical by Alan Jay Lerner and Frederick Loewe, with new songs by Andre Previn and Lerner. One can guess at one inherent problem with the picture from the very notion of starring Lee Marvin and Clint Eastwood in a musical. The soundtrack is a peculiar release; in purely musical terms, it would only be of interest to dedicated fans of Harve Presnell (who performs "They Call the Wind Maria") and Anita Gordon, who acquits herself well singing Jean Seberg's part on "A Million Miles Away Behind the Door." It is Clint Eastwood and Lee Marvin, however, who do more of the singing here, and while they might not be of much interest musically, there is a certain "Golden Throats"-type allure to their songs. Neither reveals any hidden musical talents, though Eastwood does the better job of the two on his songs, particularly "I Still See Elisa." The Nitty Gritty Dirt Band also spent time working on the movie, both on camera and on the soundtrack, but their major surviving contribution is "Hand Me Down That Can O' Beans," in which they share the spotlight vocally with Lee Marvin and a male chorus; it adds nothing to their output. Harve Presnell's rendition of "They Call the Wind Maria" brings a suitably operatic approach to the piece, but it is marred by Nelson Riddle's overly busy orchestral arrangement. The original LP came with a souvenir booklet that made it an expensive release but didn't enhance its sales—*Paint Your Wagon* was a perennial cutout album. The MCA CD sounds OK, but the souvenir booklet has been consigned to history. *—Bruce Eder*

Paris, Texas / Mar. 14, 1989 / Warner Bros. ♦♦♦♦

Suggestive of both the imagery of Wim Wenders' movie *Paris, Texas* and the desert itself, Ry Cooder's score is a peaceful, poetic journey into the soul of an acoustic guitar. "Paris, Texas," "Brothers," and "Nothing Out There" open the album as meditative blends of guitar twang and scratching ambient effects. The songs move at a pretty, slow place, and the opening track sees Cooder plucking his guitar's strings and letting that sound vibrate into thin air; it's a motif that he returns to repeatedly throughout the score. There's a bit of both humor and mystery to the stillness and the echoing, edgy sound effects that crop up. "Cancion Mixteca" includes a memorable turn on vocals by Harry Dean Stanton, singing in Spanish. "No Safety Zone" is almost completely ambient in its ethics, with fleeting experimental guitar playing, as the song works more as a mood-setter than a traditional song. "I Knew These People" begins with an extended segment of dialogue from the film before Cooder's somber guitar creeps in. The effect of the dialogue makes the track a fine, artistic statement, but the moment works better in the context of the movie than as a track on an album. The dialogue comes from a scene where the characters played by Stanton and Nastassja Kinski have a particularly emotional meeting. The majority of the score is delicate and stunningly pretty. The overall sense is that Cooder was reaching for spare, emotional movements. The score is stark, quiet, and as uplifting as it is sad. Cooder makes the music sound as modern and stylish as acoustic music can sound. The album is at once alien and organic. Since "I Knew These People" includes dialogue from *Paris, Texas*, the score works best for people who have seen the movie, but it's still a powerful and immensely evocative journey for those whose experience with the material is the album alone. *—Tim DiGravina*

Pat Garrett & Billy the Kid / Jul. 13, 1973 / Columbia ♦♦♦

The soundtrack to Sam Peckinpah's film is split between instrumentals and full-fledged songs, including the repeated "Billy." This essentially is mood music, and it's quite effective on that level, but "Knockin' on Heaven's Door"—his greatest song since "John Wesley Harding"—gives the album some weight and is the main reason for purchasing the album. While the rest of the album isn't just pleasant, it's effective, conjuring images of the mythologized wild west that the film itself evokes, it still winds up being a lesser item in his catalog, despite the presence of "Knockin' on Heaven's Door." *—Stephen Thomas Erlewine*

Return of the Magnificent Seven / 1966 / Rykodisc ♦♦♦♦♦

Although Elmer Bernstein had first laid out many of the motifs of this 1966 soundtrack in the original *Magnificent Seven* film in 1960, this sequel was by no means a pointless rehash. The first soundtrack had not even been issued on album when the sequel came out, and Bernstein's score was quite similar to what had been heard on the original *Magnificent Seven.* This included the original "Magnificent Seven" theme itself, which is *the* classic western movie theme, with its sweeping strings and staccato, mariachi-influenced horn bursts. For that cut alone this soundtrack would be significant, but the rest of the work is also adept at evoking a sunblasted, melancholic Mexican atmosphere that builds dramatic orchestral tension with more subtlety than bombast. [The CD reissue has excellent photos and notes about both the film and the score.] *—Richie Unterberger*

Return of the Magnificent Seven / Feb. 24, 1998 / Rykodisc ♦♦♦♦♦

Although Elmer Bernstein had first laid out much of the motifs of this 1966 soundtrack in the original *Magnificent Seven* film in 1960, this sequel was by no means a pointless rehash. The first soundtrack had not even been issued on album when the sequel came out, and Bernstein's score was quite similar to what had been heard on the original *Magnificent Seven.* This included the original "Magnificent Seven" theme itself, which is *the* classic western movie theme with its sweeping strings, and staccato, mariachi-influenced horn bursts. For that cut alone this soundtrack would be significant, but the rest of the work is also adept at evoking a sunblasted, melancholic Mexican atmosphere that builds dramatic orchestral tension with more subtlety than bombast. The CD reissue has excellent photos and notes about both the film and the score. *—Richie Unterberger*

Ring of Fire / Oct. 10, 2000 / Bna ♦♦♦

Appropriately, the soundtrack to the rodeo circuit drama *Ring of Fire* features songs by country, country-rock, and Southern rock artists such as Andy Griggs, Rick Derringer, Waylon Jennings, and Lynyrd Skynyrd. Asleep at the Wheel's "If I Don't Get Gone," Brooks & Dunn's "Not in Kansas Anymore," Nick Lowe's "What Lack of Love Has Done," and "On My Way" by Pam Tillis and Kenny Rogers are some of the highlights from this lively, heartfelt collection. *—Heather Phares*

Rio Grande / 1993 / Varese Sarabande ♦♦♦

The Sons of the Pioneers appeared in dozens of movies, and provided music for still more films than that, but those were all low-budget B-westerns. John Ford's *Rio Grande* was the only big-budget film in which they not only provided music but appeared on camera. Victor Young wrote the main body of the score, an alternately sentimental and rousing body of music, built around richly tonal themes and dark sonorities, reminiscent of Max Steiner's work, and that music does its job of underscoring the broader action of the film very well, marred only where Young almost pushes the sentimental side a little too hard, or roots his music depicting the Indians in some obvious Hollywood movie score cliches; even the cue "Laundresses Row" has some interesting embellishments over its traditional Irish source material. The distinguishing feature here, however, is the mix of traditional songs ("I'll Take You Home Again, Kathleen," "Down By the Glen Side," "Erie Canal" etc.), numbers by Tex Owens ("Cattle Call"), Dale Evans ("Aha, San Antone"), and originals by Stan Jones, all of it sung by the Pioneers. This is some of the better work of the period for the group, if only because, as on-screen music, much of it is devoid of the over-produced, over-orchestrated sound that marred many of the group's postwar recordings for RCA Victor—it's just them, with maybe a guitar accompaniment. The quality of their singing on the Stan Jones material, and the quality of Jones' songwriting ("Yellow Stripes," "My Gal Is Purple," "Footsore Cavalry" etc.) makes one especially sorry that the Pioneers never did an album of Stan Jones songs. The quality of the reissue is excellent, the tracks sounding far cleaner and crisper than their nearly 50-year-old origins would lead one to expect. The notes, by actor Harry Carey Jr., are very thorough-he can take credit for getting Stan Jones involved in the production-though they spend more time talking about on-screen action than the music itself. *—Bruce Eder*

Rough Riders / Nov. 18, 1997 / Intrada ♦♦♦

Say what you will about *Rough Riders*, a thundering John Milius movie for TNT, the score by Peter Bernstein (with conducting and a little compositional help from dad Elmer Bernstein, who knows a few things about movies involving men, horses, and guns) is a crackling piece of work, with rousing themes, lots of forward momentum, and the odd spot of suspenseful discord. In short, a well-done score for a period adventure. Though it seems to have been written for a small orchestra (augmented very lightly by electronics), the portions of the score included on this Intrada release are still strong and resounding, with crisp highs and a tight low end. Elmer Bernstein fans, meanwhile, will definitely *not* miss the entrance of his "G-Troop Theme." *—Steven McDonald*

The Slaughter Rule / Mar. 4, 2003 / Bloodshot ♦♦♦♦

This fantastic soundtrack to an independent coming-of-age film about a young Montana football player not only includes entries from Bloodshot Records' best and brightest (Ryan Adams, Neko Case, and Blood Oranges, for example), but a beautiful and delicate score by Uncle Tupelo's Jay Farrar. Farrar's music, which is interspersed throughout the songs, is so subtle, so emotive, it effortlessly captures the feeling of driving an old car across the bleak, two-lane roads of the Midwest. This record is the sound of traveling, or dreaming of travel at least; the sound of being stuck in the same place for too long; the sound of change. From Vic Chesnutt and Freakwater's old-timey country to Ryan Adams' freewheeling "To Be Young" (arguably his best tune), *The Slaughter Rule* is one of the greatest collections of alternative country you're apt to find. Speedy West & Jimmy Bryant add an oddity with the exotic Pacific sounds of "West of Samoa" and Neko Case grabs the prize for the record's most sublime and purely powerful cut, "Porchlight." Still, it's Farrar's strange and almost surreal, rootsy instrumentals that are really breaking new ground. *—Charles Spano*

Song of the Golden West / 1958 / London ♦♦♦♦

Cyril Stapleton's *Song of the Golden West* is a concept album of sorts, imagining the American West through music. Stapleton and his orchestra perform 14 songs designed to "make a world of people nostalgic for a place and time that 99 percent of them never even knew." Standout tracks include "Home on the Range," "Indian Summer," "Pale Moon," and "On the Alamo." Entertainment onto itself, *Song of the Golden West* was designed as an evocative radio show to transport the listener back in time. As the back jacket says, "For those who wish to sit back with their eyes closed and let all the cares of the world drop away, here are all the resources that music has to offer." —*JT Griffith*

South of Heaven, West of Hell / Oct. 2, 2001 / Warner Bros. ✦✦✦✦
As country music's favorite antihero, Yoakam has built an impressive dossier as an actor in films like *Red Rock West*, *Sling Blade*, and *The Newton Boys*. *South of Heaven, West of Hell* was his poorly received debut as a writer/director. As far as the soundtrack to this ambitious film goes, there are plenty of the fine modern/vintage country tunes that Yoakam seems to produce so effortlessly. And though none stand out as classics, songs co-written with Billy Gibbons and Mick Jagger deserve a listen. But those little dialogue snippets bridging the songs add very little. They reveal nothing interesting about the film other than its obvious plot points, and don't do much on their own either. Bekka Bramlett guests on "Who at the Door Is Standing." —*John Duffy*

☆ **Spaghetti Westerns, Vol. 2** / Oct. 17, 1995 / DRG ✦✦✦✦✦
Another two-CD compilation of spaghetti Western soundtrack music, equal to the first volume of the series in its breadth and quality. With 63 tracks from 1965-1973, there's so much ground covered that it's doubtful every selection will be to every listener's liking, even if you're a big fan of the form. A lot of these were taken from films that were never released outside of Italy, and indeed over half of the material has never been previously available on recordings. One big plus is the presence of five pieces by Ennio Morricone; "The Hellbenders," his 1966 theme to the movie of the same name, is an especially irresistibly mournful gem. The rest is given over to composers like Luis Bacalov, Piero Paccioni, and Roberto Pregadio, names which are almost unknown in the U.S. It's not just for genre specialists, though. From the unbelievably blunt, poker-faced vocalizations of ham-fisted lyrics to the dramatic orchestral vistas, there's a lot of catchy, funny, and/or just plain beautiful music here, whether you enjoy for the films it was used for or not. —*Richie Unterberger*

Spaghetti Westerns, Vol. 3 / May 18, 1999 / DRG ✦✦✦✦
This double-disc collection of spaghetti western classics features moments from movies like *Blood & Guns*, *I Don't Forget—I Kill*, *A Professional Gun* and *My Name is Nobody*. Prominent Italian film composers like Ennio Morricone, Bruno Nicolai, Carlo Savina, and Luis Bacalov created some of the most evocative, moody music ever made for films when they scored movies like these. *Spaghetti Westerns, Vol. 3* is a comprehensive tribute to their talents and a great collection for film buffs. —*Heather Phares*

Treasure of the Sierra Madre / Nov. 1, 1995 / Radiola ✦✦✦✦✦

Unforgiven / 1992 / Varese Sarabande ✦✦✦✦

☆ **Urban Cowboy** / 1980 / Asylum ✦✦✦✦✦
It includes Joe Walsh, Bob Seger, Boz Scaggs, and Dan Fogelberg, so it's obviously not strictly a country album. But the soundtrack is important because it symbolizes the country trend that grew, then faded, in the early '80s (a case can be made that J.R. Ewing had a lot more influence on the fad than the film *Urban Cowboy*). Most of the country tracks here lean toward MOR. —*Tom Roland*

Urban Cowboy 2 / 1981 / Epic ✦✦✦✦

What Am I Bid? / MGM ✦✦✦

Where the Buffalo Roam / Mar. 1980 / Backstreet/MCA ✦✦✦
Neil Young's score for this film about writer Hunter Thompson (played by Bill Murray) consists of several fragmentary instrumental and vocal performances of "Home on the Range" played by an orchestra with Young on vocals, harmonica, and distorted electric guitar (amounting to less than ten minutes of music), plus a series of rock evergreens-"All Along the Watchtower" and "Purple Haze," by Jimi Hendrix, "Papa Was a Rolling Stone," by the Temptations, "Highway 61," by Bob Dylan, "I Can't Help Myself (Sugar Pie Honey Bunch)," by the Four Tops, and "Keep on Chooglin'," by Creedence Clearwater Revival. Also, Murray strangles his way through a torturous "Lucy in the Sky With Diamonds," and there is some dialogue from the film. —*William Ruhlmann*

Wild Rovers/Great Train Robbery / Memoir Classics ✦✦✦
Two of Jerry Goldsmith's better and unfairly overlooked early-'70s movie scores. *Wild Rovers*, written for Blake Edwards' most unusual Western movie of that title, is an extraordinarily beautiful Western score, making use of traditional, folk-based material wherever possible, sometimes hauntingly so (as in its title theme)—the best parts of the score compare very favorably to such Aaron Copland works as "Rodeo," and Goldsmith is very obviously having fun working with this material in his own way. "Wild Horses" alone is worth the price of the CD. *The Great Train Robbery*, by contrast, is a freewheeling adventure yarn with a score to match, the music's brisk, lighthearted nature matching the suspense of the film itself—there is much excitement and lots of musical chills here, which show Goldsmith's writing near its peak in terms of straightforward suspense. The sound is good on both scores. —*Bruce Eder*

Essays

Country Music on Film

Bound for Glory
1976
Director: Hal Ashby
Stars: David Carradine, Randy Quaid

Adapted by Robert Getchell from Woody Guthrie's autobiography, Hal Ashby's biopic portrays a few pivotal years in the life of the celebrated folksinger and social activist. In the Depression 1930s, Midwesterner Guthrie (David Carradine) plays music locally but cannot make enough as a sign painter to support his wife (Melinda Dillon) and children. With only his paintbrushes, Woody joins the migration westward from the Dust Bowl to supposedly greener California pastures via boxcar and hitchhiking. When penniless Woody is turned back from the California border, he sneaks into the state alone and meets Luther (Randy Quaid), who takes Woody to a farm where hundreds of workers scrounge for a few ill-paid harvesting jobs. When singer Ozark Bole (Ronny Cox) arrives both to entertain and to urge the workers to unionize, Woody joins Ozark in song, fleeing with him after thugs break up the assembly. He lands a job singing with Ozark on the radio, and the two become partners in union agitation. Unable to commit in his personal life as he finds his political voice, Woody brings his family west, but his wife can't tolerate Woody's wandering ways. Reluctant to sell out his ideals for a lucrative career, Woody hits the road again, bringing his songs of freedom and protest to a nationwide audience on his own terms. Opting for atmospheric storytelling over strident polemic, the filmmakers present Guthrie as a complex individual with contradictory virtues and faults. Despite critical praise and nominations for several Oscars, including Best Picture, *Bound for Glory* proved less than glorious at the box office. —*Lucia Bozzola*

Coal Miner's Daughter
1980
Director: Michael Apted
Stars: Sissy Spacek, Tommy Lee Jones

Loretta Lynn was one of the first female superstars in country music and remains a defining presence within the genre; with her strong, clear, hard-country voice and tough, no-nonsense songs about husbands who cheat and wives who weren't about to be pushed around, Lynn introduced a feminist mindset to Nashville years before the phrase "women's liberation" became common currency. *Coal Miner's Daughter* is a screen adaptation of Lynn's autobiography, starring Sissy Spacek as Loretta Lynn. One of eight children born to Ted Webb (Levon Helm), a coal miner raising a family despite grinding poverty in Butcher Hollow, KY, Loretta married Dolittle "Mooney" Lynn (Tommy Lee Jones) when she was only 13 years old. A mother of four by the time she was 20, Lynn began singing the occasional song at local honky tonks on weekends, and at 25, she cut (at Mooney's suggestion) a demo tape that earned her a deal with an independent record label. Loretta and Mooney's tireless promotion of the record (including a long road trip through the South in which they stopped at every country radio station they could find) paid off; Loretta's first single, "Honky Tonk Girl," hit the charts and earned her a spot on the *Grand Ole Opry*. Stardom called and Loretta never looked back, but success brought with it both joy (a long string of hit records and sold-out concerts and a close friendship with Patsy Cline) and sorrow (a nervous breakdown brought on by overwork and a great deal of stress to a marriage that endured; but just barely). Sissy Spacek won an Academy award for her vivid, thoroughly natural performance as Loretta (she also did her own singing), and Levon Helm (drummer for the legendary rock group the Band) made an impressive screen debut as her father. Ernest Tubb makes a cameo appearance as himself. —*Mark Deming*

Down From the Mountain
2000
Directors: D.A. Pennebaker, Chris Hegedus, and Nick Doob

For their film *O Brother, Where Art Thou?*, set in the American South during the 1930s, filmmakers Joel and Ethan Coen collaborated with musician, songwriter, and producer T-Bone Burnett to compile a score that reflected the rich variety of musical influences of the rural South during the Depression. Burnett brought together a veritable who's who of American roots music for the project, and while the film was a moderate success, the soundtrack album to *O Brother, Where Art Thou?* was a surprise hit, topping the country charts for several weeks and helping to open the ears of a new audience to the beauty and rough-hewn poetry of bluegrass, traditional country, rural blues, and gospel music. Shortly before the film's release, Burnett assembled many of the artists who appeared on the *O Brother, Where Art Thou?* soundtrack for a special concert at Nashville's Ryman Auditorium (the original home of the *Grand Ole Opry*) to benefit the Country Music Hall of Fame and Museum; the evening was filmed, and *Down From the Mountain* documents this very special night of music that celebrates America's musical past as it points to the future. Performers include Emmylou Harris, Dr. Ralph Stanley, Alison Krauss, the Cox

Family, the Fairfield Four, the Whites, Chris Thomas King, and Gillian Welch. Holly Hunter, one of the stars of *O Brother*, makes a cameo appearance, as does noted country music enthusiast Billy Bob Thornton. Songwriter, musician, and historian John Hartford served as master of ceremonies for the concert (and the film); sadly, he died after a long bout with cancer less than two weeks before *Down From the Mountain* premiered in New York and Nashville in June 2001. —*Mark Deming*

Falling From Grace
1992
Director: John Mellencamp
Stars: John Mellencamp, Mariel Hemingway, Kay Lenz

Rocker John Mellencamp both directed and starred in this drama about a well-known musician who returns to his old home town, opening a number of old wounds in the process. Bud Parks (Mellencamp) is a country-rock star who's feeling burned out after a long stretch on the road and heads back to his hometown in Indiana for some downtime with his family and old friends for the occasion of his father's birthday. But after arriving in Indiana with his wife, Alice (Mariel Hemingway), and daughter, Terri Jo (Melissa Ann Hackman), Bud gets a reminder that the Parks family is no more happy or stable than it has ever been. Bud's wealthy father, Speck (Claude Akins), is still a self-centered womanizer; Grandpa (Dub Taylor) is a foul and hateful man; and Bud's half-brother, Ramey (Larry Crane)—the result of one of Speck's many extramarital affairs—is much better adjusted than his full brother, Parker (Brent Huff), whose loyalty to Speck has turned him into a spiritless lackey. Parker also happens to be married to P.J. (Kay Lenz), who was Bud's girlfriend in high-school, and as Alice sits on the sidelines attracting the unwanted attentions of Speck, Bud finds himself falling into an affair with P.J. As he faces his own guilt and the mixed emotions of his family and friends at his return, Bud realizes he's more like his father than he ever wanted to be. Novelist and screenwriter Larry McMurtry wrote *Falling From Grace* for Mellencamp, even spending time with the singer in Indiana to get a better feel for the locations; songwriter and Mellencamp collaborator John Prine also appears and contributes to the soundtrack. —*Mark Deming*

Honeysuckle Rose
1980
Director: Jerry Schatzberg
Stars: Willie Nelson, Dyan Cannon, Amy Irving

After displaying his easygoing charm in a number of television appearances and a showy supporting role in *The Electric Horseman*, Willie Nelson scored his first leading role in this romantic comedy-drama in which he (appropriately enough) plays a musician. Buck Bonham (Nelson) is a country singer/songwriter with a loyal following in his native Texas and the neighboring Western states. However, Buck hasn't yet had the hit record that would make him a star nationwide; in the meantime, Buck and his band keep up a busy tour schedule, much to the annoyance of his wife, Viv (Dyan Cannon), and son, Jamie (Joey Floyd), who would like to see Buck at home every once in a while. As Buck wonders if he should press on with his musical career or call it quits, his close friend and long-time guitarist Garland Ramsey (Slim Pickens) announces he's retiring, and suggests a good replacement: his daughter, Lily (Amy Irving). Lily had a crush on Buck as a child, and now as a full-grown and very beautiful woman, her infatuation has only increased with time. Consequently, Buck must choose between Viv and Lily as well as his home and his career. *Honeysuckle Rose* was written specifically for Nelson, and his character bears more than a passing similarity to Willie and his life before the album *Red Headed Stranger* made him a star; the film also earned Nelson an Academy Award nomination for the film's theme song, "On the Road Again." —*Mark Deming*

Honkytonk Man
1982
Director: Clint Eastwood
Stars: Clint Eastwood, Kyle Eastwood, John McIntire

Clint Eastwood put his tough-guy image on hold for this personal project, which follows a musician taking one final chance at the big time. Red Stovall (Eastwood) is a would-be country singer who has been bouncing around the margins of the music business for years. With nowhere in particular to go, Red arrives at the failing Oklahoma farm of his sister for an extended visit, where her son Whit (Kyle Eastwood) quickly bonds with his uncle. However, it's obvious that Red is in very poor health, drinking heavily and breathing with difficulty, and when Red is invited to audition for the Grand Old Opry in Nashville, Whit tags along for the road trip to keep an eye on his ailing uncle. En route, Red and Whit are joined by Whit's grandfather (John McIntire) and another hopeful vocalist, Marlene (Alexa Kenin), who, like Red, is chasing her own dreams of stardom on the *Opry*. Clint Eastwood performed his own vocals and guitar work for Honkytonk Man, and a number of Nashville legends appear in cameo roles, including Marty Robbins, Porter Wagoner, Ray Price, Merle Travis, and Johnny Gimble. —*Mark Deming*

Living Proof: The Hank Williams Jr. Story
1983

Director: Richard Lowry

Stars: Richard Thomas

Richard Thomas stars as country music star Hank Williams Jr. in this made-for-TV biopic, based on Williams' own memoirs. Williams wasn't yet four years old when his father, the legendary country singer/songwriter Hank Williams, died en route to a show. By the time he was eight, his mother, Audrey (Allyn Ann McLerie), had put Hank Jr. on-stage, singing his father's songs as a novelty act. As a teenager, Williams was signed to a recording contract, still specializing in his father's material. Williams made a respectable living in the music business, but he longed to create a musical identity of his own. Williams' struggle to come out from under the long shadow of his father's legacy was a difficult one, and it took a prolonged bout with alcoholism, an unsuccessful suicide attempt, and a near-fatal fall while mountain climbing before Williams was able to come to terms with his father's reputation; forging a country-rock style all his own and finding success on his own terms. *Living Proof: The Hank Williams Jr. Story* also features Williams' longtime manager and friend Merle Kilgore as himself; country star Naomi Judd also makes a cameo appearance as one of Hank's many one-night romances on the road, and a 14-year-old Christian Slater plays Hank's son. —*Mark Deming*

Nashville
1975

Director: Robert Altman

Stars: Keith Carradine, Henry Gibson, Lily Tomlin

Following 24 characters through five days in the country music capital, Robert Altman's 1975 epic presents a complexly textured portrayal (and critique) of American obsessions with celebrity and power. Among the various stars, aspirants, hangers-on, observers, and media folk are politically ambitious country icon Haven Hamilton (Henry Gibson) and his fragile star protégée Barbara Jean (Ronee Blakley); Tom (Keith Carradine), a self-absorbed rock star who woos lonely married gospel singer Linnea Reese (Lily Tomlin); Sueleen Gay (Gwen Welles), a talentless waitress painfully humiliated at her first singing gig; Albuquerque (Barbara Harris), a runaway wife with dreams of stardom; nightclub owner Lady Pearl (Barbara Baxley), who reminisces about "those Kennedy boys"; single-minded groupie L.A. Joan (Shelley Duvall); vapid BBC commentator Opal (Geraldine Chaplin); and campaign guru John Triplette (Michael Murphy), who is trying to organize a concert rally for the unseen-but-always-heard populist presidential candidate-cum-demagogue Hal Phillip Walker. Everything comes to a head during a climactic concert at Nashville's replica of the Parthenon temple, as the entertainment-hungry audience is momentarily woken out of its stupor by unexpected violence, only to be lulled into a restorative singalong to "It Don't Worry Me." —*Lucia Bozzola*

Nashville Rebel
1966

Director: Jay Sheridan

Stars: Waylon Jennings, Mary Frann

Waylon Jennings stars as an up-and-coming country singer in this low-budget musical drama. Arlin Grove (Jennings) has just finished a hitch in the Army, and decides to give a career in music a shot upon returning to civilian life. Grove starts playing shows at local honky-tonks and begins to develop a reputation as an act to watch, as well as a loyal following. Grove also attracts the attention of pretty Molly Morgan (Mary Frann), and before long the two are married. Grove is approached by a manager who promises to make him a star and get him on the *Grand Ole Opry*, but it isn't until it's too late that Grove discovers he's been working with a phony. Depressed, Grove starts hitting the bottle hard, but Molly refuses to give up on her husband and arranges for him to get a prime gig in Nashville on her own. Along with Jennings in his big screen debut, *Nashville Rebel* also features vintage performances from Loretta Lynn, Faron Young, Porter Wagoner, Tex Ritter, Sonny James, and Henny Youngman. —*Mark Deming*

The Night the Lights Went Out in Georgia
1981

Director: Ronald F. Maxwell

Stars: Dennis Quaid, Kristy McNichol, Mark Hamill

A would-be Nashville star finds himself in hot water during a stay in Georgia in this drama based (very loosely) on the hit song of the same title. Travis Child (Dennis Quaid) is a country singer looking for his big break, crisscrossing the country playing honky-tonks with his younger sister (and manager), Amanda (Kristy McNichol), in tow. Travis has a bad habit of drinking too much and putting the moves on the wrong women, leaving tough-as-nails Amanda to bail him out. One night Travis runs afoul of Seth Ames (Don Stroud), the sheriff of a small Georgia town who isn't against using his fists to teach lawbreakers a lesson; thanks to Ames, Travis ends up behind bars, but Amanda is able to persuade a sympathetic state trooper, Conrad (Mark Hamill), to help raise bail. In exchange, Travis has to work off his debt as a bartender at a local watering hole (where he hopes he might get to play a few tunes for the customers), and between drawing beers and pouring shots, he meets a beautiful local girl named Melody (Sunny Johnson). However, as romance begins to bloom between them, Travis find himself in trouble again when he discovers Melody already has a boyfriend: Seth Ames. Both Dennis Quaid and Kristy McNichol do their own singing in *The Night the Lights Went Out in Georgia*, with Quaid also writing several of his character's tunes. —*Mark Deming*

O Brother, Where Art Thou?
2000

Director: Joel Coen

Stars: George Clooney, John Turturro, Tim Blake Nelson

The writing, directing, and producing team of Joel Coen and Ethan Coen created this picaresque comedy (inspired in part by Homer's *The Odyssey*) set in the Deep South during the Depression. Suave and fancy-talking Everett Ulysses McGill (George Clooney), dim-witted Delmar (Tim Blake Nelson), and easily excitable Pete (John Turturro) are serving time together on a prison chain gang. Everett knows where $1.2 million is hidden that's theirs for the taking, and the three manage to escape; however, a stranger soon warns them that they'll find treasure, but not the sort they're looking for. As Everett and his partners hit the road, they happen upon a gluttonous bible salesman, Big Dan Teague (John Goodman); meet up with Baby Face Nelson (Michael Badalucco) as he robs a bank; encounter three Sirens doing their washing; run into Everett's estranged wife Penny (Holly Hunter), who has told everyone her husband was killed in a train wreck; find themselves in the middle of a heated campaign between political boss Pappy O'Daniel (Charles Durning) and reformist candidate Homer Stokes (Wayne Duvall); and even find time to make a hit record as the Soggy Bottom Boys. Noted songwriter T-Bone Burnett helped compile the songs (combining vintage country blues tunes with originals in the same style), while Carter Burwell composed the background score. Incidentally, the title *O Brother, Where Art Thou?* is a reference to the classic Preston Sturges comedy *Sullivan's Travels*, in which a director plans to make a serious of "message picture" with that name. —*Mark Deming*

Outlaw Blues
1977

Director: Richard T. Heffron

Stars: Peter Fonda, Susan St. James

A musician discovers that there's no such thing as bad publicity when a murder charge makes him a star in this comedy-drama. Bobby Ogden (Peter Fonda) is an ex-con trying to go straight and build a career as a country & western singer. Bobby gets the opportunity to show off some of his tunes to Nashville star Garland Dupree (James Callahan), but Garland takes Bobby's best song, "Outlaw Blues," and puts his own name to it. Suddenly, Bobby's tune is a hit, with the struggling writer getting no credit (and no royalties). An understandably angry Bobby confronts Garland, and when Garland is found shot dead shortly afterward, Bobby becomes the prime suspect. Bobby is innocent, but hardly anyone believes this outside of Garland's back-up singer Tina Waters (Susan St. James). Bobby and Tina hit the road together, and the wanted man becomes an underground hero as Bobby climbs both the *Billboard* charts and the "Most Wanted" list. Peter Fonda does his own singing in Outlaw Blues, and he croons half-a-dozen tunes, including three written for the film by Hoyt Axton. —*Mark Deming*

Payday
1972

Director: Daryl Duke

Stars: Rip Torn, Anna Capri

A musician finds his life and his career jumping off the rails in this moody, intelligent drama. Maury Dann (Rip Torn) is a singer and songwriter struggling to hold onto his footing as one of the top names in country & western music. This being 1972, long before the Nashville sound had gone "mainstream," Dann has a new Cadillac and a small entourage to show for his efforts, but most of his shows are one-nighters at beer-soaked honky tonks in the Deep South. On-stage, Maury Dann comes off as a soft-hearted good ol' boy, but off the stand, Dann is a mean-spirited hell raiser with a nearly unquenchable appetite for booze, pills, and women. Over the course of a seemingly typical day and a half, Dann steals a guy's girlfriend; ditches his longtime mistress, Mayleen (Anna Capri); picks up a naïve groupie named Rosamond (Elayne Heilveil) and gives her a crash course in life on the road; fires his guitar player (and best friend) and hires a starry-eyed teenager as his replacement; tries to bribe a disc jockey with booze and free records; has a harrowing run-in with his speed-addicted mother (Cara Dunn); discovers he's missed his son's birthday by four months; and, in cahoots with his manager, Clarence (Michael C. Gwynne), fast-talks his loyal driver, cook, and gofer, Chicago (Cliff Emmich), into taking a possible murder rap. While *Payday* earned excellent reviews (particularly for Rip Torn's superb performance as Maury Dann) and a handful of awards (Daryl Duke's direction won him a citation from the National Association of Film Critics, while Don Carpenter's screenplay received a prize from the Writer's Guild of America), the film's downbeat themes made it a tough sell. However, *Payday* gained a cult following, and more than one "outlaw" country star of the 1970s has been said to claim the film was based on his own true story. —*Mark Deming*

Pure Country
1992

Director: Christopher Cain

Stars: George Strait, Lesley Ann Warren, John Doe

The big-screen debut of country singer George Strait is a familiar tale of a star returning to his roots, a route traveled the same year by John Mellencamp in *Falling From Grace* (1992). Strait plays Dusty Chandler, one of the hottest performers in country music. Dusty feels that his elaborate stage show is overwhelming his music, a suspicion confirmed one night when he forgets several bars of a chart-topping hit and his fans don't even notice. Disillusioned, Dusty tells his manager Lula (Lesley Ann Warren) and best buddy Earl (John Doe) that he's taking a break. After shaving off his beard and cutting off his ponytail, Dusty heads for the small farm town where he grew up, visiting his wise old grandmother (Molly McClure) and ending up at the ranch of the Tucker family, where nobody recognizes him. He becomes a hired hand, earning the respect of owner Ernest (Rory Calhoun) and falling in love with Ernest's daughter, Harley (Isabel Glasser), a woman determined to save the struggling spread with victory in a Las Vegas rodeo. When Dusty learns that Lula has secretly replaced him on-stage with her boyfriend (Kyle Chandler), he stages a showdown that wins Harley's affections. —*Karl Williams*

Songcatcher
2000
Director: Maggie Greenwald
Stars: Janet McTeer, Aidan Quinn

Janet McTeer follows up her Oscar-nominated performance in *Tumbleweeds* (1999) with this period melodrama set during the 1910s. Dr. Lily Penleric (McTeer), an uptight musicologist, is furious after getting denied tenure again at an elite all-male East Coast university. She promptly quits out of protest, and having nowhere else to go, she joins her sister in a remote mountain school. Her high-minded, refined ways quickly clash with the locals, yet her academic interests are peaked when she realizes that this bucolic mountain culture is thoroughly infused with music that harkens back to traditional English and Scottish folk ballads. After retrieving some tools, including a primitive recording device, from the East Coast, she sets out collecting songs. The locals react with a mixture of amusement, bafflement, and suspicion. Meanwhile, a mining company is strong-arming the impoverished residences into selling their coal-rich land for a pittance. Lily soon realizes that the culture she's seeking to preserve is quickly being torn asunder. Aidan Quinn and David Patrick Kelly also appear in this film, which was screened at the 2000 Sundance Film Festival. —*Jonathan Crow*

Songwriter
1984
Director: Alan Rudolph
Stars: Willie Nelson, Kris Kristofferson, Melinda Dillon

A good ol' boy comedy-drama, *Songwriter* flashes enough substance between the songs and the hijinks to qualify as a sometimes astute look into the darker areas of the music business. Willie Nelson plays Doc Jenkins, the title character, who conspires with longtime pal Blackie Buck (Kris Kristofferson) to turn the tables on a shady promoter, Rodeo Rocky (Richard Sarafian), who has Doc signed to a contract that is one step short of indentured servitude. Lesley Ann Warren plays Gilda, an up-and-coming country chanteuse whom Doc is tutoring. The rest of the supporting cast is a mix of veteran character players (Rip Torn, Melinda Dillon) and musicians associated with Nelson (Mickey Raphael, Bee Spears, Jody Payne, Johnny Gimble). There are also plenty of musical numbers featuring Nelson and Kristofferson (solo and duets). The musicians/actors went on to co-star in two TV movies, *A Pair of Aces* and *Another Pair of Aces*, essentially playing the same kind of good ol' boy characters, though as detectives, not songwriters. —*Tom Wiener*

Sweet Dreams
1985
Director: Karel Reisz
Stars: Jessica Lange, Ed Harris

Patsy Cline was one of the first great female stars of country music, and her best-known hits (such as "Sweet Dreams" and "Walking After Midnight") not only broadened the audience for country but brought a new sophistication to the Nashville sound. Cline was at the peak of her popularity when she died in a plane crash in 1963, and *Sweet Dreams* is a biopic which examines her life and career, with a particular focus on her troubled relationship with her second husband, Charlie Dick. Cline (played by Jessica Lange) is unhappily married and playing small-time gigs in West Virginia when she meets Dick (Ed Harris), whose charm and aggressive self-confidence catch her attention. In time, Cline leaves her husband to marry Dick, and she gives up music to focus on raising their children. But after Dick goes into the Army, Cline begins singing again, and after joining forces with manager Randy Hughes (David Clennon), Cline becomes a rising star on the country music scene. However, Cline's success fuels her self-confidence, much to Dick's annoyance, and he becomes increasingly abusive (both physically and emotionally) as she attempts to assert her independence. Rather than attempt to recreate Patsy Cline's vocals, Jessica Lange instead opted to lip-synch with Cline's original recordings. —*Mark Deming*

Tender Mercies
1983
Director: Bruce Beresford
Stars: Robert Duvall, Tess Harper, Ellen Barkin

Mac Sledge (Robert Duvall), a once-famous country & western singer, wakes up broke, alone, and hung over in a tiny Texas motel run by widowed Rosa Lee (Tess Harper). Having nowhere else to go, Sledge takes a job at the motel, and through the kindness and faith of Rosa he changes his self-destructive ways. He marries Rosa (after he's baptized at her urging) and becomes a father/pal to her son (Allan Hubbard). Given an opportunity to make a comeback, Sledge considers leaving his new family behind, but after a reunion with his own unhappy daughter (Ellen Barkin), he vows never again to ruin anyone else's life. A simple story simply told, *Tender Mercies* is a warm, persuasive tale of redemption, with Robert Duvall giving one of his finest performances. Also appearing is Betty Buckley as Duvall's ex-wife, a Dolly Parton-type country star, and Wilford Brimley as Duvall's former manager. —*Hal Erickson*

The Thing Called Love
1993
Director: Peter Bogdanovich
Stars: River Phoenix, Samantha Mathis, Sandra Bullock

A handful of up-and-coming songwriters discover that love is as difficult to navigate as the music business in this romantic comedy-drama from director Peter Bogdanovich. Miranda Presley (Samantha Mathis) is an aspiring singer/songwriter from New York City who loves country music and has decided to take her chances in Nashville, TN, where she hopes to strike it big as a musician. After arriving in the Music City after a long bus ride, Miranda makes her way to the Bluebird Café, a local watering hole with a reputation as a showcase for new talent. The bar's owner, Lucy (K.T. Oslin), takes a shine to the shy but plucky newcomer, and gives her a job as a waitress. Before long, Miranda has gotten to know a number of other Nashville transplants who are look looking to land a gig or sell a song, among them sweet and open-hearted Kyle Davidson (Dermot Mulroney), moody but talented James Wright (River Phoenix), and spunky Linda Lue Linden (Sandra Bullock). As the four friends struggle to find their place in the competitive Nashville music scene, both Kyle and James display a romantic interest in Miranda, while she finds it difficult to choose between the two. *The Thing Called Love* features cameos from a number of noted country performers, including Trisha Yearwood, Pam Tillis, Katy Moffatt, Jo-El Sonnier, and Jimmie Dale Gilmore. Sadly, *The Thing Called Love* would be best remembered as the last film actor River Phoenix completed before his death in the fall of 1993. —*Mark Deming*

Old-Time Traditional Country

For some, the mention of "old-time traditional" country music evokes images of mountain string bands and singers vacillating somewhere between quaint and prosaic to stereotypical and cartoonish; for others, it is the ground-floor of the music at its purest and most unsullied. A genre rich in oral tradition and untainted by commercial restrictions, it exists within a clear time frame (the mountain music passed around by early American settlers in Tennessee and Virginia from the late 1800s through the early '20s, when it was first recorded) before an abrupt change into country music's next phase, the rise of the radio and recording star (better known as the singing cowboy phenomenon) of the late '20s and early '30s. That it has survived into the present time is genuinely to be admired, both as the survival of a genre and as the work of a dedicated band of preservationists. And like the preservation of any other antiquated form, it is held aloft as something from another era well worth maintaining, lest something quite valuable be lost forever in the process. Yet its very name implies its self-imposed limitations, and thus ultimately mummifies its creative progress; its traditional designs are revered for what they are, yet allowed to progress no further creatively, lest they coalesce into something else entirely. Still, the music's roots have survived, and they remain very deep roots indeed.

The history of country music stretches much further back than its beginnings in the United States, and in the ballads of the British Isles are found the music's true roots. Sometimes reaching back as far as the 17th century for their point of origin, ballads such as "The Cruelty of Barbary Allen" and "The Gypsy Lad" coalesced over time into traditional folk songs better known as "Barbara Allen" and "Black Jack David," respectively. The derivatives (and their subsequent derivatives and spinoffs) of these songs served double duty, as not only topical entertainment based on the grisliest of current events but as extensions of the oral tradition from town to village. The song would consequently develop and change, taking new shape as each singer added verse and stanza before passing it on to the next songster, ultimately making it to its best-known version. "Black Jack David" had gone through at least half a dozen title and lyrical variants, with its eventual American sobriquet having ties to both Scottish and English dialects of that period, while a love ballad like "The Lass of Loch Royal" had reached an interminable 35-verse length in its English incarnation before it was eventually trimmed to a mere three-verse stanza by its arrival on American shores as "Who's Gonna Shoe Your Pretty Little Feet." Sometimes nothing more was needed in translation between cultures than a change in town for an English murder ballad like "The Wexford Girl" to assume similar American mythic folk song proportions as "The Knoxville Girl." But songs that were rife with lyrical content of death, regret, and recrimination were more than commonplace, and survived into the new world seemingly intact.

The old-timey genre comprises many sounds and styles. While the music of the Appalachian mountains—with its high and lonesome tenor vocal stylings (later the identifying aural fingerprint of bluegrass)—played its obvious role, equally pivotal were the styles of the medicine shows of Tennessee and Mississippi, the cowboy singers of Texas, and the regional variations provided by the singers and instrumentalists of Virginia, North Carolina, Louisiana, and Georgia. In the early days, performances were of a strictly family nature, for the sole enjoyment of the musician and those within immediate earshot. Songs were sung inside the home as the day's chores were being done, and this simple, unreconstructed a cappella singing brought with it countless regional variations.

The fiddle was the dominant—and only—instrument from its arrival on American shores in the 1600s, and the fiddler and singer soon became one, keeping their own highly rhythmic beat and accompaniment going between shouted verses with no other support behind them. By the mid-1800s, the fiddle was joined by the new popularity of the banjo; an instrument of entirely African-American derivation, it was cheap and easy to make, and in the 1800s was played almost exclusively by slaves and minstrel show performers. But before long it was being mainstreamed into the mountain regions and the South, where white musicians quickly adapted to it. Initially, guitars had no place within the music's confines; that quickly changed with the invention of the steel string around the turn of the century, however, and with guitars being built by Martin and Gibson that offered stronger bracing to accommodate the added string pressure, the instrument was suddenly louder, brighter, and something that could now keep up with a flailing banjo and a fiddle. Suddenly all performers embraced the instrument in droves, and by the 1920s, the guitar—along with its smaller stylistic cousin, the mandolin—had arrived.

For a music with such a long pedigree, it still took a very longtime for documentation on records, at least in its pure, unadulterated form. Recordings of songs popularized by "hill country musicians" had been going on since the turn of the century ("Soldier's Joy," a staple fiddler's piece, was recorded by the Victor Military Band, for example), but these were versions bleached of all unvarnished regional eccentricities for a mainstream audience. Make no mistake about it: This was considered fringe music of an uneducated people, and in the social climate of the Roaring Twenties, it was believed to have almost no commercial appeal. But the twin encroachments of a downturned economy and the coming of radio made the recording industry start looking for new, previously untapped markets to peddle their wares to. Jazz was emerging, and the first blues recordings were taking place; it wasn't long before country music became the third new market to be courted by the major record labels.

In 1922, Texas fiddlers Eck Robinson and Henry Gilliland strong-armed their way into a Victor recording audition in New York. More to be rid of them than anything else, the Victor engineer recorded a handful of duets and Robinson solo sides before dispatching the duo and filing the masters away. The following year, the label had reluctantly released one of the duets, "Turkey in the Straw," as a single. Meanwhile, OKeh Records had recorded the Atlanta musician Fiddlin' John Carson, who sang along with his fiddle playing, making him the first country singer ever recorded (although history notes the producer of the session thought his voice was horrendous). His first single, "The Little Log Cabin in the Lane," was released without a catalog number, the label considering it to be little more than a vanity pressing. Soon, however, both the Robinson-Gilliland duet and the Carson single had racked up impressive sales, and suddenly the mad scramble had started within the industry to record this new, strange music.

By 1927, labels were regularly sending field units down South to record the best singers and instrumentalists, issuing the results almost as fast as they could. But in the major labels' rush to record the best fiddlers and string band practitioners, a large chunk of the music's history went unrecorded. It would take folklorists working for the Library of Congress (like Alan Lomax) another decade before solo vocal and fiddle performances were documented, with the form already a hair's breadth away from extinction. But that same year, Victor sent recording supervisor (a forerunner to today's record producer) Ralph Peer down to the border town of Bristol, TN. Armed with gigantic "portable" recording equipment and two engineers, his early flyers broadcasting his impending arrival stood him in excellent stead as far as attracting new talent.

The resulting applicants for auditions came from as far afield as West Virginia, and in a space of two weeks—recording literally around the clock—Peer had amassed over 76 masters from various participants. Some, like Ernest Stoneman, the Alcoa Quartet, and the Johnson Brothers, had minimal experience in recording and were considered at least semi-professional musicians; others showed up just for the opportunity to cut a record and make a little pocket money. This brace of masters has gone down in country music history as *The Bristol Sessions*, the first major-label documentation of old-time country in a wide variety of regional strains. Although much fine music (and invaluable historical documentation) came from these recordings, there was still no defined "star" system attached to country music. Artists like Macon, Vernon Dalhart, and Robinson & Carson all sold records in appreciable quantities, but it could honestly be said that the song started the artist, and not the other way around. But with the pivotal *Bristol Sessions*, two new acts emerged that would change the face of country music forever: A.P. Carter & the Carter Family, and the Singing Brakeman, Jimmie Rodgers.

These two new recording acts—both contemporaries of each other—attacked the new music's equations from entirely different perspectives. The Carter Family were unreconstructed Appalachian hill people solidly rooted in rural church music, shape note singing, and a traditional family-style presentation. With A.P. (Alvin Pleasant) as bass singer and leader, his wife, Sara, on autoharp and lead vocals, and the tenor vocals and guitar of sister-in-law Maybelle entwining together in song, their somewhat nasal voices nonetheless established the basic outlines of country music harmonies. A.P. was also a master at taking traditional material and adapting it into new pieces, and the Carters' first hits ("Wildwood Flower," "Keep on the Sunny Side," "Bury Me Beneath the Willow," "The Storms Are on the Ocean," "Will the Circle Be Unbroken") clearly reflect how the traditional sounds and songs were mainstreamed into easily digestible performances that would fit onto one side of a black phonograph record. Provincial in both their musical and performing demeanor, their live performance posters (declaring that "this show is morally good") solidified their image as the first great country music family act, a point not lost on other similar units who came in their wake.

But it was the rise of Jimmie Rodgers that brought old-time traditional country to its zenith in popularity. Where the Carters projected an image of rigid stoicism, Rodgers was jaunty, frolicsome, and quick with a slang expression, and while the Carter Family sang hymns, Jimmie Rodgers sang the blues with gusto, abandon, and a high-pitched yodel that quickly became his vocal trademark (although the practice itself had roots that were centuries old). He made his show business pull recasting himself as "the Singing Brakeman," a jaunty tip of the cap to both his railroading roots and the exotic, colorful image it represented to mainstream America at the time. But once success quickly came with the release of his first recordings, Rodgers just as quickly shucked the railroader's dungarees (with the rare exception of a one-reel movie short made in 1929, the only filmed record of him) and took to wearing straw hats and fancy suits. He cut records—110 of them in six years—as if nothing could possibly contain him or his irrepressible spirit, and became the biggest country star of his day in a way that had strong roots in old-time traditional music while recasting it—and his image in a way that was new and cutting-edge for the time. In other words, Rodgers was the first artist to consciously promote the idea of a country singer being something more urbane than the buffoonish image of a barefoot hick, a rube ready for the taking.

There's no telling how big Jimmie Rodgers' star would have ultimately become if he wasn't facing the inescapable fact that he was dying of tuberculosis, a disease totally incurable during his lifetime. Knowing he was on borrowed time with an audience who also knew he was on borrowed time, Rodgers fortified himself with an old show business determination to keep plugging along, damn the consequences. In a final defiant

---

Music Map

Evolution of Country Music

The following is a timeline tracing the development of country music on a decade-by-decade basis from the 1920s to the 1990s. A genre's inclusion denotes that it enjoyed popularity and prevalence during that decade; an asterisk denotes the genre's first introduction.

1920s

Old-Timey	Cowboy Songs

1930s

Old-Timey	Cowboy Songs
Honky Tonk*	Western Swing*

1940s

Cowboy Songs	Honky Tonk
Western Swing	Bluegrass*

1950s

Cowboy Songs	Honky Tonk
Western Swing	Bluegrass
Nashville Sound*	Bakersfield Sound
Rockabilly*	

1960s

Honky Tonk	Bakersfield Sound
Country-Rock*	Bluegrass
Nashville Sound/Countrypolitan*	

1970s

Country-Rock	Outlaws
Countrypolitan	Country-Pop*
Southern Rock*	Progressive*
Newgrass*	

1980s

Urban Cowboy*	New Traditionalists*
Contemporary Country*	Alternative Country*
Roots Rock*	

1990s

Contemporary Country	New Traditionalists
Alternative Country	Americana*
Alternative Country-Rock	

gesture—equal parts bravado, financial insurance, sentimentalism, and hillbilly senselessness—he traveled to New York to record one last session. Racked with uncontrollable pain but determined to leave something behind for his family, Rodgers returned to his original style, just himself and his simply picked guitar accompaniment. A cot was kept in the studio for Rodgers to lay down and rest between takes, and according to legend, there was also a bucket next for him to spit blood into. Two days later, Jimmie Rodgers drowned in his own blood from a severe internal hemorrhage. In the wake of his death, the first country tribute records appeared, all of them solemnly intoning the sadness everyone felt over "The Death of Jimmie Rodgers"; within a couple of years, "the Singing Cowboy" was the rage of country music. By the time the first country music shows started appearing on radio in the mid-'30s, the music of the Appalachian mountains was already being described as "old-timey" and "traditional"—the sound of a bygone age, forever preserved.

Recommended Recordings:

Vernon Dalhart, *Ballads & Railroad Songs* (Old Homestead)
Grandpa Jones, *28 Greatest Hits* (King)
Pee Wee King, *Pee Wee King's Country Hoedown* (Bloodshot)
Bradley Kincaid, *Favorite Old-Time Songs* (King)
Dock Boggs, *His Folkways Years (1963-1968)* (Smithsonian Folkways)
The Carter Family, *In the Shadow of Clinch Mountain* (Bear Family)
Stringbean, *Old Time Pickin' and Singin'* (Starday)
Grayson and Whitter, *Grayson and Whitter: Complete Works* (Old Homestead)
Various Artists, *Anthology of American Folk Music, Vol. 1-3* (Smithsonian Folkways)
Doc Watson, *Essential Doc Watson 2* (Vanguard)
Fiddlin' John C, *Fiddlin' John C* (Rounder)
The Carter Family, *Can the Circle Be Unbroken?: Country Music's First Family* (Columbia/Legacy)

—Cub Koda

Grand Ole Opry

The longest-running broadcast in radio history, nothing is more tied to the image of country music than the institution known as the *Grand Ole Opry*. For the last 70-plus years, the highest aspiration of all country singers has been to play the *Grand Ole Opry*. It is country music's ultimate prestige gig; to be invited to stand on its stage and sing and pick means you have arrived—only the best get to play the *Opry*. For years, its alumni were the very best the genre had to offer, and to be asked to become a member was the highest honor anyone in country music could achieve. Its Saturday night broadcasts brought a rural nation together, imparting a commonality of both community and language; it gave its audience a sense of belonging. Long before cable, car phones, and faxes entered our lives, the *Grand Ole Opry* radio show let the people of a whole rural nation know that they weren't alone.

It started life both as a accident and a knockoff of another—more successful—show. In October of 1925, radio station WSM began broadcasting in Nashville. WSM was owned by National Life and Accident Insurance Company, whose slogan "We Shield Millions" became the station's call letters. WLS in Chicago had great success with their *National Barn Dance*, and WSM had lured George D. Hay from WLS to become their station director. The *Opry* had its genesis on the night of November 28, 1925, when a preacher missed his regular broadcast and Hay grabbed a local fiddler named Uncle Jimmy Thompson to fill in the dead air time. The response from listeners was swift, immediate, and overwhelmingly positive. By December 26th, the show was a regular feature of the WSM lineup, featuring Hay as MC, with Thompson and Uncle Dave Macon on banjo as its nominal cast.

The show progressed mightily in the next year, adding local musicians like the Crook Brothers, Humphrey Bate's Possum Hunters, and the African-American harmonica wizard DeFord Bailey to the regular lineup. For the first year or so of its radio life, it went by the not-so-original handle of the *WSM Barn Dance*, but one night in 1927 (following a national radio hookup of classical music and grand opera) Hay coined the name *Grand Ole Opry*, and suddenly the show had a whole new outlook that distanced it from the competition. By the early '30s, WSM had boosted its AM signal to a whopping 50,000 watts, which, on their nightly broadcasts, beamed them into 30 of the 48 states and sections of Canada. While shows like the *National Barn Dance* and *Shreveport's Louisiana Hayride* (both precursors to the *Opry*) continued on successfully, suddenly the *Opry*—and Nashville—became the hot spot for country music. The show got larger and more varied by the decade's end, with the Delmore Brothers, Pee Wee King & His Golden West Cowboys, Bill Monroe, and Minnie Pearl all becoming regular cast members.

But no one cemented the image of the *Opry*, country music, and Nashville more than Roy Acuff. Joining the show in 1938 (a year before Monroe and two years before Minnie Pearl), Acuff was a superb athlete, his baseball playing skills earning him a spring-training tryout with the New York Yankees. But a severe bout with sunstroke in 1929 put those aspirations to rest forever. He concentrated on fiddling, learning his trade as part of a medicine show that traveled the Smoky Mountains (where he was born and raised). It was show-business training you couldn't buy for a million dollars, and Acuff soaked it up like a sponge; here he learned how to work a crowd, how to do train-whistle imitations, and how to balance his fiddle on his nose. All this showmanship led to his first radio spot, on Knoxville's WROL. His backup combo was called the Tennessee Crackerjacks, but Acuff's unbridled enthusiasm with the group caused the station announcer to redub them "Roy Acuff & His Crazy Tennesseans." When they inherited a song called "The Great Speckled Bird," Acuff's emotionally charged performance was strong enough to nail them a recording contract and a chance to audition for the *Opry*. The response from the radio audience was overwhelming, and Acuff and his band—with their new, *Opry*-applied name, the Smoky Mountain Boys—quickly became synonymous with the image of the show.

Acuff's tenacity toward keeping his music mountain-influenced and down to earth cost him several bandmembers, but it proved to be his perfect forum when the show began national broadcasting over NBC in 1939. At a time when everybody wanted to be either a cowboy singer or a Western swing band, Acuff was already an anachronism, with an audience that mirrored his beliefs every note of the way. He was the first modern-day star of country music, with hit records under his belt ("Wabash Cannonball," "Wreck on the Highway," "Fireball Mail," "The Precious Jewel"), crowds of adoring fans at his personal appearances, and an overall popularity—especially with American servicemen during World War II—commensurate with pop performers like Frank Sinatra. He continued to influence and shape country music both as a music publisher (one of Nashville's first and most successful) and defender of older styles and their practitioners. His constant presence on the *Opry* assured the audience that as long as Roy Acuff was still there, certain traditions would always be in place.

The *Grand Ole Opry* grew bigger and more popular during the wartime years of the 1940s, eventually overtaking WLS' *National Barn Dance* in popularity as the country music program of choice. It stayed traditional, neither allowing drums or references to liquor on its stage. It also moved with the times, bringing such new stars into the fold as Ernest Tubb, Eddy Arnold, and, by the decade's end, the biggest of them all, Hank Williams. In early 1943 the show took up residence at the Ryman Auditorium, a huge tabernacle located in downtown Nashville. The inside of the place suited the music and the down-home image of the show perfectly. It was a big old church and virtually no attempts were made to renovate it, keeping its past alive as well. It was cold and drafty in the winter and hot as hell in the summer. It was unprepossessing and charming all at once—or, as one performer put it, "not so big, just so famous." Soon the old church would be welcoming Little Jimmy Dickens, Hank Snow, Moon Mullican, and comic Rod Brasfield to the show's roster.

Since WSM (and National Life) knew they had a good thing going with this enterprise, they protected their interests by having its cast members booked through the station's artist service bureau. One of the strictest enforcements by the *Opry* was that cast members appear a set number of Saturdays a year, giving up lucrative show dates for union scale. The first artist to leave the fold (others had been fired for missing radio broadcasts) was Eddy Arnold, who bucked the system and went on to even greater success. Although artists like Cowboy Copas, Carl Smith, and Porter Wagoner were early-'50s stars seemingly tailor-made for the show's musical makeup, the face of the *Opry* was changing. New *Opry* managers Jim Denny and Jack Stapp had wrested control of the show away from George D. Hay, as the "Solemn Old Judge" was in failing health by the early '50s. They planned to modernize the show (less mountain-style string bands, more Nudie-suited recording star singers) while clinging tenaciously to the program's etched-in-stone conservative values (no references to alcohol on-stage and no drums). The older stars had their traditional spots, with old-timers like Acuff and Hank Snow boosted up to hosting their own segments of the three-hour radio broadcast. The "give the public what they want" modernization only went so far, and the two managers missed the boat completely when rockabilly and rock & roll—themselves both clear outgrowths of country music—came to prominence in the mid-'50s. The story of Denny telling Elvis to go back to driving a truck after his lone *Opry* appearance is legendary, and while shows like the *Louisiana Hayride* welcomed the new music (and its upstart practitioners), when Carl Perkins sat atop all three music charts with "Blue Suede Shoes," his *Opry* appearance left his drummer sitting in the car, listening to the show on the radio. It would be decades before a drum set was unpacked and set up on the stage of Ryman Auditorium.

But the *Opry* was on a more youth-oriented kick, adding artists like Stonewall Jackson, Roy Drusky, Jimmie C. Newman, Charlie Louvin, Bobby Helms, Jean Shepard, and Don Gibson to its already burgeoning roster. By the late '60s, the youth movement was even more pronounced with the additions of Bill Anderson, David Houston (himself a former rockabilly artist), George Jones, Connie Smith, Jack Greene, and the woman who would become the queen of country crossover, Dolly Parton. With a fresh stable of artists and its staid traditions still firmly in place, the radio show went out every Saturday night like clockwork, establishing Nashville as country music's world headquarters and drawing tourists by the Grey Line bus full. While this massive influx of tourism bade well for the city and the industry, it spelled the end of the Ryman Auditorium. The old church—with its straight church pews for seating still in place—simply was never equipped for this many people, either in the cast or in the audience. Sometime in the late '60s, National Life stepped in and started making plans for the *Opry* to be moved to a bigger facility, the centerpiece of an amusement park to be called Opryland. The final *Grand Ole Opry* show in the Ryman was held on March 9, 1974, and without missing a beat, the inaugural broadcast from Opryland was on the air the following week. But the following decades saw the *Opry* diminish in omnipresence, weathering the onslaught of country-pop crossover artists and rock & roll's unflagging influence infiltrating through the ranks. No longer was the *Grand Ole Opry* the only game in town or the only way a country artist could truly become a big name; by the end of the 1960s, the chart-topping success of West Coast stars like Buck Owens and Merle Haggard had already proven that point.

Though its popularity stayed as high as always and tourists still flocked to Opryland from around the world, it went through yet another makeover, from cream-of-the-crop cutting-edge country to its current incarnation as a solid standard bearer of country's past and rich traditions. Finally coming to terms with its old nemesis rock & roll, the show has also dropped its restrictive booking practices, making *Opry* cast members out of many of today's superstars, with the requirement of so many appearances a year no longer keeping artists away from joining the show. Its very traditionalism has, oddly enough, attracted many of the new breed to its fold as a matter of pride and validation as well, its current membership including Vince Gill, Ricky Skaggs, Randy Travis, Alison Krauss, and Alan Jackson, with new ones coming every day. Although you can now make your fortune in country music by other means and routes, the *Grand Ole Opry* is still the ultimate prestige gig.

—Cub Koda

Singing Cowboys and Their Songs

Strictly speaking, cowboy songs—the "western" part of country & western music—should stand on their own, separate from country music. They come from a tradition far older than commercial country music, and derive from origins unique in the history of the United States. Apart from the power of their melodies and words, much of their original appeal lay in their nostalgic connection with a specific era in American history that had long since passed. The songs have been grouped with country music mostly due to the fact that the original instrumentation of the two genres was similar (acoustic guitars, fiddles, harmonicas, upright bass, and concertinas), the sentiments and orientations of both were distinctly rural (or, at least, non-urban), and some of the same people who played cowboy songs also played country songs.

The music's roots lay in the expansion of the United States, especially the migration of the white European-spawned population beyond the boundaries of the original 13 states. Before any songs surfaced that would take a lasting hold on the imagination, there were stories, legends, and folktales, some of them quite grisly. When the country moved west, the songs that people knew went west with them. The basic problem for anyone traveling west was the open space beyond the Mississippi and Missouri rivers; just getting anywhere took months. Mostly, it was music conceived to overcome loneliness—to fight the monotony, families would sing together to break up their days' unyielding routine. A song might spread one farm or ranch at a time, town by town or county by county, from saloon to saloon, getting altered along the way by bad memories and the better-or-worse musical talents that were applied to playing them. Other than that most common of instruments, the human voice, the usual means of playing this material were the most portable of instruments: guitar, banjo, harmonica, fiddle, and concertina. In the early days, spinets and upright pianos were a rarity in saloons, and anything larger than that was virtually unknown.

Cowboys constituted virtually a separate society unto themselves. Most were drifters, and they came mostly from the East or the South (after the Civil War, they even included a significant number of freed black men). They brought the music they knew with them, and it became the raw material around which the new songs of the West were built, reflecting the new surroundings and environment in which the singers were working and living. It was only at the dawn of the 20th century that anyone seemed to have thought of collecting and writing down the tunes in any serious way. It was a cowboy, N. Howard Thorp, who printed a 23-song collection called *Songs of the Cowboys* in 1908. This was followed two years later by *Cowboy Songs and Other Frontier Ballads*, edited by John A. Lomax—the same man who was to discover Leadbelly some 20 years later—a much more ambitious work containing 122 songs.

The Thorp and Lomax books sold well, but not in enormous numbers. There was little new interest in the music of the West at the time, but public fascination did grow. Ironically, all of this activity was taking place just at the time that the reality behind the songs was passing into history; by the turn of the century, the cowboy had begun to slowly fade from the West, though he never disappeared entirely. As early as 1925, Western songs had become a mainstay of radio; among the singers who recorded cowboy songs during this era were Carl T. Sprague, Harry "Mac" McClintock, Goebel Reeves (aka the Texas Drifter), and Jules Van Allen. Sprague's "When the Work's All Done This Fall" became an enormous hit in 1925, selling 900,000 copies; in 1927, McLintock's "The Old Chisholm Trail" also sold in the hundreds of thousands. California was an especially fertile land for Western groups, including Len Nash & His Country Boys, which included future Sons of the Pioneers Hugh and Karl Farr; Sheriff Loyal Underwood's Arizona Wranglers; and Jack LeFevre & His Texas Outlaws. In 1929, a young Texan named Gene Autry came to New York to try his hand at a recording career; in 1931, he had his first major hit with "That Silver-Haired Daddy of Mine."

In Hollywood, Westerns had long been a staple of the film industry, and in 1933 producer Nat Levine of Mascot Pictures began producing features starring the former silent cowboy actor Ken Maynard. In Maynard's earlier movies, the actor had sung a song or two that seemed to go over well—not only did the songs break up the tension and add variety to the movies' tempos, but the audiences seemed to like the movies better. Maynard was no singer, and Levine reasoned that if he could make a song work, then a professional singer might make even more of a difference in the popularity of a film. After a screen test, Autry and another ARC artist, comic/singer/songwriter Smiley Burnette, were brought out to Hollywood to appear in a barn dance sequence in the Maynard movie *In Old Santa Fe.*

Autry and Burnette only appeared in one scene in the film, but they proved the most popular elements in the movie. The next step was for Levine to try building an entire film around Autry. These Westerns proved a gold mine—Autry's singing, coupled with his personality in front of the cameras, drew people by the millions into theaters to see his movies, which further helped his record sales. By 1936, he was virtually unrivaled as a Western film star and had no peer as a recording artist. In the meantime, every small studio wanted to release its own series of B-Westerns. Columbia signed up ex-football star Charles Starrett as *The Durango Kid,* but Starrett didn't sing, so the studio signed up the highly popular Sons of the Pioneers to appear in his films and provide the music. The fledgling Grand National studios got Tex Ritter, and even John Wayne, still making his way in B pictures, was pressed into service in the part of the lawman Singin' Sandy, his

voice dubbed by a professional. In 1937, Autry and Republic Pictures found themselves at loggerheads over a contract dispute, and the singer failed to report for the shooting of his next scheduled film. The studio began looking for a substitute, and found one in Leonard Slye, a founding member of the Sons of the Pioneers, who made his debut as Autry's replacement in *Under Western Stars* (1937) with his new screen name, Roy Rogers. Autry's dispute with the company was settled soon after, but Republic now had two Western stars on its roster.

During World War II, Rogers continued making Westerns, while Autry joined the armed forces. By the end of the war, Rogers was the undisputed king of the movie cowboys, and Autry returned from military service to resumed his career. At the same time, a new generation of singing cowboys had come along, led by Jimmy Wakely and Rex Allen, who began their own series of B-Westerns spiced with songs. The days of the B-Western were numbered, however, by change in the population and the way that it looked at entertainment. World War II had cost Autry and Rogers much of the adult portion of their audience—the country came out of the war a lot less rural than it had gone in, and without the problems of the Great Depression to send millions of people looking for simple stories and solutions in movie theaters for a few hours at a time.

And then came television. As soon as audiences were able to stay home on Saturdays and see action films for free on TV, the attendance for B-Westerns, serials, and other low-budget film entertainment declined rapidly. Autry and Rogers, who owned their own properties (Rogers had taken legal ownership of the Roy Rogers name and all merchandising rights associated with it during the early '40s), saw the handwriting on the wall and, by the end of the 1940s, had shifted their activities to the new medium. It was here that the Western song was preserved in popular culture. While there were no singing cowboys on television after Autry's and Rogers' respective retirements in the mid-'50s, there were lots of cowboy songs around. It seemed like every late-'50s adult Western had to have a title song, and while few of these songs were hits in commercial release, all were well-known enough to keep the cowboy song alive in popular culture.

The following decades saw the deaths of many of the most important original singers of cowboy songs from the first commercial wave, including most of the founding Sons of the Pioneers. Others were on hand by then, however, to pick up the tradition. Apart from the newer generation of the Sons of the Pioneers and veteran singer/songwriters such as Johnny Western and Rex Allen Sr., younger solo artists such as ex-folksinger Ian Tyson, cosmic cowboy songster Michael Martin Murphey, established country stars like Emmylou Harris, and even Allen's son, Rex Allen Jr., carried on, and groups such as the Riders in the Sky and the Sons of the San Joachin have made entire careers singing about the West.

Recommended Recordings:
Various Artists, *When I Was a Cowboy, Vol. 1* (Yazoo)
Various Artists, *When I Was a Cowboy, Vol. 2* (Yazoo)
Various Artists, *Saddle Up!* (Rounder)
Various Artists, *The Singing Cowboys* (K-Tel)
Various Artists, *The Singing Cowboys* (CEMA)
Various Artists, *Home on the Range* (Pavilion)
Various Artists, *Silver Screen Cowboys* (Sony Music)
Various Artists, *Small Screen Cowboy Heroes* (Sony Music)
Various Artists, *Songs of the West* (Rhino)
Gene Autry, *Back in the Saddle Again* (Sony Music)
Sons of the Pioneers, *Country Music Hall of Fame Series* (MCA)
Marty Robbins, *Gunfighter Ballads* (Sony Music)
Johnny Western, *Gunfight at the O.K. Corral* (Bear Family)

—Bruce Eder

Western Swing

Western swing is the genre of country music where string band sounds mesh with jazz stylings to produce a form uniquely its own. A diverse and interesting amalgam, its form draws on everything from blues to pop tunes (complete with crooner-style vocals reminiscent of Bing Crosby) to fiddle breakdowns to jazz standards with a big-band swing beat underpinning it all. Completely southwestern in its derivation—coming from the twin musical geographical wellsprings of Texas and Oklahoma—the beginnings of the style can be traced back to one singular source point.

The group generally credited for giving the style its first creative forum was the Fort Worth-based Wills Fiddle Band, later to become the Aladdin Laddies, who even later became the Light Crust Doughboys. Not unlike bluesman Muddy Waters' famous first electric blues band—loaded with brand-name players like Little Walter who went on to stardom of their own—the Doughboys featured the twin fountainheads of this new music, fiddler Bob Wills and vocalist Milton Brown. Originally a trio (with guitarist Herman Arspiger the third member), the group started broadcasting over station WBAP by 1930, changing its name every time it changed sponsors. They also started experimenting with the music early on, especially when they played dances at the Crystal Springs Pavilion on the edge of town. The development of this musical hybrid was directly tied to the patrons' tastes and what they wanted to hear. Although old-time fiddle tunes expertly played were still great crowd-pleasers, folks in a modern-thinking metropolis like Fort Worth liked to dance to hot jazz, then the style in vogue. Wills and Brown adjusted their set list to accommodate this stylistic addition, and soon started bringing more musicians into the group with similar eclectic tastes. The seeds of a distinct style were being planted with an audience that was responding to it, thus shaping it as well.

But the next pivotal move in the music's development came when the station management at WBAP handed down the edict that the Doughboys had to give up their

Music Map

Western Swing

Influences
Jig-Dancing • Itinerant Music
(early 20th century)

Old-Time Music
Jimmie Rodgers • The Carter Family
(1920s–1930s)

Big Band Jazz
(1930s)

Early Development
Light Crust Doughboys
(1930–1933)

First Inclusion of Amplified Steel Guitar
Milton Brown & His Musical Brownies
Bob Wills & the Texas Playboys
(1934–1935)

Early Recordings
Bob Wills • Art Satherly
(1935–WWII era)

California Era
Bob Wills • Spade Cooley • Hank Penny
(1940s–mid-'50s)

Swing Revival
Merle Haggard • Asleep at the Wheel • Dan Hicks & His Hot Licks
Big Sandy & His Fly-Rite Boys
(late '60s–present)

---

appearances at Crystal Springs. Milton Brown resigned from both band and station, immediately starting up his own outfit, Milton Brown & His Musical Brownies. He landed a noontime slot on rival station KTAT and moved into the Doughboys' old slot with his new band, playing at Crystal Springs four nights a week. Brown's vision for the music was more cutting-edge—at least at first—than Wills', and he was the first to get on record, cutting an eight-song session for Bluebird in 1934. Whereas Wills was content to take older fiddle breakdowns and the like and jazz them up with the new beat, Brown would take the current hits of the day and do them up in the new hybrid string band style. Although Brown did not play an instrument, his smooth, honey-toned vocals—equal parts Crosby, Cab Calloway, and Emmett Miller—were also highly influential with other country singers.

While both bands featured the twin-fiddle sound that would become the connecting thread of Western swing, the Brownies' true secret weapon was Bob Dunn. Dunn brought the first amplified steel guitar into the genre, and although the instrument was crude by modern standards (a cheap Mexican guitar with a warped neck and a homemade pickup stuck on it), it was state-of-the-art for the time and the sounds he produced on it changed country music forever. Dunn's jazzy, hornlike leads combined with a jagged dissonance in his approach was featured front and center on all of the Brownies' records for the next year of their existence. It was a sound that sent shock waves throughout country music, and soon Wills was ordering up an amplified steel for his guitarist, Leon McAuliffe. The Brownies were seminal in the creation of several bands concocted in their own image, their influence reaching as far as Louisiana Cajun country and Alabama. The future for the band was looking extremely bright when, suddenly, Brown was killed in a car accident in April 1936. His younger brother assumed leadership of the band, but soon its key

players scattered to several territory bands (primarily Cliff Bruner's Texas Wanderers and Dunn's Vagabonds), spelling an end to this innovative outfit.

Meanwhile, up in Tulsa, OK (after moving from Fort Worth to Waco to Oklahoma City), Bob Wills had settled in at Cain's Ballroom and spent all of 1934 and 1935 almost single-handedly redefining the new form while simultaneously stretching the boundaries of acceptable country instrumentation. By now the new aggregation was called Bob Wills & His Texas Playboys, and by 1934 the group featured two fiddles, two guitars, banjo, piano, string bass, and the vocals of Tommy Duncan, a holdover from the Light Crust Doughboys. Wills hired violinist Jesse Ashlock away from Milton Brown, letting Ashlock (a disciple of jazz great Joe Venuti) play all the "hot" breaks, while he did the traditional breakdowns. Adding a trumpet, trombone, and a saxophone to this string band lineup, Wills further instructed his musicians to play jazz lines as much as possible, trying to imitate the horn section of Fletcher Henderson's band on stringed instruments. Realizing he needed a bigger beat to go with this bigger sound, Wills broke with convention (again) and became the first country band to have a drummer in it, a former Dixieland player named Smokey Dacus.

Above all, Wills was simply a superb bandleader, with a keen eye for talent and how best to utilize it. While a tough taskmaster with definite ideas about how he wanted his music played and presented, he promoted a family atmosphere within the ranks, making him someone you wanted to play your heart out for. Above all, he prized music loaded with feel, and would let mistakes slide if the groove was right. When the Texas Playboys locked into the right spirit of the selection, Wills would start shouting encouragement, usually capped off with his trademark holler of "a-ha!" He never assigned solo spots, merely pointing his fiddle bow at whoever he wanted to take it or hollering out their name a scant moment or two before they were to start. While Tommy Duncan is to commended for keeping a straight face while Wills constantly interjected nonsensical patter between his vocal lines, a quick listen to the group's *Tiffany Transcription* recording of "Are You from Texas?" proves that this wasn't always the case: No one could ever accuse the Bob Wills band of being boring or too somber in its approach.

By 1935, he had assembled his first great version of the Texas Playboys and was ready to record. At their first session, the producer—Arthur Satherly, who had cut hits on everyone from Ma Rainey to Gene Autry—admonished Wills for hollering too much, claiming it was drowning out the music. Wills was ready to yank the band out of the studio right then and there, and when Satherly tried to placate him was promptly told in so many words, "You want Bob Wills, you get Bob Wills, and Bob Wills hollers anytime he wants." Satherly let Wills follow his muse and by the second session in Chicago the following year was fully converted, letting the bandmembers play and yell their heads off. The big hit from this session was "Steel Guitar Rag," a modern-style swing tune that featured Wills' admonition, "Ah, take it away, Leon" with McAuliffe providing the rest of the fireworks. Wills kept adding more horns to the band in the late '30s and brought aboard Eldon Shamblin as electric lead guitarist and occasional arranger. The 1940s brought Wills his greatest successes on records with hits like "San Antonio Rose," "Time Changes Everything," "Corrine, Corrina," "Take Me Back to Tulsa," "Cherokee Maiden," and "Stay a Little Longer."

The Second World War broke up this configuration of the band, the draft leaving only Wills and Tommy Duncan behind. Wills reorganized the unit and moved it to California, finding an enthusiastic audience of transplanted Texans and Okies who had moved there to work in the defense plants. This proved to be the last great hurrah for Bob Wills & His Texas Playboys and for the Western swing movement as well. Hollywood had been co-opting the style for a spate of low-budget cowboy movies, using the more modern-sounding genre to "upscale" the music behind their sometimes nominal stars. Even singing cowboys like Gene Autry were augmenting their old-timey string bands with trumpet and accordions. In the wake of Wills' arrival in California, territory bands started springing up like wildfire, kicking off the entire California country movement, which reached its commercial and creative apex with the Bakersfield sound of the 1960s. The most successful of these was led by Spade Cooley (himself a transplanted Oklahoman), whose band featured vocalist Tex Williams, who would later go on to a successful solo career of his own. Wills stripped his horn section down to a single trumpet, hired the jazzy guitar of Junior Barnard and the electric mandolin of Tiny Moore, and scored his final hit in 1950 with the classic "Faded Love."

By the mid-'50s, the heyday of Western swing was over. Mirroring its decline in popularity was the decline in health and success of Bob Wills himself. The crowds got smaller, Wills kept drinking, the band got smaller, Wills kept drinking, the record companies got smaller, and Wills kept drinking until he drank himself into two heart attacks by 1962 and 1964. Five years later, he suffered a massive stroke, and spent his remaining days confined to a wheelchair. His final session, reuniting him with several of the original Texas Playboys, was organized by longtime fan Merle Haggard with Wills still cuing the soloists and hollering "a-ha!" from his wheelchair.

The music went through a renaissance of sorts in the '70s through the hippie revivalist efforts of bands like Commander Cody & the Lost Planet Airmen, Dan Hicks & His Licks, and most notably Asleep at the Wheel. Led by visionary Ray Benson, the group's sound and spirit is much more than mere revivalism and has survived numerous personnel changes to become part of the country music firmament itself. In mainstream country, the sound reverberates as well in the music of Junior Brown, George Strait, Merle Haggard, and Willie Nelson, making Western swing accessible to yet another generation of fans.

Recommended Recordings:
Bob Wills: *Anthology* (Rhino)
Milton Brown & His Musical Brownies: *Pioneer Western Swing Band* (MCA), *Cliff Bruner's Texas Wanderers* (Texas Rose)
Spade Cooley: *Spadella!: The Essential Spade Cooley* (Columbia/Legacy)
Tex Williams: *Capitol's Collector Series* (Capitol)
Merle Haggard: *A Tribute to the Best Damn Fiddle Player in the World (Or My Salute to Bob Wills)* (Capitol/Koch International)
Asleep at the Wheel: *Texas Gold* (Capitol)
Various Artists, *Hillbilly Fever, Vol. 1.: Legends of Western Swing* (Rhino)

—*Cub Koda*

Honky Tonk

One of the most enduring of all of country's myriad genres, the history of honky tonk music boasts several anomalies that make it unique. For one, the form—unlike bluegrass—is one of the few in country music that doesn't come from a "folk" background, its sound and style being almost fully a byproduct of rural people living in the cities, Southern cities though they may be. Two, while other trends have briefly dominated country music with great commercial success (countrypolitan, Western swing, etc.) only to be swept aside when public favor waned, as long as there's been a country band playing in a bar somewhere, honky tonk music has survived and—in many ways—developed and prospered.

While the first documented instance of the phrase being used goes back to a newspaper article published in 1891, the terminology didn't enter the country music vocabulary until the mid-'30s. The man responsible for bringing it to the genre was singer/songwriter Al Dexter. Dexter had operated a honky tonk in Texas since the early '30s (although he always referred to it as a tavern), but his friend and fellow songwriter James Paris turned him on to the phrase—one describing "those beer joints up and down the road"—and the

two of them parlayed it into the genre's first hit, "Honky Tonk Blues." From the very beginning, the style celebrated both the good-times inherent in the Friday payday night kick-up-your-heels experience and the wages of sin and guilt extracted from those good-times. There was no such thing in country as "cry-in-your-beer music" until honky tonk came along.

The Second World War years led to the growth and development of honky tonk music. The mood in the country, especially among the rural Southerners who had rafts of family and loved ones fighting overseas, was perfectly suited to the twin themes of celebration and sin that were part and parcel of the music. Here was a country that had every reason to celebrate—if only to cast off its wartime woes—yet couldn't really commit to wholesale revelry because of the religion-tinged guilt and despair that came as a payoff for partying too hard and too loosely.

If honky tonk didn't develop lyrically beyond those two themes, it was because it didn't really have to. There was gold aplenty in those two ideas and, not unlike the canon that there's always a new way to say "I love you" in a song, a million lyrical twists and turns to be derived from them. Whether it was just an uptempo celebration of a hillbilly Saturday night dancing a sprightly jig while getting loaded on cheap liquor or the poor average Joe with a cold one in hand lamenting his sorry lot in life, the form was elastic as all get-out. Not only did honky tonk music change the face of country music, but perhaps its greatest contribution is how it changed the face of country songwriting forever. No longer were songs about trains, dead dogs, and Mama going to get the job done anymore.

The sound of honky tonk was a break with country music's past as well. The main culprit for this change in the sound was electricity and the different, more highly evolved type of player who embraced that change. Electric instruments, still quite a new phenomenon on the music scene, started creeping into country bands and soon the sound of the amplified steel guitar became the linchpin of the honky tonk style. Bob Dunn, of Milton Brown & His Musical Brownies, was country music's first amplified steel player, and his jagged, swooping jazz-inspired lines set the pace on the new instrument. When Brown was killed in an automobile accident in 1936, the bandleadership role fell to a 20-year-old Texas fiddler named Cliff Bruner. Starting his own band, Bruner's Texas Wanderers, he soon enlisted the services of Dunn on steel guitar and pianist/singer/songwriter Moon Mullican. The Texas Wanderers took the honky tonk even further uptown, featuring numerous electric instruments in the band (including an amplified mandola, a descendant of the mandolin family) and a synergy with other Texas bands that led to further developments in the style.

Above all, they had great songs, and on September 13, 1938, the band committed to wax (literally, as magnetic tape hadn't been invented yet) the first great classic of the honky tonk genre, "It Makes No Difference Now." The tune was written by Floyd Tillman, one of country music's most successful songwriters, himself at the time a member of the Blue Ridge Playboys, another Texas band that worked the circuit with Bruner's outfit. Sung by the Texas Wanderers' guitarist, Dickie McBride, the song and performance were astounding in their simplicity and directness, tapping a raw nerve of emotion hitherto unexplored in country music. Given the state that songwriting royalty collection was in back then, Tillman sold the song outright for 300 dollars to singer Jimmie Davis, who would later turn his back on honky tonk and "lewd music" when he ran for governor of Louisiana, making the mawkish "You Are My Sunshine" his theme song. Following the mega-success of "It Makes No Difference Now" (it was the first song to be listed at number one on *Billboard*'s new country charts), Tillman left the Playboys and struck out on his own, eventually becoming a mainstay one-man hit-writing machine of the Nashville firmament.

But Nashville aside, the music in its formative years was almost entirely of Texas invention and derivation, with a few notable exceptions. Singer Buddy Jones and steel guitarist Ted Daffan called Louisiana home, but both made notable contributions to the music. Jones' songs were full of the honky tonk wild-side-of-life spirit, and while Daffan was no match for Dunn's inventive steel work, his enduring classic "Born to Lose" ensured his name in the history books forever. Mirroring the despair of wartime thoughts, "Born to Lose" was a massive hit, even during wartime shellac rationing. The only country record that outsold it in 1943-1944 was Al Dexter's "Pistol Packin' Mama," a hammy piece of lighthearted honky tonk that became a huge crossover pop hit and the first of its kind to be featured on *Your Hit Parade*, the weekly radio (and later TV) show that presented a fixed troupe of singers doing the popular songs of the day.

But no one brought a Texas-sized sensibility to the music or moved the form into its next phase more than Ernest Tubb. Originally a Jimmie Rodgers clone of the highest order, Tubb quickly found his own voice and recast it in the new sound of the Texas honky tonks. His band, the Texas Troubadors, became the model honky tonk combo, spawning several solo careers over the years. Tubb's plodding, ordinary-sounding voice became the standard that the drunk at the bar could always claim that he could sing better than while simultaneously shoveling nickels into the jukebox to play one Ernest Tubb record after another to make his point. His style never really altered or changed, and by his death in 1982 he was ensconced as one of country music's most noble and gentle figures, a true legend.

But it was the music of Hank Williams Sr. that finally gave honky tonk its true voice. One critic has opined that if it were not for Williams' volume of classic songs, the sound of honky tonk bands (with everyone taking a shot at "Your Cheatin' Heart" sooner or later) would have stopped decades ago. Certainly Williams' music—and his legend—is the ghost that still hangs over country music, held up as the icon of everything that is "pure" about the style. His music—with his band, the Drifting Cowboys, doing much to establish the integral role of each bandmember within the style's framework—was equal parts religious guilt and torment, self-pity, and recrimination, with the other side of the coin mirroring the best Saturday night party anyone could ever attend. Love, true love, was something ever elusive, something that was always lost along the way, and the ache

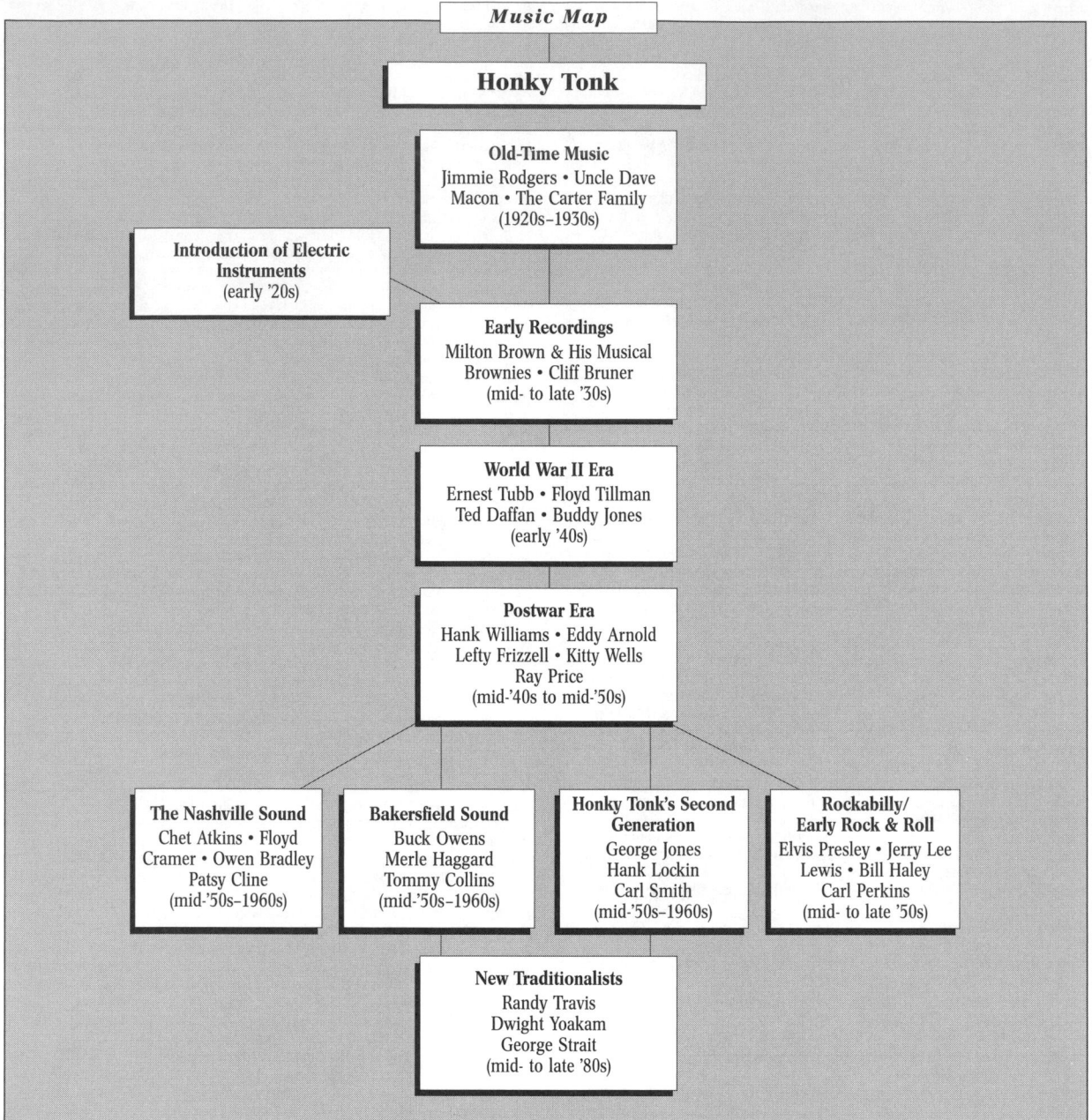

Music Map

Honky Tonk

Old-Time Music
Jimmie Rodgers • Uncle Dave
Macon • The Carter Family
(1920s–1930s)

**Introduction of Electric
Instruments**
(early '20s)

Early Recordings
Milton Brown & His Musical
Brownies • Cliff Bruner
(mid- to late '30s)

World War II Era
Ernest Tubb • Floyd Tillman
Ted Daffan • Buddy Jones
(early '40s)

Postwar Era
Hank Williams • Eddy Arnold
Lefty Frizzell • Kitty Wells
Ray Price
(mid-'40s to mid-'50s)

The Nashville Sound
Chet Atkins • Floyd
Cramer • Owen Bradley
Patsy Cline
(mid-'50s–1960s)

Bakersfield Sound
Buck Owens
Merle Haggard
Tommy Collins
(mid-'50s–1960s)

**Honky Tonk's Second
Generation**
George Jones
Hank Lockin
Carl Smith
(mid-'50s–1960s)

**Rockabilly/
Early Rock & Roll**
Elvis Presley • Jerry Lee
Lewis • Bill Haley
Carl Perkins
(mid- to late '50s)

New Traditionalists
Randy Travis
Dwight Yoakam
George Strait
(mid- to late '80s)

of it—and for it—would last a lifetime, until your dying day. Or you could just jump in your old jalopy with your honey, go into town, and order up two bowls of chili, as was his description of the hillbilly highlife in "Settin' the Woods on Fire." Either way, Hank Williams raised the level of honky tonk music—all of country songwriting, for that matter—to new artistic heights. To call his stark, lyrical work poetry would not be laying it on too thick.

Of all the honky tonkers who followed after Hank's death on New Year's Eve 1953, no one defined it better than Lefty Frizzell. With Frizzell's clear, melodic voice in stark contrast to the rough nasality of Williams and Tubb, the best of his music ("If You've Got the Money, I've Got the Time," "Always Late (With Your Kisses)") freezes a moment in time at the style's creative peak. Others contributing classics to the genre included Webb Pierce ("Slowly," "There Stands the Glass," "Back Street Affair"), Hank Thompson ("The Wild Side of Life," "A Six Pack to Go"), and Ray Price, whose rough-edged turns on tunes like "Release Me" and "Crazy Arms" would later seem at odds with his later move to pop crossover material.

It was George Jones who brought honky tonk into its next glorious phase, once again reinventing country music in the process. No country singer has ever possessed a greater voice, a better interpretation of commonplace lyrics, or a more effective means of putting those sentiments over while making the hair on the back of your neck standup. From his early Texas sides to his later overblown Nashville sides (with Billy Sherrill burying him under a sea of strings and ooh-wahing choruses), no amount of alcohol, less-than-stellar backup, mundane tunes, or overwrought production could dilute his message. That he is revered today as country music's last pure singer is testimony enough to his art. Meanwhile, in Bakersfield, CA, a new strain of honky tonk was developing, raucous and more electric (and more tied to rock & roll, '50s style), primarily pioneered by singer Wynn Stewart. Stewart would help launch the careers of Buck Owens and Merle Haggard, Bakersfield's two greatest exports of the '60s honky tonk sound. Both racked up hit after hit, and the guitar work of Don Rich with Buck's Buckaroos and Roy Nichols with Haggard's Strangers popularized the trebly Fender Telecaster as the must-have sound on any honky tonk record or bandstand. Also a noteworthy contributor to the form was the late-'60s comeback of rocker Jerry Lee Lewis, whose run of hits on the country charts was distilled from the purest of honky tonk essence.

One of the goals of the batch of new traditionalists who invaded country in the 1980s was a determination to restore the music back to its rootsier and rougher side. Part of that return fully embraced honky tonk's sound and pioneers. You could hear the new breed's nod to their heroes in their style and sound and draw straight lines back to the original source points: Randy Travis (George Jones), Dwight Yoakam (Buck Owens), George Strait (Jones and Hank Williams), and Junior Brown (Ernest Tubb). Bluegrass musician turned roadhouse rocker Marty Stuart has successfully brought the form even further into a contemporary groove while sacrificing none of the basic elements of the genre.

The chart-topping successes of Alan Jackson's "Don't Rock the Jukebox" and Stuart's "Honky Tonkin's What I Do Best" prove once again that there's always another great honky tonk song in the making and, best of all, that the form is alive and well as country music enters the 21st century.

Recommended Recordings:
Milton Brown & His Musical Brownies, *Pioneer Western Swing Band* (MCA)
Cliff Bruner, *Texas Wanderers* (Texas Rose)
Floyd Tillman, *Country Music Hall of Fame* (MCA)
Jimmie Davis, *Country Music Hall of Fame* (MCA)
Ernest Tubb, *Country Music Hall of Fame* (MCA)
Webb Pierce, *Wandering Boy* (Bear Family)
Hank Williams, *40 Greatest Hits* (Polydor)
Lefty Frizzell, *Best Of* (Rhino)
George Jones, *Best Of* (Rhino)
Jerry Lee Lewis, *The Mercury Years, Vol. 1* (Mercury)
Buck Owens, *Collection* (Rhino)
Hank Thompson, *Capitol Collector's Series* (Capitol)

—Cub Koda

Country Duos/Close Harmonies

The tradition of duet singing in country music, in all likelihood, extends back far beyond the birth of country styles. Before the dawn of the 20th century, American families would gather in their parlors, or in their churches, to sing both secular and religious tunes. These were musical family values in the purest sense, an expression of deep blood bonds, community recreation, and religious devotion.

When country music began to be recorded for commercial audiences in the 1920s and 1930s, it made sense that many of the best harmony teams tended to be from the same families. Genetics ensured that the vocal blends between brother and brother, sister and sister, brother and sister, and so forth would be more pleasing and natural than those between singers without common ancestry. Just as crucially, many harmony teams from the same family had been singing together since they were children. This gave their harmonies a deep-seated telepathy, ironed and perfected over years of experience, that would be almost impossible to develop between singers that had been raised in different households.

Not all of the great early country harmony teams were duets. The Carter Family, perhaps the most influential of all, was a trio; they were indeed all family, but they weren't even siblings. It was the Carters who would, to a large degree, be responsible for synthesizing old-time Appalachian music, gospel, and pop into early country music with wide commercial appeal. Indeed, along with Jimmie Rodgers, they were vital in the transformation of commercial country music into a vocal product, as opposed to an instrumental one.

As the commercial country market began to develop in the 1930s, brother teams in particular became popular items. It's not hard to divine the reasons for their appeal; close, tight harmonies more than doubled the impact of hearing a singer on his own, and many of the choices in their repertoire would be familiar to their audiences as traditional hymns or folk tunes. As Billy Altman writes in his liner notes to *Are You from Dixie?: Great Country Brother Teams of the 1930s*, "Certainly in no place and at no time was the country duet ever more prominent than in the southeastern United States in the 1930s. Spurred on at the close of the previous decade by both the national recording successes of the Carter Family and Jimmie Rodgers as well as the enormous rise in demand for live radio performers, countless numbers of home-trained brother teams who previously never envisioned themselves as anything more than, at best, local celebrities suddenly found themselves before far-ranging audiences."

The most notable of the brother teams to make an impact in this period were the Dixon Brothers, the Delmore Brothers, the Monroe Brothers, and the Blue Sky Boys (the last of whom were comprised of the brothers Bill & Earl Bolick). These duet teams were notable not just for their singing, but wide repertoires that encompassed gospel, sacred hymns, folk, and even blues. What's more, most of them were talented and prolific songwriters, able to draw on all of these influences to come up with something more original and slightly more modern. Backed only with guitars and other simple string instruments, the basic arrangements ensured that the emotional qualities of their singing would be at the forefront of the records. The homespun, gut-level sincerity of the harmonies—whether celebrating simple pleasures, mourning tragedies, or offering supplications to loved ones or the Almighty—have ensured that the recordings continue to appeal to contemporary listeners, despite the relatively primitive fidelity of the performances.

Two of these brother acts would have an influence that extended well beyond pre-World War II popular music. The Delmore Brothers would take the blues influence to further extremes between the mid-'40s and early '50s by adding boogie beats, harmonica, and thumping rhythms. This new kind of hillbilly music helped pave the way for the fusion of blues and country that became rockabilly, though the Delmores' contribution in this area is still underappreciated. Whether singing proto-rockabilly or sacred hymns, the Delmores always featured great harmony singing. Alton & Rabon Delmore were rarities in country music for switching high and low harmony parts from song to song, or even within the same tune.

One of the Monroe Brothers was Bill Monroe, who would become known as the father of bluegrass after World War II. In the 1930s, however, he recorded over 50 tracks with his brother Charlie before the siblings split to form separate bands in 1938. Whether or not one views bluegrass as central to the mainstream country tradition, it would be hard not to argue that bluegrass helped the duet/close harmony style survive in the 1940s and 1950s, as the focus of country music shifted toward solo singers and Western swing bands.

Bluegrass owes much of its famed "high and lonesome" qualities to the harmonic blends of the vocals, which hadn't changed much since the family recordings of the 1930s, except that now they were more professionally recorded. The most notable of these acts happened, again, to be brother teams. The Stanley Brothers were one of the most tradition-based bluegrass acts, though their instrumental approach was influenced by the more modern vision of Bill Monroe. Jim & Jesse, usually billed without any last names given, were brothers Jim & Jesse McReynolds. As Bill Malone writes in *Country Music, U.S.A.*, "If Jesse was the instrumental mainstay of the duo, Jim was the key to their heralded vocal blend. His smooth and deceptively effortless tenor was sometimes reminiscent of Ira Louvin, but without the latter's sharp edge. He was probably the least strident of bluegrass singers, and on some slow songs his voice assumed a plaintiveness that recalled the singing of Bill Bolick. Jim & Jesse brought a mellow, soft tone to bluegrass singing, and a receptivity to songs from other genres, that gave them an audience which extended well beyond the borders of their adopted musical field."

Duet harmonies weren't ghettoized to the country field. The Louvin Brothers, Charlie and Ira, owed a lot to gospel and bluegrass traditions. But they also made some effort to make their material more palatable to wider country and pop audiences, even employing Chet Atkins as electric guitarist for some sides. Johnnie & Jack (who were not relatives) also did their part to link old-time music with more modern elements.

Perhaps the most notable of the relatively few female harmony teams were the Davis Sisters, who had one huge hit, "I Forgot More Than You'll Ever Know," before Betty Jack Davis died in a car crash in 1953. Actually, the Davis Sisters were not sisters, but close friends, one of whom was actually named Mary Frances Penick. Penick changed her name to Skeeter Davis for professional services, and, after the death of Betty Jack, attempted to keep the act going for a while with Betty Jack's sister, Georgie. Skeeter would eventually find success as a solo act. The Davis Sisters' recordings owed less to old-time music or bluegrass than the more traditional older acts that had begun recording in the 1930s. Some of their sides feature a young Chet Atkins, and their most boisterous material anticipates rockabilly. Their material continues to interest listeners as early showcases for harmony singing within a relatively modern country music format.

It could be said that the brothers in the most influential country duet team weren't country singers at all. Phil & Don Everly were raised with old-time country music; their father was a respected country guitarist, and the brothers started performing professionally before their teens. Their first recordings (in 1955) were straight country music, but when they started to cut hits in 1957, they were rock & rollers. The country influence was always strong in their peerless soaring harmony vocals, though, which essentially modernized the best of Appalachian/old-time country duet singing for the pop/rock market.

The Everlys could thus be seen as the link in the chain that finally brought the magic of country harmony singing to a wide international pop audience. In the process they weren't playing country music anymore, although you could hardly say they sold out, given that they made some of the finest rock and pop records of the late '50s and early '60s. Their influence was immense on the Beatles, the Hollies, Simon & Garfunkel, and many other rock and pop acts of the last several decades that built their sound around close harmonies.

Within mainstream country music itself, duet harmony acts, family or otherwise, were becoming less prevalent. Perhaps that's due, in part, to social changes in the 20th century that were eroding the sort of family structures in which close harmony singing thrived. After World War II, families didn't gather in the parlor that often (if they had a parlor at all) to sing together. There were other distractions for providing entertainment, like television and other mass media. Instead of creating music themselves, families could turn on their radios and record players. And increased mobility meant that families were moving around more frequently and staying together for shorter periods of time, if they were staying together at all.

The duet/close harmony tradition survived, most frequently, via collaborations between male and female stars. These are too numerous to mention in a paragraph or two, but some of the most prominent of these would be Porter Wagoner-Dolly Parton, Merle Haggard-Bonnie Owens, and Conway Twitty-Loretta Lynn. George Jones likes to record duet albums, perhaps as a boost to his apparent quest to release more material than any other popular singer. His most celebrated partnerships, however, have been with Melba Montgomery and ex-wife Tammy Wynette (he also recorded little-noticed duets with pop/rock singer Gene Pitney in the mid-'60s). Male-male duets were not unknown either; Willie Nelson recorded albums with Waylon Jennings, Merle Haggard, Webb Pierce, Kris Kristofferson, and Hank Snow, though most fans would agree that Nelson's forte is solo singing, not harmonizing.

But by and large, these duets were not permanent, or even long-running, partnerships. They were side projects of celebrities whose individual careers were far more important concerns than building inspiring artistic collaborations. It would not be fair to dismiss them entirely as marketing gimmicks, but they could also not be truly compared to the

Music Map

Country Duos/Close Harmonies

Early Country Stars
The Carter family

Early Bluegrass Harmonizers
The Stanley Brothers
Jim & Jesse

Brother Teams of the 1930s
The Delmore Brothers
The Monroe Brothers
The Blue Sky Boys
The Dixon Brothers

Early '50s Harmony Teams
The Louvin Brothers • The Davis Sisters

The Everly Brothers

Male-Female Duet Partners
Porter Wagoner-Dolly Parton
Merle Haggard-Bonnie Owens
Conway Twitty-Loretta Lynn
George Jones-Melba Montgomery
George Jones-Tammy Wynette

The Nashville Sound

Commercial Country Brothers Acts
The Statler Brothers
The Gatlin Brothers

Rockabilly

Modern-Day New Traditionalists, and No Depression Country Harmony
Gram Parsons-Emmylou Harris
Dolly Parton-Emmylou Harris-Linda Ronstadt
The Judds • Ricky Skaggs & Tony Rice
Barry & Holly Tashian • Freakwater

decades-long relationships, musical and otherwise, that had built up with the best pre-1960 duet harmony teams. Some brother acts (the Statler Brothers, the Gatlin Brothers) built long-running careers, but shed some of the purity of their gospel-country roots by absorbing middle-of-the-road country-pop influences.

Close harmonies weren't entirely neglected by the commercial country market in the '80s and '90s. The Judds put a twist into the family blend by offering a mother-daughter duo (as opposed to a sibling one). They weren't a duo, but Dolly Parton, Emmylou Harris, and Linda Ronstadt came up with an interesting side project on their 1987 *Trio* album that emphasized tight harmonies.

The best close harmony recordings of recent teams have tended to originate from outside the country mainstream. Gram Parsons and Emmylou Harris began a promising vocal partnership in 1973 on Parsons' *G.P.* and *Grievous Angel* albums. Unfortunately, Parsons died in late 1973, before the collaboration could be taken any further. With hindsight, it seems doubtful that Harris would have delayed her solo career for long, but she did do enough duets with various partners to generate an entire compilation of them in 1990. While moving from bluegrass stardom to mainstream country success, Ricky Skaggs took the time to do some old-school country harmonies with Tony Rice on *Skaggs & Rice*. Of course, the high and lonesome harmonic sound survives in innumerable contemporary bluegrass recordings.

And for the most outstanding close harmony act of the alternative rock-influenced *No Depression* movement, check out the female harmonies of Freakwater, a band that reaches back into the spirit of Appalachia for its brand of country-folk. Freakwater's popularity with an underground rock audience seems to indicate that the beauty of sparsely adorned close harmony singing will always retain its appeal. Its acceptance by listeners seeking a cutting edge also seems to indicate that the more things change, the more they remain the same.

Recommended Recordings:
The Carter Family, *Country Music Hall of Fame* (MCA)
Various Artists, *Are You From Dixie?: Great Country Brother Teams of the 1930s* (RCA)
Various Artists, *Something Got a Hold of Me: A Treasury of Sacred Music* (RCA)
Various Artists, *Anthology of Country Music: Early Country Harmony 1930s* (ACM)
Various Artists, *Anthology of Country Music: Early Country Harmony 1940s* (ACM)
The Blue Sky Boys, *There'll Come a Time/Can't You Hear That Nightbird* (Blue Tone)
The Delmore Brothers, *Sand Mountain Blues* (County)
The Stanley Brothers, *Complete Columbia Recordings* (Columbia/Legacy)

Jim & Jesse, *1952-1955* (Bear Family)
The Louvin Brothers, *When I Stop Dreaming: The Best of the Louvin Brothers* (Razor & Tie)
The Davis Sisters, *Memories* (Bear Family)
The Everly Brothers, *Cadence Classics: Their 20 Greatest Hits* (Rhino)
George Jones & Melba Montgomery, *Vintage Collection Series* (Capitol)
Porter Wagoner & Dolly Parton, *The Essential Porter Wagoner and Dolly Parton* (RCA)
Gram Parsons, *G.P./Grievous Angel* (Reprise)
Ricky Skaggs & Tony Rice, *Skaggs & Rice* (Sugar Hill)
Dolly Parton, Linda Ronstadt, & Emmylou Harris, *Trio* (Warner Bros.)
The Judds, *Greatest Hits* (RCA)
Emmylou Harris, *Duets* (Reprise)
Freakwater, *Dancing Under Water* (Amoeba)

—*Richie Unterberger*

Country Comedy

Probably no form of humor has been as enduring—and constantly defiled by highbrow critics—as what is collectively known as country comedy. It covers as wide a field of genres—and the similar development of those genres—as any strain of the music itself. From gentle, homespun storytellers to outrageous cartoonish characters playing the "rube" to Southern standup comics hip enough to work north of the Mason-Dixon Line, it becomes readily apparent that comedy has been at the core of country music almost from its inception.

Comedy has always been part of the presentation in a live country appearance, whether through a few well-placed jokes by the star of the show, a straight comedy act added to the bill to provide laughs, or a baggy pants, toothless bass player in the star's backup band doing a standup turn. Country comedy is also a style of humor that is profoundly Southern in derivation and outlook, never originally intended to play to any other audience than the ones who came out to country music live performances or tuned into country radio shows. Its broadness and rural folksiness were grooved perfectly for the white Southerners who listened and laughed. The audience at a typical country music show generally consisted of straight-laced, conservative churchgoing folks who would titter at the wheeziest old punchlines, seemingly unable to distinguish between good comedy and bad. Indeed, one of the charges leveled against country comedy by its

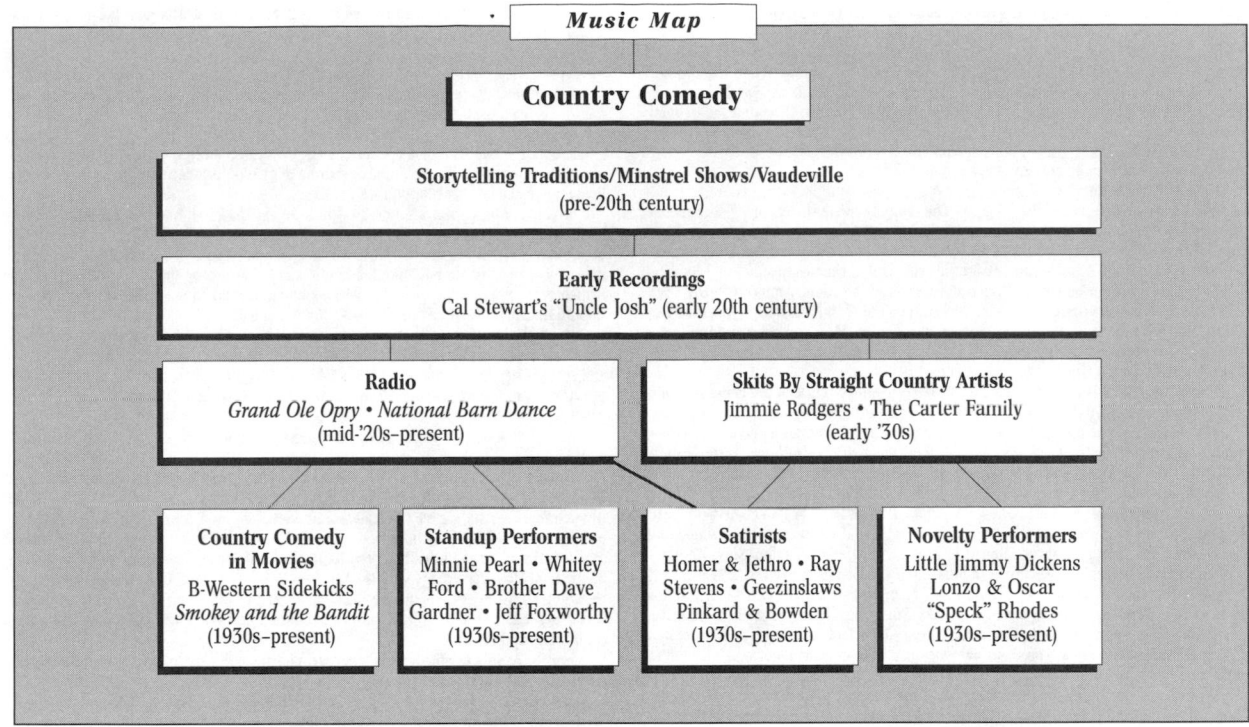

detractors is that the genre is little more than bad vaudeville jokes told with a hillbilly accent. But to be fair, that same audience in question has never been quite as square—or stupid—as its critics have made it out to be.

However, certain social and show business proprieties had to be observed if country comedians were going to work on the same show where the cast would "gather 'round the microphone and sing an old-time hymn." George Burns once asked veteran country standup Pat Buttram how he got away for years with essentially ribald material in front of audiences generally acknowledged to be living on the buckle of the Bible Belt. Buttram's answer not only drills to the essence of what fuels the genre, but provides an excellent example of it as well: "We could do anything we wanted with animals, crops, fields, outhouses, as long as we stayed out of the bedroom. Once I told the story about a husband and wife who were invited to a masquerade party. They looked around the farmhouse and found some skin and horns, so she dressed as a cow and he dressed as a bull. On the way to this party their car broke down and they decided to cut across an open pasture. They got halfway across when this old bull started charging down the hill towards them. Well, this husband and wife were really scared, and the wife said, 'What'll we do, what'll we do?' 'Well, honey,' the husband said, 'I'm gonna munch grass. You better brace yourself.'"

This folksy, good old boy approach obviously had much milder beginnings and only changed marginally over the years as social mores loosened a bit. Its documentation on record goes back to the turn of the century with Cal Stewart's very successful "Uncle Josh" series of 78s, early Southern storytelling at its best. It was certainly a broad characterization that Stewart employed, but its general easygoing style set the stage for almost everything that came afterwards.

Certainly incorporating bits of comedy into your act was the mark of a well-rounded performer, and most everybody took a stab at it at one time or another. But for those fans and historians with a taste for the surreal mixed in with their early country, they would do well to check out the comedy skit recordings of Jimmie Rodgers with the Carter Family, neither of them exactly noted for the mirth-inducing qualities of their respective musical styles. Comedy was a stretch to say the least, honestly mirrored in their clumsy and wooden delivery of even the most mundane of lines, but these recordings are an important indicator of its integral role in country music's makeup, even back then.

The rise of radio brought country music into homes nationwide, and with it a new spate of country comics. With national broadcasts like the *National Barn Dance* on WLS and WSM's *Grand Ole Opry*, country comedy entered its first popular phase. Lum & Abner was one of the new medium's most popular early series, paving the way for later movie and television "hillbilly family" comedies. The popular blackface duo Jam Up & Honey worked the *Opry* and the Southern vaudeville circuit, while the aforementioned Pat Buttram regaled audiences both on-stage and on radio. The Hoosier Hot Shots, with their appearances on *the Uncle Ezra Show* and *National Barn Dance*, also broke new ground by proving that the music itself could be played and sung in a wild and humorous way. Dorothy Shay, known as "the Park Avenue Hillbilly," played slow drawling comedic foils on a number of radio shows with hit recordings into the mid-'40s.

And of course, the movies played a substantial role in showcasing country comedy to a wider audience. Westerns were a staple of the so-called "poverty row" studios, which ground them out like sausage for Depression-era audiences starved for any form of escapism. It seemed as if every Western movie cowboy of the 1930s and 1940s had to have a funny sidekick. The best of the lot were undoubtedly Gene Autry's: Smiley Burnette and ventriloquist Max Terhune. A great female country comic of the period who scored big with audiences was Judy Canova, whose movie career took off with a series of country corn films for Republic Pictures, home to low-budget John Wayne Westerns and the like. Meanwhile, back on the radio, the *National Barn Dance* on WLS found a gold mine in the duo of Homer & Jethro, whose broad musical satires of pop tunes would keep their careers prospering well into the late '60s. Novelty material was always big with country audiences, and this niche was easily filled on the *Opry* with loud, exciting acts like Little Jimmy Dickens (Skeets McDonald also mined similar turf with tunes like "The Tattooed Lady"), Grandpa Jones, and Lonzo & Oscar. Lonzo & Oscar's secret weapon was the instrumental comedy work of their steel guitar player, Cousin Jody, who had just come from a tenure with Roy Acuff. He looked funny, he acted funny, and most interestingly of all, he played funny. While the *Grand Ole Opry* was host to some of country music's best pickers, a player like Cousin Jody was worth his weight in comedic gold. Having a player in your band who could do comedy was a distinct plus for any traveling outfit, and this role usually fell on the shoulders of the string bass player. Besides doing the standard shtick of riding the instrument like a horse, it became comedy protocol for the bassman to don the most ridiculous "rube" outfit available, black out his teeth if necessary, and make with the corn. Every major band seemed to have one of these, and certainly nobody was better at it than "Speck" Rhodes, who started in Memphis in his brother Slim's band, moving on to national prominence later with Porter Wagoner.

Meanwhile, a new batch of standups was making its presence felt on WSM's airwaves, most notably "the Gal from Grinder's Switch," Minnie Pearl. Her talents were voluminous, and Minnie could be plugged in anywhere the show needed her; she could sing, do monologues, work with another comic or singer (usually her favorite foil in two-person skits was sad sack comedian Rod Brasfield), as well as MC the whole proceedings if need be. Another comic who hit pay dirt on the *Opry* was Whitey Ford, who told old-time folksy one-liners as "the Duke of Paducah," always closing with his trademark line, "I'm going back to the wagon boys, these shoes are killin' me!"

While it's hard to imagine television legend Andy Griffith making his show business entry as a country stand-up, that's exactly what happened in the early '50s. Griffith came to national prominence with a spate of recorded standup routines, including the big hit, "What It Was, Was Football." The success of his comedy recordings secured him film work and guest shots on TV. When he portrayed a country sheriff named Andy Taylor on an episode of *the Danny Thomas Show*, his future was secured.

Probably the most important and influential country comedian of the late '50s was Brother Dave Gardner. He started as a singing drummer and, as time went on, started peppering his stage routine with more and more bits until the drums were relegated to a solo spot in his show if they were needed at all. Brother Dave's comedic approach was equal parts jazz hipster and hell-and-brimstone radio preacher wed to the then-current crop of '50s "sick" comics. His albums were extremely successful, and the early '60s found him making the rounds of all the big TV variety and talk shows. While the Duke of Paducah and his ilk worked the gymnasiums and country fairs down South, Gardner—because of his hipness—was one of the few country comedy artists (Homer & Jethro being the other) who could work to a northern audience with no dilution or change to his act. His influence was almost incalculable; one line from a Brother Dave routine would resurface years later as a complete Ray Stevens song!

But for all of Gardner's new-breed hipness, Americans still liked their country humor as broad and as corny as they could get it. The ongoing mega success of TV sitcoms like *the Beverly Hillbillies* and *Green Acres* (with veteran Pat Buttram playing a central role as Mr. Haney) drove that point home as only successful television ratings can. There was still plenty of room in country comedy for the same "rube" characterizations and good old boy one-liners, proven by the multi-decade success of the country music/comedy show *Hee Haw.* Not only did the show make national stars out of its hosts Buck Owens and Roy Clark, but brought new life to the careers of veterans Minnie Pearl, Grandpa Jones, George "Goober" Lindsay, and Archie Campbell, as well as up-and-comers like Junior Samples and rotundo singer/comedian Kenny Price.

As the '70s and '80s brought new awareness of country music to the general public, new standups emerged on the scene. Jerry Clower, an ordained minister from Louisiana, brought a proud-to-be-country aspect to his stories and found an audience for it that bridged effortlessly between young and old. Working a similar track was Justin Wilson, noted for his "Cajun Cooker" TV shows, whose impenetrable Louisiana accent made northern audiences sometimes wish he came with subtitles.

If every comic wants to play Shakespeare, then perhaps there beats a comedian's heart in many country singers as well. Autry Inman, who had cut several chart singles for Decca, issued no less than three albums of him doing straight standup. Sheb Wooley—who had played on the TV Western *Rawhide* and had a '50s novelty hit with "The Purple People Eater"—found an alter ego for himself in the personage of "Ben Colder," doing tipsy drunk parodies of country hits, while the Statler Brothers' parody of a less-than-marginally-talented country band (Lester Moran, "the Old Roadhog," & His Cadillac Cowboys) spread their tonal mayhem over a couple of albums and the occasional television appearance.

Ray Stevens started in rock & roll but over the years gravitated toward the country field, where his numerous Brother Dave Gardner-meets-Spike Jones-inspired takeoffs upped the ante in the novelty record sweepstakes. Pinkard & Bowden have also carved out a niche in this still fertile turf with their Cousin Bubba character and a run of successful song parodies based on current country hits. Novelty material still does well in the genre; witness the work of the Geezinslaw Brothers or the one-off success of Elmo & Patsy with the Christmas perennial, "Grandma Got Run Over By a Reindeer."

Virtually impossible to categorize despite the rigidness of their format, Riders in the Sky's presentation stands right on the precipice between satire and loving tribute. Certainly comedy is a large part of their stage persona, but their rhythmic drive and fine harmonies reveal serious musicianship underneath the chaps and ten-gallon hats. And of course, no mention of the current state of country comedy would be complete without a mention of Jeff Foxworthy, the young standup who parlayed his "you might be a redneck if" routine into a national catch phrase. Foxworthy has logged in a series of best-selling albums and videos, culminating with an NBC self-titled sitcom. With a new century now beginning, the state of country comedy remains very much alive and well.

Recommended Recordings:

Homer & Jethro, *America's Song Butchers: The Weird World of Homer & Jethro* (Razor & Tie)

Jerry Clower, *Jerry Clower's Greatest Hits* (MCA)

Ray Stevens, *Best of Ray Stevens* (Rhino)

Ben Colder, *Eskimos, Mean Old Queens and Little Bitty Steers* (Bear Family)

Jeff Foxworthy, *You Might Be a Redneck If…* (Warner Bros.)

Jim Stafford, *Greatest Hits* (Curb)

Geezinslaws, *World Tour* (Step One)

Minnie Pearl, *Best of Minnie Pearl* (Nashville)

Kinky Friedman, *Lasso from El Paso* (Varese)

Jerry Clower, *Live From Dollywood* (MCA)

Brother Dave Gardner, *Rejoice, Dear Hearts!/Kick Thy Own Self* (Collector's Choice Music)

Cledus T. Judd, *I Stoled This Record* (Razor & Tie)

—Cub Koda

Bluegrass

For those who value popular music at its most authentic, it may appear on the surface that no style could serve their needs as well as bluegrass. Relying mostly or entirely upon acoustic instruments, it reaches back for centuries into Appalachian and Anglo-Celtic traditions for the foundations of its sound. The vocals place a high premium upon harmony and emotional expressiveness. The lyrics are usually as down-to-earth as they come, celebrating family, the land, and the simple pleasures of life. There is also a strong religious/spiritual thread running through most of the material, even among bluegrass bands that most likely don't go to church every Sunday.

Yet upon closer examination, it's a bit of a stretch, if not ridiculous, to characterize bluegrass as an "authentic" music. Like all strains of pop music, it's drawn and bastardized from a multitude of genres. Although it's often associated with rural life and generations-old mountain traditions, in fact it's only been in existence since about World War II, and

is not even the oldest country-related sub-genre. Though it acts as a bastion of traditional musical values, it's changed and evolved over the years like everything else in modern times.

Anyone who tries to master this supposedly "simple" music knows that it can demand as much in the way of instrumental virtuosity, complex harmonics, and tricky time signatures as the most intricate jazz. At times it's spilled onto the pop charts, and indeed pop culture, whether in the incidental music to *the Beverly Hillbillies,* or the obligatory bluegrass soundtrack for B-movie car chase scenes. It's never been the most profitable sector of country music, but it's maintained a strong degree of influence on the form, and even made a noticeable impact upon rock & roll.

The roots of bluegrass were bred in (but not exclusively limited to) the Appalachian Mountains, which stretch over 1,500 miles from Quebec to Alabama. Here, even more than other areas of the South, music was a vital family and social activity. It was dominated by string instruments like the banjo, and informed by the folk traditions of the British Isles, where many of the musicians had ancestral roots. On top of the old-time "mountain music" styles came the early country music of giants like the Carter Family, the gospel music of the churches in this most religious region, and the early duos and harmony acts of country music, which were often composed of brother teams. As radio and records began to bring the region into closer contact with external influences, the musicians also became exposed to early jazz, Western swing, country blues, and Tin Pan Alley pop.

It's difficult to detect the exact origins of most pop and country styles. Not so, however, with bluegrass, in which it's easy not only to pinpoint the first bluegrass performer, but the way the music got named. The source of all bluegrass that followed, of course, was Bill Monroe, who earned the title of "father of bluegrass," and whose backup band, the Blue Grass Boys, soon gave the style a moniker of its own. Monroe made his first few records—quite a few of them, in fact—as half of one of the best brother teams in country music in the 1930s, with his brother Charlie. By 1938, he was working on his own, and he made his first recordings with the Blue Grass Boys in 1940. Over the next few years he would cultivate and popularize the style known as bluegrass. As the name infers, it was to some degree a combination of rural country and the blues, but it was a bit more complex than that.

Monroe not only established the basic string-driven, five-piece format of the bluegrass ensemble, but also made sure his bands escaped from the limited formats—namely, the C, D, and G keys—that dominated most traditional country music. The fast, rhythmic drive of his mandolin playing was clearly influenced by urban forms of jazz and blues; he made sure his bands were as disciplined as any ensemble in country, or any kind of music. He helped set the prototype for the "high, lonesome" sound that typified bluegrass vocals. That particular "high, lonesome" phrase may have become a cliché, but it does ring true to a large extent. Bluegrass singers usually need a wide range; it's hard to imagine, for instance, Johnny Cash or Kris Kristofferson tackling the music successfully.

As James Rooney writes in his biography of Monroe in the book *Bossmen,* "His singing was high and clear as a bell, his mandolin cut through on solos and supplied a driving beat behind the others, the fiddle would swing into its breaks like a frightened deer, and when they all sang together on gospel numbers, the harmonies with Bill way on top gave people the shivers. This was not just another old-time band. It was driving and together. It brought the audience up to a new level of musical experience. They instinctively recognized a special musical excellence that was part of their culture, that was theirs to share. They realized that there was more to their music than a few laughs and a whoop. It said something to them stronger and deeper than music had before. This new mixture of lonesome, blue, old-time, jazzy, religious music hit country people inside."

As Mark Humphrey observes in his liner notes to Rhino's *Appalachian Stomp* collection, when Monroe began recording for Columbia, "The old-time string band music of Appalachia was radically streamlined; it attained a tighter ensemble sound and a newly improvisational character that demanded high levels of musicianship. Complex vocal harmonies and piercing high-register leads (the high, lonesome sound) likewise became trademarks of this new music, and its effect was electrifying. In short order, hosts of Southern bands enthusiastically followed Monroe's lead."

Monroe's band is also vastly important for another reason, though it's not one that gave him much satisfaction at the time. After Monroe had established himself as a country star in the mid-'40s, two of his best sidemen—mandolinist Lester Flatt and banjo player Earl Scruggs—split to form their own phenomenally successful act. Scruggs pioneered a three-finger form of banjo playing that began to get picked up by other acts, such as Ralph Stanley, who switched from a clawhammer style to three-fingered playing after hearing Scruggs. Monroe, it seems, was unaware of just how influential his work had been; in his eyes, imitators were trying to muscle in on his territory. When Columbia signed the Stanley Brothers at the end of the 1940s, Bill was upset enough to leave for another company.

Yet by 1950, bluegrass music had gathered such a head of steam that its format was starting to become codified. In the words of Frank & Marty Godbey, writing in *The Blackwell Guide to Recorded Country Music:* "Bluegrass is an ensemble music, generally played by five or six people, using guitar, five-string banjo, mandolin, fiddle, and bass, although Dobro (a raised-string resonator guitar noted with a steel bar) and multiple fiddles are sometimes included, and an electric bass guitar occasionally replaces the acoustic bass. The delimiting characteristic of bluegrass, however, is not instrumentation but 'timing,' in which the downbeat of guitar and bass is balanced by the offbeat mandolin 'chop' and the driving roll of three-finger-style banjo. Lead singing in bluegrass is often 'high lonesome,' but varies according to the range of the singer; two or three voices combine in bluegrass harmony, usually on choruses, but frequently throughout an entire song. In bluegrass quartets, primarily of a religious nature, a vocal bassline is added. Topics of bluegrass songs may be nostalgic (home and mother, idyllic life), personalized statements

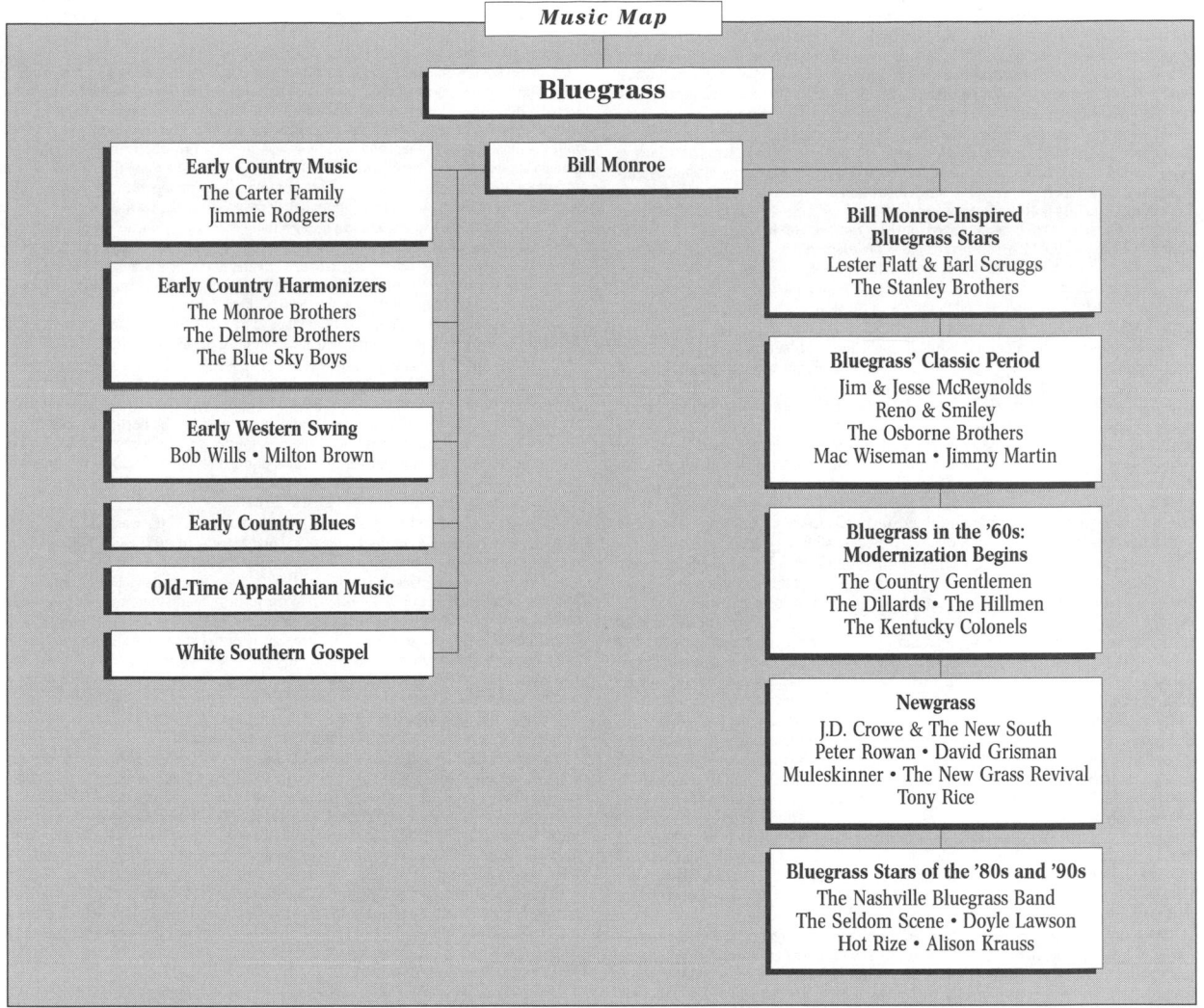

Music Map

Bluegrass

Bill Monroe

Early Country Music
The Carter Family
Jimmie Rodgers

Early Country Harmonizers
The Monroe Brothers
The Delmore Brothers
The Blue Sky Boys

Early Western Swing
Bob Wills • Milton Brown

Early Country Blues

Old-Time Appalachian Music

White Southern Gospel

**Bill Monroe-Inspired
Bluegrass Stars**
Lester Flatt & Earl Scruggs
The Stanley Brothers

Bluegrass' Classic Period
Jim & Jesse McReynolds
Reno & Smiley
The Osborne Brothers
Mac Wiseman • Jimmy Martin

**Bluegrass in the '60s:
Modernization Begins**
The Country Gentlemen
The Dillards • The Hillmen
The Kentucky Colonels

Newgrass
J.D. Crowe & The New South
Peter Rowan • David Grisman
Muleskinner • The New Grass Revival
Tony Rice

Bluegrass Stars of the '80s and '90s
The Nashville Bluegrass Band
The Seldom Scene • Doyle Lawson
Hot Rize • Alison Krauss

(love lost, love found, regret for past actions), sentimentality (death of child, sweetheart, or other loved one, broken heart), or reworking of 'murder ballads' and traditional songs."

Bluegrass would never be the majority taste of the country audience, however. More than most styles, it staunchly resisted radical modernization, which made it sound somewhat passé to some ears and radio programmers as country slowly became more urbanized in the '50s and '60s. The widespread popularity of rock & roll was another obstacle to consistent chart success for bluegrass acts, though the speed and drive of rockabilly owed a certain something to the bluegrass pioneers. The B-side of Elvis Presley's first single, in fact, was a rockabilly cover of one of Bill Monroe's biggest hits, "Blue Moon of Kentucky." Monroe was sparked by the success of this young upstart to record a rockabilly-influenced remake of the tune just a couple of months after Elvis' version had appeared on Sun Records. For the most widely known close mating between bluegrass and rockabilly, check out the Fendermen's one-shot hit version of "Mule Skinner Blues" from 1960, which was as wild as rock got during a year that found rock's very existence threatened by the onslaught of teen idols.

Bluegrass' evolution over the past five-plus decades has been slow and subtle, but the form did begin to modify from the 1950s onward. Jesse McReynolds, of the duo Jim & Jesse, developed a "cross-picking" banjo style that approximated the style of Earl Scruggs using a flat pick. Mac Wiseman established himself as bluegrass' most renowned solo singer; the Stanley Brothers built a body of original material that sounded, as much as we hate to use the word, as "authentic" as any traditional mountain tune.

The Osborne Brothers helped introduce changes in bluegrass harmonizing that gave the style more flexibility. As Bill Malone explains in his *Country Music USA:* "Most bluegrass and country groups had typically put their harmony lines above the lead singer who sang the melody. In bluegrass trio singing, for example, someone usually sang a tenor just above the lead, and another voice either sang a baritone just below the lead or went up above the tenor into what was called a high baritone. The Osborne Brothers, on the

other hand, put the two harmony voices below Bobby's high lead. They made this change in order to take advantage of Bobby's unusual tenor range and to make singing with him more comfortable for Sonny [Osborne] and Red Allen. Other bluegrass groups, though, were charmed by the style's uniqueness and found that it permitted a wider range of vocal arrangements and choice of keys."

By the 1960s, faced with the twin assaults of the Nashville sound and rock, bluegrass was becoming a pretty specialized market; a niche that, with occasional exceptions, it still occupies today. At the same time, however, the early '60s folk revival welcomed bluegrass masters onto the folk circuit, throwing a lifeline that enabled its practitioners to survive and sometimes thrive when their records weren't selling in huge quantities. There were occasional fluke bluegrass hits, like Flatt & Scruggs' "Ballad of Jed Clampett," or Eric Weissberg & Steve Mandell's "Dueling Banjos," although these usually had to ride onto the radio airwaves on the back of massive television/movie exposure ("Ballad of Jed Clampett" was the theme for *the Beverly Hillbillies*, "Dueling Banjos" was used in the popular 1972 movie *Deliverance*).

In pure musical terms, bluegrass had the image of being the most conservative of styles, yet in some respects it was more progressive than any other country micro-genre. Bands like the Country Gentlemen were opening up the bluegrass repertoire beyond old-time and country songs. The Country Gentlemen, the Dillards, and the Hillmen were among the first acts of any sort to cover Bob Dylan material, at a time when mainstream country acts wouldn't touch him (with the exception of Johnny Cash). The Hillmen's young mandolin prodigy, Chris Hillman, became the bassist for the Byrds; eventually, Kentucky Colonels guitarist Clarence White would join the same group. Buffalo Springfield drummer Dewey Martin had served a short stint in the Dillards. You could occasionally hear bits of bluegrass in straight rock bands, such as the tunes Hillman penned for the Byrds' 1967 *Younger Than Yesterday* album, "Time Between" and "The Girl With No Name." More unlikely examples include the Beatles' "I've Just Seen a Face,"

Buffalo Springfield's "Bluebird," and the Doors' bizarre bluegrass-soul concoction, "Runnin' Blue." There was even a bit of movement in the other direction, when the Dillards broadened their repertoire to such an extent that it became difficult to tag them as a bluegrass group. *Wheatstraw Suite* (1968) was certainly a triumph in illustrating just how much a bluegrass group could change with the times, although ultimately it's much more suitably categorized as a country-rock album than a bluegrass one.

Rock music would eventually have a hand in the creation of progressive bluegrass, or "newgrass," in the 1970s, not so much in actual sound as approach. Musicians such as Peter Rowan and David Grisman—who had once played together in the Boston psychedelic band Earth Opera—were not so much interested in creating a bluegrass-rock fusion as making bluegrass itself more open and diverse. These musicians were not dilettantes, even though they may have outraged purists; Rowan, for instance, had served an apprenticeship in Bill Monroe's band before broadening his scope. What "newgrass" meant was an increased tolerance for electric instrument; bluegrass covers of material from rock, blues, jazz, and other outside sources; some jam-like sense of instrumental improvisation; and the freedom to collaborate with musicians who didn't have strict traditional backgrounds.

Rowan, Grisman, and Clarence White brought the rock "supersession" vibe to their collaboration in Muleskinner, although Muleskinner's album was far more disciplined and respectful of tradition than any all-star counterpoint in the rock world. Grisman would collaborate with Jerry Garcia of the Grateful Dead, and espouse a form of "dawg" music, a jazz-influenced brand of bluegrass that, as the name implies, didn't try to take itself too seriously. A newgrass ensemble that was more influential upon the straight country scene was J.D. Crowe & the New South, a breeding ground for budding solo acts. The two most famous of these were Ricky Skaggs and the late Keith Whitley, who both went on to stardom in the straight country market. Not all Crowe alumni went in this direction; Tony Rice, for instance, has stuck to largely acoustic sounds, and teamed up with fellow Crowe vet Skaggs for a well-received duet album.

In recent decades, bluegrass has largely been confined to independent labels, college and noncommercial radio stations, and a thriving live circuit that includes several major festivals. Bluegrass is to some degree an insular culture of own, with devotees planning vacations around festivals, and aspiring musicians hanging around parking lots at bluegrass events for impromptu jam sessions and workshops where they might pick up a few pointers. The increased level of instrumental virtuosity in the bluegrass community has led to a proliferation of ensembles that have taken the musicianship to a more intense level, such as the Nashville Bluegrass Band, the New Grass Revival, and Hot Rize.

It's no use pretending that most bluegrass stakes out much territory beyond the tried and true. If diversity and adventurousness are your prime musical targets, you're better off concentrating on another field. Old-time gospel music remains a large part of most bands' repertoires, some groups (such as Doyle Lawson and Quicksilver) emphasizing this feature more than others. Other acts with broad tastes sometimes craft gospel/spiritual-only albums to attract a particular market or concentrate upon a certain aspect of their set. Stylistic bluegrass radicals, like mandolinist Niles Hokkanen—who would insert licks from Jimi Hendrix's "Purple Haze" into a cover of "Orange Blossom Special"; played in a band called the Flaming Grassholes; wrote tunes like "Help I'm Married to a Houseplant"; and once described his wilder work as sounding like a cross between Dan Hicks, Syd Barrett, and Nick Drake—are rare indeed.

Bluegrass' very conservatism, however, gives it a sturdier foundation than other minority tastes that's enabled it to survive, albeit with a low commercial profile, more readily than most other styles. It's an exciting music to watch live, for one thing, which guarantees a lot of concert work for many ensembles that sell only a few thousand records. In the 1990s, bluegrass-bred innovators like fiddler Mark O'Connor and banjoman Béla Fleck brought bluegrass sensibilities into other fields. Fleck in particular became a gadfly, moving into jazz and new acoustic music without ever entirely shedding his bluegrass roots. The mid-'90s, to the surprise of many, saw the first bluegrass-pop crossover in many a moon when fiddler Alison Krauss went into the Top Ten with *Now That I've Found You.* Though her most commercial recordings may owe as much to pop and country as bluegrass, her success was a doubly important milestone for bluegrass as a whole, as she's both one of the few performers to achieve pop stardom in the style, and one of the few female performers in a pretty male-dominated field.

Recommended Recordings:

Various Artists, *Appalachian Stomp: Bluegrass Classics* (Rhino)
Bill Monroe, *The Essential Bill Monroe (1945-1949)* (Columbia/Legacy)
Bill Monroe, *Country Music Hall of Fame* (MCA)
Flatt and Scruggs, *The Complete Mercury Sessions* (Mercury)
The Stanley Brothers, *Complete Columbia Recordings* (Columbia/Legacy)
Jim and Jesse, *1952-1955* (Bear Family)
Mac Wiseman, *The Mac Wiseman Story* (CMH)
The Osborne Brothers, *The Osborne Brothers* (Rounder)
The Country Gentlemen, *Country Songs Old and New* (Smithsonian/Folkways)
The Dillards, *There Is a Time (1963-70)* (Vanguard)
The Kentucky Colonels, *Appalachian Swing!* (Rounder)
Muleskinner, *Muleskinner* (Warner Bros.)
J.D. Crowe & the New South, *J.D. Crowe & the New South* (Rounder)
David Grisman, *The David Grisman Quintet* (Rhino)
The New Grass Revival, *Best of New Grass Revival* (Liberty)
Alison Krauss, *Now That I've Found You: A Collection* (Rounder)

—Richie Unterberger

The Nashville Sound

For some country fans, the rise of the Nashville sound in the mid-'50s signaled the end of country music's first golden age. With its sweet choruses and string sections sanding off all the rough edges in an effort to reach a crossover pop audience, the Nashville sound can also be seen as country music's first acknowledgement of the existence of a world outside of its own. The attempts to fuse pop music sensibilities to a country lilt—sometimes only the most tenuous connection to its roots was present—brought the music for the first time to audiences who had previously viewed the genre as little more than a joke. While it's commonplace nowadays to see a Garth Brooks album on top of the pop charts, this separation of marketplaces was no more in evidence than in the early '50s.

At this stage of the game, there was no such thing as crossover music; if a pop audience was going to hear Hank Williams' latest hit (which had already sold thousands of copies in the country market), they were going to hear a crooner like Tony Bennett or Frankie Laine sing it. You didn't hear "Sixteen Tons" by Merle Travis on pop radio, you heard Tennessee Ernie Ford's pop version of it. Not unlike the R&B field, country music was denied access to the big national audience (and the big money to be made from it); conversely, its traditionalism became even more entrenched as it continued preaching to the converted.

But by the mid-'50s, country music was in a bit of a tailspin. The undeniable influence of rock & roll—led by Elvis Presley, a man kicked off the stage of the *Grand Ole Opry*—had made several inroads into its core audience. Suddenly, the younger-generation country audience wanted something newer and more uptown. Some artists like Marty Robbins and Webb Pierce took a stab at the new music, while others waited for it all to blow over. But something happened in the meantime that forever changed the course of country music in how it was presented and how it was played: Crossover, handed over to country music via the success of Presley, had arrived.

Although this broader basing of the audience had its seeds in the work of Eddy Arnold and the genre-bending recordings of Les Paul and Mary Ford, 1957 and 1958 were banner years in the roots of country-pop fusion. Johnny Cash's "Ballad of a Teenage Queen," Ferlin Husky's "Gone," George Hamilton IV's "A Rose and a Baby Ruth," and Marty Robbins' "A White Sport Coat" all catered to the teenage market and met with far more success than the hardcore honky tonk sounds that were still topping the country charts. By the late '50s, the sound of a fiddle sawing away or the keening wail of a steel guitar could barely be heard on mainstream country records. If an "authentic" country record was going to crash the upper regions of the pop charts, it would be more on the order of novelty tunes like Johnny Horton's "Battle of New Orleans" or Stonewall Jackson's "Waterloo," hillbilly singalongs fortified with a big beat. In the meantime, the sound of country records was becoming more and more homogeneous.

This pasteurization of the music had a lot to do with Nashville's emergence as the center of the country music universe. All of the major labels had offices there, all of the important studios, producers, and song publishers were there, and the *Grand Ole Opry* was still an omnipresent figure in dictating the pecking order in the genre's star system. Also important was the rise to prominence of Nashville session players, musicians who didn't tour with regular bands and seldom recorded under their own names. By the mid-'50s there was a solid core of reliable players who were used on almost every session, regardless of label affiliation or stylistic diversions. A great many of these players possessed talents that were far beyond the scope of what they were laying down behind country artists, and several of them indeed had inclinations toward jazz and smoother sounds. If Nashville was going to become a part of the big mainstream music picture, somebody was going to have to do something.

One picker who was in a position to do something was guitarist Chet Atkins. A guitarist with chops to spare and a wide range of musical tastes running from the Carter Family to jazz to classical, Atkins had risen to prominence both as a session player and as a solo recording artist. By 1957, his profile as a link to these musicians and as a forward-thinking individual led to his installation as chief of RCA Victor's country division in Nashville. Atkins set out to create a style that would still preserve some elements of country music while simultaneously removing all lyrical references to rural life and any hard twang still present in the sound. A group of players with whom he would often jam in *Printer's Alley*—Floyd Cramer on piano, Buddy Harman on drums, Bob Moore on bass, and Boots Randolph on tenor saxophone—would end up on the majority of sessions cut in what was now beginning to be known as "Music City, U.S.A." Also moving things along in a similar direction was the work of producer and studio owner Owen Bradley. Working almost exclusively with Decca artists, Bradley's sharp ear for sonics, great players (guitarists Hank Garland, Grady Martin, Ray Edenton, and pianist Hargus "Pig" Robbins were first-call regulars on his sessions), and commercial sounds helped to move country into this new style. The ultimate in sweetening came with the vocal choruses added to so many of these sessions by groups like the Anita Kerr Singers and the Jordanaires, who edged the music closer to mainstream pop with every breath.

Both Atkins and Bradley found that this new synthesis was just the ticket in reaping a bigger market share for the music, and many RCA Victor and Decca artists were plugged into the new machine. But the Nashville sound was only accessible to singers who could adapt to the sound; Atkins brought pop success to singers like Don Gibson ("Oh Lonesome Me" and "I Can't Stop Loving You"), Skeeter Davis ("The End of the World"), the Browns ("Three Bells"), and, most significantly, Jim Reeves, who managed to hit the inside corner of the plate with every release and simultaneously appealed to both pop and country audiences. Bradley was making similar inroads with his recasting of big-voiced honky tonk singer Patsy Cline into a pop hitmaking machine, changing the role of women in country music forever. Another artist eminently qualified to take on the new music was Marty Robbins, whose countrypolitan stylings served him in good stead right up until his death in 1983.

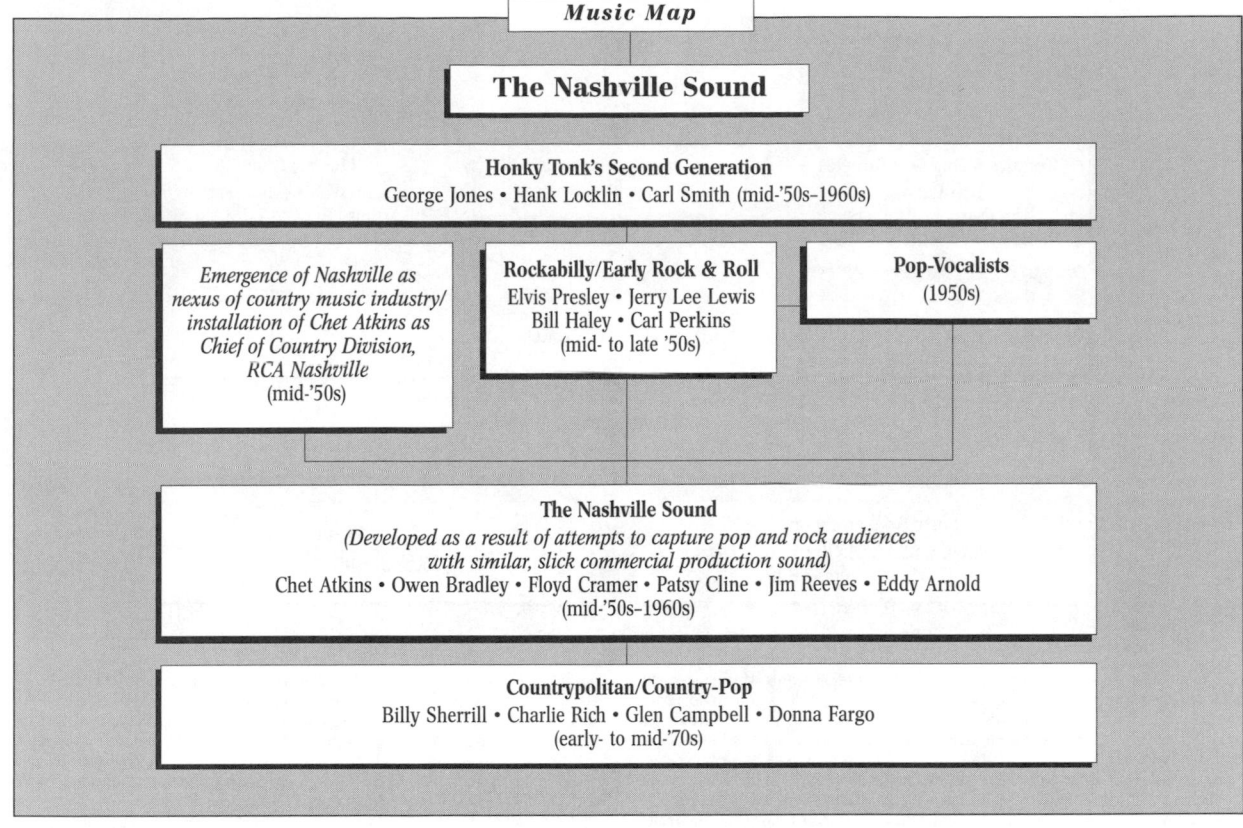

Music Map

The Nashville Sound

Honky Tonk's Second Generation
George Jones • Hank Locklin • Carl Smith (mid-'50s–1960s)

Emergence of Nashville as nexus of country music industry/ installation of Chet Atkins as Chief of Country Division, RCA Nashville (mid-'50s)

Rockabilly/Early Rock & Roll
Elvis Presley • Jerry Lee Lewis
Bill Haley • Carl Perkins
(mid- to late '50s)

Pop-Vocalists
(1950s)

The Nashville Sound
(Developed as a result of attempts to capture pop and rock audiences with similar, slick commercial production sound)
Chet Atkins • Owen Bradley • Floyd Cramer • Patsy Cline • Jim Reeves • Eddy Arnold
(mid-'50s–1960s)

Countrypolitan/Country-Pop
Billy Sherrill • Charlie Rich • Glen Campbell • Donna Fargo
(early- to mid-'70s)

But not everyone in Nashville approved of these stylistic changes. There was a backlash in the country community—both with its core audience and the older performers— and the battle lines were drawn. While a former honky tonker like Ray Price was now standing in front of an orchestra with a string section, older artists like Porter Wagoner made only marginal concessions to the style, seeing the Nashville sound as an artistic compromise necessary for making records. Meanwhile, the Texas-California contingent— who had moved the music forward in the previous decade with the birth of Western swing—was developing its own strain of honky tonk music that would soon signal the line where hard country started and countrypolitan ended. Honky tonker Buck Owens issued a publicity-grabbing proclamation in the mid-'60s trying to get authentic genre artists to declare that they "will not sing a song that is not a country song," even as his twangy guitar and big beat-driven Bakersfield sound was making country far more accessible to rock & rollers than the music now coming out of Nashville.

By the late '60s and early '70s, all recordings coming out of Music City were dubbed as having "that Nashville sound." The next backlash against the style came with the rise of "outlaw music," a return to rougher sounds led by Willie Nelson and Waylon Jennings, themselves Nashville artists dissatisfied with the system and its one-sound-fits-all production values. Mainstream country took another sock in the jaw in the mid-'80s—some point to this period as the true end of the Nashville sound—with the rise in popularity of several youth-oriented performers with strong stylistic ties to country's past. Singers like Randy Travis and George Strait recalled the glory of George Jones, and Dwight Yoakam recast Buck Owens' Bakersfield sound in a move that looked forward and backward at the same time. Hank Williams Jr. came up with his own rocking hybrid that wed the honky tonk sound to the more rocked-out sensibilities of Southern rock bands like Lynyrd Skynyrd. But a new audience was coming to country music that grew up on rock & roll, turning to younger and more rock-oriented country acts like Garth Brooks when they no longer heard music on rock stations that they could identify with.

But in the end, country will evolve once again and, in an odd way, the genre has the rise of the Nashville sound to thank for it. Its success, while alternately broadening and dividing its fan base, has provided the music with its essential stylistic yin and yang. There couldn't have been any radical movements in the music ('60s honky tonk, outlaw music, neo-traditionalism) or conservative bastions clinging to older styles if the Nashville sound had not created the center from which to provide these alternatives.

Recommended Recordings:
Jim Reeves, *Welcome to My World: The Essential Jim Reeves Collection* (RCA)
Patsy Cline, *12 Greatest Hits* (MCA)
Don Gibson, *A Legend in His Time* (Bear Family)
Marty Robbins, *The Essential Marty Robbins: 1951-1982* (Columbia/Legacy)

The Browns, *20 of the Best* (RCA)
Skeeter Davis, *The Essential Skeeter Davis* (RCA)
Ray Price, *The Essential Ray Price (1951-1962)* (Columbia/Legacy)
Porter Wagoner, *The Thin Man from West Plains* (Bear Family)
Porter Wagoner & Dolly Parton, *The Essential* (RCA)

—Cub Koda

Rockabilly

If rock & roll can be called the child of R&B and country & western music, no style is a purer blend than rockabilly. The first form of rock & roll performed by white musicians, its duration of mass popularity was brief, but the best of it remains among the most exciting and frenetic rock & roll ever waxed.

Even in the segregated American South of the early 20th century, blacks and whites often had cause to interact with each other on a daily basis. The interaction carried over to music, and white hillbilly country performers have reflected the influence of the blues and other African-American music since they began recording, as a listen to Jimmie Rodgers will attest. Just as blues became jazzier, faster, and more electric throughout the 1940s and early '50s, so did country, through swing bands like Bob Wills & His Texas Playboys and the Maddox Brothers. The Delmore Brothers, starting as a more traditional hillbilly harmony act, anticipated much of rockabilly's mania when they added a thumping country boogie beat to the equation on their finest recordings in the late '40s. Nearly forgotten performers like Arthur Smith and Hardrock Gunter laid down country boogie sides that brought the guitar to the forefront.

Considering that most rockabilly musicians of importance came from the South, it's ironic that the first records that could be termed as honest to God rockabilly were issued by a Northerner, Bill Haley. The Philadelphian had been pursuing a hillbilly career with generally dismal results until 1951, when he covered Jackie Brenston's "Rocket '88'" (which is often cited as one of the very first rock & roll records). Although they aren't nearly as well-known as his huge rock & roll hits like "Rock Around the Clock," the sides he cut for the small Essex label between 1951 and 1954 are groundbreaking early rockabilly; the 1952 single "Rock the Joint," in fact, is almost identical in melody and arrangement to "Rock Around the Clock." Haley was no Elvis vocally, and the steel guitars and jump beats of his Comets betrayed lingering influences of hillbilly and swing music. But he was undoubtedly the first to bring together R&B and country & western with such force, although nobody knew quite what to call the music at the time.

There were certainly numerous musicians in the South experimenting with primitive rockabilly-like sounds by mid-1954. Sam Phillips and his Memphis record label, Sun Records, were chiefly responsible for honing the sound and capturing it on vinyl.

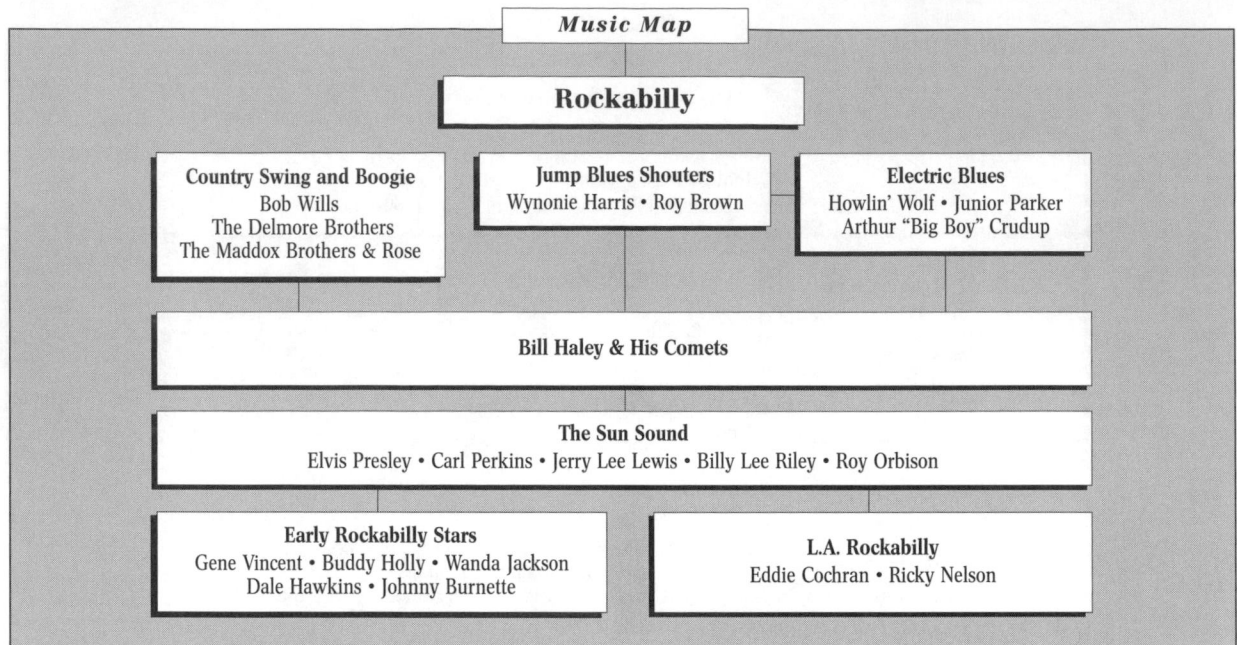

Often quoted as having said that he could make a fortune with a white singer who sounded black (though he has denied saying this in such explicit terms), Phillips found the perfect vehicle for doing so with Elvis Presley, who recorded five singles for Sun between mid-1954 and the end of 1955. Supported by guitarist Scotty Moore and bassist Bill Black, this was rockabilly, if not rock & roll, at its best and purest; as great as his subsequent achievements were, by critical consensus this handful of 45s ranks as Elvis' finest work.

As has already been noted by some conscientious historians, it would be inaccurate to say that Elvis simply whitewashed the blues for the mass market. Look at the Sun singles themselves: They usually pair a blues/R&B cover with a rocked-up rendition of a country tune. "Blue Moon of Kentucky," the flip side of his debut 45, "That's All Right Mama," was a cover of a Bill Monroe composition. "You're a Heartbreaker," "I'm Left, You're Right, She's Gone," and "I Forget to Remember to Forget"—these are all, essentially, country songs given a rockabilly treatment. Also, in his Sun days, Elvis was really thought of as a country, or hillbilly, performer—the term "rock & roll" had hardly been applied to any white performers yet, for one thing. Elvis played the country circuit in the South, where he shared the stage with such mainstream country stars as Hank Snow, and was signed to a management deal with Colonel Tom Parker, who had worked with Snow and Eddy Arnold. When his records began to chart, first locally and then nationally, they were on the country listings, not the pop ones. Before Elvis had ever dented the pop charts, "Baby Let's Play House" and "I Forgot to Remember to Forget" were nationwide country hits, the latter reaching number one in 1955.

Presley didn't set off a mass wave of imitators right away; he was primarily a regional sensation until his contract was bought by RCA. Sam Phillips used the money from the sale to develop his own formidable stable of rockabilly performers. Carl Perkins' "Blue Suede Shoes" almost beat Elvis' "Heartbreak Hotel" to the top of the charts, and although Perkins was never able to duplicate Elvis' success, Sun generated a wealth of great rockabilly hits and misses over the next few years by Jerry Lee Lewis, Billy Lee Riley, Sonny Burgess, Carl Mann, and Roy Orbison. The Sun sound—echo-chamber vocals, crisp electric guitar leads, and slapback bass—became the standard of rockabilly excellence, often imitated, never recaptured.

Almost all of the rockabilly singers had been playing country music before they caught the rockabilly fever, whether or not they recorded before the rockabilly explosion. (There were a few black rockabilly singles here and there, such as the Jerry Lee Lewis-like outings of Big Al Downing from Oklahoma, but these were quite rare.) Listen, for instance, to the early Sun outtakes of Elvis Presley, which show a far tamer, more countrified vocalist (not to mention one who was also considerably influenced by pop ballads). Carl Perkins, prior to recording "Blue Suede Shoes," laid down some pure country with "Tennessee," complete with fiddle. Even some rockabilly stars who made their recording debuts after 1955 would sometimes ooze pure country, as on Jerry Lee Lewis' debut single, "Crazy Arms" (a cover of a Ray Price song), or Gene Vincent's delicately crooned "Important Words."

But rockabilly, and Elvis Presley in particular, was so exciting—and commercially viable—that many young country singers didn't need much prodding to change their style. Bob Luman, who would make both rockabilly and country records, described an early Elvis Presley show in Paul Hemphill's *The Nashville Sound*: "This cat came out in red pants and a green coat and a pink shirt and socks, and he had this sneer on his face and he stood behind the mike for five minutes, I'll bet, before he made a move. Then he hit

his guitar a lick, and he broke two strings. I'd been playing ten years, and I hadn't broken a total of two strings. So there he was, these two strings dangling, and he hadn't done anything yet, and these high-school girls were screaming and fainting and running up to the stage, and then he started to move his hips real slow like he had a thing for his guitar."

"That was Elvis Presley when he was about nineteen, playing Kilgore, Texas. He made chills run up my back, man, like when your hair starts grabbing at your collar. For the next nine days he played one-nighters around Kilgore, and after school every day me and my girl would get in the car and go wherever he was playing that night. That's the last time I tried to sing like Webb Pierce and Lefty Frizzell."

By 1956, even such old-school country stars as Webb Pierce would be jumping onto the rockabilly bandwagon, either to keep up with trends or to try reviving flagging careers. George Jones, Rose Maddox, the Delmore Brothers, Patsy Cline, Marty Robbins, Tex Williams, and Buck Owens—all of these artists are thought of as country giants, not rock singers. Yet all of them recorded rockabilly in the 1950s, sometimes quite well, and sometimes (as with Marty Robbins' cover of "That's All Right Mama") with some commercial success. George Jones was so reluctant to sing the music that he recorded some rockabilly under the pseudonym of Thumper Jones. Johnny Cash probably would have been just as happy not to do any rockabilly at all, but as he was recording for Sam Phillips at Sun, hits like "I Walk the Line" bore just enough traces of the slapback echoed beat to bleed into the rockabilly margins.

Presley mania overran the country in 1956, instigating a wave of rockabilly recordings, nationally and (more often) regionally distributed, that was similar in some respects to the garage band explosion of a decade later. Hundreds of performers found their way into studios in Tennessee, Texas, California, and other locales, embracing the new sound with a hepped-up enthusiasm that often bordered on mania. The singles were usually crudely recorded and extremely basic and derivative, their not inconsiderable saving grace being their infectious energy.

While the Sun sound was the pinnacle of rockabilly, several performers became legends outside of Sam Phillips' studio. Gene Vincent's 1956 sides, featuring his breathy vocals and the speed-of-light guitar of Cliff Gallup from Vincent's backing band, the Blue Caps, were usually brilliant. Eddie Cochran brought a sophisticated brand of teenage rebellion to his rockabilly hits, which helped pioneer the use of overdubbed guitars and vocals. Ricky Nelson recorded first-class rockabilly pop in Hollywood with the help of ace guitarist James Burton. Johnny Burnette and his trio recorded some of the raunchiest Elvis-derived rock & roll of the time, including the first rock version of "Train Kept A-Rollin.'" Dale Hawkins cut a crackling classic with "Susie Q," and Wanda Jackson's raspy rockabilly sides rank as the finest rock & roll recorded by a female singer in the 1950s.

Rockabilly began to fade as a commercial force around 1958, not just because of fickle popular taste, but because of the rapid evolution of rock & roll itself. One of the greatest rockabilly singers, Buddy Holly, displayed a facility for melodic invention that branched into all forms of pop/rock, and had a far-reaching influence on all of pop that extended to the British Invasion. Along with the Everly Brothers and Ricky Nelson, he began gravitating toward a more gentle, melodic sound that was less structurally limited, if not as energetic, as pure rockabilly. Elvis himself was moving toward more straightforward rock material, and then toward pop after his hitch in the Army.

Those performers who stuck with the basic rockabilly sound faced diminishing returns. Some, like Gene Vincent, simply vanished from the charts, although they maintained loyal audiences, especially overseas. Roy Orbison, never comfortable as a rockabilly singer in the first place, reinvented himself as a masterful crooner of pop/rock ballads. Jerry Lee Lewis' career was crippled by scandal. Eventually he would find success in the country & western mainstream, a path followed by many other singers who had achieved limited success with rockabilly.

The list of those who "returned" to country & western from rockabilly is substantial, though it varied in degrees. Wanda Jackson, Brenda Lee, Conway Twitty, and quite a few other rockabilly artists did mostly country after the early '60s. The Everly Brothers and Ricky Nelson tried to have their cake and eat it too by helping pioneer country-rock in the late '60s. Most of the first wave of rockabilly singers—Carl Perkins, Roy Orbison, and Elvis Presley himself—would occasionally sing quite a bit of straight country on their recordings, without ever redefining themselves as country artists. Sometimes these singers reverted to country music as a matter of personal choice, and at any rate, having grown up with country music, they could have been expected to always maintain a country influence.

But often it was also a matter of survival. Rockabilly was passé after the 1950s, and all-country radio formats were becoming increasingly common. Some felt compelled to record country records in order to get airplay, which was necessary to keep the live work coming. In many cases, country music may have represented the best (or only) option. It's also true that some artists who dallied in rockabilly, such as George Jones, Jack Scott, Marty Robbins, and Waylon Jennings, were at heart country artists all along.

Rockabilly never returned to the charts in a significant way after the '50s, though several acts have scored big hits in the style, such as Billy Swan and the Stray Cats. Some obscure rockabilly singers from the old days, like Ronnie Dawson, Sleepy LaBeef, and Ray Campi, enjoyed a considerably more widespread following in later decades as part of mini-rockabilly revivals. Others who weren't around for the first wave of rockabilly have carved a career for themselves as rockabilly artists playing for small and specialized audiences, such as Shakin' Stevens in Britain, and, much more recently, Big Sandy.

A huge influence on the early Beatles, Creedence Clearwater Revival, and others, rockabilly was instrumental in establishing the focus of rock & roll on the electric guitar/bass/drums combination, with a simple joy and force that has helped inspire generations of musicians. The influence of rockabilly upon country itself is harder to ascertain. Ex-rockabilly artists like Jerry Lee Lewis and Charlie Rich always kept some hell-raising tunes in the wings, whether for album tracks or live gigs. Some of the more frenetic straight country singers, like Lewis' cousin Mickey Gilley, have a trace of muted rockabilly in some of their material. Sometimes a big country star will drag out an old rockabilly-related tune (as Alan Jackson did on his hit treatment of Eddie Cochran's "Summertime Blues"), although the results usually have a lot more to do with standard Nashville pop than real rockabilly. Of more recent country stars, Marty Stuart may be the one whose style bears the most visible influence of rockabilly, although Stuart has not gone into rockabilly in an all-out way.

If rockabilly is a part of contemporary country music, it's by and large kept in the closet, just as some politicians attempt to smother all evidence of their wild drug-taking days in order to woo middle-of-the-road voters. There are a few artists who approach rockabilly from a country footing (as opposed to a rock one), though outings such as Doc Watson's mid-'90s rockabilly album (*Docabilly*) are relatively rare. The best of these mavericks may be Rosie Flores, who brought it all home by recording some material with rockabilly queen Wanda Jackson, who came home to the music herself, making her first all-rockabilly tour of the U.S. in the mid '90s.

Recommended Recordings:
Elvis Presley, *King of Rock 'n' Roll: Complete '50s Masters* (RCA)
Buddy Holly, *Buddy Holly Collection* (MCA)
Gene Vincent, *Capitol Collectors Series* (Capitol)
Carl Perkins, *Original Sun Greatest Hits* (Rhino)
Jerry Lee Lewis, *18 Original Sun Greatest Hits* (Rhino)
Johnny Burnette, *Tear It Up* (Solid Smoke)
Eddie Cochran, *Legendary Masters* (EMI)
Ricky Nelson, *Legendary Masters* (EMI)
Wanda Jackson, *Rockin' With Wanda* (Capitol)
The Collins Kids, *Introducing Larry and Laurie* (Epic)
Bill Haley & His Comets, *Rock the Joint!* (School Kids)
Various Artists, *Rock This Town, Vols. 1-2* (Rhino)
Recommended Books:
Good Rockin' Tonight: Sun Records and the Birth of Rock 'n' Roll, by Colin Escott with Martin Hawkins (St. Martin's, 1991)
Last Train to Memphis, by Peter Guralnick (Little, Brown & Co., 1994)
Elvis: The Illustrated Record, by Roy Carr & Mick Farren (Harmony, 1982)
Remembering Buddy: The Definitive Biography of Buddy Holly, by John Goldrosen & John Beecher (Da Capo, 1996)
The Day the World Turned Blue: A Biography of Gene Vincent, by Britt Hagarty (Blandford Press, U.K., 1984)
Ricky Nelson: Idol for a Generation, by Joel Selvin (Contemporary, 1990)

—*Richie Unterberger*

The Bakersfield Sound

Because Nashville has long been uncontested as the house and home of country music, the idea of the working-class town of Bakersfield, CA, being a country music hot spot was a surprise, to say the least—and likely, at least in the minds of more than a few Music Row executives, sacrilege. In the late '50s and '60s, the development of the Nashville sound meant that the majority of charting hits were softer, smoother, and easier to

swallow. So for a bona fide blue-collar, hard country movement to spring up some 2,000 miles west—and for several of these West Coast artists to eventually be recognized by the establishment and played on country radio—was something close to a revolution, albeit a short-lived one.

The so-called Bakersfield sound probably wouldn't be remembered—or even exist as such—if not for the huge and lasting success of two specific artists: Merle Haggard and Buck Owens. But it's also likely that those two country singers might not have become superstars if not for the rich music scene that thrived in the city during the 1950s and '60s. The development of Bakersfield's honky tonk style is indirectly tied to the region's natural resources. Located at the southern end of California's San Joaquin Valley and 100 miles northeast of Los Angeles, Bakersfield became a boom town in the mid- to late 1800s thanks first to gold (in Kern River Canyon) and, more significantly, to oil. It also grew into a major regional market and distribution center for all sorts of agricultural goods. Thanks to the Dust Bowl, the Depression, and World War II, Bakersfield saw a huge influx of Okies in the 1930s, '40s, and '50s. Coming to pick California's fruit and cotton and to work its oil fields, these rural transplants brought their love of country music, and turned Bakersfield into a musical boomtown as well. The city's growing number of dancehalls, bars, and honky tonks became, then, fertile ground for performers who understood the hard-edged, traditionally rooted dancing and drinking music these working people craved every weekend ("loud music that plays until all hours," as Bakersfield singer Wynn Stewart tells it in his song "How the Other Half Lives").

A series of bars and clubs actually sprouted all up and down the state, creating a California country music circuit that would feed the careers of many West Coast-based singers as well as countless touring acts. But it was Bakersfield, the biggest city in the southern San Joaquin, that became the hub for cultural life in the region. It was here that, in the 1950s, country artists such as Tommy Collins, Johnny Bond, Ferlin Husky, the Maddox Brothers & Rose, and bandleaders like Bills Woods and Billy Mize played regularly, and earned reputations as solid acts with large draws.

While the music in nearby Los Angeles was often urban and swanky, Bakersfield was home to a less sophisticated crowd. Attempting to erase the working-class angst of the weekend revelers in the area honky tonks, the Bakersfield sound is marked by the sharp, loud, high-end sound of the electric and steel guitars, fiddles, and lead and harmony vocals—influenced by rock & roll and rockabilly as well as traditional country. It was simple in structure and designed to be heard over the din of the average honky tonk. This was a direct contrast with the production style of the Nashville sound, at the time filling the country airwaves with crooning voices, lush string arrangements, and background choruses.

If anyone deserves to be called the king of Bakersfield, it's Buck Owens. Though born in Texas and raised in Arizona, Owens and his family moved to Bakersfield in 1951 because there was work to be had in the city's nightclubs. He played in a house band at the Blackboard with bandleader Bill Woods, and soon landed session work at Capitol Records with Tommy Collins, Wanda Jackson, Gene Vincent, and others. Owens' style was influenced by rock & roll as well as traditional country, and his guitar playing (on his Fender Telecaster) stood out for its sharp, punchy sound. Soon Owens was signed to Capitol himself, and his 1960 version of his friend Harlan Howard's song "Above and Beyond" catapulted him into the national spotlight. Like most of his numerous hits, it's an immediately bright and lively song, sharp, upbeat, and cut to be noticed.

One of Nashville's top songwriters, Howard got his start while living in L.A. in the 1950s. His songs are loosely tied to the Bakersfield crowd via Owens and, to a less degree, Wynn Stewart, who recorded a version of "Above and Beyond" six months before Owens. Stewart's version failed to catch; other songs of his ("How the Other Half Lives," a duet with Howard's wife, Jan, and the superb "Wishful Thinking") also failed to make Stewart much of a household name, yet today they stand out as some of the classic recordings of the era. In particular, "Wishful Thinking" is a clear-minded, hard-driving song packed with energy that grabs hold from the very first notes. Like much of Owens' material, Stewart's songs were usually far more aggressive in tone and approach than the work of crooners like Jim Reeves and Patsy Cline—even more so than the honky tonk being made back east at the time by Ray Price and George Jones.

Stewart was a mainstay and highly successful performer on the region's club circuit. He was also responsible for giving a job to another upstart musician, Merle Haggard, who played in his band for a year. In 1963, Haggard recorded a version of Stewart's "Sing a Sad Song" for the Bakersfield-based Tally label, and it became his first charting record; his 1964 hit, the Liz Anderson song "(My Friends Are Gonna Be) Strangers," led to his being signed to Capitol. (Anderson, who lived for a while in California, also penned the Haggard hit "I'm a Lonesome Fugitive.")

Haggard was the only artist associated with Bakersfield who was actually born there. His style matured into something far more personal and individualistic than his honky tonk surroundings, yet his San Joaquin roots remained in his soul, and he's never forgotten them. He wrote a song paying tribute to his friend, Bakersfield mainstay Tommy Collins ("Leonard"), and covered that artist's material many times ("High on a Hilltop," "Carolyn"). Haggard's album *Someday We'll Look Back* recalls the field work of his youth (his parents were Okie migrants), and includes the Dallas Frazier song "California Cotton Fields," probably the best picture of the migrant workers' life ever written in song.

Frazier grew up in Bakersfield and got his start in the business thanks to Ferlin Husky, who was a regular on the region's club circuit in the 1950s. Frazier soon moved to Nashville, however, where he became another of Music Row's top songwriters from the 1960s onward. (His song "Elvira" was a smash for the Oak Ridge Boys.) Collins (born Leonard Raymond Sipes) worked in and out of Bakersfield's live music circuit in the 1950s and '60s. Collins also got help from Husky—in this case for a Capitol recording contract. Collins' cutesy 1952 song "You Better Not Do That" (with Owens on lead guitar) was

Music Map

The Bakersfield Sound

Folk/Dust Bowl Ballads
Woody Guthrie (1930s)

Honky Tonk
Hank Williams
Lefty Frizzell
Ernest Tubb
(1930s–1950s)

Bakersfield Pioneers
Maddox Brothers and Rose • Wynn Stewart
(late '40s–early '50s)

Bakersfield Sound
Buck Owens • Merle Haggard • Tommy Collins
(mid-'50s–1960s)

Bakersfield Revival—First Wave
Dwight Yoakam • Pete Anderson
(mid- to late '80s)

Bakersfield Revival—Second Wave
Scott Joss • Kathy Robertson • Cody Bryant
(1990s)

his biggest hit, but he had others. Haggard wasn't the only artist to have recorded Collins' material over the years; his song "If You Ain't Lovin'," for instance, was a hit for Faron Young in 1955 and George Strait in 1988. The national success of Bakersfield's artists owes significant thanks to Los Angeles-based Capitol Records. Owens, Haggard, Husky, Collins, and Stewart were all members of the Capitol roster at one time or another, signed and produced by Ken Nelson, who was head of the label's country music division from the mid-'50s through the '70s. (Capitol, a major player in the country music industry, was also home to Hank Thompson, Jean Shepard, Faron Young, Wanda Jackson, Freddie Hart, and many others.)

The strength of Bakersfield's country music scene eventually tapered off as Owens and Haggard shifted their focus in other directions—and as the town's economy began to falter. Today, few reminders of the old club scene remain in Bakersfield, and southern California's country music community is based in and around Los Angeles, with Dwight Yoakam being the figurehead. Yoakam—whose hard-edged, rocked-up approach is the closest today to the once-proud Bakersfield sound—deliberately moved to California instead of Nashville because it was home to individualists like Owens. He even brought his idol out of retirement to cut a duet version of Owens' 1972 song "The Streets of Bakersfield," which hit number one in 1988.

Recommended Recordings:
Tommy Collins, *Words and Music Country Style* (Capitol)
Dallas Frazier, *Singing My Songs* (RCA)
Ferlin Husky, *Gone* (Capitol)
Merle Haggard, *Someday We'll Look Back* (Capitol)
Merle Haggard, *Down Every Road* (Capitol)
Buck Owens, *The Buck Owens Collection, 1959-1990* (Rhino)
Buck Owens, *Buck Owens Sings Harlan Howard* (Capitol)
Wynn Stewart, *California Country: The Best of the Challenge Masters* (AVI)
Various Artists, *A Town South of Bakersfield, Vols. 1-2* (Restless)
Dwight Yoakam, *Buenas Noches from a Lonely Room* (Reprise)

—*Kurt Wolff*

Country-Pop

If Chet Atkins' countrypolitan was the sound of mainstream country during the '60s, Billy Sherrill's lush, string-laden productions defined the country-pop of the '70s. Though Atkins and Sherrill appeared to work the same ground, Sherrill's approach was considerably different. Sherrill produced country records as if they were pop/rock singles, adapting Phil Spector's "Wall of Sound" for the genre. Instead of relying on standard country instruments like steel guitars and fiddles, he recorded with string sections and vocal choruses, often overdubbing parts to give the music a grandiose, epic sound. Some critics complained that his style wasn't pure country, yet there is no denying that he helped bring

country music to a wider pop audience during the late '60s and '70s with the recordings he made with George Jones, Tammy Wynette, Charlie Rich, and Johnny Paycheck, as well as many, many others. In his wake, numerous other producers—including Nashville sound predecessors like Owen Bradley—adapted Sherrill's sweeping, melodic technique, often bringing in even more overt rock & roll influences in order to make the records appealing to mainstream AM pop radio.

Initially a rock & roll and R&B musician, Sherrill became interested in country music in 1962 when an unknown Nashville country artist cut one of his songs. Encouraged by the unannounced royalty check, he moved to Nashville. Upon his arrival, Sherrill was hired by Sam Phillips to oversee Sun Records' Nashville studios. After Sun and Phillips went bankrupt the following year, Epic Records' Nashville division hired him as an in-house producer, and he was assigned to record any artist who all of the label's other producers had already rejected. At that time, he was unfamiliar with many of country music's production techniques and musical conventions. Instead of heeding the advice of the studio musicians he was working with, Sherrill forged ahead and created his own style, telling the professional musicians what to play. Basing his sound on the work of Spector, Atkins, Bradley, and Don Law, he began pushing the boundaries of the Nashville sound of the '50s and early '60s by making the productions bigger and grander. Sherrill also decided to select the songs that his artists would record, often co-writing the songs to suit the singer's style and his own production.

Sherrill's first major hit arrived in 1965, when David Houston took his song "Livin' in a House Full of Love" to number three late that year. The following year, Houston recorded the Sherrill/Glenn Sutton song "Almost Persuaded," which spent nine weeks at number one. "Almost Persuaded" quickly became a standard, becoming the subject of cover versions by artists as diverse as Louis Armstrong, Louis Prima, and Etta James. The success of "Almost Persuaded" launched Sherrill's career as much as it did Houston's, and Sherrill found his first superstar the following year when he discovered Tammy Wynette, an Alabama hairdresser and waitress. Wynette had previously approached several other record labels but had been rejected. Sherrill signed her, co-writing "Your Good Girl's Gonna Go Bad" with Sutton with her specifically in mind. The single became a hit upon its early-1967 release, launching a very successful career for Wynette.

By 1968, Sherrill had begun to develop a distinctive sound that was highlighted by his detailed production; nevertheless, he hadn't landed on his unique, near-operatic blend of orchestration and sound effects. In fact, he kept fairly close to the honky tonk roots of Wynette, while letting Charlie Rich explore his idiosyncratic fusion of jazz, blues, R&B, and country. Over the next two years, he slowly pushed Wynette toward string-laden country-pop arrangements, the kind he explored on Barbara Mandrell's early Columbia records.

By the early '70s, it became apparent that Sherrill's sleek, urban production was catching on, as AM pop radio embraced hits that sounded quite similar to his own productions.

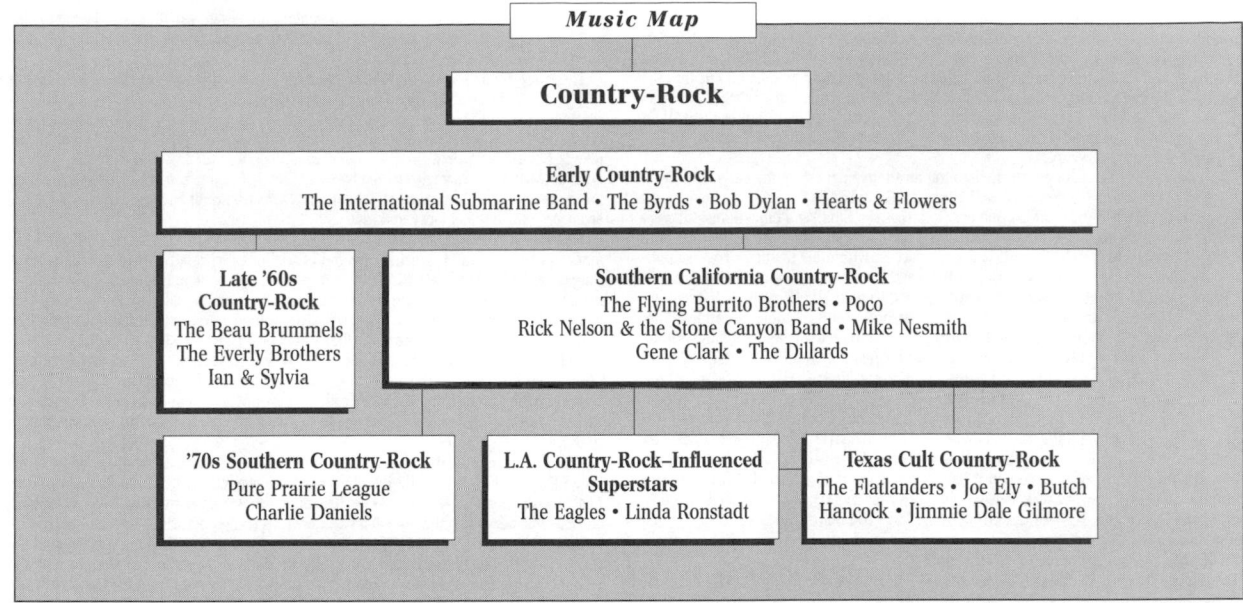

Music Map

Country-Rock

Early Country-Rock
The International Submarine Band • The Byrds • Bob Dylan • Hearts & Flowers

Late '60s Country-Rock
The Beau Brummels
The Everly Brothers
Ian & Sylvia

Southern California Country-Rock
The Flying Burrito Brothers • Poco
Rick Nelson & the Stone Canyon Band • Mike Nesmith
Gene Clark • The Dillards

'70s Southern Country-Rock
Pure Prairie League
Charlie Daniels

L.A. Country-Rock–Influenced Superstars
The Eagles • Linda Ronstadt

Texas Cult Country-Rock
The Flatlanders • Joe Ely • Butch Hancock • Jimmie Dale Gilmore

---

Simultaneously, artists like B.J. Thomas and Glen Campbell were carving out a country-pop sound that was simpler and more direct than Sherrill's. Both musicians had extensive backgrounds in pop, rock, and folk, and their recordings reflected their past endeavors. Soon, a number of singers developed a compromise between the sound of Campbell and Sherrill, and these records—Donna Fargo's "The Happiest Girl in the Whole U.S.A.," Lynn Anderson's "Rose Garden"—began receiving heavy airplay on AM pop radio. Before long, Sherrill and his artists were having crossover hits, most notably in the form of Rich's "Behind Closed Doors" and "The Most Beautiful Girl" in 1973.

For the remainder of the '70s, this lush, pop-ready form of country-pop dominated mainstream country music. By the middle of the decade, pop had turned away from the style, yet many country artists continued to record singles in this vein. George Jones, who began recording with Sherrill in 1971, made some of his very best recordings during this era, as did Conway Twitty, who recorded with Bradley. Toward the end of the decade, country-pop had lost much of its appeal, and major artists like Jones and Twitty were beginning to expand its boundaries. Still, the sound of country-pop remained popular until the beginning of the '80s, when *Urban Cowboy* and its more pronounced soft rock influences came along. *Urban Cowboy* smoothed out the remaining edges in country-pop, making it more appealing to the emerging adult contemporary radio format, while co-opting the outlaw image to create a pop culture sensation. In its wake, country-pop began to fade, yet there were several artists who pursued the distinctively lush Nashville sound during the course of the '80s.

Recommended Recordings:
George Jones, *Anniversary* (Epic)
Conway Twitty, *20 Greatest Hits* (MCA)
Charlie Rich, *Behind Closed Doors* (Epic)
Loretta Lynn, *20 Greatest Hits* (MCA)
Don Williams, *20 Greatest Hits* (MCA)
Tammy Wynette, *Anniversary* (Epic)
Glen Campbell, *The Essential Glen Campbell* (Razor & Tie)
B.J. Thomas, *The Best of B.J. Thomas* (Rhino)
Donna Fargo, *Best of Donna Fargo* (Varese)

—*Stephen Thomas Erlewine*

Country-Rock

Country-rock is one of the hardest rock & roll styles to map and define. Country music, of course, was integral to the birth of rock & roll, and has continued to exert a huge influence on rock until the present. You can find innumerable examples of rock & roll performers who are heavily soaked with country, from Elvis Presley to Elvis Costello. As a label and as a movement, however, country-rock is primarily identified with a school of bands in the late '60s and early '70s that brought the modern and irreverent qualities of rock to the more traditional musical values of country music.

There are many antecedents to country-rock; the close harmonies and acoustic guitars on much of the Everly Brothers' material foreshadows much of it. In the mid-'60s, Del Shannon recorded an entire album of Hank Williams tunes, George Jones and Gene Pitney teamed up for an LP of duets, and the trashy British R&B/punk band the Downliners Sect recorded a bizarre straight country album that was unnoticed commercially and unsuccessful artistically. Several of the '60s top groups dallied successfully with countrified rock & roll at times, such as the Beatles (especially around the *Beatles for Sale* period, on tracks like "I Don't Want to Spoil the Party"), the early Byrds ("Satisfied Mind,"

"Mr. Spaceman," "Time Between"), and Buffalo Springfield ("Go and Say Goodbye," "Kind Woman"); all of these bands placed a premium on close harmonies, and could incorporate country signatures into their sound with natural ease when the spirit moved them.

The term "country-rock" actually began to get used and thrown around in 1968, when most of the major rock acts were retreating from their psychedelic experiments into a "back to basics" approach. Bob Dylan, who had never embraced psychedelia in the first place, led the way with his *John Wesley Harding* album. Dylan had recorded in Nashville before, but this early 1968 effort was far more basic in instrumentation and far more country in tone. In 1969, he would largely eschew his inscrutable wordplay for basic homilies on *Nashville Skyline*, as well as recording an entire unreleased LP with one of his chief mentors, Johnny Cash.

The true god of country-rock, though, was guitarist and singer Gram Parsons. As the leader of the International Submarine Band, he recorded an album in 1967, *Safe at Home*, that prominently used pedal steel guitar. The LP is seen by some scholars as the first true country-rock record, although it was little noticed upon its release. Shortly afterwards, Parsons joined the Byrds and was almost single-handedly responsible for altering the band's focus from folk-rock to country-rock. Byrds leader Roger McGuinn had been entertaining the idea of an ambitious double album with heavy use of electronics, but the project was scuttled in favor of *Sweetheart of the Rodeo*. The 1968 release is almost universally hailed as one of the first and best country-rock efforts.

The Byrds' country-rock era was short; Parsons left the band after a year. Longtime Byrds bassist Chris Hillman left the group around the same time, and the pair quickly teamed to form the nucleus of the Flying Burrito Brothers; Parsons only stayed with the band for a couple albums, but these works, also prominently featuring Sneaky Pete Kleinow on pedal steel, are the purest and most influential country-rock hybrids, and among the few major country-rock recordings that are not in reality closer to rock than country.

Country music may have sprung from the Southern states, but country-rock primarily flourished in southern California. Other country-rock acts of note in the late '60s included the little-known Hearts & Flowers, which actually surfaced before 1968 but was classified as folk-rock at the time, and Poco, featuring former Buffalo Springfield members Richie Furay and Jim Messina. In northern California, the New Riders of the Purple Sage established themselves as a more countrified and laid-back cousin of the Grateful Dead in the early '70s.

Some veteran acts primarily associated with other forms of rock and folk became country-rockers for a time in the late '60s. Folk-rock pioneers the Beau Brummels went to Nashville to record *Bradley's Barn* at the legendary studio of the same name; the Everly Brothers' *Roots* was their most critically acclaimed post-early-'60s work; Ian & Sylvia moved from contemporary folk to country as a duo and leaders of the band Great Speckled Bird; Rick Nelson had an artistic renaissance while fronting the Stone Canyon Band, which featured future Eagle Randy Meisner. Former Byrd Gene Clark recorded country-rock on his own and as part of Dillard & Clark. The Dillards themselves, primarily known as a bluegrass act before the late '60s, had already acted as important figures in folk-rock by helping teach the Byrds harmony vocals, and employing Dewey Martin on drums before he left to join Buffalo Springfield. On 1968's *Wheatstraw Suite*, they became one of the few noted country-rock performers to move into the style from country rather than rock.

Country-rock wasn't big commercially, and may have made its greatest impact as an influence on other performers. The Band, the Grateful Dead, Creedence Clearwater

Revival, and George Harrison, for instance, could not be called country-rock performers by any means, but all recorded some impressive country-rock material on their late-'60s and early-'70s albums. Gram Parsons was a big influence on the Rolling Stones around this time, and on Keith Richards in particular, though it should be pointed out that the Stones had fused country and rock as far back as 1966 on "High and Dry." Still, their *Let It Bleed* and *Sticky Fingers* albums had quite a few country licks, most famously on "Wild Horses" (which appeared as a cover by the Flying Burrito Brothers before the Stones released their own version).

Country-rock hasn't gotten much attention as a movement since the early '70s. Commercially, it found its greatest success in the mid-'70s on hits by the Eagles (who featured ex-members of the Burritos, Poco, and the Stone Canyon Band) and Linda Ronstadt, who absorbed country-rock into their brands of soft rock and pop. Southern bands like Pure Prairie League and Charlie Daniels had some success with more Southern-fried sounds, and Southern rock bands like the Allman Brothers, the Ozark Mountain Daredevils, and Lynyrd Skynyrd recorded some country-influenced material, although their focus remained blues-rock and hard rock. In the 1980s and 1990s, it could be argued that Nashville was a lot more successful in borrowing from rock than the other way around.

Country-rock arguably never recovered from the death of Gram Parsons in 1973, but it's remained alive and kicking, if hardly omnipresent. Elvis Costello made an all-out country album, albeit a commercial flop, in 1981 with *Almost Blue*; country music informs much of Neil Young's work, in whatever decade he's working in; alternative rockers like the Meat Puppets and the Jayhawks have leaned heavily on country-rock at times. Texas eccentrics Joe Ely, Butch Hancock, and Jimmie Dale Gilmore (all of whom have played with each other at some point) have formed a sort of extended family for their brand of maverick country-rock. Once in a while a country-rock band will get a big push, like Lone Justice, but the hybrid seems to resist huge commercial success.

Recommended Recordings:

The Byrds, *Sweetheart of the Rodeo* (Columbia)
The Flying Burrito Brothers, *Farther Along: The Best of the Flying Burrito Brothers* (A&M)
The International Submarine Band, *Safe at Home* (Rhino)
Hearts & Flowers, *Now Is the Time* (Bam Caruso, U.K.)
The Beau Brummels, *Bradley's Barn* (Edsel, U.K.)
Poco, *Pickin' Up the Pieces* (Epic)
The Everly Brothers, *Roots* (Warner)
The Dillards, *Wheatstraw Suite* (Elektra)
Bob Dylan, *John Wesley Harding* (Columbia)
Various Artists, *Hillbilly Fever, Vol. 5* (Rhino)
The Flatlanders, *More a Legend than a Band* (Rounder)
Neil Young, *Harvest Moon* (Reprise)

Recommended Books:

Gram Parsons: A Music Biography, by Sid Griffin (Sierra, 1985)
Hickory Wind: The Life and Times of Gram Parsons, by Ben Fong-Torres (Pocket Books, 1991)

—Richie Unterberger

Outlaw Country

While country music is full of outlaws—many who have done real jail time—the term "outlaw" also refers to a period during the early to mid-'70s. It was a time when the '60s generation began to have its effect on the Nashville establishment, and the long reign of the staid, crooner-oriented Nashville sound finally came to an end.

The term "outlaw" began as a nickname for the music (and lifestyles) of Waylon Jennings, Tompall Glaser, Willie Nelson, and their compatriots and hangers-on, but it soon became a marketing and publicity tool that helped RCA and other major labels cross over into the rock & roll market and sell more albums than the country industry ever had before. Nonetheless, the work these artists produced during this period is some of the freshest and most viscerally exciting in modern country music history.

The origin of the name more or less originated with a song by Lee Clayton, "Ladies Love Outlaws," that became the title track of a 1972 Waylon Jennings album. Soon after, Jennings grew a beard, his hair got longer, and coupled with his penchant for denim and leather clothes, he certainly looked the part. Journalists picked up on the catchy name, and publicist Hazel Smith also used the term to promote the Glaser Brothers.

To many Music Row executives, "outlaw" meant an unwanted infusion of self-important longhaired singers—roughnecks who mixed dope with their drink and wore biker gear instead of Nudie suits—into the comfortably conservative establishment. But as record sales quickly showed, singers like Jennings, Nelson, Glaser, Kris Kristofferson, and Billy Joe Shaver were loaded with talent, and they possessed exactly the kind of youthful energy the stiff-collared industry needed. These and others of the outlaw ilk not only reinforced the bridge that was beginning to appear between country and rock & roll audiences—magazines like *Rolling Stone* began paying serious attention to Nashville for the first time—but showed an honest love and reverence for country music's history. Despite their ragged lifestyles and rock & roll associations, the music these artists created was far more traditional—more "country"—than almost anything that had come out of Nashville during the previous decade.

That's because the outlaw movement wasn't about long hair and cheap drugs, it was about creative control for the artists in the recording studio. This was fairly standard practice for rock musicians, but in the world of country music, under the guidelines of the Nashville sound, producers were in the driver's seat; they hired the band and picked most of the songs. All a singer needed was his or her voice, which was often shaved of its rough edges to fit the mold of the smooth, pop-oriented countrypolitan sound that was the radio-friendly norm of the time. So when Waylon Jennings, fed up with being told what to play and how to play it, argued for the right to choose his own producers and bring his road band into the studio, he was attacking an entire industry standard.

He struck, though, at the right time. Not only was the industry ripe for a shakeup, but Waylon himself was a successful singer—he'd been so since the mid-'60s. He was also becoming more and more outspoken about his beliefs, so rather than lose this lucrative artist (and probably also to shut him up), his longtime label, RCA, eventually met his demands. His 1973 album *Lonesome, On'ry and Mean* was the first featuring his own production work (the title track, written by Steve Young, became something of a theme song for the genre), and it's marked by bigger beats, an absence of background choruses, and arrangements that feel loose and raw.

However, it's really the following collection, *Honky Tonk Heroes*, that is Waylon's landmark "outlaw" album. Featuring nine out of ten songs written by up-and-coming Texas songwriter Billy Joe Shaver, the record's informal production and spare, simple arrangements brought the lyrics and melodies out into the open air in a way that country fans had rarely heard in well over a decade. (The album cover, which featured Jennings, Shaver, and their shaggy cohorts in the studio, also caused a stir.) The catchy, rock-inflected song "Are You Sure Hank Done It This Way?" on Waylon's 1975 album, *Dreaming My Dreams*—the second masterpiece of his career, co-produced by the legendary Jack Clement (who founded the first independent recording studio in Nashville)—is as clear a statement as any he made of his struggle to break free of the industry's countrypolitan confines.

Thanks to the critical acclaim of *Honky Tonk Heroes*, as well as the support of his friend Kris Kristofferson, Billy Joe Shaver got the chance to record his first album, *Old Five and Dimers Like Me*, in 1973 for Kristofferson's label, Monument. Shaver, for various reasons, never saw the financial success of his contemporaries—a rambling cowboy by nature, he wasn't so good on self-promotion—but his records remain classics of the genre. Kristofferson himself was never really an "outlaw" by name, but when he took the podium in long hair and jeans to receive his songwriter's award from the Country Music Association in 1970 for "Sunday Mornin' Comin' Down," he signaled Music Row that the new generation's musical revolution was underway.

Willie Nelson was in a bind similar to Waylon's. He'd been a hugely successful songwriter since the early '60s ("Night Life," "Crazy"), but as a singer, his career had failed to take off. While it's hard to comprehend that a man now considered one of country music's finest singers would have such trouble getting attention, the blame again goes to the era's production methods, which downplayed the personality of his dusty-sweet baritone voice.

As a performer, though, Nelson, a native Texan, always did well in his home state. His eventual move in 1971 from the Nashville area to a ranch outside of Austin was another signal to the establishment that change was in the air. Fate had played a hand here: Nelson's Nashville house had burned down a few months earlier, and his second wife, Shirley, had left him. Combined with the seeming lack of support for his singing career, Nelson decided to move to where he was better appreciated. What he found in Austin—an audience of both long-haired hippies and rednecked cowboys who were wild for the kind of rock and folk-influenced country that became known as "progressive" (Jerry Jeff Walker, Michael Martin Murphey, Commander Cody)—reinvigorated him.

In 1972, Nelson put together the first of several infamous outdoor music showcases in Dripping Springs, TX, which mixed young and old country singers and fans. These Woodstock-like Fourth of July picnics also served as grassroots promotion machines for Willie and his pal Waylon's brand of country music, showcases for countrified rockers like Leon Russell, and launching pads for singer/songwriters like Shaver.

RCA finally dropped Nelson in 1972, but soon after he was signed to Atlantic's new country division by legendary R&B producer Jerry Wexler. The results included the albums *Shotgun Willie* and *Phases and Stages*, two of the finest works of his career and the beginning of the turnaround of his sales figures. In 1975, he switched to Columbia Records and released *The Red-Headed Stranger*. This became his landmark album for two reasons: First, he argued for creative control to keep the mostly acoustic arrangements sparse and quiet, and he got it; second, it sold massively, and turned out two number-one hits.

It's ironic that the most outgoing outlaw of them all, Tompall Glaser, is the least remembered today. Not only was he a successful singer/songwriter at the time, but the studio he ran with his brothers, Chuck and Jim—dubbed "Hillbilly Central"—became the meeting hall and focal point for all things "outlaw" in Nashville. Several years earlier, the brothers had caused a stir by forming their own publishing company; Nashville's old boy network got a hearty shake when one of their songs, John Hartford's "Gentle on My Mind," became a smash hit. Now, the Glasers had their own fortress.

When Glaser Studios opened in 1969, Tompall had been the lead voice in the folk/country singing group Tompall & the Glaser Brothers for more than a decade. When the brothers split up in the early '70s, Tompall began recording as a solo artist, and "outlaw" became his badge of honor. He, too, had been fed up with Nashville's old-fashioned attitudes and old boy networks. His way of fighting was to take a businessman's angle and start his own production company, a tactic that worked wonders for him financially and allowed him the creative control he desired. Tompall made several excellent albums in the 1970s, but his first, *Charlie* (1973), is his undisputed best, deserving a history-book spot alongside *Honky Tonk Heroes* and *The Red-Headed Stranger*.

Ex-con singer David Allan Coe didn't wait for an invitation to jump onto the outlaw bandwagon, even writing a song called "Willie, Waylon and Me." Many of Coe's ragged, rocked-up songs, however, deserve greater recognition. Johnny Paycheck also joined the club when he grew a beard and renamed himself "John Austin Paycheck" on his 1976 album, *11 Months and 29 Days*.

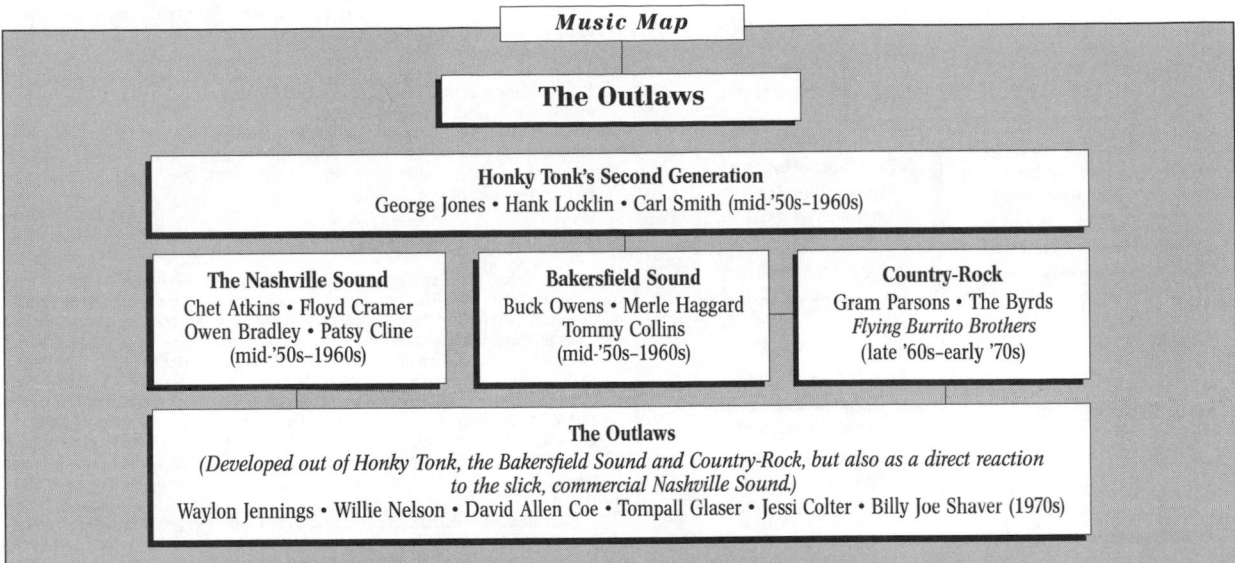

Music Map

The Outlaws

Honky Tonk's Second Generation
George Jones • Hank Locklin • Carl Smith (mid-'50s–1960s)

The Nashville Sound
Chet Atkins • Floyd Cramer
Owen Bradley • Patsy Cline
(mid-'50s–1960s)

Bakersfield Sound
Buck Owens • Merle Haggard
Tommy Collins
(mid-'50s–1960s)

Country-Rock
Gram Parsons • The Byrds
Flying Burrito Brothers
(late '60s–early '70s)

The Outlaws
(Developed out of Honky Tonk, the Bakersfield Sound and Country-Rock, but also as a direct reaction to the slick, commercial Nashville Sound.)
Waylon Jennings • Willie Nelson • David Allen Coe • Tompall Glaser • Jessi Colter • Billy Joe Shaver (1970s)

Further singer/songwriters associated to varying degrees with the era include Guy Clark, Sammi Smith (her version of Kristofferson's "Help Me Make It Through the Night" was a major hit in 1970), Kinky Friedman, Johnny Rodriguez, and even Jimmy Buffett. Two other songwriters turned singers, Mickey Newbury and Tom T. Hall, may have been clean-cut Music Row favorites for the hits they'd written, but they associated aesthetically and philosophically with what the outlaw movement stood for.

The movement culminated in the 1976 album *Wanted! The Outlaws*, which compiled previously recorded material by Waylon, Willie, Jessi Colter (Waylon's wife and the voice behind the hit "I'm Not Lisa"), and Tompall. Waylon's record company (RCA) had decided the time was right to exploit the outlaw moniker, and they were right: Less than a musical landmark, the album is best remembered for being the first country album to sell over a million copies. After the success of *Wanted! The Outlaws*, however, "outlaw" quickly became an overused label. And when Waylon was arrested for cocaine possession in 1977, he reacted by recording the song "Don't You Think This Outlaw Bit Done Got Out of Hand?" The party, it seemed, was finally winding down.

Recommended Recordings :
David Allan Coe, *The Mysterious Rhinestone Cowboy* (Columbia)
Jack Clement, *All I Want to Do in Life* (Elektra)
Tompall Glaser, *Charlie* (MGM)
Kris Kristofferson, *Kristofferson* (Monument)
Waylon Jennings, *Dreamin' My Dreams* (RCA)
Waylon Jennings, *Honky Tonk Heroes* (RCA)
Willie Nelson, *A Classic and Unreleased Collection* box set (Rhino)
Willie Nelson, *Red-Headed Stranger* (Columbia)
Billy Joe Shaver, *Old Fiver and Dimers Like Me* (Monument)
Sammi Smith, *Help Me Make It Through the Night* (Mega)
Steve Young, *Renegade Picker* (RCA)
Various Artists, *Wanted! The Outlaws: Twentieth Anniversary Edition* (RCA)
—Kurt Wolff

The Lubbock Country Scene

It's one of the great ironies of country music that one of the most conservative regions of America has been responsible for some of the most progressive country sounds of the late 20th century. Lubbock, TX, 300 miles west of Dallas, is so far into the western region of the state that it's just an hour or two drive's away from New Mexico. It's still a "dry" county where liquor is hard to come by, with more churches per capita than in any other midsize city in the U.S. As recently as 1928, a city ordinance was passed that prevented residents with more than one-tenth of African-American blood from living west of Avenue D.

Yet this is also the city that gave the world Buddy Holly, who makes anyone's list as one of the three or four most important pioneers of early rock & roll. In the late '50s, a young Waylon Jennings had a show on a radio station here. He was touring with Holly's band in early 1959 when Buddy died in a plane crash; if the Big Bopper hadn't convinced Waylon to give up his seat and take the bus instead, Jennings himself would have been on that plane as well. Not that the city itself was too proud of its prodigal sons, refusing to serve Holly's Puerto Rican wife at a local diner, and not erecting a statue in Buddy's memory until about 20 years after his death.

Much less well-known than Holly are the maverick country singer/songwriters who emerged from the city in the 1970s and 1980s. If Joe Ely, Jimmie Dale Gilmore, Butch Hancock, and Terry Allen are influenced by Holly, it's more a matter of attitude than

actual sound. All of the aforementioned Lubbockites are stone-cold country, even if their records and arrangements bear some rock and folk influences. They're too stone-cold country, actually, for either Nashville or most of the mainstream country audience. And their lyrics are way too eccentric for either pop or country listeners. It's been no coincidence that Lubbock's major country talents have established themselves outside of Lubbock, usually in the more liberal and tolerant musical and political climates of the state capital, Austin.

It was the tension between the endlessly flat west Texas landscape and these performers' fiery imaginations that fueled the innovations of their music. As Terry Allen once wrote in the notes to a Texas Tech Museum exhibit called Nothin' Else to Do, "Lubbock is so flat in every direction that if you grew up in it (and are blessed with any curiosity at all), your attention just naturally runs to the horizon, the edge ... I don't think the music comes so much from 'nothin' else to do' as really from just nothin' better to be done."

Any discussion of modern-day Lubbock country music must begin with the Flatlanders, a Lubbock supergroup of sorts that recorded one album, *More a Legend Than a Band*, in 1972. At the time, the appellation "supergroup" was most inappropriate. The band's three singer/songwriter/guitarists—Butch Hancock, Joe Ely, and Jimmie Dale Gilmore—were unknown, and would largely remain so for years. The record was released on a tiny independent label (it has now been reissued), and would be the outfit's sole recorded legacy before the bandmembers scattered to solo careers. Yet these three performers, individually and collectively, were almost solely responsible for carving a mini-genre of their own within country music.

Gilmore and Ely had been working toward a fusion of country music and rock sensibilities since the mid-'60s. When the Flatlanders finally got around to recording, however, the music owed more to country-folk than psychedelic rock. There was no drummer; the guitars were supported by fiddle, dobro, and Steve Wesson's strange musical saw. From contemporary rock, the group members borrowed a willingness to play by their own rules, addressing eerily personal concerns without heed for commercial success. In *The Rolling Stone Album Guide*, David McGee wrote that it was "beholden on one hand to the entire sweep of country and mountain folk music of an Appalachian nature, on the other to nothing save the sort of brutal honesty that cuts into souls in the dark heart of a lonesome night.... real outlaw music, years ahead of its time and years behind; it is the first blow of the new traditionalist movement, sharper and more penetrating than the anguished (and justly acclaimed) sides the late Gram Parsons produced in 1973."

Joe Ely was the first of the trio to taste solo success on his own. He is also the most rock-influenced of the three, though much of his solo output could be more aptly categorized as modern honky tonk music. The influence of his former colleagues was not just symbolic; Ely popularized several Hancock and Gilmore compositions at a time when these guys were without record deals. He also utilized the talents of two musicians, Lloyd Maines (pedal steel) and Ponty Bone (accordion), whose rootsy touches are now identified with the Lubbock/progressive Texas sound as a whole. Ely never found great commercial success, but he did make inroads into the rock audience when the Clash, to the surprise of many onlookers, tapped him as an opening act on one of their tours.

Hancock is simultaneously the most tradition-bound of the trio, and the most eccentric. His very earliest solo recordings are a gold mine for those who love very early Bob Dylan; like the early-'60s Dylan, he updates the Woody Guthrie aesthetic with close-to-the-bone original folk tunes, featuring guitar and harmonica. These solo albums, which started appearing in the late '70s on his own Rainlight label, suffered from such microscopic distribution that they were almost unknown outside of Austin, unless you happened to catch one of Butch's gigs. By the mid-'80s he had several albums under his belt,

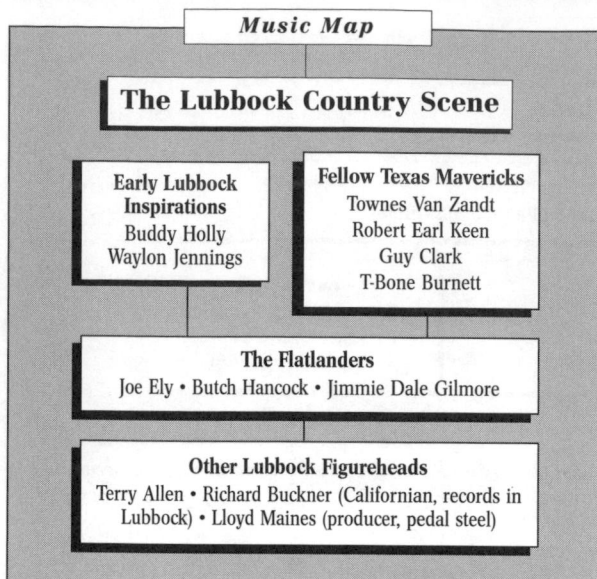

Music Map

The Lubbock Country Scene

Early Lubbock Inspirations
Buddy Holly
Waylon Jennings

Fellow Texas Mavericks
Townes Van Zandt
Robert Earl Keen
Guy Clark
T-Bone Burnett

The Flatlanders
Joe Ely • Butch Hancock • Jimmie Dale Gilmore

Other Lubbock Figureheads
Terry Allen • Richard Buckner (Californian, records in Lubbock) • Lloyd Maines (producer, pedal steel)

but was, perversely, far more appreciated in England, where he was able to tour to critical acclaim. In his homeland, he was not as much neglected as unfound; even top specialist record stores didn't carry his releases. In time his albums became more slickly produced, though for Butch, as is usually the case with such talents, less is definitely more. Getting the word out about Hancock remains a problem to this day, as most of his catalog is still only available on his tiny Rainlight label (sometimes on cassette only), although Sugar Hill has picked up some material for wider distribution.

Ultimately, however, it was Jimmie Dale Gilmore who would fare best in the critical sweepstakes. While Ely and Hancock were beginning to build their catalogs, Gilmore was missing in action, forgoing professional music to live in Colorado and study metaphysics. In the 1980s he moved to Austin, always a sympathetic climate for roots music oddballs. He finally made his solo debut in 1988, moving to a major label and year-end placings in pop/rock critic polls by the 1990s, inspiring purple prose usually reserved for the likes of Neil Young and R.E.M. *The Spin Alternative Record Guide*, for instance, hails his "encompassing spirituality" and "reconfiguration of rural music's tug between sin and salvation that speaks not of a judging god but of connections between people, the flexibility of time and space, the relative triteness of the ego." Maybe so. For many listeners, however, the chief pleasure of Gilmore's records is his voice, which delivers some of the most expressive pure country singing of recent times.

Even by Lubbock standards, singer/songwriter Terry Allen is very much a cult figure, and perhaps the weirdest of the lot. Actually, this Renaissance man has experienced far greater success as an internationally acclaimed artist than as a musician. His resumé includes NEA grants and a Guggenheim fellowship; he's worked in painting, film, sculpture, poetry, theater, and video. He wrote songs for David Byrne's *True Stories* soundtrack and Little Feat, and wrote a new national anthem with Gilmore, Ely, and Hancock. But Allen is also a recording artist whose material is perhaps the most sociopolitical and left-leaning to be found in all of country; he crafts concept albums that affectionately satirize small-town life, or assembles a set of songs (as on *Juarez*) reflecting images of Mexico. He is not afraid to mince words, make fun of the "hats" dominating Nashville, or tackle tough topics like teenage runaways. Indeed, part of the reward of listening to Allen is the sheer pleasure of finding a country performer who not only has genuinely left-of-center politics, but makes no bones about expressing them within the songs themselves—a true rarity in contemporary country music.

That also means that those with more centrist beliefs, and more mainstream musical tastes, will have no truck with the likes of Allen or his Lubbock buddies. As some critics quip, the Lubbock sound is too country in orientation to even get played on country radio. That's why much, and perhaps most, of the audience for Lubbock country music is found not in traditional country circles, but in alternative rock or folk ones. The Lubbockites certainly have a greater affinity with the contemporary No Depression country-rock bands than with the average Nashville star (or Nashville songwriter). In the mid-'90s, Californian Richard Buckner, a singer/songwriter with a rock-oriented background, even went to the extent of recording his solo debut in Lubbock. With Lloyd Maines—who has worked with Hancock, Ely, Gilmore, and Allen—producing, the resulting effort sounded as authentically Lubbock as anything by Buckner's obvious inspirations.

The Lubbock sound's influence within country itself, however, has not been negligible. Certainly other progressive country musicians in Texas seemed to have been influenced by the Lubbock performers, including Guy Clark, Townes Van Zandt, Nanci Griffith, Robert Earl Keen, Lyle Lovett, and T-Bone Burnett (though it's fair to point out that the interchange went both ways). It would seem to be a long shot that Lubbock can consistently

produce more first-rate talent, especially as its major figureheads are well into middle age. For the time being, though, it functions as a repository of a sort for the best of the new traditionalism.

Recommended Recordings:
The Flatlanders, *More a Legend Than a Band* (Rounder)
Joe Ely, *Honky Tonk Masquerade* (MCA)
Butch Hancock, *Own and Own* (Sugar Hill)
Terry Allen, *Lubbock on Everything* (Sugar Hill)
Jimmie Dale Gilmore, *After Awhile* (Elektra/Nonesuch)
Richard Buckner, *Bloomed* (Dejadisc)

—*Richie Unterberger*

Austin in the '70s

Located three hours south of Dallas and 80 miles north of the Alamo, with LBJ's ranch to the west and numerous dry towns to the east, Austin, TX, has long enjoyed a reputation as an oasis for free thinkers in a state known for its conservative politics, strict religious practices, and traditional values. Like any city, Austin—which straddles a river called the Colorado (different from the one that runs through the Grand Canyon)—has its ghettos, its downtown traffic, and its suburban housing developments. But it's also grown into a cultural crossroads that thrives on its diversity. The town's liberal attitude is in large part due to the university located here that each year brings a new roster of young, eager, and largely open minds. And with the city's diverse cultural background comes all sorts of music, drifting in from every direction—Cajun, conjunto, and German oompah music; honky tonk, blues, folk, and R&B; and all sorts of cowboy country and ribald rock & roll.

Over the last few decades, Austin has drifted in and out of fashion as a musical Mecca. In the 1970s, the city found itself in the national spotlight thanks to the success of singers like Willie Nelson, Jerry Jeff Walker, and Michael Martin Murphey, and since the mid-'80s, it gets pounced on each spring by thousands of fans, bands, and music industry reps who fill up on Shiner beer, greasy enchiladas, and late-night concerts during the annual South By Southwest Music Conference. But whether they're "hip" in the eyes of the visiting press or not, Austin's residents have continued to nurture and enjoy their town's reputation as a lively, friendly, and creative place for musicians and fans—individualistic folks who like their culture outside the mainstream—to get together, hang out, and grow.

Austin was always a good town for all sorts of music, but in the 1970s, it became known for a country-rock mixture called "progressive country" (thanks to radio station KOKE) or sometimes "redneck rock" (from the title of a book by Jan Reid, *The Improbable Rise of Redneck Rock*). It was a country-fried sound that mixed West Coast psychedelic rock influences with traditional cowboy ballads and honky tonk numbers, and put ropers and dopers in the same room at the same time, grooving to the same music.

This intergenerational convergence had been happening for at least a decade previously at Threadgill's, a former gas station on Austin's north side that was converted to a bar and makeshift music venue in 1933 by country singer Kenneth Threadgill. By the 1960s, university students were mixing regularly with the country-folks at Threadgill's shows, which often featured traditional country acts but also nurtured the talents of young unknown singers, including the club's most famous discovery, Janis Joplin. In the 1970s, Threadgill became regarded as the patriarch of the town's burgeoning music community.

Radio station KOKE may have coined and then publicized the moniker "progressive country," but the center point (though not the only point) of much of this convergence was the Armadillo World Headquarters, a converted National Guard armory that opened in 1970 as a rock & roll venue and haven for the town's hippie community. It was large enough to attract big-name national acts that might otherwise have passed Austin by—and soon became a favorite stop on the tour circuit—yet it was also a principal base for the town's homegrown music. The armadillo itself—a creature of the area's desert landscape—was a clear example of how the local counterculture had successfully adopted cowboy and Western imagery as its identity.

The country-rock scene was already swinging in Austin when Willie Nelson moved there in 1971. An established songwriter in Nashville but a frustrated performer, Nelson had met some bad luck that year when his house burned down. It was time to regroup his thoughts, and so the Fort Worth native moved back home to Texas, a place where his concerts had always met with enthusiasm. He quickly became the town's star attraction, and his local performances probably brought more cowboys and longhairs together than ever before; on one hand he was a traditional country singer, on the other a casually dressed, shaggy-haired friend of the counterculture. It was Willie's concerts—his appearances at the Armadillo or his numerous outdoor "picnics" in Dripping Springs (where singers like Roy Acuff, Tom T. Hall, Billy Joe Shaver, and Leon Russell often shared the bill)—that provided the colorful stories of wide-eyed, gray-haired ranch couples dancing side by side with freaky youngsters and encountering pot smoke for the first time.

Another of Austin's famous residents is Jerry Jeff Walker, a hard-partying folksinger best known for his song "Mr. Bojangles." Despite his strong Texas identity, however, Walker was no native; he was born in upstate New York, recorded his first several albums in New York City, and didn't move to Austin until 1971. He's remained a major figure in the area ever since, though, helping confirm the progressive country movement with his informal folk-inspired albums and loose, party-friendly performances, which frequently turned into "drunken clown shows," as writer John Morthland once put it. (He's long since cleaned up his act, however.)

Walker used to write nearly all his songs, but in Austin he began championing the work of up-and-coming writers like Guy Clark and Ray Wylie Hubbard. In 1972, Walker recorded two of Clark's songs—"L.A. Freeway" and "That Old Time Feeling"—on his self-titled MCA album. On Walker's best-known record, *Viva Terlingua*, which he recorded in 1973 in the tiny Texas town of Luckenbach (turning the place into a tourist attraction in the process), he created a loud-mouthed hippie anthem out of Hubbard's good-natured but sharp-edged "Up Against the Wall, Redneck Mothers." It became an answer song of sorts to Merle Haggard's "Okie from Muskogee."

Walker knew Clark and fellow singer/songwriter Townes Van Zandt from years before in Houston. Clark was never technically an Austin artist—he moved to California and then Nashville—but his songs are frequently associated with the scene there. He was born in west Texas, and many of his best songs center around his days growing up there. After years playing live around the state, Clark's excellent debut album, *Old No. 1*, was finally released by RCA in 1975. He's since become a successful songwriter deeply respected by his peers. Like Clark, Van Zandt drifted in and out of Texas over the years (a young Jimmie Dale Gilmore once picked him up hitchhiking), becoming one of Austin's favorite singer/songwriter figures and an influence on many generations of musicians yet to come.

Hubbard tried to turn the success of "Redneck Mothers" into a viable solo career, but with more than one record company, he encountered many of the same difficulties (overproduction and a refusal to allow his road band, the Cowboy Twinkies, in the studio) that had plagued Waylon Jennings and other Nashville artists for years, and had been the basis for the "outlaw" movement. Hubbard's best album just might be his 1994 comeback, *Loco Gringo's Lament*, an acoustic collection of country-folk material. Michael Martin Murphey, meanwhile, was the town's "cosmic cowboy" folksinger. He was a Dallas native who'd moved to California and earned a career as a successful songwriter ("Calico Silver" for the First Edition, among others), but like so many others he tired of the city grind and eventually moved back home, landing in Austin. He was soon a star of the local scene. Early albums of his such as *Geronimo's Cadillac* are loose country-rock affairs, but by the time his song "Wildfire" became a huge national hit in 1975, Murphey's music had turned far too precious.

Kinky Friedman was the infamous self-dubbed "Texas Jewboy" whose shows brimmed over with his biting satirical songs (though he also showed his penchant for serious observation when he wrote one of the best fallen-cowboy songs of the modern era, "Sold American"), while Asleep at the Wheel brought the region's Western swing history back to life when the band moved to Austin from Berkeley in 1974. Other singer/songwriters associated with the local cowboy-folk-rock scene include B.W. Stevenson, Willis Alan Ramsey, Gary Nunn, Steve Fromholz, Bill & Bonnie Hearne, and Bobby Bridger. Some made albums of their own, and most had songs recorded by Walker, Murphey, and other compatriots. Some of the best performances, though, of these and other Texas artists were captured on time-capsule compilations like *Texas Folk & Outlaw Music*, which features live performances at the nearby *Kerrville Folk Festival* from 1972 to 1976.

If Willie Nelson is the country embodiment of Austin's musical mishmash and Jerry Jeff Walker its most famous folkie, then Doug Sahm is the blustery rock & roller. He's also the artist who best embodies the city's (and the state's) wide range of musical influences, from blues and rock to conjunto, R&B, and hardcore honky tonk. A San Antonio native, Sahm achieved fame in the 1960s as leader of the Sir Douglas Quintet. The band was based in San Francisco during the Haight-Ashbury heyday, but in the early '70s, Sahm got tired of the hippie trip and moved back home to Texas to rediscover his roots, recording *The Return of Doug Saldaña* with the Quintet. This and subsequent albums like 1976's *Texas Rock for Country Rollers* are some of the most country-oriented—and best—albums of Sahm's career. In 1973, producer Jerry Wexler snatched him up, and Sahm recorded a rootsy album with a famous guest list (*Doug Sahm and Band*). Sahm's career, however, never took off like Wexler hoped, and by the end of the decade, restless as ever, he was shifting labels and heading off in new musical directions.

Like any scene, Austin eventually got over-hyped, and national attention shifted elsewhere. But the music never stopped in the town's numerous clubs, and by the mid-'80s and '90s, the city's reputation for solid, individualistic performers (non-mainstream, in other words) was back on track—thanks in large part, certainly, to the South By Southwest Music Conference. Jimmie Dale Gilmore, Joe Ely, and Butch Hancock are some of the stars of this latest generation (and Lucinda Williams, whenever she's in town), and Junior Brown, Robert Earl Keen, Dale Watson, and Jo Carol Pierce are also country favorites who are loaded with talent. But some things never change. The names Walker and Nelson have never left the vernacular (Walker's birthday concerts are still some of the town's most popular events), and Threadgill's has expanded into a thriving restaurant business, still home to regular music shows.

Recommended Recordings:
Asleep at the Wheel, *Texas Gold* (Capitol)
Guy Clark, *Old No. 1* (RCA)
Joe Ely, *Joe Ely* (MCA)
Kinky Friedman, *Sold American* (Vanguard)
Butch Hancock, *West Texas Waltzes & Dust-Blown Tractor Tunes* (Rainlight)
Michael Murphey, *Geronimo's Cadillac* (A&M)
Willie Nelson, *Shotgun Willie* (Atlantic)
Doug Sahm, *Texas Rock for Country Rollers* (ABC/Dot)
Various Artists, *Texas Folk & Outlaw Music* (Adelphi Records)
Jerry Jeff Walker, *A Man Must Carry On* (MCA)

—Kurt Wolff

Urban Cowboy

Urban cowboy was the (perhaps) inevitable culmination of the two most popular country genres of the '70s—polished Nashville country-pop and outlaw country. For most of the decade, country had been moving further into the mainstream, with country-pop making inroads on pop radio stations and outlaw singers winning the hearts of rock &

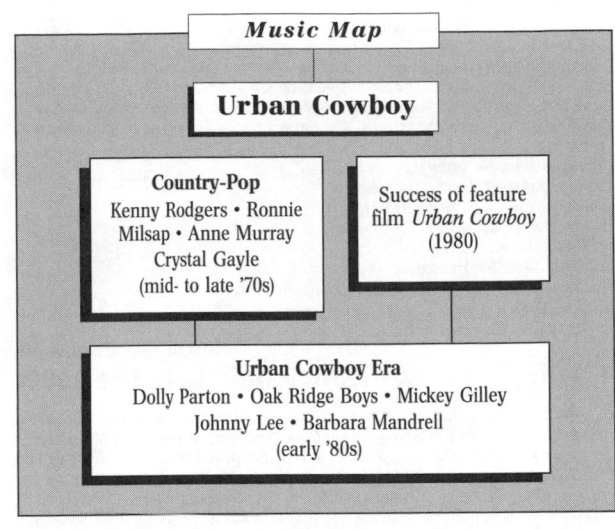

Music Map

Urban Cowboy

Country-Pop
Kenny Rodgers • Ronnie Milsap • Anne Murray Crystal Gayle
(mid- to late '70s)

Success of feature film *Urban Cowboy* (1980)

Urban Cowboy Era
Dolly Parton • Oak Ridge Boys • Mickey Gilley
Johnny Lee • Barbara Mandrell
(early '80s)

roll fans. Urban cowboy fused those two audiences, taking the hooks of country-pop and crossing them with the working-class, down to earth image of outlaw country. Urban cowboy was considerably slicker than outlaw, but it was designed to appeal to an audience that had been reluctant to embrace country—urban professionals and soft rock fans. As the '80s progressed, the sound of urban cowboy gravitated toward adult contemporary pop, as the grittier stance and sound of outlaw was adopted by both roots rockers and new traditionalists. However, the sound and style of urban cowboy—with its slick productions, light rock flourishes, and hummable melodies—set the pace for mainstream country music for the remainder of the decade.

The sound of urban cowboy had been evolving since the mid-'70s, when honky tonkers like Mickey Gilley began injecting touches of country-pop and rock & roll into their sound. Nevertheless, it didn't emerge as a full-fledged musical style until 1980, when the music was packaged as the soundtrack to the hit John Travolta film *Urban Cowboy*. Based on a 1979 *Esquire* article about a group of Houston oil workers who spent their free time in roadhouse nightclubs like Gilley's, the film sparked a pop culture sensation. Not only was the film a blockbuster, but it inspired numerous other films about contemporary country life (*Honeysuckle Rose, Coal Miner's Daughter*) and provided the basis for the popular *Dukes of Hazzard* television series. The movie popularized various country dances and fashion, as well as the pastime of riding mechanical bulls.

What the pop culture phenomenon signaled was how country music had adapted itself to the modern age; it was no longer rural music, but it was music for big-city dwellers as well, no matter if they were blue or white-collar workers. And nowhere was this more evident than on the soundtrack to *Urban Cowboy* itself. Comprised of material from country-pop crooners like Kenny Rogers, watered-down honky tonk from Mickey Gilley and Johnny Lee, country-rock from the Eagles and Linda Ronstadt & J.D. Souther, Southern rock from the Charlie Daniels Band, and straight-ahead rock & roll from Bob Seger, Bonnie Raitt, and Joe Walsh, the album blurred the lines between country and rock & roll, opening up a whole new audience for country music in the process. For rock & roll fans, country music no longer seemed like the province of rednecks; for country fans, the lexicon of rock & roll began to inch its way into their music, slowly beginning to undermine its traditions. For instance, before *Urban Cowboy*, the Eagles were considered a straight rock & roll act, but a decade after the album's release, the group had influenced more country singers than rock bands.

Over the course of the '80s, the impact of *Urban Cowboy* became apparent. Between 1980 and 1983, country was a dominant force in the American pop marketplace. Rock & roll artists continued to comprise the bulk of the album charts, but country-pop had completely infiltrated the upper reaches of the pop Top 40, with singers like Kenny Rogers, Dolly Parton, Barbara Mandrell, Juice Newton, and Charlie Daniels all scoring significant pop hits. Perhaps more importantly, the country industry—an industry which has always been driven by fads and product—devoted itself to the pursuit of crossover hits. During the '70s, Billy Sherrill's grandiose, string-laden productions had received criticisms for their over the top orchestrations, but those seemed like pure honky tonk compared to the sound of post-*Urban Cowboy* country music. By 1983, the tempos in country-pop had become quite slow, the productions were slick, smooth, and filled with synthesizers, and there was no difference between pop-oriented country and adult contemporary AM pop—Kenny Rogers and Dolly Parton had the biggest single of their respective careers with their duet "Islands in the Stream," a song written by the Bee Gees and produced by Barry Gibb.

During 1983, country-pop was swept off mainstream pop radio by the twin forces of MTV-sponsored new wave and Michael Jackson's *Thriller*, but the sound of mainstream country didn't change at all. Over the next five years, country-pop was ruled by the polished sounds of post-*Urban Cowboy* country-pop. A few performers, such as George Strait, Ricky Skaggs, and Randy Travis, broke through with their hard-edged, updated take on traditional country, but it wasn't until the late '80s that the appeal of the urban cowboy style faded for many country fans. During the latter half of the decade, a wave of new traditionalists inspired by Strait and Skaggs captured the attention of the country audience, bringing country back closer to its roots. Yet urban cowboy hadn't completely left the consciousness of many country audiences, and a fusion of its slick, pop-oriented sensibilities and the hard-edged music of new traditionalists dubbed new country enjoyed crossover success in the early '90s, ten years after *Urban Cowboy* conquered the pop charts.

Recommended Recordings:
Various Artists, *Urban Cowboy* (Asylum)
Various Artists, *Urban Cowboy II* (Asylum)
Kenny Rogers, *25 Greatest Hits* (Liberty)
Alabama, *Greatest Hits* (RCA)
Mickey Gilley, *Ten Years of Hits* (Epic)
Barbara Mandrell, *The Best of Barbara Mandrell* (MCA)
Charlie Daniels Band, *A Decade of Hits* (Epic)
Dolly Parton, *Greatest Hits* (RCA)

—Stephen Thomas Erlewine

Nashville's New Traditionalists in the 1980s

At the same time that outlaw fever was sweeping Nashville in the mid-'70s, another trend was stirring feathers among the city's traditionalists; an infiltration into Music City by pop singers like Olivia Newton-John, Linda Ronstadt, and John Denver. Not only were these lightweight vocalists hitting the tops of the country charts, but they were winning Country Music Association awards. (When, in 1975, presenter Charlie Rich opened the envelope containing the name of the CMA's Entertainer of the Year and found the winner was John Denver, he burned the envelope right then and there; a moment that may have been shameful at the time, but is now legendary.)

By the close of the decade, outlaw chic was pretty much played out; and it was clear that, as strong as the back-to-the-basics music of Waylon Jennings and Willie Nelson had been, it wasn't going to eradicate the country music industry's interest in playing footsie with the pop music market. Rising superstar Kenny Rogers showed the powerful crossover potential of watered-down country when "The Gambler" hit in 1978. Dolly Parton had her first big crossover hit, "Here You Come Again," a year earlier, and seemed to be giving up the traditional country she'd grown up singing (her partnership with Porter Wagoner "broke up" a couple of years later). By the turn of the decade, names like Mac Davis, Anne Murray, the Little River Band, and Barbara Mandrell were appearing on the country charts more and more often.

This was also the era when country went Hollywood. Nelson, Parton, and Kris Kristofferson enjoyed prominent movie roles, and Mandrell had a glitzy "uptown" TV show that had little to do with country music's hillbilly past (which had been ghettoized on *Hee Haw*). But it was *Urban Cowboy* in 1980 that marked the peak of the industry's love affair with soft-country gaudiness; and also marked the point of market saturation. Greed for bigger and bigger pop hits had been rampant, and now it was clear that national sales figures were not keeping up with industry spending. The pop-country infatuation was headed for a fall.

Which is why it was so refreshing to hear the plain, unadorned voice of Texan George Strait hit the airwaves in 1981 with "Unwound." As a singer, Strait hardly matches someone like George Jones, but there was a sincerity in his voice that was immediately refreshing. And his music had nothing to do with pop; it was a back-to-basics, neo-traditional approach in arrangements and instrumentation that had hardly been heard since the outlaw days. Instead of trying to hide his music's hillbilly roots, Strait celebrated them; he had no crossover aspirations. Some of Strait's most enduring songs released throughout the mid-'80s include "Amarillo By Morning," "Right or Wrong," and "Does Fort Worth Ever Cross Your Mind." (Strait's big cowboy hat may at the time have been a genuine mark of his rural background, but some ten years down the road it would inspire the "hat act" look and become an overused prop among a whole new breed of male country stylists.)

Another singer making his mark at the time was John Anderson, a Florida native who'd come to Nashville in 1971 and recorded his first single in 1974. He didn't, though, get major attention until early in the following decade with the release of "1959" and "I'm Just an Old Chunk of Coal." The latter was a Billy Joe Shaver song from the '70s, which helps connect the dots between the two decades. Anderson has lots of Lefty Frizzell in his voice, and, like Strait, his music was at the opposite (traditional) end of the musical spectrum from someone like Mandrell (who was CMA's Entertainer of the Year in 1980 and 1981, the years of Anderson and Strait's breakthroughs). In 1982, Anderson had his first number one with "Wild and Blue," a great, punchy song that speaks frankly of sexual tension and became something of a modern classic (the Mekons even recorded a version of it); a year later, Anderson's popularity was cemented by the huge success of "Swingin'."

Ricky Skaggs was perhaps the most "traditional" of this slowly-forming group of "new traditionalist" singers. A mandolin prodigy in his early childhood—though also skilled on fiddle and guitar—Skaggs played for several years with bluegrass legend Ralph Stanley (joining when he was 15), and later with Emmylou Harris' Hot Band. So it was natural that his solo country records would feature an exciting mix of traditional bluegrass and country. His debut album, *Waitin' for the Sun to Shine* (1981), produced several hit songs, and Skaggs became one of the most popular country artists of the early '80s. The Judds were a mother-daughter duo (Naomi and Wynonna) from Ashland, KY, who started by making early-morning appearances on Ralph Emery's radio show, and ended up one of the most popular country acts of the decade. Their music was simple and had mass appeal, but it was far more traditional than anything on Dolly Parton's records at the time.

They released their first single in 1983, and the following year won a Grammy for "Mama He's Crazy."

It's hard to say what exactly makes the doors in Nashville open a bit wider every once in a while—allowing individualists and oddballs a chance they otherwise might never get—but that's exactly what happened in the mid-'80s. Perhaps it was the popularity of people like Strait, Anderson, and Skaggs, but whatever the cause, record contracts (and substantial promotion to boot) were suddenly available for artists like Steve Earle, the O'Kanes, and Lyle Lovett, superb talents who spiced up the "straight" world of country music considerably. The year 1986 turned out to be a magic one, as Earle, Lovett, Dwight Yoakam, and Randy Travis each released their debut albums. Unlike the outlaws a decade earlier, each of these artists came from different musical (and geographical) directions and worked independently of the others; there was no clique or scene—no "Hillbilly Central"—to hang out in.

Earle proved himself the rocker of the bunch, perhaps the closest in spirit to the classic work of Waylon Jennings. Earle looked rather clean cut on his debut, *Guitar Town*—as hard and up-front a country album to have come out of Nashville in years, and much more aggressive than anything George Strait ever recorded—but he soon showed his true ragged-glory colors with *Copperhead Road* two years later. That album's title track did have a twangy mandolin intro, but once it got going, it almost felt like heavy metal. Lovett's music is strongly rooted in Texas folk and country, especially on his self-titled debut (which featured the classic "This Old Porch," co-written with his buddy Robert Earl Keen). But as later albums have shown, the world of country music couldn't contain this diverse talent. His third release (*Lyle Lovett & His Large Band*) was marked by arrangements that had been jazzed up considerably, including a snazzy, big-band-style cover of "Stand By Your Man." By this point, Lovett had moved away from traditional country and was off in new, refreshing directions.

Travis' 1986 debut album, *Storms of Life*, was a beautiful showcase for his strong, versatile, George Jones-inspired vocal work, and contained great catchy songs like "Digging Up Bones" and "1982." He quickly turned into one of the most popular country stars of the decade (his follow-up album, 1987's *Always and Forever*, stayed on top of the country charts for nearly a year). Yoakam was something of an outsider, having settled in L.A. instead of Nashville. On the West Coast, he hooked into the rockabilly-revival and punk-rock communities, and his debut album, *Guitars, Cadillacs, Etc., Etc.*—with its hard, honky tonk sound and Yoakam's pure, strong voice—was immediately popular with rock & rollers as well as a large number of country crowd. Yoakam's later association with Buck Owens showed his affinity for the Bakersfield sound. Another group that released their debut album in 1986 was the O'Kanes, a catchy country duo comprised of Jamie O'Hara and Kieran Kane (the latter of whom would go on to found the Dead Reckoning record label a decade later). Their music was based around spare, folk-inspired melodies and arrangements which featured fiddle, mandolin, and accordion; and gentle, pleasant harmonies.

Toward the end of the decade, more names had cropped up that were associated with "new traditionalism," which was now more visible as a genre. Ricky Van Shelton was one of the most prominent, a guy who inspired the "hunk" look of the 1990s but also had a penchant for material that was more or less traditionally based. He even recorded a gospel album. Keith Whitley (a pal of Ricky Skaggs) died at an early age, but his mark as a strong, distinct vocalist and modern honky tonk stylist has proved indelible. And Kentucky native Patty Loveless, who emerged in the late '80s, proved herself not just one of the strongest female solo artists of the era (though that title probably should go to Reba McEntire based on popularity and hard work alone), but someone who truly feels the soul in country's roots. By the 1990s, however, "new traditionist" had become an all-too-common buzzword, as such labels inevitably do. And the accoutrements that went with this back-to-basics music—big hats and hunky, fresh-faced singers in clean white T-shirts—were images that contributed to the big new boom in country music's popularity. It's likely, though, that it's because of the success of artists like George Strait, Randy Travis, and even Steve Earle that we get singers like Alan Jackson and Marty Stuart at the top of the charts today.

Recommended Recordings:
John Anderson, *Wild & Blue* (Warner Bros.)
Rosanne Cash, *King's Record Shop* (Columbia)
Steve Earle, *Guitar Town* (MCA)
The Judds, *The Greatest Hits* (RCA)
Patty Loveless, *If My Heart Had Windows* (MCA)
Lyle Lovett, *Lyle Lovett* (MCA/Curb)
The O'Kanes, *The O'Kanes* (Columbia)
Ricky Skaggs, *Waitin' for the Sun to Shine* (Epic)
George Strait, *Does Fort Worth Ever Cross Your Mind* (MCA)
Randy Travis, *Storms of Life* (Warner Bros.)
Keith Whitley, *I Wonder Do You Think of Me* (RCA)
Dwight Yoakam, *Guitars, Cadillacs, Etc., Etc.* (Reprise)

—Kurt Wolff

Roots Rock

Roots rock was one of the more curious trends of the '80s. In the previous two decades, there were always back-to-basics movements in rock & roll, whether it was the periodic rockabilly revivals or the punk explosion of the late '70s, but roots rock was a different beast entirely. Growing out of the tangled web of post-punk in the early '80s, roots rock was equally indebted to underground, American indie rock as it was to country-rock. It functioned outside of the mainstream of the industry, building up a cult following through constant touring and a steady stream of records. Roots rock occasionally roared

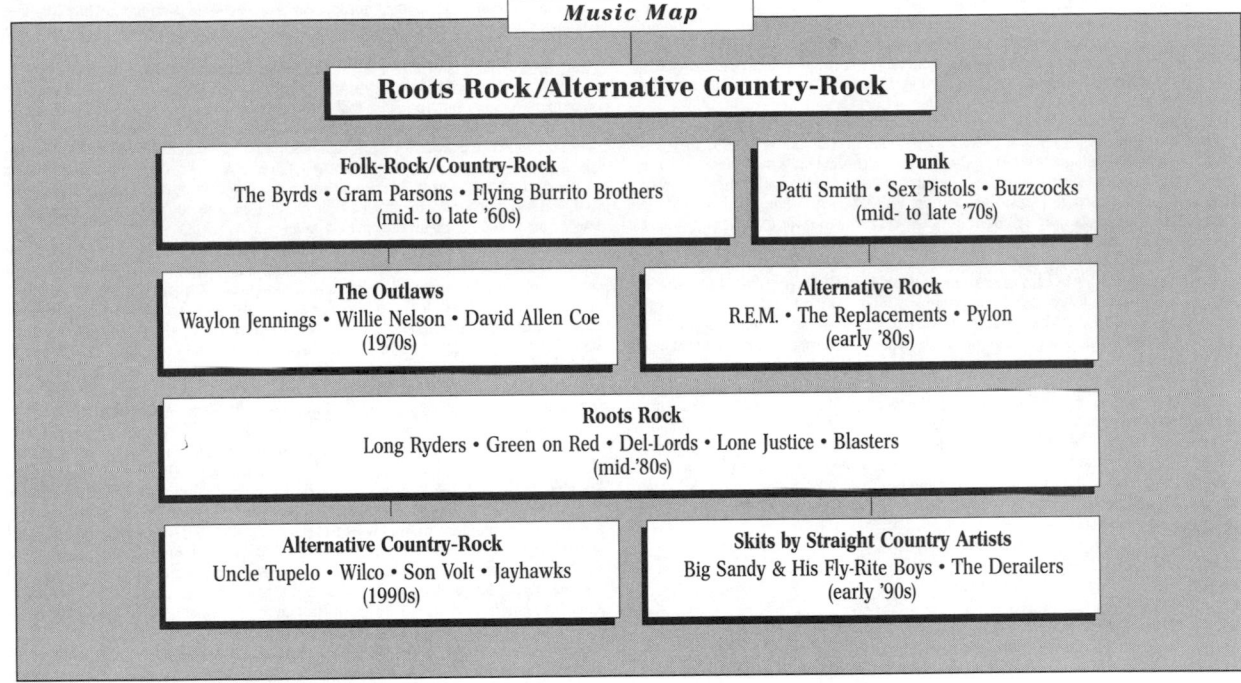

Music Map

Roots Rock/Alternative Country-Rock

Folk-Rock/Country-Rock
The Byrds • Gram Parsons • Flying Burrito Brothers
(mid- to late '60s)

Punk
Patti Smith • Sex Pistols • Buzzcocks
(mid- to late '70s)

The Outlaws
Waylon Jennings • Willie Nelson • David Allen Coe
(1970s)

Alternative Rock
R.E.M. • The Replacements • Pylon
(early '80s)

Roots Rock
Long Ryders • Green on Red • Del-Lords • Lone Justice • Blasters
(mid-'80s)

Alternative Country-Rock
Uncle Tupelo • Wilco • Son Volt • Jayhawks
(1990s)

Skits by Straight Country Artists
Big Sandy & His Fly-Rite Boys • The Derailers
(early '90s)

with punk energy, but its sensibilities were out of the country-rock movement of the late '60s and early '70s. No roots rock band broke into the mainstream—the Del Fuegos came the closest, but that was only in the form of a beer commercial—but they laid the groundwork for the Americana and alternative country/country-rock boom of the '90s. Indeed, many of its alumni were still active in Americana or alternative country during the '90s.

While most of roots rock bands were heavily influenced by the raunchy swagger of the Rolling Stones and the hard twang of Gram Parsons, it is unlikely many of them would have existed without R.E.M. Though the Athens-based band only occasionally delved into country-rock, R.E.M. ushered in an era of simple, garage-based pop and rock in the mid-'80s. By wiping out the synth-pop of new wave and the arty post-punk experiments of the early '80s, the group allowed both neo-psychedelic rockers and roots rockers grab the spotlight. Before R.E.M., the Los Angeles-based Blasters had played an edgy variation of roots rock and punk, while X had flirted with rockabilly (the Stray Cats had a couple of new wave pop hits with their kitschy rockabilly revival, as well), but roots rockers did not appear until after R.E.M.

Once the roots rockers appeared, they quickly divided themselves into two camps: edgy cowpunk bands like Jason & the Scorchers and the Beat Farmers, and straight-forward country-rockers like the Long Ryders and Del Fuegos. Over the course of the mid-'80s, the groups steadily built up strong followings. Country audiences paid no mind to the bands, but alternative country artists like Dwight Yoakam and k.d. lang came to prominence through this movement; both musicians adhered to country traditions more than even the Gram Parsons-devoted Long Ryders, but the conservative Nashville establishment ignored them, leaving the roots rock circuit as their only option.

During the late '80s, roots rock began to splinter. None of the bands had sold many records, and the climate of American indie rock was beginning to change. No longer were rootsy garage rockers and jangling guitar-pop bands like R.E.M. hip currency, as grunge and artsy post-punk bands began to earn larger audiences. As a result, many roots rock bands broke up during the last three years of the '80s. Most musicians left the industry. Some, like Syd Griffin, worked behind the scenes as a journalist. Some kept performing, eventually carving out their own niche as a singer/songwriter on such labels as Hightone Records.

Many roots rockers got a second chance in the '90s, when alternative country-rock became a hip underground movement. Bands like Jason & the Scorchers re-formed, while the leaders of other bands carved out solo careers. Much of the alternative country movement was inspired by the original roots rockers. Though roots rock rarely offered any sonic innovations, it kept the spirit of the music alive during an era when hard country had virtually disappeared.

Recommended Recordings:
R.E.M., *Reckoning* (IRS)
Jason & the Scorchers, *Essential, Vol. 1 (Are You Ready for the Country)* (Capitol)
The Blasters, *The Blasters Collection* (Slash)
Beat Farmers, *Tales of the New West* (Rhino)
Lone Justice, *Lone Justice* (Geffen)
The Long Ryders, *Two-Fisted Tales* (Island)
Del-Lords, *Johnny Comes Marching Home* (EMI)

Green on Red, *Gas Food Lodging* (Enigma)
The Del Fuegos, *The Longest Day* (Slash)
True Believers, *True Believers* (EMI)
The Silos, *Cuba* (Record Collect/Watermelon)

–Thom Owens

New Country

The unprecedented crossover success of Garth Brooks in the early '90s was the sign that new country had come into its own. A blend of new traditionalist sensibilities and the slick, pop-savvy crossover potential of urban cowboy, new country not only appealed to fans of hard-edged, honky tonk-derived traditional country, but also a wide variety of urban pop fans; including both teenagers and maturing baby boomers. The music owed as much to the mainstream arena rock of the '70s as it did to country music—Brooks himself was an avowed fan of not only George Strait, but also the Eagles, Kiss, and Billy Joel—which gave it a crossover appeal unmatched even by urban cowboy. Depending on the artist, new country either sounded like an updated version of country-boogie or twangy power ballads, which meant that it appealed to both rock and country audiences equally. New country had an even more powerful impact on the country audience than urban cowboy did in the previous decade; by the mid-'90s, new country artists ruled the airwaves completely, leaving older artists in the dust.

Given the ultimate result of new country, it is somewhat ironic that its roots lay in the revival of traditional country values represented by such singers as George Strait and Randy Travis. During the mid-'80s, Strait and Travis—along with singers like Dwight Yoakam and k.d. lang, who both functioned outside of Nashville's mainstream—were two of only a handful of new vocalists who refused to bend to the pop inclinations of post-urban cowboy country radio, instead choosing to adhere to the traditions of George Jones, Merle Haggard, and Lefty Frizzell. Both Strait and Travis were considerably successful, which led the industry to believe that there was an audience for harder-edged country.

For a while, new traditionalists dominated the country charts during the latter half of the '80s, signaling that the genre was experiencing a kind of artistic rebirth. But it wasn't until the early '90s that this burgeoning movement broke through into the mainstream, in the guise of new country singers like Clint Black, Travis Tritt, and, of course, Garth Brooks. None of these three vocalists were traditionalists like Strait and Travis; they adapted the rootsy tendencies of their immediate predecessors, melding them into a sound that demonstrated more rock and pop influences. Not only did the sound of new country crib heavily from the rock industry, so did the image. No longer was the country industry working from rural roots, doing its best to hide the redneck past of their artists. Instead, it groomed a breed of attractive, good-looking vocalists that on the surface had very little to do with either the down-home appeal of George Jones and Hank Williams, or the rugged redneck image of outlaw singers like Waylon Jennings and Hank Williams Jr. New country singers were clean, well-groomed and non-threatening; ideal for crossover success.

That crossover success happened when Garth Brooks' *No Fences* gained momentum in 1991. Brooks had enough cowboy in him to appeal to the new traditionalists, but also enough pop savvy to appeal to a generation of baby boomers weaned on the Californian country-rock of the Eagles and Linda Ronstadt. As a result, he became a pop music phenomenon: *No Fences* went platinum 13 times over; while its successor, 1991's *Ropin' the Wind*, spent 18 weeks at the top of the pop charts and sold over 11-million albums. In the process, it ushered in a whole new generation of country singers to the charts. There were both one-hit wonders like Billy Ray Cyrus and more substantial acts like Brooks & Dunn that followed Brooks to the top of the charts.

During the first half of the '90s, the new country boom was extraordinary. In the previous decade, country artists were lucky if they went gold, but during the '90s, they regularly went multi-platinum. Country radio changed according to its new audience. Since there were so many new listeners to country radio unfamiliar and impatient with such older stars as George Jones, Dolly Parton, Willie Nelson, Johnny Cash, and Merle Haggard, the old artists were removed from the play lists in favor of newer musicians. Soon, veteran artists were not heard on the radio at all, and their record sales dried up. In no time, edgier country artists were phased out of rotation as well.

By the middle of the decade, new country completely dominated the country charts and radio, and while it was harder than the post-urban country music, it nevertheless owed more to pop than country. Shania Twain, the biggest star of the mid-'90s, was produced by Robert "Mutt" Lange—who made his name by working with heavy metal acts like AC/DC and Def Leppard, as well as new wave rockers like the Cars—and her music appropriately resembled slightly rootsy AOR pop/rock. Though Twain's *The Woman in Me* sold eight-million copies, it was the last of the country blockbusters. In 1996, the country audience declined drastically, partially because the music was becoming too similar, and partially because its fans had found other genres to listen to. True country fans listened to the edgy sound of alternative country-rock, while baby boomers found themselves leaning toward the adult alternative sounds of pop radio. By the end of 1996, the sales of country albums were approaching the levels of the pre-Garth days.

Recommended Recordings:

Garth Brooks, *Ropin' the Wind* (Liberty)
Garth Brooks, *The Hits* (Liberty)
Brooks & Dunn, *Brand New Man* (Arista)
Clint Black, *Greatest Hits* (RCA)
Shania Twain, *The Women in Me* (Mercury)
Alan Jackson, *Greatest Hits Collection* (Arista)
Vince Gill, *Souvenirs* (MCA Nashville)
Reba McEntire, *Greatest Hits, Vol. 2* (MCA)
Wynonna Judd, *Collection* (MCA)
Travis Tritt, *Greatest Hits: From the Beginning* (Warner Bros.)
Lorrie Morgan, *Greatest Hits* (BNA)
Tim McGraw, *All I Want* (Curb)
John Michael Montgomery, *John Michael Montgomery* (Atlantic)
Trisha Yearwood, *Thinkin' About You* (MCA)

—Stephen Thomas Erlewine

Alternative Country in the '90s

In 1990, a band called Uncle Tupelo from Belleville, IL—a small town just north of East St. Louis—released their debut album. Titled *No Depression*, it featured a rough but captivating mixture of raucous punk-rock songs, but it also added something different: several toned-down, acoustic ballads that had a distinct country flavor. And the title track itself was even a cover of a Carter Family song from the 1930s.

A few years later, when Uncle Tupelo's music began catching on among indie rockers with a taste for old-time country, that simple little song and album title became the name of an Internet fan club and chat group. But it didn't stop there: in 1995, a magazine of the same name went into publication, and "No Depression" soon became the leading moniker for a burgeoning alternative country movement. Other names include "insurgent country" (coined by Chicago label Bloodshot, which put out a couple of acclaimed "alternative country" compilations), "Americana," or simply "alt.country," the latter reminding us of the role the Internet has played in the growth and publicity of this movement (a development that is distinctly separate from the growth of the music itself).

For the most part, No Depression or alt.country bands weren't much of a threat to the sales figures of mainstream Nashville country artists. But the speed with which this music (and its various nicknames) caught on showed that a substantial number of people were fed up with the overproduced pop trends of 1990s mainstream country music, and the limited range of styles and sounds that were typically played on country radio stations. When an average rock fans thinks country, they think Garth Brooks; this, say No Depression fans, is a crime and a damn shame.

Alternative music in any genre is nothing new. As long as there's been a mainstream, there have been other, less obvious artists struggling to get their brand of music noticed. In country music's recent past, names like Gram Parsons, Waylon Jennings, and Willie Nelson—and practically anything that came out of Austin, TX—are frequently-cited examples of people who struggled for the chance just to play music the way they wanted. In addition, the blending of country and rock music is as old as Elvis Presley's recording of Bill Monroe's "Blue Moon of Kentucky" in 1954. Johnny Cash and Bob Dylan helped tear down the walls between the two genres with their famous collaborations in the 1960s; Gram Parsons took the Byrds all the way to the *Grand Ole Opry*; Waylon Jennings covered Rolling Stones songs and got a standing ovation opening for the Grateful Dead in the 1970s; and Neil Young let hippies singing "Are You Ready for the Country" while Merle Haggard's "Okie from Muskogee" was still fresh in most Americans' minds. Jennings may be a favorite of many No Depression fans, but it's Parsons who is considered the patron saint of this movement; a guy who grew up a rocker but always had a

love of pure, traditional country music. He was an outsider looking in, while "outlaw" Jennings was an established country singer trying to make more room for himself in a claustrophobic industry.

But there is something about this No Depression movement that's genuinely distinct from past country-rock trends. Maybe it's the fact that a good number of the fans grew up on punk rock, and came to realize that many of the old-time country outfits were musically untrained and express a similar do-it-yourself philosophy shared by many punk bands (as well as a penchant for fast rhythms, rough-edged guitar licks, and unadorned lyrics). Or maybe these same punks simply got tired of loud, brash rock bands. Or maybe it's the fact that people were finally realizing that country music is a big, wide world unto itself that had much more to offer than Top 40 radio stations and the industry bigwigs on Music Row would let the average person believe.

Many of the artists at the top of the No Depression and insurgent country rosters are indeed bands who play in rock & roll clubs, not at county fairs. The fact that they can get young punk-rock fans bobbing their heads to straight-up covers of songs by Tom T. Hall or the Louvin Brothers—a group few would know by name—is proof enough that this music is able to reach beyond the traditional boundaries of the country and rock genres. While Uncle Tupelo and its offshoot bands, Wilco and Son Volt—both formed in the wake of UT's breakup—are the centerpieces of the No Depression movement, to say that the '90s alternative country scene began with this single Uncle Tupelo album isn't really correct. The music itself already existed; it simply didn't have such a visible umbrella under which to fall.

The country roots of L.A. punk legends X, for instance, began showing in their later albums, and they even recorded a full-on country album in 1985 under the name the Knitters. Southern California, long a haven for individualistic country artists (Merle Haggard, for instance), even spawned an entire "cowpunk" crowd (Rank and File, Lone Justice), not to mention a rockabilly revival scene (the Blasters, Big Sandy) that remained strong into the 1990s. Jason & the Scorchers' debut album, *Lost and Found* (1985), was an electrified inspiration to many rock fans who liked their twang on the loud side. And the raucous British punk group the Mekons became, on later albums, more and more fixated on American roots music; singer Jon Langford went on to front a far more countrified side project called the Waco Brothers.

Souled American was a late-'80s Chicago band that mixed country and folk influences into their quirky rock songs. On their third album, *Around the Horn*, the twang got thicker and deeper, and they twisted the country genre in their own way by taking the rhythms down to a slow, mesmerizing crawl. Unfortunately, Souled American never received the recognition it deserved (partly because the band's label, Rough Trade, went bankrupt). The Blood Oranges spiked their excellent albums with country-inspired ballads (often featuring the beautiful voice of Cheri Knight) and heavy doses of bluegrass. Go to Blazes played barroom rock & roll laced with country and blues (and a few choice Charlie Rich and Hank Williams Jr. covers). Freakwater is an acoustic group inspired by Carter Family songs and other old-time mountain folk ballads, and despite being fronted by two women who grew up in the punk scene of Louisville, KY, they were one of the most "traditional" country acts of the 1990s. Lambchop is a lush, arty Nashville band that claims '70s pop producer and songwriter Billy Sherrill as their idol.

Rock is certainly the background of most No Depression fans and artists, but the community also became extremely fond of artists like Haggard and George Jones, country music legends who were more and more finding themselves shunned by an industry (one with an shockingly short memory) that became obsessed with sales figures and a flurry of young, fresh-scrubbed singers. Steve Earle was once one of these fresh faces himself (though not too well-scrubbed), but his confrontational, "bad boy" attitude kept him at a distance from Nashville almost since his debut, *Guitar Town*. In 1996, he graced the cover of No Depression magazine, and has been an alt.country hero ever since. Another favorite is Dale Watson, a straight-up honky tonker based in Austin, TX, who was one of the strongest country artists working today, yet on a West Coast indie label, Hightone, and, like his idols (Haggard, Buck Owens, Johnny Paycheck), is virtually ignored by Nashville. Acclaimed singer/songwriters like Townes Van Zandt, Guy Clark, Lucinda Williams, Billy Joe Shaver, and Jimmie Dale Gilmore—many of them Texas artists, showing that Austin's colorful, off-center musical history has much in common with the No Depression scene as well—also are icons of the alt.country genre. And all sorts of musicians and fans continue to back further still for inspiration, to artists like the Louvin Brothers, Bill Monroe, Rose Maddox, and the Carter Family.

Recommended Recordings:

Dave Alvin, *Blue Blvd.* (Hightone)
Blood Oranges, *The Crying Tree* (East Side Digital)
Steve Earle, *I Feel Alright* (E-Squared)
Freakwater, *Old Paint* (Thrill Jockey)
Geraldine Fibbers, *Lost Somewhere Between the Earth and My Home* (Virgin)
Jimmie Dale Gilmore, *After Awhile* (Elektra Nonesuch/American Explorer)
Go to Blazes, *Waiting Around for the Crash* (East Side Digital)
Joe Henry, *Short Man's Room* (Mammoth)
Jayhawks, *Blue Earth* (Twin Tone)
Lambchop, *How I Quit Smoking* (Merge)
Palace Brothers, *There Is No-One What Will Take Care of You* (Drag City)
Scud Mountain Boys, *Massachusetts* (Sub Pop)
Shaver, *Tramp on Your Street* (Zoo/Praxis)
Son Volt, *Trace* (Warner Bros.)
Souled American, *Around the Horn* (Rough Trade)
Uncle Tupelo, *Anodyne* (Reprise)
Townes Van Zandt, *Live at the Old Quarter, Houston, Texas* (Tomato)

Dale Watson, *Cheatin' Heart Attack* (Hightone)
Wilco, *Being There* (Reprise)
Lucinda Williams, *Lucinda Williams* (Rough Trade)

—Kurt Wolff

Bakersfield Revival

There are those who continue to claim that only Nashville can be the home of country & western music. In truth, the West Coast was recording and promoting country & western music a full decade before Nashville caught on. It was out in the wilds of the West that Western swing, honky tonk, bluegrass, mountain music, hillbilly, and country & western were first given a foothold beyond the clutches of the Big Apple. Los Angeles was the place, and due to its thriving movie industry, entertainments of all kinds were sought out. A hearty percentage of the population of California were immigrants from Arkansas, Oklahoma, Missouri, Kentucky, and, yes, even Tennessee and Texas. They brought with them their culture and, more importantly, their music.

It was only natural that as the 20th century progressed through two World Wars, a Dust Bowl, and Depression, something had to give. In California's San Joaquin Valley, it was the music, where a sound was starting to take shape that was distinctly a melding of all the different musics that had come together in this region. Carried upon the shoulders of Missouri fiddle players and Dust Bowl Okies who made their daily bread as migrant farm workers, day laborers, and, later, as factory workers, the music settled in and took root in the fertile soil of Bakersfield. Once an agricultural crossroads that also found affluence in oil and gold mining the century before, Bakersfield was suddenly a cultural axis that captured the imaginations of players, writers, singers, and fun seekers, all craving the hard-edged, wild, and loud honky tonk sound.

Prior to the boom years of the 1950s and '60s, Bakersfield had something boiling beneath its surface. Bill Woods and his Orange Blossom Playboys were playing at the infamous Blackboard as the house band before Buck Owens even set foot within the Bakersfield city limits. Tommy Collins and Billy Mize were already making waves before the 1950s brought attention to Bakersfield, and Capitol Records decided to take a chance on the hillbillies who were creating such a revolutionary sound. The boom years saw Bakersfield cement its reputation as the center of all West Coast country & western music activity. Recording, performing, and access to Los Angeles were all in its favor, as was the local population. Famed guitarist and songwriter Roy Nichols came from Fresno just as the Maddox Brothers and Sister Rose moved south from Modesto. Others, like Buck and Bonnie Owens, came from Arizona, while some made their way from Texas and other points east, north, and south.

Ferlin Husky, Jean Shepard, Harlan Howard, Dallas Frazier, Jan Howard, Wynn Stewart, and Lefty Frizzell all owe Bakersfield a debt of gratitude. Others who found their way and made names for themselves include Ralph Mooney, Tom Bramley, Don Rich, Norm Hamlin, Jim Shaw, Henry Sharp, Don Markham, Doyle Holly, Roy Hays, and many more. Bonnie Owens, sometimes referred to as "the Queen of Bakersfield," and songwriter Red Simpson created a place for themselves after taking up residence in Bakersfield. It was the working class who paved the path that lead directly to the Bakersfield sound. Those who worked a five or six day week at minimum wage with no future found sustenance and a form of communication that defined their lives and their own emotions within the music. Almost mythical in proportion, the sound and the scene fueled a whole new generation of traditionalists beyond its glory years. Dwight Yoakam makes no bones about the fact that he too was a disciple of the Bakersfield sound, even though he grew up in Ohio and the hollers of Kentucky, where his grandparents exposed him to the hillbilly culture so many others had taken with them on their quest for a better life in California.

Today the boom town may be gone, but the sound remains. Its expansion into Los Angeles, the San Fernando Valley, Orange Country, and beyond allowed the Bakersfield sound to continue to prevail between the 1970s and the mid-'80s explosion generated by the compilation project *A Town South of Bakersfield*. Kept alive by the rebel bands that found a camaraderie with Don Rich, the '70s was a time for the meshing together of country and roots rock, the result being the New Riders of the Purple Sage, Commander Cody and his Lost Planet Airmen, the Flying Burrito Brothers, Poco, and the Eagles.

The success of *A Town South of Bakersfield* generated a renewed interest in the country & western music coming from the West Coast. The major-label interest given to Dwight Yoakam added fuel to the fire as the Lonesome Strangers, Syd Straw, the Neon Angels, the Plowboys, Sid Griffin, Kathy Robertson, Rosie Flores, Larry Dean, Katy Moffatt, Dale Watson, Patty Booker, James Intveld, Dave Alvin, Ronnie Mack, and a slew of other talent took up the cause. L.A. sought out the energy and tradition of their musical heritage and, because of their foresight, a quiet Bakersfield Renaissance began to unfold as the mid-'90s rolled around.

By 1996, the renaissance was catching on in Texas, Chicago, Portland, and North Carolina, and even Nashville was beginning to feel the force that was once again rising out of the West. Artists and bands like the Derailers, Junior Brown, Robbie Fulks, the Backsliders, BR5-49, and Rebecca Kilgore found the Bakersfield spirit alive and well within their own music. Bakersfield band Big House was signed by MCA and another hometown outfit, the Wichitas, continued to move forward with their contribution to the Bakersfield sound in the recording studio.

The evidence was mounting. Herb Pedersen and Chris Hillman recorded the tribute *Bakersfield Bound*, which featured exceptional versions of classic tunes including "Playboy." Former Haggard apprentice Scott Joss, who was just a teenager when he began his career as a member of the Strangers, released his first solo effort, *Souvenirs*, which honored Bakersfield and Joss' mentors Tiny Moore, Roy Nichols, and Merle Haggard. And, too, there are those who have carefully nurtured the sound, passing it on to the next generation. Larry Dean, who came from Idaho because he heard the call of Bakersfield

decades ago, was mentored by Nichols and in turn mentored newcomer Michael Dart. Cody Bryant and Kathy Robertson counted Red Simpson as their teacher and friend, and Bonnie Owens always reached out to younger players and singers in the hopes of giving them a hand. The next generation includes the many who came to sit at Red's feet on any given Monday night when he held court at Trout's.

With an influx of pilgrims comes an increase in business and the need for venues, including the opening of Buck Owens' Crystal Palace Museum and Theatre. Other venues are being remodeled, restored, and reopened. The grand old Fox Theatre went through a five-year reconstruction project. Trout's remains the old lady of distinction, and it continues to support the local musicians as well as welcoming the many who make the two-hour drive from Los Angeles. Some of the clubs in L.A. are jumping on the bandwagon and giving the Bakersfield Revolution a push. The Foothill Club, just south of L.A., is still operating and booking more country & western acts. Thrown to the punk crowd in the '70s and '80s, this legendary honky tonk is looking to the future and feeling optimistic. It is the place that the real honky tonkers want to play when they come to the City of Angels. Just as important, the Bakersfield Revolution has spread to non-country clubs; Jacks Sugar Shack, once known for blues and rock, now seeks out country and roots music.

It is interesting to note that our great-grandparents, grandparents, and parents who trudged out from the Ozarks, the Appalachians, and the Dust Bowl set into motion a cultural phenomenon that is still vibrant and meaningful 70 and 80 years later. This is their legacy and ours as we look toward a future filled with unknowns. Those who continue to be purveyors of the Bakersfield sound carry with them the strength of a past they are deeply connected to and the seeds that will be planted once again in a still farther off, distant future. Because they are the Bakersfield bards whose perseverance in the face of greed and convention has no limits, no one will ever forget what took place in the little town north of Los Angeles. In fact, they will more than likely seek out the Bakersfield sound time and time again, hunting for the joy and sustenance that their forebearers found in that special music when the the initial strains of fiddle, guitar, and pedal steel joined together in perfect harmony, ringing through the starry western night, calling out to the faithful.

Recommended Recordings:
Tommy Collins, *Words and Music Country Style* (Capitol)
Dallas Frazier, *Singing My Songs* (RCA)
Ferlin Husky, *Gone* (Capitol)
Billy Mize, *This Time and Place* (Imperial)
Merle Haggard, *The Lonesome Fugitive: The Anthology (1963-1977)* (Razor & Tie)
Buck Owens, *The Buck Owens Collection, 1959-1990* (Rhino)
Wynn Stewart, *The Best of the Challenge Masters* (AVI)
Various Artists, *A Town South of Bakersfield, Vols. I, II, & III* (Restless)
Various Artists, *Hillbilly Fever, Vol. 4: Legends of the West Coast* (Rhino)
Jean Shepard, *Classic Capitol Recordings, 1952-1964* (CMF)
Hank Penny, *Rompin', Stompin', Swingin'* (Bear Family)
Joe & Rose Lee Maphis, *Dim Lights, Thick Smoke* (CMH)
Lefty Frizzell, *Lefty Frizzell* (Columbia)
Molly Bee, *Good Golly Ms. Molly* (Granite)
Freddie Hart, *The Best of Freddie Hart* (Harmony)
Johnny Bond, *That Wild, Wicked but Wonderful West* (Starday)
Larry Dean, *Outside Chance* (USA Music Group)
Dwight Yoakam, *Guitars, Cadillacs, Etc., Etc.* (Reprise)
Desert Rose Band, *Running* (MCA/Curb)
Rick Shea, *Buffalo Show* (Major Label Records)
Kathy Robertson, *At the Cantina* (Kitty LA Tour)
Cody Bryant, *Big Dose of Country* (Wagon Wheel)
Mark Insley, *Good Country Junk* (Country Town Records)
James Intveld, *James Intveld* (Bear Family)
Neil Mooney, *Ranchdressing* (Strawdog)
Scott Joss, *Souvenirs* (Little Dog)
The Lonesome Strangers, *The Lonesome Strangers* (HighTone)
Chris Gaffney, *Loser's Paradise* (HighTone)

—Jana Pendragon

Country Albums by Rock Artists

Country music has always gotten a lot of lip service from rock musicians, whether it's to praise the vocals of George Jones and the songwriting of Hank Williams, or just to enthuse wildly over artists like the Carter Family and Tammy Wynette. It's relatively rare, however, that artists who define themselves as rock musicians will take their admiration into action by recording an entire country album. To do so means alienating a good many of their fans, for one thing. More importantly, liking a music and playing it are two entirely separate things. Making a detour into country music is a risky venture that has led to extremely erratic results, ranging from inspired fusions and landmark albums to ill-advised experiments that are best forgotten.

Country music was a big part of the chemical equation that gave birth to rock & roll, and naturally its influence has been felt, to small and large degrees, within rock music for the past 40 years. The first generation of rockabilly singers usually came from straight country backgrounds. Many of them would record country tunes at roughly the same time they were getting established as rockers; see Jerry Lee Lewis' "Crazy Arms," Carl Perkins' "Tennessee," and much of Wanda Jackson's early Capitol output for easy reference. And many rockabilly singers would redefine themselves as country singers after rockabilly passed out of fashion in the 1960s.

However, this essay is concerned not with artists who have balanced rockabilly and country music (see separate piece on rockabilly for a more in-depth discussion of those), but with musicians who dallied with country after firmly establishing themselves as rock performers. The first of them to do so on a large scale was Ray Charles, who surprised audiences with his *Modern Sounds in Country & Western Music* album in early 1962. Charles had only recently established himself as a pop star, after a decade or so of gospel-infused R&B hits that were instrumental to the birth of soul. Now the voice behind "I Got a Woman" and "What'd I Say" was covering songs identified with white country singers like Hank Williams, Eddy Arnold, and Don Gibson. Add to this the MOR flavor of some of the strings and backing singers, and it seemed that Charles ran a great risk of alienating his constituency.

The record, however, became a huge commercial success, reaching number one on the LP charts and yielding two massive hit singles, "I Can't Stop Loving You" and "You Don't Know Me." Almost as successful was *Modern Sounds in Country & Western Music, Vol. 2*, released at the end of 1962. Charles' move to country sounds is more understandable when considering the eclecticism of his career as a whole. He may have been principally known as an R&B/rock singer, but before 1960 he had also played straight jazz and, at the very beginning, straight pop. He did not think of himself so much as an R&B singer as a singer, period, who could handle a wide repertoire. Like many Americans, he had developed an appreciation for country music by listening to the *Grand Ole Opry* while growing up.

The crossover success of the *Modern Sounds* albums, however, was probably due to the fact that they were at least as much pop as country. Indeed, they weren't entirely successful on pure aesthetic grounds; Charles' vocals were perennially soulful, but the arrangements were often quite mushy exercises that would have found a more comfortable home with Ray Conniff. Charles never went to the extent of identifying himself as a country singer, though he has continued to insert country items into his repertoire ever since the early '60s. Nor did his country outings inspire other black soul singers to do the same. Charles' talents were perhaps too singular to generate an imitative trend, though it's worth noting that in the early '80s B.B. King did an MOR country album, *Love Me Tender*. Many fans judge this to be the worst mistake of his career, despite the disingenuous sleeve note, in which B.B. himself claims that this is the album he's always wanted to make.

Prior to the inception of country-rock in the late '60s, there were a few odd attempts by rock singers to work in the country idiom that stick out more as curiosities than innovations. Gene Pitney and George Jones teamed up for a bunch of duets in the mid-'60s that, despite some decent tracks, wouldn't rate among the highlights of either men's career. Pitney also did some recording with one of Jones' other duet partners, country singer Melba Montgomery. Pitney, Jones, and Montgomery happened to all record for the same label (Musicor), leading some historians to suspect that the Pitney duets might have been more of a convenient marketing exercise than an experimental artistic enterprise.

Around the time that Pitney was cutting his country duets, Del Shannon paid tribute to one of country's legends with *Del Shannon Sings Hank Williams*. It's hard to figure exactly who this would have been pitched to: not the fans who bought his hard-driving rock singles like "Keep on Searchin'," one would think, nor the somewhat older straight country fans, who might not have been familiar with Shannon in the first place. The album was not as interesting as you might guess. It sounds, well, exactly like you would think Shannon would sound singing Hank Williams tunes, with competent but unexciting interpretations that neither add much to the originals nor stretch Shannon's vocals in unexpected directions. Another Hank Williams tribute album was offered by Charlie Rich, who in the mid-'60s had yet to firmly identify himself as a country artist, playing the field with rock and soul at least as often. Considering his enormous interpretive gifts, Rich's *Sings the Songs of Hank Williams* is also a disappointment, relying far more upon predictably reverent, lukewarm covers than canny reinvention.

Prior to the late '60s, self-contained rock groups—who had become the pacesetters of rock music since the Beatles achieved international stardom in 1964—made very few serious nods in the direction of country. There were some very interesting individual tracks by top rock groups that fairly stank of country pie: the Beatles' own "I Don't Want to Spoil the Party" and "Baby's in Black," for instance, or "I've Just Seen a Face," which can be rearranged into a bluegrass cover with very little effort. The Rolling Stones covered Hank Williams' "I'm Movin' On," and wrote a down-home country tune of sorts for *Aftermath*, "High and Dry." On "Go and Say Goodbye" and especially "Kind Woman," Buffalo Springfield put folk-rock harmonies and arrangements to material that was country to the core. But there were no entire country albums by rock groups, save for the Downliners Sect's bizarre *The Sect Sing Country Songs*, by a little-known mid-'60s British group. The Downliners Sect were much more noted for sloppy punk/R&B in the mold of the Rolling Stones and the Pretty Things; their country LP, which suffered from poor execution, is best considered as a novelty rather than a groundbreaking creative endeavor. (Even more of a novelty was Nancy Sinatra's *Country My Way*, which did little to enhance her career in either the country or pop markets.)

A sort of "back to basics" year for rock arrived in 1968, and Bob Dylan's predominantly acoustic *John Wesley Harding* helped point the compass toward country sounds as well. *John Wesley Harding* was recorded (as much of *Blonde on Blonde* was) in Nashville, and the last cut in particular, "I'll Be Your Baby Tonight," was straight country, complete with steel guitar. The album still featured much of Dylan's oblique wordplay, but that was largely discarded on his follow-up, *Nashville Skyline*, on which Dylan for the first time could be said to be more of a country artist than a folk or rock one. The record still sold well, partly because of its hit single "Lay Lady Lay," and partly because Dylan had such a large, adoring following that listeners were willing to follow him into unexpected waters. Much of Dylan's audience, though, was disappointed with the record overall, not necessarily because of the country textures, but because the record itself was rather

uninspired, and because Dylan had substituted country clichés for ambitious poetry. Dylan would never immerse himself as deeply in country again.

Several major rock groups helped ignite country-rock in 1968 by recording country albums, most notably the Byrds. Their *Sweetheart of the Rodeo* is often acclaimed as one of the greatest country-rock records, and introduced Gram Parsons to a wide audience. The Byrds' country phase was not entirely unexpected, given that back in 1966 they had covered a Porter Wagoner song ("A Satisfied Mind"), that bassist Chris Hillman had originally been a bluegrass musician, and that some of their best originals had a strong country feel ("Mr. Spaceman," "Time Between"). It was quite a switch from their electric folk-rock era, and they even played the *Grand Ole Opry* before Gram Parsons, who had only been in the band for about six months, left, eventually forming the Flying Burrito Brothers with Hillman. The Byrds had always been about change, and nothing else they did was as pure country as *Sweetheart*.

The year 1968 also saw interesting country albums by the Beau Brummels (*Bradley's Barn*) and the Everly Brothers (*Roots*). The Everlys had always maintained strong ties to country in their vocal style, and their late-'50s album *Songs Our Daddy Taught Us* could even be considered a country record if you stretched things (though it might be more appropriately classified as a folk disc). The Everlys weren't the only early rock & roll stars to dabble in country. In the late '60s, Rick Nelson made country-flavored albums with the Stone Canyon Band, although these are perhaps more notable for the musicians (including future members of the Eagles, Little Feat, and the Desert Rose Band) than the music. There were also a host of acts that played country-rock from the start, like the Flying Burrito Brothers, Michael Nesmith, Poco, Hearts & Flowers, and former Byrd Gene Clark. As they always considered country a main staple rather than a side dish, they are described in more depth in a separate country-rock essay (as are latter-day country-rockers such as Son Volt and Uncle Tupelo, who are covered as part of the *No Depression* movement).

By the early '70s, the influence of country-rock had spread to rock acts that would never be principally identified as country-rock musicians. The Rolling Stones, probably as a result of their friendship with Gram Parsons, recorded some country-ish material in the late '60s and early '70s, with "Wild Horses" being the most successful and famous example. There was too much folk, blues, and muted psychedelia in the Grateful Dead's *American Beauty* and *Workingman's Dead* for those to be considered country-rock albums, but there was a great deal of country in the songwriting, musicianship, and especially the harmonies. George Harrison made some relatively little-noticed forays into country on the *All Things Must Pass* cuts "Behind That Locked Door" and "If Not for You," which featured ace pedal steel player Pete Drake. Less successful was Ringo Starr's *Beaucoups of Blues*, cut in Nashville with some of the city's session men, including Drake, whose publishing company also supplied the ex-Beatle with material for the record.

Of the California-based singer/songwriters who appropriated some of country-rock's laid-back feel, Neil Young has delved into country with the greatest depth. Country and folk influences pepper all of his acoustic-oriented (and some of his electric) work. They truly came to the forefront on 1972's *Harvest*, which went to number one and netted him a number one pop single, "Heart of Gold," that featured a weepy steel guitar. It was his most countrified album for quite some time, until he decided in the mid-'80s to go the whole nine yards with *Old Ways*, which could be safely considered a country album, as opposed to a country-influenced rock record. Waylon Jennings and Willie Nelson contributed guest vocals, just in case anyone doubted that Young was serious.

Young had always flip-flopped between musical styles (and political viewpoints), and at the time he inferred that he would be happy to leave the rock world completely and pursue country music full-time. That didn't happen, of course; by 1990 he was making eardrums bleed again with *Ragged Glory*. Just to keep everybody on their toes, *Harvest Moon* (1992) was another right turn into a predominantly country-folk mood, although Young's lyrics (and image) are too eccentric to find their way onto country playlists or the collections of mainstream country listeners.

When the country-rock trend began to die down after the early '70s, such unabashedly country-ish outings became rarer. The punk/new wave movement of the late '70s made them rarer still. The musical conservatism of much country music, and its frequent reflection of mainstream, family-oriented values, were among the last things that interested the safety-pin-and-torn-T-shirts crowd. Elvis Costello, who owed much of his success to that crowd, tried to defy audience expectations by releasing an album of country covers in the early '80s, *Almost Blue*. Recorded in Nashville, it may be the most notorious example of a rock star turning into a country singer with little or no notice.

Actually, Costello's country experiment would not have been a surprise for those paying extremely close attention to his career. Before he made records, Costello had occasionally sung in bar bands that played country music; he had also penned enthusiastic liner notes for a George Jones reissue. *Almost Blue*, however, sold poorly and was panned by most critics, and not just because they might have been too close-minded to give it a chance. No one can doubt that Costello's affection for country music was (and is) sincere. Whether he actually had the ability to make good country music himself, despite his obvious desire to, was another question entirely; the opinion was nearly universal that Costello was a major rock/new wave artist, and a non-event as a country vocalist.

Generally, the same disparity in results afflicts other rock artists who decide to make all-out country albums. If they were really meant to sing country, it can be reasonably asked, why have they been singing rock for all these years instead? Marianne Faithfull may claim to have been deeply influenced by Waylon Jennings, but she sounded ill-suited for outlaw territory on her *Faithless* country album, recorded just before she reoriented herself to the new wave crowd with *Broken English*. Jonathan Richman, who has adapted doo wop and Spanish music to his own idiosyncratic child-rock

Weltanschauung, did the same with *Jonathan Goes Country*, which was more colored by the naïveté of Richman himself than the time-honored traditions of country & western. Better left unexamined is the *Rhythm Country and Blues* compilation, which paired a bunch of well-known country and soul singers for an album of celebrity duets. But it looked more like a marketing exercise to the adult contemporary audience than a convincing aesthetic project.

In the mid-'90s, the The, much more noted for dark modern English rock than anything rootsy, tore a page out of the Del Shannon songbook by recording a tribute album to Hank Williams. It attracted more notice than some of the The's original material had in the States, though the results weren't as strange as one might have anticipated. The point seemed to be that Matt Johnson (who is, essentially, the core of the The) was able to make Hank Williams songs sound like fodder for modern rock playlists—which, in the eyes of many music fans, is not so much making a point as being pointless. In the *AMG to Rock*, Stephen Thomas Erlewine aptly summarized, "Strangely enough, it works better than several the The records, since Hank Williams is a better songwriter than Matt Johnson."

One way to get around the thorny issue of trying to sell country albums to a rock following is for rock musicians to release country records as side projects, particularly within the alternative world, where there's generally more freedom for flexibility in this regard. John Doe and Exene Cervenka of X, with assistance from Dave Alvin, formed the Knitters to offer country-flavored music on *Poor Little Critter on the Road*, which was still poorly received, but at least didn't alienate X fans who wanted brittle underground rock. Janet Bean, drummer/singer of the fairly straightforward alternative rock band Eleventh Dream Day, formed an acoustic band, Freakwater (in which she sings and plays guitar), for the purposes of playing country-folk music. Ironically, the Appalachian-flavored musings of Freakwater may well prove to be more enduring than those of the rock band from which Bean sprung.

Then there's the approach that purists may find most offensive—to treat the whole issue of rock artists slumming in country as something of a joke. The Mekons, a long-lived British alternative band of considerable eclecticism, often offer a brand of cowpunk that seems equal parts reverence and iconoclastic satire. More blatantly satirical is Eugene Chadbourne, the avant rock guitarist, who often uses C&W forms to advocate adamantly left-wing politics that would find no comfortable home on Music Row. On 1980's *There'll Be No Tears Tonight*, he devoted the whole set to avant-garde interpretations of country standards. And if you want to make sure there's country & western in the house to offend anyone regardless of political orientation, there's Ween's *12 Golden Country Greats*, in which the most successful comedy rock group of the 1990s marries its juvenile wit to straight MOR country backing.

Recommended Recordings:

Ray Charles, *Modern Sounds in Country & Western Music* (Rhino)
Bob Dylan, *Nashville Skyline* (Columbia)
The Byrds, *Sweetheart of the Rodeo* (Columbia)
The Everly Brothers, *Roots* (Warner Bros.)
The Beau Brummels, *Bradley's Barn* (Edsel)
The Grateful Dead, *American Beauty* (Warner Bros.)
Elvis Costello, *Almost Blue* (Rykodisc)
Neil Young, *Old Ways* (Geffen)
The The, *Hanky Panky* (550 Music/Epic)
Ween, *12 Golden Country Greats* (Elektra)

—Richie Unterberger

Essential Artists

Alternative Country

Pete Anderson
● Junior Brown
Richard Buckner
● Guy Clark
● Iris DeMent
● Steve Earle
● The Flatlanders
Jimmie Dale Gilmore
Butch Hancock
Wayne Hancock
Robert Earl Keen, Jr.
● k.d. lang
● Lyle Lovett
Dale Watson
Gillian Welch
● Dwight Yoakam

Alternative Country-Rock

Bad Livers
Beachwood Sparks
Big Sandy & His Fly-Rite Boys
The Blood Oranges
Blue Rodeo
● The Bottle Rockets
Cowboy Junkies
● Freakwater
Giant Sand
Golden Smog
Health & Happiness Show
● The Jayhawks
Lambchop
Shelby Lynne
Maria McKee
● Old 97's
● Palace
Scud Mountain Boys
Son Volt
● Uncle Tupelo
The Waco Brothers
● Whiskeytown
● Wilco

Americana

● Ryan Adams
Dave Alvin
● Neko Case
Iris DeMent
Fred Eaglesmith
● Steve Earle
Joe Ely
● Alejandro Escovedo
Rosie Flores
Grant Lee Buffalo
Butch Hancock

Wayne Hancock
Joe Henry
● John Hiatt
Walter Hyatt
● The Jayhawks
Freedy Johnston
The Mavericks
Delbert McClinton
James McMurtry
Jeb Loy Nichols
Old 97's
Amy Rigby
● Doug Sahm
● Billy Joe Shaver
Son Volt
Uncle Tupelo
Townes Van Zandt
● Gillian Welch
● Lucinda Williams

Alternative Country-Rock

Johnny Bond
Tommy Collins
Dick Curless
Dave Dudley
● Merle Haggard
Harlan Howard
Ferlin Husky
Bonnie Owens
● Buck Owens
Susan Raye
Don Rich
● Jean Shepard
Red Simpson
● Wynn Stewart
Hank Thompson
Dwight Yoakam

Bluegrass-Gospel

Dry Branch Fire Squad
Five for the Gospel
The Greenbriar Boys
Laurel Canyon Ramblers
● The Louvin Brothers
● Bill Monroe
Charlie Moore
● Ricky Skaggs
● Ralph Stanley

Close Harmony

Anglin Brothers
Armstrong Twins
● The Bailes Brothers
The Bailey Brothers

The Blue Sky Boys
● The Delmore Brothers
● The Everly Brothers
● Jim & Jesse
● Johnnie & Jack
Kalin Twins
● The Louvin Brothers
● Osborne Brothers
The Whitstein Brothers
York Brothers

Contemporary Bluegrass

The Cantrells
● Béla Fleck
The Gibson Brothers
Bobby Hicks
● Alison Krauss
Phil Leadbetter
● Nickel Creek
Todd Phillips
Art Stamper
Ernie Thacker
● Rhonda Vincent

Contemporary Country

Trace Adkins
● Alabama
John Berry
● Clint Black
Suzy Bogguss
● Brooks & Dunn
● Garth Brooks
Tracy Byrd
Mary Chapin Carpenter
Carlene Carter
Deana Carter
Rosanne Cash
Joe Diffie
● Dixie Chicks
Ty England
Vince Gill
Nanci Griffith
● Faith Hill
● Alan Jackson
Wynonna Judd
The Judds
● Toby Keith
Sammy Kershaw
Tracy Lawrence
The Mavericks
Reba McEntire
● Tim McGraw
Jo Dee Messina
John Michael Montgomery
K.T. Oslin

● Indicates top pick in that category.

LeAnn Rimes
Sawyer Brown
SHeDAISY
● George Strait
Marty Stuart
Aaron Tippin
Travis Tritt
Tanya Tucker
● Shania Twain
Steve Wariner
● Trisha Yearwood

Country Boogie

Charline Arthur
Chet Atkins
Molly Bee
Martha Carson
The Delmore Brothers
● Al Deeter
● Tennessee Ernie Ford
Hardrock Gunter
● Johnny Horton
● Sid King
Arthur Guitar Boogie Smith
● Hank Snow
● Merle Travis

Country Comedy

Boecar Willie
Jethro Burns
● Jerry Clower
Ben Colder
Dick Feller
Jeff Foeworthy
Kinky Friedman
The Geezinslaws
● Homer & Jethro
● Hoosier Hot Shots
● Ferlin Husky
● Grandpa Jones
● Cledus T. Judd
● Minnie Pearl
Pinkard & Bowden
Junior Samples
Jim Stafford
● Ray Stevens
Honey Wilds
Sheb Wooley

Country Gospel

Allen Brothers
E.C. and Orna Ball
The Blackwood Brothers
Martha Carson
● Johnny Cash
Chuck Wagon Gang
● Red Foley
● Tennessee Ernie Ford
The Goldens
The Happy Goodman Family
● George Jones
The Lewis Family
The Oak Ridge Boys
Connie Smith
● The Statler Brothers
Carl Story
The Whites

Country-Folk

● Bobby Bare
Mary Chapin Carpenter
Beth Nielsen Chapman
● Guy Clark
Iris DeMent
Fred Eaglesmith
Tennessee Ernie Ford
Jimmie Dale Gilmore
● Nanci Griffith
● Tom T. Hall
George Hamilton IV
Butch Hancock
● Waylon Jennings
Robert Earl Keen, Jr.
Kathy Mattea
Hugh Moffatt
Katy Moffatt
Dolly Parton
Gretchen Peters
Cheryl Wheeler
● Slim Whitman

Country-Pop

● Bill Anderson
Lynn Anderson
● Eddy Arnold
Hoyt Aeton
The Bellamy Brothers
● Glen Campbell
Mac Davis
Donna Fargo
Janie Fricke
Gatlin Brothers
● Crystal Gayle
● Bobbie Gentry
● Don Gibson
George Hamilton IV
● David Houston
Ferlin Husky
Sonny James
George Jones
● Barbara Mandrell
● Ronnie Milsap
Anne Murray
Juice Newton
The Oak Ridge Boys
K.T. Oslin
Dolly Parton
Ray Price
● Charley Pride
Jeanne Pruett
Eddie Rabbitt
● Jim Reeves
● Charlie Rich
Marty Robbins
● Kenny Rogers
Connie Smith
The Statler Brothers
B.J. Thomas
Mel Tillis
Tanya Tucker
● Conway Twitty
● Porter Wagoner
Dottie West
Don Williams
Tammy Wynette

Country-Rock

● The Amazing Rhythm Aces
American Flyer
● The Band
The Beau Brummels
● Brinsley Schwarz
Buffalo Springfield
Jimmy Buffett
● The Byrds
Gene Clark
Commander Cody
Charlie Daniels
● Dillard & Clark
The Dillards
● Bob Dylan
● The Eagles
The Everly Brothers
Firefall
● The Flying Burrito Brothers
The Grateful Dead
Hearts & Flowers
The International Submarine Band
Nick Lowe
The Marshall Tucker Band
● Rick Nelson
Michael Nesmith
The Nitty Gritty Dirt Band
Ozark Mountain Daredevils
● Gram Parsons
● Poco
● Pure Prairie League
Linda Ronstadt
Doug Sahm
Billy Swan
Neil Young

Cowboy

Jules Verne Allen
● Ree Allen
Rosalie Allen
● Eddy Arnold
Bob Atcher
● Gene Autry
Bill Carlisle
Cliff Carlisle
Wilf Carter
Johnny Cash
Yodeling Slim Clark
Vernon Dalhart
● Al Deeter
Don Edwards
Dale Evans
Pee Wee King
Chris LeDoue
Waddie Mitchell
● Patsy Montana
Tee Owens
● Riders in the Sky
● Tee Ritter
● Marty Robbins
Kenny Roberts
● Roy Rogers
● Hank Snow
● The Sons of the Pioneers
Sons of the San Joaquin
Carl T. Sprague
Red Steagall
Jimmy Wakely
Johnny Western

Slim Whitman
Sheb Wooley

Honky Tonk

John Anderson
● Moe Bandy
Jim Ed Brown
Tommy Collins
Cowboy Copas
Ted Daffan
Dave Dudley
Stoney Edwards
Red Foley
● Lefty Frizzell
● Mickey Gilley
Merle Haggard
Johnny Horton
Stonewall Jackson
● George Jones
● Jerry Lee Lewis
Loretta Lynn
Skeets McDonald
Roger Miller
Moon Mullican
Buck Owens
● Johnny Paycheck
Webb Pierce
● Ray Price
Jean Shepard
● Carl Smith
● Thompson
● Floyd Tillman
● Ernest Tubb
Kitty Wells
Hank Williams
● Faron Young

Instrumental Country

● Chet Atkins
● Jimmy Bryant
James Burton
Roy Clark
● Floyd Cramer
Jimmy Day
Buddy Emmons
Johnny Gimble
Bill Keith
● Joe Maphis
Tiny Moore
● Moon Mullican
Mark O'Connor
Boots Randolph
● Jerry Reed
● Merle Travis
Frank Wakefield
● Speedy West

Nashville Sound/Countrypolitan

Bill Anderson
Lynn Anderson
● Eddy Arnold
● Chet Atkins
The Browns
● Glen Campbell
● Patsy Cline
● Floyd Cramer
Skeeter Davis
Jimmy Dean

Little Jimmy Dickens
Donna Fargo
Tennessee Ernie Ford
● Don Gibson
Connie Hall
George Hamilton IV
Johnny Horton
● David Houston
● George Jones
Hank Locklin
Loretta Lynn
Roger Miller
George Morgan
Willie Nelson
Ray Price
● Jim Reeves
Charlie Rich
● Marty Robbins
● Conway Twitty
Porter Wagoner
Kitty Wells
Dottie West
● Tammy Wynette

Neo-Traditionalist Country

Ace in the Hole Band
● Asleep at the Wheel
● BR5-49
Junior Brown
● Carlene Carter
● Rosanne Cash
● Rodney Crowell
Lacy J. Dalton
Iris DeMent
Rosie Flores
● Danny Gatton
Gosdin Brothers
Wayne Hancock
James Intveld
Hal Ketchum
● k.d. lang
Chris LeDoue
● Lorrie Morgan
Michael Martin Murphey
Daryle Singletary
Steve Wariner

New Traditionalist

Trace Adkins
● John Anderson
● Clint Black
● Garth Brooks
Marty Brown
Tracy Byrd
Mark Chesnutt
Joe Diffie
● Steve Earle
● Vince Gill
● Alan Jackson
Toby Keith
Sammy Kershaw
Martina McBride
John Michael Montgomery
Collin Raye
Ricky Skaggs
● George Strait
Marty Stuart
Aaron Tippin
● Randy Travis

● Travis Tritt
Clay Walker
● Keith Whitley
● Dwight Yoakam

Old-Timey

● Allen Brothers
● The Bailey Brothers
● Bashful Brother Oswald
The Blue Sky Boys
● Dock Boggs
Camp Creek Boys
The Carolina Tar Heels
Fiddlin' John Carson
● The Carter Family
Sara & Maybelle Carter
Coon Creek Girls
Wilma Lee Cooper
The Delmore Brothers
Grayson & Whitter
● Hoosier Hot Shots
Aunt Molly Jackson
Ledford String Band
● Wilma Lee & Stoney Cooper
● Uncle Dave Macon
J.E. Mainer
● Emmett Miller
The New Lost City Ramblers
Charlie Poole
Riley Puckett
The Red Clay Ramblers
Carson Robison
The Stonemans
Stringbean
● Gid Tanner
● Doc Watson

Outlaw Country

Guy Clark
● David Allan Coe
Jessi Colter
● Tompall Glaser
● Waylon Jennings
● Willie Nelson
Mickey Newbury
● Johnny Paycheck
● Billy Joe Shaver
Jerry Jeff Walker
Hank Williams, Jr.

Progressive Bluegrass

Eddie Adcock
Mike Auldridge
● Austin Lounge Lizards
Russ Barenberg
Byron Berline
● Norman Blake
The Bluegrass Cardinals
Sam Bush
● The Country Gentlemen
● J.D. Crowe
Rodney Dillard
● The Dillards
Jerry Douglas
Béla Fleck
Vern Gosdin
David Grisman
Hot Rize

Bill Keith
- The Kentucky Colonels
- Alison Krauss
John McEuen
- New Grass Revival
- Mark O'Connor
- Tony Rice
Peter Rowan
The Seldom Scene
- Ricky Skaggs
- Tony Trischka
- Clarence White

Progressive Country

- Bobby Bare
- Guy Clark
Lee Clayton
- David Allan Coe
- Joe Ely
Steven Fromholz
Jimmie Dale Gilmore
- Tompall Glaser
Nanci Griffith
- Tom T. Hall
Butch Hancock
Emmylou Harris
- John Hartford
Dan Hicks
Chris Hillman
Ray Wylie Hubbard
- Waylon Jennings
Robert Earl Keen Jr.
- Kris Kristofferson
Michael Martin Murphey
- Willie Nelson
- Mickey Newbury
The Nitty Gritty Dirt Band
Dolly Parton
Jerry Reed
- Charlie Rich
- Doug Sahm
Billy Joe Shaver
Ricky Skaggs
Gary Stewart
- Townes Van Zandt
- Jerry Jeff Walker
Steve Young

Rockabilly

- Sonny Burgess
- Johnny Burnette
James Burton
- Johnny Cash
Joe Clay
- Eddie Cochran
The Collins Kids
Ronnie Dawson
- Charlie Feathers
Dale Hawkins
Ronnie Hawkins
- Buddy Holly
Johnny Horton
- Wanda Jackson
Sleepy LaBeef
Jerry Lee Lewis
Carl Mann
Scotty Moore
- Rick Nelson
Roy Orbison

- Carl Perkins
- Elvis Presley
Charlie Rich
- Billy Lee Riley
Jack Scott
Ronnie Self
- Warren Smith
- Gene Vincent

String Bands

- The Carolina Tar Heels
Fuzzy Mountain String Band
The Greenbriar Boys
- Hackberry Ramblers
Ledford String Band
J.E. Mainer
- Mississippi Sheiks
- The New Lost City Ramblers
- Charlie Poole
The Red Clay Ramblers
- Gid Tanner

Traditional Bluegrass

Norman Blake
- Stoney Cooper
J.D. Crowe
- Flatt & Scruggs
Lester Flatt
- Jim & Jesse
The Johnson Mountain Boys
- The Kentucky Colonels
Doyle Lawson
- Jimmy Martin
The McCoury Brothers
Del McCoury
The Monroe Brothers
- Bill Monroe
Old & In the Way
Osborne Brothers
Reno & Smiley
Reno Brothers
Don Reno
Earl Scruggs
Ricky Skaggs
- The Stanley Brothers
- Ralph Stanley
Carl Story
The Whites
Mac Wiseman

Country Boogie

- Roy Acuff
- Eddy Arnold
Chet Atkins
Gene Autry
Bobby Bare
Jim Ed Brown
Cliff Bruner
- The Carter Family
- Johnny Cash
Roy Clark
- Patsy Cline
Jimmie Davis
Skeeter Davis
The Delmore Brothers
Little Jimmy Dickens
Red Foley
- Tennessee Ernie Ford

- Lefty Frizzell
Don Gibson
Mickey Gilley
- Merle Haggard
Homer & Jethro
Johnny Horton
- Waylon Jennings
Johnnie & Jack
- George Jones
Claude King
- Hank Locklin
- The Louvin Brothers
- Loretta Lynn
Uncle Dave Macon
- Roger Miller
George Morgan
- Willie Nelson
- Buck Owens
Dolly Parton
Johnny Paycheck
Webb Pierce
- Ray Price
Charley Pride
Jerry Reed
Charlie Rich
- Marty Robbins
- Jimmie Rodgers
Carl Smith
- Hank Snow
- Hank Thompson
Floyd Tillman
Merle Travis
Don Williams
Bob Wills
- Tammy Wynette
Faron Young

Truck Driving Country

- Dick Curless
- Dave Dudley
- Terry Fell
Jimmy Martin
Del Reeves
- Red Simpson
Red Steagall

Urban Cowboy

- Glen Campbell
- Earl Thomas Conley
- Charlie Daniels
Gatlin Brothers
- Crystal Gayle
Terri Gibbs
Mickey Gilley
Jim Glaser
Nicolette Larson
- Johnny Lee
- Barbara Mandrell
Louise Mandrell
C.W. McCall
- Ronnie McDowell
- Ronnie Milsap
Juice Newton
- Eddie Rabbitt
- Kenny Rogers
- T.G. Sheppard
Sylvia

Western Swing

- Milton Brown
- Cliff Bruner
- Spade Cooley
  Tommy Duncan
  Johnny Gimble
  Jimmy Heap
  Pee Wee King
- The Light Crust Doughboys
  Leon McAuliffe

Hank Penny
- Hank Thompson
  Tee Williams
- Bob Wills
  Johnnie Lee Wills

Western Swing Revival

- Asleep at the Wheel
- Commander Cody

- Merle Haggard
- Dan Hicks
  Don McCalister Jr.
  Lee Roy Parnell
  Prairie Oyster
  Riders in the Sky
- Carl Smith
- George Strait
  Don Walser

Essential Albums

Alternative Country

Junior Brown, **Guit with It** (1993)
Guy Clark, **Cold Dog Soup** (1999)
Iris Dement, **Infamous Angel** (1992)
Derailers, **Full Western Dress** (1999)
The Flatlanders, **More a Legend Than a Band** (1990)
Rosie Flores, **Rosie Flores** (1987)
Jimmie Dale Gilmore, **After Awhile** (1991)
Wayne Hancock, **That's What Daddy Wants** (1997)
Robert Earl Keen, Jr., **No Kinda Dancer** (1984)
k.d. lang and the Reclines, **Absolute Torch and Twang** (1989)
k.d. lang, **Shadowland** (1988)
Lyle Lovett, **Lyle Lovett** (1986)
Lyle Lovett, **Pontiac** (1987)
The Waco Brothers, **Cowboy in Flames** (1997)
Gillian Welch, **Revival** (1996)
Gillian Welch, **Time (The Revelator)** (2001)
Dwight Yoakam, **Buenos Noches from a Lonely Room** (1988)
Dwight Yoakam, **Guitars, Cadillacs, Etc., Etc.** (1986)
Various Artists, **Insurgent Country, Vol. 3: Nashville–The Other Side of the Alley** (1996)

Alternative Country-Rock

Bad Livers, **Delusions of Banjer** (1992)
Blue Rodeo, **Casino** (1991)
Bottle Rockets, **The Brooklyn Side** (1995)
BR5-49, **BR Five Four Nine** (1996)
Neko Case & Her Boyfriends, **Furnace Room Lullaby** (2000)
Cowboy Junkies, **The Trinity Session** (1988)
Alejandro Escovedo, **A Man Under the Influence** (2001)
The Jayhawks, **Hollywood Town Hall** (1992)
The Jayhawks, **Tomorrow the Green Grass** (1995)
Shelby Lynne, **I Am Shelby Lynne** (2000)
Old 97's, **Too Far to Care** (1997)
Palace Brothers, **There Is No-One What Will Take Care of You** (1993)
Scud Mountain Boys, **Massachusetts** (1996)
Uncle Tupelo, **Anodyne** (1993)
Uncle Tupelo, **March 16-20, 1992** (2003)
The Walkabouts, **Satisfied Mind** (1993)
Whiskeytown, **Stranger's Almanac** (1997)
Wilco, **Being There** (1996)

Americana

Ryan Adams, **Heartbreaker** (2000)
Dave Alvin, **Blackjack David** (1998)
Blue Rodeo, **Casino** (1991)
Neko Case & Her Boyfriends, **Furnace Room Lullaby** (2000)
Fred Eaglesmith, **Lipstick, Lies & Gasoline** (1997)
Joe Ely, **The Best of Joe Ely** (2000)
Alejandro Escovedo, **Gravity** (1992)
Rosie Flores, **Rosie Flores** (1987)
Joe Henry, **Short Man's Room** (1992)
John Hiatt, **Bring the Family** (1987)
John Hiatt, **Slow Turning** (1988)
Walter Hyatt, **King Tears** (1990)
The Jayhawks, **Hollywood Town Hall** (1992)
Freedy Johnston, **Can You Fly** (1992)
The Mavericks, **What a Crying Shame** (1994)
James McMurtry, **Too Long in the Wasteland** (1989)
Katy Moffatt, **The Evangeline Hotel** (1993)
Old 97's, **Too Far to Care** (1997)
Billy Joe Shaver, **Restless Wind: The Legendary Billy Joe Shaver 1973–1987** (1995)
Gillian Welch, **Revival** (1996)
Lucinda Williams, **Car Wheels on a Gravel Road** (1998)
Lucinda Williams, **Sweet Old World** (1992)

Bakersfield Sound

Tommy Collins, **Leonard** (1992)
Dave Dudley, **20th Century Masters—The Millennium Collection: The Best of Dave Dudley** (2002)
Dave Dudley, **Truck Drivin' Son-Of-A-Gun** (1965)
Merle Haggard, **The Lonesome Fugitive: The Merle Haggard Anthology (1963–1977)** (1995)
Merle Haggard & the Strangers, **Sing Me Back Home** (1968)
Merle Haggard & the Strangers, **Swinging Doors** (1966)
Harlan Howard, **All Time Favorite Country Songwriter** (1965)
Buck Owens, **The Buck Owens Collection (1959–1990)** (1992)
Buck Owens, **Buck Owens Sings Harlan Howard** (1961)
Buck Owens, **I've Got a Tiger by the Tail** (1965)
Buck Owens, **Together Again/My Heart Skips a Beat** (1964)
Susan Raye, **16 Greatest Hits** (1999)
Jean Shepard, **Honky Tonk Heroine: Classic Capitol Recordings, 1952–1962** (1995)
Red Simpson, **The Best of Red Simpson: Country Western Truck Drivin' Singer** (1999)
Red Simpson, **The Man Behind the Badge/Roll, Truck, Roll** (1999)
Wynn Stewart, **The Very Best of Wynn Stewart 1958–1962** (2001)
Wynn Stewart, **California Country: The Best of the Challenge Masters** (1995)
Hank Thompson, **The Best of Hank Thompson: 1966–1979** (1996)
Hank Thompson, **Dance Ranch/Songs for Rounders** (1999)
Hank Thompson, **Vintage** (1996)
Dwight Yoakam, **Guitars, Cadillacs, Etc., Etc.** (1986)
Dwight Yoakam, **Hillbilly Deluxe** (1987)
Various Artists, **Hillbilly Fever, Vol. 4: Legends of the West Coast** (1995)

Bluegrass-Gospel

J.D. Crowe & the New South, **The Model Church** (1969)
Doyle Lawson, **Winding Through Life** (1999)
The Louvin Brothers, **Satan Is Real** (1960)
Ricky Skaggs and Kentucky Thunder, **Soldier of the Cross** (1999)
The Stanley Brothers, **Hymns and Sacred Songs** (1959)
Ralph Stanley, **Almost Home** (1992)
Various Artists, **Bluegrass from Heaven** (1995)
Various Artists, **Stained Glass Hour: Bluegrass and Old-Timey Gospel Music** (1992)

Close Harmony

The Bailey Brothers, **Early Days of Bluegrass, Vol. 6—Have You Forgotten?** (1976)
The Blue Sky Boys, **Presenting the Blue Sky Boys** (1966)
The Blue Sky Boys, **There'll Come a Time/Can't You Hear That Nightbird Crying?** (1936)
The Blue Sky Boys, **Within the Circle/Who Wouldn't Be Lonely** (1937)
The Delmore Brothers, **Freight Train Boogie** (1993)
The Delmore Brothers, **When They Let the Hammer Fall** (1984)
The Everly Brothers, **Cadence Classics: Their 20 Greatest Hits** (1986)
The Everly Brothers, **Songs Our Daddy Taught Us** (1959)
Jim & Jesse, **Jim & Jesse: 1952–1955** (1992)
Jim & Jesse, **Y'All Come: The Essential Jim & Jesse** (1998)
Johnnie & Jack, **All the Best of Johnnie and Jack** (1970)

Kalin Twins, **When** (1984)

The Louvin Brothers, **Close Harmony** (1992)

The Louvin Brothers, **Satan Is Real** (1960)

The Louvin Brothers, **When I Stop Dreaming: The Best of the Louvin Brothers** (1995)

The Osborne Brothers, **The Best of the Osborne Brothers** (1975)

Osborne Brothers and Mac Wiseman, **The Essential Bluegrass Album** (1979)

The York Brothers, **16 Great Country & Western Hits** (1963)

Various Artists, **Anthology of Country Music: Early Country Harmony 1940s**

Contemporary Bluegrass

Blue Highway, **Blue Highway** (1999)

The Country Gentlemen, **Sugar Hill Collection** (1995)

J.D. Crowe & the New South, **J.D. Crowe & The New South** (1975)

Alison Krauss, **I've Got That Old Feeling** (1990)

Alison Krauss, **Now That I've Found You: A Collection** (1995)

Alison Krauss & Union Station, **So Long So Wrong** (1997)

Del McCoury, **Deeper Shade of Blue** (1993)

The Nashville Bluegrass Band, **Waitin' for the Hard Times to Go** (1993)

The Seldom Scene, **New Seldom Scene Album** (1976)

Rhonda Vincent, **Back Home Again** (2000)

Contemporary Country

Alabama, **For the Record** (1998)

Clint Black, **Killin' Time** (1989)

Brooks & Dunn, **Greatest Hits** (1997)

Garth Brooks, **No Fences** (1990)

Garth Brooks, **Ropin' the Wind** (1991)

Tracy Byrd, **Keepers: Greatest Hits** (1999)

Mary-Chapin Carpenter, **Come on Come On** (1992)

Deana Carter, **Did I Shave My Legs for This?** (1995)

Rosanne Cash, **Interiors** (1990)

Rosanne Cash, **Seven Year Ache** (1981)

Rodney Crowell, **Diamonds & Dirt** (1989)

Joe Diffie, **16 Biggest Hits** (2002)

Dixie Chicks, **Fly** (1999)

Dixie Chicks, **Wide Open Spaces** (1998)

Vince Gill, **Souvenirs** (1995)

Faith Hill, **Breathe** (1999)

Alan Jackson, **Greatest Hits Collection** (1995)

Alan Jackson, **Who I Am** (1994)

Wynonna Judd, **Tell Me Why** (1993)

The Judds, **The Greatest Hits** (1988)

Toby Keith, **How Do You Like Me Now?!** (1999)

Reba McEntire, **Greatest Hits** (1987)

Reba McEntire, **Whoever's in New England** (1986)

Tim McGraw, **Greatest Hits** (2000)

George Strait, **Does Fort Worth Ever Cross Your Mind** (1984)

George Strait, **Strait Out of the Box** (1995)

Randy Travis, **Storms of Life** (1986)

Randy Travis, **Trail of Memories: The Randy Travis Anthology** (2002)

Travis Tritt, **Greatest Hits: From the Beginning** (1995)

Tanya Tucker, **Greatest Hits 1990–1992** (1993)

Shania Twain, **Come on Over** (1997)

Shania Twain, **The Woman in Me** (1995)

Steve Wariner, **Greatest Hits** (1987)

Trisha Yearwood, **Songbook: A Collection of Hits** (1997)

Dwight Yoakam, **Hillbilly Deluxe** (1987)

Country Boogie

Chet Atkins, **Guitar Legend: The RCA Years** (2000)

Molly Bee, **Swingin' Country** (1967)

Tennessee Ernie Ford, **The Ultimate Collection (1949–1965)** (1997)

Hardrock Gunter, **Boogie Woogie on a Saturday Night** (1984)

Johnny Horton, **16 Biggest Hits** (1999)

Sid King & the Five Strings, **Gonna Shake This Shack Tonight** (1991)

Arthur Smith, **Original Guitar Boogie** (1964)

Hank Snow, **Yodelling Ranger: Young Hank Snow 1936–1943** (1999)

Merle Travis, **The Best of Merle Travis: Sweet Temptation 1946–1953** (2000)

Various Artists, **Hillbilly Boogie** (1994)

Various Artists, **Hillbilly Boogie** (2002)

Various Artists, **The Sun Story** (1987)

Country Comedy

Jerry Clower, **Jerry Clower's Greatest Hits** (1994)

Ben Colder, **Golden Hits** (1979)

Ben Colder, **Wacky World of Ben Colder** (1973)

Dick Feller, **No Words on Me** (1975)

Jeff Foxworthy, **You Might Be a Redneck If...** (1994)

Kinky Friedman, **Lasso from El Paso** (1976)

The Geezinslaws, **The Kooky World of the Geezinlaw Brothers** (1963)

Homer & Jethro, **America's Song Butchers: The Weird World of Homer & Jethro** (1997)

Hoosier Hot Shots, **Rural Rhythm** (1992)

Ferlin Husky, **Country Music Is Here to Stay: The Complete Simon Crum a.k.a. Ferlin Husky on Capitol** (2002)

Grandpa Jones, **Country Music Hall of Fame Series** (1992)

Cledus T. Judd, **Did I Shave My Back for This?** (1998)

Cledus T. Judd, **I Stoled This Record** (1996)

Minnie Pearl, **The Best of Minnie Pearl** (1996)

Ray Stevens, **The Best of Ray Stevens** (1997)

Sheb Wooley, **The Very Best of Sheb Wooley** (1965)

Country Gospel

E.C. Ball/Orna Ball & The Friendly Gospel Singers, **E.C. Ball with Orna Ball & the Friendly Gospel Singers** (1996)

The Blackwood Brothers, **Gospel Classics Series** (1998)

Johnny Cash, **God** (2000)

Johnny Cash, **Hymns by Johnny Cash** (1959)

Chuck Wagon Gang, **Golden Gospel Greats, Vol. 1** (1987)

Chuck Wagon Gang, **Golden Gospel Greats, Vol. 2** (1995)

Red Foley, **He Walks with Thee** (1958)

Red Foley, **Songs of Devotion** (1961)

Tennessee Ernie Ford, **Book of Favorite Hymns** (1962)

Merle Haggard, **The Land of Many Churches** (1971)

George Jones, **The Gospel Collection** (2003)

George Jones, **Homecoming In Heaven** (1962)

George Jones, **In a Gospel Way** (1974)

Willie Nelson, **The Troublemaker** (1976)

Buck Owens, **Dust on Mother's Bible** (1966)

Elvis Presley, **Peace in the Valley: The Complete Gospel Recordings** (2000)

Charlie Rich, **Silver Linings** (1976)

Connie Smith, **Connie Smith Sings Great Sacred Songs** (1966)

The Statler Brothers, **Holy Bible/New Testament** (1975)

The Statler Brothers, **Today's Gospel Favorites** (1993)

Various Artists, **The Best of Nashboro Gospel** (1993)

Various Artists, **Jubilation, Vol. 3 (Country Gospel)** (1992)

Country-Folk

Bobby Bare, **The Best of Bobby Bare** (1994)

Bobby Bare, **The Streets of Baltimore** (1966)

Mary-Chapin Carpenter, **Come on Come On** (1992)

Guy Clark, **Old #1** (1975)

Iris Dement, **Infamous Angel** (1992)

Jimmie Dale Gilmore, **After Awhile** (1991)

Nanci Griffith, **The Last of the True Believers** (1986)

Nanci Griffith, **Other Voices, Other Rooms** (1993)

Tom T. Hall, **Ballad of Forty Dollars** (1969)

Tom T. Hall, **In Search of a Song** (1971)

George Hamilton IV, **Folk Country Classics** (1967)

Butch Hancock, **Own & Own** (1989)

Waylon Jennings, **Folk Country** (1966)

Robert Earl Keen, Jr., **No Kinda Dancer** (1984)

Kathy Mattea, **Lonesome Standard Time** (1992)

Katy Moffatt, **The Evangeline Hotel** (1993)

Dolly Parton, **Coat of Many Colors** (1971)

Country-Pop

Bill Anderson, **Bill Anderson's Greatest Hits** (1967)

Eddy Arnold, **The Best of Eddy Arnold [RCA]** (1967)

Glen Campbell, **By the Time I Get to Phoenix** (1968)

Glen Campbell, **Capitol Years: 1965–1977** (1999)

Glen Campbell, **Gentle on My Mind** (1967)

Mac Davis, **The Best of Mac Davis** (2000)

Donna Fargo, **The Best of Donna Fargo** (1995)

Bobbie Gentry, **The Capitol Years: Ode to Bobbie Gentry** (2000)

Don Gibson, **RCA Country Legends** (2001)

Sonny James, **Young Love: The Classic Hits** (1997)

George Jones, **Anniversary: Ten Years of Hits** (1982)

Barbara Mandrell, **The Best of Barbara Mandrell** (1979)

Ronnie Milsap, **40 #1 Hits** (2000)

Anne Murray, **Greatest Hits** (1980)

Dolly Parton, **Ultimate Dolly Parton** (2003)

Ray Price, **The Essential Ray Price (1951–1962)** (1991)

Charley Pride, **RCA Country Legends** (2000)

Eddie Rabbitt, **All Time Greatest Hits** (1991)

Jim Reeves, **The Essential Jim Reeves** (1995)

Charlie Rich, **Behind Closed Doors** (1973)

Jeannie C. Riley, **The Best of Jeannie C. Riley** (1996)

Marty Robbins, **All-Time Greatest Hits** (1972)

Kenny Rogers, **25 Greatest Hits** (1987)

Connie Smith, **The Essential Connie Smith** (1996)

The Statler Brothers, **Flowers on the Wall: The Essential Statler Brothers** (1996)

B.J. Thomas, **Greatest Hits** (1990)

Tanya Tucker, **The Upper 48 Hits: 1972–1997** (2002)

Conway Twitty, **Conway Twitty's Greatest Hits, Vol. 1** (1972)

Porter Wagoner, **The Essential Porter Wagoner** (1997)

Don Williams, **Anthology** (2000)

Tammy Wynette, **Anniversary: 20 Years of Hits** (1987)

Country-Rock

The Amazing Rhythm Aces, **Stacked Deck/Too Stuffed to Jump** (2000)

American Flyer, **American Flyer** (1976)

The Band, **The Band** (1969)

The Beau Brummels, **Bradley's Barn** (1968)

Brinsley Schwarz, **Surrender to the Rhythm** (1991)

Buffalo Springfield, **The Best of Buffalo Springfield...Retrospective** (1969)

Jimmy Buffett, **Songs You Know By Heart** (1985)

The Byrds, **Ballad of Easy Rider** (1969)

The Byrds, **Sweetheart of the Rodeo** (1968)

Gene Clark, **Flying High** (1998)

Commander Cody & the Lost Planet Airmen, **Too Much Fun: Best of Commander Cody** (1990)

Elvis Costello & the Attractions, **Almost Blue** (1981)

Charlie Daniels Band, **Fire on the Mountain** (1975)

Dillard & Clark, **The Fantastic Expedition of Dillard & Clark/Through the Morning, Through the Night** (1989)

The Dillards, **There Is a Time (1963–70)** (1991)

Bob Dylan, **Nashville Skyline** (1969)

The Eagles, **Their Greatest Hits (1971–1975)** (1976)

The Everly Brothers, **Roots** (1968)

Firefall, **Firefall** (1976)

The Flying Burrito Brothers, **The Gilded Palace of Sin** (1969)

The Flying Burrito Brothers, **Hot Burritos! The Flying Burrito Brothers Anthology: 1969–1972** (2000)

The Grateful Dead, **American Beauty** (1970)

The Grateful Dead, **Workingman's Dead** (1970)

Emmylou Harris, **Anthology: The Warner/Reprise Years** (2001)

The International Submarine Band, **Safe at Home** (1968)

Nick Lowe, **The Impossible Bird** (1994)

The Marshall Tucker Band, **The Best of the Marshall Tucker Band: The Capricorn Years** (1995)

Ricky Nelson, **Bright Lights & Country Music/Country Fever** (1998)

Rick Nelson, **Stay Young: The Epic Recordings** (1993)

Michael Nesmith/The First National Band, **Complete** (1993)

Michael Nesmith, **Magnetic South** (1970)

Gram Parsons, **G.P./Grievous Angel** (1973)

Gram Parsons, **Sacred Hearts and Fallen Angels: The Gram Parsons Anthology** (2001)

Poco, **Ultimate Collection** (1998)

Pure Prairie League, **Greatest Hits** (1999)

Linda Ronstadt, **Heart Like a Wheel** (1974)

Doug Sahm, **The Best of Doug Sahm (1968–1975)** (1991)

Neil Young, **Harvest** (1972)

Various Artists, **Heroes of Country Music, Vol. 5: Legends of Country Rock** (1996)

Cowboy

Rex Allen, **Boney Kneed, Hairy Legged Cowboy Songs** (1984)

Rosalie Allen, **Songs of the Golden West** (1957)

Gene Autry, **The Essential Gene Autry** (1992)

Johnny Bond & His Red River Valley Boys, **Johnny Bond & His Red River Valley Boys** (2001)

Elton Britt, **Ridin' with Elton** (2000)

Wilf Carter, **Cowboy Songs** (1997)

Pee Wee King and His Golden West Cowboys, **Pee Wee King and His Golden West Cowboys** (1995)

Montana Slim, **The Dynamite Trail: The Decca Years** (1960)

Patsy Montana, **The Best of Patsy Montana** (2001)

Tex Owens, **Cattle Call** (1995)

Riders in the Sky, **The Best of the West** (1988)

Tex Ritter, **High Noon** (1992)

Marty Robbins, **All-Time Greatest Hits** (1972)

Roy Rogers, **Happy Trails: The Roy Rogers Collection 1937–1990** (1999)

Hank Snow, **Yodelling Ranger: Young Hank Snow 1936–1943** (1999)

The Sons of the Pioneers, **Country Music Hall of Fame** (1991)

Sons of the San Joaquin, **A Cowboy Has to Sing** (1992)

Carl T. Sprague, **Classic Cowboy Songs** (1988)

Red Steagall, **Born to This Land** (1993)

Jimmy Wakely, **Vintage Collections Series** (1996)

Various Artists, **American Cowboy Songs** (1983)

Various Artists, **Cowboy Songs from Folkways** (1991)

Various Artists, **Don't Fence Me In: Western Music's Early Golden Era** (1996)

Various Artists, **Legendary Songs of the Old West**

Various Artists, **Songs of the West, Vol. 1** (1994)

Various Artists, **Songs of the West, Vol. 2** (1994)

Various Artists, **Songs of the West, Vol. 3** (1994)

Various Artists, **When I Was a Cowboy, Vol. 1** (1996)

Various Artists, **When I Was a Cowboy, Vol. 2** (1996)

Honky Tonk

Moe Bandy, **Honky Tonk Amnesia: The Hard Country Sound of Moe Bandy** (1996)

Moe Bandy, **I Just Started Hatin' Cheatin' Songs Today/It Was Always So Easy (To Find An Unhappy Woman)** (2002)

Lefty Frizzell, **Look What Thoughts Will Do** (1997)

Mickey Gilley, **Room Full of Roses/Gilley's Smokin'** (2003)

Mickey Gilley, **Ten Years of Hits** (1984)

Merle Haggard, **The Lonesome Fugitive: The Merle Haggard Anthology (1963–1977)** (1995)

Johnny Horton, **Honky Tonk Man: The Essential Johnny Horton 1956–1960** (1996)

George Jones, **The Best of George Jones (1955–1967)** (1991)

Jerry Lee Lewis, **Another Place Another Time/She Even Woke Me Up to Say Goodbye** (2002)

Loretta Lynn, **Honky Tonk Girl: Collection** (1994)

Roger Miller, **Golden Hits** (1965)

Buck Owens, **The Very Best of Buck Owens, Vol. 1** (1994)

Johnny Paycheck, **The Real Mr. Heartache: The Little Darlin' Years** (1996)

Ray Price, **The Essential Ray Price (1951–1962)** (1991)

Carl Smith, **The Essential Carl Smith (1950–1956)** (1991)

Hank Thompson, **The Best of Hank Thompson: 1966–1979** (1996)

Hank Thompson, **Vintage** (1996)

Floyd Tillman, **Best of Floyd Tillman** (1999)

Ernest Tubb, **The Definitive Ernest Tubb Hits Collection** (2001)

Charlie Walker, **Pick Me Up on Your Way Down** (1999)

Kitty Wells, **God's Honky Tonk Angel: The First Queen of Country Music** (2000)

Hank Williams, Sr., **40 Greatest Hits** (1978)

Faron Young, **The Complete Capitol Hits of Faron Young** (2000)

Various Artists, **Columbia Country Classics, Vol. 2: Honky Tonk Heroes** (1984)

Various Artists, **Heroes of Country Music, Vol. 2: Legends of Honky Tonk** (1996)

Instrumental Country

Chet Atkins, Guitar Legend: The RCA Years (2000)

Chet Atkins/Les Paul, **Masters of the Guitar: Together** (1989)

Chet Atkins, **Me & Chet/Me & Jerry** (1998)

Jimmy Bryant, **Guitar Take-Off** (1989)

Roy Clark, **The Lightning Fingers of Roy Clark** (1963)

Buddy Emmons, **Amazing Steel Guitar: The Buddy Emmons Collection** (1997)

Mark O'Connor/Ma/Marsalis/Taylor, **Liberty** (1997)

Jerry Reed, **Pickin'** (1999)

Merle Travis, **The Best of Merle Travis: Sweet Temptation 1946–1953** (2000)

Merle Travis, **Travis Pickin'** (1981)

Speedy West & Jimmy Bryant, **Flamin' Guitars** (1997)

Speedy West, **Steel Guitar from Outer Space** (1989)

Speedy West & Jimmy Bryant, **Stratosphere Boogie: The Flaming Guitars of Speedy West & Jimmy Bryant** (1995)

Speedy West & Jimmy Bryant, **Swingin' on the Strings: The Speedy West & Jimmy Bryant Collection, Vol. 2** (1999)

Various Artists, **Swingwest!, Vol. 2: Guitar Slingers** (1999)

Nashville Sound/Countrypolitan

Lynn Anderson, **Golden Classics Edition** (1997)

Eddy Arnold, **The Best of Eddy Arnold** (1967)

Chet Atkins, **Guitar Legend: The RCA Years** (2000)

Jim Ed Brown & the Browns, **The Essential Jim Ed Brown & the Browns** (1996)

Glen Campbell, **The Capitol Years: 1965–1977** (1999)

Patsy Cline, **The Ultimate Collection** (2000)

Tennessee Ernie Ford, **16 Tons of Boogie: The Best of Tennessee Ernie Ford** (1990)

Don Gibson, **RCA Country Legends** (2001)

George Jones, **Anniversary: Ten Years of Hits** (1982)

Loretta Lynn, **Country Music Hall of Fame Series** (1991)

Roger Miller, **Golden Hits** (1965)

Willie Nelson, **Nite Life: Greatest Hits and Rare Tracks, 1959–1971** (1989)

Ray Price, **For the Good Times** (1970)

Jim Reeves, **Welcome to My World: The Essential Jim Reeves Collection** (1993)

Charlie Rich, **Behind Closed Doors** (1973)

Charlie Rich, **Greatest Hits: The Best of Charlie Rich**

Conway Twitty & Loretta Lynn, **The #1 Hits Collection** (2000)

Porter Wagoner, **The Essential Porter Wagoner** (1997)

Porter Wagoner, **The Essential Porter Wagoner and Dolly Parton** (1996)

Tammy Wynette, **Anniversary: 20 Years of Hits** (1987)

Various Artists, **Columbia Country Classics, Vol. 4: The Nashville Sound**

Various Artists, **Heroes of Country Music, Vol. 3: Legends of Nashville** (1996)

Neo-Traditionalist Country

Asleep at the Wheel, **Greatest Hits: Live & Kickin'** (1991)

Asleep at the Wheel, **Western Standard Time** (1988)

BR5-49, **BR5-49** (1996)

Junior Brown, **Guit with It** (1993)

Carlene Carter, **Hindsight 20/20** (1996)

Rosanne Cash, **Interiors** (1990)

Rosanne Cash, **Seven Year Ache** (1981)

Lacy J. Dalton, **Crazy Love** (1991)

Rosie Flores, **Honky Tonk Reprise** (1996)

Rosie Flores, **Rosie Flores** (1987)

Danny Gatton, **88 Elmira St.** (1991)

Wayne Hancock, **Thunderstorms and Neon Signs** (1995)

James Intveld, **James Intveld** (1996)

k.d. lang and the Reclines, **Angel With a Lariat** (1987)

Chris Ledoux, **20 Greatest Hits** (1999)

Reba McEntire, **Greatest Hits** (1987)

Reba McEntire, **Greatest Hits, Vol. 2** (1993)

Lorrie Morgan, **Greatest Hits** (1995)

Michael Martin Murphey, **Wildfire 1972–1984** (1998)

Steve Wariner, **Burnin' the Roadhouse Down** (1998)

New Traditionalist

John Anderson, **The Essential** (1998)

Clint Black, **Greatest Hits** (1996)

Clint Black, **Killin' Time** (1989)

Garth Brooks, **The Hits** (1994)

Garth Brooks, **No Fences** (1990)

Garth Brooks, **Ropin' the Wind** (1991)

Rodney Crowell, **Diamonds & Dirt** (1989)

Steve Earle, **The Very Best of: Angry Young Man** (1999)

Janie Fricke, **Anthology** (1999)

Vince Gill, **When I Call Your Name** (1989)

Alan Jackson, **Greatest Hits Collection** (1995)

Alan Jackson, **A Lot About Livin' (And a Little 'Bout Love)** (1992)

Ricky Skaggs, **Country Gentleman: The Best of Ricky Skaggs** (1998)

George Strait, **Does Fort Worth Ever Cross Your Mind** (1984)

George Strait, **Greatest Hits, Vol. 2** (1987)

Randy Travis, **Storms of Life** (1986)

Randy Travis, **Trail of Memories: The Randy Travis Anthology** (2002)

Travis Tritt, **Greatest Hits: From the Beginning** (1995)

Keith Whitley, **I Wonder Do You Think of Me** (1989)

Dwight Yoakam, **Buenos Noches from a Lonely Room** (1988)

Dwight Yoakam, **Guitars, Cadillacs, Etc., Etc.** (1986)

Old-Timey

Allen Brothers, **Allen Brothers, Vol. 3: 1932–1934** (2001)

The Bailey Brothers, **Early Days of Bluegrass, Vol. 6—Have You Forgotten?** (1976)

Bashful Brother Oswald, **Brother Oswald** (1972)

Bashful Brother Oswald, **Don't Say Aloha** (1998)

The Blue Sky Boys, **Blue Sky Boys on Radio, Vol. 1** (1996)

The Blue Sky Boys, **There'll Come a Time/Can't You Hear That Nightbird Crying?** (1936)

Dock Boggs, **Country Blues: Complete Early Recordings (1927–1929)** (1997)

Dock Boggs, **His Folkways Years (1963–1968)** (1998)

The Original Carter Family, **Can the Circle Be Unbroken?: Country Music's First Family** (2000)

The Carter Family, **In the Shadow of Clinch Mountain** (2000)

Coon Creek Girls, **Early Radio Favorites** (1982)

The Delmore Brothers, **Freight Train Boogie** (1993)

Pee Wee King, **Pee Wee King's Country Hoedown** (1999)

Uncle Dave Macon, **Country Music Hall of Fame Series** (1992)

Riley Puckett, **Red Sails in the Sunset** (1988)

Gid Tanner & His Skillet Lickers, **The Skillet Lickers** (1996)

Doc Watson, **The Best of Doc Watson: 1964–1968** (1999)

Doc Watson, **Doc Watson** (1964)

Various Artists, **16 Down Home Country Classics** (1998)

Various Artists, **Anthology of American Folk Music, Vol. 4** (2000)

Various Artists, **Anthology of American Folk Music, Vol. 1-3** (1997)

Various Artists, **Classic Country Music, Vol. 1** (1990)

Various Artists, **Mountain Music of Kentucky** (1996)

Various Artists, **Ragged But Right: 30's Country Bands**

Various Artists, **Roots 'n' Blues: The Retrospective 1925–1950** (1992)

Various Artists, **Stars of the Grand Ole Opry 1926–1974**

Outlaw Country

Bobby Bare, **The Columbia Years: Bare's Picks** (2000)

Ed Bruce, **The Best of Ed Bruce** (1995)

Guy Clark, **Old #1** (1975)

David Allan Coe, **For the Record: The First 10 Years** (1985)

David Allan Coe, **The Mysterious Rhinestone Cowboy/Once Upon a Time** (1993)
Joe Ely, **Honky Tonk Masquerade** (1978)
The Flatlanders, **More a Legend Than a Band** (1990)
Tompall Glaser, **The Best of Tompall Glaser & the Glaser Brothers** (2001)
Tompall Glaser, **Charlie** (1973)
Tompall Glaser, **The Outlaw** (1977)
Waylon Jennings, **Dreaming My Dreams** (1975)
Waylon Jennings, **Honky Tonk Heroes** (1973)
Waylon Jennings, **Lonesome, On'ry and Mean** (1972)
Waylon Jennings, **The Taker/Tulsa** (1970)
Kris Kristofferson, **Kristofferson** (1970)
Kris Kristofferson, **The Silver Tongued Devil and I** (1971)
Willie Nelson, **Phases and Stages** (1974)
Willie Nelson, **Red Headed Stranger** (1975)
Willie Nelson, **Shotgun Willie** (1973)
Willie Nelson & Waylon Jennings, **Wanted: The Outlaws!** (1976)
Mickey Newbury, **The Sailor** (1979)
Johnny Paycheck, **The Soul & the Edge: The Best of Johnny Paycheck** (2002)
Johnny Paycheck, **Take This Job & Shove It** (1978)
Billy Joe Shaver, **Old Five and Dimers Like Me** (1973)
Billy Joe Shaver, **Restless Wind: The Legendary Billy Joe Shaver 1973-1987** (1995)
Jerry Jeff Walker, **The Very Best of Jerry Jeff Walker** (1980)
Hank Williams, Jr., **Hank Williams, Jr.'s Greatest Hits** (1982)

Progressive Bluegrass

Austin Lounge Lizards, **Creatures from the Black Saloon** (1984)
Alison Brown, **Twilight Motel** (1992)
Sam Bush, **Glamour & Grits** (1996)
Vassar Clements, **Hillbilly Jazz** (1975)
The Dillards, **There Is a Time** (1963-70) (1991)
Jerry Douglas, **Slide Rule** (1992)
Béla Fleck & the Flecktones, **Flight of the Cosmic Hippo** (1991)
David Grisman Quintet, **David Grisman Quintet** (1977)
Hot Rize, **Hot Rize** (1979)
Alison Krauss & Union Station, **So Long So Wrong** (1997)
The Nashville Bluegrass Band, **Waitin' for the Hard Times to Go** (1993)
New Grass Revival, **The Best of New Grass Revival** (1994)
Mark O'Connor, **Retrospective** (1990)
Tony Rice Unit, **Backwaters** (1982)
The Seldom Scene, **The Best of Seldom Scene, Vol. 1** (1987)
Tony Trischka, **Dust on the Needle** (1988)

Progressive Country

Bobby Bare, **The Best of Bobby Bare** (1994)
Bobby Bare, **Bobby Bare Sings Lullabys, Legends and Lies** (1973)

Bobby Bare, **Singles: 1959-1969** (2001)
Guy Clark, **Essential** (1997)
Guy Clark, **Old #1** (1975)
Lee Clayton, **Lee Clayton** (1973)
David Allan Coe, **For the Record: The First 10 Years** (1985)
David Allan Coe, **Once Upon a Rhyme** (1974)
Joe Ely, **Honky Tonk Masquerade** (1978)
Jimmie Dale Gilmore, **After Awhile** (1991)
Tompall Glaser, **The Best of Tompall Glaser & the Glaser Brothers** (2001)
Tom T. Hall, **The Essential Tom T. Hall: Story Songs** (1988)
Tom T. Hall, **In Search of a Song** (1971)
Butch Hancock, **Own & Own** (1989)
Emmylou Harris, **Elite Hotel** (1975)
John Hartford, **RCA Country Legends** (2001)
Waylon Jennings, **Honky Tonk Heroes** (1973)
Waylon Jennings, **Only Daddy That'll Walk the Line: The RCA Years** (1993)
Kris Kristofferson, **Kristofferson** (1970)
Kris Kristofferson, **The Silver Tongued Devil and I** (1971)
Michael Murphey, **Blue Sky—Night Thunder** (1975)
Willie Nelson, **Red Headed Stranger** (1975)
Willie Nelson, **Stardust** (1978)
Willie Nelson, **The Troublemaker** (1976)
Willie Nelson, **Yesterday's Wine** (1971)
Mickey Newbury, **'Frisco Mabel Joy** (1971)
Mickey Newbury, **Harlequin Melodies: The Complete RCA Recordings Plus** (2003)
Mickey Newbury, **The Sailor** (1979)
The Nitty Gritty Dirt Band, **Dirt, Silver & Gold** (1976)
Dolly Parton, **Mission Chapel Memories 1971-1975** (2001)
Charlie Rich, **Feel Like Going Home: The Essential Charlie Rich** (1999)
Billy Joe Shaver, **Old Five and Dimers Like Me** (1973)
Tanya Tucker, **What's Your Mama's Name/Would You Lay With Me (In a Field of Stone)** (1999)
Townes Van Zandt, **Our Mother the Mountain** (1969)
Jerry Jeff Walker, **Jerry Jeff Walker** (1972)
Steve Young, **Lonesome On'ry & Mean** (1997)

Rockabilly

Sonny Burgess, **The Classic Recordings 1956-1959** (1991)
Johnny Burnette and the Rock & Roll Trio, **Rockabilly Boogie** (1989)
Johnny Carroll, **Rock Baby Rock It: 1955-1960** (1996)
Johnny Cash, **The Sun Years** (1990)
Eddie Cochran, **Somethin' Else** (1960)
Eddie Cochran, **Somethin' Else: The Fine Lookin' Hits of Eddie Cochran** (1998)
The Collins Kids, **Rockin'est** (1998)
Charlie Feathers, **Get With It: The Essential Recordings (1954-1969)** (1998)
Dale Hawkins, **Oh Suzy Q** (1995)
Ronnie Hawkins & The Hawks, **The Best of Ronnie Hawkins & the Hawks** (1990)

Buddy Holly, **Greatest Hits** (1996)
Wanda Jackson, **Queen of Rockabilly** (2000)
Sleepy LaBeef, **Early Rare & Rockin'** (1980)
Jerry Lee Lewis, **18 Original Sun Greatest Hits** (1984)
Carl Mann, **Mona Lisa: The Very Best of Carl Mann** (1999)
Rick Nelson, **Rockin' With Ricky** (1996)
Roy Orbison, **Sun Years** (1989)
Carl Perkins, **Original Sun Greatest Hits** (1986)
Elvis Presley, **Sunrise** (1999)
Charlie Rich, **Lonely Weekends: Best of the Sun Years** (1996)
Billy Lee Riley, **Classic Recordings, 1956-1960** (1990)
Ronnie Self, **Bop-A-Lena** (1990)
Warren Smith, **The Classic Recordings 1956-59** (1992)
Gene Vincent, **The Screaming End: The Best of Gene Vincent** (1997)
Various Artists, **Ain't I'm a Dog: 25 More Rockabilly Rave-Ups** (2000)
Various Artists, **Complete Sun Singles, Vol. 5** (1998)
Various Artists, **Get Hot or Go Home: Vintage RCA Rockabilly '56-'59—Vols. I & II**
Various Artists, **King Federal Rockabillys**
Various Artists, **Rock This Town: Rockabilly Hits, Vol. 2** (1991)
Various Artists, **Rock This Town: Rockabilly Hits, Vol. 1** (1991)
Various Artists, **The Sun Records Collection** (1994)
Various Artists, **Sun Records: 25 All-Time Greatest Hits** (1999)
Various Artists, **The Sun Story** (1987)
Various Artists, **That'll Flat Git It!, Vol. 1** (1992)
Various Artists, **That'll Flat Git It!, Vol. 2** (1992)
Various Artists, **That'll Flat Git It!, Vol. 3** (1992)
Various Artists, **Whistle Bait: 25 Rockabilly Rave-Ups** (2000)

String Bands

Fuzzy Mountain String Band, **Summer Oaks and Porch** (1973)
Hackberry Ramblers, **Cajun Boogie** (1992)
J.E. Mainer, **A Legendary Family from the Blue Ridge Mountains** (1963)
The New Lost City Ramblers, **The Early Years (1958-1962)** (1991)
The New Lost City Ramblers, **There Ain't No Way Out** (1997)
Charlie Poole & the North Carolina Ramblers, **Charlie Poole & the North Carolina Ramblers 1926-1930**
The Red Clay Ramblers, **Twisted Laurel/Merchants Lunch** (1991)
Gid Tanner & His Skillet Lickers, **The Skillet Lickers** (1996)
Various Artists, **Cajun String Bands 1930's: Cajun Breakdown** (1997)
Various Artists, **Fresh Oldtime String Band Music** (1988)
Various Artists, **Georgia String Bands (1928-1930)** (1992)

Various Artists, **Hokum Blues (1924–1929)** (1995)

Various Artists, **The Music of Kentucky: Early American Rural Classics 1927–1937, Vol. 1-2** (1995)

Various Artists, **Ragged But Right: 30's Country Bands**

Various Artists, **Roots 'n' Blues: The Retrospective 1925–1950** (1992)

Traditional Bluegrass

Flatt & Scruggs, **The 'Tis Sweet to Be Remembered: Essential Flatt & Scruggs** (1997)

Lester Flatt/Earl Scruggs/The Foggy Mountain Boys, **The Complete Mercury Recordings** (2003)

Jim & Jesse, **Jim & Jesse: 1952–1955** (1992)

The Kentucky Colonels, **Long Journey Home** (1964)

Jimmy Martin, **The King of Bluegrass** (2001)

Bill Monroe, **16 Gems** (1996)

Bill Monroe, **Anthology** (2003)

Bill Monroe, **RCA Country Legends** (2002)

The Osborne Brothers, **The Best of the Osborne Brothers** (1975)

Reno & Smiley, **Good Old Country Ballads** (1959)

The Stanley Brothers, **Angel Band: The Classic Mercury Recordings** (1995)

The Stanley Brothers, **Complete Columbia Recordings** (1996)

Eric Weissberg/Steve Mandell/Marshall Brickman, **Dueling Banjos from Deliverance** (1973)

Mac Wiseman, **The Mac Wiseman Story** (1976)

Various Artists, **24 Greatest Bluegrass Hits** (1989)

Various Artists, **Appalachian Stomp: Bluegrass Classics** (1995)

Various Artists, **Appalachian Stomp: More Bluegrass Classics** (1999)

Various Artists, **Bluegrass at Newport** (1959)

Various Artists, **The Country Gentlemen**

Various Artists, **Roots 'n' Blues: The Retrospective 1925–1950** (1992)

Traditional Country

Roy Acuff, **The Essential Roy Acuff (1936–1949)** (1992)

Eddy Arnold, **The Best of Eddy Arnold** (1967)

Gene Autry, **The Essential Gene Autry** (1992)

The Original Carter Family, **Can the Circle Be Unbroken?: Country Music's First Family** (2000)

Johnny Cash, **At Folsom Prison** (1968)

Johnny Cash, **The Essential Johnny Cash** (2002)

Patsy Cline, **The Ultimate Collection** (2000)

Red Foley, **Country Music Hall of Fame** (1991)

Tennessee Ernie Ford, **The Ultimate Collection (1949–1965)** (1997)

Lefty Frizzell, **Look What Thoughts Will Do** (1997)

Don Gibson, **RCA Country Legends** (2001)

Merle Haggard, **The Lonesome Fugitive: The**

Merle Haggard Anthology (1963–1977) (1995)

Johnny Horton, **Honky Tonk Man: The Essential Johnny Horton 1956–1960** (1996)

Waylon Jennings, **RCA Country Legends** (2001)

George Jones, **The Best of George Jones (1955–1967)** (1991)

Jerry Lee Lewis, **Another Place Another Time/She Even Woke Me Up to Say Goodbye** (2002)

Hank Locklin, **RCA Country Legends** (1998)

The Louvin Brothers, **When I Stop Dreaming: The Best of the Louvin Brothers** (1995)

Loretta Lynn, **Country Music Hall of Fame Series** (1991)

Roger Miller, **All Time Greatest Hits** (2003)

Willie Nelson, **Greatest Hits (& Some That Will Be)** (1981)

Buck Owens, **The Buck Owens Collection (1959–1990)** (1992)

Webb Pierce, **King of the Honky-Tonk: From the Original Master Tapes** (1994)

Ray Price, **The Essential Ray Price (1951–1962)** (1991)

Charley Pride, **RCA Country Legends** (2000)

Jerry Reed, **RCA Country Legends** (2001)

Charlie Rich, **Feel Like Going Home: The Essential Charlie Rich** (1997)

Jimmie Rodgers, **The Essential Jimmie Rodgers** (1997)

Roy Rogers, **Happy Trails: The Roy Rogers Collection 1937–1990** (1999)

Hank Snow, **The Essential Hank Snow** (1997)

The Statler Brothers, **Flowers on the Wall: The Essential Statler Brothers** (1996)

Hank Thompson, **Vintage** (1996)

Floyd Tillman, **Best of Floyd Tillman** (1999)

Merle Travis, **The Best of Merle Travis: Sweet Temptation 1946–1953** (2000)

Ernest Tubb, **The Definitive Ernest Tubb Hits Collection** (2001)

Porter Wagoner, **The Essential Porter Wagoner and Dolly Parton** (1996)

Porter Wagoner, **The Essential Porter Wagoner** (1997)

Don Williams, **Anthology** (2000)

Hank Williams, Sr., **40 Greatest Hits** (1978)

Bob Wills & His Texas Playboys, **Anthology 1935–1973** (1991)

Tammy Wynette, **Anniversary: 20 Years of Hits** (1987)

Faron Young, **The Complete Capitol Hits of Faron Young** (2000)

Various Artists, **Columbia Country Classics, Vol. 3: Americana** (1990)

Various Artists, **Columbia Country Classics, Vol. 1: The Golden Age** (1990)

Various Artists, **Hillbilly Music: Thank God!, Vol. 1** (1989)

Various Artists, **Roots 'n' Blues: The Retrospective 1925–1950** (1992)

Truck Driving Country

Dick Curless, **Drag 'Em off the Interstate, Sock It to Em: The Hits of Dick Curless** (1998)

Dick Curless, **Hard Hard Traveling Man** (2000)

Dick Curless, **A Tombstone Every Mile** (1973)

Dave Dudley, **20th Century Masters—The Millennium Collection: The Best of Dave Dudley** (2002)

Terry Fell, **Truck Drivin' Man** (1993)

Red Simpson, **The Best of Red Simpson: Country Western Truck Drivin' Singer** (1999)

Red Simpson, **The Man Behind the Badge/Roll, Truck, Roll** (1999)

Red Sovine, **The Best of Red Sovine** (1995)

Red Steagall, **Truck Driving Man**

Various Artists, **Truck Driver's Boogie: Big Rig Hits Vol. 1: 1939–1969** (2001)

Urban Cowboy

Glen Campbell, **Rhinestone Cowboy-/ Bloodline** (2002)

Earl Thomas Conley, **The Essential** (1996)

Charlie Daniels Band, **A Decade of Hits** (1983)

The Gatlin Brothers, **The Best of the Gatlins: All the Gold in California** (1996)

Mickey Gilley, **Ten Years of Hits** (1984)

Johnny Lee, **Greatest Hits** (1983)

Barbara Mandrell, **The Best of Barbara Mandrell** (1979)

Ronnie McDowell, **Older Women and Other Greatest Hits** (1987)

Ronnie Milsap, **40 #1 Hits** (2000)

Juice Newton, **Greatest Hits (And More)** (1984)

Eddie Rabbitt, **The Essentials** (2003)

Kenny Rogers, **Through the Years: A Retrospective** (1999)

T.G. Sheppard, **The Best of T.G. Sheppard** (1992)

Various Artists, **Urban Cowboy** (1980)

Western Swing

Milton Brown and the Brownies, **Daddy of Western Swing** (2003)

Cliff Bruner, **Cliff Bruner's Texas Wanderers** (1983)

Vassar Clements, **Hillbilly Jazz** (1975)

Spade Cooley, **Spadella: The Essential** (1994)

Tommy Duncan, **Texas Moon** (1996)

Johnny Gimble, **Still Swingin': Johnny Gimble and the Texas Swing Pioneers** (1976)

Pee Wee King, **Pee Wee King's Country Hoedown** (1999)

The Lightcrust Doughboys, **Light Crust Doughboys 1936–39** (1982)

Leon Mcauliffe & His Western Swing Band, **Columbia Historic Edition** (1984)

Hank Penny, **Crazy Rhythm: The Standard Transcriptions** (2000)

Hank Thompson, **Dance Ranch** (1958)

Hank Thompson, **Hank Thompson & His Brazos Valley Boys (1946–1964)** (1996)

Hank Thompson, **Vintage** (1996)

Tex Williams, **Vintage Collections Series** (1996)

Bob Wills & His Texas Playboys, **Anthology 1935–1973** (1991)

Bob Wills & His Texas Playboys, **Tiffany Transcriptions, Vol. 1** (1982)

Bob Wills & His Texas Playboys, **Tiffany Transcriptions, Vol. 2** (1986)

Bob Wills & His Texas Playboys, **Tiffany Transcriptions, Vol. 3** (1986)

Bob Wills & His Texas Playboys, **Tiffany Transcriptions, Vol. 4** (1986)

Various Artists, **As Good As It Gets: Western Swing** (2000)

Various Artists, **Heroes of Country Music, Vol. 1: Legends of Western Swing** (1996)

Various Artists, **Hillbilly Fever, Vol. 1: Legends of Western Swing** (1995)

Various Artists, **OKeh Western Swing**

Various Artists, **Texas Music, Vol. 2: Western Swing & Honky Tonk** (1994)

Western Swing Revival

Asleep at the Wheel, **Ride With Bob** (1999)

Asleep at the Wheel, **Western Standard Time** (1988)

Commander Cody & The Lost Planet Airmen, **Too Much Fun: Best of Commander Cody** (1990)

Commander Cody & The Lost Planet Airmen, **We've Got a Live One Here** (1976)

Merle Haggard & the Strangers, **A Tribute to the Best Damn Fiddle Player in the World (Or My Salute to Bob Wills)** (1970)

Dan Hicks & His Hot Licks, **Return to Hicksville: The Best of Dan Hicks & His Hot Licks – The Blue Thumb Years 1971–1973** (1997)

Joe & Eddie, **The Best of Joe & Eddie** (1967)

Riders in the Sky, **The Best of the West** (1988)

Don Walser, **Down at the Sky-Vue Drive-In** (1998)

Essential Songs

Alternative Country

"Honky Tonk Song," BR5-49
"My Wife Thinks You're Dead," Junior Brown
"Broken Hearted People," Guy Clark
"Lover's Lie," Derailers
"Copperhead Road," Steve Earle
"Guitar Town," Steve Earle
"Dallas," The Flatlanders
"Tonight I Think I'm Gonna Go Downtown," The Flatlanders
"West Texas Waltz," Butch Hancock
"Think It over One Time," Robert Earl Keen, Jr.,
"Big Boned Gal," k.d. lang
"I'm Down To My Last Cigarette," k.d. lang
"God Will," Lyle Lovett
"If I Had a Boat," Lyle Lovett
"L.A. County," Lyle Lovett
"What a Crying Shame," The Mavericks
"I'm Not Afraid to Die," Gillian Welch
"Guitars, Cadillacs," Dwight Yoakam
"Honky Tonk Man," Dwight Yoakam
"Thousand Miles from Nowhere," Dwight Yoakam

Alternative Country-Rock

"Fools Like You," Blue Rodeo
"Welfare Music," The Bottle Rockets
"Blue Moon Revisited (Song for Elvis)," Cowboy Junkies
"Sweet Jane," Cowboy Junkies
"Binding Twine," Freakwater
"Hero/Heroine," Freakwater
"Blue," The Jayhawks
"Waiting for the Sun," The Jayhawks
"For Which We Are Truly Thankful," Lambchop
"Barrier Reef," Old 97's
"Timebomb," Old 97's
"You Will Miss Me When I Burn," The Palace Brothers
"Drown," Son Volt
"Game of Broken Hearts," Tarnation
"Two Wrongs Won't Make Things Right," Tarnation,
"Anodyne," Uncle Tupelo
"Chickamauga," Uncle Tupelo
"No Depression," Uncle Tupelo
"Whiskey Bottle," Uncle Tupelo
"Excuse Me While I Break My Own Heart Tonight," Whiskeytown
"I Got You (At the End of the Century)," Wilco
"I Must Be High," Wilco
"Outtasite (Outta Mind)," Wilco

Americana

"My Winding Wheel," Ryan Adams
"Fourth of July," Dave Alvin
"Are You Gettin' Tired of Me," BR5-49
"Porchlight," Neko Case
"Set Out Running," Neko Case
"After You're Gone," Iris Dement
"I Like Trains," Fred Eaglesmith
"Devil's Right Hand," Steve Earle
"Goodbye's All We've Got Left," Steve Earle
"She Never Spoke Spanish To Me," Joe Ely
"Tonight I Think I'm Gonna Go Downtown," Joe Ely
"Baby's Got New Plans," Alejandro Escovedo
"Love and Danger," Rosie Flores
"West Texas Waltz," Butch Hancock
"Have a Little Faith in Me," John Hiatt
"Thing Called Love," John Hiatt
"Waiting for the Sun," The Jayhawks
"O What a Thrill," The Mavericks
"(Is Anybody Going To) San Antone," Doug Sahm
"Georgia on a Fast Train," Billy Joe Shaver
"Anodyne," Uncle Tupelo
"I'm Not Afraid to Die," Gillian Welch
"16 Days," Whiskeytown
"Car Wheels on a Gravel Road," Lucinda Williams
"Passionate Kisses," Lucinda Williams
"Sweet Old World," Lucinda Williams

Bakersfield Sound

"So Round, So Firm, So Fully Packed," Johnny Bond
"High on a Hilltop," Tommy Collins
"If You Can't Bite, Don't Growl," Tommy Collins
"You Better Not Do That," Tommy Collins
"(My Friends Are Gonna Be) Strangers," Merle Haggard
"Bottle Let Me Down," Merle Haggard
"Mama Tried," Merle Haggard
"Sing a Sad Song," Merle Haggard
"Sing Me Back Home," Merle Haggard
"Heartaches by the Number," Harlan Howard
"Gone," Ferlin Husky
"I've Got a Tiger by the Tail," Buck Owens
"Love's Gonna Live Here," Buck Owens
"Streets of Bakersfield," Buck Owens
"Under Your Spell Again," Buck Owens
"L.A. International Airport," Susan Raye
"Dear John Letter," Jean Shepard
"Second Fiddle (To an Old Guitar)," Jean Shepard
"Highway Patrol," Red Simpson
"Truck Drivin' Man," Red Steagall

(continued)

"Above and Beyond," Sly & Sal
"Big Big Love," Sly & Sal
"Wishful Thinking," Wynn Stewart
"How Cold Hearted Can You Get," Hank Thompson
"Humpty Dumpty Heart," Hank Thompson
"Wild Side of Life," Hank Thompson
"Guitars, Cadillacs," Dwight Yoakam
"Honky Tonk Man," Dwight Yoakam
"Streets of Bakersfield," Dwight Yoakam

Bluegrass-Gospel

"I Saw the Light," Bill Monroe
"Gospel Way," Dry Branch Fire Squad
"Touch the Hem of His Garment," Dry Branch Fire Squad
"Hallelujah I'm Ready," Five for the Gospel
"Let Me Introduce You to Jesus," Five for the Gospel
"Christian Life," The Louvin Brothers
"Satan Is Real," The Louvin Brothers
"Can't You Hear Me Calling," Bill Monroe
"Going up Home to Live in Green Pastures," Ralph Stanley

Close Harmony

"You Can't Go Halfway (And Get In)," The Bailes Brothers
"Take Me Back to Happy Valley," The Bailey Brothers
"I'm Just Here to Get My Baby Out of Jail," The Blue Sky Boys
"Kentucky," The Blue Sky Boys
"Blues Stay Away from Me," The Delmore Brothers
"Freight Train Boogie," The Delmore Brothers
"Long Time Gone," The Everly Brothers
"Roving Gambler," The Everly Brothers
"Are You Missing Me?," Jim & Jesse
"Gosh, I Miss You All the Time," Jim & Jesse
"When I Stop Dreaming," Jim & Jesse
"(Oh Baby Mine) I Get So Lonely," Johnnie & Jack
"Poison Love," Johnnie & Jack
"Three Ways of Knowing," Johnnie & Jack
"Cash on the Barrelhead," The Louvin Brothers
"Christian Life," The Louvin Brothers
"I Don't Believe You've Met My Baby," The Louvin Brothers
"Satan Is Real," The Louvin Brothers
"When I Stop Dreaming," The Louvin Brothers
"You've Got the Look of a Perfect Diamond," The McCoury Brothers
"Kentucky Waltz," Osborne Brothers

"Rocky Top," Osborne Brothers

"I Wonder How the Old Folks Are at Home," Mac Wiseman

"Midnight Flyer," Mac Wiseman

Contemporary Bluegrass

"Sailin' Shoes," Sam Bush

"Wayfaring Stranger," Sam Bush

"Fields Have Turned Brown," The Country Gentlemen

"Legend of the Rebel Soldier," The Country Gentlemen

"Ride," Jerry Douglas

"Why Don't You Go Back to the Woods," Jerry Douglas

"Bill Cheatham," Béla Fleck

"Flight of the Cosmic Hippo," Béla Fleck

"Sinister Minister," Béla Fleck & The Flecktones

"My Yesterdays Look Better Every Day," The Gibson Brothers

"Earl's Breakdown," Josh Graves

"Angel's Waltz," Bobby Hicks

"Constant State of Grace," Irene Kelley

"Love You in Vain," Alison Krauss

"So Long, So Wrong," Alison Krauss

"When You Say Nothing at All," Alison Krauss

"Carolyn the Teenage Queen," The Lonesome River Band

"Love's Come over Me," The Lonesome River Band

"Moonlighter," Claire Lynch

"Lighthouse's Tale," Nickel Creek

"Out of the Woods," Nickel Creek

"City of New Orleans," The Seldom Scene

"Darling Corey," The Seldom Scene

"Been There and Back," Stockwell Brothers

"Black Mountain Rag," Tony Trischka

"Goofing off Suite," Tony Trischka

"Country Rain," Rhonda Vincent

"I Do My Cryin' at Night," Rhonda Vincent

Contemporary Country

"Closer You Get," Alabama

"Mountain Music," Alabama

"Killin' Time," Clint Black

"Boot Scootin' Boogie," Brooks & Dunn

"Brand New Man," Brooks & Dunn

"Friends in Low Places," Garth Brooks

"Shameless," Garth Brooks

"Ten Rounds with Jose Cuervo," Tracy Byrd

"He Thinks He'll Keep Her," Mary Chapin Carpenter

"Every Little Thing," Carlene Carter

"Strawberry Wine," Deana Carter

"I Don't Know Why You Don't Want Me," Rosanne Cash

"Bubba Shot the Jukebox," Mark Chesnutt

"Third Rock from the Sun," Joe Diffie

"Goodbye Earl," Dixie Chicks

"Wide Open Spaces," Dixie Chicks

"What Mattered Most," Ty Herndon

"This Kiss," Faith Hill

"Chasin' That Neon Rainbow," Alan Jackson

"Don't Rock the Jukebox," Alan Jackson

"Tell Me Why," Wynonna Judd

"Rockin' With the Rhythm of the Rain," The Judds

"Lonely Days, Lonely Nights," Patty Loveless

"Whoever's in New England," Reba McEntire

"Indian Outlaw," Tim McGraw

"80's Ladies," K.T. Oslin

"Blue," LeAnn Rimes

"Ocean Front Property," George Strait

"Whiskey Ain't Workin'," Marty Stuart

"Forever and Ever, Amen," Randy Travis

"T-R-O-U-B-L-E," Travis Tritt

"Any Man of Mine," Shania Twain

"Whose Bed Have Your Boots Been Under?," Shania Twain

"Life Turned Her That Way," Ricky Van Shelton

"She's in Love With the Boy," Trisha Yearwood

Country Boogie

"Galloping on the Guitar," Chet Atkins

"Yakety Axe," Chet Atkins

"Pistol Packin' Mama," Al Dexter and His Troopers

"Mule Train," Tennessee Ernie Ford

"Shotgun Boogie," Tennessee Ernie Ford

"Honky Tonk Man," Johnny Horton

"I'm a One Woman Man," Johnny Horton

"Let 'Er Roll," Sid King & The Five Strings

"I'm Movin' On," Hank Snow

"Divorce Me C.O.D.," Merle Travis

Country Comedy

"Where's The Dress?," Moe Bandy & Joe Stampley

"Coon Huntin' Story," Jerry Clower

"Almost Persuaded No. 2," Ben Colder

"Fifteen Beers Ago," Ben Colder

"You Might Be a Redneck If...," Jeff Foxworthy

"They Ain't Makin' Jews Like Jesus Anymore," Kinky Friedman

"Help, I'm White and I Can't Get Down/Son's Love," The Geezinslaws

"(How Much) Is That Doggie in the Window?," Homer & Jethro

"Battle of Kookamonga," Homer & Jethro

"I'm My Own Grandpaw," Homer & Jethro

"Mr. Sandman," Homer & Jethro

"From the Indies to the Andies in His Undies," Hoosier Hot Shots

"Country Music Is Here to Stay," Simon Crum

"Cledus Went Down to Florida," Cledus T. Judd

"Did I Shave My Back for This?," Cledus T. Judd

"If Shania Was Mine," Cledus T. Judd

"Convoy," C.W. McCall

"Chug-A-Lug," Roger Miller

"Dang Me," Roger Miller

"Lou's Got the Flu," Roger Miller

"Spiders and Snakes," Jim Stafford

"Gitarzan," Ray Stevens

"Streak," Ray Stevens

"15 Beers Ago," Sheb Wooley

Country Gospel

"Great Speckled Bird," Roy Acuff

"Church in the Wildwood," E.C. Ball

"Satisfied," Martha Carson

"It Was Jesus," Johnny Cash

"The Old Account," Johnny Cash

"When the Roll Is Called up Yonder," Chuck Wagon Gang

"Peace in the Valley," Red Foley

"What a Friend We Have in Jesus," Tennessee Ernie Ford

"Lighthouse," The Happy Goodman Family

"Wings of a Dove," Ferlin Husky

"Someone's Watching Over You," George Jones

"Old Time Religion," Jerry Lee Lewis

"Amazing Grace," Charlie Rich

"How Great Thou Art," George Beverly Shea

"Do You Know You Are My Sunshine," The Statler Brothers

"Key to the Kingdom," The Whites

"I Saw the Light," Carl Story

Country-Folk

"500 Miles Away from Home," Bobby Bare

"Detroit City," Bobby Bare

"Houston," Bobby Bare

"Passionate Kisses," Mary Chapin Carpenter

"Life Holds On," Beth Nielsen Chapman

"Broken Hearted People," Guy Clark

"Dublin Blues," Guy Clark

"Would You Lay with Me (In a Field of Stone)," David Allan Coe

"Our Town," Iris Dement

"Seven Shells," Fred Eaglesmith

"You've Never Seen Me Cry," The Flatlanders

"Sixteen Tons," Tennessee Ernie Ford

"Dallas," Jimmie Dale Gilmore

"Gulf Coast Highway," Nanci Griffith

"Lone Star State of Mind," Nanci Griffith

"That's How I Got To Memphis," Tom T. Hall

"Old Dogs, Children and Watermelon Wine," Tom T. Hall

"Year That Clayton Delaney Died," Tom T. Hall

"Abilene," George Hamilton IV

"Look into My Teardrops," Waylon Jennings

"Front Porch Song," Robert Earl Keen, Jr.

"Love at the Five and Dime," Kathy Mattea

"My Tennessee Mountain Home," Dolly Parton

"Quarter Moon," Cheryl Wheeler

"Cattle Call," Slim Whitman

Country-Pop

"Rose Garden," Lynn Anderson

"Make the World Go Away," Eddy Arnold

"Let Your Love Flow," The Bellamy Brothers

"Gentle on My Mind," Glen Campbell

"Rhinestone Cowboy," Glen Campbell

"Baby Don't Get Hooked on Me," Mac Davis

"Happiest Girl in the Whole U.S.A.," Donna Fargo

"Don't It Make My Brown Eyes Blue," Crystal Gayle

"Ode to Billie Joe," Bobbie Gentry

"Oh, Lonesome Me," Don Gibson

"Grand Tour," George Jones

"Wolverton Mountain," Claude King

"Sleeping Single in a Double Bed," Barbara Mandrell

"(There's) No Gettin' over Me," Ronnie Milsap

"Stranger in My House," Ronnie Milsap

"Snowbird," Anne Murray

"Always on My Mind," Willie Nelson
"Queen of Hearts," Juice Newton
"Have You Never Been Mellow," Olivia Newton-John,
"Elvira," The Oak Ridge Boys
"Here You Come Again," Dolly Parton
"For the Good Times," Ray Price
"Kiss an Angel Good Morning," Charley Pride
"Step by Step," Eddie Rabbitt
"Most Beautiful Girl," Charlie Rich
"Singing the Blues," Marty Robbins
"Gambler," Kenny Rogers
"Ruby, Don't Take Your Love to Town," Kenny Rogers
"Flowers on the Wall," The Statler Brothers
"(Hey Won't You Play) Another Somebody Done Somebody Wrong Song," B.J. Thomas
"Hello Darlin,'" Conway Twitty
"Satisfied Mind," Porter Wagoner
"I Believe in You," Don Williams
"Tulsa Time," Don Williams

Country-Rock

"Third Rate Romance," The Amazing Rhythm Aces
"Weight," The Band
"Country Girl," Brinsley Schwarz
"Goin' Back," The Byrds
"Hickory Wind," The Byrds
"Hot Rod Lincoln," Commander Cody & His Lost Planet Airmen
"Lay Lady Lay," Bob Dylan
"Desperado," The Eagles
"Take It Easy," The Eagles
"Take It to the Limit," The Eagles
"Christine's Tune (A.K.A. Devil in Disguise)," The Flying Burrito Brothers
"Farther Along," The Flying Burrito Brothers
"Hot Burrito No. 1," The Flying Burrito Brothers
"Hot Burrito No. 2," The Flying Burrito Brothers
"Sin City," The Flying Burrito Brothers
"Friend of the Devil," The Grateful Dead
"Sugar Magnolia," The Grateful Dead
"Listen to the Band," Michael Nesmith & the First National Band
"Mr. Bojangles," The Nitty Gritty Dirt Band
"Will the Circle Be Unbroken," The Nitty Gritty Dirt Band
"$1000 Wedding," Gram Parsons
"Brass Buttons," Gram Parsons
"Luxury Liner," Gram Parsons
"Return of the Grievous Angel," Gram Parsons
"Song for You," Gram Parsons
"Crazy Love," Poco,
"Pickin' up the Pieces," Poco
"Amie," Pure Prairie League
"Garden Party," Rick Nelson & the Stone Canyon Band
"Pancho and Lefty," Townes Van Zandt
"Polk Salad Annie," Tony Joe White
"Heart of Gold," Neil Young

Cowboy

"Last Roundup," Rex Allen
"Streets of Laredo," Rex Allen

"Wide Rolling Plains," Rosalie Allen
"Cattle Call," Eddy Arnold
"Back in the Saddle Again," Gene Autry
"Yellow Rose of Texas," Gene Autry
"Don't Take Your Guns to Town," Johnny Cash
"Pistol Packin' Mama," Al Dexter and His Troopers
"Cowboy's Song," Don Edwards
"I Want to Be a Cowboy's Sweetheart," Patsy Montana
"I Ride an Old Paint," Riders in the Sky
"High Noon (Do Not Forsake Me)," Tex Ritter
"Big Iron," Marty Robbins
"El Paso," Marty Robbins
"West Ain't What It Used to Be," Carson Robison
"Happy Trails," Roy Rogers
"I've Sold My Saddle for an Old Guitar," Roy Rogers
"Home on the Range," Roy Rogers & The Sons of the Pioneers
"I'm an Old Cowhand (From the Rio Grande)," Roy Rogers & The Sons of the Pioneers
"Cool Water," The Sons of the Pioneers
"Tumbling Tumbleweeds," The Sons of the Pioneers
"When the Work's All Done This Fall," Carl T. Sprague

Honky Tonk

"I Just Started Hatin' Cheatin' Songs Today," Moe Bandy
"Pop A Top," Jim Ed Brown
"Born to Lose," Ted Daffan
"If You've Got the Money (I've Got the Time)," Lefty Frizzell
"Just Can't Live That Fast (Any More)," Lefty Frizzell
"Look What Thoughts Will Do," Lefty Frizzell
"Bottle Let Me Down," Merle Haggard
"Swinging Doors," Merle Haggard
"Honky Tonk Man," Johnny Horton
"I'm a One Woman Man," Johnny Horton
"Window up Above," Ralph Stanley
"Why Baby Why," George Jones
"She Even Woke Me Up To Say Goodbye," Jerry Lee Lewis
"What's Made Milwaukee Famous," Jerry Lee Lewis
"Room Full of Roses," George Morgan
"Under Your Spell Again," Buck Owens
"Honky Tonk Song," Webb Pierce
"There Stands the Glass," Webb Pierce
"Crazy Arms," Ray Price
"Heartaches by the Number," Ray Price
"Dear John Letter," Jean Shepard
"I Overlooked An Orchid (While Searching for a Rose)," Carl Smith
"Hey Joe!," Carl Smith
"Wild Side of Life," Hank Thompson
"Drivin' Nails in My Coffin," Johnny Bush
"Slipping Around," Floyd Tillman
"This Cold War With You," Floyd Tillman
"Walking the Floor over You," Ernest Tubb
"Waltz Across Texas," Ernest Tubb
"You're the Only Good Thing (That's Happened to Me)," Ernest Tubb

"Close All the Honky Tonks," Charlie Walker
"Pick Me Up on Your Way Down," Charlie Walker
"It Wasn't God Who Made Honky Tonk Angels," Kitty Wells
"Honky Tonk Blues," Hank Williams
"You Win Again," Hank Williams
"Your Cheatin' Heart," Hank Williams
"Hello Walls," Faron Young
"Live Fast, Love Hard, Die Young," Faron Young

Instrumental Country

"Country Gentleman," Chet Atkins
"Galloping on the Guitar," Chet Atkins
"Little Rock Getaway," Jimmy Bryant
"Malagueña," Roy Clark
"Steel Guitar Rag," Jimmy Day
"Texas Playboy Rag," Jimmy Day
"Raisin' the Dickens," Buddy Emmons
"Black and White Rag," Johnny Gimble
"Fort Worth Drag," Shot Jackson
"Fire on the Strings," Joe Maphis
"I'll Sail My Ship Alone," Moon Mullican
"Yakety Sax," Nashville Sax
"Yakety Sax," Boots Randolph
"Cannonball Rag," Merle Travis
"Steel Guitar Rag," Merle Travis
"Foggy Mountain Breakdown," Frank Wakefield
"Frettin' Fingers," Speedy West
"Speedin' West," Speedy West
"Stratosphere Boogie," Speedy West

Nashville Sound/Countrypolitan

"Still," Bill Anderson
"Make the World Go Away," Eddy Arnold
"What's He Doing in My World," Eddy Arnold
"Three Bells," The Browns
"Galveston," Glen Campbell
"I Fall to Pieces," Patsy Cline
"She's Got You," Patsy Cline
"Walkin' After Midnight," Patsy Cline
"Last Date," Floyd Cramer
"End of the World," Skeeter Davis
"Blue Blue Day," Don Gibson
"Oh, Lonesome Me," Don Gibson
"Rose and a Baby Ruth," George Hamilton IV
"Gone," Ferlin Husky
"She Thinks I Still Care," George Jones
"Walk Through This World With Me," George Jones
"Please Help Me I'm Falling," Hank Locklin,
"Husbands and Wives," Roger Miller
"Candy Kisses," George Morgan
"Funny How Time Slips Away," Willie Nelson
"Night Life," Willie Nelson
"Four Walls," Jim Reeves
"He'll Have to Go," Jim Reeves
"Welcome to My World," Jim Reeves
"White Sport Coat (And a Pink Carnation)," Marty Robbins
"Green, Green Grass of Home," Porter Wagoner
"Just Someone I Used to Know," Porter Wagoner
"D-I-V-O-R-C-E," Tammy Wynette
"I Don't Wanna Play House," Tammy Wynette

Neo-Traditionalist Country

"House of Blue Lights," Asleep at the Wheel
"Drive South," Suzy Bogguss
"Honky Tonk Song," BR5-49
"Highway Patrol," Junior Brown
"Cry," Carlene Carter
"Blue Moon With Heartache," Rosanne Cash
"Runaway Train," Rosanne Cash
"I Couldn't Leave You If I Tried," Rodney Crowell
"She's Crazy for Leaving," Rodney Crowell
"Takin' It Easy," Lacy J. Dalton
"There's Your Trouble," Dixie Chicks
"Love and Danger," Rosie Flores
"Crazy over You," Radney Foster
"Let's Kill Saturday Night," Robbie Fulks
"That's What Daddy Wants," Wayne Hancock
"Blue Blue Day," James Intveld
"Small Town Saturday Night," Hal Ketchum
"Miss Chatelaine," k.d. lang
"Big Big Love," k.d. lang & the re-clines
"I Thought We Had a Deal," Jim Lauderdale
"What'cha Gonna Do With a Cowboy?," Chris LeDoux
"Here Comes the Rain," The Mavericks
"What a Crying Shame," The Mavericks
"Little Rock," Reba McEntire
"Til a Tear Becomes a Rose," Lorrie Morgan
"Highway 40 Blues," Ricky Skaggs
"Diggin' up Bones," Randy Travis
"Honky Tonk Man," Dwight Yoakam
"Little Ways," Dwight Yoakam

New Traditionalist

"Black Sheep," John Anderson
"Swingin'," John Anderson
"Better Man," Clint Black
"Killin' Time," Trace Adkins
"Ain't Goin' Down (Til the Sun Comes Up)," Garth Brooks
"Friends in Low Places," Garth Brooks
"Lifestyles of the Not So Rich and Famous," Tracy Byrd
"Honky Tonk Attitude," Joe Diffie
"Don't Let Our Love Start Slippin' Away," Vince Gill
"Don't Rock the Jukebox," Alan Jackson
"She's Got the Rhythm (And I Got the Blues)," Alan Jackson
"National Working Woman's Holiday," Sammy Kershaw
"Rope the Moon," John Michael Montgomery
"Does Fort Worth Ever Cross Your Mind," George Strait
"Ocean Front Property," George Strait
"Now That's Country," Marty Stuart
"Whiskey Ain't Workin'," Marty Stuart
"1982," Randy Travis
"Diggin' Up Bones," Randy Travis
"When You Say Nothing at All," Keith Whitley

Old-Timey

"Carry Me Back to the Mountains," Bashful Brother Oswald
"Kentucky," The Blue Sky Boys
"Pretty Polly," Dock Boggs
"Will Sweethearts Know Each Other There?," Dock Boggs
"Black Jack David," The Carter Family
"Can the Circle Be Unbroken (Bye and Bye)," The Carter Family
"Keep on the Sunny Side," The Carter Family
"Worried Man Blues," The Carter Family
"Tom Dooley," Grayson & Whitter
"Moving in Jungletown," Hoosier Hot Shots
"Backwater Blues," Uncle Dave Macon
"Way Down the Old Plank Road," Uncle Dave Macon
"Lovesick Blues," Emmett Miller
"Big Bad Bill (Is Sweet William Now)," Emmett Miller & His Georgia Crackers
"Cumberland Gap," The New Lost City Ramblers
"Goodbye Liza Jane," Charlie Poole
"Soldier's Joy," Riley Puckett
"How Can a Poor Man Stand Such Times and Live?," Blind Alfred Reed
"Darling Cora," Mike Seeger
"Broken Down Gambler," The Skillet Lickers
"Molly Put the Kettle On," The Skillet Lickers
"Life's Railway to Heaven," The Stonemans
"Black Mountain Rag," Doc Watson
"Omie Wise," Doc Watson

Outlaw Country

"Texas Cookin'," Guy Clark
"Mona Lisa Lost Her Smile," David Allan Coe
"You Never Even Called Me by My Name," David Allan Coe
"Storms Never Last," Jessi Colter
"Tonight I Think I'm Gonna Go Downtown," The Flatlanders
"Charlie," Tompall Glaser
"Put Another Log on the Fire (Male Chauvinist National Anthem)," Tompall Glaser
"Texas Law Sez," Tompall Glaser
"Are You Sure Hank Done It This Way," Waylon Jennings
"Black Rose," Waylon Jennings
"Good Hearted Woman," Waylon Jennings
"Honky Tonk Heroes," Waylon Jennings
"Lonesome, On'ry and Mean," Waylon Jennings
"Help Me Make It Through the Night," Kris Kristofferson
"Loving Her Was Easier (Than Anything I'll Ever Do Again)," Kris Kristofferson
"Pilgrim, Chapter 33," Kris Kristofferson
"Sunday Morning Coming Down," Kris Kristofferson
"Taker," Kris Kristofferson
"Bloody Mary Morning," Willie Nelson
"Me and Paul," Willie Nelson
"Whiskey River," Willie Nelson
"I'm the Only Hell (Mama Ever Raised)," Johnny Paycheck
"Take This Job and Shove It," Johnny Paycheck
"I'm Just an Old Chunk of Coal (But I'm Going to Be a Diamond Someday)," Billy Joe Shaver
"Ride Me Down Easy," Billy Joe Shaver
"L.A. Freeway," Jerry Jeff Walker
"Up Against the Wall, Redneck Mother," Jerry Jeff Walker

"Whiskey Bent and Hell Bound," Hank Williams, Jr

Progressive Bluegrass

"Bethesda," Mike Auldridge
"Car Hank Died In," Austin Lounge Lizards
"Cowboy Calypso," Russ Barenberg
"Salt Creek," Norman Blake
"Wayfaring Stranger," Sam Bush
"Fields Have Turned Brown," The Country Gentlemen
"Mr. Engineer," J.D. Crowe & The New South
"Hey Boys," The Dillards
"Hymn of Ordinary Motion," Jerry Douglas
"Flight of the Cosmic Hippo," Béla Fleck
"I Ain't Broke (But I'm Badly Bent)," David Grisman
"Dawg's Rag," David Grisman Quintet
"When You Say Nothing at All," Alison Krauss
"On the Boulevard," New Grass Revival
"First Whippoorwill," Peter Rowan
"Macedonia," Strength in Numbers,
"Robot Plane Flies over Arkansas," Tony Trischka
"Bury Me Beneath the Willow," Clarence White
"Farewell Blues," Clarence White

Progressive Country

"(Margie's At) The Lincoln Park Inn," Bobby Bare
"500 Miles Away from Home," Bobby Bare
"Texas Cookin'," Guy Clark
"Would You Lay with Me (In a Field of Stone)," David Allan Coe
"She Never Spoke Spanish To Me," Joe Ely
"Tonight I Think I'm Gonna Go Downtown," Jimmie Dale Gilmore
"Streets of Baltimore," Tompall Glaser
"Wicked California," Nanci Griffith
"Love at the Five and Dime," Nanci Griffith
"Ballad of 40 Dollars," Tom T. Hall
"Cloudy Day," Butch Hancock
"That's How I Got To Memphis," Tom T. Hall
"Year That Clayton Delaney Died," Tom T. Hall
"Beneath Still Waters," Emmylou Harris
"Boulder to Birmingham," Emmylou Harris
"Cedartown, Georgia," Waylon Jennings
"Taker," Waylon Jennings,
"Front Porch Song," Robert Earl Keen, Jr.
"Help Me Make It Through the Night," Kris Kristofferson
"Loving Her Was Easier (Than Anything I'll Ever Do Again)," Kris Kristofferson
"Pilgrim, Chapter 33," Kris Kristofferson
"Sunday Morning Coming Down," Kris Kristofferson
"Bloody Mary Morning," Willie Nelson
"Blue Eyes Crying in the Rain," Willie Nelson
"American Trilogy," Mickey Newbury
"San Francisco Mabel Joy," Mickey Newbury
"She Even Woke Me up to Say Goodbye," Mickey Newbury
"(Is Anybody Going To) San Antone," Doug Sahm
"I'm Just an Old Chunk of Coal (But I'm Going to Be a Diamond Someday)," Billy Joe Shaver

"Pancho and Lefty," Townes Van Zandt

"Desperados Waiting for the Train," Jerry Jeff Walker

"Mr. Bojangles," Jerry Jeff Walker

"Seven Bridges Road," Steve Young

Rockabilly

"Red Headed Woman," Sonny Burgess

"Train Kept A Rollin'," Johnny Burnette

"Get Rhythm," Johnny Cash

"Duck Tail," Joe Clay

"C'mon Everybody," Eddie Cochran

"Twenty Flight Rock," Eddie Cochran

"Whistle Bait," The Collins Kids

"Susie-Q," Dale Hawkins

"Forty Days," Ronnie Hawkins & The Hawks

"Mary Lou," Ronnie Hawkins & The Hawks

"That'll Be the Day," Buddy Holly

"I'm a One Woman Man," Johnny Horton

"Fujiyama Mama," Wanda Jackson

"Let's Have a Party," Wanda Jackson

"Believe What You Say," Rick Nelson

"Stood Up," Rick Nelson

"Waitin' in School," Rick Nelson

"Blue Suede Shoes," Carl Perkins

"Dixie Fried," Carl Perkins

"Honey Don't," Carl Perkins

"Matchbox," Carl Perkins

"Baby Let's Play House," Elvis Presley

"Good Rockin' Tonight," Elvis Presley

"Mystery Train," Elvis Presley

"That's All Right," Elvis Presley

"Lonely Weekends," Charlie Rich

"Flyin' Saucers Rock and Roll," Billy Lee Riley

"Red Hot," Billy Lee Riley

"Leroy," Jack Scott

"Ubangi Stomp," Warren Smith

"Be-Bop-A-Lula," Gene Vincent & His Blue Caps

"Lotta Lovin'," Gene Vincent & His Blue Caps

"Race With the Devil," Gene Vincent & His Blue Caps

String Bands

"Peg and Awl," The Carolina Tar Heels

"Sally Ann," Fuzzy Mountain String Band

"Old Pipeliner," Hackberry Ramblers

"Old and in the Way," J.E. Mainer

"Sitting on Top of the World," Mississippi Sheiks

"Goodbye Liza Jane," Charlie Poole

"Merchants Lunch," The Red Clay Ramblers

"Molly Put the Kettle On," The Skillet Lickers

"Soldier's Joy," The Skillet Lickers

Traditional Bluegrass

"Flint Hill Special," Flatt & Scruggs

"Foggy Mountain Breakdown," Flatt & Scruggs

"Roll in My Sweet Baby's Arms," Flatt & Scruggs

"Ballad of Jed Clampett," Lester Flatt

"Great Speckled Bird," Jim & Jesse

"Get Down on Your Knees and Pray," The Johnson Mountain Boys

"Blue Moon of Kentucky," Bill Monroe

"Kentucky Waltz," Bill Monroe

"Mule Skinner Blues," Bill Monroe

"Uncle Pen," Bill Monroe

"Rocky Top," Osborne Brothers

"Ruby (Are You Mad)," Osborne Brothers

"I'm Using My Bible for a Roadmap," Reno & Smiley

"How Mountain Girls Can Love," The Stanley Brothers

"Man of Constant Sorrow," The Stanley Brothers

"Orange Blossom Special," The Stanley Brothers

Traditional Country

"Wabash Cannonball," Roy Acuff

"Wreck on the Highwayk," Roy Acuff

"Cattle Call," Eddy Arnold

"What's He Doing in My World," Eddy Arnold

"Yellow Rose of Texas," Gene Autry

"I Walk the Line," Johnny Cash

"Ring of Fire," Johnny Cash

"Crazy," Patsy Cline

"I Fall to Pieces," Patsy Cline

"Walkin' After Midnight," Patsy Cline

"You Are My Sunshine," Jimmie Davis

"Sixteen Tons," Tennessee Ernie Ford

"Saginaw, Michigan," Lefty Frizzell

"I Can't Stop Loving You," Don Gibson

"Oh, Lonesome Me," Don Gibson

"(My Friends Are Gonna Be) Strangers," Merle Haggard

"Battle of New Orleans," Johnny Horton

"Honky Tonk Man," Johnny Horton

"Gone," Ferlin Husky

"Only Daddy That'll Walk the Line," Waylon Jennings

"Race Is On," George Jones,

"White Lightning," George Jones

"Please Help Me, I'm Falling," Hank Locklin

"Cash on the Barrelhead," The Louvin Brothers

"Don't Come Home a Drinkin' (With Lovin' on Your Mind)," Loretta Lynn

"King of the Road," Roger Miller

"Hello Walls," Willie Nelson

"Cryin' Time," Buck Owens

"In the Jailhouse Now," Webb Pierce

"Crazy Arms," Ray Price

"Sittin' and Thinkin'," Charlie Rich

"High Noon (Do Not Forsake Me)," Tex Ritter

"El Paso," Marty Robbins

"Mule Skinner Blues (Blue Yodel No. 8)," Jimmie Rodgers

"T for Texas (Blue Yodel No. 1)," Jimmie Rodgers

"I'm Movin' On," Hank Snow

"Tumbling Tumbleweeds," The Sons of the Pioneers

"Wild Side of Life," Hank Thompson

"Walking the Floor over You," Ernest Tubb

"Waltz Across Texas," Ernest Tubb

"Hello Darlin'," Conway Twitty

"Green, Green Grass of Home," Porter Wagoner

"It Wasn't God Who Made Honky Tonk Angels," Kitty Wells

"Honky Tonk Blues," Hank Williams

"I'm So Lonesome I Could Cry," Hank Williams

"You Win Again," Hank Williams

"Your Cheatin' Heart," Hank Williams

"New San Antonio Rose," Bob Wills & His Texas Playboys

"Stay a Little Longer," Bob Wills & His Texas Playboys

"Stand by Your Man," Tammy Wynette

"Hello Walls," Faron Young

Truck Driving Country

"Gear Bustin' Sort of Feller," Bobby Braddock

"Truck Driver's Blues," Cliff Bruner

"Chick Inspector (That's Where My Money Goes)," Dick Curless

"Drag 'Em off the Interstate, Sock It to 'Em J.P. Blues," Dick Curless

"Tombstone Every Mile," Dick Curless

"Travelin' Man," Dick Curless

"Six Days on the Road," Dave Dudley

"There Ain't No Easy Run," Dave Dudley

"Truck Drivin' Son-of-a-Gun," Dave Dudley

"Two Six Packs Away," Dave Dudley

"Truck Drivin' Man," Jimmy Martin

"Widow Maker," Jimmy Martin

"Convoy," C.W. McCall

"Truck Drivin' Cat With Nine Wives," Jim Nesbitt

"Diesel Smoke (Dangerous Curves)," Doyle O'Dell

"Girl on the Billboard," Del Reeves

"Looking at the World Through a Windshield," Del Reeves

"Give Me Forty Acres," Red Simpson

"Highway Patrol," Red Simpson

"I'm a Truck," Red Simpson

"Roll, Truck, Roll," Red Simpson

"Phantom 309," Red Sovine

Urban Cowboy

"Closer You Get," Alabama

"Baby I Lied," Deborah Allen

"Country Boy (You Got Your Feet in L.A.)," Glen Campbell

"Rhinestone Cowboy," Glen Campbell

"Southern Nights," Glen Campbell

"Fire and Smoke," Earl Thomas Conley

"Devil Went Down to Georgia," Charlie Daniels

"Houston (Means I'm One Day Closer to You)," Larry Gatlin

"Lady Takes the Cowboy Everytime," Larry Gatlin

"I'll Get over You," Crystal Gayle

"Somebody's Knockin'," Terri Gibbs

"Room Full of Roses," Mickey Gilley

"You Don't Know Me," Mickey Gilley

"Lotta Love," Nicolette Larson

"I Was Country When Country Wasn't Cool," Barbara Mandrell

"Sleeping Single in a Double Bed," Barbara Mandrell

"Paradise Tonight," Charly McClain

"You're Gonna Ruin My Bad Reputation," Ronnie McDowell

"(There's) No Gettin' over Me," Ronnie Milsap

"Stranger in My House," Ronnie Milsap

"Queen of Hearts," Juice Newton

"Drivin' My Life Away," Eddie Rabbitt,

"I Love a Rainy Night," Eddie Rabbitt
"Two Dollars in the Jukebox," Eddie Rabbitt
"Coward of the County," Kenny Rogers
"Gambler," Kenny Rogers
"I Loved 'Em Every One," T.G. Sheppard
"Only One You," T.G. Sheppard

Western Swing

"Brownie's Stomp," Milton Brown
"Who's Sorry Now," Milton Brown
"That's What I Like About the South," Cliff
   Bruner
"It Makes No Difference Now," Cliff Bruner &
   The Texas Wanderers
"Crazy 'Cause I Love You," Spade Cooley
"Shame on You," Spade Cooley
"Steel Guitar Rag," Jimmy Day
"Tennessee Waltz," Pee Wee King
"Pussy, Pussy, Pussy," Lightcrust Doughboys
"Columbus Stockade," Leon McAuliffe
"Beaumont Rag," Hank Thompson
"Driving Nails In My Coffin," Hank Thompson

"Wild Side of Life," Hank Thompson
"Smoke! Smoke! Smoke! (That Cigarette)," Tex
   Williams & the Western Caravan
"Milk Cow Blues," Johnny Lee Willis
"Big Beaver," Bob Wills & His Texas Playboys
"Cherokee Maiden," Bob Wills & His Texas
   Playboys
"Miss Molly," Bob Wills & His Texas
   Playboys
"New San Antonio Rose," Bob Wills & His Texas
   Playboys
"Right or Wrong," Bob Wills & His Texas
   Playboys
"Roly Poly," Bob Wills & His Texas Playboys
"Stay a Little Longer," Bob Wills & His Texas
   Playboys
"Take Me Back to Tulsa," Bob Wills & His Texas
   Playboys
"Texas Playboy Rag," Bob Wills & His Texas
   Playboys
"Time Changes Everything," Bob Wills & His
   Texas Playboys
"Rag Mop," Johnnie Lee Wills

Western Swing Revival

"My Shoes Keep Walking Back to You," Ace in
   the Hole Band
"Boogie Back to Texas," Asleep at the Wheel
"Cherokee Boogie," Asleep at the Wheel
"Choo Choo Ch'Boogie," Asleep at the Wheel
"House of Blue Lights," Asleep at the Wheel
"My Window Faces the South," Commander
   Cody
"Smoke! Smoke! Smoke! (That Cigarette),"
   Commander Cody
"Faded Love," Tompall Glaser
"Cherokee Maiden," Merle Haggard
"Old Man from the Mountain's Coming Home,"
   Merle Haggard
"Right or Wrong," Merle Haggard
"Time Changes Everything," Merle Haggard
"My Old Timey Baby," Dan Hicks & His Hot
   Licks
"Bob Wills Is Still the King," Waylon Jennings
"Stay A Little Longer," Willie Nelson
"(Ghost) Riders In The Sky," Riders in the Sky
   (1988)

Index

Coria, Enrique 300
Corn Sisters 128, 468
Corneal, Jon 206, 347, 366
Cornelison, Buzz 238
Cornelius, Helen 91, **174**, 208
Cornells 504
Cornor, Randy 386
Correia, Amy 494
Corson, Roger 365
Costello, Elvis 101, 104, 118, 134, 137, 339, 352, 386, 413, 455, 456, 581, 661, 686, 702, 880, 882, 893, 915, 916, 924, 925
Cotner, Carl 35
Cotten, Elizabeth 869
Cotton, Carolina 871
Cotton, James 885
Cotton, Paul 598
Counting Crows 101, 179, 374, 893
Country Boys 204, 406, 814, 842
Country Cooking 54, 757, 809
Country Gazette 60, 105, **174**, 207, 253, 518, 519
Country Gentlemen 3, 4, 77, 153, **175**, 209, 211, 215, 232, 242, 431, 542, 690, 866, 909, 910
Country Joe & the Fish 562
Country Pardners 873
Country Rockers **176**
Country Store 369
County Line 747, 846
Courville, Sady 19
Cousin Emmy 878
Cousin Jody 907
Coutch, Frank 68
Covelle, Buddy 887
Cowan, John 105, **176**, 542, 887
Coward, Buster 766
Cowboy Jazz 477
Cowboy Junkies **176**, 177, 403, 779
Cowboy Nation **178**
Cowboy Ramblers 79, 793
Cows 374
Cox Family 68, **178**, 179, 865, 872, 880
Cox, Billy 42
Cox, Evelyn 178
Cox, Jim 4
Cox, Sidney 178, 179
Cox, Suzanne 178
Cox, Willard 178
Coyne, Wayne 259, 433, 633, 804
Crabtree, Mike 121
Craddock, Billy Bixby Crash **179**
Craig, Francis 59
Crain, Edward L. 889
Cramer, Floyd 24, 27, 154, **179**, 192, 196, 324, 402, 407, 434, 444, 594, 620, 680, 866, 910
Crary, Dan 60, 111, **180**
Crase, Noah 9
Craven, Joe 300
Cravens, Red **180**
Cravens, Red & the Bray Brothers 180
Craver, Mike 625
Crawford, Blackie 264
Crawford, Bob 575
Crawford, Ed 813
Cray, Robert 875
Crazy Horse 77, 671, 857
Cream 111, 461
Creed, Kyle 112, 268
Creedence Clearwater Revival 79, 707, 895, 913, 915
Cregan, Jim 241
Crenshaw, Marshall 101, 782, 783
Crickets 184, 351, 352, 353, 872
Crider, Doug 73
Critchlow, Slim **180**
Crockett, G.L. 868
Croker, Brendan 557
Croker, Glenn 306
Crook Brothers 696, 867
Cropper, Steve 598
Crosby & Nash 174

Crosby, Bing 104, 184, 202, 217, 315, 349, 396, 630, 652, 703, 750, 791, 901
Crosby, Bob 192, 296
Crosby, David 107, 108, 145, 347, 491, 492, 511, 532, 882
Crosby, Stills & Nash 82, 97, 108, 598, 673, 707, 857
Crosby, Stills, Nash & Young 269, 857
Cross, Hugh 614, 738
Crouch, Dennis 525
Crow, Alvin 688, 886
Crow, Sheryl 136, 459, 494, 511, 882
Crowbar 863
Crowe Brothers 651
Crowe, J.D. 9, 71, 77, 105, **180**, 181, 431, 447, 471, 635, 865, 867, 910
Crowe, J.D. & the Kentucky Mountain Boys 181, 431
Crowe, J.D. & the New South 211, 447, 635, 690, 818, 910
Crowell, Rodney 51, 89, 137, 144, **181**, 182, 261, 275, 280, 324, 428, 429, 511, 690, 707, 783, 815, 887
Crudup, Arthur "Big Boy" 601, 877
Crum, Simon 363, 887
Crumit, Frank 651
Crumm, Chad 143
Crutchfield, Jerry 84, 174, 539
Cryner, Bobbie **183**
Cryque, Boenzee 597
Crystal Springs Ramblers 194, 880, 889
Cuddy, Jim 69
Cuevas, Bill 739
Culture Club 49
Cumberland Ridge Runners 255
Cumberland Three 723
Cunha, Rick 337
Cuomo, Jim 890
Cupids 662
Cupit, Jerry 495
Curless, Dick **183**
Curtis, Ken 704
Curtis, Mac 868, 877
Curtis, Sonny **184**, 351
Cushnie, Scott 46
Cymbala, Carol 128
Cyrus, Billy Ray 163, **184**, 185, 629, 922

D

D., Chris 11
Dacus, Smokey 836, 837, 902
Dadmun-Bixby, Denny 293
Daffan, Ted 11, 95, 264, 886, 903
Dag 374
Daily, Pappy 50, **186**, 387, 499, 562, 686, 871, 885
Dale, Denny 351
Dale, Dick 875
Dalhart, Vernon **186**, 464, 614, 651, 712, 899
Dallas County Line 287
Dalton, Lacy J. **187**, 505, 686, 739
Daly, Mike 280, 813
DAmbrosio, Joey 315
Damned 455
Dando, Evan 3
Danelli, Dino 295
Dangerous Toys 260
Danheim, Eric 351
Daniel, Clay 741
Daniel, Davis **187**
Danko, Rick 46, 47, 331
Daniels, Charlie 145, 167, **187**, 188, 212, 409, 476, 510, 641, 760, 827, 866, 920
Daniels, Charlie Band 869
Daniels, Clint **190**
Daniels, Jack 120, 344
Daniels, Jeff 882
Danko, Rick 46, 47, 331
Danny & the Juniors 877
Darbone, Luderin 306, 868
Darby & Tarlton **190**
Darby, Tom 190
Darin, Bobby 51, 113, 402, 491

Darling, Helen **190**
Darnell, Larry 836
Darrell, Johnny **190**, 191, 589, 748
Darrow, Chris **191**, 554
Daryll, Ted 739
Dave & Deke Combo **191**
Dave and Sugar 663
David, Bobby 685
David, Hal 276, 648
Davidson, Clay 565
Davidson, Donna 369
Davies, Cyril 314
Davies, Gail **191**
Davies, Ray 135
Davies, Ron 191
Davis Sisters **192**, 195, 905, 906
Davis, Andon T. 645
Davis, Art 79
Davis, Betty Jack 192, 195, 905
Davis, Clifford 882
Davis, Danny **192**
Davis, Don 166
Davis, Drusilla 144
Davis, Eddie 869
Davis, Frank 570
Davis, Gail 570, 884
Davis, Gene 20
Davis, Hank 133, 869, 870
Davis, Hugh 581
Davis, Jeff 12
Davis, Jimmie 11, 95, **192**, 193, 284, 295, 296, 386, 510, 623, 734, 750, 892, 893, 903, 905
Davis, Linda **193**
Davis, Link **193**, 194, 881, 885, 886
Davis, Link Jr. 194
Davis, Lynn 561, 562, 865
Davis, Mac **194**, 476, 655, 733, 877, 920
Davis, Miles 635
Davis, Paul 571
Davis, Sammy Jr. 78, 752
Davis, Skeeter 57, 153, 192, **195**, 244, 407, 863, 866, 869, 905, 910, 911
Dawson, David 337
Dawson, John 545
Dawson, Julian 196
Dawson, Ronnie **196**, 210, 864, 913
Day, Doris 590
Day, Jimmy **196**, 197, 230, 756
Dayton, Jesse **197**
Dea, Roy 225
Dead Kennedys 851
Deakin, Paul 474
Dean, Billy **197**
Dean, Eddie **197**, 198, 692, 837
Dean, Freddie 706
Dean, Ira 756
Dean, James 819
Dean, Jimmy 75, 149, 197, **198**, 244, 273, 289, 356, 809, 866, 887
Dean, Larry **199**, 923
Dean, Melissa 663
deCarle, Russell 601
Decker, Carol 159
Decker, Shane 159
DeCourville, Joachim Thibault 19
Dee, Johnny 449
Dee, Kathy 809
Def Leppard 767, 922
DeFrancesco, Joey 273
DeHaven, Penny 629
Deisler, Conrad 34
Del Fuegos 735
Del Lords 14, 214, 921
Delaney & Bonnie 101, 170, 256, 414
Delevante, Bob 199
Delevante, Mike 199
Delevantes **199**
Delmore Brothers 19, 70, 75, 190, 192, **200**, 233, 297, 346, 384, 428, 442, 447, 450, 451, 452, 462, 590, 621, 696, 748, 752, 805, 845, 854, 871, 879, 882, 888, 905, 906
Delmore, Alton 200, 395, 696, 882, 905

Delmore, Rabon 200, 395, 905
Delorme, Dennis 601
DelPesco, Nino 447
Delta Boys 240
Delta Rhythm Boys 384
DeLugg, Milton 557
Demarcus, Jay 622
DeMent, Iris 201, 881, 888, 892
Dengler, Jerry 471
Dennis, Jeff 41
Denny, Jim 264, 594
Denson, Lee 102, 886
Denunzio, Vinny 336
Denver, John 104, 244, 266, 385, 552, 590, 638, 648, 685, 737, 920
Depeche Mode 137
Depp, Johnny 366
Derailers 11, 56, **201**, 788
Derek & the Dominos 408, 707
Derringer, Rick 894
Desaulniers, Stephen 677
Deschamps, Kim 69
Desert Rose Band 108, **202**, 347, 397, 398, 491, 590, 707, 923
DeShannon, Jackie 552, 624, 739, 876
Devonie, Nova 620
DeWilde, Brandon 365
DeWitt, Lew 717
Dexter, Al **202**, 868, 875, 903
Diadem, David 663
Diamond Rio 112, 173, **202**, 203, 238
Diamond, Neil 58, 136, 685
Dickens, Hazel 54, **203**, 277, 863, 865, 879, 880, 883, 884
Dickens, Little Jimmy 24, 75, 96, 106, 120, 150, **204**, 210, 232, 264, 578, 621, 648, 717, 748, 813, 819, 865, 875, 889, 900, 907
Dickerson, Dave 191
Dickerson, Lance 166
Dickey, Tom 349
Dickson, Jim 347
Dictators 14
Diddley, Bo 46, 235, 314, 352
Diffie, Joe **204**, 205, 398, 747, 756, 867
DiGregorio, Joel "Taz" 187
Dilks, Johnny **205**
Dill, Danny 51, 264
Dillard & Clark 60, 145, 174, **205**, 206, 207, 221, 915
Dillard-Hartford-Dillard 206
Dillard, Dottie 407
Dillard, Doug 60, 72, 145, 205, **206**, 207, 266, 327, 590
Dillard, Doug Band 72, 206
Dillard, Rodney 206, 207
Dillards 60, 78, 97, 205, **206**, 207, 327, 337, 489, 590, 635, 645, 740, 865, 867, 909, 910, 915, 916
Dillon, Dean 158, **208**, 721, 805
Dillon, John 576
Dimmery, Ira 375
DiMucci, Dion 402
Dinning, Delores 478
Dino, Desi & Billy 333
Dio, Ronnie James 887
Dion, Celine 208
DiPiero, Bob 749
Dire Straits 280, 557, 775
Dirt Band 489, 554, 555
Dirty Dozen Brass Band 12
Disco Brothers 455
Dittrich, John 633, 634
Dixiana 208
Dixie Chicks 145, **208**, 263, 398, 443, 497, 683, 747, 776, 871
Dixie Gentlemen **209**, 740
Dixie Ramblers 206, 868, 877
Dixieliners 696
Dixon Brothers 881
Dixon, Dorsey 884
Dixon, Mark 261
Dixon, Willie 256

More ALL MUSIC GUIDES from BACKBEAT BOOKS

All Music Guide
Fourth Edition

"The most useful single volume your money can buy." –*Mojo*

From rock to rap, country to reggae, avant-garde jazz to folk—and all the sounds in between—this definitive record guide offers expert advice for every style of music. With over 20,000 album reviews, 4,000 artist biographies, educational essays, and music maps, this is the one essential guide for music lovers.
Softcover, 1,491 pages, 8 charts, ISBN 0-87930-627-0, $34.95

All Music Guide to Jazz
Fourth Edition

"An indispensable resource for any jazz record collector." –*Los Angeles Times*

This entertaining, easy-to-use reference reviews and rates more than 20,000 top recordings by over 1,700 musicians in all jazz styles and eras—from New Orleans jazz to swing, bebop, cool, hard bop, Latin jazz, fusion, and beyond. Fully updated to cover the latest new releases, plus notable reissues and compilations.
Softcover, 1488 pages, 52 charts, ISBN 0-87930-717-X, $32.95

All Music Guide to Soul

"Extremely valuable and exhaustive." –*The Christian Science Monitor*

This comprehensive guide reviews and rates 8,450 recordings by 1,550 artists in all styles of the genre, and helps readers find new music to explore. Informative biographies, essays, and music maps trace R&B's growth from its roots in blues and gospel, its flowering in Memphis and Motown, to its many branches today.
Softcover, 912 pages, 12 charts, ISBN 0-87930-744-7, $26.95

All Music Guide to the Blues
Third Edition

"Easily the best blues guide to hit the market." –*Real Blues*

This fully updated and expanded guide reviews 8,900 recordings by 1,200 artists—from 1920s Delta blues to 1990s electric. It includes sections on the blues influence in jazz, and great gospel performers and recordings.
Softcover, 768 pages, 30 charts, ISBN 0-87930-736-6, $24.95

All Music Guide to Hip-Hop

This latest volume in the definitive All Music Guide series offers entertaining and informative reviews that lead readers to the best recordings by their favorite artists and help them find new music to explore. Informative biographies, essays, and music maps trace hip-hop's growth from its roots in urban soul and "old school" MCs and DJs, to its mainstream breakout during the '90's and the myriad branches that thrive today.
Softcover, 656 pages, 12 charts, ISBN 0-87930-759-5, $24.95

AVAILABLE AT FINE BOOK AND MUSIC STORES EVERYWHERE, OR CONTACT:

Backbeat Books • 6600 Silacci Way • Gilroy, CA 95020 USA • **Phone Toll Free: (866) 222-5232**
Fax: (408) 848-5784 • E-mail: backbeat@rushorder.com • Web: www.backbeatbooks.com